# WHO'S WHO AMONG AFRICAN AMERICANS

# WHO'S WHO AMONG AFRICAN AMERICANS

**32ND EDITION**

**Foreword by**
Jessie Carney Smith
Dean of the Library and
Camille Cosby Distinguished Chair in the Humanities
Fisk University

**Edited by**
Jeffrey Muhr

**Who's Who Among African Americans, 32nd Edition**

Project Editor: Jeffrey Muhr

Editorial: Katherine H. Nemeh

Editorial Support Services: Natalyia Mikheyeva

Composition and Electronic Prepress: Mobius365 Knowledge Services

Manufacturing: Rita Wimberley



*Gale*
27500 Drake Rd.
Farmington Hills, MI, 48331-3535

ISBN-13: 978-1-4103-2533-4

ISSN 1081-1400

Printed in the United States of America
1 2 3 4 5 6 7 20 19 18 17

# Advisory Board

# Contents

# Foreword

Since this series began publication over forty years ago, it has been issued under different titles, yet it remains unique as one of the most extensive and current sources of easily–accessible biographical information on African Americans. The lives of the entrants remind us of luminaries from our past who pioneered and achieved against seemingly insurmountable odds, or who opened what were thought to be impenetrable pathways, who enhanced the cultural life of a people, or who crafted new ways of knowing. It is easy to still see among living African Americans traces of the great work of those long departed, such as the political protest of women like abolitionist Sojourner Truth, the oration of reformer Frederick Douglass, the activism and scholarship of Pan-Africanist W. E. B. Du Bois, the creative genius of poet Phillis Wheatley, or the pioneering and educational leadership of school founder Mary McLeod Bethune. A lingering query, however, is how these pioneers succeeded against the backdrop of the world in which they lived. President Barack Obama showed us that black people can still achieve in this modern day. We have among us those who continue to pursue their vision, who extend the frontiers of knowledge, and who labor hard to remove what some identify as the "effects of neglectful times."

The *Who's Who among African Americans* series is always rich with those who make our history happen, who make literary talent blossom. It is enriched by those who shape public policy, the ones who educate our children, the ones who account for the entrepreneurial development of our communities, those who provide cultural enlightenment, pioneers and champions of racial equality, and so on. Their lives document the fact that African Americans voice their concern for self-expression, which, knowingly or not, makes their dreams come true. Now that the leader whom black America has cherished for eight years leaves his position at the White House, it is appropriate to revisit the words of President Obama in his book, *Dreams from My Father*, who writes about coming of age, the "awkward steps toward manhood," of being a black man with a funny name, of living long enough to see some of the ills of history return with a vengeance, the "desperation and disorder of the powerless," and finally about the power of constant love and support of family and love and respect for them. His book is a collection of stories, of tales handed down in a family. And that characterizes much of what African American life is all about. As we close the curtain on President Obama and his main stage of public life, we know that the spotlight will remain on him and his work, possibly more so than any other entrant in *Who's Who among African Americans.*

For each edition of this "who's who" we continue to cast our nets widely and in return have a bountiful catch of African American achievers. Perhaps it is appropriate to begin with the inclusion of Kevin Young: the writer, poet, educator, curator of rare books, and the new director of Harlem's Schomburg Center for Research in Black Culture—a place where the work of African Americans is collected, recorded, preserved, and made available for public use. Like the other repositories of our history—Hampton, Howard, Fisk, Clark Atlanta, and Tuskegee universities—this is a place where the scholarship of the race is continually available for analysis and interpretation. In the arts, much praise and discussion centers on the Broadway play *Hamilton.* Among its stars, we focus on actors/singers Victor Dixon Brandon and Leslie Odom Jr. Also in the arts we cite the highly-touted Taraji P. Henson, a star in the hit television musical drama *Empire* and the movie *Hidden Figures*; actor/singer Tituss Burgess, who continues to appear in Broadway musicals, and comedian Leslie Jones, a hit on the popular television show *Saturday Night Live.* Already established in the arts field is singer/actor Audra McDonald, a Tony-award-winner who has appeared in ten Broadway productions.

In education, several of our entrants have distinguished themselves to the extent that they now head colleges and universities. Those at historically black colleges and universities include James E. Clark, president of South Carolina State University; Herman J. Felton Jr., president of Wilberforce University; Forrest Eliot Harris, president of American Baptist College, the most recently-acclaimed four-year HBCU; and Harold Martin, president of North Carolina A&T State University. In mainstream America, Swarthmore College now has is first African American president and educator Valerie Smith. Some of our entrants have achieved in the public sector schools. Nashville, Tennessee, boasts its first African American superintendent of public schools in the selection of educator Shawn Joseph.

African Americans have been characterized as a religious people. Those who continue to ensure that we wear that title with pride include Jamal Harrison Bryant, named by *Time* magazine as one of the key figures to move this generation forward; Judy Fentress-Williams, professor of Old Testament at Virginia Theological Seminary and minister at historic Alfred Street Baptist Church in Alexandria, Virginia; Sharma Lewis, first African American woman elected bishop by the North Georgia Conference of the United Methodist Church; Byron E. Thomas, pastor of Atlanta's Ben Hill United Methodist Church; and Dorien Warren, pastor and activist of Alfred Street Baptist Church.

African Americans continue to excel in sports, including events such as the 2016 Summer Olympics held in Brazil. The nation cheered Simon Biles, gymnast and the first African American to win all-around title at three consecutive World Championships. Since 1908, when track and field icon

John Taylor won Black America's first Olympic gold medal at the Summer Games held in London, African Americans have continued to excel in that sport. Allison Felix is another sports champion who achieved in track and field at the London games, winning silver in the 400-meter relay. American sabre fencer Ibtihaj Muhammad, the first black American woman to complete in the Olympics in fencing, acquitted herself well at the 2016 Summer Games, becoming an Olympic bronze medalist. She represented America's fencing team and was also the first U.S. female athlete to wear traditional Muslim covering, or a hijab, while competing in an Olympic event. Previously, she won bronze while competing in the Fencing World Cup in Athens.

African Americans have been engaged locally, nationally, and even internationally as entrepreneurs, corporate executives of major firms, and journalists. In this year some kept alive the tragedies that led to the founding of the movement Black Lives Matter. As an example, in Ferguson, Missouri, known for a white police officer's shooting of unarmed black teenager Michael Brown on August 9, 2014, Delrish Moss was hired as the town's police chief, the first African American to hold that position. Their lives round out the new entrants in WWAA.

Although not a new entrant, we cite the achievement and update the biography of Carla Hayden, who became the fourteenth Librarian of Congress and the first African American woman to hold that post. Her noteworthy achievement won the praise of women, librarians, and African Americans.

For those who passed on in 2016, the results of their labor planted a seed in their honor to signal a life well lived, a new spirit awakened, a path untouched. When giants depart, the void that they leave is enormous, and so are the memories and recounts of their accomplishments. Among these legends were singer/song-writer and pop icon Prince; newsmaker Gwen Ifill; boxing champion Muhammad Ali; professional football coach, player and football executive Dennis Green; and Edward Temple, women's track coach for Tennessee State University's Tigerbells and several U.S. women's track teams, including Olympic winners.

The much-used phrase, "history repeats itself," is still an established fact; so is the fact that the WWAA series continues to identify and present to the public new people and new facts that may be identified as "living history." The importance and necessity of the series is omnipresent.

Jessie Carney Smith
Dean of the Library
Camille Cosby Distinguished Chair in the Humanities
Fisk University

# Introduction

Now in its thirty-second edition, *Who's Who Among African Americans (WWAFA)* is your guide to more than 18,785 men and women who have changed today's world and are shaping tomorrow's. The biographical entries you will find on these pages reflect the diversity of African-American achievement by documenting the contributions of leaders in all fields of endeavor. Together these entries make *Who's Who Among African Americans* the most comprehensive publication devoted to recording the accomplishments of African Americans.

## Compilation Methods

The selection of *WWAFA* listees is based primarily on reference value. In order to identify noteworthy new achievers and monitor significant events in the lives of current listees, the editorial staff scans a wide variety of books, magazines, newspapers, and other material on an ongoing basis. Associations, businesses, government offices, and colleges and universities were also contacted for their suggestions. Users, current listees, and members of the *WWAFA* Advisory Board continue to provide their recommendations as well.

These candidates become eligible for inclusion by virtue of positions held through election or appointment to office, notable career achievements, or outstanding community service. Black persons who are not American citizens are considered eligible if they live or work in the United States and contribute significantly to American life. Such broad coverage makes *Who's Who Among African Americans* the logical source for you to consult when gathering facts on a distinguished leader or a favorite celebrity, locating a colleague, contacting an expert, recruiting personnel, or launching a fund-raising effort.

Once this identification process is complete, we make an effort to secure information directly from biographees. In absense of this, we gather information from reliable sources. Those candidates whose achievements merit inclusion proceed through the remaining stages of entry compilation.

In an almost simultaneous process, current listees receive copies of their entries from the most recent edition in which they appeared. They then update their biographies as necessary to reflect new career positions, address changes, or recent awards and achievements.

Sometimes potential and current listees decline to furnish biographical data. Recognizing that this does not satisfy your need for comprehensiveness, we have compiled selected entries from a variety of secondary sources to help ensure that the people you want to see in *WWAFA* are indeed listed. These entries are marked by an *asterisk (*)*, indicating that the listees have not personally provided or reviewed the data, but you still benefit from having basic biographical information at your fingertips.

## Important Features

To complement its thorough coverage, *Who's Who Among African Americans* uses these important features to help you locate the information you need:

- **Boldface Rubrics** allow quick and easy scanning for specifics on personal data, educational background, career positions, organizational affiliations, honors and awards, special achievements, military service, home address, business address, and telephone number.

- **Obituaries Section** provides you with entries on recently deceased newsworthy African Americans. This section provides a full entry plus date and place of death, when available.

## Indexing

*Who's Who Among African Americans* features two indexes, both of which make quick work of your searches:

- **Geographic Index.** Locate biographees by specific city, state, and country of residence and/or employment. (Only those listees who agree to allow their addresses to be printed in the directory will appear in this index.)

- **Occupation Index.** With more than 150 categories, this index allows you to identify listees working in fields ranging from accounting to zoology.

## Acknowledgments

The editors wish to thank the Advisory Board members whose names appear at the front of this volume for their advice and encouragement as we compiled this edition of *Who's Who Among African Americans.*

We would also like to thank the many individuals and organizations who nominated achievers for consideration in this edition.

## Available in Electronic Formats

***Licensing.*** *Who's Who Among African Americans* is available for licensing. The complete database is provided in a fielded format and is deliverable on such media as disk or CD-ROM. For more information, contact Gale's Business Development Group at 1-800-877-GALE, or visit our website at http://gale.cengage.com/bizdev.

***Online.*** *WWAFA* is accessible online as part of the Gale Biographies (GALBIO) database accessible through LexisNexis, P.O. Box 933, Dayton, OH 45401-0933; phone: 937-865-6800; toll-free: 800-227-9597.

## Suggestions Welcome

Comments and suggestions from users on any aspect of *WWAFA* are cordially invited to write:

The Editor

*Who's Who Among African Americans*

Gale

27500 Drake Road

Farmington Hills, MI 48331-3535

# Key to Biographical Information

▮1▮ **MATNEY, WILLIAM C., JR. [In Memoriam]**
▮2▮ Federal official (retired), communications consultant. ▮ 3 ▮ **Personal:** Born Sep 02, 1924, Bluefield, WV; died June 13, 2001, La Plata, MD; son of William C Matney Sr and Jane A Matney; widowed; children: Alma, Angelique, William III. ▮ 4 ▮ **Educ:** Wayne State Univ, 1940-42; Univ of Michigan, BA, 1946. ▮ 5 ▮ **Career:** The Michigan Chronicle, reporter, sports editor, city editor, mng editor, 1946-61; Detroit News, reporter, writer, 1962-63; WMAQ-NBC, TV and radio reporter, 1963-65; NBC Network Television, correspondent, 1966-72; ABC Network News, correspondent, 1972-78; Who's Who among Black Americans, founding editor, 1974-88, consulting editor, 1988-93; US Bureau of the Census, sr public affairs coord, 1979-93. ▮ 6 ▮ **Orgs:** Mem, Big Ten Championship Track Team, 1943; pres, Cotillion Club, 1962-63; mem, NAACP, AFTRA; Alpha Phi Alpha; Natl Acad of Television Arts and Sciences. ▮ 7 ▮ **Honors/Awds:** Natl Achievement Award, Lincoln Univ, 1966; Man of the Year, Intl Pioneers, 1966; Sigma Delta Chi Citation, 1967; Outstanding Achievement Citation (Emmy), Natl Acad of Television Arts and Sciences, 1967; Natl Award, Southern Press In st, 1976; Hon Dr Jour, Benedict Coll, 1973; Outstanding TV Correspondent, Women in Media, 1977; Outstanding Natl Corres Serv Award, Michigan Minority Business Enterprise Assn, 1977; Natl Advisory Comm, Crisis Magazine, NAACP, 1981-91. ▮ 8 ▮ **Special Achievements:** First Black exec sec, Michigan State Ath Assn, 1950-61; First Black reporter, Detroit News, 1960-63; First Black network news correspondent, NBC-News, 1965-70; First Black correspondent permanently assigned to the White House, Washington NBC News, 1970-72. ▮ 9 ▮ **Military Serv:** USAAF, 1943-45. ▮ 10 ▮ **Business Addr:** Former Sr Public Affairs Specialist, US Bureau of the Census, Washington, DC 20233.

## Description

▮ 1 ▮ Name of biographee.
▮ 2 ▮ Occupation.
▮ 3 ▮ Personal data.
▮ 4 ▮ Educational background.
▮ 5 ▮ Career information.
▮ 6 ▮ Organizational affiliations.
▮ 7 ▮ Honors/Awards.
▮ 8 ▮ Special Achievements.
▮ 9 ▮ Military Service.
▮ 10 ▮ Home and/or business address and telephone number (at listee's discretion).

Biographees are listed alphabetically by surname. In cases where the surnames are identical, biographees are arranged first by surname, then by first and middle names, and finally by suffixes such as Jr., Sr., or II, III, etc. Surnames beginning with a prefix (such as Du, Mac, or Van), however spaced, are listed alphabetically under the first letter of the prefix and are treated as if there were no space. Other compound surnames, hyphenated names, and names with apostrophes, likewise, are alphabetized as if there were no space or punctuation. Surnames beginning with Saint, Sainte, St., or Ste. appear after names that begin with Sains and before names that begin with Sainu.

# Abbreviations Table

|  |  |
|---|---|
| AK | Alaska |
| AL | Alabama |
| Apr | April |
| AR | Arkansas |
| Aug | August |
| AZ | Arizona |
| CA | California |
| CO | Colorado |
| CT | Connecticut |
| DC | District of Columbia |
| DE | Delaware |
| Dec | December |
| Feb | February |
| FL | Florida |
| GA | Georgia |
| HI | Hawaii |
| IA | Iowa |
| ID | Idaho |
| IL | Illinois |
| IN | Indiana |
| Jan | January |
| Jul | July |
| Jun | June |
| KS | Kansas |
| KY | Kentucky |
| LA | Louisiana |
| MA | Massachusetts |
| Mar | March |
| MD | Maryland |
| ME | Maine |
| MI | Michigan |
| MN | Minnesota |
| MO | Missouri |
| MT | Montana |
| NC | North Carolina |
| NH | New Hampshire |
| NJ | New Jersey |
| NM | New Mexico |
| Nov | November |
| NUL | National Urban League |
| NV | Nevada |
| NY | New York |
| Oct | October |
| OH | Ohio |
| OK | Oklahoma |
| OR | Oregon |
| PA | Pennsylvania |
| PR | Puerto Rico |
| PUSH | People United to Save Humanity |
| RI | Rhode Island |
| SC | South Carolina |
| SCLC | Southern Christian Leadership Conference |
| SD | South Dakota |
| Sep | September |
| TN | Tennessee |
| TX | Texas |
| UT | Utah |
| VA | Virginia |
| VI | Virgin Islands |
| VT | Vermont |
| WA | Washington |
| WI | Wisconsin |
| WV | West Virginia |
| WY | Wyoming |

# Biographies

# A

## AARON, HENRY LOUIS (HANK AARON)

Baseball player, executive. **Personal:** Born Feb 5, 1934, Mobile, AL; son of Edwin Caldwell and Pearl Caldwell; married Billye Williams; children: Ceci; married Barbara Lucas; children: Gail, Hank, Lary, Gary (deceased) & Dorenda. **Educ:** Josephine Allen Inst, attended 1951. **Career:** Prof baseball player (retired), baseball executive; Mobile Black Bears, right fielder; Indianapolis Clowns, Negro Am League, prof baseball player, right fielder, 1952; Milwaukee Braves, Eau Claire, right fielder, 1954-65, vpres player develop, 1975-76; Atlanta Braves, right fielder, 1954-74; Milwaukee Brewers, 1975-76; Atlanta Nat League Baseball Club Inc, farm syst dir, 1976-90, vpres, spec asst pres, 1990, sr vpres & mem bd dir, currently; Hank Aaron Automotive Group Inc, pres, currently; 755 Restaurant Corp, owner, currently; CNN Airport Network, bd dirs, vpres bus develop, currently; Medallion Financial Corp, bd dir, 2004-. **Orgs:** Sponsor, Hank Aaron Celebrity Bowling Tourn Sickle Cell Anemia, 1972; Negro Am Leagues Indianapolis Clowns; pres, No Greater Love, 1974-; nat sports chmn, Nat Easter Seal Soc, 1974; nat chmn, Friends Fisk Athletes; state chmn Wis Easter Seals Soc, 1975; Atlanta Comt Progress, 2004. **Honors/Awds:** NL batting title, Nat League, 1956, 1959; NL home run champion, Nat League, 1957, 1963, 1966, 1967; World Series champion, 1957; Most Valuable Player Award, Nat League, 1957; Gold Glove Award, 1958, 1959, 1960; Lou Gehrig Memorial Award, 1970; Gerogia Sports Hall of Fame, 1975; Gold Glove Award; MLB Hall of Fame, 1982; Presidential Citizens Medal; Presidential Medal of Freedom, 2002; Hank Aaron State Trail, Milwaukee, Wisc, named in honor, 2006. **Special Achievements:** Hank Aaron BMW ranked 87, BE Top 100 Auto Dealers, 2001; One of Most Influential Atlantans, Atlanta Bus J, 2004; Broke Babe Ruth's home run rec April 18, 1974; Holds 18 maj league rec; holds 9 Nat League rec; co-author autobiography, I Had a Hammer, Harper, 1991; dedicated, Hank Aaron-Chasing the Dream, to Baseball Hall of Fame, 2009. **Business Addr:** President, Co-Founder, Hank Aaron Automotive Enterprises LLC, 4171 Jonesboro Rd, Union City, GA 30291-2251, **Business Phone:** (770)969-0755.

## ABADEY, NASAR

Musician. **Educ:** State Univ NY, Buffalo; Howard Univ; Univ DC. **Career:** Songs: "Mirage", Amosaya Records; "Better Days", Karen Francis& Virgo Rising Records; "Secrets of the Soul", Sendy Brown& Po Tolo Music; "Steppin' Out", Sandra Y. Johnson& SYJ Productions; "Finally", Sharon Clark; "Rising Day Star", Malachi Thompson & Delmark Records; "NewStandards", Malachi Thompson & Delmark Records; "Spirits", Malachi Thompson & Delmark Records; "The Jaz Life", Malachi Thompson & Delmark Records; "47th Street", Malachi Thompson & Delmark Records; "Freebop Now!", Malachi Thompson & Delmark Records; "Timeline", Malachi Thompson & Delmark Records; "Songbook", Gerry Eastman & WMC Records; "Native Son", Gerry Eastman & WMC Records; "My Real Self", Gerry Eastman & WMC Records; "Today's Nights", Joe Ford & Mesa Records; "Yoka Boka", Jeff Majors; "Keyto Nowhere", Brother Ah & Sounds of Awareness & Divine Records; "Free Spirits", Birthright& Freelance Records; "Breathe of Life", Birthright & Freelance records; "Timbre Tambre", Rey Scott & Planetary Lights Records; "Sweet Heritage", Jaman Quartet & Mark Records. Brown Univ, artist in residence, 1981-82; Young Audiences, Wash, DC, 1984-04; Levine Sch Music, artist in residence, 1988-90; Creative Arts Performance, 1989-93; Birthright, band co-founder & co-leader; Prince George's Arts Coun & Thelonious Monk Inst Jazz, teacher & performer, 1995-99; Smithsonian Jazz Camp, artist in residence, 2001-02; Savoy Elem Sch, Wash, DC, artist in residence, 2004; John Hopkins Univ, Peabody Inst, fac, 2006-07; The Rough, DPC, 2011; Supernova, band founder, leader, currently. **Orgs:** Panelist, Mid Atlantic Arts Found; Panelist, Nat Endowment Arts & Humanities; Panelist, DC Comn Arts; bd mem, Wash Area Lawyers Asn; artist-in-residence, Honda Dream Lab Proj, Wash, DC; Int Asn Jazz Educr; Int Musicians Union Local, 161-710, Wash, DC; Prince Georges Arts Coun; bd mem, Area Lawyers Arts. **Honors/ Awds:** Creative Artist Performance Service Award, NY State composition; Creative Communities Initiative Grant Award, Community Found Nat Capital Region; Prince Georges Arts Council Grant Award. **Special Achievements:** Capital Bop-Complete DC Jazz Guide Selected one five Top CDs 2010. **Business Addr:** Jazz Musician, SuperNova, 6200 Kilmer St, Cheverly, MD 20785, **Business Phone:** (301)341-5255.

## ABBOA-OFFEI, ABENAA

Vice president (organization). **Personal:** married John Udochi. **Educ:** Syracuse Univ, BS, journalism, 1991; Am Health Ins Plans, managed care exec cert. **Career:** Am Broadcasting Co., advert & publicity mgr, 1991-93; First Baptist Community Develop Corp., pub affairs dir 1993-95; Abenaa Abboa-Offei Pub Rels Inc, founder; Affinity Health Plan, from vpres, customer serv & pub affairs to exec dir State Govt Progs & chief mkt Officer 2003-. **Orgs:** Bd mem, New York Mission Soc; bd mem, YouthBridgeNY; New York Coalition 100 Black Women; Pub Affairs Coun. **Honors/Awds:** "The Network Journal: Black Professionals & Small Business Magazine", 25 Influential Black Women, 2009. **Business Addr:** Affinity Health Plan Inc, 2500 Halsey St, New York City, NY 10461, **Business Phone:** (718)794-7700.

## ABBOTT, LEANDRA

Public utility executive. **Career:** Cosmopolitan mag, staff mem; Newsweek mag, reporter, 1967-69; Community News Serv, reporter; Zambia Times, reporter; Consol Edison NY Inc, asst dir community rels & corp philanthropy, asst vpres community rels & consumer rels, currently. **Orgs:** Exec vol, United Way NY; Am Asn Blacks in Energy. **Honors/Awds:** All-Star, NY Women's Agenda, 1994; Lifetime Service Award, Consol Edison Inc, 2001. **Special Achievements:** First black female staff in Cosmopolitan Magazine. **Business Addr:** Assistant Vice President, Consol Edison Inc, 701 Westchester Ave Suite 300 E, White Plains, NY 10604, **Business Phone:** (914)286-7000.

## ABDUL-JABBAR, KAREEM (FERDINAND LEWIS ALCINDOR, JR.)

Athletic coach, basketball player, writer. **Personal:** Born Apr 16, 1947, New York, NY; son of Ferdinand Lewis Alcindor Sr and Cora Lillian; married Habiba; children: Habiba, Sultana & Kareem Jr; married Cheryl Pistono; children: Amir & Adam. **Educ:** Univ Calif, Los Angeles, BA, hist, 1969. **Career:** Basketball player, basketball coach, actor, producer (retired); National Basketball Association Milwaukee Bucks, 1969-75; Los Angeles Lakers, 1975-89, spec asst coach, 2005-11; Alchesay High Sch, White Mountain Apache Reservation, asst coach, 1999; Los Angeles Clippers, asst coach; Ind Pacers & Seattle Supersonics, player consult; USBL Okla Storm, coach, 2002; NY Knicks, player consult & scout; Phil Jackson, spec asst; Los Angeles Lakers, spec asst coach, 2006-; Producer: co-exec producer, "Vernon Johns Story", 1994; Shoulders Giants, 2007. Books: Giant Steps: An Autobiography Kareem Abdul-Jabbar, 1983; Kareem, 1990; Black Profiles Courage: A Legacy African Am Achievement, 1996; A Season Reservation: My Sojourn with Mountain Apaches, 2000; Bros Arms: Epic Story 761st Tank Battalion, 2004; Shoulders Giants: My Journey Through Harlem Renaissance, 2007. Tv Series: "Mannix", 1971; "Emergency!", 1974; "Man from Atlantis", 1977; "Tales from the Darkside", 1985; "Diff'rent Strokes", 1982-1985; "Bustin' Loose", 1987; "Jake Spanner, Private Eye", 1989; "21 Jump Street", 1990; "Amen", 1991; "Uncle Buck", 1991; "Matrix", 1993; "The Critic", 1994; "Martin", 1996; "Saved by the Bell: The New Class", 1998; "Guys with Kids", 2013. **Orgs:** Founder, Skyhook Found, 2010. **Business Addr:** Special Assistant Coach, Los Angeles Lakers, 555 N Nash St, El Segundo, CA 90245, **Business Phone:** (310)426-6000.

## ABDUL-MALIK, DR. IBRAHIM

Executive director, counselor, educator. **Personal:** Born New York, NY. **Educ:** City Univ NY, BS, 1952, MA, 1954; Harvard Univ, EdD, 1971; Grad Theol Found, PhD, 2007. **Career:** Teacher & asst prin & staff developer, 1954-65; Bank St Col, Educ Resource Ctr, dir, 1965-68; Harlem Sch NYC, prin, 1968-69; New York Urban Educ, Develop Div Ctr, dir, 1971-72; New York Bd Educ, Bd Examiners, vice chmn, 1972-74, educ planner, 1974-76, sci assoc, 1976-79; curric spec col, univ fac; educ coun, admin, res, writer, health counr, pract, nutrit consult; Ctr Higher Sec Educ, prin; City Univ New York, City Col, adj prof; Baruch Col, adj prof; UN Summer Internship Prog, assoc dir; Fairleigh Dickinson Univ, Metrop Campus, Islamic chaplain; Grad Theol Found, prof Am Muslim hist & cult, currently; Ctr Empowerment & Personal Growth, dir, currently. **Orgs:** Bd dir, Harlem Neighborhood Asn, 1968-70; Community Serv Soc; Family Life Educ Comn, 1966-70; overseas sci adv, Univ Educ, Sci & Cult Org, 1979-81; Nat Asn Bilingual Educ; Am Asn Sch Personnel Admin; Int Coun Educ Teaching; Kappa Delta Pi; Phi Delta Kappa; consult, Grad Theol Found, Muslim Educ Coun Clergy Am; sci advisor, Un Educ Sci & Cult Orgn; neuro-ling programming practr, World Health Community; fel NSF; co-founder, Imams Coun New York. **Special Achievements:** Book: "The Joys and Rewards of Prayer-A Guide for Beginners, A Reminder for Believers". **Home Addr:** 315 W 70 St, New York, NY 10023. **Business Addr:** Professor, Graduate Theological Foundation, The Dodge House, Mishawaka, IN 46544, **Business Phone:** (574)255-3642.

## ABDUL-RAHMAN, TAHIRA SADIQA

Real estate agent. **Personal:** Born Dec 15, 1947, Shreveport, LA; daughter of Albert Maurice Moody Sr and Estella Martin; married Mustafa; children: Jamilla, Zainab, Naeema, Ibn & Ismail. **Educ:** Howard Univ, BA, 1968; Howard Univ Sch Soc Work, MSW, 1970; Adams Inst Mkt Shreveport, LA, attended 1990; Baker's Prof Real Estate Col, Shreveport, LA, attended 1990. **Career:** New Careers Prog, specialty instr, 1970-71; Parent & Child Ctr, supvr, 1971-72; Morgan Univ, assoc prof, 1972-74; Assoc Comm Training Inc, dir homemaker prog, 1984-86; Marak Realty, Shreveport, LA, realtor & assoc, 1986-90; Family Ctr Asn Community Training Inc, dir, 1987-88; Tahira & Assoc Realty, Shreveport, LA, realtor, broker, property mgr, chief exec officer & owner, 1990-. **Orgs:** Pres, PTA West Shreveport Elem Sch, 1982-84; exec bd mem, Dist Parent Teachers Asn, 1984-85; guest columnist, Shreveport Sun, 1985-87; vpres, PTA Booker T Wash High Sch, 1986-87; steering comt, YMCA Annual Awareness Banquet, 1986; guest speaker, Annual Luncheon Sr Citizens Union Mission Baptist Church, 1987; Delta Sigma Theta Sorority Inc, Polit Action Community Delta Sigma Theta Sor Inc; pres, Booker T Wash High Sch Alumni Found, 1990-; chairperson, fundraiser comt, Nat Asn Women Bus Owners, Shreveport Chap, 1991-; pres, Shreveport/Bossit Chap Women's Coun Realtors, 2001-; pres-elect State Chap Women's Coun Realtors, 2004; bd mem, LA Realtors; Nat Asn Prof Women, 2014-. **Honors/Awds:** Certificate of Appreciation, W Shreveport Sch, 1980-87; Honorary Life Member, La State PTA, 1984; Outstanding Leadership Award, W Shreveport Sch PTA, 1984; Outstanding Realtor/Asniate, Marak Ralty, 1988; Emerging Young Leader, YWCA Allendale Br, Shreveport, 1989; Outstanding Service Award, BTW Alumni Found, 1990; Outstanding Leadership, 1995; Business Award, Shreveport African-Am Chamber Community; Outstanding Business Woman of the Year Award, Shreveport-Bossier African Am Chamber of Com, 2009; Award of Excellence, City Shreveport, 2009. **Home Addr:** 9203 Midvale Dr, Shreveport, LA 71118. **Business Addr:** Owner, Broker & Chief Executive officer, Tahira & Associates Realty Inc, 449 Stoner Ave, Shreveport, LA 71101-4120, **Business Phone:** (318)425-2707.

## ABDUL-RAUF, MAHMOUD (CHRIS WAYNE JACKSON)

Basketball player, clergy. **Personal:** Born Mar 9, 1969, Gulfport, MS; son of Jacqueline Jackson; married Kim; children: 5. **Educ:** La State Univ, attended 1989. **Career:** Basketball player, Imam; Denver Nuggets, guard, 1990-96; Sacramento Kings, 1996-98; Fenerbahce, EuroLeague, 1998-99; Vancouver Grizzlies, 2000-01; Ural Great basketball team, Russia, 2003-04; Sedima Roseto, Italy, 2004-05; Aris Thessaloniki, Greece, 2006-07; Al Ittihad Jeddah, 2007-08; Kyoto Hannaryz, 2009-11; Masjid al-Haqq, imam, currently. **Business Addr:** Imam, Masjid al-Haqq, Suite 229 45 Hardy Ct, Gulfport, MS 39507.

## ABDUL-WAHAD, TARIQ (OLIVIER SAINT-JEAN)

Basketball coach, basketball player. **Personal:** Born Nov 3, 1974, Val de Marne; son of George Goudet and Luc Saint-Jean; married Khadijah Ibn Lahoucine; children: Amine, Hind & Anas. **Educ:** Univ Mich, attended 1995; San Jose State Univ, BA, hist, 1997, MA, hist, 2009. **Career:** Basketball player (retired), basketball coach, executive; Univ Mich; Alm Evreux, France, 1990-93; Sacramento Kings, forward & guard, 1997-99; Orlando Magic, 1999-2000; Denver Nuggets, 2000-02; Dallas Mavericks, 2002-07; Dar Sohane/Dar Al Wafa, partner, 2006-; Saul Productions, partner, 2006-; 610 Brasil, partner, 2008-; BlueSox Basketball, dir opers, 2010-; Cal State Monterey Bay, asst coach, 2011-12; Abraham Lincoln High Sch, San Jose, Calif, coach, 2012-. **Orgs:** Seed Acad. **Business Addr:** Head Coach, About Abraham Lincoln High School, 2162 24th Ave, San Francisco, CA 94116, **Business Phone:** (415)759-2700.

**ABDULLAH, DR. LARRY RICHARD BURLEY**
Dentist. **Personal:** Born Apr 17, 1947, Malvern, AR; children: Zakkiyya, Jeffery, Kerry, Larry II & Najla. **Educ:** Univ Ariz, BS, 1968; Meharry Med Col, DDS, 1972; Govs State Univ, MHA, 1996, PhD. **Career:** Pvt pract dent surgeon. **Orgs:** Guardian PPO; Am Dent Asn, 1974-, Chicago Dent Soc, 1974-, Ill Dent Asn, 1974-, Acad Gen Dent, 1974-, Am Straight Wire Orthod Soc, 1982-; Health Vols Overseas, 1994-. **Honors/Awds:** Fel, Acad Gen Dent, 1987. **Home Addr:** 22715 Torrence Ave, Chicago Heights, IL 60411. **Business Addr:** Dentist, Private Practice, 7013 S W Ave Suite 1, Chicago, IL 60636-3121, **Business Phone:** (773)476-0600.

**ABDULLAH, DR. MAKOLA**
Educator. **Personal:** married Ahkinyala; children: Mikaili & Sefiyetu. **Educ:** Howard Univ, BS, civil engineering, 1990; Northwestern Univ, MS, civil engineering, 1991, PhD, civil engineering, 1994. **Career:** Northwestern Univ, Dept Civil Engineering, res & teaching asst, 1990-94; Chicago State Univ, Dept Chem & Phys, adj prof, 1994-96; Jackson & Tull Chartered Engrs, Wash, DC, proj mgr, 1994-96; Fla A&M Univ, Div Engineering Tech, asst prof, 1996-98, Dept Civil Engineering, from asst prof to prof, 1996-2011, assoc vpres res, 2005-08, dir diversity prog, Technol & Agr, dean, 2008-11, dir, prof civil & construct engineering technol, Wind Hazard & Earthquake Engineering Lab, advisor; NSF; Boeing; NASA; Fla Memorial Univ, provost & vpres acad affairs, 2011-13; Bethune-Cookman Univ, provost & chief acad officer, 2013-. **Orgs:** Nat Soc Black Engrs, 1986-; Am Soc Civil Engrs, 1988-; Tau Beta Pi Engineering Hon Soc. **Special Achievements:** Recognized as the youngest African American to ever receive a PhD in engineering from Northwestern University. **Home Addr:** 1912 Wahalaw Ct, Tallahassee, FL 32301, **Home Phone:** (850)309-1509. **Business Addr:** Provost, Chief Academic Officer, Bethune-Cookman University, Thomas White Hall, Daytona Beach, FL 32114, **Business Phone:** (386)481-2042.

**ABDULLAH, MUSTAFA (MUSTAFA ROCKS)**
Executive, designer. **Career:** Original Afro Wear Inc, co-founder, 1996-. **Business Addr:** Co-Founder, Original AfroWear Inc, 1560 E 61st St Suite 2 E, Chicago, IL 60637-3049, **Business Phone:** (773)437-5425.

**ABDULLAH, RABIH FARD**
Football player. **Personal:** Born Apr 27, 1975, Martinsville, VA; son of Shahid; married Nichole. **Educ:** Lehigh Univ, BA, intl bus, 1998. **Career:** Football player (retired); Lehigh Univ, player, 1993-97; Tampa Bay Buccaneers, running back & fullback, 1998-2001; Chicago Bears, running back, 2002-03; New Eng Patriots, running back, 2004.

**ABDULLAH, DR. SAMELLA BERRY**
Educator, psychotherapist, consultant. **Personal:** Born Mar 9, 1934, Chicago, IL; daughter of Samuel and Addie Berry; children: Tracey Everett-Carter, Makola M & G Noora. **Educ:** Howard Univ, BS, psychol, sociol & educ, 1955, MSW, psychiat social work, 1959; Univ Pittsburgh, community probs rehab, 1956; Heed Univ, PhD, coun psychol, 1978. **Career:** Legal Aid Soc, social worker, 1962-63; Northwestern Univ Med Sch, med social worker, 1964-69; City Chicago, Ment Health admin, social worker to ctr dir, 1973-77; Chicago Bd Health, Ment Health Bur, coordr: c & adolescent serv & intake to-ctr dir, 1973-77; Abdullah & Assocs, owner, counr, consult & chief therapist, 1979-; Ill Sch Prof Psych, prof, 1987-95; FL A&M Univ, adj prof, 2001, 04; United Health Care, provider, 2004-09; Afi Coun Assoc, owner & primary psychotherapist & state qualified supvr, 2005-09; Home Based Consultative Serv, independent writer/speaker, 2009-12. **Orgs:** Nat Asn Black Social Workers, 1969-; nat bd dir, Asn Black Psychologists, 1985-87, 1996-97; life mem & nat secy, Asn Black Psychologists, 1986-88; nat pres, Asn Black Psychologists 1998-99; co-founder, Chicago Coalition Against Violence Inst; Nat Asn Social Workers; partner, Alliance Childhood; Am Psychol Asn; ed bd, Ethical Human Psychol & Psychiat. **Home Addr:** 1402 Nancy Dr, Tallahassee, FL 32301, **Home Phone:** (850)309-0728. **Business Addr:** Owner, Therapist, Abdullah & Associates, 2892 E Pk Ave Suite 1 C, Tallahassee, FL 32301-2729, **Business Phone:** (850)339-3723.

**ABDULLAH, SHARIF (VAUGHN ALLEN GOODWIN)**
Public speaker, businessperson, philanthropist. **Personal:** Born Jan 1, 1968, Philadelphia, PA; son of Alfred and Mary. **Educ:** Temple Univ, Philadelphia, PA; Morehouse Col, Atlanta, GA; Lancaster Univ; Islamic Teaching Ctr. **Career:** Temple Univ, Philadelphia, PA, asst dean students, 1988-89; Am Friends Serv Comt, stud consult; Vine Memorial Baptist Church, Philadelphia, PA, youth minister; Morehouse Col, Du Bois Hall, resident asst; Am Family Financial Servs, mortgage financial planner, currently; Ummah Int Found: A Muslim Investment Group, chief exec officer & founder. **Orgs:** Exec mem, Youth Sect, Dem Socialists Am; founder & pres, Temple Progressive Nat Asn Advan Colored People, 1988; speechwriter & speaker, Jesse Jackson Campaign, 1988; founder & chmn, Stud Coalition Racial Equality; Martin Luther King Int Chaplain Asst; Int Asn Fin Planning; Islamic Soc N Am; Metro-Atlanta Chamber Com; Speakers Bur; Consumer Credit Coun Serv Metro Atlanta; Ga Bankers Asn. **Honors/Awds:** Outstanding Scholastic Achievement, 1985; ACTSO Winner, Nat Asn Advan Colored People, 1985-86; Oratorical Contest Winner, Black History Month, 1985; Seniors of Pennsylvania Service Award, Outstanding Service, 1989; License, Nat Baptist Conv, 1990; Certificate of Outstanding Service, African Fel Fund; Certificate of Achievement, Islamic Teaching Ctr ISNA. **Special Achievements:** Young African-American Males in the 21st Century, 1994; Contributing author and editor: Towards 2000. **Home Addr:** 6901 Roosevelt Hwy, College Park, GA 30337, **Home Phone:** (404)767-5536. **Business Addr:** Mortgage Financial Planner, American Family Financial Services, 3565 Piedmont Rd Bldg 3 Suite 715, Atlanta, GA 30305, **Business Phone:** (404)814-1660.

**ABDULLAH, TALIB Z.**
Chief executive officer, screenwriter. **Personal:** Born Aug 10, 1973, Rochester, NY; married Mona; children: Basheer & Kamal. **Educ:** Buffalo State Col, BA, sociol; Clark Atlanta Univ, MSW. **Career:** Producer, currently; TV series: "Being Bobby Brown", assoc producer, 2005; TZA Assocs, founder, pres & chief exec officer, currently. **Orgs:** Chair, exec team, Nat Young Adult Asn; active mem, Masjid Nu'Man, pres, Muslim Stud Asn; active mem, Atlanta Masjid Al-Islam; ASM Islamic Affairs Coun; chair, pres, Am Soc Microbiol New York Acad Art; Chair, Masjid's young adult orgn; vice chair, Am Soc Muslims Nat Young Adult Asn's S E Sectional Rep. **Business Addr:** President, Chief Executive Officer & Founder, TZA Associates, 8328 Mission Dr Apt B, Rosemead, CA 91770.

**ABDULLAH-MUSA, OMALAWA**
Manager, architect. **Personal:** married Melissa Glasgow. **Educ:** City Univ NY, BA, archit, 1998. **Career:** New York Housing Authority, Design Dept, asst architect, 1997-99; DaSilva Black Calcagni Chesser, jr architect, 1999-2000; Larsen Shien Ginsburg & Magnusson LLP, capt, 2000-02; Magnusson Archit & Planning PC, architect, assoc, 2002-11; Stephen B Jacobs Group PC, proj mgr, 2011-13; Goldstein Hill & W Architects LLP, proj mgr, 2013-. **Business Addr:** Project Manager, Goldstein, Hill & West Architects LLP, 11 Broadway Suite 1700, New York, NY 10004, **Business Phone:** (212)213-8007.

**ABDULMAJID, IMAN MOHAMED**
Fashion model, actor, chief executive officer. **Personal:** Born Jul 25, 1955, Mogadishu; daughter of Mohamed and Marian; married Spencer Haywood; children: Zulekha; married David Bowie; children: Alexandria Zahra Jones. **Educ:** Univ Nairobi, Kenya, polit sci; NY Univ. **Career:** Wilhelmina Model Inc, 1975; Vogue, model, 1979; Film: The Human Factor, 1979; Jane Austen in Manhattan; 1980; Exposed, 1983; Out of Africa, 1985; Back in the World, 1985; No Way Out, 1987; Surrender, 1987; In the Heat of the Night, 1988; Love At First Sight, 1988; LA Story, 1991; House Party 2, 1991; Star Trek VI: The Undiscovered Country, 1991; The Linguini Incident, 1991; Remember the Time, 1992; Exit to Eden, 1994; The Deli, 1997; Omikron: The Nomad Soul, 1999; Project Runway Canada, host, 2007 & 2009; The Fashion Show: Ultimate Collection, host, 2010; TV series: "Miami Vice", 1985, "The Cosby Show", "Dream On", "In the Heat of the Night", 1989; "Heart of Darkness", 1994; Iman Cosmetics, chief exec officer & founder, 1994-. **Orgs:** C's Defense Fund; Action Against Hunger; All Kids Found. **Honors/Awds:** Fashion Icon Lifetime Achievement Award, Coun Fashion Designers Am, 2010. **Special Achievements:** Feb 29, 1980 declared Iman Day in NYC; Appeared in music video for Micheal Jackson's "Remember the Time", 1992; documentary creator, Somalia Diary, 1992; Autobiography, I Am Iman, 2001; The Beauty of Color: The Ultimate Guide for Skin of Color. **Business Addr:** Founder, Chief Executive Officer, Iman Cosmetics, 363 7th Ave Suite 8, Chantilly, VA 20151, **Business Phone:** (212)560-9906.

**ABDUR-RAHIM, SHAREEF**
Basketball player, president (organization), basketball coach. **Personal:** Born Dec 11, 1976, Marietta, GA; son of William and Aminah; married Delicia; children: Jabri & Samiyah. **Career:** Basketball player (retired), basketball coach; Vancouver Grizzlies, forward, 1996-2001; Atlanta Hawks, 2001-04; AVF Inc (now Abdur-Rahim Enterprises), Atlanta, Ga, pres, 2003-; Portland TrailBlazers, 2004-05; Sacramento Kings, forward, 2005-08, dir, asst gen mgr, asst coach, currently. TV Series: "Hang Time", 1997; "The Sport Jerks", 1998; "The Jamie Foxx Show", 1998; "NBA All-Star Game", 2002. **Orgs:** Founder, Future Found, 2001-. **Business Addr:** Founder, Future Foundation, 1892 Wash Rd, East Point, GA 30344, **Business Phone:** (404)766-0510.

**ABDUS-SALAAM, SHEILA**
Judge, lawyer. **Personal:** Born Washington, DC. **Educ:** Barnard Univ, BA, econs, 1974; Columbia Univ Law Sch, JD, 1977. **Career:** NY State Atty Gen's Off, Civil Rights Bur, lawyer; NY State Atty Gen's Off, Real Estate Fin Bur, lawyer; City NY, Dept Contract Compliance, gen coun; NY City Civil Ct, lawyer; Brooklyn Legal Servs, staff atty, 1977-80; NY Dept Law, asst atty, 1980-88; New York Off Labor Serv, gen coun, 1988-91; Civil Ct City New York, judge, 1992-93; NY State Supreme Ct, First Judicial Dist, judge, 1993-2009, justice, 1994-2012, Appellate Div, First Judicial Dept, assoc justice, 2009-13; Ny Ct Appeals, assoc judge, 2013. **Orgs:** NY Bar Asn, 1978; DC Bar Asn, 1979; Chair, Women's Housing & Econ Develop Corp, currently; asst atty Gen, civil Rights & Real Estate Financing Bureaus, 1980-88; gen coun, New York Off Labor Serv, 1988-91; senate, Ny; vice chair, Columbia Law Sch, currently. **Home Addr:** , New York, NY 10001. **Business Addr:** Associate Justice, New York State Supreme Court, 27 Madison Ave, New York, NY 10010, **Business Phone:** (212)340-0400.

**ABE, DR. BENJAMIN OMARA A.**
Educator. **Personal:** Born Nov 19, 1943, Gulu; married Joan B White; children: Daudi John & Peter Okech. **Educ:** Carleton Col, BA, social anthrop, 1968; Wash State Univ, MA, anthrop, 1970; Faith Grant Col, LLD. **Career:** N Seattle Community Col, Anthrop Dept, prof, 1970-, E African Study Tour Prog, dir, 1978-; Trans World Trading Corp, pres & chmn bd, 1974-75; BAS Assoc Int, managing gen partner, 1975-; phys anthropologist, currently. **Orgs:** Am Anthrop Asn; pres, Soc Anthrop Community Cols, 1999-2000; hon consult Uganda to Wash St; founder & chmn, African Chamber Com; Univ Dist Rotary Club Seattle; vol, Polio immunization works & clean water Proj Ethiopia; vpres & bd mem, Ugandan N Am Asn. **Home Addr:** 827 38th Ave, Seattle, WA 98122. **Business Addr:** Professor, North Seattle Community College, 9600 Col Way N, Seattle, WA 98103-3599, **Business Phone:** (206)934-3709.

**ABEBE, RUBY**
Civil rights activist. **Personal:** Born Apr 19, 1949, Waterloo, IA; children: Yeshimebet Marie, Tsehaynesh Eugena & Saba DyAnn. **Educ:** Univ IA, BA, 1972; Univ Northern. **Career:** Dept Agri, citizen adv to secy, 1991; Iowa City, civil rights coordr, 1994; Water 1st, owner, currently. **Orgs:** State chair, Nat Black Repubans, IA, 1984-; adhoc, Govt Branstad Black Adv Bd, 1985; adv bd, Sr Vol Prog, 1985; comnr, Iowa Civil Rights Comn, 1986-94; ABC; comnr, State IA Family Youth & C; Abebe Int; Adv Bd Blacks, State IA; IA City UN Asn USA; Affirmative Action Adv Bd, Oakdale Med Classification Ctr, Black Resource Guide. **Business Addr:** Owner, Water 1st, 621 Independence Ave, Waterloo, IA 50703-4114, **Business Phone:** (319)234-2389.

**ABEL, RENAUL N.**
Administrator, executive director, manager. **Personal:** Born Dec 28, 1940, Philadelphia, PA; son of William J and Revender C Strother; married Patricia Fenner; children: Sean & Damien. **Educ:** Cent State Univ, Wilberforce, OH, BS, biol, 1962; Ohio State Univ, Columbus, OH, 1972. **Career:** Anheuser-Busch Inc, Newark, NJ, Columbus, Ohio, asst plant mgr, mgr beer packaging & shipping, mgr packaging, mgr warehouse & shipping, asst mgr indust rels, coord tech serv opers dept, qual control lab supvr, Tampa, FL, beer packaging & shipping mgr, asst plant mgr, plant mgr, dir dispute resolution prog, 1965-. **Orgs:** Bd mem, Greater Tampa Urban League; Pinellas Co Urban League, Boy Scouts Am, Gulf Ridge Coun, Hillsborough Community Col Found; Pebble Creek Civic Asn; Master Brewers Asn; Beer & Beverage Packaging Asn; Boys & Girls Clubs Am; Greater Tampa Chamber Com; mentor, Hillsborough Community Col, Minority Affairs; bd mem, Tampa Marine Inst Inc, 1991-; chmn, busretention comn; Greater Tampa Chamber Com Comt 100, 1991-; bd mem, Univ SFla Inst Black Life, 1984-; minority devel coun, Greater Tampa Chamber Com, 1991-. **Home Addr:** 9124 Regents Pk Dr, Tampa, FL 33647, **Home Phone:** (813)973-2012. **Business Addr:** Director, Anheuser-Busch Inc, 1 Busch Pl 202 7, St. Louis, MO 63118, **Business Phone:** (314)577-3356.

**ABERCRUMBIE, DR. PAUL ERIC**
School administrator. **Personal:** Born Jun 14, 1948, Cleveland, OH; son of Margaret Louise Taylor-Nelson; married Claudia Marie Colvard; children: Paul II & Erica Marie. **Educ:** Eastern Ky Univ, BA, sociol, 1970, MA, coun, 1971; Univ Cincinnati, PhD, 1987. **Career:** Princeton City Sch Dist, adv specialist, 1971-72; Univ Cincinnati, resident counr, 1972-73, spec serv counr, 1973-75, Ethnic Progs & Serv, African-Am Cult & Res Ctr, dir, 1975-, asst adj prof, currently, Africana Studies, adj fac, currently; John DO'Bryant Nat Think Tank Black, pres; Black Man Think Tank, founder. **Orgs:** Omicron Delta Kappa Hon Soc, Univ Cincinnati, 1974; Omega Psi Phi Frat Inc; bd mem, Dr Martin Luther King Jr Coalition; coach, Athletic Asn; Nat Asn Advan Colored People; exec bd mem, Dr Martin Luther King Jr Coalition, 1980-. speaker, EASFAA; Whos Who Among Black Americans, 1986. **Home Addr:** 10301 Giverny Blvd, Cincinnati, OH 45241-3280, **Home Phone:** (513)681-8493. **Business Addr:** Adjunct Faculty, University of Cincinnati, 555 Steger Student Life Ctr, Cincinnati, OH 45221-0092, **Business Phone:** (513)556-6008.

**ABERNATHY, REV. RALPH DAVID, III**
State government official, executive, business owner. **Personal:** Born Mar 19, 1959, Montgomery, AL; son of Ralph David II Sr and Juanita Odessa; married Annette; children: Ralph David IV Christiana Ahlayah & Micah. **Educ:** Morehouse Col, eng & ling, 1981. **Career:** Ga Gen Assembly, state rep, 1988-92, state sen, 1992-98; Ga State Prison, staff, 2000-01, 2002-03; Ga House Representatives, 38th Dist, sen; CleanAir Industs, owner & chmn; Ralph David Abernathy III Found, chmn, pres, chief exec officer, 2007-. **Orgs:** Vice chmn, Senate Retirement Comn; vice chmn, Ins & Labor Comn; chmn, Interstate Coop; Legis Black Caucus & Policy Comn, Senate Dem Caucus; chmn, Sunshine Litigation Study Comn; Senate Electrology Study Comn; bd dir, Consumer Credit Coun Serv; bd dir, Big Bros & Big Sisters; Underground Adv Comn; chmn, Sub-Comt Pension Funds; Influential Appropriation & Rules Comts. **Business Addr:** President, Chief Executive Officer, Ralph David Abernathy III Foundation, 2785 ENGLE RD NW, ATLANTA, GA 30318.

**ABERNATHY, RONALD LEE**
Basketball coach, association executive. **Personal:** Born Dec 13, 1950, Louisville, KY; son of Ben W and Juanita. **Educ:** Morehead State Univ, BA, soc, 1972; La State Univ, MA, admin, 1979. **Career:** Shawnee HS La KY, teacher, head basketball coach, 1972-76; La State Univ Baton Rouge, asst basketball coach, 1976-83, assoc head coach, 1983-89; Belg All Star Team, Namur Belg, head basketball coach, 1981; LA Assoc Basketball Coaches All-Star Game, exec dir, 1981; S&R Oilfield Serv Co, pres, 1981-; Tenn State Univ, head basketball coach, 1989; Lane Col, athletic dir, currently, head basketball coach, currently. **Orgs:** Dir & lead singer, Gospel Chorus Gr Salem Baptist Church, 1954-76; bd mem, Morehead Rec Comns, 1971-72; Nat Asn Basketball Coaches, 1976-; lead singer, Young Adult Choir Shiloh Baptist Church, 1976-; big bro prog, Family Ct Baton Rouge, LA, 1982; asst basketball coach, Nat Asn Basketball Coaches All-Star Game, 1982; LA Pageant Judges & Entertainers Asn, 1983-. **Honors/Awds:** Teacher of the Year, Shawnee HS Louisville KY, 1976; High School Coach of the Year, Louisville Urban League, 1976; Runner-up State of KY High School Coach of the Year, 1976; Houston Post Top Ten Assistant Coaches America, 1980; Final Four Basketball Team Philadelphia, PA coach, 1981; LAs 10 Best Dressed Men, 1983; LA's Most Eligible Bachelors, 1983; Baton Rouge's Most Fashionable Man, 1983; Final Four Basketball Team Dallas, TX coach, 1986; Recruiter of the Year, Sporting Mag. **Special Achievements:** First black appointed to full time coaching position Louisiana State University. **Home Addr:** 1319 Arbor Ridge Dr, Antioch, TN 37013. **Business Addr:** Athletic Director, Head Coach, Lane College, 545 Lane Ave, Jackson, TN 38301, **Business Phone:** (731)426-7500.

**ABERNATHY, TENISHA.** **See TAYLOR, TENISHA NICOLE.**

**ABIBIO, NANA ESSIE.** **See JEFFRIES, DR. ROSALIND ROBINSON.**

**ABIF, KHAFRE KUJICHAGULIA**
Librarian, library administrator. **Personal:** Born Jun 6, 1966, McKeesport, PA; son of Jackie and Barbara J Page; children: Amenhotep Kazembe Ture. **Educ:** Fla A&M Univ, attended 1989; Univ Pittsburgh, BA, 1992, MLS, 1993. **Career:** Dist Columbia Pub Libr, c librn, 1993-95; Montclair Pub Libr, youth serv librn, 1995-98; Mt Vernon Pub Libr, head, c serv, 1998-99; Brooklyn Pub Libr, mgr, c serv, 1999-2001; C Defense Fund/Haley Farm, dir, Langston Hughes Libr, dir, 2002; Cleveland Pub Libr, br mgr, currently. **Orgs:** Pub Libr Asn, 1996-; Asn Libr Serv C, 1996-; ALA, Black Caucus exec bd, 1996-98; 1999-2001; Spectrum Initiative Steering Comm, 1997-2000; C Bk Coun, 1997-99

& 1999-2001; Global Awareness Team, 1998, coun, 2001-05. **Honors/Awds:** Miracle Award, Family & Children's Services, Miracle Makers Inc, 1999. **Home Addr:** 5800 Cent Ave Pke Suite 4003, Knoxville, TN 37912. **Business Addr:** Branch Manager, Cleveland Public Library, 2820 E 116th St, Cleveland, OH 44120, **Business Phone:** (216)623-7046.

### ABNEY, ALBERT
Commissioner. **Career:** York Col, Remanufacturing Ctr, dir; Gov Dist 7250; City Planning Comn, comnr, NY, 1996-01. **Orgs:** Pres, Rotary Club Jamaica; chmn, bd Cent Queen YMCA; NY city Planning Comn; Nat Found Teaching Entrepreneurship. **Honors/Awds:** Gift Life Inc. **Home Addr:** 10935 196th St, Hollis, NY 11412-1705, **Home Phone:** (718)479-4914. **Business Addr:** Director, York College, 94-20 Guy R Brewer Blvd Rm 2F01, Jamaica, NY 11451, **Business Phone:** (718)262-2452.

### ABNEY, ROBERT
Playwright, school administrator, consultant. **Personal:** Born Jul 2, 1949, Washington, DC; son of Robert Sr and Willie Mae Carson. **Educ:** DC Teachers Col, BS, educ psychol, 1972. **Career:** First Georgetown Adv DC, vpres, 1981-82; Windstar Ltd, DC, pres, 1981-; Washington, DC, advert consult, 1982-; Creative Connection, DC, dir mkt & advert, 1982-83; Southwest Neighborhood Assembly, bd mem, 1984-88; Channel 48 Cable TV, Vol's Forum, host, independent video producer; DC Pub Schs, coord home study prog, dir homework centers, 1988-93; Fannie Mae Found, prog dir & mentor coordr, 1993-99; Child & Family Servs Agency, planning specialist, 2000-11; Self Employed Independent Consult, consult, 2011-; Concerned Black Men Nat, regional prog mgr CBM Cares Nat Mentoring Initiative, 2013. **Orgs:** Chmn, SNEA Human Rels Coun, Nat Educ Asn, DC, 1970-71; Clearing house mgr, DC Pub Lib Comt Info Serv DC, 1976-81; consult, US Dept Comn DC Pub Sch Syst, 1983-; pres, Amidon Ele PTA, 1984-86; Int Platform Asn; Nat Leadership Conf; Honor Book; bd dir, Southwest Neighborhood Assembly; bd dir, Southwest House, 1989-90. **Honors/Awds:** Special Award, 1969; Award for Artistic Achievement, 1978; Riggs National Bank Community Achievement Award, 1990, 1991; Resident Initiatives Award. **Special Achievements:** "Jaycee's Vol Citation", 1969; "Headstart Volunteer Citation", 1977-84. **Home Addr:** 421 Gallatin St NW, Washington, DC 20011-4061, **Home Phone:** (202)829-5140. **Business Addr:** Consultant, Self Employed, 3346 Erie St SE, Washington, DC 20020-1228.

### ABRAHAM, CLIFTON EUGENE, JR.
Football player. **Personal:** Born Dec 9, 1971, Dallas, TX. **Educ:** Fla State Univ, attended 1994. **Career:** Football player (retired); Tampa Bay Buccaneers, 1995; Chicago Bears, 1995-96; Carolina Panthers, 1997; Toronto Argonuats, 1998-99, 2001; Los Angeles Extreme, XFL, 2001. **Honors/Awds:** All-Am Honorable Mention, United Press Int, 1993; First Team All-Am, Am Football Coaches Asn, 1994; All-Am Honorable Mention, United Press Int, 1994; 1st Team All-Am, The Sporting News, 1994; 1st Team All-Am, Assoc Press; Walter Camp; 1st Team All-Am, Football News; 1st Team All-Am, Walter Camp; All-Am, Scripps Howard.

**ABRAHAM, DONNIE.** **See ABRAHAM, NATHANIEL DONNELL.**

### ABRAHAM, JEANETTE M.
Chief executive officer, business owner. **Educ:** Wayne State Univ, BA, interdisciplinary studies, 1989; Cent Mich Univ, MA, human resource, 1998. **Career:** Gen Motors Corp, purchasing mgr, 1968-2000; Detroit Heading LLC, pres, chief exec officer & owner, 2001-08; JMA Logistics LLC, founder, pres & chief exec officer, 2001-. **Orgs:** Nat Asn Black Automotive Suppliers; Nat Asn Advan Colored People; Detroit Rescue Mission. **Business Addr:** Founder, President, JMA Logistics LLC, 28301 Schoolcraft Rd Suite 360, Livonia, MI 48150, **Business Phone:** (734)762-4830.

### ABRAHAM, NATHANIEL DONNELL (DONNIE ABRAHAM)
Football player, businessperson. **Personal:** Born Oct 8, 1973, Orangeburg, SC; married Tunisia; children: Devin Isaiah, Alivia & Micah. **Educ:** E Tenn State Univ, BS, bus mgt. **Career:** Football player (retired), exec; Tampa Bay Buccaneers, right cornerback, 1996, left cornerback, 1997-2001; NY Jets, left cornerback, 2002, 2004, defensive back & left cornerback, 2003, cornerback & right cornerback, 2004; bus exec, 2005-; IMG Acad, defensive coordr, currently. **Honors/Awds:** Pro Bowl, 2000. **Home Addr:** 128 Waterford Pky, Orangeburg, SC 29118-9039, **Home Phone:** (803)536-1841. **Business Addr:** Defensive Coordinator, IMG Academy, 5650 Bollettieri Blvd, Bradenton, FL 34210, **Business Phone:** (941)755-1000.

### ABRAHAM, SHARON L.
School administrator, executive director. **Educ:** Univ Mich, BA, orgn behav & indust rels, 1980, MBA, 1984, PhD. **Career:** City Detroit, urban renewal asst, 1980-82; Int Bus Mach, mkt rep, 1984-87; Ameritech, mgr, 1987-94; Oakland Univ, off diversity & compliance, dir, 1996-2002, Pub Sch Academics & Urban Partnerships, dir, 2002-04; Abraham & Assocs, founder, pres, 2004-06; Roosevelt Thomas Consult & Training, trainer, 2004-06; Eastern Mich Univ, dir diversity affirmative action human resources, 2006-, title ix coordr, 2014-15. **Orgs:** Arbitrator, Better Bus Bur, 1989-94; finance comm chair & vice bd chair, Head Start Agency, 1989-94; Nat Black MBA Asn, 1990-; vol coordr, Heidelberg Proj, 1995-97; Leadership Detroit XIX, 1997; Leadership Oakland IX, 1998-; Celebration Race Rels Task Force; co-chair, Ann Martin Luther King; Mich Diversity Coun Mem; Soc Human Resources; Mich Indust Liaison Group. **Honors/Awds:** LGBT Resource Ctr Role Model & Mentor Award, Eastern Mich Univ; Research Award, Mich Col & Univ Personnel Asn, 1999-; Diversity Champion, Birmingham Bloomfield Task force Race Rels, 2000. **Home Addr:** 26336 Lathrup Blvd, Lathrup Village, MI 48076-4612, **Home Phone:** (248)559-1501. **Business Addr:** Director of Diversity, Affirmative Action Human Resources, Eastern Michigan University, 140 McKenny, Ypsilanti, MI 48197, **Business Phone:** (734)487-3430.

### ABRAHAM, YOHANNES
Government official, presidential aide. **Educ:** Yale University, Bachelor's in Political Science, 2007. **Career:** White House Office of Legislative Affairs; Organizing for America, National Political Director; Obama for America 2012, Deputy National Political Director; White House, Special Assistant to the President and Chief of Staff for the Office of Public Engagement and the Office of Intergovernmental Affairs, 2013-. **Honors/Awds:** "Forbes," 30 Under 30; "The Root" Magazine, The Talented Ten, 2009, The Root 100 Honorees, 2013.

### ABRAHAMS, ANTHONY D.
Executive. **Educ:** Va State Univ, BS, acct; Harvard Bus Sch, MBA. **Career:** Coopers & Lybrand LLP, auditor; Peabody & Co, investment banker, 1990-95; Ernst & Young LLP, finance exec, 1995-98; Lucents New Ventures Group, chief financial officer, 1998-; New Venture Partners LLC, adv bd, indust recognition, corp partners, chief financial officer & partner, 2001-08; RRL Finance LLC, founder, chief exec officer, 2010-. **Orgs:** Bd advisor, Technol Ventures Incubator, Stevens Inst Technol. **Business Addr:** CFO, Partner, New Venture Partners LLC, 98 Floral Ave, Murray Hill, NJ 07974, **Business Phone:** (908)464-0900.

### ABRAMS, KENNETH RODNEY
Marketing executive, association executive. **Personal:** Born Dec 31, 1970, Baltimore, MD; son of Titus Robertson and Sheila Jones; married Denise Reid; children: Khalil. **Educ:** Towson State Univ, BS, bus concentration mkt, 1992. **Career:** Baltimore Orioles, comn rels rep, 1992-95; Trahan Burden & Charles, acct exec, 1995-97; Baltimore Ravens, proms & advert mgr, mgr corp commun partnerships & dir community rels, 1997-2009; Abrams Ins Agency, agt, currently. **Orgs:** Publicity chair, United Negro Coll Fund, MD, 1995-97; diversity comn, Advert Asn Baltimore, 1995-97; celebrity auction chair, Woodholme Found, 1996-97. **Honors/Awds:** Black Achiever Award, Druid Hill YMCA, 1993. **Special Achievements:** Coordinate Stars Early Black Baseball event 1993 MLB All Star Game. **Home Addr:** 3824 Collier Rd, Randallstown, MD 21133, **Home Phone:** (410)922-1186. **Business Addr:** Agent, Abrams Insurance Agency, 110 E 25th St, Baltimore, MD 21218, **Business Phone:** (410)727-0800.

### ABRAMS, KEVIN R.
Football player. **Personal:** Born Feb 28, 1974, Tampa, FL. **Educ:** Syracuse Univ, attended 1996. **Career:** Football player (retired); Detroit Lions, 1999-2000, defensive back, 1997, right corner back, 1998. **Honors/Awds:** All-American, 1995-96.

### ABRAMSON, DR. JOHN J., JR.
Government official, consultant. **Personal:** Born Aug 26, 1957, Brooklyn, NY; son of John J Sr and Norine; children: John III, Jason, Monae & Kiara. **Educ:** Univ Del, BS, 1979; NH Col, MS, int community econ develop, 1991; Union Inst, PhD, 1996. **Career:** Gov VI, energy dir, 1981-87; Legal asst, 1985; Legis VI, chief staff, 1987-89, 1991-92, Sen Judy M Gomez, consult, 1992-94, supvr elections, 1995-; Energy Resources Int, caribbean rep, 1988-90; Pvt Indust Coun, inr, consult, 1989-90; Parliamentarian, 1989; US Small Bus Admin, doc examr, 1990; Election Syst VI, supvr elections, 1995-; consult, 2013-. **Orgs:** Adv bd chair, VI Dept Health, 1983-84; chap pres, Opp Fraternity, 1985-89; cot & parental com chair, VI Bd Educ, 1986-88; Int Basketball Fed, 1986-93; chair, Resource Conserv & Develop Coun, 1988-90; VI Tourism Awareness Link, 1988-90; inspector gen, U.S. Election Assistance Comn. **Home Addr:** PO Box 55, Frederiksted00841-0055, **Home Phone:** (340)772-4066. **Business Addr:** Supervisor of Elections, Election Syst VI, Lagoon Complex, St. Croix00851-1499, **Business Phone:** (340)773-1021.

### ABSTON, DR. NATHANIEL, JR.
Clinical psychologist. **Personal:** Born Jul 18, 1952, Mobile, AL; son of Nathaniel Sr and Minnie L; married Elverna McCants; children: Jamila Aziza & Khalid Amir. **Educ:** Univ S Ala, BA, 1975, MS, 1978; Univ Southern Miss, PhD, biol & biomed sci, 1984. **Career:** Mobile Youth Ct, stud social worker, 1971-74; Mobile Ment Health Ctr, counr, 1974-76; Univ S Ala, lectr, 1978-; Biloxi VA Med Ctr, internship, 1983; Va Outpatient Clin, Mobile, Ala, staff clin psychol, 1984-; lic psychol, Miss, 1984-; Lic Psychol, Ala, 1998-; Gulf Coast Vet Health Care Syst, Biloxi, Miss, internship, Ment/Behav Health, staff psychol, currently; Univ S Ala, prof psychol, currently; Ment Health Clin, clin psychologist. **Orgs:** Alpha Phi Alpha Fraternity; Am Psychol Asn; Ala Psychol Asn; Miss Psychol Asn; Urban League Mobile. **Honors/Awds:** Psi Chi Hon Psychol Club, Univ S Ala Chap, 1975-; USA Res Grant Award, Univ S Ala, 1978-79. **Special Achievements:** Several scientific publications & presentations. **Home Addr:** 13789 Roberts Rd, Chunchula, AL 36521-6203. **Business Addr:** Staff Psychologist, VA Gulf Coast Veterans Health Care System, 400 Veterans Ave, Biloxi, MS 39531, **Business Phone:** (228)523-5000.

### ABUBAKR, RASHIDA ISMALI
Writer. **Personal:** Born Jan 1, 1941?, Cotonou; children: Daoud Samir. **Educ:** New York Col Music, BA, music; New Sch Social Res, MA, social psychol; State Univ NY, PhD, psychol. **Career:** Academia, lectr, counr & adminr; Pratt Inst, assoc dir Higher Educ Opportunity Prog, 2000; Galleria Africa, owner; Wilkes Univ, Wilkes-Barre, Pa, fac mem, Creative Writing MA & MFA dept, currently; Poem: SHAMING OF AN OLIVE TREE, 2001; Geraldine Dodge Poetry Festival, 2002; Festival Fall Semester, 2003; Univ Ghana, vis scholar, 2004; Nat Ghana Dance Ensemble, the Ghanaian Women Writers; New Online Master Creative Writing Prog, fac mem; Rice Keepers' just out, 2006. **Orgs:** WEB Du Bois Found, 1999; founding mem, Orgn Women Writers Africa; second vpres, Pen & Brush all-womens prof artists orgn. **Honors/Awds:** Travel lecture series in the Nederland Antilles, 2004. **Special Achievements:** First Writers Conference at Wilkes University, 2004. **Home Addr:** 1851 Adam Clayton Powell Jr Blvd Apt 4, New York, NY 10026-3642, **Home Phone:** (212)222-8631. **Business Addr:** Faculty Member, Wilkes University, 84 W S St, Wilkes-Barre, PA 18766, **Business Phone:** (570)408-4235.

### ACKERMAN, DR. PATRICIA A.
Educator. **Personal:** Born Feb 6, 1944, Cleveland, OH; daughter of Amos Abraham (deceased) and Minnie Ruth Glover. **Educ:** Ohio Univ, Athens, OH, BA, eng, 1966; Cleveland State Univ, OH, MEd, admin, 1974; Kent State Univ, OH, PhD, admin, 1983. **Career:** Cleveland Bd Educ, Ohio, teacher, 1966-72; Beachwood Bd Educ, Ohio, teacher, 1972-74; Lima City Schs, Ohio, dean girls, 1974-75; Cleveland Heights-Univ Heights Bd Educ, Ohio, coordr, 1975, high sch asst prin, 1975-87, prin taylor acad, 1987, dir curric, 1993; Taylor Acad, founder & prin; Chalkdust Inc, founder, pres & chief exec officer. **Orgs:** Pres, Nat Alliance Black Sch Educ, 1987-89; Leadership Cleveland, 1988-89; from adv to chmn, Nat Gov's Asn, 1989; from chmn to bd trustee, Ohio St Univ, 2000-04; bd mem, Greater Cleveland Delta Found Life Develop Ctr; active mem, Delta Sigma Theta Sorority Inc; chair, Educ Braintrust, Int Womens Air & Space Mus. **Home Addr:** 456 Rushmore Dr, Richmond Heights, OH 44143-2548, **Home Phone:** (216)531-1837. **Business Addr:** Chief Executing Officer, President, Chalkdust Inc, PO Box 46516, Bedford, OH 44146-0516, **Business Phone:** (440)439-5924.

### ACKORD, MARIE MALLORY
Educator. **Personal:** Born Jan 5, 1939, Bronwood, GA; daughter of Clarence and Lula Perry; married Ronald A; children: Monique Patrice Campbell. **Educ:** Bethune-Cookman Col, BS, math, 1960; Nova Univ, Ft Lauderdale, FL, MS, admin & supv, 1982. **Career:** Educator (retired); Carver High Sch, Naples, FL, 1960-64; Dunbar High Sch, math teacher, 1964-66; N Ft Myers High Sch, math teacher, 1966-70, 1973; Dunbar Mid Sch, head math dept & teacher, 1970-73, varsity cheer leading, sponsor, 1976-77; Sch Bd Lee County, N Ft Myers, FL, human rel specialist, 1980-83, math teacher, 1983; Ft Myers Comm Rels Commin, commr. **Orgs:** Past charter pres, vpres, Ft Myers Alumnae Chap Delta Sigma Theta Sorority Inc, 1965-70, 1979-81, 1999-2003; secy, Ft Myers Alumnae Chap Delta Sigma Theta, 1975-77; dept elections clerk, Lee County, 1987-; NCNW; treas, vpres, chmn, charter mem & charter pres, Ft Myers Alumnae Chap Delta Sigma Theta, 1991-; bd clin social work, Marriage & Family Ther & Ment Health Coun, 1991-98; primary advisor, Tau Sigma Chap Delta Sigma Theta Sorority Inc, Fla Gulf Coast Univ, 2004-10; Southwest Fla Community Found, 2009; Phi Delta Kappa Educ Fraternity, secy, bd dir, Delta Life Develop Ctr; consumer mem, State Fla, Agency Health Care Admin; secy, Caribbean Continental Social Club; bd mem, Clavary Am Methodist Episcopal Church; Sch Community Adv Com; NCTM Fla Math Teachers; Lee County Teachers Math, Delta Sigma Theta Inc; Nat Asn Advan Colored People; adv bd, Dunbar Day Care; Collier County Alumnae Chap Delta sigma Theta Sorority Inc; chairperson, N Ft Myers High Sch-Sch Adv Comt. **Honors/Awds:** Elected Beta Kappa Chi, 1960; Teacher of the Month, N Ft Myers High Sch, 1976; Nom Lee Co Woman of the Year, 1976-77; Woman of the Year, Zeta Phi Beta Minority; Cert of Appreciation from Gov Bob Graham, 1986; Staff Member of the Month, N Ft Myers High Sch, 1990, 1995; Trailblazer Award, Zeta Phi Beta Sorority Inc, 2014; Fortitude Award, Fla Deltas Epitome; Golden Apple Award, Finalist-Lee County; Ida S. Baker Distinguished Educator Award; Florida Department of Health-Exemplary Service Award; American Legion Post 192-Community Service Award. **Home Addr:** 1921 SE 8th St, Cape Coral, FL 33990-1628, **Home Phone:** (239)574-2120.

### ACKRIDGE, FLORENCE GATEWARD
Administrator. **Personal:** Born Jun 14, 1939, Philadelphia, PA; married John C; children: Anthony, Antoinette & Angelo. **Educ:** Temple Univ, BSW, 1977. **Career:** Norris Brown & Hall, legal secy, 1965-68; Rentex Systs, off asst, 1968-69; Philadelphia Urban Coalition, secy, 1969-71; Rebound Med Group, clerical supvr, 1971-73; Young Men's Christian Asn, Youth Leadership Inst, prog coordr, 1973-74; Philadelphia City, Dept Human Serv, social worker, currently. **Orgs:** Vol, Consult Prisoners Rights Coun; social worker, Walton Village; Nat Coun Black Child Develop; Black Social Workers Alliance; W Oak Lane Comn Group; Black & Non-White Young Men's Christian Asn; Model Legis Plan Com Model Judicial Plan Comn; vol, Christian St Young Men's Christian Asn Mem Dr. **Home Addr:** 6713 Gratz St, Philadelphia, PA 19126, **Home Phone:** (215)276-2535. **Business Addr:** Social Worker, Department of Human Services, 1515 Arch St, Philadelphia, PA 19102, **Business Phone:** (215)683-4347.

### ACREY, AUTRY
School administrator. **Personal:** Born Mar 20, 1948, Frederick, OK; son of William and Mildred Thomas. **Educ:** Jarvis Christian Col, BS, educ, 1970; Tex Christian Univ, MA, 1972; N Tex State Univ. **Career:** Jarvis Christian Col, Hawkins, Tex, instr hist, 1973-76, asst prof hist, 1976-, asst dean, 1976-79, assoc dean, 1981-89, vpres acad affairs, 1994, Instnl Res, Planning & Assessment, Off Pres, actg dir, currently, Instnl Res & Planning, regist & vpres instnl effectiveness, currently, historian, cur. **Orgs:** Dir, Consortium Res Training, 1974-76; secy, Mu Rho Lambda Chap, Alpha Phi Alpha, 1978; dir, Coop Educ, 1981-; dir, E Tex Res Coun, 1983-84. **Home Addr:** 1011 N Francis, Hawkins, TX 75765-0351, **Home Phone:** (903)769-2972. **Business Addr:** Registrar, Acting Director, Jarvis Christian College, PO Box 1470, Hawkins, TX 75765, **Business Phone:** (903)730-2451.

### ADAIR, ALVIS V.
Educator. **Personal:** Born Jul 19, 1940, Hare Valley, VA; son of Eddie and Sereta; married Deloris; children: Almaz Sande & Poro. **Educ:** Va State Col, BS, 1962, MS, 1964; Univ Mich, PhD, psychol, 1971; Monrovia Col Liberia W Africa, LLD, 1973. **Career:** US Peace Corps, teacher & community develop, 1965-68; Allen Univ, assessor & dir spec exp progs, 1968-69, asst prof, 1971, assoc prof, 1972, chmn soc res, 1973, pres, 1977-79; Howard Univ, asst to dean res develop, 1979-84, Sch Soc Work, Coun Int Prog, dir, prof, 2004-. **Orgs:** Bd mem, Social Work Abstracts; Hill crest C Ctr; DC Comn Aging; hon mem, Cross roads Africa, 1966; State Planning Comn White House Conf Families & Aging, 1980-81; co-chmn, Asn Black Psychologists; trustee, St Paul AME Church; Asn Univ Prof, Social Workers, Black Soc Workers, Psychologists; chmn, DC Nursing Home Adv Comn, 1988-90; DC Bd Psychol, 1990-; Bd Psychol Inc. **Home Addr:** 711 Quackenbos St NW, Washington, DC 20011. **Business Addr:** Professor, Howard University, 601 Howard Pl NW, Washington, DC 20059, **Business Phone:** (202)806-7300.

**ADAIR, ANDREW A.**
Chief executive officer, lawyer. **Personal:** Born Aug 5, 1933, Chicago, IL; children: Andrew Jr & Suzanne. **Educ:** Morehouse Col, BS, 1965; Univ Toledo, Col Law, JD, 1969. **Career:** Nat Urban League, assoc dir, field oper, 1971-72, assoc dir progs, 1973-74; Mauy Develop Ctr, dir, 1975-79, actg gen coun, 1978-79, dir cent region, 1979-. **Orgs:** Legal couns Ctr Stud Rights Dayton, 1969-70; bd mem, Human Rights Comn Dayton, 1969-71; bd mem, ACLU Dayton Chap, 1969-71; Ind Bar Asn; Fed Bar US Dist Ct; Nat Bar Asn, 1971; secy, nat coun exec dir, Nat Urban League, 1971-72; nat adv & coun, Nat Coun Urban League Guilds, 1972-79; bd mem, Coun Econ Educ NY, 1975-78; Am Bar Asn, 1976. **Home Addr:** 400 Roselawn Pl, Charlotte, NC 28211-4163. **Business Addr:** Director Central Region, National Urban League, 36 S Wabash Ave, Chicago, IL 60603, **Business Phone:** (773)451-3535.

**ADAIR, GWEN (GWEN FARRELL)**
Judge. **Personal:** daughter of Lovie Yanceymarried Frank; children: 4. **Career:** Calif Athletic Comn, referee & judge, 1980-; actress. **Orgs:** Calif Referees Asn. **Honors/Awds:** Inducted into the Calif Boxing Hall Fame, World Boxing Hall Fame, 2005. **Special Achievements:** First African American & only woman referee to officiate a world championship heavyweight bout; Films: Lady Sings the Blues; The Poseidon Adventure; Billy Jack Goes to Washington, 1977; TV appearance: "MASH". **Home Addr:** 15204 Dickens St, Sherman Oaks, CA 91403-3331, **Home Phone:** (818)788-6617. **Business Addr:** Referee, Judge, California Athletic Commission, 1424 Howe Ave Suite 33, Sacramento, CA 95825-3217, **Business Phone:** (916)263-2195.

**ADAIR, JAMES E.**
Lecturer, artistic director. **Personal:** married Marjorie P Spellen; children: Andrea Denice & Tonja Michelle. **Educ:** Mrehouse Col, sec educ & teaching, 1957; Ft Valley State Col, BS, 1962. **Career:** Adair's Art Gallery Atlanta, dir, 1963-64; Barber-Scotia Col Concord, art instr, 1964-66; Parks Jr High Sch, Atlanta, art instr, 1967-69; Morris-Brown Col Atlanta, art lectr, 1970-; J AdairArtwork LLC, artist dir, 2007-. **Honors/Awds:** Executed Murals, Ft Valley State Col, 1962; Annual Negro Exhibition 1st Place Award, 1969; Fine Arts Gallery Atlanta, 1964, 1968. **Home Addr:** 2904 Arrowwood Dr, Atlanta, GA 30344, **Home Phone:** (404)349-5229. **Business Addr:** Art Lecturer, Morris Brown College, 643 Martin Luther King Jr Dr, Atlanta, GA 30314, **Business Phone:** (404)739-1012.

**ADAIR, DR. ROBERT A.**
Physician, writer, health services administrator. **Personal:** Born Jun 27, 1943, New York, NY; married Ella; children: Kai & Robert A. **Educ:** Univ Pa, BA, 1965; Howard Univ Col Med, MD, 1969; Columbia Univ, MPH, 1972. **Career:** Staten Community Col, adj prof, 1970; Met Hosp, med intern, 1970; E Harlem Alcoh Anony Asn, spec consult, 1970; NY City Dept Health, actg dist health officer, Cent Harlem, 1970-71; Bd Educ Harlem Pub Sch, consult, 1970-71; Narcot Addict & Ven Dis Mt Morr Presb Chap, spec consult, 1970-72; Morrisania Youth Ctr, consult physician, 1970-72; NY City Dept Corrections, physician, 1971; WNBC-TV, med consult & co-producer TV films, 1971-72; Pub Health Nurses New Pub Health, sch syst, spec consult & instr, 1971-72; Sydenham Hosp NY City, dir ambul serv, 1972, Dept Health New York, pub health residency, 1972; Manhattanville Col, spec health course pub health, 1972; pvt pract physician, 1980-; Holy Name Hosp, med dir community rels, 2002; Englewood Hosp & Med Ctr. **Orgs:** Fel Am Pub Health Asn, 1969; NY Co Med Soc; NY State Med Soc; Nat Med Asn; Black Am Med & Dent Asn Stud; Black Caucus Health Workers; AMA; med adv bd, Found Res & Educ Sick Cell Dis; sec adv counc, pres & med bd, NY City Health & Hosp Corp; bd pres, med bd Sydenham Hosp; bd dir, Physic Inc; chmn, Health Comn 10 Black Men; consult Health Dept Englewood NY; bd Elig, Am Acad Pub Health & Prevent Med, 1972; admis comnr, Bio-Med Prog City Col, NY, 1973-; Nat Asn Advan Colored People; Harlem Alli May Org Task Force; Duke Elling Jazz Soc; Elder Mt Morris Unit Presby Chap; Sub-area health Plan Body Mod Cit; financial comn, Mt Morris Fed Cred UN; bd trust, Mary Holmes Col; bd trust, Harl Interf Couns Serv; First Aid Com Red Cross Asn; adv coun, NY Urban League Manhat; bd, Sherm Terr Corp; Am Soc Bariatric Physicians; chmn, Prevent Med Sect Nat Med Conv, 1973. **Honors/Awds:** Woodrow Wilson Academic Scholar, 1961-65; dipl, Nat Med Bd, 1970; hon disc, 1974. **Special Achievements:** Author of several publications. **Business Addr:** Physician, Private Practice, 699 Teaneck Rd Suite 101, Teaneck, NJ 07666, **Business Phone:** (201)837-2111.

**ADAMS, DR. AFESA M.**
Educator, vice president (organization). **Personal:** Born Feb 20, 1936, Greenwood, MS; daughter of Annie Miller and Eddie; married Allan Nathaniel; children: Suzanne Bell-Brown, Steven A Bell & David C Bell. **Educ:** Weber State Col, BA, psychol, 1969; Univ Utah, MS, psychol, 1973, PhD, social psychol, 1975. **Career:** Univ Fla, asst prof, behav studies, 1974-79, actg chmn, behav studies, 1976-78, assoc prof psychol, 1976-80; Univ Utah, Dept Family & Consumer Studies, chmn, 1980-83, assoc vpres, acad affairs, 1984-89, assoc prof, family & consumer studies, adj assoc prof, dept psychol, assoc vpres acad affairs, 1984-89; Univ N Fla, Col Arts & Sci, dean, 1989-92, prof psychol, 1993, Fla Inst Educ, sr res assoc, prof emer psychol, currently. **Orgs:** Am Psychol Asn; Utah Coun Family Rels; Nat Coun Negro Women Inc; Southeastern Psychol Asn; Am Psychol Asn; bd dir, Gainesville Womens Health Ctr; adv bd, State Utah, Div C, Youth & Families Day Care, 1980-83; Gov's Comm Exec Reorganization, 1983-85; Gov's Task Force, study financial barriers health care, 1983-84, employer sponsored child care, 1984; bd dir, Daniel Memorial Inst Inc, 1989; Jacksonville Womens Network, 1989-; adv coun, Raines High Sch, 1989-; Andrew Jackson High Sch, accreditation team, 1989-; chmn, Implementation Community: JCCI Young Black Males Study, 1989-; Nat Coun Family Rels, 1989-; Popular Cult Asn, 1989-; Am Asn High Educ, 1989-93; Advocates Better Jacksonville, 1989-, bd dir, Jacksonville Art Mus, 1990-93; bd dir, Hubbard House Progs Spouse Abuse, 1992-94; bd dir, 1993, pres, bd dir, 1997-98, Jacksonville Community Coun Inc; Leadership Jacksonville Class, 1994; bd dir, LJ, 1994-95; bd dir, Fla Theatre, 1994-, vpres, 1996-; UNFNW Link: A Serv Learning Monitoring Prog, 1995-; Phi Kappa Phi. **Home Addr:** 4543 Harbour N Ct, Jacksonville, FL 32225, **Home Phone:** (904)642-7972. **Business Addr:** Senior Research Associate, Professor Emeritus of Psychology, University of North Florida, 1 Univ N Fla Dr, Jacksonville, FL 32224-2678, **Business Phone:** (904)620-1000.

**ADAMS, DR. ALICE OMEGA**
Physician. **Personal:** Born Apr 28, 1951, Washington, DC; children: Sharon & Leslie Wilbanks. **Educ:** Univ DC, BS, 1974; Howard Univ Grad Sch, PhD, 1979; Howard Univ Col Med, MD, 1984. **Career:** Dc Hosp, resident; Univ DC, teaching asst, 1972-74, asst prof, 1979-81; Childrens Hosp Nat Med Ctr, res assoc, 1975-77; Howard Univ, grad teaching asst, 1976-79, med stud tutor, 1978-79, asst prof neurol, 1989-; C's Hosp, med tech, 1977-81; Howard Univ Hosp, resident physician internal med, 1984-85, fel, clin neurophysiology, 1989, Neurol dept, clerkship dir med students. **Honors/Awds:** Outstanding Achievement, DC Med Chirolurgical Soc, 1983; Outstanding Achievement, Howard Univ Dept of Internal med, 1984; Outstanding Achievement, Alpha Omega Alpha Honor Med Soc, 1984. **Home Addr:** 2056 Merrifields Dr, Silver Spring, MD 20906-1256, **Home Phone:** (301)598-0645. **Business Addr:** Assistant Professor, Howard University Hospital, 2041 Georgia Ave NW Suite 5B-01, Washington, DC 20060, **Business Phone:** (202)865-1546.

**ADAMS, ALMA**
Congressional representative (U.S. federal government). **Personal:** Born May 27, 1946, High Point, NC; children: Linda Jeanelle Lindsay & Billy E II. **Educ:** NC Agr & Tech State Univ, BS, 1968, MS, art educ, 1972; Ohio State Univ, PhD, art educ & multicultural educ, 1981. **Career:** Bennett College, faculty member in art history, 1972-2012; Greensboro, North Carolina, School Board, member, 1984-86; Greensboro, North Carolina, City Council, member, 1987-94; North Carolina house of representatives, member, 1994-2014; US House of Representatives, member, 2014-. **Orgs:** Alpha Kappa Alpha sorority; Art Caucus; Congressional Bipartisan HBCU Caucus; Congressional Progressive Caucus; Diabetes Caucus; Medicaid Expansion Caucus; Women's Caucus. **Special Achievements:** First African-American woman elected to the Greensboro City Council, 1987; chair of the North Carolina Legislative Black Caucus; vice president of the Democratic Caucus for the 114th Congress' freshman class; regional whip for the Democratic Caucus; founder of the first Congressional Bipartisan HBCU Caucus. **Business Addr:** U.S. Representative, U.S. House of Representatives, 222 Cannon House Off Bldg, Washington, DC 20515-3312, **Business Phone:** (202)225-1510.

**ADAMS, ANNE CURRIN**
Consultant, educator, social worker. **Personal:** Born Jun 28, 1942, Hackensack, NJ; daughter of Charles Colbert and Etta Greer; married Thomas E; children: Tracey Anne. **Educ:** Keuka Col, NY, BA, 1964; Rutgers Univ, Grad Sch Social Work, MSW, 1970, PhD, educ & sociol. **Career:** Nj Bur Childrens Serv, caseworker, activ dir, 1966-70; Newark Nj Bd Educ, sch social worker, 1970-72; Newark Eng Col, adminr asst to eop dir, 1971-72; Rutgers Grad Sch Social Work, State Univ Nj, asst prof, 1972-86, consult, trainer, human serv delivery, 1986; Brandeis Univ, Heller Grad Sch, Ctr Youth & Communities, sr prog assoc, 1992-2004, res assoc, currently; Strumpf Assocs, sr assoc, interim WIB dir. **Orgs:** Prog dir, YWCA, youth & teenagers, 1964-66; Shiloh Baptist Church, Cascade, VA; Nat Coun Negro Women; mem fac, Tier III training; Skillman Found; Community Family Planning Coun; Tech Assistance Team Summer Youth Employ Progs; Ctr Youth & Communities; New Jersey Div Youth & Family Serv; NewJersy Bd Educ; Community Family Planning Coun New York; Newark. **Home Addr:** 4024 Livingstone Pl, Durham, NC 27707-5540, **Home Phone:** (919)489-9036. **Business Addr:** Research Associate, Brandeis University, Ctr for Youth & Communities, Waltham, MA 02454, **Business Phone:** (781)736-2000.

**ADAMS, ARMENTA ESTELLA (ARMENTA ADAMS HUMMINGS)**
Pianist. **Personal:** Born Jun 27, 1936, Cleveland, OH; daughter of Albert and Estella Mitchell; married Gus Lester; children: Amadi, Gus Jr, Martin & Marcus. **Educ:** New Eng Conserv, prep div, 1953; Juilliard Sch Music, BM, MM, 1960; London, eng, post-grad study, 1963. **Career:** Juilliard Sch Prep Div, piano teacher, 1967-69; Harlem Sch Music, piano teacher, 1968-69; Fla A&M Univ, piano fac, 1965-66; Urban Arts Winston-Salem, artist-in-residence, 1983-84; Winston-Salem State Univ, instrument fac, 1984-85; NC A&T Univ, piano fac, 1987-88; Martha Baird Rockefeller Aid to Music Grant; Int Inst Educ grant; Gateways Music Festival, founder & artistic dir, 1993-; Univ Rochester, Eastman Sch Music, distinguished community mentor, assoc prof music, 1994-. **Orgs:** Artistic Progs Comt. **Honors/Awds:** First prize, Musicians Club, NY, 1956; John Hay Whitney grant; Martha Baird Rockefeller grant; First prize, Nat Asn Negro Musicians; Special prize, Int Competition Leeds England; Freida Loewenthal Eising Award; Musical Am Musician of the Year Award; Special Prize, Leeds Int Competition. **Special Achievements:** Recording: Music That Feeds The Soul, extensive concert tours throughout the world US State Dept, 1963-67, performance at Univ MD Int Piano Festival Great Performer Series, 1985. **Home Addr:** 2012 Milford St, Winston Salem, NC 27107. **Business Addr:** Artistic Director, Founder, Gateways Music Festival Inc, 26 Gibbs St, Rochester, NY 14604, **Business Phone:** (585)232-6106.

**ADAMS, BENNIE**
Basketball executive. **Personal:** Born Apr 8, 1967, New Orleans, LA. **Educ:** Southern Univ & A&M Col, BS, math, attended 1990, MS, math, attended 1993. **Career:** Southern Univ, math instr, 1993-95; NBA, referee, currently. **Business Addr:** Referee, National Basketball Associaiton, Olympic Tower, New York, NY 10022-5986, **Business Phone:** (212)826-7000.

**ADAMS, BETTY PHILLIPS. See Obituaries Section.**

**ADAMS, DR. BILLIE MORRIS WRIGHT**
Pediatrician, administrator, executive director. **Personal:** Born Bluefield, WV; daughter of William; married Frank M; children: Frank M Jr. **Educ:** Fisk Univ, BS, 1950; Ind Univ, MA, zool, 1951; Howard Univ, MD, 1960; Am Bd Pediat, dipl, 1964. **Career:** Univ Ill Coll Med, Sickle Cell Comprehensive Ctr, oper consult; Links Inc; Cook Co Hosp Hekutoen Inst, rotating intern, 1960, pediat residency, 1961-63, hematol fel, 1963-64, res assoc hematol dept, 1965-67; Chicago Med Sch, clin instr, 1967; Martin Luther King Ctr, pediatrician, 1967-68; Michael Reese Hosp, attend pediat dept, 1970; Pediat Hematol Clin Mercy Hosp, pediathematologist, chief; Pediat Assocs, pvt practice physician, currently; Health Power Infant & Child Health Channel, ed, currently; Univ Ill, Dept Pediat, clin asst instr, clin assoc prof, 1976, coordr, 2006-; US Dept Health & Human Serv, proj dir, 1980; Mercy Hosp & Med Ctrs Dept Pediat, asst prog dir, 1981-87; Cook County Hosp, med stud training prog, coordr; Chicago Dept Health, bur chief. **Orgs:** Nat Med Asn, 1962; Pediat Asn, SC; Am Acad Pediat, 1963; Am Soc Hematol, 1968; pres, Chicago Pediat Soc; Alpha Gamma Pi, 1972; appl chairperson, StateIll Comt Sickle Cell Anemia, 1972; med adv comt, Planned Parenthood, 1972-75; Cook Co Physicians Asn, 1974-; med adv comt, Chicago Bd Health'sC & Maternal Comn; AMA; Chicago Inst Med; Chicago Med Asn; IllState & Med Soc; bd dir, Midwest Asn; Art Inst Chicago; Lyric Opera Guild; bd mem, Ounce Prev; Delta Sigma Theta; bd dir, S Side Community Art Ctr; Friends Carter G Woodson Libr; exec comt, Ounce Prev; Robert Taylor Boys & Girls Clubs; Bronzeville C Mus; bd dir, Michael Reese Health Trust; pres, Chicago Pediat Soc; gardner trustee, Michael Reese Health Trust, 2004-; chmn, Nat Med Asn; Bur Community & Comprehensive Personal Health. **Honors/Awds:** Archibald Hoyne Award, Chicago Pediat Soc; Grace James Award, Nat Med Asn; Honoree, Alpha Gamma Pi, 1973; PUSH Woman of the Year, 1975; Congress District Award in Medical, 1985; United Negro College Fund Star, 1986; Pediatrician of the Year, Ill, Chap Am Acad Pediat, 1997; Public Service Award, Chicago Med Soc, 1999; Timuel Black Community Service Award, Jazz Inst Chicago, 2012. **Special Achievements:** First to win Cong Dist Award in Med, 1985; One of the Best Doctors in America and honored at the University of Illinois at Chicago in 2005-06. **Home Addr:** 2011 E 75th St Suite 101, Chicago, IL 60649-3646, **Home Phone:** (773)288-4824. **Business Addr:** Co-Ordinator, University of Illinois, 1301 W Green St, Urbana, IL 61801, **Business Phone:** (217)333-1216.

**ADAMS, DR. CAROL LAURENCE**
Socialist, government official, educator. **Personal:** Born May 11, 1944, Louisville, KY; daughter of William and Lora; children: Nia Malika Augustine. **Educ:** Fisk Univ, BA, sociol, 1965; Boston Univ, MA, sociol, 1966; Univ Chicago; Union Grad Sch, PhD, sociol, 1976. **Career:** Northeastern Ill, Univ Ctr Inner City Studies, res dir, 1968-69; asst dir, 1969-78, tenured assoc prof, exec dir, 2000; Neighborhood Inst, dir res & planning, 1978-81; Loyola Univ Chicago, Afro-Amer studies, dir, 1981-88, assoc prof sociol, 1981, prof; Kennedy-King Col, dean, 1988-89; Chicago Housing Authority, dir resident serv & progs, 1989-96; Int House Blues Found, exec dir, 1997; Ill Dept Human Serv, secy, 2003-09, chief, Rep Africa; DuSable Mus African Am Hist, pres & chief exec officer, 2009-14. **Orgs:** Nat Asn Blacks Criminal Justice; African Heritage Studies Asn; Am Sociol Asn; bd mem, Ebony Talent Creative Arts Found; Asn Advan Creative Musicians; bd dir, Cable Access Corp; Nat Coun Black Studies; Ill Coun Black Studies. **Honors/Awds:** Phi Beta Kappa Fisk Univ, 1965; George Edmund Hayes Social Sci Award, Fisk Univ, 1965; Community Achievement Award, Hubame Assoc; Leadership in Ed Award, YMCA Metrop Chicago; Govrs Award Arts; Black Bus Award, Black Book Dir; Achievement Award, Ill Bd Higher Educ. **Home Addr:** 6929 S Crandon 3A, Chicago, IL 60649, **Home Phone:** (773)955-6291.

**ADAMS, CECIL RAY**
Banker. **Personal:** Born Feb 15, 1948, Crockett, TX; son of Leo and Verna Davis (deceased); married Myra Bliss; children: Jennifer, Kraig & Andrew. **Educ:** Univ N Tex, Denton, TX, BA, polit sci, econ, 1970; Univ Houston, TX, MS, accountancy, 1982. **Career:** First City Nat Bank, Houston, TX, vpres, 1973-85, sr vpres, 1985-86; Union Bank, Los Angeles, CA, vpres, 1986-88; Unity Nat Bank, Houston, TX, pres & chief exec officer, 1988-90; Imp Bank, Costa Mesa, CA, vpres, 1990-95; Community Bank Bay, Oakland, CA, pres & chief exec officer, 1995-97; Founders Nat Bank, chief operating officer, 1991-2001, sr vpres, 2000-03; Pac Mercantile Bank; Gilmore Bank, sr vpres & chief credit officer, 2013-. **Orgs:** Bd mem, Hester House Community Ctr, 1978-80; dir, Oakland Pvt Indust Coun; Peoples Workshop Performing Arts; bd mem, Houston Sun Literacy Acad, 1988-90; Julia C Hester House Community Ctr; City Hope Med Ctr; City Oakland Loan Comt; adv bd, Calif Organized Ins Network; chmn, Corp Econ Develop Harris County; N Am Air Defense Command; bd mem, S Cent YMCA, 1988-90; bd mem, Professions & Finance Assocs, 1990-93; bd mem, Nat Monetary Fund. **Honors/Awds:** Bank of the Year, Black Enterprise Mag, 1990; Founders Award, YMCA, 1990. **Home Addr:** PO Box 3971, Walnut Creek, CA 94598-0845. **Business Addr:** Senior Vice President, Chief Credit Officer, Gilmore Bank, 110 S Fairfax Ave, Los Angeles, CA 90036, **Business Phone:** (323)549-3621.

**ADAMS, DR. CHARLES GILCHRIST**
Clergy. **Personal:** Born Dec 13, 1936, Detroit, MI; son of Charles Nathaniel and Clifton Verdelle Gilchrist; married Agnes Hadley; children: Tara Hancock Washington & Charles Christian. **Educ:** Fisk Univ, attended 1956; Univ Mich, BA, 1958; Harvard Divinity Sch, MDiv, 1964. **Career:** Concord Baptist Church, pastor, 1962-69; Hartford Memorial Baptist Church, sr pastor, 1969-; Boston Univ, Homiletics & black Church Studies, lectr; Andover Newton Sch Theol; Cent Baptist Sem; Lliff Sch Theol; Ecumenical Theol Sem, prof preaching, 2000-07; Harvard Divinity Sch, william & lucille nickerson prof pract ethics & ministry, 2007-12. **Orgs:** Pres, Detroit Br, Nat Asn Advan Colored People, 1984-86; Baptist World Alliance; pres, Black Alumni-Nat Asn Harvard Divinity Sch, 1988-94; pres, Progressive Nat Baptist Conv, 1990-94; cent comn, World Coun Churches, 1991, planning comm, 1994; Nat Coun Churches, 1992; conf preacher, Hampton Univ Ministers Conf, 1993-94; ed columnist, Mich Chronicle; chair, Ecumenical Urban Strategy Comn; bd trustee, Morehouse Col, bd trustee, Morris Col; Cong Nat Black Churches; bd dir, First Independence Bank; Phi Mu Alpha; Omega Psi Phi; Rockefeller fel Harvard Univ; Doctoral fel Union Theol Sem; Merrill Theol fel Harvard Univ; pres, Sophomore Class, Fisk Univ; vpres, Stud Coun. **Honors/Awds:** Doctor of Divinity, Morehouse Col, 1984; Doctor of Laws, Dillard Univ, 1985; Doctor of Humane Letters, Marygrove Col, 1985; Doc-

tor of Humanities, Univ Mich, 1986; Doctor of Divinity, Morris Col, 1980; Rabbi Marvin Katzenstein Award, Harvard Div Sch, 1992; 15 Greatest Black Preachers, Ebony Mag, 1994. **Special Achievements:** Spoke before United Nations, 1989; World Congress of the Baptist World Alliance, Speaker, 1990; Top 100 Influential Black Americans, Ebony Mag, 1990-94; Seventh General Assembly of the World Council of Churches, speaker, 1991; Spoke before President Clinton at the White House, 1992; He has been awarded twelve honorary doctorates from such institutions as Morehouse College, Marygrove College, Dillard University, Morris College, Kalamazoo College, and University of Michigan. Author: Drunk on the Eve of Reconstruction, Judson Press, 2001-02; Power in the Pulpit, John Knox Press, 2002; First Nickerson Prof of the Pract of Ethics and Ministry at Harvard Divinity Sch in 2007. **Home Addr:** 19472 Suffolk, Detroit, MI 48203, **Home Phone:** (313)368-5448. **Business Addr:** Pastor, Hartford Memorial Baptist Church, 18900 James Couzens Fwy, Detroit, MI 48235, **Business Phone:** (313)861-1300.

## ADAMS, DEBORAH ROSS

Judge. **Personal:** married Anthony; children: Ashley, Arin (deceased) & Aric. **Educ:** Univ Mich, BA, 1975; Georgetown Univ Law Ctr, JD, 1979. **Career:** City Detroit Law Dept, sr asst corp coun, 1983-94; Mich 36th Dist Ct, magistrate, 1994-97; 3rd Circuit Ct, Mich, judge, 1997-2013; Circuit Ct bench, 2006. **Orgs:** State Bar Mich; Wolverine Bar Asn; Nat Asn Advan Colored People; Georgetown Law Alumni Asn; Tabernacle Missionary Baptist Church, Detroit; Campaign Steering Comt, United Way Community Serv. **Honors/Awds:** Women of Excellence, The Michigan Chronicle, 2009. **Business Addr:** Judge, 3rd Circuit Court, 2 Woodward Ave, Detroit, MI 48226, **Business Phone:** (313)224-5261.

## ADAMS, DON L. See Obituaries Section.

## ADAMS, EDWARD ROBERT

Lawyer. **Personal:** Born Nov 1, 1943, Jamaica, NY; son of Anna Mae Nelson. **Educ:** Queens Col, BA, 1971; Rutgers Univ, Sch Law, JD, 1977. **Career:** NY State Dept Law, asst atty gen, 1996-; Fifteenth Dist NY, US Cong rep, 1996. **Orgs:** Macon B Allan Black Bar Asn, 1979-; NY Co Lawyers Asn, 1980-; chair, Third World Lawyer's Caucus, 1981-; bd dir, BRC Human Serv Corp, 1982-; NY City Community Bd 12, chair laws comn, 1984-89; regional rep, Nat Bar Asn, 1988-; Metrop Bar Asn, 1989-; comn mem, NY Comn Qual Care Ment Disabled, 1993-. **Honors/Awds:** Two Student Achievement Awards, Queens Col, 1971. **Home Addr:** 100 W 93rd St Apt 30D, New York, NY 10025-7598, **Home Phone:** (212)316-4842. **Business Addr:** Assistant Attorney General, New York State Department of Law, 120 Broadway Suite 25, New York, NY 10271, **Business Phone:** (212)416-8080.

## ADAMS, DR. ELAINE PARKER

Library administrator, educator. **Educ:** Xavier Univ La, BA, span educ, 1961; La State Univ, MS, libr sci, 1966; Univ Southern Calif, PhD, libr sci, 1973; Harvard Univ, mgt develop prog, 1986, Inst Educ Mgt, attended 1989; Univ Houston-Clear Lake, Houston, TX, MA, behav sci psychol, 2000. **Career:** Educator (retired); Orleans Parish Sch Syst, librn, teacher, 1961-68; Xavier Univ, New Orleans, La, ref librn, 1966-67; Grossmont Union HS Dist, dist catalog librn, 1971; Upper St Clair Sch Dist, librn, 1972-73; Univ Md, vis asst prof, 1973; Univ Southern Calif Health Sci Campus, media specialist, 1974-75; Tex Southern Univ, coord learning resource ctr, 1976-80; co-ed, Media & Young Adult, Chicago Ala, 1981; Getty Oil Co Res Ctr, supvr libr serv, 1980-83; Prairie View A&M Univ, assoc vpres, acad serv & planning, 1983-85, vpres stud affairs, 1985-89; Tex Higher Educ, Coord Bd, asst comnr, 1989-91; Houston Community Col Syst, NE, founding pres, 1991-96, vice chancellor, 1997-99, Houston Community Col, SW, psychol prof, founding pres, 1999-2006; State Tex, asst comnr educ opportunity planning. **Orgs:** Alpha Kappa Alpha Sor, 1967-; fel HEA Title II USC, 1968-71; Am Libr Asn, 1970-; chairperson, Calif Librns Black Caucus, Southern Area, 1975; area rep, Youth Understanding Int Stud Exchange, 1979-82; Spec Libr Asn, 1981-84; rec secy, Nat Coalition 100 Black Women Houston, 1984-86; adminr & counr, Nat Asn Women Deans, 1985-89; Nat Asn Stud Personnel Admin, 1986-89; accreditation team mem, Mid States Asn Col & Univ, 1987-91; pres, Xavier Univ Alumni Asn, 1989-91; bd trustee, Xavier Univ, 1990-95; accreditation team mem, Southern Asn Col & Sch, 1991-92; Am Coun Educ, Comn Leadership, 1994-96; pres, Houston YWCA; presiding officer, Tex Traumatic Brain Injury Adv Coun, 2006-11; bd mem, Disability Rights Tex, 2006-12; W Houston Assistance Ministries. **Home Addr:** , Houston, TX.

## ADAMS, EUGENE BRUCE

Funeral director. **Personal:** Born May 6, 1953, Atlanta, GA; son of John Wesley (deceased) and Eunice Hines; children: Amari Alexander. **Educ:** More house Col, Atlanta, BA, bus admin, 1974, BS, biol, 1982; Gupton Jones Col Mortuary Sci, attended 1975. **Career:** Guyton Bros Funeral Home, co-owner, 1974-78; Sellers Bros Funeral Home, gen mgr, 1978-84; Williams & Williams Funeral Home, gen mgr, 1984-86; Moffett-Speed & Smart Funeral Home, from gen mgr to owner, 1986-. **Orgs:** Kappa Alpha Psi Fraternity Inc, 1973-; Epsilon Nu Delta Mortuary Fraternity, 1975-; Nat Funeral Dir & Morticians Asn, 1975-; vpres, First District Ga Funeral Serv Practitioner Asn, 1986-; pres, Ga Funeral Serv Practitioners Asn, 1992-. **Honors/Awds:** Boy Scouts of America, Eagle Scout, 1970; Appointed by Governor Ga, Joe Frank Harris, Ga State Bd Funeral Serv, 1984, pres, 1988-90; Appointed by Govenor Ga, George Bus bee, Juvenile Justice Comt, 1980-84. **Home Addr:** 637 E 37th St, Savannah, GA 31401, **Home Phone:** (912)236-8871. **Business Addr:** General Manager, Secretary, Speed and Smart Funeral Home Inc, 224 Houston St, Savannah, GA 31401, **Business Phone:** (912)236-7881.

## ADAMS, DR. EUGENE WILLIAM

Educator, college teacher. **Personal:** Born Jan 12, 1920, Guthrie, OK; son of Clarence Leon and Lucille Evelyn Owens; married Myrtle Louise Evans; children: Eugene W Jr, Clyde & Michael. **Educ:** Wichita State Univ, attended 1941; Kans State Univ, DVM, 1944; Cornell Univ, MS, 1957, PhD, 1962. **Career:** US Dept Agr, St Louis, Mo, pub health vet, 1944-51; Tuskegee Univ, prof, assoc dean, vice provost & dir, 1951-89, prof emer, currently; Ahmadu Bello Univ, Zaria, Nigeria, prof, 1970-72. **Orgs:** Nat Resources Res Coun, NIH, 1974; Africa Bur Steering Comt Agr Educ, USAID, Africa Bur, 1984; Adv Panel, Off Technol Assessment, 1987; chmn, Trustee Bd Southeast Corsortium Inter Develop, 1987-89; bd dir, Inst Alternative Agr, 1990; Sigma Xi, Kappa Alpha Psi; Phi Zeta; Phi Boule; Kans State Univ. **Home Addr:** 704 Patterson St, Tuskegee, AL 36088, **Home Phone:** (334)727-8174. **Business Addr:** Professor Emeritus, The Tuskegee University, 1866 S Lane, Decatur, GA 30033, **Business Phone:** (404)679-4500.

## ADAMS, EULA L.

Executive. **Personal:** Born Feb 12, 1950, Tifton, GA; son of Thelma Billington; married Janet C; children: Kevin B. **Educ:** Morris Brown Col, BS, 1972; Harvard Bus Sch, MBA, 1976. **Career:** Deloitte & Touche, acct, 1972-73, partner, 1972-91; Am Express Info Serv, Denver, exec vpres finance & admin, 1991; First Data Corp, First Data Teleservices subsi, exec vpres finance & admin, 1991-94, exec vp & gen mgr, 1994-97, sr exec vp & chief operating officer, 1997-98, First Data Merchant Serv, pres, 1997-2000; First Data Resources, pres, 2000-04; First Data Resources, sr exec vpres, 1991-2003; Storage Technol Corp, vpres, global serv, 2004; NetBank Inc, bd dir, 2003-07; Solidus Networks Inc, chief operating officer & dir; Sun Microsystems Inc, Data Mgt Group & Delivery Serv, vpres, 2004-07; Xcore Corp, Pres, 2007-13; MasterCard Int, bd dir; Wells Fargo Merchant Servs, bd dir; Pay By Touch, chief operating officer, currently; Neuromonics, chief exec officer, 2013-. **Home Addr:** 18 Red Tail Dr, Highlands Ranch, CO 80126, **Home Phone:** (303)791-4212. **Business Addr:** Chief Executive Officer, Neuromonics, 2810 Emrick Blvd, Bethlehem, PA 18020.

## ADAMS, FLOYD, JR. See Obituaries Section.

## ADAMS, FLOZELL JOOTIN

Football player. **Personal:** Born May 18, 1975, Chicago, IL. **Educ:** Mich State Univ. **Career:** Football player (retired); Dallas Cowboys, right guard & offensive tackle, 1998, left tackle, 1999-2009; Pittsburgh Steelers, right tackle, 2010-11. **Orgs:** Activenumerous charities. **Honors/Awds:** Big Ten Offensive Lineman of the Year, 1997; Pro Bowl, 2003, 2004, 2006, 2007, 2008; All-Am hons; Champion, Asian Football Confederation, 2010. **Home Addr:** , Flower Mound, TX.

## ADAMS, GINA FERGUSON

Lobbyist, vice president (organization). **Personal:** married Eugene A; children: Spenser. **Educ:** Am Univ, BS; Georgetown Univ, Law Ctr, MS, int & comparative law; Howard Univ, Sch Law, JD. **Career:** US Dept Transp, atty hons prog, Off Gen Coun; FedEx Corp, managing atty int regulatory affairs off, 1992, staff dir, staff vpres int regulatory affairs, vpres, sr vpres govt affairs, 2001-, lobbyist; Nat Comn to Ensure a Strong Competitive Airline Indust, presidential appointee, 1993. **Orgs:** Bd mem, Am Univ; bd mem, Alvin Ailey Am Dance Theater; bd mem, Nat Mus Women Arts; bd mem, Wash Performing Arts Soc; bd mem, DC Pub Educ Fund; immediate chair, DC Chamber Com; bd mem, Town Hall Educ Arts & Recreational Campus (THEARC); chairwoman, Knock Out Abuse: Benefitting Victims Domestic Violence, 2009; Beauvoir Sch. **Home Addr:** , Washington, DC. **Business Addr:** Corporate Vice President for Government Affairs, FedEx Corp, 942 S Shady Grove Rd, Memphis, TN 38120, **Business Phone:** (901)369-3600.

## ADAMS, JUDGE GREGORY ALBERT

Lawyer. **Personal:** Born Jun 10, 1958, Atlanta, GA; son of Enoch Q Sr and Emily E Jackson; married Wanda Marie Crutchfield. **Educ:** Ga State Univ, Atlanta, BS, criminal justice, 1981; Univ Ga, Sch Law, Athens, JD, 1983. **Career:** Ga State Univ, Atlanta, supvr, 1977-81; Athens Off Dist Atty, law clerk, 1982-83; Inst Continuing Judicial Educ, Athens, Ga, researcher, 1983-84; Off Dekalb Co Solicitor, Decatur, Ga, sr asst solicitor, 1984-87; Dekalb County Juv Ct, dep chief asst dist atty, judge, 1987-94; DeKalb County Govt, chief judge, 1994-2004, DeKalb County Super Ct, judge, 2005-; State Ga, Super Ct, Stone Mountain Judicial Circuit, Super Ct judge, 2005-12, chief super ct judge, chief & admin judge, 2013-16; Inst Continuing Judicial Educ Ga, chmn bd trustees, 2008-10. **Orgs:** Alpha Phi Alpha Fraternity, 1980-; Asn Trial Lawyers Am, 1984-88; State Bar Ga, 1984-; Dekalb Lawyers Asn, 1984-, pres, 1994-95; pres, Scarbrough Sq Homeowners Asn, 1986-87; bd dir, Scarbrough Sq Community Asn, 1986; Dekalb County, Nat Asn Advan Colored People, 1987-; bd mem, Decatur-Dekalb Bar Asn, 1988-89; parliamentarian, Alpha Phi Alpha Fraternity, 1988-90; vpres, Dekalb Jaycees, 1989-; bd dir, Grad Leadership DeKalb, 1990; Chief Justice Comn Prof, 1994-; Rotary Int, 1995-; bd chmn, Leadership DeKalb, 1996; Atlanta Attorneys; Gate City Bar Asn; Univ Ga Sch Law Alumni; Nat Ctr State Ct; chmn trustee bd, Inst Continuing Judicial Educ; State Disciplinary Bd State Bar Ga; formal adv opinion bd, State Bar Ga; adv bd, Andrew Young Sch Policy Studies Ga State Univ; Chief Justice Ga Supreme Cts Comn; Blue Ribbon Comn; pres, DeKalb Bar Asn. **Honors/Awds:** Serv Award, Dekalb Br Nat Asn Advan Colored People, 1988; Merit Award, Dekalb Lawyers Asn, 1988; Legion of Honour, Dekalb-Atlanta Voters Coun, 1988; Outstanding Pub Serv, Dunwoody Rotary Club, 1990; Champion of Community Excellence Award, New Life Ministries Inc, 2005; Community Service Award, DeKalb Coun Arts, 2006; Justice Benham Community Service Award, State Bar Ga, 2006; Whitney M Young Service Award, Boy Scouts Am, 2007; Spirit of Scouting Award, Boy Scouts Am, 2007; Distinguished Leadership Award, Community Leadership Asn, 2008; Outstanding Jurist Award, Gate City Bar Asn, 2009; Distinguished Alumni Community Service Award, Ga State Univ Alumni Asn, 2009; Distinguished Service Award, DeKalb Hist Ctr, 2010; Living legend Award, Greater Travellers Rest Baptist Church, 2011. **Special Achievements:** First African American Jurist to have portrait displayed in a DeKalb County Building. **Home Addr:** 5285 Kingsgate Close, Stone Mountain, GA 30088, **Home Phone:** (770)469-7192.

## ADAMS, GREGORY KEITH, SR.

Meeting planner. **Personal:** Born Apr 9, 1958, Philadelphia, PA; children: Jasmine & Gregory II. **Educ:** Rutgers Univ, econs & bus, 1981. **Career:** Hyatt Hotels Corp, sales mgr, 1981-83; Westin Hotels Corp, sales mgr, 1983-85; Radisson Corp, asst dir sales, 1985; Bayard Rustin Alliance, founder & exec dir; Gay & Bi Equal Rights & Liberation, media dir, 1993; Westchester Co, bldg inspector planning, 2003-; Stop Renting Inst Md & Am, founder & chief exec officer, 1996-; ReMax Greater Metro, assoc broker, 1997-; Golden Triangle Inc, chief exec officer, From Bankruptcy 2 Bounty - Unlimited, pres, 2009-. **Orgs:** Nat conf dir, Nat Asn Advan Colored People, 1985; Greater Wash Soc Assoc Execs; Nat Assoc Expos Mgrs; Omega Psi Phi Frat; Prince Hall Master Mason; bd mem, Nat Coalition Black Meeting Planners; steering comm, Baltimore Black Enterprise Prof Exchange; bd mem, Port Chester Carver Ctr; Village Port Chester. **Home Addr:** 2019 Madison Ave, Baltimore, MD 21217. **Business Addr:** President, From Bankruptcy to Bounty, 22 W Rd, Baltimore, MD 21204, **Business Phone:** (888)616-2324.

## ADAMS, H. LESLIE, JR. (DR. HARRISON LESLIE ADAMS)

Composer. **Personal:** Born Dec 30, 1932, Cleveland, OH; son of Harrison Leslie Sr and Jessie B Manease. **Educ:** Oberlin Col, BS, biomed engineering, 1955; Calif State Univ, Long Beach, Calif, MMus, 1967; Ohio State Univ, PhD, 1973. **Career:** Karamu House, Cleveland, Ohio, assoc musical dir, 1964-65, composer-in-residence, 1979-80, resident composer, 1980-82; N Mex Sec Sch, vocal music supvr & choir dir, 1966-67; Kaleidoscope Players, musical dir, 1967-68; Fla A & M Univ, Tallahassee, Fla, asst prof music, 1968; Univ Kans, Lawrence, Kans, assoc prof music, dir univ choir, dir choral clin, 1970-78; Yaddo Artist Colony, Rockefeller Found, 1977, composer fel, 1980-84; Accord Assocs Inc, founder & pres, 1980-86, exec vpres & composer residence, 1986-92; Cuyahoga Community Col, guest composer, 1980; Martha Holden Jennings Found, artist-in-residence, 1981-83; Cleveland Music Sch Settlement, resident composer, 1981-82; Grace Presby Church, music/choir dir, 1996-; Creative Arts Inc, pres & artist-in-residence, 1997-; Univ Md, Col Pk, Md, guest composer, 2000; Shasta Col, Shasta, Calif, guest composer, 2000; Seifullah Gallery, artist-in-residence, 2011-. **Orgs:** life mem, Phi Kappa Phi, 1965-; life mem, Pi Kappa Lambda, 1972-; life mem, Phi Mu Alpha Sinfonia, 1973-; life mem, Phi Delta Kappa, 1974-; Ohio Chamber Orchestra, 1981-82; Am Composers Alliance, 1984-; Borg-Warner Found, 1985; Ctr Black Music Res, 1989; Cleveland Chamber Symphony, 1991; life mem, Am Organists Guild, 1992-; Cleveland Orchestra, 1994; Hist First Presby Church, 1997; Lakewood Presby Church; life mem, Am Choral Dirs Asn; life mem, Music Arts Asn. **Honors/Awds:** Winner composition competition, Nat Asn Negro Women, 1963; Nat Award, Choral Arts Inc, 1974; KC Composers Forum winner choral composition competition, 1974; Competition Award, Nat Choral Comp, 1974; Nat Endowment for the Arts, 1979; Fellowship Award, Rockefeller Found, 1979; Yaddo Artists Fellowship Award, 1980-84; Cleveland Orchestra Commissioned Composer, 1995; NANM 2004 Composer Award; Composer Legacy Award, Nat Opera Asn, 2006; Distinguished Alumnus Award, Calif State Univ, Long Beach, Calif, 2006; Gems of Cleveland Award, 2007. **Business Addr:** President, Composer-in-residence, Creative Arts Inc, 9409 Kempton Ave, Cleveland, OH 44108-2940.

## ADAMS, DR. HOWARD GLEN

Educator. **Personal:** Born Mar 28, 1940, Pittsylvania County, VA; son of Daniel Boone and Delsia Mae Waller; married Eloise Christine Davis; children: Stephanie Glenn. **Educ:** Norfolk State Univ, BS, biol, 1964; Va State Univ, MS, biol, 1968; Syracuse Univ, PhD, 1978. **Career:** Jacox Jr High Sch, teacher, gen sci, 1964; Norfolk City Pub Schs, biol/gen sci teacher, 1964-70; Norfolk State Univ, alumni affairs dir, 1970-73; vpres stud affairs, 1974-77; Nat Consortium GEM, exec dir, 1978-94; GEM, ecevutive dir, Minorities Engineering & Sci Inc, Nat Inst Mentoring, dir; H G Adams & Assocs Inc, founder & pres, 1995-; Books: Get Up with Something on your Mind! Lessons for Navigating Life, 2002. **Orgs:** Nat Teachers Sci Fel, 1964-65; Nsf In-Serv Fel, 1970; Comn serv bd, YMCA, 1979-85; bd trustee, Meadville/Lombard Theol Sch, 1980-87; corp adv bd, Nat Assoc Equal Opportunity Higher Educ, 1981-; consult, Black Collegian Publ, 1984-91; coun econ Priorities, bd dir, 1986-93; US Cong Task Force Women, Minorities & Handicapped Sci & Tech, 1987-90; Col Indust Partnership Div, Am Soc Engineering Educ, bd dir, 1988-; Nat Adv Coun Environ Tech Transfer, US Environ Protection Agency, 1988-90; Sci & Engineering Rev group, Waste Policy Inst, US Dept Energy, 1990-; Women Engineering Prog Advocates Network, Wash, DC, 1990-92; Col Engineering, Univ Mich, Nat Adv Comn, 1992-95; bd mem, Am Asn Blacks Higher Educ; fac mem, AABHE's Leadership & Mentoring Inst. **Special Achievements:** One of the first recipients of the Presidential Awards for Excellence in Science, Mathematics, Engineering and Mentoring. **Home Addr:** 361 Willow Glenn Ct, Marietta, GA 30068, **Home Phone:** (770)578-6813. **Business Addr:** Founder, President, HG Adams & Associates Inc, 361 Willow Glenn Ct, Marietta, GA 30065, **Business Phone:** (770)578-6813.

## ADAMS, JEAN TUCKER

Government official. **Personal:** Born Baltimore, MD; children: Stuart Randall & Scott Hamilton. **Educ:** Coppin State Teachers Col, BS, 1958; Univ Md, MSW, 1972. **Career:** Baltimore City, teacher, 1958-64; Health & Ment Hygiene Juvenile Serv Admin, asst reg dir, 1965-76; Pvt pract, psychotherapist, 1975-; Off Mayor Baltimore Md, dep dir, 1976-80; State House Gov Off, exec asst. **Orgs:** Consult, Pvt Pub, 1975-; Nat Asn Soc Workers, 1975-; legislative adv, Exec & Prof Women's Coun MD, 1980-; vpres, United Serv Orgn, 1982-; bd mem, Sudden Infant Death Syndrome Inst, 1983-. **Honors/Awds:** Mayor's Citation, Baltimore City, 1979; Governor's Citation, State Md, 1984; Scroll Appreciation, Wiesbaen Germany Military Comn, 1984; Social Worker of the Year, Nat Asn Soc Workers, 1984. **Home Addr:** 5820 Stuart Ave, Baltimore, MD 21215.

## ADAMS, BISHOP JOHN HURST

Clergy. **Personal:** Born Nov 27, 1927, Columbia, SC; son of E Avery and Charity Nash; married Dolly Jacqueline Desselle; children: Gaye Desselle, Jann Hurst & Madelyn Rose. **Educ:** Johnson C Smith Univ, AB, hist, 1947; Boston Univ Sch Theol, STB, 1952, STM, 1956; Union Theol Sem NY; Payne Theol Sem, DD, 1956; Wilberforce Univ, LLD, 1956; Paul Quinn Col, HHD, 1972; Harvard Univ. **Career:** Clergy (retired); Bethel African Methodist Episcopal Church, Lynn, MA, pastor; Payne Theol Sem, sem teaching fac, 1952-56; Paul Quinn

Col Waco, pres & campus pastor, 1956-62; First African Methodist Episcopal Church, Seattle, sr pastor, 1962-68; Grant African Methodist Episcopal Church, Los Angeles, CA, sr pastor, 1968-72; African Methodist Episcopal Church, sr bishop, 1988-04. **Orgs:** Chair, Cent Area Civil Rights Comt; Chmn bd, Paul Quinn Col; chmn, Comn Higher Educ Am Church; dir, Am Income Life Ins Co; chmn, Am Church Serv & Develop Agency, 1978; dir, Fund Theol Educ; vpres, Nat Black United Fund; chmn, Cong Nat Black Church; dir, chmn, trustee, Interdenominational Theol Ctr; trustee, Allen Univ; trustee, Edward Waters Col; trustee, Morris Brown Col; chmn bd trustee, Atlanta Univ Ctr; founder chmn emer, Cong Nat Black Churches, 1978; initiator exec mgt training, Black Church Leaders; chmn, Inst Church Admin & Mgt; Joint Ctr Polit & Econ Studies; Transafrica; Nat Black United Fund; King Ctr Develop Bd; Alpha Phi Alpha Fraternity; King Ctr Develop Bd; Alpha Phi Alpha Fraternity. **Special Achievements:** First pastor of African Methodist Episcopal Church. **Home Addr:** 2500 Peachtree Rd NW Suite 206N, Atlanta, GA 30305, **Home Phone:** (404)467-8533.

### ADAMS, ESQ. JOHN OSCAR

Educator, executive, engineer. **Personal:** Born Apr 3, 1937, Chattanooga, TN; son of John M and Queen M. **Educ:** Wayne State Univ, BS, 1962; Loyola Univ, Los Angeles, CA, JD, 1970. **Career:** Detroit Publ Sch, instr, 1962-64; Pasadena City Col, lectr, 1964-65; IBM LA, mgr, sys engr & instr, 1964-70; IBM Corp Hq, atty antitrust, 1970-72; US Senate Small Bus Comm, minor coun, 1972-75; City Los Angeles, dep city atty, 1975-76; Wallace & Wallace, spec coun, 1975-80; Adams Industs Inc, Calif, CA, pres & bd chmn, 1978-82; atty at law, 1982-; art dealer, 1985-; judge pro term, 1995-; US Bankruptcy Ct, Cent Dist Calif, bd mediators, currently; Adams & Alexander, managing Partner, currently. **Orgs:** Chmn & bd dir, Hollywood Chamber Com; bd dir, Hollywood Arts Coun; Supreme Ct; Wash DC Bar Asns, Calif, NY; Hollywood Kiwanis; bd regents, Loyola Marymount Univ; Cent Dist Consumer Bankruptcy Attorneys Asn. **Honors/Awds:** Special Achievement Award, Los Angeles Urban League, 1970; Saturday Review Commen Issue, 1975; Men of Achievement. **Special Achievements:** Author, "Notes of an Afro-Saxon", "Future Hope for the US". **Home Addr:** 8880 Appian Way, Los Angeles, CA 90046, **Home Phone:** (323)650-8879. **Business Addr:** Managing Partner, Adams & Alexander, 8383 Wilshire Blvd Suite 919, Beverly Hills, CA 90211, **Business Phone:** (323)966-5533.

### ADAMS, JONATHAN, III

Actor. **Personal:** Born Jul 16, 1967, Pittsburgh, PA; married Monica Farrell; children: Sydney & Monica. **Educ:** Carnegie-Mellon Univ. **Career:** Theater: "Danger: Memory"; "The Taming of the Shrew"; "A Midsummer Night's Dream"; "Cymbelline"; Films: Two Evil Eyes; Heartstopper, 1991; Air Bud: Golden Receiver, 1998; Planetfall, 2005; Midground, 2009. TV Series: "Frasier"; "City of Angels"; "Walker, Texas Ranger"; "Felicity"; "The American Embassy", 2002; "American Dreams", "Bones"; NBC, 2004; "The Unit", 2006; "The Closer", 2007; "Navy NCIS: Naval Criminal Investigative Service", 2007; "Women's Murder Club", 2007-08; "Boston Legal", 2008; "The Cleaner", 2009; "The Philanthropist", 2009; "NCIS: Los Angeles", 2009; "The Deep End", 2010; "Desperate Housewives", 2010; "Miami Medical", 2010; "No Ordinary Family", 2010; "The Avengers: Earth's Mightiest Heroes", 2010-12; "Hellcats", 2010-11; "Memphis Beat", 2011; "The Glades", 2011; "Fanboy and Chum Chum", 2011; "Burn Notice", 2011; "Harry's Law", 2011; "Castle", 2011-14; "Green Lantern: The Animated Series", 2011-13; "Up All Night", 2012; "Revenge", 2012-13; "America's Book of Secrets", 2012-13; "Last Man Standing", 2012-14; "Pair of Kings", 2013; "Nikita", 2013; "Uncle Grandpa", 2013; "Hulk and the Agents of S.M.A.S.H.", 2013-14; "The Legend of Korra", 2013-14; "Crisis", 2014; "Drop Dead Diva", 2014; "Dallas", 2014.

### ADAMS, JOSEPH LEE

Manager, president (organization), educator. **Personal:** Born Jan 5, 1944, Kansas City, MO; son of Joseph L Sr and Thelma V O; married Nancy; children: Lee, Heather, Joseph III & Patrick. **Educ:** Univ Mo, Kans City, BA, 1970, MA, 1971; Wash Univ, St Louis, post grad, 1979. **Career:** Prof (retired); IBM, data ctr suprv, 1968-70; Univ Mo, Kans City, teaching asst, 1970-71; Univ City, councilman, 1974-95, mayor, 1995-2010; Meramec Comm Col, assoc prof hist; St Louis Community Col, prof hist, 1971-2003; Whitfield Cong, campaign mgr, 2012-. **Orgs:** Oc Hist Asn, Nat League Cities; bd dir, Mo Mcpl League, vpres, 1998-99, pres, 1999-2000; St Louis Cty Munic League; Episcopalian Church, Univ Dem; Mo Comn Intergovernmental Coop, 1985-; steering comt transp community, Nat League Cities, 1982-; vice chmn, Transp& Commun Steering Comt, 1988; chmn, Telecommunication Subcomt Transp & Commun, Nat League Cities, 1991; bd dir, Nat League Cities, 1991-93, adv coun, 1993-, vice chair, 1997; adv coun, Nat League Cities, 1993; bd dir, Citizens Mod Transit, 1994-97; mayor, Univ City, 1996; Secy, Loop Trolley Bd dir; adv bd, State Hist Rec; pres, Regional Mayors Orgn; pres, State League; bd dir, Nat League Cities. **Home Addr:** 924 Wild Cherry Lane, University City, MO 63130, **Home Phone:** (314)862-7877.

### ADAMS, DR. JULIUS GREGG

Dean (education), executive director, educator. **Personal:** Born Oct 4, 1957, Buffalo, NY; son of Peter William and Evelyn; married Carmon Grigsby. **Educ:** State Univ NY, Buffalo, BA, educ psychol, 1978, MA, psychol, 1985, PhD, educ psychol, 1988. **Career:** St Univ NY Col, Fredonia, Sch Educ, asst prof, 1988, assoc prof, 1994, dir, 1997, assoc prof & dir, 1997-2001; Univ Bufflalo, Grad Sch Educ, assoc dean teacher educ, 2002-06, Educ Opportunity Ctr, exec dir, currently; Off Univ Prep Progs, interim exec dir; Buffalo Pub Schs, psychologist; Ralph C Wilson Jr Sch Educ, St John Fisher Col, assoc dean, 2006-, dir sch educ, assoc prof educ; Daemen Col, chair, assoc dean spec progs. **Orgs:** Western New York Educ Serv Coun; pres, Ny Asn Teacher Educr. **Business Addr:** Executive Director, State University of New York, 465 Wash St Rm 426, Buffalo, NY 14203-1707, **Business Phone:** (716)849-6727.

### ADAMS, KATHERINE J.

President (organization). **Personal:** Born Oct 16, 1952, Pittsburgh, PA; married Herman L Jr; children: H Dean. **Educ:** Malone Col, commun, 1972; Kent State Univ, commun, 1974; Cleveland State Univ, commun; Wayne State Univ, BA, 1993; Our Savior Lutheran, Bronx, BS, interdisciplinary studies. **Career:** WJKW-TV Storer Broadcasting, desk asst, 1974-75, reporter trainee, prod asst, 1976-77, news anchor, reporter & host, 1977-82; WDIV, news anchor; Katherine Enterprises Inc, owner, 1989-, pres & chief exec officer, 1996-2011; A&M Automotive Transp, pres & owner, 2001-11; Big Bros Big Sisters Metrop Detroit, dir corp & found rels, 2007-12. **Orgs:** Comn comnr, Cleveland Chap, Nat Asn Advan Colored People; hostess, Focus Black-Pub Serv Prog; City Cleveland Comm Rels Bd; adv bd, Salvation Army Hough Multi Purpose Ctr. **Honors/Awds:** Salute to Black Clevelanders Award, Greater Cleveland Interchurch Coun, 1980; Emmy Award. **Business Addr:** President, A & M Automotive Transport Company LLC, 645 Griswold Suite 1300, Detroit, MI 48226, **Business Phone:** (313)237-6857.

### ADAMS, KATHY J.

President (organization), television journalist. **Educ:** Wayne State Univ, attended 1993. **Career:** WDIV Channel 4, TV news anchor; Katherine Enterprises Inc, pres & chief exec officer, 1996-11; A& M Automotive Transp, owner & pres, 2001-11; J & M Automotive Transp Co LLC, pres. **Orgs:** Dir Corp & Found Rels, Big Bros Big Sisters Metrop Detroit, 2007-12. **Business Addr:** President, A & M Automotive Transport, 645 Griswold St Suite 1300, Detroit, MI 48226, **Business Phone:** (313)237-6855.

### ADAMS, KAWEEDA G.

School principal, educator, administrator. **Personal:** married Eric J Sr; children: Eric J Jr (Ashley) & Katelynn Elizabeth. **Educ:** Univ New Orleans, BA, Eng educ; Univ Nev, Las Vegas, MEd, educ admin & higher educ, 2010. **Career:** St Augustine Pvt Cath High Sch, teacher; O'Callaghan Mid Sch, asst prin; Duane D Keller Mid Sch, asst prin; Bob Miller Mid Sch, Clark County, prin; Clark County Sch Dist, dean students, asst prin, prin, human resources dir, asst chief stud achievement officer, facil admin, currently, dir instr unit, currently; Regis Univ, Denver, Colo, fac, currently. **Orgs:** Alpha Kappa Alpha Theta, Las Vegas Chap. **Home Addr:** 8228 Mountain Heather Ct, Las Vegas, NV 89149, **Home Phone:** (702)658-8488. **Business Addr:** Director of Instruction & Facilities Administration, Clark County School District, 5100 W Sahara Ave, Las Vegas, NV 89146, **Business Phone:** (702)799-5000.

### ADAMS, LEON

Administrator, executive director. **Career:** Ohio Civil Rights Comn, mediation adminr, currently. **Orgs:** Exec dir, Ohio Civil Rights Comn. **Home Addr:** 618 Eastmoor Blvd, Columbus, OH 43209-2253, **Home Phone:** (614)235-4791. **Business Addr:** Mediation Administrator, Ohio Civil Rights Comn, 1111 E Broad St Suite 301, Columbus, OH 43205-1379, **Business Phone:** (614)466-2785.

### ADAMS, LEONARD E., JR.

Executive, business owner. **Career:** Adams Home Improvement, owner, prin, pres, currently. **Business Addr:** Owner, President, Adams Home Improvement, 4265 Brandon Ridge Dr NE, Marietta, GA 30066-2107, **Business Phone:** (770)924-1062.

### ADAMS, LILLIAN LOUISE TOLBERT

Teacher. **Personal:** Born Aug 8, 1929, Greenwood, SC; married David H; children: Hannah Lucille Iula Shaper (deceased), David H Jr & Debra A Montgomery. **Educ:** Fisk Univ, AB, 1951; SC State Col, MEd, 1970. **Career:** Gordon High Sch, teacher, 1951-53; Lincoln High Sch, 1955-57; Willow Creek Elem, 1957-68; Harllee Elem Sch, 1968-. **Orgs:** Florence Co Educ Asn; Asn Classroom Teacher; Cumberland United Methodist Church; chmn, Stewardship Comn; pres, Am Legion Aux. **Home Addr:** 600 W Sumter St, Florence, SC 29501, **Home Phone:** (843)662-1605. **Business Addr:** Teacher, Harllee Elem School, 408 E Pine St, Florence, SC 29501.

### ADAMS, LUCINDA WILLIAMS

Educator, athlete. **Personal:** Born Aug 10, 1937, Bloomingdale, GA; daughter of David and Willie M; married Floyd; children: Kimberly. **Educ:** Tenn State Univ, BS, 1959, MS, 1961; Univ Dayton, attended 1979; Ohio State Univ, attended 1984. **Career:** Educator (retired); Dayton Pub Schs, teacher, 1960-73, curric supvr, 1975, assoc dir; Dayton Div Parks & Recreation, recreation leader, 1968-70; Natl Assoc for Sports & Physical Edn, pres, 1994-95. **Orgs:** AKA Sorority Inc, 1958-; pres, Midwest Dist Asn Health, Phys Educ, Recreation, Dance, 1958-, 1990; Ohio Asn Health, Phys Educ, Recreation, Dance, 1970-; Phi Delta Kappa, 1979; Am Alliance Health, Phys Educ, Recreation & Dance, 1983-; adv bd, Univ Dayton Phys Educ, 1983-; Ohio Spec Olympic Brd, 1989-; Dayton Chap Ronald McDonald's Charities Brd, 1991; pres, Nat Asn Sports & Phys Educ, 1994; US Olympian Soc. **Home Addr:** 5049 Coulson Dr, Dayton, OH 45417-6032, **Home Phone:** (937)268-2377.

### ADAMS, DR. MELBA K.

Dentist. **Educ:** Meharry Med Col, DDS, dent, 1973. **Career:** Pk Plaza Periodont, dentist, 1976-. **Business Addr:** Dentist, Park Plaza Periodontics, 1213 Hermann Dr Suite 265, Houston, TX 77004, **Business Phone:** (713)523-0502.

### ADAMS, NELSON EDDY

Police detective, president (organization), association executive. **Personal:** Born Aug 11, 1945, Southport, NC; married Yvonne McKenzie; children: Nelson Demond & Marius Anton. **Educ:** Cape Fear Tech Inst, rec admin, 1972, nondestructive testing, 1973; Convair Sch, Nondestructive Testing, 1974; Southeastern Comt Col, police sci, 1975; Northwestern Univ, super police personnel, 1976. **Career:** Brown & Root Const Co, qual control inspector, 1974; Brunswick Co Sheriff's Dept, jailer patrolman sgt detective, 1974-80; Int Long shoremans Asn, pres; City Southport, aldermen ward 2. **Orgs:** Steward Mt Carmel AME Church; Pythagoras Lodge No 6 F&AM; South port Lions Club; city alderman South port Bd Aldermen 2nd 4 year term; former adv, Nat Asn Advan Colored People Youth Coun, 1967-69. **Honors/Awds:** Cert Appreciation pres elect S Brunswick Middle Sch PTO, 1982-83; Cert of Appreciation pres S Brunswick Middle Sch PTO, 1984. **Business Addr:** Aldermen Ward 2, City of Southport, 303 W 10th St, Southport, NC 28461, **Business Phone:** (910)457-6557.

### ADAMS, OLETA ANGELA

Singer, songwriter. **Personal:** Born May 4, 1953, Seattle, WA; daughter of preacher; married John Cushon. **Career:** Tears for Fears's Seeds of Love album, backup singer, 1989; opened tour for Michael Bolton, singer, 1992; Solo albums: Going on Record, 1983; Circle of One, 1990; Evolution, 1993; Come Walk with Me, 1997; All the Love, 2001; Ultimate Collection, 2004, Christmas Time with Oleta, 2006; Lets Stay here, 2009. Singles: "Rhythm of Life", 1990; "You've Got to Give Me Room", 1991; "Don't Let the Sun Go Down on Me", 1991; "Window of Hope", "I Just Had to Hear Your Voice", 1990; "Easier To Say Goodbye", 1994; "My Heart Won't Lie", 1994; "Never Knew Love", 1995; "Life Keeps Moving On", 1995; "We Will Meet Again", 1996. William Morris Agency, singer, currently. **Special Achievements:** Debut album, Circle of One, earned a certified gold record, 1991. **Business Addr:** Singer, William Morris Agency, 1 William Morris Pl, Beverly Hills, CA 90212, **Business Phone:** (310)859-4000.

### ADAMS, RICHARD MELVIN

School administrator. **Personal:** Born May 13, 1951, Pittsburgh, PA; son of Richard M Sr and J Marion; married Judy Duck; children: Amena C & Marcus T. **Educ:** Bowdoin Col, BA, govt & Afro-Am studies, 1973; Univ Pittsburgh, Grad Sch Pub & Int Affairs, attended 1974; Jones Int Univ, MA, bus commun, 2005. **Career:** GMAC, field rep, 1974-75; Homewood-Brushton Community Improv Asn, field rep, 1975-76; Oper Better Block Inc, community develop specialist, 1976-85; Community Col Allegheny County, asst exec dean, S campus, 1985-97, from asst pres to pres, 1998, actg asst dean homewood-brushton, pres diversity & equity, asst vpres, currently, exec dir, community rels & outreach, 2010, pub info officer; Off Instnl Diversity & Equity, head, currently; radio talk show, host. **Orgs:** Primary Care Health Serv Inc, vice chair, 1978-2000, pres, 2000-; bd mem, Dist I Pittsburgh Pub Schs, 1985-; bd dir, Nat Asn Neighborhoods, 1985-; bd mem, NE Region Coun Black Am Affairs, 1985-; bd dir, Am Asn Sch Adminr; Nat Asn Advan Colored People, Oper PUSH, Trans Africa; state chmn, Pa Nat Rainbow Coalition, 1986-; co-convener, W Pa Black Polit Assembly; Pittsburgh Human Rels Comn; Pittsburgh Sch Bd; exec comt, Inst Black World 21st Century; assoc mem, Nat Asn Diversity Officers Higher Educ. **Home Addr:** 700 N Sheridan Ave, Pittsburgh, PA 15206. **Business Addr:** Assistant Vice President, Acting Assistant Dean of Homewood-Brushton, Community College of Allegheny County, 808 Ridge Ave, Pittsburgh, PA 15212, **Business Phone:** (412)237-2511.

### ADAMS, ROBERT EUGENE

Educator. **Personal:** Born May 14, 1946, Richmond, VA; son of Thomas S and Daisy W; married Kathye J Gary; children: Shannon Marie. **Educ:** Norfolk State Univ, AS, 1969; Va State Univ, BS, 1972, MEd, 1990. **Career:** Imp Plz, asst food serv mgr, 1972-73; Marriott Corp, mgr food serv, 1973-82; Creative Cuisine, owner & mgr, 1982-88; Northern Va Community Col, instr restaurant mgt prog, 1989-90; Va State Univ, instr, recruiter, 1990-2000; Morris Brown Col, instr, bus & hospitality admin dept, 1992-, interim chmn, 1994-96. **Orgs:** Am Dietetic Asn; Coun Hotel, Restaurant & Instnl Educ; Omega Psi Phi Frat, Psi Alpha Alpha Chap; secy, Int Food Execs Asn; Hist & Predominantly Black Col & Univs. **Home Addr:** 5112 Hunterest Dr SW, Mableton, GA 30126, **Home Phone:** (770)948-2995. **Business Addr:** Instructor, Morris Brown College, 643 Martin Luther King Jr Dr NW, Atlanta, GA 30314, **Business Phone:** (404)739-1000.

### ADAMS, DR. RUSSELL LEE

Educator. **Personal:** Born Aug 13, 1930, Baltimore, MD; son of James Russell and Lilly B; married Eleanor McCurine; children: Sabrina & Russell Lowell. **Educ:** Morehouse Col, BA, polit sci, 1952; Univ Chicago, MA, polit sci, 1954, PhD, polit sci, 1971. **Career:** Cook County, probation officer, 1958-64; NC Cent Univ, asst prof & chairperson dept polit sci, 1965-69; Newark-New Castle-Marshalton McKean Sch Dist, Jackson Pub Schs, consult, 1969-71; Fed City Col, assoc prof & actg chairperson div humanities, 1969-71; Howard Univ, Dept Afro-Am Studies, prof & chair, 1971-2005, prof emer, 2005-; Univ Pittsburgh, Ctr Deseg, consult, 1976-. **Orgs:** Chmn, Comm Status Blacks Prof Am Polit Sci Asn, 1974-77; Nat Asn Advan Colored People; bd ed, Prince Georges County, Curr Eval Pool, 1976-; consult, Wilmington DE Pub Schs, 1977; lectr & consult, US Info Agency, 1977; Nat Conf Black Polit Scientists; Nat Asn Study Afro-Am Life & Hist; assoc ed, Ed Bd. **Honors/Awds:** George Washington Honor Medal, 1966; lect, Univ Md, Columbia Univ, Georgetown Univ, Rutgers Univ & Harvard Univ. **Special Achievements:** Author of "Great Negroes Past & Present, 1963-69", 1972, "Leading American Negroes", 1965, "Perceptual Difficulties Dev Political Science Varia", Spring 1976, publisher of "Black Studies Movement, Assessment Journal of Negro Education", 1977. **Home Addr:** 2414 Fairhill Dr, Suitland, MD 20746-2302, **Home Phone:** (301)423-5739. **Business Addr:** Professor Emeritus, Howard University, Rm 316 2400 6th St NW Founders Lib Bldg, Washington, DC 20059-0002, **Business Phone:** (202)806-7242.

### ADAMS, SAM AARON, JR.

Business owner, football player. **Personal:** Born Jun 13, 1973, Houston, TX; son of Sam Sr; married Erika; children: Sam, Terin & Tea Alexis. **Educ:** Tex A&M Univ, agr econs. **Career:** Football player (retired); Seattle Seahawks, left defensive end, 1994, left defensive tackle, 1995-99; Baltimore Ravens, left defensive tackle, 2000-01; Oakland Raiders, defensive tackle, nose tackle, 2002; Buffalo Bills, defensive tackle, left defensive tackle, 2003-05; Cincinnati Bengals, left defensive tackle, 2006; Denver Broncos, left defensive tackle, 2007; Everett Hawks, Nat Indoor Football League, owner. **Honors/Awds:** Consensus All-American, 1993; American Football Conference Pro Bowl, 1997; Pro Bowl, 2000, 2001, 2004; Hall of Fame, Texas A&M, 2001; American Football Conference champion, 2000, 2002; Super Bowl champion, XXXV. **Business Addr:** CO.

**ADAMS, SAMUEL LEVI, SR.**
Journalist, educator. **Personal:** Born Jan 25, 1926, Waycross, GA; son of Joe Nathan (deceased) and Viola Virgil (deceased); married Elenora Willette Grimes; children: Carol W, Bruce L & Samuel L Jr. **Educ:** WVa State Col, BA, Eng & fine arts, 1948; Wayne State Univ, AB, 1950; Univ Minn, MA, jour, 1954. **Career:** Educator, journalist (retired); Atlanta Daily World, reporter, 1954-56; Des Moines Regis, copy ed, 1956-57; Gibbs-St Petersburg Jr Col, dir pubrels, 1958-60, part-time teacher, 1960-64; St Petersburg Times, reporter, 1960-65, investigative reporter, 1967-68; Univ Wis, Russell Sage Fel Behav Sci Writing, 1965-66; Southern Regional Coun, dir res, 1965-66; Wis St Jour, corr, 1966-67; Univ Wis, vis prof, 1968-69, vis prof jour, 1985-87; Univ S Fla, asst prof, 1969-71; Dem Nat Comm, asst dir Minorities Div & asst pres sec, 1970-72; Univ KS, assoc prof jour, 1972-2000; Hampton Univ, distinguished vis prof, 1981-82; vis prof jour, 1982-83; Univ KS Sch Jour & Mass Commun, assoc prof journalism, prof emer; Univ Vi. **Orgs:** Founder, dir Continuing Acad Cult Enrich Prog, 1962-64; first vpres, Greater St Petersburg Coun Churches, 1963-65; prog dir, div & jointsessions San Diego Conv, 1974; Asn Educ Journ Head Minorities Div, 1974-75; dir, Gannett-AEJ Proj Enrichment Jour Educ, 1975-80; pres & bd chmn, Nat Youth Commun Inc, 1977-82; dir, Newspaper Fund's Nat Minority Internship Prog, 1979-80; KU Tenure Study Task Force; Task Force Univ Outreach; Minority Affairs Adv Bd; Am Asn Univ Prof; bd dir & educ resource chmn, Jones Holloway-Bryan Found, 1986-; consult commun, AmnestyInt USA, 1988-92. **Honors/Awds:** Regional Award, Nat Conf Christians & Jews, 1962; Pulitzer Prize Award, nominee in journ, 1964-65; Lane Bryant Awards, semi-finalist outstanding volunteer serv, 1966; Hampton Jr Col Award, 1966; Green Eyeshade Sweepstakes Award, Sigma Delta Chi Atlanta, 1969; Award for Distinguished Service, A&T State Univ, 1978; Ida B Wells Award, 1983; Blackening in the Media, NUL's State Black America, 1985; Highways to Hope, St Pete Times & Hohenburg's The New Front Page, 1965; Partners in Progress Award, Nat Asn Black Journalists, 1990; Distinguished Service Journalism Award, United Minority Media Asn, 1996; Lifetime Achievement Award, Nat Asn Black Journalists, 1997; UMMA Hall Media Fame, 1998; Ida B Wells Award, 2002. **Home Addr:** 1304 McDonald St, Waycross, GA 31501, **Home Phone:** (912)283-5089.

**ADAMS, SHEILA J.**
Association executive. **Personal:** Born Jun 1, 1943, Cincinnati, OH; children: Ariana; married Alexander; children: Derek & Brian. **Educ:** Univ Cincinnati, BA, sociol, 1964. **Career:** Association executive (retired); City Cincinnati, Employ & Training div, chief planner, 1971-81; Pvt Indust Coun, pres, 1982-89; Urban League Greater Cincinnati, pres & chief exec officer, 1990-2003. **Orgs:** Deleg Pres Clinton Summit Am Future, 1997; bd mem, Key Bank, Choice Care Found; Downtown Cincinnati Inc; United Way Found; Cincinnati Youth Collab; Advocates Youth Educ; Family & C First Exec Comn; Black Career Women Inc; Cincinnati Links; dir emer, Health Found Greater Cincinnati; chair, Ohio Coun Urban league; New Covenant Missionary Baptist Church. **Honors/Awds:** Notable Black Alumni, Univ Cincinnati, 1984- 1997; Hall of Fame, Withrow High Sch, 1991; Delta Sigma Theta Econ Empowerment Award, 1995; Gem Award, Asn Women Commun Cincinnati Chap, 1997; Dr MLK Jr Dream Keeper Award, 1998; Distinguished Black Women Award, Black Women Sisterhood Action, 1999; President of the Decade Award, Nat Urban League Youth Orgn, 1999; Bridges Award, Cincinnati Bell Bldg, 2000; Joseph A Hall Award, Promoting Diversity; Urban League of Greater Cincinnati Heritage Award. **Special Achievements:** Adams is the first woman to head the organization.

**ADAMS, DR. SHEILA MARY**
Teacher, consultant, president (organization). **Personal:** Born Jun 7, 1947, Chicago, IL; daughter of Frank Ricks and Delores Lawrence Wasmund; married Alvin; children: Lara, Kristina, Stefani & Susan. **Educ:** DePaul Univ, Chicago, IL, BA, music educ, 1979; Off Ministry Formation, Chicago, IL, lay ministry, 1983. **Career:** Chicago Police Dept, Chicago, Ill, jr clerk, 1968-71; US Treas Dept, Chicago, Ill, clerk, 1973-74; Archdiocese Chicago, Ill, elem teacher, 1979-90, Off Black Cath Ministries, exec, 1990-91, Off Ethnic Ministries, 1991-2000, African Am consult, 1991-98, African Am Ministry, dir, 1998; Off Black Cath, Chicago archdiocesan consult, dir African Am consult, currently; Black Cath Chicago.org, co founder & events ed, currently. **Orgs:** Bishops Nat Adv Coun, 1985-90; chair, Spirituality Com Archdiocesan Pastoral Coun, 1986-88; deleg; Nat Black Cath Cong VI, 1987; chair, Bishop's Nat Adv Coun, 1989; regional coordr, Nat Black Cath Cong VII, VIII, IX, 1990-2002; Nat Black Cath Cong VII, 1992; Nat Black Cath Cong VIII, 1998; secy, Nat Asn Black Cath Adrs, 1996-99; dir, Off Black Cath; dir, African Am Ministries. **Honors/Awds:** Archdiocesan Honoree; Fr Augustus Tolton Hon Award, 1987-88, Sr Thea Bowman Award, 1994; Dei Gloriam Award, 1999. **Home Addr:** 10149 S Crandon Ave, Chicago, IL 60617-5618, **Home Phone:** (773)721-0869. **Business Addr:** African American Consultant, Office of Black Catholics, 155 E Superior St 2nd Fl, Chicago, IL 60611, **Business Phone:** (312)534-5325.

**ADAMS, STEPHAN**
Entrepreneur. **Educ:** Univ Calif, Berkeley, BS, sociol; Wright Inst, PhD, psychol, 1985. **Career:** Adamation Inc, pres & chief exec officer, founder, 1984-2003, managing partner, 2012-; Curacin Global, prin, 2003-06; KANA Software, exec bus develop, 2006-10; ValenciaVentures, gen partner, 2011-12; Artiful.net, founder, 2012-. **Business Addr:** Managing Partner, Adamation Inc, 1940 Webster St Suite 250, Oakland, CA 94612, **Business Phone:** (510)452-5252.

**ADAMS, T. PATTON**
Government official, consultant, executive director. **Personal:** Born Feb 16, 1943, Columbia, SC; married Jacquelyn Hackett Culbertson; children: Thomas, John & Lucas. **Educ:** Wash & Lee Univ, BA, 1965; Univ SC, JD, 1968. **Career:** Columbia Zoning Bd Adjustments, bd mem, 1974-76; City Columbia, city coun mem, 1976-86, mayor, 1986-90; Army SC secy, civilian aide, 1986-2001, civilian aide emer, 2001-05; SC Comn Indigent Defense, exec dir, 2005-; pvt consult. **Orgs:** SC Bar Asn; Richland Co Bar Asn; SC Chamber Com; Columbia Visitors & Conv Bur; Nat Asn Criminal Defense Lawyers, Nat Legal Aid & Defender Asn; Am Legion; SC Off Indigent Defense; bd advisor, Charleston Sch Law, currently; chmn, Sc Youth Advocate Prog; chmn, City Columbia Govt Restructure Study Comn; Sc Veterans Memorial Pk Comn. **Honors/Awds:** Distinguished Service Award, Munic Asn SC, 1987; Nat Distinguished Service Award, Asn AUS; States Order of the Palmetto. **Business Addr:** Executive Director, South Carolina Commission on Indigent Defense, 1330 Lady St Suite 401, Columbia, SC 29201, **Business Phone:** (803)734-1343.

**ADAMS, V. TONI**
Executive. **Personal:** Born Dec 13, 1946, Oakland, CA; married James L Robinson; children: Karla, Doyle, Todd & Vikki. **Educ:** Mills Col, BA, 1968; Oxford Univ, Eng, attended 1976; Calif State Univ, MPA, econs & pub policy, 1976; Golden Gate Univ, DPA. **Career:** UC Berkeley, cont ed spec, 1968-77; City Oakland, spec asst to mayor, 1977-84; Builders Mutual Suriety Co, chief finance officer, 1982-83; Alameda Co Off Educ, bd chmn & dir stud progs & serv, county coordr, currently. **Orgs:** Grand juror, Alameda County Super Ct, 1973-74; bd dir, Calif Alcoholism Found, 1975-77; Alameda County Juv Delinq Prev, 1976-78; bd mem, Displaced Homemakers Ctr, 1983-; bd dir, Oakland Conv Ctr Mgt Inc, 1983-; pres, founding mem, Oakland Conv & Visitors Bd; treas, Nat Forum Black Pub Adminrs, bd mem, currently; vpres tourism, Nat Asn Black & Minority Chamber Com; bd mem, Playworks, 2002-; bd dir, Visit Oakland, currently. **Honors/Awds:** Outstanding Service Education, Col Bounders Oakland, 1979; Outstanding Young Women of America, 1981, 1983; Dick Spees Award for Tourism Promotion, 2005. **Business Addr:** Board of Director, Visit Oakland, 481 Water St, Oakland, CA 94607, **Business Phone:** (510)839-9000.

**ADAMS, VASHONE LAVEY**
Football player. **Personal:** Born Sep 12, 1973, Aurora, CO. **Educ:** Eastern Mich, grad. **Career:** Football player (retired); Cleveland Browns, defensive back & free safety, 1995; Baltimore Ravens, defensive back, 1996; New Orleans Sts, defensive back, 1997; Kans City Chiefs, 1998; Dallas Cow boys, 1999.

**ADAMS, DR. VERNA MAY SHOECRAFT**
School administrator, educator. **Personal:** Born Jul 1, 1928, Toledo, OH; daughter of John Henry and Ogrietta Lee; married Fred Sr; children: Jacqueline O Redd, Fred A Jr, Douglas F & Cynthia V McBride. **Educ:** Toledo Univ, St Francis Col, BS, 1962, MS, educ, 1964; Ball State Univ, EdD, 1979. **Career:** Educator (retired); Ft Wayne Comm Schs, teacher, 1961-67, guid couns, consult teacher, 1966-68, elem teacher, 1967-71, elem prin, 1971-80, dir title I prog, 1980-82, dir federally funded Chap I prog, Suppl Instrnl Prog, dir, 1982-89; Harmar Elem Sch, first grade classroom teacher, 1961, sixth grade teacher; St Francis Col, instr, lectr, 1964-74; Whitney Young Elem Sch, prin; Croniger Elem Sch, sixth grade teacher, Adult Basic Educ prog, counr; Smart Elem Sch, prin. **Orgs:** Bd dir, Parkview Hosp; bd dir, Ft Wayne Found; bd dir, Ft Wayne Philharmonic; Ft Wayne Philharmonic Outreach Comm; develop comm, Turner Chapel AME; trustee, Int Links Inc; Nat Asn Advan Colored People, Urban League, Phi Delta Kappa Ft Wayne Chap; Nat Alliance Black Sch Educ; cofounder, Ft Wayne Alliance Black Sch Educ. **Honors/Awds:** Woman of the Year, Ft Wayne Urban League, 1964; Woman of the Year, Kappa Alpha Psi Ft Wayne, Alumni Chap, 1976; Verna M. Adams educ financial asst prog excellence teacher educ, Lincoln Nat Bank & Fort Wayne Comm Sch, 1989; Verna M. Adams Scholarship, FWCS, named in honor, 1989; Woman of the Year, Zeta Phi Beta, Ft Wayne Chap; Service Award in the field of Education, Dr Martin Luther King Jr Club Comm, 2002. **Special Achievements:** Scholarship named Verna M Adams Educ Financial Asst Prog for Excellence in Teacher Educ, First African American woman lecturer and instructor St. Francis College, 1964-74; First African American woman prin, Ft. Wayne Community Sch, 1971; First African American woman director in the FWCS department of instruction, 1980; First African American woman elementary consultant teacher for FWCS, 1987; First African American to enter many doors in the field of education in Fort Wayne. **Home Addr:** 3524 Autumn Lane, Ft Wayne, IN 46806-4385, **Home Phone:** (260)456-6376.

**ADAMS, DR. WILLIE, JR.**
Government official, executive, medical scientist. **Personal:** Born Apalachicola, FL; married Constance Lee; children: 4. **Educ:** Fla A&M Univ; Meharry Med Col, Nashville, MD. **Career:** Hurley Hosp, internship; Emory Univ, Sch Med, residency; Pvt practr, Obstet & Gynec, 1973; Dipl Am Bd of Obstet & Gynec; Am Col Obstet & Gynec; Gov's Coun Maternal & Infant Care; City Albany, mayor, 2004-12; Albany State Univ, Col Sci & Health Professions, prof. **Orgs:** Pres, Stud Govt Asn, Fla A&M Univ; founder & dir, First Nat Bank S Ga; Albany Dougherty Inner City Authority; Dougherty County Bd Educ; Dougherty Aviation Comn; Ga Chamber Com; Phi Beta Sigma Fraternity; Adv Bd Salvation Army; bd dir, Mag Mutual Ins Co; Shiloh Baptist Church; Am Asn Gynec Laparoscopists; Am Med Asn; Am Fertil Soc; Ga State Med Soc; bd mem, Ga Dept Community Affairs, 2005-; adv bd mem, Albany State Univ, nursing prog. **Home Addr:** 320 W 2nd Ave, Albany, GA 31701, **Home Phone:** (229)439-7721. **Business Addr:** Board Member, Georgia Department of Community Affairs, 60 Executive Pk S NE, Atlanta, GA 30329, **Business Phone:** (404)679-4940.

**ADAMS, YOLANDA YVETTE**
Gospel singer. **Personal:** Born Aug 27, 1962, Houston, TX; married Tim Crawford Jr; children: Taylor Ayana; married Frank Fountain; children: 1. **Educ:** Teaching degree & cert; Howard Univ, divinity stud. **Career:** Gospel music rec artist, 1987-; Albums: Just as I Am, 1987; Through the Storm, 1991; Save the World, 1993; Bring It to Jesus, 1993; More Than a Melody, 1995; Yolanda.Live in Washington, 1996; Songs From the Heart, 1998; Mountain High Valley Low, 1999; The Best of Yolanda Adams, 1999; Christmas with Yolanda Adams, 2000; The Experience, 2001; Believe, 2001; The Praise and Worship Songs of Yolanda Adams, 2003; Day by Day, 2005; The Essential Yolanda Adams, 2006; What a Wonderful Time, 2007; Becoming, 2011; The Yolanda Adams Morning Show, radio host, currently. **Honors/Awds:** SGMWA Execellence Award, 1991, 1993, 1994 & 1997; Stellar Award, 1992, 1995; 1996; 1997, 2001, 2002 & 2003; Soul Train Lady of Soul Award, 1996, 2000, 2001 & 2002; Grammy Nomination, Yolanda. Live in Washington, 1996; Grammy Award, 1999, 2001 & 2006; Soul Train Music Award, 1999, 2001; Image Award, Nat Asn Advan Colored People, 2001; American Music Award, 2001; BET Award, 2003, 2004; Gospel-Indust Stellar Awards; Grammy Award, Victory, 2007. **Special Achievements:** Author: Points of Power, 2010. **Business Addr:** Gospel Singer, Mahogany Entertainment, 12201 Pleasant Prospect, Upper Marlboro, MD 20775.

**ADAMS-DUDLEY, LILLY ANNETTE**
Educator, consultant. **Personal:** Born Jun 7, 1950, Lochgelly, WV; daughter of James Alfred Adams Sr and Jerlena Paulanne Williams; married Jerry Lee Dudley Sr; children: Jerry Jr. **Educ:** Canisius Col, BA, 1972, MA, 1976, MS, 1984. **Career:** Hampton City Schs, Eng teacher, 1972-73; Buffalo Pub Schs, eng teacher, 1974-75; Canisius Col, lang arts specialist, 1975-78, asst dir, 1978-80, writing lab instr, 1982-84, reading & study skills instr, 1981-, consult, Canisius Opportunity Progs Educ, dir, 1980-& assoc dean, currently. **Orgs:** Policy bd mem, Consortium Niagara Frontier, 1980-; treas & campus rep, AJCU Conf Minority Affairs, 1980-81; Buffalo & Rochester regional rep, HEOP Prof Orgn, 1980-; Am Asn Black Women Higher Educ; Am Soc Training & Devel; Am Asn Univ Women; Nat Asn Female Execs; sem developer & co-leader, Today's Prof Woman, Develop Attitudes for Success; Self-Esteem & Your Success; Prof Black Women & Success; Am Soc Prof & Exec Women, 1986-. **Home Addr:** 92 Davidson Ave, Buffalo, NY 14215, **Home Phone:** (716)833-6762. **Business Addr:** Associate Dean, Director, Canisius College, 2001 Main St, Buffalo, NY 14208, **Business Phone:** (716)888-2575.

**ADAMS-ENDER, CLARA LEACH**
Military leader, entrepreneur. **Personal:** Born Jul 11, 1939, Willow Springs, NC; daughter of Otha and Caretha Bell Sapp; married F Heinz; children: Sven Ingo. **Educ:** NC A&T Univ, BS, nursing, 1961; Univ Minn, MS, med surg nursing, 1969; Army Command & Gen Staff Col, MS, mil arts & sci, 1976. **Career:** Military leader (retired), executive; AUS Nurse Corps, second lt; AUS, career officer, 1961-93, 121st evacuation hosp, staff nurse, 1963; Ft Sam Houston, med-surg nursing instr, 1964; Ft Belvoir, comndg gen, Mil Dist, Wash, DC, dep comndg gen, 1991-93; Georgetown Univ, adj prof; Oakland Univ, adj prof; Caring About People with Enthusiasm Assocs Inc, founder, pres & chief exec officer, currently. **Orgs:** Fel Am Acad Nurses; Defense Adv Comt Women Servs, 1994-; mil aide-de-camp, State Va, 2003-; chairperson & bd dir, Andrews Fed Credit Union; charter mem & bd visitorsUS Marine Corps Univ; mem, Defense Adv Comt Women Serv; Delta Sigma Theta sorority. **Special Achievements:** First woman to earn a Master of Military Art and Science degree at the Army Command & General Staff College; First female in the Army to be awarded the Expert Field Medical Badge, 1967. Published her autobiography, My Rise to the Stars: How a Sharecropper's Daughter Became an Army General, 2001. **Business Addr:** President, Chief Executive Officer, Caring About People with Enthusiasm Associates Inc, 3088 Woods Cove Lane, Woodbridge, VA 22192, **Business Phone:** (703)497-3088.

**ADAMS-GASTON, DR. JAVAUNE**
Executive director, educator. **Educ:** Univ Dubuque, BS, biol, psychol & gen sci; Loras Col, MS, appl psychol; Iowa State Univ, PhD, psychol. **Career:** Univ Md, staff psychologist coun ctr, Dept Intercollegiate Athletics, asst athletic dir, Undergrad Studies, assoc dean acad affairs, equity adminr, div stud affairs, Lett & Sci Dept, dir, Univ Career Ctr, exec dir, currently, Coun & Personnel Serv Dept, affil asst prof; Ohio Univ, vpres stud life, 2009-, assoc dean, acad affairs, asst athletic dir & equity adminr. **Orgs:** Grad fac, Md Univ. **Business Addr:** Vice President for Student Life, University of Ohio, 3034 Ohio Union 1739 N High St, Columbus, OH 43210, **Business Phone:** (614)292-9334.

**ADAMS-MAILLIAN, AUBREY**
Public relations executive. **Career:** Essence Mag, dir corp pub rels; Andrea Jovines fashion line, pub rels dir; R&R Entertainment & Consult, speaker, currently. **Business Addr:** Speakers Bureau, R&R Entertainment & Consulting, PO Box 020777, Brooklyn, NY 11202, **Business Phone:** (718)638-5082.

**ADDAMS, ROBERT DAVID**
Lawyer, college teacher. **Personal:** Born Feb 12, 1957, Chicago, IL. **Educ:** Princeton Univ, AB, 1978; Columbia Univ Grad Sch Jour, MSJ, 1980; Columbia Univ Sch Law, JD, 1982. **Career:** Goodman, Eden, Millender & Bedrosian, assoc atty, 1982-86; Nat Conf Black Lawyers, assoc dir, 1986; City Col NY, revson prof, 1986-87; Asn Legal Aid Atty, exec dir, 1986-92; Inst Mediation & Conflict Resolution, chief exec officer & pres, currently; Brooklyn Col, vis distinguished prof, Belle Zeller, 1994-. **Orgs:** State Bar Mich, 1982-92; Nat Lawyers Guild, 1982-86; Am Bar Asn, 1982-84; Nat Bar Asn, 1982-84; Wolverine Bar Asn, 1982-86; bd dir, Nat Conf Black Lawyers, 1985-87; Metrop Black Bar Asn, 1992; bd dir, NY State Mediation Asn, 1993-94. **Home Addr:** 137 Cent Pk N, New York, NY 10026, **Home Phone:** (212)222-2984. **Business Addr:** President & Chief Executive Officer, Director, Institute Mediation & Conflict Resolution, 505 8th Ave 2nd Fl, New York, NY 10018, **Business Phone:** (212)643-0711.

**ADDEI, ARTHELLA HARRIS**
Teacher, educator, school administrator. **Personal:** Born St. Louis, MO; daughter of Jesse K and Iona L; married Kwabena A; children: D'Asante. **Educ:** Harris Teachers Col, St Louis, MO, BA; Columbia Univ, NY, MA; City Univ NY, MS. **Career:** New Perspectives WWRL Radio NYC, producer & moderator; Essence Mag, contrib ed; NY Pub Schs, guid counr; Manpower Prog NYC, supvr counr; St Louis Pub Sch, teacher; Community Sch Dist 19 NY Pub Schs, dist supvr; Long Island Univ, prof dipl educ admin supv; NY Pub Sch Syst, prin; Ethan Allen Elem Sch, prin; CUNY, educ coun & guid stud; Dept Sch Admin, adj prof, currently. **Orgs:** Mayors Task Force Early Childhood, 1989-90; prog chmn, NY St Div Youth Adv Bd & Youth Serv Action Team; Alpha Kappa Alpha Sor; Womens Auxiliary Nassau Co Med Soc AMA; Womens Auxiliary Nat Med Asn; CSA Coun Supvrs & Admins, NY City; NYESPA Prins Asn; leader, New York educ syst. **Home Addr:** 475 Glen Cove Rd, Roslyn, NY 11576, **Home Phone:** (516)626-1112. **Business Addr:** Principal, Ethan Allen Elementa-

ry School, 970 Vermont St, Brooklyn, NY 11207, **Business Phone:** (718)649-3155.

### ADDERLEY, HERB ANTHONY (HERBERT ALLEN ADDERLEY)

Football player, executive. **Personal:** Born Jun 8, 1939, Philadelphia, PA; son of Charles and Rene (White); married Bell; children: Toni. **Educ:** Mich State Univ, BS, educ, 1961. **Career:** Football player (retired), executive; Green Bay Packers, corner back & left corner back & kick returner, 1961-69; Dallas Cowboys, corner back & left corner back, 1970-72; Giant Step Rec Co, vpres; Temple Univ, broadcast; Philadelphia Eagles, broadcast. **Orgs:** Charter mem, Sigma Chap Omega Psi Phi Fraternity. **Honors/Awds:** Super Bowl, 1967, 1968, 1971; All-Star Game, 1963-67; Pro Bowl, 1963-67; Pro Football Hall of Fame, 1980; Green Bay Packers Hall of Fame. **Home Addr:** 1058 Tristram Cir, Mantua, NJ 08051-2204.

### ADDERLY, T. C., JR.

Manager. **Personal:** Born Miami, FL; son of Bertha L and T C Sr; children: Beth, Andrew, Janine & Ashlee. **Educ:** Miami Dade Community Col, Miami, Fla, AA, 1980; Univ Miami Sch Bus, MBA, strategic mgt & leadership, 1991. **Career:** Fl Power & Light, Miami, Fla, customer serv & sales supvr & employee rels mgr, 1975-83, orgn training & develop instr, 1975-91, southern div human resources mgr, 1983-91; Y's Men Intl, pres, 1979-83; City Miami Beach, Dept Human Res, Fla, human res dir, 1992-2004; Fla Memorial Univ, adj prof, 2009-; City Opa-locka, FL, human resources dir, 2013-15; City Lauderdale Lakes, asst city mgr, 2015-. **Orgs:** Bd mem, Family Christian Asn Am Inc, 1979-, vice chmn, treas, currently; mentor chmn, Ocean Reef Mentor Prog, 1986-91; Amigos De Ser, 1983-; scholar chmn, Miami dade Chamber Com, 1981-; African Am Success Found. **Honors/Awds:** Americas Best & Brightest Young Business & Professional, Dollars & Sense, 1989; Leadership Miami, Greater Miami, Chamber, 1980; Member Chairman Appoint Award, Family Christian Asn Am Inc, 1990; Black Achiever, Family Christian Asn Am Inc, 1984. **Home Addr:** 18850 NW 14 Av Rd, Miami, FL 33169-3615. **Business Addr:** Adjunct Professor, Florida Memorial University, 15800 NW 42nd Ave, Miami Gardens, FL 33054, **Business Phone:** (305)626-3600.

### ADDISON, ADELE

Singer. **Personal:** Born Jul 24, 1925, New York, NY; married Norman Berger. **Educ:** Westminster Choir Col, BMus, 1946; Berkshire Music Ctr; Univ Mass, DHV, 1963. **Career:** Town Hall New York City, recital debut, 1952; State Univ NY, voice teacher; Eastman Sch Music, voice teacher; Aspen Music Festival & Sch, voice teacher; Aspen Music Festival, fac artist, 1956; New Eng City Ctr Wash Opera Co; orchestral & engagements w/symphonies Boston, Cleveland; NY Philharmonic, Nat Chicago, Pittsburgh, Indianapolis, LA, SF; World Premiere performances Incl John La Montaigne's Fragments, Song of Songs w/New Haven Symphony, 1959, Porgy & Bess Original, film soundtrack, 1959; Foss' Time Cycle w/NY Philharmonic, 1960; Poulenc's Gloria w/Boston Symphony, 1961; Philharmonic Hall Lincoln Ctr, soloist, 1962; US, Can, Soviet Union, recital tours, 1963; Aspen Music Inst, pvt voice lessons, 1975; Foss, Time Cycle; Phorion; Song of Songs, 1997; Mahler, Symphonies Nos 2, 5 & 8, 1997; Bach Clavierubung Part 3 (ii), 1999; Bach, Mass in Bminor, 1999; Bach, St Matthew Passion, 1999; Debussy, Le Martyre de St Sebastien, 1999; Handel, Messiah, 1999; Handel, Ode for St Cecilia's Day, 1999; The Essential Beethoven, 1999; Albums: Porgy & Bess, 1958; Beethoven, Symphony No 9, 1988; Beethoven, Symphony No 9 Fidelio Ov, 1991; Beethoven, Symphonies & Overtures, 1992; Gershwin, 1994; Vaughan Williams, Orchestral Works, 1994. **Orgs:** Am Acad Teachers Singing; chmn, Voice dept, Manhattan Sch Music. **Honors/Awds:** Honorary Doctorate, Manhattan Sch Music, 2001. **Home Addr:** 98 Riverside Dr, New York, NY 10024, **Home Phone:** (212)874-0557.

### ADDISON, CAROLINE ELIZABETH

College teacher, dean (education). **Personal:** Born Nov 14, 1938, Brooklyn, NY; married Wallace O Kelly Peace; children: Douglas K & Rock P. **Educ:** Bronx Community Col, AAS, 1964; Long Island Univ, BSN, 1972, MS, 1974; NY Univ, MPA, 1976; Walden Univ, PhD, 1978; Wayne State Univ, EdD, 1986. **Career:** St Joseph's Col, dean fac, 1976-78; Passaic Community Col, dir nursing & allied health prog, 1978-80; Va State Univ, dean & dir nursing, 1980-81; Univ Detroit, dir & chair nursing educ, 1981-; Univ Phoenix, Mich Campus, dir. **Orgs:** Nat League Nursing, 1964-; Am Nursing Asn, 1964-; Mich Asn Cols Nursing, 1981-; Mich Holistic Asn, 1983-; League Women Voters, 1984-; Wellness Network, 1986. **Special Achievements:** Selected Factors Related to Admission and Retention of Adult Registered Nurses. **Home Addr:** 29264 Franklin Hills Dr, Southfield, MI 48034-1149. **Business Addr:** Director, University of Phoenix, Michigan Campus, Southfield, MI 48076-4174, **Business Phone:** (248)262-3003.

### ADDISON, JAMES DAVID

Business owner, automotive executive. **Personal:** Born Jan 8, 1949, Shelby, NC; son of Inez Mildred and Jimmie Lee; married Marie Yolene Pierre; children: Jessica Marie & Jennifer Maureen. **Career:** Addison Auto Parts, pres & owner, 1987-; Auto parts salesman; mgr. **Home Addr:** 4202 12th Rd S, Arlington, VA 22204-3775. **Business Addr:** President, Addison Auto Parts, 3908 Pa Ave SE, Washington, DC 20020, **Business Phone:** (202)581-2900.

### ADDISON, RAFAEL

Basketball player, college teacher, basketball coach. **Personal:** Born Jul 22, 1964, Jersey City, NJ; married Xanda; children: Ashley & Antonio. **Educ:** Syracuse Univ, BA, commun, 1986. **Career:** Basketball player (retired), basketball coach, teacher; Phoenix Suns, forward, 1986-87; Libertas Livorno, Italy, 1987-91; NJ Nets, forward, 1991-93; Benetton Treviso, Italy, 1994; Detroit Pistons, forward, 1994-95; Charlotte Hornets, forward, 1995-97; PAOK Thessaloniki, Greece, 1997; alma mater high sch, coach & teacher, 1998; Snyder High Sch, head basketball coach, 2002-05; Jersey City St Univ, lectr, currently. **Orgs:** Vol, Spec Olympics; Fannie Mae Found; US Olympic Basketball Team, 1982. **Business Addr:** Lecturer, New Jersey City University, 2039 Kennedy Blvd, Jersey City, NJ 07305, **Business Phone:** (888)441-6528.

### ADDISON, TERRY HUNTER, JR.

School administrator. **Personal:** Born May 15, 1950, Memphis, TN; son of Terry Sr and Carsaunder Goosby; married Michele Ann Walker; children: Terry III & Matthew Kenneth; married L Alessandra V LaReaux. **Educ:** Univ Minn, Minneapolis, BA, 1971, MA, 1973. **Career:** ABC Prog Carleton Col, instr, 1972; Macalester Col, Eng Dept, instr, 1972; Augsburg Col, Minority Prog dir, 1972-73; Minneapolis Urban League St Acad, instr, 1979-81; Macalester Col, coord minority prog, 1981-84; Univ Ri, Multicultural Stud Serv, dir, 1983-93, minority stud serv, 1984; Multicultural Stud Serv, dir, 1984-93; Ctr Non-Violence, Coun Ctr, asst dir, dir, 1993-95; Kent County YMCA, Greater Providence YMCA, assoc exec dir, 1995-97; Intown Providence YMCA, Greater Providence YMCA, exec dir, 1997-2000; Johnson & Wales Univ, dean students, 2000-04; Brown Univ, Stud Life Off Stud Life, assoc dean stud life, 2004-. **Orgs:** Bd dir, Leadership RI; bd dir, Sojourner House; Omega Psi Phi Frat; Urban League, Nat Asn Advan Colored People; Asn Prof YMCA, 1976-; Kent County YMCA, bd dir, 2000-; Nat Asn Sch Personnel, NASPA, 2000; Asn Stud Judical Affairs, 2001; Warwick City Affirmative Action Equal Employ Opportunity, comnr. **Honors/Awds:** Positive Image Award, Minneapolis Urban League, 1984; Henry L Williams Memorial Award, Univ Minnesota; Awareness Award, 1987, Leadership Award, 1989, USN Recruiting Dist, Boston; Leadership Rhode Island, Lambda Class, 1991; Inductee Golden Key Nat Honor Soc, 1992; Inductee Order of Omega Nat Honor Soc, 1992; Leadership RI, David L Sweet Award, 1996; Man of the Year, Omega Psi Phi, Sigma Nu Chap, 2000. **Home Addr:** 46 Saxony Dr, Warwick, RI 02886, **Home Phone:** (401)739-8618. **Business Addr:** Associate Dean, Brown University, 20 Benevolent St, Providence, RI 02912, **Business Phone:** (401)863-9579.

### ADDY, DR. TRALANCE OBUAMA

Executive. **Personal:** Born Aug 24, 1944, Kumasi; son of Matthew Biala (deceased) and Docea L Baddoo (deceased); married Jo Alison Phears; children: Nii Mantse, Miishe, Dwetri & Naakai. **Educ:** Swarthmore Col, BA, chem, BS, mech engineering, 1969; Univ Mass, Amherst, MSME, PhD, 1974; Harvard Bus Sch, advan mgt prog, 1987. **Career:** Scott Paper Co, Philadelphia, PA, sr res proj eng, 1973-76, res scientist, 1976-79, prog leader, 1979-80; Surgikos Inc, Johnson & Johnson, Arlington, Tex, dir appl res, 1980-86, dir technol venture develop, 1986-88; ASP div, vpres, gen mgr, 1988-95, ASP, pres, 1992-98, int vpres, 1998-2001; Johnson & Johnson Med Inc, vpres, 1999-2001; Water Health int, pres, chief exec officer, 2001-09; Plebys Int LLC, founder, pres & chief exec officer, 2001-; Phyto-Riker Pharmaceut, bd; Johns Hopkins Ctr Talented Youth; Stanford Univ, Exec Dir, 2012-15. **Orgs:** Teacher, Upward Bound, 1967-73; Am Soc Mech Eng, 1979-; Am Asn Advan Sci, 1983-; Black & Jewish Dialogue Dallas, 1986-92; chmn, co-chmn, Surgikos United Way Campaign, 1985-86; fel, Am Inst Med & Biol Engineering, 1997; bd dir, United Way; bd mem, Sickle Cell DisAsn Am; adv bd, Univ NC, Kenan-Flagler Bus Sch, Ctr Sustainable Enterprise; Johnson & Johnson, Global Mgt Comn; Sigma Xi. **Home Addr:** 8 Palomino, Trabuco Canyon, CA 92679-4837, **Home Phone:** (949)546-0867. **Business Addr:** Founder, President & Chief Executive Officer, Plebys International LLC, 9 Orchard Rd Suite 111, Lake Forest, CA 92979, **Business Phone:** (949)716-5792.

### ADEGBILE, DR. GIDEON SUNDAY ADEBISI

Physician. **Personal:** Born May 18, 1941, Iree; son of Rev John Bimpe and Sarah Oyefunke; married Doris Mae Goodman; children: Lisa, Titilayo & Babalola. **Educ:** Va Union Univ, BS, cum laude, 1966; Meharry Med Col, MD, 1971. **Career:** Good Samaritan Hosp, resident, intern, 1971-72; Drexel Health Ctr, community health physician, 1972-73; PEG Inc, emergency physician, 1972-75; pvt pract physician, 1973-; Wright State Univ, Sch Med, clin instr, 1975-79, from asst clin prof to clin prof, 1979-92; Free Pke Med Ctr, Gen & Family Pract, currently. **Orgs:** Med dir, Christel Manor Nursing Homes, 1973-80; chmn bd, Dayton Contemp Dance Co, 1977-79; pres, Gem City Med Dent & Pharm Soc, 1978-80; chmn, Horizon Med Prog, 1978-; trustee, Montgomery County Med Soc, 1978; bd mem, Adv Ment Health Bd, Good Samaritan Hosp & Health Ctr, 1979-85; mem advan bd, Miami Valley Child Devel Ctr Inc, 1979; chmn, Long Term Care Community Region II Med Rev Corp, 1979-81; secy, Buckeye Med Asn, 1980-82; House Deleg Nat Med Asn, 1980-91; chmn, Qual Assurance Comt, St Elizabeth Med Ctr, 1980-82, 1984; bd mem, Region II Rev Corp, 1981-84, exec bd mem, 1982-84; Am Acad Family Physicians; Ore Acad Family Physicians; Ohio State Med Asn; Nat Med Asn; Montgomery County Med Soc; Nat Asn Advan Colored People; Alpha Phi Alpha Fraternity; Sigma Pi Phi Fraternity; Dem Bapt; Miami Valley Racquet Club; bd mem, Dayton Area Health Plan, 1985-92; pres, Selectmen, 1986-87; secy, Montgomery County Med Soc, 1987; chmn, Dept Family Pract, GSH & Health Ctr, 1987-88; pres, Buckeye Med Asn, 1987-89; chmn, Credentials & Accreditation Comt, St Elizabeth Med Ctr, 1987-88, 1995-96, chief staff, 1993-94, bd mem, PHO, 1994-; med dir, Dept Archaeol & Hist Preserv, 1994-; bd mem, Dayton Area Am Red Cross, 1994-. **Honors/Awds:** Certificate of Appreciation, Christel Manor Nursing Home, 1977. **Home Addr:** PO Box 133, Dayton, OH 45406-0133. **Business Addr:** Physician, Private Practice, 3033 Kettering Blvd Suite 100, Moraine, OH 45439, **Business Phone:** (937)293-2133.

### ADELEKAN, DR. TAHIRA GITTENS

Physician, pediatrician. **Educ:** DePauw Univ, BA; Univ Tex Health Sci Ctr, San Antonio, TX, MD, 1999. **Career:** State Univ New York Health Sci Ctr, Brooklyn, NY, internship, resident pediat, 1999-2003. **Orgs:** Rep, Res Action Group; Comm Interns & Residents; Team of Scientists & Health Care Profs Investigating Down Syndrome; Delta Sigma Theta Sorority Inc; C's Hosp Philadelphia, develop & behav Pediat, fel, 2007-. **Honors/Awds:** Doris Millman Award for excellence, State Univ NY Health Sci Ctr. **Home Addr:** 6627 Lotus Rd, Philadelphia, PA 19151-2345, **Home Phone:** (215)477-1805. **Business Addr:** Developmental & Behavioral Pediatric Fellow, Childrens Hospital Philadelphia, Childrens Seashore House, Philadelphia, PA 19104, **Business Phone:** (215)590-1000.

### ADESUYI, DR. SUNDAY ADENIJI

Chairperson, educator, chemist. **Personal:** Born Jun 27, 1948, Igbajo, OY; son of Jacob Owolabi (deceased) and Mary Ojuolape. **Educ:** Howard Univ, Wash, DC, BS, 1974, PhD, 1980. **Career:** Howard Univ, Chem Dept, teaching asst, 1974-75, teaching fel, 1974-78, instr, 1978-79; St Paul's Col, Sci & Math Dept, asst prof, 1979-83, Pan-Hellenic, coun, 1986-2001, 2002-, interim provost, acad vpres, actg pres, 1988, interim vpres acad affairs & provost, 1999-2000, Dept Natural Sci & Math, prof & chair, 2001-, fac, Athletics Rep, currently; Med Col Va, Dept Pharmacol, res assoc, 1983-84; First Baptist Church, ordained minister & assoc pastor; Cent Intercollegiate Athletic Asn, fac athletic rep; Nat Newsletter Nat Asn Minority Med Educr, ed chief. **Orgs:** Pres, Grad Stud Asn, 1976-78; exec bd mem, US Stud Asn, 1977-78; co-chmn, Teaching Effectiveness Sub Comn; Howard Univ's Steering Comn Self-Study, 1977-79; coordr, Sci & Math Fair, St Paul's Col, 1980-82; Am Chem Soc, 1976-; coordr, Ann Proj, Serv Elderly People, Lawrenceville, VA, 1981-; founder & adv, Xi Rho Chap & Phi Beta Sigma, 1983-; adv, Sci & Math Club, St Paul's Col, 1984-; fac rep to bd trustees, Presidential Search Comn, St Paul's Col, 1985-88 & 1996-98, 1986; adv, Pan-Hellenic Coun, St Paul's Col, 1986-; adv, Int Stud Asn, St Paul's Col, 1986; chmn, Provost Search Comn, St Paul's Col, 1987; Steering Comt, Self-Study, St Paul's Col, 1987-80 & 1998-; chmn, Inst Purpose Comn, Self-Study, St Paul's Col, 1987-80; chmn, Educ Prog Comn, 1998-; chmn, Athletic Comn, St Paul's Col, 1988-; fac Athletic Chair, Cent Intercollegiate Athletic Asn, 1988-; vpres, Northern Div, Cent Intercollegiate Athletic Asn, 1992-94; Southern Asn Col & Sch Vis Team Erskine Col, 1992; Miles Col, 1993; Campbellsville Col, 1994; Berea Col, 1995; Anderson Col, 1997; Our Lady Lake Col, 1998; deacon & trustee bd, First Bapt Church; Sigma Pi Phi Fraternity, exec comt, Cent Intercollegiate Athletic Asn Basketball Tournament Comn, 1990-2010; parliamentarian, Cent Intercollegiate Athletic Asn Fac Athletics Rep Assoc, 1994-, pres, 1997-; mem bd dirs, Nat Asn Med Minority Educrs Inc, 1994-98; chair, Nat Comnunications, ed-in-chief newsletter, 1994-98; SACS Vis Teamto Huston-Tillotson Col, 2000; pres, Cent Intercollegiate Athletic Asn Conf, 2002-; Div II Mgt Coun, Nat Col Athletic Asn, 2002-; admin rev sub Comn, Nat Col Athletic Asn, 2002-, Comn, 2002-, res comn, 2002-; vis team to Erskine Col, Southern Asn Col & Sch, 2002; fel African Sci Inst, currently; pres, historically black insts. **Honors/Awds:** Most Outstanding Graduate Student, Grad Student Asn, Howard Univ, 1978; Presial Silver Award, Howard Univ Stud Asn, 1978; Appreciation Award, Sophomore class, St Paul's Col, 1979-80; Student Merit Award, Student Body, St Paul's Col, 1982, 1983; Most Outstanding Dept Faculty Member, Sci & Math Club, St Paul's Col, 1982; First Supporter Award, Tennis Team, St Paul's Col, 1982; Appreciation Award, Sr Class, St Paul's Col, 1983; Presidential Medal, Outstanding Contributions to St Paul's Col, 1988; Excellence in Academy Advising Award, St Paul's Col, 1990; Sears-Roebuck Faculty of the Year, 1990-91; UNCF Distinguished Leadership Award, 1991, Meritorious Service Award, 1992; Sunbelt Video Sports & CIAA Partnership Award, 1993; CIAA Outstanding Service Award, 1994; Appreciation Award, SPC Athletic Dept, 1995; Certificate Of Appreciation, St Paul's Col, 1998; Appreciation Award, US Dept Com, 1999; 20-Year Service Award, St Paul Col, 1999; 15-Year Service Award as Department Chair, St Paul Col, Dept Natural Sci & Math, 1999; Certificate of Appreciation, UNCF, 1999, 2000; Leadership & Encouragement Award, St Paul's Col, Upward Bound Prog, 2000; Most Outstanding Science Faculty Award. **Home Addr:** PO Box 71, Lawrenceville, VA 23868-0071, **Home Phone:** (434)848-4264. **Business Addr:** Professor, Chairman, St Pauls College, 115 College Dr, Lawrenceville, VA 23868, **Business Phone:** (434)848-3111.

### ADEYEMI, BAKARI (DESMOND MURRAY)

Chief executive officer, founder (originator), educator. **Personal:** Born Apr 21, 1960, Queens, NY; son of James Murray and Elizabeth; married Sandra Alexander; children: Deyami & Alexis Alexander. **Educ:** State Univ NY, New Paltz, BA, 1982. **Career:** New Paltz Sch Dist, teacher, 1985-87; DJ Realization & DJ Unique, mgr; Marist Col, asst dir heop prog, 1987-90, asst dir field experience, 1990-, Affirmative Action adv comm chmn, currently; Blue Ice Entertainment, founder, chief exec officer, pres. **Orgs:** Promotions dir, Ambiance Productions; adv bd, Poughkeepsie Jour, multi cult affairs community; pub rels chair, African Am Mens Asn; co-founder, Poughkeepsie Unity B-Ball Classic, 1985; founding mem, Simba, 1991-; Order Feather Fraternity; Order Bonnet Fraternity. **Home Addr:** 9 Waldorf Pl, Poughkeepsie, NY 12601, **Home Phone:** (845)473-7370. **Business Addr:** Assistant Director of Field Experience, Marist College, 3399 N Rd, Poughkeepsie, NY 12601, **Business Phone:** (845)575-3226.

### ADEYIGA, DR. ADEYINKA A.

Educator, college administrator. **Personal:** Born Jan 20, 1948, Irolu; son of Alhaja Oladunni Apadiya-Osinbowale and Alhaji; married Abidemi Adibi; children: Adeleke, Adebunmi & Adetayo. **Educ:** Tenn Tech Univ, Cookeville, BS, chem engineering, 1974; Univ Mo, Columbia, MS, chem engineering, 1976; Okla State Univ, Stillwater, PhD, chem engineering, 1980. **Career:** Okla State Univ, Fluid Properties Res Inc, res asst, 1979-80; EI DuPont De Nemours Co, res engr, 1981-82; Shell Oil Co, reservoir engr, 1982-83; Va State Univ, asst prof, 1984-85; Hampton Univ, assoc prof chem engineering, head engineering, prof chem engineering & dir DOE-Massie Chair Excellence, 1985-; Shell Petrol, reservoir engr; Padson Engineering, Nigeria, chief consult. **Orgs:** Founding chair, Dept Engineering, Hampton Univ; chief consult, Padson Engineering Co, 1983-84; Engineering Deans Coun HBCU, 1986-; State Va Engineering Dean Coun, 1986-; Am Inst Chem Engrs; Am Chem Soc; AAAS; Omega Chi Epsilon; Soc Petrol Engrs; fel Am Soc Engineering Educ; fel, African Sci Inst; fel, Am Inst Chem Engrs; Dept Energy; NASA; Nsf; Am Inst Chem Engrs, Am Socs Engineering Educ; Am Chem Socs; fel, Am Soc Engineering Educ; fel, African Sci Inst; fel, Am Inst Chem Engrs. **Home Addr:** 126 Chinquapin Orchard, Yorktown, VA 23693-2321, **Home Phone:** (804)868-0929. **Business Addr:** Professor of Chemical Engineering, Director of DOE-Massie Chair of Excellence, Hampton University, Olin Engineering Bldg Suite 318J, Hampton, VA 23668, **Business Phone:** (757)727-5289.

### ADEYIGA, DR. OLANREWAJU MUNIRU

Physician. **Personal:** Born Sep 30, 1949, Irolu; married Mosekunola Omisakin; children: Adebowale, Oladunni & Temitope. **Educ:** Southern Ill Univ, Edwardsville, BA, 1973, MSc, 1975; Howard Univ, Col Med, MD, 1979; Nat Bd Med Exam, dipl, 1981. **Career:** SIP Prog, Southern Ill Univ, vis lectr, 1976-77; Howard Univ, residency obstet & gynec, 1979-84; Howard Univ Hosp, instr, attend, 1985-86; Columbia

Hosp Women, attend, 1985-; Wash Hosp Ctr, attend, 1985-; Group Health Asn, physician; Howard Univ Hosp, Dept Obstet & Gynec, dir & asst prof, currently, chair, 2002- 06. **Orgs:** AMA, 1976-; fel Am Col Obstetricians & Gynecologists, 1986-. **Home Addr:** 126 Chinquapin Orchard, Yorktown, VA 23693-2321. **Business Addr:** Associate Professor, Director, Howard University Hospital, 2041 Georgia Ave NW Suite 3200, Washington, DC 20060, **Business Phone:** (202)865-4164.

## ADIELE, DR. MOSES NKWACHUKWU

Executive director, government official. **Personal:** Born Jun 22, 1951, Umuahia; son of Robert and Virginia; married Vickie I Eseonu; children: Elizabeth, Bobby & Casey. **Educ:** Ga Inst Tech, BSHS, 1976; Howard Univ, MD, 1980; Johns Hopkins Univ, MPH, 1981; Uniformed Serv Univ Health Sci, Bethesda, MD, cert armed forces combat casualty care course, 1990; Acad Health Sci, San Antonio, TX, cert officer advan course, 1990; Ft Leavenworthe, KS, AUS command & gen staff officer course, 1993; Prev Med Pub Health & Gen Prev Med, cert, 1999. **Career:** Baltimore City Health Dept, internship, pub health clinician, 1980-81; Howard Univ, Hosp & Affilated Hosps, internship, med house officer residency family pract, 1981-84, Col Med, adj fac, 1983-85; Richmond City Health Dept, asst dir pub health, 1984-86; VI State Health Dept, dist health dir, 1986-90; Va Dept Med Assistance Serv, Richmond, dir med support, 1990-; Fed Licensure Examr Med Bd, Dipl Nat Bd, Med Examr. **Orgs:** Pres, bd dir, Asn African Physicians N Am, 1981-84; prof mem, fel Am & VI Asn Family Physicians, 1982-; bd adv, Int United Black Fund, 1984-89; Richmond Med Soc, 1984-90; VI Pub Health Asn, 1984; Richmond Acad Med, 1986-90; US Mil Res Officers Asn, 1988-; fel Am Acad Family Physicians, 1991; fel Am Col Med Qual, 1992; Am Col Physician Exec, 1998-; fel Am Col Prev Med, 1999. **Home Addr:** 1305 Ceder Crossing Trail, Midlothian, VA 23114-3148, **Home Phone:** (804)794-0801. **Business Addr:** Director, Virginia Department of Medical Assistance Services, 600 E Broad St Suite 1300, Richmond, VA 23219, **Business Phone:** (804)786-8052.

## ADJAYE, DAVID

Architect. **Personal:** Born Sep 1, 1966?; married Ashley Shaw-Scott. **Educ:** S Bank Univ, London, BA, 1990; Royal Col Art, MArch, 1993. **Career:** Chassay Architects, architect, 1988-90; David Chipperfield Architects, 1991; Eduardo Souto de Moura Architects, 1991; Adjaye & Russell, partner, 1994-2000; founded Adjaye Assoc, London, 2000- ; Princeton Univ Sch Archit, vis prof, currently; Univ Pa, vis prof; Harvard Grad Sch Design, Kenzo Tange Prof Archit. **Orgs:** Trustee, Archit Educ Trust; bd mem, Greenwich Dance Agency; advisor, LDA Thames Gateway Design Panel; fel Royal Acad; trustee, S London Gallery; hon fel Am Inst Archit; foreign hon mem, Am Acad Arts & Lett; sr fel Design Futures Coun; chartered mem, Royal Inst Brit Architects; adv bd, London Sch Econs; adv coun, Barcelona Inst Archit. **Business Addr:** 415 Broadway 3rd Fl, New York, NY 10013, **Business Phone:** (212)965-8420.

## ADKINS, BILL. See ADKINS, WILLIAM.

## ADKINS, LEROY J.

Law enforcement officer. **Personal:** Born Jun 17, 1933, St. Louis, MO; son of Alfred J and Fannie E; married Glenda Jane Watt; children: Kevin L & Alfred J. **Educ:** Forest Park Community Col, AA, 1976; Columbia Col, attended 1978; Webster Univ, MA, 1979. **Career:** Law enforcement officer (retired); St Louis Police Dept, dep chief, 1958-92; St Louis Homicide Div, comdr, capt; St Louis Airport Police Dept, chief, 1992-96. **Orgs:** Local treas, Nat Orgn Black Law Enforcement Exec, 1976-; Omega Psi Phi, 1980; Int Asn Chiefs Police, 1984; Mo Police Chiefs, 1992; Newstead Missionary Baptist Church. **Home Addr:** 9760 Grandview Dr, St. Louis, MO 63132, **Home Phone:** (314)991-3598.

## ADKINS, RODNEY C.

Vice president (organization). **Personal:** Born Aug 23, 1958, Miami, FL; son of Wauneta and Archie; married Michelle Collier; children: Rodney Adkins II & Ryan Adkins. **Educ:** Rollins Col, BA, physics, 1982; Ga Inst Technol, BS, 1981, MS, elec engineering, 1983. **Career:** IBM, engr, 1981-86, mgt, 1986-95, com desktop systs vpres, 1995-96, Desktop Systs, gen mgr, 1996-98, UNIX Server Div, gen mgr, 1998-2001, Pervasive Comput Div, gen mgr, 2001-03, Systs & Technol Group, vpres develop, 2003-07, sr vpres, 2007-, sr vpres develop & mfg, 2009. **Orgs:** Dir, Pitney Bowes Inc; Nat Acad Engineering (NAE); Exec Leadership Coun; Nat Soc Black Engrs (NSBE); bd dir, Nat Action Coun Minorities Engineering (NACME); bd mem, PeopleClick Inc; bd mem, Pitney Bowes, 2007-; Obama Am; bd dir, United Parcel Serv; nat bd mem, Smithsonian Inst; Ga Tech Found; bd trustees, Rollins Col; bd visitors, Univ Md Baltimore County; vis comt, Univ Miami Col Engineering. **Honors/Awds:** National Society of Black Engineers (NSBE), Golden Torch Award for Lifetime Achievement in Industry, 2001; "Fortune," Most Powerful Black Executives in America, 2002; Top Blacks in Technology, 2004; Black Engineer of the Year, 2007; "Black Enterprise," The 100 Most Powerful Executives in Corporate America, 2010; Hon doctor degrees, Ga Inst Technol; Hon doctor degrees, Univ Md Baltimore County.

## ADKINS, WILLIAM (BILL ADKINS)

Automotive executive. **Personal:** Born Chicago, IL. **Educ:** Univ Md, Bus Col, bus admin & mkt, 1984; Gen Motors Inst, cert, automotive mgt, 1985. **Career:** First Nat Bank; Gen Motors Corp, Finance Div; Pontiac Motors, serv part & sales mgr; Volkswagen Am Inc, Regional Mkt & Training Mgr, 1980-84; Adkins Chevrolet Buick Oldsmobile, pres, owner & gen mgr, 1985-89; Adkins & Assocs, pres, owner & gen mgr, 1989-94; Bayview Lincoln Mercury, pres & gen mgr, 1990-92; Ford Motor Co, consult; Gen Motor Corp, consult; Palanker Chevrolet, pres & gen mgr, 1994-2003; Nat Automobile Dealers Asn, mgt instr, 2004-14; State Univ New York, bd dir, vice chmn; Adelphi Univ, adj prof; automotiveMastermind LLC, strategic bus develop mgr, 2014-. **Orgs:** Suffolk Co Community Col; Harbor Country Day Sch; bd dir, Gen Motors Minority Dealers Asn; bd dir, vice chmn, Greater New York Automobile Dealers Asn; Long Island United Way; Nat Advan Asn Colored People; prin, Day Prog; active supporter, United Negro Col Fund; bd trustee, Island Aquarium; mgt instr, Nat Automobile Dealers Asn, 2004-; bd dir, Mentoring Partnership Long Island; bd dir, Long Island Univ; bd dir, Breath Life; bd dir, Nat Asn Minority Automobile Dealers; bd dir, Cath Health Serv Long Island; bd dir, Heckscher Mus Art; Asn Finance & Ins Prof; Gen Motors Inst Alumni; bd dir, Stud Achievements; bd dir vice chmn, SUNY Old Westbury Univ. **Special Achievements:** NADA Annual Convention Workshop Speaker, 2014. **Business Addr:** Strategic Business Development Manager, automotiveMastermind LLC, 222 Bdwy Ninteenth Fl, New York, NY 10038.

## ADKINS-GREEN, SHERYL

Marketing executive. **Personal:** married Geoff; children: Landon & Colton. **Educ:** Univ Wis, BS, retailingExec Leadership Coun; Cosmetic Exec Women; Network Exec Women; Harvard Grad Sch Bus, MBA. **Career:** Kraft Foods, bus dir, 1985-96; Citigroup, Regional Pres, 1996-2002; Snapple Beverage Group at Cadbury Schweppes, sr vpres mkt, 2002-04; Pro-Line Int, Div Alberto-Culver, gen mgr & vpres, 2004-08; Mary Kay Inc, vpres global brand develop, 2009-, chief mkt officer, 2011-. **Orgs:** Exec Leadership Coun; Cosmetic Exec Women; Network Exec Women. **Honors/Awds:** 25 Most Influential Black Women in Business, 2008; Global Marketer Award, Acad Mkt Sci, 2012. **Business Addr:** Vice President of Global Brand Development, Chief Marketing Officer, Mary Kay Inc, 16251 Dallas Pkwy, Addison, TX 75001-6801, **Business Phone:** (800)627-9529.

## ADOLPH, GERALD STEPHEN

Management consultant, association executive. **Personal:** Born Dec 30, 1953, New York, NY; son of Leroy and Beryl. **Educ:** Mass Inst Technol, BS, chem engineering, 1976, BS, mgt & orgn psychol, 1976, MS, chem engineering, 1981; Harvard Bus Sch, MBA, 1981. **Career:** Polaroid Corp, engr, 1976-81, Chem Mfg Div; Booz Allen & Hamilton, assoc, 1981-83, sr assoc, 1983-85, prin, 1985-88, partner, 1988-99, sr partner, 1999-, sr vpres & dir, currently, worldwide chem pract leader, worldwide consumer & health pract leader & global mergers & restructuring pract leader; Cintas Corp, dir, 2006-; Strategy & part PwC network, prin, 2015-16. **Orgs:** Corp adv bd chair, Univ Mich Bus Sch; bd dir, chair, Exec Leadership Coun; bd dir, Nat Am Advan Colored People Legal Defense Fund; bd dir, Hellen Keller Worldwide; bd mem, Archbishop's Leadership Proj; bd mem, Nat Am Advan Colored People Legal Defense & Educ Fund; bd mem, Booz Allen Hamilton; bd mem, cintas, 2006-. **Business Addr:** Senior Vice President, Cintas Corp, 6800 Cintas Blvd, Cincinnati, OH 45262, **Business Phone:** (513)459-1200.

## ADOM, DR. EDWIN NII AMALAI

Psychiatrist. **Personal:** Born Jan 12, 1941, Accra; son of Isaac Quaye and Juliana Adorkor Brown; married Margaret Odarkor Lamptey; children: Edwin Nii Nortey Jr & Isaac Michael Nii Nortei. **Educ:** Univ Pa, BA, 1963; Meharry Med Col, MD, 1968; Royal Soc Health, Eng, FRSH, 1974; Am Bd Psychiat & Neurol, dipl, 1978. **Career:** Pa Hosp, internship, 1968-69; Thomas Jefferson Univ, residency, 1969-72; W Philadelphia Consortium, staff psychiatrist, 1972-; Univ Pa Sch Med, fac, clin asst prof psychiat, 1972-74; State Pa, cons psychiatrist, Bur Visually Handicap & Blindness, 1974-, Bur Disability Determination, 1975-; Parents Preparing Parenthood, Philadelphia, Pa, cons psychiatrist, 1975-76; Grad Hosp, Philadelphia, cons psychiatrist, 1976; St Joseph Hosp, Philadelphia, cons psychiatrist, 1976-80; Stephen Smith Home Aged, Philadelphia, cons psychiatrist, 1976-80; Mercy Douglas Human Serv Ctr, Philadelphia, cons psychiatrist, 1977-79; St Ignatius Home Aged, Phildelphia, cons psychiatrist, 1978-85; Philadelphia Psychiat Ctr, attend psychiatrist, 1987-; Horizon House Rehab Ctr, Pa, cons psychiatrist, 1987-89; Hosp Univ Pa, cons psychiatrist, 1989-; W Philadelphia Community Ment Health Consortium, Philadelphia, Pa, med dir, 1991-, psychiatrist. **Orgs:** Am Psychol Asn; Nat Med Asn; MSEP; Black Psych Am, World Fedn Ment Health; Royal Soc Health; NY Acad Sci, 1987-; Am Acad Psychiat & Law, 1990-; Am Soc Clin Psychopharmacology; fel Royal Soc Health Eng; fel Thomas Bond Soc Pa Hosp, 1994; Am Bd Psychiat & Neurol. **Honors/Awds:** Citizens Citation Chapel of 4 Chaplins, Philadelphia; African-Am Wallof Fame, 1995; Black Americas Achievement, 1995; Astra Merck & the Medical Society of Eastern Pennysylvania Excellency Award for Mentorship, 1995. **Special Achievements:** Nation's first black blind physician & psychiatrist. **Home Addr:** 3801 Mkt St Suite 201, Philadelphia, PA 19104, **Home Phone:** (215)596-8100. **Business Addr:** Psychiatry, Med Tower Bldg 255 S 17th St Suite 2704, Philadelphia, PA 19103-6228, **Business Phone:** (215)545-5116.

## ADONA, ALISA

Photographer. **Career:** Tilford Art Group, photogr, currently. **Orgs:** Break Cycle. **Special Achievements:** CUBA, Reflections of Life series; "Lost Tribe" photographic exhibition. **Business Addr:** Art Photographer, Studio 109, 1230 N June St Suite 109, Los Angeles, CA 90038, **Business Phone:** (323)461-5050.

## ADRINE, RONALD BRUCE

Judge. **Personal:** Born Apr 21, 1947, Cleveland, OH; son of Russell T (deceased). **Educ:** Wittenberg Univ, attended 1966; Fisk Univ, BA, hist, 1969; Cleveland Marshall Col Law, JD, 1973. **Career:** Cuyahoga County, asst pros atty, 1974-76; Adrine & Adrine, partner, 1976-78; US House Reps, staff coun, 1978-81; Adrine & Adrine, partner, 1979-82; Cleveland Munic Ct, judge, 1981-, chmn & secy, admin & presiding judge, currently. **Orgs:** Trustee, Urban League Greater Cleveland, 1972; comn, Cuyahoga Metro Housing Auth, 1981; Mayor's Citizen Charter Rev Comn, 1983; African Am Leadership Network; African Am Family Cong; cofounder, Black Male Agenda Ohio Inc; Nat Leadership Inst Minorities Ohio Inc; bd trustee, Shaker Heights High Sch Alumni Asn; bd trustee, Opportunities Industrialization Coun; bd trustee, Ohio Community Corrections Orgn; bd trustee, Norman S Minor Bar Asn; bd trustee, Exodus Prog; bd trustee, Transitional Housing; bd trustee, Proj Second Chance; adv bd, Resocializing African Am Males; Omega Psi Phi Fraternity; bd trustee, Harambee Servs Black Families; Fisk Alumni Asn; bd trustee, Cleveland Bar Asn; Cleveland-Marshall Law Alumni Asn; Cleveland State Univ Alumni Asn. **Honors/Awds:** Man of the Year, Omega Psi Phi Fraternity fourth Dist, 1983. **Special Achievements:** First chmn, Cleveland Domestic Violence Coordinating Coun; Ohio Bar Medal, Ohio State Bar Association. **Home Addr:** 13515 Drexmore Rd, Cleveland, OH 44120, **Home Phone:** (216)561-6777. **Business Addr:** Administrative and Presiding Judge, Cleveland Municipal Court, 1200 Ont St, Cleveland, OH 44101-4894, **Business Phone:** (216)664-4974.

## AGEE, BOBBY L.

Funeral director, county commissioner. **Personal:** Born Oct 28, 1949, Maplesville, AL; son of Clara M; married Emily Wilson; children: Anthony, Antionette, Bobby II, Ahzeezee, Ngozi, Jabari & Awlahjaday. **Educ:** Ky Sch Mortuary Sci, Ky, mortician, 1973; Sch Govt Serv, Auburn, Ala, attended 1989; Auburn Univ, Ala Co Comnrs Col, Ctr Govt Serv, attended 1992. **Career:** Agee Bros Funeral Home, Clanton, Ala, owner, 1975-; Chilton Co Comnr, comnr, 1989-92; Chilton Co Ala, conventioneer, currently. **Orgs:** Deacon, Union Baptist Church, 1983-; Clanton Eve Lions Club, 1986-89; chmn, W End Pk Bd, 1989-; Zoning Bd City Clanton, 1989-; 4H & FHA Bd Chilton, Co, 1990-; vice chmn, Mid Ala Area Agency Aging, 1992-. **Honors/Awds:** Certificate of Merit, Booker T Wash Bus Col, 1988; Certificate of Merit, Clanton Evening Lions Club, 1988; Certificate of Merit, Auburn Univ, 1989; Certificate of Merit, Middle Ala Area Agency Aging, 1990. **Home Addr:** 905 Samaria Rd, Clanton, AL 35045, **Home Phone:** (205)755-5026. **Business Addr:** Mortician, Owner, Agee Brothers Funeral Home, 905 Samaria Rd, Clanton, AL 35045-8841, **Business Phone:** (205)755-5075.

## AGEE, THOMAS LEE (TOMMIE AGEE)

Football player. **Personal:** Born Feb 22, 1964, Chilton, AL; married Anchylus; children: Tyler, Torey & Angelique. **Educ:** Auburn Univ, BA, criminal justice. **Career:** Football player (retired), executive; Seattle Seahawks, 1988; Kansas City Chiefs, 1989; Dallas Cowboys, running back, 1990-94, fullback, 1990; Juv Community Serv Coordr; Opelika's Parks & Recreation Dept, asst dir, currently. **Orgs:** Speaker, Fel Christian Athletes & Athletes Action groups, Ala. **Honors/Awds:** Super Bowl champion (XXVII, XXVIII). **Business Addr:** Assistant Director, City of Opelika, 204 S 7th St, Opelika, AL 36801, **Business Phone:** (334)705-5558.

## AGGREY, HON. ORISON RUDOLPH GUGGISBERG. See Obituaries Section.

## AGINS, TERI

Journalist, writer. **Personal:** Born Nov 14, 1953, Kansas City, KS. **Educ:** Wellesley Col, BA, eng/polit sci, 1975; Univ Mo, MA, jour. **Career:** The Kansas City Star, intern, 1972; "The Boston Globe", intern, 1973; Fairchild Publications, writer, 1974-77; "The New York Times" "Time" and Fairchild News Service, freelance writer and stringer in Brazil, 1978-83; "Wall Street Journal", reporter and business column writer, 1984-89, developed fashion beat, 1989-95, senior special writer, 1995-2009, freelance writer, 2009-. **Special Achievements:** Author of "The End of Fashion: How Marketing Changed the Clothing Business Forever" (William Morrow, 1999); author of "Hijacking the Runway: How Celebrities Are Stealing the Spotlight from Fashion Designers" (Gotham, 2014); contributed to numerous periodicals including "Vogue", "Town & Country", "O: The Oprah Magazine", and "Essence". **Business Addr:** Wall Street Journal, 1211 Avenue of the Americas, New York, NY 10036.

## AGNEW, RAYMOND MITCHELL, JR. (RAY AGNEW)

Administrator, football player. **Personal:** Born Dec 9, 1967, Winston-Salem, NC; married Katherine; children: Ray III, Malcolm Lamar & Keenan. **Educ:** NC State Univ, BA, hist. **Career:** Football player (retired), administrator; New Eng Patriots, right defensive end, 1990, left defensive end, 1991-92, defensive tackle, 1993-94; NY Giants, 1997, right defensive tackle, 1995, defensive tackle, 1996; St Louis Rams, left defensive tackle, 1998-99, defensive end, defensive tackle, left defensive tackle, 2000; dir player develop & team pastor, 2001-04; sports ed, Sch's newspaper; St Louis Rams, pro scout, currently. **Orgs:** Nat Honor Soc. **Honors/Awds:** Super Bowl champion. **Home Addr:** 2215 Cline St, Winston-Salem, NC 27107, **Home Phone:** (271)072-2411. **Business Addr:** Pro Scout, St Louis Rams, 1 Rams Way, St. Louis, MO 63045, **Business Phone:** (314)982-7267.

## AGUIRRE, MARK ANTHONY

Basketball player, basketball coach. **Personal:** Born Dec 10, 1959, Chicago, IL; married Angela Bowman; children: 4. **Educ:** De Paul Univ, attended 1982. **Career:** Basketball player (retired), basketball coach; Dallas Mavericks, 1981-89; Detroit Pistons, 1988-93; Los Angeles Clippers, 1993-94; Life Cast, chmn & chief exec officer, 1999-2001; Ind Pacers, spec asst, 2001-02, asst coach, 2002-03; New York Knicks, asst coach, 2004-08. TV Series: "NBA All-Star Game", 1984, 1987-88; 'Back in the Day", 2006; "Quite Frankly with Stephen A Smith", 2006; "30 for 30", 2014. **Orgs:** Big Bros & Big Sisters; Nat Basketball Asn.

## AGURS, DONALD STEELE (DON AGURS)

Journalist. **Personal:** Born Jun 1, 1947, Rock Hill, SC; married Brenda Louise Crenshaw; children: Renda & Chris. **Educ:** Howard Univ, attended 1967 & 1977; DC Teachers Col, attended 1971; Fed City Col, attended 1972. **Career:** Westinghouse Broadcasting Co, newsman, 1970-71; WHUR-FM, newsman & producer, 1972; WSOC Radio & TV, newsman, 1973; 236 Housing Proj, admin, 1973-75; WGIV, newscaster, 1975; WHUR-FM, NBN, White House, corresp, 1975-78; Sheridan Broadcasting Network, White House, corresp. **Orgs:** PAG, 1973-74; bd dir, Mecklenburg Co Pub Access, 1974-75; Am Fedn TV & Radio Artists; Nat Asn Black Journalists; Wash press Club, Cong Corresp Asn; White House Corresp Asn; Nat Asn Advan Colored People; Laytonsville Golf Club; Pinetuck Golf Club. **Home Addr:** 315 T St NW, Washington, DC 20001.

## AGWUNOBI, DR. ANDREW C.

Executive, activist, chief executive officer. **Personal:** Born Scotland; married Elizabeth Nega; children: Hannah. **Educ:** Howard Univ Teaching Hosp, pediatrician, 1995; Stanford Bus Sch, MBA, 2001; Univ Jos, Jos, Nigeria, MD. **Career:** Qual Life Health Serv, 1995-97;

Harvard Vanguard Med Assocs, chief & instr, 1997-99; S Fulton Med Ctr, chief operating officer, chief execofficer & pres, 2001; Tenet S Fulton Hosp, pres & chief exec officer, 2001-03; Grady Health Syst, pres & chief exec officer, 2003-06; St Joseph Health Syst, exec vpres & chief operating officer, 2006-07; Fla's Agency Health Care Admin, secy, 2007-08; Providence Health & Serv, chief exec officer & hon vpres, 2008-11; Berkeley Res Group LLC, dir, 2011-; UConn Health, interim exec vice pres. **Orgs:** Bd adv & bd dir, Ga State Univ Col Health & Human Sci; Ga Chamber Com; 191 Club Bd Gov; Cent Atlanta Progress Inc; Atlanta Regional Health Forum Inc; Nat Asn Pub Hosp & Health Syst; Arthur M Blank Family Found & Better Beginnings Adv Coun; Atlanta Fulton Family Connection; Metro Atlanta Chamber Com; Ga Hosp Asn Bd; Ga Alliance Community Hosp; Am Col Healthcare Execs; Ga Asn Healthcare Execs; Partners Int Develop; Hosp Exec Coun; Leadership Ga Class 2005; 100 Black Men Atlanta; Rotary Club Atlanta; fel Acad Pediat; chmn bd & opers adv, Health-e-Sta Adv Bd; bd mem, Cath Healthcare W; bd mem, Dignity Health. **Business Addr:** Chief Executive Officer, Providence Health & Services, 3901 E Main Ave, Spokane, WA 99202-4736, **Business Phone:** (509)534-4300.

### AHANOTU, CHIDI OBIOMA

Executive, football player. **Personal:** Born Oct 11, 1970, Modesto, CA; son of Austin; children: Ijechi Woodrow & Mayan. **Educ:** Univ Calif, Berkeley, BS, integrative biol, 1993. **Career:** Football player (retired), executive; Tampa Bay Buccaneers, defensive end & left defensive end & left defensive tackle, 1993-2000, 2004; Magellan Talent Mgt Inc, chief exec officer, 1993-; Magellan Entertainment Inc, founder, pres & cheif exec officer, 1999-; St. Louis Rams, 2001; Buffalo Bills, 2002; San Francisco 49ers, 2003; Miami dolphins, 2004; NFL Players Asn, vpres tampa retired chap, 2007-11; Legends Energy Group, regional exec dir, 2011-. **Orgs:** Active with Big Bros & Big Sisters, Save a Child & Ahanotu Found; fla chmn, Nat Parents Orgn, 2013-; Nat Football League Ambassador, Nat Football League, 2013-. **Special Achievements:** Films: Euphoria, 2009; Adventure Scouts, 2010. **Business Addr:** Founder, President, Magellan Entertainment Inc, 301 Platt St Suite 443, Tampa, FL 33606, **Business Phone:** (813)786-6690.

### AHART, THOMAS I.

Executive. **Personal:** Born Apr 3, 1938, Detroit, MI; son of Greek and Eula; married Menda Britton; children: Pamela M & Thomas B. **Educ:** Wayne State Univ, BA, jour, 1962. **Career:** Ford Motor Co, indust rel adminr, 1967-70; Am Bankers Asn, dir, 1970-77; Nat Min Purch Coun, exec dir, 1977-78; Dyma Assocs, pres, 1978-87; Networks Solutions, Control Data Corp, consult, 1984; Export-Import Bank US, consult, 1985; Customer Opers, supvr; A & M Grp, pres, 1987-98; Nations Bus Grp, nat proj dir, proj dir emerging markets, currently; Ahart Grp Inc, pres, 1995-; Ahart Alpha Stratgies LLC, pres, 2012-; Family & Youth Advocacy Ctr Inc, exec dir, 2013-. **Orgs:** Omega Psi Phi; dir, Crispus Attucks Inst, 1990; pres, S Lakes HS PTA, 1992; consult, US Com Dept, 1995-; chmn, Hughes PTA Human Rels; Nat Asn Advan Colored People; Inter Fraternity Coun. **Special Achievements:** Numerous publications including "Bankers and Urban Affairs", "Future of Comm Bnkg Praeger", 1976; "Poems" Rustlings, Reston Publishers, 1975. **Home Phone:** (703)620-3875. **Business Addr:** President, The Ahart Group Inc, 12385 Copenhagen Ct, Reston, VA 20191-2509, **Business Phone:** (571)263-1458.

### AHMAD, JADWAA W.

Lawyer. **Personal:** Born Jul 23, 1935, Detroit, MI; married Ruth Joyce; children: Jamar H, Jadwaa W & Jamil O. **Educ:** W Mich Univ; E Mich Univ, BS, 1957; Detroit Col Law, JD, 1970. **Career:** City Detroit, jr chemist, 1957-59; Stroh Brewery Co, Detroit, chemist, 1959-70; Wayne City Neighborhood Legal Serv, atty trainee, 1970-71; Gragg & Gardner Detroit, atty, 1970-72; Terry Ahmad & Bradfield Detroit, atty; pvt pract atty, currently. **Orgs:** Legal Frat Sigma Nu Phi; Kappa Alpha Psi; State Bar Mich; Wolverine Bar Asn; Nat Bar Asn; Detroit Bar Asn; Am Bar Asn; House Coun Peace, 1972-. **Honors/Awds:** NAACP Recipient of Scholastic Awards, E Mich Univ, 1954-57. **Home Addr:** 17607 Pennington Dr, Detroit, MI 48221-2616, **Home Phone:** (313)341-9717. **Business Addr:** Attorney, Jadwaa Ahmad, Highland Park, MI 48203-3539, **Business Phone:** (313)865-3608.

### AHOTO, YAO

Business owner. **Career:** Karibu Bks, co-owner, 1993-. **Orgs:** Hurston-Wright Found, Nat Med Asn, Nat Coun Negro Women. **Special Achievements:** Nation's largest Black black store chain. **Business Addr:** Co-owner, Karibu Books Bowie, Town Ctr, Bowie, MD 20716, **Business Phone:** (301)352-4110.

### AIKEN, CAROL ANN. See AMIN, KARIMA.

### AIKEN, KIMBERLY CLARICE (KIMBERLY CLARICE AIKEN COCKERHAM)

Columnist, fashion model, accountant. **Personal:** Born Oct 11, 1975, Columbia, SC; daughter of Charles and Valerie; married Haven Earl Cockerham Jr; children: 2. **Educ:** Univ NC; Univ SC; NY Univ, grad. **Career:** Ernst & Young LLP, pub acct; Pageantry Mag, columnist, currently; Aikens Community Care Home Inc, founder, currently; Homeless Educ & Resource Orgn, founder, pres, currently; image consult & motivational speaker. **Orgs:** Delta Sigma Theta Sorority Inc; HERO; Habitat Humanity. **Honors/Awds:** Order of the Palmetto; Miss America, 1994; Miss Columbia; Miss SC, 1994; "Fifty Most Beautiful People in the World", People Magazine. **Special Achievements:** First African American to win the Miss SC contest, 1994; Fifth African American to win the Miss America pageant; Second African American winner to have later served as a judge in the pageant. **Business Addr:** Founder, President, Aikens Community Care Home Inc, 216 Cora Dr, Columbia, SC 29203, **Business Phone:** (803)754-4468.

### AIKEN, WILLIAM

Executive. **Personal:** Born Mar 11, 1934, New York, NY; son of Eugene Sr and Ida Brown; married Joyce Blackwell; children: Adrienne, William Jr, Candice, Nicole & Sharla. **Educ:** City Col, BBA, pub accountancy, 1963; City Univ NY, Baruch Col, MBA, finance & investments, 1970. **Career:** NY State Ins Dept, state ins examr, 1963-67; Arthur Young & Co, sr acct, 1967-72; Aiken & Wilson CPA, 1972-78; NY City Human Resources Admin, asst dep comnr, 1978-80; Main Hurdman, NY, partner, 1980-87; KPMG Peat Marwick Main & co, New York, NY, partner, 1987-88; Medger Evers Col, adj prof; Long Island RR Co, Jamaica, NY, vpres finance; Jewish Child Care Asn NY, chief financial officer; USMC. **Orgs:** Bd chmn, Nat Asn Black Accountants, 1971-73; NY State Bd Pub Accountancy, 1974-; Am Inst Cert Pub Accountants, 1975-78; treas, Assoc Black Cities, 1990-; past pres& mem exec bd, NY Soc Cert Pub Accountants, Manhattan Bronx Chap, dir, 2012-; Accountants Club Am; 100 Black Men; comn mem, Ins Cos & Agencies Acct; NC Agr & Tech Univ, Cluster Prog; bus develop coun, NC Cent Univ; Nat Bus League Comn Nat Policy Rev; Nat Urban League Black Exec Exchange Prog; past pres, Nat Asn Black Accountants; Westchester Minority Bus Asst Org; Ethical Fieldson Fund; Studio Mus Harlem; asst dep comnr, New York Human Resources Admin. **Honors/Awds:** Achievement Award, Jackson State Chapter, Nat Asn Black Accountants, 1972; Ebony Success Libr, 1974; Annual Achievement Award, Nat Asn Black Accountant, 1975. **Special Achievements:** Author of "The Black Experience in Large Public Accounting Firms", 1971; First black to receive appointment to New York State Board for Public Accountancy in 1974. **Home Addr:** 5640 Netherland Ave, Riverdale, NY 10471. **Business Addr:** Director, New York State Society of Certified Public Accountants, 14 Wall St 19th Fl, New York, NY 10005, **Business Phone:** (800)537-3635.

### AIKENS, ALEXANDER E., III

Banker, educator. **Personal:** Born Feb 22, 1949, Chicago, IL; son of Alexander E Jr and Ruth Lane; married Jean Murgida; children: Talia C & Felicia. **Educ:** Brandeis Univ, BA, econ, 1971; Northeastern Law Sch, JD, 1974; Harvard Bus Sch, Prof Mgt Develop Prog, 1986. **Career:** Chase Manhattan Bank, NA, New York, NY, second vpres, 1974-80; First Nat Bank Boston, Boston, MA, group sr credit officer, Global Banking Group, 1987-91, Div Exec Multinational, 1992-95, Emerging Markets Investment Banking, managing dir; Brandeis Univ, Int Bus Sch, bus prof, asst men's basketball coach, adj prof, 2000-, Grad Sch Int Econs & Finance, prof, currently; Landon Sch, Bus Sch, prof, bus leader, atty. **Orgs:** Mass Bar Asn, 1974; bd mem, Boston Acoust Inc, 2001-04; bd mem, trustee, Wheelock Col; bd mem, Pension Retirement Investment Mgt Bd, Commonwealth Mass. **Honors/Awds:** Alexander Aikens Award, Landon Sch, 2005. **Special Achievements:** First black student to graduate from Landon School. **Home Addr:** 31 Hampshire Rd, Wellesley, MA 02481, **Home Phone:** (781)235-1694. **Business Addr:** Adjunct Professor, Brandeis University, Sachar Int Ctr 11B, Waltham, MA 02453, **Business Phone:** (781)736-2250.

### AIKENS-YOUNG, DR. LINDA LEE

School administrator, educator. **Personal:** Born Nov 5, 1950, Conyers, GA; daughter of Willie Melvin Lee and Genoulia Minter Lee; married W Roger; married William Roger; children: Konswello & Jimmneka. **Educ:** Spelman Col, Atlanta, GA, BA, 1972; Ga State Univ, Atlanta, GA, MA, elem educ, 1975, specialist, elem educ, 1976, specialist, educ admin, 1979, PhD, 1988, MEd, EdS. **Career:** Rockdale County Schs, Conyers, Ga, headstart, summers, 1972-77, classroom teacher, 1972-81, lead teacher, 1981-89; Conyers Mid Sch, asst prin, 1989-91; Salem High Sch, asst prin, 1991-92; CJ Hicks Elem Sch, prin; Brenau Univ, asst prof educ, currently. **Orgs:** Wesley Chapel United Methodist Church; bd dir, Ga Asn Educr, 1979-82; exec comt, Rockdale County Dem Party, 1980-; state dir, Nat Educ Asn Bd dir, 1983-89; trustee, Nat Educ Spec Servs, 1986-92; bd trustee, Brenau Univ & Acad, 2007. **Home Addr:** 1869 Farmer Rd NW, Conyers, GA 30012-3407, **Home Phone:** (706)483-0207. **Business Addr:** Assistant Professor of Education, Brenau University, 500 Washington St SE, Gainesville, GA 30501, **Business Phone:** (770)718-5337.

### AIRALL, DR. GUILLERMO EVERS

Dentist, educator, army officer. **Personal:** Born Apr 17, 1919, Paraiso; son of Josiah C Sr (deceased) and Rosetta Letitia Christian; married Clara; children: Zoila Erlinda, Angela & Sheldon. **Educ:** Panama Univ, BS, 1946; Howard Univ, DDS, 1953. **Career:** Pub Health Detroit, dentist, 1953; AUS, dentist, 1953-74; 252nd Med Detachment Thailand, comdr, 1963-64; dentist, pvt pract, 1972-; Temple Univ, Philadelphia, asst prof, 1978-82. **Orgs:** Pres, Little League BB, Ger, 1969-71; vpres, Boy Scout Ger, 1969-71; pres, Lions Club Willingboro, NJ, 1979-80; Burlington Chamber Com, 1982-; admin bd & stewardship bd, United Methodist Church, 1983-; vpres & pres elect, Chi Delta Mu Fraternity Philadelphia, 1984-; vpres elect & pres, Chi Delta Mu Fraternity, Nu Chap, 1984-87; chmn, Church & Soc, 1988; co-chmn, outreach, St Paul United Methodist Church, 1989; Alpha Phi Alpha Fraternity Kappa Iota Lambda Chap, 1989-. **Special Achievements:** Author: "Silver and Gold: Untold Stories of the Immigrant Life in the Panama Canal Zone", 2014. **Home Addr:** , Durham, NC, **Home Phone:** (919)765-9021. **Business Addr:** Dentist, Private Practice, 28 Windsor Lane, Willingboro, NJ 08046-3413, **Business Phone:** (609)871-4088.

### AIRALL, ZOILA ERLINDA

School administrator. **Personal:** Born Jan 21, 1951, Washington, DC. **Educ:** Douglass Col Rutgers Univ, BA, US hist & sociol, 1973; Columbia Univ Teachers Col, MA, 1974, EdM, coun & human develop, 1975; Univ PA, PhD, anthrop educ, 1996. **Career:** Pemberton Twp HS, guid counr, 1975-81; Zurbrugg Hosp, ment health therapist, 1981; Bethany Col, asst dean, coordr coun testing serv & dir coun, 1981-84, assoc dir, 1990-95; Univ Pa, asst dean residence, 1984-88, assoc dir, 1988-96; Bryn Mawr Col, dir instrnl diversity, 1996-2002; Duke Univ, asst vpres stud affairs & adj assoc prof, 2002-. **Orgs:** Pres, basileus Beta Theta Omega-Alpha Kappa Alpha, 1978-; organist, Cove United Presby Church, 1983-; Fels Menniger Found, 1984; Acad Integrity Coun, 2006-07; Alpha Kappa Alpha Sorority Inc; Durham Bk Club Epworth Methodist Church. **Honors/Awds:** Grad Fellowship Columbia Univ, 1973 & 1974; Keynote Speaker Annual Breakfast, Bethany Col, 1984; Outstanding Young Women publication, 1984. **Home Addr:** PO Box 215, Bethany, WV 26032. **Business Addr:** Assistant Vice President For Campus Life, Duke University, 101 Bryan Ctr 125 Sciencel Dr, Durham, NC 27708, **Business Phone:** (919)684-3737.

### AKANDE, BENJAMIN OLA

President (organization), dean (education), educator. **Personal:** son of Samuel Ola; married Bola; children: Moyosola, Anjola & Reni. **Educ:** Wayland Baptist Univ, BS, bus admin, 1983; Univ Okla, MPA, pub admin, 1984, MA, econs, 1990, PhD, econs, 1995; John F Kennedy Sch Govt Exec Prog, Harvard Univ, post doctoral. **Career:** Univ Okla, grad res asst, 1984; Okla Senate & House Representatives, res legal & fiscal staff, economist policy analyst, 1986; Dallas Baptist Univ; Univ Okla, grad teaching asst, 1984-92, res asst, 1989-91; Okla City Univ & DeVry Inst; Benjamin Akande Group, 1992-95; UN Develop Prog, econ consult, 1993; World Bank, econ consult, 1995-96; Wayland Baptist Univ, chief acad officer, chief, assoc prof, spec asst to pres, dean, Sch Bus, Tx, 1995-2000; Webster Univ, Sch Bus & Technol, dean & prof, 2000-, chief, 2010-15; Newberry Group, bd dir; Xiolink Corp; Pvt Bank St Louis; Ralcorp Corp, dir, 2010-13; Westminster Col, pres, 2015. **Orgs:** Trustee, Mary Inst & St Louis Country Day Sch, exec comt bd & chair, schs investment comt, 2004-11; bd advisors, Dean & Provost, 2007-; Hungarian-Mo Educ Partnership, 2008-; co-chair, Websters Instnl Plng Comt, 2008-2009; bd, Vandiver Grp, 2009-; bd, Rx Outreach, 2010-; vice chair, Beyond Housing, 2008-13; bd mem, Pvt Bank St Louis; World Affairs Coun; FDC, 2011-; Bellerive Country Club, 2011-; bd mem, Mo Baptist Med Ctr, 2011-; bd mem, Jefferson Nat Parks Asn, 2012-; Mo Coun Better Econ, 2013-; bd mem, St Louis Art Mus, 2013-; bd mem, Forest Pk Forever, 2013-; bd mem, St Louis Club, 2013-; vice chair, Argent Capital, 2013-; bd mem, Enterprise Bank & Trust, 2014-. **Home Addr:** 2480 Town & Country Lane, St. Louis, MO 63131, **Home Phone:** (314)692-2645. **Business Addr:** President, Westminster College, 501 Westminster Ave, Fulton, MO 65251, **Business Phone:** (573)592-5315.

### AKBAR, DR. NA'IM (LUTHER BENJAMIN WEEMS, JR.)

Psychologist, educator, founder (originator). **Personal:** Born Apr 26, 1944, Tallahassee, FL; son of Luther B Weems and Bessie G Weems; married Renee V Beach; children: Shaakira, Mutaqee & Tareeq. **Educ:** Univ Mich, BA, 1965, MS, 1969, PhD, clin psychol, 1970. **Career:** Morehouse Col, Dept Psychol, assoc prof & dept head, 1970-75, chmn; Norfolk State Univ, assoc prof, 1977-79; Fla State Univ, vis prof, 1979-81, Dept Psychol, clin fac, 1981-2008; J Black Psychol, assoc ed, 1980-85; Mind Prod & Assocs, owner, pres, 1980-; J Black Studies, ed bd, 1981-95; auth: Chains & Images Psychol Slavery, 1984; The Community of Self, 1985; Know ThySelf, 1989; Visions Black Men, 1991; Light from Ancient Africa, 1994; Natural Psychology & Human Transformation, 1995; Breaking the Chains of Psychological Slavery, 1996; Akbar Papers in African Psychology, 2003. **Orgs:** Bd mem, Off Human Develop Am Muslim Mission, 1975-77; bd mem, Nat Black Child Develop Inst, 1978-81; bd dir, Nat Asn Black Psychologists, 1983-84, 1986-89, pres, 1986-87; bd dir, J Black Studies, 1981-95. **Honors/Awds:** Annual Member Award, Asn Black Psychologists, 1980; Martin Luther King Jr Distinguished Scholar Award, Fla State Univ, 1983; Distinguished Black Psychologists, Nat Asn Black Psychologists; Honorary Doctorate of Humane Letters, Edinboro Univ Pa; One of the world's preeminent psychologists & a pioneer in the development of an African-centered approach in modern psychology, Essence Magazine. **Special Achievements:** First Black psychology course and eventually developed probably the first Black psychology program at a Historically Black College or University; Oprah Winfrey Show; The Geraldo Show. **Home Addr:** 503 Famcee Ave, Tallahassee, FL 32310, **Home Phone:** (850)574-9039. **Business Addr:** Founder, Mind Productions & Associates, 324 N Copeland St, Tallahassee, FL 32304, **Business Phone:** (850)222-1764.

### AKINS, DR. DANIEL L.

Educator. **Educ:** Howard Univ, BS; Univ Calif, Berkeley, PhD, phys chem, 1968. **Career:** Fla State Univ, Inst Molecular Biophys, post-doctoral assoc, 1968-69, vis asst prof chem, 1969-70; Univ S Fla, from asst prof to assoc prof, 1970-77; Nat Bur Stds, Laser Chem Sect, guest scientist, 1977-79; Nat Sci Found, Dynamics Prog, phys chem subsection, prog dir chem dynamics, 1977-79; Polaroid Corp, sr scientist, 1979-81; City Univ NY, City Col, prof phys chem, 1981-, Ctr Anal Struct & Interfaces, dir, 1988-, distinguished serv prof chem, 1996-; Grad Sch, doctoral fac & Univ Ctr's PhD Prog chem engineering, 2001-. **Orgs:** Am Chem Soc; Soc Appl Spectros; Sigma Pi Sigma Physics Soc, 1962; Phi Beta Kappa, 1963; Soc Sigma Xi, 1963. **Business Addr:** Professor, Director of Center for Analysis of Structures, City University of New York, Rm J-1120 138th St Convent Ave, New York, NY 10031, **Business Phone:** (212)650-6953.

### AKINYEMI, DR. NURUDEEN B.

College teacher, educator. **Educ:** State Univ NY, Buffalo, BA, polit sci, 1985; Southern Univ, Baton Rouge, MA, polit sci, 1986; Univ SC, PhD, int studies, 1994. **Career:** Kennesaw State Univ, African & African Diaspora Studies prog, coord, Ctr African & African Diaspora Studies, asst dir, interim dir, Dept Polit Sci & Int Affairs, prof, assoc prof & comt chair, currently. **Home Addr:** 1351 Rhododendron Dr NW, Acworth, GA 30102, **Home Phone:** (770)590-9357. **Business Addr:** Associate Professor of Political Science & International Affairs, Committee Chair, Kennesaw State University, SO 5052 1000 Chastain Rd, Kennesaw, GA 30144-5591, **Business Phone:** (770)499-3346.

### AKOREDE, AYO (AYOBAMI S AKOREDE)

Educator. **Personal:** Born Jan 24, 1971; son of Sholape and Salawadeen; children: Sholape. **Educ:** Nova Univ, BS, 1993; Nova Southeastern Univ, MBA, 1995, mgt info sys, 1995. **Career:** St Atty's Off, legal asst, 1993-94; Nova Southeastern Univ, grad asst, 1993-95; Savannah St Univ, stud affairs adv, 1995-, asst dir & event coordr, 1996-12, asst advisor, 2004-06. **Orgs:** Adv, Peer Counr Org, 1995-; vol, Union Mission, 1995-; adv, Phi Alpha Delta, 1996-; Nat Orientation Dir Asn, 1998-; Nat Acad Advising Asn, 1998-; adv, Savannah St Univ, Stud Govt Asn, 1999-; Nat Asn Stud Affairs Personnel, 1999-2000; Savannah Chatham County Coun Disability Issues, 1999-. **Home Addr:** 7717 N Marshfield Ave Suite 1, Chicago, IL 60626-1107.

### AL'UQDAH, WILLIAM MUJAHID

Lawyer. **Personal:** Born Oct 29, 1953, Cincinnati, OH; son of William Henry Jones Sr and Helen G Jones; married Deborah Russell,

Oct 30, 1976; children: William M Ibn III, Shareefah N & Nadirah A. **Educ:** Univ Cincinnati, BS, 1982; Salmon P Chase Col Law, JD, 1987. **Career:** Hamilton Co Welfare Dept, prog adminr, 1974-88; Univ Cincinnati, adj prof, 1987; Hamilton Co Prosecutors Off, asst dist atty, 1988-94; WCIN 1480 AM Radio, sports dir & air personality, 1992; Harmon, Davis & Keys Co, LPA, sr assoc, 1994-96; Lawson & Gaines, atty. **Orgs:** Capt Ohio Army Nat Guard, 1979-; pres, Black Law Stud Asn Am, 1985-86; first exec dir, Black Male Coalition, 1988-89; pres, Ohio Rep Coun, Cin, 1990; Cincinnati Bar Asn. **Honors/Awds:** Scholarship, Black Prof, 1986. **Home Addr:** 2177 Crane Ave, Cincinnati, OH 45207, **Home Phone:** (513)221-0690. **Business Addr:** Attorney, 830 Main St Suite 1000, Cincinnati, OH 45202, **Business Phone:** (513)684-0057.

### AL-MATEEN, DR. CHERYL SINGLETON
Physician, educator. **Personal:** Born Aug 26, 1959, Washington, DC; daughter of Israel Benjamin and Carole Waters; married Kevin Bakeer; children: Benjamin & Katherine. **Educ:** Howard Univ, Col Lib Arts, BS, 1979; Howard Univ, Col Med, MD, 1983. **Career:** Howard Univ Hosp, transitional Med internship, 1983-84; Hahnemann Univ Hosp, psychiat residency, 1984-87, child psychiat residency, 1987-89; Va Commonwealth Univ, Med Col Va, sch med, asst prof, 1989-96, assoc prof psychiat & pediat, 1996-, clerkship dir, currently. **Orgs:** Vpres, admin Howard Univ Col Med Class, 1982-; component mem, Am Psychiat Asn, 1985-98, 2001-; ed-in-chief Spectrum, Am Psychol Asn, 1986-87; co-chair, Am Acad Child & Adolescent Psychiat, 1987-; dir, Inpatient Serv, Va Treat Ctr C; chair, Multicultural Affairs Comt; chair, Clin Subcomt Curric Coun. **Home Addr:** 5306 Clipper Cove Rd, Midlothian, VA 23112-6235, **Home Phone:** (804)739-6891. **Business Addr:** Associate Professor, Virginia Commonwealth University, 515 N 10th St, Richmond, VA 23219, **Business Phone:** (804)828-3129.

### AL-MATEEN, DR. KEVIN BAKEER
Physician. **Personal:** Born Aug 31, 1958, Pasadena, CA; son of Eddie Jr and Margaret Janet Strain; married Cheryl Singleton; children: Benjamin. **Educ:** Univ Calif, Davis, attended 1980; Howard Univ, Col Med, MD, 1984; Va Commonwealth Univ, MS, 1999. **Career:** Pres, Howard Univ, Col Med; St Christopher's C Hosp, Pa, resident pediat; Med Col Va, Dept Neonatology, asst prof pediat, dir, Neonatal ECMO prog; Swift Creek Pediat, Physician, currently; Va Commonwealth Univ, mem fac. **Orgs:** Chesterfield Co Republican Comt. **Honors/Awds:** Malcolm X Scholar & Service Citation, Howard Univ, Col Med, 1984. **Home Addr:** 5306 Clipper Cove Rd, Midlothian, VA 23112-6235, **Home Phone:** (804)739-6891. **Business Addr:** Physician, Swift Creek Pediatrics, 13700 St Francis Blvd Suite 501, Midlothian, VA 23114, **Business Phone:** (804)378-4420.

### ALBERS, KENNETH LYNN
Actor, movie director. **Personal:** Born Jan 24, 1944, Eureka, IL; son of Mildred and Clarence; married Catherine L; children: Elizabeth & Matthew. **Educ:** Ill Wesleyan Univ, BFA, 1967; Univ Minn, MFA, 1969. **Career:** LaCross Community Theater, managing dir, 1969-71; Case Western Res Univ, assoc prof, 1971-84; Cleveland Play House, actor & dir, 1974-82; Freelance, actor & dir, 1974-97; Am Player's Theatre, actor & dir; Actors Co Cleveland, actor & dir; New Am Theater, actor & dir; Nat Theater Deaf, actor & dir; Deaf W Theater Co, actor & dir; Milwaukee Repertory Theater, actor & dir, 1984-94; Ore Shakespeare, actor & dir, 1997-. **Orgs:** Soc Stage Dirs & Choreographers; Independent Labor Union. **Honors/Awds:** Six Cleveland Critics Circle Awards; IL Wesleyan, Alumni Award, 1985; LA Ovation Award, 1995; Dramalogue Award, 1996. **Special Achievements:** Worked with deaf theater companies including Natl Theater of the Deaf and Deaf West Theater Co. **Home Addr:** 569 Scenic Dr, Ashland, OR 97520-1587, **Home Phone:** (541)488-1008. **Business Addr:** Actor, Oregon Skakespeare Festival, 15 S Pioneer St, Ashland, OR 97520, **Business Phone:** (541)482-2111.

### ALBERT, CHARLES GREGORY
Lawyer. **Personal:** Born May 12, 1955, Chicago, IL; son of Essie L and Eugie. **Educ:** Princeton Univ, AB, 1976; Harvard Law Sch, JD, 1979. **Career:** Bell Boyd & Lloyd, assoc, 1979-86, partner, 1987-92; Albert Whitehead PC, atty, pres, 1992-, sr partner, currently. **Orgs:** Trial Bar US Dist Ct Northern Dist Ill, 1983-; dir, Better Boys Found, 1986-; dir, Young Execs Polit, 1986-; dir, Proj Skil, 1986-90; St Gregory's Episcopal Choir Sch, 1990-; Ill Asn Defense Trial Coun; Chicago Bar Asn; Am Bar Asn; Nat Asn Rr Trial Coun; Am Nat Cook County; Nat Asn Rr Trial Coun. **Home Addr:** 1215 E 54th St, Chicago, IL 60615, **Home Phone:** (312)288-4478. **Business Addr:** Senior Partner, Albert Whitehead PC, 10 N Dearborn St Suite 600, Chicago, IL 60602, **Business Phone:** (312)357-6300.

### ALBERT, DONNIE RAY
Opera singer. **Personal:** Born Jan 10, 1950, New Orleans, LA; son of Etta Mae Hatter; married Gwendolyn Veal; children: Dimitri Rholas & Domenic Raoul. **Educ:** La State Univ, BM, 1972; Southern Meth Univ, MM, 1975. **Career:** Can Opera, 1986; Houston Grand Opera, 1986-87; Theater des Westens, Berlin, 1988-89; Florentine Opera Co, 1989; Miami Opera, opera debut, 1990; Salome, Sao Paulo, Brazil, 2004; Dallas Opera's LA Vida Breve, 2004; Austin Lyric Opera, Flying Dutchman, 2004; Opera Pac, I Pagliaci, 2004; Florentine Opera, IL Trovatore, 2004; Los Angeles Philharmonic; Dallas Symphony; Grant Park Music Festival; Kolner Philharmoniker; Munich Symphony; Minn Symphony; Nat Symphony Orchestra; Jerusalem Symphony; Chicago Symphony; Houston Symphony; Jouston Symphony; Seattle Symphony; Israel Symphony; Alvin Ailey Dance Co; Brucknerhaus, Linz; St. Paul Chamber Orchestra; Charleston Symphony; Palm Beach Symphony; Madison Symphony; recordings: Donnie Ray Albert In Recital; Tearless; Porgy & Bess; The Horse I Ride Has Wings; Eine Florentinische Tragodie; Cymbeline-Suite: Ein Tanzpoem; A Clear Midnight; Baltimore Opera, Cincinnati Opera, Dallas Opera, Ft Worth Opera, New Orleans Opera, Portland Opera and Tulsa Opera; LA Opera, performer, 2007-08; Austin, int performer, 2012-. Albums: Dustbowl; Border Line; Night: Four Songs; . Burden; Grave Yard; Poppy Flower; Gypsy Melodies; Fragments; The Lynching; To the White Fiends; Vorfruehling. **Orgs:** Am Guild Musical Artists; Actors Equity; Am Fedn TV & Radio Artists; artist in residence, Ctr Black Music Res, 1989-. **Home Addr:** 515 Wentworth Dr, Richardson, TX 75081, **Home Phone:** (972)231-4963. **Business Addr:** Opera Singer, Pinnacle Arts Management, 889 9th Ave 2nd Fl, New York, NY 10019, **Business Phone:** (212)397-7915.

### ALBRIGHT, GERALD ANTHONY
Singer. **Personal:** Born Aug 30, 1957, Los Angeles, CA; son of Mattie Pearl and William Dudley; married Glynis; children: Selina Marie & Brandon Terrell; married Glynis. **Educ:** Univ Redlands, BS, bus mgt, 1979. **Career:** Studio rec musician, 1980-; Atlantic Rec, rec artist, 1987-99; Albums: Just Between Us, Bermuda Nights, 1988; Live At Birdland West, 1991; Smooth, 1994; Giving Myself to You, 1995; Live To Love, 1997; Pleasures of the Night, 1998; Groovology, 2002; Kickin' It Up, 2004; New Beginnings, 2006; Sax for Stax, 2008; Gerald Alston Sings Sam Cooke, 2008; Gerald Alston Sings Sam Cooke with Gerald Alston, 2008; Pushing the Envelope, 2010; Film: Living Out Loud, 1998; Fire & Ice, 2001. **Orgs:** Alpha Phi Alpha Fraternity, 1978-; Hon spokesperson, InstBlack Parenting, beginning 1989. **Honors/Awds:** Best Jazz Artist Award, Black Radio Exclusive, 1988; Recognition Award, Boy's Club of Am, 1991. **Special Achievements:** Film Score, Devlin; performance, Passenger 57; two-time Grammy Award nominee, 1989, 1990; performance, Hank Gathers Story, 1991-92; performer dat Pres Bill Clinton's Inaguration Ceremony, 1993. **Business Addr:** Singer, c/o Concord Music Group Inc, PO Box 15096, Beverly Hills, CA 90209, **Business Phone:** (800)551-5299.

### ALBRIGHT, DR. ROBERT, JR.
School administrator, president (organization). **Personal:** Born Dec 2, 1944, Philadelphia, PA; married Linda Diane Pittman; children: Keia Lorriane & Lance Robert. **Educ:** Lincoln Univ, AB, 1966; Tufts Univ, MA, 1972; Kent State Univ, PhD, 1978. **Career:** School administrator, president (retired); Lincoln Univ, dir, 1969-71, vpres, 1972-76; Consortium RR Morton Memorial Inst Wash, dir, 1977-79; US Dept Ed Wash, spec asst asst secy, 1979-81; Univ NC Charlotte, vice chancellor, 1981-83; Johnson C Smith Univ Charlotte, pres, 1983-94, pres emer, currently; Educ Testing Serv, exec vpres, 1983-94; NC Consortium, chmn bd dir; Harvard Univ Summer Inst Cambridge, MA, instr; Va Union Univ, dir upward bound morton. **Orgs:** Consult, US Off Ed, Wash, 1970-79, Pa Dept Ed, Harrisburg, 1972-79, Res Triangle Inst; ed, Stud Serv Issues Probs & Opportunity J, 1983; Urban League, 1983; bd visitors, Univ NC, 1983; Rotary; bd dir, Duke Power Co; bd dir, Nat Bank NC; bd trustee, Educ Testing Serv; bd trustee, Southern Educ Found; bd dir, trustee, Warren Wilson Col; trustee, Southern Educ Found; Educ Develop Ctr; bd dir, United Negro Col Fund; Nat Consortium Educ Access; bd Visitors, Lenior-Rhyne Col; trustee, Educ Testing Serv; chmn, bd dir, NC Consortium Int & Intercultural Educ; State Dept Task Force; leadership fel Japan Soc New York. **Honors/Awds:** Sec's Cert Appreciation, US Dept Educ, 1981; W K Kellog Leadership Fel, Nat Asn Equal Opportunity Higher Educ, 2003; Distinguished Service Award, Nat Advan Asn Colored People; Hope Award, Mult Sclerosis Soc; President's Award, NASPA; Received Honorary doctorate, Lenoir-Rhyne Col. **Special Achievements:** First African American to serve as the Chairman of the Board of Directors of the American Council of Education; Fulbright Scholar, 1984; Published numerous articles relating to higher education. **Business Addr:** President Emeritus, Johnson C Smith University, 100 Beatties Ford Rd, Charlotte, NC 28216, **Business Phone:** (704)378-1010.

### ALBRIGHT, WILLIAM DUDLEY, JR.
Executive, executive director. **Personal:** Born Dec 1, 1949, Los Angeles, CA; son of William Dudley Sr and Mattie Pearl Dabner; children: Anterine Penee & Jackson. **Educ:** Univ Redlands, Redlands, CA, BS, chem, 1971; Calif State Univ, Dominguez Hills, CA, MBA, 1974. **Career:** Director (retired); Aerospace Corp, El Segundo, head personnel & security, 1972-78; MITRE Corp, McLean, corp dir human resources mgt, dir, qual work life & benefits, 1978-2012, dir human resources mgt, 1999. **Orgs:** Life mem, Alpha Phi Alpha Fraternity Inc, 1968-; bd mem, Grad Eng Minorities Inc, 1981-. **Home Addr:** 821 Still Creek Lane, Gaithersburg, MD 20878-3218, **Home Phone:** (301)855-3126. **Business Addr:** VA.

### ALBRITTON, DAVID
Businessperson, executive. **Educ:** US Naval Acad, BS, 1988; Naval Postgrad Sch, MS, 1993. **Career:** Sears, Roebuck & Co, sr pub rels mgr, 1998-2000; Hewlett Packard Co/Compaq Comput Corp, dir pub rels, 2000-04; United Way Am, vpres field & media commun, 2004-05; Caraway Group, sr vpres commun, 2005-06; Raytheon Co, dir media rels-Wash, 2006-08; ITT Defense & Info Solutions, vpres commun, 2008-11; Exelis, vpres & chief commun officer, 2011-15; Gen Motors, exec dir global prod develop commun, 2015-. **Orgs:** Kappa Alpha Psi; Exec Leadership Coun, 2012-; mem bd dirs, Points Light, 2012-; mem bd dirs, Final Salute Inc., 2013-; mem bd trustees, Arthur W. Page Soc, 2015-. **Honors/Awds:** Top 100 Most Influential Blacks in Corporate America, SAVOY Magazine, 2014. **Business Addr:** General Motors, PO Box 33170, Detroit, MI 48232-5170.

### ALCINDOR, FERDINAND LEWIS, JR. See ABDUL-JABBAR, KAREEM.

### ALDREDGE, PROF. JAMES EARL
Educator. **Personal:** Born May 1, 1939, Gilmer, TX; son of Lonnie and Ida B; married Daisy Rae. **Educ:** Fresno City Col, AA, bus, 1959; Calif State Univ, BA, therapeut recreation, 1964, MPA, pub admin, 1976; Golden Gate Univ, PhD, pub admin, 1985. **Career:** Fresno Cty Econ Opportunities, prog coord 1965; City Fresno, city mgr, 1985-89; Calif St Univ, prof, 1990-2002, Cent Valley Health Policy Inst, adv coun, currently, prof emer, 2002-; CEN-CAL Bus Finance Group, bd dir, dir, 2004-; Kings View Behav Health, bd dir, dir, 2005-; HAW Develop Group, partner; Fresno Unified Sch Dist Safety Comn, bd dir, dir, 2007; St. Agnes Hosp, bd dir, dir. **Orgs:** Bd mem, Fresno Cty United Way, CA State Univ, Fresno; bd mem, St Agnes Med Ctr, Fresno; bd trustee, Calif Sch Prof Psychol; Fresno Pac Univ, bd dir, dir, 2001-; Kings View Behav Health, 2005; chair, Fresno Unified Sch Dist Safety Comn, 2007. **Home Addr:** 5555 N W Ave, Fresno, CA 93711-2368, **Home Phone:** (559)440-9953.

### ALDRIDGE, ALLEN RAY, JR.
Teacher, football player. **Personal:** Born May 30, 1972, Houston, TX; son of Allen Sr and Cleotha William. **Educ:** Univ Houston, BA, sports admin. **Career:** Football player (retired), teacher; Denver Broncos, linebacker, right linebacker, mid linebacker, 1994-97; Detroit Lions, linebacker, right linebacker, left outside linebacker, 1998-2001; Houston Texans, 2002; George Bush High Sch, teacher, currently; Philadelphia Eagles, vol asst coach. **Orgs:** Fel Christian Athletes; vol, Pontiac Rescue Mission. **Honors/Awds:** Defensive MVP, Blue-Gray All-Star Game, 1993; Super Bowl XXXII; Championship Game Defensive MVP, 1999. **Business Addr:** Teacher, George Bush High School, 6707 FM 1464, Richmond, TX 77469, **Business Phone:** (281)634-6060.

### ALDRIDGE, DR. DELORES PATRICIA
Editor, educator, sociologist. **Personal:** Born Jun 8, 1941, Tampa, FL; daughter of Willie Lee and Mary Ellen; married Kwame Essuon; children: Kwame G Essuon & Aba D Essuon. **Educ:** Clark Col, BS, sociol & psychol, 1963; Atlanta Univ, MA, social work, 1966; Univ Ireland-Dublin, cert child psychol, 1967; Purdue Univ, PhD, sociol, 1971; Univ Ghana-Legon, attended 1972; Georgetown Univ, PG, 1979; Bryn Mawr, advan cert educ mgt, 1980. **Career:** Tampa Urban League, assoc dir, 1966; St John God Bros Child Guid Clin, supvr & family therapist, 1966-67; Comprehensive Community Ment Health Ctr, actg chief social work, 1967-68; Purdue Univ, Dept Sociol, teaching asst, 1968-70; Summer Nat Defense Educ Act fel, 1969; Greater Lafayette Community Ctrs Inc, dir community develop div, 1969, exec dir, 1969-71; Emory Univ, Dept Sociol, asst prof, founding coordr, 1971-75, Inst Lib Arts, adj prof, 1973-75, assoc prof, coordr Black Studies, 1976-78, Ctr Res Social Chg, res assoc, 1977-85, assoc prof sociol, 1978-87, prof social, 1988-, Grace Towns Hamilton, prof sociol & african Am Studies, 1990-; Am Forum Int Study fel, 1972; Spelman Col, vis lectr, 1972-74; USDA Forest Serv, policy analyst, 1980-81; Nat Coun Black Studies, dir res component grants, 1988-93; Clin Eval Serv, Prog Res Women's Health Care, assoc dir, 1994-; State Ga, Social & Econ Contrib Women Ga, proj dir, 1997-; Univ Ghana, vis distinguished prof, 1997-; Author: A Battle Unfinished, 1974; Coping with Conflict: The Natural Resource Agency, 1983; Racial Ethnic, 1987; Black Male-Female Relationships: A Resource Book, 1989; Toward Integrating Africana Women into Africana Studies, 1992; Focusing: Black Male Female Relationships, 1994; Every Black Woman Should Wear A Red Dress, 2003; Editor: River of Tears: The Politics of Black Womens Health, 1993; Out of the Revolution: The Development of Africana Studies, 2000. **Orgs:** Delta Sigma Theta Sorority; Asn Social & Behav Scientists; Int Black Women's Cong; Asn African Am Life & Hist; dir, Nat Coun Black Studies, 1988-93; Asn Black Sociologists; Societas Doctas; Care Int-Atlanta; Decatur Alumnae Chap Delta Sigma Theta Sorority'Ga; Ankh Maat Wedjau Hon Soc; co-founder, KESS NSONA Health & Educ FOUND, 2000; chair, Int Black Women's Cong, 2008; Am Sociol Asn; Southern Sociol Soc; bd trustee, Clark Atlanta Univ, 2008; pres, vice-chair, Ga Develop Authority. **Special Achievements:** First African American woman faculty member of Emory University and founding director of the first African American and African Studies degree-granting program in the South, which she administered until 1990; First sociologist to serve as a policy analyst with the U.S. Forest Service. **Home Addr:** 2931 Yucca Dr, Decatur, GA 30032-5836, **Home Phone:** (404)289-0272. **Business Addr:** Professor, Emory University, 228 Tarbutton Hall, Atlanta, GA 30322, **Business Phone:** (404)727-0534.

### ALDRIDGE, KAREN BETH (KAREN B ALDRIDGE-EASON)
Government official, association executive. **Personal:** Born Oct 19, 1952, Flint, MI; daughter of Avery and Mildred Light; married Spencer Sims. **Educ:** Univ Mich, Ann Arbor, MI, BA, spec educ, 1975; Western Mich Univ, Kalamazoo, MI, MPA, 1985. **Career:** Nat Baptist Foreign Mission Bd, Liberia, W Africa, prin & mgr, 1975-77; Mich State Senate, Lansing MI, legis asst, 1977-83; Mich Dept Com, Lansing, Mich, sr budget analyst, 1984-87, actg budget dir & dep budget dir, 1987-88; City Flint, Mich, budget dir, 1988-92; Charles Stewart Mott Found, prog dir, 1994-2003; Mich Dept Mgt & Budget, div budget dir, dir off health & human servs, 1992-94; Harwood Inst, community coach consult, 2008-10. **Orgs:** Treas, bd, mem, Am Soc Publ Admin, Flint & Saginaw Valley Chap, 1983-; bd mem, 1989-, treas, Visually Impaired Ctr, 1990-91; adv bd mem, Baker Col, 1989-; bd mem, Int Inst Flint, 1990-; dir, Youth Div, Nat Baptist Cong; found liaison, Charles Stewart Mott Found, 2003-, Off Gov Jennifer M Granholm, State Mich 2006-, prog dir, 1994-03; bd mem, Tapology inc, 2006-11; bd dir, Genesys Inc, 2008-. **Home Addr:** 1534 S Franklin Ave, Flint, MI 48503, **Home Phone:** (313)232-8573. **Business Addr:** Foundation Liaison, Program Director, Charles Stewart Mott Foundation, Mott Foundation Bldg 503 S Saginaw St Suite 1200, Flint, MI 48502-1851, **Business Phone:** (810)238-5651.

### ALDRIDGE, KITA. See ALDRIDGE, MARKITA.

### ALDRIDGE, MARKITA (KITA ALDRIDGE)
Loan officer, basketball player, executive. **Personal:** Born Sep 15, 1973, Detroit, MI; daughter of Adele; married Woods. **Educ:** Univ NC, Charlotte, BS, financial mgt, 1996. **Career:** Basketball player (retired), executive; Portland Power, guard, 1996-97; Colo Xplosion, 1996-97; Philadelphia Rage, 1997-98; NE Blizzard, 1998; Columbus Quest, 1998-99; Wash Mystics, 1999-2001; Atlanta Justice, 2000-01; Charlotte 49ers, 2008; WestStar Mortgage, sr loan officer, 2002-15; Gold Star Mortgage Financial Group, sr loan officer, 2015-. **Orgs:** Founder, Markita Aldridge Found; Realtor Asn Prince William; Nat Asn Real Estate Brokers. **Business Addr:** Senior Loan Officer, Gold Star Mortgage Financial Group, 12726 Directors Loop, Woodbridge, VA 22192, **Business Phone:** (703)929-2274.

### ALDRIDGE-EASON, KAREN B. See ALDRIDGE, KAREN BETH.

### ALERS, ROCHELLE
Writer. **Personal:** Born New York, NY. **Educ:** John Jay Col Criminal Justice, City Univ NY, BA, 1974. **Career:** Empire State Med Equip Dealers Asn, exec asst, 1987-91; Nassau County Dept Drugs & Al-

cohol Addiction Serv, community liaison specialist, 1991-. Author: "Careless Whispers", 1988; "Happily Ever After", 1994; "Holiday Cheer-First Fruits", 1995; "Hideaway", 1995; "Holiday Cheer", 1995; "Home Sweet Home", 1995; "Vows", 1997; "Reckless Surrender", 1997; "Love Letters-Hearts of Gold", 1997; "Heaven Sent", 1998; "Gentle Yearning", 1998; "Hidden Agenda", 1998; "Harvest Moon", 1999; "Rosie's Curl and Weave", 1999; "Summer Magic", 1999; "Just Before Dawn", 2000; "Dellas House of Style", 2000; "Island Magic", 2000; "Welcome to Leos", 2000; "Private Passions", 2001; "Going To The Chapel", 2001; "Tis The Season", 2001; "My Love's Keeper", 2001; "Twilight Mood", 2002; "Island Bliss", 2002; "No Compromise", 2002 & 2007; "Living Large", 2003; "Renegade", 2003; "Secrets Never Told", 2003; "Hideaway Saga", 2004; "Very Private Duty", 2004; "Four Degrees of Heat", 2004; "Lets Get It On", 2004; "The Long Hot Summer", 2004; "Lessons of a Lowcountry", 2004; "All My Tomorrow", 2005; "A Younger Man", 2005; "Beyond Business", 2005; "Best Kept Secrets", 2006; "A Time To Keep", 2006; "A Season of Miracles", 2006; "Stranger In My Arms", 2007; "Hideaway Legacy", 2007; "Pleasure Seekers", 2007; "Taken by Storm", 2008; "The Sweetest Temptation", 2008; "Long Time Coming", 2008; "After Hours", 2008; "Naughty", 2009; "Secret Agenda", 2009; "Bittersweet Love", 2009; "The Best Men Trilogy", 2009; "Man of Fate", 2009; "Man of Fortune", 2009; "Man of Fantasy", 2009; "Because of You", "Twice the Temptation"; "Breakaway", 2010; "Black Expressions". **Orgs:** Freeport Exchange Club, 1990-; co founder, pres, Women Writers Color, 1990-94; Long Island Quilters Soc, 1996; Iota Theta Zeta Chap Zeta Phi Beta Sorority Inc. **Home Addr:** 90 Kingston Ave, Floral Park, NY 11001, **Home Phone:** (516)775-0790.

### ALEX, GREGORY K.

Clergy, administrator, executive director. **Personal:** Born Nov 30, 1948, Seattle, WA; son of Joseph P and Delores. **Educ:** Univ Wash, BA, urban planning/archit, 1971; Seattle Univ, Sch Theol, MA, theol, 1996. **Career:** Housing & Urban Develop, Wash, DC, urban planner, 1971-75; Seattle Housing Authority, dir target proj prog, 1975-78; A&R Imports Inc, pres, 1978-80; Matt Talbot Ministry, Seattle, Wash, minister, exec dir & founder, 1985-. **Orgs:** Yale Univ Black Environ Studies Team Curric Comn; comnr judo, Goodwill Games, 1988-90; African Am Reach & Teach Health Ministry. **Honors/Awds:** Black Athletic Alumni Award, 1971; Outstanding Achievement Award, Housing & Urban Develop, 1972; Outstanding Achievement Award, Univ WA; Master TKD, Chang Moo Kwan, Seoul, Korea, 1989; Fran Nordstrom Vol Year, King County Boys & Girls Clubs, 1986; Community Service Award, Downtown Human Serv Coun, 1986. **Home Addr:** 2313 3rd Ave, Seattle, WA 98122. **Business Addr:** Founder, Executive Director, Matt Talbot Center, 2313 3rd Ave, Seattle, WA 98121-1712, **Business Phone:** (206)256-9865.

### ALEXANDER, ARIKA

Marketing executive, manager. **Personal:** Born Bronx, NY. **Educ:** Univ N Tex, attended 1997. **Career:** Reach Media Inc, mkt mgr, affil mkt mgr, currently; Peewees 2 Pros, owner, currently. **Orgs:** ASD. **Home Addr:** 14400 Montfort Dr, Dallas, TX 75254, **Home Phone:** (972)385-9277. **Business Addr:** Affiliate Marketing Manager, Reach Media Inc, 13760 Noel Rd Suite 750, Dallas, TX 75240, **Business Phone:** (972)371-5846.

### ALEXANDER, BILLYE J.

Executive. **Educ:** Univ Pac, Stockton, BA, fr. **Career:** Executive (retired); Sears, Roebuck & Co, exec, 1970, Weberstown Mall Store, div mgr, 1971, dist gen mgr, 1992, NW Region, sr vpres commun, 2002, Midwest Region, vpres & gen mgr, 2003, Dept Multicultural Mkt, vpres, 2004. **Orgs:** John McLendon Memorial Minority Blue Ribbon Comn.

### ALEXANDER, BLAIR E.

Executive. **Career:** Oper Urgent Fury, plt ldr; United Negro Col Fund Spec Progs Corp, Dept Defense Tech Asst Prog, prog dir, currently. **Home Addr:** 3424 Red Adm Ct, Edgewater, MD 21037, **Home Phone:** (410)798-7753. **Business Addr:** Program Director, United Negro College Fund Special Programs, 2750 Prosperity Ave Suite 600, Fairfax, VA 22031, **Business Phone:** (703)205-7631.

### ALEXANDER, BRENT (RONALD BRENT ALEXANDER)

Football player, teacher, football coach. **Personal:** Born Jul 10, 1971, Detroit, MI; married Mari; children: Corey & Myles. **Educ:** Tenn State Univ, grad. **Career:** Football player (retired), teacher, football coach; Ariz Cardinals, right cornerback, 1994, free safety, 1995-97; Carolina Panthers, free safety, 1998, strong safety, 1999; Pittsburgh Steelers, free safety, 2000-03; New York Giants, free safety, strong safety, 2004-05; Pope John Paul II High Sch, Tenn, math teacher, football coach, currently.

### ALEXANDER, REV. CEDRIC V.

Chief executive officer, chairperson. **Educ:** Howard Univ, BA, int rels; San Francisco State Univ, BS, bus admin with an emphasis acct; Univ Calif, PhD. **Career:** First AME Church, pastor; Seventeenth Episcopal Dist, exec asst; Col Financial Planning, adj fac mem; Williams, Adley & Co, LLP, audit sr; Peat Marwick, Mitchell & Co, staff acct; Am Express Financial Advisors, personal & bus financial advisor; Waddell & Reed Inc, financial planning, assoc mgr; Primerica Financial Serv, sr vpres; Blaylock Robert Van LLC, sr vpres, financial planning & chief compliance officer; Demanco Brokerage Serv Inc, founder, chmn & chief exec officer, currently; Primerica Inc, sr vice pres & regist prin; Demanco Technol Serv Inc, chmn & chief exec officer. **Orgs:** Orange County Bar Asn; Richard Banyard Inns Ct; Nat Bar Asn; Financial Planning Asn; Nat Asn Black Accountants; Calif Conf Ministerial Alliance, AME Church; Int Fraternity Delta Sigma Pi. **Business Addr:** Chairman, Chief Executive Officer, Demanco Brokerage Services Inc, 2030 Franklin St Suite 220, Oakland, CA 94612-2006, **Business Phone:** (510)435-1780.

### ALEXANDER, DR. CHARLES

College administrator. **Educ:** State Univ NY Col, Cortland, NY, BA, sociol, 1974; Univ Nebr, Omaha, NE, MA, sociol, 1977; Ohio State Univ, Stud Coun & Personnel Serv, attended 1980; Marquette Univ, PhD, educ, 1988. **Career:** Marquette Univ, Multicultural Concerns, dir, 1996; Univ Calif, San Francisco, CA, Sch Dent, assoc dean admin & stud affairs, 1996-2006, Los Angeles, CA, assoc vice provost stud diversity, 1996-, Acad Advan Prog, dir & adj assoc prof, currently. **Orgs:** Pres, Nat Asn Med Minority Educr, 1998; UCLA Coun Diversity & Inclusion 2011-; Alpha Phi Alpha; Advocates. **Home Addr:** 760 Arguello Blvd, San Francisco, CA 94118, **Home Phone:** (415)750-9496. **Business Addr:** Associate Vice Provost, AAP Director, University of California Los Angeles, 1232 Campbell, Los Angeles, CA 90095-1541, **Business Phone:** (310)206-1551.

### ALEXANDER, CHARLES FRED, JR.

Football player, executive. **Personal:** Born Jul 28, 1957, Galveston, TX; married Yvette; children: Nicole. **Educ:** La State Univ, BS, gen studies, 1980. **Career:** Football player (retired), executive; Cincinnati Bengals, running back & fullback, 1979-85; Whitco Supply LLC, sr proj mgr, 2013-; LSU's Tiger Athletic Found, asst dir; Charlie 4 Strong Seasoning Inc, owner, founder, 2011. **Honors/Awds:** All-Am, La State Univ; Athletic Hall of Fame, La State Univ, 1989; Col Football Hall Fame, 2012. **Special Achievements:** Only La State Univ player to ever account for 4000 or more yards in a career. **Business Addr:** Owner, Founder, Charlie 4 Seasoning Inc, 5003 Lockridge Sky Lane, Sugar Land, TX 77479, **Business Phone:** (713)822-6327.

### ALEXANDER, CLIFFORD LEOPOLD, JR.

Management consultant, lawyer, president (organization). **Personal:** Born Sep 21, 1933, New York, NY; son of Clifford L and Edith A; married Adele Logan; children: Elizabeth & Mark Clifford. **Educ:** Harvard Univ, BA, 1955; Yale Univ, LLB, 1958. **Career:** New York County, asst dist atty, 1959-61; Manhattanville Hamilton Grange, exec dir, 1961-62; HARYOU Inc, exec prog dir, pvt pract law, 1962-63; Nat Security Coun, staff mem, 1963-64; Pres Lyndon, dep spec asst, 1964-65, Pres Johnson, assoc spec coun, 1965-66, dep spec coun, 1966-67; Independence Swaziland, spec ambassador, 1968; Equal Employ Opportunity Comn, chmn, 1967-69; Arnold & Porter, partner, 1969-75; TV news commentator, 1972-76; Howard Univ, prof law, 1973-74; DC, mayor, 1974; Verner, Liipfert, Bernhard, McPherson & Alexander, partner, 1975-76; Dept Army, secy, 1977-81; Alexander & Assocs Inc, pres & founder, 1981-; Maj League Baseball, consult; IMS Health, bd dir, 1998-2002; MCI Corp, dir; Georgetown Univ, adj prof; Dun & Bradstreet Corp, chmn & chief exec officer; Moody's Corp, chmn. **Orgs:** Chmn, US Equal Employ Opportunity Comn, 1967-69; pres, Comn Income Maint Progs, 1967-68; pres, Comn Observation Human Rights, 1968; bd dir, Mex-Am Legal Def & Educ Fund; Nat Asn Advan Colored People Legal & Educ Fund; bd overseers, Harvard Univ, 1969-75; trustee, Atlanta Univ; host & co-producer, TV prog Cliff Alexander, Black White, 1971-74; chmn, Comm Food & Shelter; chmn, Dance Theatre Harlem, 1995-; dir, Pa Power & Light Co; dir, Dreyfus Third Century Fund; dir, Dreyfus Gen Money Mkt Fund; dir, Dreyfus Common Stock Fund; dir, Dreyfus Govt Sec Fund; dir, Dreyfus Tax Exempt Fund; Am & DC Bar Asns; dir, Equitable Resources Inc; Bd Gov, Am Stock Exchange; Omega Psi Phi fraternity; bd dir, Am Home Prod Corp; bd dir, MCI Worldcom; bd dir, Mutual Am. **Honors/Awds:** Ames Award, Harvard Univ, 1955; Named Honorable Citizen, Kansas City, Mo, 1965; Frederick Douglass Award, 1970; LLD, Malcolm X Col, 1972; LLD, Morgan State Univ, 1972; LLD, Wake Forest Univ, 1978; LLD, Univ Md, 1980; Outstanding Civilian Service Award, Dept Army, 1980; Distinguished Public Service Award, Dept Def, 1981; LLD, Atlanta Univ, 1982. **Special Achievements:** Rep pres, Kingdom of Swaziland, 1968; First African-American Secretary of the Army. **Home Addr:** 512 A St SE, Washington, DC 20003-1139, **Home Phone:** (202)544-8223. **Business Addr:** President, Founder, Alexander & Associates Inc, 400 C St NE, Washington, DC 20002-5818, **Business Phone:** (202)546-0111.

### ALEXANDER, CORNELIA

Beautician, government official, public speaker. **Personal:** Born Winona, MS; daughter of George Thompson and Emma Trotter Thompson; married John Sr; children: Margaret McLaughlin, John Jr, Leslie B Hardy, Charles, Carl E Hardy & Constance E Hardy Atkins. **Educ:** Vestal Labs, cert, 1969; Youngstown State Univ, cert, 1977. **Career:** Alexander's Garage, off mgr, 1959-77; Salem City Hosp, laundry mgr, 1965-80; Mary Kay Cosmetics, beauty consult, 1979; NCSC Sr Aide Prog, sr aide, 1982-83; Salem City Coun, coun woman, 1984-89; pub speaker, 1986; Columbiana County Recorder's Off, dep recorder, 1982. **Orgs:** Mt Zion AME Church, 1957-82; Salem YWCA, 1968-; dir, Salem YWCA, 1971-75; bd dir, Mobile Meals Salem, 1978; dem precinct comn, 1980; Bus & Prof Women, Lisbon, OH, 1981-83; Am Cancer Soc, 1982-83; Believer's Christian Fel, 1982-; spec exec, Salem YWCA, 1982-85; chmn, Fed & State Funding Comn City Coun; nienth coun comn; Columbiana County Community Corrections Planning Bd, 1984; vpres, pres, Human Serv Dept Adv Bd, 1991; Salem Bus & Prof Women Orgn; corresp secy, Salem Women's Aglow, 1992; bd mem, Salem Area Habitat Housing Humanity, vpres, 1992-95; Salem Sr Citizens Orgn; pres, Salem Women's Dem Club; Salem Hist Soc; E Liverpool African Am Hist Mus; sr companion vol, Dept Eldercare, State Fla, 1998-. **Honors/Awds:** Senior Citizen of the Year, Columbiana County, 1992; Community Service Award, Fed Prison Bd; Black Achievers Award, State Rep, 2000. **Special Achievements:** First among 3 nominees Chosen as Democrats of the Year, 1985; First African American to obtain a seat on the City Coun of Salem; "Local Heroes/They Made a Difference in 1992", The Vindicator, Jan 3, 1992; Salem News, June 8, 1992, May 17, 1993; Ohio's Heritage, Autumn 1994; Yesteryears, January 14, 1995. **Home Addr:** 115 3rd St Suite 908, Jacksonville Beach, FL 32250, **Home Phone:** (904)270-1710.

### ALEXANDER, CORY LYNN

Basketball player, basketball coach. **Personal:** Born Jun 22, 1973, Waynesboro, VA. **Educ:** Univ Va, BA, psychol, 1995. **Career:** Basketball player (retired), executive; San Antonio Spurs, guard & point guard, 1995-98; Cory Alexander Basketball School, owner & president, 1995-; Denver Nuggets, point guard, 1998-2000; Orlando Magic, point guard, 2000-01; Roanoke Dazzle, NBA Develop League, 2002-03, 2004-05; Virtus Roma, Italy, 2003-04; Charlotte Bobcats, guard & point guard, 2004-05; ACC Network/ESPNU, TV color analyst, 2009-. **Honors/Awds:** Silver Medal, FIBA U20 Americas Championship, 1993; Gold Medal, FIBA U21 World Championship, 1993. **Special Achievements:** Flim: Eddie, 1996. **Business Addr:** Commentator, ACC Network, 1900 W Morehead St, Charlotte, NC 28208, **Business Phone:** (704)378-4400.

### ALEXANDER, DAWN

Marketing executive, president (organization). **Educ:** Oberlin Col, BA, 1982; Harvard Univ JFK Sch Govt, cert, 1985; Yale Sch Mgt, MBA, 1987. **Career:** Morgan Stanley, syst analyst, 1982-84, data ctr oper supvr, 1984-85; Drew-Dawn Enterprises, pres, 1984-85, chair & chief exec officer, 1997-; DFS Dorland Worldwide, asst acct exec, 1986; Pepsi-Cola Co, from asst assoc to sr assoc, mkt mgr, 1987-90; Colgate-Palmolive, prod mgr, 1990-91; Uniworld Grp, acct supvr, 1991, reg acct dir, 1991-92, vpres mgt supvr, 1992-95; Compuserve, sr prod mgr, 1995-96, promos grp mgr, 1996-97; MosaicLink, chairperson; IBM, sr prod mgr, 1997; Image Mkg Solutions Inc, pres, 1996-; Aether Systs, dir mkt, 2000-01; SafeNet Inc, mkt mgr, mkt dir, dir worldwide prod mkt; InfraGard, pres Baltimore chap, works, bd mem; SecureNet Solutions Inc, dir sales & mkt, vpres sls & mkt, currently; Univ Md, adj fac mem, bus & mgt unit, currently. **Orgs:** Alumni admis rep, Oberlin Col, 1982-; Nat Black MBA Asn, 1986-; bd mem, Dance Theatre Workshop, 1993-95; chairperson, Oberlin African Am Alumni Grp, 1996-; bd mem, Oberlin Col Alumni Asn, 1996-; Women Sports Found, 1996-2001; Women Basketball Coaches Asn, 1996-2001; bd mem, Gateway, Ga AV Revitalization Corp, 1999-2000; Am Mkt Asn; Am Advert Fedn & Advert Club Metrop DC; bd mem, Rockville Chamber Com, 1999-2000; comnr, chair, develop comt, Montgomery Co Celebration, 2000. **Special Achievements:** Served as first vice president of Maryland InfraGard chapter. **Home Addr:** 8205 Grubb Rd, Silver Spring, MD 20910. **Business Addr:** Vice President of Sales & Marketing, SecureNet Solutions Inc, 761 Silver Spring Ave Suite B, Silver Spring, MD 20910, **Business Phone:** (301)565-0001.

### ALEXANDER, DERRICK L.

Football coach, football player. **Personal:** Born Nov 13, 1973, Jacksonville, FL. **Educ:** Fla State Univ, grad. **Career:** Football player (retried), coach; Minn Vikings, defensive end & right defensive end & left defensive end, 1995-98; Cleveland Browns, right defensive end & defensive end & right defensive tackle, 1999-2000; Bishop McLaughlin Cath High Sch, head football coach, 2011-13. **Honors/Awds:** Inducted into the Florida State Hall of Fame, 2007. **Business Addr:** Head Football Coach, Bishop McLaughlin Catholic High School, 13651 Hays Rd, Spring Hill, FL 34610, **Business Phone:** (727)857-2600.

### ALEXANDER, DERRICK SCOTT

Football player, systems engineer. **Personal:** Born Nov 6, 1971, Detroit, MI. **Educ:** Univ Mich, BA, sports mgt & commun, 1994. **Career:** Football player (retired), system engineer; Cleveland Browns, wide receiver, 1994-95; Baltimore Ravens, wide receiver, 1996-97; Kans City Chiefs, wide receiver, 1998-2001; Minn Vikings Football LLC, wide receiver, 2002-03; Cerner Corp, syst engr, 2011-. **Home Addr:** , Kansas City, MO. **Business Addr:** System Engineer, Cerner Corp, 2800 Rockcreek Pkwy, North Kansas City, MO 64117, **Business Phone:** (816)221-1024.

### ALEXANDER, DOROTHY DEXTER

Educator. **Personal:** Born Jun 17, 1929, Chattaroy, WV; daughter of William (deceased) and Georgia (deceased); married Robert D; children: Robert D Jr & Doncella Darice. **Educ:** WVa State Univ, BMus, 1950; Pikeville Col, attended 1957; Marshall Univ, attended 1962; Ohio State Univ, attended 1964. **Career:** Educator (retired); WV Mingo County Educ Bd, social studies & music teacher, 1950-63; Franklin County Child Welfare Bd, OH, teacher, 1963-66; Educ Bd, Columbus, OH, vocal music teacher, 1966-88; Shiloh Baptist Church, minister music, 1992-97 & 2008-15; Greater Columbus Conv Ctr, mgr. **Orgs:** Local vpres, AKA Sorority Inc, 1950, 1984, local secy music, 1982-92, chmn awards luncheon, 1983; collector, UNF, 1979-88; Mid-Ohio & Franklin County Health Planning Fedn, 1979-80; pres, Aesthetics Social Club, 1980-84; accompanists, Columbus Boychoir, 1985-88; community rept, educcomt, Franklin County Child Develop Coun, 1988-92; NCW, 1989-; regional music dir, Great Lakes, 1990; chmn scholar comt, Lunch Bunch, 1991-92; Nat Coun Negro Women; Nat Asn Advan Colored People; Federated Women's Club; Worthy Matron Esther Chap No 3, OES PHA; Friends Arts Community Enrichment; Dir Sr, Choir Shiloh Baptist Church. **Special Achievements:** Produced outstanding piano students in Mingo County West Virginia; Vocal Music Director, Promoting Talented Youth of Franklin County, Ohio. **Home Addr:** 2187 Liston Ave, Columbus, Columbus, OH 43207-2835, **Home Phone:** (614)444-1658. **Business Addr:** Choir Director, Shiloh Baptist Church, 720 Mt Vernon Ave, Columbus, OH 43203, **Business Phone:** (614)253-7946.

### ALEXANDER, DR. DREW W.

Physician, dean (education). **Personal:** Born Dec 21, 1948, Peoria, IL. **Educ:** Earlham Col, BA, 1966; Med Col Ohio, MD, 1973. **Career:** Albert Einstein Col Med, resident & intern, 1973-76; Univ Tex, Health Sci Ctr, Dallas, adolescent med fel, 1976-77, asst prof pediat, 1977; W Dallas Youth Clin, health team leader, 1977; Southwestern Med Sch, asst dean, Minority Stud Affairs, currently; Adolescent Health Assoc, physician, currently. **Orgs:** Educ comt, Soc Adolescent Med, 1976-; asst med dir, Dallas City Juv Detention Clin, 1977-; consult, Multidisciplinary Adolescent Health Training Proj, 1977-; admis comn, Univ Tex, Dallas, 1978-; coordr, Minority Affairs, 1979-; vol, Big Bros & Big Sisters, 1976-; bd mem, Child Care Asn Metrop, Dallas, 1978-. **Business Addr:** Assistant Dean Community Affairs, UT Southwestern Medical School, 5323 Harry Hines Blvd, Dallas, TX 75390-9003, **Business Phone:** (214)648-2509.

### ALEXANDER, DR. EDWARD CLEVE

Scientist, educator. **Personal:** Born Nov 20, 1943, Knoxville, TN; son of Robert W and Gladys Clardy; married Edwina Carr; children: Everett, Erika & Efrem. **Educ:** City Univ NY, BS, 1965; State Univ NY, Buffalo, NY, PhD, 1969. **Career:** Lowa State Univ, post doctoral fel, 1969-70; Calif Univ, San Diego, Third Col Sci & Technol Prog, asst prof chem & coordr, 1970-78, lectr, 1978-82, vis assoc prof; BOOST Prog, San Diego, supvr dept math & sci, 1982-89; USN Broadened

Opportunity Officers Selection & Trng Prog, supvr math & sci, consult; San Diego Mesa Col, fac, 1989-, chmn chem, 1995-, chair, 1996-99, prof chem, Bridges Prog dir, currently. **Orgs:** Consult, Nat Insts Health; fel Am Chem Soc, 1965-; bd dir & exec bd, San Diego Urban League, 1972-76; Minority Bio med Support Bd, 1974-78; IBM, San Jose, CA, 1976; fel House Plan; fel Baskerville Chem Socs; fel African Sci Inst. **Home Addr:** 3381 Lone Jack Rd, Encinitas, CA 92024-7014, **Home Phone:** (858)756-5412. **Business Addr:** Professor, Bridges Program Director, San Diego Mesa College, I-214 7250 Mesa Col Dr, San Diego, CA 92111-4998, **Business Phone:** (619)388-2618.

### ALEXANDER, ERIKA L.

Administrator. **Personal:** married Tracy Barbour. **Educ:** Univ Va, BA; George Mason Univ, MBA. **Career:** Residence Inn, sales mgr, brand dir; TownePlace Suites, dir opers, brand vpres; Marriott Int Inc, market mgmt, sales rep to regional vpres, area vpres, 1989-. **Orgs:** Bd mem, Memphis Conv & Visitors Bur; trustee, Ron Clark Acad; trustee, Leadership Atlanta; Atlanta C's Shelter; Int Women's Forum; exec comt, Metro Atlanta Chamber Com; Tenn Women's Forum; fel, International Women's Forum Leadership Foundation, 2002. **Business Addr:** Area Vice President, Marriott International Inc, 10400 Fernwood Rd, Bethesda, MD 20817, **Business Phone:** (301)380-3000.

### ALEXANDER, DR. ESTELLA CONWILL

Educator, poet. **Personal:** Born Jan 19, 1949, Louisville, KY; children: Patrice Sales & Dominic. **Educ:** Univ Louisville, BA, 1975, MA, 1976; Univ Iowa, PhD, 1984. **Career:** Univ Iowa, instr/dir black poetry, 1976-79; Grinnell Col, asst prof, 1979-80; Ky State Univ, prof eng, poet, currently; Hunter Col City Univ NY, prof eng. **Home Addr:** 3323 Dumesnil St, Louisville, KY 40211.

### ALEXANDER, F. S. JACK

Firefighter, state government official, commissioner. **Personal:** Born Dec 7, 1930, Iola, KS; son of James Floyd and Agnes Marie Stewart; married Tillie Marie Simon; children: Patricia M, Jack Jr, Stephanie R & Terrell L. **Educ:** Washburn Univ, BA, 1954. **Career:** Commissioner (retired), state govt off; Topeka Bd Educ, stockroom mgr, 1948-51 (retired); Goodyear Tire & Rubber Co, qual control, 1951-85; Topeka City, water commr, 1973-85, pres, 1983; State Kans Oilfield & Environ Geol, consult, 1985-86; Kans dept health & environ, 1985-89; Gov Legis Affairs, 1989-91; Kans Corp Comn, comnr, 1991-96; State Fire Marshal, 2004-. **Orgs:** Ex-com & bd, NLC, 1975-85; Econ & Com Develop Comn, 1975-85; vpres, Topeka United Way Bd, 1975-85; pres, Topeka City Comn, 1975-85; trustee, St Vail Hosp Bd, 1976-85, 1992-; State Water Authority, 1981-86; exec comn, Nat Asn Advan Colored People (Nat Asn Advan Colored People); past pres, Kans League Munic, 1983-84. **Honors/Awds:** Pub Serv Shawnee Co Comm Asst, 1972-83; Outstanding Public Officer Award, Topeka Comm Develop, 1976; Award, USA 501 Dir Assoc, 1977; Award, Reg 7 Comm Action, 1979. **Home Addr:** 2509 Fillmore St, Topeka, KS 66611-1251, **Home Phone:** (785)232-5715. **Business Addr:** State Fire Marshal, Kansas State Fire Marshal, 700 SW Jackson St Suite 600, Topeka, KS 66603, **Business Phone:** (785)296-3401.

### ALEXANDER, FLEX (MARK ALEXANDER KNOX)

Comedian, actor. **Personal:** Born Apr 15, 1970, New York, NY; son of Alethia Knox and Robert Whitehead; married Shanice Wilson; children: Imani Shekinah Knox & Elijah Knox. **Career:** Films: Juice, 1992; Money Train, 1995; City of Industry, 1997; The Sixth Man, 1997; Modern Vampires, 1998; She's All That, 1999; Out Cold, 2001; Out Cold, 2001; Sweet Oranges, 2003; Her Minor Thing, 2005; Love. & Other 4 Letter Words, 2006; Snakes on a Plane, 2006; The List, 2007; The Hills Have Eyes 2, 2007; Poor Boy's Game, 2007; My Sister's Wedding, 2013. TV series: "The Uptown Comedy Club", writer, 1992; Def Comedy Jam, writer, 1995; "One on One", actor & co-exec producer, 2001-06; "Gas", 2004; "Man in the Mirror: The Michael Jackson Story", 2004; "Waiting for Huffman", 2005; "One on One, One Oh Oh", 2005; "House Dad", 2005; "Money's Tight & So Are My Abs", 2005; "Cuts", 2005; "Keeping It Real", 2005; "Missing the Daddy Express", 2006; "Nice Girls Don't Get the Corner Office", 2007; "Love & Other 4 Letter Words", 2007; "The Hills Have Eyes II", 2007; "Deep Freeze", 2007; "CSI: Miami", 2007; "Blue Bloods", 2010; "It Takes Two", 2011; "Single Ladies", 2012; "The Client List", 2013; "Masters of Sex", 2013; "Flex & Shanice", 2014. **Orgs:** Phi Beta Sigma fraternity. **Business Addr:** Actor, c/o One on One, 9346 Civic Ctr Dr, Beverly Hills, CA 90210.

### ALEXANDER, GARY ROBERTS

Basketball player. **Personal:** Born Nov 1, 1969, Jacksonville, FL. **Educ:** Univ Southern Fla, attended 1992. **Career:** Basketball player (retired); Gaiteros del Zulia, Venezuela, 1992; Maccabi Haifa, 1992; Miami Heat, power forward, 1993; Elecon Desio, Italy, 1993-94; Cleveland Cavaliers, power forward, 1994; Strasbourg IG, France, 1994-95; Estudiantes, Spain, 1995; Dragons Rhondorf, Ger, 1996; Besiktas Istambul, Turkey, 1996-97; Breogan Lugo, Spain, 1996-98; SSA Trefl Sopot, Poland, 1997, 2001-02; BCM Gravelines, France, 1998-2001; Prokom Trefl Sopot, Poland, 1998; Caceres, Spain, 2001-02; Gran Canaria, Spain, 2002; Prokom Trefl Sopot, Poland, 2002; STB LeHavre, France, 2003-04; Chorale Roanne, France, capt, 2004-06.

### ALEXANDER, HUBBARD LINDSAY. See Obituaries Section.

### ALEXANDER, JAMES, JR.

Lawyer. **Personal:** Born Oct 7, 1945, Charlotte, NC. **Educ:** Columbia Univ, BA, 1967; Case Western Res Univ, JD, 1970; Nat Col Crim Defense Lawyer, cert, 1974. **Career:** Hough Area & Develop Corp, Cleveland, gen coun, 1971-72; Cuyahoga Co, asst co pro secy, 1972; Tolliver Nimrod & Alexender, atty, 1972-75; Hardiman Alexander Buchanan Pittman & Howland Co LPA, atty; Darryl E Pittman & Assocs, atty. **Orgs:** Cleveland Bar Asn; Am Acad Trial Layers; Nat Bar Asn; Cuyahoga Bar Asn; Nat Conf Black Lawyers Asn; pres, Hough Community Coun; treas, Columbia Univ Club, Cleveland, 1972; bd trustee, Un Torch Serv; Fed Community Plan Bd; Goodrich Soc Settle Bd; vpres, Legal Aid Soc Cleveland; pres, Hough Area Develop Corp; Ohio State Bar Asn. **Honors/Awds:** President Award, 1972; Martin Luther King Award. **Business Addr:** Attorney, Darryl E Pittman and Associates, 2940 Noble Rd Suite 202, Cleveland, OH 44121, **Business Phone:** (216)291-1005.

### ALEXANDER, JAMES ARTHUR (JIM ALEXANDER)

School administrator, executive director. **Personal:** Born Aug 22, 1953, Memphis, TN; son of Calvin and Katherine; married Vicki Marshall. **Educ:** Yale Univ, BA, 1975, JD, polit sci, 1978. **Career:** Lord Bissell & Brodk, assoc atty, 1978-84; Chicago State Univ, exec asst to pres, 1985-86, vpres, admin, 1986-89; Ill State Univ, vpres, bus & finance, 1989-93; Govs State Univ, 1993-99; Nat Louis Univ, exec vpres, 2001-02, 2003-; Admin & Planning, Univ Pk, Ill, vpres. **Orgs:** Exec dir, Inner City Teaching Corps, 2003-09; vpres Strategic Planning & Execution, Ill Action C, 2009-; Am Bar Asn; CBA; CCBA; NACUBO; Leadership Greater Chicago, NACUA. **Special Achievements:** He has received numerous awards and recognitions and, in 1985, was selected to the first class of Leadership Greater Chicago. **Home Addr:** 6818 S Euclid Ave, Chicago, IL 60649, **Home Phone:** (773)363-8883. **Business Addr:** Vice President of Strategic Planning & Execution, Illinois Action for Children, 1340 S Damen Ave, Chicago, IL 60612, **Business Phone:** (312)823-1100.

### ALEXANDER, JAMES BRETT

Journalist. **Personal:** Born Nov 19, 1948, Boston, MA. **Educ:** Northeastern Univ, BA, 1971. **Career:** NE Univ, Div Instr Community Urban Confrontation, producer, dir 1968; Northeastern's radio, prod dept; CBS, corp diversity comm; Christian Sci Monitor Boston, staff writer, 1968-71; Random House Inc Lang Arts Div, ed asst, 1972-73; Manhattan Community Col, dir, publs New York, 1973-74; NY Post, staff reporter, journalist, 1994; Real Malcolm X, producer, dir & writer; CBS News Prods, exec producer, 2001; Harvard Univ, Lucius W. Neiman Fel. **Orgs:** Dir, publ No Am Reg Ford Found Fel 1966-69; Ford Found grants, 1966; Exp Int Living, 1969-; Am Forum Intl Study; Boston Black United Front, 1969-70; Int Peace Acad, 1972-; Sixth Pan-African Cong. **Home Addr:** 59 Livingston Hall St, Brooklyn, NY 11201.

### ALEXANDER, JAMES EDUARD (JIM ALEXANDER)

U.S. attorney, writer. **Personal:** married Toian Bowser. **Educ:** St Mary's Univ, San Antonio, Tex; Sch Aviation Med; Whittier Law Sch; Ind Univ, BS, broadcast mgt. **Career:** Attorney, writer & lecturer; Armed Forces Radio & TV sta, Greenland, sta mgr; Defense Info Sch, sr instr broadcasting; Time Life Broadcasting Co; McGraw-Hill Broadcasting Co; Combined Commun; US Sen, press secy re-election campaign; ABC Network, videotape operator; Adams & Alexander, partner, 1991-03, atty, 1999-2005; Value varies with no of bks sold, no of manuscrips & legal brief written, owner. **Orgs:** Bar Supreme Ct US; US Circuit Ct Appeals, Ninth Circuit; US Dist Ct; State Bar Calif. **Special Achievements:** Author "Half Way Home From Kinderlou"; Published "If I should Die Before I wake What Will Happen to My Stuff?", 2009. **Business Addr:** Owner.

### ALEXANDER, JOHN WESLEY, JR.

School administrator, college teacher. **Personal:** Born May 17, 1938, Salem, OH; son of John Wesley and Virgina. **Educ:** Southern Colo State Col, AA, 1958; Boston Univ, BS, math, 1961; Bowling Green State Univ, MA, 1965; Boston Univ, EdD, math educ, 1985; Calif Coast Univ, MBA, 1987, PhD, mgt sci & opers res, 1989. **Career:** Model Cities Col Consortium, acad dean, 1969-70; W African Reg Math Prog, math adv, 1970-77; Ed Develop Ctr, consult ed, 1977-78; Boston Univ, asst, 1977-78; CT Mutual Life Ins Co, acturial analyst, 1978-81; Futures Group, chief statistician, 1981-82; Wentworth Inst Tech, assoc prof, 1982, prof math, 1982-84; Col Arts & Sci, dean, 1984-90; Univ DC, fac, 1990-97, Dept Math, chmn, 1992-95; Nat Acad Sci, Bd Math Sci, prog officer, 1995-96, dir bd, 1996-97; Spelman Col, chmn & prof math, 1998-2002; Miami Dade Community Col, assoc prof, prof, 2005-. **Orgs:** Fel Bowling Green State Univ, 1964-65; Campaign chairperson, United Combined Health Appeal, Conn Mutual Life Ins Co, 1981; pres, Nat Asn Mathematicians, 1994-, pres emer; pres, Nat Asn Math, 1994-. **Honors/Awds:** Athletic scholar, Southern Colo & Boston Univ, 1956-60; Award of Excellence, Conn Mutual Life Ins Co, 1981. **Home Addr:** 9739 Country Meadows Lane Apt 2A, Laurel, MD 20723, **Home Phone:** (443)280-0929. **Business Addr:** Professor, Miami Dade Community College, N Campus, Miami, FL 33167-3418, **Business Phone:** (305)237-8307.

### ALEXANDER, JOSEPHINE

Registered nurse. **Personal:** Born Tuskegee, AL; daughter of P and Daisy Menefee. **Educ:** Tuskegee Univ, Tuskegee, BSN, 1958; Univ Calif, Los Angeles, MSN, 1972; US Dept Veterans affairs, cert, clin nurse specialist. **Career:** Veterans Admin Med Ctr, Los Angeles, staff nurse, 1958-60, nurse mgr, 1960-72, psychiat clin specialist, 1972-, primary adult care nurse practr, 1977-. **Orgs:** Life mem, Chi Eta Phi; Am Nurses Asn; Nat League Nursing; Nat Coun Negro Women; historian, 1974-84, first vpres, 1980-84, pres, 1985-89, Chi Eta Phi sorority; Sigma Theta Tau Hon Soc; ANA Found; Black Women Forum; asst parliamentarian, Tuskee Nat Alumni Asn. **Honors/Awds:** Outstanding Leadership Award, Chi Eta Pi, Southwest Region, 1987; Outstanding Service Award, Tuskegee Univ Alumni Asn, Los Angeles Chap, 1988; Black Woman Achievement Award, NAACP Legal Defense & Educ Fund, 1989. **Home Addr:** 1238 S Carmona Ave, Los Angeles, CA 90019-2530, **Home Phone:** (323)734-0288. **Business Addr:** Clinical Nurse Specialist, VA Greater Los Angeles Healthcare System, 11301 Wilshire Blvd, Los Angeles, CA 90073, **Business Phone:** (310)478-3711.

### ALEXANDER, HON. JOYCE LONDON

Judge, executive, administrator. **Personal:** Born Sep 1, 1949; daughter of Oscar London and Edna London; married Johnny Ford. **Educ:** Howard Univ, BA; New Eng Law Sch, JD, 1972. **Career:** Judge (retired); Greater Boston Legal Assistance Proj, staff atty, 1972-74; Reginald Heber Smith Community, law fel; Youth Activ Comn, legal coun, 1974-76; Tufts Univ, asst prof, 1974-75; Mass Bd Higher Educ, vice chancellor & gen coun, 1976-79; WBZ-TV Boston, on-camera legal ed, 1978-79; US Dist Ct, Dist Mass, magistrate judge, 1979-95, chief US magistrate judge, 1996-2009. **Orgs:** Urban League Eastern Mass; pres emer, Nat Coun US Magistrates, 1979; First Circuit dir; chair, MA Black Judges Conf, 1985-87; chair, Nat Bar Asn Judicial Coun, 1987-88; bd mem, Joint Ctr Polit & Econ Studies, 1996; ABA Sect Int Law; Cameras Courtroom Comt; chmn, Nat Policy Comn Links Inc; bd overseer, Boys & Girls Club Greater Boston; Alpha Kappa Alpha Sorority. **Honors/Awds:** William Robert Ming Award, Nat Asn Advan Colored People; Equal Justice Award, Nat Bar Asn; William Hastie Award, Nat Bar Asn; Raymond Pace Alexander Award, Nat Bar Asn; Martin Luther King Jr Drum Major for Justice Award, Southern Christian Leadership Conf, 1985; C Francis Stadford Award, Nat Bar Asn, 1997; Thurgood Marshall Award, Natl Bar Asn, 2004; LLD, North Eastern Univ Law Sch; LLD, Bridgewater St Col; LLD, Suffolk Univ; LLD, NC Cent Univ. **Special Achievements:** Ten Outstanding Young Leaders of Massachusetts, Boston Jaycees, 1980; One of Ten Outstanding Young Women in American; Honored as a "Living Legend", Museum of Afro-American History, 2004; New England Law Review dedicated its entire summer edition; First African-American Chief United States Magistrate Judge; First African-American woman Chief Judge of any court in Massachusetts. **Home Addr:** 230 Garden St, Cambridge, MA 02138. **Business Addr:** Chief Magistrate Judge, US District Court District of Massachusetts, Rm 932 John Joseph Moakley US Courthouse, Boston, MA 02109, **Business Phone:** (617)748-9238.

### ALEXANDER, JULIUS J., JR.

Executive. **Personal:** Born Jan 1, 1937?, Tuskegee, AL; married Jo Ann Sims; children: Patrick, Julie, Karen & Carmen. **Educ:** Morehouse Col, BA, eng, 1959. **Career:** Executive (retired); Luther Judson Price High Sch, Atlanta Pub Sch Syst, teacher, eng; O Keef Booker T. Wash & Brown High Schs, aviation instr; WAGA TV, CBS affil, tv news reporter & photogr, 1974; Lockheed Martin Aerospace Corp, Spokesman, tv newsman, ground instr, asst dir pub rel, sr pub rel rep, chief instr, 1997; Aviation Career Enrichment Inc, owner. **Orgs:** Aviation Career Education program; founder, chief exec officer, chief instr, bd mem, Aviation Career Enrichment Inc, 1980-. **Special Achievements:** First civilian African American flight instructor to train students at Atlanta's Fulton County Airport. In 1970, he wrote a major article for Science Activities Magazine, entitled, "Wings for the Black Ghetto". **Business Addr:** Founder, Chief Executive Officer, Aviation Career Enrichment Inc, 3952 Aviation Cir NW Suite 300, Atlanta, GA 30336, **Business Phone:** (404)691-0441.

### ALEXANDER, REP. KELLY MILLER, JR.

Funeral director. **Personal:** Born Oct 17, 1948, Charlotte, NC; son of Kelly Sr (deceased) and Margaret; children: Kelly M III. **Educ:** Univ NC, Chapel Hill, NC, BA, polit sci, 1970, MPA, 1973. **Career:** NC Personnel Dept, admin intern, 1971-72; Charlotte Area Fund, planner, 1972-74; Alexander Funeral Home Inc, vpres, 1973-94, vpres & chief finance officer, 1994-; Mecklenburg County Dem Party, rep, 2008-. **Orgs:** Exec vpres, US Youth Coun, 1976-85; trustee, Nat Asn Advan Colored People Spec Contrib Fund, 1985-98; pres, NC Nat Asn Advan Colored People, 1985-96; chmn, Mothers Murdered Offspring, 2003-; Gov Comn Workforce Preparedness; past vpres, Nat Asn Advan Colored People; chmn, Nat Asn Advan Colored People Econ Develop Fair Share Community; NC House Dist; Airport Adv Comt; fel Schs Bldg Solutions Comt; fel Charlotte-Mecklenburg Planning Comn; fel Friendship Community Develop Corp; chief operating officer, Nc Transp Mus; Univ Pk Neighborhood Asn; bd dir, Greater Charlotte Chamber Com; Z Smith Reynolds Adv Bd; NC Martin Luther King, Jr.Comn; chair, New Brooklyn Initiative; co-founder, Proj Uplift; Acad Polit Sci; bd visitor, UNC Chapel Hill. **Honors/Awds:** UNCF Labor Dept Res Grant, 1977; Harvey E Beech Outstanding Alumni Award, UNC Chapel Hill; Numerous awards for civil rights & economic development. **Home Addr:** 2128 Sr Dr, PO Box 36468, Charlotte, NC 28216-4302, **Home Phone:** (704)392-6775. **Business Addr:** Vice President, Chief Finance Officer, Alexander Funeral Home Inc, 1424 Statesville Ave, Charlotte, NC 28236-3007, **Business Phone:** (704)333-1167.

### ALEXANDER, KHANDI

Actor. **Personal:** Born Sep 4, 1957, New York, NY; daughter of Alverina and Henry. **Educ:** Queens bor Community Col, BA. **Career:** Films: Street walkin, 1985; A Chorus Line, 1985; Maid to Order, 1987; CB4, 1993; Joshua Tree, 1993; Menace II Society, 1993; What's Love Got to Do with It, 1993; Poetic Justice, 1993; House Party 3, 1994; Sugar Hill, 1994; Greedy, 1994; No Easy Way, 1996; Thick as Thieves, 1998; There's Something About Mary, 1998; Fool Proof, 2002; Emmett's Mark, 2002; Dark Blue, 2002; First Born, 2006; Rain, 2006; First Born, 2007; The Assault, 2014. TV series: "The Motown Revue Starring Smokey Robinson", 1985; "Shameful Secrets", 1993; "To My Daughter with Love", 1994; "Terminal", 1996; "Spawn", 1997; "Soul Sacrifice", 1998; "Kids", 1997; "TV Episode Twins", 1997; "Bill Moves On", 1998; "X-Chromosome", 1999; "Cosby-The Awful Truth", 1999; "Partners", 1999; "The Corner", 2000; "Third Watch", 2000; "Life's a Bitch", 2003; "Perfect Strangers", 2004; "CSI: Miami", 2002-09; "Better Off Ted", 2009; "Body of Proof", 2012; "Treme", 2010-13; "Scandal", 2013-14. **Honors/Awds:** Black Reel Award, 2001; Image Award, Nat Asn Advan Colored People, 2005; Vision Award, Nat Asn Multi-ethnicity Commun, 2011. **Business Addr:** Actress, CBS TV Network, 51 W 52nd St, New York, NY 10019, **Business Phone:** (212)975-4321.

### ALEXANDER, LARRY

President (organization), chief executive officer. **Personal:** married Kitt; children: Carson. **Educ:** Univ Houston, attended 1974. **Career:** Westin Hotels & Resorts, managing dir, 1974-97; The Westin Miyako, San Francisco, GM; Detroit Metro Sports Comn, founder; Detroit Metro Conv & Visitors Bur, pres & chief exec officer, 1999-. **Orgs:** Exec comt, owners adv comt, chmn finance comt & vice-chair, bd dir, Metrop Detroit Conv & Visitors Bur; bd dir, Mich Hotel, Motel & Resort Asn; Greater Detroit Chamber Com; Kidney Found Mich; Detroit Riverfront Conservancy; Auto Nat Heritage; Super Bowl XL Host Comt; Parade Co; New Detroit Inc; foud, Detroit Metro Sports Comn; app by Detroit Mayor Dennis Archer, Detroit Master Plan Task Force, 1994; bd dir, Automobile Nat Heritage Area; Detroit 300 celebration comt. **Business Addr:** President, Chief Executive Officer,

Detroit Metro Convention & Visitors Bureau, 211 W Fort St Suite 1000, Detroit, MI 48226, **Business Phone:** (313)202-1800.

### ALEXANDER, DR. LAURENCE BENEDICT

Journalist, educator. **Personal:** Born Oct 31, 1959, New Orleans, LA; son of Garland and Dorothy; married Veronica Wicker; children: Brandon Keith, David Laurence & Tyler Christian. **Educ:** Univ New Orleans, BA, drama & commun, 1981; Univ Fla, MA, jour & commun, 1983; Tulane Univ, Sch Law, JD, 1987; Fla State Univ, PhD, higher educ. **Career:** Times-Picayune, New Orleans, staff writer, 1981, 1982-85; Houma Courier, staff writer, 1982; Univ New Orleans, dir, jour prog, asst prof, jour, 1987-88, coordr jour eng dept; Temple Univ, dir, news ed sequence, asst prof, commun, 1988-91; Philadelphia Inquirer, summer copy ed, 1989-92; Univ Fla, McKnight doctoral fel, asst prof, jour, 1991-94, chmn, dept jour, 1994-98, assoc prof, 1994-2003, prof, jour, 2003-, assoc dean, dean, 2006, Off Grad Minority Progs, dir, fac senate; Nsf, co-prin Investr; Univ Ark, Pine Bluff, chancellor, currently. **Orgs:** Provost admin fel Univ Fla; Am Bar Asn, 1987-; La State Bar Asn, 1987-; Asn Educ Jour & Mass Commun, 1989-; Soc Prof Journalists, 1989-; Nat Asn Black Journalists, 1989-; Int Commun Asn, 1992-; AEJMC Exec bd; chmn, 2000-01, AEJMC Prof Freedom & Responsibility Comt; chmn & bd dir, 2001-, Campus Commun Inc; bd dir, Univ Athletic Asn; chmn, Grad Curric Comt, univ fla, Nat Alumni Asn; Fla A&M Univ Grad Fel Feeder Prog; Nsf LSAMP Bridge; Ann Grad Stud Grants & Fels Conf; Univ Fla Acad Distinguished Teaching Scholars; Univ Fla Res Found Prof; chmn, Bd dir Independent Fla Alligator; fel, Southeastern Conf Acad Consortium's Acad Leadership Develop Prog, 2012-13. **Home Addr:** 4548 NW 36th Ave, Gainesville, FL 32606, **Home Phone:** (352)374-7997. **Business Addr:** Chancellor, University of Arkansas, 1200 N Univ Dr, Pine Bluff, AR 71601, **Business Phone:** (870)575-8000.

### ALEXANDER, DR. LENORA COLE

Executive, association executive. **Personal:** Born Mar 9, 1935, Buffalo, NY; daughter of John L and Susie Stamper; married Theodore M Sr. **Educ:** State Univ Col, Buffalo, NY, BS, elem educ & educ except c, 1957; State Univ NY, Buffalo, NY, MEd, educ admin, policy & orgn develop, 1969, PhD, educ admin & policy & orgn develop, 1974. **Career:** Bd Educ, Chicago, IL, teacher, 1957-68; State Univ NY, res asst, 1968-69, asst vpres stud life, 1969-73; Am Univ, vpres stud life, 1974-77; Univ DC, vpres stud affairs, 1978-81; US Dept Labor, dir womens bur, 1981-86; George Mason Univ, commonwealth vis prof pub admin, 1986-89; LCA & Assocs Inc, pres, 1989-; US Agency Int Develop, Off Hr, Div Labor Rels, staff, 1990-; Univ Md, adj prof, 2004-; Inst Womens Policy Res, bd chair, currently. **Orgs:** Bd dir, Delta Sigma Theta Sorority, 1976-; bd dir, DC Chamber Com, 1979-81; US Rep Working Party Role Women Econ, Orgn Econ Develop & Coop Paris France, 1981-86; Alpha Kappa Alpha Sorority Inc, 1982; adv comt mem, Women Veterans Affairs US Vet Admin, 1983-86; us rep, Conf Int Comn Status Women Cartegena Colombia, 1983; bd mem, Girl Friends Inc, 1983-; conf, Vienna Austria, 1984; US Del UN Decade Women Conf Nairobi Kenya, 1985; bd dir, Jerusalem Int Forum Am Israel Friendship League, 1987-89; Defense Adv Comt Women Servs, 1989-92; DC Bd Elections & Ethics, 1998-2000, 2003-; DC Bd Elections & Ethics, 2000-; bd dir, McAuley Inst; bd dir, Found Except C; Adv bd, Black Womens Fashion Mus; bd dir, IWPR; bd trustee, Legal Aid Soc; secy & bd dir, Woodley House, Wash, Va. **Honors/Awds:** Special Citation Award, Comn Womens Affairs Off Gov Puerto Rico, 1982; Salute for Contributions Award, Club Twenty Wash, 1983; Distinguished American and Humanitarian Coahoma, Jr Col, 1983; Distinguished Alumnus Award, State Univ NY, 1983; Pauline Weeden Maloney Award, Nat Trends & Serv, Links Inc, Philadelphia, 1984; Gratitude for Success Award, Unit Church Usher's League, Chicago, 1984; Distinguished Service Citation, Nat Black MBA Asn Inc, Wash, 1984; Outstanding Women Award, Progressive DC Chap Federally Employed Women Washington, 1984; Outstanding Political Achievement Award, Nat Asn Minority Polit Women, 1985; Woman Achievement Award, Womens City Club Cleveland, 1986; Outstanding CareerWoman Award, Alpha Phi Alpha. **Home Addr:** 3020 Brandywine St NW, Washington, DC 20008, **Home Phone:** (202)686-0512. **Business Addr:** Board of Chair, Institute for Women, 1707 L St NW Suite 750, Washington, DC 20036, **Business Phone:** (202)785-5100.

### ALEXANDER, DR. LIVINGSTON

Administrator. **Personal:** Born Breaux Bridge, LA; married Evelyn; children: Erika, Jason & Alicia. **Educ:** St Joseph Sem Col, Wash, DC, AB, philos; Univ Houston, MEd, curric, EdD, educ psychol. **Career:** Univ Tenn-Knoxville, am coun educ fel, higher educ admin; Western Ky Univ, from asst prof to prof, psychol, dir grad stud, 1990-94; Troy State Univ, Montgomery, vpres acad affairs, 1994-98; Ga Southern Univ, dept head, assoc vpres, acad affairs; Kean Univ, Union, NJ, provost & vpres acad affairs & prof psychol, 1998; Univ Pittsburgh, Bradford, PA, pres, 2003-, Titusville, pres, 2012-. **Orgs:** Fac mem & sem leader, Am Coun Educ, bd dir, currently; chmn, Nj Coun Chief Acad Officers; bd dir, Am Asn Univ Adminr; NCAA Div III Presidents Coun; Millennium Leadership Initiative Steering Comt; nominating comt, Am Asn State Cols & Univs; bd mem, Upper Allegheny Health Systs; bd dir, Continental One; bd dir, Ctr Rural Pa; trustee, Hilbert Col, Hamburg, NY; bd gov, Renaissance Group; Nat asn presidents, provosts, & deans; chmn, Col Bound Adv Coun, State Nj. **Business Addr:** President, University of Pittsburgh, 300 Campus Dr, Bradford, PA 16701-1087, **Business Phone:** (814)362-7501.

### ALEXANDER, LIYONGO PATRISE

Football player. **Personal:** Born Oct 23, 1972, Galveston, TX. **Educ:** Univ La, Lafayette. **Career:** Football player (retired); Wash Redskins, linebacker & defensive tackle, 1995-98; Philadelphia Eagles, 1999; Orlando Rage Xtreme Football League, linebacker, 2001; Dallas Desperadoes Arena Football League, 2002-03; Austin Wranglers, 2004.

### ALEXANDER, DR. LYDIA LEWIS

School administrator. **Personal:** Born Aug 21, 1938, Bessemer, AL; daughter of Clinton E and Flora Laird; married Judson T Sr; children: Judson T Jr. **Educ:** Talladega Col, Talladega, AL, BA, hist, 1958; Ind Univ, Bloomington, MAT, 1964; Auburn Univ, Auburn, AL, PhD, EdD, 1972. **Career:** Educator (retired); Wenonah High Sch, Birmingham, Ala, eng instr, 1959-66; Lawson State Jr Col, Birmingham, AL, speech & eng instr, 1966-70; Auburn Univ, Auburn, AL, asst prof, sch educ, 1972-74; Univ Ala, Birmingham, asst prof, sec educ, 1974-79, asst vpres, 1980-84, biomed sci prog dir, 1982-84, dir genstudies, 1984-89, asst dean, 1989-94, assoc prof educ leadership. **Orgs:** Pres, Omicron Omega Chap, Alpha Kappa Alpha Sorority Inc, 1978-82; nat pres, Holidays, 1987-91; pres, Birmingham Chap Links, 1988-89; pres, Univ Ala Birmingham Fac & Staff Benevolent Fund Coun, 1990; Asn Supv &Curric Develop; Am Asn Col Teacher Educ. **Home Addr:** 1141 Posey Ave, Bessemer, AL 35022, **Home Phone:** (205)424-7953. **Business Addr:** AL.

### ALEXANDER, MARCELLUS WINSTON, JR.

Executive, president (organization). **Personal:** Born Oct 3, 1951, Austin, TX; son of Juanita Smith and Marcellus Sr; married Linda Carter; children: Ehrin, Andrea & Marcellus III. **Educ:** Southwest Tex State Univ, San Marcos, TX, BS, speech & jour, 1973; Western Med Col, PhD, 1995. **Career:** Am Broadcasting Co, Detroit, Mich, gen sls mgr, 1982-84, vpres & gen mgr, 1984-86; Silver Star Commun, Detroit, Mich, chief operating officer, part owner, 1986; Grp W Broadcasting, Philadelphia, Pa, sta mgr, 1987-89; Grp W Broadcasting, Baltimore, Md, vpres & gen mgr, 1999-2002; Nat Asn Broadcasters, EVP, TV, 2002-, NAB Educ Found, pres, 2004-. **Orgs:** Nat Asn Black Journalists, 1987-; bd mem, Baltimore Urban League, 1989-; bd mem, Advert Asn Baltimore, 1989-; bd mem, Kennedy Inst, 1989-; bd mem, Advert & Prof Club, 1989-. **Home Addr:** 5103 Cape Cod Ct, Bethesda, MD 20816-2907, **Home Phone:** (301)320-0622. **Business Addr:** Executive Vice President, Television, National Association of Broadcasters, 1771 N St NW, Washington, DC 20036, **Business Phone:** (202)429-5365.

### ALEXANDER, DR. OTIS DOUGLAS

Librarian, executive director. **Personal:** Born Jun 1, 1949, Norfolk, VA; son of Gilbert and Vivian Bell. **Educ:** Fed City Col, Wash, DC, BA, urban studies & music, 1972, MS, media sci, 1974; Atlanta Univ, GA, attended 1982; Ball State Univ, Muncie, IN, MLS, libr sci, 1983; Oberlin Conserv Music Voice Performance Pedag; Int Univ Grad Studies St Kitts, WI; Harvard Grad Sch Educ Leadership Inst; Southeastern Univ. **Career:** Dept Educ, VI St John, interant librn, 1976-77; Bur Libr Mus & Archeol Serv, Christiansted St Croix US VI, juv serv librn, 1977-78; Cuttington Univ Col Liberia W Africa, asst librn & lectr c, 1978-79; Dept Educ VI, info spec, 1979-83, sec music, 1990-2001; Atlanta Univ, scholar, 1982; fel USDOE, 1982-83; Bur Libr & Mus, head librn, 1983-85; St Dunstans Episcopal Sch, St Croix VI, lit teacher, 1985-90; St Theatre Dance Ensemble, fdr/drr, 1986-2000; Howard Reed Int Scholar, 1992; Southeastern Univ, Randolph E Meyer Mem Libr, dir; Danville Pub Libr, dir. **Orgs:** Dir, St John Ethnic Theatre, 1976-77; Childrens Theatre, St Croix, 1977-78; dir, perCuttington Cult Troop W Africa, 1978-79; Am Libr Asn, 1983-; artistic dir, St Theatre, 1986-97; bd dir, Univ DC Alumni Asn, 1991-93; chap adv, Phi Delta Kappa; Am Fedn Teachers; St Croix Fedn Teachers; Omega Psi Phi Fraternity. **Home Addr:** 609 Obendorfer Rd, Norfolk, VA 23523, **Home Phone:** (757)478-8272.

### ALEXANDER, PAMELA GAYLE

Judge. **Personal:** Born Sep 25, 1952, Minneapolis, MN; daughter of Robert W Bellesen and Frances L Smith; married Albert G; children: 2. **Educ:** Augsburg Col, BA, 1974; Univ Minn Sch Law, JD, 1977. **Career:** Neighborhood Justice Ctr & Legal Rights Ctr, Law Clerk, 1974; First Bank, Minneapolis, trust admnr, 1977-78; Legal Rights Ctr Inc, criminal defense atty, 1978-81; Hennepin Co Atty Off, prosecutor criminal div, 1980; Hennepin County Munic Ct, 1983; State Minneapolis, county ct judge, 1983-86; Hennepin Co Dist Co, dist ct judge, 1986-96, asst chief judge, 1996-98; Juv Div, Coun Crime & Justice, Pres, 2008; Hennepin Co Dist Ct, dis ct judge, currently. **Orgs:** Charter mem, former vpres, Minn Minority Lawyers Asn; trustee, Greater Friendship Missionary Bapt Church, 1980-84; Nat Bar Asn Judicial Coun; parliamentarian, treas Minneapolis & St Paul Links; chmn governance comt, exec comt, Minneapolis Found; bd dir, Emma Howe Memorial Found Esther V Crosby Girl Scout Comt; pres, Hennepin County Bar Asn. **Honors/Awds:** Special Recognition Award, Phi Beta Sigma Frat, 1982; Constance B Motley Award, TCB-WTC Comn, 1982-83; Community Service Award, Inner City Youth League, 1983; Loft Teen Ctr, 1983; Distinguished Service Award, Hennepin Co Atty Off, 1983; Community Service Award, Kappa Alpha Psi Fraternity, 1992; BIHA The Comm Award, 1993; Omega Citizen of the Year Award, 10th Dist, 1993; Chauncey Eskridge Distinguished Barrister Award, Southern Christian Leadership Conf, 1993; Freedom Fund Award, Nat Asn Advan Colored People, Minneapolis br, 1993; Humanitarian Award, Metrop Community Col, 1995; Profiles in Courage Award, Minnesota Minority Lawyers Asn, 1995; Esther V Crosby Award, Greater Minneapolis Girl Scouts; Jurist Award, Nat Bar Asn Women Lawyers Div, 1997; Woman of the Year Award, Iota Phi Lambda; Star Performer Award, Hennepin County, 1998; Torchbearer's Award, Rainbow Push Coalition, 2000; Profiles in Courage Award, Nat Bar Asn, 2001; C & L award, 2006. **Special Achievements:** First African-American judge in Hennepin County in 1983. **Home Addr:** PO Box 15712, Minneapolis, MN 55415, **Home Phone:** (612)942-8004. **Business Addr:** Judge, Hennepin County District Court, 626 S 6th St, Minneapolis, MN 55415, **Business Phone:** (612)348-4822.

### ALEXANDER, PRESTON PAUL

Labor relations manager. **Personal:** Born Apr 20, 1952, Bronx, NY; son of Preston Sr and Sylvia; children: Drew Philip & Jason Ross. **Educ:** Fairleigh Dickinson Univ, BA, psychol, 1973, MPA, 1980; Univ Mass Lowell, grad fel, community col leadership, ethics & chg mgt, 2014; Univ Mich, cert, strategic leadership, strategic leadership; Univ Md, cert, critical incident & stress mgt (cism) counr; NY Ctr Mediation & law, cert, mediation; Am Heart Asn, cert, basic life support & CPR instr; Nat Registry & NJ State Dept Health, cert, emergency med technician. **Career:** Teaneck Vol Ambulance Corps, sunday eve crew chief, 1972-; Midlantic Nat Bank Citizens, internal auditor, 1973-74; Fairleigh Dickinson Univ Cent Admis, dir admis rel, 1974-79, Silberman Col Bus, adj instr, 2008-10; Nat Asn Col Admis Counr, vpres human rel, 1978-79; Citibank NA, dir human resources, 1979-90; Alexander's Surg Supply Co, co-owner, 1989-91; Joseph E Seagram & Sons Inc, human resources dir, 1993-98; Oxford Health Plans, regional dir human resources, 1998-2000; Pitney Bowes Inc, vpres human resources, 2000-06, vpres workforce rel, 2003; human resources consult, currently; Columbia Univ Med Ctr, assoc vpres human resources, 2006-08; Roxbury Community Col, chief human resources & affirmative action officer, 2010-14; Tufts Univ, human resources bus partner, 2015-16; Cape Cod Community Col, assoc vpres & chief human resources officer, 2016-. **Orgs:** Soc Human Res Mgt, 1995-; bd trustee, Shelter Our Sisters; Palm Beach (FL) Workforce Develop Coun, 1995-97; critical incident counr, Phoenix Emergency Serv, 1999-; Stamford Emergency Med Serv, 2001-03; Griffin Hosp, 2004-. **Honors/Awds:** Outstanding Distinguished Service Award, Fairleigh Dickinson Univ, 1978. **Business Addr:** Vice President Workforce Relations, Pitney Bowes Inc, 335 Griggs Ave, Teaneck, NJ 07666-3101.

### ALEXANDER, MAJOR GEN. RICHARD C.

Association executive, military leader, government official. **Personal:** Born Jun 26, 1935, Cleveland, OH; married LaVera; children: Jeff, Ronald & Gail. **Educ:** Franklin Univ, BA; Ohio Nat Guard Officer Sch, attended 1965; Army Command & Gen Staff Studies Course, 1977; Army War Col, attended 1983. **Career:** Military leader (retired), exe; USMC, 1954; Army Nat Guard, second lt, 1965, first lt, 1967, capt, 1969, maj, 1973, lt col, 1978, brig, 1988, maj gen, 1992-98; Ohio Nat Guard, adj gen; Dept Defense Res Forces Policy Bd, 1993-96; Nat Guard Asn US, Columbia, Ohio, pres, 1996-98, exec dir, 1999-; Am Bus Develop Group, sr consult. **Orgs:** Nat Asn Advan Colored People; Gov's Cabinet. **Honors/Awds:** Meritorious Service Medal; Army Commendation Medal; Army Achievement Medal; Good Conduct Medal-Marine Corps; Army Research Component Achievement Medal; National Defense Service Medal; Humanitarian Service Medal; Armed Forces Res Medal; Army Service Ribbon; Army Res Component Overseas Training Ribbon; Defense Super Service Medal; Legion Merit; Ohio Award Merit; Gen Raymond S McLain Medal, Assn of the AUS. **Special Achievements:** First African-American president and executive director of NGAUS. **Business Addr:** Executive Director, The National Guard Association of the United States, 1 Massachusetts Ave NW, Washington, DC 20001, **Business Phone:** (202)789-0031.

### ALEXANDER, RONALD BRENT. See ALEXANDER, BRENT.

### ALEXANDER, S. TYRONE

Executive, vice president (organization), founder (originator). **Educ:** Va Polytech Inst, State Univ, BS, polit sci; Lake Forest Grad Sch Mgt, MS, finance, MS, mgt; George Washington Univ, PhD, human resource. **Career:** Empire Blue Cross Blue Shield, NY, sr vpres, human resources & serv; Highmark Blue Cross, Human Resources & Admin Servs, exec vpres, currently. **Orgs:** Bd dir, Inst Supply Mgt; CIGNA Healthcare; DuPont; Sara Lee; Pitney Bowes; Corning; Epilepsy Found Bd; bd Inst Supply Mgt; chmn, Pa Bus Leadership Network; chmn, Pittsburgh Disability Employ Proj Freedom; Pittsburgh Ballet; Three Rivers Workforce Investment Bd; Socs Human Resource Mgt; Human Resources Exec Roundtable; comnr, Penn Workforce Invest Bd, currently; Human Resource Inst. **Business Addr:** Senior Vice President, Highmark Blue Cross Blue Shield, 120 5th Ave Suite 3012, Pittsburgh, PA 15222-3099, **Business Phone:** (412)544-4017.

### ALEXANDER, VIC

Vice president (organization). **Personal:** married Rose Cornell. **Educ:** Cent Mich Univ, grad; Univ Cincinnati. **Career:** Cent Mich Univ, commun coordr; Steelworkers Local 87, vpres; Delphi Chassis Automotive, vpres, currently. **Orgs:** Local Union No 87, United Steel Workers Am. **Business Addr:** Vice President, United Steel Workers of Amercia, 21 Abbey Ave, Dayton, OH 45417, **Business Phone:** (937)268-6646.

### ALEXANDER, VINCENT J.

Teacher. **Personal:** Born Oct 19, 1958, Ft. Wayne, IN; son of John and Dorothy Logan; married Gail; children: Vince II, Colin & Gavin. **Educ:** Vincennes Univ, AS, broadcast prod technol, 1979; Ind State Univ, BS, commun, 1981; Ball State Univ, transition teaching cert, eng, 1983; Butler Univ, MS, educ, 2006. **Career:** WMRI-WGOM, Marion, radio announcer & reporter, 1982-85; Chronicle-Tribune, sports writer, 1985-90; Ft Wayne Newspapers, sports writer, 1990; J-Gazette, sports writer, 1990-96; High Sch, sports ed, 1990-97; Sports Page Mag, founder, 1997; It's All Good Inc, pres, chief exec officer, 1997-99; Indianapolis Pub Schs, teacher, 1999-2001; Coleman Mid Sch, teacher, 2001-04; Ben Davis High Sch, Wayne Twp, Indianapolis, 2004-05; Perry Meridian Mid Sch, teacher, 2005-07; Craig Mid Sch, teacher, 2007-11; Dipl Plus Sec Acad, teacher, 2010-11; Belzer Mid Sch, Indianapolis, Ind, teacher, 2011-. **Home Addr:** 5512 Skyridge Dr, Indianapolis, IN 46250. **Business Addr:** Teacher, Belzer Middle School, 7555 E 56th St, Indianapolis, IN 46226, **Business Phone:** (317)964-6200.

### ALEXANDER, WARDINE TOWERS

Health services administrator. **Personal:** Born Jul 26, 1955, Birmingham, AL; daughter of Ward Towers Jr and Thelma Otey Towers; married Gregory Bernard Sr; children: Gregory Bernard II. **Educ:** Univ Ala, Birmingham, AL, BS, 1978. **Career:** Am Red Cross, Birmingham, AL, ref lab technologist, 1977-84, asst dir, tech serv, 1984-90, dir hosp serv, 1990-; Hosp/Tech Serv, reg mgr, 1994-; Am Red Cross Blood Servs, educ mgr, training mgr, 1975-99; BioLife Plasma, training supvr, currently. **Orgs:** Am Asn Blood Banks, 1977-; Ala State Asn Blood Banks, 1977-; Am Soc Med Technologist, 1977-; Am Soc Clin Pathologist, 1977-; publicity comt chair, Alpha Kappa Alpha Sorority Inc, 1982-; pres, Ala State Asn Blood Banks, 1994-95. **Home Addr:** 161 Highland Crest Pkwy, Hoover, AL 35226-4106, **Home Phone:** (205)834-8648. **Business Addr:** Training Supervisor, BioLife Plasma, 1 Daxter Pkwy, Deerfield, IL 60015, **Business Phone:** (847)948-2000.

### ALEXANDER, WILLIE JAMES

Football player, executive, insurance executive. **Personal:** Born Sep 21, 1949, Montgomery, AL; children: 3. **Educ:** Alcorn A & M Univ, BBA. **Career:** Football player (retired), executive, chartered life underwriter & health insurance councilor; Houston Oilers, right cornerback, 1971, 1973, left cornerback, 1972, 1974-79, career consult, 1981-

86, dir player rels, 1987; W J Alexander & Assocs PC, founder & pres, 1980-. **Orgs:** Nat Adv Coun, Univ Houston; chair, Greater Houston Partnership Educ; chmn, Houston Forum; chmn, Heritage Socs; chmn, Ronald McDonald House, Houston; chmn, Mem Serv Comt; bd mem, Amegy Bank Nat Asn; bd mem, S Tex Col Law; bd mem, Tex Childrens Hosp; bd mem, Houston Mus African-Am Cult; bd mem, Wolff Found; Socs Financial Servs Professionals; rep, Financial Indust Regulatory Authority Inc. **Business Addr:** Founder, President, W J Alexander & Associates PC, 50 Briar Hollow St Suite 320 E, Houston, TX 77027, **Business Phone:** (713)802-0900.

### ALEXANDER-WHITING, HARRIETT

Educator. **Personal:** Born Charlotte, NC; daughter of James Alexander Sr; married Robert W. **Educ:** Northern Ill Univ, BS, 1968; Kent State Univ, MA, 1970. **Career:** Va Regional Med Prog, asst allied health off, 1971-72; Emory Univ, instr, 1972-74; Ala Inst Deaf & Blind, Talladega Col, prog coord/supv teacher, 1974-80, asst vis prof, 1976-79; Gallaudet Univ, speech lang path & coord of commun unit & lab, 1980-84, prog supvr, 1985-96, asst dir, support serv, 1996, dir, stud serv team, currently. **Orgs:** Am Speech Lang & Hearing Assoc, 1971-; bd trustee, Ala Assoc Retarded Citizens, 1977-79; Nat Accreditation Coun Site Team, 1978; Nat Task Force Deaf-Blind US Dept Educ, 1979; Nat Comn Develop Disabilities; Am Speech Lang & Hearing Asn, 1980-82; Mid States Accreditation Team, 1983; task group, Mayor's Comn Early Childhood, 1987; Nat Comm Deafness Am Speech Lang & Hearing Asn, 1987-90; Conf Educr & Admin Serv Deaf, 1992-; Gallaudet Univ, Child Develop Ctr Adv Coun, 1993-2000; Nat Task Force Equity in Testing, 1997-; treas, AHA Found. **Home Addr:** 11304 Kencrest Dr, Mitchellville, MD 20721, **Home Phone:** (301)262-6675. **Business Addr:** Director, Student Services Team, Gallaudet University, 800 Florida Ave NE, Washington, DC 20002-3695, **Business Phone:** (202)651-5000.

### ALEXANDRE, DR. JOURNEL

Physician. **Personal:** Born Jul 14, 1931, Arcahaie; children: Cibe & Colette. **Educ:** Lycee Toussaint Louverture, BS, 1952; Univ Mex, MD, 1960; Am Bd Surgery, dipl, 1968. **Career:** St Joseph Hosp, physician; Mercy Cath Med Ctr, physician; Douglass Hosp, resident gen surg, 1961-65; Hahnemann Univ Hosp, resident, 1964; Montgomery Hosp, physician, 1965-66, resident clin path, 1966; pvt pract physician. **Orgs:** Penn & Montgomery Co Med Soc, 1967; Int Col Surgeons; fel Am Col Surgeons, 1969. **Business Addr:** Physician, Private Practice, 1701 Pheasant Lane, Norristown, PA 19403-3333, **Business Phone:** (610)539-8500.

### ALEXIS, DR. CARLTON PETER

Physician, administrator, government official. **Personal:** Born Jun 29, 1929, Port-of-Spain; married Ogbonia M; children: Carla, Anthony & Lisa. **Educ:** NY Univ, BA, 1953; Howard Univ, MD, 1957; Haiti, DHC, 1972; Georgetown Univ, DSc, 1980. **Career:** Physician, administrator (retired); Walter Reed Army Hosp, intern, 1957-58; Bronx VA Hosp, res int med, 1961-63; Georgetown Univ Hosp, fel endocrinol, 1963-64; Freedmens Hosp, pres med-dent staff, 1968-69; Howard Univ, instr prof med, 1964; HowardUniv, vpres health affairs, 1969, exec vpres, interim pres, 1989; Am Col Physicians, fel. **Orgs:** Nat Med Asn; AMA; Am Col Phys; Am Soc Int med; Asn Acad Health Ctr; Med Soc DC; Med Chirurgical Soc DC; chmn, Gov Bd, DC Gen Hosp; Mayors Task Force Reorganization, Dept Human Resources DC; adv comn community, IRS; Mayors Comn Drug Abuse; Ed Bd Jour Med Educ. **Honors/Awds:** Elected Alpha Omega Alpha; Outstanding Teacher, Howard Univ, Col Med, 1966. **Home Addr:** 444 M St SW, Washington, DC 20024, **Home Phone:** (202)554-2310.

### ALEXIS, DORIS VIRGINIA

Administrator. **Personal:** Born Jul 10, 1921, Brooklyn, NY; married Joseph; children: Neal Howe & Priscilla Rand. **Educ:** Hunter Col, attended 1946; Univ Calif, Los Angeles, attended 1960; Univ Calif, Davis, cert, prog mgmt, 1976. **Career:** Calif Dept Motor Vehicles, dep dir, 1977-83, first woman & first career, dir, 1977-85; Nat Traffic Safety Inst, sr consult, currently. **Orgs:** Bd trustee, Sacramento Safety Council, 1978-79; bd dir, Am Asn Motor Vehicle Admin, 1979-; bd dir, Sacramento Safety Coun, 1979-; pres, bd trustee, Commonwealth Equity Trust, 1979-; Women's Forum, 1977-; past pres, bd dir, Youth Women's Christian Asn, 1978-; Nat Asn Advan Colored People, 1978-; Urban League, 1978-; adv coun, Californians Drug Free Youth; Travellers Aid Sacramento; Motor Vehicle Managers Asn; Calif State Employee Asn; Coalition Women State Serv. **Honors/Awds:** Planning & Implementation, DVM Child Care Ctr C State Employees, 1975; Grand Masters Award, MW Prince Hall Grand Lodge F & AM; Honoree Coalition of Women in State, SVC; First CA Official, nominated, membership Women's Forum. **Home Addr:** 7623 Bridgeview Dr, Sacramento, CA 95831. **Business Addr:** Senior Consultant, National Traffic Safety Institute, 15 1st Ave NW, Issaquah, WA 98027, **Business Phone:** (425)369-9000.

### ALEXIS, ELOISE ABERNATHY

Administrator, vice president (organization). **Educ:** Spelman Col, BA, eng; Vanderbilt Univ, MEd, higher educ admin. **Career:** Spelman Col, asst dir, dir, 1991; dir alumnae affairs & ann giving, vpres col rels, currently. **Orgs:** Jr League Atlanta; Alpha Kappa Alpha Sorority Inc; vpres, Nat Alumnae Asn Spelman Col; bd mem, Spelman Col; bd mem, Coun Advan & Support Educ. **Business Addr:** Vice President for College Relations, Spelman College, 350 Spelman Lane SW, Atlanta, GA 30314-4399, **Business Phone:** (404)270-5040.

### ALFONSO, PEDRO

Executive. **Personal:** Born Jun 28, 1948, Tampa, FL; son of Eugenio and Florencia; married Kimberley; children: Gabrielle & Alexandra. **Educ:** Howard Univ Sch Bus, BA, 1973. **Career:** IBM Corp, Fed Syst Div, systs engr, 1969-75; Seymore Systs, mkt mgr, 1975-76; Gen Elec Co, Info Systs Bus Div, acct mgr, 1976-79; Dynamic Concepts Inc, co-founder, chmn, pres & chief exec officer, 1979-. **Orgs:** Pres & bd mem, DC Chamber Com, 1985-2001; bd mem, Leadership Wash, 1987-90; chair & bd mem, YMCA Metrop, 1990-; bd & exec comm, Fed City Coun, 1995-; bd & exec comn, Nat Small Bus United, 1995-; bd trustee, Southeastern Univ, 1995-; co-founder & bd mem, DC Techno Coun, 1998-2000; bd dir, Georgetown Hosp, 1999-; BICSI; bd mem, Greater Southeast Community Hosp; boards, Metrop Wash USO; Girl Scout Coun Nation's Capital; vice chair bd, DC Pub Access Corp; Bldg Indust Consult Serv Int; Int Trade Asn Info Technol Professionals; bd comnr, DC Housing Authority; bd chmn, DC Pvt Indust Coun; Greater Wash Ibero Am Chamber Com. **Home Addr:** 1809 Parkside Dr NW, Washington, DC 20012, **Home Phone:** (202)291-2619. **Business Addr:** President, Chief Executive Officer, Dynamic Concepts Inc, 1730 17th St NE, Washington, DC 20002, **Business Phone:** (202)944-8787.

### ALFORD, BRENDA

Association executive, executive director, manager. **Personal:** Born Jan 27, 1947, Atlanta, GA; daughter of James and Rosette. **Educ:** TN State Univ, BS, 1969; Univ Pittsburgh, MSW, 1975. **Career:** Nat Inst Ment Health, fel, 1973-75; City Houston, prog mgr human res, 1975-78; US Dept Health & Human Servs, pub health adv, 1978-83; Am Asn Black Women Entrepreneurs Inc, nat pres & exec dir, 1982-; RABA Inc, exec vpres, 1981-84; Brasman Health & Bus Res, pres, 1985-. **Orgs:** Nat Asn Soc Workers, Am Pub Health Asn, treas, Wash Urban League Guild, 1980-82; Silver Spring Chamber Comt, Fedn Republican Women, Nat Asn Smal Res Co; pres, Asn African-Am Women Bus Owners. **Honors/Awds:** Edited, Predicted Kilograms Quantities Med & Res Needs Controlled Substances, 1980-81. **Home Addr:** 815 Thayer Ave Apt 1628, Silver Spring, MD 20910, **Home Phone:** (301)565-0527. **Business Addr:** National President, American Association Black Women Entrepreneurs, PO Box 13858, Silver Spring, MD 20911, **Business Phone:** (301)230-5583.

### ALFORD, BRIAN WAYNE

Football player. **Personal:** Born Jun 7, 1975, Oak Park, MI. **Educ:** Purdue Univ, BS, orgn leadership & supv, 1998; Wayne State Univ, MA, teaching & sports admin, 2010. **Career:** Football player (retired); New York Giants, wide receiver, 1998-99; Miami Dolphins, wide receiver, 2000; Ind Firebirds, offensive specialist, 2003; Grand Rapids Rampage, offensive specialist, 2006; Ferndale Sch Dist, col transition specialist, 2012-14; Ferndale Public Schools, adminr stud & family affairs, 2014-. **Honors/Awds:** Most Valuable Player, Purdue, 1996; All-American, Sporting News, 1997; Big Ten track sprint champion. **Special Achievements:** Ranked Second in the Big Ten & twenty second in the NCAA in pass receptions; Ranked Second in Purdue career receiving touchdowns. **Business Addr:** Administrator of Student & Family Affairs, Ferndale Public Schools, Harding Admin Ctr, Ferndale, MI 48220, **Business Phone:** (248)586-8848.

### ALFORD, HARRY C.

Executive. **Personal:** Born CA; children: 2. **Career:** Exec, var orgn: Procter & Gamble, Johnson & Johnson & Sara Lee Corp; US Chamber Com, bd dir, currently; Nat Black Chamber Com, pres, chief exec officer & co-founder, currently. **Orgs:** Nat Adv Coun; Small Bus Admin; bd dir, Studs Free Enterprise; bd dir, Nat 4H Coun; bd dir, Nat Newspaper Publishers Asn Found. **Home Addr:** , MD. **Business Addr:** President, Chief Executive Officer, The National Black Chamber of Commerce, 4400 Jenifer St NW Suite 331, Washington, DC 20015, **Business Phone:** (202)466-6888.

### ALFORD, THOMAS EARL

Librarian. **Personal:** Born Mar 5, 1935, McKeesport, PA; son of Horace and Della Slade; married Kay Alice Taylor; children: Thomas E Jr & Elaine Kay. **Educ:** Eastern Mich Univ, Ypsilanti, Mich, BS, 1958; Univ Mich, Ann Arbor, Mich, MALS, 1964. **Career:** Mideastern Mich Libr Cooper, Flint, Mich, coordr, young adult serv, 1967-69; Berrien Co Libr League, Benton Harbor, Mich, dir, 1969-74; Benton Harbor Pub Libr, dir, 1969-74; Libr Cooper Macomb, Mt Clemens, Mich, dir, 1974-80; Macomb Co Libr, Mt Clemens, Mich, dir, 1974-80; Los Angeles Pub Libr, Los Angeles, Calif, asst city librn, 1980-; Queens Bor Pub Libr, dep lib dir, cust serv & asst dir, currently. **Orgs:** Mich Libr Asn, 1960-80; Am Libr Asn, 1960-; co-chair, Mich Deleg White House Conf Libr Info & Servs, 1979-80; Mich Libr Asn, 1960-80; Calif Libr Asn, 1980-. **Honors/Awds:** Librn, Libr USA NY World Fair, 1964; Author, chapter, Black Librarian Am, Scarecrow, 1970, What Black Librarian Are Saying, Scarecrow, 1972, Libraries Political Process, Scarecrow, 1980. **Home Addr:** 955 Roxbury Dr, Pasadena, CA 91104, **Home Phone:** (626)398-1296. **Business Addr:** Deputy Director, Queens Borough Public Library, 89 11 Merrick Blvd, Jamaica, NY 11432, **Business Phone:** (213)612-3333.

### ALFRED, RAYFIELD

College teacher, firefighter. **Personal:** Born Jul 11, 1939, Ville Platte, LA; married Cynthia A Patterson; children: A LaChelle, Shaun C, Raphael W & Jonathan K. **Educ:** Univ Va, attended 1975; Univ DC, AA, 1977, BS, 1981; Okla State Univ, attended 1981, 1983; US Fire Acad, attended 1983, 1984. **Career:** College teacher (retired); Univ DC, asst prof, cardiopulmonary resuscitation, 1980-81; DC Fire Dept, consult, pub info officer, fire chief, 1988-94; Jacksonville Fire Dept, 1995-2003. **Orgs:** Instr trainer, Am Heart Assoc, 1977; adv neighborhood comm, DC Govt, 1981-84; adv sub comt facil & bd trustee, Univ DC, 1982-83; emergency cardiac comm, Am Heart Asn, 1983-84; prof adv comt, Greater SE Comm Hosp, 1983-85; bd dir, Leadership Wash; bd dir, Anthony Bowen, YMCA; bd dir, DC St Acad; chmn bd, Greater DC Cares; Nat Fire Protection Asn. **Home Addr:** 1437 35th St SE, Washington, DC 20020, **Home Phone:** (202)582-1081.

### ALI, DR. GRACE L.

Executive, chief financial officer. **Personal:** Born May 27, 1952, Georgetown; daughter of Joseph Moore and Victoria Nurse Moore; married Oscar; children: Asgar & Rasheed. **Educ:** Univ Mass, Amherst, MA, MBA, 1973; Univ Miami, Miami, FL, MBA, 1987, PhD. **Career:** Peat, Marwick, Mitchell, New York, NY, internal analyst, 1973-76; Peat, Marwick, Main, Miami, Fla, sr auditor, 1976-79; Air Fla Syst, Miami, Fla, vice pres finance & admin, 1979-80; Air Fla Europe, London, Eng, vpres finance, 1980-83; Univ Miami, Miami, Fla, sr assoc dean admin & fac affairs, 1983-89; Fla Memorial Col, Miami, Fla, vice pres bus & fiscal affairs, 1989; Fla A&M Univ, chief financial officer & vice pres fiscal affairs; Miami-Dade Pub Schs, chief financial officer, 2007-. **Orgs:** Am Inst CPAs, 1984-; Fla Inst CPAs, 1984-; bd mem, 1987-, comt chmn, 1987-89, Fla Inst CPAs-S Dade; mem finance comt, United Way Dade Co, 1990-. **Home Addr:** 10920 SW 125 St, Miami, FL 33176, **Home Phone:** (305)251-4791. **Business Addr:** Chief Financial Officer, Miami-Dade County Public Schools, 1450 NE 2 Ave Suite 456, Miami, FL 33132, **Business Phone:** (305)995-1000.

### ALI, DR. KAMAL HASSAN

Educator. **Personal:** Born Sep 3, 1944, Springfield, MA; son of Edwin Harold Marshall Sr and Stella Abrams Bridges-Marshall; married Ayesha; children: Ahmed Hassan, Quesiyah Sana & Ibrahim Suhnoon. **Educ:** Hunter Col, attended 1964; NY Univ, attended 1965; Univ Mass, Amherst, MA, MEd, 1977, EdD, 1981. **Career:** Human Resources Admin, sr human resource specialist, 1967-71; Harlem E-Harlem Model Cities, proj liason, 1971-74; Univ Mass, Amherst, gradres & teaching asst, 1974-78; Vantage Consult, Hartford, Conn, training prog developer, 1978-79; Westfield State Col, dir, minority & bilingualvoc teacher educ prog, 1980-81, dir minority affairs, 1981-, asst dean acad affairs, prof, World Lang, Multicultural & Gender Studies, 1993-. **Orgs:** Vpres, Islamic Soc Western Mass, 1983-; chmn, bd dir, 1984-86, chmn, New Bldg Comm, 1986-; bd mem, Dunbar Community Ctr; YaSin Mosque's Dar ul-Islam movement; first Imam, Ludlow Correctional Facil, Mass, currently; dir res & develop, Can Dawah Asn. **Home Addr:** 698 Alden St, Springfield, MA 01109-2665, **Home Phone:** (413)783-1590. **Business Addr:** Assistant Professor, Westfield State College, Wilson Hall 235, Westfield, MA 01086, **Business Phone:** (413)572-5388.

### ALI, LAILA AMARIA

Television show host, boxer. **Personal:** Born Dec 30, 1977, Miami Beach, FL; daughter of Muhammad and Veronica Porche Anderson; married Curtis L Conway; children: Curtis Jr & Sydney; married Johnny McClain; children: 3. **Educ:** Univ Southern Calif Bus Sch, Santa Monica Col, BA, bus mgt. **Career:** Boxer (retired), TV show host; Nail Salon, owner; prof boxer, 1999-2007; CBS The Early Show, health & lifestyle correspondent, 2007-; NBC's "American Gladiators", co-host, 2008, "Stars Earn Stripes", 2012; ABC's "Everyday Health", co-host, currently. Author: Reach!: Finding Strength, Spirit and Personal Power, 2002; TV: "One on One", 2001; "The Parkers", 2001; "Sheena", 2001; "Strong Medicine", 2003; "Diamond Life", 2005; "The N's Student Body", 2008; "Cubed", 2010; "Real Husbands of Hollywood", 2013; "All in with Laila Ali", 2013; Films: All You've Got, 2006; Falcon Rising, 2014. **Orgs:** Founder, Reach Found. **Home Addr:** 4801 Azucena Rd, Woodland Hills, CA 91364-4039. **Business Addr:** Co-Host, ABC, 7 Lincoln Sq, New York, NY 10023, **Business Phone:** (212)456-7777.

### ALI, MAAJID F.

Clergy. **Career:** Masjid Jihad, imam, currently. **Home Addr:** 1 Castello Ave, Savannah, GA 31419-2456. **Business Addr:** Imam, Masjid Jihad, 117 E 34th St, Savannah, GA 31401-8101, **Business Phone:** (912)236-7387.

### ALI, MAHERSHALA (MAHERSHALALHASHBAZ GILMORE)

Actor. **Personal:** Born Feb 16, 1974, Oakland, CA; married Amatus Sami-Karim. **Educ:** St Mary's Col Calif, BA, 1996; NY Univ, MFA, 2000. **Career:** Actor, 1996-; California Shakespeare Festival, apprentice, 1996; The Gavin Report, spin recorder, 1996. Television: Crossing Jordan, 2001-02; Haunted, 2002; NYPD Blue, 2002; CSI: Crime Scene Investigation, 2003; The Handler, 2003; Threat Matrix, 2003-04; The 4400, 2004-07; Lie to Me, 2009; Law & Order; Special Victims Unit, 2009; The Wrong Man, 2010; All Signs of Death, 2010; Lights Out, 2011; Treme, 2011-12; Alphas, 2011-12; Alcatraz, 2012; House of Cards, 2013-16; Luke Cage, 2016. Film: Making Revolution, 2003; The Curious Case of Benjamin Button, 2008; Crossing Over, 2009; Predators, 2010; The Place Beyond the Pines, 2012; Go for Sisters; Supremacy, 2014; The Hunger Games: Mockinjay: Part 1, 2014; The Hunger Games: Mockinjay: Part 2, 2015; Kicks, 2016; Free State of Jones, 2016; Moonlight, 2016. Stage: Blues for an Alabama Sky; The School of Scandal; A Lie of the Mind; A Doll's House; Monkey in the Middle; The Merchant of Venice; The New Place; Secret Injury, Secret Revenge; The Great White Hope, Arena Stage, Washington, D.C.; Jack and Jill; Smart People, 2016. **Honors/Awds:** Special Jury Award, Gotham Awards, 2016. **Business Addr:** IFA Talent Agency, 8730 Sunset Blvd Suite 490, Los Angeles, CA 90069.

### ALI, MUHAMMAD (CASSIUS MARCELLUS CLAY, JR.)

Boxer, activist, social worker. **Personal:** Born Jan 17, 1942, Louisville, KY; son of Cassius Marcellus Clay Sr and Odessa Grady Clay; married Veronica Porsche, Mar 13, 1977, (divorced 1986); children: Hana, Khaliah, Miya & Laila; married Yolanda, Nov 19, 1986; children: Asaad Amin & Rasheda; married Belinda Boyd, Aug 17, 1967, (divorced 1977); children: Maryum, Jamillah, Rasheda & Muhammad Jr. **Career:** Boxer (retired), polit activist, lect, philanthropist; prof boxer, 1960-81; Muhammad Ali Ctr, founder & owner, 2005-; Muhammad Ali Enterprises LLC, partner, 2006-. **Orgs:** World Community Islam; conducts missionary work; World Orgn Rights, Liberty & Dignity. **Home Addr:** PO Box 187, Berrien Springs, MI 49103-0187. **Business Addr:** Founder, Owner, Muhammad Ali Enterprises LLC, 650 Madison Ave 15th Fl, New York, NY 10022, **Business Phone:** (212)407-9173.

### ALI, SHAHRAZAD

Writer, executive. **Personal:** Born Apr 27, 1954, Brooklyn, NY; daughter of Lucy Marshall and Harry Levy; married Solomon; children: 3; married Yahya. **Educ:** Xavier Univ, Cincinnati, OH; Ga State Univ, Atlanta, Ga. **Career:** Cincinnati Herald, Call & Post, Cincinnati Enquirer & Hi-Lites Mag, feature contrib ed, 1966-71; med transcriptionist, 1977-83; Clark Col, asst to vpres, 1983-85; Civilized Publ, Atlanta, Ga, 1985-; Ali's Unlimited Accessories, exec asst, 1986-89; Temple Univ, PASCEP Prog for Independent Publ, teacher, 1987. **Orgs:** Advisory bd mem, Ford Recreation Center, Philadelphia, Pa, 1988-89; advisory bd mem, Pennsylvania Bd of Probation & Parole, Philadelphia, Pa, 1988-89; public relations director, Mayor's Comn on Women, Philadelphia, PA, 1987-88; published author, Moonstone

Black Writers Asn, Philadelphia, PA, 1987-88. **Honors/Awds:** Alpha Phi Alpha Literary Award, 1987; Mayor's Proclamation for Writing, New Orleans, La, 1987, Detroit, Mich, 1990; Third Place, Top Georgia Authors of Atlanta Public Library, 1985; Author, How Not to Eat Pork, 1985; Author, The Blackman's Guide to Understanding the Blackwoman, 1989; 1 book on Black Best Selling List for 40 weeks, 1990; The Blackwoman's Guide to Understanding the Blackman, 1992; Blackman's Guide on Tour Video, 1992; Are You Still a Slave?, 1994; Things Your Parents Should Have Told You, 1998; Urban Survival for the Year 2000/Y2K, 1999; Day by Day, 1996; Honorary doctoral, journalism, UHURU Univ, 1995. **Special Achievements:** Promotional activities include appearances on Donahue, Geraldo, Sally, Montel, Larry King, Jerry Springer, Ricki Laker, Judge for Yourself, Gordon Elliot, Rolonda, Our Voices-BET, Tony Brown's Journal; Author: How To Tell If Your Man Is Gay or Bisexual, 2003, Urban Survival, 2000, How not to eat pork, blackmans guide to understanding blackwoman, Things your parents should have told you, Blackwoman's guide to understanding Blackman, How not to eat pork or Life without pig, Are you still a slave. **Business Addr:** Owner, Civilized Publications, 2023 S 7th St, Philadelphia, PA 19148, **Business Phone:** (215)339-0061.

### ALI, TATYANA MARISOL (TY TATY)

Singer, actor. **Personal:** Born Jan 24, 1979, Atlanta, GA; daughter of Sheriff and Sonia Enieda. **Educ:** Harvard Univ, anthrop, 2002. **Career:** Theatre performance: Fences, 1987; Orfeo del Campo; Sugar Hill; TV Series: "Sesame Street", 1984-88; A Man Called Hawk, The Cosby Show, 1989; Getting By, "Star Search"; "Brains & Brawn", co-host, 1993; "Are You Afraid of the Dark?", 1994; "In the House", 1995; "Living Single", 1996; "Fresh Price of Bel Air", 1990-96; "Fall Into Darkness", 1996; "Foster's Field rip"; "413 Hope Street", 1997; "Fastlane", 2002; "Half & Half", 2003; "On the Lot", 2007; "The Young and the Restless", 2007-13; "The Jeffrey Henderson Show", 2009; "Buppies", 2009-10; "Love That Girl!", 2010-14; "Second Generation Wayans", 2013; "Dear Secret Santa", 2013; "The Divorce", 2014. Albums: Kiss the Sky, Everytime, 1999; "Day Dreamin", Boy You Knock Me Out, 1998. Films: Eddie Murphy Raw; Jawbreakers; Brother, 2000; National Lampoon Presents Dorm Daze, 2003; Nora's Hair Salon, 2004; Back in the Day, 2005; Glory Road, 2006; The List, 2007; Hotel California, 2008; Mother and Child, 2009 Privileged, 2010; MJJ Music, vocal artist, currently. **Honors/Awds:** Junior Vocalist Champion, 1987; Young Artist Award, 1991; YoungStar Award, 1997; BET Award, 2005; Image Award, Nat Asn Advan Colored People, 1996, 2011-14. **Special Achievements:** Appeared on Star Search & won twice receiving a 4 star rating when she appeared for a 2nd time; ranked 6th in Billboard 100 Hot Singles; Ranked seventy fourth in VH1 100 Top Child Stars, 2005; Gold Album: "Daydreamin". **Business Addr:** Vocal Artist, c/o Sony Music, 550 Madison Ave, New York, NY 10022, **Business Phone:** (212)833-8000.

### ALI-JACKSON, KAMIL

Lawyer, administrator. **Personal:** Born Mar 4, 1959, El Paso, TX; daughter of John Ali and Ruth; married Michael Stephen; children: Ross (deceased), Kendall & Kamryn. **Educ:** Princeton Univ, AB, polit, 1981; Harvard Law Sch, JD, 1984. **Career:** Mc Carter & Eng, assoc, 1984-86; Pepper, Hamilton & Scheetz, assoc, 1986-90; Merck & Co Inc, asst Coun, 1990-98; Endo Pharmaceut Inc, assoc gen coun & vpres, 1998-2000; Care soft Inc, gen coun & chief privacy officer, 2000-01; Dr Reddys Lab Inc, assoc gen coun & vpres legal, 2004-06; Legal Consultant, Pharmaceut Company, 2011-14; Ception Therapeut Inc, gen coun & secy; chief legal officer, Ceptaris Therapeutics Inc, 2011-13; chief legal officer, currently. **Orgs:** Nat Bar Asn, 1986-92; Philadelphia Bar Asn, 1986-92; Pa Bar Asn; bd mem, Zoning Hearing. **Home Addr:** 143 Hart Ave, Doylestown, PA 18901. **Business Addr:** Chief Legal Officer, Ceptaris Therapeutics Inc, 101 Lindenwood Dr Suite 400, Malvern, PA 19355, **Business Phone:** (610)975-9290.

### ALICE, MARY (MARY ALICE SMITH)

Actor. **Personal:** Born Dec 3, 1941, Indianola, MS; daughter of Sam and Ozelar Jurnakin. **Career:** Theatrical appearances: A Rat's Mass, 1969; The Duplex, 1972; Miss Julie, 1973; House Party, 1973; Black Sunlight, 1974; Terraces, 1974; Heaven andHell's Agreement, 1974; In the Deepest Part of Sleep, 1974; Cockfight, 1977; Nongogo, 1978; Player No 9, Spell No 7, NY Shakespeare Festival, 1979; Zooman and the Sign, 1980; Open Admissions Long Wharf Theatre, 1982; A Raisin in the Sun, 1984; Glasshouse, 1984; Take Me Along, 1984; Fences, Goodman Theatre, Chgo, 1986; 46th St Theatre, NYC, 1987; TheShadow Box, 1994; Films: The Education of Sonny Carson, 1974; Sparkle, 1976; Teachers, 1984; Brat Street, 1984; To Sleep With Anger, 1990; Awakenings, 1990; Bonfire of the Vanities, 1990; A Perfect World, 1992; Life with Mikey, 1993; The Inkwell, 1994; Heading Home, 1995; Bed ofRoses, 1996; Down in the Delta, 1998; Catfish in Black Bean Sauce, 1999; The Wishing Tree, 1999; The Photographer, 2000; Sunshine State, 2002; TheMatrix Revolutions, 2003; The Matrix Recalibrated, 2004; The Burly ManChronicles, 2004; The Matrix Online, 2005. TV movies: "The Sty of the Blind Pig", 1974; "Just an OldSweet Song", 1976; "This Man Stands Alone", 1979; "Joshua's World", 1980; "The Color of Friendship", 1981; "The Killing Floor", 1984; "ConcealedBurmies", 1984; "Charlotte Forten's Mission: Experiment on Freedom", 1984; "The Women of Brewster Place", 1989; "Laurel Avenue", 1993; "The Mother", 1994; "The Vernon Johns Story", 1994; "The Last Brickmaker in America", 2001; TV series: "Sanford and Son", 1972; "A Different World", 1988-89; "I'll Fly Away", 1991-93; "Oz", 2002; "Lineof Fire", 2004; "The Jury", 2004; "Kojak", 2005; Narrator Crime Scene USA, 2000-09. **Orgs:** Am Fedn TV & Radio Artists; Screen Actors Guild; Actor's Equity Asn. **Honors/Awds:** Obie Award, Village Voice, 1979; Antoinette Perry Award; Drama Desk Award, 1987; Tony Award, 1987; Emmy Award, 1993; Nominated for Black Reel Award, 2004. **Special Achievements:** Tony Award nominee, Having Our Say: The Delany Sisters' First 100 Years. **Business Addr:** Actress, Terri Kelly & Associates, 8949 Sunset Blvd, West Hollywood, CA 90069, **Business Phone:** (310)275-0172.

### ALLAH, RAKIM (WILLIAM MICHAEL GRIFFIN, JR.)

Rap musician. **Personal:** Born Jan 28, 1968, Long Island, NY. **Career:** Eric B & Rakim, group mem; All-Pro Football 2K8, com spokesman, currently; Albums: Paid in Full, 1987; Follow the Leader, 1988; Let the Rhythm Hitem, 1990; Dont Sweat the Technique, 1992; The 18th Letter, 1997; oh mygod; The Master, 1999; The Archive: Live, Lost & Found, 2008; The Seventh Seal, 2009; The Hunting Party, 2014. Singles: "Holy Are You", 2009; "Walk These Streets", 2009; "Don't Call Me", 2013; "Guilty All the Same", 2014. **Honors/Awds:** The Greatest MCs Of All Time, #4 MTV. **Special Achievements:** Raekwon of the Wu-Tang Clan dedicated a tribute to Rakim entitled "Rakim Tribute"; Tupac Shakur also pays tribute to Rakim in a song called "Old School". **Business Addr:** Rap Artist, c/o Universal Records, 1325 Ave of the Americas, New York, NY 10019, **Business Phone:** (212)373-0600.

### ALLAIN, STEPHANIE

Movie producer. **Personal:** Born Oct 30, 1959, New Orleans, LA; daughter of Charles and Gwen Miller; married Mitch Marcus; children: Wade & Jesse; married Stephen Bray; children: 3. **Educ:** Univ Calif, Santa Cruz, BA, lit & creative writing. **Career:** Creative Artists Agency, script reader, staff reader, 1985-87; 20th Century Fox, story analyst, 1987-88; Warner Bros, analyst, 1988; Columbia Pictures, analyst, creative exec & vpres prod, 1989-96; Jim Henson Pictures, pres prod, 1996-2000; 3Arts Entertainment, proj developer, 2000-03; Homegrown Pictures, founder, 2003-; Producer: Boyz N the Hood, 1991; Poetic Justice, 1993; El Mariachi, 1994; Higher Learning, 1994; Desperado, 1994; A Boy Called Hate, 1995; I Like it Like That, 1995; The Craft, 1995; Buddy, 1997; The Adventures of Elmo in Grouchland, 1999; Muppets from Space, 1999; Rat, 2000; 40, 2002; Good Boy!, 2003; Craig Brewer, 2003; Hustle & Flow, 2003; Biker Boyz, 2003; Hustle & Flow, 2005; Something New, 2006; Black Snake Moan, 2007; Hurricane Season, 2009; Granny on Family, Bobby on Art, 2010; We the Peeples, 2011; "John Oliver's New York Stand-Up Show", lightening tech, 2010; Films: A Boy Called Hate, 1995; Peeples, 2013; Dear White People, 2013; Una Y Otra Y Otra Vez, 2013; Blackbird, 2014; Serial: "New York Stand-Up Show". **Orgs:** Producers Guild Am; bd mem, Proj Evolve IFP. **Honors/Awds:** Audience Award at Sundance, Academy Award for Best Original Song, 2005. **Special Achievements:** Nominated for Black Reel Awards and Black Movie Awards. **Business Addr:** President of Production, Jim Henson Pictures, **Business Phone:** (323)802-1500.

**ALLEN, BENJAMIN P, III. See Obituaries Section.**

### ALLEN, BERNESTINE

Economist, government official. **Personal:** Born Aug 20, 1944, Soperton, GA. **Educ:** Ft Valley State Col, BS, bus admin, 1967; Northeastern Univ, MA, econs, 1968. **Career:** Dept Labor, Wash, econ analyst, 1967; NSF grant, 1967; Gen Elec Co, financial analyst, 1968-69; Dept Transp, Wash, economist, 1969-71; Airport & Airway Cost Allocation Study, asst prog dir, 1971-73; Int Aviation Policy, economist, 1973-75; US Dept Transp, int transp specialist, 1975-80, sr int transp specialist, 1980-87, int coop div & secretarial chief, 1987-95, int coop & trade div chief, 1995-97, dep dir & actg dir off int transp trade, 1997-2000, dir off int transp, 2000-. **Orgs:** Pres, Delta Sigma Theta Inc, 1966-67, 1972-74; Am Econ Asn; Am Fedn Govt Employees, 1970-72; Women Ex-Offenders Prog, 1973; bd dir, DST Telecommunications Inc, 1976-81; Nat Econ Asn; Am Acad Polit & Soc Sci; Bus & Prof Women's League; DC Asn Retarded Citizens; exec comt, March Dimes, Nat Capital Area Chap, 1988-91; Garfield Home Sr Citizens; Proj Women; Nat Coun Negro Women; Nat Asn Advan Colored People; Nat Urban League; exec bd, financial secy, Nat Pan-Hellenic Coun Inc, 1991-95; Int Freedom Found; active mem, First Baptist Church; Delta Sigma Theta Sorority. **Home Addr:** 2034 Woodshade Ct, Mitchellville, MD 20721. **Business Addr:** Director, US Department of Transportation, 400 7th St SW Rm 10300, Washington, DC 20590, **Business Phone:** (202)366-4398.

**ALLEN, BETTIE JEAN. See Obituaries Section.**

### ALLEN, BILLY R.

Consultant. **Personal:** Born Mar 16, 1945, Crossroads, TX; son of Fannie M; married Clare Dickerson; children: Sheldon C, Sean L & Kristy B. **Educ:** Henderson County Jr Col, attended 1965; Univ N Tex, BS, polit sci & psych, 1968. **Career:** New York Life Ins, field underwriter, 1970-72; Pitney Bowes, acct rep, 1971-73; Minority Search Inc, pres, chief exec off, chmn, 1975-2004; Unique New Visions Inc, owner, 1975-. **Orgs:** Soc Int Bus Fel, 1986; Nat Recreation & Pk Asn, vice chmn, 1986-92; Dallas Ft Worth Airport Bd, comt chmn, 1988; Dallas Assembly; Dallas Black Chamber Com; Comt 100; bd visitor, Univ N Tex, 1990; Concord Missionary Baptist Church, elder, currently. **Honors/Awds:** Dallas Chamber Com, 1976; YMCA Achievement, 1984; Outstanding Ex-Stud, Henderson Co Jr Col, 1985; Willow Award, Dallas Black Chamber, 1986; Nat Asn Community Leadership Orgn, Distinguished Leadership Award, 1986. **Home Addr:** 830 Misty Glen Lane, Dallas, TX 75232, **Home Phone:** (214)374-8607. **Business Addr:** Owner, Unique New Visions Inc, 830 Misty Glen Lane, Dallas, TX 75232, **Business Phone:** (214)374-8607.

### ALLEN, DR. BRENDA FOSTER

Educator, teacher. **Personal:** Born Jan 24, 1947, Gloucester, VA; married Robert P; children: Tameka D. **Educ:** Va State Univ, BS, 1969; NC State Univ, MS, 1976, EdD, 1985. **Career:** Cornell Univ, Coop Exten Serv, county 4-H agt, 1969, youth develop specialist, 1971-72; Nat 4-H Found, Div Leadership Develop, prog specialist, 1972-75; NC State Univ, Sch Educ, res asst, 1975-76, Div Stud Affairs, coordr, 1976-80, asst dir, 1980-83, Off Provost, coordr, 1983-85, Agr Exten Serv, prog specialist, 1985-, Col Textiles, coordr African-Am advising, currently; Shaw Univ Sem Ext Prog, teacher, 1984-86. **Orgs:** Task force mem, Image NC State Univ Seminars, 1978-79, facilitator, 1979-80, grad stud's assoc adult educ exec bd, Hewlett Fel; NCSU comt Recruitment & Retention Black Studs, 1982-83; facilitator, Gov's Conf Women & Econ, 1983; NC Home Econs Ext Prog Comn, 1983-84; Youth Motivation Task Force, 1985-86; NC 4-H Vol Task Force, 1986; NC Home Econ Volunt Task Force, 1986; NC coordr, Women & Chronic DisTeleconference, 1988; Epsilon Sigma Phi, Nat Hon Exten Fraternity, 1989; Nat 4-H Found, staff develop & training comt, vols' forum planning comt; Task Force Prog Develop 4-H vols; Nat Teen Leaders' Symp Planning Comt; Am Home Econs Asn; Nat 4-H Asn; Kappa Omicron Phi. **Honors/Awds:** Infant Mortality Grant from United Church of Christ, 1989. **Special Achievements:** Publications: "Making Incentives Work for You", 1976; "Competencies Needed by 4-H Volunteers for the Effective Use of Incentives - A Needs Asessment Study", 1976; "Criteria for Selection, Evaluating or Developing Learning Modules", 1976; "Are Your Reading Habits a Liability?", 1977; "Video tapes Help University Students Learn How to Learn", 1981; "Build Up One Another", 1986; "Women, Builders of Communities and Dreams", 1986; "Rural Minority Women As Community Volunteers", 1986. **Home Addr:** 2025 Rabbit Run, Raleigh, NC 27603-2783, **Home Phone:** (919)832-6136. **Business Addr:** Coordinator of African-American Advising, North Carolina State University, 2401 Research Dr, Raleigh, NC 27695, **Business Phone:** (919)515-2194.

### ALLEN, BYRON (BYRON ALLEN FOLKS)

Entertainer. **Personal:** Born Apr 22, 1961, Detroit, MI; married Jennifer Lucas; children: Chloe Ava, Olivia Rose & Lucas Byron. **Career:** TV Series: "Case Closed", 1988; "Jammin'", actor & dir, 1992; "The American Athlete", dir, 1996; "Global Business People", dir, 1999; "Every Woman", dir, 2000; "Recipe TV Featuring the World's Greatest Chefs", dir, 2002; "Beautiful Homes & Great Estates", dir, 2002; "Urban Style", dir, 2003; "Designers Fashions & Runways", dir, 2004; The Best of Comics Unleashed with Byron Allen, dir, 2008; "The Young Icons", dir, 2010; America's Court with Judge Ross", dir, 2010-13; "The First Family", 2013. Executive producer: Real People", host, 1979-84; "Every Woman", 2000; "Beautiful Homes & Great Estates", 2002; "Designers Fashions & Runways", 2004; "Comics Unleashed", 2006; Are U Serious?: Best of Shawn Morgan, 2008; "ES.TV HD", 2009; "The Byron Allen Show", 1989-92; "Comics Unleashed", currently; Film: America's Sweethearts, 2001; Entertainment Studios, chmn & Chief Exec Officer, 2004-. **Honors/Awds:** Daytime Emmy Award, 2012. **Business Addr:** Chairman, Chief Executive Officer, Entertainment Studios, 9903 Santa Monica Blvd Suite 418, Los Angeles, CA 90212, **Business Phone:** (310)277-3500.

### ALLEN, CAROL WARD

Executive director, politician. **Personal:** Born Oakland, CA; daughter of Claude. **Educ:** Nova Southeastern Univ, PhD; San Jose State Univ, BA, art, MBA; Univ Paris, Sorbonne, France, post grad; Fourah Bay Col Univ; Univ Ile-Ife; Univ Kumasi; Univ Nairobi. **Career:** Professor (retired); Oakland Port Authority, pres; Laney Col, fac mem, 1970, Community Servs Off, dir, 1993; Oakland Bd Port Commissioners, pres, 1990-92; Col of Alameda, prof; Peralta Community Col, dir, mkt & asst vchancellor; Peralta Fedn Teachers Polit Action Comt, pres, 2002-04; CWA Partners LLC, chief exec officer, 2015. **Orgs:** Supvr, Sr Vols Prog; past-pres, Calif Comn Status Women, 1980-85; found & pres, Bay Area Women Entrepreneurs; bd mem, Child Abuse Prev; bd mem, Oakland Lyric Opera; bd mem, Bay Area Dance Ser; adv, Phi Theta Cappa Hon Soc, Laney Col; Nat Women's Polit Caucus; Black Women Organizers Polit Action; Nat Orgn Women; Emily's List, listee; bd dir, Bay Area Rapid Transit (BART); bd vpres, 2004, pres, 2005. **Business Addr:** Director, Laney College, 900 Sallon St, Oakland, CA 94607, **Business Phone:** (510)834-5740.

### ALLEN, CAROLE GENEVA WARD

Teacher, educator. **Personal:** Born Jan 14, 1943, Phoenix City, AL. **Educ:** Sorbonne, attended 1963; Calif State Univ, San Jose, BA, 1965, MA, 1973; Univ Calif, attended 1970; Int Comm Col, PhD; Univ Ile-Ife Nigeria, attended 1970; Univ Sci & Tech, attended 1970; Kumasi Ghana Forah Bay Col, Sierra Leone, attended 1970. **Career:** Educator (retired); Andrew Hill High Sch, 1965-69; airline stewardess, 1966-68; Calif Col Arts Cabrillo Col, 1970; Laney Col, ethnic studies, chairwoman, 1970-, prof; Goddard Col, mentor consult teacher masters degree stud, 1973-74; Oakland Bd Port Commissioners, pres, 1990-92; San Francisco Bay Area Rapid Transit Dist, bd dir, gen mgr, 1998-, vpres, 2005, pres, 2006; Col Alameda, prof; CWA Partners LLC, chief exec officer. **Orgs:** Bay Area Black Artists, 1972-; Nat Conf Artists, 1973-74; Bay Area Rapid Transp Admin, vice chairperson; Fruitvale Policy Comt, chair personl Oakland Airport connector Liaison Comt; Metrop Transp Comn AB 842; Alameda County Trap Improve Authority; pres, Peralta Fedn Teachers Union. **Honors/Awds:** Purchase Award, 27th Annual SF Art Festival, 1973; Outstanding Black Woman Award, Alpha Phi Alpha, 1974; CJ Walker Business and Community Recognition Award, National Coalition of 100 Black Women, 2005; Thirty Most Influential African Americans, City Fight Mag; COMTO Award; Hall of Fame, Alameda County Women's. **Special Achievements:** Published Images of Awareness Pan Africanist Mag, 1973; Afro-Am Artists Bio-Biographical Dir Theres Dickason, 1973; black artist on Art Vol 2 by Samella Lewis Ruth Waddy, 1970; First African American to serve as president of the California Commission on the Status of Women in 1983; First woman to serve as general manager or CEO of the entire BART organization; Dem Party; President's Award, Laney Col. **Home Addr:** 121 Embarcadero W, Oakland, CA 94607-3789, **Home Phone:** (510)350-7456. **Business Addr:** Board of Director, Laney College, 900 Fallon St, Oakland, CA 94607-4808, **Business Phone:** (510)464-3198.

### ALLEN, CATHY H.

Executive. **Educ:** Stephen F Austin State Univ, BBA, 1981, MEd, 1989; Human Resources Cert Inst, Sr Prof Human Resources, cert. **Career:** Tex Tech Univ, vice chancellor community & multicultural affairs, 1997-2006; Vol Ctr Lubbock, vol speaker & trainer, 2004-07; Covenant Health Syst, vpres human resources, 2006-08; Gibraltar Group, vpres human resources, 2010-13; Tex Tech Univ T-STEM Ctr, assoc dir, 2013, sr dir, 2013-; HR Consult, owner, 2008-. **Orgs:** Bd dir, Tex Ct App Spec Advocates; historian & regional dir, Leadership Tex Alumnae Asn; treas, Lubbock Housing Finance Corp; vice chair, Grants Comt, LISD Found Excellence; backpack buddies, Jr League Lubbock; chair, Women Excellence Comt, YWCA; secy, Camp Rio BlanCo. **Business Addr:** Senior Director, Texas Tech University, PO Box 43103, Lubbock, TX 79409-3103, **Business Phone:** (806)742-3451.

### ALLEN, CHARLES CLAYBOURNE

Consultant. **Personal:** Born Sep 21, 1935, Newport News, VA; son of John C and Margaret C; married Sallie Tucker; children: Charles II, John IV & Sallie Monique. **Educ:** Hampton Inst, BS, archit, 1958; Columbia Univ, MSUP, 1963. **Career:** Clarke & Rapuano Inc, urban planner, 1963-68; Dept Develop & Planning Gary, dir, 1968-75; Soul City Col, vpres & gen mgr, 1974-75; Wendell Campbell Assoc Inc, sr vpres, 1975-88; Newport News, Dept Planning & Develop, dep dir, VA, 1988-91, consult urban planning, 1991-; City Newport News, vice mayor, 1996. **Orgs:** Kappa Alpha Psi Fraternity, 1955-; bd mem, Am Soc Planning off, 1971-73; bd mem, Am Planning Asn, 1979-82, charter mem, 1979-; chmn, joint AIP & ASPO Comn Min Affairs, 1973-78; pres, Nat Asn Planners, 1976-80; Am Inst Planners, 1977-78; charter mem, Am Inst Cert Planners, 1979; pres, Nat Hampton Alumni Asn, 1987-89; bd mem, Ray Graham Asn, 1988-89; Newport News City Coun, 1992-; Adv Comn Intergovernmental Rels, 1992-; Hampton Roads Planning Dist Comn, 1994-; Commonwealth Va Adv Comn Inter govt Rels, 1997-; bd mem, Urban League Hampton Roads, 1998-; Transp Comn Hampton Roads, 1999-; chmn, Visual Qual Comt, 2000-; Sigma Pi Phi Fraternity, 2003; fel Am Inst Cert Planners, 2004; chair, ACIR Comt Visual Qual; bd mem, Hampton Roads; Va Munic League, Gen Laws Comt; Lambda Alpha; bd dir, Newport News Pub Art Found. **Honors/Awds:** Distinguished Kappa Award, Kappa Alpha Psi Fraternity, 1971; Good Government Award, Gary Jaycees, 1973; Department Head of the Year, City Gary, 1973; Outstanding Government Award, Gary Jaycees, 1974; Public Service Award, Gary Chapter Frontiers, 1974; City Councilor, Gary City Co, 1974; Outstanding 20 Year Alumnus, Hampton Inst, 1978; Outstanding Person, DuPage Co, Nat Asn Advan Colored People, 1978; Award of Achievement, Hampton Newport News, Alumni Chap, Kappa Alpha Psi Fraternity, 1992; Distinguished Citizen Award, Zeta Lambda Chap, Alpha Phi Alpha Fraternity, 1992. **Home Addr:** 97 28th St Apt K, Newport News, VA 23607-3954, **Home Phone:** (757)247-7556. **Business Addr:** Director, Newport News Public Art Foundation, 735 Thimble Shoals Blvd Suite 100, Newport News, VA 23606, **Business Phone:** (757)369-3014.

## ALLEN, CHARLES EDWARD, JR. (CHARLES E ALLEN)

Real estate developer, executive, association executive. **Personal:** Born Feb 22, 1948, Atlanta, GA; son of Charles Sr and Ruby Collins; married Elizabeth Ann Glover; children: Charles Phillip, David Kennedy & Rebecca Ann. **Educ:** Morehouse Col, Atlanta, GA, BS, bus admin, 1970; Univ Chicago, IL, MBA, 1972; Benedict Col, honorary doctor, 1996. **Career:** First Nat Bank, Chicago, Ill; Bank Calif, vpres, mgr, 1976-78; First Bank Nat Asn, pres, chief operating officer, 1978-80; United Nat Bank, Wash, DC, exec vpres, chief admin officer, 1980-81; Marakon Assocs, financial controller; AAA, spokesman, pres, dir, 1987, chmn, 1992-94; Gartmore, asst acct; First Ind Nat Bank, pres, chief exec officer, 1981-88; MIG Realty Adv, vpres, regional mgr, 1988; Graimark Realty Adv Inc, co-founder, pres, chmn, chief exec officer, currently; Gartmore Variable Ins Trust, chmn, chief exec officer. **Orgs:** Bd dir, AAA Mich & Affil Ins Co, 1987-; former corp dir, Blue Cross/Blue Shield Mich; pres, Nat Bankers Asn; former dir, Mus Afro-Am Hist; former chmn bd, Benedict Col; former dir, 7th Fed Res Bank, Detroit Br; bd mem, Preferred Provider Orgn Mich; Mutual Funds Nationwide Ins Co; Detroit Econ Club; United Negro Col Fund; adv bd mem, Woodlands Conservancy; trustee, Gartmore Variable Ins Trust; trustee, Gartmore Mutual Funds; bd, Auto Club Group; chmn, Automobile Club Mich; chmn, nations trade asn African-Am & women-owned com banks. **Honors/Awds:** Black Achievers Award, 1976; Outstanding Young Men of America, YMCA, 1981; Alpha Theta Young Mens Christian Association Sorority, 1981; Citizen of the Year, Hartford Ave Baptist Church, 1982; Boy Scouts Am, 1984; Mayors Award Merit, 1984; Americas Best & Brightest Young Men & Women, 1987; hon DL, Benedict Col, 1996; During tenure, First Ind Natl Bank featured as Bank of the Year, Black Enterprise Mag, profiled in Minority Bus Entrepreneur Mag; Outstanding Business Leader, Northwood Univ, 2003. **Special Achievements:** First African American elected AAA Chairman from Michigan Chronicle. **Home Addr:** 8162 E Jefferson Ave Apt 15B, Detroit, MI 48214-2611, **Home Phone:** (313)823-1005. **Business Addr:** Chairman, Co-Founder, Chief Executive Officer & President, Graimark Realty Advisors Inc, 500 River Pl Dr Apt 5105, Detroit, MI 48207, **Business Phone:** (313)259-9479.

## ALLEN, CHARLES EDWARD (CHARLES E ALLEN, III)

Manager, public relations executive, association executive. **Personal:** Born Jul 21, 1973, New Orleans, LA; son of Charles E Jr and Rosemarie. **Educ:** Xavier Univ La, BS, biol, 1995; Tulane Univ, MSPH, environ policy, 1998. **Career:** New Orleans Pub Sch Syst, substitute teacher, 1995-97, admin asst, 1997; La Off Pub Health, asst prog coordr, 1998, admin intern, 1998; Tulane Xavier Univ, Ctr Bioenvironmental Res, educ & outreach coord, 1999-, pub rel off, 2000-, prog mgr, currently, asst dir, external rels, assoc dir, 2008-. **Orgs:** Capt, Times-Picayune Christmas Doll & Toy Fund, 1987-; Knights Peter Claver, 1994-; commt co-chair, Omega Psi Phi, Rho Phi chap, 1995-; La Environ Roundtable, 1999-; advisor, Coastal & Environ Affairs; dir, Coastal & Environ Affairs, New Orleans; chmn, vice chmn, pres, Holy Cross Neighborhood Asn; actg dir, Lower 9th Ctr Sustainable Engagement & Develop, 2010; bd mem, REACH-NOLA; bd dir, La/Haiti Sustainable Village Proj; La Gov's Adv Comn Coastal Restoration & Protection; secy, CSED, currently. **Honors/Awds:** Cert Merit, New Orleans City Coun, 1996, 1997, 2000; Brother of the Year, Omega Psi Phi, Rho Phi chap, 1997; Excellence in Total Quality Mgt, John McDonogh Sr HS, 1997; Dean's Leadership Award, Tulane Univ Sch Public Health, 1998; Certificate of Merit, Jefferson Parish Off Environ Affairs, 2000, 2001. **Home Addr:** 7107 Martin Dr Apt 229, New Orleans, LA 70126, **Home Phone:** (504)240-0880. **Business Addr:** Program Manager, Assistant Director, Tulane University, Health & Environ Res Bldg, New Orleans, LA 70118, **Business Phone:** (504)862-8000.

## ALLEN, CHERYL L.

Judge. **Personal:** Born Dec 16, 1947, Pittsburgh, PA; daughter of Robert and Corrine Davis; married Jim Skipwith; children: Jason, Justin & Frederick. **Educ:** Penn State Univ, Pittsburgh, PA, BS, elem educ, 1969; Univ Pittsburgh, PA, grad studies, 1972, JD, 1975. **Career:** Pittsburgh Pub Schs, Pittsburgh, Pa, teacher, 1969-72; Col Arts & Scis, Univ Pittsburgh, acad adv, 1973-75; Neighborhood Legal Servs, Northside Off, staff atty, 1975-76; Pa Human Rels Comn, asst gen coun, 1976-77; Allegheny County Law Dept, asst county solicitor, 1977-90; self-employed lawyer, 1980-90; Allegheny County Disadvantaged & Women's Bus Enterprise Appeal Bd, admin hearing officer, 1988-90; Allegheny County Common Pleas Ct, Criminal Div, judge, 1990-92; Allegheny Co Crt Pleas, Family Div Juv Sec, judge, 1992-99; supv judge, 1999-2003; judge, 2003-; Pt Pk Univ, Criminal Justice Dept, assoc prof, 2001-06; Super Ct Pa, judge. **Orgs:** Bd mem, Pittsburgh Leadership Found; bd mem, Communities Schs; bd mem, Child Watch; bd mem, Lydia's Pl; bd mem, Theotherapy; Faith, Law & Morality Comt Nat Cncl Juv/Family Ct Judges; Juv Ct Judges Comn, PA Comn Crime & Delinq; Juv Ct Judges Comn; bd mem, Cornerstone Tv; Hosanna House; trustee, Waynesburg Univ; adv bd mem, Nat Regional Church CARE. **Honors/Awds:** Alumni of the Year, Univ Pittsburgh, 1999; Woman of the Year, Univ Pittsburgh, Women's Law Asn, 2002; Message Carriers 1st Annual Tree of Hope in Life Award, 2003; Jubilee Intl Ministries-Catalyst for Change Award; Every Child Permanency Award; Rankin Christian Center-Community Unity Service Award; Sojourner Award; 3 Rivers Youth Nellie Leadership Award; Juvenile Court Judges Commission Award, 2004; Women of Standard Award, Second Chance Inc, 2004; Pennsylvania Commission for Women's History Month Award, 2005; Tribute to Women Award, Greater Pittsburgh YWCA, 2006; Second Chance Inc, Woman of Standard Award; New Pittsburgh Couriers Women of Excellence Award, 2008; Pennsylvania Law Weekly Women of the Year, Legal Intelligencer, 2008; Celebrate & Share Woman of Achievement Honor Award, 2008. **Special Achievements:** The first black woman to serve on the state Supreme Ct; Univ PA Women's Law Asn Women Yr; University of Pittsburgh's Alumni of the Year. **Home Addr:** 1535 Fairmont St, Pittsburgh, PA 15221, **Home Phone:** (412)247-3530. **Business Addr:** Judge, Allegheny County Court Common Pleas, 3333 5th Ave, Pittsburgh, PA 15213, **Business Phone:** (412)578-8261.

## ALLEN, CHRIS

Health services administrator. **Personal:** children: 2. **Educ:** Wayne State Univ, BA, jour, 1976; Univ Mich, MA, health serv admin, 1980; Highland Park Community Col, AA, lib arts. **Career:** Detroit Osteop Hosp Corp, Oak Pk, Mich, exec asst; Detroit Osteop Hosp, Highland Pk, Mich, adminr; Hurley Med Ctr, Flint, Mich, asst dir; Detroit Med Ctr, Hutzel Hosp, exec vpres, vpres mgt serv, corp vpres mgt serv, 1989-91; Hutzel Womens Hosp, exec vpres, chief exec officer & chief operating officer, 1991-95; Health Authority, exec dir & chief exec officer; Health First Partners Inc, founder, pres & chief exec officer; Family Rd Care Ctrs, founder, pres & chief exec officer, 1995-; Detroit Wayne County Health Authority, exec dir & chief exec officer, currently. **Orgs:** Bd dir, Christus Health, 1999-; bd dir, Sisters Charity Health Care Syt; Nat Arthritis & Musculoskeletal & Skin Dis Adv Coun, Nat Insts Health, 2000-; bd dir, Am Nat Red Cross, currently; chair, Fache; bd mem, Cath Med Mission Bd; Michuhcan; fel, Am Col Health Care Execs; Am Red Cross; Cath Health Asn; Nat Arthritis Found. **Home Addr:** 16865 Edinborough Rd, Detroit, MI 48219, **Home Phone:** (313)794-5883. **Business Addr:** President, Chief Executive Officer, Family Road Care Centers, 19440 Bretton Dr, Detroit, MI 48223, **Business Phone:** (313)535-6009.

## ALLEN, DR. CLAUDE ALEXANDER, JR.

Government official, health services administrator. **Personal:** Born Oct 11, 1960, Philadelphia, PA; married Jannese Mitchell; children: Claude III, Lila-Cjoan & Christian Isaiah. **Educ:** Univ NC, BA, 1982; Duke Univ Law Sch, master, law, int & comparative law, JD, 1990. **Career:** Baker Botts Assoc, assoc, 1991-95; Va Off Atty Gen, coun gen, dep atty gen, 1995-98; Va state govt, secy health& human resources, 1998-2001; US Dept Health & Human Serv, dep secy, 2001; White House, Domestic Policy, asst to pres & dir, 2005-06. **Orgs:** Durham Guardian Ad Litem Program; bd dir, CARAMORE; Legal Coun Elderly & Street Law Program, DC; bd dir, Peacemaker Ministries Inc; Chi Psi Fraternity. **Home Addr:** 7217 Cliff Pine Dr, Gaithersburg, MD 20879-5703, **Home Phone:** (301)208-3769.

## ALLEN, CLYDE CECIL

Marketing executive, president (organization). **Personal:** Born Jan 29, 1943, Youngstown, OH; son of Eugene and Frances; married Gayle Thigpen; children: Michael Clyde & Brett Donaldo. **Educ:** Kent State Univ, BS, microbiol, 1965; Rutgers Univ, MS, indust rels, 1977. **Career:** Schering Corp, sr microbiologist, 1965-70, personnel admin, 1970-72; Ind Community Ctr, exec dir, 1972-74; Johnson & Johnson, sr personnel admin, 1974-75, sr comps admin, 1975-76, mgr, human resource planning, 1976-78; M & M Mars Inc, dir, compensation & benefits, 1978-80; JE Seagram Inc, corp mgr eeo, 1980-83, dir community rels, 1983-87, dir pub rels & event mkt, 1987-; Allen & Partners Inc, pres & founder, 1994-. **Orgs:** Chmn bd, exec dir, Nat Alliance Mkt Developers; chairs corp adv bd, Nat United Merchants Beverage Asn; Sigma Pi Phi Fraternity; Mu Boule Chap. **Business Addr:** President, Founder, Allen & Partners Inc, 620 Sheridan Ave, Plainfield, NJ 07060, **Business Phone:** (908)561-4062.

## ALLEN, DEBBIE (DEBORRAH KAYE ALLEN)

Actor, singer, dancer. **Personal:** Born Jan 16, 1950, Houston, TX; daughter of Arthur and Vivian Ayers; married Winfred Wilford; married Norman Nixon; children: Vivian Nicole & Norman Jr. **Educ:** Howard Univ, Sch Fine Arts, BA, hons, class greek lit, speech & drama, 1971. **Career:** Works: Ti-Jean & His Brothers, New York, 1972; Purlie, 1972; Raisin, 1973; Aint Misbehavin, 1978; The Illusion & Holiday, 1979; West Side Story, 1980; Louis, 1981; The Song is Kern, 1981; Parade of Stars Playing the Palace, 1983; Sweet Charity, 1986; JoJo Dancer, 1985; Brothers of the Knight, 1998; Pearl, 2003; "Fame", choreographer, 1982-87, 2003; "A Different World", 1988-93; "In the House", 1995; "The Debbie Allen Show", 1989; "Sunday in Paris", 1991; "The Old Settler", PBS, 2001; Amistad, exec producer, 1997; Harriet's Return, play, 1998; Ragtime; Michael Jordan: An American Hero, 1999; The Old Settler, 2001; Debbie Allen Dance Acad, Los Angeles, CA, artistic dir, founder & owner, 2001-; C's Musical, Pearl, writer, dir & choreographer, 2003; "All of Us", 2004; Tournament of Dreams, 2006; Tournament of Dreams, 2007; Confessions of an Action Star, 2008; Next Day Air, 2008; Fame; 2009. Director: "Fame", 1982-87; Family Ties; 1982; Polly, 1989; Fresh Prince of Bel Air, 1990; Stompin at the Savoy, 1992; Girlfriends; The Sinbad Show, 1993; Between Brothers, 1997; Cool Women, 2000; "The Old Settler", 2001; Everybody Hates Chris; Life Is Not A Fairy Tale; That's So Raven; A Different World; The Fresh Prince of Bel-Air; Family Ties; "The Game", 2008. Flim: The Fish That Saved Pittsburgh, 1979; Jo Jo Dancer, Your Life is Calling, 1986; Blank Check, 1994; Mona Must Die, 1994; Out of Sync, 1995; Everythings Jake, 2000; All About You, 2001; The Painting, 2002; Director: Hellcats; Greys Anatomy, 2005-13; The Parkers; The Twilight Zone; Polly: Coming Home; Family Ties; The Fresh Prince of Bel-Air; A Different World; The Jamie Foxx Show; That's So Raven; Life Is Not a Fairy Tale; All of Us; Everybody Hates Chris; Girlfriends. **Orgs:** Actors Equity Asn; Screen Actors Guild; Am Fedn TV & Radio Artists; founder, Debbie Allen Dance Inst; Delta Sigma Theta Sorority Inc. **Business Addr:** Founder, Artistic Director, Debbie Allen Dance Academy, 3791 Santa Rosalia Dr, Los Angeles, CA 90008, **Business Phone:** (310)280-9145.

## ALLEN, DR. EDNA ROWERY

School administrator, educator. **Personal:** Born Jul 20, 1938, Carrollton, AL; married Robert H; children: Robin, Dawn & Robert Jr. **Educ:** Lincoln Univ, BS, coun, 1960; Univ Ill, MS, counr educ, 1970, cert, admin; Edward sville Ill, attended 1974; McMurray Col, Doctor Humanities hon degree, 1983. **Career:** Rock Jr Higher Sec Sch, teacher, 1962-70, counr, 1970-71; E St Louis Libr Bd, dir gifted prog, 1971-. **Orgs:** Chmn, social action, Delta Sigma Theta Sorority Inc; bd dir, Nat Asn Gifted C, 1973-83; bd dir, E St Louis Pub Libr, 1974-83; bd trustee, State Comn, Col E St Louis, 1975-78, 1985-99; pres, St Ann's Sodality St Patrick's Ch; vpres, Concerned Citizens Comn; chmn, social action, Top Ladies Distinction; chmn, Status Women Comn; Top Ladies Distinction; Phi Delta Kappa; E St. Louis Bd Election Commissioners, vice chmn, currently. **Honors/Awds:** Service Award, State Comn Col, 1978; Merit Award, ML King Jr High Sch, ESt Louis, 1979; Recognition Award, Delta Sigma Theta Sorority Inc, 1984; Hon Doctorate, Mac Murray Col, Jacksonville, Ill, 1983. **Home Addr:** 664 N 33rd St, East St. Louis, IL 62205. **Business Addr:** Vice Chairman, East St Louis Board of Election Commissioners, 301 River Pk Dr Suite 300, East St. Louis, IL 62201, **Business Phone:** (618)482-6672.

## ALLEN, EUGENE, JR.

President (organization), chief executive officer, executive. **Personal:** Born Nov 7, 1937, Chicago, IL; son of Eugene Sr and Pearl; married Ledell Fields; children: Sheryl, Karla, Nicole & Eugene III. **Educ:** Ill Inst Technol, BS, 1969; Univ Chicago Grad Sch, MBA, 1976. **Career:** LSherwin-Williams Co, paint technologist, chemist, 1963-67; Libby McNeil & Libby, mat mgr, engr, 1967-69; Avon Prod Inc, div mgr, 1969-76; Hub States Corp, sr vpres, 1976-79; Clinitemp Inc, pres, 1979-81; Aquamint Labs Inc, pres, chief exec officer, 1981-; Allen Industs Inc, chmn, pres & chief exec officer, 1981-; Allen Chem Inc, pres, 1989-; Consol Cleaning Systs Inc, pres, 1990-. **Orgs:** Chmn bd, Indianapolis Bus Develop, 1986-90; bd mem, Jr Achievement, 1986-96; bd mem, Dist Export Coun, 1979-91. **Home Addr:** 10615 Stormhaven Way, Indianapolis, IN 46256-9524, **Home Phone:** (317)842-2272. **Business Addr:** Chairman, President, Allen Industries Inc, 6874 Hawthorn Pk Dr, Indianapolis, IN 46220-3909, **Business Phone:** (317)595-0730.

## ALLEN, DR. GLORIA MARIE

Physician, pediatrician. **Personal:** Born Washington, DC; daughter of Archie and Viola Childs; married William Henry Toles; children: William Henry III & Allen Wesley. **Educ:** Howard Univ, BS, 1947, Med Sch, MD, 1951. **Career:** Harlem Hosp, asst attend physician, 1954-56; Jamaica Hosp, asst attend physician, 1963-; Carter Comm Health Ctr, chief pediat, 1974-85; Linden Cs Servs, pvt med pract physician, 1985-. **Orgs:** Med Soc Co Queens, 1964-; pres, Omega Wives Long Island, 1964-; Delta Sigma Theta Sorority, 1964-; bd dir, Queens Urban League, 1970-; nom comt, Young Men's Christian Asn New York, 1974-75; secy, Empire State Med Asn, 1975-; chmn, Merrick Young Men's Young Women's Christian Asn Day Care Ctr, 1975-77; treas & charter mem, Susan S McKinney Smith Med Soc, 1976-; Clin Soc Queens & Long Island. **Honors/Awds:** Woman's World Award, Bethel Temple, 1958; Senior Youth Community Award, Queens Young Women's Christian Asn, 1973; Community Award, Queens Fresh Air Fund, 1978; Appointed by Mayor Koch, Comnr Comn Status Women, 1979. **Home Addr:** 10427 192nd St, Jamaica, NY 11412-1160, **Home Phone:** (718)479-3135. **Business Addr:** Physician, Linden Childrens Services, 14504 97th Ave, Jamaica, NY 11435-4426, **Business Phone:** (718)657-6085.

## ALLEN, HERBERT J.

Social worker. **Personal:** Born May 19, 1922, Jersey City, NJ; son of Benjamin and Jeanetta Casey; children: Deborah. **Educ:** Univ Cincinnati Teachers Col, BS, 1946; Case Western Res Univ, MSSW, 1948; Nat Cincinnati, admin & mgmt Training Prog. **Career:** Ohio State Univ, Sch Soc Work, clin instr; Cincinnati Gen Hosp, sr caseworker; Montgomery City Child Welfare Bd, supvr, 1952-64; Barney C Med Ctr, dir social serv, 1964-66; Good Samaritan Hosp, dir soc serv, 1966-67; Univ Cincinnati Med Ctr, adj assoc prof, dir soc work, 1970-89; Human Resources, asst adminr, 1990-. **Orgs:** Acad Cert Soc Workers; pres, Miami Valley Chap Dayton Nat Asn Social Workers, 1969; pres, Ohio Valley Chap Nat Asn Soc Workers, 1972-74; chmn, Community Action Comn, 1974-77; trustee, Cent Community Health Bd Hamilton City Inc, 1976-77; Soc Serv, Asn Gr Cincinnati; pres, Child Health Asn; pres, Mt Auburn Health Ctr, 1975-; Manpower Serv Adv Coun City Cincinnati, 1975-; Cincinnati Gen Hosp Med Audit Comt, 1975; Col Med Expanded Deans Conf, 1977; pres, Ohio Valley Chap; soc dir, Hosp Soc Work Depts. **Honors/Awds:** Certificate of Outstanding Social Worker Year, Nat Asn Soc Workers, 1973; Award Gold Medal, Cincinnati Gen Hosp Emp Arts & Crafts, 1973; CertificateLeadership Training Prog, Soc Workers Mental Health Nat Asn Soc Workers, 1974; nominee, Soc Worker Year, 1974; Certificate of Appreciation, Mt Auburn Community Coun, 1975; Certificate of Appreciation, Lincoln Heights Health Ctr Inc, 1975; Merit Award Gold Medal, 1975; nominee, Outstanding Citizen Award, 1976; University of Cincinnati Humanitarian Award, 1990; Community Service Award, Kappa Alpha Psi, Cincinnati AlumniChapter, 1990. **Home Addr:** 144 Dorsey St, Cincinnati, OH 45202, **Home Phone:** (513)381-0062.

## ALLEN, DR. HERMAN

President (organization), dentist. **Career:** Pvt pract, dentist. **Orgs:** Nat Dent Asn; pres, Dade County Dent Soc. **Home Addr:** 921 NW 35th Ave, Lauderhill, FL 33311, **Home Phone:** (954)584-9694. **Business Addr:** Dentist, President, Dade County Dental Society,

2323 NW 19 St Suite 1, Ft. Lauderdale, FL 33311, **Business Phone:** (954)484-8780.

### ALLEN, JACOB BENJAMIN, III
Counselor. **Personal:** Born Sep 20, 1927, Raleigh, NC; son of Jacob Benjamin Jr and Fannie Williams; married Shirley K. **Educ:** Shaw Univ, attended 1955; Springfield Col, grad cert, 1962. **Career:** NC Dept Voc Rehab, Human Resources Dept; NC Dept Ment Health; Patterson Ave Br Young Men's Christian Asn; Voc Eval Facil, voc rehab counr, currently. **Orgs:** Nat Black Achievers Asn; Raleigh Mayor's Eastside Neighborhood Task Force; Shaw Univ Alumni Asn; NC Rehab Counr Asn; AEAONMS Inc, Prince Hall Shrine; comdr chief, Boyer Consistory No 219; United Supreme Coun Ancient & Accepted Scottis Rite Masonary 33 Degree; chair, exec bd, Garner Rd Family Young Men's Christian Asn; NC State Employees Asn; ruling elder, Davie St Presby Church; chmn & potentates, Kabala Temple No 177, AEANMS Inc. **Special Achievements:** Achieved independent status as a counselor. **Home Addr:** 2509 Firelight Rd, Raleigh, NC 27610-5813, **Home Phone:** (919)828-6854.

### ALLEN, JAMES
Football player. **Personal:** Born Mar 28, 1975, Wynnewood, OK; children: Hayden. **Educ:** Univ Okla, grad. **Career:** Football player (retired); Chicago Bears, running back, 1998-2001; Houston Texans, running back, 2002; sports trainer. **Home Addr:** , Houston, TX.

### ALLEN, JERRY ORMES
Lawyer. **Personal:** Born Dec 16, 1953, Cleveland, OH; son of Luther Ormes and Netty L Cooper; married Jacqueline L; children: Danielle Y & Jerry Ormes II. **Educ:** Capital Univ, BA, gen, bus admin & mgt, 1975; Capital Univ Law Sch, JD, 1984; NY Univ Law Sch, LLM, taxation, 1987. **Career:** Chief Coun, IRS, staff atty, 1984-86; Bricker & Eckler, partner, atty, 1987-. **Orgs:** Nat Bar Asn; co-chair, Am Bar Asn; Ohio Bar Asn; Columbus Bar Asn; bd pres, Martin Luther King Arts Complex; past trustee, bd mem, trustee, Columbus Zoo; bd mem, pres, Hospice Riverside Hosp; bd mem, vice chmn, Greater Columbus Arts Coun; bd trustee, Columbus Mus Art; bd coun, Capital Univ Law Sch; bd trustee, New Albany Community Arts Ctr; bd trustee, Columbus Col Art & Design; mem bd dir, Ohio Asn Nonprofit Orgn; mem bd dir, Jeanne B. McCoy Community Ctr Arts. **Honors/Awds:** Recipient, Community Service Award, Columbus Bar Asn, 1996; Listed in Best Lawyers in America, 2005-13; David D. White Award, Capital Univ Law Sch, 2013; Columbus Lawyer of the Year, Best Lawyers in America, 2014. **Special Achievements:** Author, "Taxation of Investment Income From Offshore Trusts and Other Foreign Entities", Offshore Finance USA, 1999; "Residency of Asset Protection Trusts: IRS Issues New Regulations", Offshore Finance USA, 1999; "Look Before You Leap - The Tax Consequences of Golden Parachute Payments", International Legal Strategy, 2000; "Solving The Low Income Tax Credit Housing Partnership Dilemma", Exempt Organization Tax Review, 2005; "Helping Physicians Obtain Medical Malpractice Insurance Furthers Charitable Purposes, IRS Rules," Exempt Organization Tax Review. **Home Addr:** 3751 Prestwould Close, New Albany, OH 43054, **Home Phone:** (614)933-0066. **Business Addr:** Partner, Bricker & Eckler, 100 S 3rd St, Columbus, OH 43215-4291, **Business Phone:** (614)227-8834.

### ALLEN, KAREN B.
Manager, vice president (organization). **Career:** Comerica Bank, vpres & civic affairs mgr, currently. **Special Achievements:** First vice president of Civic Affairs in Comerica Bank history. **Business Addr:** Vice President of Civic Affairs, Comerica Bank, 188 N Old Woodward, Birmingham, MI 48009-3371, **Business Phone:** (248)544-9955.

### ALLEN, DR. KAREN M.
Administrator, educator, nursing home administrator. **Personal:** Born Aug 31, 1956, Ypsilanti, MI; daughter of George Moses Jr and Claudia M Moses; married Clifford L; children: Claudia & Clifford Jr. **Educ:** Andrews Univ, BS, nursing, 1979, MS, nursing admin, 1983; Univ Ill, Chicago, PhD, nursing sci, 1992; RN, FAAN. **Career:** US Ctr Substance Abuse Treat, res consult; Univ MD, asst & assoc prof; Andrews Univ, fac, 1988, prof nursing, chair nursing dept & dir DNP progs, currently. **Orgs:** Pres, Int & Nat Nurses Soc Addictions, 1996-2000; fel Am Acad Nurses; Sigma Theta Tau Int Nursing; Phi Kappa Phi, Nat Hon Soc; Ed adv bd, US Substance Abuse & Ment Health Serv Admin's Ctr Substance Abuse Treat; adv coun; Treat Improv Protocols; Nat Coord Ctr Off Addiction Technol Transfer Centers; Ed Adv Bd, US Substance Abuse & Ment Health Serv. **Special Achievements:** Books: Nursing Care of the Addicted Client; Women's Health Across the Lifespan: A Comprehensive Perspective. **Home Addr:** 4137 Courtney St, St. Joseph, MI 49085-9678, **Home Phone:** (269)556-0394. **Business Addr:** Professor of Nursing, Chair of Graduate Nursing Program, Andrews University, Marsh Hall Rm 200 100 US 31, Berrien Springs, MI 49104-0200, **Business Phone:** (269)471-3364.

### ALLEN, LARRY CHRISTOPHER, JR.
Football player. **Personal:** Born Nov 27, 1971, Los Angeles, CA; married Janelle; children: Jayla, Loriana & Larry III. **Educ:** Sonoma State Univ, attended 1994. **Career:** Football player (retired); Dallas Cowboys, guard, right tackle, 1994, right guard, 1995-97, left tackle, 1998, left guard, 1999-2001, 2003-05, left guard & right tackle, 2002; San Francisco 49ers, guard & left guard, 2006-07. **Honors/Awds:** NFL 1990s All-Decade Team, All-Rookie Team, 1994; Pro Bowl, 1995-07; All-Pro selection, 1995-01; Strongest Man Award, ESPN, 2006; Super Bowl champion; Dallas Cowboys Ring of Honor, 2011; Pro Football Hall of Fame, Nat Football League, 2013.

### ALLEN, LECESTER L.
School administrator. **Personal:** Born Feb 27, 1944, Pickens, AR; son of Joe and Rebecca; married Mattie; children: Dana Nicole & Aaron Matthew. **Educ:** Wayne State Univ, BS, 1966, pursuing MA. **Career:** Do Re Mi Learning Ctrs, chief exec officer; Acad Detroit Sch, pres, currently. **Orgs:** Pres, Mich Asn Childcare Ctrs, 1974-80; pres, Optimist Club Cent Det, 1976-77; chmn summer funding comn, United Comn Servs, 1979-82; pres, Booker T Wash Bus Asn, 1980-82; pres, Don Bosco Home Boys, 1982-86; co-chair/funding mem, Citizens Better Gov, 1982-; Mich State Job Training Coun, Appt Govr Mich, 1983-85; pres, Lawton Sch; pres, Charter Sch Admin Serv; bd mem, nominating com, Metrop YMCA, 1988-. **Home Addr:** 45 Orchard Lane, Bloomfield Hills, MI 48304, **Home Phone:** (810)642-7101. **Business Addr:** President, Academy of Detroit Schools, 18330 George Wash Dr, Southfield, MI 48075, **Business Phone:** (248)569-7787.

### ALLEN, MARCUS LEMARR
Football player, sports manager. **Personal:** Born Mar 26, 1960, San Diego, CA; son of Harold and Gwendolyn; married Kathryn. **Educ:** Univ Southern Calif. **Career:** Football player (retired), sports executive; Los Angeles Raiders, running back, 1982-92; Kansas City Chiefs, running back, 1993-97; CBS Sports, commentator, studio analyst; Nat Football League Network, analyst, currently. **Orgs:** Spokesperson, Ronald McDonald Children's Charities; Laureus World Sports Acad, 2007. **Honors/Awds:** Chic Harley Award, Nat Col Athletic Asn, 1981; Maxwell Award, Nat Col Athletic Asn, 1981; TSN Player of the Year, 1981; College Player of the Year, Walter Camp, Maxwell Club & Football News, 1981; Walter Camp Award, Nat Col Athletic Asn, 1981; Unanimous All-American, 1981; Player of the Year, United Press Int, 1981; Heisman Trophy, 1981; Pac-10 Player of the Year, 1981; Pro Bowl, 1982, 1984, 1985, 1986, 1987, 1993; Rookie of the Year, National Football League, 1982; Most Valuable Player, Super Bowl, 1983; Chief Most Valuable Player, National Football League, 1985; Most Valuable Player, Prof Football Writers Asn & Asniated Press; Player of the Year, Sporting News & Football News, 1981; College Football Hall of Fame, 2000; Missouri Sports Hall of Fame, 2001; Offensive Player of the Year, United Press Int; National Football League Hall of Fame, 2003; Price water house Coopers Doak Walker Legends Award, 2007. **Special Achievements:** Executive producer for a film, Searching for Angela Shelton, 2004. **Home Addr:** , Kansas City, MT. **Business Addr:** Commentator, CBS Sports, 7800 Beverly Blvd, Los Angeles, CA 90036.

### ALLEN, MARK S.
Government official, executive, association executive. **Personal:** Born Mar 18, 1962, Chicago, IL; son of Minor Sr and Ollie; children: DaNia & Markus. **Educ:** Western Ill Univ, BA, mass commun, 1986. **Career:** Citizen Action-Midwest Acad, asst, nat co-dir, 1986-87; Push Excellence, Chicago Off, proj dir, 1987-88; Jesse Jackson Pres 88, nat youth coordr & nat field staff, 1988; Oper Push, interim chief staff & spec proj coordr, 1988-89; Chicago Urban League, voter educ & govt rels specialists, 1989-92; Chicago Rehab Network, field coordr, 1993; Ill Dept Human Rights, human rights investr, 1994-; Rainbow & PUSH, field dir, 1995-2003; Chicago Communicator, independent consult newspaper columnist; AJ Wright & Assocs Ltd, field dir, currently; S St J Newspaper, Assoc Ed, 2006-. **Orgs:** Task Force Black Polit Empowerment, 1986-; Kappa Alpha Psi Fraternity, 1987; founder & pres, Black Leadership Devel Inst, 1989-; local coordr, Nat Coalition Black Voter Participation, 1989-; vice chair, Chicago Sch Bd Nominating Comn, 1989-; Black elected Officials Ill, 1990-; Chicago Urban Policy Inst, 1991. **Honors/Awds:** America's Best & Brightest, Dollars & Sense Mag, 1989; Man of the Year, United Am Progress Asn, 1989; Kool Achiever Awards, Chicago Area Finalist, 1990; Community Service Award, Monroe Found, 1994; Outstanding Young Men of America. **Special Achievements:** Voices of the Electorate, Nat PBS TV Documentary on 92 Presidential Elections; Analyst, Live Broadcast "Front and Center" Chicagoland TV News on Urban Violence, 1994; Co-host/urban affairs correspondent, "Omnibus Roundtable", Chicago Cable Access; Motivational speaker/trainer. **Home Addr:** 2800 W Seipp, Chicago, IL 60652, **Home Phone:** (773)925-4797. **Business Addr:** Associate Editor, The South Street Journal Newspaper, 449 E 35th St, Chicago, IL 60616, **Business Phone:** (312)624-8351.

### ALLEN, MARTHA
State government official. **Educ:** Chicago Teachers Col, BS; Northwestern Univ, Medill Sch Jour, MS, jour. **Career:** Chicago pub sch, teacher; Chicago Reporter, journ, 1985-86; Channel 2 Anchorman Walter Jacobson, investigative prod, 1986-89; Channel 2 Political Ed Mike Flannery, political prod, 1989-92; Dept C & Family Servs, chief commun, 1993-97; Ill Dept Human Serv, press secy, 1997-99; Dept C & Family Servs, dir external affairs, 1999, chief staff, 2001-07. **Orgs:** Nat co-chair, Am Pub Human Serv Asn's Child Welfare Task Force, 2000. **Business Addr:** IL.

### ALLEN, MARVA
Executive, vice president (organization). **Personal:** Born Feb 21, 1954, Sav-LaMar; daughter of Enid Moulton and Hedley Moulton; children: Kenneth R. **Educ:** Staffordshire Gen Infirmary, Eng, BS, biol, 1975; Univ Mich, BS, biol, 1979; Univ Detroit, MS, bus & health admin, 1982. **Career:** Author; Univ Mich Hosp, nurse, 1975-76; Upjohn Pharmaceut, res, 1977-80; Girlstown Found, med coordr, 1980-82; Universal Solutions Inc, pres, exec vpres & co-founder, co-owner; Hue-Man Bookstore & Cafe, founder & owner, chief exec officer, managing partner & co-owner, 2004-. Books: Protegee, 1993; Camouflage, 2000, If I Should Die Tonight. **Orgs:** Nat Asn Women Bus Owners; bd trustee, St Francis Assisi Sch; Eastern Mich Univ, Hospitaliy Comt; Women Corp Bds Comt; dir, Melvin Van Peebles Found; bd dir, LitWorld, mem bd trustee, St Hope Leadership Acad; mem bd trustee, Riverside Theater Oppressed, mem bd trustee, Neighborhood Charter Sch. **Business Addr:** Managing Partner, Hue-Man Bookstore and Cafe, 2319 Frederick Douglass Blvd, New York, NY 10027, **Business Phone:** (212)665-7400.

### ALLEN, DR. MAXINE BOGUES
School administrator. **Personal:** Born Jul 31, 1942, Portsmouth, VA; daughter of Raymond A Bogues (deceased) and Essie M Kemp; married George Stanley; children: Vanya A Belk. **Educ:** Norfolk State Univ, BS, 1966; Hampton Univ, MA, 1972; Va Polytech Inst & State Univ, EdD, 1976. **Career:** School administrator (retired); Portsmouth City Schs, math dept, head, 1966-74; Norfolk State Univ, prof math, 1976-79, dir, instnl res & planning, 1980, dir, inst res AA/EEO, 1980-86, exec asst, pres, dir instr sch, 1986-87, assoc vpres acad affairs, 1987, vice-chmn bd. **Orgs:** Alpha Kappa Alpha Sorority, 1974; consult, A&T Univ, 1978-79; consult, Inst Serv Educ, 1982; bd trustee, SE Univ Res Assoc, 1984; pres, Suffolk Chap Links Inc, 1985-92; bd dir, WHRO Educ TV, 1986-92; vice chair schbd, Suffolk City, 1986-92; Moles Inc, 1990-. **Honors/Awds:** Presidential Citation, Asn Equal Opportunity, 1988; Administrator of the Year, Norfolk State Univ, 1996. **Home Addr:** 12760 Indian Rocks Rd, Largo, FL 33774-2300, **Home Phone:** (727)595-7378.

### ALLEN, DR. MITCHELL
Educator. **Educ:** Tex Southern Univ, BS; Prairie View A&M Univ, MS; Univ Houston, EdD, 1978. **Career:** Tex Southern Univ, Col Sci & Technol, assoc prof technol & interim dean, currently. **Orgs:** Am Coun Indust Arts Teacher Educ; Am Design & Drafting Asn; Epsilon PiTau; Nat Asn Indust Technol; bd mgr, Alief YMCA; trustee, Gamma Pi Chap Epsilon Pi Tau; Strategic Planning Steering Comt, Tex Southern Univ. **Business Addr:** Interim Dean, Associate Professor, Texas Southern University, 3100 Cleburne St, Houston, TX 77004, **Business Phone:** (713)313-7071.

### ALLEN, NANCY A.
Executive. **Career:** Urban Solutions Inc, founder, bd dir & pres, currently. **Orgs:** Prog chair, Fashion Extravaganza, March Dimes; exec dir, Charles H Wright Mus African Am Hist; NY Asn HIV over Fifty. **Home Addr:** 4708 Bedford St, Detroit, MI 48224, **Home Phone:** (313)640-1324. **Business Addr:** Founder, President & Board of Director, Urban Solutions Inc, 269 Walker St Suite 124, Detroit, MI 48101, **Business Phone:** (313)567-2251.

### ALLEN, OTTIS EUGENE, JR.
College administrator, librarian. **Personal:** Born Feb 2, 1953, Fletcher, NC; son of Georgia Bradley and Eugene; married Vanessa R Northcutt; children: Dawn, Ottis III & Eboni. **Educ:** Appalachian State Univ, BA, sociol, 1975, MA, educ media, 1976. **Career:** Coun Ministries United Methodist Church, field coord, 1981; Radio Shack Corp, salesman, 1982-; Spartanburg Methodist Col, asst librn, dir, audio-visual serv, assoc librn & dir multimedia serv, currently. **Orgs:** SC Libr Asn, 1977-; Allocation Comt United Way Piedmont; Piedmont Libr Asn, 1980-; Mt Moriah Baptist Church, 1980-; chmn, Sound Comm Mt Moriah Baptist Church, 1983-2004; bd trustee, Mt Moriah Baptist Church, 1983-; United Way Allocation Community Spartanburg, 1986-; Epsilon Nu Chap Omega Psi Phi Fraternity, 1987-; pres, PTA Jesse Bobo Elem; Spartanburg Human Rels Community, 1999; vice chmn bd, Zoning appeals, Spartanburg, SC, 2002. **Home Addr:** 208 Sheffield Dr, Spartanburg, SC 29301-1314, **Home Phone:** (864)574-0700. **Business Addr:** Associate Librarian, Director Multimedia Services, Spartanburg Methodist College, 1000 Powell Mill Rd, Spartanburg, SC 29301, **Business Phone:** (864)587-4248.

### ALLEN, PERCY, II
Hospital administrator, executive. **Personal:** Born Apr 7, 1941, New Orleans, LA; son of Esther Anderson and Percy Sr; married Zennia Marie McKnight; children: Merrily Marie Littlejohn & Percy III; married Fay Malcolm. **Educ:** Delgado Trade & Tech Inst, attended 1965; Oakland Univ, Rochester, MI, BA, econ, 1973; Cornell Univ, Grad Sch Bus & Pub Admin, MPA, 1975. **Career:** Executive, Hosp Administrator (retired); Gr New Mt Moriah Baptist Church, Detroit, Mich, youth dir, summer camp founder & dir, 1968-74; Chrysler Corp, Detroit, Mich, qual control supvr, 1968-70; Oakland Univ, Rochester, Mich, residence hall dir, 1972-73; Cornell Univ, Ithaca, NY, prog consult, 1973-75; Parkview Memorial Hosp, Ft Wayne, Ind, asst hosp adminr, 1975; Nat Urban League Black Exec Exchange Prog, Vis Prof, 1978-92; Sinai Hosp, asst adminr, 1982-85; New York Health & Hosps Corp, 1986-89; Univ Hosp Brooklyn, chief exec officer & vpres hosp affairs, 1989-99; Bon Secours Baltimore Health Syst Inc, chief exec officer, 1999-2006. **Orgs:** First vpres, Ft Wayne Urban Leag, 1976-; bd mem, Am Cancer Soc, 1977-; exec comt, NE Ind Emergency Med Serv Comn, 1977-; Emrgcy Med Serv Comn Ind Hosp Asn, 1978-; first vpres Allen Co Oppor Indstrlztn Ctr, 1978-; bd mem, United Way Allen Co, 1979-; Counc Health Care Dlvry Syst Ind Hosp Asn, 1979-; pres, Nat Asn Health Serv Execs; fel Am Col Healthcare Execs; prog develop comt mem, Greater New York Hosp Asn; bd mem, Col S Brooklyn Houses Inc; bd trustee, Mt Moriah Baptist Church. **Home Addr:** 250 S President St Apt 1104, Baltimore, MD 21202.

### ALLEN, QUINCY L.
Executive. **Personal:** Born Mar 28, 1960, Quonset Point, RI. **Educ:** Northeastern Univ, BS, elec engineering, 1982; Univ Rochester, MBA, 1993. **Career:** Xerox Corp, elec engr, 1982, Worldwide Customer Serv Strategy, vpres, 1999, N Am Serv & Solutions, sr vpres, 2001-03, Xerox Bus Group Opers, sr vpres, 2003-04, corp vpres, bd dir, 2004-, vpres, Xerox Prod Syst Group, pres, 2004-09, pres, global bus & strategic mkt group, 2009-; Gateway Inc, bd dir, 2006-; Worldwide Customer Serv Strategy, vpres; Prod Systs Group, pres; NCR Corp, dir, 2009-12; Global Bus & Strategic Mkt Group, pres; Vertis Inc, chief exec officer, 2009-10; Vertis Holdings Inc, chief exec officer & pres, 2010; Unisys Corp, chief mkt & strategy officer & sr vpres, 2012-. **Orgs:** Dir, mem spec comt, mem corp governance & nominating comt, Gateway Inc, 2006-; bd mem, Nat Action Coun Minorities Engineering Inc; bd mem, Electronic Doc Systs Found; trustee, Northeastern Univ. **Business Addr:** Unisys Corp, 801 Lakeview Dr Suite 100, Blue Bell, PA 19422, **Business Phone:** (215)986-4011.

### ALLEN, QUINCY L.
Chief executive officer, president (organization), vice president (organization). **Educ:** Northeastern Univ, BS, elec engineering, 1982; Univ Rochester, MBA, mkt & entrepreneurship, 1993. **Career:** Xerox, elec engr, 1982, sr tech & mgt staff, pres, Worldwide Customer Serv Strategy, vpres, 1999, Bus Group Opers, sr vpres, 2003-04, corp vpres, 2004, Prod Systs Group, pres, 2004-09, Global Bus & Strategic Mkt Group, pres, 2009-; N Am Serv & Solutions, sr vpres, 2001-03; Gateway Inc, dir, 2006-; Vertis Commun, chief exec officer, 2009-10; Unisys, sr vpres, chief mkt & strategy officer, 2012-. **Orgs:** Bd mem, Nat Action Coun Minorities Engineering Inc; bd mem, Electronic Doc Systs Found; bd dir, IBM; dir, NCR Corp, 2009-12; trustee, Northeastern Univ. **Honors/Awds:** "Black Enterprise," The 100 Most Powerful Executives in Corporate America, 2010. **Business Addr:** Chief Mar-

keting and Strategy Officer, Unisys, 11720 Plaza America Dr, Reston, VA 20190, **Business Phone:** (703)439-5000.

## ALLEN, ROBERT G.

Law enforcement officer. **Career:** Captain (retired); City Indianapolis Police Dept, asst police chief, capt. **Business Addr:** Captain, City of Indianapolis Police Department, 50 N Ala St, Indianapolis, IN 46204, **Business Phone:** (317)327-3911.

## ALLEN, ROBERT LEE

Editor, writer, teacher. **Personal:** Born May 29, 1942, Atlanta, GA; son of Robert Lee and Sadie Sims; married Janet Carter; married Pamela Parker; children: Casey Douglass. **Educ:** Univ Vienna, attended 1962; Morehouse Col, BS, 1963; Columbia Univ, attended 1964; New Sch Social Res, New York, NY, MA, 1967; Univ Calif, San Francisco, CA, PhD, sociol, 1983. **Career:** Guardian Newsweekly NYC, staff reporter, 1967-69; San Jose State Col, asst prof new col & black studies dept, 1969-72; Black Scholar Mag, ed; Mills Col, Oakland, CA, from lectr to asst prof ethnic studies, 1973-84; Guggenheim fel, 1977; Wild Trees Press, gen mgr, 1984-90; Black Scholar, sr ed, 1990-; Univ Calif-Berkeley, African Am Studies & Ethnic Studies, vis prof, 1994-2003, adj full prof, 2003-; Author: Black Awakening in Capitalist Amer, Doubleday, 1969; A Guide to Black Power in America: An Historical Analysis, 1970; Reluctant Reformers, The Impact of Racism on Amer Social Reform Movements, Howard Univ Press, 1983; contributor to periodicals; The Port Chicago Mutiny, Warner Books, 1989; Brotherman Ballantine, co-editor, 1999; Strong in the Struggle: My Life as a Black Labor Activist, co-author, 2001; Honoring Sergeant Carter, HarperCollins, co-author, 2003. **Orgs:** Vpres, Black World Found; Am Sociol Asn; Am Hist & Cult Soc; Asn Black Sociologists; Pac Sociol Asn; Coun Black Studies; Bay Area Black Journalists; bd mem, Oakland Mens Proj, 1986-96; bd mem, San Francisco Bk Coun; adv bd, Family Violence Prev Fund, 1998-; adv bd, San Francisco Writers Corps, 1999-; adv comm, African Am Fac Oral Hist Proj, UC Berkeley, 2002-. **Home Addr:** 1130 3rd Ave suite 1104, Oakland, CA 94606. **Business Addr:** Professor Emeritus, University of California, Berkeley, CA 94720.

## ALLEN, RON

Journalist, broadcaster. **Personal:** Born Jan 1, 1957, Jersey City, NJ; son of Lindsay L Jr and Shirley; married Adaora Udoji, Oct 5, 2002; children: 1. **Educ:** Univ Pa, BA, polit sci, MA, Am govt & polit, 1979. **Career:** CBS News, nat corresp, 1988-92; ABC News, foreign corresp, 1992-96; NBC News, corresp, 1996-. **Orgs:** Bd Overseas Press Club; Leadership Coun Comt to Protect Journalists; Univ Pa Bd Overseers. **Honors/Awds:** Six Overseas Press Club Awards; Five Emmys; Two Robert F. Kennedy Awards; Two George Foster Peabody Awards; Two Alfred I. DuPont-Columbia Awards; National Association of Black Journalists, Journalist of the Year, 1996.

## ALLEN, ROSCOE, JR.

Business owner. **Career:** Roscoe Allen Co, chief exec officer, owner & pres, currently. **Honors/Awds:** Georgia Small Business Person of the Year, 1998; Nat Small Business Person of the Year, 1998; Cong Rec Recognition; Featured in numerous books and magazines including Black Enterprise Mag & Ga Trend. **Home Addr:** Pine Hill Ests, Douglas, GA 31533, **Home Phone:** (912)384-8465. **Business Addr:** Owner, President, Roscoe Allen Co, 213 Alapaha Hwy, Ocilla, GA 31774-2339, **Business Phone:** (229)468-9540.

## ALLEN, S. MONIQUE NICOLE (S MONIQUE ALLEN)

Publisher. **Personal:** Born Dec 20, 1964, New York, NY; daughter of Charles and Sallie Tucker. **Educ:** Princeton Univ, Princeton, NJ, AB, 1986. **Career:** Tucker Publs Inc, Lisle, IL, ed, 1989-. **Orgs:** Rec secy, Links. **Home Addr:** 1600 Hinman Ave 1B, Evanston, IL 60201, **Home Phone:** (708)969-3809. **Business Addr:** Editor, Tucker Publications, 5823 Queens Cove, Lisle, IL 60532-0580, **Business Phone:** (630)969-0221.

## ALLEN, SAMUEL WASHINGTON. See Obituaries Section.

## ALLEN, SANFORD

Violinist. **Personal:** Born Feb 26, 1939, New York, NY; married Madhur Jaffrey. **Educ:** Juilliard Sch Music; Mannes Col Music. **Career:** Rutgers Univ, Livingston Col, fac mem; NY Philharmonic, violinist, 1962; Columbia Co's Leaf Peeper Ser, Clarion Concerts, dir, currently; Albums: The Many Facets Of David Newman, 1969; Chap Two, 1970; A New Era, 1971; Soul Is... Pretty Purdie, 1972; Exten Of A Man, 1973; Prepare Thyself To Deal With A Miracle, 1973; Song Of The New World, 1973; Felix Cavaliere, 1974; 10 Yrs Hence: Recorded Live At Keystone Korner, San Francisco, 1975; Circle Of Love, 1975; From Disco To Love, 1975; Hermeto, 1975; The Choice 4, 1975; Lena & Michel, 1976; On The Town, 1976; Pastels, 1976; After The Dance, 1977; Babyface Strikes Back, 1977; Babyface Strikes Back, 1977; Bionic Boogie, 1977; Dune, 1977; Encounters Of Every Kind, 1977; From The Beginning, 1977; La Catedral Y El Toro, 1977; Star Wars And Other Galactic Funk, 1977; Tailgunner, 1977; The Mysterious Flying Orchestra, 1977; All Things Beautiful, 1978; Concrete Jungle, 1978; Easy, 1978; Lemon, 1978; The Path, 1978; Z-licious, 1978; B. Baker Chocolate Co., 1979; Come Into My Life, 1979; Let Me Be Your Fantasy, 1979; Carnaval, 1980; Christmas In The Stars: Star Wars Christmas Album, 1980; Fame - The Original Soundtrack From The Motion Picture, 1980; Get It Right, 1983; Late Night Guitar, 1983; Beat St Vol 2, 1984; Beat St: Original Motion Picture Soundtrack - Vol 1, 1984; inside Moves, 1984; They Said It Couldn't Be Done, 1984; Songs From Liquid Days, 1986; DancePieces, 1987; Basic Blythe, 1988; Double Time, 1988; Powaqqatsi, 1988; Trilogy: Past, Present & Future, 1988; Follow Me, 1989; Heat / Jungle Fire, 1992; Malcolm X: The Original Motion Picture Score, 1992; Jesus' Blood Never Failed Me Yet, 1993; Please Yourself, 1993; Walk The Dog & Light The Light, 1993; Zappa's Universe, 1993; Clockers, 1995; Sophisticated Lady, 1995; Beneath The Surface, 1996; Birth Of The Cool Funk, 1998; Snake Eyes, 19898; Oops!...I Did It Again, 2000; Girlfriend, 2002; Dangerously In Love, 2003; Glassworks, 2003; The Diary Of Alicia Keys, 2003; Untinted (Sources For Madlib's Shades Of Blue, 2003; So Amazing:, 2005; The Phoenix, 2006; Introducing Joss Stone, violinist, 2007. **Orgs:** Adv panel, York State Arts Coun; vice chmn adv comm, High Sch Performing Arts Fed Music Clubs Award; exec bd, Kennedy Ctr Nat Black Music Colloquium & Competition; juror, adv bd mem, Sphinx Orgn. **Honors/Awds:** Koussevitzky International Recording Award, High Fidelity Mag, 1974. **Special Achievements:** First Black musician ever to become a regular member of the NY Philharmonic, 1962; has appeared in var: Quebec, Baltimore, Detroit Symphonies, NY Philharmonic; recorded Cordero Violin Concerto with Detroit Symphony on Black Composers Series; gave a premiere performance of Sir Roland Hanna's Sonata for Violin and Piano at the Kennedy Center in Washington; first African-American to gain a regular place with the New York Philharmonic, 1962. **Home Addr:** 101 W 12th St Apt 14n, New York, NY 10011-8127, **Home Phone:** (212)924-6287. **Business Addr:** Director, Columbia County's Leaf Peeper Series, Chatham, NY 12037.

## ALLEN, SAUNDRA C.

Chairperson. **Career:** Coun DC, Dem Ward 8, Comt Human Serv, chairperson, 2003. **Orgs:** Comt Consumer & Regulatory Affairs; Comt Pub Serv. **Business Addr:** Chairperson, Coun DC, 1350 Pa Ave NW, Washington, DC 20004, **Business Phone:** (202)724-8045.

## ALLEN, SHIRLEY JEANNE

**Personal:** Born Dec 19, 1941, Tyler, TX; daughter of Theressa Carter McDonald and Ralph C. **Educ:** Talladega Col, music, 1960; Jarvis Christian Col, Hawkins, TX, music, 1963; Gallaudet Col, Wash, DC, BA, Eng lit, 1966; Howard Univ, Wash, DC, MA, couns, 1972; Univ Rochester, EdD, guid & coun educ, 1992. **Career:** Educator (retired); US Peace Corp, classification clerk, 1964-65; US IRS, ed clerk; US Post Off, dist clerk, 1966-67; Gallaudet Col, Wash, DC, couns instr, 1967-73; Rochester Inst Technol, assoc prof gen educ, 1973-2001. **Orgs:** Nat Asn Deaf; Conf Am Instr Deaf; Nat Asn Women Educ; Nat Black Deaf Advocates. **Honors/Awds:** National Deaf Woman of the Year, Quota Int, 1993; Inducted into the Jarvis Christian College Pioneer Hall of Fame, 1994; Black Deaf Advocates Achievement Award, Calif State, Dept Rehab & Los Angeles, 1994; Special Achievement Award, Campbell Alumni Asn. **Special Achievements:** Author: "What are the factors considered in the selection of vocationalgoals by persons-with differing degrees of hearing ability?", 1972; Received BA, MA, & EdD after becoming deaf, 1962; The first Black deaf female to earn a doctoral degree, 1992; One of the 20 most influential black deaf persons in America, 2003. **Home Addr:** 395 Ravenwood Ave, Austin, TX 14619-1509.

## ALLEN, STANLEY M.

Airplane pilot. **Personal:** Born Dec 6, 1941, Washington, DC; married Josita E Hair; children: Khyron Shane & Kesha Lynette. **Educ:** Howard Univ, BA, 1965. **Career:** Howard Univ Football, co-capt, 1964; Eastern Airlines Inc, airline pilot, first officer. **Orgs:** Airline Pilots Asn; sr class pres, Fairmont Heights High Sch, 1960. **Honors/Awds:** Md State High Hurdles Champion, 1960. **Home Addr:** 5388 Graywing Ct, Columbia, MD 21045-2328, **Home Phone:** (301)596-6887. **Business Addr:** Airline Pilot, Eastern Airlines Inc, Washington, DC 20001.

## ALLEN, TAJE LAQAYNE

Football player. **Personal:** Born Nov 6, 1973, Lubbock, TX; married Gladys. **Educ:** Univ Tex, sports mgt. **Career:** Football player (retired); St Louis Rams, 1998, defensive back, 1997, linebacker, Right Cornerback, 1999, cornerback, 2000; Kans City Chiefs, 2001-02. **Home Addr:** 1209 Valorie Ct, Cedar Park, TX 78613-4023, **Home Phone:** (512)394-7275.

## ALLEN, TERRELL ALLISON, III

Administrator, association executive, executive. **Personal:** Born Feb 10, 1959, Washington, DC; married Lorna; children: 3. **Educ:** Howard Univ, BS, elec engineering, 1982; Univ Pa, MBA, finance, 1987. **Career:** Eastman Kodak Co, coop educ stud, 1978-81; Howard Univ, electronics lab asst, 1980-82, assoc dir finance, 2008-14, Athletics Dept, 2011; Commonwealth Edison Co, gen engr, 1982-85; Coopers & Lybrand, consult; MCI WorldCom, sr mgr, 1992-97; George Washington Univ, Bus Mgt & Anal Group, sr assoc, 2014-. **Orgs:** Vpres, Phi Beta Sigma Fraternity Inc Alpha Chap, 1981-82; comt chmn, Chicago Jr Asn Com & Indust, 1982-85; sci club dir, Chicago Adopt-A-Sch Prog, 1982-85; pres, Nat Black MBA Asn. **Honors/Awds:** Outstanding Young Men America, 1984; Leadership Award, Johnson & Johnson Family Co, 1985. **Home Addr:** 1701 Albert Dr, Bowie, MD 20721-2250, **Home Phone:** (301)390-0393. **Business Addr:** Senior Associate, George Washington University, 2121 I St NW, Washington, DC 20052, **Business Phone:** (202)994-1000.

## ALLEN, TREMAYNE AUBREY

Football player. **Personal:** Born Aug 9, 1974, Nashville, TN. **Educ:** Univ Fla, BS, bldg construct. **Career:** Football player (retired); Real estate agt; Chicago Bears, tight end, 1997-98; Scottish Claymores, tight end, 2000-01; Los Angeles Xtreme Roster, tight end, 2001.

## ALLEN, TY W.

Executive. **Personal:** Born Jun 27, 1961, Denver, CO; son of Elijah and Carleen Matis. **Educ:** Univ Colo, Denver, CO, eng, polit sci, 1983. **Career:** Burlington Northern Air Freight, sales, 1982-85; C F Air Freight, sales, 1985; Worldwide Air Freight, pres, 1985-88; AFI Int Forwarding, founder, 1988-. **Home Addr:** 16462 E Berry Pl, Aurora, CO 80015-4053, **Home Phone:** (303)321-9159. **Business Addr:** Founder, Director, AFI International Forwarding Inc, 700 S Colo Blvd, Denver, CO 80206, **Business Phone:** (888)276-4405.

## ALLEN, DR. VAN SIZAR

School administrator. **Personal:** Born Apr 2, 1926, Edwards, MS; son of Van and Edna Sizar; married Mary Frances Cartwright; children: Van S Jr & Nathaniel B. **Educ:** Tougaloo Col, BA, 1950; Univ Mich, MS, 1952; Yale Univ, cert, 1955; Univ NC, MPH, 1962, PhD, 1969. **Career:** School administrator (retired); Univ Mich, John Hay Whitney Opportunity fel, 1950; Bennett Col, assoc prof, 1952-68; Guilford Co Anti-Poverty Prog, dep dir, 1966-68; Southern Regional Educ Bd, assoc dir, inst higher educ opportunity, 1969-71; TACTICS, exec dir, 1971-80; Tougaloo Col, vpres acad affairs, 1980-85; Paul Quinn Col, vpres acad affairs, 1985-87, 1989-90, vpres & ceo, Waco Campus, adminr; Cent Tex Cancer Network Prog, dir, 1988-89. **Orgs:** Pres, Tougaloo Col Nat Alumni Asn, 1978-80; chmn, Tougaloo Col Nat Alumni Fundraising Campaign, 1980-84; Am Asn Univ Prof; Beta Kappa Chi Sci Soc; Nat Inst Sci; AAAS; John Hay Whitney Opportunity Fel Org; Phi Delta Kappa Nat Educ Fraternity; NC Community Develop Asn; Omega Psi Phi Frat; Sigma Pi Phi Frat; Nat Asn Advan Colored People; Soc Pub Health Educ. **Home Addr:** 225 Garrison St, Waco, TX 76704-2310, **Home Phone:** (254)753-6063.

## ALLEN, W. GEORGE

Lawyer, association executive. **Personal:** Born Mar 3, 1936, Sanford, FL; son of Lessie Mae Williams and Fletcher; married Enid Meadows; children: Timothy, Frederick, Amy & Jonathan. **Educ:** Fla A&M Univ, BS, polit sci, 1958; Univ Fla Law Sch, JD, 1962. **Career:** FL Human Rels Comn, comnr; pvt pract atty, 1963-. **Orgs:** Comn Fla Ethics Comt; Fla Adv Comn, US Civil Rights Comn, Govs prop Rights Study Community; pres, Nat Bar Asn, 1975-76; pres, Fla Bar Asn, 1988-89; Broward City Bar Asn; Am Trial Lawyers Asn; Fla Acad Trail Lawyers; Broward Criminal Defense Asn; Nat Asn Crim Defense Lawyers; Nat Asn Advan Colored People; Alpha Phi Alpha Fraternity Inc, Elks; YMCA; Fla A&M Univ Alumni Asn, State Fla; bd dir, Univ Fla Found Inc; Urban League Broward Co; bd trustee, Fla A&M Univ, 2005. Chair Bd, OIC Broward; pres, Broward County Bar Asn. **Honors/Awds:** Distinguished Alumnus Award, Univ Fla, 2000; Silver Medallion Award, Nat Conf Community & Justice, 2001 & 2003; Inducted Hall of Fame, Nat Bar Asn, 2005. **Special Achievements:** First African American to graduate from the University of Florida. **Home Addr:** 777 Bayshore Dr Apt 1104, Ft. Lauderdale, FL 33304, **Home Phone:** (954)566-2889. **Business Addr:** Attorney, W George Allen Law Office, 800 SE 3rd Ave Penthouse, Ft. Lauderdale, FL 33316-1152, **Business Phone:** (954)463-6681.

## ALLEN, WALTER R.

Educator. **Personal:** Born Allendale, SC; married Mary Clay; children: Walter Jr, Jeffrey & Brian. **Educ:** Beloit Col, BA, sociol, 1971; Univ Chicago, MA, sociol, 1973, PhD, sociol, 1975; Univ NC, Sch Pub Health, Postdoctoral Study, psycho-social epidemiol, 1978. **Career:** Shoals High Sch, asst prin; Univ Ga, asst prof; Faulkner State Jr Col, Dept Fine Arts, art instr, currently; Nat Inst Child Health & Human Develop, postdoctoral fel, 1971-74; Univ NC, Dept Sociol, from instr to asst prof, 1974-79; Howard Univ, vis fac, 1975, 2008; Duke Univ, vis fac, 1976; Nih, postdoctoral fel, 1978-79; Univ Mich, Dept Sociol & Ctr Afroamerican & African Studies, from asst prof to prof, 1979-91, Ctr Afroamerican & African Studies, assoc dir, 1987-89; Rockefeller Found, postdoctoral fel, 1982-83; Univ Zimbabwe, vis fac, 1984-88, sr fulbright lectr, 1984, 1987-88; Wayne State Univ, vis fac, 1988; Univ Ill Urbana-Champaign, Allerton lectr, 1988; Univ Calif, Los Angeles, Dept Sociol, prof, 1988-, Sch Med, assoc dir, Robert Wood Johnson Clin Scholars Prog, 1993-97, Inst Social Sci Res, dir, 1998-, Grad Sch Educ & Info Studies, Dept Educ, Allan Murray Cartter prof, 2004-, distinguished prof sociol, 2008-; St. Petersburg State Univ, Russia, vis fac, 2004-07; consult. **Orgs:** NIH, 1978-79; coun, Am Sociol Asn, 1991-94; Sociol Res Asn, 1991-; pres, Asn Black Sociol, 1992-93; Am Educ Res Asn, 2000; Kappa Alpha Psi; Phi Delta Kappa; Kappa Kappa Psi; Thirty second Deg Mason; Am Psychol Asn; Nat Asn Musicologists; educr, Haile Selassie Ethiopia; social psychologist, musician & adminr, Hundred Percenters Orgn; Hill First Baptist Church; Nat Asn Advan Colored People; Free Lance Musician; Asn Grad Schs; Cong Black Caucus Found; Int Sociol Asn; Nat Asn Educ Young C; Nat Coun Black Studies; Nat Coun Family Rels; Pop Asn Am; Soc Res Child Develop; Soc Study Social Probs; Southern Sociol Soc; Caribbean Studies Asn; Am Asn Advan Sci; Am Pub Health Asn; Nat Asn Black Journalists. **Honors/Awds:** Achievement Award, Kappa Alpha Psi; Hundred Percenters Award; Educators Award; Phi Delta Kappa Award; Nat Asn Musicologists; Kappa Kappa Psi Award; Distinguished Leadership Award, United Negro Col Fund, 1985; Faculty Recognition Award, Univ Mich, Ann Arbor, 1987; Distinguished Scholar Award, Am Educ Res Asn, 1987; Research Excellence Award, Am Educ Res Asn, 1993; Distinguished Career Award, Asn Black Sociologists, 1995; Harriet & Charles Luckman Distinguished Teaching Award, Univ Calif LosAngeles, 1996; Ellis Joseph Distinguished Scholar Award, Univ Dayton, 1997; Special Merit Award, Asn Study Higher Edu, 2002; DuBois-Johnson-Frazier Award, Am Sociol Asn, 2002; Presidential Citation, Am Educ Res Asn, 2008; AERA Fellows Award, Am Educ Res Asn, 2009. **Special Achievements:** Contributed numerous publications. **Home Addr:** 297 Davis St, Athens, GA 30606-5048, **Home Phone:** (706)353-4009. **Business Addr:** Allan Murray Cartter Professor, University of California, 3101A Moore Hall 405 Hilgard Ave, Los Angeles, CA 90095-1521, **Business Phone:** (310)206-7107.

## ALLEN, WALTER RAY, JR.

Actor, association executive, basketball player. **Personal:** Born Jul 20, 1975, Merced, CA; son of Flora; married Shannon; children: Tierra, Ray Ray, Walker, Wynn & Wystan. **Educ:** Univ Conn, attended 1996. **Career:** Basketball player (retired); Milwaukee Bucks, shooting guard, 1996-2003; SeattleSuperSonics, shooting guard, 2003-07; Boston Celtics, shooting guard, 2007-12; Miami Heat, shooting guard, 2012-14. **Orgs:** Founder, Ray Hope Found, 1997; All-Star Adv Coun; Bd mem, Back9Network; Team USA 2000 Olympics. **Honors/Awds:** USA Basketball's Male Athlete Yr, 1995; Gold medal, Summer Universiade, 1995; Big E Player Yr, 1996; UPI Player Yr, 1996; NBA All-Star, 2000-02, 2004-09, 2011; Gold medal, Sydney olympics, 2000; NBA, Three-Pt Shootout Champion, 2001; Joe Dumars Sportsmanship Award, 2003; NBA Sportsmanship Award, 2003; Gold medal, FIBA Americas Championship, 2003; NBA champion, 2008, 2013; NBA Community Assist Award, 2010; NBA all-time leader three-pointers made. **Special Achievements:** Movie: He Got Game, 1998; Harvard Man, 2001. Named Sporting News "Good Guy" 2000, 2001 & 2005; Love Blind, Producer, 2013. Appeared TV ser. **Business**

**Addr:** Founder, PO Box 746, Beaverton, OR 97075, **Business Phone:** (503)208-3088.

### ALLEN, WILL D.
Football player. **Personal:** Born Aug 5, 1978, Syracuse, NY; son of Will Sr and Carolyn; married Roshonda; children: Jasmine, Will Jr & Blake. **Educ:** Syracuse Univ, econ. **Career:** New York Giants, left cornerback, 2001-05; Miami Dolphins, left cornerback, 2006-11, cornerback, 2007, 2011, defensive back, free safety, 2011; New Eng Patriots, cornerback, 2012. **Orgs:** Ronald McDonald House, Giants Found Golf Outing; Nat Football Found. **Home Addr:** 2325 SW 105th Terr, Davie, FL 33324-7608, **Home Phone:** (954)577-3064.

### ALLEN, DR. WILLIAM BARCLAY
Educator, dean (education), chairperson. **Personal:** Born Mar 18, 1944, Fernandina Beach, FL; son of James P and Rosa Lee Johnson; married Carol Michelle Pfeiffer; children: Danielle Susan & Bertrand Marc. **Educ:** Pepperdine Col, BA, 1967, MA, 1968; Claremont Grad Sch, PhD, 1972. **Career:** Sears, Roebuck Inc, Calif, Elec Supplies, sales & asst mgr, 1965-66; Radio Sta KMPC, Hollywood, news ed, 1966-68; Fernandina Beach High Sch, instr Am hist, phys sci & bus math, 1968-69; Pepperdine Col, Am Polit Theory, instr, 1969; Univ de Rouen, lectr, 1970-71; Fulbright fel, 1970-71; Am Univ Sch Gov & Pub Admin, asst prof, 1971-72; Harvey Mudd Col, from asst prof to prof, 1972-94; St John's Col Grad Inst, vis tutor 1977-; Liberty Fund Inc, Bicentennial Ser, prog admin & co-organizer, 1982-90; Earhart Found res grant, 1986-87; Pac Res Inst Pub Policy, mem Civil Rights Task Force, 1988-90; US Comn Civil Rights, chmn, 1988-89; Bicentennial Educ Grant Prog, Comn Bicentennial US Const, 1988-89; Mich State Univ, James Madison Col, dean, 1993-98, Dept Polit Sci, prof polit philos, 1993-, dir Prog Pub Policy & Pub Admin, 1998-99, 2002-05, Working Group Improv Undergrad Educ, chmn, 2004-06; State Coun Higher Educ Va, dir, 1998-99; Yorktown Univ.com, adj prof, currently; Inst Responsible Citizenship, sr fel, currently; Princeton Univ, James Madison Prog, Ann & Herbert W Vaughan Vis fel, 2006-07. **Orgs:** Pres, Claremont Unified Sch Dist Bd, 1981-84; bd mem, Calif Assembly Fel Prog, 1982-92; prog dir, Liberty Fund Inc, 1982-89; chmn, Calif Scholars Reagan, 1984; bd mem, LeRoy Boys Home; Nat Coun Humanities, 1984-87; fel Kellogg Found, 1984-87; Academie Montesquieu; US Civil Rights Comn, Calif State Adv Comt, 1985-87; chmn, US Comn Civil Rights, 1988-89; trustee, Hoover Inst, Stanford Univ, 1995-98; chmn emer, George Wash Soc, Calif; dir Youth Ministry, Westwood Baptist Church, Richmond, Va, 1998-2000; co-chmn, Anniversary Comt, 2003, co-chmn, Stewardship Comt, 2003, trustee, 2005-, Union Missionary Baptist Church, Lansing, Mich; Pi Sigma Alpha, Sigma Alpha. **Business Addr:** Professor, Michigan State University, 307 S Kedzie Hall, East Lansing, MI 48824-1032, **Business Phone:** (517)355-6590.

### ALLEN, DR. WINSTON EARLE
Executive, entrepreneur. **Personal:** Born Jan 1, 1930, New York, NY; married Ruby; children: Vaughn & Julie. **Educ:** NY Univ, Wash Sq, Col Arts & Sci, BA, 1955; City Col NY, MA, 1958; Fordham Univ, PhD, 1971. **Career:** NY City Bd Educ, teacher econ, 1956-68; Fordham Univ, asst prof, 1970-72; Xerox Corp Educ Planning & Develop, mgr, 1972-82; George Wash Univ & Am Univ, adj prof, mgt sci dept, 1974-75; Creative Investor Serv Inc, pres; Innovative Health Prod Inc, founder, owner, pres, 1993-. **Orgs:** Bd mem, US comn UNICEF, 1972-82; phi delta kappa; bd dir, sunrise rotary westport, CT; chmn, westport conserv comn, 1989-93; zoning bd appeals, westport, CT; pres elect, westport rotary, 1997-98; Winston E. Allen Found Inc (WEAF), pres, founder, 1999; Rotary Dist Gov, 2000-01. **Home Addr:** 4 Burritts Landing N, Westport, CT 06880, **Home Phone:** (203)227-4897. **Business Addr:** Owner, President, Innovative Health Products Inc, 4 Burritts Landing N, Westport, CT 06880-6403, **Business Phone:** (203)227-4897.

### ALLEN-HOWARD, MARQUITA W.
Municipal government official, police officer, manager. **Career:** City NY, Dept Invest, dep inspector gen, admin mgr, currently. **Business Addr:** Deputy Inspector General, Administrative Manager, City of New York, 80 Maiden Lane 16th Fl, New York, NY 10038, **Business Phone:** (212)825-2421.

### ALLEN-JONES, PATRICIA ANN (PATRICIA JONES)
Journalist. **Personal:** Born Nov 9, 1958, Pittsburg, CA; daughter of William J and Bettye J; married George Wallace Jr. **Educ:** Calif State Univ, BA, 1981. **Career:** Neighbor News, reporter, 1981-83; Suncoast News, reporter, 1983-84; Fla Sentinel Bull, reporter, 1984-86; Leesburg Com Newspaper, reporter, 1986-88; Herald-Tribune Newspaper, reporter, 1988-; N Suncoast Chap FICPA, pres. **Orgs:** St Martha's Cath Church, 1988-; Adult Black Achievers, 1992-. **Honors/Awds:** Media Award, Eastern Seal Soc SW Fla, 1992. **Home Addr:** 2703 24th St, Sarasota, FL 34234. **Business Addr:** Reporter, Herald-Tribune Newspaper, 1741 Main St, Sarasota, FL 34236, **Business Phone:** (941)361-4800.

### ALLEN-MEARES, PAULA G.
Educator, school administrator. **Personal:** Born Buffalo, NY; daughter of Joseph N Allen and Mary T Hienz; married Henry; children: Tracey, Nichole & Shannon. **Educ:** State Univ NY, BS, 1969; Univ Ill, Urbana-Champaign, Jane Addams Sch Social Work, MSW, child welfare, 1971, PhD, social work & educ admin, 1975; Harvard Univ, Mgt Inst, cert, 1990; Univ Mich, Bus Sch, cert, mgt mgr, 1993. **Career:** State Univ New York, res asst, 1966-69; Univ Ill Sch Social Work, Urbana-Champaign, Ill, fac, 1978-84, assoc prof, 1983-89, dir doctoral prog, 1985-89, prof & dean, chancellor, 1990-93; Univ Mich, Sch Social Work, prof & dean, 1993-2008, Norma Radin Col prof social work, prof educ, prof emer & dean emer, 2009-; Univ Ill, Chancellor, 2009-. **Orgs:** Human rels dir, Urbana Educ, 1973-1975; bd dir, develop serv Champaign County, 1973-1975;;regional adv bd, 1977-1978; planning comt Ill March Dimes, 1978; bd dir, Vol Action Ctr Champaign County, 1978-1980; chmn nomination comt, ad hoc comt bd policy; Prog comt Girls Club Champaign, 1978-1981, adv bd, Ambulatory Care Ctr, Mercy Hosp, 1981-82; mem policy comt Regional Ill C's Home & Aid Soc, 1980-84; chmn, Comn Educ, Nat Asn Black Social Workers, 1982-88; Dept C & Family Serv, 1984; moderator, black adoptions C's Home & Aid Soc Ill; mem Champaign county child placement rev comt Champaign County Circuit Ct, 1985-93; ed chief, J Social Work Educ, Nat Asn Social Workers, 1989-93; steering comm, Group Advan Doctoral Educ, 1987-88; Bd dir, Coun Social Work Educ, 1989-91; bd dir, Family Serv Champaign County, 1988-89; commun Bd mem, Nat Asn Social Workers, 1990-; trustee, William Thomas Grant Found; chmn, nomination comt, 2004-07; chmn, New York Acad Med's Nat Adv Panel, currently; Inst Med Nat Academies; bd trustee, William T Grant Found; pres, Soc Social Work & Res; Phi Delta Kappa; Delta Mu, Delta Kappa Gamma; fel Royal Acad Med. **Business Addr:** Dean Emerita, Professor Emeritus of Social Work & Education, University of Michigan, SSWB 1080 S Univ Rm 3851, Ann Arbor, MI 48109, **Business Phone:** (734)647-2547.

### ALLEN-NOBLE, PROF. ROSIE ELIZABETH
School administrator, executive director, educator. **Personal:** Born Jun 22, 1938, Americus, GA; daughter of Velma Douglas and Ulysses Grant Allen; children: Antoinette Celine Webb. **Educ:** Albany State Col, BS, 1960; Atlanta Univ, MS, 1967; Rutgers Univ, MS, 1974, DEd, 1991. **Career:** Rutgers Univ, instr, 1970-76; Vision Builders Nat Conf, grant proposal writer, 1970-; Seton Hall Univ, vis asst prof, 1972-78; Univ Med & Dentist, NJ, instr, 1972; Univ Med & Dent, NJ, consult, 1972-; Soroptomist Int, 1974-; Fairleigh Dickinson Univ, asst prof, 1974-80; Upsala Col, Sci Enrichment Prog, dir, 1976; Montclair State Col, Health Careers Prog, dir, 1979; Univ Conn, consult & evaluator, 1981-83; Hobart William Smith Col, consult, 1983; Long Island Univ, 1984; Wichita State Univ, 1984; Univ Med & Dent NJ, Sch Health Related Professions, consult, 1986-; Gwynedd-Mercy Col, consult, 1987-; HPPI, proj dir; Med Col Ga, assoc prof & assoc dean spec acad progs, 1995-2004; Allen Noble Assocs LLC, owner, 1999-. **Orgs:** Alpha Kappa Alpha Sorority, 1959; Am Asn Univ Women, 1969-; NJ Chap Albany State Col Alumni Asn, 1974; Nat Asn Med Minority Educ, 1980; Omicrom Xi Omega, 1984; Eval Comt Higher Educ Mid State Asn Eval Team, 1984; Nat Asn Pre-Prof Advs, 1984; nat treas, Nat Asn Med Minority Educ Inc, 1984; NE regional dir, Nat Asn Med Minority Educr, 1988-90, bd dir, 1990; bd dir, Nat Legacy Found Inc. **Honors/Awds:** Merit Award for Outstanding Service, Montclair State Col, 1982 & 1987; Outstanding Leadership & Service, Upsala Col, 1982; NSF Grants; Outstanding Service Award, Montclair State Col, 1984-85; Numerous Fed, State & Private Found Fellowship Grants over the past 20 years. **Home Addr:** 364 Orange Rd C5, Montclair, NJ 07042, **Home Phone:** (706)721-2522. **Business Addr:** Owner, Allen Noble Associates LLC, 397 Bakers Ferry Trl, Martinez, GA 30907, **Business Phone:** (706)651-9275.

### ALLEN-RASHEED, JAMAL RANDY
Association executive, judge. **Personal:** Born Dec 15, 1953, Memphis, TN; married Jacquline Carlotte Gipson; children: Randy D. **Educ:** Southern Ill Univ, Carbondale, BS, jour, 1980; Prairie View A&M Univ, MA, sociol, 1986; Newburgh Theol Sem, PhD, African Am Ministry, 2012; N Lake Col, AAS, media technol, 2014. **Career:** KEWC-AM/FM Radio, disc jockey & reporter, 1975-76; WPHD-NBC TV, news asst, 1979-80; Black Observer Newspaper, managing ed, 1979-80; WLS-ABC Network, prod engr, 1980; Lackland Tailspinner Airforce Pub, reporter, 1981; Forward Times Newspaper, asst circulation mgr, 1982-83; Sam Houston State Univ/Housing, pub rels dir, 1983-84; Martin Luther King Jr Ctr Nonviolent Social Chg Inc, community develop asst, 1984; Tex Dept Corrections, correctional officer, 1984-86; Dallas County Adult Probation, adult probation officer, currently; Dallas County Juv Prog, admin; state dir. **Orgs:** Alpha Epsilon Rho Hon Radio/TV, 1978-80; nat bd dir, Alpha Phi Alpha Frat Inc, 1978-79; Sigma Delta Chi Prof Journalist, 1979-80; pub rels dir, Black Affairs Coun SI U-C, 1979-80; founder & dir, Martin Luther King Jr Inst Afro-Am Studies/Soc Chg, 1985-86; bd dir, Hillvale Educ Asn Substance Abuse, 1986-; Blacks Soc, Blacks Journ, Blacks Criminal Justice; 32 Degree Ancient & Accepted Scottish Rite Masonary Prince Hall Affil; John M Harlan Alumni Asn; dep supreme master, Knight KOP Prog; Ellis County African Am Hall Fame Mus, 2012-. **Home Addr:** 36 W 103rd Pl, Chicago, IL 60628-2610, **Home Phone:** (773)941-4039. **Business Addr:** Adult Probation Officer, Dallas County Adult Probation, 2600 Lone Star Dr, Dallas, TX 75212, **Business Phone:** (214)698-2200.

### ALLENSWORTH, JERMAINE LAMONT
Baseball player. **Personal:** Born Jan 11, 1972, Anderson, IN. **Educ:** Purdue Univ, W Lafayette, IN. **Career:** Baseball player (retired); Pittsburgh Pirates, outfielder, 1996-98; Kans City Royals, 1998; NY Mets, 1998-99; Boston Red Sox, outfielder, 2000; Milwaukee Brewers, outfielder, 2004; Joliet Jack Hammers, 2004-05; Gary S Shore Rail Cats, 2006; Schaumburg Flyers, 2008; free agt, currently.

### ALLEYNE, REV. EDWARD D.
Clergy. **Personal:** Born Jun 14, 1928, Brooklyn, NY. **Educ:** Cath Univ Am, BA, 1956. **Career:** Clergy (retired); Mother Savior Sem, instr, 1960-67; Var Parishes Diocese Camden, assoc pastor, 1968-84; St Monica's Church, pastor, 1984; Queen Heaven Church, pastor, 1993-2004. **Orgs:** Diocesan Bd Educ, 1969-; dir, Parkside Cath Ctr, 1971-75; Diocesan Ecumenical Comn, 1971-; Camden Region Moderator Diocesan PTA, 1971-; Diocesan Campaign Human Develop Comn, 1971-; Diocesan Soc Justice Comn, 1972-; financial coordr, Consol Cath Sch, Camden, 1972-75; chaplin, Knights Columbus Coun; dir, Off Black Ministry; priests coun; priest personnel bd.

### ALLIGOOD, DOUGLASS LACY
Executive. **Personal:** Born Feb 15, 1934, St. Louis, MO; son of Forest D and Countess M Murphy; children: Donna L Johnson, Craig F, Debra Alligood White & Douglas L Jr. **Educ:** Bradley Univ, Peoria, IL, BFA, com & advert art, 1956. **Career:** Seymour Leatherwood & Cleveland Inc, Detroit, MI, staff artist & copywriter, 1956; Black Owned Advert Agency; Radio Sta WCHB, Detroit, MI, merch dir, 1959-62; Batten Barton Durstine & Osborn Inc, Detroit, MI, acct exec, 1962-64, sr acct exec, 1964-71; RCA Corp, NY, dir corp adv, 1971-83; UniWorld Grp Inc, New York, NY, pres, 1983-84; BBDO Worldwide Inc, acct exec, 1962-71, sr vpres horizontal mkt, 1984-; Univ Fla, A P Phillips, lectr, 1989. **Orgs:** Dir adv coun, Int Film & TV Festival NY, 1976-; bd dir, speaker, Advert Educ Found, 1985-; Am Asn Advert Agencies EOO Comn, 1986-93; chmn adv coun, Ethnic Perspectives Comn, 1991-93; chmn, Health Watch Info & Prom Serv, 1995-99; hon dir, Advert Coun Inc; chmn diversity coun, BBDO, 2006-, bd dir. **Honors/Awds:** Five To Watch Award, Am Women Radio & TV, Detroit, 1964; CEBA Advert Campaign Award, 1980-82; Black Achievers in Industry, Harlem Br YMCA Greater New York, 1990; BBDO Founders Award, 1993; Bradley University Centurion, 1994; 2-Year Service Award, Adv Coun, 1996; Institute Award, Nat Eagle Leadership, 1998; All Star-Research, Mediaweek, 1998; Distinguished Service Award, Health Watch, 1999; AAF Diversity Achievement Award, 2005; BBDO Dillon Prize, 2007; hon dir, Advert Coun Inc. **Special Achievements:** An Analysis of Black Audience Primetime Network Viewing Preferences, 1984-; Media Opportunities Newsletter, 1991; Special Markets Media Guidebook, 1993; An Analysis of Hispanic Audience Primetime Network Viewing Preferences, 1993-; Spindex Media Star, Advertising Age, 1997-00; Crains Top 100 Minority Executive, 1998, 2003; Co-author of "Color Television: Fifty Years of Images of African Americans and Latinos on Prime Time Television, 2005. **Home Addr:** 131 Woodlands Ave, White Plains, NY 10607-2807, **Home Phone:** (914)693-2599. **Business Addr:** Senior Vice President, Chairman of Diversity Council, BBDO Worldwide Inc, 1285 Avenue of the Americas, New York, NY 10019-6028, **Business Phone:** (212)459-5000.

### ALLISON, CAROLYN C.
President (organization). **Educ:** Univ Chicago, IL, BS & MPH, pub health. **Career:** Queens Hosp Ctr, New York, NY, sr assoc dir; C.W. Williams Community Health Ctr, pres; Northern New York Rural Health Care Alliance, Watertown, NY, exec dir; Kaiser Permanente, med off adminr; Metrolina Comprehensive Health Ctr Inc, chief exec officer & exec dir; Youfirst Healthcare Solutions, pres, exec consult, currently. **Orgs:** Bd mem, Uptown Shelter; bd mem, Nc Community Health Ctr Asn. **Business Addr:** Executive Consultant, Youfirst Healthcare Solutions, PO Box 782062, San Antonio, TX 78278, **Business Phone:** (866)227-5750.

### ALLISON, DR. E. LAVONIA
Executive. **Educ:** Hampton Inst; NY Univ. **Career:** Durham County Govt, chmn durham commt affairs black people. **Orgs:** Univ's Bd trustee; dir, N Carolina Health Careers Access Prog.

### ALLISON, VERNE
Singer. **Personal:** Born Jun 22, 1936, Chicago, IL. **Career:** Dells, tenor vocalist; Albums (with Dells): There Is, 1968; Love Is Blue, 1969; The Dells' Musical Menu/Always Together, 1969; The Dells' Greatest Hits, 1970; Like It Is, Like It Was, 1971; Freedom Means, 1971; Sweet As Funk Can Be, 1972; The Dells Sing Dionne, 1972; Give Your Baby a Standing Ovation, 1976; The Dells, 1973; The Mighty Mighty Dells, 1974; The Dellsvs. The Dramatics, 1975; The Dells' Greatest Hits Volume 2, 1975; We Got To Get Our Thing Together, 1975; No Way Back, 1976; They Said It Couldn't Be Done But We Did It, 1977; Love Connection, 1977; New Beginnings, 1978; Face to Face, 1979; I Touched a Dream, 1980; Whatever Turns You On, 1981; One Step Closer, 1984; The Second Time, 1988; On Their Corner, 1992; I Salute You, 1992; Dreams of Contentment, 1993; Bring Back the Love: Classic Dells, 1996; I Touch a Dream/Whatever Turns, 1998; Reminiscing, 2000; Open Up My Heart: The 9/11 Album, 2002; Hott, 2003; (with MichaelRoss): We Finally Meet, 1995; Last Love Letter, 1996; Dells, mem, currently. **Honors/Awds:** Rock and Roll Hall of Fame, Original Dells, 2004; Vocal Group Hall of Fame, Original Dells, 2004. **Business Addr:** Singer, The Original Dells Inc, 10112 S La Salle St, Chicago, IL 60628, **Business Phone:** (708)474-1422.

### ALLISON, VIVIAN L.
Executive. **Personal:** Born Aug 27, 1936; children: 1. **Educ:** Fisk Univ, attended 1953; Wayne State Univ, BS, chem, 1958. **Career:** Robeson-Tubman Community Devel Corp, 1970-79, bd dir, 1979-85, chairperson, 1981-85; Off US Congman John Conyers, cong asst, 1980-93; Off Wayne County Exec William Lucas, exec asst, 1983-86; Mich Dept Licensing & Regulation, from admin asst to dir, 1987-90; City Detroit, Consumer Aff Dept, dep dir, 1991, interim dir, currently. **Orgs:** Nat Asn Advan Colored People; Am Med Technologists; Nat Asn Black Substance Abuse Workers; Nat Clearinghouses Licensure, Enforcement & Regulation; Int Asn Transp Regulators; Greenacres-Woodward Civic Asn; Nat, State, 14th Dist Dem Party. **Home Addr:** 20159 Warrington Dr, Detroit, MI 48221-1357, **Home Phone:** (313)863-8127. **Business Addr:** Interim Director, City of Detroit, 1010 Woodward Ave, Detroit, MI 48226-1906, **Business Phone:** (313)224-3270.

### ALLOTEY, VICTOR P.
Football player, executive. **Personal:** Born Apr 8, 1975, Brooklyn, NY. **Educ:** Univ Ind. **Career:** Buffalo Bills, guard, 1998-2000; Kans City Chiefs, 2001-03, free agt; Main St Multiplex & Emerald House, 2003-04; Studio 69 Restaurant & Lounge, owner & head chef, 2004-05; Black Card Catering, owner & head chef, 2007-; Black Card Travel, co-owner & travel specialist, 2008-; CK Entertainment Productions Inc, found & pres, currently. **Business Addr:** President, Founder, CK Entertainment Production Inc, 5846 S Flamingo Rd Suite 354, Ft. Lauderdale, FL 33330-3026, **Business Phone:** (954)436-1230.

### ALLOY, DR. VALERIE
Psychologist. **Personal:** married Phillip; children: 1. **Educ:** Ohio Univ, BA, MEd; Univ Toledo, MA, PhD, clin psychol, 2001. **Career:** Pvt prac, psychol, currently; State Ohio, counr; Ohio Dept Ment Health Recovery Demonstration Grant, proj mgr & consult, ment health adminr, 2013-. **Orgs:** Nat bd, Women's Philanthropy Inst, 2003-; Catherine Eberly Ctr Women; minoriy Asn comt, Am Heart Asn; bd trustee, Maumee Valley Country Day Sch; bd dir, Planned Parenthood Northwest Ohio. **Home Addr:** 8463 W Bancroft St, Toledo, OH 43617, **Home Phone:** (419)829-4882. **Business Addr:** National Board, Women's Philanthropy Institute, 550 WN St Suite 301, Indianapolis, IN 46202-3272, **Business Phone:** (317)278-8990.

**ALLSTON, THOMAS GRAY, III**
Executive, consultant. **Personal:** Born Jul 13, 1954, Stoneham, MA; son of Thomas G II and Zeola Belle. **Educ:** Hampton Inst, BA, Eng, 1977; Hampton Univ, MS, bus mgt, 1994; Capella Univ, EdD, leadership & mgt, 2016. **Career:** Burson-Marsteller, New York, asst acct exec, 1977-78; Hampton Univ, asst dir pub rel, 1979-85, internal consult, asst dir, spec events consult, adj instr, 1991-98; Hill & Knowlton Inc, acct exec, 1985-87; Renaissance Comm, vpres, 1987-91; Allston Commun Inc, prin, pres & chief exec officer, 1987-; Newport News, pres, chief exec officer, 1991-; Oakwood Univ, exec dir pub rels, 1998-2001, lead mkt, recruitment consult, 2010-11, servant leader, dir pub rels, 2011-13; Madison Res Corp, bus develop specialist, 2006; Directv, customer retention, tech, customer serv rep, 2007-10. **Orgs:** Calvary Seventh day Adventist Church, 1973-; life mem, Alpha Phi Alpha Fraternity Inc, 1974-; Nat ampton Alumni Asn, 1977-; Pub Rel Soc Am, 1977-; former bd mem, Leadership Huntsville, 2000-01; Accredited Pub Rels Soc Am, 2001; former bd mem, Pub Rels Coun Ala Grad; Soc Adventist Communicators Founding Mem; 100 Black Men Am Inc; chap life mem, Great Huntsville; Nat Hampton Alumni Asn Former Mem; Nat Speakers Asn. **Honors/Awds:** Silver Anvil Award, Pub Rels Soc Am, 1978; Outstanding Communications Achievement, John W Hill Award, Hill & Knowlton, 1986. **Special Achievements:** Publication: "Managing Editor's Notes", Regional Voice Magazine, 2016. **Business Addr:** President, Principal, Allston Communications Inc, PO Box 22252, Huntsville, AL 35814-2252, **Business Phone:** (256)837-5452.

**ALLY, DR. AKBAR F.**
Educator. **Personal:** Born Aug 23, 1943, Wismar Demerara; son of Beraspratt and Lucille Ward; married Ellen Mason; children: Antonius & Kristina. **Educ:** St Lawrence Univ, BA, 1967; Hunter Col, MA, 1972; Univ Wis, Milwaukee, PhD, urban social studies, 1981. **Career:** Chase Manhattan Bank, New York, int adjuster, 1970; Metrop Life Ins, New York, NY, claims adjuster, 1970-72; Brooklyn Col, lectr, 1973-75; Bronx Community Col, New York, NY, lectr, 1975; Univ Wis-Milwaukee, dir & coordr, 1975-82; Univ Wis-Madison, asst dean stud affairs, 1982-89, asst to provost, asst to vice chancellor, asst vice chancellor stud affairs, 1989-2001, emer asst vice chancellor, 2002-. **Orgs:** Caribbean Hist Soc, 1972-; Nat Asn Advan Colored People, Madison, 1985-; Madison Urban League, 1985-. **Home Addr:** 5914 Meadowood Dr, Madison, WI 53711, **Home Phone:** (608)278-7083. **Business Addr:** Emeritus Assistant Vice Chancellor, University of Wisconsin-Madison, Bascom Hall 500 Lincoln Dr Suite 121, Madison, WI 53706, **Business Phone:** (608)262-3571.

**ALOMAR, ROBERTO VELAZQUEZ**
Baseball player. **Personal:** Born Feb 5, 1968, Ponce; son of Sandy Sr and Maria Velazquez; married Kim Perks; children: Lourdes Maria; married Maripily Rivera. **Career:** Baseball player (retired); San Diego Padres, 1988-90; Toronto Blue Jays, 1991-95; Baltimore Orioles, 1996-98; Cleveland Indians, 1999-2001; NewYork Mets, 2002-03; Chicago White Sox, 2003, 2004; Ariz Diamondbacks, 2004; Tampa Bay Devil Rays, 2005. **Honors/Awds:** All-Star, 1990-2001; American League Gold Glove Award, 1991, 1992-2001; Silver Slugger Award, 1992, 1996, 1999, 2000; Most Valuable Player, Am League Championship Series, 1992; World Series champion, 1992, 1993; All-Star Game Most Valuable Player, 1998; Baltimore Orioles Hall of Fame; National Baseball Hall of Fame, 2011. **Special Achievements:** Won more Gold Gloves (10) than any other second baseman in history.

**ALOMAR, SANDY, SR. (SANTOS ALOMAR CONDE, SR.)**
Baseball player, athletic coach. **Personal:** Born Oct 19, 1943, Salinas; married Maria; children: Sandia, Sandy Jr & Roberto. **Career:** Baseball player (retired), coach; Milwaukee Braves, infielder, 1964-66; New York Mets, infielder, 1967, Willie Randolph's, bench coach, 2004-05, 2008-, first base bench coach, 2005-07, third base coach, 2007-09; Chicago White Sox, 1967-69; Calif Angels, infielder, 1969-74; New York Yankees, 1974-76; Tex Rangers, infielder, 1977-78; Puerto Rican Nat Team, coach, 1979-84; San Diego Padres, third base coach, 1986-90; Cleveland Indians, coach, 1990; Iowa Pac Coast League, interim mgr, 1991; Latin Am coordr, 1991-94; mgr rookie-level affiliate, 1995-96; roving minor league instr; San Juans, gen mgr, 1999-2000; Chicago Cubs, bull pen coach, 2000-01, first base coach, 2002; Colo Rockies, third base coach, 2003-04. **Orgs:** Chicago Cubs Orgn, 1991-2003.

**ALOMAR, SANDY, JR. (SANTOS VELAZQUEZ ALOMAR, JR.)**
Baseball player, athletic coach. **Personal:** Born Jun 18, 1966, Salinas; son of Sandy Sr; married Christie Solis; children: Marcus Xavier & Marissa Daniele; married Kelly Donovan; children: 1; married Margred; children: Leanna April, Brianna Maria & Isabela Simone. **Career:** Baseball player (retired), athletic coach, executive; San Diego Padres, prof baseball player, 1988-89, Cleveland Indians, prof baseball player, 1990-2000, first base coach, 2009, bench coach, 2011-, 2013-, mgr, 2012; Chicago White Sox, 2001-02, 2003-04, 2006; Colo Rockies, 2002; Tex Rangers, 2005; Los Angeles Dodgers, 2006; New York Mets, 2007, catching instr, 2008-09. **Honors/Awds:** Minor League Co-Player of the Year, Sporting News, 1988, Minor League Player of the Year, 1989; Player of the Year, Pac Coast League, 1989; American League Rookie Player of the Year, 1990; Gold Glove, American League, 1990; American League Rookie of the Year, Baseball Writers Asn Am, 1990; Baseball America Minor League Player of the Year Award, 1990; Major League Baseball All-Star Game MVP, 1997; inducted, The Cleveland Indians hall of fame, 2009. **Home Addr:** PO Box 367, Salinas, PR 00751. **Business Addr:** Catching Instructor, New York Mets, Shea Stadium, Flushing, NY 11368, **Business Phone:** (718)507-6387.

**ALONZO, JENNY**
Consultant, president (organization). **Personal:** children: 2. **Educ:** St John's Univ, BS, commun, 1987. **Career:** NBC Universal, coordr, on-air Promotions, 1989-91; WNBC-TV On-Air Prom, mgr, creative serv, 1990-93; Lifetime Tv, sr vpres, prod & prom planning, 1994-2006; Nat Asn Multi-Ethnicity Commun, pres, bd chair, bd dir, 2002-04; FCC, adv coun, 2002-10; Ford Motor Co's Premiere Automotive Group, adv coun, 2004-07; MIO TV, co-found, exec vpres & chief exec officer, 2007-09; The Nielsen Co, co-chair, hisp latino adv coun; 2007-;St John's Univ, adv coun, col of prof studies, 2009-; Girl Scouts of the USA, nat bd; Nat Bd Develop Comt, 2009-; Pvt Consultancy, Consult / Entertainment, 2009-; NUVOtv, Head of Mkt, 2012-2013. **Orgs:** Adv coun, FCC, 2002-10; Adv Coun, Ford Motor Co's Premiere Automotive Group, 2004-07; co-chair, Hisp Latino Adv Coun, Nielsen Co, 2007-; nat bd dir, Girl Scouts USA, Nat Bd Develop Comt, 2009-. **Business Addr:** Board Director, Girl Scouts of the USA, 420 5th Ave, New York, NY 10018-2798, **Business Phone:** (212)852-8000.

**ALSTON, BETTY BRUNER**
Educator. **Personal:** Born Jul 5, 1933, Concord, NC; daughter of Buford Sr and Ethel Torrence; married Henry Clay; children: Henry Clay Jr & Terry Verice. **Educ:** Barber-Scotia Col, BS, 1955; A&T State Univ, attended 1957; Appalachian State Univ, attended 1969. **Career:** Educator (retired); PTA/Odell Elem Sch, secy, 1979; PTSA/Northwest Mid Sch, secy, 1980, 1981; Northwest High Sch Booster Club, secy, 1982, vpres, 1983; Briarwood, Sch teacher, 1983-93. **Orgs:** NC Asn Educrs; elder, organist First United Presby Church; bd dir, Stonewall Jackson Sch, 1988, adv Coun, 1988, vice chair, 1991, Cabarrus County Bd Educ; second vpres, Dem Womens Orgn, 1989; Concord, Cabarrus Chamber Com, pres club, 1994; chmn, Cabarrus County Bd Educ, 1993-94; pres, Dem Women, 1993; adv coun, Stonewall Jackson Sch, 1995; bd trustee, Barber-Scotia Col, 1995; ambassador, Cabarrus Regional Chamber Com, 1996; bd mem, Am Red Cross, Cabarrus County chp, 2000. **Home Addr:** 1216 Crossbow Cir, PO Box 5091, Concord, NC 28027, **Home Phone:** (704)720-0706.

**ALSTON, DERRICK SAMUEL**
Basketball player. **Personal:** Born Aug 20, 1972, Bronx, NY. **Educ:** Duquesne Univ, attended 1994. **Career:** Basketball player (retired), coach; Philadelphia 76ers, ctr, 1994-96; Atlanta Hawks, ctr, 1996-97; Efes Pilsen, Turkey, 1996-97; TDK Manresa, Spain, 1997-98; FC Barcelona, Spain, 1998-2000; Boston Celtics, 2002; Pamesa Valencia, Spain, 2000-02; Real Madrid, Spain, 2002-03; Lleida, Spain, 2003-05; BCM Gravelines, France, 2005-06; Ural Great Perm, Russia, forward, 2006; Turk Telekom, Turkey, 2006-07; Nz Breakers, 2007-08; Libertad de Sunchales, Arg, 2008-09; Boca Juniors, Arg, 2009-10; La Union de Formosa, Arg, 2010, 2011-12; Houston Rockets, asst coach, 2012-15; Westchester Knicks, asst coach, 2015-. **Honors/Awds:** NBA Draft, 1994; Spanish League Finals Most Valuable Player, 1999. **Business Addr:** Assistant Coach, Westchester Knicks, Westchester County Ctr, White Plains, NY 10606, **Business Phone:** (914)559-6888.

**ALSTON, GERALD**
Singer. **Personal:** Born Nov 8, 1951, Henderson, NC; son of John and Geraldine Boyd; married Edna Chew; children: Kyle & Tod M. **Educ:** Kittrell Col. **Career:** New Imperials, mem; The Manhattans, lead singer, 1971-88; Motown band, singer; Albums: Where Did We Go Wrong, 1986; Gerald Alston, 1988; Open Invitation, 1990; Always in the Mood, 1992; First Class Only, 1994; Gerald Alston Sings Sam Cooke, 2008; Singles: "Take Me Where You Want To", 1988; "I Can't Tell You Why", 1989; "You Laid Your Love On Me", 1989; "Slow Motion", 1990; "Getting Back Into Love", 1991; "Tell Me This Night Won't End", 1991; "Hell Of A Situation (Backroom Conversation)", 1992; "Send For Me", 1993; "Stay The Night", 1994; "Devote All The Time", 1995. **Honors/Awds:** Grammy Winner for Shining Star, 1980. **Special Achievements:** Nominee, Am Music Award, 1980. **Business Addr:** Singer, Scotti Bros Records, 2114 Pico Blvd, Santa Monica, CA 90405, **Business Phone:** (212)662-2990.

**ALSTON, DR. KATHY DIANE**
Physician. **Personal:** Born Mar 29, 1958, Staten Island, NY. **Educ:** Univ Va, BA, 1980; Howard Univ Col Med, Md, 1984. **Career:** Martin Luther King Gen Hosp, physician, currently; emergency med, pvt practr, currently. **Orgs:** Asn Black Women Physicians, 1985-86; dorm coun, Joint Coun Interns & Residents, 1986-87. **Honors/Awds:** Nat Health Serv Corp Scholarship, 1980-83. **Home Addr:** 5850 S Main St, Los Angeles, CA 90003, **Home Phone:** (323)846-4104. **Business Addr:** Physician, Private Practitioner, 115 W Calif Blvd Suite 151, Pasadena, CA 91105, **Business Phone:** (626)585-8998.

**ALSTON, KWAKU**
Photographer, business owner. **Personal:** Born Feb 19, 1971, Philadelphia, PA. **Educ:** Rochester Inst Technol, BFA, 1994. **Career:** New York Times Mag, Sony Music, Rolling Stone, Photogr; rep music, entertainment & adv; Kwaku Alston Photog Inc, Owner, 1995-. **Business Addr:** Owner, Kwaku Alston Photographer Inc, 1346 Abbot Kinney Blvd, Venice, CA 90291, **Business Phone:** (310)392-9957.

**ALSTON, DR. PAMELA SUSAN ARBUCKLE**
Dentist. **Personal:** Born Mar 12, 1955, Oakland, CA; daughter of Ruby Arbuckle. **Educ:** Laney Col, AS, 1975; Univ Calif, BA, econ, 1977, MA, pub policy, BS, DDS, 1982, MPP, 1984. **Career:** Univ Calif, teaching asst, 1982-83; Cong Res Serv, policy analyst summer, 1983; San Francisco Gen Hosp, staff dentist, 1983-91; Alameda County Health Care Serv Agency, Cent Health Ctr, staff dentist, dir, 1983-; Johnson Bassin & Shaw Inc, consult, jobs corps health support proj, 1987-95; Prison Health Serv Inc, 1988-96; San Francisco Community Provider, dent consult, AIDS proj, 1990-93; Humanitas Inc; Job Corps Health Support Proj, consult; Eastmont Wellness Ctr, dent dir. **Orgs:** Secy, Nat Dent Soc Bay Area, 1983-84; comnr, Emeryville Community Develop Adv Comn, 1983-85; bd mem, Holy Names HS Alumnae Bd, 1983; Alameda City Bd Suprvs Subcomt Dent Health, 1983-85; prog comm mem, Bay Area Black Consortium Qual, 1983-85; ed, Network Black Health Prof newsletter, 1984-85; bd mem, Berkeley Head Start Health Adv Bd, 1984-85; counr, UC CA Alumni Asn, 1984-87; bd mem, City Berkeley Maternal Child & Adolescent Health Bd, 1985-86; vpres, Calif Chap Nat Dent Asn, 1985; Univ Calif Black Alumni Club; Nat Asn Advan Colored People, 1985; Alameda County Dent Soc; Am Dent Asn; Calif Dent Asn. **Honors/Awds:** Regents Scholar, Univ Calif, 1978-84; Williard Fleming Scholar, Univ Calif, 1979; Community Dentistry Service Award, Univ Calif, 1982; Certificate of Appreciation, SF Area Health Educ Ctr, 1984; Rosalie Stern Award, Community Serv, Univ Calif, 1990; Public Health Hero Award, Univ Calif, Berkeley Sch Pub Health, 1999; Women's Hall of Fame, Alameda County, 2012. **Home Addr:** 1262 Ocean Ave, Emeryville, CA 94608. **Business Addr:** Dentist, Alameda County Medical Center, 1411 E 31st St, Oakland, CA 94602, **Business Phone:** (510)437-4091.

**ALVES, PAGET L.**
Executive. **Personal:** Born Jan 1, 1955?. **Educ:** Cornell Univ, BS, indust & labor rels, 1976; Cornell Law Sch, JD. **Career:** IBM Corp, atty & sr mgr; Muratec Am, exec vpres & chief Operating officer; Sprint Commun Bus Serv Group, pres sales & support, 1996-2000; PointOne Telecommun, pres & chief exec officer, 2000-05; Centennial Commun Corp, pres & chief oper officer, 2002-03; Sprint Nextel Corp, pres strategic markets, 2003-06, chief financial officer, regional pres sales & distrib, 2006-08, pres bus markets group, chief sales officer, 2012-; Int Bus Mach Corp, Atty; Int Game Technol, dir, 2010-. **Orgs:** Bd mem, Higher M-Pact; bd mem, Kans City Area Develop Coun; dir, Int Game Technol, 2010-; GTECH Holdings Corp, bd dir, 2005-; Herman Miller Inc, bd dir, 2007-10. **Business Addr:** Director, GTECH Holdings Corp, 55 Technol Way, West Greenwich, RI 02817, **Business Phone:** (401)392-6980.

**ALVES, PAGET L.**
President (organization), chief executive officer. **Educ:** Cornell Univ, BS, labor & indust rels, 1978; Cornell Law Sch, JD, 1982. **Career:** Murata Bus Syst, exec vpres & chief operating officer, 1988-96; Pointe Telecommunications, pres & chief exec officer, 2000-01; Centennial Commun, pres & chief operating officer, 2002-03; Sprint Nextel, Wholesale Group, vpres sales & mkt, 1996-97, pres, 1998-99, Bus Serv Group, co-pres, 1999-2000, Strategic Markets, pres, 2003-05, Enterprise Markets, sr vpres, 2005-06, S Region, pres, 2007-08, pres sales & distrib, 2008-09, Bus Markets Group, pres, 2009-12, chief sales officer, 2012-13. **Orgs:** Dir, GTECH Holdings Corp, bd mem, mem audit comt, 2005-07; dir, Gtech Corp; dir, Int Game Technol, 2010-; dir, chair compensation comt, bd mem & chair capital deployment comt, 2010-; dir, Herman Miller Inc, 2007-10, bd mem, mem compensation comt, 2007-09; IGT; Synchrony Financial, 2015-. **Honors/Awds:** National Eagle Leadership Institute, CareerFOCUS Eagle Award, 2008; "Black Enterprise," The 100 Most Powerful Executives in Corporate America, 2010.

**ALWAN, MANSOUR**
Government official, engineer. **Personal:** children: 5. **Career:** Chesilhurst, NJ, mayor, 1975-83; Electronic engr & consult, currently. **Orgs:** Adenu Allah Arabic Asn; exec dir, Chesilhurst Coalition Youth & Family Develop. **Home Addr:** 3 6th Ave, Waterford Works, NJ 08089-1115, **Home Phone:** (856)809-1853. **Business Addr:** Member, Chesilhurst Coalition For Youth & Family Development, 511 Edwards Ave, Waterford Works, NJ 08089-1115.

**AMADO, JOSEPH S.**
Executive, vice president (organization). **Personal:** Born Yonkers, NY. **Educ:** Winston-Salem State Univ, BA, 1978. **Career:** Nestle; Philip Morris USA, comput analyst, 1986, systs supvr, 1989, info technol mgr, 1992, Pioneer Philip Morris USA, SAP Competency Ctr, 1994, info technol dir info servs sls orgn, 1997, info technol dir ops, 1998, IT Orgn, exec sponsor, col recruiting efforts, currently; Altria Group Inc, sr vpres info systs & chief info officer, altria client serv, currently. **Orgs:** Bd dir, Greater Richmond Technol Coun; bd dir, Greater Richmond Chamber Found; bd dir, FRIENDS; bd dir, Asn C, Richmond, Va; trustee, bd dir Winston-Salem State Univ, currently; bd dir & secy, Altria Co Employee Community Fund, currently. **Business Addr:** Senior Vice President of Information, Chief Information Officer, Altria Group Inc, 521 Gotham Pkwy, Carlstadt, NJ 07072-2404.

**AMAKER, HAROLD TOMMY**
Basketball coach, basketball player. **Personal:** Born Jun 6, 1965, Falls Church, VA; son of Alma; married Stephanie Pinder. **Educ:** Univ Harvard, econ, 1987. **Career:** Basketball player (retired); Duke Univ, asst coach, 1988-97; Seton Hall Univ, head men's basketball coach, 1997-2001; Univ Mich, head men's basketball coach, 2001-07; Harvard Univ, coach, 2007-. **Orgs:** Black Coaches Asn; USA Basketball. **Business Addr:** Head Coach, Harvard Uniersity, Holyoke Ctr 3rd Fl, Cambridge, MA 02138, **Business Phone:** (617)495-1000.

**AMAN, MARY JO PARKER**
Educator. **Personal:** Born Sep 6, 1938, Portsmouth, OH; daughter of Ronald F and Goldia M Parker; married Mohammed M; children: David. **Educ:** Fisk Univ, BA, 1960; Clark Atlanta Univ, MSLS, 1962. **Career:** Brooklyn Pub Libr, asst coordr, c's serv; Viking Press, dir, libr prom; Naussau Libr Syst, coor dr, c's servs; Univ Wis, Milwaukee, bus librn, 1983-86, head, curric collection, 1986-98, outreach specialist, 1998-2001, dir, tech stud affairs, 2001, sr outreach specialist, Div Outreach & Continuing Edu, currently; New Directions in the Middle East Vol. 2, ed; Digest of Middle East Studies, assoc ed; Post Arab Spring: Middle East Reviews, ed. **Orgs:** Am Libr Asn, 1962-; Wis Lib asn, Am libr Asn Coun, 1996-2000. **Home Addr:** 4020 W Mequon Rd, Mequon, WI 53092, **Home Phone:** (262)242-9031. **Business Addr:** Director, Senior Outreach Specialist, University Wisconsin-Milwaukee, 161 W Wis Ave Suite 6000, Milwaukee, WI 53203, **Business Phone:** (414)227-3232.

**AMAN, DR. MOHAMMED**
Dean (education), educator, library administrator. **Personal:** Born Jan 3, 1940, Alexandria; son of Mohammed and Fathia Ali al-Maghrabi; married Mary Jo Parker; children: David. **Educ:** Cairo Univ, Egypt, BA, 1961; Columbia Univ, MS, 1965; Univ Pittsburgh, PhD, 1968; NY Univ, post grad studies, 1970. **Career:** Univ Pittsburgh, res asst, 1965-66; Duquesne Univ, Pittsburgh, Pa, ref libr, 1966-68; Pratt Inst, Brooklyn, NY, asst prof; St John's Univ, New York, NY, from asst prof to assoc prof, 1969-73, dir & prof, 1973-76; Long Island Univ, Greenvale, Long Island, NY, dean & prof, 1976-79; Univ Wis-Milwaukee, Wis, Sch Info studies, dean & prof, 1979-202; IT2000 MITEC Progs, princ investr & dir, 2000-05, Sch Educ, interim dean, 2000-02. **Orgs:** Egyptian Am Scholars Asn, 1971-; info mgt consult, Un Indust Develop Orgn, 1978-; Unesco, 1982-, US-AID, 1984-96; chmn, Int Rels Comt, Am Lib Asn, 1984-86; life mem & founding exec bd mem, Nat Asn Advan

Colored People, 1984-; Asn Lib & Info Sci Ed, 1985-86; Am Soc Info Sci Int Rel Comt; chair, Int Issues Info Spec Interest Group; bd mem, Wisc African Relief Effort, 1986-89; founder & bd mem, Interfaith Dialogue, WI; bd mem, Wisc African Hist Soc Mus, 1988-91; Audience Develop Comt, Milwaukee Art Mus; founder, Milwaukee Leader's Forum, 1991-; bd mem, Am Black Holocaust Mus, 1998-2001; bd mem, Coun Eyptian-Am Rels, 2000-; bd mem, Clarah Mohammad Sch; life mem, Archons Colophon; Beta Phi Mu; bd mem, Assn Mid Eastern Pub Policy & Admin; bd mem, Am Univ Dubai; bd mem, Arab Union Catalog; bd mem, Online Learning J (Wiley/PSO); hon vpres, Policy Studies Orgn. **Special Achievements:** Obtained first national ALA accreditation for the St. John's University Division of Library and Information Science in 1979; introduced the first doctoral program at C. W. Post Center of Long Island University; Introduced the first BS and PhD in Information Science at University of Wisconsin-Milwaukee; Grants received at University of Wisconsin-Milwaukee-SOIS exceeded two million during Dr. Aman's tenure as dean. Author of 200+ articles and 15 books in his areas of expertise. Editor-in-Chief, Digest of Middle East Studies (DOMES), published by Wiley-Blackwell; EIC, Middle East Media & Book Reviews, published by the University of Wisconsin-Milwaukee. **Home Addr:** 10200 W Bluemound Rd Suite 819, Mequon, WI 53226, **Home Phone:** (414)229-3315. **Business Addr:** Professor, University of Wisconsin-Milwaukee, PO Box 413, Milwaukee, WI 53201, **Business Phone:** (414)229-3315.

**AMARO, MORA, SR.** See AMARO, RUBEN, SR.

### AMARO, RUBEN, SR. (MORA AMARO, SR.)
Baseball manager, baseball executive, baseball player. **Personal:** Born Jan 6, 1936, Veracruz, VC; son of Santos and Josefina Mora; married Judy; children: David & Ruben Jr; married Lilia Machado; children: Luis Alfredo & Ruben Andres. **Career:** Baseball player, baseball coach (retired), baseball executive; St Louis Cardinals, 1958; Philadelphia Phillies, shortstop, 1960-65, coach minor leagues, 1970-71, scout, 1972-74, Latin Am, coordr, asst to Dallas Green, Minor Leagues Scouting, dir, 1974-77, scout develop supvr, 1977-79, minor league coach, 1980-81, scout, 1982; New York Yankees, shortstop, 1966-68; Calif Angels, shortstop, 1969; Chicago Cubs, coach, 1982-87, caribbean area scout, 1988; Detroit Tigers, scout, 1989-96; Chicago Cubs, minor league mgr, Aguilas del Zulia, asst gen mgr, currently. **Orgs:** Chicago Cubs; Maj League Baseball-Baseball Assistance Team. **Home Addr:** 4098 Cinnamon Way, Weston, FL 33331-3810, **Home Phone:** (954)349-3478.

### AMBEAU, KAREN M.
Marketing executive, executive director. **Personal:** Born Jul 4, 1956, Berkeley, CA; daughter of Mildred Anthony and Lucien; married Michael McClendon. **Educ:** Tuskegee Univ, Tuskegee, AL, BSEE, 1981. **Career:** Pac Gas & Elec, Hayward, Calif, acct rep, 1981-, sr prog mgr, San Francisco, Calif, IDSM progs, 2006-, supvr; Nat NBS Asst Ski, coach, Western Region Ski, head, youth dir. **Orgs:** McGee Ave Church Educ Aid, 1982-; corresp sect, Delta Sigma Theta Sorority, 1987-89, chairperson & fund-raiser, 1990; Bus Prof Women's Club, 1987-90; dir, All Seasons Youth Ski Club; Head Western Region Ski, Coach; Nat NBS Asst Ski, Coach. **Honors/Awds:** Outstanding Young Careerist, Bus & Prof Womens, 1987; Miss Tuskegee, Tuskegee Univ, 1977. **Home Addr:** 20715 Waterford Pl, Castro Valley, CA 94552-3753, **Home Phone:** (510)538-3368. **Business Addr:** Sr Program Manager, Pacific Gas & Electric Co, Rm 697D 245 Mkt St, San Francisco, CA 94105-1126, **Business Phone:** (415)973-3329.

### AMBERS, MONIQUE
Basketball player, basketball coach. **Personal:** Born Dec 21, 1970, Hayward, CA; daughter of Robert and Linda. **Educ:** Ariz State Univ, BS, family resources & human develop, 1994. **Career:** Basketball player (retired), basketball coach; George Wash Univ, asst coach, 1994-97; Phoenix Mercury, forward, 1997; Kalamarias-Thessoloniki, Greece, 1997-98; Hali, Wolfenbuettel, Ger, 1999-2001; Wuppertal, Wuppertal, Ger, 2001-02; Sacramento Monarchs, asst coach, 2002-09; Shinsegae, Seoul, Korea, 2002-03; Chen Nen, Harbin, China, 2004-06; New York Liberty, asst coach, 2010-12; State Farm Ins, Agt Intern, 2014; State Farm, Owner, 2014-. **Business Addr:** Assistant Coach, New York Liberty, 4331 Truxel Rd Suite G3, Sacramento, CA 95834-1944, **Business Phone:** (916)928-4747.

### AMBROSE, ASHLEY AVERY
Football player, football coach. **Personal:** Born Sep 17, 1970, New Orleans, LA; married Melanie; children: Aisha & A J. **Educ:** Miss Valley State Univ, attended. **Career:** Football player (retired), coach; Indianapolis Colts, defensive back, 1992-95; Cincinnati Bengals, cornerback, 1996-98; New Orleans Saints, cornerback, 1999, 2003-04; Atlanta Falcons, cornerback, 2000-02; Colo Buffaloes, defensive tech intern, 2008-09, wide receivers coach, 2010-11; Calif Golden Bears, defensive backs coach, 2011-12; Boise State Broncos, defensive backs coach, 2016-. **Honors/Awds:** AFC Defensive Back of the Year, NFL Players Asn, 1996; Pro Bowl, 1996. **Business Addr:** Defensive Backs Coach, Boise State Broncos, 2035 Corte del Nogal Suite 250, Carlsbad, CA 92009.

### AMBROSE, DR. ETHEL L.
Government official, social worker. **Personal:** Born Dec 18, 1930, Perryville, AR; children: Ethel M Harris, Derek S Brown & Lakeitha Brown. **Educ:** Highland Park Community Col, attended 1975; Southeastern Univ, BS, sociol, 1980. **Career:** Government official, social worker (retired); City Highland Pk, spec asst mayor, 1969-76; Univ Mich, lic social worker, 1973; Detroit Adult Ed, substitute teacher, 1978-79; Diversified Health Ctr, social worker, 1979-80; Alpha Annex Nursing Ctr, social worker. **Orgs:** Citizen Interest Scholar Comt, 1967-; life mem, Highland Pk Caucus Club, 1973-; bd pres, Wayne Metrop Community Servs Agency, 1983-84; trustee, Highland Pk Bd Ed/Community Col, 1983-; pres, ACCT Minorities Affairs/Cent Region, 1984-; Nat Polit Cong Black Women, 1984; Mich Ctr Urban African Am Aging Res; sr aide, bd mem, Healthier Black Elders Ctr Community Adv Bd, Wayne State Univ. **Home Addr:** 352 Courtland, Highland Park, MI 48203. **Business Addr:** Board Member, Wayne State University, 87 E Ferry St 226 Knapp Bldg, Detroit, MI 48202, **Business Phone:** (313)664-2634.

### AMENKHIENAN, DR. CHARLOTTE
Counselor. **Personal:** Born Nov 15, 1958, Warri, BE. **Educ:** Va Tech, PhD. **Career:** VA Polytech Inst & State Univ, staff counr, currently. **Orgs:** Coordr, multicultural & progs eval, Cook Coun Ctr; Peer Assistance Learning. **Business Addr:** Staff Counselor, Outreach Services, Cook Coun Center Va Tech, 240 McComas Hall, Blacksburg, VA 24061-0108, **Business Phone:** (540)231-6557.

### AMERICA, RICHARD F.
Educator. **Personal:** son of Richard F Sr and Arline; married Diane Salin. **Educ:** Pa State Univ, BS, econs, 1960; Harvard Univ, MBA, 1965. **Career:** SRI Int, Develop economist, consult, 1965-69; Univ Calif, Berkeley, Calif, lectr & dir urban progs, 1970-72; Stanford Bus Sch, vis lectr, 1970-72; Joint Ctr for Polit and Econ Studies, consult, 1972-73; Cong Budget Off, consult, 1976; House Comt on Banking, consult, 1976; US Dept of Com, dir, 1978-90; Small Bus Admin, sr policy advisor, sr prog mgr & dir, Prog Eval, 1980-97; Bank of Am; Stanford Res Inst; americaconsulting, prin, 1996-; Georgetown Univ, McDonough Sch Bus, prof, 1999-2012, adj lectr, currently; Africa Bus Group, consult, 2011-. Books: Developing the Afro-American Economy; Moving Ahead: Black Managers in American Business; The Wealth of Races, ed; Paying the Social Debt; Philanthropy and Economic Development, ed; Soul in Management: How African American Managers Thrive in the Competitive Corporate Environment. **Orgs:** Founder & pres, Nat Econ Asn, 1970; San Francisco Local Develop Corp, 1972-73; Unitarian Affordable Housing Corp; Northern Va Vis Nurse Asn, 1989-95; bd trustee, W Africa Socs On Bus Ethics, 2013-; bd adv, Global Bus Sch Network, 2013-. **Business Addr:** Adjunct Lecturer, Georgetown University, 3700 O St NW, Washington, DC 20057, **Business Phone:** (202)687-0100.

### AMIE, GWEN E.
School administrator. **Personal:** Born May 5, 1956, Las Vegas, NV; children: Justina. **Educ:** Univ Nev, Las Vegas, BS, educ, 1978, master, coun, 1982; Nat Univ, MA, admin, 1986. **Career:** CCSD, math teacher, 1979-85, counselor, 1985-92, dean of students, 1992-97, asst principal, 1997-; Sierra Vista High Sch, asst prin, currently. **Orgs:** Delta Sigma Theta, 1976-; Western regional tournament comn, Nat Bowling Asn, 1980-, nat scholarship chair, 1999-; Western States Golf Asn, 1986-; Nat Asn Secondary Sch Prin, 1992-; Clark Co Asn Sch Admin, 1992-; debutante advisory comn, Les Femmes Douzer, 1996-; bd mem, Southern Nev Bowling Asn, 2000-; chairperson, Nat Bowling Asn Inc, 2003. **Home Addr:** 904 Woodbridge Dr, Las Vegas, NV 89131, **Home Phone:** (702)648-8530. **Business Addr:** Assistant Principal, Sierra Vista High School, 8100 W Robindale Rd, Las Vegas, NV 89113, **Business Phone:** (702)799-6820.

### AMIJI, HATIM M.
Educator. **Personal:** Born Jun 11, 1939. **Educ:** London, BA, hons, 1964; Princeton Univ, MA, PhD. **Career:** Trinity Coll Nabingo, Uganda, lectr, 1964; Nairobi Univ, Kenya, res assoc hist, 1967-68; Princeton Univ, lectr, 1969-70; Boston Univ, lectr, Dept Hist & Centre African Studies, 1972; Univ Mass, assoc prof hist. **Orgs:** Sec gen, Zanzibar Youth League, 1960; dir, African Studies Workshop World Affairs Coun, Boston, 1972; Mid Eastern Studies Assoc; fel African Acad; African Studies Assoc, US; ed bd, Gemini Rev; founder, Pan-African Univ Org; Prince Agakhan Shia Imami Ismaili Coun Kenya. **Home Addr:** 7 Treadway Rd, Boston, MA 02125. **Business Addr:** Associate Professor, University of Massachusetts, Harbor Campus, Boston, MA 02125, **Business Phone:** (617)287-5000.

### AMIN, KARIMA (CAROL ANN AIKEN)
Educator, storyteller, activist. **Personal:** Born Jun 1, 1947, Buffalo, NY; daughter of Harvey Aiken and Bessie Mabry; children: Abdur Rahman, Takiyah Nur & Sabriyah. **Educ:** State Univ NY, Buffalo, BA, Eng, 1969, MEd, urban educ/curric develop, 1974. **Career:** Buffalo Pub Schs, lan arts sec teacher, 1969-92; multicultural lit specialist, 1992-94; prof storyteller, social justice advocate & auth, 1994-. **Orgs:** Treas & secy, Taara Zakkiyya Islamic Strhd, 1975-82; Nat Coun Teachers Eng, 1982-86; bd dir, Afro-Am Hist Asn Niagara Frontier, 1984-86; co-founder, Spin-a-Story Tellers Western New York, 1984-; Nat Storytelling Network, 1984-; Nat Asn Black Storytellers, 1986-; We All Storytellers, 1987-; Nat Comn Storytelling, 1987-90; Erie County Community Corrections Adv Bd, 1988-; Comn Preserv Multicultural Lit Am, 1988-90; consult, Proj Reach, 1989-; bd dir, EPIC Nat, 1994-2005; nat adv bd, MacMillan McGraw-Hill Publ, 1994-96; Tradition Keepers: Black Storytellers Western New York, 1995-; 50 Women Vision Inc, 1996-; bd dir, Squeaky Wheel Media Arts Org, 1999-2007; bd mem, Crossroads Storytelling Ctr, 2003-; founder & dir, Prisoners Are People Too Inc, 2005-; co-chair, Erie County Prisoners Rights Coalition; Partnership Pub Good. **Honors/Awds:** Black Educators of the Year, Black Educators Asn Western New York, 1977; Teacher of Tomorrow Award, Buffalo Bd Ed, 1978; William Wells Brown Award, Afro-Am Historical Asn, 1984; Award, Eng Speaking Union Western New York, 1986; Achievement Award, Nat Asn Negro Bus & Prof Women's Clubs, 1994; Apple for the Teacher Award, Iota Phi Lambda Sorority Inc, Beta Phi Chap, 1994; Community Service Award, Alpha Kappa Alpha, 1997, Outstanding Artist Award, 2000; Community Leadership Award, Niagra Univ, 2001; Daisy Lampkin Award, Links Inc Eastern Region, 2001; Uncrowned Queen Award, Pan-Am Exposition, 2001; Parents Choice Foundation Gold Award, 2005; Storytelling World Winner Award, 2006; Distinguished Humanitarian, Univ Buffalo, 2009. **Special Achievements:** Co-wrote Black Lit for HS Studs, NCTE, 1978; Publication: "You Can Say That Again!, Galactic Multimedia", 1994; "Adventures of Brer Rabbit and Friends, Dorling-Kendersley (UK)", 1999; contributor, "African American Children's Stories: A Treasury of Tradition & Pride", 2001; "My First Treasury: Grandma Loves You", 2003; "You Can Say That Again!", re-mastered 2004 by S'Wanye. **Home Addr:** 389 Millicent Ave, Buffalo, NY 14215. **Business Addr:** Founder, Director, Prisoners Are People Too Inc, Pratt-Willert Community Ctr 422 Pratt St, Buffalo, NY 14204, **Business Phone:** (716)834-8438.

### AMMONS, DR. JAMES H.
Educator. **Personal:** son of James Henry and Agnes; married Judy; children: James III. **Educ:** Fla A&M Univ, BS, polit sci, 1974; Fla State Univ, MS, pub admin, 1975, PhD, govt, 1977. **Career:** Univ Cent Fla, asst prof pub policy & admin, 1977-83; Fla A&M Univ, asst prof polit sci, 1983-84, asst vpres acad affairs, 1984-89, assoc vpres, dir, 1989-93, prof, 1993-95, provost, vpres acad affairs, 1995, chancellor, pres, 2007-12; Univ Wis, Madison, Booth Ferris fel, 1993; NC Cent Univ, chief adminr, chancellor, 2001-07. **Orgs:** Fel Am Coun Educ, 1986-87; CIGNA Found, 1986-87; Comn Col Southern Asn Col& Sch; Am Asn State Col & Univ Task Force; Joint Comn Accountability Reporting; chmn, Compliance & Report Comt, Comt Col Coun Advan & Support Educ; bd mem, Am Asn Cols Teacher Educ. **Business Addr:** President, Florida A & M University, 1601 Martin Luther King Jr Blvd Suite 400, Tallahassee, FL 32307, **Business Phone:** (850)599-3000.

### AMORY, DR. REGINALD L.
Chairperson, educator, engineer. **Personal:** Born Jul 17, 1936, Peekskill, NY; married Marion Rose Boothe; children: Reginald & Susan. **Educ:** NY Univ, BCE, 1960; Clarkson Univ, MCE, 1963; Rensselaer Polytech Inst, PhD, 1967. **Career:** Westinghouse Labs, sr engr; Gen Elec Res Labs, res engr; B&M Technol Serv, chief scientist corp res; RMS Sci & Technol, pres; US Dept Energy, Spec Asst; Energy Res & Develop Admin, consult; US Dept Transp, consult; Nat Acad Engineering, consult; Nat Sci Found, consult; Mobil Oil Corp, consult;Throop & Feiden, engr, 1960-61; Abbott, Jerkt & Co, engr, 1961-63; RPI, tech asst, 1963-64, instr, 1965-66; Northeastern Univ, Dept Civil Eng, asst prof, 1966-68, prof, 1974; NC Agri & Tech Univ, dean, 1968-74; ALCOA Found, prof civil engineering; Morgan State Univ, Dept Civil Eng, fac, prof & chair, 1996-. **Orgs:** Educ Develop Corp; SC Commn Higher Educ; Tenn State Univ; Robert Charles Assoc; proj bd, vpres, exec bd, Am Soc Engr Educ; fel Am Soc Civil Engrs; Int Asn Bridge & Struct Engrs; Nat Soc Prof Engrs; AAAS; bd trustee, St Augustine's Col; adv bd, Nat Urban League; Sigma Psi Phi; fel Lambda Alpha Int Hon Soc; fel Am Socs Civil Engrs; mem adv bd, Ctr Advan Microwave Res & Applications; New York Acad Sci. **Special Achievements:** First African American to receive a PhD in engineering from Rensselaer Polytechnic Institute. **Home Addr:** 806 Morris Tpke Suite 3F, Short Hills, NJ 07078-2604. **Business Addr:** Professor, Chairperson, Morgan State University School of Engineering, 1700 E Cold Spring Lane, Baltimore, MD 21251, **Business Phone:** (443)885-4220.

**AMOS, CATHYE ROSS.** See ROSS, CATHYE P.

### AMOS, DONALD E.
Lawyer. **Personal:** Born Aug 2, 1953, Buffalo, NY; son of Edward Jr and Ann; children: Sharnele, Lauren & Amber. **Educ:** Chicago State Univ, BS, 1975; DePaul Univ, JD, 1984. **Career:** IRS Criminal Invests Div, spec agt, 1975-87; US Environ Protection Agency, spec agt, 1994-2007; DC Govt, US EPA Off Inspector Gen, spec agt & dir, squad 1, 2007-; Law Off Donald E. Amos, owner. **Home Addr:** 187 8th St Suite 3, Brooklyn, NY 11215, **Home Phone:** (202)646-0323. **Business Addr:** Special Agent, Director, Squad 1, District of Columbia Government, 717 14th St NW Suite 500, Washington, DC 20005-3211, **Business Phone:** (202)727-2540.

### AMOS, JOHN A., JR.
Actor. **Personal:** Born Dec 27, 1939, Newark, NJ; son of John Sr and Annabelle P; married Noel J Mickelson; children: 2; married Elisabete De Sousa; children: 2; married Lillian Lehman; children: 2. **Educ:** Colo State Univ. **Career:** Social worker; advert copywriter; TV series: "Mary Tyler Moore", 1970-77; "The Dist", 2000; "All About the Andersons", 2003; "Men in Trees, 2006; "My Name Is Earl", 2008; "The Law", 2009; "Two and a Half Men", 2010; "Royal Pains", 2010; "30 Rock", 2010; "Lie to Me", 2010; "Untitled Martin Lawrence Project", 2012; "NYC 22", 2012; "The Bob Show", 2012. Films: Touched by Love, 1980; The Beastmaster, 1982; Am Flyers, 1985; Coming to Am, 1988; Lock Up, 1989; Die Hard 2, 1990; Ricochet, 1991; Clippers, 1991; Mac, 1992; Night Trap, 1993; The Black Cat, 1993; Hologram Man, 1995; For Better or Worse, 1996; A Woman Like That, 1997; The Player's Club, 1998; All Over Again, 2001; The Watermelon Heist, 2003; My Baby's Daddy, 2004; Lichnyy nomer, 2004; Boy s tenyu, 2005; Voodoo Moon, 2005; Dr. Dolittle 3, 2006; Ascension Day, 2007; Tamales and Gumbo, 2008; Perfect Sunday, 2010; Zombie Hamlet, co-producer, 2012; Madea's Witness Protection, 2012; Strawberries for the Homeless, 2014; Act of Faith, 2014. **Honors/Awds:** Golden Gloves boxing champion; Groundbreaking Show, 2004; Impact Award, 2006; Anniversary Award, TV Land Awards, 2004, 2006 & 2007. **Business Addr:** Actor, c/o Michael Mesnick & Associates, 11300 Olympic Blvd Suite 610, Los Angeles, CA 90064.

### AMOS, KENT B.
Chief executive officer, sales manager, founder (originator). **Personal:** Born May 21, 1944, Washington, DC; son of Benjamin F and Gladys C; married Carmen. **Educ:** Del State Col, BS, 1970. **Career:** Xerox Corp, salesperson, sales mgr, 1975-76, area mgr, 1976-77, ISG Affirm Action, mgr, 1977-78, dir corp affirm action, EEO, 1978-82; Triad Group, pres; Community Acad Pub Charter Sch, founder, prin, chief exec officer & acad leader; Kids House, founder, 1994. **Orgs:** Alpha Kappa Mu Nat Hon Soc, 1968-69; Corp Few, 1971-79; Big Bros, 1971-74; Inside & Outside, 1972-; bus consult, Cong Black Caucus, 1975-79; Bus Policy Rev Comn, 1977-79; Nat Asn Advan Colored People; Nat Urban League; Nat Coun Negro Women; Del St Col Alumni Asn; Coolidge High Sch Alumni Asn; Omega Psi Phi; bd dir, Boys & Girls Club Greater Wash, 1990-; adv bd mem, I Have a Dream Found, 1990-; chmn, Shiloh Community Develop Corp; founder, Urban Family Inst, 1991, pres, currently. **Honors/Awds:** Black Hist Week Awards, WMAL Radio & TV Sta, 1974; Merit Awards for Job Performance, Xerox Corp; Pres Sales Recognition Award, Xerox Corp; Chair's Award, Cong Black Caucus, 1979; Nat Asn Equal Opportunity Higher Educ; Legacy Award, Nat Coun Negro Women; Image Award, Nat Asn Advan Colored People; Whitney Young Award, Urban League; Roy Dykes Mem Award, Xerox Corp; Citizen of the Year, Omega Psi Phi; Man of the Year, Shiloh Baptist Church; Alumnus of the Century, Delaware State Col; Alumnus of the Year, Calvin Coolidge High Sch; Alumnus of the Year, Del State Col; scholar funds created in his name at Calvin Coolidge High Sch & Del State Col;

Annual Serv Youth Award, Big Brothers Nat Capea, 1990; Thanks giving Tuesday Award, Distinguished Community Serv, Catholic Univ Am & Madison Natl Bank, 1990. **Home Addr:** 2720 Unicorn Lane NW, Washington, DC 20015, **Home Phone:** (202)966-6620. **Business Addr:** President, Founder, Urban Family Institute, 1400 16th St NW Suite 101, Washington, DC 20036, **Business Phone:** (202)234-5437.

### AMOS, RALPH
Executive director. **Educ:** Ohio State Univ, BS, 1986; Ohio Univ, MPA, 2004; PhD. **Career:** Ohio State Univ, Alumni Asn, staff, 1990-98, Off alumni rel, asst vpres & exec dir, 1998-2007; Univ Calif, Los Angeles, Alumni Asn, exec dir, 2007-, External Affairs, asst vice chancellor alumni rels, 2007-13, chief constituent serv officer, 2007-13; Univ Md, exec dir, 2013-14; exec dir mkt & spec events, currently. **Business Addr:** Executive Director, Assistant Vice Chancellor, University California Los Angeles Alumni Association, 10920 Wilshire Blvd Suite 1400, Los Angeles, CA 90095-6516, **Business Phone:** (310)794-2345.

### AMPY, DR. FRANKLIN R.
Educator. **Personal:** Born Jun 22, 1936, Dinwiddie, VA; son of Preston and Beatrice Tucker. **Educ:** Va State Col, Petersburg, BS, 1958; Ore State Univ, Corvallis, MS, PhD, biostatistics & genetics, 1962. **Career:** Ore State Univ, Corvallis, res asst, 1958-62; Am Univ Beirut, asst prof, Lebanon, 1962-68; Univ Calif, Davis, postdoctorate, 1968-70, Educ Oppor Prog, assoc dean, 1970-71; Howard Univ, assoc prof zool, actg chmn zool, 1973-75, 1984-86, prof biol, 2003-, interim chmn, currently; NASA Am Moffett Fields, fel, 1976. **Orgs:** Evaluator, Va Talent Search, 1980-; consult, Nat Inst Health, 1981, 1983; treas, Howard Chap Am Assoc Univ Prof, 1983-84; Proj Thirty, Carnegie Found NY, comm. **Home Addr:** 5630 16th St NW, Washington, DC 20011, **Home Phone:** (202)829-9590. **Business Addr:** Professor, Interim Chairman, Howard University, Ernest Just Hall Rm 126 415 Col St NW, Washington, DC 20059, **Business Phone:** (202)806-6933.

### ANASAZI, TYR. See COBB, KEITH HAMILTON.

### ANCRUM, ALBERTA E.
Municipal government official, police chief. **Career:** City NY, Dept Invest, asst inspector gen, spec investgr, 2001, Inspector Gen Office, dep inspector gen, asst comnr, dir, chief Firearms instr; Grand Central Partnership, dep dir, currently. **Business Addr:** Deputy Director, Grand Central Partnership, 122 E 42nd St Suite 601, New York, NY 10168, **Business Phone:** (212)883-2420.

### ANDERS, KIMBLE LYNARD
Football player, football coach. **Personal:** Born Sep 10, 1966, Galveston, TX. **Educ:** Univ Houston, MA, athletic admin, 1989. **Career:** Football player (retired), football coach; Kans City Chiefs, 1991, running back, 1992, 1999 & 2000, full back, 1993-98; Avila Univ, running back coach; Mid Am Nazarene Univ, running back coach, 2006; Northeast H.S, head football coach, 2009-; Mo Sch Dept, athletic dir; Galveston Ball High Sch, athletic dir, head football coach, 2013-. **Orgs:** Founder, Running Back Giving Back Found, 2000; Kans City Chiefs Ambassadors. **Honors/Awds:** Unsung Hero Achievement Award, 1997; Pro Bowl, 1995, & 1996 & 1997; "All Time Leading Receiver", kans city chiefs. **Business Addr:** Blue Springs, MO.

### ANDERS, RICHARD H.
Athletic coach, educator. **Personal:** Born Jul 29, 1925, Arcadia, CA; son of James and Nettie; married Charlotte King; children: Kenneth, Keith & Rosalind. **Educ:** Fla A&M Univ, BS, 1947; Ind Univ, MS, 1963. **Career:** Dunbar High Sch, Ft Myers, athletic dir coach, 1947-48; Richardson High Sch, Lake City, 1948-69; part time city recreation asst, 1968-; Columbia High Sch, suprv educ health, 1973-75, dir, 1970-. **Orgs:** Polemarch Gainesville Alumni, Chap Kappa Alpha Psi Frat, 1968-69, 1972-73, pres, 1989-91; adv bd, N Cent Fla Phys Educ Clin, 1970-; vpres, Columbia Educ Asn, 1974-75; secy, Gateway Serv Unit, Fla Educ Asn, 1974-75; CEA Exec Bd; pres, Fla A&M Alumni Gateway Chap Lake City, 1974-; Lake City Optimist Club; Emerg Med Training Comt; Versiteers Soc Club; Masonic Fraternal Order Shiloh 619; pres, chorister New Bethel Bapt Ch, 1990-; chmn, Columbia County Sch Bd, 1988, 1992-. **Honors/Awds:** Football Championships, 1947, 1951, 1953, 1959 & 1963-65; runner up, 1955-56, 1961-62; Coach of the Year Award, 1963, 1966; Florida Interscholastic Coaches Association Award, 1967; Life Memorial Award, FL Athletic Coaches Asn, 1970; Music Director Trophy, 1974; Education Achievement Award, NAACP, 1985; Versiteers Presidential Award, Versiteers Club, 1987-89; Achievement Award, Girl Scout Troop 117, 1989; SABO Service Award, Sothern Asn Basketball Official, 1991; Kappa Founders Day Award, Kappa Alpha Psi Fraternity, 1991. **Home Addr:** 1072 W Jefferson St, Lake City, FL 32055, **Home Phone:** (386)752-0959. **Business Addr:** Intramural Director, Columbia HS, Lake City, FL 32055.

### ANDERSON, ABBIE H.
Military leader, administrator. **Personal:** Born Jun 3, 1928, Terrell, TX; son of James C and Abbie Gill; married Frances R Morgan; children: Donna R, Rosalind T, Abbie H Jr & Michael EC. **Educ:** Tuskegee Inst, BS, 1953; Lincoln Univ, MEd, 1966. **Career:** Administrator (retired), brigade exec officer; Vietnamese Chief Reg Forces, Popular Forces, dist sr adv, asst prof mil sci, mem gen staff, Auto Weapons Sec, chief, Marksmanship Unit, co comdr, rifle platoon leader & weapons & platoon leader, co exec officer; NY Life Ins Co, ins salesman; Terrell Ind Sch Dist, pres, currently. **Orgs:** Dallas Asn Life Underwriters, 1971-; pres, Am Heart Asn Kaufman County, 1983-85; Nat Asn Advan Colored People; treas, Tuskegee Alumni Club Dallas; sch bd mem, Terrell Ind Sch Dist; bd mem, Rosehill Water Coop; Cath Ch; Omega Psi Phi Frat; grand knight Father Vincius Coun 6887 Knights Columbus; chmn bd, Jackson Comm Hosp; bd mem, Terrell Comm Hosp. **Honors/Awds:** Rookie of the Year, NY Life Ins Co.

### ANDERSON, ADUKE AREMU-GWENDOLYN. See AREMU, DR. ADUKE.

### ANDERSON, REV. DR. AL H., JR.
Entrepreneur, marketing executive, association executive. **Personal:** Born May 1, 1942, Winston-Salem, NC; son of Albert H Sr and Gladys H; married Jeanette Robbins; children: April & Albert H. **Educ:** Morehouse Col, BS, 1964; Rutgers Univ, attended 1971. **Career:** C&S Nat Bank, mgt trainee, 1967-68; Citizens Trust Bank, vpres, 1968-70; Entreprises Now Inc, exec dir, 1970-72; Anderson Commun, chief exec officer, founder & chmn, 1971-; United Repub Tanzania, hon consulate. **Orgs:** Vpres, Black Pub Rels Soc; African-Am Mkt & Media Asn; Nat Asn Mkt Developers; pres, Am Med Team Africa; chmn & founder, Black Health Now. **Honors/Awds:** Outstanding Agency Award; hon Doctorate Degree, AAF. **Special Achievements:** Speaker at numerous seminars, Univs & confs. creator of the three award winning nationally syndicated programs: "Inspirations Across America", a two-hour weekly program of contemporary gospel music which is currently aired in more than 107 cities; "Focus on Women" a daily program that addresses issues affecting African-American women; & "Power Minutes". **Business Addr:** Chief Executive Officer, Chairman, Founder, Anderson Communications Inc, 2245 Godby Rd, Atlanta, GA 30349, **Business Phone:** (404)766-8000.

### ANDERSON, ALFRED ANTHONY
Executive, football player. **Personal:** Born Aug 4, 1961, Waco, TX; married Monica; children: Alfred Jr & Adrian Craig. **Educ:** Baylor Univ, BS. **Career:** Minn Vikings, running back, 1984-91 (retired); Gen Nutrit Ctr, owner, 1993-; AAA Sports Mgt, pres. **Orgs:** Arlington S Rotary Club; Optimist Club; Baylor Alumni Orgn; Arlington Mus Art Adv Bd; Adv Coun Arlington Police Dept. **Home Addr:** 2006 Weymouth Ct, Arlington, TX 76013-4822, **Home Phone:** (817)461-4437. **Business Addr:** President, AAA Sports Management, 4101 W Green Oaks Blvd Suite 305 No 531, Arlington, TX 76016, **Business Phone:** (817)300-8600.

### ANDERSON, DR. AMEL L.
School administrator. **Personal:** Born Nov 17, 1936, Hazlehurst, MS; children: Reynaldo, Terrence & Robert. **Educ:** Jackson State Univ, BS, 1962; Univ Houston, MS, 1969; Va Polytech Inst & State Univ, EdD, 1976. **Career:** School administrator (retired); Va Polytech Inst State Univ, res asst, 1975-76; Univ Md, Div Agr & Life Sci, asst to provost, 1976-86, Jr Sci & Humanities Symp, asst dean. **Orgs:** NSF fel Univ Houston, 1967; vol & instr, Receiving Home C Wash, DC, 1977-79; pres, Jackson State Univ Alumni Chap, 1978-79; pres, PTA Happy Acres Elem Sch, 1978-80; Md Asn Coun & Develop, 1980-81. **Home Addr:** 6504 Maureen Ct, Cheverly, MD 20785-1436, **Home Phone:** (301)773-5267.

### ANDERSON, AMELIA VERONICA
Marketing executive. **Personal:** Born Mar 13, 1947, New York, NY; daughter of Howard A and Bernardine Turbee Grissom. **Educ:** Bernard M Baruch Col, BBA, 1969. **Career:** Bloomingdales, dept mgr & personnel rep, 1967-74; Essence Mag, dir sales prom & merchandising, 1974-83; Playboy Enterprises Inc, Games Mag, prom mgr, 1983-84, Playboy Mag, prom mgr, 1985-87; Mary Gilliatt Interiors Ltd, design asst & off mgr, 1987-88; Anderson-Rooke Designs, partner, 1988-90; AVA Co, owner, 1991; Times Mirror Mag, prom mgr, corp sales, 1993-96; Creative Health Concepts, mkt dir. **Honors/Awds:** CEBA Award Excellence, 1980; Outstanding Achievements Commun, BESI Inc, 1982; CEBA Award Merit, 1983; CEBA Award Excellence, 1983. **Home Addr:** 155 E 93rd St Apt 6C, New York, NY 10128-3769, **Home Phone:** (212)427-8256.

### ANDERSON, ANTHONY
Actor. **Personal:** Born Aug 15, 1970, Los Angeles, CA; son of Sterling Bowman and Doris; married Alvina; children: Kyra & Nathan. **Educ:** Hollywood High Sch Performing Arts Ctr; Howard Univ. **Career:** Films: Life, 1999; Trippin', 1999; Liberty Heights, 1999; Romeo Must Die, 1999; Big Momma's House, 2000; Urban Legends: Final Cut, 2000; Me Myself & Irene, 2000; Kingdom Come, 2001; See Spot Run, 2001; Exit Wounds, 2001; Two Can Play That Game, 2001; Barbershop, 2002; Kangaroo Jack, 2003; Cradle 2 the Grave, 2003; Malibu's Most Wanted, 2003; Scary Movie 3, 2003; My Baby's Daddy, 2004; King's Ransom, 2005; The Departed, 2006; The Last Stand, 2006; Transformers, 2007; Steppin: The Movie, 2009; The Back-Up Plan, 2010; Scream 4, 2011; The Big Year, 2011; You Laugh But It's True, exec producer, 2011; Scary Movie 5, 2012; Goats, 2012; The Little Penguin Pororo's Racing Adventure, 2013; The Power of Few, 2013; Grudge Match, 2013; The Town That Dreaded Sundown, 2014. TV series: "Hang Time", 1995; "All About the Andersons", producer, writer, 2003; "Veronica Mars", 2005; "The Shield", 2005; "Campus Ladies", 2006; "'Til Death", 2006; "K-Ville", 2007; "Samantha Who?", 2008; "Law & Order", 2008-10; "Golf in America", 2010; "Shameless", 2011; "Reed Between the Lines", 2011; "Matumbo Goldberg" exec producer, 2011; "Psych", 2012; "Raising Hope", 2012; "Treme", 2012; "Guys with Kids", 2012-13; "The Soul Man", 2013; "Rake", 2014; "Black-ish", exec producer, 2014. **Honors/Awds:** Rising Star Award, Acapulco Black Film Festival, 2001; WAFCA Award, Wash DC Area Film Critics Asn, 2002; Black Movie Award, 2005; NBR Award, Nat Bd Rev, 2006; COFCA Award, Cent Ohio Film Critics Asn, 2007; Satellite Award, 2006. **Home Addr:** 17133 Albers St, Encino, CA 91316, **Home Phone:** (818)385-0667. **Business Addr:** Actor, William Morris Agency, 17328 Ventura Blvd, Encino, CA 91316, **Business Phone:** (323)469-5155.

### ANDERSON, ANTONIO KENNETH
Football coach, football player. **Personal:** Born Jun 4, 1973, Brooklyn, NY. **Educ:** Syracuse Univ, grad. **Career:** Football player (retired), football coach; Dallas Cowboys, defensive tackle & right defensive tackle, 1997-98; Dallas Cowboys Hempstead High Sch, coach, 2004; ASA Jr Col (NY), coach, currently. **Honors/Awds:** All Rookie, Pro Football Weekly, 1997. **Business Addr:** Coach, ASA Junior College (NY), 81 Willoughby St, Brooklyn, NY 11201, **Business Phone:** (718)522-9073.

### ANDERSON, DR. ARNETT ARTIS
Dentist. **Personal:** Born Apr 1, 1931, GA; married Delores C Perry; children: Angela C & Andrea C. **Educ:** Savannah State Col, BS, 1953; Grad Sch, Howard Univ, attended 1957; Howard Univ, DDS, 1962; Univ Mich, MS, 1965. **Career:** Inst Health, nutrit & endocrinol res mem, 1956-58; Howard Univ, cardiovasc res, 1960-62, pedodontics & instr, 1962-63; C's Orthod Clin, dir, 1964-65; Howard Univ Col Dent, assoc prof, 1965-69; pvt pract dentist, Wash, DC, 1966-. **Orgs:** Orthod consult, Community Group Health found, St Elizabeth Hosp Wash; DC; NE Regional Bd Dent Examr; DC Bd Dent Examr; Am Asn Orthodontists; Mid Atlantic Soc Orthodontists; Am Col Dent; Am Asn Dent Examr; Nat Dent Asn; Am Dent Asn; Int Asn Dent Res, Am Soc Dent C; Robert T Freeman Dent Soc; SW Neighborhood Assembly; Alpha Phi Alpha Fraternity; Omicron Kappa Upsilon Nat Hon Dent Soc; Sigma Xi Hon Sci Soc; Beta Kappa Chi; Alpha Kappa Mu. **Honors/Awds:** Best Thesis Award, Univ Mich Sch Orthodontics, C Edward Martin Award, 1965; First Place, Int competition Dent Res Edward H Hetton Award, 1966. **Home Addr:** 519 G St SW, Washington, DC 20024, **Home Phone:** (202)554-5465. **Business Addr:** Dentist, 635 G St SW, Washington, DC 20024, **Business Phone:** (202)554-5800.

### ANDERSON, DR. AVIS OLIVIA
Educator. **Personal:** Born Aug 27, 1949, Vivian, WV; daughter of Harvey Fails and Naomi T Fails; married Weldon Edward. **Educ:** Bronx Community Col, AAS, 1970; Herbert H Lehman Col, BS, 1971; Hunter Col, MS, 1973; NY Univ, PhD, bus educ, 1986. **Career:** Bronx Community Col, lab tech, 1971-72; Herbert H Lehman Col, adj instr, 1972-73; LaGuardia Community Col, full time instr, 1973-75, asst prof, assoc prof, fac acct & mgr studies, currently, prof, 1975-. **Orgs:** Morrisania Educ Coun, 1972-; exec bd mem, Bus Educ Assoc, 1978-; pres, Col Bus Educr, 1981-82; Charismatic Prayer Group, 1985-; Conf Coordr, SUNY Off Tech & Secretarial Educr, 1986-87; second vpres, Bus Educ Assoc, 1986-87; pres, Gregg Shorthand Teachers Assoc, 1986-87. **Home Addr:** 100-39 Francis Lewis Blvd, Queens Village, NY 11429, **Home Phone:** (718)465-2191. **Business Addr:** Professor, LaGuardia Community College, 31-10 Thomson Ave, Long Island City, NY 11101, **Business Phone:** (718)482-7200.

### ANDERSON, BARBARA LOUISE
Librarian, social worker. **Personal:** Born Jan 5, 1933, San Diego, CA; daughter of Lorenzo and Louise Morgan; children: Sean Allen. **Educ:** San Diego State Col, BS, 1954; Kans State Teachers Col, MS, LS, 1955. **Career:** Librn (retired); LA Pub Libr, br young adult librn, 1956-59; San Diego Pub Libr, br libr, ref young adult librn, 1959-64; AUS Europe, admin librn, 1964-69; Serra Reg Libr Systs, San Diego, ref proj coordr, 1969-71; Riverside Pub Libr, head reader serv, 1972-74; San Bernardino County Libr, County librn & dir, 1974-94. **Orgs:** Am CA Libr Asns; Nat Asn Advan Colored People, Alpha Delta Chi; pres, Calif Soc Librns, 1974-75; Riverside Ment Health Asn, 1975-79; deleg, White House Conf Info Sci, 1979-; bd dir, Inland Empire Symphony, 1982-84; deleg, OCLC, Users Coun, 1983-88; bd dir, Ywca, San Bernardino, 1988-89; Rec Blind & Dyslexic, 1992-; bd supvr, San Bernardino Co, 1994; US House Reps, 1994; vol, Riverside Co Arch Comn, 1996; vpres, sunshine chair, Nat Asn Advan Colored People, 1997-; adv bd, Riverside County Libr, 1997; Lake Elsinore Woman's Club, 1997; pres, Black Art & Cult Club, Lake Elsinore; Riverside Co Libr adv comt, 1998-; Riverside Co Libr Adv Comt, 1998-99; bd mem, Riverside Ment Health; bd mem, Calif Youth Authority Libr Asn; chair, Inland Libr Syst Admin Coun; bd mem, Univ Southern Calif Sch Lib & Info, Nat Coun Negro Women Serv; pres, Am Asn Univ Women, 1976-77; bd trustee, Univ Ill; Am Libr Asn; Calif Libr; Black Caucus Calif Libr Asn; Cong Pub Libr Asn; Online Comput Libr Ctr Users Coun, 1984-88; Bus & Prof Women San Bernardino. **Home Addr:** 304 N Lewis Ave, Lake Elsinore, CA 92530, **Home Phone:** (951)674-7096.

### ANDERSON, DR. BARBARA STEWART JENKINS
Pathologist, educator. **Personal:** Born Chicago, IL; daughter of Carlyle F and Alyce Walker; married Sidney B Jenkins; children: Kevin C Jenkins, Judith Jenkins Kelly MD, Sharolyn Jenkins Sanders, MarcJ Jenkins & Kayla S Jenkins French; married Arthur E. **Educ:** Univ Mich, BS, 1950; Wayne State Med Sch, MD, 1957. **Career:** Wayne Co Hosp, 1966-70; Wayne State Med Sch, assoc prof, 1970, staff pathologist, adj assoc prof clin lab sci, currently; Detroit Receiving Hosp, chief path, 1988, assoc prof, assoc syst med dir, Path Dept, med dir, currently; DMC Univ Labs, admin med dir; Wayne State Univ, prof & vice chmn clin path; Detroit Gen Hosp, dir clin lab; Pt Serv Labs, med dir; Wayne State Univ Allied Health Progs, med dir. **Orgs:** Elected, Alpha Omega Alpha, 1956; Wayne Co Med Soc; Mich State Med Soc; AMA; Detroit Med Soc; Wolverine Med Soc; Nat Med Soc; Col Am Path; Am Soc Clin Pathol; Minority Recruitment Comt; Wayne Med Sch; Careers Club HS Studs. **Honors/Awds:** Alexander McKenzie Campbell Award, 1957; Pathfinders in Medicine Award, Wayne State Univ, 2004. **Home Addr:** 6920 Nashway Dr W, West Bloomfield, MI 48322-3213, **Home Phone:** (248)661-3650. **Business Addr:** Associate System Medical Director, Chief Pathology, Detroit Receiving Hospital, 4201 St Antoine 3E UHC, Detroit, MI 48201, **Business Phone:** (313)745-4571.

### ANDERSON, DR. BELINDA C.
Dean (education). **Educ:** Radford Univ, BS, 1976, MA, hist, 1977; Va Tech Univ, EdD. **Career:** Portsmouth Pub Sch Syst, teacher; Norfolk Pub Sch Syst, teacher; Radford Univ, dir acad advising serv; Norfolk State Univ, sch gen & continuing educ, dean & prof; VA Union Univ, vpres acad affairs, 2000-03, interim pres, 2003-04, pres, 2004-09; Norfolk State Univ, Col Lib Arts, dean, 2012-. **Business Addr:** Dean, Norfolk State University, NEAB Rm 223, Norfolk, VA 23504, **Business Phone:** (757)823-8118.

### ANDERSON, DR. BENJAMIN STRATMAN, JR.
Physician, chairperson. **Personal:** Born Feb 23, 1936, Dothan, AL; son of Benjamin Sr and Lula Sutton; married Sandra C Wright; children: Benjamin III, Kevin & Carita. **Educ:** Fisk Univ, BS, 1957; Meharry Med Col, MD, 1962; Am Bd Family Pract, dipl, 1975, recert, 1981, 1987, 1995. **Career:** Homer G Phillips Hosp, intern; Polk Gen Hosp, staff pres, 1969-70, 1978-79, 1988-89, 1991-93; GA Bd Human Resources, secy, 1972-86; GA State Med Asn, exec bd, 1973-; Polk County Emergency Med Servs, med dir, 1977-99; fel Am Acad Family Physicians, 1979; Polk Co Bd Health, 1979-; chmn, 1985-; Brentwood Pk Nursing Home, med dir, 1988-93; Coosa Valley Res-

idential Substance Abuse Prog, dir med servs, 1989-2002; Anderson Med ctr, physician, currently. **Orgs:** Life mem, Kappa Alpha Psi Fraternity, 1970-; adv coun, Cedartown City Comn, 1970-86; health serv dir, proj Head start, Tallatoona EOA Inc, 1974-79; life mem, Nat Asn Advan Colored People, 1975-; vice speaker, House Delegates GA Acad Family Physicians, 1975-77; bd dir, Cedartown Little League, 1976-85; consult, preceptor, Polk Co Primary Care Proj, 1981-83; Cedartown Comm Rels Coun, 1986-; consult, Wayside Inn Alcohol & Drug Residential Rehab Prog, 1986-92; bd dir, GA Asn Minority Entrepreneurs, 1988-90; Am Soc Addiction Med, 1989-2003; Cedartown Recreation Comn, 1990-95; bd adv, Columbia Polk Gen Hosp, 1996-, chair, 1998-. **Honors/Awds:** Service Award, Atlanta Med Asn, 1973; Service Award, GA State Med Asn, 1975; President's Award, GA County Welfare Asn, 1982; Businessman of the Yr, Northwest GA Minority Business Asn, 1986; Community Service Award, Polk County Nat Asn Advan Colored People, 1987; Community Service Commendation, GA House Reps, 1988; Service Award, Polk Co EMS, 1999. **Home Addr:** 105 Hill St, PO Box 508, Cedartown, GA 30125-4056, **Home Phone:** (770)748-7136. **Business Addr:** Physician, Anderson Medical Center, 812 S Main St, Cedartown, GA 30125, **Business Phone:** (770)748-3006.

### ANDERSON, BERNADINE M.
Beautician. **Personal:** Born Dec 1, 1942, New York, NY; daughter of Benjamin Tonsler and Sarah Brown; children: Sherri Bruce & Jacqueline Brown. **Educ:** NY Univ, BA, 1963. **Career:** Trouble Man, make-up artist, 1972; Together Bros, makeup artist, 1974; Fun with Dick & Jane, makeup artist, 1977; Julia, 1makeup artist, 977; Coming Home, makeup artist, 1978; Comes a Horseman, makeup artist, 1978; The China Syndrome, makeup artist, 1979; The Elec Horseman, makeup artist, 1979; Cicely Tyson, head make-up artist, 1979-81; Jane Fonda Movies, 20th Century Fox, personal make-up artist, 1980-84; Nine to Five, makeup artist, 1980; "Hallmark Hall of Fame", makeup artist, 1981; Stevie Wonder, head make-up artist, 1981-82; Rollover, makeup artist, 1981; The Buddy Syst, makeup artist, 1982; A Soldier's Story, makeup artist, 1984; Fast Forward, makeup artist, 1985; The Alan King Show, makeup artist, 1985; Eddie Murphy Movies, Paramount, head make-up artist, 1985-94; Lionel Ritchie, head make-up artist, 1986-87; "Amen", makeup artist, 1986-87; "Head of the Class", makeup artist, 1986-87; Coming to Am, head makeup artist, 1988; Police Acad 6: City Under Siege, makeup artist, 1989; Harlem Nights, makeup artist, 1989; Laurence Fishburne, Touchtone, personal make-up artist, 1990-93; Boomerang, makeup artist, 1992; What's Love Got to Do with It, makeup artist, 1993; Angela Basset Movies, Paramount, head of dept, 1994-95; Vampire in Brooklyn, makeup dept supvr, 1995. **Orgs:** IASE Local 706, SAG-SEG, 1970-. **Honors/Awds:** Academy Awards, Emmy Nomination, Am 4 times, 1987-89; Academy Award Nomination, Filmmakers Acad, Best Make-Up, 1990; Inductee, Black Filmmakers Hall Fame, 1991. **Special Achievements:** Roots, 1976; A Soldiers Story, 1982; Another 48 Hours, 1985; What's Love Got To Do With It, 1991; Bad Company, 1993. **Home Addr:** 9600 Orchid Bay Dr, Las Vegas, NV 89123, **Home Phone:** (702)451-8207. **Business Addr:** Make-up Artist, Self Employed, 4559 Don Richardo Dr, Los Angeles, CA 90008, **Business Phone:** (213)296-5891.

### ANDERSON, DR. BERNARD E.
Educator. **Personal:** Born Philadelphia, PA; son of William and Dorothy Gideon; children: Melinda D & Bernard E II. **Educ:** Livingstone Col, BA, econ, 1959; Mich State Univ, MA, econ, 1961; Univ Pa, PhD, bus & appl econ, 1969. **Career:** US Bur Labor Statist, economist, 1963-66; Wharton Sch, Univ Pa, from asst to assoc prof indust, 1969-75, prof, 1978-83, Whitney M Young term prof, 2001-, pract prof mgt, currently; MDRC Corp, bd dir, 1977-93, vchmn, 1988-93; Swarthmore Col, lectr; Rockefeller Found, dir social sci, 1979-85; Urban Affairs Partnership, mng partner, 1987; Provident Mutual Life Ins Co, bd dir, 1988-; US Dept Labor, asst secy, 1994-2001; Overseas Pvt Investment Corp, bd dir, 1995-; Anderson Group, pres; US Dept Labor, asst sec emp stand admin, currently. **Orgs:** Philadelphia Urban League, 1970-76; pres, Nat Econ Asn 1970-; bd mem, Nat Asn Advan Colored People, Spec Contrib Fund, 1976-80; brd trustee, Livingstone Col, 1980-94; bd econs, Black Enterprise Mag, 1981-93; consult, Ford Found, 1985-93; Woodrow Wilson Sch, Princeton Univ, vis fel, 1985; Natl Comn Jobs & Small Bus, 1986; United Bank Philadelphia; chmn bd trustee, Lincoln Univ, 1987-93, chmn, 1989-93; chmn, Pa Intergovernmental Coop Authority, 1991-94; co-chmn, Northeast Region Sigma Phi Fraternity; Am Econ Asn; vice chmn, Manpower Demonstration & Res Corp; exec bd, Indust Rels Res Asn; Mayors Adv Comn, Construct Indust Diversity; vice chmn, bd trustee, Tuskegee Univ, currently. **Home Addr:** PO Box 576, Wayne, PA 19087, **Home Phone:** (215)878-4239. **Business Addr:** Assistant Secretary Employment Standards Admin, US Department Labor, Francis Perkins Bldg 200 Constitution Ave NW, Washington, DC 20210.

### ANDERSON, BETTY KELLER
Journalist, editor. **Personal:** Born Dec 13, 1951, Pineville, LA; daughter of Arthur D Keller Sr and Helen L; children: Tamara Renee & Travis Randolph. **Educ:** Univ NMex, Albuquerque, NM, BA, jour, 1973. **Career:** Albuquerque Jour, summer intern, 1971; Tacoma News Tribune, reporter/copy ed, 1974-85; Houston Chronicle, copy ed, 1985-86; Seattle Times, copy/design ed, 1986-. **Orgs:** Pres, Black Journalist Asn Seattle, 1988-90; dep regional dir, Region 10, Nat Asn Black Journalists, 1990-91; regional dir, NABJ, 1991-93; supvr, Editing & Publ Ministry, Tacoma Christian Ctr, 1994-. **Honors/Awds:** Fel, Editing Prog Minority Journalists, Inst Jour Educ, 1984. **Home Addr:** 6514 N Pkwy, Tacoma, WA 98407, **Home Phone:** (253)756-1051. **Business Addr:** Copy Editor, The Seattle Times, 1120 John St, Seattle, WA 98109, **Business Phone:** (206)464-2050.

### ANDERSON, BRYAN N.
Administrator, executive. **Personal:** Born Jun 18, 1955, New Haven, CT. **Educ:** Univ Conn, attended 1977. **Career:** Sen Weicker, staff asst; Vir Legis Improv Proj, St Thomas, US Vir, proj dir; Conn State Senate, admin asst chief dep minority leaders; Harlem mayor; Hamden, CT, constable, 1973-80; Pace Advert, coordr client serv. **Orgs:** Bd mem, State Bd Higher Educ; dist leader, Hamden Rep Town Comn; Hamden Arts Coun; Hamden League Women Voters; Ripon Soc Nat Gov Bd. **Honors/Awds:** Hamden Outstanding Youth Award, 1971; Comm Involvement Award, Greater New Haven Urban League, 1973. **Home Addr:** 469 Newhall St, Hamden, CT 06517.

### ANDERSON, CADILLAC. See ANDERSON, GREGORY WAYNE.

### ANDERSON, CAREY LAINE, JR.
Architect. **Personal:** Born Jan 12, 1950, Louisville, KY; married Karen Elizabeth White; children: Latrice. **Educ:** Univ Ky, BArch, 1973. **Career:** Arrasmith Judd Rapp & Assoc Architects, architect & draftsman, 1973-77; Robert F Crump Architects, proj architect, 1977-78; Ky Bd Regist Architects, pres; City Louisville Pub Works Dept, city architect, 1978-79; Larry E Wright & Assocs Architects, assoc & proj architect, 1979-80; C L Anderson Archit LLC, architect, 1980-; ARC Honsortium LLC, prin, currently. **Orgs:** Prog chmn, Cent Ky Chap Am Inst Architects; Construct Specif Inst; Ky Soc Architects; Nat Asn Advan Colored People; Phi Beta Sigma Fraternity Inc; adv bd, Greater Louisville CVB; Louisville Urban League. **Special Achievements:** First Black Architect License in Kentucky in 1977; First Black Architect to establish architecture firm in Kentucky. **Home Addr:** 1275 Pky Gardens Ct Apt 209, Louisville, KY 40217-1295, **Home Phone:** (502)634-4040. **Business Addr:** Architect, C L Anderson Architecture LLC, 455 S 4th St Suite 546, Louisville, KY 40202-2554, **Business Phone:** (502)585-9750.

### ANDERSON, CARL EDWARD
Judge, business owner. **Personal:** Born Jan 8, 1939, Pendleton, SC; son of Wilhelmina and Amos; married Etta Humphrey; children: Carl Wendell. **Educ:** Tri Co Tech Col, criminal justice, 1975; SC Criminal Justice Acad. **Career:** Sangamo Elec Co, 1965-70; Anderson County Sheriff's Off, dep chief, 1970-; Anderson County Summary Ct, chief magistrate & judge, 1989-2000; CEAS Investigative Agency, owner, pvt investr, 2000-08; Criminal Invests Div, criminal investr. **Orgs:** Tri County Judicial Asn; SC Summary Ct Educ Comn; Anderson Jr Assembly Adv Bd; SC Summary Ct Asn; SC Human Affairs Comnr; SC Asn Legal Investigators; Investigative agency; Anderson County Law Enforcement Ctr; Prof Stand Div; Sch Resource Officer Unit; Forensics & Community Serv Unit; chief investr, Invests Bur. **Home Addr:** 1313 Cherry St Exten, Pendleton, SC 29670, **Home Phone:** (803)646-7134. **Business Addr:** Deputy Chief, Anderson County Sheriff's Office, 305 Camson Rd, Anderson, SC 29625, **Business Phone:** (864)260-4400.

### ANDERSON, DR. CARL EDWIN
School administrator, government official. **Personal:** Born Sep 29, 1934, St. Louis, MO; son of Raymond W and Elizabeth Hooper; married Ida L Bass; children: Carl Jr, Rhonda L Speight & Sherri Cherry. **Educ:** Southern Ill Univ, BA, govt, 1956, MS, col personnel admin, 1958; Univ Md, EdD, admin higher educ, 1969. **Career:** School administrator, government official (retired); Howard Univ, head resident, cooke hall, 1960, dir stud activ, 1964, assoc dean stud, 1964-69, actg dean stud, 1969, vpres stud affairs, 1969-90; consult; US House Rep, Post Off & Civil Serv Comn, prof staff, 1991-95. **Orgs:** Bd dir, Am Asn Univ Admin; Southern Ill Univ Found; Howard Univ Found; Nat Asn Stud Personnel Admin; Am Asn Coun & Develop; Nat vpres Stud Affairs Org; evaluator, Mid States Asn & Sec Sch & Col; Nat Urban League; Nat Asn Advan Colored People; pres, Kappa Scholar Endowment Fund; Kappa Alpha Psi Frat; Sigma Pi Phi Frat; bd dir, William L Clay Scholar &Res Fund, 1988-; Nat Asn Personnel Workers; Eastern Asn Col Deans; Pi Sigma Alpha Hon Soc Polit Sci; Psi Chi Hon Soc Psychol; Phi Delta Kappa Hon Soc Educ; Wash DC Bd Educ Adv Comt. **Home Addr:** 2100 Yorktown Rd NW, Washington, DC 20012, **Home Phone:** (202)291-8494.

### ANDERSON, DR. CAROL BYRD (CAROL M ANDERSON)
Economist, educator. **Personal:** Born Jun 7, 1941, Kansas City, MO; daughter of Hartwell and Elmira; married Winston Anthony; children: Laura Elisabeth & Lea Elmira. **Educ:** Col St Teresa, BA, 1962; Boston Col, MA, 1964, PhD, 1969. **Career:** Economist, educr, banker (retired); Bur Labor Statist, gen economist, 1963-64; Fed Res Boston, economist, 1969-70; First Nat Bank Chicago, staff officer, 1970-75; Howard Univ Wash, DC, assoc prof, 1975-76; Fed Res Wash, DC, economist, 1976-86. **Orgs:** Am Econ Asn, 1960-; Social Econ, 1960-; Nat Econ Asn, 1975-; trustee, Col St Teresa, 1975-81. **Home Addr:** 1629 Hopefield Rd, Silver Spring, MD 20904-4111, **Home Phone:** (301)384-0727.

### ANDERSON, DR. CAROLYN H.
Administrator. **Educ:** Morgan State Univ, BA; Johns Hopkins Univ, MS; NC State Univ, EdD, adult & community col educ. **Career:** N Lake Col, asst dir, human resources; Broome Community Col, dean acad serv div; Cincinnati State Tech & Community Col, exec vpres, currently. **Orgs:** Bd mem, Nat Coun Black Am Affairs; bd mem, Baltimore Workforce Investment bd; pres, co vpres, mem, Morgan State Univ Community Col; bd mem, Northeast Region Nat Coun Black Am Affairs; interim pres, Baltimore City Community Col. **Business Addr:** Executive Vice President, Cincinnati State Technical & Community College, 3520 Cent Pkwy, Cincinnati, OH 45223-2690, **Business Phone:** (513)569-1515.

### ANDERSON, DARREN HUNTER
Football player, scout. **Personal:** Born Jan 11, 1969, Cincinnati, OH; married Robyn. **Educ:** Univ Toledo. **Career:** Football player (retired), scout; Tampa Bay Buccaneers, corner back, 1992-93; New Eng Patriots, 1992; Kans City Chiefs, corner back, 1994-97; Atlanta Falcons, corner back, 1998; Detroit lions, regional scout, currently. **Home Addr:** 7328 Overland Pk Ct, West Chester, OH 45069-5560, **Home Phone:** (513)642-7100. **Business Addr:** Regional Scout, Detroit Lions, 222 Repub Dr, Allen Park, MI 48101, **Business Phone:** (313)216-4000.

### ANDERSON, DR. DAVID ATLAS
Educator, storyteller. **Personal:** Born Apr 28, 1930, Cincinnati, OH; son of Willie David and Mary Alice; married Ruth Joanine; children: David M, Kenwood M & Joanine C. **Educ:** Rochester Inst Tech, BFA, 1960; Syracuse Univ, MA, 1962; Union Inst, PhD, educ admin, 1975. **Career:** Action a Better Community Inc, assoc dir, 1965-67; Urban League Rochester, assoc dir, dep exec dir, 1967-70; State Univ NY, Brockport, lectr Afro-Amer studies; Rochester City Sch Dist, supvr, parent & comm involvement, 1970-92, storyteller, currently; Rochester Inst Tech, vis asst prof, 1981-, dir parent educ; Tex Educ Agency, cheif coun; African Am Studies, teacher; Nazareth Col, vis community scholar, 2007-. **Orgs:** Assoc Comn Health, Univ Rochester Med Sch, 1970-82; vpres, Ment Health Asn, 1980-86; founder, Blackstorytelling League, 1981-; Correctional Inst, Sonyea & Oatka, NY, 1983-85; bd dir, Rochester Mus & Sci Ctr, 1986-90; Nat Asn Black Storytellers, 1988-89; chmn, Rochester-Monroe County Freedom Trail Comn. **Home Addr:** 181 Royleston Rd, Rochester, NY 14609, **Home Phone:** (585)482-5192. **Business Addr:** Visiting Community Scholar, Nazareth College, 4245 E Ave GAC 367, Rochester, NY 14618, **Business Phone:** (585)389-5140.

### ANDERSON, JUDGE DAVID TURPEAU
Government official. **Personal:** Born Aug 9, 1942, Cincinnati, OH; son of Florida Turpeau and Randall Hudson; children: David M & Daniel M. **Educ:** Univ Cincinnati, BS, 1963; George Washington Univ, JD, 1972. **Career:** Congressman Robert Taft Jr, cong staff asst, 1967-69; Housing & Urban Develop, asst cong rels, 1970; Am Hosp Asn, asst legis, 1971-73; Stanley, Durham & Johnson, assoc, 1972-76; City Philadelphia, asst city solicitor, 1976-81; US Dept Housing & Urban Develop, chief admin judge, 1981-2007. **Orgs:** Bar, Commonwealth Pa, Nat Press Club; Philadelphia Bar Asn; Nat Bar Asn; Inter-Am Bar Asn; Sr Executives Asn. **Home Addr:** PO Box 23084, Washington, DC 20026. **Business Addr:** Director, Office of Hearings & Appeals, Rm B-133 401 7th St SW, Washington, DC 20410, **Business Phone:** (202)254-0000.

### ANDERSON, DEREK LAMONT
Executive director, basketball player. **Personal:** Born Jul 18, 1974, Louisville, KY. **Educ:** Ohio State Univ, attended 1994; Univ Ky, pharm, 1997. **Career:** Basketball player (retired), executive; Derek Anderson Found, pres, 1988-; Cleveland Cavaliers, guard, 1997-99; Stamina Sch, pres, 1998-; Los Angeles Clippers, 1999-2000; San Antonio Spurs, 2000-01; Portland Trail Blazers, guard, 2001-05; Houston Rockets, 2005-06, free agt; Miami Heat, Guard, 2006; Charlotte Bobcats, 2006-08; Loyalty Media Group, chief exec officer & founder, 2008-; Derek AndersonWorks, founder & chief exec officer, 2009; Stamina Found, founder & pres, 2009-; DerekAndersonWrites, screen writer & producer, 2010-; Loyalty Media Group LLC, producer & screen writer, 2013-; free agt, currently; D A Enterprises, owner & operator; Victory H2O Global Opers, pres; Loyalty Clothing Co, designs & operator; Loyalty Home & Auto Concierge, owner & operator; Anderson Develop, owner & operator; Hotels, owner & operator. **Special Achievements:** Book: Stamina. **Business Addr:** Founder, Chief Executive Officer, Loyalty Media Group, 675 Metrop Pky SW, Atlanta, GA 30310, **Business Phone:** (678)927-9896.

### ANDERSON, DR. REV. DERRICK RUSHON
Clergy. **Personal:** son of Bishop Hermon L and Ruth R; married Margaret R; children: Michael, Rashana Benjamin & Adria. **Educ:** Hampton Univ, BA, sociol, 1973; Univ Louisville, MS, community develop, 1975; Livingstone Col, Hood Theol Sem, MDiv, 1983; Asbury Theol Sem, DDiv, 1995. **Career:** Jefferson County Circuit Ct, ct clerk, 1973; Louville Home Fed, br mgr, 1973-80; Soldier's Memorial AME Zion Church, youth pastor, 1980-81; Bethel AME Zion Church, 1981-82; Shady Ridge AME Zion Church, 1982-86; E Stonewall AME Zion Church, sr pastor, 1986-96; St Paul AME Zion Church, pastor, 1996-. **Orgs:** Jeffersontown Chamber Com, 1978-80; bd mem, Uptown Homeless Shelter, 1990-91; co-founder & bd mem, Ministry Recovery, 1990-91; bd mem, Human Servs Coun, 1992-94. **Home Addr:** 1901 Chicago Blvd, Detroit, MI 48206, **Home Phone:** (313)865-8502. **Business Addr:** Senior Pastor, St Paul AME Zion, 11359 Dexter Ave, Detroit, MI 48206-1424, **Business Phone:** (313)933-1823.

### ANDERSON, DOREATHA MADISON
Manager. **Personal:** Born Apr 3, 1934, Lynchburg, VA; children: Wanda M Taylor, Rae L Madison, Raymond B Madison Jr (deceased), Doretha L Madison & Octavia D Madison-Colmore. **Educ:** Va Sem Col, BS, 1968; Va Union Univ, BA, 1984. **Career:** Juv Detention Home, youth care worker, 1968-82; Bags Unlimited Inc, pres, 1982-; Nat Asn Advan Colored People, finance chmn, 1982-84; Comm Educ Employ Svcs, prog mgr, 1985-86; Youth Develop Svcs, prog mgr, 1986-. **Orgs:** Diamond Hill Baptist Ch; Usher Bd; Ch Aid; rec secy, Daughter Elk Chap 181 IPOEW, 1975-82; Eastern Star, 1980-82; pres, Missionary Circle; asst treas, Variety Garden Club Hill City Chap; Am Bus Women Assoc, 1983; United Way, 1986; Nat Assoc Female Exec Inc, 1986. **Home Addr:** 2114 Indian Hill Rd, Lynchburg, VA 24503, **Home Phone:** (434)384-9105. **Business Addr:** Training Coordinator, 1310 Church St, Lynchburg, VA 24504, **Business Phone:** (804)846-8731.

### ANDERSON, DORIS J.
Teacher. **Personal:** Born Oct 16, 1933, Reagan, IN; married Franklin D; children: Deborah, Daryl F & Caleb. **Educ:** BA, 1962; MEd, 1966. **Career:** Teacher, 13 yrs; Bastian Sch, counr. **Orgs:** Nat Educ Asn; Tex State Troopers Asn; Tex Classrm Teachers Asn; Health Technol Assessment; Am Pub Gardens Asn; Tenn Valley Gamers Asn; Humane Socs Calumet Area; Am Sch Counr Asn; Nat Voc Guid Asn; Am News Women's Club; Tex Pecan Growers Asn; TACES; Sigma Gamma Rho Sor, 1962; treas, Houston Teachers Asn, 1974-75; pres, Houston Sch Counr Asn, 1975; Ct Vol WICS Vol; Phi Delta Kappa, 1975; Nat Coun Negro Women; Gamma Phi Beta. **Home Addr:** 803 W 20th St, Houston, TX 77008-3509, **Home Phone:** (713)861-1512.

### ANDERSON, EDDIE LEE, JR.
Athlete, football player. **Personal:** Born Jul 22, 1963, Warner Robins, GA. **Educ:** Ft Valley State Univ. **Career:** Football player (retired),

football coach; Seattle Seahawks, defensive back, 1986; Los Angeles Raiders, 1987-97; Oakland Raiders, safety, 1995-97; coach Middle Georgia Stallions, 2003-05; Oakland Raiders, 2009-12; FBU defensive back coach, 2013-.

## ANDERSON, ELIZABETH M.

Association executive, government official. **Personal:** Born Paris, TX; daughter of Walter Mason and Emma McClure; married Harold; children: Andrew, Patricia Roper, Theresa Danzy & Portia Tucker. **Educ:** Draughon Bus Col, attended 1958; Tulsa Univ, attended 1974. **Career:** Okla Tax Comn, Tulsa, Okla, dir personnel supvr acct; Anderson Amusement Corp, Tulsa, Okla, dir personnel. **Orgs:** Nat Asn Advan Colored People Tulsa Chap, 1949-89; Tulsa Urban League, 1950-89; pres, Jack & Jill Am, Tulsa Chap, 1952-71 & 1984-86; exec bd, Tulsa Pastors Wives Coun; nat bd, Nat Coun Negro Women, Wash, DC; nat coun, Assault Illiteracy, New York; exec bd, YWCA, Tulsa, OK; southern regional dir, Eta Phi Beta Sorority, chief exec officer & vpres, nat pres, 1986-90. **Home Addr:** 1724 Mohawk Blvd, Tulsa, OK 74110, **Home Phone:** (918)425-7717.

## ANDERSON, EUGENE

Government official, executive. **Personal:** Born Mar 9, 1944, Diffee, GA; son of Velver Sr and Velma; married Mamie Jewel Sapp; children: Timothy E, Tamara E & Melanie J. **Educ:** Wichita Tech Inst, radio & tel commun, 1971. **Career:** State Kans, state rep, 1973-76; Congressman Dan Glickman, dist aide, 1976-78; Kans Comn Civil Rights, chairperson, 1979-83; K Black Dem Caucus, S, secy, 1982-85; Rollin & Smokin Bar-B-Que Hut, owner & operator; Kans Legis, sen, rep, currently. **Orgs:** Pres, Optimist Club NE Wichita, 1974-75; treas, State Dem Party, KS, 1985-87; Masonic Lodge, Nat Asn Advan Colored People; Fed & State Affairs; Confirmations Comt, Ed Comt, Pub Health & Welfare Comt, Midwestern Conf Coun State Govts, Adv Coun Aging, Legis Ed Planning Comt. **Honors/Awds:** Sommunity Service Award, Police Neighborhood Serv Ctr, 1976; Coach of the Year Award. **Home Addr:** 1832 N Poplar Ave, Wichita, KS 67214-2134, **Home Phone:** (316)685-2666. **Business Addr:** Representative, Kansas Legislature, 300 SW 10th Ave Suite 551, Topeka, KS 66612-1504, **Business Phone:** (785)296-2391.

## ANDERSON, FLIPPER. See ANDERSON, WILLIE LEE, JR.

## ANDERSON, FRED

Music director. **Personal:** Born Jun 3, 1962, Lima, OH; son of Lucious Upshaw and Mary. **Educ:** Northeastern Bus Col. **Career:** Mid Bus Inc, prod, currently; Rudolph Foods, processing, currently. **Orgs:** Choir dir. New Morning star Church. **Home Addr:** 473 E 4th St, Lima, OH 45804, **Home Phone:** (419)225-7842. **Business Addr:** Production, Mid Bus Inc, 505 E Jefferson St, Bluffton, OH 45817-1398, **Business Phone:** (419)358-2500.

## ANDERSON, GARRET JOSEPH

Baseball player. **Personal:** Born Jun 30, 1972, Los Angeles, CA; married Teresa Arciniega; children: Brianne & Bailey. **Career:** Baseball player (retired); Calif Angels, outfielder, 1994-96; Anaheim Angels, outfielder, 1997-2004; Los Angeles Angels Anaheim, outfielder, 2005-08; Atlanta Braves, outfielder, 2009; Los Angeles Dodgers, outfielder, 2010. **Orgs:** Boy Scouts Am recruiting campaign & Responsible Fatherhood Campaign; Calif Dept Social Serv; Los Angels City Championship baseball team, 1989. **Business Addr:** Baseball Player, Atlanta Braves, Turner Field 755 Hank Aaron Dr, Atlanta, GA 30315, **Business Phone:** (404)522-7630.

## ANDERSON, GARY

Artistic director. **Educ:** Wayne State Univ, BFA, directing, 1996, MFA, directing. **Career:** Plays: Woza Albert; Zooman & Sign; Pill Hill; Piano Lesson; Buses; I Am A Man; Two Trains Running; Plowshares Theatre Co, dir, co-founder & producing artistic dir, 1989-; BTN's Black Voices, ed, 1990-94; Western Mich Univ, interim instr, 1991; Univ Mich, vis prof, 1994-95; WTVS Detroit Pub Tv, segment host, 1997-2002; Arts Centered Educ, proj dir, 1995-2001; Wayne State Univ, exec dir, 1995-2002; Wayne County Community Col, Humanities Dept, 2005-instr, 2006-13; Plymouth United Church Christ, deacon, 2011-. **Orgs:** Dana Found; Black Theatre Network, 1989-; bd trustee, Plowshares Theatre Co, 1989-; Nat Conf African Am Theatre, 1991-92; bd mem, Theatre Commun Group, 2000-06, vpres, 2002-06, bd dir; bd mem, Cult Alliance Southeastern Mich, 2007-; Art X Detroit, 2009-10; bd mem, Mich Equity Theatre Alliance, 2010-. **Business Addr:** Producing Artistic Director, Co-Founder, Plowshares Theatre Co, 3663 Woodward Ave Suite 150, Detroit, MI 48202-3146, **Business Phone:** (313)744-3181.

## ANDERSON, GARY WAYNE

Football coach. **Personal:** Born Apr 18, 1961, Columbia, MO; married Ollie; children: Antisha & Gary Jr. **Educ:** Univ Ark, attended 1983. **Career:** Football player (retired); Tampa Bay Bandits, 1983-85; San Diego Chargers, running back, 1985-88, punt returner, 1986, kick returner, 1986-87; Tampa Bay Buccaneers, running back, 1990-92, kick returner, 1991-92, punt returner, 1993; Detroit Lions, running back, 1993; Memphis Mad Dogs, 1995. **Honors/Awds:** 1985 USFL Season Awards, 1985; Pro Bowl, 1986; Arkansas Sports Hall of Fame, 2003; All-Rookie First Team, UPI, Football Digest & Pro Football Writers. **Special Achievements:** Film: 1981 Gator Bowl, 1981.

## ANDERSON, GEORGE A.

Manager, executive. **Personal:** Born Nov 15, 1923, Chicago, IL; children: George Jr. **Educ:** Howard Univ; Roosevelt Univ; Cent YMCA Col, Chicago. **Career:** Draper & Kramer Chicago Real Estate Firm, br off mgr, vpres; Lake Meadows Apts Chicago, mgr; prairie appartment complex, asst mgr. **Orgs:** Chicago Real Estate Bd; Nat Real Estate Bd; Inst Real Estate Mgt; Apt Bldg Owners & Mgrs Asn; S Side Planning Bd; supports La Rabida C Hosp; Jane Dent Home Aged. **Special Achievements:** Nation's black first certified property manager. **Home Addr:** 4800 Lake Shore Dr, Chicago, IL 60615.

## ANDERSON, DR. GEORGE ALLEN

Lawyer. **Personal:** Born Sep 11, 1941, Zanesville, OH; son of Louis B and Cenna M; married Brenda; children: Kim & George A Jr. **Educ:** SC State Univ, BS, 1962, JD, 1966. **Career:** Aiken-Barnwell CAC Inc, chief exec officer, 1966-, exec dir, currently; Anderson & Assocs Aiken PA, owner, currently. **Orgs:** Am Bar Asn; Nat Bar Asn; Southeastern Lawyers Asn; Sc Bar Asn; Lower Savannah Coun Governments; Zoning Bd Adjustments, City Aiken; Cumberland AME Ch, Aiken; Aiken County Bar Asn; SC State Col Alumni Asn. **Honors/Awds:** Sch Law Award, SC State Col. **Home Addr:** 724 Barnwell Ave NE, Aiken, SC 29801-4414, **Home Phone:** (803)649-7572. **Business Addr:** Owner, Anderson & Assocs of Aiken PA, 302 Pk Ave SE 2nd Fl, Aiken, SC 29801-4508, **Business Phone:** (803)648-0797.

## ANDERSON, DR. GLENN B.

College teacher. **Personal:** son of Bennie and Zetta; married Karen; children: Danielle & Jamaal. **Educ:** Gallaudet Col, BA, psychol, 1968; Univ Ariz, MS, rehab coun, 1970; NY Univ, PhD, rehab coun, 1982. **Career:** LaGuardia Community Col, prog coordr, 1975-82; NY Univ, assoc res scientist; Univ Ark, Rehab Res & Training Ctr, prof, dir training, 1982-2008; Univ Ark at Little Rock, asst prof, currently; consult, currently. **Orgs:** Chmn, Gallaudet Univ Bd trustee; Nat Coun Disability; Ark Rehab Coun; coord, RSA-funded deafness rehab Counspecialization; Nat Adv Coun Rehab Cult Diversity proj; Ark Rehab Coun; bd dir, Nat Black Deaf Advocates. **Home Addr:** 22 Bellegarde Dr, Little Rock, AR 72223-9185, **Home Phone:** (501)831-4685. **Business Addr:** Associate Professor, University of Arkansas at Little Rock, 2801 S Univ Ave, Little Rock, AR 72204, **Business Phone:** (501)246-8294.

## ANDERSON, DR. GLORIA LONG

Educator. **Personal:** Born Nov 5, 1938, Altheimer, AR; daughter of Charley Long (deceased) and Elsie Foggie Long (deceased); married Leonard Sinclair; children: Gerald L. **Educ:** AM&N Col, BS, chem, 1958; Atlanta Univ, MS, org chem, 1960; Univ Chicago, PhD, phys org chem, 1968. **Career:** SC State Col, instr, 1961-62; Morehouse Col, instr, 1962-64; Univ Chicago, teaching & res asst, 1964-68; SC State Col, summer sch, prof, 1967; Morris Brown Col, assoc prof & chmn, 1968-73, Callaway prof & chmn, 1973-84, actg vpres, acad affairs, 1984-85, dean acad affairs, 1984-89, Fuller E Callaway prof chem, 1990-, interim pres, 1992-93, 1995-97, 1998, dean sci & technol, 1996-, Dept chem, Fuller E Callaway prof & chmn, 2003, fac rep bd, 2004, vpres acad affairs, 2007-; Lockheed GA Corp, NSF res fel, 1981, res consult, 1982; Edwards Afb Calif, Air Force Rocket Propulsion Lab, SCEEE fac res fel, 1984; UNCF, distinguished scholar, 1989-90; Am Inst Chemists, cert prof chemist, 1992-. **Orgs:** Educ consult, US Dept Educ, 1976-88; fel Am Biog Inst, 1977; ad hoc technol rev group, Nat Cancer Inst, 1986; NIADA, contract reviewer, 1990-91; fel Am Inst Chemists; fel Am Chem Soc; fel Ga Acad Sci; fel NY Acad Sci; AASI; Nat Sci Teachers Asn; Am Asn Univ Profs; Delta Sigma Theta Sorority Inc; Nat Inst Sci; Atlanta Univ Sci Res Inst; Nat Asn Educ Broadcasters; Nat Asn Advan Colored People; Asn Comput Mathand Sci Teaching. **Honors/Awds:** Alpha Kappa Mu Honor Trophy Col All Expense Scholar Highest Average in Freshman Class, 1955; vchair, Corp Pub Broadcasting's Bd Dirs, 1972-79; AR AM&N Col Nat Alumni Asn, 1973; "Breaking NewGround", Atlanta Chap Delta Sigma Theta Sor Inc, 1974; gov's appointee Pub Telecommunications Task Force, 1980; Arkansan Achievement Education, 1985; United Negro Col Fund Distinguished Scholar, 1985; National Alumni Award, 1986; All-Star Excellence in Education Award, Univ Arkansas, PlineBluff Alumni, 1987; Alpha Kappa Mu Natl Honor Soc; Beta Kappa Chi Sci Honor Soc; 30 other honors and awards. **Special Achievements:** Author of numerous science publications; "Atlanta's Best and Brightest Scientists", Atlanta Mag, 1983. **Home Addr:** 560 Lynn Valley Rd SW, Atlanta, GA 30311, **Home Phone:** (404)691-5146. **Business Addr:** Vice President of Academic Affairs, Fuller E. Callaway Professor of Chemistry, Morris Brown College, 643 Martin Luther King Jr Dr NW, Atlanta, GA 30314, **Business Phone:** (404)458-2003.

## ANDERSON, GRANVILLE SCOTT

School administrator. **Personal:** Born Jul 25, 1947, Honolulu, HI; son of Granville P and Olga Edna Jones; married Jennifer Sachie Kato. **Educ:** Ruskin Col, Oxford, Eng, cert, 1970; Queensborough Community Col, AAS, 1971; Queens Col, BA, 1972; Baruch Col, Master's degree. **Career:** City Univ New York, exec asst, 1972-82, exec officer, 1982-87, coordr res found, 1987-90, dep dir admis, 1990-; Town Squash Inc, squash prof, 1980-; BMCC dir human resources, labor designee & dean fac & staff rels, 1994, vpres admin & planning, 2000-. **Orgs:** Univ Chancellor's Scholar Study UK, 1969-70; Oscar Wilde Speaker's Tour Belfast, N Ireland, 1969; adminr, City Univ NY Pamela S Galiber Scholar Fund, 1976-86; exec bd, Metro Squash Racquets Asn, 1977-80; Sports Mgt Consult, 1977-; chmn, Referees Comm MSRA, 1978; pres, Queens bor Community Col Alumni Asn, 1979-86; NY Aikido Club, 1990-. **Honors/Awds:** John F Kennedy Award, 1968; Nationally ranked amateur squash player, US Squash Racquets Asn. **Home Addr:** 3 Stuyvesant Oval, New York, NY 10009, **Home Phone:** (212)674-7063. **Business Addr:** Vice President Of Administration & Planning, Borough of Manhattan Community College, 199 Chambers St, New York, NY 10007, **Business Phone:** (212)220-8000.

## ANDERSON, GREGORY WAYNE (CADILLAC ANDERSON)

Basketball player. **Personal:** Born Jun 22, 1964, Houston, TX; married Tammie; children: Greg Jr, Geia, Gabrielle & Geremy. **Educ:** Univ Houston, attended 1987. **Career:** Basketball player (retired); San Antonio Spurs, ctr forward, 1987-89; Milwaukee Bucks, ctr forward, 1989-91; NJ Nets, ctr forward, 1991; Denver Nuggets, ctr forward, 1991-92; Juvecaserta Basket, 1992-93; Phonola Caserta, Italy, ctr forward, 1992-93; Detroit Pistons, ctr forward, 1993-94; Atlanta Hawks, ctr forward, 1994-95; San Antonio Spurs, ctr forward, 1995-97; Atlanta Hawks, ctr forward, 1997-98; Belgrano de San Nicolas, 1999-2000.

## ANDERSON, HAROLD A.

Manager, executive. **Personal:** Born Oct 12, 1939, New York, NY; married Alice Campbell; children: Joi & Dwight. **Educ:** Morehouse Col, attended 1963; Queens Col, BA, 1966; NY Univ, attended 1969. **Career:** NY Life Ins Co, pub rels asst, 1967-69; Interracial Coun Bus Opers, dir pub rels, 1969-70; ITT News Serv, writer, 1970-74; ITT News & Pub Affairs, adminr, 1974-76; ITT, mgr pub affairs, 1977-86; NY Pub Libr, Schomburg Ctr Res Black Cult, contribr, pub rels officer, 1986-, dir pub rels, 2000; Nat Urban League Black Exec Exchange Prog Coord, vis prof; singer; rec artist; song writer. **Orgs:** Provide Addict Care Today; Rutgers Minority Invest; Harlem Consumers Educ Coun; Nat Urban Affairs Coun; Pub Rels Soc Am; 100 Black Men; OIC NY Tech Adv Comm; Nigerian Am Friendship Soc; Youth Motivation Task Force Living Witness Prog; consult, Nat Urban League; Col Awareness Prog; bd mem, Harlem YMCA, Greater NY; award comm, CBS TV's "Living Dream" Awards; hon mem, YMCA Black Achiever Indust; Citations US Dept Treas; save our scholar comm, Dillard Univ Louise Wise Serv. **Special Achievements:** Black Achiever, ITT, 1976; Book: "A Memorial Tribute to Jean Blackwell Hutson, Memorial Tribute Comt", 1998. **Home Addr:** 11827 227th St, Cambria Heights, NY 11411-2125, **Home Phone:** (718)949-0817. **Business Addr:** Director, Public Relations Officer, New York Public Library, 515 Malcolm X Blvd, New York, NY 10037-1801, **Business Phone:** (212)491-2259.

## ANDERSON, HELEN LOUISE

Consultant, executive, association executive. **Personal:** Born Feb 23, 1941, Luxora, AR; daughter of Mack and Ruby Lee Evans Nunn. **Educ:** Syracuse Univ, attended 1961; Fashion Inst Tech, attended 1967. **Career:** Eastern Airlines, flight attend, 1965-67; Fashion Barn, exec vpres, 1967-88; Anderson & Assoc Financial Consult Inc, chairperson & nat rep, pres & consult, region deleg, 1988-; A.G. Anderson & Assocs Ltd, assoc. **Orgs:** Dir, bd mem, Fred J Rogers Memorial Found; Princess Grace Found, exec Women NJ; Coalition 100 Black Women; Cornell Univ Med Sch Comm Benefit Minority Stud, BRAG; Nat Asn Black Journalists; bd dir, Fashion Barn, 1987-; bd mem, Support Network Inc; bd dir, Can Pension & Benefits Inst; Can Pension & Benefits Inst. **Honors/Awds:** Twin Award, Nat Bd of the YWCA, 1986; National Volunteer of the Year Award, CPBI Atlantic Region, 2010. **Home Addr:** 1 Lincoln Plz Apt 12b, New York, NY 10023-7131, **Home Phone:** (212)799-4161. **Business Addr:** President, Delegate, Anderson & Associates Financial Consulting Inc, 2624 Windsor St, Halifax, NS B3L 4G5, **Business Phone:** (902)454-7338.

## ANDERSON, HENRY L. N.

School administrator. **Personal:** Born May 23, 1934, Ogeechee, GA; son of Egister Lee and Louise Burns Lonon; married Margie N Johnson; children: Brenda Ivelisse, Ileana La Norma & Henry Lee Norman. **Educ:** Earlham Col, Richmond, IN, 1954; Cheyney Univ, PA, BSEd, 1957; Univ Calif, Los Angeles, EdD, 1972; Yale Univ, MAR, 1973. **Career:** Los Angeles County Schs, teacher, 1961-66; Los Angeles Unified Schs Dist, instr & adminr, 1967-68; Univ Calif, Los Angeles, dir, Dept Spec Educ Prog, assoc dir, 1968-69; Loyola Univ, Grad Sch Educ Prog, asst prof, 1968-72; Eval & Mgt Int Inc, dir, chairperson, chief exec officer, 1971; Calif St Univ Grad Sch Educ, supvr stud teachers, 1972-73; Windsor Univ, Los Angeles, CA, vpres, 1973-75; Fruitarian & Wellness, lectr; financial consult; real estate developer & entrepreneur; African-Am Community Trust, chief exec officer; Lonon Classic Motorcars, chief exec officer; City Univ Los Angeles, founder, dean, pres, 1974-2011, chancellor, emer, currently. **Orgs:** Yale Club Southern Calif; life mem, Nat Asn Advan Colored People; life mem, Univ Calif Los Angeles Alumni Asn; founder, Org Wellness Crusade Network; pres, Phi Delta Kappa. **Home Addr:** 4647 Presidio Dr, Los Angeles, CA 90008-4825, **Home Phone:** (323)296-1566. **Business Addr:** President, Chancellor, City University Los Angeles, 3960 Wilshire Blvd Suite 501, Los Angeles, CA 90045-5227, **Business Phone:** (310)341-5205.

## ANDERSON, J. MORRIS

Television producer, entrepreneur, publisher. **Personal:** Born Jul 6, 1936, Greenville, SC; children: J Morris Jr, Gracelyn, Aleta & Kathy. **Educ:** Am Univ, BA, 1961. **Career:** Miss Black Am Beauty Pageant, founder, 1968-; Little Miss Black Am, staff; Tiny Miss Black Am, staff; Miss Black Am Teenager, staff; Miss Black Am, staff; Mrs Black Am, staff; Miss Third World, founder & exec producer. **Orgs:** Pres, Success Seekers Sem; chmn & founder, Black Am Radio & TV Network; chmn, Miss Black Am Beauty Ctrs; exec dir, Rehab Inst Am; founder, J Morris Anderson Asn Investments Stocks & Bonds; Omega Psi Phi. **Business Addr:** Founder, Miss Black America Pageant, PO Box 25668, Philadelphia, PA 19144, **Business Phone:** (215)844-8872.

## ANDERSON, JAMAL SHARIF

Executive, football player, broadcaster. **Personal:** Born Sep 30, 1972, El Camino Real, CA; son of Zenobia. **Educ:** Utah Univ, BS, sociol, 1994. **Career:** Football player (retired), exec; Jam Entertainment, owner, 1996-; Atlanta Falcons, running back, 1994-95, running back, 1996-2001; Entertainment & Sports Programming Network, analyst, 2002-09; Hardcore Sports Radio, phone-guest, 2009; Cable News Network, contribr, sports & entertainment, 2010-. **Honors/Awds:** Pro Bowl, 1998; Rushing Leader, Nat Football League, 1998. **Business Addr:** Owner, Jam Entertainment, 1000 Peachtree Industrial Blvd, Suwanee, GA 30024.

## ANDERSON, JAMES

Executive, vice president (organization). **Educ:** Denison Univ, BA, theater, 1985; Univ Calif, Los Angeles, Anderson Sch Mgt, NAMIC exec leadership prog, 2009. **Career:** Carsey-Werner Co, prod asst, 1985-87, asst to producer, 1987-89, pub rels coordr, 1989-91, mgr, dir pub rels, 1991-93, vpres publicity, pub rel, 1993-97, sr vpres, corp publicity & pub rels, 1997-2005; EMMY mag, ed advisor; Turner Broadcasting Syst Inc, Cartoon Network, vpres pub rels, 2005-, sr vpres commun, 2007-. **Orgs:** Tv Publicity Exec Comt; TV Cares; Gov Ball comt; Entertainment Publicists Prof Socs; bd mem, Los Angeles Chap Sickle Cell Anemia; bd trustee, Denison Univ; bd dir, Securities Indust & Financial Markets Asn; bd dir, Alliance Theater; bd gov, Acad Tv Arts & Sci, 2001-05; Nat Asn Multi-Ethnicity Commun; Pub Rels Soc Am; Dad's Garage Theater Adv Bd. **Business Addr:** Senior Vice President Communications, Vice-President Public Relations, Turner Broadcasting System Inc, 1 CNN Ctr, Atlanta, GA 30303, **Business Phone:** (404)885-4205.

**ANDERSON, DR. JAMES ALAN**
Educator, school administrator. **Personal:** Born Dec 13, 1948, Washington, DC; married Nancy; children: 3. **Educ:** Villanova Univ, BA, psychol, 1970; Cornell Univ, PhD, 1980. **Career:** Xavier Univ, asst prof psy chol, 1976-80, chmn, dept psychol & assoc prpsychol, 1980-83; Ind Univ PA, assoc prof psychol 1983-87, prof psych, 1987-92; NC State Univ, Undergrad affairs, vice provost, 1992-2003; Tex A&M Univ, Off Inst Assessment & Diversity, assoc provost & vpres, 2003-05; Univ Albany, vpres, 2005-. **Orgs:** Asn Black Psychologists 1982-; Asn Black Women Higher Educ, 1983-; Am Fedn Teachers 1983-; dir, Benjamin E Mays Acad Scholars IUP, 1985-; ed Benjamin E Mays Acad Scholars Monogr Ser, 1986-; Am Psychol Soc; Nat Asn Develop Educ; bd trustee, Southern Asn Cols & Schs; bd dir, United Way Cumberland County; chmn, Sustainability Communities Found. **Home Addr:** 1128 School St, Indiana, PA 15701. **Business Addr:** Vice President, University Albany, 1400 Washington Ave, Albany, NY 12222, **Business Phone:** (518)442-3300.

**ANDERSON, JAMES W., JR.**
Business owner, consultant, real estate agent. **Educ:** Univ Mich; Wilberforce Col. **Career:** Bank Ann Arbor, bd dir, 2004-; Anderson Assocs, owner & pres, currently; Arbor Bancorp Inc, dir emer, currently. **Orgs:** Bd trustee, Washtenaw Community Col; Washtenaw Tech Mid Col; bd dir, NEW Ctr; bd dir, Ann Arbor Chamber Com; Ann Arbor Area Bd Realtors, 2006-; Another Ann Arbor; bd mem, NEW Ctr; bd mem, Bank Ann Arbor. **Business Addr:** Owner, The Anderson Associates Inc, 2160 Huron Pkwy, Ann Arbor, MI 48104, **Business Phone:** (734)677-4300.

**ANDERSON, JOSEPH B., JR.**
Administrator. **Personal:** Born Jan 1, 1943?, Topeka, KS. **Educ:** US Mil acad, BS, math & engineering, 1965; Univ Calif, Los Angeles, CA, MA, 1973; AUS & Gen Staff Col, attended 1984. **Career:** US Com Dept, from asst to secy, 1977-79; Gen Motors Corp, plant mgr, dir, gen dir, 1979-92; Composite Energy Mgt Systs Inc, pres, chief exec officer & chmn, 1992-93; Chivas Industs LLC, chmn & chief exec officer, 1994-2002; TAG Holdings LLC, chmn & chief exec officer, 2001-; Vibration Control Technologies LLC, chmn & chief exec officer, 2002-; A&D Technologies LLC, chmn & chief exec officer, 2003-; US Mil Acad, prof, social sci; Great Lakes Assemblies, chmn & chief exec officer, 2005-. **Orgs:** Fel White House, 1977-78; bd mem, Quaker Chem Corp, 1992-; bd mem, Meritor Automotive, 1997-2000; bd mem, R.R. Donnelley & Sons, 1998-; bd mem, Arvin Meritor Inc, 2000-; bd mem, Sierra Pac Resources, 2005-; bd mem, Rite Aid Corp, 2005-; bd mem, Valassis commun, 2006-; bd gov, Ctr Creative Leadership; trustee, Boys & Girls Clubs Am; bd dir, Detroit Econ Club; bd dir, Nat Recreation Found; Original Equip Suppliers Asn; Soc Automotive Engrs Found; Soc Automotive Engrs Int; Exec Comt, Nat Asn Black Automotive Suppliers; adv bd, Horizons Upward Bound; trustee, Kettering Univ. **Business Addr:** Chairman, Chief Executive Officer, TAG Holdings LLC, 2075 W Big Beaver Rd Suite 500, Troy, MI 48084-3442, **Business Phone:** (248)822-8056.

**ANDERSON, JULIUS J., JR.**
Electrician, president (organization), administrator. **Educ:** Ivy Tech Col, attended 1984. **Career:** JJ Elec, electrician, owner, 1985-; Ball State Univ, supvr, 1990-; Muncie Community Sch Bd, vpres, pres, councilman, 2009-. **Orgs:** Bd mem, Habitat Humanity; Am Heart Asn; Whiteley Neighborhood Asn; Buley Ctr Bd. **Home Addr:** 1809 E Carver Dr, Muncie, IN 47303-4009, **Home Phone:** (765)289-6639. **Business Addr:** Councilman 6th District, City of Muncie, Muncie City Hall 300 N High St 3rd Fl, Muncie, IN 47305, **Business Phone:** (765)747-4845.

**ANDERSON, KATHLEEN WILEY**
Government official. **Personal:** Born May 22, 1932, Kansas City, KS; married Harvey L; children: Harvey, H Delon & Doryanna. **Educ:** Univ Kans, Lawrence, KS, BS, 1954, MS, 1955; Univ Southern Calif, MPA, 1974; Wharton Sch, Univ Pa, attended 1979. **Career:** Government official (retired); Kans City, high sch teacher, 1954-56; Sch Deaf, teacher, 1958-63; Calif Inst Women, adminr, 1963-74, supt, 1976-80; Correctional Training Facil, assoc supt act dep supt, 1974-76; CalifInst Men, supt. **Orgs:** United Black Correctional Workers Asn; Calif Black Correctional Coalition; Nat Advan Asn Colored People; Am Correctional Asn; Alpha Kappa Alpha Sor; Eastern Star; Links Inc; guest instr, Simon Fraser Univ Banbury Brit Columbia, Wharton Sch; instr, Int Women Corrections. **Honors/Awds:** Ford Found Fellowship Fisk Univ, Univ Kans, 1948-55; Ina B Temple Fellowship, Univ Kans; Notable Women, 1977-87; Inductee, Hall of Fame, African-Am Criminal Justice. **Special Achievements:** First female correctional admin in a male facility; First female correctional supervisor in CA; First black women heads in prison. **Home Addr:** 4795 Boyd Ct, Riverside, CA 92507-5601, **Home Phone:** (951)781-6988.

**ANDERSON, KEISHA DAWN**
Basketball player. **Personal:** Born May 17, 1974. **Educ:** Univ Wis-Madison. **Career:** Basketball player (retired), trainer; Colo Xplosion, guard, 1998-2000; Wash Mystics, 1999-2000; Atlanta Justice, 2000-01; Charlotte Sting, 2001-02; Springfield Spirit, 2002-03; Chicago Blaze, guard, 2003-04; Dallas Fury, 2004; San Antonio Silver Stars, 2005; ASA Jerusalem, 2006-07; Istanbul Univ, 2007-08; Keisha Dawn Anderson Charities, trainer & owner, currently.

**ANDERSON, KENNETH RICHARD**
Engineer, electrical engineer, manager. **Personal:** Born Aug 4, 1936, Philadelphia, PA; son of William and Dorothy; married Dorothy; children: Pamela & Veronica. **Educ:** Drexel Univ, BSEE, 1968; Cent Mich Univ, BA, 1975, MA. **Career:** Engineer (retired); Inselek, mgr test engr, 1971-75; Aeroneutronic Ford, super comp engr, 1975-76; RCA Gov Systs Div, mgr rel & test, 1976-79; Siemens RTL, mgr IC design & test, strategic planning, anal & design mfg syst; Widener Univ, adj prof, 1982. **Orgs:** Bd mem, Willingboro NJ Sch Dist, 1971-74; gov bd, IEEE Comp Soc, 1979-, 2nd vpres chmn, tech activ, 1987, pres, 1988-90, gov bd, 1999-2000; Asn Dept Heads Comp & Info Sci & Eng; chmn, IEEE Comput Socs's Test Technol Tech Comt. **Honors/Awds:** Distinguished Service Award, US Jaycees, 1972; Computer Society Meritorious Service Award, 1981, 1982, 1983, 1984, 1985. **Home Addr:** 158 Camber Lane, Mount Laurel, NJ 08054-3333, **Home Phone:** (856)273-0091.

**ANDERSON, KENNY (KENNETH ANDERSON)**
Basketball player, basketball coach. **Personal:** Born Oct 9, 1970, Queens, NY; son of Joan (deceased); married Tami Akbar, Jan 1, 1994, (divorced 2001); children: Lyric & Jazz; married Tamiyka R Lockhart, Jan 1, 1998, (divorced 2004); children: Kenneth Jr; married Natasha, Jan 1, 2007. **Educ:** Ga Inst Technol, attended 1993. **Career:** Basketball player (retired), basketball coach; NJ Nets, guard & point guard, 1991-96; Charlotte Hornets, 1995-96, 2003; Portland Blazers, point guard, 1996-98; Boston Celtics, point guard, 1998-2002; Seattle Super Sonics, 2002-03; Ind Pacers, point guard, 2003-04; Atlanta Hawks, 2004-05; Los Angeles Clippers, 2004-05; Zalgiris Kaunas, pt guard, 2005-06; Atlanta Krunk, Continental Basketball Asn, head coach, 2007-08; slamball, head coach, 2008; David Posnack Jewish Day Sch, coach, 2011-. **Orgs:** Kenny Anderson Found. **Honors/Awds:** Silver Medal, FIBA World Championship, 1990; Consensus first-team All-American, 1991; Silver Medal, Goodwill Games, 1990; All-Star, Nat Basketball Asn, 1994; New York City Basketball Hall of Fame, 2008. **Special Achievements:** NBA Draft, First round pick, No 2, 1991. **Business Addr:** Coach, 5810 S Pine Island Rd, Davie, FL 33328, **Business Phone:** (954)583-6100.

**ANDERSON, LESLIE BLAKE**
Lawyer. **Personal:** Born Sep 14, 1966, Port Jefferson, NY; daughter of Alphonso and Andrea. **Educ:** Univ Endinburgh, Scotland, 1986; State Univ NY, Albany, BA, 1987; Albany Law Sch Union Univ, JD, 1990. **Career:** Suffolk Co Dist Atty Off, asst dist atty, dist ct bur, 1991-92, case adv bur, 1993, maj crime bur, 1993-97, asst dist atty, Gang Unit Chief, 1998-2002; Suffolk County Dist Atty, asst dist atty, 1991-2002; JLC Assocs NY LLC, partner, 2003-; Appellate Div, 2nd Dept, prin atty, 2003-; Judicial Dist, Grievance Comt, 10th, prin atty. **Orgs:** NY Dist Attys Asn, 1991-; Boy Scouts Am, Eagle Scout comm, 1993-; comnr, Suffolk Co Human Rights Comn, 1996; African-Am Adv Bd, Cong man Rick Lazio, 1996; E Coast Gang Investrs Asn; parliamentarian & coun, bd dir, Long Island Head start; exec bd, Opportunities Industrialization Ctr Inc; Suffolk County Community Col, found bd mem, 2012-13. **Honors/Awds:** Advocate Award, Suffolk Co Exec, 1996; Advocacy Award, Nat Asn Advan Colored People, 1997; Cong Recognition Award, 1997, 1998; Republican of Distinction, Afro-Am Republican Club, 1997; Guardian of the Year, Suffolk Co Police Depart Guardians, 1999; Zonta Woman of the Year, 1999. **Home Addr:** 64 Feller Dr, Central Islip, NY 11722, **Home Phone:** (516)582-6499. **Business Addr:** Principal Attorney, Appellate Division, 45 Monroe Pl, Brooklyn, NY 11201, **Business Phone:** (718)875-1300.

**ANDERSON, MADELINE**
Television producer, administrator. **Personal:** Born Lancaster, PA; daughter of William and Nellie; married Ralph Joseph; children: Adele, Rachel, Laura & Ralph Jr. **Educ:** New York Univ, BA, 1956. **Career:** WNET-TV, film ed, assoc producer, producer & dir, 1964-69; CTV Workshop, supv ed & prod dir, 1971-75, TV producer, 1985-87; Onyx Prod, founder, pres, 1975-; Infinity Factory Educ Develop Ctr, exec producer, 1976-77; Off Black Ministry, Diocese Brooklyn/Queens, assoc dir, 1995-2000; TV series: The Cool World assistant to dir continuity, 1964; "AlManaahil", 1986; Movies: Integration Report 1, 1961; I Am Somebody, dir, 1970; Infinity Factory, 1977; Sisters in Cinema, 2003. **Orgs:** Bd trustee, Int Film Seminars, 1974-77; film panelist & bd mem, NY Coun Arts, 1975-79; Nat Acad TV Arts & Sci; bd mem, Women Make Movies, 1986-88; bd mem, NY Film Coun. **Honors/Awds:** Woman of the Year, Sojourner Truth Festival Arts, 1976; Grand Prize, Media Women, 1977; Grants, NYSCA, WNET Doc Fund, Nat Endowment Arts & Am Film Inst; Indie Award, 1985; Lifelong Achievement Award, Asn Independent Video & Filmmakers; Unsung Heroine of Local 1199, 1969; Office of Black Ministry Diocese of Brooklyn, 1995; Humanitarian Award, NAWBPW Baisley Park Club, 1999; Gallery of the Greatest, Miller Brewing Co, Year 2000 Calendar; Award for Outstanding Contributions As A Documentary Filmmaker, African-Am Cinema Conf, 2000; Award for Willingness to Share Love & Knowledge of Black Catholic Heritage, Kuienga Youth Diocese Brooklyn. **Special Achievements:** First African-American woman to executive produce a TV series; inducted into the Black Filmmakers Hall of Fame, 1992; became the First African-American woman to executive produce a television series with Infinity Factory. **Home Addr:** 83 Sterling St, Brooklyn, NY 11225, **Home Phone:** (718)469-4682. **Business Addr:** President, Onyx Productions, 2355 Westwood Blvd, Los Angeles, CA 90013, **Business Phone:** (323)692-9830.

**ANDERSON, DR. MARJORIE**
Public relations executive, association executive, executive. **Personal:** Born Detroit, MI. **Educ:** Univ Detroit, BBA. **Career:** US Govt, EEO counr, staff adv; D-Sace Charm Sch Comn, pub rel; Urban League Youth Assembly, pub rel dir; St Paul's Ch, pub rel dir; Afboney Mod & Fin Sch, pub rel dir; CANAC, pub rel dir. **Orgs:** Bd mem, Det Soc Adv Cultur & Educ; bd mem, Fisher YMCA; pres, FEMS Fisher YMCA; corr secy, media coord Det Urban League Guild; Red Cross vol; coordr, child hops Sickle Cell Anemia prog; columnist Spirit Det Tarcom Newspaper; bi-centennial chmn, Det Urban League Guilds Fund Raising Proj; nat historian Gamma Phi Delta Sor Inc; ed chief, Basileus Delta Nu Chap GPD Sor; youth dir, Delta Nu's Rosebud Youth Group; US Govt coord, Equal Oppty Day Upward Mobility Race Relat Unit Found Progs. **Honors/Awds:** President of the Year, Gamma Phi Delta, 1973; Nat Pres, Outstanding Basileus GPD, 1974; Commission Service Award, GPD Sor, 1976; Commission Service Award, Det Urban League; Most Value Member Award, Urban League Guild, 1976; Bi-Centennial Award, Delta Nu's Youth Group 1976. **Business Addr:** President, Notable Printing & Products, 20034 Prest Dr, Detroit, MI 48235.

**ANDERSON, MARLON ORDELL**
Broadcaster, baseball player. **Personal:** Born Jan 6, 1974, Montgomery, AL; married Shadia Tilahun; children: Zoe, Hannah & Caleb. **Educ:** Univ S Ala. **Career:** Baseball player (retired), baseball coach; Philadelphia Phillies, second baseman, 1998-2002, color analyst, 2014; Tampa Bay Devil Rays, 2003; St Louis Cardinals, 2004; New York Mets, 2005, 2007-09; Wash Nationals, 2006; Los Angeles Dodgers, 2006-07, free agt, currently; Newark Bears independent Atlantic League, 2009; Potomac Nationals, hitting coach, 2012; Hagerstown Suns, hitting coach, currently; Comcast SportsNet, analysts, currently. TV Series: "Sunday Night Baseball", 1990; "National League Championship Series", 2004; "Island Song", 2013. **Business Addr:** Hitting Coach, Potomac Nationals, 7 County Complex Ct, Woodbridge, VA 22192, **Business Phone:** (703)590-2311.

**ANDERSON, MARSHA C.**
Educator. **Personal:** married Terrance. **Career:** Abraham Baldwin Agr Col, admin coordr, dir stud support serv, 2005. **Business Addr:** PREP & MAP Coordinator, Abraham Baldwin Agriculture College, ABAC 50 2802 Moore Hwy, Tifton, GA 31793-2601, **Business Phone:** (229)386-5100.

**ANDERSON, MARVA JEAN**
Government official, president (organization). **Personal:** Born May 9, 1945, Morrilton, AR; children: Tamikko Afresa Green. **Educ:** Los Angeles Trade Tech Col, AA, 1970; Calif State Univ, Dominguez Hills, BA, 1973; Univ Calif Los Angeles, MSW, 1978. **Career:** Communicative Arts Acad, admin asst, 1972-76; Spec Serv Groups, asst dir prog develop, 1976-82; YWCA Women Shelter, dir, 1982-84; Los Angeles County Dept C Serv, spec asst, 1984; Mus of Sci & Indust, dir, corp & fdn rels. **Orgs:** Asn Black Social Workers Greater Los Angeles, 1976-; vpres, 1980-81, pres, 1982-83, treas, 1984-87, Nat Asn Black Social Workers Los Angeles Chap; nat rep, Nat Asn Black Social Workers, 1984-87; comt mem, 1984-86, bd mem, 1987, Image Awards; Nat Asn Advan Colored People Hollywood Chap, 1984-86; bd mem, Jenesse Domestic Violence Shelter, 1985-; vpres, Jenesse Inc, 1986-88; Lambda Kappa Mu Sorority, 1990-; sponsor, Black Womens Forum, 1990-. **Home Addr:** 919 W 49th St, Los Angeles, CA 90037-2933, **Home Phone:** (323)752-3412.

**ANDERSON, MARY ELIZABETH**
Teacher. **Personal:** Born Andersonville, GA. **Educ:** Va Union Univ, BS; Chicago Col Com; Am Univ; USDA Grad Sch. **Career:** Off Educ, fiscal officer, 1965-70; US Dept Health Educ & Welfare, specialist, 1970-, women's prog coordr, 1975-; Union High Sch, teacher; Va Union Univ Dept Women's Nat Adv Coun, counr, 1976-. **Orgs:** Affil Nat Alliance Black Sch Educs; life mem, Nat Asn Advan Colored People, exec bd mem, 1975-77; DC Women's Polit Caucus; Friends Frederick Douglass Mus African Art; Alpha Kappa Alpha. **Home Addr:** 6111 Brandy Hall Ct, Oxon Hill, MD 20745. **Business Addr:** Specialist, US Department of Health Education & Welfare, 400 Maryland Ave SW, Washington, DC 20202, **Business Phone:** (202)205-8435.

**ANDERSON, MICHAEL WAYNE**
Public relations executive. **Personal:** Born Feb 24, 1942, Wilmington, DE; married Yvonne Gloria Copeland; children: Kima-Joi Michaele. **Educ:** George Washington HS, grad, 1960; Calif State Univ, Los Angeles, CA, BS, bus admin, 1974. **Career:** YMCA Youthmobile Metro Los Angeles, dir, 1971-73; A Better Chance Inc, sr prog mgr, 1973-2004, western states reg dir, 1973-2004, recruitment coordr; Calif Fair Plan Asn, mgr pub affairs, 1989-93; self employed consult, 2004-. **Orgs:** Crenshaw Br Young Mens Christian Asn Metro Los Angeles, exec dir, 1975-77; Calif Arson Prevent Comt, 1977-80; pres, Los Angeles chap, Nat Asn Mkt Developers, 1978-80; San Francisco Arson Task Force, 1979-80; chmn, speakers bur Pub Club Los Angeles, 1979-80; eligible comt chmn, Pub Rel Soc Am, 1980; res secy, PIRATES, 1980; bd dir, Angeles Girl Scout Coun, 1980; pres, Toastmasters Int, 1980; Los Angeles Mayor's Arson Suppression Task Force; Los Angeles Chap, Nat Asn Advan Colored People; Los Angeles Chap Urban League; Crenshaw Neighbors. **Home Addr:** 5958 Overhill Dr, Los Angeles, CA 90043.

**ANDERSON, MILLER R.**
Social worker. **Personal:** Born Chicago, IL. **Educ:** Ill State Univ, BS, sociol & anthrop, 1975; Univ Ill, MSW, 1984. **Career:** Ill Dept C & Family Serv, case mgr, Northern Region, regional admin; Cs Home & Aid Soc Ill; Child Care Asn Ill, assoc dir; Habilitative Systs Inc, Child Welfare Serv, dir; Chicago Youth Ctrs, pres, chief exec officer; Chicago State Univ, Sch Social Work, adj prof; Ill Dept C & Family Serv, Div Monitoring, dep dir, 2008-12; MRA Consult, consult, 2004-; Human Resources Devlopment Inst Inc, chief operating officer, 2013-. **Orgs:** Dir, Midwest Regional, Child Welfare League Am; Child Welfare; Youth Develop; Syst Chg & Policy Developemnt Areas C; Youth & Families. **Honors/Awds:** City Partner Award, Univ Ill, 2003. **Business Addr:** Deputy Director, Illinois Department Children & Family Service, 100 W Randolph St 6-200, Chicago, IL 60601, **Business Phone:** (312)814-6847.

**ANDERSON, MONROE, III**
Writer. **Personal:** Born Apr 6, 1947, Gary, IN; son of Monroe Jr; married Joyce Owens; children: Scott & Kyle. **Educ:** Ind Univ, Bloomington, BA, jour & eng lit, 1970. **Career:** Newsweek mag; Chicago Tribune, polit columnist; WBEZ-FM, commentator; Post-Tribune, 1969; Nat Observer, staff writer, 1970-72; Johnson Publ Co, asst ed, 1972-74; Ebony Mag, asst ed, 1972-74; Chicago Tribune, columnist, reporter, 1974-85; Columbia Col-Chicago, adj prof, 1984-88; Newsweek Mag, midwest corresp, 1985-88; Mayor's Off, press secy, 1988-89; WBBM-TV, dir sta serv & community affairs, host, exec prod, 1989-202; CBS News, dir Sta Serv & Community Affairs, 1989-202; N'DIGO, ed; Savoy Mag, ed, 2003-04; Savoy Mag, ed, 2004-05; Chicago Sun-Times, freelance op-ed page columnist, 2006-07; Ebonyjet.com, contrib columnist, 2007-09; Columbia Col, adj prof, 2009. **Orgs:** NABJ; dir, Region V; Ill Broadcasters assoc; IL Arts Found; bd dir, Keep Chicago Beautiful, 1989-; Nat Acad TV Arts & Sci, Chicago Chapt; Trotter Group; bd dir, Ill Arts Alliance, 1995-; bd dir, Gilda's Club Chicago, 1998-. **Home Addr:** 2100 N Clifton Ave, Chicago, IL 60614-4116, **Home Phone:** (773)327-7217.

### ANDERSON, NATHANIEL (NATE ANDERSON)

Educator, school administrator. **Personal:** Born Sep 15, 1950, St. Louis, MO; son of Noble and Rosie; married Tanya E; children: Shunique Oliver & Nichelle Womack. **Educ:** Eastern Ill Univ, BS, recreation, 1973, MS, educ, 1977; Southeast Mo State Univ, specialist, educ, 1991; Ill State Univ, doctorate, educ admin, 1998. **Career:** Decatur Recreation Dept, pk leader, 1977; Mac Arthur High Sch, counr & teacher, suspension counr, phys ed instr, football & track asst coach, 1977-82; Stephen Decatur High Sch, dean stud, 1982-88; Cairo High Sch, prin, 1988-90; Dwight D Eisen hower High Sch, prin, 1990-93; Rock Island & Milan Dist 41, high sch prin, asst supt, 1993-98; E St. Louis Sch Dist 189, supt, 1998-2004; Rock Island/Milan Sch Dist 41, Coordr/Consult, 2005-06, Prin, 2006-08; Univ Ill Springfield, asst prof & educ leadership, 2004-07; Lindenwood Univ, Adj Prof, 2008-; Southeast Mo State Univ, Adj Prof/Consult, 2009-; St. Clair County Regional Off Educ, Statewide Syst Support, Coach McKinney-Vento Homeless Liaison Truancy Hearing Off, 2009-. **Orgs:** Bd dir, Eastern Ill Univ Alumni Asn, 1992-93; adv bd, Educ Admin Comt, Eastern Ill Univ, 1992-93, chair & bd trustee, hon lifetime mem; dir, Decatur Parks Found, 1992-93; bd mem, Decatur Respect, 1992-93; bd dir, W End Coalition, 1992-93; secy & treas, vpres, Big 12 Athletic Conf, 1992-93; Rock Island Youth Concerns Group Comn, 1992-93; bd dir, Bethany Home, 1992-93; bd dir, Quad Cities Scholars, 1992-93; Ill Asn Sch Adminrs; Nat Asn Secy Sch Principals; Ill Principals Asn; Asn for Supv & Curric Develop; Phi Delta Kappa; Ill High Sch Asn; Omega Psi Phi Fraternity; Nat Asn Advan Colored People; John C Ellis Masonic Lodge; Eastern IL Club-Athletic Boosters; founder, Base Runners Athletic Team; Optimist Int, Rock Island, IL; Nat Asn Black Sch Educrs; Mt Zion Baptist Church, E St Louis. **Home Addr:** PO Box 69, Glen Carbon, IL 62034, **Home Phone:** (618)394-9381. **Business Addr:** Professor of Educational Leadership & Master Teaching, University of Illinois, Brookens 390 1 Univ Plz, Springfield, IL 62703-5407, **Business Phone:** (217)206-6247.

### ANDERSON, NICHOLAS CHARLES

Executive director, salesperson, association executive. **Personal:** Born Feb 7, 1953, Gaston County, NC; son of Nicodemus (deceased) and Fannie Mae Moses; married Darlene Davis; children: Takecia Kamari, Brandye Nicole & Michelle Darlene; married Marionette. **Educ:** Cent Piedmont Community Col, Charlotte, NC, 1972; Wayne State Univ, Detroit, MI, BA, 1981. **Career:** Am Tobacco Co, sales rep, 1974-76, dist sales mgr, 1976-81; Com Freddie G Burton Jr, legis aide, 1983-87; Detroit Urban League, pres & chief exec officer, 1987-94, 1997-; City Detroit, Dept Human Servs, exec dir, 1994-97. **Orgs:** Youth prog dir, Detroit Br, Nat Asn Advan Colored People, 1981-83, Mid w region III, dir, 1983-87; Econ Club Detroit, 1988-; bd dirs, Oper ABLE, 1990-97; adv bd, NBD Community Develop Corp, 1990-95; bd dirs, CATCH, 1991-; bd dirs, Mich Black Caucus, 1991-96; trustee, Mich Non-Profit Forum, 1991-; Detroit Compact Community Partners Comn; Detroit Pub Sch City-Wide Community Orgn; secy & trustee, Luellen Hannah Found; bd trustees, chair, Pub Responsibility Comn, Henry Ford Health Syst; bd dir, Health Alliance Plan; vice chmn, bd dir, Schs 21st Century; bd Police comnr, Testimonial Resolution, 1994; bd dirs & pres, WSU Alumni Asn, 1996-97; Detroit Bd Educ, 1997-98; chmn bd, Health Alliance Plan, Detroit. **Honors/Awds:** Regional III Service, Nat Asn Advan Colored People, 1988; Man of the Year, Minority Women's Network, 1992. **Special Achievements:** Co author "The State of Black Michigan: 1993". **Home Addr:** 18232 Fairfield St, Detroit, MI 48221, **Home Phone:** (313)342-5907. **Business Addr:** President, Detroit Urban League, 208 Mack Ave, Detroit, MI 48201, **Business Phone:** (313)832-4600.

### ANDERSON, NICK (NELISON ANDERSON)

Basketball player, basketball executive. **Personal:** Born Jan 20, 1968, Chicago, IL; son of Robert and Alberta; married Kenyarda Higgins; children: 3. **Educ:** Univ Ill, attended 1989. **Career:** Basketball player (retired), basketball exec; Orlando Magic, forward-guard, 1989-99, Sacramento Kings, 1999-2001; Memphis Grizzlies, 2001-02; Illini Men's Basketball All Century Team, 2004; Mem community rels dept, Orlando Magic, 2006-. **Business Addr:** Member of Community Relations Department, Orlando Magic, RDV Sportsplex 8701 Maitland Summit Blvd, Orlando, FL 32810, **Business Phone:** (407)916-2400.

### ANDERSON, NORMAN BRUCE

College teacher, executive, psychologist. **Personal:** Born Oct 16, 1955, Greensboro, NC; son of Charles W and Lois J; married Elizabeth. **Educ:** NC Cent Univ, BA, clin psychol, 1976; Univ NC, Greensboro, MA, clin psychol, 1979, PhD, clin psychol, 1983. **Career:** Brown Univ, clin psychol intern; Duke Univ, assoc prof, 1985-95; Nat Inst Health, assoc dir, 1995-2000; Harvard Univ Sch Pub Health, prof, 2000-; Am Psychol Asn, chief exec officer & exec vpres, 2003-; Books: ed in chief, Encyclopedia of Health and Behavior, APA's flagship journal, American Psychologist; Emotional Longevity: What Really Determines How Long You Live. **Orgs:** Founding dir, Off Behav & Social Sci Res; pres, bd dir, Starbright Found; Nat Adv Coun, Nat Inst Drug Abuse; Soc Psychol Study Ethnic Minority Issues; Soc Behav Med; Acad Behav Med Res; fel Am Psychol Asn; AAAS. **Special Achievements:** APA's first African-American CEO. **Business Addr:** Chief Executive Officer, Executive Vice President, American Psychology Association, 750 1st St NE, Washington, DC 20002-4242, **Business Phone:** (202)336-6080.

### ANDERSON, PATRICIA HEBERT

Activist, executive, president (organization). **Personal:** Born Aug 28, 1945, Houston, TX; daughter of Emma Jean Pope and Aldaah Augusta; married Adolphus Anderson Jr; children: Renee, Reginald, Adolphus III, Ruthalyn, Victor, Albert, Michael & Miriam. **Educ:** Tex Southern Univ, attended 1963, MS, 1997, doctoral stud; Gulf Coast Bible Col, AA, theol, 1975; COGIC, nat evangelist prog, 1987; Union Baptist Bible Col & Sem, BTh, 1992; Arts & Sci Social Work, TSU, attended 1995; Union Baptist Sem & Bible Col, Coun & Rel Ed, MS, 1995. **Career:** Harris City Dem Exec Comn, precinct comnr, 1976-; Glen Manor Weyburn Pl Civic Col, pres, 1979-; Gulf Coast Community Serv, sec, bd dir, 1980; N Forest ISD, sec, bd dir, 1981; Nat Black Caucus Sch Bd, sec, 1982, 1984, bd dir, 1984; Pleasant Green Bapt Church, active church musician; Star Faith Grand Chap, OES 55 grand musician; N Forest Sch Dist, trustee; N Forest Sch Dist Bd Educ, pres, 1988-89; Harris County Dem Party, precinct chair, currently. **Orgs:** Community coordr, NE Community Proj Fund, 1972; chairwoman, New Hope Baptist Church Missionary Affairs, 1975; pres, Glen Manor Weyburn Pl, 1979-; alt person, City Comnr Jim Fontero, 1980; sec, Gulf Coast Community Serv, 1981; bd dir, BATTS, 1982; admin asst, City Comn EA Squattylyons, 1982; Harris County Black Elected Officers, 1986; bd mem, Evangelistic Bible Days Revival Church; secy, Nat Caucus Black Sch, bd mem, 1986-; Houston Cent Young Women Christian Coun, 1987-89; bd mem, Greater ParkHill Church God Christ Evangel Bd, 1987-; pres, Sewing Circle, 1988-; pres, Young Women Christian Coun, 1988-; Houston Cent Dist Church God Christ; Mt Sinai Grand Lodge, AF & AM, grand matron; Greater Pk Hill Church God Christ. **Honors/Awds:** Community Service Award, City Houston Mayor Whitmire, 1983; Hon, Nat Black Caucus Sch Bd Mem, 1983; Woman of the Year, New Hope Baptist Church, 1983; Honor Award, Gulf Coast Community Serv, 1983; High Achievement, NE Community Proj, 1984; Merit of Achievement, Legis Black Caucus State RepHarol Dutton, 1986; Mother of the Year, New Hope Baptist Church, 1986; Outstanding Black Elected Official, Wayside Church of Christ, 1986; Juneteenth Freedom Award, Nat Am Advan Colored People, 1987; Nat Dean'sList, Tex Southern Univ, 1989-90; Outstanding Leadership, Bd Educ, North Forest ISD, 1992; TSU, Deans List, Nat, 1993-95. **Home Addr:** 7539 Carothers St, Houston, TX 77028, **Home Phone:** (713)631-8213. **Business Addr:** Precinct Chair, Harris County Democratic Party, 1445 N Loop W Suite 110, Houston, TX 77008, **Business Phone:** (713)631-8213.

### ANDERSON, PERRY L., JR.

Police chief, commissioner. **Personal:** Born Aug 6, 1944, Miami, FL; children: 1. **Educ:** Miami-Dade Community Col; Fla Int Univ; Univ La Southern Police Inst. **Career:** Miami Police Dept, police officer to chief police, 1969-88; Cambridge Police Dept, comnr, 1988-91. **Orgs:** Pres, Nat Orgn Black Law Enforcement Off. **Special Achievements:** The second black chief of the Miami Police Department. **Business Addr:** Chief, Miami Beach Police Department, 400 NW 2nd Ave, Miami, FL 33101, **Business Phone:** (305)603-6640.

### ANDERSON, RACHEL

Educator. **Educ:** Stanford Univ, BA, commun; St Mary's Col, CA, MA, coun. **Career:** Kent State Univ, Off Adult Serv, co-pres & dir ctr adult & veteran serv, currently, life coordr, currently; Cuyahoga Community Col, asst dean stud affairs. **Business Addr:** Director, Kent State University, 181 Michael Schwartz Ctr Kent Campus, Kent, OH 44242-0001, **Business Phone:** (330)672-7933.

### ANDERSON, DR. RACHELL

Educator, administrator. **Personal:** Born Jan 1, 1942, Tunica, MS; children: 3. **Educ:** Philander Smith Col, BA; Sangamon State Univ, MA; Northern Ill Univ, MS; Adler Sch Prof Psychol, PhD. **Career:** Prof (retired): Pvt clin pract, 1974-2008; Univ Ill, Human Serv prog, chmn, 1999-2006; Women & Gender Studies, assoc prof & dept chair, prof, Dept Human Serv, teacher; vpres, chair, N Am Soc Adlerian Psychol; Cent Ill Soc Adlerian Psychol, co-pres; Okla, juv probation counr; E St Louis, placement counr; Adult educ ctr, sch counr; Books: Before Our Eyes, The Legacy Continues: Writing Healing Stories, The Legacy Continues: Writing Healing Stories. **Orgs:** Founder, Cent Ill Soc Adlerian Psychol; co pres, Cent Ill Psychol Soc; Am Asn Black Psychologists; Nat Orgn Human Serv; Am Psychol Asn; N Am Soc Adlerian Psychol; bd trustee, Northwest Miss Community Col; Church Health Ctr; bd trustee, Miss Writers Guild; AM Psychol Asn; Nat Org Human Serv; pres, Alliance group; . **Home Addr:** 2075 S 5th St, Springfield, IL 62703, **Home Phone:** (217)753-3764.

### ANDERSON, RICHARD CHARLES

Lawyer. **Personal:** Born Nov 25, 1945, Vallejo, CA; son of Walter and Margaret; married Rosalynn; children: Walter. **Educ:** Kennedy King Jr Col, AA, 1972; Univ Chicago, BA, 1973; Northwestern Univ, Sch Law, JD, 1977. **Career:** CNA Ins Co, acct exec, 1980-81; Cook County State's Atty, asst state atty, 1981-84; pvt pract atty law, 1984-86, 1995-; Chicago Housing Authority, dep gen coun, 1986-95. **Orgs:** Chmn, Volunteers Housing, 1971-76; Nat Pub Housing Mus. **Special Achievements:** Regenald Heber Smity Community Lawyer Fellowship, 1977; Published article, "I Love My Son Walter As He Is," in Exceptional Parent Magazine, 1991; Published article, "Walter At 10," in book entitled Uncommon Fathers Reflections on Raising a Child with a Disability, Woodline House, 1995. **Home Addr:** 518 W 62nd St, Chicago, IL 60621-3206, **Home Phone:** (773)994-5154.

### ANDERSON, RICHARD DARNOLL (RICHIE ANDERSON)

Football player, football coach. **Personal:** Born Sep 13, 1971, Olney, MD; children: Richie II & Reginald. **Educ:** Pa State Univ, grad. **Career:** Football player (retired), football coach; New York Jets, running back, 1993-2002; Dallas Cowboys, running back, 2003-04, coach, 2007; New York Jets, asst wide receivers coach, 2005-06; Ariz Cardinals, wide receivers coach, 2006; Kans City Chiefs, wide receivers coach, 2009-11. **Honors/Awds:** NFLPA Byron Whizzer White Award, 2000; Maryland Player of the Year, USA today. Pro Bowl, 2000.

### ANDERSON, RONALD GENE (RON ANDERSON)

Basketball player. **Personal:** Born Oct 10, 1958, Chicago, IL; married Gail; children: 2. **Educ:** Calif State Univ, Fresno, attended 1984. **Career:** Basketball player (retired); Cleveland Cavaliers, 1983-85; Ind Pacers, 1985-88; Philadelphia 76ers, 1988-93; NJ Nets, 1993; Rochester Renegade, 1993-94; Wash Bullets; 1994; Montpellier Basket, 1994-95; Maccabi Natanya, Israel, 1995-96; Atlantic City Seagulls, 1996; Le Mans SB, France, 1996-97; Montpellier Basket, 1997-99; Angers, 1999-2000.

### ANDERSON, ROSALAND GUIDRY

Manager, association executive. **Personal:** Born Jan 27, 1959, Lake Charles, LA; daughter of Calvin and Theresa; married David T Jr; children: David III & Theresa Camille. **Educ:** Tex Southern Univ, BS, math, 1978; Univ Houston, MS, math, 1979. **Career:** IBM Corp, systs engr, 1988-90, systs eng mgr, 1990-94, solution serv mgr, 1994-95, availability serv mgr, 1995-97, AS & 400 area mgr, nat bp prog mgr, 1999-, nat oper mgr, opers manger americas. **Orgs:** Jack & Jill Am, nat rec sec, 1985-; Leadership Tex Alumni; bd mem, Bexar County Oppor Industrialization Ctr, 1987-; bd mem, Cath Families & Charities, 1987-; bd mem, UT Pre Freshman Engineering, 1987-; jr counr girls, Knights St Peter Claver, 1987-. **Honors/Awds:** Eagle Award, IBM, 1979, Regional Awards, 1983, 1985, 1987; BCOIC, Top Citizens Award, 1992; Profiles in Leadership Award, Mission City Business & Professional Women, 1999. **Home Addr:** 15507 Dawn Crest, PO Box 691195, San Antonio, TX 78248, **Home Phone:** (210)492-3658. **Business Addr:** National Business Partner Program Manager, IBM Corp, 911 Cent Pkwy N Suite 100, San Antonio, TX 78232, **Business Phone:** (210)403-1014.

### ANDERSON, S. A.

Basketball player, basketball coach, executive. **Personal:** Born May 31, 1935, Ennis, TX; married Betty Blaine; children: Monetta Kaye, Madeline Joyce & Arthur Girard. **Educ:** Prairie View Agr & Mech Univ, BS, 1956; Atlanta Univ; Tex Southern Univ; Univ Okla. **Career:** Coach (retired); basketball player, 1953-56; Pemberton High Sch, teacher & coach, 1958-69. **Orgs:** Nat Urban League; E Tex Coaches & Officials Asn, 1958-69; Asn Black Soc Workers; Order Arrow Boy Scouts Am, 1962; Am Soc Pub Admin; Tex Asn Comm Action Agencies; chmn, Nat Asn Advan Colored People, 1970-75; Nat Asn Comm Develop; exec dir, Nat Comm Action Agency Asn; bd dir, E Tex Legal Serv Corp; Alpha Phi Alpha Frat; SW Baseball Umpires Asn; Am Asn Retired Persons. **Home Addr:** 308 E Freeman St, Ennis, TX 75119-2518.

### ANDERSON, SHANDON RODRIGUEZ

Basketball player. **Personal:** Born Dec 31, 1973, Atlanta, GA; son of Willie and Dorothy; children: Kori, Dorothy & Willie. **Educ:** Univ Ga, attended 1996. **Career:** Basketball player (retired); Utah Jazz, shooting forward, 1996-99; Houston Rockets, small forward, 1999-2000, shooting guard, 2000-01; New York Knicks, shooting guard, 2001-05, small forward, 2002-03; Miami Heat, small forward, 2004-06. **Orgs:** Founder & pres, Shandon Anderson Found, 2003-. **Honors/Awds:** NBA champion, 2006. **Business Addr:** Founder, The Shandon Anderson Foundation, 595 Piedmont Ave NE Suite 320-115, Atlanta, GA 30308, **Business Phone:** (786)777-4328.

### ANDERSON, STEVIE DARRELL

Football player, spokesperson, golfer. **Personal:** Born May 12, 1970, Monroe, LA. **Educ:** Grambling State Univ. **Career:** Football player (retired), speaker, model; New York Jets, wide receiver, 1994; Ariz Cardinals, wide receiver, 1995-96; prof golfer, model & youth motivational speaker, currently. **Business Addr:** Professional Golfer, Youth Motivational Speaker.

### ANDERSON, SUNNY

Radio host, business owner, television show host. **Personal:** Born Apr 9, 1975, Lawton, OK. **Career:** KCJZ & KONO-FM (San Antonio), radio personality; WYLD-FM & KUMX (Ft Polk, LA), radio personality; WJWZ (Montgomery, AL), radio personality; WDTJ (Detroit), radio personality; WQHT (New York), radio personality, 2001-03; Sunny's Delicious Dishes (Jersey City, NJ), owner, 2003-05; "Hip Hop Weekly" Magazine, food & lifestyle ed, 2006-07; Food Network, "Gotta Get It", "Cooking for Real", "How'd That Get on My Plate?", and "The Kitchen", TV host, 2007-. **Special Achievements:** Author of Sunny's Kitchen: Easy Food for Real Life, Clarkston Potter (2013).

### ANDERSON, DR. THOMAS JEFFERSON

Teacher, musician. **Personal:** Born Aug 17, 1928, Coatesville, PA; son of Thomas J and Anita Turpeau; married Lois Ann Field; children: T J III, Janet & Anita. **Educ:** WVa State Col, BMus, 1950, DMus, 1984; Pa State Univ, MEd, 1951; Univ Iowa, PhD, compos, 1958; Holy Cross Col, DMA, 1983; Bridgewater State Col, DMus, 1991; St Augustine's Col, DMA, 1996; Northwestern Univ, DMus, 2002; Bates Col, DMA, 2005; Tufts Univ, DMus, 2007. **Career:** Treemonisha, 1972; Opera: Soldier Boy, Soldier, 1982; High Pt City Pub Sch, teacher, 1951-54; Wva State Col, instr, 1955-56; Langston Univ, prof music & chmn, 1958-63; Tenn State Univ, prof music, 1963-69; Atlanta Symphony Orchestra, composer-in-residence, 1969-71; Morehouse Col, Danforth vis prof music, 1971-72; Tufts Univ, prof music & chmn, 1972-80, Austin Fletcher prof music, 1976-90, Austin Fletcher prof emer music, 1990-; Univ Salvador, artistic residency, 1988; John Simon Guggenheim Found, fel, 1988-89; Univ Minn, Minneapolis, Hill Distinguished Vis Prof, 1990; Calif State Univ, Chicago, Distinguished Vis Prof, 1991; Univ Mich, Vis Prof, 1993; Nat Humanities Ctr, Res Triangle Pk, NC, assoc, 1996-97; DeKalb Univ, Dept Fine Arts, prof, 1998-. **Orgs:** Fel MacDowell Colony, 1960-83; fel Yhaddo, 1970-77; founder & pres, Black Music Caucus MENC; bd mem, Elma Lewis Sch Fine Arts, 1975-; chair, Comt Status Minorities, Col Music Soc, 1976-80; Harvard Musical Asn, 1976-; hon mem, Phi Beta Kappa, 1977; Music Coun Arts & Humanities, 1978-81; St Botolph Club, 1980; adv bd, MeetComposer, 1980; fel Pa State Univ, 1982; NEA Artists Educ Panel, 1983-85; InstArts, 1983-85; bd mem, Harvard Musical Asn, 1989; fel Va Ctr Creative Arts, 1989; Am Asn Univ Professors; Phi Mu Alpha Sinfonia; fel Nat Humanities Ctr, Res Triangle Pk, 1996-97. **Honors/Awds:** Copley Foundation Award, 1964; Fromm Foundation Award, 1964 & 1971; Distinguished Achievement Award, Nat Assoc Negro Musicians, 1979; Leadership Award, Nat Black Music Caucus, MENC, 1980; Col of the Holy Cross, 1983; Honorary degree, Wva State Col, 1984; Distinguished Alumnus Award, Col Arts & Archit, Penn State Univ, 1990; Mary Hudson Onley Award, 1991; Distinguished Alumni Award, Univ Iowa, 2006. **Special Achievements:** Over 50 published compositions; 60th Birthday Concert, Videmus, Harvard University, 1989; Anderson was singularly honored when Bruce Alfred Thompson devoted his Ph.D. dissertation at Indiana University to an analysis of his works; First president of the National Black Music Caucus with concert of his music, 1997. **Home Addr:** 111 Cameron Glen Dr, Chapel Hill, NC 27516-2333. **Business Addr:** Professor, Dekalb College, 555 N Indian Creek Dr, Clarkston, MI 30021, **Business Phone:** (404)299-4136.

### ANDERSON, TONY
Insurance executive. **Personal:** Born Jun 14, 1947, Dillon, SC; son of Mary Agnes; married Westley A Smith; married Rosalyn L; children: Christopher Michael & Natasha Clevette. **Educ:** Western Conn State Col, Danbury, Conn, BA, 1979; Univ New Haven, W Haven, Conn, MBA, 1989. **Career:** N J Natural Gas Co, duplication clerk, Asbury Park, 1968-72; City Trust, Bridgeport, Conn, comput operator, 1972-76, security trader, 1976-80; Equitable Life Assurance Soc, NYC, security trader, 1980-81, mgr, money mkt trading, 1981-82, asst treas, 1982-83, asst vpres, 1983-88, vpres, 1988-; Equitable Credit Union, NYC, dir, 1988. **Orgs:** NASD, 1977-; dir, Equitable Credit Union, 1988-. **Honors/Awds:** Ford Found Scholar, 1976. **Home Addr:** 6 Button Rd, Shelton, CT 06484, **Home Phone:** (203)926-9986. **Business Addr:** Vice President, Equitable Financial Co, 787 7th Ave Suite 41N, New York, NY 10019, **Business Phone:** (212)554-3100.

### ANDERSON, TONY
Executive. **Personal:** Born Oct 29, 1950, Washington, DC; son of William and Frances; married Antoinette; children: Angela, William, Nathan & Aja. **Career:** Track Rec Studio, rec engr, 1971-73; Warner Elektra Atlantic Distrib, mktg coordr, 1974-75; Jonas Cash Promotions, independent prom rep, 1975-82; Motown Rec, nat R&B prom dir, 1982-85; Arista Rec, vpres, R&B prom, 1985-91; Mercury Rec, exec vpres & gen mgr, 1991-93; Columbia Rec, sr vpres & black music, currently. **Business Addr:** Senior Vice President, Columbia Records, 550 Madison Ave, New York, NY 10022-3211, **Business Phone:** (212)833-8000.

### ANDERSON, TYFINI CHENCE
Manager. **Personal:** Born Jan 9, 1978, Cincinnati, OH; daughter of Edward and Avis. **Educ:** Wilberforce Univ, BS, psychol. **Career:** Vols Am, case mgr, 2000-. **Orgs:** Alpha Kappa Mu Hon Soc; Wilberforce Bk Club, 1997; pres, Imani Dance Troope, 1998-99; vpres, Kappa Theta Epsilon Hon Soc, 1999-2000. **Honors/Awds:** Belle Hogan Roberts Award, Wilberforce Univ, 1999; Employee of the Month, Vols Am, 2000. **Home Addr:** 2140 Rockdell Dr Suite 10, Fairborn, OH 45324. **Business Addr:** Case Manager, Volunteers of America, 1931 S Gettysburge Ave, Dayton, OH 45408, **Business Phone:** (937)262-8876.

### ANDERSON, WARREN E.
Executive, president (organization). **Personal:** Born Ypsilanti, MI; son of Edward and Dorothy. **Educ:** Univ Mich, BS, 1974, MS, 1976. **Career:** Acct exec; nat & local sales mgr; gen sales mgr; Anderson-Dubose Co, gen mgr, co-founder, chief exec officer & pres, 1991-. **Orgs:** Young Pres; Playhouse Sq Found; Cuyahoga Community Col Found; Leadership Cleveland; Shoreby Club; Pres's Coun. **Business Addr:** President & Co- Founder, Chief Executive Officer, Anderson Dubose Co, 6575 Davis Indust Pkwy, Solon, OH 44139, **Business Phone:** (440)248-8800.

### ANDERSON, WILLIAM
Art collector, educator. **Personal:** Born Aug 30, 1932, Selma, AL; son of William James Sr and Minnie B; married Peggy Rambo; children: Bridgette Lucas, Barbara Erwin & William Harrington. **Educ:** Ala State Col, BS, 1959; Layton Sch Art, Univ Wis, BFA, 1962; Instituto Allende, San Miguel, Mex, MFA, 1968. **Career:** Univ Wis, prof, 1963-64; Alcorn Col, prof, 1964-69; Knoxville Col, fac, 1970-71; Univ Tenn, fac, 1970-71; Savannah State Col, fac, 1971-80; Dallas County Performing Arts Ctr, 1981-82; Ala Arts Coun, 1982-90; pvt instr, 1982-90; Morehouse Col, assoc prof art, bus admin, sculptor, musician, painter & photogr, Dept Arts & Hist, prof art, currently. **Orgs:** C-Natural Music Club, Wis, 1957-; Ga Art Asn, 1970-; Savannah Art Asn, 1971-80; Telfair Acad Art, 1971-80; Nat Conf Artists. **Home Addr:** 1997 King George Lane SW, PO Box 310025, Atlanta, GA 30331-4929, **Home Phone:** (404)349-1432. **Business Addr:** Professor of Art, Morehouse College, Wheeler Hall 101 830 Westview Dr SW, Atlanta, GA 30314, **Business Phone:** (404)681-2800.

### ANDERSON, WILLIAM GILCHRIST
Physician, surgeon, association executive. **Personal:** Born Dec 12, 1927, Americus, GA; son of John D Sr and Emma Gilchrist; married Norma Dixon; children: A Laurita Faison, W Gilchrist II, V Jeanita Henson, Frank L, Darnita Dawn & Hill. **Educ:** Ala State Col, BS, 1949; Univ Osteop Med, DO, 1956; Art Ctr Hosp, attended 1984. **Career:** Art Ctr Clin Group, staff surgeon, 1967-71; Zieger Clin Group, attend surgeon, 1971-74; Detroit Surg Asn, sr attend surgeon & consult, 1974-84; Mich Healthcare Corp, exec vpres & chief med officer, 1984-86; Detroit Osteop Hosp, dir govt affairs, 1986-92; Detroit Riverview Hosp, dir med educ, 1992-; Kirksville Col Osteop Med, assoc dean, 1996-; Detroit Osteop & Riverview Hosp, physician, currently; Mich State Univ Col Osteop Med, clin prof. **Orgs:** YMCA, dir, 1970-; Univ Osteop Med, dir, 1974-; Citizens Trust bank, dir, 1974-; Wayne County Osteo Asn, dir, 1968-, pres, 1977, exec dir, 1993-; Mich Asn Osteo Physicians, dir, 1975-, pres, 1981; Am Osteop Asn, deleg, 1980-, trustee, 1981-, pres, 1994-95; life mem, Nat Asn Advan Colored People; trustee, Hartford Memorial Baptist Church Detroit. **Honors/Awds:** Patenge Meritorious Service Award, Mich State Univ, 1982; Phillips Meritorious Service Award, Ohio Univ, 1986, Doctor of Humane Letters, 1990; Doctor of Humane Letters, Univ New England, 1992; Doctor of Science, W VA Sch Osteo Med, 1993; Doctor of Humane Letters, Univ Osteo Med, 1994; Distinguished Service Award, Am Osteopathic Asn, 2001. **Special Achievements:** Publications: Abnormal Uterine Bleeding after Tubal Ligation, MI Journal of Osteo Med, 1957; Von Redkling hausen's Disease of the Mesentery, MIJournal of Osteo Med, 1965; Choledocholithiasis After Cholecystectomy, Journal of AOA, 1973; Osteopathic Physician Looks at Quality, DO Magazine, 1984; first black surgical resident in Detroit history, 1964; first African American to serve as president of the AOA, 1994. **Home Addr:** 24535 N Carolina, Southfield, MI 48075, **Home Phone:** (810)557-8147. **Business Addr:** Medical Education, Detroit Riverview Hospital, 7733 E Jefferson Ave Suite 2201, Detroit, MI 48214, **Business Phone:** (313)499-4000.

### ANDERSON, WILLIE AARON
Football player, executive. **Personal:** Born Jul 11, 1975, Mobile, AL; son of Mary Steele; children: Jair. **Educ:** Auburn Univ, mkt educ. **Career:** Football player (retired), owner; Cincinnati Bengals, left tackle, 1996, right tackle, 1997-2001, right tackle & offensive tackle, 2002 right tackle & tackle, 2003-07; Baltimore Ravens, offensive tackle, 2008; Think B.I.G. Inc, owner; Fatburger Restaurants, owner. **Honors/Awds:** Pro Bowl, Cincinnati Bengals, 2003 & 2004 & 2005 & 2006. **Special Achievements:** Wears biggest shoe size (19-EEE) in Bengals history.

### ANDERSON, WILLIE LEE, JR. (FLIPPER ANDERSON)
Football player, clergy. **Personal:** Born Mar 7, 1965, Paulsboro, NJ; children: Dres. **Educ:** Univ Calif, Los Angeles. **Career:** Football player (retired), clergy; Los Angeles Rams, wide receiver, 1988-94; Indianapolis Colts, wide receiver, 1995; Wash Redskins, wide receiver, 1996; Denver Broncos, wide receiver, 1997; Yes to Life Ministries, clergy. **Honors/Awds:** NFL Record, 1989; NFC Championship Game, 1989. **Business Addr:** Clergy, Yes to Life Ministries, 5525 Foothill Blvd, Oakland, CA 94605, **Business Phone:** (510)706-0259.

### ANDERSON-BUTLER, CAROLYN
Dean (education). **Educ:** Morgan State Univ, BA; Johns Hopkins Univ, MLA, MS; NC State Univ, EdD. **Career:** Broome Community Col, dean acad serv, 2001-. **Business Addr:** Dean of Academic Services, Broome Community College, PO Box 1017, Binghamton, NY 13902, **Business Phone:** (607)778-5210.

### ANDRADE, MERY
Basketball player, basketball coach. **Personal:** Born Dec 31, 1975, Lisbon. **Educ:** Old Dom Univ, BA, health & phys educ, 1999. **Career:** Cleveland Rockers, forward, 1999-2002; Napoli Vomero, 2003-06; Charlotte Sting, forward, 2004-06; Reyer Venezia, 2006-10; Umana Venezia, 2006-07, 2009-10; Le Mura Lucca, 2010-13; Quinta dos Lombos, 2013-14; Dike Naples, 2014-15; San Diego Toreros, coach, 2015-; pro basketball player, currently. **Business Addr:** Professional basketball player, Quinta dos Lombos, Feitoria St, Cascais2775-568, **Business Phone:** (351)21458-58.

### ANDREW, MILTON
School principal. **Educ:** Dillard Univ, BA; Wayne State Univ. **Career:** Detroit Pub Schs, prin, asst, supt; Wilkins Elem Sch, prin, 1997. **Business Addr:** Principal, Wilkins Elementary School, 12400 Nashville St, Detroit, MI 48205-3848, **Business Phone:** (313)852-8600.

### ANDREWS, CARL R.
Executive director, association executive. **Personal:** Born Apr 20, 1926, Williamsport, PA; son of Carl M and Georgie Bannister; married Jeanette M White; children: Carl R Jr, Keith R & Cheryl Y. **Educ:** Lycoming Col, attended 1948; Howard Univ, attended 1950; Howard Univ Sch Soc Work, attended 1952; Rutgers Univ, adj urban fel prog, 1964; Yale Univ Drug Dependence Inst, attended 1971. **Career:** Boys' Club Newark, NJ, club dir, 1952-66; Boys' Club Am Nat Prog & Training Serv, asst dir, 1966-73; Boys' Club Asn, Indianapolis, Ind, exec dir, 1973-89; Boys & Girls Clubs Indianapolis, hon dir, currently. **Orgs:** Kiwanis Int; Ind Juv Justice Task Force; Witherspoon Presby Church; Alpha Phi Alpha Fraternity; Exec Serv Corps; Boys & Girls Clubs, Indianapolis; Nat Scholastic Hon Soc. **Honors/Awds:** New Jersey Afro-American Newspaper Award, 1959; Man of the Week Award, Prudential Ins Co, 1966; Midwest Region Heart & Soul Award, 1978; Paul Lemmon Administrator of the Year Award, 1977; President Award, E Orange Comm Day Nursery, 1973; Career Award, Kiwanis Club, Indianapolis, 1980; Sagamore Wabash, State Indiana, 1989; Lifetime Achievement Award, Exec Serv Corps. **Home Addr:** 602 Lions Head Lane, Indianapolis, IN 46260, **Home Phone:** (317)475-0109. **Business Addr:** Honorary Director, Boys & Girls Clubs of Indianapolis, 2236 E 10th St Suite 200, Indianapolis, IN 46201, **Business Phone:** (317)920-4700.

### ANDREWS, DR. CHARLES CLIFTON, JR.
Media executive. **Personal:** Born Dec 16, 1939, San Antonio, TX; son of Charles Clifton; married Thelma W; children: Charles III & Michael. **Educ:** Lincoln Univ; Incarnate Word Col; Harvard Bus Sch. **Career:** Bexar County, archivist; Sch Aerospace Med, Brooks Afb, lab technician, physiol training officer; Andrews Bros, pres & chief exec officer, 1979-89; Entermercial Inc, pres; KSJL-FM, host, pres & gen mgr; Inner City Broadcasting Corp, pres, 1982-. **Orgs:** Bd mem & secy, AfriCom Telecommunications Ltd, 1990-; bd dir, San Bernardino Child Advocacy Prog; chmn, San Antonio Housing Authority; dir, Inst Texan Cultures Develop Bd; dir, Alamo Pub Telecommunications Coun; dir, San Pedro Playhouse; dir, Inner City Broadcasting Corp; United Negro Col Fund; San Antonio Air Force Community Coun; San Antonio Bus League; Alamo Plaza Asn; Greater San Antonio Crime Prev Comn; Nat Asn Advan Colored People. **Honors/Awds:** Outstanding Texan Award; Man of the Year, Elks, 1993; Links-Western Regional Man of the Year, 1993; Doctor Law, Univ Tex at San Antonio. **Business Addr:** President, Inner City Broadcasting Co, 217 Alamo Plz Suite 200, San Antonio, TX 78205, **Business Phone:** (210)558-0938.

### ANDREWS, DONNOVAN
Advertising executive, executive. **Educ:** St Bonaventure Univ, BA, polit sci, jour & mass commun, 1996; Univ Pa, Wharton Exec Educ Prog, cert finance & acct. **Career:** DDB Worldwide, advert; Compaq, advert; Lockheed-Martin, advert; Reuters, advert; McDonalds, advert; Tanqueray, advert; iMedia Agency Summit; iMedia Brand Summit; Fast Co; Rethink Media, founder; Bank Am; FortuneCity Inc, dir bus develop; Ziff Davis Publ, dir bus develop; Sportgenic Inc, adv bd; Performance Bridge Advert, pres, 2002-; Tribal Fusion, vpres strategic develop, 2009-. **Orgs:** Advert Club New York; co-founder & bd mem, Xenium Found; founder, Red Wagon Found; 212 NYC. **Honors/Awds:** Media & Future of the Internet lect, Columbia Bus Sch, New York, Sci Po Univ, Paris, Univ Paris Dauphine, Paris. **Special Achievements:** Andrews is currently develop a book about the changing landscape of Am polit, relig, demographics, educ and cult. **Business Addr:** Vice President of Strategic Development, Tribal Fusion Inc, 2200 Powell St Suite 600, Emeryville, CA 94608, **Business Phone:** (510)250-5500.

### ANDREWS, ELEANOR
President (organization). **Educ:** Calif State Univ; Univ Alaska. **Career:** State Ak, Dep Comnr & Comnr Admin; Municipality Anchorage, dir human resources; Andrews Group Inc, pres & chief exec officer, 1987-; Tryck Nyman Hayes Inc, dir; Eyak Technol LLC, dir, 2002. **Orgs:** Bd dir, 2002; bd officer, Anchorage Chamber Com, Anchorage Neighborhood Housing Serv, Anchorage Munic Housing Asn; adv bd, Univ Alaska, Small Bus Develop Ctr; Alaska Black Caucus; Anchorage Neighborhood Health Ctr; Anchorage E Rotary Club; United Way; dir, Premera Blue Cross. **Home Addr:** PO Box 241845, Anchorage, AR 99524. **Business Addr:** President, Chief Executive Officer, Andrews Group Inc, 2627 C St 99503, Anchorage, AK 99524-1845, **Business Phone:** (907)276-1454.

### ANDREWS, EMANUEL CARL
Government official, politician. **Personal:** Born Sep 9, 1956, New York, NY. **Educ:** Medgar Evers Col, BA, 1978; Albany State Univ, MA, 1981. **Career:** Black & Puerto Rican Caucus NYS Legis, asst exec dir, 1980-81; US Congressman Maj Owens, spl asst, 1982-84; NY State Assembly, spec asst state assembly; Gov Rel NYS Sen Minority, dir; Ny House Rep, 11th Dist, cand, 2006; US Congressman. **Home Addr:** 1185 Carroll St, Brooklyn, NY 11225-2245, **Home Phone:** (718)467-3982.

### ANDREWS, GEORGE G., III
Executive. **Personal:** married Janice; children: 3. **Educ:** Morehouse Col, BS, bus admin; Clark Atlanta Univ; La State Univ, Sch Banking S. **Career:** Nat Bank Ga, area br mgr; Capitol City bank Trust Co, founder, head capital formation & strategic, treas, dir, pres, chief exec officer; Capitol City Bancshares, dir, chief financial officer, pres & chief exec officer, 1994-2013; Independent Community Bankers Am, Secy. **Orgs:** Nat Bankers Asn; Independent Community Bankers Am; coordr, United Way; bd trustee, Atlanta Workforce Develop Agency; Community Bankers Asn Ga; bd mem, Metrop Atlanta Transit Authority; dir, W End Merchant Asn; dir, Adams Parks Neighborhood Asn; bd dir, Urban Residential Develop Corp, Urban Ministerial Alliance. **Business Addr:** President, Chief Financial Officer & Chief Executive Officer, Capitol City Bancshares Inc, 562 Lee St SW, Atlanta, GA 30311, **Business Phone:** (404)752-6067.

### ANDREWS, JAMES
Entrepreneur, business owner. **Personal:** Born San Jose, CA; married Sherrelle; children: 2. **Educ:** Ventura Col, 1990; Univ Calif, Los Angeles, 1992. **Career:** Immortal Rec, sr dir mkt, 1992-94; Columbia Rec, sr direct mkt, 1994-98; Ecko Unlimited exec vpres, 1998-99; SoulPurpose.com, founder, 1999; Urban Box Off, exec vpres, 1999-2000; Brand Influence, chief digital storyteller, 2000-07; Isobar Global, global client dir, 2007; Ketchum Digital Social Media, vpres-dir interactive, 2007-09; Everywhere, co-founder, 2009-10; Social People, founder, 2010-14; True Story Agency, founder & chief narrative designer, 2014-; Ebola Deeply, co-founder & transmedia strategist, 2014-. **Orgs:** Bd dir, GCAPP; bd dir, Startup Atlanta; bd dir, Women At Frontier; bd dir, Univ Miami, Frost Sch Music. **Special Achievements:** Contributor to FastCompany.com; regular contributor to CNN. **Business Addr:** 931 Monroe Dr., Atlanta, GA, **Business Phone:** (678)707-8557.

### ANDREWS, DR. JAMES E.
Educator, psychologist. **Personal:** Born Aug 6, 1943, Pensacola, FL; son of C and Emma; married Pat; children: Lisa & Marcus. **Educ:** Compson Col, AA, 1970; Calif State Dom Hill, BA, 1972; Univ Calif, Los Angeles, MA, 1974; Nova Univ, EdD, 1977. **Career:** Compson Unified Sch, psychologist, 1973-75; consult, Dept Rehab, 1975-; Pomona Unified Sch, psychologist, 1975-79; Psychol Assessment Lab, owner, 1977-; Mt San Antonio Col, psychologist, 1979-; consult, Calif Poly, 1981-. **Orgs:** Pres, Southern Calif Asn Black Psychologists, 1975-76. **Home Addr:** 5690 Avenida Barcelona, Yorba Linda, CA 92886-3517, **Home Phone:** (714)777-1148. **Business Addr:** Psychologist, Mt San Antonio College, 1100 N Grand Ave, Walnut, CA 91789, **Business Phone:** (909)594-5611.

### ANDREWS, JAMES EDWARD
Labor activist, president (organization), chief executive officer. **Personal:** Born Sep 29, 1948, Norlina, NC; son of Merlin and Bettie Hargrove; married Audrey P; children: Timothy, Annisha & LaTonya. **Career:** Perfect Packed Prod Co, Henderson, NC, 1971-75; NC State AFL-CIO, proj outreach dir, 1975-84, actg secy & treas, 1984, secy & treas, 1985, chief exec officer, 1991, pres, 2002-; Nat A Philip Randolph Inst grant. **Orgs:** Pres, Warren County Nat Asn Advan Colored People, 1971-75; exec bd mem, NCAPRI, 1975-; exec comt & bd mem, Nat APRI, 1978-; regional rep, APRI southern Region, 1978-; pres, NC State AFL-CIO, 1997-; fel OPEIU. **Honors/Awds:** Tar Heel of The Week, News & Observer; recipient of the Purple Heart. **Special Achievements:** First full-time elected African-American state federation president in the country's history; A Vietnam veteran. **Home Addr:** 1309 Lions Way, Raleigh, NC 27604-2319, **Home Phone:** (919)755-0871. **Business Addr:** President, North Carolina State AFL-CIO, 1408 Hillsborough St, Raleigh, NC 27605, **Business Phone:** (919)833-6678.

### ANDREWS, JUDIS R.
Lawyer. **Personal:** Born Aug 27, 1941; married Cheryl D. **Educ:** Ariz State Univ, JD, 1972. **Career:** Ariz Civil Rights Comn, asst dir, 1964-67; Ariz Real Estate Comn; Govs Adv Comn; Phoenix Col, instr, 1967-68; Ariz State Univ, admin asst to pres, 1968-69; Joshua M Bursh II firm Cunningham Goodson Tiffany & Weltch, law clerk, 1968-69; Maricopa County, pub defense atty, 1984; Andrews & Tinsley, atty; pvt pract atty, currently. **Orgs:** Pres, Negro Polit Action Asn Ariz State, 1966-67; dir, Summer Youth Proj, Phoenix, OIC, 1969; dir, Spec Serv Maricopa Co Community Action Prog, 1969; spec asst to dir, Housing Ariz State Univ, 1969-70; dir, Progs & Opers Seattle Oppors Indus Ctr Inc, Seattle, 1972-73; bd dir, Ariz Comn Post Sec Educ, 1974-75; bd

dir, Ariz State Alumni Asn, 1975; State Bar Ariz; founding mem, first secy to bd dir, Wm F Patterson Lodge IBPOE No 47; founding mem & initial bd mem, Civil E Neighborhood Coun; Nat Asn Advan Colored People Youth Pres Pinal Co; chmn, vice chmn, secy, treas, CORE; pres & founder, 50 Bus Man Club; Omega Psi Phi Frat Ariz State Univ Scholar Comn. **Honors/Awds:** Man of the Year, 50 Bus Man Club, 1967-68; Man of the Year, Negro Polit Action Asn Ariz, 1968; Scholar Award, Martin Luther King Ctr Disadvantaged Youth Seeking Educ Oppors. **Business Addr:** Attorney, Andrews & Tinsley, 710 W Roosevelt St, Phoenix, AZ 85007-2104, **Business Phone:** (540)955-1574.

## ANDREWS, MARK ALTHAVEAN

Singer, actor. **Personal:** Born Nov 9, 1978, Baltimore, MD; son of Alonzo and Carolyn Andrews; children: Shaione. **Educ:** Baltimore City Col, attended 1994. **Career:** Mem group Dru Hill; Albums Dru Hill: Dru Hill, 1996; Enter the Dru, 1998; Solo Albums: Unleash the Dragon, 1999; Return of the Dragon, 2001.TV Series: "Sisqo's Shakedown", 2000; "Linc's", 2000; "Sabrina, the Teenage Witch", 2001; "Gone Country", 2008; "I Love the New Millennium", 2008; "Keith Sweat's Platinum House", 2009; "Celebrity Big Brother 2010", 2010. Films: Get Over It, 2001; Snow Dogs, 2002; Pieces of April, 2003; Surf School, 2006. Singles: "It's All About Me", 1998; "Got to Get It", 1999; "Thong Song", 2000; "Unleash the Dragon", 2000; "What These Bitches Want", 2000; "Incomplete", 2000; "How Many Licks", 2000; "Lap Dance", 2001; "Can I Live", 2001; "Dance For Me", 2001; "Who's Ur Daddy", 2007; "Perfect Christmas", 2007; "Gone Country", 2008; "Last Dragon Promo", 2008. DVDs: The Thong Song Uncensored Dragon, 2000; 24 Hours with Sisqo, 2001; Dru Hill Hits: The Videos, 2005. Mixtape songs: "This is the Heart", 2001; "In da Club", 2003; "One Love", 2004; "Really Real", 2004; "One Finger", 2005; "Go Dumb", 2006; "Let Me Hump On You", 2008; "Set It Off", 2009; "Put Me On", 2009; "So Bad", 2009; "Caught Up", 2009; "See It To Believe It", 2013. Other songs: "I Miss U", 2007; "Pop That", 2008; "Club On Fire", 2009; "Already Know", 2009; "Huff&Puff", 2009; "Billie Jean (Dragon Remix)", 2010; "Boy Shorts", 2010; "Bounce", 2010; "O", 2010; "Sexual", 2010; "Star", 2010; "All Night", 2013; "Earthquake", 2014; "Let's Get Down Tonight", 2014; "Like A Mothaf*cker", 2014; "You The Finest", 2014; "I Let That Money Go", 2014; "The One", 2014; "A-list", 2014; "Lips", 2014; "Breathtaker", 2014. Music Group, owner, currently. **Honors/Awds:** Numerous awards including 6 Billboard Awards, 5 MTV Video Music Award, 4 Grammy Awards, 3 MOBO Awards, 2 Radio Music Awards, 2 American Music Awards, a Source Award, & World Music Award. **Business Addr:** Singer, c/o Richard De La Font Agency Inc, 4845 S Sheridan Rd Suite 505, Tulsa, OK 74145, **Business Phone:** (918)665-6200.

## ANDREWS, MELANIE CURTIS

College administrator. **Career:** Compton Community Col, bd mem, currently. **Orgs:** Compton Community Col, pres bd trustee, currently. **Business Addr:** President of Board of Trustees Member, Compton Community College, 1111 E Artesia Blvd, Compton, CA 90221, **Business Phone:** (310)900-1600.

## ANDREWS, NELSON MONTGOMERY

Statistician. **Personal:** Born Jul 9, 1951, Winston-Salem, NC; son of Frances and Clem Sr; married Sharon Millicent Parrish; children: Elenora & Ava. **Educ:** Johnson C Smith Univ, physics, math, 1973; Purdue Univ, statist, MSD, 1977. **Career:** BF Goodrich, statistician, 1977-78; Bell Labs, NJ, statistician, 1978-82; Bellcore Community NJ, statistician, 1982-84; GTF Deer Valley Ariz, sr orgn statistician, 1985-87; NEC Am Inc, mgr, qual statist, currently. **Orgs:** Phi Beta Sigma Frat, 1971-; partic, Gistault Inst Career Develop Prog, 1978; career recruiter, Bell Labs, Bellcore, NJ, 1980-84; Affirmative Action Educ Career Developer, 1982-84; charter mem, Boule, Sigma Pi Phi Frat, 1986-. **Honors/Awds:** Pres, Beta Kappa Chi, Phi Beta Sigma, Johnson C Smith Univ; speaker on statist abstracts, Joint Statist Meeting, 1986; speaker, Int Commun Meeting, Tokyo, Japan, 1987. **Home Addr:** 3676 Garden Brook Suite 14100, Farmers Branch, TX 75234. **Business Addr:** Statistician, NEC America Inc, 6555 N State Hwy 161, Irving, TX 75039-2402, **Business Phone:** (214)262-2000.

## ANDREWS, PHILLIP

Executive. **Personal:** Born Jun 8, 1963, Brooklyn, NY; son of Frank and Daphine; married Chriscelle S Seldon; children: Phillip & Chriscelle II. **Educ:** Int Career Inst, paralegal dipl, 1985; John Jay Col Criminal Justice, 1990. **Career:** NYC Dept Correction, correction officer, 1984-; Hair Cut Hut, vpres, 1990-; Envogue I Beauty Salon, co owner; C & B Bks Distrib, pub rels dir, 2002-; Haircut Hut, vpres & mkt dir; Blackbusinesscircle.com, pub rels dir, currently; Power Networking Bus Sem Ser, currently. **Orgs:** Chair, Majestic Eagles Long Island, Speaker's Bur, 1990-; Black Unity Day Comt, 1990-91; chair, One Penny a Day Self Help Movement, 1991-; bd mem, Roosevelt Chamber Com, 1992-; bd mem, Roosevelt Kiwanis Club, 1992-; pub rels comt, 100 Black Men Nassau & Suffolk Inc; Barber Cult Asn Long Island Queens, vpres, cosmetologist; exec comt, Hempstead Nat Asn Advan Colored People; bd mem, W Indian Am COC; ed bd, Econ Forum Newspaper; W Indian Am COC; Nassau County Coun Chambers; chmn, United Black Men Queens Inc; New York Asn Black Journalist, Nat Black Pub Rels Soc New York; Urban League Long Island Young Professionals; mem visionary, Caribbean-Am Chamber Com & Indust Inc; pub rels comt, New York Metro MBA Asn, currently; pub rel dir, West Indian Am Chamber Com. **Home Addr:** 38 Va Ave, Hempstead, NY 11550, **Home Phone:** (516)485-0015. **Business Addr:** Public Relations Director, C & B Books Distribution, PO Box 357, New York, NY 10030, **Business Phone:** (718)602-7797.

## ANDREWS, REAL (ANTONIO CAMERON DAVIS)

Actor. **Personal:** Born Jan 31, 1963, North Vancouver, BC; married Michele Viscasso; children: 2. **Career:** General Hospital, 1963; "Days of Our Lives", 1965; "Step by Step", 1994; Family of Cops, 1995; "Side Effects", 1995; Mad Dog Time, 1996; "Viper", 1996; "Nash Bridges", 1996; "Highlander"; The End of Innocence, 1996; Expect No Mercy, 1996; Balance of Power, 1996; "The Sentinel", 1996; Port Charles, 1997-2003; "Soldier of Fortune", 1997; "Breach of Faith: Family of Cops II", 1997; "PSI Factor: Chronicles of the Paranormal", 1997; Lookin 'Italian, 1998; "The Girl Next Door", 1998; "Beyond Belief: Fact or Fiction"; "Port Charles", 1998; "General Hospital", 2002-03; "As the World Turns", 2003-04; Lost in Plainview, 2004; Blood, 2004; "Law & Order", 2006; "Damages", 2007; Films: Iceman, 1984; Wild Thing, 1987; Born on the Fourth of July, 1989; Under Surveillance, 1991; No Escape, No Return, 1993; Rocky V; Expect No Mercy, 1995; Simon Says, 1998; As the World Turns, 2003-04; Lost in Plainview, 2005; The Picture of Dorian Gray, 2006. **Honors/Awds:** Trained as 100-meter sprinter for the 1984 Olympics. **Business Addr:** Actor, CBS Television Network, 51 W 52nd St, New York, NY 10019, **Business Phone:** (212)975-3247.

## ANDREWS, SHARONY S.

Painter (artist), journalist, writer. **Personal:** Born Jan 28, 1967, Miami, FL; daughter of Estela Meyers and Garcia; married Grant Green Jr. **Educ:** Univ Miami, BS, polit sci & broadcast jour, 1989; Univ NC, Greensboro, MS, dance & related studies. **Career:** Miami Herald, reporter, 1989-92; Detroit Free Press, reporter & asst nat ed, 1993, writer, 1997-, painter, 1997-; Columbus Ga Ledger-Enquirer, bus ed; Books: Cuttin the Rug Under the Moonlit Sky, 1997; Essence mag, freelancer, currently. **Orgs:** Alpha Kappa Alpha Sorority, 1986-; vpres print, S Fla Asn Black Journalists, 1991-92; Jour & Women's Symp, 1992-. **Honors/Awds:** Greater Miami Achievers Goldendrum Scholar, Univ Miami, 1985; Soc Prof Journalists Scholar, 1985; Scholar, Alpha Kappa Alpha, Gamma Zeta Omega Chap, 1985; Grant Green, Rediscovering the Forgotten Genius of Jazz Guitar, 1999. **Special Achievements:** Paintings exhibited in various galleries included: Peligro Gallery, Red Piano Too Gallery, Zeitgeist Gallery & House of Blues; Books: Cutting the Rug Under the Moonlit Sky: Stories and Drawings About a Bunch of Women Named Mae, 1997. **Business Addr:** Freelancer, Essence Magazine, 135 W 50th St 4th Fl, New York, NY 10020, **Business Phone:** (800)274-9398.

## ANDREWS, WILLIAM PERNELL

Educator, psychotherapist, manager. **Personal:** Born Mar 24, 1947, Richmond, VA; son of William and Rena Thompson; married Michele Evans; married Michele Evans; children: Oronde K, Joshua T & Kayla S. **Educ:** Univ Calif, Santa Cruz, BA, 1980; Boston Univ, attended 1981; Cambridge Col, EdM, 1989. **Career:** Staff asst, constrn budget prog, Pac Tel Co; pharm sales rep, Progress Labs Inc, 1970-74; coun psychologist intern, Boston State Hosp; counsellor intern, Santa Cruz Coun Ctr, 1979-80; Boston City Hosp, staff psychologist narcotics addiction, 1981-83; Mass Dept Corrections, clin coordr, psychologist, 1983-92; Roxbury Youth Works Inc, exd, 1992-93; Dimock Comn Health Ctr, dir family coun, 1993-95; Northeastern Univ, JDOAAI, asst dir, 1995-; Bur Substance Abuse Serv, Dept Pub Health, regional mgr, currently. **Orgs:** Am Counselors Asn, 1986-92; Am Ment Health Counselors Asn, 1986-92. **Home Addr:** 1812 Leslie Lane, Richmond, VA 23228-1528, **Home Phone:** (617)244-1095. **Business Addr:** Regional Manager, Bureau of Substance Abuse Services, Dept Pub Health, Boston, MA 02108-4619, **Business Phone:** (617)624-5111.

## ANDREWS, WILLIAM PHILLIP

Executive. **Personal:** Born Jan 9, 1938, Kansas City, MO; son of William and Florence; married Dolores Caesar; children: Phillip, Steven & Jeffrey. **Educ:** Lincoln Univ, Jefferson City, MO, BS, 1961. **Career:** Anheuser-Busch Inc, Houston, Tex, nat coordr, ethnic sales mgr, 1967-. **Orgs:** Kappa Alpha Psi, 1958-. **Home Addr:** 4823 McDermed Dr, Houston, TX 77035, **Home Phone:** (713)283-0381. **Business Addr:** Ethnic Sales Mgr, Anheuser-Busch Inc, 1800 W Loop S Suite 1100, Houston, TX 77027, **Business Phone:** (713)622-2400.

## ANDREWS-MCCALL, DR. MAXINE RAMSEUR

Executive, educator. **Personal:** Born Fayetteville, NC; daughter of Patsy Evans and Emory Adolphus; children: Sabrina Andrews Molden, Gigi & Thurman J III. **Educ:** Fayetteville State Univ, BS, elem educ & teaching, 1956; NC Cent Univ, MEd, admin & curric develop, 1963; E Carolina Univ, Eds, educ admin & supv, 1975; Univ NC, Greensboro, EdD, educ admin & supv, 1985. **Career:** Educator (retired); Lewis Chapel Sch, teacher, 1956-66, sch social worker, 1966-69; Elizabeth City State Univ, dir fed prog & title III coord, 1969-71; Cumberland County Schs, curric supvr, 1971-91; Cumberland County Schs, elem supvr, 1971-84, supvrsec educ, 1984-90; Fayetteville State Univ, adj prof, 1985, asst prof & coord sec educ, coord educ admin & curric instr, dir, teaching felsprog, Mc Callcoord, master sch admin degree prog, 1999; Col Lakes Elem, asst prin, 1991; MSA Prog, coord, 1996-99, adj asst prof, 1999, Masters Educ Leadership, prog coordr, 1991-2005. **Orgs:** Pres, 1987-90, sec, 1988-91, NC Asn Supv & Curric Develop; Master Sch Admin, Fay State Univ, coord, 1997-; NC Charmettes Inc; Nat Educ Asn; Asn Supv & Curric Div; NC Asn Educrs; Phi Delta Kappa; NC Asn Admin; Delta Sigma Theta Sor; NC Hist Preserv Soc; Fayetteville State Alumni Asn; Alpha Mu Hon Soc; Who's Who Am; Presidential Citation Nat Asn Equal Opportunity Higher Educ, Entrepreneur; Sincerely Yours Writing Serv; Alpha Kappa Mu. **Honors/Awds:** Distinguished Alumnae Fayetteville State Univ, Nat Asn Equal Opport Higher Educ, 1986. **Special Achievements:** Sincerely Yours Writing & Specialty Services, 1986. **Home Addr:** 5637 Mumcreek Lane, Fayetteville, NC 28304, **Home Phone:** (919)423-1727.

## ANGAGAW, ASTER

Vice president (organization), marketing executive. **Educ:** Eastern Univ, BA, orgn mgt; Temple Univ, MBA. **Career:** Sodexo, sr vpres mkt develop & corp serv, global head sales, bus develop & health care segment. **Orgs:** Sodexo's African Am Leadership Forum; Sodexo's Women's Network Group; bd mem, Meals Wheels Del; corp adv bd mem, Temple Univ, Fox Sch Bus; active mem, Exec Leadership Coun.

## ANGLEN, REGINALD CHARLES

Journalist, public relations executive. **Personal:** Born Feb 20, 1952, Cleveland, OH; son of Howard and Barbara. **Educ:** Ohio State Univ, BA, 1989; Columbus Tech Inst, grantsmanship cert. **Career:** Ohio State Sch Blind, pub rels dir, 1973-75; St Stephen's Community House, caseworker, 1979-85; WCKX, dir & producer; OH State Univ, commun specists, Pub Rels Coordr, 1989-. **Orgs:** Phi Beta Sigma Fraternity, 1972-; Nat Asn Black Journalists, 1989-; pres, Columbus Asn Black Journalists; Columbus Area Leadership Prog. **Honors/Awds:** Delegate, White House Coun Youth, 1970; Martin Luther King Jr Humanitarian Award, 1996; Columbus Citizen J, 1 10 Outstanding Young Man, 1974; Ohio Jaycees, 1 5 Outstanding Ohioans, 1974; Friend of Education Award, CEA, 1996. **Special Achievements:** One of Five Outstanding Ohioans, Ohio Jaycees, 1974; One of Ten Outstanding Young Man, Columbus Citizen Journal, 1974. **Home Addr:** 2525 Avalon Pl, Columbus, OH 43219, **Home Phone:** (614)253-1368. **Business Addr:** OH.

## ANOKWA, KWADWO

Chairperson, educator. **Educ:** Univ Wis, Milwaukee, BA, 1975; Univ Wis'Madison, MA, 1977; Mich State Univ, PhD, 1991. **Career:** Ghana, broadcast journalist; Butler Univ, Eugene S Pulliam Sch, Dept Jour, assoc prof & chair, dir, prof, retired, LAS emer. **Orgs:** Asn Educ Journalism & Mass Commun. **Special Achievements:** Publication: International Communication: Concepts and Cases. **Home Addr:** 5941 Ann Marie Way, Indianapolis, IN 46254-5087, **Home Phone:** (317)329-6942. **Business Addr:** Professor Emeritus, Eugene S Pulliam School, Butler University, 218 Fairbanks Ctr 4600 Sunset Ave, Indianapolis, IN 46208, **Business Phone:** (317)940-9674.

## ANSA, TINA MCELROY

Editor, writer, novelist. **Personal:** Born Nov 18, 1949, Macon, GA; daughter of Walter J and Nellie McElroy; married Jonee. **Educ:** Spelman Col, attended 1971. **Career:** Brunswick Col, freelance journalist, newspaper columnist & writing workshop instr, 1982; Spelman Col, writer-in-residence, 1990; DownSouth Press, 2007-; Atlanta Const, copy desk, copy ed, makeup ed, layout ed, entertainment writer, features ed & news reporter; Charlotte Observer, ed & copy ed; freelance journalist; newspaper columnist; Brunswick Col, Emory Univ, Spelman Col, writing workshop instr; Sea Island Writers Retreat, writer, currently; Novels: Baby of the Family, 1989; Harcourt Brace Jovanovich, 1989, 1993; Ugly Ways, 1993; The Hand I Fan With, 1996; Doubleday, 1996; You Know Better, 2002; William Morrow, 2002; Taking After Mudear, 2007; Short Story: Willie Bea & Jaybird: A Love Story. **Orgs:** S African African-Am SisterLove Sisters Sharing Bk Prog; adv comt mem, Ga Ctr Bk; host comt mem, Flannery O'Connor Awards; founder, Good Lil' Sch Girl Found. **Honors/Awds:** Georgia Authors Series Award, 1989; Stanley W Lindberg Award, 2005; Int Lit Hall of Fame Writers African Descent, Gwendolyn Brooks Ctr, Chicago State Univ; Notable Book of the Year, New York Times; Top 25 books Every Georgian Should Read; Best Books for Young Adults, Am Libr Asn; best fiction, African American Blackboard List, 1994-95. **Special Achievements:** First black woman hired by The Atlanta Const; produced and directed the 1989 Georgia Sea Island Festival. **Business Addr:** Writer, Novelist, Sea Island Writers Retreat, PO Box 20602, Saint Simons Island, GA 31522.

## ANTHONY, BERNARD WINSTON

Manager. **Personal:** Born Mar 20, 1945, St. Maurice, LA; son of Lee and Ica O Wade; married Marion D Sherman; children: Alaric B, Timothy W, Corwin S, Shelley D, Christopher M, Dante Harris & Tanesha M Harris. **Educ:** Bakersfield City Col, AA; Fresno City Col, 1992; Merced Col, 1996; Calif State, Bakersfield, 1996. **Career:** Pac Gas & Elec Co, supt gas & elec construct, maintenance & opers, 1965. **Orgs:** Teacher, trustee, deacon, coordr, dir, St Peter Miss Baptist Church, 1965-; pres, Black Employees Asn, Bakersfield, 1983-; Black Employees Asn, Fresno, 1986-; Nat Asn Advan Colored People, Fresno, 1987-; mentor, facilitator, Fresno Unified Sch Dist, 1988-; tax preparer, Enrolled Agents Am, 1988-; Black Employees Asn, Yosemite Div, adv; mentor & dir, Tassel Prog Merced High Sch Dist, 1992-; Pres, Nat Asn Advan Colored People, currently. **Honors/Awds:** Community Service Award, Pacific Gas & Elec Co, 1989-90; Service Award, Fresno Unified Sch Dist, 1989-90. **Home Addr:** 11115 Open Trail Rd, Bakersfield, CA 93311-2865, **Home Phone:** (661)663-9528. **Business Addr:** President, National Association for the Advancement of Colored People, PO Box 70101, Bakersfield, CA 93387-0101.

## ANTHONY, BRENDA TUCKER

Executive. **Personal:** Born Java, VA; daughter of James P and Beulah E; married Edward French. **Educ:** Cent State Univ, BS, 1969; Univ Dayton, MBA, 1974. **Career:** NCR Corp, financial analyst, 1969-76; Gen Motors Corp, acct, 1976-87; Johnson Energy Co, finance mgr, 1987-90; EFA & Assoc Inc, comptroller. **Orgs:** AKA, 1967-; NCP, 1969-; Cent State Univ Alumni Asn, 1969-; Nat Black MBA Asn, 1970-; Nat Asn Female Exec, 1973-; Nat Coun Negro Women, 1974-. **Home Addr:** 8916 Winged Foot Dr, Tallahassee, FL 32312, **Home Phone:** (513)275-2442.

## ANTHONY, CLARENCE EDWARD

Consultant, mayor, president (organization). **Personal:** Born Oct 10, 1959, Belle Glade, FL; son of Bill and Irene; children: Reidel V. **Educ:** Palm Beach Jr Col, AA, 1979; Fla Atlantic Univ, BA, soc sci, 1981, MPA, pub admin, 1982. **Career:** S Fla Water Mgt Dist, intern res asst; Treas Coast Regional Planning Coun, regional planner; Comnr Ken Adams Dist Va, admin asst; Dept Equal Opportunity, dir; Palm Beach Co Bd Comnrs, county comnr; Anthony & Assocs, pres; S Bay Fla, mayor, 1984-08; Emerge Consult Corp, pres, 1996-2004; PBS&J, sr vpres, dir govt rels & nat bus develop, chief mkt officer, 2006-09; Anthony Govt Solutions Inc, pres & chief exec officer, 2009-; CH2M Hill, dir client mgt southeast. **Orgs:** Pres, Fla Atlantic Univ Alumni Asn; bd dir, Big Bros & Big Sisters; Dist IX Ment Health Drug Abuse Planning Coun; bd dir Leadership Palm Beach County; bd dir, Hisp Human Resources, Glades Area Retarded Citizens; FL League Cities Urban Admin Comm; bd dir, FL Inst Govt; pres & founder, FAU Black Alumni Asn; Omega Psi Phi Fraternity; chmn, FlaLeague Cities Fin & Taxation Comm; bd mem, Palm Beach County Area Planning Bd; pres, Nat League Cities; bd dir, PBS&J's Corp Diversity Adv Coun; bd dir, PBS&J Found; bd dir, PBS&J Int; pres, Fla League Cities; pres, Nat League Cities; bd dir, GEO Group Inc; treas, United Cities & Local Govt; Fed Govt Ecosystems Task Force; Fla Const Rev Comn; bd dir, Nat Conf Black Mayors, 1994-08; CentraCore Properties Trust, 1998-2007; bd dir, Fla State Univ. **Home Addr:** 310 SE 3rd Ave, South Bay, FL 33493, **Home Phone:** (561)992-9404. **Business Addr:** President, Chief Executive Officer, Anthony Government Solutions Inc, 1665 Palm Beach Lakes Blvd Suite 520, West Palm Beach, FL 33401, **Business Phone:** (561)310-8877.

**ANTHONY, DR. DAVID HENRY, III**
Educator. **Personal:** Born Apr 28, 1952, Brooklyn, NY; son of David H Jr and Carolyn; married Allison Anitra Sampson; children: Adey Tabita Frances & Djibril Senay Frederick William. **Educ:** NY Univ, BA, eng & hist, 1972; Univ Wis Madison, MA, hist, 1975, PhD, hist, 1983. **Career:** YMCA Greater New York, 1963-64; WORT FM Back Porch Radio, programmer, 1975-80; Dept State, Fulbright fel & res assoc, 1976-77; Univ Dar es Salaam Tanzania, res assoc, 1976-77; Clark Univ, vis asst prof, 1978-79; Coppin St Col, instr hist, 1980-84; Towson St Univ, Hist Dept, vis prof, 1982-83; Univ Ore, Eugene, asst prof hist, 1984-88; Nat Univ Lesotho, vis lectr hist, 1987-88; Univ Calif, Presidents humanities fel, 1990-91; Toadal Fitness, 1996-13; Univ Calif, Oakes Col, Santa Cruz, provost, 1996-2002, asst prof, Dept Hist, assoc prof, currently; Inner light ministries, 2007-09. **Orgs:** YMCA Greater New York, 1963-64; Curr spec, Madison Metro Sch Dist, 1977-78; consult, Swahili AnteiroPietila Helen Winternitz, 1980; Fulbright Alumni Asn, 1981-; res affil, Univ Fla Ctr African studies, 1982; judge, Gr Baltimore Hist Fair, 1982-84; Phi Alpha Theta, 1983-; KUSP 88.9 FM Radio Pataphysical Broadcasting Media, 2006-10; Santa Cruz Film Festival, 2007-10; KUSP Film Gang, 2009-14; Church St John Coltran, 2011; Church St John Coltrane; One Life Inst, 2012. **Home Addr:** 225 Dickens Way, Santa Cruz, CA 95064-1059, **Home Phone:** (831)425-7523. **Business Addr:** Associate Professor, University of California, 532 Humanities 1, Santa Cruz, CA 95064, **Business Phone:** (831)459-4028.

**ANTHONY, EMORY, JR.**
Judge. **Personal:** Born Jan 1, 1953, Birmingham, AL; married Felicia; children: 2. **Educ:** Ala A&M Univ, BA, 1974; Miles Sch Law, JD, 1979. **Career:** Jefferson County Dist Atty Off, prosec, 1979; Mun judge to Mayor Bernard Kincaid, 1999; Miles Sch Law, dean; Jefferson County Progressive Dem Coun, pres; Birmingham Munic Ct, judge & defensive lawyer; Guster Law Firm LLC, mentor, currently. **Orgs:** Deacon, Tabernacle Baptist Church; bd mem, Metrop Develop Bd Birmingham City; bd commissioners, Housing Authority Birmingham City, currently. **Business Addr:** Mentor, Guster Law Firm LLC, 505 20th St N, Birmingham, AL 35203, **Business Phone:** (205)581-9777.

**ANTHONY, ERIC TODD**
Executive, baseball player. **Personal:** Born Nov 8, 1967, San Diego, CA. **Career:** Baseball player (retired), executive; Houston Astros, Tex, outfielder, 1989-93; Seattle Mariners, 1994; Cincinnati Reds, 1995-96; Colo Rockies, 1996; Los Angeles Dodgers, 1997; Yakult Swallows, 1998; Big League Baseball Acad, coach; Solarverse Technologies Inc, founder, chmn, chief technol officer, 2003-. TV Series: "Little Big League", 1994; "Sunday Night Baseball", 1990; "1995 National League Championship Series", 1995. **Business Addr:** Chairman, Founder, Solarverse Technologies Inc, 3516 Hwy 6, Sugarland, TX 77478, **Business Phone:** (281)850-6443.

**ANTHONY, GREGORY CARLETON**
Basketball player. **Personal:** Born Nov 15, 1967, Las Vegas, NV; married Chere Lucas; children: 4. **Educ:** Univ Portland, attended 1987; Univ Nev, Las Vegas, NV, BA, polit sci, 1991. **Career:** Basketball player (retired), game analyst; New York Knicks, pt guard, 1991-95; Vancouver Grizzlies, pt guard, 1995-97; Seattle Supersonics, pt guard, 1997-98; Portland Trailblazers, pt guard, 1998-2001; Chicago Bulls, pt guard, 2001-02; Milwaukee Bucks, pt guard, 2001-02; CBS Sports, col basketball analyst, 2008, tv analyst, currently; ESPN, analyst, NBA coverage, currently; Yahoo! Sports, col basketball analyst; Turner Sports, studio analyst. **Orgs:** Vice chmn, Nev's Young Republicans. **Business Addr:** Analyst, ESPN, ESPN Plz 935 Middle St, Bristol, CT 06010, **Business Phone:** (860)766-2000.

**ANTHONY, JEFFREY CONRAD (JEFF ANTHONY)**
Consultant. **Personal:** Born Jun 3, 1949, Washington, DC. **Educ:** Georgetown Univ, BA, pub admin & music, 1976; Univ Pittsburgh, BA, pub admin & music. **Career:** United State Marine Corp, 1967-76; Nat Endowment Arts, jazz prog specialist, 1980-85; Capital City Jazz Festival Wash, DC, assoc producer, 1982-85, sr producer, 2004-14; Brooklyn Acad Music, dir comn rels, 1986-87; Freelance Entertainment Indust, freelance event prod, 1986-99; Hist Lincoln Theatre, gen mgr; United Serv Org, tour mgr, 2001-10; JBV Prod, operating partner, owner, 2000-13, sr producer, tech producer, 2000-14, co-founder, 2000-; Event Prod Serv, jeff anthony productions, 2013-. **Orgs:** Assoc mem, Smithsonian Inst; Nat Assoc Jazz Educrs; bd mem, New Music Distrib Servs; assoc mem, Mgt Nat Jazz Serv Orgn. **Honors/Awds:** Certificate of Merit Outstanding Young Men American, 1983; Sustained Superior Performance, Nat Endowment Arts, 1984; Special Act & Service Award, 1984; Certificate of Appreciation, 1985. **Special Achievements:** Producer "Dance Africa" Brooklyn NY, 1986; assoc producer "Black Family Reunion Celebration", Wash DC, Atlanta GA, Los Angeles CA, Detroit MI, 1986-87; producer "first Annual DIVA Found Awds" Kennedy Center, Wash DC, 1987; tech producer, Cong Black Caucus Found, 1998-2013. **Home Addr:** 6701 14th St Suite 107, Washington, DC 20012, **Home Phone:** (202)723-1483. **Business Addr:** Co-Founder, JBV Production, 427 3rd St NE, Washington, DC 20002, **Business Phone:** (202)688-1334.

**ANTHONY, REIDEL CLARENCE**
Football player, football coach. **Personal:** Born Oct 20, 1976, Pahokee, FL; son of Clarence E. **Educ:** Univ Fla. **Career:** Football player (retired), coach, free agt, analyst; Tampa Bay Buccaneers, wide receiver, kick returner, 1997-2001; free agt; Wash Redskins, wide receiver, 2002; Trinity Cath High Sch, receivers coach; GatorCountry.com, contrib writer, offensive analyst, currently; Glades Cent High Sch, coach, currently. **Honors/Awds:** SEC Championship, 1994-96; Bowl Alliance National Championship, 1996; Athletic Hall of Fame, Univ Fla, 2009; Florida-Georgia Hall of Fame. **Business Addr:** Coach, Glades Central High School, 1001 SW Ave M, Belle Glade, FL 33430.

**ANTHONY, VERNICE DAVIS**
President (organization), health services administrator. **Personal:** Born Jan 10, 1945; daughter of Leonard Chambers and Vernice Bradford Chambers; married Eddie; children: Dana, Dara & Todd. **Educ:** Wayne State Univ, BS, nursing, 1970; Univ Mich, Ann Arbor, MPH, 1976. **Career:** City Detroit, serv, chief, pub health nursing, field prog, 1971-79, Detroit Dept Health & Wellness Prom, dir, pub health officer, 2012-; State Mich, Develop & Eval, local health serv admn, community health field, 1979-83; Wayne Co, co health officer chief, off policy, 1983-91; State Mich, Mich Dept Pub Health, dir, 1991-95; St John Health Syst, Corp Affairs & Community Health, sr vpres, 1995-2001; Western Mich Univ, vice chairperson, pres; Greater Detroit Area Health Coun, pres & chief exec officer, 2002-12. **Orgs:** Chair bd trustee, Western Mich Univ; Cyberstate Orgn Bd; Mich Res Coun; Mich Neighborhood Partnership; exec bd, Voices Detroit; S E Mich Health Improv Coun; Immunization Safety Rev Comt Inst Med; Mich Dept Community Health & Health Plans Adv Coun; bd govs & gov emer, Wayne State Univ; chairperson, Ctr Health Prom; Mich Women's Found. **Honors/Awds:** Distinguished Alumni Award, Wayne St Univ; Distinguished Alumni Award, Univ Mich Sch Pub Health; Distinguished Service Award, Mich Pub Health Asn; Women of Wayne Headliner Award; Girls Role Model Award; Professor Women Award, Mich Asn Bus; Humanitarian Award, Michigan Womens Found; Anti Defamation League Humanitarian Award; Detroit Bus Most Influential Women & Most Influential Blacks Top 100, Crane; Detroit Free Press Shining Light Award; Professional Women Award; Women of Achievement Award, Anti-Defamation League's. **Home Addr:** 196 Keelson, Detroit, MI 48215. **Business Addr:** Director, Public Health Officer, city of Detroit, 3245 E Jefferson, Detroit, MI 48207, **Business Phone:** (313)876-4000.

**ANTHONY, VERNICE DAVIS**
Chief executive officer. **Personal:** Born Mobile, AL. **Educ:** Wayne State Univ, BS, nursing, 1970; Univ Mich, MPH, pub health, 1976. **Career:** Mich Dept Pub Health, dir, 1991-95; John Health Syst, Corp Affairs & Community Health, sr vpres, 1995-2002; St. John Health Syst, sr vpres, 1995-2001; Western Mich Univ, pres, 2001; Greater Detroit Area Health Coun Inc, pres & chief exec officer, 2002-12; Wayne State Univ, gov emer, currently; City Detroit, pub health officer, 2012-. **Orgs:** Molina Healthcare Inc; bd trustee & chair, Western Mich Univ. **Business Addr:** President, Chief Executive Officer, Greater Detroit Area Health Council, 333 W Fort St Suite 1230, Detroit, MI 48226, **Business Phone:** (313)963-4990.

**ANTHONY, REV. DR. WENDELL**
Clergy, association executive, activist. **Personal:** Born Jan 1, 1950, St. Louis, MO; son of James and Ida; married Monica G; children: Tolani, Maia, Meagan & Wendelaya. **Educ:** Marygrove Col, MA, pastor alministry, 1974, PhD; Wayne State Univ, BA, polit sci, 1976; Univ Detroit, black theol. **Career:** Detroit Black News & Detroit Black J Pub TV News Show, commentator, 1972-76; WNEC 4 Radio, news commentator; Fel Chapel, assoc pastor, 1983-86, pastor, 1986; Community Health Forum TV Show, Channel 62, host, 1985-86; "A New Vision", radio prog, WCHB Radio, host & producer; Isuthu Inst & Intonjane Inst, founder, currently; lectr, motivationalist & writer; Holt, Rinehart & Winston Publ Inc, educ consult; Fel Chapel Health Clin, Cape Coast, Ghana, W Africa, founder, 1996-; Detroit Br-NAACP, pres, currently. **Orgs:** New Detroit Inc; adv bd, Mich Coalition Human Rights & Minority State Health Policy; chmn, Interfaith Coun Relig & Civic Leaders; trustee, Gen Retirement Syst Bd, City Detroit; chmn, New Stadia Develop Task Force Comerica Pk & Ford Field; co-chmn, Detroit Comm, Amalgamated Clothing &Textile Workers Union; founder, Fannie Lou Hamer Polit Action Comn; co-chmn, City Detroit Million Man March Comn; Detroit Bldg Authority, 1994; founder, Detroit Relief Effort Aid Mozambique, Zimbabwe & S Africa; co-chair, Detroit Fair Banking Alliance; pres, Detroit Bd Nat Asn Advan Colored People, 1993-; bd dir, First Independence Nat Bank; Nat Asn Securities Professionals-Detroit; chmn & founder, Freedom Inst for Econ Social Justice and People Empowerment. **Business Addr:** President, Detroit Branch-NAACP, 8220 2nd Ave, Detroit, MI 48202, **Business Phone:** (313)871-2087.

**ANTHONY-PEREZ, DR. BOBBIE M.**
Educator, psychologist. **Personal:** Born Nov 15, 1923, Macon, GA; daughter of Solomon Richard Cotton Sr (deceased) and Maude Alice Lockett Cotton (deceased); married Andrew; children: Freida M Chapman. **Educ:** Univ De Paul, BS, 1953, MS, 1954, MA, 1975; Univ Ill, Urbana, MS, 1959; Univ Chicago, PhD, 1967. **Career:** Chicago Pub Sch, math teacher, 1954-68; Univ Chicago, math consult, 1965; Worthington Hurst, psychiat Head Start, 1971-72; Howard Univ, Inst UrbanAffairs res coordr, 1977; Chicago State Univ, prof psychol, 1968-95, actg coordr black studies, 1981, coordr black studies, 1990-94, prof emer, currently. **Orgs:** Conf presenter, Int Asn Appl Psychol, 1974, 1982, 1986, 1988; Local rep, Midwestern Psychiat Asn, 1979-97; Am Educ Ress Asn, 1980-; presenter, United Am Prog Asn, 1980-; chpbus rels, Chatham Avalon Pk Comm Coun, 1982-; conf presenter, Int AsnCross-Cult Psychol, 1986, 1988, 1990, 1992, 1994; communs chair, Communs Ingleside Whitfield Parish, 1989-91, 1994-96; Midwestern Educ Res Asn, conf presenter, 1989, 1990, 1992; asst secy & bd mem, Chicago Chap, Asn Black Psychologists, 1990-92, pres, 1995-96; Asian Regional, 1992; Int Cong Psychol, confpresenter, 1992; Nat Coun Teachers Math; Pi Lambda Theta; Educ Hon Asn; Asn Black Psychologists, Midwestern Educ Res Asn; elder, Int Asn Black Psychol, 1994-; life mem, DODO chap Tuskegee Airmen; feature writer & reporter, DODO newsletter, 1998-; vpres, Ladies Aux, Tuskegee Airmen, 2000-01; chair, mem & Outreach, United Methodist Women Ingleside Whitfield Parish, 2000-; chair, Friends Blackwell, Blackwell Mem Church, 2000-; co-advisor, Black Students Psychol Asn. **Home Addr:** PO Box 19104, Chicago, IL 60619, **Home Phone:** (312)783-4424. **Business Addr:** Professor Emeritus of Psychology, Chicago State University, Education Bldg, Chicago, IL 60628, **Business Phone:** (773)995-2598.

**APEA, JOSEPH BENNET KYEREMATENG**
Engineer, executive, president (organization). **Personal:** Born Aug 19, 1932, Aburi; son of Madam Nancy Ofeibea Norman and Nana Esumgyima II; married Agnes Johanna Hinson; children: Kathleen Kyerewa, Adwoa Ofeibea, Abena Otwiwa & Akua Nyam. **Educ:** Ill Inst Tech, BSCE, 1968; Univ IL, Arch. **Career:** Westen hoff & Novic Inc, Chicago, civil engr, 1961-64; Kaiser Engrs, Chicago, struct engr, 1964-65; Sargent & Lundy Engrs, Chicago, struct engr, 1965-72; Samuels, Apea & Assoc Inc, pres, 1972-80; Joseph Apea & Assocs Inc, Consult Engrs, pres, 1981-86; Apian Int Ltd, pres, 1986-; Cosmic Petrol Inc, pres & financier, African countries, currently. **Orgs:** Nat Soc Prof Engrs; Am Soc Civil Engrs; Ill Asn Struct Engrs; Framework reconstruction Ghana Citizens Org USA & Canada; chmn, DBE/WBE Adv Coun Ill Dept Transp, 1986-88. **Special Achievements:** Positive attitude toward progress, The Talking Drums, UK, 1985. **Business Addr:** President, Apian International Ltd, 2650 Wern Ave, Park Forest, IL 60466, **Business Phone:** (708)747-2552.

**APPLEBY-YOUNG, SADYE PEARL**
Educator. **Personal:** Born Dec 18, 1927, Gainesville, GA; married Harding B; children: Sybil Bernadette, Harding G, Angela & Gregory. **Educ:** Tuskegee Inst, BS, 1945; Cornell Univ, MS, child develop, 1946; Ga State Univ, PhD, educ & psychol, 1974. **Career:** Educator (retired); Univ Ark Pine Bluff, div dir, 1946-57; NC Cent Univ Durham, interim div dir, 1958-60; Spelman Col Atlanta, Ga, dept chmn, 1961-78; Morris Brown Col, div dir, educ & psychol, 1978-89. **Orgs:** Alpha Kappa Mus Nat Hon Soc, 1943-; secy, Pi Lambda Theta Hon Soc, 1978; fac secy, Omicron Delta Kappa Nat Hon Leadership Soc, 1983-89; St Paul Cross Roman Cath Church; rep, Cath Sch Bd Educ; Acad Coun Work Related, Morris Brown Col. **Home Addr:** 1735 Childress Dr SW, Atlanta, GA 30311.

**APPLETON, CLEVETTE WILMA**
Social worker. **Personal:** Born Louisville, KY; daughter of Cleve and Wilma Henry. **Educ:** Ky State Univ, BA, 1971; Ky Sch Social Work, Univ Louisville, MSSW, 1974. **Career:** Neighborhood Youth Corp, teacher asst, 1966-67; Louisville Free Pul Libr, clerk, 1968-70; Ky Dept Human Resources, soc worker, 1971-73; Metro Soc Serv Dept, stud soc worker, 1974; Bridge haven, stud soc worker, 1974; Ky Dept Human Resources, soc worker grad I, 1975-77; River Region Serv, sr social worker, 1977-78; Univ Louisville Sch Med, sr social worker, 1978-91; Bryce Hosp, social worker II, 1991-92; Indian Rivers Community Ment Health, Ment Retard Ctr, asst trainer, 1993. **Orgs:** Coun Nephrology Soc Workers Network 9; Nat Kidney Found Metro Louisville. **Honors/Awds:** Nat Hon Soc Sec Schs, 1965; Maude Ainslie Scholar, 1967; Miss Wesley Club, Ky State Univ, 1971; Ky Dept Human Resources, Grad Sch Stipend, 1973. **Business Addr:** 1108 14th Ave Suite 325, Tuscaloosa, AL 35401-3078, **Business Phone:** (205)345-6016.

**APPLEWHAITE, LEON B.**
Educator, lawyer. **Personal:** Born Sep 4, 1927, Brooklyn, NY; married Louise J Harley. **Educ:** NY Univ, BA, 1948; Brooklyn Law Sch, JD, 1951; Brooklyn Univ Law Sch, LLM, 1961. **Career:** US Social Security Admin, claims authorizer, 1955-59; Justice Francis E Rivers, legal secy, 1959-63; NY Comn Human Rights, field rep; NY Bd Mediation, labor arbit & mediator, 1964-67; NY Workmen's Comp Bd, assoc coun, 1967-68; NY Pub Employee Rels Bd, supv mediator regional rep; atty, currently; NY Pub Employ Rels Bd, chief regional mediator, 1968-79; arbitrator; Cornell Univ ILR Sch, adj prof, 1971-; Labor Col, fac; Hofstra Univ, fac; Pace Univ, fac; State Univ New York, asst prof, currently. **Orgs:** Asn Bar City NY; Nat Acad Arbitrators; Indus Rels Res Asn; Nat Bar Asn; Am Arbit Asn; Soc Prof Dispute Resolution; New York County Lawyers Asn; Harlem Lawyers Asn; Indust Rels Res Asn; NJ State Bd Mediation; NY Comn Human Rights, 1963-64, 1967; Fed Labor Rels Authority. **Home Addr:** 7 Lawrence Ave, Rockville Ctr, NY 11570, **Home Phone:** (516)766-1384. **Business Addr:** Attorney, 1110 Fidler Lane, Silver Spring, MD 20910-3425, **Business Phone:** (301)608-8182.

**ARAUJO, DR. NORMAN**
Educator, writer. **Personal:** Born Mar 22, 1933, New Bedford, MA; son of Jose Joao and Julia Coracao; married Barbara Cartmill. **Educ:** Harvard Col, AB, 1955; Univ d'Aix-Marseille, cert d'etudeslitteraires, 1956; Harvard Univ, AM, 1957, PhD, 1962. **Career:** Univ Mass, Amherst, Mass, asst prof, 1962-64; Boston Col, asst prof, 1964-68, assoc prof Fr, 1968-; fulbright fel; Nat Defense Act, fel. **Orgs:** Mod Lang Asn Am, 1976-; chief advisor, Cape Verdean News; Phi Beta Kappa. **Special Achievements:** Book: A Study of Cape Verdean Literature, 1966. **Home Addr:** 60 Old Post Rd, East Walpole, MA 02032-1428, **Home Phone:** (508)668-8067. **Business Addr:** Associate Professor, Boston College, Lyons Hall 302C, Chestnut Hill, MA 02467-3804, **Business Phone:** (617)552-3820.

**ARBERRY, MORSE, JR.**
Chief executive officer, real estate executive, government official. **Personal:** Born Mar 1, 1953, Berkeley, CA; married Carol I Daniels. **Educ:** Cent Ariz Col, AA; Northern Ariz Univ, BS, eng; Univ Nev, Las Vegas, MBA. **Career:** Assembly man, bus exec; Nev Legis Coun Bur, Carson City Nev, state assemblyman, Dist 7, 1985-2005; Alt, mem, Legis Comn, 1985-86, 1991-92; Nev Assembly, Legis Comn, mem, 1987-2005; Nev Assembly, Interim Finance Comt, vice chair, 1993-95, 1997-99, 2001-03, 2005-07, chair, 1995-97, 1999-2001, 2003-05, 2007-09, co-chair, 1995-96, vice chmn, 1993-94, 1997-98 & 2001-02; Clark Co Assembly, dem, currently; Neighborhood Serv Offices, mgr; Mortgage Co, pres & chief exec officer, currently. **Orgs:** Nat Asn Advan Colored People; Nat Black Caucus State Legislators; Clark County Cent Dem Comt; Western Legis Conf; Coun State Governments; Nat Conf State Legislatures; Jodie Cannon Prince Hall Mason; Dr Martin Luther King Jr Comn; Order Elks Lodge; Order Eastern Star; Opportunity Village Bd; W Charleston Lions Club; Lied Discovery C's Mus Bd; Am Legis Exchange Coun; Urban Chamber Com, Las Vegas; Las Vegas Chamber Com; Gov's Comn Martin Luther King Jr Holiday; Valley Hosp Bd Gov; Nat Asn Mortgage Brokers; chmn, KCEP Radio Sta; Dem Club N Las Vegas; Econ Opportunity Bd Clark County; Greater Las Vegas Urban League; Gov's Comn Martin Luther King Jr. Holiday; Overall Econ Develop Comt; Black Chamber Com; Nat Asn Mortgage Brokers. **Home Addr:** 2551 S Ft Apache Rd Suite 102, Las Vegas, NV 89117-8700, **Home Phone:** (702)646-4211. **Business Addr:** President, Chief Executive Officer, Mortgage Co, 5300 W Spring Mountain Rd Suite 212D, Las Vegas, NV 89146-8721, **Business Phone:** (702)325-8599.

**ARBUCKLE, JOHN FINLEY, JR.**
Financial manager. **Personal:** Born Jan 16, 1938, Peoria, IL; son of John F Sr and Florence (Netter) A; married Janet M Johnson; chil-

dren: Elana L & Andrea D Parker. **Educ:** Bradley Univ, attended 1956, 1985; Life Underwriter Training Coun, grad, 1962; Peoria Chamber Com, leadership Sch, grad, 1977; Am Bankers Asn, Grad Sch, Univ Okla, 1985. **Career:** Chicago Metrop Mutual Assurance, asst dist mgr, 1958-66; Metrop Life Ins Co, sales consult, 1966-75; First Am Bank, asst vpres, bus lender & vpres, 1975-97; AT & Investor Serv, sr investment analyst & shareholder rels, 1996-2001; Farmers Home Fire Ins Co, secy, treas, chmn & pres. **Orgs:** Ill Valley Yacht & Canoe Club, 1970-; corp mem, Peoria Area Chamber Com, 1975-; Sons Union Vets Civil War, 1976-77; pres, Florence Crittenton Home, 1980; proj mgr, Ctr Study, Res & Learning, 1981-; life mem, Nat Asn Advan Colored People, 1984-; pres, Minority Bus Mgt Conf Bd, 1990-; Phoenix Bus Awareness Asn, 1992-93; pres, S W Kiwanis Club; bd mem, Peoria Pub Sch Dist 150. **Honors/Awds:** Inducted, African Am Hall Fame Mus Inc, 1992; Man of the Year, Peoria Dist Met-Life, 1969. **Special Achievements:** Chmn, Am Freedom Train, City of Peoria, 1974-75; Chicago Urban Lie, article on "Negro New Breed," 1962. **Home Addr:** 7330 N Andover Pl, Peoria, IL 61614-2002, **Home Phone:** (309)689-0628. **Business Addr:** Chairman, President, Farmers Home Fire Insurance Co, 122 S Jefferson St, Lewisburg, WV 24901-1315, **Business Phone:** (304)645-1975.

### ARBUCKLE, RONALD LEE

Engineer, police officer, manager. **Personal:** Born Jul 13, 1945, Newark, NJ; son of Robert Lee and Mary Alice White; married Helena Yvonne Patrick; children: Ronald L Jr. **Educ:** Rutgers Univ, Newark, NJ, 1973; AT&T Corp Schs; Newark Police Acad, NJ Inst Real Estate. **Career:** AT&T, Edison, NJ, customer eng, 1963-; Newark Spec Police, Newark, NJ, pres, 1971; Sweet Temptations Lingerie Co, E Orange, NJ, sales, 1986-88; Maylock Realty Corp, Newark, NJ, asst sales mgr, 2000-. **Orgs:** Pres, Fed Afro Am Police Officers, 1976-99; bd dir, Theater Universal Images, Newark, NJ, 1985-; pres, Newark Spec Police Asn, 1988-94; vpres, Neighborhood Housing Servs Newark, 1988-91; conf chairperson, Nat Black Police Asn, Northeast Region, 1988-92. **Honors/Awds:** Class A Valor Award, Newark Spec Police Asn, 1978; Member of the Year, Nat Black Police Asn, Northeast Region, 1985; Rookie of the Year, Sweet Temptations, 1986; Member of the Year, Newark Spec Police Asn, 1988; Outstanding Service Award, Nat Black Police Asn, Northeast Region, 1990. **Home Addr:** 21 Porter Ave, Newark, NJ 07112-2405, **Home Phone:** (973)923-3480. **Business Addr:** Assistant Sales Manager, Maylock Realty Corp, 252 Chancellor Ave, Newark, NJ 07112, **Business Phone:** (973)923-6200.

### ARCHAMBEAU, LESTER MILWARD, III

Football player. **Personal:** Born Jun 27, 1967, Montville, NJ; married Kathleen; children: Lester IV, Kellyn & Carsyn. **Educ:** Stanford Univ, BS, indust engineering, 1990. **Career:** Football player (retired), exec; Green Bay Packers, defensive end, 1990-92; Schneider Nat, mgr, 1991; Atlanta Falcons, defensive end & right defensive end & left defensive end & defensive tackle, 1993-99; Bank Am, proj mgr intern, 1994 Denver Broncos, defensive end, 2000; Sportstars Inc, nat football league agt, 2003-12; Harvard Football Players Study, advisor, 2014-currently. **Orgs:** Exec bd mem, Nat Football League Players Asn, 1993-2000, regional dir, 2012-. **Honors/Awds:** SuperBowl, 1999; Hall of Fame, Montville Twp High Sch; Unsung Hero Award, Players Inc, 1999. **Home Addr:** 10520 Montclair Way, Duluth, GA 30097-1840. **Business Addr:** Regional Director, National Football League Players Association, 1133 20th St NW Suite 600, Washington, DC 20036, **Business Phone:** (800)372-2000.

### ARCHAMBEAU, SHELLYE L.

Chief executive officer, executive director. **Personal:** Born Jul 6, 1962, Washington, DC; daughter of Lester and Mera; married S Clarence Scott; children: Kethlyn & Kheaton. **Educ:** Univ Pa, Wharton Sch, BS, 1984; IBM Bus Mgt Inst, 1995. **Career:** IBM, gen mgr, pub sector asia pac & other positions, 1984-99; Keystone Serv Syst Inc, 1989-, chair finance comt, 1991-93, vice chair bd, 1993; Blockbuster Inc, e-com div, pres, 1999-2000; N Pt Commun, chief mkt officer & exec vpres, 2000-01; Loudcloud Inc, chief mkt officer & exec vpres sales, 2001-03; Metric Stream Inc, wharton econ summit, chief exec officer, 2003-; Arbitron Inc, dir, 2005-13; IBM, var exec sales& mkt positions; CSW Res Ltd, dir, 2013; Verizon, dir, 2013-; Nordstrom, dir, 2015-. **Orgs:** Bd dir, Nation's Capital Girl Scout Coun, 1995-97; Nat Asn Women Bus Owners, 1995-97; Coun Foreign Rels, 1997-; Am Chamber Com, Tokyo, Japan, 1998-99; Girls Inc, 2000; trustee, Coun Women, Univ Pa; Mentium, 2001-; USPS, mktg adv bd, 2002; bd dir, Watermark, 2005-; bd dir, Silicon Valley Leadership Group, 2007-; bd dir, Info Technol Sr Mgt Forum, 2008-13; Forum Women Entrepreneurs; Women's Coun Bd trustee Univ Pa. **Home Addr:** 4016 Purdue Ave, Dallas, TX 75225, **Home Phone:** (214)750-7278. **Business Addr:** Chief Executive Officer, MetricStream Inc, 2600 E Bayshore Rd, Palo Alto, CA 94303, **Business Phone:** (650)620-2900.

**ARCHER, DR. CHALMERS, JR.** **See Obituaries Section.**

### ARCHER, CHRIS (CHRISTOPHER ALAN ARCHER)

Baseball player. **Personal:** Born Sep 26, 1988, Raleigh, NC; son of Ron and Donna. **Career:** Baseball player; Burlington Indians (Rookie), pitcher, 2006-07; Lake County (A), pitcher, 2007-08; Peoria (A), pitcher, 2009; Daytona (A), pitcher, 2010; Tennessee (AA), pitcher, 2010; Montgomery (AA), pitcher, 2011; Durham (AAA), pitcher, 2011-13; Tampa Bay Rays, pitcher, 2012-. **Special Achievements:** Drafted by Cleveland Indians in the fifth round of the 2006 amateur draft; traded to Chicago Cubs, 2008; traded to Tampa Bay Rays, 2011. **Business Addr:** Tampa Bay Rays, 1 Tropicana Dr, St. Petersburg, FL 33705.

### ARCHER, DENNIS WAYNE

Lawyer. **Personal:** Born Jan 1, 1942, Detroit, MI; son of Ernest James and Frances Carroll; married Trudy DunCombe; children: Dennis Wayne Jr & Vincent DunCombe. **Educ:** Wayne State Univ, attended 1961; Western Mich Univ, BS, 1965; Detroit Col Law, JD, 1970, LLD, 1988; Univ Detroit Sch Law, LLD, 1988, John Marshall Law Sch, LLD, 1991. **Career:** Gragg & Gardner PC, trial lawyer, 1970-71; Hall Stone Allen & Archer, trial lawyer, 1971-73; Detroit Col Law, Detroit MI, assoc prof, 1972-78; Charfoos Christensen & Archer, trial lawyer & partner, 1973-85; Wayne State Univ Law Sch, Detroit MI, adj prof, 1984-85; Mich Supreme Ct, assoc justice, 1985-93; Dickinson Wright PLLC, partner, 1991-93, chmn, 2002-09, chmn emer, currently. City Detroit, mayor, 1994-2001; Dennis W. Archer PLLC, chmn & chief exec officer. **Orgs:** Bd dir, Detroit Bar Asn, 1973-75; Detroit Bar Asn; fel Intl Soc Barristers; pres, Wolverine Bar Asn, 1979-80; Old Newsboys Goodfel Fund, 1980-97; pres, State Bar Mich, 1984-85; bd dir, MI Cancer Found, 1985-92; pres, life mem, Nat Bar Asn; Am Judicature Soc; Alpha Phi Alpha; Fel Am Bar Asn; life mem, Nat Asn Advan Colored People; bd trustee, Olivet Col, 1991-94; US Conf Mayors, 1994; Intergovernmemtal Policy Adv Comt US Trade Rep, 1994; Nat Conf Black Mayors, 1994; Nat Comt Crime Control & Prev, 1995; Dem Conv Platform Comt, 1996; pres, Nat Conf Dem Mayors, 1996-99; vice chair, pres, Nat League Cities, Comt & Econ Develop Policy Comt, 1997; Brookings Inst, 1997; Nat Res Coun, Steering Comt Harnessing Technol Am Econ Future, 1997; US Dept Housing & Urban Develop, Joint Ctr Sustainable Communities, 1998; Fannie Mae, Nat Adv Coun, 1998-99; Compuware, 2001-; pres-elect, 2002, pres, 2003-04, Am Bar Asn; bd mem, Johnson Controls, 2002-13; pres, Mich Bar; chmn & bd dir, Detroit Reg Chamber, 2006-07; Int Socs Barristers; Am Mich Trial Lawyers Asn; life mem, Sixth Circuit Judicial Conf; life mem fel am bar found, life mem fel mich state bar found; Fel Int Soc Barristers; bd mem, InfiLaw, 2010-13; chmn & bd trustee, Western Mich Univ, 2011-14; fel Litigation Coun Am; cochair, Nat Transp Policy Proj, Bipartisan Policy Ctr. **Honors/Awds:** Distinguished Achievement Award, NAACP Detroit Br, 1985; Spirit of Excellence Award, Am Bar Asn, 1996; Newsmaker of the Year, Engr News-Record mag, 1998; Public Official of the Year, Governing mag, 2000; Distinguished Achievement Award, Tuskegee Airmen Natl Hist Mus, 2001; Award of Excellence. **Special Achievements:** Author: Blackballed-A Case Against Private Clubs Barrister, 1983; Named one of the 100 Most Influential Black Americans, Ebony magazine 1984; citedin Nat Law Journal as one of the 100 most powerful attorneys in the US, 1985; Named 25 Most Dynamic Mayors in America by Newsweek magazine, November 1996; Most Respected Judge in Michigan, Michigan Lawyers Weekly, 1990; Listed in Michigan Super Lawyers, 2009, Listed in Best Lawyers in America; First African American to serve as President of the American Bar Association; First African American President of the Michigan Bar. **Home Addr:** 9240 Dwight, Detroit, MI 48214. **Business Addr:** Chairman Emeritus, Dickinson Wright PLLC, 500 Woodward Ave Suite 4000, Detroit, MI 48226-3425, **Business Phone:** (313)223-3500.

### ARCHER, DR. JUANITA A.

Educator, physician. **Personal:** Born Nov 3, 1934, Washington, DC; daughter of Roy E Hinnant and Anna Blakeney; married Frederick I; children: Frederick II. **Educ:** Howard Univ, Wash, DC, BS, 1956, MS, 1958, MD, endocrinol, 1965. **Career:** Freedman's Hosp, intern, 1965-66; Howard Univ, resident, 1966-68, fel, 1970-71, instr, 1971-75; Diabetes Investigative Group, dir, Endocrine Metab Lab, 1972-; Endocrine & Metab Dis Sect, asst prof med, 1975-79, assoc prof med, 1980-; Howard Univ, emer assoc prof endocrinol. **Orgs:** Gen Clin Res Comt NIH, 1976-86; Consult, Ariz Res Coun, 1986-87; DC Med Soc; Am Diabetes Asn; Sigma Xi; Beta Kappa Chi; Am Fedn Clin Res; Endocrine Soc; NY Acad Sci; Delta Sigma Theta; Biohazards & Biosafety Comt, Howard Univ; Am Asn Clin Endocrinologists. **Honors/Awds:** Josiah Macy Faculty Fel, 1974-77; Physician's Recognition Award, 1983-86; Am Red Cross Award, 1988; Moses Wharton Young Research Award, 1988; Nat Podiatry Med Award, 1989; Public Relations Award, Howard Univ Hosp, 1990; Physicians Recognition Award, Am Med Asn. **Special Achievements:** Numerous publications including: P Gorden & J Roth, Defect Insulin Binding Receptors Clin Invest 55, 166-175, 1975; "Clinical Diabetes Update 11" Upjohn Monograph, 1980. **Home Addr:** 4305 Ranger Ave, Temple Hills, MD 20748-1829, **Home Phone:** (301)423-8105. **Business Addr:** Emeritus Associate Professor, Howard University Hospital, 2041 Georgia Ave NW Suite 5000, Washington, DC 20060, **Business Phone:** (202)865-1516.

### ARCHER, MICHAEL EUGENE

Singer. **Personal:** Born Feb 11, 1974, Richmond, VA; married Angie Stone; children: Michael Jr & Imani. **Career:** Albums: Brown Sugar, 1995; Live at the Jazz Cafe, 1998; Voodoo, 2000; YODA: The Monarch of Neo-Soul, 2007; The Best So Far, 2008; Remix albums: Voodoo DJ Soul Essentials, 2000; Singles: "U Will Know", 1994; "Lady", 1996; "Devil's Pie", 1998; "Left & Right", 1999; "Feel Like Makin' Love", 2000; "Be Here", 2002; "So Far To Go", 2007; "I Found My Smile Again", 2008; "Glass Mountain Trust", 2010. **Honors/Awds:** Grammy Awards, 2000. **Special Achievements:** Named in the list of 50 Bands To See Before You Die in Q magazine in 2002. **Business Addr:** Vocalist, Virgin Records, 150 5th Ave 7th Fl, New York, NY 10011-4311, **Business Phone:** (212)786-8200.

### ARCHER, SUSIE COLEMAN

Educator, administrator. **Personal:** Born Mar 29, 1946, Pembroke, KY; married Dennis. **Educ:** BS, 1968; MA, 1969; Vanderbilt Univ, PhD. **Career:** Austin Peay State Univ, supvr women's dormitories, 1969-74, teacher, 1969-75; Univ Md, Europ Br, W Berlin, Ger, instr, 1975-77; Salt Lake City Sch Dist, supvr counr, 1978-80; UT Tech Col, Salt Lake, dir regist & admin, 1980-87; Vanderbilt Univ, assoc univ registr, 1987, asst to provost & dir, asst provost acad affairs, Strategic Process Enhancement Enrollment Mgt, dir, currently. **Orgs:** Fac adv, Phi Alpha Theta, 1971-72; fac adv, Sr Class League, 1973-; Altrusa Club, 1979; bd dir, Travelers Aid Soc, 1979-; Acad Governance Comt; Discrimination & Unfair Grading Practices Comm; Affirmative Action Comm; Comt Revise Prom & Tenure Policies; Comn Union Women's Rights; Mid Tenn Educ Asn; APSU Women's Club; fac adv, Alpha Mu Gamma; fac adv, Circle K; fac adv, Alpha Phi; fac adv, Int Students Asn; Am Asn Col Registrars & Admis Officers, 1980-; pres, Univ Tenn Asn Col & Admis Officers, 1985-86; Tenn Southern Asn Col Registrars & Admis Officers, 1987-; pres, Southern Asn Col Registrars & Admis Officers; Clearing Adv Comt. **Home Addr:** 865 Bellevue Rd A-14, Nashville, TN 37221, **Home Phone:** (615)662-0118. **Business Addr:** Director, Strategic Process Enhancement Enrollment Management, Vanderbilt University, 2201 W End Ave, Nashville, TN 37235, **Business Phone:** (615)322-7311.

### ARCHER, HON. TRUDY DUNCOMBE

Judge, mayor. **Personal:** married Dennis W; children: Dennis Wayne Jr & Vincent DunCombe. **Educ:** Eastern Mich Univ, BS; Wayne State Univ, master, educ, guid & coun; Detroit Col Law, JD. **Career:** Judge (retired), Executive; Detroit Bd Educ, teacher; Detroit Col Law, asst dean; Mich, 36th Dist Ct, judge, 1989-2006; Detroit, mayor, 1994-2001; Detroit Inst of Arts, dir emer, currently. **Orgs:** Pres, Am Bar Asn; life mem, Nat Asn Advan Colored People; Millionaires Club Mus African Am Hist Detroit; dir emer, Detroit Inst Arts; Greening Detroit, Community Found Southeastern Mich Dennis W. Archer Found; C's Ctr; Community Found Southeastern Mich; Women's Comt Detroit Inst Arts; C's Hosp Mich Pediat Clin Serv Bd; Jr League Detroit; African Am Parent Mag. **Business Addr:** Director Emeritus, Detroit Institute of Arts, 5200 Woodward Ave, Detroit, MI 48202, **Business Phone:** (313)833-7900.

### ARCHIBALD, B. MILELE

Lawyer, educator. **Personal:** Born Jul 4, 1945, New York, NY; married Faruq Muhammad; children: Nyota. **Educ:** Bronx Community Col, AAS, 1968; City Univ, Hunter Col, BA, eng, 1973; Univ Calif, Sch Law, JD, 1976. **Career:** Chief Judge DC, Ct Appeals, law clerk, 1976-77; Fed Trade Comt, WA, staff atty, 1977-78; Overseas Pvt Investment Corp, spec asst pres; Womens Health Ctr, dir; Martin Community Col, Small Bus Ctr, dir, 1997-2002; Alamance Community Col, Small Bus Ctr, dir, 2002-13. **Orgs:** Wash DC Bar Asn, 1977-; Nat Asn Black Women Atty, 1978; N Carolina Community Col Adult Educr Asn; bd mem, United Way Alamance County; bd mem, Burlington Downtown Corp; bd mem, OE Enterprises Inc; bd mem, Alamance County Area Chamber Com; bd mem, Womens Resource Ctr.

### ARCHIBALD, NATHANIEL (TINY ARCHIBALD)

Basketball player, basketball coach. **Personal:** Born Sep 2, 1948, New York, NY; son of Big Tiny and Julia. **Educ:** Univ Tex, El Paso, TX, attended 1970; Fordham Univ, MA, 1990, dipl, supv & admin, 1994; Calif Coast Univ, doctorate, 2000. **Career:** Basketball player (retired), basketball coach; Cincinnati Royals, basketball player, 1970-76; New York Nets, basketball player, 1976-77; Buffalo Braves, basketball player, 1977-78; Boston Celtics, 1978-83, Milwaukee Bucks, 1983-84; Univ Ga, asst basketball coach; Univ Tex, El Paso, asst basketball coach; Harlem Armory Homeless Shelter, athletic dir, 1991; Nat Basketball Develop League, head coach, 2001-02; Nat Basketball Asn Community Rels Dept, 2002. **Orgs:** Alpha Phi Alpha Fraternity Inc. **Home Addr:** 2920 Holland Ave, Bronx, NY 10467. **Business Addr:** Member, Alpha Phi Alpha Fraternity Inc, 2313 St Paul St, Baltimore, MD 21218-5234, **Business Phone:** (410)554-0040.

**ARCHIBALD, TINY.** **See ARCHIBALD, NATHANIEL.**

### ARCHIE, SHIRLEY FRANKLIN

Association executive, educator, consultant. **Personal:** Born Apr 15, 1944, Philadelphia, PA; married Robert Lewis Archie Jr; children: Keita T & Kweli I. **Educ:** Cheyney State Col, BA, 1966; Howard Univ, attended 1969; Temple Univ, Urban Educ, 1981. **Career:** DC Sch Syst, educator, 1967-70; Philadelphia Sch Syst, educator, 1976-; Temple Univ, instr, 1983-85; Sigler Travel Serv Inc, travel consult; Nat Asn Bench & Bar Spouses, nat pres. **Orgs:** Links Inc; Alpha Kappa Alpha; Jack & Jill Am; Women's Leaders Team, African-American Inst Zimbabwe; bd dir, Girl Scouts Am; First woman mayor Atlanta, bd trustees, Springside Sch; comn Camden City, Comn Women, 1983; comn Philadelphia, Major's Comn Women, 1985. **Honors/Awds:** Distinguished Service Award, Girl Scouts Am, 1982; Commendation Outstanding Teacher, Philadelphia Systems, 1982, 1984; Teacher of the Year Delaware Valley, Daily News & Inquirer, 2002. **Home Addr:** 400 W Hortter St Apt 603, Philadelphia, PA 19119-3642. **Business Addr:** Educator, School District of Philadelphia Education Center, 440 N Broad St, Philadelphia, PA 19130, **Business Phone:** (215)400-4000.

### ARCHIE-HUDSON, MARGUERITE

School administrator. **Personal:** Born Nov 18, 1937, Yonges Island, SC; married Hudson. **Educ:** Talledega Col, BA, psychol, 1958; Harvard Univ, MA, educ & coun, 1962; Univ Calif, Los Angeles, CA, PhD, higher educ admin, 1980. **Career:** Burke High Sch, Charleston, SC, counr, 1958; Inst Psychol Servs, IL Inst Technol, psychometrist, 1959-69; City Chicago, test writer, 1960; Univ Chicago, Lab Sch, counr, 1962-66; Upward Bound, Occidental Col, dir, 1966-68; Locke High Sch, Los Angeles, dir col coun, 1968-71; Calif State Univ, dir Educ Opportunities Prog, 1971-72; US Congresswoman, Yvonne Brathwaite Burke, dist staff dir, 1972-78; Dept HUD, Los Angeles, 1978-79; Off CA Assemblyman Willie Brown, staffer, 1980; Free All, TV host, 1980-98; Calif State Govt, Assemblywoman Dist 48, 1990-96; Talladega Col, pres, 1998-2001; Crystal Stairs, consult, 1997; Col Charleston, dept polit sci, vis asst prof & instr, 2002-. **Orgs:** Bd trustee, Los Angeles Community Col Dist; vpres, Calif Mus Sci & Indust Found; bd trustee, Los Angeles SW Col Found; bd trustee, Jenesse Ctr; Crystal Stairs, bd trustee; State Bar CA; Delta Sigma Theta Sorority; chairperson, March Dimes, Talladega; United Way; bd trustee, Los Angeles Southwest Col Found; State Bar Calif; Comn Judicial Nominees Evaluations; Calif Comt Bar Examiners; City Los Angeles Comn Charter Reform; Dem Nat Comt; bd dir, Talladega Col Chamber Com; Calif State Legis. **Special Achievements:** First Women President of Talladega College, Alabama. **Business Addr:** Visiting Assistant Professor, College of Charleston, 114 Wentworth St Rm 101, Charleston, SC 29424, **Business Phone:** (843)953-8138.

### ARD, REV. ROBERT

Clergy. **Career:** Christ Church San Diego, pastor, 2002; United African Am Ministerial Action Coun, chmn. **Orgs:** Bd dir, treas, Ecumenical Coun San Diego County; exec bd, Interfaith Comt Worker Justice; chmn, United African Am Ministerial Action Coun. **Business Addr:** Pastor, Christ Church San Diego, 1355 Fern St, San Diego, CA 92101, **Business Phone:** (619)264-7240.

### ARDREY, DR. SAUNDRA CURRY

Educator. **Personal:** Born Aug 26, 1953, Louisville, GA; daughter of Earle and Estella; married William McCarty; children: Chris

& Lindsey. **Educ:** Winston-Salem State Univ, BA, 1975; Ohio State Univ, MA, 1976, PhD, 1983. **Career:** Univ NC, Chapel Hill, vis lectr, 1979-80; Univ Ky, Jefferson Community Col, instr, 1980-81; Furman Univ, asst prof, 1983-88; WKU Inst Citizenship & Social Responsibility, co-founder, co-dir; fac leader; coordr; TWC nat Adv Bd; Western Ky Univ, Dept Govt, from asst prof to assoc prof, 1988-99, spec asst to provost fac recruitment, 1999-2000, Dept Govt, head, 2000-, Dept Polit Sci, head, African-Am Studies Dept, dir, currently. **Orgs:** Am Polit Sci Asn Womens Sect Comt, 1975-87; Nat Conf Black Polit Sci, 1978-; Southern Polit Sci Asn, 1983-87; Am Asn Univ Prof, 1983-85; bd mem, Greenville City Urban League, 1983-87; Greenville City United Way, 1983-84; exec community mem, Greenville City Dem Party, 1984-85; pres, Greenville City Young Dem, 1984-85; fac teaching fel Republican & Dem Nominating Conventions, 1988-2012; Alpha Kappa Alpha Sorority, 1989-; Nat Asn Advan Colored People; Bowling Green Br, 1990-; pres, Bowling Green/Warren County NOW; campaign mgr, Dem party exec comt; pres, exec secy, Ky Polit Sci Asn; chair, Bowling Green/Warren County Nat Asn Advan Colored People, currently. **Special Achievements:** The only African American department head at Western Kentucky University in Bowling Green, Kentucky; First African American to serve as president and as executive secretary of the Kentucky Political Science Association; Organizing and coordinating the first ever Africana/African American Studies Conference in Turkey at Bilkent University. **Home Addr:** 833 Albemarle Dr, Bowling Green, KY 42103-1573, **Home Phone:** (270)781-8975. **Business Addr:** Associate Professor, Department Head, Western Kentucky University, 1906 College Heights Blvd, Bowling Green, KY 42101-3576, **Business Phone:** (270)745-4558.

## ARDS, DR. SHEILA DIANN

Educator, president (organization). **Personal:** Born Jun 30, 1960, Houston, TX; daughter of James Ed and Rosie M; married Samuel L Myers Jr; children: Andrea & Angela. **Educ:** Univ Tex, Austin, 1981; Carnegie Mellon Univ, MA, pub mgt, 1983, PhD, pub policy, 1990. **Career:** Urban Inst, res scholar; Univ Md, asst prof; Univ Minn, assoc prof, Humphrey Inst Pub Affairs, assoc vpres community partnerships & develop, 2002-06; Benedict Col, vpres, community develop, currently, Dept Soc Sci & Criminal justice, assoc prof, currently, Ctr Excellence, dir, currently. **Orgs:** Pi Sigma Alpha Exec Coun, 1995-; bd dir, Nat Leadership Inst, 1995-; pres, Nat Conf Black Polit Scientists, 1997; vpres, APPAM, 1998; pres, Nat Econ Assoc, 2004. **Home Addr:** 9 Island View Lane, North Oaks, MN 55127-2614, **Home Phone:** (651)482-8752. **Business Addr:** Vice President of Community Development, Director, Center of Excellence, Benedict College, 1600 Harden St, Columbia, SC 29204, **Business Phone:** (803)253-5000.

## AREMU, DR. ADUKE (ADUKE AREMU-GWENDOLYN ANDERSON)

Founder (originator), educator, writer. **Personal:** Born New York, NY; daughter of Robert and Frances Holmes; married W Calvin Anderson; children: Hakim, CJ, Mimi & Tricia. **Educ:** Hunter Col, BA, commun & theatre, 1968, MS, educ & theatre, 1973; Col New Rochelle, supv & admin; NY Univ, PhD, theatre. **Career:** Dept Educ New York; Dept Educ Conn; Dept Educ Westchester County; Star Acad, founder; Int Arts Bus Sch, Wingate High Sch; Essex County Col, prof, 1974-79; Urban Coalition, consult, 1979; Bor Manhattan Community Col, prof, 1981-83; Sch Syst New York, 1981-99; Col New Rochelle, prof, 1985-87; Medgar Evers Col, prof, 1993-98; Sch Syst New Rochelle, 1999-; Dove LLC, chief exec officer & owner, currently; Elite Dove Enterprise LLC, co-owner, currently. **Orgs:** Zeta Phi Beta Sorority, 1975-; founder, New Dove Promotions Inc, 1985-; founder, New York Youth Consortium Inc, 1985-; Hunter Col Alumnus Asn; Audel Co, New York, NY, 1998-; Stud Empowerment Prog, 1999-; Educ Comt, Nat Asn Advan Colored People, 1999-; adminr, Harlem C's Theatre; consult, Nat Educ Asn, Wash; consult, Ny Coun Arts. **Honors/Awds:** Theatre Award, Audelco, 1979; Woman of the Year, Caribbean-Am Chamber Com, 1998; Creativity Award, Kwanzaa Found New York, 1998; Congressional Awards, Retired Congressman Edolphus Towns; Playwright/Producer Award, Nigerian Consul Gen New York; Producer Awards, Dept Cult Jamaica, Trinidad & Barbados. **Special Achievements:** Published: Reaching Out With Love, 1981; "Hannibal and The Culture Carnival", 1995; Plays: "The Liberation of Mother Goose", 1977; "Babylon II", 1981; "Bum Sonata", 1991; "Kwanzaa-A Musical Play", 1996. **Business Addr:** Co-owner, Elite Dove Enterprise LLC, 226 Cedar Trl, Jonesboro, GA 30238, **Business Phone:** (678)439-6393.

## ARGRETT, LORETTA COLLINS

Government official. **Personal:** Born Oct 7, 1937, Carlisle, MS; daughter of Joseph Daniel Collins Sr and Katie Marie C; married James H Argrett Jr; children: Lisa Argrett Ahmad & Brian E; married Vantile E Whitfield. **Educ:** Howard Univ, BS, chem, 1958; Howard Univ, attended 1967; George Washington Univ, attended 1968; Inst Fur Organische Chemie, Technische Hoch Sch; Harvard Law Sch, JD, tax law, 1976. **Career:** Chemist Nat Insts Health, 1958-59, 1959-61; Duval County Bd Instr, Fla, teacher, 1961-62; Chemist Hazleton Labs, Reston, Va, 1965-66; Food & Drug Admin, 1966-68; Chemist, supvr lab Walter Reed Army Inst Res, 1968-73; Stroock & Stroock & Lavan, Wash, 1978-79; Summer assoc Mahoney, Hadlow, Chambers & Adams, Jacksonville, Fla, summer 1975; Arent, Fox, Kintner, Plotkin & Kahn, Wash, summer 1975; assoc, 1976-78; Legis atty, Joint Comt Taxation Us Cong, 1979-81; Partner Wald, Harkrader & Ross, Wash, 1981-86; Secy bd meetings opportunity funding corp, 1984-93; Pvt pract, 1986; assoc prof, prof Sch Law, Howard Univ, 1986; adj prof, Georgetown Law Ctr, Wash Col Law, 1986-88; adj prof, Am Univ, 1988; Georgetown Univ law schs, fac; Am Univ law schs, fac; ABA Sect Taxation, gov coun; US Cong, Joint Comt Taxation, atty; US Justice Dept, Tax Div, asst atty gen, 1993-99; Santa Fe Group, consult, currently. **Orgs:** Adv comt mem, Univ Baltimore Law Sch, Grad Tax Prog, 1986-; vis comt mem, Harvard Law Sch, 1987-93; life fel Am Bar Found, 1993-; comt mem, Dist Columbia Bar Legal Ethics, 1993-97; Am Bar Asn, Standing Comn Ethics & Prof Responsibility, 1998-; joint comn, mediator, Am Bar Asn, currently; bd dir, Am Bar Retirement Asn, currently; elected mem, Am Law Inst, 2001-. **Business Addr:** Elected Member, American Law Institute, 4025 Chestnut St, Philadelphia, PA 19104, **Business Phone:** (215)243-1600.

## ARGRETTE, JOSEPH M.

Executive, president (organization), chief executive officer. **Personal:** Born Apr 1, 1931, New York, NY; son of Joseph Jr and Mariah Tucker Dawson; children: Kendelle Ruth. **Educ:** Long Island Univ, Brooklyn, NY, BS, psychol, MS, psychol, 1954; Yeshiva Univ, PhD, clin psychol. **Career:** Nat Alliance Businessmen, Wash, DC, dir community rels, 1968-69; Econ Manpower Corp, founder & vpres, 1969-72; Rapadco Industs, founder & vpres mkt & sales, 1972-77; Ny Assembly, consult, 1977; Argrett Enterprises Corp, New York, NY, pres & chief exec officer, 1977-89; JMA Concrete Co, pres & chief exec officer, 1986-97; Riverside Hosp, Bronx, NY, dir voc coun; Fed Govt Off Equal Opportunity, Off Inspections, Wash, DC, dir region 2; Stone Craft Int, New York, NY, pres; JMA Concrete Construct Co Inc, pres & chief exec officer, 1997-; Argrette & Assocs LLC, prin, 2009-. **Orgs:** Asn Gen Contractors Am, 1980-89; dir, vpres, emer bd, Nat Asn Minority Contractors, 1985-89; dir, Gen Bldg Contractors-Asn Gen Contractor; exec comt mem, Gen Contractors Asn, NYC; Eagle Scout, Boy Scouts Am; bd dir, second vpres, Asn Minority Enterprises New York; founder, Ny Asn Minority Contractors; Nat Asn Advan Colored People; exec comt, Gen Contractors Asn New York Inc. **Home Addr:** 61 Townsend Rd, Crompond, NY 10517. **Business Addr:** President, Chief Executive Officer, JMA Concrete Construct Co Inc, 920 Lester Ave, Mamaroneck, NY 10543, **Business Phone:** (914)777-6400.

## ARKHURST, JOYCE COOPER

Librarian. **Personal:** Born Oct 20, 1921, Seattle, WA; daughter of Felix and Hazel James; married Frederick; children: Cecile. **Educ:** Univ Wash, Seattle, WA, BA, 1944; Columbia Univ, MLS, 1957. **Career:** Librarian (retired); New York Pub Libr, c's librn, 1947-58; Chicago Pub Lib, c's librn, 1967-69; Fieldston Sch, Bronx, NY, librn, 1971-74; Elisabeth Irwin Sch, New York, NY, 1978-83; New York Bd Educ, libr teacher, 1983-93. **Orgs:** Delta Sigma Theta Sorority, 1943-; Am Libr Asn, 1983-85; New York Black Librns Caucus, 1983-; NAACP, 1984-88; Schomburg Corp, 1988-; Countee Cullen Libr Support Group, 1988-; Am Asn Univ Women, 1991-. **Honors/Awds:** Mortar Bd, Sociology Honorary, Univ Washington, 1944; Author, The Adventures Spider, 1964, More Adventures Spider, 1971. **Home Addr:** 2235 5th Ave 10C, New York, NY 10037, **Home Phone:** (212)368-8605.

## ARMANO, KWADWO JONES

Lawyer. **Educ:** Bradley Univ, BA, 1985; St Louis Univ, JD, 1988. **Career:** Kwadwo J Armano LLC, atty, currently. **Orgs:** Mo Bar. **Business Addr:** Attorney, Kwadwo J Armano LLC, 34 N Brentwood Blvd Suite 212, St. Louis, MT 63105-3746, **Business Phone:** (314)721-5211.

## ARMISTEAD, MILTON

Lawyer. **Personal:** Born Jun 19, 1947, Indianapolis, IN; son of Mitchell and Margarette; children: Jeff & Milton. **Educ:** Pasadena City Col, AA, 1967; San Jose State Col, BA, 1969; Univ Southern Calif, MS, 1972, JD, 1974. **Career:** Milton Armistead Law Off, atty, currently. **Orgs:** Calif State Bar, 1977-; pres, Wiley Manual Law Soc, 1979-; corresp, Sacramento Observer, 1981; Defense Res Inst, 1983; pres, Toastmasters Capital Club, 1984; bd dir, Sacramento Claims Asn, 1984; vpres, Sacramento Black Chamber Comn, 1985-; chmn, Vols Am, 1985; Black Ins Prof Asn, 1985; Calif Trial Lawyers Asn. **Honors/Awds:** Best Speaker Toastmasters, 1984; Competent Toastmaster Award, 1987; Lawyer of the Year, Wiley W Manuel Bar Asn, 2010. **Business Addr:** Attorney, Milton Armistead Law Office, 11409 Gold Hill Ct, Gold River, CA 95670-7219, **Business Phone:** (916)257-1525.

## ARMOUR, DR. CHRISTOPHER E.

Physician. **Personal:** Born Nov 1, 1959, Columbus, GA; son of John Henry Crowder III and Mildred L; married Jacqueline L; children: Jonathan R & Kristen M. **Educ:** Univ Ga, BS, 1982; Morehouse Sch Med, MD, 1987. **Career:** Southwest Hosp, med resident physician, 1987-90; Smyrna Med first, med dir & physician, 1990-94; Aetna Health ways Family Med Ctr, staff physcian, 1995-; Wellstar Physician Group, 1998; Pkwy Med, physician; Southeat Permanente Med Group, 2003-. **Orgs:** Am Acad Family Physicians, 1990-; Ga Acad Family Physicians, 1990-; Nat Med Asn, 1991-; AMA, 1994. **Home Addr:** 2725 Thornbury Way, Atlanta, GA 30349-7119. **Business Addr:** Physician, Kaiser Permanente, 1175 Cascade SW Pkwy, Atlanta, GA 30311, **Business Phone:** (404)365-0966.

## ARMOUR, DR. LAWRENCE

Educator. **Educ:** Southern Univ New Orleans, BS, 1989; Univ New Orleans, MS, 1994, PhD, 1998. **Career:** Southern Univ New Orleans, asst prof, currently. **Orgs:** Fel, UNO, 1996-98; exec bd, Southern Baptist Conv, 2002-; treas, GNOAEYC. **Business Addr:** Assistant Professor, Southern University New Orleans, 6400 Press Dr, New Orleans, LA 70126, **Business Phone:** (504)286-5000.

## ARMSTEAD, JESSIE WILLARD

Football player. **Personal:** Born Oct 26, 1970, Dallas, TX; married Channon; children: Jessica & Jaya. **Educ:** Univ Miami, criminal justice, 1993. **Career:** Football player (retired), owner; New York Giants, 1993-94, linebacker, 1995, 1999, 2000-01, left linebacker, 1996-99, strong safety, 1999, spec asst & consult, 2008-; Wash Redskins, 2002-03; Carolina Panthers, linebacker, 2004; Hamilton Honda, owner, 2008-; Englewood cliffs Cadillac, owner, 2008-. **Orgs:** Founder, Armstead Found New York community; Wash Community. **Honors/Awds:** National Football Conference Special Teams Player of the Week, 1993; National Football Conference Special Teams Player of the Month, 1993; Rookie of the Year, NY Giants, 1993; Defensive Most Valuable Player, 1996; Most Valuable Player, 1997; Pro Bowl, 1997-01; All-Pro, 1997-2000; Nat Football Conf Defensive Player of the Month, 1999; Nat Football Conf Defensive Player of the Week; Top 25 team hon, USA Today; Jessie's Giant Hoop Team; New York Giants Ring of Honor. **Special Achievements:** TV appearence: Pros vs Joes, Spike TV, 2008. TV Series: Arli$$, 2000. Film: Super Bowl XXXV, 2001. **Business Addr:** Owner, Hamilton Honda, 655 US Hwy 130, Hamilton, NJ 08691, **Business Phone:** (609)528-2600.

## ARMSTEAD, RON E.

Social worker, city planner. **Personal:** Born Apr 12, 1947, Boston, MA; son of Leemon Smith and Ruby Smith; children: Tod, Kaili & Ronni. **Educ:** Boston Univ Metro Col, attended 1974; Boston State Col, BA, 1979; Harvard Univ, Grad Sch Design, cert, 1983; Mass Inst Technol, Cambridge MA & MCP, 1989. **Career:** Teen Educ Ctr, educ counr, 1970-73; Model Cities Admin, community planner, 1970-74; Boston State Col, campus organizer, 1975, Stud Govt Asn, pres; Vet Ctr Vet Admin, readjustment counr, social worker, 1979-87; Amistad Asn, pres; Cong Black Caucus Vet Braintrust, exec dir, 1988-. **Orgs:** Bd dir, William Joiner Ctr Study War & Social Consequences; conf issue coordr Speakers Conf Vietnam Vet; co-chmn, Nat Black Vet Working Group; coord, Mass Black Vet Think Tank Group; Appropriations Subcomt Mil Construct & Veterans Affairs; Soc Traumatic Stress Studies; fel Mass Inst Technol, 1987; pres & bd dir, Vet Benefits Clearinghouse Inc, 1975-85; Nat Asn Social Workers, 1980-; Nat Asn Black Social Workers; Asn Study Afro-Am Life & Hist, 1985-; Sen John F Kerry's Black Adv Comt, 1989; consult, Secy Jesse Brown's Adv Comt Minority Veterans. **Honors/Awds:** Commendation, Vet Admin, 1982; Commendation, Gov Michael L Dukakis, 1983; coordinated Black Vet Workshops at Cong Black Caucus Legis Weekends, 1985, 1987 & 1988; Salute Award, Chelsea Soldiers Home, 1986; Scholar Award, Mass Inst Technol, 1987; Certificate Award, Mass Off Affirmative Action, 1989; presented Stress & Trauma Workshops, Nat Asn Black Social Workers Conf, 1987-89; Spec Cong Recognition Award; Boston Neighborhood Fels Award; Outstanding Veterans Achievement Award; Drylongso Award. **Home Addr:** 86 Thornton St, Boston, MA 02119, **Home Phone:** (617)442-5691. **Business Addr:** Executive Director, Congressional Black Caucus Veterans Braintrust, PO Box 54158, Washington, DC 20032-9998, **Business Phone:** (202)331-4497.

## ARMSTEAD, WILBERT EDWARD, JR.

Administrator, association executive, army officer. **Personal:** Born Jun 23, 1934, Baltimore, MD; son of Wilbert Edward and Mary Josephine Hill; married Erma Shirley Cole; children: Barbara E, Valerie, Sheryl J, Joann C, Jeri L Connelly & Angela M Bernard. **Educ:** Johns Hopkins Univ, BA, elect engr, 1955. **Career:** RCA Missile & Surface Radar, assoc mem engr staff, 1955-58, mem engr staff, 1958-62, sr mem engr staff, 1963-74, unit mgr, 1974-86; GE, Moores town, NJ, mgr, 1986-93; Martin Marietta Prin Prog, ctrs pecialist, 1993-95; Lockheed Martin GES, prog mgr, 1995-. **Orgs:** Vpres, 1979, pres, 1980-86, Moorestown Twp Bd Educ; Community Serv Club Blue Chips, 1975; ed comn, Baptist Ch Moorestown, 1977, NJ State Fed Colored Women, 1981; pres & newsletter ed, Moorestown Improv Asn; bd trustee, Burlington City Family Serv; adv bd, Moorestown Citizens; Low & Moderate Income Housing, 1994-97; Moorestown Zoning Bd; Republican Comt man, 10th Dist, Moorestown NJ, 1997-; Moorestown Improv Asn. **Honors/Awds:** Citizen of the Year, Moorestown NJ Combined Serv Clubs, 2000; Star of Excellence Award Citizen of the Year, Lockheed Martin Corp, Naval Electronics and Surveillance Systems Div, 2000. **Home Addr:** 325 Farmdale Rd, Moorestown, NJ 08057, **Home Phone:** (856)235-1359. **Business Addr:** Program Manager, Lockheed Martin, Mail Stop 116 302, Moorestown, NJ 08057.

## ARMSTER-WORRILL, CYNTHIA DENISE

President (organization), school administrator, educator. **Personal:** Born Aug 7, 1960, Tokyo; daughter of Dorothy L and Franksin; married Conrad W Worrill; children: Sobeenna Armster Worrill. **Educ:** Emporia State Univ, BS, 1982, MS, 1983. **Career:** Emporia State Univ, job develop coordr, 1982-83; Northern Ill Univ, counr, minority prog, 1983-85; George Williams Col, dir acad support, 1985; Chicago State Univ, dir freshmen serv, 1986-; City Col Chicago, assoc vice chancellor stud affairs, currently; pres, ABWHE Inc. **Orgs:** Chair, Minority Personnel Concerns Comn, 1984-85; prog chair, 1985-86, mem chair, 1986-87, Am Col Personnel Asn; pres, rec secy, Alpha Kappa Alpha Sor Inc, 1986-87; Nat Black United Front, 1986-87; YWCA Chmn, Monarch Awards Found, 1989; Asn Black Women Higher Educ. **Home Addr:** 7414 S Chappel 2nd Fl, Chicago, IL 60649, **Home Phone:** (312)947-9661. **Business Addr:** Associate Vice Chancellor of Student Affairs, City Colleges of Chicago, 226 W Jackson Blvd 9th Fl, Chicago, IL 60606-6997, **Business Phone:** (312)553-2931.

## ARMSTRONG, B. J., JR. (BENJAMIN ROY ARMSTRONG)

Basketball player, executive, vice president (organization). **Personal:** Born Sep 9, 1967, Detroit, MI. **Educ:** Univ Iowa, Iowa City, IA, 1989. **Career:** Basketball player (retired) executive; Chicago Bulls, guard, 1989-95, 1999-2000; Golden State Warriors, guard, 1995-97; Toronto Raptors, 1996; Charlotte Hornets, guard, 1997-98; Orlando Magic, 1998-99; Chicago Bulls, 1999-2000, asst gen mgr, 2000-03, gen mgr, 2003, spec asst exec vpres basketball oper, 2005; ESPN, basketball analyst, 2005-; Wasserman Media Group LLC, vpres basketball mgt, 2006-. **Orgs:** Nat Basketball Asn; Wasserman Media Group, 2006; Entertainment & Sports Programming Network; Calif prof athletes & entertainers. **Home Addr:** 14636 Martha St, Sherman Oaks, CA 91411, **Home Phone:** (818)997-6168. **Business Addr:** Vice President Basketball Management, Wasserman Media Group LLC, 12100 W Olympic Blvd Suite 200, Los Angeles, CA 90064-1052, **Business Phone:** (310)440-2811.

## ARMSTRONG, BRUCE CHARLES

Football player, executive. **Personal:** Born Sep 7, 1965, Miami, FL; married Melinda Yvette; children: Candace Lynne & Nicholas Charles. **Educ:** Univ Louisville, BA, polit sci. **Career:** Football player (retired), executive; New England Patriots, right tackle, 1987-89, left tackle, 1990-2000; salon owner, currently. **Honors/Awds:** Pro Bowl, 1990-91, 1994-97; Rookie of the Year, 1776 Quarterback Club of New England, 1987; All-American Honorable Mention; Most Outstanding Lineman. **Home Addr:** 12543 Brookwood Ct, Davie, FL 33330-1207.

## ARMSTRONG, DARRELL EUGENE

Basketball coach, basketball player. **Personal:** Born Jun 22, 1968, Gastonia, NC; married Deidra; children: Arkia, Mayliah & Darrell Jr. **Educ:** Fayettville State Univ, attended 1991. **Career:** Basketball player (retired), coach; Atlanta Trojans, Us Basketball League, 1991-94; Capitol Reign Pontiacs, Continental Basketball Asn, 1992-93; S Ga Blues, Global Basketball Asn, 1992-93; Pezoporikos Larnaca, Cyprus, 1993-94; Ourense Baloncesto, Spain, 1993-95; Coren Orense, Spain, 1994-95; Orlando Magic, guard & point guard, 1995-2003; New Orleans Hornets, guard & point guard, 2003-04; Dallas Mavericks, guard & point guard, 2004-06, asst coach, 2009-; Ind Pacers, point guard, 2006-07; NJ Nets, point guard, 2007-08. **Orgs:** Pres, Darrell Armstrong Found Premature Babies Inc. **Honors/Awds:** Cyprus Basketball Player of the Year, 1994; Alumni Hall of Fame, Boys & Girls Clubs Am, 1998; Rich and Helen DeVos Community Enrichment Award, 1998, 2000; Sixth Man of the Year, Nat Basketball Asn, 1999; Most Improved Player, Nat Basketball Asn, 1999; Hometown Hero Award, 1999; Champion, Nat Basketball Asn, 2011. **Business Addr:** Assistant Basketball Coach, Dallas Mavericks, 2909 Taylor St, Dallas, TX 75226, **Business Phone:** (214)658-7100.

## ARMSTRONG, DR. EARL MAGNUS

Physician. **Educ:** Univ Chicago, Pritzker Sch Med, MD, 1973. **Career:** Johns Hopkins Hosp, Baltimore, Md, internship, 1973-76, resident, 1976-78, fel pulmonary disease, 1976-78; Providence Hosp, physician; Wash Hosp Ctr, physician, currently; Pulm Critical Care Assoc, physician, currently; Armstrong & Polk, physician, currently. **Honors/Awds:** Named one of the Top Doctor in Providence Hospital, Washingtonian Magazine, 2008. **Business Addr:** Physician, Armstrong & Polk, 1160 Varnum St NE Suite 214, Washington, DC 20017, **Business Phone:** (202)526-5491.

## ARMSTRONG, ERNEST W., SR.

**Personal:** Born May 1, 1915, Soper, OK; son of Giles and Vinnie; children: Earl M & Everett W. **Educ:** Dillard Univ, AB, 1942; Howard Univ, MDiv, 1946, MA, 1947; Univ Heidelberg, Ger, cert, 1954; Univ Okla, MEd, 1969; Santa Barbara Univ, PhD, 1974; Prince Georges Community Col, AA, 1979, 1981. **Career:** Educator, real estate agent (retired); Nat YMCA, NY Army-Navy Dept, stud sec, 1944-45; Howard Univ, 1946-48; Shiloh Baptist Church, asst pastor, 1946-48; Savannah State Col, Col chaplain & asst prof social sci, 1948-49; Triton Community Col, Reiver Grove IL, counr & instr, 1969-70; Enon Baptist Church, Baltimore, MD, asst pastor, 1970-72; Catonsville Community Col, counr, 1970-72; Livingstone Col, Salisbury NC, counr, 1972-73; Annapolis MD Sr High Sch, counr, 1973-77; real estate broker, 1977-92. **Orgs:** Am Pub Gardens Asn; Am Col Personnel Asn; AAMFC; MPGA; MCPA; Nat Asn Black Psychol; Omega Psi Phi Frat; Prince Hall Masons thirty third degree; US Chess Fedn. **Honors/Awds:** Publ Army Chaplain in Korea "The Oracle", Omega Psi Phi Frat Inc, 1952; Distinguished Alumni Award, Dillard Univ, 1983; hon Dr, Faith Grant Col, 1995. **Special Achievements:** Published autobiography, The Joy of Living at 85, 2000; Omega Man of the Year Frankfort, Germany/Theta Rho Tau Chap 1962; Mason of the Year, 1962; OK Prince Hall Grand Lodge. **Home Addr:** 4046 Hilton Rd, Baltimore, MD 21215-9123, **Home Phone:** (410)367-5383.

## ARMSTRONG, JANET (JAZZ ARMSTRONG)

Fashion designer. **Educ:** Howard Univ, BA, fine arts, 1972; Ray-Vogue Col Design, AA, fashion, design, draping, pattern making, 1974; Art Inst Chicago, attended 1976. **Career:** Tommy Hilfiger, sr dir tech design, 1996-2002; Polo Jeans Co, sr dir tech design, 2002-04; Ltd Brands, sr dir tech design, 2004-07; Creative Design Studio NY, sr dir tech design, 2008-; Creative Design Studios L & T, sr dir tech design, currently; MESH Brands, tech design dir. **Business Addr:** Senior Director of Technical Design, Creative Design Studio, 601 W 26th St, New York, NY 10001-1101, **Business Phone:** (646)416-8000.

## ARMSTRONG, JOAN BERNARD

Judge, teacher. **Personal:** Born New Orleans, LA; married Andrew; children: David M & Anna K. **Educ:** Xavier Univ, BA, 1963; Loyola Univ Sch Law, JD, 1967; Nat Col Juv Justice, col cert, 1974. **Career:** Orleans Parish, teacher; Orleans Parish Juv Ct, judge, 1974-84; 4th Circuit Ct Appeal, judge, 1984, chief judge, 2003-11. **Orgs:** Pres, Community Rels Coun, 1972-74; pres, La League Good Govt, 1972-74; Criminal Justice Coord Coun New Orleans, 1975-86; Vis Comm Loyola Univ; charter mem, Nat Asn Women Judges; trustee, Loyola Univ S; Bar Asn; Am Red Cross; Legal Aid Bur; Nat Coun Juv & Family Ct Judges; La Asn Ment Health; Crisis Care Ctr. **Honors/Awds:** Outstanding Young Woman, New Orleans Jaycees, 1974; Hon mem, Alpha Kappa Alpha, 1974; Silver Bowl Award, Greyhound Co; Clay Award, The C Bureau, New Orleans; Special Jurist Award, Nat Bar Asn. **Special Achievements:** First woman elected to the bench in the state of Louisiana; First black woman to serve as an appellate court judge in Louisiana. **Home Addr:** 4701 Lafon Dr, New Orleans, LA 70126, **Home Phone:** (504)241-5155. **Business Addr:** Judge, 4th Circuit Court of Appeal, 400 Royal St, New Orleans, LA 70130, **Business Phone:** (504)412-6030.

## ARMSTRONG, REP. JOE E.

State government official, politician. **Personal:** Born Nov 30, 1956, Knoxville, TN; married LeTonia; children: 4. **Educ:** Univ Tenn, Col Bus Admin, BS, bus admin, 1981. **Career:** Knox County, TN, comnr, 1986-88, vice chair, 1982-88; ins mgr, currently; State Tenn, Tenn Gen Assembly, 15th Dist, state rep, 1988-; ins mgr, currently. **Orgs:** Chmn, House Health & Human Resources Comt; House Calendar & Rules Comt; House Fin Comt; vice Chair, Tenn House Dem Caucus; exec comt mem, Nat Black Caucus State Legislators, pres, 2010-; bd mem, Nat Dem Leadership Found; Nat Ins Asn; life mem, Nat Asn Advan Colored People; life mem, Omega Psi Phi Frat; Knoxville Urban League; Tenn Black Alumni Asn; Univ Tenn Alumni Asn; lifetime mem, Beck Cult Exchange Ctr; E side Optimist Club; Knoxville Col Alumni Asn; Mens Health Network; bd mem, St Marys Health Care Ctr; Knoxville Nat Asn Advan Colored People; E side Ymca; bd mem, Mercy Health Partners; Knoxville Col Boosters Club; Health Equity Comn. **Honors/Awds:** Appreciation Award, Tenn Reflexologist Asn, 2002; Legislator of the Year Award, County Officials Asn Tenn, Tenn Asn Human Resource Agencies, Nat Alliance Ment Ill, 2003, Tenn Men's Health Network, 2006 & 2008, Nat Black Caucus State Legislators, 2006; Hardest Working Volunteer Award, Tom Joyner Found, 2004; Humanitarian Award, Nat Conf Community & Justice, 2004; Legislative Champion Award, AARP, 2004; Health Disparities Leadership Award, NBCSL/NBCHL, 2005; Legislator of the Year Award, Tenn Men's Health Network, 2005; Crystal Gavel Award, Nat Black Caucus State Legislators, 2012; MLK Distinguished Award, Dr. Martin Luther King Jr Commemorative Comn, 2013. **Home Addr:** 4708 Hilldale Dr, Knoxville, TN 37914, **Home Phone:** (865)523-6374. **Business Addr:** State Representative, House of Representatives, 301 6th Ave N Suite 33 Legis Plz, Nashville, TN 37243-0115, **Business Phone:** (615)741-0768.

## ARMSTRONG, KEVIN

Vice president (organization), executive. **Educ:** Rutgers Univ; Rutgers Univ Law Sch, JD; Univ St Thomas. **Career:** Prudential Securities, mgt; Thomson McKinnon Securities Inc, mgt; NY Stock Exchange, sr mkt analyst; Nat Asn Securities Dealers, sr compliance examr; First Mich Corp, vpres, dir compliances; Fleet Fin Grp, sr vpres, functional dir compliance, 1998; US Bancorp, PowerTrack, dir, 2000-09, vpres, sr vpres & gen mgr, currently; Syncada, prod mgr, 2009-; Pershing Advisor Solutions LLC, a BNY Mellon co, dir & managing coun. **Orgs:** NJ State Bar Asn; Pa State Bar Asn; Am Bar Asn; Nat Bar Asn; Bond Mkt Asn; Securities Indust Asn. **Business Addr:** Senior Vice President, General Manager, US Bancorp, US Bancorp Ctr, Boston, MN 55402, **Business Phone:** (612)872-2657.

## ARMSTRONG, MARIO

Founder (originator), television show host. **Personal:** married Nicole Armstrong; children: one son. **Educ:** University of Maryland, Communications, 1996. **Career:** System Source (Hunt Valley, MD), Tech Trainer, 1997-00; Ciena, IT User Support Specialist, 1999-01; Mayor's Office City of Baltimore, Mayor's Technology Advisor (Martin O'Malley), 2001-06; TechTechBoom, Founder, 2004-10; XM Satellite Radio, Sirius XM, Host and Owner of "Daily Talk" show, 2004-12; Mario Armstrong Media LLC, Owner, 2003-; National Public Radio, On-air Contributor for shows "Morning Edition" and "Tell Me More," 2005-; CNN, On-air Guest, 2009-; NBC, On-air Contributor, 2010-; HLN, On-air Contributor, 2011-; Fuse TV, On-air Guest, 2013-. **Orgs:** Boys & Girls Club, Member; Kappa Alpha Psi, Member; Urban League of Baltimore, Member. **Honors/Awds:** Legislative Black Caucus of Maryland, Hope for Today, Visions for Tomorrow Award; Urban League, Technology Advocate of the Year; Rotary Club of Maryland; "Baltimore Times," Top 25 Young Rising Stars; Career Communications Group, Modern-Day Technology Leader; "Baltimore Business Journal," Top 40 Under 40 Emerging Leaders; "Daily Record VIP List," Successful before 40; Emmy Award, Best TV Show Host of Informational Program, 2011; TheGrio.com, 100 Making History Today, 2010, 2011, 2012.

## ARMSTRONG, REGINALD DONALD, II

Editor. **Personal:** Born Jul 28, 1958, Long Beach, CA; son of Reginald D and Marie Roque; married Sandra Achue; children: Omari Hasan & Sarou Bakila. **Educ:** Univ Calif, San Diego, LaJolla, CA, attended 1977; Morehouse Col, Atlanta, GA, attended 1977; Univ SC, Columbia, BA, 1979. **Career:** Nat Asn Advan Colored People/Crisis Mag, Brooklyn, NY, ed asst, 1983-85; Village Voice, New York, NY, asst ed, 1985-88; Times Mirror/Sports Inc, New York, NY, copy chief, 1988-89; Gen Media/Omni, asst managing ed, 1989; Emerge Mag, New York, NY, asst managing ed, 1989. **Orgs:** Nat Asn Black Journalists, 1990-. **Home Addr:** 930 St Nicholas Ave, New York, NY 10032, **Home Phone:** (212)283-1529. **Business Addr:** Assistant Managing Editor, Emerge Magazine, 599 Broadway, New York, NY 10012, **Business Phone:** (212)941-8811.

## ARMSTRONG, RICH (RICHARD L ARMSTRONG)

Executive. **Personal:** married Cheri; children: Jason Hellwich & Dylan Hellwich. **Career:** Executive (retired); Hygrade Food Prod, supt, 1975-82, prod scheduler, 1982-85; plant mgr, 1985-87, gen mgr, 1987-90; Hillshire Farm & Kahns New London, Wis, gen mgr, 1990-93; King Cotton Foods, Memphis, chief exec officer, 1993-94; Galileo Foods, chief exec officer, 1994-2001; Sara Lee Corp, vice pres & chief supply chain officer, 2001-05; Sara Lee Corp, Downers Grove, vice pres & chief supply chain officer, food & beverage. **Orgs:** Bd dir, Am Meat Inst; bd dir, Ohio Urban League.

## ARMSTRONG, ROBB

Cartoonist or animator, illustrator, artist. **Personal:** Born Mar 4, 1962, Wynnefield, PA; son of Dorothy (deceased); married Sherry West; children: Tess & Rex Alexander. **Educ:** Syracuse Univ, BA, fine arts, 1985. **Career:** Var ad agencies, art dir; syndicated cartoonist, 1988-; Savannah Col Art & Design, vis prof, 1997; United Media, syndicated cartoonist, currently. **Orgs:** Syracuse Univ Alumni Bd. **Honors/Awds:** Wilbur Award, Relig Pub Rels Coun, 1995; Men of Courage Award, Nestle; hon Doctor Humane Lett degree, Holy Family Univ. **Special Achievements:** Articles about him & his comic strip Jump Start, appeared in Time, Ebony, The New York Times, Black Enterprise & People among others; contributed cartoons to national magazines including The New Yorker; Featured guest, Good Morning America, MSNBC, numerous local & national TV shows. **Business Addr:** Cartoonist, United Media, 200 Madison Ave, New York, NY 10016, **Business Phone:** (212)293-8500.

## ARMSTRONG, SAUNDRA BROWN

Judge. **Personal:** Born Mar 23, 1947, Oakland, CA. **Educ:** Merritt Col, AA, 1967; Calif State Univ, Fresno, BA, 1969; Univ San Francisco Sch Law, JD, 1977. **Career:** Oakland Police Dept, Oakland, Calif, policewoman, 1970-77; Calif Ct Appeals, judicial extern, 1977; Alameda County, Calif, dep dist atty, 1978-79, 1980-82; Calif Assembly Comt Criminal Justice, sr consult, 1979-80; US Dept Justice, Pub Integrity Sect, trial atty, 1982-83; Consumer Prod Safety Comn, comnr, 1983-86; US Parole Comn, comnr, 1986-89; Alameda Super Ct, Calif, judge, 1989-91; US Dist Ct, Northern Calif, fed judge, sr dist judge, 1991-. **Special Achievements:** First African-American policewoman; First African-American female prosecutor in the Alameda County District; First African-American woman to serve on the United States District Court for the Northern District of California. **Business Addr:** Senior District Judge, United States District Court, Oakland Courthouse Courtroom 1, Oakland, CA 94612, **Business Phone:** (510)637-3562.

## ARMSTRONG, TYJI DONRAPHEAL

Football player, executive. **Personal:** Born Oct 3, 1970, Inkster, MI; married Jeannie. **Educ:** Iowa Cent Community Col, attended; Univ Miss, attended. **Career:** Football player (retired), executive; Tampa Bay Buccaneers, tight end, 1992-95; Dallas Cowboys, 1996; St Louis Rams, 1998; Chicago Enforcers, 2000-01; Jakona Rhodesian Ridgebacks, owner, currently. **Home Addr:** PO Box 657, Balm, FL 33503, **Home Phone:** (813)746-1103. **Business Addr:** Owner, Jakona Rhodesian Ridgebacks, 12934 CR 672, Balm, FL 33503, **Business Phone:** (813)746-1103.

## ARMSTRONG, VANESSA BELL

Gospel singer. **Personal:** Born Oct 2, 1953, Detroit, MI; daughter of Jesse Bell; children: 5. **Career:** Gospel vocalist, Albums: Peace Be Still, 1983; Chosen, 1984; Following Jesus, 1986; Vanessa Bell Armstrong, 1987; Wonderful One, 1990; The Truth About Christmas, 1990; Something on the Inside, 1993; The Secret Is Out, 1995; Desire of My Heart: Live in Detroit, 1998; A Brand New Day, 2001; Walking Miracle, 2007; The Experience, 2009. Actress: Don't Get God Started; The Women of Brewster Place; Compilations: Greatest Hits, 1990; The Best of Vanessa Bell Armstrong, Verity, 1999; Sing To Glory, 2005; Praise & Worship, 2006. **Orgs:** Sigma Gamma Rho Sorority Inc. **Honors/Awds:** Best Soul Gospel Performance, Female for Peace Be Still, 1983; Best Soul Gospel Performance, Female for Chosen, 1985; Best Soul Gospel Performance, Duo, Group, Choir or Chorus for Choose Ye, 1986; Best Soul Gospel Performance, Female for Pressing On, 1988; Gospel Music Hall of Fame, 2001. **Business Addr:** Gospel Vocalist, EMI Gospel, 101 Winners Circle, Brentwood, TN 37024, **Business Phone:** (615)371-6800.

## ARMSTRONG, WILLIAM

President (organization), automotive executive. **Career:** Armstrong Toyota, pres & owner, 1994-; Hollywood Ford, pres, currently. **Orgs:** Exec bd, Nat Asn Minority Automotive Dealers; bd mem, Beacon Coun; Greater Miami Chamber Com; Dade Community Found; Broward Red Cross & Broward Employ Training Admin; pres, Ford Motor Minority Dealers Asn, currently; bd mem, Jobs Miami, currently; asst treas, Carnival Ctr Performing Arts, currently. **Honors/Awds:** Citizen of the Year, 2006. **Business Addr:** President, Hollywood Ford, 1200 N Federal Hwy, Hollywood, FL 33020, **Business Phone:** (954)921-6800.

## ARMSTRONG, WILLIAM F.

Government official. **Personal:** Born Aug 13, 1942, York, PA; son of Jesse C and Mary L; married Carolyn Ann; children: Nadine M Walker, Paulette, Darnell L, DeAnna R McKoy, Darleen L Smith & Daryl J (deceased). **Educ:** Univ Md, Eastern Shore, BS, 1970; Catholic Univ Am, MA, 1971; CPM; APP. **Career:** Univ Md, College Park, Dept Procurement & Supply, asst dir & mgr, MBE progs, 1982-98; Prince George's County govt, Off Cent Serv, dep dir, 1998; Md Dept Gen Serv, dir procurement & logistics. **Orgs:** Nat Asn Purchasing Mgt; Purchasing Mgt Asn Md; Md Pub Purchasing Asn; Nat Inst Govt Purchasing; Nat Asn Black Procurement Profs; Univ Syst Md Found; pres, Black Fac & Staff Asn; chair, Purchasing Month Comt. **Home Addr:** 601 Concerto Lane, Silver Spring, MD 20901-5009, **Home Phone:** (301)593-8122.

## ARNELLE, HUGH JESSE

Basketball player, executive, lawyer. **Personal:** Born Dec 30, 1933, New Rochelle, NY; son of Hugh and Lynn; married Carolyn; children: Nicole, Paolo & Michael. **Educ:** Pa State Univ, BA, 1955, Dickinson Sch Law, JD, 1962; Hastings Law Sch, dipl. **Career:** Basketball player, lawyer (retired), executive; AU State Univ, All-Am Basketball, 1952-54; Nat Basketball Asn, Ft Wayne Piston, 1955-56; Nat Football League Baltimore Colts, 1957-58; Dept Labor, atty, 1962-63; Peace Corps, from assoc dir to dir, 1963-66, staff, 1966-67; FPC, asst to gen coun, 1967-68; Morrison Foerster Holloway, atty, 1971-73; US Dist Ct, asst fed pub defender; pvt pract, 1973-85; Hastings Law Sch Criminal Trial Advocacy, fac, 1977; Arnelle, Hastie, McGee, Willis & Greene, civil litigation & pub finance atty, sr partner, 1985-97; Waste Mgt Inc, dir, 1992-; Womble Carlyle Sandridge & Rice, coun, 1997-2005; Textron Corp, dir, 1993-2008; Armstrong World Indust Inc, dir, 1995-; Eastman Chem Co Inc, dir, 1994-2004; Gannett Co, dir, 1999-; Union Pac & Resources Inc, staff; Metrop Life Ser Fund, dir, 2002; URS Inc, dir, 2004-10; admitted to pract CA, PA, US Supreme Ct; WFC Holdings Corp, dir, 1990-; RME Holding Co, dir, 1995-; FPL Group Inc, dir, 1990-2006; Armstrong Holdings Inc, dir, 1995-2006; WMX Technologies Inc, dir; Fla Power & Light, bd mem. **Orgs:** IDEA Inc Chas F Kettering Found, 1968-69; Col Civil Trial Advocacy, 1976; Hall Fame NY, 1977; comnr, San Francisco Redevelop Agency; bd dir, San Fransisco Boys Club, 1981; Am Bd Criminal Trial Lawyers, 1982; exec comnr, bd trustees, San Francisco World Affairs Coun, 1983; bd trustee, Pa State Univ; vice chmn, Pa State Bd Trustees, 1993; vice chmn, Pa State Univ Bd Trustee, 1992-95, vice chmn, 1996-98; Nat Football Found Hall Fame, 1993; vpres, Pa State Univ, 1993-95, pres, 1996-98; dir, pres, co-founder, Renaissance Fund Pa State Univ; Charles Houston Bar Asn; Nat Bar Asn; Bar Pa; Bar US Supreme Ct; Nat Panel Arbit, Am Trial Lawyers Asn; Westchester Co Hall Fame; pres, Afro-Am Hist Soc; bd dir, San Francisco Opportunity; bd dir, Bay Area UNICEF; Univ Governance; bd mem, Wells Fargo Bank; Boys & Girls Clubs Am; State Bar Calif; San Francisco Bar Asn. **Honors/Awds:** Honory mention, All-Am Football, 1953-54; Dr Martin Luther King Jr Medal for Outstanding Professional Service, George Washington Univ, 1995; Lion's Paw Award, Dr laws, Dickinson Sch Law, 2000. **Special Achievements:** Ranks among the top 10 bond council in the state; First African-American student body president in 1955; One of the top 12 African-American law firms in the country in 1987. **Business Addr:** Director, Armstrong World Industries Inc, PO Box 3001, Lancaster, PA 17604, **Business Phone:** (717)397-0611.

## ARNETTE, EVELYN

President (organization), entrepreneur. **Educ:** Wells Col, NY, BA, criminal justice, 1982; Mercer Univ Atlanta, MBA, mkt, 1993. **Career:** BellSouth, staff sls & customer serv; Atlanta Tribune, customer serv writer; A Customers Pt View Inc, founder, chief exec & pres, 1997-. **Orgs:** Delta Sigma Theta Sorority; past pres, Int Asn Serv Evaluators. **Honors/Awds:** Creative Style Award, Atlanta Bus League,

2001. **Special Achievements:** Featured nationally in Black Enterprise Magazine, Who's Who in Black Atlanta, Good Day Atlanta Morning Television Show; Nominated for SBAs Small Business Person of the Year Award; A Customer's Point of View was selected to participate in the Georgia Governor Mentor/Protege program, 2003-04. **Business Addr:** Founder, President, A Customers Point of View Inc, 815 Pavilion Ct, McDonough, GA 30253, **Business Phone:** (770)288-2717.

### ARNEZ, DR. NANCY L.

Teacher, lecturer, school administrator. **Personal:** Born Jul 6, 1928, Baltimore, MD; daughter of Emerson Milton Levi and Ida Barbour Rusk. **Educ:** Morgan State Col, AB, eng, 1949; Columbia Univ, MA, eng, 1954, EdD, educ admin, 1958. **Career:** Teacher, lecturer (retired), school administrator; Baltimore Pub Sch, Eng teacher, 1949-58, dept head, 1958-62; Morgan State Col, dir stud teaching, 1962-66; Harvard Univ, post doctoral, 1962; Loyola Col, post doctoral, 1965; Northeastern Ill Univ, assoc prof & asst dir, Ctr Inner City Studies, 1966-69, prof & dir Ctr Inner City Studies, 1969-74, co-founder, Cult Ling, Follow Through Early Childhood CICS, 1969-74; Howard Univ Sch Educ, assoc dean, 1974, actg dean, 1975, prof, 1976-13, dept chmn, 1980-86, coordr, prof emer, 2013-; Nat Alliance Black Sch Educr, ed, 1981-84; Pub Sch Systs, Black Female Supt, 1982. **Orgs:** Cong African People, 1968-70; Am Asn Sch Admin, 1968-87; Black Child Develop Inst DC, 1971-74; Asn African Historians Chicago, 1972; Asn Study Afro-Am Life & Hist, 1972-77; bd dir, memship secy, African Heritage Studies Asn, 1973-77; Nat Alliance Black Sch Educr; Am Asn Sch Admin Resolutions Community, 1973-75; African Info Ctr Catalyst Chicago, 1973-77; bd dir, DuSable Mus Chicago, 1973-74; Black Women's ComnDevelop Found, DC, 1974; ed bd, J Negro Educ, 1975-80; Phi Delta Kappa Howard Univ Chap; Am Asn Col Teachers Educ, 1977; Nat Coun Negro Women, 1977; prof, ed bd, Am Asn Sch Adminr, 1981-84; ed, NatAlliance Black Sch Educr Newsbrief, 1984-86; DC Alliance Black Sch Educr, 1984-86, pres, 1986-88. **Honors/Awds:** Alpha Kappa Alpha Sor Service Award, 1971; Association African Histroy Service Award, 1972; Distinguished Faculty Research Award, Howard Univ, 1983; Outstanding Res Award, Phi Delta Kappa's biennial, 1985. **Home Addr:** 3122 Cherry Rd NE, Washington, DC 20018-1612, **Home Phone:** (202)529-6198. **Business Addr:** Professor Emeritus, Howard University, 2400 6th St NW, Washington, DC 20059, **Business Phone:** (202)806-6100.

### ARNOLD, ALISON JOY

Lawyer, association executive. **Personal:** Born Apr 26, 1960, Seattle, WA; daughter of James A and Janice M. **Educ:** Brown Univ, BA, biol, 1982; Wesleyan Univ, MA, soc studies, 1988; Univ Pa Law Sch, JD, mkt, 1991. **Career:** Univ Mich, res scientist, 1983-84; Bristolmyers, Squibb, res scientist, 1984-88; Fish & Neave, assoc, 1991-2000, partner, 2000-; King & Spalding LLP, partner & atty; Univ Pa Law Sch, assoc ed; Sheppard Mullin Richter & Hampton LLP, partner & atty; Heller Ehrman LLP, atty, Currently. **Orgs:** Am Bar Asn; Nat Bar Asn; Am Intellectual Property Law Asn; Federal Circuit Bar Asn; Ny Bar, 1992-. **Special Achievements:** Numerous articles published in scientific journals. **Home Addr:** 4141 46th St Apt 4A, Sunnyside, NY 11104, **Home Phone:** (718)786-9381. **Business Addr:** Partner, Fish & Neave, 1251 Avenue of the Americas, New York, NY 10020, **Business Phone:** (212)596-9140.

### ARNOLD, CLARENCE EDWARD, JR.

School administrator, army officer. **Personal:** Born May 18, 1944, Eastville, VA; son of Clarence Edward Sr and Nicey Press; married Kateena Davenport; children: Sherri Mignon & Chelsea N Davenport. **Educ:** Va State Univ, BS, 1970, MEd, 1973; Howard Univ, attended 1979; Univ Va, EdD, 1990. **Career:** Petersburg High Sch, home sch coordr, 1970-71; McGuffy Educ Ctr, teacher, 1971-72; 16th Dist Ct Serv Unit, counr juv & domestic rel, 1973-74; J Sargeant Reynolds Community Col, instr & coordr audio visual serv dept, 1974-80; Va St Univ, teacher educ, TV prodn & photogr, 1977-78; CE Arnold Photog Serv, freelance photogr, 1980-81; Va St Univ, instr & coordr mass communs prog, 1981-88; Danville Conn Col, dir learning resource ctr, 1988-91; Chancellor's fel, Va Conn ClearingSystem, 1990-91; Univ Va, doctoral internship, 1991, fel, 1991-93; Norfolk State Univ, part-time teacher, 1994-. **Orgs:** Vpres, Richmond Br Nat Asn Advan Colored People, 1976-82; bd dir, Va StateConf Nat Asn Advan Colored People, 1976-82; Community Col Asn Instr & Technol, 1976-80; Va Tv Reps Higher Educ, 1976-80; Black AdvisoryCoun, WTVR TV AM & FM, 1979-83; Va Educ Asn; Va State Univ Educ Asn, 1981-88; pres, Richmond Media Soc, 1986-87; Va Community Col Asn, 1988-; Va Lib Asn, 1988; Nat Educ Asn; Kappa Alpha Psi Frat Inc; Asn Educ Communs & Technol; Va Educ Media Asn. **Honors/Awds:** R P Daniel Award & Trophy for Outstanding Mil Leadership & Scholastic Achievement in ROTC, Va State Univ, 1966; Grant NDEA Educ Media Instr for Trainers of Teachers, Va State Univ, 1972-73; Black Arts Award for VisualArts, BOTA, 1981; Chancellor's Fel, Va Conn Clearing System, 1990-91; Univ Va, Fel, 1991-93. **Home Addr:** 500 Emmet St Suite B6, Charlottesville, VA 22903-2506, **Home Phone:** (804)977-3814.

### ARNOLD, CRAIG

Chairperson, executive. **Educ:** Calif State Univ, BS, psychol; Pepperdine Univ, MBA, bus admin & mgt, gen. **Career:** Gen Elec Corp, vpres & pres, 1983-2000; GE Plastics, Structured Prod Europe, managing dir, 1995-97, vpres & pres, Greater China, 1998-99; GE Appliances, Asia vpres & pres, 1997-98; GE Lighting Serv Ltd, vpres & pres, 1999; Eaton Corp, Indust Sector, sr vpres, 2000-08, vice chmn & chief operating officer, 2009-15, chmn & chief exec officer, 2016-; Fluid Power Group, pres. **Orgs:** Dir, mem audit comt, Unocal Corp, 2004-; bd dir, Medtronic Inc, 2015-; dir, Covidien Ltd; bd dir, Univ Hosps Health Systs, Cleveland; adv bd mem, Salvation Army Greater Cleveland; bd dir, Greater Cleveland Partnership; United Way Greater Cleveland. **Honors/Awds:** "Black Enterprise," The 100 Most Powerful Executives in Corporate America, 2010; "Wall Street Journal," Hot Prospects: 12 Coveted Executives, 2011. **Business Addr:** Chairman, Chief Executive Officer, Eaton Corp, Eaton Ctr, Cleveland, OH 44114, **Business Phone:** (216)523-5000.

### ARNOLD, DAVID

Opera singer. **Personal:** Born Atlanta, GA; son of Charles. **Educ:** Ind Univ, BA, 1968, MA, 1970; New Eng Conserv, artist dipl, 1974. **Career:** Performances: Opera Co, Boston; Metrop Opera; Boston Symphony; New York Opera; Eng Nat Opera; Komische Opera Berlin; Am Symphony; San Francisco Opera; Am Composer Orchestra; Atlanta Symphony; Wolf Trap Festival; Baltimore Symphony; Chatauqua Festival; Spoleto Festivals; Nashville Symphony; Tanglewood Festival; Chicago Symphony; Cincinnati May Festival; Concertge bouw; Tulsa Opera; Musica Sacra New York; Boston Baroque; Handel & Haydn Soc, Boston; Am Symphony New York; Metrop Opera, baritone singer; Komische Opera, Berlin, leading baritone; Recordings: "Gurrelieder"; "The Magic World"; "Full Moon in March"; "Walpurgisnacht"; "Beethoven Ninth Symphony"; "Mozart Requiem"; "Haydn's Lord Nelson Mass"; Temple Univ, artist-in-residence, currently. **Honors/Awds:** Metrop Auditions Winner; Sullivan Foundation Music Award; New York Opera Gold Debut Award, 1980; Shoshana Foundation Award. **Special Achievements:** Guest appearances at the White House on the occasion of a state dinner honoring Prime Minister Margaret Thatcher and at musical events for President Clinton. **Home Addr:** 309 Wood St, Burlington, NJ 08016, **Home Phone:** (609)386-3933. **Business Addr:** Artist in Residence, Temple University, 1515 Market St, Philadelphia, PA 19122, **Business Phone:** (215)204-8303.

### ARNOLD, ETHEL N.

Executive. **Personal:** Born Dec 20, 1924, Stillwater, OK; children: Nishua Bell, Renay Thigpen, Booker Jr, Myron & Geino. **Educ:** Langston Univ, ICS Bus Col; Northwestern Col, BBA. **Career:** Cleve Cell & Post, news columnist; Picker Corp, tax specialist, 1968; Harshaw Chem, asst tax mgr, 1970; Diamond Shamrock, accts asst, 1973; Ohio Cell Podiatry Med, dir community rels, 1976-84; Avant-Garde Models Inc, Modeling Sch & Agency, owner; R & E, pres & owner. **Orgs:** Nat pres, Nat Asn Career Womens Civic Club, 1964-88; chmn, Nat Asn Negro Bus Prof Womens Club, Cleveland, 1984-85; Human Res Comn. **Home Addr:** 3571 Gridley Rd, Cleveland, OH 44122. **Business Addr:** President, R & E, 14402 Kinsman Rd, Cleveland, OH 44120.

### ARNOLD, JAHINE AMID

Football player. **Personal:** Born Jun 19, 1973, Rockville, CT. **Educ:** Fresno State Univ. **Career:** Football player, (retired); Pittsburgh Steelers, kick returner, 1996, wide receiver, 1997-98; Green Bay Packers, 1998-99; Memphis Maniax, 2001; Tampa Bay Storm, 2002; Los Angeles Avengers, 2003; Austin Wranglers, 2004. **Home Addr:** 4534 W Beachway Dr, Tampa, WI 33609-4234.

### ARNOLD, DR. JOHN RUSSELL, JR.

Administrator. **Personal:** Born Sep 13, 1954, Detroit, MI; son of John Russell Sr and Christene Ford; married Cheryl Anne Young; children: John R III. **Educ:** Univ Detroit & Mercy, attended 1975; Univ Mich, BA, polit sci, 2000, MA, lib studies & sociol, 2001; Wayne State Univ, PhD, mass commun & media studies, 2007. **Career:** WERD, prog dir, 1974-76; WABX, disc jockey, 1976-78; WCHB Radio-Bell Broadcasting Co, music dir, 1976-87, radio host, 1991-94; WFXY, prog dir, 1987-89, host & exec producer, 1989-97, Martin Lawrence Show, TV Consult, 1992; WCXI/WWWW, dj, staff announcer, 1988-89, disc jockey, 1990-91; Barden Cable, advert sls, 1989-90; WWJ News-Radio-950, Radio Co host, 1993-98; Continental Cable tv, Co-host, 1994-99; Broadcasting Systs Radio Network, host, 1995-2000; WJBK-TV, co-producer, writer & host, 1995-2000; Detroit Bell Broadcasting Syst, nat radio talk show host, 1995-2001, founder; Metro Detroit Broadcasting Corp, John Arnold Show, host, producer, newscaster & vpres affil rels & prog distrib, 1995-2001; WOL-1450 AM & XM Satellite Radio, host, 2000-; Univ Mich, lectr, 2003-06; Wayne State Univ, asst prof, 2003-06, grad teaching asst, 2008-; Howard Univ, asst prof, 2006-08; Lane Col, div chair, 2012-15. **Orgs:** Inkster, MI City Plng Comnr, 1990-94; founder, Black Men Inc, 1992-; founder, Black Women Inc, 1992-; Talk Radio Host Am, 1994-; Talkers, 1995-; Am Asn Talk Show Host; Nat Asn Broadcasters; Blacks Advert, Radio & TV; Mich Asn Teachers; Mich Asn Broadcasters; Ad Crafters; Thursday Luncheon Grp; Booker T. Wash Businessmens Asn; Nat Commun Asn; Mich Acad Arts lett & Sci; Midwest Polit Sci Asn; Southern Polit Sci Asn; Nat Asn Black Journalist. **Business Addr:** Dearborn, MI.

### ARNOLD, DR. LIONEL A.

Dean (education). **Personal:** Born Aug 30, 1921, Greenville, SC; son of J P and Gertrude Dowe. **Educ:** BA, 1943; Anderson Col, BTh, 1944; Oberlin Grad Sch, MA, BD, 1947; Harvard Univ, STM, 1955; Drew Univ, PhD, 1969. **Career:** LeMoyne-Owen Col, Col pastor, 1947-64, dean, 1964-71; OK State Univ, prof humanistic studies & eng, 1971-86, prof emer. **Honors/Awds:** DHL, Thiel Col Greenville, PA, 1964. **Home Addr:** 2132 W University Ave, Stillwater, OK 74074, **Home Phone:** (405)372-0103. **Business Addr:** Professor Emeritus Religious Standards, OK State University, Stillwater, OK 74078.

### ARNOLD, MONICA DENISE (MONICA DENISE BROWN)

Singer. **Personal:** Born Oct 24, 1980, Atlanta, GA; daughter of MC Jr and Marilyn Best; married Rodney R Hill; children: Rodney Ramone Hill III & Romello Montez; married Shannon. **Career:** Rowdy Rec, 1993; Albums: Miss Thang, 1995; The Boy is Mine, 1998; All Eyez on Me, 2002; After the Storm, 2003; The Makings of Me, 2006; Still Standing, 2010; New Life, 2012. Songs: "For You I Will"; "Don't Take It Personal", 1995; "The Boy is Mine", 1998; "Angel of Mine", 1999; "So Gone", 2003; "Knock Knock/Get It Off", 2003; "U Should've Known Better", 2004; "Everytime tha Beat Drop", 2006; "A Dozen Roses", 2006; "Sideline Ho", 2007; "Hell No", 2007; "Trust", 2009; "Everything to Me", 2010; "Love All Over Me", 2010; "Anything", 2011; "Until It's Gone", 2011; "It All Belongs to Me", 2012; "Without You", 2012. Films: Boys and Girls, 2000; ATL, 2006; Pastor Brown, 2009; TV Series: "Living Single", 1996; "Love Song", 2000; "Felicity", 2001; "American Dreams", 2003; "Keyshia Cole: The Way It Is", 2006-08; "The Single: Monica", 2008. **Honors/Awds:** Billboard Music Awards, 1996, 1998; Grammy Award, 1999. **Special Achievements:** Became the youngest recording act to ever have two consecutive chart-topping hits on the U.S. Billboard Top R&B Singles chart; nominated for numerous awards. **Business Addr:** Vocalist, c/o Arista Records, 6 W 57th St 5th Fl, New York, NY 10019.

### ARNOLD, NANCY

Registered nurse. **Educ:** Univ Minn, RN; Cent Mich Univ, RN. **Career:** Fairlane Nursing Ctr, regist nurse, 2003; AAA Mich, coordr; John J Pershing VA Med Ctr, med ctr dir, currently. **Orgs:** Adv comt mem, Foster Care Rev Bd; Franklin Wright Settlement House Mus African Am. **Honors/Awds:** Nursing Award Excellence, 2003; MHA Visionary Leadership Award, 2005. **Business Addr:** Director, John J Pershing VA Medical Center, 1500 N Westwood Blvd, Poplar Bluff, MO 63901-3318, **Business Phone:** (573)686-4151.

### ARNOLD, HON. RUDOLPH P.

Lawyer, banker. **Personal:** Born May 24, 1948, Harlem, NY; married Linda J Kelly; children: Preston & Rebecca. **Educ:** Howard Univ, BA, 1970; Univ Conn, JD, 1975; NY Univ, LLM, 1976. **Career:** Aetna Life & Casualty, 1971-72; Legal Aid Soc Hartford City, atty, 1976-81; Arnold & Hershinson, atty, 1982-84; Bd Pres, Arnold & Assoc, atty, 1985-, vpres, pres, currently; Soc Savings Bancorp Inc, dir & chmn, 1991-93. **Orgs:** Conn Bar Asn; Hartford Bar Asn; Pub Int Lawyer-Law, 1974; pres, nine-mem City Coun; bd dir, Urban League, 1977-79; dep mayor, Hartford City Coun, 1979-83; Nat Bar Asn, 1980-; bd dir, World Affairs Ctr, 1983-88; chmn, Hartford Community TV, 1986-89; bd dir, Soc Savings, 1987-93; Am Bar Asn; lifetime mem, Nat Asn Advan Colored People; dir, Nat Coun Int Visitors, 1989-92; bd dir, Hartford Pub Libr, 1994-; Nat Asn Bond Lawyer; Nat Asn Securities Prof; George Crawford Law Soc; Nat Campaign Human Develop; Hartford World Affairs Coun; bd mem, Farmington Ave Alliance, currently; bd mem, Conn Nat Asn Housing & Redevelopment Off; Community Partners Action & FannieMae Con Partnership Adv Comt. **Home Addr:** 132 Terry Rd, Hartford, CT 06105, **Home Phone:** (203)233-1431. **Business Addr:** Attorney, President, Arnold & Associates, 80 Cedar St, Hartford, CT 06106, **Business Phone:** (860)728-0037.

### ARNOLD, WALLACE C.

Executive, army officer, association executive. **Personal:** Born Jul 27, 1938, Washington, DC; son of George W and Lydia Gibson; married Earlene Costner; children: Sheila & Stephanie. **Educ:** Hampton Inst, BS, indust educ, 1960; George Washington Univ, MA, personnel mgt & admin, 1965; Naval War Col, Newport, RI, 1977; Campbell Univ, Buies Creek, NC, hon doctor law degree, 1990. **Career:** Army officer (retired), executive; AUS, maj gen, 1961-95, Wash, DC, mil asst & exec officer, off under secy army, 1979-81, USA Europe, inspector gen, VII corps Europe, 1981-82, comdr, 69th air defense artil brigade, 1982-84, dir/officer personnel & admin Europe, 1984-87, Ft Bragg, NC, comndg gen, 1st ROTC reg, 1987-90, Ft Monroe, Va, comndg gen, ROTC cadet command, 1990-93, Wash, DC, asst dep chief staff Personnel, maj gen, 1995; Info Technol Solutions Inc, exec vpres & chief Admin off, 1995; Comput Sci Corp, Hampton, Va, regional dir bus develop; Hampton Rotary Club, pres; Hampton Univ Tech Data Mgt Lab, dir, Currently; Cheyney Univ Penn, interim pres, 2004-07, dir, currently. **Orgs:** Chmn, Boy Scout Dist, Boy Scouts Am Coun, Raleigh, NC, 1987-90; deacon, Second Baptist Church, Falls Church, Va, 1977-81; chmn, budget comm, Second Baptist Church, Falls Church, Va, 1977-81; pres, Northern VA Chap, Nat Hampton Univ Alumni Asn, 1979-81; chmn, Europ Sch Coun, DOD Dependent Sch Syst, 1984-87; past pres, Hampton Rotary Club; Commonwealth Va Comn Vet Affairs; Base Closure Task Force; Ft Monroe Credit Union; bd dir, Piney Woods Sch; deacon, First Baptist Church; bd dir, Massanutten Mil Acad; bd dir, Achievable Dream Sch Inc; Indust Develop Authority; City Hampton Fed Area Develop Authority; City Hampton Fed Area Develop Authority; bd dir, Greater Hampton Roads Boys' & Girls' Clubs; Hampton (City) Strategic Planning Oversight Comt; Gov's Pa Mil Opers Comt; Va Comn Veterans' Affairs; Base Closure Task Force. **Honors/Awds:** Hampton Univ Outstanding Alumni Award, 1985; Roy Wilkins Meritorious Serv Award, Nat Asn Advan Colored People Inc, 1990; Douglas MacArthur Distinguished Serv Award, Asn US Army; Paul Harris Fel, Rotary Intl; Distinguished Alumni Award, Hampton Univ. **Home Addr:** 10100 Fairfax Dr, Ft. Belvoir, VA 22060, **Home Phone:** (703)799-3178. **Business Addr:** Interim President, Cheyney University of Pennsylvania, 1837 Univ Cir, Cheyney, PA 19319-0200, **Business Phone:** (610)399-2275.

### ARNWINE, BARBARA R.

Activist, lawyer, executive director. **Personal:** Born Jan 1, 1951, Claremont, CA; daughter of Vera Pearl Carter; children: Justin Daniel Almiri. **Educ:** Scripps Col, BA, 1973; Duke Univ Sch Law, grad, JD, 1976. **Career:** Durham Legal Assistance Prog, Reginald Huber Smith fel, 1976-79; NC Legal Serv, dir, 1979-83; Boston Lawyers Comm Civil Rights, exec dir, 1983-89, 1989-; Nat Off Lawyers Comm Civil Rights Under the Law, exec dir, 1989-; Network Black Women Justice, founder, currently; Transformative Justice Coalition, exec dir, 2015-. **Orgs:** Bd mem, New Perimeter; exec dir, pres, Lawyers Comt Civil Rights Under Law, 1989-; exec comt, leader, Nonpartisan Election Protection Coalition, 2004; Rockwood Inst Leadership Fel, 2008; Nat Bar Asn; Environ Defense Fund, Nat Asn Advan Colored People; Black Women's Roundtable. **Home Addr:** , MD. **Business Addr:** Executive Director, President, Lawyer, 1401 New York Ave NW Suite 400, Washington, DC 20005, **Business Phone:** (202)662-8600.

### ARRINGTON, DR. HAROLD MITCHELL

Physician. **Personal:** Born Apr 9, 1947, Detroit, MI; son of Robyn and Irene. **Educ:** Adrian Col, BS, 1968; Univ Mich Med Sch, MD, 1972; Am Bd Obstetrics & Gynec, dipl, 1978. **Career:** Wayne State Univ Hosp, resident obstet & gynec, 1972-76; pvt pract obstet & gynec, Mich, 1976-; Planned Parenthood League Inc, med dir, 1976-93; Detroit Bd Educ, med dir, 1978-93; Mich, state surgeon, 1998-; Sinai Grace Hosp, Northwest Women's Care, currently. **Orgs:** Fel Am Col Obstet & Gynec, 1980; Iota Boule Sigma Pi Phi, 1988-; Nat Asn Advan Colored People; LPN adv comt, AMA; Nat Med Asn; Nat Guard Asn US; fel Int Col Surgeons; Wayne Co Med Asn. **Special Achievements:** Commercial instrument pilot's license, 1979. **Home Addr:** 3800 Woodward Ave Suite 502, Detroit, MI 48201-2065, **Home Phone:** (313)831-1060. **Business Addr:** Physician, St John Hospital & Medical Center, 7815 E Jefferson Ave, Detroit, MI 48214, **Business Phone:** (313)499-4170.

## ARRINGTON, LLOYD M., JR.

Executive, manager. **Personal:** Born Dec 12, 1947, Montgomery, AL; son of Lloyd Madison Sr and Annie M; children: Briana & Bianca. **Educ:** Fisk Univ, BA, 1970; Stanford Univ, MBA, 1973. **Career:** Fisk Univ, T J Watson fel, 1970-71; Stanford Univ, C E Merrill fel, 1972-73, COGME fel, 1971-73; Bankers Tr NY Corp, asst treas, 1973-77; Asn Integration Mgt, proj dir, 1974-75; Pfizer Inc, mgr strategic planning, 1978-79; US Small Bus Admin, asst adv, 1979-81; US Dept Comt MBDA, chief capital develop, 1981-82; Inst Am Bus, vpres, 1983-84; Ferguson Group, sr consult, 1985-88; Entrepreneurial Appl Inc, exec vpres, 1985-; Arrington & Co, pres; Columbia Capital Group, pres. **Orgs:** Chmn, MD Small Bus Develop Finance Authority, 1986-93; investment assoc, Econ Develop Finance Corp, 1988-90, vpres, 1990-92; pres, 1992-; pres, Econ Develop Corp, 1990; Nat Black MBA Asn; Omega Psi Phi; WA Soc Investment Analyst. **Home Addr:** 1602 Pebble Beach Dr, Bowie, MD 20721, **Home Phone:** (301)336-6063. **Business Addr:** President, Economic Development Finance Corp, 1660 L St NW Suite 308, Washington, DC 20036, **Business Phone:** (202)775-8815.

## ARRINGTON, JUDGE MARVIN S., SR.

Executive, lawyer, judge. **Personal:** Born Feb 10, 1941, Atlanta, GA; son of George Robert and Maggie Andrews; married Jones; children: 2. **Educ:** Clark Atlanta Univ, BA, sociol, 1963; Emory Univ Sch Law, JD, 1967. **Career:** Judge (retired); Atlanta Bd Aldermen, mem, 1969-73; Atlanta City Coun, pres, 1980-96; Ga Sen Leroy Johnson, staff; Arrington & Hollowell law firm, sr partner; Fulton County Super Ct, judge, 2002-12. Book: Making My Mark: The Story of a Man Who Wouldn't Stay in His Place, 2008. **Orgs:** Nat Bar Asn; Am Bar Asn; State Bar Ga; Lawyers Club; Gate City Bar Asn Hall Fame; Kiwanis Int; pres, Atlanta City Coun; Big Bethel African Methodist Episcopalian Church; Soc Int Bus Fels; Am Trial Lawyers Asn; Ga Asn Criminal Defense Lawyers; Kappa Alpha Psi; bd trustee, Clark Atlanta Univ; bd trustee, Emory Univ Law Sch, currently. **Business Addr:** Board of Trustee, Emory University School of Law, Gambrell Hall 1301 Clifton Rd, Atlanta, GA 30322-2770, **Business Phone:** (404)727-6802.

## ARRINGTON, DR. PAMELA GRAY

Vice president (organization), college teacher. **Personal:** Born Feb 28, 1953, Montgomery, AL; daughter of Willis E Gray and Martha (Davenport) Gray; married Richard III; children: Gray, Julian & Justin. **Educ:** Spelman Col, BA, psychol, 1974; Univ Mich, MA, 1975; George Mason Univ, DA, 1987, PhD, 1995. **Career:** Talladega Col, counr, 1976-77; Northern VA Community Col, counr, 1977-80, co-ordr affirmative action & grants devel, 1980-88; Bowie State Univ, Human Resource Devel, prof, 1988-; Coppin State Univ, assoc vpres Planning & Accreditation, 2004-, dir Off Planning & Accreditation, chief of staff, 2005; Troy Univ, assoc dean, prof develop & res prof, 2009-. **Orgs:** Asn Talent Develop; HRD Profs Network, Wash Metro Area; Am Asn Univ Prof; dir, Nat Retention Proj, Am Asn State Cols & Univs, 1993-; Alpha Kappa Alpha Sorority; HBCU Summit Steering Comt, 2006; Nat Col Athletic Asn; Bd dir, Am Conf Acad Deans. **Home Addr:** 5720 Avondale Dr, Bowie, MD 20715-4382. **Business Addr:** Board of Directors, American Conference of Academic Deans, 1818 R St NW, Washington, DC 20009, **Business Phone:** (202)884-7419.

## ARRINGTON, RICHARD, JR.

Educator, government official. **Personal:** Born Oct 19, 1934, Livingston, AL; son of Richard Sr and Ernestine; married Rachel; children: Anthony, Kenneth, Kevin, Angela & Erika Lynn. **Educ:** Miles Col, BA, 1955; Univ Detroit, MS, biol, 1957; Univ Okla, PhD, 1966, PhD, zool, biochem; Harvard Univ, Postdoctoral Work, Higher Educ Admin; Univ Mich, Postdoctoral Work, Higher Educ Admin. **Career:** Miles Col, prof, 1957-63, counr men, 1962-63, dir summer sch & actg dean, 1966-67, dean Colacad, 1967-70; Univ Okla, spec instr, 1965-66, prof, 1966-; Univ Ala, assoc prof part-time, 1971-72, chair, Natural Scis Dept; Ala Ctr Higher Educ, dir, 1970-79, Ctr Urban Affairs, Ctr Urban Affairs, vis prof pub serv, currently; City Birmingham, AL, councilman, mayor, 1979-99; Univ Detroit, grad asst. **Orgs:** Birmingham City Coun, 1971-79; Am Inst Biol Sci; Okla Acad Sci; AAAS; Am Soc Zoologists; Phi Sigma Nat Biol Soc; Soc Sigma Xi; Am Asn Col Deans; adv bd, Family Coun Asn Jefferson County; Alpha Phi Alpha; bd trustee, Univ Ala; officer, Thespian Club. **Honors/Awds:** Ortenburger Award for Outstanding Work in Biology, Univ Okla, 1966; Man of the Year, Alpha Phi Alpha, 1969; Achievement Award for Outstanding Community Service, Alpha Phi Alpha, 1971; Man of the Year Award, Ala Fedn Civic Leagues, 1971; Community Civic Service Award, Druid Hill-Norwood Civic League, 1972; Charles A Billups Community Service Award, 1972; Community Achievement Award, 1972; Distinguished Alumni Award, Miles Col Alumni Asn, 1972; Freedom Achievement Award, Emancipation Asn, 1973; Public Service Award, Birmingham Chap Delta Sigma Theta, 1974; Outstanding Educator Award, Friends Miles Col, 1973; Presidential Commendation Award, Miles Col Alumni Asn, 1974; Distinguished Community Service Award, Birmingham Oppor Indust, 1974; One of the 100 Most Influential Black Americans, Ebony Mag, 1980-2000; Alabama Administrator of the Year, Alabama Society of Public Administrators, 1982; number-one leader in Birmingham by polls of corporate and civic leaders, The Birmingham News and The Birmingham Post-Herald, 1984, 1990; one of the top 20 city officials in the nation, U.S. News & World Report; one of the Nation Best Mayors, U.S. News & World Report, 1987; Most Distinguished Mayor, National Urban Coalition, 1988; lpha Phi Alpha Fraternity's Thurgood Marshall Award; National Alliance Against Racist and Political Repression's Human Rights Award, 1991. **Special Achievements:** First African American to be elected as mayor of Birmingham, Alabama. **Home Addr:** 1245 Mims St SW, Birmingham, AL 35211. **Business Addr:** Visiting Professor, University of Alabama, 1715 9th Ave S, Birmingham, AL 35294-1270, **Business Phone:** (205)934-3500.

## ARRINGTON, WARREN H., JR.

President (organization). **Personal:** Born Jul 10, 1948, Raleigh, NC; son of Warren H and Lois B; married Annie Hilliard; children: Janssen, Jamaine & Jarrodd. **Educ:** Livingstone Col, BS, math, 1970; Hardbarger Bus Col, acct & bus, 1979; NC State Univ, sociol. **Career:** Arrington Warren H Jr Enterprises Inc, pres, 1985-; Am Safety Prod, owner. **Orgs:** Dir, Touch-A-Teen Found Wake Co, 1985-; Piedmont Minority Supplier Develop Coun, 1990-91; exec bd, Minority Bus Enterprises Input Comt, 1991-; vpres, Livingstone Col Alumni Asn; bd dir, Greater Raleigh Chamber Com, 1993-96; state dir, Touch-A-Teen Found NC, 1993-; vpres, small bus bd, 1994-; adv bd, MCI small bus ctr, 1994-; bd trustee, Livingston Col & Hood Theol Sem. **Home Addr:** 4929 Bartwood Dr, Raleigh, NC 27613-7002, **Home Phone:** (919)848-1346. **Business Addr:** President, Warren H Arrington Jr Enterprises Inc, 3200 Glen Royal Rd Suite 105, Raleigh, NC 27617-7419, **Business Phone:** (919)571-7822.

## ARRINGTON-JONES, LORRAINE

Executive, association executive. **Personal:** married Robert Cannon Sr. **Career:** People Econ Reform, chief exec officer. **Business Addr:** Chief Executing Officer, People For Economic Reform, 1350 Moore St, Toledo, OH 43608, **Business Phone:** (419)727-4245.

## ARROYO, PROF. MARTINA

Opera singer, educator, association executive. **Personal:** Born Feb 2, 1937, New York, NY; daughter of Demetrio and Lucille Washington; married Michel Maurel; married Emilio Poggioni. **Educ:** City Univ NY, Hunter Col, BA, romance lang, 1954. **Career:** Singer (retired), educator; Opera: Aida; Madame Butterfly; Un Ballo Maschera; Cavalleria Rusticana; La Forza del Destino; Macbeth; Don Giovanni; La Gioconda; Trovatore; Andrea Chenier; Metrop Opera; Vienna State Opera; Paris Opera; Covent Garden, London; Teatro Colon, Buenos Aires; Hamburg Staatsoper; La Scala, Milan; Munich Staatsoper; Berlin Deutsche Opera; Rome Opera; San Francisco, Chicago & all maj opera houses; soloist New York, Vienna, Berlin, Royal & London, Paris Philharmonics, San Francisco, Pittsburgh, Philadelphia, Chicago, Cleveland Symphonies; Ind Univ, Bloomington, prof emer. **Orgs:** Trustee, Nat Endowment Arts; trustee, Carnegie Hall; trustee emerita, Hunter Col Found, currently; fel Am Acad Arts & Sci; pres, Martina Arroyo Found Inc; bd dir, Metrop Opera Guild; Ambassador Arts, WA; bd dir, Col Chorale; bd overseas mem, Harvard Col Cambridge. **Honors/Awds:** Received numerous awards including: Outstanding Alumna; Dr Honoris Cause of Human Letters, Hunter Col; The President Award, Lehman Col City Univ New York; Distinguished Professor, Indiana Univ; Distinguished Achievement, Opera Index New York; Verdi Medal, Amici di Verdi London, NEA Lifetime Achievement for Opera. **Special Achievements:** First soprano in thirty years to sing three opening nights for the Met, 1970, 1971, 1973; co-authored the Task Force report of music education in the United States, published by the NEA, Washington, DC, has made more than 50 recordings for EMI, Decca, Philips etc; first black person to portray, 1968. **Home Addr:** , NY. **Business Addr:** President, Martina Arroyo Foundation Inc, 57 W 57th St 4th Fl, New York, NY 10101-2015, **Business Phone:** (212)315-9190.

## ARTERBERY, DR. V. ELAYNE

Educator, oncologist. **Educ:** Stanford Univ, Palo Alto, CA, BS, biol; Univ Mich, MD, med, MHSA, health mgt & policy, 2008; Harvard Univ. **Career:** Mem Sloan Kettering Cancer Ctr, resident radiation oncol, 1989-94; Johns Hopkins Sch Med, Dept Radiation Oncol, Baltimore, instr, 1993-95; Crittendon Hosp, Karmanos Cancer Inst, assoc prof radiation Oncol & interim assoc chair radiation oncol, clin chief, currently; Swed Tumor Inst, vis prof; Gershenson Radiation Oncol Ctr, dir prostate brachy ther, currently; Wayne State Univ, Detroit Med Ctr, dir, 1997-2004, radiation oncologist, 1999-2007, vice chmn, dept radiation Oncol, 2000-01, specialist chief, dept radiation Oncol, 2013-; Northwest Prostate Tumor Inst, lectr. **Orgs:** Detroit Symphony Orchestra; pres, Univ Mich Med Ctr Alumni Soc; Am Brachy ther Soc; Harvard-Westlake Alumni; Johns Hopkins Med Insts Alumni Network; Stanford Univ Alumni. **Home Addr:** 134 Arden Pk Blvd, Detroit, MI 48202-1366, **Home Phone:** (313)974-7641. **Business Addr:** Director & Professor, Interim Associate Chairman, Crittendon Hospital, 1101 W Univ Dr, Rochester, MI 48307, **Business Phone:** (248)650-4580.

## ARTERBERY, VIVIAN J.

Executive. **Educ:** Howard Univ, BA, 1958; Univ Southern Calif, MLS, 1965. **Career:** Space Tech Labs; Aerospace Corp, Calif, 1960-79; RAND Corp, Santa Monica, libr dir, 1979-86, corp secy, 1988-; US Nat Comn Libr & Info Sci, exec dir, 1986-88. **Orgs:** Consult, US Off Educ, 1974-76; pres, Spec Libr Asn, 1984-85; SLA rep, Am Libr Asn US Dept Educ Accreditation Proj, 1985-86; fel Spec Libr Asn, 1988; adv bd mem, Calif Libr Asn Counr Univ Southern Calif Libr Sch; bd dir, Santa Monica YMCA; treas, Nat Conf Christians Jews, Santa Monica Chap; bd dir, Santa Monica YWCA; bd dir, Santa Monica Col Found, 1995-99; adv bd, Salvation Army, 1996-98; Links Inc; Alpha Kappa Alpha. **Business Addr:** Corporate Secretary, Rand Corp, 1776 Main St, Santa Monica, CA 90401-3208, **Business Phone:** (310)393-0411.

## ARTEST, RONALD WILLIAM, JR. (METTA WORLD PEACE)

Basketball player. **Personal:** Born Nov 13, 1979, Queensbridge, NY; son of Ron Sr and Sarah; married Kimsha; children: Sadie, Ron III & Diamond. **Educ:** St John's Univ, math, 1999. **Career:** Chicago Bulls, 1999-2002; Ind Pacers, defense, 2002-06; Sacramento Kings, guard, 2006-08; Houston Rockets, 2008-09, Los Angeles Lakers, guard, 2009-13; Artest Media Group, chief exec officer & mgr, 2010-; New York Knicks, 2013-14; Sichuan Blue Whales, 2014;Pallacanestro Cantu, currently; Los Angeles Lakers; currently; Film Actor: Mr Immortality: Life & Times Twista, 2011; All Wifed Out, 2012; Think Like a Man, 2012; Grind, 2014. **Orgs:** Xcel Univ, founder, 2007-; Artest Found, consult, 2012-. **Business Addr:** Basketball Player, Los Angeles Lakers, 555 N Nash St, El Segundo, CA 90245, **Business Phone:** (310)426-6000.

## ARTHUR, GEORGE KENNETH

Administrator. **Personal:** Born Jun 29, 1934, Buffalo, NY; son of William E and Jayne M Potter; married Frances Bivens; children: George K Jr, Janice M & Hugh. **Educ:** Empire State Col, polit sci, 1977. **Career:** Government official (retired); Erie Cty Bd Suprvs, supvr, 1964-67; City Buffalo, councilman, 1970-77; city Buffalo, councilman large, 1978-84, common coun, 1984; city coun, pres, 1984-96. **Orgs:** Bd dir, Better Bus Bureau, Buffalo Philharmonic Orch, Kleinhans Music Hall, Nat Asn Advan Colored People Life Mem; Jr Warden St John Lodge 16; First Shiloh Baptist Church. **Honors/Awds:** Man of the Year, The Buffalo Club, 1970; Man of the Year, Afro Police, 1973; Medgar Evers Award, NAACP, 1984; Jackie Robinson Award, YMCA, 1985; Red Jacket Award, Erie County Hist Soc, 2007. **Home Addr:** 154 Roebling Ave, Buffalo, NY 14215-3308, **Home Phone:** (716)896-6188.

## ARTIES, LUCY ELVIRA YVONNE

Educator. **Personal:** Born Pittsburgh, PA; daughter of William Walter Eugene Jr and Catherine Lillian Holland (deceased). **Educ:** Oakwood Col, Huntsville, AL, 1958; Univ DC, BA, 1972, attended 1989; Howard Univ, Wash, DC, attended 1974; George Washington Univ, attended 1984. **Career:** Dept Navy, pres spec, 1964-69; Fed City Col, Wash DC, staff asst, 1969-72; Dept Housing & Urban Develop, Wash DC, educ specialist, 1973-74; Wash DC Pub Sch, educr, 1974-; Kinder-Care Learning Ctr, Bowie, Md, teaching, 1991-92. **Orgs:** Oakland Col Alumni Assoc, 1958-; Univ DC Alumni Assoc, 1981-; Wash DC Chamber Com, 1985; DC/DECA DC Pub Sch, 1985; secy, Wash Metrop Area, 1991-; chaplain, Botsmota Club, 1992-. **Home Addr:** Doreen 5950 14th St NW, Washington, DC 20011, **Home Phone:** (202)723-7991. **Business Addr:** Teacher, Our Lady of Lourdes Catholic School, 7500 Pearl St, Bethesda, MD 20814, **Business Phone:** (301)654-5376.

## ARTIES, WALTER EUGENE, III

Television producer, administrator. **Personal:** Born Nov 12, 1941, Pittsburgh, PA; married Beverly Ruth Deshay. **Educ:** Faith Col, Birmingham, LHD, 1977. **Career:** Walter Arties Chorale La, dir & arranger, 1961-71; Little Richard Gospel Singer Penniman, arranger, 1961-63; Webber Button Co, off head, 1961-71; Billy Graham Crusades Asn Minneapolis, guest tenor soloist; KHOF-TV & FM Radio, comm serv dir, 1971-74; Breath Life Telecast, prod coordr & founder, 1974, evangelism & field serv dir, 2001; Oakwood Col, media exec; Voice Prophecy, mgr & treas; Adventist Media Ctr, Simi Valley, Calif, human resources dir, 1975-; Ariz Conf Corp African-Am Ministries, asst to pres & dir, 2011-. **Orgs:** Baseball partic La, Dept Rec Univ, SDC Chap, LA, 1966-67; bd trustee, Seventh Day Adventist Radio & TV Film Ctr, Thousand Oaks, CA, 1974-; exec mem, N Am Adv Comm, Wash, DC; SDA Radio Film Ctr, Thousand Oaks, CA, 1974-; bd dir, RV Opers, Thousand Oaks, CA, 1974-; singing partic, World Evangilization Lusanne Switz, 1974. **Honors/Awds:** Outstanding Music Accomplishment Award, Grant Theol Sem Birmingham, 1977; Musical Contributions Singing Award, Port Albernia, BC, Canada, 1977; Outstanding Production Coordination Award, Breath Life Comm, Wash, DC, 1980; Religion in Media Award. **Special Achievements:** Album: "Peace", "I'm Gonna Sing", "Softly and Tenderly", "Almost Over", "Gentle Exhortations", "Sincerely Yours", "Spirituals Collection" & "Hymns Collection". **Home Addr:** 270 Thompson Ave, Chatsworth, CA 91311-7023. **Business Addr:** Assistant to President, Director, Arizona Conference African-American Ministries, PO Box 12340, Scottsdale, AZ 85267-2340, **Business Phone:** (480)991-6777.

## ARTIS, ANTHONY J.

Musician, musical instrument maker. **Personal:** Born Jan 11, 1951, Kokomo, IN; son of Myrle E and Yvonne S; married Iris Rosa; children: Andre Antonio & Claudia Lizet. **Educ:** Miami Univ, Oxford, OH, Sch Archit & Design, bachelor, environ design, 1975; Ind Univ, Bloomington, IN, folklore & ethnomusicology, 2007. **Career:** Apprentice architect, 1974-79; founder, Artis Envirionments, environ design & preserv, 1979-99; founder, Coal Bin Productions, 1987-; Arts Learning Ind, teaching artist, 1994-; Teaching Artist w/Art Mix Ind, 1997-2001, master artist, 2001-; founder, Amoah's African Drum Works, 2000-. **Orgs:** Youth adv coun Ctr Leadership Devel, 1979-89; speaker & mem, Exhib Comt Minorities Eng, 1979-82; Meridian Kessler Neighborhood Asn, 1981-82, 2012-13; Nat Trust Hist Preserv, 1983-; vol staff, Indianapolis City Ctr, 1983-84; Indianapolis Chamber Com, 1984-88; bd dir, Neighborhood Housing Serv Indianapolis, 1985-87; bd devel corp, Meridian-Kessler Neighborhood Asn, 1996-97. **Special Achievements:** Indianapolis Arts Council Creative Renewal Arts Fellow, 1999 & 2007; Indiana Arts Commission Individual Artist Grant, 2001. **Business Addr:** Owner/Operator, Coal Bin Productions, Indianapolis, IN 46205.

## ARTIS, JENNIFER

Executive director, president (organization), chief executive officer. **Career:** Southland Health Careers, bd dirs, pres, 2006-; St James Hosp & Health Ctrs, dir pub affairs, currently; Star columnist, currently; Southland Health Care Forum, founder, chief exec officer, currently. **Orgs:** Community health develop & advocacy, 1982; Family Health Socs; 1996; founder, Crossroads Coalition, 1997; LeClaire Courts Housing Develop, 1998; Sr Provider Network, 2006; dir, Community Serv, Pub Affairs Franciscan St. James Hosp; mayors & managers, S Suburban; Southland Chamber Com. **Business Addr:** Founder, Chief Executive Officer, Southland Health Care Forum, 30 E 15th St Suite 405, Chicago Heights, IL 60411, **Business Phone:** (708)756-1000.

## ARTISON, RICHARD E.

Law enforcement officer, educator, government official. **Personal:** Born Jun 9, 1933, Omaha, NE; married Charleszine; children: Lisa (Von), Richard Jr & Kelli. **Educ:** Drake Univ, BA, sociol & psychol, 1954; Univ NE Law Sch, attended 1955; Cornell Univ, Ed, pub mgt, 1974. **Career:** AUS Counter Intelligence, spec agt, 1955-58; Omaha NE Police Dept, police officer, 1958-62; US Treas Secret Serv, spec agt, 1963-67; Milwaukee Off Secret Serv, spec agt in-charge, 1974-83; Milwaukee Co, sheriff, 1983-95; Penn St Univ, Dept Justice, trainer, currently. **Orgs:** Exec bd mem, Milwaukee City Boy Scouts; bd dir, Boys & Girls Clubs Greater Milwaukee; past pres, Fed Officials Asn; vpres, Milwaukee Frontiers Int; Milwaukee City Metro Police Chiefs; charter mem, Fed Criminal Invest Asn. **Honors/Awds:** Exemplary Achievement Kappa Alpha Psi; High Quality Award, US Treas Dept; Law Enforcement Exec of the Year Award, Wisc Atty Gen, 1992; First African American Sheriff for Milwaukee Country. **Business Addr:** Trainer, University of Pennsylvania, 211 Oswald Tower, Philadelphia, PA 16802-6207, **Business Phone:** (215)898-5000.

**ARTISST, ROBERT IRVING, SR.**
Teacher. **Personal:** Born Jul 13, 1932, Washington, DC; children: Tawnya Alicia, Robert Irving II & Kevin Frederick. **Educ:** Howard Univ, BA, 1959, MA, 1969; Univ DC, MA, 1971; Fed City Col, MA, 1977; George Washington Univ, PhD, 1994. **Career:** Appalacian Reg Comm, pub info & visual specialist, 1966-71; Urban Inst, dir pub, 1972-71; Nat Asn Black Mfg Inc, exec liaison officer, 1972-73; Coop Exten Serv WTI, pub info & comm coord, 1973-76; Univ Wash DC, assoc prof media; Mary Mt Univ, assoc prof, currently. **Orgs:** Comm Adv, Neighborhood Comn, 1975-85; vice chmn, Neighborhood PlanningCoun, 1976-79; pres, Brookland Civic Asso Inc, 1977-84; vpres, DC Citizens Better Pub Ed, 1977-84; comm, Dept C Human Rights Comn, 1978-84; chm bd, DC Capitol Head Start, 1983-85; comnr, Dem Clinton Deleg, 1988-. **Honors/Awds:** Special Accomadation, Mayor of the City for Services, 1976-77, speccitation, 1978-79; Special Award, Youth Operation Rescue, 1982-84; President Special Award for Citizen Service, 1993; Special Award by PhiDelta Kappa. **Special Achievements:** Ed & Writer, Handbook for Teachers of Adult, 1971-72. **Home Addr:** 1353 Otis St NE, Washington, DC 20017, **Home Phone:** (202)529-7953. **Business Addr:** Associate Professor, Marymount University, 2807 N Glebe Rd, Arlington, VA 22207, **Business Phone:** (703)522-5600.

**ARTOPE, WILLIAM**
Executive, advertising executive. **Personal:** Born Apr 2, 1950, New York, NY; son of James and Warnetta Mays; married Linda Young; children: Westley, Tamara, George M & William. **Educ:** NY Univ Film Sch, attended 1972; NY Inst Technol, attended 1974. **Career:** Columbia Prep Sch, teacher, 1965-69; J Walter Thompson, producer, 1970-79; W B Donner & Co, Head Broadcast Prod, 1980-81; DDB Chicago, exec producer & vpres, 1981; Wild-Eyed Entertainment, exec producer & owner, 2004-. **Orgs:** Chap chief, Nichiren Shoshu Soka Gakkai Am. **Home Addr:** 2222 S Figueroa St Ph 30, Los Angeles, CA 90007-6605, **Home Phone:** (213)741-2303. **Business Addr:** Executive Producer, Wild Eyed Entertainment, 3929 Flower St, Los Angeles, CA 90037-1310, **Business Phone:** (213)741-9301.

**ASANTE, DR. MOLEFI KETE**
Educator. **Personal:** Born Aug 14, 1942, Valdosta, GA; son of Arthur L Smith Sr and Lillie B Wilkson; married Ana Yenenga; children: Eka, Molefi K Jr & Mario. **Educ:** S Western Christian Col, AA, 1962; Okla Christian Col, BA, 1964; Pepperdine Univ, MA, 1965; Univ Calif, Los Angles, PhD, commun, 1968; L'Universite Catholique de lOuest, CIDEF, Angers, 2002. **Career:** Inst Study Intercultural Commun, dir; Calif State Poly tech Col, instr, 1967; Calif State Univ, Northridge, instr, 1968; Purdue Univ, Dept Commun, asst prof, 1968-69; Pepperdine Univ, vis prof, 1969; Univ Calif, Los Angeles, asst prof, 1968-69, Ctr Afro-Am Studies, dir, 1970-73, assoc prof speech, 1969-73; Fla State Univ Tallahassee, vis assoc prof, 1972; State Univ NY, Buffalo, Commun Dept, prof & chair, 1973-82; State Univ NY, Buffalo, Dept Black Studies, prof & chair, 1977-79; Ctr Positive Thought Buffalo, cur; Univ Ibadan, Univ Nairobi, external examr, 1976-80; Howard Univ, vis prof, 1979-80, 1995; Zimbabwe Inst Mass Commu, Fulbright prof, 1981-82; Temple Univ, African Am Studies Sect, prof & chmn, 1984-96; Zhejiang Univ, vis prof, Hangzhou, China, 2007-; Molefi Kete Asante Inst Afrocentric Studies, founder; Afrocentricity Int, co-founder. **Orgs:** Initial mem, Asn Study Class African Civilizations; Spec Black Nat Commun Asn, 1969-; Rhet County Probation Dept, La, 1969-; vpres, African Heritage Studies Asn, 1970-; charter mem, World Univ, 1973-82; bd eds, Black Man Am; adv bd, Black J; Int Soc Gen Semantics; Int Asn Symbolic Anal; Am Educ Res Asn, 1973-77; pres, Soc Inter cult Educ, Training & Res, 1975-76; bd mem, Proj Daytime Tv, 1975-79, pres & vpres, Int Commun Asn, 1978-80; Western Speech Asn; Cent State Speech Asn; S Speech Asn; Nat Asn Dramatic & Speech Arts; Mod Lang Asn, 1981; African Studies Asn, 1984-; Am Acad Polit & Social Sci, 1979-84; Int Sci Comn FESPAC, 1986-87; chairperson, IMHOTEP, 1987-; vice chair & pres, Nat Coun Black Studies, bd mem, 1988-90 & 2003-08; Am Studies Asn, 1988; founder & pres, Nat Afrocentric Inst, 1989-; vice chair, Institut des Peuples Noirs, Comn II, Ouagadougou Burkina Faso, 1990; pres, Asn Nubian Kemetic Heritage, 1995-2008; pres & chairperson, African Writers Endowment Found, 2000-; African Comt African Intellectuals, 2003-04; Coord Coun Intellectuals Africa Diaspora, 2009-. **Honors/Awds:** Christian Ed Guild Writer's Awards, 1965; LHD Univ New Haven, 1976; Outstanding Community Scholar, Jackson State Univ, 1980; Ehninger Award for Outstanding Rhetorical Scholar, NCA, 2003. **Special Achievements:** Author: "The Afrocentric Idea", 1987; "Afrocentricity", 1987; "Kemet, Afrocentricity and Knowledge", 1990; "Historical & Cultural Atlas African-Ams", 1991; "African Am Hist: A Journey of Liberation, 1995; Love Dance", 1996; "African Intellectual Heritage", 1996; "African American Names", 1998; "Egyptian Philosophers", 2002; "Egypt v Greece in the American Academy", 2003; "Erasing Racism", 2003; "Encyclopedia of Black Studies", 2005; "Handbook of Black Studies", 2006; "Race, Rhetoric and Identity", 2006; "The History of Africa", 2007; "Encyclopedia of African Religion", 2008; "Maulana Karenga: An Intellectual Portrait", 2009. Published 81 books as of 2016. **Home Addr:** 1600 Arch St Suite 613, Philadelphia, PA 19103, **Home Phone:** (215)782-3214. **Business Addr:** Professor, Chair, Temple University, 1115 W Berks Mall 615A Gladfelter Hall, Philadelphia, PA 19122, **Business Phone:** (215)204-4322.

**ASBURY, WILLIAM W.**
Football player, college president, school administrator. **Personal:** Born Feb 22, 1943, Crawfordville, GA; son of William J and Ida B McLendon; married Leslee Diane Swift; children: Keleigh, Kristin & Kimberly. **Educ:** Kent State Univ, Kent, OH, BS, 1966, MA, sociol, 1973. **Career:** President emeritus (retired); NFL Pittsburgh Steelers, 1966-69; Sanford Rose Assoc, Akron, Ohio, sr consult, 1969-70; City Akron, Ohio, contract compliance off, 1970-74; Kent State Univ, Kent, Ohio, dir human resources, 1974-76; Penn State Univ, Univ Pk, Pa, affirmative action off, 1976-83, exec asst pres, 1983-87, asst to provost, vpres stud affairs, 1987-2003, emer vpres stud affairs, 2003. **Orgs:** Pres, 1991-92, exec coun secy, NASULGC Stud Affairs Coun; Am Asn Higher Educ; Nat Asn Stud Personnel Adminr; pres, Penn Black Conf Higher Educ; Forum Black Affairs, Penn State Univ; hon mem, Nat Residence Hall Hon; Quarterback Club; hon chmn, Penn State 4-H Ambassador Prog; life mem, Kent State Univ Alumni Asn; pres, Kiwanis Club State Col; NASPA Found, mem, bd dir, Spec Olympics; chair, Eual Opportunity Planning Comt; bd dir, pres, Int Leadership Coun, Golden Key Int Hon Soc; dir, Robert Lynch Stud Leadership Dev Inst. **Home Addr:** 119 Wildernest Lane, Port Matilda, PA 16870-0517, **Home Phone:** (814)238-3246. **Business Addr:** Vice President of Student Affairs Emeritus, Pennsylvania State University, 206 Old Main Bldg, University Park, PA 16802, **Business Phone:** (814)865-0909.

**ASEME, DR. KATE NKOYENI**
Surgeon. **Personal:** Born Nov 20, 1944; daughter of Justice; married Larry Winborne; children: Jeffrey, Isah Paul & Heidi S. **Educ:** Bennett Col, BS, 1967; Howard Univ Col Med, MD, 1970. **Career:** Harlem Hosp Ctr, resident gen surg; Surg & Med Assoc, Hattisburg, pvt pract, 1977-98; Hattisburg Clin, group pract, 1998-2001; Forrest Gen Hosp, med dir, trauma servs, 2000-, med dir, surg servs, 2001-. **Orgs:** Fel Am Col Surgeons, 1981-; fel Int Col Surgeons, 1981; Southern Med Asn; Miss State Med Asn; S Miss Med Soc; bd trustee, Forest Gen Hosp, 1990-93; Miss State Bd Health, 1995-2001; community bd, Bancorp S, 1996-; risk mgt comm, Med Asn Miss, 1997-; Am Med Asn; Eagle Club; Int Col Surgeons; Univ Southern Miss; Miss bank. **Home Addr:** 416 Bay St, Hattiesburg, MS 39401-3552, **Home Phone:** (601)544-3464. **Business Addr:** Medical Director, Forrest General Hospital, 6051 US Hwy 49, Hattiesburg, MS 39401, **Business Phone:** (601)288-2690.

**ASH, RICHARD LARRY**
Hotel executive, manager, executive. **Personal:** Born Mar 23, 1959, Newark, NJ; son of Richard Jr and Daisy Pugh; married Kathy W; children: Alexandra Erin. **Educ:** Snow Col, Ephraim, UT, attended 1983; Rutgers Univ, Newark, NJ, attended 1985. **Career:** McDonald's Corp, crew person, 1978-80, restaurant mgr, 1983-85; Ana Serv, Bedminster, NJ, banquet sized catering mgr, 1985-87; Chelsea Catering, Newark Airport, NJ, asst food prod mgr, 1987-89; Marriott Host, Newark Airport, NJ, asst food & beverage mgr, 1989-90; Harrisburg Hilton & Towers, PA, dir human resources, 1990-. **Orgs:** Nat Job Corps Alumni Asn, 1982-; vpres, Nat Asn Black Hospitality Professionals, 1988-. **Honors/Awds:** Numerous National & Regional Debate Awards, 1980-83; Silver Hat Award, McDonald's Corp, 1984. **Home Addr:** 19th N 4th St, Harrisburg, PA 17101, **Home Phone:** (717)233-5187. **Business Addr:** Director Human Resources, Harrisburg Hilton and Towers, 1st N 2nd St, Harrisburg, PA 17101, **Business Phone:** (717)233-6000.

**ASHBURN, VIVIAN DIANE**
Executive. **Personal:** Born Oct 7, 1949, Kansas City, KS; daughter of Alvin M Patterson and Margaret V Patterson; married Richard R; children: Aaron Cedric & Joseph Elliott. **Educ:** Ohio State Univ, BA, indust rels, 1972; IBM Systs Eng Inst, attended 1974. **Career:** Int Bus Mach, syst engr, 1972-77; Ashburn Pizza Dominos, vpres, 1977-85; Stark Tech Col, 1984-88; Univ Akron, lectr, 1990-; VDP Assocs Inc, pres, 1990-. **Orgs:** Alpha Kappa Alpha Sorority, 1970-; vpres, Black Data Processing Assocs, 1986-; chair, prog planning, Portage Pvt Indust Coun, 1985-; exec dir, Franklin Mills Mediation Coun, 1989-91; bd mem, W VIZ Radio, 1987-88; Minority Bus Coun, Ohio Chap, 1989-91. **Home Addr:** 305 E Archwood Ave, Akron, OH 44301, **Home Phone:** (330)773-4494. **Business Addr:** President, VDP Assocs Inc, 2633 State Rt 59 Suite B, Ravenna, OH 44266, **Business Phone:** (216)384-7169.

**ASHBY, LUCIUS ANTONE**
Executive, consultant, certified public accountant. **Personal:** Born Feb 1, 1944, Des Moines, IA; son of Lucius A Sr and Ruth M Moore; married Victoria Lacy; children: Anand; married Penny Ware; children: Felecia & Wind. **Educ:** Univ Colo, Denver, BS, acct, 1969; Harvard Univ, OPM 10, 1985. **Career:** Great Western Sugar Co, mgt trainee prog, 1968-69; Arthur Andersen & Co, sr acct, 1969-72; Ashby Armstrong & Co, chmn, chief exec officer, managing partner, 1973-91; Ashby Jackson Inc, investor, consult, chmn bd, 1991-; Software Develop Co, consult & investor; DECIS, co-founder, mkt mgt software serv, DC; Jackson Ashby & Goldstine PC, assoc, owner, cert pub acct & partner, 2003-; IAM Smart Technol Inc, dir, 2010-. **Orgs:** Treas, Colo State Dem Party; Am Inst CPA's; bd dir, Colo Soc CPAW's Denver Partnerships; Asn Black CPA Firms; Leadership Denver Asn; pres, Colo State Bd Accountancy, 1984; bd dir, Salvation Army, 1988-; bd dir, Downtown Denver Inc; chmn bd, Colo Invesco Inc, 1988-; Red Shield Community Ctr, 1988-; Rotary Club Denver Club 31, 2003-; bd dir, Denver Kids Inc; Denver Rotary, currently; bd mem & treas, Denver Rotary Found, currently; trustee, Colo Golf Asn; Colo Christian Fel currently; chmn, Deacon Bd; Minority Bus Adv Coun. **Honors/Awds:** Barney Ford Eastside Action Movement Award, 1975; Achievement Award, Nat Asn Black Accountants, 1979; Entrepreneur Award, United Negro Col Fund, 1980; Colorado Gospel Music Academy Award. **Home Addr:** 3861 S Rosemary Way, Denver, CO 80237-1350, **Home Phone:** (303)773-3665. **Business Addr:** Partner, Certified Public Accountant, Jackson, Ashby & Goldstine PC, 655 Broadway Suite 565, Denver, CO 80203, **Business Phone:** (303)825-4072.

**ASHE, DR. CLIFFORD, III**
Clergy. **Personal:** Born Youngstown, OH; married Audree; children: 2. **Educ:** Mich State Univ, BA; Philadelphia Col Bible; Geneva Col. **Career:** Willie Richardson Christian Stronghold Baptist Church, Philadelphia, Pa, assoc minister, 1982- 87, fulltime staff, 1987-91; Geneva Col, adj prof; DaySpring Ministries, sr pastor & founder, 1992-; Mighty Men of Valor, pres, currently; Arms Around Communities, chief exec officer, currently. **Orgs:** Dir, Christian Educ; Deacon; sch teacher, Young Adult Sunday; sch teacher, Adult Sunday; coordr, Men's Breakfast; instr, ETTA. **Honors/Awds:** DDiv, Vision Int Col & Univ, Ramona, Calif, 2005; Received numerous awards for the impact DaySpring Ministries on region from the Gov PA, Mayor Harrisburg, State Rep & Nat Orgn Black Law Enforcement Execs. **Special Achievements:** Written a "Job Enrichment" manual that has been used since 1982 to successfully enhance & improve employ status and promotability of thousands worldwide. **Business Addr:** Senior Pastor, Founder, DaySpring Ministries, 1600 Spring Garden Dr, Middletown, PA 17057, **Business Phone:** (717)939-9500.

**ASHFORD, EVELYN**
Businessperson, athlete. **Personal:** Born Apr 15, 1957, Shreveport, LA; daughter of Samuel and Vietta; married Ray Washington; children: Raina Ashley Washington. **Educ:** Univ Calif, Los Angeles. **Career:** Athlete (retired), businessperson; track & field runner; businessperson, currently; TV: "World Class Women", sports commentator, 1986. **Orgs:** Bd dir, US Anti-Doping Agency, 2003-. **Business Addr:** Board of Director, United States Anti-Doping Agency (USADA), 1330 Quail Lake Loop Suite 260, Colorado Springs, CO 80906-4651, **Business Phone:** (719)785-2000.

**ASHFORD, JOHN**
Business owner, artist. **Personal:** Born Silver Spring, MD. **Educ:** Va Commonwealth Univ, BFA. **Career:** Artist, painter, currently. Tv Series: "For Your Love"; "Malcolm & Eddie", "The Parkers"; John Ashford Art Collection, owner, currently; hundred mid sch, teaches art. **Home Addr:** , Bronx, NY. **Business Addr:** Artist, The John Ashford Art Collection, 1527 Metropolitan Ave Suite 7E, Bronx, NY 10462, **Business Phone:** (212)386-2163.

**ASHFORD, L. JEROME**
Executive. **Personal:** Born Aug 7, 1937, Woodville, MS; son of Mazie Iola Moore and Littleton Perry; married Joyce Linebacker; children: Wesley Jerome, Maurice Eugene, Dwayne Perry & Jerome; married Alicestine D. **Educ:** Boston Univ Sch Mgt, Boston, BS, MA, bus admin mgt, 1968; Univ Southern Calif, Los Angeles, CA, MA, pub admin, 1979; Stanford Univ, Exec Develop Prog Sch Bus, cert; Del Univ & US Chamber Com, Cert Asn Mgt, Inst Orgn Mgt. **Career:** US Dept Health & Human Serv, Wash, DC, expert consult, sr res fel, 1978-82; IPM Health Plan, Vallejo, Calif, pres, 1982-88; Kaiser Permanente, Colo Region, Denver, Colo, vpres & health plan mgr, 1988-90; Kaiser Permanente, Southern Calif Region, Pasadena, Calif, vpres & health plan mgr, 1990-94; Ashford Miller Moore Health Care Consult, pres, 1994-; Jerome Ashford Llc, pres, 1994-; Univ Miss, prof & dir, int progs, 1997-2000, adj prof, health mgt & informatics, clin prof, currently, Sch Med, Int Acad Health Mgt Informatics, dir, 1999; Univ Miss, Nat Ctr Managed Care Admin Sch Bus, sr fel. **Orgs:** Exec dir, Nat Asn Community Health Ctr, 1973-78; USC Alumni Asn; bd dir, Los Angeles March Dimes; life mem, Nat Asn Advan Colored People; Strategic Alignment Health Care Orgn; Nat Med Asn; Easter Seals Disability Serv; exec dir, Fla Comprehensive Health Asn, 2007-. **Business Addr:** Adjunct Professor, University Missouri -Columbia School of Medicine, 304 Clark Hall, Columbia, MO 65211-4380, **Business Phone:** (573)882-6178.

**ASHFORD, MARY E.**
Educator. **Personal:** Born Jul 15, 1945, Barnwell, SC; daughter of Bernice Wright; married Jesse; children: Angela & Eric. **Educ:** Austin Community Col, AA, 1974; Huston-Tillotson Col, BA, elem educ & teaching, 1981; Univ Tex, MLS, 1995. **Career:** Austin Independent Sch Dist, teacher, 1981-87; Huston-Tillotson Col, pres, dir, alumni affairs, 1992-. **Orgs:** Nat Asn Advan Colored People, 1981-; Nat Coun Negro Women, 1990-; Asn Prof Fundraisers, 2000-; Travis County Hist Comm, 2000-02; pres, Sigma Gamma Rho sorority, 2002-; bd dir, Nat Alumni Coun, 2008-. **Business Addr:** Director of Alumni Affairs, Huston-Tillotson College, 900 Chicon St, Austin, TX 78702, **Business Phone:** (512)505-3074.

**ASHFORD, ORLANDO D.**
Executive, vice president (organization). **Educ:** Purdue Univ, BS, orgn leadership, MS, indust technol, 1993. **Career:** Prin/ Partner, Oliver Wyman-Delta Orgn and Leadership, 1999-2003; Ameritech & Andersen Consult; Delta Consult Group (now Mercer Delta Consult); VP Human Resources Strategy and Orgn Develop, Motorola, 2004-05; VP Corp Ctr Human Resources and Cult Transformation, Coca-Cola Co, 2005-06; Coca-Cola Co, human resource mgt, 2005-08; Marsh & McLennan Co Inc, sr vpres, chief human resource & commun officer, 2008-12; Pres, Talent Bus Segment, Mercer, 2013-14; Pres, Holland Am Line, 2014-. **Orgs:** Managing partner, ITT Corp; bd dir, Exec Leadership Coun; bd dir, Streetwise Partners; adv bd mem, Purdue Univ, Sch Technol; adv bd mem, NFL Players Asn; adv bd mem, Ladders.com; Managing Partner, Mercer, 2012. **Business Addr:** President, Holland America Line, 300 Elliott Ave, West Seattle, WA 98119.

**ASHHURST-WATSON, CARMEN**
Executive, activist, movie producer. **Career:** Filmmaker; fundraiser; Def Jam Rec, pres & chief operating officer, 1990; Hip Hop Indust, exec; Rush Commun, pres, 1991-. **Honors/Awds:** Black Radio Exclusive President's Award. **Special Achievements:** One Hundred Most Promising Black Women in Corporate America, Ebony Mag; Selling My Brothers, writer. **Business Addr:** President, Rush Communication, 980 Avenue of the Americas Suite 401, New York, NY 10018, **Business Phone:** (212)380-2433.

**ASHLEY, DWAYNE**
President (organization), executive. **Educ:** Wiley Col, BS, bus mgt; Univ Pa Fel Sch Govt, MS, govt admin; Univ DC, PhD, 2001. **Career:** United Way Tex Gulf Coast, campaign mgr, 1990-91; United Negro Col Fund, area dir, 1991-96; Thurgood Marshall Col Fund, pres, chief exec officer, 1999-2000; Generations Develop Co, interim managing dir, 2009-10; Success Kids, chief exec officer global opers, 2010-11; Jazz Lincoln Ctr, vpres, develop, 2011-; Fed Judicial Ctr. **Orgs:** Bd dir, Asn Fundraising Professionals, Philadelphia, 1994-96; exec dir & chief prof officer, 100 Black Men Am Inc, 1996-99; bd dir, Asn Fundraising Professionals, New York, 2000-03; Coun Foundations, 2003-09; Asn Black Found Execs, 2003-09; bd dir, Gallup Orgn, 2005-09; Independent Sector, 2006-09; bd dir, Evidence Dance Co, 2006-13; comnr, City Newark-Hist Preserv Comn, 2007-09; United Negro Col Fund & United Way; bd dir, Newark Pub Libr; Asn Historically Black Cols & Univs; life mem, Phi Beta Sigma Fraternity; Wiley Col Alumni Asn. **Honors/Awds:** Phi Beta Sigma Fraternitys Image Award, 2003. **Special Achievements:** Author: "I'll Find A Way or Make One" & "Dream Internships! It's Not Who You Know, It's What You Know", Amistad Harper Collins, 2004; "Eight Steps to Raising Money: Measuring Your Fundraising Impact", Word Word Publ, 2008; "8 Winning

Steps to Creating a Successful Special Event", Word Word Publ, 2009. **Business Addr:** Vice President, Development, Jazz at Lincoln Center, 3 Columbus Cir 12th Fl, New York, NY 10019, **Business Phone:** (212)258-9800.

### ASHLEY, MAURICE
Chess player. **Personal:** Born Mar 6, 1966, St. Andrew; married Michele; children: Nia & Jayden. **Educ:** City Col NY, BA, creative writing, 1999. **Career:** Prof Chess Grand Master, currently; Raging Rooks Harlem, coach, 1991; Dark Knights, coach, 1994-95; Commentator: Man vs Mach chess match, 1996, Kasparov vs Deep Blue chess rematch, 1997. ESPN's broadcast, 2003. **Orgs:** Founder, Harlem Educ Activ Fund. **Honors/Awds:** Nat Jr High Sch Championships, 1991; Nat Champions, 1994 & 1995; Grandmaster of the Year Award, US Chess Fed, 2003; Named Community Educator of the Year, 2004; Organizer of the Year Award, 2005. **Special Achievements:** First ever African Am Int Master in Us hist, 1993; Finished First pl in the prestigious Enhance Int, 1993; Designer, award-winning instrnl CD-ROM; Maurice Ashley Teaches Chess; Became the first & only African-Am to attain the coveted title Int Grand Master Chess in 1999; Only back-to-back winner in Foxwoods Open hist, 2001; First African-Am in 157 yrs to qualify the US Championship, 2002; First African-Am Int Grandmaster incl Time mag, USA Today, New York Times, Sports Illus, London Times, Ebony, Investors Bus Daily, New York Daily News, Jet, New York Newsday, New York Post, Emerge & a host other papers around the world served by the Assoc Press & Reuters; TV shows: Charlie Rose Show, CBS News This Morning, Nat Pub Radio, Today New York (W-NBC), CNN, Bloomberg Radio & a no radio shows around the US; Authored essay :The End the Draw Offer?; Chess for Success, 2005; First GM to ever participate in a tournament in that country; Featured in an interview the CNN doc Black in Am, 2008. **Home Addr:** 117-21 201 Pl, Saint Albans, NY 11412, **Home Phone:** (718)528-3006. **Business Addr:** Founder, Harlem Educational Activities Fund Inc, 2090 7th Ave 10th Fl, New York, NY 10027, **Business Phone:** (212)663-9732.

### ASHLEY-WARD, AMELIA
Editor, publisher, business owner. **Personal:** Born Sep 17, 1957, Magnolia, MS; daughter of Louise James and Amile; children: Evan Carlton. **Educ:** San Jose State Univ, BA, jour & photojournalism, 1979. **Career:** Sun-Reporter Publ Co, reporter & photojournalist, 1979-85, Managing Editor, 1985-94, publ & editor-in-chief, owner, currently; People mag; Jet mag; Sepia; San Jose State Univ, universitys Journalism dept, commencement speaker, 2004; adv bd, St Marys Col, currently. **Orgs:** Nat Newspaper Publ Asn; life mem, Nat Coun Negro Women; life mem, Nat Asn Advan Colored People; founder, Sun-Reporter Found, 2004; founding pres, Young Adult Christian Movement; San Francisco Conv & Visitors Bur; bd mem, San Francisco br Nat Asn Advan Colored People, currently. **Business Addr:** Owner & Publisher, Editor-in-chief, Sun Reporter Publ Co, 1791 Bancroft Ave, San Francisco, CA 94124, **Business Phone:** (415)671-1000.

### ASHMORE, DARRYL ALLAN
Football player. **Personal:** Born Nov 1, 1969, Peoria, IL. **Educ:** Northwestern Univ, BS, bus. **Career:** Football player (retired); Los Angeles Rams, right tackle, 1993, tackle, 1994; St Louis Rams, right tackle, 1995; Wash Redskins, tackle, 1997; Oakland Raiders, 2000, tackle, 1997-98, right guards, right tackle, 1999, right tackle, 2001. **Honors/Awds:** Scholar Athlete of the Year, Tri-County Area. **Home Addr:** 8695 Thornbrook Terrace Pt, Boynton Beach, FL 33473, **Home Phone:** (561)654-1395.

### ASKA, JOSEPH (JOE ASKA)
Football player. **Personal:** Born Jul 14, 1972, St. Croix. **Educ:** Cent Okla, grad. **Career:** Football player (retired); Oakland Raiders, running back, 1995-97; Indianapolis Colts, 1999; New York Hitmen, 2001; NJ Hitmen, 2001.

### ASKEW, BONNY LAMAR
Government official, association executive, commissioner. **Personal:** Born Mar 4, 1955, Rome, GA; married Adrianne Denise Smith. **Educ:** US Naval Acad, attended 1973; West Ga Col, BA, polit sci, 1977. **Career:** GA Kraft Co, laborer, 1977-; 2nd Ward City Rome, comnr, 1982-84. **Orgs:** Thankful Baptist Church; S Rome Comm Asn; Starlight Lodge 433 FAAYM; co-founder, S Rome Comm Assoc; comt mem, Ga Munic Asn Comm Develop, 1983-84; comt mem, Nat League Cities Comm Develop, 1983-84; Nat Black Caucus Local off, 1983-84; Ga Asn Black Elected Off, 1983-84; vchmn, Rome Coun Human Rels; treas, dir, Univ Ga, Alumni Asn. **Home Addr:** 503 Cotton Ave, Rome, GA 30161, **Home Phone:** (706)436-5453. **Business Addr:** Director, University of West Georgia Alumni House, 1601 Maple St, Carrollton, GA 30118, **Business Phone:** (678)839-6582.

### ASKEW, VINCENT JEROME
Basketball coach, basketball player. **Personal:** Born Feb 28, 1966, Memphis, TN. **Educ:** Memphis State Univ, attended 1987. **Career:** Basketball player (retired), basketball coach; Philadelphia 76ers, shooting guard, 1987-88; Savannah Spirits, 1987-88; Albany Patroons, 1988-90; Arimo Bologna, 1989; Memphis Rockers, 1989; Emmezeta Udine, Italy, 1990-91; Golden State Warriors, 1991-92; Sidis Reggio Emilia, Italy, 1992; Sacramento Kings, guard, 1992; Seattle Supersonics, shooting guard, 1992-96; Denver Nuggets, 1996-97; NJ Nets, guard, 1996-97; Ind Pacers, guard, 1996-97; Portland Trailblazers, guard, 1997-98; Idaho Stampede, 1998; Cocodrilos de Caracas, Venezuela, 1998-99; Elliston Baptist Acad, head coach; Rossville Christian Acad, head coach, 2004-05; Tacoma Navigators, Am Basketball Asn, head coach, 2005-07; Albany Patroons, Continental Basketball Asn, head coach, 2007-08; Ky Mavericks, Am Basketball Asn, coach, 2008-. **Honors/Awds:** Most Valuable Player, Continental Basketball Asn, 1990, 1991. **Special Achievements:** TV appearance: The 1996 NBA Finals, 1996. **Business Addr:** Head Coach, Albany Patroons, Washington Ave Armory, Albany, NY 12210, **Business Phone:** (518)694-7160.

### ASKINS, KEITH BERNARD
Basketball player, basketball coach. **Personal:** Born Dec 15, 1967, Athens, AL; married Paulina; children: Franco & Vicente. **Educ:** Univ Ala, attended 1990. **Career:** Basketball player (retired), basketball coach; Miami Heat, guard-forward, 1990-99, asst coach, 1999-2013, advan scout, 2000-02, dir col & pro scouting, 2013-. **Business Addr:** Director, Miami Heat, 601 Biscayne Blvd, Miami, FL 33132, **Business Phone:** (786)777-3008.

### ASMA, THOMAS M.
Artist. **Educ:** Layton Sch Art, attended 1968; Col Lake Co, Lib Arts, 1975; Univ Ill, attended 1976. **Career:** Layson Prods, com artist, 1970-71; Carlson Studios, com artist, 1971-72; Lake County Regional Planning Comn, planning tech, 1972-73; Lake County Safety Comn, graphic artist, 1973-74; BALL Corp, palletizer gen factory, 1976-78; Kitchens Sara Lee, prod sanit, 1978-80; Am Heritage Indust, custom artist, 1980-. **Home Addr:** 3170 W Monroe St Apt 313, Waukegan, IL 60085-3066, **Home Phone:** (847)263-7512. **Business Addr:** Custom Artist, Am Heritage Indust, 3400 W Grand Ave, Waukegan, IL 60085.

### ASOM, DR. MOSES T.
Scientist. **Personal:** Born Jul 27, 1958, Gboko Benue; son of Ikyutor and Lydia. **Educ:** Univ DC, BSc, physics, 1980; Howard Univ, MSc, 1982, PhD, elec eng, 1985; Univ Pa, Wharton Sch, MBA, 1994. **Career:** Univ DC, Wash, instr, 1984; Howard Univ, Wash, res asst, 1981-85; AT&T Bell Labs, Murray Hill, NJ, MTS, 1986-89, SSTC, 1990-94; Optoelectronics, mkt mgr; AT&T Microeletronics, Asia/Pac, Japan & S Am, prod mgr, 1994; Lucent New Ventures Grp, dir; SyChip Inc, co-founder, pres, chief operating officer & sr vpres mkt & bus develop, currently. **Orgs:** Comn mem, Educ Affairs, Am Soc Mat; Inst Elec & Electronics Engrs; Am Phys Soc; Nat Tech Asn; Am Vacuum Soc; Mat Res Soc; Nat Orgn Adv Black Chemists & Chem Engrs; strategic adv bd, Covera Ventures. **Honors/Awds:** NASA-HBCU, NASA, 1989; Black Engineer of the Year, 1989; 2 patents awarded; Most Promising engineer, 1989. **Special Achievements:** Holds 3 patents; Publ & presented over seventy tech papers & seminars. **Business Addr:** Co-founder, Senior Vice President Of Marketing, SyChip Inc, Pkwy Centre II, Plano, TX 75093, **Business Phone:** (972)202-8888.

### ATCHISON, BR. CALVIN O.
Executive. **Personal:** Born Sep 15, 1920, Millry, AL; married Amanda Rosetta McFadden; children: Antoinette & Calvin II. **Educ:** Ala A&M Col, BS, 1944; Columbia Univ, MA, 1949; Ind Univ, PhD, psychol, 1958. **Career:** Charlotte City Schs, sch psychol, 1949-53; Tenn State Univ, assoc prof, 1953-58, prof & coord grad studies & res, 1958-64, prof psychol & asst grad dean, 1964-67, actg dir res & develop, 1968-69, develop officer, 1969-72, vpres res planning & develop, 1981-82; Tenn State Univ Found, exec dir & vpres, 1986; Metrop Nashville Head Start Admin, vice chmn, 2003-; US Dept Educ, consult; Nat Asn Black Sch Edu, consult. **Orgs:** Am psychol Asn; Soc Study Proj Tech; Psy Chi; Nashville Ment Health Asn; Better Bus Bur Nashville; Metro Nashville Housing & Urban Devel; Coun Advan & Study Educ; bd dir, Meharry metal Health Ctr; Tau Lambda Chap; bd trustee, Tau Lambda Educ Found. **Honors/Awds:** Danforth Teacher, 1956-57; Outstanding Educator, 1972-73; Admin Year, 1985. **Home Addr:** 940 TS Jackson Ave, Nashville, TN 37209, **Home Phone:** (615)320-7574. **Business Addr:** Vice Chairman, Metrop Clerk's Office, 225 Polk Ave, Nashville, TN 37203, **Business Phone:** (615)862-6770.

### ATCHISON, LEON H. See Obituaries Section.

### ATKINS, BRENDA JOYCE
School administrator, government official. **Personal:** Born Jan 25, 1954, Washington, DC. **Educ:** Loyola Marymount, BA, 1975; Georgetown Univ Law Ctr, JD, 1978. **Career:** Lawy Com Civil Rights Educ Proj, researcher, 1976; US Dept Justice, Tax Div, law clerk, 1977; White House Off Coun, pres, law clerk, 1977-78; Am Crim Law Rev, managing ed, 1977-78; Georgetown Univ Law Ctr, asst dean, 1978-. **Orgs:** Nat Conf Black Lawyer; Nat Bar Asn. **Special Achievements:** Author of "US Tax For & For Tax Art", 1980. **Home Addr:** 1070 S La Brea Ave, Los Angeles, CA 90019, **Home Phone:** (323)936-8251. **Business Addr:** Attorney at Law, Georgetown University Law Center, 1070 S La Brea Ave, Los Angeles, CA 90019, **Business Phone:** (323)936-8251.

### ATKINS, DR. CARL J.
Educator, arts administrator, musician. **Personal:** Born Jul 4, 1945, Birmingham, AL; son of James Spencer and Kathryn Watson Woods; married Deborah Little; children: Kathryn-Louise & Leslie Stevens Dowdell. **Educ:** Cent State Col, Wilberforce, OH, 1963; Ind Univ, Bloomington, IN, BM, 1967; New Eng Conserv, Boston, DMA, MM, 1975; Univ Rochester, Eastman Sch, Rochester, NY, DM, 1982. **Career:** Am Nat Opera Co, Boston, Mass, orchestra, 1967-68; New Eng Conserv Boston, Mass, fac, 1968-78; Univ Rochester Eastman Sch, conducting fel, 1978; Hochstein Music Sch, Rochester, NY, dean, 1979-81; Univ Rochester, Rochester, NY, asst prof, 1981-84; David Hochstein Memorial Music Sch, Rochester, NY, pres, 1984-91; Rochester Philharmonic Orchestra Inc, pres & chief exec officer, 1991-93; Carl Atkins & Assoc, pres, 1993-; Thelonious Monk Inst Jazz New Eng Conserv, Boston, Mass, co-dir, 1995-; Thelonius Monk Inst, prog dir; Rochester Inst Tech, Rochester, NY, Dept Fine Arts, prof & dir music prog, currently. **Orgs:** Am Fedn Musicians, 1960-; Col Band dir Nat Asn, 1981-; Nat Guild Comm Schs Arts; Bd Nat Guild Community Arts Educ, 1993-98; Northeastern Univ; Univ Rochester; adv dir, Hochstein Sch Music & Dance; Eastman Sch Music; pres, Acad Community Music, currently. **Home Addr:** 53 Mt Morency Dr, Rochester, NY 14612-3631. **Business Addr:** Professor, Director of the Music Program, Rochester Institute of Technology, 1 Lomb Memorial Dr, Rochester, NY 14623-5603, **Business Phone:** (585)475-4439.

### ATKINS, CHUCK
Vice president (organization), manager, executive. **Career:** Clear Channels Urban AC KMJM-FM, prog dir; Urban KATZ-FM; Urban KATZ-FM, prog dir; Chaz Saunders; Clear Channel Commun, vpres, oper mgr & prog dir, 1987-2006; Urban AC 860 WNOV Milwaukee's Hertiage Sta, oper mgr & prog dir; Atkins Commun, owner, currently; Emanon Entertainment & Consult LLC, owner, 2006-; Cost Plus World Mkt, supvr sales, 2014-. **Business Addr:** Supervisor of Sales, Cost Plus World Market, 200 4th St, Oakland, CA 94607, **Business Phone:** (510)893-7300.

### ATKINS, EDMUND E.
City planner. **Personal:** Born Dec 6, 1944, Winston-Salem, NC; married Vera J Clayton; children: Damien. **Educ:** Grinnell Col, BA, 1966; Univ Okla, MRCP, 1972. **Career:** San Francisco Redev Agency, asst planner, 1969; Oakland Model Cities, chief phys planner, 1970-71; US Dept HUD, urban planner, 1971-74; City Berkeley, city planner, 1974, US Consulate Gen Rio de Janeiro, Brazil, consul gen, 2004-06. **Orgs:** Assoc mem, Am Inst Planners; vpres, Nat Asn Planners; pres, Bay Area chap New Niagra Movement Demo Club; treas, Oakland Citizens Comt Urban Renewal, 1976-; Alameda Co Human Serv Coun, 1976-; CA Land Use Taks Force; life mem, Nat Asn Advan Colored People; vpres, Youth Coun. **Home Addr:** 1642 Myrtle St NW, Washington, DC 20012-1130.

### ATKINS, HON. EDNA R.
Lawyer, judge. **Personal:** Born Jan 22, 1945, Sicily Island, LA. **Educ:** Univ Nebr, BA, 1967; Creighton Law Sch, JD, 1970. **Career:** Judge (retired); Legal Aid Soc Omaha, Coun Bluffs Inc, staff atty, 1970-81; State Nebr County Ct, 4th Judicial Dist, Douglas County, judge, 2001, 2003, retired. **Orgs:** NE State Bar Asn; Nat Bar Asn; Am Bar Asn; Nat Asn Black Women Atty; Nat Asn Advan Colored People, 1970; gen coun, CARE Prog Inc, 1973; founding mem, Midlands Bar Asn; fel Nebr State Bar Found.

### ATKINS, ERICA (ERICA MONIQUE ATKINS)
Gospel singer, actor. **Personal:** Born Jan 1, 1972?, Inglewood, CA; daughter of Eddie and Thomasina; married Warryn Campbell; children: 1. **Career:** TV Series: "What's Hot in Music", 2000, "Trackers", 2000, "Whassup with Heyyy?", 2000, "The Parkers", 2000, "Soul Food", writer, 2000; "An Evening of Stars: A Celebration of Educational Excellence", 2001, "Top of the Pops", 2001, "9th Annual Soul Train Lady of Soul Awards", 2003; "The Big Bitter Shower Episode", 2003, "Half & Half", 2003, "Gospel Fest 2004", 2004, "Higher Ground: Voices of Contemporary Gospel Music", writer, 2004; "Living It Up with Patti La Belle", 2004, "Tavis Smiley", 2005-09, "Episode #35.2", 2005, "Soul Train", 2005, " Showtime at the Apollo", 2005; "The 10th Annual Soul Train Lady of Soul Awards", 2005; "2005 American Music Awards", 2005; "Tavis Smiley", 2005-09; "BET Awards 2006, 2011", 2006; "21st Annual Stellar Gospel Music Awards", 2006; "22nd Annual Stellar Gospel Music Awards", 2007; "The Mo'Nique Show", 2011; "The Hot 10", 2011; "The Wendy Williams Show", 2011-12; "Mary Mary", 2012; Movies: Sister Act II: Back in the Habit, 1993; Writer: Doctor Dolittle, 1998. **Orgs:** Duo Mary Mary. **Honors/Awds:** New Artist of the Year & Contemporary CD of the Year, 2001; 4 Stellar awards. **Special Achievements:** Wrote songs appearing on secular and sacred CDs & on Dr Dolittle & The Prince of Egypt soundtracks. **Business Addr:** Gospel Singer, The Firm, 911 Wilshire Blvd Suite 400 W, Los Angeles, CA 90212.

### ATKINS, FREDD G.
City commissioner. **Personal:** Born Jun 19, 1952, Sarasota, FL; son of Glossie; married Sheila Hammond; married Luethel Chochran; children: Carol, Nilaja, Amina, Baraka, Dumaka & Zakia. **Educ:** Manatee Jr Col, Bradenton, FL, AA, soc welfare, 1979; Univ Southern Fla, Sarasota, FL, BA, interdisciplinary soc scis. **Career:** Storefront Newtown Community Ctr, Sarasota, FL, asst dir, 1982-85; Genus Enterprises Inc, Sarasota, FL, dir mkt, 1985-87; City Sarasota Comn, FL, comnr, 1985-95, Dist 1, vice mayor, 2003-; Cent Life Ins, Tampa, FL, vpres, 1988-89. **Orgs:** Nat Black Family Found; Nat Forum Black Administrs; Southwest Fla Regional Planning Coun; Fla League Cities; founder & pres, Newtown Little League; founding bd mem, Greater Newtown Community Redevelop Corp; pres, Booker High Sch Boosters; chair, Booker Mid Sch Adv Comt; Southwest Fla Regional Planning Coun; Metrop Planning Orgn; econ develop bd, Sarasota County; Tourist Develop Coun; Urban Admin Comt Fla League Cities; bd trustee, Out Door Acad; educ chmn, Sarasota County Nat Asn Advan Colored People; Fla Adv Coun HUD. **Honors/Awds:** Political Academic Award, Kappa Alpha Psi, 1987; Martin Luther King Award for Service to Youth, 1988; NAACP Achievement Award, 1988; Human Rights & Achievement Award, Interdenomi Nat Ministerial Alliance, 1988. **Home Addr:** 1598 29th St, Sarasota, FL 34234-4712, **Home Phone:** (941)359-9018. **Business Addr:** Vice Mayor, Commissioner, City Sarasota, 1565 1st St Rm 101, Sarasota, FL 34236, **Business Phone:** (941)954-4115.

### ATKINS, JAMES CURTIS
Football player. **Personal:** Born Jan 28, 1970, Amite, LA; married Nicole. **Educ:** Univ La Lafayette, grad. **Career:** Football player (retired); Seattle Seahawks, tackle, 1994 & 1997, left tackle, 1995-96; Baltimore Ravens, left tackle, 1998, right tackle, 1999; Detroit Lions, tackle, 2000.

### ATKINS, JEFFREY. See JA RULE.

### ATKINS, HON. MARYLIN E.
Judge, lawyer. **Personal:** Born Jan 1, 1946, Detroit, MI. **Educ:** Saginaw Valley State Univ, BA, psychol, 1973; Univ Detroit Sch Law, JD, 1980. **Career:** Mich Employ Security Comn, asst dir labor rels, 1973-80; Mich Legis Serv Bur, staff atty, 1980; US Dist Ct, Eastern Dist, asst atty gen, 1980-83, Worker's Compensation Appeal Bd, mem, 1983-85, chair, 1985-91; State Mich, 36th Dist Ct, asst atty gen, magistrate, 1994-99, chief judge pro tem, 1999, chief judge, 2000-. **Orgs:** Chmn, Workers Compensation Appeal Bd, 1985-91; Wolverine Bar Asn; State Bar Mich; Mich Black Judges Asn; Detroit Bar Asn; Nat Asn Advan Colored People; Optimist Club; bd dir, Interim House, YMCA; adv bd, Benjamin E Mays Male Acad; Kiwanis Club 1 Detroit; bd dir, Eastern Wayne Div, Am Heart Asn; Metrop Bar Asn; Mich Coun Chief Judges; Asn Black Judges Mich; bd mem, Nat Coun Alcoholism & Drug Dependency Greater Detroit Area; chmn, Mich Legis Black Caucus & Detroit Urban League. **Special Achievements:** First

African American women headed the Workers Compensation Appeal Board in its fifty year history. **Business Addr:** Chief Judge, State of Michigan, 421 Madison Ave, Detroit, MI 48226, **Business Phone:** (313)965-4158.

## ATKINS, PERVIS R., JR.
Executive, football player, actor. **Personal:** Born Nov 24, 1935, Ruston, LA; son of Pervis and Mattie; children: Gerald, Christine, Gregory & Gayle. **Educ:** NMex State Univ, BA, sociol, 1962. **Career:** Football player (retired), executive, actor; NMex State Univ, football player; Los Angeles Rams, wide receiver, 1961-63; Wash Redskins, wide receiver, 1964-65; Oakland Raiders, wide receiver, 1965-66; KIIX, TV sports commentator; Ashley-Famous Talent Agency; TV Series: "Police Woman", 1975-77; "Desperate Miles", 1975; "Ellery Queen", 1976; "Delvecchio", 1977; ABC-TV, dir develop motion pictures; Artist Career Mgt, vpres; Atkins & Assocs, pres, owner, currently. **Orgs:** Pop Warner Football League; Kwanza Adv Bd. **Honors/Awds:** Consensus, All Am Football, 1960, 1961; Outstanding Citizen of Ruston, 1961; Inducted in College Football Hall of Fame, 2009. **Business Addr:** Owner, Atkins & Associates, 208 S Beverly Dr, Beverly Hills, CA 90212.

## ATKINS, RICHARD
Executive, architect. **Personal:** Born Feb 9, 1949, Stephens, AR; son of Robert and Clemmine Ferguson; married Diane Williams; children: Gregory & Gary R. **Educ:** Forest Park Community Col, attended 1971; Wash Univ, attended 1970; Howard Univ, BA, arch, 1975; Lindenwood Col, MBA, 1982. **Career:** Stottler, Stagg & Assoc, engr technician II, 1972-74; Gordon H Ball Inc, engr technician & draftsman, 1974; Itzig Heine Construct, engr technician & draftsman, 1974-75; Peckham-Guyton Inc, architect-in-trng, 1975-77; JG Randle & Assoc, proj architect, 1977-78; Environ Seven Ltd, off mgr, proj architect, 1978-80; TDP & St Louis Inc, chief archit, owner, pres, 1980-. **Orgs:** Nat Orgn Minority Architects; pres, 100 Black Men St Louis; Scholar found; chmn, Boy Scouts Am, 1991. **Home Addr:** 12884 Patridge Run, Florissant, MO 63033, **Home Phone:** (314)741-0039. **Business Addr:** Owner/President, Architect/Principal, TDP/St Louis Inc, 3101 Olive St, St. Louis, MO 63103-1212, **Business Phone:** (314)533-1996.

## ATKINS, RUSSELL
Writer, composer. **Personal:** Born Feb 25, 1926, Cleveland, OH; son of Perry Kelly and Mamie Belle Kelley. **Educ:** Cleveland Sch Art, scholar, 1944; Cleveland Music Sch Settlement, prischolar, 1943; Cleveland Inst Music, attended 1945; Pvt Music Study, 1954. **Career:** Editor, poet, writer, lecturer & composer; Free Lance Mag, ed & co-founder, 1950-79; Univ Iowa, Iowa Workshop, affil, 1953-54; Sutphen Sch Music, asst dir, 1957-60; Poets & Lectr Alliance, lectr, 1963-65; WVIZ-TV, consult, 1969-72; Karamu Writers Conf, consult, 1971; Karamu House, writing instr, 1972-86; Cleveland Bd Educ, consult, 1972-73; Cuyahoga Community Col, writer-in-residence, 1973; Ohio Prog Humanities, instr, 1978; writer, currently. **Orgs:** Bread Loaf Writers Conf, 1956; Artists-in-Schs Prog, Ohio Arts Coun & Nat Endowment Arts, 1973-; lit adv panel, Ohio Arts Coun, 1973-76; Cleveland State Univ Poetry Forum; Coord Coun Lit Mag, Nat Endowment Arts; Int Platform Asn, 1976-77; trustee, Poets League Greaster Cleveland, 1978; Comt Small Mag Ed & Publishers; Poets League Greater Cleveland. **Honors/Awds:** Honorary PhD, Cleveland State Univ, 1976; Individual Artist grant, Ohio Arts Coun, 1978; Lifetime Literary Achievement, Poetic League, 1997. **Special Achievements:** Books: A Podium Presentation, 1960; Phenomena, 1961; Objects, 1963; The Abortionist and The Corpse, 1963; Objects 2, 1963; Spyrytual, 1966; Objects For Piano, 1967; Heretofore, 1968; Presentations, 1969; Sounds & Silences: Poetry for Now, 1969; Nail, 1970; Maleficium, 1971; Here in The, 1976; Celebrations, 1977; Whichever, 1978; Juxtapositions: A Manifesto, 1991; Contributor to anthologies including An Ear to the Ground, 1989; Beyond the Reef, 1991; Scarecrow Poetry, 1994; The Garden Thrives, 1996; Voices of Cleveland, 1996; Letters to America, 1995. Contributions to Periodicals including Marrahwannah Quarterly, Silver Cesspool. **Home Addr:** 6005 Grand Ave, Cleveland, OH 44104, **Home Phone:** (216)431-7116.

## ATKINS, SHARIF
Actor. **Personal:** Born Jan 29, 1975, Pittsburgh, PA; son of David and Jacqueline. **Educ:** Northwestern Univ, BA, theatre/speech, 1997. **Career:** Victoria's Secret stock boy, waiter; TV Series: "The More You Know", 1989; "The Fourth Carpathian", 1998; "Cashier and Number One with a Bullet", "Turks", "Early Edition", 1999; "That's Life", "The District", 2001; "Arli$$", 2002; "Hawaii", 2004; "ER", 2001-04; "Eve", 2005-06; "The 4400", 2005; "In Justice", 2006; "Numb3rs", "Close to Home", 2007; "Raising the Bar", 2008; "My Manny", "Criminal Minds", "Cold Case", "The New 20s", "CSI Miami", 2009; Films: Light It Up, 1999; The Big Time, 2002; Something for Nothing, exec producer, 2004; Paved with Good Intentions, 2006; Privacy Policy, 2007; Preacher's Kid, 2010; The Good Wife, White Collar, 2009-10. **Orgs:** Kappa Alpha Psi Fraternity Inc. **Business Addr:** Actor, NBC Productions, 30 Rockefeller Plz, New York, NY 10112.

## ATKINS, TINA (TRECINA EVETTE CAMPBELL)
Gospel singer. **Personal:** Born May 1, 1975, Inglewood, CA; daughter of Thomasina and Eddie; married Teddy Campbell; children: Laiah Simone, Meela Jane & Ted Jr. **Career:** Albums: THankful, 2000; Incredible, 2002; Heaven, 2005; The Real Party, 2005; Mary Mary, 2005; A Mary Mary Christmas, 2006; The Sound, 2008; Something Big, 2011; Go Get It, 2012. Songs: "Shackles Praise You", 2000; "I Sings", 2000; "Thank You", 2001; "In the Morning", 2002; "Heaven", 2005; "Yesterday", 2006; "Love Him Like I Do", 2008; "Get Up", 2008; "I Worship You", 2008; "God in Me", 2009; "We Are the World 25 for Haiti", 2010; "Walking", 2011; "Survive", 2011. **Honors/Awds:** Grammy Award, 2000; Four Stellar Awards, including New Artist of the Year & Contemporary CD of the Year, Thankful, 2001; Dove Award; American Music Award; Best Inspirational/Christian Contemprary Artist, 2005; Nominee, Favorite R&B/Soul or Hip-Hop New Artist Award, 2001; Best Gospel Artist Award, 2009.

## ATKINSON, EUGENIA CALWISE
Administrator, association executive, social worker. **Personal:** Born Jan 16, 1943, Laurens, SC; married Richard W; children: Najuma, W Omari, Akilah & Jamila. **Educ:** Youngstown State Univ, BA, 1971; Hiram Col, BA, 1989. **Career:** Hon Nathaniel R Jones Judge US Dist Ct, secy, 1960-63; Youngstown Sheet Tube Co, supvr sec-steno pool, 1969-74; Youngstown Area Com Action Coun, admin asst, 1974-76, dir WIC prog, 1976-79; Western Res Transit Auth, pres bd trustee; Youngstown Civil Serv Comn, chmn; Home Savings & Loan Co, dir, 1999-2013; Metro Housing Authority, dir admin, exec dir, 2000-07; United Community Financial Corp, dir, 2005-13; Youngstown State Univ Found, trustee, currently; Western Res Care Div Forum Health, dir, currently; Mahoning Valley Community Corp, dir, currently; Better Bus Bur Youngstown, dir, currently. **Orgs:** Bd trustee, Youngstown State Univ, 1989; OHI mlk Holiday cms; Scholarshipcom chmn, Youngstown Chap Ohio Black Womens Leadership Caucus, 1977-80; pres, YWCA, 1981-81; Leadership Warren-Youngstown Alumni Asn; Yo AlumnaeChapter Delta Sigma Theta; Nat Afro-Am Mus Plng Coun, 1978-80; bd trustee, Career Develop Ctr Women, 1979-80; Youth Area Urban league; Nat Asn Advan Colored People; Income Distrib/Appointing Comt, Walter E. Watson Found; Youngstown Alumni Chap Delta Sigma Theta Sorority; Leadership Mahoning Valley Alumni Asn. **Honors/Awds:** Dedication Commitment Award, Freedom Inc Youngstown OH, 1972; Outstanding Admin Performance, OH Dept Health Cols OH, 1978; Downtown Improvement Com Service, Youngstown Bd Trade, 1980. **Home Addr:** 265 Redondo Rd, Youngstown, OH 44504. **Business Addr:** Executive Director, Metro Housing Authority, 131 W Boardman St, Youngstown, OH 44503-1329, **Business Phone:** (330)744-2161.

## ATKINSON, REGINA ELIZABETH
Social worker. **Personal:** Born May 13, 1952, New Haven, CT; daughter of Samuel Griffin and Virginia Louise Griffin. **Educ:** Univ Conn, BA, 1974; Atlanta Univ, MSW, 1978. **Career:** Palm Beach Co Health Dept, med social worker, 1978-81; Glades Gen Hosp, dir social serv, 1981-95; Palm Beach County Community Servs, sr servs, case mgr, 1996-. **Orgs:** AHA Soc Hosp Soc Work Dirs; Comn Action Coun; Fla Pub Health Asn Inc; Glades Area Asn Retarded Citizens; Nat Asn Black Social Workers Inc; Nat Asn Social Workers Inc; Fla Asn Health & Social Serv; Nat Chamber Com Women Inc; Nat Asn Female Exec; Area Agency Aging Adv Coun, Nat Asn Advan Colored People. **Honors/Awds:** American Legion Award; Whitney Young Fellowship; DHEW Pub Health Service Scholarship. **Home Addr:** 525 12 SW 10th St, Belle Glade, FL 33430. **Business Addr:** Case Manager, Palm Beach County Community Services, 850 Belle Glade Gdns, Belle Glade, FL 33430, **Business Phone:** (561)996-9708.

## ATLAS, DR. JOHN WESLEY
Educator. **Personal:** Born Aug 15, 1941, Lake Providence, LA; son of Francis Joseph (deceased) and Willie Mae Gibson (deceased); married Arthurlean Johnson; children: Mavis, Candace Latrice, Jamila & Amina. **Educ:** Grambling Col, BS, 1963; Wayne State Univ, MEd, 1968, EdD, 1972. **Career:** LA Schs, music teacher, 1963-65; Detroit Pub Schs, music teacher, 1965-67, guid counr, 1967-70, asst prin, 1970-72; Gov State Univ, prof, 1972-73; Oakland Univ, assoc prof, 1973. **Orgs:** Am Personnel & Guid Asn; Asn Non-White Concerns Personnel & Guid; Omega Psi Phi Frat; Topical Conf Career Educ Handicapped Indiv, 1979. **Home Addr:** 9212 W Outer Dr, Detroit, MI 48219, **Home Phone:** (313)531-6373. **Business Addr:** Associate Professor, Oakland University, 2200 N Squirrel Rd, Rochester, MI 48309.

## ATTLES, ALVIN AUSTIN, JR. (AL ATTLES)
Basketball coach, basketball player, basketball executive. **Personal:** Born Nov 7, 1936, Newark, NJ; married Wilhemina Rice; children: Alvin III & Erica. **Educ:** NC A&T State Univ. **Career:** Basketball player (retired), executive; Philadelphia Warriors, guard, 1960-72; San Francisco Warriors, guard, 1962-71, head coach, 1970-71; Golden State Warriors, guard, head coach, 1979-83, gen mgr, 1983-84, vpres & asst gen mgr, currently.TV Series: "Inside Moves", 1980; "Whatever Happened to Micheal Ray", 2000; "Black Magic", 2008. **Business Addr:** Vice President, Assistant General Manager, Golden State Warriors, 1011 Broadway, Oakland, CA 94607, **Business Phone:** (510)986-2200.

## ATWATER, STEPHEN DENNIS
Football player, executive. **Personal:** Born Oct 28, 1966, Chicago, IL; married Letha; children: Stephen Jr, DiAndre, Paris & Malaysia. **Educ:** Univ Ark, BS, finance & banking, 1989. **Career:** Football player (retired), exec; Denver Broncos, safety, 1989-98; New York Jets, free safety & return specialist, 1999-2000; E Coast, nat dir player develop. **Honors/Awds:** All-SW Hons; All-American Hons; Pro Bowl, 1990-98; NFL 1990s All Decade Team; Ring of Fame at Invesco Field at Mile High; Super Bowl championship, 1997-98; Sports Hall of Honor, Univ Ark, 1998; Broncos Ring of Fame, 2005. **Home Addr:** 2424 Sapling Ridge Lane, Brookeville, MD 20833-1833.

## ATWATER, DR. TONY K.
Educator. **Personal:** Born Jan 1, 1952?, Nashville, TN; married Beverly Roberts. **Educ:** Va Western Community Col, AAS, 1972; Hampton Univ, BA, mass media arts, 1973; Mich State Univ, PhD, commun res, 1983; Harvard Univ, Grad Sch Educ, mgt develop prog cert, 1995, inst mgt leadership educ cert, 2001, inst educ mgt cert, 2002; Carnegie Mellon Univ, HJ Heinz Sch Pub Policy & Mgt, Col Mgt Prog, 1996. **Career:** WTOY Radio, Roanoke, Va, asst news dir & reporter, 1971-72; WSLC Radio, Roanoke, Va, news reporter, 1973-74; WPVR-FM Radio, Roanoke, Va, news dir, 1975-76; WSET-TV, Lynchburg, Va, assignment ed, news reporter, 1976-78; Va Polytech Inst & State Univ, Blacksburg, Va, radio & TV specialist, 1978-79; Mich State Univ, teaching asst & instr, 1982-82, from asst prof to assoc prof, 1983-91, asst dir, 1988-91; Univ Mich, Dept Commun, postdoctoral, 1989; Rutgers Univ, New Burnswick, NJ, Dept Jour & Mass Media, chairperson & prof, 1991-94; Univ Conn, spec asst to provost & vpres acad affairs, 1994-95; Univ Toledo, prof commun & assoc vpres acad affairs, 1995-99; Northern Ky Univ, dean, col prof studies & educ, 1999-2001; Youngstown State Univ, provost vpres acad affairs, 2001-05; Ind Univ Pa, pres & chief exec officer, 2005-10; Norfolk State Univ, pres, 2011-13. **Orgs:** Am Asn Higher Educ; Int Commun Asn; Broadcast Educ Asn; Soc Prof Journalists; Ky Gov Task Force Youth & Substance Abuse Prev; bd trustee, Northwest Ohio Pub Tv Found; Leadership Cincinnati, 2000-01; adv bd, Key Bank, OH; Youngstown Bus Incubator; pres, Asn Educ Jour & Mass Commun; adv bd, Pa Econ League Southwestern Pa; bd dir, Int Stud Exchange Prog; Am Coun Edu's Comn Lifelong Learning; bd dir, Ind County Chamber Com; Ind County Ctr Econ Opers; Rotary Club Ind; Greater Ind Revitalization Steering Comt; Ind County Tourist Bur Bd; Postdoctoral fel, Ford Found; bd dir, Ind County Tourist Bur Bd; bd dir, Urban League Pittsburgh; gov bd mem, Mid-Atlantic Consortium-Ctr Acad Excellence, currently. **Business Addr:** Governing Board Member, Mid-Atlantic Consortium-Center for Academic Excellence, 1700 E Cold Spring Lane, Baltimore, MD 21251, **Business Phone:** (443)885-4516.

## AUBESPIN, MERVIN R.
Journalist. **Personal:** Born Jun 30, 1937, Opelousas, LA; son of Henry and Blanche Sittig Earsery; children: Eleska. **Educ:** Tuskegee Univ, BA, indust arts, 1958; Ind State Univ, postgrad, 1960; Columbia Univ, Minority Jour Prog, 1971. **Career:** Journalist (retired); Courier Jour, artist, 1965-72, assoc ed develop, 1969-2002, dir minority recruitment, spec asst exec ed, reporter, 1972-84; Louisville Times, artist, dir minority recruitment, spec asst exec ed; "Two Centuries of Black Louisville: A Photographic History", co-ed, Butler Books, 2011. **Orgs:** Pres & founder, Louisville Asn Black Commun, 1979-80; dir reg & pres, Nat Asn Black Journalist, 1979-81; bd mem, Overseers Bellarmine Col, 1980-81; vpres, 1981-83, pres, 1983-85; Minorities Comn Am Soc Newspaper Ed, 1985; chair, Minorities Comn & Human Resource Comn; Am Soc & Newspaper; co-chmn, Indust Wide Minority Issues Steering Comt, 1985-; chmn, Ida B Wells Jury, 1986-88; bd mem, Mid Am Press Inst, 1995; Sch Journ, Howard Univ, Univ KY, Western KY Univ; adv bd, Black Col Commun Asn; Univ Ky, Ky. **Home Addr:** 733 Southwestern Pkwy, Louisville, KY 40211.

## AUDAIN, DR. LINZ
Educator, lawyer, physician. **Personal:** Born Jul 13, 1959, Port-au-Prince; daughter of Fenelon B and Georgette Nicoleau. **Educ:** Southern Col, BA, 1979; Univ Tenn, pyschol, 1979; Univ Miami, MBA & MA, 1981; Fla Int Univ, MS, finance, 1982; Univ NC, 1984; Univ Chicago, JD, 1987; Duke Univ, PhD, 1991; Howard Univ, MD, 1997. **Career:** Univ of Miami Sch of Bus, Instr of Econs, 1981; Miami Dade Community Col, instr of Econs, 1981-82; Var univs, part time instr econ, 1981-86; Duke Univ, res Asst, 1982-84; Nc A & T State Univ, asst Prof, 1984; The Univ of Chicago Law Sch, res Asst, 1985; U. S. Environ Protection Agency, law clerk, 1985; Keller Grad Sch of Mgt, part time instr, 1985-86; Hartunian, Futterman & Howard, atty & assoc, 1987-88; Loyola Univ Chicago, instr econ, 1988-89; Wash Col Law, Am Univ, asst & assoc prof law, 1989-95; Mandate Corp, chief exec officer, 1992; Northwest internists com. George Wash Univ, Internal Med, resident; Linz Audain, MD LLC, Prin, 2002-; Good Samaritan Hosp, hospitalist, 2012-. **Orgs:** Adv Bd, Next Millenium Consult, 1998-99. Am Bar Asn; Ill Bar Asn; Nat Bar Asn; Hisp Nat Bar Asn; Law & Soc Asn; Am Econ Asn; Am Soc Law & Med; Radio & TV News Dir Asn; Am Law & Econs Asn; Am Med Asn; Nation Med Asn. **Home Addr:** 4924 Wealding Wy, Oxon Hill, MD 20745. **Business Addr:** Internal Medicine Physician, Sibley Memorial Hospital, 5255 Loughboro Rd NW, Washington, DC 20016.

## AUGMON, STACEY ORLANDO
Basketball player. **Personal:** Born Aug 1, 1968, Pasadena, CA; son of Vernett. **Educ:** Univ Nev, Las Vegas, attended 1991. **Career:** Basketball player (retired), basketball coach; Atlanta Hawks, forward & shooting guard, 1991-95, small forward, 1996; Detroit Pistons, shooting guard, 1996-97; Portland Blazers, shooting guard, 1997-98, 1999-2001, small forward, 1999; Charlotte Hornets, shooting guard & forward, 2001-04; New Orleans Hornets, guard & small forward, 2003-04; Orlando Magic, forward & small forward, 2004-06; Denver Nuggets, player develop coach, 2007-11; Dave Rice, asst coach, currently; UNLV Runnin' Rebels, asst coach, 2011-16. **Orgs:** Pres, Bike Club. **Honors/Awds:** Bronze Medal, Olympic Games, US Basketball Team, 1988; Big West Player of the Year, 1989; Defensive Player of the Year, Nat Asn Basketball Coaches, 1989, 1990, 1991; NBA All-Rookie first team, 1992; Hall of fame, Univ Nev, Las Vegas, 2002. **Special Achievements:** NBA Draft, First round pick, No 9, 1991. **Business Addr:** Player Development Coach, Denver Nuggets, 1000 Chopper Cir, Denver, CO 80204, **Business Phone:** (303)405-1100.

## AUGUSTE, DONNA M.
Businessperson, chief executive officer, social worker. **Personal:** Born Sep 11, 1958, Beaumont, TX; daughter of Willa Mae Fruge. **Educ:** Univ Calif, Berkeley, CA, BS, elec eng & comput sci, 1980; Carnegie-Mellon Univ, MS, comput sci, 1983; Aspen Inst, Henry Crown Fel Prog. **Career:** Newton Personal Digital Asst prod family Apple Comput, engineering mgr; WomenCompute.com, bus newsletter, ed; Intelli corp, engr, 1986-90; Apple Comput, sr eng mgr, 1990-93; US W Advan Technologies, sr dir, multimedia systs eng & develop, 1994-96; Freshwater Software Inc, found & chief exec officer, 1996-2001; LLR Gospel Music, founder, pres & chief exec officer, currently. **Orgs:** Inst Elec & Electronic Engrs Internet Comput Ed Bd; Colo Comn Sci &Technol; found & chief exec officer, Leave Little Rm Found, 2001-; Cure D Ars Roman Cath Church; vol, c's orgn. **Home Addr:** 145 Ramona Ave, El Cerrito, CA 94530-4142, **Home Phone:** (303)393-2699. **Business Addr:** Founder, Chief Executive Officer, Leave Little Room Foundation, 9350 Paradise Lane, Broomfield, CO 80020, **Business Phone:** (303)449-5024.

## AUGUSTINE, CYNTHIA
President (organization), executive. **Personal:** children: 2. **Educ:** Sarah Lawrence Col, BA; Rutgers Sch Law, Newark, JD, 1982. **Career:** New York Times Co, sr atty, 1986-93; Sabin, Bermant & Gould, partner, 1993-98; New York Times Co, sr vpres & pres Broadcast Group, 1998-2005; New York Times Broadcast Group, pres, 2000-04; Time Warner Inc, sr vpres talent mgt, 2004-05; Scholastic Corp, sr vpres human resources, 2007-11; FCB Worldwide Inc, global chief talent officer, 2011-; Local TV LLC, pres. **Orgs:** New York Bar Asn; NJ Bar Asn; pres, Nat Asn African Americans Human Resources, 2010-11; HRPS; Soc Human Resource Mgt; Nat Asn Mutual Ins Co; bd trustee, Save C, 2014-. **Business Addr:** Board of Trustee, Save the Children,

501 Kings Hwy E Suite 400, Fairfield, CT 06825, **Business Phone:** (203)221-4000.

**AUGUSTINE, FRANK. See THOMAS, FRANKLIN A.**

### AUGUSTINE, HILTON H., JR.
Chief executive officer, chairperson. **Personal:** children: 4. **Educ:** Univ Wis-Madison, BS, elec & comput engineering, 1982. **Career:** Int Bus Mach, elec engr, 1983-85, mfg mgr, 1986-87, sales & mkt exec, 1988-90; Custom Command Systs, engr, 1988-89; Global Mgt Syst Inc, chmn, pres & chief exec officer, 1988-; Englare, chief angel, 2011-. **Orgs:** Bd dir, Wis Alumni Asn; adv bd, UW Madison Indust Engineering; chmn bd, Atvantec, 1998-2001; bd dir, WAA, 2007; founder, Global Mgt Syst Inc; OneVest.com; Angel.co; Dingman Ctr Angles; Angel Capital Asn; Inst Elec & Electronics Engrs; Wis Black Engineering Stud Soc; Nat Soc Black Engrs. **Business Addr:** Chairman, Chief Executive Officer, Global Management System Inc, 2201 Wis Ave Suite 300, Washington, DC 20007, **Business Phone:** (202)471-4674.

### AUGUSTINE, MATTHEW
Executive. **Personal:** Born Nov 11, 1944, Macon, GA; married Rita V Guillory; children: Malcolm & Karanja. **Educ:** Univ Southwestern La, BS, 1969; Harvard Univ, Cambridge, MBA, 1971. **Career:** RBA Bd Bus, secy; Adage Polaroid; Eltrex Industs Inc, chief exec officer & pres, 1976-; prof, Rochester Inst Technol, 1992-93; Ny Inc, Dir, Bus Coun; RCSB Financial Inc, 1994-; Adage, dir mgt info systs. **Orgs:** Regional vice-chair, dir, Bus Coun NY State Inc; chmn, Urban League Black Scholars Scholar Endowment Prog; mem bd, Rochester Bus Alliance; Boy Scouts Am-Otetiana Coun; Rural Opportunities Inc; Sojourner House; Progressive Neighborhood Fed Credit Union; HSBC Rochester Region; fel Oak Hill Country Club; Alpha Phi Alpha; pres, Sigma Pi Phi Fraternities; pres, Rochester Black Bus Asn, 1994; pres, Rochester Bus Opportunity Corp; chmn, Suny Brockport Bus Indust Ctr; United Way Greater Rochester; Urban League Rochester; Greater Rochester YMCA; Buffalo New York Fed Res Bank; Hochstein Music Schoo; Rochester Downtown Develop Corp; bd mem, Rochester Community Savings Bank; Rochester Jr Achievement Rochester Area Community Found; Small Bus Coun; Blue Shield Rochester; Rochester Chamber Com; chmn, Pvt Indust Coun. **Business Addr:** Chief Executive Officer, President, Eltrex Industries Inc, 65 Sullivan St, Rochester, NY 14605, **Business Phone:** (585)454-6100.

### AUGUSTUS, FRANKLIN J. P.
Airplane pilot. **Personal:** Born Mar 6, 1950, New Orleans, LA; son of Henry Jr and Annie Cooper; children: Brandi. **Educ:** NC State Univ; AUS, Mil Police, MPI, CID Narcotic Agt; NCSBI Sch & Conf. **Career:** Terrebonne Parish Sheriff's Off, res dep, instr acad; New Orleans Recreation Dept, La, head martial arts dept; Franklin JP Augustus Detective Agency Inc, New Orleans, La, pres; Orleans Parish Civil Sheriff's Off, res duty; Super Air Shows Int Inc, New Orleans, La, pres, dir. **Orgs:** Pres, Black Wing Pilots Asn; Exp Aircraft Asn, New Orleans & Slidell Area Chapters Exp Aircraft Asn, Negro Airmen Int, Int Aerobatic Club, Int Coun Air Shows; charter, Cajun Chap No 72 Int Aerobatic Club, Crescent City Aviators; accident prev counr, FAA, 1985-. **Honors/Awds:** Aerobatic license, FAA Unlimited Low Level; private license earned, 1977; Commercial license earned, 1978; Flight instructor certificate, 1979; Certified in Scuba, NOSD School, 1977-; Master of Martial Arts; Movie Stuntman; Logged over 8000 flight hours. **Special Achievements:** World's Only African-American Professional Aerobatic Stunt Pilot. **Home Addr:** 3429 LaSalle St, New Orleans, LA 70115, **Home Phone:** (504)897-2718. **Business Addr:** President, Director, Super Air Shows International Inc, 1 Level St, Abita Springs, LA 70420, **Business Phone:** (504)897-2718.

### AULD, ALBERT MICHAEL
Artist. **Personal:** Born Aug 15, 1943, Kingston; married Rose A Powttatan; children: Ian, Alexei & Kiros. **Educ:** Howard Univ, BFA, 1966, MFA, 1980. **Career:** Lindo, Norman, Craig & Kummel, designer illusr, 1966-67; Nat Ed Asn, designer illusr, 1967-73; USDA Grad Sch, instr, 1967; Sidwell Friends Sch, art teacher, 1973-77; Howard Univ, Dept Art, lectr, 1977-82; Dist Columbia Pub Schs, 1982-; Auld Powhatan, co-founder, writer & researcher indigenous caribbean cultures; Vietnam Metro Sta, 1982; Jamestown Festival Pk, Va, sculptural installations sect, 1995. **Orgs:** Writer & illusr, Self Syndicated Publ Comic Strip, 1967-72; co-founder & dir, A & B Assoc Adv, 1973-79; co-founder & dir, Opus 2 Gallery, 1973-77; freelance Ill designer, Design Co, 1977-; cult chmn, Caribbean Am Intercutl Orgn, 1975-79; Africobra Nat Artists Coop, 1977-; Int Sculpture Conf, 1983-; Nat Art Educrs Asn, 1984-; Artists Equity, Nat Conf Artists, 1986-; bd dir, Fondo del Sol Mus & Cult Ctr, 1986-; chmn, Humanities Bd Fondo del Sol Mus, Wash DC; chmn, Visual Arts Dept, Duke Ellington Sch Arts. **Honors/Awds:** Research Grant, Cafrit Z Found; Research Grant, DC Comm Arts. **Special Achievements:** Published articles: "Taiano Survival In Caribbean: A Focus on Jamaica", "Dead Languages", article on Africobra Artists Black Colegian 1967-, exhibited widely as a sculptor 1967-, Folkloric Article titled Ananesempub in Jamarca Journal 1983, lectured on African Retentions in Ams Oberlin, Smithsonian Inst, Nat Conf Artists, NY Univ, Bronx Museum, NBCHs Tony Brown at Daybreak, local & overseas radio networks, Sculptural Works acclaimed by NY Times, Wash Post, Wash Times, lecturer on Indigenous people Caribbean, Howard Univ, NY Museum Natural History. **Business Addr:** Instructor of Visual Arts, Duke Ellington School of Arts, 1519 Monroe St NW, Washington, DC 20010.

### AUSBROOKS, BETH NELSON
Educator. **Personal:** Born May 18, 1930, Philadelphia, PA; daughter of David Nelson and Phoebe Novotny Nelson; children: Dawna Rogers & Gregory Rogers. **Educ:** Howard Univ, WA, DC, BA, 1952, MA, 1956, PhD, 1971. **Career:** Howard Univ, Wash, DC, assoc prof, 1971-72; Univ NC, Chapel Hill, assoc prof, 1972-74; Univ Md, Baltimore, MD, assoc prof, 1974-75; Univ DC, Dept Urban Affairs, Social Sci & Social Work, prof, 1975-. **Orgs:** Minority Group Rev Comt, Nat Inst Ment Health, 1975-79; bd dir, Provident Hosp, Baltimore, MD, 1980-83; resident adv bd, DC Dept Housing, 1987-; extramural assoc, Nat Inst Health, 1999; Am Polit Sci Orgn; Coun Univ Inst Urban Affairs; Am Sociol Asn; Nat Conf Black Polit Scientists, UDC Chap, Phi Delta Kappa. **Home Addr:** 4986 April Day Garth, Columbia, MD 21044-1329, **Home Phone:** (301)596-3869. **Business Addr:** Professor, University of the District of Columbia, 4200 Conn Ave NW Bldg 41 Rm 400-05, Washington, DC 20008, **Business Phone:** (202)274-5000.

### AUSTIN, DR. BOBBY WILLIAM
School administrator, writer, lecturer. **Personal:** Born Dec 29, 1944, Bowling Green, KY; son of Herschel and Mary E; married Joy L Ford; children: Sushama Meredith Cleva, Julian Sanjay Ford, Leah Mary Sajova & Aviana Joy Lalita. **Educ:** Western Ky Univ, BA, econs & sociol, 1966; Fisk Univ, MA, sociol, 1968; McMaster Univ, PhD, 1972; Harvard Univ, dipl, 1986. **Career:** Georgetown Univ, asst prof, 1971-72; Georgetown summer term, Dept Sociol, chmn, 1972; W.K. Kellogg Found, prog dir, 1986-98; Univ DC, exec asst to pres, asst bd trustee; Nat Urban League, Urban League Rev, founder & ed; Housing & Urban Develop Secy Patricia Roberts Harris, speechwriter; Mayor Wash, D.C. Sharon Pratt Kelly, speechwriter; Austin Ford Assocs, pres; EducationThinkTank, managing dir; Village Found, pres & chief exec officer, currently. **Orgs:** Mahatma M.K. Gandhi fel Am Acad Polit & Social Sci, 2000; Nat Coun Accreditation Teachers Educ; Am Soc Asn; Groves Conf Marriage & Family; Alpha Phi Alpha Frat; Nat Cong Black Prof; Voice; Alphi Phi Omega Nat Serv Fraternity; Peoples Congregational Church; Hannover Proj, Ger; Acad Coun UN Systs; Global Co-Oper Better World; UN Asn, DC Chap; fel Kellogg Nat; Nat Housing Trust; Nat Inst Urban Wildlife; Atlantic Coun US; Global Educ Asn; Am Cult Asn; Am Sociol Asn; chmn, Yr African-Am Male; Co-Convener Secretariat African Am Civil Soc Leaders; Coun Advan Adult Literacy; former chmn planning comt, Status African Am Men; African Am Young Men & Boys Am Soc. **Honors/Awds:** Honorary Doctorate for Public Service, Cent Mich Univ; Kellogg National Fellowship Award. **Special Achievements:** Author of numerous publications; paper presented at the Association for the Study of Afro-American Life & History, New York, 1973; Smithsonian Inst, 1976; published National Black Opinion ACRA Inc, 1977; co-author of Repairing the Breach; listed in Who's Who in Black America, Outstanding Young Men of America and Men of Achievement; First African American full time professor at Georgetown University. **Business Addr:** President, Chief Executive Officer, Village Foundation, 66 Canal Ctr Plz Suite 501, Alexandria, VA 22314, **Business Phone:** (703)548-3200.

### AUSTIN, HON. CARRIE M.
Government official. **Personal:** married Lemuel; children: 7. **Career:** US Rep Mel Reynolds, dep dist dir, 2nd Cong dist; City Chicago, alderman, 34th ward, 1994-; State Cent comt woman, 2000-; Cook County Dem Party, Ill, vice chair; Cent State, committeeman. **Orgs:** Dem Orgn 34th Ward, 1972-; chmn, Comt Budget & Govt Opers; vice chair, Comt Comts, Rules & Ethics; Comt Energy, Environ Protection & Pub Utilities; Comt Finance; Comt Health; Comt Housing & Real Estate; Comt Police & Fire; Comt Zoning; Logos Baptist Assembly Church; Messiah Temple; chmn, Comt Budget & Govt Opers, 2007; chair, City Chicago Black Caucus, secy-. **Special Achievements:** Selected as one of Chicago's 100 Most Influential Women. **Business Addr:** Alderman 34th Ward, City of Chicago, 507 W 111th St, Chicago, IL 60628, **Business Phone:** (773)928-6961.

### AUSTIN, DALLAS
Executive. **Personal:** Born Dec 29, 1970, Columbus, GA. **Career:** Songwriter, Music producer & Musician; Rowdy Rec, pres & chief exec officer, 1992-; Albums: "Push Button", Sugababes; "Ugly", Sugababes; "Trick Me", Kelis; "Blowin Me Up", JC Chasez; "Keep It Down", Kelis; "Secret", Madonna; "Sanctuary", Madonna; "Don't Stop", Madonna; "Survival", Madonna; "Power Good-Bye, Dallas' Low End Mix" Madonna; "Your Honesty", Madonna; "Demand", Tex; "Stuck", Stacie Orrico; "Secrets", Eternal; "Cool", Gwen Stefani; "Crash", Gwen Stefani; "Danger Zone", Gwen Stefani; "Hit 'Em Up Style, Oops, Blu Cantrell?; "Don't Let Me Get Me", Pink; "Just like a Pill", P!nk; "Left Outside Alone", Anastacia; "Sick & Tired", Anastacia; "Creep", TLC; "Case Fake People", TLC; "Unpretty", TLC; "Silly Ho", TLC; "If They Knew", TLC; "Shout", TLC; Executive producer: Drumline, 2002; ATL, 2006; 8Dazeaweakend (director), 2009; Acid Girls, 2014; Warner Bros Studios, producer, currently; Dallas Austin Rec Proj, owner. **Business Addr:** Producer, Warner Bros Studios, 4000 Warner Blvd, Burbank, CA 91522, **Business Phone:** (818)954-3000.

### AUSTIN, DR. DEBRA
Chancellor (education), college administrator, vice president (organization). **Personal:** children: Kimberly & Kendrea. **Educ:** Mich State Univ, BA, eng; Univ Fla, MA, eng; Fla State Univ, master degree, bus admin, PhD, higher educ. **Career:** Lake-Sumter Community Col, eng instr; Tallahassee Community Co, div head, chief acad officer, actg Pres, exec vpres, 2000-; Fla State Univ, asst vpres acad affairs & provost; State Univ Syst Fla, chancellor, 2003-05; chancellor col univ, 2003-; Fla A & M Univ, provost & vpres acad affairs, 2005-; Lake-Sumter Community Col, eng instr. **Orgs:** Bd dir, Tallahassee Mem Health Care, 2003-04; Delta Sigma Theta Sorority; Leadership Fla; Knight Found Community Adv Comt; second vpres & bd dir, Tallahassee Urban League; Fel Bethel A.M.E. Church; bd gov mem, State Univ Syst Fla; bd gov mem, Fla Bd Gov Found Inc; staff, Fla Bd Gov; pres, FAMU chap United Fac Fla; TMH Bd's Planning Comt; Nsf; bd mem, Tallahassee Memorial. **Business Addr:** Provost & Vice President of Academic Affairs, Florida A&M University, Foote-Hilyer Administration Ctr Suite 301, Tallahassee, FL 32307, **Business Phone:** (850)599-3276.

### AUSTIN, DR. DORIS
College president. **Career:** Tallahassee Community Col, interim pres, currently. **Home Addr:** 2216 Keith St, Tallahassee, FL 32310, **Home Phone:** (850)574-7451. **Business Addr:** Interim President, Tallahassee Community College, 444 Appleyard Dr, Tallahassee, FL 32304, **Business Phone:** (850)488-9200.

### AUSTIN, DR. ERNEST AUGUSTUS
Physician, educator. **Personal:** Born Nov 26, 1932, Brooklyn, NY; son of Augustin and Elrica Mildred Davidson; married Margaret P Byrd; children: Vivian, Jean & Alan. **Educ:** St Johns Univ, BS, 1953; Howard Univ, MD, 1957. **Career:** Physician, educator(retired); Suny, clin instr surg, 1962-69; Fordham Hosp, chief surg, 1966-69; Bowman Gray Sch Med, asst prof surg, 1969-72; Reynolds Meml Hosp, dir surg, 1969-72; Univ MD Sch Med, asst prof surg, 1972-79; Provident Hosp, chief surg, 1972-73; D Univ MInst Emergency MedShock Traum Ctr, chief surg & traumatology, 1974-76, 1978-79; Univ MD Hosp, dir emergency serv, 1977-78; Cooper Med Ctr Camden NJ, chief traumatology, dir emergency med serv, 1979-84; CMDNJ-Rutgers Med Sch, assoc prof surg, 1979-84; Prudential Ins, Horsham, PA, dir med serv, 1989-92, 1994-97; Intracorp, Plymouth Meeting, PA, sr physician adv, 1992-93. **Orgs:** Founding mem, Am Trauma soc; bd dir, Am Cancer Soc Forsyth Unit NC; bd dir, Nat Found Forsyth-Stokes Chap NC; bd dir, Am Trauma Soc MD Chapt; dipl Am Bd Surg; fel Am Col Surgeons. **Home Addr:** 131 Paisley Pl, Hainesport, NJ 08036-2787, **Home Phone:** (609)265-2928.

### AUSTIN, ISAAC EDWARD (IKE AUSTIN)
Basketball coach, basketball player. **Personal:** Born Aug 18, 1969, Gridley, CA; married Denise. **Educ:** Ariz State Univ, attended 1991. **Career:** Basketball player (retired), basketball coach; Utah Jazz, ctr, 1991-93; Continental Basketball Asn, Okla City Cavalry, ctr, 1993-94; Philadelphia 76ers, ctr, 1994; CRO Lyon, France, ctr, 1994-95; Tuborg Izmir, Turkey, ctr, 1995-96; Miami Heat, ctr, 1996-98; Los Angeles Clippers, ctr, 1999; Orlando Magic, ctr, 1999; Wash Wizards, ctr, 2000; Vancouver Grizzlies, ctr, 2000-02; Memphis Grizzlies, ctr, 2001-02; Ulkerspor, Turkey, 2002; Xinjiang Flying Tigers, China, 2003; Jersey Squires, Am Basketball League, 2004; Utah Snowbears, owner & head coach, 2004-05. **Honors/Awds:** Most Improved Player, Nat Basketball Asn, 1997. **Business Addr:** Owner, Chief Executive Officer, Utah Snowbears, 180 S 300 W Suite 140, Salt Lake City, UT 84101, **Business Phone:** (801)533-2327.

### AUSTIN, JAMES N., JR.
President (organization). **Personal:** married Gloria. **Educ:** Howard Univ, Wash, DC, BA, bus, 1976. **Career:** Am Express, mgr; Austin Co, owner & broker, currently; National Cowboys Color Museum & Hall Fame, founder, currently. **Orgs:** Nat Asn Realtors; comnr, Tex Real Estate Comn. **Honors/Awds:** Good Neighbor Award, 2003. **Business Addr:** Broker, Owner, Austin Co, 2401 Scott Ave, Fort Worth, TX 76103-2228, **Business Phone:** (817)923-9305.

### AUSTIN, JOYCE PHILLIPS
Lawyer. **Personal:** Born Sep 10, 1923, New York, NY; daughter of Fitzgerald and Kathleen Miller; married Rodman W. **Educ:** Hunter Col, City Univ NY, BA, 1943; Fordham Univ Sch Law, JD, 1945. **Career:** Lawyer (retired); Off Price Stabilization, atty adv, 1951-53; NY State Dept Comn, exec secy, Women's Coun, 1956-57, asst dep comnr, 1957-59; City NY, asst mayor, 1959-65; Off Econ Opportunity, exec asst regional dir, 1966-68; Sheltering Arms C Serv, asst dir, 1968-75; Fedn Protestant Welfare Agencies Inc, exec vpres, 1974-86. **Orgs:** Episcopal Diocese NY, Bishops Cross, 1983; trustee, Helen Keller, Worldwide; bd mem, Consortium Endowed Episcopal Parisher; Am Bar Asn; NY Lawyers Asn; Fordham Law Alumni Asn; Nat Asn Advan Colored People; Nat Coun Negro Women; Union Black Episcopalians; Cosmopolitan Club; Nat Arts Club; trustee, Gen Theol Sem. **Honors/Awds:** Keystone Award, Fedn Protestant Welfare Agencies, 1986; Hall of Fame, Hunter Col; John H Finley Award, City Col Alumni Asn. **Home Addr:** 510 E 23rd St Apt 7A, New York, NY 10010-5019, **Home Phone:** (212)674-2903.

### AUSTIN, LUCIUS STANLEY
Newspaper editor. **Personal:** Born Jul 3, 1960, Batesville, MS; son of Sherman E Sr and Glennie V Cox; married Laurie Scott; children: Rebekah Hope & Joshua T S. **Educ:** Jackson State Univ, attended 1982; Univ Memphis, BA, jour, 1982; Univ Mo, jour, 1987. **Career:** Belleville News Dem, reporter, 1983-84; St Louis Am, city ed, 1984-85; Kans City Times, copy ed, 1985-86, makeup ed, 1986-87; Kans City Star, asst bus ed, 1987. **Orgs:** Alpha Phi Alpha Fraternity, 1980-; Nat Asn Black Journalist, 1983-; Kans City Asn Black Journalist, 1985-; Soc Am Bus Ed & Writers, 1992-. **Home Addr:** 11712 E 87th St, Raytown, MO 64138-3560.

### AUSTIN, MARY JANE
School administrator. **Personal:** Born Apr 24, 1935, Orange, NJ; daughter of George W Jr and Louise Margaret Street; married Harry Lester; children: Sharon Milora & Sherrill Ruth. **Educ:** Newark State Col, BS, 1957; Bank St Col Parsons Sch Design, MA, art educ, 1983. **Career:** Educator (retired); Elizabeth Pub Sch, art educr, 1957-87; Roosevelt Jr Sch, art consult, 1970-73; Elizabeth Bd Educ, layout artist, 1973-78; William F Halloran Alternative Sch Gifted & Talented, art educr, 1979-87; Irvington Bd Educ, supvr art educ, 1987-2000. **Orgs:** Arts Educr NJ; Nat Art Educ Asn, 1979-86; Independent Orders Foresters, assoc supv & curric develop; Asn Supv & Curric Devel, 1987-89; treasr, Citizen Awareness Group/Cranford, 1989-90; chairperson, Women's Day, 1989-90; Prin Supvr Asn. **Home Addr:** 15 Wall St, Cranford, NJ 07016, **Home Phone:** (908)276-5926.

### AUSTIN, PATTI
Singer. **Personal:** Born Aug 10, 1950, Harlem, NY; daughter of Gordon and Edna. **Career:** Albums: End of A Rainbow, 1976; Havana Candy, 1977; Live at the Bottom Line, 1979; Body Language, 1980; Every Home Should Have One, 1981; In My Life, 1983; Patti Austin, 1984; Getting Away With Murder, 1985; The Real Me, 1988; Love Is Gonna Getcha, 1990; Carry On, 1991; Live, 1992; That Secret Place, 1994; Jukebox Dreams, 1996; In & Out of Love, 1998; Street of Dreams, 1999; On the Way to Love, 2001; For Ella, 2002; Avant Gershwin, 2007; An Inspirational Holiday, 2008; Sound Advice, 2011; TV shows: The Kennedy Center Honors: A Celebration of the Performing Arts, 2001; Pyramid, 2003; Apollo at 70: A Hot Night in Harlem, 2004; Q Prod Inc, singer, currently; Compliations: The Very Best Of Patti Austin, 2001; Collection, 2002; Baby Come To Me & Other Hits, 2003; Intimate Patti Austin, 2007. **Business Addr:** Singer, Q Production Inc, 236 W Portal Ave Suite 396, San Francisco, CA 94127.

**AUSTIN, RAYMOND DEMONT (RAY AUSTIN)**
Football player. **Personal:** Born Dec 21, 1974, Greensboro, NC. **Educ:** Univ Tenn, grad. **Career:** Football player (retired); New York Jets, defensive back, 1997-98; Chicago Bears, defensive, 1998-99; Chicago Enforcers, 2001. **Special Achievements:** Acted in 11 commercials.

**AUSTIN, DR. SENIOR REE B.**
Accountant. **Career:** DC Pub Sch Systs. **Business Addr:** Accountant, DC Public School Systems, 1258 Oates St NE, Washington, DC 20002, **Business Phone:** (202)399-8186.

**AUSTIN, DR. WANDA M.**
Engineer. **Personal:** Born New York, NY; daughter of Murry Pompey and Helen; married Wade Jr; children: 2. **Educ:** Franklin & Marshall Col, BA, math, 1975; Univ Pittsburgh, MS, systs engineering & math, 1977; Univ Southern Calif, PhD, systs engineering, 1987. **Career:** Aerospace Corp, gen mgr, electronic systs div, 1979-, pres & chief exec officer, 2008; Engineering & Tech Group, sr vpres, 2001-03; Nat Systs Group, sr vpres, 2004-07. **Orgs:** Fel Am Inst Aeronaut & Astronaut, 1980-; Nat Acad Engineering, 2008-; Int Acad Astronaut; Am Acad Arts & Sci; Space Found; bd trustee, Univ Southern Calif; Nat Geog Soc; advisors sci & technol, Defense Sci Bd, 2010. **Honors/Awds:** Herndon Black Image Award, Aerospace Corp, 1984; Outstanding Business & Professional, Dollars & Sense, 1993; Outstanding Achievement, Women Aerospace, 1996; Service & Leadership Award, Int Coun Systs Engineering, 1996; Upward Mobility Award, Soc Women Engrs, 2002; National Reconnaissance Office Gold Medal, 2004; Women in Technology InterNat Award, 2007; Special Achievement Award, 100 Black Men of Los Angeles, 2008; National Intelligence Medallion for Meritorious Service Award; Air Force Scroll of Achievement Award; Von Braun Award for Excellence; NDIA Peter B. Teets Industry Award, 2012; USC Viterbi Distinguished Alumni Award, 2014. **Special Achievements:** Publ: Austin W & Khoshnevis B, Qualitative Modeling Using Natural Language: An Application in Systems Dynamics; Qualitative Simulation Modeling & Analysis, Springer Verlag, Spring, 1991; First female, first black sr vpres Aerospace Corp's Engineering & Technol Group, 2001; First female, first black President and CEO of major Aerospace company. **Home Addr:** , Hawthorne, CA. **Business Addr:** President, Chief Executive Officer, The Aerospace Corp, 2350 E El Segundo Blvd, El Segundo, CA 90245-4691, **Business Phone:** (310)336-5000.

**AUTRY, HARRINGTON DARNELL**
Executive, football player. **Personal:** Born Jun 19, 1976, Wiesbaden. **Educ:** Northwestern Univ, BA, commun & theatre, 1997. **Career:** Football player (retired); Chicago Bears, running back, 1997; Philadelphia Eagles, running back, 2000; Team Autry Productions, chief exec officer, currently. **Special Achievements:** Film: "The Eighteenth Angel", 1997. **Business Addr:** Chief Executive Officer, Team Autry Productions, 4822 S Heather Dr, Tempe, AZ 85282-7373, **Business Phone:** (480)244-9969.

**AVANT, CLARENCE**
Music producer, executive, president (organization). **Personal:** Born Feb 25, 1931, Climax, NC; son of Gertrude; married Jacqueline Alberta Gray; children: Nicole & Alexander Devore. **Career:** Exec Producer: Save the Children, 1973; Deliver Us from Evil, 1975; Stalingrad, producer, 1990; Jason's Lyric, 1994; Avant Garde Enterprises Inc, pres, 1962-; Clarama Music Inc, pres, 1968; Avant Garde Broadcasting, founder, 1971-; Tabu Productions Inc, founder, 1976; Interior Music Publ, pres, 1983-; Motown Rec, pres & chief exec officer, 1993-97; Urban Box Off Network Inc, chmn, 1999. **Orgs:** Pres, Neighbors Watts, 1975; chmn, NOW mem, 1974; Int Mgt Bd, Polygram, 1997; Nat Asn Advan Colored People Legal Defense Fund; Pepsi-Cola African-Am Adv Bd; bd dir, Int Stud Ctr, Univ Calif, Los Angeles. **Business Addr:** President, Interior Music Publishing, 5757 Wilshire Blvd Rm335, Los Angeles, CA 90036, **Business Phone:** (323)933-5952.

**AVENT, JACQUES MYRON**
Manager, government official. **Personal:** Born Nov 13, 1940, Washington, DC; son of Charles Alexander Sr (deceased) and Virginia Hartwell (deceased); married Loretta Taylor; children: James Edward. **Educ:** Howard Univ, BS, 1963. **Career:** Fed Elec Corp, Jobs Corp, Wash, Nj, field rep, job counr, 1965-67; Wash Metrop Area Jobs Coun, asst dir, 1967-69; Nat Asn Regional Couns, field dir, 1969-71; Nat Urban Coalition, asst dir field opers, 1971-72; NLC USCM, prog mgr, 1972-74; League CA Cities, Berkeley, spec proj assoc, 1974-75; Human Serv Inst, exec dir, 1975-76; NLC, asst dir mem serv, 1976-77, dir off mem serv, 1977-86; Security Pac Nat Bank, vpres munic finance, 1986-88; City Phoenix, exec asst to city coun, 1989-90, exec asst to city mgr, 1990-92, dep city mgr, 1992. **Orgs:** Urban Exec Prog, Sloan Sch MIT, 1973; Am Soc Pub Admin, 1978-; bd mem, Nat Forum Black Pub Admin, 1983-; Nat Asn Securities Professionals; secy, Nat Forum Black Pub Admin, 1985; mem dir, Nat League Cities; Nat Forum Black Pub Admin; bd mem, Phoenix Lisc; adv bd, Phoenix Salvation Army; bd mem, Valley Sun United Way; Cent Ariz Chap, NFBPA; ICMA; Gov Finance Officers Asn Clubs. **Home Addr:** 3538 E Modoc Ct, Phoenix, AZ 85044, **Home Phone:** (480)496-9430. **Business Addr:** AZ.

**AVERY, BYLLYE Y.**
Association executive, college teacher. **Personal:** Born Oct 20, 1937, DeLand, FL; married Ngina Lythcott. **Educ:** Talladega Univ, BA, psychol, 1959; Fla State Univ, MEd, spec educ & teaching, 1969; Univ Fla, PhD, 1969; State Univ NY, attended 1990; Bowdoin Col, DHL, 1993; Bates Col, LHD, 1995. **Career:** Raising Women's Voices Health Care We Need, co-founder; Gainsville Women's Health Ctr & Birthplace, co-founder; Nat Black Women's Health Imperative, founder & pres, 1981-92; Columbia Univ, Ctr Bioethics, external adv bd; Nat Insts Health, advisor; Harvard Sch Pub Health, vis fel; Columbia Univ, Mailman Sch Pub Health, clin prof pop & family health, currently; Avery Inst Social Chg, founder, 2002-11. **Orgs:** Fenway Health Ctr, Boston, 2002; bd mem, Global Fund Women; bd mem, Int Women's Health Coalition; bd mem, Boston Women's Health Bk Collective; bd mem, Adv Comt Kellogg Int Fel Prog; bd visitors, Tucker Found, Dartmouth Col; Dana Farber Cancer Adv Bd; Charter Adv Comt, Off Res Women's Health, NIH; vis fel, Harvard Sch Pub Health; Am Pub Health Asn; Nat Women's Health Network; founder, Black Women's Health Imperative; Am Pub Health Asn; Nat Women's Health Network; LLuminari & Be Well health expert network. **Home Addr:** , Provincetown, MD. **Business Addr:** Founder, Ex-officio, Black Women's Health Imperative, 1726 M St NW Suite 300, Washington, SC 20036, **Business Phone:** (202)548-4000.

**AVERY, CHARLES E.**
Photographer, writer. **Personal:** Born Jan 1, 1938. **Educ:** Sch Visual Arts, attended 1964; Germain Sch Photog, attended 1968; Essex Co Col, attended 1974. **Career:** Piscataway Libr, sr asst librn bookmobile, 1988; Piscataway Dept Pub Works, traffic asst, 1989; auth currently; Books: Everybody Has Feelings/ Todos Tenemos Sentimientos, auth; Todos Tienen Emociones, auth & photogr. **Home Addr:** 37 Grove St, Plainfield, NJ 07060, **Home Phone:** (908)754-8259. **Business Addr:** Author, Open Hand Publishing Inc, PO Box 22048, Seattle, WA 98122, **Business Phone:** (206)447-0597.

**AVERY-BLAIR, LORRAINE**
Banker. **Personal:** children: Nina, Lanita & Martina. **Educ:** Univ Wis. **Career:** First Financial Bank, sr vpres, currently. **Orgs:** Pres, bd dir, Woodland Girl Scouts Coun; pres & bd mem, WI Automated Clearing House, WACHA; bd chair, EFTI & Access 24 ILL Regional Electronic Funds Network; bd vis, Univ WI, Stevens Pt; adv comn, Tyme Regional Electronic Funds Network; pres, Zonta, Cent WI Chap; United Way Campaign Portage County, chair; Accountability Measures, gov's task force, Univ WI, 1993-. **Honors/Awds:** Am Best & Brightest Bus Women, Dollars & Sense Mag, 1993; Outstanding Women Color Educ Award, Univ Wis. **Home Addr:** 3346 Sandy Acres Dr, Plover, WI 54467, **Home Phone:** (715)344-1167.

**AVILES, DORA**
Educator. **Personal:** Born Oct 12, 1960, Puerto Cortes; daughter of Juan; children: Karima Raimundi, Atrion Raimundi & Crayg Springer. **Educ:** Lehman Col. **Career:** Bronx Community Col, Stud Govt Activies, secy, 1991-93; Citizen's Adv Bur, head teacher infant, toddler rm, 1995-2000; City Univ New York, Lehman Col, Res Found, admin asst, asst educ, res asst. **Orgs:** Network Orgn Bronx Bus Women, 1995-; bd mem, NW Bronx Neighborhood Orgn, 1997-; bd mem, Youth Comt, 2000-02, Bronx Community Bd-7; COBRA, 2000-; bd mem, Truman High Leadership Team, 2000-02; bd mem, PS 94 Leadership Team, 2000-02. **Home Addr:** 3351 Reservoir Oval W Suite 2A, Bronx, NY 10467, **Home Phone:** (718)325-1825.

**AWKARD, LINDA NANLINE**
Lawyer. **Personal:** Born Nov 21, 1948, Harrisonburg, VA; daughter of Joseph C Jr and Julita C; married Edward C Maddox Jr; children: Edward C Maddox III. **Educ:** Fla State Univ, BA, BS, chem, 1970; Fordham Univ Sch Law, JD, 1978; Harvard Law Sch, grad cert, 1982. **Career:** Pan Am Airways, int flight attend, 1970-79; Legal Servs Corp, spec asst pres, 1979-83; Awkard & Assocs Chartered, owner, pres, 1984-. **Orgs:** NY State Bar Asn, 1979-; Am Bar Asn, 1979-; comt mem, Nat Bar Asn, 1979-; Nat Bus League, 1984-; bd mem, Nat Chamber Litigation Ctr; bd dir, US Chamber Com; bd mem, Americans Transp Mobility. **Honors/Awds:** NBL Merit Citation, Nat Bus League, 1991. **Special Achievements:** Founder of one of the few minority & female owned law firms in the US specilizing in commercial transactional law with emphasis on financing of automobile, marine vehicle, and commercial real estate development transactions; first female to serve as general counsel of the 93 year-old Nat Bus League; First African-American to graduate from Florida StateUniv with a degree in chemistry & mathematics. **Home Addr:** 3805 Longford Dr, Tallahassee, FL 32309. **Business Addr:** President, Awkard & Associates Chartered, 4201 Cathedral Ave NW Suite 1416, Washington, DC 20016.

**AXAM, JOHN ARTHUR**
Consultant, librarian, writer. **Personal:** Born Feb 12, 1930, Cincinnati, OH; married Dolores Ballard. **Educ:** Cheyney State Univ, BSE, 1953; Drexel Univ, MSLS, 1958. **Career:** Free Libr Philadelphia, librn, 1958-64, head stas dept, 1964-78, area adminr, 1978-91; Employ Rels & Strategies Unit, consult, 2003. **Orgs:** Am Libr Asn; Pa Libr Asn; United Way Southern Pa; United Methodist Church; Pub Lib Asn Goals, Guidelines & Stand Comt, 1971-77; pres, Pa Libr Asn, Alternative Educ Prog Sect, 1980; Mkt Pub Lib Serv Comm, 1983-84. **Honors/Awds:** Various articles, Library Prof Publ; Chapel of the Four Chaplains Award; Cert Merit, Pa Libr Asn, 1988; Harry Hosier Award, Black United Methodist Preachers. **Special Achievements:** Author: "The Free Library of Philadelphia Reader Development Program, Report for the Period June 12, 1967 - June 30", 1968. **Home Addr:** 1803 W Chew St, Philadelphia, PA 19141-1201, **Home Phone:** (215)549-6485.

**AYCOCK, ANGELA LYNNETTE**
Basketball player, clergy. **Personal:** Born Feb 28, 1973, Dallas, TX; daughter of Charles Williams and Albertine. **Educ:** Univ Kans, 1995. **Career:** Basketball player (retired), clergy; SC Alcamo-Banca Don Rizzo, 1995-96, Seattle Reign, guard forward, 1996; Panathinaikos AC, Phoenix Mercury, 1999; Seattle Storm, Minnesota Lynx, 2000; Nun, Russ Orthodox Church, currently. **Honors/Awds:** Kodak All-American, 1995; USBWA All-American, 1995.

**AYERS, DR. GEORGE WALDON, JR.**
Dentist. **Personal:** Born Sep 23, 1931, Lake City, FL; married Marjorie E; children: Dwayne M, Marva, Damian & Donald. **Educ:** Fla A&M Univ, BS, 1956; Meharry Med Col, Sch Dent, DDS, 1966. **Career:** Alachua Co Health, 1969-70; Sunland Ctr, dent dir, 1972-. **Orgs:** Alachua Co Dent Soc; Cent Dist Dent; Fla Dent Asn; Am Dent Asn; Fla Pub Health Asn; S Asn Int Dentist. **Honors/Awds:** Senior Sental Student Recognition Award, 1966. **Home Addr:** 1224 SE 12th Ave, Gainesville, FL 32641-8115. **Business Addr:** Dental Director, Sunland Center, 1621 NE Waldo Rd, Gainesville, FL 32601, **Business Phone:** (352)955-5000.

**AYERS, RANDY (RANDALL DUANE AYERS)**
Basketball coach. **Personal:** Born Apr 16, 1956, Springfield, OH; son of Frank and Betty Basey; married Carol Denise Peery; children: Ryan Vincent & Cameron Alexander. **Educ:** Miami Univ, BS, educ, 1978; Miami Univ Ohio, MA, educ, 1981. **Career:** Basketball player (retired), basketball coach; Miami Univ, grad asst, 1978-81; Army, asst coach, 1982-84; US Mil Acad, W Pt, coach, 1982-84; Ohio State Univ, basketball coach, 1984-97; Philadelphia 76ers, asst coach, 1997-2003, 2009-10, head coach, 2003-04; Orlando Magic, asst coach, 2005-07; Wash Wizards, asst coach, 2007-09; New Orleans Hornets / Pelicans, asst coach, 2010-, lead asst, 2011. **Business Addr:** Assistant Coach, New Orleans Pelicans, 5800 Airline Dr, Metairie, LA 70003, **Business Phone:** (504)593-4700.

**AYERS, ROY**
Musician. **Personal:** Born Sep 10, 1940, Los Angeles, CA. **Career:** Ubiquity, founder; musician, currently; Evolution: The Polydor Anthology, two-cd compilation, 1995; Smooth Jazz, 1999; Albums: West Coast Vibes, 1963; Stoned Soul Picnic, 1968; Ubiquity, 1971; Change Up The Groove, 1974; Mystic Voyage, 1975; Vibrations, 1976; Red, Black & Green, 1976; Everybody Loves The Sunshine, 1976; You Send Me, 1978; No Stranger To Love, 1979; Love Fantasy, 1980; Music Of Many Colors, 1980; Africa-Centre Of The World, 1981; Feelin Good, 1982; Lots Of Love, 1983; Silver Vibrations, 1983; Drivin On Up, 1983; In The Dark, 1984; You Might Be Surprised, 1985; I'm The One, 1987; Drive, 1988; Wake Up, 1989; Fast Money, 1990; Searchin, 1991; Double Trouble, 1992; Hot, 1992; Good Vibrations, 1993; The Essential Groove - Live, 1994; Vibesman, 1995; Naste, 1995; Spoken Word, 1998; Smooth Jazz, 1999; Juice, 1999; Live At Ronnie Scott's - London 1988, 2001; Our Time is Coming, 2001; For Cafe Apres-midi, 2002; Good Vibrations, 2003; Snoop, 2003; Virgin Ubiquity: Unreleased Recordings, 1976-81, 2004; Mahogany Vibe, 2004; Sunshine Man, 2005; Virgin Ubiquity II, 2005; Virgin Ubiquity Remixed, 2006; Perfection, 2006; Roy Ayers Ubiquity Inc, founder, currently. **Business Addr:** Musician, Roy Ayers Productions Co, PO Box 1219, New York, NY 10023.

**AYERS, HON. TIMOTHY F. (TIM AYERS)**
Mayor, insurance agent. **Personal:** Born Nov 19, 1958, Springfield, OH; son of Franklin and Betty Rae Basey; married Lisa J Henry; children: Katheryne; married Robin Brown; children: Joseph & Perry. **Educ:** Capital Univ, Columbus, OH, polit sci, 1981. **Career:** Ohio House Reps, Columbus, OH, legis page, 1979, legis message clerk, 1980-84; Ohio House Campaign Comn, Columbus, OH, 1982; Clark County Community Action Corp, Springfield, OH, 1984-86; City Springfield, OH, mayor & city comnr, 1984-90; Ohio Dept of Agr, spec asst, 1990; Lic ins agt, OH; Reach Out Youth Inc, Springfield, OH, foster care social worker; Equitable, Springfield, OH, agt; Chamber of Com, Nashville, Tenn, small bus mgr, staff, exec dir; Centers DisControl, N Nashville, exec dir; N Nashville Community Develop Corp, bus owner, dir, exec dir, 2000; Tenn State Democrative Exec Committeemen, 2000; teacher. **Orgs:** Truman Kennedy Club; Clark County Democratic Exec Comm; bd mem, Am Red Cross. **Honors/Awds:** Outstanding Young Man in America, 1984, 1985. **Special Achievements:** Selected one of Kentuckys Minority Educator and Retention Award winners. **Home Addr:** 334 Fair St, Springfield, OH 45506, **Home Phone:** (513)322-2888.

**AYERS-ELLIOTT, CINDY**
Executive. **Personal:** Born Aug 12, 1956, Ashland, MS; daughter of Annie Mae Ayers Jackson; children: Lagrand & Eric. **Educ:** Rust Col, Holly Springs, MA, BA, 1980; Univ Mass, Boston, MA, MBA, 1988. **Career:** Sen Campaign, Jackson, Mass, field coordr, 1984-85; Gov Off, Jackson, Mass, prog specialist, 1985-86, nat rural fel, 1986-87; State Treas Off, Jackson, Mass, admin asst, 1988-96; Grigsby Brandford & Co Inc, vpres; Chapman Capital Mgt Inc, vpres mkt, 1994; Sun-Delta Capital Access Ctr Inc, pres, currently. **Orgs:** Nat deleg, Dem Nat Conv, 1984-96; nat comt woman, Miss Young Dem, 1986; track deleg, Dem Nat Conv, 1988; state coordr, Presidential Election, 1988; treas, Young Dem Am, 1989-; vice chairperson & bd dir, Miss Home Corp, 1989; chairwoman, First Am bank; founder, Miss First African-Am Bank; Nat Bankers Asn; Miss Bankers Asn; Nat Asn Advan Colored People; Nat Rural Fel; vice chair, Delta Found; vice chair, Miss Home Corp, 1990; Leadership Jackson Class, 1991; bd, Miss Food Network, 1995; treas, Miss Head Start Asn; adv bd, Jackson State Univ; sr vpres, Wall St Investment Banking Firm. **Home Addr:** 4945 S Dr, Jackson, MS 39209, **Home Phone:** (601)922-8395. **Business Addr:** President, Sun-Delta Capital Access Center Inc, 819 Main St, Greenville, MS 38701, **Business Phone:** (662)335-5291.

**AYERS-JOHNSON, DARLENE**
Government official. **Personal:** Born Feb 28, 1943, Oakland, CA; daughter of Ernest and Thelma; married Perry Oliver; children: Cynthia Maria. **Educ:** Holy Names Col, BA, bus admin-econs, 1983; Golden Gate Univ, BA, human rels, 1997. **Career:** Stand Regist Co, Oakland, group exec, mkt, 1972-85; A F Smith Trading Ltd, Bermuda Bus Mach, gen mgr, mkt mgr, 1985-88; AMBER Printing Co, chief exec officer & owner, 1989-91; Oakland Bd Port Commissioners, comnr, pres, 2000-08; Friends Faith Inc, exec dir, 2004-07; Interagency Support Div, Dept Gen Servs, dep dir, chief dep dir; Port Oakland, sec vpres, 2007-; Ayers-Johnson & Assocs, founder; Pac Rim Regional Adminr US Gen Serv Admin, sr advisor, 2007-09; Northern Calif div advert firm Clear Channel Airports, consult & community develop expert 2011-; CAbi Clothing, Independent CAbi Fashion Styllst, 2013-. **Orgs:** Ford's Consumer Appeals Bd; speaker house, Emergency Bus Enterprises Comn, 1992; Calif Comn Status Women, 2006-10. **Home Addr:** 11001 Lochard St, Oakland, CA 94605-5442, **Home Phone:** (510)568-2656. **Business Addr:** Consultant, Community Development Expert, Clear Channel Airports, 555 12th St Suite 950, Oakland, CA 94607, **Business Phone:** (510)835-5900.

**AZIBO, DR. DAUDI AJANI YA**
Educator. **Personal:** Born Washington, DC. **Educ:** Xavier Univ, BS; Rider Univ, MS, 1978; Wash Univ, PhD, psychol. **Career:** Temple Univ, asst prof, Africana studies, 1987-1992; State Univ New York, New Paltz, NY, fac Africana studies; Fla A & M Univ, Dept Psychol, assoc prof; Grambling State Univ, Dept Sociol & Psychol, assoc prof

psychol, currently. **Orgs:** Eval Rev Panel, Off Asst Secy Planning & Eval. **Business Addr:** Associate Professor of Psychology, Grambling State University, 105 Woodson Hall, Grambling, LA 71245, **Business Phone:** (318)274-2240.

**AZIZ, KAREEM A.**
School administrator, executive director. **Personal:** Born Dec 15, 1951, Dayton, OH; married Vernetta Nini Oseye; children: 3. **Educ:** Cent State Univ, BA, polit sci & govt, 1975; Univ Dayton, MPA, pub admin, 1976; Morgan State Univ, doctoral stud, 1984; Union Inst & Univ, ABD, doctoral stud, educ leadership & appl info technol, 2004. **Career:** Comprehensive Manpower Ctr, admin asst exec dir, 1975-77; Clark Co Employ & Trng Off, coord comm PSE prog, 1977-78; YMCA Springfield OH, exec dir, 1978-80; YMCA Baltimore, Md, exec dir, 1980-81; Sojourner Douglass Col, Inst Res & Plng, field supvr, 1981-85, instr, 1981-, coord, 1981-, local coordr, 1994-95, dir, inst res & planning, 1995-, admin, 2005-, dir, currently; Co Investr, Minority Univ Space Interdisciplinary Network, NASA, currently. **Orgs:** Co chair, Nat Communs Community Nat Black Independent Polit Party, 1983-; consult, New Day Asn, 1985; bd mem, pres, Inst Black World; Leader Campus Fire Dept; Stud Govt Commun Coordr; Stud Coordr State-wide Conf African Liberation Struggles; Alpha Phi Alpha Fraternity; bd dir, Inst Black World 21st Century; chmn, Rites Passage Prog Comt; chmn, Thurgood Marshall Dist Baltimore Area Coun Boy Scouts Am. **Honors/Awds:** Key Statistics About Minorities in the Dayton Area, Dayton Human Relations Council, 1973. **Home Addr:** 8548 Stevenswood Rd, Windsor Mill, MD 21244-2217, **Home Phone:** (410)521-4045. **Business Addr:** Director, Sojourner Douglass College, 500 N Caroline St, Baltimore, MD 21205, **Business Phone:** (410)276-0306.

**AZOULAY, KATYA GIBEL. See MEVORACH, KATYA GIBEL.**

# B

**BAAKO, SEKOU MOLEFI. See JACKSON, ANDREW PRESTON.**

**BAAQEE, DR. SUSANNE INEZ**
Dentist. **Personal:** Born Nov 24, 1952, Boston, MA; daughter of Inez and Everett; married Melvin Bilal; children: Shakir, Aneesah & Mikal. **Educ:** Simmons Col, BS, biol, 1974; Tufts Dent Sch, DMD, dent, 1978; Harvard Sch Dent Implantology, 1987; Simmons Grad Sch Mgt, MBA, 1995. **Career:** C's Hosp Med Ctr, hemat asst, 1972-75; Harvard Biol Labs, res asst, 1974; Roxbury Community Health Clin, family dentist, 1979-81; Implant & Family Dent Prac, dentist, 1980-; Baaqee Susanne, dentist, currently. **Orgs:** MASJID Al-Quaran, 1965-; Mass Women's Dent Soc, 1975-; Mass Dent Soc, 1979-; Am Dent Asn, 1979-; bd mem, Dorchester Coun Serv, 1983-86; treas, Am islamic EID Asn, 1983-87; vpres, Mattapan Community Concern Group, 1984; New Eng Soc Clin Hypn, 1985-; Am Acad Implant Dent, 1987-; Am Dent Assoc; Fla Dent Asn; Am Assoc Cosmetic Dent; fel Int Cong Oral Implantologists; Acad Gen Dent; Doctors Oral Conscious Sedation. **Honors/Awds:** Scholastic Achievement, Nat Honor Soc, 1967-70; Girl of the Year Award, 1970; Alpha Kappa Alpha, 1975-77; Links Soc, 1976-78; HAJJ, 1980, 1990. **Business Addr:** Dentist, Baaqee Susanne, 1764 E Silver Star Rd, Ocoee, FL 34761, **Business Phone:** (407)293-3002.

**BABATUNDE, OBBA**
Actor, teacher, singer. **Personal:** Born Dec 1, 1951, Queens, NY. **Educ:** Brooklyn Col. **Career:** Metrop Brass Ensemble; Negro Ensemble Theater, performer; Harriet Tubman Sch, teacher & admin, 1974-76; Theater: Guys and Dolls, 1976; Timbuktu, 1977-78; Dream girls, 1982; Golden Boy, 1984; Grind, 1985; Jelly's Last Jam, 1991; Chicago, 1997-98; TV series: "All My Children", 1987; "Dawson's Creek", 1999-2000; "Soul Food", 2000; "Half & Half", 2002; "One Life To Live", 2005; TV movies: "MANTIS", 1994; "The Cherokee Kid", 1996; "The Tomorrow Man", 1996; "Miss Evers' Boys", 1997; "Temptations", 1998; "Introducting Dorothy Dandridge", 1999; "The Apartment Complex", 1999; "Redeemer", 2002; "The Great Commission", 2003; Films: Short Eyes, 1977; Married to the Mob, 1988; Miami Blues, 1990; Silence of the Lambs, 1991; Dead Again, 1991; Importance Of Being Earnest, 1992; Undercover Blues, 1993; Philadelphia, 1993; Conversations, 1994; A Reason to Believe, 1995; Born To Be Wild, 1995; Carpool, 1996; Multiplicity, 1996; That Thing You Do!, 1996; Fatal Pursuit, 1998; Life, 1999; The Visit, 2000; How High, 2001; John Q, 2002; The Wild Thorn berrys Movie (voice), 2002; MVP, 2003; The Great Commission, 2003; After the Sunset, 2004; The Manchurian Candidate, 2004; Kangaroo Jack, 2004; After The Sunset, 2004; Material Girls, 2006; The Celestine Prophecy, 2006; The Black Man's Guide To Understanding Black women, 2006; Stage: "Secret Place", 1970; "Timbuktu!", 1978; "Sing Happy", 1978; "Liza Minnelli in Concert", 1979; "Baryshnikov on Broadway", 1980; "Esau, Reggae: A Musical Revelation", 1980; "Dreamgirls", 1981-85; "Grind", 1985; "ittle Ham", 1987; "Golden Boy", 1989; "The Roar of the Greasepaint, Smell of the Crowd", 1989; "Blues in the Night", 1991; Album: "Dream girls", 1982; Song: "Throw Down", 1985; TV series: Partner, "TV in Black: The First 50 Years,"; "Oscar Black Odyssey: From Hattie to Hallie"; "Dorthy Dandridge: An American Beauty". **Orgs:** Bill Picket All Black Rodeo. **Special Achievements:** Earned Emmy and Cable ACE Award nominations for his role as "Willie Johnson" in HBO's "Miss Evers' Boys," and a NAACP Image Award nomination for his portrayal of "Harold Nicholas" in HBO's "Introducing Dorothy Dandridge"; was nominated for Broadway's 1982 Tony Award as Best Actor. **Business Addr:** Actor, c/o Stone Manners, 8436 W 3rd Suite 740, Los Angeles, CA 90048, **Business Phone:** (323)655-1313.

**BABB, DR. VALERIE M.**
Writer, educator. **Personal:** Born May 6, 1955, New York, NY; daughter of Lionel S Duncan and Dorothy L. **Educ:** City Univ NY, Queens Col, New York, NY, BA, 1977; State Univ NY, Buffalo, NY, MA & PhD, 1981. **Career:** Georgetown Univ, Wash, DC, from asst prof to prof; Middlebury Col, Bread Loaf Sch Eng, fac, currently; Univ Ga, Franklin Col Arts & Sci, prof Eng & dir Inst African Am Studies, currently. Books: Ernest Gaines, 1991; Whiteness Visible: The Meaning of Whiteness in American Literature, 1998; Black Georgetown Remembered: A History of Its Black Community. **Orgs:** Cambridge Univ Press, hist African Am novel. **Business Addr:** Professor, University of Georgia, 312 Holmes Hunter Acad Bldg, Athens, GA 30602-2556, **Business Phone:** (706)542-5197.

**BABBS, DR. JUNIOUS C., SR.**
Education reformer. **Personal:** Born Aug 15, 1924; married Bobbie; children: Junious C Jr, Dwayne (deceased) & Jade. **Educ:** BS, MS, EdS, 1971; EdD, 1984. **Career:** Cotton Plant Pub Schs, coach, sci teacher, rec dir, prin, supt sch; educ consult; motivational speaker, 1989-; Little Rock Sch Dist, asst supt, assoc supt, currently. **Orgs:** Chmn bd trustees, Ash Grove Bapt Church; secy, ECOEO; County Health Comn; City Adv Comn; City Coun; chmn, Finance Comn; NEAAA, AEA, State Prin Orgn Admin; NCA State Comm; Adv Coun Sec Ed, City Exten Bd; dir, Cotton Plant Clin; Ariz State Admin Asn, 32 Deg Mason, NAC; bd dir, DAD; secy, Ment Health Bd; deacon Ash Grove B Church; State Adv Comt Chap II State Bonds & Facil Comn; Chair, Woodruff Co Local Planning Group, Ark Dept Human Servs; bd dirs, Wilber D Mills Ed coop; State Health Comn; Dr Martin Lihing Comn, govt appointment, 1993; Nat Community Serv Comn, govt appointment, 1993; dir, Little Rock Rotary Club, 2002-03. **Honors/Awds:** Coach of the Year, 1953, 1956, 1960-62; Biology Teacher Award, 1960-61; Man of the Year Award, 1969 & 1973; Service Award, City Cotton Plant, 1989; State Service Chapter I Award, 1990; Man of the Year Award, Am Biographic Inst, 1990; Distinguished Service Award, N Ark Serv, 1994. **Home Addr:** 400 Gum St D 10, Cotton Plant, AR 72036, **Home Phone:** (870)459-3779. **Business Addr:** Associate Superintendent, Little Rock School District, 808 Dr Martin Luther King Jr Dr, Little Rock, AR 72202-3646, **Business Phone:** (712)475-3311.

**BABER, DR. CEOLA ROSS**
Educator. **Personal:** Born Nov 30, 1950, Selma, AL; married Willie L; children: Lorenzo DuBois, Tylisha Marie & Cheickna St Clair. **Educ:** Calif State Univ, Sacramento, BA, 1972; Stanford Univ, MA, 1975; Purdue Univ, PhD, 1984. **Career:** Sequoia Union High Sch Dist, teacher, 1974-78; Tuskegee Univ, Ala, proj coordr, instr, 1979-80; Purdue Univ, Ind, res assoc, 1980-81, grad asst, 1982-84, dir, asst prof, 1984-89; Univ NC, Greensboro, Sch Educ, Sec Social Studies Licensure Prog, from asst prof to assoc prof, 1989-2005, coordr, 1989-, from actg assoc dean to assoc dean, 1999-2004; UNCG Sch Educ, Teacher Educ & Sch Relationships, assoc dean, 1999-2004, interim assoc vice provost, undergrad educ, 2007-08; NC Agr & Tech State Univ, dean, 2008-10, Leadership Studies, Sch Educ, prof, currently. **Orgs:** UNC-Greensboro Dept Curric & Instr, 1989-2008; Am Asn Col Teacher Educ; Am Educ Res Asn; Nat Asn Multicultural Educ; Nat Coun Social Studies; Phi Delta Kappa; Kappa Delta Pi Int Educ Hon Soc; Delta Kappa Gamma Int Educ Soc; Nat Coun Accreditation Teacher Educ Bd Examiners. **Home Addr:** 1512 Forest Hill Dr, Greensboro, NC 27410. **Business Addr:** Professor, NC Agr & Tech State University, 1601 E Mkt St, Greensboro, NC 27411-0001, **Business Phone:** (336)334-7500.

**BABINEAUX-FONTENOT, CLAIRE**
Vice president (organization). **Personal:** daughter of Warren Babineaux Jr and Mary Alice; married Barry J; children: Barry J Jr & Sydney Alyce. **Educ:** Univ La, BS; Southern Methodist Univ Sch Law, LLM, taxation; Southern Univ Law Ctr, JD; Kellogg Sch Mgt, exec training prog. **Career:** Univ La, Lafayette, libr asst; La Dept Revenue, tax atty; Off Legal Affairs, asst secy; La Dept Civil Serv, admin law judge; PriceWaterhouseCoopers, dispute pract group leader; Adams & Reese, partner-in-charge; Wal-Mart Stores Inc, vpres audit & tax policy, 2004-07, sr vpres & chief tax officer, 2007-, exec vpres & treas, currently. **Orgs:** Ct App Spec Advocates (CASA); Natl Coun Adoption; Natl Asn Black Accountants; Am Bar Asn; Coun Taxation; bd mem, Tax Coun Policy Inst; bd mem, Greater Baton Rouge Chamber Com; asst secy off legal affairs, La Dept Revenue; bd mem, Pub Affairs Res Coun & Cath Community Serv. **Home Addr:** , Springdale, AR. **Business Addr:** Executive Vice President, Treasurer, Wal-Mart Stores Inc, 702 SW 8th St, Bentonville, AR 72716-0160, **Business Phone:** (800)925-6278.

**BABINEAUX-FONTENOT, CLAIRE**
Vice president (organization), executive, government official. **Personal:** married Barry; children: Barry Jr & Sydney. **Educ:** Univ La, Lafayette; Southern Univ Law Ctr, Baton Rouge, JD; Southern Methodist Univ Sch Law, Dedman Sch Law Dallas, LLM, taxation; Kellogg Sch Mgt Training Prog. **Career:** La Dept Revenue, tax atty, asst secy off legal affairs, La Dept Civil Serv, admin law judge; Southwest Region PriceWaterhouseCoopers LLP, dispute resolution pract group leader; Adams & Reese (Baton Rouge, LA), partner-in-charge; Wal-Mart Stores Inc, exec vpres, vpres audits & tax policy, 2004, sr vpres & chief tax officer, 2007, Asst Secy, currently. **Orgs:** Bd dir, Thurgood Marshall Col Fund. **Honors/Awds:** The Links, Baton Rouge Chapter, Louisiana Role Model, 2008; "Black Enterprise," The 100 Most Powerful Executives in Corporate America, 2010; Women Worth Watching, Diversity J, 2011; Dave Jackson Trailblazer Award; Diversity Champion, Diversity Edge mag; Inducted SULC Hall of Fame in 2012. **Business Addr:** Assistant Secretary, Wal-Mart Stores Inc, 702 SW 8th St, Bentonville, AR 72716-6299, **Business Phone:** (479)273-4000.

**BACKSTROM, DON**
Investment banker. **Personal:** Born Jun 4, 1941, Los Angeles, CA; son of Walter and Julia Carter; married Jacquelyn Webster; children: Kellye Dion. **Educ:** Am Inst Banking, Los Angeles, CA, cert, 1975; El Camino Community Col, Torrance, CA, attended 1975; Calif State Univ, Dominguez Hills, CA, attended 1978. **Career:** Bank Am, Los Angeles, CA, bank mgr, 1964-73; Bank Finance, Los Angeles, CA, bank mgr, 1973-75; Home Bank, Compton, CA, bank mgr, 1975-76; Imp Bank, Los Angeles, CA, vpres, 1976-77; Mech Bank, bank mgr, 1977-78; State Calif, Sacramento, LA, mgr CAL-VET housing prog, 1978-84, Calif State Treas's Off, exec dir CIDFAC, 1984-90; Salomon Smith Barney, Harris Upham & Co Inc, vpres, pub finance div, 1991-98; John Nuveen Co, 1998-99; Chapman Co, sr vpres, 1999-2002; Compton Community Col Dist, financial advisor; Backstrom Mccarley Berry & Co LLC, managing dir & prin, 2002-. **Orgs:** Dir, Calif Statewide Cert Develop Corp, 1988-. **Home Addr:** 966 Eve Shade Dr, San Pedro, CA 90731-1453, **Home Phone:** (310)221-0640. **Business Addr:** Managing Director, Principal, Backstrom Mccarley Berry & Co LLC, 115 Sansome St Mezzanine A, San Francisco, CA 94104, **Business Phone:** (310)221-0640.

**BACKUS, BRADLEY**
Executive. **Personal:** Born Sep 12, 1950, Kings County, NY; son of Thomas and Bernice Smith; married Stephanie George; children: Crystal Olivia. **Educ:** Lincoln Univ, Oxford, PA, BA, 1972; George Washington Univ, Nat Law Ctr, JD, 1975. **Career:** Executive (retired); Metro Life Ins Co, New York, consult advan underwriting, 1977-80, dir estate planning, 1980-82, sr bus & estate consult, 1983-93, agency mgr training, field mgt training. **Orgs:** Pres, Bedford-Stuyvesant Lawyers Asn, 1980-81; bd mem, Bedford-Stuyvesant Community Legal Serv Corp, 1980-89; pres, Metrop Black Bar Asn, 1986-89; vpres, MBBA Scholarship Fund, 1987-; bd mem, Comt Modern Cts, 1988-; comnr, NY State Judicial Comn Minorities, 1988-90; comnr, NY City Korean Vet Memorial Comn, 1988-90; comnr, NY State Comn Improve Availability Legal Serv, 1988-90; bd mem, Legal Aid Soc, 1988-; regional dir, Nat Bar Asn, 1990-91 & 1994-. **Home Addr:** 52 Herkimer St, Brooklyn, NY 11216-2707, **Home Phone:** (718)856-8066.

**BACOATE, MATTHEW V., JR.**
Executive. **Personal:** Born Feb 10, 1930, Asheville, NC; son of Matthew Sr and Osie; children: Matthew III. **Educ:** Med Admin Sch, attended 1951; Univ SC, USAFI, bus admin, 1955; Western Carolina Univ, bus admin, 1971; NC State Univ CEU's, 1975. **Career:** Executive (retired); Asheville Chamber Com, clerk, writer & gen mgr; Afram Inc, founder, mgr & later bus owner; Asheville Comun Enter Inc, gen mgr; M Bacoate Disposable's Inc, pres; Western Mtn Sci Inc, pres. **Orgs:** NC Minority Bus Comn, 1969; appeal officer, Asheville City Schs Free Lunch Prog, 1969-95; adv comt, Sen Robert Morgan, 1974, 1980; steering comt, Gov Jim Hunt, 1976-92; bd dir, NC Econ Dev, 1977; Small Bus Adv Coun, 1978; Daniel Boone Coun Boy Scouts Am, 1978; bd dir, Gov Western Residence Asn, 1978; Pvt Indust Coun, 1979, 1988; NC Small Bus Advocacy Coun, 1979; Employ Security Adv Coun, 1979; Cent Asheville Optimist Club, 1979; bd mem, Asheville Area Chamber Com, 1981; adv coun, US Small Bus Admin, 1981; chmn bd, Victoria Health Care Ctr, 1981-; co-founder, Black Bus & Prof League, 1983; adv comt, AB Tech Small Bus, 1986; Sen Terry Sanford Adv Comn, 1986; Smky Mountain Minority Purchasing Coun, 1986; bd dir, YMI Cult Ctr, 1987, chmn, 1992; City Asheville Minority Bus Comn, 1989; chmn, Minority Loan Pool, 1990; Buncombe County Sheriffs Transition/Rev Comn, 1990; chmn, Minority Loan Pool, 1990; bd dir, Pack Pl Inc, 1991; NC Sheriff Asn, 1991; chmn Bd, YMI Community Develop Corp, 1992; bd dir, Western NC Regional Econ Develop Comn, 1993; chmn bd, Black Mountain Ctr Found, 1994; founder & co-chmn, Comt Prog; bd vis, Western Carolina Univ; Comm Int & Comt WLOS-TV; bd dir, Asheville Chap Am Red Cross; steering comt, Martin L King Prayer Break; bd dir, Comn Mus Fire Equip. **Honors/Awds:** Look Magazine Recognition, 1970; National Audience, Exemplifying Accomplishments, documentary "Help" ABC, 1970; Appreciation Service Phalany Fraternity, Market St YMCA, 1972; Boss of the Year, Asheville Jaycees, 1976; Cert Appreciation Asheville Buncombe Tech Inst, 1977; White House invitation, Pres Jimmy Carter, 1979; Cert Recognition, City Winston-Salem, NC, 1980; Award Ashville Area Chamber Com, 1981; Cert Recog, Western Carolina Univ, 1983; Outstanding Service Inducted Chamber Echoes Cent Asheville Optimist, 1984; Cert City Asheville, 1988; Outstanding Service Recognition, City Asheville, 1993; Appreciation Leadership & Dedication to the Region, Advantage West WNCREDC, 1993-97; Appreciation Outstanding Leadership, Black Mountain Ctr Found, 1995-96; Outstanding Service Award, Buncombe County Sheriff Dept. **Home Addr:** 67 Clingman Ave, Asheville, NC 28801, **Home Phone:** (828)254-6773.

**BACON, DR. ALBERT S.**
Dentist. **Personal:** Born Mar 1, 1942, LaGrange, GA; son of Albert Stanley Sr and Julia Spain. **Educ:** Howard Univ, BS, 1963, DDS, 1968; cert Orthodontics, 1971. **Career:** Va Hosp, staff dentist, 1969; Community Group Health Found, staff dentist, 1970; Howard Univ, asst prof, 1971; pvt pract orthod, 1971-; Dept Comm Dent, actg chmn, 1972; Univ Dent Asn, chief dent, currently. **Orgs:** Am Nat Soc MD Dent Asn; Robert T Freeman Dent Soc; Am Asn Orthodontists; Mid Atlantic Soc Orthodontists; Am Acad Group Dent Pract; Chi Delta Mu Frat; Young Adults Wash; St Albans Soc; Canterbury Club; Howard Univ Alumni Asn. **Business Addr:** Chief Dentist, University of Dental Associates, 6101 16th St NW Suite 2, Washington, DC 20011-1751, **Business Phone:** (202)291-5000.

**BACON, BARBARA CRUMPLER**
School administrator, administrator. **Personal:** Born Sep 7, 1943, Youngstown, OH; daughter of Robert Crumpler (Deceased) and Jessie McCray Irby (Deceased); married Oscar; children: Robert & Jessica. **Educ:** Youngstown State Univ, BA, sociol, 1980; Univ Akron Sch Law, Akron, OH, attended 1990. **Career:** Smithsonian Inst, EEO spec, 1972-78; Mahoning City Transitional Homes, affirm action consult, 1980, search tech instr, 1980-81; Youngstown State Univ, asst to pres affirm action, dir affirmative action. **Orgs:** Bd mem, Assoc Neighborhood Ctrs, 1984-92; Young Women's Christian Asn, 1985-92; Links Inc, 1985-; bd mem, Gateways to Better Living, 1985; Design Rev Comn; bd mem, Help Hotline; bd mem, Burdman Group. **Home Addr:** 2020 Guadalupe Ave, Youngstown, OH 44504, **Home Phone:** (216)742-3370.

**BACON, DR. GLORIA JACKSON**
Poet, physician, singer. **Personal:** Born Sep 21, 1937, New Orleans, LA; daughter of Henry Johnson and Vina V; married Frank C Bacon Jr; children: Constance Jackson, Judith Jackson, Phillip, Geoffrey &

Stuart. **Educ:** Xavier Univ, BS, 1958; Univ Ill Col Med, MD, 1962, Sch Pub Health, MPH, 1984. **Career:** Mt Sinai Hosp-Med Ctr, resident; Altgeld Inc, founder & dir, 1970-2001; Health & Hosp Gov Comn, Cook County, med dir, 1979; Clin Assocs Chicago Ltd, pres, 1982; Provident Hosp & Med Ctr, vpres, 1985; Metro Care HMO, med dir, 1986-87; TCA Healthier health-care ctr, founder; Chicago Orchestra Hall, soloist; ETA Theater, soloist, currently; Proj 18, founder, 2004. **Orgs:** Bd trustee, Fisk Univ, 1980-85; Gannon & Proctor Comn, 1982-83; Nat Med Asn; Robert Wood Johnson Found; fel Am Acad Family Physicians; bd trustee, Univ Ill, 1990-97; steering comt, Lincoln Net; pres, Altgeld Community Found; founder, Clin Altgeld Inc, med dir. **Honors/Awds:** Woman of the Year, PUSH, 1975; Candace Award, Nat Coalition 100 Black Women, 1984; UIC City Partner Award, 1998. **Special Achievements:** Publication: "Is Love Ever Enough?" A Finial Press Campaign IL, 1987. **Business Addr:** Soloist, 6910 S Bennett Ave, Chicago, IL 60649, **Business Phone:** (312)955-1995.

## BACON, DR. ROBERT JOHN, JR.

Psychiatrist. **Personal:** Born Nov 20, 1948, Houston, TX; son of Robert Sr (deceased) and Bernice Narcisse; children: Robyn, Kristen & Angelle. **Educ:** Stanford Univ, BA, hist, 1970; George Wash Univ Med Sch, attended 1971; Meharry Med Col, MD, 1975. **Career:** Howard Univ Hosp, resident, 1975-77; Univ Tex, Houston, resident, 1977-78; Univ Tex Health & Sci Ctr Psychiat, Hermann Hosp, Geriat, head, 1977-78; Harris County MHMRA, Harris County Forensic Treat Unit, clin consult, 1979-81; Tex Med Found, physician adv, 1982-88; Univ Tex-Houston, clin asst prof, 1984-90; Ben Taub Gen Hosp, dir psychiat emergency serv, 1984-88; Baylor Col Med, clin asst prof & asst prof psychiat, 1984-90; Tex Dept Corrections, consult, 1985-86; Riverside Gen Hosp, Total Care & Stress Unit, psychiat sect chief, dir, 1987-90; Chrysalis Ctr, Chem Dependency Treat, med dir, 1989-90; Charter Coun Ctr Pasadena, med dir, 1990; Charter Hosp Kingwood, clin dir adult psychiat, 1989-94; NBA Aftercare Network Team, network provider, 1989-93; Houston Recovery Campus, Day Treat, physician, 1992-; CHOICES Prog, acupuncture consult, 1992-; Comprehensive Therapies & Servs, psychiat med dir, 1994-; Friends Mind, psych med dir, 1997-; Silveridge Community Care Ctr, psychmed dir, 1998; Glory Partial, psych med dir, 1998; Waymaker, psych med dir, 1998; Bacon Psychiat Assocs, pvt pract, currently; Pk Plaza Hosp. **Orgs:** Clin consult Harris Co Forensic Treatment Unit, 1979-81; Sum Arts; Am Bd Qual Assurance & Utilization Review Physicians, diplomat; Am Psychiatric Asn; Harris County Psychiat Soc; Tex Med Asn; Harris County Med Soc; Med Forum. **Honors/Awds:** Riverside Hospital Black Achievement Awards; Physicians Recognition Award, 1989. **Special Achievements:** Developed the Therapeutic Community of Howard Univ Hosp, Dept Psychiat, 1975-76; article: "The Single Parent-Helping the Children Adjust", Your Health, Texas Health Plan, June 1980; "Providing Mental Health Services with Meager Resources: The Experience of Riverside General Hospital", presented at annual meeting of Black Psychiatrist Assn, Bahamas, 1986; Seminars: "Coping with Stress: Teenagers, Drugs & Suicide", Nat Medical Assn, 1981; "Job Stress", US Customs Service, Federal Woman's Program, 1979; symposiums: On Family Therapy, Washington Institute of Psychiatry, Washington, DC, 1977; On Psychiatric Problems of College Students, Conf College Health Administrators, TX Southern Univ, 1980. **Home Addr:** 5151 Katy Fwy Suite 203, Houston, TX 77007, **Home Phone:** (713)655-9410. **Business Addr:** Psychiatrist, Bacon Psychiatric Associates, 1919 N Loop W Suite 224, Houston, TX 77008, **Business Phone:** (713)869-4500.

## BACON, DR. WILLIAM LOUIS

Surgeon. **Personal:** Born Dec 3, 1936, Austin, TX; son of William and Louise; married Donna Marie Harbatis; children: Tyra, William II, Donna, Mary Schroeder, Jesse, Louise, Jonathan & Nicholas. **Educ:** Morehouse Col, BS, biol gen, 1956; Meharry Med Col, attended 1962. **Career:** Fitzsimons Gen Hosp, intern, 1962-63; Ireland Army Hosp, surgeon, 1963-64; Brooke Army Med Ctr, 1964-67; Wash, DC, course dir, 1972-74; Miami, surgeon, 1975; pvt pract physician, 1975-94; Univ Miami, guest lectr, 1976; Mt Sinai Med Ctr, Cedars Leb Hosp, Vict Hosp, Jack Memorial Hosp, staff mem; Metrop Nashville Gen Hosp & Meharry Med Ctr, chief orthop surg, 1994-2005, chief orthop & rehab, currently. **Orgs:** Cert Am Bd Ortho Surg, 1970; Am Col Surg, 1971; Am Acad Ortho Surg, 1972; staff consult, Friedman's Hosp & Howard Univ; mem bd, Cedars Leb Hosp; Dade Co Med Asn, Fla Med Soc, Am Med Asn, Miami Ortho Soc, Fla Ortho Soc; Am Bd Ortho Surg, 1983; Soc Black Am Surg. **Honors/Awds:** Merit Service Medical, 1970, 1974; Examiner, Am Bd Ortho Surg, 1978-84. **Home Addr:** 6028 Deer Trace Dr, Nashville, TN 37211, **Home Phone:** (615)315-9863. **Business Addr:** Physician, Meharry Medical College, 1005 DB Todd Blvd, Nashville, TN 37208, **Business Phone:** (615)327-4663.

## BACON-BERCEY, JUNE ESTHER (JUNE ESTHER GRIFFIN)

Meteorologist, lecturer, consultant. **Personal:** Born Oct 23, 1932, Wichita, KS; married George W Brewer; children: Dail ST Claire & Dawn-Maire; married Walker; married John. **Educ:** Univ Calif, BS, mathematics & meteorol, 1954, MS, meteorol, 1955; Univ Southern Calif, MPA, 1979. **Career:** Nat Weather Serv, meteorologist, 1956-62; Sperry Rand Corp, 1962-74; Nat Broadcasting Co, 1970-73; prof lectr, 1974-75; Nat Weather Serv, meteorologist, broadcaster, 1975-78, forecasting training officer, 1982-89; Nat Oceanic & Atmospheric Agency, pub affairs specialist, chief broadcast serv, chief tv serv, 1979-81, radar meteorologist; chief adminr tv activ; consult & educr, 1990-. **Orgs:** Bd mem women & minorities, Am Meteorol Soc, 1975; chair, N Calif Chap, 1985; Women Sci & Eng; Am Geophys Union; Am Asn Pub Admins; NY Acad Sci; Aec; founding member, Am Meteorol Soc's Bd. **Honors/Awds:** Seal of Approval, Am Meteorol Soc, 1972; Certificate of Recognition for Sustained Superior Performance, Nat Oceanic & Atmospheric Admin, 1982-84; Outstanding Contribution to Furthering the Mission of National Oceanic and Atmospheric Administration, Nat Oceanic & Atmospheric Admin, 1984-92. **Special Achievements:** The First African American woman to earn a meteorology degree in the 1950; The first female broadcaster in the country in Buffalo, New York, 1970; Bacon-Bercey was the first woman, as well as the first African-American to be awarded the American Meteorological Society's Seal of Approval for excellence in television weather casting; Minority Pioneer for Achievements in Atmospheric Science, Nat Sci Found & Nat Aeronauts & Space Admin, 2000. **Home Addr:** 160 Bella Vista Dr, Hillsborough, CA 94010-6261.

## BADEJO, DR. DIEDRA L.

Administrator, educator, association executive. **Personal:** Born Corona, CA. **Educ:** Los Angeles City Col, AA, eng, fr, 1971; Univ Southern Calif, BA, Eng/Afro-Am, 1973; Univ Calif, Los Angeles, African Area Studies, MA, 1977, PhD, comparative lit, 1985. **Career:** African & Afro-Am Literatures & Area Studies, URI, asst Prof, 1984-89; Eng & Res & Grad Studies (URI, UL, KSU), grad fac, 1985-2008; African/Afro-Am Literatures & Area Studies, URI, Assoc Prof, 1989-90; Pan-African Lit & Area Studies, Univ Louisville, assoc prof, 1990-95, chair dept, 1998-2007; Univ Louisville, African World Literatures & Cult Histories, prof, 1991-96; Kent State Univ, African World Literatures & Cult Histories, prof, 1996-2008; Klein Family Sch Commun Design, prof, Currently. **Orgs:** Bd mem, Nat Coun Black Studies; ACE Fel prog, Kent state Univ; featured speaker, Ky Humanities Coun; humanities consult & speaker, Nc Ctr Advan Teaching; La Humanities Coun; Ri Humanities Coun; Ri State Libr Serv. **Special Achievements:** One of 37 scholars chosen to serve in the ACE Fellow program. **Business Addr:** Professor, University of Baltimore, 1445 MD Ave, Baltimore, MD 21201, **Business Phone:** (410)837-5683.

## BADGER, BRENDA JOYCE

Counselor. **Personal:** Born May 10, 1950, Camden, AR; daughter of Woodrow and Lizzie Mae Frazier; married David; children: Kreya Jackson & Keith Jackson. **Educ:** Wayne State Univ, BS, criminal justice, 1982, MA, guid & coun, 1987. **Career:** Wayne County Community Col, secy, 1970-92; Community Informant, ed, columnist, 1988-; Pontiac/Hazel Pk Schs, part-time adult educ counr, 1988-89; "Did You Know?" producer, host, 1989-; Lawrence Technol Univ, counr, 1991-, dir, HELP prog, 1994-; Am Couns Asn, Red Cross, disaster ment health counr/instr, 1992-. **Orgs:** Am Coun Asn, 1985-; founder & pres, Spirit, Ambition, Vigor, & Enthusiasm SAVE, 1986-; Juv Teen & Violence Comt, Detroit City, 1986-; Asn Marriage & Family Coun, 1992-; Am Col Coun Asn, 1992; mem sch bd, Detroit Acad Schs, Westland Sch, 1996-; bd trustee, Cent Mich Univ, 2001; Fin & Investment Rev Comt. **Honors/Awds:** Strong Achiever Award, WJLB-FM Radio, 1991. **Special Achievements:** Author, "Teachers Still Work Miracles," Detroit Free Press, 1984; State Counseling Licensee, 1991; "Did You Know?" song, 1992; licensed counselor, selected nationwide for training, 1992; "The Alto," poem, 1993; wrote a proposal for the Buddy System, which was approved for funding. **Home Addr:** 23764 Riverside Dr, Southfield, MI 48033, **Home Phone:** (248)354-4058. **Business Addr:** Counselor, Lawrence Technological University, 29540 Meadowlane Dr, Southfield, MI 48075-1058, **Business Phone:** (248)204-4113.

## BADGER, DR. LEONARD MICHAEL

Dentist. **Personal:** Born Oct 17, 1962, Jacksonville, FL; married Madelyne Woods; children: Montana S Williams & Michael Bryce. **Educ:** Fla A&M Univ, BS, 1985; Meharry Med Col, DDS, 1990. **Career:** Pvt pract dentist, currently; DellagioDentist.com, gen dentist, 2009-; Badger Ctr Mod Dent PA, owner, currently. **Orgs:** Nat Dent Asn; Am Dent Asn; fel Acad Gen Dent; Fla Dent Asn; Kappa Alpha Psi Frat; Dent Soc Greater Orlando; Am Acad Implant Dent; Int Cong Oral Implantologists. **Honors/Awds:** Fel Acad Gen Dent, 1999. **Home Addr:** , FL. **Business Addr:** General Dentist, DellagioDentist.com, 8060 Via Dellagio Way Suite 202, Orlando, FL 32819, **Business Phone:** (407)351-4104.

## BADGER, MADELYNE WOODS

Television news anchorperson, television show host, publicist. **Personal:** Born Oct 10, 1965, Washington, DC; daughter of Lloyd Woods and Mary Kittrell; married L Michael; children: Montana Symone Woods Williams & Michael Bryce. **Educ:** Univ Md, College Park, MD, BS, broadcast jour, 1986; Howard Univ, Wash, DC, MA, mass commun, 1987. **Career:** WHMM TV 32, Wash, DC, host, 1987-88; WJWJ TV 16, Beaufort, SC, news reporter, 1988-89; WCIV News 4, Charleston, SC, news reporter, 1989-90; Black Entertainment TV, Wash, DC, news anchor, 1990, freelance anchor reporter, 1993-96; WJLA TV, Wash, DC, news reporter, 1996-97; Walt Disney World, mkt & media rel, 1997-99; Fox Am's Health Network, host, news anchor, 1999; WCFB, news community affairs dir, currently. **Orgs:** Nat Asn Black Journalists, 1987-; Wash Asn Black Journalists, 1987-; Nat Acad Arts & Scis, 1987-88. **Home Addr:** 9672 Camberley Cir, Orlando, FL 32836-5754. **Business Addr:** News Director, Community Affairs Director, WCFB, 4192 N John Young Pkwy, Orlando, FL 32804, **Business Phone:** (407)297-0945.

## BADU, ERYKAH (ERICA ABI WRIGHT)

Singer, actor, songwriter. **Personal:** Born Feb 26, 1971, Dallas, TX; daughter of William Jr and Kolleen; married The DOC; children: Puma & Mars Merkaba; children: Seven & Sirius. **Educ:** Grambling State Univ, dance & theatre. **Career:** S Dallas Cult Ctr, drama & dance teacher; Erykah Free, founder & drama teacher, 1993-; Universal Rec, currently; Albums: Funky Cousins; Baduizm, 1997; Live, 1997; Mama's Gun, 2000; Worldwide Underground, 2003; New Amerykah Part One, 2008; New Amerykah Part Two, 2010. Songs: "On & On", 1997; "Next Lifetime", 1997; "Other side of the Game", 1997; "Apple Tree", 1997; "Tyrone", 1997; "Southern Gul", 1999; "Bag Lady", 2000; "Didn't Cha Know?", 2000; "Cleva", 2001; "Love of My Life", 2002; "Danger", 2003; "Back in the Day", 2004; "Honey", 2007; "Healer"; "Soldier"; "The Wire", 2008; "window seat", 2010; "Q.U.E.E.N.", 2013. Films: Blues Brothers, 2000, 1998; The Cider House Rules, 1999; New Amerykah Part One, 2008; New Amerykah Part Two, 2010; House of D, 2004; Dave Chappelle's Block Party, 2006; Before the Music Dies, 2006; Say My Name, 2009; Teenage Paparazzo, 2010; Re: Generation Music Project, 2012; Diary of a Decade: The Story of a Movement, 2012; They Die by Dawn, 2013; What Difference Does It Make? A Film About Making Music, 2014. TV series: "The Tonight Show with Jay Leno", 2002; "Real Husbands of Hollywood", 2013. **Orgs:** Beautiful Love Inc Non Profit Develop. **Honors/Awds:** Soul Train Lady of Soul Awards, Best New Artist, Best Album, Best Single, Best Song, 1997; Blockbuster Awards, Favorite Female New Artist, Favorite Female R&B Artist, 1997; American Music Awards, Favorite New Artist Soul & Rap, Favorite Soul Album, 1998; Outstanding New Artist, Outstanding Female Artist, NAACP Image Awards, 1998; Danish Grammy Awards, Best International Newcomer, Best International Female Artist, 1998; Soul Train Music Awards, Best R&B/Soul Single-Female, Best R&B & Soul Album-Female, Best R&B & Soulor Rap Album of the Year, Best R&B/Soul or Rap New Artist, 1998; Black Reel Award, 2000, 2003. **Special Achievements:** People magazine's 50 Most Beautiful People, 1999; VH1's 100 Greatest Women of Rock N Roll. **Business Addr:** Singer, Universal Records, 1325 Avenue of the Americas, New York, NY 10019, **Business Phone:** (212)373-0600.

## BAETY, EDWARD L., SR.

Lawyer, judge. **Personal:** Born Mar 13, 1944, Jacksonville, FL. **Educ:** Morris Brown Col, BS, 1965; Howard Univ Sch Law, JD, 1968. **Career:** Atlanta Leg Aid Soc, staff atty, 1968-71; Equal Employ Opportunity Comn, dist coun, 1971-72; Hill Jones & Farr, assoc coun, 1972-74; Hill Jones & Farr, part, 1974-76; Pro Mac Vice Themunicioal Ct Atlanta, atty; City Ct Atlanta, assoc judge 1976, chief judge, currently. **Orgs:** Atlanta Bar Asn; Gate City Bar Asn; State Bar Asn Ga; Atlanta Bus League; Vol Leg Serv Atty; pres, Atlanta Spart Ath Club; vpres, Phi Beta Sigma Fraternity Inc; Black Consort. **Special Achievements:** First black fill-time municipal traffic judge. **Home Addr:** 1827 Kanawha Trl, Stone Mountain, GA 30087-2132, **Home Phone:** (770)939-8299. **Business Addr:** Chief Judge, City Court of Atlanta, 104 Trinity Ave SW, Atlanta, GA 30303-3686, **Business Phone:** (404)658-6987.

## BAEZA, DELLA BRITTON

President (organization). **Personal:** Born Pittsburgh, PA; married Mario L; children: 3. **Educ:** Princeton Univ, BA, 1975; Columbia Law Sch, JD, 1978. **Career:** Covington & Burling Wash DC Law Firm, atty, 1978-81; Am Broadcasting Co Inc, coun & Asst Gen Atty, 1981-86; Hillside Broadcasting LLP, pres, 1990-97; AJM Rec, pres, 1998-2004; Jackie Robinson Found, pres & chief exec officer, 2004-. **Orgs:** Consult, Nat Black Arch Film & Broadcasting, 1987-89, Ford Found Proj; chairperson, Dance Theatre Harlem Bd dir, 1988-91; Inwood Settlement House; Nat Urban League Black Exec Exchange Prog; NY Times Instnl Task Force; Lawyers Comt Civil Rights under Law; Nat Urban League Black Exec Exchange Prog. **Business Addr:** President, Chief Executive Officer, Jackie Robinson Foundation, 75 Varick St 2nd Fl, New York, NY 10013-1917, **Business Phone:** (212)290-8600.

## BAFFOE, NANA KWAME, II. See KIRKLIN, DR. PERRY WILLIAM.

## BAGBY, RACHEL L.

Educator, writer, composer. **Personal:** Born Feb 11, 1956, Philadelphia, PA; daughter of William H and Rachel Edna Samiella Rebecca Jones; married Martin Neal Davidson. **Educ:** NC AT&T State, Greensboro, NC, attended 1974; Univ Pittsburgh, Pittsburgh, PA, BA, 1977; Stanford Law Sch, Stanford, CA, JD, 1983. **Career:** V Pittsburgh, Chancellor's Teaching Fel, 1975; Wall St Jour, San Francisco, Calif, writer, 1979; Stanford, Calif, freelance composer & writer, 1979-; Philadelphia Community Rehab Corp, Philadelphia, Pa, asst dir, 1980-82; Stanford Univ, African & Am Studies, prog coordr, 1983-85; Comm Black Performing Arts, Stanford, Calif, prog coordr, 1983-85; Martin Luther King Jr, Papers Proj, Stanford, Calif, assoc dir, 1985; Bobby McFerrin's Voicestra, San Francisco, Calif, composer & performer, 1989-; Outta Box Recs, pres, 1989, Vallecitos Mountain Refuge, bd dir, 2000-; Satyana Inst, consult, currently; Composer: "Grandmothers' Song?; "A Power of Numbers?; "Healing the Wounds", 1989; "Daughters of Growing Things?"; "Reach Across the Lines?"; Produced: Full, 1993; Co-produced: Becoming Consciously Vibralingual. **Orgs:** Calif Lawyers Arts, 1982-; consult, Calif Arts Coun, 1984-86; consult, Nat Black Womens Health Prog, 1986-; codir, Woman Earth Inst, 1986-; bd, Ctr Contemplative Mind & Soc; bd, Vallecitos Mountain Refuge. **Home Addr:** PO Box 5101, Charlottesville, VA 22905-5101, **Home Phone:** (434)244-2502. **Business Addr:** Board of Directors, Vallecitos Mountain Refuge, 1219E Gusdorf Rd, Taos, NM 87571, **Business Phone:** (505)751-9613.

## BAGLEY, GREGORY P., SR.

Engineer, association executive, air force officer. **Personal:** Born Sep 19, 1930, New York, NY; son of Garrett P and Carrie A; married Helen Smith; children: Gregory Jr, Carole & John. **Educ:** Johns Hopkins Univ, BES, 1958; Adelphi Univ, MS, 1969. **Career:** Engineer (retired): Hazeltine Corp, elec engr, 1958-62; Sperry Gyroscope Cty, sr elec engr, 1962-68; Assoc Univ, Brookhaven Nat Lab, res engr, 1968-93. **Orgs:** Secy, bd deacon, Union Baptist Church Hempstead, 1962-98, Sunday Sch Supt, 1985-96; bd, Pk Lake Develop Fund Corp, 1970-98; vpres, Franklin PTA, 1972-73; African Sci Inst. **Honors/Awds:** Tau Beta Pi, Eta Kappa Nu Hon Engr Soc. **Home Addr:** 4550 Chaucer Way Suite 403, Owings Mills, MD 21117-6614, **Home Phone:** (410)998-4275.

## BAGLEY, DR. PETER B. E.

Educator, conductor (music). **Personal:** Born May 22, 1935, Yonkers, NY; married Bythema Byrd; children: Margaret R. **Educ:** Crane Sch Music, State Univ NY, BS, 1957; Ind Univ, Sch Music, Bloomington, IN, MM, chorus conductor, 1962, DM, chorus conductor, 1968. **Career:** Greenwich Conn Pub Sch, vocal music teacher, 1957-61; First Baptist Church, dir music, 1964-66; SUNY New Paltz, assoc prof music, 1966, prof music, 1968-84; New Paltz Concert Choir & Chamber Singers, conductor, 1966-; All State Choruses W Va, 1970-71, Nh, 1972, Conn, 1976, Vt, 1978; New Eng Festival Chorus, guest conductor, 1980; State Univ New York, prof music; Univ Conn, Dept Music, prof music, prof emer music & spec asst to dean, 2003-. **Orgs:** Am Choral Dir Asn; Am Choral Found; Music Educr Nat Conf; Music Libr Asn; Nat Asn African-Am Educ; Natl Asn Afro Am Edn; bd dir, Chorus Am; Nat Black Music Caucus; NY Sch Music Asn; Am Choral dir Asn; bd mem, Chorus Am; bd mem, Hall Johnson Inst. **Home Addr:** 206 Foster Dr, Willimantic, CT 06226, **Home Phone:** (860)456-8761. **Business Addr:** Professor Emeritus of Music, Special Assistant to the Dean, University of Connecticut, 1295 Storrs Rd Suite 1012, Storrs, CT 06269-1012, **Business Phone:** (860)486-2000.

**BAGLEY, REV. STANLEY B.**
Chaplain. **Personal:** Born Sep 7, 1935, Trenton, NJ; son of Dr Semuel M and Leomae Walker; married Ruth McDowell; children: Bernard, Sharon, Bryant & Brett. **Educ:** Morehouse Col, BA, 1958; Crozer Theol Sem, BD, 1961; Univ OK, grad study, 1967; Ashland Theol Sem, MDiv, 1973; Asn Ment Health Clergy, cert prof ment health clergy, 1976; Century Univ, PhD, 1994; Dept VA Nat Black Chaplin Asn, cert clin chaplain, 1996. **Career:** Galilee Baptist Chruch Trenton, NJ, asst pastor, 1961-65; Calvary Baptist Chruch, pastor, 1965-67; Baptist Campus Ministry Langston Univ, dir, 1967-70; Hough Chruch, minister educ comn, 1970-71; VA Med Ctr, Brecksville, OH, chaplain, 1971-; Lakeside Baptist Chruch E, Cleveland OH, pastor, 1972-79. **Orgs:** E Cleveland Ministerial Alliance, 1975; Asn Ment Health Clergy, bd cert chaplain, 1974; Ohio Health Care Chaplains; Am Protestant Hosp Asn; Col Chaplains; chmn, Evangelism Com Bapt Minister's Conf Cleveland OH; Dept Metropolitian Ministry Cleveland Baptist Asn; life mem & golden heritage life mem, Nat Asn Advan Colored People; Omega Psi Phi Fraternity Inc; Am Asn Christian Counrs; Asn Christian Marriage Counrs; life mem, Asn prof Chaplains.; life mem, Morehouse Col; Nat Alumni Asn. **Honors/Awds:** Christian Leadership Citation, Bapt Student Union Langston Univ, 1969; Outstanding Young Man, Outstanding Am Found, 1970; 33 Degree Free Mason; United Supreme Council 33 Degree Ancient & Accepted Scottish Rite Freemasonry Prince Hall Affiliation; loaned executive, VAMC Combined Federal Campaign, 1988; Crozer Theological Seminary, Crozer Scholar, 1989 & 1995. **Home Addr:** 2361 Traymore Rd, Cleveland, OH 44118, **Home Phone:** (216)932-0085.

**BAGNERIS, ESQ. MICHELE CHRISTINE BEAL (MICHELE BAGNERIS)**
Lawyer, executive. **Personal:** Born Mar 7, 1959, Los Angeles, CA; daughter of M Meredith and Rohelia; married Jules S III; children: Monet Christine, Jules S IV & Mariana. **Educ:** Stanford Univ, AB, int rels, 1980; Boalt Hall Sch Law, Univ Calif, Berkeley, JD, 1983. **Career:** Richards Watson & Gershon, atty, 1983-92, partner, 1992-; City Monrovia, Calif, city atty, 1992-99; Pasadena City, atty, 1997-. **Orgs:** Asst secy, Los Angeles Urban League Bd, 1985-91; State Bar Comn Human Rights, 1987-90; bd mem, San Fernando Legal Serv Corp, 1989-; LA City Atty Criminal Justice Panel, 1991-; dir missionary educ, AME Church, S Calif Conf Women's Missionary Soc, 1992-93; Langston Bar Asn; Black Women Lawyers Los Angeles. **Honors/Awds:** Medal of Excellence from Women at Work, Humanitarian Award, Alkebu-lan Cult Ctr; Woman of Excellence, YWCA. **Home Addr:** 1701 Buckingham Rd, Los Angeles, CA 90019, **Home Phone:** (213)939-7482. **Business Addr:** Attorney, Pasadena City Attorney, City Prosecutors Off, Pasadena, CA 91109, **Business Phone:** (626)744-4141.

**BAILER, BONNIE LYNN**
President (organization), art consultant, association executive. **Personal:** Born Oct 11, 1946, New York, NY; daughter of Lloyd Harding and Marvelyne Amanda (Matthews); married Philmore; children: Miles Bailer Armstead. **Educ:** City Univ NY, Queens Col, BS, Fr, 1968, MS, educ, 1975; Columbia Univ Sch Law, JD, law, 1992. **Career:** Intermediate Sch, teacher, 1968-75; New York Pub Sch Syst, Jr High Sch, Foreign Lang Dept, chmn, 1970-75; Yellow-Go-Rilla Productions Ltd, co-founder & vpres, 1975-78; Manhattan Bor Pres Campaigns, polit campaign admin, 1977; Gilbert Jonas Co Inc, prof fund raiser, vpres, corp develop officer, 1978-86; Morningside Montessori Sch, dir, 1979-82; Talk Shop Foreign Lang Prog C, founder & pres, 1981-; UN Asn USA, dir capital campaign, 1986-88; Bailer Studios, artists agt & prof fund raising consult, 1988-; Jones, Day, Reavis & Pogue, legal intern, 1991; Bet Tzedek Legal Serv, atty, 1992-93; Pub Coun, directing atty, 1994-99; Northridge Hosp Med Ctr, Ctr Healthier Communities, dir, 1999-. **Orgs:** Mem consult, Nat Asn Advan Colored People, 1978-79, life mem; bd mem, Morning side Montessori Sch, 1979-82; cert bldg mgr, City New York, 1979; pres, coordr, Ann Westside Community Conf, 1979-; consult, Minisink City Mission Soc, 1984; Grinnell HouseDefense Corp, 1984-; comn mem, Cathedral Sch, 1984-; Nat Asn Female Exec; Nat Soc Fund raising Exec; Women Fin Develop, Planned Giving Group; Black Law Students Asn, Columbia Univ, 1989-; bd dir & vpres, Connections C; bd mem, Connections C, 1998-2011; bd dir & pres, Valley Care Community Consortium, 2008-11. **Home Addr:** 1620 Herrin St, Redondo Beach, CA 90278-2826, **Home Phone:** (310)245-7530. **Business Addr:** Director, Northridge Hospital Medical Center, 18300 Roscoe Blvd, Northridge, CA 91328, **Business Phone:** (818)885-8500.

**BAILEY, DR. ADRIENNE YVONNE**
Teacher, consultant, educator. **Personal:** Born Nov 24, 1944, Chicago, IL; daughter of Leroy and Julia Spalding. **Educ:** Mundelein Col, BA, 1966; Wayne State Univ, MA, 1969; Northwestern Univ, PhD, 1973. **Career:** Chicago Bd Educ, Deneen Elem Sch, teacher social studies, Eng, Fr, math, 1966-67; So Shore YMCA, Chicago, neighborhood youth corps supvr, 1967; Circle Maxwell YMCA, Chicago, prog coordr, 1967-68; Detroit Bd Educ, substitute teacher, 1968-69; Govt Off Human Resources, Chicago, educ coordr, 1969-71; Northwestern Univ, Northwestern Comn Educ Proj, univ coordr, 1972-73; Chicago Comn Trust, Chicago, sr staff assoc, 1973-81; Col Bd New York, NY, vpres acad affairs, 1981; US Dept Educ, peer reviewer, 1994; educ consult; Harvard Univ, Exec Leadership Prog Urban Educ, 2007-10; Working Behalf Kids, sr consult, 2011-12; SCOPE/LEADS, Sch Educ, Stanford Univ, leads liaison/sr consult, 2010-13; Panasonic Found, strategic consult & sr consult, 2012-. **Orgs:** IL State Bd Educ, 1974-81; steering comn, exec comn, comn, Educ Comn States, 1974-79, 1975-77, 1978-79, 1981; bd dir, Asn Black Found Exec, 1975-87; Nat Assessment Educ Prog Policy Comn, 1976-80; task force Desegregation Strategies Proj, 1976-81; policy comn Sch Educ Northwestern Univ; bd trustees, Hazen Found, New Haven CT, 1977-87; vis comn Grad Sch Educ Harvard Univ, 1977-83; Nat Task Force State Efforts Achieve Sex Equity, 1980-83, chmn, adv comn Coun Found Internship & Fel Prog Minorities & Women, 1980-82; adv comn, Inst Educ Fin & Govt Stanford Univ, 1980-85; Career Develop Adv Comn Nat Urban League, 1982; Govt Educ Advan Comt, 1983-87; Nat Comt Sec Schooling Hispanics, 1983-85; adv panel Phi Delta Kappa Gallup Poll Pubs Attitudes Toward Pub Educ, 1984; bd dir, Coun Found, 1986; META, 1986; bd dir, Negro Ensemble, NY; bd trustees Mary mt Col, 1988-89; ed bd, Kappan (Phi Delta Kappan); co chmn, Gov's Adv Comn Black Affairs, NY, Educ sub-Comt; bd trustee, So Educ Found, Atlanta GA; bd trustee, Found Ctr; vpres, Nat Asn State Bds Educ. **Honors/Awds:** MDEA Inst french, Univ ME, 1966; Image Award, League Black Women, 1974; Recognition Award, Black Achiever Indust YMCA Metro Chicago, 1974; 1 of 100 Outstanding Black Women in America Award, Operation PUSH, 1975; 1 of 10 Outstanding Young Persons Award, IL Jaycees, 1975; Community Motivation Award, HU MA BE Karate Assoc, 1975; 1 of 10 Outstanding Young Citizens Award, Chicago Jaycees, 1976; Distinguished Service Award, Ed Comn State, 1977; Outstanding Achievement Award, YWCA Metro Chicago, 1978; Kizzy Award, Outstanding Contributions, 1979; Salute IL Serv, Federal Savings & Loan Bank, 1980; Meritorious Service Award, Educ Comn State NAEP, 1980; Human Relations Award, IL Educ Asn, 1980; Certificate of Recognition, Phi Delta Kappa NW Univ Chap, 1980; Merit Award, NW Alumni Asn, 1981; Diamond Jubilee Recognition, Phi Delta Kappa, 1981; Agenda for Action, Educ Leadership, 1984; Top 100 Black Bus & Prof Women, Dollars & Sense Magazine, 1985; Special Service Award, Nat Alliance Black Sch Educr, 1987. **Home Addr:** 2951 S King Dr Apt 911, Chicago, IL 60616-3344, **Home Phone:** (312)225-0079. **Business Addr:** Senior Consultant, Strategic Consultant, Panasonic Foundation, 2 Riverfront Plz 11th Fl, Newark, NJ 07102, **Business Phone:** (201)392-4132.

**BAILEY, ANTOINETTE M.**
President (organization), lecturer, teacher. **Personal:** Born Oct 4, 1949, St. Louis, MO; daughter of Jack D and Margurie Brown; married George E; children: Dara Braddock & Errin Braddock. **Educ:** Southern Ill Univ, BA, philos, 1972; Mich State Univ, MA, coun, 1975. **Career:** Mich St Univ, grad asst, 1973-75; E Lansing High Sch, MI, teacher, 1973-74; Panama Canal Co, Balboa Heights, CZ, EEO specialist investr, 1976-77; Narcotics Serv Coun, St Louis, super counr, 1978-80; Mo Div Voc Rehab, Olivette, sr counr deaf, 1980-84; McDonnell Douglas Corp, St Louis, dir training & devt, 1984-, vpres community rels; Boeing-McDonnell Found, pres, 1984-2006; Boeing Co, Community & Educ Rels, vpres, 1984-2006, pres, 2000; Bailey Consult, pres, 2006-; Wash Univ, adj prof, 2006-; Webster Univ, adj prof, 2009-. **Orgs:** Bd mem, Urban League Metrop St Louis; bd mem, Regional Com & Growth Asn; bd mem, Comn Bot Garden Subdistrict, Metrop Zool Park & Mus, St. Louis; bd mem, Mo Hist Soc, YWCA Metrop Soc. **Honors/Awds:** Nat Inst Ment Health Fel, 1972-75; Counselor of the Year, Mo Nat Rehab Asn, 1983; Presenteeism Award 1, McDonnell Douglas, 1985-86, 1986-87; Leadership Award, YMCA, 1988; Leadership St Louis Participant, Class, 1991-92. **Business Addr:** Adjunct Professor, Webster University, 470 E Lockwood Ave, St. Louis, MT 63119-3141.

**BAILEY, ARTHUR**
Administrator, gospel singer. **Personal:** Born Wilkinsburg, PA; son of William Henry and Winifred Townsend. **Educ:** Pittsburgh Acad, attended 1949; Carnegie Inst Tech, attended 1955; Dept Agr, Grad Sch Wash, DC, attended 1956; Dept Interior, mgt training prog, 1956. **Career:** Downtown Chorale, singer, tenor, 1949-58; Dept Interior Bur Mines, admin asst, 1956-58, purchasing agt, 1958-60; Holmes & Narver Inc, secy, 1964-65; NASA Pasadena, contract asst, 1966-68; Social Security Admin, claims rep, 1968-73, field rep, 1974-81, claims rep, 1981-93, social ins specialist, 1993-. **Orgs:** Actor Pittsburgh Playhouse, 1958-59; field rep journalist, pub speaker Social Security Admin, 1974-83; dir pub, rel Black Porsche Inc, 1976-78; Parliamentarian, 1979-82, historian, 1983-84; BPI, 1973-; Porsche Club Am, 1981-; bd dir, 1986-88, treas & bd dir, 1989-90, secy & bd dir, 1991-92, Fed Employees West Credit. **Honors/Awds:** Sustained Superior Performance Award, Corps of Engrs, 1960-61; Outstanding Performance Award, Social Security Admin Huntington Park, 1976; Superior Performance Award, Social Security Admin Los Angeles, Calif, 1984; Outstanding Performance Award, Univ Village Office, Los Angeles, Social Security Admin, 1988; Public Service Award in Recognition of 40 years of service in the govt of USA, Commr of Social Security, 1988; Outstanding Performance Award, Social Security Admin, Univ Village Off, Pittsburgh, 1992; Outstanding Performance Award, Univ Village Office, 1992-93. **Home Addr:** 444 S Kingsley Dr Apt 343, Los Angeles, CA 90020-3262. **Business Addr:** Social Insurance Representative, Social Security Administration, 1115 W Adams Blvd, Los Angeles, CA 90007.

**BAILEY, CARLTON WILSON**
Football player. **Personal:** Born Dec 15, 1964, Baltimore, MD; married Karen Buscaglia; children: Justin. **Educ:** Univ NC, BA, sociol, 1988. **Career:** Football player (retired); Buffalo Bills, linebacker & right inner linebacker, 1988-92; New York Giants, left inner linebacker, 1993-94; Carolina Panthers, right inner linebacker, 1995-97.

**BAILEY, CAROL A.**
Air traffic controller. **Career:** Air force specialist (retired); US Dept Transp, Fed Aviation Admin, Detroit Metrop Air Traffic Control, supvry air traffic control specialist, 1981-2004. **Orgs:** Prof Women Controllers. **Special Achievements:** First African American female supervisory air traffic control specialist at the Detroit Metropolitan Air Traffic Control. **Business Addr:** Supervisory Air Traffic Control Specialist, Detroit Metrop Air Traffic Control, Bldg 801 Suite 104, Detroit, MI 48242, **Business Phone:** (313)955-5000.

**BAILEY, DR. CLARENCE WALTER**
Business owner, manager, executive. **Personal:** Born Sep 25, 1933, Longview, TX; married Mavis Lean Blankenship; children: Sherry Lenel Smith. **Educ:** Wiley Col, BS, 1954; Drake Univ, MS, 1959. **Career:** Wiley Col, emer, 1954; C W Bailey Ins Agency Inc, mgr, owner, 1966-. **Orgs:** Dir, Oil Belt Asn Life Underwriters, 1967-; life mem, Million Dollar Round Table, 1973-; Civitan Club, 1978-; dir, Jr Achievement, 1984-; secy, LISD Sch Bd, 1984-; dir, Good Shephard Med Ctr, 1983-; bd trustee, Wiley Col, 2000-03. **Honors/Awds:** Top ten prod, President Coun NWL, 1971-; Outstanding Citizen Award, Nat Asn Advan Colored People, 1978; Silver Beaver Award, BSA, 1980; Phi Delta Kappa, 1981-; Hon Doctorate Degree, Wiley Col, 1995. **Home Addr:** 2307 Lilly St, Longview, TX 75602-3703, **Home Phone:** (903)753-6663. **Business Addr:** Owner, C W Bailey Insurance Agency Inc, 2411 SE Monroe, Longview, TX 75601, **Business Phone:** (903)753-8636.

**BAILEY, CURTIS DARNELL**
Consultant, educator. **Personal:** Born May 21, 1954, Philadelphia, PA; son of Helena. **Educ:** Temple Univ, BA, 1976; Clark/Atlanta Univ, MBA, 1978. **Career:** Benton & Bowles Inc, asst acct exec, 1978-79; Atochem Corp, advert mgr, 1979-84; DuPont Co, mkt commun specialist, 1984-87; mkt & commun consult, 1987; Rowan Univ, prof mgt/mkt, 1990-93; Eastern Col, prof fast-track MBA prog, 1997-. **Orgs:** Kappa Alpha Psi Fraternity, 1983-; fac fel Dept Higher Educ, State NJ, 1993. **Home Addr:** 1601 E Mt Pleasant Ave, Philadelphia, PA 19150-1208, **Home Phone:** (267)297-7608.

**BAILEY, CYNTHIA**
Fashion model, business owner, television actor. **Personal:** Born AL; married Peter Thomas, Jul 24, 2010; children: Noelle Forde Robinson. **Career:** Wilhelmia Models NYC, model; Bailey Agency Sch Fashion, founder; Bravo cable channel's "Real Housewives of Atlanta" and "Watch What Happens: Live", actor, 2010-14. **Special Achievements:** Appearances: Movie "Without You I'm Nothing" (1990); "The Cosby Show," (1990); 2011 Soul Train Awards (2012) and 20th Annual Trumpet Awards (2012). **Business Addr:** Owner, The Bailey Agency School of Fashion, 924 Garrett St, Atlanta, GA 30316, **Business Phone:** (404)622-1791.

**BAILEY, DR. DARLYNE**
Educator. **Educ:** Lafayette Col, BA, psychol, 1974; Columbia Univ, MS, social work, 1976; Lenox Hill Hosp, cert psychoanal psychother, 1981; Case Western Res Univ, PhD, orgn behav, 1988. **Career:** Weatherhead Sch of Mgt, prof; Case Western Res Univ, Mandel Sch Appl Social Scis, dean & prof, 1988-2002; Columbia Univ, Teachers Col, vpres acad affairs & dean, 2002-, interim pres, 2003; Univ Minn, Col Educ & Human Develop, founding dean, 2006-08; Bryn Mawr Col, Grad Sch Social Work, Social Res, spec asst to pres community partnerships, dean, prof, currently. Books: Strategic Alliances Among Health and Human Services Organizations, Sage Publ; Managing Human Resources in the Human Services, Oxford Univ. **Orgs:** Bd mem, Lorraine Monroe Leadership Inst; chair, gov secretariat, Mandel Ctr; Cleveland's Bond Accountability Comn, currently; Cleveland Comn on Econ Partnerships & Inclusion; W.K.Kellogg Found Fel, 1994; Salzburg Sem Fel, 1996. **Business Addr:** Dean, Vice President for Academic Affairs, Columbia University, 122 Main Hall 525 W 120th St, New York, NY 10027-6696, **Business Phone:** (212)678-3000.

**BAILEY, DR. DERYL FLYNN**
Founder (originator), counselor, educator. **Educ:** Campbell Univ, BS, social serv, 1982, MED, guid & coun, 1984; Univ Va, EDS, counr educ, 1995, PhD, counr educ, 1999. **Career:** Pinecrest High Sch, Counr, 1984-87; Southern High Sch, Counr, 1987-89; Asheville High Sch, Counr, 1989-94; Univ Ga, Col Educ, Dept Coun & Human Develop Serv, dir, 1989-, asst prof, 1999-2005, dir, 1999-, int res fel, 2001, assoc prof, 2005-, admis coordr; Off Youth Staunton, Va, interim dir, 1997-99; Univ N Fla, vis asst prof, 2002; Univ Buffalo, Ctr Am Educ Singapore, vis asst prof, 2003, 2005; Author: Increasing multicultural understanding, 2013. **Orgs:** Am Coun Asn; Asn Specialists Group Work; Asn Counr Educ & Supvn; Asn Multicultural Coun & Develop; founder & dir, Empowered Youth Progs; Am Sch Coun Asn; Asn Counr Educ & Supv; pres, Southern Asn Counr Educ & Supv, 2005-06; Ga Sch Counr Asn; Asn Specialists Group Work; Coun Asn Humanistic Educ & Develop; Chi Sigma Iota; Int Asn Coun; pres, Asn Counr Educ & Supv, 2011-12. **Business Addr:** Counseling Professor, Admissions Coordinator, University of Georgia, 408K Aderhold Hall, Athens, GA 30602, **Business Phone:** (706)583-0126.

**BAILEY, DR. DIDI GISELLE**
Psychiatrist. **Personal:** Born Mar 14, 1948, New York, NY; daughter of William Buster and Gertha Jones Smith; children: Jordan Eleanor Pete. **Educ:** Howard Univ, BS, 1968, MD, 1972; Howard Univ Hosp, attended 1975. **Career:** DC Govt, forensic psychiatrist, 1974-79, med consult disability dept, 1979-80; Howard Univ Hosp, resident psychiat, 1975; pvt pract psychiatrist, 1975-; State Calif, med consult disability dept, 1981-85; Urban Behav Assocs PA, psychiatrist, currently. **Orgs:** Adv bd, Alameda County Ment Health, 1981-89; pres, Nat Coalition Black Women Physicians Asn, 1990-93; counr, Golden State Med Asn, 1990-93; mem exec comt, Sinkler Miller State Med Asn, 1991-92. **Honors/Awds:** Commendation, Alameda Co Bd of Supvrs, 1989. **Home Addr:** 4324 Rilea Way Suite 35, Oakland, CA 94605-3720. **Business Addr:** Psychiatrist, Urban Behavior Associates PA, 2310 N Charles St, Baltimore, MD 21218, **Business Phone:** (410)230-0028.

**BAILEY, DORIS JONES (DORIS BAILEY-REAVIS)**
Secretary (office), association executive, activist. **Personal:** Born May 16, 1927, Port Chester, NY; daughter of Robert Leon and Alice M Randall; married Alfred K; children: Alethia Joy Streeter. **Educ:** Immanuel Lutheran Col, assoc degree, educ, 1947. **Career:** Dept Army-Pentagon, clerk; New York State, secy; New York Bd Coop Educ Serv, soc worker asst, admin asst. **Orgs:** Pres, Immanuel Lutheran Col Alumni Asn, 1985-; pres, Port Chester Rye Nat Asn Adv Colored People, 1990-; bd mem, Carver Community Ctr, 1990-; bd mem, Coun Community Serv, 1992-; mus adv comt mem, State Univ NY, 1992-; Sno-burners, Ski & Sports Asn. **Home Addr:** 325 King St, Port Chester, NY 10573-4050, **Home Phone:** (914)937-6613.

**BAILEY, DUWAIN**
Administrator, manager, broker. **Personal:** Born May 29, 1957, Chicago, IL; son of McWillie and Arlena Sanders; married Jocelyn Kyle; children: Branden & Kyle. **Educ:** Southern Ill Univ, Carbondale, IL, BA, polit sci & govt, 1980. **Career:** State Ill, Springfield, Ill, tech mgr/safety proj mgr, 1980-84, tech mgrl II/pub transp mgr, 1984-85; City Chicago, Chicago, Ill, supv budget anayst, 1985-87, dir finance, 1987-88, dep comnr finance & admin, 1988-98, first dep comnr, 1998-2000; Chicago Housing Authority, chief opers, 2000-08, exec advisor, 2008-14; New W Realty Inc, real estate broker, 2009-; Primerica Financial Serv, dist mgr, 2013-. **Orgs:** Treas, bd dir, Nat Forum Black Pub Adminr, Chicago Chap, 1989-; chmn, social action comt, Phi Beta Sigma Fraternity-Upsilon Sigma, 1990-; asst financial secy, Phi Beta Sigma Fraternity-Upsilon Sigma, 1991-; advisor, S Shore High Sch Clg Club;

Apostolic Church God; partic, Chicago Asn Com & Indust Youth Motivation Prog; bd mem, Nat Forum Black Pub Admin, 2004-12; Chicago Asn Realtors; Nat Asn Housing & Redevelop Officials; SIU Col Bus Minority Adv Coun; Blue & White Educ Found; City Club Chicago. **Home Addr:** 12538 S Princeton, Chicago, IL 60628. **Business Addr:** Real Estate Broker, New West Realty Inc, 1440 W Taylor St, Chicago, IL 60607-4623, **Business Phone:** (312)829-2100.

### BAILEY, EUGENE RIDGEWAY
Military leader. **Personal:** Born Oct 1, 1938, Painter, VA; son of James Hatton and Alma Cleo Jacobs; married Juanita Hicks; children: Denise & Duane. **Educ:** Va State Univ, Petersburg, VA, BS, 1960; US Int Univ, San Diego, CA, MA, 1976, DBA, 1986. **Career:** Military leader (retired); USS Fort Fisher, LSD-40, San Diego, Calif, exec officer, 1977-79; Amphibious Squadron, San Diego, Calif, chief staff, 1979-81; USS Racine, LST-1191, Long Beach, Calif, commanding officer, 1981-83; Telecommunications, CMD, Wash, DC, div dir, 1983-85; USS Juneau, LPD-10, San Diego, Calif, commanding officer, 1985-87; Naval Recruiting HDQ, Arlington, Va, dep, 1987-89; San Diego, Calif, captain/commanding officer; Eugene R Bailey & Assoc, founder. **Orgs:** Greater San Diego Chamber Com; Nat Naval Officers Asn, 1977-91; Calif Continuing Milit Educrs Asn, 1990-91; bd dir, Jackie Robinson, YMCA, San Diego, 1987-91, bd mgr, currently. **Home Addr:** 6206 Lake Lucerne Dr, San Diego, CA 92119-3034, **Home Phone:** (619)463-7313. **Business Addr:** President, Eugene R Bailey & Associates, 6206 Lake Lucerne Dr, San Diego, CA 92119, **Business Phone:** (619)463-7671.

### BAILEY, PROF. GARY
Social worker, educator. **Personal:** Born Oct 9, 1955, Cleveland, OH; son of Samuel Jr and Lucille; married Richard D McCarthy. **Educ:** Tufts Univ, Eliot Pearson Sch Child Study, BA, 1977; Boston Univ, Sch Social Work, MSW, 1979. **Career:** Social worker, 1979-84; Family Serv Asn Greater Boston, unit supvr, 1984-92; Univ Mass, Col Pub & Commun, lectr, 1984-93; Family Serv Greater Boston, Serv Older People, asst dir, 1986-90, Spec Proj, dir, 1990-91, dir boston social serv, 1991-93; Boston Univ Sch Social Work, adj asst prof, 1989-, coordr, 1990-92, adj prof pub health, 1993-; Parents & C Serv, exec dir, 1993-99; Simmons Col Sch Social Work, adj assoc prof, 1994-99, vis prof, 1999-2002, asst prof, 2002-05; Simmons Col Sch Social Work, asst prof & coord racism & oppression sequence, prof pract, Urban Leadership Prog, dir, 2005-; Policy, Advocacy & Representation Comn, Inaugural Chair, 2006. **Orgs:** Past Pres, AIDS Action Community Inc, 1992-; pres, Mass Chap Nat Asn Social Workers, 1993-95; treas, Nat Asn Social Workers, Wash, DC, 1995-97; Wang Ctr Performing Arts, 1994-; Phillips Brooks House Asn, Harvard Univ, 1996; bd dir, Nat Asn Social Workers, vpres, 2000-02, pres, 2003-05; pres, N Am Region Int Fedn Social Workers, 2003-06; pres, Int Fedn Social Workers, 2010; Coun Social Work Educ Global Comn, 2010; bd mem, Leadership Coun, United Way Mass Bay; bd mem, Comnrs Prof Adv Comt, Mass Dept Soc Serv; bd mem, Mass Dept Ment Health Prof Adv Comt, Child & Adolescent Serv; Mass Educ Finance Authority; Design Indust Found AIDS; Wang Ctr Performing Arts; mem & bd dir, Community Benefits Adv Bd, C's Hosp; mem rels comt, Tufts Health Plan; United Homes C Dorchester; Nat Asn Social Workers Wash; Black Admin Child Welfare; Asn Black Social Workers, Mass Chap; N Am & Caribbean Asn Schs Social Work; bd mem, Fenway High Sch; Governance & Facil Comts; bd dir, Mass Educ Financing Authority; bd ambassadors, Gay & Lesbian Advocates & Defenders; AIDS Action Adv Coun; trustee, Union United Methodist Church; chmn, Nat Social Work Pub Educ Campaign; Nat Asn Social Workers Found Bd Dirs. **Honors/Awds:** Social Worker of the Year, Nat Asn Social Work Mass Chap, 1988; Boston Gerontology Center Community Award, Univ Mass, 1993; Congressman Gerry Studds Visibility Award, 1944; Alumni Asn Award, Boston Univ Sch Social Work, 1995; Multicultural AIDS Coalition Wayne S Wright Advocacy Award, 1997; Massachusetts Bayard Rustin Spirit Award, 1997; Visibility Award, Fenway Community health Ctr, Congressman Gerry Studs, 1996; Social Worker of the Year, NASW, 1998; Social Work Pioneer, NASW, 2005; Legacy of Caring Award, Devereux-Massachusetts, 2007; Man of the Year, Union United Methodist Church, 2012; Recipient of Numerous Awards & Honors. **Special Achievements:** Named a Social Work Pioneer by the NASW Foundation; In 2008 was the Cecil and Ida Green Honors Professor, at Texas Christian University; Received the State Directors Award for Excellence in Social Work Leadership from the South Carolina Office of Public Health. Author of Several Books. **Home Addr:** 300 Fenway, Boston, MA 02115, **Home Phone:** (617)521-3977. **Business Addr:** Assistant Professor, Professor of Practice, Simmons College, Rm P-404J 300 Fenway, Boston, MA 02115, **Business Phone:** (617)521-3977.

### BAILEY, DR. GRACIE MASSENBERG
School administrator. **Personal:** Born Feb 25, 1936, Waverly, VA; daughter of Maxine Stith and Ernest R; married Erling Sr; children: LaVetta B Goldsborough & Erling Jr. **Educ:** Va State Col, BS, 1958, comput mgt, 1969, MEd, 1970; Va Polytech Inst & State Univ, EdD, 1983. **Career:** VA St Col, sec, 1958-62; Amelia City Sch Bd, teacher, 1958-60; Hartford Variable Annuity Life Ins Co, salesperson, 1960-79; Sussex City Sch Bd, teacher, 1961-63; Dinwiddie City Sch Bd, bus educ teacher, 1963-74; Richard Bland Col, dir personnel, assoc prof bus, asst to pres AA/EEO, 1974, registr, 1986-88, assoc provost stud serv, 1988-90, assoc provost, 1990, assoc prof emer, currently. **Orgs:** Sussex Ed Assoc, 1961-63; Dinwiddie Ed Assoc, 1963-74; sec, treas, Erling Baily Elect Contr, 1966-85; Am Bus Women Assoc Dinwiddie Charter Chap, 1971-84; Am Asn Univ Profs, 1974-79; Am Asn Affirmative Action, 1976-; Advcoun Educ Comput St Va, 1976-80; Col & Univ Personnel Assoc, 1978-; Nat & Va Asn Women Higher Ed 1978-; rec sec, Va Admis Coun Black Concerns, 1984-; Human Rights Comn Hiram Davis Med Ctr, 1986-; Va Assoc Col Registrars & Admis Officers, Southern Asn Col Registr & Admis Officers; Am Asn Col Registr & Admis Officers, 1986-; vpres, Budget, Allocation & Fund Raising, UnitedWay Serv, 1988-89; chairperson, Sside Opers Bd, 1990; bd mem, Petersburg Festival Chorus Inc, 1990-; chairperson, Girl Scouts Va, 1991-94. **Home Addr:** 1900 Birdsong Rd, Petersburg, VA 23805, **Home Phone:** (804)861-8182. **Business Addr:** Associate Professor Emeritus, Richard Bland College, 11301 Johnson Rd, Petersburg, VA 23805, **Business Phone:** (804)862-6226.

### BAILEY, HARRY AUGUSTINE, JR.
Government official, educator, editor. **Personal:** Born Dec 19, 1932, Ft. Pierce, FL; son of Harry Augustine and Ruth; married Mary L; children: Harry III & Larry B. **Educ:** Fla A&M Univ, BA, 1954; Univ Kans, MA, 1960, PhD, 1964. **Career:** Government official (retired), educator (retired), editor; Univ Kans, asst instr, 1960-62, asst instr, Western Civilization, 1962-64, instr sociol, 1964; Temple Univ, Dept Polit Sci, from asst prof to prof, 1964-75, Dept Polit Sci, chmn, 1970-73, prof & dir, Masters Prog Pub Admin, 1975-80, chmn grad studies, 1985-90; Charles Merrill Publ, Negro Polit Am, ed, 1967; Book: The Politics of the Southern Negro, rev auth; Charles Merrill Publ, co-ed, Ethnic Group Polit, 1969; J Polit, ed bd, 1975-76; Moore Publ Co, ed, Classics Am Pres, 1980; Dorsey Press, co-ed, Am Pres, 1988; FE Peacock Publ, co-ed, State & Local Gov & Polit, 1993. **Orgs:** Am Polit Sci Asn; Am Soc Pub Admin; C Study Pres; Pi Sigma Alpha; Pa Polit Sci & Pub Admin Asn, 1970-72; pres, Pa Polit Sci Asn, 1970; vpres, Northeastern Sci Asn, 1971-72; pres, bd gov, Temple Univ Fac Club, 1972-73; Danforth Asn, 1975-81; chmn, Civil Serv Comn, City Philadelphia, 1983-91; Zoning Bd Adjust, City Philadelphia, 1992-. **Home Addr:** 18 Appletree Ct, Philadelphia, PA 19106.

### BAILEY, HILTRON
Photographer. **Personal:** married Elizabeth. **Educ:** Hope Int Univ; Penn Valley Community Col. **Career:** Eurweb/Electronic Urban Report, photo journalist, currently; freelance photogr, currently; Hiltron Bailey Photog, owner, currently. **Business Addr:** Photographer, Eurweb.com/Electronic Urban Report, PO Box 412081, Los Angeles, CA 90041, **Business Phone:** (323)254-9599.

### BAILEY, DR. JOSEPH ALEXANDER, II
Educator, physician. **Personal:** Born Jul 22, 1935, Pine Bluff, AR; son of Joseph A Sr and Angeline Elaine Davis; children: Ryan, Jana, Joseph III, Johathan, Jerad & Jordan. **Educ:** Univ Mich, Ann Arbor, MI, orthopaedics, 1955; Morehouse Col, Atlanta, GA, BS, orthopaedics, 1957; Meharry Med Sch, MD, orthopaedics, 1961; Am Bd Ortho Surgeons, dipl, 1971. **Career:** Riverside Seventh Day Adventist Hosp, Nashville, TN, externship, 1959-60; Los Angeles Co Gen Hosp, internship, 1961-62; Sloan Bettering Memorial Hosp, New York, NY, externship, 1961-62; Hahnemann Hosp Phil, PA, chiefres, 1964-66; DuPuy Mfg Co, consult, 1966-74; St Hosp Crippled C, PA, chief researcher, 1966-68; Hosp Joint Dis, New York, NY, Orthopaedic Residency, 1967-68; Orthopaedic Genetics Hosp Joint Dis & Med Ctr, New York, NY, consult, 1968-2000; Med Gen John Hopkins Hosp, fel, 1968-69; Ortho Sur John Hopkins Hosp, Baltimore, fel, 1968-69; Univ Conn Health Ctr, Hartford, CT, asst prof Orthopaedic Surg, 1969-71; Veterans Admin Hosp Newington, CT, chief orthopaedic surg, 1969-71; Pediat Orthpaedics, Newington, CT, consult staff, 1969-71; Univ Conn, Sports Dept, Storrs, CT, team physician, 1969-71; Univ Calif, Riverside, asst clin prof, clin instr, 1986-; San Bernardino Co Gen Hosp, assoc staff, prof; St Calif, independent med examr; St Benardines Hosp, assoc staff; Univ New Am Communities Prog, endowed chair; Teaching Inner City Youth Los Angeles & San Bernardino, CA, 1986-; Calif State Polytech Inst, mentor prog mem, 1989-; Los Angeles Conserv Corp, Dir & Instr, 1993-; Black Voice News, 1995-. Publications: Disproportionate Short Stature Diagnosis and Management, 1973; The Handbook for Worker's Compensation Doctors, 1994; The Concise Dictionary of Medical-Legal Terms, 1996; Rational Thinking, 1997; Preparing to Prepare, 2000. **Orgs:** Chief gen secy, Acad Ortho-Neuro Soc; Omega Psi Phi Fraternity, 1954; founding owner, JAB II Lifeskills Found CA, 1964-; diplomats, Am Bd Orthopaedic Surgeons, 1971; Fel Am Col Surgeons, 1971-; pres, Orthopaedic Sect Nat Med Asn, 1972; pres, Med Legal Comt, San Bernardino Co Med Socs, 1973; Community Leader Award, Noteworthy Americans, 1978; hon mem, Orthopaedic Technicians, 1978; African Elder Chair at 19th Ann African Holocaust Commemoration, 2010. **Business Addr:** Founding Owner, JAB II Lifeskills Foundation, 1699 Ctr St, Colton, CA 92324, **Business Phone:** (909)824-2252.

### BAILEY, KENETTA
Executive, vice president (organization). **Educ:** Northwestern Univ, BA; Northwestern Univ Medill Sch Jour, MBA, broadcast jour; Northwestern Univ, Kellogg Sch Mgt, MBA, mkt & strategy; CTAM Univ, Harvard Bus Sch; WICT Betsy Magness Leadership Inst; Univ Calif Los Angeles Anderson Sch Bus, NAMIC exec develop leadership prog. **Career:** Golin/Harris Commun, sr acct exec; Allstate Ins Co, Ill, corp rels rep; Kraft Foods, brand mgr, 1992-97; Pepsi-Cola Co, mkt mgr, 1997-99; BMG Entertainment, dir youth mkt progs, RCA Recs, sr dir strategic bus, 1999-2002, vpres strategic mktg, 2003; NBC Universal's Telemundo Network, group mkt dir, 2003-06; franchise owner, 2003-05; BMG Music, vpres Strategic Mkt, 2004-06; AMC Networks, 2006-11; Women's Entertainment TV, sr vpres mkt, 2006-; TV One, chief mkt officer & exec vpres, 2011-. **Orgs:** Women Cable Telecommunications, 2006-; nat bd mem, Nat Asn Multi-Ethnicity Commun, 2007-; Cable & Telecommunications Asn Mkt, 2007-; Advert Women New York, 2010-. **Business Addr:** Chief Marketing Officer, Executive Vice President, TV One, 1010 Wayne Ave, Silver Spring, MD 20910, **Business Phone:** (301)755-0400.

### BAILEY, LEE
President (organization). **Personal:** married Diane Blackmon. **Career:** Radio programming, 1970; Disc jockey; LeeBailey Communs Inc, pres, 1979-; Bailey Broadcasting Services, founder, 1983-. **Business Addr:** President, Lee Bailey Communications Inc, 3151 Cahuenga Bl W Suite 205, Los Angeles, CA 90068-1768, **Business Phone:** (213)969-0011.

### BAILEY, LILICIA
Executive, vice president (organization). **Educ:** Spelman Col, BA, psychol; Keller Grad Sch, MA, human resources mgt; Pepperdine Univ, MBA. **Career:** Home Depot, dir inclusion & orgn effectiveness; Cox Enterprises, dir orgn develop, sr vpres; Manheim, sr vpres & global chief people officer, 2004-; Belk Inc, exec vpres & chief people officer, 2013. **Orgs:** Bd mem, Cobb Family Resources; bd mem, Girl's Inc; bd mem, Communities Schs Ga; Leadership Atlanta Class 2010; chair-elect, Communities Schs Ga; Human Resources Planning Soc; Int Soc Human Resource Mgt; human resources coun mem, Girl Scouts Atlanta.

### BAILEY, LINDA F. (LINDA F GLOVER)
Government official. **Personal:** Born Oct 1, 1951, Emerson, AR; daughter of Edmond Glover and Alberta Washington Glover; married Fred E; children: Janelle Nicole & Jocelyn Briana. **Educ:** S Ark Univ, Magnolia, AR, BME, 1973; Univ Mo, Kans City, MO, MPA, 1978. **Career:** Social Security Admin, Kansas City, Mo, Social Ins Claims Examiner, 1973-79; US Small Bus Admin, Kansas City, Mo, equal opportunity officer, 1979-82, bus develop spec, 1982-90, asst dist dir bus dev, 1990-94, chief, 1994, econ develop specialist, sr lender rels specialist, currently. **Home Addr:** 9713 Harvard Ave, Kansas City, MO 64134, **Home Phone:** (816)966-8759. **Business Addr:** Senior Lender Relations Specialist, US Small Business Administration, 323 W 8th Suite 501, Kansas City, MO 64105-1500, **Business Phone:** (816)374-6762.

### BAILEY, MONA HUMPHRIES
School administrator, consultant. **Personal:** Born Dec 14, 1932; married William Peter; children: Peter Govan & Christopher Evans. **Educ:** Fla A&M Univ Tallahassee, BS, chem, 1954; Ore State Univ, Corvalis, MS, sci educ, 1962; Univ Wash, PhD, educ admin. **Career:** Meany-Madrona Mid Sch, Seattle Wash, prin, 1970-73; Univ Wash, instr, 1973-74; State Wash, asst state supt pub instr, 1974-86; Eckstein Mid Sch, Seattle Wash, prin appointee, 1974-75; Wash State Supt Pub Instuction, asst supt, 1974-86; Seattle Pub Sch, dist asst supt, 1986-90, dep supi, 1990-94; Nat Fac Western Region, dir, 1995-98; Forest Ridge Sch Sacred Heart, head, 1998-2000; Seattle Sch Dist, prin, personnel adminr, high sch counr & sci teacher; Univ Wash, Ctr Educ Renewal, sr assoc, currently; independent consult, currently. **Orgs:** Comn mem, Gov's Comn Criminal Justice, 1974-; bd trustee, Pac Sci Ctr, Seattle, 1975-; bd dir, Totem Girl Scout Coun Seattle, 1977-; chmn, adv comn, Seattle Oppors Industrialization Ctr, 1978; adv bd, United Negro Col Fund Inc, Seattle, 1978-; nat pres, 1979-83, Delta Sigma Theta, 1980; pres, Delta Res & Educ Found, 2002-06; Nat Network Sacred Heart Sch; Forest Ridge Sch; assoc, Pac Sci Ctr Found; Nat Bd Trans Africa; Mary McLeod Bethune Memorial Mus Found; Am Civil Liberties Union Nat Adv Comt; Wash State Vendor Rates Adv Comt; bd, Wash State Crime & Delinq; bd, Seattle's Univ Prep Acad; bd, Pac Sci Ctr; City Seattle Adv Comt, African Am Heritage Mus; bd dir, Wash Spec Olympics; Pac Sci Ctr Found Adv Comt; chair, State Bd Wash MESA Prog; Assoc Pac Sci Ctr Found; Roads Puget Sound; Mothers Against Violence; Northwest Regional Lab's Adv Comt Educ Profession & Improving Outcome Schooling; bd mem, Wash State Bd Educ; YWCA Communities Color Adv Comt; Black Educ Strategy Roundtable Bd Dirs; Seattle Art Mus Educ & Community Adv Comt; United Way King County's Community Bldg Comt; co chair, HB2722 State Adv Comt, Close Achievement Gap African Am Students, State Wash. **Honors/Awds:** Distinguished Service Field of Education Inner City Award, Carnation Co, 1973-74; Achievement Award, Les Dames Bridge Club Seattle, 1974; Distinguished Achievement Service to Youth Award, Links Inc, Twentieth Nat Asn Seattle, 1976; Distinguished Community Service Award, Benefit Guild Seattle, 1978; Hundred most influential FAMUANS of the century, 1999; Meritorious Achievement Award, Florida A&M Univ; Centennial Medallion, Florida A & M Univ; Mary Church Terrell Award, Delta Sigma Theta Sorority; One of the one hundred outstanding FAMUANS selected to receive the Centennial Medallion. **Home Addr:** 4708 E Mercer Way, Mercer Island, WA 98040, **Home Phone:** (206)232-9451. **Business Addr:** Senior Associate, University of Washington, 315A Miller Hall, Seattle, WA 98195-3600, **Business Phone:** (206)543-6230.

### BAILEY, MYRTLE LUCILLE (MYRTLE BAILEY)
Real estate agent, business owner, manager. **Personal:** Born Jul 11, 1954, St. Louis, MO; daughter of George Wendell and Mildred Turrentine; married R Mark Odom; children: Jared Michael. **Educ:** Lutheran High Sch N, dipl, col prep, 1972; Dillard Univ, BA, psychol & bus admin, 1975; St Louis Univ, MA, urban affairs, 1977; Dartmouth Col, Minority Bus Exec Prog, 1991. **Career:** Cent Med Ctr, dir mkt, 1977-80; Greater St Louis Health Systs Agency, planning assoc, 1980-81; Catalyst, consult, 1981-84; Catalyst Pub Rels Inc, owner, cheif exec officer, 1981-2000; Harris-Stowe Col, dir pub rels, 1984-87; Real Estate Agt; Child Day Care Asn, develop dir, 2002-07; Coldwell Banker Gundaker CWE, owner; Cent Realty, realtor, 2003-05; Bricke, Mortor & Clay Realty, realtor, 2005-07; Brown-Kortkamp Realty, realtor, 2007-11; FPD Mgt Inc, site mgr, 2011-13; Yarco Co, community mgr, currently. **Orgs:** Bd mem, Catholic cms on Housing, 1990-; bd mem, Provident Sch, 1990-; St Louis Convention & Vis, 1991-; bd mem, Paraquad, 1992-; pres, City-wide fed Republican Women, 1992-; RCGA, 1992-; exec comt, Nat Asn Advancement Colored People, 1992-; bd dir, Women's Self Help Ctr; comt mem, Urban League Metrop St Louis, 2000-11; St.Louis/Mo/Nat Assoc REALTORS; Cert Short Sale & Foreclosure Resource/Specialist; Int Right Way Assoc-CH37; Cert Course Coordr IRWA; bd dirs/Criteria & Allocations Comt; St. Louis Philathropic Orgn. **Honors/Awds:** Appreciation Student Gover, Harris Stowe State Col, 1987; Silver Microphone Award We Wish to Plead Our Own Cause, 1989; Outstanding Business Man, St Louis Develop Agency, 1992; Top Listing Agent, 2005; Agent of the Month, 2009 & 2010; Second Highest Producing Agent in Office, 2009; Agent of the Quarter, 2010; Registered HUD Agent; Certified Short Sale & Foreclosure Resource Specialist; Approved Negotiator, Missouri. **Special Achievements:** Dedication & Service Alumni Asn, 1987; Lincoln Univ Student Gov Asn, Participation-Youth Motivation Task Force, 1988; Annie Malone Children's Home, Special Contribution, 1990. **Home Addr:** 6040 W Cabanne Pl, St Louis, MO 63112, **Home Phone:** (314)726-2989. **Business Addr:** Realtor, Brown-Kortkamp Realty, 4709 Delmar Blvd, St. Louis, MO 63108-1705, **Business Phone:** (314)367-4709.

### BAILEY, PHILIP
Singer, actor. **Personal:** Born May 8, 1951, Denver, CO; married Krystal; children: 1; married Janet; children: 5. **Career:** Phoenix Horns, vocalist; Earth Wind & Fire, singer, 1972-84 & 1987-; Albums: Last Days & Time, 1972; Head to the Sky, 1973; Open Our Eyes, 1974; Another Time, 1974; Spirit, 1975; Gratitude, 1975; All 'N All, 1977; Sing a Song, 1977; I Am, 1979; Faces, 1980; Raise!, 1981; Secret Messages, 1982; Powerlight, 1983; Electric Universe, 1983; Continuation, 1983; The Wonders of His Love, 1984; Chinese Wall, 1984; Triumph, 1986; Inside Out, 1986; Touch the World, 1987; Family Affair, 1989; Chinese Wall, 1990; Heritage, 1990; The Best of Philip Bailey: A Gospel Collection, 1991; Philip Bailey, 1994; Life and Love, 1995; Dreams,

1999; Soul on Jazz, 2002. Films: That's the Way of the World, 1975; Full Metal Jacket, 1987. TV series: "Matlock", 1987; "The Tonight Show with Jay Leno", 1999; "Earth Wind and Fire Live at the Venetian", 2013. **Honors/Awds:** Grammy for Best R&B Vocal Performance By a Duo, Group or Chorus (With Earth, Wind & Fire), 1975, 1978, 1979, 1982; Grammy for Best R&B Instrumental Performance (With Earth, Wind and Fire), 1978, 1979; Grammy Award for Gospel Male, 1986; Rock & Roll Hall of Fame, 2000. **Business Addr:** Singer, c/o Bret Steinberg, 2000 Ave of the Stars, Los Angeles, CA 90067, **Business Phone:** (424)288-2000.

## BAILEY, DR. RANDALL CHARLES

Clergy, educator. **Personal:** Born May 26, 1947, Malden, MA; son of Charles C and Lorraine Margolis; married Dorothy Jean Lewis; children: Omari & Imani Akilah. **Educ:** Brandeis Univ, Waltham, BA; Univ Chicago, IL, AM, social serv admin; Candler Sch Theol, Atlanta, GA, MDiv, 1979; Emory Univ, Atlanta, GA, PhD, relig, 1987. **Career:** PCSAP Loop Col, Chicago, Ill, dir educ prog, 1972-73; Shelby County Develop Coord Dept, Memphis, Tenn, assoc dir, 1973; Atlanta Univ Sch Social Work, Atlanta, Ga, asst prof, 1973-81; Xavier Univ, Inst Black Cath Studies, fac; First Cong Church, UCC, Atlanta, Ga, asst minister, 1980-81; Interdenominational Theol Ctr, instr, 1981-87, asst prof, 1987-90, assoc prof, Atlanta, Ga, 1990-, Andrew W Mellon prof Hebrew Bible, retired; Memphis Theol Sem, adj prof, 2005-06. **Orgs:** Fel United Negro Col Fund, 1984-85; Black Theol Proj, 1986-; co-chair, Afro-Am Theol & Bibl Hermeneutics Soc Bibl Lit, 1987-94; co-chair, Unity Renewal Study, COFO NCCCUSA, 1988-92; Div Educ & Min NCCCUSA, 1988-91; chair, Bible Transl & Utilization Comm DEM NCCCUSA, 1988-, Soc Study Black Relig, 1988-; mem exec bd, NCCCUSA; consult, Balm in Gilead Inc; ed bd, Semeia Jour; Ebenezer Baptist Church; ed bd, Semeia; bd, Atlanta Interfaith AIDS Network; consult, Balm Gilead Inc; exec bd, Nat Coun Churches Christ; bd, J Relig Abuse Black Theol. **Honors/Awds:** Distinguished Service Award, Atlanta Nat Assn Black Social Workers, 1978. **Special Achievements:** Author: "Wash Me White as Snow: When Bad is Turned to Good, Race, Class and the Politics of Bible Translation," Seneia 76, 1996; "The Redemption of Yhwh: A Literary Critical Function of the Songs of Hannah and David," Biblical Interpretation, 1995; "'Is That Any Name for a Nice Hebrew Boy?' - Exodus 2:1-10: The De-Africanization of an Israelite Hero," The Recover of Black Presence: An Interdisciplinary Exploration, Abingdon, 1995; "They're Nothing but Incestuous Bastards: The Polemical Use of Sex and Sexuality in Hebrew Canon Narrative," Reading From This Place: Social Location and Biblical Interpretation in the United States, Fortress, 1994; "And Then They Will Know That I Am YHWH: The P Recasting of the Plague Narratives," JITC, 1994; "What Price Inclusivity?: An Afrocentric Reading of Dangerous Biblical Texts," Voices from the Third World, 1994; "Cobb Clergy's Gay Stance Loses Punch in Biblical Debate," Atlanta Journal/Constitution, p F2, June 26, 1994; "A De-politicized Gospel: Reflections on Galatians 5:22-23," Ecumenical Trends, 22 No 1, Jan 1993; "Doing the Wrong Thing: Male-Female Relationships in the Hebrew Canon," We Belong Together: The Churches in Solidarity with Women, Friendship Press, 1992; Yet With a Steady Beat: U.S. Afrocentric Biblical Interpretation (Semeia Studies); The Church With AIDS: Renewal in the Midst of Crisis; David in Love and War: The Pursuit of Power in a Samuel 10-12, Sheffield, 1990; numerous other publications. **Home Addr:** 2473 Glenrock Dr, Decatur, GA 30032, **Home Phone:** (404)284-0512. **Business Addr:** Andrew W Mellon Professor of Hebrew Bible, Interdenominational Theological Center, 700 Martin Luther King Jr Dr SW ClassRm Bldg 308B, Atlanta, GA 30314-4143, **Business Phone:** (404)527-7754.

## BAILEY, RICHARD

Historian. **Personal:** Born Oct 29, 1947, Montgomery, AL; son of Raymond and Lottie; married Judy; children: Judy, Valerie, Richard Jr & Karen. **Educ:** Ala State Univ, BS, 1971, MEd, 1972; Atlanta Univ, MA, 1973; Kans State Univ, PhD, 1984. **Career:** Hist Res Agency, Maxwell AFB, Ala, tech info specialist, 1982-83; Exten Course Inst, Gunter AFB, Ala, educ specialist, 1983-85; Air Univ Press, Maxwell AFB, Ala, res & writer spec, 1986; Univ Ala, consult Ctr Pub TV; Pyramid Publ, Inc, prin, currently. **Orgs:** Pres, Phi Delta Kappa, 1985-; Ala Hist Asn, 1986-; Ala Hist Comn, 1995; Ala Humanities Found; bd mem, Chesapeake Bay Writers. **Honors/Awds:** State Volunteer of the Year, 1991; National Volunteer of the Year, 1991; Maxwell Air Force Base Angel Award, 1994. **Special Achievements:** Neither Carpetbaggers nor Scalawags: Blacks Officeholders during the Reconstruction of Alabama, 1867-1878, 1991, reprint, 1997; Author: "Neither Carpetbaggers Nor Scalawags"; The Too Call Alabama Home: African American Profiles, 1800-1999, 1999. **Home Addr:** PO Box 1264, Montgomery, AL 36102-1264, **Home Phone:** (334)272-4826. **Business Addr:** Principal, Pyramid Publishing Inc, PO Box 230144, Montgomery, AL 36123, **Business Phone:** (334)272-4675.

## BAILEY, ROBERT (ROBERT MARTIN LUTHER BAILEY)

Football player, executive. **Personal:** Born Sep 3, 1968, Barbodas; married Wylidra; children: Kharee. **Educ:** Univ Miami, Fla, BS, sci. **Career:** Football player (retired), executive; Los Angeles Rams, 1991, left cornerback, 1992, defensive back, 1993-94; Wash Redskins, 1995; Dallas Cowboys, 1995; Miami Dolphins, 1996; Detroit Lions, 1997-98, 2001, left cornerback & right cornerback, 1999; Baltimore Ravens, 2000; Rosenhaus Sports Representation, head mkt div, 2002, pres, currently. **Orgs:** Spokesperson, SaveEarth Found. **Honors/Awds:** Super Bowl champion, XXX, XXXV. **Special Achievements:** Film: Super Bowl XXXV, 2001. The only current Lion to have won Super Bowl titles with two different teams. **Business Addr:** President, Rosenhaus Sports Representation, 6400 Allison Rd, Miami, FL 33141, **Business Phone:** (305)936-1093.

## BAILEY, ROBIN A.

Administrator. **Career:** Am Postal Workers Union, admin asst. **Business Addr:** Administrative Assistant, American Postal Workers Union, 1300 L St NW, Washington, DC 20005, **Business Phone:** (202)842-4248.

## BAILEY, RONALD T.

Planner, consultant. **Personal:** Born May 21, 1938, Chicago, IL; son of Claude and Leona Z Smith Alexander; married Florentine Kelly; children: Darlene, Ronald Jr & Charles. **Educ:** Univ Wis, BS, 1962; Northeastern IL Univ, MEd, 1972; Univ Mich, mgt obj, 1978; John Marshall Law Sch, cert, community law, 1979; Loyola Univ, master's jurisp, child & family law, 2001. **Career:** Dayton YMCA, Dayton, youth prog dir, 1964-67; Off Econ Opportunity, Cayton, exec dir, 1967-70; Wasco County Planning Off, planning dir, 1973-82; Josephine County Planning Comn, planning dir, 1976-82; City Vancouver, Wash, dir planning & develop, 1982-88; Lancaster Co Planning Comn, exec dir, 1988-2005; Franklin & Marshall Col, sr res fel, 2006; Chester County Planning Comn, exec dir, 2006-15; Chicago Youth Ctrs, assoc exec dir; Northeastern Ill Univ, instr; United Way Chicago, planner; City Chicago, child care mgr; Cook Co Ill, manpower planner; United Way Dade Co, sr consult, prog mgr, Community Renewal Soc; State Ill, DCFS, Gov State Univ, caseworker trainer. **Orgs:** Chicago Urban League, 1970-88; co-founder, chmn, Chicago Black Child Develop, 1978-; Black Child Dev Inst Wash, 1978-; Wash State Shorelines Hearing Bd, 1983-88; Chicago Blacks Philanthropy, 1984-; Asn Black Fund Raising Execs, 1984-; People United Save Humanity, 1984-88; Asn Black Fund raising Execs, 1986-88; bd mem, Provident St Mel Develop Corp, 1990-; bd mem, Provident StMel Sch, 1990-; vpres, Roosevelt PTA; Steering Comm Neighborhood Capitol Budget Group; Chicago Coun Urban Affairs, Chicago Workshop Econ Dev, Chicago Mgt Assistance Prog; Village Bellwood, Ill, bd health; Canaan AME Church, steward; bd mem, Chicago Area Tech Assist Providers; bd mem, LEAD; coord, Black Caucus, Family Resource Coalition, Chicago; Statewide Family Preserv, Statewide Task Force, Ill Dept C & Family Serv; consult, Ill Dept C & Family Serv; consult, Fishers Men Proj, a male mentoring prog, Chicago; consult, Proj 2000+, Gov State Univ, Ill; consult, Coun Accreditation Serv Families & C Inc; LancasterProspers Planning Comt. **Honors/Awds:** Superior Supervisor Award, SCOPE, 1969-70; Executive of the Year, Chicago Youth Center, 1980. **Home Addr:** 125 Rice Ave, Bellwood, IL 60104-1240, **Home Phone:** (708)544-5140. **Business Addr:** Executive Director, Lancaster County Planning Commission, 50 N Duke St, Lancaster, PA 17608-3480, **Business Phone:** (717)299-8000.

## BAILEY, DR. SHARON BROWN

Administrator, teacher, government official. **Personal:** married John T; children: Musa, Ramu & Kamau Y. **Educ:** Princeton Univ, BA, 1975, teacher cert; Univ Colo, MA, interdisciplinary social sci, 1980; Univ Colo, PhD, pub admin, 1997. **Career:** Princeton mid sch, teacher; Metrop State Col, adminr; Univ Colo, minority stud advisor, presidential intern; Western Interstate Comn Higher Educ, policy assoc II, 2001-04; Pathways Col Network, SPIDO, policy analyst; City Council District 8, Office Auditor City & County Denver, Acct, Finance & Policy, cand & dir, currently. **Orgs:** Pres, Int Black Women's Cong; mem, Denver Sch Bd; dir, Princeton Community House; dir, Univ Colo, Health Careers Sci Prog, 1980; Denver Pub Schs Bd Educ; DPS Bd Educ; bd liaison, Colo legis; City Coun District 8, City-Schs Coord Coun; co-chair, Coun Great City Schs Nat Task Force Urban Educ; bd mem & pres, Int Black Women's Cong, 1980; consult, Educ Comn States, consult, Colo Comn Higher Educ; consult, Chicago Pub Schs; consult, Region VIII Desegregation Assistance Ctr; consult, Colo Dept Educ; Univ Colo's Blue Ribbon Comn Diversity. **Home Addr:** 3570 Monaco Pkwy, Denver, CO 80207-1440, **Home Phone:** (303)297-9106. **Business Addr:** Director, City Council District 8, 3280 Downing St, Denver, CO 80205, **Business Phone:** (720)337-8888.

## BAILEY, THOMAS R., JR.

Economics historian. **Educ:** Harvard Univ, BA, 1976; Mass Inst Technol, PhD, econs, 1983. **Career:** White Motors, int div, mgr admin; Housing Info Serv, Cuyahoga Plan Ohio, Inc, dir; Northland Res Corp, pres, 1982-; Books & non-fiction: Urban Residential Real Estate Mkt Analyst; Snake Walkers. **Orgs:** 100 Black Men Am; dir, Community Col Res Ctr. **Special Achievements:** Wrote "The Double Helix of Education and the Economy", "Manufacturing Advantage", "Working Knowledge: Work-Based Learning and Education Reform", and "Defending the Community College Equity Agenda". **Business Addr:** Director, Columbia University Teachers Col, PO Box 174, New York, NY 10027, **Business Phone:** (212)678-3091.

## BAILEY, THURL LEE

Television broadcaster, songwriter, basketball player. **Personal:** Born Apr 7, 1961, Seat Pleasant, MD; married Sindi; children: 3; children: Thurl Jr, Tevaun & Chonell. **Educ:** NC State, commun, 1983. **Career:** Basketball player (retired), broadcast analyst, songwriter; exec; Utah Jazz, forward, 1983-91, 1999, broadcast analyst, 2000-; Big T Productions, chmn, Inspirational & Motivational Speaker, 1984-; Minn Timber wolves, 1991-94; Ital League, 1995-98; Univ Utah, broadcast analyst, currently; inspirational speaker, currently; Album: Faith In Your Heart, 1998; The Gift Christmas, 2001; I'm Not The Same, 2002; Big TLC, founder; Fertile Earth, chmn; FourLeaf Films, chmn; Black Clover, vip & corp partnerships, 2010-. **Orgs:** Nat Basketball Retired Players Asn, vice chmn bd, 2009-. **Business Addr:** Broadcast analyst, Utah Jazz, 301 W S Temple, Salt Lake City, UT 84101-1216, **Business Phone:** (801)325-2500.

## BAILEY, DR. WELTMAN D., SR.

Dentist. **Personal:** Born Jan 26, 1927, Harveil, MO; married Margaret Barber; children: Sandra, Weltman Jr, Peter & Robert. **Educ:** Univ Wiscon, BS, 1950; Meharry Med Col, DDS, 1956; Univ Mo, MPA, MPH, 1973. **Career:** Pvt pract dentist, 1958-; Weltman D Bailey & Assoc Inc, dr. **Orgs:** Trustee, Baptist church, 1967-; Rehab Inst; Reg Health Welfare Coun, 1969-70; bd dir, Mid-Am Comprehensive Health Planning Agency, 1970-71; med adv bd, Mo Div Family Health, 1974-; fel Royal Soc Health; Acad Gen Dent; Alpha Phi Alpha Fraternity; YMCA; Urban League; Nat Am Dent Asn; Am Pub Health Asn; Am Soc Pub Admin; Nat Rehab Asn; Am Asn Hosp Dentists. **Home Addr:** 10433 Grand Ave, PO Box 16272, Kansas City, MO 64114-4726, **Home Phone:** (816)942-6227. **Business Addr:** General Dentist, Weltman D Bailey & Associates Incorporation, 4301 Paseo Blvd, Kansas City, MO 64110, **Business Phone:** (816)924-1190.

## BAILEY-REAVIS, DORIS. See BAILEY, DORIS JONES.

## BAILEY-THOMAS, SHERYL K.

Publisher, executive, chief executive officer. **Personal:** Born Jul 29, 1958, Palmer, AK; daughter of Algian R and Evelyn D; children: Mykal Jabari. **Educ:** Univ Alaska, AAS, electronics technol, 1978, BA, bus mgt, 1988; MED, coun & guid sec educ, 1998; adult educ & career develop, MA, 1998. **Career:** National Weather Serv, technician, 1979-80; Multi vision Cable TV, AV technician, 1980-85; State of Alaska, AV technician, 1988-; Abram Abraham Prod & Mgt Inc, pres & chief exec officer. **Orgs:** Founder, organizing comt, UCAAN; BIG, 1990-92. **Special Achievements:** FCC, Radio-Telephone License, 1978; Anchorage Gazette, The African-Am Voice of Alaska, assoc ed, 1992-93; African-American in Alaska, a Black Community Booklet & Calendar of Events, publ, 1990-93; Alaska Resource Guide, 1994-99. **Home Addr:** PO Box 201741, Anchorage, AK 99520-1741. **Business Addr:** President, Chief Executive Officer, Abram Abraham Productions & Management, PO Box 201741, Anchorage, AK 99520-1741.

## BAIN, LINDA VALERIE

Educator, management consultant. **Personal:** Born Feb 14, 1947, New York, NY; daughter of Carlton L and Helen Boyd; married Samuel Green. **Educ:** City Col NY, BA, sociol, 1974; Cambridge Col, MEd. **Career:** New York Dept Labor, secy, 1965-66; New York Dept Social Serv, exec secy, 1966-70; Manhattan St Hosp, prog coordr, 1970-73; Donchian Mgmt Serv, sr consult, 1980-85; Bain Assocs Inc, founder & pres, 1985-; Health Power, external affairs liaison; New York Dept Educ, Off Adult & Continuing Educ, counr & educr. **Orgs:** Assoc dir, Nat Coun Negro Women's Ctr Educ & Career Advan, 1973-79; Nat Asn Female Exec, 1980; Am Soc Training & Develop, 1981; Nat & NY Org Develop Network, 1981; bd dir, NY Friends Alvin Ailey, 1985; chairperson, bd dirs, Friendly Pl, 1989; Corp Women's Network; Bks Kids Found, 1992; Alvin Ailey Am Dance Ctr Sch Comt; Lincoln Ctr Arts Educ Inst; bd mem, Manhattan Valley Townhouses. **Honors/Awds:** Coalition of 100 Black Women, 1971; Mary McLeod Bethune Achievement Award, Nat Coun Negro Women. **Business Addr:** President, Bain Associates Inc, 23 W 104th St, New York, NY 10025, **Business Phone:** (212)864-5811.

## BAINES, HAROLD DOUGLAS

Baseball player, athletic coach. **Personal:** Born Mar 15, 1959, Easton, MD; son of Linwood and Gloria; married Marla Henry; children: Antoinette, Britni, Harold Jr & Courtney. **Career:** Baseball player (retired), baseball coach; Chicago White Sox, outfielder, 1980-89, 1996-97, 2000-01, bench coach, 2004-05, first base coach, currently; Tex Rangers, outfielder, 1989-90; Oakland Athletics, outfielder, 1990-92; Baltimore Orioles, outfielder, 1993-95, 1997-99, 2000; Cleveland Indians, outfielder, 1999. **Orgs:** Cook County Teen Democracy; Nat Asn Down Syndrome. **Home Addr:** PO Box 10, St Michaels, MD 21663. **Business Addr:** First Base Coach, Chicago White Sox, US Cellular Field 333 W 35th St, Chicago, IL 60616, **Business Phone:** (312)674-1000.

## BAINES, DR. REV. HENRY T., SR.

Executive. **Personal:** Born Wilson, NC. **Educ:** Howard Univ Sch Divinity, MA; United Technol Sem, Dayton, OH, DMin. **Career:** Baines Stop Shop & Save Food Mkts, pres & chief exec officer, currently. **Orgs:** Acad Achievement Awards Found Inc. **Business Addr:** President, Chief Executing Officer, Baines Stop Shop & Save Food Markets, 200 S Arlington Ave Suite 300, Baltimore, MD 21223-2672, **Business Phone:** (410)783-8180.

## BAINES, DR. TYRONE RANDOLPH

Association executive. **Personal:** Born Feb 22, 1943, Exmore, VA; son of Hilton and Clarease Dillard; married Shereatha; children: Tyrone R II & Tonita. **Educ:** Morgan State Univ, AB, 1965; Univ Pa, MSW, 1967; Univ Md, MA, 1971, PhD, pub admin, 1972; Harvard Bus Sch, cert, educ mgt. **Career:** Community Progs Inc, consult, 1971-72; Md Sch Syst, consult, 1972; Fed Exec Inst, sr fac mem, 1974-75; NC Cent Univ, prof pub admin, dir pub admin, 1975-78, dir publ admin prog, 1979-82, NC Cent Univ, Univ Rels, vice-chancellor, exec asst chancellor, 1985-88, sr fel, 2006-, prof pub admin, currently; Harvard Univ Inst Educ Mgt, fel, 1977; W K Kellogg Found, Battle Creek, prog dir; Kellogg Youth Initiatives Prog, dir; Cent Intelligence Agency, Dept Defense; Environ Protection Agency; Univ Southern Calif, prof; Univ NC, Chapel Hill, prof; Southern Ill Univ, prof; Univ Va, prof. **Orgs:** Omega Psi Phi Fraternity, 1965-; Social worker C's Serv Inc, 1967; capt, AUS Med Serv Corp, 1967-69; consult, US Cong House Rep, 1969-70; grad teaching asst, Univ Md, 1969-70; personnel rels spec, Off Econ Opport, 1970-71, prog mgr, consult; exec coun, Nat Asn Schs Pub Affairs & Admin, 1985; bd trustee, Durham Acad, 1986; ed bd, Polit Sci, Southern Rev Pub Admin, 1986; Citizens Adv CommDurham Bd Educ, 1987; Nat Forum Black Pub Adminrs, 1989-; bd trustee, Mt Zion AME Church, 1989-; bd dir, Nat InstPub Mgt; chmn, Battle Creek Goodwill Industs Bd; bd dir, Battle Creek Youth Women's Christian Asn, 1990-; bd mem, NC Inst Minority Econ Develop; Mich City Comn; Nat Asn Advan Colored People; fel Nat Acad Pub Admin; chmn bd trustee, St Paul's Col; chmn, Nat Resource Ctr Healing Racism; fel Woodrow Wilson; fel Am Coun Educ; fel W K Kellogg Found. **Honors/Awds:** Superior Performance Duty Award, 1969; Nat Award, Conf Minority Pub Admin, 1975; Am Coun on Educ Fellow, Educ Admin, 1978; Certificate of Recognition, US Dept Labor, Atlanta Reg, 1979; Kellogg Nat Fellow Kellogg Found, 1982-85; Honorary doctor humane letters, Medgar Evers Col, 1997; Honorary doctor of public service, Bowie State Univ. **Home Addr:** 177 Minges Hills Dr, Battle Creek, MI 49015, **Home Phone:** (269)979-1605. **Business Addr:** Professor of Public Administration, Senior Fellow, North Carolina Central University, 1801 Fayetteville St, Durham, NC 27707, **Business Phone:** (919)530-6100.

## BAIOCCHI, REGINA A. HARRIS

Composer, writer, musician. **Personal:** Born Jul 16, 1956, Chicago, IL; daughter of Elgie Jr and Lanzie Mozelle Belmont; married Gregory. **Educ:** Roosevelt Univ, BM, 1978; Ill Inst Technol, attended 1986; Northwestern Univ, attended 1992; NY Univ, pub rels cert, 1991; De Paul Univ, MA, music, 1995. **Career:** Composer, numerous pieces for instrument & voice, 1978-; Dunbar Voc HS, teacher, 1979; St Bride's Jr HS, teacher, 1979-81; St Thomas the Apostle Jr HS, teacher, 1983-86; Telaction Corp, audio qual control analyst & writer, 1986-89; Cath Theo Union, pub rels dir, 1989-94; Ill Arts Coun grant, 1995; Steppen wolf Theater, composer & dir, 1997; Nat Endowment Arts Regional Artists Prog grant, 1997; Ravinia Music Festival, Music Illum Prog, artistic dir, 1997-99; Art Inst Chicago grant, 1997; Roots & Wings concert, artist dir, 1998; E W Univ, lectr, 2000-, Dept Eng & Comm, instr, part-time fac, currently; Columbia Col, Chicago, adj prof, currently; composer, poet & writer, currently. Poems: Teeter Totter, Ghetto Child, Chicago Tribune Mag. short story: Mama's Will, 1988. novel: Indigo Sound, 2003. numerous music compositions, 1978-; Compositions: Two Piano Etudes, 1978; Chase For Wind Sextet, 1979; Realizations 1979; Father, We Thank You, 1986; Two Zora Neale Hurston Songs, 1989; Miles per Hour, 1990; We Real Cool, 1990; Autumn Night, 1991; Foster Pet, 1991; Crystal Stair, 1991; Orchestra Suite, 1991; Shadows, 1992; Legacy, 1992; A Few Black Voices, 1992; Bwana's Libation, 1992; Sketches for Piano Trio, 1992; Mason Room, 1993; Much in Common, 1993; Ain't Nobody's Child, 1993; Teddy Bear Suite, 1994; QFX, 1994; Liszten, My Husband Is Not a Hat, 1994; Three Pieces For Greg, 1994; Deborah, 1994; Best Friends, 1994; Ancestor's Medley, 1994; Much In Common, 1994; After The Rain, 1994; Say No To Guns, 1994; Good New Falls Gently, 1995; Darryl's Rose, 1995; Friday Night, 1995; Dream hoppers, 1997; Gbeldahoven: No One's Child, 1997; African Hands, 1997; Nikki Giovanni, 1997; Skins, 1997; Muse, 1997; Message To My Muse, 1997; Dream Weaver 1997; Azuretta, 2000; Ask Him, 2000; Cycles, 2000; HB4A, 2000; Lovers & Friends, 2000; Psalm Cat, 2000; Litany for Hale Smith, 2000. **Orgs:** Am Soc Composers, Authors & Publ; Nat Endowment Randolph St Gallery; Ill Arts Coun. **Home Addr:** 40 E 9th St Suite 1816, PO Box 450, Chicago, IL 60605, **Home Phone:** (312)458-9898. **Business Addr:** lecturer, East-West University, 816 S Michigan Ave, Chicago, IL 60605, **Business Phone:** (312)939-0111.

### BAIRD, SR. ANITA PRICE
Executive director, president (organization). **Personal:** Born Feb 8, 1947, Warrensburg, MO; daughter of Robert Price Jr and Marcella Hill Price. **Educ:** DePaul Univ, BA, sociol; Loyola Univ-Chicago, Mundelein Col, MA, relig studies. **Career:** Archdiocese Chicago, St Sabina Church, Chicago, Ill, word ministry team leader, exec asst archbishop; St Paul, regional super, Chicago, currently; St Louis communities Daughters Heart Mary, dir, 2000-; Archdiocese Chicago's Off Racial Justice, dir, 2000-. **Orgs:** Nat Black Sisters Conf, 1982-, pres, 2001-03; Relig Congregation Socs Daughters Heart May; preaching staff; team leader, Word Ministry; chief spokesperson & rep, areas racial justice & human rels. **Home Addr:** 1029 Wash Blvd 302, Oak Park, IL 60302. **Business Addr:** Director, Archdiocese Chicago, 155 E Super St, Chicago, IL 60611-2911, **Business Phone:** (312)751-5200.

### BAIRD, DR. KEITH E.
Editor, educator, college teacher. **Personal:** Born Jan 20, 1923; children: Diana Baird N'Diaye & Marcia Baird-Johnson. **Educ:** Columbia Univ, BS, 1952; Union Grad Sch, PhD, 1982. **Career:** Educator (retired), editor; Freedom ways, assoc ed & writer, 1961-85; Hunter Col, prof & dir afro-am studies, 1969-70; Ford Found, travel sem grant, 1969; Hofstra Univ, prof humanities, 1970-73; State Univ NY, Bufflalo, Old W bury, prof humanities, 1973-75; State Univ NY, Buffalo, chair african am studies, assoc prof anthrop, 1975-; Univ Jena, US GOR Friendship Comt, summer scholar grant, 1981; Clark Atlanta Univ, Dept Soc Sci, prof; freelance ed, currently. **Orgs:** Assoc fel Ctr Afro-Am Studies, Atlanta Univ, 1973-; consult, Gullah Lang, Sea Island Ctr, 1977; State Univ NY Chancellor's Task Force Afro Studies, 1984; pres emer, NY African Studies Asn; assoc ed, Freedom ways; ed bd, J Black Studies, African Urban Quart; co-founder, Kush Mus African & African-Am Art & Antiq; Hutkaptah Soc. **Special Achievements:** Publisher of "Names from Africa", 1972. **Home Addr:** 218 E Trinity Pl Apt 913, Decatur, GA 30030, **Home Phone:** (404)758-3623.

### BAISDEN, MICHAEL
Radio host, writer. **Personal:** Born Jun 26, 1963, Chicago, IL; children: 2. **Career:** Writer, motivational speaker & talk show host; Bks: "Never Satisfied: How & Why Men Cheat", 1997; "Men Cry Dark", 1999; "Maintenance Man: It's Midnight, Do You Know Where Your Woman Is?", 2000; "God's Gift to Women", 2003; "Do Men Know What They Want?", 2011; "Maintenance Man II", 2012; "The Maintenance Man Collectors Edition", 2012; "Raise Your Hand If You Have Issues", 2014; Chicago Transit Authority, train driver, 2003; writer, 1993-2001; Legacy Publ, ceo, 2001; Tribune Broadcasting, TV Talk Show Talk or Walk, host, 2001; Tribune Entertainment, radio host, 2001; 98.7 KISS FM, noon dr-time host, 2003; Radio Host: WKSP, Todays R&B & Old Sch; WHUR, Sounds Like Wash; WQQK, Adult Choice!; WDAI, R&B & Old Sch; WZKS, Southern Soul & Today's R&B; WKZJ, Big Sta K92.7; WLPZ, Goove 93; WFUN, Best Variety R&B; ABC Radio Network, radio host, 2004; Legacy Publ & Happilysingle.com, founder. **Orgs:** Founder, Michael Baisden Found Literacy & Technol.

### BAITY, GAIL OWENS
Manager, educator, consultant. **Personal:** Born May 20, 1952, New York, NY; daughter of Ruth Owens and George A Owens; married Elijah A; children: Allen J. **Educ:** Spelman Col, BA, psych, 1974; Univ WI, Madison, MA, indust labor rels, 1976; Gestalt Inst Cleveland, cert int orgn systs. **Career:** Corning, Corp Labor Rels Div, placement specialist, 1976, Consumer Prod Div, prdn suprv, 1978, Info Serv Div, personnel dev spec, 1978-80, R&D Div, personnel suprv, 1980-82, Consumer Prod Div, personnel suprv, 1982-83, Career Devel Coun, consult, 1982-, Personnel Div, human resource consult; Elmira Col, instr, 1980; Corning Glass Works, human resource consult, 1983-87; Workforce Develop & Learning, dir, 2000-15. **Orgs:** Vpres, Soc Black Prof, 1982, 1986; treas, Elmira Corning Nat Asn Advan Colored People, 1982-83; chmn policy comm, Corning Childrens Ctr, 1986-87; bd mem, Career Develop Coun, 1988-; bd dir, Corning Inc, 2015-; leadership develop consult, Asn Talent Develop, 2015-; Am Socs Educ & Training; Nat Black MBA Asn; bd mem, Greater Steuben Chap Am Red Cross; Great Lakes Region Nominating Comt Alpha Kappa Alpha Sorority; Community Found Elmira-Corning; Finger Lakes Inc; regional bd trustee, Corning Community Col; Orgn Develop Network. **Home Addr:** 2817 Forest Hill Dr, Corning, NY 14830-3691, **Home Phone:** (607)962-4167. **Business Addr:** Leadership Development Consultant, Association for Talent Development, 1640 King St, Alexandria, VA 22314, **Business Phone:** (703)683-8100.

### BAJOIE, DIANA E.
President (organization). **Personal:** daughter of Olander B Sr. **Educ:** Southern Univ, BA. **Career:** La House Reps, pub serv, 1976; adult educr; New Orleans City Coun, sen; La State, rep dist 9, 1976-91, sen dist 5, 1991-2008, pres pro tempore, 2004, sen dist five, currently. **Orgs:** Founder & chmn, La Legis Black Caucus & La Legis Women's Caucus; pres, Nat Org Black Elected Legis Women; La House Representatives, 1975; coun mem, New Orleans City Coun Dist B, 2012-13; dir, LSU Health Sci Ctr; legislator, Minority Health Care Comn; mem, La State Legis. **Home Addr:** , LA. **Business Addr:** Senator, New Orleans City Council, City Hall Rm 2W10 1300 Perdido St, New Orleans, LA 70112, **Business Phone:** (504)658-1020.

### BAKER, ALTHEA R.
Judge, lawyer, educator. **Personal:** Born Dec 24, 1949, San Francisco, CA; daughter of Vernon Ross and Ethel Ross; married Bruce Mitchell; children: Chase Brendan. **Educ:** Pepperdine Univ, BA, 1970, MA, clin psychol, 1981; Loyola Univ, Sch Law, JD, 1984. **Career:** La Community Cols, prof, coun & psychol, 1975-89; Lic marriage family child therapist, 1976-84; Law Off Althea Baker, atty, 1984-93; Los Angeles Community Col, chief negotiator, 1985-89; La Super Ct, judge pro team, Sylmar Juv Courthouse Dept 275, referee hearing officer; Traffic Ct Referee, currently. **Orgs:** Black Women Lawyers Los Angeles; trustee, Los Angeles Community Cols, 1989-2001; Mediator & arbit, 1990-01; bd mem, Southern Calif Mediation Asn, 1990-92; Pepperdine Univ Grad Sch Educ & Psychol Bd, 1990-92. **Home Addr:** 1059 Glen Arbor Ave, Los Angeles, CA 90041, **Home Phone:** (323)254-5014. **Business Addr:** Referee, Los Angeles Super Court, 16350 Filbert St, Sylmar, CA 91342, **Business Phone:** (818)364-2187.

### BAKER, ANITA DENISE
Songwriter, singer, musician. **Personal:** Born Jan 26, 1958, Toledo, OH; married Walter Bridgforth Jr; children: Walter Baker Bridgforth & Edward Carlton Bridgforth. **Career:** Vocalist, several Detroit bars & nightclubs; lead vocalist, Chap Eight, 1978; receptionist, Detroit law firm; Chapter 8, soloist, 1979; Albums: Ariola, 1979; The Songstress, 1983; A Night of Rapture Tour, 1986; Giving You The Best That I Got, 1988; Compositions, 1990; Rhythm of Love, 1994; Fireside Love Songs, 2003; My Everything, Blue Note Records, 2005; Christmas Fantasy, 2005; Why Did I Get Married?, 2007; Live Performances: with singer AlJarreau, Montreaux Jazz Festival, Switzerland, 1988; Bermuda Music Festival, 2004; An Evening with Anita Baker Tour, 2008; The BET Honors, actress, 2009; 21st Century Love, 2011. **Honors/Awds:** NAACP Image Award, Best Female Vocalist & Best Album of the Year; Soul Train Music Award, 1987, 1989 & 2010; American Music Award, 1988, 1990, 1995; Grammy Awards, 1987-88, 1989-90 & 1996; Hollywood Walk of Fame, 1994; Grammy Awards: Best Rhythm & Blues Vocal Performance - Female won, 1995; Best Rhythm & Blues Album Nominee, 2005; International Artist of the Year, Can Smooth Jazz Award, 2005; Best Traditional R&B Vocal Performance, nominee, 2005; Best Traditional R&B Vocal Performance, Nominee, 2006; Legend Award, 2010. **Home Addr:** , Grosse Pointe, MI. **Business Addr:** Singer, Blue Note Records, 75 Rockefeller Plz, New York, NY 10011, **Business Phone:** (212)786-8600.

### BAKER, DR. BERYLE I.
Educator. **Educ:** Univ Madras, int studies; Norfolk State Univ, VA, BA, hist; Cent Mo State, MEd; Auburn Univ, AL, EdD; Univ Madras, India, int study; Univ Ga, cert. **Career:** Ga Perimeter Col, assoc prof educ, prof educ, currently. **Business Addr:** Associate Professor, Georgia Perimeter College, 555 N Indian Creek Dr, Clarkston, GA 30021-2361, **Business Phone:** (678)891-3362.

### BAKER, ESQ. BEVERLY POOLE
Lawyer. **Personal:** Born Jan 14, 1944, Birmingham, AL; daughter of Grafton C and Minda Ingersoll; married James K; children: Paige, Paula & Leslie. **Educ:** Univ Ala, Birmingham, BA, urban studies, 1982; Samford Univ, Cumberland Sch Law, Birmingham, AL, JD, 1985. **Career:** McMillan & Spratling, Birmingham, AL, atty, 1985-86; Haskell Slaughter & Young, Birmingham, AL, assoc, 1986-89, partner, 1989-2002; Miller, Hamilton, Snider & ODOM LLC, Birmingham, AL, Atty, 2002-; Ogletree, Deakins, Nash, Smoak & Stewart PC, shareholder, 2006-12, lawyer, arbitrator & coun, mediator, atty coun, 2006-14; Beverly P Baker LLC, lawyer, 2014-. **Orgs:** Comnr, Am Bar Asn; Standing Comt Lawyers Pub Serv Responsibility; co-chair, Equal Opportunity Comt Litigation Sect; Nat Bar Asn; Nat Asn Bond Lawyers; Ala State Bar Asn, ADR Comt; Magic City Bar Asn; Birmingham Bar Asn; bd dirs & alumni coun, First Class Leadership Ala; Leadership Birmingham; Jefferson County Med Examr Comn; Res Coun Ala; adv bd, Cumberland Sch Law; Birmingham Leadership Coun; Univ Ala; arbitrator, Am Arbit Asn; arbitrator, Nat Arbit Forum; arbitrator, Nat Arbit Mediation; roster neutrals, Alliance Cornell Univ; mediator & appellate mediator, US Dist Ct Northern Dist Ala; comnr, Comn Opportunities Minorities Profession; Coun Litigation Sect ABA; fel Am Asn Univ Women, 1985; Birmingham Bar Asn; Magic City Bar Asn; fel Col Labor & Employ Lawyers; life fel Ala Law Found; Ala Lawyers Asn; Charter fel Litigation Coun Am; founding bd mem, Pub Affairs Res Coun Ala; Cumberland Sch Law Adv Bd; Fedn Defense & Corp Coun; Nat Employ Law Coun; bd mem, Meyer Found; Women Lawyers Alliance; Ala Bar Asn; Mem's Coun Leadership Birmingham; Nat Asn Women Lawyers; Birmingham Inns Ct; fel Am Asn Women Lawyers; Nat Acad Distinguished Neutrals, 2013. **Honors/Awds:** Dean's Award, Univ Ala, 1981, 1982; Perceptions & Propinquity on Police Patrol, SE Sociological Asn, 1982; Privacy in a High-Tech World, 1985; The Age Discrimination in Employment Act & Termination of the Public Sector Employee, Ala Bar Inst Sem, 1989; Basic Wage & Hour Law in AL, NBI, 1996; Employment Arbitration Basics for Legal Services Professionals, Ala State Bar Asn, 2004; listed in the Best Lawyers in America; inducted into the Alabama Law Foundation (limited to one percent of lawyers in the State of Alabama). **Special Achievements:** First African American in Alabama listed in the prestigious Red Book. **Home Addr:** 224 Cahaba Lake Cir, Helena, AL 35080, **Home Phone:** (205)426-3504. **Business Addr:** Lawyer, Beverly P Baker LLC, 2960 Pelham Pkwy Suite 100, Pelham, AL 35214, **Business Phone:** (205)540-3985.

### BAKER, C. C.
School administrator. **Personal:** married Gene. **Educ:** Ala State Univ, attended 1954. **Career:** Ala State Univ, from teacher to asst state supt of educ, prof & adminr, interim pres, 1991-94.

### BAKER, CAROLETTA A.
Administrator. **Career:** Wake County Pub Sch Syst, Elem Sch Serv, Spl Educ Serv Dept, sr adminr elem, currently. **Orgs:** Wake County Bd Educ. **Home Addr:** , NC. **Business Addr:** Senior Administrator, Wake County Public School System, 3600 Wake Forest Rd 2114, Raleigh, NC 27611-8041, **Business Phone:** (919)850-1600.

### BAKER, DR. DARRYL BRENT, SR.
Executive. **Personal:** Born May 5, 1955, Detroit, MI; son of Elliott D Sr and Mary L Scott; children: Darryl Jr, Donnathon & Lakeisha. **Educ:** Gen Motors Inst Tech, attended 1973; Mott Community Col, AS, 1983; Univ Mich, 1988; Baker Col, Flint, MI, BA, bus leadership, 1995, MBA, bus admin, 1999; Wayne State Univ, bus, qual, 2008; Univ Phoenix, DBA, 2009. **Career:** Boy Scouts, cub scout & boy scout leader dist exec, 1975-77; Primary Sch, football & basketball coach, 1981-82; Little League & Pee Wee League Baseball Teams, mgr, 1987; Gen Motors, Flint, Metal Fab, stockbroker, financial consult, auditor, mach repairer, supvr, 1978-2009; Baker Financial Serv, owner, pres, stockbroker, chief exec officer, 1992-2009; Baker Col, adj prof, 1999-2005; Global Paradigm Solutions, bus consult, owner, 2009-; Calif Col San Diego, prof, 2010-11; Univ Phoenix, adj prof, 2010-; video & youth music, producer. **Orgs:** Exec bd mem, unit chmn, UAW Local 659, 1993-2001; chmn, UAW Black Leadership Caucus, Local 659, 1993-2001; pres, Nat Asn Black Acct, Flint, 2000; exec bd mem, vp, Black Caucus Genessee Cty; exec bd mem, Millionth Man; Genessee Cty Bd Canvassers; Vernon Chapel AME Ch; Owner income tax serv; Ebony & Ivory Enterprises investment consult serv; Order Arrow; life mem, Nat Asn Advan Colored People; Univ Phoenix Alumni Asn. **Honors/Awds:** Life Accident Health Insurance License and Securities Series 7, Investment License, 1988; Business Award, Top Gun, 1989; Flint Journal, Top 10 Personality of Flint, 1994; Honored in Edition of Cambridge "Who's Who" Registry of Business Leaders, 1996-97; Scouting Wood Badge Award. **Special Achievements:** Authored a weekly financial strategies newspaper column, 1992-93; Featured on Lou Dobbs Money-line national TV broadcast, 1998; A featured speaker on CNBC national televised money show broadcast, 2001; Featured on the BBCA international broadcast, 2009. Publication; "Life After Job Loss", ProQuest LLC, 2009. **Home Addr:** 2217 Wolcott St Suite 1, Flint, MI 48504-4029, **Home Phone:** (810)235-5798. **Business Addr:** Professor, University of Phoenix, 180 Otay Lakes Rd Suite 100, Bonita, CA 91902, **Business Phone:** (619)267-2960.

### BAKER, DAVE E.
Educator, baseball executive. **Personal:** Born Jun 18, 1943, Manhattan, KS; married Janice; children: Sherri Ann. **Educ:** Emporia St Col, BS, phys educ, 1968, MS, phys educ, 1969. **Career:** Emporia St Col, phys educ, grad asst, asst baseball coach, 1969; Lib Community Jr Col, head track coach, asst basketball coach, instr phys educ, 1970; Creighton Univ, instr phys educ, asst basketball coach, asst baseball coach, 1971-75, head baseball coach, 1972-77. **Orgs:** Phi Delta Kappa; Nat Collegiate Athletic Asn; Col World Ser Games Comm, 1972-75. **Business Addr:** Instructor, Creighton University, 2500 Calif Plz, Omaha, NE 68178, **Business Phone:** (402)280-2700.

### BAKER, DAVID NATHANIEL, JR.
Musician, composer, educator. **Personal:** Born Dec 21, 1931, Indianapolis, IN; married Lida Margret Belt; children: April Elaine. **Educ:** Sch Jazz, Lenox, MA; Ind Univ, Bloomington, IN, BME, MME, BM, 1953, MM, 1954; New Eng Conserv Music. **Career:** W Coast orchestras, 1956; Boston Sym Evansville, Philharmonic, soloist; Indianapolis Sym, guest conductor; Indianapolis Civic Orch, guest conductor, Ind Univ Sym, guest conductor; George Russell Sextet, mem; Ind Univ, Jazz Dept, chmn, 1966, Sch Mus distinguished prof, currently; Smithsonian Inst, artistic dir & conductor, sr consult music progs, currently. Books: A Comprehensive Method of Study for All Players, 1969; Techniques of Improvisation, ed, 1971; The Black Composer Speaks, 1978. **Orgs:** Chmn, Nat Endowment Arts; bd dir, Nat Music Coun; Am Asn Univ Professors; Nat Asn Negro Musicians; Nat Coun Arts; pres, Nat Jazz Serv Org, currently; chmn, Jazz Studies Dept, Ind Univ Sch Music; pres, vpres, Int Asn Jazz Educ, 2002-04; bd mem, Am Symphony Orchestra League. **Home Addr:** 1901 E Marilyn Dr, Bloomington, IN 47401-6064, **Home Phone:** (812)336-1940. **Business Addr:** Distinguished Professor, Chairman of the Jazz Department, Indiana University, 107 S Indiana Ave, Bloomington, IN 47405-7000, **Business Phone:** (812)855-8546.

### BAKER, DELBERT WAYNE
Editor, educator, association executive. **Personal:** Born Jan 25, 1953, Oakland, CA; son of Paul Thomas and Amelia A; married Susan M Lee; children: David Mathias, Benjamin Joseph & Jonathan Michael. **Educ:** Oakwood Col, BA, ministerial theol, 1975; Andrews Univ Sem, MDiv, 1977; Howard Univ, PhD, commun, 1992. **Career:** Pastor, Mich, Va, OH, 1975-85; Messsage Mag, ed chief, 1985-92; Howard Univ, instr, 1990-91; consult, 1990; Loma Linda Univ, from asst to pres, dir diversity, assoc prof, 1992-96; Oakwood Col, pres, 1996-2010; Adventist Univ Africa, vice chancellor, 2015-; Books: The Unknown Prophet, author, 1986; From Exile to Prime Minister, author, 1988; Profiles of Service, author, 1990; Communication & Change in Religious Organization, author, 1992; Secret Keys, author, 1993; Make Us One, author, 1995; Telling the Story, author, 1996. **Orgs:** Clergy's Black Caucus, 1985; bd mem, Rev & Herald Pub Asn, 1985; bd mem, San Mars C Home, 1986-89; bd mem, Human Rels Coun Gen Conf Seventh-day Adventist Church, 1987; contribr video, Africa Continent Explosive Growth, 1987; United Negro Col Fund; Asn Latin Am Stud, 1993; Black Fac Forum, 1993; Hisp Fac Forum, 1995; Huntsville Hosp Bd; Huntsville City Chamber Com; vpres, Gen Conf Seventh-day Adventists, 2010. **Honors/Awds:** Alumnus of the Yr, Oakwood Col, 1985; Ed Jour Awards, Ed Int, 1988-90; White House

Spec Comt on HBCUs, 2006. **Home Addr:** 2141 Hill Ct, Colton, CA 92324. **Business Addr:** Vice Chancellor, Adventist University of Africa, Next To Advent Hill Primary00503, **Business Phone:** (254)733-3334.

### BAKER, DUSTY (JOHNNIE B BAKER, JR.)
Baseball manager, baseball player, broadcaster. **Personal:** Born Jun 15, 1949, Riverside, CA; son of Johnnie B Sr and Christine; married Alice Lee; children: Natosha; married Melissa Esplana; children: Darren. **Educ:** Am River Jr Col, Sacramento, CA. **Career:** Baseball player, manager (retired); Atlanta Braves, outfielder, 1968-75; Los Angeles Dodgers, outfielder, 1976-83; San Francisco Giants, outfielder, 1984; Oakland Athletics, outfielder & first baseman, 1985-86; Minn Twins, 1990; San Francisco Giants, mgr, 1993-2002; Chicago Cubs, mgr, 2003-06; ESPN analyst, MLB Postseason; Cincinnati Reds, mgr, 2008-13.TV Series:"Sunday Night Baseball", 1990; "Rooster", 1982; Hank Aaron: Chasing the Dream, 1995. **Orgs:** Sacramento C's Home Abused Youth; Am Sports Inst; Calif Campaign Libr; Spec Olympics; Swords Into Plowshares; Nat Muscular Dystrophy Asn; chairperson, Fourth Ann ALS; Nat Adv Bd, Positive Coaching Alliance, currently. **Home Addr:** 40 Livingston Ter Dr, San Bruno, CA 94066.

### BAKER, DR. GAIL F.
Vice president (organization), college administrator, educator. **Personal:** children: 2. **Educ:** Northwestern Univ Medill Sch Jour, BS, jour, 1976; Roosevelt Univ, MS, mkt commun, 1980; Univ Mo-Columbia, PhD, jour, 1991. **Career:** Chicago Daily Defender, reporter & ed; IBM; Int Harvester Corp; Univ Mo-Columbia, Advert Dept, chmn & dir, Knight Found Off Minority Recruiting & Retention, 1983-95; Univ Fla, Col Jour & Commun, dir commun, assoc prof & chmn pub rels dept, 1995-2005, vpres pub rels, spec asst to pres diversity, 2004-05; Univ Nebr, Omaha, Col Commun, Fine Arts & Media, dean & prof, 2006-. **Orgs:** Fel Pub Rels Soc Am; mem col fellows, Multicultural Commun Sect; bd dir, Mildred D Brown Memorial Study Ctr. **Honors/Awds:** Professional of the Year Award, Fla Pub Rels Asn, 1999; William T Kemper Award for Excellence, Univ Mo; Emmy Award for Excellence in Documentary Writing, 2006 & 2011. **Special Achievements:** Author: Advertising & Marketing to the New Majority; Co-author: Exploding Stereotypes: Milestones in Black Newspaper Research. **Business Addr:** Dean, Professor, University of Nebraska, 6001 Dodge St WFAB 314, Omaha, NE 68182, **Business Phone:** (402)554-2232.

### BAKER, GREGORY D.
Executive. **Personal:** Born Mar 2, 1948, Kansas City, MO; son of Richard A and Lacy B; married Janet L Carlson; children: Kimberly R, Timothy P, Chad G, Sydney L & Aaron Mitchell. **Educ:** Rockhurst Univ, BA, psychol, MPA, pub admin, 1973; Univ Ky, cert rational behav therapist; Univ Kans, MPA, pub admin, 1981. **Career:** DC Refugee State, coordr; Community Develop Int Bus, mgr; Kans City Minority Developer Supplier Coun, pres,; Miss Gas Energy, vpres of Community Leadership, 1996-98; LeadTeam LLC, founding chief exec officer; Minority Bus Capital Corp, chmn, currently; Negro Leagues Baseball Mus, pres, 2008-10; Mainstream Minority Commonwealth LLC, pres, chief exec officer, 2011-. **Orgs:** Pres, Kans City Consensus, 1981; State Refugee Resettlement Coordr/ Dir EEOC, Dept Health & Human Serv, 1980-82; Chamber Com Greater Kans City, MO, Mgr Community Develop/ Int/ Agribusiness, 1982-84; Minority Supplier Develop Coun, Founding Exec Dir, 1983-96; vpres, Jr Achievement, 1991-; bd dir, Leukemia Soc, 1991-; bd dir, Truman Med Ctr, 1990-; bd dir, CORO, Metrop Orgn Counter Sexual Assault; bd dir, Citizens Asn; bd mem, Metrop Energy Ctr; bd mem, Metrop Community Col Trust Fund; Asst City Mgr, City Kans City, MO, 2001-08; City Damascus, Ore, City Mgr, 2012-13; Multi-Cult Liaison & Advisor, N Am Div Interfaith Peace Bldg Initiative (IPI). **Home Addr:** 11200 Summit, Kansas City, MO 64114, **Home Phone:** (816)941-3277. **Business Addr:** Executive Director, Blanchet House of Hospitality, Damascus, OR.

### BAKER, DR. GWENDOLYN CALVERT
President (organization), educator, socialist. **Personal:** Born Dec 31, 1931, Ann Arbor, MI; daughter of Burgess Edward and Viola Lee; married James Grady; children: JoAnn, Claudia & James Jr. **Educ:** Univ Mich, Ann Arbor, MI, BS, elem educ, 1964, MA, educ admin, 1968, PhD, educ, 1972. **Career:** Ann Arbor Pub Schs, Ann Arbor, Mich, teacher, 1964-69; Wines Elem Sch, teacher; Univ Mich, Ann Arbor, Mich, asst/assoc prof, 1969-76, dir affirmative action, 1976-78; Nat Inst Educ, Wash, DC, chief, minorities & women's prog, 1978-81; Bank St Col, New York, NY, vpres & dean grad & c's progs, 1981-84; Young Women's Christian Asn USA, New York, nat exec dir, 1984-93; US Comn UNICEF, pres, chief exec officer, 1993-97; Calvert Baker & Assocs, pres, 1997-; Am Educ Res Asn, dir soc justice, 2005. **Orgs:** Pres, NY City Bd Educ, 1986-92, pres, 1991-92; Alpha Kappa Alpha Sorority; Am Asn Univ Women; bd, Nat Coalition 100 Black Women; bd, US Olympic Comt, 1984-2000; bd, US Comn UN Develop Fund Women; NYC Women's Forum; NY Alliance Black Sch Educr; Women's City Club NY. **Home Addr:** 7118 La Ronda Ct, Sarasota, FL 34238, **Home Phone:** (941)923-2481. **Business Addr:** President, Calvert Baker & Associates Inc, 118 Laronda Ct, Sarasota, FL 34238.

### BAKER, DR. HOUSTON ALFRED, JR.
Educator. **Personal:** Born Mar 22, 1943, Louisville, KY; son of Alfred Sr and Viola Elizabeth Smith; married Charlotte Pierce; children: Mark Frederick. **Educ:** Howard Univ, BA, eng lit, 1965; Univ Calif, Los Angeles, CA, MA, victorian lit, 1966, PhD, victorian lit, 1968; Univ Edinburgh, Scotland, doctoral work, 1968. **Career:** Howard Univ, instr, 1966; Yale Univ, instr, eng, 1968-69, asst prof, eng, 1969; Univ Va, Ctr Advan Studies, from assoc prof to prof, 1970-73, prof Eng, 1973-74; Univ Penn, dir, Dept Afro-Am Studies, 1974-77, prof Eng, 1977-99, Lit and Lit Theory, 1979-82, 1988, Prof of Human Rels, 1982-89, Ctr for the Study of Black Lit and Cult, founder & dir, 1987-99; Mod Lang Asn, Pres, 1992; Duke Univ, Susan Fox & George D Beisher, prof eng & african am studies, 1999-2006; Vanderbilt Univ, distinguished univ prof & prof Eng, 2006-. **Orgs:** Fel Ctr Advan Study Behav Sci, 1977-78; fel Nat Endowment Humanities, 1977-78; fel John Simon Guggenheim, 1978-79; Inst Advan Study, 1980-81; Fel Nat Humanities Ctr, 1982-83; fel Rockefeller Res Fel Prog Minority Group Scholar, 1982-83; Coun Humanities, 1991-92; pres, Mod Lang Asn, 1992; fel Fulbright 50th Anniversary Distinguished, 1996; fel Breckenridge Distinguished, 1999; Fel Sch Criticism & Theory, 1999; fel Sch Criticism & Theory, Cornell Univ, 1996-2006; ed, Am Lit, 1999-2006; Humanities Ctr, Univ Ill Chicago, 2008; MLA Exec Coun; assoc ed, BALE; com Scholarly Worth, Howard Univ Pres. **Business Addr:** Distinguished University Professor, Professor of English, Vanderbilt University, 223 Buttrick Hall, Nashville, TN 37235, **Business Phone:** (615)343-7355.

### BAKER, JACQUELINE J.
Educator. **Personal:** Born Jun 13, 1952, Cleveland, OH; daughter of R C and Ora Lee; children: Jody James & Dayairre Zeleeka. **Educ:** Univ Minn, BS, arts, 1984; Univ St Thomas, MA, educ, 1998. **Career:** Fed Res, banker, 1973-89; NW Airlines, 1989-94; Minn Pub Schs, 1994-. **Home Addr:** 2823 Lyndale Ave N, Minneapolis, MN 55411-1449, **Home Phone:** (612)668-1530. **Business Addr:** Teacher, Minneapolis Public Schools, 1250 W Broadway St, Minneapolis, MN 55411-2533, **Business Phone:** (612)668-0000.

**BAKER, JOHNNIE B, JR.** **See BAKER, DUSTY.**

### BAKER, KIMBERLEY RENEE
Journalist. **Personal:** Born Sep 26, 1965, Houston, TX; daughter of Melvin Lavoisier and Diane Denise Randolph. **Educ:** Univ Tex, Austin, BA, jour, 1988. **Career:** Bellaire Texan, Houston, community reporter, 1981-84; Houston Sun, Houston, gen assignments intern, 1987; Amarillo Globe-News, Amarillo, lifestyles reporter, 1988-93; City Austin, media prog mgr; Tex Dept Econ Develop Bus, community assistance & small bus, currently. **Orgs:** Issue staff, Daily Texan, UT-Austin, 1984-87; publ liaison, Afro-Am Cult Comm, UT-Austin, 1984-88; chairwoman commun week, Commun Coun, UT-Austin, 1985-88; second vpres, Delta Sigma Theta Sorority, UT-Austin, Amarillo, 1987-; Nat Asn Black Journalists, 1987-88 & 1990-94; bd mem, Tex Stud Publ, UT-Austin, 1987-88; community serv reporting, United Way, 1988-93; Provisional Class Jr League Amarillo, 1993; Nat Asn Black Journalists; Asn Women Commun. **Honors/Awds:** Texas Student Publication Board Award, UT-Austin, 1987-88; Plaque for helping the handicapped, Goodwill Indust, 1988-93; Opportunity Symposium Series Award, Austin, 1992 & 1993; Hon Big Sisters, Big Brothers/Big Sisters, 1993-94; Outstanding Alumnus, Delta Sigma Theta Sorority, Amarillo Alumnae, 1993-94. **Home Addr:** 1415 Marsh Harbour Dr, Round Rock, TX 78664-7260, **Home Phone:** (512)990-7911. **Business Addr:** Community Assistance & Small Business, Texas Department of Economic Development Business, 1700 N Cong Ave Suite 200, Austin, TX 78711-2728, **Business Phone:** (512)936-0211.

### BAKER, LAVOLIA EALY
Insurance executive, business owner, manager. **Personal:** Born Nov 11, 1925, Shreveport, LA; married Luchan G; children: Paul, Ronald & Luchan Jr. **Educ:** Univ Calif, Berkeley, CA, attended 1968; Contra Costa, AA, 1970; Golden Gate Univ, attended 1974; Univ San Francisco, BS, 1998. **Career:** L Baker Ins, owner & mgr, 1974, fire & casualty ins broker, currently. **Orgs:** Founder, Church By Side Rd, 1955; chairperson, Oakland Metro Enterprises; chmn, Wis Asn Prof Agr Consults; BOWOPA & E Bay Area Dem Club, 1972; dir, Sojourner Truth Housing Corp, 1974; dir, San Francisco Indep Agents Asn, 1975; dir, Black Brokers & Agents Asn; vpres, Nat Asn Negro Bus & Prof Womens Club; pres, bd chmn, Alpha Phi Alpha Wives Aux; life mem, Nat Asn Advan Colored People; Bay Area Urban League. **Honors/Awds:** Business Woman of the Year. **Home Addr:** 737 Balra Dr, El Cerrito, CA 94530-3302, **Home Phone:** (510)528-5147. **Business Addr:** Member, Church by the Side of the Road, 2108 Russell St, Berkeley, CA 94704, **Business Phone:** (510)644-1263.

**BAKER, LEE, JR.** **See BROOKS, LONNIE.**

### BAKER, MAXINE BEATRICE
Executive director, executive, association executive. **Personal:** Born Feb 29, 1952, Homestead, PA; daughter of Evan Posey and Maxine Reynolds; married Mark McIntosh; children: Morgan & Jill. **Educ:** Emerson Col, BS, speech communs, 1973; Univ Md, grad study; Southeastern Univ, grad study. **Career:** Pac Consults, asst vpres admin; Urban Inst, mgr staff support serv; Freddie Mac Corp, vpres admin & corp properties, vpres human resources, dir admin serv, mgr procurement & regional admin serv, contracts & budget admin, vpres community rels, 1997-2007; SASSY by maxie, prin. 2010-. **Orgs:** Pres & chief exec officer, Freddie Mac Found; Cong Coalition Adoption Inst; Wash Regional Area Grantmakers; Metrop Wash Boys & Girls Club & Voices Am's C; pres, African Am Nonprofit Network, 2008-09; immediate past chair bd, Leadership Greater Wash; sr vpres impact area progs, AARP Found, 2012-. **Honors/Awds:** National Merit Scholarship, Emerson Col, Boston. **Special Achievements:** First African American engineer and boat builder in Pennsylvania; The First president of the African American Nonprofit Network. **Business Addr:** Senior Vice President of Impact Programs, AARP Foundation, 601 E St NW, Washington, DC 20049, **Business Phone:** (888)687-2277.

### BAKER, MYRON TOBIAS (MYRON BAKER)
Football player. **Personal:** Born Jan 6, 1971, Haughton, LA. **Educ:** La Tech Univ. **Career:** Football player (retired); Chicago Bears, linebacker, 1993-95; Carolina Panthers, linebacker, 1996-97.

### BAKER, ROBERT N.
Executive. **Personal:** Born Sep 15, 1943, Cleveland, OH; son of Ora Lee Pettit and R C; children: Schaaron & Brionne. **Educ:** Univ Minn, Minneapolis, MN, course work, photog, psychol, 1977; Henry Ford Community Col, statist, 1987. **Career:** Werner Continental Transp, cent dispatcher, 1969-73; Glendenning Motorways, mgr linehaul transp, 1973-77; Gateway Transp, mgr labor & indust rels, 1977-82; Transportation Logistics, owner & warehouse mgr, 1982-89; Regency Air Freight Inc, co-owner, 1982-83; Baker Motor Freight Inc, owner, 1983-86; Astro Air Express Inc, regional vpres, 1986-89; Shippers Air Freight Express Inc, pres, owner, chief exec officer, 1989-99. **Orgs:** Better Bus Bur, Detroit, Mich, arbitrator, 1986-89; Better Bus Bur, Minn, sr arbitrator, 1989-. **Home Addr:** 4018 Dupont Ave N, Minneapolis, MN 55412, **Home Phone:** (612)339-9093.

**BAKER, ROLAND CHARLES.** **See Obituaries Section.**

### BAKER, SHANA V.
Transportation consultant, founder (originator). **Personal:** Born Feb 27, 1971, Baltimore, MD; daughter of Gordon and Vera. **Educ:** Bethune-Cookman Col, BA, 1993; Univ Akron, MA, urban planning, 1995; Loyola Univ Md, MS, pastoral coun, 2015. **Career:** Akron Metrop Regional Transit Authority, transportaton planner, 1995-96; Fed Hwy Admin, transp planner, scenic byway dir, 1996-; Wellbeing Inc, founder, exec dir, Currently. **Orgs:** Alpha Kappa Alpha Sorority Inc; Women's Transp Sem, Am Planning Asn. **Home Addr:** 2616 Amanda Ct, Woodstock, MD 21163. **Business Addr:** Transportation Planner, US Department Transportation, 400 7th St SW, Washington, DC 20590, **Business Phone:** (202)366-4000.

### BAKER, DR. SHARON SMITH
Government official. **Personal:** Born Oct 13, 1949, Boston, MA; daughter of Howard William and Elnora Clark; married Donald. **Educ:** NC Cent Univ, Durham, NC, BA, 1971; NC Cent Univ Law Sch, Durham, NC, JD, 1975; Duke Univ, Durham, NC, 1975. **Career:** Paul C Bland Law Firm, Durham, NC, paralegal, 1978-81; City Durham, Durham, NC, affirmative action dir CETA, 1979-80, admin asst II, 1982-85, asst to city mgr, 1985-87, dir employ & training prog, Community Health Coalition, dir admin & develop/proj coordr, currently; Pub Tech Inc, Wa, DC, mem officer, 1987-88; Pt Res, owner, currently. **Orgs:** Nat Asn Advan Colored People, Durham, N C, 1985-; vpres, NC Triangle Area Chapter Nat Forum Black Pub Adminrs, 1989-91; parish coun bd mem, Holy Cross Catholic Church, 1989-; NC Black Child Develop, 1990-91; NC Job Training Adminrs Asn, vpres, 1992-94. **Business Addr:** Owner, Chief Executive Officer, On Point Research, 106 W Geer St, Durham, NC 27701-2219, **Business Phone:** (919)688-2386.

### BAKER, SHAUN
Actor. **Personal:** Born New York, NY; married Julie; children: 2. **Career:** TV Series: "Cop Rock", 1990; "You Take the Kids", 1991; "The Fresh Prince of Bel-Air", 1991; "In the Heat of the Night", 1991, "Family Matters", 1992; "Dinosaurs", 1992; "A Different World", "Where I Live", 1993; "Bakersfield P.D.", 1993-94; " Statistically Speaking", 1995; "Too Something", 1995; "Buddies", 1996, "The Show", "Martin", 1996; "Oddville, MTV", 1997; "Chicago Hope", 1997, " Living Single", 1994-97; "The District", 2002, "NYPD Blue", 1994-2002; "V.I.P.", 1998-2002; "Blowing Smoke", 2004; "CSI: Miami", 2007; "Medium", 2010; "The Protector", 2011; Chosen, 2013; Film: House Party, 1990; Grand Canyon, 1991; In the Line of Duty, The Price of Vengeance, 1993; Banged Out, 2002; Full Clip, 2006; Cuttin Da Mustard, 2008; There But Not There, 2009; Kissed by the Devil, 2011. **Business Addr:** Actor, Columbia TriStar Domestic Television, 2859 Paces Ferry Rd SE Suite 1130, Atlanta, GA 30339, **Business Phone:** (770)434-5400.

### BAKER, THURBERT E.
Lawyer, government official. **Personal:** Born Dec 16, 1952, Rocky Mount, NC; son of Mary Baker High; married Catherine; children: Jocelyn & Chelsea. **Educ:** Univ NC, Chapel Hill, BA, polit sci, 1975; Emory Univ Sch Law, JD, 1979. **Career:** US Environ Protection Agency, lawyer; Law Firm Baker & Shivers, sr partner, 1985-97; Ga State House, rep, 1989-97; Gov Zell Miller, from asst floor leader to floor leader, 1990-93; state Ga, atty gen, 1997-2011; Univ S Fla, Harrell Ctr, adv, currently; Dentons US LLP, partner, currently. **Orgs:** Ga Bar Asn; Kiwanis; Nat Med Soc-Emory Univ; Perimeter Col Bd; adv, Harrell Ctr Stud Domestic Violence, Univ S Fla; adv, State Bar Ga bd Gov; Judicial Nominating Cms; exec comt, pres, chmn, Nat Asn Attorneys Gen, 2006-07; Am Bar Asn House Del; mem coun, Foreign Rels; bd mem, DeKalb County Libr; trustee, Ebenezer Baptist Church; mem bd, Nat Med Soc Emory Univ & DeKalb Col Found; Emory Law Sch Coun; bd visitor, Emory Univ; mem bd gov, State Bar Ga; Judicial Nominating Comn; chmn, NAAG's Conf Violence Against Women; trustee, Metro-Fair Housing Bd; Convener, Civil Rights Comt, Nat Asn Attorneys Gen; Omega Psi Pi; chair, Southern Regional Conf Attorneys Gen; trustee, Martin Luther King Jr. Charitable Found. **Special Achievements:** First African American attorney general for the state of Georgia. **Home Addr:** , Stone Mountain, GA. **Business Addr:** Partner, Dentons US LLP, 303 Peachtree St NE Suite 5300, Atlanta, GA 30308, **Business Phone:** (404)527-8480.

**BAKER, VERDENIA C.** **See CRUTCHFIELD-BAKER, VERDENIA.**

### BAKER, VIN (VINCENT LAMONT BAKER)
Basketball player, president (organization). **Personal:** Born Nov 23, 1971, Lake Wales, FL; son of James and Jean; married Shawne Pagan; children: 4. **Educ:** Univ Hartford, mass commun, 1993. **Career:** Milwaukee Bucks, forward, 1993-97; Seattle SuperSonics, 1997-2002; Boston Celtics, 2002-04; NY Knicks, 2004-05; Houston Rockets, 2005; Los Angeles Clippers, forward, 2005-06; MN Timberwolves, 2006; Stand Tall Found, founder, 1998-; St. Bernard School in Uncasville, asst coach, 2011; Vin Baker Enterprises, pres, currently. **Business Addr:** President, Vin Baker Enterprises, 10 Springbrook Rd, Old Saybrook, CT 06475, **Business Phone:** (860)395-1383.

### BAKER, WILLIE L., JR.
Labor activist, executive. **Personal:** Born May 21, 1941, Sanford, FL; son of Willie Sr and Ila Jessie Harris (deceased); married Madeline Dennis; children: Kim & Keith. **Educ:** Univ Md Eastern Shore, Princess Anne, BA, 1965. **Career:** United Food & Com Workers Int Union, Local 56, Bridgeton, NJ, rec sect, 1974-80, asst bus agt, 1974-85, legis, S Jersey, 1974-85, vpres, 1980-85, affairs dept, dir, 1989, civil rights & community rels Dept, dir, field opers, dir. **Orgs:** Bd mem, Community Serv Comn AFL-CIO, 1986-95; Univ Md Eastern Shore

Nat Alumni Asn, 1987-91; former vpres, Consumer Fedn Am Exec Comn, 1990-95; Dem Nat Comm, 1990-95; Nat Asn Advan Colored People; Coalition Labor Union Women; bd mem, Food Res & Action Ctr; bd mem, TransAfrica; vice chmn, Labor Roundtable Nat Black Caucus State Legislators; exec vpres emer, Coalition Black Trade Unionists. **Honors/Awds:** Presidential Citation, Nat Asn Equal Opportunity Higher Educ, 1981; Alumnus of the Year Award, Univ Md Eastern Shore, 1986; Retiree of the Year, UFCW Minority Coalition, 2006. **Special Achievements:** NBCSL recognized as Nation Builder. **Business Addr:** Executive Vice President Emeritus, Coalition of Black Trade Unionists, 1155 Conn Ave Suite 500, Washington, DC 20036, **Business Phone:** (202)778-3318.

### BAKER-KELLY, DR. BEVERLY

Lawyer, educator. **Personal:** Born Nov 2, 1942, Detroit, MI; daughter of Robert Edwoods and Cornelia Lewis; married A Paul; children: Traci Allyce & Kara Gisele. **Educ:** Howard Univ, attended 1962; Univ Mich, BA, 1964; Columbia Univ, MA, 1966, MEd, 1970, Sch Int Affairs, cert, African studies, 1970, EdD, 1973; Univ Calif, Berkeley, JD, 1976; Harvard Univ, MA, 1977, PhD, 1978; Johns Hopkins Univ, attended 1986; London Sch Econ, attended 1992. **Career:** Columbia Univ, co-dir, African-Am Summer Studies Prog, 1970; Univ Windsor, sociol instr, 1971-73; Greenberg & Glusker, law clerk, 1974; Dunn & Cruthcer, law clerk, 1975; Legal Aid Soc, law clerk, 1976; Calif St Univ, assoc prof, 1976-82; Mayr, Galle, Weiss-Tessback, und Ben Ibler, Attorneys Law, stagiaire, 1978-79; UNESCO, stagiaire, 1979-80; Univ Md, AUS Bases, lectr & facilitator, 1980; Southern Poverty Law Cent, assoc, 1981; Univ Calif, Dir Acad Support Prog, lectr, 1982-84; Res Mgt Servs, partner & dir, Int Law Div, 1984-86; Focus Int Consultancy, dir, 1986-93; Pvt Immigration Law Pract, 1991-93; Focus Legal Consultancy, lawyer, 1991-; Howard Univ, vis assoc prof, 1993-; Golden Gate Univ, Sch Law, 1996, 1997; Int Criminal Tribunal Rwanda, dep registr, 1999-2000; Golden Gate Univ, adj fac, currently. **Orgs:** Union Int Des Advocates; vpres & bd dir, Boalt Hall Fund Diversity, 1988-91; chair, Nat Bar Asn, Int Law Sect, 1994-96; Comn Judicial Nominees Eval, 2001-; deleg, African Judicial Network, Bamako, Mali, 2003; Calif State Bar, 1991-. **Honors/Awds:** Presidential Award, Natl Bar Assn, 1992, 1993 & 1995. **Special Achievements:** Editor: Assoc Ed, California Law Review; Articles Editor, Black Law Journal; Co-author: "The African-American Encyclopedia of Education", 1994; "A Study of the Degree of Trans nationalization of College & Non-College Educated Blacks", Columbia Univ; "Housing Conceptions & Satisfactions of Residents in Federally Subsidized Lower-Middle Income Housing", Harvard Univ; "US Immigration: A Wake up Call", Howard Law Journal, 1995; Participant, Fulbright Seminar for Intl Law Professors on McDougal-Lasswell Jurisprudence. **Home Addr:** 2983 Burdeck Dr, Oakland, CA 94602, **Home Phone:** (510)530-9331. **Business Addr:** Adjunct Faculty, Golden Gate University, 536 Mission St, San Francisco, CA 94105-2968, **Business Phone:** (415)442-7000.

### BAKER-PARKS, SHARON L.

Executive, social worker. **Personal:** Born Jan 18, 1958, New York, NY; daughter of Willie Baker Jr (deceased) and Lee Baker (deceased); married Brainard J; children: Kendra. **Educ:** Univ NC Charlotte, BA, sociol, Afro-Am & African studies, 1979; Columbia Univ, Sch Social Work, MSW, 1983; Baruch Col, Sch Continuing Studies, cert bus, 1986. **Career:** Steinway Child & Family Develop Ctr, social worker, 1983-84; S Bronx Ment Health Coun Inc, psychiat social worker, 1984; Bedford Stuyvesant Community Ment Health Ctr Inc, psychiat social worker & recreation coord, 1985; Victim Serv Agency, casework supvr, 1985-86; Bronx-Lebanon Hosp Ctr, psychiat social worker, 1986-89; New York Bd Educ, sch social worker, 1989-. **Orgs:** Nursing home chair, Delta Sigma Theta Sorority Inc, 1977-; Nat Asn Social Workers, NYC Chap, 1981-; Workshop Bus Opportunities Alumni Asn, 1985-; Girl Scout Coun Greater NY; Vol Troop Leader, 1996-. **Honors/Awds:** NY State Certification in Social Work (CSW), 1986; NY State Sch Social Work, License, NY City Sch Social Work, Lic, Sch Social Work Specialist Credential; President's Volunteer Service Awards, Bronze level, 2011. **Home Addr:** 880 Colgate Ave Apt 11L, Bronx, NY 10473-4862, **Home Phone:** (718)617-4106. **Business Addr:** School Social Worker, New York Bd Education, 1070 Castle Hill Ave, Bronx, NY 10472-6314, **Business Phone:** (718)822-5345.

### BALDON, JANICE C.

Lecturer, college teacher, administrator, administrator. **Personal:** Born Jun 5, 1955, Louisville, KY; daughter of Virgil and Willana; married Gutter. **Educ:** Univ Louisville, BS, com, 1977, MS, human resource educ, human resources; Bellarmine Col, MBA, human resources, mgt, 1987, mgt & orgn develop; Human Resources Cert Inst, prof human resources cert. **Career:** DuPont Dow Elastomers, off coord, 1978-; Univ Louisville, Adj Instr, macro & micro econs, 1990-2008; Online Facilitator, 2006-11; Learning House; prof develop adminr, 2012-. **Orgs:** Nat Coun Negro Women, 1994; Million Man March Comt Adv; Alpha Kappa Alpha; Ky Alliance Against Racism/Repression. **Business Addr:** Professional Development Administrator, The Learning House Inc, 427 S 4th St Suite 300, Louisville, KY 40202, **Business Phone:** (502)589-9878.

### BALDWIN, ARTHUR L.

Manager. **Personal:** married Cynthia A; children: 2. **Educ:** Univ Pittsburgh, BS, microbiol, 1969, MA, org chem, 1976, PhD, org chem; Duquesne Univ, MBA. **Career:** Nat Energy Technol Lab, US Dept Energy, regional mgr & sr-level off, currently; Pittsburgh Energy Technol, US Dept Energy, prog coordr; Baldwin Investment Mgt Group, LLC, pres. **Orgs:** African Am Chamber Com; Penn State Eberly Col Sci Alumni Soc; bd dir, Heinz Hist Ctr; adv bd, Penn State Univ Undergrad; bd dir, Opportunity Industrialization Ctr Pittsburgh; bd dir, McKeesport Br Pittsburgh Urban League; adv bd, Salvation Army; Am Inst Chem Engrs; Am Chem Soc; Air & Waste Mgt Asn; Nat Tech Asn; Sigma Pi Phi Fraternity. **Honors/Awds:** Alumni Fellow Award, Penn State Univ, 2011; DOE's Service to Society Award. **Business Addr:** Regional Manager, US Department of Energy, 626 Cochrans Mill Rd, Pittsburgh, PA 15236-0940, **Business Phone:** (412)386-6011.

### BALDWIN, CAROLYN H.

President (organization), chief executive officer, executive. **Personal:** married Anthony; children: 2. **Educ:** Fisk Univ, BA, econs, bus admin; Univ Chicago, MBA. **Career:** Citibank, NA, acct officer, sr acct officer; Coca-Cola Co, sr financial analyst, 1977; Latin Am treas serv, treas specialist, asst treas & mgr; Coca-Cola Financial Corp, pres, 1991; Schweppes Beverages, Human Resource dir, 1999; Coca-Cola N Am, Finance, Info Systs, Human Resources & Tech, human resources dir, Global Mkt Div, Human Resource dir, vpres, human resources; Global Tech Financial, chmn, chief exec officer, 2000; ReliaStar Financial Corp, dir; RARE Hospitality Int Inc, chmn, chief exec officer. **Orgs:** Leadership Atlanta, Soc Int Bus Fels; dir, Exec Leadership Found; dir, Consumer Credit Coun serv; vice chmn, Teachers Retirement Syst Ga; bd trustee, Fisk Univ; bd dir, RARE Hospitality Int; treas, MESBIC. **Business Addr:** Chief Executive Officer, chairman, RARE Hospitality Int Inc, 8215 Roswell Rd, Atlanta, GA 30350.

### BALDWIN, CYNTHIA A.

Judge, educator. **Personal:** Born Feb 8, 1945, McKeesport, PA; daughter of James A (deceased) and Iona Meriweather (deceased); married Arthur L; children: James A & Crystal A. **Educ:** Pa State Univ, Univ Park, PA, BA, eng, 1966, MA, Am lit, 1974; Duquesne Univ Sch Law, Pittsburgh, PA, JD, 1980. **Career:** Pa State Univ, McKeesport, PA, asst dean stud affairs, 1976-77; Hollinhead & Mendelson, law clerk, 1979; Neighborhood Legal Serv, McKeesport, PA, staff atty, 1980-81; Off Atty Gen, PA, dep atty gen, 1981-83, atty-in-charge, 1983-86; Palkovitz & Palkovitz, McKeesport, PA, atty; Duquesne Univ Law, Pittsburgh, PA, adj prof, 1984-86, vis prof, 1986-87, adj prof, 1989-99; Duquesne Univ, bd dir, 1996-; Allegheny Co Ct Common Pleas, Family Div & Part-time Civil Div, judge, 1999-; Pa State Univ, vice chmn bd, 2001-03, chmn bd; Supreme Ct Pa, justice, 2005-08; Duane Morris LLP, pvt pract, 2008-; Pa State Univ, gen coun & chief legal officer, 2010-. **Orgs:** Exec comt mem, Homer S Brown Law Asn, 1980-97; Allegheny Co Bar Asn, 1980-; vpres & bd dir, Neighborhood Legal Serv Asn, 1986-88; pres, Pa State Alumni Asn, 1987-88; vice chair & bd dir, Greater Pittsburgh YMCA, 1987-89; Greater Pittsburgh Comn Women, 1987-89; Int Asn Women Judges Pa Bar Asn, 1988-; Pa Bar Asn House Delegates, 1988-99; pres, Pa State Alumni Asn, 1989-91; vice chair & gubernational appointee, Pa State, 1995-; bd trustee, Pa State, 2004-07; Pa Comn Crime & Delinq. **Special Achievements:** Avoiding Abuse, 1994; All About Family Court, 1999; Combating Judicial Corruption in Uganda, 2009. **Home Addr:** 2009 McClintock Rd, Mc Keesport, PA 15131, **Home Phone:** (412)678-0943. **Business Addr:** Chief Legal Officer, General Counsel, Pennsylvania State University, 777 W Harrisburg Pke, Middletown, PA 17057, **Business Phone:** (814)865-4700.

### BALDWIN, GEORGE R.

Lawyer, executive. **Personal:** Born Oct 4, 1934, Brunswick, GA; children: Kirk & Goldie. **Educ:** Lincoln Univ, BA, econs, 1955; Brooklyn Law Sch, LLB, JD, 1964; NY Univ Law Sch, LLM, 1976. **Career:** Pvt pract, New York, atty, 1966-67; Danch, Rivers & Baldwin Westbury, NY, partner, 1967-71; Legal Aid Soc New York, Comn Defender Off, atty-in-charge, 1971; atty, currently. **Orgs:** Nat Bar Asn; Nat Conf Black Lawyers; 100 Black Men Inc; JFK Dem Club; Metro AME Church. **Home Addr:** 221 Canal St Lobby, New York, NY 10013, **Home Phone:** (212)226-8990. **Business Addr:** Attorney, 78 80 Mott St Suite 300, New York, NY 10013, **Business Phone:** (212)226-8990.

### BALDWIN, JAMES J., JR.

Baseball player, baseball manager. **Personal:** Born Jul 15, 1971, Southern Pines, NC; children: James III. **Career:** Baseball player (retired), baseball coach; Chicago White Sox, pitcher, 1995-2001; Los Angeles Dodgers, 2001; Seattle Mariners, 2002; Minn Twins, 2003; New York Mets, pitcher, 2004; Baltimore Orioles, 2005; Tex Rangers, 2005; Toronto Blue Jays, 2006; Pinecrest High Sch, pitching coach, 2006-. **Business Addr:** Pitching Coach, Pinecrest Baseball, 250 Voit Gilmore Lane, Southern Pines, NC 28387, **Business Phone:** (910)692-6554.

### BALDWIN, LEWIS V.

Educator, writer, clergy. **Personal:** Born Sep 17, 1949, Camden, AL; son of L V and Flora Bell; married Jacqueline Loretta Laws; children: Sheryl Boykin-Robinson. **Educ:** Talladega Col, Talladega, AL, BA, hist, 1971; Colgate-Rochester Divinity Sch, Rochester, NY, MA, black church studies, 1973, Mdiv, theol, 1975; Northwestern Univ, Evanston, IL, PhD, hist Christianity, 1980. **Career:** Wooster Col, vis asst prof relig, 1981-92; Colgate Univ, asst prof philos & relig, 1982-84, vis asst prof, church hist, 1983-84, Colgate-Rochester Divinity Sch; Fisk Univ; Am Baptist Col; Vanderbilt Univ, asst prof relig studies, 1984-90, assoc prof, 1991-2000, prof relig studies, 2001-, dir, african am studies, emer prof. Books: Invisible Strands in African Methodism: A History of the African Union Methodist Protestant and Union American Methodist Episcopal Churches 1805-1980, 1983; The Mark of a Man: Peter Spencer and the African Union Methodist Tradition, 1987; There is a Balm in Gilead: The Cultural Roots of Martin Luther King Jr, 1991; To Make the Wounded Whole: The Cultural Legacy of Martin Luther King Jr, 1992; Freedom is Never Free: A Biographical Portrait of E.D. Nixon Sr, 1992; Toward the Beloved Community: Martin Luther King Jr and South Africa, 1995; Between the Cross and the Crescent: Christian and Muslim Perspectives on Malcolm and Martin, 2002; Plenty Good Room Student: A Bible Study Based on African-American Spirituals, 2002; The Voice of Conscience: The Church in the Mind of Martin Luther King Jr, 2010; Never to Leave Us Alone: The Prayer Life of Martin Luther King Jr, 2010; "Thou, Dear God": Prayers that Open Hearts and Spirits, 2013; "In a Single Garment of Destiny": A Global Vision of Justice (King Legacy), 2014. **Orgs:** Nat Asn Advan Colored People, 1980-; Soc Study Black Relig, 1981-; Am Acad Relig, 1981-; Am Soc Church Hist, 1981-; Southern Christian Leadership Conf, financial supporter, 1986-. **Home Addr:** 651 Harpeth Bend Dr, Nashville, TN 37221, **Home Phone:** (615)646-6524. **Business Addr:** Professor, Vanderbilt University, 2301 Vanderbilt Pl 300 Garland Hall, Nashville, TN 37235-1585, **Business Phone:** (615)322-4885.

### BALDWIN, LOUIS J.

Manager, association executive, executive. **Personal:** Born New York, NY. **Educ:** Ithaca Col, BA, bus admin, 1970. **Career:** Ithaca Col, asst dir admis, 1970-72; Am Arbit Asn, asst dir, 1972-73; Union Carbide Corp, adminr, recruitment & placement, 1974-77; Allied Corp, supvr employee rels, 1977-83; Staten Island Cable, mgr human resources, 1984-85; Amerada Hess Corp, personnel admin, 1985-86; Time Warner Cable, mgr human resources, 1986-91; Cablevision Systs Corp, dir human resources & area dir, 1992-99, area dir employee rels, 1999-2005; Seeking Opportunity, Human Resources Mgt, 2005-. **Orgs:** Adv, Jr Achievement New York, 1976; EDGES Group Inc, 1977-; Nat Asn Advan Colored People, 1978-; bd mem, Forum Advan Minorities Eng, 1980-82; loaned exec, United Way, 1982; Nat Asn Minorities Cable, 1984-; secy/bd mem, Harlem Dowling, Westside C & Family Ctr Serv, 1986-; New York Urban League, 1986-; One Hundred Black Men Inc, 1990-; bd dir, Ithaca Col Alumni, 1996-99. **Home Addr:** 19727 Foothill Ave, Hollis, NY 11423-1609, **Home Phone:** (718)217-7123.

### BALDWIN, MITCHELL CARDELL

Executive, systems analyst, president (organization). **Personal:** Born Aug 22, 1958, Birmingham, AL; son of Bernard and Ezell Caldwell Barnes; married Gennia; children: Mitchell Jr. **Educ:** Jacksonville State Univ, Jacksonville, AL, BS, comput sci, 1980. **Career:** Life-changing speaker; author; corporate consultant; executive coach, real estate entrepreneur; Am Intermedial Resources, Birmingham, AL, comput prog, 1980-82; Fed Res Bank, Birmingham, AL, comput analyst, 1982-84; Ala Power Co, Birmingham, AL, systs analyst & coordr, 1984-93; Baldwin Real Estate Investment & Property Mgt, prin, 1984-; CHAMP Inc, founder & chmn bd, 1989-2005; Smart Talk with MCB, pres & owner, 1993-. Author: Surviving Corporate Downsizing with Dignity & Grace. **Orgs:** Educ comt, AABE; trustee, First Baptist Church; Birmingham City Schs Parent & Community Task Force; River Run Neighborhood Asn; Basketball Coach-Vestavia Hills Recreation League. **Home Addr:** 4121 Riverview Cv, Birmingham, AL 35243, **Home Phone:** (205)970-0828. **Business Addr:** President, Owner, Smart Talk with M C B, PO Box 11404, Birmingham, AL 35202-1404, **Business Phone:** (205)970-0828.

### BALDWIN, OLIVIA MCNAIR

Government official. **Personal:** Born Mar 30, 1943, Cleveland, OH; daughter of Merdic McNair Jr and Carrie Mae Head McNair; married Otis L; children: Omar L. **Career:** Government official (retired); St Lukes Hosp, Cleveland, Ohio, food serv supvr, 1962-65; Sumby Hosp, River Rouge, Mich, pur asst, 1965-66; City Detroit, Detroit, Mich, typist, 1970-75, asst mkt master, 1975-90; Mich Real Estate agt, 1998; James Grant Realty, Real Estate agt, currently. **Orgs:** Order Eastern Star, 1980-; second vpres, Local 808-M, SEIU, 1989-; Ways & Means Comt, Am Bus Womens Asn, treas, 1990-. **Honors/Awds:** First female asst market master, first female market master, City Detroit, Bureau Markets; Unity Bap Church, Sr Ursher Bd, Busy Bee. **Home Addr:** 6 Lakeside Pl E, Palm Coast, FL 32137. **Business Addr:** Real Estate Agent, James Grant Realty, 1254 Westgate Pkwy, Dothan, AL 36303, **Business Phone:** (334)803-1555.

### BALL, BRENDA LOUISE

Insurance executive, association executive, executive. **Personal:** Born May 26, 1951, Springfield, OH; daughter of John W and Virginia L Davis; married Richard Nixon; children: Majenni Nixon & Johnathan Nixon. **Educ:** Sinclair Community Col, ABA, 1971; Univ Cincinnati, BBA, 1973; State Mich, cert pub accountants, 1975; Univ Detroit, MBA, 1988. **Career:** Arthur Andersen & Co, sr auditor, 1973-78; Ford Motor Co, fin analyst, 1978-79; Fed-Mogul Corp, bank & pension fund mgr, 1979-81, staff controller, 1982-86, internal audit, 1986-88; Blue Cross & Blue Shield Mich, vpres & controller, 1988-95, vpres & dep treas, 1995-96, vpres & treas, 1996-2003, Ronrich Corp, exec vpres fin, currently; B L Ball Consulting, owner, currently. **Orgs:** Fin Execs Inst; Econs Am, bd dirs; Liberty BIDCO, bd dirs; Richard Austin Scholar Comn, Wayne State; United Way, Community Servs Community Priority Review Comt; Nat Asn Black Accts; Univ Detroit-Mercy, bd dirs; Luella Hannan Mem Found, bd dirs; Vista Maria, adv & fin comts; Am Hear Asn, women & heart disease comt; Leadership Detroit, trustee; invest comt, Wayne State Univ Found; bd trustee, Kettering Univ. **Honors/Awds:** Nat & Local Achievement Awards, Nat Asn Black Accts; Wall Street Journal Award; Links Inc, Scholar; Ford Found, Scholar. **Home Addr:** 2300 W Long Lake Rd, West Bloomfield, MI 48323-3076, **Home Phone:** (810)932-1008. **Business Addr:** Executive Vice President of Finance, Ronrich Corp, 22400 Lucerne Dr Suite 201, Southfield, MI 48075, **Business Phone:** (248)448-8400.

### BALL, CLARENCE M., JR.

Nursing home administrator, chief executive officer. **Personal:** Born Dec 23, 1949, New Braunfels, TX; son of Clarence and Clarice Coleman; married Charlesetta Owens; children: Sean Terrell, Kevin Denard & Cherise Montre. **Educ:** Tex A&M Univ, Kingsville, TX, attended 1970; SW Tex State Univ, San Marcos, TX, BA, 1972; N Tex State Univ, attended 1974. **Career:** Vari-Care Inc, Rochester, NY, adminr, 1974-84; Ball Healthcare Servs Inc, Mobile, Ala, pres & chief exec officer, 1983-. **Orgs:** Ala Nursing Home Asn, 1988-; pres, Am Col Nursing Home Adminrs, 1982; pres, Montgomery Area Coun Nursing Home Adminrs, 1980; bd mem, Young Men's Christian Asn, Mobile, AL, 1987-; chmn bd, Mobile Housing bd; second vice chmn, Ala St Port Authority, 2000. **Honors/Awds:** Small Business of the Month, Mobile Area Chamber Com, 1987; Alumnus of the Year Award, N Tex State Univ, 1989; Minority Business Service Award, Mobile Minority Bus Ctr, 1990; Community Service Award, Mobile Chap, Nat Asn Black Social Workers, 1990; Benefactor of Youth Award, Mobile Young Men's Christian Asn, 1990. **Business Addr:** President, Chief Executive Officer, Ball Healthcare Services Inc, 1 Southern Way, Mobile, AL 36619, **Business Phone:** (251)433-9801.

### BALL, DREXEL BERNARD

College administrator. **Personal:** Born Apr 30, 1948, McClellanville, SC; son of Lucille Garrett; married Brenda Petty; children: Tyler Anderson. **Educ:** Morehouse Col, Atlanta, GA, BA, 1972; NC A&T State Univ, Greensboro, NC, MS, 1986. **Career:** Greensboro Daily News, Greensboro, NC, reporter, 1972-82; NC A&T State Univ, Greensboro, NC, asst dir pub rel, 1982-89; Delaware State Univ, Dover, Del, dir pub rels, 1989-93, exec asst pres, 1992-2006; Lincoln Univ Commonwealth Penn, Off Commun & Pub Rel, dir, 2006-08; Claflin Univ, exec vpres, currently. **Orgs:** Pres, Gate City Morehouse Alumni Chap, 1985-89; Sigma Delta Chi; Nat Asn Black Journalist; Steering Comt, Delaware Chicken Festival, 1991; PR Specialist, Cent Delaware United Way

Campaign, 1991; chmn, Dev Comt, Dover Arts Coun; co-dir, Col Proj, Dover Art League. **Home Addr:** 210 Chelsea Way, Dover, DE 19904-5396, **Home Phone:** (302)674-3408. **Business Addr:** Executive Vice President, Claflin University, 400 Magnolia st, Orangeburg, SC 29115, **Business Phone:** (800)535-5000.

## BALL, JANET M.

Executive director. **Educ:** Univ Ariz, MA, libr sci, 1995. **Career:** Circulation clerk; inter libr loan clerk; libr asst; asst libr dir; libr mgr; libr dir; Ariz State Libr, continuing educ coordr & Arch & Pub Rec, Libr Develop Div consult; Copper Queen Libr, Bisbee, Ariz, librn, facilitator & dir, currently. **Business Addr:** Director, Facilitator, Copper Queen Library, 6 Main St, Bisbee, AZ 85603-1857, **Business Phone:** (520)432-4232.

## BALL, JERRY LEE, JR.

Entrepreneur, football player. **Personal:** Born Dec 15, 1964, Beaumont, TX; married Michelle; children: Faren, Lindsey & Halle. **Educ:** Southern Methodist Univ. **Career:** Football player (retired), business owner; Detroit Lions, nose tackle, 1987-92; Cleveland Browns, Left defensive tackle, 1993-94, 1999; Los Angeles Raiders, Left defensive tackle, 1994-96; Oakland Raiders, 1996, nose tackle & Left defensive tackle, 1995; Minn Vikings, nose tackle & Left defensive tackle, 1997-98, 1999; Ice Box Sportswear Inc, pres & owner, currently. **Orgs:** mem, Omega Psi Phi Fraternity Inc. **Honors/Awds:** Pro Bowl, 1989-91. **Home Addr:** , Pontiac, MI, **Home Phone:** (810)335-4500. **Business Addr:** President, Owner, Ice Box Sportswear Inc, 1045 Beaubien St, Detroit, MI 48221, **Business Phone:** (313)963-4433.

## BALL, RICHARD E.

Law enforcement officer. **Personal:** Born Jul 18, 1918, Springfield, IL; married Dolores Edwinton Raiford. **Educ:** NY Univ, BS, 1946, MBA, 1948; Brooklyn Law Sch, LLB, 1954, JD, 1967. **Career:** New York Housing Authority; Dept Welfare; New York Bd Educ; St Augustine's Col, chmn & prof; NC Cent Univ, bd trustees & actg pres & bus mgr; Nat Asn Advan Colored People, atty & legal ed, coun & consult; Episcopal Church, lay reader. **Orgs:** Masons, shriners; Consistory; life mem, Alpha Phi Alpha; life mem, Am Nat Bar Asn; NC, Mass, State Bar Asn; Nat Mgt Asn; pres, Alpha Phi Lambds Chap. **Honors/Awds:** Cand, Super Court Judge. **Home Addr:** 1509 Summerville Cir, Raleigh, NC 27610. **Business Addr:** Odd Fels Bldg Suite 304, Raleigh, NC 27601.

## BALL, RICHARD ERWIN

Zoologist. **Personal:** Born Sep 24, 1946, Zanesville, OH; son of Evelyn T; children: Jennifer Giodano & Michael. **Career:** Paradise Pk, opers mgr, 1969-76; Honolulu Zoo, animal keeper I, 1976-88, working foreman II, 1988-90, animal specialist III, 1990-. **Orgs:** Am Zoo Asn; Am Asn Zoo Keepers; Sierra Club. **Home Addr:** 1115 Liku St, Kailua, HI 96734, **Home Phone:** (808)262-8779. **Business Addr:** Mammal Specialist, Curator, Honolulu Zoo, 151 Kapahulu Ave, Honolulu, HI 96815, **Business Phone:** (808)971-7171.

## BALL, ROGER

Vice president (organization), business owner. **Personal:** Born Feb 19, 1961, Ashtabula, OH; son of E Peter and Helen R; married Trenisha G Moore; children: Demetrius A D & Quinton T. **Educ:** Am Bankers Asn, bank mkt, 1984; Ohio State Univ, Max M Fisher Col Bus, BS & BA, 1985, MBA,1994; Bus people Inst, cert, prof & personal leadership & exec leadership, 2009; Northwestern Univ, Kellogg Sch Mgt, cert, exec mgt, 2011. **Career:** Evcor Bus Syst, govt acct mgr, 1986-87; TBS, Ohio, nat acct mgr, 1987-88; Dispatch Consumer Serv Inc, acct exec, 1988-89; B&B Comput Serv Inc, founder & owner, pres, 1986-2000; Sophisticated Syst Inc, dir hardware & software sales, 1997-2000; VERITAS Software, sr acct exec pub sector, 2000-03; Strategic Educ Solutions Inc, pres, 2003-07; Century Industs Inc, chief operating officer, 2007-10, pres & chief exec officer, 2010-; Three Leaf Productions, exec vpres, currently. **Orgs:** Omega Psi Phi Frat; OSU, Black Alumni Soc, treas & steering comt, 1991; OSU Advocate, 1991; Nat Black MBA Asn; Ohio State Univ Pres Club bd; Mentoring Stud Athletes. **Honors/Awds:** Outstanding Community Serv, Columbus City Coun, 1985; Community Service, Ohio House Representatives, 1986; Student Leadership, Ohio State University, 1985, Pace Setter Award, 1985. **Special Achievements:** Volunteer speaker for OSU Young Scholars Program, 1992. **Home Addr:** 730 Hunters Glen Dr, Columbus, OH 43230, **Home Phone:** (614)471-6841. **Business Addr:** Executive Vice President, Three Leaf Productions, 250 E Wilson Bridge Rd, Worthington, OH 43085, **Business Phone:** (614)447-2100.

## BALL, DR. WILFRED R.

Educator. **Personal:** Born Jan 3, 1932, Chicago, IL; son of Wilfred Sr and Mary Sanders; married Jane Lee; children: Janet, Carol, Wendy & Cris. **Educ:** Morehouse Col, BS, 1952; Atlanta Univ, MS, 1955; Ohio State Univ, PhD, 1965. **Career:** Educator (retired); Southern Univ, instr, 1955-60; Alcorn Col, asst prof, 1960-61, 1968-69; Knoxville Col, assoc prof, 1969-70; Wilberforce Univ, assoc & prof, 1972, Natural Sci Div, chair, 1991-96. **Orgs:** Fel, Nat Sci Found, 1960-62; Beta Kappi Chi Hon Sci Soc; Beta Beta Beta Biol Soc; Kappa Alpha Psi Fraternity. **Home Addr:** 1395 Corry St, Yellow Springs, OH 45387-1313, **Home Phone:** (937)767-5781.

## BALL, WILLIAM BATTEN

Accountant, lawyer. **Personal:** Born Aug 28, 1928, San Antonio, TX; son of William Henry (deceased) and Lillian Edna Young (deceased); married Charlie Mae Cooper; children: Jeffrey Christopher, Kathleen Lorraine & William Eric. **Educ:** Woodrow Wilson Jr Col, attended 1945; Roosevelt Univ, BS, commun, 1955, MBA, 1960; Chicago Kent Col Law, Ill Inst Technol, JD, 1968. **Career:** IRS, revenue officer, 1955-57; Supreme Life Ins Co, acct, jr exec, 1957-59; State Ill Dept Labor, auditor, 1959; Internal Revenue Serv, agt, 1959-67, appellate appeals officer, 1967-86, mgt coordr, 1972-73; pvt pract atty, 1986-. **Orgs:** Cook Co Bar Asn; Nat Bar Asn; chmn, admin bd, St Mark United Meth Church, 1973-77; troop comtman, BSA; Order Arrow Nat Fraternity Scout Hon Campers; Order Brotherhood; Kappa Alpha Psi Fraternity Inc; bd dir, Community Ment Health Coun, 1982-87; Chicago Bd Educ; W cott Local Sch Coun, 1989-93; chmn, Bylaws Comm, Sub dist Coun Rep, 1989-93. **Honors/Awds:** Various Awards & Honors, BSA; Outstanding Performance Award, Internal Revenue Serv; masters thesis, Ins Co Ann Statement Prep & Instrs, Roosevelt Univ, 1960; Silver Beaver Award, Chicago Area Boy Scouts Coun, 2000; Chicago Sch Reform Act, created by Ill State Legisative. **Business Addr:** Attorney at Law, 8355 S Perry Ave, Chicago, IL 60620, **Business Phone:** (773)874-0311.

## BALL-REED, HON. PATRICE M.

State government official. **Personal:** Born Sep 16, 1958, Chicago, IL; daughter of Arthur and Portia; married Roy L Reed; children: Candace, Alexis, William & Darion. **Educ:** Trinity Col, BA, econs, 1980; John Marshall Law Sch, JD, 1984. **Career:** Wash, Kennon, Hunter & Samuels, law clerk, 1984-85, assoc atty, 1985-88; Patricia Banks & Assocs, independent contractor, 1988-89; Cook County State's Atty Off, asst state's atty, 1989, dep supvr Real Estate Property Tax Unit, sr trial supvr child support enforcement div, dep atty gen child support, 2003-08; Assoc Judge, Cook County Circuit Ct, 2008-. **Orgs:** Assembly, family sect coun, women & minority participation comt, Bd Govs; Bar Publ bd, Ill State Bar Asn, 2010-; Women's Bar Asn; bd dir, Black Women Lawyer's Asn Greater Chicago, treas, scholar found; Cook County Bar Asn; Nat Polit Women's Caucus; bd dir, John Marshall Alumni Asn; regist agt, treas, Nat Black Prosecutors Asn; Scholar Ill Residents Trinity Col. **Home Addr:** 1631 N Nashville Ave, Chicago, IL 60707, **Home Phone:** (773)745-6438. **Business Addr:** Associate judge, Cook County Circuit Court, 50 W Washington St Suite 1001, Chicago, IL 60602, **Business Phone:** (312)603-5030.

## BALLARD, DR. ALLEN BUTLER, JR.

Dean (education), educator. **Personal:** Born Nov 1, 1930, Philadelphia, PA; son of Robert Sr and Olive Robinson; married Raisa; children: John & Alayna. **Educ:** Kenyon Col, BA, 1952; Univ Bordeaux, attended 1953; Harvard Univ, MA, 1957, PhD, 1962. **Career:** Police officer, prof; Harvard, fel, 1955-57; Dartmouth Col, lectr, 1960; Boston Univ; City Col NY, lectr, 1961, asst prof, 1962, asst dean, 1965-67, assoc dean, 1967-69, assoc prof, 1967, dean fac, 1973-76, prof, 1969-86, prof emer, 1986; Cornell Univ, vis prof, 1962, 1964; St Univ New York, Albany, NY, prof hist, polit sci & Afro-Am studies, 1986-. **Orgs:** Ford Found; Nat Humanities Ctr; Moton Ctr Grants; Fulbright Fel, Univ Bordeaux, France, 1952-53; Phi Beta kappa; Black Caucus Am Libr Asn. **Home Addr:** 15 Cobble Ct, Clifton Park, NY 12065, **Home Phone:** (518)371-9193. **Business Addr:** Professor, State University of New York, 1400 Wash Ave, Albany, NY 12222, **Business Phone:** (518)442-5300.

## BALLARD, DR. BILLY RAY

Physician, educator, dentist. **Personal:** Born Aug 15, 1940, Bossier City, LA; married Rose M Carter; children: Rachel & Percy. **Educ:** Southern Univ, BS, 1961; Meharry Med Col, DDS, 1965, MD, 1980. **Career:** 1967-70; State Univ NY, Buffalo, Dept Oral Path, asst prof oral path, 1971-74; Univ Miss Med Ctr, Dept Path, assoc prof, 1982, dir minority stud affairs, 1982; Surg Path & Cytopathology fel, 1982-85; Meharry Med Col, assoc prof path, 1974-82, assoc prof & chmn oral path, 1981-82, Grad Med Col, assoc dean, prof & dept chair, 1982-2009, interim dean & vpres health affairs, 2009; Am Soc Clin Pathologists fel, 1986-; Univ Tex Med Br, assoc vpres stud affairs & assoc dean stud affairs & med sch admis; Col Am Pathologists fel, 1986-; Am Acad Oral Path fel; Vanderbilt Univ Med Ctr, Dept Path, Microbiol & Immunol, prof, currently. **Orgs:** Lay reader & vestry St Philips Episcopal Church; Nat Asn Advan Colored People; Urban League, Am Acad Oral Path, Am Asn Dent Schs; Am Asn Med Col; Am Dent Soc; Ama; Am Soc Clin Pathologists; Am Soc Cytol; Cent Miss Med Soc; Int Acad Path; Int Asn Dent Res, Miss Med & Surg Asn; bd dir, Miss Div Am Cancer Soc; Am Bd Oral Path; Am Bd Path; fel Nat Insts Health; fel Nat Cancer Inst; Alpha Omega Alpha Hon Med Soc; Omicron Kappa Upsilon Hon Dent Soc. **Honors/Awds:** Humanism Medicine Award, 2004; Bd Cert, Am Bd Dent; Harris L Kempner Award; Martin Luther King Award, Univ Tex Med Br; Distinguished Service Award, Tex Asn Advisors Health Professions; Alumni Achievement Award, Meharry Med Col. **Special Achievements:** First African American Board Certified Oral Pathologist. **Home Addr:** 120 Waycross Ct, Jackson, MS 39206. **Business Addr:** Professor, Vanderbilt University Medical Center, 1211 Med Ctr Dr, Nashville, TN 37232, **Business Phone:** (615)322-5000.

## BALLARD, DR. BRUCE LAINE

Physician, psychiatrist. **Personal:** Born Dec 19, 1939, Waverly Hills, KY; married Eleanor Glynn Cross; children: Tracy & Timothy. **Educ:** Yale Univ, BA, 1960; Columbia Univ, Col Physicians & Surgeons, MD, 1964. **Career:** Michael Reese Hosp, internship, 1964-65; Ny Psychiat Inst, resident; Harlem Hosp Ctr, Dept Psychiat, assoc dir training, 1970-76; NY Hosp-Westchester Div, assoc dir, adult out patient dept, 1976-81, coordr residency prog; Travelers Summer Res Fel Prog, 1981-; Weill Med Col, Cornell Univ, assoc dean stud affairs & equal opport progs, 1981-, assoc prof clin psychiat, 2001. **Orgs:** Chmn, selection & adv comn, APA-Nat Inst Ment Health fel prog, Am Psychiat Asn, 1974-80, fel, 1976; chmn, comn black psychiatrists, 1982-86; Am Psychiat Asn Assembly Rep, 1994-02; chair, Group Stud Affairs, Asn Am Med Cols, 1992-93; fel NY Acad Med; bd mem, NY Community Trust. **Honors/Awds:** Alumni Fel, Weill Med Col, 2001; Nancy C A Roeske MD Award, Am Psychiat Asn, 2001; Distinguished Life Fel, Am Psychiat Asn, 2003; Pioneers In Diversity Award, Excellence in Mentorship, Off Fac Diversity, 2011. **Home Addr:** 191 Sprain Rd, Scarsdale, NY 10583, **Home Phone:** (914)693-1097. **Business Addr:** Associate Dean for Student Affairs & Equal Opportunity Programs, Associate Professor of Clinical Psychiatry, Weill Medical College Cornell University, 445 E 69th St Rm 110, New York, NY 10021, **Business Phone:** (212)746-1057.

## BALLARD, GREGORY (GREG BALLARD)

Basketball player, basketball coach. **Personal:** Born Jan 29, 1955, Los Angeles, CA; married Donna; children: Lawrence, Gabrielle & Gregory Jr. **Educ:** Univ Ore, BA, social work & polit sci, 1977. **Career:** Basketball player (retired), basketball coach; Wash Bullets, prof basketball player, 1977-85; Golden State Warriors, 1985-87; VL Pesaro, 1987-88; Il Messagero Roma, asst coach, 1989-90; Continental Basketball Asn; Seattle Supersonics, 1989; Libertas Forli, Italy, 1989; Burghy Roma, Ital League, asst scout; Dallas Mavericks, asst coach; Minn Timberwolves, asst coach, 1994-2003; MikeWoodson, 2004-05; Atlanta Hawks, asst coach & advan scout, 2003-. **Business Addr:** Assistant Coach, Atlanta Hawks, Centennial Tower, Atlanta, GA 30303, **Business Phone:** (866)715-1500.

## BALLARD, DR. HAROLD STANLEY

Hematologist, college teacher. **Personal:** Born Nov 25, 1927, New Orleans, LA; son of Dan and Lillie; married Gail; children: Harold Jr & Kevin. **Educ:** Univ Calif, AB, 1948; Meharry Med Col, Sch Med, Nashville, TN, MD, 1952. **Career:** Brooklyn Hosp Ctr, resident; Queens Hosp Ctr, internship; Vet Affairs Med Ctr, resident; Natl Heart Lung & Blood Inst, consult; New York Va Hosp, asst chief, physician; NY Univ Col, clin prof med, currently; Columbia Univ, Dept Clin Med, Div Hemat & Oncol, prof, 1979-. **Orgs:** NIH Coun Thrombosis; Am Heart Asn; Am Brd Int Med; chmn policy brd, Hemat Oncol Natural Hist Study Sickle Cell Anemia; Cent Tex Med Found. **Home Addr:** 423 E 23rd St, New York, NY 10010, **Home Phone:** (212)951-3484. **Business Addr:** Professor of Clinical Medicine, Columbia University, 350 1st Ave Apt 7F, New York, NY 10010, **Business Phone:** (212)951-3484.

## BALLARD, DR. JAMES M., JR.

Psychologist. **Personal:** Born May 19, 1938, Petersburg, VA; married Natalie Dandridge; children: Tresa Melinda & James III. **Educ:** Va State Col, BS, 1963, MS, 1964; Ind Univ; George Wash Univ; Univ Minn, PhD, soc psychol, 1971. **Career:** Mid-Level Community Clin Psychol Prog, dir; Howard Univ, assoc prof; Univ Man, assoc prof; Bowie State Col, Inst Res & Eval, first dir; Crownsville State Hosp, staff psychol; Behav & Soc Systs Inc, founder & pres; pvt pract psychiatrist, 1975-. **Orgs:** SE Psychol Asn; Am Educ Res Asn; Asn Black Psychologists; pres, Eta Lambda Chap Alpha Phi Alpha Frat; Psi Chi Psychol Hon Soc, 1964; HeroesFight, 2008. **Honors/Awds:** Cited for Service, Inspiration & Support, Nat Asn Advan Colored People; Certificate of Appreciation, 1974. **Home Addr:** 2839 Piscataway Run Dr, Odenton, MD 21113-4019. **Business Addr:** Psychiatrist, Private Practice, 102 Green Valley Rd, Arnold, MD 21012, **Business Phone:** (410)647-3147.

## BALLARD, MYRTLE ETHEL (MYRTLE G BALLARD)

Government official. **Personal:** Born Apr 20, 1930, Shreveport, LA; daughter of Henry Jr and Roxanna Turner Gammage; married Thomas A; children: Thomas A Jr, Roxane R Johnigan, Michael S & Alexandria Alicia. **Educ:** St Mary's Col, Moraga, CA, BA, pub mgt, 1978. **Career:** Government official (retired); Calif State Employ Develop, Oakland, Calif, off mgr, 1967-2003; Northern Alameda County, Workforce Investment Bd, mandated partner. **Orgs:** Secy, Int Asn Personnel Security, 1971-73; secy, Black Personnel Mgt Asn, 1972-75; pres, Calif State Employees Asn, 1973-75; secy, Money works; bd mem, Calif Coun C & Youth, 1973-75; bd mem, Lincoln Child Ctr, 1975-; bd chairperson, Sickle Cell Anemia Res & Educ, 1982-84; regional dir, Zeta Phi Beta Sorority, 1986-92; loan exec, United Way, 1988; bd mem, Lincoln Child Ctr, 1990-, chair, regional exec bd, 1992-96; bd mem, Bayarea consortium Qual Health Care; Staff Pastor, Parish comt Taylor; United Methodist Church, 2003-; regional bd mem, Panhellenic coun; chair, Nat Trustee Bd; Zeta Capital Campaign. **Home Addr:** 2239 Dexter Way, Hayward, CA 94541-4441, **Home Phone:** (510)538-0584.

## BALLARD, SHAREESE RENEE

Singer. **Personal:** Born Jan 1, 1978, Philadelphia, PA. **Educ:** Temple Univ, Philadelphia. **Career:** Album: How I Do, 2001; Singles: "Golden Boys", 2001; "Ice King", 2001; "They Say Vision", 2002; "Sittin' Back", 2002; "There's No Way", 2007; "Black Girls Rock!", 2009; "Party Robot", 2009; "Habit of the Heart", 2011; "A Box of Chocolates", 2011; "ReFried Mac Ep", 2013. **Business Addr:** Recording Artist, c/o MCA, 100 Universal City Plz, Universal City, CA 91608.

## BALLENTINE, KRIM MENELIK

Military leader, politician. **Personal:** Born Oct 22, 1936, St. Louis, MO; son of Habib Dickey and Rose Mae Grimes; married Rosalie Erica Simmonds; children: Taraka T & Jabriel S. **Educ:** Wayne State Univ, BS, criminal justice, 1980; Univ Va, Quantico Continuing Educ Prog, cert, 1980; Univ VI, MA, educ coun, 1999. **Career:** Mil leader (retired), politician; Pinkerton Nat Detective Agency, spec investr, 1958-60; St Louis Airport Police, patrolman, 1960-66; US Marshals Serv, chief dep, 1966-95; 902d AUs Res. MI Intell Agt, chief warrant officer three, 1979-96; St Thomas-St John Crime Comn, exec dir, 1984-85; ICOP Invests, exec officer, 1984-; Minority Bus Develop Ctr, bus counr, 1987-88; CBS Affil, talk show radio host, 1987-88; Univ VI, teacher, 1996; VI Police Dept, asst comnr, 2007-08; Repub Party, Wash, DC, politician, currently; Radio Talk Show Host, 'Ulama-'One who knows', 2013-. **Orgs:** Charter mem, Nat Orgn Black Law-Enforcement Exec; Int Asn Chiefs Police; Mo Peace Officers Asn; FBI Acad Asn; Rotary Int; life mem, Disabled Am Veterans; Int Platform Asn; Int Asn Law Enforcement Intelligence Analysts; Northeast Regional Boy Scout Comt; VI Republican Territorial Comt; chmn, Gov Comn Crime & Violence, Criminal Justice Inst; hon mem, Mark Twain Soc. **Home Addr:** PO Box 305396, St. Thomas00803, **Home Phone:** (803)776-0581. **Business Addr:** Politician, Republican Party, 310 1st St SE, Washington, DC 20003.

## BALTHROPE, DR. JACQUELINE MOREHEAD

Educator. **Personal:** Born Philadelphia, PA; married Robert G Sr; children: Robert G Jr, Yvonne G & Robin B. **Educ:** Cent State Univ, BS, 1949; Case Western Res Univ, MA, 1959; John Carroll Univ, hon PhD; Bowling Green State Univ, hon PhD; Cleveland State Univ, hon PhD. **Career:** Principal(retired), writer, columnist: Cleveland Call Post, free-lance writer & columnist; Chicago Defender, freelance writer & columnist; Pittsburgh Courier Afro-Am, free-lance writer & columnist, 1960-69; Cleveland Pub Sch Syst, teacher & supvr stud teachers; Cleveland Bd Educ, Oliver Hazard Perry Elem Sch, prin; Consult, educ. **Orgs:** Hon mem, Entre Nous Club; officer, Royal Hearts Bridge Club; Pair Ables Vol Homes Aged & Juv; active mem

& off, Alpha Kappa Alpha Soc, 1946-; Nat SorPhi Delta Kappa, 1960; Delta Kappa Gamma Soc, 1972; Eta Phi Beta Soc, 1972; Nat Coun Negro Women; Cleveland Chap CaratsInc; Cleveland Squaws; Jr League; local, state, nat Elem Sch Prin; active church worker, St John AME Ch; vol Heart, Cancer, March Dimes; UNICEF; Ment Health; United Negro Col Fund; Girl Scouts Campaigns; Retarded Child; active mem & off, League Women Voters; Nat Asn Advan Colored People; YWCA; Phillis Wheatley Asn; Forest Hosp; Urban League & Guild; Phi Delta Kappa Nat Frat; organizer, Top Ladies Distinction; Chums Inc; Proj Friendship; Pi Lambda Omega; Am Assoc Univ Women. **Home Addr:** PO Box 938, Ashland, AL 36251-0938.

**BALTIMORE, CHARLI (TIFFANY LANE)**
Rap musician. **Personal:** Born Aug 16, 1974, Philadelphia, PA; children: India & Sianni. **Educ:** Pierce Col, fine arts. **Career:** Singles: "Money", 1998; "Feel It", 1998; "Stand Up", 1999; "Horse and Carriage (Remix)", 1999; "Everybody Wanna Know", 2000; "Diary", 2002; "Hey Charli", 2002; "Nobody Does It Better", 2002; "Lose It", 2008; "P.S.", 2008; "Come Test Us", 2010; "Machine Gun (Remix)", 2011; "All Lies", 2012; "Philly Stand Up", 2012; "B.M.B", 2013; "Hunnids", 2014. Albums: Cold As Ice, 1999; : The Diary (You Think You Know), 2003; TBA: True Lies. Albums appearances: "Me & My Boo", 1998; "Walk On By", 1998; "Blak is Blak", 2000; "Last Temptation", 2002; "No One Does It Better", 2002; "We Still Don't Give a Fuck", 2002; "I Am", 2007; Featured Singles: "Horse & Carriage", 1998; "Down 4 U", 2002; "Spending Time", 2002; "Down Ass Bitch", 2002; "Rain on Me (Remix)", 2003; "Portrait of Love (Remix)", 2008. Films: Bamboozled, 2000; Snipes, 2001; Crime Partners, 2003; Gang of Roses 2: Next Generation, 2012; Changing the Game, 2012. **Honors/Awds:** Grammy Award nominee, Best Female Rap Solo Performance, 2002.

**BALTIMORE, AMBASSADOR RICHARD LEWIS, III**
Executive, consultant, ambassador. **Personal:** Born Dec 31, 1947, New York, NY; son of Richard Lewis Jr and Lois Madison; married Eszter Anna; children: Krisztina, Josephine, Natalie & Vanessa. **Educ:** MacMurray Col, ND, int affairs, 1967; George Washington Univ, BA, int polit & econs, 1969; Harvard Law Sch, JD, law, 1972. **Career:** Ambassador (retired), executive; US Dept State, ambassador foreign serv officer, 1972-2005; US Embassy Lisbon, Port, polit & econ officer, 1973-75; US Embassy, Pretoria, S Africa, polit officer, 1976-79; Dept State, spec asst to state secy, 1979-81; US Embassy Cairo, Egypt, polit officer, 1981-83; US Embassy, Budapest, Hungary, polit chief, 1984-87, dep chief mission, 1990-94; Bur Near E & S Asian Affairs, dep dir, Off Reg Affairs, 1987-88, dir, 1988-90; U.S. Embassy Budapest, Hungary, dep chief mission, 1990-94; Europ Can affairs, sr polit adv asst sec, 1994-95; Sr Sem, class pres, 1995-96; US Embassy, San Jose, Costa Rica, dep chief mission, 1996-99; US Consulate Gen, Jeddah, Saudi Arabia, coun gen, 1999-2002; Sultanate Oman, ambassador, 2002-06; US Embassy, Kabul, Afghanistan, counr rule law, 2006; Int Consult Blue City, Oman, 2007-; SASLO Law Off, consult, sr mgr, 2008-11; SASLO Legal Trng Ctr, prin, 2009-11; Oman Tourism Develop Co, adv to bd dir, 2011-. **Orgs:** bd dirs, Omran. **Honors/Awds:** Salgo Award, Polit Reporting, 1986; Group Honor Award, 1997; Meritorious Honor Award for Rule of Law performance in Afghanistan, 2006. **Special Achievements:** First Black Political Officer to serve in apartheid South Africa. **Home Addr:** PO Box 1492, Al AzaibaPC 130, **Home Phone:** (968)9544-400. **Business Addr:** Adviser, Oman Tourism Development Co, PO Box 991, Al AzaibaPC 130, **Business Phone:** (968)2439-120.

**BALTIMORE, ROSLYN LOIS**
Executive, real estate developer. **Personal:** daughter of Richard Jr and Lois; married John Ervin; children: Richard. **Educ:** Boston Univ, AB, 1964; Harvard Grad Sch Educ, EdM, 1970; Harvard Bus Sch, MBA, 1972. **Career:** Paul Sack Prop, asst develop, 1972-73; Wells Fargo Bank, asst vpres, 1973-77; RL Baltimore Co, pres, 1977-; San Francisco Planning Comn; Baltimore Mortgage Co Inc, owner & pres, 1989-; Crescendo LLC, real estate developer, 2005-. **Orgs:** Bd mem, Reality House W, 1978-; dir, Bay Area Rapid Transit; Access Appeals Bd, 1983-; pres, Handicapped Access Appeals Bd, 1985; hon mem, Sigma Gamma Rho, 1986; SF Planning Comn, 2000. **Honors/Awds:** Business Woman of the Year, Savvy Mag, 1984; proclamation, Mayor San Francisco, 1985; Key to the City, Evansville, Ind, 1985. **Home Phone:** (415)242-5702. **Business Addr:** President, RL Baltimore Mortgage Co Inc, PO Box 193422, San Francisco, CA 94119-3422, **Business Phone:** (415)242-7888.

**BALTON, DR. JUANITA J.**
Educator. **Personal:** Born Oct 28, 1933?; married Kirkwood R (deceased); children: Adriene Y Balton Topping (W Frank). **Educ:** EdD. **Career:** Educator (retired). **Orgs:** Women's Fund Greater Birmingham; hon mem, Alys Robinson Stephens Performing Arts Ctr. **Home Addr:** 408 10th Ct W, Birmingham, AL 35204, **Home Phone:** (205)252-3908. **Business Addr:** Honorary Member, Alys Robinson Stephens Performing Arts Center, 1200 10th Ave S, Birmingham, AL 35294, **Business Phone:** (205)975-9540.

**BAMBAATAA, AFRIKA (KEVIN DONOVAN)**
Disc jockey, music producer. **Personal:** Born Apr 10, 1960, South Bronx, NY. **Career:** Bronx River Proj, leader; Albums: Death Mix, 1983; Sun City, 1985; Planet Rock: The Album, 1986; Beware, 1986; Death Mix Throwdown, 1987; Return to Planet Rock, 1999; Hydraulic Funk, 2000; Theme Of The United Nations w DJ Yutaka, 2000; Electro Funk Breakdown, 2001; Looking for the Perfect Beat: 1980-85, 2001; Lovage: Music To Make Love To Your Old Lady By, 2001; Dark Matter Moving at the Speed of Light, 2004; Metal, 2005; Metal Remixes, 2005; Death Mix 2, 2006; Discography: Unity, Tommy Boy, 1984; Shango Funk Theology, Celluloid, 1984; Planet Rock, Tommy Boy, 1986; Beware Tommy Boy, 1987; The Light, CapitolEMI, 1988; Decade of Darkness: 1990-2000, EMI, 1991; Thy Will B Funk!, Planet Rock Music, 1992; Jazzin by Khayan, ZYX, 1996; Lost Generation, Hot, 1996; Zulu Groove, Hudson Vandam, 1997; Electro Funk Breakdown, DMC, 1999; Hydraulic Funk, Strictly Hype, 2000; Electro Funk Breakdown 2001, DMC, 2001; Vanilla Sky Warner Bros, 2001. **Honors/Awds:** The Source Hip Hop Music Award; Pioneer Award, 1999. **Business Addr:** Producer, Profile Records, 740 Broadway 7th Fl, New York, NY 10003.

**BANDELE, ASHA**
Writer. **Personal:** Born Jan 1, 1970; married Rashid; children: Nisa. **Educ:** City Univ, New Sch Social Res, NY, BA; Bennington Col, MFA. **Career:** Essence mag, writer, 2000-04, ed, currently; Columbia Univ, Revson fel, 2004-; author: Absence in the Palms of My Hands (poetry), 1996; Absence in the Palms of My Hands, 1996; The Prisoner's Wife: A Memoir, 2000; Daughter, 2003; Brown Sugar 4, 2005: Secret Desires, 2005; The Subtle Art of Breathing, 2005; Something Like Beautiful, 2009. **Orgs:** Dep dir, Pub Policy Drug Policy Alliance; fel Columbia Univ. **Business Addr:** Writer, c/o Charles Scribners Sons, 300 Pk Ave S 9th Fl, New York, NY 10010.

**BANDELE, DR. SAFIYA**
College administrator. **Career:** Medgar Evers Col, City Univ New York, Ctr Women's Develop, dir, 2011. **Home Addr:** 396 Stuyvesant Ave, Brooklyn, NY 11233, **Home Phone:** (718)756-5827. **Business Addr:** Director, Medgar Evers College-City University of New York, 1650 Bedford Ave Bedford Campus Rm 1032P, Brooklyn, NY 11225-2010, **Business Phone:** (718)270-5155.

**BANFIELD, ANNE L.** **See Obituaries Section.**

**BANFIELD, DR. EDISON H.**
Surgeon. **Personal:** Born Jun 25, 1924, Baltimore, MD; married Julia; children: Ava, Yvonne, Stephen & Edison Jr. **Educ:** Howard Univ, BS, chem, 1950, MD, 1954. **Career:** Physician (retired); Freedman's Hosp, resident; DC Gen Hosp, surgeon; St Joseph's Hosp, staff; Citizens Gen Hosp, staff; Riverside Gen Hosp, staff; St Elizabeth's Hosp, staff; Baylor Col Med, instr surg; pvt pract physician & surgeon; Methodist Hosp, staff; Ben Taub Hosp, staff. **Orgs:** Fel Am Col Surgeons, 1963. **Home Addr:** 7467 Brompton St, Houston, TX 77025-2263, **Home Phone:** (713)664-6204. **Business Addr:** TX.

**BANKETT, WILLIAM DANIEL**
Government official. **Personal:** Born Dec 8, 1930, Oak Grove, VA; son of William and Edna Weeden; married Evelyn Robinson; children: Wendell & Kevin. **Educ:** W Va State Col, Inst WVa, BS, 1954; George Washington Univ, Wash, DC, 1958; Hampton Inst, Hampton, VA, 1961; Mass Inst Technol, Boston, MA, cert urban exec, 1972. **Career:** Nat Security Agency, Wash, DC, 1954-55; Dept Agr, Minneapolis, MN, exam, 1955-57; W moreland Co Sch, Oak Grove VA, prin, 1957-62; Prince William Co Schs, Manassas, VA, prin, 1962-67; Southeast House, Wash, DC, exec dir, 1967-68; Southwest Community House, Wash, DC, exec dir, 1968-70; Redevelop Land Agency, H St area dir; Dept Housing & Community Develop, spec asst, H St area dir, 1970-; Dan Man Mustangs Inc, chief exec officer, 1973-. **Orgs:** Vpres, Elem Prins Asn, 1960-65; Mayor's Econ Task Force, 1970-78; VOICE, 1970-79; Anacostia Econ Develop Corp, 1970-80; Marlton Swim Asn, 1972-; Mustang Club Am, 1980-; Dept Housing & Community Develop Asn, 1985-; vpres, Johnson Alumni Asn 1986-. **Home Addr:** 12119 Old Colony Dr, Upper Marlboro, MD 20772-5047, **Home Phone:** (301)627-2940.

**BANKHEAD, PATRICIA ANN**
Educator. **Personal:** Born Dec 30, 1947, Los Angeles, CA; married Lynn Burton. **Educ:** Calif State Univ, Los Angeles, BS, sociol, 1972; Pepperdine Univ, MS, sch mgt, 1976; San Jose State Univ, cert aerospace educ, 1983. **Career:** Los Angeles Unified Sch Dist, elem teacher, 1973-76; Calif Lutheran Col, lectr, 1977; Los Angeles Southwest Col, instr, 1977-80; Los Angeles Unified Sch Dist, prog coordr, 1977-80; State Calif, mentor & teacher, 1984-87; Alta Loma Elem, teacher, 2004-06. **Orgs:** Sponsor Black Women's Forum, Los Angeles, 1980-87; adv bd, United NegroCol Fund, 1981-87; off hostess, City Los Angeles, 1983-87; Nat Asn Advan Colored People, 1984-87; Mentor Adv Bd, LA Unified Schs, 1984-87; Calif Aerospace Asn, 1985-87; Delta Kappa Gamma Int, 1987; Nat Coun NegroWomen, 1987; mayor, City Inglewood, Human Affairs Comn, 2003-06. **Home Addr:** 3771 Olmsted Ave, Los Angeles, CA 90018. **Business Addr:** Mentor Teacher, Los Angeles Unified School District, 1745 Vineyard Ave, Los Angeles, CA 90019, **Business Phone:** (213)939-2113.

**BANKS, ALICIA**
Columnist, executive, radio producer. **Personal:** Born Aug 10, 1963, Chicago, IL. **Educ:** Univ Ill, Urbana-Champaign, BA, speech commun pre-law, 1984; Univ Ark, Little Rock, MA, interpersonal & orgn & commun, 2001. **Career:** WUHS Radio, gen mgr, announcer, newscaster, 1979-80; WPGU Radio, vocal prod talent, copy writer, 1980-82; WBML Radio, founder, gen mgr, prog dir, host, producer, dj, sales agt, 1982-84; WRFG Radio, producer, host, dj, engr, non-profit fund raiser, subscription sales, 1989-96; WIGO Radio, producer, talk show host, copywriter, vocal prod talent, sales agt, 1993-95; Friends Mag, columnist, 1994-96; Eloquent Fury Website, webmaster, columnist, 1994-; WGST Radio, talk show host, 1995-96; Hues Mag, columnist, 1996; KPFA/KPFB/KFCF Radio, producer, host, engr, 1996-98; KABF Radio, producer, currently. **Home Addr:** PO Box 55622, Little Rock, AR 72215, **Home Phone:** (501)580-3211. **Business Addr:** Producer, KABF, 2101 S Main St Suite 200, Little Rock, AR 72206, **Business Phone:** (501)372-6119.

**BANKS, ANDREW J.**
President (organization). **Educ:** Cleveland State Univ, BA, econ; Baldwin Wallace Col, MBA, bus admin. **Career:** Mgt consult div Deloitte & Touche, mgr, 1986; LTV Steel, bus systs analyst; Caterpillar Tractor Co, planner; Mid-Am Consult Group Inc, founder, chmn, pres & chief exec officer, currently. **Orgs:** Trustee, Kent State Univ. **Business Addr:** President & Chief Executive Officer, Founder & Chairman, Mid-America Consult Group Inc, 25800 Sci Pk Dr Suite 225, Beachwood, OH 44122, **Business Phone:** (216)292-2800.

**BANKS, ANTHONY LAMAR.** **See BANKS, TONY.**

**BANKS, BEATRICE**
Executive. **Personal:** Born Jul 24, 1936, Uniontown, AL; daughter of Robert. **Educ:** Wayne State Univ, BS, 1963. **Career:** Detroit Bd Educ, teacher; Residential & consumer Serv, adv, 1963-71, asst supvr, 1971-72; Detroit Wayne Div Customer Mkt Serv, asst mgr, 1972-74, mgr, 1974-75, dir mkt serv, 1975-79; Detroit Edison Co, Customer & Mkt Serv, Macomb Div, dir, 1979-84, asst mgr, 1980-. **Orgs:** Women's Econ Club; Eng Soc Detroit; Greater Detrioit C C; Proj Pride Bd; Corp Urban Forum; bd dir, Don Bosco Home Boys; chairperson, Mich Civil Rights Comn, 1983; Dearborn & Greater Detroit Chambers Com; exec comt, Nat Asn Advan Colored People; Booker T. Wash Bus Asn; Am Asn Blacks Energy; adv bd, Horizon Upward Bound; adv bd, Black Family Develop. **Honors/Awds:** Headliner Award, Women Wayne State Univ, 1976; YMCA Minority Achievement Award, 1982. **Home Addr:** 6981 Indian Creek Dr, West Bloomfield, MI 48322-3118, **Home Phone:** (248)788-0852. **Business Addr:** Assistant Manager, Director, Detroit Edison Co, 2000 2nd Ave, Detroit, MI 48221, **Business Phone:** (313)235-4000.

**BANKS, CARL E.**
Football player, broadcaster. **Personal:** Born Aug 29, 1962, Flint, MI. **Educ:** Mich State Univ, attended 1984. **Career:** Football player (retired), broadcaster; New York Giants, linebacker & left outside linebacker, 1984-92, radio broadcast analyst, 2007-; Wash Redskins, left linebacker, 1993; Cleveland Browns, left linebacker, 1994-95; New York Jets, dir player develop, 1993-97; Banks Commun, chmn; GIII Apparel Group, pres sports lic; Sirius NFL Radio, host, currently; WFAN, host, 2005; WNBC, color analyst; FOX5, co-host. **Orgs:** Arena Football League's Nj Red Dogs. **Honors/Awds:** NFC Championship Game, 1986; Pro Bowl, 1987. **Business Addr:** Radio Broadcast Analyst, New York Giants, Giants Stadium, East Rutherford, NJ 07073, **Business Phone:** (201)935-8111.

**BANKS, CARLTON LUTHER**
Accountant. **Personal:** Born Apr 9, 1958, Bronx, NY; married Creecy Seymore; children: Regina & Attallah. **Educ:** Morgan State Univ, BA, polit sci, 1980; NY Univ, dipl direct mkt, 1986; Columbia Univ, Grad Sch Archit Planning & Preserv, MS, real estate develop, 1996. **Career:** TroCar Realty Inc, vpres, 1981-85; Greek Gallery, pres; NY Life Ins Co, regist financial adv, 1988-; Talented Tenth Invests Inc, pres, chief exec officer, prin, currently; Global Financial Network, cert sr advisor, 2009-10, prin, 2006-. **Orgs:** Omega Psi Phi Fraternity, 1977; Direct Mkt Club, NY, 1986; Nat Asn Advan Colored People, 1987; Keeper fin, 1987. **Business Addr:** Principal, Global Financial Network, 274 Malcolm X Blvd, New York, NY 10027, **Business Phone:** (866)963-0427.

**BANKS, CAROLINE LONG**
City council member, executive, association executive. **Personal:** Born Oct 30, 1940, McDonough, GA; daughter of Ralph A and Rubye Carolyn Hall; children: April Lynn & James H Jr. **Educ:** Clark Col, Atlanta GA, BA, 1962; Univ HI, 1963; Ga State Univ, MA, 1973. **Career:** HI Bd Educ, eng teacher, 1963-64; Atlanta Bd Educ, eng teacher, 1967-69; Rich's Depart Store, Corp Credit Servs, from mgt trainee to mgr, 1973-89; Atlanta City Coun, 1980-97, pub safety comn, finance comn, chair, 1992, comn coun, exec & community develop comns, city councilwoman, currently; Minority Training & Assistance Partnerships Inc, chief exec officer, 1990-. **Orgs:** Atlanta League Women Voters, 1980-; bd dir, Black Women's Coalition, 1980-; Ga Coalition Black Women, 1980-; Nat League Cities, 1980-, bd dir, 1981-, adv coun, 1990-; Delta Sigma Theta Sorority Inc, Golden Life mem, 1980-; Nat Black Caucus Local Elected Off, 1981-, bd dir, 1981-, pres, 1992; Ga Munic Asn, 1980-, bd dir, 1990-92, domestic violence task force, 1990-92; Nat Forum Black Pub Adminrs, 1983-; Nat Purchasing Coun; Atlanta Regional Minority Purchasing Coun; Atlanta Chamber Com; panelist, Nat Cong Black Women, 1989; Leadership Atlanta Alumni Asn; Atlanta Bus League; life mem, Nat Asn Advan Colored People; St. Paul Cross Cath Church. **Honors/Awds:** Bronze Woman of the Year, Iota Phi Lambda, 1980; Cummings Forsyth Optimist Club & Forsyth Co Sch Syst, 1987; Outstanding Community Awards, Human Econ Love Plan Atlanta Jamaican Asn, Gamma Theta Chap, 1987; Outstanding Contribution, Port-of-Spain People-to-People Exchange, 1987; Outstanding Achievement Award, Clark Col, 1988. **Special Achievements:** First African American woman appointed to Atlanta City Council, 1980; Democratic Nat Part Conv delegate, 1984; panelist, Atlanta Historical Soc Educ Series: 150 Years of Key Civil Rights Decisions, 1990; First African American woman to serve on the citys Board of Aldermen; First African American fashion buyer for Richs department store. **Home Addr:** 1275 Fair St SW, Atlanta, GA 30314, **Home Phone:** (404)758-4482. **Business Addr:** City Councilwoman, Atlanta City Council, 55 Trinity Ave SW Suite 2900, Atlanta, GA 30303, **Business Phone:** (404)330-6030.

**BANKS, CECIL JAMES**
Lawyer, business owner. **Personal:** Born Sep 27, 1947, Des Moines, IA; married Margot H; children: Kimberly, Imani & Jamaal. **Educ:** Sophia Univ, Tokyo, Japan; Duquesene Univ, BA, 1970; Univ Pittsburgh, MPA, 1974; Rutgers Univ Sch Law, JD, 1976. **Career:** Mc Carter & Enguisir Esq, assoc, 1976; Newark Bd Educ, gen coun, 1978-82; City Orange, legis coun, 1980-84, city atty, 1984; Leaguers Inc, asst treas, 1986; Sills Beck Cummis, Zuckerman Radin Tischman & Epstein, partner; City Orange, atty, currently; Banks Erlanger A Prof Corp, partner, currently. **Orgs:** Legis coun, Orange City Coun, 1980-84; active dem fund raiser, 1996; bd dir, Essex Legal Serv Inc; bd trustee, bd dir, United Commun Corp; chmn & founder, Young Lawyer's Com Essex Co Bar Asn; bd dir, Nat Asn Advan Colored People Nat Bar Asn, Am Bar Asn & Nat Asn Bond Lawyers; bd mem, Nat Asn Sch Law Attorneys; bd dir, Community Coop Develop Found, Bridgeport, Conn; pres, Advice & Consent US Senate; bd dir, African Develop Found; bd dir, United Hosps Found; Essex County; Am & Nat Bar Associations; Nat Asn Munic Bond Lawyers. **Honors/Awds:** Service Award, United Commun Corp; Service Award, United Clergy Oranges. **Home Addr:** 238 Elmwynd Dr, Orange, NJ 07050, **Home Phone:** (973)672-4424. **Business Addr:** Partner, Banks Erlanger A Professional Corp, 1 Gateway Ctr, Newark, NJ 07102-5311, **Business Phone:** (973)648-0800.

**BANKS, CERRI ANNETTE**
College teacher, college administrator. **Educ:** Monroe Community Col, AA; Syracuse Univ, BA, 1997, MS, PhD, 2006. **Career:** Syracuse Univ, grad instr & adj prof, 2001-07; William Smith Col, asst prof, 2005-10, interim dean, dir Pres's Comn Inclusive Excellence & dean, 2008-10; Mt Holyoke Col, vpres stud affairs & dean col, 2011-16; Skidmore Col, vpres stud affairs & dean students, 2016-. **Honors/Awds:** Monroe Community College Hall of Fame, inductee. **Special Achievements:** Author, Black Women Undergraduates, Culture Capital, and College Success, 2009; Intersectional Pedagogy and Transformative Learning, 2012. **Business Addr:** Office of the Dean of Students and Vice President for Student Affairs, 311 Case Ctr, Saratoga Springs, NY 12866, **Business Phone:** (518)580-5760.

**BANKS, CHARLIE**
Chief executive officer, business owner. **Personal:** Born Aug 11, 1931, Little Rock, AR; son of George and Lela Ervin Williams; married Mary Caster Catherine; children: Charles, Lamarr & Daphne. **Educ:** Chicago Tech Col, BSEE, Chicago, IL, 1955; Western State Univ, Law, Fullerton, CA, 1975. **Career:** Rockwell Int, Downey, Calif, engineering, logistics, 1960-75; Rockwell Int, Pittsburgh, Pa, purchasing mgr, 1975-79; Gould Inc, Rolling Meadows, Ill, purch dir, 1979-83; Mitchell S Watkins Assoc, Chicago, Ill, vpres, 1981-83; City Chicago, Chicago, Ill, first dep PA, 1983-85; Prod Dynamics Chicago Inc, Ill, pres & secy, 1985-, chief exec officer & owner, currently. **Orgs:** Omega Psi Phi, 1959-; Am Mgt Asn, 1960-75; Purch Mgt Asn, 1975-79. **Business Addr:** President, Chief Executive Officer, Owner, Production Dynamics of Chicago Inc, 455 W N Ave, Chicago, IL 60610, **Business Phone:** (312)440-0800.

**BANKS, DWAYNE MARTIN**
Educator. **Personal:** Born Apr 7, 1961, Newport News, VA. **Educ:** Norfolk State Univ, BS, 1985; Old Dom Univ, MEd, 1992. **Career:** NEA, Crittenden Mid Sch, technol teacher, currently. **Orgs:** Bd mem, SCA, 1986-87; PTA, 1986-87; Alpha Phi Alpha Fraternity Inc. **Home Addr:** 604 S Ave, Newport News, VA 23601. **Business Addr:** Technology Teacher, Crittenden Middle School, Rm 300 6158 Jefferson Ave, Newport News, VA 23605, **Business Phone:** (757)591-4900.

**BANKS, ELLEN**
Painter (artist). **Personal:** Born Jan 1, 1938, Boston, MA. **Educ:** Mass Col Art, BA; Sch Mus, fine arts. **Career:** Dunbarton Galleries, painter & exhibs, 1962; Boston Mus Fine Arts, 1970; Smith-Mason Gallery, 1971; Sch Mus Fine Arts, Boston, MA, instr, 1974-96. **Orgs:** Nat Ctr Afro-Am Artists. **Honors/Awds:** Prix De Paris, 1967; Blanche E Coleman Award, 1972. **Home Addr:** 4260 58th St, San Diego, CA 92115-6126, **Home Phone:** (619)287-7746.

**BANKS, EUGENE LAVON.** **See BANKS, GENE.**

**BANKS, FRED L., JR.**
Judge, businessperson. **Personal:** Born Sep 1, 1942, Jackson, MS; son of Violet Mabery and Fred L; married Pamela Gipson; children: Rachel, Jonathan & Gabrielle. **Educ:** Howard Univ, BA, acct, 1965, Sch Law, JD, 1968. **Career:** Nichols Attys & Pred, partner, 1968-84; Town Fayetten, atty, 1970-75; Miss Col Sch Law, adj prof law; Miss House Rep, Judiciary Comt, 1976-84; Banks Owens & Byrd Attys, 1985; Circuit Ct Dist Miss, circuit judge, 1985-91; Miss Supreme Ct, justice, 1991-2000, presiding justice, 2000-01; Phelps Dunbar LLP, sr partner & atty, 2001-; US Dist Ct, Southern Dist Miss; US Supreme Ct; US Ct Appeals Fifth Circuit; US Dist Ct, Northern Dist Miss. **Orgs:** Pres, 1971-82, nat bd dir, 1982-, Nat Advan Asn Colored People, Jackson Br; pres, State Mutual Fed Savings & Loan Asn, 1979-89; Magnolia Bar Asn; Nat Bar Asn; Am Bar Asn; Charles Clark Inn Am Inns Ct; Sigma Pi Phi Fraternity; Miss Bd Bar Admis, 1978-80; DC Bar Asn; fel Miss Bar Found; nat adv, Community Educ Disadvantaged C, 1978-80; Jackson Goodwill Industs, 1985-91; chair, Capitol City Conv Ctr Comn; chair, Miss Ctr Justice; Community Found Greater Jackson, 2000-; Phi Beta Sigma, Beta Gamma Boule; pres, Am Inns Ct; Am Law Inst; chair, House Ethics Comt; chair, House Judiciary Comt; chair, Miss Legis Black Caucus. **Home Addr:** 976 Metairie, Jackson, MS 39209, **Home Phone:** (601)354-0786. **Business Addr:** Senior Partner, Attorney, Phelbs Dunbar LLP, 4270 I-55 N, Jackson, MS 39211-6391, **Business Phone:** (601)360-9356.

**BANKS, GENE (EUGENE LAVON BANKS)**
Basketball player, basketball coach. **Personal:** Born May 15, 1959, Philadelphia, PA; married Isabelle; children: 5. **Educ:** Duke Univ, BS, 1981. **Career:** Basketball player (retired), basketball coach; San Antonio Spurs, 1981-85; Chicago Bulls, 1985-87; Arimo Bologna, 1988-89; La Crosse Catbirds, 1989-90; Maccabi Rishon LeZion, Israel, 1990-92; Bnei Herzeliya, 1992-93; Hapoel Herzliya, Israel, 1992-93; Hapoel Gvat & Haemek, 1993-94; Bluefield State Col, Lady Blues, head basketball coach; Wash Wizards, asst coach, 2009-12. **Business Addr:** Assistant Coach, Washington Wizards, 601 F St NW, Washington, DC 20004.

**BANKS, GEORGE S.**
Chief executive officer, executive, president (organization). **Educ:** Univ Liberia, Liberia, training & cert, 1990; Community Col RI Providence, RI, AA, arts gen studies, 1992; RI Col, Providence, RI, BA, justice studies & criminal justice, 1994; George Washington Univ, Wash, DC, Web Mgt Grad Cert Prog; Protection Prof, cert. **Career:** Journalism & Pub Rels, chief staff & spec asst; Liberian News Agency, Liberia, News Reporter, 1981-83; Welcome to Liberia Mag, publ, 1983-85; Interim Nat Assembly, Liberia, Admin Secy, chmn com tlabor, 1985-86; Capital City Monrovia Liberian Senate, chief staff & spec asst to sen, 1986-90; Guardsmark Inc, Boston, MA, security officer & site supvr, 1990-92, asst to br mgr, 1993, inve str, 1995, acct supvr, 1995-96; Johnston Police Dept, Johnston, RI, Criminal Justice Intern, 1993; Super Ct, Wash, DC, Regist Pvt Criminal Justice Act Inve str, 1996-99; Sentry Security Int Inc, chmn, pres & chief exec officer, 1999-. **Orgs:** White House Community Empowerment; Black Enterprise Inc; pres, bd dir, St James Int Community Church USA; Am Soc Ind Security; Comn African Affairs, Gov dist Columbia. **Business Addr:** President, Chief Executive Officer, Sentry Security International Inc, 1425 K St NW Suite 350, Washington, DC 20005, **Business Phone:** (202)291-8030.

**BANKS, JAHSHUWAN-JESSEAN**
Educator. **Personal:** Born Sep 1, 1990?. **Career:** Clark Atlanta Univ, psychol prof, 2004-. **Home Addr:** 653 Beckwith St SW, Atlanta, GA 30314, **Home Phone:** (404)880-3537. **Business Addr:** Professor of Psychology, Clark Atlanta University, 223 James P Brawley Dr SW, Atlanta, GA 30314, **Business Phone:** (404)880-8000.

**BANKS, PROF. JAMES ALBERT**
Writer, educator, college teacher. **Personal:** Born Sep 24, 1941, Marianna, AR; son of Matthew and Lula; married Cherry Ann McGee; children: Angela Marie & Patricia Ann. **Educ:** Chicago City Col, AA, 1963; Chicago St Col, BA, elem educ & social sci, 1964; Mich State Univ, MA, 1967, PhD, 1969. **Career:** Joilet Ill Pub Schs, teacher, 1965; Francis W Parker Sch, teacher, 1965-66; Univ Wash, Seattle, from asst prof to assoc prof, 1969-73, prof educ, 1973-, chmn curric & instr, 1982-87, Kerry & Linda Killinger prof, chmn, diversity studies, dir ctr multi cult educ, Russell F Stark prof, 2001-06; Univ Mich, vis prof educ, 1975; Kent St Univ, distinguished scholar lectr, 1978; Univ Ariz, vis prof, 1979; Univ Guam, vis prof, 1979; Va State Univ, eminent scholar lectr, 1981; Brit Acad, UK, vis lectr, 1983; Ind Univ, Bloomington, vis prof, 1983; Monash Univ, Australia, vis prof educ, 1985; Humboldt State Univ, vis prof, 1989; Calif State Univ, Fullerton, distinguished vis lectr, 1989; Univ NC, Chapel Hill, vis prof, 1989; Syracuse Univ, Harry F & Alva K Ganders Memorial Fund Distinguished Lectr, 1989; Univ Minn, Twin Cities, James J Hill vis prof, 1991; Howard Univ, Charles F Thompson lectr, 1995; Columbia Univ, Teachers Col, sachs lectr, 1996, Tisch distinguished vis prof, 2007; Fla State Univ, Mack & Effie Campbell Tyner Eminent scholar, 1998; Books: Teaching Strategies Ethnic Studies, 8th Ed; Multicultural Educ: Issues & Perspectives, 7th ed; Cult Diversity & Educ: Foundations, Curric & Teaching, 4th ed; An Introd to Multicultural Educ, 3rd ed; Multicultural Educ, Transformative Knowledge & Action; Educating Citizens a Multicultural Soc; Diversity & Citizenship Educ: Global Perspectives; Race, Cult & Educ: Selected Works James A. Banks; Teaching Strategies Ethnic Studies, 4th ed, 1987; Multiethnic Educ Theory & Pract, 2nd ed, 1988; Multicultural Educ: Issues & Prespectives, 6th ed, 1989; Teaching Strategies Ethnic Studies, 8th ed; Cult Diversity & Educ: Foundations, Curric & Teaching, 5th ed. **Orgs:** Nat Defense Educ Act; Nat Acad Educ, 1973-76; bd dir, Nat Coun Social Studies, 1973-74, 1980-85, chmn task force, Ethnic Studies Curric Guidelines, 1975-76, vpres, 1980; pres, Nat Adv Coun Ethnic Heritage Studies, 1975-79, 1982; bd dir, Social Sci Educ Consortium, 1976-79; bd dir, Asn Supv & Curric Develop, 1976-79; Nat fel W K Kellogg Found, 1980-83; Rockefeller Found fel 1980; vpres, Nat Coun Social Studies, 1980, bd dir, 1980-84, pres, 1982; bd mem, Nat Res Coun comt, 1996-97; pres, Am Educ Res Asn, 1997-98; bd mem, Inst Med, Nat Acad Sci; spencer fel, Ctr Advan Studies Behav Sci, Stanford, CA, 2005-06. **Home Addr:** 1333 NW 200 St, Seattle, WA 98177, **Home Phone:** (206)546-1625. **Business Addr:** Kerry & Linda Killinger Professor of Diversity S, Director, University Washington, 110 Miller Hall, Seattle, WA 98195-3600, **Business Phone:** (206)543-3386.

**BANKS, JEFFREY**
Fashion designer. **Personal:** Born Nov 3, 1953, Washington, DC. **Educ:** Pratt Inst, Brooklyn, NY, attended 1974; Parsons Sch Design, BFA, 1977. **Career:** Ralph Lauren Polo, design asst to pres, 1971-73; Calvin Klein & Calvin Klein Ltd, design asst to pres, 1973-76; Nik-Nik Clothing & Sportswear, designer, 1976-77; Jeffrey Banks Ltd, 1977-; Alixandre, designer, 1980; Boyswear collection, 1980; Merona Sports, head designer, 1980; Parson's Sch Design, design critic; Jeffrey Banks Int, 1980-; Hartz & Co, NY, 1984; Takihyo Inc, Hong Kong, 1988; Bloomingdale, NY, menswear consult, 1993; Johnnie Walker, 1998; Haggar Clothing Co, design consult, 2004-. **Orgs:** Designers Collective; sr bd mem, Fashion Inst Technol; mem exec bd, Coun Fashion Designers Am. **Honors/Awds:** Coty Fashion Critics Award, Men's Furs; Special Coty Award, Men's Furs, 1977; Harvey's Bristol Cream Tribute to Black Designers, Excellence in Men's Wear Design, 1978-80; Earnie award, 1980; Special Coty Award, Menswear, 1982; Cutty Sark Award, Outstanding US Designer, 1987. **Home Addr:** 12 E 26th St, New York, NY 10010. **Business Addr:** Designer, Haggar Clothing Co, 2nd Colinas Crossing, Dallas, TX 75234, **Business Phone:** (214)352-8481.

**BANKS, JUNE SKINNER**
Pathologist. **Personal:** Born Jun 5, 1936, Norfolk, VA; daughter of Solomon Kermit and Gaynell Clanton; married John L; children: Junelle S Letha. **Educ:** Fisk Univ, BA, Eng, 1956; NY Univ, MA, speech educ, 1966; Old Dom Univ; Norfolk State Univ; Univ Va. **Career:** Pathologist (retired); Am Mil Sec Sch, Eng Dept, chair, 1968-69; Old Dom Univ, instr, 1969-70; JRE Lee High Sch, eng teacher, 1956-57; Norfolk Pub Schs, eng teacher, 1957-67, speech & langpathologist, 1967-93, speech eligibility liaison, 1989-93, teacher spt, 1993-95. **Orgs:** Nat mem-at-large & found bd, The Links Inc, 1990-94; trustee bd, Mt Zion Baptist Church, Norfolk, 1993-; local bd, Coalition 100 Black Women, 1992-94; local social action comn, Delta Sigma Theta Sorority Inc, 1991-2002; parlimentarian, Dejouir Inc, 1988-90; Moles Inc, 1981-94, vpres, Norfolk Chap, 1990-94; pres, Chums Inc, Norfolk Chap, 1998-2002; chair, Nat Nominating Comn, 2002; chair, Nat Scholar Comt, 2002; localpubity dir, Chums Inc, 1994-96; Am Speech & Hearing Asn; chair, Speech & Hearing Asn VA, Multicultural Interest Group, 1994-95; Pinochle Bugs Inc, 1972-; vpres, VA Br Chap, 2002-; Nat Hon Soc. **Honors/Awds:** Professional Award, Norfolk Metropolitan Club, Nat Asn Negro Bus & Prof Women's Clubs Inc; Apple for Teacher Award, Iota Phi Lambda Sorority, 1989; Distinguished Service Award, Links Inc, 1984; Nat Serv Award, Dejouir Inc, 1996. **Home Addr:** 1052 Lockwood Ct, Virginia Beach, VA 23464, **Home Phone:** (757)424-2591.

**BANKS, DR. LAURA NOBLES**
School administrator. **Personal:** Born Jun 29, 1921, Tucson, AZ; daughter of James Nobles Sr and Missouri Johnson Nobles; married Jack Leonard. **Educ:** Univ Ariz, BS, 1943, MA, 1966, EdS, 1970, EdD, educ admin, 1980; Univ Southern Calif, cert, elem educ. **Career:** School Administrator (retired); Univ Ariz, 5 summers, asst teacher workshops; Cavett Elem Sch, elem teacher & prin; Tucson Pub Sch Dist No 1, coord reading progs K-12; Mari Mac Corp, pub rels dir; Jacks Original Bar-B-Q, Tucson, AZ, owner, 1950-92; Links Inc, parliamentarian & nat sec, 1970-76, nat rec secy, 1974-78; adv coun, Col Social & Behav Scis, Univ Tex San Antonio, 1999-2002; coordr, Neighborhood Youth Corp; Peace Corp lectr, dist reading coordr & prin, Univ Ariz; Tucson Unified Sch Dist, asst supt; LNB Enterprises, pres & owner. **Orgs:** Nat Coun Women Admin; TEA; AEA; Nat Educ Asn; chairperson, Elem Prin Group; Ariz Admin Asn; Golden Heritage mem, Nat Asn Elem Prin; nat bd, YWCA, 1965-76; Nat Asn Advan Colored People; pres, Tucson Urban League, 1979-81; Palo Verde Ment Health Found; bd dir, Alumni Bd Univ Ariz; organizer, pres local chap, far western reg dir, nat secy & nat prog chmn, local pres, Alpha Kappa Alpha; Nat Coun Negro Women; Model Cities Neighborhood Housing Task Force; bd mem, Coun United Way; Pima Col Exec Comm Comm Affairs; adv bd, Resources Women, bd dir, 1984-94; pres, Women at Top, 1985-94; hon mem, Soroptomist Int; bd dir, Univ Ariz Pres Club, Comm Housing Resource Bd; Rotary Int; community adv bd, Tucson Jr League, 1990-94; Tucson Rotary Club, 1990-94; planned giving com, Univ Ariz Black Alumni, 1992-94; Coalition 100 Black Women-San Antonio, TX; Neighborhood Youth Corp; Nat Coun Women Adm; AZ Juv Justice Planning Adv Comm; Tucson Civil Serv Rev; bd mem, Big Sisters Inc; advisor, Jr League Tucson; ational Secy Alpha Kappa Alpha Inc; charter mem, San Antonio Chap; Coalition 100 Black Women; 2nd Baptist Church. **Home Addr:** 9438 Gray Sage, Helotes, TX 78023, **Home Phone:** (210)695-3424. **Business Addr:** President, Owner, LNB Enterprises, 5250 E 22nd St, Tucson, AZ 85711, **Business Phone:** (520)750-1280.

**BANKS, DR. LULA F.**
Government official. **Personal:** Born Feb 23, 1947, Tallahassee, FL; daughter of Harry E Sr and Elizabeth Gaines Richardson; children: Felicia A Williams & Deanna M Williams. **Educ:** Tallahassee Community Col, FL, AA, 1985; Fla State Univ, Tallahassee, FL, BS, social sci, 1992; Fl A&M Univ, Tallahassee, MEd, FL, 1995; Argosy Univ, Sarasota, FL, EdD, 2004. **Career:** Harris Corp, Melbourne, FL, 1978; Indian River Co Sch Bd, Vero Beach, teacher adult educ, 1978; Brevard Co Sch Bd, Melbourne, FL, teacher adult educ, 1979; Leon Co Bd Comnrs & Leon Co Sch Bd, Tallahassee, FL, purchasing agt, 1980-85, purchasing dir, 1985-90; City Tallahassee, purchasing adminr, 1990-96; Pinellas County BOCC, purchasing depart, dir, 1996-01; Hillsborough County BOCC, Dept Procurement Serv, Dept Purchasing, dir, 2001-. **Orgs:** Exec mem, Small Bus Week Comn; Fla Asn Pub Prof Purch Officers; Am Soc Pub Admin; COMPA/ASPA; Nat Forum Black Pub Admin &grad Exec Leadership Inst, 1994; PACE, Sch-to-Work Comn, Workforce Dev Bus& Ed Comn, Leadership Pinellas Alumni; NIGP Nat Ed Comn; NFBP Nat Prog Comn; Delta Sigma Theta Sorority; Tampa Bay Area NIGP Chap; Pinellas County Sch-to-Work Comt; Petersburg Col Corp Training Comt; Fla State Univ Black Alumni; Grievance Mediation & Fee Arbit Comt, Fl Bar Asn; logistic chief & Master Instr, bd mem, Nat Inst Govt Purchasing. **Honors/Awds:** Chairman's Award-MEDCOP of Tampa Bay, Public Admin-Fla State Univ; Certificate of Outstanding Performance for Excellence in Government-Hillsborough County; Certificate of Extra Mile Award-Hillsborough County; Certificate of Leadership & Excellence-NIGP. **Home Addr:** 214 Nestlebranch Dr, Safety Harbor, FL 34695-4726. **Business Addr:** Director, Department of Purchasing, Hillsborough County, County Ctr 18th Fl, Tampa, FL 33602, **Business Phone:** (813)272-5790.

**BANKS, MANLEY E., SR.**
Executive. **Personal:** Born Oct 12, 1913, Anniston, AL; married Dorothy M Jones; children: Manley E Jr & Jacquelyn A. **Educ:** Ala State Univ, BS, 1937; Howard Univ, LLB, 1949. **Career:** Perry Co Sch Union town AL, asst prin coach, 1937-42; Afro Cab Co Inc Enterprises, co-founder & vpres, 1946-51; teacher, 1949-52; Banks Bicycle Shop, owner, currently. **Orgs:** Treas deacon clerk, United Church Christ, 1949-69; Human Rels Coun, 1964-70; adv bd, City Water & Sewer Bd, 1965-; dist adv bd, Salvation Army, 1972-; elected chmn, City Water & Sewer Bd, 1976; exec bd, Alpha Phi Alpha Fraternity Inc; Boy Scout Coun; mem legal adv, Calhoun County Improv Asn; Nat Asn Advan Colored People. **Special Achievements:** First African American appointed to the City Advisory Board. **Home Addr:** 1204 Cobb Ave, Anniston, AL 36201-4456, **Home Phone:** (256)237-4596. **Business Addr:** Owner, Banks Bicycle Shop, 112 W 10 St, Anniston, AL 36201.

**BANKS, MARGUERITA C.BANKS**
Journalist. **Personal:** Born Sep 13, 1946, New York, NY; married Alfred Quarles. **Educ:** Notre Dame Col, Cleveland, BA, eng & fr lit, 1967. **Career:** Journalist (retired); Cleveland Press, reporter, 1967-69, ed comm page, 1969-70; WEWS-TV Scripps Howard Broadcasting, gen assignment reporter & consumer troubleshooter, host "Black Black", 1970-87; WEWS-TV Scripps Howard Broadcasting, co-host Ed Five, 1986-87. **Orgs:** Exec bd mem, Am Sickle Cell Anemia Assoc, 1972-; adv bd mem, Notre Dame Col, 1978-; exec bd mem, Harambee Serv Black C, 1979-; bd trustee, Big Bros Greater Cleveland; bd trustee, Urban League Cleveland; bd trustee, Blacks Commun, NE Young Women's Christian Asn; Womens Equity Action League, Sigma Delta Chi; ed, Gamma Phi Delta Sor; ballet & mod dance teacher, local art ctrs; leadership Cleveland Class. **Home Addr:** 1552 Burlington Rd, Cleveland Heights, OH 44118. **Business Addr:** Reporter Co-Host, WEWS-TV Scripps Howard Broadcasting, 3001 Euclid Ave, Cleveland, OH 44115, **Business Phone:** (216)431-5555.

**BANKS, HON. PATRICIA**
Lawyer, judge. **Personal:** Born Feb 6, 1949, Marianna, AR. **Educ:** Univ Ill, BA, 1969; Univ Wis, JD, 1972. **Career:** US Dept Labor Chicago Region, staff atty, 1972-73; Leadership Coun Met Open Comt, atty, 1973-74; Sears Roebuck & Co, 1974-78; pvt pract atty, 1978-80; State Ill, Cook Co Circuit Ct, judge, currently. **Orgs:** Nat Bar Asn; Cook County Bar Asn; Chicago Bar Asn; Delta Sigma Theta Sorority; chmn, Nominating Comt, Ill Judicial Coun; rec secy & treas, Nat Judicial Coun Nat Bar Asn; chmn, Judicial Coun, Nat Bar Asn, 2002-03. **Home Addr:** 3361 S Ind Ave, Chicago, IL 60616, **Home Phone:** (312)603-4347. **Business Addr:** Judge, State of Illinois, Richard J Daley Ctr, Chicago, IL 60602, **Business Phone:** (312)603-4347.

**BANKS, PAULA A.**
Executive. **Personal:** Born Chicago, IL. **Educ:** Loyola Univ, math & psychol; Univ Ill; Harvard Univ, int advan mgt prog. **Career:** Sears, Roebuck & Co, dir pub rels, human resources dir, mgr, labor rel, store opers & merchandising mgr; Global Social Investment, BP, vpres, 1996-; PepsiCo Inc, sr vpres, global diversity & orgn partnership, currently. **Orgs:** Bd, Fisk Univ; pres, Exec Leadership Coun; corp adv bd, Conf Bd; Pub Educ Network; Nat Coun Negro Women. **Business Addr:** Senior Vice President, PepsiCo Inc, 700 Anderson Hill Rd, Purchase, NY 10577, **Business Phone:** (914)253-2000.

**BANKS, PERRY L.**
Executive. **Personal:** Born Apr 15, 1955; son of Josie Greer and Walter; married Shirley; children: Patrice & Chinua. **Educ:** Shaw Bus Col, Detroit, MI, 1976; Nat Inst Technol, Detroit, MI, AS, 1981. **Career:** Gen Tel AE, Northland, Ill, test engr II, 1981-84; Rotelcom Bus Systs, Rochester, NY, technician, 1984-86; Tele commun Bank Inc, Rochester, NY, pres & chief exec officer, 1986-. **Orgs:** Trustee, Greater Rochester Metro Chamber Com, 1990-92; vpres, Black BusAsn Chamber Com, 1991-. **Home Addr:** 552 Clay Ave, Rochester, NY 14613-1028, **Home Phone:** (585)647-1784. **Business Addr:** President, Chief Executive Officer, The Telecommunication Bank Inc, 274 N Goodman St, Rochester, NY 14607, **Business Phone:** (585)442-2040.

**BANKS, PRISCILLA SNEED**
Federal government official. **Personal:** Born Jul 13, 1941, Washington, DC; daughter of Mabel Sneed and Excell Sneed; children: Monica Greene. **Educ:** Am Univ. **Career:** Low Income Housing, tech instr; Low Rent Occupancy; US Dept Housing & Urban Devel, task force desegregate pub housing, housing prog specialist, housing specialist, currently; Anti-Drug Prog Pub Housing; Civil Rights Act 1964 & Title VIII, 1988; Vidor Housing Authority, chair. **Orgs:** Nat Asn Advan Colored People; Wash Urban League; Nat Welfare Mothers; Nat Asn Housing & Redevelop Officials. **Honors/Awds:** Public Service Awards; Miss Houisng & Urban Develop, 1972; Special Achievement, 1975-76 & 1978; Sustained Superior Performance, 1969 & 1980; 2nd Highest Award, US Dept Housing & Urban Develop, 1984; Outstanding Performance Award, 1984. **Home Addr:** 5003 Odessa Rd, College Park, MD 20740-1127, **Home Phone:** (301)345-5929. **Business Addr:** Housing Specialist, US Department of Housing and Urban Development, 451 7th St SW, Washington, DC 20410, **Business Phone:** (202)708-1420.

**BANKS, RICHARD EDWARD**
Lawyer. **Personal:** Born Jan 5, 1960, St. Louis, MO; son of Vincent A and Laura M Gillispie; children: Jessica Ruth & Richard Edward Jr. **Educ:** Howard Univ, BBA, 1982; Tex Southern Univ, Thurgood Marshall Sch Law, Houston, JD, 1986. **Career:** State Farm Ins Co, St Louis, Mo, claims atty, 1986-88; Vickers, Moore & Wiest, St. Louis, Mo, assoc atty, 1988-89; Banks & Assocs PC, St. Louis, Mo, managing partner & founder, 1989-; KMOV-TV, legal consult; KPLR-TV, legal consult; KSDK-TV, legal consult; KMOX Radio; pvt pract atty & counr law, currently. **Orgs:** MO & Ill Bar Asn, 1988-; Bar Asn Metrop St. Louis, 1988-; Am & Nat Bar Asn, 1988-; MO Trial Lawyers Asn, 1989-; Chicago Bar Asn, 1989-; MO Bar Disciplinary Bd, 1995-; vpres, Am Bar Asn; vpres, Nat Bar Asn; bd mem, Grand Ctr Inc; bd mem, Urban League St Louis; vpres, Mound City Bar Asn; chmn, Mo Bar Disciplinary Comt; chmn, Community Orgn Comt; co chair, Ann Richard E Banks Charity Golf Classic; founding bd mem, Maj Broadcasting Network; founding bd mem, Weinman Ctr Abused Women & C; St Alphonsus Cath Church. **Honors/Awds:** Leaders Conf, C's Defense Fund, 1990; 50 Leaders of the Future, Ebony Mag, 1990; Judicial Selection Comt, MO Bar, 1990; Outstanding Business Leader Award, St Louis Sentinel Newspaper, 1996; Young Democrats Community Service Award, 1998; Corporate Citizen Award, Better Family Life, 2000; Trailblazer Award, St Charles Lwanga Cath Ctr, 2001; Martin Luther King Outstanding Businessman of the Year Award, MO Gov's Office. **Home Addr:** 308 S 21st St, St. Louis, MO 63103, **Home Phone:** (314)721-4040. **Business Addr:** Attorney, Counselor at Law, Banks & Associates, Huntleigh Financial Ctr 8000 Md Ave Suite 1260, Saint Louis, MO 63105-3752, **Business Phone:** (314)721-4040.

**BANKS, RONALD**
Executive, president (organization). **Personal:** Born Jun 19, 1951, Chicago, IL; son of Geneva Martin and Earl; married Vera D Lott; children: Janel & Lauren. **Educ:** Loyola Univ, Chicago, IL, BA, 1973. **Career:** Montgomery Ward Chicago, buyer, 1973-82; Sherwin Williams Co Cleveland, buyer, 1982-84; Parks/Carver Tripp Cos, regional vpres 1984-91; Mkt 2000, mgr & owner, 1991-. **Home Addr:** 2919 MacFarlane Cres, Flossmoor, IL 60422, **Home Phone:** (708)799-1542. **Business Addr:** Owner, Manager, Marketing 2000 Inc, 1939 Miller Ct, Homewood, IL 60430, **Business Phone:** (708)922-0391.

**BANKS, RONALD TRENTON (RON BANKS)**
Educator, school administrator. **Personal:** Born Sep 20, 1947, Knoxville, TN; son of Ralph and Clara; children: Rashondra Trenia & Brianna Jene. **Educ:** Tenn State Univ, BS, 1970, MS, 1976; Meharry Med Col, cert ment health, 1971. **Career:** Meharry Med Col, ment health tech trainees, pres, 1970-71; Ky State Police, drug & alcohol consult, 1976; Ky State Univ, founder & dir, Dial A Job prog, co-chair rotating staff adv bd, vpres, 1983-84, career planning & placement, assoc dir, career planning & placement serv, dir, currently; Ky Teachers Network, 1984-85; Coop Educ Handicap Comt, nat co-chairperson, 1985-86. **Orgs:** Frankfort Comn, dir crisis serv, 1977-; Kappa Alpha Psi; United Way, 1978; YMCA, Sr Citizens, Blind, Juv Deliq Ment Health Vol, 1978; Coop Educ Asn Ky, Awards Comn, 1988-89; Coop Educ Asn; pres, mem retention dir, YMCA, 1992-. **Home Addr:** 120 Turnberry Dr, Frankfort, KY 40601-3664, **Home Phone:** (502)227-9744. **Business Addr:** Director of Career Counseling & Placement Services, Kentucky State University, 400 E Main St, Frankfort, KY 40601, **Business Phone:** (502)597-5998.

**BANKS, SHARON P.**
Lawyer, educator. **Personal:** Born Sep 21, 1942, Washington, DC. **Educ:** Morgan State Col, BA, 1964; Howard Univ Law Sch, JD, 1967. **Career:** Neighborhood Legal Serv Prog, 1967-72; Howard Univ, part-time teacher, 1969-72, full-time teacher, 1972-, Off Pres, sr assoc gen coun, title ix coordr, currently; pvt pract atty, 1972-. **Orgs:** DC Bar Asn; Howard Univ Law Alumni Asn; bd dir, DC ACIU; Kappa Beta Pi Legal Sorority. **Home Addr:** 6908 32 St NW, Washington, DC 20015, **Home Phone:** (202)362-1920. **Business Addr:** Senior Associate General Counsel, Howard University, Rm 402 Off Gen 2244 10th St NW, Washington, DC 20059, **Business Phone:** (202)806-2650.

**BANKS, DR. TAZEWELL**
Physician, educator. **Personal:** Born Jan 7, 1932, Washington, DC; son of Cora Page and Seldon; married Myrtle Marie Trescott; children: Andrea, Gregory & Kelley. **Educ:** Howard Univ, BS, chem, 1953; Howard Med Col, MD, 1957. **Career:** Vet Affairs Med Ctr, resident, fel; Wm Beaumont Army Med Ctr, resident; Howard Med Col, clin instr, 1966-68, from asst prof to assoc prof, 1968-76, prof med, vol fac, 1976-; Cent Heart Sta DC Gen Hosp, dir. **Orgs:** Phi Beta Kappa Howard Univ, 1953; Alpha Omega Alpha Howard Med Col, 1957; bd dir, Wash Heart Asn, 1983-87; Asn Black Cardiologists, chair, nutrit comt; Chmn, Stud Res Comn, Wash Heart Asn; Am Bd Internal Med. **Honors/Awds:** Meritorious Service, DC Gen Hosp, 1970; Citizens Advisory, Comn DC Bar, 1972-76; Outstanding Teacher Student Council Award, Howard Med, 1977; Golden Apple Award, Wash Heart Asn, 1983; Outstanding Physician Award, DC Gen Hosp, 1985-86. **Special Achievements:** Published over 50 articles on cardiovascular diseases; Presented over 300 talks on cardiovascular diseases. **Home Addr:** 1925 Varnum St NE, Washington, DC 20018-3339, **Home Phone:** (202)529-1960. **Business Addr:** Professor of Medicine, Volunteer Faculty, Howard Medical College, 520 W St NW, Washington, DC 20059, **Business Phone:** (202)806-6270.

**BANKS, TONY (ANTHONY LAMAR BANKS)**
Football player. **Personal:** Born Apr 5, 1973, San Diego, CA; married Yolanda. **Educ:** Mich State Univ, Mesa Community Col. **Career:** Football player (retired), reporter; St Louis Rams, quarterback, 1996-98; Baltimore Ravens, quarterback, 1999-2000; Wash Redskins, quarterback, 2001; Dallas Cowboys, quarterback, 2001; Houston Texans, quarterback, 2002-06; Big Ten Network, football sideline reporter. **Honors/Awds:** Super Bowl champion XXXV. **Business Addr:** Football Sideline Reporter, Big Ten Network LLC, Chicago, IL.

**BANKS, TYRA LYNNE**
Actor, fashion model, television broadcaster. **Personal:** Born Dec 4, 1973, Inglewood, CA; daughter of Donald and Carolyn Johnson. **Career:** Actress & Talk show host; TV series: "Fresh Prince of Bel-Air", 1993; "Felicity", 1999; "Just Shoot Me!", 1999; "Mad TV", 2000; "America's Next Top Model", 2003-; "American Dreams", 2004; "All of Us", 2004; "Marple: The Body in the Library", 2004; The Tyra Banks Show, host, 2005-10; Entertainment tonight, 2006-09; "Gossip Girl", 2009; "Mexico's Next Top Model", 2011; "Vietnam's Next Top Model", 2012; "Shake It Up", 2012; "Top Model po-russki", 2012; "Asia's Next Top Model", 2012; "Glee", 2013; Films: Higher Learning, 1995; A Woman Like That, 1997; Love Stinks, 1999; Coyote Ugly, 2000; Love & Basketball, 2000; Life-Size, 2000; Halloween:Resurrection, 2002; Eight Crazy Nights; 2002; Larceny, 2004; Mr Woodcock, 2007; Tropic Thunder, 2008; Hannah Montana: The Movie, 2009; Songs: "Shake Ya Body, " 2004; Nike, fashion model; Pepsi, fashion model; Tommy Hilfiger, fashion model; Ralph Lauren, fashion model; Dolce & Gabbana, fashion model; Swatch, fashion model; Cover Girl, fashion model; Ty Ty Baby Prod, founder & chief exec officer, currently; CW TV Network, talk show host, currently. **Orgs:** Spokesperson, Ctr C & Families; founder, T-Zone. **Honors/Awds:** Michael Award, 1997; Won, Teen Choice Award, 2007, 2008; Won Daytime Emmy Award, 2008. **Special Achievements:** Listed in "50 Most Beautiful People in the World", People mag, 1994, 1996; First African-American model on cover of Sports Illustrated & the Victoria's Secret catalog, 1997; Co-author of Tyra's Beauty Inside & Out, Harper Collins, 1998; first black woman to sign for a cosmetic company at the age of 23; one of only four African Americans and seven women to have repeatedly ranked among the world's most influential people by Time magazine; Author of Modell and, 2010. **Business Addr:** Host, Singer, CW Television Network, 3300 W Olive Ave Suite 3, Burbank, CA 91505, **Business Phone:** (818)977-2500.

**BANKS, ESQ. VANITA M.**
**Personal:** married James R Bly. **Educ:** Purdue Univ, BA, polit sci, 1977; Valparaiso Univ, JD, 1980; DePaul Col Law, LLM, taxation; Menttium. **Career:** US Dept Health & Human Serv; DePaul Univ Sch Law, fac; Caldwell & Hubbard; Allstate Insurance Co, coun; Purdue Univ, old master, 2006. **Orgs:** Pres, Nat Bar Asn, 2002, vpres mem, chief exec officer & spokesperson, Hurricane Katrina Task Force, co-chair, Corp Law Sect, chair, Exec Comt, spec coun, Issues & Resolutions Comt, chair, Finance & Fundraising Comt, chair, Strategic Planning Comt, chair; founding mem, Allstate Law & Regulation Dept Diversity Comt; Law & Regulation Info Technol; fel Life Mgt Inst; bd mem, Nat Bar Inst; Am Bar Asn; Cook County Bar Asn; Black Women Lawyers Chicago; N Shore Labor Coun; Alpha Kappa Alpha Sorority Inc; Links Inc; Hawthorn Woods Women's Club; bd dir, Black Women's Agenda; bd dir, Coun Legal Educ Opportunity. **Honors/Awds:** Women Making History Award, Nat Coun Negro Women; Legacy Diversity Award, Coun Legal Educ Opportunity; All-state Chairman's Quality Award. **Business Addr:** President, National Bar Association, 1225 11th St NW, Washington, DC 20001, **Business Phone:** (202)842-3900.

**BANKS, DR. WALDO R., SR.**
Educator, executive, consultant. **Personal:** Born Mar 30, 1928, Beaumont, TX; married Anice D; children: Monica Diane, Natalie Anice & Waldo R. **Educ:** Bishop Col, BA, 1951; Prairie View Univ, attended 1952; Tex Southern Univ, MA, 1957; Ind Univ, EdS, 1964; Claremont Grad Sch Educ, PhD, 1975. **Career:** Educator (retired), association executive; S Pk Ind Sch Dist, psychol consult instr, 1952-54; Orange Ind Sch Dist, psychol consult instr, 1954-56; Tex Southern Univ, instr coun, 1957-58; Ind Univ, admins researcher, 1958-59; Knoxville Col, dean, dir & asst prof, 1959-61; Gary Pub Sch, dir scholar, 1961-65, dir consult, 1961-65; Los Angeles Bd Educ, instr & couns, 1965-66; Los Angeles City, Human Rel Bur, asst prof couns & dir, 1965-67; PACE Proj, prof researcher writer, 1967-69; Compton Unified Sch Dist, adminr & dir, 1967-75; Univ Calif Los Angeles, instr, 1971-76; Global Oil Co Inc, pres, 1975-77; Imp Health Ctr Inc, dir, 1975-77; Natl Employ Ctr, pres, 1975-77; Am Educ Econ Found, pres, 1970-80; Dept Health, Educ & Welfare, consult; Calif St Univ, consult. **Orgs:** Am Soc Mil Hist Los Angeles; Nat Adv Counc Educ Prof Devel; Harry Walker; Am Prog Bur; UN Speaker Bur; Am Asn Col Registr & Admis Officers; Am Asn Col & Univ Deans; Am Asn Sec Sch Prin; Am Asn Sch Admin; Am Asn Univ Profs; Am Col Personnel Asn; Am Fed Teachers; Am Jr Col Asn; Am Personnel & Guid Asn; Am Polit Sci Asn; Am Sociol Soc; Am PsycholAsn Boys Club Am; BSA; BPOE; Calif Asn Prog Dem; Calif Fed Teachers; Calif Person & Guid Asn; Calif St Teachers Asn; Int Platform Asn; Masonic Lodge; Nat Asn Advan Colored People; Nat Adv Coun EPDA; Nat Cong Parents & Teachers; NEA; Nat Urban League; Phi Delta Kappa; S Christian Leadership Conf; YMCA. **Honors/Awds:** Dr Joseph J Rhoads Schlrshp, Grant Bishop Col, 1946-50; Admin Res Grant, Ind Univ, 1957-58; educ grant, Claremont Grad Sch Educ, 1972-74; pres USA appointee Nat Adv Coun Educ Prof Devel, 1972-75; grant Nat fel Fund Atlanta, 1974-75; numerous publications, research programs and projects; Nat Prof Serv Citation Pres Ford USA. **Home Addr:** 1806 E Turmont St, Carson, CO 90746, **Home Phone:** (310)898-1008.

**BANKS, DR. WILLIAM JASPER, JR. (WILLIE J BANKS)**
Physician, educator. **Personal:** Born Jul 4, 1944, Richmond, VA; son of W J and C E. **Educ:** Va Univ, BS, 1965; Va Commonwealth Univ, MS, 1966; Howard Univ, MD, 1970; Univ Edinburgh McMasters Col, MA, 1986. **Career:** DC Gen Hosp, med officer, 1977-, vpres med staff, 1981-82; Howard Univ Hosp, chief orth clinics, 1979-; Howard Univ, instr surg, 1977-80, sec divorth surg, asst prof surg, 1980, assoc prof; Veterans Admin Hosp, chief Dept Orthop; pvt pract, currently. **Orgs:** Fel Am Col Surgeons, Am Acad Ortho Surgeons, Int Col Surgeons; Am Med Asn; DC Med Soc; Southern Med Soc; Arlington Hosp Found; Intl Oceanog Found; secy, Capital City Orth Found; fel Royal Col Surgeons Edinburgh, Nat Geog Soc Navl Inst; Southern Orth Soc, Eastern Orth Soc, Sigma Xi, Am Asn Advan Sci; NY Acad Sci; Am Philos Soc; Pan Am Orth Group; Soc Clin Investrs. **Home Addr:** 2300 24th Rd S Off, Arlington, VA 22206, **Home Phone:** (703)979-6913. **Business Addr:** Private Practice, Veterans Admin Med, Veterans Affairs Medical Center, 50 Irving St NW, Washington, DC 20422, **Business Phone:** (202)745-8166.

**BANKS, DR. WILLIAM MARON, III**
Educator, association executive. **Personal:** Born Sep 22, 1943, Thomasville, GA; son of William and Hattie; children: David, Tracey, Trey & Shane. **Educ:** Dillard Univ, attended 1963; Univ Ky, EdD, 1967. **Career:** Attebury Job Corps Ctr, supr counr & psychol, 1967; Howard Univ, counr psychol, 1967-70, dept chairperson, 1972-75; Univ Calif, Berkeley, prof, 1970, Undergrad Affairs, provost, 1987-89; Univ Calif, Berkeley, prof emer african am studies, currently. **Orgs:** Soc Psychol Study Soc Issues; Soc Study Soc Probs; Am Personnel & Guid Asn; chairperson, Univ Calif Afro-Am Studies Consortium, 1979-81; Asn Black Psychologists; fel Nat Humanities Ctr; fel Ctr Advan Study Socialand Behav Sci; fel Univ Calif Regents. **Honors/Awds:** Summer Scholars Award, US Civil Serv Comn; Instructional Improve Grant; num scholarly articles & monographs pub on effects of racial differences in psychotherapy & counseling; American Book Award, 1996. **Special Achievements:** Published, Black Intellectuals. **Home Addr:** 837 Santa Ray Ave, Oakland, CA 94610. **Business Addr:** Emeritus Professor, University of California Berkeley, 660 Barrows Hall 6th Fl, Berkeley, CA 94720-2572, **Business Phone:** (510)642-7084.

**BANKS, WILLIE ANTHONY**
Executive, baseball player. **Personal:** Born Feb 27, 1969, Jersey City, NJ. **Career:** Baseball (retired), executive; Minn Twins, pitcher, 1991-93; Chicago Cubs, pitcher, 1994-95; Los Angeles Dodgers, pitcher, 1995; Fla Marlins, pitcher, 1995; Philadelphia Phillies, pitcher, 1995-97; NY Yankees, pitcher, 1997-98; Ariz Diamondbacks, pitcher, 1998; Orix BlueWave, pitcher, 1999; Boston Red Sox, pitcher, 2001-02; Newark Bears, 2004, 2005; Triple Crown Baseball Acad, instr; pub speaker & consult, currently. **Orgs:** Nat League Western Div champion Los Angeles Dodgers, 1995; World Ser champion New York Yankees, 1998. **Honors/Awds:** World Series champion, 1991. **Business Addr:** Baseball Player, The Newark Bears, Bears & Eagles Riverfront Stadium, Newark, NJ 07102, **Business Phone:** (973)848-1000.

**BANKSTON, ARCHIE M. See Obituaries Section.**

**BANKSTON, CHARLES E.**
Automotive executive. **Career:** Village Ford Lewisville Inc, pres, owner & chief exec, 1996-. **Home Addr:** 5006 Village Pl, Dallas, TX 75248. **Business Addr:** Owner, Chief Executive, Village Ford Of Lewisville Inc, 1144 N Stemmons FWY, Lewisville, TX 75067, **Business Phone:** (214)434-1855.

**BANKSTON, MICHAEL KANE**
Consultant, football player. **Personal:** Born Mar 12, 1970, East Bernard, TX; married Kimberly; children: Michael Jr & Mikaela. **Educ:** Sam Houston State Univ, BA, bus mgt, 1992. **Career:** Football player (retired), coach, consultant; Community League, Baseball, Basketball, Football, Soccer, Tennis, Roller Hockey, coach, 1992-; Phoenix Cardinals, nose tackle, 1992, left defensive end, 1993; Ariz Cardinals, left defensive end, 1994-97; Cincinnati Bengals, left defensive end, 1998, defensive end, 1999-2000; Wash Redskins, defensive end, 2001; High Sch, players rep; Bankston Ventures Group Inc, pres & chief exec officer, 2002-; Brahma Investments, owner, 2004-07; Wash Mutual, loan consult, 2006-07; Charles Schwab, stock broker, 2007-08; Canyon State Rite Passage, head coach, 2012-; YMCA progs, coach; Charles Schwab, broker. **Orgs:** Black Chamber Com, 2002-; bd mem & vice chair, Future KIDS, 2009-; Sam Houston Black Alumni Asn; Nat Football Asn; stud coun mem, Nat Hon Soc; Nat Football League Prof Asn; Taste Phoenix. **Honors/Awds:** All American Winner; Blue Chip All American Award Winner. **Business Addr:** Vice Chair, Future for KIDS, 6991 E Camelback Rd Suite D301, Scottsdale, AZ 85251, **Business Phone:** (480)947-8131.

**BANNERMAN-RICHTER, GABRIEL**
Educator. **Personal:** Born Oct 28, 1931, Oyo; married Jane Harvey Ewusie; children: Anna, Jessica, Gabriel Jr, Matilda & Elizabeth. **Educ:** Calif State Univ, Sacramento, BA, 1969, MA, eng lang & lit & lett, 1970; Univ Calif, Davis, attended 1972. **Career:** Sacramento City Col, instr, 1969-80; Univ Calif, Davis, instr, 1972-75; Univ Cape Coast Ghana, vis assoc prof, 1976-77; Calif State Univ, Sacramento, prof eng & ethnic studies, 1996-2002, prof emer. **Orgs:** Pub Gabari Pub Co, 1982-. **Honors/Awds:** National Endowment For The Humanities Scholar, Nat Endowment Humanities Inst, Univ Ind, 1985. **Special Achievements:** Author, "Practice of Witchcraft in Ghana", 1982; "Don't Cry My Baby, Don't Cry", 1984; "Mmoetia, The Mysterious Dwarfs", 1985. **Home Addr:** 1125 Evergreen Ct, Rosamond, CA 93560-6607, **Home Phone:** (661)258-9021.

**BANTON, LINDA WHEELER**
Executive, vice president (organization). **Personal:** Born Mar 28, 1948, Akron, OH; daughter of James and Jane Wheeler; children: Brooks. **Educ:** Univ Akron, BS, bus admin, 1979; Harvard Univ, John F Kennedy Sch Govt, attended 1998. **Career:** Goodyear Aerospace, bus devel rep, 1980-85; Sunohio Co, govt laison mgr, 1985-86; Honeywell, govt rels mgr, sr mkt rep, 1986-88; Alliant Techsyst, mgr govt rels, 1988-92; Lockheed Martin, vpres legis affairs, 1992-99; Honeywell, vpres aerospace govt rels, 1999; Russell Reynolds Assocs Aerospace & Defense Pract, sr exec search consult; Lockheed Martin, vpres legis affairs; Henry L Stimson Ctr, bd dir, 2001-. **Orgs:** Women Gov Rels, secy, 1988-; exec Comt, Wash Indust Roundtable, 1996-; Aerospace Indust Asn, Wash rep, 1999-; Electronic Indust Alliance, bd govs, 1999-; bd govs, Va Commonwealth Space Flight Authority. **Home Addr:** 1227 Roundhouse Lane, Alexandria, VA 22314. **Business Addr:** Board of Director, The Henry L Stimson Center, 1111 19th St 20th Fl, Washington, DC 20036, **Business Phone:** (202)223-5956.

**BANTON, DR. WILLIAM C., II**
Executive, military leader, physician. **Personal:** Born Nov 9, 1922, Washington, DC. **Educ:** Howard Univ, Col Lib Arts & Sci; Howard Univ Col Med, MD, 1946; John Hopkins Univ Sch Hyg & Pub Health, attended 1970; St Louis Univ Sch Med; USAF Sch Aviation Med; USPHS; Sch Aerospace Med; USN Med Sch; Armed Forces Inst Pathol; Wash Univ Sch Med; Def Atomic Support Agy; Sch Aerospace Med; Boston U; Harvard U; Tufts Univ Sch Med; Indust Col Armed Forces. **Career:** Homer G Phillips Hosp, 1946-47; Robert Koch Hosp, 1947-49; USAF Gen Hosp, 1950-52; Mitchell AFB NY, med officer internal med; 2230th AFR Floyd Bennett Naval Air Sta, flight surgeon, 1951-52; St Louis Health Div Chest & TB Svc; pvt pract internal med; 8711th USAFG Hosp Scott AFB, comdr & flight surgeon, 1954-71; Hq USAF/SG Forrestal Bldg Wash, asst surgeon gen, 1971-; served short active duty tours So Vietnam, 1968-69; HQ Strategic Air Command, surgeon gen; City St Louis, health comnr; Dept Community Health & Med Care, St Louis County, Mo, dir, 1973; St Louis Univ Sch Med, asst clin prof internal med emer; pvt pract, currently. **Orgs:** Res Officer's Asn; Air Force Asn; life mem, Alpha Phi Alpha; Chi Delta Mu; Howard Univ Alumni Asn; life mem, Nat Asn Advan Colored People; bd dir, Koch Welfare Asn; Friends City Art Mus St Louis; Nat Geog Soc; St Louis Zoo Asn; John Hopkins Univ Alumni Asn; Homer G Phillips Hosp Intern Alumni Asn. **Honors/Awds:** WW II Victory Medal; Am Campaign Medal; Nat Def Serv Medal; Good Conduct Medal; Expert Marksman Medal; Armed Forces Longevity Serv Award; Award Forces Res Medal; S Vietnam Campaitn Medal. **Special Achievements:** First African-American Brigadier General in USAF Reserves. **Business Addr:** Private Practice, 13634 Peacock Farm Rd, St. Louis, MO 63131, **Business Phone:** (314)965-1204.

**BAPTISTE, HANSOM PRENTICE, JR.**
Educator, teacher. **Personal:** Born Jan 18, 1939, Beaumont, TX; married Mirabelle; children: 7. **Educ:** Lamar State, Col, BS, 1961; Univ Calif, attended 1962; Univ Notre dame, attended 1964; Ind Univ, Math, 1966, EdD, 1968. **Career:** Cuero Independent Sch Dist, 1961-63; Beaumont Independent Sch Dist, teacher, 1963-65; Ind Univ, asst prof, 1968-72; Off Educ Title III, grant training fac, doctorate level, 1973-75; NMex State Univ, distinguished prof curric & instr, currently; Univ Houston, assoc prof. **Orgs:** Many workshops & seminars, 1971-75; Ind Univ Alumni Asn; Nat Sci Teachers Asn; Nat Cong Parents & Teachers; Phi Delta Kappa. **Honors/Awds:** Valedictorian Scholar, 1957-58; Outstanding Teacher Award, 1969-70. **Special Achievements:** Authored or Edited Six Books as well as Numerous Articles & Papers. **Home Addr:** 4300 Bay Area Blvd Suite 212, Houston, TX 77058-1103. **Business Addr:** Distinguished Professor of Curriculum and Instruction, New Mexico State University, Rm 102E MSC 3CUR O'Donnell Hall, Las Cruces, NM 88003-8001, **Business Phone:** (575)646-4820.

**BAQUET, DEAN**
Editor. **Personal:** Born Jan 1, 1957; married Dylan; children: Ari. **Educ:** Columbia Univ, BA, eng. **Career:** States-Item & Times-Picayune, New Orleans; Chicago Tribune, chief investigative reporter, assoc metrop ed, reporter, 1984-90; New York Times, investigative reporter, 1990-95, nat ed, 1995-2000, managing edidor, 2011-; Los Angeles Times, mng ed, vpres & ed, 2005-. **Orgs:** Bd dir, Comt Protect Journalists; nat judge, Livingston Awards, currently. **Honors/Awds:** Pulitzer Prize, Chicago City Coun, 1988; Peter Lisagor Award, 1988; William H. Jones Award, Chicago Tribune, 1987-89. **Business Addr:** Judge, The Livingston Awards, Wallace House, Ann Arbor, MI 48104, **Business Phone:** (734)998-7575.

**BARAKA, AMINA (SYLVIA ROBINSON)**
Writer, actor, teacher. **Personal:** Born Oct 7, 1934, Newark, NJ; daughter of Leverette Jones and Anna Lois; married Amiri; children: Kellie Jones, Lisa Jones, Dominque DiPrima, Maria Jones, Shani, Obalaji, Ras, Ahi, & Amiri. **Educ:** Rutgers Univ, philos & relig; Columbia Univ, philos & relig; comparative lit; Howard Univ; New Sch Social Res. **Career:** Actor, teacher, theater director, producer, writer & activist; Blue Ark: Word Ship, ensemble mem, currently; Kimako's Blues People, co-dir, currently; Rutgers Univ, prof; Poems: Preface to a Twenty Volume Suicide Note, 1961; Blues People: Negro Music in White America, 1963; Black Magic, 1969; It's Nation Time, 1970; Hard Facts, 1975; Poetry for the Advanced, 1979; reggae or not!, 1981; The Music: Reflections on Jazz & Blues, 1987; Wise, Why's Y's, 1995; Transbluesency, 1995; Funk Lore, 1996; Billy Harper: Blueprints of Jazz, 2008; Ancient Music; Novels: Dutchman & The Slave, 1964; The System of Dante's Hell, 1965; Home: Social Essays, 1965; Raise Race Rays Raize, 1965 & 1971; A Black Mass, 1966; Tales, 1967; Four Black Revolutionary Plays, 1969; Slave Ship, 1970; Daggers & Javelins, 1974-79, 1984; The Motion of History & Other Plays, 1978; Confirmation: An Anthology of African American Women, 1983; The Autobiography of LeRoi Jones/Amiri Baraka, 1984; Somebody Blew Up America, 2001; The Book of Monk, 2005; Tales of the Out & the Gone, 2006; Film Appearances: One P.M, 1972; Fried Shoes Cooked Diamonds, 1978; Black Theatre: The Making of a Movement, 1978; Furious Flower: A Video Anthology of African American Poetry 1960-95, Volume II: Warriors, 1998; Bulworth, 1998; Pinero, 2001; Strange Fruit, 2002; Ralph Ellison: An American Journey, 2002; Chisholm '72: Unbought & Unbossed, 2004; Keeping Time: The Life, Music & Photography of Milt Hinton, 2004; Hubert Selby Jr: It/ll Be Better Tomorrow, 2005; 500 Years Later, 2005; The Ballad of Greenwich Village, 2005; The Pact, 2006; Retour a Goree, 2007; Polis Is This: Charles Olson & the Persistence of Place, 2007; Revolution '67, 2007; Turn Me On, 2007; Oscene, 2007; Corso: The Last Beat, 2008; The Black Candle, 2008; Ferlinghetti: A City Light, 2008; Motherland, 2009; editor. **Orgs:** Guggenheim Found fel; Nat Endowment for the Arts fel. **Honors/Awds:** Langston Hughes Award, City Coll New York; Rockefeller Foundation Award for Drama; Inducted into the American Academy of Arts & Letters; Lifetime Achievement Award, Before Columbus Found; Poet Laureate of New Jersey. **Business Addr:** Writer, Poet, Kimako's Blues People, 808 S 10th St, Newark, NJ 07108, **Business Phone:** (201)242-1346.

**BARANCO, HON. GORDON S.**
Judge. **Personal:** Born Feb 25, 1948, Oakland, CA; son of Arnold and Lillian; married Barbara N Gee; children: Lauren Barbara Gee & Brandon Michael Gee. **Educ:** Univ Calif, BA, 1969, JD, 1972. **Career:** Calif State Attys Off, Grad Legal Coun; San Francisco, asst dist atty, 1974-77; Neighborhood Legal Asst, managing atty, 1977-80; Oakland, asst city atty, 1980; Oakland Munic Ct, judge, 1980-84; Alameda Co Super Ct, judge, currently. **Orgs:** Vice chair, Access & Fairness Adv Comt, currently; chair, Community Focused Ct Planning Comt. **Honors/Awds:** Judicial Distinguished Service Award, Alameda County Bar Asn, 2002; Benjamin Aranda III Access to Justice Award, 2009. **Home Addr:** 4300 Sequoyah Rd, Oakland, CA 94605, **Home Phone:** (510)569-5363. **Business Addr:** Judge, Superior Court of California, 1221 Oak St Dept 15, Oakland, CA 94612, **Business Phone:** (510)272-6124.

**BARANCO, GREGORY T.**
Automotive executive, president (organization). **Personal:** married Juanita Powell. **Career:** Baranco Lincoln-Mercury Inc, Duluth, Ga, chief exec officer; Acura Tallahassee, Tallahassee, Fla, pres & owner; Baranco Automotive Group, Lilburn, Ga, pres, chief exec officer, currently. **Orgs:** Bd mem, trustee, Morehouse Sch Med Inc; Nat Minority Supplier Develop Coun; pres, Gen Motors Minority Dealers Asn; bd dir, Kaiser Found Health Plan Ga; Metrop Atlanta Automobile Dealers Asn; Ga Automobile Dealers Asn; DeKalb Chamber Com; pres coun, Spelman Col; Atlanta Bus League; emer trustee, Ga Res Alliance; DeKalb Develop Authority; 100 Black Men DeKalb; United Way; DeKalb County Task Force Efficiency; chmn, First Southern Bank; chmn bd First Southern Bancshares; chmn bd, Atlanta Life Ins Co; bd mem, Tour De Ga. **Business Addr:** President, Baranco Automotive Group, 4355 Hwy 78, Lilburn, GA 30047-4523.

**BARANCO, DR. JUANITA POWELL**
Vice president (organization), executive. **Personal:** Born Mar 19, 1949, Washington, DC; married Gregory T; children: Gregory Jr. **Educ:** La State Univ, BS, JD. **Career:** Legal Coun, co-owner; State GA, asst atty gen, 1970; Fed Res Bank Atlanta, bd dir; Baranco Automotive Group, exec vpres, chief operating officer & co-owner, 1978-; John H Harland Co, dir; First Union Bank, dir; Clark Atlanta Univ, chair, currently; Ga Power Co, bd dir, 1997-2006; Cox Radio, bd dir, 2003-; Southern Co, bd dir, 2006-. **Orgs:** Chair & bd regents Univ Syst, GA; chmn, DeKalb Co Educ Task Force; Ga State Bd Educ, 1985-91; chmn, Educ Comn, 1996 Olympics; exec comt mem, Ga Chamber Com; chmn, Sickle Cell Found Ga; Am Bar Asn; State Bar Asn Ga; La State Bar Asn; Govs Human Rels Comt; trustee, Clark Atlanta Univ; bd mem, DeKalb Chamber Com; Delta Sigma Theta Sorority; bd trustee, Clark Atlanta Univ; chair bd regents, Univ Syst Ga; bd dir, Woodruff Arts Ctr; Gore 2000; Hillary Clinton Pres; Metro Atlanta Chamber Com. **Home Addr:** 4070 Sandy Lake Dr, Lithonia, GA 30038. **Business Addr:** Board Member, Southern Co, 30 Ivan Allen Jr Blvd NW, Atlanta, GA 30308, **Business Phone:** (404)506-5000.

**BARANCO, DR. RAPHAEL ALVIN**
Dentist. **Personal:** Born Nov 19, 1932, Baton Rouge, LA; married Terry Bryant; children: Angela, Rachel & Raphael. **Educ:** Xavier Univ, BS, 1956; Meharry Med Col, DDS, 1961. **Career:** Jersey City Med Ctr, intern, 1961-62; Meharry Med Col, instr prosthetic dent, 1963-64; Va Hosp, Tuskegee, AL, dir clin dent, 1964-68; pvt pract dent, 1968-. **Orgs:** Lafayette Coun Human Rels, 1968-; Sheriff's Adv Comn, 1968-; pres, bd dirs, Holy Family Sch, 1971-; chmn, Lafayette Parish Comt Action Coun, 1971; Nat Asn Advan Colored People; Alpha Phi Alpha; Alpha Phi Omega; Chi Delta Mu; Am Dent Asn; Lafayette Parish Sch Bd; Lafayette Parish Coun Govt; bd dirs, Tri-Parish Comt Action Agency; United Givers Fund. **Home Addr:** 200 Alfred St, Lafayette, LA 70501, **Home Phone:** (337)232-1468. **Business Addr:** Dentist, Individual Practice, 701 N Pierce St Suite 3, Lafayette, LA 70501, **Business Phone:** (337)232-8397.

**BARBER, ATIIM KIAMBU HAKEEM-AH. See BARBER, TIKI.**

**BARBER, DR. HARGROW DEXTER**
Dentist, oral surgeon. **Personal:** Born Aug 29, 1956, Alameda, CA; son of Hargrow Dexter Sr and Jessie Singleton; married Kimberly Higgins DDS. **Educ:** Univ Calif, BA, 1978; Meharry Med Col, DDS, 1983. **Career:** Pvt pract, dentist, 1983-85; Highland Gen Hosp, oral maxillofacial surgeon resident, 1985-89; Cooper Univ Hosp, physician surg, currently; Oral Surg Residency Highland Hosp, 1989; Mercy Suburban Hosp; Temple Univ C's Med Ctr. **Orgs:** Nat Dent Asn, 1979-; Am Acad Oral Med, 1983; Calif Dent Asn, 1986; Am Asn Oral & Maxillofacial Surgeons, 1986; Am Dent Asn, 1986-; Md State Dent Asn, 1988; Am Dent Soc Anesthesiol, 1989; Am Bd Oral Implantology. **Honors/Awds:** Outstanding Achievement Award, Am Acad Oral Med, 1983; Honor Scholarship Award, Meharry Med Col Sch Dent, 1983; Hospital Dentistry Award, Meharry Med Col, 1983; Golden State Achievement Award, 1988. **Special Achievements:** Second black person accepted into the Oral & Maxillofacial Residency Program at Highland General Hospital in its fifty year history; published "Double Degree Oral Surgeons", Journal of Oral & Maxillofacial Surgery, Oct 1989, & "Orbital Infections",Journal of Oral & Maxillofacial Surgery, Nov 1989. **Home Addr:** 2142 66th Ave, Oakland, CA 94621, **Home Phone:** (510)562-1046. **Business Addr:** Physician Surgery, Cooper University Hospital, Bunker Hill Plaza 2 Plaza Dr Suite 203, Sewell, NJ 08080, **Business Phone:** (856)270-4100.

**BARBER, JAMAEL ORONDE. See BARBER, RONDE.**

**BARBER, JAMES W.**
Educator. **Personal:** Born Sep 17, 1937, Alexandria, VA; married Doris; children: Laura & Tracy. **Educ:** BS, 1964; MS, 1975. **Career:** High Meadows Conn State Treat Ctr, dir educ & group life; Ala Ctr Higher Educ, sr group training consult, 1972; Southern Conn State Univ, fac, exercise & sci, 1969-70, dir comm & minority affairs, 1976-81, dir, AAIEEO, 1981-89, dir stud support Serv, 1989-, Women's Track & Field, head coach, currently. **Orgs:** Awards chair, New Haven Scholar Fund Inc; Nat Asn Advan Colored People; bd dir, Regional Workforce Develop; bd dir, Enterprise Empowerment Zone; dir, AA-IEEO, 1981-89; dir, Stud Support Serv, 1989-. **Home Addr:** 65 Vista Terr, New Haven, CT 06515, **Home Phone:** (203)397-3391. **Business Addr:** Director of Student Support & Services, Director of Community Engagement, Southern Connecticut State University, 501 Cres St Engleman Hall Rm 34, New Haven, CT 06515-1355, **Business Phone:** (203)392-5200.

**BARBER, DR. JANICE DENISE**
Dentist. **Personal:** Born Nov 6, 1952, Alameda, CA; daughter of Hargrow and Jessie Singleton; married Russell J Frazier. **Educ:** Mills Col, BA, 1974; Meharry Med Col Dent Sch, DDS, 1979. **Career:** Hubbard Hosp, gen pract resident, 1981-82, asst instr hosp dent, 1981; NY City, assoc dentist, 1983-86; Sydenham NFCC & Harlem Hosp, attend dentist, 1984-86; Harlem Hosp, clin fl coordr, 1985-86; Oakland, Calif, assoc dentist, 1986-; Highland Gen Hosp, 1990; pvt pract, dentist, currently. **Orgs:** Delta Sigma Theta; Acad Gen Dent; Am Dent Asn. **Honors/Awds:** Employee of the Year, Harlem Hosp Dent Clin, 1985; Employee of the Month, Harlem Hosp, 1985; Attending of the Year Dental Clinic, Harlem Hosp, 1986. **Special Achievements:** Abstract: "The Mental Foramen Injection", The NY J Dentistry, 1983; "Cosmetic Dentistry" Harlem Hosp Ambulatory Newsletter, 1986. **Home Addr:** 2930 Peabody Ave, Columbus, GA 31904-8237, **Home Phone:** (706)576-6733. **Business Addr:** Dentist, Private Practice, 5325 Broder Blvd, Dublin, CA 94568, **Business Phone:** (925)551-6740.

**BARBER, MICHAEL LENARD**
Football player. **Personal:** Born Nov 9, 1971, Edgemore, SC. **Educ:** Clemson Univ, grad. **Career:** Football player (retired); Seattle Seahawks, linebacker, 1995-97; Indianapolis Colts, linebacker & mid linebacker, 1998-99.

**BARBER, ORNETTA M.**
Consultant, television producer, executive. **Personal:** Born Mar 14, 1949, St. Louis, MO; daughter of James Ornett and Edna Morales; married R Gregg Dickerson; married Bobby L Wilkerson. **Educ:** Calif State Univ, Los Angeles, Calif, BA, radio & TV broadcasting, 1978. **Career:** Greater Los Angeles Community Action Agency, community activist; KHJ TV, Frankly Female, assoc prod, 1977-86; Elektra & Asylum Rec, Nat Mkt Res, sr dir, 1979-86; WEA Corp, Black Music Mkt, nat dir, 1986-87, vpres, 1987; Hidden Beach Recordings, consult, currently; WithaSong Inc, pres, currently; Best & Brightest 100 Women Corp Am, Ebony Mag, 1990. **Orgs:** Avalon Carver Community Ctr, 1976-; Westminster Neighborhood Assoc, 1976-; Nat Assoc Rec Arts & Sci, 1979-; Yes Jobs Prog, 1987-; Inst Black Parenting, 1989-; Thurgood Marshall Scholar Fund, 1990-; 331 Found, 1991-; chair, Int Asn African-Am Music, 1993; Nat Asn Black Female Execs Music & Entertainment. **Honors/Awds:** Original 13 Award, Jack the Rapper, 1990; Women's Networking Award, Impact Mag, 1990; Heritage Award, Black Radio Exclusive, 1991; Black Woman Achievement, Nat Am Advan Colored People Legal Defense Fund, 1991.

**BARBER, RONDE (JAMAEL ORONDE BARBER)**
Broadcaster, football player. **Personal:** Born Apr 7, 1975, Roanoke, VA; son of James and Geraldine Brickhouse; married Claudia Patron; children: Yammile Rose & Justyce Rosina. **Educ:** Univ Va, BA, com, 1997. **Career:** Football player (retired); Tampa Bay Buccaneers, 1997, right cornerback, 1998-2011, left cornerback, 2003, 2007, cornerback & free safety, 2012; Fox Sports, color analyst; Nat Football League Games, broadcaster, currently. **Orgs:** Phi Eta Sigma Hon Soc; fel Christian Athletes; Phi Eta Sigma Hon Soc; co-chair, Read Across Am Day, 2005. **Honors/Awds:** Best Sportscast, Assoc Press; Soc Prof Journalist Award; Freshman of the Year; 50 Most Beautiful People, People Mag, 2001; Women's Sexiest Male Athletes, Sports Illustrated, 2001; Interception Leader, Nat Football League, 2001; Nat Football League 100 Best Players, The Sporting News, 2003; Champion, Super Bowl XXXVII, 2003; Hall of Fame, Univ Va, 2005; Interception Touchdown Leader, Nat Football League, 2006; Ed Block Courage Award, 2011; Virginia Sports Hall of Fame, 2014. **Special Achievements:** Co-host, Sunday Sports Extra, WFLA News Channel; Co-writter: By My Brother's Side, 2004; Game Day, 2005; Teammates, 2006; Kickoff!, 2007; Go Long!, 2008; Wild Card, 2009; Red Zone, 2010; Goal Line, 2011. **Home Addr:** , Keystone, FL. **Business Addr:** Broadcaster, National Football League, 345 Pk Ave, New York, FL 10154, **Business Phone:** (212)450-2000.

**BARBER, SHAWN WILLIAM (SHAWN BARBER)**
Football player, football coach. **Personal:** Born Jan 14, 1975, Richmond, VA. **Educ:** Univ Richmond, 1998. **Career:** Football player (retired), coach, show host; Wash Redskins, linebacker, 1998-2001; Philadelphia Eagles, linebacker, 2002, 2006, coaching intern, 2010-; Kans City Chiefs, 2005, linebacker, right outside linebacker, 2003-04; Houston Texans, linebacker, 2007; Comcast Sports Network, fantasy analyst; Baker Univ, running backs coach, currently. **Honors/Awds:** Defensive Player of the Year, Atlantic 10 Conference, 1997; Eagles Ed Block Courage Award, 2002. **Business Addr:** Running Backs Coach, Baker University, 618 8th St, Baldwin City, KS 66006, **Business Phone:** (785)594-6451.

**BARBER, TIKI (ATIIM KIAMBU HAKEEM-AH BARBER)**
Executive, football player, broadcaster. **Personal:** Born Apr 7, 1975, Roanoke, VA; son of James and Geraldine Brickhouse; married Ginny Cha; children: Atiim Kiambu Jr, Chason, Riley & Ella; married Traci Lynn Johnson. **Educ:** Univ Va, grad. **Career:** Football player (retired), host, broadcaster, executive; New York Giants, running back, 1997-2002, 2004-05, fullback, running back, 2003, running back, touchback, 2006; OBeverages, partner & investor; Sports broadcaster; LLCWFAN & WCBS, New York, host, 2007; NBC News corres, 2007; NBC's Football Night Am, analyst, 2007; NBC Universal, host; Tiki Ventures; "Fox & Friends", host; Sirius Satellite Radio, Barber Shop, host; WFAN radio, broadcaster; WCBS, New York, news broadcaster; MSNBC, 2008 summer olympics broadcaster; Yahoo! sports, commentator; BBC's Super Bowl XLV, studio pundit; www.thuzio.com, co-chmn & co-founder; CBS Sports Radio, host, currently. **Orgs:** Bd, MMRF; chmn, co-founder, Tiki Ventures LLC. **Honors/Awds:** Three All-Pro, 2002-05; Three ProBowls, 2004-06; BBI Giant of the Year Award, 2005; Super Bowl Appearance, XXXV; 10, 000 Rushing Yards Club; New York Giants All-Time Leading Rusher; New York Giants Ring of Honor. **Special Achievements:** Wrote a book "My Life and the Game Beyond ", 2007; "Tiki Barber's Pure Hard Workout", 2008. **Business Addr:** Chairman and Co-Founder, Tiki Ventures LLC, 546 Fifth Ave 6th Fl Circle, New York, NY 10036, **Business Phone:** (212)869-1100.

**BARBER, VAUGHN J.**
Lawyer. **Educ:** DePaul Univ, JD, 1981. **Career:** Vaughn J Barber Law Off, pvt pract atty, currently. **Orgs:** Treas, Retired Teachers Asn, Chicago, 2006, bd mem, vpres, pres, 2009-10; bd trustee, Chicago Teacher's Pension Fund, 2007. **Honors/Awds:** Armstrong Award, 2014. **Business Addr:** Attorney, Vaughn J Barber Law Office, 1525 E 53rd St Suite 431, Chicago, IL 60615-4575, **Business Phone:** (773)363-9049.

**BARBER, WILLIAM, JR.**
Construction worker. **Personal:** Born Jan 4, 1942, Morristown, NJ; married Anita C; children: William III. **Educ:** Univ Nebr, BE, 1967. **Career:** Town Morristown, recreational dir; M&M Mars, employ & comm rels rep; NJ Morris Cath HS, wrestling coach, coach, 1967-73; Urban 4H, social comt worker, 1967-73; Morristown Neighborhood House, social rec dir, 1967-; Int Harvester, sales trainee, sch comt worker, social case & guid counr, 1967-73; Barber Maintenance Cleaning Contractor, pres; AT&T, mgr bldg opers, mgr pub rels, bldg serv; Passaic Tech Voc Educ, intervention instr, phys health educ instr; St Clare Riverside Med Ctr, ment health counr; Passaic Juv Detentions, phys ed teacher, 1990, 1998. **Orgs:** Counr After Care Clin Drug Rehab Regions Clergy Coun; chmn Juv Conf Bd; Morristown YMCA; Morris Community Col; Plainfield Nat Asn Advan Colored People, 1974; Human Civil Rights Comn; Morristown Kiwanis Club, Morris City Nat Asn Advan Colored People, 1980; Morristown Mem Hosp; parole bd State NJ; Int Group Friendship Force; Morris Habitat Humanity; NJ Sch Soc Workers Coun; Hands Across Morristown; SCI Club; Charles Menninger; Notary Pub NJ; Radio Hist Soc. **Honors/Awds:** Jaycees Distinguished Service Award, 1969; Outstanding Citizen 4-H Club Award, 1970; Morris County Human Resource Award, 1978; Nat Asn Advan Colored People Community Service Award; Community Service Award Ike Martin Book of Honors, 1987. **Special Achievements:** First African American wrestling coach; First African American volunteer fireman in Morristown; Developed a private library with antique radios. **Home Addr:** 22 Tulip Lane, Randolph, NJ 07869, **Home Phone:** (973)895-9921. **Business Addr:** Instructor, Passaic Co Tech Institute, 45 Reiwhardt Rd, Wayne, NJ 07470, **Business Phone:** (201)790-6000.

**BARBOZA, ANTHONY**
Photographer, artist. **Personal:** Born May 10, 1944, New Bedford, MA; son of Anthony and Lillian; married Laura Carrington; children: Leticia, Laryssa, Danica, Alexio & Lien. **Career:** Kamoinge Workshop, photog, 1964; US Navy, photogr, 1965-68; free-lance photogr, 1969-; Int Ctr Photog, lect, 1975; Mass State Coun Arts, lect, 1982; Columbia Col Photog, lect, 1983; Int Ctr Photog, lect, 1983; Ohio Univ, lect, 1985; Ri Sch Design, lect, 2001; Tisch Sch Arts, lect, 2005; Columbia Col Photog, lect, 2007; Tisch Sch Arts, lect, 2011; Barboza Studio.com, photogr, currently; artist, historian, writer; Art Pubs: Songs My People, Little Brown, 1992; Flesh & Blood; Picture Proj, 1992; Shooting Stars: Stuart, Tabori & Chang, 1992; African-Ams, Viking, 1993; Day Life Israel, Viking, 1994; Books: "Black Borders", 1980; "Piano Days", "Black Bk Lists", 1998. Exhibitions: Pensacola Art Mus, 1966; Emily Lowe Gallery, 1967; Morgan State Col, 1968; Jacksonville Art Mus, 1969; Swain Sch Design, 1969; Studio Mus Harlem, 1971; Addison Gallery Am Arts, 1971; Studio Mus Harlem, 1971; Mus Mod Art, 1978; Studio Mus Harlem, 1982; Drew Univ, One-Man Show, 1989; Songs My People, Time Life Tour, 1990; Cinque Gallery, NY, 1990; Brooklyn Mus Art, Committed to Image A Half Century Black Photog, 2001; Day Life Africa, 2002; Day Life Armed Forces Around World, 2003; Sheldon Art Gallery, 2006; African Am Mus Nassau County, 2009; Posing Beauty Hamilton Art Gallery, 2010; We Want Miles Montreal Mus Fine Arts, 2010; Black Dreams/ White Sheets, Bill Hodges Gallery, 2010. **Orgs:** Panelist-judge, Ny Coun Arts, 1973; panelist-judge, Mass State Coun Arts, 1978; panelist-judge, Nat Endowment Arts, 1981; assoc cur photog, Contemp Black Photogr Brooklyn Mus, 1998-00. **Honors/Awds:** Awarded New York Council of the Arts grants, 1974, 1976; National Endowment for the Arts grant, 1980; Int Group Exhibitor of Photogr, 1997; Achievement Award, Cape Verdean Film Festival, 1998; New York Foundation for the Arts grant, 2000, 2002. Lectures, Int Ctr Photog, NYC, 1975, 1983; Mass State Coun Arts, 1982; Columbia Col Photog, Chicago, IL, 1983, 2007; Ohio Univ, Athens, 1985; Oberlin Col, 1986; Lowell Univ, Lowell, MA, 1989; Rochester Inst Technol, Rochester, NY, 1991; Ri Sch Design, Providence, RI, 2001; Wadsworth Anthenum, Hartford, CT, 2002; New York Univ, Tisch Sch Arts, Black Portrait Symp, 2005, 2010; Nassau Community Col, Long Island, NY, 2009. **Business Addr:** Photographer, Barboza Studio Com, 915 Gloucester Ct, Westbury, NY 11590, **Business Phone:** (516)876-1939.

**BARBOZA, STEVEN ALAN**
Writer. **Personal:** Born Jul 20, 1952, New Bedford, MA; son of Lillian Barros and Anthony Canto; married Regina Lewis. **Educ:** Boston Univ, BA, 1976; Columbia Univ, Gradute Sch Journalism, MSJ, 1979. **Career:** Doubleday etc, Auth, 1987-98; Barboza Commun, owner, 1988-; Author:Door of No Return, 1994; American Jihad, 1994; The African American Book of Values, 1998; M Booth, sr writer, 1998-08; Euro RSCG Magnet, sr writer, 2003-05. **Orgs:** Founder & pres, Black Drama Collective Writer. **Honors/Awds:** Golden Globe winner; Emmy Award. **Home Addr:** 245 Ave C 11E, New York, NY 10009, **Home Phone:** (212)995-5921. **Business Addr:** Owner, Barboza Communications, 522 Henderson Dr, South Orange, NJ 07079-2411, **Business Phone:** (973)313-1688.

**BARCLIFF, MELVIN**
Rap musician. **Personal:** Born Jul 12, 1973, Norfolk, VA. **Career:** Vocalist, 1997-; Albums: Welcome to Our World, 1997; Tim's Bio: Life From Tha Bassment, 1998; Indecent Proposal, 2001; Under Construction, 2003; The Best Of, 2004; Timbaland & Magoo Present : Greatest Hits, 2005. Singles: "Beep Me 911", 1997; "Up Jumps Da Boogie", 1997; "Luv 2 Luv U[Remix]", 1997; "Here We Come", 1998; "We At It Again", 2000; "Drop", 2001; "All Y'all", 2002; "Cop That Disc", 2003; "Indian Flute", 2003; Respect M.E., 2006; Shock Value, 2007. **Orgs:** DeVante Swing's Swing Mob. **Business Addr:** Rap Artist, c/o WEA Corp, 111 N Hollywood Way, Burbank, CA 91505, **Business Phone:** (818)843-6311.

**BAREFIELD, DR. JAMES E., II**
Chemist. **Career:** Los Alamos Nat Labs, Anal Chem, laser chemist, res scientist, currently. **Home Addr:** 111 Lane Vista Dr, Los Alamos, NM 87544, **Home Phone:** (505)672-9527. **Business Addr:** Laser Chemist, Research Scientist, Los Alamos National Laboratory, PO Box 1663 MS J565, Los Alamos, NM 87544, **Business Phone:** (505)665-5195.

**BAREFIELD, DR. OLLIE DELORES.** **See Obituaries Section.**

**BARFIELD, CLEMENTINE**
Association executive, executive director. **Personal:** Born Aug 19, 1950, Lexington, MS; daughter of Tolbert and Malinda Baugh; married John J; children: John, Ollie, Malinda, Derick (deceased) & Roger. **Educ:** Wayne State Univ, Detroit, MI, BS, 1981. **Career:** Save Our Sons & Daughters, Detroit, Mich, founder & pres, exec dir, 1987-04. Tv progs: "Oprah Winfrey"; "Phil Donahue"; "Geraldo Rivera"; "20/20". **Orgs:** Am Humanics, Wayne St Univ; comnr, Detroit City Coun-Youth Adv Commn; bd mem, Proj Start; bd mem, Mich Victim Alliance; Nat Org Victim Assistance; admin asst, Am Red Cross, 2010-; admin asst, Nashville Area Red Cross, currently. **Home Addr:** 16896 Tracey, Detroit, MI 48235, **Home Phone:** (313)863-5147. **Business Addr:** Administrative Assistant, Nashville Area Red Cross, 2201 Charlotte Ave, Nashville, TN 37203.

**BARFIELD, DEBORAH DENISE**
Journalist. **Personal:** Born Jul 6, 1963, St. Albans, NY; daughter of William and Carrie Montgomery. **Educ:** Univ Md, College Park, MD, BS, col jour, 1985. **Career:** Black Explosion, Col Pk, Md, reporter, 1983-85; Star-Dem, Easton, Md, sportswriter, 1985-87; Times Herald Rec, Middletown, NY, reporter, 1987-89; Providence J-Bull, reporter, 1989-, Newsday, wash corresp, 2004. **Orgs:** Nat Assoc Black Journalists, 1987-; Sigma Circle Omicron Delta Kappa, 1984-; Sigma Delta Chi, Soc Prof Journalist, Univ Md, 1983-85. **Honors/Awds:** Best in Show, "How Far Have We Come", Maryland, Delaware, DC Press Asn, 1985; NAACP Service Awards, 1987-88; National Awards for Education Reporting, 1988. **Home Addr:** 1113 Md Ave NE, Washington, DC 20002-5331, **Home Phone:** (202)467-2417. **Business Addr:** Correspondent, Newsday, 235 Pinelawn Rd, Melville, NY 11747-4250, **Business Phone:** (631)843-4000.

**BARFIELD, JON E.**
Executive. **Personal:** Born Jan 1, 1952?, Ypsilanti, MI; son of John W; married Betty; children: Jon & Aaron; married Vivian Carpenter; children: 4. **Educ:** Princeton Univ, BA, 1974; Harvard Law Sch, JD, 1977. **Career:** Univ Mich, janitor; Janitorial Serv; Princeton Univ, Janitorial Serv; Sidley, corp & security law; Austin, corp & security law; Brown & Wood, Chigago, Ill, corp & security law; Bartech Group, chief exec officer, chmn & pres, 1981-2012; Barfield & Assoc, consult; Barfield Co, chief exec & pres, 1981, chmn, 1995; First Am Bank Corp, dir; Tecumseh Prod Co, dir, 1993-2006; Granite Broadcasting Corp, dir, 1999-2006; LJ Holdings Investment Co LLC, pres & chief exec officer, 2012-. **Orgs:** Ypsilanti Chamber Com, 1993; bd mem, Eastern Mich Univ Col Bus; pres, Nat Tech Servs Asn; bd trustee, Kettering Univ; bd trustee, Detroit Renaissance; bd dir, Dow Jones & Co, 2006-07; trustee emer, Princeton Univ; trustee, Henry Ford Mus; dir, Blue Cross Blue Shield; bd dir, Nat City Corp, 1998-; bd dir, BMC Software; bd dir, CMS Energy, 2005-. **Business Addr:** President, Chief Executive Officer, LJ Holdings Investment Company LLC, **Business Phone:** (850)299-4200.

**BARFIELD, DR. RUFUS L.**
Teacher. **Personal:** Born Nov 14, 1929, Hickman, NE; married Emma Crawford; children: Rufus Jr, Sheila & Joselyn. **Educ:** Ky State Univ, BA, 1952; Univ Ky, MA, 1956; Univ Cincinnati, MEd, 1966; Ohio State, adv grad work, 1967; Miami Univ, PhD, 1972. **Career:** Educator (retired); Rosenwald High Sch, Ky, teacher, 1952-55; Lincoln Heights Schs, OH, teacher, 1955-56; Hoffman Schs, Cincinnati, OH, teacher, 1956-64; Schiel Schs, Cincinnati, OH, teacher, 1964-66, asst prin, 1966-69; Colum Schs, prin, 1969; Burton Schs, Cincinnati, OH, prin, 1969-71; Ky State Univ, admin asst pres, 1972-74; Acad Affairs Univ AR, vice chancellor, 1977-78; Acad Affairs Ky State Univ, vpres, 1974-77; Bowie State Univ, pres, 1978-83; Montgomery Co Pub Sch, pup personnel admin. **Orgs:** Nat Educ Asn; Am Asn Sch Admin; Phi Delta Kappa; Nat Orgn Legal Prob Educ; Soc Res Admin; Ky Coun Higher Educ; Comn Higher Educ Ky comn child servs. **Honors/Awds:** Merit Award Service, YMCA, 1964; Certificate Award for Outstanding service, Corryville Community Coun, Cincinnati, 1967. **Home Addr:** 11801 Chantilly Lane, Bowie, MD 20721, **Home Phone:** (301)464-0802.

**BARGE, GAYLE S. COLSTON**
Executive. **Personal:** Born Jun 9, 1951, Columbus, OH; daughter of Ervin M Colston (deceased) and Geneva Laws Colston; married Carlos H; children: Darron & Mario. **Educ:** Ohio Univ, attended 1971; Wright State Univ, attended 1972; Minot State Univ, BA, 1981; Seton Hall Univ, MA, 2007; Pepperdine Univ, EdD, 2011. **Career:** City Columbus, pub educ spec, 1976-78; KBLE Ohio, admin mgr, 1978; JC Penney Ins Co, customer serv rep, 1978-80, from underwriter to sr underwriter, 1980-82; JC Penney Co, syst proj coordr, 1982-83, mkt pub affairs coordr, 1983-88, field pub affairs coord dir, 1988-90, field pub affairs mgr, sr community rels proj mgr; Barge Group, pres, 1995-98; Countrywide Home Loans, Mkt & Pub Rels, vpres, 1998-2001; Landsafe, vpres, 1998; Accor N Am, Corp Commun, dir, 2001-02; Pepperdine Univ, Grad Sch Edu & Psychol, staff, currently; Parker Col Chiropractic, chief mkt officer, 2003-04; Tex Southern Univ, Mkt & Commun, dir, 2005-07; Winston-Salem State Univ, asst vice chancellor & chief mkt & commun officer, currently officer, 2007-08; Kaleidoscope Commun, prin strategist, 2008-; Cent State Univ, dir univ pub rels, 2012. **Orgs:** Bd dir, M L King Performing Arts Ctr, 1986-88; comnr, State Ohio Job Training Partnership Act Comn, 1987-88; comm chair, 500 Inc montage & auction, 1988; co-chair, Dallas Black Dance atre Gala Comm, 1990; class mem, Leadership Dallas, 1992-93; mem nat comt, Delta Sigma ta Sorority, 1993-97; exec comm, Links Inc, Plano Chap, 1995; bd mem, Bryan's House, 1995; bd mem, Dallas Women's Found, 1998. **Business Addr:** Principal Strategist, Kaleidoscope Communications, Dallas, TX, **Business Phone:** (937)376-6216.

**BARGONETTI, JILL (DR. JILL BARGONETTI CHAVARRIA)**
Biologist, educator. **Personal:** Born NY; daughter of Arthur and Adah Askew; married Nicholas Chavarria; children: Carlo & Miles. **Educ:** State Univ NY Purchase, BA, 1985; NY Univ, MS, 1987, PhD, molecular biol, 1990; Columbia Univ, postdoctoral work, 1994. **Career:** City Univ NY, Hunter Col, from asst prof to assoc prof, biol, 1999-2006, prof, 2007-, cancer researcher, currently; City Univ NY, Grad Ctr, Molecular, Cellular & Develop PhD Subprogram, chair, currently. **Orgs:** Bd mem, Nat Cancer Policy Bd, 2002-05. **Honors/Awds:** Presidential Early Career Award, 1997; Cathy Keeton Mountain Top Award, NAACP NY Branch, 1997; Felix Gross Endowment Award, 1998; NY Voice Award, 1998; Research Award, NIH SCORE, 2000; New York Mayors Award, 2001; Outstanding Woman Scientist Award, Asn Women Sci, 2001; NYU & SUNY Purchase Distinguished Alumni Award, 2005; Young Investigator Award, mayor of New York; Breast Cancer Research Foundation Award; Alumnae Achievement Award, NYU Grad Sch Arts & Sci, 2015. **Special Achievements:** Numerous publications including, "Mdm2 Associates with Chromatin in the Presence of p53 and is Released to Facilitate Activation of Transcription", Cancer res, 2006; "Phospholipase D Elevates the Level of MDM2 and Suppresses DNA Damage-Induced Increases", 2004. **Business Addr:** Professor of Biology, Hunter College, Rm 942 N 695 Pk Ave, New York, NY 10021, **Business Phone:** (212)650-3519.

**BARHAM, WILBUR STECTSON**
Executive. **Personal:** Born Como, NC; son of Lincoln and Jessie Mae Cowper; married Sonia Arlene Guy. **Educ:** NC Cent Univ, Durham, NC, BS, 1977; Univ Wis Madison, Madison, WI, MBA, 1980. **Career:** Prudential Ins Co, Wash, DC, assoc investment mgr, 1980-83; Ky Fried Chicken, Hanover, Md, real estate mgr, 1983-88; Cardinal Industs, Glen Burnie, Md, real estate rep, 1988; HMS Host Corp, Bethesda, Md, dir govt affairs, 1988; Fed Aviation Admin, external prog specialist, dir Nat Airports Civil Rights Policy & Compliance, currently. **Orgs:** Nat Forum Black Pub Adminr; First Baptist Church, Glenarden, MD; Airport Mny Adv Coun. **Home Addr:** 1214 Kings Heather Dr, Bowie, MD 20721-2015, **Home Phone:** (301)390-9457. **Business Addr:** Director of National Airport Civil Rights Policy & Compliance, Federal Aviation Administration, 800 Independence Ave SW, Washington, DC 20591, **Business Phone:** (202)267-3484.

**BARKER, JUDY**
Executive. **Personal:** Born Feb 5, 1941, Burlington, NC; daughter of Thelma Ferguson; children: Lesa & Lori. **Educ:** Ohio State Univ; Franklin Univ; Xavier Univ, HHD, 1986. **Career:** Key Bank Found, Cleveland, OH, sr vpres, chairwoman; Avon prod, global vpres, pres, currently; KeyCorp, Cleveland, OH, sr vpres, civic affairs & corp contrib. **Orgs:** Pres, Borden Found; United Negro Col Fund; Paine Col; Women's Forum & Proj People Found, NY; bd dir, Coun Better Bus Bur Foundations; bd dir Columbus Airport Authority; mem Afro-Am adv bd Columbus; bd dir Pub/Pvt Ventures, Ohio State Univ Hosps; mem Sch Home Econs adv bd Ohio State Univ; mem corp adv comt Philan; Secy, bd dir ABC Quilts, Northwood, 2003. **Business Addr:** President, Avon Products Foundation Inc, 1345 Avenue of the Americas, New York, NY 10105-5515, **Business Phone:** (212)282-5516.

**BARKLEY, CHARLES WADE**
Basketball player, television sportscaster. **Personal:** Born Feb 20, 1963, Leeds, AL; son of Frank and Charcey Glenn; married Maureen Blumhardt; children: Christiana. **Educ:** Auburn Univ, bus mgt, 1984. **Career:** Basketball player (retired), sports commentator, executive; Philadelphia 76ers, forward, 1984-92, Phoenix Suns, forward, 1992-96; US Olympic Basketball team, 1992, 1996; Houston Rockets,

1996-2000; Turner Network TV, NBA sports commentator, 2000-12; Gordon & Taylor, it guy & ringer, 2012-. **Business Addr:** Sports Commentator, Turner Network Television, 1050 Techwood Dr NW, Atlanta, GA 30318, **Business Phone:** (404)827-1717.

### BARKLEY, MARK E.

Executive, government official. **Personal:** Born Oct 2, 1932, Alpine, AL; son of Simon W Stamps and Ruby Bledsoe; married Arrie Ann Morton. **Educ:** Ala State Univ, BS, 1957; Ohio State Univ, attended 1960; Atlanta Univ, attended 1963; Wash Univ, DSC, 1976; Oper Res, Comput Sci, Stats, 1976. **Career:** AUS Aviation Systs Command, S & CA, mathematician, 1969-70, S&CA & P&P, oper res analyst, 1970-72, Plans & Anal, supr oper res analyst, 1972-77, Black Hawk, proj mgr, supr oper res analyst, 1977-86; Prog Innovators Inc, St Louis, pres, vpres, 1973-; Chm, bd dirs, 1972-. **Orgs:** Asn Comp Mach, 1968-; Oper Res Soc Am, 1972-; Nat Sci Found fel Ohio St Univ, Columbus, OH; secy, bd dirs, Gateway Fed Employees CU, 1976-87, chmn, bd dirs, 1987-91; Soc Logistics Engrs, 1977-; Army Aviation Asn Am, 1972-; deacon, Antioch Bapt Church, St Louis, MO, 1972; Cedar Vly Est Trustees, 1983-; Free & Accepted Masons, AL, 1960; Beta Kappa Chi Sci Hon Soc, 1956-. **Honors/Awds:** Hons grad, Ala St Univ, 1957; long term training, USAF & AUS, 1967-68, 1975; Commanders Award for Civil Service, TSARCOM St Louis, MO, 1983; Exceptional Performance Award, AUS Aviation Systs Command, Black Hawk, 1984; Super Performance Award, 1967. **Home Addr:** 104 Camden Cir, Madison, AL 35758-3609, **Home Phone:** (256)461-0796. **Business Addr:** Budget Officer, United States Army Aviation Systems Command, 4300 Goodfellow Blvd, St. Louis, MO 63120.

### BARKLEY, RUFUS, JR.

Fashion designer. **Personal:** Born Jan 11, 1949, New York, NY; son of Rufus Sr and Sally Virginia Motron. **Educ:** Parsons Sch Design, New York City, 1970. **Career:** Teal Traina, New York, designer; Oscar de la Renta Int, asst designer; Geoffrey Beene Bag & Beene Shirt Bazaar, NY City, designer, 1973-74; Mollie Parnis Boutique & Couture NY City, asst designer, 1975-78; Beldoch Industs, NY City, designer Pierre Cardin blouses, 1982-83; Sherry Cassin & Co Ltd, freelance fashion illusr, currently; Ri Sch Design, adj fac apparel design, currently, lectr/critic. **Honors/Awds:** Don Simonelli Crit Award; JC Penney Sports Award; participant, Ebony Fashion Fair, 1969-79. **Special Achievements:** New Face of '72, article in Women's Wear Daily, 1972; dress design, Bazaar Mag, 1972; Soul on Seventh Ave, article in Time magazine, Aug 7, 1972; 'Designer of the Month', Essence Mag, 1972; dress design, cover of Cosmopolitan mag, 1973. **Home Addr:** 760 W End Ave Apt 8E, New York, NY 10025. **Business Addr:** Adjunct Faculty, Rhode Island School Of Design, 2 College St, Providence, RI 02903, **Business Phone:** (401)454-6100.

### BARKSDALE, CHUCK

Singer. **Personal:** Born Jan 11, 1935, Chicago, IL. **Career:** The Marquees, mem; The Cats & the Fiddle, mem; The Dells, mem, currently; Albums (With the Dells): Oh What a Night, 1957; It's Not Unusual, 1965; There Is, 1968; Love Is Blue, 1969; The Dells' Musical Menu/Always Together, 1969; The Dells' Greatest Hits, 1970; Like It Is, Like It Was, 1971; Freedom Means, 1971; Sweet As Funk Can Be, 1972; The Dells Sing Dionne, 1972; Give Your Baby a Standing Ovation, 1976; The Dells, 1973; The Mighty Mighty Dells, 1974; The Dells vs. The Dramatics, 1975; The Dells' Greatest Hits Volume 2, 1975; We Got To Get Our Thing Together, 1975; No Way Back, 1976; They Said It Couldn't Be Done But We Did It, 1977; Love Connection, 1977; New Beginnings, 1978; Face to Face, 1979; I Touched a Dream, 1980; Whatever Turns You On, 1981; One Step Closer, 1984; The Second Time, 1988; On Their Corner, 1992; I Salute You, 1992; Dreams of Contentment, 1993; Bring Back the Love: Classic Dells, 1996; I Touch a Dream/Whatever Turns, 1998; Reminiscing, 2000; Open Up My Heart: The 9/11 Album, 2002; Hott, 2003. **Honors/Awds:** Rock & Roll Hall of Fame, The Dells, 2004; Vocal Group Hall of Fame, 2004. **Business Addr:** Singer, The Original Dells Inc, PO Box 1113, Harvey, IL 60426, **Business Phone:** (708)474-1422.

### BARKSDALE, REV. LEONARD N., III

Clergy, lawyer. **Personal:** Born Nov 11, 1948, Galveston, TX; son of Leonard N II and Joan Pendergraff; married Gladys Glass; children: Lea N & Anita J. **Educ:** Univ Houston, BA, 1969; Thurgood Marshall Sch Law, JD, 1974; Houston Grad Sch Theol, MA; Col Bibl Studies, Houston, ABS; Dallas Theol Sem, CGS. **Career:** Boys Scouts Am, Eagle Scout, 1964; Us Judge Advocate Gen, Pentagon, Wash, DC, legal intern, 1972; Reginald Legal Aid Soc, Louisville, atty, 1974; Houston Legal Found, atty, 1975; Houston Community Col, law instr, 1975-85; Pvt pract law, sr atty, 1976-; Fifth Ward Missionary Baptist Church, minister, 1992-, pastor, 1994-. **Orgs:** Omega Psi Phi, 1970-; State Bar Tex, 1974-; Phi Alpha Delta, 1974; The Nat Bar Asn, 1975-; secy, Houston Lawyers Asn, 1975-; vpres, Cent High Sch Alumni Asn, 1988-; bd dir, Houston Habitat Humanity, 1988-92; Nat Asn Advan Colored People, 1990-; chmn bd trustee, Col Bibl Studies Houston. **Honors/Awds:** Heber Smith Fellow, 1974-75; Leadership Award, Boy Scouts Am, 1987; Men on the Move in the 90's, Sigma Gamma Rho Sorority, 1992. **Special Achievements:** Scout show chairman, W L Davis Dist of Boy Scouts of America, 1980-81; Continuing legal education lecturer, Gulf Coast Black Women Lawyers Association, 1992; Frequent speaker at church, civic & legal functions. **Home Addr:** 16402 Quail Pk Dr, Missouri City, TX 77489-5705, **Home Phone:** (713)438-2451. **Business Addr:** Pastor, Fifth Ward Missionary Baptist Church, 4300 Noble St, Houston, TX 77020, **Business Phone:** (713)675-5111.

### BARKSDALE, MARY FRANCES

Executive, manager, association executive. **Personal:** Born Apr 5, 1934, Richmond, IN; daughter of Charles Woodson and Mary Ardelia Mitchell; married Wayne Edward; children: Wayne E Jr, Stacey L McCampbell & Vickki A Morgan. **Educ:** Earlham Col, attended 1953; Ind Univ, attended 1981. **Career:** Manager (retired); Int Harvester Co, employ asst, 1969-74, employ supvr, 1969-77, labor rels supvr, 1977-81, human resources mgr, 1981-83; Navistar Int Corp, compensation & develop mgr, 1984-90, mgr human res, 1990-99. **Orgs:** Bd mem, Parkview Mem Hosp, 1970-73, 1974-77, 1985-91, 1995-98; bd adv, Ind Univ, Purdue Univ, 1976-89; bd mem, Urban League, Ft Wayne, 1979-85; 1979-92, Links Inc, pres, 1989-91; bd sch trustee, E Allen Co Schs, 1979-92; bd mem, United Way Allen Co, 1983-86; bd mem, Leadership Ft Wayne, 1983-91; bd mem, Ft Wayne Mus Art, 1991-93; bd mem, Local Educ Fund, 1989-93; bd mem, Ft Wayne Med Found, 1992-95; bd dir, Foellinger Found, 1997-2008, vice chmn & secy, currently; Midwest Alliance Health Educ, 1997-. **Honors/Awds:** Commander of the Garrison Award Community Service, Robert E Armstrong Mayor, City Ft Wayne, 1979; Recognized for Community Service, Kappa Alpha Psi Fraternity, 1981; Community Service to City of Ft Wayne, Gent's Club, 1983; Humanitarian Award, Fort Wayne Urban League, 1985; Helene Foellinger Award, Outstanding Contributions, 1989; Fort Wayne Rotary, Paul Harris Fel, 1992; Executive Director Award, Fort Wayne Urban League, 1994. **Home Addr:** 3424 Mono Gene Dr, Ft. Wayne, IN 46806, **Home Phone:** (219)447-6108. **Business Addr:** Vice Chairman, Secretary, Foellinger Foundation, 520 E Berry St, Ft. Wayne, IN 46802, **Business Phone:** (260)422-2900.

### BARKSDALE, ROSA KITTRELL

Executive. **Personal:** Born Apr 5, 1936, Mt. Vernon, NY; daughter of Fred and Edna; married Leroy; children: Marion Rudy Davis Jr & Kellye Jan Davis. **Educ:** Davis High Sch, AB; Long Island Hosp, Sch Nursing, 1957; Col New Rochelle, BA, 1975. **Career:** New York Bd Ed, nurse, drug abuse & health teacher; Gould Statham, sls rep; Abbott Labs, prof hosp rep; Barksdale Home Care Serv Corp, founder, chief exec officer, 1982-. **Orgs:** New York Health Care Facil Workers Compensation Trust, chair, bd trust, 1998-; adv bd, Visting Nurse Serv Westchester; bd trustee, Col New Rochelle; active mem, Westchester County Black Nurses Asn; New York Asn Health Care Providers; Westchester HELP Mt Vernon; Delta Sigma Theta; adv coun mem, Mt Vernon High Sch; investment bd, chair, youth coun, Westchester Putnam Workforce; bd dir, Am Red Cross Westchester County; bd dir, Nat Conf Community & Justice; African Am Chamber Com, Westchester Rockland County; Westchester Alumnae Chap Delta Sigma Theta Sorority Inc; bd mem, Westchester Rockland County Workforce Investment Bd; County Execs Blue Ribbon Task Force; Zonta Int Westchester County. **Home Addr:** 2 Greens Way, New Rochelle, NY 10805-1222, **Home Phone:** (914)632-0278. **Business Addr:** Chief Executive Officer, Barksdale Home Care Services Corp, 327 5th Ave, Pelham, NY 10803, **Business Phone:** (914)738-5600.

### BARKSDALE, WAYNE E., JR.

Vice president (organization), manager, executive. **Educ:** Purdue Univ, BS, indust mgt, 1976; Univ Mich. **Career:** Eaton Corp, corp indust engr, 1985-89; Westinghouse Elec Corp, Indust Engineering mgr, 1989-92, bus develop rep, 1992-94; prod mgr, 1994-96; Weil-McLain/SPX Corp, dir mfg opers, 1996-2007, vpres opers, 1999-2007; DRS Technologies, vpres opers, 2007-08; StandAero, A Dubai Aerospace Enterprise, dir opers, 2010-. **Home Addr:** 9801 Regatta Dr, Cincinnati, OH 45252-1974. **Business Addr:** Director, Operations, StandardAero, 11550 Mosteller Rd, Cincinnati, OH 45241, **Business Phone:** (513)618-9588.

### BARLEY, TRACY HICKS

Lawyer. **Personal:** Born Roanoke Rapids, NC; married Lesley; children: Leslie. **Educ:** Winston-Salem State Univ, BA, Eng, 1983; NC Agr & Tech State Univ, Grad Sch, MS, adult educ, 1990; NC Cent Univ Sch Law, JD, high hons, 1993. **Career:** Winston-Salem State Univ, 1983-90; NC Cent Univ Sch Law, Durham, 1993-96, clin asst prof; Pillmon Daye & Barley Attorneys Law, Durham, NC, 1995-98; Tracy Hicks Barley & Assocs PA, atty, 1998-2010; Oper Breakthrough Inc, Durham, NC, 2010; Diverse Insulation LLC, 2011; Greensphere LLC, 2011-. **Orgs:** Union Baptist Church Durham; bd mem, Women In Action Inc, pres, N Cent Legal Assistance Prog; Legal Aid NC Durham Adv Bd; comnr, NC Social Serv Comn; Delta Sigma Theta Inc; legal coun, Winston-Salem State Univ, currently. **Home Addr:** 4412 Cumberland Dr, Durham, NC 27705, **Home Phone:** (919)768-8953. **Business Addr:** Attorney, Tracy Hicks Barley & Associates PA, 800 N Mangum St Suite 201, Durham, NC 27701, **Business Phone:** (919)956-9440.

### BARLOW, REGGIE DEVON

Football player, football coach. **Personal:** Born Jan 22, 1973, Montgomery, AL; married Tracy Kidd; children: Erica, Reggie Jr & Simone. **Educ:** Ala State Univ, grad. **Career:** Football player (retired); football coach; Ala State, 1992-95, quaterback coach, 2005-06, coach, 2007-; Jacksonville Jaguars, 1996, 2000, punt returner, 1997, kick returner & punt returner, 1998, wide receiver, 1999; Oakland Raiders, 2001; Tampa Bay Buccaneers, tight end, 2002, 2003; Ala State Hornets, head coach, 2007-; Denver Broncos, asst; Johnnie Carr Mid Sch, coach, currently. **Honors/Awds:** Super Bowl ring for Super Bowl XXXVII Award, winner. **Special Achievements:** Films: 1996 AFC Championship Game, 1997; 1999 AFC Championship Game, 2000. **Business Addr:** Head Coach, Alabama State Hornets, 915 S Jackson St, Montgomery, AL 36101, **Business Phone:** (334)229-4444.

### BARLOW, WILLIAM B.

Educator, college teacher, consultant. **Personal:** Born Feb 25, 1943, Ft. Rucker, AL; son of John Earl and Dorothy Goodman. **Educ:** San Francisco State Univ, BA, 1968; Univ Southern Calif, Santa Cruz, MA, 1974, PhD, 1983. **Career:** Mt Vernon Col, asst prof, 1976-80; Howard Univ, prof, 1980; Univ Miss, Nat Endowment Humanities fel, 1986; Schomburg, Nat Endowment Humanities fel, 1991-92; Smithsonian Inst, Blues Found, consult; Pacifica Radio, music programmer & producer; Barlow Systs, owner, currently. **Orgs:** Union Dem Commun Steering Comt, 1977-; Int Asn Study Popular Music Steering Comt, 1989-; Int Asn Mass Commun Res, 1986-. **Home Addr:** 19 E Curtis Ave, Alexandria, VA 22301, **Home Phone:** (703)519-7894. **Business Addr:** Owner, Barlow Systems, 6640 Camp Bowie Blvd, Ft. Worth, TX 76116, **Business Phone:** (817)732-1489.

### BARNARD-BAILEY, DR. WANDA ARLENE (WANDA BARNARD-BAILEY)

Social worker, manager. **Personal:** Born Jan 29, 1962, Norfolk, VA; daughter of James Webster and Wilhelmina Phillips; married Kevin Bernard. **Educ:** Univ NC, Chapel Hill, BA, recreation admin, 1984, MSW, clin & adminstration, 1986; PhD, social work. **Career:** Albemarle Home Care, hospice social worker coordr, 1986-87; Currituck Co Bd Educ, alcohol & drug & dropout prev coordr, 1987-92; Navy Family Advocacy Prog, clin social worker, 1992-2005, regional dir, 2001; Chesapeake City, Human Develop & Community Initiatives, dep city mgr, 2005-. **Orgs:** Nat Asn Social Workers, 1984-; bd dir, NC Dropout Prev Asn, 1987-92; NC Sch Social Work Asn, 1987-92; bd dir, Albemarle Home Care Hospice, 1988-92; bd dir, Am Cancer Soc, 1988-92; bd, Albemarle Hopeline, 1991-92; dep city mgr, Va Local Govt Mgt Asn. **Honors/Awds:** Volunteer Award, Currituck Co Schs, 1988-91. **Business Addr:** Deputy City Manager, City of Chesapeake, 306 Cedar Rd 6th Fl, Chesapeake, VA 23322, **Business Phone:** (757)382-6166.

### BARNER, SHARON R.

Executive, association executive. **Educ:** Syracuse Univ, BS, psychol, 1979; Univ Mich, JD, law, 1982. **Career:** US Patent & Trademark Off, Dep Dir, 2009-11; Us Dept Com, dep under secy, 2009-11; Foley & Lardner LLP, partner, 2011-12; Cummins Inc, vpres & gen coun, 2012-; Patent Properties Inc, dir, 2013-. **Orgs:** Chair, Foley & Lardner LLP, Chicago Intellectual Property Group, 1998-2009, Intellectual Property Litigation Group, 2003-06; Ill State Bar Asn, currently; Nat Bar Asn, currently; Fed Am Bar Asn, currently; bd, Grateful Hand Found, currently; trustee, La Rabida C's Hosp, currently; independent dir, Walker Innovation Inc, 2013-. **Honors/Awds:** The 50 Most Influential Minority Lawyers in America, Nat Law J, 2008; Women of Vision Award, Women's Bar Asn Ill, 2011. **Home Addr:** 321 N Clark St, Chicago, IL 60610, **Home Phone:** (312)832-4569. **Business Addr:** Vice President, General Counsel, Cummins Inc, 500 Jackson St, Columbus, IN 47201, **Business Phone:** (812)377-5000.

### BARNES, ADIA OSHUN

Basketball player, radio broadcaster, basketball coach. **Personal:** Born Feb 3, 1977, San Diego, CA; daughter of Pete and Patricia Mcrae; married Salvo Coppa. **Educ:** Univ Ariz, sociol, 1998. **Career:** Basketball player (retired); Sacramento Monarchs, 1998; Minn Lynx, forward, 1999; Cleveland Rockers, 2000-01; Seattle Sonics & Storm, forward, 2002-05; Adia Barnes Found, pres, 2003-; Houston Comets, forward, 2005-06; Women's Nat Basketball Asn Seattle Storm, radio & tv color analyst & mc, 2006-; Dynamo Kiev, Ukraine; Broadcaster, 1150 AM KKNW, color analyst, 2007-; Seattle Acad, dir player & coach develop, 2010; Fox Sports, color analyst, 2011; Univ Wash, asst women's basketball coach, 2011-. **Orgs:** Girl Power; Barnes Found; Adia's Dreams Action. **Home Addr:** 3556 Apollo St, San Diego, CA 92111. **Business Addr:** President, Adia Barnes Foundation, PO Box 9671, Seattle, WA 98109.

### BARNES, REV. ANNE T.

Executive, businessperson. **Personal:** Born Mar 10, 1940, Pitt County, NC; children: Darryl & Anita. **Educ:** Corrine Brooks Hair Design Inst, dipl, cosmetology, 1958; Norfolk State Univ, BA, 1964; Nat Beauty Culturist League Inc, BA, 1965, MA, 1969; Va Union Univ Sch Theol, cert, 1979; Gulf Coast Sem, BTh, 1985. **Career:** La Baron Hairstyling Salon, stylist, 1958-61; Bett's Hairstyling Salon, stylist, 1961-67; Anne Barnes Inc, pres, 1967; Anne's Beauty Acad, pres, 1975; Makubi II Corp, pres, currently. **Orgs:** Bd dir, Tidewater Tele Adv Coun; assoc min, Garretts Community Church; bd dir, 100 Black Women Coalition; bd mem, United Christian Front Brotherhood; bd mem, Hal Jackson Talented Teen; Nat Beauty Culturists League, 1959-; bd mem, Church St Merchant Assoc, 1982-; bd mem, Nat Teachers Educ Coun, 1983-. **Honors/Awds:** Businessperson of the Year, TABCA, Norfolk; Award of merit, STOIC, Norfolk, 1981; Outstanding Citizen Award, Iota Phi Lambda Sor Inc, 1984; Black Businesswoman of the Year, Norfolk J & Guide Newspaper, 1984; Outstanding Businessperson of the Year, WRAP radio st, Norfolk, 1984. **Home Addr:** 1506 Covel St, Norfolk, VA 23523-1808, **Home Phone:** (757)543-5403. **Business Addr:** President, MAKUBI II Corp, 701 Tidewater Dr, Norfolk, VA 23504, **Business Phone:** (757)622-7721.

### BARNES, ANTHONY L.

Entrepreneur, government official, real estate agent. **Personal:** Born Jan 1, 1950?; married Mildred Prather; children: 5. **Career:** Realtor, 1983-; Anthony L Barnes & Assocs, pres & chief exec officer, 1989-; Ala's Real Estate Comnr. **Orgs:** Leadership Birmingham Class, 1986; Birmingham Planning Comn, 1991; chmn, bd dir, Water Works & Sewer Bd, Birmingham, 1991-; Metrop Develop Bd; bd, Birmingham Asns Realtors; bd, Ala Asns Realtors; bd Mem Ala Housing & Finance Authority. **Special Achievements:** First African American elected as chairman of the Water Works board in 1998. **Business Addr:** President, Chief Executive Officer, Barnes & Associates PC, Realtors, 660-C Univ Blvd, Birmingham, AL 35233, **Business Phone:** (205)328-3330.

### BARNES, DR. BOISEY O., JR.

Cardiologist. **Personal:** Born May 16, 1943, Wilson, NC; married Bernadine. **Educ:** Johnson C Smith Univ, BS, 1964; Howard Univ, MD, 1968. **Career:** Howard Univ Hosp, Noninvasive Echocardiography Lab, dir, 1974-77, Cardiac Clin, dir, asst prof med, 1976-77; Am Heart Asn, lectr, 1975-77; Shaw E Corp, staff; Boisey O Barnes, pres; pvt pract cardiologist, currently. **Orgs:** Pres, Beta Kappa Chi Hon Soc, 1963-64; DC Med Soc Dipl Am Bd Int Med, 1972; keeper rec & seals, Omega Psi Phi Frat, 1975-77; Am Inst Ultrasound, 1975-77; Am Soc Echo Cardiography, 1977; adv bd, Anacostia Cong Hghts Sect Red Cross, 1977; Vascular Biol Working Group. **Honors/Awds:** Outstanding Young Men American, 1970. **Special Achievements:** Honorary Mention Department Prize International Medicine & Pediatrics, Howard Univ, 1968; Publ "Echo cardiographics Findings in Endocarditis inHeroin Addicts" Amer Journ Card 1977; "Echo cardiography Abstracts, Echo cardiography in Hypertensive Patients" "Echo cardiography in Amyloidosis". **Business Addr:** Physician, Private Practice, 413 G St SW, Washington, DC 20024, **Business Phone:** (202)554-2679.

### BARNES, DR. DELORISE CREECY

Educator, consultant, executive director. **Personal:** Born Apr 2, 1947, Hertford, NC; daughter of William O and Easter Lillian; married James M; children: Victor, Timothy, Stephen & Jonathan. **Educ:** Livingstone Col, BS, 1969; Univ Tenn, MS, 1970, EdD, Voc Tech Educ,

 

1978; Univ Tenn, Knoxville, US Off Educ Fel, 1976. **Career:** Creecy's Poultry Farm, owner, 1962-65; Oak Ridge Pub Health & Welfare Dept, analyst, survr summer, 1965; Eureka Ctr Roane Co Schs, head off admin, 1970-75; Oak Ridge Schs, adult ed instr, 1973-76; Roane State Community Col, prof bus & Sub-Coun Rep, 1975-. **Orgs:** Nat Bus Educ Asn, 1969-; advisor, Phi Beta Lambda RSCC, 1976-; appt gov tn mem, Sec TN CommissHuman Develop, 1977-79; consult, Univ Tenn, Ctr Govt Training, 1980-87, Knoxville Prof Sec Int, 1983-87; Oak Ridge Schs, 1983-88; Martin Marietta Energy Syst Inc, 1984-; pres, Alpha Kappa Alpha Xi Iota Omega; bd dir, Big Bro Big Sisters, 1985-88; chmn-organized, Homework Hot Lines Oak Ridge Schs, 1986-87; Am Bus Comn Asn; Delta Pi Epsilon; resource person, Youth Enrichment Ctr; secy, Crown Monarch, Auxillary Girls Club, 1988-; legis liaison chmn, Tenn Bus Educ Asn, 1988-; pres, Oak Ridge Chap AKA Sorority, 1990-92; pres, Tenn Chap Am Asn Women Community Cols; first vpres, Monarch Inc. **Honors/Awds:** USOE grant, Univ Tenn, Knoxville, 1975-77; Grant for a Model Office, Univ Tenn, 1976; led a round table discussion at NBEA conv; Dedicated Prof, Phi Beta Lambda, RSCC chap, 1988; Publication Award, Writing Ctr, RSCC, 1989; Leadership Award, AKA Sorority Inc, 1990; Businesswoman of the Year Award, Bus & Prof Women's Orgn, 1989; Consortium of Doctors Honoree, Ga Univ Syst, 1991. **Special Achievements:** Changes in Business Education Programs in Tenn public sr high schools since the passage of the Nat Voc Educ Act of 1963, 1978; Published six articles in major publications between 1979-84; "Mobilizing for the Minority Teacher Educ Shortage" in The Balance Sheet, 1988; numerous other articles; presented papers at Am Bus Commun Asn, SE & Midwestern regionals, 1989. **Home Addr:** 126 Barrington Dr, Oak Ridge, TN 37830-7669, **Home Phone:** (865)483-1913. **Business Addr:** Professor, Roane State Community College, 276 Patton Lane, Harriman, TN 37748-5011, **Business Phone:** (865)882-4600.

### BARNES, DIANE
Police officer. **Personal:** Born Jul 4, 1961, Ridgeland, SC; daughter of Leroy and Sally Mae; children: Trameka Lashond Wade. **Educ:** Miami Dade Community Col N, Miami, FL, criminal justice; Nova Seastern Univ, elem educ, 1996. **Career:** Johnson Model City Ins, Miami, Fl, ins underwriter, 1977-79; Metro-Dade Police Dept, Miami, Fl, loan servicing clerk, 1979-80, police rec specialist, 1981; City Miami Police Dept, Miami, Fl, commun oper, 1981-84, police officer, 1984-. **Orgs:** Head Orgn Newsletter, Miami Community Police Benevolent Asn, 1985-; exec bd mem, Miami Community Police Benevolent Asn, 1985-; pres, Miami Community Police Benevolent Asn, 1985; Nat Black Police Asn, 1985-; Fla Women Law Enforcement, 1990-. **Honors/Awds:** Training Adverse Award, Basic Law Enforcement Classes, 1987-89; President's Award, Miami Community Police Benevolent Asn, 1990-91; Community Service Award, People United Lead Struggle, 1990. **Home Addr:** 12289 Pembroke Rd Suite 148, Pembroke Pines, FL 33025-1725, **Home Phone:** (305)433-9587. **Business Addr:** Police Officer, Miami Police Department, 400 NW 2nd Ave, Miami, FL 33128, **Business Phone:** (305)603-6640.

### BARNES, DR. ELSIE M.
College administrator, educator. **Educ:** NC A&T Univ, BS, polit sci; Ind Univ, MA, teaching polit sci; Lehigh Univ, DA; Univ NC, pub admin. **Career:** Norfolk State Univ, prof, polit sci, currently. **Orgs:** Am Soc Pub Admin; Am Polit Sci Asn; Conf Minority Publ Adminr; Va Network. **Business Addr:** Professor, Professor of Political Science, Norfolk State University, B-207 Brown Memorial Hall 700 Pk Ave Suite 460, Norfolk, VA 23504, **Business Phone:** (757)368-4146.

### BARNES, FANNIE BURRELL
Librarian. **Personal:** Born New Orleans, LA; married Richard Alexander; children: Erica Arnetta & Maria Monique. **Educ:** Dillard Univ, AB, 1945; Atlanta Univ, MS, 1950. **Career:** Gilbert Acad New Orleans, teacher eng, 1945-49; Atlanta Univ, asst libr summer, 1950-67; Claflin Col Orangeburg, SC, head libr, 1950-54; Clark Col Atlanta, head libr, 1954-, teacher C lit, 1957-; Atlanta Pub Libr Bookmobile, c libr summer, 1961. **Orgs:** Am Libr Asn; Nat Educ Asn; Nat Asn Advan Colored People; Alpha Kappa Alpha. **Home Addr:** 1981 Valley Ridge Dr SW, Atlanta, GA 30331.

### BARNES, JOHNNIE DARNELL
Football player. **Personal:** Born Jul 21, 1968, Suffolk, VA. **Educ:** Hampton Univ, grad. **Career:** Football player (retired); San Diego Chargers, wide receiver, 1992-94; Pittsburgh Steelers, wide receiver, 1995.

### BARNES, DR. JOSEPH NATHAN
Lawyer, association executive, executive. **Personal:** Born Nov 29, 1950, Hermondale, MO; son of John Wesley and Lillie Mae; children: Julius. **Educ:** Ibadan Univ Nigeria, cert int econs, 1971; Antioch Col, BA, econs & polit sci, 1973; Univ Pa, MBA, 1977, Sch Law, JD, 1977; Wharton Sch Bus, MBA. **Career:** Spearman & Sterling, assoc atty, 1977-81; Zimet Haines Moss & Friedman, assoc atty, 1981-82; Barnes & Williams, partner, 1982-85; Barnes & Darby, sr vpres, partner, 1985; Grigsby & Assocs Inc, managing dir, investment banker; PNC Investments LLC, Bus Banker III, vpres; Old Pt Nat Bank, Chesapeake city exec; Barnes, McGhee, Neal, Poston & Segue, founding partner, currently. **Orgs:** Fel Nat Fel Found, 1973 & 1974; Nat Bar Asn, 1981-87; dir, Black Entertainment & Sports Lawyers Asn, 1983-88; bd mem, Urban League Manhattan Br, 1985-87; Metro Black Bar Asn, 1986-87, Nat Asn Securities Profs, 1986-87; NY chmn, telethon United Negro Col Fund, 1986, 1987, 1988; Nat Asn Advan Colored People. **Honors/Awds:** Rockefeller Grant, 1968 & 1973. **Special Achievements:** First Black NY Law firm listed in Directory of Municipal Bond Dealers, 1987. **Home Addr:** 150 W End Ave Suite 19M, New York, NY 10023, **Home Phone:** (212)724-6015. **Business Addr:** Founding Partner, Barnes, McGhee, Neal, Poston & Segue, 1114 Avenue of the Americas, New York, NY 10036, **Business Phone:** (212)944-1095.

### BARNES, LIONEL, JR.
Football player. **Personal:** Born Apr 19, 1976, New Orleans, LA. **Educ:** Univ La, Monroe. **Career:** Football player (retired); St Louis Rams, defensive tackle & defensive end, 1999-2000; Indianapolis Colts, defensive end, 2000-01; Jacksonville Jaguars, defensive end & right defensive end, 2003-04.

### BARNES, MATTHEW MOLENA, JR.
Community activist. **Personal:** Born Jan 28, 1933, Homer, LA; son of Matthew Molena Sr and Addie Mae; married Clara Mae Lee; children: Danette LaTrise Perry. **Educ:** Contra Costa Community Col; Calif State Univ; Hayward Univ; Univ Calif. **Career:** Mare Island Naval Shipyard, marine machinist, 1951-55, machinist, 1955-63, foreman machinist, 1963-64, equip spec, 1964-65, engr tech methods & stand, 1965-66, foreman machinist, 1966-73, eng tech prev maint, 1973-81, prog mgr, 1981-88; Sunday Sch, supt. **Orgs:** Mare Island Super Asn; Super Toastmasters Club; pres, Richmond Br, Nat Asn Advan Colored People; vpres, Northern Area Conf, officer, Calif State Conf; choir bd, Stewarts Davis Chapel CME Church; chmn, Scholar Com Davis Chapel CME Church; Richmond City Human Rel Speakers Bur; chmn bd, Richmond City Youth Serv Bur; Shipyard Comdr Equal Employ Opp Adv Com; pres, Original 21'ers Club; staff mem, state assembly mem Bob Campbell; pres, Greater Richmond Community Devlop Corp, Nat Asn Advan Colored People, currently, community activist. **Honors/Awds:** First Black Supervisor Mare Island Naval Shipyard. **Home Addr:** 2811 Moyers Rd, Richmond, CA 94806-2728, **Home Phone:** (510)223-6731. **Business Addr:** Community Activist, President, National Association for the Advancement of Colored People, 338 11th St, Richmond, CA 94801, **Business Phone:** (510)236-1166.

### BARNES, MELODY
Government official. **Personal:** Born Apr 29, 1964, Richmond, VA; married Marland Buckner Jr. **Educ:** Univ NC, BA, 1986; Univ Mich, LLB, 1989. **Career:** Shearman & Sterling, atty; Served Asst Coun to House Judiciary Subcomt Civil & Const Rights, where she helped enact into law voting rights Improv Act, 1992; Equal Employ Opportunity Comn, dir legis affairs; Sen. Edward M. Kennedy, chief coun, 1995-2003; Ctr Am Progress, exec vpres, 2003-08; White House Domestic Policy Coun, dir, 2008-, adv; Us House Judiciary Subcomt Const, asst coun; New York univ, vice provost global stud leadership initiatives, currently; Pres Obama, strategic advice, 2009-12. **Orgs:** NY Bar Asn; DC Bar Asn; bd dir, Const Proj; bd mem, EMILY'S List; Maya Angelou Pub Charter Sch; adv bd, Obama-Biden Presidential Transition Team, 2003-08; chair, Aspen Inst, Forum Community Solutions; sr fel Robert F. Wagner Grad Sch Pub Serv, currently. **Business Addr:** Senior Fellow, Robert F. Wagner Graduate School of Public Service, 295 Lafayette St, New York, NY 10012, **Business Phone:** (212)998-7400.

### BARNES, MILTON, JR.
Automotive executive, president (organization). **Educ:** Xavier Univ; Univ Cincinnati. **Career:** Yorba Linda, dealer; Gen Motors Co; Classic Chevrolet, pres & cheif exec officer, 1996-. **Orgs:** Nat Automobile Dealers Asn Acad, 1999-. **Business Addr:** President, Chief Executive Officer, Classic Chevrolet, 1001 N Weir Canyon Blvd, Anaheim, CA 92807, **Business Phone:** (714)283-5400.

### BARNES, N. KURT
Chief financial officer. **Personal:** Born Jan 11, 1947, Washington, DC; son of Norman H and Doris Boyd. **Educ:** Yale Col, BA, econs, 1968; Harvard Univ, MA, econs, 1973. **Career:** Rand Corp, assoc economist, 1968-73; Fortune Mag, assoc ed, 1973-75; Time Inc, asst ed, fin analyst, 1975-77; Inco Ltd, fin analyst, dir investor rels & pres, 1977-98; Marquest Investment Coun Ltd, chmn, 1989-91; Morgan Stanley Dean Witter Investment Mgt, vpres, 1999-; Hale House Ctr, chief financial officer, 2002; Amnesty Int USA, interim dep exec dir; Episcopal Church USA, treas & chief financial officer, 2003-. **Orgs:** Treas, Hale Found, 1974-; Friends Legal Defense Fund; treas, Episcopal Charities New York; bd dir, Episcopal Relief & Develop. **Honors/Awds:** John Hay Whitney Fel, 1970, 1971; Harvard Graduate Prize Fel, 1971, 1972, 1973. **Home Addr:** 1 Sherman Sq, New York, NY 10023-4301, **Home Phone:** (212)595-3568. **Business Addr:** Treasurer, Chief Financial Officer, The Episcopal Church, 815 2nd Ave, New York, NY 10017, **Business Phone:** (212)922-5296.

### BARNES, PAUL DOUGLAS
Government official. **Personal:** Born Dec 20, 1946, Henderson, TN; married Faye L Rainey; children: Richard, Michael & Felica. **Educ:** Lane Col, BS, 1968; Univ Southern Calif, MPA, 1977; Harvard Univ. **Career:** Soc Sec Admin, Columbia, TN, claims rep, 1968-70, admin officer, 1970-73, prog analyst, 1973-77, area dir, 1977-79, regional comnr, 1990-96; Social Security Admin, Atlanta, pep comnr human res, 1997, regional comnr, 2002-; Southeastern Prog Serv Ctr, dir, Chicago Region, regional comnr. **Orgs:** Am Soc Pub Admin; Omega Psi Phi Fraternity; lifetime mem, Nat Asn Advan Colored People; chmn, Atlanta Fed Exec Bd, 2004; United Methodist Church; bd dir, United Way Metrop Atlanta; Sr Exec Serv; lifetime mem, Lane Col Nat Alumni Asn. **Honors/Awds:** Special Achievement Award, 1971 & 1974; Superior Performance Award, 1975-92; Leadrship Award, Social Security Admin, 1992; Meritorious Service Award, Pres Bush, 1992; Distinguished Executive Award, Pres Clinton, 1995; Federal Executive of the Year, Fed Exec inst Alumni Asn, 1997; Meritorious Service Award, Pres Clinton, 1998; Federal Hispanic Heritage Month Excellence Award, Secy Labor, 1999; Distinguished Executive Award, Pres Clinton, 2000; National Public Service Award, NAPA, ASPA, 2001; Roger W. Jones Award, Am Univ, 2001; Equal Employment Opportunity Award, Secy Dept Health & Human Servs; first recipient of the Social Security Commissioner's Personal Achievement Award, 2002; Commissioner's Trailblazer Award, 2005; National Leadership Award; National Combined Federal Campaign Hero Award, 2009; Presidential Rank Award; Hammer Award; Outstanding Young Men in America; Who's Who in Black America; SSA Commissioner's Citation. **Home Addr:** 10014 Village Green Dr, Woodstock, MD 21163. **Business Addr:** Regional Commissioner, Social Security Administration, Atlanta Fed Center, Atlanta, GA 30303-8907, **Business Phone:** (800)772-1213.

### BARNES, QUACY (QUACY TIMMONS)
Basketball coach, basketball player. **Personal:** Born Sep 26, 1976, Benton Harbor, MI; daughter of John and Sonia Wright; married Desmond; children: Trenell Domonic Bell & Taryn. **Educ:** Ind Univ, phys educ, 1998. **Career:** Basketball player (retired), basketball coach; Sacramento Monarchs, 1998; Cleveland Rockers, 1999; Seattle Storm, 2000-01; Phoenix Mercury, ctr, 2002; Ind Univ Womens Basketball, asst coach, 2003-05; Austin Peay, asst coach, 2005-06; Eastern Ill Univ Panther Athletics, Women's Basketball, asst coach & recruiting coordr, 2006-; Tuskegee Univ, coach, 2015-. **Orgs:** Fel, NCAA Div II; Columbus State Univ; NCAA Div I. **Business Addr:** Assistant Coach, Recruiting Coordinator Women's Basketball, Eastern Illinois University Panther Athletics, 600 Lincoln Ave, Charleston, IL 61920, **Business Phone:** (217)581-8505.

### BARNES, RONALD LEWIS
Chief executive officer. **Personal:** Born May 2, 1951, Farmville, NC; son of Carlillia Bethea; married Dannie Edwina; children: Tiffany Monique. **Educ:** NC A&T State Univ, BS, econ, sociol, 1972; Trinity Univ, MS, urban studies, 1974. **Career:** ATE Mgt Serv Co Inc, assoc, 1973-74, gen man, 1974-88Ate Management & Service Co Inc; Greater Lynchburg Transit Co, dir mktg, pre & plan, 1974-76; B'ham & Jefferson Cty Transit Authority, asst resident mgr, 1976-80; Transit Mgt Wayne & Oakland Ctys Inc, gen mgr, 1980-81; Western Res Transit Authority, exec dir, gen mgr, 1981; Madison Metro Transit, gen mgr, 1982-88; Gr Cleve Regional Transit Authority, dep gen mgr, 1989-; Cent Ohio Transit Authority, pres & chief exec officer, currently, Veolia Transp, regional vpres, 2006-08; Steer Davies Gleave, bus strategist, 2008-10; Total Transit Inc, nat busines develop leader-pub transp, 2009-14; Md Transit Admin, sr dep adminr & chief operating officer, 2014-. **Orgs:** Conf Minority Transit Officials; Am Pub Transit Asn Scholar Found; Western Res Hist Soc; Greater Cleve Coun Boy Scouts Am; pres, Black Professionals Asn Charitable Found; Nat Forum for Black Pub Adminr; Blacks In Mgt; dir, Prof on Move. **Home Addr:** 7670 Fulmar Dr, Dublin, OH 43017, **Home Phone:** (614)791-8484. **Business Addr:** President, Chief Executive Officer, Central Ohio Transit Authority, 1600 McKinley Ave, Columbus, OH 43222, **Business Phone:** (614)275-5800.

### BARNES, ESQ. STEPHEN DARRYL
Lawyer. **Personal:** Born May 29, 1953, Los Angeles, CA; son of John J and Marian E. **Educ:** Univ Southern Calif, BA, 1978; Harvard Law Sch, JD, 1981.Univ Southern Calif, BA, 1978; Harvard Law Sch, JD, 1981. **Career:** Covington & Burling, assoc, 1981-86; Weissmann Wolff et al, assoc, 1986-87; Strange & Nelson, partner, 1987-89; Bloom, Hergott, Cook, Diemer& Klein, partner, 1989-; Barnes Morris Klein Mark Yorn Barnes & Levine, partner, 2002-, atty, currently. **Orgs:** Local Spiritual Assembly Baha'i Faith, 1981-; Calif Bar Asn; Am Bar Asn. **Business Addr:** Attorney, Partner, Barnes Morris Klein Mark Yorn Barnes & Levine, 2000 Ave of the Stars 3Fl Ntwr, Los Angeles, CA 90067, **Business Phone:** (310)319-3900.

### BARNES, THOMAS V.
Mayor, lawyer. **Personal:** Born Apr 23, 1936, Marked Tree, AR; son of Ollie Garfield and Thelma Louise Brooks; married Francis Jean Carroll; children: Paul Matthew. **Educ:** Purdue Univ, BS, 1958; DePaul Univ, JD, 1972; AUS Command & Gen Staff Col. **Career:** Pvt pract, atty, Gary, 1972-88; City Gary, mayor, 1988-95; pvt pract, currently. **Orgs:** Bd mem, Retired Ind Pub Employees Asn, 1998; life mem, Nat Asn Advan Colored People; founding mem, James G Kimbrough Law Asn; life mem, Res Officers Asn; AMVETS; Lions Clubs Int, Dunes Chap; hon bd dir, Bro's Keeper; St Monica-Luke Cath Church; Alpha Phi Alpha. **Home Addr:** 1345 Bigger St, Gary, IN 46404-1839, **Home Phone:** (219)944-9946.

### BARNES, VIVIAN LEIGH
Government official, secretary (office), commissioner. **Personal:** Born Aug 9, 1946, Wilkinson, WV; daughter of James Wilder and Margaret Lawson Anderson; married Leroy P; children: Charles Pershon, Jamila Kali & Nathifa Oni. **Educ:** Delta Col; SaginaWVAlley State Univ, BA, sociol, commun, 1996. **Career:** Greater Omaha Community Action Youth Prog, asst dir, 1969-71; Opportunity Indust Ctr, exec secy, 1974-76; Delta Col, Univ Ctr, admin sec, 1977-79; Buena Vista Charter Twp, twp clerk, 1980-90, trustee, 1991-92. **Orgs:** Exec bd mem, Saginaw City Dem Party, 1980-, vice chair, Mich Dem Black Caucus, 1980-; alt deleg, Mich Dem State Cent, 1980-; comnr, Mich Econ & Social Opportunities Comn; bd mem, Saginaw County Community Action Agency. **Honors/Awds:** Community Service Delta Col Black Honors Award, 1983. **Home Addr:** 151 Barbara Lane, Saginaw, MI 48601-9469, **Home Phone:** (989)752-4917.

### BARNES, WILLIAM L.
Lawyer. **Personal:** Born Nov 28, 1936, Benton Harbor, MI; married Patricia Jean; children: Barbara. **Educ:** Los Angeles City Col, AA, 1962; Van Norman Univ, BS, 1965; Univ Southern Calif, JD, 1969. **Career:** Litton Syst, analyst, 1963-65; Northrop Corp, buyer & contracts admin, 1965-69, workmen's comp specialist, 1969-71; Fibre-Therm, gen coun & vpres; Barnes & Grant, atty, 1971-. **Orgs:** Nat Bar Asn; Am Bar Asn; Nu Beta Epsilon Nat Law; Am Trial Lawyers Asn; Calif Lawyers Criminal Justice; Los Angeles Trial Lawyers Asn; Kappa Alpha Psi; Shriners, Free Mason Scottish Rite. **Honors/Awds:** Scholarship, Balwin-Wallace Col, 1953. **Home Addr:** 10319 Ruthelen St, Los Angeles, CA 90047.

### BARNES, ESQ. WILLIE R.
Lawyer. **Personal:** Born Dec 9, 1931, Dallas, TX; married Barbara Bailey; children: Michael, Sandra, Traci, Wendi & Brandi. **Educ:** Univ Calif, Los Angeles, BA, polit sci, 1953, Sch Law, JD, 1959. **Career:** State Calif, Dept Corps, var atty positions, 1960-68, supvr corps coun, 1968-70, asst comnr, 1970-75, comnr corps, 1975-79; Am Shared Hosp, dir, 1984; Leveraged Real Estate Task Force Inst Financial Planners, chmn, 1985-86; Manatt Phelps Rothenberg & Phillips, sr partner, 1979-88, chmn corp & securities dept; Wyman Bautzer, Kuchel & Silbert, sr partner, 1989-91; Katten, Muchin, Zavis & Weitzman, sr partner, 1991-92; Musick, Peeler & Garrett LLP, sr partner, 1992-; GE Capital Franchise Finance Corp, dir, 1995-2001; Spirit Finance Corp, dir, 2003-; investment adv, broker-dealer, representation clients, Securities & Exchange Comn, Calif Dept Corp. **Orgs:** Exec comt, Bus & Corps Sec, 1970-86; vpres & dir, Univ Calif, Los Angeles, Law Alumni Asn, 1971-73, gen coun, dir, 1984-86; chmn, SEC Liasion Comn,

1974-78; chmn, Real Estate Investment Comn, 1974-78; chmn, Knox Keene Health Care Serv Plan Comn, 1976-79; pres, Midwest Securities Community Asn, 1978-79; first vpres, state securities regulator, N Am Securities Admin Asn, 1978-79; co-managing ed, Calif Bus Law Reporter, 1983; bd govs, Century City Bar Asn, 1982-84; vice chair, exec comt, Bus Law Sec, Calif State Bar, 1983-86; chmn, Leveraged Real Estate Task Force, 1985-86; chmn, bd trustee, Wilshire United Methodist Church, 1986-91; dir pub coun, 1988-90; Independent Comn Los Angeles Police Dept, 1991; Calif Senate Comn CRE Governance; Independent Comn Rev Los Angeles Police Dept; adv bd, Inst CRE Coun; exec comn, Corp & Com Law Sec, Beverly Hills Bar Asn; vice chmn, Comn Corp; Corp Banking & Bus Law, Fed Regulation Securities, Commodities, Franchises & State Regulation Comts; Am Bar Asn; vice chmn, Oil Investment Comn; active leadership directing Securities Reg Prog Calif; Comn Real Estate Franchises Mutual Funds; Ad hoc Comt, Corp Governance Bus Law Sect Calif State Bar; Fed Regulation Securities Comt; State Regulation Securities Comt; Futures Regulation Comt. **Honors/Awds:** Certificate of Appreciation, Practicing Law Inst, 1973; Law School, Alumnus of the Year, Univ Calif, Los Angeles, 1976; Resolutions of Commendation, Calif State Senate & Assembly, 1979; Specialist in Real Estate Securities, Real Estate Securities and Syndication Institute, 1983. **Special Achievements:** The Best Lawyers in America for the last 21 years. **Business Addr:** Partner, Musick Peeler & Garrett LLP, 1 Wilshire Blvd Suite 2000, Los Angeles, CA 90017, **Business Phone:** (213)629-7600.

## BARNES, WILSON EDWARD

Military leader, marshal. **Personal:** Born Jun 9, 1938, Richmond, VA; son of Ora Henderson; married Barbara A Jones; children: Kaye, Lynette & Kimberly. **Educ:** Va State Univ, BS, Biol, 1960, MS, 1971; Univ Southern Calif, Doctoral Studies. **Career:** Military leader, Marshal (retired); AUS 18th Battalion 4th Training, comdr, 1976-78; Richmond Recruiting Battalion, comdr, 1978-80; Area IV First ROTC Region, comdr, 1982-84; Hq Dept Army ROTC Study Group, dir, 1984-86; US Cent Command, Dep J-1, col, 1986-88. Fla Supreme Ct, marshal, 1990-2005. **Orgs:** Asn AUS; Va State Univ Alumni Asn; Nat Asn Advan Colored People; Retired Officer's Asn; Urban League. **Home Addr:** 1949 Setting Sun Trl, Tallahassee, FL 32303-2636, **Home Phone:** (850)562-1025.

## BARNES, YOLANDA L.

Government official. **Personal:** Born Aug 15, 1961, Cleveland, OH; daughter of Ellis Clancy and Henrietta; married James A; children: Alayna. **Educ:** Cleveland State Univ, BA, 1983; Cleveland Marshall Col Law, JD, 1987. **Career:** Ohio Bur Workers Compensation; Indust Comn OH; Ohio Atty Gen Off, asst atty gen, appellees Indust Comn, Ohio. **Orgs:** Ohio State Bar Asn, workers compensation comm. **Home Addr:** 5664 Bull Run Ct, Columbus, OH 43230, **Home Phone:** (614)473-0460. **Business Addr:** Assistant Attorney General, Administration section, Ohio Atty Gen Off, 30 E Broad St 17th Fl, Columbus, OH 43215-5148, **Business Phone:** (614)466-4320.

## BARNETT, AMY DUBOIS

Editor. **Personal:** Born Sep 1, 1969, Chicago, IL; daughter of Stephen and Marguerite Ross; married Nathaniel Newell John Grant; children: Max. **Educ:** Brown Univ, BA, polit sci, 1991; Parsons Sch Design, fashion merchandising, 1993; Columbia Univ, NY, MFA, creative writing, 1998. **Career:** Fashion Almanac Mag, managing ed, 1996-98; Essence Mag, lifestyle ed, 1998-2000; Honey Mag & Website, ed in chief, 2000-03; Teen People Mag & Website, managing ed in chief, 2003-05; Time Inc, managing ed; Harper's Bazaar Mag & Website, dep ed in chief, 2007-08; Polymath Media, pres, 2008-10; Ebony Mag, editor-in-chief, 2010-; Books: "Get Yours How to Have Everything You Ever Dreamed of & More", 2007. **Orgs:** Nat Asn Black Journalists; Am Socs Mag Ed; Girls Inc New York; Brown Alumni Monthly Mag; Delta Sigma Theta. **Home Addr:** 605 Pk Ave Suite 15B, New York, NY 10065-7018. **Business Addr:** Managing Editor, Time Inc, 1 Time Warner Ctr, New York, NY 10019-8016, **Business Phone:** (212)484-8000.

## BARNETT, CARL L., SR.

Automotive executive. **Educ:** Mott Jr Col, journeyman millwright apprenticeship, 1973; Gen Motors Dealer Develop Acad, attended 1987; Ark AM&N Col, Hon LLD, 1967. **Career:** Gen Motors Corp, assembly line employee, 1967-74, supvr, 1974-81, gen supvr, 1981-86; Paris Ford Lincoln & Mercury, owner, 1994-; Gulf Freeway Pontiac GMC Truck, owner & pres, 1991; Barnett Auto Group, pres, 1989-. **Orgs:** Bd dir, Houston Automobile Dealers Asn; bd dir, Nat Automobile Dealers Asn; bd dir, Gen Motors Minority Dealers Asn, 1993-97. **Honors/Awds:** Ranked 34 on list of top 100 auto dealers, Black Enterprises, 1994; Ranked 31 on list of top 100 auto dealers, Black Enterprises, 1999; Ranked 18 on list of top 100 auto dealers, Black Enterprises, 2000; Time Quality Dealer Award, 2005; Lifetime Achievement Award, NAMAD, 2012; Honorary Doctorate, Univ Ark, 2013. **Business Addr:** President, Barnett Auto Group, 10200 Hartsook St, Houston, TX 77034, **Business Phone:** (713)941-2730.

## BARNETT, ETHEL S.

Government official. **Personal:** Born Mar 7, 1929, Macon, GA; children: Prentis Earl Vinson. **Educ:** Pioneer Bus Sch, attended 1950; Cheyney State Col. **Career:** Government official (retired); Supreme Lib Life Ins Co, ins agt, 1954-55, City Philadelphia Police Dept, police officer, 1961-71; Commonwealth Pa, civil serv comnr; State Civil Serv Comn, chmn, 1991-98. **Orgs:** Vpres, treas, Nat dir resource develop, Am Found Negro Affairs, 1972, 1976, 1978, 1987, 1992, 1998; bd dir, Women Greater Philadelphia, 1978-; first Black reg dir, Pa Fedn Dem Women; nat dir, Educ Dept, 1978-; consult, PECO Elec Co, 1979-; Int Personnel Mgr Asn; PUSH; Elks; Nat Asn Advan Colored People; Nat Asn Female Execs. **Honors/Awds:** Community Service Award, N Philadelphia Chap, Nat Asn Advan Colored People, 1973; Humanitarian Award, Bell Tel Co Pa, 1976; Outstanding Woman of the Year, Bright Hope Bapt Church, 1977; Patriots Bowl, City Philadelphia, 1980. **Special Achievements:** First African American regional director to Pennsylvania Federation of Democratic Women; First Black Women Member of the Civil Service Commission. **Home Addr:** 1901 John F Kennedy Blvd Apt 509, Philadelphia, PA 19103-1503, **Home Phone:** (215)569-1011.

## BARNETT, FRED LEE, JR.

Football player, executive. **Personal:** Born Jun 17, 1966, Gunnison, MS. **Educ:** Ark State Univ, grad. **Career:** Football player (retired), executive; Philadelphia Eagles, wide receiver, 1990-95; Miami Dolphins, wide receiver, 1996-97; Barbecue Restaurant, owner, currently. **Honors/Awds:** Pro Bowl, 1992; Eagles Ed Block Courage Award recipient, 1994. **Special Achievements:** Films: "1990 NFL Draft", 1990, The Complete History of the Philadelphia Eagles, 2004, Leaf, 2008; "Where's Daddy?", 2017. **Business Addr:** Owner, Barbecue Restaurant.

## BARNETT, KENNETH LYDELL

Business owner. **Personal:** married Helene Morgan; children: Camille & Nydia. **Educ:** Wesleyan Univ. **Career:** Geffen Playhouse Inc, staff; Landmark Partners Inc, staff; Lagniappe Bed & Breakfast, innkeeper, currently. **Business Addr:** Innkeeper, Lagniappe Bed & Breakfast, 1925 Peniston St, New Orleans, LA 70115-5355, **Business Phone:** (504)899-2120.

## BARNETT, DR. LORNA

Executive, chiropractor. **Personal:** Born Sep 5, 1951, Trinidad; daughter of Theodora J; children: Ki Joy, Sophia & Angelika Morris. **Educ:** Brooklyn Col, attended 1978; Pratt Inst, attended 1987; NY Chiropractic Col, Doctor Chiropractic, 1991; City Univ NY Col, MS, educ, 2010. **Career:** New York Tel, supvr, comput opers, 1982; Barnett Wellness Ctr, 1991-; chiropractor & kinesiologist, 1991-; self-employed, massage therapist. **Orgs:** NYZS; New York Chiropractic Coun. **Home Addr:** 67 Manhattan Ave Apt 14C, Brooklyn, NY 11206-3113, **Home Phone:** (718)387-3478. **Business Addr:** Chiropractor, Massage Therapist, Barnett Chiropractic & Wellness, 115 Joralemon St, Brooklyn, NY 11201-4007, **Business Phone:** (718)399-1709.

## BARNETT, ROBERT

Government official, lawyer. **Personal:** Born Apr 21, 1938, Fayetteville, GA; son of Robert and R C Hightower; married Bessie Pearl Burch; children: Robert Terrance. **Educ:** Morris Brown Col, BA, 1961; Ga State Univ, MA. **Career:** Atlanta Housing Auth, admin intern, 1966-67, bus relocation adv, 1967-69, proj coordr, 1969-71, asst dir redevelop, 1971-75, dir redevelop, 1975-; HUD, Atlanta, Ga, regional rehab mgt officer, 1981-; Barnett & Assocs, Pa, atty, managing dir, pres & owner, currently. **Orgs:** Basketball & football referee, S Conf Off Asn, 1965-; Nat Asn Housing & Redevelop Officials, 1966-; Ford Fel Scholar, Ga State Univ, 1970; Resurgens, 1971-; vice chmn, Salvation Army Adv Coun, 1974-; Leadership Atlanta, 1978-; vpres, W Manor Elem Sch PTA, 1979-; pres, Capitol City Officials Asn, 1980-; pres, Morris Brown Col Athletic Found, 1985-; bd trustee, Morris Brown Col, 1989-. **Honors/Awds:** Annual Housing Award, Interfaith Inc, Atlanta, 1976; Certificate of Appreciation for Outstanding Performance, Atlanta Housing Authority, 1977; Inducted, Hall of Fame, Morris Brown Col, TAY Club, 1978; Federal Employee of the Year, Civic & Community Servs, Fed Exec Bd, 1989; Atlanta Univ Ctr Hall of Fame, Extra Point Club Inc, 1990. **Home Addr:** 3317 Spreading Oak Dr SW, Atlanta, GA 30311-2931, **Home Phone:** (404)696-0041. **Business Addr:** President & Managing Director, Principal Owner, Barnett & Associates PA, 1000 N Ashley Dr, Tampa, FL 33602, **Business Phone:** (813)224-9510.

## BARNETT, DR. SAMUEL B.

Police officer. **Personal:** Born May 5, 1931, Philadelphia, PA; son of Solomon and Jennie; married Dorothy; children: Diane, Avonna, Christopher, Samuel, Donna & Betty. **Educ:** Temple Univ, AA, BS; Kean Col, MA; Rutgers Univ, EdD; Univ Pa, Fels Inst; Woodrow Wilson Sch Princeton Univ; Southeastern Univ, PhD, 1979. **Career:** City Philadelphia, PA, police officer, 1957-62; Philadelphia Area Delinquent Youth Prog, proj dir, 1965-67; German Town Settlement, Philadelphia, PA, youth work counr, 1965-68; State Pa, parole officer, 1967-68; Social Learning Lab Educ Testing Serv, prof assoc res div, 1968-82; Veterans Admin, Philadelphia, PA, benefits counr, 1985-86. **Orgs:** Am Personnel & Guidance Asn; Am Soc Criminol; Nat Coun Measurement Educ; Nat Asn Blacks Criminal Justice Syst; bd dirs, Timberlake Camp Charities Inc. **Honors/Awds:** Chamber of Commerce Award, City Philadelphia; Pop Warner All-American Football Player, 1950; Police Dept Commemdation Bravery, City Philadelphia, 1959, Badge & Key Award, 1959; Award for Outstanding ServiceYouth, 1967. **Home Addr:** 849 E Rittenhouse St, Philadelphia, PA 19138, **Home Phone:** (215)849-4497. **Business Addr:** Princeton, PA.

## BARNETT, TEDDY

Association executive, accountant, executive. **Personal:** Born Mar 12, 1948, Freeport, NY; married Carol Ann Grier; children: Joell Carol, Jason Theodore & Jordan Dai. **Educ:** Boston Univ, BS, 1970. **Career:** Price Waterhouse & Co, sr acct, 1970-75; Bedford Stuyvesant Restoration Corp, dir int audit, 1976-78, dir fin admin, 1978-79, vpres fin & admin, 1980-81, exec vpres, 1981-82, pres, 1982. **Orgs:** Bd dir, Enock Star Restoration Housing Develop Fund; Stearns Pk Civic Asn; Nat Asn Accountants; Nat Asn Black Accountants; bd dir, Brooklyn Arts Coun; Am Red Cross, Greater NY Brooklyn Chap. **Honors/Awds:** Black Achievers in Industry Award, 1974; American Achievement Award, Key Woman, 1984. **Home Addr:** 267 Moore Ave, Freeport, NY 11520-1004.

## BARNETT-REYES, SAUNDRA

Psychiatrist. **Educ:** State Univ New York Upstate Med Univ, attended 1973; Am Bd Psychiat & Neurol, cert. **Career:** State Univ NY Upstate Med Univ Hosp, intern, 1973-74, resident, psychiat, 1974-77; St Joseph's Hosp Health Ctr, psychiat, currently. **Orgs:** Am Bd Psychiatry & Neurol. **Home Addr:** 614 S Salina St 2nd Fl, Syracuse, NY 13202, **Home Phone:** (315)422-2700. **Business Addr:** Psychiatry, St Josephs Hosp Health Center, 301 Prospect Ave, Syracuse, NY 13203-1898, **Business Phone:** (315)448-5111.

## BARNETTE, NEEMA

Television director, college teacher, movie director. **Personal:** Born Dec 14, 1949, New York, NY; married Reed R McCants; children: 1. **Educ:** City Col NY, BA; NY Univ, Sch Arts, MFA; Am Film Inst. **Career:** Urban Arts Corps, actress & dir; Hope Entertainment, founder & owner, 1990-; Univ Calif Los Angeles, prof, 1999-; Univ Southern Calif, assoc prof, 2002-; Live Theatre Gang, exec dir. Stage director, "The Blue Journey", Public Theatre, New York City; "The Talented Tenth", Manhattan Theatre Club; television director, "To Be a Man", ABC, "One More Hurdle", 1984, "Silent Crime", NBC, "What's Happening Now", 1986, "Frank's Place", 1987, "It's a Living", 1988, 1989; "The Robert Guillaume Show", 1989; "Hooperman", 1989, "The Cosby Show", 1989, 1990, 1991, "China Beach", 1990, "Zora Is My Name", 1990, "A Different World", 1990, 1991, "The Royal Family", 1991, "Different Worlds: An Interracial Love Story", 1992, "Better Off Dead", Showtime, 1993; "The Sinbad Show", 1993, "Scattered Dreams", 1993, "Sin & Redemption", CBS, 1994, "The Cosby Mysteries", 1994, 1995, "Diagnosis Murder", 1994, 1998, "Deadly Games", 1996, "Run for the Dream: The Gail Devers Story, 1996, "Close to Danger, 1997, "Seventh Heaven", 1998, "The PJs", 2000, "The Gilmore Girls", 2003, "Miracle's Boys", 2005, "Being Mary Jane", 2015; Film director: "Sky Captain", 1985; "The Fig Tree" "Spirit Lost", 1997; "Civil Brand", 2002; "All You've Got", 2006; "Super Sweet 16: The Movie", 2008; "Heaven Ain't Hard to Find", 2010, "Woman Thou Art Loosed: On the 7th Day", 2012. Film producer: "Sky Captain", 1985; "The Fig Tree"; "Civil Brand", 2002, "Woman Thou Art Loosed: On the 7th Day", 2012. Screenwriter: "Sky Captain" 1985, "The Fig Tree". **Orgs:** Dirs Guild Am, mem African Am Steering Comt; Black Filmmakers Found, founding mem; Am Film Inst Independent Film Comt, panel mem; Writers Guild Am. **Special Achievements:** First African American woman to sign a deal with a major studio; first African American woman to direct a sitcom on a major U.S. TV network. **Business Addr:** UCLA School of Theater, Film and Television, 102 E Melnitz Hall, Los Angeles, CA 90095-1622, **Business Phone:** (310)206-2736.

## BARNEY, LEMUEL JACKSON (LEMUEL JOSEPH BARNEY)

Executive, football player, baptist clergy. **Personal:** Born Sep 8, 1945, Gulfport, MS; son of Lemuel Sr and Burdell; married Benny; married Martha; children: Lemuel III & LaTrece; married Jacci. **Educ:** Jackson State Univ, BS, 1967. **Career:** Football player (retired), clergy; Detroit Lions, cornerback, 1967-77; Black Entertainment TV, sports analyst, 1992; Mich Con, community activ specialist, 1992-93; Mel Farr Automotive Group, finance dir, 1993-2001; Springhill Missionary Baptist Church, Assoc Pastor, currently. **Orgs:** Kappa Alpha Psi Fraternity Inc; bd dir, Prison Fellowship Ministries. **Special Achievements:** The Black 6, Actor, 1973. **Business Addr:** Baptist Minister, Springhill Missionary Baptist Church, 19321 Greenfield Rd, Detroit, MI 48235, **Business Phone:** (313)837-1080.

## BARNEY, WILLIE J.

Executive, president (organization). **Personal:** Born Oct 10, 1927, Parkdale, AR; married Hazel Willis; children: Ronald, Reginald, Raymond & Reynaldo. **Career:** WISEC C, pres & founder, 1967-70; Consol Rec Distrib, pres, 1968-; Pyramid Int, pres 1953-66; Barney's Rec Inc, pres, 1953-96. **Orgs:** Sr warden Masons Masonic Chicago, 1959-69; Westside Bus Asn, 1973-75; Mkt & Com Black Music Asn, 1978-; treas, Operation Brotherhood, 1979-. **Home Addr:** 1326 S Troy St, Chicago, IL 60623. **Business Addr:** President, Barney's one stop records, 3145 W Roosevelt Rd, Chicago, IL 60612-3939, **Business Phone:** (773)521-6300.

## BARNWELL, ANDRE

Educator, fashion designer. **Educ:** Univ Houston, bus admin, 1983; Howard Univ, BBA, mkt, 1986. **Career:** Andre Barnwell Frangrances Inc, pres & fragrance designer, 1992-; Fashion Inst Design & Merchandising, adj prof, instr, 1998-, col rep, 2007-, guest beauty blogger, 2011-; Saw Elephant Entertainment, producer/dir, 2002-; 3 Days Fashion, host & emcee, 2012-; Armory Ctr Arts, instr Web TV, 2013-. **Orgs:** John Muir High Sch Adv Bd; Omega Psi Phi Fraternity Inc. **Special Achievements:** Book: Saw the Elephant Books. **Business Addr:** Faculty, Fashion Institute of Design & Merchandising, 919 S Grand Ave, Los Angeles, CA 90015-1421, **Business Phone:** (213)624-1201.

## BARNWELL, DR. HENRY LEE

Clergy. **Personal:** Born Aug 14, 1934, Blountstown, FL; married Shelie Yvonne Whiley; children: Aubrey, Cassandra, Timothy & Darlene. **Educ:** Univ Md; Ariz Col, BA, 1978; St Stephens Col, MS, 1979; Carolina Christian Univ, doctorate ministry, 1984; Grand Canyon Col; Talbot Theol Sem, Biola Univ; Lacy Kirk Williams Minster's Inst, Bishop Col. **Career:** First New Life Missionary Baptist Church, pastor emer; Maricopa City Personnel, admin aide, 1977-80; Bishop Can & 1st State Bishop Ariz, pastor, currently; Zion Rest Dist Asn, bible inst. **Orgs:** Chmn, Evangelism Bd Area I AB PSW, 1970-83; exec bd mem, Phoenix AZ PUSH Inc, 1979-; chaplain, Juv Dept Corrections, 1980-; exec bd mem, Phoenix OIC, 1980-; moderator, Area I Am Baptist Pac SW, 1984-; pres, Interdenominational Ministerial Alliance, 1984-; reg dir, Nat Evangelism Movement, 1984-; relig adv coun mem, Maricopa City Sheriff Dept, 1984-; Libr Cong; bd dir, St. Mary Food Bank; fel Nat Asn Advan Colored People; bd dir & gen chmn, Martin Luther King Jr.Candlelight Serv. **Home Addr:** 11633 N 49th Dr, Glendale, AZ 85304-2910, **Home Phone:** (602)938-1835. **Business Addr:** Pastor, 1st State Bishop Arizona.

## BARR, WENDEL

Vice president (organization), executive. **Educ:** DeVry Inst Technol, Phoenix, AZ, BS, elec engineering, 1984; Nat Univ, San Diego, CA, MBA, bus, 1987. **Career:** GE Healthcare, Field Engineering Prog, 1984-85, field support engr w region, 1985-89, area serv mgr northwest dist, 1989-90, mgr serv progs, 1990-93, serv mkt Latin Am mgr, 1993-95, Parts & Accessories Bus, mgr, 1995-97, gen mgr, 1997-2000; Marconi Med Systs, global vpres & gen mgr; Marconi Med Serv, vpres & gen mgr; Covance Labs, exec vpres & chief operating officer, 1997-2011, corp vpres & gen mgr, 2000-03, Early Develop Labs, corp sr vpres & pres, 2003-07; Synteract Inc, chief exec officer, 2011-. **Honors/Awds:** "Black Enterprise," The 100 Most Powerful Executives in Corporate America, 2010. **Business Addr:** Chief Executive Officer, SynteractHCR, 430 Davis Dr Suite 500, Morrisville, NC 27560, **Business Phone:** (919)674-8080.

### BARR-BRACY, ADRIAN (ADRIAN E BRACY)
Vice president (organization), sports agent. **Personal:** married Vernon; children: Donovan. **Educ:** Morgan State Univ, Baltimore, BA, acct; Nova SE Univ, Ft Lauderdale, Fla, MBA. **Career:** Baltimore Sun, acct, 1983-86; athletic player, athletic dir (retired); Wake Forest Univ, sports marketer & acct exec, 1989, dir community progs, 1991-94, asst athletic dir, 1995-99; Bowie State Univ, athletics dir, 2000-02; NC A&T State Univ, athletics dir, 2002-04; St. Louis Rams, vpres finance, currently; Ariz Cardinals, dir finance; Miami Dolphins; Joe Robbie Stadium Corp. **Honors/Awds:** Dolphins & Pro Player Stadium, dir finance, 1995-99; St. Louis Business Journals Most Influential Business Women Award, 2006; YWCA Metro St. Louis Leader of Distinction Award in Corporate Management, 2006; 50 Most Powerful Black Women in Business, 2006. **Special Achievements:** Only black female CFO with an NFL team. **Business Addr:** Director Finance, Arizona Cardinals, PO Box 888, Phoenix, AZ 85001, **Business Phone:** (602)379-0101.

### BARR-DAVENPORT, LEONA
President (organization). **Personal:** Born Nov 30, 1957, Hemingway, SC; daughter of Luther Rufus and Mary Leona; married Jewel L. **Educ:** Leadership Ga, attended 1999; Benedict Col, BS, bus admin & econ; MBA, mkt concentration, 2001; Leadership Atlanta grad, attended 2002; Diversity Leadership Acad, currently. **Career:** Atlanta Bus League, dir, pres & chief exec officer, 1998-. **Orgs:** Co-chair, Atlanta Red Cross, 2002; adv bd, Clark Atlanta Univ Community, 2002-03; adv bd, Goodwill Industs Atlanta Inc; secy, Minority Entrepreneurship Educ Inc; Antioch Baptist Church N; advisor, Southwest Atlanta Youth Bus Orgn, currently; Metro-Atlanta Opportunities Industrialization Ctr; Atlanta Inter-Alumni Coun United Negro Col Fund; bd dir, Atlanta Bus League; Voter Educ Proj Inc; workforce investment bd, State Ga; Atlanta Develop Authority; Workforce Develop Fulton County; Boy Scouts Am; Nat Leadership Coalition; Atlanta Coalition 100 Black Women, bd, Crossroads Community Ministries, currently; bd, Econ Develop Corp Fulton County, currently; Nat Bus League. **Business Addr:** President, Chief Executive Officer, Atlanta Business League, 931 Martin Luther King Jr Dr NW, Atlanta, GA 30314, **Business Phone:** (404)584-8126.

### BARRETT, AUDRA (AUDRA BARRETT SHIVERS)
Business owner. **Personal:** Born Mar 12, 1967, Richmond, VA; daughter of William and Barbara; married Roderic A. **Educ:** Southern Ill Univ, BS, jour, 1989. **Career:** Richmond-Times Dispatch Newspaper, advert rep, 1989-90; Pharmaceut Mfrs Am, commun asst, 1992-93; Paralyzed Veterans Am, communs asst, 1993-98; communs consult, 1998-99; Howard Univ, staff writer, 1999-02; Barrett Bks, lit agt, founder, 1999-. **Orgs:** Black Pub Rels Soc, 1996-98; dir, Marlborough Condominium Bd, 1997-2002, pres, 2002-; Women's Nat Bk Asn, 2001-02; Nat Asn Black Journalists, 2002-03. **Honors/Awds:** Outstanding Intern, The Voice Newspaper, 1988. **Special Achievements:** Selected as county correspondent for the Washington Afro Newspaper, 1998. **Home Addr:** 4707 Col Dent Ct, Upper Marlboro, MD 20772-2880, **Home Phone:** (301)627-2104. **Business Addr:** Literary Agent, Founder, Barrett Books, 12138 Cent Ave Suite 183, Mitchellville, MD 20721, **Business Phone:** (301)627-2104.

### BARRETT, IRIS LOUISE KILLIAN
Educator, executive, founder (originator). **Personal:** Born Aug 28, 1962, Hickory, NC; daughter of James C and Dorothy Booker; married Jathan. **Educ:** Univ NC, Chapel Hill, NC, BSPH, 1984; Duke Univ, MBA, 1986; Regent Univ, Ded, 2012. **Career:** Duke Univ Fuqua Sch Bus, grad fel, 1984-86; Am Med Int, summer assoc, 1985; Corning Cable Systs, training specialist, 1986-88, prod supvr, 1988-89, supvr training dept telecommuns cable plant, 1989-92, qual & educ mgr, 1992-97, Wildacres Leadership Initiative Friday Fel, 1997-99, staffing & develop, mgr, 1997-2001, human res dir, cable div, 2002; Christian Community Outreach Ministries Hickory, bibl counr, 2002-; Word My Life Training Ministry, founder & owner, 2002-; Mountain State Univ, fac, adj prof, 2008-12; Regent Univ, adj prof adult educ, 2012-; Catawba Valley Community Col, instr, 2015-16; Christ Alive Church Bible Col, dir & advisor, 2015-. **Orgs:** Am Bus Women's Asn, 1990-94; Grace Pentecostal Holiness Church, 1994-; bd mem, Econo Force, 1994-2000; bd mem, Chamber Com, 1995-97; vol, Hospice, 2000-; bd dir, Grace Church, 2001-; bd mem, Bank Granite,1998-2004; Maiden Chapel Faith Ctr; former trustee, Catawba Valley Community Col, mem, Adult Sunday Sch Teacher & Intercessory Prayer; Catawba Valley Community Col; Am Asn Christian Counselors. **Honors/Awds:** Outstanding Business Woman of Catawba County, 1993; Girl Scout Woman of Distinction Award, 1999; Beazley Scholarship Recipient, 2011-12. **Home Addr:** 603 29th Ave NE, Hickory, NC 28601-0552, **Home Phone:** (828)327-7848. **Business Addr:** Founder, Owner, The Word is My Life Training Ministry, PO Box 1771, Hickory, NC 28603, **Business Phone:** (828)327-7848.

### BARRETT, JACQUELYN HARRISON
Sheriff, association executive. **Personal:** Born Nov 4, 1950, Charlotte, NC; daughter of Cornelius Harrison Sr (deceased) and Ocie P Harrison; married Gene Washington; children: Kimberly & Alan. **Educ:** Beaver Col, BA, sociol; Clark-Atlanta Univ, MA, sociol; Arcadia Col, LLD, 2001. **Career:** Ga Peace Officer Stand & Training Coun, curric specialist; Fulton County Pub Training Safety Ctr, dir; Fulton County, sheriff, 1992-2004; Cascade United Methodist Church, dir progs; W Ga Col; Spelman Col. **Orgs:** bd mem, Ga Ctr C; bd mem, Ga Int Law Enforcement Exchange; Adv Bd, Fulton County Emergency Med Serv/911; St. Jude's Recovery; Nat Sheriffs Asn, Accreditation & Educ & Training Comts; Pres, Nat Orgn Black Law Enforcement, 1997-98; Ga Comn Family Violence; State Judicial Nominating Comt. **Honors/Awds:** Atlanta YMCA's Academy of Women, 1995; Officer of the Year, Ga Women Law Enforcement; Jean Young Community Service Award; Trumpet Award, Turner Broadcasting System, 1998; Martin Luther King Jr Drum Major for Justice Award; Triple Crown Award, 2003. **Special Achievements:** The nation's first African-American female sheriff, Fulton County, 1992; first woman to serve as president of National Organization of Black Law Enforcement Executives. **Business Addr:** Fulton County Courthouse, 185 Central Ave, Atlanta, GA 30303, **Business Phone:** (404)730-5100.

### BARRETT, JAMES A.
City commissioner. **Personal:** Born Dec 2, 1932, Cleveland, OH; married Edith Ransby; children: Zina & Jurena. **Educ:** Ky St Univ; Cleveland St Univ. **Career:** E Cleveland City, app city commnr, 1969, elected, 1970-72; E Cleveland Civil Serv, app commnr, 1972-76; E Cleveland Pub Libr, app trustee, 1974-80; Blue Cross NE Ohio, rep labor affairs, mgr govt affairs, 1976-. **Orgs:** E Cleveland Cits Adv Comn, 1968-69; former bd mem, E Cleveland, YMCA, 1972-73; trustee, E Cleveland PA, 1974; past pres, Chamber May fair League. **Home Addr:** 13605 Graham Rd, East Cleveland, OH 44112. **Business Addr:** Representative Labor Affairs, Blue Cross Northeast Ohio, 2066 E 9th St, Cleveland, OH 44112.

### BARRETT, MATTHEW ANDERSON
Executive. **Personal:** Born Nov 13, 1947, Roanoke, VA. **Educ:** Va Commonwealth Univ, BS, bus admin, 1974. **Career:** Univ Ford Motor Co, salesman, 1969-70; Stand Drug Stores Inc, asst mgr, 1970-72; Va Commonwealth Univ, comput prog, 1972-76; Sem Walk Unit Owners Asn, pres, 1986-89; 3M Co, acct rep, currently. **Orgs:** Speaker, Richmond Pub Sch Speakers Bur, 1970-74; big bro Big Bros Richmond, 1970-75; treas, Huntington Club Condominiums, 1980-84; aircraft, Owners & Pilots Assoc, 1981-; scuba diver, NAUI, 1982-; Sem Walk Condominium Asn, pres, 1986-90. **Honors/Awds:** Salesman of the Year, 3M Co, 1979-80, Apogee Award, 1989; Prod Award, 3MCo, 1979; Salesman of the Year, 1987. **Home Addr:** 53 Skyhill Rd Suite 304, Alexandria, VA 22314, **Home Phone:** (703)370-2888. **Business Addr:** Account Representative, 3M Co, 1101 15th St NW, Washington, DC 20005, **Business Phone:** (202)331-6900.

**BARRETT, DR. RONALD KEITH.** See Obituaries Section.

### BARRETT, REV. WALTER CARLIN, JR.
Clergy. **Personal:** Born Sep 30, 1947, Richmond, VA; son of Walter Carlin Sr (deceased) and Elizabeth Norrell. **Educ:** St John Vianney Sem, dipl; St Mary's Sem Col, Catonsville, BA, philos, MDiv, theol. **Career:** Roman Cath Diocese Richmond, priest, 1975-; St Mary's Cath Church, assoc pastor, 1975-77; St Gerard's Cath Church, Roanoke VA, pastor, 1977-85; Basilica St Mary, Norfolk, Va, rector, 1985-2000; Holy Rosary Cath Church, Richmond, Va, pastor, 2001-; St Mary Annuciation Parish, Caroline Co, pastor, 2009-. **Orgs:** Nat Asn Advan Colored People; Nat Black Cath Clergy Caucus; Black Cath Comn; Black Cath Clergy Conf; Diocesan Pastoral Coun; Diocesan Priest Coun; founder, Richmond Black Cathc Caucus, 1971-74; Exec Comn Priests Coun. **Honors/Awds:** Recognized for Outstanding Service, Roman Catholic Diocese, Richmond, 1985; St Mary's a Minor Basilica, 1991; Named "Prelate of Honor", 1996. **Home Addr:** 1201 N 36th St, Richmond, VA 23223-7711. **Business Addr:** Pastor, Holy Rosary Catholic Church, 3300 R St, Richmond, VA 23223, **Business Phone:** (804)222-1105.

### BARRINGTON, DR. EUGENE L.
Educator. **Educ:** Rutgers Univ, MEd; Syracuse Univ, MPh, PhD. **Career:** Tex Southern Univ, facilitator, assoc prof, prof, 2009-11, pub admin, currently. **Orgs:** Adv bd, Southern Conf African Am Studies Inc, 2008-; Am Asn Behav & Social Sci. **Business Addr:** Associate Professor of Public Administration, Texas Southern University, SPA/COLABS Bldg Fac 3100 Cleburne St Suite 402Z, Houston, TX 77004, **Business Phone:** (713)313-6700.

### BARROIS, LYNDON J.
Administrator, cartoonist or animator. **Personal:** Born Jun 6, 1964, New Orleans, LA. **Career:** TV movie: PJs, dir, 1999; Film: Parasite Eve, 1998; Kung Pow: Enter Fist, 2002; Scooby-Doo, 2002; Matrix Reloaded, 2003; Matrix Revolutions, 2003; Karate Dog, 2004; I, Robot, 2004; Matrix Recalibrated, 2004; Elektra, 2005; Lion, Witch & Wardrobe, 2005; appy Feet, 2006; Night at Mus, character supvr, 2006; Happy Feet, 2006; Rhythm & Hues, animator supvr, currently; Alvin & Chipmunks, animation dir, 2007; Speed Racer, animator, 2008; Sucker Punch, animation dir, animation supvr, 2011; Tree Life, animation supvr, 2011; Thing, animation supvr, 2011; R.I.P.D, animation dir, 2013. Tv series: "The PJs", dir, 2000; The Lift, dir, writer, producer, 2011. **Business Addr:** Animator Supervisor, Rhythm & Hues, 5404 Jandy Pl, Los Angeles, CA 90066, **Business Phone:** (310)448-7500.

### BARRON, REGINALD
Automotive executive. **Career:** Barron Chevrolet-Geo Inc, Danvers, Mass, chief exec officer, 1984-. **Orgs:** Bd mem, Judge Baker C's Ctr. **Business Addr:** Chief Executive Officer, Barron Chevrolet-Geo Inc, 90 Andover St, Danvers, MA 01913, **Business Phone:** (978)273-8155.

### BARRON, WENDELL
Automotive executive. **Personal:** married Marta; children: Elena, Randall & Steven. **Educ:** Howard Univ, BS, mech engineering, 1966. **Career:** Fotor Motors, Buffalo, NY, engr, Dearborn, Mich; Campus Ford Inc, Okemos, Mich, owner & pres, 1985-2005; Courtesy Ford, vpres & owner, 2005-. **Orgs:** Pres, Mich Automobile Dealers Asn, 1997; bd mem, Sparrow Hosp; fel Trinity AME Church; fel Lansing Regional Chamber Com; Emeritus. **Business Addr:** Vice President, Owner, Campus Ford Inc, 1830 W Grand River, Okemos, MI 48864, **Business Phone:** (888)719-9553.

### BARROS, DANA BRUCE
Business owner, basketball player. **Personal:** Born Apr 13, 1967, Boston, MA; married Veronica; children: Jordan. **Educ:** Boston Col, MA, 1989. **Career:** Basketball player (retired), coach, bus owner; Seattle SuperSonics, guard, pt guard, 1989-93; Philadelphia 76ers, pt guard, 1993-95; Boston Celtics, pt guard, 1995-2000, 2004; Detroit Pistons, pt guard, 2000-02; Dana Barros Sports Complex, owner; Northeastern Univ men's basketball team, asst coach; City Boston, dir recreation; New Eng Sports Network, basketball insider; Celtics, media rels, currently; Dana Barros Basketball Club, head Coach & prog dir, currently. **Honors/Awds:** NBA Draft, First round pick, 1989; NBA Most Improved Player, 1995; NBA All-Star Game, 1995. **Business Addr:** Head Coach, Program Director, Dana Barros Basketball Club, 6 Kiddie Dr, Avon, MA 02322, **Business Phone:** (508)857-2962.

### BARROW, JOE LOUIS, JR.
Executive. **Personal:** Born May 28, 1947, Mexico City; son of Joe Louis and Marva Spaulding; married Susan. **Educ:** Univ Denver, BA, 1968. **Career:** United Bank Denver, trust off, asst vpres, 1968-76; US Dept Energy, Off Commercialization Conserv, Solar Energy, dir, 1978-81; Wood Bros, vpres, corp mkt, 1981-82, vpres reg mkt, dir, 1982-85; Ronald H Brown, dir spec proj, sr adv; Izzo Systs, pres & chief exec officer; First Tee, exec dir & chief exec officer, 1997-; World Golf Found, sr vpres, currently. **Orgs:** IZZO Systs Inc; IZZO Ltd, UK; bd mem, Franklin & Eleanor Roosevelt Inst; Planned Parenthood Rocky Mountains; bd mem, Nat Golf Found; bd mem, Colo Golf Asn; Am Jr Golf Asn; Planned Parenthood Fed Am; Mile High United Way; bd fellows, Univ Denver; chmn, Colo Health Facil Finance Authority; chmn, Urban League Colo; Big Bros Metro Denver; Piton Found Community Dev Proj; Denver Metro Chamber Comm; Colo Jr Golf Comt; chmn, Rails-to-Trails Conservancy; Baptist Health Systs, Jacksonville; Nat Minority Golf Found; Jacksonville Urban League; Jacksonville Econ Develop Comn. **Business Addr:** Executive Director, Chief Executive Officer, The First Tee, World Golf Village 425 S Legacy Trail, Saint Augustine, FL 32092, **Business Phone:** (904)940-4300.

### BARROW, MICHEAL COLVIN
Football player, football coach. **Personal:** Born Apr 19, 1970, Homestead, FL; married Shelley; children: Mikenzi, Kaleb, John & Michael. **Educ:** Univ Miami, BS, acct, 1992. **Career:** Football player (retired), coach; Houston Oilers, linebacker, 1993, right linebacker, 1994, 1996, mid linebacker, 1995; Carolina Panthers, left outside linebacker, 1997, right inside linebacker, 1998, linebacker, 1999; New York Giants, mid linebacker, 2000-03; Wash Redskins, 2004; Dallas Cowboys, 2005; Homestead High Sch, asst head coach & defensive coordr, 2006; Miami Hurricanes, linebackers coach & spec teams coach, 2007-13; Univ Miami, coach, 2007-; Seattle Seahawks, linebackers coach, 2015-. **Honors/Awds:** Starting linebacker on national championship teams at Miami, 1989, 1991; All-America as a senior, 1992; Big East Defensive Player of the Year, 1992; Seventh in voting for the Heisman Trophy, 1992; Second-round draft choice of the Houston Oilers in 1993; NFC champion, 2000; NFC Combined Tackles Leader, 2003; Defensive Rookie of the Year and Freshman, Atlantic Coast Conf, 2008. **Business Addr:** Coach, University of Miami, 1320 S Dixie Hwy, Coral Gables, FL 33124, **Business Phone:** (305)284-2211.

**BARROW, REV. WILLIE T.** See Obituaries Section.

### BARRY, HARRIET S.
Executive, executive director. **Educ:** Northwestern Univ, Kellogg Sch Mgt, MBA, 1979. **Career:** Gen Foods, mkt & brand mgt; Kimberly Clark; Soft Sheen Corp, dir mkt, 1983-96; Urban Ministries Inc, gen mgr, 1999-2006; Communion Source, pres, gen mgr, 1999-2006; HS Barry Consult, consult, 2007-10; Univ Medicines Int, exec vpres; It Tastes Like Love, pres, 2008-. **Business Addr:** President, It Tastes Like Love LLC, 15 W 100 Plainfield Rd, Hinsdale, IL 60522-0385, **Business Phone:** (630)880-2417.

**BARRY, MARION SHEPILOV, JR.** See Obituaries Section.

### BARRY, REV. RICHARD L.M.
Church historian. **Personal:** Born Nov 14, 1940. **Career:** St Agnes Episcopal Church, rector; Hist St Agnes Episcopal Church, priest, rector, pastor. **Business Addr:** Rector, Historic Saint Agnes Episcopal Church, 1750 NW 3rd Ave, Miami, FL 33136, **Business Phone:** (305)573-5330.

### BARTEE, KIMERA ANOTCHI
Baseball player, athletic coach. **Personal:** Born Jul 21, 1972, Omaha, NE. **Educ:** Creighton Univ. **Career:** Baseball player (retired), baseball coach; Perth Heat, 1995; Bowie Baysox, outfielder, 1995; Detroit Tigers, outfielder, 1996-99; Cincinnati Reds, 2000; Colo Rockies, 2001; Baltimore minor league orgn, 2005-07; Delmarva Shorebirds, field coach, 2005-07, Pittsburgh Pirates, roving instr, outfield & base running coordr, coach, 2008-11; State Col Spikes, mgr; Warrior's Baseball Academy, instrs, currently. **Business Addr:** Instructor, Warrior's Baseball Academy, **Business Phone:** (602)793-1016.

### BARTHELEMY, SIDNEY JOHN
Mayor, executive, executive director. **Personal:** Born Mar 17, 1942, New Orleans, LA; son of Lionel and Ruth (Fernandez) B; married Michaele Thibodeaux; children: Cherrie Ann, Bridget & Sidney Jr. **Educ:** Epiphany Apostolic Jr Col, attended 1963; St Joseph Sem, BA, philos, 1967; Tulane Univ, MSW, 1971. **Career:** Total Community Action, admin asst, 1967-68, asst dir, 1969; Adult Basic Educ Prog, guid counr & interim dir, 1968-69; New Careers Prog, asst dir, 1969; Parent-Child Ctr, dir, 1969-71, dir social serv, 1971-72; Labour Educ Advan Prog, Urban League, coordr, 1969-72; City New Orleans Welfare Dept, dir, 1972-74; Xavier Univ, assoc prof sociol, 1974-86; La Legis, state sen, 1974-78; New Orleans City Coun, councilman-at-large, 1978-86; City New Orleans, mayor, 1986-94; Dem Nat Party, vice chmn voter regist, 1988-89; Nat League Cites, second vpres, 1988; La Conf Mayors, second vpres, 1989-93; Kennedy Sch Gov, adj prof; Tulane Univ Sch Pub Health, adj prof; Univ New Orleans Col Educ, adj prof; HRI Properties, dir gov affairs, vpres civic affairs, vpres gov rel, currently. **Orgs:** vice pres, Comm Org Urban Polit; Orleans Parish Dem Exec Comt; chmn, Youth Assistance Coun; bd dir, Cent City Fed Credit Union; bd dir, Family Serv Soc; bd dir, St Bernard Neighborhood Comt Ctr; Comm Serv Ctr; City Pk Comn; Dem Nat Comn; pres, Labor Educ Advan Prog, La Conf Mayors; La Munic Asn; Miss-La-Ala Transit Comn; Nat Asn Advan Colored People; Nat Asn Black Mayors; Nat Asn County Officials; pres, Nat Asn Regional Councils, 1987-88; Nat Black Couns Local Elected Officials; Nat Inst Educ; New

Orleans Asn Black Soc Workers, US Conf Mayors; first vice pres, Nat League Cities, 1989-90, pres, 1990; Nat Asn Regional Councils. **Honors/Awds:** Purple Knight Award, St Augustine High Sch, 1960; Outstanding Alumnus, Tulane Univ Sch Social Welfare, 1986; Social Worker of the Year, La Chap, Nat Asn Soc Workers, 1987; American Freedom Award, Third Baptist Church Chicago, 1987; Certificate of National Merit, Dept Housing and Urban Develop, 1988; American Spirit Award, USAF Recruiting Serv, 1989; President's Award, La Conf Black Mayors, 1989; Daniel E. Byrd Award, Nat Asn Advan Colored People Award, 1990; National League of Cities Leadership Award, 1994; B'nai B'rith Torch of Liberty Award. **Home Addr:** 4445 Franklin Ave, New Orleans, LA 70122-6107, **Home Phone:** (504)283-4200. **Business Addr:** Vice President of Government Relations, HRI Properties, 812 Gravier St Suite 200, New Orleans, LA 70112, **Business Phone:** (504)566-0204.

### BARTLETT, LORRIE
Talent agent. **Personal:** Born Jan 1, 1963?; daughter of Robert Bartlett. **Educ:** Occidental College, 1981. **Career:** William Morris Agency, Agent; The Gersh Agency, Agent, 1992-08; International Creative Management (ICM) Partners, Partner and Co-head of Talent, 2008-. **Honors/Awds:** "Hollywood Reporter," Women in Entertainment Power 100, 2011, 2012, 2013. **Special Achievements:** First African America to lead a major agency's talent department. **Business Addr:** Partner, 10250 Constellation Blvd., Los Angeles, CA 90067.

### BARTLEY, DR. WILLIAM RAYMOND
Physician, surgeon. **Personal:** Born Dec 9, 1944, Daytona Beach, FL; married Freddye; children: Diallo & Rashida. **Educ:** Knoxville Col, BA, 1968; Meharry Med Col, Md, 1975. **Career:** Equal Opportunity Agency, staff; Little Rock Va Hosp, Lee Co Co-op Clin, part time staff; Erlanger Hosp, intern, 1975; USAF Sch Aerospace Med, 1976; USAF, flight surgeon; US Pub Health Serv; Alton Multispecialists, internist; St Anthony's Health Ctr; St Luke'S Med Ctr; pvt pract internal med, currently. **Orgs:** Little League Sports. **Honors/Awds:** National Medical Fellows Award, 1970-72. **Home Addr:** 210 Blue Ridge Dr, Glen Carbon, IL 62034, **Home Phone:** (618)288-9095. **Business Addr:** Physician, Alton Multispecialists, 1 Prof Dr Suite 230, Alton, IL 62002, **Business Phone:** (618)463-8626.

### BARTON, RHONDA L.
Engineer, lawyer. **Personal:** Born Dec 10, 1966, Wilmington, DE; daughter of Lyndon and Olive. **Educ:** Howard Univ, Wash, DC, BS, mech engineering, 1989; Univ Md, Sch Law, JD, 1998. **Career:** Pac Gas & Elec Co, San Francisco, gas distrib engr, 1989; Arent Fox, assoc patient pract, assoc, currently. **Orgs:** Nat Soc Black Engrs Alumni Ext, 1989-; Pac Coast Gas Asn, 1991-; Am Intellectual Property Law Asn; Dist Columbia Bar; Md State Bar Asn; Dc Bar. **Home Addr:** 350 Wayne Pl Suite 1, Oakland, CA 94606, **Home Phone:** (510)839-0161. **Business Addr:** Associate, Lawyer, Arent Fox LLP, 1717 K St NW, Washington, DC 20036-5339, **Business Phone:** (202)857-6000.

### BARTON, WAYNE DARRELL
Chief executive officer, law enforcement officer. **Personal:** Born Feb 21, 1961, Ft. Lauderdale, FL; son of Burnett and Willie; children: Tarsheka D & Sharque. **Educ:** Palm Beach Jr Col, attended 1992. **Career:** Police Officer (retired), social worker; Boca Raton Police Dept, police aid, from motorcycle patrol to narcotics invests, 1980-81, police officer, 1981; Barton's Boosters, founder & chief exec officer, currently. **Orgs:** Salvation Army; March Dimes; Child Watch; Visions, 2002; Boca Raton Jaycees; founding mem: I Have Dream Found; Law Day Found; Boca Raton Lions Club; numerous others. **Business Addr:** Chief Executive Officer, Founder, Barton Boosters, 269 NE 14th St, Boca Raton, FL 33432, **Business Phone:** (561)620-6203.

### BARZEY, DR. RAYMOND CLIFFORD, II
Government official. **Personal:** Born New York, NY; son of Raymond C and Elva Waters. **Educ:** City Col, City Univ NY, BA, 1967; Atlanta Univ, MS, 1968; State Univ NY, MA, 1970; NY Univ, PhD, 1980; Seton Hall, JD, 1983. **Career:** Sterns Dept Store, asst buyer, 1965-67; MN Mining & Mfg, prod analyst, 1968-71; Urban Develop Corp, assoc economist, 1971-73; Housing Develop Corp, asst exec dir, 1974; Urban Develop Corp, assoc economist, 1975; Harlem Urban Develop Corp, dir commercial develop, 1976; Co La, sr budget analyst; City Univ New York, Baruch Col, New York, adjunct asst prof, 1981-87; New York off Econ Develop, 1982; q, 1983-; Dep Atty Gen, asst chief, currently. **Orgs:** Am Asn Univ Profs; Am Econ Asn; Am Inst Planners; Am Libr Asn; Am Soc Planning Officials; Nat Asn Housing & Re development Officials; Nat Econ Asn Amnesty Int; Hosp Audience; Nat Trust Historic Preserv; Nat Urban League; 100 Black Men; Am Bar Asn; NJ Bar Asn; Asn City New York; New York County Lawyers Asn. **Home Addr:** 65 W 90th St, New York, NY 10024, **Home Phone:** (212)877-1396. **Business Addr:** Assistant Chief, Deputy Attorney General, Hughes Justice Complex, Trenton, NJ 08625-0112, **Business Phone:** (609)984-3900.

### BASIL, RICHARD
Football coach, football player. **Personal:** Born Sep 28, 1967, Demopolis, AL; married Mary Diase. **Educ:** Savannah State Univ, grad, 2001. **Career:** Football player, asst coach (retired); Detroit Tigers, quarterback, 1988-89; Tennessee State, quarterback, 1994-95; Savannah State Univ, asst coach, 1993-95, asst coach, 1997-2003, head coach, 2003-05; Johnson C Smith & Tenn State, asst coach, 1994-2006; Jump Start Youth Initiative Prog, founder & exec dir. **Honors/Awds:** Offensive Player of the Year honors, SIAC, 1988; George H. Hopson Offensive Back of the Year, 1988; Volunteer Service Award, 2009; Hall of Fame, Savannah State Univ Athletics, 2011. **Home Addr:** , Stockbridge, GA.

### BASKERVILLE, DR. LEZLI
Executive, judge, association executive. **Personal:** Born Montclair, NJ; daughter of Charles W and Marjorie. **Educ:** Rutgers Univ, Douglas Col, BA; Howard Univ Sch Law, JD, 1979; Shaw Univ & Benedict Col, LLB; Northwestern Univ Kellogg Sch, exec mgt prog. **Career:** Cong staffer; DC Ct Appeals, law clerk; pvt pract lawyer; Baskerville Group, founder & mem; Col Bd, Wash Off, chief exec officer, vpres govt rels, 1999-2003; Nat Asn Equal Opportunity Higher Educ, pres & chief exec officer, 2004-; Historically Black Cols & Univs, liaison; DC, admin appeals judge. **Orgs:** Nat legis coun, Nat Asn Advan Colored People; exec dir, Nat Black Leadership Round table; Nat Appellate Litigation Team, Lawyers Comt Civil Rights Under Law; nat co-chair, Pathways Col Network; Douglass Soc. **Honors/Awds:** Honorary Doctorate of Laws, Benedict College; 100 Women Leaders in STEM, STEMConnector; 25 Women Making a Difference, Diverse Issues Higher Educ; Top 10 Black Women in Higher Education, AOL Blackvoices; America's Top 100 Most Influential Association Leaders, Ebony Mag; Inducted, Hall of Fame, Rutgers Univ. **Special Achievements:** Mem, NAFEO brief writing teams in the landmark Supreme Ct affirmative action cases of Bakke, Weber & Fullilove; primary ed, Nat Dialogue Stud Financial Aid; first woman president of the National Association for Equal Opportunity in Higher Education. **Home Addr:** 611 H St SW, Washington, DC 20024-2727, **Home Phone:** (202)488-5860. **Business Addr:** President, Chief Executive Officer, National Association for Equal Opportunity in Higher Education, 209 3rd St SE, Washington, DC 20003, **Business Phone:** (202)552-3300.

### BASKERVILLE, PENELOPE ANNE. See Obituaries Section.

### BASKERVILLE, HON. RANDOLPH
Lawyer, district court judge. **Personal:** Born Jul 22, 1949, Henderson, NC; married Sarah McLean; children: Latoyia & Nathan. **Educ:** Fayetteville State Univ, BS, 1971; NC A&T State Univ, MS, 1972; NC Cent Univ Sch Law, JD, 1976. **Career:** Admin Off Courts, asst, 1979-84; Dept Social Serv, staff atty, 1985-86; pvt pract, lawyer, 1985; Judicial Dist 9B, NC, dist judge, 2005-. **Orgs:** Nat Bar Asn, 1977-; Am Cancer Soc, 1984-; dir, Ymca, 1984-85; pres, Charles Williamson Bar Asn, 1985-86; dir, NCNB Bank, 1985-; dir, C C, 1986-; NC Asn Trial Lawyers; Vance County Bar Asn; mem, N Carolina Bar Asn; mem, N Carolina Asn Trial Lawyers; mem, Vance County Bar Asn. **Home Addr:** 424 N William St, PO Box 793 A, Henderson, NC 27536, **Home Phone:** (252)438-2044. **Business Addr:** District Court Judge, District 9B, PO Box 2448, Raleigh, NC 27602-2448, **Business Phone:** (252)738-9101.

### BASKERVILLE, DR. SAMUEL J., JR.
Physician. **Personal:** Born Mar 2, 1933, Charleston, WV; son of Samuel Sr and Geraldine W Ashe. **Educ:** Howard Univ, Wash, DC, BS, 1953; Meharry Med Col, MD, 1958. **Career:** Detroit Receiving Hosp, intern, 1958-59; Kern Co Gen Hosp, res internal med, 1959-62, chief res internal med, 1961-62; Mercy Hosp Bakersfield, Calif, chief staff, 1973; pvt pract, physician, currently. **Orgs:** Bd dir, Kern Co Med Soc, 1964-67; Calif Med Asn, 1964; Am Med Asn, 1964; Nat Med Asn, 1967; Am Soc Internal Med, 1968; Omega Psi Phi Fraternity; bd dir, Mercy Hosp Bakersfield, 1979-81, 1986-90; Kern Co Sheriff's Adv Coun, 1988-90; Bakersfield Memorial Hosp; Independence Med Group. **Honors/Awds:** Civil Serv Comn Kern Co, 1969-77; Kern Co Heart Asn, 1991. **Home Addr:** 2008 Hasti Acres Dr, Bakersfield, CA 93309, **Home Phone:** (661)832-8963. **Business Addr:** Physician, Private Practice, 815 Dr Martin Luther King Jr Blvd, Bakersfield, CA 93307, **Business Phone:** (661)322-3905.

### BASKETT, KENNETH GERALD (KEN BASKETT)
Vice president (organization), army officer, educator. **Personal:** Born Nov 18, 1942, Kansas City, MO; son of W Cletus and Rosella Kelly King; children: Charmel, Adrienne & Tiffany. **Educ:** Tuskegee Inst, BS, acct, 1972; Ala A&M Univ, MS, personnel mgt, 1975; Command & Gen Staff Col, masters, 1979. **Career:** Ala A&M Univ, asst prof, 1972-75; Lincoln Univ, prof, 1982-85; Lt Col USA, educr; Micro GLOBE LLC, vpres com markets, currently; Col's Complete Choice, pres, 2005-12; Furtah Prep Sch, dean & fac, 2007-10; Fundamental Focus Inc, vpres bus develop & sr consult, 2012-. **Orgs:** Bd mem, Optimist Club Jefferson City, 1982-85; Atlanta City Country Club; Alpha Phi Alpha Frat, 1989; pres, Pi Gamma Lambda Chap, Alpha Phi Alpha Frat Inc, bd dir, BridgeMill Community Asn Inc; bd mem, ITTS Found Inc; Hopewell Baptist Church. **Home Addr:** 4584 Jamerson Forest Pkwy, Marietta, GA 30066-1102, **Home Phone:** (770)928-1630. **Business Addr:** Vice President of Commercial Markets, Micro GLOP[illegible] LLC, 75 5th St Suite 430, Atlanta, GA 30308, **Business Phone:** ([illegible])630-1268.

### BASKETTE, ERNEST E., JR.
Association executive, executive director, consultant. **Personal:** Born Apr 24, 1944, Lumpkin, GA; son of Ernest E and Julia Williams; married Stephanie R Bush; children: Damien B. **Educ:** City Univ NY, City Col, BA, sociol & early childhood educ, 1972; City Univ NY, Hunter Col, MS, urban planing, city & regional planning, 1974. **Career:** Town Islip, Islip, NY, urban planner, 1974-75; City New Rochelle, New Rochelle, NY, urban planner, 1975-77; NHS Newark, Newark, NJ, exec dir, 1977-80; Neighborhood Housing Serv Am, sr vpres, 1980-2010; Front Porch Strategies, sr consult, 2011-. **Orgs:** Bd mem, SEW & Lorraine Hansbury Theatre, 1985-87; bd dir & treas, Ventura County Community Develop Corp. **Home Addr:** 80 Lakeshore Ct, Richmond, CA 94804, **Home Phone:** (510)237-2748. **Business Addr:** Senior Consultant, Front Porch Strategies, PO Box 2524, Kernersville, NC 27285.

### BASKIN, ANDREW LEWIS
Editor, college teacher. **Personal:** Born Feb 28, 1951, Maryville, TN; son of Eloise and Jimmy; married Symerdar Lavern Capehart; children: Thalethia Elois & Thameka La Cape. **Educ:** Berea Col, BA, hist, 1972; Va Tech, MA, Am hist, 1975. **Career:** Ferrum Col, asst prof, 1975-83; Berea Col, Black Cult Ctr, dir, 1983-, dir, 1983-95, Dept African & African Am Studies & Gen Studies, assoc prof, currently; Appalachian Col Asn, fel, coordr, 1995-2000; Berea Col, Gen & African & African Am Studies, chair, assoc prof, 2000-, interim dir Black Studies, 2002-04; The Griot: The Journal of African American Studies, co-ed. **Orgs:** Phi Alpha Theta, 1975-; treas, Coun So Mts, 1983-84; bd dir, Mt Maternal Health League, 1984-86; bd dir, Berea Col Credit Union, 1985-91; bd dir, Ky Humanities Coun, 1990-97; bd ed, Berea Independent Sch Syst, 1991-99, chairperson, 1996-99; vice chmn, Ky African Am Heritage Comn, 1994-2006; chair bd dir, Ky River Foothills Develop Corp, 1994-97; chairperson bd dir, Ky Humanities Coun, 1995-97; Phi Kappa Phi, Berea Col, 2002; bd trustee, Lincoln Found, 2008-. **Home Addr:** 105 Cherry Rd, Berea, KY 40403, **Home Phone:** (859)986-1430. **Business Addr:** Associate Professor, Berea College, Hafer-Gibson Rm 107, Berea, KY 40404, **Business Phone:** (859)985-3781.

### BASKINS, DR. LEWIS C.
Executive, dentist. **Personal:** Born Jul 16, 1932, Springfield, AR; married Amanda J; children: Duane, Brian, Kevin & Holli. **Educ:** Ark Agr, Mech & Normal Col, BS, 1956; Univ Ill, DDS, 1961. **Career:** Fuller Products Co, vpres, pres; pvt pract dentist, currently. **Orgs:** Pres, Chicago Chap AR AM & N Alumni; Chicago, Lincoln Dent Soc; Omega Psi Phi Fraternity; Mt Zion Baptist Church. **Special Achievements:** Book: "Uncover The Missing Peace: How to Dissolve Resentment and Avoid Anger", 2015. **Home Addr:** 840 E 87th St, Chicago, IL 60619-6248, **Home Phone:** (773)994-9300. **Business Addr:** Dentist, Private Practitioner, 701 W 111th St, Chicago, IL 60628, **Business Phone:** (773)995-1234.

### BASRI, GIBOR
Educator, scientist. **Personal:** Born May 3, 1951, New York, NY; son of Phyllis and Saul; married Jessica Broitman; children: Jacob. **Educ:** Stanford Univ, BS, physics, 1973; Univ Colo, PhD, astrophys, 1979. **Career:** Univ Colo, res asst, 1974-79; Univ CA, postdoctoral fel, 1979-82, asst res astronr, 1981-82, asst prof, 1982-87; Univ Calif Berkeley, assoc prof, 1988-94, prof astron, 1994-, actg chair astron dept, 2006-07, vice chancellor, Equity & Inclusion, 2007-; Ames Res Ctr, nasa fac fel, 2002; Books: Observations of Brown Dwarfs, 2000; Brown Dwarfs: Up Close and Physical, 2004; What is a Planet?, auth. **Orgs:** Am Astron Soc 1979; Int Astron Union, 1984; Astron Soc Pac, 1984; Nat Socs Black Physicists. **Home Addr:** 2940 Forest Ave, Berkeley, CA 94705. **Business Addr:** Vice Chancellor, Professor of Astronomy, University California, 102 Calif Hall MC 3411, Berkeley, CA 94720-1508, **Business Phone:** (510)642-8198.

### BASS, ANTHONY EMMANOLE
Football player. **Personal:** Born Mar 27, 1975, St. Albans, WV. **Educ:** Bethune-Cookman Univ, grad. **Career:** Minn Vikings, 1998, defensive back, strong safety, free safety, 1999.

### BASS, HARRY S., JR.
Dean (education), chancellor (education), educator. **Personal:** Born Apr 15, 1954, Farmville, VA; son of Harry S Sr. **Educ:** Va Union Univ, BS, 1976; Atlanta Univ, MS, 1979, PhD, 1985. **Career:** Notre Dame Univ, fel, 1985-86; Mehary Med Col, fel, 1986-89; Va Union Univ, assoc prof, 1989, chair, div nat sci, 1990-93, chair, dept biol& natural sci & math, 1993, admin dir, currently; Nsf, prog off, 2007-09; Elizabeth City State Univ, dean sch mst, 2009-, interim assoc vice chancellor, currently. **Orgs:** Am Parasotology Soc, 1980; Trans Am Micros Soc, 1980; AAAS, 1989; dir, Mid-Eastern Alliance Minority Participation; Nat Sci Found, 2007-2009. **Home Addr:** PO Box 25596, Richmond, VA 23260, **Home Phone:** (804)230-0345. **Business Addr:** Dean, Interim Associate Vice Chancellor, Elizabeth City State University, 400 Jimmy R Jenkins, Elizabeth City, NC 27909, **Business Phone:** (252)335-3189.

### BASS, DR. HERBERT H.
Educator, consultant. **Personal:** Born Dec 26, 1929, Warsaw, NC; married Carrie L Ruff; children: Lori. **Educ:** Shaw Univ, BA, 1955; Antioch Univ, MEd, coun, 1972; Union Grad, PhD, 1980. **Career:** Supreme Liberty Life Co, ins agent, 1956; Philadelphia Sch Dist, teacher, 1957; City Philadelphia, gang control worker, 1959; Pa Dept Pub Asst, social worker, 1960; Philadelphia Dept Welfare, recreation supvr, 1960; Philadelphia Sch Dist, counr special educ, 1961; Provident Life Ins Co, consult, 1965; Leeds & Northrup Co, coord counseling, 1968-. **Orgs:** Vice chmn & trustee, New Bethlehem Bapt Church; comnr, Boy Scouts Am; CounExceptional C; Nat Advan Asn Colored People; YMCA. **Home Addr:** 1122 E Sydney St, Philadelphia, PA 19150-2910, **Home Phone:** (215)247-2723. **Business Addr:** Coordinator of Counseling, Leeds & Northrup Co, Sumneytown Pke, North Wales, PA 19454.

### BASS, JAMES F., JR.
Superior court judge. **Educ:** Rider Univ Lawrenceville, BA, hist, 1972; Cornell Univ Ithaca, NY, PhD, 1977. **Career:** Beach Inst Hist Neighborhood Asn, 1981-83; Male Initiative & Fatherhood Progs Equal Opportunity Authority Savannah Inc, advisor, 1993-98; Super ct judge, 1995; Coun Super Ct Judges, 2000-08; Ga State Comn Family Violence, 2006-09; Ga Supreme Ct Comt Equality, Ga Supreme Ct Comn Drug Courts, 2006-09, Ga Supreme Ct Comn Marriage, C & Family Law, 2007-09; Chatham County, Ga, Drug Ct, 2001, super ct judge, currently. **Orgs:** Beta Phi Lambda Chap Alpha Phi Alpha Fraternity, 1985-; Mandatory Continuing Judicial Educ Comt; Spec Comt Drug Courts Coun Super Ct Judges; Tidelands Ment Health/Ment Retardation & Substance Abuse Community Serv Bd, 1991-94; bd dir, Am Diabetes Asn Savannah, 1996-98; bd dir, Coastal C Advocacy Ctr Inc, 1994-95; Union Mission Soc, 1997-2000; Adv Bd Ralph Mark Gilbert Civil Rights Mus, 2001-02; Savannah Area Health Collab, 2005-08; Young Men Hon Prog Spencer Elem Sch, 100 Black Men Savannah, currently; life mem, Alpha Phi Alpha Fraternity Inc, currently; Frogs Club Inc, currently; Sigma Pi Phi Fraternity Inc, currently; Temple Glory Community Church under pastorate Bishop Matthew M. Odum, currently. **Honors/Awds:** Reginald Huber Smith Fellowship in Community Service Law Award, 1977. **Special Achievements:** Named Man of the Year by the Beta Phi Lambda Chapter of Alpha Phi Alpha Fraternity, 1995. **Home Addr:** 21 Twelve Oaks Dr, Savannah, GA 31410, **Home Phone:** (912)655-7154. **Business Addr:** Superior Court Judge, Chatham County, Rm 421 Chatham County Courthouse, Savannah, GA 31401, **Business Phone:** (912)652-7154.

### BASS, JOSEPH FRANK
Administrator, transportation consultant. **Personal:** Born Jan 10, 1938, Phoenix, AZ; married Jenean Brantley; children: Terence, Ste-

ven & Sandra. **Educ:** Hartnell Col, AA, 1958; Carnegie-Mellon Univ, cert transp, 1972; Univ Santa Clara, cert mgt, 1977; Harvard Univ, cert state & local gvt, 1981. **Career:** City Salinas, eng draftsman, 1958; City San Jose, civil engr, 1962, sr civil engr, 1967, prin civil engr & head transp planning, 1975-80, dir dept traffic, 1980-92. **Orgs:** Regis civil engr CA, 1966; Inst Traffic Engrs, 1970; Am Pub Works Asn, 1975; regis traffic engr CA, 1977; Nat Asn Advan Colored People, 1980; Black Coalition Local Govt Employ, 1980; No Calif Coun Black Prof Engrs, 1980; 100 Black Men, 1990. **Home Addr:** 6025 Susan Ct, San Jose, CA 95123-4545, **Home Phone:** (408)972-2453.

## BASS, KAREN
Congressional representative (U.S. federal government). **Personal:** Born Oct 3, 1953, Los Angeles, CA; daughter of DeWitt Bass and Wilhelmina Bass; children: Emilia Bass-Lechuga. **Educ:** Calif State Univ, Dominguez Hills, BA, 1990; Univ Southern Calif, PA. **Career:** Physician's asst; Univ Southern Calif, clin instr Physician Asst Prog; Calif State Assembly, mem, 2005-10, majority floor leader, 2006-08, speaker, 2008-10; US House Representatives, rep from Calif's 33rd Cong Dist, 2011-13, rep from Calif's 37th Cong Dist, 2013-. **Special Achievements:** Community Coalition, founder and executive director, 1990-2004; Majority Floor Leader, California State Assembly, 2005-10; first African-American woman to serve as the Speaker for the California State Assembly, 2008-10; House Committee on Foreign Affairs Committee, member, 2011-; America Jobs Act, co-sponsor, 2013; House Judiciary Committee, member, 2013-; Congressional Black Caucus, secretary for the 114th Congress; Congressional Caucus on Foster Youth, co-founder; Congressional Coalition on Adoption, co-chair; Steering and Policy Committee, member; Subcommittee on Africa, Global Health, Global Human Rights, and International Organizations, ranking member. **Business Addr:** U.S. House of Representatives, 408 Cannon House Off Bldg, Washington, DC 20515, **Business Phone:** (202)225-7084.

## BASS, KEVIN CHARLES
Executive, baseball player. **Personal:** Born May 12, 1959, Redwood City, CA; married Elaine; children: Garrett, April Brittany & Justin. **Career:** Baseball player (retired), executive; Milwaukee Brewers, outfielder, 1981-82; Houston Astros, outfielder, 1982-89, 1993-94; San Francisco Giants, outfielder, 1990-92; New York Mets, 1992; Baltimore Orioles, 1995; Onyx Motion & Media LLC, prin, currently. **Home Addr:** 1971 Byers Dr, Menlo Park, CA 94025, **Home Phone:** (650)325-2392. **Business Addr:** Principal, Onyx Motion & Media LLC, 10711 Cobleskill Lane, Houston, TX 77099-4512, **Business Phone:** (281)564-7673.

## BASS, DR. LAURENT
Physician. **Educ:** Tuskegee Univ, BASc, DVM, vet med. **Career:** RLM Vet Serv, vet, 1988-2003, pres, owner, 2002-. **Business Addr:** President, RLM Veterinary Services, 2805 N State Hwy 3, North Vernon, IN 47265, **Business Phone:** (812)346-8008.

## BASS, DR. LEONARD CHANNING
Physician. **Personal:** Born Jul 23, 1941, Live Oak, FL; married Janet. **Educ:** Fla A&M Univ, BA, 1962; Meharry Med Col, MD, 1966. **Career:** Genessee Hosp, intern, 1967; Leonard C Bass, MD, PA, pvt pract physician, 1969-2007; Plantation Gen Med Hosp, Dept Family Pract, chief serv, 1986-90; Broward Gen Med Ctr; Westside Regional Med Ctr; Fla Dept Corrections, physican, 2008-09; Arleen Richards, MD, PA, physician, 2009-11; Your Doctor Med Ctr, staff physician, 2012-. **Orgs:** Fla Med Dent & Pharm Asn; Nat Med Asn; Fla Med Asn; Broward Co Med Soc; pres, Fla St Med Asn; vpres, Am Heart Asn, 1976; co-chmn, prof conf, Am Heart Asn, 1976; Fla Med, 1982-86; life mem, Alpha Phi Alpha Frat; dir, Minimally Invasive Plastic Surg Inst Reconstructive Plastic Surg; fel Am Acad Family Pract. **Honors/Awds:** Distinguished Service Award, Med Fla Dent & Pharm Asn, 1977; Vietnam Commendation Medal, USAF. **Home Addr:** 9750 NW 45th Manor, PO Box 8273, Pompano Beach, FL 33065-1514, **Home Phone:** (954)753-9877. **Business Addr:** Physician, Your Doctor Medical Center, 2323 NW 19th St Suite 3, Ft. Lauderdale, FL 33311, **Business Phone:** (954)484-9590.

## BASS, MARSHALL BRENT
Consultant, executive. **Personal:** Born Goldsboro, NC; son of Estella and Marshall; married Celestine Pate(deceased); children: Brenda & Marsha. **Educ:** Univ Md, College Park, BS; Fla A&M Univ, DH; Kings Memorial Col, DHL; St Augustine Col, DHL; Livingstone Col, DHL; Winston-Salem State Univ, DHL; Voorhees Col, DHS; NC Cent Univ, JD; St Augustine Col, JD; Tenn Sch Relig, DDiv, Detroit. **Career:** Winston-Salem State Univ, vis prof; NC Cent Univ, adj prof bus; RJ Reynolds Tobacco Co, mgr personnel develop, 1968-70; RJ Reynolds Industs, corp mgr, 1970-76, corp dir, 1976-82, vpres, 1982, sr vpres, 1986-91; RJR Nabisco, sr vpres, 1991; Marshall B Bass & Assocs, pres, 1997-. **Orgs:** Bd dir, Piedmont Fed Savings & Loan Asn; former mem, Nat Comn Working Women; former bd dir, Winston-Salem/Forsyth Co, YMCA; indust adv coun, Nat Newspaper Publishers Asn; bd visitors, NC Cent Univ; chmn, bd dir, Winston-Salem State Univ Found; former mem, bd trustee, NC A&T State Univ; Phi Beta Sigma Frat Inc; Gamma Kappa Boule Sigma Pi Phi; sr warden St Stephen's Episcopal Church; lay leader chalice bearer Episcopal Diocese NC; bd trustee, Nat Asn Advan Colored People Spec Contrib Fund; chmn, bd trustee, St Augustines Col, Raleigh; chmn, Adv Bd Consortuim, Grad Studies Mgt; bd dir, Piedmont Triad Horizon; chair, bd trustee, Vorhees Col; chmn, Marshall B. Bass C Fund; chmn, Best Choice Ctr Bass Endowment Fund, Winston-Salem, Nc; bd dirs, Hospice Found; found bd dirs, Forsyth Tech Community Col; bd trustees, Nc Baptist Hosp Inc; dir, Winston-Salem Exp Self-Reliance; former, dir Greater Winston-Salem Chamber Com. **Honors/Awds:** Black book Nat Outstanding Business & Professional Award, 1984; Several Honorary Degrees: Doctor of Civil Law, St Augustines Raleigh; Doctor of Humane Letters, Florida A&M Univ, Tallahasse, Fla; Doctor of Divinity, Tenn Sch Relig, Detroit, Mich Div; LLD, Dr of Humane Letters, NC Cent Univ, St Augustine Col, Raleigh, NC, King Memorial Col, Columbia, SC, Livingston Col, Salisbury NC, Winston Salem State Univ. **Home Addr:** 3726 Spaulding Dr, Winston-Salem, NC 27105, **Home Phone:** (336)724-6852. **Business Addr:** President, Marshall B Bass & Associates, 1324 Ashley Sq, Winston-Salem, NC 27114-4338, **Business Phone:** (336)659-7898.

## BASS, PATRICK HENRY
Book editor. **Career:** Time Inc, ed proj dir, 2000-; New York Univ, adj prof, 2006-09; Takeaway, sr ed & contribr, 2008-13; CNN, creative consult, 2012-13; Essence Mag, ed proj dir, currently; New York Times, ed; Brooklyn Bridge, ed; The Washington Post, ed; Entertainment Weekly, ed; Publishers Weekly, ed; Blacxk Issues Book Rev; Quart Black Rev Books; Am Visions; Black Enterprise; Notorius; Time Out New York; YSB; BET Weekend; Like A Mighty Stream: The March on Wash, August 28, 1963, auth; Treasures African Am Traditions, Journeys & Icons, auth; The Obamas: Portrait of Americas New First Family, ed, 2009; The Obamas in The White House, ed, 2010; A Salute to Michelle Obama, ed, 2013; LEDISI Better Than Alright: Finding Peace, Love & Powerm ed, 2013; The Zero Degree Zombie Zone, auth, 2014. **Orgs:** New York Asn Black Journalists; Nat Asn Black Journalists. **Business Addr:** Senior Editor, Essence Magazine, 135 W 50th St 4th Fl, New York, NY 10020, **Business Phone:** (800)274-9398.

## BASSARD, DR. YVONNE BROOKS
Administrator, health services administrator. **Personal:** Born Oct 27, 1937, Oakland, CA; married Edward Lee Jr; children: Edward Lee Jr, Margot Denise Walton, Daryl Lamont & Alicia Yvonne. **Educ:** Patten Bible Col, BS, theol, 1973; St Stephens Col, MA, health sci, 1975, PhD, 1978. **Career:** Parks AFB Hosp, nurse, 1956-57; Eden Hosp Castro Valley, Calif, nurse, 1960-62; St Rose Hosp, Hayward, Calif, nurse, 1962-63; Bassard Rehab Hosp, owner, admin & nurse, 1963-2007; Patten Sch Relig, sch nurse, 1976-. **Orgs:** Am Col Nursing Home Adminr, 1976-; Lic Voc Norses League, 1977-; Consumer Aging Comn, Calif Asn Health Fac, 1978-80; Smithsonian Inst. **Honors/Awds:** Heart Award, Patten Bible Col, 1969. **Home Addr:** 24606 Fairview Ave, Fairview, CA 94542.

## BASSETT, ANGELA EVELYN
Actor. **Personal:** Born Aug 16, 1958, New York, NY; daughter of Daniel Benjamin and Betty; married Courtney B Vance; children: Slater Josiah & Bronwyn Golden. **Educ:** Yale Univ, BA, African-Am studies, 1980, Yale Sch Drama, MFA, 1983. **Career:** Films: City of Hope, 1991; Boyz N the Hood, 1992; Malcolm X, 1992; The Jacksons, 1992; Passion Fish; What's Love Got to Do With It?, 1993; Waiting to Exhale, 1995; Contact, 1997; How Stella Got Her Groove Back, 1998; Music From the Heart, 1999; Supernova, 2000; Boesman & Lena, 2000; The Score, 2001; Sunshine State, 2002; Masked & Anonymous, 2003; Mr 3000, 2004; Mr & Mrs Smith, 2005; Akeelah & the Bee, 2006; Meet the Robinsons, voice, 2007; Gospel Hill, 2008; Of Boys & Men, 2008; Meet the Browns, 2008; Nothing But the Truth, 2008; Notorious, 2009; Green Lantern, 2011; Jumping the Broom, 2011; I Aint Scared Of You, 2012; This Means War, 2012; Olympus Has Fallen, 2013; Black Nativity, 2013; White Bird in a Blizzard, 2014; Curious George 3: Back to the Jungle, 2015; Survivor, 2015; Chi-Raq, 2015; London Has Fallen, 2016. HBO movie, Unchained Memories: Readings from the Slave Narratives, reader, 2003; Plays: Joe Turner's Come & Gone; Macbeth; Authorized Personnel Only: Part 1, 2005. TV Series: "Ruby's Buckey of Blood", actress & producer, 2001; "The Rosa Parks Story", actress & exec producer, 2002; "Our America", exec producer, 2002; "The Index", 2005; "The Descent", 2005; "Search & Rescue", 2005; "Before the Flood", 2005; "Time Bomb", 2006; "ER", 2008-09; "The Simpsons", 2010; "Identity", 2011; "Rogue", 2012; "Betty and Coretta", 2013; "American Horror Story", 2013-16; BoJack Horseman, 2015; Whitney, 2015; American Horror Story: Hotel, 2015; Close to the Enemy, 2016. **Orgs:** Royal Theater Boys & Girls Club; hon mem Delta Sigma Theta, 2013. **Honors/Awds:** Golden Globe Award, 1994; Muse Award, 1995; Image Award, Nat Asn Advan Colored People, 1995-96, 1999-2003, 2009 & 2014; Crystal Award, 1996; Saturn Award, Acad Sci Fiction, Fantasy & Horror Films, 1996; Black Film Award, Acapulco Black Film Festival, 1999; Black Reel Award, 2002; Black Movie Award, Outstanding Performance by an Actress in a Supporting Role, 2006; Star on the Walk of Fame, 2008; Icon Award, 2009; Pioneer Award, LA Femme Film Festival, 2010; LA Femme Filmmaker Award, LA Femme Int Film Festival, 2010. **Business Addr:** Actress, c/o Ambrosio Mortimer, 1127 High Ridge Rd Suite 119, Stamford, CT 06905-1203.

## BASSETT, DENNIS
Executive. **Personal:** Born Dec 12, 1947, Gary, IN; son of Leonard Sr and Ruby; married Carmen Johnson; children: Dennis LaShun & Dawn Lashae. **Educ:** Knoxville Col, BA, eng, 1970; Pa State Univ; Univ Chicago, exec mgt progrs. **Career:** Eastman Kodak, Wash, DC, sales rep, copy prod, 1977, mkt educ specialist, 1979, sales mgr, 1980, Chicago Ill, dist sales mgr, 1982, Rochester NY, prog dir, worldwide training, 1985, staff asst sr vpres, 1986, Mid Atlantic, regional sales mgr, 1987, Restructuring Proj, proj leader, 1989, dir intercultural develop progs, 1990-94; Bausch & Lomb Corp, regional dir, 1994, vpres field sales, conact lens div, 1995, leader collab sales & commun, dir sales & customer progs, currently. **Orgs:** Pres, Network Nstar, Black Networking Org Ek, 1992; bd dir, Kappa Alpha Psi, Rochester Chap; bd chmn, Monroe Community Col Found, 2002; chmn, OMNI; Health assoc Inc; Rochester Community Found. **Home Addr:** 291 Genesee Pk Blvd, Rochester, NY 14619, **Home Phone:** (585)235-3469. **Business Addr:** Board Chairman, Monroe Community College Foundation, Damon City Campus, Rochester, NY 14604, **Business Phone:** (585)262-1500.

## BASSEY, MORGAN
President (organization), chief executive officer. **Personal:** married Supang. **Educ:** Purdue Univ, BS; Univ Colo, MBA, MS, finance; Univ Denver Col Law, JD. **Career:** Harvestons Securities Inc, owner, pres & chief exec officer, 1993-; City & County Denver, Single Family Mortgage Financing, co-financial adv, currently. **Orgs:** Co-chair, Nuisance Abatement Ordinance Oversight Comt. **Business Addr:** President, Chief Executive Officer, Harvestons Securities Inc, 8301 E Prentice Ave Suite 305, Greenwood Village, CO 80111-2906, **Business Phone:** (303)832-8887.

## BATAILLE, DR. JACQUES ALBERT
Physician. **Personal:** Born Jul 11, 1926. **Educ:** State Univ Haiti, Faculty Med Haiti, MD, 1953. **Career:** Physician (retired); Provident Hosp, resident pediat, jr asst, 1955-56; Homer G Phillips Hosp, resident Internal Medi, 1956-57; Cumberland Hosp, resident, 1957-58; Bronx Munic Hosp Ctr, resident; Albert Einstein Med Col, 1958-59; Port-Au-Prince, pvt pract, 1960-69; Muscata tuck State Hosp, staff physician, 1971-73, med dir, 1974; pvt pract physician, 1974-77; Sharon Gen Hosp, 1974. **Orgs:** AMA; Nat Asn Advan Colored People; Shenango Valley CC; Mercer Co Heart Asn; Pa med Soc; Smithsonian Inst. **Honors/Awds:** Sharon Gen Hosp Continuing Educ Award, Am Med Asn; Am Citizen, 1973. **Home Addr:** 1808 Mcdowell St, PO Box 1329, Sharon, PA 16146-3830, **Home Phone:** (724)981-1981.

## BATCH, CHARLIE (CHARLES D DONTE BATCH)
Radio host, executive, football player. **Personal:** Born Dec 5, 1974, Homestead, PA; son of Lynne Settles. **Educ:** Eastern Mich Univ, BS, criminal justice, 1997; Wash & Jefferson Col, DPS, 2013; La Roche Col, DHL, 2014; Eastern Mich Univ, DPS, 2015; Pt Pk Univ, DH, 2016. **Career:** Football player (retired), executive; Detroit Lions, quarterback, 1998-2001; Pittsburgh Steelers, quarterback, 2002-13; motivational speaker, 2006-; NFL Players Asn, player rep, 2006-09; Batch Develop Co Inc, pres, 2007-; Nat Football League Players Asn, Exec Comt, vpres, 2009-14; The Trust, sr capt, 2013-; Champs Sports Network-High Sch, basketball & football color commentator, 2012-; TechVibe Radio, Pittsburgh Technol Coun, co-host, 2013; Champs Sports Network, color analyst; XFINITY, Comcast-High Sch, football tv color commentator, 2013-; KDKA-TV, pre-game analyst, 2013-, color commentator, 2015-; XFINITY, Comcast-High Sch, Basketball TV, color commentator, 2014-; Harvard Univ, player advisor, 2014-; WDVE, co-host, 2014; Impellia, co-founder, managing mem, 2015-. **Orgs:** Mem, Phi Beta Sigma Fraternity Inc; United Way Allegheny County; Riedel & Cody Fund Inc; spokesman, Canned Food Dr; pres & founder, Best Batch Found, 2000-; bd dir, Youth Futures Comn Steering Comt, 2007-; bd dir, Landmarks Community Capital Corp, 2008-09; vpres, Nat Football League Players Asn, 2009-14; exec comt mem, Nat Football League Players Asn, 2010; basketball off, Pa Interscholastic Athletic Asn, 2010-; bd dir, Strong Women Strong Girls Pittsburgh Adv Coun, 2011-; bd dir, Urban League Greater Pittsburgh, 2011-; bd dir, Western Pa Humane Soc, 2012-; bd dir, Imani Christian Acad Adv Coun, 2013-; Paul Harris fel Rotary Found, 2014; bd dir, Pittsburgh Three Rivers Marathon, 2014-; prof mem, Nat Speakers Asn, 2014-; bd dir, United Way Southwestern PA, 2015-; bd dir, University of Pittsburgh Brain Institute Advisory Council, 2015-; bd dir, Pittsburgh Musical Theater, 2016-. **Honors/Awds:** Super Bowl XL; Super Bowl XLIII; Eastern Michigan Outstanding Alumnus Award, 2005; First Jerome Bettis Award, 2006; Humanitarian and Community Award, Bus Stops Here Found, 2006; Walton Payton Man of the Year, Pittsburgh Steelers, 2006; Outstanding Service Award, Boys & Girls Club, 2007; 40 Under 40 Award, Pittsburgh Urban Magnet Project, 2009; Hall of Fame, Eastern Mich Univ, 2010; Pulse Award, Nat Football League Players Asn, 2011; Dignity & Respect Champion, 2012; Hall of Fame, Steel Valley, 2012; Humanitarian of the Year, Syria Shriners, 2013; Courage Award, Pittsburgh Circle, 2013; Conference Award, Baptist Ministries, 2013; Judge Homer S. Brown Award, Nat Asn Advan Colored People, 2013; Byron Whizzer White Award, Nat Football League Players Asn, 2013; Outstanding Campaign Volunteer of the Year, United Way of Allegheny Co, 2013; Pennsylvania Sports Hall of Fame, Western Chapter, 2014; Children Award, Macedonia FACE Friend, 2014. **Business Addr:** Founder, President, Best of the Batch Foundation, 2000 West St, Munhall, PA 15120, **Business Phone:** (412)326-0119.

## BATCHELOR, REV. ASBURY COLLINS
Executive. **Personal:** Born Nov 26, 1929, Leggett, NC; married William Ethel Stephen; children: Marlon Diane Whitehead. **Educ:** NC Agr & Tech State Univ, Greensboro, attended 1956; NC Cent Univ, Durham, attended 1957; AUS Intelligence Sch, attended 1958. **Career:** NC Mutual Life Ins Co, agt, 1957-61, sales mgr, 1961-80, asst to agency dir, 1980-; Western Dist Union, dir training, 1970-; Rocky Mt Develop Corp, secy, 1973-. **Orgs:** Am Legion Post, 1965; chmn & treas, Rocky Mt Opportunity Industrializ Ctr, 1974-; chmn pub rel, Big Bros/Big Sisters, 1978; Rocky Mt Rotary Club, 1979. **Honors/Awds:** Man of the Year Award, Mt Lebanon Masonic Lodge, 1960; Staff Manager of the Year, NC Mutual Life Ins Co, 1963; Appreciation Award, Coastal Plain Heart Fund Asn, 1968; Citation for Meritorious Service, Am Legion Post, 1979. **Home Addr:** 502 Greenwood Blvd, Tarboro, NC 27886, **Home Phone:** (252)823-4667. **Business Addr:** Assistant to Agency Director, North Carolina Mutual Life Insurance Co, Mutual Plz, Durham, NC 27701.

## BATEMAN, CELESTE
Talent agent, business owner. **Personal:** Born Sep 1, 1956, Newark, NJ; daughter of William and Elma; married Carter Mangan; children: Jamil & Carter Jr. **Educ:** Rutgers Univ, BA, theatre arts & speech, 1978; Montclair State Univ, MA, comm arts. **Career:** New Community Corp, Newark, NJ, prog dir, 1978-79; Port Authority New York & Nj, secy, 1981-84; Newark Mus, Newark, NJ, prog coordr, 1984-87; City Newark, Div Recreation/Cult Affairs, Newark, NJ, cult affairs supvr, 1987-97; exec dir, Newark Arts Coun, 1997-99; Celeste Bateman & Assoc, prin & founder, 1997-. **Orgs:** Alpha Psi Omega, 1978; Alpha Epsilon Rho, 1978; selection comm mem, Newark Black Film Festival, 1984-87; Asn Performing Arts Presenters, 1984-87; Friends Newark Symphony Hall, 1985-88; mem adv coun, Newark Symphony Hall, 1987-89; Asn Am Cultures, 1987-90; ex-officio mem, Newark Festival People; Am For The Arts, 1987-96; bd dir, WBGO-FM Jazz Radio, 1989-95; bd mem, Gov Sch, NJ, 1991-92; bd dir, Newark Jazz Festival, 1991-97. **Honors/Awds:** NAACP Image Award, 2003. **Special Achievements:** Author: We've Got the Victory; Fall Back and Let the Universe Catch You; Short Story: "Rebirth of William" in Tavis Smiley's Keeping the Faith, 2002. **Home Addr:** 68 Shephard Ave, Newark, NJ 07112. **Business Addr:** Principal, Founder, Celeste Bateman & Associates, PO Box 4071, Newark, NJ 07114-4071, **Business Phone:** (973)705-8253.

**BATEMAN, PAUL E.**
Lawyer. **Personal:** Born Feb 28, 1956, Highland Park, IL; son of Joel and Tyree; married Sylvia L; children: Paul Jr, Philip & Preston. **Educ:** Ill State Univ, BS, polit sci & govt, 1976; Univ Mich Law Sch, JD, 1980. **Career:** Nat Labor Rels Bd, trial atty, 1980-84; Friedman & Koven, assoc, 1984-86; Sachnoff & Weaver, shareholder, 1986-93; Burke, Warren & MacKay, shareholder, 1993-2000; Littler Mendelson PC, labor, employ law counr, litigator, shareholder & atty, 2000-. **Orgs:** Am Bar Asn, 1980-; US Ct Appeals, First, Fourth, Eighth, Ninth, Tenth & Eleventh DC Circuits, 1981; adv bd, Civic Fedn Chicago, 1989-; regional liasion, Univ Mich Black Law Alumni, 1991-; club master, Boy Scouts Am, 1992-; DC Bar; Ill State Bar; Labor & Employ & Litigation Sections; mem bd dir, Ill Inst Continuing Legal Educ; mem adv bd, Coord Advice & Referral Prog Legal Serv; former mem, Chicago Coun United Way Metrop Chicago. **Special Achievements:** Illinois Institute of Continuing Legal Education, Age Discrimination, 1996; Investigations, Testing & Privacy, 1990. **Home Addr:** 324 N Jefferson St Apt 106, Chicago, IL 60661-1248, **Home Phone:** (312)795-3224. **Business Addr:** Attorney, Shareholder, Littler Mendelson PC, 321 N Clark St Suite 1000, Chicago, IL 60654, **Business Phone:** (312)372-5520.

**BATES, BARBARA ANN**
Executive, fashion designer. **Personal:** Born Jun 27, 1955, Chicago, IL; daughter of Elvin Hicks and Vera; children: Eugene & Kristopher. **Career:** First Nat Bank Chicago, secy; corp secy, 1986; Bates Design Inc, chief exec officer & pres, 1986-. **Orgs:** Founder, Barbara Bates Found. **Business Addr:** Chief Executive Officer, President, Bates Design Inc, 2031 S Ind, Chicago, IL 60616, **Business Phone:** (312)808-8091.

**BATES, DR. CLAYTON WILSON, JR.**
Educator, electrical engineer. **Personal:** Born Sep 5, 1932, New York, NY; son of Clayton Sr and Arline Walker; married Priscilla Suzanne Baly; children: Katherine Arline, Christopher Thomas & Naomi Elizabeth. **Educ:** Manhattan Col, BS, elec engineering, 1954; Brooklyn Polytech Inst, MS, elec engineering, 1956; Harvard Univ, MS, elec engineering, 1960; Wash Univ, St Louis, MO, PhD, physics, 1966. **Career:** RCA, elect engr, 1955; Ford Inst Co, 1955; Sylvania Elec Prod, 1955-57; AVCO, 1960; Varian Assoc, sr res engr, 1966-72; London Univ, vis prof, 1968; Princeton Univ, visitng fel, 1978-79; Stanford Univ, Departments Mat Sci & Engineering & Elec Engineering, assoc prof, 1972-76, elec eng & mat sci eng, emriti prof, 1976-94; Howard Univ, Dept Elec & Comput Engineering, assoc dean Grad Educ & Res, 1995-2004, prof, 1994-; Harvard Univ, fel. **Orgs:** Optical Soc Am; sr mem, Inst Elec & Electronics Engrs, 1980; fel Am Phys Soc, 1982; AAAS; Am Asn Univ Profs; Soc Photo-Optical Instr Engrs; Sigma Xi; Eta Kappa Nu; Sigma Pi Sigma; Am Ceramic Soc; chmn, Affirm Action CommSch Engr, fac, adv Soc Black Scientists & Engrs, resident fel 1973-76, Stanford Univ; mem, bd dir, Jr Achievement; mem, Nat Acad Sci Eval Panel; NSF; Demeter Agency San Francisco. **Home Addr:** 339 Kellogg Ave, Palo Alto, CA 94301. **Business Addr:** Professor, Howard University College of Engineering, Architecture & Computer Science, 2300 6th St NW, Washington, DC 20059, **Business Phone:** (202)806-6565.

**BATES, GEORGE ALBERT**
Consultant. **Personal:** Born May 30, 1954, Charlottesville, VA; son of Otto L and Lucy H. **Educ:** Princeton Univ, BA, 1976; Univ Va, JD, 1980; Mediate Tech Inc, gen mediation cert, 1994. **Career:** Princeton Univ Food Serv, asst mgr, 1972-76; Univ Va, grad asst track coach, 1976-80, assoc dean off afro-am affairs, 1987; State Farm Ins Co, automobile liability underwriter, 1976-77; US Dept Labor, law clerk-judge Roy P Smith, 1980-81; Law Off George A Bates, proprietor, 1983-2005; Gen Coun N Am Van Lines, norcross trans, 1990-94; EEO & Diversity consult, mediator. **Orgs:** Alpha Phi Alpha Fraternity, 1977-2005; bd mem, Old Dom Bar Asn, 1985-2005; pres, Coop Exten Serv Bd Va State Univ, 1985-96; Cent Va Minority Bus Asn, 1987-2005. **Honors/Awds:** NJ State Col Champ Triple Jump Winner, 1973-76; Track Team Keene-Fitzpatrick Award, 1975; Heptagonal Track Meet All-Ivy, Triple Jump, 1975; Co-Capt Track Team, Princeton Univ, 1976; Affairs Warrior Award, Univ Va Off Afro-Am, 1987; Humanitarian Service Award, Va State Univ, Cooperative Extended Service, 1987; Humanitarian Service Award, Saint Paul's Col, 1988. **Special Achievements:** Co-ed/Prof Kenneth R Redden, "Punitive Damages" Michie Co, 1980; Organized the first legal advocacy workshop for the Old Dominion Bar Assn, 1988; Organized the first Employment Law Seminar for the NAACP, 1993; Journalist for five local newspapers & manuscript in progress on "The History of Bid Whist"; mem of the Ministerial Training Program, Charlottesville Church of Christ-Worldwide Bible Way, 1997. **Business Addr:** Consultant, 644 Maxfield Rd, Keswick, VA 22947, **Business Phone:** (804)293-8724.

**BATES, KAREN GRIGSBY**
Journalist, writer. **Personal:** married Bruce W Talamon; children: 1. **Educ:** Wellesley Col, BA; Univ Ghana; Yale Univ, Sch Orgn & Mgt, post-grad coursework. **Career:** NY Times, staff; Wash Post, staff; Essence & Vogue, journalist; Los Angeles Times, contrib columnist; ABC's Nightline, host; CBS Eve News, guest; People mag, writer & news reporter; Nat Pub Radio, corresp, 2002-; Tavis Smiley Show, alt host, 2002-, Day to Day, corresp, 2003-. **Special Achievements:** First correspondent and alternate host for The Tavis Smiley Show; co-author: Basic Black: Home Training for Modern Times, 1996; Author: Chosen People; Plain Brown Wrappers, 2001; Contributor: Mothers Who Think: Tales of Real-Life Parenting, 1999; Gumbo: An Anthology of African American Writing, 2002; co-author, Basic Black: Home Training for Modern Times. **Business Addr:** Correspondent, National Public Radio, 635 Mass Ave NW, Washington, DC 20001, **Business Phone:** (202)513-2000.

**BATES, LIONEL RAY, SR.**
Diver. **Personal:** Born Oct 21, 1955, New Orleans, LA; married Karen M; children: Nicole M Brown & Lionel R Jr. **Educ:** Com Dive Ctr, cert, air/mixed gas, 1979. **Career:** Anatole's Garage, auto mech, 1965-78; Sub-Sea Int, tender, 1979-80, com diver. **Orgs:** Bible stud & minister Inst, Divine Metaphys Res Inc, 1980-. **Honors/Awds:** People & Places, Ebony Mag, Jan, 1984. **Special Achievements:** First Black to Graduate from Com Dive Center, 1979; First Black to do saturation diving to depth of 450 feet, 1985. **Home Addr:** 2025 Portola Via, Harvey, LA 70058-2940, **Home Phone:** (504)368-3160. **Business Addr:** Commercial Diver, Subsea Intl, 1808 Engineers Rd, Belle Chasse, LA 70037.

**BATES, LOUISE REBECCA**
Business owner, executive. **Personal:** Born Sep 16, 1932, Cairo, IL. **Educ:** Wilson Jr Col, AA, 1957. **Career:** Executive (retired); Gold Blatt Bros Inc, clerk & buyer, 1952-75; Evans Inc, buyer, 1976-77; Chicago Dept Health, hearing & vision technician, 1980-98; Louise Bates Jewelry Store, mgr, pres & owner; Ytb, 2013-. **Orgs:** Nat Asn Advan Colored People, Oper Breadbasket Urban League; WTTW TV; United Negro Col Fund; pres, Jr Hostess Coun & Ed newsletter USO; vol, work Better Boys Found hostess Kup's Purple Heart Cruises; vol work & guest lectr, Audy Juv Home Prog & Chicago Pub Sch; AFSCME Coun 31, 1998-. **Home Addr:** 7944 S Sangamon St, Chicago, IL 60620.

**BATES, MARIO DONIEL**
Football player. **Personal:** Born Jan 16, 1973, Tucson, AZ. **Educ:** Ariz State Univ. **Career:** Football player, (retired); New Orleans Saints, running back, 1994-97; Ariz Cardinals, kick returner & running back, 1998-99; Detroit Lions, running back, 2000.

**BATES, MICHAEL DION**
Football player. **Personal:** Born Dec 19, 1969, Victoria, TX; married Kethera. **Educ:** Univ Ariz. **Career:** Football player (retired); Seattle Sea hawks, kick returner, 1993-94; Cleveland Browns, 1995; Carolina Panthers, kick returner, 1996-2000, 2002; Wash Redskins, 2001; Dallas Cowboys, 2003; New York Jets, 2003. **Honors/Awds:** Olympic Bronze Medal, 1992; Pro Bowl selection, 1996-2000; All-Pro selection, 1996-2000; NFL Alumni Kick Returner of the Year, 1996; NFL 1990s All-Decade Team.

**BATES, NATHANIEL RUBIN (NAT BATES)**
Government official, politician. **Personal:** Born Sep 9, 1931, Cason, TX; son of Viola Hill; married Shirley Christine Adams; children: Michael (deceased), Gale, Larry & Steven. **Educ:** San Francisco State Univ, BA, 1963; Calif State-Hayward, teachers cert, 1975. **Career:** City Richmond, councilman, 1967-, mayor, 1971-72, 1976-77, vice mayor, 1975-76, 2000-01, 2008; Alameda Co, Probation Dept, unit superv, 1963-93; State Sen Dan Boatwright, Contra Costa Co, Calif, field rep. **Orgs:** Chmn, Contra Costa Co Mayors Conf, 1971-72; pres, E Bay Div League Calif Cities, 1972-73; bd dir, League Calif Cities, 1973-75; US Conf Mayors, 1972-74; Bay Area Sewage Serv Agency, 1973-; bd dir, Nat League Cities, 1973-80, 1980-; vice chmn, Human Resources Comn; Richmond Port Auth, 1976-; Richmond Housing Auth, 1976-; Richmond Redevel Comn, 1976-; Black Probation & Parole Asn; Nat Black Elected Officials Adv Bd; Nat Coun Alcoholism Contra Costa Co; Regional Coun Criminal Justice; Adv bd Mt Diablo Coun Boys Scouts Am, Camp Fire Girls, Richmond Boys Club; pres, Richmond Dem Club, 1986-89; bd dir, ElSobrante Girls Club, 1986-89; W Co Young Men Christain Asn, 1986-89; Salesian Boys Club, 1986-87; Nat Black Conf League Elected Officials; Citizen Civic Club; Calif Apt Asn; Richmond Police Officers Asn. **Honors/Awds:** Father of the Year, Easter Hill Doris Cluster, 1988; Richmond Democratic Club Honors, 1990; Bethel Temple POA Church Honors, 1990; Resolution Honors, Senator Dan Boatwright, 1983, 1988, 1990-97; Resolution Honors, Assembly man Bob Campbell, 1983, 1988, 1990; Man of the Year Award, Richmond Dem Club, 1999; Don Bosco Award, 2004; Contra Costa College Hall of Fame, 2011; Judge Carroll Community Impact Award, BAPAC, 2012; El Cerrito High School Hall of Fame, 2012. **Home Addr:** 4038 Mozart Dr, Richmond, CA 94803-2748. **Business Addr:** Council Member, Richmond City Hall, 450 Civic Ctr Plaza 1401 Marina Way S, Richmond, CA 94804, **Business Phone:** (510)620-6743.

**BATES, DR. PERCY**
School administrator, educator. **Personal:** Born Jul 8, 1932, Pensacola, FL; son of Gladys Travis Graves and Percy; married Cheryl Proctor; children: Allison & Nathan. **Educ:** Cent Mich Univ, Mt Pleasant, MI, BS, biol, 1958; Wayne State Univ, Detroit, MI, MA, voc rehab, 1961; Univ Mich, Ann Arbor, MI, PhD, educ psychol, 1968. **Career:** Detroit Pub Sch, Spec Educ, teacher, 1959-61; Ypsilanti Pub Sch, Prog Educable Ment Impaired, psychologist & dir, 1961-64; Boys' Training Sch, Whitmore Lake, Mich, psychologist, 1963-64; Univ Mich, Ann Arbor, Mich, from asst prof to assoc prof educ, 1965-73, assoc prof & chairperson, 1969-73, asst dean, 1973-80, dir div, 1984-87, prof educ & dir, currently, Sch Educ, dir progs educ opportunity, 1987-; US Dept Educ, Wash, DC, dep asst secy & dir, 1980-81. **Orgs:** Chair, Nat Alliance Black Sch Educ; Tech Assistance Parent Progs, 1986-; co-chair, TAPP Select Comt, 1986-; chair, Perry Nursery Sch, 1987-; founding bd mem & chmn, Higher Educ Comn, Nat Alliance Black Sch Educr, 1989-93; Nat Coun Proj Equal Educ Rights, 1991-; exec bd, Father Patrick Jackson House, Ann Arbor, Mich, 1997-; Secy Educs Title IX Comn Opportunities Athletics, 2002-03; Am Asn Ment Retardation; Am Educ Res Asn; Am Psychol Asn; Coun Except C; Mich Psychol Asn; Univ Mich & Nat Stud Athlete Adv Comt; bd mem, Control Intercollegiate Athletics, Univ Mich; Nat Col Athletic Asn Exec Comt; pres, Fac Athletics Rep Asn. **Home Addr:** 2244 Pinegrove Ct, Ann Arbor, MI 48103, **Home Phone:** (734)665-8341. **Business Addr:** Professor of Education, Director, University of Michigan, Rm 4043 School of Education Bldg, Ann Arbor, MI 48109-1259, **Business Phone:** (734)647-1666.

**BATES, ROBERT E., JR.**
Manager. **Personal:** Born Oct 12, 1934, Washington, DC; son of Robert E and Alice M; children: Dawne E Collier, Brandon R & Hillman M. **Educ:** Univ Ill, AB, 1955. **Career:** US Census Bur, statistician, 1958-69; US Off Econ Opportunity, mgt info analyst, 1967-69; Sen Edward Kennedy, legis asst, 1969-77; Mobil Oil Corp, staff, 1993, mgr govt rels, financial analyst; Medco Med Supply, dir admin serv, 2006-. **Orgs:** Bd dir, Am Lung Asn; bd mem, Everybody Wins; bd mem, Am Asn Blacks Energy; corp secy, Mobil Corp; mem bd trustee, RAND Corp. **Honors/Awds:** JES Award. **Home Addr:** 6970 Kim Lane, Friendship, MD 20758-9765, **Home Phone:** (301)855-2036. **Business Addr:** Director of Administrative Services, Medco Medical Supply, 10305 Round Up Lane, Houston, TX 77064, **Business Phone:** (713)956-5288.

**BATES, WILLIAM J.**
Architect. **Personal:** Born Oct 5, 1952, Canonsburg, PA; son of George C and Laura Ethel Andersen; married Margaret M McDermott; children: Meaghan A, Owen P & Nora K. **Educ:** Univ Notre Dame, BA, Notre Dame, IN, 1975; Pa State Univ, grad, construct mgt; Harvard Univ, Grad Sch Design. **Career:** Shields Construct Co, Pittsburgh, PA, designer, 1975; Celento & Edison Archits, Pittsburgh, PA, intern archit, 1976, partner, 1978-84; Selck Minnerly Group Inc, Pittsburgh, PA, proj archit, 1976-78; Westinghouse Elec Corp, Pittsburgh, PA, consult, 1984-88, design mgr, 1988-93; PNC Bank, Pittsburgh, PA, vpres, 1993-95; Fore Systs Inc, Pittsburgh, PA, dir, real estate & facil, 1995-99; Marconi Inc, vpres, real estate & bldg servs, 1999-02; Eat'n Pk Hospity Group, Eat N Pk Restaurants, vpres, real estate & bldg servs, 2002-, sr vpres, currently. **Orgs:** Pres, Pittsburgh Archits Woskshop, 1980-85; Partnerships Educ Speakers Bur, 1980; pres, Community Design Ctr Pittsburgh, 1985; founder, Allegheny Trails Archit Career Explorer Post, 1983; pres, Pittsburgh chap Am Inst Architects, 1987; chmn, Minority Resource Comt Am Inst Architects, 1990; Allegheny County Airport Develop Comn, 1989-91; pres, Pa Soc Architects, 1991 & 2011; Leadership Pittsburgh, 1989; organizer, Int Remaking Cities Conf, 1988; Allegheny County Parks Comn, 2002-; Parks & Recreation Comn, 2003-; pres, bd Green Bldg Alliance, 2003-; bd Presby SeniorCare, 2004-; adv bd, Assoc Artists Pittsburgh, 2004-; mem a bd, Pittsburgh Hist & Landmarks Found, 2004-, vice chair, 2010-; secy, bd Allegheny County Parks & Recreation Found, 2007-; bd mem, Allegheny Land Trust; Am Inst Architects, tres, 2007-. **Home Addr:** 57 Marlin Dr W, Pittsburgh, PA 15216, **Home Phone:** (412)341-2640. **Business Addr:** Senior Vice President, Eat N Park Restaurants, 285 E Waterfront St, Homestead, PA 15120, **Business Phone:** (412)461-2000.

**BATES, WILLIE EARL.** **See Obituaries Section.**

**BATES, YASMIN T.**
Banker, vice president (organization). **Educ:** Univ Ill, BS, bus admin. **Career:** Harris NA, com banking trainee, 1976, banking officer, cash mgt sales & consult, team leader, asst vpres, 1981, sect mgr sales & consult; Harris NA, Metrop Banking Div, vpres & div adminr, 1991; Harris Chicago Community Bank, pres, 1994-; Harris Bank's City Region, pres, 1998; Harris Trust & Savings Bank, Chicagoland, S Div, exec vpres, 2003-, sr vpres com loans; Harris Financial Corp, sr vpres & head community affairs & econ develop. **Orgs:** Bd mem, Chicago Equity Fund; Community Investment Corp; Glenwood Sch Boys; Network Real Estate Prof; adv bd, Univ Ill Bus Adv Coun; Univ Chicago's Vis Forum; Urban Bankers Forum Chicago; Spec Allocations Comm, United Way Chicago; Comprehensive Housing Affordability Strategy Comt, Chicago City; Fannie Mae Nat Adv Bd; Am Bankers Asn; Community Develop Comt; bd mem, Shedd Aquarium. **Business Addr:** Executive Vice President, Harris Trust & Savings Bank, 111 W Monroe St Fl 17, Chicago, IL 60603-4096, **Business Phone:** (312)461-2121.

**BATH, DR. PATRICIA ERA**
Educator, executive, surgeon. **Personal:** Born Nov 4, 1942, Harlem, NY; daughter of Rupert and Gladys; married Beny J Primm; children: Eraka Patty (Alexandre Michel Louis Fortuit). **Educ:** Hunter Col NY, BS, chem, 1964; Howard Univ Med Col, MD, 1968; NY Univ, specialty training; Columbia Univ, specialty training. **Career:** Sydenham Hosp NYC, asst surg, 1973; Flower & Fifth Ave Hosp NYC, asstsurg, 1973; Metro Surg NYC, asst surg, 1973-74; NY Med Col Dept Ophthalmol, clin instr, 1973-74; UCLA Ctr Health Scis, asst attend, 1974-93; UCLA Sch Med, asst prof opthal, 1974-93; Charles R Drew Postgrad Med Sch, asst prof opthalmol, 1974-, asst prof surg, 1974-; Martin L KingJr Gen Hosp Los Ageles, dir clin serv & asst chief, Div Ophthal, 1974-; Univ Nigeria Med Sch, visit prof surg, 1976-; Jules Stein Eye Inst Dept Ophthal, prog dir ophthalmic asst, 1977-93; UCLA MedCtr, chair, ophthal residency training prog, 1983; Dept Ophthal, UCLA Med Ctr, chair, 1983-86; Howard Univ Sch Med, dir telemedicine prog, 2001-; Charles R Drew Postgrad Med Sch Los Angeles, asst prof dept community med int health sect; Howard Univ Hosp, prof telecommunications; St George's Univ, Grenada, prof telecommunications; Am Inst Prev Blindness, partner. **Orgs:** Am Med Asn, 1973-75; Nat Med Asn, 1973-; Am Soc Contemp Ophthal, 1974-; Am Pub Health Asn, 1975-; Int Agency Prev Blindness, 1975-; Soc Eye Surg Int Eye Found, 1976-; fel Am Col Surgeons, 1976-; fel Am Acad Ophthal & Otolaryngology, 1976-; pres, Am Inst Prevent Blindness, 1976-; White House consult, Nat & Int Blindness Prevention Prog USA, 1977-78; consult, Food Drug Admin Ophthalmic Devices Panel, 1979-; NSF, 1959; Med Soc Co NY; UCLA Jules Stein Eye Inst. **Honors/Awds:** Merit Award, Mademoiselle mag, 1960; Scholar Alpha Kappa AlphaSor, 1965; NIH Fel, 1965; NIMH Fel, 1965; NIMH Fel, 1966; Fel Dept HEWChildrens' Bur, 1967; NIH Fel Dept Ophthal Howard Univ, 1968; Outstanding Stud Endocrinol, Dept med, Howard Univ, 1968; Outstanding Stud Pulmonary Dis, Dept Med, 1968; Outstanding Stud Ophthal Prize, Dept Surg, 1968; Hall of Fame, Hunter Col, 1988; Howard UnivPioneer Acad Med, 1993; Hall of Fame. Int Women Med, 2001; Am Med Women's Asn, 2001. **Special Achievements:** First African American woman doctor to receive a patent for a medical invention; first African-American woman surgeon at the UCLA Medical Center; Dr. Patricia Bath was the first woman opthalmologist to be appointed to the faculty of the University of California at Los Angeles School of Medicine Jules Stein Eye Institute; First African American resident in ophthalmology at new York University's School of Medicine; First woman chair and first female program director of a postgraduate training program in the United States. **Business Addr:** Director, Howard University, 520 W St NW, Washington, DC 20059, **Business Phone:** (202)806-6270.

**BATINE, DR. RAFAEL**
Lawyer, teacher. **Personal:** Born Jul 20, 1947, Santurce, PR; married Patricia Estelle Pryde; children: Rafael Pablo. **Educ:** St John's Univ, Col Bus Admin, BS, 1969; St John's Univ, Sch Law, JD, 1974. **Career:** Westbury Pub Sch, NY, math teacher, 1969-73; Covington Howard

Hagood & Holland, NY, law clerk, 1973-74; Queens Dist Attys Off, asst dist atty, 1974-75; Rutledge Holmes Willis Batine & Kellam NY, pvt law pract, 1975-78; Ga Off Fair Employ, gen coun, dep adminr, 1978-79; US Dept Labor, Off Solicitor, atty, sr trial atty, currently. **Orgs:** Martin Luther King Scholar, St John's Univ, Sch Law, 1971-74; Admitted pract law, NY, 1975, US Supreme Ct, 1977, Ga, 1983. **Home Addr:** 4355 Valley Lake Terr, Atlanta, GA 30349, **Home Phone:** (404)767-0324. **Business Addr:** Senior Trial Attorney, United States Department of Labor, Sam Nunn Atlanta Fed Ctr, Atlanta, GA 30303-8916, **Business Phone:** (404)562-2057.

## BATISTE, KIMOTHY EMIL
Baseball player. **Personal:** Born Mar 15, 1968, New Orleans, LA. **Career:** Baseball player (retired); Philadelphia Phillies, third baseman & shortstop, 1991-94; San Francisco Giants, third baseman & shortstop, 1996; Atlantic City Surf, 1999, 2003. **Home Addr:** 16163 Aikens Rd, Prairieville, LA 70769-4903, **Home Phone:** (225)673-3776.

## BATTEN, REV. GRACE RUTH
Clergy, chairperson. **Personal:** Born Mar 22, 1943, Harbeson, DE; daughter of Jacob Brittingham Sr and Virginia Brittingham Sr; children: Earl William Jr. **Educ:** Del Tech & Comn Col, AAS, 1976; Burke Bible Col, BTh, 1977; Wilmington Col, BS, 1986; Light Univ, dipl bibl coun, 2007. **Career:** Adult Educ Satellite Prog, admin; Nat Youth Conf, educ chair, 1980-84; Mt Sinai Farm Develop Comn, chair, 1985-87; Mt Sinai Holy Church Am Inc, pastor & pres admin, currently; Mt Zion Bible Inst, founder & dir, 1988-; Milton Pub Libr, vpres. **Orgs:** Nat Coun Negro Women; bd mem, Del Asn A & C Educ; coun woman, secy, Milton Town Coun; Am Soc Notaries; vice chmn, pres bd dir, Sussex Co Red Cross Inc, currently; Nat Asn female Execs; bd mem, People Pl II Coun Ctr; vice mayor, Milton Town Coun; bd dir, Chesapeake Bay Girl Scout Coun; bd dir, Am Red Cross Delmarva Peninsula. **Special Achievements:** First African American woman mayor in Sussex County. **Home Addr:** 111 Orchard St, Milton, DE 19968, **Home Phone:** (302)684-4332. **Business Addr:** President of the Board of Directors, Sussex County Senior Services, Inc., 546 S Bedford St, Georgetown, DE 19947, **Business Phone:** (302)856-5187.

**BATTIE, DEMETRIUS ANTONIO.** **See BATTIE, TONY.**

## BATTIE, TONY (DEMETRIUS ANTONIO BATTIE)
Basketball player, basketball executive. **Personal:** Born Feb 11, 1976, Dallas, TX; son of Dell. **Educ:** Tex Tech, commun, 1997. **Career:** Basketball player (retired), executive; Denver Nuggets, ctr-forward, 1997-98; Boston Celtics, ctr-forward, 1998-2003; Cleveland Cavaliers, ctr-forward, 2003-04; Orlando Magic, ctr-forward, 2004-08; Nj Nets, 2009-10; Philadelphia 76ers, free agt, 2010-12; Orlando Magic, analyst, currently. **Business Addr:** Analyst, Orlando Magic, 8701 Maitland Summit Blvd, Orlando, FL 32810, **Business Phone:** (407)916-2400.

## BATTIES, DR. PAUL TERRY
Physician, cardiologist. **Personal:** Born Jul 22, 1941, Indianapolis, IN; son of Paul A and Louise Terry B. **Educ:** Ind Univ, BA, 1962; Ind Sch Med, MD, 1965. **Career:** Detroit Gen Hosp, internship, 1965-66; Wayne State Univ, resident internal med, 1966-69, chief med resident, 1969; Univ KY, Cardiol fel, 1971-73; pvt practr physician; Paul Terry Batties Inc, cardiologist. **Orgs:** Founding mem, bd dir, Asn Black Cardiologists; past bd, Marion Co Heart Asn; pres, Aesculapian Med Soc, 1982-84; chmn, Hypertension Comn; Kappa Alpha Psi Frat; Univ United Meth Ch; pres, Ind Soc Int Med, 1990-91; pres, Am Heart Asn, 1990, chmn; AMA; Ind State Med Asn; life mem, Nat Advan Asn Colored People, fel Am Col Cardiol; Am Soc Internal Med; Ind Univ Alumni Asn. **Honors/Awds:** Distinguished Citizens Award, Ind, 1976. **Special Achievements:** First African American Physician appointed to the City Hospital Surgical Staff. **Home Addr:** 10316 Coral Reef Way, Indianapolis, IN 46256. **Business Addr:** Cardiologist, Paul Terry Batties Incorporation, 1633 N Capitol Ave Suite 510, Indianapolis, IN 46202, **Business Phone:** (317)924-1001.

## BATTIES, THOMAS L.
Chief executive officer, president (organization). **Career:** Enterprise Fed Savings Bank, pres & chief exec officer, 1999-2003; Independence Fed Savings Bank, actg pres & chief exec officer, 2003-06. **Business Addr:** DC.

## BATTISTE, AUDREY ELAYNE QUICK
Librarian. **Personal:** Born Aug 24, 1944, Norfolk, VA; daughter of Oscar S Jr and Geneva Shokes; married Eugene Wilson Tyler; married Auggeretto. **Educ:** SC State Univ, Orangeburg, SC, BS, 1965; Univ Okla, Norman, Okla, attended 1965; John Carroll Univ, Cleveland Heights, OH, attended 1966; Atlanta Univ, Atlanta, Ga, MSLS, 1968. **Career:** Librarian (retired); Dept Welfare, Bronx, NY, caseworker, 1966-67; Bristol Myers Res Labs, E Syracuse, NY, librn, 1968-70; Atlanta Pub Libr, Atlanta, Ga, librn, 1972-74; SC State Col, Orangeburg, SC, instr, 1975; Atlanta Fulton Pub Libr, Atlanta, Ga, libr adminr, 1977-90, mgr libr human resources, 1985-99; Fulton Co Super Ct, Atlanta, Ga, proj dir, 1990-97. **Orgs:** Chair, prof develop comt, 1984-86, Black Caucus, Ala; treas, bd dir, ACIP, 1985-87; chair, nominations comt, 1985-90, nat vpres, 1986-89, nat pres, 1989-93, SC State Univ Nat Alumni Asn; pres, bd dir, Atlanta Coun Int Prog, 1987-89; bd dir, SC State Univ Educ Found, 1989-; African Am Family Hist Asn; vol, Fulton Co Juv Ct, Citizens Rev Panel; Delta Sigma Theta Sorority, Inc; Who's Who Among Students; Sec, y Stud Govt Asn, Assoc ed, collegian. **Honors/Awds:** Bulldog Award, SC State Univ Almni Asn. **Special Achievements:** First Attendant to Miss South Carolina State University. **Home Addr:** 1421 S Gordon St SW, Atlanta, GA 30310-2331, **Home Phone:** (404)753-5564.

## BATTLE, DR. CONCHITA Y. (CONCHA Y BATTLE)
Administrator, public speaker. **Personal:** Born Feb 8, 1963, Philadelphia, PA; daughter of Turner C III and Yvonne M Minnick; children: Amethyst Jai. **Educ:** Talladega Col, Talladega, AL, BA, 1987; Jacksonville State Univ, MPA, pub adminr, 1981; Univ Pa, EDD, 1999. **Career:** Talladega Col, dir equal opp employ, 1991-92, instr, 1990-92, actg dept head/asst dir teacher ed prog, 1990-92; Univ PA, res assist, 1994-95; Philadelphia Sch Readiness Proj, res assoc prog develop, 1995-96; Lincoln Univ, assist vp, Acad Affairs, 1995-98; Univ MD, assist dir admin, acad achievement progs, 1997-2001; CA State Univ, Northridge, dir advising resource ctr & eop, 2001-, CA State Libr, assembly speaker, 2004-08; Simi Valley High Sch, asst varsity coach, 2014-. **Orgs:** Phi Delta Kappa; NACADA; Am Asn Higher Ed; Am Asn Univ Prof; Am Coun Ed; United Negro Col Fund; Coun Opportunity Ed; Nat Asn Women Ed; Nat Asn Equal Opp Higher Ed; Nat Consortium Sports Asn, Nat Acad Advising Asn; Alpha Kappa Alpha. **Home Addr:** 4212 E Los Angeles Ave, Simi Valley, CA 93063, **Home Phone:** (805)527-4270. **Business Addr:** Director, California State University, 18111 Nordhoff St, Northridge, CA 91330, **Business Phone:** (818)677-1200.

## BATTLE, GLORIA JEAN
County government official. **Personal:** Born May 23, 1950, Deerfield Beach, FL; daughter of Joyce and Eugene. **Educ:** Bennett Col, Greensboro, NC, BA, 1972; Howard Univ, Washington, DC, MUS, 1976; Fla State Univ, Tallahassee, FL, PhD, 1985. **Career:** Social Systs Intervention, Wash, DC, res analyst, 1973-76; Mark Battle Asn, Wash, DC, consult, 1976; Child Advocacy Inc, Ft Lauderdale, Fla, planner, 1977-79; Fla Int Univ, Miami Fla, dir, 1979-80; Cult & Human Interaction Ctr, dir, 1979; Broward County Govt, Ft Lauderdale Fla, dir human rels div, 1981-2000; Fla Asn Realtors, 1987; City Deerfield Beach, Dist 2, comnr, 2009; Us Census Bur, sr partnership specialist, 2008; Rep Gwyndolen Clarke-Reed, community outreach coordr. **Orgs:** Pres, Nat Asn Human Rights Workers, 1981-, pres, Deerfield Child Develop Ctr, 1981-82; Community Housing Resource Bd, 1983-86; first vpres, Nat Asn Advan Colored People, N Broward Chap, 1984-85; Int Asn Human Rights Off; Forum Black Pub Admin, 1984-; Deerfield Beach Community Rels Bd; Deerfield Beach Ethics Comt; Alpha Kappa Alpha Sorority Inc, currently; Our Lady Mercy Cath Church, currently. **Home Addr:** 1240 SW 6th Way, Deerfield Beach, FL 33441, **Home Phone:** (954)428-2233. **Business Addr:** Commissioner, City of Deerfield Beach, 115 NE 2 Ave, Deerfield Beach, FL 33441.

## BATTLE, JACQUELINE
Banker. **Personal:** Born Sep 7, 1962, Columbus, GA; daughter of Myrtis Mahone Porter; married Gregory; children: Gregory II & James. **Educ:** Columbus Col, Columbus, Ga, 1982; Tuskegee Inst, Tuskegee, Ala, attended 1984; Atlanta Inst Real Estate, real estate banking & financing cert, 1994. **Career:** Atlantic Mortgage, Columbus, Ga, loan off, 1983-84; Money Express, Columbus, Ga, pres, underwriter, 1984-93; Lincoln Seervices Inc, title examr, 1993-96; Pub Res Inc, qual control mgr, 1996-. **Orgs:** Am Bus Women's Asn; Coordr Sus Women's Commn; clerk, Seventh-day Adventist Church; dir, C Praise; pres, Money Youth Pathfinders orgn; mem bd relators, Columbus; Harmonius Vision Singers; Am Bus Women; Criminal Justice Club; Columbus Chamber Com. **Honors/Awds:** Future Leader of America, Ebony Magazine, Nov, 1989; Leader of teen support group; Million Dollar Club. **Home Addr:** 210 Whipoorwill Lane, Columbus, GA 31903, **Home Phone:** (404)689-9770. **Business Addr:** Manager, Public Research Inc, 679 Criscoe Circle, Union Grove, AL 35175-5218, **Business Phone:** (334)375-4838.

## BATTLE, PROF. JUAN
President (organization), educator. **Educ:** York Col, PA, AS, law enforcement, 1988, BS, corrections & sociol, 1989; Univ Mich, MA, sociol, 1991, PhD, sociol, 1994. **Career:** City Univ New York, Hunter Col & Grad Ctr, prof sociol, pub health & urban educ, currently; Africana Studies Cert Prog, coordr; Univ Klagenfurt, fulbright fistinguished chair gender studies, fulbright sr specialist; Univ Wi, Inst Gender & Develop Studies, affil fac; Hunter Col, Sociol dept, prof. **Orgs:** Organizer, Race/Sex/Power: New Movements Black & Latina/o Sexualities; co-investr, Interdisciplinary Curric Urban Health Res; researcher, Returning Educated African Am & Latino Men to Empowered Neighborhoods; reviewer, NIH; reviewer, NSF; Am Found AIDS Res; reviewer, Contemp Sociol; Sociol Quart; Western J Black Studies; J Negro Educ; J Poverty; lead co-ed, Free At Last: Black Am Twenty-First Century, 2006; pres, Asn Black Sociologists, 2006-07; Nat Gay & Lesbian Task Force; Ctr Lesbian & Gay Studies; pres, Am Sociol Asn; Black Sexualities: Probing Powers, Passions, Practices, & Policies, 2010; YMCA; bd scholar fund, Camp Shohola Boys. **Business Addr:** Professor, City University of New York Graduate Center, 365 5th Ave, New York, NY 10016-4309, **Business Phone:** (212)817-8775.

## BATTLE, KATHLEEN DEANNA
Opera singer. **Personal:** Born Aug 13, 1948, Portsmouth, OH. **Educ:** Univ Cincinnati Col Conserv, BA, 1970, MA, 1971. **Career:** Requium, Cincinnati May Festival, singer, 1972; Festival of Two Worlds in Spoleto, Italy, performer, 1972; NY Metrop Opera, singer, 1980-94; regular guest soprano with orchestras in NY, Chicago, Boston, Philadelphia, Cleveland, Paris & Berlin & at major opera houses including the Metrop, Paris, Vienna & the Royal Opera/Covent Garden; Albums: Christmas Celebration, 1986; Salzburg Recital, 1987; Ariadne auf Naxos, 1987; Sings Mozart, 1995; So Many Stars, 1995; Angels' Glory, 1996; Greatest Hits, 2002; Kathleen Battle, 2002; Classic Battle: A Portrait, 2002; First Love, 2004; Best of Kathleen Battle: 20th Century Masters/The Millennium Collection, 2004; The Lord's Prayer, 2008. **Honors/Awds:** Nat Achievement Scholar; Laurence Olivier Award, 1985; Salz burg Recital; Candace Award, Nat Coalition100 Black Women, 1992; Hall of Fame, NAACP Image; five-time Grammy Award winner; Emmy Award, 1991; Honorary Doctorate, Univ Cincinnati; Honorary Doctorate, Westminster Choir Col; Honorary Doctorate, Ohio Univ; Honorary Doctorate, Xavier Univ; Honorary Doctorate, Amherst Col; Honorary Doctorate, Seton Hall Univ; Image Hall of Fame, Nat Asn Advan Colored People, 1999.

## BATTLE, ROXANE MORRISON
Television news anchorperson. **Personal:** Born St. Paul, MN; children: 1. **Educ:** Univ Minn, BA, jour; Univ Mo, Columbia, MA, jour. **Career:** KOMU-TV, Columbia, MO, reporter & anchor, 1987-88; WJXT-TV, Jacksonville, FL, reporter & anchor, 1988-90; WDAF-TV, Kans City, MO, reporter & ancho, 1990-91; KARE-11, Minneapolis, MN, gen assignment reporter, 1992; KAFE KARE, host, weekend anchor, 1998-2000, KARE 11 Today Show, co-host & anchor, 2000-06; WCCO-TV, Tv host, 2009-10. **Orgs:** Media dir/exec producer, Speak Word Church International, 2007-; bd mem, CycleHealth, 2015-. **Special Achievements:** Book: Pockets of Joy, 2015. **Business Addr:** Reporter, Co-Host, Kare-11, 8811 Olson Memorial, Minneapolis, MN 55427, **Business Phone:** (763)546-1111.

## BATTLE, DR. STANLEY F.
Vice president (organization), educator, president (organization). **Personal:** Born Jun 12, 1951, Springfield, MA; son of Henry and Rachel Williams; married Judith Lynn Rozie; children: Ashley Lynn. **Educ:** Springfield Col, BA, sociol, 1973; Univ Conn, MSW, 1975; Univ Pittsburgh, MPH, 1979, PhD, 1980; Harvard Univ, Inst Educ Mgt, attended 2002. **Career:** Educator, authr; Univ Minn Sch Social Work, asst prof, 1980-84; Boston Univ Sch Social Work, assoc prof, 1984-87; Sch Med Pediat, sr res, 1984-89; Univ Conn, Sch Social Work, prof, 1987-93, Sch Med-Community Med, sr lectr, 1987-93, assoc dean res & devel, 1991-93, Sch Allied Health, adj prof, 1996-98; Eastern Conn State Univ, assoc vpres acad affairs, 1993-98; Schs Social Welfare & Educ, sullivan spaights distinguished profship, 1998-2001; Univ Wis-Milwaukee, vice chancellor stud & multicultural affairs, 2000-03; Coppin State Univ, pres, 2003-06; chancellor, NC Agr & Tech State Univ, 2007-09; Southern Conn State Univ, interim pres, 2010-11. **Orgs:** Chair, Univ Planning Coun, Coppin State Univ; Cent Conn State Univ, 2012-13; dir, Univ St Joseph; Meriden Chamber Com; New Haven Chamber Com; bd mem, Conn Campus Compact. **Home Addr:** 4000 Hazel Lane, Greensboro, NC 27408, **Home Phone:** (336)286-3435. **Business Addr:** President, Southern Connecticut State University, 501 Crescent St, New Haven, CT 06515, **Business Phone:** (203)392-8047.

## BATTLE, DR. THOMAS CORNELL
Librarian, administrator. **Personal:** Born Mar 19, 1946, Washington, DC; son of Thomas Oscar and Lenora Thomas; children: Brima Omar, Idrissa Saville & Mensah Lukman. **Educ:** Howard Univ, BA, hist, 1968; Univ Md, MLS, info studies, 1971; George Washington Univ, PhD, Am studies, 1983. **Career:** Fed City Col, Sr Media Intern, 1969-71; DC Pub Libr, readers adv, 1971; Howards Moorland-Spingarn Res Collection, librn, 1972; MSRC, ref librn, 1972-74; Sierra Leone Lib Bd, exchange librn, 1972-73; Howard Univ, Moorland Spingarn Res Ctr, cur manuscripts, ref librn, 1972, founding cur, manuscript div, 1974-86, dir, 1986-2009, univ archivist, teacher; Univ Md; Amherst Univ; Donna M. Wells, ed, 2007; Mt. Pleasant Pub Libr. **Orgs:** Field reviewer & panelist, Nat Endowment humanities, 1976-; bd mem, DC Libr Asn, 1978-80; bd mem, mus City Wash, 1978, 1981-90; exec bd, Black Caucus Am Libr Asn, 1980-92; chair, African & Caribbean Task Force Black Caucus Am Libr Asn, 1980-82; councillor at large, 1980-83, treas, 1983-85; bylaws comt, Metro Wash Caucus Black Librns, 1982-83; chair, task force minorities, Soc Am Archivists, 1982-86; bd mem, Nat Hist Day, 1983-85; consult, Nat Park Serv, 1983-85; prog comn, 1986, Mid Atlantic Regional Arch Conf, nominating comn, 1987; fel prog comn, Soc Am Archivists, 1987; Am Libr Asn Mid-Atlantic Regional Arch Conf; African Am Mus Asn; chair, nominating comn; exec coun asn, Study African Am Life & Hist; founder, Black Hist Month. **Honors/Awds:** Title IIB Higher Educ Acct fel, 1970-71; Beta Phi Mu Iota Chap, 1971; Certified Archivist, Academy Certified Archivists, 1989; author of: "Howard University: Heritage and Horizons", Academic Affairs Bulletin, Howard Univ, v. 2, no. 1, February, 1977; "Research Centers Document the Black Experience", History News, February, 1981; "Behind the Marble Mask", The Wilson Quarterly, New Year's, 1989; James Partridge Award, Univ Md Col Info Studies, 2006. **Special Achievements:** Co-edited the book "Legacy: Treasures of Black History", 2007. **Home Addr:** 13004 Chalfont Ave, Ft Washington, MD 20744, **Home Phone:** (301)292-9359.

## BATTLE, DR. TURNER CHARLES, III
Educator, executive director, teacher. **Personal:** Born Jan 1, 1926; son of Turner and Annie Evelyn McClellan; married Carmen H Gonzalez Castellanos; children: Anne E (McAndrew), Turner IV, Conchita & Carmen Rosario; married Marion. **Educ:** Oakwood Col, BA; Temple Univ, MFA; Columbia Univ; NY Univ; Columbia Pac Univ; Wiley Col, HHD. **Career:** Oakwood Col, instr; USN Dept, auditor & acct; Philadelphia Sch Syst, teacher, 1955-65; Elmira Col, asst prof, 1968-70; Moore Col, assoc prof, 1968-70; La Salle Col, dir spec progs; New York Univ, teaching fel, 1970-72; Westminster Choir Col, dir, coun, 1974-74; United Negro Col Fund Inc, asst exec dir, 1974, corp sec, vpres; Educ Develop Serv, pres. **Orgs:** Oakwood Col Alumni Asn; Temple Univ Alumni Asn; vis comn educ, Metro Mus Art; Am Soc Asn Exec; Sierra Club; Am Mus Nat Hist; Smithsonian Inst; Am Asn Higher Educ; Phi Delta Kappa. **Home Addr:** 1519 W Turner St, Allentown, PA 18102-3634, **Home Phone:** (610)740-9440.

## BATTLE-BUMPERS, KATRINA
Businessperson. **Personal:** Born Miami, FL. **Career:** Benford Brown & Assocs LLC, managing partner, currently. **Business Addr:** Managing Partner, Benford Brown & Associates LLC, 8334 S Stony Island Ave, Chicago, IL 60617, **Business Phone:** (773)731-1300.

## BATTLES, SHERYL Y.
Executive. **Personal:** married Curt; children: Kendall. **Educ:** Stanford Univ, BA, human biol. **Career:** Pitney Bowes Inc, vpres, corp commun, 2004-. **Orgs:** Bd dir & exec comt, Stamford Ctr Arts; Bd dir & exec comt, Stamford Partnership; Stamford Norwalk Chap Jack & Jill Am Inc; Fairfield County Chap Links Inc; Arthur W Page Soc; Pub Rels Soc Am; Stanford Univ Alumni Asn; Stanford Nat Black Alumni Asn; bd trustee, Johnson C Smith Theol Sem; Sem Comt PR Sem; Fairfield County Alumnae Chap Delta Sigma Theta Sorority Inc; deacon, First Presby Church Stamford. **Business Addr:** Vice President of Corporate Communications, Pitney Bowes Inc, 1 Elmcroft Rd, Stamford, CT 06926-0700, **Business Phone:** (203)351-6808.

## BATTS, ALICIA J.
Lawyer. **Educ:** Harvard Col, BA, soc studies, 1987; Columbia Univ Law Sch, JD, 1990. **Career:** Skadden, Arps, Slate, Meagher & Flom LLP, assoc, antitrust & com litigator, 1990-96; Howrey Simon Arnold

& White LLP, anti trust & com litigator, assoc, 1996-98; Fed Trade Comnr Mozelle W. Thompson, atty adv, 1998-2000; Foley & Lardner's Litigation Dept, partner, 2000-04; Dickstein Shapiro Morin & Oshinsky, Litigation & Dispute Resolution Group, atty & partner, 2004-07; Proskauer Rose LLP, partner, 2007-16; Squire Patton Boggs, partner, 2016-. **Orgs:** Vice chair, Am Bar Asn Antitrust Sec Bus Torts & Civil RICO Comt, 1990-2012; bd dir, Appleseed Found, 1995-2016; Active mem sect antitrust law, Am Bar Asn; DC Bar Asn; ed bd, Antitrust Law Jour. **Honors/Awds:** Listed in Black Enterprises Americas Top Black Lawyers. **Special Achievements:** Author: "Prudenceis the Best Policy for Standard-Setters", Merger Review in a Sluggish Economy. **Business Addr:** Partner, Squire Patton Boggs, 2550 M St Northwest, Washington, DC 20037, **Business Phone:** (202)457-6335.

### BATTS, NIA
Mass media specialist, executive, foundation executive. **Personal:** Born Jan 1, 1985?. **Educ:** Columbia Univ, New York, BA, film studies; Harvard Bus Sch, exec educ cert; NY Univ, cert producing. **Career:** Island Def Jam Music Group, intern to pres, 2003-04; Warner Music Group, asst to exec vpres, 2004-06; Viacom, coordr mkt coun, 2007-08, sr mgr mkt coun & strategic partnerships, 2008-09, dir strategic partnerships & social impact, 2010-13, sr dir strategic partnerships & social innovation, 2013-15; Def Jam, working Kevin Liles; Telescope Collective, founder & chief exec officer, 2015-. **Orgs:** E Harlem Sch, Young Vols exec bd; bd dir, Louis Carr Internship Found. **Honors/Awds:** Hello Beautiful, 30 Under 30, 2011; "Black Enterprise," Rising Stars 40 & Under, 2014. **Business Addr:** Director, Viacom Inc, 1515 Broadway, New York, NY 10036.

### BAUGH, ESQ. EDNA Y.
Lawyer, administrator. **Personal:** Born Aug 22, 1948, Orange, NJ; daughter of George W and Pauline E. **Educ:** Hartwick Col, BA, econs, 1970; Vt Law Sch, JD, 1983. **Career:** Williams, Caliri, Miller & Otley firm; City E Orange, assst corp coun, corp trial coun, 1986-94; Medvin & Elberg, assoc atty, 1988-98; Stephens & Baugh LLC, founding mem, managing mem & co-chmn, 2000-; Ruters Law Sch, asst dir clin admin, 2004-. **Orgs:** Nat Bar Asn, 1986-; dir, pres, Garden State Bar Asn, 1986-; Girl Scout Coun Greater Essex & Hudson Counties, 1986-, pres, 1995-2001; bd trustee, Essex-Newark Legal Servs, 1993-; secy, bd trustee, Essex County Col, 1997-; NJ State Bar Asn; trustee, Essex County Bar Asn; vice chmn, NJ Supreme Ct Disciplinary Rev Bd, currently; NJ Supreme Ct Comt Tax Ct; chmn, Essex County Col Found Bd, currently; bd trustee, Vt Law Sch. **Special Achievements:** First African-American President of the Girl Scout Council of Greater Essex and Hudson Counties. **Home Addr:** 142 S Clinton St, East Orange, NJ 07018-3011. **Business Addr:** Co-Chairperson, Managing Member, Stephens & Baugh LLC, 2040 Millburn Ave Suite 305, Maplewood, NJ 07040-3716, **Business Phone:** (973)762-9400.

### BAUGH, FLORENCE ELLEN
Administrator. **Personal:** Born Feb 2, 1935, Beaver Dam, KY; daughter of William C Jackson and Glendora Fant Birch; married Dallas A Baug; children: Delandria, Dallas, Christopher, Orville & Lynne. **Educ:** State Univ NY, Millard Fillmore Col, BA; Empire State Col; CCAP cert, 1995, 2003. **Career:** Comm Action Org, Erie Co, comn aide, 1965-70; YWCA, dir racial justice pub affairs, 1971-72; Comn Action Org, Erie Co, Neighborhood Servs Dept, dir, 1972-2001, New Venture Housing Inc, mgr, 1988-2001; Sr Serv & Community Rels Dept, dir, 2001-04, Providence Baptist Church, church clerk, chmn bd trustee & church organist, currently. **Orgs:** Trustee, Sheehan Mem Emer Hosp, 1974-86; Buffalo Bd Educ, 1973-89; dir pres, Ellicott Houses Inc, 1978; Univ Buffalo CAC; bd mem, We NY Art Inst; sec treas, Coun Grt City Sch Bds, 1978-89; trustee, D'Youville Col, 1980-88; Gov's appointee, Dist Judicial Rev Comn, 1986-94; organist, clerk, trustee, Providence Bapt Ch; pres, Coun Great City Sch, 1988-89; State Univ Buffalo Community Adv Coun, 1989-91; pres, State Univ Buffalo CAC; bd mem, EPIC; co-chmn, Irene Bellam Scholar Fund; Nat Black Child Develop Inst; Nat Caucus & Ctr Black Aged Inc; Nat Mus Women Arts; nat bd dir, EPIC, 1989-92; Erie County Dept Social Serv Adv Bd, comnr, 1991; Concerned Citizens Against Violence Coalition, 1991; trustee, Theodore Roosevelt inaugural site; Cert Housing Counr, 1995; Cert Community Action Prof, 1995; bd trustee, Villa Marie Col, 1995; bd dir, City Buffalo, Enterprise Zone, 1995; Buffalo & Erie County Workforce Develop Bd, 2002; Canisius Col Sports Comt; pres, Ny Conf Large Cities Boards Educ. **Honors/Awds:** Commission Service Award, Afro-Am Policeman's Asn, 1972; Buffalo Chapter Negro Bus & Prof Women Commission Service Award, 1973; Black Educators Association Education Service Award, 1974; Citizen of the Year, Buffalo Evening News, 1975; Woman of the Year, Nat Org PUSH, 1975; Citizen of the Year, Buffalo Kiwanis Club, 1976; Buffalo Urban League Family Life Award, 1976; President Distinguished Medal, Buffalo St Teacher Col, 1978; University Alumni Award, Univ Buffalo, 1982; National Conference Christians & Jews Educatin Award, 1982; Medal Excellence, NY State Univ, Bd Regents, 1984; honorary chairman, Week of the Young Child; Vernie Mulholland Friend of Education Award, Delta Kappa Gamma, 1986; Distinguished Citizen Award, St Univ Syst of NY St, 1986; Everett R. Dwyer Award, 1987; Empire State Fed of Women's Clubs Commission Service Award; YMCA Community Service Award, 1989; Ebony and Ivory Award, Erie Community Col, 1997; Western NY Women Hall of Fame, 1997; Buffalo Queens, 2001; Southern Christian Leadership Conference Community Service Award, 2004; honorary doctorate degrees: Canisius Col, 1976; Medaille Col, 1985; appointed Governor Cuomo NY State Sch & Bus Alliance. **Home Addr:** 45 Woodward Ave, Buffalo, NY 14214, **Home Phone:** (716)835-7394. **Business Addr:** Chairman of the Board of Trustees, Church Clerk, Providence Baptist Church, 2 Kermit Ave, Buffalo, NY 14215, **Business Phone:** (716)896-6032.

### BAUGH, PROF. JOYCE A.
Political scientist. **Personal:** Born Jul 19, 1959, Charleston, SC; daughter of Jeff and Ella Jones; married Roger D Hatch. **Educ:** Clemson Univ, Clemson, SC, BA, 1981; Kent State Univ, Kent, OH, MA, 1983, PhD, 1989. **Career:** Kent State Univ, Kent, OH, grad asst, 1982-83, teaching fel, 1984-88, David B. Smith fel, 1986-87; Cent Mich Univ, Mt Pleasant, MI, from asst prof to assoc prof, 1988-98, Affirmative Action Coun, 1990-95, Dept Polit Sci, chmn, 1995-2001, prof, 1998-, Fac Asn, bd dir, 1991-95, 2000-04, res prof, 1999-2000, Acad Senate, exec bd, 2004-05; Saginaw News, guest columnist, 2005. **Orgs:** Secy, Womens Aid Serv, 1990-2004; secy, Midwest Women's Caucus Polit Sci, 1990-91; co chmn, Affirmative Action Coun, 1992-94; Am Polit Sci Asn; Midwest Polit Sci Asn; Am Acad Relig; bd dir, Mich Conf Polit Scientists, 2006-09. **Honors/Awds:** Harry S Truman Scholar, Truman Found, 1979; Outstanding Graduate Student Teaching Award, Kent State University, 1984; Excellence in Teaching award, Cent Mich Univ Col Humanities & Social & Behav Sci, 2009. **Home Addr:** 711 Hopkins Ave, Mount Pleasant, MI 48858, **Home Phone:** (989)773-2589. **Business Addr:** Professor, Central Michigan University, 247 Anspach Hall, Mount Pleasant, MI 48859, **Business Phone:** (989)774-3475.

### BAUGH, LYNNETTE B.
Executive. **Personal:** Born Feb 22, 1949, Charleston, WV. **Educ:** WVa State Col, BA, 1971; Univ Pittsburgh, MPA, 1972. **Career:** City Chicago Pub Works Dept, planning anal, 1973-74; IL Dept Local Govt Affairs, area rep, 1974-76, area supvr, 1976-77; City Tacoma Comn Develop Dept, asst dir, 1978-; Dept Pub Utilities, mgt anal, 1984-89, Customer Finance & Admin Serv, asst dir, 1989-; Tacoma Inter Govern Affairs Off, dir. **Orgs:** Delta Sigma Theta Sorority, 1968-; vice chmn, APPA Perform Mgt Comt, 1989-91, chmn, 1991-93; Title 9 Sex Equity Adv Comt; bd mem, Pierce Co Growth Policy Asn; exec com & vpres, NAHRO Puget Sound Chap NAHRO; Altrusa Int; Kiwannianne; APPA Comn Perform Mgt; Women Govern; Acct Adv Comt; Tacoma Rotary Club; bd mem, Tacom Urban League; Nat Asn Advan Colored People; vpres, Tacoma Alumnae Chap Delta Sigma Theta Sorority; RK Mellon Fels. **Special Achievements:** Named Wash Potential Black Leader 1980's NW Conf Black Pub Officials. **Home Addr:** 5413 Chinook Dr NE, Tacoma, WA 98422-1985, **Home Phone:** (253)924-1120. **Business Addr:** Assistant Director of Customer Finance & Administrative Services, City of Tacoma, Tacoma Munic Bldg 747 Mkt St, Tacoma, WA 98402, **Business Phone:** (253)591-5000.

### BAUGH, DR. REGINALD F.
Executive, physician. **Personal:** Born Jun 12, 1956, Grand Forks, ND; son of Gerald R and Virginia; married Bobbie Hafford; children: Brandon & Aaron. **Educ:** Univ Iowa, BS, biol sci, 1977; Univ Mich Med Sch, MD, MEd, 1981, surg, 1983, otolaryngol, 1987; Am Bd Otolaryngol, cert, otolaryngol. **Career:** Univ Mich Med Ctr, oto resident, 1983-87, internship; Univ Lowa, training, Gen Sci; Kans City Veteran's Hosp, chief otolaryngol, 1988-90; Univ Kans Med Sch, asst prof, 1988-90; Kaiser Permanente, chief otolaryngol, 1990-93, res mgt, dir, 1991-93; Henry Ford Health Syst, gen surg resident, med dir, hosp utilization, 1993-2000; clin res improv, med dir, 1995-98, clin serv, med dir, 1996-; Tex A&M Univ, vice chmn, dept surg, 2005-08, prof & chair, otolaryngol, 2005-08; Scott & White, Div Otolaryngol, dir, 2005-; New Grace Apostolic Church, deacon & Sunday Sch teacher; Univ Toledo, prof & chair, otolaryngol, 2009-. **Orgs:** Am med Asn; coun, AMAP Performance Measurement Comn; House Delegates, Am Med Group Asn; pres, treas, Nat Med Assn, Otolaryngol Sect; Mich State Med Soc; Mich Inst Med Qual; chair, Reimbursement Comt, Am Acad Otolaryngol; Aetna US Healthcare, Mich, Credentialing/Performance Mgt Comt, Qual Oversight Comt; trustee, Onika Ins Co; trustee, Henry Ford Health Syst/Henry Ford Med Group/Herny Ford Hosp; Am Col Physician Exec; treas, Barnes Soc; Walter P Work Soc; exec comt, Healthy Detroit. **Home Addr:** 256 Barton Shore Dr, Ann Arbor, MI 48105. **Business Addr:** Chair-College of Medicine Council, Professor, The University of Toledo, 2801 W Bancroft, Toledo, OH 43606-3390, **Business Phone:** (419)530-4636.

### BAULDOCK, GERALD, SR.
Writer, chemical engineer, inventor. **Personal:** Born Aug 5, 1957, Trenton, NJ; son of Dalbert and Ora; married Alveria; children: Gerald Jr, Justin & Jacob. **Educ:** Bucknell Univ, Lewisburg, PA, BS, chem engineering, 1979; Villanova Univ, Philadelphia, PA, MS, chem engineering, 1986. **Career:** Rohm & Haas, Bristol, PA, process engr, 1979-90; B-Dock Press, Willingboro, NJ, pres; B-Dock Educ Products, chief exec officer & vpres, currently; Sybron Chemicals, Birmingham, NJ, sr process engr; WL Gore & Assocs, process engr; Author: Reaching for the Moon; Say It Loud. I'm Smart, Black & Proud, 2003; "Racial Profiling in Kindergarten!", "Arrested by Officer Dan Polo Jr!", Kids for Chemistry; Inventor, Kids for Chemistry: The Game; The PI Wheel; The CosSin Calculator; The Cylinder Calculator. **Honors/Awds:** Achievement Award, Optimist Club Philadelphia, 1990; Achievement Award, Bus Women Atlantic City, 1990; The Carl T Humphrey Memorial Award, Villanova Univ, 1992. **Business Addr:** Chief Executive Officer, Vice President, B-Dock Educational Products, PO Box 8, Willingboro, NJ 08046, **Business Phone:** (609)871-3932.

### BAUTISTA, DANNY (DANIEL ALCANTARA BAUTISTA)
Baseball player. **Personal:** Born May 24, 1972, Santo Domingo. **Career:** Baseball player (retired); Detroit Tigers, outfielder, 1993-96; Atlanta Braves, outfielder, 1996-98; Fla Marlins, outfielder, 1999-2000; Ariz Diamondbacks, outfielder, 2000-04; Tampa Bay Devil Rays, left-forward, 2005; York Revolution, Atlantic League Prof Baseball; Camden Riversharks; Mex Red Devils, currently.

### BAXTER, A. D.
Educator. **Career:** Univ Tenn, Nat Asn Advan Colored People, chap adv, currently; 2TOR & 2T Cent, Off Minority Stud Affairs, tutorial prog coordr, currently; Black Fac & Staff Asn, exec comt. **Home Addr:** 9401 Barrington Rd, Knoxville, TN 37922, **Home Phone:** (865)693-1140. **Business Addr:** Tutorial Program Coordinator, University of Tennessee, 812 Volunteer Blvd, Knoxville, TN 37916, **Business Phone:** (423)974-6861.

### BAXTER, DR. CHARLES F., JR.
Physician. **Personal:** Born Apr 23, 1959, Brooklyn, NY; son of Charles F Sr and Bernice Kinand. **Educ:** City Col NY, BS, 1981; Meharry Med Col, MD, 1986. **Career:** Col Physicians & Surgeons Columbia Univ, assoc fell surg; Columbia Univ Col Physicians & Surgeons, surg resident; Harlem Hosp Ctr, surg resident, 1986-92; Sloan-Kettering Memorial Hosp, New York, NY, surg presoncol, 1989; McHarry Med Col, vis instr, dept anat, 1990; Portsmouth Naval Hosp, staff gen surgeon, 1990-94; USS George Wash, ship surgeon, 1992-94; US Naval Hosp, Yokosuka, Japan, staff gen surgeon, 1995-; DOD, 7th fleet surgeon, 2004-06, Navy cent command surgeon, 2006-08; Us Pac Fleet, pac fleet surgeon, 2008-10; US Embassy Viet Nam, US Dept State, health attache, 2010-. **Orgs:** Am Med Asn; Am Chem Soc; New York Acad Sci; Asn Mil Surgeons US; Am Col Surgeons, Cand Group; Med Soc Ny; Am Asn Clin Chem; Nat Naval Officers Asn; Nat Naval Inst. **Honors/Awds:** Baskerville Chemical Award, City Col New York, 1981; Navy Commendation Medal, 1994. **Home Addr:** 110 W End Ave, New York, NY 10023, **Home Phone:** (212)874-6917. **Business Addr:** Staff General Surgeon, USNH-Yokosuka, PSC 475, Yokosuka96350-1620.

### BAXTER, FREDERICK DENARD (FRED BAXTER)
Football player. **Personal:** Born Jun 14, 1971, Brundidge, AL; son of Brittany and Kellan; married Lisa. **Educ:** Auburn Univ, grad. **Career:** Football player (retired); NY Jets, tight end, 1993-2000; Chicago Bears, tight end, 2001-02; New Eng Patriots, 2002-03. **Orgs:** Founder, Fred Baxter Found, 2000. **Honors/Awds:** NY Jets, Most Valuable Player, 1996-2000; Super Bowl, New England Patriots, 2003. **Business Addr:** Owner, Fred Baxter Foundation Inc, PO Box 14, Brundige, AL 36010, **Business Phone:** (609)410-9092.

### BAXTER, KALA LYNN
Theatrical director. **Career:** Lincoln Univ, dir theater arts. **Business Addr:** Director of Theatre Arts, Lincoln University, Ware Center 122, Lincoln Univ, PA 19352, **Business Phone:** (267)257-5282.

### BAXTER, REV. NATHAN DWIGHT
Educator, school administrator, bishop. **Personal:** Born Nov 16, 1948, Coatesville, PA; son of Elder Belgium Nathan and Augusta Ruth Byrd; married Mary Ellen Walker; children: Timika Ann & Harrison David. **Educ:** Lancaster Theol Sem, homiletics & Christology, 1976, DMin, 1984; Dickinson Col, Carlisle, PA, sexually transmitted infection, 1990; St Paul's Col, Lawrenceville, VA, DD, 2000; Messiah Col, Grantham, PA, Dept Sci & Technol, 2001; York Col, PA, DHL, 2002; Colgate Univ, Hamilton, NY, DD, 2003. **Career:** Bishop (retired); St. John's Episcopal Church, curate, 1976-78; St. Cypman's Episcopal Church, rector, 1978-84; St. Paul's Col, chaplain, prof relig studies, 1984-86; Lancaster Theol Sem, dean, assoc prof, 1986-90; Col Preachers, fel, 1990; Episcopal Divinity Sch, dean, assoc prof, 1990-91; Wash Nat Cathedral, dean, 1991-2003; Diocese Cent Pa, Episcopal Church, bishop, 2006-14; Author: Visions for the Millennium: Thoughts on Christian Living. **Orgs:** Bd, Episcopal Cathedral Telecommunications Network; Metrop Dialogue WA; Am Soc Order St John Jerusalem; Urban League; Epsilon Boule Sigma Pi Phi; life mem, Nat Asn Advan Colored People; chief admin officer, Protestant Episcopal Church Found; bd dir, Faith & Polit Inst, 1996; lectr, Medina Sem Princeton Univ, 1997-2002; preacher, Chautaugua Inst, New York, 1997-2002; bd mem, Univ Va Ctr Relig & Democracy, 2002; bd dir, Riggs Nat Bank, 2002. **Special Achievements:** Ordained Episcopal Church, 1977. **Business Addr:** Bishop, Episcopal Diocese of Central Pennsylvania, 101 Pine St, Harrisburg, PA 17101, **Business Phone:** (888)236-5959.

### BAXTER, HON. WENDY MARIE
Judge, executive, lawyer. **Personal:** Born Jul 25, 1952, Detroit, MI; married David Ford Cartwright Jr; children: Samantha. **Educ:** Eastern Mich Univ, BBA, 1972; Univ Detroit Sch Law, JD, 1978; Nat Judical Col, CLE, Acct & Finance, Bus Valuation, Electronic Discovery, 2013. **Career:** Judge (retired); Gen Motors, oil lease analyst, 1977; Wayne Cty Criminal Bond, investr, 1978; Recorder's Ct, ct docket admin, 1979; State Appellate Defender's Off, atty, 1980; Pvt pract, atty, 1982; Thirty Sixth Dist Ct, judge; Recorder's Ct, judge, 1982-86; Wayne Co Circuit Ct, judge, 1986-97; Third Circuit Ct judge, 1997-2013; Nat Judicial Col, guest lectr; WinWin Facilitation PLLC, Atty Mediator, 2013-. **Orgs:** Women Lawyers Asn, 1981; bd dir, Wolverine Bar Asn, 1981; rules & forms comt woman, Dist Judges Asn, 1982; bd dir, Women's Judges Fund Justice, 1986-90; seventh dist prog dir, Nat Asn Women Judges, officer 1987-1990; pres, Asn Black Judges Mich, 1986; Nat Asn Advan Colored People; Nat Bar Asn; Mich Asn Black Judges; State Bar Mich; organizer, Sherwood Forest Neighborhood Asn, 2005; Jim Dandies Ski Club; bd, Detroit Metrop Bar Asn, 2014. **Honors/Awds:** Spirit Detroit Detroit City Coun, 1981; Adoptive Parent Detroit Pub Sch, 1985; Women of Excellence Award, 2013; Legacy in Motion Award Salute to Leadership Award, 2013; Advocacy Award, 2014. **Home Addr:** 17546 Birchcrest, Detroit, MI 48221. **Business Addr:** Attorney Mediator, WinWin Facilitation PLLC, 333 W Fort St, Detroit, MI 48226, **Business Phone:** (313)224-5261.

### BAYE, BETTY WINSTON
Writer, columnist. **Personal:** Born Brooklyn, NY; daughter of George Washington and Betty Jane Brown. **Educ:** Hunter Col, City Univ NY, BA, commun; Columbia Univ Grad Sch Jour, MA. **Career:** Courier-J, gen assignment reporter, 1984, ed writer & columnist, currently; Author: Black Am & Bill Clinton, 25 Am Best Black Columnists Speak Their Minds, My cup runneth over, Africans, Blackbird, C Dream & Work Sister Work; Black exec Leadership Inst. **Orgs:** Nieman Fel, Harvard Univ, 1990-91; Poynter Inst; Trotter Group; vpres, Nat assoc Black Journalists & NY assoc Black Journalists, fel William Monroe Trotter Grp; founder, Black Alumni Network, Columbia Univ Sch Journalism; Delta Sigma Theta Sorority Inc, Ed Gordon Nat Pub Radio. **Honors/Awds:** Best of Gannett; National Association of Black Journalists Region VI Hall of Fame Award. **Special Achievements:** First the Africans novel was published, 1983; Black Achiever of the Chestnut Street, Young Mens Christian Association. **Home Addr:** 3721 Hurstbourne Ridge Blvd, Louisville, KY 40299-6532. **Business Addr:** Editorial Writer, Columnist, The Courier-Journal, 525 W Broadway, Louisville, KY 40202, **Business Phone:** (502)582-4011.

### BAYE, DR. LAWRENCE JAMES J.
Educator, writer. **Personal:** Born Oct 10, 1933, Houston, TX; son of Frank Claude and Bernice Margrett Navy; children: Elizabeth Lenoa & Ursula Frances. **Educ:** Tex Southern Univ, BS, 1956, MS, 1957; Univ Tex, Austin, PhD, chem, 1963. **Career:** Educator (retired); Tex

Southern Univ, Houston, asst prof chem, 1961-64; Knoxville Col, TN, assoc prof & head, Dept Chem, 1964-67; Univ Tex, Austin, post doctoral res, 1964; Univ Tenn, Knoxville, post doctoral res, 1966; Huston-Tillotson Col, Austin, Tex, prof chem, 1967. **Orgs:** Am Chem Soc; Sigma Xi; Beta Kappa Chi; Phi Beta Sigma Fraternity, 1955-; Black Citizens Task Force, 1978-; Nat Org Prof Adv Black Chemists & Chem Eng, 1980-. **Honors/Awds:** Recepient Robt A Welch Found Res Grants; NASA Grant Fluorocarbon Polymer Res, 1995-97. **Special Achievements:** Author of 14 publications; "Journal of American Chemical Society & other Major Chemistry Journal, 1956; Outstanding educator of America, 1971. **Home Addr:** 1729 E 38th 1/2 St, Austin, TX 78722-1211, **Home Phone:** (512)477-8998.

### BAYLISS, JOCELYN KELLY
Engineer. **Educ:** Univ Tenn, BS, 1991. **Career:** Corning Cable Systs, engr, 2001. **Orgs:** Nat Soc Black Engrs.

### BAYLOR, DONALD EDWARD (DON BAYLOR)
Baseball player, baseball manager, athletic coach. **Personal:** Born Jun 28, 1949, Austin, TX; son of George and Lillian Brown; married Rebecca Giles; children: Don Jr; married Jo Cash; children: Don Jr. **Educ:** Blinn Jr Col. **Career:** Baseball player (retired), baseball coach, executive; Baltimore Orioles, 1970-75; Oakland Athletics, 1976, 1988; Calif Angels, 1977-82; New York Yankees, 1983-85; Boston Red Sox, 1986-87; Minn Twins, 1987; Milwaukee Brewers, hitting coach, 1990-91; St Louis Cardinals, hitting coach, 1992; Colo Rockies, mgr, 1993-98, hitting coach, 2009-10; Atlanta Braves, hitting coach, 1999; Chicago Cubs, mgr, 2000-02; New York Mets, bench coach, 2003-04; Seattle Mariners, hitting coach, 2005; Ariz Diamondbacks, player & mgr, hitting coach, 2011-13; Mid-Atlantic Sports Network, Nats Xtra, co-host, currently; Los Angeles Angels Anaheim, hitting coach, 2013-. **Orgs:** Cystic Fibrosis Found, 1979. **Home Addr:** 56-325 Riviera, La Quinta, CA 92253. **Business Addr:** Hitting Coach, Los Angeles Angels of Anaheim, Angel Stadium 2000 Gene Autry Way, Anaheim, CA 92806, **Business Phone:** (714)940-2000.

### BAYLOR, ELGIN GAY
Sports manager, basketball coach, executive. **Personal:** Born Sep 16, 1934, Washington, DC; married Elaine; children: Krystle. **Educ:** Col Idaho, attended 1955; Seattle Univ, attended 1958. **Career:** Basketball player (retired), basketball coach, basketball exec; Minneapolis Lakers, player, 1958; New Orleans Jazz, asst coach, 1974-77, head coach, 1976-77; Los Angeles Clippers, exec vpres & gen mgr, vpres basketball opers & gen mgr, 1986-2008. **Orgs:** Kappa Alpha Psi Fraternity.

### BAYLOR, EMMETT ROBERT, JR.
Government official. **Personal:** Born Oct 18, 1933, New York, NY; son of Emmett (deceased) and Lilliam (deceased); married Margaret; children: Kathryn R, Gladys E, Emmett R III & Steven G. **Educ:** Wayne County Community Col, pub admin; Mercy Col, pub admin, 1991. **Career:** Maidenform Inc, sales rep, 1963-75; Metrop Life Ins, rep, 1975-79; City Detroit, dir detroit house correction, 1977-85; Mich Dept Corrections, warden & dep warden, 1985-93; Scott Correctional Facility, dep warden, 1992; City Detroit, exec asst mayor & pub safety dir. **Orgs:** Asn, 1968-; detroit chap, Trans Africa, 1970-; founder Soc Detroit Inst Arts, 1970-; Wardens & Superintendents N Am, 1985-93; Am Correctional Asn, 1985-93; Am Jail Asn, 1985-93; Mich Correctional Asn, 1985-93; Nat Asn Advan Colored People. **Home Addr:** 4815 W Siesta Way, Laveen, AZ 85339-4228, **Home Phone:** (602)237-0244.

### BAYLOR, HELEN
Gospel singer. **Personal:** Born Jan 8, 1953, Tulsa, OK; married James; children: 4. **Career:** Toured with muscial Hair, 1970; R&B grp Side Effect, 1976; Albums: Highly Recommended, 1990; Look A Little Closer, 1991; Start All Over, 1993; Live Experience, 1995; Love Brought Me Back, 1996; Live, 1999, 2002, 2011; My Everything, 2002; Diadem Music, 2003; Full Circle, MCG Rec, 2006; Definitive Gospel Collection, 2008. **Orgs:** Adv coun, Elizabeth Home Unwed Mothers, 2000-; bd mem, St Dominic's Home Unwed Mothers, 2000-; Crenshaw Christian Ctr; fel Inner-City Word Faith Ministries. **Honors/Awds:** Soul Train Lady Soul Award, Best Gospel Album, 1995; 3 Stellar Awards; 4 Grammy nominations; 2 Dove Awards; Hon Doctorate, Friends Int Christian Univ, 1995; Oklahoma Jazz Hall of Fame, 2000. **Special Achievements:** Ordained to Christian ministry, 1993; Autobiography: No Greater Love: The Helen Baylor Story. **Home Addr:** , Las Vegas, NV 89101. **Business Addr:** Singer, MCG Records, PO Box 2154, Alpharetta, GA 30023, **Business Phone:** (770)667-4970.

### BAYLOR, HON. MARGARET E.
Government official. **Personal:** Born Jan 1, 1937. **Educ:** Hunter Col, BA; Wayne State Univ, MA, educ; Detroit Col Law, JD. **Career:** Wayne County Community Col, prof, 1972-92; Chair Disciplinary Appeals Subcomm, Bd Police Comnr, 36th Dist Ct, magistrate, 1994-. **Orgs:** Bd dir, Mich Coalition Human Rights, 1986-91; co chair, Nelson Mandela Detroit '90 Comt, 1990; pres, Asn Black Judges Mich, 1999-2000; Wolverine Bar Asn; treas, Am Fedn Teachers; Mich Asn Dist Ct Magistrates, 2000-01; State Bar Mich; Nat Bar Asn; Wolverine Bar Asn; Am Judges Asn; co chair, Int Trends Comt. **Business Addr:** Magistrate, 36th District Court, 421 Madison St Suite 2027, Detroit, MI 48226-2358, **Business Phone:** (313)965-5025.

### BAYLOR, SANDRA JOHNSON
Executive. **Educ:** Southern Univ, BS, elec engineering; Stanford Univ, MS, elec engineering; Rice Univ, PhD, elec engineering. **Career:** Int Bus Mach Corp, Thomas J Watson Res Ctr, res staff mem, 1988-2000, mgr, 2000-02, IBM Silicon Valley Lab, San Jose, Calif, WebSphere Database Develop, mgr, 2001, senior technical staff, 2002-04, chief technology officer & senior technical staff, 2004-11, IBM bus develop exec, United Arab Emirates, 2011-12, chief technology officer, 2012-14; Int Bus Mach Linux Technol Ctr, mgr, 2002; SKJ Visioneering LLC, founder & chief exec officer, 2014-; Books: Linux Performance Tuning, editor in chief; Inspirational Nuggets, author; Gregory: Life of a Lupus Warrior, co-author. **Orgs:** Inst Elec & Electronics Engrs fel; Asn Comput Mach; Women Technol Int; Soc Women Engrs; Delta Sigma Theta Sorority Inc. **Special Achievements:** First African-American woman to get a PhD in electrical engineering in the United States.

### BAYNE, CHRIS (CHRISTOPHER OLIVER BAYNE)
Football player. **Personal:** Born Mar 22, 1975, Riverside, CA; son of Ralph and Deborah. **Educ:** San Bernardino Valley Jr Col; Fresno State Univ, BS, biol, 1993. **Career:** Football player (retired); Atlanta Falcons, defensive back, 1997-98; Scottish Claymores, 2000; Miami Dolphins, 2000; LasVegas Outlaws, 2001; Fresno Frenzy, 2002; Hamilton Tiger-Cat, 2003.

### BAZEMORE, TERESA A BRYCE
President (organization). **Educ:** Univ Va, BA; Columbia Univ, JD. **Career:** Piper & Marbury, assoc; New Jersey Supreme Ct, law clerk; Bank Am Mortgage, gen coun; PNC Mortgage Corp; Prudential Home Mortgage Co, vpres & assoc gen coun; Nexstar Financial Corp, gen coun, sr vpres, secy; Gse Systs Inc; MBNA Home Finance, dir, legal & corp affairs; Radian Guaranty Inc, exec vpres, gen coun & corp secy, 2006-07, chief risk officer, 2007-08, pres, 2008-; Pub Media Co, bd dir; Mortgage Ins Bus, pres, 2008-. **Orgs:** Bd dir & adv comt, Mortgage Bankers Asn, 2001-04, 2005, 2006, 2009; adv coun, Fed Res Bank Philadelphia; bd dir & nat adv coun, Fannie Mae, 2004-; trustee & bd chair, Res Inst Housing Am; vice chair, Legis Steering Comt; Ethics Task Force; Habitat Humanity Comt; Univ Vas Alumni Asn; bd dir, Home Builders Inst; exec comt, Philadelphia Chamber Com; bd dir, Am Red Cross; bd dir, Univ Va Col Found. **Business Addr:** President, Radian Group Inc, 1601 Mkt St, Philadelphia, PA 19103, **Business Phone:** (877)723-4261.

### BAZIL, RONALD
Teacher. **Personal:** Born Mar 10, 1937, Brooklyn, NY; married Bonnie; children: Lance & Tami. **Educ:** Springfield Col, BS, 1958; Brooklyn Col, MS, health, phys edu & recreation, 1964. **Career:** US Mil Acad, coach; Health Educ, teacher, 1959-68; Adelphi Univ, asst dean stud, 1968-69, dean mem, 1969-70, assoc dean studs, 1970-72, dir inter col athel, 1972; Tulane Univ, head coach, 2002-. **Orgs:** Exec coun, ECAC; pres exec coun, ICA; Concerned City Westbury, NCAA Div I Men's & Women's Track & Field Comt, 1994. **Honors/Awds:** Indoor Track coach of the Year, USTFF, 1972, 1974; Cross Country Coach of the Year, Dist II, 1993; Louisiana Cross Country Coach of the Year, 1995; Conference USA Freshman of the Year, 1996. **Home Addr:** 2220 Brighton Pl, Harvey, LA 70058, **Home Phone:** (478)476-0456. **Business Addr:** Head Coach, Tulane University, 6823 St Charles Ave, New Orleans, LA 70118, **Business Phone:** (504)865-5000.

### BAZILE, LEO
Administrator. **Educ:** Merritt Col; Stanford Univ; Univ Calif, Berkeley, Boalt Law Sch. **Career:** City Coun Dist 7, Oakland, Calif, coun mem, 1983-92; City Oakland, Calif, vice mayor, mayor; Friendly Cab, Oakland, Calif, gen mgr, 2002; Oakland, Calif, atty; chmn, Oakland Bus Develop Corp; Community Econ Develop Adv Comn, Oakland, chmn; Harrison, Taylor & Bazile Law Pract, partner, currently; Task Force African Am Educ, atty; KSBT Channel 37, TV host; Merritt Col, lectr; Secy Legis Affairs, asst. **Orgs:** State Bar mem, 1977-2001; Community Policing Adv Bd; City Loan Rev Comt, Oakland; adv bd mem, City Oakland; Task Force African Am Educ; chmn, Local Organizing Comt; chmn, bd mem, Housing Authority; Bus Develop Corp; adv bd, Community Econ Develop, & Community Policing; city loan rev comt; mayor educ cabinet; Oakland Sharing Vision Inc.; 5th Century Develop Corp; Traveller's Aid Soc Alameda; E Bay Perinatal Coun. **Business Addr:** Attorney, Harrison Taylor & Bazile, 1940 Embarcadero, Oakland, CA 94606-5213, **Business Phone:** (510)434-0140.

### BEACH, GEORGE
Advertising executive. **Personal:** Born Aug 14, 1936, New York, NY; son of James H and Ethel McKinnon; married Mary; children: 2. **Educ:** Univ Arts Philadelphia, BFA, 1958. **Career:** Artist Guild Del Valley, pres, 1967; Beach Advert & Beach Graphics, chmn & chief exec officer, 1974-. **Orgs:** Am Numis Asn; founder, Af Am Commemorative Soc; bd, Alliance Aging Res; Philadelphia Af Am Mus; Hist Philadelphia Inc; Philadelphia Conv & Visitors Bur; Nat Arthritis Found; W Philadelphia Cult Alliance; Univ Arts. **Honors/Awds:** Addy, Neographic Art Director Club Award; Best Category Award, Printing Industs Am. **Special Achievements:** First African American pres of the Artist Guild of Delaware Valley. **Home Addr:** 522 Mohawk St, Sayre, PA 18840-1447, **Home Phone:** (570)888-0432. **Business Addr:** Chairman, Chief Executive Officer, Beach Advertising & Beach Graphics, 1613 Spruce St, Philadelphia, PA 19103-6306, **Business Phone:** (215)735-4747.

### BEACH, MICHAEL ANTHONY
Actor. **Personal:** Born Oct 30, 1963, Roxbury, MA; married Tracey E; children: Tyler, Alex, Quincey & Roarke; married Elisha Wilson. **Career:** Films: Streets of Gold, 1986; Lean On Me; One False Move; White Man's Burden; Waiting to Exhale, 1995; A Family Thing, 1996; Soul Food, 1997; Johnny Skid marks, 1998; Dr Hugo, 1998; A Room Without Doors, 1998; Asunder, 1998; Made Men, 1999; Crazy As Hell, 2002; First Sunday, 2008; Hell Ride, 2008; Stargate: The Ark of Truth, 2008; Play Dead, 2009; Pastor Brown, 2009; Relative Stranger, 2009; Gimme Shelter, 2010; Night & Day, 2010; Justice for Natalee Holloway, 2011; Partners, 2011; Red Dawn, 2011; Things Never Said, 2012; Insidious: Chapter 2, 2013; Scrapper, exec producer, 2013; Shaker Pointe, 2014. TV series: "ER", 1996-97; "Spawn", 1997; "Ms Scrooge", 1997; "Ruby Bridges", 1998; "Third Watch", 1999; "Critical Assembly", 2003; "Justice League Unlimited", 2006; "Brothers & Sisters", 2006; "Shark", 2007; "Stargate: Atlantis", 2007; "Numb3rs", 2009; "The Cleaner", 2009; "Lie to Me", 2010; "Sons of Anarchy", 2010-14; "Grey's Anatomy", 2011; "Criminal Minds: Suspect Behavior", 2011; "The Closer", 2011; "Partners", 2011; "The Game", 2011-13; "NCIS", 2012; "A Gifted Man", 2012; "Southland", 2013; "Notes from Dad", 2013; "The Client List", 2013; "Crisis", 2014. **Honors/Awds:** Drama Award, 1984; New York Shakespeare Festival Award; Volpi Cup, 1993; Golden Globe Award, 1994; Image Award, Nat Asn Advan Colored People, 2003. **Special Achievements:** Nominated for Image Awards, Black Film Award and Black Reel Awards. **Business Addr:** Actor, c/o Paradigm, 10100 Santa Monica Blvd 25th Fl, Los Angeles, CA 90067, **Business Phone:** (310)277-4400.

**BEACH, WALTER G, II. See Obituaries Section.**

### BEADY, DR. CHARLES H., JR.
School administrator, president (organization). **Personal:** Born Adel, GA. **Educ:** Mich Univ, BA, advert, MA, urban coun, PhD, coun educ. **Career:** Morgan State Univ, asst prof; Johns Hopkins Univ, postdoctoral res, Inst Urban Res, sr res scientist; Johns Hopkins Univ, res affil, Ctr Social Orgn Sch, prof cartoonist; Piney Woods Country Life Sch, provost, 1984-85, pres, 1985. **Business Addr:** President Emeritus, Piney Woods Country Life School, 5096 Hwy 49 S, Piney Woods, MS 39148, **Business Phone:** (601)845-2214.

### BEAL, DR. ANNE C.
Pediatrician. **Educ:** Brown Univ, AB; Cornell Univ Med Col, MD; Columbia Univ, MPH. **Career:** Albert Einstein Col Med, intern, resident; Montefiore Med Ctr, Bronx, NY, intern, resident, NRSA fel; Mass Gen Hosp, Ctr Child & Adolescent Health Policy, health serv researcher, Gen Pediat, pediatrician, Multicultural Affairs Off, assoc dir; Harvard Med Sch, instr pediat; Essence Mag, Am Baby Show, ABC News & NBC News, med corresp, currently; Commonwealth Fund, sr prog officer, asst vpres, chief patient officer, currently; Patient-Centered Outcomes Res Inst, chief operating officer. **Orgs:** Reviewer, Agency Health care Res & Qual; Am Acad Pediat; co chair, Nat Qual Forum; chair, NY Minority Health Coun, currently; pres, Aetna Found. **Special Achievements:** Auth: The Black Parenting Book: Caring for Our Children in the First Five Years; The Changing Face of Race: Risk Factors for Neonatal Hyperbilirubinemia, 2006; numerous prof articles in Pediat, Ambulatory Pediat, Health Affairs. **Business Addr:** Chief Patient Officer, The Commonwealth Fund, 1 E 75th St, New York, NY 10021, **Business Phone:** (212)606-3800.

### BEAL, BERNARD B.
Investment banker. **Personal:** Born Jan 1, 1954?, New York, NY; married Valerie Rose; children: Manning & Mae. **Educ:** Carleton Col, BA, econs, 1976; Stanford Univ, Grad Sch Bus, MBA, 1979. **Career:** Jack Box Restaurant, Bronx, NY, co-owner & part-time mgr; Shearson Lehman Hutton Inc, Munic & Corp Finance Div, sr vpres, 1979-88; MR Beal & Co, owner, founder, chmn & chief exec officer, 1988-. **Orgs:** NY Metrop Transp Authority; Securities Indust Asn; Pub Securities Asn; Nat Asn Securities Professionals; Carleton Col; Nat Found Affordable Housing; bd chair, A Better Chance; vchmn & dir, Securities Indust & Financial Markets Asn; co-chair, Securities Indust Asn's Comt Diversity. **Special Achievements:** Listed as one of 25 "Hottest Blacks on Wall Street" and company ranked third on BE Investment Bank list, Black Enterprise, 1992, ranked #6, 2000. **Home Addr:** 249 E 48th St, New York, NY 10017-1529, **Home Phone:** (646)669-8441. **Business Addr:** Chief Executive Officer, Chairman, M R Beal & Co, 14 Wall St 17th Fl, New York, NY 10005, **Business Phone:** (212)983-3930.

### BEAL, BERNARD B.
Founder (originator), chief executive officer, association executive. **Personal:** Born Jan 1, 1954?; married Valerie Rose. **Educ:** Carleton Col, BA, 1976; Stand Univ Sch Bus, MBA, 1979. **Career:** E.F. Hutton, bond trader, sr vpres Corp Finance Div, 1979-88; M.R. Beal & Co, founder & chief exec officer, 1988-; Blaylock Beal Van LLC, chmn, 2014-. **Orgs:** Bd chair, A Better Chance; treas, Securities Indust & Financial Markets Asn (SIFMA); co chair, Securities Indust Asn. **Honors/Awds:** "Black Enterprise", 75 Most Powerful Blacks on Wall Street, 2011. **Business Addr:** Chairman, Blaylock Beal Van LLC, 600 Lexington Ave, New York, NY 10022, **Business Phone:** (212)715-6600.

### BEAL, LISA SUZANNE
Association executive, executive. **Personal:** Born Sep 2, 1963, Paris. **Educ:** Hampton Univ, BS, marine & environ sci, 1987; Univ Phoenix, MBA, bus, 2002; Harvard Exten Sch, cert, corp sustainability & innovation, 2016. **Career:** Geo Recource Consults, info specialist, 1990-92; Am Trucking Asn, environ specialist, 1990-95; Hazardous Waste Mgt Asn, mgr transp & safety, 1995-96; Interstate Sanit Comn, compliance inspector; Interstate Nat Gas Asn Am, dir environ & construct policy, 1996-2009, vpres environ & construct policy, 2010-15; Dominion, Gas Regulatory Policies, environ proj advisor, 2016-. **Orgs:** Adv bd mem, EnvironMentors, 1993-; Nat Coun Sci & Environ; secy, INGAA Found Inc; Women's Coun Energy & Environ; chair, Am Asn Blacks Energy, 2012-14; chair, Youth Scholar & Mentoring Prog; Hampton Univ, class reunion comt, co-chair, 2007-; bd mem, Natural Gas Training Coun, 2015-. **Home Addr:** , Washington, DC. **Business Addr:** Vice President, Interstate Natural Gas Association of America, 20 F St NW Suite 450, Washington, DC 20001, **Business Phone:** (202)216-5900.

### BEALS, YVONNE
Government official. **Personal:** daughter of Melvin L and Marietta; married Vincent Rogers. **Educ:** Calif State Univ, BS, criminal justice, MS, pub admin & pub policy. **Career:** City Calif, legis secy & dist field rep; Port Oakland, govt affairs specialist, 2000; City Pittsburg Calif, coun mem, 2000-04, mayor, 2003; Exec Bd Yahweh Enterprises, chief financial officer; Pub Health Found Enterprises Inc, policy coordr, 2006-07; Calif State Senate, field rep, 2007-08; John Muir Health Community Health Alliance, community outreach coordr/health educr, 2008-09; Food Bank Contra Costa & Solano, agency rels coordr, 2002-05, community rels mgr, 2005-06, community rels dir, currently; Ctr Educ & Info Serv, prog dir, 2010-. **Orgs:** Co-chmn, Black Am polit Asn Calif; Kennedy-King Memorial Col Scholar Fund Ltd; Sigma Gamma Rho; exec br secy & exec comt mem, E County br, Nat Asn Advan Colored People, bd mem, 4AC. **Special Achievements:** First African American woman to be elected to the city council; First Black female mayor of the 100-year-old city, Pittsburg, CA. **Business Addr:** Community Relations Manager, Community Relations Director, Food Bank of Contra Costa and Solano, PO Box 271966, Concord, CA 94527-1966, **Business Phone:** (925)676-7543.

**BEAMON, ARTHUR LEON**
Lawyer. **Personal:** Born Jan 1, 1942. **Educ:** USAF Acad, BS, 1965; George Washington Univ, MA, 1970; Univ Chicago Law Sch, JD, 1972; Harvard Univ Prog Instr Lawyers, cert, 1981. **Career:** Law enforcement officer (retired), attorney; Fed Deposit Ins Corp, atty, 1972-78, sr atty, 1978-80, coun, 1980-84; asst gen coun, 1984-89, Compliance & Enforcement, Legal Div, assoc gen coun. **Orgs:** Bd mem, treas, 1996-; rep, Ad Hoc Home Owners Asn Comn, 1997-; Tuckerman Sta Condominium Asn; outreach comm, St Mark Presby Church; Dist Bar Asn; Am Bar Asn; Nat Bar Asn. **Honors/Awds:** Sustained Superior Performance Awards, 1980-97; Annual Performance Bonus Awards, 1989-97. **Home Addr:** 2475 Va Ave NW 328, Washington, DC 20037-2639, **Home Phone:** (202)625-2632.

**BEAMON, BOB. See BEAMON, ROBERT.**

**BEAMON, ROBERT (BOB BEAMON)**
Executive, athlete. **Personal:** Born Aug 29, 1946, Queens, NY; son of James and Naomi Brown; married Milana Walter; children: Deanna. **Educ:** Adelphi Univ, BA, sociol, 1972. **Career:** Atheletic (retired), executive; Youth Serv Metro-Dade, dir, 1982-95; Bob Beamon Commun Inc, pres, 2001; Fla Atlantic Univ, dir athletic develop, currently. **Orgs:** Chair, S Fla Inner City Games, 1994-96; Orange Bowl Community, 1994-; pres, US Olympic Comt Alumni, 1996-; bd trustee, United Way, Dade City; chmn, Bob Beamon Golf Tennis Classic; chief exec oficer, Art Olympians Mus, Fla, currently. **Business Addr:** Director of Athletic Development, Florida Atlantic University, 777 Glades Rd, Boca Raton, FL 33431, **Business Phone:** (561)297-0032.

**BEAN, DR. BOBBY GENE**
Librarian, educator. **Personal:** Born Jan 15, 1951, Houlka, MS; son of Deacon Dan (deceased) and Mary Bess (deceased); married Mattie Marie Kitchen; children: Bobby Gene II. **Educ:** Southeast Mo State Univ, BSE, 1974; Southern Ill Univ, MSE, 1979, EDS, 1981; Lael Univ, EDD, 1983; Atlanta Univ, MSLS, 1987; Inter denominational Theol Ctr, MDiv, 1989; Univ Sarasota, EDD, cand, 1998. **Career:** Sikeston Pub Sch, high sch librn asst, 1972-73; E St Louis Pub Sch, 6th grade teacher, 1974-82, Jr high math teacher, 1982-83, Jr high librn, 1983-87; Atlanta Pub Sch, John Hope Elem, media specialist, 1988-; Atlanta Univ Ctr, R W Woodruff Libr, ref librn, 1988-; Interdenominational Theol Ctr, instr, 1992-, Therrell High, Crim Eve Col, media specialist, 2003; CH Mason Theol Sem, instr, currently. **Orgs:** Atlanta Univ, Beta Phi Mu Libr Sci Hon Fraternity, 1987; United Negro Col Fund Scholar, 1989; Theta Phi, 1989; Am Libr Asn; Ga Libr Asn; Am Asn Sch Librn; Ga Chaplain Asn. **Honors/Awds:** Honorable Mention Those Who Excel, Sch Media Serv, 1987; Research Board Advisor, Am Biog Inst, 1990; Distinguished Leadership Award, ABI; Man of Achievement Award, Am Biographical Inst. **Special Achievements:** Author of the book "This is The Church Of God in Christ", 2001. Author of Numerous Books. **Home Addr:** 1208 Muirfield Dr, Stone Mountain, GA 30088, **Home Phone:** (770)498-1071.

**BEANE, DOROTHEA ANNETTE**
Educator. **Personal:** Born Mar 30, 1952, Plainfield, NJ; daughter of Floyd and Mary. **Educ:** Spelman Col, attended 1972; Drew Univ, BA, 1974; State Univ NJ, Newark Col Law, JD, 1977. **Career:** US Dept Justice, Civil Div, Torts Br, trial atty, 1977-81; Law Firm Robinson & Geraldo, assoc atty, 1981-82; Mid Dist Fla, Jacksonville Div, asst US atty, 1983-90; Gen Civil Litigation, asst us atty, 1983-90, sr civil litigating atty, 1985-90; US Dept Justice, asst US atty; Stetson Univ Col Law, asst prof, 1990-, prof law, 1996-, fac mem, 2001, Law Tribunal proj dir, 2004-, prog dir, 2005, Inst Caribbean Law & Policy, co-dir, currently; Wash & Lee Univ, vis assoc prof law, 1995-96. **Orgs:** Am Bar Asn, 1990-; fac adv, Black Law Stud Asn, 1990-; acad master, Sarasota County Am Inns Ct, 1990-; house rep, Asn Am Law Sch, 1991; rep, Stetson Univ Sen, 1992-; Am Col Legal Med, 1992-; fac mem, Samford Univ, Cumberland Sch Law, 1994; exec comt, Asn Am Law Schs, 2003-; NJ Bar Asn; Fed Bar Asn; Am Soc Int Law; exec comt, Nat Bar Asn, 2003-; Am Caribbean Law, exec comt, 2004-. **Home Addr:** 7912 Sailboat Key Blvd, South Pasadena, FL 33707, **Home Phone:** (813)367-8138. **Business Addr:** Professor of Law, Stetson University College Law, 1401 61st St S Rm 211, St Petersburg, FL 33707-3299, **Business Phone:** (727)562-7800.

**BEANE, PATRICIA JEAN**
Educator, teacher. **Personal:** Born Jan 13, 1944, Massillon, OH; married Frank Llewellyn; children: Frank Clarence II & Adam Tyler. **Educ:** Ashland Col, OH, BS, 1966. **Career:** Akron City Schs, teacher, 1966-67; Massillon City Schs, teacher, 1967-2003. **Orgs:** Nat Educ Asn, 1966-76, 1979-; Ohio Educ Asn, 1966-76, 1979-; E Cent Ohio Teachers Asn, 1966-76, 1979-; Massilon Educ Asn, 1966-76, 1979-2003; Akron Symphony Chorus, 1966-67; Canton Civic Opera Chorus, 1969-79; secy, bd trustee, Massillon YWCA, 1972-76; Massillon Bus & Prof Women's, 1977-80; Ohio Asn Colored Women's Clubs, 1978-98; Nat Asn Colored Women's Clubs, 1978-98; Doris L Allen Minority Caucus, 1984; bd trustee, Massillon Youth Ctr, 1984; secy & bd trustee, regional & local women's clubs, Massillon Pub Libr; comt chmn, Cult Diversity, 2005-. **Home Addr:** 1134 3rd St SE, Massillon, OH 44646. **Business Addr:** Secretary of Board of Trustees, The Massillon Public Library, 208 Lincoln Way E, Massillon, OH 44646, **Business Phone:** (330)832-9831.

**BEANE, ROBERT HUBERT**
County government official. **Personal:** Born Mar 4, 1947, New York, NY; son of Sidney and Lorraine Braithwaite; children: Craig J. **Educ:** Fordham Univ Col Lincoln Ctr, BA, 1974, Fordham Univ Grad Sch Social Serv, MSW, 1976. **Career:** Mt Vernon Community Action Group; Westchester Community Opportunity Prog, exec dir, 1970-73; Westchester Urban Coalition, prog dir, 1973-74; Alcohelp Prog, res & eval specialist, 1974-76; Westchester Co, prog specialist, 1976, Dept Ment Health, ctr adminr, 1976-79, asst to comnr, 1979-83, dir community serv, 1983-00. **Orgs:** Community Protection Human Sub NY Med Col, 1980-96; trustee, City Yonkers Bd Educ, 1983-93, vpres, 1988-90, pres, 1992-93, 1995-97; Youth Shelter Prog Westchester, 1996; Westchester County Sick Bank. **Home Addr:** 1658 S Hidden Hills Pkwy, Stone Mountain, GA 30088, **Home Phone:** (770)323-7285.

**BEARD, ALFRED BUTCH, JR. See BEARD, BUTCH, JR.**

**BEARD, BUTCH, JR. (ALFRED BUTCH BEARD, JR.)**
Basketball player, basketball coach. **Personal:** Born May 5, 1947, Hardinsburg, KY. **Educ:** Louisville Col, attended 1969. **Career:** Basketball player, head coach (retired); Atlanta Hawks, player, 1969-70; Cleveland Cavaliers, player, 1970-71, 1975; Seattle Supersonics, player, 1971-72; Golden State Warriors, player, 1973-75; New York Knicks, player, 1975-79, asst coach, 1978-82, color analyst, 1980, broadcaster, 1982-87; Atlanta Hawks, broadcaster, 1987-88; NJ Nets, asst coach, 1988-90, head coach, 1994-96; Howard Univ, head coach, 1990-94; Dallas Mavericks, asst coach, 1996-98; Morgan State Bears, head coach, 1998-2006; Wash Wizards, asst coach, 1999-2000. **Honors/Awds:** Kentucky Mr. Basketball, 1965; All-Star Game, Nat Basketball Asn, 1972; Champion, Nat Basketball Asn, 1975; Coach of the Year, Mid Eastern Athletic Conf.

**BEARD, DARRYL H.**
Security consultant, executive, executive director. **Educ:** John Jay Col Criminal Justice, NY, BS, criminal justice, 1992; Seton Hall Univ, S Orange, NJ, MA, educ, supv & admin, 1999; Am Soc Indust Security, cert, protection prof, prof investr, phys security prof; Acad Security Educr Trainers, cert, security trainer; NJ State Police Training Comn, police Instr. **Career:** Integrated Security & Training Consult Inc, chief exec consult, vice chmn; Williams Assocs LLC, prin security consult, currently, sr assoc; Univ Pa, dir security. **Orgs:** Am Soc Indust Security; Int Asn Black Security Professionals; Prof Security Consults Int; Trans-Continental Pub Safety Consults; John Jay Col Alumni Asn; Seton Hall Univ Alumni Asn. **Honors/Awds:** Outstanding Young Man of America Award, 1996; Walter Lawson Award, Nat Orgn Black Law Enforcement Execs, 2001; Outstanding Achievement in Community Service, Motorola Corp, 2001; Regional Award of Achievement, Am Soc Indust Security, 2002; Vanguard Award, Brother Officers Law Enforcement Soc, 2002; ASIS International Regional Award of Achievement, 2002. **Special Achievements:** Holds the highest American Society of Industrial Security and International Certification for security professionals. **Home Addr:** 84 Elderberry Lane, Willingboro, NJ 08046. **Business Addr:** Principal Security Consultant, Williams Associates LLC, 1175 Marlkress Rd, Cherry Hill, NJ 08034, **Business Phone:** (609)280-9787.

**BEARD, JAMES WILLIAM, JR.**
Lawyer, educator. **Personal:** Born Sep 16, 1941, Chillicothe, OH; married Gail LaVerne Rivers; children: James III, Ryan Jamail & Kevin Jarrard. **Educ:** Hardin-Simmons Univ, BS, 1967; Tex Southern Univ, Thurgood Marshall Sch Law, JD, 1973; Univ Tex, LLM, 1976. **Career:** Tex Southern Univ, Thurgood Marshall Sch Law, assoc prof law, 1974-, spec admin asst to dean, 1976-79, assoc dean acad affairs, 1979-80, dir fed tax clin, 1984-92; Earl Carl Inst Legal & Social Policy Inc, pres, 2002-. **Orgs:** Nat Asn Advan Colored People, 1968-; trustee, Houston Legal Found, 1972; Speaker, Liability Nurses Nursing Homes & Hosps, Rehab Ctr, 1979; Golden Age Manor, 1980; Riverside Gen Hosp, 1982; bd gov, chmn & Ed Tax Newsletter, Sect Taxation, Nat Bar Asn, 1983-86; Deleg, Dem State Conv, 1984, 1988; Moderator Community Forum Sidewalks, Schs & Community Develop, Houston, 1985; Legal Counr, Martin Luther King Ctr, Houston, 1985-86; Tex Coalition Black Dem, 1986; legal adv, S Union Civic Club, 1987-91; coordr, Thurgood Marshall Sch Law Econ Conferences, 1988-89; election judge, Briargate Community Improv Asn, 1991-92; coordr, Studs Tax Testimonies Hearings Before Comt Ways & Means, House Rep, 1991; Bus & Prof Men's Club, 1991; chair, Legal Add Comt, Ft Bend Co Nat Asn Advan Colored People, 1991; bd gov, Ft Bend County Subsidence Dist, 1992-94; founder, DADs Club, Mo City Mid Sch, FBISD, 1993-94; Tex Hosp Licensing Adv Coun, 1994; founder, E Ft Bend Alliance Educ, 1994-95; Am Bar Asn; State Bar Tex; bd dir, Tex War Drugs. **Home Addr:** 7410 W Fuqua Dr, Missouri City, TX 77489-2415, **Home Phone:** (713)313-7111. **Business Addr:** Associate Professor of Law, Texas Southern University, Thurgood Marshall Law Sch Bldg, Houston, TX 77004, **Business Phone:** (713)313-7111.

**BEARD, DR. LILLIAN MCLEAN**
Physician, consultant. **Personal:** Born Jan 1, 1943, New York, NY; daughter of Woodie McLean and Johnie Wilson; married DeLawrence. **Educ:** Howard Univ, Col Lib Arts, BS, 1965, Col Med, MD, 1970. **Career:** Childrens Nat Med Ctr, resident pediat, 1970-73, Child develop, 1972-73, fel, 1973, Child Develop, consult-dir, 1973-75; Howard Univ Col Med, asst clin prof, 1979-; George Washington Univ, Sch Med, Dept Pediats, staff, assoc clin prof, 1982-; pvt practr, pediatrician, 1973-; Good Housekeeping Mag, "Ask Dr Beard", column, authored, 1989-95, contrib ed; ABC TV-7 News, med & health news contribr, 2000-05; C's Pediatricians & Assocs, sr physician, 2002-; Child Health Commun consult to industs; Fel C's Hosp Natl Med Ctr. **Orgs:** Spokesperson, Fel Am Acad Pediat; Nat Med Asn; Links Inc; Girl Friends Inc; dipl, Nat Bd Med Examnrs; dipl, Am Bd Pediat; fel Am Med Women's Asn; fel Nat Med Asn. **Honors/Awds:** Physician Recognition Awards, Am Med Asn, 1973-2000; Hall of Fame Award, Nat Med Asn, 1994; Howard Univ Charter Day-Distinguished Alumni, 1996; Women of Courage, 1998; Award of Merit, Global Initiative For Telemedicine, 1998; Top Doctors, Washington Magazine, 2002; Md's Top 100 Women, The Daily Record, 2003; Am's Top Doctors, Consumers' Research Council, 2007; Leadership Award, Nat Asn Equal Opportunity Higher Educ. **Special Achievements:** Outstanding Young Women of America, 1979; Publisher: "Beyond Chicken Soup, 2005; Salt in Your Sock and Other Tried-and-True Home Remedies, 2003. Published & Authored several articles/books. **Home Addr:** 10517 Alloway Dr, Potomac, MD 20854, **Home Phone:** (301)983-4222. **Business Addr:** Physician Director, Children's Pediatricians and Associates, 10801 Lockwood Dr Suite 230, Silver Spring, MD 20901, **Business Phone:** (301)593-5566.

**BEASLEY, AARON BRUCE**
Football player, executive. **Personal:** Born Jul 7, 1973, Pottstown, PA. **Educ:** WVa Univ, BA, phys educ, 2006. **Career:** Football player (retired), exec; Jacksonville Jaguars, left cornerback, 1996-2000, right cornerback, 1999-2001; New York jets, right cornerback, 2002-03; Atlanta Falcons, corner back & right cornerback, 2004; Fever energy drink co, co founder, currently. **Honors/Awds:** All-American, 1995; West Virginia University Sports Hall of Fame, 2009. **Home Addr:** , Pasadena, MD.

**BEASLEY, ARLENE A. (PHOEBE BEASLEY)**
Teacher, executive, artist. **Personal:** Born Jun 3, 1943, Cleveland, OH; married Louie Gene Evans Jr. **Educ:** Ohio Univ, BFA, painting, 1965; Kent State Univ, MA, 1969. **Career:** Cleveland Bd Educ, teacher, 1965-69; Sage Pub, artist, 1969-70; KFI & KOST Radio, acct exec, 1970; solo exhibs, artist, 1976-. "Morning Glory", Paramount Television pilot, artwork, 1989; 20th Anniversary Essence Magazine, artwork poster, 1990; Los Angeles Co Arts comn, pres, 2002-03; Phoebe Beasley Art Studio, artist, currently; Oprah Winfrey, series of lithographs and paintings based on television mini-series "The Women of Brewster Place", artist; private collections for: Andre and Linda Johnson-Rice, Robert and Nancy Daly, Joel and Marlene Chaseman, Attorney Tyrone Brown, Attorney Reginald Govan, Edward and Bettiann Gardner, William and Carol Sutton-Lewis, Maya Angelou, Anita Baker, Gordon Parks, Oprah Winfrey. **Orgs:** Bd trustee, Savannah Col Art & Design; adv bd, New Regal Theater, Chicago; bd dir pres & hon bd trustee, Mus African-Am Art; curric adv bd, Calif State Univ, Long Beach; county comnr, Pvt Indust Coun; exec adv bd, United Negro Col Fund, Los Angeles; bd dir, Story Proj Found; bd mem, Prologue Soc Los Angeles; bd dir, Story Proj Found; bd, Transp Found Los Angeles; trustee, Southern Calif Women's Forum; Calif Arts Coun, 2015. **Honors/Awds:** Merit Award, Am Women Radio & TV, 1975, Achievement Award, Genii Award; selected to design the prestigious International Tennis Trophy and Medal, Summer Olympic Games, 1984; named Official Artist, Los Angeles Marathon, 1987; chosen to design the national poster, Sickle Cell Disease Campaign; "Clinton Inaugural", 1989 & 1993; Inauguration of former President Bush, artwork, official poster, 1989; Woman of the Year, Los Angeles Sentinel, 1989; Black Women of Achievement Award, Nat Asn for the Advan of Colored People Legal Defense & Educ Fund, 1991; named the "Official Artist" for the Democratic National Convention, 2000; Medal of Merit, Ohio Univ, 2003; Honorary Doctorate of Fine Arts, Ohio Univ, 2005; Lifetime Achievement Award for Visual Arts & Arts Advocacy, Calif African Am Mus, 2013; The Legacy Ladies Torch Award; Southern California Freedoms Sister Award, Mus Tolerance, Ford Motor Co; The Jenesse Center Silver Rose Award. **Special Achievements:** First African-American female president, American Women in Radio & TV, 1977-78; only artist to twice receive the Presidential Seal; Beasley was one of 44 artists commissioned to create a collage on a life-size bust of the 44th President Barack Obama; First African American female president of the Los Angeles County Arts Commission. **Business Addr:** Artist, Phoebe Beasley Art Studio, 6110 El Canon, Woodland Hills, CA 91367, **Business Phone:** (818)888-5525.

**BEASLEY, EDWARD**
City manager. **Personal:** Born Omaha, NE; son of Edward Jr and Bessie Chandler. **Educ:** Pittsburgh State Univ, Pittsburgh, PA, 1977; Loyola Univ, BA, polit sci/bus law, 1980; Univ Mo, Kansas City, MPA, 1983; Pioneer Community Col, Kansas City, attended 1984. **Career:** Jolly Walsh & Gordon, Kans City, Mo, legal clerk, 1982-84; Fed Govt, Wash, DC, aid, Sen Thomas Eagleton, 1983; City Kans, Mo, mgmt trainee, 1984-85; City Flagstaff, Flagstaff, Ariz, admin asst city mgr, 1985-88; City Eloy, city mgr, 1988-91; Pinal County, asst county mgr & dir pub work, 1991-92; Wyandotte County Kans City, asst county adminr & dir health/ human serv, 1992-94; City Glendale, asst city mgr, 1994-2001, city mgr, 2002-12, owner; Beasley Assocs LLC, pres & chief exec officer, 2012-; Colliers Int, vpres govt solutions, 2013-14. **Orgs:** Bd mem, United Way Northern Ariz, 1988, bd mem, Ctr Against Domestic Violence, 1988; chmn, Comt Workplace Diversity, 1990-91; Conf Planning Comt, 1991,1994,1996; life mem, pres, Ariz City/County Mgt Asn, 1997-98; First-Time Adminr Task Force, 1997-99; Nominating Comt, 1998-99; Task Force Mem Connection, 2001-02; bd mem, Impact Crisis Funding, 1988; Credentialed Mgr, 2003; vpres, exec bd, ICMA Mountain Plains Region, 2003-06; Comt Prof Conduct & Ethics, 2004; Int City Mgrs Asn; bd dir, Nat Forum Black Pub Admin; bd dir, Am Cancer Soc, Pinal County, AZ; Ariz ICMA Endowment Fund Comt; Nat Forum Black Pub Adminr; Int Hisp Network; bd mem, Greater Phoenix Econ Coun; Mem Gov's African-Am Adv Coun; Ariz Physician's Rev Bd - Gov App; Ariz Supreme Ct to Judicial Rev Bd Ariz; Growing Smarter Plan State AZ - Gov App; Athletic Training Comn - Gov App; bd mem, Downtown Urban Kids Prog; NAACP Exec Bd Mem; Pop Warner Football Coach; YMCA Basketball, Soccer, Football & Basketball Coach; CCV Stars Youth Football Coach. **Honors/Awds:** John J Jack Debolske Professional Excellence Award, Ariz City & Co Mgt Asn, 2001; Work Force Diversity Prof Develop Award, Int City Mgrs Asn, 2004; Martin Luther King Leadership Diversity Award, 2005; Roy Wilkins Freedom Award, Maricopa Co Nat Asn Advan Colored People, 2005; Economic Engines Arizona Award, Arizona Business, 2006; Lincoln J Ragsdale Outstanding Director Award; 100 Black Men of Phoenix Inc; African American Achievement Award; Superior Service Award for Individual Contributions, Am Soc Pub Adminr; Received Numerous Awards. **Home Addr:** 6647 W Robin Lane, Glendale, AZ 85310, **Home Phone:** (623)561-9463. **Business Addr:** City Manager, City of Glendale, 5850 W Glendale Ave, Glendale, AZ 85301-2563, **Business Phone:** (623)930-2870.

**BEASLEY, DR. EULA DANIEL**
Educator. **Personal:** Born Sep 16, 1958, Oxford, NC; daughter of Benjamin Daniel III and Helen Pettiford Daniel; married Robert E; children: Lydia E & Benjamin W. **Educ:** Univ NC, Chapel Hill, NC, BS, pharm, 1981; PharmD, 1983. **Career:** Orange-Chatham Comprehensive Health Serv, Carrboro, NC, proj pharmacist, 1983-84; Univ NC, Chapel Hill, NC, clin asst, prof, 1983-84; Wash Hosp Ctr, Wash, DC, clin pharmacist, 1984-85, 1987, clin serv mgr, 1990, clin coordr med; Howard Univ, Col Pharm, Wash, DC, asst prof, 1985; Pharm Dir, Shady Grove Adventist Hosp, 2005-12; Corp Dir, Medstar Health, 2012-. **Orgs:** Phi Lambda Sigma Pharm Leadership Soc, 1978;

Rho Chi Pharm Hon Soc, 1980; Fac rep, Stud Info Network, 1986-89; Am Soc Hosp Pharmacists, 1981; DC Soc Hosp Pharmacists, 1985-. **Home Addr:** 232 Mowbray Rd, Silver Spring, MD 20904, **Home Phone:** (301)384-1388.

### BEASLEY, FREDERICK JEROME
Football player. **Personal:** Born Sep 18, 1974, Montgomery, AL; married Jackie; children: 5. **Educ:** Univ Auburn, psychol. **Career:** Football player (retired); San Francisco 49ers, 1998, fullback, 1999-2005, running back & wide receiver, 2001; Miami Dolphins, practice & squad member, 2006; Wash Redskins, pract & squad mem, 2007; Pk Crossing High Sch, suspension officer & asst football coach, currently. **Honors/Awds:** Pro Bowler Selection Once, 2003; All Pro Selection Twice, 2002-03. **Special Achievements:** Two-time All-State honoree & one-time AAU National decathalon champion; named an All-American by Parade Magazine. **Business Addr:** Suspension Officer, Assistant Football Coach, Park Crossing High School, 8000 Pk Crossing, Montgomery, AL 36117, **Business Phone:** (334)260-8121.

### BEASLEY, JAMAR
Soccer player. **Personal:** Born Oct 11, 1979, Ft. Wayne, IN. **Career:** New Eng Revolution, 1998-2001; Chicago Fire, 2001; Ital club, Puteolana, 2002; Ind Blast, 2003; Carolina Dynamo, 2003; Charleston Battery, 2003; Milwaukee Wave United, 2004; Kans City Comets, forward, 2003-05; US Nat Futsal Team, 2004-; St Louis Steamers, 2005-06; maj indoor soccer league, Detroit Ignition, 2006-08; Rockford Rampage, 2008-10; Kans City Wizards, 2010; Mo Comets, 2010-12; Wichita Wings, 2011-12; Syracuse Silver Knights, 2012-13; St Louis Ambush, 2013-14; Seattle Impact FC, 2014-15; Ontario Fury, 2015-. **Honors/Awds:** MLS Player of the Week, 2000; Most Improved Player, Kansas City Comets, 2003-04. **Business Addr:** Professional Soccer Player, Ontario Fury, 4000 E Ont Ctr Pkwy, Ontario, CA 91764, **Business Phone:** (909)457-0252.

### BEASLEY, DR. JESSE C.
Optometrist, president (organization). **Personal:** Born Mar 11, 1929, Marshall, TX; married Ruth Adella Evans; children: Jesse II, Joseph & Janice. **Educ:** La City Col, AA, Ophthal Optics, 1952; La Col Optom, OD, 1956; Univ Calif, MPH, 1971. **Career:** Assoc pract, 1957; pvt practr optometrist, 1957-; Manchester Optom Ctr, optometrist, 2001-. **Orgs:** CA Optom Asn; Optom Health Ctr; Optom Vision Care Coun; Comp Health Planning Comt Southern Calif Optom Soc; Am Optom Comt; Div Pub Health Optom; Am Pub Health Asn; Los Angeles Optom Soc; Calif Optom Asn; Am Optom Asn; bd pres, Calif State Bd Optom, 1982, 1984. **Honors/Awds:** Has published & presented many papers on optometry; Appointed to Calif State Bd of Optometry by Gov Edmund G Brown Jr, 1978-86. **Home Addr:** 10211 Darby Ave Apt 2, Inglewood, CA 90303-5063. **Business Addr:** Optometrist, Founder, Manchester Optom Eye Care Center, 10024 S Vermont Ave 2, Los Angeles, CA 90044, **Business Phone:** (323)756-1114.

### BEASLEY, MYRLIE LOUISE. See EVERS-WILLIAMS, DR. MYRLIE LOUISE.

### BEASLEY, DR. PAUL LEE
School administrator, executive director. **Personal:** Born Jan 10, 1950, East Point, GA; married Pamela Simmons; children: Deanna Estella & Erin Michelle. **Educ:** Earlham Col, BA, 1972; Trenton State Col, MEd, 1973; Univ Tenn, EdD, 1988. **Career:** Trenton State Col, dormitory dir, 1973-74; Emory Univ Upward Bound, dir, 1974-75; US Off Educ, educ prog specialist, 1975-78; Univ Tenn Chattanooga, dir spec serv, 1978-89; Univ SC, TRIO, dir, 1989-. **Orgs:** State rep, SE Asn Educ Opportunity Prog Personnel, 1979-; comm chmn, Tenn Asn Spec Prog, 1978-; usher & bd mem, First Baptist Church Chattanooga, 1979-; Toastmasters Int, 1979-; pres, SAEOPP, 1989-91. **Honors/Awds:** Outstanding Young Men of America, 1979; Outstanding Upward Bounder, US Off Educ, 1976; Award for Distinguished Service, SE Asn Educ Opportunity Prog Personnel, 1977; Walter O Mason Award, Coun Opportunity Educ, 2003; Paul L Beasley Leadership Award, named in honor. **Home Addr:** 707-B Mansion Cir, Chattanooga, TN 37405. **Business Addr:** Director, University of South Carolina, 1400 Wheat St, Columbia, SC 29208, **Business Phone:** (803)777-5125.

### BEASLEY, PHOEBE. See BEASLEY, ARLENE A.

### BEASLEY, VICTOR MARIO
Lawyer. **Personal:** Born Feb 13, 1956, Atlanta, GA; son of Willie J and Mary L Ferguson; married Linda Kaye Randolph; children: Cea Janay. **Educ:** Morehouse Col, BA, 1979; GA Inst Tech, attended 1975; GA State Col Law, attended 1985. **Career:** City Atlanta Planning Bur, planning asst, 1977-78; Atlanta Bur Corrections, sgt & officer, 1980-83; Atlanta Munic Ct, clerk & bailiff, 1983-85; Atlanta Pub Defender's Off, resr, investr, 1985-; SOAR Songs Inc, Douglasville, pres, 1989-; State Ga Bd Pardons & Paroles, parole officer, 1991. **Orgs:** Region I mem, Morehouse Col Alumni Asn, 1985; publ, songwriter, Broadcast Music Inc, 1989-. **Honors/Awds:** Scholarship, Atlanta Fellows & Interns, 1977-78. **Home Addr:** 217 Lakeridge Dr, Temple, GA 30179-4304, **Home Phone:** (770)562-8974. **Business Addr:** President, Soar Songs Inc, 6794 Alexander Pkwy, Douglasville, GA 30135-3581.

### BEATTY, BRYAN E., SR.
Secretary general, commissioner. **Personal:** Born Mar 10, 1958, Englewood, NJ; married Rhonda; children: Bryan Jr, Nicole & Michael. **Educ:** State Univ NY, Stony BrooK, BA, polit sci, 1980; NC State Bur Invest Acad, Salemburg, NC, attended 1981; Univ NC, Sch Law, JD, 1987. **Career:** State Bur Invest, spec agt, 1981-84, dir, 1999-2001; NC Dept Crime Control & Pub Safety, secy, 2001-09; Gov Terrorism Preparedness Task Force, chmn; Johnson, Toal & Battiste, Columbia, SC, practised law; Dept Justice; UNC Hosp Syst, assoc atty; Motor Vehicles Sect, assoc atty gen; NC Utilities Comn, comnr, 2009-. **Orgs:** Chair, State Emergency Response Comn; NC Lottery Comn; Gov's Crime Comn; bd dir, Criminal Justice Info Network; chair, Gov's Terrorism Preparedness Task Force. **Honors/Awds:** Harvey E. Beech Outstanding Alumni Award, Univ NC, 2002; Distinguished Service to State Govt Award, Nat Gov Asn, 2003; Charles Dick Medal of Merit Award, Nat Guard Asn, 2005; Distinguished Civilian Service Award, State NC, 2005; Order of the Long Leaf Pine, Gov Mike Easley, 2008. **Special Achievements:** First black director of State Bureau of Investigation. **Home Addr:** 2400 Millstone Harbor Dr, Raleigh, NC 27603-3966, **Home Phone:** (919)771-1173. **Business Addr:** Governor, Commissioner, North Carolina Utilities Commission, 4325 Mail Service Ctr, Raleigh, NC 27699-4325, **Business Phone:** (919)733-7328.

### BEATTY, CHRISTINE ROWLAND
Social worker, government official. **Personal:** Born May 1, 1970; married Lou; children: 2; married Kwame Kilpatrick. **Educ:** Howard Univ, BA, social work, 1993; Wayne State Univ, MA, social work, 1996. **Career:** Orchards C Serv; Judson Ctr; Ninth Dist State House campaign, mgr, 1996; City Detroit, Mayor Off, dist dir, legis chief staff, dep campaign mgr, chief of staff, 2002-08. **Orgs:** Mayor's Cabinet, 2002-. **Business Addr:** MI.

### BEATTY, MARTIN CLARKE
Athletic coach, educator. **Personal:** Born New Haven, CT; son of Eunice Clarke and Raszue Willis; married Barbara Conger; children: Pierson & Parker. **Educ:** Middlebury Col, Middlebury, VT, BA, art hist, criticism & conserv, 1984; Trinity Col, Hartford, CT, hist, 1987. **Career:** Trinity Col, Hartford, Conn, grad fel, asst football & track coach, 1985-87; Middlebury Col, asst coach, 1987, Cook Commons Fac Head, track coach, head coach, 1988-. **Orgs:** Fac adv, Middlebury Col Activ Bd, 1987-88; Minority Issues Group, 1989-; African-Am Alliance, Commons Fac Assoc; Community Rel Adv Sexual Harassment. **Honors/Awds:** Coach of the Year, US Track Coaches Asn, NCAA Division III New Eng, 1998, 2000; Men's Coach of the Year, New Eng Small Col Athletic Conf, 2005. **Home Addr:** 629 Happy Valley Rd, Middlebury, VT 05753, **Home Phone:** (802)388-9931. **Business Addr:** Head Coach, Track Coach, Middlebury College, M&W Track & Field, Middlebury, VT 05753, **Business Phone:** (802)443-5956.

### BEATTY, OTTO B., JR.
State government official, lawyer. **Personal:** Born Jan 26, 1940, Columbus, OH; son of Otto Sr and Myrna; married Joyce H; children: Otto III & Laurel. **Educ:** Howard Univ, Wash, DC, BA, bus admin, 1961, MA, bus admin; Ohio State Univ Col Law, Columbus, OH, JD, 1965. **Career:** Ohio House Representatives, state rep, 1980-99; Beatty & Roseboro, Columbus, OH, founder & sr partner; Otto Beatty Jr & Assocs, owner & atty, 2004-; Black Elected Dem Ohio, atty; State Atty Gen, spec coun. **Orgs:** Am Arbit Asn; Am Bar Asn; Am & Ohio Trial Lawyers Asn; Black Elected Dem Ohio; Columbus Area Black Elected Officials; Ohio State Consumer Educ Asn; Nat Bar Asn; Nat Asn Advan Colored People; Oper PUSH; Nat Conf Black Lawyers, Columbus Chap; Columbus Apt Asn; Chamber Com; Hunger Task Force Ohio; Ohio Alliance Black Sch Educrs; Nat Black Programming Consortium; Black Chamber Com; Columbus Asn Black Journalists; Ohio Asn Real Estate Brokers; Eastern Union Missionary Baptist Asn; pres, Franklin County Trial Lawyers Asn; chmn, Ohio Comn Minority Health; Nat Asn Defense Lawyers; Ohio House Representatives; Am & Columbus Bar Asn; Finance & Appropriations; Health, Retirement, & Aging; Rules & Ref; Agr & Develop Subcomt. **Home Addr:** 1421 Taylor Corners Cir, Blacklick, OH 43004-9770, **Home Phone:** (614)856-9007. **Business Addr:** Attorney, Owner, Otto Beatty Jr & Associates, 233 S High St Suite 300, Columbus, OH 43215, **Business Phone:** (614)221-2400.

### BEAUBIEN, GEORGE L.
Executive director. **Personal:** Born Nov 10, 1937, Hempstead, NY; married Lois Ann Lowe; children: Jacqueline II. **Educ:** Compton Col, AA, 1956; Pepperdine Col, BA, 1958. **Career:** Golden State Mutual Life Ins Co, staff mgr, 1960-64; IBM Corp, legal mkt rep, 1964-65, mkt mgr, 1965-71; Self-Employed, gen ins agency all line sins, 1971-76; Mayor's Off, Small Bus Asst, exec dir, 1976-85; A & S Resources Inc, pres, 1985. **Orgs:** Dir, pres, Alpha Phi Alpha Fraternity; dir, La fire Dept Recruitment Prog; consult, Nat Bank United Fund Wash, DC, Norfolk; chmn bd, La Brotherhood Crusade, 1968; pres, New Frontier Dem Club, 1969; pres, La Bd Fire Comnr, 1973-77. **Home Addr:** 4123 Don Luis Dr, Los Angeles, CA 90008, **Home Phone:** (323)292-5383.

### BEAUCHAMP, PATRICK L.
Executive, president (organization), chief executive officer. **Career:** Beauchamp Distributing Co, Compton, Calif, founder, chief exec officer & pres, 1973-. **Business Addr:** President, Chief Executive Officer, Beauchamp Distributing Co, 1911 S Santa Fe Ave, Compton, CA 90221-5306, **Business Phone:** (310)639-5320.

### BEAUVAIS, GARCELLE
Actor. **Personal:** Born Nov 26, 1966, St. Marc; daughter of Axel Jean Pierre and Maria Claire Beauvais; married Daniel Saunders; children: Oliver; married Michael Nilon; children: Jax Joseph & Jaid Thomas. **Career:** Eileen Ford modeling agency; Video: R. Kelly: The R. in R&B - The Video Collection, 2003; tv guest appearances: "Miami Vice", 1984-85; "The Cosby Show", 1986; "Family Matters", 1991-96; "Dream On", 1992; "The Fresh Prince of Bel-Air", 1992-95; "Hangin' with Mr Cooper", 1993; "Models Inc", 1994-95; TV series: "Down the Shore", 1992; "The Wayans Bros.", 1995; "The Jamie Foxx Show", 1996-2001; "Arli$$ ", 1999; "Opposite Sex", 2000; "Titans", 2001; "NYPD Blue", 2001-04; "Inside 'NYPD Blue': A Decade on the Job", 2002; "The Bernie Mac Show", 2003; "Curb Your Enthusiasm", 2004; "Life with Bonnie", 2004"; "Eyes", 2005-07; "CSI: Miami", 2006; "Women in Law ", 2006; "Crash", 2009; "Human Target", 2010; "State of Georgia ", 2011; "Franklin & Bash", 2011-12; "Psych", 2013; "Arrested Development", 2013; "Necessary Roughness", 2013; "Playing House", 2013. TV movies: "Second String", 2002; "10.5: Apocalypse", 2006; "The Cure", 2007; "Girlfriends' Getaway", 2014. Films: Manhunter, 1986; Coming to America, 1988; Every Breath, 1994; Wild Wild West, 1999; Double Take, 2001; Bad Company, 2002; Barbershop 2: Back in Business, 2004; American Gun, 2005; I Know Who Killed Me, 2007; Women in Trouble, 2009; Flight, 2012; White House Down, 2013; And Then There Was You, 2013; Small Time, 2014. Mini short: "Man eater", 2009; Short: "Eyes to See ", 2010. **Honors/Awds:** Emmy Award, Outstanding Supporting Actress Drama Series, 1993; Honorary Award, Motion Picture Asn Haiti, 2013. **Business Addr:** Actress, c/o United Talent Agency, 9465 Wilshire Blvd Suite 405, Beverly Hills, CA 90212, **Business Phone:** (310)273-6700.

### BEAVER, JOSEPH T., JR.
Publisher, writer. **Personal:** Born Sep 22, 1922, Cincinnati, OH; son of Joseph and Eva; married Helen Mae Greene; children: Joseph T III, James Paul, Northe Lejana Olague & Wendla Tarascana Helene Coonan. **Educ:** Univ Cincinnati, lib arts, 1941; Univ Wis Ext, econ, 1947; Univ Teuerife Spain, econ geog, 1951; Foreign Serv Inst, lang labor confs pub speech consular officers courses, 1954, 1961, 1968, sr exec sem course, 1967; Col Desert Palm Desert CA, jour micro. **Career:** US foreign serv, 26 yrs; Span interpreter; Int Rev Third World Cult & Issues, publ, ed. **Orgs:** Life mem, Nat Asn Advan Colored People; bd mem, Western States Black Res Ctr; bd mem, Coachella Econ Develop Corp; Palm Springs Chamber Com; Citizens Freedom; Affirmative action cr Coalicion Politica de la Raza; DEMAND; founder, Friends Jesse Jackson Coalition, 1985; exec dir, Black Hist & Cult Soc Coachella Valley; chmn, Martin Luther King Commemoration Comm Palm Springs; pres, Jesse Jackson Demo Club Coachella Valley; Col Desert Adv Comt; Educ Alert Comt; Coachella Valley African Am Chamber Com; hon mem, Greater Palm Springs Hisp Chamber Com; co-chair, Col Desert Extended Opportunity Prog Serv, EOPS; Col Desert Diversity Task Force; bd dir, Black Am Cinema Soc; ed bd, Desert Sun; bd dir, Palm Springs Conv Ctr; organizer, Friends Cuba, Coachella Valley Br; co-pres, Coachella Valleywide Kwanzaa Celebration Ceremonies, 1993-94; bd dir, Cabazon Indian Cult Ctr, 1996; adv bd, Que Nuevas Newspaper, 1997. **Home Addr:** 450 E Laurel Cir, Palm Springs, CA 92262-2236, **Home Phone:** (760)327-4983. **Business Addr:** Publisher, Editor, International Review of 3rd World Culture, PO Box 1785, Palm Springs, CA 92263, **Business Phone:** (619)327-4983.

### BEAVERS, REV. NATHAN HOWARD, JR. See Obituaries Section.

### BECHET, JENNIFER BORUM. See BORUM, JENNIFER LYNN.

### BECHET, RONALD (RON J BECHET)
Artist, educator. **Personal:** Born Jul 22, 1956, New Orleans, LA; son of Ronald Sr and Yvonne. **Educ:** Univ New Orleans, BFA, 1979; Yale Univ, MFA, 1982. **Career:** Southern Univ, New Orleans, Dept Fine Arts & Philos, actg chmn; Xavier Univ, LA, Dept Art, chmn, asst prof, prof fine arts & artist, currently; Imagining Am Arts, co-prin. **Orgs:** Founding mem, Porch Cult Arts Orgn; co-dir, Home New Orleans Proj. **Home Addr:** 3824 Gentilly Blvd, New Orleans, LA 70122, **Home Phone:** (504)947-1032. **Business Addr:** Professor, Chairman, Xavier University of Louisiana, Rm 102 Bldg 39 1 Drexel Dr, New Orleans, LA 70125, **Business Phone:** (504)520-7553.

### BECK, COREY LAVEON
Basketball player. **Personal:** Born May 27, 1971, Memphis, TN. **Educ:** Univ Ark, attended 1995. **Career:** Basketball player (retired); Charlotte Hornets, guard, 1995-99; Sioux Falls Skyforce (CBA), 1995, 1996-97, 1998-99, 1999-2000; Detroit Pistons, guard, 1998-99; Zalgiris Kaunas, Lithuania, 2000; Memphis Houn'Dawgs (ABA), 2000-01; Toros de Aragua (Venezuela), 2001; Fila Biella, guard, 2001; Roseto Basket, 2001; Euro Roseto, 2001.

### BECK, SAUL L.
Government official, mayor. **Personal:** Born Jul 11, 1928, Greenwood, MS; married Elaine; children: 5. **Educ:** Chicago Tech Col. **Career:** City Councilman, 1964-72; E Chicago Heights Ill, mayor, 1973-, city councilman, 1991-95; Sch Dist No 169, Village Ford Heights, dir bldg & grounds, mayor, currently. **Orgs:** Int Brotherhood Elec Workers; Ill Bd Community & Econ Develop; bd mem, Prairie State Jr Col; educ counr mem, Nat Conf Black Mayors, 1976; Ill Chap Nat Conf Black Mayors; deleg, Dem Nat Conv, 1980; bd dir, Ill Munic League; NBC LEO; Nat Asn Advan Colored People; PUSH; bd mem, Community Econ Develop Asn Inc. **Honors/Awds:** Appreciation Award Order of Eastern Star; Humanitarian Award Fel for Action; Community Service Award, CEDA. **Business Addr:** Mayor, Ford Heights, 1343 Ellis Ave, Ford Heights, IL 60411, **Business Phone:** (708)758-3131.

### BECKETT, EVETTE OLGA (EVETTE BECKETT-TUGGLE)
Marketing executive. **Personal:** Born Sep 1, 1956, Glen Cove, NY; daughter of Arthur Dean and Ollie Leone Hall; married Reginald Tuggle; married J Barrington Jackson; children: Lauren, Karleena & Regine. **Educ:** Tufts Univ, BA, Eng, drama, 1978; Columbia Univ Grad Sch Bus, MBA, mkt & finance, 1981. **Career:** Random House Inc, prod asst, 1978-79; Bankers Trust Co, casst treas, orp lending officer, 1981-82; Avon Prod Inc, merchandising planner, dir mkt/investor rels, 1982-84, asst merchandising mgr, 1984-85, merchanding mgr, 1985-86, mgr fragrance mkt, 1986-89, dir fragrance mkt, 1989-92, Speciality Gift Bus, gen mgr, 1992-, dir investor rels; Tambrands Inc, dir global mkt, 1995-97; Citibank, vpres global mkt, 1997-2000; Global Music Network, chief mkt officer, 2000; Essence Mag, chief mkt officer, 2000-01; Dowling Col, asst vpres, 2002-05; Nassau Co Off Econ Develop, exec dir, 2006-11; Carolinas Minority Supplier Develop Coun, pres & chief exec officer, 2012; Noble Woman Enterprises, pres & chief exec officer, 2012-15; All About Parenting, host, 2014-15; Agilant Group LLC, prin consult, 2015-. **Orgs:** Nat Asn Female Exec, 1986-87; bd mem, Coalition Black Prof Orgn, 1986-87; Cosmetic Exec Women, 1987; prog chmn, NY Chap Nat Black MBA Asn, 1987; vpres, oper, Nat Black MBA Asn, New York Chap, 1987-88; bd dir, C House, 1988-; prog chmn, 100 Black Women Long Island, 1987-, bd dir, 1990-; bd dir, Glen Cove Boys & Girls Club, 1990-; adv comt, Carolina Theatre, 2014-; bd dir, Harvey B. Gantt Ctr African-Am Arts + Cult, 2014-; chair, peer adv bd facilitator, chief exec officer, coach, bus advisor, growth consult, Vistage, 2015-; Long Island Womens Agenda; Women Econ Developers Long Island; Alpha Kappa Alpha Sorority; Theta Iota Omega; pres, Nassau Co Chap Jack & Jill Am; vpres, Wom-

ens League Mem Presby Church; fel Coun Advisors Community Develop Corp LI. **Honors/Awds:** Billie Holiday Performing Arts Award, Tufts Univ, 1978; Outstanding Volunteer Award, Avon Products Inc, 1984; Top 100 Black Bus & Prof Women, Dollars & Sense Mag, 1988; Black Achievers Award, Harlem YMCA, 1989; Crain's NY Bus 40 People Under 40 to Watch in the, 1990; On The Move, Fortune Magazine, 1990; Essence Magazine 10 Corp Women, 1991; Marketer of the Month Sales & Marketing Management, 1991. **Special Achievements:** Publications: The Phenomenal Coach, Coaching Perspectives IV, 2014. Fourth African-American to graduate from the Quaker college. **Business Addr:** Principal, The Agilant Group LLC, 9935-D Rea Rd Suite 234, Charlotte, NC 28277, **Business Phone:** (704)575-8829.

## BECKETT, JUSTIN F.

Association executive, founder (originator), chief executive officer. **Personal:** Born Apr 5, 1963, Boston, MA; son of Herbert and Eleanor. **Educ:** Duke Univ, BA, polit sci & hist, 1985. **Career:** E F Hutton, acct exec, 1985-86; NCM Capital Mgt Group Inc, exec vpres, 1986; New Africa Advs, pres & chief exec officer, 1992-; Sloan financial group, exec vpres, prin; Music Gaming Inc, founder & chief exec officer, 2000; SkillJam Technologies, founder; Fluid Audio Networks, chmn & chief exec officer & founder, 2004-08; Muse Media Inc, founder & chief exec officer, currently; Skilljam Technologies, founder & ceo, 2000-04; Intermix Media/MySpace, exec dir, 2001-04; Sloan Financial Group, exec vpres, 1986-2000; LIVEWELL Care Inc, vice chmn, 2004-; Generosity Water, chmn, 2007-; Engage Play Technologies, chmn & chief exec officer, 2008-; BeLike, chmn, 2013-. **Orgs:** Secy & treas, Nat Investment Mgrs Asn, 1988-92; Nat Asn Securities Profs, 1988-; adj prof, Southern Univ New Orleans, 1989-92; advocacy comn, Nat Minority Suppliers Develop Coun, 1989-93; Duke Univ Black Alumni Connection, 1990-; trustee, Elizabeth City State Univ, 1992-94; bd mem, Fluid Music; bd mem, Aptilon, 2008-; bd mem, Kangaroo Media, 2007; bd mem, GNO Healthcare Serv; bd mem, Consonus Technologies Inc. **Home Addr:** 6720 Pauline Dr, Chapel Hill, NC 27514-9781, **Home Phone:** (919)489-5357. **Business Addr:** Chief Executive Officer, Chairman, Engage Play Technologies, 5301 Beethoven St Suite 200B, Los Angeles, CA 90008, **Business Phone:** (310)736-4711.

## BECKETT, SYDNEY ANN

Artist, educator. **Personal:** Born Nov 20, 1943, Philadelphia, PA. **Educ:** Temple Univ, BA, 1965, MEd, 1967, PhD. **Career:** Philadelphia Sch Dist, elem teacher, 1965-66; IBM, mkt support rep, 1967-73; Pa Comm Status Women, comnr app govn, 1972-; EI Dupont, training & develop, 1974; Silver Horse Artists Creations, artist. **Orgs:** Delta Sigma Theta Sor, 1962; bd dir, Alumni Asn, Temple Univ, 1967; bd dir, SW Belmont Young Women Christian Asn, 1970; Am Soc Training & Develop, 1974; Am Asn Univ Women, 1977; Phi Delta Gamma; bd mem, Philadelphia Singers. **Honors/Awds:** Outstanding Woman of the Year, Temple Univ, 1970; Community Service Award, IBM, 1970-72; Dale Carnegie Inst 2 awards; Sr Recognition Award of Pres & Faculty; Outstanding Sr Templar Yearbook; Greek Woman of the Year, Temple Univ; Vol Service Award; Treble Clef Alumnae Award. **Home Addr:** 6430 Wayne Ave, Philadelphia, PA 19119, **Home Phone:** (215)843-1965. **Business Addr:** Artist, Silver Horse Artists Creations, 2118 Co Hwy 33, Cooperstown, NY 13326, **Business Phone:** (607)547-2107.

## BECKETT-TUGGLE, EVETTE. See BECKETT, EVETTE OLGA.

## BECKFORD, ORVILLE

Automotive executive. **Career:** Orville Beckford Ford-Mercury Inc, chief exec officer, prin & dealer, Owner, 1987-. **Business Addr:** Chief Executive Officer, Principal, Orville Beckford Ford-Mercury Inc, 6400 Hwy 90 W, Milton, FL 32570, **Business Phone:** (850)623-2234.

## BECKFORD, TYSON CRAIG

Fashion model, actor. **Personal:** Born Dec 19, 1970, Bronx, NY; children: Jordan. **Career:** Ralph Lauren, lead model, actor; "Make Me A Supermodel", host, currently; Bethann Hardison/Bethann Mgt Co Inc, model, currently; Films: Punks; Boricua's Bond, 2000; Zoolander, 2001; Shottas, 2002; Pandora's Box, 2002; Gully, 2002; Biker Boyz, 2003; Gas, 2004; Searching for Bobby D, 2004; Into the Blue, 2005; Dream Street, 2006; Kings Of the Evening, 2008; Hotel California; actor & producer, 2008; Dream Street, 2010; Addicted, 2014. TV Shows: "Superbikes", "Americas Next Top Model"; "Project Runaway"; "Candy Girls"; Music Videos: "Unbreak My Heart"; "Ice Cream", "21 Questions"; "Toxic"; "Anything"; "Say How I Feel"; "Go West"; "China Wine"; "One More Chance"; "How It Was Supposed To Be"; "Go Hard"; "Whatcha Gonna Do"; "Raise the Roof". TV series: "My Wife and Kids", 2002; "Half & Half", 2003; "Video on Trial", 2005; "SWV Reunited", 2014. **Honors/Awds:** Hottest Male Model, Man of the Year, VH-1, 1995. **Special Achievements:** First African American to be featured with Ralph Lauren/Polo; 50 MostBeautiful People in the World, People Magazine, 1995; appeared on variousmagazines: Essence & Paper; Vogue; GQ; Details; Men's Health; Vibe & TheNY Times; TV appearances include Toni Braxton; Mia X; Notorious BIG; Shaquille O'Neal; Jay Leno; Oprah; Rosie O'Donnel; Vibe; The Magic Hour; Good Morning Am; Keenan Ivory Wayans; Mad TV; Nickelodeon; EntertainmentTonight; E! Entertainment; Video Soul; Teen Summit. **Business Addr:** Model, c/o Bethann Management, 36 N Moore St, New York, NY 10013, **Business Phone:** (212)925-2153.

## BECKHAM, BARRY EARL

Publisher, writer, educator. **Personal:** Born Mar 19, 1944, Philadelphia, PA; son of Mildred Williams and Clarence; married Betty Louise Hope, Feb 19, 1966, (divorced 1977); children: Brian Elliott & Bonnie Lorine; married Monica L Scott, Oct 23, 1997; married Geraldine Lynne Palmer, Jan 1, 1979?, (divorced 1983). **Educ:** Brown Univ, AB, eng lit, 1966; Columbia Univ Law Sch. **Career:** Prof (retired), founder, pres & writer; Chase Manhattan Bank, pub rels, consult, 1966-67, urban affairs assoc, 1969-70; Nat Coun YMCAs, pub rels assoc, 1967-68; Western Elec Co, pub rels assoc, 1968-69; Brown Univ, vislect, 1970-72, asst prof, 1972-78, assoc prof eng, 1979-87, dir grad creative writing prog, 1980-87; Gary Lives, Writer, 1973; Hampton Univ, prof, 1987 (retired); Publ: My Main Mother, 1969; Runner Mack; Double Dunk, 1981; Will You Be Mine; Beckhams Guide to Scholarships for Black & Minority Students, 1982; The Col Selection Work book; The Black Students guide to col, 1982; The Col Selection Workbook, 2nd ed, 1987; You Have a Friend: The Rise & Fall & Rise of Chase Manhattan Bank, serialized on Internet, 1998; Plays: Garvey Lives! 1972; Articles: "Listen to the Black Graduate, You Might Learn Something", Esquire, 1969, "Ladies & Gentlemen, NoSalt-Water Taffy Today", Brown Alumni Monthly, 1970 & "Why It Is Right to Write", Brown Alumni Monthly, 1978; Ed: The Black Student's Guide to Cols, 1997; The Black Student's Guide to Scholarships, 1999; Beckham Publ Group, pres, 1997-, founder, currently; Nat Endowment Arts, fel. **Orgs:** Bd dir, Authors Guild; Authors League Am; bd dir, PEN; Ri Coun Arts, lit panel; judge, Hurston Wright Found, 2005. **Home Addr:** 13619 Cedar Creek Lane, Silver Spring, MD 20904, **Home Phone:** (301)384-1118. **Business Addr:** Founder, President, Beckham Publications Group, 13619 Cedar Creek Lane, Silver Spring, MD 20904, **Business Phone:** (301)384-7995.

## BECKLES, BENITA HARRIS

Human services worker. **Personal:** Born Feb 21, 1950, Chicago, IL; daughter of Felicia Mason Williams; married Lionel L; children: Lionel E & Jefferson. **Educ:** Hampton Univ, BA, 1971; George Washington Univ, MA, 1977. **Career:** Author & publisher; Potential Plus, human potential consult, 1996; Detroit Pub Libr, employee develop coordr, 1998-, human resources mgr, currently; Tuskegee Airmen Inc; White House fel; Books: Back to Basics Life Strategies for Success. **Orgs:** Delta Sigma Theta Sorority, Inkster Alumni Chap. **Home Addr:** 18810 Alhambra, Lathrup Village, MI 48076, **Home Phone:** (313)559-8714. **Business Addr:** Human Resources Manager, Detroit Public Library, 5201 Woodward Ave, Detroit, MI 48202, **Business Phone:** (248)497-1522.

## BECKLES, IAN HAROLD

Football player, broadcaster. **Personal:** Born Jul 20, 1967, Montreal, QC; married Dayle; children: Zayna & Marques. **Educ:** Ind Univ, BS, bus. **Career:** Football player (retired), football coach, exec; Tampa Bay Buccaneers, guard, 1990-96; Philadelphia Eagles, 1997-99; New York Jets, 1999-2000; Denver Broncos, 2000; Sports Radio 620 WDAE, sportscaster, "The Ron & Ian Show", currently. **Business Addr:** Sportscaster, WDAE 620, 4002 W Gandy Blvd Suite A, Tampa, FL 33611, **Business Phone:** (813)832-1000.

## BECKLES, INGRID

Vice president (organization). **Educ:** Univ Md Col Park, BS, acct/technol & mgt; Northwestern Univ, Kellogg Sch Mgt, exec cert prog; Mass Inst Technol, Sloan Sch Mgt, exec cert prog, reinventing bus strategy & develop a leading edge opers strategy; Univ Va, pre-med, 1981. **Career:** BF Saul Mortgage; PNC Mortgage Corp Am, vpres chief underwriter, 1991-98, vpres customer focused initiatives, 1998-99, vpres consol credit policy, qual assurance & appraisal policies div, 1999-2001; Freddie Mac, vpres credit strategy & opers, mortgage serv div, 2001-03, vpres & head default asset mgt, servicing & asset mgt, 2003-08, sr vpres default asset mgt, 2008-10; Velocity Capital Defense, pres, 2010-11; Beckles Collective LLC, founder & chief exec officer, 2011-. **Orgs:** Nat Inst Housing Strategy; Nat Mortgage Bankers Asn; Nat Asn Prof Women; coun mem mortgage banking, Gerson Lehrman Group, 2010-; bd mem, Family Health & Birth Ctr; bd mem, DC Youth Orchestra; bd dir, Nat Capital YWCA, 2011-; bd dir mem & regulatory policy comt chair, Nat Asn Women Real Estate Bus, 2012-14. **Business Addr:** Founder, Chief Executive Officer, The Beckles Collective LLC, 10 G St NE Suite 710, Washington, DC 20002, **Business Phone:** (202)248-5023.

## BECKLEY, DR. DAVID LENARD

College president. **Personal:** Born Mar 21, 1946, Shannon, MS; married Gemma Douglass; children: Jacqueline B Abdulah & Lisa B Roberts. **Educ:** Rust Col, BA, 1967; Univ Miss, MEd, higher educ admin, 1975, PhD, higher educ admin, 1986. **Career:** Rust Col, dir pub rels, 1967-77, purchasing agt, 1968-69, dir develop, 1977-81, interim provost, 1984, dir advan, 1984, pres, 1993-; Wiley Col, pres, 1987-93. **Orgs:** Bd dir, Holly Springs Miss Chamber Com, 1980-86; consult, UN Negro Col Fund, Lilly Endowment, 1981-84; secy, Indust Develop Authority, Marshall City, 1985-87; chair, Methodist LeBonheur Healthcare Found, 1999-2000; chair, Mem Presidents United Negro Col Fund, 2002; United Methodist Sr Serv Miss Inc, 1999-2008; Comn Cols Southern Asn Cols & Schs, 2002-08; chair, Miss Asn Independent Cols; pres, Miss Asn Cols; NCAA Div III Presidents Coun; pres, Nat Asn Schs & Cols United Methodist Church; bd dir, Methodist Health Systs Inc, Memphis, Tenn; Univ Senate, United Methodist Church; chair, Black Col Coun; chair, SERVE Bd; chair, Yocona Area Coun Boy Scouts Am; Black Methodist Church Renewal; CREATE Bd; Miss Inst Arts & Lett; Asbury United Methodist Church; Phi Delta Kappa Educ Fraternity; Alpha Phi Omega Nat Serv Fraternity; Sigma Pi Phi Prof Men's Fraternity; Omega Psi Phi Nat Fraternity Inc; 33 Mason. **Honors/Awds:** Omega Man Year, Omega Psi Phi Frat Phi Rho Chap, 1983; Kappan Year, Phi Delta Kappa Educ Frat, 1984; Man of Excellence Award, Tri-State Defender Newspaper, 2010; Silver Beaver Award, Boy Scouts Am; Outstanding Education Alumni Award, Univ Miss; Outstanding Alumni Achievement Award, Nat Asn Equal Opportunity Higher Educ; Citizen of the Year, Omega Psi Phi Fraternity Inc; Service Award, Nat Col Athletic Asn; President of the Year, Nat Asn African Am Hons Progs; New Conference Center renamed in honor as David L. Beckley Conference Center. **Special Achievements:** Third alumnus to serve his alma mater as president. **Home Addr:** PO Box 481, Holly Springs, MS 38635. **Business Addr:** President, Rust College, McCoy Admin Bldg 150 Rust Ave, Holly Springs, MS 38635, **Business Phone:** (662)252-8000.

## BECKWITH, REV. DR. MICHAEL BERNARD

Clergy, executive. **Personal:** married Rickie Byars. **Career:** Agape Int Spiritual Ctr, founder, 1986, spiritual dir & sr minister, currently; Ernest Holmes Inst Sch Ministry, dir, currently. **Orgs:** int co-chair, Gandhi King Season Nonviolence, 1998; Co-founder, pres, Asn Global New Thought; co-chair, Season Nonviolence; Twilight Brigade. **Honors/Awds:** Africa Achievement Peace Award, 2004; Humanitarian Award, Nat Coun Community & Justice; "Prime Minister of the Children's Diplomatic Corp" Award, United World Inter Nat Protection Children's Rights; Martin Luther King Jr, Bd Preachers Morehouse Col; Excellence in Spiritual Leadership & Community Development Award; Congress of Racial Equality Award as one of the top ten ministers in Los Angeles; Gold Medal Nautilus Book Award; Martin Luther King Peace Award. **Special Achievements:** Author: Spiritual Liberation; Inspirations of the Heart; Forty Day Mind Fast Soul Feast, A Manifesto of Peace; Living from the Overflow; Life Visioning; TranscenDance Expanded; Film: The Secret, 2006; Raw for Life & Raw for 30 days. **Business Addr:** Founder, Spiritual Director & Senior Minister, Agape International Spiritual Center, 5700 Buckingham Pkwy, Culver City, CA 90230, **Business Phone:** (310)348-1250.

## BECOTE, FOHLIETTE W.

Banker, executive, vice president (organization). **Personal:** Born Dec 28, 1958, Burgaw, NC; daughter of Arlander and Ola Mae; married Lawen J II. **Educ:** Univ NC, Chapel Hill, NC, BA, 1981; NC Cent Univ, Durham, NC, MBA, 1985. **Career:** NC Cent Univ, Durham, NC, grad asst, 1983-84; Mech & Farmers Bank, Durham, NC, anal clerk, 1983-84, asst comptroller, 1984-88, asst vpres, 1987-88, vpres & comptroller, 1988-96, sr vpres & comptroller, 1997-2000, sr vpres, chief financial officer & corp secy, 2000-05; M&F Bancorp Inc, secy & treas, 1999-2005. **Orgs:** Treas, Salvation Army Adv Bd, 1985-88; Nat Asn Accts, 1986-90; treas, Durham Child Advocacy Comn, 1987-88; secy, Bankers Educ Soc Inc, 1987-88; Leadership Durham Alumni Asn, 1990-; Univ NC Educ Found; Univ NC Gen Alumni; Alpha Kappa Alpha; Delta Sigma Pi Alumni; Wake County Ind Facil & Pollution Control Financing Authority. **Honors/Awds:** Hundred Most Promising Black Women in Corp Am, Ebony, 1991; YWCA Women of Achievement Award, YWCA, 198 Fohliette5. **Home Addr:** 1005 Devonhurst Ct, Apex, NC 27502-5224, **Home Phone:** (919)362-0739. **Business Addr:** Senior Vice President & Chief Financial Officer, Corporate Secretary, Mechanics & Farmers Bank, 2705 Durham Chapel Hill Blvd, Durham, NC 27702-2800, **Business Phone:** (919)687-7835.

## BECTON, LT. GEN. JULIUS WESLEY, JR.

School administrator. **Personal:** Born Jun 29, 1926, Bryn Mawr, PA; son of Julius Wesley Sr and Rose Inez; married Louise Thornton; children: Shirley McKenzie, Karen Johnson, Joyce Best, Renee Strickland & J Wesley III. **Educ:** Prairie View A&M Col, BS, math, 1960; Univ Md, MA, econ, 1967; AUS Command & Gen Staff Col; Armed Forces Staff Col; Nat War Col, attended 1970; Muhlenberg Col, Allentown, PA. **Career:** Military service (retired), dir, educ adminr; First CavalryDiv, comndg gen, 1975-76; AUS, Oper Test & Eval Agency, commandinggen, 1976-78; VII US Corps, comndg gen, 1978-81; USA Training DctrnCommand, dep comndg gen & Army inspector training, 1981-83; US Agency Int Develop, Off Foreign Disaster, asst dir, 1984-85; Fed Emergency Mgt Agency, dir, 1985-89; Prairie View A&M Univ, pres, 1989-94; DC PubSchs, supt, pres, 1996-98; Am Coastal Industs, chief oper officer. **Orgs:** Dir, Nat Asn Uniformed Serv, 1969-71; vpres, US Armor Asn, 1982-91; Ret Officers Asn, 1983-85; Fairfax Coun Red Cross, 1983-84; USO World BdGov, 1985-90; Am Red Cross bd gov, 1986-90; bd trustee, Valley Forge MilAcad & Jr Col, 1988-90; bd, Fund Improv Post-Sec Educ, 1990-93; bd dir, Marine Spill Response Corp, 1990-01; vice chair & dir, SouthernRegional Educ Bd, 1991-94; Community Col Southern Asn Col & Schs, 1991-94; bd dir, Nat Asn Equal Oppor Higher Educ, 1992-94; bd dir, Wackenhut Corp, 1993-02; adv coun, Citadel Bd Visitors, 1994-99; bd dir, GenDynamics, 1997-2002; bd adv, First Cavalry Div Asn; bd visitors, DefenseEqual Opportunity Mgt Inst; five star coun mem, Libr Cong Veterans HistProj; adv bd, Resolution Trust; Long Range Planning & Oversight Comn, FedDist Ct, Knight v Ala; bd dir, Greater Wash Urban League; vice chair coun trustee, Asn AUS; bd trustee, George C Marshall Found; Am Battle Monument Comn, 2001-05; FAMU Bd trustee, 2001-04; bd dir, IllTool Works Inc, 2002. **Special Achievements:** First African American to command a Corps in the United States Army. **Home Addr:** 7737 Jewelweed Ct, Springfield, VA 22152, **Home Phone:** (703)644-5771.

## BECTON, RUDOLPH

Business owner, executive, association executive. **Personal:** Born May 21, 1930, Eureka, NC; married Annie Veronia Wilson; children: Karen L. **Educ:** Green County Training Sch, dipl, 1950; Harris Barber Col dipl, 1956; Sampson Tech Inst, cert, 1979; NC Agr Exten, cert, 1984. **Career:** UNC Chapel Hill, emergency med serv, 1976 & 1978; James Sprunt Inst, communi & patrol, 1978; Winston Salem State Univ, hair styling & cutting tech, 1979; James Sprunt Tech Col, fire apparatus & house pract, 1983; Becton Barber Shop, owner & operator, currently. **Orgs:** Humanitarian Magnolia Civic League, 1968-73; comt mem, Farmer's Home Admin, 1970-73 & 1977-80; Human Rels Duplin Co Good Neighbor Coun, 1973; town comnr, Town Magnolia; vol fireman & rescue, Town Magnolia; bd mem, Duplin & Sampson Ment Health; mayor pro team, Town Magnolia; bd mem, Magnolia Fire Dept; pres, Dupenza; Pres, Magnolia Civic League; African Am Heritage Found Wilmington. **Honors/Awds:** Trailblazer Boy Scouts Am, 1968; Distinguished Citizen, Crouton III Boy Scouts of Am, 1979; Good Conduct Medal. **Special Achievements:** First African American business in Magnolia, North Carolina. **Home Addr:** 410 S Railroad St, PO Box 86, Magnolia, NC 28453, **Home Phone:** (910)289-2288. **Business Addr:** Owner, Becton Barber Shop, Hwy 117, Magnolia, NC 28453, **Business Phone:** (910)289-2288.

## BEDELL, DR. FREDERICK DELANO

School administrator. **Personal:** Born Apr 13, 1934, New York, NY; married Gail Smith; children: Karin, Kevin & Keith. **Educ:** NY Univ, BS, 1957, MA, 1965; Univ MA, EdD, 1984. **Career:** Rockaway Beach, chief life guard, 1953-56; White Plains Pub Schs, 1957-68, asst prin, 1968-69, asst supt Pub Serv, 1984-; Bd Coop Educ Serv, prin, 1969-76; NY State Div Youth, dir educ, 1983-84; NY State Dept Corrections, asst comnr & dir Correctional Industs, 1983-84; Del-K Educ Consult Serv, pres, 1993. **Orgs:** Chmn, Equal Opportunity Educ Comt, White Plains Teacher Asn, 1966-68; dep mayor & village trust Ossining, 1973-76; vice chmn, Ossining Urban Reveval Bd, 1973-76; vpres Cage Teen Ctr; bd mem, St Mary's Field Sch; sec, treas & bd dir, High Meadow Coop; NY State Cong Parents & Teachers. **Honors/Awds:** Jaycees Award. **Home Addr:** 9750 N Monterey Dr Apt 19, Fountain Hills, AZ 85268-6736, **Home Phone:** (480)836-9352. **Business Addr:** President, Del-K Educ Consult Serv, 8 Rolling Brook Dr, Clifton Park, NY 12065, **Business Phone:** (518)371-3673.

**BEDOYA, ADRIANA. See SYKES, WANDA Y'VETTE.**

**BEE, QUEEN. See JONES, KIMBERLY DENISE.**

## BEHRMANN, SERGE T.

Executive. **Personal:** Born Jun 9, 1937, Port-au-Prince; children: Rachelle, Daphne, Serge J, Alex & Sophia. **Educ:** Col Simon Bolivar, attended 1955; Wis Univ, struct fabricating engineering, 1973; Purdue Univ, struct fabricating engineering, 1974. **Career:** Feinstein Iron Works, 1959-66; Behrmann Iron Works, struct fabricator. **Orgs:** Pres, Ferrum Realty Corp, New York. **Home Addr:** 627 Powells Lane, Westbury, NY 11590. **Business Addr:** Structural Fabricator, Behrmann Iron Works Inc, 832 Dean St, Brooklyn, NY 11238.

## BELAFONTE, HARRY (HAROLD GEORGE BELAFONTE, JR.)

Singer, television producer, actor. **Personal:** Born Mar 1, 1927, Harlem, NY; son of Harold George Sr and Malvene Love Wright; married Marguerite Byrd, Jan 1, 1948, (divorced 1957); children: Adrienne & Shari; married Julie Robinson, Mar 8, 1957; children: David & Gina; married Pamela Frank, Mar 1, 2008. **Educ:** Manhattan New Sch Soc Res Dramatic Workshop, attended 1948. **Career:** Broadway appearances: Almanac, 1953, Three for Tonight, 1955; Films: Bright Road, 1953; Carmen Jones, 1954; Island in the Sun, 1957; The Heart of Show Business, 1957; The World: the Flesh & the Devil, 1959; Odds Against Tomorrow, 1959; The Angel Levine, 1970; Buck & the Preacher, 1972; Uptown Saturday Night, 1974; Der Schonste Traum, 1984; We Shall Overcome, 1989; White Man's Burden, 1995; Hank Aaron: Chasing the Dream, 1995; Jazz '34, 1996; Kansas City, 1996; Scandalize My Name: Stories from the Blacklist, 1998; Fidel, 2001; XXI Century, 2003; Conakry Kas, 2003; Ladders, 2004; Mo & Me, 2006; Bobby, 2006; Motherland, 2009; Sing Your Song, 2011; Hava Nagila: The Movie, 2013; TV series: "TV Specs", prod; "A Time of Laughter", 1967, "Harry & Lena", 1969; "Tonight with Belafonte", 1960; "Strolling Twenties TV", prod; "Beat St", co-prod, 1984; "Tanner on Tanner", 2004; "That's What I'm Talking About", 2006; "When the Levees Broke: A Requiem in Four Acts", 2006; "Speakeasy, interviewing Carlos Santana", 2015; "Lip Sync Battle", Belafonte Enterprises Inc, pres, currently. **Orgs:** Bd dir, Trans Africa Forum Bd; hon mem, Phi Beta Sigma fraternity, 2014. **Honors/Awds:** Tony Award, 1953; Emmy Award, 1960; Honorary Doctor of Humanities, Park Col, 1968; Honorary Doctor of Arts, New Sch Social Res, 1968; Martin Luther King Jr Nonviolent Peace Prize, 1982; ABAA Music Award, 1985; Grammy Award, 1985; Honorary Doctorate, Spel man Col, 1990; Nat Medal of Arts Award, White House, 1994; Freedom in Film Award, 2000; Bishop John T Walker Distinguished Humanitarian Service Award, Africare, 2002; Humanitarian Award, BET, 2006; Hollywood Film Award, 2006. **Special Achievements:** Received an appointment to UNICEF as a goodwill ambassador since 1987; The first African-American television producer, working on numerous musical shows. **Business Addr:** President, Belafonte Enterprises Inc, PO Box 650189, Fresh Meadows, NY 11365.

## BELAFONTE, SHARI LYNN (SHARI BELAFONTE HARPER)

Actor, fashion model. **Personal:** Born Aug 22, 1954, New York, NY; daughter of Harry and Marguerite Byrd; married Robert Harper; married Sam Behrens. **Educ:** Hampshire Col, BA; Carnegie-Mellon Univ, BFA, 1977. **Career:** Actress, producer, photographer, writer & fashion model; Hanna Barbera Prod, publicist asst; fashion model; TV series: "ABC Weekend Specials", 1981; "Misadventures of Sheriff Lobo", 1981; "Hart to Hart", 1981; "If You Could See What I Hear", 1982; "Trapper John", 1982; "Diff'rent Strokes", 1982; "Hotel", 1983-88; "Family Feud", 1983; "Battle of the Network Stars", 1984; "Velvet", 1984; "The Love Boat", 1984; "The Midnight Hour", 1985; "Matt Houston", 1985; "Kate's Secret", 1986; "Square One TV", 1987; "The Women of Brewster Place", 1989; "Gravedale High", 1990; "Beyond Reality", 1991; "French Silk", 1994; "The Heidi Chronicles", 1995; "Hey Arnold!", 1996; "The Real Adventures of Jonny Quest", 1997; "Babylon 5: Third space", 1998; "The Octopus Show", 2000; "Loving Evangeline", 2001; "The District", 2001; "Sonic the Hedgehog", 2003; "It's Christopher Lowell", 2003; "The Oprah Winfrey Show", 2004; "Nip/Tuck", 2008; "Miami Medical", 2010. Photographer: The Big Empty, 2003; Betrunner, 2004; Betty's Treats, photographer & producer, 2004; Lonesome Matador, 2005; Efflorescе, 2014. Films: Time Walker, 1982; Feuer, Eis & Dynamit, 1990; Murder by Numbers, 1990; Mars, 1997; Harlequin's Loving Evangeline, 1998; Teacher of the Year, 2014. **Honors/Awds:** Bambi Award, 1985. **Special Achievements:** Appeared on more than 200 magazine covers. **Business Addr:** Actress, Blanchard Nina Agency, 957 N Cole Ave, Los Angeles, CA 90038, **Business Phone:** (213)462-7274.

## BELARDO DE O, LILLIANA

Senator (U.S. federal government), politician, association executive. **Personal:** Born Jan 11, 1944, Christiansted; daughter of Gil Belardo Sanes and Paula Mendez Agosto; married Humberto; children: Carlos Gill Ortiz. **Educ:** Inter-Am Univ, BA, 1963; Univ Mich, MSW, 1969; Calif State Univ; Univ PR; Univ Miami, PhD. **Career:** Dept Social Welfare, social worker, 1964, probation worker, 1970; Dept Social Welfare Girls Training Sch, dir, 1971; State Calif, youth authority worker, 1975; Dept Educ, sch guid counr, 1976; Legis VI, legislator, 1981, sen; Republican Party VI, nat comt woman, currently. gift shop, owner, currently; Paradise Sunset Beach Hotel, co-owner, currently. **Orgs:** Bd dir & chair, Am Red Cross, St Croix Chap, 2015; League Women Voters; St Croix Lioness Club; Asn Social Workers Bus & Prof Women; Phi Delta Kappa. **Special Achievements:** first elected as the national committeewoman for the Republican Party of the Virgin Islands, 1987. **Home Addr:** 53 Dlagr Princess Cisted, PO Box 3382, St Croix00820, **Home Phone:** (809)773-6543. **Business Addr:** National Committee Woman, The Republican Party of the Virgin Islands, 6067 Questa Verde, St. Croix00820-4485, **Business Phone:** (340)332-2579.

## BELCHER, DR. JACQUELYN M.

School administrator, president (organization), chief executive officer. **Personal:** married Lew. **Educ:** Marymount Col, Salina, KS, BS, nursing; Univ Wash, MA, psychosocial nursing & psychol, 1971; Univ Puget Sound, Tacoma, WA, JD, nursing, psychol, bus, law, 1984; Inst Mgt Lifelong Educ. **Career:** Minneapolis Community Col, pres, 1990-95; Ga Perimeter Col, dist pres, 1995-2005, pres emer, 2005-. Options Unlimited LLC, pres & chief exec officer, 2005-. **Orgs:** Exec coun & chair, AACC; bd mem, Metro Atlanta Chamber Com; Metro Atlanta Boys & Girls Clubs; Atlanta Bus League; Carter Ctr; Seamless Educ Comt; vice chair, Ga Human Rels Comn; vice chair, Knowledge Works Found, Partnership Pub Serv; vice chair, Gateway to Col Nat Network; pres, KnowledgeWorks Found; vice chair, Ga Human Rels Comn; bd mem, Atlanta Educ Telecommunications Collab Inc; Coastline Community Col. **Business Addr:** President Emeritus, Georgia Perimeter College, 3251 Panthersville Rd, Decatur, GA 30034, **Business Phone:** (678)891-2300.

## BELCHER, DR. LEON H.

Educator. **Personal:** Born Aug 8, 1930, Mineral Springs, AR; married Mary S Randall; children: 2. **Educ:** Univ Ark, BS, 1955, MA, 1957; Univ Northern Colo, PhD, 1961. **Career:** State Ark, teacher, jr high sch counr, 1955-60; Ala A&M Univ, Dean Studs, prof, 1961-66; Princeton Univ, res psychologist, 1966-67; Tex Southern Univ, dir testing, dir inst res & prof, 1967-71, Dept psychol & philos, prof & chair, currently. **Orgs:** Alpha Kappa Mu, 1955; Phi Delta Kappa, 1960; Am Psychol Asn; Am Personnel & Guid Asn; Am Educ Res Asn; Am Col Personnel Asn; ed bd, Col Stud Personnel J; ed bd, Asn Inst Res; Tex State Bd Examiners; Cult Affairs Comt, Houston Chamber Com; Houston Coun Boys Scout Am. **Home Addr:** 4305 Fernwood Dr, Houston, TX 77021, **Home Phone:** (713)643-4500. **Business Addr:** Professor, Chair, Texas Southern University, 3100 Cleburne St ED B02A, Houston, TX 77004-4501, **Business Phone:** (713)313-7011.

## BELIZAIRE-SPITZER, JULIE

Social worker. **Personal:** Born Dec 23, 1969, New York, NY; daughter of Gabriel and Simone; married Andrew; children: 3. **Educ:** Albany Univ-SUNY, BA; Hunter Col-CUNY, MSW. **Career:** Citizens Advice Bur, prog dir, HRAP, 1997, asst dir, Homeless Prev, 1998, prog dir, sr servs, 1999-, Citizens Adv Bur, actg dir; BronxWorks, Homelessness Prev Dept, dir, 2005-. **Orgs:** Zeta Phi Beta, 1990-; Girls Club, New York, 1992; bd dir, Bronx Regional Inter-Agency Coun Aging, 2000. **Home Addr:** 263 Genesee Ave, Englewood, NJ 07631, **Home Phone:** (201)871-4969. **Business Addr:** Program Director - Homelessness Prevention Program, BronxWorks, 60 E Tremont Ave, Bronx, NY 10453, **Business Phone:** (646)393-4000.

## BELL, ALBERTA SAFFELL

Publisher. **Personal:** Born Sep 25, 1944, Knoxville, TN; daughter of Alfred J Saffell Sr and Mildred J; married C Gordon; children: Tiffany M & C Gordon II. **Educ:** Tenn State Univ, BS, 1966, MS, 1968; Howard Univ, DDS, 1976. **Career:** Gardner News, vpres, 1989-92, publ & pres, 1992-; Nashville Pub Sch; Mass Newspapers, publ, 1992. **Home Addr:** 123 Willis Rd, Gardner, MA 01440-2449, **Home Phone:** (978)630-2215. **Business Addr:** President, Publisher, The Gardner News, 309 Cent St, Gardner, MA 01441-0340, **Business Phone:** (978)632-8000.

## BELL, DR. CARL COMPTON

Psychiatrist, medical researcher. **Personal:** Born Oct 28, 1947, Chicago, IL; son of William Yancey Jr and Pearl Debnam; children: Cristin, Briatta & William. **Educ:** Univ Ill, Chicago Circle, Ill, BS, biol, 1967; Meharry Med Col, MD, 1971. **Career:** Goldberger Fel, 1969; Meharry Med Col, Matthew Walker Comp Health Ctr, bio statistician, 1970-72; Ill Dept Ment Health, resident physician, 1971-74; pvt pract psychiatrist, 1972-; Jackson Pk Hosp, consult, 1972-74; Ill State Psychiat Inst, Chicago, Ill, psychiat resident, 1974; Chicago Med Sch, clin instr psych, 1975; Psychiat Emergency Serv Prog, dir, 1976-77, assoc dir div behav & psychodynamic med, 1979-80; Human Correctional & Serv Inst, staff psychiatrist, 1977-78; Chatham Avalon Ment Health Ctr, staff psychiatrist, 1977-79; Chicago Bd Educ, staff psychiatrist, 1977-79; Community Ment Health Coun & Found Inc, Day Treat Ctr, staff psychiatrist, 1977-79, med dir, 1982-87, pres & chief exec officer, 1987-, prin investr; Univ Ill, Sch Med, clin prof psychiat & pub health, 1983-, Sch Pub Health, prof, 1995, dir, currently; WVON-AM, Chicago, Ill, radio talk show host, 1987-88; WJPC-FM, Black Couch, radio talk show, 1992-93. **Orgs:** Falk Fel Am Psychiat Asn Participate Coun Nat Affairs, 1972, 1973; dipl bd examr, Am Bd Psychiat & Neurol, 1976; Am-Indian Asian-Pac Am/Black & Hisp Core Ment Health Discipline Adv Comn, Howard Univ Sch Social Work, 1980-83; Nat Comn Correctional Health Care, 1983, chmn, 1992; chmn, Nat Med Asn Sect Psych, 1985-86; bd dir, Am Asn Community Ment Health Ctr Psychiatrists, 1985-89; fel Am Psychiat Asn, 1985; Shorei Goju Karate Soc-Rank 6th Degree Black Belt; Black Belt Med Soc Physicians Martial Arts Asn; secy, treas, Nat Coun Community Ment Health Ctr, 1986-87; Am Col Psychiat, 1987; bd dir, Ill Coun against Handgun Violence, 1990-; co-investr, African-Am Youth Proj, Univ Il Sch Pub Health, 1994-; ed bd, Jour Infant, Child & Adolescent Psychother, 1997-; fel Am Col Psychiatrists, 1998; Ill State Atty's Comn Violent Young Offenders, 1998; ed adv bd, Clin Psychiat News, 2000; Pres's Distinguished Speakers Prog, Univ Ill, 2000; Am Psych Asn; Res Planning Work Groups DSM V, Nat Inst Ment Health, 2000-02; Inst Med, Bd Neuroscience & Behav Health Study Psychopath & Prev Adolescent & Adult Suicide, 2000-02; Am Col Psych Bd Regents, 2006-11; NIMH Nat Ment Health Adv Coun, 2008-11; founder, Inst Prev Violence; Alpha Omega Alpha Med Hon Socs; pres & chief exec officer, Community Ment Health Coun, currently; vpres, newsletter ed, Black Psychiatrists Am. **Honors/Awds:** Citation of Merit, Disabled Am Veterans, 1971; Mosby Scholar Book Award, Scholastic Excellence Med, Meharry Med Col, 1971; Plaque, Ill Shaolin Karate & Kung-Fu Asn, 1975; Certificate of Appreciation, Chatham-Avalon Community Ment Health Ctr, 1979; Gamma TN Chap Alpha Omega Alpha, 1980; Scholastic Achievement Award, Chicago Chap, Nat Asn Black Social Workers, 1980; Monarch Award Medicine, Alpha Kappa Alpha, 1986; Ellen Quinn Memorial Award for Outstanding Individual Achievement in Community Mental Health, 1986; Social Action Award, Chicago Chap Black Social Workers, 1988; Mental Health Award, Englewood Community Health Orgn, 1988; Outstanding Young Doctor Award, Dollars & Sense Mag, 1991; Alumnus of the Year, Meharry Med Col 20 Yr Reunion, 1991; EY Williams Distinguished Senior Clinical Scholar Award, Sect Psychiat & Behav Sci Nat Med Asn, 1992; Annual Award of Excellence in Community Mental Health, Am Asn Community Psychiatrists, 1992; President's Commendation for work on violence, Am Psychiat Asn, 1997; Blanche F Ittleson Award for lifetime contributions, Am Orthopsychiatric Asn, 1999; Presidential Award, Am Psychiat Asn; Minority Service Award, Am Psychiat Found, 2004; Special Presidential Commendation, Am Psychiat Asn, 2012; Agnes Purcell McGavin Award, Am Psychiat Asn, 2012. **Special Achievements:** Creator & producer of animation "Book Worm", PBS 1984; Top Doctor, Chicago Magazine, 2001, 2007. **Home Addr:** 5328 S Hyde Pk Blvd, Chicago, IL 60615-5927. **Business Addr:** President, Chief Executive Officer, Community Mental Health Council & Foundation Inc, 8704 S Constance Ave, Chicago, IL 60617, **Business Phone:** (773)734-4033.

## BELL, CHARLES SMITH

Educator, teacher. **Personal:** Born May 21, 1934, Capeville, VA; son of James A Sr and Martha Robinson; married Sallie Annette Parker; children: Charlette LaVonne, Mia Sallie & Angel Monique. **Educ:** Va Union Univ, BS, biol, 1957, 1970; Old Dom Univ, attended 1972; Norfolk State Univ. **Career:** Educator (retired); Northampton Co Sch Bd, teacher, 1960-90; Dist Dep, Grand MW Prince Hall Masons Inc, 1960-85; Northampton Co Bd Super, Eastville Magisterial Dist, teacher. **Orgs:** Exec bd, Northampton Co Br Nat Asn Advan Colored People, 1960-85; Northampton Co Voter's League, 1960-85; Northampton Ed Asn, 1960-85; Va Ed Asn, 1960-85; Nat Ed Asn, 1960-85; Eastern Shore VA & MD Baptist Asn, 1960-85; master, chmn bd deacons, First Baptist Church Capeville, 1960-85; chmn, scholar comm, Club Chautauqua, 1961-85; chaplain, Northampton Co Bd Super, 1982-85; chmn, Accomack-Northampton Co Planning Dist Comn. **Honors/Awds:** Teacher of the Year, Northampton High Sch, 1980-82. **Home Addr:** PO Box 554, Eastville, VA 23347-0554. **Business Addr:** Board Of Member, First Baptist Church-Capeville, 25283 Lankford Hwy, Cape Charles, VA 23310, **Business Phone:** (757)331-4315.

## BELL, CHRISTOPHER (CHRIS BELL)

Clergy. **Educ:** Western Ill Univ, BS, 1994, MS, 1996; Lincoln Christian Col & Sem, MDiv, 1998. **Career:** Celebration Community Church, pastor, 1996-2002; Baypoint Community Church, pastor, 2002-03; Naperville Christian Church, pastor, 2003-06; Checkmate Tactical Systs, owner & head instr, 1994-08; Orchard, team, 2006-08; Ridge Faith Community, pastor, 2008-; Chris Bell Int, owner & chief instr, 2009-. **Business Addr:** Pastor, Naperville Christian Church, 25W530 75th St, Naperville, IL 60565-1547, **Business Phone:** (630)983-5600.

## BELL, COBY SCOTT

Actor. **Personal:** Born May 11, 1975, Orange County, CA; son of Michel; married Aviss Pinkney; children: Serrae, Jaena, Quinn & Eli. **Educ:** San Jose State Univ. **Career:** Reggae band, musician & songwriter; TV series: "Smart Guy", 1997; Buffy contre les vampires, 1997; Urgences, 1997; "ER: Good Touch, Bad Touch", 1997; "Buffy the Vampire Slayer: Reptile Boy", 1997; "LA Doctors", 1998; "ATF", 1999; New York 911, 1999-2005; "Third Watch", 1999; "Weakest Link", 2001; "Half & Half", 2005; "CSI: Miami", 2007; "The Game", 2006-14; "Archer", 2010; "Burn Notice", 2010-13; "Hot in Cleveland", 2014. Film: The Parent 'Hood, 1997; "Drifting Elegant", co-producer, 2006; Showdown at Area 51, 2007; Ball Don't Lie, 2008; Flowers and Weeds, 2008; Dream Street, 2010. **Orgs:** Mentor, Big Bros Am. **Home Addr:** , NY. **Business Addr:** Actor, c/o NBC, 30 Rockefeller Plz, New York, NY 10112.

## BELL, DARRYL M.

Actor. **Personal:** Born May 10, 1963, Chicago, IL; son of Travers J Jr. **Educ:** Syracuse Univ, attended 1986. **Career:** TV series: "A Different World", 1987-93; "Homeboys In Outer Space", 1996; "Cosby", 1997; "For Your Love", 1999; "Beverly Hills S.U.V.", 2004; "Househusbands of Hollywood", 2009. Films: School Daze, 1988; Mr. Write, 1994; New Jersey Turnpikes, 1999; Brother, 2000; The Dark Party, 2013. **Orgs:** Alpha Phi Alpha Fraternity fictional fraternity. **Special Achievements:** Was awarded the Chancellor's Citation from Syracuse for prominent alumni. **Business Addr:** Actor, 1750 S Hauser Blvd, Los Angeles, CA 90019.

## BELL, DEREK NATHANIEL

Baseball player. **Personal:** Born Dec 11, 1968, Tampa, FL. **Career:** Baseball player (retired); Toronto Blue Jays, outfielder, 1991-92; San Diego Padres, outfielder, 1993-94; Houston Astros, outfielder, 1995-99; New York Mets, outfielder, 2000; Pittsburgh Pirates, outfielder, 2001. **Honors/Awds:** Most Valuable Player Award, South Atlantic League Myrtle Beach Blue Jays, 1988; Most Valuable Player Award, Int League, 1991; Minor League Player of the Year, Baseball Am Mag, 1991; World Series champion, 1992.

## BELL, DORIS E.

Educator, school administrator, nurse. **Personal:** Born Nov 25, 1938, Oak Ridge, MO; daughter of James W Lenox and Oma A Wilson Lenox; married Charles A. **Educ:** Harris Teachers Col, AA, 1957; Homer G Phillips Hosp Sch Nursing, dipl, 1960; Wash Univ, BSN, 1963, MSN, 1965; St Louis Univ, PhD, 1979. **Career:** Barnes Hosp, staff nurse, 1960-63; St Luke Hosp, staff nurse, 1963; MSR Baptist Hosp, staff nurse, 1964-65; KAS Neurol Inst, dir, nursing serv, 1965-69; Marymont Col, psychiat nurse inr, 1967-68; Res Hosp, ment health crd, 1969-70; SIUE Sch Nursing, psychiat nurse inr, 1970-72, inr, crd, psychiat ment health nursing, 1972-73, asst prof, 1973-81, assoc prof, 1981-88, prof, nursing, 1988-2004, chairperson area II nursing, prof emer, currently; St Louis Univ Med Sch, vis fac, 1981-2004; E Cent COT Col, inr, 1981-2004. **Orgs:** Am Asn Personnel & Guid; Am Asn Univ Profs; Am Nurses Asn; Nat League Nursing; Sigma Phi Omega; Black Nurses Asn; MSR Nurses Asn; Sigma Theta Tau, Delta Lambda Chap; Asn Black Fac Higher Educ; Phi Kappa Phi;Fel Ill Comt Black Concerns Higher Educ, Acad Admin, 1985-86. **Home Addr:** 5249 Longhorn Trl, Florissant, MO 63033, **Home Phone:** (314)355-0047. **Business Addr:** Professor of Nursing, Southern Illinois University, 1220 Lincoln Dr, Edwardsvillie, IL 62901, **Business Phone:** (618)453-2121.

**BELL, EDNA R.**
Government official. **Personal:** Born Mar 9, 1944, Detroit, MI; daughter of Theodore and Edna Rush; married James; children: Alisha Y & Sonja. **Educ:** Wayne State Univ, BS, 1989. **Career:** Commissioner (retired); Mich Bell Phone Co, mgr; Wayne County Govt, comnr, 1999-2002. **Orgs:** Chair, Environ Task Force, Southeastern Mich Coun Gov; vice chair econ & sustainable leadership team, Nat Asn Counties; Nat Orgn Black County Officials; bd dir, Boscoe Home Boys; Nat Alliance Black Educr; Nat Asn Negro Bus Prof Women; Optimist Club Cent Detroit; bd dir, Metro Detroit YWCA. **Home Addr:** 9439 Cloverlawn St, Detroit, MI 48204-2759, **Home Phone:** (313)834-0492. **Business Addr:** MI.

**BELL, ELDRIN A.**
Civil servant, government official. **Personal:** Born GA; married Kathy Pepino Guarini; children: Terry, Elizabeth, Terry, Ashley, Michael, Val, Albert, Adrion, Allyson, Gregory & Justin. **Educ:** Morris Brown Col, Atlanta, GA; Ga State; Atlanta Univ; Harvard Univ Law Sch; Northwestern Univ Traffic Inst. **Career:** Police Chief (retired), govt officer; Atlanta Police Dept, police chief, 1990; Clayton County Bd Comnrs, actg dir planning, chmn, 2004-. **Orgs:** Gate City Bar Asn; Nat Org Black Law Enforcement Officers; Ga Int Law Enforcement Exchange; Clayton County Nat Asn Advan Colored People; Govs Martin Luther King Holiday Comn; minister, Salem Baptist Church, Atlanta. **Home Addr:** 2600 Creek Indian Trl, Jonesboro, GA 30236-4006, **Home Phone:** (770)210-3532. **Business Addr:** Chairman, Clayton County Board of Commissioners, 121 S McDonough St County Courthouse, Jonesboro, GA 30236, **Business Phone:** (770)477-3208.

**BELL, DR. ELLA L. J. EDMONSON**
Educator. **Educ:** Mills Col Educ, BA, elem educ, 1971; Columbia Univ, MA, urban educ, 1973; Case Western Res Univ, PhD, orgn behav, 1987. **Career:** Univ NC, Charlotte, Belk Col Bus Admin, assoc prof orgn behav; Mass Inst Technol, Sloan Sch Mgt, asst prof orgn studies; Yale's Sch Mgt, fac, 1986-91; Univ Mass Amherst, 1990-91; Radcliffe Col, Bunting Inst, vis scholar; Harvard Univ, vis scholar; Salomon Smith Barney, consult; Proctor & Gamble, consult; Gen Elec, consult; Merridan Bank, consult; Gen Foods, consult; Southern New Eng Tel Co, consult; New York Pub Libr, consult; United Way Serv, consult; Dept Labor, consult; Union County Pub Schs & Loyola Col, consult; Tuck Sch Bus, Dartmouth, assoc prof bus admin, currently; Work balance, inquiring issues, currently. **Orgs:** Founder & pres, ASCENT-Leading Multicultural Women to Top, currently. **Special Achievements:** Co-author, Our Separate Ways, Black and White Women and the Struggle for Professional Identity, 2001. **Business Addr:** Associate Professor, Business Administration, Tuck School of Business Dartmouth, 100 Tuck Hall, Hanover, NH 03755, **Business Phone:** (603)646-0619.

**BELL, GEORGE**
Administrator. **Personal:** Born Pittsburgh, PA; children: George Jr, Christian & Kofi. **Educ:** Cheyney State Col, BS; Univ Detroit, MA. **Career:** Friends Select Sch Phila, teacher; Philadelphia Pub Schs, teacher; Harvou-Act Inc NYC, actg dir; United Ch Christ, asst to dir & prog coord comn racial justice; Shaw Col, chmn, div soc sci; Mayor City Detroit, exec asst. **Orgs:** Dir, Child & Family Ctr, City Detroit; chmn, Reg One Bd Educ, City Detroit; pres, Central Bd Educ, City Detroit; chmn, bd trustee, Wayne Co Comm Col. **Home Addr:** 495 W Willis, Detroit, MI 48202.

**BELL, GEORGE ANTONIO (JORGE ANTONIO BELL MATHEY)**
Baseball player. **Personal:** Born Oct 21, 1959, San Pedro de Macoris; married Marie Louisa Beguero; children: Christopher & George Jr; married Melida; children: Dean, Shadelyn, Michael & Brainel. **Career:** Baseball player (retired); Toronto Blue Jays, outfielder, 1981, 1983-90; Chicago Cubs, outfielder, 1991; Chicago White Sox, 1992-93. **Home Addr:** Bario Rest Cle T Suite 179, San Pedro de Macoris809.

**BELL, GORDON PHILIP**
Executive, financial manager. **Personal:** Born Jan 1, 1961, Brooklyn, NY; son of Elver Joseph Jr and Betty Ann; married Sherrie Curette; children: Dandridge & Elver III. **Educ:** Harvard Col, AB, 1983; Univ Mex, rotary scholar, 1984; Harvard Bus Sch, MBA, 1988; Chartered Financial Analyst, 1993. **Career:** Lehman Bros, trader, 1988-90; Prudential Capital Corp, vres, 1990-93; UCP, asset mgr, prin, 1993-97; JP Morgan, client adv, 1997-98; Citi group Asset Mgt, Salomon Smith Barney, dir, vpres, portfolio mgr, 1999-; Insts & High Net-worth Persons Pvt Portfolio Group, vpres, portfolio mgr & dir; Legacy Growth Partners, LLC, sr advisor, 2004-. **Orgs:** Asn Investment Mgt & Res, 1993-; NY Soc Security Anal, 1993-; bd, Lit Partners, 1998-; bd, Rudel Scholar Fund, 1998-; bd, Gen Hosp, 2003-; Foreign Rels; bd mem, Literacy Partners. **Honors/Awds:** The 40 Achievers Under 40, Network J, 2001; hon AB, Harv Col. **Business Addr:** Director, Portfolio Manager, Citi Group, 399 Pk Ave 4th Fl, New York, NY 10022, **Business Phone:** (212)559-0880.

**BELL, GREG**
Labor activist, secretary (office). **Career:** Bakery, Confectionery, Tobacco Workers & Grain Millers Int Union, Local 232, financial secy, 2004; Am Postal Workers Union, Indust Rel, dir, 1995, exec vpres, 2010; Am Fedn Labor & Cong Indust Orgn. **Orgs:** Pres, Philadelphia PA Area Local; chmn, Nat Presidents Conf; Rank-&-File Bargaining Adv Comt, 1987, 1990, 1994, pres, NALC; pres, Mail Handlers Union. **Business Addr:** Director Industrial Relations, Executive Vice President, American Postal Workers Union, 1300 L St NW, Washington, DC 20005-4128, **Business Phone:** (202)842-4200.

**BELL, HAROLD KEVIN**
Radio host, association executive. **Personal:** Born May 21, 1938, Washington, DC; son of Alfred and Mattie; married Hatti Thomas. **Educ:** Winston-Salem State Univ, attended 1963. **Career:** United Planning Orgn, 1964-66; DC Recreation Dept, Roving Leader Prog, 1966-69; Dept Defense, sports & recreation specialist, 1969-71; Proj Build, job placement specialist, 1971-74; Hb Sports Promotions & Mkt Inc, founder & pres, 1972-95, consult; WOOK Radio, sportscaster & talkshow host, 1974-78; Anheuser-Bush, mkt & sports rep, 1978-80; Nike Shoes, sports promotions rep, 1980-82; WUST Radio, sports dir & talk show host, 1986-94; WINX Radio, sportscaster & talk show host, currently; Kids Trouble, pres & founder, currently. **Orgs:** Founder, Hillcrest C's Ctr Saturday Prog, 1969; coordr, Send A Kid To Camp, 1970; founder, first halfway house juv delinquents amilitary base, "Bolling Boys Base", 1971; media coordr, Nat Asn Advan Colored People, 1976; consult, SE Youth Develop Prog, 1979; consult & celebrity fund raiser, United Negro Col Fund, 1980; bd mem, Nat Jr Tennis League, 1982; bd mem, Sonny Hill/John Chaney Summer League, 1984; bd mem, DC Sch Syst Community Task Force, 1988. **Honors/Awds:** Cited in Congressional Record by Rep Louis Stokes, 1975; Washingtonian of the Year, Wash Mag, 1980; Cited for Work with the Youth, President Richard M. Nixon, 1970; Founder of First Half Way House, Dept Defense, 1971; Community Person of the Year, Phi Delta Kappa, Howard University, 1988; Image Award, Pioneering/San Francisco, 1995. **Special Achievements:** Media pioneer & First African-American to host and produce own radio sports talk show in Washington, DC, 1974; First to host and produce own TV sports special on NBC affiliate WRC-TV4, 1975; First sports media personality to create a media round table to discuss current issues in the sports world, by inviting radio, TV, and print media personalities to participate on "Inside Sports", once monthly; cited in Congressional record by Sen Bob Dole, 1994; Included in the Richard M. Nixon Library inYoba Linda, CA. **Home Addr:** 16010 Excalibur Rd Apt A109, Bowie, MD 20716-3930, **Home Phone:** (240)245-3008. **Business Addr:** President, Founder, Kids in Trouble, 2322 Wood Bark Lane, Suitland, MD 20746, **Business Phone:** (301)568-8036.

**BELL, HUBERT THOMAS**
Government official. **Personal:** Born Jul 9, 1942, Mobile, AL; son of Hubert Thomas Sr and Theresa; married Satwant Kaur; children: Naydja Maya, Nileah Shanti, Anthony Anand & Andrew Amrit. **Educ:** Ala State Univ, Montgomery, AL, BS, 1965. **Career:** Agt incharge, Vice Presidential Protective Div; Agt in charge, Honolulu, Hawaii, field office; US Secret Serv, Wash, DC, Off Invests, dep asst dir, Off Protective Operations, asst dir, Off Inspection, exec dir, Work Force Planning & diversity mgt; Progressive Govt Inst, Nuclear Regulatory Comn, inspector gen, 1996-. **Orgs:** Kappa Alpha Psi Fraternity, 1963-; vpres, Va chap, Region II, 1977-; Int Asn Chiefs Police, 1988-; pres, Fraternal Order Police, 1991; pres, Nat Org Black Law Enforcement Execs, 1994-95; bd dir, Nat Ctr Missing & Exploited C; past nat pres, Nat Org Black Women Law Enforcement; Nat Asn Regulatory Utility Comners. **Home Addr:** 5906 Reservoir Heights Ave, Alexandria, VA 22311-1010, **Home Phone:** (703)671-2556. **Business Addr:** Inspector General, US Government Nuclear Regulatory Commission, 11545 Rockville Pke, Rockville, MD 20852, **Business Phone:** (301)415-5930.

**BELL, JAMES A.**
Executive director, association executive, executive. **Personal:** Born Jun 4, 1948, Los Angeles, CA; son of Clyde and Mamie. **Educ:** Calif State Univ, Los Angeles, BA, acct. **Career:** Rockwell Int, acct, 1972, corp sr internal auditor, acct mgr, mgr gen & cost acct, 1996; Boeing Rocketdyne unit, Space Sta Elec Power Syst, dir bus mgt; Boeing Co, vpres contracts & pricing, space & commun, 1996-2000, sr vpres finance & corp controller, 2000-04, actg chief financial officer, 2003-12, exec vpres, 2003-12, exec vpres finance, 2004-, interiem pres & chief exec officer, corp pres, 2008-12, pres & chief financial officer, 2009-. **Orgs:** Joint Leadership Coun; bd dir, Chmn Audit Committe, Dow Chem Co, 2005-; bd dir, Chicago Infrastructure Trust; bd trustee, Rush Univ Med Ctr; dir, Joffrey Ballet; Chicago Urban League; dir, World Bus Chicago; Chicago Econ Club; New Leaders New Schs, bd dir, Boeing Co, 2004; trustee, Ctr Strategic & Int Studies Inc; dir, JP Morgan Chase & Co, 2011-. **Business Addr:** Executive Vice President of Finance, Boeing Co, 100 N Riverside Plz, Chicago, IL 60606-1596, **Business Phone:** (312)544-2000.

**BELL, JAMES L., JR.**
Civil engineer, government official. **Personal:** Born Aug 4, 1921, Buffalo, NY; son of James L Sr (deceased) and Madie G Nelson (deceased); married Jessal Holland; children: James L III. **Educ:** Howard Univ, BSCE, 1954; Univ Buffalo, cert mech engineering, 1949; Dept Transp Wash DC, cert bridge inspector, 1973. **Career:** Tenn Valley Authority, civil engr, div power opers, 1954-63, mech engr & asst mech maint supvr, Widows Creek Steam Plant, 1963-64, prin civil engr, div oil spill prev & control coordr, 1964-67; Tenn Valley Authority Off Power, chief bridge inspector, 1967-82; Air Pollution Control Bur, lowly secy, currently. **Orgs:** Chattanooga Engr Club; chmn, fel comt, Equal Empl Opport, United Way Comt chmn; Tenn Valley Authority Engrs Asn; Am Soc Civil Engr, Chattanooga Br, Tenn Valley Sect; Am Concrete Inst; Physiog Judge Chattanooga Area Regional Sci & Engineering Fair; engineering career guid couns, Chattanooga HS; chmn, Credit Com; bd dir, Chattanooga Tenn Valley Authority Employees Fed Credit Union; Tenn Valley Authority Chattanooga Community Rels Comt; keeper rec & seals, 5th dist Omega Psi Phi Frat Inc; basileus, Kappa Iota Chap, Omega Psi Phi Frat Inc; Dist Comnr, Cherokee Area Coun Boy Scouts Am; chmn, Planning Comn; Chattanooga Br Nat Asn Advan Colored People; bd dir, Chattanooga Hamilton Co Speech & Hearing Ctr; chmn, Indust Audiol Com; Ruling Elder Renaissance Presb Ch; pres, Chattanooga Chap Pan-Hellenic Coun Inc; Boy Scout Adv; Alpha Phi Omega Frat Boy Scouts Am; dist comnr, Cherokee Area Coun; mem-at-large, Merit Badge Coun; Chmn Vet Comt, Chattanooga Nat Asn Advan Colored People; Chattanooga Area Urban League; bd dir & bd secy, Chattanooga, Hamilton County Air Pollution Control Bur; bd mem, Interfaith Elderly Assistance Agency, 1989-; Chattanooga Afro-Am Mus; Chattanooga Sr Neighbors; bd mem, Chattanooga Memorial Soc. **Honors/Awds:** Silver Beaver Award; Arrowhead Honor Commissioners Key Award, Order Arrow; 35 yr Vet Award; People-to-People Award, Nat Engr Week Comt, 1984; Citation Plaque, Chattanooga State Tech Community Col, 1977; Service Recognition Plaque, Fairview Presbyterian Church, 1987; Recognition Plaque, Alpha Phi Omega Fraternity, 1978; Recognition/Certificate, Chattanooga Br, Am Soc Civil Engrs, 1984. **Home Addr:** 606 Mooremont Terr, Chattanooga, TN 37411-2924, **Home Phone:** (423)624-9648. **Business Addr:** Board Member, Air Pollution Control Bureau, 6125 Preservation Dr, Chattanooga, TN 37416, **Business Phone:** (423)643-5970.

**BELL, JANET SHARON**
College administrator, counselor. **Personal:** Born Jun 27, 1947, Chicago, IL; children: Lenny. **Educ:** Chicago State Univ, BS, educ, 1972; Ill State Univ, MS, educ, 1978. **Career:** Chicago Pub Sch, teacher, 1972-74; State Farm Ins, coordr, 1974-76; Ill State Univ, acad adv, 1981, counr spec serv prog, 1981-86, asst coordr minority stud serv, 1986-88, asst dir, financial aid off, 1988-92. **Orgs:** Ill Asn Educ Opportunity Prog Personnel, 1977-86; Mid-Am Asn Educ Opportunity Prog Personnel; vpres, Asn Black Acad Employ, 1985-87; Mid W Asn Stud Fin Aid Adminr; chmn, Community Rels Comt, Ill Asn Fin Aid Adminr, 1990-92; co-chair, Ill Coun Col Attendance, Prof Develop Comt; Ind State Bar Asn. **Home Addr:** 28 Gloucester Cir, Bloomington, IN 61704, **Home Phone:** (309)663-5629.

**BELL, JIMMY**
Educator. **Personal:** Born Jan 4, 1944, Indianola, MS; married Clara Mcgee; children: Sonya, Arlinda, Meredith & Rasheda. **Educ:** Miss Valley State Univ, BS, 1966; Miss State Univ, MA & ABD, 1969; NY Univ, Albany, 1978. **Career:** Miss Valley State Univ, Dept Sociol, chmn, 1969; Jackson State Univ, Dept Criminal Justice & Sociol, founding chair, prof, asst prof, 1970, vpres, criminal justice coordr, 1972-80, prof & interim chmn, currently; Jackson Police Dept, consult lectr, 1974-80; Lexington Bks DC Health, writer, 1977-79; Nat Coalition Community Researchers Inc, founder. **Orgs:** Nat fel Nat Inst Ment Health, 1966-70; dir res proj, SCAN, Indianola, Miss, 1969; consult, IT&T, 1970; chmn, Black Caucus Southern Sociol Soc, 1973; exec comm mem, Nat Asn Blacks Criminal Justice, 1973-76; consult, Nat Inst Law Enforcement, 1975-77. **Home Addr:** 1832 Northwood Cir, Jackson, MS 39213, **Home Phone:** (601)366-8590. **Business Addr:** Chairman, Criminology Professor, Jackson State University, 1400 John R Lynch St, Jackson, MS 39217, **Business Phone:** (601)979-2121.

**BELL, DR. JOSEPH N.**
Executive. **Personal:** Born Aug 15, 1948, Wilmington, NC; married Carolyn Hodges. **Educ:** Shaw Univ, BS, 1970; Univ GA; Armstrong St Col; Am Inst Banking; BSA. **Career:** Shaw Univ, hd lncch, 1970; Cental Trust Co, sr anal, 1971; Carver State Bank, exec vpres & cashier; Savannah City Coun, alderman-at-large. **Orgs:** Dir, Savannah Area C C; dir, Savannah Bus Leag; dir, Savannah Trbn; Am Cancer Soc; Grnbr C Ctr; Cit Adv Com Chthm Urban Trans; Chthm Co Asn Rtrd C; Savannah Area Mnrty Cntrctrs; Better Bus Bur; Nat Asn Advan Colored People; Omega Psi Phi Frat; Dcn tst Cnnrs Temp Bapt Ch; exec dir, Chatham Asn Educr. **Honors/Awds:** Man of the Year, Shaw Univ, 1969. **Home Addr:** 210 E Bolton St, Savannah, GA 31401, **Home Phone:** (912)232-3436. **Business Addr:** Executive Vice President, Carver State Bank, 701 Martin Luther King Jr Blvd, Savannah, GA 31415, **Business Phone:** (912)233-9971.

**BELL, KARL I.**
Banker. **Personal:** Born Jan 29, 1960, Atlanta, GA; son of Henry and Naomi; married Pamela; children: Alexis, Kristina & Cameron. **Educ:** Morehouse Col, BA, bus admin, 1981; Univ Wisc-Madison, MBA, fInance & mkt, 1983; Grad Sch Banking, 1997. **Career:** Lockheed Co, Ga, 1981; IBM Corp, 1982; NBD Bank, vpres, 1983-98; LaSalle/Stand Fed Bank, vpres, 1999-2004; Fifth Third Bank, vpres, sr managing dir, 2004-06; Invest Detroit, sr vpres, 2006-. **Orgs:** Bd dir, Southfield Symphony Orchestra, 1987-88; dir, Morehouse Alumni Asn, Detroit, 1988-90; pres, Urban Bankers Forum, 1994-; Detroit Econ Develop Task Force, 1994-95; trustee, New Detroit Inc, 1996-98; Mich Metro Girl Scout Coun, finance comn, 1997. **Honors/Awds:** Fel Consortium for Grad Sch Study, 1981; Student of the Year, Trust Co Bank, 1981; Banking School Fellow, Nat Asn Urban Bankers, 1994. **Home Addr:** 4580 Rolling Ridge Rd, West Bloomfield, MI 48323-3340, **Home Phone:** (248)851-5076. **Business Addr:** Senior Vice President, Invest Detroit, 600 Renaissance Ctr Suite 1710, Detroit, MI 48243-1802, **Business Phone:** (313)259-6368.

**BELL, DR. KATIE ROBERSON**
Librarian, educator. **Personal:** Born Jun 14, 1936, Birmingham, AL; daughter of Alex and Blanche Davis; married Leroy Bell Jr; children: Cheryl Kaye, Mada Carol & Janet E. **Educ:** Ala State Col, BS, 1956, EdS, 1977; Wayne State Univ, MSLA, 1973; Univ Ala, PhD, 1982. **Career:** Educator, librarian (retired), board member; Tuskegee Inst HS, libr, 1956-59; Parker HS, asst libr, 1959-70, libr, 1970-73; AL State Univ, asst ref libr, 1973-74, coordr, user serv, 1974-75, coordr, libr educ, 1975-, retired; So AL Reg Inserv Educ Ctr, dir, 1985; AL State Univ, prof libr educ, 1985; Montgomery City-Co Pub Libr, trustee, libr Bd, currently. **Orgs:** Consult, ESAA Task Force ASU & Mobile Sch Syst, 1979-82; Comt Tutorial Prog & links Inc, 1982-84; evaluator Nat Coun Accreditation Teacher Educ, 1983-; bd mem, pres elect AL Instrnl Media Asn, 1984-; counr, Nu Epsilon Chap Kappa Delta Pi, 1984-; evaluator S Asn Schs & Cols, 1985-; bd mem, Montgomery Comn Coun United Way, 1985-; area dir, Links Inc. southern area dir, 1991-94; Ala Pub Libr Serv. **Honors/Awds:** Certificate Honor, Birmingham Classroom Teachers Asn, 1970; Educator of the Year Area of Instructional Leadership, Univ AL, 1981; Identification Activities Staff Capstone Journal, 1982; Develop Progs Sec Educ Teachers; Women Distinction Luncheon, 2005. **Home Addr:** 3613 Winterset Ct, Montgomery, AL 36111-3361, **Home Phone:** (334)284-1800. **Business Addr:** Library Board of Trustee, Montgomery City County Public Library, PO Box 1950, Montgomery, AL 36102-1950, **Business Phone:** (334)240-4300.

**BELL, KENDRELL ALEXANDER**
Football player. **Personal:** Born Jul 2, 1980, Augusta, GA; son of C B Jim Marsalis; married Tahira Locke; children: Caleb. **Educ:** Univ Ga, child & family develop. **Career:** Football player (retired); Pittsburgh Steelers, right inside linebacker, 2001-04, linebacker, 2002; Kans City Chiefs, right outside linebacker, 2005-07. **Honors/Awds:** Defensive Rookie of the Year, Nat Football League, 2001; Steeler Rookie of the Year, 2001; Joe Greene Great Performance Award, 2001; Pro Bowl,

2001. **Home Addr:** 2501 S Ocean Dr Apt 204, Hollywood, FL 33019-2665.

**BELL, REV. KENNETH M, SR.** See Obituaries Section.

**BELL, LAWRENCE A.**
Government official, president (organization). **Educ:** Univ Md, College Park, BA, 1983. **Career:** Baltimore City Coun, pres, 1995-99; Radio 860 AM WBGR, The Lawrence Bell Show, host, currently. **Orgs:** Founder & pres, Nat Black Anti-Defamation League; Baltimore Worldwide Speakers Bur; Southern Christian Leadership Conf. **Honors/Awds:** Baltimore Best Councilman, Baltimore Mag, 1994. **Special Achievements:** Ebony Magazine named Bell as one of "30 leaders of the future", 1988; Youngest person ever elected as City Council President. **Business Addr:** President, Founder, National Black Anti-Defamation League, 4410 Mass Ave NW Suite 209, Washington, DC 20016-0000, **Business Phone:** (800)999-9999.

**BELL, LAWRENCE F.**
Business owner. **Personal:** Born Dec 1, 1958, Philadelphia, PA; son of Marian Green and Furman. **Educ:** Temple Univ, Pa, BBA, 1979; Wharton Sch, Univ Pa, MBA, 1989. **Career:** Mellon Bank, sr auditor, 1979-81; PPG Indust, sr auditor, 1981-87; IU Int, audit supvr, 1987-88; Wharton Sch, sr consult, 1988-89; Bell & Assocs, owner, 1989; Pepsi Cola, finance mgr, 1991-94. **Orgs:** Treas, Uptown Community Resource Ctr, 1987; mgr, W Philadelphia Enterprise Ctr, 1989-, partnership, 1995; treas, W Philadelphia Neighborhood Enterprise Ctr, 1990. **Honors/Awds:** Black Accountant's Entreprenuer of the Year, 1991. **Home Addr:** 5625 Montrose St, Philadelphia, PA 19143, **Home Phone:** (215)476-6164.

**BELL, REV. LEON**
Clergy, manager, business owner. **Personal:** Born Jul 14, 1930, Liberty, MS. **Educ:** Miss Bapt Sem, ThB, 1957; Jackson State Univ, BS, 1959; Wheaton Col, pursued grad studies, 1966; Univ Southern Miss, MS, coun & eng, 1969; Univ Southern Miss, postgrad studies, eng & writing. **Career:** Springhill Priestly Chap Fairview Bapt Church, Pilgrim Br Bapt Church, Monticello First Bapt, pastor, 1954-68; Miss Baptist Sem, state dirvacation Bible schs, 1958-59; MS Bapt Sem, dean cent ctr, 1959-67; Jackson State Univ, chaplain, 1965-69, dir stud actvts, 1967-69, relig adv, instr, 1969-75; Hyde Pk Bapt Churches, pastor, 1967-91; New Mt Zion Baptist Church, pastor, 1969-; Jackson Dist Mission Bapt Asn, moderator, 1976-82; Miss Baptist Cong Christian Educ, instr bible hist; Bell's Robes & Worship Aids, proprietor & mgr, currently. **Orgs:** Chmn, Jackson Bicent City-wide Simultan Rev, 1976; org Bell's All-Faith Lit Supplies, 1975; chmn, Curric Com Convert Natchez Jr Col into four yrs Bible Col, 1976; moderator, Jackson Dist Mission Bapt Asn, 1976-82, 1994-96; Jackson Ministrial Allian; bd mem, Miss Bapt Sem; vpres, Gen Bapt State Conv Miss; dir, Youth Oratorical & Musical Contest, Gen Missionary Bapt State Conv Miss, 1993-; asst dir, Oratorical Contest, Nat Baptist Conv, USA Inc, 1980-94; VFW; Nat Asn Advan Colored People; Masons; Smithsonian Inst; bd mem, Southern Christian Leadership Conf, Jackson Mschap, 1995-; instr homiletics, Metropolitan Ministerial Fel Jackson Miss, 1996-. **Honors/Awds:** Ambass Life Mag, 1966; Miss Baptist Sem, Honorary DDiv, 1973; Most Outstanding Minister Community Affairs, Jackson Mississippi Chap Nat Bus League, 1985. **Special Achievements:** Author: "Top Notch Introductory Essays all Occasions, 1983"; "Prog Outlines Spec Occasions Church, 1987". **Home Addr:** 4322 Beacon Pl, Jackson, MS 39213, **Home Phone:** (601)362-7279. **Business Addr:** Owner, Bell's Robes & Worship Aids, 3200 Medgar Evers Blvd, Jackson, MS 39283, **Business Phone:** (601)982-7112.

**BELL, DR. MARION L.**
Educator. **Educ:** BS, MEd, EdD. **Career:** Prof (retired); Wayne State Univ, Bennett Col, VA Tech; Univ Nev, Las Vegas, prof; Africa Univ, Zimbabwe, Africa, prof. **Orgs:** Pres, Nat Alumnae Asn; asst, Western Reg Rep & vpres, pub Rels, Nat Alumni Coun, United Negro Col Fund, 2006-. **Home Addr:** 8757 Castle View Ave, Las vegas, NV 89129. **Business Addr:** President, Bennett College, 8757 Castle View Ave, Las Vegas, NV 89129, **Business Phone:** (702)255-6987.

**BELL, MELVYN CLARENCE**
Executive. **Personal:** Born Dec 13, 1944, Los Angeles, CA; married Eliza Ann Johnson. **Educ:** Calif State Univ, Los Angeles, BS, 1971; Univ Southern Calif, MBA, 1973. **Career:** Security Pac Nat Bank, vpres, 1971; KFOX Radio Inc, co-owner & vpres, 1979; Los Angeles Community Develop Bank; Comerica Bank Calif, Long Beach, Calif, vpres. **Orgs:** Univ Soc Cal MBA Asn; Nat Asn Black MBAs; Kappa Alpha Psi Fraternity; Nat Asn Advan Colored People; Los Angeles Urban League; Los Angeles Black Bus Mens Asn; bd dir, Los Angeles Soc Area Boys Club; pres, Kappa Alpha Psi Fraternity Upsilon Chap Los Angeles. **Home Addr:** 5032 Inadale Ave, Los Angeles, CA 90043.

**BELL, MICHAEL P.**
Firefighter. **Personal:** Born Jan 1, 1955, LA; son of Norman and Ora. **Educ:** Univ Toledo, BA, 1978. **Career:** Toledo Fire Dept, Water Rescue Diver, Fire Recruiter, Paramedic Shift Supr & Training Officer, Training Capt, 1980-90, chief, 1990-2007; Joint Reg Terrorism Task Force, Lucas County, Ohio, chmn, 2001-; Ohio Fire Dept, ohio fire marshall, 2007-; City Toledo, OH, Mayor, 2010-14. **Orgs:** True Vine Baptist Church Toledo; Joint Terrorism Task Force, Lucas Co, OH, 2001-; life mem, Nat Asn Advan Colored People; Boys & Girls Club; Am Red Cross; Am Liver Found; Boy Scouts Am & Salvation Army; Am Cancer Soc; Int Fire Chief's Asn; True Vine Missionary Baptist Church. **Honors/Awds:** President's Recognition Award, Int Asn Fire Chiefs, 2000; Woodward HS Hall of Fame; Boys and Girls Club of Toledo's Hall of Fame. **Special Achievements:** Selected to carry the Olympic Torch in June 1996 through the City of Toledo as a community leader; first African-American to be appointed to the position of Chief in the history of the Toledo fire service; First such person to helm a major fire department in the state of Ohio; First wave of firefighters hired after the department was placed under a consent decree to increase its minority staffing levels. **Business Addr:** Fire Marshall, Ohio Fire Dept, 8895 E Main St, Reynoldsburg, OH 43068, **Business Phone:** (614)752-8200.

**BELL, MYRON COREY**
Football coach, football player. **Personal:** Born Sep 15, 1971, Toledo, OH; children: Corey & Kennedy. **Educ:** Mich State Univ, grad. **Career:** Football player (retired), football coach; Pittsburgh Steelers, 1994, 2000, strong safety, 1995, 1997, defensive back, 1996, strong safety, 2001; Cincinnati Bengals, defensive back, 1998; strong safety, 1999; Northside Christian Acad, asst coach, currently; W Mecklenburg High Sch, security guard, currently. **Orgs:** City Toledo. **Honors/Awds:** All-American 1st team Big Ten; All-American 1st team in the state of Ohio; Ohio Hall of Fame. **Business Addr:** Assistant Coach, Northside Christian Academy, 333 Jeremiah Blvd, Charlotte, NC 28262, **Business Phone:** (704)596-4074.

**BELL, NGOZI O.**
Executive, executive director. **Personal:** Born May 10, 1967, Enugu; daughter of E Obikwerc; married Dwane A; children: Yamira & Zaneta. **Educ:** Univ Port Harcourt, Nigeria, BS, physics & electronics, 1988; Fla State Univ, Col Eng, MS, elec engineering, 1992. **Career:** Fla Agr & Mech Univ, Col Eng, res asst, 1990-92; RW Beck, consult engr, 1992-95; AT&T Bell Labs, Lucent Technol, design engr, 1995-97, mkt mgr, 1997-2000; Agere Systs, optical networking solutions group, sr mkt mgr, 2001, Access & Transp Group, segment mgr, 2002, Enterprise & Networking Div, dir mkt, 2004-07, dir, 2007-09; Birchmere Ventures, vpres, 2008; Fed Govt, Small Businesses, regional III advocate, 2010-. **Orgs:** Zita Sigma Hon Soc, 1984-88; vpres, Nat Asn Physics Studs, 1985-86, pres, 1986-88; chmn, Sch Involv Lucent Tech, 1996-97; co-chmn, Lucent Diversity Comt, 1997-; bd mem, Camp Pl, Allentown, 1997-; co founder, Nigerian Am orgn, 2005. **Home Addr:** 3781 Ranee St, Easton, PA 18045-3038, **Home Phone:** (610)438-2257. **Business Addr:** Vice President, Birchmere Ventures, 2835 E Carson St Suite 208, Pittsburgh, PA 15203, **Business Phone:** (412)322-3300.

**BELL, RICKY (RICARDO BELL)**
Singer, entertainer. **Personal:** Born Sep 18, 1967, Roxbury, MA; son of Daniel and Dorothy. **Career:** Albums: Hey There Lonely Girl; School; One More Day; I'm Still In Love With You; All for Love, 1985; Christmas All Over the World, 1985; Heart Break, 1989; Poision, 1990; WBBD-Boot city, 1991; Above the Rim, 1993; Hootie Mack, 1993; Ricardo Campana, 2000; BBD, 2001; When Will I See You Smile Again; Songs: "The Album", 2000; "Spanish Fly"; "Please Don't Cry"; "Pretty Little Girl"; " Bobby"; New Edition, founder & singer, 1983-; Bell Biv Devoe, soloist; Featured songs: Candy; Phenomenon; CD Baby, 2000; So So Def/Geffen, 2008. **Honors/Awds:** Golden Note Award, Am Soc Composers, Authors & Publishers, 2008. **Special Achievements:** Debut album Poison reached Billboard's Top Ten, 1990. **Business Addr:** Singer, c o MCA Records Inc, 70 Universal City Plaza Fl 3, Universal City, CA 91608, **Business Phone:** (818)777-4000.

**BELL, DR. ROBERT L.**
Physician. **Personal:** Born May 10, 1934, Bastrop, LA; married Mattye M; children: Allison E & Millicent P. **Educ:** Tex Southern Univ, BA, 1953; Univ Tex, MA, 1955, PhD, 1961; Univ Tex Sch Pub Health, MPH, 1980. **Career:** Va Hosp Waco, clin psychologist, 1961-66; Baylor Univ, adj prof psychol, 1965-66; Va Hosp, psychologist, 1966-72; Rice Univ, consult, 1970-72; Va Hosp Houston Drug Abuse Prog, asst dir, 1970-72; Tex Southern Univ, assoc prof, 1972; Riverside Gen Hosp Drug Abuse Prog, psychologist, 1972; Coun Ctr Vassar Col, clin psychologist, 1972-73; Rice Univ Houston, dir stud advising & prof psychol, 1973-79, adj prof, 1979-80; Pvt Pract, clin psychol, currently. **Orgs:** Asn Black Psychologists; Am Psychol Asn; SW Psychol Asn; Tex Psychol Asn; Houston Psychol Asn; Am Group Psychother Asn; Houston Group Psychother Soc; SW Inst Personal & Orgn Develop; Nat Inst Appl Behav Scis; Alpha Phi Alpha Fraternity; Ethnic Arts Ctr Hope Develop Inc. **Honors/Awds:** Super Performance Award, Vets Admin, 1964; Special Service Performance Award, Vets Admin, 1968; Cattell Fund Award, Am Psychol Asn, 1969; Outstanding Alumnus Award, Tex Southern Univ, 1972. **Business Addr:** Clinical Psychologist, 11410 Ribstone Dr, Houston, TX 77016.

**BELL, ROBERT MACK**
Judge. **Personal:** Born Jul 6, 1943, Rocky Mount, NC. **Educ:** Dunbar High Sch, Baltimore, MD; Morgan State Col, BA, hist & polit sci, 1966; Harvard Univ Law Sch, JD, 1969. **Career:** Piper & Marbury, assoc, 1969-74; Dist Ct MD, Dist 1, Baltimore City, assoc judge, 1975-80; Baltimore City Circuit Ct, 8th Judicial Circuit, assoc judg, 1980-84; Md Ct Appeals, 6th Appellate Circuit, judge, 1991-, chief judge, 1996-, Md Judicial Conf Judicial Compensation Comt, 1993-, chmn, 1996-, Judicial Coun, chmn, 2000, Exec Comt, mem, 1996-2000, Dept Juv Serv, Judges Masters & Juv Justice Comt, mem, 1996-, Comt Bldg Pub Trust & Confidence Justice Syst, chmn, 1998-99, State Comn Criminal Sentencing Policy, mem, 1999-2000, Technol Oversight Bd, chmn, 1999-, Juv Justice Coord Coun, chmn, 2000-02, Pub Trust & Confidence Implementation Comt, 2000-, Judicial Cabinet, chmn, 2000-; Task Force Study Criminal Offender Monitoring Global Positioning Systs, 2004-05; Conf Chief Justices, first vpres, 2004-05, pres elect, 2005-06, pres, 2006-07. **Orgs:** Bd dir, Legal Aid Bur; grader MD St Bar Examr, 1973-75; bd dir, Afro Am Newspaper, 1973-74; bd dir, Neighborhood Adolescent & Young Adult Drug Prog Inc, 1974-75; Grievance Comt, exec comt & chmn Baltimore City Bar Asn; Md State Bar Asn; chmn, Bar Asn; Bail Bond Comn, 1973-77; Ct Appeals Standing Comt Rules Pract & Procedure, 1977-82; bd dir, Villa Julie Col, 1978-85; Am Bar Asn; Nat Bar Asn; Monumental City Bar Asn; bd dir, Sojourner-Douglass Col, 1982-91; bd dir, Comn Revise Annotated Provident Hosp, 1983-84; African-Am Community Found, bd dir, 1994-; Univ Md Sch Law, Bd Visitor, 1994-; chmn, Advan Sci & Technol Adjudication Resource Ctr; bd trustee, Johns Hopkins Med, 2000-; Adv Bd, chmn, Md Mediation & Conflict Resolution Off, 2001-; State Comn Pub Safety Technol & Critical Infrastructure, 2002-05; Task Force Child Welfare Syst Accountability, 2003-04; bd dir, Nat Ctr State Courts, 2004-05; Alpha Phi Omega. **Home Addr:** 2528 E Chase St, Baltimore, MD 21213. **Business Addr:** Chief Judge, Md Ct Appeals, 634 Courthouse E 111 N Calvert St, Baltimore, MD 21202, **Business Phone:** (410)333-6396.

**BELL, ROBERT WESLEY**
Construction worker. **Personal:** Born Apr 10, 1918, Bethlehem, GA; married Louvenia Smith. **Educ:** Welders & Mech Sch, attended 1940. **Career:** Afro Am Life Ins Co, agt, 1955-75; State Ga, selective serv, 1972-; Am Legion, first black dist domdr, 1973-74; first black chmn c & youth div, 1974-80; Econ Opportunity Atlanta, mem fin comn, 1980-84; Buford City Sch, elected mem bd educr, 1981-85, vice chmn bd educr; People's Bank Buford, first black mem bd dir, 1983-85; Bell Bros Construct Co, part owner. **Orgs:** Deacon bd, Poplar Hill Baptist Church, 1940-85; church clerk, Poplar Hill Baptist Church, 1950-85; supt, Sunday Sch Poplar Hill Baptist Church, 1950-85; asst clerk, Hopewell Baptist Asn, 1974-85; staff mem, Boys State Am Legion, 1976-85; appt mem, Planning & Zoning City Buford, 1979-85; chmn, Boy Scouts State Ga, 1980-82; Gwinnett Clean & Beautiful Citizens Bd, Gwinnett County, 1980-83; am chmn, Am Legion State Ga, 1982-85. **Honors/Awds:** National Achievement Award, Nat Am Legion, 1966; Man of the Year, Buford Comm Orgn, 1974; Gwinnett Clean & Beautiful Award, Gwinnett County Citizens Bd, 1980; Asiatic Pacific Service Medal, AUS; World War II Victory Medal, AUS; Am Service Medal, AUS; European-African Middle East Service Medal & Two Bronze Stars, AUS. **Home Addr:** 620 Bona Rd, Buford, GA 30518, **Home Phone:** (678)945-9443.

**BELL, ROSALIND NANETTE**
Marketing executive, vice president (organization). **Personal:** Born Dec 1, 1958, Panama City, FL; daughter of Stanley J and Bettye Price; married Jacob R Miles III. **Educ:** Wash Univ, BA, bus, 1980; Northwestern Univ, MBA, bus admin, 1981. **Career:** Dow Chem, Merrell Dow Pharmaceut, sls, asst prod mgr, 1981-84; Kraft Foods, Dairy Grp, asst prodmgr, assoc prod mgr, 1984-86; Pillsbury Co, assoc prod mgr, pizza new prod develop, 1986-88, sr mkt mgr, 1991-95, grp mktg, 1996-97; Gillette, Lustrasilk div, from assoc prod mgr to sr prod mgr, actg dir, 1988-91; Cult MGR, Exchange Gallery, mng dir, 1991; Six Flags Amusement Parks, vp mkt, 1997-98; Avado Brands Inc, vpres mkt, 1998-99; optel inc, vpres mkt, 1999-; Urban cool network inc, dir, 1999, mkt consul, 2000-. **Orgs:** bd dirs, Arlington Conv & Visitors Bur, 1997-78; Jr League, Minneapolis; Nat assn Black MBA, 1981-87; Minneapolis & St Paul Chap Links; Ordway Theater Adv comn, 1998-99; Family & C's Serv; Hennpin Unit AM Cancer soc, 1997. **Honors/Awds:** Merrill Dow-Pace Setter Award; Gillette-Marketing Excellence Award, 1990; Dell-Q2 FY04 Healthcare Marketing Employee of the Quarter; Dell-Q3 FY04 Public Marketing Employee of the Quarter; Dell-Q3 FY05 Public Sector Peer-to-Peer Award; Dell-Q2 FY05 K12 Marketing Employee of the Quarter; Dell-Q3 FY05 Marketing Employee of the Quarter; Dell-Q3 FY05 Public Sector Marketing on the Spot Award; Dell-FY05 K12 Marketing Employee of the Year; Dell-FY05 Impact Award; Dell-FY06 Office of the Chair & Dell Microsoft Summit Meeting, 2005; Dell-FY06 MVP Channel Marketing Award; Dell-FY06 K12 Marketing Employee of the Year; Dell-Q4 FY07, Vice President Impact Award; Dell Value Proposition Community Service Award; Dell-Q1 FY09 Certificate of Excellence. **Home Addr:** 3416 Hightimber Dr, Grapevine, TX 76051-6334, **Home Phone:** (817)329-6259. **Business Addr:** Director, Sandlot Solutions, 1701 River Run Suite 902, Ft Worth Tex, TX 76107, **Business Phone:** (800)370-1393.

**BELL, SANDRA WATSON**
Executive, vice president (organization). **Personal:** Born May 30, 1955, San Francisco, CA; daughter of Adell Rogers Watson; married Phillip; children: Phillip Jr & Lauren. **Educ:** San Jose State Univ, San Jose, CA, BS, bus admin, 1976. **Career:** Fairchild, Mountain View, Calif, mgr syst software, 1976-83; Masstor Systs, Santa Clara, Calif, vpres human resources & admin, pres, data ctr, mgr, 1983, dir, admin & corp data ctr, currently; Bay Equity LLC, sr mortgage loan officer. **Home Addr:** 120 Tehama Ct, San Bruno, CA 94066, **Home Phone:** (650)794-1646. **Business Addr:** Director of Administration & Corporate Center, Masstor Systems Corp, 5200 Great Am Pkwy, Santa Clara, CA 95052-8017, **Business Phone:** (408)988-1008.

**BELL, SHEILA TRICE**
Lawyer, executive, vice president (organization). **Personal:** Born Aug 25, 1949, Pittsburgh, PA; daughter of William Benjamin and Mildred Moore; married Howard W Jr; children: Mayet Maria, Annora Alicia & William Howard. **Educ:** Wellesley Col, BA, biol sci, 1971; Harvard Law Sch, JD, 1974. **Career:** Pine Manor Jr Col, fac mem, 1972-74; Hutchins & Wheeler, assoc lawyer, 1973-77; Pvt Legal Prac, atty, 1977-79; Fisk Univ, univ coun, 1979-83; J Col & Univ Law, ed bd, 1982-83; Northern Ky Univ, actg univ coun & affirmative action officer, 1984-85, univ legal coun, 1985-96; dep dir, Sharon Murphy; Bell & Trice Enterprises Inc, exec vpres, co-owner, 2000-11, exec vpres, gen coun, co-owner, 2013-. **Orgs:** Equal Rights Amendment Comn Commonwealth, MA, 1976; bd mem, Family & C Serv, Nashville, TN, 1981-83; Mayor's Spec Task Force Union Sta, Nashville, TN, 1982-83; vpres, Links Inc, Cincinnati Chap, 1984-89; Jack & Jill Inc, Cincinnati Chap, 1984-90; bd dir, secy, Nat Asn Col & Univ Attys, 1985-88, exec dir, chief exec, 1996-2000; bd mem, Prog Cincinnati, 1986-88; bd mem, Bethesda Hosp Inc, 1990-; MA, TN, KY Bars; Am Bar Asn; US Dist Ct, MA; Mid Dist TN & Eastern Dist KY, US Ct Appeals Sixth Circuit; exec dir & chief exec officer, Nat Asn Col & Univ Attorneys, 1996-2000; bd dir, United Educr; bd dir, Am Coun Educ; Bd Gov, Colo State Univ Syst; Bd Channel 48, Western Interstate Comn Higher Educ; Comt Accreditation Am Psychol Asn; Wash Higher Educ Secretariat; Co-Founder, Proj Future Inst, 2014. **Home Addr:** 800 McCeney Ave, Silver Spring, MD 20901-1453, **Home Phone:** (301)681-9329. **Business Addr:** Executive Vice President, Co-owner, Bell Trice Enterprises Inc, 1875 Eye St NW Suite 500, Washington, DC 20006, **Business Phone:** (202)467-8050.

**BELL, THEODORE JOSHUA, JR.**
Financial manager. **Personal:** Born Jan 8, 1961, Berkeley, CA; son of Theodore J and Beverly Russ. **Educ:** St Mary's Col, BA, 1983; Calif Sch Arts & Crafts, attended 1984; Heald Bus Col, Oakland, dipl career bus, 1985; Berkeley Sch Comput Graphics, attended 1989. **Career:** Marriott Boykin Corp, graphic illustr banquet waiter, 1981-85; Equite Financial Group, acct, 1985-88; McCue Systs Inc, prod support analyst, 1994-, sr bus analyst, currently; First Am Title Inc, escrow acct. **Orgs:** Donator & supporter, St Mary's Col Alumni, 1983-; illusr & vol, Work Love Prog, 1984-85; admin mem, Heald Col Bus Club, 1985; adv

viewer, Kron TV Adv Bd, 1985-; supporter, Nat Urban League, 1986-; organizer & developer, TBELL Visual, 1988-; facilitator & speaker, Excel Net Customer First Prog, 1990-. **Honors/Awds:** Berkeley Marriott Employee of the Year Award, 1984; Commitment to Excellence Equitec Award, 1986; Investment in Excellence Award, Equitec Financial Group, 1986; Customer First Award, First Am Title, 1990; 100 Steps Award, First Am Title, 1990. **Home Addr:** 2777 Pk St, Berkeley, CA 94702-2314, **Home Phone:** (510)644-1123. **Business Addr:** Senior Business Analyst, McCue Systems Inc, 111 Anza Blvd Suite 310, Burlingame, CA 94010-1932, **Business Phone:** (650)348-0650.

## BELL, THERON J.

Government official, management consultant, manager. **Personal:** Born Jun 2, 1931, Junction City, KS; married Sonya M Brown; children: Kirk, Mark, Joy Pinell, Kimberly Good, Margo Goldsboro & Michele Brown. **Educ:** Jct City Sr High Sch, grad, Col/Univ Prep & Advan High Sch/Sec Dipl Prog, 1949; Wayne State Univ, bus admin, mgt & gen, 1951; Los Angeles City Col, attended 1955; Tuck Sch Bus Dartmouth, exec educ, 1992; US Civil Serv Comn, cert, introd to supv & sem advancing managers; Va Exec Inst, cert; Fed Exec Inst, cert; Nat Defense Educ Inst, cert, mkt & selling to govt agencies; LaSalle Exten Univ, bus admin & mgt, gen. **Career:** AK Rr Housing Dept, janitor, 1951-53; AUS Corps Engs, acct, 1953-55; Masseyl Bell Trucking Co, partner, 1953-55; Westward Motor Co, bus mgr, 1955-60; Blue Largo & Easy St nightclubs, partner, 1958-60; Independent Ins Agency, 1960-61; N Am Life & Casualty Co, agt, 1961-63; Fed Automotive Servs, bus mgr, 1963-66; Calif Govt Ronald Reagan's cabinet, 1967-69; Calif Off Econ Opportunity, dir, 1967-68; Volt Info Sci, dir govt rels, 1968-70; Chrysler Motors Corp, exec, 1970-72; Kenmore Chrysler-Plymouth, pres, gen mgr, 1971-72; Action Agency, var exec & sr mgt, 1972-81; Minority Bus Devel Agency, US Dept Com, nat dep dir, 1981-89; US Dept Interior, Off Surface Mining, asst to dir, 1989-91; Troy Systs Inc, vpres bus planning & develop, 1991-92; Walcoff & Assocs, bus devel mgr, 1992-94; Va Dept Labor & Indust, comnr, 1994-98; Va Employ Comn, chief dep comnr, 1998-99; adv to Co Lt Gov Joe Rogers, 1999-2000; AARP, CO state off, state coord cot opers, 2000-01; US EPA, cot rels coord, 2001-02; Off Surface Mining, dir external affairs; Olympus Group, pres, 2000-; Colo Dept Pub Health & Environ, vice chmn minority health adv comn, 2005-12. **Orgs:** Calif Asn Health & Welfare, 1967-69; Calif Job Training & Placement Coun, 1968-69; Erie Cty NY Environ Mgt Coun, 1970-71; bd dir, Lafayette Fed Credit Union, 1976-81; VA Emergency Response Coun, 1994-99; Commonwealth VA Competition Coun, 1995-99; bd dir, Latin Am Res & Serv Agency, 2000-02; bd dir, CO Republican Bus Coalition, 2000-02; bd dir, Colo Neurol Inst, 2004-10; Foothills Found; life mem, Jefferson County Coun Aging, 2012; bd dir, John W Nick Found Inc, 2013-; Alexandria VA Human Rights Comn; Fed Interagency Comn Fed Activ Alcohol Abuse & Alcoholism; Alexandria VA Republican City Comn, CA Republican State Cent Comt; life mem, Republican Nat Comn; Alexandria VA Republican City Comn; Navy League US, Am Legion, dir, Fredrick Douglass Coalition; comnr, Colo Minority Health Adv Comn; Reagan Alumni Asn; Bush-Quayle Alumni Asn; Republican Nat Comt; Colo Breast Cancer Coalition. **Honors/Awds:** Top Producer for One Year, consistently among the top producers for N Am Life & Casualty Co San Francisco. **Home Addr:** 1811 S Harlan Cir Unit 119, Lakewood, CO 80232-7099, **Home Phone:** (720)981-2101. **Business Addr:** Vice Chairman, Colorado Department of Public Health & Environment, 4300 Cherry Creek Dr S C-1, Denver, CO 80246-1530, **Business Phone:** (303)692-2000.

## BELL, THOM RANDOLPH

Songwriter, performing arts administrator. **Personal:** Born Jan 27, 1943, Kingston; married Sybell; children: 4; married Vanessa; children: 4. **Career:** Gamble's harmony grp, 1959; Chubby Checker, conductor, arranger & band leader, 1962-65; Cameo Pkwy Rec, musician, 1966-68; Avco Rec, 1971-74; Atlantic Rec, 1974; Recordings: Closer Than Close; Gentlemen of Soul, 2003-; Gamble Huff & Bell, mng partner, currently; Philadelphia Int Rec, producer, currently; songs: "La La Means I Love You", 1968; "Ready or Not Here I Come ", 1969; "Didn't I Blow Your Mind This Time", 1970; "Hey Love", 1971; "Stop, Look, Listen To Your Heart", 1971; "You Are Everything", 1971; "Betcha by Golly, Wow", 1971; "People Make the World Go Round", 1972; "I'm Stone in Love with You", 1972; "I'll Be Around", 1972; "Could It Be I'm Falling in Love", 1972; "Break Up to Make Up", 1972; "I'm Doing Fine Now", 1973; "One of a Kind", 1973; "Ghetto Child", 1973; "You Make Me Feel Brand New", 1974; "Mighty Love", 1974; "Then Came You", 1974; "They Just Can't Stop It the", 1975; "The Rubberband Man", 1976; "Are You Ready for Love", 1979; "Mama Can't Buy You Love", 1979; "It's Gonna Take a Miracle", 1982; "I Don't Have the Heart", 1990; other: Sound Philadelphia, chief architect; Uptown Theatre, pianist; Chubby Checker, musical dir. **Orgs:** Pres, Mighty Three Music; Am Fedn Musicians; Thom Bell Songwriter Workshop. **Business Addr:** Producer, Philadelphia International Records, 309 S Broad St, Philadelphia, PA 19107.

## BELL, VICTORY

Executive, government official. **Personal:** Born Mar 7, 1934, Durant, MS; son of Gladys Thompson Parker and Bea; married Carol Banks; children: Jeffrey, Gregory, Victor, Michele McAlister, Caryle & Bradley. **Career:** Ill Bell, Rockford, IL, installer tech, 1953-70, asst mgr, 1956-86; City Coun, alderman, 1971-; Cwans Corp, Rockford, IL, pres, 1986-. **Orgs:** Region coordr, Ill Statewide Black Caucus, 1990-; bd mem, Winnebago Co Health Dept, 1990-; bd mem, Southwest Ideas Today & Tomorrow, SWIFTT, 1990-; pub rep, US Census, 2000; App mayor's, Econ Develop Comn C C; Pilgrim Baptist Church; Nat Asn Advan Colored People; Rockford Citizen Adv Bd Sch, bd mem; chmn, Coun Sub Comm Soc Serv Prog; chair, Community Develop Comn, Rockford; vice chmn, Fair Housing Bd, Planning & Develop Comm. **Special Achievements:** First African-American to serve on the Rockford City Council. **Home Addr:** 2597 Meadow View Lane, Rockford, IL 61102-2516, **Home Phone:** (815)963-1075. **Business Addr:** Vice Chairman, Fair Housing Board, 425 E State St, Rockford, IL 61101, **Business Phone:** (815)987-5600.

## BELL, VIVIAN

Broker. **Career:** Int Bus mach, mgr; Alpha-Omega Properties, broker, currently. **Home Addr:** 6400 McNeil Dr, Austin, TX 78729, **Home Phone:** (512)335-8708. **Business Addr:** Broker, Alpha-Omega Properties Inc, 3131-F E 29th St, Bryan, TX 77802, **Business Phone:** (979)774-7820.

## BELL, DR. WILLIAM A., SR.

Mayor, president (government), politician. **Personal:** Born Jun 1, 1949; married Sharon Carson; children: 2. **Educ:** Univ Ala, Birmingham, MA, psychol & guidance coun; Miles Law Sch, JD. **Career:** Birmingham City Coun, pres, 1987-97, mayor, 2011-; Dist 5 City Coun, councilor, 2005-. **Orgs:** Kappa Alpha Psi; Rotary Club; Our Lady Fatima Cath Church; Comt, Transp & Commun; Comt, Pub Safety. **Home Addr:** 1437 Highland Dr, Birmingham, AL 35235, **Home Phone:** (205)854-7710. **Business Addr:** Councilor, District 5 City Council seat, City Hall, Birmingham, AL 35203-2216, **Business Phone:** (205)254-2294.

## BELL, WILLIAM JERRY

Government official. **Personal:** Born Apr 18, 1934, Chicago, IL; son of William and Kathlyn. **Educ:** Univ Ill; Roosevelt Univ, BS, com, 1958; Univ Chiago, Pa. **Career:** Ill Bur Budget, sr budget anal, 1969-72; Ill Dept Labor, mgmt specialist, 1972-75, financial res, 1975-79, asst comm, unemploy ins; IDES, doc control mgr, 1980-90. **Orgs:** Consult, Small Bus Asn, 1968-69; Bell & Assoc Ins Agency, 1970-83; founder & chmn bd, Talent Asst Prog, 1976-77; adv, Univ Ill Sch Art & Design, 1981-83; bd mem, Southside Comt Art Ctr, 1985; bd dir, Citizenship Educ Fund; Rainbow & Push. **Home Addr:** 2645 Michgan Ave, Chicago, IL 60616, **Home Phone:** (312)842-7891.

## BELL, WILLIAM MCKINLEY

Secretary of the navy, administrator. **Personal:** Born Aug 31, 1926, Grand Rapids, MI; son of William M (deceased) and Mentie N Moore (deceased); married Patsy Ann Kelley. **Educ:** Univ Mich, BA, 1948, MBA, 1954. **Career:** Johnson Publ Co, salesman & merchandising rep, 1956-57; William M Bell & Assoc, pres, 1958-75; Equal Employ Opportunity Comn, consult, 1975-76; Bold Concepts, Inc, pres, 1976-82; Legal Serv Corp, legis asst dir. **Orgs:** Omega Psi Phi Fraternity, 1947; Univ Mich, Sch Bus Alumni Asn, 1982; Shiloh Baptist Church, 1986-. **Honors/Awds:** Optimist of the Year, Optimist Club, 1981; Special Tribute Award, State Mich, 1981. **Home Addr:** 1515 S Jefferson Davis Hwy Apt 504, Arlington, VA 22202, **Home Phone:** (703)413-4402.

## BELL, WILLIAM VAUGHN

Mayor, engineer, government official. **Personal:** Born Jan 3, 1941, Washington, DC; son of William B and Willie M Mullen; married Judith Chatters; children: William V II, Tiffany Anne, Anjanee Nicole & Kristen Vaughn. **Educ:** Howard Univ, BS, elec engineering, 1961; NY Univ, MS, elec engineering, 1968. **Career:** Senior engineer (retired), mayor, executive; Martin Marietta Corp, jr engr, 1961; AUs Electronics Command, proj engr, 1963-68; Int Bus Mach Corp, mgr, 1968-83, tech asst, 1983-85, elect engr, 1985-96, sr engr, 1996; Durham County, comnr, 1972-94, 1996-2000, chmn, 1982-94; City Durham, mayor, 2001-; NC Metrop Mayors Coalition, chmn; UDI Community Develop Corp, exec vpres & chief operating officer, currently. **Orgs:** Inst Elec & Electronics Engrs, 1961-; UDI/CDC, pres & bd dir, 1970-83, exec vpres & chief operating officer, 1996-; bd dir, NC Sch Sci & math, 1979-; city comn, Durham City Bd Comn, 1972-; Durham Bd County Comner, 1972-94, 1996-2000; chmn bd, Durham City Bd Comn, 1982-94; dir, Durham Chamber Comm, 1982-; bd trustee, Durham County Hosp Corp, 1984-; adv bd, Duke Univ Hosp, 1987-; chair, Mutual community Savings Bank; Triangle Transit Authority; Trinity Pk Neighborhood Asn; Mayors Against Illegal Guns Coalition. **Honors/Awds:** Community Service Award, State NC, 1981; Outstanding Citizen, Durham Comt Affairs Blacks, 1985; Community Service Award, Durham Chap Kappa Alpha Psi, 1985; Outstanding Alumnus, Howard Univ Club Res Triangle Park, 1985; Outstanding Citizen Award, Omega Psi Phi, Durham NC, 1986; Alumni Award for Distinguished Post-Graduate Achievement, Howard Univ, 1988; Service to Mankind Award, James E Shephard Sertoma Club, 1989. **Special Achievements:** First elected mayor of Durham in 2001. **Home Addr:** 1003 Huntsman Dr, Durham, NC 27713-2384, **Home Phone:** (919)544-5597. **Business Addr:** Mayor, City of Durham, 101 City Hall Plz, Durham, NC 27701, **Business Phone:** (919)560-4333.

## BELL, DR. WINSTON ALONZO

Pianist, educator. **Personal:** Born Mar 24, 1930, Winchester, KY; son of Edward C and Margaret Hansbro; married Marlita Peyton; children: Taimia Danielle & Chase. **Educ:** St Louis Inst Music, St Louis, MO, 1947; Fisk Univ, BA, 1951; Univ Mich, mus, 1955; Columbia Univ, EdD, 1963; Gen Theol Sem, St B, 1964. **Career:** Elizabeth City State Univ NC, instr piano, 1953-55; NY City Sch Syst, teacher, 1955-60; Music Studio Nyack NY, pianist & teacher, 1955-60; St Augustine Chapel NYC, curate, 1963-64; St James Less Jamaica NY, rector, 1964-71; Winston Salem State Univ, Winston-Salem, NC, chmn dept music, 1972-; Real Estate Broker, 1981-; Exec Enterprises, Winston Salem, NC, found & chief exec officer, 1984; Livingstone Col, adj lect African-Am studies, currently. **Orgs:** Bd dir, Organist Holy Family Cath Church; Winston Salem Symphony, Piedmont Opera Soc; Suzuki Assoc Am, MENC, Phi Mu Alpha Sinfonia, Omega Psi Phi Frat, Col Music Soc; Reynolda House Chamber Music Soc; Knights Columbus; One Hundred Black Men. **Home Addr:** 2263 Sedgemont Dr, Winston Salem, NC 27103, **Home Phone:** (336)765-6652. **Business Addr:** Chairman, Winston-Salem State University, Columbia Hts, Winston Salem, NC 27101, **Business Phone:** (336)750-2520.

## BELL, YVONNE LOLA

Restaurateur, talk show host. **Personal:** Born Dec 25, 1953, New York, NY; daughter of Henry and Gladys Greene. **Career:** Flowers by Yvonne, owner & mgr, 1980-84; Pesca Restaurant, mgr, 1981-84; Ribbons & Rolls, owner & mgr, 1982-84; Lola Restaurant, owner & mgr, 1985-91, LolaBelle Restaurant, owner & mgr, 1992-94; Valentine's Day "Live Your Fantasy" night, theater show; Caribbean/soul food restaurant, co-owner, hostess, currently. **Special Achievements:** Starting a TV cooking talk show, "Lunch with Lola". **Home Addr:** 4940 N Hiawassee Rd, Orlando, FL 32818-1306. **Business Addr:** Owner, Manager, LolaBelle Restaurant, 206 E 63rd St, New York, NY 10021, **Business Phone:** (212)420-1111.

## BELL-SCOTT, DR. PATRICIA

Writer, educator, editor. **Personal:** Born Dec 20, 1950, Chattanooga, TN; daughter of Louis Wilbanks and Dorothy Graves; married Charles Vernon Underwood Jr. **Educ:** Univ Tenn, Knoxville, BS, 1972, MS, 1973, PhD, 1976. **Career:** Univ Tenn, Child & Family Study, fac, 1974-76, asst dir black studies & asst prof, 1976-79; JFK Sch Govt Harvard, Pub Policy Prog, fel & res assoc, 1979; Psychol Women Quart, New Directions Women, guest ed, 1982-83, J Nat Asn Women Deans & Admins, ed, 1979-81; Wellesley Col Ctr Res Women, res assoc, 1980-84; Mass Inst Technol, asst equal opportunity officer, 1982-84; J Negro Educ, ed bd, 1983-; Women Power, A J Feminism & Power, staff, 1984; John F. Kennedy Sch Govt, post-doctoral fel; W.E.B. DuBois Inst, Harvard Univ, post-doctoral fel; Jane & Harry Willson Ctr, Univ Ga, post-doctoral fel; Univ Conn, Sch Family Studies, assoc prof, 1985-91; Ms.Mag, contrib ed; SAGE: A Scholarly J Black Women, co-founding ed; Univ Ga, Dept Child & Family Studies, Womens Studies Prog & Psychol Dept, prof, 1991, adj prof, 1999, emer prof, currently; author: Life Notes: Personal Writings by Contemporary Black Women; Flat-footed Truths: Telling Black Womens Lives; Double Stitch: Black Women Write about Mothers and Daughters; All the Women Are White, All the Blacks Are Men, But Some of Us Are Brave: Black Womens Studies; The Firebrand and the First Lady: Portrait of a Friendship: Pauli Murray, Eleanor Roosevelt and the Struggle for Social Justice. **Orgs:** Chair, Nat Coun Family Rels, Family Action Sect, 1974-76, nominating comt, 1991-92; chairwoman, AWA, Black Womens Community Comn, 1975-77; bd mem, Black Community Develop Inc, Knoxville, 1975-77; social action comt mem, Delta Sigma Theta, Alumnae Chap, Knoxville, 1977-78; co-convener, Coord Coun, Nat Womens Studies Asn, 1977-78; Consult Womens Prog Off Educ, 1978; nat exec bd, Nat Asn Women Deans Adminr & Counrs, 1978-80; consult, Nat Adv Comn Black Higher Educ, 1979; vpres, Nat Asn Women Deans & Admins, 1980-82; bd mem, Col Express Found, 1989-; contrib ed, Ms Mag, 1995-. **Honors/Awds:** Citation for Outstanding Service, UTK Chap Mortar Bd, 1977; Regional Finalist White House Fel Prog, 1977-78; Cited for Outstanding Service to the University of Tennessee, Knoxville Black Studs Asn, 1978; Award for Outstanding Contribution to Feminist Scholarship, Nat Inst Women Color, 1982; Fourth Curriculum Materials Award, Women Educrs, 1983; Distinguished Educator in Connecticut Award, Conn Chap Coalition 100 Black Women, 1986; Citation of Outstanding Contribution to the Psychology of Black Women, Div 35, Am Psychol Asn, 1988; Esther Lloyd-Jones Distinguished Service Award, Nat Asn Women Deans, Counrs, 1989; Letitia Woods Brown Memorial Book Prize, Asn Black Women Historians, 1992; Women of Achievement Award, Nat Asn Women Educ, Ethnic Women's Caucus, 1992; Archive of Achievement Alumnae Award, Univ Tenn, 1994; Cited at 20th Anniversary of the Wellesley Col Center for Research on Women, 1995; Centennial Leader Award, Univ Tenn, 1997. **Special Achievements:** Author of over 25 arts and four books; First book, But Some of Us Are Brave: Black Women's Studies. **Home Addr:** 225 Cedar Springs Dr, Athens, GA 30605-3411. **Business Addr:** Emeritus Professor, University of Georgia, Gilbert Hall 210 Herty Dr, Athens, GA 30602-3622, **Business Phone:** (706)542-2846.

## BELLAMY, ANGELA ROBINSON

Government official. **Personal:** Born Nov 25, 1952, Miami, FL; daughter of Leon Giddings and Helen Peavy; married Gregory Derek; children: Gregory Robinson & Evan Matthew Robinson. **Educ:** Fisk Univ, Nashville, TN, BA, 1974; Vanderbilt Univ, Owen Grad Sch Mgt, Nashville, TN, MBA, 1976; Harvard Univ, John F Kennedy Sch Govt, Prog Sr Execs State & Local Govt, 1986; Nat Forum Black Adminrs Exec Leadership Inst, cert, 1991. **Career:** Government official (retired); City Miami, admin asst, 1976-77, personnel officer, 1977-78, sr personnel officer, 1978-79, personnel supr hr, 1979, asst city mgr, 1979-81, asst dir hr, 1981-84, dir, personnel mgt, 1984, asst city mgr, 1988, dir, dept human res, 2002. **Orgs:** Sec, IPMA S FL Chapt, 1978, vpres, 1979; co-ch host comn, IPMA Int Conf, 1983-84; area coord, FL Pub Personnel Asn, 1984-85; chair, IPMA Human Rights Comn, 1985-86; Nat Forum Black Pub Admin; IPMA Nomination Comm, 1987; pres, Delta Sigma Theta, Dade Co Alumnae Chap, 1991-93; Soc Human Resource Mgt; Personnel Asn Greater Miami; Int Found Employee Benefit Plans; Am Mgt Asn; Int City Mgt Asn; Fla Pub Personnel Asn; pres, Greater Miami Chap, 2010; bd mem, pres, Links Inc, 2006-10; S Miami Chap, Jack & Jill Am Inc; chair bd, Urban League Greater Miami. **Home Addr:** 16601 Sw 88 Ct, Palmetto Bay, Miami, FL 33157, **Home Phone:** (305)253-9866. **Business Addr:** DC.

## BELLAMY, BILL

Comedian, actor. **Personal:** Born Apr 7, 1965, Newark, NJ; married Kristen Baker. **Educ:** Rutgers Univ, BS, econs, 1988. **Career:** Rep, Tobacco sales; MTV Jams, deejay; Films: Joey Breaker, 1993; Who's The Man?, 1993; Fled, 1996; Love Jones, 1997; How to Be a Player, 1997; Love Stinks, 1999; Any Given Sunday, 1999; The Brothers, 2001; Buying the Cow, 2002; Host, MTV Jams; The Real Mario Grey, 2005; Never was, Getting Played, 2005; Lottery Ticket, 2010; Noobz, 2012; 10 Rules for Sleeping Around, 2013; TV series: "Bowen A'i Bartner", 1985; "MTV Beach House", 1993; "The Bill Bellamy Show", 1996; "Austin Powers' Electric Pussycat Swingers Club", 1997; "Cousin Skeeter", 1998-2001; "The Jamie Foxx Show", 2000; "Men, Women & Dogs", 2001-02; "Fastlane", 2002-03; "Half & Half", 2004; "Back to My Roots", writer, 2005; "Who's Got Jokes?", exec producer, 2006; "Caerdydd", 2006; "Getting Played", 2006; "Amy Coyne", 2006; "Def Comedy Jam", writer, 2006; "October Road", 2007-08; "Castle", 2010; "Royal Pains", 2010; "BlackBox TV", 2012; "Bill Bellamy: Crazy Sexy Dirty", exec producer, 2012; "White Collar", 2013; "Bill Bellamy's Ladies Night Out Comedy Tour", exec producer, 2013; "Mr. Box Office", exec producer, 2012-13; "Hot in Cleveland", 2014. **Honors/Awds:** Image Award for Outstanding Performance in a Youth or Children's Series/Special, 1998; Image Award for Outstanding Actor in a Drama Series, 2002; Teen Choice Award for Choice TV Actor - Drama/Action Adventure, 2002.

## BELLAMY, PROF. EVERETT

Educator, lawyer. **Personal:** Born Dec 29, 1949, Chicago, IL; son of William T and Emma M. **Educ:** Univ Wis, BS, 1972, MS, 1974; Cleveland State Univ JD, 1980; Cleveland-Marshall Col Law. **Career:** Univ Wis, grad asst; Cleveland State Univ, cord stud activ; Charles Hamilton Houston Pre-Law Inst, instr & asst exec dir; Georgetown

Univ, Law Ctr, sr asst dean & adj prof, 1980-; Howard Univ Small Bus Develop Ctr, Babson Col, guest lectr. **Orgs:** Phi Alpha Delta Law Fraternity Int, 1980-; chmn, Nat Conf Black Lawyers, DC Chap, 1981-83; Am Bar Asn, 1984-; Bd Gov, Nat Bar Asn, 1986-; Hon degrees Commt Georgetown Law; fac adv, Moots Ct George Town Law; co-chmn, Law Professors Div, Nat Bar Asn; co-chmn, Nat Bar Asn Law Professors Div, 1990-; Gov Nat Bar Asn. **Home Addr:** 11706 Sherbrooke Woods Lane, Silver Spring, MD 20904, **Home Phone:** (301)622-2416. **Business Addr:** Adjunct Professor of Law, Georgetown University, 600 NJ Ave Rm 352, Washington, DC 20001, **Business Phone:** (202)662-9039.

## BELLAMY, IVORY GANDY

Educator, health services administrator. **Personal:** Born Feb 21, 1952, Tuscaloosa, AL; daughter of Iverson Sr; married Kenneth N; children: Cinnamon & Cecily. **Educ:** Stillman Col, BA, 1974; Fla Int Univ, Miami; Nova Univ. **Career:** Dade County Pub Schs, instr, 1978-79; Miami Dade Community Col, prog coordr, 1979-85; Univ Miami, prog dir Minority Admis, 1985-89; Fayette County Schs, eng teacher, 1990-; "Life is a Million Good-byes", auth, 2010. **Orgs:** Southern Asn Admis Counrs; bd dir, Rainbow House, 1991-. **Home Addr:** 9117 Jenni Cir, PO Box 2243, Jonesboro, GA 30237, **Home Phone:** (770)472-4560. **Business Addr:** Teacher, Flat Rock Middle School, 325 Jenkins Rd, Tyrone, GA 30290, **Business Phone:** (404)969-2830.

## BELLAMY, JAY (JOHN JAY BELLAMY)

Football player. **Personal:** Born Jul 8, 1972, Perth Amboy, NJ. **Educ:** Rutgers State Univ, sociol. **Career:** Football player (retired); Seattle Sea hawks, 1994-96, strong safety, 1997-98, free safety, 1999-2000; New Orleans Saints, free safety, 2001-02, safety, 2002, strong safety, 2003-06, safety, 2004, defensive back, 2007. **Business Addr:** Professional Football Player, New Orleans Saints, 5800 Airline Dr, Metairie, LA 70003, **Business Phone:** (504)733-0255.

## BELLAMY, WERTEN F. W., JR.

Lawyer. **Personal:** married Kellye L Walker; children: Werten, Matthew & Erica. **Educ:** Princeton Univ, BA, 1986; Univ Va Law Sch, JD, 1989. **Career:** Wyeth-Ayerst Pharmaceut, atty, corp trans & technol licensing; CYOC, co-founder, 1998; Celera Genomics Group, gen coun, chief legal coun, 2000-02; Stakeholders Inc, pres & founder, 2007-; Leadership Coun Legal Diversity, consult, 2010-; Health & Centers DisControl & Prev, asst secy; TRSG Inc, vpres intellectual property, consult; Merck & Co Inc, atty, joint ventures & technol licensing; Blackwell Igbanugo PA, adv, currently, managing partner, chmn & shareholder; Genetics Inst Inc; Wyeth Pharmaceut Inc. **Orgs:** Chmn, Lewis & Munday Corp & Technol Pract Group, 2002-; bd dir, St. Benedict's Prep Sch; bd dir, Phillips Exeter Acad Gen Alumni Asn; adv bd mem, Ultimate Law Guide Ltd. **Honors/Awds:** The Chairman's Award, Nat Bar Asn, 1999; Excellence in the Corporate Practice Award, Am Corp Coun Asn, 2000; Trailblazer Award, CYOC Found. **Special Achievements:** Publication: The Path to Indispensable, Am Bar Asn Publ, 2013; Relationship-Building Skills: The Pathway from the Zone of Indifference, NALP Bulletin, 2014. **Home Addr:** , Philadelphia, PA. **Business Addr:** President, Founder, Stakeholders Inc, 1100 Pa Ave, Washington, DC 20004, **Business Phone:** (202)756-5040.

## BELLE, ALBERT JOJUAN (JOEY BELLE)

Baseball player. **Personal:** Born Aug 25, 1966, Shreveport, LA; son of Albert Sr and Carrie Jean Giles; married Melissa; children: Cecila Marie. **Educ:** La State Univ, BA, acct, 1987. **Career:** Baseball player (retired); Cleveland Indians, leftfielder, 1989-96; Chicago White Sox, leftfielder, 1997-98; Baltimore Orioles, leftfielder, 1999-2000. **Honors/Awds:** Most Valuable Player, South 1 Regional Tournament, 1986; Silver Slugger Award, 1993-96, 1998; Major League Baseball All-Star Game, 1993-96, 1998; Sporting News Player of the Year, 1995; Baseball Digest Player of the Year, 1995; Home Run Champion, Maj League, 1995; inducted, Louisiana Sports Hall of Fame, 2005. **Special Achievements:** First player to ever hit 50 HR and 50 Doubles in a single season, 1995; one of only six players in major league history to have nine consecutive 100-RBI seasons. **Home Addr:** 321 Katey Rose Lane, Euclid, OH 44143.

## BELLE, CHARLES E.

Journalist, executive. **Personal:** Born Sep 2, 1940, Chicago, IL; son of Charles Douglas and Ella; married Rita Cummings; children: Cynthia Maureen & Charles Escobar. **Educ:** Roosevelt Univ, BS, 1963; Harvard Grad Sch Bus, MBA, 1973. **Career:** Harvard Univ, Cogme fel, 1971-73; Drexel Burnham Lambert Inc, asst vpres, 1973-80; Brookings Inst, econ journalist, 1978; Nat Endowment Humanities, journalist, 1979; Prudential Bache Securities Inc, vpres & investment mgt adv, 1989; AG Edwards Sons Inc, investment broker. **Orgs:** Bus ed, Nat Newspaper Publ Asn, Wash, DC, 1973-; prof lectr, Golden Gate Univ, San Francisco, 1975-80; chmn, Mayors Adv Comm Community Develop San Francisco, 1983-85; bd dir, San Francisco Conv Vistors Bur; bd gov, Nat Conf Christians Jews, Northern Calif Region; dir, Australian Am Chamber Com. **Honors/Awds:** Best Column, John Ryan Motoring Press Asn, 1993-94, 1998-99. **Home Addr:** 270 Francisco St, San Francisco, CA 94133-2012, **Home Phone:** (415)391-2030. **Business Addr:** Investment Broker, AG Edwards & Sons Inc, 1 N Jefferson Ave, St. Louis, MO 63103, **Business Phone:** (314)955-3000.

**BELLE, JOEY. See BELLE, ALBERT JOJUAN.**

## BELLE, REGINA

Singer, actor. **Personal:** Born Jul 17, 1963, Englewood, NJ; daughter of Eugene and Lois; married John S Battle; children: Winter, Sydni Milan, Tiy Chreigna, Jayln Nuri & Nyla. **Educ:** Manhattan Sch Music, opera & class music; Rutgers Univ, acct & hist. **Career:** Singer, currently; Albums: All By Myself, 1987; Stay With Me, 1989; Better Together: The Duet Album, 1992; Passion, 1993; Reachin Back, 1995; Baby Come to Me, 1997; Believe In Me, 1998; This Is Regina!, 2001; Dont Let Go, 2002; Lazy Afternoon, 2004; Love Songs, 2006; Love Forever Shines, 2008; Higher, 2012; The Day Life Began, 2016. Singles: "You Got the Love", 1986; "Show Me The Way", 1987; "So Many Tears", 1987; "Without You", 1988; "How Could You Do It To Me", 1988; "All I Want Is Forever", 1989; "Good Lovin", 1989; "Make It Like It Was", 1990; "This Is Love", 1990; "What Goes Around", 1990; "A Whole New World", 1992; "If I Could", 1993; "Dream in Color", 1993; "Quiet Time", 1993; "The Deeper I Love", 1994; "Don't Let Go", 1998; "I've Had Enough", 1998; "Oooh Boy", 2001; "For the Love of You", 2004; "God Is Good", 2008; "I Call on Jesus", 2008, "Make An Example Out Of Me", 2012. Film: The Brewster Project, 2004; The Walk, 2005. **Honors/Awds:** Grammy Award for Pop Duo & Group, 1993; Grammy Award; Oscar, 1994. **Special Achievements:** Headliner, Avery Fisher Hall, NY; Am Music Awards, nomination, Best R&B Female Singer, 1991. **Business Addr:** Singer, c/o Miles Ahead Entertainment Inc (MAE), 380 Piermont Ave, Hillsdale, NJ 07642, **Business Phone:** (201)722-1500.

## BELLEGARDE-SMITH, DR. PATRICK

Educator, association executive. **Personal:** Born Aug 8, 1947, Spokane, WA; son of Jasper Benton and Simone Cecile. **Educ:** Syracuse Univ, BA, polit sci, 1968; Am Univ, MA, Latin Am studies, 1970, PhD, int studies, 1977. **Career:** Howard Univ, Dept Fr & Span, lectr, 1977; Howard Univ, Moorland-Springarn Res Ctr, consult, 1980; Bradley Univ, Inst Int Studies, assoc prof, 1978-86, tenured fac, 1983-84; Univ Wis, Milwaukee, Dept Africology, assoc prof, 1986-2005, chair, 1987-90, 1994-95 & 2005-06, prof africology, 2005; Univ Wis, Milwaukee, Dept Africology, prof emer, currently; Haitian Inst Cult & Sci Res, bd mem, 1991-; Univ Calif, Santa Barbara, Ctr Black Studies, scholar-in-residence, Dept Relig Studies, instr & vis prof, 2000-01; J Haitian Studies, assoc ed, 2001-. **Orgs:** Founding mem, Ill Coun Black Studies, 1979; bd dir, Third World Conf Found, Chicago, 1983-84; founding mem, Progressive Latin Am Network, 1985; founding mem, Nat Cong Black Fac, 1988; founding mem, Brazilian Studies Asn, 1993; founding mem, Cong Santa Barbara, 1997; Am Asn Univ Profs; African Studies Asn; life mem, Caribbean Studies Asn; mem & exec bd, Nat Coun Black Studies, 1991-92 & 1996-97; Nat Conf Black Polit Scientists; life mem, Asn Caribbean Historians; Latin Am Studies Asn; Scholarly Asn Study Haitian Vodou; vpres, Gens de la Caraibe; vpres, Haitian Studies Asn; Am Asn Relig. **Honors/Awds:** Barnett J Frank Award, Outstanding Social Science Student, Univ Vi, 1964-66; Lifetime Achievement Award for Scholarship, Haitian Studies Asn, Brown Univ, 2010. **Special Achievements:** Edited "Fragments of Bone: Neo-African Religions in a New World, Univ Ill Press", 2005; published numerous books and articles. **Business Addr:** Professor Emeritus of Africology, University of Wisconsin-Milwaukee, 221 Mitchell Hall, Milwaukee, MI 53201, **Business Phone:** (414)229-4155.

## BELLINGER, HAROLD

School administrator, educator. **Personal:** Born Mar 28, 1951, New York, NY; son of Lionel Jordan and Naomi Jordan. **Educ:** State Univ NY, Farmingdale, AAS, 1972; Rochester Inst Technol, BS, social work, 1974; Univ Pittsburgh, master, pub & int affairs, 1975; NY Exec Chamber NYS Affirmative Action Progs, cert, 1982; St John Univ, JD. **Career:** Legis Comn Expenditure Rev, sr assoc, 1976-79; Ny Senate Fin Comm Minority, legis budget analyst, 1979-81; Ny Dept Corrections, bus affairs & contract compliance mgr, 1981-82; Ny Correctional Indust, Indust asst dir mkt sls, 1982-84; Econ Opportunity Comn Nassau County, asst dir Youth proj, 1984-85; State Univ New York, asst pres affirmative action, 1985-89; Nassau Community Col, affirmative action & diversity, 1989-, asst pres, currently. **Orgs:** Asn Minority Bus Enterprises, 1981-82; Albany Chamber Com, 1981-82; course instr, Ny Budget Process sponsoring w/AL 1982; bd dir, Econ Opportunity Comn Nassau County, 1984-89; UN Asn USA Mid Long Island Chap, 1986-91; Minority Access Lic Professionals, Long Island Reg Comt, 1986-90; 100 Black Men Nassau, Suffolk Chap, 1991-96, 2001-; bd dir, Urban League Long Island, 1991-93; Am Asn Affirmative Action Officers, 1996. **Special Achievements:** Nominee, US President's, Volunteer Action Award, 1991. **Home Addr:** 1191 Little E Neck Rd, West Babylon, NY 11704-2409, **Home Phone:** (631)920-2477. **Business Addr:** Assistant to the President, Nassau Community College, 1 Educ Dr Twr Bldg Rm 818, Garden City, NY 11530-6793, **Business Phone:** (516)572-7121.

## BELLINGER, REV. MARY ANNE ALLEN (BIBI TALIBA MSHONAJI)

Consultant, clergy, administrator. **Personal:** Born Jul 16, 1939, Cincinnati, OH; daughter of George W Allen and Mary Jane Banks Allen; children: Georgiana, Teresa Lynn, Lawrence Wesley, Maurice & Sheila Renee Kinnard. **Educ:** Andover Newton Theol Sch, Boston, MA, Mdiv, basic studies, 1981. **Career:** Wellesley Col, Wellesley, Mass, asst chaplain, 1975-80; Andover Newton TheolSch, Boston MA, adj fac, 1978-80; ordained Baptist clergy woman, minister, 1980; BigBethel AME Church, assoc pastor, 1984-85; ordained intinerant elder AMEchurch, itinerant, 1984; St Stephens AME Church, pastor, 1985-87; Grady MemorialHosp, chaplain intern, 1986-87; Newberry Chapel AME Church, pastor, 1987-89; VISION House Inc, group home, founder & dir, 1987-; Atlanta Voice Newspaper, columnist/ed, 1988-89; elected Atlanta Bd Educ, vpres largerep, 1989-93; Think About This Inc, Atlanta, Ga, pres, 1994; Atlanta PubSch, substitute teacher, 1994-96; Black Women Church & Soc, prog assoc, 1997-; Interdenominational Theol Ctr, proj coordr, 1997-2000, adj prof; consult, currently. **Orgs:** SE regional vpres, Partners Ecumenism Nat Coun Churches, 1984-90; fac, first Year Class, AME Church Ministerial Prep, 1987-89; bd dir, Christian Coun Metrop Atlanta, 1987-91; chairperson, Ecumenical Celebrations & Church Women United, 1987-88; chairperson, Racial Justice Working Group, Nat Coun Churches Sea Islands Comt, 1989-92; secy, Racial Justice Working Group; Ga Network Against Domestic Violence, 1988-89; Nat Asn Advan Colored People; Concerned Black Clergy Atlanta; secy & bd dir, Exodus, Atlanta Cities Schs; adv comt, Success Six Atlanta United Way, 1990-94; Atlanta Fulton Comn C & Youth, 1990-96; judge, organizing comt, Hearts Youth Salute, 1990-96; parliamentarian, Beulah Baptist Church Gospel Choir; asst minister, Beulah Bapt Church, Vine City; assoc, First African Presby Church, 1998-. **Business Addr:** Consultant, 6232 Austin Dr, Mableton, GA 30126-4308, **Business Phone:** (770)819-2647.

## BELSER, JASON DAKS

Football player, athletic director. **Personal:** Born May 28, 1970, Kansas City, MO; son of Caesar; married Sarita Garrison. **Educ:** Univ Okla, BA. **Career:** Football player (retired); Indianapolis Colts, defensive back, 1992-2000; Kans City Chiefs, 2001-02; NFL Players Asn, sr dir, currently. **Orgs:** NFL Plyoff Team, 1995. **Business Addr:** Regional Director, NFL Players Association, 2021 L St NW, Washington, DC 20036, **Business Phone:** (202)463-2200.

## BELSON, JERRY

Manager, government official. **Personal:** Born Mar 1, 1949, Lafayette, LA; son of Joseph and Elrose; married JoAnn St Clair; children: Dedrick, Abayomi, Farisa, Aisha & Jonathan. **Educ:** Southern Univ, AA, music educ, 1970; Sulross State Univ, BS, criminal justice, 1980. **Career:** Government official (retired); Amistad Nat Recreation Area, dist ranger, 1973-85; Tuskegee Inst NHS, supt, 1985-87; Nat Park Serv, Ft Frederica Nat Monument, supt, 1987-89, Martin Luther King Jr Nat Hist Site, supt, 1990-91, Yosemite Nat Park, dep supt, 1991-94, Southern Arz Group, gen supt, 1994-95, Atlanta, dep regional dir, 1995-96, southeast regional dir, 1996-2004. **Orgs:** Bd mem, Trust Pub Land, 1990-92; bd dir, Nat Assoc Interpreters, 1992-; bd dir, Atlanta Conv & Viss Bur, 1992-95; bd dir, Atlanta Olympic Comt, 1995-96; bd mem, Round table Assoc, 1996-98. **Honors/Awds:** Meritorious Service, Nat Park Serv, 1995. **Home Addr:** 3060 Birchton St, Alpharetta, GA 30022-7623, **Home Phone:** (770)650-2096.

## BELTON, C. RONALD

Chief executive officer, president (organization). **Personal:** Born Aug 28, 1948, Jacksonville, FL; son of Clarence A Jr and Bettye Ruth Taylor. **Educ:** Hampton Inst, BS, Sociol, 1970. **Career:** Jacksonville Urban League, assoc dir, 1970-76; Tucker Bros, mortgage broker 1972-; Merrill Lynch Inc, sr fin consult, 1976-96; St. Johns Investment Mgt Co Inc, vpres; Riverplace Capital Mgt Inc, exec vpres, prin, compliance officer, 1998-2011, Riverplace Analytics LLC, chief exec officer & pres, 2006-11; Univ Chicago Harris Sch, asst to mayor, chief financial officer. **Orgs:** Chmn bd, Jacksonville Urban League, 1983-84; life Nat Asn Advan Colored People; Nat Eagle Scout Asn; chmn, Jacksonville Downtown Develop Authority, 1987-90; bd gov, Jacksonville Chamber Com, 1988-91; bd mem, Jacksonville Symphony Asn, 1988-91; adv bd, Univ N Fla Sch Bus, 1988-91; fin comt, Jacksonville Community Found, 1990-92; Sigma Pi Phi Fraternity; State Bd Community Cols; bd trustee, Memorial Hosp Jacksonville, 2003-12; chmn bd, Boys & Girls Club Northeast Fla, 2003-10; bd mem, Bus Coun Univ N Fla; chief financial officer, Sigma Pi Phi Fraternity, 2011. **Home Addr:** 2970 St Johns Ave, Jacksonville, FL 32205, **Home Phone:** (904)388-2582. **Business Addr:** Assistant to the Mayor, Chief Financial Officer, University of Chicago Harris Schoo, 1155 E 60th St, Chicago, IL 60637, **Business Phone:** (773)702-8400.

## BELTON, HOWARD G.

Educator, administrator. **Personal:** Born Mar 22, 1934, Muskogee, OK; son of Louis and Jonella; married Ann Rempson; children: Consandra Denise & Sheryl Anne. **Educ:** Mich State Univ, BA, MS. **Career:** Mich Dept Social Serv, case worker, 1960-64; Lansing Mich Sch Dist, teacher, 1964-69; Mich Educ Asn, human rel consult, 1969-72; Nat Educ Asn, orgn specialist, 1972-73, dir employee rels, 1973-85, dir internal opers; HG Belton Photog, Photogr. **Orgs:** Nat Asn Advan Colored People; Chicago Chap Oper PUSH; Urban League, Proj Equality; Prof Photogr Soc Greater Wash. **Home Addr:** 14017 Breeze Hill Lane, Silver Spring, MD 20906, **Home Phone:** (301)460-0760. **Business Addr:** Photographer, HG Belton Photography, New Mkt, Silver Spring, MD 20904, **Business Phone:** (240)602-8951.

## BELTON, SHARON SAYLES

Government official, college administrator. **Personal:** Born May 13, 1951, St. Paul, MN; daughter of Bill and Marian Sayles; married Steve; children: Kilayna, Jordan & Coleman. **Educ:** Macalester Col, biol & sociol, 1973. **Career:** Minn Dept Corrections, parole officer; Minn Prog Victims Sexual Assault, asst dir; Minnapolis City Coun, coun mem, 1983, pres, 1990; City Minneapolis, mayor, 1994-2001; Univ Minn, Hubert H Humphrey Inst Pub Affairs, Roy Wilkins Ctr Human Rels & Social Justice, sr fel, currently. **Orgs:** Minneapolis Youth Coord Bd; Bd Estimates & Taxation; Heritage Bd; pres, Harriet Tubman Shelter Battered Women; co-founder, Harriet Tubman Shelter Battered Women, 1978; pres, Nat Coalition Against Sexual Assault; Metrop Task Force Develop Disabilities; bd mem, Minneapolis Youth Diversion Prog; Minn Women Elected Officials; C's Theater & Turning Pt; bd mem, Bush Found, 1991-; bd mem, United Way Minneapolis, 1997-; Am Bar Asn; US Conf Mayors. **Special Achievements:** The first African American and woman to be elected the Mayor of Minneapolis. **Business Addr:** Senior Fellow, University of Minnesota, 258 Humphrey Ctr, Minneapolis, MN 55455, **Business Phone:** (612)626-8910.

## BELTON, Y. MARC

Vice president (organization), executive. **Personal:** Born Jan 1, 1959?, West Hempstead, NY; married Alicia. **Educ:** Dartmouth Col, BS, econ & environ studies, 1981; Univ Pa, Wharton Sch Bus, MBA, mkt & finance, 1983. **Career:** Yoplait USA; Gen Mills Can Corp; New Bus Develop; Gen Mills, mkt asst, 1983-91, vpres, 1991-94, Worldwide Health, Brand & New Bus Develop, sr vpres, 1994-2006, pres, 2002-, exec vpres, 2006-, Snacks Unlimited, 1994-97, New Venture, 1997-99, Big G cereals, pres, 1999-2002, Global Strategy, Growth & Marketing Innovation, exec vpres, 2006-. **Orgs:** Leadership bd, Promise Keepers, 1995; Audit Comt, Fin Comt, Compensation Comt & Governance Comt; bd dir, Navistar Int corp, 1999-2009; bd dir, Guthrie Theater & Urban Ventures, 2004; Exec Leadership Coun; vice chairman & bd trustee, NW Bible Col; co-chair, Capital Campaign, Minneapolis Salvation Army; bd dir, US Bancorp, 2009-. **Business Addr:** Executive Vice President, Global Strategy, Growth & Marketing Innovation, General Mills Inc, 1 Gen Mills Blvd, Minneapolis, MN 55440, **Business Phone:** (763)764-7600.

## BEMBRY, JERRY E.

Journalist. **Personal:** Born Sep 18, 1962, Brooklyn, NY; children: Ashley. **Educ:** Ohio Wesleyan Univ, BA, journ, broadcasting, 1984.

**Career:** Courier-News, reporter, 1984-85; The Baltimore Sun, police reporter, 1985-90, sports reporter, 1993-99, High Sch Sports Show, host, 1998-99; ESPN The Mag, NBA ed, 1999-04, sr writer, 2004-09; ESPN, ESPNU, color analyst; WYPR, sr video producer; Morgan State Univ, commun studies, lectr, currently. **Orgs:** Nat Asn Black Journalists, 1984-; pres, Asn Black Media Workers, 1985-; New York Asn Black Journalists; pres, Baltimore Asn Black Media Works; Prof Basketball Writers Asn. **Honors/Awds:** Award for Series News, SPJ, 1988; Award for Local Govt, 1988; Award for Feature Writing Sports, 1999; Feature Writing Award, Pro Basketball Writers Asn, 1999; The 2007 Best Feature Award. **Special Achievements:** First African American to hold senior writer position at ESPN The magazine. **Business Addr:** Lecturer Communication Studies, Morgan State University, 1700 E Cold Spring Lane Commun Ctr 221, Baltimore, MD 21251, **Business Phone:** (443)885-1591.

### BEMBRY, LAWRENCE
Government official. **Personal:** Born Nov 29, 1946, Columbus, OH; son of Richard and Willie B Matthews; married Carol Flax; children: Steve Lakin, Lisa Lee Steptoe, Ross Lakin & Laura Jean. **Educ:** Am Int Col, BS, indust mgt & acct, 1967; Univ Del, 1973; Lewis & Clark Univ, attended 1991. **Career:** US Merit Systs Protection Bd, admin dir, 1979-82; US Equal Employ Opportunity Comm, admin mgt dir, 1982-85; US Dept Agr forest serv, Equal Opportunity dir, 1985-86, dir, 1986-89, dep reg forester, 1989-91, natural resources prog dir, 1991-94; Los Padres Nat Forest, forest supvr, dep regional forester; Bur Land Mgt, serv ctr dir, 1993-95, spec asst dep dir, 1995-98, sr adv dir, 1998-, dir serv ctr, currently. **Orgs:** Tau Epsilon Phi Fraternity, 1963; B'nai B'rith, 1982-93; Hebrew Educ Alliance; cfo, HEAR Now, 1994-99. **Honors/Awds:** Presidential Rank Awards, 1986, 1988 & 1989; Meritorious Service Awards, US Merit Syst Protection Bd, USAF & US Dept Interior. **Special Achievements:** First African-American and Orthodox Jew in the agency. **Home Addr:** 4204 E Lark Sparrow St, Highlands Ranch, CO 80126-5234, **Home Phone:** (303)683-9016. **Business Addr:** Director Service Center, US Bureau Land Management, 303 W Colfax Ave, Denver, CO 80204, **Business Phone:** (303)534-0412.

### BEMPONG, DR. MAXWELL A.
Educator. **Personal:** Born Sep 14, 1938, Oda; married Jacqueline B; children: Jeffrey Eugene & Kwabena Alexander. **Educ:** Mich State Univ, BS, MS, PhD, 1967. **Career:** Mich State Univ, res asst ship, 1965-67; Univ Nev Reno, teaching fel, 1970; J Basic & Appl Sci, Nat Inst Sci Trans, ed-in-chief; Norfolk State Univ, dir biomed res, head interim, dept chair, 1999-2003, Dept Biol, prof biol, currently. **Orgs:** Fel Phelps-Stokes Found, 1962-64; fel Cocoa Mkt Bd, 1964-67; Am Genetic Asn; Am Col Toxicol; AAAS; Environ Mutagen Soc; Torrey Bot Club; Nat Inst Sci; Sigma Xi; Beta Kappa Chi; Alpha Pi Zi; Am Soc Plant Biologists. **Honors/Awds:** Outstanding Faculty Award, Commonwealth Va, 1990; Prestigious Teaching Award, State Coun Higher Educ, 1990. **Home Addr:** 3746 Brennan Ave, Norfolk, VA 23502-4304, **Home Phone:** (757)466-9252. **Business Addr:** Professor, Norfolk State University, 700 Pk Ave, Norfolk, VA 23504, **Business Phone:** (757)823-8600.

### BENDOLPH, LAURIE
Executive. **Career:** Charter Capital LLC, owner & partner, pres, 1998-. **Business Addr:** Owner, Partner, Charter Capital LLC, 43 Golec Ave, Shelton, CT 06484-4017, **Business Phone:** (203)924-0851.

### BENDY, MELINDA
School administrator, educator. **Career:** McAuliffe Elem Sch, prin, dir, currently. **Business Addr:** Director, Principal, McAuliffe Elementary School, 13540 Princedale Dr, Dale City, VA 22193-3845, **Business Phone:** (703)680-7270.

### BENEFIELD, MICHAEL MAURICE, JR.
Vice president (organization), government official. **Personal:** Born Jan 22, 1968, Washington, DC. **Educ:** Univ NC, Chapel Hill, NC, BA, polit sci, 1990; Univ Del, MPA, 1998. **Career:** US Sen William V Roth Jr, staff asst, 1990-91; New Castle Co Chamber Com, mgr city & state govt rels, beginning 1991; State Del, spec asst to lt gov, 1992-96, div dir, 1996-2000; MBNA Am, vpres, 2000-08; Bank Am, vpres, 2008-10, vpres, corp audit, 2011-; Del Dept Labor, Div Employ & Training, US Dept Labor, dir, currently. **Orgs:** Bd dir, Christina Educ Endowment Fund, 1992; adv coun, Pub Allies Del. **Home Addr:** 2127 Hollowbrooke Way NW, Acworth, GA 30101, **Home Phone:** (678)594-4759. **Business Addr:** Director, Delaware Department of Labor, Div Employ & Training, Wilmington, DE 19809-0828, **Business Phone:** (302)761-8000.

### BENET, ERIC (ERIC BENET JORDAN)
Singer. **Personal:** Born Oct 15, 1966, Milwaukee, WI; married Halle Berry; children: India; married Manuela Testolini; children: Lucia Bella. **Career:** Vocalist; Benet, 1990-96; solo artist, 1996-; Albums with Benet: Benet, 1992; Warner Bros, 1994-2004; Solo Albums: True to Myself, 1996; Let's Stay Together, 1996; Spiritual Thang, 1996; Femininity, 1997; True To Myself, 1997; A Day inthe Life, 1999; Georgy Porgy, 1999; Spend My Life With You, 1999; When YouThink Of Me, 2000; Glitter, 2001; Love Don't Love Me, 2001; I Wanna BeLoved, 2005; Hurricane, 2005; Pretty Baby, 2006; Where Does The Love Go, 2006; Love & Life, 2008, The Hunger, 2008; Chocolate Legs, 2009; Sometimes I Cry, 2010; Never Want to Live Without You, 2010; Lost in Time, 2010; Real Love, 2012; Harriett Jones, 2012; The One, 2012; Jordan House, 2011-; TV Episode: "For Your Love", 1998-2002; Burden of Truth, 2000; Half& Half, 2002-06; The Big Who's Wooing Who Episode, 2005; Soul Train, 2006; "Kaya", 2007; Trinity Goodheart, 2011; "Real Husbands of Hollywood ", 2013. **Business Addr:** Recording Artist, Warner Brothers Records Inc, 3300 Warner Blvd, Burbank, CA 91505, **Business Phone:** (818)846-9090.

### BENFORD, EDWARD A.
Executive, president (organization). **Career:** Benford & Assoc Inc, founder & mgr, 1989-, pres, currently. **Business Addr:** President, Benford & Associates Inc, 3000 Town Ctr Suite 1333, Southfield, MI 48075, **Business Phone:** (248)351-0250.

### BENFORD-LEE, ALYSSIA
Auditor, executive, association executive. **Educ:** Fla Agr & Mech Univ, BA, acct. **Career:** Deloitte & Touche LLP, sr auditor; Motorola Inc, regional adv bd, leader; Benford Brown & Assocs LLC, cert pub acc & co-founding partner, currently. **Orgs:** Am Inst Cert Pub Acct; Ill Cert Pub Acct Soc; Nat Asn Black Acct; bd dir, United Way Progs & Allocations Comt; bd dir, Bolingbrook Police Pension Bd; treas, Bolingbrook Chamber Com; treas, Bolingbrook Rotary Int. **Honors/Awds:** Entrepreneur of the Year, Bolingbrook, 2005. **Business Addr:** Co-Founding Partner, Benford Brown & Associates LLC, 343 N Schmidt Rd, Bolingbrook, IL 60440, **Business Phone:** (630)679-9424.

### BENHAM, DR. ROBERT
Judge. **Personal:** Born Sep 25, 1946, Cartersville, GA; son of Clarence and Jesse Knox; married Nell Dodson; children: Corey Brevard & Austin Tyler. **Educ:** Tuskegee Univ, BS, polit sci, 1967; Univ Ga, Lumpkin Sch Law, JD, 1970; Univ Va, LLM, 1989; Harvard Univ, attended. **Career:** Atlanta Legal Aid Socs Inc, trial atty; State Ga, spec asst atty gen, 1978-84; Ga Ct Appeals, judge, 1984-89; Ga Supreme Ct, judge, 1989-; Ga Supreme Ct, chief justice, 1995-2001; justice, currently. **Orgs:** Bd dir, Cartersville Chamber Com, 1976; bd chnm, Coosa Valley APDC, 1978; pres, Cartersville Bar Asn, 1981-82; vpres, Ga Conf Black Lawyers; bd mem, Fed Defender Prog, 1983-84; Am Judicature Soc; Ga Hist Soc; pres, Bartow County Bar Asn; Gov's Southern Bus Inst; pres, Soc Alternative Dispute Resolution; Nat Criminal Justice Asn; Ga Asn Trial Lawyers; Alpha Phi Alpha; Lawyers' Club Atlanta; Ga Bar Found; trustee, Ga Legal Hist Found; Scribes-Am Socs Writers Legal Subjects; bd mem, Fed Lawyers Asn; chmn, Gov's Comn Drug Awareness & Prev; State Bar Task Force Involvement Women & Minorities Profession; Ga Comn C & Youth; Nat Asn Ct Mgt; Nat Conf Chief Justices; Fed-State Jurisdiction Comt; pres, Socs Alternative Dispute Resolution; chmn, Judicial Coun; chmn, Chief Justice's Comn Professionalism; Gov Southern Bus Inst; Demosthenian Lit Soc; Lawyers' Club Atlanta; Am Soc Writers Legal Subjects; chmn, Gov's Comn Drug Awareness & Prev; State Bar Task Force Involvement Women & Minorities; Ga Comn C & Youth; Nat Asn Ct Mgt; Nat Conf Chief Justices; Fed-State Jurisdiction Comt; Alpha Phi Alpha fraternity. **Home Addr:** 205 Old Mill Rd, Cartersville, GA 30120, **Home Phone:** (770)382-7209. **Business Addr:** Justice, Supreme Court of Georgia, 244 Wash St Rm 572, Atlanta, GA 30334, **Business Phone:** (404)656-3470.

### BENJAMIN, ALBERT W.
Educator. **Personal:** Born New York, NY; son of Alfred W and Olivia E; married Goldie; children: Albert II, Scott & Candace. **Educ:** Brooklyn Col, BA, 1953, MS, 1958; Columbia Univ, prof dipl, 1964, Fordham Univ, PhD, 1976. **Career:** City NY Bd Educ, teacher, 1953-60, asst prin, 1964-68, from exec asst to asst supt, 1964-69; consult, 1968-; Exp Elem Prog, cent coordr, 1969-72; Career Educ, Develop & Implementation, dir, 1972-73, prin, 1973-78; bd examiners, supv asst examr, 1978-90; Brooklyn Col, adj prof, 1980-; Bur Teacher Test Develop & ADM, dir, 1990-2002. **Orgs:** Alpha Phi Alpha, 1952; Phi Delta Kapa, 1963; Fellow, Ford Found, 1968; Kappa Delta Pi, 1971; NY Acad Pub Educ, 1974; life mem, NCP. **Home Addr:** 17234 133rd Ave Apt 11C, Jamaica, NY 11434, **Home Phone:** (718)723-1102.

### BENJAMIN, ARTHUR J., JR.
Executive, executive director. **Personal:** Born Feb 8, 1938, Wagener, SC; married Dorothy Carrington; children: Lisa Simone, Cecily Lyn & Stacy Elisabeth. **Educ:** Nat Bus Col, jr acct cert, 1955; Tenn State Univ, BS, 1959; Univ Colo, attended 1960; NY Univ, attended 1964. **Career:** Franklin Bk Progs, sr acct, 1962-67; Am Home Prod Corp, asst comptroller, 1967-68; Whitehall Labs, asst treas, 1968-72; ITT, sr financial analyst, 1972-77; Wallace & Wallace Ent, vpres, controller, 1977-82; Unity Broadcasting Network, dir corp finance, currently. **Orgs:** Pres, Jamaica Serv Prog Older Adults, 1979-81; chmn bd, Queensborough Soc Prev Cruelty C, 1981-83. **Honors/Awds:** Black Achievers Harlem Br YMCA, 1978; Tenn State Univ Sch Bus Award, 1978. **Home Addr:** 115101 222nd St, Cambria Heights, NY 11411-1230, **Home Phone:** (718)528-9893. **Business Addr:** Director of Corporate Finance, Unity Broadcasting Network, 10 Columbus Cir, New York, NY 10019.

### BENJAMIN, COREY DWIGHT
Basketball player. **Personal:** Born Feb 24, 1978, Compton, CA; son of Steward. **Educ:** Ore State Univ, attended 1998. **Career:** Basketball player (retired); Chicago Bulls, guard, 1998-2001; Sutor Montegranaro, 2001-02; Southern Calif Surf, 2001-02; N Charleston Lowgators, 2002-03; Atlanta Hawks, guard, 2003; Chalonnais, 2003-04; Xinjiang Flying Tigers, 2003-04; Charlotte Bobcats, guard, 2004-05; Guaros de Lara, 2005-06; Conquistadores de Guaynabo, 2006; NBA Develop League Enterprises LLC, D-League; Benfica, 2006-07; Guaynabo, Pr, forward, 2007; Daegu Orions, 2007-08.

### BENJAMIN, FLOYD G.
Executive. **Personal:** married Floretta; children: Floyd Jr. **Educ:** NC Cent Univ, BS, biol, MS, microbiol. **Career:** Lyphomed, sr vpres sci affairs; McGaw; Abbott; Neocrin, chief exec off; Biotech Startupneocrin Inc, pres & chief exec officer, 1992-93; Pasadena Res Lab, consult, 1993-94, pres & chief exec officer, 1994-96; Taylor Pharmaceut Inc, pres, 1996-98; Akorn Inc, pres & chief exec officer, 1998-2001, vice chmn, 2001; Keystone Pharmaceut, chief exec off, owner & dir, 2002-; Cenomed, bd dir, 2005-. **Business Addr:** Chief Executive Officer, Chairman, Keystone Pharmaceuticals Inc, 26072 Merit Cir Suite 101, Laguna Hills, CA 92653, **Business Phone:** (949)348-7770.

### BENJAMIN, MICHAEL L.
Health services administrator. **Personal:** married Marva P. **Educ:** Tex Southern Univ, Houston, BA, psychol; Yale Univ, Sch Med, MPH, ment health admin, 1972; Am Soc Asn Exec, CAE, 2006; Am Soc Asn Exec, cert asn exec, 2006. **Career:** Norteast Community Ment Health Ctr, exec dir; Nat Asn counties, human serv & prog dir, assoc legis dir; Nat Inst Ment Health, health scientist adminr; Community ment health ctr, exec dir; Employee Assistance Profs Asn, chief operating officer; US Dept Health & Human Serv, Substance Abuse & Ment Health Serv Admin; Inst Ment Health Initiatives, exec dir; Nat Coun Family Rels, Minneapolis, MN, exec dir, 2006; Family, Career & Community Leaders Am, exec dir, 2006-13; Exec Dirs & chief exec officers Wash DC Metro Area, founder, chief exec officer & exec dir, 2013-. **Orgs:** Bd mem, Child Care Works; Univ Minn Family Social Sci Adv Bd; adv bd mem, NC A&T State Univ Human Environ & Family Sci Adv Bd; Am Soc Asn Execs; Am Pub Health Asn. **Home Phone:** (612)747-9562. **Business Addr:** Executive Director, Family, Career & Community Leaders of America, 1910 Asn Dr, Reston, VA 20191, **Business Phone:** (703)476-4900.

### BENJAMIN, DR. REGINA M. (REGINA MARCIA BENJAMIN)
Physician, founder (originator). **Personal:** Born Oct 26, 1956, Mobile, AL; daughter of Millie and Clarence. **Educ:** Xavier Univ, BS, chem, 1979; Morehouse Sch Med, 1982; Univ Ala, Birmingham, MD, 1984; Med Ctr Cent GA, Macon GA, residency, 1987; Tulane Univ, MBA, 1991. **Career:** Bayou La Batre city, pvt pract; Bayou La Batre Rural Health Clin, founder & chief exec officer, 1990-; Univ S Ala, Col Med, Mobile, AL, assoc dean rural health, admnr; USPHS, vice adm, surgeon gen, 2009-13. **Orgs:** Delta Sigma Theta sorority; Bd mem, Bd Health, Mobile County Health Dept, 1992-97; Ala Bd Censors MASA, bd med examr, bd pub health, 1992-97; Fel Kellogg Nat, 1993-96; Gov's Health Care Reform Task Force, 1994-95; past vice chair, Gov's Comn Aging, 1994-95; adv comt, Clin Lab Improv, 1994-; bd trustees, Ama, 1995-98; past pres, Educ & Res Found, Coun Ethical & Judicial Affairs; Coun Grad Med Educ, 1997; pres, bd dir, bd trustees, Mobile County Med Soc, 1997; pres, Med Asn State Ala, 2002-; Nat Acad Sci Inst Med; Dipl, Am Bd Family Pract; fel, Am Acad Family Physicians; past bd mem, Physicians Human Rights; exec comt, Forum Med Affairs; Southern Rural Access Prog; vpres, Deep S Girl Scout Coun; bd trustees, Eastern Mercy Health Syst; bd trustees, United Way Mobile; State Comt Publ Health Ala; bd trustees, Mobile Area Red Cross; bd trustees, Mobile Chamber Com; bd trustees, Mobile 200; bd trustee, Morehouse Sch Med. **Honors/Awds:** American Medical Association's Unsung Hero Campaign advertisement, 1990; Angel in a White Coat, New York Times, 1995; Person of the Week, ABC's World News, 1995; Woman of the Year, CBS This Morning, 1996; Nelson Mandela Award for Health & Human Rights, 1998; hon Nat Gov Asn, 2003; Rockefeller Next Generation Leader; Woman of Achievement award, Mobile Press Register; Pro Ecclesia et Pontifice Award, Pope Benedict XVI, 2006; 100 Most Trusted People in America. **Special Achievements:** First physician under age 40 and the first African-American woman to be elected to AMA's board trustees; Time Magazine, One of the 50 Future Leaders Age 40 & Under, 1994; National Forum, The Phi Kappa Phi Journal, "Feeling Poorly: The Troubling Verdict on Poverty & Health Care in America", 1996; American Medical Association Board of Trustees first African-American woman to be elected. **Home Addr:** 318 N Patrician Dr, Spanish Fort, AL 36527, **Home Phone:** (334)626-0394. **Business Addr:** Founder, Chief Executive Officer, Bayou La Batre Rural Health Clinic, 13833 Tapia Lane, Bayou La Batre, AL 36509, **Business Phone:** (334)824-4985.

### BENJAMIN, RONALD
Auditor, accountant. **Personal:** Born Dec 31, 1941, New York, NY; married Carmen E Hodge; children: Nicolle, Danielle & Christopher. **Educ:** Bronx Community Col, AAS, 1966; Pace Col, BBA, pub accountancy, 1968; Bernard M Baruch Col, MBA, comput methodology, 1974. **Career:** Main LaFrentz & Co CPA's, sr acct, 1968-71; Union Camp Corp, sr auditor, 1971-74; Ross Stewart & Benjamin PC CPA's, dir, 1974-; Bronx Lebanon Hosp, vice chmn & treas, currently; Hostos Comm Col, adj prof; NY Soc State Cert Pub Accountants, treas, 1999; Ernst & Young LLP, audit partner; Mitchell & Titus LLP, audit partner, currently. **Orgs:** NY State Health Care Trustees, 1999; Am Inst Cert Pub Accountants; bd dir, NY St Soc Cert Pub Accountants; NJ Soc Cert Pub Accountants; co-founder, Nat Asn Black Accts; William Patterson & Essex Co Col; Mitchell & Titus Qual Control Comt. **Home Addr:** 555 Kappock St Apt 23E, Bronx, NY 10463-6433. **Business Addr:** Audit Partner, Mitchell & Titus LLP, 1 Battery Pk Plz 27th Fl, New York, NY 10004-1461, **Business Phone:** (212)709-4500.

### BENJAMIN, ROSE MARY
Government official, vice president (organization). **Personal:** Born Apr 28, 1933, Pueblo, CO; married Orville B; children: Darryl Kevin, Darwin Craig, Duane Carter & Benjamin Jr. **Career:** Educator (retired); Inglewood Unified Bd Educ, pres, 1982; Southern Calif Regional Occup, clerk, v pres, 1983-84; Calif Urban Asn Sch Dist, secy exec brd, 1985; Inglewood Sch Brd, v pres, 1988. **Orgs:** Chmn, Coaltition Black Sch Bd, 1983-84; dist chairperson coalition, Advocating Reform Educ, 1984; secy exec, March Dimes Bd dir, 1984; rep, March Dimes, Inglewood Coun PTA, 1984; bd dir, Centinela Child GuidClinic, 1984; comt mem, Calif Sch Brd. **Home Addr:** 8711 3rd Ave, Inglewood, CA 90305.

### BENJAMIN, STEPHEN K.
Politician, lawyer. **Personal:** Born Dec 1, 1969, Queens, NY; son of Sam and Maggie; married DeAndrea Gist; children: Bethany & Jordan Grace. **Educ:** Univ SC, BA, polit sci, 1991; Univ SC, Sch Law, JD, 1994; Francis Marion Univ, DHH. **Career:** McNair Law Firm (Columbia, SC), Admin & Regulatory Pract, assoc; Carolina Power & Light Co, mgr corp affairs; Int Paper Co, regional mgr pub affairs; Benjamin Law Firm, LLC, prin; Gov Jim Hodges' Cabinet, Dept Probation, Parole & Pardon Serv, dir app, 1999-2002; Richland County Dem Party, chmn; S Carolina's Fourth Judicial Circuit, asst prosecutor; Dem Party Nominee, atty gen, 2002; Columbia, SC, mayor, July, 2010-; Parker Poe, atty; Ogletree, Deakins, Nash, Smoak & Stewart P.C. (Ogletree Deakins), coun, 2010-. **Orgs:** NAACP's S Carolina Youth & Col Div, former Pres; USC Sch Law, Stud Govt & Stud Bar Asn, former pres; Columbia Urban League, Bd Dirs; Benedict Col, Bd Mem; Greater Columbia Chamber Com, Bd Dirs; Eau Claire Promise Zone, Founding Bd Mem; Choose C First, Founding Mem; Univ S Carolina Develop Found, Bd Mem; S Carolina Sch Law Partnership, Bd Mem; S Carolina Chamber Com, Bd Dirs; Jr Achievement S Carolina, Bd Dirs; Habitat Humanity Midlands, Bd Dirs; Univ S Carolina C's Ctr, Bd Dirs; Nat Bank S Carolina (NBSC), former mem Bd Dirs;

Kappa Alpha Psi fraternity. **Honors/Awds:** National Bar Association, National Young Lawyer of the Year, 1999; University of South Carolina School of Law, Compleat Lawyer Award, 2000; South Carolina Bar Association, Young Lawyer of the Year Award, Co-recipient, 2001; Greater Columbia Chamber of Commerce, Athena Award, 2001; "Ebony" Magazine, 30 Leaders of the Future; Columbia, SC Urban League's Lincoln C. Jenkins, Jr. Award, Recipient; "The State Newspaper" (Columbia, SC), 20 Business Leaders Changing Columbia, 2005, 10 Top Movers and Shakers to Watch in Government and Politics, 2005-06; Liberty Fellow, 2007; Richland County (SC) Bar Association, Civic Star Award, 2007; "Best Lawyers in America," 2008-09; Aspen Rodel Fellowship, Recipient; "The Washington Post," The Root 100 List: The 100 Most influential African Americans in 2011; U.S. Conference of Mayors, Trustee, 2012. **Special Achievements:** First African-American mayor in Columbia's history. **Business Addr:** Mayor, PO Box 147, Columbia, SC 29217, **Business Phone:** (803)545-3075.

**BENJAMIN, DR. TRITOBIA HAYES. See Obituaries Section.**

**BENNETT, ALONZA**
Chief executive officer, automotive executive. **Personal:** Born MS; married Yvonne. **Career:** Al Bennett Ford Inc, Flint MI, chief exec. **Home Addr:** 5470 Ali Dr, Grand Blanc, MI 48439-5172. **Business Addr:** Chief Executive, Al Bennett Ford Inc, 5510 Clio Rd RD, Flint, MI 48504, **Business Phone:** (810)789-1511.

**BENNETT, ANN. See NESBY, ANN.**

**BENNETT, ARTHUR T.**
Judge. **Personal:** Born Feb 3, 1933, Corapeake, NC; married Josephine Adams. **Educ:** Norfolk State Col, cert, 1957; Howard Univ, BA, 1959; Howard Univ, Sch Law, LLB & JD, 1963; Univ Houston, Nat Col Dist atty, grad, 1972. **Career:** Judge(retired); BL Hooks, AW Willis Jr, RB Sugarmon Jr & IH Murphy Memphis, Tenn, assoc atty, 1963-65; pvt pract, atty, 1964; Dist Atty's Off, prosecutor, 1965; Nat Col Dist Atty, fac adv, 1973; Shelby Co, Tenn Gen Sessions Ct, judge, 1975; State Tenn, Criminal Ct, 30th Judicial Dist, Shelby Criminal Justice Complex, judge, 1976-06. **Orgs:** Memphis & Shelby Co Bar Asn; Nat Bar Asn; legal dir & exec bd mem, Nat United Law Enforcement Officers Asn; Nat Asn Advan Colored People; bd dir, Memphis Br, Nat Asn Advan Colored People; Memphis Chap Asn Study Afro-Am Life & Hist; Title XX State Adv Coun Dept Human Servs; Nat Dist Atty Asn. **Home Addr:** 1334 W Crestwood Dr, Memphis, TN 38119, **Home Phone:** (901)685-8383.

**BENNETT, BELINDA**
Ship captain. **Personal:** Born Jan 1, 1977?. **Career:** RMS St. Helena, deck cadet, third officer & second officer, 1994-2003; SS Delphine, chief officer, 2004-05; Isle Man Steam Packet co, chief officer, 2004-05; Windstar Cruises, second officer & chief officer, 2005-, master, 2016-. **Special Achievements:** First black woman to serve as the captain of a commercial cruise ship. **Business Addr:** Windstar Cruises, 2101 4th Ave Suite 210, Seattle, WA 98121, **Business Phone:** (206)733-2703.

**BENNETT, BETTY B.**
College administrator. **Educ:** MSN, CS. **Career:** Savannah State Univ, Harris-McDew Stud Health Serv, admin dir, currently. **Business Addr:** Administrative Director, Savannah State University, 3219 Col St, Savannah, GA 31404, **Business Phone:** (912)358-4778.

**BENNETT, BRANDON PURRELL**
Football player, executive. **Personal:** Born Feb 3, 1973, Greenville, SC. **Educ:** Univ SC, BS, 1995. **Career:** Football player (retired), executive; Cincinnati Bengals, running back, 1995, 1998-2003; Cleveland Browns, 1995; Chicago Bears, 1995-96; Miami Dolphins, 1996-97; Carolina Panthers, running back, 2004; Tampa Bay Buccaneers, 2004; Bethlehem Baptist Church Christian Acad, phys educ teacher, currently; Carolina High Sch & Acad, dean students, currently; Sprint, Greenville, SC, acct exec, 2010-; Southside Christian Sch, Dir Intramural Sports. **Honors/Awds:** Good Guy, National Football League, 2003; Hall of Fame, Univ SC, 2004; Southeastern Conference Football Legend, 2011. **Home Addr:** , Simpsonville, SC. **Business Addr:** Account Executive, Sprint, 3275 N Pleasantburg Dr, Greenville, SC 29609, **Business Phone:** (864)631-6915.

**BENNETT, CHARLES JAMES**
Manager. **Personal:** Born Aug 17, 1956, Shreveport, LA; son of Charles Sr and Emma M Fountain. **Educ:** Wiley Col, Marshall, Tex, BA, Educ. **Career:** Coors Brewing Co, ield mgr, 1979-, dir, environ affairs, currently. **Orgs:** Bd dir, Brass Found, 1989-; recruitment comt, Chicago Urban League, 1989-; bd, Coors African Am Asn; NCP; comt mem, S Side Br. **Honors/Awds:** Being Single Magazine Pinnacle Award, Achievement Bus & Prof Excellence, 1988; Chicago Race for Literacy Campaign, Chicago Pub Schs. **Special Achievements:** America's Best & Brightest Business and Professional Men, Dollars & Sense Mag, 1989. **Business Addr:** Director Environmental Affairs, Coors Brewing Co, 900 Circle 75 Pkwy Suite 1080, Atlanta, GA 30339.

**BENNETT, CORNELIUS O'LANDA**
Football player. **Personal:** Born Aug 25, 1965, Birmingham, AL; son of Lino; married Kimberly. **Educ:** Univ Ala, attended 1986. **Career:** Football player (retired); Buffalo Bills, left outside linebacker, 1987-94, right inside linebacker, 1995; Atlanta Falcons, left linebacker, 1996-98, Indianapolis Colts, linebacker, 1999-2000. **Honors/Awds:** All-American, 1984-86; SEC Player of the Year, 1986; Lombardi Award, 1986; SEC Player of the Year honors, 1986; Vince Lombardi Trophy, 1986; AFC Defensive Player of the Year, 1988, 1991; Pro Bowl, 1988, 1990-93; Rookie the Year, Sports Illus, 1990; Super Bowl, 1990-93; Col Football Hall Fame, 2005; Alabama Sports Hall of Fame; Lombardi Award. **Special Achievements:** First-team All-Pro selection, 1988, 1991-92; All-America Selection, 1984-86. Films: 1986 John Hancock Sun Bowl, 1986; 1987 NFL Draft, 1987; 1988 AFC Championship Game, 1989; 1990 AFC Championship Game, 1991; Super Bowl XXV, 1991; 1991 AFC Championship Game, 1992; Super Bowl XXVI, 1992; 1992 AFC Championship Game, 1993; Super Bowl XXVII, 1993; Super Bowl XXVIII, 1994; 1998 NFC Championship Game, 1999; Super Bowl XXXIII, 1999; The Top 5 Reasons You Can't Blame, 2006. **Home Addr:** , Hollywood, FL.

**BENNETT, COURTNEY AJAYE**
Educator. **Personal:** Born Nov 17, 1959, New York, NY. **Educ:** HS Music & Art, dipl, music, 1976; Wagner Col, BS, 1980. **Career:** Health Ins Plan Greater NY, mkt rep, 1983; Ralph Bunch Sch, sci coord, teacher. **Orgs:** Partner, JBR Discount Corp; bd dir, Sigma Phi Rho Frat, 1978-80, nat pres, 1992-94; 100 Young Black Men, 1985; founder, Phoenix Sorority, 1994; chair, Harlem Tobacco Community Action Bd; founder, Repertory Theatre.

**BENNETT, DAINA T.**
Writer. **Educ:** Southwest Tex State, jour. **Career:** Chelsea House, Scholastic Publ; Educ Mat distribrs, chief exec officer, currently. **Orgs:** Co-chair, African-Am Parent Coun, 1987-91; chair, African-Am Community Improv Found, 1991-92; bd mem, Country Doctor, 1991-92. **Home Addr:** 5550 17th Ave S, Seattle, WA 98108, **Home Phone:** (206)763-1036. **Business Addr:** Chief Executive Officer, Educational Materials distributors, 1424 4th Ave Suite 4A, Seattle, WA 98101, **Business Phone:** (206)853-8230.

**BENNETT, DEBORAH MINOR**
Consultant, executive. **Personal:** Born Aug 13, 1951, Long Branch, NJ; daughter of Leonard and Caroline; married Harvey. **Educ:** Montclair State Col, BA, 1973, MA, 1976; NY Univ; Stevens Inst Tech, org develop coursework. **Career:** Neptune Sr HS, humanities instr, 1974-75; Webster Hall Res Hall Montclair State, dir, 1975-76; Upward Bound, dir, 1976-78; Stevens Tech Enrichment Prog, dir, 1978-83; WBDC's Child Care Bus Initiative, coordr, 2000-02; Chicago Area Pre-Col Eng Prog, exec dir; Right Source Inc, owner, currently. **Orgs:** Represented Women's Bus Develop Ctr, 2007; Bd mem, treas, Asn Equality & Excel Educ; bd mem, NJ Asn Black Educrs; bd mem, Educ Opportunity Fund Dir Asn; steering comt, Nat Asn Multicultural Eng Prog Advocate Inc; dir, Nat Asn Pre-Col; Asn Supvr & Curric Develop; Coalition Keep Sch Open; bd mem, Ill Fair Schs Coalition Blacks Develop; pres, Partners Profit; Youth move Christ; vice chmn, Chicago Inst Urban Poverty; Haye's Educ Leg Adv Coun; vice-chair, bd mem, Chicago Inst Urban Poverty; Sustain environ commun group. **Special Achievements:** Published Article, "Overcoming Barriers"-Winning The Retention Battle, NSBE Journal, Dec 85/Jan 86. Published article, "Case for Retention Programs". **Home Addr:** 1423 E 68th St, Chicago, IL 60637-4828, **Home Phone:** (773)363-0977. **Business Addr:** Owner, The Right Source Inc, 1423 E 68th St Suite 3, Chicago, IL 60637, **Business Phone:** (773)324-1834.

**BENNETT, REV. DEBRA QUINETTE**
Clergy, editor. **Personal:** Born Feb 10, 1958, New York, NY. **Educ:** Wagner Col, BA, eng, 1980; Bexley Hall Sem, Mdiv. **Career:** Asn Ship Brokers & Agts, asst exec dir, 1980; Newsweek Mag, res & reporter, 1981-82; Mamaroneck Daily Times, reporter, 1981; Sci Am Mag, proofreader & copy ed; Grace Episcopal Church, sunday sch teacher, 1984-; St Pauls Episcopal Church, priest-in-charge; Church Our Saviour, priest-in-charge, 2012-. **Orgs:** Managing ed, Sigma Phi Rho Frat Newsletter, 1981-; Zeta Phi Beta Sorority Inc. **Home Addr:** 16010 89th Ave Suite 12M, Jamaica, NY 11432, **Home Phone:** (718)658-8290. **Business Addr:** Priest-in-Charge, Church of Our Saviour, 471 Crosby St, Akron, OH 44302, **Business Phone:** (330)535-9174.

**BENNETT, DELORA**
Executive. **Career:** Genesis Personnel Serv Inc, pres & chief exec officer, 1984-. **Business Addr:** President, Chief Executive Officer, Genesis Personnel Service Inc, 10921 Reed Hartman Suite 226, Cincinnati, OH 45242, **Business Phone:** (513)891-4433.

**BENNETT, DELORES M.**
Community activist, social worker. **Personal:** Born Clarksville, TN; daughter of Will Henry and Carrie B Barbee; married Eugene Sr; children: Ronda J, Eugene Jr, Mary King & Michelle. **Career:** Wayne Co, Mich, Wayne Co comnr, 1978-82; N End Youth Improv Coun, founder & exec, currently. **Orgs:** Founder & exec dir, Northend Youth Improv Coun, 1964-; bd trustee, Henry Ford Hosp; chair by-laws comm, Detroit Health Dept Substance Abuse Adv Coun; bd dir, United Community Serv; lifetime mem, Nat Asn Advan Colored People; bd assembly, United Found; Detroit Rctrn Partners; Considine Adv Coun; Concerned Citizens Coun; Afro-Am Mus Detroit; Nat Coun Negro Women Inc; Team Organizer, Police Athletic League; adv mem, Henry Ford Hosp; Metro Youth Coun; Neighborhood Legal Serv; Northern Community Coun Sch Edu; Am Bus Womens Ass; St. John CME Church; United Way Serv; Adopt A Pk; Oper Green Thumb; Adopt-A-Child Christmas; Pride Inc. **Honors/Awds:** Resolution Service, Detroit Bd Educ, 1982; Proclamation of Dolores Bennett Day, Mayor City Detroit, 1982; Michigan State Senate Resolution, MI State Senate, 1982; Jefferson Award, Am Inst Pub Serv, 1987; Michiganian of the Year, The Detroit News, 1988; Mental Health Clothing Drive, Northend Youth Improv Coun; Operation Green Thumb, North end Youth Improv Coun; Jobs for Youth Conference, North end Youth Improv Coun; North end Youth Improv Coun Youth Against Drugs; America's Award Hero, Positive Thinking, 1990; WWJ Radio 95 Citizen, WWJ Radio, 1990; The Erma L. Henderson Distinguished Community Service Award, The Safe Center Inc; Lifetime Achievement Award, Youth Sports and Recreation Comn; Community Service Award, Afro American Sports Hall of Fame & Gallery; Youth Service Award FBI, Community Outreach Award Prog; Gertrude Powe Community Service Award; The Detroit Old Timers Inc. **Special Achievements:** First elected to the Wayne County Board of Commissioners from the 8th District in 1978. **Home Addr:** 20498 Yonka St, Detroit, MI 48234-1834, **Home Phone:** (313)368-0997. **Business Addr:** Founder, Executive Director, Northend Youth Improvement Council, 111 King St, Detroit, MI 48202-2126.

**BENNETT, DONNELL, JR.**
Football player, football coach. **Personal:** Born Sep 14, 1972, Ft. Lauderdale, FL; married Adrienne; children: Matthew, Donnell III, Coleman & Caden. **Educ:** Univ Miami, grad. **Career:** Football player (retired), coach; Kans City Chiefs, 1994-2000, running back, 1995, 1997-99, fullback, 2000; Wash Redskins, fullback, 2001; Coral Springs Christian Acad high sch, head coach; Northeast High Sch, head coach, currently. **Business Addr:** Head Coach, Coral Springs Christian Academy, 2251 Riverside Dr, Coral Springs, FL 33065, **Business Phone:** (954)752-2870.

**BENNETT, EDGAR, III**
Executive, football coach, football player. **Personal:** Born Feb 15, 1969, Jacksonville, FL; son of Juanita; married Mindy; children: Edgar IV & Elyse Morgan. **Educ:** Fla State Univ, BA, polit sci & sociol. **Career:** Football player (retired), football coach; Green Bay Packers, running back, 1992, 1996, fullback, 1993-95, dir player develop & dir player prog, 2001-04, running backs coach, 2005-, wide receivers coach, 2011-, offensive coordr, 2015-; Chicago Bears, running back, 1998-99, fullback, 1999. **Orgs:** March Dimes, 2003; Fund C with Cancer. **Honors/Awds:** Hall of Fame, Green Bay Packers, 2005; Nice Guy Award, Doug Jirschele Sports Awards Banquet Clintonville, 2006; Florida State Athletic Hall of Fame; Super Bowl XLV, Super Bowl XXXI Champions, Green Bay Packers. **Home Addr:** , Green Bay, WI. **Business Addr:** Running Backs Coach, Green Bay Packers, 1265 Lombardi Ave, Green Bay, WI 54307-0628, **Business Phone:** (920)496-5700.

**BENNETT, REV. GORDON D.**
Bishop, school principal, clergy. **Personal:** Born Oct 21, 1946, Denver, CO. **Educ:** Loyola Univ, Los Angeles, CA, grad; Loyola Marymount Univ, MEd; Gonzaga Univ, BA, philos; Jesuit Sch Theol, Berkeley, CA, MDiv, 1975; Loyola Marymount Univ, MEd, sec sch admin, 1979; Fordham Univ, dipl, admin. **Career:** Bishop (retired); Loyola High Sch, Los Angeles, Calif, prin, 1980-88, pres, 1996-98; St Ignatius Col Prep, San Francisco, Calif, asst prin campus ministry; Jesuit Novitiate Santa Barbara & Culver City, Calif, rector & master novices; Diocese, Baltimore, Md, auxiliary bishop, 1998; Diocese, Mandeville, Jamaica, bishop, 2004-08, bishop emer, 2008-. **Special Achievements:** Guest "Black Cath, Yes!", WIMG 1300 AM. **Home Addr:** 20 Perth Rd, PO Box 8, Mandeville21201, **Home Phone:** (876)962-5162. **Business Addr:** Bishop Emeritus, Diocese, 59 Main St, Mandeville21201, **Business Phone:** (876)962-1269.

**BENNETT, IVY H.**
Marketing executive, association executive, executive director. **Personal:** Born Oct 30, 1951, Waterbury, CT. **Educ:** Hampton Univ, BA, 1973; Univ Mich, Ann Arbor, MPH, 1975; Harvard Bus Sch, MBA, 1982. **Career:** Quaker Oats Co, brand mkt assoc, 1982-84; Kraft Foods, mkt brand mgr, 1984-89; Allstate Ins Co, asst vpres mkt, 1989-2002; Univ Chicago Hosp, vpres & chief mkt officer, 2002-06; Harris Bank, chief mkt officer, exec vpres, mkt & customer strategies, sr vpres advert res mkt serv, 2006-13. **Orgs:** bd mem, Harris Bank Nat Asn, 2004-13. **Special Achievements:** Charted Property Casualty Underwriter, CPCW, insurance designation, 1995. **Home Addr:** 5050 S Lake Shore Dr Apt 415, Chicago, IL 60615-3240. **Business Addr:** Senior Vice President, Harris Bank, 111 W Monroe St, Chicago, IL 60603, **Business Phone:** (312)461-6475.

**BENNETT, DR. JAMES L.**
College administrator. **Educ:** Macalester Col, BA, eng/lang arts teacher educ, 1969; Minn State Univ, Mankato, MA, higher educ/higher educ admin, curric develop, minority studies, 1977; Univ Wash, PhD, higher educ, 1988. **Career:** Metrop Community Col, Minneapolis, St Paul, Minn; Bellevue Community Col, Bellevue, Wash, counr, Minority Affairs Prog, 1978-2011, Eng-as-a-Second Lang & Lang Arts, instr, dean instr, 1990-2011, vpres equity & pluralism, 2006-11. **Orgs:** Chmn, Task Forces Develop Educ; Wash Voc Techn Coun; Joint Comt Assessment; pres-elect, bd dir, Nat Coun Black Am Affairs; Western Region Coun Black Am Affairs; United Way King County Employ Impact Coun; Lake City Rotary; N Seattle Boys & Girls Club.

**BENNETT, JOSSELYN**
Executive director. **Personal:** married Bruce; children: 2. **Educ:** Capital Univ, BA, social work, 1973; Ohio State Univ, MSW, social work, 1988. **Career:** Advocate; Proj Linden Coun Ctr, exec dir, 1975-88; Evangel Lutheran Church Am, 1988-91, Age-Span Ministries, dir, 1991-2003, dir educ & prog resources, Div Church Soc, currently, dir poverty ministry, justice congregational & synodical mission, currently. **Orgs:** Am Soc Aging; Nat Coun Churches Christ Comt Justice C; Comt Human Sexuality & Family Ministry; chair, Deleg Coun NICA, 1996-99, secy, 2003-05; NCC Educ & Leadership Ministries Comn; Manual Black Family Ministry. **Business Addr:** Director, Evangelical Lutheran Church America, 8765 W Higgins Rd, Chicago, IL 60631-4101, **Business Phone:** (800)638-3522.

**BENNETT, JOYCE ANNETTE**
Research scientist. **Personal:** Born Apr 18, 1941, Columbia, NC; daughter of Henry and Polly Bryant (deceased); married Robert L; children: Roderick, Roberta, Rhonda J Banks, Juancara, Robert & Chet. **Educ:** Wash Tech Inst, AA, acct, 1974; Univ DC, BBA, acct, 1989. **Career:** Raleigh Haberdasher, acct technician, 1970-72; Riggs Nat Bank, bank teller, 1972-73; Fed Res Bd, statist asst, 1973-79, sr statist asst, 1979-94, res asst, 1994-; Bennett Beauty Inst Inc, Sch Cosmetology, Barbering & Manicuring, owner; Bennett Careet Inst, owner & pres, currently. **Orgs:** Chair, Greater Mt Calvary Holy Church, trustee bd, 1985-; Pastor's Aid, 1985-; Women Virture, 1992-. **Home Addr:** 1813 Newton St NW, Washington, DC 20010, **Home Phone:** (202)232-3305. **Business Addr:** Research Assistant, Board of Governors of the Federal Reserve Board, 20th St Const Ave NW, Washington, DC 20551, **Business Phone:** (202)452-3000.

**BENNETT, KANYA A.**
Government official. **Educ:** Univ Ill, Urbana-Champaign, BS, jour, 1999; Univ NC Law Sch, JD, 2002. **Career:** US Dept Educ, law clerk,

2000; Lawyers' Comt Better Housing, legal intern, 2000; O'Donnell, Schwartz & Anderson, summer assoc, 2001; NC Jour Law & Technol, stud ed, 2001-02; Charter High Sch, tutor; US House Rep Comt Judiciary, Wash, DC, minority legal coun, 2003-11; Am Const Soc, dir progs criminal & civil justice, 2011-14; ACLU, legis coun, 2014-. **Orgs:** Cong Fel, Cong Black Caucus Found, 2002-03; Comt House Adminr; coun judiciary comt, US House Representatives, 2003-11; bd mem, Humanities Coun Wash DC. **Business Addr:** Legislative Counsel, ACLU Washington Legislative Office, 125 Broad St, New York, NY 10004.

### BENNETT, KAREN
President (organization). **Personal:** Born Jan 1, 1956, Richmond, VA; married Leroy; children: Jabari & Asha. **Educ:** Howard Univ, BS, phys ther, 1979; Ga State Univ, MS, exercise physiol, 2008; Emory Univ, Mdiv, 2008. **Career:** Ga Gen Assembly, State Rep Dist 94; Phys therapist; Metro Ther Providers Inc, owner & pres, 1990-; African Methodist Episcopal Church, ordained itinerant elder, 2009; New St Mark AME Church Ga, pastor, 2010; New Hope AME Church Hoschton Ga, pastor, currently. **Orgs:** Chmn & bd dir, DeKalb Bus Incubator, bd dir, Phys Ther Asn Ga; Alpha Kappa Alpha Sorority Inc; 100 Black Women DeKalb County; assoc minister, New Bethel AME Church Ga; chmn bd dir, New Bethel Sr Ctr. **Business Addr:** President, Owner, Metro Therapy Providers Inc, 3760 Lavista Rd Suite 102, Tucker, GA 30084-5615, **Business Phone:** (404)248-0415.

### BENNETT, LERONE, JR.
Writer, editor, historian. **Personal:** Born Oct 17, 1928, Clarksdale, MS; son of Lerone Sr and Alma Reed; married Gloria Sylvester; children: Alma Joy, Constance, Courtney & Lerone III. **Educ:** Morehouse Col, BA, jour, 1949. **Career:** Ed, writer, journalist; Atlanta Daily World, journalist, 1949-52; Jet Mag, city ed, 1952-53; Ebony Mag, assoc ed, sr ed, 1953-87, exec ed, 1987-2005, exec ed emer, 2005-; Northwestern Univ, vis prof hist, 1968-69; Bks: Pioneers Protest, 1968; What Manner Man: A Biog Martin Luther King, Jr., 1976; Before Mayflower: A Hist Black Am 1619-1962, 1984; Shaping Black Am: Struggles & Triumphs African Americans, 1619-90s, 1993; Forced Into Glory: Abraham Lincoln & White Dream, 2000; Great Moments Black Hist: Wade Water, 2000; Black Voices: An Anthology African-Am Lit, 2001. **Orgs:** Sigma Delta Chi; Kappa Alpha Psi; Phi Beta Kappa; trustee, Chicago Hist Soc, Morehouse Col, Columbia Col. **Honors/Awds:** Book of the Year Award, Capital Press Club, 1963; Patron Saints Award, Soc Midland Authors, 1965; DHum, Wilberforce Univ, 1977; Academic Institute Literature Award, Acad Arts & Lett, 1978; DLitt, Marquette Univ, 1979; LHD, Univ Ill, 1980; LHD, Lincoln Col, 1980; LHD, Dillard Univ, 1980; DLitt, Morgan St Univ, 1981; DLitt, Voorhees Col & Morgan St Univ, 1981; DLetters, Morris Brown Univ, 1985; DLetters, SC Univ, 1986; DLetters, Boston Univ, 1987; named to Pres Clinton's Comn Arts & Humanities; Trumpet Award, Turner Broadcasting Syst, 1998; Lifetime Achievement Award, Nat Asn Black Journalists, 2002; Carter G. Woodson Lifetime Achievement Award, Asn Study African Am Life & Hist, 2003. **Home Addr:** 1308 E 89th St, Chicago, IL 60619. **Business Addr:** Executive Editor Emeritus, Johnson Publishing Co, 820 S Mich Ave, Chicago, IL 60605, **Business Phone:** (312)322-9200.

### BENNETT, LONNIE M.
Chief executive officer, automotive executive, president (organization). **Career:** Champion Ford; Champion Mitsubishi; Rountree Hyundai, pres & dir, currently; Rountree Olds-Cadillac Co Inc, pres & chief exec officer, currently. **Orgs:** Comm One Hundred; adv bd, Cadillac; GM Minority Asn. **Special Achievements:** Black Enterprise's list of Top 100 Auto Dealers, ranked no 11, 2000. **Home Addr:** 8660 Fern Ave Suite 200, Shreveport, LA 71105, **Home Phone:** (318)798-7150. **Business Addr:** President, Chief Executive Officer, Rountree Olds-Cadillac Co Inc, 8600 Fren Suite 200, Shreveport, LA 71105, **Business Phone:** (318)798-5565.

### BENNETT, MARIAN C.
Lawyer, government official. **Educ:** Radcliffe Col, BA; Univ Pa Law Sch, JD, 1972. **Career:** Nat Labor Rels Bd, investr, field atty; US Dept Energy, var positions; Off Inspector Gen, sr atty; US Info Agency, inspector gen, 1993-96; Off Civil Rights, spec asst, Transp Security Admin, atty, currently, dir, currently. **Orgs:** Nat Labor Rels Bd; Bullis Bd trustee, 2003-. **Business Addr:** Attorney, Director, Office of Civil Rights, 800 N Capitol St NW Suite 500, Washington, DC 20536.

### BENNETT, MAYBELLE TAYLOR
City planner. **Personal:** Born Oct 19, 1949, Washington, DC; daughter of Raymond Bernard Taylor and Ruby Elizabeth Mills Taylor; married Robert Alvin; children: Rebeccah Leah. **Educ:** Vassar Col, Poughkeepsie, NY, AB, 1970; Columbia Univ, Grad Sch Archit, Planning & Preserv, New York, NY, MSUP, 1972. **Career:** Lagos State Develop & Property Corp, Lagos, Nigeria, town planning officer, 1972-75; Joint Ctr Polit Studies, Wash, DC, proj mgr, 1975-78; Working Group Community Develop Reform, dir res, 1978-81; Nat Comn Against Discrimination Housing, asst dir prog serv, 1982-84; DC Zoning Comn, comnr & chmn, 1982-98; Coalition Human Needs, dir res, 1984-91; Howard Univ, Off Pres, asst community rels & planning, 1991-; Howard Univ, dir community rels, 1996-. **Orgs:** Alpha Kappa Alpha Sorority, 1968; Lambda Alpha Land Econs Soc, 1986-; Leadership Wash, 1991-; Eckankar, 1994. **Honors/Awds:** Maryland Vassar Club Scholar, Maryland Vassar Club, 1966; Carnegie-Mellon Fel Grad Studies, Carnegie-Mellon Found, 1970-71; HUD Work-Study Fel Grad Study, US Dept HUD, 1971-72; William Kinne Fellows Travel Fel, Columbia Univ Sch Archit, 1972. **Special Achievements:** Author, Community Development Versus Poor Peoples' Needs: Tension in CDBG, 1981, Citizen-Monitoring-A How-To Manual: Controlling Community Resources through Grass Roots Research & Action, 1981, Private Sector Support for Fair Housing: A Guide, 1983, Block Grants: Beyond the Rhetoric, An Assessment of the Last Four Years, 1986, 1987, Block Grants: Missing the Target, An Overview of Findings, 1987. **Home Addr:** 2806 2nd St SE, Washington, DC 20032, **Home Phone:** (202)563-5357. **Business Addr:** Director, Howard University Community Association, 2731 Ga Ave NW, Washington, DC 20059, **Business Phone:** (202)806-4771.

### BENNETT, MICHAEL
Boxer. **Personal:** Born Mar 26, 1971, Chicago, IL; son of Calvance and Aileen Brock. **Educ:** Univ NC, BS, finance, 2000. **Career:** Boxer (retired); Bank Am, banking assoc, 1999-2000; prof boxer, 2001-03. **Honors/Awds:** Champion, Nat Police Force Athletic League, 1993, 1996, 1998; Silver medal, US Nat Championships, 1997, 1998, 1999, gold medal, 1999; Nat Golden Gloves, champion, 1998; Champion, US Challenge, 1999; National Amateur Heavyweight Boxing Champion, Sydney, 2000. **Home Addr:** 1000 E 53rd St, Chicago, IL 60615, **Home Phone:** (773)324-7291.

### BENNETT, MICHAEL
Football player. **Personal:** Born Aug 13, 1978, Milwaukee, WI; married Katie Salzano; children: 4. **Educ:** Univ Wis, BS, consumer sci. **Career:** Football player (retired); Minn Vikings, running back, 2001-05; New Orleans Saints, 2006; Kans City Chiefs, running back, 2006-07; Tampa Bay Buccaneers, 2007-08; San Diego Chargers, 2008-09; Oakland Raiders, 2010. **Orgs:** Twin Cities community. **Honors/Awds:** Pro Bowl, 2002. **Business Addr:** CA.

### BENNETT, PATRICIA A.
Judge. **Personal:** children: Shandra Elaine. **Educ:** Col Guam Agana, GU, 1961; Riverside City Col, Riverside, CA, 1970; Univ Calif, BA, 1973; Hastings Col Law San Francisco, CA, 1976. **Career:** Judge(retired), attorney; State Ohio, Dept Finance, asst supr pay roll div, 1962-66; UCR Comput Ctr, prin clk, 1967-71; Stanislaus Co Dist Atty's Off, legal researcher, 1974; State Calif, Dept Water Resources, legal researcher, 1975; Contra Costa County, Dist Attys Off, Martinez, Calif, law clerk, 1976-77; State Pub Utilities Comm, atty, 1978-88; Calif Pub Utilities Comn, admin law judge; Tenn, atty, currently. **Orgs:** Urban League Guild, 1970; Univ Calif Riverside Stud Coun, 1971-72; vol, San Francisco Co Legal Asst Prog, San Bruno, Calif, 1973; Coun Legal Educ Opportunity Scholar, 1973-76; vol, San Francisco Int Visitors, 1980-83; Assembly man Walter Ingalls, Sacramento, Calif, Polit Sci Intern, 1973; Nat Dist Atty Asn Intern, 1974; Charles Houston Bar Asn, 1976-; Nat Bar Asn, 1979-. **Home Addr:** 2701 Maxwell Ave, Oakland, CA 94619. **Business Addr:** Attorney, Pvt Pract, 712 Wyntree N, Hermitage, TN 37076, **Business Phone:** (615)885-2168.

### BENNETT, PATRICIA W.
Educator. **Personal:** Born Forest, MS. **Educ:** Tougaloo Col, BA, 1975; Miss Col Sch Law, JD, 1979. **Career:** Small Bus Admin, atty, 1979-80; Miss Atty Gen, spec asst atty gen, 1980-82; Seventh Circuit Ct Dist, asst dist atty, 1982-87; Dist Atty Hinds County, asst dist atty, 1982-87; US Atty, asst US atty, 1987-89; Harvard Law Sch Trial Advocacy Prog, vis prof, 1990, 1993, 1995; Univ Ark Sch Law, Little Rock, Summer Trial Advocacy Prog, vis prof, 1991-94 & 1996; Emory Univ Sch Law Trial Tech Prog, vis prof, 1992-93, 1995-96, 1999-2000; Nat Inst Trial Advocacy, instr, 1993-; Hinds & Yazoo Counties, Miss, MS, spec asst dist atty, 1993-98; Miss Col Sch Law, prof law, currently. **Orgs:** Secy, Cent Miss Legal Servs Corp Bd, 1989-; bd dir, YMCA, 1991-; Smith Robertson Mus Bd, 1992; comnr, Miss Bd Bar Comners, 1992; fel Miss Bar Found, 1997-, trustee, 2000-03, 2012-; Supreme Ct Miss Task Force Gender Fairness, 1998; mediator, Cert with Miss Bar, 1999-; Exec Comt Am Inn Ct, Charles Clark Chap, 1999-; Miss Supreme Ct Adv Comt Rules, 2000-08; Miss Bar Ct Liaison & Judicial Admin Comt, 2000-10; gov, Fifth Circuit Fed Bar Asn, 2001-, pres, 2006-08; pres, Hinds County Bar Asn, 2001-02; bd mem, Leadership Jackson Alumni Asn, 2004-06; Miss Bar Resolution Fee Dispute Comt, 2004-10; Miss Bar Asn; Am Bar Asn; Magnolia Bar Asn; Miss Women Lawyers Asn; Metro Jackson Black Women Lawyers Asn; Capital Area Bar Asn; prog chair, Am Inn Ct, Charles Clark Chap, 2012-. **Business Addr:** Professor of Law, Mississippi College School of Law, 151 E Griffith St, Jackson, MS 39201-1391, **Business Phone:** (601)925-7154.

### BENNETT, REV. ROBERT AVON, JR.
Executive, college teacher. **Personal:** Born Jan 11, 1933, Baltimore, MD; son of Robert Sr (deceased) and Irene Julie Harris (deceased); married Marceline M Donaldson; children: Elise Frazier, Mark, Malica Aronowitz, Ann, Michelle & Jacqueline. **Educ:** Kenyon Col, AB, 1954; Gen Theol Sem, New York, BS & MS, divinity, 1959, STB, 1958, STM, 1966; Harvard Univ, PhD, 1974; Johns Hopkins Univ, MS, semitic lang. **Career:** Educator (retired); Episcopal Diocese MAR, ordained priest, 1959; Episcopal Theol Sch & Divinity Sch, instr, asst prof, 1965-74, prof, 1974-94; Int Theol Ctr, Atlanta, vis prof, 1973-77; Episcopal Divinity Sch, prof Old Testament, 1974-94; Boston Univ Sch Theol, vis prof, 1975, 1982; Princeton Theol Sem, vis prof, 1975, 1983, 1986; Harvard Divinity Sch, vis prof, 1976; Hebrew Univ, Jerusalem, Israel, fld arch staff supvr, 1984. **Orgs:** Archon Fraternity; Trustee, bd mem, Int Theol Ctr, Atlanta, 1973-77; vice chair, Standing Lit Comn Episcopal Church, 1982-; Nat Coun Churchs Christ, 1982-; final selection comt, Fund Theol Educ, 1984; Univ Copenhagen, Denmark, fulbright fel; Phi Beta Kappa; Pan-Hellenic council. **Honors/Awds:** Kenyon Col, 1953; Fulbright Scholar, Univ Copenhagen, Denmark, 1954-55; vis res scholar, Am Res Ctr, Cairo, Egypt, 1979-80; res scholar, Univ Khartoum, Sudan, 1980; Israel Hebrew Univ, 1984. **Special Achievements:** Author: "Africa & the Bibl Period", 1971; "The Bible for Today's Church", 1979; "Howard Thurman & The Bible, God & Human Freedom", 1983; "Black Episcopalians, The Episcopal Diocese of Massachusetts", 1784-1984, 1984; "Black Experience and the Bible, African Am Relig Studies", 1989; "Africa, Oxford Companion to the Bible", 1993; "The Book of Zephaniah, The New Interpreter's Bible, vol 7", 1996. **Home Addr:** PO Box 380367, Cambridge, MA 02238-0367.

### BENNETT, DR. RODNEY D.
College president, educator. **Personal:** Born Jan 1, 1966?; married Temple Bennett; children: Colby & Logan. **Educ:** Mid Tenn State Univ, BS, mass commun, EdS, educ admin, MEd, educ admin; Tenn State Univ, PhD, educ admin. **Career:** Mid Tenn State Univ, Murfreesboro, TN, assoc dean stud life; Winthrop Univ, Rock Hill, SC, dean students; Univ Ga, dean students, interim assoc provost instnl diversity, vpres stud affairs; Univ Southern Miss, pres, 2013-. **Orgs:** Chair, Univ Ga's Athletic Asn NCAA Recertification; on-site comt mem, Southern Asn Cols & Schs. **Business Addr:** President, University of Southern Mississippi, 118 College Dr, Hattiesburg, MS 39406-0001, **Business Phone:** (601)266-1000.

### BENNETT, DR. SYBRIL M.
Television journalist, educator. **Educ:** Marquette Univ, BA, broadcast & electronic jour, 1990; Loyola Univ, Chicago, IL, MEd, 1993; Vanderbilt Univ, PhD, higher educ admin, 1999; Harvard Univ, Mgt Develop Prog, 2007. **Career:** WISN-TV, assignment desk news trainee, 1989-90, assoc producer, 1991; Loyola Univ Chicago, Grad Asst, 1991-93; WBBM-TV, desk asst & fill-assignment ed, 1993-94; WTVF-News Channel 5, assoc producer & weekend assignment ed, 1994-95, freelance news writer & assignment ed, 1995-98, 1999-2000; Vol State Community Col, adj prof, 1995-98; Tenn State Univ, adj prof, 1995-97, MARC Prog, res assoc, 1997-99; Vanderbilt Univ, res asst, 1995-96, teaching asst, 1996, Media Rels, spec asst vice chancellor & sr pub officer, 1998-99; Mid Tenn State Univ, asst prof elec media jour, 1999-2000, sr pub affairs officer; Black Collegian & Music & Ministry Mag, freelance writer, 1999-2001; WNPT-PBS affil, producer & reporter, 1999-2000, Telethon vol host, 2003-; News Channel 5 Network, gen assignment reporter & anchor, 2000-03, freelance reporter, 2003-; Belmont Univ, New Century Jour Prog, asst prof jour, 2003-07, exec dir, 2003-09, assoc prof jour, 2007-19, Prof, 2013-; Coop Ctr Study Abroad, study abroad instr, 2006. **Orgs:** Nat Asn Black Journalists; Broadcast Educ Asn; Radio & Tv News dir Asn; Soc Prof Journalists; bd mem, Nashville Area Chap Am Red Cross, 1995-97, comt mem, pub rels, 1999-2000; chair, Grad Stud Higher Educ Fac Search Comt, 1998; bd dir, Vanderbilt Univ Stud Commun Inc, 2003-; Grant Comt, Fifteenth Ave Baptist Church Child Learning Ctr, 2003-05; coordr, Belmont-Nashville Asn Black Journalists, 2004-05; Nashville Conv & Visitors Bur, 2004; adv bd, Greater Nashville Chap MBA Asn, 2005; R. H.Boyd Leadership Soc, 2005; Rotary Club, 2006; Leadership Nashville Alumni Asn, 2006-; Nashville Area Chap Nat Asn Advan Colored People, 2007. **Home Addr:** 135 Canton Ct, Goodlettsville, TN 37072-2173, **Home Phone:** (615)851-9909. **Business Addr:** Executive Director, Assistant Professor of Journalism, Belmont University, 1900 Belmont Blvd, Nashville, TN 37212-3757, **Business Phone:** (615)460-6000.

### BENNETT, TONY LYDELL
Football player. **Personal:** Born Jul 1, 1967, Alligator, MS. **Educ:** Univ Miss. **Career:** Football player (retired); Green Bay Packers, right outside linebacker, 1990-93; Indianapolis Colts, right defensive end, 1994-97. **Home Addr:** , Fort Lauderdale, FL.

### BENNETT, WILLIAM RONALD
Teacher, president (organization), educator. **Personal:** Born Jan 1, 1935, Parkersburg, WV; son of William D and Pearl C; married Sarah L Clarkson; children: Denise Renee, Diane Elizabeth & Douglas Eugene. **Educ:** Hampton Univ, BS, 1956; John Carroll Univ, MEd, 1972. **Career:** Cleveland Clnc, res teacher, 1960-62; Cleveland Bd Educ, sch admin, 1962-72; Mt Vernon Nazarene Univ, registr & assoc prof emer educ, 1968-91; Cleveland State Univ, dir financial aid, 1972. **Orgs:** Dir, Inroads N E Ohio, 1983-; pres, Friendly Town, 1983-; CEEB Comm Pre Col Guid & Coun, 1984-; pres, Nat Asn Stud Fin Aid Admin, 1984-85; treas, Inner City Renewal Soc, 1985; trustee, Antioch Baptist Church, 1985-88; pres, Midwest Asn Stud Fin Aid Admin, 1988-89. **Honors/Awds:** Man of the Year, Alpha Phi Alpha Fraternity, 1982, 1986, 1988; James W. White Award, Ohio Asn Stud Financial Aid Adminr, 1992; Distinguished Services Award, Nat Asn Stud Financial Aid Adminr; Alan Purdy Distinguished Service Award, Nat Asn Stud Financial Aid Adminr. **Home Addr:** 55 W Orange Hill Cir, Orange, OH 44022. **Business Addr:** Associate Professor Emeritus of Education, Mount Vernon Nazarene University, 800 Martinsburg Rd, Mount Vernon, OH 43050, **Business Phone:** (740)392-6868.

### BENNETT-ALEXANDER, DAWN DEJUANA
Educator, lawyer. **Personal:** Born Jan 2, 1951, Washington, DC; daughter of William H Sr and Ann Pearl Frances Liles; children: Jenniffer, Anne Alexis & Tess. **Educ:** Defiance Col, attended 1970; Fed City Col, BS, sociol, 1972; Howard Univ, Sch Law, JD, 1975. **Career:** Oreg State Dept Justice, Solicitor's Off, law clerk, 1974; DC Ct Appeals, law clerk, Hon Julia Cooper Mack, 1975-76; White House Domestic Coun, from asst to assoc dir & coun, 1976-77; US Fed Trade Comn, atty, 1977-79; Antioch Sch Law, Nat Farmworker Paralegal Training Prog, instr, 1979-81; Fed Labor Rels Authority, atty, adv, 1981-82; Univ N Fla, assoc prof, bus & employ law, 1982-87; McKnight Found, Fla Endowment Fund, McKnight Jr fac fel, 1984; Fla Pub Employee Rel Comn, labor arbitrator, 1985-91; Employ Law & Diversity Consult, consult, 1985-; Univ Ga, assoc prof, legal studies, 1988-. **Orgs:** DC Bar, 1979-; co-chmn, Am Acad Legal Studies Bus, 1982-; Nat Coun Negro Women, 1983-; bd mem, Consumer Credit Coun Servs NE Fla, 1983-84; bd mem, Girls Clubs Jacksonville, 1983-85; Nat Org Women, 1985-; bd mem, Friends Athens Creative Theater, 1990; Pres, Southeastern Acad Legal Studies Bus, 1992-93; pres, co-chmn Employ Law Sect, 1992-94; Beta Gamma Sigma Nat Hon Soc, 1992; Ga Polit Action Comt PAC, 1993-94; treas, Ga Now, 1993-95. **Special Achievements:** Co-authored first-ever Employment Law text for colleges of business that established the discipline; Best-selling Employment Law text in country, Employment Law for Business, McGraw-Hill publication, 1994-; Co-authored first Legal, Ethical, and Regulatory Environment of Business text that fully integrated diversity issues, McGraw-Hill publication, 2011. **Home Addr:** 175 St James Dr, Athens, GA 30606-3944, **Home Phone:** (706)338-2293. **Business Addr:** Associate Professor, Employment Law & Legal Studies, University of Georgia, 202 Brooks Hall, Athens, GA 30602-6255, **Business Phone:** (706)542-3438.

### BENNETT-MURRAY, DR. JUDITH
Registered nurse. **Educ:** CUNY, NY City Tech Col, AAS, RN; CUNY, Hunter Col, BSN, MSN; Columbia Univ Teachers Col, Med. **Career:** Nassau Community Col, assoc prof, dean, currently. **Orgs:** Co chair, Alpha Phi Chap. **Honors/Awds:** Shirley Chisolm Award, Brooklyn Mus, 2000; Award for Excellence in Nursing Education. **Business Addr:** Associate Professor, Nassau Community College, Nassau Hall 308 1 Educ Dr, Garden City, NY 11530-6793, **Business Phone:** (516)572-7098.

### BENNING, DR. EMMA BOWMAN
Educator. **Personal:** Born Oct 5, 1928, Columbus, GA; daughter of Ralph Bowman and Tinella Bowman; married Calvin C; children:

Sheryl Ann Thomas, Nathaniel A & Eric A. **Educ:** Cleveland State Univ, Cleveland, OH, BS, MEd; Case Western Res Univ, Cleveland, OH; Kent State Univ, Kent, OH; LaSalle Univ, Mandeville, LA, PhD. **Career:** Educator (retired); Cleveland Pub Schs, Cleveland, Ohio, prin; Benjamin Franklin Elem, 1975-77, prin, planner, 1979, dir, elem schs, 1979-80, cluster dir, 1980-85, area supt, 1985-87, asst supt curric & instr, 1987-90; Cleveland State Univ, supvr teachers; Cleveland State Univ, supvr stud teachers. **Orgs:** Trustee, bd dir, C's Serv, 1969-76; pres, bd dir, Karamu House, 1976-80; pres, Ludlow Community Asn, 1979-80; vpres, Jack & Jill Am Found, 1977-85, nat pres, 1985-96; Shaker Heights; Human Rels Comn, 1991-96; Delta Sigma Theta; Nat Sorority Phi Delta Kappa; Links Inc; charter mem, Imani Temple Ministries; trustee, Rainbow Babies & C's Hosp; pres, bd trustee, Shaker Heights Pub Libr; women's coun, Cleveland Mus Art; pres, Shaker Heights Ludlow Community Asn; C's Defense Fund Wash DC; CMA African Am Community Task force. **Home Addr:** 3143 Ludlow Rd, Shaker Heights, OH 44120, **Home Phone:** (216)991-2563. **Business Addr:** Charter Member, Imani Temple Ministries, 2463 N Taylor Rd, Cleveland Heights, OH 44118, **Business Phone:** (216)231-9902.

### BENOIT, DAVID
Basketball coach, basketball player. **Personal:** Born May 9, 1968, Lafayette, LA; married Aline; children: Deseree & David Jr. **Educ:** Tyler Jr Col, 1988; Univ Ala, phys educ, 1990. **Career:** Basketball player (retired), basketball coach; Unicaja Malaga, Spain, 1990-91; Utah Jazz, forward & small forward, 1991-96, 2000-01; NJ Nets, forward & small forward, 1996-98; Orlando Magic, forward & small forward, 1998; Maccabi Tel Aviv, Israel, 1998-99; Shanghai Sharks, China, forward, 2001-02; Hitachi Sunrockers, Japan, forward, 2003-04; Hitachi SunRockers, 2002-04; Utah Snowbears, Am Basketball Asn, 2004-05; Saitama Broncos, Japan, forward, 2005-07, head coach, 2007-09.

### BENOIT, EDITH B.
Nurse. **Personal:** Born Mar 7, 1918, New York, NY; married Elliot; children: Barbara & Lloyd. **Educ:** Hunter Col, AB, 1938; Harlem Hosp Sch Nursing, RN, 1942; Teachers Col Columbia Univ, MA, 1945, prof dipl, 1959. **Career:** Harlem Hosp, instr, supvr, asst supt nurses, 1942-51, dir nursing serv, 1967; VA Hosp Brooklyn, supvr, instr, asst chief nurse res, coordr, 1951-64; VA Hosp E Orange, assoc chief nursing serv educ, 1964-65; VA Hosp Bronx, asst chief nursing serv, 1965-67; Columbia Univ, asst prof; Pace Univ, adj asst, prof. **Orgs:** Am Nurses Asn, 1942; chmn, NY State Asn Comn Study Nurse Pract Act, 1970; bd dir, Nat League Nursing; Open Curric Comn, NLN, 1972; Hunter Col Alumnae Asn; bd mgr, Minisink Town House, NY City Mission Soc, 1972-77; bd dir, Nat League Nursing, 1973-77. **Home Addr:** 926 Brush Hollow Rd, Westbury, NY 11590. **Business Addr:** Director, Harlem Hospital, 506 Lenox Ave, New York, NY 10037, **Business Phone:** (212)939-1000.

### BENSON, DR. ANGELA
Educator, writer. **Personal:** Born AL. **Educ:** Spelman Col, BS, math, 1982; Ga Inst Tech, BS, indust engineering, 1982, MS, opers res, 1984, MS, human res develop, 1997, PhD, instrnl tech, 2001; Univ Ga, PhD, instrnl technol. **Career:** AT&T Bell Lab, systs engr, 1982-90; Bell S Telecommunications Indust, res engr, 1990-95; Univ Ill, urbana campaign, asst prof educ technol dept human resource educ, 2001-06; Univ Manchester, sch educ, Manchester, UK, hon res fel & fac humanities, 2006; Univ Ala, assoc prof instrnl technol, 2006-, prog coordr dept educ leadership, policy & technol Studies, 2010-12; Novels: Bands Gold, 1994; All Time, 1995; Between Lines, 1996; A Family Wedding, 1997; Way Home, 1997; Nicest Guy Am, 1997; Second Chance Dad, 1997; Awakening Mercy, 2000; Abiding Hope, 2001; Amen Sisters, 2005; Pastors Wife, 2005; Up Pops Devil, 2008; Sins Father (Avon A), 2009. **Orgs:** Acad human ers develop; Am Educ Res Asn, 1998-; Int Socs Technol Educ, 2001-; Ed Bd, J Res Technol Educ, 2002-; reviewer, Human Res Develp Rev, 2002-; HRE Dept Adv Comt, 2003-; Asn Advan comput Educ; early career scholar award comt, Acad human Res Develop, 2004-; vpres, pres, Immediate pres, bd dir, Asn Educ Commnu & technol, 2001-10; Acad Human Resource Develop, 2001-06; Educ Technol Bd, Univ Ill, Urbana Champaign, 2005-06; Mid-S Educ Res Asn, 2006-; Am Cancer Soc; Nat Breast Cancer Coalition; fel, McNair Scholars Prog, Univ Ala, 2007; bd mem, McNair Scholars Prog, 2008-. **Home Addr:** PO Box 360571, Decatur, GA 30036. **Business Addr:** Associate Professor of Instructional Technology, The University of Alabama, 328F Graves Hall, Tuscaloosa, AL 35487-0302, **Business Phone:** (205)348-7824.

### BENSON, DARREN
Football player. **Personal:** Born Aug 25, 1974, Memphis, TN. **Educ:** Trinity Valley Community Col; Ark State Univ. **Career:** Football player (retired); Dallas Cowboys, defensive tackle, 1995-98. **Honors/Awds:** Super Bowl Champion.

### BENSON, GEORGE
Jazz musician, songwriter, singer. **Personal:** Born Mar 22, 1943, Pittsburgh, PA; married Johnnie Lee; children: Keith Givens (deceased), Robert, Marcus, Christopher, George Jr & Stephen. **Career:** Pittsburgh night club, singer & dancer; Verve Music Group, guitarist, performer, singer, composer, currently; Composer: The Greatest; The Switchor How to Alter Your Ego, 1974; Saturday Night Live, 1977; Mike Hammer, 1986; Albums: George Benson/Jack McDuff, The New Boss Guitar, 1964; Benson Burner, Its Uptown, 1965; The George Benson Cookbook, Willow Weep for Me, 1966; Blue Benson, 1967; Giblet Gravy, Goodies, 1968; Shape of Things to Come, Tell It Like It Is, The Other Side of Abbey Road, 1969; Here Comes the Sun, 1969; I Got a Woman & Some Blues, 1970; Beyond the Blue Horizon, 1971; White Rabbit, 1972; Jazz on a Sunday Afternoon, Vol. 1, Jazz on a Sunday Afternoon, Vol. 2, Witchcraft, 1973; Body Talk, 1974; Bad Benson, 1975; Good King Bad, Benson & Farrell, Breezin, 1976; In Concert-Carnegie Hall, In Flight, 1977; Space Album, Weekend in L A, 1978; Livin Inside Your Love, Take Five, 1979; Cast Your Fate to the Wind, Give Me the Night, 1980; GB, The George Benson Collection, 1981; In Your Eyes, Pacific Fire, 1983; 20/20, Live in Concert, 1984; The Electrifying George Benson, 1985; While the City Sleeps, 1986; Collaboration (with Earl Klugh), 1987; Twice the Love, 1988; Tenderly, 1989; Round Midnight, 1989; Big Boss Band, 1990; Midnight Moods, 1991; The Essence of George Benson, 1992; Love Remembers, 1993; The Most Exciting New Guitarist on the Jazz Scene, 1994; The Best of George Benson, 1995; California Dreamin, Lil Darlin, That's Right, 1996; Standing Together, Masquerade, 1998; The Masquerade Is Over, 1999; Live at Casa Caribe, Absolute Benson, 2000; All Blues, 2001; Blue Bossa, 2002; After Hours, 2002; Irreplaceable, 2003; The Greatest Hits of All, 2003; Golden Legends Live, 2004; Jazz After Hours with George Benson, 2005; Best of George Benson Live, 2005; Givin' It Up, 2006; Live from Montreux Immortal, 2007; Songs And Stories, 2009; Guitar Man, 2011; Inspiration: A Tribute to Nat King Cole, 2013. Singles: Supership, 1975; This Masquerade, Breezin, 1976; Everything Must Change, Nature Boy, Gonna Love You More, The Greatest Love of All, 1977; On Broadway, Lady Blue, 1978; Love Ballad, Unchained Melody, 1979; Give Me the Night, Love X Love, 1980; Love All the Hurt Away, Turn Out the Lamplight, Whats On Your Mind, Turn Your Love Around, 1981; Never Give Up on a Good Thing, 1982; Inside Love (So Personal), Lady Love Me (One More Time), Feel Like Makin' Love, In Your Eyes, 1983; Late At Night, 20/20, 1984; Beyond The Sea (La Mer), I Just Wanna Hang Around You, New Day, 1985; Kisses in the Moonlight, Shiver, 1986; Teaser", 1987; Let's do it again, Twice the Love, 1988; Standing Together, 1998; Cell Phone, 2004. **Honors/Awds:** Grammy Award for Record of the Year, 1976; Grammy Award for Best R&B Instrumental Performance, 1977, 1981; Grammy Award for Best Pop Instrumental Performance, 1977, 1984, 2007; Grammy Award for Best Record of the Year, 1977; Grammy Award for Best Instrumental Performance, 1977; Grammy Award, Best R&B Male Vocal Performance, 1979, 1981; Grammy Award, Best Jazz Vocal Performance Male, 1981; Multi-platinum Album: Breezin; Platinum Albums: Give Me the Night, In Flight, Weekend in LA; Gold Albums: 20/20, In Your Eyes, Livin Inside Your Love, The George Benson Collection, Collaboration; Honorary Doctorates in Music, Berklee Sch of Music, Morris Brown Col; recipient of a "Hollywood Walk of Fame" star; World Music Award, Legend Award, 2003; Best Traditional R&B Performance, 2007. **Home Addr:** 365 Ave de los Arboles Suite 220, Thousand Oaks, CA 91360, **Home Phone:** (207)278-3331. **Business Addr:** Jazz Musician, Verve Music Group, 1755 Broadway Fl 3, New York, NY 10019, **Business Phone:** (212)373-0600.

### BENSON, GILBERT O.
Administrator, counselor. **Personal:** Born Nov 1, 1930, Paterson, NJ; son of Walter and Hattie; children: Michelle & Gilda. **Educ:** Howard Univ, Wash, DC, BS; William Paterson Col, Wayne, NJ, MA. **Career:** Administrator (retired); Family Planning Admin Youth Serv, welfare caseworker & youth worker, 1960-74; Passaic Community Comn Col, EOF counr & admin; Coun Probs Living, counr & adminr; Bergen County Shelter Homeless, supvr; Paterson Bd Educ, E side HS, Paterson, NJ, counr; jazz vocalist. **Orgs:** Omega Psi Phi Fraternity, 1985; deleg assembly, Nat Educ Asn, 1987-90; chmn, Paterson Nat Asn Advan Colored People; affirm action chmn, NJ State Nat Asn Advan Colored People; chmn, head, Paterson Coalition Media Changes; chmn, Passaic Co Citizens Vs Passaic Co Voc Sch Bd; Now Theater Paterson, NJ; Black Male Caucus Paterson, NJ; past chmn, Greater Paterson Arts Coun. **Honors/Awds:** Coun Service Award, Passaic County Col, 1976; Adminrs Merit Award, Passaic County Co, 1978; Commission Service Award, Nat Asn Advan Colored People; Salute Black Men & Women Duke Ellington Award Arts, 1985; JFK High Sch Award Contribution Arts, 1990. **Home Addr:** 34 Hennessy Pl, Irvington, NJ 07111, **Home Phone:** (973)345-2143.

### BENSON, HAYWARD J., JR.
President (organization), chief executive officer, mayor. **Personal:** Born Aug 29, 1936, Mt. Dora, FL; son of Hayward J Sr and Emily Smith; married Mattie Jo Alexander; children: Stephan & Cameron. **Educ:** Fla A&M Univ, Tallahassee, FA, BS, elem educ, 1958; Univ Ariz, Tucson, AZ, MEd, educ, 1965; Univ Fla, cert admin & supv, 1968; Fla Atlantic Univ, Boca Raton, FA, EdD, 1985. **Career:** Univ Fla, Gainesville, FA, fel; Sch Bd St Lucie County Ft Pierce, FA, teacher, 1958-59; Fla Educ Syst, educr & admin, 1958-83; Broward County Sch Bd, teacher, 1961-65, ITV Utilization, specialist, 1966, prin, 1968-70; Comprehensive Planning Equal Opportunities, exec dir, 1971-75, dir, 1975-83; Nova Univ, adj prof, 1975; Broward County Sch Bd, admin asst to supt sch, 1977-83; Lauderhill City, councilman, 1982-84; Broward County Govt, Pub Serv Dept, dir, 1983; Broward County Bd County Comnrs, dir, 1983-89; Nat Alliance Black Sch Educ, prof & vpres; Airocar Inc, chief exec officer; Airocar Inc, Gray Line, Ft Lauderdale, vpres, 1990-91, chief exec officer, 1991-93, pres, 1993-95; Gaddis Corp, vpres; Universal Meeting Makers Inc, owner & pres, 1995-2000; City Lauderhill, FA, comnr & dep vice mayor, 2006-; Broward County Charter Rev Comn, comnr, 2006-08; Southeastern Consult Group, dir, currently; Equal Access Sch Bd, classroom teacher, sch prin & dir; Ben-Alex Group Inc, owner, pres & chief exec officer, currently. **Orgs:** Fla Asn Health & Social Serv; Broward County Human Rels Div; State Univ Syst EEO Adv Comn Bd Regents, Dem Exec Comn; bd dir, Areawide Coun Aging; Am Red Cross; chmn, bd dir, Nova Univ Clin; pres, Fla Asn Community Rels; libr adv bd, Broward County, 2004-; bd mem, City Nat Bank, Miami; Estates Inverrary Home Owners Asn; Inverrary Home Owners Asn; bd dir, Am Cancer Soc, Broward County; comnr, Fla Comn Tourism, Tallahassee, FA; bd trustee, Pine Crest Sch, Ft Lauderdale, FA; bd mem, Fla Tourism Indust Mkt Corp, Tallahassee, FA; bd chair, bd gov, Tower Club, Ft Lauderdale, FA; Kiwanis Club Cent Broward, Ft Lauderdale, FA; bd mem, Susie C. Holley Cradle Nursery Inc, Ft Lauderdale, FA; vice chair, Planning & Zoning Bd, City Lauderhill, FL; bd mem, Fla Educ Fund Inc, Tampa, FA, vice chair; pres, Broward Elem Sch Principals Asn, Ft Lauderdale, FA; pres, Fla Motor Coach Asn, State Fla; bd mem, Sistrunk Hist Festival Inc; exec bd mem, Lauderhill Chamber Com; bd trustee, Lauderhill Police Retirement Syst; Omega Psi Phi; pres, Fla Black Caucus, Local Elected Officials. **Business Addr:** Vice Mayor, City of Lauderhill Florida, 5581 W Oakland Pk Blvd Suite 410, Lauderdale, FL 33313, **Business Phone:** (954)777-2044.

### BENSON, DR. JAMES RUSSELL
Educator, administrator. **Personal:** Born Jan 19, 1933, Marks, MS; son of Escar and Tressie V; married Madgeolyn Warren; children: Barry Ray & Agnela Davis. **Educ:** Ala State Univ, BS, 1963; Claremont Grad Col, MA, 1972, PhD, 1977. **Career:** Radio Sta WRMA Montgomery, Ala, news dir, 1960-63; Urban League, dir teenpost, 1963-64; Lincoln High Sch, human rels dir, 1964-66; Gow-Dow Experience, pres, 1968-; Pomona Unified Sch Dist, dir music; Calif Polytech, Pomana; Palomares Jr High Sch, vice prin. **Orgs:** Bd dir, JoAnn Concert Dance Corp, 1984-85; bd dir, Nat Asn Advan Colored People, 1986-87; dir, MESA, 1986-87; chmn, ACT-CO/Acad Excellence Prog, 1989-91; Nat Alliance Black Sch Educators. **Home Addr:** 1044 Vanderbilt Ave, Claremont, CA 91711, **Home Phone:** (909)621-2848. **Business Addr:** Vice Principal, Palomares Junior High School, 2211 N Orange Grove Ave, Pomona, CA 91767, **Business Phone:** (909)397-4539.

### BENSON, LILLIAN
Movie editor. **Educ:** Pratt Inst, BFA. **Career:** Film: The Promised Land, 1990; Alma's Rainbow, 1994; The Revolutionary War, 1995; A Century of Living, 1999; Soul Food, 2000; The Old Settler, 2001; Smothered: The Censorship Struggles of the Smothers Brothers Comedy Hour, 2002; Eyes on the Prize, LightWave Pictures, dir, 2004; Au Pair Chocolat, 2004; All Our Sons: Fallen Heroes 9 & 11, 2004; Troop 1500, 2005; Life Is Not a Fairytale: The Fantasia Barrino Story, 2006; God In America; Wounded Knee, We Shall Remain; Beyond the Steps-Alvin Ailey American Dance Theater; Craft In America; Death by Hanging and Out at Work; Motown 40th; Celebrate! Christmas with Maya Angelou; The Massachusetts 54th Colored Infantry. **Orgs:** Bd dir, Am Cinema Ed; Int Doc Asn; Acad TV Arts & Sci; Editing Peer Group comt TV Acad. **Special Achievements:** First African American woman elected to the American Cinema Editors Assn, 1991; Emmy Nomination. **Home Addr:** 11151 Aquavista St, Studio City, CA 91604, **Home Phone:** (818)705-5338. **Business Addr:** Director, LightWave Pictures, 2918 Santa Monica Blvd Suite D, Santa Monica, CA 90404-2430, **Business Phone:** (310)315-7130.

### BENSON, ROMONA RISCOE
Association executive, president (organization). **Personal:** Born Sep 18, 1959, Brooklyn, NY; daughter of Alfonso Riscoe and Mary Crawford. **Educ:** Univ Pittsburgh, speech communs, 1981; Antioch Univ, BA, human serv admin, 1988; Univ Colo, Boulder, cert mus mgt. **Career:** Abraxas Found, Abraxas Group, mkt liaison, fac dir, regional dir, vpres; NJ state Aquarium, dir, visitor servs & com rels, 1991-93; Philadelphia Multicultural Affairs Cong, exec dir, 1993-97; Riscoe & Assocs, pres & chief exec officer, 1997-. **Orgs:** Am Soc Exec Asn; Nat Coalition Black Meeting Planners; African Am Travel &Tourism Asn; chair, Meeting Planners Int Initiative; Philadelphia Urban League; Philadelphia Int Airport Bd; bd mem, Black Family Reunion Cult Ctr; Philadelphia Conv & Visitors Bur Bd; pres & ceo African Am Mus, 2005-; Meeting Professionals Int; Pub Rels Socs Am; Americans Arts; Nat Asn Female Execs; Southern Poverty Law Ctr; adv, Nat Asn Advan Colored People's Econ Reciprocity Lodging Initiative; chair, Nat Multicultural Tourism Adv Coun; MPI Found Bd trustee; fundraiser, Nat Mult Sclerosis Socs; pres & chief exec officer, African Am Mus Philadelphia, 2005-. **Business Addr:** President, Chief Executive Officer, Riscoe & Associates, 2 Bala Plz Suite 300, Philadelphia, PA 19004, **Business Phone:** (800)906-0673.

### BENSON, RUBIN AUTHOR, JR.
Graphic artist, educator, executive. **Personal:** Born Feb 8, 1946, Philadelphia, PA; son of Calvin and Mable S Skinner (deceased); married Janet Wicks; children: Rubin, Heather & Badeerah. **Educ:** Cheyney Univ, Cheyney, PA, BS, 1969; Univ Pa, Philadelphia, PA, 1971; Parsons Sch Design, New York, NY, 1972. **Career:** Philadelphia Sch Dist, Philadelphia, Pa, graphic arts teacher, 1969-; Philadelphia Int Recs, art dir, 1982-84; First Impressions Design Group, Philadelphia, Pa, owner, 1976-. **Orgs:** Judge, CEBA Awards, 1980-. **Business Addr:** President, First Impressions Design Group, 4920 Hazel Ave, Philadelphia, PA 19143-2005, **Business Phone:** (215)476-3397.

### BENSON, WANDA MILLER
Publisher. **Personal:** Born Jul 15, 1956, Washington, DC; daughter of William Miller and Rosetta; married Steve; children: Brandon & Connor. **Educ:** Tenn State Univ, BA, 1980. **Career:** IRS, union rep, 1975-86; Contempora Brides, publ, 1986-. **Orgs:** Nat Asn Advan Colored People Personnel Comt, 1995-96. **Home Addr:** 548 Mill Sta Dr, Nashville, TN 37207, **Home Phone:** (615)876-8573. **Business Addr:** Publisher, Contempora Brides, 1818 Morena St, Nashville, TN 37208, **Business Phone:** (615)321-3268.

### BENT-GOODLEY, DR. TRICIA
Educator. **Personal:** Born New York, NY; children: 2. **Educ:** Queens Col, BA, sociol; Univ Pa, MSW; Columbia Univ, PhD, social policy, planning & anal, 1997. **Career:** Family violence prev progs, Harlem, USA & Jamaica, New York, dir, clinician; Harlem & Queens County, admin & practr; Howard Univ, Sch Social Work, assoc prof, prof, dir, 1998-. **Orgs:** Coun Social Work Educ; Nat Asn Black Social Workers; Nat Asn Social Workers; Am Pub Health Asn; Alpha Kappa Alpha Sorority Inc; Adminr, Harlem & Queens County; fel, Child & Family Scholars; fel, Samuel fels; fel, HISTP Prog; Howard Univ, dir Interpersonal Violence Prev Prog, dir, Univ Women Leadership Initiative. **Business Addr:** Professor, Director, Howard University, 601 Howard Pl NW, Washington, DC 20059, **Business Phone:** (202)806-4729.

### BENTLEY, HERBERT DEAN
Executive. **Personal:** Born Dec 9, 1940, DeSoto, MO; married Judy Ann Lazard; children: Herbert, Karthryn & Karyn. **Educ:** Harris Teachers Col, AA, 1958; Southern Ill Univ, BS, 1966; Am Mgt Asn, cert syst design, 1972. **Career:** New Age Fed Savings & Loan Asn, managing officer. **Orgs:** Pres, PAS Mgmt Systs Inc; bd dir, Gateway Nat Bank, 1973-; bd dir, New Age Fed Savings & Loan Asn, 1974-; bd dir, Nat Asn Black Acct, 1974-75; bd dir, Inter racial Coun Bus Opportunity, 1974-; bd mem, Nat Asn Black Acct, 1975-; bd dir, Ctr Med Ctr, 1976-; bd dir, Christian Med Ctr, 1976-; bd dir, Opportunity Industrialisation Ctr, 1976-; bd dir, Minority Bus Forum Asn, 1976-; St Louis Tax Task Force Cong US, 1977. **Honors/Awds:** Public Service Award Small Bus Admin, 1977. **Home Addr:** 503 Hinsdale Ct, St Louis, MO 63119-1531, **Home Phone:** (314)961-6994. **Business Addr:** Managing Officer, New Age Federal Savings & Loan Association, 1401 N Kings Hwy, St Louis, MO 63113, **Business Phone:** (313)361-4100.

**BENTON, ADRIENNE R.**
Executive, president (organization). **Educ:** Rutgers Univ, BA, urban studies; Univ Ala, Birmingham, MS; Seton Hall Univ, pre-legal studies. **Career:** New Media & Technol, dir, 2003; WebCTel LLC, co founder, sr exec vpres, 2003; Onyx Spectrum Technol Inc, founder, pres & chief exec officer, 2004-. **Orgs:** Am Col Healthcare Exec; Nat Asn Health Serv Exec; Men Color Against AIDS; S End Hist Soc; bd dir, Lena Pk Community Develop Corp; Boston Coalition Black Women; Adv Bd, Fleet Bank's Women's Entrepreneurs Connection; Adv Bd, Fleet Bank Nat Community; Nat Asn Rec Arts & Sci; co-chair, Women's Dinner Party. **Business Addr:** President, Chief Executive Officer, Onyx Spectrum Technology Inc, 184 Dudley St Suite 101A, Boston, MA 02119-2561, **Business Phone:** (617)407-2826.

**BENTON, ANGELA**
Entrepreneur, 001173, founder (originator). **Personal:** Born May 22, 1981, Chicago, IL; children: 3. **Educ:** Am InterContinental Univ, BFA, visual commun & specialization digital design, 2004; Savannah Col Art & Design, MFA, graphic design, 2007. **Career:** Visual i Designs, prin, 2000-08; Homes Color Mag, visual design mgr, 2003-05, freelance web ed, designer, 2005-06; Bizjournals.com, web designer, 2005-06; Hope Women Mag, creative dir, 2005-06; Lendingtree.com/RealEstate.com, front-end web developer, 2006-07; Black Web Media, chief exec officer, 2007-12; Black Web Enterprise Inc, lead designer, 2007-08, dir creative & digital strategy, 2008-09; NewME, founder, 2011-. **Honors/Awds:** Fast Company, Most Influential Women in Technology, 2010; Minority Media and Telecommunications Council (MMTC), Hall of Fame Inductee, 2010; National Urban League, Women of Power Award, 2010; "Ebony" Magazine, Power 100, 2010; "TheRoot," The Root 100, 2012; "TheGrio," TheGrio's 100, 2012; "Black Enterprise," Rising Stars 40 & Under, 2014; Goldman Sachs, 100 Most Intriguing Entrepreneurs; "Business Insider," The 46 Most Important African-Americans in Technology, 2014. **Special Achievements:** NewME was featured in CNN's documentary series "Black in America: The New Promised Land: Silicon Valley," 2011; youngest person selected to MMTC's Hall of Fame.

**BENTON, JAMES WILBERT, JR.**
Administrative court judge, lawyer. **Personal:** Born Sep 16, 1944, Norfolk, VA; son of James W (deceased) and Annie Scott; children: Laverne Aisha. **Educ:** Temple Univ, AB, 1966; Univ Va Law Sch, JD, 1970. **Career:** Judge (retired); Hill Tucker & Marsh Attys, partner, 1970-85; Court Appeals Va, judge, 1989-2007. **Orgs:** Former bd mem, Friends Asn C; bd mem, Am Civil Liberties Union; Va State Educ Ast Authority; Nat Advan Asn Colored People; former bd mem, Neighborhood Legal Aid Soc; Richmond Traffic Safety Comn; former bd mem, Va Educ Loan Authority; bd mem, Va Arts Comn; bd mem, Va Ctr Performing Arts. **Home Addr:** 5705 Regent Cir, Richmond, VA 23225-2560, **Home Phone:** (804)230-0053.

**BENTON, LEONARD D.**
Association executive, consultant. **Personal:** Born Jul 1, 1939, Chickasha, OK; married Barbara Y Pointer; children: Quincy L & Savannah. **Educ:** Grambling Stet Univ, BS, 1961; Ill Wesleyan Univ, MS, educ, 1964; Univ Pittsburgh, MPA, 1975. **Career:** Pub Sch Shreveport, La & Chicago, instr, 1961-65; Urban League, assoc dir, 1967-69; Urban League Job Ctr, dir, 1969-70; Southern Regional Off Nat Urban League, dir, 1986-88; Univ Okla, Okla Multicultural Leadership Inst, dir; Urban League, Greater Okla City, life mem, pres emer, currently; Urban League, Okla City, pres & chief exec officer; educ consult, currently. **Orgs:** NSF, 1962-64; chmn, Nat Black Luth Lay Comn; exec secy, Coalition Civil Leadership Okla City; pole march, Kappa Alpha Psi Frat Inc; gen mgr, SW Urban Develop Corp; secy coun, exec dirs, Southern Region; Nat Urban League; chmn, Soc Ministry Okla Dist Luth Church; exec dir, Southwestern Urban Found; Ntu Art Asn; Okla Hist Soc, Black Heritage Comt; Nat Asn Advan Colored People; Southwest Ctr Human Rels Studies; Okla City Northeast Indust Pk; Legal Aid Serv Okla; leader, Quayle United Methodist Church; regional dir, Nat Urban League's Southern. **Honors/Awds:** Service to Mankind Award, Seroma Club, Okla City, 1975. **Home Addr:** 3201 E Forest Pk, Oklahoma City, OK 73121, **Home Phone:** (405)424-8091. **Business Addr:** Executive Director, Southwestern Urban Foundation, 3017 N Martin Luther King Ave, Oklahoma City, OK 73136-1533, **Business Phone:** (405)424-2889.

**BENTON, NELKANE O. See Obituaries Section.**

**BENTON, PHYLLIS CLORA**
Entrepreneur, president (organization). **Personal:** Born Dec 4, 1947, Portland, OR; daughter of William T Sr and Theresa. **Educ:** Portland State Univ, BS, 1970, MSW, 1972, cert, black studies, 1974. **Career:** State Ore, C's Servs Div, social worker, 1976-77; Del Dept Health & Social Serv, Social Security Admin, claims rep, 1977-80, Off Civil Rights, investr, 1980-84, Off Child Support Enforcement, prog specialist, 1984-93; Midnight Ramble Video, owner, 1992-. **Home Addr:** 1810 NE Jarrett St, Portland, OR 97211-5552, **Home Phone:** (503)287-0319. **Business Addr:** Owner, Midnight Ramble Video, PO Box 11522, Portland, OR 97211-0522, **Business Phone:** (503)287-0319.

**BENYARD, WILLIAM B.**
Computer scientist. **Personal:** Born Nov 6, 1948, Detroit, MI; son of Willie and Frances Wilcher Tidwell; married Regenia Christine Powell; children: Erica, Brian, Clarence & Ian; married Regenia Jackson. **Educ:** Delta Col, Univ Ctr, MI, 1978; Wayne State Univ, Detroit, MI; Ind Univ, S Bend, IN. **Career:** Dow Chem USA, Midland, MI, oper analyst, 1974-80; Am Natural Serv Co, Detroit, MI, prod control analyst; Mich Consol Gas Co, Detroit, MI, programmer analyst, 1980-82; State Ohio, programmer analyst 5; AM Gen Corp, S Bend, IN, MIS analyst, 1982-85; Genesis Info Systs, Akron, OH, independent contractor, 1985; Premark Int Food Equip Group, Troy, OH, sr analyst, 1986-87; Advan Programming Resolutions Inc, Dublin, OH, MIS consult, 1987-88; Dayton Bd Educ, OH; Metters Industs, sr syst programmer opers facilitator, sr prin comput analyst; Bilgen Group, Real Estate Investments & Mkt & Distrib, partner, owner, 1988-; Toastmasters Dist 40, vpres educ, 2009-. **Orgs:** Nat rec secy, Black Data Processing Assocs, 1982-86; Nat Asn Advan Colored People, Dayton Chap, 1984; founder, Dayton Chap, Black Data Processing Assocs, 1988-90; pres, Princeton Park Neighborhood Asn, 1989-; Equity Lodge, 121 PHFAU, 1990. **Honors/Awds:** Founders Award, Black Data Processing Asns, 1989. **Home Addr:** 123 Briar Heath Circle, Dayton, OH 45415-2601, **Home Phone:** (937)276-3916. **Business Addr:** Senior Principal Computer Systems Analyst, Metters Industries Inc, 5200 Springfield Pke Suite 300, Dayton, OH 45431-1255, **Business Phone:** (513)253-3697.

**BENYMON, CHICO (THERON D BENYMON)**
Actor, rhythm and blues singer. **Personal:** Born Aug 7, 1969, Amityville, NY. **Career:** Tra-Knox, group mem; TV Series: "Moesha", 2000, 2001; "Half & Half", 2002-06; "Life Is Not a Fairytale: The Fantasia Barrino Story", 2006; Media Blitz, 2007; The Truth Hurts, 2007; "The Game", 2007; "Let's Stay Together", 2012; "Hollywood Heights", 2012; "Haunted Hathaways", 2013-; "One Love", 2014; "The Thundermans", 2014; Films: Ali, 2001; Love on Layaway, 2005; Where Is Love Waiting, 2006; Nite Tales: The Movie, 2008; See Dick Run, 2009; Steppin: The Movie, 2009; Perfect Combination, 2010; Speed-Dating, 2010; "Streets, 2010; House Arrest, 2012; Guardian of Eden, 2012; Because I Love You, 2012; The Trace, 2012; 24 Hour Love, 2013; Act Like You Love Me, 2013. Albums: Born to Reign Introducing Tra-Knox; Songs in films: Men in Black II; Black Suits Coming. **Special Achievements:** Nominated for Image Awards. **Business Addr:** Actor, United Paramount Network, 11800 Wilshire Blvd, Los Angeles, CA 90025, **Business Phone:** (310)575-7000.

**BERAKI, DR. NAILAH G. (NAILAH G BERAKI-PIERRE)**
Physician. **Personal:** Born Jun 17, 1951, New York, NY; daughter of Ina L Green; children: Omar Jackson. **Educ:** San Diego State Col, BA, psychol, 1981; Mueller's Col Wholistic Med, 1987; Lehman Col, BS, health edu, 1998; Mercy Col, MS, orient med, attend; MSEd, coun educ. **Career:** Muwasi Wholistic Health Healing Arts, practioner, massage therapist, currently; Shakeray Wellness Collab LLC, owner, mindset mentor & transformational coach, currently. **Orgs:** Int Massage Asn; Int Reflexology Asn; Nat Black Iridologist Asn; Asn Rebirthers Int; Soc Pub Health Educrs, Greater New York Chap; Nat Acupuncture Detox Asn; Nat Asn Prof Women; Nat Rehab Asn; Am Coun Asn, 2003-; Am Asn Drugless; Asn Voc Rehab Alcoholism & Substance Abuse, 2003-; Health & Nutrit, counr & educr. **Honors/Awds:** Kentucky Colonel, honored for service. **Business Addr:** Owner, Shakeray Wellness Collaborative LLC, 44 E 32nd St Suite1100, New York, NY 10016, **Business Phone:** (718)569-7840.

**BERAKI-PIERRE, NAILAH G. See BERAKI, DR. NAILAH G.**

**BERGER, NATHANIEL**
Architect. **Personal:** married Lady Washington. **Educ:** Carnegie Mellon Univ, BA, archit, Pittsburgh, Pa. **Career:** Design Experience Incl: projs NASA, IBM Corp, AUS Corps Engrs, U.S. Dept State - Off Foreign Bldg Opers, USN, Intel Corp, Motorola Semiconductor; JMGR Inc, partner, currently; Am Inst Architects, dir pub awareness, currently; Pbs & J, group mgr, prog mgr, currently; Hok, vpres, 1980-2005. **Orgs:** Am Inst Archit; bd dir, Asn Atlanta chap; bd dir, AIA Atlanta Bd Dirs. **Special Achievements:** First African American to be named a partner with JMGR Inc, the oldest architectural and engineering design firm in Memphis. **Business Addr:** Vice President, Hok, 191 Peachtree St NE Suite 4100, Atlanta, GA 30303, **Business Phone:** (404)439-9000.

**BERGER-SWEENEY, JOANNE**
College president. **Personal:** Born Jan 18, 1958?, Los Angeles, CA; married Urs V Berger; children: Clara & Tommy. **Educ:** Wellsley Col, BS, psychobiology, 1979; Univ Calif, Berkeley, MPH, environ health sci, 1981; Johns Hopkins Sch Pub Health, PhD, neurotoxicology, 1989. **Career:** Wellesley Col, asst prof, 1991, Allene Lummis Russell Prof Neuroscience, dir Neuroscience Prog, assoc dean, 2004-10; Tufts Univ, dean Sch Arts & Sci, 2010-14; Trinity Col, pres, 2014-. **Special Achievements:** First African-American and first woman president of Trinity College; involved in the creation of the Bridge to Liberal Arts Success and the Center for Race and Democracy at Tufts; contributed to the "Journal of Neuroscience", and others; authored more than 60 scientific publications; held grants from the National Institutes of Health, the National Science Foundation, and numerous private foundations; member of the Behavioral Neuroscience Review Panel of the National Science Foundation; member of the National Institutes of Health Study Selection panel; member of the editorial board of "Behavioral Neuroscience". **Business Addr:** Trinity College, 300 Summit St, Hartford, CT 06106.

**BERHE-HUNT, ANNETTE**
Librarian. **Personal:** Born Batesville, MS; daughter of Roland Cole and Adelle Toliver Cole. **Educ:** Jackson State Univ, Jackson, MS, BS, 1974; Atlanta Univ, Atlanta, GA, MLS, 1979. **Career:** Quitman Co Pub Schs, Marks, MS, teacher, 1974-77; Lemoyne-Owen Col, Memphis, TN, Hollis F. Price Libr, librn, 1982-, dir libr, currently. **Orgs:** Tutor, Memphis Literacy Coun, 1982-86; Young Women Christian Asn, 1982-90; Tenn Libr Asn, 1986; Am Libr Asn, 1987-; treas, Les Gemmes, 1989. **Honors/Awds:** Archival Training Inst, Nat Historical Pub & Record Comn, 1982. **Home Addr:** 4189 Kenosha Rd, Memphis, TN 38118, **Home Phone:** (901)368-5158. **Business Addr:** Director Library, Lemoyne-Owen College, 807 Walker Ave, Memphis, TN 38126, **Business Phone:** (901)435-1350.

**BERNARD, DONALD L.**
Artist, educator. **Personal:** Born Nov 26, 1942, Baton Rouge, LA; son of Matthew L D and Doris Lillian; children: Alecia C. **Educ:** Los Angeles City Col, attended 1968; Calif State Univ La, BA, 1974, MFA, 1997; Otis Parsons, attended 1982; Grossmont Col, Polaroid Workshop, 1999. **Career:** Artist & photographer: City Los Angeles, graphic designer & photogr, 1971-2000; "A Certain Beauty", pub Los Angeles Times, 1985; The Hist of Black Photogr from 1840-, publ & exhib; San Bernadino Valley Col, part-time photog instr, 1999; Calif State Univ Los Angeles, part-time visual literacy instr; Reflections in Black, 2000; Elem Sch C, teacher, 2000-08; Committed to the Image: Contemp Black Photogr, publ & exhib, 2001. **Orgs:** Los Angeles Photog Ctr, 1981-87; co-founder, Black Photogr CA, 1984-86; co-founder, Black Gallery, 1984-86; San Francisco Camera works, 1998-99; Friends Photog, 1999; San Diego Mus Photog, 1999; FNFOCO, 1999-2000; Exposure Group, Wash, DC, 2007-2008. **Home Addr:** 2497 Diamond Dr, Chino Hills, CA 91709-3537, **Home Phone:** (909)627-8285. **Business Phone:** (909)627-8285.

**BERNARD, LINDA D.**
Association executive, lawyer. **Educ:** Wayne State Univ, BA, 1970, Law Sch, JD, 1973; Univ Pa, LLM, 1975. **Career:** Judge (retired), attroney; Wayne Co Neighborhood Legal Serv, proj mgr, dir, pres & chief exec officer, 1999; pvt pract atty, 2001-; Thirty-Sixth Judicial Dist Ct Mich, judge, 2012-14; Linda D. Bernard & Assocs PLC, managing partner, owner; Ford Motor Co, atty; Detroit Film Off, dir; Detroit Int Productions Ltd, founder; DIP-STIK Music Publ, founder; City Detroit Law Dept, supv asst corp coun; Mass Port Authority, gen coun. **Orgs:** Vpres, Nat Asn Women Lawyers; Founding mem, State Bar's Delivery Legal Serv Comt; Mass Port Authority; bd mem, Black Sports Agents Asn; hearings referee, Mich Civil Rights Comn; Wolverine Bar Asn; Am Arbitrator Asn Arbitrator. **Special Achievements:** First African American Masters of Law recipient from the University of Pennsylvania Law School. **Business Addr:** Managing Partner, Owner, Linda D Bernard & Assocs PLC, 17144 Wildemere St Suite 1000, Detroit, MI 48221, **Business Phone:** (313)864-6785.

**BERNARD, DR. LOUIS JOSEPH**
Surgeon, educator, executive. **Personal:** Born Aug 19, 1925, Laplace, LA; son of Edward (deceased) and Jeanne Vinet (deceased); married Lois Jeanette McDonald; children: Marie Antonia Bernard Jenkins & Phyllis Elaine Bernard Robison May. **Educ:** Dillard Univ, BA, 1946; Meharry Med Col, MD, 1950. **Career:** Hubbard Hosp Nashville, intern, 1950-51, resident, 1954-56, chief resident, 1957-58; Univ Rochester, NIH res fel, 1953-54, Nat Cancer Inst, res fel, 1953-54; Memorial Ctr NY Col, resident, 1956-57; Am Cancer Soc, clin fel, 1958-59, instr surg, chmn comt; Okla City, OK, pract, med spec surg, 1959-69; Univ Okla, clin asst prof surg, 1959-69; Nashville, 1969-; Meharry Med Col, vice chair, surg dept, 1969-73, prof, chmn, surg dept, 1973-87, assoc dean, 1974-81, interim dean, 1987, dean, 1987-90, Health Serv, vpres, 1988-90, distinguished prof surg emer, 1990-; Drew Meharry & Morehouse Consortium Cancer Ctr, dir, 1990-96, assoc prof; Dillard Univ, teaching asst biol. **Orgs:** Comn Cancer Am Col Surgeons, 1974-84; bd dir, Tenn Div Am Cancer Soc, pres, 1987-88; fel Am Col Surgeons; fel Southeastern Surg Cong; Nashville Acad Med; Tenn Med Asn; Nat Med Asn; Soc Surg Oncologists; Okla Surg Asn; Okla City Surg Asn; Alpha Omega Alpha; Alpha Phi Alpha; Sigma Pi Phi; Am Asn Cancer Educ; fel Sloan-Kettering Memorial Cancer Ctr. **Honors/Awds:** St. George Award, 1985; Distinguished Prof Surgery Emer, 1990; Louis JBernard Neighbors Life Award, 1992; Humanitarian Award, Nat Am Cancer Soc, 1993; Margaret Hay Edwards Achievement Medal, Am Asn Cancer Educ, 1996. **Special Achievements:** Author of numerous books. **Home Addr:** 156 Queens Lane, Nashville, TN 37218-1826, **Home Phone:** (615)876-7117. **Business Addr:** Distinguished Professor of Surgery Emeritus, Meharry Medical College, 1005 Dr DB Todd Jr Blvd, Nashville, TN 37208, **Business Phone:** (615)327-6000.

**BERNARD, DR. MICHELLE DENISE**
Political consultant, lawyer. **Personal:** Born Jul 30, 1963, Washington, DC; daughter of Milton D and Nesta Hyacinth Grant; married Joe Johns; children: Logan Christopher & Avery. **Educ:** Howard Univ, Wash, DC, BA, philos & polit sci, 1985; Georgetown Univ Law Ctr, Wash, DC, JD, 1988. **Career:** Wash Perito & Dubuc, Wash, DC, atty, 1988; Patton Boggs LLP, partner, 1996-2000; Independent Womens Forum, sr vpres, pres & chief exec officer, 2004-10; Bernard Ctr, chmn, founder, pres & chief exec officer, 2009-; MSNBC, polit analyst, 2008-; Wash Speakers Bur, speaker, 2009-; 74 Media, columnist, 2015-; Root, individual writer & contribr, 2015-; Roll Call, columnist, 2016-; US News & World Report, columnist, 2016-. **Orgs:** Am Bar Asn, 1988-; Nat Found Black Pub Adminrs, 1990-; Md Chamber Com, 1990-; bd trustees, Hampton Univ; bd dir, Coalition Opportunity Educ; exec bd, Int Women's Forum; adv bd, Am Bd Cert Teacher Excellence; Capital City Chap Links Inc, 2012-. **Honors/Awds:** Award for outstanding contribution to the Law Center Academic Program, Georgetown Univ Law Ctr, 1988; one of three "Fast Trackers" nation's top opinion leaders, Newsmax magazine, 2008. **Special Achievements:** Authored numerous articles including: Qui Tam Litigation Under the Civiland Criminal False Claims Act, Complex Crimes Journal, 1994; RICO and the "Operation Management" Test: The Potential Chilling Effect on Criminal Prosecutions, 28 U. Rich.L. Rev. 669, 1994; co-author, Ira H. Raphaelson; Financial Institution Fraud: Congress Still Struggles to Respond Consistently, 2Bank Fraud, ABA White Collar Crime Committee, Section of Criminal Justice, 1993; co-author, Eva Marie Shivers, Maryland Environmental Law, Federal Publications, 1990 & Supp 1991; contributing author: How Women are Wealthier, Healthier, and More Independent than Ever Before, Spence Publishing; featured in several publications, including: Fast Company magazine, The Legal Times, The New York Daily News, The Washington Business Journal, The Washington City Paper, The Washington Lawyer, The Washington Post, The Washington Post Sunday Magazine, and The Washington Times and also featured in the Observer and the Gleaner, two of Jamaica's leading national newspapers; television and radio appearances include America's Black Forum, BBC Radio, CNBC's The Dennis Miller Show, C-SPAN's Washington Journal, Court TV's Catherine Crier Live, Good Morning Jamaica, MSNBC, PBS's Evening Exchange and To the Contrary, NPR's Tavis Smiley Showand KLAS FM 89, Jamaica. **Home Addr:** 3225 Grace St NW Spt 221, Washington, DC 20007-3643, **Home Phone:** (202)244-6136. **Business Addr:** President, Chief Executive Officer, Bernard Center, PO Box 59410, Potomac, MD 20859, **Business Phone:** (301)299-4092.

**BERNARD, NESTA HYACINTH**
College administrator. **Personal:** daughter of Charles Reginald and Edith Eliza Henry; married Milton Desmond; children: Michelle, Nicole, Andrea & Desmond. **Educ:** Howard Univ, Wash, DC, BA, 1975; Univ Md, College Park, MD, MS, 1977. **Career:** United Plan-

ning Orgn, chief new progs br; Howard Univ, Wash, DC, dir alumni affairs, 1983, sr dir alumni rels, asst vpres, assoc vpres univ advan, interim vpres & vpres develop & alumni rels, 2009-2015. **Orgs:** Nat Asn Fundraising Execs, 1983-; Alpha Kappa Alpha Sorority; Girl friends Links Inc. **Special Achievements:** Became only the third recipient of the prestigious Bison Pride Award, 2015. **Home Addr:** 10519 Tanager Lane, Potomac, MD 20854, **Home Phone:** (301)424-7026.

### BERNARD, NICOLE A.
Vice president (organization). **Educ:** Howard Univ, BA, broadcast jour & commun, 1987; Georgetown Univ Law Ctr, JD, 1990. **Career:** Davis Shapiro & Lewit, atty, 1993-2000; Nicole A Bernard, PC, atty, 2000-02; Uptown& MCA Rec, sr atty; Apollo Theater Found Inc, sr vpres bus develop, 2002-05; Fox Broadcasting Co, sr vpres brdcst stand & practices, 2005-11; Fox Group Fox Entertainment, audience strategy, sr vpres brdcst stand, 2011-. **Orgs:** Bd mem, Apollo Theater Found. **Business Addr:** Senior Vice President Broadcast Standards & Practice, Fox Broadcasting Co, 10201 W Pico Blvd, Los Angeles, CA 90035, **Business Phone:** (310)369-1000.

### BERNARD, PAUL
State government official. **Educ:** Georgetown Univ, Sch Foreign Serv, Int Finance, BS; Georgetown Univ, McDonough Sch Bus, MBA; Harvard Univ, Kennedy Sch Govt, MS, urban econs, pub finance. **Career:** Redevelop Authority, City Philadelphia, dir develop, 1993-95; Pub Financial Mgt, sr managment consult, 1995-98; State Mich, City Detroit, dir planning & develop, 1998-2002, dir econ develop, currently; MuniMae, prin, capital investments, 2002-08; Walker & Dunlop, sr vpres, prin investments, 2008-14; Enterprise Community Partners, vpres, enterprise advisors, 2015-. **Orgs:** Bd mem, Nat Asn Real Estate Investment Managers, 2010; bd mem, Steers Ctr Global Real Estate, 2012. **Business Addr:** Director, State of Michigan, 65 Cadillac Sq Suite 2300, Detroit, MI 48226, **Business Phone:** (313)224-6380.

### BERNARD, SHARON ELAINE
Banker, vice president (organization). **Personal:** Born Apr 19, 1943, Detroit, MI; daughter of John and Dorothea; children: Cylenthia & Sharon Gayle. **Educ:** Univ Ariz Sch Law, BSL, JD, 1969. **Career:** Banker (retired); self-employed, atty, 1970-74; Mich Nat Bank, vice chair, exec vpres, 1975; Detroit Police Dept, police comnr, 1979-84; Detroit Urban League, endowed exec. **Orgs:** Kappa Beta Pi Legal Sorority, 1968, Women's Econ Club, 1975; chairperson, C Trust Fund, 1982-88, Detroit Urban League Bd, 1984-89; dir, Nat Comt, Prev Child Abuse Bd, 1984; pres, Neighborhood Serv Orgn Bd, 1987; dir, vice chair, Ennis Ctr C Bd, 1987; dir, United Way, SE Mich Bd, 1988; dir, vice chair, United Community Serv Bd, 1989; Mich Family Planning Adv Bd, 1990; YWCA Detroit; Mich Children; Booker T Wash Bus Asn. **Honors/Awds:** Esq; Minority Achiever Indust Award, YMCA, 1980; Spirit Detroit, City Coun Detroit, 1984; Humanitarian of the Year, Optimist Youth Found, 1986; Outstanding Vol, Mich Nat Bank, 1987; Kool Achiever Award Nominee, Brown & Williamson, 1988; Mich 150 First Lady Award, State Mich, 1988; First Black Female Law Grad Award, Black Law Stud Asn, Univ Ark, 1989; Outstanding Leadership Award, Detroit Urban League, 1989; Vol Serv Award, Cent Region, Nat Urban League, 1990. **Home Addr:** 16160 Chapel St, Detroit, MI 48219, **Home Phone:** (313)863-0300.

### BERNOUDY, MONIQUE ROCHELLE
Educator, athletic director. **Personal:** Born May 18, 1960, Detroit, MI; daughter of Benjamin Joseph and Cynthia. **Educ:** Spelman Col, BS, psychol, 1983; Northern Ill Univ, MS, adult educ, 1992, EdD, higher educ admin, currently. **Career:** Univ Mich, col basket ball, 1978-80; Northern Ill Univ, asst dir admis, 1984-86, Col Bus, acad counr, 1987-92, Stud Athlete Support Serv, dir, 1999-2004, Huskie Life Skills, assoc athletics dir, 2004-10, IDSP 302, instr, 2009-12, assoc athletics dir, 2010-; Valparaiso Univ, Stud Affairs, dir multicultural progs, 1992-97; Univ Chicago, dir diversity affairs, 1997-99. **Orgs:** Adv Coun Multiracial Concerns, 1992-; Campus Parking Comn, 1992-94; coord comn, Campus Diversity, 1992-; coord comn, Heritage Festival, 1992-; Intercultural Studies Comn, 1992-; adv comn, Knight Found, 1992-; planning comn, Martin Luther King Day Observance, 1992-; Porter Co Comn Corrections Comn, 1992-; Town & Gown Comn, 1992-94; alumni bd, Valparaiso Univ, 1993-; Ind Coalition Blacks Higher Educ, 1993-; alumni bd, Multiracial Sub-Comn, 1993-, guild, 1994-; co-chair, W Side High Sch Partnership Coord Comn; William Rand lph Hearst Scholar Comn, 1994-; co-chair, Campus Coord Comn, Sexual Harassment & Assault, 1994; develop comn, Diversity Plan, 1994; Judiciary Bd Hearing Panel, 1994; Racial Harassment Advocate, 1994-; stud senate, Intercultural Comn, 1994-; Week Challenge Coord Comn, 1994; evaluator, Goshen Col, Lilly Found Grant, 1994-95; advisor, EBONY Women; Mid-Am Asn Educ Opportunity Prog Personnel, 1994-; bd dir, Mombasa Relief Initiative, 2007-; bd mem, Athletic dir Asn, 2008-10; facilitator, NCAA Career Sports Forum, 2009-11; Black Coaches & Adminr Asn; Womens Basketball Coaches Asn. **Home Addr:** 3900 W 95th Suite 304, Evergreen Park, IL 60805-1917, **Home Phone:** (815)761-6453. **Business Addr:** Associate Athletic Director, Northern Illinois University, 1425 W Lincoln Hwy, DeKalb, IL 60115-2828, **Business Phone:** (815)753-1000.

### BERNSTEIN, MARGARET ESTHER
Newspaper editor. **Personal:** Born Nov 23, 1959, Los Angeles, CA; daughter of Morris and Alice Collum; married C Randolph Keller. **Educ:** Univ Southern Calif, BA, print jour, 1993. **Career:** Wave Newspapers, Los Angeles, CA, staff writer, 1981-84; Herald-Dispatch, Huntington, WV, feature writer, 1984-87; Tucson Citizen, AR, asst city ed, 1987-89; Plain Dealer, Cleveland, OH, feature writer, columnist, 1989-92, ed, women's sect, 1992-; Plain Dealers everywoman sect, founding ed, 1993-2000; feature writer, currently. **Orgs:** Delta Sigma Theta Sorority, 1981-; bd mem, Black Journalists Asn Southern Calif, 1982-84; founder/pres, Tri-State Black Media Asn, 1986-87; comt chair, Cleveland Chap, Nat Asn Black Journalists, 1989-; Cath Big Sisters Cleveland, 1989-. **Honors/Awds:** Project Editor for "Tucson's Tapestry of Cultures", a 1988-89 newspaper series that received: Sweepstakes Award & 1st Place for In Depth News, Arizona Asniated Press, & 3rd Place, Staff Enterprise Award, Best of Gannett Competition; First Place, Ohio Excellence in Journalism Awards, Column-writing, 1992; Best in Media Award, Cleveland Services for Independent Living, 1992; Nat Big Sister of the Year, Big Brothers Big Sisters of Am, 2000; Second-place award for public service, 2005. **Special Achievements:** Co Writer: "The Bond: Three Young Men Learn to Forgive and Reconnect with Their Fathers," with the Three Doctors, 2007. **Home Addr:** 3417 Rumson Rd, Cleveland Heights, OH 44118, **Home Phone:** (216)999-4876. **Business Addr:** Feature Writer, The Plain Dealer, 1801 Super Ave, Cleveland, OH 44114-2198, **Business Phone:** (216)999-4876.

### BERNSTINE, DR. DANIEL O.
President (organization), lawyer, educator. **Personal:** Born Sep 7, 1947, Berkeley, CA; son of Annias and Emma; married Nancy Jean Tyler; children: Quincy & Justin. **Educ:** Univ Calif, Berkeley, CA, BA, polit sci, 1969; Northwestern Univ Sch Law, JD, 1972; Univ Wis, Law Sch, LLM, 1975; Howard Univ Sch Law. **Career:** Clearinghouse Rev, Northwestern Univ Sch Law, sr ed, 1971-72; US Dept Labor, staff atty, 1972-73; Univ WI Law Sch, teaching fel, 1974-75; Howard Univ Law Sch, asst prof, 1975-78; Howard Univ, asst vpres, legal affairs, 1984-87, gen coun, 1987-90, interim law sch dean, 1988-90; Univ WI Law Sch, prof, 1978-97, dean, 1990-97; Fac Law Pontificial Cath Univ Peru, Lima, Peru, prof law, 1996; Portland State Univ, Ore, pres, 1997-2007, pres emer; Law Sch Admis Coun, pres & chief exec officer, 2007-. **Orgs:** Fel Wis Law Found, 2002; bd mem, United Way Columbia-Willamette; bd mem, Portland Bus Alliance; co-chaired, LSAC Minority Affairs (now Diversity) Comt's LSAC/HBCU Work Group; LSAC Bd trustee, 2007-. **Home Addr:** 11650 SW Mil Rd, Portland, OR 97219, **Home Phone:** (503)725-2376. **Business Addr:** President, Chief Executive Officer, Law School Admissions Council, PO Box 8512, Newtown, PA 18940.

### BERNSTINE, RODERICK EARL
Football player. **Personal:** Born Feb 8, 1965, Fairfield, CA; married Stephanie Kay Smith; children: Payton Chaneln & Roderick Earl Jr. **Educ:** Tex A&M Univ. **Career:** Football player (retired); San Diego Chargers, tight end & running back, 1987-92; Denver Broncos, running back, 1993-95. **Home Addr:** 1015 W Evans Ave, Denver, CO 80223-4077, **Home Phone:** (303)699-8083.

### BERRY, BERTAND DEMOND
Football player, broadcaster. **Personal:** Born Aug 15, 1975, Houston, TX. **Educ:** Univ Notre Dame, attended. **Career:** Football player (retired), host; Indianapolis Colts, defensive end, 1997, right defensive end, 1998, 1999; Edmonton Eskimos, 2000; Denver Broncos, 2001, defensive end, 2002-03, Ariz Cardinals, defensive end, 2004-09, linebacker, 2007, right outside linebacker, 2009; Fan AM 1060 KDUS, host, 2011-12; Ariz Sports 98.7 FM, host, 2015-. **Honors/Awds:** Pro Bowl selection, 2004, 2005; All-Pro selection, 2004; NFC Champion, Nat football league, 2008. **Business Addr:** Host, Arizona Sports 98.7 FM, 7740 N 16th St Suite 200, Phoenix, AZ 85020, **Business Phone:** (602)274-6200.

### BERRY, BILL (WILLIAM E BERRY)
Basketball coach. **Personal:** Born Jan 1, 1942?, Winnemucca, NV; married Clarice; children: Pam & Ricky (deceased). **Educ:** Mich State Univ, BA, 1965, MA, phys educ, 1969. **Career:** Basketball coach (retired); Highlands High Sch, Sacramento, coach, 1966-69; MI State Univ, asst coach, 1969, 1977-79; Cosumnes River Jr Col, head coach, 1970-72; Univ Calif, Berkeley, asst coach, 1972-77; San Jose State Univ, head coach, 1979-89; Sacramento Kings, asst coach, scout, 1989-91; Houston Rockets, scout, 1991-92, asst coach, 1994-99; Chicago Bulls, asst coach, 1999-2003, interim head, 2001, coach, 2001-03, dir oper, defensive coordr, 2002-03; Wash Wizards, asst coach, 2006-07. **Business Addr:** Assistant Coach, Washington Wizards, Verizon Ctr, Washington, DC 20004, **Business Phone:** (202)661-5000.

### BERRY, CHARLES F., JR.
Auditor. **Personal:** Born May 15, 1964, Detroit, MI; son of Charles F Sr and Edna J; married D Lynn. **Educ:** Univ Mich, Ann Arbor, bachelors, 1987. **Career:** Citizens Trust Bank & Trust, bank teller, 1986-87; Plante & Moran CPA's, auditor, beginning 1987; Dutch Ventures Ltd, auditor, pres & chief exec officer, currently; Sb Realty Group LLC. **Orgs:** Toastmasters Int, pres, 1991-93; Vol Income Tax Assistance, tax preparer, 1987-92; Mich Asn Cert Pub Accts, 1987-; Nat Asn Black Accts, 1987-; Am Inst Cert Pub Accts, 1988-; United Way Health & Human Servs Allocation Comt, 1994-. **Honors/Awds:** Detroit Chamber Com, Leadership Detroit Grad, 1994. **Home Addr:** 8 Alexandria Towne St, Southfield, MI 48075-3440. **Business Addr:** Auditor, Dutch Ventures Ltd, 645 Griswold Suite 1300, Detroit, MI 48226, **Business Phone:** (313)237-8166.

### BERRY, CHUCK (CHARLES EDWARD ANDERSON BERRY)
Singer, composer, songwriter. **Personal:** Born Oct 18, 1926, St. Louis, MO; son of Henry William and Martha Bell Banks; married Themetta Toddy Suggs; children: Darlin Ingrid Berry-Clay, Melody Exes Berry-Eskridge, Aloha Isa Lei & Charles Edward Jr. **Career:** Sir Johns Trio, guitarist, 1952; solo rec artist, 1955-; Songs & Compositions: "Maybellene", 1955; "Roll Over Beethoven", 1956; "Too Much Monkey Bus/Brown Eyed Handsome Man", 1956; "Sch Day (Ring Ring Goes the Bell)", 1957; "Rock & Roll Music", composer, 1957; "Sweet Little Sixteen", composer, 1958; "Johnny B Goode/Around & Around", composer, 1958; Caraol, 1958; "Little Queenie/Almost Grown", 1959; "Nadine", 1964; "No Particular Place to Go", 1964; "Memphis/Back in the USA", composer, 1967; "My Ding-a-Ling", 1972; The Southern Air Restaurant, owner; "Sweet Little Rock & Roller", composer, 1981; "My Ding A Ling", singer, 1982; Chuck Berry Hail! Hail! Rock n Roll, producer, 1987; "Run Rudoph Run", Home Alone, singer, 1990; "The Promised Land, writer, 1997; "You Never Can Tell", writer, 1998; "Surfin USA", writer, 1998; "No particular place to go", composer, 2002; Unaccompanied Minors, 2006; Elvis Presley: Love Me Tender, 2006; Aloha from Sweden, 2006; "The Sopranos", 2006; Camping, 2006; Cars, 2006; The Shaggy Dog, 2006; The Wendell Baker Story, 2005; Ganes, 2007; Yhden tahden hotelli, 2007; Albums: Rock Rock Rock, 1957; After School Session, 1958; Berry Is On Top, 1959; Rockin At The Hops, 1960; New Juke-Box Hits, 1961; Chuck Berry Twist, 1962; Chuck Berry On Stage, 1963; St. Louis To Liverpool, 1964; Fresh Berrys, 1965; Chuck Berry In London, 1965; Live At The Fillmore Auditorium, 1967; Chuck Berry In Memphis, 1967; Chuck Berrys Golden Hits, 1967; Chuck Berrys Golden Decade, 1967; From St. Louie To Frisco, 1968; Concerto In B. Goode, 1969; Back Home, 1970; San Francisco Dues, 1971; The London Chuck Berry Sessions, 1972; St. Louie To Frisco To Memphis, 1972; Johnny B. Goode, 1972; Sweet Little Rock And Roller, 1973; Bio, 1973; Wild Berrys, 1974; Flashback, 1974; Chuck And His Friends, 1974; Chuck Berry, 1975; Rock It, 1979; Alive And Rockin, 1981; The Great Twenty-Eight, 1982; Hail Hail Rock N Roll, 1987; On The Blues Side, 1994; Roll Over Beethoven, 1996; Let It Rock, 1996; Guitar Legends, 1997; Blast From The Past, 2001. **Honors/Awds:** Triple Award, Billboard Mag, 1955; Best R & B Singer, Blues Unlimited, 1973; Nat Music Award, Am Music Conf, 1976; Grammy Award for Lifetime Achievement, 1984; Nashville Songwriters Asn Int Hall of Fame, 1982; Rock & Roll Hall of Fame, 1986; Guitar Player Mag, 1987; Hollywood Walk of Fame, 1987; Star, Hollywood Blvd Calif, 1987; Honored with a Star, Delmar Blvd, 1989; Icon Award, BMI, 2002. **Special Achievements:** First singer and songwriter of 1955; first guitarist and singer to get on Billboard charts; released his autobiography in 1987. **Home Addr:** 691 Buckner Rd, Wentzville, MO 63385, **Home Phone:** (636)327-8700. **Business Addr:** Singer, Writer, William Morris Endeavor Entertainment, 9601 Wilshire Blvd, Beverly Hills, CA 90210-5213, **Business Phone:** (310)285-9000.

### BERRY, DANTE
Journalist, activist. **Educ:** Monmouth Univ, BA, 2010. **Career:** Polit Develop Group, LLC, intern, 2010; Sch-Based Health Alliance, policy asst, 2010-11; Roosevelt Inst Campus Network, opers mgr, 2011-13; Dante Barry, freelance consult, 2012-; Roosevelt Inst, engagement ed, 2013-14; Million Hoodies Movement Justice, exec dir, 2013-; Ctr Media Justice, digital, 2014-15. **Orgs:** Pi Sigma Alpha Hon Soc; Phi Kappa Psi; Andrew Goodman Found, 2015-. Monmouth Univ Alumni Bd Dirs, past sr class pres, 2009-10. **Honors/Awds:** Martin Luther King Jr. Unsung Hero Award, 2007; named one of 100 Black Influencers by The Root. **Special Achievements:** Contributor, The Nation, MSNBC, Huffington Post, Ebony, and Truthout. **Business Addr:** Million Hoodies Movement for Justice, 330 West 42nd St Suite 900, New York, NY 10036.

### BERRY, ERIC
Administrator. **Personal:** Born Nov 16, 1952, Salem, NJ; son of Daisy and Adolphus (deceased); children: Erin. **Educ:** Cumberland County Col, AA; Glassboro State Col & Rowan Univ, BA, 1976; Rutgers Univ, MA. **Career:** Boy Scout Am, paid prof scout, 1973-76; Asgrow Seed Com, Nat acct consult, 1976-88; Food Network Sears, regional mgr, 1988-90; Retebtion Syst & Workforce, radio vpres mkt, 1990-93; Shadow Broadcasting Serv, gen sales mgr, 1993-96; TBG, mkt, commun, contract consult, 1996-98; Tri-county Action Agency, dir fund develop, 1998-99; Twp Fairfield, bus admin, currently; Willingboro Twp, dep twp mgr. **Orgs:** Millennium Comn; Am Soc Pub Admin. **Home Addr:** 301 Brighton Ct, Sicklerville, NJ 08081, **Home Phone:** (856)232-7171. **Business Addr:** Business Administrator, Fairfield Township, 70 Fairton Gouldtown Rd, Fairton, NJ 08320, **Business Phone:** (856)451-9284.

### BERRY, FREDRICK JOSEPH
Educator. **Personal:** Born May 29, 1940, Jacksonville, IL; married Quereda Ann Harris; children: Anthony & Frederick Jr. **Educ:** Roosevelt Univ, attended 1961; Southern Ill Univ, BMus, 1962, MMus, 1964; Stanford Univ, attended 1969. **Career:** Southern Ill Univ, Lab Sch, super music, 1964; Chicago Pub Sch Syst, instr, 1964-66; Stanford Univ, asst dir bands, 1966-69, Jazz Ensembles, dir, 1989-, Stanford Jazz Orchestra, dir, 1991-, Jazz Studies, lectr, currently; Col San Mateo, dir jazz ensembles, 1972-88, dir jazz prog; Nueva Learning Ctr, Hillsborough, Calif, brass specialist, 1984-94. **Orgs:** Am Fed Musicians, 1956-; San Fran 49ers Band, 1970-; Am Fed Teachers, 1970-; vpres, Am Fed Music Local 6 Credit Union, 1973; Calif Teachers Asn, 1975-85; pres, Berry Enterprises & Music Serv, 1980-; Calif Music Educ Asn, 1980-; Asn Advan Creative Music; Roscoe Mitchell Quartet. **Home Addr:** 36 Cadiz Cir, Redwood City, CA 94065, **Home Phone:** (650)595-3592. **Business Addr:** Director, Lecturer, Stanford University, 541 Lasuen Mall, Stanford, CA 94305-3076, **Business Phone:** (650)723-2109.

### BERRY, GEMERAL E., JR.
Publisher, educator. **Personal:** Born Aug 9, 1948, San Antonio, TX; son of Leotha O Sr and Gemeral E; married Elaine; children: Gemeral III. **Educ:** Univ N Tex, BA, 1974. **Career:** Our Tex Mag, publ, owner, 1991-; Univ N Tex, adj prof jour, 1996. **Orgs:** Dallas Black Chamber Com; Acres Home Citizens Chamber Com; Ft Worth Metrop Chamber; Midland Black Chamber Entreprenuers, Midland, Dallas Ft Worth/ABC Journalists; Dallas Ft Worth/Asn Black Journalists. **Business Addr:** Publisher, Owner, Our Texas Magazine, 103 N Willomet Ave, Dallas, TX 75208-5040, **Business Phone:** (214)943-7374.

### BERRY, DR. GORDON L.
Educator, lecturer, writer. **Personal:** son of Marcus and Gertrude; married G Juanita; children: Gordon Jr, Steven & Cheryl. **Educ:** Cent State Univ, BS, 1955; Univ Wis, MS, 1961; Marquette Univ, EdD, coun psychol, 1969. **Career:** Milwaukee Tech Col, coun psychologist; Marquette Univ, asst to acad vpres; Univ Calif, Los Angeles, asst dean, 1970-76, prof, prof emer, currently; TV programs: Captain Kangaroo Fraggle Rock, tech adv; Ghostwriter; Zoobilee Zoo, tech adv; Name your Adventure, tech adv; Barney & Friends, tech adv; Space Acad, tech adv; The Leopard Son, tech adv; Happily Ever After Fairy Tales for Every Child, tech adv; Fat Albert & The Cosby Kids, tech adv; SecretsIsis, tech adv; Shazam, tech adv; NBC, KCET, Nickelodeon, consult; Unic Calif Los Angeles, Commun Stud Prog, fac; Unic Calif Los Angeles, Grad Sch Educ & Info Studies, prof emer; CBS network, sr tech adv, consult, currrently. **Orgs:** Nat Asn Sch Psychologists, 1970-; Phi Delta Kappa; bd, Los Angeles Film Teachers Asn; Am Psychol Asn; Am Psychol Soc; Acad TV, Arts & Sci Found. **Honors/Awds:** Ralph Metcalfe Chair Lectr; cert hon, Acad TV, Arts & Sci; Distinguished Alumnus Award, School of Education, 2009. **Business Addr:** Professor Emeritus, University California Los Angeles, 1113 Murphy Hall 405 Hilgard Ave, Los Angeles, CA 90095-1538, **Business Phone:** (310)825-8316.

**BERRY, HALLE MARIA (HANNAH LITTLE)**
Actor. **Personal:** Born Aug 14, 1966, Cleveland, OH; daughter of Jerome and Judith; married David Justice, Jan 1, 1993, (divorced 1997); married Eric Benet, Jan 24, 2001, (divorced 2005); married Olivier Martinez, Jul 13, 2013, (divorced 2015); children: 1. **Educ:** Cleveland State Univ; Cuyahoga Community Col. **Career:** TV series: "Living Dolls", lead, 1988-89; "Knot's Landing", guest lead, 1991; TV miniseries: "Queen", 1992; Episode No 1.18, 2004; "Their Eyes Were Watching God", 2005; "The Simpsons", 2011; "Extant", 2014. Films: Jungle Fever, 1989; Strictly Business, 1990-91; The Last Boy Scout, 1991; Boomerang, 1992; Father Hood, 1993; Program, The, 1993; The Flintstones, 1994; Losing Isaiah, 1994; Solomon & Sheba, 1995; Executive Decision, 1996; Race the Sun, 1996; BAPS, 1997; Bullworth, 1998; The Wedding, 1998; Why Do Fools Fall in Love, 1998; Introducing Dorothy Dandridge, HBO, producer, 1999; X-Men, 2000; Swordfish, 2001; Monster's Ball, 2001; Die Another Day, 2002; X-Men 2, 2003; Gothika, 2003; Catwoman, 2004; Robots, 2005; Lackawanna Blues, producer, 2005; X-Men: The Last Stand, 2006; Perfect Stranger, 2006; Revlon, model; Things We Lost in the Fire, 2007; Frankie & Alice, producer, 2009; Frankie & Alice, 2010; New Years Eve, 2011; Dark Tide, 2012; Cloud Atlas, 2012; Movie 43, 2013; The Call, 2013; X-Men: Days of Future Past, 2014; Kidnap, 2016; Kingsman: The Golden Circle, 2017. **Orgs:** Spokesperson, Juv Diabetes Asn; spokesperson, C Outreach. **Honors/Awds:** Miss Teen Ohio; Miss Teen All America; Runner Up to Miss USA; Image Award, Nat Asn Advan Colored People, 1995, 2000, 2002, 2003, 2011; Golden Globe Award, 2000, 2001, 2006, 2011; OFTA Television Award, 2000; Black Reel, 2000, 2002; Best Actress in a Television Movie, 2000; Screen Actors Guild Award, 2000, 2002; NBR Award, 2001; Emmy Award; SAG Award, Best Actress, 2002; Best Actress, Berlinale Int Film Festival, 2002; Crystal Award, 2002; Academy Award, Best Actress, 2002; Essence Award, 2002; PFCS Award, Phoenix Film Critics Soc, 2002; Bambi Award, 2002; DFWFCA Award, 2002; Jupiter Award, 2002; BET Award, 2002, 2003, 2004, 2005, 2008; ShoWest Award, 2004; Teen Choice Award, 2004; Razzie Award, 2005; Primetime Emmy Award, 2005; Black Movie Award, 2005; Peoples Choice Award, 2006; Woman of the Year, Hasty Pudding Theatricals, 2006; Christopher Award, 2006; People's Choice Award, 2007; Star on the Walk of Fame, 2007; Icon Award, 2008; Desert Palm Achievement Award, 2008; Spike Guys' Choice Award, 2009; AAFCA Award, African-Am Film Critics Asn, 2010; Spotlight Award, 2011; Prism Award, 2011; Best Actress Academy Award, 2016. **Home Addr:** 8721 Sunset Blvd Suite 205, Los Angeles, CA 90069, **Home Phone:** (310)234-1992. **Business Addr:** Actress, c/o Creative Artists Agency, 9830 Wilshire Blvd, Beverly Hills, CA 90212, **Business Phone:** (310)288-4545.

**BERRY, JAY**
Journalist, television news anchorperson. **Personal:** Born Aug 5, 1950, Tulsa, OK; married Claudia; children: Carla Michelle, Kristen Lynette & Kayla Renee. **Educ:** Univ Wyo, statist; Tulsa Univ; Bishop Col. **Career:** Univ of Wyo, football player; Gulf Oil Co, 1970-73; KTUL TV, news reporter, sportscaster, 1973-74; KPRC TV Houston, news reporter, sportscaster, 1974-79; WLS-TV, sportscaster, 1979-82; WXYZ-TV Detroit, sports reporter, weekend anchor, host; sports prog: "Action News Weekend"; "UPN Detroit Action News Weekend" Channel 7's; "Sunday Sports Update". **Orgs:** Nat Asn Advan Colored People; Black Communicators; co-chair, Black United Fund. **Home Addr:** 29270 Murray Cres, Southfield, MI 48076.

**BERRY, LATIN DAFONSO**
Football player. **Personal:** Born Jan 13, 1967, Lakeview Terrace, CA. **Educ:** Univ Ore, attended 1989. **Career:** Football player (retired); Los Angeles Rams, corner back, 1990-91; Cleveland Browns, 1991-92; Green Bay Packers. **Orgs:** Kappa Alpha Psi Fraternity. **Honors/Awds:** Multicultural Leadership Award. **Home Addr:** 4247 5th Ave Apt 161, Lake Charles, LA 70607-2835, **Home Phone:** (337)562-7829.

**BERRY, LEE ROY, JR.**
Teacher, educator, lawyer. **Personal:** Born Nov 5, 1943, Lake Placid, FL; married Elizabeth Ann Hostetler; children: Joseph Jonathan, Malinda Elizabeth & Anne Hostetler. **Educ:** Eastern Mennonite Col, BA, 1966; Univ Notre Dame, MA, 1969, PhD, 1976; Ind Univ, Bloomington, Sch Law, JD, 1984. **Career:** Educator, lawyer & polit scientist; Cleveland Pub Schs, teacher, 1966-68; Goshen Col, prof, 1969-79, fac mem, 1969-2010, leader, study serv trimester, 1979-80, Dept Hist & Polit Sci, assoc prof polit sci, 1980-, atty law; Berkey Ave Mennonite, fel; Eastern Mennonite Col, pres; Downtown Goshen, atty, currently. **Orgs:** Gen bd, Mennonite Ch; chmn, High Aim Comt; Relief & Serv Comt; Mennonite Bd Missions; Peace Sect, Mennonite Cent Comt; fel John Hay Whitney, 1970-71; fel Nat Fels Fund, 1975-76. **Home Addr:** 19736 Riverview Dr, Goshen, IN 46526-9129, **Home Phone:** (574)533-5821. **Business Addr:** Associate Professor, Goshen College, WY 309 1700 S Main St, Goshen, IN 46526-4795, **Business Phone:** (574)535-7000.

**BERRY, MAJOR T., JR.**
Police chief, manager. **Personal:** married Dianna. **Educ:** Univ Cent Okla, BS, criminal justice; FBI Nat Acad. **Career:** Police chief (retired); Okla city police dept, community serv officer, 1970, chief police, 1998-2003; COUASI Interoperable Commun Subcomt, chmn; Interim Police Chief, 1991; Okla Off Homeland Security, asst city mgr, currently; Cent Okla Urban Area Security Initiative, Interoperable Commun Subcomt, chair. **Orgs:** Region 8 Coun; Okla Chap FBI Nat Acad Assocs; bd dir, Last Frontier Coun Boy Scouts Am, Am Red Cross Cent Okla; adv bd, Leadership Okla City; Int Asn Chiefs Police, Maj Cities Chiefs Asn, Nat Exec Inst Alumni Asn, Nat Orgn Blacks Law Enforcement. **Special Achievements:** First African American Chief of Police, Oklahoma City. **Business Addr:** Assistant City Manager, Okla Office of Homeland Security, PO Box 11415, Oklahoma City, OK 73136, **Business Phone:** (405)425-7296.

**BERRY, DR. MARY FRANCES**
Educator. **Personal:** Born Feb 17, 1938, Nashville, TN; daughter of George F and Frances Southall. **Educ:** Howard Univ, BA, 1961, MA, 1962; Univ Mich, PhD, hist, 1966, JD, 1970. **Career:** Howard Univ, teaching fel Am hist, 1962-63; Univ Mich, teaching asst, 1965-66, from asst prof hist to assoc prof hist, 1966-70; Univ Md, assoc prof, 1969-76; Univ Colo, Afro-Am Studies, actg dir, 1970-72, dir, 1972-74, Div Behav Social Sci, provost, 1974, chancellor, 1976-77, prof hist, 1976-80; US Dept HEW, asst secy educ, 1977-80; US Comn Civil Rights, mem, 1980-93, chair, 1993-2004; Howard Univ, Dept Hist & Law, prof, 1981-87; Univ Pa, Geraldine R Segal prof Am soc thought & prof hist, 1987-; auth, currently. **Orgs:** DC Bar Asn, 1972; consult to cur educ, Nat Portrait Gallery, Smithsonian Inst; consult, Off Policy Planning, HUD; bd mem, Afro-Am Bicentennial Corp; chmn, Md Comn Afro-Am & Indian Hist Cul, 1974; exec bd mem, pres, Orgn Am Historians, 1974-77, 1990-91; exec bd, Asn Study Afro-Am Life Hist, 1973-76; Am Hist Asn; Orgn Am Historians; Am Bar Asn; Nat Bar Asn; nat panel adv, Univ Mid-Am; bd trustees, Tuskegee Inst; bd dirs, DC Chap, ARC; chair, Pacifica Radio Found Nat Bd. co-founded, Free S Africa Movement, 1984. **Honors/Awds:** Civil War Round Table Fellowship Award, 1965-66; Honarary degree, Univ Akron, 1977; Honarary degree, Benedict Col, 1979; Honarary degree, Grambling State Univ, 1979; Honarary degree, Bethune-Cookman Col, 1980; Honarary degree, Clark Col, 1980; Honarary degree, Oberlin Col, 1983; Honarary degree, Langston Univ, 1983; Honarary degree, Haverford Col, 1984; Honarary degree, Colby Col, 1986; Honarary degree, DePaul Univ, 1987; Rosa Parks Award, Southern Christian Leadership Conf; Black Achievement Award, Ebony Magazine; Woman of the Year, Ms Mag, 1986; Lamplighter Award for Civil Rights, 2001; One of the women of the century, Women's Hall of Fame; Nat Asn for the Advan of Colored Roy Wilkins Award; Received 32 honorary doctoral degrees. **Special Achievements:** One of 75 women featured in I Dream A World: Portraits of Black Women Who Changed America; Sienna College Research Institute and the Women's Hall of Fame designated her one of "America's Women of the Century. Author of Black Resistance/White Law: A History of Constitutional Racism in America, 1971, Why ERA Failed: Women's Rights & the Amending Process of the Constitution, 1986, And Justice For All, 2009, My face is Black is True, Power in Words, 2010, We Are Who We Say We Are: A Black Family's Search for Home Across the Atlantic World, 2014, Five Dollars and a Pork Chop Sandwich: Vote Buying and the Corruption of Democracy, 2016. **Home Addr:** 2110 65th Ave, Philadelphia, PA 19138, **Home Phone:** (215)548-7925. **Business Addr:** Professor, Geraldine R. Segal Professor, University of Pennsylvania, College Hall 216E, Philadelphia, PA 19104-6379, **Business Phone:** (215)898-9587.

**BERRY, COL. ONDRA LAMON**
Police officer. **Personal:** Born Oct 3, 1958, Evansville, IN; son of Charles and Ethel Gibson Kuykendall; married Margo Curry; children: Jarel. **Educ:** Univ Evansville, Evansville, IN, BA, educ, 1980; Univ Nev, Reno, NV, MPA, 1996; Harvard Exec Leadership Develop prog. **Career:** Police Exec Res Forum, diversity trainer; Rapport Leadership Intl, cert asst instr; consult; Reno Police Dept, Reno, NV, lt, dep chief, asst chief police, admin div; Nev Air Nat Guard, comdr Mission Personnel Flight, col, maj; US Dept Justice; US Dept Educ; Police Exec Res Forum; Air Nat Guard Readiness Ctr; Guardian Quest, co-founder & owner, currently. **Orgs:** Past pres, Northern Nev Black Cult Awareness Soc; vchair, United Way Nev, 1991-97; State Job Training Coun, 1989-93; founder & partner, Guardian Quest; AIM Leadership. **Honors/Awds:** Outstanding Airman of the Year, Nev Air Nat Guard, 1988; Outstanding Law Enforcement Officer, Reno Jaycees, 1989-90; One of twelve airman selected nationwide representing the Air Nat Guard as Airman of the Year. **Special Achievements:** Author of AYOBA: Spirit of Awesomeness, 2012. **Home Addr:** 3909 Vista Crest Dr, Reno, NV 89509, **Home Phone:** (702)322-5519. **Business Addr:** Co-Founder, Partner, Guardian Quest, 123 S Evanslawn Ave, Aurora, IL 60506.

**BERRY, PAUL LAWRENCE**
President (organization), journalist. **Personal:** Born Feb 15, 1944, Detroit, MI; married Amy; children: Talley, Hudson & Paul. **Educ:** USAF Def Info Sch, Basic Med Sch, Basic Dent Sch. **Career:** WXYZ-TV, staff rep & co-anchor, 1969-72; WJLA-TV, news anchor & weekday reporter, 1972-78, on-air reporter & dir, 1978-93, daily host, 1993-94, sr news anchor, 1994-99; WMAL-TV, anchor st rep & mod, 1972-75; WMAL-TV, st rep mod & co-anchor, 1975-; Am Black Forum, panelist; Paul Berry's WA, weekend anchor & host; Paul L Berry & Assocs, pres, 2000-06; Booz Allen Hamilton, exec advisor, 2006-10; AM570 WTNT, host, currently; Armed Forces Radio & Television Services, S Viet Nam; CUNA Mutual Group, host. **Orgs:** Wash DC Mayors Ad Hock Comm Criminal Justice; DC Fed 524 Coun Except Child; Sigma Delta Chi Prof Journ Soc; bd dir, Am Dig DisAsn; Lion Club Wash, DC; bd dir, vpres, Neediest Kids, 1987-2010; bd dir, Wash Jesuit Acad; bd dir, Nat Rehab Hosp; dir & bd mem, pres, Paul Berry Acad Scholar Found, 1994-2005; bd dir, Chesapeake Bay Maritime Mus; bd dir, Leukemia & Lymphoma Soc; Nat Press Club; vpres, DC Friends Ireland; Soc Prof Journalists; pres, Nat Acad TV Arts & Sci; bd dir, Avalon Found; bd trustee, Ford Theatres, currently; comnr, Md Pub TV, currently. **Home Addr:** 6358 Lyric Lane, Falls Church, VA 22044. **Business Addr:** President, Paul Berry & Associates LLC, 1050 Thomas Jefferson St NW Suite 500, Washington, DC 20007, **Business Phone:** (202)342-6310.

**BERRY, PHILIP ALFONSO**
Executive, manager, vice president (organization). **Personal:** Born Jan 28, 1950, New York, NY; married Karen Bryan; children: Kiel & Maya. **Educ:** Manhattan Community Col, AA, mkt, 1971; Queens Col City Univ NY, BA, sociol, 1973; Columbia Univ Sch Social Work, MS, behav sci, social work, 1975; Xavier Univ, Williams Col Bus, Cincinnati, MBA, mkt/mgt, 1983. **Career:** Ford Found Fel; Int Bus Mach, prod scheduler, 1968-71; Urban League Westchester, NY, dir, 1975-78; Procter & Gamble, indust rels mgr, 1978-86; Digital Equip Corp, human resources consult, 1986-88; Triboro Bridge & Tunnel Authority, NY, vpres human resources & admin, 1988-90; Colgate-Palmolive, assoc dir orgn planning, 1990-93, HR dir Int Bus Develop Group, 1993-95, vpres HR Latin Am Div, 1995-98, Human Resources Int, vpres, Europe HR, vpres, 1998-2001, Global Employ Rels, vpres, 2001-03, Global Workplace Initiatives, vpres, 2004-08; City Univ New York, vpres, 2007-; Philip Berry Assocs, pres, 2008-15; Clinton Found, chief human resources officer, 2015-. **Orgs:** NY State Chmn Asn Black Social Workers, 1975-78; founder, pres, Housing & Neighborhood Develop Inst, 1976-78; pres, Delta Group & Berry Asn Consult, 1983-; bd mem, Cincinnati Comt Action Agency, 1985-86; dean pledges, Alpha Phi Alpha Frat Alumni Chap, 1986; chmn, indust social work, Nat Asn Social Workers, 1989-; memship comt, EDGES, 1990-; Am Soc Training & Develop; World Future Soc; pres, Black Stud Union Queens Col; Black Stud Caucus Columbia Univ; Nat Foreign Trade Coun; Columbia Univ Alumni Bd; chair, New York Dept Educ Human Resources Adv Panel, 2004-; Bd Standing Comt Fiscal Affairs; Standing Comt Fac, Staff & Admin; Dept Educ's Panel, Vice Chair; fel CUNY Bus Leadership Coun; chair actg, Vice Chmn bd trustee, City Univ New York Construct Fund; Gov David Paterson, currently-. **Home Addr:** 320 E 46th St, New York, NY 10017, **Home Phone:** (201)744-9006. **Business Addr:** President, Philip Berry Associates LLC, 100 Riverside Blvd Suite 4b, New York, NY 10069-0403, **Business Phone:** (917)208-3428.

**BERRY, REGINALD FRANCIS**
Government official. **Personal:** Born May 21, 1920, Washington, DC; son of John and Blanche; married Anna Pitts. **Educ:** George Washington Univ, attended 1948; Howard Univ, attended 1952. **Career:** Government official (retired); Coast Guard, Dept Transp, sr investr; Civil Rights Act, 1964, Titles VI & VII, adminr; USCG, US Civil Rights officer, 1970-82. **Orgs:** App Wash DC, Dioceasan Comn Racism, 1988-92; State Md, Prince George's County Cent Comn, 1994-2000. **Honors/Awds:** Twice cited by the Governor of Md for meritorious & political accomplishment to the State. **Special Achievements:** The first Episcopal African Bishop to serve the Diocese of Haiti from 1892-1911, 1975. **Home Addr:** 912 Cox Ave, Hyattsville, MD 20783-3165, **Home Phone:** (301)559-0830.

**BERRY, PROF. VENISE TORRIANA**
Writer, journalist, educator. **Personal:** Born Jan 1, 1956?, Kansas City, KS; daughter of Virgil and Jean. **Educ:** Univ Iowa, BA, jour, 1977, MA, commun stud, 1979; Univ Tex, PhD, radio, tv & film, 1989. **Career:** KFRD Radio, Tx, newscaster, 1979-80; Tex Southern Univ, instr, 1980-83; KCOH Radio, Tx, asst news dir, 1980-83; KTSU Radio, news dir, 1982-83; Tillotson Col, from asst prof to assoc prof, 1983-91, coun, 1986-91, depthead mass commun, 1989-91, spec asst to pres, 1990-91; KLBJ Radio, Tx, news reporter, 1983-84; KAZI Radio, news dir, 1983-86; Univ Tex, SchMusic, lectr, 1990-91; Univ Iowa, Sch Jour & Mass commun, asst prof, 1991-97, assoc prof, 1998-, int dir, 2001-02, assoc dir, 2004-, African Am Studies, assoc prof, 2006-; Auth: So Good, An African American Love Story, 1996; All of Me, A Voluptuous Tale, 2000; Colored Sugar Water, 2002; co-auth: The 50 Most Influential Black Films, Citadel, 2001; Mediated Messages & African-American Culture: Contemporary Issues, Sage, 1996; co-ed: Reflections on a Higher Power: Exceptional Writers Share Their Experience with Faith, Spirituality & Divine Intervention. **Orgs:** Asn Educ Jour & Mass Commun; Int Asn Study Popular Music; Nat Asn Black Journalists; Kappa Tau Alpha, Jour Hon Soc; Delta Sigma Theta, Pub Serv Sorority; trustee, co-chair, Bldg Fundraising Comt. **Home Addr:** 3432 10th St, PO Box 5411, Coralville, IA 52241-1200, **Home Phone:** (319)377-7557. **Business Addr:** Associate Professor, University Iowa, E340 AJB 100 Adler Journalism Bldg, Iowa City, IA 52242-2004, **Business Phone:** (319)335-3361.

**BERRY, WILLIAM E.** **See BERRY, BILL.**

**BERRYMAN, ESQ. MATILENE S.** **See Obituaries Section.**

**BERTELSEN, PHIL**
Writer, movie director, movie producer. **Personal:** Born NJ. **Educ:** Rutgers Univ, BA, polit sci; NY Univ, MFA, 2000. **Career:** WYBE-TV, pub affairs TV, producer & dir; Frederick Douglass Creative Arts Ctr, instr, 1998-2000; Films: Around the Time, 1997; The Sunshine, 2000; Outside Looking In: Transracial Adoption in America, 2001; Chisholm '72: Matters of Race, 2003; Unbought & Unbossed, 2004; Rock the Paint, 2005; Beyond the Steps: Alvin Ailey American Dance, 2006; Roja Productions, producer, 2001-02; Chisholm '72 Inc, producer, 2002-04; Realization Pictures 2006-; City Univ New York, prof, 2008-09; MTV Networks, dir & sr producer, 2010-12; Ark Media, producer & dir, 2012-. **Orgs:** Spike Lee Fel, NY Univ; fel Sundance Institute, 2000. **Honors/Awds:** Student Academy Award, NY Univ; Wasserman Award, NY Univ; Best Documentary; Best Short Documentary, Woodstock Film Festival; Jury Prize, Newport Int Film Festival; Roger Award, Avignon Film Festival; Director's Guild East Award; Creative Promise Award, Tribeca Film Festival, 2004. **Special Achievements:** The Sunshine, Best Doc, NY & Palm Springs Intl Short Film Festivals, Best Short Doc, Woodstock Film Festivals. **Business Addr:** Producer & Director, Writer, Ark Media, 325 Gold St Suite 602, Brooklyn, NY 11201, **Business Phone:** (718)935-9745.

**BERTLEY, FREDERIC**
Administrator, educator. **Personal:** Born Dec 18, 1970?, Montreal, QC; son of Leo and June. **Educ:** McGill Univ, BS, physiol & math, 1994, PhD, immunol, 1999. **Career:** Harvard University Medical School and Children's Hospital, postdoctoral research fellow, 2000-03; International Development Research Council, international project manager, 2003; Northeastern, educator; Roxbury Community College, director of the Louis Stokes Alliance Membership Program and the Bridges program and the Boston Science Partnership program, 2006-08; Massachusetts Institute of Technology, research affiliate; Franklin Institute, Philadelphia, PA, vpres, 2008, senior vice president of science and education, director of the Franklin Center, Franklin Awards Program and executive director of the "Journal of The Franklin Institute". **Orgs:** Bd mem, Philadelphia Biotech Life Sci Inst; bd mem, Garvey Inst Inc.; bd mem, Dudley St Neighborhood Initiative; Que Black Med Asn. **Special Achievements:** Color of Science Program, founder and director; Massachusetts Comprehensive Assessment System, founder and director; published in numerous academic scientific journals, including "Journal of Immunology" and "Nature of Medicine"; Bell Science Foundation, mentor; Science Education and Innovation, Goodwill Ambassador to Senegal; keynote or invited speaker at the United Nations, the White House, U.S. Department of Interior, National Academy of Sciences, National Science Foundation. **Business Addr:** The Franklin Institute, 271 N 21st St, Philadelphia, PA 19103.

**BESHAH, ESQ. GUENET M. M.**
Lawyer, association executive. **Educ:** Hampton Univ, BA, polit sci, 1990; Duke Univ Sch Law, JD, 1993. **Career:** Capital One, atty & assoc gen coun, corp coun off, vpres exec coaching, vpres, human resources, exec coach & dir exec coaching prog, currently; Litigation. **Orgs:** Bd trustee mem, Orchard House Sch; Old Dom Bar asn; Va State Bar; bd mem, Venture Richmond; mem sr leadership team, Legal Dept; bd mem, Metrop Bus League Inc; Va State Bar Corp Coun Sect; Richmond Bar Asn; State Old Dom Bar Asn; Va Minority Bar Prep Prog; bd comnr, Richmond Redevelop & Housing Authority, 2006-. **Home Addr:** 11124 Live Oak Cir, Midlothian, VA 23113, **Home Phone:** (804)272-1564. **Business Addr:** Vice President, Capital One Services Inc, 15000 Capital One Dr, Richmond, VA 23238-1119, **Business Phone:** (804)284-2721.

**BESSENT, DR. YVETTE E.**
Gynecologist. **Educ:** Univ NC, Chapel Hill, MD, 1991; FACOG. **Career:** Univ Cincinnati, resident; Northcross Obstet & Gynec, obstetrician & gynecologist, 2001-. **Orgs:** Am Bd Obstet & Gynec, 1997. **Home Addr:** 7821 Taymouth Lane, Charlotte, NC 28269, **Home Phone:** (704)948-9537. **Business Addr:** Obstetrician, Gynecologist, Northcross Obstetrics & Gynecology, 16455 Statesville Rd Suite 400, Huntersville, NC 28078-7140, **Business Phone:** (704)801-2130.

**BESSON, DR. PAUL SMITH**
Lawyer, vice president (organization). **Personal:** Born May 11, 1953, New York, NY; son of Frederick A and Patricia Smith; married Joyce Brewer. **Educ:** Cornell Univ, BS, human resources, labor rels, 1975, SC Johnson Grad Sch Mgt, MBA, mkt/finance, 1976; Northwestern Univ, JD, 1980; Georgetown Univ Law Ctr, LLM, 1995; George Washington Univ, EdD, human resources, 2013. **Career:** Cummins Engine Co, mkt planning analyst, 1976-77; Jewel Co Inc, labor rels coun, 1980-82, mgr personnel & labor rels, 1982-83; Nat Broadcasting Co Inc, mgr labor rels, 1984-88, dir employee rels, human resources, 1988-97, Talent Negotiations & Labor Rels dir, 1997-98; Am Com Lines LLC, sr vpres human resources, 1998-2000, sr vpres, CAO, 2000-02; GE Equip Serv, vpres human resources, 2002-07; GE Money, vpres Human Resources Global Mkt/Strategy, 2007-08; Hartford Healthcare & Hartford Hosp, sr vpres human resources, 2009-10; New-Day Solutions, arbitrator, mediator & hr legal consult, 2010-; Heritage Leadership Acad, gen coun, 2014-; Univ Md Univ Col, adj fac, currently; ABC Tv, exec coun, currently. **Orgs:** Ill Bar Asn; NY Bar Asn; DC Bar Asn; bd dir, Cornell Club Asn 1982; pres, Cornell Black Alumni Asn Chicago, 1982-83; Am Arbit Asn Panel Com Arbitrations; hearing officer, Civil Serv Commn IL; bd dir, ABE Credit Union; pres, Cornell Black Alumni Asn, Wash, DC, 1989-91; Bingham Leadership fel 2001;Capital Press Club; Wash Asn Black Journalists; mediator, US Dist Ct, Dist Columbia; adv coun, GE African Am Forum; bd dir, Louisville Urban League; bd dir, March Dimes; bd mem, State Panel, Ill Labor Bd, 2011-15; bd mem, Black Heritage Network, 2012-. **Home Addr:** 5203 Clarks Point, Louisville, KY 40207, **Home Phone:** (812)288-1886.

**BEST, GLENN**
Administrator. **Educ:** Bard Col, Simon's Rock, AA, lib arts, 1982; Old Dom Univ, bus admin, 1984; St Paul's Col, BS, bus admin mgt, 1987. **Career:** St Paul's Col, dir alumni affairs, 1995-98; Martin Luther King Jr Nat Memorial Proj Found, proj coordr, 2000-02; Tex Col, vpres instnl advan, 2002-04; Glenn Best & Assocs, pres, 2004-07; Arbor Educ & Training, supvr, training & develop, 2007-10; Urban League Essex County, dir bus develop, 2010-14; Delta-T Group, educ acct mgr, 2014-. **Orgs:** Trustee, KivaZip, 2013-; comt mem, Essex Vicinage Adv Comt Minority Concerns, 2014-; Phi Beta Lambda; Kappa Alpha Psi Fraternity Inc; Pre Alumni Coun; Pre Alumni Coun; Nat Alumni Asn. **Business Addr:** Project Coordinator, Martin Luther King Jr National Memorial Project Foundation, 401 F St NW Suite 334, Washington, DC 20001, **Business Phone:** (202)737-5420.

**BEST, JENNINGS H.**
Lawyer. **Personal:** Born Aug 5, 1925, Jacksonville, FL; married Elizabeth Blake; children: Valorie. **Educ:** Lincoln Univ, Jefferson City, Mo, BA; Fla A&M Univ, Col Law, JD, 1956. **Career:** Pvt pract lawyer. **Orgs:** DW Perkins Bar Asn; Nat Bar Asn; Phi Beta Sigma Fraternity; New Bethlehem Missionary Baptist Church; Fla Chap Nat Bar Asn; Grand Lodge. **Home Addr:** 2078 W 14th St, Jacksonville, FL 32209-4758, **Home Phone:** (904)353-5017.

**BEST, JOHN T., JR.**
Counselor, federal government official, manager. **Personal:** Born Jan 24, 1936, Philadelphia, PA; son of John Thomas and Mary Elizabeth Armwood; married Mary Anna Grady; children: Toussaint, Johanna N, Johnathan, Kevin, Deborah Stone-Patterson & LydiaTimmons. **Educ:** Henry George Sch Social Sci, NY, cert, 1972; Philadelphia Govt Training Inst, attended 1972; La Salle Univ Inst, acct, certs, 1972; Community Col Philadelphia, AGS, 1972; Rutgers Univ, BA, 1974; Univ Pa, MCP, 1976; Rutgers Univ, labor mgt, 1980; Am Mgt Asn, mgt studies, 1984; Franklin Inst, comput training, 1984; Morris Arboretum, landscape design cert, 1987; Rosemont Col, Holistic Health, cert, 1989. **Career:** City planner (retired); Best Assocs, urban planner begin, 1976; City Philadelphia, City Planner II, 1980-81; retired USPS, supvr, 1981; Radio, communicator, 1996. **Orgs:** Am Planning Asn, 1976-90; Soc Advan Mgt, 1981-90; Am Mgt Asn, 1981-91; comm mem, United Way, 1981-91; Dobbins Alumni Asn, 1990-; dist dir, Am Asn Retired Persons AARP, 1994-98; Am Legion Post 292; 101st Airborne Asn; Veteran Foreign Wars; Nat Asn Advan Colored People; Fel Philaxis Soc; Prince Hall Affil, Lemuel Googins No 129 Philadelphia PA; Community Col Philadelphia Alumni Asn; Rutgers Univ, African Am Alumni Asn; Nat Caucus & Ctr Black Aged Inc; Philadelphia Sr Ctr; Nat Asn Retired Fed Employees. **Home Addr:** 6154 W Columbia Ave, Philadelphia, PA 19151-4503, **Home Phone:** (267)275-8103.

**BEST, DR. SHEILA DIANE**
Physician. **Personal:** Born Feb 23, 1956, Sacramento, CA; daughter of Eddie and Elizabeth Best. **Educ:** Univ Calif, Riverside, BA, biol, 1978; Howard Univ Col Med, MD, 1982. **Career:** Howard Univ Hosp, intern, 1982-83, resident, 1983-85; Independent Contractor, emergency med physician, 1985-; Extended Care Facil Morrow County Hosp, emergency med physician, currently; pvt pract, currently. **Orgs:** Emergency med physician, Med Residents Asn, 1984-85; Am Col Emergency Physicians, 1985-; Action Alliance Black Managers, 1986-. **Home Addr:** 4024 Sharon Woods Dr, Powder Springs, GA 30127-2822, **Home Phone:** (770)439-7140. **Business Addr:** Emergency Medical Physician, Extended Care Facility Morrow County Hospital, 200 Allen Memorial Dr, Bremen, GA 30110, **Business Phone:** (770)537-5851.

**BEST, TRAVIS ERIC**
Basketball player. **Personal:** Born Jul 12, 1972, Springfield, MA; son of Bobbie and Leo. **Educ:** Ga Inst Tech, BA, bus mgt, 1995. **Career:** Basketball player (retired); Ind Pacers, pt guard, 1995-2002; Chicago Bulls, pt guard, 2001-02; Miami Heat, pt guard, 2002-03; Dallas Mavericks, pt guard, 2003-04; NJ Nets, pt guard, 2004-05; UNICS Kazan, Russia, 2005-06; VidiVici Bologna, Italy, 2006-07; Asseco Prokom Gdynia, Poland, 2007; Prokom Trefl Sopot, Poland, 2007; Virtus Bologna, Italy, 2007-08; La Fortezza Bologna, Italy, 2007-08; Air Avellino, Italy, 2008-09; Nuova AMG Sebastiani Basket Napoli, Italy, 2009. **Orgs:** mem, US All-Stars. **Honors/Awds:** John Lahovich Award. **Special Achievements:** Films: He Got Game, 1998; TV appearance: The 2000 NBA Finals, 2000; First three-time recipient of the John Lahovich Award.

**BEST, VANESSA**
President (organization), chief executive officer. **Career:** Precision HealthCare Consults, pres & chief exec officer, 1995-. **Business Addr:** President, Chief Executive Officer, Precision HealthCare Consultants, PO Box 1239, North Baldwin, NY 11510, **Business Phone:** (888)265-2547.

**BEST, REV. WILLIAM ANDREW, SR.**
Clergy. **Personal:** Born Sep 17, 1949, Newburgh, NY; married Sharon Gerald; children: Cleveland A, Andrew, Stephany & Shawn. **Educ:** Mt St Mary Col, BA, 1975; Western Conn State Col, MPS, 1981. **Career:** Middletown Minority Ministerial Alliance, pres, 1984-87; Church God Christ, regional pres, 1986-91; Inner Faith Coun, vpres, 1986-87; Church God Christ, Nat Pastor's & Elder Coun, secy, 1993-; Cats kill Dist Church God Christ, 2nd Ecclesiastical Jurisdiction, dist supt, 1994-; enlarged sch dist Mid town, educr, currently; St James Church God In Christ, pastor, currently. **Orgs:** Pres, Middletown State Ctr, 1985-86; Mem Kiwanis, Nat Asn Advan Colored People, 1986-87; bd mem, YMCA, 1987-; mem bd educ, Enlarged City Sch Dist Middletown, 2001-. **Home Addr:** 135 Linden Ave, Middletown, NY 10940-4734, **Home Phone:** (845)342-4773. **Business Addr:** Pastor, St James Church of God In Christ, 137-139 Linden Ave, Middletown, NY 10940, **Business Phone:** (914)342-4773.

**BEST-WHITAKER, DR. VAUGHN (VON BEST WHITAKER)**
Educator, college administrator. **Educ:** Columbia Union Col, RN, BS; Univ Md, MS; Univ NC, Chapel Hill, NC, MA, PhD, 1983. **Career:** NC A&T State Univ, asst dean & assoc prof, clin asst prof, currently. **Orgs:** Bd dir, Wesley Long Community Health Found. **Business Addr:** Assistant Dean & Associate Professor, Clinical Assistant Professor, North Carolina Agricultural & Technical State University, 1601 E Mkt St Noble Hall, Greensboro, NC 27411, **Business Phone:** (336)334-7500.

**BETHA, MASON DURRELL**
Rap musician, clergy. **Personal:** Born Aug 27, 1975, Jacksonville, FL; married Twyla; children: 1. **Educ:** Clark Atlanta Univ. **Career:** Rapper, pastor & songwriter; Albums: Harlem World, 1997; Double Up, 1999; Welcome Back, 2004; singles: Feel So Good, 1997; Lookin at Me, 1998; What You Want, 1998; Breathe, Stretch, Shake, 2004; I Wanna Go, 2004; Appears on vocals with Puff Daddy, Notorious B.I.G, Tribe Called Quest, Tina Turner, One Twelve, Tasha Holiday, Mario Winans, Brian McKnight, Mariah Carey, Jermaine Dupri, S Park, DJ Clue, others; Harlem World, The Movement, producer, 1999; Films: All That, 1998; All of Us, 2005; Mason Betha Ministries, Atlanta, founder & pastor, currently; Saving A Nation Endangered Church Int, founder & pastor, currently; El Elyon Int Church, founder & pastor, currently; B to Succeed, tv broadcast, currently. **Orgs:** Fel C Corn. **Honors/Awds:** Source Magazine Rapper of the Year, 1997; Honorary Doctorate of Theology, St Paul's Bible Inst, New York, 2002. **Business Addr:** Pastor, SANE Church International, 225 Ottley Dr, Atlanta, GA 30324, **Business Phone:** (404)873-1511.

**BETHEA, EDWIN AYERS**
School administrator. **Personal:** Born May 15, 1931, Birmingham, AL; son of Marzetta and Monroe. **Educ:** Knoxville Col, BA, 1953; Howard Univ, MSW, 1962. **Career:** United Planning Orgn, comm organizer, 1966-68; Youth Enterprises Inc, exec dir, 1968-70; Vols Int Tech Ctr, dir & regional dir, 1970-72; GA Tech Res Inst, sr res assoc & proj dir, 1972-86, assoc dir, Off Minority Bus Develop, 1987-88, dir, 1989-; Univ Ga, Small Bus Develop Ctr; Hudson Strategic Group, partner & assoc, currently. **Orgs:** Southern Indust Coun, 1974-, GA Indust Developers Asn, 1974-; GA Tech Centennial Comm, 1986. **Home Addr:** 2509 Bell Ave, Dodge City, KS 67801, **Home Phone:** (620)225-4436.

**BETHEA, GREGORY AUSTIN (GREG BETHEA)**
Government official. **Personal:** Born Sep 18, 1952, Hamlet, NC; son of Thomas J and Annie Austin; married Hope Stelter; children: Ryan Stelter & Austin Cox. **Educ:** NC Cent Univ, Durham, BA, 1974. **Career:** Forsyth Co, Forsyth Co NC, asst to mgr, sr asst to mgr, intergovernmental rels & budget anal, 1975-84; United Way, Forsyth Co NC, dep dir, 1984-85; City Durham, asst city mgr, 1985-2001, Town Pinetops, town adminr, Currently. **Business Addr:** Town Administrator, Town of Pinetops, 101 E Hamlet St, Pinetops, NC 27864, **Business Phone:** (252)827-4435.

**BETHEA-SHIELDS, KAREN LOUISE.** See SHIELDS, KAREN BETHEA.

**BETHEL, DR. AMIEL W.**
Educator, neurosurgeon. **Educ:** Princeton Univ, BS, biol, 1987; Univ Pa Sch Med, MD, neurosurg, 1991. **Career:** John hopkins hosp, fel, 1997; Univ Md Sch Med, clin dir, R Adams Cowley Shock Trauma Ctr, clin asst prof, Dept Neuro surg, currently; Greater Baltimore Med Ctr, physician, 1999-, chmn, Dept Surg, div head, currently; Union Mem Hosp, neurosurg prog, chief, 2004-; Univ Md Med Ctr, asst prof, 2010-; Baltimore Wash Med Ctr, Div Neurosurg, chief, 2013-. **Orgs:** Greater Baltimore Neurosurg Assocs; comt mem, Neurol, US Lacrosse, 1988-; Am Asn Neurol Surgeons. **Business Addr:** Chief, Baltimore Washington Medical Center, 301 Hosp Dr Suite 304, Glen Burnie, MD 21061, **Business Phone:** (410)553-8160.

**BETHEL, KATHLEEN EVONNE**
Librarian. **Personal:** Born Aug 4, 1953, Washington, DC; daughter of Frederick Errington and Helen Evonne Roy. **Educ:** Elmhurst Col, Elmhurst, Ill, BA, 1975; Dominican Univ, River Forest, Ill, MALS, 1977; Northwestern Univ, Evanston, Ill, MA, african hist, 1989. **Career:** Newberry Libr, Chicago, Ill, receptionist, 1975-77; Maywood Pub Libr, Maywood, Ill, br librn, 1977-78; Johnson Publ Co, Chicago, Ill, asst librn, 1978-82; Northwestern Univ Libr, Evanston, Ill, African Am Studies librn, 1982-; Univ KwaZulu-Natal, fulbright libr fel. **Orgs:** Am Libr Asn, 1976-; Black Caucus Am Libr Asn, 1978-; Nat Asn Advan Colored People, 1983-; Asn Study Afro-Am Life & Hist, 1985-; bd trustee, DuSable Mus African Am Hist, 1993-2007; Toni Morrison Soc, 2000-; Asn Northwestern Univ Women; fel Alice Berline Kaplan Inst; Black Caucus Am Libr Asn; Asn Study African Am Life & Hist; Black Metropolis Res Consortium. **Honors/Awds:** Scholarship, Nat Bridge Asn, 1971; Fulbright Library Fel, Univ Durban-Westville, S Africa, 1996; Libr Fel, Alice Berline Kaplan Ctr Humanities, Northwestern Univ, 1999-2000; Award Chicago Friends Amistad Res Ctr, Tulane Univ, 2003. **Special Achievements:** International non-gov observer, natl elections, Republic of S Africa, 1994; mem, research team, "Know Your Heritage" tv program, 1996-99. **Home Addr:** 1631 W Fargo Ave, Chicago, IL 60626-1720, **Home Phone:** (773)338-8722. **Business Addr:** African American Studies Librarian, Northwestern University Library, 1970 Campus Dr Rm 2622, Evanston, IL 60208-2300, **Business Phone:** (847)491-2173.

**BETHEL, DR. LEONARD LESLIE**
College teacher, minister (clergy). **Personal:** Born Feb 5, 1939, Philadelphia, PA; son of Henry W and Anna Bethel Young; married Veronica Bynum; children: Amiel W & Kama Pierce. **Educ:** Lincoln Univ, BA, 1961; Johnson C Smith Univ Sch Theol, Mdiv, 1964; NB Theol Sem, MA, 1971; Rutgers Univ, DEd, 1975. **Career:** Raritan Valley Community Col, prof, Afro-Am Studies; Wash United Presby Church, pastor, 1964-67; Lincoln Univ, Asst Chaplain, dir coun, 1967-79; Rutgers Univ, Dept African Studies, fac, staff, 1969-2011, chmn, 1970-2003, assoc prof, 1980-2011, prof emer, 2011; Bethel Presby Church, pastor, 1982-92; Woodrow Wilson fel, Princeton Univ, 1984. **Orgs:** Bd trustee, Rutgers Prep Sch, 1971-84; Am Asn Univ Pres, Rutgers Univ, 1980-; bd dir, Plainfield Br, Union County Col, 1980-86; Frontiers Int, 1980-; bd trustee, Bloomfield Col, 1980-86; Presbytery Elizabeth, 1982-; bd trustee, Lincoln Univ, 1996-2004; bd dir, UCC, 1980-87; Phi Delta Kappa. **Home Addr:** 30 Layle Lane, Doylestown, PA 18901, **Home Phone:** (215)345-8783.

**BETHEL, NIKKI**
Vice president (organization), executive, teacher. **Personal:** Born Jan 1, 1976; children: 1. **Educ:** Univ Md, College Park, BA, govt & polit, 1997; Harvard Univ, MEd, 1998. **Career:** Boston, high sch eng teacher, 1997-98; Morgan Stanley, assoc, 1998-2001; A-List, consult, 2001-03; HBO, recruiting assoc, 2003-04, mgr human resources, 2004-06, dir, 2007-08, vpres, 2008-13, sr vpres, 2006-. **Orgs:** Chmn bd, Mus Contemp African Diasporian Arts Brooklyn, 2004-; Links Inc; lifetime mem, Delta Sigma Theta Sorority Inc; hon mem, Women's League Sci & Med Inc. **Honors/Awds:** Black Enterprise, Rising Stars 40 & Under, 2014. **Business Addr:** Senior Vice President, Home Box Office Inc, 1100 Avenue of the Americas 42nd & 6th Ave, New York, NY 10036, **Business Phone:** (212)512-1000.

**BETHEL, PROF. VERONICA B.**
Educator. **Personal:** children: Amiel & Kama. **Career:** Raritan Valley Community Col, Dept Social Scis & Human Servs, prof, prof emer, currently. **Business Addr:** Professor Emeritus, Raritan Valley Community College, 118 Lamington Rd, Branchburg, NJ 08876, **Business Phone:** (908)526-1200.

**BETHEL-MURRAY, DR. KIMBERLY F.**
Physician. **Educ:** Howard Univ; Wright State Univ Sch Med, 1987. **Career:** Trot wood Physician Ctr, physician, 1990-. **Orgs:** Gem City Med, Dent & Pharmaceut Soc. **Special Achievements:** Become the first woman president of Gem City Medical, Dental and Pharmaceutical Society. **Business Addr:** Physician, Trotwood Physicians Ctr, 5630 Northford Rd, Trotwood, OH 45426, **Business Phone:** (937)208-7050.

**BETTIS, ANNE KATHERINE**
Financial manager. **Personal:** Born Jun 16, 1949, Newark, NJ. **Educ:** Jersey City State Col, BA, 1972; Columbia Univ, MBA, 1979. **Career:** Avon Prod Inc, sr ed, 1973-77; AT&T, acct exec, 1979-82, nat acct mgr, 1983-85, staff mgr, 1985-. **Orgs:** Pres, 8th Irving Park Condominium Asn, 1984-; Calvary Baptist Church; Nat Black MBA Asn. **Honors/Awds:** Achiever's Club AT&T, 1982-84. **Home Addr:** 83 Boston St, Newark, NJ 07101, **Home Phone:** (973)242-7678. **Business Addr:** Marketing Staff Manager, AT&T Information System, 1 Speedwell Ave Suite 771E, Morristown, NJ 07960, **Business Phone:** (201)898-3967.

**BETTIS, JEROME ABRAM, SR.**
Football player, broadcaster. **Personal:** Born Feb 16, 1972, Detroit, MI; son of Johnnie E and Gladys Elizabeth; married Trameka Boykin; children: Jerome Jr & Jada. **Educ:** Notre Dame Univ; Lawrence Tech Univ, PhD, 2006. **Career:** Football player (retired), host; Los Angeles Rams, running back, 1993-95; St Louis Rams, 1995; Pittsburgh Steelers, running back, 1996-2005; NBC, Football Night Am, studio com-

mentator, 2006; Jerome Bettis Grille 36, owner, 2007-; Football Night Am, Nat Broadcasting Co, studio analyst; Nat Football League Network, commentator; WPXI-TV, Jerome Bettis Show, host, currently; Entertainment & Sports Programming Network, nat football league analyst, currently. **Orgs:** Bus Stops Here Found, 1997. **Honors/Awds:** Rookie of the Year, Nat Football League, 1993; Rookie of the Year, Pro Football Writers Asn, 1993; Pro Bowl, 1993, 1994, 1996, 1997, 2001, 2004; Champion, Super Bowl, XL, 2006; Offensive Rookie of the Year, Nat Football League, 1993; Offensive Rookie of the Year, Nat Football Conf, 1993; Comeback Player of the Year, Nat Football League, 1996; Comeback Player of the Year, Pro Football Writers Asn, 1996; Most Valuable Player, Pittsburgh Steelers, 1996, 1997, 2000; Alumni Running Back of the Year, Nat Football League, 1996; Walter Payton Man of the Year, 2001; Pittsburgh Pro Football Hall of Fame, 2012; Pro Football Hall of Fame, 2015. **Special Achievements:** Published Books: "Driving Home: My Unforgettable Super Bowl Run", September 2006, Triumph Books. **Home Addr:** 1651 Randall Mill Pl NW, Atlanta, GA 30327-3136. **Business Addr:** NFL Analyst, Entertainment and Sports Programming Network, 3030 Peachtree Rd NW, Atlanta, GA 30305, **Business Phone:** (404)682-3776.

## BETTIS, LINDA JEAN

Administrator, secretary (organization). **Career:** TAP Multimedia LLC, sr partner, 2001-. **Orgs:** Nat Tele Communs & Info Admin, US Dept Com; exec secy, Strings Alliance Lincoln Camp, currently. **Business Addr:** Senior Partner, TAP Multimedia LLC, 9231 Three Oaks Dr, Silver Spring, MD 20918, **Business Phone:** (301)879-8544.

## BETTY, LISA C.

Environmental scientist. **Personal:** Born Sep 9, 1961, Bronx, NY; daughter of Warren R and Norma F Carter; married Rolf Demmerle. **Educ:** Polytechnic Univ, BSCF, 1992; City Col NY, MSCE, 2002. **Career:** NYC Govt Dept Environ Protection, asst civil engr, 1992-94; Newtown Creek Treat Plant, process engr, 1994-98; Wards IslandTreatment Plant, process engr, 1998-99; Red Hook Treat Plant, process engr, 2000; Oakwood Beach Treat Plant, process engr, 2000, mgt engr, 2001-. **Orgs:** Water Environ Fedn, operator, 1994-; NY Water Environ Asn, operator, 1994-; Us Gymnastics Fedn, gymnastics instr, 1996-. **Home Addr:** 924 Painter Lane, Stafford, NJ 08050, **Home Phone:** (609)978-1050. **Business Addr:** Engineer, NY City Department Environ Engineering, 96-05 Horrace Harding Expy 5th Fl Low Rise Bldg, Corona, NY 11368, **Business Phone:** (718)595-5136.

## BETTY, MICHAEL W., SR.

Association executive, executive. **Educ:** Ind Univ, Bloomington, Ind, BS & BA, bus mgt & African Am studies, 1985, MBA, finance, banking & bus mgt, 1987. **Career:** Fifth Third Bank, Large Corp Group, dir, vpres, corp treas mgt, dir, sales mgr, 2001-05; Wachovia, Palm Beach Com Banking, sr vpres, dir, 2005-07; BB&T, sr vpres, bancorp treas mgt sales mgr, 2008-; CU Bus Capital LLC, sr vpres, chief lending officer. **Orgs:** Bd mem, Ctr Enterprise Opportunity; adv comt mem, IBIS Partners LLC; Loyola Univ; St Paul's Col; small bus banking conf speaker, Am Banker; featured speaker, AFP Carolina Cash Adventure. **Honors/Awds:** Florida Diversity Council Multicultural Leadership Award, Fla Diversity Coun, 2012. **Special Achievements:** Managing Teams Across Time Zones, 2011. **Business Addr:** Senior Vice President, BB&T, 200 W Second St, Winston-Salem, NC 27101, **Business Phone:** (336)733-2500.

## BETTY, DR. WARREN RANDALL

Pediatrician, administrator, physician. **Personal:** Born Apr 21, 1931, Chicago, IL; son of A L Lucas and E C Brewington; married Judy A Austermiller; children: Lisa C & Michael W. **Educ:** Ind Univ, BA, 1954; Ind Univ Sch Med, Md, 1959. **Career:** Physician (retired); Albert Einstein Col Med NY, asst clin prof pediat, 1965-95; Richmond Co Prof Stand Rev Orgn, treas & bd dir, 1979-84; State Island Med Group, med dir, 1981-96; Health Ins Plan Greater NY, mem, bd dir, 1983-92, 1993-96; Group Coun Mutual Ins Co, mem, bd dir, 1983-96; Bronx Munic Hosp Ctr, resident. **Orgs:** Mem adv bd, Staten Island Urban League, 1982-90; Gov Comn Hosp Info Data, 1983; vpres, Richmond County Med Soc, 1983-84; treas & bd dir, Island Peer Rev Orgn, 1984-; Reg Adv Coun, State Div Human Rights; bd dir, Prof Med Conduct, 1994-99; comnr, Cape May Cult & Heritage Comn; treas, Greater Cape May Hist soc; historian, Shoreline RRHist Soc. **Honors/Awds:** Black Achiever Award, Harlem Br, YMCA, 1982. **Home Addr:** 4065 Bayshore Rd, Cape May, NJ 08204, **Home Phone:** (609)898-1945. **Business Addr:** Treasurer, Board Director, IPRO, 1979 Marcus Ave, Lake Success, NY 11042-1002, **Business Phone:** (516)326-7767.

## BEVERLY, CREIGS C.

Educator, social worker, school administrator. **Personal:** Born Sep 5, 1942, Selma, AL; son of Creigs Brooks and Margaret Brooks; married Olivia D; children: Cheryl, Creigs Jr & Larry. **Educ:** Morehouse Col, BA, 1963; Atlanta Univ, MSW, social work, 1965; Univ Wis, PhD, 1972. **Career:** Professor (retired): Atlanta Univ, Sch Social Work, prof, 1974-83, Atlanta Univ, Alcoholism Counr Training Prog, assoc prof Social Work, 1975; assoc dean acad affairs, 1979-88, dean, 1984-86, vpres & provost, 1986-87, Social & Behav Sci, sr prof, 1987; Univ Ghana, prof, 1983-84, actg coordr, 1984; Ctr African Life & Develop, post doctorate training, 1984; Spec asst to Maynard Jackson, Ga, Wayne State Univ, Sch Social Work, vis prof, 1987, prof, 1988-2004, prof emer, 2004-. **Orgs:** Spec asst tomayor, Carnegie Found Fel, 1976-77; fel Ctr study african family life & develop; Nat Asn Black Elected Officials; Nat Asn Social Workers; Nat Asn Black Social Workers; CSWE; ACSW; Nat Coun Black Alcoholism, 1980-82; bd dir, Coun Int Progs, 1985; planning comn, City Detroit, 1988-; Nat Asn Advan Colored People; Ga Coun Soc Welfare; Ga Chap Social Workers; Nat Asn Community Developers; Asn Social Work Ed Africa; Nat Ctr Child Abuse; Mich Coun Child Abuse; Kellogg Found Youth Initiatives Prog; mem Int comn, 2000-01; Detroit Planning Comn; bd pres, Detroit Youth Comn; Hartford Agape House; bd dir, Hwy Med Ctr. **Home Addr:** 17524 Birchcrest Dr, Detroit, MI 48221, **Home Phone:** (313)861-8876. **Business Addr:** Professor Emeritus, Wayne State University, 5557 Cass Ave, Detroit, MI 48202-3615, **Business Phone:** (313)577-2424.

## BEVERLY, ERIC R.

Executive, football player. **Personal:** Born Mar 28, 1974, Cleveland, OH; married Danielle; children: Lia. **Educ:** Miami Univ, BS, opers mgt & corp pirchasing, 1997. **Career:** Football player (retired), exec; Detroit Lions, corner & left guard, 1997-2003, tight end, 2007; Kmart Corp, intern, 2000; Atlanta Falcons, tight end, 2004-06; Univ Ga, coordr academics football & acad counr, 2008-12; Univ Tex at Austin, asst athletics dir football academics, 2012-. **Orgs:** Treas, Eric R Beverly Family Found; rep, NFL Players Asn, 2001-03. **Business Addr:** Treasurer, Eric R Beverly Family Foundation, 1475 Buford Dr Suite 403-127, Lawrenceville, GA 30043, **Business Phone:** (770)614-1779.

## BEVERLY, FRANKIE (HOWARD BEVERLY)

Songwriter, songwriter, singer, musician. **Personal:** Born Dec 6, 1946, Philadelphia, PA; children: Anthony. **Career:** Frankie Beverly & Maze, founder & lead singer, 1977-. Albums: Maze Featuring Frankie Beverly, 1977, Golden Time of Day, 1978, Inspiration, 1979, Joy & Pain, 1980, Live in New Orleans, 1980, We Are One, 1983; Cant Stop the Love, 1985; Maze Featuring Frankie Beverly Live in Los Angeles, 1986; Silky Soul, 1989; Back to the Basic, 1993; Southern Girl, 1996; Rebel 4 Life, 1998; Whats the Worst That Could Happen, 2001; Cherish, writer, 2002; Paid in Full, 2002; Bringing Down the House, 2003; Johnson Family Vacation, 2004; Get Rich or Die Tryin, 2005; ATL, 2006; Welcome Home, Roscoe Jenkins, 2008; Meet the Browns, 2008. Songs: "Running Away"; "Love Is The Key"; "Back In Stride"; "Too Many Games"; "Can't Get Over You"; "Silky Soul"; "Golden Time Of Day", writer, 1998; "Happy Feelins", writer, 2001; "What's the Worst That Could Happen?", writer, 2001; "Let Go", writer, 2003; "Before I Let You Go", writer, 2004, 2008; "Tavis Smiley", 2005; "Southern Girl", 2006; "California", 2016. **Honors/Awds:** Eight gold recs; BET Award, 2012. **Business Addr:** Singer, Capitol Records Inc, 1750 N Vine St, Hollywood, CA 90028, **Business Phone:** (213)462-6252.

## BEVERLY, HOWARD. See BEVERLY, FRANKIE.

## BEVERLY, MARIETTA SKYLES

School principal, teacher. **Career:** Michele Clare Mid Sch, prin, region 3 educ officer; Chicago Pub Sch, area 9 instr officer, Kozminski Elem Sch, teacher; Louis Writh Exp Sch, teacher; Chicago Voc High Sch, guid counr. **Orgs:** Chicago Bd Educ. **Business Addr:** Region Education Officer, Chicago Public School, 231 N Pine St, Chicago, IL 60636, **Business Phone:** (773)534-6284.

## BEVERLY, SHARON MANNING. See MANNING, SHARON.

## BEVERLY, WILLIAM C., JR.

Lawyer, judge, president (organization). **Personal:** Born Jan 23, 1943, Los Angeles, CA; married Mona Birkelund. **Educ:** Pepperdine Univ, BA, 1965; Southwestern Univ, Sch Law, JD, 1969. **Career:** Lawyer, Judge (retired), exec; Calif State Univ, Long Beach, instr bus law; DPSS, soc worker & supvr, 1965-70; pvt pract law, atty, 1970-2003, JAMS, arbitrator & mediator; Los Angeles County Comn, vpres; Long Beach Munic Ct, presiding judge, 1980-85; Los Angeles County Super Ct, judge, 1985-2003, assigned judge, 2003-; Southwest Dist Los Angeles Super Ct, supv judge; Southwestern Univ Sch Law, judicial officer, 1996; Eighth & Wall Inc, founder, pres & bd dir, currently. **Orgs:** Co chmn, Mil Law Panel, 1971; Calif & Long Beach Bar Asn; Langston Law Club; Langston Bar Asn; vpres, La County Comn Human Rels; Hist Coun Calif African Am Mus; African Am Heritage Soc Long Beach; Judges temp jurisdiction; adv bd mem, Ctr Mathand Teaching Inc; bd dir, founder, Eighth & Wall Inc; vpres, Los Angeles County Human Rels Comn; presiding judge appellate div, Los Angeles Super Ct; mem hist coun, African Am Heritage Socs Long Beach & Calif African Am Mus. **Business Addr:** President, Board of Director, Eighth & Wall Inc, 904 Silver Spur Rd Suite 317, Rolling Hills Estates, CA 90274, **Business Phone:** (310)541-1690.

## BEYER, TROY YVETTE

Actor, screenwriter, movie director. **Personal:** Born Nov 7, 1964, New York, NY; daughter of Jerrold and Hannan Wells Parks; married Mark Bug; children: 1; married Christopher Bailey; children: 2. **Educ:** City Univ NY, Sch Arts, actg & psycho biol; Univ Calif, Los Angeles, polit sci. **Career:** TV series: "Dynasty", 1986-87; "Uncle Tom's Cabin", 1987; "Three Chains O' Gold", 1994; "Murder One", 1995; "Alien Avengers", 1997; "Surviving Gilligan's Island: The Incredibly True Story of the Longest Three Hour Tour in History", 2001; "Recipe for Disaster", 2003. Films: Disorderlies, 1987; Rooftops, 1989; The White Girl, 1990; The Five Heartbeats, 1991; Weekend at Bernie's II, 1993; The Little Death, 1995; Eddie, 1996; BAPS, 1997; The Ginger bread Man, 1998; Let's Talk About Sex, 1998; Good Advice, 2001; John Q, 2002; A Light in the Darkness, 2002; Malevolent, 2002; Love Don't Cost a Thing, 2003; Mommy's Little Monster, 2012; I Really Hate My Ex, 2014. **Honors/Awds:** Newcomer of the Year Award, ShoWest; Nominated for BET Comedy Awars, 2004. **Special Achievements:** Author: Ex-Free: 9 Keys to Freedom After Heartbreak. **Home Addr:** 7357 Woodrow Wilson Dr, Los Angeles, CA 90046. **Business Addr:** Actress, c/o William Morris Agency, 151 El Camino Dr, Beverly Hills, CA 90212, **Business Phone:** (310)274-7451.

## BIAKABUTUKA, TIM (TSHIMANGA BIAKABUTUKA)

Football player, executive. **Personal:** Born Jan 24, 1974, Kinshasa. **Educ:** Univ Mich. **Career:** Football player (retired), owner; Carolina Panthers, running back, 1996-2001; Beya Jewelry Store, owner, currently; Bojangles Restaurant, owner, currently. **Honors/Awds:** Ed Block Courage Award, Carolina Panthers, 1997. **Home Addr:** , Fort Mill, SC. **Business Addr:** Owner, Bojangles Restaurant, 3412 Mike Padgett Hwy, Augusta, GA 30906, **Business Phone:** (706)798-6261.

## BIBB, DR. T. CLIFFORD

Educator. **Personal:** Born Oct 29, 1938, Montgomery, AL; son of Bennie and Alma; children: Tura Concetta. **Educ:** Ala State Univ, BS, 1960, MEd, 1961; Northwestern Univ, PhD, 1973. **Career:** Educator (retired); Rust Col, Eng Dept, chair, 1961-65; Daniel Payne Col, chair eng dept, 1965-67; Miles Col, eng coordr, 1967-71; Northwestern Univ, eng supvr, 1971-72, Upward Prog, dir, 1972-73; Ala State Univ, chmn advan studies & dir four yr plus curric prog, chmn emer, Univ Col, dean. **Orgs:** Comnr, Compos Nat Centre Technol Educ, 1973-76; secy, Peterson-Bibb Lodge 762, 1974-; fac adv, Alpha Phi Alpha, 1981-; exec comm, Nat Centre Technol Educ, 1983-88; exec sec & bd mem, Cent Montgomery Optimists, 1984-86; desoto comn State Ala, 1986-95; Nat Coun Teachers Eng, 1991-93; newsletter ed, Ala Asn Develop Ed, 1992-95; Ala State Coun Arts, 1992-; Nat Coun Ed Opportunity Asn, 1992-; table leader, Ed Testing Serv APT & ENG, 1994-; pres, Nat Asn Develop Educ, 1998-99. **Home Addr:** 877 Corona Dr, Montgomery, AL 36110, **Home Phone:** (334)462-4142.

## BIBBS, CHARLES

Business owner. **Personal:** Born San Pedro, CA; married Elaine. **Career:** Fine Artist, entrepreneur & philanthropist; B Graphics & Fine Arts Inc, owner, publ & distribr, 2004-; 626 Art Gallery Studio B, owner, currently. **Honors/Awds:** Entrepreneur Of The Year, African Am Chamber Com; Honoree Award, United Negro Col Fund; Hardy Brown Community Award; Recognition Award; Community Recognition Award, Nat Coun Negro Women; Appreciation Service Award; Honorary Citizens Award, Mayor Cleaver; Key To The City Award, City Coun Carson; Entreprenuer of the Year, Nat Asn Advan Colored People; Art Award, Links Inc; International Benny Award. **Home Addr:** , Moreno Valley, CA 92553-5235. **Business Addr:** Business Owner, B Graphics & Fine Arts, 12625 Frederick Ave Suite 1 8, Moreno Valley, CA 92553-5235, **Business Phone:** (909)697-4752.

## BIBBS, PATRICIA (PATRICIA CAGE-BIBBS)

Basketball coach. **Personal:** married Ezil; children: Sabrina & Satin. **Educ:** Grambling State Univ, BA, health & phys educ, 1972, MA, sports admin, 1977. **Career:** Grambling State Univ, head womens basketball coach, 1983-97, 2012-; Hampton Univ, basketball coach, 1997-2004; NC A&T State Univ, head womens basketball coach, 2005-. **Orgs:** MEAC Basketball Tournament Comt; Women's Basketball Coaches Asn; Black Coaches Asn; NCAA Coun, 1987; Zeta Phi Beta Sorority; St. Rest Baptist Church. **Business Addr:** Head Coach of Womens Basketball, North Carolina A&T State University, 1601 E Mkt St, Greensboro, NC 27411, **Business Phone:** (336)334-7500.

## BIBBS-SANDERS, ANGELIA

Administrator. **Personal:** Born May 7, 1961, Winona, MS; children: 2. **Educ:** Long Beach City Col, AA, 1982; Calif State Univ, bus admin, 1985. **Career:** Motown Records, dir artist rels; Radio Corp Am Records, dir mkt oper, 1988-95, vpres western region, 1997-2003; vpres mem serv, 2003-10; Jive Rec; Nat Acad Rec Arts & Sci, Los Angeles Chapter, exec dir; Los Angeles chap, vpres mem servs; Debut Group, pres & chief exec officer, currently; ABS Collective, founder & chief exec officer, 2010-. **Orgs:** Exec comt, Cedars-Sinai Brain Trust; trustee, Ctr Early Educ; exec comt, City Hope. **Business Addr:** President, Debut Group, 8770 W Bryn Mawr Suite 1300, Chicago, IL 6063, **Business Phone:** (773)867-8353.

## BIBBY, MIKE (MICHAEL BIBBY)

Basketball player, basketball coach. **Personal:** Born May 13, 1978, Cherry Hill, NJ; son of Henry and Virginia; married Darcy; children: Michael Jr, Janae, Mia & Nylah. **Educ:** Univ Ariz, attended 1998. **Career:** Basketball player (retired), coach; Vancouver Grizzlies, guard, pt guard, 1998-2001; Sacramento Kings, guard, pt guard, 2001-08; Atlanta Hawks, guard, pt guard, 2008-11; Wash Wizards, 2011; Miami Heat, 2011; New York Knicks, pt guard, 2011-12; Shadow Mountain High Sch, asst coach, 2013. **Honors/Awds:** NCAA Champion, 1997; Pac-10 Freshman of the Year, 1997; Pac-10 Player of the Year, 1998; NCAA All-American First Team, 1998; NBA All-Rookie First Team, 1999; Gold Medal, FIBA Americas Championship, 2003; Conf Player of the Week, 2005. **Business Addr:** Assistant Coach, Shadow Mountain High School, 2902 E Shea Blvd, Phoenix, AZ 85028, **Business Phone:** (602)449-3000.

## BIBLO, MARY (MARY P BIBLO)

Librarian. **Personal:** Born Dec 31, 1927, East Chicago, IN; daughter of James and Flora Chandler; married Herbert D; children: Lisa & David. **Educ:** Roosevelt Univ, Chicago, Ill, BS, 1966; Dominican Univ, River Forest, Ill, MLS, 1970; Teachers Col, Columbia Univ, 1985. **Career:** S Chicago Community Hosp, Sch Nursing, Chicago, Ill, med librn, 1966-67; Chicago Bd Educ, Chicago, Ill, sch librn, 1967-70; Univ Chicago, Labr Schs, Chicago, Ill, librn, 1970-98, Rowley Libr, librn emer, currently. **Orgs:** Am Lib Asn, 1970-; pres, C's Reading Round Table; Nat Caucus Black Librns; Nat Asn Independent Schs; vice chair, minority affairs comt, Ill State Bd Educ, 1988-90; Int Fedn Libr Asns, chair, Int Fedn Libr Asn's Round Table Women's Issues; Am Asn Sch Librn; intellectual freedom round table, social responsibility round table, Ill Libr Asn; Ill Asn Media Educ; fel Lincoln County Libr Dist, currently. **Honors/Awds:** Klingenstein fel, Columbia Univ, 1984-85; master teacher, Univ Chicago Lab Sch, 1985. **Home Addr:** 10 Mosshill Pl, Stony Brook, NY 11790-2919, **Home Phone:** (631)751-5003. **Business Addr:** Librarian Emeritus, University of Chicago, 1362 E 59th St, Chicago, IL 60637, **Business Phone:** (773)702-0583.

## BICKERSTAFF, BERNARD TYRONE, SR.

Basketball coach. **Personal:** Born Feb 11, 1944, Benham, KY; married Eugenia King; children: Tim, Robin, Cydni, Bernard & John Blair. **Educ:** Rio Grande Col, 1961; Univ San Diego, BS, 1968. **Career:** Univ San Diego, asst basketball coach, 1968-69, coach, 1969-73; Wash Bullets, asst coach, 1973-85, head coach, 1996-99; Seattle SuperSonics, head coach, 1985-90; Denver Nuggets, head coach, 1994-96, gen mgr & pres, 1990-97; St Louis Swarm, head coach & gen mgr; Charlotte Bobcats, head coach & gen mgr, 2004-07; Chicago Bulls, asst coach, 2008-10; Portland Trail Blazers, asst coach, 2010-12; Los Angeles Lakers asst coach, 2012-13; Cleveland Cavaliers, asst coach, 2013-; Wash Wizards, San Antonio Spurs, NBA.com & Sporting News Radio, TV and radio analyst. **Orgs:** Vpres, NBA Coaches Asn, 1980-90; Kappa Alpha Psi. **Business Addr:** Assistant Coach, Cleveland Cavaliers, Gund Arena 1 Ctr Ct, Cleveland, OH 44115-4001, **Business Phone:** (216)420-2000.

**BICKERSTAFF, CYNDI L.**
Executive, entrepreneur, chief executive officer. **Personal:** Born Columbia, MD; daughter of Bernie and Eugenia. **Educ:** Hampton Univ, BS, acct; Fla A&M Univ, MBA. **Career:** Entrepreneur, chief exec officer; ASCENT Sports; Denver Nuggets; Colo Avalanche & Host Communs; Bickerstaff Sports & Entertainment, founder & ceo, 2001-. **Business Addr:** Chief Executive Officer, Bickerstaff Sports & Entertainment, 4401 A Connecticut Ave NW Suite337, Washington, DC 20008, **Business Phone:** (202)832-8560.

**BICKHAM, DR. LUZINE B.**
Administrator, air force officer, association executive. **Personal:** Born Mar 2, 1923, New Orleans, CA; married Dorothy B (deceased); children: Luzine Jr & Nedra E. **Educ:** Univ Mich, BBA, 1947, MBA, 1948; Univ Tex, PhD, mkt, 1965. **Career:** Educator (retired); Dillard Univ, instr, 1949; Watchtower Life Ins Co, secy, 1950; Tex Southern Univ, instr, 1952; Tex Southern Univ Sch Bus, dean, 1970-78. **Orgs:** Am Mkt Asn; bd dirs, Std savs & Loan asn; Tex So Fin; St Eliz Hosp Found. **Home Addr:** 3422 S McGregor Way, Houston, TX 77021, **Home Phone:** (713)748-0780.

**BIDDLE, DR. STANTON F.**
Library administrator. **Personal:** Born Sep 16, 1943, Cuba, NY; son of Christopher F and Imogene M Peterson. **Educ:** Howard Univ, Wash, DC, BA, 1965; Atlanta Univ, Atlanta, GA, MS, libr sci, 1966; New York Univ, New York, NY, MS, pub admin, 1973; Univ Calif, Berkeley, CA, doctor libr & info studies, 1988. **Career:** The New York Pub Libr Schomburg Res Ctr, New York, NY, ref librn, archivist, 1967-73; Howard Univ Libr, Wash, DC, assoc dir, 1973-76; State Univ New York-Buffalo, assoc dir librs, 1979-84; Baruch Col, City Univ New York, chief librn, 1984-88; City Univ NY Cent Off, asst dean libr, 1988-89; Baruch Col, CUNY, prof, admin serv, librn, 1989-, currently. **Orgs:** Black Caucus Am Libr Asn, 1976-82, 1989-91; pres, Schomburg Collection Black Lit, Hist & Art, 1988-90; corresp secy, City Univ African Am Network, 1990-93; bd mem, Metro; founding mem, New York Chap Afro-Am Hist & Geneal Soc; treas, NY Black Librns Caucus, 1990-94; chief librn, Baruch Col; consult, New York Pub Librarys Schomburg Ctr; NYG&B; librn, Admin Serv, 1989; chair, Afro Am Studies Librn Sect, Asn Col & Res Libr, 1991-92; pres, Libr Asn City Univ NY, 1992-94; pres, Black Caucus Am Libr Asn, 1994-96; Digitization Adv Coun; Info Systs Adv Coun; fel myMETRO. **Honors/Awds:** William Wells Brown Award, Afro-Am Hist Asn, Buffalo, NY, 1984. **Home Addr:** 158 18 Riverside Dr W Suite 7B, New York, NY 10032, **Home Phone:** (212)933-1652. **Business Addr:** Professor, Librarian, Baruch College, 17 Lexington Ave, New York, NY 10010, **Business Phone:** (646)312-1653.

**BIFFLE, CURTIS**
Teacher. **Educ:** Ala A&M Univ. **Career:** Austin High Sch, adjust coordr, teacher, currently; Decatur City Schs, teacher, currently. **Orgs:** Coordr, Southeastern Consortium Minorities Engineering. **Special Achievements:** Credited by colleagues with keeping probable dropouts in school; survived impoverished childhood in rural Alabama. **Home Addr:** 108 Woodlawn Dr, Madison, AL 35758, **Home Phone:** (256)772-0082. **Business Addr:** Teacher, Austin High School, 1625 Danville Rd SW, Decatur, AL 35601, **Business Phone:** (256)552-3060.

**BIGGERS, DR. SAMUEL LORING, JR.**
Neurosurgeon, president (organization), educator. **Personal:** Born Nov 6, 1935, Crockett, TX; son of Samuel L Sr and Nelia J Martinez; married Florestine A Robinson; children: Samuel L III, Shaun Denise & Sanford Leon. **Educ:** Dillard Univ, AB, 1956; Univ Tex, Galveston, Tex, MD, 1961; Am Bd Neurol Surg, dipl, 1970. **Career:** Univ Tex Grad Sch, researcher & teaching asst, 1957-58; Orange County Gen Hosp, intern, 1961-62; Univ Southern Calif Med Ctr, instr clin, 1964-70, Los Angeles County, resident, asst prof clin, 1970-85; Calif Med Ctr, Los Angeles, chief surgeon, 1989-, vpres, med staff; Charles R Drew Med Sch, prof neuro sci, 1993-, Martin Luther King Jr Hosp, Dept Neurol Surg, vice chmn; White Memorial Med Ctr; Valley Presby Hosp; Chapman Med Ctr; Methodist Hosp Southern CA; neurosurgeon, currently; Dignity Health Hosp, currently. **Orgs:** Pres, Samuel L Biggers, John J Holly MD Inc, 1974-; bd dir, CMCLA Found, 1990-; bd dir, Unihealth Am Found, 1990-; Am Asn Neurol Surgeons; Kappa Alpha Psi; Alpha Kappa Mu; Alpha Omega Alpha; Sigma Pi Phi; bd trustee, Calif Hosp Med Ctr; bd mem, Cath Healthcare W. **Honors/Awds:** Alumnus of the Year, Dillard Univ, 1985; Humanitarian of the Year, Calif Med Ctr, 1992; Distinguished Physician Award, Minority Health Inst, 1994. **Home Addr:** 4291 Mt Vernon Dr, Los Angeles, CA 90008-4837, **Home Phone:** (323)299-3232. **Business Addr:** President, Biggers & Holly, 1414 S Grand Ave Suite 410, Los Angeles, CA 90015-3078, **Business Phone:** (213)745-5595.

**BIGGINS, J. VERONICA**
Executive, government official. **Personal:** Born Oct 19, 1946, Belmont, NC; daughter of Jacqueline McDonald and Andrew Williams; married Franklin; children: 2. **Educ:** Spelman Col, BS; Ga State Univ, MA; Duke Univ Fuqua, exec mgt prog; Harvard Univ, advan leadership prog, 2010. **Career:** Citizens & Southern Ga Corp, dir human resources, trainee; Nat Bank Corp, exec vpres corp community rels, 1994; The White House, asst to pres, dir pres personnel, 1994-95, US deleg UN Womens Conf Beijing, vchmn, 1995; Heidrick & Struggles Int Inc, Atlanta, sr partner, managing partner, 1995-2007; HNCL Search, partner, currently; Hodge Partners, managing partner, 2007-; AltoPartners, Diversified Search LLC, managing dir, 2012-. **Orgs:** Bd mem, Atlanta Life Ins Co; bd mem, Atlanta-Fulton County Recreation Authority; co-chairperson, Atlanta AIDS Walk, 1991; chmn, Czech Slovak Am Enterprise Fund; bd dir, Air Tran Airways, 2001-11; bd dir, Avnet; bd dir, Kaiser Permanente Ga; trustee, Woodruff Arts Ctr; bd vis, Savannah Col Art & Design; dir, CertusHoldings Inc, 2010-; mem emer, CDC Found Bd; SW Airlines; NDC Health; Ga Res Alliance; Downtown Atlanta Rotary; Int Aids Fund; fel Harvard Univ's Advan Leadership Initiative. **Business Addr:** Managing Director, AltoPartners, 3500 Lenox Rd Suite 1500, Atlanta, GA 30326, **Business Phone:** (404)419-2351.

**BIGGS, DR. SHIRLEY ANN**
Educator. **Personal:** Born Mar 9, 1938, Richmond, VA; daughter of Richard B Hill and Jennie; married Charles F; children: Charles F Jr & Cheryl A. **Educ:** Duquesne Univ, BEd, elem educ, 1960; Univ Tenn, attended 1969; Univ SC, MEd, reading & psychol serv, 1972; Univ Pittsburgh, EdD, lang commun, 1977. **Career:** Pittsburgh Pub Sch, teacher, 1961-68; Benedict Col, instr, 1968-72, reading specialist consult, 1972; Univ Pittsburgh, Sch Educ, Dept Instr & Learning, assoc prof, asst dean stud affairs, dir affirmative action, minority affairs, emer assoc prof educ, assoc ed, 1973-; Negro Educ Rev, exec ed & co-managing ed, 1992-. **Orgs:** Pres, Gerald A Yoakam Reading Coun, 1978-79; chmn, Res Div, Pittsburgh Literacy Coalition, 1984-; Int Reading Asn, 1973-90; dir res, Coalition Adv Literacy Pittsburgh, 1985-; chmn, Pittsburgh Peace Inst, 1997-; chmn, Col Reading Improv Group; Imani Christian Acad Bd & Educ chmn, 2001-; Nat Conf Res Lang & Literacy, 2001-; Golden Key Nat Hon Soc; Int Reading Asn/Int Literacy Asn; Am Asn Blacks Higher Educ; Nat Conf Res, Lang & Literacy. **Home Addr:** 1126 N Euclid Ave, Pittsburgh, PA 15206. **Business Addr:** Emeritus Associate Professor of Education, Associate Editor, University of Pittsburgh, 5602 Wesley W Posvar Hall, Pittsburgh, PA 15260, **Business Phone:** (412)648-2115.

**BIGHAM, RITA LACY**
Librarian, research scientist, executive director. **Personal:** Born Jan 7, 1949, Augusta, GA; daughter of Joseph Tolbertte and Ruth Jefferson; married Bruce W. **Educ:** Morris Brown Col, Atlanta, GA, BS, 1969; Atlanta Univ, Atlanta, GA, MSLS, 1970. **Career:** Atlanta Univ, Sch Libr Sci, Ford Found, fel, 1969-70; Morris Brown Col, Jordan-Thomas Libr, Atlanta, Ga, cataloger, 1970-79; Mellon Asn Col & Res Libs, intern, 1976-77; Atlanta Univ, Trevor Arnett Libr, Atlanta, Ga, head, tech servs, 1979-82; Atlanta Univ Ctr Inc, Robert W Woodruff Libr, Atlanta, Ga, dir, tech servs, 1982-87; Interdenominational Theol Ctr, Atlanta, Ga, res asst, 1987, Res & Eval, dir, currently. **Orgs:** Vpres, dean pledgees, Gamma Zeta Chap, Delta Sigma Theta Sorority, 1968-69; Am Libr Asn, 1970-; Beta Phi Mu, Int Libr Sci Hon Socs, 1970-; Nat Coun Negro Women, 1990-. **Home Addr:** 2681 Westchester Dr, East Point, GA 30344-2057. **Business Addr:** Director of Research & Evaluation, Interdenominational Theological Center, 671 Beckwith St SW, Atlanta, GA 30314, **Business Phone:** (404)527-7764.

**BIGLOW, KEITH**
Funeral director. **Personal:** married Shanda; children: Andre, Kaitlin & Kaleb. **Educ:** Cent State Univ. **Career:** House Winn Funeral Home, Okmulgee; McKay-Davis Mortuary, Inc, Okla; Jack's Memory Chapel Inc, Tulsa, Okla; Keith D Biglow Funeral Dir Inc, pres & owner, 1993-. **Business Addr:** President, Owner, Keith D Biglow Funeral Directors Inc, 1414 N Norfolk Ave, Tulsa, OK 74106, **Business Phone:** (918)592-2233.

**BILAL, JAZZ. See OLIVER, BILAL SAYEED.**

**BILES, SIMONE**
Athlete, gymnast. **Personal:** Born Mar 14, 1997, Columbus, OH; daughter of Ronald and Nellie. **Career:** Gymnast, 2002-. **Honors/Awds:** AT&T American Cup, silver medal, 2012; U.S. championships, all-around champion, 2013, 2014, 2015, 2016; U.S. championships, silver medals, vault, uneven bars, balance beam and floor exercise, 2013; World championships, floor exercise champion, silver medal vault, and bronze medal balance beam, 2013; World all-around champion, 2013, 2014, 2015; U.S. championships, gold medals floor exercise and vault, and silver medal balance beam, 2014; World championships, gold medal balance beam and floor exercise, and silver medal vault, 2014; Women's Sports Foundations' Individual Sportswoman of the Year, 2014; USOC's Female Olympic Athlete of the Year, 2014-15; AT&T American Cup champion, 2015; U.S. championships, gold medal balance beam and silver medal floor exercise; World championships, gold medals balance beam and floor exercise, and bronze medal vault, 2015; US championships, gold medals vault, balance beam, and floor exercise, 2016; Pacific Rim Championships, all-around champion, 2016; Summer Olympics, all-around champion, 2016; Summer Olympics, gold medals vault and floor exercise, and bronze medal balance beam, 2016. **Special Achievements:** Most decorated U.S. women's gymnast ever; tied record for most Olympic medals ever for U.S. gymnast, 2016; tied record for most Olympic gold medals by a female gymnast in a single games with four. **Business Addr:** USA Gymnastics, 132 E Washington St Suite 700, Indianapolis, IN 46204, **Business Phone:** (317)237-5050.

**BILLINGS, CORA MARIE**
Clergy. **Personal:** Born Feb 11, 1939, Philadelphia, PA; daughter of Ethel Lorraine Lee and Jesse Anthony. **Educ:** Gwynedd Mercy Col, Gwynedd, PA, 1963; Villanova Univ, Philadelphia, PA, BA, humanities, 1967; St Charles Borromed Sem, Philadelphia, PA, min rel studies, 1974. **Career:** WPCGHS, relig teacher, 1970-79; Nat Black Sisters Conf, Philadelphia, PA, exec dir, 1977-79; Cardinal Krol, Philadelphia, PA, dir, 1979-80; Bishop Walter F Sullivan, Richmond, VA, Va State Univ, campus minister, 1981-90; Off Black Catholics, dir, 1982-; St Elizabeth's Cath Church, pastoral coordr, 1990-2004; Diocesan Off Black Catholics, dir. **Orgs:** Inst Sisters Mercy Am, 1956-; Canon Law Soc Am, 1974-; pres, Nat Black Sisters Conf, 1975-77; Cath Campus Ministry Asn, 1981-; chair, Black-Hisp Caucus, 1986-; ed, Urban League, 1987-; dep dir, Va Human Rights Coun; chair, Richmond Chap; treas, Cath Diocese Richmond; bd mem, Va Ctr Inclusive Communities. **Special Achievements:** First African American woman to serve as Pastoral Coordinator in the diocese of Richmond, Virginia; First African American Nun to Head a Parish in The United States; First African-American to enter the Institute of the Sisters of Mercy of the Americas. **Home Addr:** 1301 Victor St, Richmond, VA 23222-3997, **Home Phone:** (804)329-4599. **Business Addr:** Director, Catholic Diocese of Richmond, 7800 Carousel Lane, Richmond, VA 23294-4201, **Business Phone:** (804)359-5661.

**BILLINGS, EARL WILLIAM**
Actor. **Personal:** Born Jul 4, 1945, Cleveland, OH; son of Willie Mae. **Educ:** Karamu House Theater, attended 1963; Cuyahoga Community Col, attended 1963. **Career:** Cleveland Summer Arts Festive, proj dir, 1967Cleveland Summer Arts Festive, proj dir, 1967; Karamu Theatre, dir performing arts, 1968-70; Ark Arts Ctr, dir performing arts, 1970-73; Free Southern Theater, artistic dir, 1973-76; New Orleans Pub Sch, artist-in-resident, 1976; actor, 1976-. Films: Stakeout, 1988; Wired, 1989; One False Move, 1992; One False Move, 1992; Jimmy Hollywood, 1994; Crimson Tide, 1995; Larger Than Life, 1996; The Fan, 1996; Con Air, 1997; Living in Peril, 1997; Antwone Fisher, 2002; Am Splendor, 2003; Mr Boats, 2003; Thank You for Smoking, 2005; Something New, 2006; Sr Skip Day, 2008; The Assignment, 2010. TV series: "What's Happening", 1976-79; "New Attitude", 1990; "S Cent", 1993; "Without a Trace", 2004; "Christmas at Waters Edge", 2004; "How I Met Your Mother", 2005; "Miss/Guided", 2008; "True Blood", 2008; "Cold Case", 2010; "Parenthood", 2010; "Raising Hope", 2010; "Free Agents", 2011; "Harry's Law", 2012. **Orgs:** Screen Actors Guild; Actors Equity Asn; Am Fedn TV & Radio Artists; Acad Motion Picture Arts & Sci. **Home Addr:** 8033 Sunset Blvd Suite 220, Los Angeles, CA 90046, **Home Phone:** (818)787-7119. **Business Addr:** Actor, 8271 Melrose Ave Suite 110, Los Angeles, CA 90046.

**BILLINGS, MAC**
Administrator. **Career:** Atlanta City Govt, Fire Safety Educ Dept, off torchbearer, 1996, fire chief, 2000. **Orgs:** Boy Scouts Am. **Business Addr:** GA.

**BILLINGS-HARRIS, LENORA**
Writer, educator, consultant. **Personal:** Born Aug 9, 1950, Newark, NJ; daughter of Wendell Kenneth and Lois Billings; married Charles Sommerville. **Educ:** Hampton Univ, BS, 1972; Univ Mich, MA, adult educ, 1977. **Career:** Ariz State Univ, adj prof; Gen Motors Corp, proj adminr; CIGNA Corp, dir human resources, 1979-85; Univ Mich, Exec Develop Ctr Grad Sch Bus, prog dir, 1970; Excel Develop Syst, founder & pres, 1986-; UbuntuGlobal, auth, int speaker, consult, 1986-; Trailblazers: How Top Business Leaders are Accelerating Results through Inclusion & Diversity, co-auth, 2010-; Averett Univ, adj prof, 2010-; Bryan Sch Bus Univ NC Greensboro, adj fac, 2002-; Global Speakers Fedn, coun mem, 2009-, dir, 2009-11, vpress, 2012-, pres, 2013-, pres & exec coun chair, 2014-. **Orgs:** Cert speaking prof, Nat Speakers Asn, 1996; bd dir, pres, 2006-07, Nat Speakers Asn, 1988-2007; bd mem, Win Win Resolutions, NC; chmn, Phoenix Women's Comn; pres, Nat Speakers Asn-Ariz Chap; bd mem, Ariz Women's Educ & Employ; trustee, Greensboro Day Sch, 2006-; Soc Human Resource Mgt; Global Speakers Fedn; Am Soc Training & Develop. **Business Addr:** consultant, speaker, UbuntuGlobal, PO Box 1628, Greensboro, NC 27402-1628, **Business Phone:** (336)282-4443.

**BILLINGSLEA, DR. MONROE L.**
Dentist. **Personal:** Born Aug 3, 1933, West Palm Beach, FL; children: Brent & Christa. **Educ:** Howard Univ Sch Dent, attended 1963. **Career:** Coney Island Hosp Brooklyn, intern oral surg, 1963-64; Minot AFB ND, chief oral surg, 1964-65; pvt pract, dentist, 1965-. **Orgs:** Nat Asn Advan Colored People; Southern Christian Leadership Conf; Kendrin Ment Health. **Honors/Awds:** Educational Achievement Award, USAF, 1954. **Special Achievements:** Author: Smoking & How to Stop, Brent House, 1978; Better Health Through Preventive Dentistry & Nutrition, Brent House Publ, 1978. **Home Addr:** 3704 Edgehill Dr, Los Angeles, CA 90018-4023. **Business Addr:** Dentist, Private Practice, 600 W Manchester Ave Suite 1, Los Angeles, CA 90044-5700, **Business Phone:** (213)753-2361.

**BILLINGSLEY, ANDREW**
School administrator, educator. **Personal:** Born Mar 20, 1926, Marion, AL; son of Silas and Lucy; married Amy; children: Angela & Bonita. **Educ:** Hampton Univ, attended 1949; Grinnell Col, AB, polit sci, 1951; Boston Univ, MS, social serv, 1956; Univ Mich, MA, sociol, 1960; Brandeis Univ, Florence Heller Sch, PhD, social policy & social res, 1964. **Career:** Wis Dept Pub Welfare, Mendota State Hosp, psychiat social worker, 1956-58; Univ Mich, Ann Arbor, dir friends int stud ctr, 1959-60; Res Asst Mass Soc Prev Cruelty C, social worker, 1960-63; Univ Calif, asst dean stud, 1964-65, assoc prof social welfare, 1964-68, asst chancellor acad affairs, 1968-70; Howard Univ, vpres acad affairs, 1970-75; Metro Appl Res Ctr, Nat Urban League NYC, fel, 1968; Morgan State Univ, pres, 1975-84; Univ Md, prof Sociol & Afro-Am studies, 1985-87, Family Sci Dept, prof, chmn, prof emer, currently; J Negro Educ, J Family Issues, ed bd, 1987; Spelman Col, vis scholar residence, adj prof sociol, 1992-95; Univ SC, Inst Families Soc, sr scholar, bd trustee, prof sociol, 1996-, prof emer, currently. Books: Yearning to Breathe Free: Robert Smalls of South Carolina and His Families, auth, 2007; Black Families in White America, auth; Climbing Jacobs Ladder:The Enduring Legacy of African American Families, auth; Children of the Storm, auth; Mighty Like a River:The Black Church and Social Reform, auth. **Orgs:** Chmn, Family Sect, Am Sociol Asn, 1972-73; chmn, Comt Mgt, Howard Univ Press, 1972-74; bd mem, Shiloh Bapt Church, Wash DC; Joint Ctr Polit Studies DC, 1972-75; Asn Black Sociologists; Nat Asn Black Social Workers; chmn adv bd, J Abstracts; chmn, Nat Asn Social Workers, 1973; Asn Black Sociologists; Nat Coun Family Rel, Groves Conf Marriage & Family. **Special Achievements:** University of South Carolina Institute for Families in Society and the University of South Carolina African American Studies Program are pleased to announce the establishment of the Andrew Billingsley Faculty Award and the Andrew Billingsley Community Leadership Award. **Home Addr:** 501 Hawkesbury Lane, Silver Spring, MD 20904, **Home Phone:** (301)622-2203. **Business Addr:** Professor Emeritus, University of Maryland, 1142 School of Public Health Bldg, College Park, MD 20742, **Business Phone:** (301)405-3672.

**BILLINGSLEY, RAY C.**
Cartoonist or animator, writer, artist. **Personal:** Born Jul 25, 1957, Wake Forest, NC; son of Henry and Laura Dunn. **Educ:** Sch Visual Arts, BFA, 1979. **Career:** Kids Mag, cartoon contribr, 1970-75; Crazy Mag, humorous artist, writer, 1975-79; Walt Disney Studios, intern, 1979; Ebony Mag, freelance cartoonist, 1979-87; Disney Prod, Orlando, FL, animator, 1979-80; United Feature Syndicate, syndicated cartoonist, 1980-82; freelance jobs (layouts, advert, mag illus, fashion), 1982-88; King Features Syndicate, syndicated cartoonist, 1988-. **Orgs:** Nat Cartoonists Soc; Int Mus Cartoon Art; African Am Lit Bk Club; Am Lung Asn; Can Lung Asn; Soc Pub Health Educ. **Honors/**

**Awds:** Pioneer of Excellence, The World Inst Black Commun, 1988; Award of Recognition, Detroit City Coun, 1989; Arts & Entertainment Achievement Award, Nat Am Advan Colored People, New Rochelle Br, 1993; Humanitarian Award, Am Lung Asn, 1999; Presidents Award, Am Lung Asn, 2000. **Special Achievements:** Started Oct 1969, at age 12, with "KIDS Mag". Possibly first Black artist to become prof at such a young age. Creator of comic strip "Curtis," King Features, the most popular minority comic strip in history. First Black artist to have a second comic strip publications; Author of Curtis & Twist & Shout, Ballantine Books; Who's Who in Black America; African-Americans in the Visual Arts; Garfield at 25:In Dog Years I'd Be Dead; Blondie's 75th Anniversary; Cartoon Success Secrets; The Comics Since 1945; 100 Years of American Newspaper Comics; Will Eisner/A Spirited Life. **Home Addr:** 260 Convent Ave, New York, NY 10031, **Home Phone:** (212)368-0127. **Business Addr:** Syndicated Cartoonist, King Features Syndicate, 888 7th Ave 2nd Fl, New York, NY 10019-4308, **Business Phone:** (212)455-4000.

## BILLINGSLY, DR. MARILYN MAXWELL

Pediatrician, educator. **Personal:** Born St. Louis, MO; daughter of Warren and Willie Mae; married Z Dwight. **Educ:** St Louis Univ, BA, biol, 1977, MD, 1981. **Career:** Cardinal Glennon Child Hsp, Pediat resident; St Louis Univ, asst prof, 1985-92, fac, 1997, Combined Internal Med Pediat Residency Prog, assoc prog dir, currently, Dept Pediat, assoc prof, Sch Med, Dept Internal Med, prof, currently; Federally Funded Community Health Ctr, med dir, 1992-97; People's Health Ctrs, med dir, 1992-97. **Orgs:** Focus Family Physicians Resource Coun, 1994-; Nat Med Asn, 1995-; Mound City Med Forum; Am Col Physicians, 1985-, pres, 1994-95; Christian Med & Dent Soc, 1995-; adv bd, Med Inst Sexual Health, 1996-; exec adv bd, St Louis Univ Sch Med, 2000-; Bioethics exec bd, 2003-; Am Acad Pediat, co-chair, 2006-; Med Staff Exec Comt, 2007-; Presidential Adv Coun, HIV/AIDS. **Business Addr:** Professor, Associate Program Director, Saint Louis University, Desloge Towers 3635 Vista Ave Grand Blvd 12th Fl, St. Louis, MO 63110-0250, **Business Phone:** (314)577-8762.

## BILLOPS, CAMILLE J.

Sculptor, printmaker, artist. **Personal:** Born Aug 12, 1933, Los Angeles, CA; daughter of Lucious and Alma Gilmore; married James V Hatch. **Educ:** La City Col, AA, 1955; Calif State Col, BA, 1960; City Col NY, MFA, 1975. **Career:** Huntington Hartford Found, fel, 1963; MacDowell Colony, fel, 1975; Hatch-Billops Col, co-founder; Afro-Am Bellwether Press, NY, ed, 1975-76; Rutgers Univ; City Col, artist, art educr & lectr; Rutgers Univ, Newark, instr art, 1975-87; Hatch-Billops Collection, pres & adminr, 1975-; Films: Older Women & Love, 1987; Suzanne, Suzanne; Finding Christa; KKK Boutique Ain't Just Rednecks; A String of Pearls, 2002. **Orgs:** Nat Conf Artists, 1972; Nat Conf Art Teachers; NY Women Film; NY State Coun Arts, 1987-88; NY Found Arts, 1989; Rockerfeller Found, 1991; Nat Endowment Arts, 1994. **Honors/Awds:** International Women's Year Award, 1975-76; Independent Focus Award, Mus Modern Art; New Directors New Films Award, Mus Modern Art; Grand Jury Award, Sundance Film Festival, 1992; James Van Der Zee Award, Brandywine Graphic Workshop, 1994; Skowhegan Award, 2000; Her prints & sculpture have been exhibited internationally in galleries & museums, including Cooper-Hewitt Museum of Design, The Chrysler Museum, Studio Museum, Harlem & The New Museum. **Special Achievements:** Her films have been shown on Public Television & at the Museum of Modern Art; author of The Harlem Book of the Dead; art articles in NY Times, Amsterdam News, Newsweek. **Home Addr:** 491 Broadway Apt 7, New York, NY 10012-4412, **Home Phone:** (212)966-3231. **Business Addr:** President, Hatch-Billops Collection Inc, 491 Broadway 7 Fl, New York, NY 10012-4412, **Business Phone:** (212)966-3231.

## BILLS, DR. JOHNNY BERNARD, JR.

Physician. **Personal:** Born Oct 3, 1949, Hickory Valley, TN; married Hilda M; children: Jacqueline, Melissa & Johnny III. **Educ:** Memphis State Univ, adv chem courses, 1970; Rust Col, Holly Springs, BS, chem & math, 1971; Univ Miss Med Sch, Jackson, MD, 1977. **Career:** Univ Hosp, resident gen surg; Ashland High Sch, math teacher, 1971-72; Rust Col, lab technician, 1972-73; Univ Miss Med Ctr, Gen Surg, resident, 1977; Univ Hosp, intern, 1977-78; Hosp Emergency Rm, physician, 1977-; Jefferson Co Hosp, staff physician, 1978-79; Madison, Yazoo, Leake Family Health Ctr, consult physician, 1979-80; Bills Med Clin, med dir, 1980-. **Orgs:** Phi Beta Sigma Fraternity, 1968-; Am Med Asn, 1977-; Jackson Med Soc, 1977-; Southern Med Asn, 1980-; chmn infection control, Methodist Hosp, Lexington, MS, 1981-; Chamber Com, 1983-; secy, Miss Med & Surg Asn, 1983-85; Nat Asn Advan Colored People; Jackson YMCA; New Hope Baptist Church; Jackson Rust Col Club; Baptist Haiti mission, World Concern. **Honors/Awds:** Alpha Beta Mu Honor Society, 1967-71; Academic Achievement Award, Science Student of Year, Rust Col, 1971; Friend of Children Citation-World Concern, United League of Holmes C Citation, 1983. **Home Addr:** 316 N Grove Cir, Brandon, MS 39047-6738. **Business Addr:** Physician, 225 Community Ave, Fayette, MS 39069, **Business Phone:** (601)786-3475.

## BILLUE, ZANA

Business owner. **Personal:** Born Feb 5, 1964, Brooklyn, NY; daughter of Windsor Rhoden and Erma. **Educ:** Temple Univ, BA, 1986; Culinary Inst Am, AOS, 1993. **Career:** Aramark corp, concept develop chef; Nestle USA, recipe develop specialist, 1996; Zana Cakes Inc, founder, pres & owner, 1998-; US Airways, customer serv agt, 2011-. **Orgs:** Retail Baker's Asn, 1998; comt mem, United Way Serv-Greater Cleveland, 1997-; comt mem, Harvest Hunger. **Honors/Awds:** Featured in Black Enterprise Magazine & Nia Online website. **Home Addr:** 7700 Stenton Ave Suite 214, Philadelphia, PA 19118-3102. **Business Addr:** Owner, President, Zana Cakes Inc, 7715 Crittenden St Suite 339, Philadelphia, PA 19118, **Business Phone:** (215)971-3390.

## BILLUPS, CHAUNCEY RAY

Basketball player. **Personal:** Born Sep 25, 1976, Denver, CO; son of Ray and Faye; married Piper Riley; children: Cydney, Ciara & Cenaya. **Educ:** Univ Colo, attended 1997. **Career:** Basketball player (retired); Boston Celtics, guard, 1997-98; Toronto Raptors, 1998-99; Denver Nuggets, 1999-2000; Orlando Magic, 2000; Minn Timberwolves, 2000-02; Detroit Pistons, 2002-08, 2013-14; Denver Nuggets, 2008-11; New York Knicks, 2011; Los Angeles Clippers, 2011-13; TV Series: "Who made you?". **Business Addr:** Guard, Detroit Pistons, 4 Championship Dr, Auburn Hills, MI 48326, **Business Phone:** (248)377-0100.

## BILLUPS, MATTIE LOU

Government official. **Personal:** Born Mar 5, 1935, Bixby, OK; married Vernon Sr; children: Jacci Love, Jocelyn Palmer, Vernon Jr, Ricci Evans & Reginald Evans, CherylLee, Robyn Evans, Murphy, Debi Cayasso, Beverly & Lesa Singleton. **Career:** Red Bird Pk Fund, treas, 1977-80; Branding Iron Saddle Club, treas, 1972-85; Town Red Bird, mayor. **Orgs:** Church Christ, 1967-; vpres, Wagoner County Dem Women, 1983-85. **Honors/Awds:** Most Outstanding Mayor for Black Mayors, Okla Conf Black Mayors, 1984. **Home Addr:** 34422 E 191st St S, Redbird, OK 74458-5040, **Home Phone:** (918)483-4724. **Business Addr:** Mayor, Town of Red Bird, PO Box 222, Redbird, OK 74458.

## BILSON, CAROLE

Executive. **Educ:** Univ Mich, BFA, indust design, 1980; Amos Tuck Sch, Dartmouth, cert strategic mkt; Univ Calif, Berkeley, Haas Sch Bus, exec develop prog; Smith Col, smith-tuck global leaders prog women. **Career:** Eastman Kodak Co, sr indust designer, proj leader & indust designer, design resource ctr, equip & softw, 1980-93, loaned exec, Rochester coordr NY statewide systemic initiative, 1994-95, worldwide mkt mgr, 1995-97, advan prod strategist, consumer imaging, 1997-98, prog mgr, 1998-2000; Pitney Bowes Inc, vpres & dir global design & usability & technol support opers, 2000-11; Strategic Chg & Innovation LLC, pres, 2012-14; Design Mgt Inst, vpres & chief opers officer, 2014, pres, 2014-, bd dir. **Orgs:** Founder, Usability Consortium Execs; adv coun, Design Mgt Inst; CEO Coun, 2007, 2008; World Design Found; ITSMF IT Sr Mgt Forum; Rochester Women's Network; Greater Fairfield County Found; Network N Star; Links. **Special Achievements:** First Black woman and one of three Black industrial designers in the U.S. holding executive positions with major corporations to lead a design and usability department. **Business Addr:** President, Vice President, Design Management Institute, 38 Chauncy St Suite 800, Boston, MA 02111, **Business Phone:** (617)338-6380.

## BINFORD, HENRY C.

Educator. **Personal:** Born May 2, 1944, Berea, OH; son of Henry F and Dorothy Johnston; married Janet Cyrwus; children: Charles & Evan. **Educ:** Harvard Univ, AB, hist, 1966, PhD, 1973; Univ Sussex, Eng, MA, 1967. **Career:** Danforth Grad, fel, 1966-72; Harvard Univ, teaching fel hist, 1969-73, asst head tutor hist, 1970-72; Samuel Stouffer Fel Harvard, Mass Inst Technol, 1971-72; Northwestern Univ, asst prof hist, 1973-79, Urban Studies Prog, dir, 1978-81, dir, Prog Am Cult, 1982-85, assoc prof hist & Urban Affairs, 1979-, MA Lib Studies Prog, dir, 1997-; Nat Humanities Ctr, Res Triangle Pk, NC, fel, 1990-91; Newberry Libr, Chicago, Lloyd Lewis nat endowment humanities fel, 1995-96; Alice B Kaplan Ctr Humanities, fel, 2001-02. **Orgs:** Speaker, Casino Club, 1974-; career advisor, North western Regional Conf, Boy Scouts Am, 1974-75; lectr, Pi Lambda Theta, Nat Teachers Orgn, 1977; bd dir, Bus & Prof People Pub Interest, 1985-; Archit Alliance Chicago Hist Soc, 1985-; bd ed, Chicago Reporter, 1988-93; Ill & Mich Canal Nat Heritage Corridor Workshop, 1991; bd trustee, Evanston Hist Soc, 1991-94; Chicago Archit Found; Sigma Pi Phi. **Home Addr:** 1110 Dobson St, Evanston, IL 60202, **Home Phone:** (847)475-7049. **Business Addr:** Associate Professor, Director, Master of Arts in Liberal Studies Program, Northwestern University, Harris Hall 202 1800 Sherman 105, Evanston, IL 60208-2220, **Business Phone:** (847)491-7262.

## BING, DAVE (DAVID BING)

Basketball player, mayor, executive. **Personal:** Born Nov 24, 1943, Washington, DC; son of Hasker and Juanita; married Yvette; children: Cassaundra, Bridgett & Aleisha. **Educ:** Syracuse Univ, BA, econs, 1966. **Career:** Basketball player, executive, politician (retired); Detroit Pistons, 1966-75, Washington Bullets, 1975-77, Boston Celtics, 1977-78; Nat Paragon Steel, mgt trainee, 1978-80; Bing Group, owner & pres, 1980-2009; Detroit City, mayor, 2009-13. **Orgs:** Sigma Alpha Mu Frat, Syracuse; bd dir, Stand Fed Bank, 1997-. **Home Addr:** 29555 Woodhaven Lane, Southfield, MI 48076-5281.

## BING, LISA A.

President (organization). **Educ:** Boston Univ; NY Univ & Teachers Col; Columbia Univ. **Career:** Brooklyn Chamber Com, vice chair, 1996-; Bing Consult Group Inc, pres & founder, 1996-; Pub Strategies Group, consult; New York Univ, adj prof, 2000-; Am Socs Training & Develop, pres. **Orgs:** Bd vice chair, exec comt, Brooklyn Chamber Com, 1996-; Concord Christfund Bd Gov. **Home Addr:** 212 Saint James Pl, Brooklyn, NY 11238-2302, **Home Phone:** (718)398-8516. **Business Addr:** President, Bing Consulting Group Inc, 212 St James Pl, Brooklyn, NY 11238-2302, **Business Phone:** (718)398-8516.

## BING, RUBELL M.

Librarian. **Personal:** Born Jan 6, 1938, Rocky Mount, NC; daughter of Lonnie and Alberta Green; married Alex Sr; children: Bonita, Tovoia, Yvonne & Alex J. **Career:** Girl Scout Coun Nation's Capital, girl scout leader, 1976-78; St Francis De Sales Sch, librn, 1977-, media specialist, corresp secy, 1982-. **Orgs:** Lifetime mem, PTA, Washington, DC, 1975; supvr, Summer Youth Prog, Brentwood Sec, 1981; reading & libr chairperson, DC Parent Assoc, 1981-82; DC Bd Election & Ethics, 1984-; bd mem, Bettie Benjamin Scholar Funds, 1984-87; St. Anthony's Gospel Choir; Betty Benjamin Scholar Fund; treas, Cath Libr Asn. **Honors/Awds:** Girl Scout Council Award, 1974; William R Spaulding Award, 1981. **Home Addr:** 1228 Brentwood Rd NE, Washington, DC 20018. **Business Addr:** Librarian, Media Specialist, St Francis de Sales School, 2019 RI Ave NE, Washington, DC 20018, **Business Phone:** (202)529-5394.

## BINGHAM, PORTER B.

Executive. **Educ:** Morehouse Col, attended 1983. **Career:** Malachi Group Inc, pres & chief exec officer, 1997-, Malachi Financial Prod Inc, owner, chief exec officer, currently; MuniDirect, pres, chief exec officer & chmn; Robinson Bingham Financial Serv, founder. **Orgs:** Exec bd mem, Nat Asn Securities Professionals. **Business Addr:** President, Chief Executive Officer, Malachi Group Inc, 75 Ponce De Leon Ave NE Suite 102, Atlanta, GA 30308, **Business Phone:** (404)237-3031.

## BINGHAM, REBECCA TAYLOR

Educator, librarian, commissioner. **Personal:** Born Jul 14, 1928, Indianapolis, IN; married Walter D; children: Gail Elaine Simmons & Louis Edward Simmons. **Educ:** Ind Univ, BS, 1950, MLS, 1969; Univ Tulsa, MA, 1961. **Career:** Alcorn A&M Col, asst librn, 1950-51; Tuskegee Inst, serials librn, 1952-55; Jarvis Christian Col, actg librn, 1955-57; Indianapolis Pub Libr, librn sch serv dept, 1957; Tulsa Jr High Sch, librn, 1960-62; Russell Jr High Sch, eng teacher, 1962-63; Jackson Jr High Sch, librn, 1963-66; Louisville Pub Sch, supvr libr serv, 1966-70, dir media serv, 1970-75; KY Pub Schs, Jefferson Co, dir media serv, 1975-00; US Nat Comn Libr & Info Sci, comnr, 1998-. **Orgs:** Alumni Bd Grad Libr Sch; chmn, Am Asn Sch Librns; Am Sch Coun Asn; Joint Media Com; pres, Ky Libr Asn, 1971; Ky Govs State Adv Coun Libr, 1971-73; AASL Nat Libr Week Com; Coun Am Libr Asn, 1972-; Ala Com Planning, 1973-; vpres, Alumni Asn Grad Libr Sch, 1973-74; Ky Lib Asn Legis Com, 1973-74; secy treas, S E Reg Libr Asn Resources & Tech Serv Div, 1973-75; exec bd, Am Libr Asn, 1974-78; pres, Alumni Bd Grad Libry Sch, 1974-75; adv com, Bro-Dart Elem Sch Lib Collection, 1975-77; Britannica Jr, 1975-76; com exec bd, Ky Asn Super & Curric Develop, 1976-77; KY Sch Supt Adv Coun Super, 1977-; World Bk, 1977-79; White House Conf Libr & Info Serv, 1978-79; pres, Am Asn Sch Librn, 1979-80; Louisville Jefferson Co Health & Welfare Coun Bd dir; pres, Southeastern Libr Asn, 1984-86; sch adminr, Jefferson Co 1985-86. **Special Achievements:** First African American president of the Kentucky Library Association. **Home Addr:** 3608 Dumesnil St, Louisville, KY 40211, **Home Phone:** (502)772-6933.

## BIOKO, TIKARI. See WINBUSH, DR. RAYMOND ARNOLD.

## BIRCH, WILLIE

Artist. **Personal:** Born Nov 26, 1942, New Orleans, LA; son of Wilson and Anna; children: Christopher, Postelle, Ama & Freedom. **Educ:** Southern Univ, attended 1961, BA, 1969; Md Inst, Col Art, MFA, 1973. **Career:** Bowie State Col, teacher, 1973; Selected Studio Mus Harlem, artist resident, 1977-78; Henry St Settlement, teacher, 1980; Henry St Settlement, artist-in-residence, 1980-81; Guggenheim Mus, teacher, 1981; visual artist fel, 1984-85; Hunter Col, teacher, 1988-96, artist, currently; Coun Arts, Nat Endowment Arts, New York, NY, visual artist fel, 1989-90; Lila Wallace, Readers Dig, int artists fel, 1992; John Simon Guggenheim, Memorial Found fel, 1993; Tamarind Inst, artist-in-residence, 2000; New Orleans Jazz & Heritage Found, artist-in-residence, 2002. **Orgs:** Arthur Roger Gallery, New Orleans; New York Metro Transit Authority, Arts Transit, Philadelphia Int Airport, 1994; Munic Collab Proj, Downtown Winston-Salem, 1995. **Honors/Awds:** Artist's Fellowship Award, painting, New York Found Arts, 1986; Minority Third World Fellowship Award, Printmaking Workshop, 1987; Mayor's Arts Award, New Orleans, 2002; Grant recipient, Joan Mitchell Found, 2006. **Home Addr:** 2022 N Villerre St, New Orleans, LA 70116-1514, **Home Phone:** (212)614-9061. **Business Addr:** Artist, Arthur Roger Gallery, 432 Julia St, New Orleans, LA 70130, **Business Phone:** (504)522-1999.

## BIRCHETTE, DR. WILLIAM ASHBY, III

Educator. **Personal:** Born May 9, 1942, Newport News, VA; children: Stacy Olivia Edwards & William Ashby Birchette, IV. **Educ:** St Augustine Col, BA, 1964; Va State Univ, MEd, 1973; Univ Va, EdD, 1982. **Career:** Educator (retired); UVA, Charles Stewart Mott Fel, 1980; Darden HS, teacher & coach; DE Tech & Community Col, teacher, Eng & Community Ed; Johnson JHS, teacher; Banneker JHS, prin; Reservoir MS, prin; Magruder MS, prin; DC Pub Sch, asst to reg supt; S Vance HS, prin; Isle Wight Cty Sch, asst supt; Spotsylvania County Sch, supvr, Eng Lang Arts; Twenty-Five Outstanding High Schs, NC Dept Educ, prin, 1991; Prince William County Pub Sch, assoc supt, 2004. **Orgs:** Omega Psi Phi; PDK; NABSE; ASCD; Optimist Club; Nat Asn Advan Colored People; exec secy, ATA; Achievable Dream; exec bd, Northern VA Workforce Investment Comm. **Home Addr:** 13010 Garden View Lane Apt Suite 106, Raleigh, NC 27614, **Home Phone:** (919)435-8659.

## BIRCHETTE-PIERCE, DR. CHERYL L.

Physician. **Personal:** Born Sep 25, 1945, New Orleans, LA; married Samuel H II; children: Samuel Howard. **Educ:** Spelman Col, AB, 1967; Meharry Med Col, MD, 1972; Harvard Univ, MPH, 1980. **Career:** Joslin Clin, patient mgt/instr, 1972-75; Lahey Clin NE Deaconess Hosp, intern resident, 1972-75; Peter Bent Brigham Hosp, ambulatory care doctor, 1973-74; Harvard Univ Med Sch, instr med, 1973-80; NE Baptist Hosp, critical care cpr physician coord, 1975-78; Roxbury Dent Med Group, med dir, 1976-80; McLean Hosp, consult internal med, 1976-80; MIT-HMO Cambridge, Mass, dir health screening physician provider, 1981-86; US Dept Health & Human Serv, pub health serv, 1982; pvt pract clinician. **Orgs:** TV/conf/health workshop appearances varied health issues, 1974-; attend physician, US Olympic Team Pan Am Games, 1975; sec house delegates third vpres, Nat Med Asn, 1983-85, 1986-; work group partic Health Policy Agenda AMA, 1985-86; Am Pub Health Asn. **Honors/Awds:** Merrill Scholarship Study & Travel Faculte de Medicine, Univ Geneva, Switzerland, 1966-67; Outstanding Young Women in America, 1973; US Dept of Health Human Serv Fel, 1980-81; Keynote/Founder's Day Speaker, Delta Sigma Theta, 1981. **Home Addr:** 2353 Manor Ave, East Point, GA 30344-1062. **Business Addr:** Physician, Private Practice, 91 Parker Hill Ave, Boston, MA 02120.

**BIRDINE, STEVEN T.**
Administrator, president (organization). **Personal:** married Andrienne R Homer. **Educ:** Univ Ill, BS, news ed jour, 1981, MS, radio tv jour, 1983. **Career:** Affirmations Action!, pres & cheif exec officer, founder, 1999-; Iota Phi Theta, grand polaris, 2001-05. **Orgs:** Nat pres, lota Phi Theta Fraternity Inc, Grand Polaris; Am Col Personnel Asn. **Home Addr:** 3001 Hewitt Ave Suite 390, Silver Spring, MD 20906, **Home Phone:** (301)460-2956. **Business Addr:** President, Chief Executive officer, Affirmations In Action, 8417 Locust Grove Dr, Laurel, MD 20707, **Business Phone:** (317)590-6484.

**BIRRU, DR. MULUGETTA**
Government official. **Personal:** Born Sep 30, 1946, Tig-Ray; son of Mizan Berbe and Birru Sibhat; married Elizabeth; children: Elizabeth, Meheret & Rahel. **Educ:** Addis Ababa Univ, BA, mgt & acct, 1970; Syracuse Univ, MA, econ, 1975, MBA, bus & int finance, 1974; Univ Pittsburgh, PhD, pub & int affairs, 1991. **Career:** Agr & Ind develop Bank, Ethiopia, sr vpres, sr proj eval & res officer, 1970-75; Ethopian Beverage Corp, dir planning & bus develop, 1975-78; Nat Chem Corp, gen mgr & chief exec officer, 1978-80; Seminole Econ Develop Corp, v pres & dir bus develop, 1980-83; Home wood-Brushton RDC, exec dir, 1983-92; Urban Redevelop Authority Pittsburgh, exec dir, 1992-2004; Allegheny County Econ Develop, exec dir, 1997-99; Greater Wayne Co Econ Develop Corp, chief exec officer, exec dir, pres, 2004-08; Nat Beverages Corp, dep chief exec officer; MGB & Assocs, pres, chief exec officer, 2009-. **Orgs:** Bd mem, Pittsburgh Downtown Partnership; bd mem, Pittsburgh Partnership Neighborhood Develop; bd mem, I Have A Dream Found, 1993; adj prof, Carnegie Mellon Univ, 1994-03; adj prof, Heinz Sch Pub Policy & Mgt. **Business Addr:** President, Chief Executive Officer, MGB & Associates, LLC, 1211 W Boston Blvd, Detroit, MI 48202, **Business Phone:** (313)492-6928.

**BIRTHA, JESSIE M.**
Librarian. **Personal:** Born Feb 5, 1920, Norfolk, VA; married Herbert M; children: Rachel Roxanne Eitches & Rebecca Lucille. **Educ:** Hampton Inst, BS, 1940; Drexel Univ, MLS, 1962. **Career:** Librarian (retired); Pa Sch St Helena Island SC, sec sch teacher, 1941-42; Norfolk, elem sch teacher, 1942-46; Free Libr Philadelphia, br librn, 1959-80; Antioch Grad Sch, lit instr, adj fac Philadelphia Ctr, 1975-76. **Orgs:** Pub consult, McGraw Hill Lang Arts Prog Am Lang Today, 1974; Am Libr Asn; Pa Libr Asn; Newbery Medal Selection Comt, 1974. **Home Addr:** 433 Glen Echo Rd, Philadelphia, PA 19119-2915, **Home Phone:** (215)248-9550.

**BISAMUNYU, JEANETTE**
Marketing executive. **Personal:** Born Kabale; daughter of Eli Nathan and Irene Rosemary. **Educ:** Makerere Univ, Kampala, Bcom, 1981; Talladega Col, BA, 1983; Atlanta Univ, MBA, 1985. **Career:** Talladega Col, stud tutor, 1981-83; Equitable Life Assurance Soc, mgt intern, 1982; Atlanta Univ, grad asst, 1984-85; Citicorp Acceptance Co, mgt intern, 1984; US W, mgr, 1985-91; Dale Carnegie Commun Course, grad asst, 1987; Environ Educ Solutions, gen mgr, 1991-; Global Insight, reg bus mgr, 2004-. **Orgs:** Vpres, Toastmasters Int, 1985-90; co-chmn bd, Nebraskans Peace, 1988-; mentor, Vision HOPE Prog, 1988-; choir dir, Church Resurrection, organist, 1991; Nat Asn Female Exec; Am Asn Univ Women; Omaha Womens Chamber Com. **Honors/Awds:** Alpha Chi, 1983; Certificate of Honor for Student with Highest GPA Business, 1983; Beta Gamma Sigma, 1985; Nebr Music Olympics, piano performance, gold trophy, 1988, 1989, 1991, bronze medal, 1990.Toastmasters Int, vpres, 1985-90; Dale Carnegie Commun Course, grad asst, 1987; Nebraskans Peace, co-chair the bd, 1988-; Vision HOPE Prog, mentor, 1988-; Church Resurrection, organist & choir dir, 1991; Nat Asn Female Exec, 1991-; Am Asn Univ Women, 1991-; Omaha Womens Chamber Com, 1991-. **Home Addr:** 181 W 135th St Apt 4e, New York, NY 10030-2900, **Home Phone:** (212)283-3178. **Business Addr:** Regional Business Manager, Global Insight USA Inc, 530 5th Ave 7th Fl, New York, NY 10036, **Business Phone:** (212)884-9513.

**BISHOP, DR. ALFRED A.**
College teacher. **Personal:** Born May 10, 1923, Philadelphia, PA; son of Samuel and Rose; children: Janet L. **Educ:** Univ Pittsburgh, BS, chem, 1950, MS, chem, 1965; Carnegie Mellon Univ, PhD, 1974. **Career:** Naval Res, engr, 1950-52; Fischer & Porter Co, engr, mgr, 1952-56; Westing house Corp, engr, 1956-65, Carnegie Mellon Univ, lectr, 1967-69; thermal & hydraul design & develop, mgr, reactor safety, 1965-70; Westinghouse Corp Nuclear Energy, consult engr, 1970-85; Univ Pittsburgh, res prof, 1970-74, assoc prof, chem engineering, dir, nuclear engineering prog, 1974-80, full prof, 1981-85, prof emer; BB Nuclear Energy Consult, partner, 1974-. **Orgs:** Am Indian Coun Architects & Engrs, 1960-; Am Soc Mech Engrs; Am Welding Soc; bd dir, United Fund, 1969-73; Am Soc Elec Engrs; bd dir, Pa Youth Ctr, 1973-; sr life master, Am Bridge Asn. **Home Addr:** 50 Belmont Ave Apt 210, Bala Cynwyd, PA 19004-2410, **Home Phone:** (610)664-5381.

**BISHOP, BLAINE ELWOOD, JR.**
Football player, football coach, radio host. **Personal:** Born Jul 24, 1970, Indianapolis, IN; married Cella Butler. **Educ:** Ball State Univ, BS. **Career:** Football player (retired), coach, host; Houston Oilers, defensive back, 1993, strong safety, 1994-96; Tenn Oilers, strong safety, 1997-2001; Philadelphia Eagles, safety, 2002; WTVF, commentator; WGFX, Three Hour Lunch, co-host, currently; Davidson Acad, defense coach, currently; KMG Sports Mgt. **Honors/Awds:** Pro Bowl, 1995, 1996, 1997, 2000. **Special Achievements:** Films: Dead Tone, exec producer, 2007; NFL Draft, 1993; AFC Championship Game, 2000; Super Bowl, 2000. **Business Addr:** Defense Coach, Davidson Academy, 1414 Old Hickory Blvd, Nashville, TN 37207, **Business Phone:** (615)860-5300.

**BISHOP, CLARENCE T.**
Administrator, executive director. **Personal:** Born Feb 19, 1959, Selma, AL; married Deidra N. **Educ:** Morgan State Univ, Baltimore, BA, maths, MA, urban planning & pub policy. **Career:** Lake Pk Day Care Ctr, coun, 1977-78; Mission Immaculate Virgin Group Home, sr counr, 1978-79, child care worker, 1980-81; Wagner Col, asst lead teacher, 1980; NY State Div Youth, asst supvr; Baltimore City Mayor Martin OMalley, chief staff; Md Dept Bus Econ Develop, dep secy, 2007-09; US Under Secy Com, asst; US Consumer Prod Safety Comn, dep exec dir; Ga Congressman, chief staff; Md Congressman, chief staff; Nat Nuclear Security Admin, assoc adminr external affairs, 2009-, dir off cong intergovernmental & pub affairs, currently. **Orgs:** Organized Lake View Pk Basketball Leaguen teenagers; founder & regional dir & advisor, Sigma Phi Rho Fraternity; bus mgr, Nat Gov Coun, Sigma Phi Rho; Hon Soc Art; Cath Youth Orgn Basketball League; Rutgers Univ Pro-Basketball League; Baltimore City Planning Comn; Baltimore Hotel Corp; Downtown Partnership Baltimore; Baltimore Develop Corp; E Baltimore Develop Inc; Nat Aquarium Baltimore; Reginald F Lewis Mus Md African Am Hist & Cult. **Honors/Awds:** New York State Division for Youth's Regional Director Award, Acad Excellence & Career Develop; Founders Achievement Award, Sigma Phi Rho Fraternity. **Home Addr:** 10001 Windstream Dr Suite 100, Columbia, MD 21044-2532. **Business Addr:** Associate Administrator for External Affairs, National Nuclear Security Administration, 1000 Independence Ave SW, Washington, DC 20585, **Business Phone:** (202)586-5000.

**BISHOP, ELLEN ELIZABETH GRANT**
Government official. **Personal:** Born Mar 25, 1949, Buffalo, NY; daughter of Herman J Grant and Verba M Myers; married George M Jr; children: Justin Mason. **Educ:** State Univ NY, Buffalo, BA, 1972, MSW, 1974, PhD, 1979; Medaille Col, DHL, Honis Causa, 1996. **Career:** Erie County Med Ctr, licensed practical nurse, 1968-74; Buffalo Gen Hosp, prog coord, dep dir & asst vpres, 1973-83, vpres, 1983-88; Buffalo Psy chiat Ctr, social worker, actg team leader, 1975-80; Cornell Univ, Ny Sch Labor Rels, instr, 1983-85; State Univ New York, dept psychiat, clin instr, 1985-; Erie County, Dept Ment Health, comnr ment health, 1988-; Sch Social Work, clin asst prof, 1990-; D'Youville Col, asst prof, 1993-; County Ment Health Ctr, admin; Health now New York Inc, vpres community affairs, 2005-; Nih, dir. **Orgs:** Acad Cert Social Workers, 1974-; NY State Cert Social Workers, 1974-; Am Col Ment Health Admin; vpres & bd mgr, Buffalo & Erie County Hist Soc, 1991-; Neighborhood House; Western New York Women's Fund; bd mem, Trocaire Col, 1992-; bd mem, State Univ New York, 1994-; pres, Ny Asn Counties, Albany, 1996-97; fel, Am Col Ment Health Adninstrs; bd dir, Buffalo Found; trustee, St. Bonaventure Univ. **Special Achievements:** Author, Managing in Black and White: A Guide for the Professional Woman of Color, 1992. **Home Addr:** 89 Huntley Rd, Buffalo, NY 14215. **Business Addr:** Vice President of Community Affairs, HealthNow New York Inc, 1901 Main St, Buffalo, NY 14240-0080, **Business Phone:** (716)887-6900.

**BISHOP, ERIC MARLON. See FOXX, JAMIE.**

**BISHOP, RONALD L. (RON BISHOP)**
Government official, executive director. **Personal:** Born Apr 24, 1949, Lewisburg, TN; son of David D and Erma L; married Sharon Wooten; children: Jennifer & Meredith. **Educ:** Fisk Univ, BS, health & phys educ, 1970; Tenn State Univ, attended 1971. **Career:** Tenn Dept Correction, assoc warden security, 1976-79, dir rehab servs, 1979-80, dir instnl progs, 1980-83, dir spec progs, 1983, asst to comnr, 1983, dep comnr, 1983-85; Tenn Bd Paroles, chmn parole bd, 1986-87, bd mem, 1988-90; Shelby Co Govt, Div Correction, dir, 1990-94, chief, 1995-98, Div Community Corrections, dir; Tenn Legis Comn, Tenn sentencing comn, mem, 1987; City Mayor WW Herenton, Transition Team, criminal justice comm, 1991; NACO, justice & pub safety steering comm, mem, 1991-95; Shelby Co Group, United Way, chmn, 1992; Mayor's Black-on-Black Crime Task Force, 1992; Fayette County, dir jail, jailer; Ky Dept Juv Justice, comnr; Jefferson County Fairgrounds, vpres; Fayette County Detention Ctr, bd mem & dir, currently; Ky Ctr Sch Safety, bd mem; Lexington Pub Safety Mus, Exec Bd, mem, currently. **Orgs:** Bd dir, Free the Cn, 1991-94; Leadership Memphis Class, 1992. **Honors/Awds:** Jonathan Jasper Wright Award, Nat Asn Blacks Criminal Justice, 1992. **Special Achievements:** Author: "Shelby Co Inmate Training Emphasizes Local Labor Market", Large Jail Network Bulletin, 1992. **Home Addr:** 2305 Fallsview Rd, Louisville, KY 40207, **Home Phone:** (502)899-5579. **Business Addr:** Director, Board Member, Fayette County Detention Center, 600 Old Frankfort Circle, Lexington, KY 40510, **Business Phone:** (859)425-2700.

**BISHOP, SANFORD DIXON, JR.**
Lawyer. **Personal:** Born Feb 4, 1947, Mobile, AL; son of Sanford D Sr and Minnie B Slade; married Vivian Creighton; children: Aayesha J Reese. **Educ:** Morehouse Col, BA, 1968; Emory Law Sch, JD, 1971. **Career:** Civil rights atty; Ga State House Reps, 1977-90; Ga State Senate, 1991-92; US House Reps, Ga second cong dist, 1993-. **Orgs:** Eagle Scout; 32nd Degree Mason; Shriner; Sigma Pi Phi Fraternity; Kappa Alpha Psi Fraternity; Urban League; Cong Black Caucus; Blue Dog Dem Conservative Coalition House; State Bar Ga; Ala State Bar; Am Bar asn; Nat Bar Asn; trustee, Mt Zion Baptist Church; House Comt Appropriations; Nat Rifle Asn; Peanut Caucus; Rural Health Care Coalition; Rural Caucus; Nat Guard & Res Components Caucus; Air Power Caucus; Depot Caucus; C's Working Group; Law Enforcement Caucus; Nat Security Caucus; Impact Aid Coalition; Vietnam Era Veterans Cong; Arts Caucus; portsmen's Caucus; Fire Serv Caucus; Fed Govt Serv Caucus; Motorsports Caucus; privately-funded res & educ orgn; Coun Foreign Rels; pres, Bishop State Community Col. **Business Addr:** Congressman, United States House of Representatives, 2429 Rayburn House Off Bldg, Washington, DC 20515-1002, **Business Phone:** (202)225-3631.

**BISHOP, SHERRE WHITNEY (SHERRE MILLER)**
Public relations executive, writer. **Personal:** Born Sep 2, 1958, Nashville, TN; daughter of Carrie Pillow and Christian Lytle; married Joseph; children: Joseph Jr. **Educ:** Tenn State Univ, BS, speech commun & theatre, 1982, MA, Eng, 1994; Am Baptist Col, ThB, bible theol, 2001. **Career:** WPTF-TV, news reporter, 1984-89; Meharry Med Col, media rel specialist, 1989-91; Black Entertainment TV, freelance reporter, 1989-94; Tenn State Univ, producer/pub info officer, 1991-94, dir pub rels currently; WVOL Radio, producer/talk show host, 1992-94; WLAC-TV, talk show host, 1993-94; WB TV Network, WB-channel 58, news brief anchor & pub affair dir, 1995-99; Christian Comedienne, corp speaker & comedienne, 2006-; Nashville Airport Authority, pub/community affairs mgr; WQQK, host; WMDB, host; WMDB, host; WQQK, host. **Orgs:** Bd mem, Int Asn Bus Communicators, 1994-; comt mem, Nashville Area Chamber Com, 1994-; comt mem, Mayor's Transp Workshop, 1994-; comt mem, Save Our Black Female Adolescents Proj, 1995-; Mt Zion Baptist Church. **Honors/Awds:** Volunteer Service Award, Bethlehem Ctr, 1991; Scholarship Award, CASE District III, 1991; Raymond Black Service Award, Nashville Peace Officers Asn, 1993; Journalistic Achievement Award, Soc Prof Journalists, 1995. **Special Achievements:** Author: "Auntie's Grace," entered Essence Magazine writing contest, 1993; Playwright: How I Got Over, 1991; Supporting actress in Ossie Daviss, "Purlie," 1991; Just Like Me (A Black History Series), 1992; The Great Train Ride, 1978; From the Motherland to the Promised Land, 2005 (an award-winning monologue chronicling the African American worship experience); Hands, 2003; and The Virtuous Woman, 2004; Certainly Lord; Gods Trombones, 2007; Films: The 6 Dollar man; Ought; The Secret Closet; Stage Play: He Can Do It!, 2008; Roosters Crow; Join Hands with the Badge; The River Niger; Purlie; The First Lady of Christian Comedy. **Home Addr:** PO Box 281321, Nashville, TN 37228, **Home Phone:** (615)963-5317. **Business Addr:** Director of Public Relations, Tennessee State University, 3500 John A Merritt Blvd, Nashville, TN 37209, **Business Phone:** (615)963-5331.

**BISHOP, VERISSA RENE**
Law enforcement officer. **Personal:** Born Nov 22, 1954, Houston, TX; daughter of Julia Lee (deceased). **Educ:** Tex Southern Univ, BA, 1987. **Career:** Foley's Dept Store, Houston, Tex, receptionist & beauty operator, 1973-75; Houston Police Dept, Houston, Tex, clerk dispatchers div, 1975-78, police officer, 1978-90, juv div sgt, 1990-. **Orgs:** Bd mem & secy, Afro-Am Police Officers League; fin secy, Nat Black Police Asn, secy & bd mem; YWCA; Phi Beta Lambda; City Wide Beauticians; Christian Hope Baptist Church; Nat Asn Advan Colored People. **Honors/Awds:** Member of Year, Afro-American Police Officers League; Member of Year, National Black Police Asn, 1990; Outstanding Member of Southern Region, National Black Police Asn. **Home Addr:** 3829 Wichita St, Houston, TX 77004. **Business Addr:** Sergeant, Houston Police Department, 61 Riesner, Houston, TX 77001, **Business Phone:** (713)880-6000.

**BISHOP, ESQ. WESLEY T.**
Lawyer. **Personal:** Born New Orleans, LA; son of Elder Willie and Margie; married Shannon Bruno; children: John. **Educ:** Southern Univ, BS, criminal justice, 1990; Univ Miss, MpA, pub admin, 1991; Ohio State Univ Law Sch, JD, 1995; Harvard Univ, Inst Educ Mgt, 2009. **Career:** Orleans Parish Dist Attys Off, law clerk; New Orleans Legal Assistance Corp, law clerk; New Orleans City Coun Res Off, legis intern; New Orleans Health Corp, chmn; Orleans Parish Dem Exec Comm, vchmn; La Dem State Cent Comt, House Dist 101, rep, 2004; Southern Univ New Orleans, chmn & asst prof criminal justice, 1998-2003, asst prof criminal justice & assoc vice chancellor acad affairs, 2007-, dean, sch grad studies, 2006-08, atty & advisor; Univ Northern Iowa, Dept Sociol, Anthrop & Criminol, vis prof, 2000-05; B Ray & Assocs Consult Group, atty & managing partner, currently; Spears & Spears, coun, currently; State LA, state rep dist 101, 2011; WesleyBishop.com, pres & chief exec officer, currently; La Legis Black Caucus, 1st vice chair, 2012-; State LA, state rep dist 99. **Orgs:** Bd dir, Am Bar Asn; bd Dir, N.O.J.A. Govs Adv Comn Equal Opportunities; bd dir, La State Bar Asn; bd dir, Nat Bar Asn; bd dir, Louis A Martinet Legal Soc; bd dir, Alpha Phi Alpha Fraternity; Beacon Light Baptist Church; Nat Speakers Asn; Acad Criminal Justice Sci; judge, New Orleans Teen Ct Prog; bd dir, Louis Armstrong Int Airport; bd dirs, LE Rabouin High Sch; bd dirs, New Orleans Charter Sch Found; Dem State Cent Comt, 101st Dist; vol atty, La Election Protection Proj; fel Comt Better New Orleans; fel, Metrop Area Comt; bd commissioners, Spring Lake Spec Taxing Dist; vpres & bd dirs, Spring Lake Neighborhood Asn. **Honors/Awds:** Outstanding Alumnus, Southern Univ New Orleans, 1997; Outstanding Orator Award, Ohio State Univ; deleg, Democratic National Convention, 2005; One of the Top 30 Leaders under 30 nationwide, Ebony Magazine; SUNO Alumnus of the Year; NCEOA and NAFEO National Alumni of the Year; SWASAP Regional Alumni of the Year; Loyola University Leader for Life Award; La Army Nat Guard Distinguished Serv Medal. **Home Addr:** 1555 Poydras St Suite 1710, New Orleans, LA 70112, **Home Phone:** (504)593-9500. **Business Addr:** Associate Vice Chancellor for Academic Affairs, Assistant Professor of Criminal Justice, Southern University at New Orleans, 6400 Press Dr Bldg 22B Admin 202A, New Orleans, LA 70126, **Business Phone:** (504)286-5326.

**BISWAS, DR. PROSANTO K.**
Educator. **Personal:** Born Mar 1, 1934, Calcutta, WB; married Joan; children: Shila. **Educ:** Univ Calcutta, BS, agr, 1958; Univ Mo, MS, hort, 1959, PhD, hort & physiol, 1962. **Career:** Univ Mo, res assoc, 1961; Tuskegee Univ, Tuskegee Inst Campus, Dept Agr & Environ Sci, prof plant & soil sci, 1962-, Tuskegee Realty, pres, 1975; head, currently. **Orgs:** Acad Personnel Comt; Fac Achievement Award Comt; Curric Comt; Macon County Bd Educ; chmn, Macon County Chamber Com. **Home Addr:** 608 S Main St, Tuskegee, AL 36083. **Business Addr:** Professor, Head, Tuskegee University, Tuskegee Institute, Tuskegee, AL 36088-1634, **Business Phone:** (334)727-8446.

**BIVENS, SHELIA RENEEA**
Nurse. **Personal:** Born Jul 10, 1954, Pine Bluff, AR; daughter of Leon J and Myrtle Jones Ervin; children: Cory, Ronnie & Ronniesha. **Educ:** Univ Ariz, Fayetteville, attended 1974; Univ AMS, Col Nursing, BSN, 1977, MNSC, 1982. **Career:** Dr C E Hyman, nurse practitioner, 1977-81; Jefferson Regional Med Ctr, charge nurse, 1981-83; Univ AMS, Univ Hosp, staff nurse, 1983-89, charge nurse, 1989-; Ark Cares, obstet gynec nurse & practr, currently. **Orgs:** Ark State Nurses Asn, 1977-; secy, state secy, Little Rock Br, Nat Asn Advan Colored People, 1983-84; chap pianist, 19 Elect Chap 5 OES, 1984; Ariz Black Nurses Asn, 1987; Ark Perinatal Asn, 1987; Sigma Theta Tau Nursing Hon Soc, 1989-; Nat Perinatal Asn; Napare. **Honors/Awds:** Outstanding Youth Award, Livingstone Col Gen Educ African Methodist Episcopal Zion Church, 1970; Outstanding Service Award, OES Electa Chap 5, 1983; Five Year Service Award, Univ AMS, 1989; Outstanding Black Employee of the Month, Univ AMS, 1989. **Home Addr:** 54 Saxony Cir, Little Rock, AR 72209, **Home Phone:** (501)568-7642. **Business**

Addr: Nurse, University Hospital, 4301 W Markham Slot 711 A, Little Rock, AR 72205, **Business Phone:** (501)661-7987.

## BIVINS, CYNTHIA GLASS

Lawyer. **Personal:** Born Dec 10, 1955, Houston, TX; daughter of Raymond and Mattye; married Demetrius K; children: Demetrius K II & Emily Jewel. **Educ:** Tufts Univ, BA, polit sci, 1978; Univ Tex, Law Sch, JD, 1981. **Career:** Harris County Dist Atty's Off, asst dist atty, 1981-83; William & MaryCol, asst vis prof, 1983; Bexar County Dist Atty Off, asst dist atty, 1984-88; Groce, Locke & Hebdon, PC, shareholder, 1988-96; Jenkens & Gilchrist, PC, shareholder, 1996-; Ogletree, Deakins, Nash, Smoak & Stewart, PC, shareholder, 2001-; Shell Oil Co, corp coun, sr coun, currently. **Orgs:** San Antonio Bar Asn, 1989-; San Antonio Black Lawyers Asn, 1989-; Bexar County Women's Bar Asn, former bd mem, 1989; Nat Bar Asn, 1989-; Am Bar Asn, 1989-; Fed Bar Asn, 1990-; Jack & Jill Am, prog chair sandboxers, 1999-, mem, 2001-02; Links Inc, 1999-; bd mem employ law comt chair, Defense Res Inst, 2001-03; State Bar Tex. **Special Achievements:** Defense Research Organization's for the Defense, 1999, 2001. **Home Addr:** 100 W Houston St Suite 1700, San Antonio, TX 78205, **Home Phone:** (210)277-3610. **Business Addr:** Attorney, Ogletree, Deakins, Nash, Smoak & Stewart PC, 191 Peachtree St NE Suite 4800, Atlanta, GA 30303, **Business Phone:** (404)881-1300.

## BIVINS, DEMETRIUS K.

Lawyer. **Educ:** Univ Tex, JD, 1982. **Career:** Lawer (retired); City Pub Serv, atty. **Orgs:** Vice chair, Grievance Oversight Comt, 2007-; Chair, African-Am Lawyers Sect, State Bar Tex; adv, Comt Ct Security; vice chair, Mil Lawyers Sect; State Comn Judicial Conduct. **Home Addr:** 9220 Marymont Pk, San Antonio, TX 78217, **Home Phone:** (210)656-2361. **Business Addr:** Vice-Chair, The Grievance Oversight Committee, PO Box 12487, Austin, TX 78711, **Business Phone:** (512)427-4108.

## BIVINS, HON. SONJA F.

Judge. **Personal:** Born Mobile, AL. **Educ:** Spring Hill Col, BS, 1985; Univ Ala, JD, 1988. **Career:** Law clerk; Mack & McLean firm; Minority Corp Coun Asn, magistrate judge; McGuireWoods, Atlanta, partner; US Dist Ct, Southern Dist Ala, fed magistrate judge, 2003-. **Orgs:** State Bar Ga; Just Beginning Found; pres, DeKalb Lawyers Asn; bd mem, DeKalb Rape Crisis Ctr; trustee, Spring Hill Col, 2007. **Business Addr:** Federal Magistrate Judge, US District Court, 113 St Joseph St, Mobile, AL 36602, **Business Phone:** (251)694-4545.

## BLACK, ALBERT, JR.

Administrator, president (organization), chief executive officer. **Personal:** Born Jul 24, 1959, Dallas, TX; son of Albert Sr; married Gwyneith; children: Oliver Victor, Albert C III & Cora Rene. **Educ:** W W Samuel High Sch, Dallas, attended; Univ Tex, Dallas, BA, bus & polit sci, 1982; Cox Sch Bus, Southern Methodist Univ, MBA, 1995. **Career:** On-Target Supplies & Logistics, pres, 1982-, chief exec officer, currently; OTSL Charities, 2006; ReadyToWork, 2006; Weblink Wireless Inc, dir, 2000-; Southern Methodist Univ, Edwin L Cox Sch Bus, dir. **Orgs:** Bd regent, Tex Southern Univ, Houston, 1977; bd dir, Cox Sch Bus; bd dir; Baylor Univ, Hankamer Sch Bus; adv bd mem, Oncor Energy; bd gov, Dallas Found; trustee, Baylor Univ Med Ctr; adv bd, Chase Bank; bd dir, Dallas-Tex; bd mem, Paul Quinn Col; Dallas Citizens Coun; Gov George Bush's Bus Coun; Omega Psi Phi; New Hope Baptist Church; chmn, Greater Dallas Chamber Com, 2000; treas, Tex State Sen Royce W.; bd advisor, JP Morgan Chase Tex; dir, Rees Assocs; Prime Source Food Equip Co; chmn, Baylor Health Care Syst, 2010; trustee, chmn, Physicians Realty Trust, 2013-; trustee, St Louis Univ; Capital One Tex Client Adv Bd; trustee, Baylor Health Care Syst Diabetes Health & Wellness Inst. **Home Addr:** 751 Kessler Lake Dr, Dallas, TX 75208, **Home Phone:** (214)941-0162. **Business Addr:** President, Chief Executive Officer, On-Target Supplies & Logistics, 1133 S Madison Ave, Dallas, TX 75208, **Business Phone:** (214)941-4885.

## BLACK, BARRY C.

Military leader, chaplain. **Personal:** Born Nov 1, 1948, Baltimore, MD; married Brenda Pearsall; children: Barry II, Brendan & Bradford. **Educ:** Oakwood Col; Andrews Univ; NC Cent Univ, MA, coun; Eastern Baptist Sem, DMin; Salve Regina Col, MA, mgt; US Int Univ, PhD, psychol. **Career:** USN, chaplain (retired); US Senate, chaplain, 2003-. **Orgs:** Nat Asn Advan Colored People. **Honors/Awds:** Meritorious Service Medals (twice); Navy & Marine Corps Commendation Medals (twice); Renowned Service Award, Nat Asn Advan Colored People, 1995; Benjamin Elijah Mays Distinguished Leadership Award, Morehouse Sch Religion, 2002; Image Award, "Reaffirming the Dream -- Realizing the Vision" for military excellence, Old Dominion Univ chap, Nat Asn Advan Colored People, 2004. **Special Achievements:** First African-American chaplain to the United States Senate; First Seventh-day Adventist to the United States Senate; First military chaplain to hold the office of chaplain to the United States Senate; First African American to serve as the U.S. Navy Chief of Chaplains; Author: "From the Hood to the Hill", 2006. **Business Addr:** Chaplain, United States Senate, Washington, DC 20510, **Business Phone:** (202)224-3121.

## BLACK, CHARLES E.

Pilot. **Personal:** Born Apr 2, 1943, Bainbridge, GA; children: Harriet & Michael. **Educ:** Purdue Univ, BS, 1964; Ga State Univ, MS, 1976. **Career:** Eastern Airlines Inc, pilot. **Orgs:** Nat Honor Soc, 1960; Alpha Phi Alpha Fraternity, 1961-65; Am Soc Pub Admin, 1971; ford fel GA State Univ, 1971-73; coord, SW Atlanta Comprehensive Comt Planning Workshops, 1974; Orgn Black Airline Pilots. **Honors/Awds:** Best All Around Student, Washington HS, 1960. **Home Addr:** 4350 Janice Dr, College Park, GA 30337. **Business Addr:** Pilot, Eastern Airlines Inc, Flight Opers Hartsfield Int Airport, Atlanta, GA 30354.

## BLACK, DANIEL L., JR.

Government official, chief financial officer. **Personal:** Born Sep 16, 1945, Sheldon, SC; son of Daniel and Susie; married Mary Lemmon; children: Carlita. **Educ:** SC State Col, bus admin, 1971; Univ SC, MBA, 1975. **Career:** Internal Revenue Serv, Jacksonville, exam group mgr, 1976-78, Atlanta, sr regional analyst, 1980-81, exam br chief, 1981-82, Okla City, chief appeals officer, 1983-85, Greensboro Dist, asst dist dir; Laguna Niguel Dist, asst dist dir; Springfield, dist dir; Off Tax & Revenue, dir opers, dep chief financial officer, 2004-. **Orgs:** Am Inst CPA's, 1977-86; Fla Inst CPA's, 1977-; Omega Psi Phi Fraternity, 1978-; Sr Execs Asn, 1985-; Beta Alpha Psi Acct Fraternity; Alpha Kappa Mu, Nat Hon Soc; Greater Wash Soc Cert Pub Accountants. **Honors/Awds:** Distinguished Alumni Award, 1985; Commissioner's Award, Internal Revenue Serv, 2002. **Special Achievements:** Author: The Wall Street Journal, The Tax Advisor, and Alternatives. **Home Addr:** 574 Benfield Rd Suite 103, Severna Park, MD 21146-2530. **Business Addr:** Deputy Chief Financial Officer, Office of Tax & Revenue, John A Wilson Bldg 1350 Pa Ave NW, Washington, DC 20004, **Business Phone:** (202)727-2476.

## BLACK, DAVID EUGENE, SR.

Educator, administrator. **Personal:** Born Nov 9, 1940, Columbus, OH; son of James E and Alberta L; married Marie Robinson; children: David E Jr & Monika L. **Educ:** Cent State Univ, BS, educ, 1964; Xavier Univ, educ admin, 1974. **Career:** Administrator (retired); Vice chmn, Columbus Pub Sch; Columbus Alternative High Sch, asst prin. **Orgs:** Pres, Cent State Alumni Asn, Columbus Br, 1991-92; Nat Alliance Black Sch Educr, 1992; Ohio Asn f Sec Sch Adminr, 1992; Nat Asn Sec Sch Adminr, 1992; Columbus Admin Asn, 1992; Lenden Community Alliance, 1992; Columbus Pub Sch, Multi-Cultured Steering Comt, 1992; vice chmn bd & chaired various comts.

## BLACK, DON GENE

Public relations executive, administrator. **Personal:** Born Sep 6, 1945, Chicago, IL; son of Uster James B and Inez Franklin-Davidson; married Glenda Camp; children: Donerik & Shronda. **Educ:** Sinclair Community Col, attended 1967; Wright State Univ, BA, mass commun & mkt, 1970. **Career:** Dayton Express News, dir pub rels, 1966-68; Monsanto Res Corp, mkt, 1968-70; Don, founder & pres, 1993-. Assoc Photog & Pub Rel Inc, founder & pres, 1970-77; Multi-Western Pub Rel & Mkt Co Inc, founder & pres, 1977-93; MWC Publ Inc, founder & pres, 1993-. **Orgs:** Bd mem, Urban Youth Asn, 1976-81; pres, Ohio Assoc Black PubRel/Advert/Mkt Co, 1983-85; pres, Dayton Chap Nat Bus League, 1983-86; adv bd, Goodwill Industs. **Home Addr:** 703 Angelia Ct, Englewood, CO 45322, **Home Phone:** (937)836-4702. **Business Addr:** President, Founder, MWC Publications Inc, 15 E 4th St Suite 601, Dayton, OH 45402, **Business Phone:** (937)223-8060.

## BLACK, FRANK S.

School administrator, educator. **Personal:** Born Feb 3, 1941, Detroit, MI; son of Frank and Zella Fisher; children: Piper L & Jason B. **Educ:** Cent State Univ, Wilberforce, OH, BS, 1967; Ohio State Univ, MA, 1969, PhD, 1972. **Career:** Columbus Ohio Pub Schs, eval asst, 1969-71; Ohio State Univ, proj dir & adj asst prof, 1972-73; Tex Southern Univ, assoc prof & dir instnl res, 1973-77, assoc prof educ, 1973-78; Murray State Univ, Col Human Develop & Learning, asst dean, 1978-84; Univ Southern Fla, Ft Myers, assoc dean acad affairs, 1984-85; Jackson State Univ, vpres acad affairs, 1985-87; Univ Tenn, Martin, TN, vice chancellor acad affairs, 1988-94, prof educ, 1994-2000, interim vice chancellor acad affairs, 2000-02, interim educ dean, 2002-. **Orgs:** Am Educ Res Asn, 1971-75; Phi Delta Kappa 1974-; mem exec comt, Asn Inst Res, 1977-79; Am Asn Col Teacher Educ, 1979; Murray KY Human Rights Comn, 1979-; adv bd, WKMS Univ Radio Sta, 1979-; adv bd, W Ky Regional Ment Health & Retarded Bd, 1979; Phi Kappa Phi, 1988-; Mid-S Educ Res Asn, 1995; Am Asn Schs, Cols & Univs, 1994. **Home Addr:** 156 Baker Rd, Martin, TN 38237, **Home Phone:** (731)588-0741. **Business Addr:** Interim Dean of Education, The University of Tennessee at Martin, 554 University St, Martin, TN 38237, **Business Phone:** (731)881-7000.

## BLACK, DR. FREDERICK HARRISON

Consultant, executive. **Personal:** Born Nov 11, 1921, Des Moines, IA; son of Frederick H and Aurora (Brooks); married Kay Browne; children: Joan Jackson, Lorna, Jai & Crystal. **Educ:** Fisk Univ, BS, engineering physics, 1949; Univ S Calif, Los Angeles, MS, physics, 1952; Pepperdine Univ, MBA, 1972; Univ MA, DEd Personnel, 1975. **Career:** Burroughs Co, field engineering mgr, 1955-59; Convair Astronaut, sr engr, 1959-60; N Am Aviation, proj engr, 1960-61; Gen Elec Co, Philadelphia, 1961-63; Aerospace corp, 1963-66; Gen Elec Co, mgr minority rels, Fairfield, Conn, 1966-73, mgr equal opportunity, minority rel, safety & security, 1973-75, mgr compliance spec interest group progs corp pub rels, 1975-86; USN, consult chief naval personnel; pres Domestic Coun, consult; Watts Indus Pk, exec dir; FH Black & Assocs, mng partner; FH Black & Assocs, prin exec, currently. **Orgs:** Dipl, Am Personnel Soc; bd pres, TRY US; mem bd, ICBO; bd trustee, Fisk Univ; bd chmn, Myerhoff Fund, 1990-; vpres, Nat Minority Jr Golf Scholar Asn, 1988-; bd dirs, Arts Coun Richmond, 1990-; pres, Bethune Mus Arch; exec dir, Watts Orgn; bd dirs, Interracial Coun, Bus Opportunities & Nat Minority Bus Campaign. **Honors/Awds:** Whitney Young Medal, Nat Urban League; Booker T Wash Award, Nat Bus League; Corp Pioneer Award, Bus Policy Rev Coun. **Special Achievements:** Published numerous articles. **Home Addr:** 13643 Prince William Dr, Midlothian, VA 23114-4532, **Home Phone:** (800)464-1746. **Business Addr:** Managing Partner, Principal Executive, FH Black & Assocs, 529 14th St Suite 1063, Washington, DC 20045, **Business Phone:** (202)588-8764.

## BLACK, GAIL M.

Executive. **Personal:** Born Aug 29, 1950, Klamath Falls, OR; married Carl B Bowles; children: Amil Christopher & Teri Ruth. **Educ:** Portland State Univ, attended 1971; Portland OIC, cert legal sec, 1977. **Career:** Clairon Defender Newspaper, asst ed & pub, 1970-; Union Pac RR Co Law Dept, litigation specialist, 1977-. **Orgs:** Dir, Jimmy Bang-Bang Walker Youth Found, 1969-; chmn, Albina Rose Festival float com prize winning floats Portland Rose Festival Parade, 1969-71; asst, Albina area coord United Good Neighbors, 1970-73; bd mem, Knockout Indust, 1971-; exec bd mem, Tenth Ave Irregulars Chap Toastmasters Int, 1979-; United Way rep Union Pac RR Co, 1979-80; parent adv com mem, NE Christian Sch, 1980-; chair, Rose City Pk Presby Church, currently. **Honors/Awds:** Dean's List, Portland State Univ, 1970-71. **Home Addr:** 6108 NE Sacramento St, Portland, OR 97213, **Home Phone:** (503)284-6221. **Business Addr:** Assistant Editor, Publisher, Clairon Defender Newspaper, 319 NE Wygant St, Portland, OR 97211-4065, **Business Phone:** (503)284-6221.

## BLACK, HAROLD ALONZA

President (organization), chairperson, educator. **Personal:** Born Jul 3, 1945, Atlanta, GA. **Educ:** Univ Ga, BBA, 1966; Ohio State Univ, MA, 1968, PhD, 1972. **Career:** Professor emeritus; HF Ahmanson & Co, Irwindale, Ca, dir; Nashville Br Fed Res Bank Atlanta, dir & chmn; Univ Fla, Dept Econ, Gainesville, FL, asst prof, 1971-75; Dept Econ Res & Anal, Off Comptroller Currency, dep dir, 1975-78; Univ NC Chapel Hill, Sch Bus Admin, NC, assoc prof finance, 1978-83; Howard Univ, Dept Finance & Ins, Sch Bus & Pub Admin, Wash, DC, prof & chmn, 1983-84; Am Univ, Dept Econ, Wash, DC, prof, 1985-87; Univ Tenn, Col Bus Admin, James F Smith Jr prof financial inst, 1987-, Dept Finance, head, 1987-95; pres, H A Black Co Inc, currently. **Orgs:** Bd mem, Nat Credit Union Admin; Savings Asn Ins Fund Adv Comt; Am Univ; Howard Univ; Univ NC; Univ Fla. **Home Addr:** 2319 Clipper Lane, Knoxville, TN 37922, **Home Phone:** (865)966-9544. **Business Addr:** Professor Emeritus, University of Tennessee, 453 Haslam Bus Bldg, Knoxville, TN 37996-4140, **Business Phone:** (865)974-5061.

## BLACK, DR. JAMES TILLMAN, SR.

Dentist. **Personal:** Born Feb 19, 1935, Guthrie, OK; married Joyce Toran; children: James Jr & Jeanine. **Educ:** Tenn State Univ, BS, biol, 1955; Michael Reese Sch Med Tech, attended 1956; Cent State Univ, MA, 1960; Loyola Univ Sch Dent, DDS, 1964; Chicago Col Dent Surg. **Career:** Los Angeles Co, pub health officer, Head Start Prog, dent coordr; Crenshaw Prof Dent Ctr, founder & dentist, currently. **Orgs:** Los Angels Co Pub Health Serv, 1964-71; Officer Los Angeles Den Soc, 1977; Nat Asn Advan Colored People; Am Dent Asn; Los Angels Dent Soc; Angel City Dent Soc; pres, Los Angeles Chap 100 Black Men Am, 1997-99; Kappa Alpha Psi Frat; Sigma Pi Phi fraternities; Xi Psi Phi Dent Frat; sire archon, Xi Boule, 2005-07; nat chmn, Health & Wellness Comt, currently; Exec Comt's mem large; Calif Dent Asn; Nat Diabetes Educ Prog; active mem, Nat Diabetes Educ Prog; nat health & wellness emer, 100 Black Men Am, currently. **Honors/Awds:** Commendation Award, Meritorious Service; Medical Technology Certification Award. **Special Achievements:** Published: 'Dentistry in a Head start Program', 1972; 'Changes in Dental Concepts', 1976; Dr. Black received the First Medical Technology Certification Award. **Home Addr:** 11920 Brentwood Grove Dr, Los Angeles, CA 90049-1505. **Business Addr:** Founder, General Dentist, Crenshaw Professional Dental Center, 3015 Crenshaw Blvd, Los Angeles, CA 90016-4264, **Business Phone:** (323)731-0801.

## BLACK, DR. KEITH L.

Physician. **Personal:** Born Sep 13, 1957, Tuskegee, AL; son of Robert and Lillian; married Carol Bennett; children: 2. **Educ:** Univ Mich Med Sch, UG, 1971, MD, 1981. **Career:** Univ Mich Med Ctr, Ann Arbor, intern gen surg & resident neurolsurg, 1982-87; Univ Calif, Los Angeles, prof neurosurg, Dept Surg, Ruth & Raymond Stotter chair, 1992, Comprehensive Brain Tumor Prog, head; Cedars-Sinai Med Ctr, Maxine Dunitz Neurosurgeon Inst & Div Neurosurg, dir neurosurg, 1997-, Ruth & Lawrence Harvey chair neuro sci, 1997-, Dept Neurosurg, prof, currently, chmn, currently. **Orgs:** Joint Am Asn Neurol Surgeons; Cong Neurol Surgeons, currently; Am Asn Neurol Surgeons, currently; Neurosurg Soc Am; Am Acad Neurol Surg, currently; founding mem, N Am Skull Base Soc; Nat Adv Neurol Dis & Stroke Coun, Nat Inst Health, 2000-04; Alpha Omega Alpha Hon Med Socs; Pituitary Socs, 2003-; comt mem, Cali Inst Regenerative Med Independent Citizens Oversight Comt, 2004-06; Nat Inst Neurol Dis & Strokes; Nat Cancer Inst; Socs Neurol Surgeons, 2007; mem bd dir, Los Angeles World Affairs Coun; Nat Brain Tumor Found; Independent Citizens Oversight Comt, Calif Inst Regenerative Med; Soc Neuro-oncol, currently. **Honors/Awds:** Westinghouse Science Award, 1975; Markley Award for Outstanding Graduate Scholarship, 1980; Jacobs Javits Award, NINDS, NIH, 2000; Essence Awards, 2001; Annual Martin Luther King, Jr. Day National Holiday Honor, 2002; Who is Really Who, 2002; The 40 Most Inspiring African Americans, Essence Magazine Special Edition, 2002; Candle Award in Science & Technology, Morehouse College, 2003; Highlight Award, 2004; Multicultural Prism Award, 2004; Southeast Symphony Humanitarian Award, Walt Disney Hall, 2005; Los Angeles Super Doctors, 2007; Thomas Bradley Unsung Hero Award, 2007; Lifetime Achievement Award, 100 Black Men of Los Angeles, 2008; Healthnetwork Foundation Service Excellence Award, 2008; Chairman's Award in Health and Wellness, 2009; International Brain Mapping and Intraoperative Surgical Planning Society Pioneer in Medicine Award, 2009. **Special Achievements:** Numerous publications and more than 100 science articles. **Home Addr:** 1233 Roberto Lane, Los Angeles, CA 90077-2304. **Business Addr:** Director of Neurosurgeon, Chairman, Cedars-Sinai Medical Center, 8631 W 3rd St Suite 800E, Los Angeles, CA 90048, **Business Phone:** (310)423-1773.

## BLACK, LEONA R.

Lawyer, administrator. **Personal:** Born Jan 5, 1924, Galveston, TX. **Educ:** Prairie View Col; Roosevelt Univ; Chicago Univ; DePaul Univ. **Career:** Cook City Dept Pub Aid, file clerk, finance clerk, head file clerk, off mgr, Chicago US Post Off, clerk supvr; Int Harvester Co, equip expeditor; AA Rayner Alderman 6th Ward, alderman's sec, admin asst; AR Langford Alderman 16th Ward, alderman's sec, admin asst; Donald Page Moore, polit org; State's Atty Cook County, polit coor dr Bernard Carrey; Fraud & Consumer Complaint Div Cook County, appt admin chief, 1972; Cook County States Atty Off, dir victim, witness asst proj, 1974-. **Orgs:** Ombudsman States Atty Off; polit activist, Nat Delegate, 1972; lobbyist, Local City State Consumer Protection Judicial Reform; advocate, Criminal Justice, Consumerism, Judicial Reform, Child Abuse, Drug Abuse, Alcoholism; youth gr dir, founder, org SCAPY; bd dir, Nat Org Victim Asn, 1976. **Home Addr:** 9800 S King Dr, Chicago, IL 60628, **Home Phone:** (773)928-5779. **Business Addr:** Director of Victim, Witness Assistant, Cook Co States Atty Off, 2600 S Calif Ave, Chicago, IL 60608.

## BLACK, DR. MALCOLM MAZIQUE (MIKE

## BLACK)

Educator, jazz musician, vice president (organization). **Personal:** Born Nov 28, 1937, Vicksburg, MS; son of Henriette Grace Smith and Fred Bell; married Emma Kern; children: Varen Delois & Karen Barron. **Educ:** Jackson State Univ, BME, 1959; Univ Wis, MME, 1967; Nova Univ, EdD, 1975. **Career:** Adminr(retired), educr, jazz musician; Fla & Miss HS, band dir, 1959-69; Fla Asn Col Registrars & Admis Officers, vpres 1979; Broward Community Col, registr, dir admis, 1969-79, dir Jazz Studies & Bands, Visual & Performing Arts dept, prof; Bronx Comm Col, dir; Broward County pub schs; Marilyn McCoo, dir. **Orgs:** Placement Comn, Am Asn Col Registrars & Admis Officers, 1975; Fla Vet Adv Coun, 1975; Fla Sch Rels Comn, 1975; vpres, Fla Asn ColRegistrars & Admis Officers, 1977; bd mem, Broward Co Housing Authority Adv Bd, 1978, Sunshine State Bank, Sistrunk Hist Festival Comt; Am Fedn Musicians; Music Educr Nat Conf; Nat Asn Jazz Educr; Kiwanis Club; S Fla Musicians Asn; Piney Grove Baptist Church; Omega Psi Phi Fraternity; Kiwanis Club; Miami-Dade Hampton House Jazz Restoration Comt; Lakeside Homeowners Asn, Jackson State Univ Alumni Asn. **Home Addr:** 2991 NW 24th Ave, Oakland Park, FL 33311, **Home Phone:** (954)731-7791.

## BLACK, VERONICA CORRELL

Executive, vice president (organization). **Personal:** Born Oct 30, 1946, Winston-Salem, NC; daughter of Vance A and Beatrice Moore; married Isiah A Jr; children: Braswell & Sandra B. **Educ:** Livingstone Col, BA, 1969; Am Bankers Assn, human resources cert, 1984; Univ NC, young exec prog, 1987; Duke Univ, Sr Mgt Dev Prog, 1996. **Career:** Executive (retired); Wachovia Corp, personnel mgr; Wachovia Bank & Trust Co, sr vpres, group exec, personnel, 1970-2001; First Wachovia Corp, personnel mgr oper serv div. **Orgs:** Regional vpres, Bankers Educ Soc, 1981-86; bd mem, YWCA, 1985-89, personnel Comn, 1986, personnel comn chmn, 1987-89; chmn, Career Serv Adv Comn, Winston-Salem State Univ, 1989; secy, Sr Servs. **Honors/Awds:** Leadership Award, Winston-Salem State Co-op Off, 1986; Positive Image Award, Minority Recruiter Newspaper, 1992. **Home Addr:** 3400 Del Rio Ct, Winston-Salem, NC 27105-6912, **Home Phone:** (336)725-5702. **Business Addr:** Secretary, Senior Services Inc, 2895 Shorefair Dr, Winston-Salem, NC 27105, **Business Phone:** (336)725-0907.

## BLACK, WALTER WELDON, JR.

Executive. **Personal:** Born Salisbury, MD; son of Walter Weldon Sr (deceased) and Dorothy Webb; married Clairdean E Riley; children: Walter III. **Educ:** Morgan State Col, BS, bus admin, 1958; Am Univ Law Sch, 1962. **Career:** Nat Assn Advan Colored People Spec Contrib Fund, urban prog dir, 1968-69; Howard Univ, mkt res analyst, 1972-76; Twenty-first Century financial Group; Alaska Assoc Inc, Flennaugh Reliable Serv, supt; Prudential Ins Co Am, spec agt; Talbot County Election bd vpres, currently. **Orgs:** Dir, Md State Conf Nat Asn Advan Colored People, 1965-68; vpres, DC Chap Morgan State Col Alumni Assoc, 1966-67; chmn bd, Pinkett-Brown-Black Assoc, 1969-72; pres, Alpha Phi Alpha; life mem, Br Legal Redress Comt & Freedom Fund Comt; exec mem, Talbot Dem Forum, Moton High Sch Alumni Asn; Blake-Blackstone Am Legion Post 77 Easton; chmn bd, Neighborhood Serv Ctr Easton; life mem, vpres State Conf chmn, Brs Legal Redress Comt; life mem, vpres State Conf chmn, Freedom Fund Comt; adv comt, US Comn Civil Rights; Pres, Md State Conf Br Nat Asn Advan Colored People; bd election, Md Manual On-Line. **Honors/Awds:** Meritorious Service Award, MD State Conf Br Nat Asn Advan Colored People, 1973. **Special Achievements:** Outstanding Achiever, Md African Am Pride Mag. **Home Addr:** 21 Lynnbrook Terr, Easton, MD 21601-4056, **Home Phone:** (410)820-9195. **Business Addr:** Board Vice President, Talbot County Government, 215 Bay St, Easton, MD 21601, **Business Phone:** (410)770-8099.

## BLACKBURN, ALPHA C.

Chief executive officer. **Educ:** Howard Univ, BA, 1961 MFA, painting & art hist, 1963. **Career:** TV host; Blackburn Architects Inc, pres & chief exec officer, currently. **Orgs:** Bd mem, Indianapolis Arts Coun; Am Pianists Asn; bd dir, Indianapolis Symphony Soc; bd trustee, Indianapolis Mus Art; chairperson bd, Ind Mus African Am Hist; bd adv, Ind Univ-Purdue Univ Indianapolis, 1999-11; bd dir, One Am Mutual Ins Holding Co; bd dir, Key Bank Regional Bd; bd dir, Indianapolis Cult Develop Comn; chmn, Ind Civil Rights Comn; tech rep & co-coordr, Indianapolis Int Airport; Healthnet Found; Pk Tudor Community Comt. **Business Addr:** President, Chief Executive Officer, Blackburn Architects Inc, 3388 Founders Rd, Indianapolis, IN 46268, **Business Phone:** (317)875-5500.

## BLACKBURN, DR. BENJAMIN ALLAN, II

Physician, dentist. **Personal:** Born Jun 10, 1940, Jackson, MS; married Sara Driver; children: Kellye, Benjamin III & Leigh. **Educ:** Morehouse Col, BS, biol & chem, 1961; Meharry Med Col, DDS, 1965; NY Univ Col Dent, postgrad cert prosthodontics, 1968. **Career:** Sydenham Hosp, intern, 1965-66; pvt pract prosthodontist, currently; Atlanta Prosthodontics, atlanta restorative dentist & prosthodontist, 1970-. **Orgs:** Fel Am Col Prosthdontist; Am Prosthodontist Soc; SE Acad Prosthodontics; Kappa Alpha Psi; Nat Asn Advan Colored People; Urban League; dipl, Am Bd Prosthodontics; founding mem, Health First Found; Fifth Dist Dent Soc; N Ga Dent Soc; Ga Dent Soc; Ga Dent Asn; bd mem, Meharry Med Col; hon fel GA Dent Asn. **Honors/Awds:** Cert Dipl, Am Bd Prosthodontics. **Special Achievements:** First African American to pass the Tennessee Specialty of Prosthodontics boards exams; First African American to teach at the Medical College of Georgia School of Dentistry; First African American to teach at Emory University's School of Dentistry. **Home Addr:** 75 Piedmont Ave NE, Atlanta, GA 30324-5207. **Business Addr:** Atlanta Restorative Dentist, Prosthodontist, Atlanta Prosthodontics, 2812 Piedmont Rd, Atlanta, GA 30305, **Business Phone:** (404)659-7696.

## BLACKBURN, CHARLES MILIGAN, II

Executive. **Personal:** Born Nov 4, 1937, Florence, AL; son of Charles M and Dovie E; children: Mary L, Charles M III & Mark E. **Educ:** Ala A&M Univ, BS, elec engineering, 1960. **Career:** Com Bank, dir; Sigma Systs Inc, pres & chief exec officer; First Combined Community Fed Credit Union, pres, chmn & bd mem, currently. **Orgs:** Packaging Mach Manufacturers Inst; Prince Georges County Community Col; Queen Anne Sch Bd; Partnership Workforce Qual Adv bd, dept bus & econ develop, Md, 2002; chmn, bd dir, First Combined Community. **Home Addr:** 10607 Manor Lake Ter, Bowie, MD 20721-2930, **Home Phone:** (301)808-2329. **Business Addr:** Chairman, Board Member, First Combined Community Federal Credit Union, 10666 Campus Way S, Upper Marlboro, MD 20774, **Business Phone:** (301)333-8442.

## BLACKMAN, ROLANDO ANTONIO

Baseball player, basketball coach. **Personal:** Born Feb 26, 1959, Panama City; married Laura; children: 4. **Educ:** Kans State Univ, BA, mkt & soc, 1981. **Career:** Basketball player (retired), basketball coach; Dallas Mavericks, 1981-92, defensive coordr, 2000, TV analyst, 2004-05, asst coach, dir player develop, 2006-; New York Knicks, 1992-94; AEK Athens BC, 1994-95; Olimpia Milano, Italy, 1995-96; CSP Limoges, 1996-97; Ger Nat Team, asst coach, 2001; Turkey Nat Basketball Team, asst coach, 2010. **Orgs:** Dallas Independent Sch Dist; Big Bros & Big Sisters; Spec Olympics; Muscular Dystrophy Asn; C's Med Ctr Dallas; Just Say No Found; Summer Basketball Camp; bd dir, Assist Youth Found; Kappa Alpha Psi Fraternity. **Home Addr:** 8223 Santa Clara Dr, Dallas, TX 75218-4449. **Business Addr:** Director of Player Development, Dallas Mavericks, 2909 Taylor St, Dallas, TX 75226, **Business Phone:** (214)747-6287.

## BLACKMON, ANTHONY WAYNE

Executive, lawyer. **Personal:** Born Feb 13, 1957, Newark, NJ; son of Bettye; married Pelicia E; children: Terry & Johanna. **Educ:** Cornell Univ, Sch Indust & Labor Rels, BS, 1979; LaSalle Law Sch, JD, 1996. **Career:** World Traditional Karate Orgn Ithaca NY, broadcaster, 1976-79; Meadow lands Sports Complex NJ, asst dir matrix opers, 1976-79; Hollywood Pk Racetrack, dir matrix oper, 1979-; Blackmon Enterprises, founder, pres, consult, 1981-. **Orgs:** Urban League; Nat Asn Advan Colored People; Black Bus Asn La; La Better Bus Arbitrator; Better Bus Bur Am, arbitrator; cert assoc, Am Bar Asn; Maricopa County Sheriffs Exec Posse. **Honors/Awds:** Youngest & only Black Director, Matrix Oper Hollywood Park Racetrack. **Home Addr:** 2812 Breezy Ridge Trl, Cordova, TN 38016-0106, **Home Phone:** (623)877-4124. **Business Addr:** President, TBE Office Business Service, 8405 W Sells Dr, Phoenix, AZ 85037, **Business Phone:** (623)849-6841.

## BLACKMON, BARBARA MARTIN (BARBARA ANITA MARTIN)

Lawyer. **Personal:** Born Dec 7, 1955, Jackson, MS; daughter of Julious Martin Sr and Willie T Martin; married Edward Jr; children: Madison Edward & Bradford Jerome. **Educ:** Jackson State Univ, BS, bus admin, 1975, MS, 1975; Univ Ala, MBA, legal educ, 1976; Univ Santa Clara Law Sch, 1979; Univ Miss Law Sch, JD, banking, corp, finance, & securities law, 1981; NY Univ, LLM, taxation, 1982. **Career:** Hinds Jr Col, instr, 1976-78; Bristol-Myers Co, assoc tax atty, 1982-83; Banks & Nichols, assoc, 1983-84; Barbara Martin Blackmon, atty-at-law, 1984-87; Blackmon, Blackmon & Evans, partner, 1987-98; Blackmon & Blackmon PLLC, managing partner & atty, 1989-; State Miss, Miss State Senate, sen, 1992-2003; Canton, Miss, city atty, 2009-13; Gen Missionary Baptist Conv, gen coun, 2011-; Claiborne County Med Ctr, county atty, gen coun, 2013-. **Orgs:** Pres, Nat Black Caucus States Inst; nat co-chair, Campaign Jackson State Univ; Magnolia Bar Asn; Miss Bar Asn; Nat Bar Asn; Ny Bar Asn; JSU Develop Found. steering comt, B.B. King Mus, Indianola; bd dir, United Way Capital Area; bd dir, Boys & Girls Club Cent Miss; bd dir, Stewpot Canton; bd dir, Am Red Cross Cent Miss; bd dir, Chap & Found Educ & Econ Develop. **Honors/Awds:** Constance Baker Motley Award, 1981; Special Executive Business Partner Award, 1991; Medgar Evers Faces of Courage Award, 1992; Honary Degree, Doctor Humane Letters, Tougaloo Col, 2003. **Special Achievements:** First Black Woman to Represent Madison, Yazoo Holmes Counties in Mississippi State Senate, 1992; First woman ever to hold that honor Democratic Nominee for Lieutenant Governor, 2003 State of Mississippi. **Business Addr:** Partner, Attorney, Blackmon & Blackmon PLLC, 907 W Peace St, Canton, MS 39046, **Business Phone:** (601)859-1567.

## BLACKMON, BRENDA

Television news anchorperson. **Personal:** Born Aug 20, 1952, Columbus, GA; daughter of Melzetta and Lorenza Hinton; children: Kelly. **Educ:** Fairleigh Dickinson Univ, BA, commun, 2001; MBA. **Career:** WWOR-TV, Channel 9, news anchor, 2005-; Brenda Blackmon Commun Inc, pres & chief exec officer, currently. **Orgs:** Nat Asn Black Narcotic Agents. **Honors/Awds:** Recogition Award, March of Dimes; Recognition Award, USN; Rosa Parks Humanitarian Award; Public Service Award, Alpha Phi Alpha, 1987; Citizen of the Year, Zeta Phi Beta Soc, 1984; Martin Luther King Jr Award; Telling Our Story Award; Emmy Award, Best Single Newscast in the New York Area, 1995-98; Associated Press Award, Best New Series, 1995; Best Sport News, 1995; Best Sport News Coverage, 1996; Best Coverage of a Continuing Story, 1996; Best Newscast, 1998; Humanitarian Award, United Hosp Fund New Leadership Group, 2002; Won numerous awards & honors for her prof expertise & community serv; 25 Most Influential Black Women in Business. **Special Achievements:** Became the First African American anchor in the city's history. **Home Addr:** 180 E Clinton Ave, Tenafly, NJ 07670, **Home Phone:** (201)541-9677. **Business Addr:** Anchor, WWOR-TV, 9 Broadcast Plz, Secaucus, NJ 07094-2913, **Business Phone:** (212)452-3962.

## BLACKMON, EDWARD, JR.

Lawyer, government official. **Personal:** Born Jul 21, 1947, Canton, MS; son of Edward Jr and Mollie; married Barbara Martin; children: Janessa, Madison, Bradford & Lawrence. **Educ:** Tougaloo Col, BA, polit sci, 1970; George Washington Univ, JD, 1973. **Career:** N Miss Rural Legal Serv, staff atty, 1973-74; Blackmon & Smith, partner, 1974-; Miss House Rep, 57th Dist, 1979-80, chmn judiciary A comt, 1984-; Blackmon & Blackmon PLLC, sr partner, 1989-. **Orgs:** Cade Chapel Missionary Baptist Church; state rep, Miss House Rep, 1979, 1984-; pres, Magnolia Bar Asn; Miss Trial Lawyers Asn; Am Bar Asn; Nat Asn Advan Colored People; bd adv, George Wash Univ Sch Law, currently; Nat Bar Asn. **Home Addr:** 377 Northwest St, PO Box 105, Canton, MS 39046, **Home Phone:** (601)859-4202. **Business Addr:** Senior Partner, Blackmon & Blackmon Attorneys At Law PLLC, 907 W Peace St, Canton, MS 39046-0105, **Business Phone:** (601)859-1567.

## BLACKMON, JOYCE MCANULTY

Consultant, executive, association executive. **Personal:** Born Nov 25, 1937, Memphis, TN; daughter of Samuel and Evelyn Simons; married Lawrence Burnett Sr; children: Lawrence B Jr & David G. **Educ:** Memphis State Univ, Memphis, Tenn, BS, 1966, MS, educ, 1970. **Career:** Memphis City Sch, Memphis, Tenn, teacher, guid co, 1959-79; Memphis Light, Gas & Water, Memphis, Tenn, sr vpres, vpres personnel & trng, vpres econ develop & external affairs & sr vpres, admin & support, 1979-96; Blackmon & Assoc, pres, 1994. **Orgs:** Alpha Kappa Alpha Sorority, 1956-; bd trustee, Tougaloo Col, 1986-92; grad, former bd mem, Leadership Memphis; Memphis Rotary, 1988-; bd dir, Mid S Pub Commun Found, WKN TV & FM, 1990-; Pres, Memphis Chap, Links Inc, 1990-92; pres, Memphis May Int Festival Inc, 1993; Child Advocacy Bd, 1995; Active mem, Miss Blvd Chruch; Memphis & Shelby County Film & Tv Comn; Nat dir, Arts Links. **Honors/Awds:** Distinguished Service Award, Nat Am Advan Colored People, Memphis Chap, 1982; Prominent Black Woman, Memphis State Chap Alpha Kappa Alpha, 1990; Dedicated Service Award, Memphis in May Int Festival Inc, 1990; Dedicated Service Award, Lemoyne-Owen Col, UNCF Dr & Ann Fund Dr, 1990; Contempora, Coping with a Crisis Award, Contempora Mag, 1991; March of Dimes; Big Bros & Sisters; Black Bus Asn; Grace Mag; United Way; Memphis Br Nat advan Asn coloured People. **Special Achievements:** First African American executive at Memphis Light, Gas & Water Division; Great Catches for the Over 40 crowd Featured. **Home Addr:** 387 Chickasaw Blf 2, Memphis, TN 38103, **Home Phone:** (901)528-0956.

## BLACKMON, HON. MOSETTA WHITAKER

Management consultant, executive. **Personal:** Born Jan 2, 1950, Homestead, PA; daughter of Garvis and Elgurtha Spruill; married Michael George; children: Jason B, Jacqueline Renee & Jenelle Laraine. **Educ:** Univ Pittsburgh, Pittsburgh, Pa, BS, lib arts, 1970; Am Univ, Wash, DC, MS, mgt sci, 1986. **Career:** Comsat Corp, Wash, DC, job analyst, 1974-76, employ mgr, 1977-79; Marriott Corp, Bethesda, Md, sr compensation analyst, 1979-80; Mitre Corp, McLean, Va, employ mgr & employ serv, 1980-96; Mitretek Syst's Inc, assoc dir human resource, dir, workforce develop, 1996; Noblis Inc, dir corp & employee outreach, 1996-2009; Endicott Interconnect Technologies Inc, human resource bus partner, 2010-13; Ev Prod Inc, sr hr bus partner, 2013-. **Orgs:** Am Compensation Asn, 1975-89; Prince Georges Couty PTA, 1986-94; bd adv, US Black Eng Mag, 1988-90; Black Human Resources Prof, 1988-95; Wash Tech Personnel Forum; Alpha Kappa Alpha; CARE Adv Comn. **Honors/Awds:** Certified compensation prof, Am Compensation Asn, 1983; Outstanding Recruiter, Career Commun Group, 1988; Human Resources Leadership Award, Mitretek Systems Inc; Community Service/Corporate Social Responsibility Award, Human Resources Award Greater Wash; Black Engineer of the Year Award. **Home Addr:** 8309b Osage Terr, Adelphi, MD 20783. **Business Addr:** Senior Human Resource Business Partner, Ev Products Inc, 373 Saxonburg Blvd, Saxonburg, PA 16056, **Business Phone:** (724)352-5288.

## BLACKMON, PATRICIA ANN

Judge. **Personal:** Born Aug 11, 1950, Oxford, MS; daughter of Willie James and Willie Mae. **Educ:** Tougaloo Col, BA, African-Am studies, polit sci & hist, 1972; Cleveland Marshall Col Law, JD, 1975. **Career:** Advocate Victim Witness, counr, 1974-76; Asst City Prosecutor, lawyer, 1976-81; Johnson Keenon Blackmon Law Firm, partner & lawyer, 1980-83; UAW Legal Servs, staff atty, lawyer, 1983-86; Cleveland City Prosecutor, chief prosecutor, 1986-90; Ohio Turnpike, staff atty, lawyer, 1990-91; Cuyahoga Co Ct Appeals, judge, 1991-; Dyke Col, prof; Victims/Witness Prog, asst dir. **Orgs:** Delta Sigma Theta Sorority, Inc, 1971-; founder, Black Women's Polit Action Comn, 1982-; Munic & Co Judges Law Enforcement & Nation's AIDS Crisis, 1986; Munic & Co Judges Domestic Violence, Nat Crisis Am, 1987; Munic & Co Judges Domestic Violence, Nat Crisis Am, 1987; bd dir, Hitchcock House, 1991-; Nat Asn Women Judges, 1992-; ct master, Am Inns Ct; Am Judges Asn; Supreme Ct Ohio, Bd Comt Grievance & Discipline, 1993-96; consumer mem, Cent Ohio, Bd Health Systs Agency, 1996-; bd dir, Downtown YMCA, 1996-; bd trustee, Ohio Judicial Col, 1999; Ohio Bar Asn; Cuyahoga Co Bar Asn; Olivet Inst Baptist Church; Woodruff Found; trustee, Lake Erie Col. **Honors/Awds:** Ohio Women's Hall of Fame, 1996; Alumna of the Year, Cleveland Marshall Col Law, 1996; Distinguished Litigation Award, Nat Asn Advan Colored People, 1983; H Jones History Award, Tougaloo Col, 1971. **Special Achievements:** Raceway Video and Bookshop Inc, v Cleveland Bd of Zoning Appeals, 118 Ohio, App 3d 529, 1997; Cleveland Police Patrolman's Assn v City of Cleveland, 95 Ohio App 3d 645, 1994; Stephens v A-Able Rents Co, 101 Ohio App 3d 20, 1995; White v Fed Res Bank, 103 Ohio App 3d 534, 1995; City of Lakewood v Town, 106 Ohio App 3d 521, 1995; First African American Woman elected to Ohio court of appeals, 1991. **Home Addr:** 11432 Cedar Glen Pkwy Suite A-1, Cleveland, OH 44106, **Home Phone:** (216)791-4014. **Business Addr:** Judge, Court of Appeals of Ohio, 1 Lakeside Ave Suite 202, Cleveland, OH 44113-1085, **Business Phone:** (216)443-6358.

## BLACKMON, ROOSEVELT, III

Football coach, football player. **Personal:** Born Sep 10, 1974, Pahokee, FL. **Educ:** Morris Brown Col, Atlanta, physical educ. **Career:** Football player (retired), football coach; Green Bay Packers, corner back, 1998; Cincinnati Bengals, defensive back & corner back, 1998-99; Glades Central, head coach, currently. **Business Addr:** Head Coach, Glades Central High School, 1001 SW Ave M, Belle Glade, FL 33430, **Business Phone:** (561)993-4403.

## BLACKSHEAR, JEFFERY LEON

Football player. **Personal:** Born Mar 29, 1969, Ft. Pierce, FL. **Educ:** Northeast La Univ, grad. **Career:** Football player (retired); Seattle Seahawks, guard, 1993-95, left guard, 1994; Cleveland Browns, 1995; Baltimore Ravens, right guard, 1996-99, guard, 1999; Kans City Chiefs, left guard, 2000; Green Bay Packers, 2002.

**BLACKSHEAR, WILLIAM**
Businessperson, journalist. **Personal:** Born Jun 1, 1935, Marianna, FL; son of William Sr and Julia; married Betty Jean Booze; children: Bruce, Angelia, Edwina, Jeffery, Jacquline & Sylvia. **Educ:** State Fla, educ cert, 1963; Gen Elec Employ Educ, 1969. **Career:** Businessperson (retired); Gen Elec Co, 1958-70; Weekly Challenger News, 1968-2002; Black Gold Inc, mgr; Lincoln Sch, pres; Tri-County Challenger, ed. **Orgs:** Consult, Black Media Inc; VAC; Black Gold Fla Inc; scout ldr, 1950-53; pres, PTA, 1960-63; pres & founder, Home Improv Comn, 1961-67; pres & founder, Lincoln Nursery Asn, 1961-67; pres, founder, Hope, 1965-67; pres & founder, SE Black Pub Asn Inc, 1978; vice chmn, OIC Sun coast; adv bd, Youth Am, Nat Asn Advan Colored People; Urban League; Southern Poverty Asn; Dem Fla. **Honors/Awds:** Outstanding Community Service, Le Cercle Des Jeunes Femmes, 1965; Citation, Outstanding Efforts, Human Rights Ridge Crest Improv Asn, 1966; Citation, Gen Elec Stud Guid Prog, 1970. **Special Achievements:** First African-American to run for office in Safety Harbor, and in Pinellas County; First Black person elected to public office in Florida since the end of Reconstruction in 1877, according to research by Gloria Gilghrest for the Pinellas County African History Museum. **Home Addr:** PO Box 12143, St Petersburg, FL 33733.

**BLACKSHIRE-BELAY, CAROL AISHA**
Educator. **Educ:** Oakland Community Col, Orchard Ridge, AA, Ger lang, 1971; Univ Mich-Ann Arbor, MI, BA, Ger ling, 1972; Princeton Univ, MA, Ger ling, 1985, PhD, Ger ling, 1989. **Career:** Univ Mich, fel, 1971-72; Univ Md, instr Ger, McGraw Kaserne, 1979-82, Lang Inst, instr Ger, 1980-81; Institut fur Deutsch als Fremdsprache, asst Instr, 1980-81; Bauer Lang Inst, Instr Ger & Eng, 1981-82; Benedict Sch, instr Eng, 1985-86; Friedrich-Ebert-Stipendium, res fel, 1985-86; Princeton Univ, asst Instr, 1986-87, fel, 1982-87; Univ PA, coordr, post-doctoral res & teaching fel, 1987-89, W W Smith fel, 1987-88, Fontaine fel, 1988-89; Ohio State Univ, instr, asst prof Ger Ling & cult studies, 1988-93; Stanford Univ, 1991; Ford Found, postdoctoral fel, 1991-92; Temple Univ, Dept African Am Studies, grad studies actg dir, 1993-96; res assoc, 1993-94 & assoc prof, 1994-96; Ind State Univ, Dept African & African Am Studies, chmn & prof, 1996-2002; Univ Wis-Green Bay, Lib Arts & Sci, dean, 2002-05, prof; Univ Wis, spec asst chancellor, 2002-05, prof; Sonoma State Univ, vice provost acad affairs & prof Mod Lang & Literatures Ger, chair, 2005-08; Fayetteville State Univ, dir spec res initiative & prof Eng & Foreign Lang-Ger, 2008-09, provost & vice chancellor acad affairs, 2008; Minn State Univ, fac, 2009-; Naropa Univ, interim provost, vpres acad affairs & prof interdisciplinary studies, 2011-. Grants: Temple Univ, res travel grant, 1995; Ind State Univ, grant instrnl training adj instrs, 1997; Ind State Univ, res grant, 1996, fac develop grant, 1997. **Orgs:** Chair, Coun Rep Col Arts & Sci at Ind State Univ, Admin Affairs Comt, 1977-88; Chair, Comt Cognate Areas Departments, Ind State Univ, 1999-2002; Chair, Gen Educ Comt Multicultural Studies, Ind State Univ, 1999-2002; vice chair, Univ Res Comt, Ind State Univ, 1999-2002. **Honors/Awds:** Delta Phi Alpha, Rho Chap, Nat Ger Hon Soc, 1987; Phi Beta Delta, Hon Soc Int Scholars, 1991; Phi Sigma Iota, Hon Soc Recognition Outstanding Ability & Attainments Field Lang & Ling, Terre Haute, IN, 2001; Phi Kappa Phi, Hon Soc Recognition Commitment to Acad Excellence, Green Bay, WI, 2002; Int Foreign Lang Hon Soc; Nat Ger Hon Soc. **Special Achievements:** Books published: "Language and Literature in the African American Imagination"; "The African-German Experience; The Germanic Mosaic"; Author, co-author, or editor of 14 books and 27 articles and book chapters. **Business Addr:** Vice President, Interim Provost, Naropa University, 2130 Arapahoe Ave, Boulder, CA 80302, **Business Phone:** (303)444-0202.

**BLACKWELL, ANGELA GLOVER**
Founder (originator), writer, chief executive officer. **Educ:** Howard Univ, BS; Univ Calif, Berkeley, JD. **Career:** Pub Advocates, partner, 1977-87; Oakland (CA) Urban Strategies Coun, founder; Rockefeller Found, sr vpres, 1996-9; PolicyLink (nat res & action inst), founder & chief exec officer, 1999-, pres. **Orgs:** Bd mem, Urban Inst; bd mem, James Irvine Found; bd mem, Found Child Develop; bd mem, Common Cause; bd mem, C's Defense Fund; bd mem, W Haywood Burns Inst; bd mem, Levi Strauss & Co; bd mem, Corp Enterprise Develop; co-chair, Ctr Am Progress, Task Force Poverty; Press Adv Comn Educ Excellence African Americans; bd mem, Sojourners. **Special Achievements:** Co-author with Manuel Pastor of "Searching for Uncommon Common Ground," W.W. Norton & Co. (2002); Contributor: "Ending Poverty in America: How to Restore the American Dream," The New Press (2007) and "The Covenant with Black America," Third World Press (2006); Commentator for "The New York Times," "Huffington Post," "Washington Post," "Salon," and CNN; Appearances on: American Public Media's "Marketplace," "The Tavis Smiley Show," "Nightline," and PBS's "Now," "Moyers & Company," "NewsHour"; Appeared on PBS special "The African Americans: Many Rivers to Cross" (November 2013); Collaborator with Center for American Progress on "All in Nation: An America that Works for All". **Business Addr:** President, Chief Executive Officer, PolicyLink, 1438 Webster St Suite 303, Oakland, CA 94612, **Business Phone:** (510)663-2333.

**BLACKWELL, ARTHUR BRENDHAL, II**
County commissioner, government official. **Personal:** Born Jun 10, 1953, Detroit, MI; son of Robert Brendhal and Florrie Love Willis; married Zenobia Weaver; children: Mosii Mays & Robert Brendhal II. **Educ:** NC A&T Univ, BA, polit sci, 1976. **Career:** Detroit Bank & Trust, Detroit, asst br mgr, 1978-79; 1980 Census, Detroit, dir field oper, 1980; Wayne Co Bd Comnr, comnr, 1980-82, chmn, 1989-94; Blackwell & Assoc, owner, 1983-86; Mayor Young's Re-election Campaign, hq coordr, 1985; Detroit Fire Dept, community admin coordr, 1986; Wayne Co Bd; Detroit-Wayne Co Port Authority, chmn, bd dir, 1999-2001; DeWay Develop Corp, pres & chief exec officer, currently; Bd Police Comnrs, chmn, 2002-. **Orgs:** Chmn, Detroit/Wayne Co Port Authority, 1988; Nat Orgn Black City Off; Mich Asn County Detroit Windsor Port Corp, 1988, first Cong Dist Dem Party; Mich Dem Party, City Resident Comn, Young Alliance; Nat League Co; Local Develop Finance Authority; Kids In Need Direction; Highland Park Caucus Club; New Detroit Inc, Govt Affairs Comn; Wayne Co Retirement Bd. **Honors/Awds:** Father/Son Outstanding Achievement Award, Northern Young Men's Christian Asn, 1981; Cert Appreciation, Wayne Co Bd Comnr, 1982; Outstanding Performance, Quarter State Music Competition, 1969. **Special Achievements:** Radio show: co-host, "Back to Back", WQBH. **Home Addr:** 1130 W Boston Blvd, Detroit, MI 48202, **Home Phone:** (313)883-2311. **Business Addr:** Chairman, Board of Police Commissioners, 2 Woodward Ave, Detroit, MI 48226, **Business Phone:** (313)224-3400.

**BLACKWELL, BOB. See BLACKWELL, ROBERT D, SR.**

**BLACKWELL, BOBBI L.**
Lawyer. **Educ:** Tex Southern Univ, JD, 1980. **Career:** Atty, currently. **Orgs:** Tex State Bar, 1980-. **Business Addr:** Attorney, 9000 W Bellfort St, Houston, TX 77271-0767, **Business Phone:** (713)774-1924.

**BLACKWELL, FAIGER MEGREA**
Executive, president (organization), chief executive officer. **Personal:** Born Dec 14, 1955, Reidsville, NC; son of Roy (deceased) and Mary A; children: Alexandria (Erik Battle) & MeGrea Blackwell II. **Educ:** Winston Salem State Univ (magna cum laude), polit admin, 1976; Univ NC, BS. **Career:** Jones Cross Baptist Ch, chmn, trustee; Caswell Nat Asn Advan Colored People; Caswell Co Voters League, pres, 1976; Blackwell Rest Home Inc, pres; Dogwood Forest Rest Home Inc, pres; Blackwell & Assocs; Carolina Pinnacle Studios, proprietor, pres, chief exec officer, owner, currently; Pinnacle Ministries Yanceyville Inc, founder, 2003. **Orgs:** Fel Inst Polit Leadership; founder, Blackwell Bros Florist; bd mem, Wiz 4-H Club; Caswell Co Planning Bd; bd mem, Caswell Nat Asn Advan Colored People; county comnr, State House Rep; deleg, Nat Conv, 1992, 1996; pres, NC Long Term Care Facil Asn; State Med Care Comn; Caswell County Sch Bd; founding bd mem, Nat Black Theatre Festival; State Bd Elections; 12th Cong Dist Congressman; bd dir, Mel Watts & BB & T-Burlington; chmn & vice chmn, Nat Black Patriots Found; chair, 2nd Dist Cong Dist; deleg, 2nd Dist Dem Caucus; Alamance & Caswell Human Rels Councils; bd dir, Caswell County Civic Ctr; Alamance Chamber Com; Caswell County Chamber Com; Greensboro Chamber Com; bd dir, YMCA; bd dir, Youth Men's Christian Asn; bd dir, Alamance Arts Coun; bd dir, Downtown Burlington Asn; dir, Alamance Community Col Found Bd; dir, Bennett Col Bd Visitors; bd advisors, Elon Univ Sch Bus; Piedmont Triad Film Coun. **Home Addr:** 2234 Lakeview Ter, Burlington, NC 27215, **Home Phone:** (336)524-0081. **Business Addr:** President, Chief Executing Officer, Carolina Pinnacle Studios, 336 W Main St, Yanceyville, NC 27379, **Business Phone:** (336)694-7785.

**BLACKWELL, FAYE BROWN. See Obituaries Section.**

**BLACKWELL, DR. HARVEL E.**
Educator, consultant. **Personal:** Born Sep 25, 1937, Hulbert, OK; son of Ruben and Lavada; married Sandra Sunday; children: Carmella C & Howard E. **Educ:** Compton Col, AA, 1959; Calif State Univ, Los Angeles, CA, BA, 1961; Univ Southern Calif, MS, physics, 1963, PhD, physics, 1968. **Career:** Southern Assn Col & Sch, consult, 1970-; Tex Southern Univ, prof physics; Inst Serv Educ, consult, 1970-75; Natl Sci Found, proposal rev; Lovanium Univ, vis prof; JSC NASA, consult, 1975-85; K-RAM Corp, bd dir, 1980-84; BSA Serv, sci & eng consult & pres, 1997-. **Orgs:** Bd dir, United Cerebal Palsy Gulf Coast, 1978-80; Nat Tech Asn; Nat Soc Black Physicists. **Business Addr:** President, BSA Services, 4010 Tidewater, Houston, TX 77045, **Business Phone:** (713)433-3921.

**BLACKWELL, JOEY**
Entrepreneur, president (organization). **Career:** VDS Off Supply, pres & chief exec officer, currently. **Business Addr:** President, Chief Executive Officer, VDS Office Supply, 4810 Fulton Indust Blvd, Atlanta, GA 30336, **Business Phone:** (404)691-9665.

**BLACKWELL, JOHN KENNETH (KEN BLACKWELL)**
Government official. **Personal:** Born Feb 28, 1948, Cincinnati, OH; son of George and Dana; married Rosa E; children: Kimberly A, Rahshann K & Kristin S. **Educ:** Xavier Univ, BS, psycol, 1970, MS, educ, 1971, MBA; Harvard Univ, Prog Sr Execs State & Local Govts, 1981. **Career:** Teacher, coach & politician; Cincinnati Bd Educ, teacher, coach, 1971; Model Cities Community Sch Assoc, educ & consult, 1973; Afro-Am Studies Univ Cincinnati, teacher; Xavier Univ, prof, 1974-91, Univ & Urban Affairs, instr, dir; Cincinnati City Coun, mem, 1977-89; City Cincinnati, vice mayor, 1977-78, mayor, 1979-80, vice mayor, 1985-87; Community Rels, assoc vpres 1980-; Cincinnati Employees Retirement Syst, vice chair, 1988; US Dept Housing & Urban Develop, dep under secy, 1989-91; Blue Chip Broadcasting Co, founding partner; UN Human Rights Comn, UNHRC, confirmed at rank ambassador, US rep, 1991-93; State Ohio, treas, 1994-99; Cert Govt Financial Mgr, 1997; US Census Monitoring Bd, co-chair, 1998-2001; Ohio State, secy, 1999-2007; gov bd, St Rita Sch Deaf; Nat Fedn Republican Assemblies, exec vpres, 2011-; Republican Nat Comt, vchmn platform comt, currently. **Orgs:** Chmn, Local Legislators Comm, 1978-79; vice chmn, Transp Comn 1979-80; Mayor Cincinnati, 1979-80; Cable TV Task Force; Int Econ Develop Task Force; steering comn, CommCities 1980; co-chmn, Labor Rels Adv Comn Nat League Cities; bd trustee, Pub Tech Inc; state & local govt bd adv, John F Kennedy Sch Govt Harvard Univ; adv comm, bd dir, Am Coun Young Polit Leaders; Jerusalem Comm; bd mem, Nat Leg Conf Arson; Rotary Int, Cincinnati Fine Arts, Inst Bd, Cincinnati Opera; trustee, Birthright Cincinnati Inc; bd mem, Greater Cincinnati Coalition People with Disabilities; bd dir, Fifth Third Bancorp Cincinnati, 1993; bd dir, Fifth Third Bank Cincinnati, 1993; bd dir, Physicians Human Rights, 1993; bd dir, Greater Cincinnati Coun World Affairs, 1993; bd dir, Int Repuban Inst, 1993; bd dir, Congional Human Rights Found, 1993; Coun Foreign Rels, New York, NY, 1994; Treas Ohio, 1994-98; Nat Asn State Treasurers; Nat Asn State Auditors, Comptrollers & Treasurers; Nat Asn Securities Profs; Nat Comn Econ Growth & Tax Reform; Greater Cincinnati Urban Bankers Asn; bd trustee, Xavier Univ; bd trustee, Wilmington Col; bd trustee, Wilberforce Univ; bd trustee, Cincinnati Tech Col; bd dir, Grant & Riverside Hosp; bd mem, Nat Taxpayers Union Ohio; task force mem, Govt Accting Stand Bd; bd gov, Nat Coalition Black & Jewish Am; Federalist Soc; sr fel, Heritage Found; nat bd adv, Wash Legal Found; chmn, policy bd, Underground Rr Found Inc; bd adv, John M. Ashbrook Ctr Pub Affairs, Ashland Univ, mem, 1997; Freemasonry; Pension & Pub Funds Comt; chmn, Nat Assoc State Auditors, Comptrollers & Treasurers, 1997; US Dept Labor Adv Coun Employee Welfare & Pension Benefit Plans, 1997; Huckabee Pres; bd dir, Nat Taxpayers Union; adv bd, C's Eduuc Opp Am Found, 1999; chair & bd adv trustee, Govt Investment Found, 1999; Univ Findlay, Nat Bd Visitors, Mazza Collection, 1999; bd trustee, Int City Mgt Asn & Retirement Corp, 1999; adv panel, Fed Election Comn, 1999; Ohio Secy State, 1999-2007; bd mem, Black Alliance Educ Options, 2000; chair, Cincinnati Riverfront Classic Jamboree, 2000-03; pres, Nat Electronic Com Coord Coun, 2002; exec bd, Youth Voter Corps, 2001; vpres, Nat Asn Secretaries State, Midwest Region, 2001; Campaign Finance Inst, co-chair, 2003; gov bd, Am Red Cross, Greater Cincinnati Red Cross; bd advisor, Ashbrook Ctr Pub Affairs; bd advisor, Close Up Found; sr fel Family Res Coun; life mem, Nat Asn Adv Colored People; Sigma Pi Phi Fraternity. **Special Achievements:** Actor, I Want Your Money, 2010; First African American to be a major-party candidate for governor in Ohio. **Home Addr:** 693 Windings Lane 5, Cincinnati, OH 43215. **Business Addr:** Vice Chairman, Republic National Committee, 310 1st St SE, Washington, DC 20003, **Business Phone:** (202)863-8500.

**BLACKWELL, KEN. See BLACKWELL, JOHN KENNETH.**

**BLACKWELL, PATRICIA A.**
Executive. **Personal:** Born Metropolis, IL; daughter of Phinis N and Minnie Allen. **Educ:** Southern Ill Univ, Carbondale, attended 1965; Howard Univ, Small Bus Develop Ctr, attended 1984. **Career:** Nat Urban League, Wash Bur, admin asst, 1971-72; John Dingle Assocs Inc, Wash rep/lobbyist, 1972-73; E H White & Co Inc, dir E coast opers, 1973-74; Unified Industries Inc, prog mgr, 1974-84; Pa Blackwell & Assocs Inc, pres, 1984-. **Orgs:** Consult, DC Dem Comt, 1974; vpres, SIMBA Assocs Inc-Fund Raiser, 1978-80; bd mem, Reg Purchasing Coun Va, 1978-; Nat Conf Minority Transp Officials, 1983-; Nat Forum Black Pub Adminr, 1984-; Nat Asn Female Execs, 1984-; tutor oper, Rescue-Wash Urban League, 1984-; Women's Transp Seminar, 1987; Nat Coalition Black Meeting Planners. **Home Addr:** 1039 Sells Ave Suite 1, St. Louis, MO 63147-1808, **Home Phone:** (314)652-1824.

**BLACKWELL, ROBERT D., SR. (BOB BLACKWELL)**
President (organization), chief executive officer. **Personal:** Born Jul 28, 1937, Eastville, VA; married Marjilee; children: 5. **Educ:** Wichita State Univ, BA, psychol, 1966. **Career:** IBM, syst eng, 1966-70, salesman, 1970-71, mktg mgr, 1976-78, br mgr, 1980-89, IBM, Greater Chicago Consult Serv, dir, 1990-92; Blackwell Consult Serv, founding partner, 1992-11, pres & chief exec officer, 2002-12, dir & chmn, 2011; Blackwell Global Consult LLC, founding partner, 2011-13; Sales & Mkt Strategies Inc, managing partner, 2013-. **Orgs:** Bd mem & chmn, ETA Creative Arts Found; bd chmn, ETA Creative Arts Found; advisor, Mayors Coun Technol Advisors; Execs Club Chicago; Econ Club Chicago; Metrop Club Chicago; pres, Joel Hall Dance Co; bd trustee, Ill Inst Technol; bd trustee, Mus Sci & Indust; bd trustee, Lakeside Bank; chief exec officer, DuSable Mus African Am Hist; chmn, Neighborhood Writing Alliance; nat dir, Black Data Processing Assocs; IT Serv Mgt Forum, 2007-11. **Special Achievements:** Author, My Evolution As An Entrepreneur - The Story Behind Blackwell Consulting. **Home Addr:** 910 S Mich Ave, Chicago, IL 60605, **Home Phone:** (312)431-9220. **Business Addr:** Managing Partner, Sales and Marketing Strategies Inc, 115 S Wells, Beverly Shores, IN 46301.

**BLACKWELL, UNITA**
Mayor, activist, politician. **Personal:** Born Mar 18, 1933, Lula, MS; married Jeremiah; children: Jeremiah Blackwell Jr (jerry). **Educ:** Univ Mass-Amherst, MA, regional planning, 1983. **Career:** Nat Coun Negro Women, community develop specist; City Mayersville, MS, mayor, 1976-; Southern Inst C & Families, chmn & pres emer, currently; Miss Dem Party, vice-chmn, 1976-80, Nat Conf Black Mayor, pres, 1990-92. **Orgs:** Pres, Nat Conf Black Mayors; pres, US China Peoples Friendship Asn, 1977-83; Dem Nat Comt; field worker, Stud Nonviolent Coord Comt. **Honors/Awds:** Southern Christian Leadership Award, 1990; Institute of Politics Fellow, John F. Kennedy School of Government, Harvard Univ, 1991; MacArthur Found Fel, 1992; APA Leadership Award, 1994. **Special Achievements:** First African-American woman to be mayor of Mayersville; Instrumental in persuading federal govt to fund a 20-unit housing develop in Mayersville & give the town a new fire truck; Book: Life Lessons from the Road to Freedom, 2006. **Business Addr:** Chairman, President Emeritus, Southern Institute on Children & Families, 500 Taylor St Suite 202, Columbia, SC 29201, **Business Phone:** (803)779-2607.

**BLACKWELL, WILLIE**
Football player, food service manager, manager. **Personal:** Born Dec 1, 1954, St. Louis, MO; son of Willie Jr and Flora Lee Williams; married Kathy Loman; children: Lamont, Crystal & April. **Educ:** Morris Brown Col, Atlanta, GA, BA, health & phys educ, 1977. **Career:** Football player (retired), manager, coach, literacy coordinator; Buffalo Bills, linebacker, 1978; Wash Redskins, linebacker, 1977; Kans City Chiefs, linebacker, 1980; Dobbs Int Serv, Atlanta, Ga, prod supvr, 1977-84, relief mgr, 1984-88, hot food mgr, 1988, Gate Gourmet, nat amtrak acct exec, literacy coordr, 1999-2004, US Foods, sales mgr, 2004-10, Frederick Douglass High School, acad coach, Blackwell Consultants, president mkt sales & opers, 2012-13, CarMax, president club sr sales consult, 2013-. **Orgs:** Nat Restaurant Asn; Bd mem, Ga Literacy Coalition, currently; adv bd mem, Southside High Sch, Atlanta, Ga, currently. **Home Addr:** 6007 Denmeade Dr NE, Atlanta, GA 30345-8001, **Home Phone:** (678)927-9507. **Business Addr:** Literacy Coordinator, Dobbs International Services, 1400 Aviation Blvd Suite 310, College Park, GA 30349-5463, **Business Phone:** (404)530-6492.

**BLACKWELL-HATCHER, HON. JUNE E.**
Judge. **Personal:** daughter of Robert Blackwell; married Jim; children: 2. **Educ:** Syracuse Univ, BA, psychol, 1974; Am Univ, JD, 1979. **Career:** Wayne State Univ, admis counr, recruiter, 1974-76; legal intern, agencies, 1977-79; Off Appeals & Rev, Dept Employ Serv, hearing & appeals examr, 1979-80, chief dept, 1981-83; Midwest Legal Serv, dir opers, 1984-88; pvt pract atty, 1988-92; Wayne County Probate Ct, Estates Div, judge, 1992-. **Orgs:** Nat Bar Asn; Mich Bar Asn; Wolverine Bar Asn; Women Lawyers Asn; vol, Meals Wheels; pres, Asn Black Judges Mich; co-chair, Adopt-A-Sch Comt; Asn Black Judges Mich. **Home Phone:** (313)868-7357. **Business Addr:** Judge, Wayne County Probate Court, 1305 Coleman A Young Munic Ctr Rm 1319, Detroit, MI 48226, **Business Phone:** (313)224-5706.

**BLACKWOOD, RONALD A.**
Executive, government official, association executive. **Personal:** Born Jan 19, 1926, Kingston; married Ann G; children: Helen Marie. **Educ:** Kingston Tech Sch, attended 1944; Kingston Com Col, attended 1946; Westchester Comn Col; Elizabeth Seton Col; Iona Col, BBA, mgt. **Career:** Mayor (retired); politician, 1967; Mt Vernon, actg mayor, mayor, 1985-95; Westchester County Brd Supervisors; Mt Vernon City, councilman; New Smyrna Beach Mid Sch, adv. **Orgs:** Nat Asn Advan Colored People; bd dir, Nat Conf Christians & Jews; Ment Health Asn Westchester Inc; United Way Westchester/Putnam; Boy Scouts Am-Westchester Putnam Coun; pres, Rotary Club New Smyrna Beach, Fla; Progressive Lodge No 64 AFM; All Islands Asn; bd dir, Westchester, 2000; Omega Psi Phi Fraternity; hon mem, Port Am Club; bd mem, Southeast Volusla Habitat Humanity; secy, Smyrna Yacht Club, vice commodore; bd dirs & bd mem, Volusia County, Coun Aging; Southeast Volusia County, Habitat Humanity; vpres, Tradewinds Condominium; vpres, Marine Discovery Ctr; New Smyrna Beach community. **Special Achievements:** First African American to be elected mayor in NY state, 1985. **Home Addr:** 5275 S Atlantic Ave Apt 408, New Smyrna Beach, FL 32169-4500, **Home Phone:** (386)427-7094.

**BLACQUE, TAUREAN (HERBERT MIDDLETON, JR.)**
Actor. **Personal:** Born May 10, 1941, Newark, NJ; children: 13. **Educ:** Am Musical & Dramatic Acad. **Career:** TV series: "What's Happening!!", 1976; "Sanford and Son", 1977; "Charlie's Angels", 1978; "Paris", 1979; "Backstairs at the White House", 1979; "Hill St Blues", 1981; "The $520 an Hour Dream", 1980; "Generations", 1989; "She Stood Alone", 1991; "Murder Without Motive; The Edmund Perry Story", 1992; "In the Heat of the Night", 1994; "Soul Survivors", 1995; "We Interrupt This Prog; The River Niger"; "Savannah", 1996-97. Films: House Calls, 1978; Beyond Death's Door, 1978; Rocky II, 1979; The Hunter, 1980; Oliver & Co, 1988; Deep Star Six, 1989; Fled, 1996; Nowhere Road, 2002; The Kudzu Christmas, 2002; The Stick Up Kids, 2008; Battle, 2011. **Special Achievements:** Nominated for the Emmy. **Business Addr:** Actor, Gores Fields Agency, 10100 Santa Monica Blvd Suite 700, LosAngeles, CA 90067.

**BLADE-TIGGENS, DENISE PATRICIA**
Police officer, lawyer, counselor. **Personal:** Born Dec 16, 1957, Chicago, IL; daughter of Marshall and Mary Lucille; married Willie Jr. **Educ:** Southern Ill Univ, BS, 1978; Chicago State Univ, MS, 1979; John Marshall Law Sch, JD, 1989. **Career:** Vols Am, counr, 1978-79; Dept Justice, correctional officer, 1979-81; Cook Co Juv Servs, caseworker, 1981-82; Chicago Police Dept, police officer, 1982-90; Hyatt Legal Serv, atty, 1990-91; Denise Blade-Tiggens & Assocs PC, partner, 1992-. **Orgs:** Consult, United Citizens Community Orgn, 1980-; Am Bar Asn, 1986-; Ill State Bar Asn, 1986-; Chicago Bar Asn, 1986-; Phi Delta Phi, 1987-. **Honors/Awds:** Scholastic Achievement Award, Int Legal Fraternity, Phi Delta Phi, 1987. **Business Addr:** Partner, Denise Blade-Tiggens & Associates PC, 4109 S Wabash Ave, Chicago, IL 60653-2122, **Business Phone:** (312)405-0085.

**BLADES, BENNIE, SR. (HORATIO BENEDICT BLADES)**
Football player, school custodian. **Personal:** Born Sep 3, 1966, Ft. Lauderdale, FL; children: Horatio Jr, Ashley, Amber, Jaylen & Bianca. **Educ:** Univ Miami. **Career:** Football player (retired), school guard; Detroit Lions, cornerback & strong safety, 1988-89, 1996, Free safety, 1990-92, 1994-95, defensive-back, 1993; Seattle Seahawks, cornerback & strong safety, 1997; Piper High Sch, security guard, currently. **Honors/Awds:** Pro Bowl, 1991; Jim Thorpe Award, 2006; College Football Hall of Fame, 2006. **Business Addr:** Security Guard, Piper High School, 8000 NW 44th St, Sunrise, FL 33351.

**BLADES, HORATIO BENEDICT. See BLADES, BENNIE, SR.**

**BLAIR, CHARLES MICHAEL**
Foundation executive, administrator, movie producer. **Personal:** Born Aug 5, 1947, Indianapolis, IN; married Margo Mills; children: Michael A & Tchad K. **Educ:** Oberlin Col, BA, mass commun, 1970; Kean Univ, MA, personnel admin, 1972. **Career:** Lilly Endowment Inc, prog evaluator, 1973, assoc prog officer, 1975, prog officer, 1977, sr prog officer, 1981; Grand Slam Inc & Interlace Mkt Inc, pres & owner, 1986-91; Sports, entertainment & Mgt, Consults; Indianapolis Recorder Newspaper, co-owner, vpres & pres, gen mgr, 1990-95; Martin Univ, fac mem, assoc dir, 1995-2005; Madame Walker Theatre Ctr, pres; Charles Blair Assoc, pres, 2001-; Metrop Ind polis Pub Broadcasting Inc, bd dir, secy, 2004-; producer, writer, 5 Stage Plays; Films: Facing Facade, exec producer; Eyewitness Century, writer; Marion, script consult; Mid Passage, Songs Creator. **Orgs:** Chmn, Asn Black Found Exec, 1980-83; founder, bd mem, Madame CJ Walker Bldg Restoration Proj; consult, Fund Raising Numerous Org; chmn bd, Blair Commun Indep Prod; bd dir, Big Bro Big Sisters Int; bd dir, founder, Youth Works Inc; bd dir, founder, Ind Black Expo Found; founder, BOS Community Develop Corp; bd sec, WFYI Channel 20; chair, Budget CommState Mus Found. **Honors/Awds:** Honored Spec Advocate Girls, Girls Club Am, New York City, 1979; Martin Luther King Award, N Ward Ctr Newark, NJ, 1982; Community Service Award, Ctr Leadership Develop Indianapolis, 1984. **Home Addr:** 4301 Aberdeen Cir, Indianapolis, IN 46226, **Home Phone:** (317)439-7134. **Business Addr:** Secretary of Board of Directors, Metropolitan Indianapolis Public Broadcasting Inc, WFYI TelePlex, Indianapolis, IN 46202-2389, **Business Phone:** (317)636-2020.

**BLAIR, CURTIS**
Basketball player. **Personal:** Born Sep 24, 1970, Roanoke, VA. **Educ:** Univ Richmond. **Career:** Basketball player (retired), Basketball Referee; Houston Rockets; Meysuspor, 1996-97; Nat Basketball Asn, referee, currently.

**BLAIR, DR. GEORGE ELLIS, JR.**
Executive, dean (education), chairperson. **Personal:** Born May 5, 1932, Braddock, PA; son of George E Sr and Edith Madden Cowans; married Eleanor Ann; children: Cheryl Ann & Stephanie Rene Warner. **Educ:** Ind Univ, BS, 1954; Adelphia Univ, Garden City, NY, MS, 1959; St John's Univ, Jamaica, NY, PhD, 1963. **Career:** Ind Pub Sch, teacher, 1953-54; Rockville Ctr Pub Sch, teacher, guid counr, adminr, 1956-66; Drug Prev, Treat & Rehabil Prog, consult; Roslyn Pub Sch, asst supt spl prog, 1965-66; NY State Dept Educ, asst comnr innovations educ, 1966-70, assoc comnr urban educ, 1970-72; Long Island Univ, vpres planning & develop, 1972-75; US Steel Co Am, arbitrator; City Univ NY, Bor Manhattan Community Col, NY City Educ Opportunity Ctr, dean educ & dir, 1975-77; State Univ NY, asst vice chancellor spec progs, 1977-78, assoc chancellor spec progs, 1978-79, dep chancellor spec progs, 1979-82, exec asst chancellor, 1982-89; Ascent Publ Co, chmn; Human Affairs Res Ctr, pres; Urban Ctr Res & Commun, pres & chmn; Summit Transp, chmn; Summit Farms, chmn; Camp Pioneer, chmn; Black World Championship Rodeo, founder & pres, 1989-93. **Orgs:** Chmn, NY City Riding Acad; Community Adv Comt, NY City Rikers Island Correctional Facil; pres, Ascent Found Inc, 1993-. **Home Addr:** RR 10, Summit, NY 12175, **Home Phone:** (518)287-1210. **Business Addr:** President, ASCENT Foundation Inc, PO Box 148, Summit, NY 12175-0148, **Business Phone:** (518)287-1210.

**BLAISE, KERLIN**
Football player, executive. **Personal:** Born Dec 25, 1974, Orlando, FL. **Educ:** Miami Univ, BA, bus admin & entrepreneurship, 1998. **Career:** Football player (retired), exec; Detroit Lions, guard & left guard & right tackle, 1998-2003; Blaze Contracting Inc, founder, currently. **Honors/Awds:** Top 100 players, Dallas Morning News. **Business Addr:** Founder, Blaze Contracting Inc, 5640 St Jean, Detroit, MI 48213, **Business Phone:** (313)361-1000.

**BLAIZE, MAVIS. See THOMPSON, DR. MAVIS SARAH.**

**BLAKE, DR. B. DAVID**
Administrator, physician. **Personal:** Born Bronx, NY. **Educ:** Howard Univ, Wash, DC, BS, zool; Morehouse Sch Med, Atlanta, GA, MD; Morehouse Sch Med. **Career:** Multi-Care Holistic Health Ctr LLC; Morehouse Sch Med, Dept Family Med, Southwest Hosp & Med Ctr, residency; Legacy Med Ctr; Regency Hosp; Family First Healthcare PC, Mableton, Ga, med dir, currently; State Ga Boxing Comn. **Orgs:** Ringside physician, Ga State Boxing Comn; ringside physician, USA Boxing; numerous regional & nat orgns; pres, chmn, Atlanta Med Asn; Ga State Med Asn; Nat Med Asn; Ga Acad Family Physicians; Am Bd Family Med; Independent Physician Asn Ga. **Home Addr:** 278 A Veterans Memorial Hwy SW, Mableton, GA 30126, **Home Phone:** (770)739-1233. **Business Addr:** Medical Director, First Family Healthcare PC, 1221 Old Powder Springs Rd SW, Mableton, GA 31026, **Business Phone:** (770)739-1233.

**BLAKE, CARL LEROY**
Teacher, pianist. **Personal:** Born Sep 25, 1951, Liberty, MO; son of William Louis and Hazel Roberson. **Educ:** Boston Univ, BM, piano performance, 1973; San Jose State Univ, MA, music, 1976; Cornell Univ, Ithaca, NY, DMA, piano performance, 1988. **Career:** City San Jose, Fine Arts Comn, music specialist, 1977-78; Bishop Col, Dallas, TX, chmn, music dept, asst prof music, 1978-79; Ohio Univ, Athens, OH, music lectr, 1980-84; Music & Arts Inst, San Francisco, CA, music instr, 1988-89; Pa St Univ, Univ Pk, PA, asst dean, Inst Arts & Humanistic Studies, assoc dir & asst prof music, 1998; Honduras Nat Sch Music, fulbright scholar, 1999; Church Fel All Peoples, San Francisco, dir music, 1999-; Victoriano Lopez Sch Music Honduras, fulbright scholar, 2006; Oakland Sch Arts, piano instr, 2007-. **Orgs:** Nat Music Hon Soc, Pi Kappa Lambda, 1973-; Am Matthay Asn, 1988-. **Business Addr:** Director of Music, Fellowship Church, 2041 Larkin St, San Francisco, CA 94109, **Business Phone:** (415)776-4910.

**BLAKE, CHARLES E.**
Clergy. **Personal:** Born Aug 5, 1940, Little Rock, AR; son of J A and Lula Champion; married Mae Lawrence; children: Kimberly Roxanne, Charles Edward II & Lawrence Champion. **Educ:** Calif Western Univ, BA, 1962; Interdenominational Theol Ctr, MDiv, 1965; Calif Grad Sch Theol, DD, 1982. **Career:** W Angeles COGIC, pastor, currently. **Orgs:** Jurisdictional prelate, First Jurisdiction Southern Calif, 1985-; gen bd, COGIC, 1988-; founder, La Ecumenical Cong, co-chair, 1992-; presiding bd, 12-mem Gen Bd COGIC; Pentecostal World Conf Adv Comn, 1999-; found & pres, Pan African Cs Fund; exec comt bd dir, chair bd dir, C H Mason Theol Sem; bd mem, bd dir, Interdenominational Theol Sem; chair cxec comt, dir bd mem, Oral Roberts Univ; mem bd dir, Int Charismatic Bible Ministries. **Honors/Awds:** William Booth Award, Salvation Army, 1997; Big Heart Award, Greenlining Inst, 1997; Whitney M Young Jr Award, La Urban League, 2000. **Special Achievements:** Selected as one of the 15 Greatest Preachers in America, Ebony magazine, 1982; Ebony has recognized Bishop Blake annually, as one of the 100+ most influential African Americans. **Business Addr:** Bishop, Chief Apostle, West Angeles COGIC, 3045 Crenshaw Blvd, Los Angeles, CA 90016, **Business Phone:** (323)733-8300.

**BLAKE, GRACE**
Foundation executive, movie producer, actor. **Career:** Actress: Mothers Men, 1997; Beloved, 1998; Producer: Gordon's War, prod secy, 1973; The Education of Sonny Carson, prod off coordr, 1974; Aaron Loves Angela, prod off coordr, 1975; The Wiz, prod off coordr, 1978; All That Jazz, prod coordr, 1979; Willie & Phil, prod coordr, 1980; Can't Stop Music, prod secy, 1980; Eyewitness, prod coordr, 1981; Tempest, prod coordr, 1982; Still Night, prod coordr, 1982; Star 80, assoc producer, 1983; Cotton Club, prod supvr, 1984; Prizzi's Hon, prod coordr, 1985; Heaven Help Us, prod coordr, 1985; Something Wild, prod coordr, 1986; Power, prod coordr, 1986; White Water Summer, prod coordr, 1987; Married to the Mob, financial rep, 1988; School Daze, exec prod, 1988; Lean Me, prod coordr, 1989; When Will I Be Loved?, line prod, 1990; The Silence of the Lambs, assoc producer & prod coordr, 1991; Boomerang, prod supvr, 1992; Who's the Man?, line prod, 1993; Spirit Lost, line prod, 1996. **Orgs:** Exec dir, Famed Apollo Theatre Found, 1995-; pres, advisor & bd dir, New York Women Film & Tv; bd dir, Mayor's Off Film Theatre & Broadcasting; bd dir, Cinema Arts Centre; bd dir, Caribbean Am Ctr New York; bd dir, 125th St Bus Improv Dist; chair, Nat Coalition 100 Black Women Long Island Chap; pres, Long Island Chap Partners. **Honors/Awds:** Dr. Martin Luther King Jr. Leadership Award, Hollywood Baptist Cathedral, 2009; NAACP Freeport Roosevelt Freedom Fund Award, 2009; Television Muse Awards; Leaders In Action Award, Bus from New Women Leadership Symp; Long Island's 50 Top Women Award. **Home Addr:** 42 Meister Blvd, Freeport, NY 11520, **Home Phone:** (516)623-5349. **Business Addr:** Executive Director, Famed Apollo Theatre Foundation, 253 W 125th St, New York, NY 10027, **Business Phone:** (212)531-5300.

**BLAKE, DR. J. HERMAN**
Educator. **Personal:** Born Mar 15, 1934, Mt. Vernon, NY; son of J Henry and Lylace E; married Emily Moore. **Educ:** NY Univ, BA, sociol, 1960; Univ Calif, Berkeley, CA, MA, sociol, 1965, PhD, sociol, 1974. **Career:** Univ Calif, from asst prof to prof, 1966-84; Univ Calif Santa Cruz, Oakes Col, founding provost, 1972-84; Tougaloo Col, pres, 1984-87; Iowa State Univ, African Am Studies Prog, dir, educ leadership & policy studies, prof social, 1998-2007, master teacher, Col Lib Arts & Sci; Med Univ SC, prof health prof & dent med, 2007-, humanities scholar residence; Univ SC, scholar residence & dir Sea Islands Inst; Ind Univ, v chancellor; Purdue Univ, v chancellor; Swarthmore Col, Eugene M Lang vis prof, social sci; Dillard Univ La, provost & vpres acad affairs, currently. **Orgs:** Am Sociol Asn; Pop Asn Am; Pac Sociol Asn; bd trustee, Save C Fedn; bd trustee, Pa Comm Serv Fel Woodrow Wilson, 1960; fel John Hay Whitney, 1963; Pop Coun, 1964; fel Dan forth Found, 1964; fel Rockefeller Found, 1965; fel Ford Found, 1970; bd trustee, Coun Assessment Experiential Learning; bd dir, Fielding Inst; bd dir, United Negro Col Fund; bd trustee, Coun Advan & Support Educ; bd trustee, Earlham Col; bd trustee, Berea Col; bd trustee, Gettysburg Col. **Home Addr:** , Swarthmore, PA. **Business Addr:** Professor, Medical University of South Carolina, Charleston, SC 29425, **Business Phone:** (843)792-6138.

**BLAKE, J. PAUL**
Educator, public relations executive. **Personal:** Born Mar 31, 1950, Neptune, NJ; son of Joseph E and Shirley T. **Educ:** Drake Univ, BA, jour, 1972. **Career:** Univ Minn, asst dir univ rels, 1976-83, asst pres, vpres stud develop, 1983-86; Pandamonium, pres, 1986-88; Seattle Univ, asst vpres, dir pub rels, Commun Dept, instr, 1989-98; Seattle Pub Utilities, commun dir, 1998-2004, community rels develop dir, 2004-, secy, currently. **Orgs:** Bd trustee, Coun Advan & Support Educ, 1982-84, 1992-94; pres, MN Press Club, 1988; bd dir, US China Peoples Friendship Asn MN Chap; vice chair, Pub Affairs Coun; Am Water Works Asn; CH2M Hill, sr mgt consult; Water Utility Coun; vice chair, Evergreen State Chap, Am Soc Pub Admin; Pub Rels Adv Bd, Seattle YMCA; Pub Rels Adv Bd, Univ Wash Pub Rels Cert Prog; bd mem, Seattle Biomed Res Inst; Black Heritage Soc Wash State; bd mem, Seattle Mgt Asn. **Home Addr:** 21121 SE 206th St, Renton, WA 98058-0246. **Business Addr:** Community Relations Development Director, Secretary, City of Seattle/ Seattle Public Utilities, Seattle Munic Twr 700 5th Ave Suite 4900, Seattle, WA 98124-4018, **Business Phone:** (206)684-8180.

**BLAKE, REV. JAMES G.**
Clergy, executive director. **Personal:** Born Dec 4, 1944, Charleston, SC. **Educ:** Morehouse Col, AB, 1965; Boston Univ Sch Theol, MTH, 1968. **Career:** Gov RI, spec asst, 1968; Interfaith City-Wide Coord Com NYC, exec dir, 1968-71; Union AME Church, Little Rock, pastor, 1971-72; Sen Hubert Humphrey, nat field coordr, 1972; SC Comm Farm Workers Inc, exec dir; Morris Brown AME Church, pastor. **Orgs:** Nat vpres, gen officer, Nat Asn Advan Colored People; select comt, US Youth Coun; deleg, World Assembly Youth Leige Belg, 1970; deleg, First Pan African Youth Festival Tunis, Tunisia, 1972; deleg, World Coun Churches, 1975; coordr, Del Black Relig Leaders Repub China, 1976. **Home Addr:** 92 Nassau St, Charleston, SC 29402.

**BLAKE, JAMES RILEY**
Tennis player, social worker. **Personal:** Born Dec 28, 1979, Yonkers, NY; son of Thomas Sr (deceased) and Betty; married Emily Snider; children: Riley Elizabeth. **Career:** US Tennis Asn, 2000-. **Orgs:** Found, The James Blake Foundation. **Honors/Awds:** Rookie of the Year, 2000; USTA Waikola Challenger, 2002; Comeback Player of the Year Award, 2005; Arthur Ashe Humanitarian of the Year, 2005. **Special Achievements:** Third African American to play for the United States in the Davis Cup; Co-Author: Breaking Back: How I Lost Everything and Won Back My Life, 2007. **Business Addr:** Professional Tennis Player, Founder, US Tennis Association, 70 W Red Oak Lane, White Plains, NY 10604-3602, **Business Phone:** (914)696-7000.

**BLAKE, JEFF BERTRAND COLEMAN**
Football player. **Personal:** Born Dec 4, 1970, Daytona Beach, FL; son of Emory; married Lewanna F; children: 4. **Educ:** E Carolina Univ. **Career:** Football player (retired); New York Jets, 1992-93; Cincinnati Bengals, quarterback, 1994-99; New Orleans Saints, quarterback, 2000-01; Baltimore Ravens, quarterback, 2002; Ariz Cardinals, quarterback, 2003; Philadelphia Eagles, 2004; Chicago Bears, quarterback, 2005. **Honors/Awds:** Pro Bowl, 1995; Most Valuable Player. **Special**

**Achievements:** One of Nine African-American quarterbacks, largest number in NFL history, 1997. **Home Addr:** 7909 Cobblestone, Austin, TX 78735-7900.

### BLAKE, JENNIFER LYNN
Activist, clergy. **Personal:** Born Mar 16, 1961, Ft. Benning, GA; daughter of James K Wall and Fannie Bea; children: Lakisha, Leroy & London. **Educ:** Pittsburgh Beauty Acad, attended 1986. **Career:** White Umbrella Ministry, chief exec officer, currently; Cosmetologist, currently. **Orgs:** Childrens Outreach Ministry; Action Christ Outreach Ministry; Prison Ministry. **Honors/Awds:** One of the Best Dressed Women in America, nominated, 1998. **Home Addr:** 2229 Rembert St, Columbia, SC 29201, **Home Phone:** (803)931-8714.

### BLAKE, JOHN PATRICK
Football coach, football player. **Personal:** Born Mar 6, 1961, Rockford, IL; married Freda; children: Jourdan. **Educ:** Univ Okla, BA, pub rels & recreation, 1986. **Career:** Footnall player (retired), football coach; Univ Okla, player, 1979-82, stud asst & defensive line, 1985, grad asst, 1986, asst coach & defensive line coach, 1989, asst coach & linebackers, 1990-92, head coach, 1996-98; Univ Tulsa, asst coach & tight ends & wide receivers, 1987-88; Dallas Cowboys, asst coach & defensive line, 1993-95; Miss State Univ, asst coach & defensive line, 2003; Nebr Cornhuskers, asst coach & defensive line, 2004-06; NC State Univ, asst head coach, 2007-10; Lamar Univ, defensive line coach, 2016; NC State Univ, defensive line coach, assoc head coach & recruiting coach, currently; Buffalo Bills, defensive line coach, 2016-. **Honors/Awds:** Super Bowl XXVIII Champions, Dallas Cowboys. **Business Addr:** Defensive Line Coach, The Buffalo Bills, 1 Bills Dr, Orchard Park, NY 14127.

### BLAKE, MILTON JAMES
Labor activist, executive director, administrator. **Personal:** Born Nov 11, 1934, Chicago, IL; married Beverly Marlene Skyles; children: Milton J Jr (deceased) & Robin S. **Educ:** Bradley Univ, Peoria, IL, BS, indust arts, 1957. **Career:** Chicago Police Dept, human rels officer, 1961-65; Continental Can Co, suprv indust rels, 1966-72; Whittaker Metals, div mgr indust rels, 1972-74; Gulf & Western Energy Prod Grp, grp mgr employee rels, 1974-78, consult eeo, 1979; Univ Wis, Affirm Action Prog, vis instr, 1977; Bunker Ramo Corp, Pub Affirm Action Prog, corp mgr eeo & compliance mgt, 1979-; Amphenol Co, dir & salary admin, org plng & develop, 1982-. **Orgs:** Youth adv comt, St James Luthern Church, 1961-66; indust rels adv comt, Univ Wis, 1971-; Oak Brook Asn Com & Indust, 1979-; bd dir, Chicago C Choir, 1980; Chicago Urban Affairs Coun, 1982; Alpha Phi Alpha; Alpha Phi Omega; Phi Mu Alpha. **Home Addr:** 1515 S Prairie Ave Suite 712, Chicago, IL 60605, **Home Phone:** (312)939-3361. **Business Addr:** Director, Salary Administrator, Amphenol Co, 900 Commerce Dr, Oak Brook, IL 60521.

### BLAKE, NEIL
Executive. **Personal:** Born Jan 1, 1962, Brooklyn, NY. **Educ:** Long Island Univ, Brooklyn Campus, BA, media arts, 1986. **Career:** Gerber Carter Inc, prod asst, 1981-82; WNYE-TV, New York, dir, 1983-87; Nat Broadcasting Co, producer, 1986-88, assoc dir, 1987; Long Island Univ, WLIU Radio, gen mgr; "A Current Affair", assoc dir, backup dir; Fox 5 TV, "Good Day New York", "10 O'clock News", assoc dir; NBC, "Positively Black", assoc producer; BlakeRadio Network, founder, 2000-; WNBC, freelancer, currently; Unlimited Ventures, owner, 2001-. **Orgs:** Dir Guild. **Business Addr:** Founder, BlakeRadio Network, PO Box 403, Massapequa Park, NY 11762, **Business Phone:** (516)557-5468.

### BLAKE, PEGGY JONES
Librarian. **Personal:** Born Jan 26, 1946, Georgetown, GA; daughter of David and Carrie Griggs. **Educ:** Tuskegee Univ, Tuskegee, AL, BS, 1968; Univ Mich, Ann Arbor, MI, AMLS, 1974. **Career:** Nat Libr Med, Bethesda, MD, librn, 1974-87; Morehouse Sch Med, Libr, Atlanta, GA, AHEC librn, 1987-89; Nat Agr Libr, ARS coordr, 1989-96, spec asst to the dir, 1996-. **Orgs:** Am Libr Asn, 1974-76, 1989-; Med Libr Asn, 1974-87; US Agr Info Network, 1989-; Black Caucus Am Libr Asn, 1990-; Assoc Nat Agr Libr; Tuskegee Univ Alumni Asn. **Honors/Awds:** Scholarship Award, Spec Libr Asn, 1972; Certification-Medical Librarian, Med Libr Asn, 1975-86; Post-Graduate Internship as Library Asniate, Nat Libr Med, 1980-81. **Home Addr:** 482 Winding Rose Dr, Rockville, MD 20850, **Home Phone:** (301)838-5541. **Business Addr:** Special Assistant to the Director, National Agricultural Library, Abraham Lincoln Bldg 10301 Baltimore Blvd Rm 205, Beltsville, MD 20705-2351, **Business Phone:** (301)504-5568.

### BLAKE, DR. WENDELL OWEN
Physician. **Personal:** Born Aug 9, 1940, Bartow, FL; married Mildred; children: Wendi & Michael. **Educ:** Howard Univ, BS, 1961; Meharry Med Col, MD, 1967. **Career:** Good Samaritan Hosp, intern, 1967-68; George W Hubbard Hosp, resident; Meharry Med Col, resident, 1968-72; Roswell Pk Memorial Inst, fel surg oncol, physician, 1974-75; Lakeland Regional Med Ctr, chief gen surg, staff mem, 1984; family pract physician, currently. **Orgs:** Soc Abdominal Surgeons; Fla Med Asn; Polk Co Med Asn Fla; Nat Med Asn; Fla Med Dent & Pharmaceut Asn; Polemarch Lakeland Alumni Chapt; dipl, Am Bd Surg; Kappa Alpha Psi Frat; pres, Boys & Girls ClubLakeland, Fla, 1993; fel Southeastern Surg Cong. **Honors/Awds:** Award for Achievement in recognition of meritorious performance of duty, US Kenner Army Hosp, 1972-74. **Special Achievements:** Has published various articles in scientific journals. **Home Addr:** 5514 Kings Mont Dr, Lakeland, FL 33813. **Business Addr:** Family Practice Physician, 505 Martin L King Jr Ave Suite 2, Lakeland, FL 33815-1527, **Business Phone:** (863)683-5567.

### BLAKE, REV. WILLIAM J.
Educator, college administrator. **Personal:** Born Akron, OH; son of William W Jr (deceased) and Maxine; married Vanessa A Drone; children: Jessyca, Janeil, William & Ashton. **Educ:** Ohio Univ, Athens, AB, polit sci, 1975; Atlanta Univ, MA, 1980; Capella Univ, PhD, currently. **Career:** First Baptist Church, Windham, Ohio, pastor; Johnson C Smith Univ, Charlotte, NC, assoc vpres stud affairs, 1990-95; Youngstown State Univ, dir stud activ, 1995-2004, dir stud diversity prog, 2004-. **Orgs:** Advisor, Stud Diversity Coun. **Business Addr:** Director of Student Diversity Programs, Youngstown State University, Tod Hall 1 Univ Plz Rm 312, Youngstown, OH 44555, **Business Phone:** (330)941-2340.

### BLAKELY, ALLISON
Educator, writer. **Personal:** Born Mar 31, 1940, Clinton, AL; son of Ed Walton and Alice; married Shirley Ann Reynolds; children: Shantel Lynn & Andrei. **Educ:** Ore State Col, Corvallis, OR, attended 1960; Univ Ore, Eugene, OR, BA, hist, 1962; Univ Calif, Berkeley, MA, hist, 1964, PhD, hist, 1971. **Career:** Professor (retired), Professor emeritus; AUS, active duty, 1966-68; Stanford Univ, Stanford, CA, instr, 1970-71; Howard Univ, Wash, DC, from asst prof to prof, 1971-01; Boston Univ, Boston, MA, prof, 2001-14, dir, african am studies prog, 2012-14, prof emer, 2014-. **Orgs:** Woodrow Wilson fel, Woodrow Wilson Found, 1962-63; Andrew Mellon fel, Aspen Inst Humanities, 1976-77; Fulbright-Hays Res fel, 1985-86; chair, Scholarly Worth Comt, Howard Univ Press, 1989-; Comt Qualifications, Phi Beta Kappa Soc, 1991-97; Am Hist Asn; Asn Advan Slavic Studies; World Hist Asn; gov senate, Phi Beta Kappa, 1994-2012, pres, 2006-09. **Special Achievements:** Obama appointee to National Humanities Council 2010-. **Home Addr:** 1 Sunnyside Rd, Silver Spring, MD 20910, **Home Phone:** (301)565-2412. **Business Addr:** Professor Emeritus, Boston University, 1 Sunnyside Rd, Silver Spring, MD 20910, **Business Phone:** (301)565-2412.

### BLAKELY, CAROLYN
School administrator. **Personal:** Born Feb 13, 1936, Magnolia, AR; daughter of James D and Mary E; married Neal Nathanial; children: Karen Joy & Earl Kevin. **Educ:** Ark AM&N Col, BA, eng, 1957; Atlanta Univ, MA, eng, 1964; Okla State Univ, PhD, eng, 1984. **Career:** Teacher, 1957-62; Grambling State Univ, 1963-66; Univ Ark, Pine Bluff, asst prof Eng, 1968-86, asst to chancellor, 1986-90, interim vice chancellor acad affairs, 1990-91, interim chancellor, 1991; Univ Ark Pine Bluff, Hons Col, chairperson dept eng, interim chancellor, interim vice chancellor, dean; Pinnacle Bus Solutions, bd dir, currently. **Orgs:** Nat Colgiate Hons Coun, 1980-; Nat Coun Teachers Eng, 1980-; pres, Southern Regional Hons Coun, 1991; pres, Nat Asn African-Am Hons Progs; bd dir, Ark Blue Cross & Blue Shield, 1988-; dir, Pinnacle Bus Solutions Inc; bd mem, Ark Community Found; Alpha Chi Hon Soc; Alpha Kappa Alpha Sorority; Alpha Kappa Mu Hon Soc. **Home Addr:** 2105 Mt Vernon Ct, Pine Bluff, AR 71603, **Home Phone:** (870)536-2513. **Business Addr:** Board Director, Pinnacle Business Solutions, 515 W Pershing Blvd, North Little Rock, AR 72114, **Business Phone:** (501)210-9000.

### BLAKELY, CHARLES
School administrator. **Personal:** Born Jan 31, 1951, Batesville, MS; son of Willie and Edna. **Educ:** Coahoma Jr Col, AA, 1972; Jackson State Univ, BS, bus admin, 1975; MS State Univ, attended 1973, Delta State Univ, attended 1982, Univ MS, attended 1984. **Career:** Jackson State Univ, stud admin clerk, 1974-75; N Panola Voc High Sch, substitute teacher, 1975-78; Northwest Jr Coll Greenhill Elem Sch, adult basic educ instr, 1981-88; Inst Comm Serv, lic social worker, 1988-; N Panola Consol Sch Dist I, Sch bd, pres, 1989-90, secy, 1991; Panola Co, Sch attendance officer, counr, 1989-; St Francis Behav Ctr, counr & consult; Path Finder, youth counr; N Panola High Sch, Continuing Educ Dept, site supvr, 1992-98, attendance officer; Miss Dept EDU, Sch attendance officer, 1998-; Como Mid & Elem Sch, sch attendance officer, currently. **Orgs:** Pres, Sardis Panola County Voters League, 1980-88; part time sunday sch teacher, mem choir, Miles Chapel CME Church, sch bd mem, 1980-92; selective serv bd mem, 1981-2000; asst supt Sunday sch, Miles Chapel CME Church, 1982-; MACE affil local bd continued educ, 1983-85; bd mem, Dem Exec Community Panola County, 1984-93; pres, N Panola Sch Bd Educ, 1989-90; pres, Job Corps Community Rels Coun, 2002-04; Cavalette Social Club; chmn, Steward Bd. **Honors/Awds:** Certificate in recognition of noteworthy performance of service, MS United Progress Black Community, 1980-81; Certificate Award Outstanding Service in the Community, Nat Asn Advan Colored People, 1982; Outstanding service, dedication & cooperation in the community, Panola County Voter League Inc, 1982; Staff of the Year, Inst Community Serv Headstart Prog, 1989; Outstanding School Board Award for Service Rendered, 1990; Certified Master Addiction Counselor, 1996-; Certified Criminal Justice Specialist, 1996-. **Home Addr:** 19324 Hwy 51 S, Sardis, MS 38666-1409, **Home Phone:** (662)487-3647. **Business Addr:** School Attendance Officer, Como Middle - Elementary School, 526 Compress Rd, Como, MS 38619-7302, **Business Phone:** (662)526-0333.

### BLAKELY, DR. EDWARD JAMES
Educator. **Personal:** Born Apr 21, 1938, San Bernardino, CA; son of Edward and Josephine Carter; married Maaike van der Slessen; children: Pieta & Brette. **Educ:** San Bernardino Valley Col, AA, 1958; Univ Calif, Riverside, BA, 1960; Univ Calif, Berkeley, MA, 1964; Pasadena Col, MA, 1967; Univ Calif, PhD, 1971. **Career:** Professor; Univ Calif, Los Angeles Ext, training dir, 1966-68; Western Community Action Training Inc, exec dir, 1968-70; US State Dept, spec asst to asst secy, 1970-71; Univ Pittsburgh, asst to chancellor, 1971-74; Univ Calif, Berkeley, dean, asst vpres, 1977-84, Sch Urban Planning & Develop, dean, 1994-99, Dept City & Regional Planning, prof, 1986-94, prof emer city & reg planning, currently; Univ Southern Calif, prof, 1994-99; New Sch Univ, Robert J Milano Grad Sch Mgt & Urban Policy, dean, 1999-2004. **Orgs:** Fel Colo Found, 1960; bd dir, YMCA, 1972-74; Nat Asn Advan Colored People, Pittsburgh, 1972-74; Community Develop Soc Am, 1976-; Int Soc Educ Planners 1977-; fel Natl Acad Pub Admin, 2002; consult, US Agency Int Develop & UN; leader, Civic Alliance Rebuilding City New York since sept 11; fel Guggenheim, 1995; fel Fulbright, Indust Policy, 1986. **Home Addr:** 2709 Alida St, Oakland, CA 94602. **Business Addr:** Professor Emeritus, University of California-Berkeley, 228 Wurster Hall Suite 1850, Berkeley, CA 94720-1850, **Business Phone:** (510)642-3256.

### BLALOCK, MARION W.
School administrator. **Personal:** Born Dec 18, 1947, East Chicago, IN; married Roger; children: Erin Juliane. **Educ:** Purdue Univ, BS, sociol, 1969, MS, coun & personnel serv, 1973. **Career:** Educator retired; Parker Career Ctr, employ counr, 1970; Family Serv Metro Detroit, family caseworker, 1970-71; Purdue Univ, grad teaching asst, 1971-73, asst dean studs, 1974-75, dir minority eng prog, 1975-2003, advs, asst, eng assoc dean, asst dean undergrad prog, 2008. **Orgs:** Fac adv & nat adv, hon mem, corp affairs mgr, pre-col advisor, Nat Soc Black Engrs, 1976-; Nat Asn Minority Eng Prog Adminrs, Am Soc Eng Educ, Black Col Develop Comm; vice chair, steering comm, Purdue Black Alumni Orgn; bd dir, Tippecanoe Area Planned Parenthood Asn, 1985-88. **Home Addr:** 997 Devon St, West Lafayette, IN 47906, **Home Phone:** (765)463-3064. **Business Addr:** National Convention & Pre-College Advisor, National Society of Black Engineers, 205 Daingerfield Rd, Alexandria, VA 22314, **Business Phone:** (703)549-2207.

### BLANC, ERIC ANTHONY-HAWKINS
Manager. **Personal:** Born Jun 10, 1969, New Orleans, LA; son of Stephen and Rosa Hawkins; married Dori; children: Kendal. **Educ:** Fla State Univ, BS, mkt, 1991. **Career:** Copitech Corp, mkt consult, 1991-92; Tropicana Field, events coordr, 1992-93; Fla Suncoast Dome, event coordr, 1992-93; Tampa Conv Ctr, facil mgt & sr events coordr, 1993-2000, event serv supvr, 1999-2000, dir sales, mkt & conv serv, 2010-; Centennial Olympic Games, Atlanta, Ga, event coordr, 1996; Fla Classic Football Weekend, Tampa, Fla; Freeman Co, Orlando, Fla, acct exec, 2000-03, nat sales mgr, 2004-10; Ortho McNeil Pharmaceut, Sales Rep, 2003; GES Expositions, sales mgr, 2003-04. **Orgs:** Adv, NAACP Youth Coun, 1991-94; host comt chair, Fla Classic Asn, 1994; Omega Psi Phi Fraternity Inc; pres, Asn Convention opers Mgt; Asn Conv Sales & Mkt Execs; Prof Conv Managers Asn; Meeting Planners Int; Nat Coalition Black Meeting Planners. **Special Achievements:** Publications: Hotel Executive.com Magazine, 2011. **Home Addr:** 2011 E Eskimo Ave, Tampa, FL 33604, **Home Phone:** (813)932-7859. **Business Addr:** Director of Sales Marketing and Convention Services, Tampa Convention Center, 333 S Franklin St, Tampa, FL 33602, **Business Phone:** (813)274-8442.

### BLAND, GLENN W.
Activist. **Personal:** Born Jan 6, 1953, Augusta, GA; son of Allen and Felton; children: Terius. **Career:** DuPoint, supvr, 1975-85; Laney-Walker Mus Inc, consult, 1976; Mayor Ed McIntyre, campaign coordr, 1982; Early Intervention Prog, consult, 1998. **Orgs:** Southern Christian Leadership Conf, 1975; Nat Asn Advan Colored People, 1980-. **Honors/Awds:** Man of the Year, Laney-Walker Mus, 1985. **Special Achievements:** Developed the first local Pilot Program to commemorate 9/11. **Home Addr:** 945 Wrightsboro Rd, Augusta, GA 30901, **Home Phone:** (706)724-5614.

### BLAND, LARCINE
Executive. **Educ:** Baptist Univ, BA, interdisciplinary studies, MA, orgn mgt, 2006. **Career:** CITGO, petrol, secy, 1973-79, mkt clerk, 1980-82, career opportunities coordr, 1983-85, career opportunities coordr, 1973-85; Southland Corp, temp labor mgr, 1985-89, urban affairs coordr, 1990-94; Southland Corp & 7-11 Inc, Urban Progs, mgr, 1985-97; 7-Eleven Inc, mgr, Urban Progs, 1985-98; Larcine Bland, mgr, Intercultural Affairs, 1998-2000; BLOCKBUSTER INC, vpres, Community Affairs & Diversity Initiatives, 1998-2009; LLB Consult, owner, 2009-. **Orgs:** Nat Asn Advan Colored People; C Miracle Network Corp Leadership Coun. **Business Addr:** Owner, LLB Consulting, 4529 Turnberry Lane, Grand Prairie, TX 75052, **Business Phone:** (972)642-5310.

### BLAND, DR. ROBERT ARTHUR
Government official. **Personal:** Born Jan 26, 1938, Petersburg, VA; married Shirley Thweatt; children: Angela Rene & Lael Gregory. **Educ:** Univ Va, BSEE, 1959; Calif State Univ, MA, 1975; Nova Univ, EdD, 1979, PhD. **Career:** Naval Weapons Ctr, proj engr 1959-71; Oxnard Comm Col, counr 1976-77, instr 1977-; Ventura Col; Aquarius Portrait Photogr, photogr, 1983-; Naval Ship Weapons Syst Eng Sta, div head, currently, Missile & Launching Systs, Calif, dept mgr, currently. **Orgs:** Instr Oxnard Comn Col 1977-; Comn, Ministry Episcopal Diocease Los Angeles, 1980-; vice chmn & adv comn, Ventura Cty Affirmative Action, 1982-; photog, Aquarius Portrait Photog, 1983-; vestry St Patricks Episcopal Church, 1985-. **Home Addr:** 3915 Crownhaven Ct, Newbury Park, CA 91320, **Home Phone:** (805)498-5682. **Business Addr:** Division Head, Naval Ship Weapon Sys Engineering, Code 4J10, Port Hueneme, CA 93041.

### BLANDEN, LEE ERNEST
School administrator, dean (education). **Personal:** Born Sep 16, 1942, Arcadia, FL; children: Teresa, Toni, Yvonne & Curtis. **Educ:** Voorhees Jr Col, AA, 1962; Lane Col Jackson, BA, elem educ, 1965; Univ Ill, MEd, admin & supv, 1970, post grad study educ admin & spur; Eastern Ill Univ, admin & sch law; Ill Asn Sch Bd, negotiations & sch law. **Career:** Voorhees Jr Col, Gen Develop Corp, 1958-60, maintenance, 1960-62; Wildwood Linen Supply, laborer summers, 1963-65; Lane Col Jackson TN, libr asst, asst varsity coach, 1965-70; Danville Dist 118, elem teacher, asst prin, 1965-70; Elem Bldg, prin, 1970-74; Danville Area Community Col, adult educ fac, 1970-74, dir personnel, 1974-80, asst to the pres, dean stud serv, 1980-85; interim supt, 1988. **Orgs:** Alpha Phi Alpha Fraternity; Omicron Lambda Beta; Danville United Fund; Am Soc Personnel Admin; bd dir, chairperson, Laura Lee Fel House; trustee bd, sanctuary chair, Second Baptist Church; ed admin, Danville Rotary Int; personnel mgr, Danville Chamber Com; master & secy, Corinthian Lodge 31 F&AM; bd dir, Ctr C Serv; bd dir, treas, Vermilion City Opportunities Indust Ctr Inc; bell ringer, Salvation Army; sch bd mem, Danville Community Consol Sch Dist 118, Bd Policy Revisions; chief negotiator, Bd Educ; consult & speaker, Nat Sch Bd Ann Conv; N Eastern Ohio Educ Asn. **Home Addr:** 4 W Bluff, Danville, IL 61832. **Business Addr:** Assistant to President, Dean, Danville Area Community College, 2000 E Main St, Danville, IL 61832, **Business Phone:** (217)443-3222.

### BLANDING, LARRY
Real estate agent, politician, association executive. **Personal:** Born Aug 29, 1953, Sumter, SC; son of Junius Sr and Rosa Lee (Williams) (deceased); married Peggy Ann Mack, Dec 24, 1977; children: Dreylan Dre' Neka. **Educ:** Claflin Col, BA, social sci, 1975; SC State Col,

MEd, educ, 1977; SC Sch Real Estate, 1988. **Career:** United Way Jacksonville, campaign assoc, 1975; United Way Richland & Lexington Co, actg dir comm planning, 1976; SC State Col, head resident, 1976-77; life-long resident, Sumter County; life-long resident, Coun Dist 6; SC Dem Party, vice chmn; SC House Rep, state rep, 1976-90; SC, state legislator; Univ SC, guest lectr, 1983; Realty World Colonial-Moses, sales assoc, 1987; Stud Govt Asn, pres; Sumter, SC, county coun chmn, councilman, 2006-; Santee Wateree Area Ment Health Ctr, asst dir, asst exec dir, currently. **Orgs:** Counr, Savage-Glover Boys Club, 1970; chmn, Nat Real Estate Comt, 1970-; Nat Caucus Black Leg, 1976-; bd dir, Sumter Learning Develop Ctr, 1977-82; Sumter Pub Awareness Assoc, 1977-; state dir, Phi Beta Sigma Fraternity Inc, 1979-83, life mem; bd mem, Sumter Co Develop Bd, 1983-; Southern Legis Conf, 1986-; bd mem, Sumter Chamber Com, 1986-; inspector gen, USCAAR 33rd degree Masons, 1986-; Local, State & Nat Bd Realtors, 1987-; vice chmn, Sumter County Coun, 2006, 2010; Nat Asn Advan Colored People; hon soc, Pi Gamma Mu Iota Chap, Orangesburg SC; chmn, SC Legis Black Caucus; St Paul Lodge 8, CC Johnson Consistory 136, Cario Temple 125; life mem, Claflin Univ Int Alumni Asn; Nat Hons Soc; pres, Stud Gov Asn; pres, Walker Cemetery Asn; bd dir, Jehovah Acad & Christian Sch, Jehovah Child Develop Ctr; vpres, B F Weston Educ Found, pres; Alumni Hall Fame; Nat Asn Counties; vpres, treas, Sc County Coun Coalition; co-chmn, Sumter Schs Consol Comt; charter mem, Pi Gamma Mu Nat Hons Soc; Citadel Bd Visitors; SC Human Affairs Comn; pres, Goodfellows Club; pres, Life Mem Gen Fraternity. **Honors/Awds:** Sigma Man of the Year, Phi Beta Sigma Frat Inc, 1977; Man of the Year, Claflin Col, 1975; Citizen of the Year, Omega Psi Phi Frat Gamma Iota Chap, 1976; Alumni Award, Claflin Col, 1987; Family Pioneer, Williams Family Reunion Comt, 1989; Claflin's Alumni Hall of Fame, 2003. **Special Achievements:** Listed as one of Fifty Future Leaders of America, EBONY Mag, 1978; First African American to hold the vice chairman position of SC Democratic party; first African American to sit on the Joint Bond Review Committee and to Chair a sub-committee of the powerful House Ways and Means Committee. **Home Addr:** 1021 Morton St, PO Box 1446, Sumter, SC 29150, **Home Phone:** (803)775-8062. **Business Addr:** Assistant Executive Director, Santee Wateree Area Mental Health Center, 215 N Magnolia St, Sumter, SC 29150, **Business Phone:** (803)775-9364.

### BLANFORD, DR. COLVIN

Clergy, educator, association executive. **Personal:** Born Feb 6, 1938, Dallas, TX; son of John Hardee and Hattie Ellen; married Margaret Ann Tyrrell; children: Colvin II & Christopher. **Educ:** San Francisco State Col, BA, 1960; Berkeley Baptist Divinity Sch, BDiv, 1963; Southern Calif Sch Theol, RelD, 1969. **Career:** Third Baptist Church San Francisco, youth & asst minister, 1956-63; Cosmopolitan Baptist Church San Francisco, pastor, 1963-70; San Francisco Youth Guid Ctr, prot chaplain, 1963-70; Brooks House Christian Serv Hammond IN, exec dir, 1970-73; First Baptist Church Gary IN, pastor, 1973-81; N Baptist Theol Sem, dir black church studies, 1974-91, assoc prof ministry, 1981-83, adj prof; Christ Baptist Church, pastor, 1981-2002, Repub SafricA, preaching missions Liberia, 1985, 1987, 1989; pastor emer, 2004-; New Life Christian Fels Int, organizing pastor, 2004-. **Orgs:** Baptist Ministers Conf, 1973-; Interfaith Clergy Coun, 1973-; bd dir, Morehouse Sch Relig, 1976-; life mem, Nat Asn Advan Colored People, 1980-; bd mem, Gary Nat Asn Advan Colored People, 1986-. **Honors/Awds:** Youth of the Year, San Francisco Sun Reporter, 1958; Sermon Public Outstanding Black Sermons, Judson Press, 1976; One Outstanding Black ministers in America, Dollars & Sense Magazine, 1981; Represented Baptist denomination participant, Baptist Lutheran dialogue meaning baptism, 1981. **Home Addr:** 717 Newton St, Gary, IN 46403, **Home Phone:** (219)938-0487. **Business Addr:** Pastor Emeritus, Christ Baptist Church, 4700 E Seventh Ave, Gary, IN 46403, **Business Phone:** (219)938-5504.

### BLANKENSHIP, GLENN RAYFORD

Government official. **Personal:** Born Aug 11, 1948, Memphis, TN; son of Elbert and Geraldine Walton; married Zita R Jackson; children: Maia & Rayford. **Educ:** Am Univ, attended 1969; Le Moyne-Owen Col, attended 1970; Syracuse Univ, attended 1971; Univ Wis, attended 1973; Univ Colo, attended 1976. **Career:** Government official (retired); US Dept Housing & Urban Develop, fed energy admin, 1974-77; US Dept Energy, 1977-79; USDA Forest Serv, 1979-97. **Orgs:** Life mem, Kappa Alpha Psi; life mem, Nat Asn Advan Colored People; Meals Wheels, St John African Methodist Episcopal Church, 1998-99; steward, St John African Methodist Episcopal Church, 2000-. **Home Addr:** 409 Eaton Rd, Birmingham, AL 35242-6450, **Home Phone:** (205)980-5380.

### BLANKS, BILLY

Entrepreneur, actor. **Personal:** Born Sep 1, 1955, Eerie, PA; son of Isaac and Mabeline; married Gayle Godfrey; children: Shellie & Billy Jr. **Career:** Actor; US Olympic Karate team, captain, 1980; Billy Blacks World Training Ctr, pres & co-founder, currently; Films: Blood Fist, 1989; Tango & Cash, 1989; Driving Force, 1990; Lionheart, 1990; The Last Boy Scout, 1991; Talons of the Eagle, 1992; TC 2000, 1993; Expect No Mercy, 1996; Balance of Power, 1996; Kiss the Girls, 1997; Lionheart; Talons of the Eagle; Back in Action; Stand Alone; Balance of Power; Dance Club: The Movie, 2007; Jack & Jill, 2011; TV appearances: S.O.F. Special Ops Force, 1997; The Parent 'Hood, 1997; Sabrina, the Teenage Witch; The Parkers; Suddenly Susan; ER, 1999; The Oprah Winfrey Show, 1999; Melrose Place; Martial Law; Street Justice; Spenser: For Hire. **Orgs:** Founder, Billy Blanks Found, 1999. **Honors/Awds:** Karate Hall of Fame, 1982. **Special Achievements:** Martial arts champion; First Amateur Athletic Union Champ in 1975; Massachusetts Golden Gloves Boxing Champion, 1984; Tri-State Golden Gloves Champion of Champions; 7-time world karate champion; He was the captain of the United States Karate Team and won over 30 gold medals in international competition; He was the number 1 or number 2 rated full-contact karate fighter in the United States for almost seven straight years; His epic battles with "Nasty" Anderson are legends among martial arts fans; He posted over 300 career victories; Inducted into the Karate Hall of Fame, 1982. Massachusetts Golden Gloves champion in the light-heavyweight class, 1984. Tri-State Golden Gloves Champion of Champions. **Business Addr:** President, Co-Founder, Billy Blacks World Training Center, 14708 Ventura Blvd, Sherman Oaks, CA 91403, **Business Phone:** (818)325-0335.

### BLANKS, CECELIA (CECELIA OLIVER)

Counselor, administrator. **Personal:** Born Galveston, TX; daughter of Ella L Oliver and Lovie L Oliver. **Educ:** Calif State Univ, San Marcos, BA, social sci, 1992; San Diego State Univ, MEd, coun, 1994. **Career:** Miramar Col San Diego, staff; Cuyamaca Col, Extended Opportunity Progs & Serv & Coop Agencies Resources Educ, counr, 2000-02; Calif State Univ, Educ Opportunity Prog, staff, 1990-, sch rel ambassador, coordr & acad counr, 2005-07, adminr, dir, 2007-11, lectr, 2011, sr assoc dir, 2011-. **Orgs:** Supportive Parents Info Network Bd. **Home Addr:** , CA. **Business Addr:** Senior Associate Director of Educational Opportunity Program, California State University, 333 S Twin Oaks Valley Rd, San Marcos, CA 92096-0001, **Business Phone:** (760)750-4861.

### BLANKS, DELILAH BOWEN

**Personal:** Born Apr 5, 1936, Acme, NC; married Eddie W; children: Sherri Ann & Rhonda Fay. **Educ:** Shaw Univ, AB, Eng & social studies, 1957; E Carolina Univ, AB, libr sci,1965; Univ NC, MSW, 1972, PhD, pub health, 1984. **Career:** Income tax consult, 1957-; pub sch teacher, 1957-65; Whiteville City Sch, teachereng, 1960-62; Wake Co Bd Educ, teacher & librn, 1963-67; Brunswick County Bd Educ, teacher & librn, 1963-67; Neighborhood Youth Corps, counr, 1965-67; Bladen County, Dept Social Serv, child welfare worker, 1967-71; NC State Dept Social Serv, community develop specialist I, 1971-72; Univ NC, asst prof sociol & social work, 1972-92; Bladen County, comnr, 1980-; NC Asn County Comnr, pres, currently; Univ NC, asst prof emer, currently. **Orgs:** Nat Coun Social Work Educ, 1974-; bd mem, NC Comn Two Party Syst, 1974; Nat Asn Social Workers, 1976-92; Bladen County Bd Comnr, 1988-; vice chmn, Four County Community Serv; bd dir, Bladen Community Col Found; NC Asn Black Elected Officials; bd dir, Bladen County Partnership C; bd dir, NC Southeast Econ Develop Comn; Delta Sigma Theta; chair, Arcadia Bd Town Counmen; Nat Asn Adv Colored People; vice chair, Bladen County Dem Exec Comn; Bladen County Improv Asn Univ Prof, 1976-92; bd mem, Wilmington New Hanover Headstart Inc; NC Asn County Commissioners. **Honors/Awds:** NC Senclander of the Month, 1974; Bladen County Citizen of the Year, 1991. **Special Achievements:** One of the Most Distinguished Women in North Carolina in 1989; Cited as Who's Who Among Black Americans for outstanding achievement in Education & Community Services; The Delilah B Blanks Social Work Education Award was established in her name. **Home Addr:** 1369 Bowen Blanks Rd, Riegelwood, NC 28456, **Home Phone:** (910)655-1615. **Business Addr:** Professor Emeritus, University of North Carolina, 5051 New Centre Dr, Wilmington, NC 28403, **Business Phone:** (910)962-2658.

### BLANKS, WILHELMINA E.

Government official, president (organization). **Personal:** Born Nov 10, 1905, Decatur, AL; married Walter T; children: Wilhelmina B Adm Balla & Muriel Inniss. **Educ:** Atlanta Univ, AB, 1927; Loyola Univ; N western Sch Journalism; Univ Chicago. **Career:** Prairie View State Col, teacher, 1927-29; Cook Co Dept Pub Aid, 1936-74, asst dist off supvr, 1974-; freelance writer. **Orgs:** Organizer, Mich Ave Adult Educ Ctr; Tutoring Proj Mothers Univ Chicago; Social Serv Guild St Edmund's Episcopal Church; bd mem, City Asn Women's Bd Art Inst Chicago; vpres, S Side Comn Art Ctr Chicago; Bravo Chap Lyric Opera Chicago; PUSH; Nat Asn Advan Colored People; Chicago Urban League; vpres, Am Friends Liberia; Citizens Comn Du Sable Mus African Am Hist. **Honors/Awds:** Distinguish Service Award, Dedication Develop Art Black Comn S Side Community Art Ctr, 1970; Award for Achievement, Pub Welfare Int Travelers Asn, 1972. **Home Addr:** 1146 E Hyde Pk Blvd, Chicago, IL 60615. **Business Addr:** Assistant District Office Supervisor, Department Public Aid, 300 W Pershing Rd, Chicago, IL 60609.

### BLANTON, DAIN

Athlete, volleyball player. **Personal:** Born Nov 28, 1971, Laguna Beach, CA. **Educ:** Pepperdine Univ, BA, phys educ, commun, pub rels, 1994. **Career:** Beach volleyball player, broadcaster, inspirational speaker, model; AVP, 1994-2008, analyst, currently; USAV, 1999-2000; BVA, 2001; FIVB Pro beach volleyball, analyst, currently; Getting-To-Gold, educ speaker, 2001-; Dain Blanton Inc, owner, 2004-; Universal Sports Network, sports broadcaster, 2005-; ABC, sports broadcaster, 2008-; NBC, sports broadcaster; ESPN, sports broadcaster; Fox Sports Net, sports broadcaster. **Special Achievements:** First ever African American to win a Major Beach Volleyball tournament. **Business Addr:** Sports Broadcaster, Woodland Hills, CA.

### BLANTON, RICKY WAYNE

Basketball player, basketball coach. **Personal:** Born Apr 21, 1966, Miami, FL. **Educ:** La State Univ, BA, 1989. **Career:** Basketball player (retired), basketball coach; Pheonix Suns, 1990; Scaini Venezia, Italy, 1991-92; Wichita Falls Texans, 1992-93; Chicago Bulls, 1992-93; Sioux Falls Skyforce, 1993; Rapid City Thrillers, 1993-94; Chalons-en-Champagne, 1993-94; Quilmes de Mar del Plata, 1994-95; Nicholls State Univ, head coach, 2002-04; Col basketball team, head coach.

### BLAYLOCK, DARON OSHAY. See BLAYLOCK, MOOKIE.

### BLAYLOCK, MOOKIE (DARON OSHAY BLAYLOCK)

Basketball player. **Personal:** Born Mar 20, 1967, Garland, TX; married Janelle; children: Zachary, Daron Jr & Domnick. **Educ:** Midland Col, attended 1987; Univ Okla, attended 1989. **Career:** Basketball player (retired); NJ Nets, guard, 1989-92, Atlanta Hawks, 1992-99; Golden State Warriors, res, 1999-2002.

### BLAYLOCK, RONALD

Founder (originator), chief executive officer. **Personal:** Born Jan 1, 1960?; married Judith Irene Byrd. **Educ:** Georgetown Univ, BS, finance, 1982; NY Univ, Stern Sch Bus & finance, MBA, finance. **Career:** CitiGroup, vpres, 1982-88; Paine Webber, first vpres, 1986-92; Utendahl Capital Partners, 1992-93; Blaylock & Co, founder, pres, chmn & chief exec officer, 1993-; Fine Host Corp, dir, 1996-; GenNx360 Capital Partners, founder & managing partner, 2006-; UBS, sr mgt; Denny's Corp, staff. **Orgs:** Bd dir, WR Berkley Ins Co, 2001-; bd dir, Radio One, 2002-; adv bd, e-Smart Technologies Inc, 2003-; bd dir, CarMax Inc, 2007-; Syncreon Int Group, 2009-; bd dir, New York Univ; bd trustee, Carnegie Hall; bd trustee, Prep Prep; New York Univ Bd Trustees; Nat Asn Basketball Coaches; independent dir, Harbourton Mortgage Corp; trustee, New York Univ; Am Ballet Theatre; Inner-City Scholar Fund; bd trustee, Georgetown Univ; Am Gen Life Ins Co; trustee, Prep Prep; bd dir, Blaylock Beal Van LLC. **Honors/Awds:** "Corporate Finance Magazine", Capital Raiser of the Year, 1999; "Black Enterprise", 75 Most Powerful Blacks on Wall Street, 2005 & 2011. **Business Addr:** Founder, Managing Partner, GenNx360 Capital Partners, 590 Madison Ave 27th Fl, New York, NY 10022, **Business Phone:** (212)257-6786.

### BLAYLOCK, RONALD EDWARD

Executive, executive director. **Personal:** Born Jan 1, 1960?; married Judith Irene Byrd; children: 3. **Educ:** Georgetown Univ, BS, finance, 1982; NY Univ, Stern Sch Bus, MBA, finance. **Career:** Citicorp, vpres, 1982-88; Citibank, capital markets, 1986; PaineWebber Group Inc, vpres, 1986-92; Utendahl Capital Partners, exec vpres, 1992-93; Blaylock & Partners LP, founder, chmn & chief exec officer, 1993-; bd mem, Harbourton Mortgage Corp; WR Berkley Corp, dir, 2001-; dir, Radio One Inc, 2002-; E-Smart Technologies Inc, Mem Adv Bd, 2003-; Nat Asn Investment Co, dir, currently. **Orgs:** Bd trustee, Georgetown Univ; bd mem, Fine Host Corp, 1996-; bd, Am Ballet Theatre; bd trustee, NY Univ; bd mem, CarMax Inc, 2007-; Bill Bradley Pres; Gore 2000; Gephardt Pres; Hillary Rodham Clinton US Senate Comt; Joe Lieberman Pres; bd dir, Nat Asn Basketball Coaches; Obama Am; Sharpton 2004. **Business Addr:** Founder, Chairman & Chief Executive Officer, Blaylock & Co, 780 3rd Ave 44th Fl, New York, NY 10017, **Business Phone:** (212)715-6600.

### BLAYTON-TAYLOR, BETTY. See Obituaries Section.

### BLEDSOE, CAROLYN E. LEWIS

Government official. **Personal:** Born Jan 31, 1946, Richmond, VA; married Earl L; children: Demetrius, Katrina L & Tanya N. **Educ:** Va State Univ, AB, 1968, MA. **Career:** King William Co Pub Schs, teacher, 1968-69; Richmond Pub Schs, teacher, 1969-71; Dept Develop Progs, res analyst, 1972-80; City Gov, sr planner, 1980-. **Orgs:** Vpres, bd dir, Commonwealth Girl Scout Coun VA Inc, 1976-84, 1979-81; secy, treas, Northern VA Baptist Ministers' Wives, 1981-83; chair scholar, Comn VA State Asn Ministers' Wives, 1981-84; King County Jobs, currently. **Home Addr:** 711 Wadsworth Dr, Richmond, VA 23236-2625, **Home Phone:** (804)320-7696. **Business Addr:** Senior Planner, Department Planning & Development, 900 E Broad St Rm 500, Richmond, VA 23219.

### BLEDSOE, JAMES L.

Government official, administrator, chief financial officer. **Personal:** Born Dec 1, 1947, Tuskegee, AL; son of Willie James and Ada M Randle; married Clara A Fisher; children: Patrice. **Educ:** Univ W Fla, Pensacola, Fla, BS, 1972, MPA, 1974. **Career:** Dept Budget, City Miami, chief mgmt analyst, 1978-86; Dept Solid Waste, City Miami, asst dir, 1986-87; Dept Budget, City Miami, asst dir, 1988; Sweet Home, Missionary Baptist church, chief financial officer, 1995-; church adminr, currently. **Orgs:** Am Soc Pub Admin, 1978-; Nat Forum Black Pub Admin, 1982-; Am Pub Works Asn, 1986-; bd mem, Selective Serv Syst, 1987-. **Home Addr:** 16022 SW 287th St, Homestead, FL 33033-1185, **Home Phone:** (305)245-6225. **Business Addr:** Church Administrator, Chief Financial Officer, Sweet Home Missionary Baptist Church, 10701 SW 184th St, Miami, FL 33157, **Business Phone:** (305)251-5753.

### BLEDSOE, MELVIN

Executive, transportation consultant. **Personal:** Born Jun 5, 1955, Memphis, TN; son of Estell; married Linda Ann; children: Monica & Carlos. **Educ:** Milwaukee Area Tech Col, attended 1980. **Career:** Graceland Tours, supvr shuttle bus, 1982-83; Grayline Tours, oper mgr, 1983-87; Blues City Tours, pres & co-owner, 1998-. **Orgs:** Bd mem, Memphis Conv Visitor Ctr, 1992; Downtown Memphis Redevelop Comn, 1993. **Home Addr:** 4800 Aspen Ave, Memphis, TN 38128, **Home Phone:** (901)384-3656. **Business Addr:** President, Co-Owner, Blues City Tours, 325 Union Ave, Memphis, TN 38103, **Business Phone:** (901)522-9229.

### BLEDSOE, TEMPESTT

Actor. **Personal:** Born Aug 1, 1973, Chicago, IL; daughter of Wilma. **Educ:** NY Univ, finance. **Career:** Actor, Currently; TV series: "The Cosby Show", 1984-92; "The Gift of Amazing Grace", 1986; "Dance Til Dawn", 1988-89; "Dream Date", 1989; "Santa & Pete", 1999; "The Expendables", 2000; "Fire & Ice", 2001; "South of Nowhere", 2006; "That Is So Not Mom", 2006; "Guys with Kids", 2012-13; "Instant Mom", 2014. Films: Bachelor Man, 2003; Rock Me Baby, 2004; Strong Med, 2005; Fingers Walking, 2005; The View, 2006; VH-1s Celebrity Fit Club; Husband for Hire, 2008; South of Nowhere, 2008; Clean House, 2011-. Others: ABC AfterSchool Specials, 1986; Monsters, 1988; Jenny, 1997; Johnny B Good, 1998; The Practice, 1998; The Parkers, 1999; Strong Medicine, 2005; Raising the Bar, 2008; The Replacements, 2008-09; Househusbands of Hollywood, 2009; N-Secure, 2010; ParaNorman, 2012. **Honors/Awds:** Young Artist Award, 1989; Nat Merit Scholar finalist; Clarence Muse Youth Award, 1992; Impact Award, 2011. **Home Addr:** PO Box 7217, Beverly Hills, CA 90212. **Business Addr:** Actress, Principato Young Entertainment, 9229 Sunset Blvd Suite 310, Beverly Hills, CA 90212, **Business Phone:** (310)274-4474.

### BLEVINS, TONY

Football player. **Personal:** Born Jan 29, 1975, Rockford, IL. **Educ:** Univ Kans, grad. **Career:** Football player (retired); Indianapolis Colts, 1998-99 defensive back, 2000; San Francisco 49ers, 1998. **Honors/Awds:** Kansas Rookie of the Year, 1998.

**BLIGE, MARY JANE (MARY JANE BLIGE)**
Singer, songwriter. **Personal:** Born Jan 11, 1971, Bronx, NY; daughter of Thomas and Cora; married Kendu Isaacs. **Career:** Albums: What's the 411, 1994; My Life, 1994; Share My World, 1996; Mary, 2000; No More Drama, 2001; Dance for Me, 2002; Love & Life, 2003; The Breakthrough, 2006; Growning pains, 2007; Stronger with Each Tear, 2009; My Life II The Journey Continues (Act I), 2011; A Mary Christmas, 2013; The London Sessions, 2014. TV series: "The Jamie Foxx Show"; "Divas Live", 1999, 2001, 2002; "Ghost Whisperer", 2007; "Entourage", 2007; 30 Rock, 2009; Betty and Coretta, actress & exec producer, 2013. Films: Prison Song, 2000; I Can Do Bad All By Myself, 2009; American Idol, 2011; Rock of Ages, 2012; Black Nativity, 2013. MCA records, vocalist, currently. **Honors/Awds:** Soul Train Music Award, 1993; New York Music Award; NAACP Image Award; Double-Platinum Album ward; Grammy Award, 1996; Am Music Award, 1998; Soul Train Lady of Soul Awards, 1997, 1998; celebrity spokeperson, MAC AIDS Fund, 2001, 2002; Grammy Award, 2003; Grammy Award, 2004, 2008, 2009; People magazine's 100 Most Beautiful People, 2008. **Special Achievements:** Grammy nomination for Best R&B Album, 1995, 1999, 2002; sold over 60million records around the world since her career began in 1991; Grammy Award, 2007-09; Black Reel Award, 2012. **Business Addr:** Vocalist, MCA Uptown Records, 70 Universal City Plz Fl 3, Universal City, CA 91608, **Business Phone:** (818)777-4000.

**BLOCK, CAROLYN B.**
Educator, executive, consultant. **Personal:** Born Sep 7, 1942, New Orleans, LA. **Educ:** Xavier Univ, BS, 1963; Boston Univ, MS, 1965, MA, 1968, PhD, 1971. **Career:** Ctr Univ Calif, psychol couns, 1970-72; Wstsd Ment Health Ctr, psychol consult, 1972-; Family & Child Cross Serv, Mt Zion Hosp, San Francisco, dir, 1972-74; Pvt Pract, San Francisco, clincal psychol, 1973-; Univ Calif, Psychol Dept, lectr, 1973-93; C Youth Serv, Wstsd Community MentalHealth Ctr, dir, 1974-77; KQED-TV, content consult, 1977-80. **Orgs:** Nat Asn Black Psychol, 1970-; fel Am Psychol Asn, 1972-75; bd mem, San Francisco Comt C's TV, 1973-77; fel Soc Psychol Study Ethnic Minority Issues, 2001; San Francisco Red Cross. **Honors/Awds:** ABPP, 1998. **Business Addr:** Clinical Psychologist, Private Practice, 1947 Divisadero St Suite 2, San Francisco, CA 94115-2532, **Business Phone:** (415)922-9013.

**BLOCK, DR. LESLIE S.**
President (organization), executive, consultant. **Educ:** Univ Pittsburgh, BA, polit sci, 1974, MPA, 1977, PhD, higher educ admin, 1982; Northwestern Univ, 1993; Univ St Thomas, MN; Nat Louis Univ, IL; Spertus Col. **Career:** Nat-Louis Univ, adj grad fac; Spertus Col, vis grad fac; Leslie S Block & Assocs, founder & pres, 1985-, owner, currently; Northwestern Univ, vis scholar, 1986-93; Chessmen Club N Shore, pres, 1987-89; Univ Pittsburgh, consult; Corp & Foundations Rels Northeastern Ill Univ, asst dir. **Orgs:** Mayoral appointee, Human Rels Comn, Youngstown, Ohio, 1974-76; majority leader, Consult House Representatives, 1975; bd dir, Citizens Info Serv, Ill, 1990; Eastern & Southern African Mgt Inst, 1994-98; exec bd, Evanston Twp High Sch, Booster Club, 1993-2001, PTSA, chmn, Legis Comt, 1997-2000; independent evaluator, Minneapolis Urban League's Client Serv Div, 2003-04; facilitator, Grantmaker's Bd Develop, 2004. **Home Addr:** 4255 Rosewood Lane N, Plymouth, MN 55442, **Home Phone:** (763)551-3640. **Business Addr:** Founder, President, Owner, Leslie S Block & Associates, 4255 Rosewood Lane N, Plymouth, MN 55442-2611, **Business Phone:** (312)473-3699.

**BLOCKER, COL. TYREE C. (TY BLOCKER)**
Police officer, executive. **Educ:** MS. **Career:** Police officer (retired), executive; Pa State Police, Bur Drug Law Enforcement, maj & dir, 2001; Silver Seals Consult, owner; 22nd Comnr Pa State Police, Currently. **Orgs:** Pres, Police Futurists Int. **Home Addr:** 598 Mt Hope Rd, New London Township, PA 19352-8912, **Home Phone:** (610)932-9377. **Business Addr:** Commissioner, Pennsylvania State Police Department, 1800 Elmerton Ave, Harrisburg, PA 17110, **Business Phone:** (717)783-5556.

**BLOUIN, ROSE**
Educator, photographer. **Personal:** Born IL. **Educ:** Univ Ill, Chicago, IL, BA, 1971; Chicago State Univ, MA, 1983. **Career:** Photogr, 1980-; Chicago State Univ, Ctr Women's Identity Studies, staff assoc, 1980-83, lectr Eng compos, 1983-87; Third World Press, assoc ed, 1983-89; City Harvey, Ill, pub rels dir, 1984-86; Columbia Col, Chicago, Ill, prof eng dept, 1986-. **Home Addr:** , Chicago, IL 60619. **Business Addr:** Associate Professor Emerita, Columbia College of Chicago, IL.

**BLOUNT, CHARLOTTE RENEE**
Educator, writer, journalist. **Personal:** Born Mar 2, 1952, Washington, DC. **Educ:** Cath Univ Scholastic Jour Inst; Ohio Univ, attended 1972; Am Univ, Wash, DC, BA, jour, 1974, grad courses, 1976. **Career:** WOUB-FM, Athens, OH, reporter & announcer, 1971-72; Wash DC Voice & Visions Prods, freelance talent, 1973-; WOOK-FM, Wash, reporter & announcer, 1973-74; WILD Boston, reporter & announcer, 1974; Securities & Exchange Comn, writer, 1974-75; George Washington Univ, assoc prof, 1978-; Mutual Black Network, White House & state dept corres. **Orgs:** Zeta Phi Beta Sor Beta Zeta Chap, Wash; nat pub rels dir, Zeta Phi Beta, 1976-78. **Honors/Awds:** Nominee, Most Outstanding Young Woman, 1976; News Woman of the Year, Nat Asn TV & Radio Artists, 1976; Young Career Woman DC, Nat Fedn Bus & Prof Women, 1976; Young Women of the Year, Prof Women's Club. **Home Addr:** 1111 19th St NW, Washington, DC 20036. **Business Addr:** Correspondent, Mutual Black Network, 1755 Jefferson Davis Hwy, Arlington, VA 22202.

**BLOUNT, CORIE KASOUN**
Basketball player, real estate executive. **Personal:** Born Jan 4, 1969, Monrovia, CA; married Nicole; children: 5. **Educ:** Santa Ana Col, attended 1991; Univ Cincinnati, attended 1993. **Career:** Basketball player (retired), coach, real estate exec; Chicago Bulls, pt forward, 1993-95, 2002-04; Los Angeles Lakers, pt forward, 1995-99; Cleveland Cavaliers, pt forward, 1999; Phoenix Suns, pt forward, 1999-2001; Golden State Warriors, pt forward, 2001; Philadelphia 76ers, pt forward, 2001-02; Toronto Raptors, pt forward & ctr, 2003-04; real estate exec, currently; Univ Cincinnati, men's asst basketball coach, 2005-. **Honors/Awds:** JUCO Co-Player of the Year. **Special Achievements:** Film Appeared: Eddie, 1996. **Business Addr:** Men's Assistant Basketball Coach, University of Cincinnati, 2600 Clifton Ave, Cincinnati, OH 45220, **Business Phone:** (513)556-6000.

**BLOUNT, HEIDI LYNNE**
Banker. **Personal:** Born Apr 6, 1964, Cleveland, OH; daughter of Gilbert L and Sue H Johnson. **Educ:** Cleveland State Univ, BBA, 1996, MBA, 1997; paralegal cert, 2001. **Career:** Key Corp, dist security officer, 1981-98; Fifth Third Bank, asset recovery mgr, 1998-; NIA Style. **Orgs:** Educ meeting chair, Am Asn Univ Women, 1996; bd trustee, Karamu House Inc, 1998-; bd trustee, Christmas in April, 1999-; Delta Sigma Theta Sorority Inc. **Home Addr:** 4165 E 187th St, Cleveland, OH 44122-6962, **Home Phone:** (216)752-0658. **Business Addr:** Asset Recovery Manager, Fifth Third Bank, 1404 E 9th St, Cleveland, OH 44114, **Business Phone:** (216)274-5302.

**BLOUNT, MELVIN CORNELL**
Activist, football player. **Personal:** Born Apr 10, 1948, Vidalia, GA; son of James and Alice; married TiAnda; children: Norris, Tanisia, Shuntel, Dedrick, Akil, Jibri & Khalid. **Educ:** Southern Univ, Baton Rouge, LA, BS, phys educ, 1970. **Career:** Football player (retired), executive; Pittsburgh Steelers, Nat Football League, prof football player, Cornerback, 1970-83; Nat Football League, dir player rels, 1983-90; Nat Football League, Comnr Player Adv Bd, consult & mem, 1990; Cobb Creek Farms, owner/oper; Mel Blount Cellular Phone Co, owner/oper; Mel Blount Youth Home Inc, founder, 1983-. **Orgs:** Bd dir, Pgh Cs Mus; policy Coun Nat Ctr Youth & their Families; bd dir, Am Red Cross; rep, Red Cross visit to Mauritania N Africa fact finding exped; Paint Horse Asn, Am Quarter Horse Asn, Nat Cutting Horse Asn. **Honors/Awds:** National Football League Leader in Interceptions, 1975; named Most Valuable Player, Pittsburgh Steelers, 1975; Player of the Year, Nat Football League, 1975; Player of the Year, Asian Football Confederation, 1945; Most Valuable Player Pro Bowl, 1976; Super Bowl champion; Pro Football Hall of Fame, 1989; Louisiana Sports Hall of Fame, 1989; Georgia Sports Hall of Fame, 1990; NFL's 75th anniversary All-Time team, 1995; World Sports Humanitarian Hall of Fame, 1997; Spirit Award, 2000; Leather Helmet and Community Service Award, 2002; Gandhi, King, Ikeda Award Community Builders Award, 2004; Life's Work Career Achievement Award, 2006; Art Rooney Award's Dinner-Bob Prince Humanitarian Award, 2007; Gwendolyn J. Elliot Lifetime Achievement Award, 2009; America Community Cornerstone Award, Greater Pittsburgh Coun Boys Scouts, 2010; Pittsburgh Pro Football Hall of Fame, 2011. **Special Achievements:** Publicaltion: "The Cross Burns Brightly", 1993; ranked number 36 on The Sporting News' list of the 100 Greatest Football Players, 1999. **Business Addr:** Founder, Mel Blount Youth Home, 6 Mel Blount Dr, Claysville, PA 15323, **Business Phone:** (724)948-2311.

**BLOUNT, SHERRI N.**
Administrator, lawyer, vice president (organization). **Personal:** married Edward W Gray Jr. **Educ:** Univ NC, BA, 1977; Howard Univ Sch Law, JD, 1980. **Career:** Howard Univ, assoc ed Law J; Howard Univ Sch Commun, adj prof; Akin Gump Strauss Hauer & Feld LLP, assoc, 1980-83; Fed Trade Comn, atty, 1983-88; Pub Broadcasting Serv, vpres, dep gen coun & corp secy, 1988-98; Fitch Even Tabin & Flannery LLP, partner, 1998-2003, law firm partner, 2008-; Morrison & Foerster LLP, partner, 2003-08. **Orgs:** US Dist Ct; DC Ct Appeals; Supreme Ct US Am; DC Bar Asn; Can Retransmission Collective; Asn de Gestion Interationale Collective des Oeuvres Audio visuelles; corp secy, atty, Pub Broadcasting Serv; vpres, Dep Gen Coun; atty advisor, Fed Trade Comnr; Consumer Protection Bur, Fed Trade Comn; gen coun, Links Inc; bd, Duke Ellington Sch Arts; bd, Wash Area Lawyers Arts. **Business Addr:** Partner, Fitch Even Tabin & Flannery LLP, 1 Lafayette Ctr 1120 20th St Suite 750 S, Washington, DC 20036, **Business Phone:** (202)419-7000.

**BLOW, CHARLES M.**
Graphic artist, columnist. **Personal:** Born Aug 11, 1970; children: Three children. **Educ:** Grambling State University, B.A. in Mass Communications. **Career:** "The Detroit News," Graphic Artist; "The New York Times," Graphics Editor, Graphics Director, Design Director for News, 1994-06; "National Geographic," Art Director; "The New York Times," Visual Op-ed Columnist, 2008-. **Honors/Awds:** "The Root" Magazine, The Root 100 Honorees, 2013. **Special Achievements:** Frequent appearances on CNN and MSNBC.

**BLOW, KURTIS (KURT WALKER)**
Rap musician, musician. **Personal:** Born Aug 9, 1959, Harlem, NY; children: 3. **Educ:** City Col NY. **Career:** Break dancer; DJ; Albums: Kurtis Blow, 1980; Deuce, 1981; Tough, 1982; Ego Trip, 1984; Rapper in Town, 1984; America, 1985; Kingdom Blow, 1986; The Breaks, 1986; Back by Popular Demand, 1988; Kurtis Blow Presents: Hip Hop Ministry, 2007; Just Do It, 2008; Father, Son, and Holy Ghost, 2009; 30th Anniversary of The Breaks CD, 2010. Singles: "Christmas Rappin'", 1979; "The Breaks", 1980; "Tough EP", 1982; "Party Time?", 1983; "Nervous", 1983; "Ego Trip", 1984; "Basketball", 1984; "The Bronx", 1986; "Back by Popular Demand", 1988; "Chillin' at the Spot", 1994. Films: Krush Groove, 1985; The Show, 1995; Rhyme & Reason, 1997; Allied Artists Entertainment Group, vpres, 2001; Disco: Spinning the Story, 2005; Breaking the Rules, 2006; Baisden After Dark, 2007; Beautiful Losers, 2008; Angel Camouflaged, 2010; It's Kind of a Funny Story, 2010; The Hip Hop Church, minister, currently; Sirius Satellite Radio, host, currently. **Special Achievements:** First rap artist to cut records with major recording label. **Business Addr:** Minister, The Hip Hop Church, 160 W 146 th St, Harlem, NY 10039.

**BLUDSON-FRANCIS, VERNETT MICHELLE**
Banker. **Personal:** Born Feb 18, 1951, New York, NY; daughter of William Benjamin and Alfreda Peace; married Robert Francis Sr; children: Robert Jr. **Educ:** New York Univ, New York, NY, BS, 1973, MPA, 1976. **Career:** Morgan Guaranty Trust, New York, NY, mgmt trainee, 1973-75; Citibank, NA, New York, NY, vpres, 1975-94; Nat Minority/Women's Vendor Prog, NY, dir, 1977-; CTI Personnel, Salesperson, 1994-. **Orgs:** Nat Urban Affairs Coun, 1984-; Nat Minority Bus Coun, 1986-; Coalition of 100 Black Women; YW/YMCA Day Care Ctr Inc, 1986-; Nat Forum Black Pub Admins; Nat Asn Advan Colored People; UBC; Black Achievers Indust Alumni Asn; Images-Wall St Chap; Cornell Univ Coop Exten Prog; Nat Asn Women Bus Owners; NY State Dept Econ Develop/Minority & Women's Div. **Honors/Awds:** Black Achievers, Citibank/Harlem YMCA, 1984; Those Who Make A Difference, Nat Urban Affairs CNL, 1985; MNY Advocate of the Year, US Dept Com MBDA Reg Off, 1985; Mary McLeod Bethune Award, NCW, 1986; Public Private-Sector Award, US Dept Housing & Urban Develop, 1986; Banker of the Year, Urban Bankers Coalition, 1987; Woman of the Year, Harlem YMCA, 1987; Cecelia Cabiness Saunders Award, New Harlem YMCA, 1987. **Special Achievements:** Co-sponsor, Exec Banking progs with NMBC, 1983, 1984 & 1985, Exec Banking Prog with Westchester MNY Contractors Asn, 1986; Career Explor summer internship prog with Hunter Col & Coalition of 100 Black Women, 1986; co-host, First Ann BAI Alumni Fundraiser, 1986; chair, NUAC Stud Develop Dinner, 1988; Top 100 Black Bus & Prof Women, Dollars & Sense Mag, 1988; sponsor, Dept Defense Symp for the Vendor Input Comn, 1988. **Home Addr:** 65 W 96th St Apt 20C, New York, NY 10025-6533, **Home Phone:** (212)864-4812. **Business Addr:** Vice President, Director, Citibank/Citicorp, 1 Ct Sq 10th Fl, Long Island City, NY 11101, **Business Phone:** (718)248-2096.

**BLUE, DANIEL TERRY, JR.**
State government official, lawyer, executive. **Personal:** Born Apr 18, 1949, Lumberton, NC; son of Daniel T Sr and Allene Morris; married Edna Earle Smith; children: Daniel Terry III, Kanika R & Dhamian. **Educ:** NC Cent Univ, BS, math, 1970; Duke Univ, JD, 1973; Nat Inst Trial Advocacy, cert, 1997. **Career:** Sanford, Adams, McCullough & Beard, Attys at Law, 1973-76; NC State House, rep, 1981-2002, 2006-09, speaker, 1991-94; Nat Inst Trial Advocacy, fac, 1983, 1985-87; Us Senate, Nc, cand, 2002; Thigpen, Blue, Stephens & Fellers, managing partner, founding partner, 1976-; NC Gen Assembly, rep, 2007; NC state senate, 2009-; Duke Univ, chmn, 2009-11; First BanCorp, dir, 2010-. **Orgs:** Elder, Davie St Presby Church; Alpha Phi Alpha Fraternity Inc; Wautauga Club, Kiwanis Club; bd dir, First Union Nat Bank NC; bd govs, NC Acad Trial Lawyers, 1982-86; Legis Black Caucus, chmn, 1984-89; pres, Nat Conf State Legislatures, 1998-99; trustee, Duke Univ, 2009-11; chair, Clinton & Gore Campaign NC; bd visitor, Duke Law Sch; Am Bar Asn; NC Bar Asn; Wake County Bar Asn; NC Asn Black Lawyers, Asn Trial Lawyers Am; dir, Exec & Loan Comt; dir, Nominating & Corp Governance Comt. **Home Addr:** 4917 Longpointe Ct, Raleigh, NC 27604-5860, **Home Phone:** (919)833-1931. **Business Addr:** Managing Partner, Thigpen, Blue, Stephens & Fellers, 205 Fayetteville St Mall Suite 300, Raleigh, NC 27601, **Business Phone:** (919)833-1931.

**BLUE, DR. GENE C.**
Executive, association executive. **Educ:** MBA. **Career:** Ariz Opportunities Industrialization Ctr, pres & chief exec officer, currently. **Orgs:** Nat bd dir, Ariz Fathers & Families Coalition; bd mem, Southwest Leadership Found Inc; bd mem, City Phoenix; bd mem, Downtown Phoenix; Opportunities Industrialization Ctr; Phoenix Conv Ctr; bd mem, HIV/AIDS Educ Partners; adv bd, Red Tuxedo; bd mem, FOX Systs Inc. **Business Addr:** President, Chief Executive Officer, Arizona Opportunities Industrialization Center, 39 E Jackson St, Phoenix, AZ 85004-2443, **Business Phone:** (602)254-5081.

**BLUE, OCTAVIA LADAWN**
Basketball player, basketball coach. **Personal:** Born Apr 18, 1976, Ft. Lauderdale, FL. **Educ:** Miami Univ, sociol & sports mgt, 1998. **Career:** Basketball player (retired), basketball coach; Los Angeles Sparks, 1998; Minn Lynx; Houston Comets, forward, 2003-04; Bnei Yehuda, Israel, 2005; Villeneuve, France; Maccabi Tel Kabir, power forward, Israel, 2006; St. Johns Univ, asst coach, 2008-09; CSTV Networks Inc, asst coach; Tenn Tech Univ, head coach; Ga Tech womens basketball, asst coach, 2009-12; Univ Miami, womens basketball asst coach, 2012-. **Business Addr:** Women's Basketball Assistant Coach, University of Miami, Ashe Bldg Rm 132 1252 Memorial Dr, Coral Gables, FL 33146, **Business Phone:** (305)284-4323.

**BLUE, VIDA ROCHELLE, JR.**
Actor, baseball player, executive. **Personal:** Born Jul 28, 1949, Mansfield, LA; son of Vida Sr and Sallie A Henderson; married Peggy Shannon; children: 6. **Career:** Baseball player (retired), baseball coach; Oakland Athletics, pitcher, 1969-77; San Francisco Giants, 1978-81, 1985-86; Kans City Royals, pitcher, 1982-83; Vida Blue Baseball Camp, Pleasanton, Calif, founder; Giants Fantasy Camp, NL pres; San Francisco Giants Baseball Camps, adult camp coach; Vida Blue Base Ball Clinics, Costa Rica, founder, currently; Comcast SportsNet Bay Area, baseball analyst, currently. **Special Achievements:** Film: Black Gunn, 1972. **Home Addr:** 1560 Locust Dr, PO Box 1449, Tracy, CA 95376-5301, **Home Phone:** (209)836-1214. **Business Addr:** Baseball analyst, Comcast SportsNet, 360 3rd St 2nd Fl, San Francisco, CA 94107, **Business Phone:** (415)296-8900.

**BLUFORD, COL. GUION STEWART, JR. (GUY BLUFORD)**
Astronaut, president (organization), air force officer. **Personal:** Born Nov 22, 1942, Philadelphia, PA; son of Lolita and Guion; married Linda Tull; children: Guion Stewart III & James Trevor. **Educ:** Pa State Univ, BS, aerospace engineering, 1964; Air Force Inst Technol, MS, aerospace engineering, 1974, PhD, aerospace engineering, 1978; Univ Houston, ClearLake, MBA, 1987; Univ Pa, Wharton Sch Bus. **Career:** Col, astronaut (retired), president; Williams AFB, Ariz, pilot training, 1966; USAF F-4C pilot, Vietnam; Sheppard AFB, Tex, T-38A, instr pilot, stand/eval officer & asst flight comdr, 1967; Squadron Officers Sch, Sch Secy Wing, 1971; Wright-Patterson AFB, staff devel engr, chief aerodynamics & airframe br, Ohio, 1974-78; NASA, astronaut, 1979-93, mission specialist, STS-8 Orbiter Challenger, August, 1983; STS 61-A Orbiter Challenger, mission specialist, 1985; STS-39 Orbiter Discovery, pt contact, generic Spacelab systs & experiments, payload safety, orbitor systs & flight software issues, mission specialist, 1991; Orbiter Discovery, mission specialist STS-53, 1992; NYMA Inc, vpres & gen mgr eng serv div, 1993; Fed Data Corp, vpres, 1997; Micro gravity, vpres R&D Opers; Northrop Grumman, vpres, 2000-02; Aero-

space Technol Group, pres, 2002-; ENSCO Inc, life dir, bd dir, 2005-. **Orgs:** Pa State Univ, Soc Distinguished Alumni, 1986-; Pa State Univ, Col Engineering, Comt Minority Activ, 1986-2006; Nat Res Coun Aeronaut & Space Engineering Bd, 1993-98; Leadership Cleveland, 1995-; Assoc fel Am Inst Aeronaut & Astronaut, bd dir, 1995-2001; Air Force Asn, Tau Beta Pi, Sigma Iota Epsilon, Nat Tech Asn & Tuskegee Airmen; bd Gov, Nat Space Club, 1997-2001; bd dir, Nat Inventors Hall Fame Found, 1997-2002; bd dir, Western Res Hist Soc, 1997-2003; bd dir, Great Lakes Sci Ctr, 1997-2003; bd trustee, Aerospace Corp, 1999-2008; US Space Found, bd dir, 2000-06; bd visitor, Hiram Col, 2004-09; bd advisor, Coalition Space Explor, 2006-2010. **Honors/Awds:** Leadership Award, Phi Delta Kappa, 1962; Nat Defense Service Medal, 1965; Vietnam Campaign Medal, 1967; Vietnam Service Medal, 1967; 3 Air Force Outstanding Unit Awards, 1967, 1970, 1972; German Air Force Aviation Badge, Fed Repub W Ger, 1969; T-38 Instructor Pilot of the Month, 1970; Air Training Command Outstanding Flight Safety Award, 1970; Air Force Commendation Medal, 1972; Mervin E. Gross Award, Instit Technol, 1974; Air Force Meritorious Service Award, 1978; Distinguished Nat Scientist Award, Nat Soc of Black Engrs, 1979; 2 NASA Group Achievement Awards, 1980, 1981; Distinguished Alumni Award, 1983, Alumni Fellow Award, 1986, Pennsylvania St Univ Alumni Asn; NASA Space Flight Medal, 1983, 1985, 1991, 1992; Ebony Black Achievement Award, 1983; Image Award, NAACP, 1983; Distinguished Service Medal, St of Pennsylvania, 1984; Whitney Young Memorial Award, New York City Urban League; Black Engineer of the Year Award, 1991; NASA Exceptional Service Medal, 1992; NASA Distinguished Serv Medal, 1994; inductee, Int Space Hall of Fame, 1997; Air Force Institute of Technology Distinguished Alumni Award, 2002; Clear Lake Distinguished Alumni Award, 2003; U.S. Astronaut Hall of Fame inductee, 2010; The Pennsylvania Society Gold Medal, 2011. **Special Achievements:** First African American to fly in space, STS-8, the eighth flight of the Space Shuttle; first African American to return to space, STS-61A, the 22nd flight of the Space Shuttle, STS-39; the 40th flight of the Space Shuttle, and STS-53, the 52nd flight of the Space Shuttle; Who's Who Among Black Americans 1975-77; logged 688 hours in space, 1995. **Home Addr:** PO Box 549, North Olmsted, OH 44070. **Business Addr:** President, The Aerospace Technol Group, 2009 Corporate Dr, Boynton Beach, FL 33426, **Business Phone:** (561)735-3533.

## BLUFORD, JAMES F.

Insurance agent. **Personal:** Born Sep 6, 1943, Windsor, ON; son of Francis J and Dorysse G; children: James Francis, Sherice S & Nataki Monique. **Educ:** Wayne County Community Col, arts, 1972. **Career:** Allstate Insurance Co, sr acct agt, currently. **Home Addr:** 23825 Rockingham St, Southfield, MI 48033-7026, **Home Phone:** (248)358-0495. **Business Addr:** Senior Account Agent, Allstate Insurance Co, 5836 N Wayne Rd, Westland, MI 48185, **Business Phone:** (734)722-0700.

## BLUITT, DR. JULIANN STEPHANIE

Dentist, school administrator. **Personal:** Born Jun 14, 1938, Washington, DC; daughter of Stephen Bernard and Marion Eugene Hughes; married Roscoe C Foster. **Educ:** Howard Univ, BS, 1958, Dent Sch, DDS, 1962; Northwestern Univ, cert, personnel admin, 1984. **Career:** Louis Ball Scholar, 1955-59; Proj Headstart, dentist, 1964-66; Chicago Bd Health, dentist pub schs, 1964-67; Northwestern Univ Dent Sch, dir dent hyg, 1967-70, asst dean auxiliary & community prog & patient rels, 1970-72, assoc dean, 1972-78, Dept Community Med, asst prof, Off Stud Affairs & Dent Admis, 1978-89, assoc dean stud affairs, 1988; Am Col Dentist, pres, 1994-95. **Orgs:** Omicron Kappa Upsilon hon dent fraternity; pres, Chicago Dent Soc, 1991-93; Am Col Dentists; Am Asn Dent Schs; Nat Dent Asn; Fed Dentaire Inte; Am Soc Dent C; Am Asn Women Dentists; bd dir, served a mem a variety. **Special Achievements:** First women president of the Chicago Dental Society; First full time African American teacher in Northwestern University Dental School. **Business Addr:** Associate Dean, Northwestern University Dental School, 633 Clark St, Evanston, IL 60208, **Business Phone:** (847)491-3741.

## BLUNT, ROGER RECKLING, SR.

Executive. **Personal:** Born Oct 12, 1930, Providence, RI; son of Harry Weeden Jr and Bertha Reckling; married DeRosette Yvonne Hendricks; children: Roger Jr, Jennifer Mari, Amy Elizabeth & Jonathan Hendricks. **Educ:** USMA, New York, BS, 1956; Mass Inst Tech, MS, civil engr, MS, nuclear engr, 1962; Univ Md, Eastern Shore, MD, PhD, 2002. **Career:** Harbridge House Int, sr assoc, 1969-71; Tyroc Construct LLC, chief exec officer, 1971; Blunt Enterprises LLC, founder, chief exec officer & chmn, 1979, Blunt & Evans Consult engr, managing partner, 1979-84, pres & chief exec officer, chmn, currently; Essex Construct LLC, pres & chief exec officer, 1985-; 97th Army Res Command, comdr, 1986; Potomac Elec Power Co & Ameritas-Acacia Mutual Holding Co, dir; Asn Gov Bds Univs & Cols, chmn bd, Univ Syst Md, bd regents, vice chmn, 1990-96; United Educ Ins Risk Retention Group Inc, dir, 1990-99. **Orgs:** Am Soc Civil Engrs; Chair, Retired Mil Officers Asn; RMOA; Adv BdPrince George's Co. Comm Col Ctr Min Bus Dev; dir, Prince George's Co; Econ Dev Corp; Baltimore Presidents' Round Table; Am Nuclear Socs; Greater Prince Georges Bus Roundtable; Socs Am Mil Engrs; bd visitor, Univ Md Univ Col; Trustee Greater Wash Res Ctr; bd dirs, Greater Wash Bd Trade; Univ Md Found; Md Water Resources Adv Comn; Elder Presbyterian Church; W Pt Soc DC; DC Chamber Com; Sigma Pi Phi; Alpha Phi Alpha. **Honors/Awds:** Bus Leadership Award, Greater Wash Bus Ctr, 1976, 1978; Distinguished Service Award, Nat Asphalt Pavement Asn, 1984; Community Service Award, Jr Citizens Corps Inc, 1985; Whitney Young Award, Boys Scouts Am; Laureate Wash Bus Hall of Fame, 2001; Maryland Business Hall Of Fame, 2005. The Distinguished Service Medal, USA, Leadership Aware, Chairman Greater Washington Business Center; Laureate, 2001 Washington Business Hall of Fame; Honorary Degree, Doctorate of Public Service, University of Maryland Eastern Shore; Founders Award, District of Columbia Contractors' Association; Centennial Medal, Univ Md Col Engineering. **Home Addr:** 5716 Kenfield Lane, Upper Marlboro, MD 20772-3943. **Business Addr:** President, Chief Executive Officer, Essex Construction LLC, 9440 Pa Ave Suite 200, Upper Marlboro, MD 20772, **Business Phone:** (240)492-2001.

## BLY, DRE' (DONALD ANDRE BLY)

Football player. **Personal:** Born May 22, 1977, Chesapeake, VA; married Kristyn; children: Trey, Jordan, Aaron & Peyton. **Educ:** Univ NC. **Career:** Football player (retired), free agent; St. Louis Rams, cornerback, 1999-2001, right cornerback, 2000-02, strong safety, 2001; Detroit Lions, right cornerback, 2003-06, cornerback, 2004, 2010; Denver Broncos, right cornerback, 2007-08; San Francisco 49ers, left cornerback, 2009; free agt, currently. **Orgs:** Founder, Dre' Bly Found, 2003. **Honors/Awds:** Consensus All-American, 1996, 1997; NFC champion, 1999, 2001; Rookie, Super Bowl XXXIV; Pro Bowl selection, 2003, 2004; NFL Fumble Return Yards Leader, 2003; College Football Hall of Fame, 2014. **Special Achievements:** TV Series: "Super Bowl XXXVI ", 2002; "Rome Is Burning", 2006, 2009. Film: Super Bowl XXXIV, 2000.First player in the history of the Atlantic Coast Conference to earn consensus All-America honors three time; First Lion since to lead the club or tie for its season high in interceptions during four consecutive years (2003-06).

## BOAFO, KWADWO I. See WILSON, REV. WILLIE FREDERICK.

## BOARDLEY, CURTESTINE MAY

Government official. **Personal:** Born Dec 3, 1943, Sandersville, GA; daughter of William N and Zena Reaves; married James E; children: Angela B & Zena Y. **Educ:** Tuskegee Inst, BS, 1965, MEd, 1967. **Career:** Tuskegee Inst, admin asst dean women, 1966-67; Howard Univ, residence country, 1967-68; Pub Sch DC, counr, 1968; Voc Rehab Admin DC, voc rehab counr & actg co ordr counr, 1968-70; Fed Community Comn, employ counr, 1970-73, equal employ opportunity dir, 1973-76; Civil Serv Comn, Off Fed equal employ opportunity, 1976-79; US Off Personnel Mgt, equal employ opportunity specialist & mgr, Off Affirmative Employ Progs, 1979-83; Strayer Col, Wash, DC, instr, 1987, 1989, mgr, personnel mgt training div, 1983-95; US Dept Agr, prog mgt analyst. **Orgs:** Am Coun Asn; Ebenezer African Methodist Episcopal Church; charter mem, vpres, Ft Wash Charter Chap; Am Bus Women's Asn; Group, Wash DC Metrop Area, 1981-; Delta Sigma Theta, 1992-. **Honors/Awds:** Meritorious Performance Award, US Off Personnel Mgt, 1985; Directors Award, 1990; Special Act Award, 1991; Sustained Superior Performance, 1992. **Home Addr:** 2902 Kingsway Rd, Ft Washington, MD 20744, **Home Phone:** (301)248-2470. **Business Addr:** Program Management Analyst, US Department Agriculture Office of Civil Rights, 1400 Independence Ave SW Rm 450, Washington, DC 20250, **Business Phone:** (202)720-1145.

## BOARDLEY-SUBER, DR. DIANNE

College president. **Personal:** married Farah; children: Nichole Reshan Lewis & Raegan LaTrese Thomas. **Educ:** Hampton Univ, BS, childhood educ & teaching, 1971; Univ Ill, Urbana, MEd, educ curric & supv, 1973; Va Polytech Inst & State Univ, Blacksburg, VA, PhD, educ leadership & admin, gen, 1995. **Career:** Educator (retired); Newport News Pub Schs, Elem & Mid Sch Prin, 1976-92; Matthew Whaley Primary Sch, prin, 1983-86; Greensboro, NC, first grade teacher; Grad Col Educ, Grad Col Educ, 1986-90; Newport News, Va, lead kindergarten teacher; Hampton Univ, Hampton, Va, dean admin serv, 1992-93, asst provost acad affairs, 1992-96, liaisongen assembly, Self Study Accreditation, dir, vpres admin serv, 1996-99; St Augustine's Col, pres, 1999-2014. **Orgs:** Pres Bush Bd Adv White House Initiative Hist Black Col & Univ; bd trustee, Triangle United Way; Cent Region bd dir, Wachovia Bank; bd dir, Cent Intercollegiate Athletic Asn; bd dir, United Negro Col Fund; bd dir, Bus & Technol Ctr; bd dir, NC Martin Luther King Jr Resource Ctr Founding; vpres & bd dir, Coop Raleigh Col; bd dir, Nat Asn Independent Col & Univ; Southeast Raleigh Improv Assembly; Livable St Comt; Triangle Family Serv; Asn Episcopal Cols; comnr, Am Coun Educ.

## BOATMAN, MICHAEL PATRICK

Actor. **Personal:** Born Oct 25, 1964, Colorado Springs, CO; son of Daniel and Gwendolyn Pugh; married Myrna Forney; children: 4. **Educ:** Western Ill Univ, BA, theatre prog, 1989. **Career:** TV series: "China Beach", 1988; "Donor", 1990; "Shades of LA", 1991; "Fourth Story", 1991; "In the Line of Duty: Street War", 1992; "Quantum Lea", 1992; "The Jackie Thomas Show", 1992-93; "House of Secrets", 1993; "Muscle", 1995; "The Larry Sanders Show", 1995; "Living Single ", 1995; "The Peacemaker ", 1997; "Arli", 1996; "Spin City", 1996-2002; "Celebrity Dish", 2000; "Less Than Perfect", 2003; "Celebrity Mole Hawaii", 2003; "Law & Order: Special Victims Unit", 2003-11; "Educating Lewis", 2004; "CSI: Miami", 2004; "Yes, Dear", 2004; "Woman Thou Art Loosed", 2004; "Once Upon a Mattress", 2005; "Play Dates", 2005; "Scrubs", 2005; "Huff", 2006; " Frangela", 2007; "Grey's Anatomy", 2007; "Hannah Montana", 2008; "Criminal Minds", 2009; "The Game ", 2009; "Warehouse 13", 2009; "Sherri", 2009; "The Good Wife", 2009-14; "White Collar", 2010; "Gossip Girl ", 2011; "The Doctor", 2011; "The Smart One", 2012; "Hornet's Nest", 2012; "Anger Management ", 2012-13; Instant Mom", 2012-; "Philadelphia: The Great Experiment", 2013-14". Films: Hamburger Hill, 1987; Running On Empty, 1988; Unbecoming Age, 1992; Naked Gun 33 1/3 The Final Insult, 1994; The Glass Shield, 1994; The Peacemaker, 1997; Walking to the Waterline, 1998; Kalamazoo, 2005; And Then Came Love, 2007; Killing of Wendy, 2009; A Secret Promise, 2009; Three Chris's, 2010; Philadelphia: The Great Experiment, 2010; The Pool Boys, 2011; Queen of Media, 2011; Bad Parents, 2012. Novels: The Red Wake; Revenant Road, Traveling in Packs, 2007; My Father's Will, 2009; Inside Out, 2010. Writer: Good Laughs When You Die, 2007; The Flinch, 2008; The Revenant Road, 2009. **Honors/Awds:** Best Supporting Actor Award; Alumni Achievement Award, Western Ill Univ, 1997; GLAAD Award, Best Supporting Actor; Nominated for Image Award, 1998-03. **Special Achievements:** Was also nominated for two NAACP IMAGE Awards; was nominated five timesfor the IMAGE Award for Best Supporting Actor in a comedy series. **Business Addr:** Actor, Baker, Winoker, Ryder, 909 3rd Ave 9th Fl, New York, NY 10022-4731, **Business Phone:** (212)582-0700.

## BOATWRIGHT, CYNTHIA

Executive. **Career:** WGFT Radio, prog dir, currently. **Business Addr:** Program Director, WGFT Radio, 20 Fed Plz W Suite T-2, Youngstown, OH 44503, **Business Phone:** (330)744-5115.

## BOATWRIGHT, DR. JOSEPH WELDON, III

Physician. **Personal:** Born Jan 4, 1949, Richmond, VA; married Evelyn Donella Durham; children: Joseph Weldon IV. **Educ:** Davis & Elkins Col, BS, 1970; Univ Va, Sch Med, MD, 1974. **Career:** Med Col Va, Grad Sch Med Educ, pediat resident, 1978, clin instr; pvt pract pediatrician, currently; State Health Benefits Adv Coun, 2000-02; St Mary's Hosp, active staff; Richmond Memorial Hosp, active staff. **Orgs:** N Chamberlayne Civic Asn; fund raising comt, Florence Neal Cooper Smith Sickle Cell Initiative; Med Soc Va. **Honors/Awds:** Honorable Scholar, Davis & Elkins Col, 1966; Scholar, Univ Va, 1970. **Home Addr:** PO Box 26591, Richmond, VA 23261-6591. **Business Addr:** Pediatrician, Private Practice, 211 E Clay St, Richmond, VA 23219-1325, **Business Phone:** (804)643-8914.

## BOAZ, DR. VALERIE A.

Physician, health services administrator. **Educ:** MD. **Career:** Memorial Healthcare Syst Inc, Chattanooga, TN, physician; Hutcheson Med Ctr, Ft Oglethorpe, Ga, physician; Grandview Med Ctr, Jasper, TN, Physician; Hamilton Med Ctr, Dalton, Ga, physician; Chattanooga-Hamilton County Health Dept, health officer, currently. **Orgs:** Bd dir, Chattanooga-Hamilton County Community Serv Agency. **Business Addr:** Health Officer, Chattanooga-Hamilton County, 921 E 3rd St, Chattanooga, TN 37403, **Business Phone:** (423)209-8000.

## BOBB-SEMPLE, CRYSTAL

Entrepreneur. **Personal:** married Walston; children: Corinne. **Educ:** Hampton Univ, BS, econ, 1991; Univ Del, MPA, metrop infrastructure, 1994. **Career:** Agenda C Tomorrow Proj, local planner, 1994-98; Nat Community Bldg Network, analyst, 1999-2001; Parlor Floor Antiques, founder & owner, 2000-; Brownstone Bks, founder & pres, 2000-; Camp Half Blood/Brownstone Lit Partners, chief exec officer, 2010-. **Orgs:** Am Booksellers Asn; bd mem, Brooklyn Movement Ctr; bd dir, Brooklyn Navy Yard Develop Corp. **Business Addr:** Owner, Chief Executive Officer, Brownstone Books Inc, 409 Lewis Ave, Brooklyn, NY 11233, **Business Phone:** (718)953-7328.

## BOBBITT, LEROY

Lawyer, manager. **Personal:** Born Nov 1, 1943, Jackson, MS; son of Leroy and Susie; married Andrea Marie James; children: Dawn & Antoinette. **Educ:** Mich State Univ, BA, 1966; Stanford Univ Sch Law, JD, 1969. **Career:** Legal Aid, atty, 1969-70; Paul, Weiss, Rifkind, Wharton & Garrison, atty, 1970-74; Loeb & Loeb, atty, 1974, partner; St Smart Pictures Inc, co chmn, 2001; Bobbitt & Roberts, partner. **Orgs:** State Bar Calif; Los Angeles Co Bar Asn; Am Bar Asn; Los Angeles Copyright Soc; pres, Black Entertainment & Sports Lawyers Asn, bd dir, Black Entertainment & Sports Lawyers Asn, 1991-94; Langston Bar Asn. **Honors/Awds:** Metropolitan News-Enterprise List of Top Black Attorneys. **Home Addr:** 5816 S Garth Ave, Los Angeles, CA 90056, **Home Phone:** (310)216-0784. **Business Addr:** Partner, Bobbitt & Roberts, 6100 Center Dr Suite 910, Los Angeles, CA 90045, **Business Phone:** (310)315-7150.

## BOBINO, DR. RITA FLORENCIA

Consultant, psychologist, association executive. **Personal:** Born Jun 18, 1934, San Francisco, CA; daughter of Arthur E Cummings and Urania Prince Cummings; married Felix Joseph Jr; children: Sharelle Denice Hagg, Michael J, Mario K, Mauricio J & Malaika J. **Educ:** Laney Col, AA, 1973; Col Holy Names, BS, sociol, 1975; Calif State Univ, Hayward, MS, 1977; Wright Inst, PhD, clin psychol, 1986. **Career:** Oakland Poverty Prog, 1960-71; C Hosp Alameda Cty, dir women infants & c's prog WIC, 1973-76; Berkeley Ment Health Youth Prog, ment health worker, 1976-77; San Francisco Streetwork Prog, counr, 1977-80; Oakland Unified Schs Youth Diversion Prog High Sch, Cities Sch dir, 1980-84; Oakland Unified Sch Sr High, counr, family therapist; oncall-sexual assault therapist Highland Emergency Hosp Oakland; Oakland Unified Sch Farwest High Sch, prin TSA, 1987-88; Oakland Unified Sch, Elmhurst Mid Sch, admin asst prin, Elmhurst Mid Sch, prin, 1995; Contra Costa Col, instr, Psychol African Am Women, 1994; Calif State Univ, Hayward, prof; Oakland, psychotherapist, counr & family therapist, currently. **Orgs:** Co-founder, dir, BWAMU, 1976-, Relationship Strategy, 1978-; Bay Area Black Psychol, 1979; Oakland Educ Asn, 1980-; lic marriage family therapist, Calif, 1980-; Nat Asn Advan Colored People, 1983-85, Juv Hall Diversion Prog Lucy King; Alpha Nu Omega Chap Alpha Kappa Alpha; Oakland Black Educr; Am Fed Sch Admin. **Honors/Awds:** Social Science Honor Award, Soc Pi Gamma Mu, 1975; "Self-Concept of Black Students Who Have Failed" masters thesis; "African Amer Fathers & Daughters" doctoral dissertation completed; Alpha Kappa Alpha Sorority sixty third Far Western Regional, The Charlene V Carodine Unique Professional Achievement Award, 1992. **Home Addr:** 6097 Claremont Ave, Oakland, CA 94618, **Home Phone:** (510)569-3267.

## BOBO, CEDRIC L.

Executive, vice president (organization). **Personal:** married Natasha. **Educ:** Univ Tenn, BS, mech engineering; Harvard Bus Sch, MBA. **Career:** Donaldson, Lufkin & Jenrette's Investment Banking Div, analyst; McCown De Leeuw & Co, assoc; DLJ Merchant Banking, assoc; Carlyle Group, prin, 2005-; Genesee & Wyoming Inc, 2012-. **Orgs:** Chmn & co-founder, Charter Bd Partners; bd dir, Greater China Indust; bd dir, ADT Korea. **Honors/Awds:** "Black Enterprise," 75 Most Powerful Blacks on Wall Street, 2011. **Business Addr:** Principal, The Carlyle Group, 1001 Pennsylvania Ave NW, Washington, DC 20004, **Business Phone:** (202)729-5626.

## BOBONIS, REGIS DARROW, JR.

Executive. **Personal:** Born Dec 8, 1960, Pittsburgh, PA; son of Regis D Sr and Hurley A (deceased). **Educ:** Marquette Univ, BA, 1983. **Career:** Hearst Broadcasting, managing ed, desk asst, 1983-85, night assignment ed, 1985-88, day assignment ed, 1988-89, assignment mgr, 1989-91, managing ed, 1991; WTAE-TV, managing ed, currently. **Orgs:** Chmn, Poise Found; chmn, Kiski Fund's Trustee Comt. **Home Addr:** 136 Centennial Ave Apt 107, Sewickley, PA 15143-1248. **Business Addr:** Managing Editor, WTAE-TV, 400 Ardmore Blvd, Pittsburgh, PA 15221, **Business Phone:** (412)242-4300.

**BOCAGE, ESQ. RONALD JOSEPH**
Executive, lawyer. **Personal:** Born Mar 18, 1946, New Orleans, LA; son of Charles L and Eva Charles; married Myrna DeGruy. **Educ:** Univ New Orleans, BA, 1968; Harvard Law Sch, JD, 1972. **Career:** Mintz, Levin, Cohn, Ferris, Glovsky & Popeo, Boston, Mass, 1972-74; John Hancock Financial Serv Inc, Boston, Mass, atty, 1974-79, asst coun, 1979-83, assoc coun, 1983-86, sr assoc coun, 1986, second vpres & coun, 1986-88, vpres & coun, 1988-, dir. **Orgs:** Am Bar Asn, 1972-; Mass Black Lawyers Asn, 1976-; Asn Life Ins Coun, 1986-. **Home Addr:** 220 Boylston St Suite 1118, Boston, MA 02116, **Home Phone:** (617)423-6989. **Business Addr:** Vice President, Counsel, John Hancock Financial Services Inc, John Hancock Pl, Boston, MA 02117-0111, **Business Phone:** (617)572-8050.

**BODDIE, ALGERNON OWENS**
Contractor, teacher. **Personal:** Born Apr 3, 1933, Demopolis, AL; married Velma Fitzmon. **Educ:** Tuskegee Inst Ala, BS, indust educ, 1954. **Career:** St Judes Educ Inst, Montgomery, AL, teacher, 1954-55; Boddie's Bldg Construct Inc, proprietor & estimator, 1963-70; FHA, Seattle, consult fee insp, 1969-71; Boddie's Bldg Construct Inc, pres, 1970-85; Tacoma Comn Develop, consult, 1976-77. **Orgs:** Tacoma Bldg & Fire Code Appeals Bd, 1969-76; Tacoma Chap Asn, Gen Contractors Am, 1974-85; pres, bd trustee, Tacoma Pub Libr, 1978-79. **Honors/Awds:** Comn Coop Award, Tacoma Pub Schs Div, Voc Rehab, 1971. **Home Addr:** 1310 S Cushman Ave, Tacoma, WA 98405-3526, **Home Phone:** (253)572-9469. **Business Addr:** President, Boddie's Building Construction Inc, 2102 S 12th St, Tacoma, WA 98405-3024, **Business Phone:** (253)627-6885.

**BODDIE, DANIEL W.**
Lawyer. **Personal:** Born Feb 10, 1922, New Rochelle, NY; son of J B; married Annie Virginia Wise; children: Cynthia L & Willis. **Educ:** Va Union Univ, AB, 1943; Cornell Law Sch, LLB, 1949. **Career:** Omega Psi Phi Fraternity Inc, Dist Counr, 1941; Dep Corp Coun, City New Rochelle, second asst, dep ct clerk; Asst Corp Coun, dep ct clerk; City Judge, law secy; pvt pract atty, 1984-. **Orgs:** Bd mem, United Way New Rochelle; chmn, New Rochelle Munic Housing Authority, 1951-65; pres, New Rochelle Bar Asn, 1971-72; chmn, New Rochelle Housing Authority; past legal & coun, New Rochelle Chap Nat Asn Advan Colored People; Omega Psi Phi; trustee, mem & bus mgr Bethesda Baptist Church; founding mem, Asn Black Lawyers; Chancel Choir; Treas, Am Baptist Conv. **Honors/Awds:** Man of the Year, Omicron Iota Chap, 1973; Bethesda Man of the Year, 1983. **Home Addr:** 364 N Ave, New Rochelle, NY 10801. **Business Addr:** Attorney, Private Practice, 358 N Ave, New Rochelle, NY 10801, **Business Phone:** (914)632-4659.

**BODDIE, GWENDOLYN M.**
Educator. **Personal:** Born Aug 4, 1957, Columbus, GA. **Educ:** Mercer Univ, BA, 1979; Tuskegee Inst, MEd, 1981. **Career:** Tuskegee Area Health Educ Ctr, prog coordr, 1981-83; Booker Wash Comm Ctr, prog coordr, 1983; Atlanta Jr Col, counr, 1983-85; Southern Univ, dir stud recruitment, 1985-. **Orgs:** United Way. **Home Addr:** 11671 N Harrells Ferry Suite 2, Baton Rouge, LA 70816. **Business Addr:** Director, Southern University, PO Box 9399, Baton Rouge, LA 70813.

**BODDIE, REV. JAMES R., JR.**
Clergy. **Educ:** St John Vianney Minor Sem. **Career:** St Pius V Cath Church, pastor, 2000; Orange Park Coun, chaplain; Diocese St Augustine, scout chaplain, St Catherine Parish, pastor, currently. **Orgs:** Bd trustee, St Vincent de Paul Reg Sem; Diocese St Augustine; Diocesan Tribunal. **Special Achievements:** First African American priest ordained in the Diocese of St Augustine & in the state of Florida. **Business Addr:** Pastor, St Catherine Parish, 1649 Kingsley Ave, Orange Park, FL 32073-4499, **Business Phone:** (904)264-0577.

**BODISON, WOLFGANG**
Actor, manager. **Personal:** Born Nov 19, 1966, Washington, DC; son of Dorothea. **Educ:** Univ Va, fine arts, 1988. **Career:** Columbia Pictures, file clerk; Castle Rock Productions, location mgr, mail room worker, 1989, prod asst, set asst, picture-car coordr; Playhouse W Sch & Repertory Theatre, artistic dir. Movie: A Few Good Men, 1992; The Big Gig, 1993; Little Big League, 1994; Criminal Passion, 1994; The Expert, 1995; Freeway, 1996; The M World, 1997; Goodbye America, 1997; Most Wanted, 1997; Blood Type, 1999; Joe Somebody, 2001; Where's Angelo, 2003; Akeelah & the Bee, 2006; Legacy, 2010; Now Here, currently; Not Another Not Another Moive, currently; The Appearing, 2014. TV Series: "Murder She Wrote", 1993; "Sirens", 1994; "ER", 1995; "Highlander", 1995; "Silver Strand", 1995; "Dark Skies", 1997; "Nothing Sacred", 1997; "Between Bros", 1997; "Nothing Sacred", 1998; "Family Law", 2000; "wedding Dress", 2001; "Charmed", 2003; "Skin Complex", 2003; "CSI: NY", 2006; "Cane", 2007. **Home Addr:** , Sherman Oaks, CA. **Business Addr:** Actor, Los Angeles, CA 90048.

**BODRICK, LEONARD EUGENE**
Educator, counselor. **Personal:** Born May 17, 1953, Orangeburg, SC; married Sharon Trice; children: Jabari Talib & Nia Imani. **Educ:** Johnson C Smith Univ, BA (cum laude), 1976; Univ Pittsburgh, MPIA, pub admin, 1979; Univ NC, Chapel Hill, PhD, 1983. **Career:** Three Rivers Youth Inc, staff counsr, 1978-79; Southern Ctr Rural & Urban Devel, training dir, 1979-80; Educ Opportunity Ctr Roxboro NC, outreach coun, 1983-85; Johnson C Smith Univ, dir, upward bound prog; City Seens LLC, prin. **Orgs:** Trans Africa, 1977-; finance chair, 1985-87, conf chair, 1987, NC Southern Area rep, 1987-89; NC Coun Educ Opportunity Progs; Am Soc Pub Adminrs, Conf Minority Pub Adminrs; founding mem, UNCF Inter-Alumni Chap; founding mem, managing ed, GSPIA Jour; founding mem, Exec Coun Black Grad & Prof Stud Caucus; Charlotte Coun C; Nat Asn Advan Colored People; SCLC, Charlotte Drop-Out Prev Collab. **Home Addr:** 3120 Airlie St, Charlotte, NC 28205, **Home Phone:** (704)537-0420.

**BOFILL, ANGELA**
Singer. **Personal:** Born May 3, 1954, West Bronx, NY; daughter of Carmen; children: Shauna. **Educ:** Hartt Col Music, attended 1973; Manhattan Sch Music, BMus, 1976. **Career:** Singer & songwriter; New Yorks All City Voices; Dance Theater Harlem, lead soloist; Live at Nite, singer. Albums: Angie, 1978; This Time I'll be Sweater; Under the Moon & Over the Sky; Angie, 1978; Angel of the Night, 1979; Something About You, 1981; Too Tough, 1983; Teaser, 1983; Let Me Be the One, 1984; Tell Me Tomorrow, 1985; Intuition, 1988; Love Is In Your Eyes, 1991; I Wanna Love Somebody, 1993; Love in Slow Motion, 1996; Eternity, 2000; Something About You [Expanded], 2002; Live from Manila, 2006; I Try; The Essential Angela Bofill, 2014. TV: Soul Train, 1938; The Pat Sajak Show, 1989. **Business Addr:** Singer, c/o Live at Nite, PO Box 1140, Maplewood, NJ 07040.

**BOGGAN, DANIEL A., JR.**
Executive, vice president (organization). **Personal:** Born Dec 9, 1946, Albion, MI; son of Daniel Sr and Ruthie Jean Crum; married Jacqueline Ann Beal; children: DeVone, Daniel III, Dhanthan & Alike. **Educ:** Albion Col, BA, hist & sociol, 1967; Univ Mich, MSW, 1968. **Career:** Alameda County Med Ctr, pres; Worldway Corp, dir; Off Mayor, Oakland, CA, chief staff; Starr Commonwealth Boys, clin supv, 1968-70; Jackson Mich, asst city mgr, 1970-72; Flint Mich, dep city mgr, 1972-74, city mgr, 1974-76; Portland, Oreg, dir mgt serv, 1976-78; San Diego Calif, asst co admin, 1978-79; Essex Co, NJ, co admin, 1979-82; Berkeley Calif, city mgr, 1982-86; Univ Calif, Berkeley, assoc vice chancellor bus & admin serv, 1986, actg vice chancellor bus & admin serv, 1986-87, vice chancellor bus & admin serv, 1987-94; Clorox Corp, dir, 1990-2015; Nat Col Athletic Asn, Educ Serv Div, chief operating officer, 1996-98, sr vpres, 1996-2003; Collective Brands Inc, dir, 1997-2012; Siebert Brandford Shank Co LLC, vpres, 2003-06; Viad Corp, dir, 2005-15. **Orgs:** Chmn, Alameda Cty Mgrs Asn, 1984-85; bd mem, Oakland Chap, 1985-94, pres, 1990-; chmn, comm minorities & women League Calif Cities, 1985-; bd mem & dir, Clorox Corp, 1990-; bd mem, Coro Found, 1990; Nat Forum Black Pub Adminrs; Nat Asn Adv Colored People; Carolina Freight Corp, 1995; bd mem, Payless ShoeSource Inc; bd mem, Admin Fed, 1999; fel Black Coaches Asn; fel Nat Urban League; bd, E Oakland Youth Develop Found; bd mem, African Am Experience Fund; chmn, Nat Youth Sports Corp, 2000-07; chmn, Calif Endowment Fund, 2004-. **Home Addr:** 12604 W 129th St, Overland Park, KS 66213, **Home Phone:** (913)851-0829. **Business Addr:** Director, Collective Brands Inc, 3231 SE 6th Ave, Topeka, KS 66607, **Business Phone:** (785)233-5171.

**BOGGER, DR. TOMMY**
Educator. **Personal:** Born May 7, 1944, Williamsburg, VA; son of Arthur Sr and Ethel Lee; married Nan H; children: Alexiss Nichole & Jared Edmund. **Educ:** Va State Col, Norfolk Div, BA, hist, 1968; Carnegie-Mellon Univ, MA, 1969; Univ Va, PhD, 1976. **Career:** Norfolk State Col, hist instr, 1969-71; Norfolk State uiv, asst & assoc prof, 1974-85; prof hist, 1985-86, dir arch, 1986-93, dean, libr sci & spec col, 1993-97, Lyman B Brooks Libr, Harrison B Wilson Arch, dir, 1997-, Libr Search Comt Norfolk State Univ, chair, Interim Libr dir, currently. **Orgs:** Mid-Atlantic Regional Arch Asn, 1978-80, 1997-; Rev bd, Va Hist Landmarks Comn, 1980-83; Southern Hist Asn, 1986-; Southern Hist Conf, local arrangements comt, 1988; Orgn Am Historians, 1990-; VA Hist Soc, 1991-; Chrysler Mus Sub-Comt Hist Houses. **Home Addr:** 5504 Vest Ct, Virginia Beach, VA 23464-2374, **Home Phone:** (757)424-2606. **Business Addr:** Interim Library Director, Norfolk State University, 700 Pk Ave, Norfolk, VA 23504-8060, **Business Phone:** (757)823-2004.

**BOGGS, DONALD W.**
Executive. **Educ:** Mich State Univ, BS, 1966; Univ Detroit, MA, 1971. **Career:** Orgn Sch Admin & Supvr, AFSA, AFL CIO, vpres, 1993-99; Metrop Detroit AFL CIO Coun, pres & chief exec officer, currently. **Orgs:** Pres, Am Fed Sch Adminr; New Detroit Adv Bd; bd dir, Am Red Cross; Nat Asn Advan Colored People; Coalition Black Trade Unionists; Indust Rel Res Asn; Nat Alliance Black Sch Educ; Vis Nurses Asn; United Way; Greater Detroit Health Coun; Health Alliance Plan; Labor & Employ Rels Asn. **Home Addr:** 44807 Broadmoor Cir S, Northville, MI 48168-8642, **Home Phone:** (734)335-7235. **Business Addr:** President, Chief Executive Officer, Metropolitan Detroit AFL-CIO Council, 600 W Lafayette Blvd Suite 200, Detroit, MI 48226, **Business Phone:** (313)961-0800.

**BOGGS, N. CORNELL, III**
Lawyer, executive, vice president (organization). **Personal:** children: 3. **Educ:** Valparaiso Univ, Valparaiso, IN, undergrad, Sch Law, JD. **Career:** US Justice Dept, trial atty; Monsanto, corp legal; Anheuser-Busch, corp legal; Intel, corp legal; Tyco Plastics, vpres & gen coun; MillerCoors LLC, chief legal officer & group vpres pub affairs, 2005-08, chief responsibility & ethics officer, 2008-12; Dow Corning, sr vpres, gen coun & corp secy, 2012-. **Orgs:** Bd dir, Valparaiso Univ; bd dir, Asn Corp Coun (ACC); Am Bar Asn, Stand Rev Comt.

**BOGLE, DONALD**
Writer, educator, movie producer. **Personal:** Born Jul 13, 1944, Philadelphia, PA; son of John D and Roslyn Woods. **Educ:** Lincoln Univ, BA, lit, 1966. **Career:** Film historian; auth; Rutgers Univ; Univ Pa; NY Univ's Tisch Sch Arts, prof; Bks: Eighty Yrs Am's Black Female Superstars, 1980; Blacks Am Film & Tv: An Illus Encycl, Simon & Schuster, 1989; Dorothy Dandridge: A Biog, Amistad Press, 1997; Primetime Blues: African Americans Network TV, 2001; TV ser: "Brown Sugar", dir, writer & producer, 1986; "Mo Funny: Black Comedy Am", 1993; "Intimate Portrait", 1998; "Inside TV Land: African Americans inTelevision", 2002; "It's Black Entertainment", 2002; "Jim Brown: AllAmerican", 2002; "Inside TV Land: Cops Camera", 2004; "N-Word", 2004; "Tavis Smiley", 2005; "20/20", 2005. **Home Addr:** , Manhattan, NY 90266. **Business Addr:** Writer, Producer & Director, Farrar, Straus & Giroux, 19 Union Sq W, New York, NY 10003, **Business Phone:** (212)741-6800.

**BOGLE, ROBERT W.**
Newspaper executive. **Educ:** Univ Pa, Wharton Sch Bus & Finance, mkt & econs, 1971; Cheyney State Col, BA, sociol, urban studies; Temple Univ; Rochester Inst Technol. **Career:** Philadelphia Tribune, publ, advert dir, 1973-77, dir mkt, 1977-81, exec vpres & treas, 1981-89, pres, 1989-, chief exec officer, chmn, currently; PRWT Serv Inc, dir; Independence Blue Cross Inc, dir, 2010-. **Orgs:** Pres, Nat Newspaper Publishers Asn, 1991-95; chmn, Hosps & Higher Educ Facil Authority Philadelphia; comnr, Del River Port Authority, 2003-; Nat Mus African Am Hist & Cult Comn, 2002; dir, bd mem, Zool Soc Philadelphia; bd mem, Workforce Invest Bd; bd mem, African-Am Chamber Com; coun trustee, Cheyney Univ; exec comt, Greater Philadelphia Chamber Com; bd mem, Kimmel Ctr Performing Arts; bd mem, Mann Music Ctr Performing Arts; bd govs, United Way Am; life mem, Alpha Psi Fraternity Inc; trustee, Cheyney Univ; bd mem, dir, Philadelphia Orchestra; Greater Philadelphia Tourism Mkt Corp; Philadelphia Conv & Visitors Bur; W Ins Agency; Philadelphia Mus Art; Pa Newspapers Asn; Nat Mus African Am Hist & Cult Comn; Alpha Boule Sigma Pi Phi Fraternity; life mem, Kappa Alpha Psi Fraternity Inc; Pa Soc; Philadelphia Community Leaders. **Honors/Awds:** Russwarm Award, NNPA, 1995, 1987, 1999; DHL, Drexel Univ, 2000; hon doctorate, Lit from Lincoln Univ. **Business Addr:** President, Chief Executive Officer, Philadelphia Tribune, 520 S 16th St, Philadelphia, PA 19146, **Business Phone:** (215)893-4050.

**BOGUES, BARRYMAN ANTHONY**
College teacher, writer. **Educ:** Union Inst, BA, polit sci, 1989; Univ W Indies, Mona, PhD, polit theory, 1994. **Career:** Univ Wi, Jamaica, asst lectr, 1994-95, lectr, 1995-2000, sr lectr, 2000-01; Brown Univ, vis assoc prof, 1999-2001, assoc prof, 2001-03; prof, 2003-, Royce Family Prof Teaching Excellence, 2004-07, Africana Studies Dept, chair, 2003-09, Harmon Family Prof Africana Studies, 2007-13, inaugural dir Ctr Study Slavery & Justice, 2012-, Lyn Crost Prof Social Sci & Critical Theory, 2013-; Univ Cape Town, SafricA, distinguished vis scholar, 2007, hon res prof, 2007-12, AB Mellon vis prof, 2010, 2012, 2013, hon prof, 2014-; Ctr Caribbean Thought, Univ Wi, Mona, assoc dir. **Orgs:** Caribbean Studies Asn; Am Philos Asn; Am Polit Sci Asn; Caribbean Social Hist Proj; Inst Commonwealth Studies; Mid-Atlantic Writers Asn; Int Soc Intellectual Hist; Caribbean Philos Asn; Am Studies Asn; Ethiopian Philos Asn. **Special Achievements:** Author of "Calibran's Freedom: The Early Political Thought of C.L.R. James" (1997); "Black Heretics and Black Prophets: Radical Political Intellectuals" (2003); "Empire of Liberty: Power, Freedom, and Desire" (2010); author of numerous essays and articles on history of criticism, critical theory, political thought, and political philosophy; member of the editorial collective for the journal "Boundary 2". **Business Addr:** Brown University, 94 Waterman St, Providence, RI 02906, **Business Phone:** (401)863-1782.

**BOGUES, MUGSSY. See BOGUES, TYRONE CURTIS.**

**BOGUES, TYRONE CURTIS (MUGSSY BOGUES)**
Basketball player, basketball coach, business owner. **Personal:** Born Jan 9, 1965, Baltimore, MD; son of Richard and Elaine; married Kimberly; children: Tyeisha, Brittney & Tyrone II. **Educ:** Wake Forest Univ, Winston Salem, NC, attended 1987. **Career:** Basketball player (retired), basketball coach, executive; RI Gulls, 1987; Wash Bullets, 1987-88; Charlotte Hornets, 1988-97; Golden State Warriors, guard, 1997-98; Toronto raptors, free agt, 1999-2001; New York Knicks, 2001; Bogues Enterprise LLC, owner; Charlotte Sting, head coach, 2005-07; Women's Nat Basketball Asn, coach, 2005; Charlotte Bobcats, ambassadors & broadcasters; United Faith Christian Acad, head coach, 2011-12; Books: "In the Land of Giants: My Life in Basketball", 1994; "Sports Stars", 1994. **Business Addr:** Head Coach, United Faith Christian Academy, 8617 Providence Rd, Charlotte, NC 28277, **Business Phone:** (704)541-1742.

**BOGUS, DR. HOUSTON, JR.**
Physician. **Personal:** Born Sep 10, 1951, Knoxville, TN; son of Houston and Louise; married Dorris Loretta Gray; children: Alisha Dione, Houston III & Alyson Gray. **Educ:** Univ TN, BA, 1973; Meharry Med Col, MD, 1979. **Career:** William Beaumont Army Med Ctr, Internship, fel, resident, 1980-85; Med Group Tex, gastroenterol; Dallas Diag Asn, physician; Baylor Med Ctr Garland, gastroenterologist, currently; Med City Hosp, gastroenterologist, currently. **Orgs:** Omega Psi Phi Fraternity; Alpha Omega Alpha Hon Med Soc; Meharry Chap; Am Col Gastroenterol. **Home Addr:** 4708 Alliance Blvd Suite 300, Plano, TX 75023-1311, **Home Phone:** (972)758-6000. **Business Addr:** Physician, Dallas Diagnostic Association, 601 Clara Barton Blvd Suite 300, Garland, TX 75042, **Business Phone:** (469)800-2000.

**BOGUS, DR. S. DIANE ADAMZ**
Educator, poet, publisher. **Personal:** Born Jan 22, 1946, Chicago, IL; married Frances J Huxie. **Educ:** Stillman Col, BA, 1968; Syracuse Univ, MA, 1969; Miami Univ, PhD, 1988; Am Int Univ, PhD, parapsychology, 1998. **Career:** Auth: Her poems, 1979; Dykehands, Woman Moon Publ, 1994; Chant Woman Magdalena, 1994; Buddhism Classroom, Woman Moon Publ, 1996; WIM Publ, auth, 1971-, founder, 1979-, publ, currently; LA Southwest Col, instr, 1976-81; Miami Univ, instr, 1981-84; Calif State Univ, prof am lit, 1986-90; De Anza Col, Cupertino, CA, instr, 1990. **Orgs:** Delta Sigma Theta Sorority, 1965-; Feminist Writer's Guild, 1980-; Nat Teachers Eng, 1981-; bd mem, Col Publ's, 1989-92; Publ Triangle, 1992-. **Home Addr:** 3465 Mesa Verde Cir, Stockton, CA 95209, **Home Phone:** (408)956-5616. **Business Addr:** Publisher, Founder, WIM Publications, PO Box 2087, San Jose, CA 95015, **Business Phone:** (408)279-6626.

**BOHANNAN-SHEPPARD, BARBARA**
Mayor, government official. **Personal:** Born Jun 15, 1950, Ornancock, VA; daughter of Robert Harry Lee (deceased) and Mary Sue Chandler; married Monroe. **Educ:** Del County Community, bus admin. **Career:** BB Educ Training & C's Servs, owner, 1986-; Local Daycare Ctr, dir; City Chester, mayor, 1992-95. **Orgs:** Hon chairwoman, Nat Polit Cong Black Women; Conf Mayors; Nat Coun Negro Women; Nat Asn Advan Colored People.

**BOHANNON, ETDRICK**
Basketball player. **Personal:** Born May 29, 1973, San Bernardino, CA. **Educ:** Univ Ariz, attended 1993; Univ Tenn, attended 1995; Auburn Univ, Montgomery, attended 1997. **Career:** Basketball player (retired); Ind Pacers, forward, 1997-98; Wash Wizards, forward, 1998-99; New York Knickerbockers, forward, 2000; Los Angeles

Clippers, forward, 2000-01; Cleveland Cavaliers, forward, 2001; Gijon Baloncesto, 2001; Sioux Falls Skyforce, 2002; Yakama Sun Kings, 2005. **Business Addr:** Professional Basketball Player, Yakama Sun Kings, 1301 S Fair Ave Shattuck Bldg, Yakima, WA 98901, **Business Phone:** (509)248-1222.

**BOI, BIG. See PATTON, ANTWAN ANDRE.**

## BOLAND, D. STEVE

Chief executive officer, executive director. **Educ:** Northwestern Univ, Sch Educ & Social Policy, BS, human develop & social policy orgn studies, 1990. **Career:** Fleet Financial Group, lending mgr; Bank Am Merrill Lynch, banking ctr mgr, 1990-92, vpres, 1995-98, Citigroup, vpres, 1992-94; ITT Financial, vpres, 1994-95; Countrywide Home Loans, vpres, 1997-2001; Midwest Consumer Markets Div, regional sr vpres, 1998-2001, LandSafe Inc, pres & chief exec officer, 2001-06, sr vpres & reverse mortgage exec, 2006-10, Global Wealth & Investment Mgt Mortgage Solutions, managing dir, 2010-12, Legacy Asset Servicing, managing dir, 2012, Secured Credit Underwriting & Fulfillment, managing dir, 2012-14, Home Loans, managing dir, 2014-15; Secured Consumer Lending, managing dir, 2015; Consumer Lending, managing dir, 2015-. **Honors/Awds:** "Black Enterprise," America's Most Powerful Players Under 40, 2005; "Black Enterprise," 75 Most Powerful Blacks on Wall Street, 2011. **Business Addr:** Managing Director, Bank of America, 100 N Tryon St Suite 170, Charlotte, NC 28202, **Business Phone:** (980)335-3561.

## BOLAND, D. STEVEN

Banker, president (organization), chief executive officer. **Educ:** Northwestern Univ, BS, human develop & social policy-orgn, 1990. **Career:** Bank Am, banking ctr mgr, 1990-92, vpres, 1995-96, 1st vpres, 1997-98, regional sr vpres, midwest consumer markets div, 1998-2001, sr vpres & reverse mortgage exec, 2006-10, managing dir, global wealth & investment mgt, 2010-12, managing dir, legacy asset servicing, 2012, managing dir, secured credit underwriting & fulfillment, 2012-14, managing dir, home loans, 2014-15, managing dir, secured consumer lending, 2015; managing dir, consumer lending, 2015-; Citigroup, vpres, 1992-94; ITT Financial, vpres, 1994-95; Landsafe Inc, bank am, chief exec officer, pres & managing dir, 2001-06. **Orgs:** Com Lending Network. **Honors/Awds:** Seventy five Most Powerful Blacks in Corporate America, Black Enterprise, 2005. **Business Addr:** Managing Director Secured Credit Underwriting and Fulfillment, Bank of America, 1415 Col Pt Blvd, College Point, NY 11356, **Business Phone:** (800)432-1000.

## BOLDEN, ALETHA SIMONE

Executive. **Personal:** Born Bronx, NY; daughter of Althea and Cornelius Cherry; married Vernie Lee; children: Avery & Vaughn. **Educ:** Univ NC, Greensboro, BFA, 1989. **Career:** Harrison Mus African Am Cult, cur, 1993-95, exec dir, 1995-. **Orgs:** Adv bd mem, Burrell Nursing Ctr, 1998-; Dumas Music Ctr Bd Comners, 2000-; bd mem, Dumas Drama Guild, 2001-; bd mem, Am Cancer Soc, 2001-; Kiwanis Club Roanoke, 2001-; bd mem, Va Asn Mus, 2001-04. **Business Addr:** Executive Director, Harrison Museum African American Culture, 523 Harrison Ave NW, Roanoke, VA 24016, **Business Phone:** (540)345-4818.

## BOLDEN, BARBARANETTE T.

Military leader. **Educ:** Ark State Univ, BA, hist, 1974, MA, hist, 1975; Howard Univ Sch Law, JD, 1978; AUS War Col, attended 1998; Carlisle Barracks, Pa, Sr Res Component Officer Course, 2007. **Career:** Engr Battalion 567th, Jonesboro, AK, 1975-78; 163rd Mil Police Battalion, Wash, DC; 171st Mil Police Battalion, Wash, DC, mil police investigative officer, 1978-79; DC Army Nat Guard, Wash, DC, tactical officer, 1979-82, personnel mgt officer, 1990-94, dir personnel, 1996-97, dir plans, 1997-99, chief staff, 1999-04, comdr, 2006-; 163rd Mil Police Battalion, Wash, DC, circulation control officer, 1982, detachment comdr, 1982-83; 163rd Mil Police Battalion, Wash, DC, 1983-86; 260th Mil Police Brigade, Wash, DC, 1986-88; 372nd Mil Police Battalion, Wash, DC, 1990; 372nd Mil Police Battalion, Wash, DC, 1994-96; US Northern Command, Colo Springs, Colo, oper dir, 2004; Armed Forces Inaugural Comt, Wash, DC, oper dir, 2004-05. **Orgs:** Alpha Kappa Alpha Sorority; Nat Guard Asn Us; Dc Nat Guard Asn; Boy Scouts Am, Troop 1005. **Honors/Awds:** Legion of Merit with 1 Bronze Oak Leaf Cluster; Defense Meritorious Service Medal; Meritorious Service Medal; Army Commendation Medal; Army Achievement Medal; Army Reserve Components Achievement Medal; National Defense Service Medal; Global War On Terrorism Service Medal; Humanitarian Service Medal; Military Outstanding Volunteer Medal; Armed Forces Reserve Medal; Army Service Ribbon; Army Reserve Components Overseas Training Ribbon; Legion of Merit with 3 Bronze Oak Leaf Clusters, DC Armory. **Special Achievements:** First woman in the National Guard 362-year history to be a chief of staff at the state level; First Female DC Guard brigadier general.

## BOLDEN, BETTY A.

Executive director, labor relations manager. **Personal:** Born Dec 24, 1944, St. Louis, MO. **Educ:** Univ Ill, BA, 1965; DePaul Univ, MA, 1969. **Career:** Fed employee (retired); US Civil Serv Commun Chicago, career intern, 1967; US Postal Serv Chicago/Wash, DC, personal mgmt specialist, 1968-75; US Civil Serv Commn, Wash, DC, personal mgt specialist, 1973-75; US Dept Labor, super personal mgt spec, 1975-76, dep dir personal, exec asst, 1976-78, fed employee, assoc dep sec labor, 1993; Out-of-Print Bks, part-time self-employed dealer, 1988-; Fed Serv Impasses Panel, exec dir, chmn, 1994-99. **Orgs:** Personnel com, Delta Sigma Theta, 1979-81; Nat Asn Advan Colored People. **Home Addr:** , DC.

## BOLDEN, CHARLES

Marine corps officer, astronaut, administrator. **Personal:** Born Aug 19, 1946, Columbia, SC; son of Ethel M Bolden; married Alexis (Jackie) Walker, Dec 23, 1998?; children: Kelly Michelle & Anthony Che. **Educ:** US Naval Acad, BS, elec sci, 1968; Univ Southern Calif, MS, systs mgt, 1977. **Career:** US Marine Corps (retired): joined, 1968; naval aviator, 1970-80; dep comndg gen 1st Marine Expeditionary Force Pac, 1997-98; comndg gen 1st Marine Expeditionary Force, 1998; dep comdr US forces Japan, 1998-2000; comndg gen 3rd Marine Aircraft Wing at Marine Copes Air Sta Miramar, San Diego, CA, 2000-02. NASA: mem Astronaut Off, 1980-94; Astronaut Off Safety Officer; Tech Asst to Dir Flight Crew Opers; Spec Asst to Dir Johnson Space Ctr, Houston, TX; Chief Safety Div, Johnson Space Ctr; lead astronaut vehicle test & checkout at Kennedy Space Ctr, FL; Asst Dep Adminr, NASA Hq; Adminr, 2009-. US Naval Acad, dep commandant midshipmen, 1994-97; Jackandpanther LLC, chief exec officer. **Special Achievements:** Flew more than 100 combat missions in North and South Vietnam, Laos, Cambodia, as a naval aviator, 1972-73; flew four space shuttle missions between 1986 and 1994, serving as commander twice and pilot twice; commanding general of the First Marine Expeditionary Force Forward in support of Operation Desert Thunder in Kuwait, 1998. **Business Addr:** NASA Headquarters, 300 E St SW Suite 5R30, Washington, DC 20546, **Business Phone:** (202)358-0001.

## BOLDEN, CHARLES E.

Labor activist. **Personal:** Born Feb 12, 1941, AL; son of Charles H and Ernestine; married Diane Nation; children: Charles R & Marva L. **Educ:** Ala State Univ, BS, 1966; LaSalle Ext Univ, LLB, 1975; Univ Phoenix, Denver, MA, arts mgt, 1984. **Career:** Nat Educ Asn Chicago, field rep, 1968-70; Nat Educ Asn Denver, org team coord, 1970-74, mgr shared staffing prog, 1974-76, orgn specialist, 1976-. **Orgs:** Chmn, Ft & Madison IA Human Rel Comn, 1967-68; Orgn Pub Sch Teachers Collective Bargaining, 1968-; Orgn Human Rights Ordinance Campaign; Sigma Rho Sigma, Omega Psi Phi Frat; bd dirs, Am Civil Libs Union PG Co MD, 1975; vpres, PTA Ft Wash Forest Elem Sch, 1975. **Honors/Awds:** Teacher Advocate Award Compton, CA, 1973; Outstanding Service Award, United Fac Fla, 1984; Appreciation Service Award, Okla Educ Asn, 1989; Friend Educ Award, Wyo Educ Asn, 1994. **Home Addr:** 12197 E Vassar Dr, Aurora, CO 80014, **Home Phone:** (303)337-6199. **Business Addr:** Organizational Specialist, National Education Association, 1401 17th St Suite 950, Denver, CO 80202-1398, **Business Phone:** (303)572-6965.

## BOLDEN, CLARENCE

Lawyer. **Educ:** Morehouse Col, BS, biol, sci, 1967; Ga State Law Sch, JD, 1981. **Career:** NEA Alaska, uniserv dir, 1991-2002; Conflict Resolution Skills Group, pres, 2002-, arbitrator, 2014-; atty, currently; Fairbanks N Star Bor Sch Dist, exec dir human resources, 2004-13. **Orgs:** Am Arbit Asn. **Home Addr:** 1234 Hillcrest Ave, Anchorage, AK 99501, **Home Phone:** (947)279-3456. **Business Addr:** Attorney, President, Conflict Resolution Skills Group, 1441 W 26th Ave Suite B-4, Anchorage, AK 99503-2378, **Business Phone:** (907)227-4566.

## BOLDEN, FRANK AUGUSTUS

Lawyer, executive, football player. **Personal:** Born Aug 7, 1942, Albany, GA; son of Augustus and Geraldine; married Carol Penelope Parsons; children: Brian & Ian. **Educ:** Univ Vt, BA, 1963; Columbia Univ, Grad Sch Bus, MBA, 1972; Columbia Univ Sch Law, JD, 1972. **Career:** Executive, football player, coach, lawyer (retired); Woodrow Wilson Found, Martin Luther King Jr fel, 1969-72; Charles Evans Hughes fel, 1971-72; Columbia Univ, asst football coach, 1971; Inst Educ Develop, consult, 1972; Cahill Gordon & Reindel, assoc, 1972-75; Inst Mediation & Conflict Resolution, dir, 1972-90; Windsor Minerals Inc, dir, 1976-87; Western Sources Inc, dir, 1979-87; Healthcare Prod Nigeria Ltd, dir, 1978-84; Chicopee, dir, 1980-84; Johnson & Johnson, atty, 1975, int atty, 1976-85, vpres corp staff, 1986, vpres serv, corp staff, 1994-2001, vpres, diversity health giant, 2002-07; Union County Col, 1983-98, vice chmn, 1989-93, chmn, 1993-95; Freshman Football Team, defensive line coach. **Orgs:** COGME Fel 1970-72; adv Consortium Met Law Sch, 1972-73; New york Bar, 1973-; Dir, Raritan Credit Union, 1976-78; dir, NJ Asn Corrections, 1980-88; trustee, Union County Col; vpres, NJ State Opera, 1984-; NJ Comn Pay Equity, 1984; adv comt, Fla A&M Sch Bus, 1986-90; Black Leadership Coun, 1988-; bd trustees, City Mkt, Nb, NJ, 1988-94; bd trustees, Crossroads Theatre Inc, Nb, NJ, 1989-94; chmn bd, Overlook Hosp, Summit, NJ, 1990-96, vice chmn, 1993-94, chmn, 1994-96; bd governers, Nat Conf Christians & Jews, 1991-, exec comt, Nat Conf Christians & Jews, 1992-; adv comt, Univ Vt Bus Sch, 1992; bd trustees, Univ Vt, 1994-2000, chmn, Univ Vt, 1998-2000; Christ Church UCC; bd trustees, Nat Med Fel 1995-; bd trustees, Atlantic Health Syst, 1996-; bd dir, NJ Chamber Com, 1999-, exec comt, NJ Chamber Com, 2001-; Nat Bar Asn; vpres, Black Am Law Students Asn; bd trustees, Moorestown Col; adv comts, Fla A&M & UVM Schs Bus. **Honors/Awds:** Outstanding Young Man of America, 1979; Distinguished Service Award, 1984; Outstanding Service Award, Nat Conf, 1984; Freedom Fund Award, Perth Amboy Nat Asn Advan Colored People, 1995; Distinguished Service Award, NJ State Opera, 1996; City News 100 Most Influential, NJ, 1996; Athletic Hall of Fame, Univ VT, 2000. **Home Addr:** 66 Old Cannon Rd, Berkeley Heights, NJ 07922, **Home Phone:** (908)464-5649.

## BOLDEN, JAMES LEE, SR.

Executive. **Personal:** Born Jun 14, 1936, Quitman, MS; married Margaret P Hardaway; children: James Jr, Sherry, Margery & Jeffery. **Educ:** Topeka State Hosp, cert, 1959; LUCT Training Inst, cert, 1976; Washburn Univ, cert, 1978. **Career:** Little Jim's Trucking Co, gen contractor, 1958-71; Bolden Radio & TV Repair, mgr, owner, 1958-66; Little Jim's Garage, mgr, owner, 1969-; Four M Develop Inc, pres, chief exec officer, 1970-; Mid-Cent Ins Consults, owner, gen agt, 1974-; Mid-Am Aviation Inc, pres & owner, currently. **Orgs:** Treas, Mt Carmel Missionary Bapt Church, 1966-; bd mem, Household Tech, 1978-; bd treas, Black Econ Coun Topeka, 1979-; chmn supvry comn, Capital City Credit Union, 1979-; Local Develop Corp, 1979-; chmn mem, comm, Nat Asn Advan Colored People, 1979-; lectr, Enroute & Terminal ATC Procedures Oper Rain Check USA Dept Trans Fed Aviation Admin, 1980; labor & indust chair, Nat Asn Adv Colored People Topeka Br, 2007-09; state chair, Kans Black Republican Coun; advisor chmn, United Black Republican Coalition. **Honors/Awds:** Certificate of Appreciation, Kans State Conf Br Nat Asn Advan Colored People, 1979; 19th Minority and Women Business Awards, Kans Dept Com Off Minority & Women Bus Develop. **Home Addr:** 830 SE 37th St, Topeka, KS 66605-2865, **Home Phone:** (785)266-7916. **Business Addr:** President, Chief Executive Officer, Four M Development Co, 6700 SW Topeka Blvd 612, Topeka, KS 66619, **Business Phone:** (785)862-2790.

## BOLDEN, JURAN T.

Football player. **Personal:** Born Jun 27, 1974, Tampa, FL; married Tina; children: Isiah. **Educ:** Miss Delta Community Col. **Career:** Football player (retired); Winnipeg Blue bombers, 1995, 2000-01, 2007-08; Atlanta Falcons, defensive back, 1996-97, left cornerback, 2002-03, right cornerback & strong safety, 2002; Carolina Panthers, defensive back, 1998; Green Bay Packers, defensive back, 1998; Kans City Chiefs, defensive back, 1999; Jacksonville Jaguars, defensive back, 2004; Tampa Bay Buccaneers, defensive back, 2005-06, left cornerback, 2006; free agt & sr acct exec, currently. **Honors/Awds:** Defensive Player of the Year; Miss Delta Defensive Player of the Year; Outstanding Defensive. **Special Achievements:** Film: 1996 NFL Draft, 1996. **Business Addr:** Free Agent, Tampa Bay Buccaneers, 1 Buccaneer Pl, Tampa, FL 33607, **Business Phone:** (813)870-2700.

## BOLDEN, RAYMOND A.

Lawyer, association executive. **Personal:** Born Dec 17, 1933, Chicago, IL; children: Kathryn, Alan & Joseph. **Educ:** Univ Ill, BS, bus, LLB, 1961. **Career:** Lawyer (retired); Intelligence Div US Treas Dept, agt, 1961-64; Will County, asst state atty, 1964-68; 12th Judicial Dist, assoc judge, 1986-2001; pvt pract atty. **Orgs:** Nat & Will County Bar Asn; pres, Nat Black Lawyers Conf, Joliet Br, Nat Advan Asn Colored People, 1964-68; bd dir, Joliet-Will County Comn Action Agency, 1967-73; Will County Legal Ast Prog; chmn, High Crime Red Ctr Comn, Joliet, 1975. **Honors/Awds:** Distinguished Citizens Service Award, Black Stud Union Lewis Univ, 1975; Nat Advan Asn Colored People, 1968. **Home Addr:** 54 N Ottawa St Suite 245, Joliet, IL 60432, **Home Phone:** (815)723-2895.

## BOLDEN, STEPHANIE T.

City council member. **Personal:** Born Aug 16, 1946, Wilmington, DE. **Educ:** Del State Univ, BA, 1969; Boston Col, MA, educ. **Career:** High Sch Alma mater, teacher, 1981; Eastside Substance Abuse Awareness Prog, exec dir; Christina Sch Dist, teacher; Wilmington City Coun, coun mem 3rd dist, 2004-. **Orgs:** Founder, Burton Phelan Memorial Scholar prog; St Joseph Cath Church; Gov Health Comt; Proj Stay Free; Howard High Sch Technol & Del State Univ Alumni Asns; Sojourner Pl; Nat Coalition 100 Black Women; Del Black Caucus; Delta Sigma Theta Sorority Inc; Knights Peter Claver. **Special Achievements:** Second African American female to serve on Wilmington City Council; Initiated the Drug Mug prog, 2004. **Home Addr:** 38 McCaulley St, Wilmington, DE 19802, **Home Phone:** (302)428-1269. **Business Addr:** Council Member 3rd District, Wilmington City Council, 800 Fr St 9th Fl, Wilmington, DE 19801-3537, **Business Phone:** (302)576-3070.

## BOLDEN, TONYA

Writer. **Personal:** Born Mar 1, 1959, New York, NY; daughter of Willie J and Georgia C. **Educ:** Princeton Univ, BA, Slavic Lang & Lit Russ focus, 1981; Columbia Univ, MA, slavic lang & lit, 1985. **Career:** Westside Repertory Theatre Grp, actor, stage mgr, asst dir; Charles Alan Inc, salesperson, 1981-83; Raoulfilm Inc, off coordr, 1985-87, res & ed asst, 1987-88; Malcolm-King Col, eng instr, 1988-89; Col New Rochelle Sch New Resources, eng instr, 1989-90, 1996-; HARKline, newsline ed, 1989-90; Quart Black Rev Bks, ed, 1994-95; freelance writer & auth, 1990-; Author: The Family Heirloom Cookbook, 1990; African American History, 1990; Mama, I Want to Sing, 1992; Notable Black American Women, 1992; Getting into the Mail-Order Business, 1994; Starting a Business from Your Home, 1993; Just Family, 1996; Strong Men Keep Coming: The Book of African American Men, 1999; Forgive or Forget: Never Underestimate the Power of Forgiveness, 1999; Rock of Ages A Tribute to the Black Church, 2001; 33 Things Every Girl Should Know About Women's History From Suffragettes to Skirt Lengths to the E.R.A., Crown, 2002; American Patriots: The Story of Blacks in the Military from the Revolution to Desert Storm, 2003; Portraits of African-American Heroes, 2003; CHAKA! Through The Fire, 2003; Wake Up Our Souls, 2004; The Champ, The Story of Muhammad Ali, 2004; Maritcha A Nineteenth-Century American Girl, 2005. **Orgs:** New York Coun Humanities Speakers Bur. **Honors/Awds:** Book for the Teenage Award, New York Pub Libr, 1992; Book for the Teenage Award, New York Pub Libr, 1998; Best Book for Young Adults, Am Libr Asn, 1998; Book for the Teenage, New York Pub Libr, 1999; Certificate for the Advance Study Soviet Union, Harriman Inst. **Home Addr:** 3034 Tieman Ave, Bronx, NY 10469-3216, **Home Phone:** (718)379-5359. **Business Addr:** Author, Marie Brown Associates, 412 W 154th St, New York, NY 10032, **Business Phone:** (212)939-9725.

## BOLDEN, VERONICA MARIE

Labor relations manager, government official. **Personal:** Born May 19, 1952, Brooklyn, NY; daughter of Arthur Greene and Ruth Mae Greene; married Fred A Jr; children: Jamal C & Jeron A. **Educ:** New York Col, AAS, 1972; Univ Rochester, BA, 1975; Univ Cincinnati, MEd, 1976. **Career:** Ohio Valley Goodwill Rehab, prog mgr & voc evaluator, 1976-78; Citizen's COM Youth, intake assessment specialist, 1978-81; Univ Cincinnati, coordr stud employ, 1981-89; Hamilton County Bd Ment Retardation, assoc dir, personnel servs, 1989-2008. **Orgs:** Black Career Women, 1981-; Ohio State Rep Stud Employ Adminrs, 1986-89; Stud Employ Adminrs Nominations Comt Chap, 1986-87; mem-at-large, Midwest Asn Stud Employ Adminrs, 1986-87 & 1987-88; Midwest Asn Stud EmployAdminrs, 1987-88; Minority Concerns Chapter, 1987-89; Ohio Asn Sch Personnel Adminrs, 1989-; Int Asn Personnel Women, 1989-; North Avondale Montessori Sch, PTA Mem Chap, 1989-90; Ohio Asn Female Execs, 1990-; Ohio Asn County Bd Ment Retardation, 1990-; Shroder JHS, 1991-92. **Honors/Awds:** Dedicated Serv Award, Univ Cincinnati, 1986; Leadership Recognition Award, Midwest Asn Stud Employ Adminrs, 1988; Outstanding Young Men/Women Am, Jaycees, 1988; YMCA Black Achiever, 1990. **Special Achievements:** Article written and published in response to the Campus Advisor, Black Collegian Magazine, 1988. **Home Addr:** 7863 Bobo Link Dr, Cincinnati, OH 45224, **Home Phone:** (513)522-4125.

## BOLDEN, DR. WILEY SPEIGHTS

Educator. **Personal:** Born Dec 18, 1918, Birmingham, AL; son of Wiley Lee Jr and Gertrude Mildred Speights; married Willie Creagh Miller; children: Millicent Ann (Eltahir Hassan), Lisa B Monette, Lelia E & Wiley Miller. **Educ:** Ala State Univ, BS, 1939; Atlanta Univ, attended 1941; Columbia Univ, Teachers Col, New York, NY, MA, psycol serv, 1947, EdD, psycol serv, 1957. **Career:** Educator (retired); Shelby County Bd Educ, Almont Jr High, Montevallo AL, prin, 1939-42; Mobile County Bd Educ, Mobile AL, teacher, 1943-44; Clark Col, Atlanta, Ga, assoc prof psychol, 1948-57, Dept Educ & Psychol, prof psychol & chmn, 1957-63, dean fac & instr, 1963-67; State Ga, licensedpsychologist, 1962; Southeastern Reg Educ Lab, Atlanta Ga, assoc dir res, 1967-69; Ga State Univ, Atlanta GA, prof educ founds, 1970-87; Ga State Univ, prof emer educ found, 1987; Savannah State Col, Savannah GA, actg pres, 1988-89; Morris Brown Col, Atlanta, Ga, actg vpres acad affairs, 1993-94. **Orgs:** Coordr res, Phelps-Stakes Fund, Coop Pre-freshman Prog, Atlanta Univ Ctr & Dillard Univ, 1959-63; study dir, Tuskegee Univ Role & Scope Study, Acad Educ Develop, 1969-70; consult, United Bd Col Develop, 1971-76; bd dir, United Bd Col Develop, 1978-82; bd dir, Atlanta chap Nat Asn Advan Colored People, 1971-73; co-chmn educ comt, Atlanta chap Nat Asn Advan Colored People, 1980-82; Educ Task Force, Atlanta Chamber Com, 1972-76; Fulton County Grand Jurors Asn, 1973-76; vpres spec proj & assoc dir Title III, Advan Inst Develop Proj, 1975-77; univ assoc & bd dir, Advan Inst Develop Proj, 1977-83; pres, Advan Inst Develop Proj, 1978-82; Southern Educ Found, 1978-90, pres, 1983-85, Southern Educ Found; Ga State Bd Examiners Psychologists; Gov Adv Comt Ment Health & Ment Retardation, 1980-83; adv comt educ & career develop, Nat Urban League, 1982-91; Am Psychol Asn; Southeastern Psychol Asn; fel Am Asn State Psychol Bd. **Special Achievements:** Dr. Wiley Bolden, Second African American Psychologist licensed in the State of Georgia. **Home Addr:** 975 Veltre Cir, Atlanta, GA 30311, **Home Phone:** (404)755-6135.

## BOLDRIDGE, GEORGE

Executive, sales manager. **Personal:** Born Apr 15, 1947, Atchison, KS; son of Adrian Sr and Decima; married Cynthia Davis; children: Eva & Tamara. **Educ:** Benedictine Col, BA. **Career:** Hallmark Cards Inc, dist sales mgr, nat acct coordr, currently. **Home Addr:** 13155 Johns Island Ct, Jacksonville, FL 32224-8417, **Home Phone:** (904)992-7339. **Business Addr:** District Sales Manager, Account Executive, Hallmark Cards Inc, 2501 McGee Trafficway, Kansas City, MO 64108, **Business Phone:** (800)425-5627.

## BOLEN, DAVID B. (DAVID BENJAMIN BOLEN)

Ambassador, consultant, athlete. **Personal:** Born Dec 23, 1923, Heflin, LA; married Betty L Gayden; children: Cynthia, Myra White & David B Jr. **Educ:** Univ Colo, BS, MS, 1950; Harvard Univ, MPA, 1960; Nat War Col, attended 1967. **Career:** Am Embassy, Monrovia, Liberia, admin asst, 1950-52, Karachi, Pakistan, econ asst, 1952-54, Accra, Ghana, chief econ sect, 1960-62; US Dept State, Com Dept, 1955-57, int economist Japan-Korea desk, 1957-58, Afghanistan desk officer, 1958-59; Asst Secy State Africa, staff asst, 1962-64; officer in-chg, Nigerian affairs, 1964-66, Bonn, W Ger, econ officer, 1967-72, Belgrade, Yugoslavia, econ counr, 1972-73, ambassador, Botswana, Lesotho & Swaziland, 1974-76, dep asst, Secry State Africa, 1976-77, E Berlin, E Ger, ambassador to Ger Dem Repub, 1977-80; E I Du Pont de Nemours & Co Inc, Wilmington, Del, assoc dir int affairs, 1981-89; consult, 1989-. **Orgs:** Foreign Serv Asn, 1950-; Nat War Col Alumni Asn, 1967-; Am Coun Ger, 1980-; vpres/dir, Wilmington World Affairs Coun, 1981-; dir, Wilmington Trust Co, 1981-; Wilmington Club, 1982-; Rodney Sq Club, 1983-; trustee, Univ Del, 1983-; dir, Urban Fund, S Africa, 1987-; Del Coun Econ Educ, 1987-; trustee, Med Ctr Del, 1987-; US Ambassador-designate, Botswana, Lesotho. **Honors/Awds:** Fourth place winner, 400 Meters, Olympic Games, 1948; Robert S Russell Memorial Awards, 1948; Dave Bolen Olympic Award, Univ Colo, 1948; Hall of Honor, Univ Colorado, 1969; Norlin Distinguished Alumni Award, Univ Colo, 1969; Superior Honor Award for Outstanding & Imaginative Performance, Dept State, 1972-73; Department Commercial Certificate of Sustained Superior Performance, 1974; Alumnus of the Century Award, Univ Colo, 1977; Distinguished Alumni Service Award, Univ Colo, 1983; Athletic Hall of Fame, Colo Univ, 2000; First African-American to serve as ambassador to a nation behind the Iron Curtain. **Home Addr:** PO Box 280, Rockland, DE 19732.

## BOLES, DONNA M.

Vice president (organization). **Personal:** married Eric Reed; children: 1. **Educ:** Upsala Col, BS, human resource mgt & psychol; Pace Univ, MBA. **Career:** BD Med, secy, 1973, vpres human resources, 2001-05, Sr vpres human resources, 2006-13. **Orgs:** Bd dir, Big Bros Big Sisters Morris, Bergen & Passaic Inc; bd dir, CST Brands Inc., 2013-. **Home Addr:** 1121 Catasauqua Ave, Allentown, PA 18102-5003. **Business Addr:** Board of Director, CST Brands, Inc., 1 Valero Way, San Antonio, TX 78249, **Business Phone:** (210)692-5000.

## BOLLES, A. LYNN

Anthropologist, college teacher. **Personal:** Born Dec 4, 1949, Passaic, NJ; daughter of George and Augusta Beebe; married James Walsh; children: Shane Walsh & Robeson James Walsh. **Educ:** Syracuse Univ, Syracuse, NY, AB, 1971; Rutgers Univ, NB, NJ, MA, 1978, PhD, 1981. **Career:** Rutgers Univ, Livingston Col, Nb, NJ, lectr & teaching asst, 1976-78, course coordr, women's studies prog, 1977; Bowdoin Col, Brunswick, ME, from asst prof to assoc prof anthrop, 1980-89, dir, afro-am studies prog, 1980-89; Univ Md, assoc prof women's studies, 1989-95, prof womens studies & affil fac, 1995-, actg chmn, Dept African Am Studies, currently. **Orgs:** Pres, Asn Black Anthropologist, 1983-84, secy-treas, 1988-91; bd dir, Asn Women Develop, 1984-86; prog chair, Asn Feminist Anthropologists, 1989-92, pres, 1999-2001, 2001-03; chair, Africa & Africa Americas Comt, 1992-93; exec coun, Caribbean Studies Asn, 1992-95, pres, 1997-98; Am Ethnol Soc, counr, 1993-96; Latin Am Studies Asn; Asn Black Women Historians; ed bd, Feminist Studies; ed & adv bd, Urban Anthrop; Alpha Kappa Alpha, Iota Lambda Omega; fel, Am Anthrop Asn; pres, Socs Anthrop N Am, 2009-11; founder, Inst Gender & Develop Studies, Univ Wi; mentor, Ronald McNair Felsprogram. **Honors/Awds:** Race Unity Day Award for Bowdoin Afro-Am studies prog, Spiritual Assembly Baha'is, 1983; Black History Maker of Maine Award, Augusta Black Community, 1984; Martin Luther King Jr, Community Service Award, ME NAACP, 1988; numerous res grants; Syracuse Univ, chancellor's citation for excellence in educ, 1989; Soc Appl Anthrop, fel; Outstanding Minority Faculty Member of the Year, Univ Md, Col Pk, 1994. **Special Achievements:** Author: My Mother Who Fathered Me & Others: Gender & Kinship in the English-Speaking Caribbean, 1988; Co-author: Shadow of the Sun, 1990; We Paid Our Dues: Women Trade Union Leaders in the Caribbean, 1996; Sister Jamaica: A Study of Women, Work and Households in Kingston, 1996. **Home Addr:** 3104 Bold Ruler Ct, Bowie, MD 20721-1281, **Home Phone:** (301)249-7454. **Business Addr:** Professor, University of Maryland, 2101 Woods Hall, College Park, MD 20742, **Business Phone:** (301)405-6879.

## BOLLING, BARBARA

President (organization). **Educ:** Kettering Univ, Flint, BA; Valparaiso Univ Sch Law, 1989. **Career:** Nat Asn Advan Colored People, In St Conf Pres; Nat Asn Advan Colored People, Pres; Nat Asn Advan Colored People, atty & pres, 2003-. **Orgs:** Exec Comt Mem, Nat Asn Advan Colored People. **Business Addr:** Attorney, President-Indiana Chapter, National Association for the Advancement of Colored People, 575 Broadway Suite 1A Gary, Gary, IN 46402, **Business Phone:** (219)886-2227.

## BOLLING, CAROL NICHOLSON

Manager, executive. **Personal:** Born Jan 28, 1952, Jamaica, NY; daughter of Paris Nicholson Jr and Miriam Nicholson; married Bruce. **Educ:** State Univ NY, BS, lib arts, 1974. **Career:** Gillette Co, group leader collections, 1976-78, group leader customer serv, 1978, asst supvr sales admin, 1978-80, supvr rec mgt, 1980-81, personnel recruiter, 1981-83, affirmative action adr, 1983-84, sr personnel rep, 1984-86, credit mgr employee rels, 1986-87; WCVB-TV, human resources mgr, 1987, community serv & human resource, currently. **Orgs:** Black Achievers Asn, 1984-86; Big Sisters Asn, 1985-88; bd mem, Robert F Kennedy Action Corp, 1987-89; Roxbury Comprehensive Health Ctr, 1987-89; Greater Boston YMCA, 1988-89; MSPCC, 1988-89; Advert Club Boston Charitable Trust Fund, 1988-; Endowment C Crisis, 1990-; founding mem, Nat Coalition 100 Black Women, 1991-; Greater Boston Broadcasters Minority Search Group, 1991-; bd mem, Vis Nurses Asn, 1992-; trustee, Dana-Farber Cancer Inst Inc; Ad Club Found. **Honors/Awds:** Young Leaders Award, Boston Jaycees, 1986; Black Achiever Award, YMCA, 1980. **Home Addr:** 64 Harold St, Roxbury, MA 02119, **Home Phone:** (617)445-3328. **Business Addr:** Director Community Services, Human Resource Manager, WCVB Channel 5, 5 TV Pl, Needham, MA 02494-2302, **Business Phone:** (781)449-0400.

## BOLLING, DEBORAH A.

Movie director, executive. **Personal:** Born Jun 18, 1957, New York, NY; daughter of David and Daisy Alston. **Educ:** State Univ NY, Old Westbury, BA, 1979. **Career:** Freelancer, video/filmmaker, currently. **Orgs:** Black Filmmakers Found, 1989-; Women Makes Movies, 1990-. **Honors/Awds:** Best Documentary, "Two Dollars and a Dream", Nat Asn Black Journalists, 1988; Production of the Decade, "Two Dollars and a Dream", Black Filmmaker Found, 1989; Award of Excellence, "Portraits in Black", CEBA, 1990. **Home Addr:** 2241 92nd St, East Elmhurst, NY 11369-1116.

## BOLT, USAIN ST. LEO

Athlete, entrepreneur. **Personal:** Born Aug 21, 1986, Sherwood Content; son of Jennifer and Wellesley. **Career:** Sprinter; Soul, Tracks & Records, Jamaica, owner, currently. **Home Addr:** . **Business Addr:** Sprinter, Usain Bolt Foundation Pace Sports Management, 6 Causeway Teddington, MiddlesexTW11 OHE, **Business Phone:** (208)943-1072.

**BOLTON, ALICE RUTH. See BOLTON-HOLIFIELD, RUTHIE.**

## BOLTON, HON. JULIAN TAYLOR

Executive, lawyer, city commissioner. **Personal:** Born Oct 28, 1949, Memphis, TN; married Joyce Walker; children: Julian II & Jared Walker. **Educ:** Rhodes Col, BA, commun, 1971; Memphis State Univ, MA, speech drama, 1973; Univ Memphis Sch Law, JD, 1992. **Career:** New Theatre S Ensemble, producer & dir, 1977-80; Shelby Co, bd comnrs, 1982, chmn; S Cent Bell, tech designer commun syst; Bell Syst, systs design cons, telecommun; LeMoyne Owen Col, assoc prof theater; Richardson Law Firm; Cochran Firm, managing partner. **Orgs:** Memphis Black Arts Coun, 1981-; rev comn, Memphis Arts Coun, 1985; Nat Asn Co Offices; treas, Memphis Black Arts Alliance; bd mem, Midtown Ment Health Ctr; Ben Jones Chap, Nat Bar Asn; Memphis Bar Asn; Ind Develop Bd eval comt; exec comt, Tenn Tombigbee Waterways Authority. **Honors/Awds:** Producer, Dir over 40 theatrical prods, 1968-80; Fellow Recipient consortium, Grad Study Bus Blacks, 1971; Black Stud Asn. **Home Addr:** 542 Magnolia Mound Dr, Memphis, TN 38103-4770, **Home Phone:** (901)527-4222.

## BOLTON, DR. LINDA BURNES

Nurse, association executive, executive. **Educ:** Ariz State Univ, BS, nursing; Univ Calif, Los Angeles, CA, MA, nursing, MA, pub health, PhD, pub health; RN; DrPH; FAAN. **Career:** Pub mem govt adv bds, staff nurse, clin nurse specialist, health care exec, comm & pub health nurse, univ fac & consult; Univ Calif, Los Angeles, fac mem; Univ Calif, San Francisco, fac mem; Cedars-Sinai Med Ctr, vpres nursing, chief nursing officer, dir nursing res, currently. **Orgs:** Pres, Nat Black Nurses Asn; Am Wrestling Asn; bd dir, Nat Black Nurses Found; pres, Am Orgn Nurse Execs, 2014; trustee, vice chair, Robert Wood Johnson Found Bd, 2012-; pres, Am Acad Nursing; Am Nurses Asn; Asn Calif Nurse Leaders; Am Pub Health Asn; Advan Nursing Sci; Nat League Nursing; trustee, Case Western Res Univ, 2006-; chair, Nat Adv comt Transforming Care Bedside; Veteran Affairs Comn Nursing. **Honors/Awds:** Fel Am Acad Nursing; Lifetime Achievement Award, Am Orgn of Nurse Execs, 2007; Distinguished Alumnae Award, Ariz State Univ, 2008. **Special Achievements:** She is the author of numerous articles, books, book chapters, videos and audiotapes and is the co-developer of the National Black Nurses Association Community Collaboration Model. A framework for improving community health, the model has been tested & is now used in more than 100 communities throughout the United States; Top 25 women in health care by Modern Healthcare magazine; Top 10 health care executives by the Los Angeles Business Journal. **Business Addr:** Vice President, Chief Nursing Officer, Cedars-Sinai Health System & Research Institute, 8700 Beverly Blvd Suite 2009, Los Angeles, CA 90048-1804, **Business Phone:** (310)423-8600.

## BOLTON, TERRELL D.

Police chief. **Personal:** Born Sep 12, 1958, MS; children: Terrell Jr; married Glenda; children: 2. **Educ:** Jackson State Univ, BA, criminal justice, 1980; Fed Bur Invest Nat Acad, Quantico, Va, Exec/Mgt Grad Class #163, 1988. **Career:** Dallas Police Dept, police patrol officer, 1980-84, sgt, 1984-88, dep chief, 1998-91, asst chief, 1991-99, chief, 2001-03; Chief Bolton & Assocs, pres, chief exec officer, 2003-; DeKalb County, Ga, chief police, 2007-09. **Orgs:** Jackson State Alumni Asn; Phi Beta Sigma Fraternity; Southwest Law Enforcement Inst Adv Bd; bd trustee, Major Cities Chiefs. **Honors/Awds:** Marksmanship Award; 10-Year Safe Driving Award; 10-Year Perfect Attendance Award; Police Commend Award; various Community Awards. **Special Achievements:** First African-American chief of Dallas Police Dept; First African American to head the Dallas Police Dept. **Home Addr:** 5141 Whispering Oaks Dr, Dallas, TX 75236-1739, **Home Phone:** (770)469-8250. **Business Addr:** President, Chief Executive officer, Chief Bolton & Associates, 5141 Whispering Oaks Dr, Dallas, TX 75236, **Business Phone:** (214)502-6228.

## BOLTON-HOLIFIELD, RUTHIE (ALICE RUTH BOLTON)

Basketball player, basketball coach. **Personal:** Born May 25, 1967, Lucedale, MS; daughter of Linwood and Leola; married Mark. **Educ:** Auburn, BA, exercise physiol, 1989. **Career:** Basketball player (retired), basketball coach; Visby (Sweden), guard, 1989-90; Tungstrum (Hungary), 1991-92; Erreti Faenza (Italy), 1992-95; Galatsaray (Turkey), 1996-97; Sacramento Monarchs, guard, 1997-2004, fan rels, 2005-; William Jessup Univ, head coach, 2004; Calif Pac Conf Sch, head coach, 2005; Vacaville Christian High Sch, head coach, currently. **Orgs:** Women's Nat Basketball Asn. **Honors/Awds:** USA Basketball Female Player of the Year, 1991; Gold Medal, World Univ Games, 1991; Bronze Medal, FIBA World Championship Women, 1994; Gold Medal, US Olympic Basketball Team, 1996; All-WNBA First Team, 1997; Gold Medal, FIBA World Championship Women, 1998; Gold Medal, US Olympic Basketball Team, 2000; Hall of Fame, Ala Sports, 2014. **Home Addr:** 10351 Jennick Way, Elk Grove, CA 95757-1604. **Business Addr:** Head Coach, William Jessup University, 333 Sunset Blvd, Rocklin, CA 95765, **Business Phone:** (916)577-2200.

## BOMMER, MINNIE L.

Executive, community activist. **Personal:** Born Feb 3, 1940, Covington, TN; daughter of Malcolm Yarbrough and Eula Ray Maclin Burrell; married John Samuel Sr; children: Monica, Gina & John Jr. **Educ:** Univ Tenn, educ, 1976; Tenn State Univ, attended 1982; Spelman Col, attended 1983; Univ Calif, Davis, rural leadership develop inst, 1989; Memphis State Univ, BPS, 1991; Antioch Univ, MA, emphasis rural develop, 1993. **Career:** Tipton Cty Hosp, lic practical nurse, 1968-73; Tipton City Human Serv, elig counr, 1974-82; Douglas Community Health Ctr Haywood County, 1982-86; City Covington, alderwoman, 1983; Douglas Health Clin, maternal infant health outreach worker, 1985; Vanderbilt Univ, Ctr Res Rural Families & Communities, community develop consult; Bommer Assocs Consult Serv; C & Family Serv, exec dir, founder, currently. **Orgs:** Chmn, Tipton County Libr Bd, 1983-85; chmn, Rural W TN African Am Affairs Coun, 1985-; bd mem, Community Resource Group, 1985-91, chair; bd dir, Tipton County Chamber Com, 1986-96; deleg, Nat Dem Conv, 1988; bd dir, Tenn Housing Develop Agency, 1988-91; life mem, Nat Asn Advan Colored People, 1990; Dyensbung State Adv Comm Tenn rep, Lower Miss Delta Ctr, 1990-; Eight Cong Rep State Bd Educ, 1990-97; vpres, TN State Nat Asn Advan Colored People; Support Ctr Disparities Eliminations; Nat Black Women's Polit Caucus, TN Women Govt; Tenn Suicide Prev Network; Canaan Baptist Church; Tenn Employee Asn; Covington Chamber Com; Dyersburg State Col Adv Bd; Fork Deer Regional Libr Bd; Rural Develop Leadership Network; Tenn Leadership Roundtable; Tenn Black Child Inst; Lea Migonette Club; Tipton County Nat Asn Advan Colored People; Six-stale Bd Fayetteville, Ark; Melanin Bk Club; Alumni Chap Delta Sigma Theta Sorority. **Honors/Awds:** Mother of the Year, Canaan Church Group, 1976; served on Resolution Advance Drafting Comn, Nat Asn Advan Colored People, 1985; Tenn Women on the Move, Tenn Political Caucus, 1987; Distinguished Service Award, Tenn Black Caucus State Legis, 1988; Thousand Points of Lights Volunteer Award, 1989; Nat Vol, Thousand Point of Light, 1989; Lifetime Membership Award, Nat Asn Advan Colored People, 1990; AKA Award for Outstanding Community Serv, 1994; TN Advocates for Children Pioneer Award, 1995; Un-Sung Hero Award, Memphis Peace & Justice Ctr, 1996; Mentie Buckman Empowerment Award, 1999; Rural Health Worker of the Year, 2000; deleg to White House Cont on Families State & Nat. **Special Achievements:** First African American and First Female to serve city of Covington, 1983. **Home Addr:** 707 Simonton St, Covington, TN 38019-1922, **Home Phone:** (901)476-8112. **Business Addr:** Founder, Executive Director, Children & Family Service Inc, 412 Alston St Naifeh Bldg, Covington, TN 38019, **Business Phone:** (901)476-2364.

**BONAPARTE, DR. ANTHONY. See BONAPARTE, DR. TONY HILLARY.**

## BONAPARTE, LOIS ANN

Social worker, psychologist. **Personal:** Born Mar 17, 1941, New York, NY; daughter of Randolph Graves and Floree Wilson; married Charles Jr; children: C Scott. **Educ:** Social Welfare, Garden City, BSW, 1980; Social Work, Garden City, MSW, 1988. **Career:** Holly Patterson Geriat Ctr, Uniondale, NY, dir sr citizen ctr, 1979-92; Sch Social Worker, 1994; Hempstead Pub Sch Dist, social worker, currently; Hempstead, psychologist. **Orgs:** Social worker, Family Serv Asn, Hempstead, NY, 1973-79; Nat Asn Social Workers, 1979-; NY State Conf Aging Inc, 1979-92; chairperson, Comt Commemoration African-Am Hist, 1984-92; rec corresp secy, Long Island Sr Citizen Dirs Asn, 1987-88; Adv coun mem, Ministry Black Catholics, 1989-; adv coun mem, St Anthony's Guid Coun, 1990-. **Honors/Awds:** Ebony Vanguard Enrichment Award, Comt Commendation African-Am Hist. **Special**

**Achievements:** Nominee, Dr Martin Luther King Jr Award, Nassau County, 1991; Certified Social Worker, 1989; originated, produced, an annual African-American history program, 8 years, county-wide. **Home Addr:** 254 Long Beach Rd, Hempstead, NY 11550-7603, **Home Phone:** (516)538-2095. **Business Addr:** Social Worker, Hempstead Public School District, 185 Peninsula Blvd, Hempstead, NY 11550, **Business Phone:** (516)292-7111.

### BONAPARTE, NORTON NATHANIEL, JR.
City manager, educator. **Personal:** Born Apr 10, 1953, New York, NY; son of Norton N Sr and Beryl; married Santa Orcasitas; children: Akia & Nathaniel. **Educ:** Worcester Polytech Inst, BS, civil engineering, 1975; Cornell Univ, Grad Sch Bus, Ithaca, NY, MPA, 1977; Harvard Univ, Sr Execs State & Local Govt Prog, grad. **Career:** City Grand Rapids, Mich, asst city mgr, 1977-81; Am Soc Pub Admin, dir prog develop, 1981-83; Inst Govt Servs, govt consult, 1984-87; E Coast Migrant Head Start Proj, asst dir, 1987-88; Auto Cleaning Ser, gen mgr & owner, 1988; chief admin officer, Md, munic corp, 1988-94; City Glenarden, city mgr, 1988-94; Twp Willingboro, twp mgr, 1995-2000; Officer NJ Munic Corp, Philadelphia Metrop Area, chief exec, 1995-2000; NJ Munic Corp, Philadelphia Metrop Area, chief admin officer, 2000-03; NJ Munic Corp, chief admin officer, 2003; Sanford's City Mgr, 2011-; Nat-Louis Univ, McLean, Va, sr adjunt instr; Kans, city mgr; NJ, city adminr plainfield; NJ, city adminr Camden; NJ, twp mgr Willingboro; Glenarden, Md, city mgr; Rutgers Univ, pub mgt fac; City Topeka, city mgr & chief exec officer, currently. **Orgs:** Pres, City & Town Adminr Dept, Md Munic League, 1991; pres, Md City & Co Mgt Asn, 1992; chair, Prof Munic Mgt Joint Ins Fund, 1998-2000; bd dir, United Way Burlington Co, 1999; chair, NJ Environ Joint Ins Fund, 1999-2000; Int City Mgt Asn; Nat Forum Black Pub Admins; bd dir, Burlington Co Red Cross Chap; bd mem & pres, NJ Munic Mgt Asn; Managers Who Teach comt; prin instr, Emerging Leaders Acad, Univ Kans; Kans Asn City & County Mgt; pres, Md City & County Mgt Asn; United Way Greater Topeka; bd dir, Kans Capital Area Red Cross; Community Adv Coun, Stormont-Vail Hosp; Downtown Topeka Rotary Club; Heartland Visioning; Nat Acad Pub Admin; bd dir, Fla City & County Mgt Asn; Fla Tri-County League Cities; Seminole County Regional Chamber Com; Sanford Rotary Club; Univ Cent Fla's Sch Pub Admin. **Business Addr:** City Manager, City of Sanford, 300 N Park Ave, Sanford, FL 32771, **Business Phone:** (407)688-5009.

### BONAPARTE, DR. TONY HILLARY (DR. ANTHONY BONAPARTE)
School administrator, educator. **Personal:** Born Jun 13, 1939, Grenada; son of Norman and Myra; married Sueli Fugita; children: Yvette. **Educ:** St John's Univ, BBA, 1963, MBA, 1964; NY Univ, PhD, 1967. **Career:** St John's Univ, asst prof, 1964-68, provost, 1993-99, exec, vpres, spec asst to pres, currently; Bus Intl Corp, res assoc, mgt syst, 1968-70; Pace Univ, vpres, dean, prof intl bus, 1968-85; Rapan Res Corp, exec dir, 1970-73; Univ Strathdyde Univ Edinburgh, vis prof, 1977; Bentley Col, vpres acad affairs & provost; St Thomas Aquinas Col, vice chmn bd trustee; Peter J Tobin Col Bus, prof. **Orgs:** Dir, Robert Schalkenbach Found, 1975-; World Trade Inst Port Arthur, 1977-; Brazil-Interpart Cabaatia Brazil, 1979-; pres, Mid Atlantic Assoc Bus Admin, 1981-82; pres, Fulbright Alumni Assoc, 1983-84; chmn, Int Affairs Comn Am Assembly, 1983-; dir, Assoc Black Charities, 1983-; Am Econ Asn; bd dir, Jamaica Bus Resource Ctr, currently. **Honors/Awds:** Fellow, Am Asn Adv Sci, 1969; Fulbright Sr Prof Col Liberia, 1973-74; Co-ed book Peter Drucker Contribs Bus Enterprise, 1970; Honor, DHL Southeastern Univ. **Home Addr:** 25 Leonard Rd, Lexington, MA 02420. **Business Addr:** Board Director, Jamaica Business Resource Center, 90-33 160th St, Jamaica, NY 11432, **Business Phone:** (718)206-2255.

### BOND, ALAN DALE
Consultant, real estate agent. **Personal:** Born Jul 16, 1945, Jefferson City, TN; son of Frederick Douglas (deceased) and Edna Coleman (deceased); married Claudette Davis; children: Melinda Bond Shreve & Clayton Alan. **Educ:** Cent State Univ, BS, bus admin, 1967; post degree studies law, bus & financial planning. **Career:** Detroit Pub Sch, instr, part time; Ford Motor Co, prod planning & invention control specialist, 1968-69; Control Data Corp, mat supr, 1969-70; Xerox Corp, 1970-71; City Detroit, police dept, 1971-73; Chrysler Corp, prod systs & mat control specialist, 1973-75; Equitable Life Assurance Soc US & other Co, ins broker, 1975-; Detroit Edison Co, corpins & real estate admin, 1978-86; Estate Enhancements, ins & real estate consult & owner, 1986-; Jack Christenson Inc, real estate specialist, currently. **Orgs:** Alpha Phi Alpha Frat, 1963-; trustee, Sanctuary Fel Baptist Church, 1970-; Nat Asn Life Underwriters, 1975-; life mem, Nat Asn Advan Colored People, 1984. **Honors/Awds:** Honorary Graduation National Sales Development Program, Xerox Corp, 1970; Elected Delegate, Wayne Co Conv Precinct Delegates, 1972-; Practical Electric Passenger, Car Prom Prog, 1982-83; Men of Achievement Director, Cambridge Univ Eng; Ford Motor Community Service Award; Spirit Detroit Awardee; received numerous public service recognition awards. **Home Addr:** 17158 Indiana St, Detroit, MI 48221-2445. **Business Addr:** Real Estate Specialist, Keller Williams Real Estate, 1700 W Big Beaver Rd Suite 100, Troy, MI 48084-3500, **Business Phone:** (313)342-3833.

### BOND, CECIL WALTON, JR.
Businessperson, transport worker, executive. **Personal:** Born Dec 30, 1937, Chester, PA; son of Frinjela P and Cecil W Sr; married Linette H; children: Tracy, Cecil III, Devon & Denzel. **Educ:** Morgan State Univ, BS; Wharton Grad Sch, mgt prog. **Career:** Cent Pa Nat Bank, vpres, 1970-80; Southeastern Pa Transp Authority, dir civil rights, asst gen mgr, revenue opers, 1994-96, asst gen mgr, safety & security, currently, commun technician, 2008-; Top Shelf Entertainment Group, owner operator/DJ, currently. **Orgs:** Urban Bankers Coalition; bd mem, Comt Accts; bd mem, Greater Philadelphia Comn Develop Corp; Greater Philadelphia Venture Capital Corp; Nat Forum Black Pub Adminr; Philadelphia Orchestras Cult Diversity Initiative; Philadelphia Young Men Chrisitian Asn, Adult Reading Prog; chmn, Am Pub Transp Asn, Minority Affairs Comt; Am Pub Transp Found. **Honors/Awds:** Minority Business Advocate Award, Greater Philadelphia Chamber Com, 1989. **Home Addr:** 169 Carlton Ave, Marlton, NJ 08053-1868, **Home Phone:** (856)596-4715. **Business Addr:** Assistant General Manager, Communications Technician, Southeastern Pennsylvania Transportation Authority, 1234 Market St, Philadelphia, PA 19107, **Business Phone:** (215)580-7800.

### BOND, CHARLES CYNTHIA V.
Insurance executive, funeral director, association executive. **Personal:** Born Feb 10, 1934, Brownsville, TN; daughter of Charles Allen and Maude Crofton; married Maltimore; children: Jo Zanice, Alan R, Andrea C Johnson & Maude Y. **Educ:** Fisk Univ, BS, 1955; NY Univ, MS, 1956. **Career:** Golden Circle Life Ins Co, personnel dir, 1957, asst secy, pres, 1987-2002; Golden Circle Ins Agency, partner, 2001-; Rawls Funeral Syst, pres, currently. **Orgs:** Bd dir, Insouth Bank; Lane Col Trustee Bd & Tenn Black Health Care Comn; State Bd Educ; Judicial Eval Comn; YMCA Local & Reg Bds; Birth Choice Adv Bd; Delta Sigma Theta Sorority; Jackson Tenn LINKS; life mem, Haywood County Nat Asn Advan Colored People Br. **Honors/Awds:** Avon N Williams Jr Living Legend Award; Alumni Achievement Award, Fisk Univ. **Home Addr:** 1101 Cynthia Dr, Brownsville, TN 38012-3204, **Home Phone:** (731)772-9662. **Business Addr:** Funeral Director, Rawls Funeral Home, 39 S Jackson Ave, Brownsville, TN 38012, **Business Phone:** (731)772-1472.

### BOND, HOWARD H. See Obituaries Section.

### BOND, JAMES G.
Politician. **Personal:** Born Nov 11, 1944, Ft. Valley, GA. **Career:** City Hall Atlanta, city coun, politician, currently. **Orgs:** S Eastern dir, Youth Citizenshp Fund, 1972; bd dir, Atlanta Legal Aid; Atlanta City Coun, 1973; Voter Educ Proj Fel 1973; chmn, Labor Educ Advan Proj, 1974; chmn, Labor Educ Advan Proj, 1974; chmn, Com Atlanta City Coun, 1975-76; chmn, Pub Safety Comt, 1977; bd resources, Highlander Ctr; adv bd, Nat Conf Alternative State & Local Pub Policies. **Home Addr:** 361 Westview Dr SW, Atlanta, GA 30310, **Home Phone:** (404)755-0614. **Business Addr:** Politician, City Hall Atlanta, Atlanta, GA 30303.

### BOND, JULIAN. See Obituaries Section.

### BOND, DR. LLOYD
Educator, scientist. **Personal:** Born Nov 17, 1941, Brownsville, TN. **Educ:** Hillsdale Col, BS, 1964; Johns Hopkins Univ, MS, 1975, PhD, psychol, 1976. **Career:** Gen Motors, personnel rep, 1966-72; Univ Pittsburgh, Dept Psych, asst prof, 1976-82, Learning R & D Ctr, assoc prof, sr scientist, 1982; Univ NC Greensboro, Educ Res Methodology, prof, 1988-02, prof emer, 2003-; Carnegie Found Advan Teaching, sr scholar, 2002-08, consult. **Orgs:** Phi Beta Kappa, 1977; spencer fel Nat Acad Educ, 1980-83; fel Am Psych Asn, 1982, 1990; bd trustee, Col Bd, 1984-88, 1997-2001; NAS Comt Math Assesment, 1990-; NAE Panel State, Nat Assessment Educ Progress, 1990-; fel, Am Psychol Asn & Am Educ Res Asn; sradv, Nat Bd Prof Teaching Stand, 1997-2002; bd trustee, Human Resources Res Orgn; Nat Acad Sci Comt. **Home Addr:** 214 Durand Way, Palo Alto, CA 94304. **Business Addr:** Professor Emeritus, University of North Carolina, 180 Mossman Bldg, Greensboro, NC 27402, **Business Phone:** (336)334-5946.

### BOND, DR. LOUIS GRANT
Lecturer. **Personal:** Born Jan 6, 1947, Baltimore, MD; children: Jordan & Meredith. **Educ:** Boston Univ, BA, 1958, EdD, 1974; Harvard Univ, MTS, 1972; Boston Col, MA; Western Univ, CA, PhD, 1977. **Career:** Boston Univ, lectr & instr, 1969-, asst dean fac, currently; Educ Develop Social Studies, dir, parent educ, teacher trainer, curric developer, 1972-74; St Andres United Meth Church, pastor, 1973-; J LU-ROB Enterprises Inc, pres; B&R Corrugated Container Corp & B&R World Oil, pres, chmn bd. **Orgs:** Black Meth Church Renewal; Nat Asn Black Sch Admins; Am Asn Jr & Community Cols; Asn Black Psychologist; Am Asn Gen Lib Studies; Phi Beta Kappa, Harvard Univ Fac Club, Nat Asn Advan Colored People; comt chairperson; GDCA Nat Specialty. **Honors/Awds:** Wm H Lemell Scholarship, 1964; Martin Luther King Jr Grant, 1970; Rockefeller Found Award, 1972; Fulbright Scholarship, 1973; Hatcher Scholarship, 1974. **Home Addr:** 167 Riverlin St, PO Box 350, Millbury, MA 01527-4146, **Home Phone:** (508)865-2828. **Business Addr:** Lecturer, Assistant Dean of Faculty, Boston University, 1 Silber Way, Boston, MA 02215, **Business Phone:** (617)353-2000.

### BOND, MICHAEL JULIAN
Government official. **Personal:** Born Jan 1, 1966?; son of Alice Clopton and Julian. **Educ:** Morehouse Col; Ga State Univ. **Career:** Atlanta City Coun, councilman, 1994-2001; pres, 2001-09, post 1 llarge, 2010-; Covenant Consult Inc, Pres & chief exec officer, 2000-; Seniors Home Reverse Mortgage, vpres mkt, 2005-. **Orgs:** St James Lodge No 4, Prince Hall affil; Empowerment Bd; GABEO; Ga Munic Asn, Atlanta Nat Asn Advan Colored People; bd, Ollie St, SE & E Lake YMCAs, Atlanta Empowerment Zone; chmn Bd, Laffapolooza, youth mentoring orgn; Leadership Atlanta & Black-Jewish Coalition's Proj Understanding; Dep Dir & Chief Prog Off, Atlanta Nat Asn Advan Colored People; Am Fed State, County & Munic Employees. **Home Addr:** 55 Maple St NW Apt 807, Atlanta, GA 30314, **Home Phone:** (404)589-1452. **Business Addr:** Post 1 at Large, Atlanta City Hall, 55 Trinity Ave SW Suite 2900, Atlanta, GA 30303-3584, **Business Phone:** (404)330-6770.

### BOND, NORMAN
Business owner, association executive, executive. **Educ:** Univ Pittsburgh, BS, bus & econs, 1986, MS, info sci, 1986. **Career:** Next Step Enterprises Inc, co-founder, 1995, publ & gen mgr, 1996-2004, chief exec officer, 2000; Nat Diversity Week, founder, 1999; Normbond & Assocs, pres, digital mkt strategist, 2005-14, chief digital officer, 2007-; Radio One Philadelphia, acct exec, 2008-09; Nat Alliance Mkt Developers, chmn, 2008-13; X2 Global Media, pr & commun mgr, 2016-. **Orgs:** Pres, Philadelphia Chap NAMD. **Honors/Awds:** Inroads; Black Women Publ; Granville Acad Nat; Lincoln Univ. **Special Achievements:** He was quoted in Nat publications including Chicago Tribune, USA Today, Philadelphia Inquirer, Black Enterprise & Business Week. **Business Addr:** PR & Communications Manager, X2 Global Media, 170/87 New Ratchadaphisek Rd, Bangkok10110, **Business Phone:** (662)648-6123.

### BOND, RONALD A.
Educator, manager. **Personal:** Born Nov 24, 1938, Chester, PA; son of Cecil W and Frinjela Powell; married Sonja; children: Ronald Jr & Lisa. **Educ:** NY Univ, Col Educ, 1958; Temple Univ, BS, educ, 1963, MEd, health educ, 1970, ABD, sports admin, 1993. **Career:** Philadelphia Pub Schs, teacher, 1964-70; Univ PA, Dept Recreation, dir, 1970-83; City Philadelphia, dep recreation comnr, stadium mgr, 1987-92; Temple Univ, guest lectr, 1987, 1989 & 2000; CA State Univ-Fulleron, assoc athletic dir, sports & phys performance complex, dir, 1994-99, guest lectr, 1996 & 1998; DE River Port Authority, proj mgr, 1999. **Orgs:** Life mem, Alpha Phi Alpha, 1960-; life mem, Nat Asn Advan Colored People; pres, Friars Sr Alumni Bd, Univ PA, 1984-86; Phys Ed, Recreation & Dance, Alumini Bd, Col Health, Temple Univ, 1990-94; pres, African-Am Fac Staff Asn, CA State Univ-Fullerton, 1994-99; bd dir, Am Heart Asn S CA, 1995-99; USTA-Mid States Col Tennis Comt & multicultural participation comt, 1996-99; Hope Int Univ Pres's Forum, 1997-99, Nat Asn Black Pub Adminrs; mem bd govs, Camp Tockwogh; mem bd trustee, Cornerstone Christian Acad; mem bd dir, Ralston & Mercy Douglass House; adv bd, Sprinturf; pres, Adrian Assocs Consults, LLC, 2003-. **Home Addr:** 2238 N 51st St, Philadelphia, PA 19131, **Home Phone:** (215)477-4430.

### BOND, VERNON, JR.
Educator. **Personal:** Born Nov 15, 1951, Windsor, NC; son of Vernon and Sadie; married Johnetta; children: Maya, Jennifer & Vernon III. **Educ:** St Augustine's Col, Raleigh, NC, BS, 1974; NC Cent Univ, Durham, NC, MS, 1976; Univ Tenn, Knoxville, TN, EdD, 1979. **Career:** NC Cent Univ, asst prof, 1979-80; Howard Univ, asst prof, 1980-85, assoc prof, 1985-89, Dept Health Human Performance & Leisure Studies, prof exercise physiol, 1996-, Natural Scis Div, chair, 2001-02; Univ Tenn, assoc prof, 1989-90; Howard Univ Hosp, dir, 1990-92; La State Univ, assoc prof, 1992-93; Univ Md, assoc prof, 1993-96. Books: Aerobic exercise attenuates an exaggerated blood pressure response in normotensive young adult African-American men, 2003; Normal exercise blood pressure response in African_American women with parenatl history of hypertension, Am J Med Sci, 2004. **Orgs:** Fel Am Col & Sports Med, 1980-; bd mem, Inst Rev Bd, Howard Univ. **Home Addr:** 10905 Battersea Ct, Ft. Washington, MD 20744-7210, **Home Phone:** (301)203-1681. **Business Addr:** Professor of Exercise Physiology, Howard University, Rm G-240 Burr Gym 6th & Girard St NW, Washington, DC 20059, **Business Phone:** (202)806-6327.

### BONDS, BARRY LAMAR
Baseball player, baseball executive. **Personal:** Born Jul 24, 1964, Riverside, CA; son of Bobby and Patricia Howard; married Liz Watson; children: Aisha; married Susann Margreth Branco; children: Nikolai & Shikari. **Educ:** Ariz State Univ, BA, criminol, 1986. **Career:** Baseball player (retired), baseball executive; Pittsburgh Pirates, outfielder, 1986-92; San Francisco Giants, 1993-2007; free agt, currently. **Home Addr:** 175 Lyndhurst Ave, San Carlos, CA 94070. **Business Addr:** Free Agent, Beverly Hills, CA 90212.

### BONDS, KATHLEEN
College administrator. **Personal:** Born Buffalo, NY. **Educ:** State Univ NY, Buffalo, BS, criminal justice; State Univ NY, Fredonia, MS, human resource mgt. **Career:** St Ann's Ctr, adminr; Community Action Orgn Erie County, adminr; State Univ New York Fredonia, Educ Develop Prog, counr, dir, 1992-. **Business Addr:** Director of Human Resources, State University of New York Fredonia, E284 Thompson Hall, Fredonia, NY 14063, **Business Phone:** (716)673-3318.

### BONDS, KEVIN GREGG
Executive. **Personal:** Born Mar 3, 1961, Lansing, MI; son of Solomon Jr and Anita Taylor. **Educ:** Community Col Air Force, AAS, 1990; Nat Univ, BBA, 1990. **Career:** USAF, personnel technician, 1981-90; Wis Physician's Serv, claims supvr, 1990-91; Wis Dept Develop, fiscal opers mgr. **Orgs:** Comnr, Affirmative Action Comn, 1992-, bd supvr, 1994-, Personnel & Finance Comt, supvr, 1994-, Housing Authority, comnr, 1994-; treas, So Madison Neighborhood Ctr, 1993-94; treas, African Am Ethnic Acad Inc, 1993-; treas, Wis Community Fund, 1994-; Dane Co Exec Off. **Honors/Awds:** America's Best & Brightest, Dollar's & Sense Mag, 1993; Outstanding African-American Role Model, Mother's Simpson St, 1994. **Special Achievements:** Depicting African-American History & Sites, 1995. **Home Addr:** 101 E Jolly Rd Apt B1, Lansing, MI 48910-6683, **Home Phone:** (517)373-5668.

### BONDY, KIM
Vice president (organization), executive. **Educ:** Univ New Orleans, BA, MBA, commun, 1988. **Career:** WCAU-TV, managing ed; WDSU, prod asst; CITV & CITN, news dir, reporter & anchor; WXIA, news producer; CNN, vpres spec programming, sr exec producer incharge & gen mgr, vpres morning programming & exec producer CNNs Am Morning, 2004-; NBC News, exec & sr producing positions; Bondy Group, founder & pres; America Tonight, sr exec producer. **Orgs:** Fel Nat Asn Minorities Commun. **Business Addr:** Vice President of morning programming, Executive Producer of CNNs American Morning, CNN/CNNs American Morning, 1 CNN Ctr SE 07, Atlanta, GA 30303, **Business Phone:** (404)827-1500.

### BONE, REV. WINSTON S.
Clergy, bishop. **Personal:** Born Apr 7, 1932, New Amsterdam; married Faye Alma O Bryan; children: Alma Lorraine Constable & Brian Winston. **Educ:** Inter Am Univ PR, BA, 1958; Waterloo Luth Sem, attended 1961. **Career:** Clergy (retired); Ebenezer Luth Church New Amsterdam Guyana, pastor, 1961-66; Luth Church Guyana, pres, 1966; Christ Luth Church Brooklyn, pastor, 1966-68; Incarnation Luth Church Queens, pastor, 1968-73; Metrop New York Synod Evangel Lutheran Church, asst bishop, 1973, bishop. **Orgs:** Chmn, Admin Coun Luth Church Guyana, 1965-66; bd trustee, Wagner Col Staten Island NY, 1969; chmn, S Queens Luth Parish, 1970-73; bd dir, Seamen & Int House NY, 1970-73; Mgt Com Div Prof Leadership, 1972-80; bd dir, Luth Theol Sem Gettysburg, 1977-. **Home Addr:** 8339

Pheasant Dr, Blaine, WA 98230, **Home Phone:** (360)371-6284. **Business Addr:** Bishop, Metropolitan New York Synod Evangelical Luth Church, 475 Riverside Dr Suite 1620, New York, NY 10115, **Business Phone:** (212)665-0732.

**BONES, RICARDO (RICKY BONES)**
Baseball player, athletic coach. **Personal:** Born Apr 7, 1969, Salinas. **Career:** Baseball player (retired), baseball coach; San Diego Padres, 1991; Milwaukee Brewers, 1992-96; NY Yankees, 1996; Kans City Royals, 1997-98; Cincinnati Reds, 1997; Baltimore Orioles, 1999; Fla Marlins, 2000-01; Los Angeles Dodgers, 2001; Buffalo Bisons, pitching coach; Binghamton Mets, pitching coach, 2009; New York Mets, bullpen coach, 2012-; Pr Nat Baseball Team, pitching coach, 2013. **Honors/Awds:** Am League All-Star Team, 1994. **Business Addr:** Coach, New York Mets, 75 Ninth Ave, New York, NY 10011, **Business Phone:** (512)434-1542.

**BONHAM, VENCE L.**
Lawyer, biotechnologist. **Educ:** Mich State Univ, James Madison Col, East Lansing, MI, BA, 1978, post grad studies, 1979; Ohio State Univ Col Law, Columbus, OH, JD, 1982. **Career:** US Dist Ct Southern Dist Ohio, Columbus, OH, stud judicial clerk, 1981-82; UAW Legal Serv Plan, Lansing, MI, staff atty, 1983-84; Eastern Mich Univ, Ypsilanti, MI, human resources assoc, 1984-85, univ atty, 1984-87; Mich State Univ, E Lansing, MI, asst gen coun, 1987-89, assoc gen coun, 1989-; project leader & co curator, NHGRI; Nat Human Genome Res Inst, Educ & Community Involvement Br, chief, currently, assoc investr, Social & Behav Res Br, currently, NHGRI Edu & Community Involvement Br, currently, sr advisor Dir Societal Implications Genomics Nat Inst Health, currently, Off Dir, NHGRI Dir Genomics & Health Disparities, sr advisor, currently; Nat Inst Health, Extramural Assocs Prog Adv Bd, chmn, 2004-07, mem, currently. **Orgs:** Bd mem, Nat Asn Col & Univ Attys; The Mich Minority Health Adv Comt, 1990-92; Mich State Bar; Nat Health Lawyers Asn; Am Soc Law & Med; Am Bar Asn; Mich Soc Hosp Lawyers; Phi Delta Kappa Fraternity; Detroit Area Hosp Couns Group; bd mem, Impressions 5 Mich Sci Mus; bd mem, Lansing Area Boys & Girls Club; fel Am Asn Med Cols Health Serv Res Fel Prog. **Special Achievements:** Author of: "Liability Issues Concerning Faculty and Staff: Academic Advising and Defamation in Context of Academic Evaluation," Am I Liable?: Faculty, Staff and Institutional Liability in the College and University Setting, 1989; "Health Law Update," Journal of the College of Human Medicine, 1990-. **Home Addr:** 544 Collingwood Dr, East Lansing, MI 48823, **Home Phone:** (517)351-3050. **Business Addr:** Chief, Associate Investigator, Senior Advisor, Director, National Human Genome Research Institute, Rm B1B55 Bldg 31, Bethesda, MD 20892-2070, **Business Phone:** (301)594-3973.

**BONILLA, BOBBY (ROBERTO MARTIN ANTONIO BONILLA)**
Baseball player, baseball executive. **Personal:** Born Feb 23, 1963, Bronx, NY; son of Roberto and Regina; married Migdalia; children: 2. **Career:** Baseball player (retired), baseball executive; Chicago White Sox, infielder, 1986; Pittsburgh Pirates, infielder & outfielder, 1986-91; New York Mets, 1992-95, 1999; Baltimore Orioles, 1995-96; Fla Marlins, 1997-98; Los Angeles Dodgers, 1998; Atlanta Braves, 2000; St Louis Cardinals, 2001; Maj League Baseball, union rep; Maj League Baseball Players Asn, spec asst exec dir, spec asst player serv, currently. **Special Achievements:** Film: Rookie of the Year, 1963. **Home Addr:** 2648 Bainbridge Ave, Bronx, NY 10458. **Business Addr:** Special Assistant Player Services, Major League Baseball Players Association, 12 E 49th St 24th Fl, New York, NY 10017, **Business Phone:** (212)826-0808.

**BONILLA, ROBERTO MARTIN ANTONIO.** **See BONILLA, BOBBY.**

**BONNER, ALICE A.**
Judge, lawyer. **Personal:** Born Apr 11, 1941, New Orleans, LA; married Al; children: Yvonne, Bernard & Lamont. **Educ:** Tex Southern Univ, BA, 1963, JD, 1966; Nat Col Judiciary; Am Acad Judiciary Educ. **Career:** Law Firm Bonner & Bonner, family law specialist, 1967-77; Munic Ct Houston, judge, 1974-77; Co Criminal Ct, Law 6, judge, 1977-78; 80th Civil Dist Ct, State Tex, judge, 1978-. **Orgs:** State Bd Specialization, 1975; State Dem Conv, 1974; mem bd govs, Nat Bar Asn, 1974-77; founder & actg pres, Black Women Lawyers Asn, 1975; bd mem, Judicial Coun Nat Bar Asn, 1975-76; bd mem, Houston Lawyers Asn, 1978; Comt Indigent, State Bar, TX, 1980; life mem, Nat Asn Negro Bus & Prof Women Inc; Phi Alpha Delta Legal Fraternity; Baptist Sister head, TX; City Wide Beauticians Houston; Nat Coun Negro Women; Blue Triangle Br, YWCA; Women Achievemnets; Eta Phi Beta Bus & Prof Sorority; Nat Asn Advan Colored People; coordr, Nat Coun Negro Women; Nat Med Asn; Nat Immunization Prog; Tex State Bar. **Home Addr:** 4111 Roseneath Dr, Houston, TX 77021, **Home Phone:** (713)748-0147. **Business Addr:** 80th Civil Dist Ct, Houston, TX 77002, **Business Phone:** (404)730-4166.

**BONNER, ALICE CAROL**
Journalist, foundation executive, educator. **Personal:** Born Dec 24, 1948, Dinwiddie, VA; daughter of James R and Doletha Edwards; married Leon Dash Jr; children: Destiny Kloi. **Educ:** Howard Univ, Washington, BA, jour, 1971; Columbia Univ, New York, NY, cert, 1972; Univ NC, PhD, sch jour mass commun, 1995; Harvard Univ, Cambridge, MA. **Career:** Wash Post, DC, reporter, ed, 1970-85; USA Today, Arlington, Va, ed, 1985-86; Gannett Co Inc, Arlington, Va, jour recruiter, 1986-89; Gannett Found, Arlington, Va, newsroom recruiter, dir educ progs, 1990-; Univ Southern Calif, lectr, 2000-01; Univ Md, Philip Merrill Col Jour, lectr, 2001-; Freedom Forum, dir, educ jour; Univ NC, Fel Freedom Forum. **Orgs:** Nieman fel, 1977-78; Nat Asn Black Jours, 1980-; bd mem, Community Hope, 1986-; Asn Educ Jour & Mass Commun, 1986-; summer prog dir, Inst Jour Educ, 1986; bd mem, Youth Commun, 1990-. **Special Achievements:** Author: First Black Female Network TV Reporter Debuted 40 Years Ago, 2012. Howard University's first journalism graduate. **Home Addr:** 3800 Powell Lane, Falls Church, VA 22041. **Business Addr:** Lecturer, University of Maryland, 1100 Knight Hall, College Park, MD 20742, **Business Phone:** (301)405-7106.

**BONNER, ANTHONY**
Broadcaster, basketball player, basketball coach. **Personal:** Born Jun 8, 1968, St. Louis, MO. **Educ:** St Louis Univ, 1990. **Career:** Basketball player (retired), basketball coach; Nat Basketball Asn, Sacramento Kings, 1990-93; Nat Basketball Asn, NY Knicks, 1993-95; Virtus Bologna, Italy, 1995-96; Nat Basketball Asn, Orlando Magic, 1996; FIBA Europe, Paok Thessaloniki Bc, Greece, 1996-97; Galatasaray, Turkey, 1997-98; Brujos de Guayama, Pr, 1998, 2000, 2006; TAU Ceramica, Spain, 1998-99; Breogan, Spain, 1999-2001; Unics Kazan, Russia, 2001-02; Nat Basketball Asn, Utah Jazz, 2002-03; Leones de Ponce, Pr, 2002, 2003, 2004-05; PAOK BC, Greece; CB Valladolid, Spain, 2002-03; Great Lakes Storm, 2003-04; Penarol, 2005-06; Capitanes de Arecibo, 2006; Maratonistas de Coamo, 2006; Virtus Bologna Italy; Vashon High Sch, St Louis, coach, currently. **Business Addr:** Coach, Vashon High School, 3035 Cass Ave, St. Louis, MO 63106, **Business Phone:** (314)533-9487.

**BONNER, HARRY J., SR.**
Administrator. **Career:** Albion Drop, asst dir, exec dir; Minority Prog Serv, sr exec dir, 1970-77; Albion Col, dir minority prog serv, youth advocate; Substance Abuse Prev Serv, exec dir; Albion & Adrian, educ coordr, 1984; Abuse Prev Agency, 1989. **Orgs:** Bd mem, founder, Minority Prog Servs; mem, Albion Drop; bd mem, Food Bank Coun Mich. **Business Addr:** Executive Director, Minority Program Services, Wyndham Woods Dr 300 B Dr N, Albion, MI 49224, **Business Phone:** (517)629-2113.

**BONNER, DR. MARY WINSTEAD**
Teacher, executive, educator. **Personal:** Born Apr 20, 1924, Nash County, NC; daughter of Charles Edward Winstead and Mason Ann Whitted; married Thomas E. **Educ:** St. Paul's Polytech Inst, BS, educ, 1946; St. Paul's Col, LhD, 1979; Va State Univ, MS, elem educ, 1952; NY Univ, attended 1967; Southern Univ, attended 1954; Okla State Univ, EdD, reading, minors social studies & engineering, 1968; Univ Calif, Berkeley, attended 1974; Instde Fililogia Satillo Mex, attended 1984. **Career:** Greensville Co, VA, instr, 1946-52; Southern Univ, instr, 1952-57; StLouis Pub Schs, instr, 1957-64; Kans State Teachers Col, educ fac, 1964, Dept Curric & Instr, fac, 1970-86; Emporia State Univ, Dept Ed, Butcher CSch, 1964-86, prof emer, 1986-; OK St Univ, grad asst, 1965-66; Univ SC, vis prof, 1968; Norfolk St Col, vis prof, 1971-73; Butcher Elem Sch, supv teacher. **Orgs:** Founder, Sigma Gamma Rho, 1969; Sigma Delta Pi, 1979; asst dir, Dist coord, 1989-90; Hosp Auxiliaries Kans; secy, Emporia Retired Teachers Asn, 1988-89; bd dir, Societas Docta; Lycon co Bd Corrections, 1990-91; Ed State Newsletter, 1991-92; Emporia Human Rels Comm, vol mentor, 2001; Am Asn Univ Women; Nat Coun Negro Women; Int Platform Asn; Panel Am Women; KS Childrens Serv League; Retired Teachers Asn; Lyon Co Planning; Emporia State Univ Fac Senate, Kans Stand Comm; fac senate, Kans Stand Comt; Nat Span Hon Soc. **Honors/Awds:** Certificate of Achievement in Spanish, Emporia State Univ, 1978; Outstanding Aluma, St Pauls Col, 1979, 1984; Unsung Heroine Award, Nat Asn Advan Coloured People, 1988; RuthSchillinger Faculty Award, 1998; Presidential Leadership in Diversity Award, Emporia State Univ, 2000; Hall of Fame, Okla State Univ's Col Educ, 2011; Hall of Fame Sigma Gamma Rho; ESU Presidential Award, Distinguished Serv Diversity. **Special Achievements:** Emporia State Univ second African American faculty. **Home Addr:** 2314 Sunset Lake Dr, Emporia, KS 66801-6636, **Home Phone:** (316)342-3621. **Business Addr:** Professor Emeritus, Emporia State University, 1200 Commercial St, Emporia, KS 66801, **Business Phone:** (620)341-1200.

**BONNER, DR. ROBERT**
Educator, dean (education). **Career:** Dean (retired); Hampton Univ, marine botanist, dean pure & appl sci, prof emer, 2002. **Orgs:** Chmn, Coop Hampton Roads Orgn Minorities Engineering, 1986; bd trustee, Sci Mus Va. **Business Addr:** Professor Emeritus, Hampton University, 100 E Queen St, Hampton, VA 23668, **Business Phone:** (757)727-5000.

**BONNETT, BERNICE CLARK**
Vice president (organization). **Educ:** Barnard Col, BA, sociol/piano performance; NY Univ-Leonard N Sch Bus, MBA, mkt. **Career:** Leo Burnett Advert, acct supvr, 1987-95; Young & Rubicam Advert, sr vpres & acct dir, 1995-2001; Saatchi & Saatchi Advert, sr vpres & group acct dir, 2001-03; Marshall Field's, vpres, mkt, 2003-06; Macy's N, vpres, mkt, 2003-08; Macy's Corp Mkt, sr vpres, merchandise mkt, 2008-09; Macy's, sr vpres, mkt, 2009-. **Orgs:** Barnard bus & prof women; NYU Stern AHBBS Alumni; bd mem, United Way NYC. **Business Addr:** Senior Vice President, Macy's Inc, 685 Market St, San Francisco, CA 94105, **Business Phone:** (800)289-6229.

**BONTEMPS, DR. JACQUELINE MARIE FONVIELLE**
Artist, educator, humanist. **Personal:** Born Savannah, GA; daughter of William Earl and Mattie Louise Davis; married Arna Alexander; children: Traci, Arna & Fanon. **Educ:** Fisk Univ, BA, 1964, MA, 1971; Ill State Univ, EdD, 1976. **Career:** Lane Col, chairperson, 1966-68; Jackson Parks & Recreation, supvr, 1968; S Side Community Ctr, dir, 1969; Fisk Univ, Dept Art, admin asst, 1971; Tenn State Univ, Dept Art, instr, 1972-73; Univ Tenn, Dept Art, instr, 1972-73, lectr, 1973; Ill State Univ, Col Fine Arts, asst to dir, 1975-76, admin asst, 1976-77, asst prof art, 1976-78, assoc prof art, 1978-84; Hampton Univ, dept chairperson, Div Arts Humanities, assoc prof, currently, Dept Fine & Performing Arts, fac, currently. **Orgs:** Trustee, Am Asn Mus; Am Asn Higher Educ; Am Coun Arts; Am Film Inst; Am Asn Univ Profs; Asn Teacher Educrs; comm mem, Int Coun Mus; Nat Coun Black Studies; Delta Sigma Theta; Phi Delta Kappa; nat arts res specialist, 1978-86, dir arts, 1982-84, nat secy, 1988-90, Links; Coun Arts Adminrs Va Higher Educ, 1984-89; Nat Blue Ribbon Panel mem, Inaugural Nat Blacks Art Festival, 1987-88; bd dir, Cult Alliance Greater Hampton Roads, 1987-91; Girl Scout Coun Colonial Coast, 2009. **Home Addr:** 323 Silver Isles Blvd Apt F, Hampton, VA 23664-1942, **Home Phone:** (757)723-7721. **Business Addr:** Associate Professor, Department of Fine and Performing Arts, Hampton University, Armstrong Hall Rm 144, Hampton, VA 23668-0101, **Business Phone:** (757)727-5402.

**BOOKER, ANNE M.**
Public relations executive, spokesperson, association executive. **Personal:** Born Spartanburg, SC; daughter of Claude C and Tallulah Jane Tanner. **Educ:** Morgan State Univ, Eng, 1971; Mich State Univ, BA, MA, 1986. **Career:** Ford Motor Co, electronic media specialist, 1977-78, pub affairs mgr, 1977-2005, corp news rep, 1978-82, publ ed, 1982-84, sr producer, 1984-86, pub affairs assoc, 1986-88, asst mgr, 1988, SE region pub affairs mgr, 1992-2005, Ford Southeast Communications, regional mgr. **Orgs:** Pub Rels Soc Am, 1978-; St Philip AME, Atlanta; Am Women Radio-TV; Press Club, 1978-; Women Commun, 1978-; Nat Black MBA Asn, 1983-; life mem, Nat Asn Advan Colored People. **Honors/Awds:** Achiever in Industry, YMCA Detroit; Aftra Golden Mike Award; Kappa Tau Alpha Grad Journalism Honor Soc. **Home Addr:** 1857 Fairpointe Trace, Stone Mountain, GA 30088-4025, **Home Phone:** (770)593-8597.

**BOOKER, CORLISS VONCILLE**
Educator. **Personal:** Born Jun 22, 1954, Stuttgart; daughter of Curtis and Vera Wrenn; children: Andrea Voncille & Gorman Lasure. **Educ:** John Tyler Community Col, AAS, 1982; Va Commonwealth Univ, BSN, 1989, MPH, 1998, PhD, 2005; Clin Pastoral Educ, cert, 2000. **Career:** Veteran's Admin, staff nurse, 1982-91; Va Commonwealth Univ, RN liaison, 1992-94, proj dir, asst prof; Educ Resource, owner. **Orgs:** Am Nurses Asn, 1982-; vice chair, State Bd Social Servs, 1994-; Nat Black Nurses Asn, 1994-; secy, bd mem, Young Women's Christian Asn, 1994-98; Oncol Nursing Soc, 1996-; vpres, Black Educ Asn, 1997-98; Med Col Va, Issues Sub-comt, 1997-99; admin coordr, 1998-2000; Outstanding Women Yr, Nominations comt, 2001; chair, Health Social Servs Coun, Cong Nat Black Churches; Susan G Komen Found, sci reviewer, 2001-04; Inst Rev Bd, VA Commonwealth Univ, 2001-02. **Home Addr:** 3620 Mineola Dr, Chester, VA 23831, **Home Phone:** (804)796-1907. **Business Addr:** Assistant Professor, Virginia Commonwealth University, 1200 E Broad St, Richmond, VA 23298, **Business Phone:** (804)828-0540.

**BOOKER, CORY ANTHONY**
Lawyer. **Personal:** Born Apr 27, 1969, Washington, DC; son of Cary Alfred and Carolyn Rose. **Educ:** Stanford Univ, BA, polit sci, 1991, MA, sociol, 1992; Oxford Univ, Rhodes Scholar, BA, US hist, 1994; Yale Law Sch, JD, 1997. **Career:** Urban Justice Ctr, New York, tenants' rights atty, 1997-98; Newark Youth Proj, prog coordr, 1998; Newark (NJ) City Coun, mem, 1998-2002; Pvt Pract, atty, 2002-06; Newark (NJ) mayor, 2006-13; US Senate (NJ), 2013-. **Orgs:** Mayors Against Illegal Guns Coalition; bd advisor, Dem Educ Reform; bd trustee, Teachers Col, Columbia Univ; former exec comt mem, Yale Law Sch; former bd trustee, Stanford Univ; sr fel Rutger's Sch Pub Policy & Planning; founding mem, Eliezer Soc; Nat Black Law Students Asn. **Honors/Awds:** Brady Center to Prevent Gun Violence, Honoree, 2009; Honorary Doctorate, Brandeis Univ, 2009; World Mayor Prize, Finalist, 2010, Candidate, 2012; DHL, Yeshiva Univ, 2010; U.S. Senator John Heinz Award for Greatest Public Service by an Elected or Appointed Official, Recipient, 2010; LLD, Williams Col, 2011; LLD, Bard Col, 2012; "Town & Country," Top 40 Bachelors, 2013; LLD, Washington Univ, 2013; Newark Now, Director. **Special Achievements:** First African American U.S. Senator from New Jersey; unsuccessful mayoral campaign featured in the 2002 documentary "Street Fight" by Marshall Curry; featured in documentary "Brick City". **Business Addr:** Senator, US Senate, Hart 141 359 Dirksen Senate Off Bldg, Washington, DC 20510, **Business Phone:** (202)224-3224.

**BOOKER, JACKIE R.**
College teacher. **Personal:** married Kathy; children: 2. **Educ:** Univ Calif, Irvine, PhD. **Career:** Claflin Univ, Dept Phil & Relig, chmn & assoc prof, currently. **Business Addr:** Chairman, Associate Professor Philosophy & Religion, Claflin University, 400 Magnolia St, Orangeburg, SC 29115, **Business Phone:** (803)535-5000.

**BOOKER, JOHN P., III**
Manager, controller, executive. **Personal:** Born Dec 28, 1947, Augusta, GA. **Educ:** Paine Col, hist maj, 1969; NC Cent Univ Law Sch, LLB, 1974; Univ RI, cert mgt, 1980. **Career:** Atty John D Watkins, legal asst, 1974-75; Augusta Human Rel Commun, EEOC investr & field rep, 1975-76; Ctr Savannah & River Area EOA Inc, equal opport ofc, 1976-77; Speidel Div Textron, employ mgr & urban affairs coordr, 1977-80; Amperex Electronic Corp N Amer Philips Co, asst personal mgr, 1980-; Old Dom Freight Line Inc, vpres & controller & chief acct officer, currently. **Orgs:** Woonsocket C C, 1980; Nat Asn Advan Colored People, 1980; co rep, local minority & civil org, 1980. **Home Addr:** 50 Garden Dr, East Providence, RI 02914, **Home Phone:** (401)438-3276. **Business Addr:** Vice President & Chief Accounting Officer, Controller, Old Dominion Freight Line Inc, 500 Old Dom Way, Thomasville, NC 27360, **Business Phone:** (336)889-5000.

**BOOKER, JOHNNIE B.**
Executive. **Personal:** children: S Courtney III. **Educ:** Hampton Univ, BS, social sci & social; Atlanta Univ, Sch Social Work, MSW, community orgn. **Career:** US Dept Housing & Urban Develop, dep asst secy, 1989-91; Resolution Trust Corp, vpres, 1991-95; Coca-Cola Co, global dir supplier diversity, 2001-11; Johnnie Booker Group, pres, chief exec officer, 2012-. **Orgs:** Nat Minority Supplier Develop Coun; US Pan-Asian Chamber Com; Bronx Community Col Found; Ashley Stewart Found; Nat Adv Bd Whitney M Young Jr Sch Social Work, Clark Atlanta Univ; Supplier Diversity Coun Conf Bd; Delta Sigma Theta Sorority; Links Inc, Dogwood City Chap; Circle-Lets; Nat Black Child Develop Inst; Nat Asn Advan Coloured People; Urban League, Big Bethel AME Church; dir, Fed Deposit Ins Corp, Off Equal Opportunity; vpres, Resolution Trust Corp; bd mem, Nat Minority Supplier Develop Coun; bd mem, Women Bus Enterprise Nat Coun; bd mem, GA Women Bus Coun. **Business Addr:** President, Chief Executive Officer, Johnnie Booker Group Inc, 1735 Peachtree St NE Suite 605, Atlanta, GA 30309.

**BOOKER, JOHNNIE BROOKS**
Government official, executive director. **Personal:** Born Jul 31, 1941, Forsyth, GA; daughter of Willie F (deceased) and Lillian B Graves; children: Sylvester Courtney III. **Educ:** Hampton Inst, BS, social sci, 1961; Atlanta Univ Sch Social Work, MSW, 1969. **Career:** Los Angeles Comn Redevelop Agency, 1969-73; Western Regional Off Nat Urban League, asst regional dir, 1974-76; Nat Urban League-Wash Opers, asst dir, 1977-78; Fed Home Loan Bank Bd, dir consumer affairs, 1978-89; Dept Housing & Urban Develop, dep asst sec, 1989-91; Resolution Trust Corp, vpres, 1991; Fed Deposit Ins Corp, Dir Off Equal Opportunity; consult; Coca-Cola Co, Dir Supplier Diversity, 2001-11; Johnnie Booker Group, pres, chief exec officer, 2012. **Orgs:** Am Soc Pub Admin; Women Housing & Finance; Women Wash; Wash Urban League; Nat Asn Advan Colored People; Delta Sigma Theta Sorority; Links, Inc, Capital City Chap, chair, mem comt; Nat Black Child Devlop Inst; Metrop AME Church. **Honors/Awds:** Bd Resolution, Dryades Savings Bank, 1994; City Kansas City, Mo Proclamation, 1994; Minority Asset Recovery Contractors Asn, 1994; Nat Bankers Asn, 1994; Nat Asn Black Accts, 1993; Dollar & Sense Mag, 1990; Outstanding Alumnus-at-Large Award, 2009. **Special Achievements:** Created unprecedented RTC contracting & investor opportunities for minorities and women; Author and publisher of an informational booklet entitled, Fair Housing: It's Your Right; Developed a system to detect discrimination in lending patterns and practices of regulated savings & loan asns. **Home Addr:** 1703 Leighton Wood Lane, Silver Spring, MD 20910, **Home Phone:** (301)565-5115. **Business Addr:** Director of Supplier Diversity, Coca-Cola Co, 800 Conn Ave NW, Washington, DC 20006-2735, **Business Phone:** (866)265-3638.

**BOOKER, KAREN**
Basketball player. **Personal:** Born Apr 10, 1965, Franklin, TN. **Educ:** Vanderbilt Univ, BS, econs, 1987. **Career:** Vanderbilt Univ, vol asst coach, 1986-87, asst coach, 1991-92; Univ Ky, asst head coach, 1988-91, assoc head coach, 1994-95; Univ Nev, asst coach, 1993-94; Cal Poly, head coach, 1995-97; Colo State Univ, asst coach, 1997-98; Utah Starzz, ctr, 1997; Action Fall tour, head coach Athletes, 1998; Sewanee, asst coach, 2000-01; Sewanee, head coach, 2001-03; WNBA Detroit Shock, vol asst coach, 2002; Colo Chill, asst coach, 2005; Gaylord Entertainment, fitness consult. **Home Addr:** 2960 Harber Lights Dr, Nashville, TN 37217-3446, **Home Phone:** (615)399-9117. **Business Addr:** Assistant Coach, Colorado Chill, Triple Crown Sports, Fort Collins, CO 80525, **Business Phone:** (970)223-6644.

**BOOKER, LORETTA L.** **See HUFF, LORETTA LOVE.**

**BOOKER, MARILYN F.**
Executive. **Personal:** Born Chicago, IL; married Walter; children: Walter Jr, Morgan & Maxwell. **Educ:** Spelman Col, BA; IIT/Chicago Kent Sch Law, JD. **Career:** Morgan Stanley Pride Networking Group, Human Resources/Diversity, global head diversity currently, managing dir, 2004; Wharton Whitney M. Young Conf, speaker, 2012. **Orgs:** Bd dir, Michael J Found, 2001-05; Morgan Stanley benefit plan admin comt; bd mem, Arthur Ashe Inst Health; trustee, Morgan Stanley Found; Morgan Stanley Residential Franchise Risk Comt; New York Urban League; Exec Leadership Coun. **Business Addr:** Managing Director, Global Head of Diversity Human Resources/Diversity, Morgan Stanley Pride Networking Group, 750 7th Ave, New York, NY 10019, **Business Phone:** (212)762-3412.

**BOOKER, MARILYN F.**
Executive, association executive, founder (originator). **Personal:** Born Chicago, IL; married Walter; children: Walter Jr, Morgan & Maxwell. **Educ:** Spelman Col, BA; Ill Inst Technol, Chicago-Kent Col Law, JD. **Career:** Morgan Stanley Smith Barney, global head diversity, 1989-2004, managing dir, 2004-, head urban markets group, currently. **Orgs:** Trustee, Morgan Stanley Found; Morgan Stanley Benefit Plan Admin Comt; Morgan Stanley Residential Franchise Risk Comt; bd mem, Arthur Ashe Inst Health; bd mem, Michael J. Berkeley Found; vice chmn, New York Urban League Bd. **Honors/Awds:** The Audrey P. Berkeley Spirit Award, Michael J. Berkeley Found, 2006. **Special Achievements:** 25 Influential Women in Business, Network J, 2003; Woman of the Year, Harvard Col, 2009; Top 100 Most Influential Blacks in Corporate America, Savoy, 2011-12; 100 Top Executives in America, Uptown Prof, 2011; Top 100 Most Influential Women in Corporate America, Savoy, 2012. **Business Addr:** Managing Director, Head, Morgan Stanley's Smith Braney LLC, Park Ave Plz 55 E 52nd St 29th Fl, New York, NY 10055, **Business Phone:** (212)893-7518.

**BOOKER, MICHAEL**
Football player, newspaper editor. **Personal:** Born Apr 27, 1975, Cincinnati, OH. **Educ:** Univ Nebr. **Career:** Football player (retired); Atlanta Falcons, defensive back, 1997-99; Tenn Titans, corner back, 2000-01; Daily Star Sunday, staff, 2002-07, dep ed, 2007-. **Business Addr:** Deputy Editor, Daily Star, Northern & Shell Bldg 10 Lower Thames St, LondonEC3R 6EN, **Business Phone:** (087)1520-742.

**BOOKER, ROBERT JOSEPH**
Educator, manager, executive director. **Personal:** Born Apr 14, 1935, Knoxville, TN; son of Willie Edward (deceased) and Lillian Allen (deceased). **Educ:** Knoxville Col, BS, 1962. **Career:** Tenn Pub Sch, Chattanooga, teacher 1962-64; Tenn, elected mem legis, 1966-72; Mayor Knoxville, TN, admin asst, 1972-74, city coun mem, exec dir; Stroh Brewery Co, Detroit, MI, mkt develop mgr, 1974-77; Beck Cult Exchange Ctr, freelance writer, exec dir, 1978-84; City Knoxville, personnel dir, 1984-88; Knoxville Jourl, weekly columnist, 1987-92; Knoxville Col, historian, alumni pres, archivist, 1998-, stud body pres, stud govt pres, pub rels dir; Howard High Sch, fr teacher; Ctr Neighborhood Develop, community organizer, interim exec dir, currently. Author: Two Hundred Years of Black Culture in Knoxville, Tennessee, 1791-1991; There Was Light!The 120 Year History of Knoxville College 1875-1995; The Heat of a Red Summer. **Orgs:** Phi Beta Sigma Frat; Nat Asn Advan Colored People; Veterans Foreign Wars; Am Legion; Martin Luther King Commemoration Comn; Knoxville Col Historian; Tabernacle Baptist Church. **Home Addr:** 2621 Parkview Ave, Knoxville, TN 37914, **Home Phone:** (865)546-1576. **Business Addr:** College Historian, Alumni President, Knoxville College, 901 Knoxville College Dr, Knoxville, TN 37921, **Business Phone:** (865)524-6525.

**BOOKER, REV. VAUGHAN P. L.**
Clergy. **Personal:** Born Sep 17, 1942, Philadelphia, PA; son of Lorenzo S and Mary E; married Portia A McClellan; children: Kimberly Nichole & Manuel B McClellan. **Educ:** Villanova Univ, BA, 1978; Va Theol Sem, MDiv, 1992. **Career:** Clergy (retired); Xerox Corp, acct exec, 1981-87; Sprint Communs, major acct rep, 1987-89; Meade Memorial Episcopal Church, rector. **Orgs:** Protestant Correctional Chaplain's Asn, 1975-80; bd mem, Offender Aid & Restoration, 1980-87; bd mem, Va CURE; adv bd, George Wash Nat Bank; Omega Psi Phi. **Honors/Awds:** Alpha Sigma Lambda, 1977; Xerox Corp, Pres's Club, 1981. **Special Achievements:** Books written: From Prison to Pulpit: My Road to Redemption, 1994. **Home Addr:** 7112 Lake Cove Dr, Alexandria, VA 22315-4221, **Home Phone:** (703)971-5332.

**BOOKER, VAUGHN JAMEL**
Football player. **Personal:** Born Feb 24, 1968, Cincinnati, OH; married Sheila; children: Vaughn Jr, Breana & DeVaughn. **Educ:** Univ Cincinnati, grad. **Career:** Football player (retired); Kans City Chiefs, defensive end, 1994, left defensive end, 1995, 1997, right defensive end, 1996; Green Bay Packers, defensive end, 1998-99; Cincinnati Bengals, defensive end, 2000-02.

**BOON, INA M.**
Association executive. **Personal:** Born Jan 6, 1927, St. Louis, MO; daughter of Clarence and Lovie. **Educ:** Oakwood Acad Huntsville, AL; Nat Bus Inst; Tucker's Bus Col; Wash Univ; Western Ill Univ. **Career:** Nat Asn Advan Colored People, St Louis br, pres, admin secy, 1962-68, life mem field dir, 1968-73, dir, Region IV, 1973; AUS Transp Corp; AUS Dept Labor. **Orgs:** Chmn, bd mem emer & bd dir, St Louis Comprehensive Health Ctr, 1983-87; organizer, cardinal chap, Top Ladies Distinction, 1987; St Louis Chap Nat Coun Negro Women; Nat Prof Women's Clu; MO Univ Adv Coun; bd mem, St Louis Minority Econ Develop Agency; secy, St Louis Ment Health Asn; second vpres, Top Ladies Distinction Inc; vpres, St Louis Chap; vpres, Nat Financial Secy; bd mem, St. Louis Black Leadership Round table, Voter Awareness Comt, chairperson; Organizer, Nat Serv Orgn. **Honors/Awds:** Woman Achievers Social Welfare, 1970; Outstanding Leadership & Admin Abilities, 1973; Human Dev Corp, 1976; Distinguished Service Award, Union Memorial United Methodist Church, 1977; Director of the Year Award, Women Action Crusaders & Nat Resource Ctr, 1990; Distinguished Service Award, Top Ladies Distinction Inc; St Louis Argus Newspaper Cancer Soc, St Louis Black Firefighters Inst Racial Equality; Sigma Gamma Rho Sor; Kansas City KS Br NAACP; Kansas City MO Br NAACP & St Louis Globe Dem; Humanitarian Award. **Home Addr:** 7335 Melrose Ave, St Louis, MO 63130, **Home Phone:** (314)725-3688. **Business Addr:** Chairperson, Board Member, St Louis Black Leadership Roundtable, 415 DeBaliviere, Saint Louis, MO 63112, **Business Phone:** (314)367-8822.

**BOONE, ALEXANDRIA JOHNSON**
Executive. **Personal:** Born May 15, 1947, Cleveland, OH; daughter of Alex Sr and Aria; children: Aria. **Educ:** Case Western Res Univ, Weatherhead Sch Mgt, MS, develop orgn develop & anal, 1981; Dartmouth Col, Amos Tuck Sch Bus Admin, Advan Minority Bus Mgt Prog, cert, 1991. **Career:** Cleveland-based PR firm, sr vpres; Fed govt, pub info officer; Marcus Garvey Acad Mid Sch, founder; GAP Commun Group Inc, owner, pres & chief exec officer, 1994-; Women Color Found, chmn & founder, 2003-; U S Black Chambers Inc, commun & spec event consult, 2012-13. **Orgs:** Nat fel Boston Univ's Sch Pub Health, 1997; Leadership Cleveland, 1988; pres, Black Profs Charitable Found; Nat Black MBA Asn, 2005-13. **Business Addr:** President, Chief Executive Officer, Gap Communications Group Inc, 1667 E 40th st, Cleveland, OH 44103, **Business Phone:** (216)391-4300.

**BOONE, DR. CAROL MARIE**
Executive director, health services administrator. **Personal:** Born Nov 22, 1945, Pensacola, FL; daughter of Benjamin J Butler and Clarice Thompson; married Robert L; children: Carlotta L & Robert L Jr. **Educ:** Fisk Univ, BA, 1966; Univ Chicago, MA, 1968; Vanderbilt Univ, EdD, 1982. **Career:** Ill C's Home & Aid Soc, adoption counr, 1968-69; Dede Wallace Ment Health Ctr, br dir, 1970-80; Tenn State, Dept Ment Health, State Employee Assistance Prog, dir, 1982-. **Orgs:** Alpha Kappa Alpha Sorority, 1965-; Nat Asn Social Workers, Nashville, 1969-; treas, Links Inc, Hendersonville Chap, 1976-; fin secy, Jack & Jill Am, Nashville Chap, 1982-; Nat Asn Employee Assistance Prof, 1982-; bd dir, First Baptist Church, Capitol Hill Homes Inc. **Home Addr:** 320 Chicksaw Trl, Goodlettsville, TN 37072-3302, **Home Phone:** (615)851-1527. **Business Addr:** Director Employee Assistance Program, Tennessee State Government, 312 8th Ave N Suite 1300, Nashville, TN 37243, **Business Phone:** (615)741-1925.

**BOONE, CLARENCE DONALD**
School administrator. **Personal:** Born Nov 23, 1939, Jackson, TN; married Louise May; children: Terrance A Beard & Torrance. **Educ:** Lane Col, BS, 1961; Memphis State Univ, MEd, 1977. **Career:** United Teaching, prof, 1961; West High Sch, prin, 2000. **Orgs:** Treas, Nat Asn Advan Colored People, 1957; Alpha Phi Alpha, 1959; Ambulance Authority, 1973, City Comn, 1977; YMCA, 1980; bd dir, Headstart, 1980-83; bd dir, United Way, 1980; JEA; bd dir, Lane Col Nat Youth Sports; United Teaching. **Home Addr:** 26 Brooks Dr, Jackson, TN 38301-4607, **Home Phone:** (731)424-3743.

**BOONE, CLARENCE WAYNE, SR.**
Executive, physician. **Personal:** Born Aug 27, 1931, Bryan, TX; son of Elmo and Mae Frances Martin Marion; married Blanche Ollie Lane; children: Terrie, Clarence W Jr & Brian K. **Educ:** Ind Univ Sch Med, BA, anat & physiology, 1953, MD, 1956. **Career:** Physician (retired), executive; Homer G Phillips Hosp, resident, 1957-61, intern, 1956-57; Pvt pract, 1964-2000; Planned Parenthood Asn, med dir; Gary Med Specialists Inc, pres, 1969; pvt pract physician, 1999. **Orgs:** Kappa Alpha Psi, 1950-; life fel Am Cong Obstetricians & Gynecologists, 1964-; Am Ferility Soc Dipl, Am Bd Obstet/gynec, 1964; Nat Med Asn, 1967-; pres, Gary Med Specl Inc, 1968-; Great Lakes Reg Med Adv Com Planned Parenthood Asn World Pop, 1974-; staff phys, Meth Hosp Gary; St Mary Med Ctr; Homer G Phillips Alumni Asn; Asn Planned Parenthood Physician; bd mem, Ind Univ Neal-Marshall Comt, 1980-; rep, Exec Coun, 1983-; Asn Am Gynec Laparoscopists; life dir, trustee, Ind Univ Found, 1990-; Ind Univ Alumni Asn; Afr Am Doc Proj; life mem, Ind Univ Neal-Marshall Alumni Club, co-founder & pres; Northwest Chancellor Soc. **Honors/Awds:** Alan Guttenmacher Distinguished Service Award, 1979; Dudley Turner Physician of the Year Award, 1990; Chancellor's Medallion, In Univ Northwest, 1998; Gary Steel City Hall of Fame, 2000; Distinguished Alumni Service Award, 2003; Alan Guttenmacher Distinguished Service Award, 2004; President Award, Ind Univ Alumni Asn, 2009. **Special Achievements:** First African American male and female graduates of IU. **Home Addr:** 2386 W 20th Ave, Gary, IN 46404-3013, **Home Phone:** (219)977-9799. **Business Addr:** Trustee, Indiana University Board of Trustees, 900 E 7th St, Bloomington, IN 47405-7000, **Business Phone:** (812)855-3762.

**BOONE, DR. ELWOOD BERNARD, JR.**
Physician. **Personal:** Born May 7, 1943, Petersburg, VA; son of Elwood B Sr; married Carol Fraser; children: Elwood III & Melanie. **Educ:** Phillips Acad, attended 1961; Colgate Univ, AB, 1965; Meharry Med Col, MD 1969. **Career:** Med Col Va, intern, 1969-70, surg resident, 1970-72, urol resident, 1972-75, clin instr, 1975-; Richmond Memorial Hosp, staff physician, 1975; Urol Specialists Va, physician, currently. **Orgs:** Omega Psi Phi, 1967; Richmond Med Soc; Old Dom Med Soc; Nat Med Soc; Richmond Urol Soc; Richmond Acad Med; Med Soc Va; Nat pres Stud Nat Med Asn, 1968-69; fel Surg Am Cancer Soc, 1973-74; Va Urol Soc; Am Bd Urol, 1977; fel Am Col Surgeons, 1979; pres, Old Dom Med Soc, 1981-82; Guardsmen, 1983-; chief surg Richmond Memorial Hosp, 1985-86; Paradigm Communs, 1991-; Am Asn Clin Urologists; Alpha Beta Boule, Sigma Phi, 1992-; Hosp Corp Am, 2008-. **Honors/Awds:** Certified American Board of Urology, 1977. **Home Addr:** 2143 Staples Mill Rd, Richmond, VA 23230, **Home Phone:** (804)355-6847. **Business Addr:** Physician, Urological Specialists of Virginia, 110 N Robinson St Suite 403, Richmond, VA 23220, **Business Phone:** (804)354-6202.

**BOONE, ELWOOD BERNARD, III**
Chief executive officer. **Educ:** Morehouse Col, Atlanta, BS, psychol, 1992; Univ Mich, Ann Arbor, MS, health servs admin, 1995; Am Col Healthcare Execs, dipl. **Career:** Chippenham/Johnston-Willis Med Ctr, chief operating officer; United Way Greater Richmond & Petersburg, Hosp Corp Am John Randolph Med Ctr, chief exec officer, currently; Metrop Methodist Hosp, chief exec officer; Parkland Med Ctr, chief exec officer; Sentara Va Beach Gen Hosp, adminr, pres, currently. **Orgs:** Fel Am Col Healthcare Execs; Nat Asn Health Serv Execs; Rotary Club San Antonio; Fedn Am Hosps Hosp Leadership Comt; Cent Bus Dist Asn; United Way Greater Richmond & Petersburg. **Business Addr:** Board Trustee, John Randolph Medical Center, 411 W Randolph Rd, Hopewell, VA 23860, **Business Phone:** (804)541-1600.

**BOONE, EUNETTA T.**
Writer, television producer, editor. **Personal:** Born Jan 1, 1955?. **Educ:** Univ Md College Park, BS, jour prog, 1982; Columbia Univ, Grad Sch Jour, MS, jour prog, 1984. **Career:** TV series: "Living Single", co-producer, 1995-96; "Lush Life", producer, 1996 "The Parent Hood", supv producer, 1997-98; "Hip-Hop 101", creator & exec producer; "The Hughleys ", 1998-2000; "One On One", creator & exec producer, 2001-06; "My Wife & Kids", co-exec producer & writer, 2001-02; "Cuts", exec producer & writer, 2006; Daddy's Girl Productions, writer & producer, currently; Paramount Network TV, exec producer. **Business Addr:** Writer, Producer, Daddy's Girl Productions, 2120 Colorado Ave Suite 200, Santa Monica, CA 90404.

**BOONE, FREDERICK OLIVER, JR.**
Pilot. **Personal:** Born Jan 21, 1941, Baltimore, MD; married Penny B Etienne; children: Vanessa, Frederick III, Kimberly, Sean & Shannon. **Educ:** Morgan State Col, BS, 1961. **Career:** Delta Airlines, flight engr, 1969-70, first officer, 1970-79, capt, delta's DC-9 fleet, 1980-86, capt, flight instr, evaluator, B727, 1986-91, chief instr, pilot, 1992. **Orgs:** Airline Pilots Asn; secy org, Black Airline Pilots, 1976-; Southern Christian Leadership Conf, 1977. **Honors/Awds:** Achievement Award, Wall St Jour. **Home Addr:** 100 Cherokee Rose Lane, Fairburn, GA 30213.

**BOONE, MELANIE LYNN**
Dentist. **Personal:** Born Oct 21, 1973, Richmond, VA; daughter of Elwood B and Carol Ann Jr. **Educ:** Univ Va, BA, 1995; Howard Univ Dent, DDS, 1999. **Career:** Dr Jull Bussey Inc, dentist, 2002-; Belvidere Med Ctr, dentist; pvt pract, 2005-. **Orgs:** Am Dent Asn, 2000-01; Nat Dent Asn, 2001-02; Peter B Ramsey Dent Soc, 2002-; Old Dom Dent Soc, 2003-; Va Dent Asn; Richmond Dent Asn. **Home Addr:** 8008 Cobblewood Terr, Richmond, VA 23227, **Home Phone:** (804)264-2654. **Business Addr:** Dentist, Melanie L Boone DDS PC, Brook Run Shopping Ctr 5734 Brook Rd, Richmond, VA 23220, **Business Phone:** (804)264-0224.

**BOONE, MICHELLE T.**
City commissioner. **Educ:** Indiana Univ, Bloomington, BA, telecommunications, 1983, MPA, nonprofit mgt, 1998. **Career:** WMAQ-TV, WLS-TV and WBBM-TV, television engineer; freelance television engineer, 1983; Capitol Records, CEMA Distribution and Orpheus Records, employee; Virgin Records, Midwest Regional Promotions Manager, 1990-92; Peace Corps, Chad, Africa, volunteer, 1994-96; WBBM-TV, television engineer for media room, 1987-2000; Gallery 37, Chicago Department of Cultural Affairs, director, 1998-2003; DePaul University, adjunct professor, 2007-11; The Joyce Foundation, senior program officer-culture, 2004-11; Chicago Department of Cultural Affairs and Special Events, commissioner, 2011-. **Special Achievements:** Wrote Chicago Cultural Plan, 2012; reviewer for the National Endowment for the Arts, the Illinois Arts Council, the Ramuson Foundation, and the Cuyahoga Arts and Culture program.

**Business Addr:** Chicago Department of Cultural Affairs and Special Events, 78 E Washington St, Chicago, IL 60602.

### BOONE, DR. ROBERT L.
Executive, educator. **Educ:** Tenn State Univ, BS, 1970, MA Ed, 1974; George Peabody Col, PhD, 1983. **Career:** Tenn State Univ, Dept Educ Admin, prof & assoc vpres acad affairs, currently. **Business Addr:** Professor, Associate Vice President of Academic Affairs, Tennessee State University, 3500 John A Merritt Blvd, Nashville, TN 37209, **Business Phone:** (615)963-5000.

### BOONE, RONALD BRUCE
Television broadcaster, basketball player. **Personal:** Born Sep 6, 1946, Oklahoma City, OK. **Educ:** Iowa Western Community Col, attended 1965; Idaho State Univ, attended 1968. **Career:** Basketball player (retired), broadcaster; Dallas/Tex Chaparrals, 1968-70; Utah Stars, 1970-75; Spirits St Louis, 1975-76; Kans City Kings, 1976-78; Los Angeles Lakers, 1978-80; Utah Jazz, radio & tv analyst, 1979-81, color commentator, currently. **Orgs:** Nat Basketball Retried Players Asn. **Home Addr:** 3877 Pheasant Ridge Rd, Salt Lake City, UT 84109. **Business Addr:** Color Commentator, Utah Jazz, 301 W S Temple, Salt Lake City, UT 84101, **Business Phone:** (801)325-2500.

### BOONE, DR. ZOLA ERNEST
School administrator. **Personal:** Born Oct 16, 1937, Wisner, LA; daughter of Zola Amond Ernest and Jesse Ernest Jr; married Arthur I; children: Monica, Denise & Ivan. **Educ:** Mt St Mary's, BA, 1957; Mich State Univ, MS, 1970, PhD, 1972; Inst Educ Mgt Harvard Univ, cert, 1975. **Career:** Baltimore Pub Sch, teacher & dept chmn, 1962-69; Mich State Univ, 1970-71, Ford fel, 1971-72; Coppin State Col, hons prog adv, 1972-73, prof & dept chairperson, 1973-75, spec asst vpres, 1975-76; Morgan St Univ, dir ctrcurric improv, 1976-79; Links Inc, pres, 1977-78; Am Coun Educ, fel, 1978-79; Morgan State Univ, SDIP Coord, spec asst pres, 1979-80; US Dept Educ, Inst Educ Leadership, Wash, DC, policy fel, 1981-82; consult, 1982-84; Bowie State Found, Bowie, Md, exec dir, 1984-; Bowie State Univ, Bowie, Md, vpres planning & develop, 1984-88, vpres develop & univ rel, 1988-96, Inst Diversity & Multicultural Affairs, vpres univ rels & planning & develop, 1996-; consult curric develop. **Orgs:** Asn Supv & Curric Develop, 1972-77; Am Asn Higher Educ, 1976-77, 1984-; Soc Col & Univ Planners, 1984-; ACE NID Planning Coun, 1984-; Md Asn Higher Educ, 1984-; Coun Advan & Support Educ, 1984-; Mid-Atlantic Regional Coun, 1989-; Phi Kappa Phi; Delta Sigma Theta; Howard Co Dem Coalition; Prince Georges Coalition 100 Black Women; Nat Polit Cong Black Women; Prince Georges County, Delta Sigma Theta Sorority; comnr, Md Nat Capital Pk & Planning Comn & Prince George's County Planning Bd. **Honors/Awds:** Outstanding Service Award, Adult Educ Coppin State Col, 1975; Legacy of Excellence Award, BSU Found, 1993; Case Comn Phil, 1996-97. **Home Addr:** 11124 Wood Elves Way, Columbia, MD 21044, **Home Phone:** (410)964-8382. **Business Addr:** Vice President for University Relations, Planning & Development, Bowie State University, 14000 Jericho Pk Rd, Bowie, MD 20715-9465, **Business Phone:** (301)860-4000.

### BOONIEH, OBI ANTHONY
Executive. **Personal:** Born Jun 27, 1957, Onitsha; married Neka Carmenta White; children: Amechi. **Educ:** Morgan State Univ, BA, 1983; Northeastern Univ Sch Law, JD, 1986. **Career:** Mangrover & Co Ltd, dir, 1979-; African Relief Fund, pres, 1982-84, dir, 1984-85; Cult Port Inc, consult & dir, 1986; Int Pollution Control Corp, dir, 1986-; First Writers Bur Inc, managing ed, 1986-. **Orgs:** Big Bros & Sisters Cent MD, 1980-83;Nat Asn Advan Colored People; Phi Alpha Delta. **Home Addr:** PO Box 13191, Baltimore, MD 21203-3191, **Home Phone:** (410)889-2958. **Business Addr:** Managing Editor, First Writers Bureau Inc, 819 E Fayette St, Baltimore, MD 21202, **Business Phone:** (410)625-2745.

### BOOSE, DORIAN ALEXANDER
Football player. **Personal:** Born Jan 29, 1974, Frankfurt. **Educ:** Walla Walla Comm Col; Wash State Univ. **Career:** Football player (retired); New York Jets, defensive tackle, 1998-2000; Wash Redskins, defensive end, 2001; Houston Texans, defensive end, 2002; Edmonton Eskimos, Can Football League, 2003-04. **Orgs:** Bd mem, Int Global Outreach. **Honors/Awds:** Strength & Conditioning Award; Grey Cup Champion, 2003.

### BOOTH, ANNA MARIE
Real estate executive, educator. **Personal:** children: 2. **Educ:** NY Univ, BA, psychol; Emory Law Sch, JD; Dc Bar, cert, bar admis, 1976; Calif Dept Educ, cert, teaching credential, 2007; Calif Dept Real Estate, cert, real estate broker, 2009; Nat Bd Prof Teaching Stand, cert, 2014. **Career:** US Sen Bill Bradley, legis aide, 1979-83; Atty; corp lobbyist; AT&T Inc, govt rels mgr, 1983-97; Nat Conf Community & Justice, exec dir, 1999-2003; San Francisco Arts Comn, comnr; Golden Gate Nat Recreation Adv Comn, comnr; San Francisco Unified Sch Dist, vpres, 2002-03, substitute teacher, 2007-; real estate broker, currently; Keynote Properties, Real Estate, agt, 2003-06; Booth Group, prin, 1983-2015, pres & chief exec officier. **Orgs:** Founder & vpres, Parent Teacher Stud Asn; Grace Cathedral, 1983-; founding gov, City Club San Francisco; United Educr San Francisco, 2007-; San Francisco Alliance Black Sch Educr, 2007-. **Home Addr:** 1801 Fillmore St, PO Box 475158, San Francisco, CA 94115-3125. **Business Addr:** Substitute Teacher, San Francisco Unified School District, 555 Franklin St, San Francisco, CA 94102, **Business Phone:** (415)241-6000.

### BOOTH, REV. DR. CHARLES E.
Clergy, community college teacher, educator. **Personal:** Born Feb 4, 1947, Baltimore, MD; son of William and Hazel (deceased). **Educ:** Howard Univ, BA, 1969; Eastern Bapt Theol Sem, MDiv, 1973; United Theol Sem, DMin, 1990. **Career:** Eastern Union Bible Col, lectr; Methodist Theol Sch, lectr; St Paul's Baptist Church W Chester PA, pastor, 1970-77; Mt Olivet Baptist Church, Columbus, Ohio, pastor, 1977, sr pastor, 1978-; United Theol Sem, prof preaching, 1987-94; Howard Univ, baccalaureate preacher, 1992; Morehouse Col, baccalaureate preacher, 1994; Trinity Lutheran Sem, prof preaching, currently; Trinity Lutheran Sem, affiliated prof preaching, affil prof homiletics, 1995-. **Orgs:** Deleg, Baptist World Youth Conf, 1984; Progressive Nat Baptist Conv; Am Baptist Churches; Baptist Global Mission Bur; founder, Mt Olivet Christian Acad; bd trustee, United Theol Sem; mem adv bd, African Am Pulpit; founder, Gloria S Friend Christian Acad, 1993-; vpres, Millennium Asn Pastors. **Honors/Awds:** Middler Scholar Award, Eastern Baptist Theol Sem, 1971; Who's Who Among Black Am, 1974-75; Dedicated Service Award, W Chester State Col, 1977; Notable Am Bicentennial Era; Outstanding Young Men of America, 1980; DDiv, VA Sem, 1980; Alpha Kappa Alpha Humanitarian Service Award, 1981; Honorable Roll of Great Preachers, Ebony Mag, 1993; First Administrator, named in honor, 1993; Who's Who Among African-Am's, 1996; Keynote speaker, Columbus Conv Ctr, 1997; James E Stamps Alumni Recognition Award, UNCF & Historically Black Insts, 1999; Vertner Woodson Tandy Award, Alpha Phi Alpha & Alpha Rho Lambda Chap, 1999; African-American Role Model Award; Martin Luther King, Jr. Humanitarian Award, Columbus Ohio Educ Asn, 2014. **Special Achievements:** Sermons: "When a Hunch Pays Off, " Outstanding Black Sermons, vol III, published by Judson Press; "The Blessings of Unanswered Prayer & Spirituality," published by Judson Press; Meditation: "A Blessed Joy," From One Brother to Another: Voices of African-American Men, published by Judson Press; Publishing his book Bridging the Breach: Evangelical Thought and Liberation in the African-American Preaching Tradition (Urban Ministries) in 2000; Wisdom of the Ages. **Home Addr:** 7877 Grandley Ct, Reynoldsburg, OH 43068. **Business Addr:** Senior Pastor, Mt Olivet Baptist Church, 428 E Main St, Columbus, OH 43215, **Business Phone:** (614)221-3446.

### BOOTH, GEORGE EDWIN
Administrator. **Educ:** Brandeis Univ, BA, sociol, 1982. **Career:** Cablevision, dir & regional gen mgr, 1983-98; Comcast Cable, vpres & gen mgr, 2000, area vpres, currently. **Orgs:** CTAM Univ Midwest Chap. **Business Addr:** Area Vice President, Comcast Cable, 7747 W Vernor Hwy, Detroit, MI 48209, **Business Phone:** (313)828-6601.

### BOOTH, KEITH EUGENE
Basketball coach, basketball player. **Personal:** Born Oct 9, 1974, Baltimore, MD. **Educ:** Univ Md, attended 1997, BS, criminol & criminal justice, 2003. **Career:** Basketball player (retired), basketball coach; Chicago Bulls, forward, 1997-99; Pk Sch Baltimore, Brooklandville, Md, baseball coach, 2003; Univ Md, Terrapins, asst coach, 2004-11; Loyola Greyhounds, women's asst coach, 2011-13, men's asst coach, 2013-. **Special Achievements:** First player from Baltimore City in several years to play for Maryland. **Business Addr:** Assistant Coach, Loyola University Maryland Athletics, 4501 N Charles St, Baltimore, MD 21210, **Business Phone:** (410)617-2767.

### BOOTH, DR. LE-QUITA
Administrator. **Personal:** Born Oct 7, 1946, Columbus, GA; daughter of Joseph Reese and Hilda Reese; married Lester J; children: Joseph P. **Educ:** Columbus State Univ, BS, finance, 1972, MBA, finance, 1977; Univ Ga, Athens, EdD, higher educ admin, 1987; Univ Fla, Gainesville, FL, Post-Doctoral Bridge Prog. **Career:** Nat Bank & Trust, com officer, 1974-78; Small Bus Admin, disaster loan specialist, 1977-78; Small Bus Develop Ctr, Univ Ga, assoc dir, 1977-87; Int Coun Small Bus, fel, 1986; Nat Sci Ctr Found, asst pres educ, 1989-93; Univ Tenn, consult, 1993-94; US Asn Small Bus & Entrepreneurship, fel; Fla A&M Univ, assoc prof, 1994-95, dir admin, 1995-2006; Ala State Univ, Disadvantaged Bus Enterprises & Supportive Serv, dir, dean, 2006-. **Orgs:** Bd dir & regional vpres, Nat Bus League, 1983-85; Ga Asn Minority Entrepreneurs, 1981-85; vpres minority small bus, Int Coun Small Bus, 1984-86. **Home Addr:** 609 Zeron Dr, Columbus, GA 31907-6418, **Home Phone:** (706)682-8020. **Business Addr:** Director Disadvantaged Business Enterprises Support Services, Alabama State University, Rm 430 600 S Ct St, Montgomery, AL 36101-0271, **Business Phone:** (334)229-4100.

### BOOZER, DARRYL
Founder (originator), president (organization). **Career:** IBS Commun Inc, founder & pres, 1983-. **Orgs:** Minority Bus Enterprise Coun. **Business Addr:** Founder, President & Chief Executive Officer, IBS Communications Inc, 1408 E Mermaid Lane, Wyndmoor, PA 19038, **Business Phone:** (215)948-3768.

### BOOZER, EMERSON (EMERSON Y BOOZER, JR.)
Administrator, sports manager. **Personal:** Born Jul 4, 1943, Augusta, GA; son of Emerson and Classie Mae; married Enez Yevette Bowins; children: Kiva. **Educ:** Univ Md Eastern Shore, BS, 1966. **Career:** Football player, football analyst, director (retired); CBS-TV, football analyst, 1976-77; New York Jets, football player, 1966-76; WLIBRadio, announcer, 1971-74, host; Long Island Cablevision, sports analyst football games; Town Huntington, NY, exec asst supvr, parks & recreation dir. **Orgs:** Pigskin ClubWash, DC; Police Athletic League; Nat Football League Players Asn. **Honors/Awds:** Rookie of the Year, Actors Guild Meth, Pittsburgh Courier, 1966; All-Am, 1964-65; Outstanding Small Col Athlete, Wash Pigskin Club, 1965; World Champion, 1968; All-Star Team, Am Football League, 1966-68; AFL champion, 1968; AFC Scoring Touchdowns Champion, 1972; The Hons Ct, Ga Sports Hall of Fame, 1991; Suffolk Sports Hall of Fame, 1996; Super Bowl champion (III); Inducted Hall of Fame, Col Football; Ring Honor, New York Jets, 2015. **Home Addr:** 25 Windham Dr, Huntington Station, NY 11746-4541.

### BORDEN, HAROLD F., JR.
Jeweler. **Personal:** Born Feb 3, 1942, New Orleans, LA; married Barbara Sullivan; children: Tony & Tina. **Educ:** La City Col, drawing; Trade Tech Col, LA, design; Otis Art Inst, LA, drawing. **Career:** Krasne Co, designer jewelry, 1969-71; Contemp Crafts, LA, exhibitor, 1972; H Borden Studios, master jeweler, sculptor, artist & owner. **Orgs:** Org Jua-Agr Ctr; design consult, Black Artists & Craftsman Guild; Am Guild Craftsman; bd mem, Jua. **Honors/Awds:** Special Achievement Award, Dept Recreation & Parks City, LA, 1972; Participation Award, City Los Angeles Day Pk, 1974. **Home Addr:** 1430 S Burnside Ave, Los Angeles, CA 90019-4014. **Business Addr:** Owner, Artist, H Borden Studios, 1255 12 S Cochran Ave, Los Angeles, CA 90019-2899.

### BORDERS, FLORENCE EDWARDS
Historian, archivist. **Personal:** Born Feb 24, 1924, New Iberia, LA; daughter of Sylvanus and Julia Gray; married James Buchanan; children: James Buchanan IV, Sylvanus Edwards & Thais Adams. **Educ:** Southern Univ, Baton Rouge, LA, BA, 1945; Rosary Col, Sch Libr Sci, River Forest, IL, BA, libr sci, 1947, MA, libr sci, 1966; LA State Univ, Baton Rouge, LA, Post Master's fel, 1968. **Career:** Univ Chicago, Chicago, Ill, libr asst, 1946; Bethune-Cookman Col, Daytona Beach, Fla, asst librn, 1947-58; Tenn State Univ, Nashville, Tenn, cataloger, 1958-59; Grambling State Univ, Grambling, La, head tech serv, 1959-70; Amistad Res Ctr, Tulane Univ, New Orleans, La, sr & ref archivist, 1970-89; Southern Univ New Orleans, Ctr African & African Am Studies, New Orleans, La, archivist, 1989-. **Orgs:** Founder & dir, Chicory Soc Afro-La Hist & Cult, 1986-; pres, Our Lady Lourdes Parish Coun, 1986-87; pres, Greater New Orleans Archivists, 1987-88; vpres, Our Lady Lourdes Parish Sch Bd, 1990-91; nominating comm, Acad Cert Archivists, 1990-91; block capt, Mayoral Campaign, 1990; Soc Am Archivists; Soc Southwest Archivists; Coalition 100 Black Women; Am Libr Asn; La Arch & Mss Asn; League Good Gov, Zeta Phi Beta Sorority; Archivists & Arch Color Roundtable. **Honors/Awds:** Certificate of Merit, Phi Beta Sigma Fraternity, 1969; Trophy, La World Expos, Afro-Am Pavilion, 1984; Certificate of Recognition, Black Chorale, 1986; Certificate of Appreciation, Equal Opportunity Adv Coun, 1986; Unsung Heroes Plaque, Crescent City Chap of Links, 1987; Callaloo Award, Univ of Va, 1988; Vital as a Heartbeat Award, Urban League, 1988; Trophy, Calvary CME Church, 1988. **Home Addr:** 2318 Gen Pershing St, New Orleans, LA 70115-6230, **Home Phone:** (504)891-8920. **Business Addr:** Archivist, Southern University New Orleans, 6400 Press Dr, New Orleans, LA 70126, **Business Phone:** (504)284-5550.

### BORDERS, MICHAEL G.
Artist, teacher. **Personal:** Born Oct 17, 1946, Hartford, CT; son of Thomas L and Marjorie Davis; married Sharon Armwood; children: Nicholas M A. **Educ:** Fisk Univ, BA, art, 1968; Skowhegan Sch Painting & Sculpture, attended 1969; Howard Univ, MFA, 1970. **Career:** Howard Univ, artist & technician, 1968-70; freelance artist, 1968-; Fisk Univ, instr, 1970-71; Fox Mid Sch, math teacher, 1971-72; S Arsenal Neighborhood Devel Sch, artist residence, 1973-78; Greater Hartford Community Col, art hist instr, 1978-79; Loomis-Chaffee Prep Sch, lectr, 1973; Trinity Col, lectr, 1973; Wash Galleries, portrait painter; billboard painter. **Orgs:** Fisk Univ homecoming brochure covers, 1967-68; First Ann Fine Arts Exhib, 1968; First Ann Congreg Art Show, 1968; Stud Exhib, Skowhegan Sch Painting & Sculpture, 1968; One-Man Show Cent Mich Univ, 1970; Joint Fac Exhib Fisk, Vanderbilt, Peabody, 1971; lobby, Phoenix Mutual Life Ins Co, 1974; Unitarian Meeting house Hartford, 1974; artist residence, Weaver, HS, 1973-74; Conn Comn Cult & Tourism. **Honors/Awds:** Two-man Show Nat Ctr Afro-Amer Artists, 1975; mural displayed in Hartford titled "Genesis of Capital City" (largest mural in New England - first permanent monument by Black Amer in Hartford); 18-month trip to Africa, Asia & Europe, 1976-77; CT State Panorama of Business & Indus, 1980; twomural panels City Hall, Hartford (2nd permanent monument by Black Amer in Hartford) 1980-85; three murals AETNA Insurance Co, Hartford, 1989; fourmurals AI Prince Regional Vocational Tech School, Hartford, 1989; manyconceptual paintings & portraits. **Business Addr:** Educator, Artist, 210 N Whitney St, Hartford, CT 06105, **Business Phone:** (203)523-8557.

### BORGES, FRANCISCO L.
Chairperson, executive, executive director. **Educ:** Trinity Col, BA; Univ Conn Law Sch, JD. **Career:** City Hartford, Conn, dep mayor; State Conn, treas; GE Capital Financial Guaranty Ins Co, managing dir; Landmark Partners Inc, chmn, chief exec officer & managing partner, 1999-; Assured Guaranty, dir, 2007-; Travelers Insurance Companies, legal counsel. **Orgs:** Bd mem, Hartford Found Pub Giving; bd mem, Conn Pub Broadcasting; bd trustee, Knight Found; bd mem, Univ Conn Health Ctr; bd dir, Davis Selected Funds; bd dir, Univ Conn, Med & Dent Sch & Health Ctr. **Honors/Awds:** "Black Enterprise," 75 Most Powerful Blacks on Wall Street, 2011. **Business Addr:** Chairman, Chief Executive Officer, Landmark Partners Inc, 10 Mill Pond Lane, Simsbury, CT 06070, **Business Phone:** (860)651-9760.

### BORGES, ESQ. SAUNDRA KEE (SAUNDRA ALICE KEE BORGES)
Government official, lawyer. **Personal:** Born Jun 21, 1959, Montclair, NJ; daughter of William Henry Jr and Edith Hope; married Peter L; children: Garrett, Julian & Adriana. **Educ:** Trinity Col, Hartford CT, BS, psychol, 1981; Univ Conn Sch Law, JD, 1984. **Career:** Legal intern; City Hartford Pension Comn, legal coun; City Hartford, Off Corp Coun, spec coun, 1984-87, asst corp coun, 1987-93, sr asst corp coun, 1993, city mgr, 1993-2001, dep corp coun, corp coun, 2010-14; bd trustees & secy, Conn Pub Broadcasting Inc; pvt pract atty, currently; Trinity Col, adj prof;; Spencers Partners LLC, partner; Kee Borges Silvestri, partner. **Orgs:** Alpha Kappa Alpha Sorority Inc, 1978-; corporator, St Francis Hosp, 1984-; corporator, Hartford Hosp, 1984-; bd mem, Univ Conn Law Sch Found, 1989-; Conn Town & City Managers Asn, 1993-; Conn Valley Girl Scouts, 1993-; bd dir, Legal Aid Soc, 1993-; mentor, 1994-, bd trustee, 1999-, Trinity Col; Christmas July, 1994-; Int City Managers Asn, 1994-; bd mem, St Timothy Mid Sch, 1999-; bd mem, Nat Forum Blacks Pub Admin, 1999-; Conn Pub TV; bd mem, Conn Woman's Hall Fame; George Crawford Law Asn; arbitrator, Am Arbit Asn, currently. **Business Addr:** Partner, Kee Borges & Silvestri, 56 Arbor St Suite 206, Hartford, CT 06106, **Business Phone:** (860)231-9664.

### BORLABI, WENDY
Consultant, psychologist. **Educ:** Southwestern Okla State Univ, BS; Ga Southern Univ, MS, 2000; Argosy Univ, PsyD, 2005. **Career:** James Madison Univ, sr staff/athletic consult, 2005-09; Us Olympic Comt, sr sport psychologist, 2009-14; Acumen Performance Group, cert sport psychol consult/prin, 2011-15; Nat Basketball Asn, group

doctor, 2015; Borlabi Consult, founder & sport psychol consult, 2015-; Chicago Bulls (NBA), performance coach, 2016-. **Orgs:** Asn Appl Sports Psychol, 2001-; Am Psychol Asn, 2008-, chairperson Div 47, Sports & Exercise Psychol, Spec Interest Comt, 2008-10. **Business Addr:** Borlabi Consulting LLC, 7115 West North Ave Suite 338, Oak Park, IL 60302.

## BOROM, LAWRENCE H.

Social worker, executive, executive director. **Personal:** Born Feb 28, 1937, Youngstown, OH; son of Clarence H Russell and Cora Mildred Lewis; married Betty J Fontaine; children: Martin Antoine & James. **Educ:** Youngstown State Univ, BS, educ, 1958; Mankato State Col, MA, urban studies, 1971; Univ Colo, Sociol, 1993. **Career:** Executive (retired); Cleveland Pub Schs, Cleveland, OH, elem teacher, 1962-63; St Paul Urban League, St Paul, Minn, employ & educ dir, 1963-66; Minn Gov Human Rights Comn, exec dir, 1966-67; St Paul Urban League, comn, exec dir, 1967-74; Human Rights & Community Rels Agency, dir; Nat Urban League, New York, NY, dir community develop, 1974-76; Urban League Metrop Denver, Colo, pres & chief exec officer, 1976-91; City & County Denver, Dir-Agency Human Rights & Community Rels, 1993-96; City Inc, pres & chief exec officer, 1996-2002; Metrop State U Denver, Affil Prof, 1978-2014; Bueno Eac, Adv Bd, mem, currently. **Orgs:** Kappa Alpha Psi Fraternity, 1956; Adv Comn, Denver Mayor's Black Adv Comt, 1985; pres, Colo Black Roundtable, 1988; Adv Comn, A World Differene Proj, 1988; bd dir, Colo African & Carribean Trade Off, 1989. **Honors/Awds:** Esquire Award, Esquire Club, 1984; Distinguished Service Award, UNCF, 1985; Distinguished Serv Award, Colo Civil Rights Comn, 1987. **Home Addr:** 355 S Oliver Way, Denver, CO 80224, **Home Phone:** (303)355-4635. **Business Addr:** Member, Advisory Board, BUENO-EAC.

## BORUM, JENNIFER LYNN (JENNIFER BORUM BECHET)

Lawyer. **Personal:** Born Mar 15, 1965, Hampton, VA; daughter of Wilbert and Ethel. **Educ:** Hampton Univ, BA, mass media arts, 1987; Harvard Univ Law Sch, JD, 1990. **Career:** US Ct Appeals 4th Circuit, law clerk, 1990-91; Cahill Gordon & Reindel, atty, assoc, 1991-93; Stillman, Friedman & Shaw, atty, assoc, 1993-96; Southern Dist NY, US Atty Off, asst US atty, 1996-2000; Hunton & Williams LLP, litigation atty, 2000-04; Bechet Commun, prin, 2004-07; Stone Pigman Walther Wittmann LLC, mem, 2007-12; Walmart, assoc gen coun, 2012-. **Orgs:** Alpha Kappa Alpha Sorority, 1985-; Shte Bar NY, 1991-; DC Bar Asn, 1993-; Commonwealth Va Bar, 2001-; Jr League Richmond, 2001-; newsletter ed, Rotary Club Richmond, 2001-; John Marshall Inn Ct, 2001-; bd dir, Big Bros Big Sisters, 2001-; past co-chair, Minority Trial Lawyer Comt, 2008-11; co-chair, Ethics & Professionalism Comt, 2011-12; div dir, Div I - Opers, 2012-15; Am Bar Asn Sect Litigation & immediate; ABA Litigation Sect's Criminal Litigation; Appellate Pract Comts; Ed bd La Bar J; New Orleans Bar Asn; La Asn Black Women Attorneys; Fed Bar Asn; Louis A. Martinet Soc; Alpha Kappa Alpha Sorority Inc; Am MENSA, Ltd; Stone Pigman Walther Wittmann LLC, 2007-12; White Collar Defense Referral Network; Soc Corp Compliance & Ethics; La State Bar Asn; pres, Toastmasters Int, 2014-15; co-chair, Class Actions & Derivative Suits Comt, 2015-. **Honors/Awds:** Presidents Award, Hampton Univ, 1987; Outstanding Achievement Award, Alpha Kappa Alpha, 1997; Outstanding Achievement Award, Hunton & Williams, 2003; Volunteer of the Year, Big Bros Big Sisters Inc, 2003; Big Sister of the Year, Big Bros Big Sisters Inc, 2004; Outstanding Twenty-Year Alumnus, Hampton Univ, 2007; Honoree, CityBusiness Women of the Year, 2011. **Special Achievements:** Author: Note, And Forgive Them Their Trespasses, Harvard Law Rev, 1990. **Home Addr:** 3849 W Weyburn Rd, Richmond, VA 23235, **Home Phone:** (804)267-6532. **Business Addr:** Associate General Counsel, Walmart, 702 SW 8th St, Bentonville, AR 72716, **Business Phone:** (479)273-4000.

## BOSCHULTE, ALFRED F.

Executive, chairperson. **Personal:** Born Sep 18, 1942, St. Thomas; married Kita. **Educ:** City Col NY, BS, mech engineering; City Univ NY, MS, engineering, opers res. **Career:** NY Tel, staff, 1964-76; AT&T, dir cross indust, 1982; Pac Bell, vpres external affairs, 1983-87; NY NEX Serv Co, vpres carrier servs, 1987-90; NY NEX Mobile Communs, pres, chmn & chief exec officer, 1990; NY NEX Corp, vpres mkt; Wireless One Corp, chmn, pres & chief exec officer; Detecon Inc, founder & chmn; Excelcomindo Pratama, managing dir; AirTouch Communs, chmn & chief exec officer; TomCom LP, chmn & pres; Sky Optix Inc, chief exec officer; Independent Wireless One Corp, chmn, pres, chief exec officer; Sky Optix Inc, chief exec officer; Advan Generation Telecom Group Inc, chmn & chief exec officer, currently; AFB Consult, pres, currently; Probe Financial Assocs Inc, chmn & sr advisor, currently; Boschulte schnee Group LLC, co-founder & chmn, currently; Excelcominda Pertama, managing dir & founder. **Orgs:** Inst Elec & Electronic Engrs; chmn, INROADS, Westchester & Fairfield; bd mem, NorthEast Utilities Corp; bd dir, Jr Achievement; bd trustee, Clark Univ; bd trustee, Boys & Girls Clubs Am; bd mem, Datum Inc; bd mem, Austron inc; vice chmn, Cellular Telecommunications Indust Asn; bd dir, United Way; bd mem, TranSwitch Corp & Symmetricom Inc; chmn, Wireless Access; bd mem, NE Utilities Corp; founding bd mem, Domanicom Inc; New York Independent Syst Operator Bd; bd mem, New York ISO; trustee, Manhattan Col; vice chmn & bd mem, VI Next Generation Network; bd mem, Global Broadband Serv. **Home Addr:** 123 Madiera Beach Blvd, Kissimmee, FL 34746. **Business Addr:** Chairman, Probe Financial Associates Inc, PO Box 286, Ironia, NJ 07845, **Business Phone:** (973)387-0443.

## BOSCHULTE, DR. JOSEPH CLEMENT

Physician, government official, psychiatrist. **Personal:** Born Feb 5, 1931, Tortola; married Rubina; children: Cheryl, Jualenda & Joseph. **Educ:** City Col NY, BS, 1954; Howard Univ Col Med, 1958. **Career:** Frdmn Hosp, intern, 1959, res fel, 1967; Wash Hosp Ctr, sr attend psychtrist, 1968-76; Prnc Grg's Hosp, 1968-75; Wash, DC, chief serv area, 1969-72; pvt pract, psychiatrist, 1972-. **Orgs:** Am Psychiat Asn; WA Psychiat Soc; AMA; fel DC Med Soc, Grant Nat insti Ment Health, 1964-67; chmn, Dept Psychiat Ctr SE Community Hosp, 1972-. **Home Addr:** 1000 Fell St Apt 616, Baltimore, MD 21231-3554. **Business Addr:** Psychiatrist, Private Practice, 3680 Warwick Rd, East New Market, MD 21631, **Business Phone:** (410)943-8108.

## BOSEMAN, CHADWICK

Actor, theatrical director, writer. **Personal:** Born Nov 29, 1976, Anderson, SC. **Educ:** Howard Univ, BFA; Brit Am Drama Acad. **Career:** Actor, writer and director. Films: "Date", 2004; "LadyLike", 2006; "The Appointment", 2007; "The Express", 2008; "The Kill Hole", 2012; "42", 2013; "Draft Day", 2014; "Get It Up", 2014; "9 Kisses", 2014. TV Series: "All My Children", 2003; "Third Watch", 2003; "Law & Order", 2004; "CSI: NY", 2006; "ER", 2008; "Cold Case", 2008; "Lincoln Heights", ABC, 2008-10; "Lie to Me", 2009; "Persons Unknown", NBC, 2010; "Detroit 1-8-7", 2011; "Justified", 2011; "Fringe", 2011. Stage: "Breath"; "Romeo and Juliet"; "Macbeth"; "Breathe"; "Learning Curve"; "ABK 4Life"; "Rhyme Deferred"; "Colored Museum"; "Bootleg Blues"; "Zooman and the Sign"; "Willie's Cut and Shine"; "Urban Transitions: Loos Blossoms", 2002. Playwright: "Hieroglyphic Graffiti"; "Deep Azure"; (co author) "Rhyme Deferred". Film director: "Blood Over a Broken Pawn". Stage director: "Dutchman"; "Wine in the Wilderness"; "Indian Summer"; "Spear in the Sun"; "Colored Museum"; "Six Hits". **Special Achievements:** "Hieroglyphic Graffiti" produced at the National Black Theatre Festival and the Hip Hop Theatre Festival; "Rhyme Deferred" included in the hip-hop theater anthology "The Fire This Time"; appeared on audio version of "Upstate" by Kalisha Buckhanon, 2005.

## BOSLEY, FREEMAN ROBERTSON, JR.

Mayor, lawyer. **Personal:** Born Jul 20, 1954, St. Louis, MO; son of Freeman Sr and Marjorie Ellen; married Darlynn; children: Sydney. **Educ:** Univ St Louis, BA, urban affairs & polit sci, 1976; Univ St Louis Sch Law, JD, 1979. **Career:** Legal Serv Eastern, Mo, staff atty, 1979-81; Bussey & Jordan, assoc, 1982-83; Circuit Ct St Louis, clerk, 1983-93; Child Support Comn, comnr, 1985-; City St Louis, mayor, 1993-97; Caldwell & Singleton LLC, atty, 1997-; Bosley & Assocs LLC, prin, 2004-; Boast & Jordan Law Firm. **Orgs:** Mound City Bar Asn, 1980; Metro Bar Asn, 1980; chmn, St Louis Dem Cent Comt, 1990-93; Bd Jury Commissioners; pres, Black Stud Alliance; pres, Black Am Law Stud Asn; bd dir, Cedric Entertainer Charitable Found. **Special Achievements:** First African American mayor of St. Louis, Missouri; First African-American chairman of the Democratic party, 1993; First African-American St. Louis Circuit Clerk for the 22nd Judicial Circuit. **Home Addr:** 3508 Palm Pl, St Louis, MO 63107-2519, **Home Phone:** (314)535-4929. **Business Addr:** Attorney, Caldwell & Singleton LLC, 1601 Olive Fl 1, St Louis, MO 63103, **Business Phone:** (314)535-4929.

## BOSLEY, THAD (THADDIS BOSLEY, JR.)

Baseball player, baseball manager. **Personal:** Born Sep 17, 1956, Oceanside, CA; married Cherry Sanders. **Educ:** Mira Costa Community Col. **Career:** Baseball player (retired), baseball coach, executive; Calif Angels, outfielder, 1977 & 1988; Chicago White Sox, outfielder, 1978-80; Milwaukee Brewers, outfielder, 1981; Seattle Mariners, outfielder, 1982; Chicago Cubs, outfielder, 1983-86; Kans City Royals, outfielder, 1987-88; Tex Rangers, outfielder, 1989-90; Oakland Athletics, coach, 1999-2002; Phoenix Devil Dogs, mgr, 2001; Bethany Univ, asst coach & head coach, 2008-09; Southwestern Col, head coach, 2009; Tex Rangers, hitting coach, 2010; Grace Univ, exec dir athletics, athletic develop & head coach new baseball prog, 2013-. **Orgs:** Exec dir, Neb.Grace Univ. **Business Addr:** Executive Director, Head Coach, Grace University, 1311 S 9th St, Omaha, NE 68108, **Business Phone:** (402)449-2800.

## BOST, FRED M.

Government official. **Personal:** Born Mar 12, 1938, Monroe, NC; married Sara B; children: Sybil, Olantunji & Kimberly. **Educ:** Bloomfield Col, BS, 1976; Cook Col, environ-health/law, 1979. **Career:** Elizabeth NJ Bd Educ, chmn title I, 1970-72; Dept Prop & Maint, asst mgr, 1976-79; Twp Irvington, comn drugs, 1977-79, councilman, 1980-2004; Essex County, comn youth & rehab comn, 1977-80; ABC Irvington, comn chmn, 1982-84. **Orgs:** Pres, Fred Bost Civic Asn, 1975-81; rep, Bur Indian Affairs, 1976-78, pubrels rep, data processing, 1977-79; pres, E Ward Civic Asn, 1979-81. **Honors/Awds:** Concerned Citizen Award, PBA, Irvington, 1980. **Home Addr:** 110 East Pkwy, Irvington, NJ 07111.

## BOSTIC, HARRIS, II

Executive. **Educ:** Morehouse Col, BA, bus admin & mkt, 1985; Ga State Univ, Andrew Young Sch Pub Policy, MS, pub policy, 1994; Calif Culinary Acad, cert, prof culinary skills, 2000; Rockwood Leadership Inst, art leadership training, 2013. **Career:** Peace Corps, vol, 1988-90, regional mgr, regional dir, 1998-2005; Atlanta Comt Olympic Games, prog mgr, off chmn, 1991-96; Summer & Winter Olympic Games Organizing Comts, consult, 1992-2006; Dem Nat Comt Conventions, sr advisor, 1996-2008; DJ Miller & Assocs, sr assoc, 1997-98; Am Red Cross Bay Area, dir prepare bay area, 2005-06; Clinton Found, assoc develop dir, 2006-08; Abyssinian Develop Corp, vpres, external affairs, 2008-12; Coaching Corps, chief operating officer, 2012-14; Schaffer&-Combs, dir, 2014-; Net Impact, chief prog officer, 2015-. **Orgs:** William J. Clinton Found; Am Red Cross; Clinton-Gore'96; Atlanta Comt Olympic Games & PaineWebber Inc; bd dir mem, Hostellers-Int; bd mem, Atlanta Habitat Humanity, 1993-98; bd dir mem, Brit-Am Proj, 1994-; bd dir mem, World Affairs Coun, 2005-06; bd dir mem, Habitat Humanity & Covenant Community Inc; sr advisor, Abyssinian Develop Corp, 2009-; bd mem. CorpsAfrica; bd mem, Hostelling Int USA, 2009-13; bd dir mem, Nat Peace Corps Asn, 2010-13. **Business Addr:** Chief Operating Officer, Coaching Corps, 310 8th St Suite 300, Oakland, CA 94607, **Business Phone:** (510)663-9200.

## BOSTIC, DR. JAMES EDWARD, JR.

Administrator, scientist, association executive. **Personal:** Born Jun 24, 1947, Marlboro County, SC; married Edith A Howard; children: James E III & Scott H. **Educ:** Clemson Univ, BS, textile chem, 1969, PhD, 1972. **Career:** Clemson Univ, fel, 1969-72, grad resident counr, 1969-72; Am Enka & Res Corp, sr res sci, 1972; Dept Agri, spec asst sec agri, 1972-73, dep asst sec agri, 1973-77; Riegel Text Corp, corp regul dir, tech analyst, 1977-81, convenience prod div, 1981-85; Com Prods & Syst Div, gen mgr, 1989-91; Ga Pac Corp, gen mgr, 1989, exec vpres, 1991-92, Environ, Govt Affairs & Commun, 1991-2005; Butler Paper & Mail-Well, vpres, 1991-92; Ga Pac Group, vpres commun paper, 1992-95, sr vpres, 1995-2001, exec vpres environ & gov affairs, 2001-05; Consumer Tissue Group, Gen Mgr, Com Prod & Systs Div, Dir, Sales & Opers; ACT Inc, bd dir, currently; Coleman Lew & Assocs Inc, partner, 2007-; HEP & Assocs, managing dir, currently; George W Bush, pres; US Agr Dept, dep asst secy. **Orgs:** Coun mem, Clemson Univ Grad Sch, 1971-72; Asn Textile Chem & Color; Am Chem Soc; Phi Psi Fraternity; Blue Key Nat Hnr Frat; Nat Acad Engrs, 1975-76; pres, Comn White House Fel Region Panel, 1975-78; bd trustee, USDA Grad Sch, 1976-77; FFA Hnr Am Farmer, 1976; US Dept Com Mgmt Labor Textile Adv Comn, 1978-85; vice chmn & chmn, SC Commn on Higher Educ, 1978-83; chmn, Career Found Bd Trustees, 1978-; chmn, Comn Higher Educ Sc, 1980; pres, Comn White House Fel, 1981-; bd trustee, Clemson Univ, 1983-; Ga State Bd Educ; dir, Clemson Univ Found; bd trustee, Tuskegee Univ; bd trustee, Clemson Univ; bd trustee, Wofford Col; bd trustee, Westminster Schs; bd mem, Carolina Power & Light, 2002-07; bd mem, Progress Energy; bd mem, Wachovia. **Honors/Awds:** Ford Found Doc Fel Black Students, 1969-70; White House Fel, 1972-73; Distinguished Service Award Greenville Jaycees, 1979; Outstanding Pub Servant Year Award, 1983; SC Asn Minorities Pub Admin. **Special Achievements:** First African-American to earn a doctorate at Clemson University. **Home Addr:** 401 Lakeside Dr, Aiken, SC 29801. **Business Addr:** Partner, Coleman Lew Associates Inc, 326 W Tenth St, Charlotte, NC 28202, **Business Phone:** (704)377-0362.

## BOSTIC, ESQ. LEE HAROLD

Lawyer. **Personal:** Born Apr 17, 1935, Brooklyn, CA; married Gayle Spaulding; children: Lisa, Staci & Lee. **Educ:** Morgan State Col, BA, 1957; Boston Univ Law Sch, LLB, 1962. **Career:** Allstate Ins Co, claims adj, 1964; Solomon Z Ferziger NYC, assoc atty, 1964-65; Queens Co, asst dist atty, 1966; pvt pract atty, 1967-. **Orgs:** New York & Queens Co Bar Asn; Nat Asn Advan Colored People; male comt man, 29 AD Reg Rep Club Queens Co; NY State Bar Asn; Macon B Allen Black Bar Asn; bd dirs, Jr Acad League Inc. **Home Addr:** 11150 178th St, Jamaica, NY 11433, **Home Phone:** (718)291-2888. **Business Addr:** Attorney, Private Practice, 22110 Jamaica Ave 2nd Fl, Queens Village, PA 11428.

## BOSTIC, RAPHAEL W.

Economist, educator. **Educ:** Harvard Univ, BA, psychol & econs, 1987; Stanford Univ, PhD, econ, 1995. **Career:** Am Univ, prof lectr, 1988; Fed Res Bd Wash, sr economist, 1998-2001, Monetary & Financial Studies Sect, economist, 1995-98; Univ Southern Calif, Sch Policy Planning & Develop, prof, 2008-, assoc prof, 2004-08, USC Lusk Ctr Real Estate, interim assoc dir, 2007-, Master Real Estate Develop Prog, former, dir, 2004-, Casden Real Estate Econs Forecast, founding dir, 2001-04; US Dept Housing & Urban Develop, spec asst, 1999, Policy Develop & Res, asst secy, 2009-12. **Orgs:** Fac fel Urban Land Inst; fel Royal Inst Chartered Surveyors; fed mem, Fed Geog Data Comt; bd mem, Mayors Indust Develop Policy Initiative Adv Bd; Am Econ Asn; Am Real Estate; Urban Econs Asn. **Honors/Awds:** Special Achievement Award, Federal Reserve Board of Governors. **Business Addr:** Assistant Secretary, US Department of Housing and Urban Development, 451 7th St SW, Washington, DC 20410, **Business Phone:** (202)708-1112.

## BOSTIC, VIOLA W.

Association executive, executive director. **Personal:** Born Oct 24, 1941, New York, NY; daughter of Peter Williams and Doris Andrews; married Raphael; children: Raphael William & Ebony Leigh. **Educ:** City Col NY, BA, hist, 1963; City Univ NY, MA, 1965; Univ Pa, MS, 1992. **Career:** NYC Schs, social studies teacher, 1963-66; Morgan State Univ, instr, 1967-68; Burlington County Col, instr, 1969-70; Courier Post, reporter, 1973-74; Rohm & Haas Co, mgr mkt servs, 1974-93; Big Bros/Big Sisters Am, asst nat exec dir, 1994-2001; Nat Fedn Community Develop Credit Union, dep exec dir, 2001-05; Chapel Four Chaplains, Philadelphia, exec dir, 2005-09. **Orgs:** Adv chair, Philadelphia Salvation Army, 1976-; Nat Asn Media Women, Philadelphia, pres, 1982-85; Nat Asn Media Women, 1983; vice chair, Moorestown Vis Nurse Asn, 1984-; chair community rels, Contact 609, 1993-94; Soc Am, 1994-; Pub Rels Soc Am, 1995-; Male Advocacy Network, 1996-; chair emer, Philadelphia Urban Coalition, Educ Task Force; Nat Assembly Pub Rels. **Home Addr:** 704 Westerly Dr, Marlton, NJ 08053, **Home Phone:** (856)988-3711.

## BOSTICK, THOMAS P.

Engineer, army officer. **Personal:** Born Sep 23, 1956, Fukuoka; married Renee Yvonne Coyle; children: Joshua James Bostick. **Educ:** US Mil Acad, BS, engineering, 1978; Stanford Univ, MSME & MSCE, 1985; AUS War Col, grad. **Career:** US Army, 1978-: 54th Battalion, V Corps, Ger, battalion maintenance officer, 1980-81, exec officer, 1981, comdr B Co, 1981-82; US Mil Acad, instr, asst prof, 1985-88, assoc prof; White House Fel, spec asst to Secy Veterans Affairs, 1989-90; Off Dep Chief Staff Engrs, US Army Europe & Seventh Army, Ger, engr opers staff officer, 1990-91; 1st Armored Div, US Army Europe & Seventh Army, Ger S-3 (opers) 40th Engr Brigade, 1991-92, then Engr Brigade, 1992-93; US Army Corps Engrs, exec officer to chief engrs, 1993-94; 1st Inf Div (mechanized), comdr 1st Engr Battalion, 1994-96; 1st Armored Div, Oper Joint Forge, Bosnia-Herzegovina, comdr Engr Brigade, 1997-99; US Army, exec officer to chief staff, 1999-2001; Nat Mil Command Ctr, J-3, Joint Staff Pentagon, dep dir opers, 2001-02; 1st Cavalry Div, Oper Iraqi freedom, asst div comdr (maneuver), asst div comdr (support), 2002-04; US Army Corps Engrs, dir mil progs & comdr Gulf Region Div, Oper Iraqi Freedom, 2004-05; US Army Recruiting Command, comndg gen, 2005-09; US Army, dep chief staff, G-1, Personnel, 2010-12; US Army Chief Engrs, 2012-; US Army Corps Engrs, comndg gen, 2012-. **Orgs:** Mem: Soc Am Mil Engrs; Asn U.S. Army; Mil Officers Asn Am; ROCKs; Pan Pac Am Leaders & Mentors Orgn. **Special Achievements:** Registered professional engineer, VA, 1988-. **Business Addr:** U.S. Army Corps of Engineers, 441 G St NW, Washington, DC 20314-1000.

**BOSTON, ARCHIE, JR.**
Arts administrator, college teacher. **Personal:** Born Jan 18, 1943, Clewiston, FL; married Juanita; children: Michael & Jennifer. **Educ:** Calif Inst Arts, BFA, advert design, 1964; Univ Southern Calif, MLA, lib arts, 1977; Calif State Univ-Long Beach, graphic design, 2008. **Career:** Hixon & Jorgensen Inc, art dir, 1965-66; Boston & Boston Design, partner, 1966-68; Cailf Inst Arts, 1966-68; Carson Roberts Inc, art dir, 1968; Botsford Ketchum Inc, sr art dir, 1968-77; Cailf State Univ, instr, 1971, tenured prof & chmn, VC Design Prog, currently; Archie Boston Graphic Design, prin, 1973-; Art Ctr Col Design, instr, 1976-77; Cailf State Univ, assoc prof, prof, 1977-2009, prof emer, currently; Design Concepts, pres, 1977-78. **Orgs:** Pres, bd dir, Art Dir Club, LA, 1973; Mt Sinai Bapt Church; bd govs, ArtDir Club, LA, 1974-; comt chmn, Graphic Arts Bicent Black Achivement. Exhibit; New York Art Dir; San Francisco & La Art Dir Club Show; Type Dir & Aiga Show; Comun Arts & Art Dir Mag Show; Graphis Annual & Typomondus 20. **Honors/Awds:** Award winner, The New York, San Francisco and Los Angeles Art Directors Club shows, Communication Arts and Art Direction Magazine shows, Western Art Director's show; Print Magazine's Regional Design Annual; The Type Directors; AIGA shows; The Los Angeles Belding Awards shows; Graphis Annual and Typomondus 20; International Exposition of the "Best Graphics of the 20th Century"; Intl Exp of "Best Graphics of the 20th Century"; Outstanding Professor of the Year, Calif State Univ Long Beach, 2003-04; Fellow Award, Los Angeles Chapter of AIGA, 2007. **Special Achievements:** First African American to receive the prestigious AIGA Fellows Award in 2007. Author: Fly In The Buttermilk: Memoirs of an African American in Advertising, Design, & Design Education, 2002; Lil' Colored Rascals in the Sunshine City, 2009. **Home Addr:** 5707 Aladdin St, Los Angeles, CA 90008-1002, **Home Phone:** (323)296-2428. **Business Addr:** Professor Emeritus, California State University, 401 Golden Shore, Long Beach, CA 90802-4210, **Business Phone:** (562)951-4000.

**BOSTON, DAVID BYRON**
Football coach, football player. **Personal:** Born Aug 19, 1978, Humble, TX; son of Byron and Carolyn; married Renee Marisa Dota; children: Alaia Gianna & Jaylen James. **Educ:** Ohio State Univ, sociol, 1999; Western Gov Univ, BS, bus mgt, 2013. **Career:** Football player (retired), trainer; Ariz Cardinals, wide receiver, 1999-2002; San Diego Charger, wide receiver, tight end, 2003; Miami Dolphins, wide receiver, 2004-05; Tampa Bay Buccaneers, wide receiver, 2006; Toronto Argonauts, 2008; IHP, prof trainer, 2011-. **Honors/Awds:** First-team All-Big Ten, twice, 1997-98; First-team All-American, 1998; Pro Bowl Selection, 2001; All-Pro selection, 2001; Paul Warfield Award, 2001. **Business Addr:** Professional Trainer, Inst Human Performance, 1950 NW Boca Raton Blvd, Boca Raton, FL 33432, **Business Phone:** (561)620-9556.

**BOSTON, DENNIS H.**
Advertising executive, accountant, salesperson. **Personal:** Born Chicago, IL. **Educ:** S Jr Col, Chicago; DePaul Univ. **Career:** Hertz Rent-A-Car, exec accounts mgr; Johnson Publ Co, advert sales rep, 1972-78, midwest advert dir, 1978-81, vpres & midwest advert dir, 1981-98, sr vpres, midwest advert dir, 1998-; Ebony Publ, sr vpres, midwest advert dir. **Orgs:** Mid Am Comm; Usher Bd; St Ailbe Church. **Business Addr:** Midwest Advertising Director, Senior Vice President, Johnson Publishing Co Inc, 820 S Michigan Ave, Chicago, IL 60605, **Business Phone:** (312)322-9200.

**BOSTON, GRETHA**
Actor. **Personal:** Born Apr 18, 1959, Crossett, AR. **Career:** Stage performer: Show Boat, 1994-97; It Ain't Nothin' But the Blues, 1999-; TV series: "Some Enchanted Evening: Celebrating Oscar HammersteinII", 1995; "Law & Order", 2001; "School Daze", 2001; "Hope & Faith", 2004; "Jury Duty", 2004; "D.A.W", 2004; "Law & Order: Criminal Intent", 2004. **Honors/Awds:** Tony Award, 1995; Hayes Award, 2000; Theater World Award. **Business Addr:** Actress, c/o Ambrosio/Mortimer & Associates Inc, 9150 Wilshire Blvd Suite 175, Beverly Hills, CA 90212, **Business Phone:** (310)274-4274.

**BOSTON, DR. HORACE OSCAR, SR.**
Dentist. **Personal:** Born Jul 27, 1934, Clarksville, TX; married Iola. **Educ:** Southern Univ, BS, 1955; Tex S Univ; Univ Okla; Univ NM; Wash Univ, DDS; Meharry Med Col, Sch Dent, 1973. **Career:** Wiley Col, asst prof; Midwestern Univ, asst prof; pvt pract dentist, currently. **Orgs:** YMCA; bd dir, Eastside Girls Club; commr, Wichita Falls Housing Authority; vpres, Wichita Dist Dent Soc; Gulf States Dent Asn; Tex Dent Asn; Kappa Alpha Psi Frat; City Coun, City Wichita Falls; Am Dent Asn; WF & Eve Lions Club. **Honors/Awds:** NSF, Grant. **Special Achievements:** Publication: "Prognathism: a Review of the Lit", 1972. **Home Phone:** (940)691-0190. **Business Addr:** Dentist, 505 Brook Ave Suite A, Wichita Falls, TX 76301, **Business Phone:** (940)723-7171.

**BOSTON, MCKINLEY, JR.**
School administrator, president (organization), chief executive officer. **Personal:** Born Nov 5, 1945, Elizabeth City, NC; son of McKinley and Lenora; married Magellia McIntyre; children: Lance & Kimberly. **Educ:** Univ Minn, attended 1968; Montclair State Col, BA, 1973, MA, 1973; NY Univ, EdD, 1987. **Career:** NY Giants, left defensive end, 1968-71; B C Lions, Can football player, 1971-73; Monclair State Col, dir stud serv, 1974-85; Kean Col, dir athletics, 1986-87; Univ Ri, dir athletics, 1989-91; Univ Minn, dir athletics, 1991-96, vpres stud develop & athletics, 1995; Harvard Univ, vis scholar, 1991-92; Mikael Blaisdell & Assocs Inc, pres & chief exec officer; NIRSA J, ed; NMex State Univ, dir athletics, 2004-14. **Orgs:** RI Statewide Task Force Anti Drug Coalition, 1989; New Eng Asn Sch & Col Accreditation, 1989-; Eastern Col Athletic Asn Coun, 1990-91; Nat Ethic fel, 1990; Atlantic 10 Conf, 1991; bd trustee, Minneapolis Boy Scouts; bd trustee, Methodist Hosp Found NCAA Mgt Coun Leadership cabinet NCAA Cert Comt; bd mem, La Casa. **Honors/Awds:** Watson Hon Award & Outstanding Alumni Award, Montclair State Col, 1991. **Special Achievements:** University of Mich, A Survey of Volunteerism in Low Income; Evolution of Intramural Program from Athletics to Physical Education to Student Activities, 1978; Institutional Racism: What is it?, 1980; Who's Boss Student Activities Program, 1981. **Home Addr:** 1559 Pa Ave N, Golden Valley, MN 55427. **Business Addr:** Director of Athletics, New Mexican State University, MSC 3HLS, Las Cruces, NM 88003, **Business Phone:** (575)646-7630.

**BOSTON, RALPH HAROLD**
Executive, athlete. **Personal:** Born May 9, 1939, Laurel, MS; son of Peter and Eulalia Lott; children: Kenneth Todd & Stephen Keith. **Educ:** Tenn State Univ, BS, MS. **Career:** Athlete (retired), executive; Nat Track & Field Team, long jumper & capt, 1960-69; Nat Track & Field, long jumper, 1960-69; Univ Tenn, Knoxville, asst dean, students, 1968-75; TV commentator, 1969; ESPN-TV, commentator, 1978-85; Integon Ins Corp, sales; S Cent Bell Adv Systs, acct exec; WKXT-TV, Knoxville, gen partner, 1988-92, ltd partner, 1992-; Ericsson-Gen Elec Inc, maj acct mgr, 1992-, dir customer rels, currently; Serv Master Serv, pres & chief exec officer; Forrest Investors Group LLC, vice chmn; Us Olympic, consult. **Orgs:** Field judge Spec Olympics E Tenn; Gov Coun Phys Fitness & Health, Tenn; chmn & bd dir, Tenn Sport Fest. **Home Addr:** 3301 Woodbine Ave, Knoxville, TN 37914, **Home Phone:** (865)546-8470.

**BOSTON, DR. THOMAS DANNY**
Educator, founder (originator), chief executive officer. **Educ:** WVa State Univ, BS, 1968; Cornell Univ, MA, 1974, PhD, econs, 1976. **Career:** Entrepreneur, educator; Clark-Atlanta Univ, Atlanta, Ga, Dept Econ, from asst to assoc prof econ, 1976-85, chmn, 1978-85; Stanford Univ, Dept Econ, vis scholar, 1983-84; Shanghai Inst Finance & Econ, vis lectr, 1983; Ind Univ Pa, Benjamin E Mays Acad, distinguished vis scholar, 1984; Ga Inst Technol, Ivan Allen Col, Sch Econs, assoc prof econ, 1985-95, prof econs, 1995-; Albany State Col, Sch Bus Admin, distinguished lectr bus, 1990-91; Rev Black Polit Econ, ed; US Senate, Joint Econ Comt Cong, Wash, DC, sr economist, 1992; Boston Res Group Inc, pres & chief exec officer, 1994-2007; EuQuant, founder, pres & chief exec officer, 1994-; WVa State Univ Bd Gov, vpres, 2006-07. **Orgs:** UN Educ, Social & Cult Orgn; USSmall Bus Admin; US Dept Com; pres, Nat Econ Asn; Black Enterprise Bd Economists; adv, Mayor Shirley Franklins Coun Econs; creator, Gazelle Index; Sigma Xi, Nat Sci Soc, 1989; Am Econ Asn, 2007; Asn Pub Policy Anal & Mgt, 2007; consult, Cong Black Caucus Found; Atlanta Fed Res Bank Adv Coun; advisor, Millennium Develop Goals. **Special Achievements:** Published numerous articles & books. **Business Addr:** Professor of Economics, Georgia Institute of Technology, Rm 237 Old CE Bldg, Atlanta, GA 30332-0615, **Business Phone:** (404)894-5020.

**BOSWELL, ANTHONY O.**
Secretary (organization), executive director, vice president (organization). **Educ:** Univ Pa, law; Univ NC, Charlotte, NC, MEd. **Career:** Exec, consult; Nat Urban Fels Inc, exec dir; Fortune 500, atty & Educr; Inst Corp Ethics & Governance, City Chicago, Prin; Laidlaw Inc, compliance officer & corp coun, vpres & corp coun, chief compliance officer & chief exec officer; AMEC, Ethics & Compliance, sr vpres; AMEC, US Govt Rels, sr vpres ethics & compliance; Inst Corp Ethics & Governance, prin bus develop, 2004-07; City Chicago, Off Compliance, exec dir, currently. **Orgs:** Fel Nat Urban league; bd dir, secy, Laidlaw Health Care Comn; bd dir, secy, Ethics & Compliance Comn; vice chmn, Laidlaw Bd. **Home Addr:** , Chicago, IL. **Business Addr:** Executive Director, City of Chicago, City Hall 121 N LaSalle St, Chicago, IL 60602, **Business Phone:** (303)519-3296.

**BOSWELL, BENNIE, JR.**
Banker, administrator. **Personal:** Born May 4, 1948, Danville, VA; son of Bennie Sr and Edith B Williams; married Helen Thomas. **Educ:** Williams Col, MA, BA, hist, 1970. **Career:** Western Res Acad Hudson, Ohio, instr, 1970-73; Williams Col, asst dir admis, 1973-75; A Better Chance Inc, assoc dir stud affairs, 1975; Wachovia Corp, sr vpres & dir community affairs, 1976-2012. **Orgs:** Am Soc Personnel Admin; black Exec Exch Prog ASTD; pres, Nat Asn Bank Affirmative Action Dir; Nat Asn Advan Colored People; bd, chmn, fel Home Winston-Salem; adv bd mem, Duke Univ LEAD Prog; exec comn, Williams Col Alumni Soc; consult, Atlanta Adopt-A-Stud prog; bd mem, Atlanta Chap Am Inst Banking; alumni admis rep, Williams Col; bd mem, Ga Am Inst Banking; vpres, Bridge; chmn, Atlanta C Shelter; bd mem, Ga Partnership Excellence Educn; asst treas, Atlanta Urban League; bd mem, Camp Best Friends; bd mem, Families First; bd mem, Res Atlanta; bd mem, Piedmont Pk Conserv; bd mem, Proj READ; bd mem, Metro Atlanta Pvt Indust Coun Ann Fund Comt Northwest Ga Coun Girl Scouts United Way Found Comn; bd mem, Community Found Northeast Ga; bd mem, Family Connection Partnership Inc; adv comt, Communities Sch Atlanta, 2007-08; bd dir, Sheltering Arms, 2007-15. **Honors/Awds:** Nat Achieve Scholar, Nat Merit Found, 1966; Lehman Scholar, Williams Col, 1967; Francis Session Mem Fel, Williams Col, 1970; Community Leadership & Philanthropy Award. **Home Addr:** 2080 Vanderbilt Pl, Lawrenceville, GA 30044-4542, **Home Phone:** (770)339-6333. **Business Addr:** Board of Director, Sheltering Arms, 385 Centennial Olympic Pk Dr NW, Atlanta, GA 30313, **Business Phone:** (404)523-2767.

**BOUIE, DR. JOSEPH, JR.**
Government official, educator, counselor. **Personal:** Born Jan 1, 1946?. **Educ:** Southern Univ, New Orleans, LA, BA; Tulane Univ, MSW; Clark-Atlanta Univ, PhD, admin & planning. **Career:** Faculty member, administrator (retired); Southern Univ New Orleans, chancellor, 2000-02, social work prof; La House Representatives Dist 97, rep, currently. **Business Addr:** Representative, Louisiana House of Representatives, 6305 Elysian Fields Ave Suite 400, New Orleans, LA 70122, **Business Phone:** (504)286-1033.

**BOUIE, DR. MERCELINE H.**
Educator, association executive, executive. **Personal:** Born Oct 18, 1929, St. Louis, MO; daughter of Ray C Morris; married Harry J; children: Ray Anthony & Pamela Sue. **Educ:** Lincoln Univ, BA, behav sci phys educ health, 1953; Webster Univ, BA, social behav sci, 1972, MA, social & behav sci, 1973; Open Univ, PhD, educ social behav sci, 1976. **Career:** Educator (retired); St Louis Archdiocese Parochial Sch Syst, elem & high sch phys educ & health teacher, 1958-64; Venice, IL Sch Syst, dept chmn, phys educ & health teacher, 1964-68; Wheeler State Sch, dept head, young adults, 1968-74; St Louis Bd Educ, resource specialist, 1974-82; St Louis Pub Sch, conductor workshops, 1979-83; psychol examr, 1982-83, learning disabled specialist, 1985; independent speaker & consult, Spec C Learning Prob; Internship Prog, coordr; Right Proud Prog, coordr; Drug Free Sch (TREND) Cleveland NJROTC High Sch, coordr, 1992. **Orgs:** AAUW; except child specialist counr, Bouies Learning Ctr, 1978-85; second vpres, Learning Disability Asn, 1976-79; adv, Mo Learning Disability Asn, 1976-80; Int Platform Asn, 1976-; St Louis Asn Retarded C, 1979-; Grand-lady, Ladies Aux Peter Claver, 1979-82; Pro-life Comt, Our Lady Good Coun Parish; adv bd, Human Rights Off Archdiocese; judge, Int Platform AsnConv, Wash, DC, 1987; adv, State Rep 56th Dist; pres, Mt Carmel Sch Bd, 1989-93; vpres, chmn, Webster Univ Alumni Bd Dir, 1989-92; coordr, Soldan Parent's Orgn, 1989-93; charter mem, World Found Successful Women, 1991; ed bd, Tenn State Univ. **Honors/Awds:** Parent Involvement, 1976; Committee Leadership, Am Asn Univ Women, 1977; Speaker's Award, Int Platform Asn, 1979; Fourth Degree Award, PeterClaver, 1981; Oryx Press, Dir Speakers, 1981, 1982; Special EducationAward, Civic Liberty Asn, 1982; Community Leadership Award, 27th Ward Alderman; American Association of Poetry Award, 1986; St Louis Symphony Ladies Association Award, 1986; Distinguished Alumni Award, Webster Univ Bd, 1991. **Special Achievements:** Article in North County Journal; published Poem of Life, 1989. **Home Addr:** 4602 Bircher Blvd, St Louis, MO 63115, **Home Phone:** (314)382-1079. **Business Addr:** .

**BOUIE, PRESTON L.**
Firefighter, government official. **Personal:** Born Jan 22, 1926, St. Louis, MO; son of Vennie and Emma Reed; married Stella M Mosby; children: Sylvia N Saddler & Sheila N Sledge. **Career:** Firefighter (Retired); St Louis Fire Dept, pvt, 1952-63, fire capt, 1963-76, battalion fire chief, 1976-78, dep fire chief, 1978-83, asst fire chief, 1983. **Orgs:** Trustee, Wash Metrop Am Zion Church, 1980-. **Honors/Awds:** Vashon High School Hall of Fame, Vashon Hall of Fame Community, 1989. **Special Achievements:** First African-Am to be promoted to Battalion Chief, 1976; First to be promoted to Dep Chief, 1978; First African-American Assistant Fire Chief, 1983; Who's Who Among Black Americans. **Home Addr:** 1 Friese Dr, St. Louis, MO 63132, **Home Phone:** (314)692-0612.

**BOUIE, REV. DR. SIMON PINCKNEY**
Clergy. **Personal:** Born Oct 3, 1939, Columbia, SC; married Willie Omia Jamison; children: Erich & Harold. **Educ:** Allen Univ, BA, 1962; Interdenomination Ctr, BD, 1966; SC State Hosp, clin ct, 1968. **Career:** Union AME Church, pastor; Metro AME Church, sr minister; Warwick Sch Boys, first Black Chaplain, 1972-74; Mother Bethel AME Church, sr minister & pastor; Emanuel Church, pastor; Zion AME Church, pastor, currently. **Orgs:** Chair, Salute Schomburg Ctr Res Black Cult; Salute Harlem Hosp; Bethel Day Cae Ctr; Ministerial Interfaith Asn Health Comn; Harlem Civic Welfare Asn Comn Bd; NY AME Ministerial Alliance Social Action Comt; N Cent Hosp Day; trustee bd, NY Ann Conf AME Church; 100 Black Men Inc; Alpha Phi Alpha Frat; NY Chap Nat Asn Advan Colored People; bd dir, NY City Coun Churches; NY Br YMCA; Bd NY State Coun Churches; pres, Prince Hall Masons; pres, Harlem Coun; pres, Richard Allen Ctr Life; Masonic Lodge 92; PUSH; pres, S Philadelphia Cluster Churches. **Home Addr:** 1135 Barringer St, Philadelphia, PA 19119. **Business Addr:** Pastor, Zion African Methodist Episcopal Church, 1600 S 21st St, Philadelphia, PA 19145, **Business Phone:** (215)468-6489.

**BOUIE, TONY VANDERSON**
Football player, executive. **Personal:** Born Aug 7, 1972, New Orleans, LA; married Allison; children: 4. **Educ:** Univ Ariz, BA, media arts, MA, literacy & educ; Ariz State Univ, MBA, 2005; Univ Akron. **Career:** Football player (retired); Tampa Bay Buccaneers, defensive back, 1995-98, prof athlete, 1995-99; Chevron, owner & operator, 1998-2001; Circle K, mkt mgr, 2002-05; Avnet, commodity specialist, 2005-06; Roadway Express, mgr, 2006; Halo Cups Inc, chmn & chief exec officer, 2006-10; Univ Akron, grad asst, 2011; Blue Stone Strategy Group, sr strategist, 2011-12; BAMfam Group, founder currently; Deer Valley Unified Sch Dist, substitute teacher. **Orgs:** Vpres, Univ Ariz Black Alumni Asn; Univ Ariz Alumni Asn; nat bd, Leukemia & Lymphoma Soc; nat bd, Nat Football League Players Asn, bd treas, Ridgeline Acad; Christ Church. **Home Addr:** , Anthem, AZ. **Business Addr:** Chief Executive Officer, Founder, BAMfam Group, 39506 N Daisy Mountain Dr Suite 122-186, Anthem, AZ 85086, **Business Phone:** (623)282-1403.

**BOUKNIGHT, DR. REYNARD RONALD**
Physician, educator. **Personal:** Born Dec 14, 1946, Washington, DC; son of Johnnie Bell DeWalt and Lue Dennis; married LaClaire Green; children: Tendai, Omari & Reynard II. **Educ:** Howard Univ, Wash, DC, BS, microbiol, 1968; Mich State Univ, E Lansing, MI, PhD, microbiol & pub health, 1974, MD, 1975; Am Bd Internal Med, cert, internal med; Mich State Univ Col Human Med, MD. **Career:** Case Western Res Univ, Cleveland, internal med residency, 1976-79, asst prof, 1979-80; Hough-Norwood Clin, Cleveland, Ohio, chief med, 1979-80; Univ Hosps Cleveland, asst physician, 1979-80; Ingham Med Ctr, active staff, 1980-; Mich State Univ, E Lansing, Mich, asst prof, 1980-85, asst dean, 1983-2000, assoc prof med, 1985-, interim chief, 1997-2001, key fac mem & dir qual improv, 2006-; EW Sparrow Hosp, courtesy staff, 1983-; CHM Grand Rounds, prog dir, 1984-87. **Orgs:** Beta Kappa Chi, 1967; Dobro Slovo Pi, 1967; Phi Beta Kappa, 1968; fel Nat Sci Found, 1968-69; Nat Med Fel, 1972-74; Mich State Med Soc, 1983-90; Am Pub Health Asn, 1987-92; vice-chairperson, Qual Intervention Comt, Mich Peer Rev Orgn, 1987-93; bd dir, Grad Med Educ Inc, 1989-97; fel Am Col Physicians, 1990; HIV/AIDS mini fel Wayne State Univ, 1998; Ingham County Med Soc; Acad Health. **Home Addr:** 2557 Dustin Rd, Okemos, MI 48864, **Home Phone:** (517)332-7683. **Business Addr:** Associate Professor of Medicine, Division Chief & Clinic Director of General Internal Medicine Clinic, Michigan State University, 804 Service Rd, East Lansing, MI 48824-1317, **Business Phone:** (517)353-4941.

**BOULDES, RUTH IRVING**
Automotive executive, manager. **Personal:** Born Nov 22, 1946, Bronx, NY; daughter of Charles and Fannye Irving-Gibbs. **Educ:** Bernard Baruch, BBA, mkt/mkt mgt, 1977; Fordham Univ, MBA, mkt/

mkt mgt, 1979. **Career:** Gen Motors, GM Overseas Group, 1965-78, GM Denmark, dist mgr, 1978-80, GM Continental, dealer orgn mgr, 1980-81, Mkt Res, asst mgr, 1981-82, Dealer Orgn & Planning, asst mgr, 1982-84, mkt area mgr, 1999, zone mgr, 2004; Chevrolet Motor Div, asst zone mgr (Detroit, Mich), 1983-84, asst zone mgr (Minneapolis, Minn), 1984-86, communs mgr, 1986-95, Total Customer Enthusiam & Orgna Learning, proj mgr, 1996-98; Maritz, consult, 2004-12; Aesthics by Ruthi, mkt mgt consult, 2013-. **Orgs:** Nat bd mem, Campfire Boys & Girls, 1993-96; pres, Art Ctr, 1996-98, immediate pres, 1998-; bd dir, Placitas Community Libr, 2015. **Home Addr:** 3224 Kent Dr, Flower Mound, TX 75022-4978, **Home Phone:** (810)598-0422. **Business Addr:** Market Area Manager, General Motors Inc, 300 Renaissance Ctr, Detroit, MI 48265-4000, **Business Phone:** (313)556-5000.

### BOULWARE, FAY D.
Educator. **Personal:** daughter of Fay Hendley (deceased) and William R (deceased); children: William H. **Educ:** City Univ NY, Hunter Col, BA; Teachers Col Columbia Univ, MA, prof dipl. **Career:** Educator (retired); Teachers Col Columbia Univ, assoc admis, 1960-64; Inst Dev Stds New York Med Col, adminr coord/inst, 1964-66; Inst Develop Studies New York Univ, dir admin & res scientist, 1966-71; Educ Studies Prog Wesleyan Univ, lectr, 1971-75; African Am Inst Wesleyan Univ, dir, 1971-75; Emmaline Prod, hist & literary researcher, 1982; Merrill Lynch, Pierce, Fenner & Smith, prof writer, 1983-92; Chuckles Prod, dir story develop & res, 1983-90. **Orgs:** Consult, St Croix VI, 1965, bd educ, Middletown, CT, 1972-73, Lansing, Mich, 1971, Atlanta, GA, 1971, Charlotte, NC, 1969-71, Model Cities, Pittsburgh, PA, 1969, Univ Hawaii, 1967, Virgin Isls Day Sch; consult, acad adv bd, Wesleyan Univ, 1971-75; consult, NY City Bd Educ, 1971-92. **Home Addr:** 25 W 132nd St Apt 9P, New York, NY 10037.

### BOULWARE, PETER NICHOLAS
Football player, politician, executive. **Personal:** Born Dec 18, 1974, Columbia, SC; son of Raleigh and Melva; married Kensy; children: 5. **Educ:** Fla State Univ, BS, MIS, 1997. **Career:** Football player (retired), politician, executive; Baltimore Ravens, 2005, left line back, 1997-2000, left linebacker, right linebacker, 2001, right linebacker, 2002-03; Fla Bd Educ; Community Leadership Acad, founder; Tallahassee Toyota dealer, vpres, owner, currently. **Orgs:** Peter Boulware Charitable Fund; UMM C's Hosp Bd; Founder, Peter Boulware Youth Tackle Football League. **Honors/Awds:** Nation's Top 50 Athletes, The Atlanta Jour-Constitution; Top 100 hons, The Dallas Morning News; Super Bowl champion; AP NFL Defensive Rookie of the Year, 1997; PFWA Defensive Rookie of the Year, 1997; Pro Bowl, first alternate, 1998; Good Guy Award, 1999; Ed Block Courage Award, 1999; Pro Bowls, 2000, 2003, 2004; Ravens Ring of Honor. **Special Achievements:** Won the Republican Primary with 84.1 Percent of the Vote; TV Series: Brother's Keeper. **Business Addr:** Politician, Peter Boulware Campaign, 443 E Col Ave, Tallahassee, FL 32301, **Business Phone:** (850)668-5808.

**BOUQUETT, TAMARA TUNIE.** See TUNIE, TAMARA RENEE.

**BOURDEAU, LUDMYA.** See LOVE, MIA.

**BOURNE, DOUGLAS.** See DOUG, DOUG E.

### BOURNE, JUDITH LOUISE
Lawyer, association executive. **Personal:** Born Jul 2, 1945, New York, NY; daughter of Gwendolyn Samuel and St Clair T. **Educ:** Cornell Univ, BA, Eng, 1966; NY Univ Law Sch, JD, 1972, LLM, int law, 1973. **Career:** NY Univ Clin Learning, com asst, 1966-67; NYC Human Resources Admin, specasst admin, 1967-68; NYC Neighborhood Youth Corps, spec consult dir summer progs, 1968; Bd Fundament Educ, prog assoc admin liaison tech training, 1968-69; Nat Coun Crime & Deliquency, legal intern, 1970-71; NY State Spec Comn Attica, ed staff, 1972; NY Univ Sch Continuing Educ, instr, 1973; Emergency Land Fund, SC state, coord, 1974; pvt pract atty, 1974-77, 1982-; Off Fed Pub Defender, asst fed pub defender, 1977-81; Int Criminal Tribunal Rwanda, lead defense coun, 1998-2000; Judith L. Bourne, atty, 1982-2003; Bourne Law Off, PLLC, atty, currently. **Orgs:** Nat Conf Black Lawyers, 1973-; Int Affairs Task Force, SC State Dir, 1973-76; Jr fel NY Univ, Ctr Int Studies, 1972-73; Nat co-chair, 1976-79; Int Com Inquiry Crimes Racist & Apartheid Regimes Southern Africa, 1976-90; chairperson, Polit Affairs Task Force, 1979-80; VI Bar Asn, 1983, treas, 1984, sec, 1985, mem bd governers, 1987; VI Bar Asn; Almeric L Christian Lawyers Asn; Caribbean Develop Coalition; chair, VI Anti-Apartheid Com, 1985-; sec, bd mem, United Way St Thomas & St John, 1987-91; bd dir, Barbados Asn St Thomas-St John, 1995-97; pres, Interfaith Coalition St Thomas/St John, 1996-97; bd mem, UN Asn, VI, 1993-, vpres, 1995-97, pres, 1998-; Nat Conf Black Lawyers; Int Asn Dem Lawyers. **Honors/Awds:** Outstanding Young Women of America, 1976. **Business Addr:** Attorney, The Bourne Law Office PLLC, 19 Norre Gade, St. Thomas00804, **Business Phone:** (340)776-1270.

### BOUTTE, ERNEST JOHN
Executive, chief executive officer, president (organization). **Personal:** Born Aug 18, 1943, Salinas, CA; son of Joseph Adbon (deceased) and Rose Ann Broussard; married Eleanor Rojas; children: Mark Joseph & Marlo Shay. **Educ:** Hartnell Col, Salinas, CA, AS, elec engineering, 1973; Univ San Francisco, San Francisco, CA, BS, bus mgt, 1983; Fresno State Univ, Fresno, CA, indust tech, 1986; Univ Idaho, Moscow, ID, Grad, exec degree prog, mgt, econs, 1989; Harvard Bus Sch, MBA, 1994. **Career:** Executive (retired); Pac Gas & Elec Co, div gen mgr, 1990-93, region dir, 1993-2004; EEEnterprises LLC, pres & chief exec officer, 2005-. **Orgs:** Pac Coast Employee Asn, 1965-; assoc mem, Pac Coast Elec Asn, 1978-; assoc mem, Am Mgt Asn, 1983-; life mem, Hisp Employee Asn, 1985; assoc mem, Am Blacks Energy, 1988-; life mem, Black Employee Asn, 1991. **Home Addr:** 999 Marshall Ave, Vacaville, CA 95688, **Home Phone:** (707)451-7332. **Business Addr:** President, Chief Executive Oficer, PACIFIC GAS & ELECTRIC CO, 4040 West Lane, Stockton, CA 95204.

### BOUTTE, MARC ANTHONY
Football player. **Personal:** Born Jul 25, 1969, Lake Charles, LA; married Tananjalyn. **Educ:** La State Univ. **Career:** Football player (retired); Los Angeles Rams, defensive tackle & left defensive tackle, 1992-93; Wash Redskins, defensive tackle & right defensive tackle, 1994-99. **Home Addr:** 906 Derby Lane, Missouri City, TX 77489-3260, **Home Phone:** (281)416-0265.

### BOUTTE, RHONDA
Artist. **Career:** Kitchen Dog Theater, artistic assoc, currently. **Orgs:** Kitchen Dog Theater Co; Undermain Theatre. **Business Addr:** Artistic Associate, Kitchen Dog Theater Co, 3120 McKinney Ave, Dallas, TX 75204, **Business Phone:** (214)953-1055.

### BOWDEN, JOSEPH TARROD, III (JOE TARROD BOWDEN, III)
Football player, football coach. **Personal:** Born Feb 25, 1970, Dallas, TX; married Malika; children: Sydney, Jaylon & Cheyenne. **Educ:** Univ Okla, commun; Alcorn State Univ, grad. **Career:** Football player (retired), football coach; Houston Oilers, 1992, right linebacker, 1993, 1995, linebacker, 1994, left linebacker, 1996; Tenn Oilers, left linebacker, 1997, mid linebacker, 1998; Tenn Titans, linebacker, 1999; Dallas Cowboys, linebacker, 2000; Scottish Claymores, intern coach, 2004; Buffalo Bills training camp, coach, 2004; Hamburg Sea Devils, defensiveasst, 2005; Alma Mater, Alcorn State Univ, Asst Football Coach, 2006; Okla City high schs, coach, 2008-11; Mt St. Mary High Sch, coach, 2008-11; Edmond Santa Fe High Sch, coach, 2008-11; Univ Cent Okla, sec coach, currently; Nat Football League, St. Louis Rams, linebacker coach, currently; San Francisco 49ers, inside linebackers coach, 2016-. **Honors/Awds:** All-American; Super Bowl. **Special Achievements:** Films: 1999 AFC Championship Game, 2000; Super Bowl XXXIV, 2000. **Business Addr:** Linebacker Coach, National Football League St. Louis Rams, 1 Rams Way, St. Louis, MO 63045, **Business Phone:** (314)982-7267.

### BOWDEN, DR. REGINA GEORGE
Educator. **Personal:** Born Mar 14, 1947, Durham, NC; daughter of Reginald C; children: Merris. **Educ:** Tenn State Univ, BS, sociol, 1968; NC Cent Univ, MA, sociol, 1972; NC A & T State Univ, MS, educ admin, 1977; NC State Univ, EdD, sociol/educ, 1989; Duke Univ, EdD, sociol/educ. **Career:** Shaw Univ, prof sociol, educ, assoc prof, dir, SociaL studies, 1990-2000; NC State Univ, Sch Educ, vis prof; Duke Univ, Focus Interdisciplinary Progs, Durham, Nc, vis prof; Syracuse Univ, Syracuse, New York, vis prof; Costa Rica Durham Pub Schs, Durham, Nc, prog coordr; Nc Cent Univ, Dept Human Sci, Durham, Nc, vis prof; Bennett Col, Greensboro, Nc, Field Instructions Coord & monitored field placement internships, dir, dept social sci; Elon Col, Elon, Nc, sociol instr; NC Univ, teacher educ liaison, vis prof, 1997-2003; NC A & T State Univ, sociol instr; Rockingham Community Col, Rockingham, Nc, Human Resource Develop, dir; Holloway Neighborhood Achievement Sch, pres, owner, 2003-; Publications: "The Effectiveness of Volunteers in Community Agencies", 1971; "Improving Minority Students: Professional Socialization Through Off-Campus Education Opportunities", 1983; "Black Owned Land Loss in North Carolina: Structural and Social Change", 1987; "Mentor Program for Teen Mothers", Department of Public Instruction Journal", 1988; "Teen Mothers", 1993; "Passing on the Culture: Poverty, Immigration and the Affect of African-Caribbean Families in Limon Province, Costa Rica", 1997. **Orgs:** Pres, black caucus, Southern Sociol Soc, 1972-, chair; Nat Sch Bd Asn, 1995-; Urban Coun Bd Educ, 1995-; Delta Sigma Theta; Pi Gamma Mu; Girlfriends Inc; vice chair, Durham County Bd Comnrs; Durham Pub Schs Bd Edu; Nat Social Sci Hon Socs; Nat Educr Asn; Am Sociol Asn; Nc Sociol Asn; pres, fac senate, Shaw Univ; chmn, Small Cols Sociol; bd mem, Contemp Sociol J. **Home Addr:** 232 Monticello Ave, Durham, NC 27707-3911, **Home Phone:** (919)490-1294. **Business Addr:** Owner, President, Holloway Neighborhood Achievement School, 405 Canal St, Durham, NC 27707.

### BOWDOIN, ROBERT E.
Executive. **Personal:** Born May 4, 1929, Los Angeles, CA; son of Alva Sherry and Vivian (Kochinsky); married Joan Merdith Howell; children: Kimberly J, Robert G & Wendy M. **Educ:** Univ Calif, Los Angeles, BS, 1951; Univ Calif, cert real estate, 1956. **Career:** Family Savings & Loan Asn, exec vpes, pres & chief exec officer, 1973-; Family Develop Corp Trustee Pitzer Col, Claremont, Calif, 1980-; Systs Planning Corp, Diversified Appraisal Corp, 1987-; Pasadena Redevel Agy, dep adminstr tech, serv redevel mgr; Bowdin Neal & Weathers, fedr; Fairway Escrow Co, LA, co-owner & mgr; Watts Savings & Loan, real estate appraiser, loan officer & escrow officer; Ginge Inc. **Orgs:** Pres, Am Savings & Loan League, 1981; bd mem, United Way; Nat Archit Engr Firm; Brotherhood Crusade; Altadna Lib Bd; bd mem, dir, Calif Savings & Loan League; US Savings & Loan League. **Home Addr:** 3631 N Canon Blvd, Altadena, CA 91001, **Home Phone:** (626)398-0758. **Business Addr:** President, Chief Executive Officer, Family Savings & Loan Association, 3683 Crenshaw Blvd, Los Angeles, CA 90016, **Business Phone:** (213)295-3381.

### BOWE, RIDDICK LAMONT (BIG DADDY)
Boxer. **Personal:** Born Oct 8, 1967, Brooklyn, NY; son of Dorothy; married Judy; children: 5; married Terri Blakney. **Career:** Heavyweight boxer (retired); US Marine Corps; Mixed Martial Arts, boxer. **Honors/Awds:** New York Golden Gloves Championship, 1984; The 178lb Novice Championship, 1985; 178lb Open Championship, 1986; Super Heavyweight Open Championship, 1987-88; Super Heavyweight Silver Medalist, Seoul Olympic Games, 1988; Heavyweight Boxing Champion, World Boxing Asn & Int Boxing Fedn, 1992-93; Heavyweight Boxing Champion, World Boxing Coun, 1992; Ring Fighter of the Year, 1992; World Heavyweight Championship, World Boxing Orgn, 1992-93, 1995-96; Seoul, Olympic medal record, Super Heavyweight, 1998. **Special Achievements:** Guest appearance on The Fresh Prince of Bel Air; Giant Steps Award; Filmography: Death of a Dynasty, 2003.

### BOWE-QUICK, DR. MARIE
School principal. **Educ:** DC Teachers Col, BS, 1974; Univ Md, MA, 1975; George Washington Univ, ESOL cert, 1990; PhD, 1992. **Career:** Godwin Mid Sch, asst prin, 1974-90; Prince William County, Godwin Mid Sch, spec educ adminr, summer sch prin, 1997; Parkside Mid Sch, prin, 1998-. **Home Addr:** 12306 Kings Valley Ct, Mitchellville, MD 20721-1924, **Home Phone:** (301)390-7234. **Business Addr:** Principal, Parkside Middle School, 8602 Mathis Ave, Manassas, VA 20110, **Business Phone:** (703)361-3106.

### BOWEN, DR. BLANNIE E.
Educator. **Personal:** Born Apr 26, 1953, Wilmington, NC; son of Herman Thomas and Beulah Mae Bryant; married Cathy Faulcon; children: Marcus & Douglas. **Educ:** NC Agr & Tech State Univ, Greensboro, NC, BS, agr educ, 1974, MS, agr educ, 1976; Ohio State Univ, Columbus, OH, PhD, agr educ, 1980. **Career:** Miss State Univ, asst assoc prof, 1980-85; Ohio State Univ, Columbus, OH, assoc prof, 1985-88; Penn State Univ, Univ Pk, PA, Grad Sch, assoc dean & sr fac mentor; Penn State Univ, Univ Pk, PA, C Lee Rumberger chair Agr, 1988-2004, assoc dean & sr fac mentor, grad sch, 1996-98, dept agr & exten educ, head, agr & exten educ col agr sci, 1998-2004, prof, vice provost acad affairs, 2004-, prof agr & exten educ, 2004-. **Orgs:** Ed, Ag Educ Mag, 1986-88; fac mem, Penn State Univ, 1988; Univ Rep, Nat Coun Agr Educ, 1990-92; ed bd, Jour Appl Commun, 1990-92; ed bd, Jour Voc & Tech Educ, 1990-95; nat secy, Minorities Agr & Related Sci, 1990-91; Comt Instnl Coop; Big Ten Conf. **Home Addr:** 2459 Chatham Ct, State College, PA 16803-2400, **Home Phone:** (814)237-5131. **Business Addr:** Vice Provost for Academic Affairs, Pennsylvania State University, 201 Old Main, University Park, PA 16802, **Business Phone:** (814)863-7494.

### BOWEN, BRUCE, JR.
Basketball executive, business owner, basketball player. **Personal:** Born Jun 14, 1971, Merced, CA; son of Bruce Sr and Dietra Campbell; married Yardley Barbon; children: Ojani & Ozmel. **Educ:** Cal State Fullerton, attended 1993, commun, 2006. **Career:** Basketball player (retired), analyst, business owner; Le Harve, France, 1993-94; Evreux, 1994-95; Ft Wayne Fury, Continental Basketball Asn, 1995; Rockford Lightning, Continental Basketball Asn, 1995-96, 1997; Besaccon, France, 1996-97; Miami Heat, forward, small forward, 1996-97, 2000-01; Boston Celtics, small forward, 1997-99; Philadelphia 76ers, small forward, 1999-2000; San Antonio Spurs, small forward, 2001-09; Entertainment & Sports Programming Network, Nat Basketball Asn, analyst, currently; Yardley's Salon & Spa, owner, currently. **Orgs:** H-E-B; Spurs Found; founder & pres, Bruce Bowen Found, currently. **Honors/Awds:** All-Defensive hons; NBA champion, 2003, 2005, 2007; NBA Defensive Player of the Year, 2005-06; Hall of Fame, Calif State Univ-Fullerton Titan Athletics, 2011. **Home Addr:** 18847 Calle Cierra, San Antonio, TX 78258-4032. **Business Addr:** Owner, Yardley's Salon & Spa, 16535 Huebner Rd, San Antonio, TX 78248, **Business Phone:** (210)479-9300.

### BOWEN, GEORGE WALTER
Educator. **Personal:** Born Dec 13, 1946, Council, NC; son of Estelle and Jesse W. **Educ:** Los Angeles, Valley Col, AA, criminal justice, 1974; Calif State Univ, Los Angeles, BS, criminal law, 1975, MS, pub admin, 1979. **Career:** Rochester City Sch Dist, managing dir, 1999-2001; Savannah-Chatham Co Pub Schs, dep interim supt, coodr, 2001-06, actg supt schs, 2004-06; Independent Educ & Bus, self employed; proj mgt & sch admin, consult. **Orgs:** Air Force Asn, 1978-; Armed Froces Commun Electronics Asn, 1978-; Chatham County ct house renovation proj, Chatham County. **Home Addr:** 46 Ramsgate Rd, Savannah, GA 31419, **Home Phone:** (912)920-1977.

### BOWEN, DR. RAYMOND COBB
College administrator, scientist. **Personal:** Born Sep 19, 1934, New Haven, CT; son of Raymond Curtis Sr and Lucille Cobb; married Joan deMarro Massalena; children: Raymond C III, Rebecca M, Ruth J & Rachel R. **Educ:** Univ Conn, BA, zool, 1956, PhD, parasitol & biochem, 1966; Univ New Mex, MS, biol, 1962. **Career:** College administrator (retired); Ohio Wesleyan Univ, post doctoral, 1966-67; Univ Ill, post doctoral, 1966-67; Cleveland State Univ, prof biol, 1968, asst pres & dean develop progs, 1968-71; City Univ New York, LaGuardia Community Col, assoc prof nat scis, 1971, assoc dean fac, 1971, dean acad affairs, 1973, pres & prof natural & appl sci, 1989-99; Community Col, Baltimore, vpres acad affairs & stud affairs, 1975-82; Shelby State Community Col, pres, 1982-89; Morgan State Univ Grad Sch, vis prof, 1999. **Orgs:** ACE, AACC, 1981; bd dir, SACJC, 1985; bd trustee, Leadership Memphis, 1985; bd dir, United Way, 1985; vice chmn & bd dir, Bio-Med Res Zone, 1985; Phelps-Stokes Fund; Am Coun Educ. **Home Addr:** 6318 Winner Ave, Baltimore, MD 21215-3119, **Home Phone:** (410)764-0896.

### BOWEN, RICHARD, JR.
Executive, educator, real estate executive. **Personal:** Born Apr 20, 1942, Colp, IL; son of Richard and Helen; married Cleatia B Rafe; children: Gerald & Chantel. **Educ:** VTI Southern Ill Univ, AA, 1966; Southern Ill Univ, BS, 1969; Purdue Univ, MS, 1971. **Career:** Restaurant Bar, owner, 1964-71; Purdue Univ, teaching asst, 1969-71; Lincoln Land Community Col, prof, 1971-78, div chmn, 1978-, bus, pub & human serv chair; Pillsbury Mills, mgt consult, 1973-75; real estate sales mgr, 1985. **Orgs:** Secy, Chrysler Customer Satisfaction Bd, 1980-87; training officer, Small Bus Admin, 1982-85, suprv comn, 1984-85; vpres, Sangamon Sch Credit Union; prog chmn, Breakfast Optimist Club, 1985; Frontiers Int Springfield Club; chair, bd, Sangamon Schs Credit Union. **Home Addr:** 26 Vivian Lane, Springfield, IL 62712-8924, **Home Phone:** (217)529-0767. **Business Addr:** Board of Member, Frontiers International Springfield Club, PO Box 3522, Springfield, IL 62708, **Business Phone:** (217)793-3505.

### BOWENS, GREGORY JOHN
Government official. **Personal:** Born Jan 7, 1965, Detroit, MI; son of Italee M; married Jeannine P; children: Langston & Zora. **Educ:** Morehouse Col, attended 1987; Wayne State Univ, attended 1992. **Career:** Automotive News, spec corresp, 1990-91; Detroit Free Press, reporter, 1991; Bus Week Mag, spec corresp, 1991-93; Cong Quarter-

ly Mag, reporter & journalist, 1993-94; Flint Jour, reporter, 1994-95; Detroit News, reporter, 1995; Detroit Housing Comn, consult-media rels, 1996; Mayor's off, deputy pres secy, 1996, dir media rels & pub affairs, 1998, press secy, 1999; Shaun Wilson & Assocs, vpres media rels & pub affairs; WilsonBowens Public Relations & Marketing, partner, currently. **Orgs:** Treas, Nat Asn Black Journalists, 1993-2001, sgt at arms, 1997-. **Home Addr:** 5074 Grayton St, Detroit, MI 48224, **Home Phone:** (313)642-1706. **Business Addr:** Vice President of Media Relations & Public Affairs, WilsonBowens Public Relations & Marketing, Troy, MI 48084, **Business Phone:** (248)273-8900.

## BOWENS, DR. JOHNNY WESLEY

Educator. **Personal:** Born Jun 2, 1946, Jacksonville, FL; married Monica Darlene Lewis; children: Torrence, Derick & Omari. **Educ:** Dillard Univ, BA, sociol, 1968; Univ Ariz, MEd, educ admin, 1973; Union Inst, PhD, community develop, 1978. **Career:** Pima Community Col, dir stud activ, 1970-86, coord financial aid, 1986-01; Univ Ariz, Africana Studies Prog, adj lectr, lectr, 2004-. **Orgs:** Allocation chair, Tucson United Way, 1985-; vpres, Tucson Br Nat Asn Advan Colored People, 1985-87. **Home Addr:** 1932 W Calle Armenta, Tucson, AZ 85745, **Home Phone:** (520)622-4072. **Business Addr:** Lecturer, The University of Arizona, 225 Learning Serv Bldg, Tucson, AZ 85721-0105, **Business Phone:** (520)621-3755.

## BOWENS, TIMOTHY L.

Football player. **Personal:** Born Feb 7, 1973, Okolona, MS; children: Camrin Deion. **Educ:** Miss State Univ. **Career:** Football player (retired); Miami Dolphins, left defensive tackle, 1994-95, 1997-2004, right defensive tackle, 1996, defensive tackle, 1999-2000. **Honors/Awds:** NFL Defensive Rookie of the Year, Assoc Press & Pro Football Weekly, 1994; Pro Bowl, 1998, 2002.

## BOWER, DR. BEVERLY L.

Educator. **Personal:** Born Sep 10, 1951, Washington, DC; daughter of James T Johnson and Bettylou C Johnson; married Jack R Jr. **Educ:** Univ Kans, BS, educ, 1973; Emporia State Univ, MLS, 1980; Fla State Univ, PhD, 1992. **Career:** Lansing Jr High Sch, reading teacher, 1973-74; Chillicothe High Sch, Fr & Eng teacher, 1974-75; Dept Defense Dependent Schs, Fr & Eng teacher, 1975-80; Pensacola Jr Col, librn, 1980-84, dir libr serv, 1985-92; Fla State Univ, fel, 1990-91; Univ SC, Col Educ, asst prof, 1993-96; Fla State Univ, Col Educ, Dept Educ Leadership & Policy Studies, from asst prof to assoc prof, 1997-2008, Hardee Ctr Women Higher Educ, dir, 2002-04, assoc dept chmn, 2003-04, prog coordr, 2005-07; Univ N Tex, Dept Coun & Higher Educ, dir, Don A Buchholz Endowed Chair & prof, 2008-. **Orgs:** Secy, W Fla Libr Asn, 1981-83; ALA-JMRT Minorities Recruitment Comn, 1982-83; community col caucus chmn & chmn elect, Fla Libr Asn, 1986-88; regional dir, Fla Asn Community Cols, 1987, pres, 1988; Phi Kappa Phi; bd dir, YWCA Pensacola, 1989-91; founding chap pres, Am Asn Women Community Cols, 1990-96; ASHE, 1991-; Am Educ Res Asn, 1994-; bd gov, Fla State Univ Hardee Ctr, 1997-2002, exec dir, 2003-, Fac Sen, 2003-05; bd mem; United Fac Fla, 2001-08; exec dir, Coun Study Community Cols, 2013-. **Home Addr:** 1500 Palo Verde Dr, Denton, TX 76210. **Business Addr:** Professor, Director, University of North Texas, 1155 Union Cir Suite 305039, Denton, TX 76203-5017, **Business Phone:** (940)369-7112.

## BOWERS, DOROTHY. See COLLINS, DOROTHY.

## BOWERS, GEORGE D.

Executive director. **Career:** Fed Maritime Comn, Off Info Resources Mgt, head, dir, 2003. **Business Addr:** Director, Federal Maritime Commission, 800 N Capital St NW, Washington, DC 20573, **Business Phone:** (202)523-5835.

## BOWERS, ESQ. GWENDOLYN RUTH

Lawyer. **Educ:** Ohio State Univ, BSBA; Univ Dayton Sch Law, JD. **Career:** Gwendolyn R Bowers Co LPA, atty, currently. **Orgs:** Ohio State Bar Asn. **Business Addr:** Attorney, Gwendolyn R Bowers Co LPA, 1712 W 3rd St, Dayton, OH 45407-6721, **Business Phone:** (937)461-9297.

## BOWERS, LAUREN JOYNER. See JOYNER, LAUREN CELESTE.

## BOWERS, DR. MIRION PERRY

Physician. **Personal:** Born Aug 25, 1935, Bascom, FL; married Geraldine Janis Nixon; children: Jasmine Anusha, Mirion Perry Jr, Jarvis Andrew & Jeryl Anthony. **Educ:** Fla A&M Univ, Tallahassee, BA, 1957; Meharry Med Col, Nashville, MD, 1963. **Career:** Ireland Army Comm Hosp, internship, 1964; Walson AUS Hosp, resident otolaryngol, 1966; Walter Reed Army Med Ctr, resident Otolaryngol, 1969; Univ Calif Los Angeles, Sch Med, Dept Surg, asst prof, 1972-73; Martin Luther King Jr Gen Hosp, Div Otolaryngol, Charles R Drew Post Grad Med Sch, asst prof & chief, 1972-73; Univ Calif Los Angeles, Sch Med, Dept Head-Neck Surg, asst clin prof, 1973-; Good Samaritan Hosp, chmn otolaryngol, 1976-, secy & treas med staff, 1976-, secy operating room comt, 1986-, bd trustee, 1989-, mem exec comt, 1989-, pres & chief exec officer, currently; Univ SC Sch Med, Dept Otolaryngol, Head & Neck, clin profile; pvt pract physician. **Orgs:** Taunus Med Soc Frankfurt, Ger, 1969-72; fel Am Acad Ophthalmol & Otolaryngol, 1970-; Am Col Surgeons, 1972-; Am Med Asn, 1972-; Nat Med Asn, 1973-; Charles R Drew Med Soc, 1973-; chmn, Otolaryngol Sect, Calif Med Ctr, 1982-85; bd dir, Fla A&M Found, 1989-; bd dir, City Nat Bank, Beverly Hills, CA, 1994-; bd dir, Braille Inst, CA, 1995-; Am Coun Otolaryngol; bd dir, Los Angeles Chap, Am Cancer Soc; Los Angeles City Med Asn; Soc Upper Tenth, Meharry Med Col. **Special Achievements:** Numerous publications. **Home Addr:** 5250 W 2nd St, Los Angeles, CA 90004-1057, **Home Phone:** (323)933-7386. **Business Addr:** Otolaryngologist, Good Samaritan Hospital, 1245 Wilshire Blvd Suite 801, Los Angeles, CA 90017-4805, **Business Phone:** (213)977-9661.

## BOWIE, DR. JANICE

College teacher, educator. **Educ:** Shaw Univ, BS, 1974; Univ NC, Chapel Hill, MPH, 1986; Johns Hopkins Univ Sch Pub Health, PhD, 1997. **Career:** Va Dept Health, dir chronic discontrol progs; Johns Hopkins Univ, Dept Health, Behav & Soc, assoc prof, currently. **Orgs:** Susan G Komen Found; chair, Ctr community adv comt. **Business Addr:** Associate Professor, Johns Hopkins University, 624 N Broadway St Hampton House Suite 743, Baltimore, MD 21205, **Business Phone:** (410)614-6119.

## BOWIE, LARRY DARNELL, JR.

Football player. **Personal:** Born Mar 21, 1973, Anniston, AL. **Educ:** Northeastern Okla A & M Col; Univ Ga. **Career:** Football player (retired); Wash Redskins, 1996, fullback, 1997, running back, 1998, 1999; St Louis Rams, 2001.

## BOWIE, OLIVER WENDELL

Certified public accountant. **Personal:** Born Jun 25, 1947, Detroit, MI; son of Ulvene Shaw; married Penelope Ann Jackson; children: Stephanie, Traci & Oliver II. **Educ:** Eastern Mich Univ, BBA, 1972; Elon Col, MBA, 1994; CPA. **Career:** Mich Dept Treas, revenue agt, 1970-73; Coopers & Lybrand, sr acct, 1973-75; Nat Bank Detroit, audit mgr, 1975-77; Wayne Co Community Col, dir acct, 1977-79; Garrett Sullivan Davenport Bowie & Grant, vpres, 1980-88; Bowie Oliver CPA, sole proprietor, 1988-94, pres, 1994-. **Orgs:** Am Inst CPA, 1975, Mich Asn CPA, 1975, NC Asn CPA, 1985, Greensboro W-S HP Airport Authority, 1985-; treas & pres, Triad Sickle Cell Found, 1985; pres, Trial Nat Asn Black Acct, 1986-; chmn, L Richardson Hosp, 1986; treas, Greensboro Br, Nat Asn Advan Colored People, 1993. **Honors/Awds:** Certificate of Appprieciation, Nat Asn Black Acct, 1977. **Home Addr:** 318 W Montcastle Dr, Greensboro, NC 27406-5827, **Home Phone:** (336)274-7077. **Business Addr:** Owner, Bowie Oliver CPA, 1014 Homeland Ave Suite 102, Greensboro, NC 27405, **Business Phone:** (336)273-9461.

## BOWIE, DR. STAN L.

Educator. **Educ:** Shippensburg Univ Pa, BA, 1976; Atlanta Univ, MSW; Barry Univ, PhD. **Career:** Univ Tenn, Col Social Work, assoc prof, currently. **Business Addr:** Associate Professor, University Tennessee, 326 Henson Hall 1618 Cumberland Ave, Knoxville, TN 37996-3333, **Business Phone:** (865)974-0692.

## BOWIE, WILLETTE

Executive, executive director. **Personal:** Born Jul 24, 1949, Memphis, TN; daughter of John and Callie Jenkins. **Educ:** Alverno Col, BA, 1984; Cardinal Stritch Col, MS, 1996. **Career:** Northwestern Mutual, employee rels specialist, 1983-91, employee rels off, 1991-95, dir employee rels, 1995-. **Orgs:** Mem comt, Nat Asn Advan Colored People, Milwaukee Br; Leadership Forum, 1997-; Financial Servs Group, 1983-; Human Resources Mgt Asn, 1983-; Top Ladies Distinction, 1986-; Alpha Kappa Alpha Soc, 1986-; Zonta Club Milwaukee, 1991-; Eta Phi Beta Soc, 1986-. **Home Addr:** 10129 N Brookdale Dr, Mequon, WI 53092. **Business Addr:** Director, Chief Negotiator, Northwestern Mutual Life Insurance Co, 720 E Wis Ave, Milwaukee, WI 53202, **Business Phone:** (414)271-1444.

## BOWLES, BARBARA LANDERS

Executive. **Personal:** Born Sep 17, 1947, Nashville, TN; married Earl S; children: Terrence Earl. **Educ:** Fisk Univ, BA, math, 1968; Univ Chicago Grad Sch Bus, MBA, finance, 1971; CFA Designation, attended 1977. **Career:** First Nat Bank Chicago, trust officer, 1974-77, asst vpres, 1977-80, vpres, 1980-81; Beatrice Co, asst vpres, 1981-84; Kraft Inc, vpres investr rels, 1984-89; Black & Decker Corp, bd dir, 1993-2010; Kenwood Group Inc, founder, pres, 1989-2000, chief exec officer, 1989-2005, chmn; Wis Energy Corp, pres, chmn, corp bd mem, 1998-; Dollar Gen Corp, dir, chm finance comt, 2000-; Ga-Pac LLC, dir, 2000; Profit Investment Mgt, vice chmn, 2005-07; Landers Bowles Family Found, pres, 2008-; Ft James Corp, dir; Hyde Pk Bank, bd dir; Wis Gas LLC, dir. **Orgs:** Pres, Chicago Fisk Alumni Asn, 1983-85; corp bd mem, Hospira Inc, 2008-; bd mem, Mus Sci & Indust, 2010-; chair bd trustee, Fisk Univ, 2013-; bd dir, Ga-Pac Corp; bd dir, Trust Co Chicago; bd dir, Chicago Urban League; Alpha Kappa Alpha Sorority; bd mem, C Mem Hosp Chicago; bd dir, C's Memorial Hosp; Univ Chicago Booth Sch Bus. **Special Achievements:** Top 100 Black Business & Professional Women, Black Book Delta Sigma, 1985; First African American female equity manager in Chicago; First African American woman to launch a mutual fund; The first African American woman to serve as vice president in First National Bank. **Home Addr:** 5020 S Ellis Ave, Chicago, IL 60615, **Home Phone:** (773)924-1913. **Business Addr:** Corporate Board Member, Wisconsin Energy Corp, 231 W Michigan St, Milwaukee, WI 53203, **Business Phone:** (414)221-2345.

## BOWLES, HOWARD ROOSEVELT

City manager. **Personal:** Born Oct 14, 1932, Roselle, NJ. **Career:** Parson Inst; Seton Hall Univ City Home Delivery Wash Post, mgr, 1977-2008; Baltimore News-Am, city mgr; Newark Eve News, dist mgr; Var Clg, auto salesman, sales mgr asst panel rep. **Orgs:** Interstate Circulation Mgrs Asn; bd dir, Wash Bus J, Jr Achievement, 2002-; commun chair, bd dir, Am Dent Group Orgn, 2015-; bd pres, Safe Haven Ministries. **Honors/Awds:** Art Award, 32nd Degree Mason Prince Hall F&AM; Mgt & Prod Awards. **Home Addr:** 1409 Varnum St NW, Washington, DC 20011. **Business Addr:** Board of Director, Communications Chair, American Dental Group Organization, 1775 Eye St NW Suite, Washington, DC 20006.

## BOWLES, DR. JAMES HAROLD, SR.

Physician. **Personal:** Born Jun 12, 1921, Goochland, VA; married Aretha Melton; children: Ruth Quarles, Jacqueline B Dandridge & James Jr. **Educ:** Va Union Univ, BS, 1948; Meharry Med Sch, MD, 1952. **Career:** Physician (retired); Georgetown Univ Hosp, Wash Hosp Ctr, resident, 1952-53; Bowles & Short MD, pvt practr, family pract; Intermediate Sunday Sch Class, teacher. **Orgs:** Vpres & pres, Goochland Recreational Ctr, 1961-81; Recognition Negro Emancipation Orgn, Louisa & Adjacent Counties, 1979; vice chmn, Goochland City Bd Supervisors; Nat Asn Advan Colored People, Goochland; exec bd, Va Asn Counties; treas, Goochland Voters League; Goochland Dem Comt; vpres, bd dir, Citizen Develop Corp; Hazardous Waste Siting Comn Va; Am Legion; Goochland City Social Serv Bd; bd dir, Goochland Br Red Cross; Caledonia Lodge 240 F&HA; Alpha Phi Alpha; pres & trustee bd, Emmaus Baptist Church; bd dir, Capital Area Agency Aging; bd dir, Sr Connections. **Honors/Awds:** Outstanding Leadership, Am Red Cross, 1969; Valuable Citizen, Goochland NAACP, 1978; Outstanding Serv, Goochland Recreational Ctr, 1979; Appreciation, Beulah Baptist Sunday Sch Conv, 1979; Appreciation, Am Heart Asn Va Affil, 1982; 23rd September proclaimed as Dr James H Bowles Sr Day. **Business Addr:** Physician, Bowles & Short MDs, 2884 Sand Hook Rd, Sandy Hook, VA 23153, **Business Phone:** (804)556-3172.

## BOWLES, JOYCE GERMAINE

Educator, school administrator. **Personal:** Born May 16, 1942, Washington, DC; daughter of Harvey Johnson and Mary Gaines; married Robert L Jr; children: Lee Robert. **Educ:** Univ Evansville, BS, nursing, 1964; Univ Md, Baltimore, MSN, 1972, College Park, PhD, 1978. **Career:** Army Nurse Corps, progressive leadership nursing, 1962-84; Bowie State Univ, Dept Nursing, chairperson, 1985-94, prof nursing, dean, sch prof studies. **Orgs:** Chi Eta Phi Nursing Sorority, Alpha Chap, 1972-; Nat League Nursing, 1974-; Sigma ta Tau Nursing Soc, Pi Chap, 1974-; first vpres, MAR League Nursing, Dist 6, 1989-91; pres, Top Ladies Distinction, Potomac Chap, 1988-92; Asn Black Nursing Fac, pres, 1996-98, nominating comt chair, souvenir prog bk chair, 1993; FACE Fel, Kellog Found, 1992-; rev bd, J ABNF, 1992-. **Home Addr:** 9 Potomac Sch Ct, Potomac, MD 20854, **Home Phone:** (301)365-2218. **Business Addr:** Dean of Professional Studies, Bowie State University, 14000 Jericho Pk Rd, Bowie, MD 20715-9465, **Business Phone:** (301)860-4705.

## BOWLING, LYSIA HUNTINGTON

Lawyer. **Personal:** children: Malik, Belkis, Fabiola, Killian & Cullin. **Educ:** Yale Univ, BA, polit sci, BA, latin Am, 1976; Univ Va Law Sch, JD, 1979. **Career:** State Tex, atty; State Fla, atty; Corp Tax Policy, Comptroller Pub Accts, staff atty; Tex Gen Land Off, Energy Resources Div, staff atty; City Austin, Tex, chief prosecuting atty; Tex Dept Ins, Agt Licensing Div, staff atty; Tex Off Atty Gen, Criminal Prosecuting Div, asst atty gen; City Harlington Tex, city atty; City Temple Tex, city atty, chief prosecutor & legal police adv; City Miami, Miami Dade State Attys Off, asst state atty; Off City Atty, Miami Police Dept, police legal adv, 2008; Miami-Dade Col, Sch Justice, law enforcement trainer & fac criminal justice prog; atty; City of San Angelo, atty, 2009-15; City of Pensacola, City Atty, 2015-. **Orgs:** Ebony Cult Soc; State Bar Tex; Tex City Atty's Asn; Austin Black Lawyers Asn; Tex Police Asn; Int Munic Lawyers Asn; pres, March Dimes; pres, Optimist Club; chmn, Ebony Cult Forum; Nat Asn Advan Colored People San Angelo Chap; Tom Green County Bar Asn; Soc Human Resource Mgt. **Honors/Awds:** Appreciation Award, Temple Police Dept, 1997; Optimist of the Year, 2000; Leader About Town, Miami Dade Col; Outstanding Black Women in the Legal Profession. **Home Addr:** 2614 Brooklawn, Temple, TX 76502, **Home Phone:** (254)770-0723. **Business Addr:** Attorney, City of Pensacola, 222 W Main St, San Angelo, TX 76903, **Business Phone:** (850)435-1615.

## BOWMAN, BUCK. See BOWMAN, DR. JANET WILSON.

## BOWMAN, DR. JACQUELYNNE JEANETTE (JACQUI BOWMAN)

Lawyer. **Personal:** Born Dec 4, 1955, Chicago, IL; married David Rentsch; children: Atticus David Bowman Rentsch. **Educ:** Univ Chicago, BA, 1976; Antioch Univ Sch Law, JD, 2000. **Career:** W Tenn Legal Servs, staff atty, 1979-84; Greater Boston Legal Servs, sr atty, 1984-87, managing atty, 1987-92, assoc dir, 1997-2000, dep dir, 2000-11, exec dir, 2011-; Mass Law Reform Inst, staff atty, 1992-97; Antioch Univ Sch Law, dep dir, 2000-; Am Bar Asn, Comn Domestic Violence, comnr. **Orgs:** Am Bar Asn, 1979-; Nat Conf Black Lawyers, 1980-; Battered Women's Working Group, 1984-93; vol, Proj Impact, 1984-93; Mass Bar Asn, 1986-; Gender Bias Community, task force dometic violence, 1992-94, juv justice community, 1992-94; Gov Community Domestic Violence, 1993-; bd mem, Mass Advocacy Ctr, 1994-; Mass Black Lawyers, 1995-; Mass Black Women Lawyers Asn, 1997; bd mem, Mgt Info Exchange, 1997-, exec comt, 2000-; bd mem, Mass Advocacy Ctr, Jane Doe Inc, 2000-; Dawe Sch PTO, by-laws chair, exec comn; bd mem, Mass Advocacy Ctr & Domestic Violence. **Honors/Awds:** Silver Key Award, ABA-LSD, 1979; Certificate of Appreciation, EACH, 1982-84; George Edmund Haynes fel, Nat Urban League, 1982-83; Public Service Award, Proj Impact, 1985, 1986; Special Appreciation Award, Diversity Coalition, 1997; Special Recognition, Mass Legal Assistance Corp, 1997; Special Friend Award, Legis Foster C Caucus, 1998; Legislative ocate Award, 1997; Legal Services Award, Mass Bar Asn, 1999-00; Volunteer Recognition, Dawe Sch, 2000. **Home Addr:** 195 Glen Echo Blvd, Stoughton, MA 02072-1068, **Home Phone:** (781)344-9577. **Business Addr:** Executive Director, Greater Boston Legal Services, 197 Friend St, Boston, MA 02114, **Business Phone:** (617)603-1805.

## BOWMAN, DR. JANET WILSON (BUCK BOWMAN)

School administrator, writer, association executive. **Personal:** Born Charleston, WV; daughter of Earl and Roberta; married Richard; children: Karen McAfee, M Earl McAfee, Chris, Cheryl & Patricia. **Educ:** Tuskegee Inst, BS, MS; Univ Calif, Berkeley, PhD, 1973; Univ Ore; Calif State Univ, San Diego. **Career:** Merritt Col, prof; Mars Hill Col, teacher; Univ Calif, seismologist, 1960-73; Carnegie Found, consult, 1972-73; Diablo Valley Col, admin, 1973-85; Compton Col, adr, 1986-94; Univ NC, clin assoc prof educ, 2006; Ashville YWCA, exec dir; auth, currently. **Orgs:** Bd mem, Meridian Nat Bank, 1979; Tuskegee Alumni Asn; UNCF Inter Alumni Coun; United Way Prog Evaluator; Black Women's Leadership Group; MOSTE, Women Target; bd dir, Memorial Mission Found; Kiwanis Int. **Honors/Awds:** George Washington Carver Fellowship; NSF Scholarship; Graduate StudentAssistantship, Univ Calif, Berkeley; Certificate of Appreciation, BusClub,

1988; Certificate of Commendation, Compton Col Bd Trustees, 1988. **Home Addr:** 24 Bevlyn Dr, Asheville, NC 28803, **Home Phone:** (828)684-7555. **Business Addr:** Executive Director, YMCA, 201 Beaverdam Rd, Asheville, NC 28804, **Business Phone:** (828)253-4706.

**BOWMAN, PHILLIP JESS**
Psychologist, educator, association executive. **Personal:** Born Feb 18, 1948, Kensett, AR; married Jacqueline E Creed; children: Phillip & Frederick Dubois. **Educ:** Northern Ariz Univ, BS, 1970; Univ Mich, MA, 1971, EdS, 1973, MA, 1974, PhD, 1977. **Career:** IRRPP, dir; Univ Mich, Inst Social Res, res investr to study dir, Postdoctoral Training Prog Surv Res, dir, Dept Psychol & Afro-Am & African Studies, from lectr to asst prof, 1977-84, Ctr Study Higher & Post sec, prof & founding dir, 2006-, Nat Ctr Inst Diversity, founding dir, 2006-, Inst Social Res Nat Poverty Ctr, fac assoc, 2006-; Northwestern Univ, Dept Human Develop & Social Policy Dept African Am Studies, assoc prof, Inst Policy Res, fac assoc, 1991-2000; Univ Ill, Chicago, prof urban planning & policy African Am Studies, Inst Res Race & Pub Policy, dir, 2000-06. **Orgs:** Am Educ Res Asn; Am Pub Health Asn; Am Psychol Asn; Asn Pub Policy & Mgt; Nat Asn Black Psychol; Nat Coun Family Rel; Soc Res Child Develop; Soc Res Adolescence; Soc Psychol Study Social Issues; adv bd, Inter-Univ Consortium Polit Social Res; adv bd, Ctrs Dis Control Prev; Prog Res Black Am; dir, Summer Acad Workshop; dir, Social-Behav Sci Scholars Prog. **Honors/Awds:** Exceptional Service Award, Ethnicity & Mental Health, 1979; Research Excellence Award, Urban League, 1987; Academic Scholarship Award, Black Stud Psychol Asn, 1993; Charles & Shirley Thomas Award, Am Psychol Asn, 2006. **Business Addr:** Founding Director, Professor, University of Michigan, Rm 3320 3338 Sch Educ Bldg 610 E Univ Ave, Ann Arbor, MI 48109-1259, **Business Phone:** (734)764-6497.

**BOWMAN, VIVIANE. See WINANS, VICKIE.**

**BOWMAN, WILLIAM ALTON**
Military leader, government official. **Personal:** Born Dec 15, 1933, Fayetteville, NC; son of William H (deceased) and Rebecca L Johnson (deceased); married Sylvia I; children: Carol, William A Jr (deceased), Arthur E, Susan Okediadi (deceased) & Brenda Jones. **Educ:** Southeast Cot Col, assoc, human serv, 2000. **Career:** Military leader (retired), govt off; Misle Imports Auto, serv writer, 1976-77; State Dept Rds, mech, 1977; Toms Car Care, mech, 1977-78; US Postal Serv, lett carrier, 1978-79, fleet mgr, 1979-90; Budget Rent Acar, shuttle driver, part time. **Orgs:** Air Force Asn, 1963; Air Force Sergeants, 1976; Nat Asn Fed Ret, 1990; bd mem, Disabled Veterans, store, 1993-; 40 & 8 Voiture 103, box car chr, star chr, 1994-; Va Hosp, vol-patient visitor, 1994; post comdr, Am Legion, 1995-96, dist 15 comdr, 1996-98; Vietnam Veterans, 1995; MADDADS; detachment historian, Sons Am Legion, currently; comdr, Disabled Veterans Chap 7, 2000-. **Home Addr:** 2134 S 48th St, Lincoln, NE 68506-5507, **Home Phone:** (402)489-6447. **Business Addr:** Detachment Historian, Sons of The American Legion, PO Box 5205, Lincoln, NE 68505-0205, **Business Phone:** (402)464-6338.

**BOWNES, FABIEN ALFRANSO**
Football player. **Personal:** Born Feb 29, 1972, Aurora, IL. **Educ:** Western Ill Univ, BS, commun. **Career:** Football player (retired); Chicago Bears, wide receiver, 1995, 1997-98; Seattle Seahawks, wide receiver, 1999-2001. **Orgs:** Bd dir, Heritage YMCA. **Home Addr:** , Aurora, IL.

**BOWRON, ELJAY B.**
Government official, vice president (organization). **Personal:** Born Detroit, MI; married Sandra; children: Brandon. **Educ:** Mich State Univ, BS, criminal justice, 1973; George Washington Univ, Sch Bus, exec develop prog, 1988. **Career:** Detroit Police Dept, officer, 1973; US Secret Serv, var positions, 1974, dir, 1993-97; Us Secret Serv, dir, 1993-; Social Security Admin, sr exec, dep inspector gen; Vance Int Inc, exec vpres, chief operating officer, 1999-; dir, Alpha Protective Serv; isekurity Inc, dir, 2011-. **Orgs:** Int Asn Chiefs Police; TorchStone Global LLC, bd chmn; iJet Travel Intelligence Inc Donna Kaye Drayton; iSekurity, bd dir; Hickey Family Found Bd, mem, 2011-; U.S. Secret Serv, spec advisor. **Business Addr:** Executive Vice President, Chief Operating Officer, Vance International Inc, 5870 Trinity Pkwy Suite 300, Centreville, VA 20120, **Business Phone:** (703)592-1400.

**BOWSER, PROF. BENJAMIN PAUL**
Educator. **Personal:** Born Aug 20, 1946, New York, NY; son of Benjamin J and Nathalia Earle; married K Deborah Whittle; children: Paul. **Educ:** Franklin & Marshall Col, Lancaster, PA, BA, sociol, 1969; Cornell Univ, PhD, sociol, 1976. **Career:** State Univ NY, Binghampton, asst prof, social, 1972-75; Cornell Univ, asst dean grad sch, 1975-82; Western Interstate Commiss Higher Ed, dir minorityed, 1982-84; Univ Santa Clara, dir black stud resources, 1983-85; Stanford Univ, from asst to dir, 1985-87; Eval & Training Network, res dir, 1985-; Calif State Univ, E Bay, Dept Sociol & Social Serv, prof, 1987, emer prof, 1987-, interim dean, 2006-08; Calif State Univ Hayward, Dept Sociol & Social Serv, from asst prof to prof, 1987-94, dept chair, currently; Bayview Hunter's Pt Found, San Francisco, CA, res dir, 1990-91; Univ Paris, Sorbonne, vis prof, 2005. **Orgs:** Res assoc, Soc Study Contemp Soc Prob, 1980-82; consult, Western Interstate Comm Higher Ed, 1981-83; Comt Appl Sociol Am Sociol Asn, 1985-87; Comt, Am Sociol Asn, Wash, DC, 1985-87; bd mem, Dr Martin Luther King, Jr Ctr Social Chg Santa Clara Valley, San Jose, Ca, 1986-89; bd mem, Peninsula Asn Black Personnel Adminr, Sunnyvale, Ca, 1987-88; alumni western adv comt, Franklin & Marshall Col, Lancaster, Pa, 1993-; bd mem, Glide Found Glide Mem Methodist Church, 1993-; rev panelist, Minority Grad Fel Prog, Nat Sci Found, Wash, DC, 1993-95; Am Social Health Asn, 1995-2002; planning comt, Nat Inst Health, Bestheda, MD, 1995-; bd chair, Am Social Health Asn, Durham, NC, 1996-03; Asn Black Sociologists; bd dir, Glide Mem Methodist Church; pres, Asn Black Sociologists, 2004-05. **Home Addr:** 7075 Elverton Dr, Oakland, CA 94611, **Home Phone:** (510)339-2192. **Business Addr:** Emeritus Professor, California State University East Bay, Meiklejohn Hall 3095, Hayward, CA 94542, **Business Phone:** (510)885-3173.

**BOWSER, HAMILTON VICTOR, SR.**
Executive, president (organization). **Personal:** Born Sep 20, 1928, East Orange, NJ; son of Edward T and Louise Pateman; married Merle Charlotte Moses; children: Hamilton V Jr, Rebecca Louise & Jennifer Lynn. **Educ:** NJ Inst Technol, BS, civil engineering, 1952, MS, civil engineering, 1956; Mass Inst Technol, Grad Sch, civil engineering, 1954; Lic prof engr, NJ, NY, PA. **Career:** Porter Urguhart Eng, struct engr, 1954-55; Louis Berger Assocs, sr bridge engr, 1955-57; PARCO Inc, sr struct engr, 1957-59; Engrs Inc, vpres, struct & proj engr, 1959-69; Evanbow Construct Co Inc, exec, pres, 1968-. **Orgs:** Men Essex NJ, 1959-, pres, 1969; pres, Nat Soc Prof Eng Essex Chap, 1966-68; fel Am Soc Civil Engrs, 1969; trustee & treas, Essex Co Col, 1971-74; chmn bd, Assoc Minority Contractors Am, 1980-82; bd dir & treas, Reg Plan Assoc NY, NJ, CT, 1981-97; bd dir & pres Nat Asn Minority Contractors, pres, 1988-89, emer bd mem, currently; Am Arbit Asn, Construct & Pub Works Panels, 1989-; bd chmn, Orange YMCA Community Mgmt; Prof Engrs, Construct Div Nat Soc Prof Engrs; Am Concrete Inst; NJ United Minority Bus Brain Trust; chmn, Mayor's Task Force Newark Econ Develop, NJ; rep, Co Solid Waste Disposal Comn; rep, White House Conf Small Bus; trustee bd, chair & Bldg Comn, Adv Coun Civil & Environ Eng, NJ Inst Technol, 1989-; vice chmn, Nj Govs Study Comn Discrimination Pub Procurement; vice chair, Regional Alliance Small Contractors NY & Nj; chmn, NAMC Liaison Comn US Corp Surety Bond Ind; chair & bd mem, Regional Plan Asn; spokesperson, minorities construct & procurement issues. **Home Addr:** 106 Christopher St, Montclair, NJ 07042. **Business Addr:** President, Evanbow Construction Co Inc, 67 Sanford St, East Orange, NJ 07018, **Business Phone:** (973)674-1250.

**BOWSER, KYLE DAMON**
Executive, television producer. **Personal:** Born Jan 1, 1958?, Philadelphia, PA; married Yvette Lee; children: 2. **Educ:** Ohio Univ, BS, 1980; Widener Univ, Sch Law, JD, 1991. **Career:** TV series: "Trial by Jury", exec producer, 1995; "Midnight Mac", exec producer, 1995; "For Your Love", consult, 1998; "NAMIC Vision Awards", exec producer, 2005; "For One Night", exec producer, 2006; "The Thing About Family"; "Color TV"; Others: Supreme Ct Pa, law clerk, 1989; NBC Bus Affairs, law clerk, 1990; Bowser, Weaver & Cousounis, law clerk, 1991; Fox Inc, creative assoc, 1991-92; Fox Broadcasting Co, mgr current programming, 1992-93; Home Box Off Independent Productions, dir creative affairs, 1993-94; Cult Heritage Comn, comnr, 2003-; Res Ipsa Media Inc, pres & founder, currently; Inspired By Media Group, exec partner, film & TV veteran, currently. **Orgs:** Black Entertainment & Sports Lawyers Asn; Black Filmmakers Asn; Nat Asn Minorities Commun; Hollyrod Found. **Business Addr:** Film & Television Veteran, Executive Partner, Inspired By... Media Group Inc, 5219 Denny Ave, North Hollywood, CA 91601, **Business Phone:** (818)979-6409.

**BOWSER, MURIEL (MURIEL ELIZABETH BOWSER)**
City council member, mayor. **Personal:** Born Aug 2, 1972, Washington, DC; daughter of Joe and Joan. **Educ:** Chatham Univ, BA, 1994; Am Univ, MPP, 2000. **Career:** Ward 4, District of Columbia, Advisory Neighborhood Commissioner, 2004-07; DC Council, council member representing Ward 4, 2007-15; Washington, D.C., mayor, 2015-. **Orgs:** Democratic Party **Business Addr:** District of Columbia, John A Wilson Bldg, Washington, DC 20004, **Business Phone:** (202)727-2643.

**BOWSER, REGINALD**
President (organization). **Educ:** George Mason Univ, BS, pub adminr, 1992; Darden Grad Sch Bus, Univ Va, MBA, mkt concentration, 1998. **Career:** Eastman Kodak Co, sales, maj acct mgt, bus analyst, 1990-96; LendingTree, vpres mkt, 1998-2000; HorizonGuide Inc, chief mkt officer, 2000-01; Rollover Syst Inc, founder, pres & chief exec officer, 2001-07; Red Bow Photo Inc, founder, pres & chief exec officer, 2008-10; Red Bow Mkt, Pres, 2010-; Entertainment Imaging LLC, chief exec officer, managing partner, 2012-. **Business Addr:** Founder, President & Chief Executing Officer, Rollover Systems Inc, 4135 S Stream Blvd Suite 500, Charlotte, NC 28217, **Business Phone:** (888)600-7655.

**BOWSER, REGINALD**
Administrator, chief executive officer, president (organization). **Personal:** married Trina. **Educ:** George Mason Univ, BS; Univ Va, Darden Grad Sch Bus, MBA, 1998. **Career:** Eastman Kodak Co, sales & mkt mgr, 1990-96; Lending Tree Inc, vpres mkt & advert, 1998-2000; Horizon Guide Inc, mem exec mgt team & chief mkt officer, 2000-01; Rollover Systs Inc, owner, pres, chief exec officer, 2001-07; Red Bow Photo Inc, founder, pres & chief exec officer, 2008-10; Red Bow Mkt, pres, 2010-; Entertainment Imaging LLC, managing partner, 2012-. **Orgs:** Coun mem, Bank Am Corp. **Business Addr:** Chief Executive Officer, Rollover Systems Inc, 2815 Coliseum Ctr Dr, Charlotte, NC 28217-1452.

**BOWSER, HON. ROBERT LOUIS**
Executive, mayor. **Personal:** Born Dec 13, 1935, East Orange, NJ; son of Edward T Sr and Louise E Pateman; married Marilyn K Ward; children: David, Lisa A & Leslie J. **Educ:** Newark Col Engr, BSCE, 1958; Northwestern Univ, cert, 1961; NY Univ, cert, 1963. **Career:** City Newark, city planner, 1958-60; Town Montclair, traffic engr, 1960-65, struct engr, 1965-68; Bowser Engrs & Assoc, pres, 1968-82; Robert L Bowser Assoc, owner, 1982-; Essex Co Col, adj prof, 1985-89; City E Orange, NJ, dir pub works & actg city planner, 1986-91; Newark Bd Educ, Design & Construct Dept, sch dist prin engr, 1991-97; City E Orange, NJ, elected mayor, currently. **Orgs:** Inst Traffic Engr, 1959-65; Nat Soc Prof Engrs, 1963; NJ Soc Prof Engrs, 1963; Land Surveyors Functional Sect, NJ, 1969; Lic Prof Land Survr, NJ, 1969; Am Cong Surv & Mapping, 1970; Lic Prof Planner, NJ, 1973; vice chmn, E Orange Rent Level Bd, 1975-76; founder & exec dir, Essex Co Touch Football League, 1975-2001; NJ Socs Prof Planners, 1976-; pres, Nat Asn Builders & Contractors NJ, 1976; NJ Planners Asn, 1978-; Pub Works Asn, 1986-; E Orange Planning Bd clerk, 1986-91; bd dir, Girl Scout Coun, 1989-93; pres, E Orange Kiwanis Club, 1990-98; E Orange Lions Club, 1989, pres, 1995; chmn, Rutgers Urban Gardening Prog Adv Bd, 1990-98, chmn, 1992-98; Citizens Adv Bd, Orange Hosp Ctr, 1994-; US Conf Mayor; bd dir, Conf Black Mayors, 1999; bd mem, NJ Conf Mayors, 2000; NJ Conf Mayors, Legis comm; NJ Urban Mayors Asn, Urban Enterprize Zone Comm; bd mem, United Way; bd mem, E Orange Salvation Army; Brick Church Lions Club; Men Essex Inc; Us Conf Mayors; bd trustee, E Orange Gen Hosp; Nat Minority Contractors Asn Inc; Actg Gov Richard Codey's Gang Land Security Task Force Adv Comt; State Nj Planning Comn; vpres, Nj State League Munic Exec Bd; chair, Gang & Youth Violence Task Force; Legis Comt; Econ Develop Comt. **Special Achievements:** First African American in the history of the city to have been elected to serve a third term. **Home Addr:** 571 Springdale Ave, East Orange, NJ 07017, **Home Phone:** (973)677-2476. **Business Addr:** Mayor, City of E Orange, 44 City Hall Plz, East Orange, NJ 07018, **Business Phone:** (973)266-5151.

**BOWSER, YVETTE DENISE LEE**
Executive, screenwriter. **Personal:** Born Jun 9, 1965; married Kyle D; children: Evan & Drew. **Educ:** Stanford Univ, polit sci & psychol, 1987. **Career:** Screenwriter, executive; TV Series: "A Different World", producer, 1987, 1991-92; "Hangin with Mr Cooper", producer, 1993; "Living Single", writer, creator & exec producer, 1993; "Lush Life", exec producer, 1996; "For Your Love", exec producer, 1998; "Half & Half", exec producer & writer, 2003-05; "The Big My Little Pony Episode", writer, 2004; "The Big Fast Track Episode", writer, 2005; "The Big Training Day Episode", writer, 2005; "The Big Frozen Assets Episode", writer, 2005; "The Big My Funny Valentine Episode", writer, 2006; "Lipstick Jungle", consult producer & writer, 2008-09; "The Exes", consult producer & writer, 2012; "Happily Divorced", consult producer & writer, 2012-13; "The Soul Man", writer, 2013; "Black-ish", consult producer & writer, 2014-2015. Sister Lee Productions, owner, pres, chief exec officer, currently; NBC Ser, consult producer. **Orgs:** Alpha Kappa Alpha; St. Bernard Proj; C's Defense Fund; HollyRod Found; Am Cancer Soc; I Have A Dream Found; A Pl Called Home; TreePeople; founder, Butterfly Found, 2003-; bd mem, C Caribbean Inc, currently. **Special Achievements:** First and youngest African-American woman to create and run her own television series. **Business Addr:** Board Member, Children of the Caribbean Inc, 9663 Santa Monica Blvd Suite 460, Beverly Hills, CA 90210, **Business Phone:** (310)651-8317.

**BOX, DR. CHARLES**
Mayor, government official. **Personal:** Born Jan 1, 1951?, Rockford, IL. **Educ:** Dartmouth Col, AB, hist, 1973; Univ Mich Law Sch, JD, 1976. **Career:** Rockford's munic admin, city adminr & legal dir; Rockford, Ill, mayor, 1989-2001; Ill Com Comn, chmn, currently. **Orgs:** Chair, Community Develop Housing Comn; co-chair, Conf Mayors Liaison Comn, Nat Asn Realtors; co-chair, Community Develop Block Grant Task Force; chair, Sub comt Enterprise Zones; Ill Growth Enterprises; Rockford Col; trustee & mem, Adv Bd US Conf Mayors. **Business Addr:** Chair, Illinois Commerce Commission, 527 E Capitol Ave, Springfield, IL 62701, **Business Phone:** (217)782-7295.

**BOXILL, JOHN HAMMOND**
Association executive. **Personal:** Born Oct 22, 1961, Chillicothe, OH; son of John and Janice; children: Zuri F & Uele N. **Educ:** Ohio State Univ, BS, zool, 1984; Methodist Theol Sch, OH, MA, alcohol & drug addictions ministry, 1998. **Career:** Columbus City, dist int specialist, 1987-88; ECCO Family Health Ctr, opers coordr, 1988-96; Arthur James Cancer Hosp, Community Develop, prog mgr, 1996-2000; Am Red Cross, Chap Servs, mgr, vol, 2000-03; New Salem Baptist Missionary Church, Admin Dept, chief operating officer, 2003-, vpres, pres, currently. **Orgs:** Deacon, New Salem Baptist Church, 1990-; United Way Franklin Cty, Vision Coun, Health, 1990-2000; minority involvement comt, Am Heart Asn, 1992-; educ chair, Alpha Phi Alpha Frat, 1995-; bd mem, Columbus Bd Health; develop comt mem, Metrop Residential Serv Bd; bd mem, Columbus Area Community Ment Health Ctr; charter me, Nat Black Leadership Initiative Cancer; bd mem, City Columbus-Health Dept, 2000-12. **Honors/Awds:** Jaycees, Ten Outstanding Young Citizens, 1997; Honorary Nurse, Columbus Black Nurses Asn, 1997; Outstanding Young Men of America, 1998; Circle of Friends, African American Cancer Support Group, 1999; President's Award, Alpha Phi Alpha Frat; President's Award, Alpha Rho Lambda, 1999; Outstanding Contributions Award, Ltd Distrib Serv; e Distinguished Diversity Award, Ohio State Univ; Circle of Friends Award, African Am Cancer Support Group. **Home Addr:** 6243 Peach Tree Rd, Whitehall, OH 43213-3419, **Home Phone:** (614)868-5979. **Business Addr:** Chief Operating Officer, President, New Salem Missionary Baptist Church, 2956 Cleveland Ave, Columbus, OH 43224, **Business Phone:** (614)267-2536.

**BOYCE, CHARLES N. See Obituaries Section.**

**BOYCE, DR. JOHN G.**
Gynecologist, educator. **Personal:** Born May 6, 1935; married Erma; children: Mindora & Jane. **Educ:** Univ BC, MD, 1962; Columbia Univ, MS, bio statist, 1971. **Career:** Kings County, chief gynec oncol, 1990-98, pres med bd, 1993-95; State Univ New York, prof Obstet & Gynec; State Univ New York, Health Sci Ctr Brooklyn, Dept Obstet & Gynec, chmn, distinguished serv prof; Hosp San Rafael, pres, chief infectious dis, hosp Epidemiol. **Orgs:** Chairperson, Am Col Obstetricians & Gynecologists; Kings County NY State Am; Nat Med Asn; Soc Gynec & Oncologists; treas, AGOS Exec Coun; pres, New York Obstet Soc. **Honors/Awds:** Cert Spec Competence Gynec Oncol, 1974; ACOG Community Service Award, Am Col obstetricians & Gynecologists, 1997-98; ACM Service Award & Hon Fels, Am Col obstetricians & Gynecologists, 1999. **Home Addr:** 100 Forest Dr, Port Washington, NY 11050, **Home Phone:** (516)883-7662. **Business Addr:** Chairperson District II, American College of Obstetricians and Gynecologists, 409 12th St SW, Washington, DC 20090-6920, **Business Phone:** (202)638-5577.

**BOYCE, JOSEPH NELSON (JOSEPH N BOYCE)**
Journalist. **Personal:** Born Apr 18, 1937, New Orleans, LA; son of John B and Sadie Nelson; married Carol Hill; children: Beverly, Leslie, Nelson & Joel. **Educ:** Roosevelt Univ, Chicago, IL, BS, biol, 1960; John Marshall Law Sch, Chicago, IL, attended 1965. **Career:** Journalist (retired); patrolman, 1961-66; Chicago Police Dept, 1965-67, Chicago Tribune, reporter, 1966-70; Time Mag, New York, NY, corresp, bur

chief, 1970-87; Times New York bur, dep chief, 1985; Wall St Jour, NY, sr ed, consult, 1987-98; Stanford Univ, lectr; Univ Kans, lectr; SC State Univ, lectr; Univ Calif, Berkeley, lectr; San Francisco State Univ, lectr; San Francisco bur, chief; Times Atlanta bur, chief; Howard Univ, lectr; Bradley Univ, lectr; Columbia Univ, adj prof, 1999; Ind Univ, adj prof, 2001-; Purdue Univ, adj prof, 2001-; Maynard Inst Jour Educ, vis fac. **Orgs:** Am Fedn Musicians, 1955-; Nat Asn Black Journalists; life mem, Nat Asn Advan Colored People; Indianapolis Asn Black Journalists; Ind Pro Chap Soc Prof Journalists; founding mem, Nat Asn Minority Media Execs; CORE, 1967-70; vis fac, Summer Prog Minority Journalist, 1986-89. **Honors/Awds:** Lincoln University Award Educational Reporting, 1976; Black Achiever, Metropolitian Young Mens Christian Association New York, 1976; Time Inc Fel, Duke Univ, 1983; lectured at Poynter Inst, 1992; Alfred Bynum award for mentoring, 2006. **Special Achievements:** First African American to join Chicago Tribune Magazine; First African American to Head bureau section of Times Magazine; First African American senior editor at the paper; First African American reporter, Chicago Tribune; Life member of the Chicago Federation of Musicians Union Local 10-208. **Home Addr:** 4 Sylvan Way, Suffern, NY 10901. **Business Addr:** Adjunct Professor, Consultant, Indiana University School of Journalism, 535 W Mich St, Indianapolis, IN 46202, **Business Phone:** (317)278-5320.

## BOYCE, ROBERT
School administrator. **Career:** Detroit Bd Educ, Bd pres. **Business Addr:** Board President, Detroit Board of Education, 5057 Woodward, Detroit, MI 48202, **Business Phone:** (313)494-1010.

## BOYCE, WILLIAM M.
Labor relations manager. **Personal:** Born Jul 9, 1928, Brooklyn, NY; son of Darnley and Luddie; married Alice M Billingsley; children: David C & Lynne M. **Educ:** Brooklyn Col, AAS, 1957; City Col NY, AAS, 1962, BBA, 1965; Fairleigh Dickinson Univ, MBA, 1976. **Career:** Kings Co Hosp Ctr, dir personnel, 1974-81; Muhlenberg Hosp, vpres human resources, 1981-85; Yonkers Gen Hosp, dir human resources, 1987-89; Boyce Consult Group, pres, currently; Passaic County Community Col, dir, human resources & labor rels, 1990-. **Orgs:** Dir, Ft Greene Neighborhood Manpower Ctr, 1966-70; dir, Manpower Taskforce New Urban & Coalition, 1970-74; chmn, Brooklyn Health Manpower Consortium, 1975-77; Asn MBA Execs, 1975-; NY Asn Hosp Personnel Admin, 1977-. **Honors/Awds:** Recipient of German Occupancy Medal AUS. **Business Addr:** President, Boyce Consulting Group, 33 Elk Ave, New Rochelle, NY 10804, **Business Phone:** (914)235-5182.

## BOYD, AUDREY B. RHODES
Executive, educator, physician. **Personal:** married Antonio. **Educ:** Benedict Col, BS, biol; Bowling Green State Univ, MS, biol, 1976; Med Col Ohio, Toledo, MD, 1980; FAAFP. **Career:** Univ SC, asst clin prof, family & prev med, 1992-; HOPE Kids, state proj dir, 1994; SC Acad Family Physicians, pres, 1996; SC Dept Ment Health, CM Tucker Jr Ctr, med sect chief, physician, 1996; SC Dept Ment Health, staff physician& clin asst prof, currently; Palmetto Health & Univ SC Sch Med, residency family med, currently; Palmetto Health, clin fac, currently. **Orgs:** Am Acad Family Physicians; pres, SC Chap; secy, Columbia Church Christ; bd mem, pres, SC Acad Family Physicians; chair, Am Acad Family Physicians Comn Health Pub; founder, pres, bd chair, HOPE Kids. **Home Addr:** 17 Sagefire Ct, Irmo, SC 29063-9199. **Business Addr:** Clinical Faculty, Palmetto Health, 1330 Taylor St, Columbia, SC 29220, **Business Phone:** (803)296-5010.

## BOYD, BARBARA JEAN
Librarian. **Personal:** Born Jul 14, 1954, Monroe, LA; daughter of Rube Robinson and Ora Lee Renfro Robinson (deceased); married Willian; children: Chaundra, Cameron & Chelsea. **Educ:** Univ Wis, Eau Claire, Wis, Oshkosh, BS, 1979, Milwaukee, Wis, MLIS, 1989. **Career:** Heritage Bank, Milwaukee, Wis, clerk, 1979-80; City Milwaukee-Legis Ref Bur, Milwaukee, Wis, LTA, 1980-89, librn, 1989-91; Houston Pub Libr, Johnson Br, mgr, Collier Reg, librn, 1991. **Orgs:** Am Libr Asn, 1987; Spec Librs Asn, 1987-89; Wis Black Librn Network, 1987-91; Spec Librs Asn, positive action prog minority groups stipend; Tex Libr Asn, 1995; Black Caucus Am Libr Asn, 1987. **Honors/Awds:** Libr Career Training Fel, UWM-Sch Libr & Info Sci, 1987-88. **Home Addr:** 3719 Country Pl Suite 103, Stafford, TX 77477. **Business Addr:** Branch Manager, Houston Public Library, 500 McKinney, Houston, TX 77002, **Business Phone:** (832)393-1313.

## BOYD, DR. CANDY DAWSON
Educator. **Personal:** Born Aug 8, 1946, Chicago, IL; daughter of Julian and Mary Ruth Ridley. **Educ:** Northeastern Ill State Univ, BA, educ, 1967; Univ Calif, Berkeley, CA, MA, reading educ, 1978, PhD, curric & instr, 1982. **Career:** Overton Elem Sch, Chicago, Ill, teacher, 1968-71; Longfellow Sch, Berkeley, Calif, teacher, 1971-73; Univ Calif, Berkeley, Calif, ext instr lang arts, 1972-79; Berkeley Unified Sch Dist, Berkeley, Calif, dist teacher trainer reading & commun skills, 1973-76; St Mary's Col Calif, Moraga, Calif, ext instr lang arts, 1972-79, lectr asst prof, 1976-83, Reading Leadership Elem Educ & Teacher Effectiveness Prog, chair, 1976-87, tenured assoc prof, 1983-91, prof, 1991-94, Masters Progs Reading & Spec Educ, chair, 1994-, dir reading & lang arts, 2007; prof reading & lang arts prog, currently; Multicultural Lit Collection, dir, currently. **Orgs:** St Mary's Col Rank & Tenure Comt, 1984-87; rev comn, Multiple Subj Waiver Progs Comt; adv comt, Multiple Subj Credential Childhood Emphasis, State Calif Comn Teacher Credentialing, 1986-87; co-founder, Common Lit Cult. **Special Achievements:** First African American to have tenure at Saint Mary's. **Home Addr:** 1416 Madrone Way, San Pablo, CA 94806, **Home Phone:** (510)237-9982. **Business Addr:** Professor, Director Multicultural Literature Collection, Saint Marys College of California, 1928 St Marys Rd, Moraga, CA 94556, **Business Phone:** (925)631-4565.

## BOYD, JUDGE DELORES ROSETTA
Lawyer. **Personal:** Born Apr 24, 1950, Ramer, AL. **Educ:** Univ Ala, BA, 1972; Univ Va, JD, 1975. **Career:** Judge (retired); US Ct Appeals 5th Circuit, fed judge; US Ct Appeals 11th Circuit, chief judge, 1975-76; Mandell & Boyd, partner, 1976-92, solo pract, 1992-2001; Montgomery Munic Ct, presiding judge, 2000-01; US Dist Ct Mid Dist Ala, US magistrate judge, 2001-; Judge John C Godbold, law clerk. **Orgs:** Ala State Bar Bd Bar Examiners, bar examr, 1979-83; chairperson, Ala Bd Bar Examiners, 1995-98, bar examr, 1979-82; bd dir, Legal Serv Corp Ala; fel Ala State Bar; master bencher, Hugh Maddox Inn Ct; Hist Comt U.S. Dist Ct; Am Bar Asn, Fed Bar Asn, Nat Bar Asn; Ala Lawyers Asn; Mt Zion African Methodist Episcopal Church; scholar, Nat Asn Advan Colored People Legal Defense Fund; bd trustee, Ala Dept Arch & Hist; Ala Trial Lawyers Asn; Montgomery County Trial Lawyers Asn; Asn Trial Lawyers Am. **Honors/Awds:** Constance Baker Motley Award, Nat Asn for the Advan of Colored People, 1975; "The New Women in Court", Time Magazine, 1983; Outstanding Alumna Award Communication Studies, Univ Ala, 2000; the Lanier Alumni Masters of Progress Hall of Fame. **Special Achievements:** Among Five of the "Best & Brightest" women trial lawyers in the country. Co-Author: "Jim Crow and Me: Stories from My Life as a Civil Rights Lawyer", New South Books, 2008; Freedom's Children: Young Civil Rights Activists Tell Their Own Stories, G.P. Putnam's Sons, 1992. **Home Addr:** 639 Martha St Cottage Hill Hist Dist, PO Box 2270, Montgomery, AL 36104-3333, **Home Phone:** (334)590-4624. **Business Addr:** Magistrate Judge, United States District Court, Frank M Johnson Jr Fed Courthouse Complex, Montgomery, AL 36104, **Business Phone:** (334)954-3740.

## BOYD, EVELYN SHIPPS. See Obituaries Section.

## BOYD, GWENDOLYN ELIZABETH
Engineer. **Personal:** Born Dec 27, 1955, Montgomery, AL; daughter of Dora McClain (deceased). **Educ:** Ala State Univ, BS, math, physics & music, 1977; Yale Univ, MS, mech engineering, 1979; Howard Univ, MDiv, 2007. **Career:** IBM, NY, engr, 1979-80; Ala State Univ, Staff Assoc, pres; Delta Res & Educ Found, nat pres & prof engr; Johns Hopkins Univ Appl Physics Lab, engr, 1980-98, submarine navig systs analyst, asst develop prog, 1998-2004, exec asst to chief staff, 2004-, prin prof staff, chair, currently. **Orgs:** Soc Women Engrs, 1980-; The Links Inc, 1983-, area parliamentarian, 1993-2002; bd dir, United Way Nat Capital Area, 1984-, chair, 1997-2001; APL Fed Credit Union; Leadership Wash, 1996-; bd dir, C's Nat Med Ctr, 1996-; nat vpres, Delta Sigma Theta Sorority Inc, 1996-2000, nat pres, 2000-04, regional dir leadership develop prog, immediate past nat pres, 2004-; Parent's Bd & C's Res Inst Bd, 1998-; Nat Coun Negro Women & Ebenezer AME Church, Ft Wash, ministerial staff; Diversity Leadership Coun; Barry Goldwater Scholar & Excellence in Educ Found, trustee; bd dir, Leadership Wash; bd dir, Bennett Col; bd dir, Nat Ctr Community Partnerships, adv coun, Tuskegee Univ; Nat Partnership Community Leadership. **Honors/Awds:** Maynard Jackson Leadership Award, Alpha Phi Alpha; United Way, Community Service Award, 1998; NAACP, Howard County, Outstanding Service Award, 1998; Special Congressional Recognition, presented by Hon Juanita Millender McDonald, 1999; Black Engineer of the Year, Outstanding Alumnus Achievement, 2000; 20 Keys to the City; Heroes in the Struggle, 2004; Women's Leadership Award, 2004; Special Recognition Award, 2004; Hon Doctorate, Lincoln Univ, 2005; Chancellor's Award North Carolina Central Univ, 2006; Hon Doctorate, Bennett Col Women, 2007; National Trio Achievers Award. **Special Achievements:** First African American female to earn a MS in mechanical engineering, Yale Univ, 1979; Black Engineer of the Year for Community Service, 1996. **Home Addr:** 7713 Stratfield Lane, Laurel, MD 20707, **Home Phone:** (301)725-7376. **Business Addr:** Executive Assistant to Chief of Staff, Principal Professional Staff, Johns Hopkins University, Rm 1 S137 11100 Johns Hopkins Rd, Laurel, MD 20723, **Business Phone:** (443)778-6031.

## BOYD, DR. GWENDOLYN VIOLA
Police chief, vice president (organization). **Personal:** Born Jun 4, 1954, Sneads, FL; daughter of Willie C Mathis and Vera Mae; married Harold James; children: Sherhonda & Lakeesha. **Educ:** Miami Dade Community Col, AA, 1974; St Thomas Univ, BA, criminal justice, 1980 ; Fla Int Univ, MPA, 1982, EDd, 1997. **Career:** City Miami Police Dept, police maj, 1974-97; City Prichard Police Dept, chief police, 1997; Fla, N Miami, chief police, 2002-; Fla Int Univ, adj prof, vpres admin & stud affairs, 2000-01; Broward Col, prof, 2010-. **Orgs:** Ed, Nat Orgn Black Law Enforcement Execs; Intl Asn Women Police; Intl Asn Chiefs Police; Am Soc Training & Develop; AL Asn Chiefs Police; Nat Asn Negro Bus & Prof Women's Club; United Way Am; Mobile Co Chiefs Police Asn; Boys & Girls Club Mobile; Exec coun, Fla Intl Univ. **Business Addr:** Professor, Broward College, 3501 Davie Rd, Davie, FL 33314, **Business Phone:** (954)201-6800.

## BOYD, HERB
College teacher, writer. **Personal:** Born Nov 1, 1938, Birmingham, AL. **Educ:** Wayne State Univ, BA, philos, 1969; Univ Iowa, 1983. **Career:** Wayne State University, instr, 1968-77; Oberlin College, instr, 1970-72; Center for Creative Studies, lectr, 1979-; Jazz Research Institute, pres, 1979; US Census Bureau, Detroit, supervisor of officer operations; "Metro Times", assoc editor; University of Iowa, lectr, 1983; College of New Rochelle, instructor of African American History, 1986; "The Black World Today", employee; City College of New York, adjunct instructor, 2005-. **Special Achievements:** Author of "Black Panthers for Beginners, Writers & Readers" (1995); "Autobiography of a People: Three Centuries of African-American History Told By Those Who Lived It" (Doubleday, 2000); "Race and Resistance: African Publishers in the 21st Century" (South End Press, 2002); "The Harlem Reader" (Crown Publishers, 2003); "We Shall Overcome: A History of the Civil Rights Movement" (Sourcebooks, 2004); "Pound for Pound: The Life and Times of Sugar Ray Robinson" (Amistad, 2005); "Baldwin's Harlem: A Biography of James Baldwin" (2008); co-author of "The Gentle Giant: The Autobiography of Yuseff Lateef" (Morton Books, 2006); co-editor of "The Odyssey of Black Men in America: An Anthology" (One World/Ballantine, 1995); contributor to "New York Amsterdam News", "Black World", "Emerge", "Essence", "Down Beat", "First World", "Black Scholar"; national and international correspondent for Free Speech TV. **Business Addr:** The City College of New York, NAC 6/109, New York, NY 10031.

## BOYD, PASTOR J. EDGAR
Clergy. **Personal:** Born Dec 7, 1947, FL; married Florence Miles; children: Eric, Jonathan Devereaux, Kimberly & Tamara Marie. **Educ:** Western Wash Univ, BA, community develop, 1979; Univ Dubuque Theol Sem, Md, 1982; Am Baptist Sem W, doctor ministry degree prog. **Career:** St John AME Church, pastor, 1971-73; Grace AME Church, pastor, 1973-75; Walker Chapel AME Church, pastor, 1975-80; Brookins AME Church, pastor, 1982-86; Bethel African Methodist Episcopal Church, Los Angeles, Calif, 1986-92, San Francisco, Calif, 1992-2012, treas, sr pastor, sr minister currently. **Orgs:** Keynote speaker, San Francisco Planning Comn; NAACP; bd trustee, Fel Acad; Alpha Phi Alpha Fraternity, Gamma Chi Lambda Chptr; clerical dean, Calif Conf, AME Church, 1992-2012. **Honors/Awds:** Received over 100 citations, awards & honor from Political, Civic, Social, Community, Religious, Educational & Financial groups & organizations from throughout the US. **Business Addr:** Senior Pastor, Senior Minister, Bethel African Methodist Episcopal Church, 916 Laguna St, San Francisco, CA 94115, **Business Phone:** (415)921-4935.

## BOYD, JAMES E., JR.
Executive. **Career:** Kmart, sr vpres restaurant ops; Bojangles, area mgr; Wendy's, gen mgr; AFC Enterprises, syst support vpres & coo; Popeyes, Franchise Owner; Popeye's Takes Command Brand, chief operating officer; Backyard Burgers, chief exec officer; Quiznos Can, pres; Dry Fried Wing Co, chief exec officer; Boyd Consult Grp LLC, pres; Java-U Restaurant & Coffee Bar, owner, currently. **Business Addr:** Chief Operating Officer, AFC Enterprises, 6 Concourse Pkwy NE Suite 1700, Atlanta, GA 30328, **Business Phone:** (770)391-9500.

## BOYD, DR. JOHN W.
Founder (originator), president (organization). **Personal:** Born Sep 4, 1965, Queens, NY; son of John W Sr and Betty J; married Kim S Hardy; children: 1. **Educ:** Southside Community Col, attended 1983; Clemson Univ, attended 1985. **Career:** Farmer, 1983-; John Boyd Agr & Technol Inst, founder, 1995-. **Orgs:** Nat Asn Advan Colored People; founder & pres, Nat Black Farmers Asn, 1995-; co-chair, Va Gov Tim Kaine's transition policy comt; Va Tobacco Indemnification & Community Revitalization Comn, 1999-2001. **Honors/Awds:** Keeper of the Flame Award, 2005. **Special Achievements:** Named ABC World News Tonights Person of the Week, 2003; 100 Most Influential Black Americans, Ebony Magazine, 2006; Nominee for the NAACPs highest honor The Springarn Award; Democratic nominee for election to Virginias 5th Congressional District, 2005. **Business Addr:** Founder, President, National Black Farmers Association, 68 Wind Rd, Baskerville, VA 23915, **Business Phone:** (434)848-1865.

## BOYD, DR. JOSEPH LEE
School administrator, dean (education), vice president (organization). **Personal:** Born Dec 20, 1947, Columbia, SC; son of Frank; married Nellie Brown; children: Joseph Christopher, Michael Steven & Adrienne Kerise. **Educ:** Univ SC, BS, acct, 1969, MA, acct, 1976, PhD, acct, 1977. **Career:** Johnson C Smith Univ, instr, 1972-74; Univ SC, asst prof, 1976-77; Univ Ill, asst prof, 1977-78; NC A&T State Univ, assoc prof, 1978-83; Norfolk State Univ, sch bus, dean, 1983-98; Benedict Col, distinguished prof acct, 2000-, sr vpres, acad affairs; Tex Southern Univ, Jesse H Jones Sch Bus, distinguished prof acct, dean, currently. **Orgs:** Beta Alpha Psi; Beta Gamma Sigma; Omicron Delta Kappa; Am Inst CPA; Am Acct Asn; NC Asn CPA; SC Asn CPA; Nat Asn Accts; Nat Asn Black Accts; Am Tax Asn; Ins Selling Practices Community; Curric Comn; Cluster Task Force; IRS Adv Group; Am Arbit Asn; Houston Urban League; Am Assembly Col Schs Bus; Houston Technol Ctr; Tex Entrepreneurs Exchange; Tex Coun Econ Educ; INROAD; Houston Area Urban League; Southern Bus Admin Asn; Beta Gamma Sigma; trustee, Nat Asn; Norfolk Chamber Com; United Way S Hampton Roads; Bank St Mem Baptist Church; Design Incentive Based Carbon Tax Syst. **Home Addr:** 3015 Covebrook Dr, Pearland, TX 77584-8731. **Business Addr:** Dean, Texas Southern University, 3100 Cleburne St 306 JHJ, Houston, TX 77004, **Business Phone:** (713)313-7215.

## BOYD, JULIA A.
Psychotherapist, writer. **Personal:** Born Apr 21, 1949, Camden, NJ; daughter of Joseph and Lavada Conyers; children: Michael Alan Jr. **Educ:** Antioch Univ, BA, psychol & coun, 1982; Pac Lutheran Univ, MEd, educ coun & guid, 1985; Seattle Univ, attended 1991; Univ Wash, ethnog interviewing & coun. **Career:** Pierce County Rape Relief, exec dir, 1985-86; Group Health Coop, psychotherapist, 1986-, Essence, Ebony, Jet & Heart & Soul Mag; Black Women's Health Bk; Seattle, pvt pract psychotherapist; Auth: Black Women & Self Esteem, Dutton, 1993; Girlfriend to Girlfriend: Everyday Wisdom & Affirmations from Sister Circle, Dutton, 1995; Embracing Fire: Sisters Talk About Sex & Relationships, Dutton, 1997; Can I Get a Witness: For Sisters When Blues is More Than a Song, Dutton, 1998. **Orgs:** Bd mem, Domestic Abuse Women's Network, 1983-85; Wash Sexual Assault Comn, Statewide Comt, 1984-86; Arts Comn, King County, 1986-89; AFA Women Forum, Western Wash State Univ, 1994. **Home Addr:** 2005 S 308th St, Federal Way, WA 98003, **Home Phone:** (253)839-6010. **Business Addr:** Psychotherapist, Group Health Cooperative, 1730 Minor Ave Suite 1400, Seattle, WA 98101, **Business Phone:** (206)287-2500.

## BOYD, KIMBERLY
Banker, executive. **Personal:** Born Jan 7, 1960, Georgetown, SC; daughter of Jack and Gertie Padgett; children: Curtis. **Educ:** Purdue Univ, cert, human resource mgt, 1998; Univ WI, Retail Banking Grad Prog, cert, 1999, 2000. **Career:** Anchor Bank, asst vpres training & develop, 1986-94; People's Bank, training dir, 1994, vpres retail banking, sr vpres admin, 2001; Peoples Bancorp NC Inc, sr vpres banking support, currently; Keokuk Savings Bank & Trust Co, vpres & sr retail officer. **Orgs:** Adv comt, NC Coop Ext Minority Women, 1999-; Hickory Metro Higher Educ Adv Coun; bd mem, Carteret Currents Swim; Catawba Valley YMCA; Catawba County Dept Social Serv. **Honors/Awds:** African-American Community Award, Catawba Valley Community Col. **Special Achievements:** Speaker, Minority Women's Conference, 1998-2000; Chamber Womens Leadership Conference, Female Resilence, 2000; NAACP Key Note MLK Celebration, 2003; speaker, MLK Catawba Valley Community Col, 2003. **Home Addr:**

704 Carrick Ct NW, Conover, NC 28613, **Home Phone:** (828)465-0680. **Business Addr:** Senior Vice President Banking Support, Peoples Bancorp of North Carolina Inc, Peoples Bancorp Ctr 518 W C St, Newton, NC 28658-4007, **Business Phone:** (828)464-5620.

### BOYD, LADONNA (LADONNA Y BOYD)

Executive, businessperson. **Personal:** Born Nashville, TN; daughter of Theophilus B Boyd III and Yvette Jean Duke Boyd. **Educ:** Spelman Col, BA; Tenn State Univ, MBA; Pepperdine Univ, EdD, 2016. **Career:** R.H. Boyd Publishing Corporation, special projects coordinator, chief operating officer, 2015-. **Orgs:** Beta Gamma Sigma; Alpha Kappa Alpha; Tennesee State Univ Econs & Finance Adv Bd. **Special Achievements:** Miss Black Tennesse, 2010. **Business Addr:** R H Boyd Publ Corp, 6717 Centennial Blvd, Nashville, TN 37209.

### BOYD, LINDA F. WHARTON

Government official, consultant, educator. **Personal:** Born Apr 21, 1961, Baltimore, MD; daughter of Rev Frank Wharton and Thelma L Kirby Wharton; children: Milton. **Educ:** Univ Pittsburgh, BA, 1972, MA, 1975, PhD, 1979; George Washington Univ, CPM, 1998. **Career:** Bowie State Univ, asst prof commun; Howard Univ, asst grad prof, 1979-85; Wash DC Off Mayor, commun consult, 1984-86; DC Dept Admin Serv, dir pub affairs, 1986-88; DC Dept Recreation, dir commun, 1988-92; Wharton Group, pres, chief operating officer, 1990-, media & pub affairs consult, 2004, exec dir, Chief Pub Affairs & Govt Rels, currently; Alcohol & Drug Abuse Serv Admin, chief criminal justice, 1992-95; DC Dept Human Serv, sr asst, dirpolicy & commun, 1996-97; Off Cable TV & Telecommunications, interim dir, 1997-98; Exec Off Mayor, dir commun, 1997-2000; DC Dept Health, Off Commun& Community Rels, dir, 1997; Off Commun, DC Dept Human Serv, 2000, Community Human Serv, dir, dep off mayor, 2000; DC Pub Schs, chief commun officer, Off Commun & Pub Info, dir, 2000-04; Univ Pittsburgh, Affinity coun dir, 2005-12; Coun DC, dir commun, 2009-10; DC Health Benefit Exchange, external affairs, dir, 2012-. **Orgs:** Delta Sigma Theta Sorority, 1970-; Nat Speech Commun Asn Black Caucus, 1975-79; bd mem, Nat Arts Prog Nat Coun Negro Women, 1979-; Pub Rels Soc Am, 1997-; consult, Nat Asn Advan Colored People Labor & Indust Sub-Comn Commun; chairperson, Joint Chap Event, Nat Coalition 100 Black Women Inc; first vpres, Black Pub Rel Soc; bd mem, Edward C Mazique Child Parent Ctr; Asbestos Abatement Community Outreach Campaign. **Honors/Awds:** Outstanding Black Women's Award, Commun Arts Creative Enterprises, 1974; Doctoral Hon Sem Prog, Howard Univ Speech Commun, 1977; Nat Public Radio Documentary Award, 1985; Bethune Legacy Award, Nat Coun Negro Women, 1986; Communicator of the Year Award, 1999. **Special Achievements:** Author: "Black Dance, It's Origin and Continuity", Minority Voices, 1977; advisor: "Stuff," children's program, NBC-TV, Washington, DC. **Home Addr:** 7215 16th St NW, Washington, DC 20012, **Home Phone:** (202)291-1640. **Business Addr:** Director, Wharton Group Inc, 7215 16th St, Washington, DC 20011, **Business Phone:** (202)291-6435.

### BOYD, LOUISE YVONNE

Software developer, manager. **Personal:** Born Jul 24, 1959, Newburgh, NY; daughter of Charles Carter (deceased) and Louise Yvonne Lewis. **Educ:** Univ Fl, BS, math, 1981; Webster Univ, attended 1999. **Career:** NASA, John F. Kennedy Space Ctr, aerospace technologist, ground software systs engr & workforce prog mgr, 1982-; Brevard Community Col, Cocoa, adj prof, 1984-88; SHARP prog Nat Aeronaut & Space Admin, mentor, 1988-90; Boyd Unlimited Event Planning Serv, owner, 1991-. **Orgs:** Pres, Nat Tech Asn, Space Coast Chap, 1987-89; region III dir, Nat Tech Asn, 1989-91; space coast div gov, Toastmasters Int, 1990-91; vpres, Space Coast Sect Soc Women Engrs, 1990-91; founder, chmn bd, Sweet Inc, 1990-; lt gov mkt, Toastmasters Int-Dist 47, 1991-92, treas, gov educ, 1992-93; treas, NASA Kennedy Mgt Asn, 1991-92. **Honors/Awds:** Hundred Black Sci Achievers, Chicago Mus Sci & Indust, 1989; 30 Leaders Future, Ebony Mag, 1989; Crystal Pyramid Award, Brevard Alumnae Chap Delta Sigma Theta Inc, 1990; Distinguished Toastmaster, Toastmasters Int, 1990; Distinguished Distrist Award, Toastmasters Int, 1992; Excellence Marketing Award, Toastmasters Int, 1992; NASA Points Light Award, 1992; NASA Exceptional Service Medal, 1998; Math Individual Tech Achiever Award, NTA Greater Houston Chap. **Home Addr:** 3515 Sable Palm Lane Apt D, Titusville, FL 32780, **Home Phone:** (407)383-0862. **Business Addr:** Software Systems Engineer, Workforce Program Manager, NASA, LPS Software Eng Div, Orlando, FL 32899, **Business Phone:** (407)861-5020.

### BOYD, REV. MARSHA FOSTER

School administrator, association executive. **Personal:** married Rev Kenneth; children: 1. **Educ:** Tufts Univ, BA; Interdenominational Theol Ctr, Atlanta, GA, MDiv; Grad Theol Union, Berkeley, PhD. **Career:** United Theol Sem, assoc prof pastoral care & coun; Payne Theol Sem, acad dean, 1998-99; Asn Theol Schs US & Can, Pastoral Care & Coun, assoc prof, Leadership Educ & Accreditation, dir, 1999, Ecumenical Theol Sem, pres, 2006-; Payne Theol Sem, acad dean; United Theol Sem, Pastoral Care & Coun, pres & prof, assoc prof, 2006-13. **Orgs:** African Methodist Episcopal Church, itinerant elder, 1978; AME Church, asst pastor; bd dir, Sky Found Inc; Arise Detroit Inc. **Special Achievements:** First African American female academic dean in American Theological Schs; Second African American Women President of an Advanced Technology Consulting Service-Accredited Seminary. **Business Addr:** President, The Association of Theological Schools United States & Canada, 10 Summit Pk Dr, Pittsburgh, PA 15275, **Business Phone:** (412)788-6505.

### BOYD, MARVIN

Banker. **Career:** Fed Res Bank, examr, 1978-88; Security BancShares Inc, chief exec officer, 1999-; Gulf Fed Bank, pres & chief exec officer, currently, chmn. **Orgs:** Nat Republican Cong Comt. **Business Addr:** President, Chief Executive Officer, Gulf Federal Bank, 901 Springhill Ave, Mobile, AL 36640-0217, **Business Phone:** (251)433-2671.

### BOYD, DR. MELBA JOYCE

Educator, writer. **Personal:** Born Apr 2, 1950, Detroit, MI; daughter of John Percy and Dorothy Wynn; children: John Percy III & Maya Wynn. **Educ:** Western Mich Univ, BA, eng, 1971, MA, eng, 1972; Univ Mich-Ann Arbor, Doctor Arts, eng, 1979. **Career:** Cass Tech High Sch, teacher, 1972-73; Broadside Press, asst ed, 1972-77, 1980-82; Wayne County Community Col, instr, 1972-82; Univ Mich, grad asst, 1978; Univ Iowa, asst prof, 1982-88; Ohio State Univ, assoc prof, 1988-89; Univ Mich, Dir, African Am Studies Prog, 1989-, poet, cult activist, educr; Wayne State Univ, distinguished prof & chmn, African Am, currently; Univ Mich, Adj Prof, Afro am & African Studies, currently. **Orgs:** African Am Studies Asn, 1982-; Ger Asn Am Studies, 1982-87; Col African Am Res, 2004-. **Special Achievements:** Foreward Award, Finalist, 2010; The National Association for the Advancement of Colored People Image Award, Finalist, Poetry, 2010. **Home Addr:** 15703 Grandvile Ave, Detroit, MI 48223, **Home Phone:** (313)610-0169. **Business Addr:** Distinguished Professor, Chair, Wayne State University, 5057 Woodward Ave, Detroit, MI 48202, **Business Phone:** (313)577-2321.

### BOYD, PATRICIA M. (PATRICIA L BOYD)

Chief financial officer, vice president (organization), administrator. **Educ:** Brooklyn Col, BS; NY Univ, MS, taxation; Am Univ. **Career:** Brooklyn Col, minority pres stud orientation comt; Arthur Andersen & Co, staff; M.R. Weiser & Co, staff; Benton & Bowles Inc, staff; Wachenheim Ltd Partners, staff; Texaco Int LLP, tax partner; Am Univ, staff; Guttenberg Found, staff; Kahn Boyd Levychin, tax partner; Ziegler Lotsoff Capital Mgt LLC, sr vpres; Arthur Andersen & Co, sr acct; Stud Orientation Comt Brooklyn Col, pres; Fiduciary Asset Mgt LLC, vpres & treas, controller, 1997-2011, svpres, chief financial officer, head instnl client serv, 2011-. **Orgs:** Nat Asn Black Accts; Urban Bankers Coalition; bd chmn, treas, Greater Harlem Chamber Com; treas, Claymore Securities Inc. **Home Addr:** 3530 Saint Joachim Lane, Saint Ann, MO 63074-2922. **Business Addr:** Vice President, Controller, Fiduciary Asset Management LLC, 8235 Forsyth Blvd, St. Louis, MO 63105, **Business Phone:** (314)446-6700.

### BOYD, ROZELLE

Educator. **Personal:** Born Apr 24, 1934, Indianapolis, IN; son of William and Ardelia. **Educ:** Butler Univ, BA, 1957; Ind Univ, MA, 1964. **Career:** Marion County, Dept Pub Welfare, caseworker, 1957; Indianapolis Pub Schs, Crispus Attucks High Sch, teacher, counr, 1957-68; Indianapolis City, councilman, 1966-2007; Ind Univ, lectr, asst dean, 1968-76, assoc dean, 1976-81, Groups Serv prog, founder & dir; Marion Co, counr, 1970-2007. **Orgs:** Dem Nat Comt man; chmn, Indianapolis Black Polit Caucus; Alpha Phi Alpha Fraternity Inc. **Honors/Awds:** Lily Fel, 1957; Freedom's Found Award; Lifetime Achievement Award, Groups Student Support Serv Prog, Ind Univ, 2004; Annual Outstanding Achievement Award, Ind Christian Leadership Conf; IUPUI Chancellors Medallion, indianapolis, 2009. **Special Achievements:** First African American man to serve as president of the city-county council. **Home Addr:** 2527 E 35th, Indianapolis, IN 46218.

### BOYD, SHEILA ANNE WILLIAMS

Manager, auditor. **Personal:** Born Apr 11, 1951, Chicago, IL; daughter of Kathryn Naomi Walker; children: Christine Williams, Kelly, Jamie & Michael Blakley. **Educ:** Olive Harvey Jr Col, assoc arts, acct high hon, 1975; Roosevelt Univ, BS & BA, acct with hon, 1977; Univ Chicago, exec MBA prog, 1992. **Career:** Ernst & Young, sr auditor, 1977-79; Amoco Corp, mgr, prof audit pract, 1979-92, Internal Audit Dept, mgr, banking coord & develop, 1993, mgr, credit coord, 1994-. **Orgs:** Bd govrs, Chicago Chap, Inst Internal Auditors, 1989-92; treas, Nat Black MBA Asn, Chicago, 1990; bd mem, Univ Chicago Exec Prog Club, 1993-. **Honors/Awds:** CPA, Ill, 1979; Certified Internal Auditor, 1983; Member of the Year, 1990; Outstanding Business & Professional Award, Dollars & Sense Mag, 1991. **Special Achievements:** Most Promising Black Women in Corporate America, Ebony Mag, 1991. **Home Addr:** 1130 Jamie Lane, Homewood, IL 60430-4134. **Business Addr:** Manager Credit Coordination, Amoco Corp, 200 E Randolph St Suite 2205, Chicago, IL 60601, **Business Phone:** (312)856-3200.

### BOYD, TERRY A.

Manager, executive. **Personal:** Born Cleveland, OH; children: 2. **Educ:** Defiance Col, BS, social work, 1978; Ohio State Univ, MS, social work admin, 1981, PhD, social policy, 1993, social police, 2003; Lake Erie Col, MBA, 2010. **Career:** Human Resources Inc, asst dir, 1981-82; Franklin Co C Servs, child welfare worker III, 1982-84; City Columbus, adminr youth servs bur, 1984-87, exec asst dir human servs, 1987-89; adminr, community servs, 1989-90, adminr, OMB, 1990-91; US Health Corp, dir human resources, 1991-97; Franklin Univ, adj instr, 1996, course mgr & fac mem & adminr mba prog, 1997-, div chair, 2007-09, assoc dean, 2009-, dir ctr continuing educ, 2012-, Appl Mgt & Entrepreneurship Bachelor SciencePrograms, chair, 2013-; Memorial Gen Hosp, Consult, Human Resource Mgt, 1998-2003; Columbus Pub Schs, Bd Educ, pres, 2006-09. **Orgs:** Pres, Franklin Co C Serv Citizens Adv Coun, 1985-92; bd mem, Ohio's C Defense Fund, 1986-92; bd mem, Alliance Coop Justice, 1985-89; COTA Transp Task Force, 1988-89; bd trustee, Franklin Co C Servs Bd, 1989-92; bd mem, Jobs Columbus Grads, 1991-92; cabinet mem, United Way Campaign, 1992; bd trustee, treas, vpres, The Alcohol Drug & Ment Health Bd Franklin Co, 1997-; pres, bd trustee, Columbus Metrop Libr Bd; leadership consult, bd mem, Nat Sch Bd Asn, 2007; campaign mem, United Way Franklin County, 2002; fel Human Resource Mgt Asn; fel Vol Mgt Asn; fel Not-for-Profit Mgt Asn. **Honors/Awds:** Service of Merit, Franklin Co Comnrs, 1992; Distinguished Service Award, Franklin Co C Serv, 1992. **Special Achievements:** "Changing Attitudes: An Anti-Drug Abuse Policy", 1989. **Home Addr:** 5646 Concord Hill Dr, Columbus, OH 43213, **Home Phone:** (614)866-0871. **Business Addr:** Associate Dean, Franklin University, 201 S Grant Ave, Columbus, OH 43215, **Business Phone:** (614)797-4700.

### BOYD, DR. THEOPHILUS B., III

Chief executive officer, executive. **Personal:** Born May 15, 1947, Nashville, TN; son of T B Jr (deceased); married Yvette Jean Duke; children: LaDonna Yvette, Shalae Shantel, T B IV & Justin Marriell. **Educ:** Tenn State Univ, BBA, 1969; Shreveport Bible Col, DD, 1980; Easonian Baptist Sem, DHL, 1983. **Career:** Nat Baptist Publ Bd, Nashville, TN, personnel dir, 1969-, head design & bldg comt, 1974, bd dirs, 1976, pres & chief exec officer, 1979-; Citizens Savings & Trust, mem bd dirs, 1978, chmn bd, 1982-; Citizens Realty & Develop Co, pres, 1982; Citizens Sav & Develop Co, pres, 1982-; Meharry Med Col, vice chair, bd dir, 1982-; United Negro Col Fund Telethon, chmn Mid Tenn, 1989-90; RH Boyd Publ Corp, pres & chief exec officer, currently. **Orgs:** Bd dirs, March Dimes Tenn Chap; comnr human develop State, TN; bd dirs, Nashville Tech Inst; pres, 100 Black Men Mid Tenn Inc; past vpres finance & treas, 100 Black Men Am Inc; past Mid Tenn chmn, United Negro Col Fund Telethon; bd mem, Nat Coun Christians & Jews; bd mem, Hundred Club Nashville; bd dirs, First Union Bank; mem bd gov, Nashville Area Chamber Com; vice chmn, Meharry Med Col Bd Trustees; life mem, Kappa Alpha Psi Fraternity Inc; Chi Boule Sigma Pi Phi Frat. **Honors/Awds:** DD, Shreveport Bible College, 1980; Doctor of Letters, Easonian Baptist Seminary, 1983; Great Seal of the United States Award; March of Dimes Man of the Year Award, 1990. **Special Achievements:** Best Dressed of Nashville. **Home Addr:** 5011 Tyne Ridge Ct, Nashville, TN 37220, **Home Phone:** (615)351-8484. **Business Addr:** President, Chief Executive Officer, R H Boyd Publishing Corp, 6717 Centennial Blvd, Nashville, TN 37209-1049, **Business Phone:** (615)350-8000.

### BOYD, THOMAS

Executive, consultant, manager. **Personal:** Born Apr 6, 1942, Philadelphia, PA; son of John and Thelma Archie; married Gwendolyn Lee. **Educ:** Temple Univ, BA, 1970. **Career:** Remington Rand Inc, personnel mgr, 1979; Comput Sci Corp, div mgr equal employ opportunity progs & mgr career develop, 1979-81; Hahneman Univ, employ mgr, 1984-88; Syracuse Univ, dir employ practices, 1988. **Orgs:** Consult, Nat Guard Bur, 1984. **Home Addr:** 201 E Palestine Blvd, Madison, TN 37115, **Home Phone:** (615)868-6836.

### BOYD, VALERIE

Writer, college teacher. **Personal:** Born Dec 11, 1963, Atlanta, GA; daughter of Roger and Laura J. **Educ:** Northwestern Univ, BS, jour, 1985; Goucher Col, MFA, creative nonfiction writing, 1999. **Career:** The Atlanta Jour-Const, Int & Nat Desk, copy ed, 1985-91, features dept, copy ed, 1988-92, reporter, 1991-92, asst arts ed & writer, 1992-95, asst ed, 1999-2000, arts ed, 2001-04; Univ SC, jour instr, 1987; Catalyst Mag, asst ed, 1989-95; Eight Rock Maga Bk, founder, ed & publ, 1990-94; Health Quest Mag, co-founder & chief ed, 1992-97; Nat Black Arts Festival, lit cur, 1997-98; Optical Data, McGraw-Hill, writer & ed, 1998-99; Brown Univ, Eliza Gardner Howard Found Res fel, 1999; Univ Ga, Grady Col, Dept Jour, asst prof, currently; Antioch Univ, assoc fac mentor, 2005-; UGA's Low-Residency MFA Program, founding director, narrative nonfiction, currently; Books: Wrapped in Rainbows: The Life of Zora Neale Hurston, 2003; Gathering Blossoms Under Fire: The Journals of Alice Walker, currently. **Orgs:** Nat Bks Critics Circle; Nat Black Arts Festival; Alice Walker Lit Soc; Asn Writers & Writing Progs; founder, Hurston & Wright. **Business Addr:** Associate Professor, Charlayne Hunter-Gault Writer in Residence, University of Georgia, Rm 225, Athens, GA 30602-3018, **Business Phone:** (706)542-0887.

### BOYD, DR. VIVIAN STALLWORTH

Educator, administrator. **Educ:** Antioch Col, BA, educ, 1960; Univ Colo, Boulder, CO, MA, educ, 1967; Univ Md, Okinawa, MA, col stud personnel, 1969, College Park, PhD, col stud personnel/coun psychol, 1975. **Career:** Walden Pvt Sch, teacher, 1961-62; Am Sch Poitiers, teacher, 1962-64; Norristown Pub Schs, teacher, 1964-66; Univ Md, Dept Coun & Personnel Serv, fac, 1966-, counr & res asst, 1972-73, grad asst, 1973-74, intern, 1974-75, staff psychologist, 1975-81, asst prof, 1975-89, intern training dir, 1978-85, actg asst dir, 1981-82, asst dir, 1982-88, actg dir, 1988-89, assoc prof educ & edir coun ctr, 1989-10, emerita dir, 2010-, prof emerita, stud affairs, coun, higher educ & spec educ; USAF Inst, psychometrist, 1969-70; Am Schs, teacher, 1970-71; Health Educ Systs Inc. **Orgs:** Am Psychol Asn, 1975; Gov Bd Comn Couns & Psychol Serv, Am Col Personnel Asn; pres, Int Asn Coun Serv, 2001-03. **Home Addr:** , MD. **Business Addr:** Emerita Director, Professor Emerita, University of Maryland, Shoemaker Bldg 4281 Chapel Lane, College Park, MD 20742-8111, **Business Phone:** (301)314-7651.

### BOYD, WILHEMINA Y.

Association executive, executive director, teacher. **Personal:** Born Sep 13, 1942, Baltimore, MD; daughter of William Woodley and Erma L Moore; married Raymond D; children: Adam & Jason. **Educ:** Morgan State Univ, Baltimore, BS, 1964; St Mary's Univ, San Antonio, MS, 1991. **Career:** Dept Defense/Heidelberg, Ger, pre-sch dir/high sch teacher, 1978-80, Ft Hood Tex, youth activ, dir, 1981-83; City San Antonio, parks & rcrtn, spec activ supv, 1983-85, events coordr, 1985-87, conv facil, facil mgr, 1987-91; City Kans City, Mo, Conv & Entertainment Ctrs, exec dir, 1992-93; City Tampa, Conv Ctr, exec dir, 1993-98; Dallas Conv Ctr, dir, 1998-2002; Roanoke Civic Ctr, dir, civic facil, currently. **Orgs:** Nat Forum Black Pub Adminr, 1993-; bd dirs, Sun coast Girl Scout Coun Inc, 1994-98; bd trustees, Int Asn Assembly Mgr. **Business Addr:** Executive Director, Roanoke Civic Center, 710 Williamson Rd, Roanoke, VA 24016, **Business Phone:** (540)853-2241.

### BOYD, HON. WILLIAM STEWART

Educator, lawyer, accountant. **Personal:** Born Mar 29, 1952, Chicago, IL. **Educ:** Univ Ill, BS, acct, 1974; Northern IL Univ Col Law, JD, 1980. **Career:** Attorney (retired), educator, judge; Arthur Anderson & Co, sr staff acct, 1974-77, 1981-83; Boyd & Grant, clerk, 1978-81; Legal Asst Found Chicago, clerk, 1979; Boyd & Boyd Ltd, atty, 1983-85; Law Offices William Stewart Boyd, 1985-87; Boyd & Crane, patrner, 1987-98; Traffic Ctr; Cook County Circuit Ct, assoc judge, 1998, 2011-; First Municl Dist, Domestic Rels Div, trial judge; Calendar C, preliminary judge; Chicago Kent Col Law, Adj Prof Law, 2003-05; DePaul Law Sch, guest lectr. **Orgs:** Young Exec Polit; Nat Bus League, 1974; Am Bar Asn, 1981; Cook Co Bar Asn, 1981; bd dir, NIA Comprehensive Ctr, 1984; Northern Ill Univ Col Law Bd Visitors; Chicago & Cook County Bar Asn; Ill Judicial Coun; guest lect, John Marshall Law Sch; Ill Judge's Asn; Ill State Bar Asn; Chicago Bar Asn; Bd dir, Grant Pk Recreation Asn. **Home Addr:** 436 W 100th Pl, Chicago, IL 60610. **Business Addr:** Associate Judge, Cook County Circuit Court, Rm 1605 50 W Washington St, Chicago, IL 60602, **Business Phone:** (312)603-4836.

### BOYD-FOY, MARY LOUISE

Executive. **Personal:** Born Jun 30, 1936, Memphis, TN; daughter of Ivory (deceased) and Mamie E (deceased); married James Arthur. **Educ:** Columbia Univ NY, BA, 1977; Boston Univ, Sch Soc Work, cert contract compliance adminr, 1989. **Career:** Executive (retired); United Negro Col Fund Inc, pub info asst, 1956-60; Foreign Policy Asn, pub info asst, 1960-70; Columbia Univ Urban Ctr, off mgr, 1971-73, asst exec dean sch engineering, 1973-77, exec asst vpres & personnel admin, 1977-78; Int Paper Co, rep northeastern sales accts, 1978-80; Ebasco Serv Inc, coord legis affairs, 1980-86, corp mgr, subcontract compliance, 1986, corp mgr. **Orgs:** Coalition 100 Black Women, 1980-; loyal lady, ruler Order Golden Circle, Long Island Assembly No 20, 1984, 1992; founder, matron, Emerald Chap No 81 Order Eastern Star, Prince Hall Affil, 1986-; Daughters Isis Abu-Bekr Ct No 74, Prince Hall Affil, 1986-; adv bd, United Negro Col Fund Inc, Queens, NY Br, 1986-; ad bd, United Negro Fund Inc, 1986-, Asn Minority Enterprises NY, 1986-; natl chmn, bd dir, Am Asn Blacks Energy, 1990-92; grand assoc matron, Eureka Grand Chap Prince Hall Order Eastern Star Inc; founding mem, former vpres, Nat Asn Univ Women, Long Island, NY Br. **Honors/Awds:** Woman of the Year, Nat Asn Univ Women, 1984; Outstanding Woman of NY State, NY Senate, 1984; Outstanding Service Certificate, United Negro Col Fund Inc, 1984; Distinguished Service Plaque, 1985-86; Recognition Award; Appreciation Award, Concerned Women Jersey City Inc, 1986; Outstanding Service Award, Asn Minority Enterprises NY, 1988; Inductee Registry of Distinguished Citizens, Queens, NY, 1989; Appreciation Award, US Dept Com, 1989; Hilda A Davis Award, Long Island Br, 1991; Nat Women Achievement Award, 1992; James E. Stewart Award, Am Asn Blacks Energy, 1995. **Home Addr:** 117 20 232nd St, Cambria Heights, NY 11411.

### BOYER, CHARLES E.

Executive. **Career:** Blue Cross Blue Shield Mich, vpres, human resources. **Orgs:** Bd dir, chmn, Am Soc Employers. **Business Addr:** Vice President, Blue Cross Blue Shield, PO Box 2888, Detroit, MI 48231.

### BOYER, JAMES BUCHANAN

Educator. **Personal:** Born Apr 3, 1934, Winter Park, FL; married Edna Medlock. **Educ:** Bethune-Cookman Col, BS, 1956; Fla A&M Univ, MEd, 1964; Ohio State Univ, PhD, 1969. **Career:** Fla A&M Univ, teacher & admin vis prof, 1969; Univ Houston, asst prof, 1969-71; Kans State Univ, assoc prof, 1971, prof curric & am ethnic studies, prof, found & adult educ, prof emer educ, currently; George Mason Univ, Multicult Res & Resource Ctr, 2004-; Fel Temple COGIC, pastor; NAME Founder, pastor. **Orgs:** Dir, Inst Multi-Cult Studies; Asn Afro-Am Life & Hist; Asn Supr & Curric; Nat Alliance Black Edu; Coun Interracial Bks C; Nat Asn Advan Colored People; Phi Delta Kappa; founder, Nat Asn Multicultural Educ; Human Rel Bd; consult ed, publ articles field; founder, Nat Asn Multicult Educ. **Honors/Awds:** Kelsey Pharr Award, 1956; Teacher of the Year, 1957; Outstanding Churchman, 1965 & 1969. **Special Achievements:** The Only African-american Professor In The College of Education and the Entire University. **Business Addr:** Professor, George Mason University, Rm 225 Stud Union Bldg I, Fairfax, VA 22030-4444, **Business Phone:** (703)993-4003.

### BOYER, MARCUS AURELIUS

Executive. **Personal:** Born Jul 10, 1945, Vado, NM; married Doris Ann Young; children: Malcolm. **Educ:** Univ NMex, BA, 1967; Wash Univ, MBA, 1972. **Career:** Small Bus Admin, trainee, 1967-68, econ dev asst, 1970, loan officer, 1971; Marine Midland Bank, asst officer, 1973-74, officer, 1974-76, asst vpres, 1976-77; Bank Am, vpres, sr acct officer, 1977-87; Resolution Trust Co, Atlanta, managing agt, oversight cluster mgr, 1990-; Nationsbank NA, sr vpres. **Orgs:** Consortium Grad Study Mgt, 1970; bd mem, Nat Black MBA Asn, 1973-76; pres, NY Chap Nat Black MBA Asn, 1975-76; Nat Asn Advan Colored People; Asn MBA Exec Fel. **Honors/Awds:** Black Achievers in Indiana Award, YMCA, 1975. **Home Addr:** 26-40 Church St Apt 10, South Orange, NJ 07079-1781, **Home Phone:** (973)763-8185. **Business Addr:** Senior Vice President, NationsBank, 101 W Friendly Ave 3rd Flr, Greensboro, NC 27401-2532, **Business Phone:** (336)370-2083.

### BOYER, SPENCER H.

Educator. **Personal:** Born Sep 23, 1938, West Chester, PA; married Prudence Bushnell; children: 6. **Educ:** Howard Univ, BS, elec engineering, 1960; George Washington Univ Law Sch, LLB, 1965; Harvard Law Sch, LLM, 1966. **Career:** IBM Endicott, elec engr, 1960-; US Com Dept, patenter, examr, 1964-65; Howard Univ, fac mem, Sch Law, prof, 1966-, assoc dean, Howard Legal Intern Prog, dir, dir grad law prog, 1966-; Fla Univ, Law Col, vis prof, 1968; Iowa Univ, vis prof; Anitoch Sch Law, Wash, DC, vis prof; George Washington Univ, exec bd ed; Antioch Sch Law, Wa, vis prof; Trans Urban E Inc, consult; Univ Buffalo Sch Law, distinguished lectr taxation & urban econ; Univ DC, adj prof, currently. **Orgs:** Co founder & co ed, Harvard Law Sch; Nat Bar Asn; DC Bar Asn; Am Coun Educ Comt; Nat Acad Sci Publishers; consult atty, CHG, 1967; com cit, Participation Model Cities, 1967-68; City Wide Nat Capitol Housing Authority, 1967-69; dir, Mid-Atlantic Legal Educ Opportunity Prog, 1970; dir, Atlanta Legal Educ Opportunity Prog, 1971, 1972; asst dev, HUMP; Asn Am Law Schs, Comt Minority Studs; Am Trial Lawyers Asn; fac adv, Entertainment Law Stud Asn; fac adv, Stud Bar Asn; fac adv, Barrister; fac adv & chmn, Howard Univ Law Sch Scroll & Howard Univ Law Jour; fac adv, Phi Delta Phi Fraternity; chmn, Admis & Financial Aid Comt; fac adv, Comput & Technol Comt; Spencer H. Boyer Scholar; Spencer H Boyer Ann Keynote Add; founding fac advisor, Bryant Inn Phi Delta Phi Fraternity. **Honors/Awds:** Outstanding Professor Award, 1973-74; Paul L Diggs Award; Outstanding Professor, 1972-73; Student Bar Association Award, Howard University Law School, 1970-71; Professor of the Year, Harvard Univ, 1998; Distinguished Faculty Author Award, Harvard Univ, 2000, 2002, 2004; Student Awards; Outstanding Alumni Award, 2002; Nat Howard Univ Sch Law Alumni Asn; Outstanding Professor Award, 2005-06; Georgetown Law Brothers Forum Award, 2008. **Special Achievements:** First African American law instructor in University of Florida. **Home Addr:** 8305 Oakford Pl, Silver Spring, MD 20910-4235, **Home Phone:** (301)588-6971. **Business Addr:** Professor, Howard University School of Law, 404 Houston Hall 2900 Van Ness St NW, Washington, DC 20008-1194, **Business Phone:** (202)806-8019.

### BOYKIN, A. WADE, JR.

Educator, association executive, government official. **Personal:** Born Feb 7, 1947, Detroit, MI; children: A Wade III & Curtis. **Educ:** Hampton Inst, BA, psychol, 1968; Univ Mich, MA, 1970, PhD, exp psychol, 1972. **Career:** Hampton Inst, psychol lab stud supvr, 1967-68; Cornell Univ, asst to assoc prof, 1972-80; Rockefeller Univ, Lab Comparative Human Cognition, adj assoc prof, 1976-77, fel, 1976-; Jour Black Psych, assoc ed, 1978-81; Res Dir Black Psychol, co-ed, 1979; Howard Univ, Dept Psychol, prof & dir, Develop Psychol Grad Prog, 1980-, Ctr Res Ed Students Placed At Risk, co-dir, 1994-2004, Capstone Inst, exec dir, currently; Millersville Univ, scholar-in-residence, 1985; Sage Publ Bk, ed bd, currently. Books: Res Directions of Black Psychologists, co ed, 1979; The Psychol of African Am Experiences: An Integrity-Based Perspective, co-auth; Promoting High Achievement for All C: Evidence-Based Progs, Practices & Procedures, co ed; Creating the Opportunity to Learn. **Orgs:** Co-found, Conf Empirical Res Black Psych; adv comt, Am Psych Asn MNY Fel Prog; Col bd Coun Inquiry & Praxis; fel Ctr Advan Study Behav Scis, 1978-79; Spencer Fel Nat Acad Educ, 1978-81; co dir, Task Force Relevence Soc Sci Black Exp, Yale Univ, 1981-86; Task Force Sci Persp Intelligence Test & Group Diff Test Scores, APA, 1995; educ bd, Jour Ed Students Placed Risk, Learning Environ Res, Am Ed Res Jour; Emergency Comt Urban C; NEA, 1996-98; pres, Nat Math Adv Panel; fel Inst Comparative Human Develop; res adv panel mem, Nat Minority Stud Achievement Network; bd dir, Proj Grad USA. **Honors/Awds:** Third District Scholar of the Year; Alpha Kappa Mu; Basileus of the Year; Omega Psi Phi, 1967-68; Disting Alumini Award, Hampton Univ; Faculty Senate Exemplary Teaching Award, Howard Univ, 2007. **Home Addr:** 915 Ray Rd, Hyattsville, MD 20783-3193, **Home Phone:** (301)559-4823. **Business Addr:** Executive Director, Howard University, Holy Cross Hall, Washington, DC 20008, **Business Phone:** (202)806-6805.

### BOYKIN, KEITH

Television show host, writer. **Personal:** Born Aug 28, 1965, St. Louis, MO; son of William and Shirley Hayes. **Educ:** Dartmouth Col, BA, govt, 1987; Harvard Univ, JD, 1992. **Career:** DeKalb County Public Schs, teacher, 1989; White House, spec asst, pres US, 1993-95; NBGLLF, exec dir, 1995-98; Am Univ, adj prof gov & instructor, 1999-2000; BET J, TV host, My Two Cents, 2006-08; The Daily Voice, ed chief, 2008-; Author: One More River To Cross, Doubleday, 1996; Respecting the Soul, 1999; Beyond The Down Low, Avalon, 2005; TV Series: "American Candidate"; "Anderson Cooper 360"; "The OReilly Factor"; "The Tyra Banks Show"; "The Montel Williams Show"; "Judge Hatchett"; "The Tom Joyner Morning Show"; Books: Beyond the Down Low: Sex, Lies and Denial in Black America; For Colored Boys Who Have Considered Suicide When The Rainbow Is Still Not Enough. **Orgs:** Pres bd, Nat Black Justice Coalition. **Honors/Awds:** Dartmouth Freshman Prize, The Dartmouth Newspaper, 1983; Alpha Kappa Alpha Ivy Award, Nu Beta Omega Chapter, 1983; William S. Churchill Prize, Dartmouth Col, 1984; Track & Field Achievement Award, Dartmouth Col, 1984-85; The Barrett Cup, Dartmouth Col, 1987; Dartmouth Black Caucus Senior Honor Roll, Dartmouth Black Caucus, 1987; Muhammad Kenyatta Young Alumni Award, Harvard BLSA, 1994; Nat Services Award, The Brotherhood of the Gentleman, Inc, 1997; Recognition from Cambridge, Mass City Coun, 1998; GMAD Angel Award, Gay Men African Descent, 1998; Audre Lorde-Joe Beam Literary Award, 1999; Lambda Literary Award, Lambda Lit, 1999; The Conscience of the Community Award, 1999; Solutions Award of Merit, Solutions DC, 1999; Nat Leadership Award, People of Color in Crisis, 2004; American Library Association Stonewall Award for Nonfiction, 2013. **Special Achievements:** Nominee, Lambda Literary Award. **Business Addr:** Author, PO Box 1229, New York, NY 10037.

### BOYKINS, AMBER

Government official. **Personal:** Born Apr 4, 1969, St. Louis, MO; daughter of Billie A and Amber; married Shaun. **Educ:** Columbia Col, Columbia, BS, bus admin, 1991; MBA, JD. **Career:** MO House Rep, 1998-, state rep dist 60, 1998, 2000, 2002 & 2004; dir, Child Develop Ctr; teachers, St. Louis Pub Sch; caseworker, Div Family Serv; aftercare worker, Hopewell Care Ctr. **Orgs:** Chair, Mo Legis Black Caucus; state dir, Women Govt; Delta Sigma Theta; state Dem Party; secy, Nat Order Black Elected Legis Women; Nat Asn Advan Colored People; Coun State Governments; Tax Increment Financing Comn. **Honors/Awds:** Yes I Can Award, St Louis Teachers & School Related Personnel Local 420; Dr. Joyce Thomas Leadership Award; Young Democrats Dedicated Leadership in Government Award; Making a Difference Award; Henry Toll Fellow, 1999. **Special Achievements:** Youngest African American woman legislator in the history of the Missouri House; 30 Women to Watch: Women at the Top of their Class. **Home Addr:** 4135 Shreve Ave, Saint Louis, MO 63115. **Business Addr:** State Representative, MO House of Representatives, 201 W Capitol Ave Rm 115A, Jefferson City, MO 65101, **Business Phone:** (573)751-4415.

### BOYKINS, EARL ANTOINE

Basketball player. **Personal:** Born Jun 2, 1976, Cleveland, OH; son of Willie Williams and Charlene Horton; children: Earl Jr. **Educ:** Eastern Mich Univ, attended 1998. **Career:** Rockford Lightning, player, 1998-99; NJ Nets, guard, 1999; Cleveland Cavaliers, 1999-2000; Orlando Magic, 1999; Los Angeles Clippers, 2000-02; Golden State Warriors, 2002-03; Denver Nuggets, guard, 2003-07; Milwaukee Bucks, guard, 2007-08; Charlotte Bobcats, 2008; Virtus Bologna, free agt, 2008-09; Wash Wizards, 2009-10; Milwaukee Bucks, 2010-11; Houston Rockets, 2012.

### BOYLAND, DORIAN SCOTT (DOE BOYLAND)

Automotive executive, baseball player. **Personal:** Born Jan 6, 1955, Chicago, IL; son of William and Alice Jones; married Denise A Wells; children: Shannon, Richard & Adriane. **Educ:** Univ Wis, Oshkosh, WI, BA, bus, 1976. **Career:** Pittsburgh Pirates, prof player, 1976-83; Ron Tonkin-Dodge, Gladstone, Ore, owner & gen mgr, 1985-86; Gresham Dodge Inc, Gresham, Ore, pres & gen mgr; Boyland properties, pres; Boyland Ins Group, pres; Boyland Auto Group Inc, chief exec officer, pres, owner, 1996-; pres, Mercedes Benz S Orlando. **Orgs:** Chmn, Performance 20 Groups; bd mem, United Negro Col Fund; Portland Urban League; Ore Arbit Bd; APA Fraternity Inc, 1974; Dodge Denter Coun; pres, Black Stud Union Asn. **Home Addr:** 16235 SW Falcon Dr, Beaverton, OR 97007, **Home Phone:** (503)579-2656. **Business Addr:** Owner, Chief Executive Officer, Boyland Auto Group, 4301 Millenia Blvd, Orlando, FL 32839, **Business Phone:** (866)835-2369.

### BOYNTON, ASA TERRELL, SR.

School administrator, vice president (organization), executive director. **Personal:** Born May 20, 1945, Griffin, GA; son of Estell and Willie; married Evelyn Josephine Jordan; children: Asa Terrell Jr, Aaron Vernard & Antoine Debue. **Educ:** Ft Valley State Col, BS, bus admin, 1967; Univ Ga, MA, pub admin, 1973; cert police instr. **Career:** Ft Valley State Univ, assoc dir pub safety, 1979; St Petersburg, Pub Safety Div, chief community rels, 1973; Univ Ga, Pub Safety Div, assoc dir, 1978, dir pub safety, assoc vpres security preparedness, currently. **Orgs:** Pres, Ga Asn Campus Law Enforcement Admin, 1976; Eta Iota Lambda, 1977; Athens Rotary Club, 1983-; pres, Athens Breakfast Optimist Club, 1984; pres, fel Int Asn Campus Law Enforcement Adminr, 1987-88; adv bd, Northeast Ga Police Acad; pres, Alpha Phi Alpha Fraternity; FBI Nat Acad; chmn, Athens Regional Med Ctr; fel, Ga Int Law Enforcement Exchange Team; fel Ga State Bd Corrections; bd dir & chmn, Leadership Ga. **Home Addr:** 470 Millstone Cir, Athens, GA 30605, **Home Phone:** (706)549-7353. **Business Addr:** Associate Vice President, University of Georgia, 212 Terrell Hall Jackson St, Athens, GA 30602, **Business Phone:** (706)542-3000.

### BOZE, U. LAWRENCE

Association executive, lawyer. **Personal:** Born Nov 1, 1949, Houston, TX; son of U L and Iva Stewart Bozes. **Educ:** Univ Houston, BS, hotel, motel & restaurant mgt, 1973; Tex Southern Univ, MBA, finance, gen, JD, 1978. **Career:** Chevron USA & Gulf Oil Corp, bankruptcy coun, 1978-87; Nat Bar Asn, pres, 1996; Tex Bar Examiners, vice chmn, 1997-; Riverside Bank, founder; Allied Bankshares Inc, vpres & bankruptcy coun; U Lawrence Boze & Assocs PC, owner, atty, currently. **Orgs:** Nat Bar Asn, 1987-96; pres, Houston Lawyers Asn, 1987; founder & pres, Tex Asn African Am Lawyers, 1991-; Omega Psi Phi Fraternity; Am Bar Asn. **Honors/Awds:** Distinguished Service to Houston Community Award, Nat Asn Advan Colored People. **Special Achievements:** First black fee atty, Fidelity Nat Title, 1994; first president of the Texas Association of African American Lawyers. **Business Addr:** Attorney, Owner, U Lawrence Boze & Associates PC, 2212 Blodgett St, Houston, TX 77004-5218, **Business Phone:** (713)520-0967.

### BOZEMAN, BRUCE L.

Lawyer. **Personal:** Born Jan 21, 1944, Philadelphia, PA; son of Hammie Winston and Herman H; married Patricia Johnson; children: Herman, Leslie, Patrick & Holly. **Educ:** Va Union Univ, BA, 1965; Howard Univ Sch Law, JD, 1968; NY Univ Sch Law, LLM, 1972. **Career:** US Dist Ct, DC, 1968; US Ct Appeals, DC, 1969; State New York, 1969; Maxwell House Div GFC, asst coun, 1969-71, Birds Eye div couns, 1971-73, beverage & breakfast foods div couns, 1973-78, dir consumer affairs, asst gen couns, 1978-81; US Supreme Ct, 1978-; Norton Simon Inc, asst gen coun, 1981-83; Commonwealth Va, 1991; US Dist Ct Southern Dist NY, 1994-; Bruce L Bozeman, PC, pres, currently; Westchester Financial Group Ltd, pres; pvt pract atty, currently; Bozeman & Trott, LLP, atty; Bozeman Law Firm LLP, sr partner & prin, partner, 1983-. **Orgs:** Charter mem, Fayetteville State Univ, Delta Mu Delta Nat Honor Soc Bus Admin, 1976; fel Consortium Grad Study Mgt, 1979-80; NCA Bar Asn, Labor & Employ Sec, 1989-91; Am Asn Blacks Energy, 1989-; Am Creative Coun Asn, 1989-92; Wake County Bar Asn, 1989-92; chair, Bar Exam Stipend Sub Community, Minorities Prof Community, 1989-92; Nat Bar Asn, 1989-92; NC Asn Black Lawyers, 1989-92; Soc Human Resource Mgt, 1992-95; Am Bar Asn; Ny Bar Asn; Westchester County Bar Asn; Nat Acad Elder Law Attorneys. **Home Addr:** 85 Miles Ave, White Plains, NY 10606. **Business Addr:** Senior Partner, Principal, The Bozeman Law Firm LLP, 6 Gramatan Ave 5th Fl, Mt Vernon, NY 10550, **Business Phone:** (914)668-4600.

### BOZEMAN, DAVID P.

Manager, vice president (organization). **Educ:** Bradley Univ, BS, mfg engineering technol & mech design; Milwaukee Sch Engineering, MS, engineering mgt. **Career:** Harley-Davidson Motor Co, Advan Mfg, vpres; Caterpillar, Specialty Prod Bus Unit, gen mgr, 2008-09, Core Components Bus Unit, vpres, 2009-10, bus unit mgr, Integrated Mfg Opers Div, vpres, 2010-13, Caterpillar Enterprise Syst Group, sr vpres, 2013-; Weyerhaeuser Co, dir, 2015-. **Orgs:** Exec Leadership Coun; bd dir, Soc Mfg Engrs Educ Found; Bradley Univ's Mfg & Indust Engineering; bd dir, Caterpillar's China Mach Components Co; bd dir, Advan Filtration Systs Inc; bd dir, Peoria Riverfront Mus; Nat Soc Black Engrs; Nat Black MBA Asn; bd trustee, Manufacturers Alliance Productivity & Innovation. **Business Addr:** Senior Vice President, Caterpillar Inc, 501 SW Jefferson Ave, Peoria, IL 61630, **Business Phone:** (888)614-4328.

**BRACEY, EARL W.** **See BRACEY, WILLIE EARL.**

### BRACEY, ESI EGGLESTON

Vice president (organization). **Personal:** married Des; children: Anura & Benoit Alec. **Educ:** Dartmouth Col, BA, engineering sci, 1991. **Career:** Proctor & Gamble, global cosmetics int, branding & oper, 1991-, mkt leader, 1991-99, mkt dir, skin & personal care, 1999-2000, mkt dir, covergirl, 2000-03, gen mgr, 2003-06, vpres, 2006-09, sr vpres, gen mgr global cosmetics, CMO, beauty brand bldg, 2009-; Covergirl, vpres, gen mgr & global vpres. **Business Addr:** Senior Vice President, General Manager, Procter & Gamble, 1 Procter & Gamble Plz, Cincinnati, OH 45202, **Business Phone:** (513)983-1100.

**BRACEY, HENRY J.**
Educator, counselor. **Personal:** Born Jan 31, 1949, Grand Rapids, MI; son of Joe and Sheba M Davis; children: Anton J, Candice G, Kwando A & Lisa K. **Educ:** Western Mich Univ, BS, 1971; Univ SC, MEd, 1981. **Career:** SC Personnel & Guid Asn, mem exec coun, 1982; SC Sch Counrs Asn, publicity comn, 1982; SC Asn Non-White Concerns, pres & bd mem, 1982; Southeastern Asn Educ Oppor Prog, personnel mgr, 1983; Midlands Tech Col, counr, 2003. **Orgs:** Pub rels dir, Ms Black Columbia Pageant, 1980-82; bd mem, Columbia Youth Coun, 1982-84; bd mem, Bros & Sisters, 1984-86; vpres, Col Pl Comt, Coun, 1985-87; SC Tech Educ Asn, 1986-87; Southern Regional Coun, Black Am Affairs, 1986-87; Omega Psi Phi; pres, Heritage Comt Prods; stud involvement coord Southern Regional Coun Black Am Affairs Conf, 1986; pres, Kuumba Circle, 1988; pres, Eau Claire Comm Coun; Eau Claire Devel Corp; Ujamaa A Concern Group Men; Nat Asn Advan Colored People; Ascac Asn study Class African Civilizations; SC Conf, Shalom Zone Ministries; pres, mem, Francis Burns United Methodist Church; staff coun pres, Midlands Tech Col; adv bd, Columbia Citizens; Pta pres, Alcorn Mid Sch, CA Johnson HS. **Home Addr:** 5016 Colonial Dr, Columbia, SC 29203, **Home Phone:** (803)735-8224. **Business Addr:** Counselor, Midland Tech College, PO Box 2408, Columbia, SC 29202, **Business Phone:** (803)738-7621.

**BRACEY, JOHN HENRY, JR.**
Educator. **Personal:** Born Jul 17, 1941, Chicago, IL; son of John H Sr and Helen Harris; married Ingrid Babb; children: Kali, Bryan & John Peter. **Educ:** Howard Univ, attended 1960; Roosevelt Univ, BA, 1964; Northwestern Univ, NDEA, 1969. **Career:** Northeastern Ill State Col, lectr, hist, 1969-71; Univ Rochester, asst prof hist, 1971-72; Univ Mass, W.E.B. Du Bois Dept Afro-Am Studies, assoc prof, 1972-94, chmn, 1974-79, African Diaspora Studies, co-dir. Publications: Black Nationalism in America, 1970; African American Women and the Vote, 1997; Strangers and Neighbors: Relations between Blacks and Jews in the United States, 1999; African American Mosaic: A Documentary History from the Slave Trade to the Twenty-First Century, 2004; SOS: Calling All Black People: A Black Arts Movement Reader, 2014. **Orgs:** Life mem, Asn Study African-Am Life & Hist; life mem, Org Am Historians, nominating comt, 1978-79; Phi Alpha Theta; Southern Hist Asn; Nat Asn Colored Womens Clubs; Nat Asn Advan Colored People. **Home Addr:** 3 Campbell Ct, Amherst, MA 01002, **Home Phone:** (413)549-3642. **Business Addr:** Professor, Co-director, University of Massachusetts, 327 New Africa House, Amherst, MA 01003, **Business Phone:** (413)545-2751.

**BRACEY, WILLIE EARL (EARL W BRACEY)**
Lawyer, school administrator. **Personal:** Born Dec 21, 1950, Jackson, MS; son of Dudley and Alvaretta (King) B; married Dianne Fullenwilder. **Educ:** Wright Jr Col, AA, 1971; Mt Senario Col, BA, sec educ, 1974; Eastern Ill Univ, MS, guid & coun, 1976; Southern Ill Univ, JD, 1979. **Career:** Southern Ill Univ, Ctr Basic Skill, instr, 1977-78, law clerk, 1978-79, Law Sch, res asst, 1977-78; Notre Dame Law Sch, teaching asst, 1977; Western Ill Univ, dir, stud legal serv, 1979-86, adj prof, col stud personnel prog, 1981-84, asst vpres, stud affairs support servs, 1986-99, assoc vpres stud serv, 1999-, adj asst prof, counr, assoc fac African Am studies; McDonough County, asst pub defender, 1983-84. **Orgs:** Nat Asn Advan Colored People, 1979-; Am Trial Lawyers Asn, 1979-90; Am Bar Asn, 1979-90; Int Bar Asn, 1979-; Mc Donough City Bar Asn, 1979-; Chicago Comt Foreign Realtions, 1986; Nat Asn Stud Personnel Admin, 1987-; Who's Who Among Black Americans, 1988, 1992; Who's WhoMidwest, 1989; fac mem Blue Key Hon Soc; Housing Comnr, Mc Donough County Housing Authority; Ill Atty Gen Date Rape Drugs Steering Comt, 1999; advisor, Phi Beta Sigma; Macomb Qual Life Comt; chair, Housing Authority McDonough County; Macomb Pk Dist Bd; Nat Legal Aid & Defender Asn; Ill Stud Atty Asn. **Honors/Awds:** Outstanding Leadership in Diversity Award, 2010. **Home Addr:** 2012 W Adams, Macomb, IL 61455. **Business Addr:** Associate Vice President for Student Services, Western Illinois University, Horrabin Hall 115, Macomb, IL 61455-1390, **Business Phone:** (309)298-1414.

**BRACKEN, CHARLES O.**
Management consultant, health services administrator. **Educ:** Wayne State Univ, Detroit, BS, acct, 1981, MBA, mgt, 1985; Inst Cert Comput Prof, Cert Data Processing; Andrews Univ, attended 1969; Stanford Univ Grad Sch Bus, cert, exec prog small co, 1992. **Career:** Multihosp corp, chief info officer; Healthcare Info & Mgt Systs Soc, exec vpres; Forum Healthcare Strategists, mem; Healthcare Strategy Inst, presenter; Harvard Sch Pub Health Conf, ann presenter; Med Econ Soc Fel, ann presenter; Super Consult Co, exec vpres, 1986-05; ACS Healthcare Solutions, managing dir, 2005-08; vpres Bus Develop, currently; VISIONIT, sr vpres, 2008-10, sr advisor healthcare solutions, 2011-12; Ingenix Consult, exec managing dir, Provider Mkt, 2010-11; Chasware Group LLC, partner, 2011-; GetixHealth, chief exec officer, 2012-. **Orgs:** Healthcare Info & Mgt Systs Soc; Nat Asn Health Serv Execs; Ctr Health Info Mgt; bd mem, Ctr Health Info Mgt; bd dir, Healthcare Financial Mgt Asn; bd dir, Super Consult Co Inc; Coibion & Assocs Inc; Peace Corps, gen acct, 1975-77. **Business Addr:** Senior Advisor of Healthcare Solutions, VisionIT, 3031 W Grand Blvd Suite 600, Detroit, MI 48202, **Business Phone:** (313)420-2000.

**BRACKENS, TONY LYNN, JR.**
Football player. **Personal:** Born Dec 26, 1974, Fairfield, TX; children: 3. **Educ:** Univ Tex, Austin. **Career:** Football player (retired); Jacksonville Jaguars, defensive end, 1996-97, 1999-2004, right defensive end, 1998. **Honors/Awds:** Pro Bowl, 1999; Ed Block Courage Award, 2003.

**BRACY, ADRIAN E.** **See BARR-BRACY, ADRIAN.**

**BRADBERRY, DR. RICHARD PAUL**
Librarian, library administrator. **Personal:** Born Dec 6, 1951, Florala, AL; son of Sam and Nettie Ruth Hightower. **Educ:** Ala State Univ, Montgomery, AL, BS, 1973; Atlanta Univ, Atlanta, GA, MSLS, 1974; Univ Mich, Ann Arbor, MI, PhD, 1988. **Career:** Auburn Univ, Auburn, AL, humanities librn, 1974-76; Langston Univ, Langston, OK, dir, librn chair librn sci dept, 1976-83; Lake Erie Col, Painesville, OH, dir libr, 1983-84; Univ Conn, W Hartford, CT, dir libr, 1984-89; Del State Col, Dover, DE, dir col libr, 1989-92; William Patterson Col, Sarah B Askew Libr, lib staff; Bowie State Univ, Thurgood Marshall Libr, dir & dean, currently. **Orgs:** Am Libr Asn, 1984-; Asn Libr & Info Sci Educ, 1988-; treas, Land-Grant Libr Dir Asn, 1989-; Del Libr Asn, 1990-; Am Asn Higher Educ, 1990-. **Honors/Awds:** Education Professions Development Act Grant, US Govt, 1973; Oklahoma State Regents Doctoral Study Grant, State Okla, 1980, 1981; Title II-B Fellowship, University of Michigan, 1980, 1981. **Home Addr:** 1300 S Farmview Dr H-31, Dover, DE 19901. **Business Addr:** Dean Library & Media Operations, Director, Bowie State University, 14000 Jericho Pk Rd, Bowie, MD 20715, **Business Phone:** (301)860-3849.

**BRADDOCK, CAROL T.**
Consultant, executive. **Personal:** Born Sep 7, 1942, Hamilton, OH; daughter of Rev Carlace A Tipton; married Robert L; children: Ryan Lawrence & Lauren Patricia-Tipton. **Educ:** Univ Cincinnati, BA, 1965, MA, 1976; Ind Univ, grad key, 1980. **Career:** McAlpins Dept Store, buyer, 1969; Vogue Care Col, instr, 1971; Taft Broadcasting, prod coordr, 1972; Fed Home Bank Bd, urban prog coordr, 1973; Col Mt St Joseph, lectr, 1973; Neighborhood Reinvestment Corp, consult, 1974; Fed Home Loan Bank Cincinnati, exec asst, 1975, vpres, com investment officer, 1978-85, asst vpres, 1978, pres; Banking-financial consult. **Orgs:** Founder & past pres, Womens Alliance, 1966; exec comm mem, WCET-TV Pub TV, 1972-79; Queen City Beauty, Cincinnati Enquirer, 1973; pres, Minority Bus Devel Coalition, 1980; trustee, Nat Trust Hist Preserv; Jr League Sustainee. **Honors/Awds:** Outstanding Serv Award, Urban Reinvestment Task Force, 1975; Black Achievers Award, YMCA, 1978; Outstanding Career Woman, 1983. **Home Addr:** PO Box 1661, Potomac, MD 20859. **Business Addr:** Founder, Women's Alliance Inc, PO Box 46386, Cincinnati, OH 45246.

**BRADDOCK, DR. MARILYN EUGENIA**
Educator, physician, dentist. **Personal:** Born Apr 25, 1955, Washington, DC; daughter of Ernest L and Rita H Glover. **Educ:** Marquette Univ, BS, 1977; Meharry Med Col, DDS, 1982; Univ NC, prosthodontic cert, 1992; Univ NC, Chapel Hill, MS, oral biol immunol, 1993. **Career:** Cook Co Hosp, GPR, 1982-83; USN Dent Corps, 1983-86, comdr, 2006-; USN Dent Corps, Periodontology fel, 1985-86; pvt pract dentist, 1986-89; Prince Georges County Md, consultant, 1986-88; fellowship Patricia Roberts Harris Foundation, 1990; Univ NC, Chapel Hill, prosthetic dent & res fel, 1992; Meharry Med Col, Sch Dent, Dept Prosthodontics, asst prof, 1992-95; COR USN Dent Corps, USS John F Kennedy, CV-67, 1995. **Orgs:** Food preparer & server, Wash & Nashville, 1984; troop leader, Girl Scouts Am, 1985-89; Delta Sigma Theta Sor Inc; Am Dent Asn; Fed Servs Asn; Am Col Prosthodontics; Omicron Kappa Upsilon; Acad Gen Dent. **Home Addr:** 9650 Santiago Rd, Columbia, MD 21045, **Home Phone:** (410)730-6020. **Business Addr:** Commander, US Navy, 1200 Navy Pentagon, Washington, DC 20350-1200.

**BRADEN, EVERETTE ARNOLD**
Judge. **Personal:** Born Nov 3, 1932, Chicago, IL; son of Zedrick Thomas and Bernice; married Mary Jeanette Hemphill; children: Marilynne M. **Educ:** Herzl Jr Col, attended 1952; Northwestern Univ, BS, polit sci, 1954; John Marshall Law Sch, JD, 1961, LLB. **Career:** Cook Co Dept Pub Aid, caseworker, 1961-66; property & inst consult, 1966-69; Cook Co Pub Defender Off, trial atty, 1969-76, supv trial atty, 1976-77; Cook Co Circuit Ct, assoc judge, 1977-78, circuit judge, 1978-94; Ill Appellate Ct, justice, 1994-96, circuit judge, 1996-2002; pvt pract, 2002-; John Marshall Law Sch, Off Alumni Rels & Devel, bd visitors, pres, Emer Bd Mem, currently. **Orgs:** Phi Alpha Delta Law; Nat Bar Asn; Ill State Bar Asn; Chicago Bar Asn; Meth Bar Asn; treas, Ill Judges Asn, 1980-81, bd dir, 1985-91; Kappa Alpha Psi; secy, Ill Judicial Coun, 1982-84, chmn, 1985-86; pres, bd dir, John Marshall Law Sch Alumni Asn, vpres, 1988-90, pres, 1990-91; charter fel, Ill Bar Found; Am Trial Lawyers Asn; Cook Co Judicial Adv Coun; bd dir, Ill Judges Found, 2009-10; pres, Cook County Bar Asn; Northwestern Univ Alumni Asn. **Home Addr:** 8948 S Jeffery Blvd, Chicago, IL 60617-2925, **Home Phone:** (773)721-8508. **Business Addr:** Emeritus Board Members, The John Marshall Law School, 315 S Plymouth Ct, Chicago, IL 60604, **Business Phone:** (312)427-2737.

**BRADFORD, ANDREA**
Executive. **Personal:** Born Huntsville, AL. **Educ:** Oberlin Col, BMus, performance, 1970. **Career:** Opera Co, singer; Opera Ebony, 1994; Right Mgt Consult, sr vpres, 1997-2008, sr orgn consult, client serv, vpres, 2003-08; JBK Assocs Inc, chief diversity officer, currently. **Business Addr:** Chief Diversity Office, JBK Associates Inc, 1 Engle St Suite 201, Englewood, NJ 07631, **Business Phone:** (201)567-9070.

**BRADFORD, DR. CHARLES EDWARD**
Clergy, educator, writer. **Personal:** Born Jul 12, 1925, Washington, DC; son of Robert Lee and Etta Elizabeth; married Ethel Lee McKenzie; children: Sharon Louise Lewis, Charles Edward Jr & Dwight Lyman. **Educ:** Oakwood Col, Huntsville AL, BA, 1946; Andrews Univ, Berrien Springs Mich, 1958, DD, 1978. **Career:** Pastor, administrator (retired), preacher, teacher; pastor, 1945-61; La & Tex, Pastor, 1946-51; Mo, Pastor, 1953-57; New York, pastor, 1959-61; Lake Region Conf, Seventh-day Adventists, pres, 1961-70; Northeastern Conf, St. Albans, dir, 1957-59; Lake Region Conf, Chicago, pres, 1961-70; Assoc secy Gen Conf, Wash, 1970-79; Seventh-day Adventist, N Am Div, pres, 1979-90; preacher & teacher, currently. **Orgs:** Trustee, Oakwood Col Andrews Univ, 1961; trustee, Loma Linda Univ, 1979; bd trustee, Fla Hosp Col Health Sci. **Honors/Awds:** Loma Linda University Diversity Leadership Award, Loma Linda Univ, 2000. **Special Achievements:** First African-American president of the North American Division of Seventh-day Adventist; Books: Pauline Epistles, Pauline Epistles, Sabbath Roots: The African Connection, 1999; stewardship. **Business Addr:** Preacher, 10178 Sleepy Willow Ct, Spring Hill, FL 34608-4211, **Business Phone:** (352)688-5125.

**BRADFORD, COREY LAMON**
Football player. **Personal:** Born Dec 8, 1975, Baton Rouge, LA. **Educ:** Jackson State Univ, grad. **Career:** Football player (retired); Green Bay Packers, 1998, wide receiver, 1999-2001, fullback, 2001; Houston Texans, wide receiver, 2002-05, ambassador; Detroit Lions, wide receiver, 2006; Wash Redskins, 2007. **Business Addr:** Ambassador, Houston Texans, 2 NRG Pk, Houston, TX 77054, **Business Phone:** (832)667-2002.

**BRADFORD, GARY C.**
Editor. **Personal:** Born May 4, 1956, Pittsburgh, PA; son of Frank M and Glenrose Beatrice Fields. **Educ:** Univ Pittsburgh, PA, BA, writing, 1979; Temple Univ, Philadelphia, PA, MA, jour, 1983. **Career:** WHCR-FM, New York, NY, vol host & producer, 1988-89; Pittsburgh Press, Pa, reporter, 1979-81; Philadelphia Daily News, Pa, copy editing intern, 1982; Pittsburgh, Pa, assoc ed, 1985; NY Times, copy ed, 1985-. **Orgs:** NY Asn Black Journalists, 1986-; Duke Ellington Soc, 1990-; 100 Black Men, 1991-. **Honors/Awds:** Publisher's Award Headline Writing, New York Times, 1987, 1988. **Home Addr:** 412 W 149th St Apt 2, New York, NY 10031, **Home Phone:** (212)690-4350. **Business Addr:** Copy Editor Metropolitan News, New York Times, 229 W 43rd St 3rd Fl, New York, NY 10036, **Business Phone:** (212)556-4428.

**BRADFORD, JAMES EDWARD**
Accountant, high school teacher. **Personal:** Born Jun 27, 1943, Jonesboro, LA; married Mae Lean Calahan; children: Roderick, Berkita & D'Andra. **Educ:** Grambling State Univ, BS, 1965; Wayne State Univ, attended 1966. **Career:** Sabine Parish Sch Bd, teacher, 1965-66; Bienville Parish Sch Bd, teacher, 1966-70; Continental Group, acct, 1970-76; Independent Consults Inc, pres, 1980-85; Bradco Sales, pres, 1984-85; Smurfit Stone Container Corp, mgr, super acct, currently. **Orgs:** Bd chmn, Pine Belt CAA, 1979-85; bd chmn, Jackson Coun Aging, 1980-85; bd mem, N Delta Regional Planning Comt, 1983-85; Asn La Lobbyists. **Home Addr:** 709 Leon Dr, Jonesboro, LA 71251, **Home Phone:** (318)259-7595. **Business Addr:** Superior Accountant, Smurfit Stone Container Corp, Mill St, Hodge, LA 71247, **Business Phone:** (318)259-4421.

**BRADFORD, LAJUANA**
Executive, vice president (organization). **Educ:** RI Col, BA, psychol; Univ NC, Wachovia Exec Leadership Prog, grad, 2007; Boston Col, Mgt Develop Prog Corp Community Involvement, grad. **Career:** SouthTrust Bank, sr vpres, community develop mgr, 1989-2004; Wachovia, sr vpres community rels exec, 2004-09; Regions Financial Corp, sr vpres risk opers, mgr external affairs, 2009-11, sr vpres corp diversity & pub affairs, 2010-. **Orgs:** Bd mem, YWCA Cent Ala; bd mem, Ala Region Am Red Cross; bd mem, Birmingham Civil Rights Inst; Leadership Birmingham, 2008; C's Hosp Comt Future; bd dir, Ala Humanities Found Bd's.

**BRADFORD, MARTINA LEWIS**
Executive, lawyer. **Personal:** Born Sep 14, 1952, Washington, DC; daughter of Martin Lewis and Alma Ashton; married William; children: Sydney. **Educ:** Am Univ, BA, 1973; Duke Univ, JD, 1975. **Career:** Southern Railways Inc, corp legal intern; Interstate Com Div Finance Div, Wash, atty, 1976-78; Comn Appropriations, US House Rep, coun, 1978-81; Interstate Com Comn, Wash, DC, chief staff to vice chmn, 1981-83; Am Univ Sch Law, adj prof, 1982; AT&T Corp, Legal Dept, NY, atty, 1983-85, atty, 1985-88, vpres govt affairs; Lucent Technologies, global pub affairs, vpres; Akin Gump Strauss Hauer & Feld LLP, partner, currently; Us Senate by Senate Majority Leader Harry Reid, Dep Sgt Arms, 2011. **Orgs:** Minority coun, US House Representatives, 1978-79, minority coun, US Sen, 1979-80; founding vpres, Women's Transp Sem, 1978; Dist Columbia Bar, 1976, Md Bar, 1983-, Women's Bar Asn, 1989; bd mem, INROADS Inc, 1989; bd trustee, Am Univ, 1996-2001; Cadmus Communs Corp, dir, 2000-, chmn, mem exec comt & corp comt; trustee, Lawyers Comt Civil Rights Under Law; NCSL Found State Legislators; bd visitors, Duke Univ. **Home Addr:** 383 Beechwood Dr, New Rochelle, NY 10804, **Home Phone:** (914)654-0520. **Business Addr:** Partner, Akin Gump Strauss Hauer & Feld LLP, 1333 NH Ave NW, Washington, DC 20036-1564, **Business Phone:** (202)887-4062.

**BRADFORD, PAUL L.**
Football player. **Personal:** Born Apr 20, 1974, East Palo Alto, CA; married Margarita; children: Bella Mae & Antonio. **Educ:** Portland State, phys educ. **Career:** Football player (retired); San Diego Chargers, defensive back, 1997, corner back, 1997-2000; Las Vegas Outlaws, corner back, 2000-01. **Honors/Awds:** Rookie of the Year, 1997. **Home Addr:** 4017 Via Barbara, Lancaster, CA 93536, **Home Phone:** (661)206-7326.

**BRADFORD, RONNIE (RONALD LEE BRADFORD)**
Football player, football coach. **Personal:** Born Oct 1, 1970, Minot, ND; married Trish; children: Anthony & Kaylee. **Educ:** Univ Colo, grad. **Career:** Football player (retired), football coach; Denver Broncos, defensive back, 1993-95, spec teams asst coach, 2003-04, spec-teams coach, 2004-07, asst defensive backs coach, 2007-08; Ariz Cardinals, right cornerback, 1996; Atlanta Falcons, right cornerback & free safety, 1997-2001; Minn Vikings, free safety, 2002; Kans City Cheif, defensive asst, 2009-10; Calif Golden Bears, admin asst, 2010-12; Univ Memphis, safeties coach, 2011; La Tech Univ, asst coach, 2013-, coach, 2016; USC, coach, 2016. **Honors/Awds:** All-Am hon, USA Today. **Business Addr:** Assistant Coach, Louisiana Tech University, PO Box 3168, Ruston, CO 71272, **Business Phone:** (318)257-3785.

**BRADFORD, STEVEN C.**
Government official. **Educ:** Calif State Univ, BA, polit sci. **Career:** IBM, mkt rep, 1983-90; LA Conserv Corps, Prog dir, 1990-94; Congresswoman Juanita Millender-McDonald's Off, dist dir; Gardena City Coun, coun mem, 1997-2009, mayor pro tem, currently; Pub Affairs Southern Calif Edison, region mgr; Calif State Assembly, candidiate, 2006, assembly mem, 2009-; Assembly Comt Utilities & Com, chair, 2009-; Assembly Select Comt Status Boys & Men Color Calif, chair, 2013-. **Orgs:** Dr Martin Luther King Jr. Cult Comt Gardena; chair, Black Hist Month celebration comt; PTA; pres, Hollypark Homeowners Asn; nat dir, Phi Beta Sigma Fraternity; Boy Scouts; Hollypark Homeowners Asn; Calif Contract Cities Asn; chair, Garde-

na Black Hist Month Celebration Comt; chair, Gardena Jazz Festival Comt; Independent Cities Asn; Parent Teacher Asn; S Calif Asn Gov; sr mem, City Coun; dir, Solid Waste; Calif Cities Self-Reliance Joint Powers Authority Independent Cities Asn; Southern Calif Asn Governments. **Home Addr:** , CA. **Business Addr:** Mayor Pro Tem, Gardena City Council, 1700 W 162nd St, Gardena, CA 90247, **Business Phone:** (310)217-9500.

## BRADFORD-EATON, ZEE

Advertising executive, association executive. **Personal:** Born Oct 10, 1953, Atlanta, GA; daughter of William Henry Davis and Betty Anthony Davis Harden; married Maynard; children: Quentin Eugene Jr & Qiana Yvonne. **Educ:** Morris Brown Col, attended 1975. **Career:** QZ Enterprises Inc, pub rels dir, 1979-83; First Class Inc, pub rels dir, 1983-84, exec vpres, 1984-. **Orgs:** Pres, Shaker Welcome Wagon, 1980-81; steering comt, Mayor's Task Force Educ; bd mem, Am Diabetes Asn; steering comt, Black Pub Rels Soc; min affairs comt, Pub Rels Soc Am, 1985-86; pr comt, Atlanta Assoc Black Journalists, 1985-86; adv bd, Martin Luther King Jr Ctr Soc Chg, 1985-86; prog dir, Jack & Jill Am, 1985-86; activ chmn, Girl Scouts Am, 1985-87; youth activ chmn, Providence Baptist Ch; prog dir, Collier Heights Elem Sch; PTA; Grade Parent, 1985-89; publicity rel comt, Am Heart Assoc, 1986-87; comn A Reginald Eaves Blue Ribbon Task Force Strenghthening Black Am Family, 1986-87; econ develop task force, Nat Conf Black Mayors; United Negro Col Fund, Nat Forum pub Admins, 1986-87; United Ways Media Develop, 1987; chmn, SME, 1987; comn YWCA Salute Women Achievement, 1987; Journalist, Jack & Jill Am, Atlant phoenix aza Chap, 1990-92; vpres, Inman Mid Sch PTA, 1991-92; Fulton County Roundtable C, comnr, Nancy Boxill; Atlantic Hist Soc; Regist Lobbyist State Ga; exec bd mem, Leadership Atlanta, 1989-92; bd mem, Atlanta Chap Ronald McDonald C Charities; pub rels comt chmn, Coalition100 Black Women Atlanta; bd mem, Charlee. **Honors/Awds:** Civic Award, United Way, 1981; Cert Merit, Atlanta Asn Black Journalists, 1984; Girl Scouts of America, 1986; Leadership, Atlanta, 1986-87; NFL & AFL CIO Community Service Award; Americans Best & Brightest Bus & Prof Men& Women, Dollars & Sense Magazine, 1991; One of Ten Outstanding Atlantans, Outstanding Atlantans Inc, 1989. **Home Addr:** 481 Hiawassee Dr SW, Atlanta, GA 30311, **Home Phone:** (404)696-0273. **Business Addr:** Executive Vice President, First Class Inc, 1422 W Peachtree St NW Suite 500, Atlanta, GA 30309, **Business Phone:** (404)892-1434.

## BRADLEY, DAVID HENRY, JR.

Educator, writer. **Personal:** Born Sep 7, 1950, Bedford, PA; son of Rev David (deceased) and Harriette Jackson (deceased). **Educ:** Univ Pa, BA, creative writing, 1972; Univ London, King's Col, MA, US studies, 1974. **Career:** JB Lippincott Co, asst ed, 1974-76; freelance writer, 1975-; Univ Pa, vis lectr, 1975-76; Temple Univ, from vis lectr to prof, 1976-96; Colgate Prof Humanities, 1988; Univ NC, Wilmington, dist found prof lit, 1989; Mass Inst Technol, vis prof, 1989; William & Mary, vis prof, 1997; City Col NY, vis prof, 1998; Univ Tex, vis prof, 2000; Austin Peay State Univ, Roy Acuff chmn, 2001; Univ Ore, vis prof, 2000, 2002-03, dir, creative writing prog, assoc prof fiction, 2003-13. **Orgs:** Writers Guild Am E; Author's Guild. **Honors/Awds:** Presidential Scholar, 1968; Thouron Exchange Scholar, 1972; PEN/Faulkner Award, 1982; Academy Award, Am Inst Arts & Lett, 1982; Guggenheim fel, 1989; Nat Endowment Arts, fel, 1991; PEN/O. Henry Prize, 2014; Notting Hill Prize, 2015. **Special Achievements:** Books: "South Street", 1975; "The Chaneysville Incident", 1981; "Short Story, You Remember the Pin Mill", 2012; Nonfiction: "The Bondage Hypothesis: Meditations on Race and History" (in progress); "Raystown" (in progress). published numerous articles. **Home Addr:** PO Box 12681, La Jolla, CA 92039, **Home Phone:** (858)552-0419. **Business Addr:** OR.

## BRADLEY, DR. JAMES GEORGE

Administrator. **Personal:** Born Sep 17, 1940, Cleveland, OH; married Lela; children: Wyette, James (Deborah), Candace (Steven) & Jason. **Educ:** Univ NMex, BEd, 1963; Carnegie Mellon Univ, Carnegie Inst Technol, BS, civil engineering, 1967; Univ Utah, MBA, 1973, PhD, 1977. **Career:** Human Resources, manpower dev spec, 1979; Clearfield Job Corps, dir, 1970; Detroit Manpower Ctr, dir, 1976-77; USDA, civil rights, 1986; WHX Corp, exec vpres, 1995-97, exec vpres, 1998-2003; Wheeling-Pittsburgh Steel Corp, exec vpres, 1995-97, pres & chief exec officer, 1998-2006, chmn, 2003-06; Koppel Steel Co, pres & chief operating officer, 1997-98; Euramax Holdings inc, dir, 2010-. **Orgs:** Adv Bd Spec Ed, 1983; pres, Nat Asn Advan Colored People, 1985. **Home Addr:** 6013 Unitas Ct NW, Albuquerque, NM 87114. **Business Addr:** Director, Euramax International Inc, 5445 Triangle Pkwy Suite 350, Norcross, GA 30092, **Business Phone:** (770)449-7066.

## BRADLEY, JEFFREY

Teacher. **Personal:** Born Jun 24, 1963, Bronx, NY; son of Harry (deceased) and Beatrice Stevens. **Educ:** Laguardia Community Col, AS, early childhood educ & teaching, 1985; Hunter Col, early childhood educ/sociol. **Career:** Merricats Nursery Sch, teacher, 1983-; Dalton Summer, head teacher, 2000-; Dribbl, head coach, 2002-. **Orgs:** Asst staff mem, Asn Benefit C, 1989-91; Aid, Variety House, 1990-91. **Home Addr:** 762 Brady Ave Apt 123, Bronx, NY 10462, **Home Phone:** (718)918-0840. **Business Addr:** Teacher, Merricats Nursery School, 419 E 86 St, New York, NY 10128, **Business Phone:** (212)845-3821.

## BRADLEY, JENNETTE B.

Government official, politician. **Personal:** Born Oct 2, 1952, Columbus, OH; married Michael C Taylor. **Educ:** Wittenberg Univ, BA, psycol, 1974. **Career:** Columbus Metrop Housing Authority, head Authority; Huntington Nat Bank, sr vpres, pub funds, 1989-02; Columbus City Coun, mem, 1991-02, chmn, City Coun's Recreation & Parks & Pub Utilities comts; State Ohio, lt gov, 2003-05, treas, 2005-07; Ohio Dept com, dir, 2003; Ohio Housing Finance Agency. **Orgs:** Am Politician Republican party; bd trustees & mem, Wittenberg Univ. **Honors/Awds:** Columbia Public Schools Hall of Fame, 2000. **Special Achievements:** First African American woman to serve on the council; Ohio's First African-American Lieutenant Governor & First African-American woman to serve as Lt.Governor in the US. **Home Addr:** 5791 Buck Run Dr, Columbus, OH 43213-2690, **Home Phone:** (614)755-9211. **Business Addr:** Treasurer, State Ohio, 30 E Broad St 9th Fl, Columbus, OH 43266-0421, **Business Phone:** (614)466-2160.

## BRADLEY, MARGARET THERESA. See GIBBS, MARLA.

## BRADLEY, MELVIN LEROY

Executive, government official, president (organization). **Personal:** Born Jan 6, 1938, Texarkana, TX; son of David Ella (Garth) B and S T; married Ruth Ann Terry; children: Cheryl, Eric, Jacqueline & Tracy. **Educ:** Los Angeles City Col, attended 1955; Compton Col, attended 1965; Pepperdine Univ, BS, 1973; Shaw Univ, LLD, 1982; Bishop Col, LLD, 1984; Lane Col, LLD, 1986. **Career:** Real estate broker, 1960-63; Los Angeles County, dep sheriff, 1963-70; St Calif, staff asst gov's off, 1970-73, asst to Gov Ronald Reagan mem gov's sr staff, 1973-75; Charles R Drew Postgrad Med Sch LA, dir pub rel, 1975-77; United Airlines, asst regional vpres & acct exec, 1977-81; US White House, sr policy advisor to pres, 1981-82, spec asst to pres, 1982-89, spec advisor; Garth & Bradley Assocs, pres, 1989-. **Orgs:** Kiwanis Club; Toastmasters Am Inc; Nat Urban League; Nat Asn Advan Colored People; Calif Water Qual Control Bd; bd dir, Home Savings & Loan Bank; bd dir, Essex Fed Savings Bank; bd dir, Strategic Med Alliances Microsystems Corp. **Honors/Awds:** Distinguished Alumni, Texarkana Independent Sch Dist, 2010; Award for Outstanding Contribution City Los Angeles; Awarded Mayor's Key to City, Riverside, CA; Award for Contribution in Field of Community Relations, Compton, CA; Community Service Award, Co Los Angeles; Honarary Doctor Degrees of Law: Bishop Col, Shaw Univ, Lane Univ Tenn; Distinguished Louisiana Award, Langston Univ. **Special Achievements:** 100 Most Influential Black Americans, Ebony Mag. **Home Addr:** 3333 K St NW Suite 210, Washington, DC 20007.

## BRADLEY, MILTON OBELLE, JR.

Baseball player. **Personal:** Born Apr 15, 1978, Harbor City, CA; son of Milton Sr and Charlena Rector; married Monique; children: 2. **Career:** Baseball player (retired); Montreal Expos, 2000-01; Cleveland Indians, 2001-03; Los Angeles Dodgers, outfielder, 2004-05; Oakland Athletics, 2006-07; San Diego Padres, 2007; Tex Rangers, 2008; Chicago Cubs, 2009; Seattle Mariners, 2010-11; free agt, currently.

## BRADLEY, PHILIP POOLE (PHIL BRADLEY)

Baseball player, athletic coach, manager. **Personal:** Born Mar 11, 1959, Bloomington, IN; married Ramona; children: Megan & Curt. **Educ:** Univ Mo, BS, 1982. **Career:** Baseball player (retired), coach, manager; Seattle Mariners, outfielder, 1983-87; Philadelphia Phillies, outfielder, 1988; Baltimore Orioles, outfielder, 1989-90; Chicago White Sox, outfielder, 1990; Yomiuri Giants, 1991; Montreal Expos, outfielder, 1992; Univ MO, softball vol asst coach, 2009-10; Maj League Baseball Players Asn, spec asst to exec dir, currently. **Home Addr:** 7840 SW 133rd Terr, Pinecrest, FL 33156-6733. **Business Addr:** Special Assistant, Major League Baseball Players Association, 12 E 49th St 24th Fl, New York, NY 10017, **Business Phone:** (212)826-0808.

## BRADLEY, WAYNE W., SR.

Police officer, executive, salesperson. **Personal:** Born Aug 20, 1948. **Educ:** Wayne State Univ, BA, 1972. **Career:** Detroit Police Dept, police officer; Cass Corridor Safety, sr proj, proj dir, 1974-75; Wayne County Community Col, instr, 1972-; Western Res Fin Serv Corp, sales rep, 1973-; Sears Roebuck & Co, security, 1973-74; Philco Ford Corp, acct receivable & payable, 1968-69; Mich Consol Gas Co, collection rep, 1969-70; Wellness Plan, Govt & Community Affairs, dir, 1980-2007; Detroit Community Health Connection Inc, bd mem, 1994-2006, pres & chief exec officer, 2007-. **Orgs:** Kappa Alpha Phi Frat; Trade Union Leadership Coun; vpres, Nat Pan Helenic Coun; Nat Asn Advan Colored People; 1st Precinct Comt Rel Asn; bd mem, ed bd, Community Reporter Newspaper; Detroit Police Officers Asn; Police Officers Asn Mich; Guardians Mich; Concerned Police Officers Equal Justice; chmn, Detroit Area Agency Aging; bd mem, Greater Detroit Area Health Coun; Northeast Guid Ctr, chmn bd; bd governor, Detroit Renaissance Club. **Honors/Awds:** Purple Heart Civilian Award, 1971; Detroit Police Dept Highest Award; Medal Valor, 1971; 12th Precinct Outstanding Service Award, 1972. **Special Achievements:** Listed in Leaders in Black Am; Detroit Police Dept Citation, 1972. **Home Addr:** 18940 Oak Dr, Detroit, MI 48221. **Business Addr:** President, Chief Executive Officer, Detorit Community Health Connection Inc, 13901 E Jefferson Ave, Detroit, MI 48215-2720, **Business Phone:** (313)821-2591.

## BRADLEY, WILLIAM B.

Educator, chairperson. **Personal:** Born Nov 28, 1926, Rushville, IN; married Pearle E Poole; children: William, Philip, Annette & Catherine. **Educ:** Ind Univ, BPE, 1949, MPE, 1955, PED, 1959. **Career:** Sumner High Sch, coach phys educ, 1955-58; Ind Univ, phys educ dir, 1957, Sch HPER, grad asst, 1958-59; Fayetteville State Univ, Dept Phys Educ, prof & chmn, 1959-60; Southern Univ, Dept Phys Educ, prof & chmn, 1960-64; Va State Univ, Dept Athletics & Phys Educ, dir, 1964-70; Western Ill Univ, Dept Phys educ, prof, coordr, sport mgt internship prog, 1970-. **Orgs:** Am Alliance Health, Phys Educ & Recreation; Ill Asn Health PE & Recreation; Va Asn Health, PE & Recreation; Am Asn Univ Profs; Phi Epsilon Kappa; Phi Delta Kappa; Ind Alumni Asn; "I Mens Asn Indiana Univ; US Olympic Weightlifting Comt, 1968; consult, Nat Youth Sports Prog Pres Coun Phys Fitness & Sports, 1970-79; bd mem, McDonough Co, YMCA, 1970-73; US Olympic Baseball Comn, 1972. **Home Addr:** 207 Meadow Dr, Macomb, IL 61455-9317, **Home Phone:** (309)837-9395.

## BRADLEY-BURNS, MELISSA LYNN

Association executive. **Personal:** Born Jan 14, 1968, Newark, NJ; daughter of Joan; children: Kitu, Gabriella, Alle, A O, MacKenzie & Madison. **Educ:** Georgetown Univ, BS, finance, 1989; Am Univ, MBA, mkt, 1993. **Career:** City Col, NewYork, adj prof, Sallie Mae, finance mkt specialist, 1989-91; Bradley Dev Inc, founder & pres, 1990-92; Entrepreneurial Develop Inst, founder & pres, 1991-; Entrepreneurial Devlop Inst, founder, currently; Re entry Strategies Inst, founder, 2005-; New Capitalist, founder, pres, managing dir, 1999-2010, 2013-; US Treas, financial regulatory affairs fel; Positive Impact, founder; Reentry Strategies Inst, founder, pres, currently; UBS Pvt Client Group, vpres; Cit Gap Funds, dir, investment serv, 2006-08; Green All, Capital Access Prog, sr strategist, 2008-10; Tides Found, chief exec officer, 2010-13; Kogod Sch Bus, au ctr innovation capital & exec residence, dir, 2015-. **Orgs:** Back Block Found, 1995-; bd mem, Mentors Inc, 1995-; bd mem, Who Cares, 1996-; bd dir, Tides Found; advisor, Renewal 2 Investment Fund, currently; bd gov, Georgetown Univ Alumni Asn; ex-officio, Social Venture Network; chair, Green Am; Creative Capital Found; Tides Network; financial regulatory affairs fel US Dept Treas; sr adv, Ctr Am Progress; regular consult, WK Kellogg Found; co-chair, Nat Adv Coun Innovation & Entrepreneurship, 2016-. **Honors/Awds:** Do Something Brick Award Winner, 1996. **Business Addr:** Director, Kogod School of Business, 4400 Massachusetts Ave NW, Washington, DC 20016, **Business Phone:** (202)885-1000.

## BRADLEY-COAR, ALFREDA

Executive. **Educ:** Univ Pa, BA, cum laude, int rels, 1986, Law Sch, JD, 1989; Northwestern Univ, Kellogg Sch Mgt, MBA, 2000. **Career:** US Bankruptcy Ct, judicial law clerk, 1989-90; Bell Boyd & Lloyd LLC, bankruptcy & com litigation assoc, 1990-92; Seyfarth Shaw LLP, bankruptcy & com assoc, 1992-94; GE Rail Serv Corp, assoc gen coun, 1994-2001; GE Ins Solutions, chief compliance & regulatory coun, 2001-05, vpres & global regulatory coun; GE Equip Serv, gen coun trailer fleet serv & modular space, 2005-06; GE Healthcare, Diag Imaging, vpres & gen coun Americas, 2006-; GE, chief legal officer, com, 2016-; Geraldson LLC. **Orgs:** Nat Officer, GE's African-Am Forum; GE Women's Network; GE's Legal Corp Exec Coun; GE's Sr Exec Band; Am Bar Asn; Am Col Healthcare Execs; Am Corp Cousel Asn; Am Kidney Fund Bd; bd mem, Marcus Ctr Performing Arts Bd; Hist Makers; Univ Pa Law Alumni Soc Bd; Econ Club Chicago; Exec Leadership Coun. **Honors/Awds:** The Network Journal: Black Professionals & Small Business Magazine, 25 Influential Black Women in Business, 2008; Legal Trailblazer Award, Corp Coun Women Color, 2012; Top Corporate Counsel Award, Milwaukee Bus J, 2012. **Special Achievements:** A Member of General Electric's Senior Executive Band which represents the top 1% of its executive ranks. **Business Addr:** General Counsel Americas, Vice President, GE Healthcare, 3135 Easton Tpke, Fairfield, CT 06828-0001, **Business Phone:** (203)373-2211.

## BRADSHAW, GERALD HAYWOOD

Executive. **Personal:** Born Dec 13, 1934, Larned, KS; married Wylma Louise Thompson; children: Kim Elaine, Gerri Lynn & Douglas Haywood. **Educ:** Kans State Teachers Col, attended 1956; Univ Colo, BS; Am Savings & Loan Inst, Denver. **Career:** Equity Savings & Loan Assoc, Denver, auditor & appraiser, 1958-67; Denver Urban Renew Authority, real estate dir, 1960-71; Colo Springs Urban Renew Effort, exec dir, 1971-76; GH Bradshaw & Assoc, pres, 1976-; BH Property Mgt Inc, owner, currently. **Orgs:** Pres, Colo Chap Nat Asn Housing & Redevelop Officials; sr mem, Nat Asn Rev Appraisors; bd dir, Urban League Pikes Peak Region; Downtown Rotary Club Colo Springs; Site Selection Comt, El Paso Community Col; sec, Denver Oppurtunity; chmn bd adv comt, Columbine Elem Sch US. **Honors/Awds:** President Certficate Award Serving on Sel Serv Bd. **Home Addr:** 411 Lakewood Cir Apt C506, Colorado Springs, CO 80910-4616, **Home Phone:** (719)596-7683. **Business Addr:** Owner, B-H Property Management Inc, 315 N Weber St Fl 3, Colorado Springs, CO 80903-1230, **Business Phone:** (719)475-0073.

## BRADSHAW, LAWRENCE A, SR. See Obituaries Section.

## BRADSHAW, WAYNE-KENT A.

Manager, executive, president (organization). **Educ:** Univ Ariz, BA, econs; Univ Southern Calif, Marshall Sch Bus, MBA, 1974. **Career:** Founders Savings & Loan Assocs, chief exec; Family Savings Bank, pres & chief exec officer, 1989-2002; Wash Mutual Bank, reg pres & nat mgr community & external affairs, 2003-09; Broadway Fed Bank, chief operating officer, 2009-12, pres, chief exec officer, 2012-; Broadway Financial Corp, Bank FSB, dir, pres, chief exec officer, 2012-. **Orgs:** Bd dir, Calif Econ Develop Lending Initiative; Calif State Univ Northridge Community; bd mem, Northridge Hosp Med Ctr; adv coun, Fed Res Bd Consumer Adv Coun; Calif Community Reinvestment Corp; CA Bankers Asn; Workforce Investment Bd; Los Angeles Urban League & Community Build. **Business Addr:** President, Chief Executive Officer, Broadway Federal Bank, 5055 Wilshire Blvd Suite 500, Los Angeles, CA 90036, **Business Phone:** (323)556-3248.

## BRADY, CHARLES A.

Lawyer. **Personal:** Born May 1, 1945, Palestine, TX; son of Thomas F Sr and Leona V; married Ida A Powell; children: Kimberly & Charles A Jr. **Educ:** Coe Col, BA, 1967; Howard Univ, Sch Law, JD, 1970. **Career:** McDaniel Burton & Brady, atty, 1971-82; Charles A Brady & Assoc, atty, 1982-; Bus Law Fed City Col, sub instr; Fed Commun Comn, vpres opers, 2004-. **Orgs:** Treas, Inner-City & Investment Asn Inc; Forensic & Legal Fraternities & Asn. **Home Addr:** 6620 6th St NW, Washington, DC 20012. **Business Addr:** Vice President of Operations, Federal Communications Commission, 445 12th St SW, Washington, DC 20554, **Business Phone:** (888)225-5322.

## BRADY, JULIO A.

Government official, judge. **Personal:** Born Aug 23, 1942, St. Thomas; married Maria de Freitas; children: Julie & Andrew. **Educ:** Cath Univ PR, BA, Eng philos, 1964; NY Law Sch, JD, 1969. **Career:** NY Legal Aid Soc, pub defender, 1969-71; VI Employ Security Agency, interviewer; Dist VI, asst US atty, 1971-73, US atty, 1974-78; Fed Progs Off, coordr, 1979-82; Lt Gov US Vi, 1983-87; Dist VI, US atty, currently; US VI Territorial Ct, judge, 1992-94; US Vi Super Ct, judge, 2006-; Republican Party Vi, chmn, 2006-; Innovative Commun Corp, lawyer; pvt practiced law. **Orgs:** Pres, VI Bar Asn, 1977; chmn, United Way Campaign, 1978; co-chmn, Judicial Conf Third Circuit, 1979; state chmn, Dem Party, 1980-82; Nat Conf Lt Gov, 1983-87. **Honors/Awds:** Am Juris Prudence Award, NY Law Sch, 1969; Ex Alumno Distinguido, Cath Univ PR, 1983; Certificates of Appreciation, Atlanta Univ, 1984, 1985. **Home Addr:** PO Box 3100, St Croix, VI 00820. **Business Addr:** Judge, Superior Court of the Virgin Islands, R H Amphlett Leader Justice Complex, Christiansted, VA 00821, **Business Phone:** (340)778-9750.

**BRADY, WAYNE ALPHONSO**
Comedian, entertainer, actor. **Personal:** Born Jun 2, 1972, Orlando, FL; married Diana Lasso; married Mandie Taketa; children: Maile Masako. **Career:** Actor: Roll Bounce, 2005; Crossover, 2006; The List, 2007; 1982, 2013. Stage shows: A Chorus Line; Fences; A Raisin in the Sun; Jesus Christ Superstar; I'm Not Rappaport; The Only Game in Town; Wayne Brady & Friends; Brady Out-Crystaled Billy Crystal; TV series: "On Promised Land", 1994; "Kwik Witz", 1996; "Vinyl Justice", 1998; "Hollywood Squares", 1998; "Whose Line Is It Anyway", 1998; "Survivor"; "The Sopranos"; "American Dreams", 2003; "The 30th Annual Daytime Emmy Awards", writer, 2003; "Kevin Hill", 2005; "Girlfriends", 2006; "30 Rock", 2007; "How I Met Your Mother", 2006-14; "Everybody Hates Chris", 2006-08; "Let's Make a Deal", 2009; "The Fran Drescher Show", 2010; "The Fresh Beat Band", 2011; "Are We There Yet?", 2011; "Cubed", 2011; "Psych", 2012; "Key and Peele", 2012; "American Dad!", 2012-13; "Baby Daddy", 2013; "TripTank", 2013-14; "Being Mary Jane", 2014; "Phineas and Ferb", 2014; "Real Husbands of Hollywood", 2014; "Sofia the First", 2014; "Whose Line Is It Anyway?", exec producer, 2014; VH-1 comedy series, host; Countdown to the American Music Awards, host; TV movie: Geppetto, 2000; The Electric Piper, 2003; writer & producer: "The Wayne Brady Show", exec producer & writer, 2001-03, exec producer, co-exec producer & writer, 2002-04; "The Brandon T. Jackson Show", exec producer & writer, 2006; "Don't forget the lyrics", 2008; "Wayne Brady Live", writer, 2009; "The BET Honors", co-producer, 2014. **Honors/Awds:** Rookie of the Year, Sak Theatre, 1992; Emmy Award, 2003; Daytime Emmy, 2003, 2004 & 2014; Best Actor in a Musical for Cotton Patch Gospel. **Special Achievements:** Performed solo at the 52nd Annual Emmy Award, 2000; scored a 2nd Emmy Awd nomination, 2002; first African American to ever host the Miss America Competition; performed at the prestigious Mark Taper Forum in its production of Blade to the Heat. **Business Addr:** Actor, ABC Inc, 3727 W Magnolia Blvd, Burbank, CA 91510-7711.

**BRAGG, ROBERT HENRY, JR.**
Educator. **Personal:** Born Aug 11, 1919, Jacksonville, FL; son of Robert Henry and Lilly Camille McFarland; married Violette Mattie McDonald; children: Robert III & Pamela. **Educ:** Ill Inst Tech, Chicago, IL, BS, physics, 1949, MS, physics, 1951, PhD, physics, 1960. **Career:** Portland Cement Asn, Res Lab, asst physicist, 1951-54, assoc physicist, 1954-56; Ill Inst Tech, Res Inst, sr physicist, 1959-61; Lockheed Res Lab, mgr phys metall, 1961-69; Lockheed Missiles & Space Co, consult; Palo Alto Res Lab, res scientist, 1961-63, sr staff scientist, 1963-69; Univ Calif, Lawrence Berkeley Lab, prin investr, Dept Mat Sci, prof, 1969-87, dept chmn, 1978-81, prof emer, 1987-; Fulbright Scholar, Nigeria, 1992-93; Robert H Bragg & Assocs, owner. **Orgs:** Fac sponsor, Black Engineering & Sci Studs Asn, 1969-87; Nat Aeronaut & Space Admin; Northern Calif Coun Black Prof Engrs, 1969-; Nat Tech Asn, 1978-2000; prog dir, Div Mat Scis, Off Energy Res, Dept Energy, 1981-82; adv comt, Div Mat Res, Nat Sci Found, 1982-88; eval panel, Res Assocs Prog, Nat Res Coun, 1984-; eval panel, Fulbright CIES, Africa Prog, 1994-; Nat Asn Advan Colored People; Am Phys Soc; Am Carbon Soc; Am Cryst Asn; Am Asn Univ Professors; Aaas; Sigma Xi; Sigma Pi Sigma; Tau Beta Pi; consult, Siemens-Allis; consult, Nat Sci Found; consult, Nat Res Coun; Calif Mus Afr Am Technol, 2006; fel Nat Socs Black Physicists. **Home Addr:** 1850 Alice St Apt 816, Oakland, CA 94612, **Home Phone:** (510)433-0522.

**BRAILSFORD, MARVIN DELANO**
Executive. **Personal:** Born Jan 31, 1939, Burkeville, TX; son of Geneva Vivian and Artie; married June Evelyn Samuel; children: Marvin D Jr, Keith A & Cynthia R. **Educ:** Prairie View A&M Univ, BS, biol, 1959; Iowa State Univ, MS, bact, 1966; Grad Sch Bus, exec prog; Univ Calif, Berkeley; Harvard Univ, John F Kennedy Sch Govt; Army War Col; AUS Command; Gen Staff Col; Chem Sch Advan Course; Armor Officer Basic Course. **Career:** Executive, lieutenant general (retired); USY, 60th ord group, comndg officer, 1982-84, 59th ord brigade, comndg gen, 1984-87, armament munitions & chem command, comndg gen, 1987-90, materiel command, dep comndg gen, 1990-92; Metters Industs Inc, pres, 1992-95; Brailsford Group Inc, chief exec officer & pres, 1995-96; Kaiser-Hill Co LLC, sr vpres, 1996-2002; Southeast Tex Community Develop Corp, 2002. **Orgs:** Exe comt, AMR Defense Preparedness ASN, 1978-; chap pres, ASN USY, 1984-87; exec bd, United Way, 1989; bd adv, Geo Mason Univ, Bus Sch, 1993-96; bd dir, Ill Tool Works Inc, 1996-; bd dir, Ages Group Inc, 1997-; bd dir, Conn's Inc, 2003-. **Home Addr:** 7445 Prestwick Cir, Beaumont, TX 77707, **Home Phone:** (409)840-2075.

**BRAITHWAITE, GORDON L. See Obituaries Section.**

**BRAITHWAITE, DR. MARK WINSTON**
Dentist. **Personal:** Born Jul 15, 1954, New York, NY; son of David N and Grace C; married Carlene V; children: Mark II. **Educ:** Bowdoin Col, BA, biol, 1976; Columbia Univ, attended 1977; State Univ NY, Buffalo, Sch Dent Med, DDS, 1982; Columbia Univ, Sch Dent & Oral Surg, postgrad periodontics, 1993; Columbia Univ, Grad Sch Arts & Scis, MA, oral biol, 1995. **Career:** Pvt pract dentist, 1983-85; NY City Dept Health Bur Dent, gen pract dent, 1984-87; Joint Dis N Gen Hosp, gen prac dent, 1985-90; Sydenham Hosp Neighborhood Family Care Ctr, attend dentist, 1987-90; Harlem Hosp Ctr, attend dent, 1987; Melvin L Morris res fel; Va Hosp, staff dent & periodontist, 1999; Conn Healthcare Syst, Dent Serv, pvt pract; Loyola Univ Med Ctr, Dept Path, asst prof, 1999; clin coordr, currently. **Orgs:** Lic & Cert NE Regional Dent Bds, 1982; Nat Dent Bd, 1982; Nat Dent Asn; Nat Soc Dent Practitioners; Dent Health Serv Corp; Harlem Dent Soc; State Univ NY Buffalo Sch Dent Med Alumni Asn; Am Dent Asn. **Honors/Awds:** Special Academy Achievement for Periodontology, 1981-82; Attending of the Year, Harlem Hosp, 1988-89; Fellowship in Cell & Molecular Biology, Lab Tumor Biol & Connective Tissue Res, 1993; Melvin L Morris Research Fellowship Award. **Business Addr:** Clinical Coordinator, 159 Midwood St, Brooklyn, NY 11225-5060, **Business Phone:** (718)287-6756.

**BRAMBLE, REV. PETER W. D.**
Clergy. **Personal:** Born Jul 24, 1945, Montserrat; son of Charles William and Margaret B; married Jocelyn Cheryl Nanton; children: Jocelyn Cara & Peter David. **Educ:** Codrington Col, Barbados, LTh, 1970; Yale Divinity Sch, MA, relig, 1972, STM, 1974; Univ Conn, Storrs, PhD, 1976. **Career:** Sch teacher, 1962-66; parish priest, 1972-73; Univ Conn, teaching asst & lectr, 1974-76; St Katherines Episcopal, rector, 1976-97; Morgan, St Marys & Western Univ, lectr, 1978-; rector, St Marks, 1997-. **Orgs:** Exec com, Caribbean African AMR Dialogue, 1992-; Gov CMS on Homelessness, 1982-86; Nat Insts Health, animal care com, 1980-; Baltimore Pub Schs, cot outreach com, 1988-, com on Afro-Centric curric; Overcome inst for Black Inst Develop, fdr. **Honors/Awds:** Junior Academy of Letters, Living Legend in Religion, 1990; Living Maker of History Award, Iota Phi Lambda Sorority, 1992; Congressional Service Award, 1986; Values Award, Caribbean AMR InterCultural organization, 1991; Eco-Fun Project, Leadership & Commitment to Children, 1992. **Special Achievements:** Books: The Overcome: A Black Passover, Fairfax, Baltimore, 1989; Baltimore Times, "Rites for Overcome", Baltimore, 1990. **Home Addr:** 1800 Madison Ave, Baltimore, MD 21217, **Home Phone:** (410)728-4817. **Business Addr:** Rector, St Mark's Church, 1417 Union St, Brooklyn, NY 11213, **Business Phone:** (718)756-6607.

**BRAMWELL, DR. FITZGERALD BURTON**
Chemist. **Personal:** Born May 16, 1945, Brooklyn, NY; son of Fitzgerald and Lula Burton; married Charlott; children: Fitzgerald, Elizabeth, Jill & Christopher. **Educ:** Columbia Univ, BA, 1966; Univ Mich, MS, phys chem, 1967, PhD, phys chem, 1970. **Career:** Esso Res & Engineering, res chemist, 1970-71; Brooklyn Col, asst prof chem, 1971-72, dep chmn grad studies, 1981-84, actg dean grad studies & res, 1989-90, dean grad studies & res, 1990-95, prof emer, 1995-; City Univ New York Doctoral Fac, asst prof chem, 1972-74, assoc prof chem, 1975-79, prof chem, 1980-95, dean grad studies & res; Univ Ky, prof biochem, 1995, vpres res & grad studies, 1995-2001; Howard Univ, assoc provost acad res; Tuskegee Univ, prof chem. **Orgs:** Col Bd Progs, Educ Testing Serv, Princeton, NJ; Bd Advisors Chem Innovation, 1985-2001; Col Chem Consults Serv, 1988-; Col Chem Consults Serv Adv Bd, 1991-98, 2001-04; Test Develop Comt, 1994-98; chair, Consult LS-AMP Rev Comt La Bd Regents, 1995-; bd dir, Ky Technol Serv, 1995-2001; bd dir, Ky Sci & Technol Corp, 1995-2001; bd dir, Oak Ridge Assoc Univs, 1995-2001; bd trustee, Southeastern Univs Res Asn, 1995-2001; chair, Alliances Minority Participation, 1998; Nat Sci Found Comt Visitors, 1998-2001; Adv Comt, NSF Dirate Edu & Human Resources, 1998-2000; Coun Res Policy & Grad Edu Exec Comt, 1999-2001; Nat Asn State Univs & Land Grant Cols; Am Chem Soc, Wash, DC; adv bd, Southern Univ HBCU-UP TEAMS, 1999-08; sr consult, Qual Edu Minorities Network, 2000-; chair, Systemic Rural Initiatives, 2001; adv bd, Ky State Univ HBCU-UP TEAMS, 2001-06; Adv Bd CCNY Ctr Res Excellence Sci & Technol, 2002-; Panel, Site Visit, & Reverse Site Visit Rev Comts, Nat Sci Found, 2002-; AAAS Consult EPSCoR Infrastructure Grants, Nmex, Idaho, 2003-05; Adv Bd San Francisco State Univ Res Minority Insts, 2003-; AAAS Consult INBRE Infrastructure Grants Del, 2004-05; chair, Am Inst Chemists, Inorg Chem Ed Rev Bd, 2004-; Empire Sci Resources LLC Mgr Mem, 2005-. **Honors/Awds:** Prof of the Year Award, Nat Black Sci Studs Orgn, 1985; Professor of the Year Award, Nat Black Sci Studs Orgn, 1989; Distinguished Service Award, Nat Black Sci Studs Orgn, 1993, 1995; Distinguished Service Award, Brooklyn Col Grad Studs Orgn, 1994, 1995; Distinguished Service Award, Brooklyn Subsection Am Chem Soc, 1995; Distinguished Service Award, TRACC City Col New York, 1995; Citation in Distinguished African American Scientists of the 20th Century, Oryx Press, 1996; Dept of Chemistry Alumni Excellence Award, Univ Mich, 1996; Lyman T. Johnson Alumni Asn Award, Univ Ky, 1996; Claude Feuss Medal, Distinguished Public Service, Phillips Academy, Andover, MA, 2000; Outstanding Leadership Award, Ky Geol Surv, 2000; Founders Award, NYC LSAMP'CUNY, 2000; Citation in African Americans in Science, Mathematics, & Invention, Facts on File, 2003. **Special Achievements:** Co-author: Investigations in General Chemistry Quantitative Techniques and Basic Principles, 1977; Instructor's Guide for Basic Laboratory Principles in General Chemistry with Quantitative Techniques, 1990; Basic Laboratory Principles in General Chemistry with Quantitative Techniques, 1990; 6 books, 35 articles, 300 abstracts and presentations in the areas of physical chemistry and chemical education; Highest ranking African American at the University of Kentucky, 1996. **Home Addr:** 2292 Stone Garden Lane, Lexington, KY 40513-1392. **Business Addr:** Professor of Chemistry, University of Kentucky, 313 Chem-Physics Bldg, Lexington, KY 40506-0055, **Business Phone:** (859)257-7058.

**BRAMWELL, PATRICIA ANN**
Social worker, physiologist, educator. **Personal:** Born May 17, 1941, Brooklyn, NY; daughter of Arthur L and Miriam June Campbell. **Educ:** Cent State Univ, BA, 1965; Fordham Univ Sch Social Serv, MSW, 1969; Hofstra Univ, cert managerial studies & labor rels; Para Legal cert; cert mediation arbit. **Career:** Social worker (retired); Soc Seamens C, Foster Home Care, 1966-70; City Col, Dept Spec Progs, SEEK Comt Course & Standing, chmn, asst coordr coun, psychol couns, 1970-2000, asst prof; E New York Ment Health Clin, grp ther, 1977; Human Rights, New York, comnr. **Orgs:** Asst secy, Chama Day Care Ctr, 1974-76; vice chairperson, Bedford Stuyvesant Dist 16 Community Sch Bd, 1975-77, founding mem; vpres, bd dir, New Horizons Adult Educ Prog, 1989; life mem, Nat Coun Negro Women; bd dir, first vpres, Fordham Univ Sch Social Serv Alumni Asn; Brooklyn Community Plng Bd 3; Community Bd Kings County Hosp; City Col Sexual Harassment Panel; vpres, City Col Chap Prof Staff Cong Union, Comnr; Cert State Soc Worker; New York Human Rights Comn; vice chair bd trustee & founding mem, Bedford Stuyvesant New Beginnings Charter Sch. **Honors/Awds:** Numerous education & community service awards. **Home Addr:** 458 MacDonough St, Brooklyn, NY 11233-1510, **Home Phone:** (718)493-2485.

**BRANCH, ANDRE JOSE**
Educator. **Personal:** Born May 12, 1959, Valhalla, NY; son of Millard and Virginia Ment Smith. **Educ:** Warnborough Col, Oxford, Eng, 1978; Inst Holy Land Studies, Jerusalem, Israel, 1979; King's Col, Briarcliff, NY, BA, 1981; Fayetteville State Univ, Fayetteville, NC, teacher's cert, 1985; NC State Univ, Raleigh, NC, MEd, 1989; Univ Wash, PhD, 1999. **Career:** CMML Sec Sch, Nigeria, W Africa, teacher, 1981-82; New Hanover County Sch, Wilmington, NC, teacher, 1983-87; City Wilmington, Wilmington, NC, counr, 1986; Wake County Pub Schs, Raleigh, NC, teacher, 1987-89; NC St Univ, Raleigh, NC, counr intern, 1988-89; Northwest Asn AHANA, prof, founder, 1989; Whitworth Col, Spokane, WA, dir, multi ethnic stud affairs, 1990; Bellevue Community Col, adj prof, 1993-95; Seattle Cent Community Col, 1996-97; Wash State Univ, adj prof & supvr, 1997-98; Long Island Univ Brooklyn, asst prof educ, 1998-99; San Diego Sate Univ, asst prof, 1999-2005, tenured assoc prof, 2005-. **Orgs:** Am Asn Coun & Dev, 1989-; Am Col Personnel Asn, 1989-; chair, 1989-, pres, 2015-, Nat Asn Advan Colored People; Black Educ Asn Spokane, 1989-; Wash Comt Minority Affairs, 1989-; Am Educ Res Asn; Nat Asn Multicultural Educ. **Home Addr:** PO Box 74, Renton, WA 98057-0074. **Business Addr:** Associate Professor, San Diego State University, 5500 Campanile Dr, San Diego, CA 92182-1153, **Business Phone:** (619)594-2722.

**BRANCH, B. LAWRENCE. See Obituaries Section.**

**BRANCH, CALVIN STANLEY**
Football player. **Personal:** Born May 8, 1974, Versailles, KY. **Educ:** Colo State; Iowa State. **Career:** Football player (retired); Oakland Raiders, 1997-98, 2000, 2005, strong safety, 1999; Berlin Thunder, 2002; Oakland Raiders, scout, currently. **Business Addr:** Scout, Oakland Raiders, 1220 Harbor Bay Pkwy, Alameda, CA 94502, **Business Phone:** (510)864-5000.

**BRANCH, DR. GERALDINE BURTON**
Physician. **Personal:** Born Oct 20, 1908, Savannah, GA; daughter of Joseph Burton and Agusta Freeman; married Robert Henry; children: Elizabeth Doggette & Robert Henry III. **Educ:** Hunter Col, BS, chem & physics, 1931; NY Med Col, MD, 1936; Univ Calif Los Angeles, MPH, 1962. **Career:** Pvt pract, physician, 1938-53; La Dept Health Serv, dist health officer, 1964-71, reg dir health serv, 1971-74; Univ SC, assoc clin prof commmed, 1966; Watts Health Found Inc, dir prev health serv, 1976-78, med dir, med consult, 2001. **Orgs:** Walter Gray Crump Fel NY Med Col, 1932-36; bd gov, La Co Med Asn, 1966-70; pres, Federated Kings Daughters Clubs, 1966-70; Nat Med Asn, 1968; bd dir, Am Lung Asn, 1970-76. **Honors/Awds:** Healing Hands Award, Univ Calif, Santa Barbara, 1992; Acad Boosters Award, King-Drew Med, 1992; Lifetime Achievement Award, Japanese Chamber Com, 2003; Lifetime Achievement Award, Drew Univ Med & Sci, 2003. **Special Achievements:** Author, "Study of Gonorrhea in Infants & Children, " Pub Health Reports, 1964; "Study of Use of Neighborhood Aides in Control of a Diphtheria Outbreak, " 1966; "Study of Use of Non-Physicians in HB Control, "Preventive Med, 1977; "Study of the Adult-Day-Health-Care Center of the Watts Health Foundation, " paper presented to the ASA, 1990; "Study of the Problems Concerning the Care of the Alzheimer's patient, " paper presentedto the Alzheimer's Society, 1992; Study of Generational gap-presented at Stanford Univ, 1996. **Home Addr:** 1615 S Victoria Ave, Los Angeles, CA 90019-5929, **Home Phone:** (323)733-7184.

**BRANCH, PROF. HARRISON**
Educator, artist. **Personal:** Born Jun 6, 1947, New York, NY; son of Harrison Sr and Marguerite Williams; married Jacqueline Susan Hyde; children: Harrison III, Alexander Hyde & Olivia Marguerite Elizabeth. **Educ:** San Francisco Art Inst, BFA, 1970; Yale Univ, Sch Art, MFA, 1972. **Career:** Educator (retired); Univ Bridgeport, guest lectr & photogr, 1970-71; Yale Univ Sch Art, Alice Kimball Travelling fel, 1972; Ore State Univ, Dept Art, from asst prof to assoc prof art, 1972-84, prof art, prof photog, 1984-2013, prof emer, 2013-, External Rels Art Dept, dir; Owens Valley Photograph Workshop, 1978-86. **Honors/Awds:** Research Grant, Ore State Found, 1974; Research Grant, Ore State Univ Grad Sch, 1976-77; listed in Who's Who in Fine Arts Academia. **Special Achievements:** Published photographs in Think Black, Bruce Publishing Co, NY, 1969, & An Illustrated Bio-Bibliography of Black Photographers, 1980-88, Garland Publishing Co, NY, photographs in collections of International Museum of Photography at George Eastman House, Rochester, NY & Bibliotheque Nationale, Paris, France. **Home Addr:** 1104 NW 29th St, Corvallis, OR 97330, **Home Phone:** (541)757-1729. **Business Addr:** Professor of Art, Professor of Photography, Oregon State University, 106 Fairbanks Hall, Corvallis, OR 97331, **Business Phone:** (541)737-5021.

**BRANCH, JE**
Accountant. **Educ:** Va State Univ. **Career:** Land America Financial Group Inc, tax acct, currently. **Business Addr:** Tax Accountant, LandAmerica Financial Group Inc, 101 Gateway Ctr Pkwy, Richmond, VA 23235-5136, **Business Phone:** (804)267-8000.

**BRANCH, OTIS LINWOOD**
School administrator. **Personal:** Born Sep 7, 1943, Norfolk, VA. **Educ:** Chicago Conserv Col, BMusEd, 1966; Roosevelt Univ, Chicago Mus Col, MMusEd, 1974. **Career:** School administrator (retired); LaGrange Park Pub Sch, music dept, chmn, 1970; Bremen High Sch, Midlothian IL, choral music & humanities, dir, 1970; Chicago Conserv Col, admis & rec, dean, 1979-82. **Orgs:** Curriculum writer, State Bd Educ Allied Arts Ill; evaluator, N Cent Asn & State Bd Educ Ill; Music Educr Nat Conf; Nat Educ Asn; Humanities Educrs Asn. **Home Addr:** 6116 S Loomis Blvd, Chicago, IL 60636.

**BRANCH, ROCHELLE**
Manager. **Career:** Bowers Mus Cult Art; Bronx Mus Arts; Mus Mod Art NY City; Craft & Folk Art Mus, dir pub prog; City Pasadena, prog mgr cult affairs mgr, currently. **Orgs:** La Public Art Comm. **Business Addr:** Program Manager Cultural Affairs, City Pasadena, 175 N Garfield Ave, Pasadena, CA 91101, **Business Phone:** (626)744-6915.

**BRANCH, WILLIAM BLACKWELL**
Playwright, television producer, college teacher. **Personal:** Born Sep 11, 1927, New Haven, CT; son of James Matthew and Lola Douglas; children: Rochelle Ellen. **Educ:** Northwestern Univ, BS, 1949; Columbia Univ, MFA, 1958; Columbia Univ, attended 1959; Yale Univ, res fel, 1966. **Career:** Actor, 1945-60; Ebony Mag, field rep, 1949-60; Theatre TV & Motion Pictures, playwright, 1951-; The Jackie Robin-

son Column NY Post & Syndication, co-auth, 1958-60; John Simon Guggenhein fel, 1959-60; Channel 13 Educ TV NYC, staff writer & producer, 1962-64; Am Broadcasting Co fel, Yale Univ, 1965-66; Columbia Sch Arts, assoc film, 1968-69; Universal Studios, screenwriter, 1968-69; NBC News, producer, 1972-73; Together for Days, screenwriter, 1972; William Br Assocs, pres, 1973-; Univ Md, vis prof, 1979-82; Luce Fel Williams Col, 1983; Cornell Univ, prof, 1985-94; Univ Calif, regents lectr, 1985; William Paterson Col, vis distinguished prof, 1994-96; Cornell Univ, pro femer africana studies, 1994-96; Ed & auth: Black Thunder: An Anthology of Contemp African-Am Drama, 1992; Crosswinds: An Anthology of Black Dramatists in the Diaspora, 1993; Auth: Nat Conf of Christians & Jews Citations for Light in the Southern Sky, 1958; FiftySteps Toward Freedom, 1959; A Lett from Booker T, 1988; Plays: A Medalfor Willie, 1951; In Splendid Error, 1954; Exp in Black, 1955; Light in the Southern Sky, 1958; Fifty Steps Toward Freedom, 1959; A Wreath for Udomo, 1960; To Follow the Phoenix, 1960; The Man on Meeting St, 1960; Baccalaureate, 1975; TV ser: "This Way", 1955; "Light in the Southern Sky", 1958; "Still a Bro: Inside the Negro Mid Class", 1968; "Afro-Amer Perspectives", 1973-74; "Black Perspectives on the News", 1978-79. **Orgs:** Consult, New York Bd Educ, 1975-77; consult, Ford Found Off Commun, 1976; nat adv bd, Ctr Bk Libr Cong, 1979-83; treas, Nat Conf African Am Theatre, 1987-91; nat adv bd, WEB DuBois Found, 1987-. **Honors/Awds:** Hannah B Del Vecchio Award, 1958; Robert E Sherwood Television Award, 1958; Blue Ribbon Award, Am Film Festival, 1969; American Book Award, 1992; AUDELCO Black Theatre Award, 2001. **Home Addr:** 53 Cortlandt Ave, New Rochelle, NY 10801, **Home Phone:** (914)235-1809. **Business Addr:** President, William Branch Associates, 53 Cortlandt Ave, New Rochelle, NY 10801, **Business Phone:** (914)235-1809.

**BRANCHE, GILBERT M.**
Police officer, executive director, government official. **Personal:** Born Mar 16, 1932, Philadelphia, PA; son of Merwin E and Wilma M Brown; married Joyce M Parks; children: Quincy & Nickkiiah; married Jean Overton; children: Andrea, Dolores & Kelle. **Educ:** Univ Pa, BS, polit sci, 1968; Pa State Police Exec Develop Course, cert, 1974; FBI Acad, cert, 1975. **Career:** Police(retired), comnr; Philadelphia Police Dept, policeman, sgt, lt, capt, 1957-74; Philadelphia Dist Atty Off, dep chief co detective, 1970-74; Philadelphia Police Dept, inspector, 1974-78; Philadelphia Dist Atty Off, chief co detective, 1978; Dep Sec Fraud & Abuse Invest & Recovery Commonwealth Penn; Nat Orgn Black Law Enforcement exec, asst exec dir. **Orgs:** Bd dir, vpres Safe St, 1968-80; police consult, Asn Consult Wash, DC1972-77; pres, Blacks in Blue, 1974-76; pres, Nat Orgn Black Law Enforce Exec, 1979-; comnr, Stand & Accred Police, 1979-; pres, Circle Noble, 1983-; Free & Accepted Mason; bd mem, Pa Comn Crime & Delinq, 2003-; PCCD Comn, 2006. **Home Addr:** 483 Sweetbriar Dr, Harrisburg, PA 17111, **Home Phone:** (717)561-1026. **Business Addr:** Board Member, Pennsylvania Commission on Crime & Delinquency, 3101 N Front St, Harrisburg, PA 17110, **Business Phone:** (717)705-0888.

**BRAND, ADOLPH JOHANNES DOLLAR. See IBRAHIM, ABDULLAH.**

**BRAND, ELTON TYRON**
001173, basketball player. **Personal:** Born Mar 11, 1979, Cortlandt Manor, NY; son of Daisy; married Shahara Simmons; children: 2. **Educ:** Duke Univ, sociol, attended 1999. **Career:** Chicago Bulls, 1999-2001; Los Angeles Clippers, point forward, 2001-08; Philadelphia 76ers, 2008-12; Film Producer: The Cookout, 2004; Rescue Dawn, 2006; Just Wright, 2010; Dallas Mavericks, 2012-13; Atlanta Hawks, 2013-15. **Orgs:** Founder, Elton Brand Found, 2000-; Home & C's Inst Int. **Business Addr:** Basketball Player, Atlanta Hawks, 1 CNN Ctr S Tower, Atlanta, GA 30303, **Business Phone:** (404)827-4229.

**BRANDFORD, NAPOLEON, III**
Executive. **Personal:** Born Feb 23, 1952, East Chicago, IN; son of Cora Lee; married Sharon Delores Bush. **Educ:** Purdue Univ, BA, int studies, 1974, MA, pub admin; Univ Southern Calif, MPA, 1978. **Career:** Union Carbide-Linde Air Div, summer intern, 1970; Stand Oil Ind, Summer intern, 1971-74; Pac Tel, asst transp coordr, 1976-78; Dade Co Finance Dept, asst finance dir, 1978-82; Shearson Lehman Bros Inc, vpres-pub finance, 1982-85; Grigsby, Brford Inc, dir, investment banking div, vicechmn & exec vpres, 1985-97; Siebert Brandford Shank & Co LLC, partner & chmn, 1997-, Southwestern & Western Regions, mgr & founding partner, currently. **Orgs:** Nat Forum Black Pub Adminrs, 1983-; exec secy, Builders Mutual Surety Co, 1984-85; bd mem, Urban Econ Develop Corp, 1984-; bd mem, Univ Southern Calif Alumni Asn, 1985; comt mem, Mayors Adv Comt Int Trade Foreign Investment Prog, 1985-; Nat Asn Securities Profs, 1987; bd dir, Alta Bates Med Ctr; trustee, San Jose Mus Mod Art; Nat Black MBAs; interim dep treas/chief financial officer, Calif Health Care Found; Southern Califs Sch Policy; bd mem & adv bd, Nat Col Athletic Asn; San Gabriel Boy Scouts Am; Los Angeles Am Heart Asn; Nat Asn Security Professionals; Western Region Boy Scouts Am; bd Counr, Univ Southern Calif's Sch Policy, Planning & Develop. **Honors/Awds:** Basketball Hall of Fame, E Chicago Roosevelt, 1975; Employee Suggestion Award, Dade County Managers Off, 1981; Recipient Leadership Miami Alumni Asn, 1982; Ebony Magazine, Young Tycoons, 1988; Men of Courage, Carnation, 1990. **Special Achievements:** Youngest African Am partner on Wall Street. **Home Addr:** , CA. **Business Addr:** Chairman, Partner, Siebert Brandford Shank & Co LLC, 1999 Harrison St Suite 2720, Oakland, CA 94612, **Business Phone:** (510)645-2245.

**BRANDON, BARBARA (BARBARA BRANDEN)**
Cartoonist or animator. **Personal:** Born Jan 1, 1960, Long Island, NY; daughter of Brumsic Jr. **Educ:** Syracuse Univ, visual & performing arts, 1980. **Career:** Mag Essence, fashion & beauty writer, 1989; Universal Press Syndicate, cartoonist, 1991-2000; Meredith, sr res ed, 2000-; Parents mag, sr res ed & res ed, 2004-, res dir, 2007-13. **Special Achievements:** First African American woman to be syndicated in more than 50 newspapers nationwide for the "Where I'm Coming From", "Where I'm Coming From Still", comic strip. **Business Addr:** Senior Research Editor, Meredith, 125 Pk Ave, New York, NY 10017-5529, **Business Phone:** (212)557-6600.

**BRANDON, CARL RAY**
Counselor. **Personal:** Born Nov 15, 1953, Port Gibson, MS; son of Alonzo and Marjorie Williams; children: Ashlea. **Educ:** Alcorn State Univ, BS, 1976, MS, 1984; Univ Southern Miss. **Career:** Thompson Funeral Home, funeral dir, 1971-; Claiborne City Pub Schs, counr, 1977-84; Southwest Ment Health Complex, case mgr II, 1984-88, therapist, 1988-. **Orgs:** Miss Asn Educ, 1977-; Miss Coun Asn, 1981-; Miss Dep Sheriffs Asn, 1982-; Miss Asn Constable, 1984-; bd dir, Grand Gulf State Pk, 1988. **Honors/Awds:** Citizenship Award, Charlie Griffin. **Home Addr:** 204 Mimosa St, Port Gibson, MS 39150. **Business Addr:** Mental Health Therapist, Southwest Mental Health Complex, PO Box 624, Port Gibson, MS 39150, **Business Phone:** (601)437-8185.

**BRANDON, DR. IDA GILLARD. See Obituaries Section.**

**BRANDON, DR. JEROME (LESLIE BRANDON)**
Educator. **Educ:** Murray State Univ, BS, health, phys educ, sociol, 1969, MS, phys educ, 1971; Univ Ill, PhD, exercise physiol, 1983. **Career:** Murray High Sch, Murray, Ky, teacher, 1969-71; Breckinridge Job Corps Ctr, counsr adv, 1977-78; Univ Ill Urbana Champaign, Phys Educ Dept, instr, 1978-79, res assoc, 1979-83; Ga State Univ, Dept Kinesiology & Health, Atlanta, asst prof to assoc prof, 1983-2003, Gerontol Ctr, Atlanta, Ga, fac & curric comm mem, 1997-, prof, 2003-; Dekalb Community Col, Dept Phys Educ, Clarkston, Ga, adj instr, 1984-86; Geriat Inst, Rehab Res & Develop Ctr, Vet Affairs Med Ctr, Decatur, Ga, res health scientist, 1991-; Emory Univ Med Sch, Dept Rehab Med, Atlanta, Ga, from clin instr to asst prof, 1992-. Books: Relationship of BMI and body fat in men and women, Int J of Fitness, 2008; The benefits of yoga for African American heart failure patients, 2010; Health perceptions of Southern African American and caucasian adults, Nat Med Asn, 2010; Skeletal muscle lipid peroxidation and insulin resistance in humans, Journal of Clinical Endocrinology & Metabolism, 2012; Phenotype and cardiovascular disease morbidity and mortality in multicultural populations, Nat Med Asn, 2013. **Orgs:** Pres, Southeast Am Col Sports Med, 2007; chair, Am Alliance Health, Phys Educ, Recreation & Dance; fel Am Col Sports Med; Robert Woods Johnson Found; Gen Mills; Nih. **Home Addr:** 5807 Giles Rd, Lithonia, GA 30058, **Home Phone:** (770)482-7141. **Business Addr:** Professor, Georgia State University, 125 Decatur St Suite Rm 173 Sports Arena, Atlanta, GA 30302-3980, **Business Phone:** (404)413-8368.

**BRANDON, LESLIE. See BRANDON, DR. JEROME.**

**BRANDON, SYMRA D.**
Government official, legislator. **Personal:** Born Jan 20, 1947, New York, NY; daughter of Robert and Doris Thomas; married Turhan V Sr; children: Turhan Jr & Taniya. **Educ:** Morgan State Col, BA, 1969; Hunter Sch Social Work, City Univ NY, MSW, 1976; Pace Univ, MPA, 1982. **Career:** Iona Col, adjunt prof; Westchester County, Dept Social Serv, staff devel specialist, 1981-87; Cornell Univ, Family Life Devel Ctr, consult & trainer, 1982; Columbia Univ, adj prof, 1983-85; Westchester County Youth Bur, prog adminr, 1992-95, UAW/GM Transition Ctr, staff develop, 1996; Westchester Co Exec, legislator, spec asst, 1998-; Yonkers City Coun, minority leader, 2000-, bd dir. **Orgs:** Vpres, Nat Asn Advan Colored People, Yonkers br; Alpha Kappa Alpha Sorority, Terr City Chap, 1995-; bd mem, Inst Responsible Fatherhood, 1997-; bd mem, Child Care Coun Westchester, 1998-; bd mem, Mt Vernon Health Care Ctr, 1998-; Cluster Adv chamn, Elejmal Ct 171, Voter Regist Comn, 1999; bd mem, Stardom Child Care Ctr, 1999; dir, Off African Am Affairs; chair, Yonkers Dem Comt, currently. **Home Addr:** 205 N Broadway, Yonkers, NY 10701, **Home Phone:** (914)377-6871. **Business Addr:** Assistant County Executive, Legislator, Westchester County, 148 Martine Ave Rm 906, White Plains, NY 10601, **Business Phone:** (914)995-2934.

**BRANDON, TERRELL (THOMAS TERRELL BRANDON)**
Business owner, basketball player, actor. **Personal:** Born May 20, 1970, Portland, OR; son of Charles and Charlotte; children: Trevor. **Educ:** Univ Ore, attended 1991. **Career:** Basketball player (retired), actor, business owner; Cleveland Cavaliers, pt guard, 1991-97; Milwaukee Bucks, pt guard, 1997-99; Minn Timber wolves, pt guard, 1999-2002; Atlanta Hawks, 2004; Terrell Brandon's Barber Shop, chief exec officer, currently; Tee Bee Enterprises, chief exec officer, currently. **Honors/Awds:** Most Valuable Player, Univ Ore, 1990; Pac-12 Player of the Year, 1991; NBA All-Rookie Second Team, 1992; NBA All-Star, 1996, 1997; NBA Sportsmanship Award, 1997; Oregon Sports Hall of Fame, 2006. **Special Achievements:** TV appearance: Eddie, 1996; 1996 NBA All-Star Game, 1996; 1997 NBA All-Star Game, 1997. **Business Addr:** Owner, Tee Bee Enterprises, 1330 NE Alberta St, Portland, OR 97211-5006, **Business Phone:** (503)460-9520.

**BRANDT, LILLIAN B. See Obituaries Section.**

**BRANGMAN, H. ALAN**
Architect, executive director. **Personal:** Born Apr 20, 1952, Hamilton; son of Oliver G Jr and Carolyn I; married Patricia A; children: Jacob, Jessica & Alaina. **Educ:** Univ NH, BArch, civil engineering, 1972; Cornell Univ, BArch, 1976; Harvard GSD, Bus Sch, real estate primer cert, 1984; Univ Pa, Wharton Sch Bus, real estate primer cert, 1985; Georgetown Univ McDonough Sch Bus, EML, leadership, 2005. **Career:** RTKL Assocs, Inc, proj dir, mgr, 1977-83; Oliver Carr Co, dir downtown develop, 1983-91; NEA-Design Arts Prog, dep dir, 1991-94; City Falls Church, mayor, 1993-98; Georgetown Univ, dir facil planning & proj mgt, 1994-96, univ architect, 1994-2010; US Govt, Gen Serv Admin, peer reviewer, 2010-; Univ Del, univ architect & campus planner, 2010-12, vpres facil, real estate & auxiliary serv, 2013-; Howard Univ, assoc vpres facil, real estate & univ architect, 2012-13; Facil Planning Georgetown Univ, exec dir, currently; State Md, lic architect. **Orgs:** Nat Orgn Minority Architects, 1983-85; Asn Univ Real Estate Officials; bd dir, Dist Curators, 1986-92; Urban Land Inst, 1988-91; chmn, Bus Adv Bd, Spingarn Sr High Sch, 1988-91; Urban Land Inst, 1990-91; chmn, Youth Comn, City Falls Church, 1990-92; bd dir, Int Stud House, 1991-94; Am Inst Architects, 1992-; Am Planning Asn, 1992-94; Archit Adv Bd, George Mason High Sch, 1992-94, 2002-; UVA/VA TECH-Northern Va Grad Ctr Task Force, 1992-94; Planning Comn City Falls Church, 1993-94; Lambda Alpha Int Real Estate Hon Soc; City Coun, City Falls Church, 1994-98; secy & treas, Wash Metrop Area Coun Governments, 1994-98; Air Qual Comt, Wash Metrop Area, 1994-98; vice chmn, Develop Policy Comt, Wash Metrop Area, 1996-98; bd mem, US Comn Fine Arts, Old Georgetown Bd, 2013-. **Special Achievements:** Alternative Careers in Architecture, AIA Video, 1990. **Home Addr:** 211 S Oak St, Falls Church, VA 22046-3905, **Home Phone:** (703)241-2862. **Business Addr:** Vice President for Facilities, Real Estate & Auxiliary Services, University of Delaware, 105 E Main St, Newark, DE 19716, **Business Phone:** (302)831-2792.

**BRANHAM, GEORGE, III**
Bowler. **Personal:** Born Nov 21, 1962, Detroit, MI; son of George William Francis II and Betty Ogletree; married Jacquelyne Phend; children: Hadley. **Educ:** Sun Valley's Polytech High. **Career:** Tenpin bowler (retired); Prof Bowlers Asn, bowler, 1984-03. **Orgs:** Prof Bowlers Asn, 1984-02. **Honors/Awds:** Southern Calif Jr Bowler of the Yr, 1983; Brunswick Memorial World Open, 1986, AC/Delco Classic, Professional Bowlers Assn Tournaments, 1987; Baltimore Open, 1993; Firestone Tournament of Champions, 1993; Cleveland Open, 1996. **Special Achievements:** First African American to win a Professional Bowlers Association title. **Home Addr:** 3838 Cent Ave, Indianapolis, IN 46205-2629. **Business Addr:** Professional Bowler, Professional Bowlers Association, 719 2nd Ave Suite 701, Seattle, WA 98104, **Business Phone:** (206)332-9688.

**BRANKER, JULIAN MICHAEL**
Automotive executive. **Career:** Mike Branker Buick-Hyundai Nissan Inc, Lincoln, Nebr, owner, chief exec officer, 1991-. **Business Addr:** Owner, Chief Executive Officer, Mike Branker Buick-Hyundai Nissan Inc, 421 N 48th St, Lincoln, NE 68504, **Business Phone:** (402)464-5976.

**BRANNEN, JAMES H., III**
Pilot. **Personal:** Born Dec 25, 1940, Queens, NY; married Wendy; children: Keree, Myia & Christopher. **Educ:** Northrop Inst Tech, BS, aero engineering, 1964; Univ Baltimore Law Sch, JD, 1975. **Career:** Conn Legis, mem, 1972-74; US Patent Off, 1966-67; United Airlines, first officer, pilot flight mgr. **Orgs:** Rep Study Com, CT; Rep Town Com, 1972-; Jaycees, 1972-; bd dir, Colchester Montessori C's House, 1973-; Can US Sen Rep Party, 1974. **Home Addr:** 18112 Diamond Cove, Tampa, FL 33647, **Home Phone:** (813)973-0180.

**BRANNON, DEBORAH DIANNE**
Entrepreneur. **Personal:** Born Feb 1, 1956, Hempstead, TX; daughter of George L Smith Jr; married Roy; children: Jason, Jina & Christina. **Educ:** CA State Univ, Sacramento, BA, jour, 1984. **Career:** Pro line Corp, key acct mgr, regional sales mgr; Greek Like Me, chief exec officer; Keystone Labs, dir sales & mkt opers. **Orgs:** Am Bus Women's Asn; Sigma Gamma Rho; auxilary bd, Girls Inc. **Special Achievements:** Launched Web site, www.greeklikeme.com, 1999. **Home Addr:** 881 Summit Pointe, Lewisville, TX 75077, **Home Phone:** (972)219-1244.

**BRANNON, DR. JAMES K.**
Physician, president (organization). **Educ:** Univ Iowa, MD, 1990. **Career:** Martin Luther King Jr/Drew Med Ctr, resident physician, 1992; Orthop Sci Inc, founder, pres & cheif exec officer, 1999-; Univ Mo, asst prof, orthop surg; Truman Med Centers Inc, currently. **Orgs:** Fel Am Acad Orthopaedic Surgeons. **Business Addr:** President, Chief Executive Officer, Orthopedic Sciences Inc, 3020 Old Ranch Pkwy Suite 325, Seal Beach, CA 90740, **Business Phone:** (562)799-5550.

**BRANNON, JAMES R.**
Executive, chief executive officer. **Personal:** Born Feb 26, 1943, Texarkana, TX; son of James and Ellen; married Dorothy Williams; children: Sherrilyn C & Deanna E. **Educ:** NC A & T State Univ, BS, bus admin, 1967; Harvard Univ, Grad Sch Bus Admin Prog Mgt Develop, cert, 1975. **Career:** Liberty Mutual Ins Co, bus lines underwriter, 1967-68; Roxbury Keypunch Training Ctr, mgr, 1968-69, com underwriter, 1969-71, coordr equal employ, 1971-78, asst vpres employ rels, sales rep & vpres; Minuteman Health Info Systs LLC, pres & chief exec officer, currently. **Orgs:** Nat Asn Advan Colored People; A & T State Univ Alumni Asn; Harvard Bus Sch Asn, Boston; Nat Urban League, Boston; bd mem, Freedom House, Boston, 1984-; comt mem, Lexington Fair Housing, 1985-; Lena Pk Community Ctr; bd mem, Lexington Metco Scholar Comt. **Home Addr:** 380 Lowell St, Lexington, MA 02420, **Home Phone:** (617)863-2035. **Business Addr:** President, Chief Executive Officer, Minuteman Health Information Systems LLC, 380 Lowell St, Lexington, MA 02420-2506, **Business Phone:** (617)861-8758.

**BRANSFORD, DR. PARIS**
Surgeon, judge. **Personal:** Born Jan 1, 1930?, Huntsville, AL; married Gladys Toney; children: Paris, Toni L & Traci. **Educ:** Tenn State Univ, BS, 1956; Meharry Med Col, MD, 1963. **Career:** Surgeon (retired); NASA Huntsville, Ala, res chem missile prog; Rvrsd Gen Hosp, chief emergency rm, 1972; N Cent Gen Hosp, bd dir chief staff, 1973-75; NC Med Bd, Physician, 2006; Srs Am Cancer Soc, lectr; Houston Independent Sch Dist, med educ; Harris County, judge, currently. **Orgs:** Vp secy, Hstn Med Firm, 1973-76; pres, Med Asn Almed Med Sq, 1973-; Alpha Phi Alpha Frat; Young Men's Christian Asn; Nat Asn Advan Colored People; Harris Co Med Asn; AMA; Tex Med Asn; Am Soc Abdominal Surg; Houston Med Forum. **Honors/Awds:** Recipient Of Service, Chap Comm Delta Theta Lambda Chaps, Alpha Phi Alpha Frat Inc, 1971; Appreciation, Kappa Psi Phramaceut Fraternity Serv Comn, 1975. **Home Addr:** 8010 Ashley Circle Dr N, Houston, TX 77071-3666. **Business Addr:** Judge, Harris County, 1001 Preston 9th Fl, Houston, TX 77002, **Business Phone:** (713)755-6306.

**BRANSFORD, PATRICIA**
President (organization). **Personal:** daughter of Marie Moss and Clarence. **Educ:** Cath Univ, Wash, DC, BS, math; NY Univ, Stern Sch Bus Admin, MBA. **Career:** IBM, econ develop consult; Nat Urban Technol Ctr, founder & pres, currently. **Business Addr:** Founder, President, The National Urban Technology Center, 80 Maiden Lane Suite 606, New York, NY 10038, **Business Phone:** (212)528-7350.

**BRANT, CHARLES TYRONE**
Lawyer. **Personal:** Born Jul 24, 1961, Savannah, GA; son of Johnny and Bernice Huff; married LaSean Z. **Educ:** Morehouse Col, BA, 1984; Ga Inst Technol, BS, 1984; Mercer Univ, JD, 1990. **Career:** DC Pub Defender Off, intern, 1990-92; City Atlanta Pub Defendr Off, defender & investr, 1992-95; Law Off Charles Brant, pvt pract, 1995-; US Mid Dist Ct, lawyer, 1998; Ellenberg, Ogier & Rothschild, lawyer, currently; Colom Law Firm, jr partner, currently. **Orgs:** Wash, DC Bar Asn, 1994-; Ga Bar Asn, 1994-; vice chair, Minority Caucus Asn Trial Lawyers Am; Zion Hill Baptist Church, Atlanta, GA; 100 Black Men Am. **Honors/Awds:** One Hundred Black Men of Atlanta, 2001-. **Business Addr:** Attorney, Junior Partner, The Colom Law Firm, 200 Sixth St N Suite 700, Columbus, MA 39703, **Business Phone:** (662)327-0903.

**BRANTLEY, CLIFFORD**
Baseball player. **Personal:** Born Apr 12, 1968, Staten Island, NY. **Career:** Baseball player (retired); Philadelphia Phillies, 1991-92.

**BRASEY, HENRY L.**
Educator, executive. **Personal:** Born Nov 25, 1937, Cincinnati, OH; married Anna; children: Darrell & Jenifer. **Educ:** BS, 1972; IBM Corp, cert. **Career:** Regional Comput, City Cincinnati, programming proj leader; Full House Inc, pres; Withrow HS Data Processing Prog, curric adv; Univ Cincinnati, asst dir comput serv & adj prof, asst prof eng anal, dir acad technol, adj instr info technol, currently. **Orgs:** Asn Comput Mach; Kennedy Heights Community Coun; Ken-Sil Athletic Club; Pleasant Ridge PTA; Cincinnati Youth Collab; dir, Community Access Technol. **Honors/Awds:** Senate President of the Year, 2003. **Home Addr:** 3776 Aikenside Ave, Cincinnati, OH 45213-2211, **Home Phone:** (513)731-8320. **Business Addr:** Adjunct Professor, University Cincinnati, 2600 Clifton Ave, Cincinnati, OH 45221, **Business Phone:** (513)556-6000.

**BRASHEAR, DONALD MAYNARD**
Hockey player. **Personal:** Born Jan 7, 1972, Bedford, IN; married Gabrielle Desgagne; children: Jordan & Jackson. **Career:** Longueuil, 1989-91; Verdun, 1991-92; Fredericton, 1992-93; Montreal Canadians, 1993-97; Vancouver Canucks, left wing, 1997-2001; Philadelphia Flyers, left wing, 2001-; Que RadioX, 2004-05; Philadelphia Flyers, 2005-06; Wash Capitals, 2006-09; New York Rangers, 2009-10; Riviere-du-Loup 3L, 2010-13. **Honors/Awds:** Pelle Lindbergh Memorial, 2003; First African-American to be certified as a Master Diver in the US Navy.

**BRASS, REGINALD STEPHEN**
Teacher, association executive, executive. **Personal:** Born Sep 6, 1958, Los Angeles, CA; son of Ernest and Mildred Jackson; children: Stephen Reginald II. **Career:** Unique Protection Serv, vpres; Bodyguard; St Anne's Maternity House, teacher & coun; Mini House, teacher & counr; My Child Says Daddy, founder & pres, 1991-. **Orgs:** Pregnant Minor Task Force Sex Equity Comn Los Angeles Unified Sch Dist; Maranatha Community Church; adv bd, Los Angeles Co; adv bd, Am coalition Fathers & C. **Honors/Awds:** Community Architect Award, Honorable Gwen Moore 47th Dist, 1994; Directors Award, Calif Dept Social Services, 1994; Yvonne Brathwaite Burke, Commendation, 1994; DHL, St Stephen's Edun Bible Col, 1996. **Home Addr:** 5724 Corbett St, Los Angeles, CA 90016, **Home Phone:** (323)936-3813. **Business Addr:** Founder, President, My Child Says Daddy, 5250 W Century Blvd Suite 448, Los Angeles, CA 90045, **Business Phone:** (310)642-8816.

**BRAUGHER, ANDRE K.**
Actor. **Personal:** Born Jul 1, 1962, Chicago, IL; son of Sally and Floyd; married Amy L Brabson; children: Michael, Isaiah & John Wesley. **Educ:** Stanford Univ, BA, theatre, 1984; Juilliard Sch, MFA, 1988. **Career:** TV series: "Homicide: Life on the Street", 1993-98; "The Tuskegee Airmen"; "Everybody Has To Shoot the Picture"; "Murder in Mississippi"; "The Court-Martial of Jackie Robinson"; "Passing Glory"; "Love Songs", dir, 1999; "Gideon's Crossing", 2000; "Hack", 2002; "10,000 Black Men Named George", exec producer, 2002; "Thief", 2006; "Men of a Certain Age", 2009-11; "House MD", 2009-12; "Miami Medical", 2010; "Law & Order: Special Victims Unit", 2011-13; "Last Resort", 2012-13; "Brooklyn Nine-Nine", 2013-14. Films: Glory, 1998; Primal Fear, 1998; Get On The Bus, 1998; City of Angels, 1998; Thick as Thieves, 1999; All the Rage, 1999; Frequency, 2000; Duets, 2000; A Better Way to Die, 2000; Salem's Lot, 2004; Poseidon, 2006; The Mist, 2007; Live!, 2007; Fantastic Four: Rise of the Silver Surfer, 2007; Andromeda Strain, 2008; Passengers, 2008; Salt, 2010; The Baytown Disco, 2012; Rosita Lopez for President, exec producer, 2012. Theatre: Henry V, King John, NY Shakespeare Festival; Othello; Folger Shakespeare Festival; The Way Of The World; Richard II; Measure for Measure; Twelfth Night; Coriolanus. **Honors/Awds:** Q Award, 1995; TCA Award, Tv Critics Asn, 1997, 1998; Primetime Emmy Award, 1998, 2006; Blockbuster Entertainment Award, 2001; Black Reel Award, 2007; Critics' Choice TV Award, 2010; Vision Award, 2012; OFTA Television Award, Online Film & Tv Asn, 2014. **Special Achievements:** One of the 50 Most Beautiful People in the World, 1997. **Home Addr:** 393 Charlton Ave, South Orange, NJ 07079-2405. **Business Addr:** Actor, c/o United Talent Agency, 9560 Wilshire Blvd F15, Beverly Hills, CA 90212, **Business Phone:** (310)273-6700.

**BRAUN, AMBASSADOR CAROL ELIZABETH MOSELEY**
Politician, president (organization), lawyer. **Personal:** Born Aug 16, 1947, Chicago, IL; daughter of Joseph and Edna; married Michael Allen; children: Matthew. **Educ:** Univ Ill, Chicago, BA, polit sci, 1969; Univ Chicago Law Sch, JD, 1972. **Career:** Mayer Brown & Platt, law clerk 1970; Rose Hardies O'Keefe Babcock & Parsons, law clerk, 1971; Davis, Miner & Barnhill, assoc 1972; US Dept Justice, asst atty, 1973-77; Jones, Ware & Grenard, coun; 26th Legis Dist, Chicago, state rep, 1978-88; Cook County, recorder deeds/registr titles, 1988-92; US Senate, sen State Ill, 1993-99; US Dept Educ, consult, 1998-99; US ambassador to Nz, 1999-2001; Morris Brown Col, vis distung prof & scholar residence, 2001-02; DePaul Univ, Col Com, bus law prof, 2002-03; Moseley Braun LLC, owner, currently; Ambassador Organics, founder & pres, 2005-. **Orgs:** Bar US Ct Appeals 7th Circuit, Bar US Dist Ct Northern Dist IL, Bar State Ill, Ill State Bar Asn, Nat Order Women Legislators, Dem Policy Comns Dem Nat Conv, Cook County Bar Asn, Chicago Coun Lawyers, Am Judicature Soc, Nat Conf State Leg; comn Cts & Justice; del Dem Nat Conv, 1984; League Black Women, Jane Addams Ctr Social Policy & Res; hon mem, Alpha Gamma Phi, Delta Sigma Theta Sorority Inc; Chicago Forum, DuSable Mus, Chicago Pub Schs Alumni Asn, IL women's Polit Caucus, Coaltion to Save S Shore Country Club Pk, Urban League, Nat Asn Advan Colored People, S Shore Comn. **Special Achievements:** Inducted, Hall of Fame, Chicago Gay and Lesbian Hall of Fame, 2007 as a Friend of the Community. **Business Addr:** Founder, President, Ambassador Organics, 1634 E 53rd St 2nd Fl, Chicago, IL 60615, **Business Phone:** (773)288-3700.

**BRAXTON, DR. BRAD R.**
Educator, clergy. **Personal:** married Lazetta R; children: Karis J. **Educ:** Univ Va, BA, relig studies, 1991; Univ Oxford, MPhil, new testament studies, 1993; Emory Univ, PhD, new testament studies, 1999. **Career:** First Baptist Church, Salem, Va, ordained minister, 1991; Douglas Mem Community Church, Baltimore, MD, sr pastor, 1995-2000; Mt Pleasant Missionary Baptist Church, interim minister, 2000-01; Wake Forest Univ Divinity Sch, Winston-Salem, NC, Jessie Ball duPont, asst prof Homiletics & Bibl Studies, 2000-04; Vanderbilt Univ Divinity Sch, assoc prof homiletics & new testament, 2004-08; Theologian Residence, 2007-; Riverside Church, New York, NY, pastoral ministry, 2008-09, sr minister; McCormick Theol Sem, distinguished vis scholar, 2010-12; Open Church, founding sr pastor, 2011-; Southern Methodist Univ, lois craddock perkins prof homiletics, 2012-14; Ford Found, prog officer, 2014-15. **Orgs:** Adv Bd, African Am Pulpit J; Faith Partnerships Inc, Raleigh, NC; Socs Bibl Lit; Acad Homiletics; Advocacy Poor, 2003-04. **Special Achievements:** First African American to come to SMU with an endowed faculty chair.

**BRAXTON, REV. EDWARD KENNETH**
Priest, educator, bishop. **Personal:** Born Jun 28, 1944, Chicago, IL; son of Cullen L Sr (deceased) and Evelyn (deceased). **Educ:** BA, 1966; St Mary Lake Sem, MA, 1968, STL, STB, 1968; M, Div, 1969; Cath Univ Louvain, PhD, relig studies, 1975, STD, syst theol, 1976. **Career:** Priest Chicago, ordained priest, 1970; Holy Name Cathedral, assoc pastor; Sacred Heart Parish Winnetka, assoc pastor, 1971-73; Harvard Univ, 1976-77; Notre Dame Univ, vis prof, 1977-78; Diocese Cleveland, chancellor theol affairs & personal theol; Archdiocese Wa, DC, chancellor theol affairs, 1978-81; Rome N Am Col, scholar residence, 1982-83; Univ Chicago, Cath Stud Ctr, dir, 1983-86; William H Sadlier Inc, off theol consult, 1986-92; winter sch lectr, SafricA, 1988; St. Catherine Sienna parish, pastor, 1992; Auxiliary Bishop St Louis, MO, 1995-2001; Bishop Lake Charles, LA, 2001-05; Bishop Belleville, IL, 2005-. **Orgs:** Am Acad Relig; Cath Theol Soc Am; Black Cath Clergy Caucus; Cath Bishop's Comt Liturgy & Doctrine; bd dir, St Mary Lake Sem, Chicago; keynote speaker, 43 Int Eucharistic Cong, Nairobi, Kenya; theol adv to bishops Africa & Madagascan, 1984; del, writer & speaker Hist, Nat Black Cath Cong, Wash, DC, 1997; USCCBs Comts Educ; Chmn, NCCB Comt Am Col Univ Louvain; NCCB's Comts Educ, Sci & Human Values, & Scripture Transl; Convenor, African Am Cath Bishops; Us Conf Cath Bishops; Senate Priests Archdiocese. **Business Addr:** Bishop, Diocese of Belleville, 222 S 3rd St, Belleville, IL 62220, **Business Phone:** (618)277-8181.

**BRAXTON, JANICE LAWRENCE (JANICE FAYE LAWRENCE BRAXTON)**
Basketball player, basketball coach. **Personal:** Born Jun 7, 1962, Lucedale, MS; married Steve. **Educ:** La Tech Univ, attended 1984. **Career:** Basketball player (retired), basketball coach; Cleveland Rockers, 1997-99; Cleveland Rockers, asst coach, 2003. **Business Addr:** Assistant Coach, Cleveland Rockers, 200 Huron Rd E, Cleveland, OH 44115, **Business Phone:** (216)420-2000.

**BRAXTON, DR. JEAN BAILEY**
Educator, dean (education), chairperson. **Personal:** Born Jan 6, 1943, Hampton, VA; daughter of Linwood and Christine; married Wendell F; children: Michael & Traci. **Educ:** Bennett Col, BS, health, phys educ & recreation, 1965; Hampton Univ, MA, phys educ, 1972, cert exec leadership summit, 2001; Univ NC, Greensboro, EdD, mod dance, 1984; Bryn Mawr Col, cert advan higher educ admin, 1994. **Career:** Attucks High Sch, phys educ teacher, 1965-70; Hampton HS, phys educ teacher, 1970-71; Hampton Univ, PE Dept, asst prof, 1971-83, dept chair, health & phys educ, 1971-88, dept chairperson, 1984-88; Norfolk State Univ, PE Dept, assoc prof, 1988-93, Sch Educ, dean, 1988-, dept chairperson, 1993-99, dept chair, health phys educ & exercise sci, 1999-2008, dean, 2000-, va dept educ, 2007-08. **Orgs:** Am Alliance Health; Am Asn Cols Teacher Educ; accreditation team mem, Va Dept Educ; bd examr, Nat Coun Accreditation Teacher Educ. **Home Addr:** 55 Bay Front Pl, Hampton, VA 23664-1797, **Home Phone:** (757)848-1504. **Business Addr:** Dean, Norfolk State University, Rm 115 Bozeman Educ Bldg, Norfolk, VA 23504, **Business Phone:** (757)823-8701.

**BRAXTON, HON. JOHN LEDGER**
Association executive, judge, educator. **Personal:** Born Feb 6, 1945, Philadelphia, PA; married Linda; children: 1. **Educ:** Pa State Univ, BS, 1966; Howard Univ Sch Law, JD, 1971. **Career:** Wolf, Block Schorr & Solis-Cohen, assoc, 1971-73; Braxton, Johnson & Kopanski, partner, 1973-76; Blue Cross Greater Philadelphia, assoc coun, 1976-78; Off Dist Atty Philadelphia, chief munic ct unit, 1978-81; Philadelphia, trial ct judge; Ct Common Pleas, judge, 1981-95; Phoenix Mgt Serv Inc, vpres; Temple Univ, Dept Law & Real Estate, adj prof, 1985-95; arbitrator & mediator, 1995-2010; Proj GRAD Philadelphia, judge, 2010-. **Orgs:** bd mem, Fel Comn, 1978-85; vice pres, Child Psychiat Ctr St Christopher's, 1976-85; bd mem, Philadelphia Citywide Devel Corp, 1981-85; bd mem, Judicial Coun Nat Bar, 1984-85; vice chair, Cradle Liberty Coun BSA; chmn, Nat Bar Asn, Judical Coun, 1992-93; pres, Homemaker Serv Metrop Area, 1995-99; Toll fel Coun State Govt; alumni fel Pa State Univ, 1996; bd gov, Am Red Cross; mem bd, Pa CASA; chmn bd, Philadelphia County, CASA, bd mem; mem bd, Cradle Liberty Coun Boy Scouts Am; mem bd, Juv Law Ctr, secy; chmn bd, Bearean Bank, 1999-2003; treas, Nat Bar Asn, 2008-; chmn bd, Penn-Jersey Region, Am Red Cross Blood Servs; chmn, Philadelphia Com Develop Corp. **Honors/Awds:** Outstanding Alumnus Award, Howard Univ; Silver Beaver Award, Boy Scouts Am, Phila Coun, 1989; Whitney M Young Service Award. **Home Addr:** 410 St John Neumann Way, Philadelphia, PA 19123. **Business Addr:** Senior Judge, Proj GRAD Philadelphia, 2855 Mangum Rd, Houston, TX 77092, **Business Phone:** (832)831-6018.

**BRAXTON, REV. STEVE**
Executive, clergy, writer. **Personal:** Born Jan 30, 1941, Natchitoches, LA; son of Thomas (deceased) and Mary (deceased); children: Jason & Girard. **Educ:** Grambling State Univ, eng lang & lit, gen, 1964; Wayne State Univ, bus admin & mgt gen, 1973; Windsor Univ, BS, bus admin & mgt, 1974; Loyola Univ, Inst Small Develop, Inst Pastoral Care & Study, cert, small group ministry, 1994; McCormick Theol Sem, post-grad study, 1998; Northern Baptist Theol Sem, Christian community develop, 2012. **Career:** Food Maker Inc, distrib supvr, 1970-73; Burger King, gen mgr corp distib, 1973-76; McDonald's Corp, area supvr; Church's Fried Chicken, dist mgr, 1976-80; Inner City Foods Pillsbury, vpres opers, 1980-82, pres, 1982-86; Health Tech Inc, vpres, co-owner, 1986-94; BRME Enterprise, pres, 1994-2000; Nat Progressive Inst, pres, 1996-2000; United Church Hyde Park, youth pastor, 1999-2000, interim sr pastor, 1999-2001; Marketplace Consult Inc, founder & pres, 1997-; Braxton Enterprise Inc, pres; Health Tech Industs, pharmaceut, co-owner; BRME Enterprise, pres, currently; Lawndale Christian Legal Ctr, mgr, 2009-12; Light IL.-COGIC, Int, asst presiding bishop, 2011-; Light Ill Diocese, bishop, 2011-; Karatbars Int, sr partner, 2015-. **Orgs:** Adv comm, Miss Black Chicago, 1980-85; bd mem, Chicago Opportunity Indust Ctr, 1980-84; bd mem, Black United Fund, Ill, 1986-; steering comt, Chicago Bus Develop Coun, 1990-99; deacon, 1990-96, ordained minister, 1997-, Progressive Community Church; bd mem, Inspired Partnerships, 1994-99; subcomt chair, State Ill, Access Capital, 1997-99; bd mem & co-chmn, Accreditation Partnership-Early Stars Prog; bd mem, trustee, Ecumenical Childcare Network, USA; coordr, United Church Hyde Pk, Chicago, Youth Mentoring & Enrichment Progs; Am Clergy Leadership Coun; Inter-relig Int Coun World Peace; Nat Black Relig Coalition Reproductive Choice; bd mem, C's Home & Aid Soc; chair bd dir, Partnership Qual Child Care, 2003; pres, bd dir, Ecumenical Childcare Network, 2003; co-convenor, United Way/ECCN Qual Partner Faith-based Child Develop Collab Cohort, 2003; founding vol bd mem, Black United Fund Ill Inc; exec comt mem, White House Coun Community Solutions, currently; exec comt, Lawndale Christian Fitness Ctr, 2009-; bd mem, Lawndale Christian Community Develop Corp, 2010-. **Home Addr:** 7411 S Wabash Ave, Chicago, IL 60619. **Business Addr:** Founder, President, Marketplace Consult Group, 3428 Nickel Creek, Plano, TX 75025, **Business Phone:** (972)208-1275.

**BRAXTON, TONI MICHELLE**
Actor, singer. **Personal:** Born Oct 7, 1967, Severn, MD; daughter of Michael Conrad Sr and Evelyn Jackson; married Keri Lewis; children: Denim Kole Lewis & Diezel Ky Lewis. **Educ:** Bowie State Univ, attended. **Career:** Labels: LaFace; Arista; Blackground; Atlantic Records; Motown. Albums: Toni Braxton, 1993; Secrets, 1996; Heat, 2000; Snowflakes, 2001; More Than A Woman, 2002; Ultimate Toni Braxton, 2003; Libra, 2005; Love & Pain, 2008; Pulse, 2010; Love, Marriage & Divorce, 2014. Films: Kingdom Come, 2001; The Oogieloves in the Big Balloon Adventure, 2012. TV: "Broadway: Beauty & the Beast", 1998-99; "Play'd: A Hip Hop Story", 2002; "Aida", 2003; "Kevin in Hill", 2005; "An Evening of Stars: Tribute to Stevie Wonder", 2006; "Dancing on Ice", 2009; "Twist of Faith", 2013. **Business Addr:** Singer, Artist, c/o Laface Recs, 1 Capital City Plz 3350 Peachtree Rd Suite 1500, Atlanta, GA 30326.

**BRAXTON, TYRONE SCOTT**
Football player, football coach. **Personal:** Born Dec 17, 1964, Madison, WI; married Elizabeth. **Educ:** NDak State Univ. **Career:** Football player (retired), coach; Denver Broncos, 1987-88, left cornerback, 1989, 1991-93, defensive back, 1990, strong safety, 1995-99; Miami Dolphins, 1994; Arvada High Sch, asst coach, currently. **Honors/Awds:** Rookie of the Year, 1987; Champion, Asian Football Confederation, 1987, 1989, 1997, 1998; Unsung Hero, Nat Football League Players Asn, 1996; Pro Bowl, 1996; Champion, Super Bowl, XXXII, XXXIII; Mackey Award, 1997; True Value Man of the Year, Denver Broncos, 1997. **Home Addr:** 1066 Rosemary St, Denver, CO 80230-7089. **Business Addr:** Assistant Football Coach, Arvada High School, 7951 W 65th Ave, Arvada, CO 80004, **Business Phone:** (303)982-0162.

**BRAY, LEROY, SR.**
Engineer. **Personal:** Born Aug 1, 1950, Norwich, CT; son of Luther and Beatrice; married Patricia Baldwin; children: Anthony, Desiree, Marquita, Tiffany & Leroy Jr. **Educ:** Howard Univ, BSEE, 1973; Cent Mich Univ, MBM, 1980; Wayne State Univ, MS, 1995. **Career:** Gen Motors, mfg, process elec engr, 1973-76; Ford Motor Co, maintenance supvr, engr, 1980-87; Owens Corning Fiberglass76-80, automotive safety prog mgr, 1987-. **Orgs:** Sr mem, Am Soc for Quality Control, 1989-. **Honors/Awds:** Certified Quality Engineer, Am Soc Quality Control, 1989; Certified Quality Auditor, Am Soc Quality Control, 1990. **Business Addr:** Automotive Safety Program Manager, Ford Motor Co, 330 Town Ctr Dr Fairlane Plz S Suite 1100, Dearborn, MI 48126, **Business Phone:** (313)323-4140.

**BRAYNON, DR. EDWARD J., JR.**
Dentist. **Personal:** Born Jan 15, 1928, Miami, FL; son of Edward J Sr and May Dell Jackson; married Ann Carey; children: Edward III &

Keith. **Educ:** Howard Univ, BS, 1949, DDS, 1954. **Career:** Dentist (retired); pvt pract dentist, 1956-87; Family Health Ctr Inc, chief dent serv, 1981-87, vpres suppl serv, 1987-96. **Orgs:** Pres, Dade County Acad Med, 1962-63; pres, Dade County Dent Soc, 1970-72; grand baseileus, Omega Psi Phi Frat, 1976-79. **Honors/Awds:** Key City Columbus, GA, 1973; Outstanding service to the community & profession, Howard Univ, Wash, DC, 1976; Key City Fayetteville, NC, 1976; Key Dade County, FL, 1976; Key City Spartanberg, SC, 1977; One of the 100 Most Influential Black Americans, Ebony Mag, 1977-79; Honorary Citizen of Louisville, Louisville KY, 1977; Honorary Citizen of New Orleans, New Orleans, LA, 1977; Distinguished Service Award, Fla Dent Asn, 1990. **Special Achievements:** Dr E J Braynon, Jr Day City Miami, Florida 1976. **Home Addr:** 2271 NE 191st St, Miami, FL 33180-2156, **Home Phone:** (305)932-7433.

## BRAZIL, DR. ROBERT D.

President (organization), educator, administrator. **Personal:** Born Mar 19, 1939, Memphis, TN; children: Patrice & Alan. **Educ:** Chicago Teachers Col, BEd, 1960; DePaul Univ, MEd, 1965; Northwestern Univ; Univ Ill. **Career:** Chicago, teacher, 1960; Tesla Sch, prin, 1966; Headstart, prin, 1966-67; US Dept Juctice, Midwest educ, consult, 1967; Parkside Sch, prin, 1971; HEW Off Educ, non fed pnlst, 1974-75; Francis Parker HS, prin, 1975; Sullivan High Sch, prin; Calumet & Manley high Schs, prin; Carver Elem Sch, prin; McGaw Grad Sch, adj prof educ; Nat Col Educ, instr; Univ Ill, asst prof; Roger Sullivan High Sch, prin; Chicago Pub Schs, Nat Bd Recertification, consult; Paideia Inst Hyde Pk, dir, pres, currently. **Orgs:** Kappa Alpha Psi Fraternity; Nat Col Educ Vols Side Community Comt; Beatrice Caffrey Youth Serv; Betty Boys Found; Marillac Comn House; U.S. Dept Justice; Instr, Nat Col Educ & Northern Ill Univ. **Home Addr:** 212 W Washington St, Chicago, IL 60606-3535, **Home Phone:** (312)364-9330. **Business Addr:** President, Director, Paideia Institute of Hyde Park, 1448 E 52nd St, Chicago, IL 60615, **Business Phone:** (773)684-5118.

## BRAZILE, DONNA L.

Political consultant, educator, association executive. **Personal:** Born Dec 15, 1959, New Orleans, LA; daughter of Jean and Lionel. **Educ:** La State Univ, BA, psychol, 1981. **Career:** Educr, auth, syndicated columnist, Polit Strategist; Nat Stud Educ Fund, nat dir, 1983; Roll Call Newspaper, columist; MSNBC's Hardball; Gephardt Pres, nat field dir, 1987; Michael Dukakis Pres campaign, nat field dir, 1988; Fox's Hannity & Colmes; Sen Mary Landrieu, media consult & grassroots organizer; US House Rep, del, Eleanor Holmes Norton, chief staff, pres secy, 1990-2000; Univ MD-Col Pk, guest lectr, sr lectr & adj prof, 1996-99; Al Gore Pres Campaign, polit dir, Dep Campaign, mgr, 1999-2000; Gore 2000, campaign Mgr; 2005 Sen Winona Lippman; Rutgers Univ Ctr Am Women Polit; Georgetown Univ, adj prof, currently; Brazile Assocs LLC, consult, currently, founder & mng dir, currently; Georgetown Univ, Women's Studies Prog, lectr, adj asst prof. **Orgs:** Pres & Life Ins; mem-at-large, Dem Nat Comt; bd dir, La Recovery Authority; chair, Dem Nat Comt's Voting Rights Inst; bd dir, Future PAC; fel Harvard's Inst Polit; bd, Joint Ctr Polit & Econ Studies. **Honors/Awds:** Congressional Black Caucus Foundation's Award; Minority Woman of Excellence Award, Wash Univ Natl Assn Advan Colored People; Hon DHL, 2005; Remarkable Visionaries, O, The Oprah Magazine, 2009; 100 Most Powerful Women Washingtonian magazine; Top 50 Women in America, Essence magazine; Honorary Doctorate, La State Univ, NC A&T State Univ, & Xavier Univ La. **Special Achievements:** Radio One, "A View From the Hill," past host, producer; "Roll Call, "columnist; "Ms." magazine, contributing writer; CNN frequent guest commentator; ABC "This Week with George Stephanopoulos", frequent guest commentator; HBO's "K Street," guest appearance; Showtime's "American Candidate," premier guest appearance; author, Cooking with Grease; Stirring the Pots in American Politics, Simon & Schuster, 2004; Washingtonian magazine's 100 Most Powerful Women in Washington, DC; First African-American to direct a major presidential campaign; Essence Magazine's 50 Most Powerful Women in America. **Home Addr:** PO Box 15369, Washington, DC 20003. **Business Addr:** Founder, Managing Director, Brazile & Associates LLC, 1001 G St NW Suite 1001, Washington, DC 20001, **Business Phone:** (202)628-8081.

## BRAZLEY, DR. MICHAEL DUWAIN

Architect, educator. **Personal:** Born Apr 6, 1951, Louisville, KY; son of William and Gwendolyn; children: Erin & Katelyn. **Educ:** Univ Ky, archit, attended 1973; Howard Univ, BA, archit, 1978; Univ Louisville, Sch Urban & Pub Affairs, PhD, urban infrastructure & environ anal, 2002. **Career:** Fed Rr Admin, Dept Transp, Mom Providence, RI, proj mgr, 1979; City Louisville, streetscape designer; Ky Air Nat Guard Airplane Hangar, architect; Eastern High Sch, renovator; Louisville & Jefferson County Metrop Sewer Dist, storm water drainage master plan implementation; Standiford Field Airport, Air Nat Guard civil engr, drainage, roadway & utility design; First Baptist Church, renovator; Mt Olive Missionary Baptist Church, designer; Greater Good Hope Baptist Church, designer; Michael D Brazley & Assoc PLLC, pres, 1987-2001; Ctr Sustainable Urban Neighborhoods Urban & Pub Affairs, grad res asst, 1996-2002; Southern Ill Univ, Sch Archit, asst prof archit & interior design, 2003-; Brazley & Brazley Inc, pres & chief exec officer. **Orgs:** Am Inst Archit; Ky Soc Archit; Construct Specif Inst; Urban Land Inst; Am Planning Asn; Kentuckiana Minority Supplier Devel Coun; Louisville Third Century; bd mem, Ky African Am Mus Coun; Kentuckiana Regional Planning & Devel Agency, mobility task force; YMCA; Louisville's Urban League; Nat Asn Advan Colored People; adv bd, Univ Louisville, Black Engrs & Technicians Asn; Howard Univ Alumni Asn; bd dir, Wesley Community House. **Home Addr:** 510 N 15th St, Murphysboro, IL 62966, **Home Phone:** (618)559-5112. **Business Addr:** Associate Professor, Southern Illinois University, 139 Quigley Hall, Carbondale, IL 62901, **Business Phone:** (618)453-3734.

## BRAZZELL, DR. JOHNETTA CROSS

Educator, college administrator, chancellor (education). **Educ:** Spelman Col, BA, polit sci, 1968; Univ Chicago, MA, 1972; Univ Mich, PhD, higher & adult continuing educ, 1991. **Career:** Education administrator (retired); Oakland Univ, Placement & Career Serv, dir, 1982-87; Univ Mich, asst assoc vpres, acad affairs & stud affairs, 1982-87; Spelman Col, fac; Univ Ariz, assoc dean students, 1990-93, interim dean stud, 1993; Oakland Univ, fac; Univ Ark, vice chancellor stud affairs, 1999-2009, adj assoc prof higher educ. **Orgs:** Northwest Ark Diversity Coun; Northwest Ark Dr Martin Luther King Jr Planning Comt; bd dir, Walton Arts Ctr. **Business Addr:** Adjunct Associate Professor of Higher Education, University of Arkansas, Fayetteville, AR 72701, **Business Phone:** (479)575-2000.

## BREAUX, TIMOTHY (TIM BREAUX)

Basketball player. **Personal:** Born Sep 19, 1970, Baton Rouge, LA. **Educ:** Univ Wyo, attended 1992. **Career:** Basketball player (retired); Sioux Falls Skyforce, 1992-93, 1996-97; Continental Basketball Asn, Sioux Falls Sky force, 1992-93, 1996-97; Tours Joue, France, 1993; Pamesa Valencia, Spain, 1993-94; Nat Football League, Europe; Houston Rockets, 1994-95; Vancouver Grizzlies, 1996-97; Milwaukee Bucks, forward, 1997; Idaho Stampede, 1997-98; Caceres, Spain, 1998; Galatasaray, Turkey, 1998-99; Dierre Massa e Cozzile, Italy, 1999-2000; Seattle Supersonics, 2000; Brand Hagen, Ger, 2000; Yakima Sun Kings, forward, 2003-04. **Home Addr:** 11944 Sheraton Dr, Baton Rouge, LA 70815, **Home Phone:** (225)274-8408.

## BRECKENRIDGE, REV. FRANKLIN EUGENE, SR.

Lawyer, clergy. **Personal:** married Cora Smith; children: Lejene, Franklin Jr & Emma Estel. **Educ:** Wabash Col, BA, Span & relig; Ind Univ, Robert H. McKinney Sch Law, BS, 1963, JD, 1968; Anabaptist Mennonite Bibl Sem, MDiv, 1999. **Career:** Lawyer (retired), pastor; Kokomo-Ctr Twp Consol Sch, teacher, 1963-65; Indianapolis Pre-Sch Inc, teacher, 1965-66; Ind Dept Revenue, admin supvr corp income tax, 1966-68; pvt pract, 1968-73; Bayer Corp, asst secy, assoc coun, 1973-96; St James AME Church, pastor, relig leader, currently; Franklin E Breckenridge Atty, prin. **Orgs:** Elkhart City Bar Asn; Ind Bar Asn, Am Bar Asn; Alpha Phi Alpha Social Fraternity; Phi Delta Phi Legal Fraternity; pres, Nat Asn Advan Colored People; Nat Bar Asn; Dem Precinct ComEklhart Co, 1975; pres, Ind State Conf Brs Nat Asn Advan Colored People, 1978-2000; chair bd visitors, IUPUI Sch Law. **Honors/Awds:** Numerous NAACP Awards; William Robert Ming Advocacy Award; Kelly M. Alexander, Sr. Award, Conference President's Award; National Bar Association Hall of Fame, 2009. **Home Addr:** 1219 Briarwood Dr, Elkhart, IN 46514. **Business Addr:** Religious Leader, Pastor, St James AME Church, 122 Doctor Martin Luther King Jr Dr, Elkhart, IN 46516, **Business Phone:** (574)294-4950.

## BREDA, DR. MALCOLM J.

Educator. **Personal:** Born Aug 14, 1934, Alexandria, LA. **Educ:** Xavier Univ La, BS, 1956; Univ Ind, MMEd, 1962; Univ Southern Miss, PhD, 1975. **Career:** NO Archdiocesan Music Prog, lectr & cons; Ala A&M Univ, instr, asst prof, 1956-64; Boys Town NE, organist, pianist resident, 1964-67; St John Prep Sch NO La, dir choral activ, 1967-73; Xavier Univ La, Dept Music, prof, 1967-2010; New Orleans Black Chorale, conductor, 1986-91, assoc conductor & organist, currently; Xavier Univ La, Dept Music, chmn, 1995-96, prof emer, currently. **Orgs:** Alpha Kappa Mu; Phi Mu Alpha, Sinfonia; Music Educrs Nat Conf; Nat Asn Sch Music. **Honors/Awds:** Sister M Cornelia Jubilee Award, 1952; Mother Agatha Ryan Award, 1956; ISSP Summer Fel, Harvard Univ, 1968; Nat Fel, 1973-75. **Home Addr:** 5707 Prince Lane, New Orleans, LA 70126-1229, **Home Phone:** (504)246-3480. **Business Addr:** Professor Emeritus, Xavier University, 1 Drexel Dr, New Orleans, LA 70125-1056, **Business Phone:** (504)520-7696.

## BREMBY, RODERICK LEMAR

Secretary (government), government official. **Personal:** Born Feb 4, 1960, Eufaula, AL; son of Johnny B and Margaret J Robinson-Johnson; married April Lynne Harris; children: Rachel & Arielle. **Educ:** Univ Kans, Lawrence KS, BA, 1982, MPA, 1983. **Career:** City Ft Worth, Ft Worth TX, mgt intern, 1983-84, admin analyst I, 1984-85, admin analyst II, 1985, admin analyst III, 1985-86, asst citymgr I, asst citymgr II, 1986-90; City Lawrence, Lawrence, KS, asst city mgr, 1990-2000; KU Work Group Health Prom & Community Develop, asst res prof, 2000-03; Kans Depart Health & Environ, cabinet secy, 2003-10; Conn Dept Social Serv, comnr, 2011-. **Orgs:** Assoc mem, Int City Mgt Asn, 1983-; Pi Sigma Alpha, 1984; pres, Urban MgtAsn N Tex, 1986; City Ft Worth Juneteenth Planning Comn, 1986-; City Forth Worth MLK Planning Comn, 1986-; secy, Nat Forum Black Pub Admin, NTex Chap, 1986-89, pres, 1989-; Leadership Ft Worth, 1987-; Forum Fort-Worth, 1988-90; vpres, Nat Forum Black Pub Adminr Coun Pres, 1990-; Nat Network to Eliminate Disparities Behav Health; Phi Beta Sigma Fraternity Inc; Am Pub Health Asn; Health Care Cabinet; bd dir, Access Health CT; Health Technol Work Group; Basic Health Plan Work Group; Conn Employ, Training Comn & Interagency Coun, Ending Achievement Gap. **Home Addr:** 1022 Ohio, Lawrence, KS 66044, **Home Phone:** (913)865-0932. **Business Addr:** Commissioner, Connecticut Department of Social Services, 25 Sigourney St, Hartford, CT 06106-5033, **Business Phone:** (860)424-4908.

## BREMER, CHARLES E.

Educator, administrator. **Personal:** Born Sep 12, 1941, New Orleans, LA; married Jocelyn. **Educ:** Ohio Univ, BS, govt & hist, 1965; Kent State Univ, cert, voc guid & counr, 1965; Southern Ill & Rutgers Univ, grad labor, 1978. **Career:** Cleveland Pub Sch, teacher, 1965; OH State Dept Labor, voc guid coun, 1966; RTP Inc-Manpower Training & Develop, dept exec dir, 1968-74; Southern Ill Univ, teacher & counr, 1967; Contini & Riffs Retails Bus, pres, 1974-78; A Philip Randolph Educ Fund & YEP, nat dr, 1978-. **Orgs:** Bd mediation Inst Mediation & Conflict Resolution, 1971-; chmn, scholarcom WC Handy Scholar Club, 1975-; bd finance, Workers Defense League, 1979-. **Home Addr:** 1115 12th St NW Apt T3, Washington, DC 20005-4653, **Home Phone:** (202)682-0237. **Business Addr:** Assistant Director, Social Act Department, 1126 16th St NW, Washington, DC 20036.

## BREVARD, ANTHONY (TONY BREVARD)

Executive, banker. **Personal:** married Angelia; children: Brittany & William. **Educ:** Citadel, BA, bus admin, 1990; E Carolina Univ, Bankers Sch, attended 2000; Mercer Univ, MBA, Int Bus, 2015. **Career:** Bank Am, Com Real Estate Lender, 1990-93, Prof African Am Banking Group, nat bus develop exec, 1995-99; First Palmetto Savings Bank, sr lender, head govt lending, 1993-94; BB&T, sr lender, dir emerging markets, 1999-2001; EEC Consult Group LLC/Joseph Conglomerate LLC, founder, 2001-08; Church Capital Direct, founder, 2008-11; Drayton Financial, Lic P&C Ins agt, 2009-11; Wells Fargo, com bus develop officer, Specialty Markets, 2011-14; NC Nat Bank; BB & T Bank, vpres emerging markets; Com Lending, vpres; Hamilton State Bank, vpres & sba bus develop officer, 2014; Atlantic Capital Bank, vpres, SBA Bus Develop, 2014-. **Orgs:** Omega Psi Phi Fraternity Inc, 1995. **Home Addr:** , Atlanta, GA. **Business Addr:** Vice President, 3280 Peachtree Rd NE Suite 1600, Atlanta, GA 30305, **Business Phone:** (404)460-4430.

**BREVARD, TONY. See BREVARD, ANTHONY.**

## BREWER, DR. ARTHELIA J.

Executive. **Personal:** Born SC. **Educ:** Fisk Univ, BA; Vanderbilt Univ, MA; Meharry Med Col, MD, MSPH, 1979. **Career:** Gen Motors Corp, plant med dir, assoc div med dir; Gen Dynamics Land Systs, div med dir; Health Servs Int PC, pres, med dir, 1995-. **Home Addr:** 1104 S Timberview Trl, Bloomfield Hills, MI 48304-1561, **Home Phone:** (248)853-7044. **Business Addr:** President, Medical Director, Health Services International PC, 5005 E 14 Mile Rd, Sterling Heights, MI 48310, **Business Phone:** (586)826-9116.

## BREWER, COREY (COREY WAYNE BREWER)

Baseball player. **Personal:** Born Mar 5, 1986, Portland, TN; son of Pee Wee and Glenda. **Educ:** Univ Fla, attended 2007. **Career:** Professional basketball player, 2007-; drafted by NBA Minnesota Timberwolves, 2007; Minnesota Timberwolves, 2007-10, 2013-14; Dallas Mavericks, 2010; Denver Nuggets, 2011-12; Houston Rockets, 2014-. **Orgs:** The Corey Brewer Foundation, founder. **Honors/Awds:** Class AA Mr. Basketball, Tenn High Sch State Basketball, 2004; Most Outstanding Player of the 2007 Final Four, 2007; SEC Co-Defensive Player of the Year, 2007. **Special Achievements:** University of Florida's all-time scoring leader in NCAA Tournament scoring; won two national championships with University of Florida, 2006, 2007. **Business Addr:** Houston Rockets, 1510 Polk St, Houston, TX 77002.

**BREWER, ERNESTINE T. See MANGUM, ERNESTINE BREWER.**

## BREWER, GREGORY ALAN

Research scientist. **Personal:** Born Feb 3, 1968, Denver, CO; son of Riley and Aileen. **Educ:** Morehouse Col, BS, physics, 1990; Univ Calif, Los Angeles, 1990. **Career:** Univ Calif, Los Angeles, GAAD Proj 88 fel, 1990, researcher, 1991-. **Orgs:** Nat Soc Black Engrs, 1986-; Inst Elec & Electronics Engrs, 1993-; Phi Beta Kappa, 1990-; school Minority Engineering program. **Home Addr:** 2568 Birch St, Denver, CO 80207-3133, **Home Phone:** (303)996-0044. **Business Addr:** Researcher, University Of California, Los Angeles, 405 Hilgard Ave, Los Angeles, CA 90024, **Business Phone:** (310)206-2573.

## BREWER, JIM (JAMES TURNER BREWER)

Basketball player, basketball coach. **Personal:** Born Dec 3, 1951, Maywood, IL; married Patsy; children: Jim & Phera. **Educ:** Univ Minn, BS, sociol, 1973. **Career:** Basketball player (retired), basketball coach; Cleveland Cavaliers, prof basketball player, 1973-79; Detroit Pistons, 1979; Portland Trail Blazers, 1979-80; Los Angeles Lakers, 1980-82; Pallacanestro Cantu, 1982-85; Cant, Italy, prof basketball player; Northwestern Univ, asst coach & recruit, 1986-89; Minn Timber wolves, recruit, dir player personnel role, 1990-91, asst coach, asst gen mgr, 1991-94; Los Angeles Clippers, lead asst coach, 1994-99; Orlando Magic, scout, 1999-2000; Toronto Raptors, asst coach & advan scout, 2000-02; Lenny Wilkens staff, asst coach, 2000-02; Harlem Globetrotters, head coach & consult, 2003-05; Boston Celtics, asst coach, 2004-06; LTD Enterprises, independent contractor, 2007-.

## BREWER, MOSES

Executive. **Personal:** Born Mar 12, 1947, Florence, AL; son of James and Ivory; married Gwendolyn. **Educ:** Northeastern Jr Col, Sterling, CO, attended 1967; Univ Denver, BA, phys educ & recreation, 1971, MA, speech commun & human rels, 1975. **Career:** Baseball Prog Denver Boys, dir, 1969; St Anne's Elem Sch, teacher, 1970; City Auditors Off, coordr microfilm, 1969-71; Univ Denver, coordr recreational activ, 1971-72; Univ Denver, asst dean stud life, 1972-73; Denver Univ, univ consult at large, 1973-; Denver Pub Sch, consult, 1974-75; Coors Brewing Co (Miller Coors LLC), dir corp rels; Adolph Coors Corp, Community Rels Dept, asst nat prog mgr, currently. **Orgs:** All-Regional 9 Basketball Team, 1966-67; Nat Asn Stud Personnel Adminr; Nat Speech Commun Asn; Pi Kappa Alpha Fraternity; United Negro Col Fund; Black Caucus; Black Alumni Asn Univ Denver; Western Regional Ombudsman Asn; bd mem, Nat Scholar Serv & Funds Negro Students; pres, Urban League Metrop Denver; bd mem, Nat Black Col Alumni Hall Fame. **Honors/Awds:** Outstanding Athlete Award, 1968; Outstanding Faculty Adminr Award, 1974; Outstanding Personality Award. **Home Addr:** 16259 E Powers Pl, Aurora, CO 80015-4313, **Home Phone:** (303)699-1991. **Business Addr:** Assistant National Program Manager, Adolph Coors Corp, 311 10th St Suite NH420, Golden, CO 80401, **Business Phone:** (303)279-6565.

## BREWER, ROSALIND G. (ROZ BREWER)

President (organization). **Personal:** Born Jan 1, 1962?. **Educ:** Spelman Col, BS, chem, 1984; Wharton Sch, advan mgt prog; Univ Chicago Sch Bus/Stanford Sch Law, grad. **Career:** Kimberly-Clark Corp, scientist, 1984-2006, Global Nonwoven Div, pres, 2004-06; Wal-Mart Stores Inc, overseeing opers regional vpres, 2006, sr vpres & div pres opers, 2006-, div pres Southeast, 2007-12, Walmart E, Sam's Club warehouse, exec vpres & pres & chief exec officer, currently; Molson Coors Brewing Co, human resources & compensation comt. **Orgs:** Johnnetta B. Cole Leadership Soc United Way; Exec Leadership Coun; bd dir, Molson Coors Brewing Co, 2006-; bd dir, Lockheed Martin Corp; bd trustee, Spelman Col, 2006-; bd trustee, Westminster Schs. **Business Addr:** President, Chief Executive Officer, Wal-Mart Stores Inc, 2101 SE Simple Savings Dr, Bentonville, AR 72716-0745, **Business Phone:** (479)464-2547.

**BREWER, DR. ROSE MARIE**
Educator, sociologist. **Personal:** Born Oct 30, 1947, Tulsa, OK; daughter of Wilson and Cloviece; married Walter Griffin; children: Sundiata Brewer Griffin. **Educ:** Northeastern St Col, BA, 1969; Ind Univ, MA, 1971, PhD, 1976; Univ Chicago, PhD, 1983. **Career:** Ford Found fel, 1972-73; Rice Univ, vis lectr, 1976; Univ TX, asst prof, 1977-80, 1983-86; NIMH res fel, 1981-83; Univ Chicago, fel, 1981-83; Wiepking Distinguished vis prof, Miami Univ Ohio, 1996; Univ MN, asst prof; Univ Minn, Abrigail Quigley McCarty Ctr Women & Women's Studies, Col St Catherine, dir under grad studies, 1998-2001, assoc prof, dir, prof, currently; Dept African Am & African Studies, dir undergrad studies, 2001; Souls J, contrib ed; Nat & Int J Distinguished Scholars, contrib ed; The Color of Wealth: The Story Behind the US Racial Wealth Divide, co-auth. **Orgs:** Bd dir, vpres, Big Bros & Big Sisters Austin, 1984-; bd dir, vpres, Soc Study Social Probs, 1985-88; coun mem, Sect Racial & Ethnic Minorities, 1985-88; comt mem, Am Sociol Soc, 1986-87; chair, Comt Status Racial & Ethnic Minorities Asn, 1986-87; bd dir, Midwest Sociol Soc, 1990-92; Comt Freedom Teaching & Res, ASA; Afro-Am & African Studies, chair, 1992-; CIC Leadership Fel, 1993-94; exec bd mem, Oakland Pvt Indust Coun, 1994; exec bd mem, Contra Costa Pvt Indust Coun, 1995-; chair, Rhonda Williams Award Comt, Int Asn Feminist Economists; chair, Univ Minn, Col Lib Arts, 1991-2001; Univ Minn, Stud Fees adv Comt, 1991-2001 & 2000-02; fac senate, Univ Minn, 1998-2001; Univ Minn, Col Lib Arts, CLA Leadership Col, 1999-2001; interim chair, Univ Minn, Dept African Am & African Studies, 1999-2001; Univ Minn, President's Distinguished Fac Mentor Prog, 1999-2000; Dept African Am & African Studies, Community Outreach Comt, 2000-01; co-founder & core group mem, Freire Ctr, Minneapolis, 2001; mem planning comt, African Geneal Ser, 2001-02; Univ Minn, Dept African Am & African Studies, Strategic Planning Comt, 2001-02; adv panel, Univ Minn, Civic Engagement Task Force, 2001; chair, Univ Minn, African Am & African Studies, Merit Comt, 2001-02; Univ Minn, Col Lib Arts, Stud Acad Affairs Comt, 2002-03; bd trustee, St Paul Acad & Summit Sch; editoral bd, Contemp Sociol. **Home Addr:** 4716 1st Ave S, Minneapolis, MN 55419-5604, **Home Phone:** (612)822-0617. **Business Addr:** Professor, University of Minnesota, 810 Soc Sci Bldg 267 19th Ave S, Minneapolis, MN 55455, **Business Phone:** (612)624-9305.

**BREWER, HON. WEBSTER L.**
Judge. **Personal:** Born May 11, 1935, Clarksville, TN; son of Marvin and Margie Brodie; married Patricia Freeman; children: Elaine, Pamela & Webster Jr. **Educ:** Ind Univ, BS, 1957; Ind Univ Sch Law, JD. **Career:** Judge (retired); Marion County Welfare Dept, caseworker, 1957-58; Marion County Juv Ct, probation officer, 1958-60; US Bur Prisons, parole officer, 1960-64; United Dist Ct Southern Dist Ind, probation officer, 1964-68; Indianapolis Lawyers Comn, exec dir, 1968-70; Ind Univ Sch Law, sem instr, 1970; Brewer Budnick & Sosin, lawyer pvt pract, 1970-75; Marion County Super Ct no 2, sr judge. **Orgs:** Am Bar Asn; Indianapolis Bar Asn; Ind St Bar Asn; Nat Bar Asn; nat officer, Phi Alpha Delta Legal Frat; group leader, Christamore Settlement House, 1958-60; Juv Ct Adv Comn, 1960-64; chmn bd, Nat Asn Advan Colored People, 1963-64; chmn, Labor & Indust Comn, Indianapolis Chap, 1964-66; bd mem, Forward Inc, 1968-70; bd mem, Indianapolis Legal Serv Orgn, 1970-75; F & AM, PHA; Sigma Pi Phi Frat, 1971; bd mem, trustee & chmn, Ways & Means Comt, Bethel AME Church, 1973-; bd mem, Marion County Child Guid Clin, 1973-; bd mem, Marion County Youth & Serv Bur, 1974-76; bd mem, Indianapolis Family Serv Agency, 1977-; spec proj dir, Ind Judicial Study Ctr; Kappa Alphsi Frat; Trinity Lodge 18. **Home Addr:** 1619 Thomas Woods Trl, Indianapolis, IN 46260-4487, **Home Phone:** (317)253-7666.

**BREWINGTON, DONALD EUGENE**
Clergy. **Personal:** Born Aug 29, 1954, San Antonio, TX; son of James B Bradley and Margie M. **Educ:** Sam Houston State Univ, Huntsville, BA, educ, 1977; Interdenominational Theol Ctr, MDiv, 1986. **Career:** Greater Corinth Baptist Church, minister youth/outreach, 1986-89; Ernest T Dixon United Methodist Church, pastor, 1989-92; Huston-Tillotson Col, church rels officer, col chaplain, campus minister, 1992-. **Orgs:** Tex Coun Churches, 1992-; Wesley Found Partnership Ministries, 1992-; bd higher educ, United Church Christ, 1992-; Southwest Tex Conf, 1992-; Church World Serv, Walk Hunger, 1992-; sponsor, Huston-Tillotson Col Gospel Choir, 1992-; Huston-Tillotson Col Concert Choir, 1992-; Pres, Nat Asn Col & Univ Chaplains; active mem, Austin community; United Methodist Church. **Home Addr:** 5403 Kings Hwy, Austin, TX 78745-2820, **Home Phone:** (512)443-3044. **Business Addr:** Campus Minister, Huston-Tillotson College, 900 Chicon St, Austin, TX 78702, **Business Phone:** (512)505-3054.

**BREWINGTON, RUDOLPH W.**
Journalist, association executive. **Personal:** Born Nov 2, 1946, New York, NY. **Educ:** Fed City Col, MA, adult educ, 1972; Bowie State Univ, Col Southern Nev, bus admin. **Career:** WUST Radio, news reporter, 1969-70, news anchor; Washington, DC, bus operator, 1969; WOOK Radio, news dir, 1970-71; WWDC Radio, news reporter & sportscaster, 1971-75; WRC & NBC Radio News Washington, DC, reporter, 1975-, news anchor & corresp; Nat Synd ctd TV Prog "Am's Black Forum", res dir & pnlst, 1978-79; Nat Syndctd Radio Prog "The Black Agenda Reprts", co-founder, pres & exec prod, 1979-80; Asso Prsnl Inc, Washington, DC, dir pub rels, 1980; USNR, LIFE Lines Serv Network, pub affairs officer & content mgr, dir, 1994-; B&B Productions, co-founder; Us chap Amnesty Int, commun adminr, 1988. **Orgs:** Am Fedn TV & Radio Artists; Nat Naval Officers Asn; Am Legion; Veterans Foreign Wars; Tuskegee Airmen Inc; Vietnam Veterans Am. **Honors/Awds:** EMMY Award; Chesapeake AP Spot News Award; Virginia AP Spot News Award; Recipient Robt F Kennedy Journalism Award Citation for "Diagnosis, Desperate, A Report on Minority Hlth Care", 1973; fel, APHA Ray Bruner Sci Writing, 1974. **Home Addr:** 3312 6 St SE, Washington, DC 20032. **Business Addr:** Director, LIFELines Services Network, Rm 104 720 Kennon St SE Bldg 36, Washington, DC 20374-5046, **Business Phone:** (202)433-3865.

**BREWINGTON, DR. THOMAS E., JR.**
Ophthalmologist. **Personal:** Born Oct 12, 1943, Dunn, NC; married Janice; children: Kathryne, Mitchelle, Tracy & Brea. **Educ:** Morehouse Col, Atlanta, GA, BS, biol, 1965; Meharry Med Col, Nashville, TN, MD, 1969; NC Cent Univ, Durham, JD, 1998. **Career:** Homer G Phillips Hosp, intern, 1969-70, resident, 1970-73; AUS, Moncried Army Hosp, staff ophthalmologist, 1973-75, chief EENT Clin, 1974-75; pvt pract opthalmologist, 1976-; Moses Cone Health Syst, med staff, currently. **Orgs:** Dipl, Am Bd Ophthal; fel Am Acad Ophthal; fel Am Col Legal Med; Nat Med Asn; NC State Med Soc; Guilford Co Med Soc; Greensboro Acad Med; Greensboro Med Soc; Old N State Med Soc; Phi Beta Sigma Fraternity; bd dir, Easter Seal Soc, 1978-80; bd dir, St James Nursing ctr, 1980-84; Nat Asn Advan Colored People; Sigma Pi Phi Boule; Greensboro Mens Club; Nat Bar Asn; AMA; Am Bar Asn; NC State Bar; Greensboro Bar Asn; NC Asn Black Lawyers; Spirtual Renaissance Singers Greensboro. **Honors/Awds:** Commendation Medal. **Home Addr:** 2601 Wilpar Dr, Greensboro, NC 27406-9493, **Home Phone:** (336)273-4070. **Business Addr:** Ophthalmologist, Moses Cone Health System, 807 Summit Ave, Greensboro, NC 27405, **Business Phone:** (336)272-5628.

**BREWINGTON-CARR, SHERESE**
Chairperson, government official, management consultant. **Educ:** Univ Del, cert; NC Cent Univ, BA, polit sci; Lincoln Univ, MS. **Career:** Conn Dept Corrections, warden/dep warden, 1991-95; Del Dept Corrections, IV-Multi-Purpose Criminal Justice Facil, warden, 1995-98; Dept Serv C, Youth & Their Families, Del Youth Rehabilitative Serv, dir, 1998-2001; Dept Labor, adminr, 2001-; Substance Abuse & Ment Health Serv Admin (SAMHSA), consult, 2005-; QSB Solutions, chief exec officer, 2014-. **Orgs:** Pub Policy Chair, NCBW Del Chap, 1995-; Ezion Carmel United Methodist Church, 1995-; Pub Policy Co-Chair, Nat Coalition 100 Black Women Inc, 1996-; Chair, Del Comn Women, 2009; mem bd dir, Del Financial Literacy Inst, 2010-; pres, Forum Exec Women Del, 2012-; chmn bd, Del Acad Pub Safety & Securit, 2016. **Special Achievements:** First African American to serve as Chair of the Delaware Commission for Women. **Business Addr:** Consultant, Substance Abuse & Mental Health Services Administration, 5600 Fishers Lane, Rockville, MD 20857, **Business Phone:** (877)726-4727.

**BREWSTER, LUTHER GEORGE**
Executive, airline executive. **Personal:** Born Dec 16, 1942, Manhattan, NY; son of Alethia Samuels and Donald F; married Theresa Maria Smart; children: Maria, Luther Jr & Renee. **Educ:** Bronx Community Col, Bronx, NY, 1972; Col Aeronaut, Queens, NY, AAS, 1974; Lehman Col, Bronx, NY, 1987; N Cent Col, Naperville, IL, 1988; Olivet Nazarene Univ, Kankakee, IL, BS, appl sci & mgt, 1995. **Career:** Pratt & Whitney Aircraft, Hartford, Conn, engine mech, 1964; Pan Am, New York, NY, aircraft & engine mech, 1965-77; Seaboard World Airlines, Frankfurt, W Ger, maintenance rep, 1977; Am Airlines, Chicago, Ill, div mgr aircraft maintenance, 1977-95, managing dir, eastern div aircraft maintenance, 1995-2005; Air Jamaica Ltd, sr vpres maintenance & eng, 2005-. **Orgs:** Inst Cert Eng Tech; Aviation Maintenance Found; Am Mgt Asn; bd dir, Mt Sinai Hosp. **Home Addr:** 10565 Palacio Ridge Ct, Boynton Beach, FL 33473. **Business Addr:** Senior Vice President Maintenance & Engineering, Air Jamaica Ltd, 8300 NW 33rd St Suite 440, Miami, FL 33122, **Business Phone:** (305)670-3222.

**BREWTON, DR. BUTLER E.**
Educator, poet, writer. **Personal:** Born Feb 7, 1935, Spartanburg, SC; son of J M and W O; married Blanca; children: Seneca, Monica & Catrina. **Educ:** Benedict Col, BA, 1956; Montclair State, MA, 1970; Rutgers Univ, PhD, Eng lang & lit, 1978. **Career:** SC State Col, NDEA fel, 1965; Montclair State Col, assoc prof eng, 1970, prof emer, 1996-; McGraw Hill Int Press, consult, 1972; Mod Century Encyclopedia, ed; Articles: "A Diploma Must Mean What It's Supposed to Mean", New York Times, 1986; "At the General Store"; "We Children", 1992; "Grandpa's", 1992; "Rafters", 1992; "Indian Summer", 1997; Books: South & Border States; Richard Wrights Thematic Treatment of Women; Poems: Tramp; Lady of the Evening; 5PM; Discovered; Pattern; Barren; Southbound; Idol; Yesterday Hangs; The Custodial Hour; Democracy; The Kiss; For A Reprieve; Peach Orchard; Full Measure. Furman Univ, adj prof eng, 2012; SC State Univ, Dept Eng, assoc prof, prof, currently. **Orgs:** Poet-in-residence, NJ State Coun Arts, 1970-76; speaker, Nat Coun Teacher Educ, Kans City, 1978. **Honors/Awds:** First prize winner, Essence Mag poetry contest, 1993. **Special Achievements:** Has more than seventy-five poetry publications in literary journals and magazines, including Pulpsmith, Lips, Footwork, Midway Review, Nimrod & Essence. **Home Addr:** PO Box 183, Moore, SC 29369, **Home Phone:** (803)604-0557. **Business Addr:** Professor, South Carolina State University, Rm 339 Turner Hall D Wing 3rd Fl, Orangeburg, SC 29117, **Business Phone:** (803)536-8355.

**BRICE, DR. BARBARA GOHANNA**
Educator. **Personal:** Born Feb 28, 1927. **Educ:** St Phillips Sch Nursing, Med Col, Richmond, VA, 1944; Clark Col, BS, 1975; Emory Univ, cert, 1975; Cent Mich Univ, MA, 1978; Ga State Univ, PhD, 1992; Rutgers Univ. **Career:** Coligny Day Care Ctr, dir, 1966; St Joseph Hosp, staff nurse intensive care, 1968-72; Atlanta Job Corp, staff nurse & dir nursing serv, 1972-74; W End Med Ctr, dir med rec & admiss, 1974-81; Clark Col, instr, 1977-81; Kean Col, assoc prof, 1981-83; Clark Col, asst prof, 1983-88; Clark Atlanta Univ, assoc prof, 1988, adj fac, currently. **Orgs:** Am & GA Info Mgt Asn, 1975-; GA Soc Allied Health Profs, 1977-80, 1990-93; Nat Sci Fac Atlanta Univ Ctr, 1978-79; Minority Women Sci, 1980-81; Kappa Delta Pi, Omicron Gamma Chapt Hon Soc Educ, 1988-; African Am Women Against Domestic Violence, 1989-2001; Delta Sigma Theta Sorority, 1992-; Atlanta Proj Wa Cluster, 1992-; Nat Insts Health, NIDCD, CAU Stud & Mentor, 1995-2000; GA Nonpublic Post Sec Comn Accreditation Team, 1997; AUC Cath Ctr Adv Comt, 1997-2001; St John Cath Church Hospitality Comt, 1999-2001; adv bd, Atlanta Area Tech Sch LPN, 2000-02; Fulton County Juv Ct Citizen Rev Panel, 2000-. **Business Addr:** Adjunct Faculty, Clark Atlanta University, Vivian Wilson Henderson Ctr Rm 121, Atlanta, GA 30314, **Business Phone:** (404)880-8000.

**BRICE, PERCY A., JR.**
Musician, drummer. **Personal:** Born Mar 25, 1923, New York, NY; married Pearl Minott. **Educ:** Music Sch; Kingsborough Community Col, attended 1986. **Career:** Luis Russell Orchestra, 1944; Benny Carter Orchestra, 1945-46; Mercer Ellington, 1947; Eddie Vinson, 1947-51; Tiny Grimes Show Group, 1951-52; Billy Taylor Trio, 1954-56; George Shearing Quintet, 1956-58; Harry Belafonte Troupe, 1961-68; New Sound, leader. Albums: The Midnight Spec; The Many Moods Of Belafonte; Ballads, Blues & Boasters, 1964; An Eve With Belafonte/Mouskouri; An Eve With Belafonte/Makeba; Belafonte On Campus; Belafonte At The Greek Theatre; The Big Beat. Musicals: Bubbling Brown Sugar; Eubie; Ain't Misbehavin'; Ghost Cafe. **Orgs:** Masonic Order, 1949-; Famous Friendly 50 Club. **Home Addr:** 1245 Langdon Blvd, Rockville Center, NY 11570, **Home Phone:** (516)536-7915.

**BRIDGEFORTH, ARTHUR MAC, JR.**
Journalist. **Personal:** Born Sep 18, 1965, Pittsburgh, PA; son of Arthur Mac Sr and Gwendolyn Holland. **Educ:** Mich State Univ, E Lansing, BA, jour, 1988. **Career:** Crain's Detroit Bus, Detroit, Mich, ed asst, 1988-89; Ann Arbor News, Ann Arbor, Mich, bus reporter, 1989-; Wayne State Univ, media contact, currently. **Orgs:** Detroit Chap, Nat Asn Black Journalists, 1988-; Nat Asn Black Journalist, 1989-; Mich State Univ Alumni Asn, 1988-. **Home Addr:** 19511 Greenfield Rd Suite 3, Detroit, MI 48235-2016, **Home Phone:** (313)837-8432. **Business Addr:** Media Contact, Wayne State University, 5700 Cass Ave 3100 Acad Admin Bldg, Detroit, MI 48202, **Business Phone:** (313)577-2150.

**BRIDGEMAN, DEXTER ADRIAN**
Executive. **Personal:** Born Jan 5, 1961, Grenada; son of Donald E and Phylis Alexander. **Educ:** Hofstra Univ, BS, polit sci, 1984; State Univ NY, Stonybrook, 1985. **Career:** Ivac Corp, sales exec; GE Medical Syst, sales exec; Motorala sales exec; Velobind Inc, sales exec; Allnet Communications, sales exec; Mentor Mag, pres; Diversified Communications Group Inc, pres, currently. **Orgs:** Bd mem, Opportunities Industrialization Ctrs Am; creative adv coun, Nat Youth Develop Prog; adv bd, Nat Inner City Leadership Coun; adv bd, YACT; Alpha Phi Alpha Frat Inc; Concerned Black Men Am; Outstanding Young Men Am, 1996; Urban Bding Sch Fund; Nat Asn Black Minority Consultants. **Home Addr:** 416 W 146th St, Mount Vernon, NY 10031, **Home Phone:** (917)507-8124. **Business Addr:** President, Chief Executive Officer, Diversified Communications Group Inc, 416 W 146th St Suite 2, Ardsley, NY 10031, **Business Phone:** (917)507-8124.

**BRIDGEMAN, DONALD EARL**
Banker, manager, government official. **Personal:** Born Mar 14, 1939, Grenville; son of Julien Anthony and Madonna Theresa Hall; married Rosemary Malcolm; children: Winston, Selwyn, Joie & Edelyne. **Educ:** Erdiston Teachers Col, AA, educ, 1960; Howard Univ, BSc, econs & social sci, 1968; Northwestern Univ, cert Mortage Banker, 1973; Southeastern Univ, MBPA, 1976. **Career:** Teacher; Found Coop Housing, dir housing spec inst, 1969-72; Howard Univ, dir ctr housing & real estate, 1975-77; US Dept Housing & Urban Develop, employee develop spec, 1977-84; Prince George's County, dep personnel officer, 1984-91, off human resources mgt, dir, 2004-11; SWAADA Imports, pres, 1988-, MBA Group, pres, 1991-. **Orgs:** United Way Health & Welfare Coun, Wash, DC, 1965-76; co-founder, CHG Fed Credit Union Wash DC; co-founder, Nat Asn Housing Specialists, 1971; conf dir, Joint Ann Minority Housing Conf, 1974-80; consult, Winston-Salem State Univ, Southern Univ, Tex Southern Univ, Temple Univ, develop housing mgt curricula, 1975-77; pres, Housing Specialists Inst, 1977-81 & 1993-; pres, Local Govt Personnel Asn Baltimore-Wash Metro Area, 1986-91; pres, Caribbean Coun Prince George's County, 1989-; vpres, Coun Caribbean Org, WA, DC, 1991-93; Nat Forum Black Pub Adminrs, 1990-; Southern Md Bus League, 1991-; Caribbean-Am Intercultural Orgn; Nat Coalition Caribbean Affairs. **Honors/Awds:** Samuel E Sessions Award, Nat Asn Housing Specialists Inst, 1975; Realist of the Year Award, Wash Real Estate Brokers Asn, 1976; Personnelist of the Year, Intl Personnel Mgt Asn, Eastern Region, 1989; Intl Exchange Fel, Eng's SOCPO, Intl Personnel Mgt Asn-US, 1987; Spec Achievement Award, Local Govt Personnel Asn Baltimore-Wash, 1991. **Special Achievements:** First foreign-born to serve in a County Executive's Cabinet in the Prince George's County. **Home Addr:** 600 Dwyer Pl, Upper Marlboro, MD 20774, **Home Phone:** (301)336-8326. **Business Addr:** Director, Office Of Human Resources Management, 1400 McCormick Dr Suite 351, Largo, MD 20774, **Business Phone:** (301)883-6344.

**BRIDGEMAN, JUNIOR (ULYSSES LEE BRIDGEMAN)**
Basketball player, businessperson, executive. **Personal:** Born Sep 17, 1953, East Chicago, IN; married Doris; children: Justin, Ryan & Eden. **Educ:** Univ Louisville, BS, psychol, 1975. **Career:** Basketball player (retired), businessperson, executive; Milwaukee Bucks, 1975-84, 1986-87; Los Angeles Clippers, 1985-86; Bridgeman Foods Inc, chief exec officer & pres, 1988-; Jackson Hewitt Tax Serv Inc, dir, 2004-; Louisville Arena Authority Inc, dir; Kindred Healthcare Inc, dir; Manna Inc, owner & pres; PGA Tour Inc, dir; ERJ Inc, owner & pres, currently; B.F. FT. Myers Inc, pres, currently; Fifth Third Bancorp, dir, 2007-; Pres, Bridgeman Foods LLC, currently. **Orgs:** Alpha Phi Alpha; co-chmn, African Am Heritage Found; bd mem, MACC Fund. **Business Addr:** Chief Executive Officer, President, Bridgeman Foods Inc, 2025 W S Br Blvd, Oak Creek, WI 53154, **Business Phone:** (414)302-5650.

**BRIDGEMAN, LEEA NASH**
Vice president (organization), foundation executive, association executive. **Educ:** Harvard Univ, BA, cum laude, 2000, MBA, 2005. **Career:** Bridgeman Family Found, exec dir & trustee; Churchill Downs, vpres bus develop. **Orgs:** Bd dir, Harvard Alumni Asn, 2015-18. **Honors/Awds:** Black Enterprise, Rising Stars 40 & Under, 2014. **Business Addr:** Executive Director, Trustee, Bridgeman Family Foundation, Louisville, KY.

**BRIDGEMAN, ULYSSES LEE.** See BRIDGEMAN,

JUNIOR.

## BRIDGEMAN-VEAL, JUDY

Executive, engineer. **Educ:** Gen Motors Inst, BS, elec eng; Ga Inst Technol, MS, elec eng & biomed eng. **Career:** GiGi Hunter Collection, engr; Ford Motor Co, proj mgr, spokeswoman, pension specialist, Software Dept Head, asst chair. **Orgs:** Asst chairperson, SAE Int. **Business Addr:** Spokeswoman, Ford Motor Co, 1 American Rd, Dearborn, MI 48126, **Business Phone:** (313)322-3000.

## BRIDGES, CHRISTOPHER BRIAN. See LUDACRIS.

## BRIDGES, DR. JAMES WILSON

Physician. **Personal:** Born Feb 16, 1935, Valdosta, GA; son of Leslie and Ora Lee; married Earnestine Bryant; children: Sabrina, Lloyd & Mark. **Educ:** Cent State Col, BS, 1956; Meharry Medical Col, MD, 1960. **Career:** Physician (retired); Hmr G Phillips Hosp, intern, 1961, chief resident, 1966; Univ Miami, resident, 1967; Miami's Jackson Memorial Hosp, resident obstet & gynec; Pvt pract, physician; Univ Miami, clin asst prof; Cedars Lebanon Health Care Ctr, chief; Christian Hosp, chief. **Orgs:** Dipl, Am Bd Obstet & Gynec, 1969; fel Am Col Obstet & Gynec, 1970; bd trustee, Christian Hosp, 1973-76; bd dir, Fla Div Am Cancer Soc, 1972-77, Fla Physicians Ins Rec, 1985, Fla Physicians Ins Co, Fla Polit Action Comn; chmn, Fla Div United Cancer Task Force, 1975-77; Beta Beta Lambda Chap; Alpha Phi Alpha; Nat Asn Advan Colored People; Comm Minority Affairs, Univ Miami Sch Med; Fla Bd Med, 1996-97; chmn bd, N Shore Medical; pres, bd dir, Dade County Med Asn, 1998-99. **Honors/Awds:** Scholar, Fla State Med Col, 1959-60. **Special Achievements:** First African American senior resident in Obstetrics & Gynecology in Miami's Jackson Memorial Hosp; First African American Fellow of the American College of Obstetrics & Gynecology, Florida; First African American president of the Dade County Medical Association. **Home Addr:** 8340 NE 2nd Ave Suite 222, Miami, FL 33150-2064, **Home Phone:** (305)758-9215.

## BRIDGES, LEON

Architect, executive, educator. **Personal:** Born Aug 18, 1932, Los Angeles, CA; son of James Alonzo and Agnes Zenobia Johnson; married Eloise Avonne Jones; children: Vanessa Joy, Elise Gay, Leon Jr & Elliott Reynolds. **Educ:** E Los Angeles Jr Col; Los Angeles City Col; Univ Calif, Los Angeles; Univ Wash, BArch, 1960; Urban Syst, post grad studies; Loyola Col MD, MBA, 1984. **Career:** Intern asst city, planner, draftsman, 1956; Gotteland & Kocarski, draftma, 1961-63; Leon Bridges Arch, owner, 1963-66; Bridges Burke Arch & Planners, partner, 1966-72; Hampton Inst, vis prof, 1971, 1973, 1975; Prairie View A&M, vis prof, 1972; Archit Res Collabor Inc, partner, 1976-; Leon Bridges Co, owner, 1972-87; Morgan State Univ, assoc prof, 1985-88, lectr, currently; TLBC Inc, pres, 1989-; Leon Bridges Chartered, prs, currently; Obsidian Group, chief financial officer & partner, 2001-. **Orgs:** KAP, 1954; Exec Comm Planned Parenthood/World Pop, 1968-74; particip, Tuskegee Inst Comm Arch Design Charette, Endowment, 1971; nat dir, Amrerican Inst Architects, 1971; co-founder, AIA Ford Minority Scholar fund, 1976; Guild Relig Archit; panelist, Ment Health Ctr Design, AIA & NIMH; Nat Urban League; MD State Arts Coun, 1980-; bd dir, Lutheran Hosp, 1980-; bd dir, MD MNY Contractors Asn, 1981; chmn, Morgan State Univ Urban Dev Comm, 1981; bd dir, Roland Pk Pl, 1981; bd adv, Univ Knoxville TN, 1981-; bd dir, Sch Deaf, 1981; bd dir, Am Inst Architects, 1984-86; pres, Nat Org Minority Architects, 1979-80. **Honors/Awds:** Honor Award, Am Soc Landscape Architects, 1980; Black Pages Award, 1981; Merit Award, Am Inst Architects, Wash, DC; Design Excellence Award, Nat Org Minority Architects, 1983; Design Excellence Award, Am Inst Architects, 1985; Design Excellence Award, NOMA, 1985; Grand Conceptor Award, Am Consult Engrs, 1986; Baltimore City Coun Presidential Citation, 1995; Baltimore City Mayor's Citation, 1995; Md State Legis Off Citation, 1995; State Md Gov Citation, 1995; Nat Citation Design Excellence Seattle Urban Design, 1971; Richard Upjohn Fel, Am Inst Architects, 1990; Valued Honors Award, Fullwood Found, 1995, 1999; Whitney M Young Junior Award, Am Inst Architects, 1998; Man of the Year, Nat Asn Negro Bus & Prof Womens Clubs, 1978; Dr Lillie Carroll Jackson Award, Baltimore City Br, NCP, 1991; Victor Frenkil Achievement Award, 1973; Conf MNY Transp Offs Annual FDRs Award, 1984; NCP Baltimore City Branch Hall of Fame Parren J Mitchell Award, 2001; Harlow Fullwood, Jr Serv Above Self Award, 2002. **Special Achievements:** First Registered African American Architect in Maryland; Founder of the second African American owned firm in Seattle. **Home Addr:** 6101 Smith Ave, Baltimore, MD 21209-3640, **Home Phone:** (410)542-6101. **Business Addr:** Lecturer, Morgan State University, 1700 E Cold Spring Lane, Baltimore, MD 21251, **Business Phone:** (443)885-3333.

## BRIDGES, RUBY NELL

Association executive, activist, founder (originator). **Personal:** Born Sep 8, 1954, Tylertown, MS; daughter of Abon and Lucille; married Malcolm Hall; children: 4. **Educ:** Tulane Univ, hon degree, 2012. **Career:** Travel agt; Ruby Bridges Found Inc, chair, founder, 1999-. **Honors/Awds:** Made an honorary US Marshall, 2000; Presidential Citizens Medal, 2001; elementary school named in Honor, 2006. **Special Achievements:** First African-American child to attend William Frantz Elementary School; First African-American child to attend an all-white elementary school in the South. Subject of Norman Rockwell painting, The Problem We All Live With, 1964. **Business Addr:** Founder, Chair, Ruby Bridges Foundation Inc, PO Box 870248, New Orleans, LA 70187.

## BRIDGES, SHEILA

Interior designer. **Personal:** Born Jul 7, 1954, Philadelphia, PA. **Educ:** Brown Univ, attended 1986; Parsons Sch Design. **Career:** Bloomingdale's; Shelton, Mindel, & Assoc, interior designer; Rebby B Salzman Interiors, interior designer; Sheila Bridges Design Inc, pres, chief exec officer, chmn, 1994-; www.thenestmaker.com, publ & creative dir, currently. **Honors/Awds:** Americas Best Interior Designer, CNN & Time Mag. **Special Achievements:** Author: Furnishing Forward: A Practical Guide to Furnishing for a Lifetime, 2002; She is also an author of several books, including her new memoir, The Bald Mermaid: A Memoir; host, Sheila Bridges Designer Living on the Fine Living, Network; Numerous national and international publications including The New York Times, The Wall Street Journal, O The Oprah Magazine, Martha Stewart Living, Ebony, Essence, House & Garden, Traditional Home & Black Enterprise; Gotham and New York magazines Top Interior Designer's lists; Elle Decor's 2011, 2012 & 2013. **Business Addr:** President, Chief Executive Officer, Sheila Bridges Design Inc, 1925 7th Ave 8M, New York, NY 10026, **Business Phone:** (212)678-6872.

## BRIDGES, TODD ANTHONY

Actor, writer, movie producer. **Personal:** Born May 27, 1965, San Francisco, CA; son of James Sr and Betty Bridges; married Dori Smith; children: Spencer Todd; children: Spencir. **Career:** TV series: "Katherine", 1975; "Barney Miller", 1975; "Fish", 1977-78; "Roots", 1977; "The Waltons", 1977-78; "Little House on the Prairie", 1977; "Different Strokes", 1978-86; "The Facts of Life", 1979 & 1981; "High School U.S.A.", 1983; "She's Out of Control", 1989; "Son of the Beach", 2001; "Busted", 1996; A Devil Disguised, cinematographer, 1997; "The Waterfront", 1998; producer, dir, actor, Building Bridges, 1999; "The Young and the Restless", 2002. Films: Flossin, 2001; Inhumanity, 2001; Dumb Luck, 2001; Pacino Is Missing, 2002; The Beach House, 2002; The Climb, 2002; Welcome to Am, 2002; Scream at the Sound of the Beep, 2002; Baby of the Family, 2002; Black Ball, 2003; May Day, 2003; Alien Express, 2005; "Everybody Hates Chris", 2009; TV Films: After Different Strokes: When the Laughter Stopped, 2000; The Darkling, 2000; Ghost Dog: A Detective Tail, 2003; Hollywood Horror, 2004; Treasure in tha Hood, 2005; I Got Five on It, 2005; Alien Express, 2005; The Damned, 2006; Last Call, 2006; Death Row, 2007; Big Ball'n, 2007; Foster Babies, 2007; Frankie D, 2007; Darkroom, 2008; Hollywood Horror, 2009; See Dick Run, 2009; I Got Five on It Too, 2009; Big Money Rustlas, 2010; Tyler Perry's House of Payne, 2011; That's My Boy, 2012; Turning Point, 2012. **Orgs:** Founder, Todd Bridges Youth Found, 1992-. **Special Achievements:** Ranked No 40 in VH1's list of the "100 Greatest Kid Stars". **Business Addr:** Actor, Little Bridge Productions, 7550 Zambo Ave Suite 1, Van Nuys, CA 91440.

## BRIDGEWATER, ALBERT LOUIS

Government official. **Personal:** Born Nov 22, 1941, Houston, TX; son of Albert and Rita Narcisse; married Juanita Edington; children: Ramesi & Akin. **Educ:** Univ Calif, BA, physics, 1963; Columbia Univ, NY, MA, 1967, PhD, physics, 1972. **Career:** Government Official (retired), consultant; Univ Calif, post-doctoral fel, 1970-73; Elem Particle Physics, asst prof officer, 1973-74; Nat Sci Found, exec asst, 1973-76, spec asst, 1976-86, actg asst dir, 1983-85, dep asst dir, 1981-86, sr staff assoc, 1986-01; Minority-Serv Inst Forum, pres, exec dir, 2001; recipient an NSF grant, 2003-04; MDB Inc, sr educ & res progs advisor, consult, 2008-; NSF, exec asst, actg prog mgr, dep asst dir & actg asst dir. **Orgs:** Am Geophys Union; AAAS; adv bd, LBL/SSU/AGMFF Sci Consortium, 1986-88; Indian Soc Tech Educ; Adv Bd Ana G Mendez Educ Found; Lawrence Berkeley Lab Sci Consortium; Jackson State Univ; Lawrence Berkeley Lab Sci Consortium; sr exec advisor, NSF. **Home Addr:** 3705 S George Mason Dr, Falls Church, VA 22041, **Home Phone:** (703)845-3646. **Business Addr:** Senior Education & Research Programs Advisor, MDB Inc, 1101 Conn Ave NW Suite 550, Washington, DC 20036, **Business Phone:** (202)331-0060.

## BRIDGEWATER, DEE DEE. See GARRETT, DENISE EILEEN.

## BRIDGEWATER, DR. REV. HERBERT JEREMIAH, JR.

Radio host, educator, journalist. **Personal:** Born Jul 3, 1942, Atlanta, GA; son of Herbert (deceased) and Mary Sallie Clark Hughes. **Educ:** Clark Col, BA, bus admin, 1968; Atlanta Univ, attended 1968; Univ Ga, attended 1978; Atlanta Area Tech Sch, cert, 1980; Fed Law Enforcement Training Ctr, 1980; Spelman Col Inst Continuing Educ, attended 1984. **Career:** Atlanta Pub Sch Syst, teacher, bus & eng community, 1964-67; Atlanta Housing Authority, relocation & family serv consult, 1967-70; Fed Trade Comn, consumer protection specialist & dir pub affairs, 1970-83; Bridgewaters Personnel Serv, owner, 1971-75; Confrontation, host, 1974-; Atlanta Area Tech Sch, teacher, 1978-; Bridging Gap, host, 1981-; Clark Col, assoc prof, 1983-; Delta Airlines Inc, customer sales & serv, 1984-; Atlanta Daily World Newspaper, Unsung Heroes, Facts, Consumers, columnist, currently. **Orgs:** Bd mem, Ga Chap, Epilepsy Found Am; bd mem, Mid-Atlanta Unit Am Cancer Soc; bd chmn, Atlanta Dance Theatre; task force, Just US Theater; founding mem, Int Asn African Heritage & Black Identity; Atlanta Jr Chamber Comt; Big Bros Coun Atlanta; Nat Urban League; United Negro Col Fund; City Atlanta Water & Sewer Appeals Bd; Martin Luther King Ctr Non-Violent Social Chg; Martin Luther King Ecumenical Holiday Comt; assoc minister, New Calvary Baptist Church; police chaplin, Atlanta Police Dept zone 6. **Honors/Awds:** Outstanding Atlanta, 1977; Meritorious Service Award, Ga Chap, Epilepsy Found Am, 1981 & 1985; Outstanding Service Award, Am Red Cross, 1981; Outstanding Serv, Atlanta Fed Exec Bd Minority Bus Opportunity Comn, 1981; Distinguished & Dedicated Service Award, Greater Travelers Rest Baptist Church, Decatur, GA, 1981; Outstanding Community Service Award, SW Career Coun; Dr Herbert J Bridgewater Jr Day, Atlanta, named in hon, 1982; Best Talk Show Host on Radio, Atlanta Chap Nat Asn Black Journalists, 1983; Distinguished Supporter Top Star Award, Nat Asn Black journalists, 1983; Outstanding Service Award, Martin Luther King, Jr Ctr Social Chg, 1984; Dr. Herbert J. Bridge water Jr Day, State Ga, 1985; Cong Achievement Award, Congressman Wyche Fowler, 1985; Outstanding Commun Silver Voice Award, Bronner Bros Int Beauty & Trade Show Conv, 1989; Proclamation From Mayor Maynard Jackson. **Special Achievements:** Individually won the struggle to have Black College athletic scores airedon TV stations in GA 1966; assisted the City of Atlanta & Consumer Affairs Office in preparing proposed Consumer Protection Ordinance for the City of Atlanta, ordinance currently in existence; host/master of ceremonies of numerous pageants. **Home Addr:** 2963 Duke of Windsor, Atlanta, GA 30344-5606, **Home Phone:** (404)209-7287. **Business Addr:** Journalist, Atlanta Daily World, 145 Auburn Ave NE, Atlanta, GA 30303-2503, **Business Phone:** (404)659-1110.

## BRIDGFORTH, GLINDA

Financial manager, writer. **Personal:** Born Jan 1, 1952, Detroit, MI; daughter of Walter and Opal. **Educ:** Western Mich Univ, BS, 1974. **Career:** Calif Bank, asst vpres; Bridgforth Financial Mgt Group, founder, pres, chief exec officer, 1994-, currently. **Special Achievements:** Author: A Sister's Guide to Healing Your Bank Account and Funding Your Dreams in Seven Simple Steps, 2000; Co-Author: Girl, Make Your Money Grow!, 2004; Girl, Get Your Money Straight! and Girl, Get Your Credit Straight!, 2007. **Business Addr:** Founder, President, Bridgforth Financial Management Group, 1300 Lafayette E Suite 2302, Detroit, MI 48207, **Business Phone:** (313)566-0026.

## BRIDGFORTH, WALTER, JR.

Entrepreneur, real estate developer. **Personal:** Born Detroit, MI; married Anita Baker; children: Walter Baker & Edward Carlton. **Educ:** Western Mich Univ, degree finance, 1979. **Career:** IBM, salesman, 1979-89; self-employed mgr of residential properties; Int House Pancakes, owner; Brisson Develop, developer, currently; real estate developer, currently. **Business Addr:** Owner, Brisson Development Inc, 22417 Marine St, Eastpoint, MI 48021, **Business Phone:** (810)778-3038.

## BRIEVE-MARTIN, ILA CORRINNA

Educator. **Personal:** Born Mar 20, 1939, Newark, NJ; married Robert H Dean. **Educ:** Bloomfield Col, BA, 1964; Rutgers Univ, Grad Sch Educ, EdM, 1972, EdD, 1975. **Career:** Cent High Sch, span teacher, 1964-67, title I coordr, 1967-70; US Dept Justice, Community Rels Dept, consult, 1968-70; Rutgers Univ Grad Sch Educ, asst prof, 1970-74; Va Commonwealth Univ Richmond, asst educ dean, 1975-80; Univ Ala, fel, 1979; Va St Univ, assoc prof, Dept Educ Leadership, 1984; Univ DC, dean educ. **Orgs:** Vpres, Bus & Prof Women, 1967-69; Phi Delta Kappa, 1973-; bd dir, Richmond Area Progs Minorities Engineering, 1977-; bd dir, Greater Richmond Transit Co, 1978-80. **Home Addr:** 1505 Regency Woods Rd Apt 204, Richmond, VA 23233.

## BRIGANCE, ORENTHIAL JAMES

Football player, executive director. **Personal:** Born Sep 29, 1969, Houston, TX; married Chanda. **Educ:** Rice Univ, BA, managerial studies, 1992. **Career:** Football player (retired), executive; BC Lions, linebacker, 1991-93; Baltimore Stallions, linebacker, 1994-95; Miami Dolphins, linebacker, 1996-99; Baltimore Ravens, linebacker, 1999-2000, dir player develop, 2003-, sr advisor player engagement, 2010-; St Louis Rams, linebacker, 2001-02; New Eng Patriots, linebacker, 2002. **Orgs:** Habitat Humanity; Cystic Fibrosis Found; Daily Food Bank; Brigance Brigade. **Business Addr:** Senior Advisor to Player Development, Baltimore Ravens, 1 Winning Dr, Owings Mills, MD 21117, **Business Phone:** (410)701-4000.

## BRIGGINS, CHARLES E.

Educator, army officer. **Personal:** Born Nov 6, 1930, Helena, AL; married Mary Jones; children: Charles, Anthony & Tonya. **Educ:** Ala A&M Univ, BS, 1956, MS, 1961. **Career:** Educator (retired); KY State Col, instr, 1956-68; Decatur City Schs, teacher coord, 1958-71; Huntsville City Schs, diversified occup coord; Huntsville Ala, vctnl T&I coord; SR Butler HS. **Orgs:** Ala Educ Asn; Ala Voc Asn; Am Voc Asn, 1958; Alpha Phi Alpha; RE Nelms Elks Lodge, 1977; Masn; VFW; Am Legion. **Home Addr:** 3645 Marymont Dr NW, Huntsville, AL 35810-2857, **Home Phone:** (256)859-4868.

## BRIGGS, CAROL J.

School principal. **Career:** Dusable High Sch, prin & pvt art collector; Alfred David Kohn Elem Sch, prin, currently. **Home Addr:** 8217 S Champlain Ave, Chicago, IL 60619, **Home Phone:** (773)723-5363. **Business Addr:** Principal, Alfred David Kohn Elementary School, 10414 S State St, Chicago, IL 60628, **Business Phone:** (773)535-5497.

## BRIGGS, GREG

Football player. **Personal:** Born Oct 1, 1968, Meadville, MS. **Educ:** Tex Southern Univ, grad. **Career:** Football player (retired); Dallas Cowboys, 1992, 1995; Cleveland Browns, 1993; Frankfurt Galaxy, 1995; Chicago Bears, 1996; Minn Vikings, 1997-99; speaker at churches. **Orgs:** Men's Christian fel; Christian Athletes. **Honors/Awds:** Super Bowl Champion, 1992; World Bowl Champion (III); Vince Lombardi Trophy, 1995.

## BRIGGS, DR. HAROLD E.

Educator. **Educ:** Morehouse Col, BA, sociol, 1977; Univ Pittsburgh, MA, sociol, 1978; Univ Chicago, Sch Social Serv Admin, MA, social treat, 1980, PhD, social develop, 1988. **Career:** Found I Ctr Human Develop, Prog develop specialist, 1979-81; Southwest Community Action Coalition, Clin Serv & Psychotherapist, Clin Serv & Psychotherapist, coordr, 1981-83; Wyman Gordon Pavilion Ingalls Mem Hosp, psychiat social worker, 1982-83; S Cent Community Serv, adminr, 1983-84; Habilitative Systs Inc, assoc exec dir, 1984-90; Portland State Univ, Grad Sch Social Work, from asst prof to assoc prof, 1990-2004, prof, 2004-12; Univ Ga, Sch Social Work, assoc dean & prof social work, 2012-15, Dir Res/Sponsored Proj & Prof, 2015-. **Orgs:** Tech assistance, Family Advocacy Orgn, 1990-93; Sc Continuum Care, Columbia, Sc, 1992-93; Ore Tech Assistance Ctr, 1992-93; consult, Hawaii Dept Health, 1993-94; Ctr Community Ment Health, 1993-94; tech asst, Ctr Ment Health Serv, Bethesda, Md, 1995; consult, MAC-RO Int, Atlanta, Ga, 1995; consult, Parents Behaviorally Different C, Albuquerque, Nmex, 1995-2002; consult, African Am Health Coalition, 1996-98; tech assistance, Simply Empowering Inc, Oakland, Calif, 2000-; consult, PGE-Econ Community Collab, 2000-02; chair's off, Multnomah County Comn, 2001-; African Am Alliance, Ment Health Sub Comt, 2001-; consult, Albina Ministerial Alliance Inc, 2001-03; African Am Ment Health Comn, 2002-; Int Asn Psychosocial Rehab; Asn Behav Anal; tech assistance, Hawaii's Youth Develop Initiative Entrepreneurial Community Collab, 2005-; Soc Social Work Res, 2007-; Coun Social Work Educ, 2007-; Nat Asn Social Workers.. **Business Addr:** Professor, Director of Research, University of Georgia, Tucker Hall 310 E Campus Rd, Athens, GA 30602-7016, **Business Phone:** (706)542-3364.

**BRIGHAM, FREDDIE M.**
Banker. **Personal:** Born Mar 23, 1947, Minneapolis, MN; daughter of Fred W and Mary L Lewis; children: Matthew W, Michael F & Jaime M. **Educ:** Metropolitan Community Col, attended 1982; Nat Univ, attended 1988. **Career:** Pillsbury Co, from exec sec to dir, 1973-84; Bank Am Nev, exec secy controller, 1988-93, mgr info processing, 1993-. **Orgs:** N Las Vegas Literacy Coun, 1990-92. **Home Addr:** 5101 E Twain Ave Suite 130, Las Vegas, NV 89122.

**BRIGHT, ALFRED LEE**
Artist, educator. **Personal:** Born Jan 9, 1940, Youngstown, OH; son of Henry and Elizabeth Lockhart Daniels; married Virginia Deanne Newell; children: Leslie, Alfred Jr, Nichole & Steven. **Educ:** Youngstown Univ, BS, 1964; Kent St Univ, MA, 1965. **Career:** Professor (retired); Youngstown State Univ, distinguished prof artist, 1965, black studies prog dir, 1970-87, prof artist, prof emer, currently; Ann Arundel Community Col, Canton Mus Art fel, 1990. **Orgs:** Alpha Phi Alpha Fraternity; St Dept Edn, Adv Com Arts; exec mem, Ohilo Arts Coun; Nat Humanities Fac; pres, Youngs town Area Arts Coun, 1979-80; exec bd, Ohilo Arts Coun, gov appointment, 1973-78; Phi Kappa Phi; Phi Beta Delta; Golden Key Nat Hon Soc. **Honors/Awds:** Best Of Show Haber-Gall, 1966; 1st & 2nd awards, oils Village Ctr Fine Art Exhib, Niles, OH, 1964-67; ; pvt cols, perm cols dev, "Total Walk-In Environ Rooms", 1st & Hon Ment Award, Butler Art Inst, Youngstown, 1967; Outstanding Grad Achiever, Nat Jr Achievement Inc, 1975; consult, Nat Humanities Fac, 1977-; Distinguished Prof Award, Youngstown State Univ, 1980, 1985-96; aid to individual artist, Ohio Arts Coun, 1980; painted with live jazz music: Art Blakey & Winton Marsalis, 1980, Jimmy Owens, 1985; Best of Show Butler Inst Am Art, 1984; Butler Inst Am Art, 1985; 1st pl AAA Exhib Butler Inst Am Art, 1985, 1994; Harmon-Meek Gallery, Naples, Fla, 1986, 1991; Roanoke Mus Fine Arts, 1986; Cleveland Playhouse Bolton Gallery, solo exhibs, 1990; Malcolm Brown Gallery, 1990; Solo exhibs: Cincinnati Art Mus, 1991; Beachwood Mus, 1992; Art Educator of the Year, The Ohio House Reps, 1992; The Harmon & HarrietKelly Collection African Am Art (San Antonio, Tex); Numerous solo exhibs; William Holmes McGuffey Historical Society Pioneer Award. **Special Achievements:** Co-author: "An Interdisciplinary Introd Black Studies", 1978. First African-American Professor at Youngstown State University. **Home Addr:** 697 Colonial Dr, Youngstown, OH 44505, **Home Phone:** (216)759-3972. **Business Addr:** Professor, Youngstown State University, 410 Wick Ave, Youngstown, OH 44555-0001, **Business Phone:** (303)941-3627.

**BRIGHT, ANDREW KIRK. See BRIGHT, KIRK.**

**BRIGHT, DR. HERBERT L.**
Clergy, executive. **Personal:** Born Aug 20, 1941, Shelbyville, TN; son of Henry H and Alvirleen Buchanan; married Dzifa Killings; children: Troy, Sonja, Yolonda, Herbert Jr, Kristi & Kenji Horton. **Educ:** Thornton Jr Col, Harvey, IL; Seton Hall Univ, S Orange, NJ; Inst Bible Studies, PhD; Andersonville Baptist Sem, Camilla, GA, BA, Christian educ, MA, ministry; Shiloh Theol Sem, Stafford, VA, DDiv; Tabernacle Bible Col & Sem, PhD, relig philos, 2001. **Career:** Nabisco Brands Inc, gen clerk, sr clerk, 1963-65, opers mgr, 1968-72, asst acct off mgr, 1972-73, personnel policies specialist, 1973-75, corp equal opportunity mgr, 1975-79, sr mgr personnel servs, 1979-83, dir personnel practices, 1983-87, dir personnel servs, 1987-89; dir minority affairs & bus develop, 1989-92; Faith Tabernacle Church, Faith Tabernacle Outreach Ministries Inc, sr pastor & founder, presiding bishop, currently; Bright Light Community Serv Inc, pres & chief exec officer, currently; Charles Reid Bible Col & Sem, chancellor; Plainfield Police Dept, chaplain, currently; Plainfield Pub Sch bd educ, elected off; Concern Urban Clergy Plainfield, pres; Triumphant Life Community Church, sr pastor, 2008-. **Orgs:** Pres, bd dir, Nabisco Brands Employee Credit Union; pres, bd dir, Morris County Urban League; US Chaplins Asn; Nat Asn Advan Colored People; Opportunities Industrialization Ctrs Am; Tom Skinner Assocs Ind & Labor Coun; Nat Urban League Com & Ind Coun; Am Soc Personnel Admin; bd dir, Union County Urban League; Va Union Univ Cluster; Howard Univ Cluster; Felician Col Bus Adv Bd; charter mem, Nat Urban League; 100 Black Men NJ; bd dir, Carter Woodson Found; bd dir, Nat Black United Fund; bd dir, NJ Black United Fund; bd dir, Plainfield Teen Parenting Prog; bd regents Tabernacle Bible Col & Semi; Christian Fel Coun Worldwide; Int Communion; Joint Col African-Am Pentecostal Bishops Cong; bd dir, Greater Cent Jersey Clergy Asn; bd dir, COO Kings Temple Ministries; Hisp Corp Coun; Nat Black Caucus State Legislators; Nat Minority Suppliers Develop Coun; NY & NJ Minority Purchasing Coun; Grant Ave Community Ctr; Plainfield Health Ctr; Plainfield Sch Bd Educ; eastern regional chaplain, Nat Orgn Black Law Enforcement Execs; US Chaplains Asn. **Home Addr:** 640 Sherman Ave, Plainfield, NJ 07060, **Home Phone:** (908)754-4665. **Business Addr:** Bishop, Faith Tabernacle Outreach Ministries, PO Box 548, Trenton, NJ 08604-0548, **Business Phone:** (609)392-2885.

**BRIGHT, JEAN MARIE**
Educator, writer. **Personal:** Born Sep 25, 1915, Rutherfordton, NC; daughter of John W Sr and Lollie. **Educ:** NC Agr & Tech State Univ, Greensboro, NC, BS, 1939; Columbia Univ, NY, MA, eng, 1953. **Career:** Adj gen's off, clerk-typist, 1942; Windsor Community Ctr, dir recreation; NC Agr & Tech State Univ, Greensboro, NC, prof Eng, 1953-78; NC Humanities Comt, lectr, 1977-79; Bks: Images Negro Am, co-ed, 1965; Voices from Black Experience, co-ed, 1972. **Orgs:** Am Red Cross, 1944-46; African Lit Asn; Col Lang Asn; pres, Bright Forest Enterprises Inc, 1980-89; Harvard Coop. **Home Addr:** 1008 S Benbow Rd, Greensboro, NC 27406, **Home Phone:** (336)272-9992.

**BRIGHT, KIRK (ANDREW KIRK BRIGHT)**
Executive. **Personal:** Born Jan 25, 1943, Louisville, KY; son of Lois S; married Shela; children: Greg, Yvette, Brett & Yvonne. **Educ:** Howard Univ. **Career:** IBM, customer engr, 1966-71; Bright's Dist Co, pres, 1971-89; Louisville Conv & Visitors Bur, conv sales mgr, 1990-2003; Louisville Cent Develop Corp, dir, microbusiness develop Bus Plus, 2003-. **Home Addr:** 3803 Barbour Lane, Louisville, KY 40241, **Home Phone:** (502)429-3678. **Business Addr:** Director, Louisville Central Development Corp, 1407 W Jefferson St Suite 200, Louisville, KY 40203, **Business Phone:** (502)583-8821.

**BRIGHT, WILLIE S.**
Consultant, chief executive officer. **Personal:** Born Feb 7, 1934, Houston, TX; son of Nathaniel Williams (deceased) and Ovida Y Johnson (deceased); married Mildred Ball; children: Develous A & Nicole O. **Educ:** Tuskegee Inst, Tuskegee, AL, 1953; Tex Southern Univ, Houston, TX, BS, govt, 1955, MEd, guid & coun, 1964. **Career:** Houston Independent Sch Dist, Houston, Tex, teacher, 1959-66; Crescent Found, Houston, Tex, counr, 1966-67; Concentrated Employ Prog, Houston, Tex, training officer, 1967-68; Forera Southeastern Inc, Houston, Tex, dir, 1968-71; Urban Placement Serv Inc, Houston, Tex, founder, owner, chief exec officer, 1970-07; Off Hearing & Appeal, Social Security Admin, expert witness, 1975-80. **Orgs:** Vice polemarch, bd mem, Kappa Alpha Psi Ferternity, Houston Alumni, 1954-, life mem, 1974-; Nat Asn Personnel Consult, 1971-; vpres, dir, Houston Area Asn Personnel Consult, 1971-; bd dir, Ment Health Asn, Houston, Harris County, 1974-80; bd mem, Citizens Good Sch, 1976-78; Nat Asn Mkt Developers, Houston Chap, 1978; Univ Oaks Civic Club, 1979-; Kiwanis Int, Houston Metrop Chap, 1985-; Houston Area Pan Hellenic Coun, 1986-; vice chmn, PPR Comn, Mt Vernon United Methodist Church, 1989; vpres & bd dir, 2016 Main Condo, 2009-. **Home Addr:** 4375 N MacGregor, Houston, TX 77004, **Home Phone:** (713)741-8347. **Business Addr:** Owner, Chief Executive Officer, The Urban Placement Serv, 602 Sawyer St Suite 460, Houston, TX 77007-7510, **Business Phone:** (713)880-2211.

**BRINKLEY, CHARLES H., SR.**
Educator, executive. **Personal:** Born Nov 13, 1942, Gallatin, TN; son of Ellen and Hutch; married Gloria Johnson; children: Katrena, Angela & Charles II. **Educ:** Tenn State Univ, MA, educ, 1985; Miss Vally State Univ, BS, MS; Tenn Tech Univ. **Career:** Educator (retired), principal; St Training Sch, Dept Corrections, teacher, 1967; NSF, fel grant, 1968; Taft Youth Ctr, prin, 1968-70; Sumner County Election Comn, 1983-89, chmn, 1985; TPSEA Unit, Tenn Prep Sch, pres; Charles H Brinkley, prin, currently. **Orgs:** Vice chmn, Gen Cent Comt, 1975-77; Dep Sheriff Command, 1975; C C, 1975; notary pub, State Tenn, 1975-78; Deacon, 1975-; chmn, Deacon's Bd, 1985-; pres, Nat Asn Adv Colored People Gallatin Br, 1996; First Baptist Church; Local rep, TPS Educ Asn; Mid Tenn Coun Asn; Tenn Sheriff's Asn; NEA; MTEA; TEA; TPSEA. **Honors/Awds:** Outstanding Serv Presidential Award, TPS Educ Asn, 1972; Outstanding Service Award, Nat Asn Adv Colored People, 1989, 1996. **Home Addr:** 213 Ellington Pl, Madison, TN 37115-5154, **Home Phone:** (615)866-9166. **Business Addr:** Principal, Charles H Brinkley, 155 Alpha Dr, Gallatin, TN 37066, **Business Phone:** (615)452-6435.

**BRINKLEY, NORMAN, JR.**
Dean (education), school administrator, air force officer. **Personal:** Born Jul 7, 1931, Edenton, NC; son of Norman and Adell; married Pearl A Rozier; children: Franklin, Cassandra, Norman T, Carmellia & Christa A. **Educ:** NC Agr & Tech Col, BS, 1954, MS, 1974. **Career:** City Piladelphia, youth counr, 1959-61; State Pa, youth supvr, 1961-63; CServ Inc, caseworker, 1963-64; Child Care Serv Media, social worker, 1965-69; Lincoln Univ, asst dir & community coordr, 1969-70; Miss Valley State Univ, dean studies affairs, 1970-; M WStringer Grand Lodge F & AM, officer, 1976-80; Miss NASPA, state dir, 1979-80. **Orgs:** Voters League, 1970-80; Miss Stud Personnel Admin, 1970-80. **Honors/Awds:** Community Rels Award, Univ Miss, 1971; Develop Inst Award, Univ Wis, 1972-73; Supvr Leadership Skills Award, Southern Ill Univ, 1975. **Home Addr:** 103 Winston Dr, Itta Bena, MS 38941, **Home Phone:** (601)254-9369. **Business Addr:** Dean of Student Affairs, Mississippi Valley State University, PO Box 1239, Itta Bena, MS 38941, **Business Phone:** (601)254-9041.

**BRISBY, VINCENT COLE**
Football player. **Personal:** Born Jan 25, 1971, Houston, TX; children: Donovan Herbert & Chloe. **Educ:** Univ Louisana, grad. **Career:** Football player (retired); New Eng Patriots, wide receiver, 1993-99; New York Jets, wide receiver, 2000; Northeast La Univ, wide receiver. **Orgs:** Phi Beta Sigma. **Honors/Awds:** Miller Lite Player of the Game, 1998. **Special Achievements:** Films: 1993 NFL Draft, 1993; Super Bowl XXXI, 1997.

**BRISCO-HOOKS, VALERIE ANN**
Track and field athlete, athletic coach. **Personal:** Born Jul 6, 1960, Greenwood, MS; married Alvin, Jan 1, 1981; children: Alvin Jr. **Educ:** Long Beach Comm Col; Calif State Univ, Northridge. **Career:** Athletic player (retired); coach; Athletic Cong Natl Championships, 1984; Olympic Games, Los Angeles, 1984, Seoul, Korea, 1988; UCLA Invitational, 1984; Bruce Jenner Meet, SanJose CA, 1984; Europ Track Circuit, 1984, 1985; Millrose Games, 1985; Sunkist Invitational, Los Angeles, 1985; Times-Herald Invitational, Dallas, Tex, 1985; LA Times-Kodak Games, Inglewood, Calif, 1985; W Los Angeles Col, coach, currently; Bob Kersee Group Athletes, coach, currently. **Orgs:** Valerie Brisco-Hooks Sports Found Inc. **Honors/Awds:** Three Gold Medals, Olympics, 1984; Los Angeles; Silver Medal, Olympics, Seoul, Korea, 1988; Outstanding Mother's Award, Natl Mother's Day Comm, 1986; co-chairperson, Minnie Riperton Cancer Week, 1986, 1987; World Championships Bronze Medal, 1987; USA Track & Field Hall of Fame, 1995. **Special Achievements:** TV Series: "The Cosby Show", 1986. First female asked to compete in Australia's Stalwell Gift Race, 1987; First Olympian to win gold medals in both the 200-meter and 400-meter races at a single Olympics. **Home Addr:** 1138 W 71st St, Los Angeles, CA 90044-2502. **Business Addr:** Valerie Brisco-Hooks Sports Foundation Inc, 1138 E 71st St, Los Angeles, CA 90001.

**BRISCOE, GAYLE**
Real estate agent. **Personal:** Born Suffolk, VA; children: 1. **Educ:** Hampton Univ, BS, psychol; Univ Md, Sch Social Work & Community Planning, MSW. **Career:** Greater Baltimore Bd Realtors, pres, 1995; Otis Warren & Co, vpres, 1997; Coldwell Banker Residential Brokerage, assoc broker, sales assoc, currently. **Orgs:** Life mem, Real Estate Million Dollar Asn. **Honors/Awds:** Outstanding African-American leader, The African Am Real Estate Prof, 2003; Maryland's Top 100 Women, Warfield's Magazine; 500 Most Powerful Women in Real Estate & Relocation, Nat Relocation & Real Estate Mag; Valued Hours Award, Wayland Baptist Church; Governor's Citation, Maryland's Gov; Received Governor's Citation, Maryland's Governor for noteworthy contributions to the real estate industry in Maryland; Received citations from Mayor & City Council of Baltimore for outstanding service in real estate to the citizens of Baltimore. **Special Achievements:** First African Am woman to be elected president for Greater Baltimore Bd of Realtors, 1995. **Home Addr:** , Ellicott City, MD 21041, **Home Phone:** (410)788-8087. **Business Addr:** Sales Associate, Coldwell Banker Residential Brokerage, 9380 Baltimore Nat Pke Suite 113, Catonsville, MD 21228, **Business Phone:** (410)480-1314.

**BRISCOE, MARLIN OLIVER**
Football player, teacher, executive. **Personal:** Born Sep 10, 1945, Oakland, CA; children: 1. **Educ:** Univ Nebr, Omaha. **Career:** Football player (retired), teacher, executive; Denver Broncos, 1968; Buffalo Bills, wide receiver, 1969-71; Miami Dolphins, wide receiver, 1972-74; SanDiego Charger, 1975; Detroit Lions, 1975; New England Patriots, 1976-77; Los Angeles area, teacher; Los Angeles Watts & Willowbrook Boys & Girls Club, asst proj mgr & fundraiser; Boys & Girls Club, dir. **Home Addr:** 675 Coronado Ave, Long Beach, CA 90814-1439, **Home Phone:** (562)434-2268. **Business Addr:** Director, Boys & Girls Club, 3635 Long Beach Blvd, Long Beach, CA 90807, **Business Phone:** (562)595-5945.

**BRISKER, LAWRENCE W. See Obituaries Section.**

**BRISTER, BISHOP DARRYL SYLVESTER**
Clergy. **Personal:** Born Sep 26, 1966, New Orleans, LA; son of Earlie Mae; married Dionne Flot; children: 5. **Educ:** McKinley Theol Sem, BTh, 1992; Friends Inst Christian Univ, MA, bible studies, 1995, DMin, PhD, 1998. **Career:** Greater St Stephen, Full Gospel Bapt Church, asst pastor, 1992-94; Beacon Light Bapt Church, sr pastor, 1993-; Darryl S Brister Bible Col & Theol Sem, pres & founder, 1999-. **Orgs:** Pres, Beacon Light Christian Acad, 2002; chief exec officer & pres, DSB Int Ministries; exec secy, Full Gospel Baptist Church Fel Int. **Home Addr:** PO Box 1526, Harvey, LA 70059, **Home Phone:** (504)296-8175. **Business Addr:** President, Founder, Darryl S Brister Bible College & Theological Seminary, 5134 Paris Ave, New Orleans, LA 70122, **Business Phone:** (504)283-8752.

**BRISTOW, DR. LONNIE ROBERT**
Physician. **Personal:** Born Apr 6, 1930, New York, NY; son of Lonnie H and Vivian W; married Marilyn H; children: Robert E & Elizabeth E; married Margaret Jeter; children: Mary. **Educ:** Morehouse Col; Col City NY, BS, 1953; NY Univ, Col Med, MD, 1957. **Career:** San Francisco City & County Hosp, intern, 1958; USVA Hosp, San Francisco, resident internal med, 1960; Francis Dela field Hosp, Columbia Univ Serv, 1960; USVA Hosp, Bronx, 1961; Univ Calif, San Francisco Sch Med, residency, occup med, 1981; pvt pract internist; consult, currently. **Orgs:** Alameda-Contra Costa Med Asn, 1968-; E Bay Soc Internal Med, pres, 1969; Federated Coun Internal Med, 1976-78; pres, Calif Soc Internal Med, 1976; fel master, Am Col Physicians, 1977, 1995; pres, Am Soc Internal Med, 1981-82; bd trustees, 1985-, chair, 1993-94, pres, AMA, 1995-96; exec comm sect, Community Off Lab Assessment, 1989-91; comnr, Joint Community Accreditation Health care Orgn, 1990-92; Nat Med Veterans Soc; Calif Med Asn; chair, Uniformed Serv Univ Health Sci, 1996-; Emer Mem, Ed Adv Bd Med World News; co-chair, Sullivan Alliance to Transform Am's Health Professions. **Honors/Awds:** Board Certification, Am Bd Internal Med, 1969; Parket Health Memorial Lecturer, 1982; Contra Costa Humanitarian of the Year, Contra Costa Bd Supvr, 1989; California Most Distinguished Internist, CA Society IM, 1990; Honorary Degree, Morehouse Sch Med, 1994; Honorary Degrees, Wayne State Univ Sch Med, 1995, City Col City Univ New York, 1995, Univ Md & Dent Nj, Morehouse Col Sch Med. **Special Achievements:** First Black to lead the nation' s largest medical group AMA; Publications: "The Myth of Sickle Cell Trait", medical opinion, The Western Journal of Med, 1974; "Shared Sacrifice-The AMA Leadership Response to the Health Sec Act" JAMA, 1994; "Mine Eyes Have Seen, "Journal of the AMA, 1989; first African American President of the American Medical Association. **Home Addr:** 3324 Ptarmigan Dr Apt 3B, Walnut Creek, CA 94595-3157, **Home Phone:** (925)943-7326. **Business Addr:** Co-chair, The Sullivan Alliance to Transform America's Health Professions, 3324 Ptarmigan Dr Apt B3, Walnut Creek, CA 94595, **Business Phone:** (925)933-2733.

**BRITT, DONNA**
Journalist, columnist. **Personal:** Born Jan 1, 1954, Gary, IN; daughter of Thomas and Geraldine; married Kevin Merida; children: Justin Britt-Gibson, Darrell Britt-Gibson & Skye Merida. **Educ:** Hampton Univ, BA, mass media, 1976; Univ Mich, MA, jour, 1979. **Career:** Charlotte Observer, internships; Ann Arbor News, internships; Detroit Free Press, gen assignment reporter, staff writer, 1978-85; USA Today, ed, staff writer, Los Angeles, bur chief & co-movie critic, 1985-89; Wash Post, features & style sect writer, 1989, Metro sect columnist, 1990-2008, columnist, 1991-; Polit Daily, columnist, 2009-10; Publications: Brothers (& Me): A Memoir of Loving and Giving, 2011. **Orgs:** Trotter Group. **Special Achievements:** Britt was nominated by the Washington Post for the Pulitzer Prize in journalism in 1990. **Business Addr:** Columnist, The Washington Post, 1150 15th St NW, Washington, DC 20071-0070, **Business Phone:** (202)334-6037.

**BRITT, L. D.**
Surgeon, college teacher, physician. **Personal:** Born Jun 28, 1951, Suffolk, VA; son of White and Claretta; married Charlene; children: Avery. **Educ:** Univ Va, BA, 1972; Harvard Med Sch, MD, 1977; Harvard Sch Pub Health, MPH, 1977. **Career:** Univ Il, Dept Surg, clin instr, 1983-85; Bethany Hosp, active staff, asst dir emergency med, 1984-85; Md Inst Emergency Med Serv Systs, chief admin surg fel, 1985-86; Coveted Raven Soc; Eastern Va Med Sch, asst prof surg, 1986-89, Div Trama& Critical Care, chief, 1987-97, assoc prof surg, 1989-93, Dept Surg, Henry Ford prof & vice chair, 1993-95, Dept Surg, prof & chmn, 2004-; Edward Brick house, Dept Surg, chair, 1994-; Sentara Norfolk Gen Hosp, Dept Surg, chief, 1997-99; Shock Trauma Ctr, from asst med dir to med dir, 1986-97; Am Col Surgeons, pres, 2010-11; Howard Univ, Va, vis prof; St Louis Univ, vis prof; Annals Surg, ed bd; J Am Col Surgeons, ed bd, dep ed; Am J Surg, ed bd, assoc ed; Arch Surg, ed

bd; Shock, ed bd; J Surg Educ, ed bd; Current Surg, ed bd; J Trauma, ed bd; Fr Acad Surg & Cols Med S Africa, hon fel, 2012. Books: 224 peerreviewed scientific publications, auth; 52 chapters/non-peer-reviewed articles, auth; Acute Care Surgery, ed. **Orgs:** Senate Joint Sub comt, EMS Personnel Training & Retention, 1988-91; adv bd, EMS, 1988-94; bd visitors, Norfolk State Univ, 1988-96; exec bd mem, Boy Scouts Am, 1989-; chair, Va State Comt Trauma, 1991-97; bd trustee, Sentara Health Syst, 1992-94; bd dir, Asn Prog dir Surg, 1996-; Cols Comt Trauma, 1997-2005; assoc examr, Am Bd Surg, 1997-; nat comt trauma, Am Col Surgeons, 1998-2002; bd mgr, Pan Am Trauma Soc; Sci Res Soc; Alpha Omega Alpha Hon Soc; bd regents, Am Col Surgeons; Am Asn Med Col; Am Surgeons Asn; ACGME, Residency Rev Comt; Halsted Soc; fel Royal Soc Med Eng; fel Am Asn Surg Trauma; fel Am Col Critical Care Med; Nat Insts Health SOH Study Rev Panel; Southeastern Surg Cong; Halsted Soc; Nat Med Asn Surg Sect; Soc Black Acad Surgeons; bd trustee, Va Capitol Found; Soc Surg Chairmen; Southern Surg Asn; Robert Wood Johnson Clin Scholar Prog Nat Adv Comt; bd mgr, 1993, bd adv, 2015, Univ Va; bd regents, Uniformed Serv Univ Health Sci. **Special Achievements:** First African-American in the country to have an endowed chair in surgery. **Home Addr:** 1213 Botetourt Gardens, Norfolk, VA 23507, **Home Phone:** (757)627-3366. **Business Addr:** Brickhouse Professor, Chairman, Eastern Virgina Medical School, Hofheimer Hall, Norfolk, VA 23507-1912, **Business Phone:** (757)446-8964.

### BRITT, PAUL D., JR.

School administrator, school principal. **Personal:** Born Feb 3, 1951, Franklin, VA; married Priscilla Harding; children: Pauleatha Clara & Taene Renita. **Educ:** Norfolk State Univ, BA, social serv, 1974; Va State Univ, MA, educ admin, 1984. **Career:** Southampton Co Schs, teacher & coach, 1975-79; Franklin City Schs, teacher, coach & social studies dept, chmn, 1979-84; Smithfield High Sch, asst prin; Roanoke City Pub Schs, exec for human resources; Petersburg City Pub Schs, Vernon Johns Middle Sch, prin. **Orgs:** Deacon First Baptist Ch, Franklin, 1979; coun mem, Franklin City Coun, 1982. **Home Addr:** 405 Pine St, Franklin, VA 23851.

### BRITT, SHARON FRIES. See FRIES, DR. SHARON LAVONNE.

### BRITTAIN, BRADLEY BERNARD, JR.

Engineer, editor. **Personal:** Born Mar 22, 1948, Arlington, VA; son of Bradley B Sr; married Lenora C Robinson Freeman; children: Kandakai Freeman, Kini Freeman & Zina Freeman. **Educ:** Howard Univ. **Career:** Am Broadcasting Co Inc, engr ed, newsfilm ed, apprentice film ed desk asst, 1972-; freelance photogr, 1976-77. **Orgs:** Life mem, Nat Asn Advan Colored People; Nat Rifle Asn; Nat Geog Soc; Radio & TV Corr Asn; Friends Nat Zoo; Smithsonian Resident Assocs, 1978-; Nat Capital Velo Club; Capitol Hill Correspondents Assoc, 1978-; Asn Corcoran; Nat Acad TV Arts & Sci, 1983-85; White House News Photogr Asn, 1983-85; pub rels comn, Northern Va Gun Club, 1983-85. **Home Addr:** 1314 S Poe St, Arlington, VA 22204-4731, **Home Phone:** (703)920-0496. **Business Addr:** Engineer, American Broadcasting Co, 1717 DeSales St NW, Washington, DC 20036.

### BRITTAIN, JOHN C.

College teacher, educator. **Educ:** Howard Univ, BA, 1966, JD, 1969. **Career:** N Miss Rural Legal Serv, Oxford, MS, regin ald Heber Smith fel & staff atty, 1969-71; Lawyers Comt Civil Rights Under Law, Jackson, MS, staff atty, 1971-73, chief coun & sr dep dir; pvt pract atty, San Francisco, CA, 1973-77; Univ Conn, Sch Law, Hartford, CT, prof law, 1977-99; Tex Southern Univ, Thur good Marshall Sch Law, Houston, TX, dean, 1999-2002, prof law, 2002-; Univ Dist Columbia, prof law, 1999-; David A Clarke Sch Law, tenured prof, currently.; Univ Conn Sch Law, veteran law prof. **Orgs:** Chairperson, ACLU Acad Freedom Comt, 1985-88; Conn State Labor Rels Bd, 1990-95; Pres Nat Lawyers Guild, 1991-93; bd dir, Hartford Found Pub Giving, 1995-99; bd mem, Am Civil Liberties Union, 1998-99 & 2001-; sr fel Am Leadership Forum, 2002; Soc Am Law Teachers; Nat Conf Black Lawyers; Int Asn Jurists; Int Asn Dem Lawyers; Nat Bar Asn; Charles Houston Bar Asn; George W Crawford Asn; Magnolia Bar Asn; Am Bar Asn; Houston Bar Asn; Houston Lawyers Asn; bd dir, Hartford Community Found; chair, Norflet Fund Cy Pres, currently. **Business Addr:** Professor of Law, University of the District of Columbia, 4200 Conn Ave NW, Washington, DC 20008, **Business Phone:** (202)274-6443.

### BRITTON, BARBARA

Publishing executive, vice president (organization). **Career:** Essence Mag, nat sales dir, 1988, vpres & assoc publ sales, nat advert dir, publ adv; AMBERmag.com, publ consult, britton mkt & sales. **Business Addr:** Publishing Advisor, Essence Magazine, 1500 Broadway 6th Fl, New York, NY 10036, **Business Phone:** (212)642-0600.

### BRITTON, DR. CAROLYN B.

Educator. **Educ:** NY Univ, Sch Med, MD, 1975. **Career:** Harlem Hosp Med Ctr, resident internal med; Columbia Univ Med Ctr, Neurol Inst NY, NY Presby Hosp, resident & fel; Columbia Presby Med Ctr, fel, 1984; Columbia Univ Med Ctr, Neurol Inst NY, assoc prof neurol, currently. **Orgs:** Pres, Nat Med Asn, 2008-; chmn neurol/neurosurg sect, chair finance comt, chmn bd trustee, pres, Nat Med Asn; chmn, Doctor's Pvt Off Comt; chmn, NY Presby Hosp. **Business Addr:** Associate Professor, Columbia University Medical Center, 710 W 168th St Rm 232, New York, NY 10032-2603, **Business Phone:** (212)305-5220.

### BRITTON, ELIZABETH

Nurse. **Personal:** Born Jul 18, 1930, Gary, IN; children: Darryl T Gillespie, Tamara A Gillespie, John G Gillespie, Lisa M Roach, Anthony L & Alycyn M. **Educ:** Mayfair-Chicago City Col, AA, 1969; Purdue Univ, BSN, 1974; Portland State Univ, MS, 1982. **Career:** Nurse, instructor (retired); Chicago Maternity Ctr, nursing serv admin, 1970-73; Beverly Learning Ctr, health educ instr, 1972-74; Univ Ore Health Scis Ctr Sch Nursing, instr, 1976-81; Ore Health Scis Univ Minority Stud Affairs, asst prof, 1981. **Orgs:** Pres, Willamette Valley Racial Minorities Consortium; Nat Asn Med Minority Educr; bd dir, N Portland Nurse Practer Community Health Clin; anti-basileus, Alpha Kappa Alpha Sor Zeta Sigma Omega; Ore Alliance Black Sch Educr; bd dir, Ore Donor Prog; Links Inc; Portland Chap, 1988. **Honors/Awds:** Nat Honor Soc Nursing Sigma Theta Tau, 1976; Spec Contrib Indian Educ, 1981, 82, 83; Cert of Appreciation, Ctr Black Studies Portland State Univ, 1983; Outstanding AKA Woman, Zeta Sigma Omega Chapter, 1986. **Home Addr:** 2730 Orchard Hill Pl, Lake Oswego, OR 97035, **Home Phone:** (503)246-2500. **Business Addr:** Director of International Ethnic Affairs, Oregon Health Sciences University, 3181 SW Sam Jackson Pk Rd, Portland, OR 97229, **Business Phone:** (503)494-8311.

### BRITTON, JOHN HENRY, JR.

Journalist. **Personal:** Born Jul 21, 1937, Nashville, TN; son of John Henry Sr and Martha Marie Parish; married Cherrie Alvilda Dean; married Betty; children: John III. **Educ:** Drake Univ, BS, jour, 1958; Syracuse Univ, MS, jour, 1962. **Career:** Atlanta Daily World, reporter, 1958-62; Jet Mag, asso ed, asst managinged, 1962-66; US Civil Rights Comn, asst info officer, 1966-67; Civil Rights Doc Proj Wash, assoc dir, 1967-68; Jet Mag, managing ed, 1968-71; Motown Rec Corp Detroit & La, pub rel mgr, 1971-73; Joint Ctr Polit Studies, pub affairs dir, 1973-76; Encore Mag, columnist, 1974-75; Wash Post, pub rel mgr, 1976-78; Univ DC, pub affairs dir, 1978-97; Bowie St Univ, pub rel dir, 1997-98; Meharry Med Col, assoc vpres mkt & commun, 1998-2002, spec asst to pres, 2002-2009. **Orgs:** Black Pub Rel Soc Wash; Nat Adv Comt, Nat Black Media Coalition; life mem, Nat Asn Advan Colored People; Nat Asn Black Journalists; Alpha Phi Alpha Fraternity. **Home Addr:** 116 Spring Pl Way, Nashville, TN 21401, **Home Phone:** (410)263-5112.

### BRITTON, AMBASSADOR THEODORE R., JR.

Government official. **Personal:** Born Oct 17, 1925, North Augusta, SC; son of Theodore R Sr and Bessie B Cook; married Ruth B A Baker; children: Theodore (deceased), Renee, Warren, Sharon & Darwin; married Vernell Elizabeth Stewart. **Educ:** NY Univ, BA, banking & finance, 1952. **Career:** Government official (retired); Carver Savings Bank, mortgage officer, 1955-64; Am Baptist Mgt Corp, pres, 1966-71; Dept Housing & Urban Dev, Res & Technol, dep asst secy, 1971-73, act asst secy res & tech, 1973, asst secy int affairs, 1981-89, NY, dep regional adminr, 1983-84, Newark, mgr, 1990-92; Barbados & Grenada, ambassador, 1974-77; Assoc States Caribbean, spec rep, 1974-77; United Mutual Life Ins Co, NY, pres & chief exec officer, 1978-79; mgt consult, 1979-80; D Parke Gibson Int Ltd, sr consult, 1979; Logical Tech Serv Corp, exec vpres & secy; Nat Housing Ministries, vpres, 1994-99; Lect ser: Caribbean, Gas world famed Emory Univ. **Orgs:** Deacon, trustee, Riverside Church, NY, 1965-77; chmn, New York Urban Renewal Mgt Corp, 1968-71; vice chmn, Sector Group Urban Environ Orgn Econ Coop & Develop, 1971-74, 1981-84, chmn, 1985-87; chair US & China Agreement Housing, 1981-89; vice chmn, 1982-84, chmn, 1985-87, OECD Group Urban Affairs; Inst Real Estate Mgmt; Nat Asn Realtors; Am Baptist Rep; bd dir, Freedom Nat Bank, 1978; exec secy, US Agreement Housing & Urban Develop with Can Mex & USSR; Asn Former Intelligence Officers & Second Marine Div; pres, Asn Black Am Ambassadors; bd dir, Coun Am Ambassadors, 1983; comnr, vice chair chmn, Housing Authority County Dekalb, GA, 2002; bd trustee, 2000, bd dir, People to People Int, 2001; bd mem, Ga Coun Int Visitors; chrm, Kristal Univ; hon consul gen, Repub Albania, 2006; chmn, Kristals Ctr Albanian Am Studies, 2007; Ambassador Peace, S Korean-based Universal Peace Federatio; Mid E Peace Initiative Isral & palestine, 2007; life mem, Montford Pt Marine Asn, Second Marine Div, currently; life mem, Asn Intelligence Officers, currently; hon chmn, Kristal Univ Tirana. **Honors/Awds:** J Wallace Paletou Award, Institute of Real Estate Management, 1987; Distinguished Service Award, HUD, 1989; Thurgood Marshall Award, University Bridgeport Black Law School Student Asn, 1990; degree of Doctor of Laws Honoris Causa, Kristal University, Tirana, Albania; veterans comprising sixteen nations, S Korea Nat Assembly, 2008; Hon LLD, 2009. **Home Addr:** 310 Somerlane Pl, Avondale Estates, GA 30002, **Home Phone:** (404)299-1267. **Business Addr:** Member, Council of American Ambassadors, 888 17th St NW Suite 901, Washington, DC 20006-3307, **Business Phone:** (202)296-3757.

### BROACH, S. ELIZABETH JOHNSON. See Obituaries Section.

### BROADBENT, HYDEIA

Activist. **Personal:** Born Jun 14, 1984, Las Vegas, NV; daughter of Loren and Patricia. **Educ:** Col Southern Nev, commun. **Career:** Int HIV/AIDS activist & motivational speaker, 1989-; guest panelist. **Orgs:** Founder, Hydeia L Broadbent Found, 1993-. **Honors/Awds:** A Time for Heroes Award, Pediatric AIDS Found; MLK Jr Drum Major Award; Humanitarian Spirit Award, Amer Red Cross; Grandma's House Award; CDC Award; Frederick Douglass Caring Award; AIDS Action Foundation Award; Millenium Dreamers Award, Disney; Pedro Zamora Memorial Award, Youth Advocacy; named one of Top Ten Female Role Models of the Year, Ms Fndn, 1999; American Red Cross Spirit Award, 1999; honored Essence Award, 1999; one of the Most Influential African Americans, Ebony Magazine, 2008. **Special Achievements:** Co-author: You Can Get Past the Tears, 2000. **Business Addr:** Founder, Hydeia L Broadbent Found, 1425 N Sierra Bonita Ave Suite 411, Los Angeles, CA 90046-4198, **Business Phone:** (323)874-0883.

### BROADNAX, DR. WALTER DOYCE

Government official, president (organization). **Personal:** Born Oct 21, 1944, Star City, AR; son of Walter and Mary Lee; married Angel LaVerne Wheelock; children: Andrea Alyce. **Educ:** Wash Burn Univ, BA, 1967; Kans Univ, MPA, 1969; Syracuse Univ, Maxwell Sch Citizenship & Pub Affairs, PhD, 1975. **Career:** Ny Dept Correctional Serv, staff consult, 1974-75; Joint Int City Mgt Asn/Nat Asn Schs Pub Affairs & Admin, co-dir, 1976; Fed Exec Inst, prof pub admin, 1976-79; State Kans, Serv C, Youth & Adults, dir, 1979-80; Dept Health, Educ & Welfare, Health & Human Serv, prin dep asst secy, 1980-81; Brookings Inst, Advan Study Prog, sr staffmem, 1981; Harvard Univ, JFK Sch Gov, Pub Mgt & Pub Policy, lectr, 1981-87; NYK State Civil Serv Comn, comnr, pres, 1987-90; Univ Tex, LBJ Sch Pub Affairs, vis lectr, 1989; Cleveland State Univ, Col Urban Affairs, eminent pub adv lectr, 1989; Ctr Goval Res Inc, pres, 1990-93; Pres-Elect Bill Clinton Transition Team, transition team leader, 1992; Am Univ, dean & prof pub admin, sch pub affairs, 1992-2002; Univ Md, prof, pub policy & mgt, dir, bur govt res & chair, social policy concentration, sch pub affairs, 1996-99; US Dept Health& Human Serv, chief operating officer, dep secy, 1993-96; Clark Atlanta Univ, pres, 2002-08; Syracuse Univ, prof pub admin & int affairs; Syracuse Univ, distinguished prof, 2008-. **Orgs:** Nat Comn Innovations State & Local Gov, Ford Found, Howard Univ, 1987-89; fel Nat Acad Pub Admin, 1988; Woodrow Wilson Nat Fel Found, Nat Adv Comn, 1989; S Africa Prog, Harvard Univ, 1992; bd dir, Key Corp, 1991-93; bd dir, Nat Civic League; adv comt mem, Ctr Study States, CASE Comn, Phase II; State Adv Coun; Nat Comn Am State & Local Pub Serv; spec adv bd, NYK State Comn Cost Control, 1991-93; bd dir, Rochester Gen Hosp; bd dir, Medecision, 1996-2004; Ford Found fel; bd trustee, Syracuse Univ, 1999-2008. **Home Addr:** 256 Coun Rock Ave, Rochester, NY 14610, **Home Phone:** (716)244-2472. **Business Addr:** Distinguished Professor, Syracuse University, 900 S Crouse Ave, Syracuse, NY 13244.

### BROADUS, CORDOZAR CALVIN, JR. See DOGG, SNOOP.

### BROADWATER, TOMMIE, JR.

Business owner, government official, executive. **Personal:** Born Jun 9, 1942, Washington, DC; married Lillian; children: Tommie III, Tanya, Jackie & Anita. **Educ:** Southern Univ; Prince Georges Community Col. **Career:** Broadwater Bonding Corp, owner; Ebony Inn, owner, 1974-; Md State, Prince George's County, sen, 1975-84; Prince Georges Community Bank, vpres, 1976-77, co founder. **Orgs:** Counman, City Glenarden, 1968-72; Prince Georges Chamber Com; Dem Cent Comt, 1970-74; treas, Md Legislators Black Caucus; bd dir, Prince George Community Bank; 25th Alliance Civic Group; Nat Asn Advan Colored People; Sr Citizens Adv Coun; Subcomt Corrections & Transp, 1974-83; vice-chair, Rules Comt, 1974-83 Comn Intergovernmental Coop, 1974-83; Senate, 1974-83; Budget & Taxation Comt, 1974-83; Joint Oversight Comn Corrections, 1974-83; Joint Oversight Comn Transp, 1974-83; Gov Juvenile Justice Adv Comt, 1974-83; Gov Housing Task Force, 1974-83; Gov Task Force Youth Employ, 1980-82 Plough man & Fisherman Democratic Club; Boys & Girls Club, Glenarden; Bondsmen's Asn. **Honors/Awds:** Outstanding Alumni Award, Fairmont Heights Sch, 1976; Outstanding Leader, Prince Georges Co Civic Groups, 1977. **Special Achievements:** First African American senator elected outside of Baltimore. **Home Addr:** 3309 Hayes St, Glenarden, MD 20706, **Home Phone:** (301)773-9462. **Business Addr:** Owner, Ebony Inn, 5367 Sheriff Rd, Fairmont Heights, MD 20743, **Business Phone:** (301)773-8858.

### BROCK, DR. ANNETTE K.

School administrator. **Personal:** married Otis Greet. **Educ:** Savannah State Col, BS, 1962; Duke Univ, MEd; Univ SC, PhD. **Career:** Savannah State Col, pres, 1991-93, vpres, 1997-2004, prof emer, currently. **Orgs:** Founding mem, Savannah Coun World Affairs; chair, Savannah Chap Am Red Cross; Ga Coun Humanities; Hospice Savannah Found; Bd Savannah Hospice; Ga Hist Rec Adv Bd; Savannah Music Festival; Savannah Chamber Com; chairwoman bd, King-Tisdell Cottage Found. **Business Addr:** Professor Emeritus, Savannah State University, 3219 College St, Savannah, GA 31404, **Business Phone:** (912)358-4778.

### BROCK, GERALD

Judge. **Personal:** Born Aug 23, 1932, Hamtramck, MI; married Jacqueline B Holmes. **Educ:** Eastern Mich Univ, BS, 1953; Detroit Col Law, LLB, 1961. **Career:** Flint Pub Sch, teacher, 1953-57; Wayne County Training Sch, teacher, 1957-61; Pvt Pract, atty, 1961-81; 36th Dist Ct, judge, 1982-. **Business Addr:** Judge, 36th District Court, 421 Madison Ave, Detroit, MI 48226, **Business Phone:** (313)965-8716.

### BROCK, LORRAINE

Vice president (government). **Personal:** children: 3. **Career:** Nationwide Ins, vpres diverse markets & urban mkt develop, 2004; Get Organized!, founder & pres, 2007-. **Orgs:** Adv coun, eWomenNetwork Inc; ASPIRA; Habitat Humanity, LISC; Nat Asn Advan Colored People; NFHA; Nat Hisp Corp Coun; Nat Hisp Scholar Fund; Nat Urban League; Neighborhood Reinvestment Corp; Urban Ins Partners Inst. **Honors/Awds:** Donald H McGannon Award, Nat Urban League. **Business Addr:** Vice President of Diverse Markets, Nationwide Insurance, 1 Nationwide Plz, Columbus, OH 43215-2220, **Business Phone:** (614)249-7111.

### BROCK, ROSLYN MCCALLISTER

Civil rights activist, health services administrator, executive. **Personal:** Born May 30, 1965, Ft. Pierce, FL; married Randall Eugene (deceased). **Educ:** Va Union Univ, BS, 1985; George Washington Univ, MHSA, 1989; Northwestern Univ, Kellogg Sch Mgt, MBA, 1999; Va Union Univ, Samuel DeWitt Proctor Sch Theol, divinity, 2009. **Career:** US Aid Rosslyn, prog asst, Health Mgt Fel Ny Dept Health; Conv Planning Comt, chmn, 1999-2009; Bon Secours Health Syst, exec, vpres, advocacy & govt rels, 2001-; Nat Asn Advan Colored People Centennial Comt, chmn, 2005-09; Nat Bd, vice chmn, 2001-10, chmn currently. **Orgs:** NAACP, Va Union Univ, 1984; vice chmn, Nat Asn Advan Colored People Health Comt; chmn, Conv Planning Comt, 1999; vice chmn, Nat Asn Advan Colored People Nat Bd dir, 2001; vice chmn & chmn, Nat Bd, 2010-; W K Kellogg Found; Alpha Kappa Alpha; diamond Life Mem, Nat Asn Advan Colored People; Assoc Minister, Alfred St Baptist Church; bd trustee, George Wash Univ; bd Advisors, Milken Inst Sch Pub Health; adv bd, Kellogg Sch Mgt, Northwestern Univ; trustee, Cath Health Asn; Am Pub Health Asn; Am Col Healthcare Execs, Asn Healthcare Philanthropy; Black Women's Roundtable; Links Inc. **Business Addr:** Director of System Fund Development, Bon Secours Health Systems Inc, 1505 Marriottsville Rd, Marriottsville, MD 21104, **Business Phone:** (410)442-5511.

### BROCK, TARRIK JUMAAN

Baseball player, baseball executive. **Personal:** Born Dec 25, 1973, Goleta, CA; married Kanika; children: Tarrik Jr & Christopher. **Educ:**

Benetton Treviso. **Career:** Baseball player (retired), coach, executive; Seattle Mariners, 1999; Chicago Cubs, out fielder, 2000; New York Mets, 2000; Los Angeles Dodgers, 2002-03, hitting coach, 2006-07; Ogden Raptors, coach, 2006; Miami Marlins LP, outfield & base running coordr, 2006-; Fla Marlins, interim first base coach, 2010; Cardio Grind, co-owner.

### BROCKETT, CHARLES A.
Educator. **Personal:** Born Jan 24, 1937, Princess Anne County, VA; married Annette Lee; children: Troy Christopher. **Educ:** Va State Col, BS, 1961; Old Dominion Univ, MS, 1972; Univ Va, Norfolk State Col. **Career:** School administrator (retired); Booker T Wash High Sch, Norfolk, VA, asst prin, asst football coach, 1963-67, biol teacher, 1963-70; Lake Taylor High Sch, Norfolk VA, 1979-86; Norview High Sch, asst prin; Granby High Sch, asst prin, 2001. **Orgs:** Nat Asn Sec Prin; Sec Prin Asn Norfolk; VA Asn Sec Prin; vpres, Dist LPrin Asn; nat bd mem, Nat Black United Fund; pres, Black United Fund Tidewater; Kappa Alpha Psi; Chesapeake Men Progress; Chesapeake Forward; civic reg dir, Kappa Alpha Psi Guide Right Prog; Eastern Reg pres Kappa Alpha Psi planning comt, Alpha Phi Alumni Reunion. **Honors/Awds:** Outstanding Service Award, Kappa Alpha Psi; Outstanding Community Service Award, 1973; Outstanding Community Service, 1986. **Home Addr:** 4515 Miarfield Arc, Chesapeake, VA 23321-4266, **Home Phone:** (757)686-9533.

### BROCKINGTON, DONELLA P.
Executive, association executive. **Personal:** Born Nov 8, 1952, Washington, DC; daughter of Harriet Brown and Josiah Armstrong. **Educ:** Clark Univ, BA, math & psychol, 1973; Howard Univ Sch Ed, MS, guid & coun, 1974, educ & urban sys engineering, 1976. **Career:** Health Sys Agency N VA, sr health sys analyst, 1976-80; DC Govt Off City Admin, sr oper analyst, 1981-85; DC Govt Dept Admin Serv, dep real prop admin, 1985-87, assoc dir real property, 1987-88; Lockheed Datacom, vpres nat mkt, 1988-91; Lockheed Martin IMS, Wash, vpres mkt, 1991-96, regional vpres, 1996-99, vpres, opers, 1997-2003; ACS State & Local Solutions, vpres munic mkt, 1988, vpres, co opers, 2001-04, vpres bus develop, 2004-12; Xerox, vpres, 2012-. **Orgs:** Coord McKinley High Sch Alumni Orgn, 1980; secy, Capital Ballet Guild Inc, 1982; Nat Forum Black Pub Admin, 1982-; Nat Asn Female Exec, 1986-; Mt Jezreel Baptist Church, 1990-2014; secy, Girl Scout Coun Nation's Capital, 1993-96, first vpres, 1996-99, chair, 1999-2005; bd dir, Hoop Dreams Scholar Fund; Nat Asn Prof Women; Leadership Greater Wash, 1999-; vice chair, US Tennis Asn mem comt; co-chair, Women's Adv Bd Girl Scout Coun; vpres, Affiliated Comput Serv, 2001-10; bd dir, DC Chamber Com, 2006-; chair, Posse Found, 2014-. **Honors/Awds:** Distinguished Public Service Award, DC Govt, 1982; Salute to African-American Business & Professional Women, Dollars & Sense Mag, 1989; President's Award, Lockheed Martin IMS, 1998; Lifetime Achievement Award, Women Technol, 2001; Inaugural Heroines in Technology Lifetime Achievement Award, March Dimes, 2001; Lifetime Achievement Award, ACS State & Local Solutions, 2003. **Home Addr:** 4405 13th Pl NE, Washington, DC 20017-2730, **Home Phone:** (202)526-4813. **Business Addr:** Vice President, Xerox Corp, 45 Glover Ave, Norwalk, CT 06856-4505, **Business Phone:** (800)275-9376.

**BROCKINGTON, EUGENE ALFONZO. See Obituaries Section.**

### BRODERICK, JOHNSON
Movie producer, president (organization). **Personal:** Born Athens, GA; married Jennifer Johnson; children: 3. **Educ:** Princeton Univ. **Career:** Producer; Films: Love Is All There Is, co producer, 1996; Lost & Found, 1999; My Dog Skip, 2000; Dude, Where's My Car?, 2000; The Affair of the Necklace, 2001; Insomnia, 2002; Love Don't Cost a Thing, 2003; Chasing Liberty, 2004; Racing Stripes, 2005; Sisterhood Traveling Pants, 2005; Whole Pemberton Thing, 2005; P S I Love You, 2007; One Missed Call, 2008; The Sisterhood of the Traveling Pants 2, 2008; The Blind Side, 2009; The Book of Eli, 2010; Lottery Ticket, 2010; Something Borrowed, 2011; Dolphin Tale, 2011; Joyful Noise, 2012; Chernobyl Diaries, exec producer, 2012; Beautiful Creatures, 2013; Prisoners, 2013; Transcendence, 2014; The Good Lie, 2014; Dolphin Tale 2, 2014; Point Break, forthcoming; Bastards, forthcoming; Salomon Bros, quant analyst; Alcon Entertainment LLC, co-pres & co-founder, 1997-. **Special Achievements:** Nominated, The Blind Side, Oscar Award, 2009. **Home Addr:** 1836 Virginia Rd, Los Angeles, CA 90019-5937. **Business Addr:** Co-Chief Executive Officer, Co-founder, Alcon Entertainment LLC, 10390 Santa Monica Blvd Suite 250, Los Angeles, CA 90404, **Business Phone:** (310)789-3040.

### BROGDEN, ROBERT, JR.
Automotive executive, president (organization). **Personal:** Born Feb 13, 1958, Roswell, NM; son of Robert Sr and Billie; married Kathy; children: Robert III & Anna. **Career:** K-G Men's Store, salesperson; Auto Dealership, sales mgr, 1982-92; Gen Motors, 1992-93; Robert Brogden's Olathe Pontiac-Buick-GMC Inc, pres, owner & dealer, 1993-. **Orgs:** Bd dir, Ola Chamber Com, 1995-; chair, Johnson Countys Bd Comn. **Home Addr:** 11431 Ga Ave, Kansas City, KS 66109, **Home Phone:** (913)721-1637. **Business Addr:** President Owner, Dealer, Robert Brogden Olathe Pontiac-Buick-GMC Inc, 1500 E Santa Fe St, Olathe, KS 66061, **Business Phone:** (913)782-1500.

### BROMELL, LORENZO ALEXIS
Football player. **Personal:** Born Sep 23, 1975, Georgetown, SC. **Educ:** Ga Mil Col, AA, gen studies, 1996; Clemson Univ, BA, sociol, 2006; Charis Bible Col, MA, bible training prog, 2014. **Career:** Football player (retired), executive; Miami Dolphins, defensive end, 1998-2002; Minn Vikings, defensive end, 2002-03; Oakland Raiders, defensive end, 2003-04; New York Giants, defensive end, 2004-05; Bromell & Assocs LLC, chief exec officer & chmn, 2007-13; Sports Mgt Worldwide, sport agt advisor, 2007-11; Offense Defense Football Camps, defensive line coach, 2009-11; Elite Gladiators Football Camps, founder, 2013-. **Orgs:** Chmn, Emergency Patient Care, 2007-2008; vice chmn, Nat Caucus & Ctr Black Aged Inc; Prof Athlete Network; Christian Professionals Worldwide. **Business Addr:** Founder, Elite Gladiators Football Camps, PO Box 5381, Niceville, FL 32578, **Business Phone:** (850)778-5391.

### BROMERY, KEITH MARCEL
Television journalist, school administrator. **Personal:** Born Sep 19, 1948, Washington, DC; son of Cecile Trescott and Randolph Wilson (deceased); married Susan Stanger; children: Marc Russell. **Educ:** Wash Jour Ctr, Wash, DC, cert, 1972; Univ Mass, Amherst, MA, BA, Am hist, 1972. **Career:** Chicago Daily News, Chicago, Ill, reporter, 1972-75; CBS News, New York, NY, writer, 1975-77; WBBM-AM Radio, Chicago, Ill, anchor/reporter, 1977-83; WMAQ-TV, Chicago, Ill, writer/reporter, 1983-84; Chicago Headline Club, writer, 1983-; WLS-TV, Chicago, Ill, reporter, 1984-, Ameritech Comed Entergy & GPU, Dir & Mgr; dir commun & media rels, Ft Lauderdale; Chicago Pub Schs, chief commun officer, 2000-02; Broward County Pub Schs, dir commun, 2003-09; Atlanta Pub Schs, dir media rels, 2009-12; Fla State Univ, dir commun & media rels, 2012-13; E Baton Rouge Parish Sch Syst, exec dir commun, 2013-15. **Orgs:** Soc Prof Journalists, 1983-; Nat Asn Black Journalists, 1987-; Chicago Asn Black Journalists, 1987-. **Home Addr:** 1623 N Vine St, Chicago, IL 60614-5117, **Home Phone:** (312)750-7103. **Business Addr:** Reporter, Director, WLS-TV, 190 N State St Suite 1100, Atlanta, GA 30303.

### BROMFIELD, CASSANDRA
Executive, fashion designer, business owner. **Career:** Cassandra Bromfields Co, pres & owner, currently. **Special Achievements:** Writer: Newsletter-Let's Get Married!. **Business Addr:** President, Owner, Cassandra Bromfield's Co, 25 Boeurm St 15B, Brooklyn, NY 11206-2314, **Business Phone:** (718)388-2055.

### BRONNER, BERNARD
Executive. **Personal:** son of Nathaniel H Sr; married Sheila; children: 5. **Educ:** Ga State Univ, BS, bus admin. **Career:** Upscale Magazine, publ, 1989-; Bronner Bros. Inc, cashier, beauty salesman, acct, vpres mkt, pres & chief exec officer, 1993-; Rainforest Films, partner. **Orgs:** Dir, Citizens Bancshares Corp, 1998. **Home Addr:** 465 Carondelett Cv SW, Atlanta, GA 30331-8353, **Home Phone:** (404)472-2908. **Business Addr:** President, Chief Executive Officer, Bronner Bros Inc, 2141 Powers Ferry Rd Suite 300, Marietta, GA 30067, **Business Phone:** (770)988-0015.

### BRONNER, SHEILA
Editor. **Personal:** married Bernard; children: 5. **Career:** Upscale Mag, ed-in-chief & owner, currently. **Home Addr:** 246 Willis Mill Rd SW, Atlanta, GA 30311-1728, **Home Phone:** (404)758-9066. **Business Addr:** Editor-in-Chief, Upscale Magazine, 2141 Powers Ferry Rd Suite 300, Marietta, GA 30067, **Business Phone:** (770)988-0015.

### BRONSON, REV. DR. FRED JAMES, SR.
Dentist, clergy. **Personal:** Born Jan 10, 1935, Cincinnati, OH; son of William; married Barbara Dobbins; children: Fred Jr, Mark, Stefanie, Shellie, Shawn & Sharon. **Educ:** Miami Univ, Oxford, OH, BA, 1958; Howard Univ, Wash, DC, DDS, 1962. **Career:** Ky Dent Col, instr, 1973-76; Cincinnati Dent Soc, chmn peer rev, 1979-81, vpres, 1980, pres elect, 1981, pres, 1982; Temple Church Christ Written Heaven, pastor, sr paster, currently; pvt pract dentist, currently. **Orgs:** Alpha Phi Alpha, 1957; deleg & trustee, Nat Dent Asn, 1962; deleg, Ohio Dent Asn, 1978-; fel Int Col Dentists, 1978; chmn, Dentist Concerned Dentists, 1980; Am Col Dentists, 1983; Pierre Fauchard Acad, 1988. **Honors/Awds:** Distinguished Service, Residents Lincoln Heights, OH, 1969. **Home Addr:** 4935 Paddock Rd, Cincinnati, OH 45237-5548, **Home Phone:** (513)821-2448. **Business Addr:** Pastor, Temple Church of Christ Written In Heaven, 9700 Wayne Ave, Lincoln Heights, OH 45215, **Business Phone:** (513)563-0624.

### BRONSON, DR. OSWALD PERRY, SR.
College president, executive. **Personal:** Born Jul 19, 1927, Sanford, FL; son of Flora Hollingshed and Uriah Perry; married Helen Carolyn Williams; children: Josephine Suzette, Flora Helen & Oswald Perry Jr. **Educ:** Bethune-Cookman Col, BS, 1950; Gammon Theol Sem, BD, 1959; N Western Univ, PhD, 1965; St Paul's Col, DD. **Career:** Pastor, 1950-66; Methodist Mission & Leadership Schs, lectr & teacher; Interdenominational Theol Ctr, dir field educ, 1964-68, vpres, 1966-68, pres, 1968-75; Bethune-Cookman Col, pres emer, 1975-2004; Edward Waters Col, pres, 2004-07. **Orgs:** Vice chmn, chmn, United Negro Col Fund; Am Asn Theol Schs; Fla Asn Cols & Univs; Nat Asn Advan Colored People; Sch Bd, Volusia Co; Fla Gov's Adv Coun Productivity; exec comt mem, Southern Regional Educ Bd; adv comt mem, Fla Sickle Cell Found; bd, Inst Black World, Wesley Community Ctr; Martin Luther King Ctr Social Chg; Am Red Cross; United Way; Nat Asn Equal Opportunity Higher Educ, United Methodist Comt Relief; bd dir, Fund Theol Educ; bd dir, Int Soc Theta Phi; Alpha Kappa Mu Hon Soc; Sigma Pi Phi Fraternity; Phi Delta Kappa; pres, chmn & bd dir, Relig Educ Asn US & Can. **Honors/Awds:** Herbert M Davidson Community Service Award, 2004; The Shafts of Light & Distinguished Alumnus Awards, Gammon Theol Sem, Bethune-Cookman Col; Crusade Scholar; United Negro College Fund Award; Keys to the Cities of Orlando, Ormond Beach, Lakeland, St. Petersburg, Jacksonville, Ft. Lauderdale, Florida; Appreciation Award, Nat Black Am Law Student Asn; Distinguished Service Award, United Beauty School Owners & Teachers Asn; Distinguished Asbury Award, The United Methodist Church; Dedicated Educational and Community Service Award, American Judges of the State of Florida, 2003; Lifetime Achievement Award, Alpha Phi Alpha, 2003; Citizen of the Year Award, March of Dimes of Volusia, 2003; Enterprise Award for Community Service, Halifax Area Chamber Commerce, 2004; J. Saxton Lloyd Distinguished Service Award, Civic League of Daytona and Halifax Area, 2004; Leadership and Accomplishment Award, St. Petersburg Chap B-CC Alumni Asn, 2004; Silas Tillman Award for Distinguished Service, 2004; State of Florida Congressional Resolution, 2004; ONYX Award in Education, Onyx Magazine Publishing Co, 2004; Herbert M. Davidson Memorial Award for Community Service, 2004; Education and Community Award for Service, Miami-Dade Chap B-CC Alumni Asn, 2004; Years of Service Award, Volusia County Police Chiefs & Sheriffs, 2004; DDiv, Saint Pauls Col; Doctor of Laws, Stetson Univ; Doctor of Laws, Albion Col. **Home Addr:** 107 Pine Cone Ct, Daytona Beach, FL 32119, **Home Phone:** (904)252-8667.

### BRONSON, ROBERT ZACK
**Personal:** Born Jan 28, 1974, Jasper, TX. **Educ:** McNeese State Univ, grad. **Career:** Football player (retired); San Francisco 49ers, defensive back, 1997-2003; St Louis Rams, free safety, 2004. **Honors/Awds:** Rookie of the Year, 1997.

### BRONZ, HON. LOIS GOUGIS TAPLIN
Government official, educator. **Personal:** Born Aug 20, 1927, New Orleans, LA; daughter of Alex Gougis and Elise Cousin; married Charles; children: Edgar, Francine Shorts & Shelly; married Chuck. **Educ:** Xavier Univ, BA, 1948; La State Univ, attended 1954; Wayne State Univ, MEd, 1961; Houston Tillotson Col, attended 1962; Col New Rochelle, attended 1974. **Career:** Orleans Parrish Sch Bd, classroom teacher, 1948-61; Xavier Univ, admr, 1960-66; Nat Merit Comm, consult, 1965-67; Civil Serv Comn, 1966; Manhattan ville Col, 1968-73; Greenburgh Cent 7 Sch Dist, teacher, 1968-82; Town Greenburgh, councilwoman, 1975-91; Westchester County Bd Legislators, legislator dist 8, 1993-, vice chair, 1996-2001, chmn, 2002-04. **Orgs:** Founder, League Good Gov, New Orleans, LA; League Women Voters, Greenburgh New York; Greenburgh Housing Coun; Community Facil Comn; Woodhill Neighborhood Asn; Xavier Univ Admis Comn; Inter-Alumni Coun United Negro Col Fund; Black Dems Westchester City; Afro-Am Found; co-chairperson, Westchester Womens Coun; bd dirs, United Way Westchester; bd dir, Union Child Day Care Ctr, Westchester Coalition; pres, Westchester Community Opportunity Prog; White Plains-Greenburgh, Nat Asn Am Colored People; Westchester Cty Penitentary; treas, Greenburgh Teachers Asn Ware Bd; founding mem, charter & exec mem, Westchester Black Womens Polit Caucus; Xavier Univ Nat Alumni Asn; Childrens Village Dobbs Ferry; Child Care Coun Westchester; Alpha Kappa Alpha; Pi Iota Omega; adv bd mem, Lois Bronz C Ctr; Westchester Arts Coun; Hudson Valley Coun Sr Citizens. **Honors/Awds:** Woman of the Year Award, Westchester County, 1990; Lifetime Achievement Award, Westchester Music Am, 1999; Lifetime of Courage Award, Omega Psi Phi, 2002; Leadership Award, Union Child Day Care Ctr, 2002; Appreciation Award, Fair view Fire Dept, 2002; Woman of the Year, Stroke Persons Westchester, 2002; Old Guard of White Plains Award, 2003; Senator Clinton African American Heritage Award, 2003; Greens burgh Educational Foundation Award, 2003; Fathers & Children Together Award, 2003; Achievement Award, Kappa Alpha Psi, 2003; American Asn University Women Award, 2003; Nat Asn Negro Business & Professional Womens Club Awareness Award; Black Democrats of Westchester Political Awareness Award; Westchester Black Women's Political Caucus Award; Westchester Advocate Newspaper Achievement Award; New York State Women's Political Caucus Award; Community Service Award, Westchester Black Lawyers Asn; Public Official of the Year, Westchester Chapter Nat Asn Social Workers; Westchester Senior Citizens Hall of Fame. **Special Achievements:** First African American woman elected to the Westchester County Board of Legislators, 1994. **Home Addr:** 282 Old Tarrytown Rd, White Plains, NY 10603-2823, **Home Phone:** (914)428-0449. **Business Addr:** Advisory Board Member, Lois Bronz Childrens Center, 30 Manhattan Ave, White Plains, NY 10607, **Business Phone:** (914)761-6134.

**BROOKE, EDWARD WILLIAM, III. See Obituaries Section.**

### BROOKER, MOE ALBERT
Educator, artist. **Personal:** Born Sep 24, 1940, Philadelphia, PA; son of Mack Henry and Lumisher Campbell; married Cheryl McClenney; children: Musa & Misha. **Educ:** Tyler Sch Fine Art, Temple Univ, BFA, 1970, MFA, 1972; Pa Acad fine Arts, cert, painting. **Career:** Cleveland Inst Art, assoc prof, 1976-85; Individual Artist fel, State Pa, 1989; Pa Acad Fine Arts, prof, 1985-91; Cleveland Arts fel, Womens Comm Cleveland, 1985; Parson Sch Design, chairperson found dept, 1991-93; Moore Col Art & Design, assoc prof, 1995-, Found Dept, chmn, 2004-12, Penny & Bob Fox distinguished prof, 2011-13, prof 2D fine arts & basics, currently. **Orgs:** Bd mem, New Orgn Visual Arts, 1978-85; panelist, Ohio Coun Arts, 1980; Mayo's Comm Arts, City Philadelphia, 1985-; Pa Coun Arts, State Pa, 1985-87; artist adv bd, Fabric Workshop, 1985-; Fine Arts Comm Pa Conv Ctr, 1990-93; adv bd, Mainline Ctr Arts, 1990-; chair, Phil Art Comn, 2008-. **Honors/Awds:** Commissioned by UNESCO, 1980; Artist Giant to China, City Philadelphia, China, 1987; Van Der Zee Award, Brandy wine Workshop; Van Der Zee Lifetime Achievement Award, 2003; Medal of Achievement from the Philadelphia Art Alliance, 2009; Artist of the Year Award, Govs Awards Arts, 2010. **Home Addr:** 6221 Greene St, Philadelphia, PA 19144-2617, **Home Phone:** (215)843-2557. **Business Addr:** Chairman, Professor, Moore College of Art & Design, 20th St & The Pkwy, Philadelphia, PA 19103-1179, **Business Phone:** (215)965-4093.

### BROOKS, AARON LAFETTE
Football player. **Personal:** Born Mar 24, 1976, Newport News, VA; married Tisa; children: 3. **Educ:** Univ Va, anthrop, 1998. **Career:** Football player (retired); Green Bay Packers, quaterback, 1999; New Orleans Saints, quarter back, 2000-05; Oakland Raiders, quaterback, 2006; land developer, currently. **Honors/Awds:** Named starting quarterback, New Orleans Saints, 2001; NFC Passing Touchdowns Leader, 2002; Hall of Fame, New Orleans Saints, 2014.

### BROOKS, ALVIN LEE
Government official. **Personal:** Born May 3, 1932, North Little Rock, AR; son of Chester Brooks and Estell; married Carol Rich; children: Ronall, Estelle, Carrie, Diane, Rosalind & Tameisha. **Educ:** Univ Mo, Kansas City, BA, hist & govt, 1959, MA, sociol, 1973. **Career:** Kans City Police Dept, detective & police officer; Kans City Sch Dist, home sch coordr, 1964-66; Neighborhood Youth Corp, Cath Diocese, Kans City, St Joseph, dir, out sch proj, 1966-67; Kans City, coordr pub info & com interpr, 1967-68; Human Rels Dept, Kans City, dir, 1968-73, 1980-, asst city mgr, 1973-80, rep; Ad Hoc Group Against Crime, pres, chief exec officer, bd mem, currently. **Orgs:** Nat Asn Human Rights Workers, 1968-; Int Asn Off Human Rights Agencies, 1969-; past

vpres, Bd Regents Ctr, Mo State Univ, 1975-82; chmn, Mo Comn Human Rights, 1975-82; convenor, Ad Hoc Group Against Crime, 1977, pres, 1991-; chmn, Mo Black Leadership Asn, 1979-82; vpres, Prime Heal Inc, 1987; St Joseph Cath Church. **Honors/Awds:** Man of the Year, Ivanhoe Club, 1969; Outstanding Citizen of the Year, Beta Omega Chap, Omega Psi Phi, 1972; Outstanding Citizen of the Year, Young Progressives, 1973; Alumni Achievement Award, Univ Mo, Kans City, 1975; Kans City Tomorrow, 1988; Nat Conf Christians & Jews, 1989; Press Nat Drug Adv Coun, 1989-92; UMKC Alumnus of the Year, 2009. **Special Achievements:** Recognized by former Drug Czar, William Bennet, as being one of the nation's "el3frontline soldiers in our war against drugs; " honored by Pres George Bush in November, 1989, for his work with Ad Hoc. **Home Addr:** 3717 Southern Hills Dr, Kansas City, MO 64137, **Home Phone:** (816)761-2116. **Business Addr:** Board Member, Ad Hoc Group Against Crime, 414 E 12th St 24th Fl City Hall, Kansas City, MO 64106, **Business Phone:** (816)513-1602.

## BROOKS, ARKLES CLARENCE, JR.

Salesperson. **Personal:** Born Aug 25, 1943, Detroit, MI; son of Arkles Clarence Sr; married Sarah L; children: Arkles III, Ira David, Alice Ruth & Sharon Louise. **Educ:** Southern Ill Univ, BA, 1967; Wayne State Univ, MA, 1976, educ specialist, gen admin, supv, 1999. **Career:** Nat Bank Detroit, asst br mgr, 1968-70; Aetna Life & Casualty, career agt, 1970-72; Detroit Bd Educ, math sci teacher, 1971-73; Upjohn Co, hosp sales specialist, 1973-; Allstate Ins, Southfield, Mich, sales assoc, 1987-; Dey L P Inc Distribr, Mich Dist, sales mgr, 1996-. **Orgs:** Wayne Co Notary Pub, 1968-; Nat Asn Life Underwriters, 1970-; pres, Varsity Club Inc, 1971-; corp treas, secy, Gospel Chapel Detroit Inc, 1972-, assoc pastor, 1985-, exec vpres, 1989-, pastor, pres, 1999-, sr pastor; bd mem, Circle Y Christian Camp; bd mem, corp secy, Int Christian Ministries, pres, chief exec officer, Transplus Ministries; African Americans Missions. **Home Addr:** 30436 Embassy Dr, Detroit, MI 48224, **Home Phone:** (313)642-6237. **Business Addr:** President, Senior Pastor, Gospel Chapel, 16241 Harper Ave, Detroit, MI 48224, **Business Phone:** (248)642-6236.

## BROOKS, AVERY FRANKLIN

Movie director, educator, actor. **Personal:** Born Oct 2, 1948, Evansville, IN; son of Samuel Leon and Eva Lydia Crawford; married Vicki Bowen; children: Ayana, Cabral & Asante. **Educ:** Ind Univ; Oberlin Col; Rutgers Univ, Nb NJ, BA, MFA, 1976. **Career:** Rutgers Univ, assoc prof theater, 1976-; Nat Black Arts Festival, artistic dir, 1993-96; Films: Solomon Northup's Odyssey, actor, 1984; Quest for Life, 2000; 15 Minutes, 2001; Star Trek: Legacy, 2006; TV series: "Solomon Northup's Odyssey ", 1984; "Uncle Tom's Cabin ", 1987; "Roots: The Gift ", 1988; "A Man Called Hawk", 1989; "Track down", 1991; "The Ernest Green Story ", 1993; "Spenser: For Hire?; "A Man Called Hawk"; "X: The Life & Times of Malcolm X"; "Othello"; "Star Trek: Deep Space Nine", actor & dir, 1993-99; "Gargoyles", 1996; "Jesus: The Complete Story", 2001; "Ancient Evidence", 2003; "Russell Simmons Presents Def Poetry", 2005; Mason Gross Sch Arts, prof theater, currently; jazz & blues covers, 2009. **Honors/Awds:** Hon Degrees, Oberlin Col, Tougaloo Univ, State Univ NY, Buffalo, Indiana Univ; Rutgers University Hall of Distinguished Alumni, 1993; OFTA Television Award, Online Film & Tv Asn, 1997. **Special Achievements:** First African-American to receive an MFA in acting and directing from Rutgers University; ACE Award nomination; First African-American women to earn a master's degree in music at Northwestern University; The Bible's Greatest Secrets, 2013. **Home Addr:** , Princeton, NJ. **Business Addr:** Professor of Theater, Mason Gross School of the Arts, 33 Livingston Ave, New Brunswick, NJ 08901-1959, **Business Phone:** (732)932-9360.

## BROOKS, BARRETT CHARLES

Football player. **Personal:** Born May 5, 1972, St. Louis, MO; married Sonji; children: Romel, Jasmine Johnson, Asia Johnson, Izreal & Chyna. **Educ:** Kans State Univ, grad. **Career:** Football player (retired); Philadelphia Eagles, left tackle, 1995-96, right tackle, 1997, tackle, 1998; Detroit Lions, right tackle, tackle, 1999, tackle, 2000; Green Bay Packers, 2002; New York Giants, 2002; Pittsburgh Steelers, tackle, 2003-06. **Orgs:** Omega Psi Phi fraternity; Delta Delta chap. **Home Addr:** 11 Berkshire Dr, Voorhees, NJ 08043-3448. **Business Addr:** Member, Delta Delta Chap, 851 E 15th Ave, Eugene, OR 97401.

**BROOKS, BARRY MACEY.** **See BROOKS, MACEY.**

## BROOKS, BERNARD W.

Executive, artist. **Personal:** Born Sep 6, 1939, Alexandria, VA; married Gwendolyn Aqui. **Educ:** Univ Md, attended 1960; Philadelphia Music Col Art, attended 1961; Corcoran Gallery Sch Art, BA, fine arts, 1962; Howard Univ, attended 1965. **Career:** A&B Assoc, Wash, DC, assoc dir; Howard Univ, Col Dent, chief med illusr, 1970-95; Opus 2 Galleries, assoc dir; Just Lookin gallery, artist, currently; Van Heusen Shirt Co, asst art dir; Grand Union Food Co Inc, Landover, Md, asst advert mgr, technician; Atlantic Res Corp, Alexandria, Va, tech illusr; Bernard W Brooks Studio, owner & dir; DC Art Asn, vpres; St. Croix, half time resident; B & B Assocs, owner, 2008-. **Orgs:** Publ artist, Am Chem Soc, Wash, DC; Wash Water Color Asn; pub rels dir, Nat Conf Artists. **Honors/Awds:** George F Muth Award, Howard Univ. **Home Addr:** 2920 Rittenhouse St NW, Washington, DC 20015. **Business Addr:** Artist, Just Lookin Gallery, 40 Summit Ave, Hagerstown, MD 21740, **Business Phone:** (301)714-2278.

## BROOKS, BRIAN A.

Executive, business owner, association executive. **Educ:** Franklin Univ, MBA, 2003. **Career:** EE Ward Moving & Storage Co LLC, pres & owner, currently. **Orgs:** Bd dir, Better Bus Bur, currently. **Honors/Awds:** Human Services Award, 2016. **Business Addr:** Board of Director, Better Business Bureau, 1169 Dublin Rd, Columbus, OH 43215-1005, **Business Phone:** (614)486-6336.

## BROOKS, CARL

Executive. **Personal:** Born Aug 1, 1949, Philadelphia, PA; son of Nathaniel and Sarah Lee Williams; married Drena Hastings; children: Tarik & Karima. **Educ:** Hampton Univ, BS, 1971; Southern Ill Univ, MBA, 1976; Univ Iowa, exec develop prog, 1981; Dartmouth Col, Amos Tuck Sch Bus Admin, Tuck exec prog, 1990. **Career:** Jersey Cent Power & Light Co, Morristown, NJ, corp mgr contracts, 1977-86; GPU Serv Corp, NJ, vpres, mats & serv, 1990-96; Allenhurst, NJ, shore div, div dir, 1986-90; GPU Generation Inc, vpres finance & admin; Howard Univ, Sch Bus Admin, hon chair; GENCO, chief mkt officer; GPU Energy, Human & Tech Resources, vpres; Exec Leadership Found, chair, 1999-2001; Exec Leadership Coun, pres & chief exec officer, 2001-10. **Orgs:** Exec bd dir, Nat Minority Supplier Devel Coun; chmn, Advocacy Comn; chmn, corp fund-raising, United Way, 1986-90; chmn, Leadership NJ; African Relief Fund; bd dir, Red Cross; Red Bank Chamber Com, 1986-; YMCA; Franklin Little League; Am Soc Asn Exec; Nat Asn Corp Dir; DaimlerChrysler Financial Serv Diversity Coun; Am Socs Asn Execs; Nat Black MBA Asn; Nat Urban Leagues Best Diversity Practices Study Adv Coun; Nat Minority Golf Scholar Fund; Va High-Tech Partnership; Princeton Ctr Leadership Group; Chamber Com; bd Visitor, Howard Univ; bd advisor, vice chair, Hampton Univ; chmn, GPU Diversity Action Coun; Childrens Home Reading; Princeton Leadership Group; Northern NJ INROADS Inc. **Home Addr:** 1905 S Lynn St, Arlington, VA 22202-1653, **Home Phone:** (703)920-0819. **Business Addr:** President, Chief Executive Officer, Executive Leadership Council Foundation, 1010 Wisc Ave NW Suite 520, Washington, DC 20007, **Business Phone:** (202)298-8226.

## BROOKS, CAROL LORRAINE

Government official, administrator. **Personal:** Born Nov 23, 1955, Brooklyn, NY. **Educ:** Univ Vt, BA, 1977; Rutgers Univ, attended 1979; Sch Int Training, attended 1975. **Career:** Walter Russell Scholar, 1977; CBS News Inc, proj coordr, 1978-81; NJ Off Gov, spec asst, 1981-85; NJ Dept Environ Protection, spec asst, 1982-90, admin, 1985-. **Orgs:** Bd dir, Family Serv Asn Trenton & Hopewell Valley, 1983-; comt mem, NJ Martin Luther King Jr Commemorative Comn, 1985-; Urban League Guild Metrop Trenton, 1986-. **Home Addr:** 15 Winthrop Rd, Lawrenceville, NJ 08648, **Home Phone:** (609)896-1970. **Business Addr:** Administrator, New Jersey Environmental Protection, 440 E State St, Trenton, NJ 08625, **Business Phone:** (609)984-9749.

## BROOKS, DR. CAROLYN BRANCH

Educator, college administrator. **Personal:** Born Jul 8, 1946, Richmond, VA; daughter of Charles W and Shirley Booker; married Henry M; children: Charles T, Marcellus L, Alexis J & Toni A. **Educ:** Tuskegee Univ, Tuskegee, AL, BS, biol, 1968, MS, biol, 1971; Ohio State Univ, Columbus, OH, PhD, microbiol, 1977. **Career:** Bullock County Bd Educ, Union Springs, Ala, sci teacher, 1968-69; Macon County Bd Educ, Tuskegee, Ala, sci teacher, 1971-72; Va Hosp, Tuskegee, Ala, res technician, 1972-73; Ohio State Univ, Columbus, OH, grad teaching asst, 1975-77; Ky State Univ, Frankfort, Ky, prin investr & prog dir, 1978-81; Univ Md Eastern Shore, Land-Grants Prog, res dir, asst prof, 1981-87, assoc prof, 1987-96, prof, 1996-, dept chmn, Sch Agr & Natl Sci, dean, dir, Agr Exp Sta, currently. **Orgs:** Salvation Army Youth Club Coun; Nat Asn Advan Colored People; Nat Asn Univ Women; Nat Res Coun, 1993; chair, Assoc res dir; Minorities Agr, Natural Resources, Related Serv; Am Soc Microbiol, Mult Sclerosis Coun, 1994-95; Nat Acad Sci Comt; bd dir, LEAD21. **Home Addr:** 30173 Stoneybrooke Dr, Salisbury, MD 21804, **Home Phone:** (410)546-3414. **Business Addr:** Director, Professor, University Maryland Eastern Shore, Early Childhood Res Ctr, Princess Anne, MD 21853, **Business Phone:** (410)651-6072.

## BROOKS, CHRISTOPHER A.

Biographer, writer, educator. **Educ:** Univ Md, College Park, BA, 1978; Univ Mich, MA, 1980; Univ Tex, Austin, PhD, 1989. **Career:** Va Commonwealth Univ, Col Humanities & Sci, prof & coordr Anthrop Prog, 1990-; Mich State Univ, prof, 1992; Univ Md, prof, 1995-98; Arrupe Jesuit col, lectr, 1999-2000. **Honors/Awds:** Fulbright Scholarship, recipient, 1999-2000. **Special Achievements:** "The Souls of Black Folk 100 Years Later," Contributor (University of Missouri Press, 2003); "African and African-American Religions, Religions, and Religion and War," Contributor (Routledge, 2001 and 2003); "Encyclopedia of African American Culture," Contributor (Greenwood Press, 2010); "The African American Almanac," General Editor, (Cengage/Gale, 2011); "I Never Walked Alone: The Autobiography of an American Singer," Author (with the late Shirley Verrett) (John Wiley, 2003); "Follow Your Heart: Moving with the Giants of Jazz, Swing and Rhythm and Blues," Author (with Joe Evans) (University of Illinois Press, 2008); "Dangerous Intimacy: Ten African American Men with HIV," Author (with Christopher Coleman) (Linus Publications, 2009); "Through the Voices of Men: South African Men Speak About HIV," Author (Linus Books, 2013); "Roland Hayes: An American Legacy Restored," Author (with Robert Sims) (Indiana University Press, 2014). **Business Addr:** Professor, Virginia Commonwealth University, Rm 213 Lafayette Hall, Richmond, VA 23220, **Business Phone:** (804)827-1232.

## BROOKS, REV. CLYDE HENRY

Labor relations manager, manager, executive director. **Personal:** Born Sep 5, 1941, Danville, IL; son of George and Venie. **Educ:** Western Ill Univ, BS, 1958, MS. **Career:** Harper Community Col, fac; Chicago Metro Chap S Christian Leadership Conf, pres, 1972-; Chicago Comn Youth Welfare, sch teacher, high sch counr. **Orgs:** Probation officer, Juv Ct Cook Co Chicago, 1959-61; teacher, Wendel Phillips Eve Sch, 1959-65; neighborhood worker, Chicago Comn Youth Welfare, 1961-64; coun, Marillac Settlement House, 1963-66; employ coun, Ill State Employ Serv Chicago, 1964; coun, Crane HS Chicago, 1964; supvr, Dept Ed JOBS Proj Chicago 1964-65; dir, Sears Roebuck Community Coop Proj Chicago, 1965-66; teacher, St Mary Lake Sem Mundelein, IL, 1965; area dir, Cook Co Off Equal Opport Inc Chicago, 1966-67; assoc & exec dir & manpower dir, Cook Co Off Equal Opport Inc Chicago, 1968-73; coun, Ill Drug Abuse Prog, 1969-71; pres & bd chmn, Behav Res Action Soc Sci, Chicago, 1969-71; ho n, Ed Labs IElk Grove Village, IL, 1969-71; cvis prof, Harper Col, 1970-77; field work instr, Univ Chicago, 1972-; chmn & chief exec officer, Minority Econ Resourses Corp 1972-; nat mem, dir, Nat Equal Employ Opport & Employee Rels Blue Cross & Blue Shield Asns, 1973-; Chicago C C & Indust, 1973-; Ill State C C, 1973-; Ill Parole Bd, 1993-; mem, Ill Prisoner Rev Bd; mem, Ill Human Rights Comn; Mt Prospect Fire & Police Comn; retired chmn, chief exec officer, founder, Minority Econ Resources Corp; Interfaith Church Coun Mt Prospect; pres, Ill Comn Diversity & Human Rels or Suburban Human Rels Comn; nat bd mem, Southern Christian Leadership Conf; consult, Scott Foresman Publ Co. **Special Achievements:** First African American to teach African American History at St Mary of the Lake Seminary. **Home Addr:** 1240 S Elmhurst Rd Apt 107, Mount Prospect, IL 60056. **Business Addr:** President, Chief Executive Officer, Suburban Human Relations Commission/Illinois Commission On Diversity & Human Relations, 1502 Kendal Ct, Arlington Heights, IL 60004, **Business Phone:** (847)253-7538.

## BROOKS, CORNELL WILLIAM

Executive director, lawyer, president (organization). **Personal:** Born Jan 1, 1961?, El Paso, TX; married Janice; children: Cornell II & Hamilton. **Educ:** Jackson State Univ, BA, polit sci; Boston Univ, MDiv; Yale Univ, JD. **Career:** US Dept Justice, trial atty; Fed Commun Comn (FCC), sr coun; NJ Inst Social Justice, pres & chief exec officer; US Ct Appeals Fourth Circuit, judicial clerkship; Fair Housing Coun Greater Wash, exec dir; NJ Pub Broadcasting Authority, vice-chair; Nat Asn Advan Colored People (NAACP), pres & chief exec officer, 2014-. **Orgs:** Exec dir, Fair Housing Coun Greater Wash; Lawyers' Comt Civil Rights Under Law, trial atty; bd trustee, vice chair, E Orange Gen Hosp, 2008; Nj, Comt Homeland Security & Corrections, 2010; trustee, Common Cause, Nat Gov Bd, 2012-. **Special Achievements:** In 1998, ran for the U.S. Congress for the 10th District of Virginia's Democratic nominee position. **Business Addr:** President, National Association for the Advancement of Colored People, 4805 Mt Hope Dr, Baltimore, MD 21215, **Business Phone:** (410)580-5777.

## BROOKS, DR. DAISY M. ANDERSON

Child care worker, business owner, executive director. **Personal:** children: Yolanda Denise, Wadell Jr & Cassandra Annette. **Educ:** Nat Inst Practical Nursing, Chicago, practical nurses training; Northwestern Med Sch, Chicago, training med tech; Pac Western Univ, MA, human resources develop; Faith Grant Col, EdD. **Career:** Tots & Toddlers Day Care Ctr Inc, Waukegan, Ill, co-owner, gen contractor, 1975; Victory Mem Hosp, med tech, Phys & Surg Lab, Waukegan, Ill, supvry med techl; Daisy's Nursery, co-owner & exec dir, Daisy's Resource & Develop Ctr, chief exec officer, pres, currently. **Orgs:** Worthy Matron Order Eastern Star, 1974; officer, Golden Circle 59 Deaconess Shiloh Baptist Church; pres, Music Dept; N Chicago Br, Nat Asn Advan Colored People; pres, Progressive Comt Organ N Chicago; secy, Cent Grade Sch PTA; treas, N Chicago Black Caucas; bd dir, Altrusa Int Clb/Day Care Crisis Coun State Ill; Citizen Adv Comt, Lake Co Area Voc Ctr; N Chicago HS Voc Adv Comt; vpres, N Chicago Great Lakes Va C C; vpres, Day Care Crisis Coun St Ill/Citizens Adv Comt, N Chicago Comn Block Develop; chairperson, Scholar Comn; Mt Sinai Baptist Church; pres, N Chicago Dist 64 Band Parents Asn. **Honors/Awds:** Bus Person of the Year; Citizen of the Year; Humanitarian of the Year. **Home Addr:** 1920 Sherman Ave, North Chicago, IL 60064-2318, **Home Phone:** (847)689-3010. **Business Addr:** Chief Executive Officer, President, Daisys Resource Development Center, 1919 Dr Daisy M Brooks Dr, North Chicago, IL 60064, **Business Phone:** (847)473-4898.

## BROOKS, DR. DANA DEMARCO

Dean (education). **Personal:** Born Aug 1, 1951, Hagerstown, MD. **Educ:** Hagerstown Jr Col, Hagerstown, MD, AA, 1971; Towson State Col, Towson, MD, BS, 1973; WVA Univ, Morgantown, W VA, MS, 1976, EdD, 1979. **Career:** Wash County, teacher, 1974; W V Univ, grad teaching asst, 1974-78, from instr phys educ to assoc prof phys educ, 1978-88, provost off, minority recruitment, retention coordr, 1986-87, actg asst dean phys educ sch, 1986-87, actg chairperson, sport dept, 1987, Phys Educ Sch, prof, 1988-, actg dean, 1988, assoc dean, 1987-92, actg grad coordr, 1991, interm dean, 1992-93, dean, 1993-. **Orgs:** WVa Asn Health, Phys Educ, Recreation, Dance, 1983-84; vpres, 1987-88, Midwest Dist, Health, Phys Educ, Recreation, Dance; Phi Delta Kappa; N Am Soc Sport Sociol; pres, Am Alliance Health; Phys Educ, Recreation, Dance, 2009-10; fel, Am Acad Kinesiology & Phys Educ. **Honors/Awds:** Outstanding Teacher of the Year School of Physical Education, W Va Univ, 1979-83, 1986-87; Young Professional Award, Mid W Dist, Health, Physical Education, Recreation, Dance, 1982; Honor Award, W Va Asn, Health, Physical Education, Recreation, Dance, 1985; Social Justice Award, W Va Univ, 1992; Ray O Duncan Award, W Va Asn Health, Physical Education, Recreation, Dance, 1991; Rev Dr Martin Luther King Jr, Achievement Award, 1997; Outstanding Alumnus Award, Hagerstown Jr Col, 50th Anniversary; Towson Univ Dean's Recognition Award, 1999; Hagerstown Community Col Sports Hall of Fame, 2003; Midwest AAHPERD Honor Award, 2004-05; E.B. Henderson Award, 2006, AAKPE Fellow, AAHPERD pres, 2009-10; Fellow of the North American Society of HPERSD Professionals, 2008; Living the Dream Award. **Home Addr:** 811 Timberline, Morgantown, WV 26505, **Home Phone:** (304)599-8815. **Business Addr:** Dean, Professor, West Virginia University, 258 Coliseum, Morgantown, WV 26506-6116, **Business Phone:** (304)293-0826.

## BROOKS, DERRICK DEWAN

Football player, executive, radio host. **Personal:** Born Apr 18, 1973, Pensacola, FL; son of Geraldine Mitchell; married Carol; children: Brianna Monai, Denice, Derrick Jr & Darius. **Educ:** Fla State Univ, BA, bus commun. **Career:** Football player (retired), analyst, exec; Tampa Bay Buccaneers, linebacker & right line backer, 1995-2008, 2009-10; ESPN, football analyst, currently; Sirius NFL Radio, cohost, currently; Tampa Bay Storm, Arena Football League, co-owner & pres, 2011-. **Orgs:** Founder, Brooks Bunch Found; founder, youth scholar found; bd trustees, Fla State Univ, 2003. **Honors/Awds:** Consensus All-American, 1993 & 1994; Tampa Tribune People's Champion Award, 1998; Florida Sports Awards, 2000, 2001; Walter Payton Man of the Year Award, 2000; Defensive Player of the Year, Nat Football League, 2002; EDDIE Award, Hillsborough Education Found, 2002; Alumni Linebacker of the Year, Nat Football League, 2002; Bart Starr Award, 2003; Byron "Whizzer" White Man of the Year Award, Nat Football League, 2003; Most Valuable Player, Pro Bowl, 2005; Champion, Super Bowl, XXXVII; Florida Sports Hall of Fame; Pro Football Hall of Fame, 2014. **Special Achievements:** TV Series: "The Road to Canton: Warren Sapp - Relentless", 2013; Utopia: The Temple of Paradise, 2013. **Business Addr:** Co-Host, Sirius NFL Radio, 1221 Avenue of the Americas, New York, NY 10020.

### BROOKS, DIANE K.
Executive director. **Educ:** Howard Univ, Wash, DC, BA, psychol; Gallaudet Univ, MA. **Career:** Nat Tech Inst Deaf, assoc dir, 2003-, Northeast Tech Assistance Ctr, dir, assoc dean outreach & tech assistance, currently. **Orgs:** Postsecondary Educ Progs Network; Rochester Sch Deaf; Conf Educ Adminr Schs & Progs; NTID Ctr Outreach; bd mem, CEASD; bd mem, PEPNet; bd mem, Netac Technol Co Ltd. **Business Addr:** Associate Dean for Outreach & Technical Assistance, Director, National Technical Institute for the Deaf, 52 Lomb Memorial Dr, Rochester, NY 14623, **Business Phone:** (585)475-6700.

### BROOKS, DON LOCELLUS
Executive. **Personal:** Born Galveston, TX; married Charlotte; children: Eric, Don Jr & Chris. **Educ:** Galveston Col, AA, mgt, 1975; Univ Houston, BS, mkt & mgt, 1977; Univ Tex, Austin, finance leadership, 1978. **Career:** Guaranty Fed Savings & Loans, mgt trainee, 1976-78, reg savings coordr, 1978-80, asst vpres, 1980-81, vpres savings, 1981. **Orgs:** Founder, Galveston Col Key Club, 1975; bd trustee, Galveston Park Bd, 1982-; bd dir, Family Serv Ctr, 1984-85; exec comn, United Way Inc, Galveston, 1984-85, Legis Comt Galveston, 1984-; coun rep, City Galveston, 1984-; chmn, Fiscal Auditing & Ins Comn, City Galveston Park Bd trustee, 1984-85. **Home Addr:** 5506 Ave Pl, Galveston, TX 77550.

### BROOKS, FABIENNE
Law enforcement officer, president (organization), commander. **Personal:** children: 4. **Educ:** FBI Acad, grad; Western Wash Univ, attended 1971; Pac Northwest Command Col, grad. **Career:** Commander (retired); King County Sheriffs Off, officer, sergeant, lt, capt, precinct comdr, chief, 1978-2004; Atlantic fel pub policy, London, Eng, 1996; Wash Chap, FBI Nat Acad Assoc Inc; Brooks SAC Inc, pres, 2004-; City Seattle, policy advisor, 2012-13; Touchstone Productions, content expert. **Orgs:** Int Asn Women Police; dir, community proj coordr, Nat Coalition Bldg Inst, 2004-; consult, Ctr C & Youth Justice; Seattle Univ Criminal Justice Adv Coun; Bellevue Police Dept Diversity Coun; King County Sexual Assault Resource Ctr; First AME Church; Domestic Abuse Womens Network; Pk Lake/White Ctr Boys & Girls Club; pres, Black Law Enforcement Asn; Wash State Chap FBI Nat Acad Assocs; Wash State Chap Nat Orgn Black Law Enforcement Execs; secy, FBI NA Wash Chap; secy, Wash State Chap NOBLE, 2007-; life mem, NOBLE; life mem, Nat Asn Advan Colored People; bd mem, Seattle Neighborhood Group. **Home Phone:** (425)641-6273. **Business Addr:** Law Enforcement Program Director, National Coalition Building Institute, 8403 Colesville Rd Suite 1100, Silver Spring, MD 20910, **Business Phone:** (202)785-9400.

### BROOKS, GOLDEN AMEDA
Actor. **Personal:** Born Dec 1, 1970, San Francisco, CA. **Educ:** Univ Calif, Berkeley, BA, lit & sociol; Sarah Lawrence Col, MA. **Career:** Films: Drive by A Love Story, 1997; Hell's Kitchen, 1998; Timecode, 2000; Impostor, 2002; Motives, 2004; Beauty Shop, 2005; Something New, 2006; A Good man is hard to find, 2008; Polish Bar, 2010; The Inheritance, 2010; The Perfect Gift, 2011; A Beautiful Soul, 2012; The Great Divide, 2012; The Marriage Lover, 2013. TV series: "Linc's", 1999; "The Parkers", 2000; "Girlfriends", 2000-08; "Moesha, 2001; "Haunted", 2002; "Star Trek: Enterprise", 2004; "Eve, 2005; "CSI: Miami", 2008; "The Exes", 2011; "In Sickness and in Health", 2012; "Hart of Dixie", 2012-13. **Orgs:** Vol, Pediat AIDS Found; vol, AIDS Proj, Los Angeles. **Honors/Awds:** BET Comedy Award, 2004; Nominee, Image Award, 2008; Grand Jury Prize, Am Black Film Festival, 2010. **Special Achievements:** Nominated for Outstanding Actress in a Comedy Series, Image Award, 2003; Black Reel Award for Best Actress, 2005. **Business Addr:** Actress, United Paramount Network (UPN), 11800 Wilshire Blvd, Los Angeles, CA 90025, **Business Phone:** (310)575-7000.

### BROOKS, GEN. HARRY W., JR.
Executive, army officer, chief executive officer. **Personal:** Born May 17, 1928, Indianapolis, IN; son of Harry W Sr and Nora E; married June Hezekiah; children: 4. **Educ:** Univ Nebr, Omaha, BA, 1962; Univ Okla, MA, 1973; AUS War Col, Carlysle, PA; Army Command & Gen Staff Col, Army War Col. **Career:** Major general (retired), chairperson; USAR, 1962-65; Command & Gen Staff Col, stud officer, 1965-66; 72nd Field Artil Group, comdr, 1970-72; 2nd Div, Korea, asst comdr, 1973-74; AUS, pvt maj gen, 1947-76, comndg gen, 25th Inf Div, HI, 1974-76; Amfac Inc, sr vpres & pub affairs dir, 1978-82, exec vpres & chmn hort group, 1982-84; Advan Consumer Mkt Corp, chmn & chief exec officer & founder, 1985-96; Gurney Seed & Nursery Corp, chmn & chief exec officer, 1984-90; Gurney Wholesale Inc, chmn & chief exec officer, 1985-90; Western Comput GroupInc, chmn & chief exec, 1985-90; Brooks Intl, pres, 2004, chmn, currently. **Orgs:** Trustee, Freedom Forum, 1976-; dir, Occup Med Corp Am, 1985-96; trustee, San Mateo Easter Seals, 1988-89; dir, San Francisco Opera, 1988-92; Seven Air Medale, 1967; advisor, SpaceVest Ltd; dir, Int Diplomacy Coun; bd mem, TopArtist Inc. **Home Addr:** 3212 Malibu Vista St, Las Vegas, NV 89117, **Home Phone:** (702)304-4454. **Business Addr:** Chairman, Brooks Intl, 763 Santa Fe Dr, Denver, CO 80204, **Business Phone:** (303)825-8700.

### BROOKS, DR. HENRY MARCELLUS
School administrator, executive director. **Personal:** Born Oct 16, 1942, Tuskegee, AL; son of Ruth Jackson and Ewing Tipton; married Carolyn D Branch; children: Charles Tipton, Marcellus Leader, Alexis Janine & Toni Andrea. **Educ:** Tuskegee Univ, Tuskegee, Ala, BS, 1965, MEd, 1966; Ohio State Univ, Columbus, OH, PhD, 1975. **Career:** Auburn Univ, Union Spring, Ala, exten farm agt, 1967-73; Ky State Univ, Frankfort, Ky, exten specialist & asst admin, 1975-80; Univ Md Eastern Shore Exten, Princess Anne, exten admin, 1980-, Coop Exten Serv, adminr, assoc dir, assoc prof & coordr, currently, Agr Exp Sta, asst dir, currently. **Orgs:** Sigma Pi Phi; Kappa Alpha Psi; bd dir, Nat 4-H Cong; bd dir, J Exten. **Honors/Awds:** Eastern Shore President's Award, Univ Md, 1992; Pres Delegate Assembly, Mid-Eastern Athletic Conf, 1992, honored at an African American History Month ceremony, 2008; Black Caucus Award. **Home Addr:** 30173 Stoneybrooke Dr, Salisbury, MD 21804-2486, **Home Phone:** (410)546-3414. **Business Addr:** Extension Administrator & Associate Professor, Associate Director, University of Maryland Eastern Shore, Rm 2122 Richard A Henson Ctr, Princess Anne, MD 21853, **Business Phone:** (410)651-6206.

### BROOKS, JAMES ROBERT
Football player, executive, actor. **Personal:** Born Dec 28, 1958, Warner Robins, GA; married Simone Renee; children: James Darnell & Tianna Renee. **Educ:** Auburn Univ, attended 1980. **Career:** Football player (retired); San Diego Chargers, running back, kick returner, punt returner, 1981-83; Cincinnati Bengals, running back, 1984-91; Cleveland Browns, running back, 1992; Tampa Bay Buccaneers, running back, 1992; GSI Com, warehouse assoc, currently. Films: 1981 NFL Draft, 1981; 1981 AFC Championship Game, 1982; 1988 AFC Championship Game, 1989; Super Bowl XXIII, 1989; What the Frock?, 2007; Casa Hollywood, 2015. **Honors/Awds:** All-Am, Auburn Univ; High School All-American Nat Champion, Warner-Robins, Ga team; All Pro; played in Pro Bowl, 1986, 1988, 189, 1990. **Special Achievements:** Led the NFL in total yards, rushing, receiving, punt & kickoff returns, 1981-82. **Business Addr:** Warehouse Associate, GSI Commerce, 40 Logistics Blvd, Walton, KY 41094, **Business Phone:** (859)292-1200.

### BROOKS, JAMES TAYLOR
Military leader. **Personal:** Born Mar 3, 1945, Memphis, TN; son of Booker T and Elizabeth P; married Jacqueline D; children: Bryant O, Brandi C & Kamaroon A. **Educ:** Memphis Univ, BS, 1976. **Career:** Firestone Tire & Rubber Co, prod supvr, 1968-83; Albright Chemical Co, sales mgr, 1983-86; Mich Air Nat Guard, recruiting & retention supt, 1986-. **Orgs:** NCOA Grad Asn, 1983-; Nat Guard Asn Mich, 1986-; Cummings St Baptist Church, 1989-; Wade A McCree Jr Scholar Prog, 1990-; Big Brother & Big Sister, 1994-; Tuskegee Airmen, Detroit Chap, 1995-; Nat Asn Advan Colored People. **Honors/Awds:** Service Award, Wade A McCree Jr Scholarship Program, 1995. **Home Addr:** 2500 S Wash Ave, Lansing, MI 48913-5101. **Business Addr:** Recruiting & Retention Superintendent, Michigan Air National Guard, 25 S Wash, Lansing, MI 48913, **Business Phone:** (517)372-8767.

### BROOKS, JOHN S.
Manager. **Personal:** Born Mar 4, 1951, Greenwood, MS; son of John J and Bernice; married Barbara E; children: Jason S. **Educ:** ITT Tech Inst, Indianapolis, AA, elec & elec engineering technol, 1971; Ind Wesleyan Univ, BS, bus mgt, 1992; Anderson Univ, MBA, 1996. **Career:** JS Brooks Realty, owner; Delphi Automotive, prod worker, 1969-71, lab technician, 1972-83, supvr eng labs, 1983-87, mgr prod eng labs, 1987-88, supvr switch eng, 1988-91, mgr, switch eng, 1992, test & facil mgr, 1992, chief engr, 2006; Western & Southern Financial Group, sales rep, 2008-10, sales mgr, 2010-11; Battles & Assocs, advisor, 2011-12; J S Brooks Agency, founder & advisor, 2012-; ClemCorp, trustee, 2013-; Brooks Advisors LLC, advisor, 2013-. **Orgs:** Anderson Zion Baptist Church, 1962-; past master, Peerless Lodge No 32 Masonic, 1980-; life mem, NAACP, 1983-; scholar comt, Prince Hall Grand Lodge Ind, 1984-; bd chmn, Wilson Boys & Girls Club, 1994-96; qual comt mem, St Johns Hosp, 1996-; coun pres, Ind Area Coun, Boys & Girls Clubs Am, 1997-; rep, Ind & Ky, Nat Area Coun; Boys & Girls Clubs Am, 1997; trustee, Boys & Girls Club Dayton, 2004-11; trustee, Frank Callen Boys & Girls Club Savannah, 2015-, vpres. **Honors/Awds:** US Patent Off, US patent No 4, 481, 925, 1984; Worshipful Master of the Year, Prince Hall Grand Lodge Ind, 1984. **Home Addr:** 85 Royal Troon, Springboro, OH 45066-8900, **Home Phone:** (937)748-9767. **Business Addr:** Test & Facility Manager, Delphi-E General Motors, 2900 S Scatterfield Suite 6A, Anderson, IN 46013, **Business Phone:** (765)646-7210.

### BROOKS, JOSEPH
City planner. **Educ:** San Jose State Univ, BA, bus & econs; Univ Calif, Berkeley, MA, city & regional planning. **Career:** Emergency Land Fund, Atlanta, Ga, pres; Rev Black Polit Econ, New York, NY, ed; San Francisco Found, prog exec neighborhood & community develop; PolicyLink, vpres civic engagement, currently. **Orgs:** Nat co-chair, Neighborhood Funders Group; vice chair, Asn of Black Found Execs. **Honors/Awds:** New Commitment to Vitality Oakland Tribune, Op-ed, 2003; A Convoy Hope Men & Boys Color San Francisco Chronicle, Op-ed, 2007. **Business Addr:** Vice President for Civic Engagement, Policy Link, 1438 Webster St Suite 303, Oakland, CA 94612, **Business Phone:** (510)663-2333.

### BROOKS, JOYCE RENEE WARD
Systems analyst. **Personal:** Born Sep 9, 1952, Kansas City, MO; married John L; children: Carmen R & Leah V. **Educ:** Washington Univ, BS, bus admin, 1974. **Career:** Mobil Oil Corp, programmer & analyst, 1972-73; Southwestern Bell Tele Co, acct off supv, 1974-78, acct mgr, 1978-80, asst staff mgr, 1980-85, systs analyst, 1985. **Home Addr:** 12844 Stoneridge Dr, Florissant, MO 63033-4623, **Home Phone:** (314)355-0377.

### BROOKS, BRIGADIER GEN. LEO AUSTIN, SR.
Military leader, executive. **Personal:** Born Aug 9, 1932, Alexandria, VA; married Naomi Ethel Lewis; children: Leo Jr, Vincent Keith & Marquita Karen. **Educ:** Va State Univ, BS, instrumental mus educ, 1954; Cent St Univ, Wilbeforce, OH, bus admin additional study, 1962; George Washington Univ, Wash, DC, MS, finance mgt, 1966; AUS Command & Gen Staff Col; Nat War Col; Res Officers' Training Corps, distinguished mil grad. **Career:** Military leader (retired); Hq Dept Army, Wash, DC, cong coordr, 1967-70; Joint Chiefs Staff, Wash, DC, Cambodian desk officer, 1972-74; Sacramento Army Depot, comndg officer, 1974-76; 13th Corps Sport Command, Ft Hood, TX, comndg officer, 1976-78; US Cong Off Dep Chief Staff Logistics, HQDA, budget liaison; AUS, Qm Corps, second lt, 2nd Inf Div Alaska, platoon leader, Troop Support Agency, Ft Lee, VA, comndg gen, 1978, maj gen, 1984, brig gen; City Philadelphia, managing dir, 1985. **Orgs:** Master, Acacia Lodge 32 Prince Hall, F&A Masons, VA, 1967-; bd dir, United Urban League, Sacramento, CA, 1974-76; bd dir, Gr Sacramento United Way, 1974-76; chmn bd, Advis Jesuit High Sch, Sacramento, CA, 1974-76; bd dir, United Serv Auto Asn, 1978-; pres, Fed Exec Asn, 1979-; Am Bar Asn Coun Legal Educ & Accreditation law schs. **Honors/Awds:** Fame of the Year, Freedom Found, Forge, PA, 1980; Hon doctor laws degree, New Eng Sch Law. **Special Achievements:** First African American Army General with two sons who have attained the rank of General.

### BROOKS, LEROY
Government official. **Career:** Lowndes County, county supvr dist 5, currently. **Orgs:** Nat Asn Counties; bd supervisors, Lowndes County, Dist 5. **Home Addr:** 214 12th St N, Columbus, MS 39701, **Home Phone:** (662)328-0032. **Business Addr:** Supervisor, Lowndes County, County Courthouse, Columbus, MS 39703-1364, **Business Phone:** (662)329-5871.

### BROOKS, LONNIE (LEE BAKER, JR.)
Musician. **Personal:** Born Dec 18, 1933, Dubuisson, LA; children: Ronnie Baker & Wayne Baker. **Career:** Laborer, Port Arthur, TX; professional musician, 1955-. **Special Achievements:** Recorded songs with Red Hot Louisiana Band, "Family Rules" and "The Crawl"; recorded songs "Roll, Roll, Roll", "Big Boss Man", and "Two Headed Man" (1978); recorded albums "Broke an' Hungry" (Capitol, 1969), "Sweet Home Chicago" (Black & Blue, 1975), "Bayou Lightening" (Alligator, 1979), "Turn on the Night" (1981), "Hot Shot" (1983), "Wound Up Tight" (1986), "Live from Chicago" (1988), "Satisfaction Guaranteed" (1991), "Roadhouse Blues", and "Lone Star Shootout" (1999); appeared at the San Francisco Blues Fest, Montreaux Jazz Festival; co-author "Blues for Dummies". **Business Addr:** Alligator Records, PO Box 60234, Chicago, IL 60660.

### BROOKS, MACEY (BARRY MACEY BROOKS)
Football player, football executive. **Personal:** Born Mar 2, 1975, Hampton, VA. **Educ:** James Madison Univ, BS, health serv admin. **Career:** Football player (retired), exec; Dallas Cowboys, wide receiver, 1997; Chicago Bears, exec dir; Dallas Cowboys, exec dir; Oakland Raiders, exec dir; Elite Sports Performance, chief exec officer & co-owner, exec dir, currently; Chicago Bears, 1998-2000; Kane County Dawgs, wide receiver coach, co owner, 2012. **Orgs:** Oakland Raiders; Dallas Cowboys; Chicago Bears. **Business Addr:** Owner, Executive Director, Elite Sports Performance, 1517 Mitchell Dr, Oswego, CA 60543.

### BROOKS, NORWARD J.
Government official, college administrator. **Personal:** Born Sep 10, 1934, New Iberia, LA; son of Cleo Spencer and Ivory; married Violet Caldwell; children: Norward Jr, Cleoanna & David Eric Spencer. **Educ:** Southern Univ, BS, 1955; Seattle Univ, MBA, 1971; Univ Wash, PhD, 1989. **Career:** Boeing Co Seattle, fac, 1959-69; United Inner City Develop Found, exec dir, 1969-70; King Co Govt Seattle, dir rec & elections dept, 1970-73; Wash State Employ Sec Dept, comnr, 1973-77; Univ Wash, dir admin data proc, 1977-81; Model Capitol Corp, pres 1979-; Wash State Employ Security Dept, comnr, 1981-85; City Seattle, comptroller, King County, assessor; Seattle Univ, adj prof, 1988-; Seattle Voc Inst, dir, 1995, exec dean, currently, pres; Rec & Elections King County, dir. **Orgs:** Pres, Coun Minority Bus Enterprises Wash State, 1969-70; pres, Seattle Econ Oppor Bd, 1971-72; Govt Adv Coun Voc Educ; chmn, Wash Occup Info Consortium; trustee, Wash State Asn Co Off, 1971-72; co-chmn, Wash State Co Auditors Educ Comt, 1971-72; pres, Int Thunderbird Little League Asn; chmn, Minority Bd adv, Bus Develop Comn, Seattle Chamber Com; King Co Boys Club Bd Dir; United Way; bd dir, Nat Conf Christians & Jews; First African Methodist Episcopal Church; Alpha Phi Alpha; reg pres, Blacks Govt, 1982-85; pres, Black Elected & App Offs, Region X, 1986-; pres, Nat Black Caucus, Govern Financial Officers Asn, 1990-; US Comn Civil Rights Western Region, 1992-; bd mem, Seattle Voc Inst; bd mem, Rec; bd advisors mem, Greater Seattle Chamber Com. **Honors/Awds:** Magna Cum Laude Southern Univ, 1955; Golden Acorn Award, Newport Hills PTA, 1971; Affirmative Action Award, Urban League, 1985; Employment Security Administrator of the Year, 1985; One of 100 Outstanding Alumni, Seattle Univ, 1991. **Home Addr:** 11044 Durland Ave NE, Seattle, WA 98125-5905, **Home Phone:** (206)361-8688. **Business Addr:** Executive Dean, Seattle Vocational Institute, 2120 S Jackson St, Seattle, WA 98144, **Business Phone:** (206)587-4940.

### BROOKS, PATRICK, JR.
Educator. **Personal:** Born Jun 8, 1944, Newark, NJ; son of Patrick Sr and Ethel Fields; children: Lisa M Ware, Chrisham & Patrick III. **Educ:** Lane Col, Jackson, TN, AB, 1967; Tex Southern Univ, Houston, MEd, 1970; Univ Minn, advan studies; NY Univ, advan studies; Jersey City State Univ, NJ, MA; Trenton State Univ, advan studies; Lydon State Univ, VT, advan studies. **Career:** Wildwood Consolidate Sch, Wildwood, NJ, crisis intervention counr; NY Housing Authority, NY, asst dist supvr; Essex County Col, Newark, NJ, instr sociol & counr; Kent State Univ, Frankfurt, KY, dir stud activ; Tex Southern Univ, Houston, asst resident hall dir & counr; Houston Urban League, Houston, Tex, asst dir; coach: girls cross country, basketball, boys track, wrestling; Rutgers Univ, NJ, regional workshop dir & counr voc educ, 1982. **Orgs:** NJ Prof Counr Asn; NJ Career Counr Asn; NJ Counr Non-White Concerns; Cape May County; county adv, Stud Against Drunk Driving; trustee, NJ Youth Correctional Bd; County Ment Health Advocate Bd; County Prosecutors; Supts Task Force Drug & Alcohol Abuse; S Jersey Coaches Asn; NJ Correctional Bd trustee Penal Youth Prisons; County Ment Health, Drug & Alcohol Bd; County Prosecutor's County Supt Sch Alliance Drug Abuse; Mayors Coun Drug Abuse; NJ Sch Counr Asn, mid sch adv coun; City St Rd Improv, Comnr, 1987; comnr, Wildwood Hist Soc, 1988; Stud Personal Servs, Alcohol Drug Counr. **Home Addr:** 321 W Garfield Ave, Wildwood, NJ 08260-1908. **Business Addr:** Councilor, Wildwood High School, 4300 Pacific Ave, Wildwood, NJ 08260, **Business Phone:** (609)522-7922.

### BROOKS, PAULINE C.
President (organization), chief executive officer, executive. **Educ:** George Washington Univ, BA, 1972; Fiche Inst Data Processing,

comput cert; Entrex Sch Programming, comput cert; USDA Grad Sch, comput cert; Univ Md, comput cert. **Career:** Natl Oceanic & Atmospheric Admin, prog mgr; UN Fed Nat Mortgage Asn; Lloyds London City Comput Ctr; Automated data processing firm, vpres opers & exec vpres; Dynamic Data Processing, exec vpres, 1972-85; Mgt Technol Inc, founder, owner, pres & chief exec officer, 1985-. **Orgs:** Entrepreneur Yr Inst; Nat Asn Female Exec; Comn Women Prince, George's Co, Md; bd mem, Mitchellville Sch; sr mananagement, Un & Fed Nat Mortgage Asn. **Home Addr:** 3384 Hewitt Ave Apt 201, Silver Spring, MD 20906-5418, **Home Phone:** (301)603-0387. **Business Addr:** Chief Executive Officer, President, Management Technology Inc, 7700 Old Br Ave Suite C200, Clinton, MD 20735, **Business Phone:** (301)265-8900.

## BROOKS, PHILLIP DANIEL

Executive. **Personal:** Born Mar 2, 1946, Charlottesville, VA. **Educ:** Norfolk State Col, BA, 1969; VA Commonwealth Univ, MA, 1971. **Career:** Norfolk Comm Hosp, admin, asst admins, 1971; Norfolk State Univ Athletics Found, treas, 2007-08; Norfolk Community Health Ctr, pres, currently. **Orgs:** Bd dir, Blue Cross Blue Shield, VA; Tidewater Hosp Coun; Am Hosp Asn; VA Hosp Asn; Am Col Hosp Admin; Nat Asn Health Serv Execs; Tidewater Regional Polit Asn; United Comn Fund Allocation Liaison Team, 1977; chmn, adv com, Hal Jacksons Miss US Talented Teen Pageant. **Honors/Awds:** Award of Recognition Norfolk Comm, 1976; Health Mgmt Achievement Award, Nat Asn of Health Serv Execs, 1976. **Home Addr:** 2901 Mapleton Ave, Norfolk, VA 23504. **Business Addr:** President, Norfolk Community Health Center Inc, 2539 Corprew Ave, Norfolk, VA 23504-3909, **Business Phone:** (757)628-1400.

## BROOKS, ROBERT DARREN

Minister (clergy), football player, business owner. **Personal:** Born Jun 23, 1970, Greenwood, SC; married Diana, Nov 4, 1997; children: Robert, Elisha & Austin. **Educ:** Univ SC, BSc, retailing. **Career:** Football player (retired), business owner, minister; Green Bay Packers, wide receiver, 1992, 1994-98, kick returner, 1993, punt returner, 1994; Denver Broncos, 2000; Shoo-in four Life Rec Inc, pres, currently; Robert Brooks Football Camp, owner, currently; Trendsetters Church, RBM Ctr, Phoenix, minister, currently. **Honors/Awds:** Comeback Player of the Year, Nat Football League, 1997; Super Bowl XXXI Champion. **Special Achievements:** Films: 1992 NFL Draft, 1992; 1995 NFC Championship Game, 1996; 1997 NFC Championship Game, 1998; Super Bowl XXXII, 1998. TV Series: "The NFL on NBC", 1992; "ESPN's Sunday Night Football", 1992-98; "NFL Monday Night Football", 1993-98; "TNT Sunday Night Football", 1994; "NFL on FOX", 1994-95. **Business Addr:** Owner, Robert Brooks Football Camp, 2430 Sugarloaf Club Dr, Duluth, GA 30097, **Business Phone:** (800)807-8282.

## BROOKS, ROBIN C.

Chief executive officer, chairperson. **Personal:** Born Jan 1, 1954?; married Frank. **Educ:** Smith Col, BA, econ; Northwestern Univ, JL Kellogg Grad Sch Mgt, MA, finance & econ. **Career:** Williamette Mgt Assocs; Deloitte & Touche; Arthur D Little Valuation Inc; Gen Elec Credit Corps Asset Based Lending & Acquisition Funding Group; Am Nat Bank; Brooks Food Group Inc, chief operating officer & treas, chmn & cheif exec officer; Chicago Corp, sr advisor, currently. **Orgs:** Dir, United Enterprise Fund; Commonwealth Inst; founding bd mem, tres, MultiCultural Foodservice & Hospitality Alliance, 2002-04; Comt 200; treas, dir, Women's Foodservice Forum; treas, bd advisor, Commonwealth Inst S Fla; bd advisor, SBA Nat Adv Coun. **Business Addr:** Senior Advisor, The Chicago Corporation, 135 S LaSalle St Suite 2130, Chicago, IL 60603, **Business Phone:** (312)283-0825.

## BROOKS, RODNEY ALAN

Journalist. **Personal:** Born May 29, 1953, Baltimore, MD; son of William F and Mattie Bell Crosson; married Sheila Smith; children: Rodney Alan Jr, Tahira & Andre. **Educ:** Cornell Univ, Ithaca, NY, BS, commun arts, 1974; Georgetown Univ, exec cert financial planning, 2010. **Career:** Ithaca Jour, Ithaca, NY, reporter, 1974-77; Asheville Citizen-Times, Asheville, NC, bus ed, 1977-80; The Bull, Philadelphia, Pa, fin writer, 1980-81; Philadelphia Inquirer, Philadelphia, Pa, asst bus ed, asst city ed, bus writer, 1981-85; USA TODAY, McLean, Va, Money Sect, assignment ed, dep managing ed, 1985-; Northwestern Univ, McCormick-Tribune fel, 2008; Brookings Prog Econs Journalists; Univ Mo, Multi-Cult Mgt Prog; USA TODAY, Dep Managing Ed/Personal Finance & columnist, 2010-. **Orgs:** Co-founder & chmn, NABJ Bus Writers Task Force, 1989-93; City New Carrollton Adv Planning Comn, 1990-93; bd dir, Nat Asn Minority Media Execs, 1990-93, treas, 1991-93; Financial Planning Asn; bd govs, Soc Am Bus Ed & Writers, 1993-96; bd dir, Nat Asn Black Journalists, Col Pk, MD, treas, 1994-98, chair, finance comt, 2005-07; chmn, Strategic Planning Comn, 1994; bd dir, Creative Writing Alliance, Hyattsville, MD, 2007-. **Honors/Awds:** Outstanding Contributions, Inroads Baltimore, 1994; Outstanding Contributions, Greater Ithaca Activ Ctr; President Award, NABJ, 2007. **Home Addr:** 201 Flannery Lane, Silver Spring, MD 20904-1271, **Home Phone:** (301)879-1839. **Business Addr:** Deputy Managing Editor, USA Today, 7950 Jones Br Dr, McLean, VA 22107, **Business Phone:** (703)854-3496.

## BROOKS, RODNEY NORMAN

Teacher, executive, chief executive officer. **Personal:** Born Jun 6, 1954, Asbury Park, NJ; married Mary Jane Carroll; children: Sheena Monique & Anneka LeChelle. **Educ:** Bowling Green State Univ, BS, Eng, 1976; Kent State Univ, attended 1981; Atlanta Univ, attended 1984. **Career:** Massillon Bd Educ, sub teacher, 1977-78; Supreme Life Ins Co, debit mgr, 1977-78; Canton Urban League Inc, proj dir, 1978-83; Planned Parenthood Stark Co, dir, 1984-; Massillon Urban League, pres & chief exec officer; Urban League Metro Harrisburg Inc, pres & chief exec officer; Hamilton Health Ctr, Capital Region Health Syst, Cares Proj, prog dir, currently. **Orgs:** Dir, Westcare Ment Health Ctr, 1984-; dir, Social Plng Coun, United Way W Stark, 1984-; worshipful master, Simpson Lodge 1, IF & AMM, 1985; pres, Grand Rapids Urban League, 1993-95. **Honors/Awds:** Outstanding Young Men of America, 1988. **Home Addr:** 2131 Francis Ave SE, Grand Rapids, MI 49506. **Business Addr:** Program Director, Hamilton Health Center Inc, 1821 Fulton St, Harrisburg, PA 17110, **Business Phone:** (717)232-9971.

## BROOKS, ROSEMARIE

Educator. **Personal:** Born Aug 6, 1949, Detroit, MI; daughter of Leonard Richard and Bertha Corrine; children: Wilbert O'Neil Barnes II & Sesmone Lanette Barnes-Cox. **Educ:** Univ Detroit, BA, 1980, teachers cert, 1997; Ferris State, voc educ cert, 1997; Cambridge Col, MEd, 1997. **Career:** WXYZ-TV-7, producer & host, 1980-90; Sprint Communs, sales mgr, 1982-87; Detroit Bus Inst, placement dir, 1987-90; Brooks Right Price Convenience Plz, chief exec officer, 1990-93; Detroit Pub Schs, Placement Specialist, 1993-; Shar Inc, assessment counr, 1995-97; Davenport Univ, fac, 1997-; Breithaupt Career & Tech Ctr, placement specialist, 1999-. **Orgs:** Nat Asn Advan Colored People, 1977-; bd, Joint Apprenticeship Community, 1995-; Sex Equity & Diversity Proj, 1995-; Mich Ed Apprenticeship & Training Asn, 1997-; Detroit Workforce Develop, 1999-. **Home Addr:** 1300 E Lafayette Blvd 1810-11, Detroit, MI 48207, **Home Phone:** (313)866-9623. **Business Addr:** Placement Specialist, Breithaupt Career & Tech Center, 9300 Hubbell, Detroit, MI 48228-2325, **Business Phone:** (313)866-9623.

## BROOKS, ROSEMARY BITTINGS

Publisher, educator. **Personal:** Born Jan 2, 1951, East Orange, NJ; daughter of Patrick and Ethel Fields; children: Haven Michael, Ebony Mekia & Deja Renee. **Educ:** Claflin Univ, BA, 1971; Seton Hall Univ, MA, 1976; Kean Col, commun cert, 1978; Rutger's Union, MA, phys fitness specialist, 1983. **Career:** E Orange Drug Ctr, substance abuse counr, 1975; Essex Valley Sch, Bridge W, dir, 1981-82; Second Chance Coun Ctr, dir, 1982-83; NJ Black Caucus Legislators, lobbyist, 1984-87; Staying Fit Exercise Prog NJ Network, host, dir, 1984-86; Irvington Bd Educ, guid counr, dir hist & law, educr hist, 1984-; NJ Chap Parents Joint Custody, lobbyist, 1985-87; Irvington High Sch NJ Law & Psychol, instr hist, 1985-87; Essex Co Fitness Prog, specialist, 1986-87; NJ Careers Coun, Irvington High, coordr, 1986-87; Person Person Greeting Cards, pres, writer, 1988-, guid counr, 1994-. **Orgs:** Educ comn chmn, SOMAC Comn Coun, 1979-86; Gov's Coun Educ, 1982-87; NJ State Bd Lobbyists, 1982-87; NJ State Bd Fitness Specialist, 1984-87; proj chmn, Maplewood PTA, 1985-86; dir, Afro-Hist Soc Irvington High Sch, 1983-87; treas, Irvington Awareness Coun, 1986-87; writer, consult, Sands Casino, Atlantic City NJ, 1988-89; writer, consult, Planned Parenthood NJ, 1988-89; NJ state deleg, Nat Conv, 2000-01; vice chair, Maplewood Dem Party, 2001; Minority Comt chmn local & state NJ; State Instrnl Comt, NJ Educ Asn; Guid Counr Irvington Sch Dist; appointee govs comm, Adolescent Justice & Anti-Violence; State Bd Educ, State NJ, lobbyist. **Home Addr:** 95 Parker Ave, Maplewood, NJ 07040, **Home Phone:** (201)761-1678. **Business Addr:** Director, Irvington Board of Education, 1034 Clinton Ave, Irvington, NJ 07111, **Business Phone:** (973)373-3900.

## BROOKS, SHEILA DEAN

Entrepreneur, television journalist. **Personal:** Born Jun 24, 1956, Kansas City, MO; daughter of Stanley Benjamin Smith and Gussie Mae Dean Smith; married Rodney Alan Sr; children: Andre Timothy. **Educ:** Univ Wash, Seattle, WA, BA, broadcast jour, 1978; Seattle Univ, WA, 1980; Howard Univ, MA, 1998. **Career:** KCTS-TV, Seattle, Wash, reporter & producer, 1978-81; KREM-TV, Spokane, Wash, reporter & anchor, 1981-83; KAMU-TV/FM, Col Sta, Tex, news dir & anchor, 1984-85; Dallas Morning News, Dallas, Tex, exec mgt prog, 1985-88; Vanita Prods, Baltimore, Md, sr producer, 1988-89; SRB Prods Inc, Wash, DC, pres & chief exec officer, 1988-; WTTG-TV Channel 5, Wash, DC, exec producer, 1989-90; Crowe Chizek & Co LLC, corp adv bd, currently; adv bd, MassMutual Financial Group. **Orgs:** Exec bd officer & secy, 1986-91, chairwoman scholar comm, 1987-90, chairwoman internship comm, 1990-91, Nat Asn Black Journalists; bd dir, Archbishop Carroll High Sch, 1990-95; bd dir, New Carrollton Cablevision Inc, 1990-92; exec bd & pres, 1996-97, bd dir, 1994-, pres, 1997, Nat Asn Women Bus Owners, Wash, DC; bd govs, Nat Acad TV Arts & Sci, NATAS-DC, 1996-; exec bd officer. Md Dist Columbia Minority Supplier Develop Coun, 1994-; bd dir, 1994-96, adv bd, 1996-, Women Film & Video, Wash, DC Chap; The Presidents' Roundtable. **Honors/Awds:** Emmy Awards 1979, 1980; Texas Asn Broadcasters Radio Award, 1984; First Place CEBA Award of Excellence, Best Documentary in the Country, CEBA--World Inst Commun Inc, New York, 1990; Emmy Award Nomination, Best Local Documentary, 1990, Emmy Award Nomination, Best Local Information-Oriented Show, Nat Acad TV Arts & Sci, Wash, DC, 1990; First Place (RTNDA) Regional Award, Radio-TV News Dirs Asn, Wash, DC, 1990; Honorable Mention NABJ Award, Nat Asn Black Journalists, 1990; Supplier of the Year, Md Dist Columbia Minority Supplier Develop Coun, 1995; Telly Awards, 1995, 1996; Advocate of the year, Women Bus. **Home Addr:** 8403 Longfellow St, New Carrollton, MD 20784, **Home Phone:** (301)306-9143. **Business Addr:** President, Chief Executive Officer, SRB Productions Inc, 1990 K St NW 2nd Fl, Washington, DC 20006, **Business Phone:** (202)775-7721.

## BROOKS, SUZANNE R.

School administrator. **Personal:** Born Jan 20, 1941, Philadelphia, PA; daughter of Rayetta Ortiga and John Lemon. **Educ:** LaSalle Univ, Philadelphia, PA, BS, educ/eng, 1975; Wash State Univ, Pullman, WA, MA, eng, 1979, adv lang studies, summers, 1979, 1981; Univ Nev-Reno, grad courses, summers, 1982, 1983; Pa State Univ, Univ Park, PA, doc prog, 1985. **Career:** Philadelphia Police Dept, Philadelphia, Pa, policewoman, 1968-72; Philadelphia High Sch Girls, Philadelphia, Pa, teaching practicum, 1974; Pa Adv Sch, Philadelphia, Pa, vol teacher, 1975; Wash State Univ, Pullman, WA, teaching apprentice, 1975-76, res asst, 1978-79, teaching asst, 1978-79, grad asst, 1978-79, dir sci support servs, 1979-82; GED instr, 1980, bi-lingual ESL instr, 1980-81; Andrew V. Kozak Fel, Pa State Univ Chap, Phi Delta Kappa; Univ Nev Reno, affirmative action officer, 1982-84; Danforth Fel; Pa State Univ, Philadelphia, Pa, affirmative action officer, 1984-89; Sign Lang Systs, co-owner & educ design/develop specialist, 1986-; Creative Concepts/Systs, owner, 1989, chief exec officer, currently; Calif State Univ, Sacramento, Calif, dir Multi-Cult Ctr, 1990; Pa State Univ, affirmative action officer. **Orgs:** Planning comt, Ctr Women Policy Studies; Nat Asn Bus & Prof Women, State Col Chap; Nat Coun Negro Women; adminrs & counrs, Nat Asn Women Deans; Col& Univ Personnel Asn; bd mem, Nat Inst Women Color; chair, Founds Comt, State Col Bus & Prof Women's Asn; Affirmative Action Comt, Dem Party Ctr County; chief exec officer, pres & founder, Int Asn Women Color Day. **Home Addr:** 7295 Gloria Dr, Sacramento, CA 95831, **Home Phone:** (916)421-7824. **Business Addr:** Owner, Chief Executive Officer, Creative Concepts/Systems, 3325 Northrop Ave, Sacramento, CA 95864, **Business Phone:** (916)483-9804.

## BROOKS, DR. TODD FREDERICK

Physician. **Personal:** Born Sep 1, 1954, New York, NY; son of Delaney and Effie C. **Educ:** Drew Univ, BA, 1976; Meharry Med Col, MD, 1980; Univ Tenn Health Sci, PhD, 1984. **Career:** Univ Tenn, clin instr, 1984-; pvt pract obstet & gynec, 1984-; Memphis Health Ctr, consult, 1984-. **Orgs:** Bluff City Med Soc; chmn, Univ Tenn Obstet/Gynec Soc; fund raiser, Boy Scouts Am. **Special Achievements:** Publ "Perinatal Outcome", Journal of Ob/Gyn, 1984. **Home Addr:** 220 S Claybrook St Suite 202, Memphis, TN 38104, **Home Phone:** (901)276-4895. **Business Addr:** Physician, Private Practitioner, 200 S Claybrook St Suite 202, Memphis, TN 38104, **Business Phone:** (901)276-4895.

## BROOKS, TYRONE L., SR.

State government official. **Personal:** Born Oct 10, 1945, Warrenton, GA; son of Mose and Ruby Cody; married Mary; children: Tyrone Jr, Nahede Teresa & Matthew. **Educ:** Howard Univ; Albany State Col; Atlanta Univ. **Career:** Tyrone Brooks & Assoc, nat pres, 1973-; Universal Humanities & Visions Literacy, founder & chmn, currently; African Am Bus Systs, pres; Ga State House Rep, Dist 54, state rep, 1980-2015. **Orgs:** Ga Legis Black Caucus; Southern Christian Leadership Conf, 1967-79; Nat Asn Advan Colored People; Am Civil Liberties Union; adv bd, Gate City Bar Asn; pres, Ga Asn Black Elected Offs, 1993-; Rainbow Coalition; W Hunter St Baptist Church. **Home Addr:** 1315 Beecher St SW, Atlanta, GA 30310-0185, **Home Phone:** (404)753-3361. **Business Addr:** State Representative, Georgia House Representative, Legis Office Bldg 18 Capitol Sq Suite 511H, Atlanta, GA 30334, **Business Phone:** (404)656-6372.

## BROOKS, VINCENT K.

Army officer. **Personal:** Born Oct 24, 1958, Anchorage, AK; son of Leo A Sr and Naomi; married Carol P Brooks. **Educ:** US Mil Acad, BS, 1980; Sch Advanced Mil Studies, MMAS. **Career:** US Army, 1980-: held command & staff positions Us, Ger, Korea, Kosovo & Mid E; served 82d Airborne Div a lt; 1st Inf Div (forward) a capt; 1st Cavalry Div a maj & later a brig gen; 2d Inf Div a lt col; 3rd Army Cent (with duty Hq, Coalition Joint Task Force-Kuwait) & 3d Inf Div (with duty Nato-Kosovo Forces) a col; Hq, Us Cent Command, Hq, 1st Cavalry Div (with duty Hq, Multi-Nat Div-Baghdad) & Hq, III Corps & Ft Hood a brig gen; Hq, 1st Inf Div (with duty Hq US Div-S) a maj gen; 3rd Aus/AUs Cent (ARCENT), comndg gen Kuwait, Qatar, Afghanistan, Bahrain, Jordan & United Arab Emirates; Joint Chiefs Staff, dep dir war terrorism, 2003-04; US Army, dep chief pub affairs, 2004, chief, 2004-05; Multi-Nat Div-Baghdad, Iraq & 1st Calvary, dep comdr, 2006-08; 1st Inf Divison nat elections & transition from Iraqi Freeedom to Red Dawn, comndg gen, 2010-11; Third Army & Army Forces Cent, 2011-13; U.S Army Pac, comndg gen, 2013-. **Special Achievements:** First African-American top-rated cadet (valedictorian) in the U.S. Corp of Cadet his senior year at the U.S. Military Academy; part of only African-American family to have three U.S. Army generals within two generations. **Business Addr:** United States Army Pacific, Fort Shafter, HI 96858-5100.

## BROOKS, WADELL, SR.

Secretary (organization), executive, labor relations manager. **Personal:** Born Jan 20, 1933, Lexington, MS; married Daisy Anderson; children: Yolanda, Wadell Jr & Cassandra. **Educ:** Ill State Norm Univ, BS, bus educ, 1957. **Career:** Labor relations manager (retired), president, secretary, treasurer, director; VA Hosp, educ therapist, 1957-68; Naval Training Ctr, Great Lakes Naval Base, educ specialist, 1968-70, dir housing assignment & referral, 1970-79; Rufus Mitchell Lodge 107, master, 1972; Tots & Toddlers Day Care Ctr Inc, pres, 1974-; Pub Works Ctr Naval Base, Great Lakes, IL, dep equal employ opportunity officer, 1979-90; Daisy's Nursery Infant & Resource Develop Ctr, secy & treas, 1988; Gurnee Village Bd, currently; Feed C, vol, currently; Daisys Resource Ctr, bd dir, currently. **Orgs:** Pres, Am Asn Rehab Ther, 1970; pres & life mem, Nat Asn Am Colored People, 1976-80; bd dir, Great Lakes Credit Union Naval Base Great Lakes, IL, 1980-90; chmn, Lake Co Race Unity Task Force, 1993-; First Midwest bank Community Reinvestment Coun, 1995-2001; pres, Natl Alumni Asn Faith Grant Col, 1996; pres, N Chicago Chamber Com, 1997-99; bd dir, Navy League; Lake Co Urban League; chmn, Ctr's Bd Dirs. **Honors/Awds:** Super Performance Award, VA Hosp, 1967; Non-Fed Contribution Award, Pub Works Ctr, Great Lakes, IL, 1979; Mason of the Year, Rufus Mitchell Lodge 107, 1987; Super Achievement Award, We Do Care Orgn, Chicago, 1990; Faith Grant College Aluminus of the Year, 1996; Past E. Burton Mercier Service Award, 1996; The Bahai National Spiritual Assembly Award, 2002. **Special Achievements:** The most influential African Americans in Lake County. **Home Addr:** 1932 Sherman Ave, PO Box 468, North Chicago, IL 60064, **Home Phone:** (847)473-5663. **Business Addr:** Board Director, Daisy's Resource Center, 1919 Sherman Ave, North Chicago, IL 60064, **Business Phone:** (847)689-3766.

## BROOKS, WILLIAM C.

Chief executive officer, air force officer, businessperson. **Personal:** children: 3. **Educ:** Long Island Univ, BA; Univ Okla, MBA; Harvard Bus Sch, advan mgt prog, 1985. **Career:** Gene Motors Corp, froup dir personnel, 1978-89, vpres, community & urban affairs, 1993-97; US Dept Labor, asst secy, 1989-90; Entech Human Resources, chmn, 1997-98; Brooks Group Int, chmn; United Am Healthcare Corp, chmn, 1998-2008, pres & chief exec officer, 2002-10, dir, 1997-11; Caraco Pharmaceut Labs Ltd, dir, 2004-05; CSC Covansys Corporation, bd dir, 1998-; Louisiana Pacific Corp, dir, 1996-2003. **Orgs:** Bd dir, La Pac Corp; asst secy labor, Soc Security Adv Bd, 1996-98; chmn bd, Lason, Detroit, 2001; dir, United Am Healthcare Corp, 1997-2002; Gen Motors Dey Exec; Fla A&M Univ; Nat Inst Ed Adv Panel Employability; chmn & bd dir, 70001 Training & Employ; bd dir, Nat Coalition Black Voter Participtation Inc; Ohio State Univ, Nat Ctr Res & Voc Ed; State Ohio Pub Employ Adv & Coun; dist chmn, Boy Scouts Am; chmn, adv bd, Detroit Pub Schs Bd Educ; bd mem,

Detroit Regional Chamber Com; DTE Energy; bd trustee, Rand Valley State Univ; bd trustee, Univ Detroit Mercy; trustee, Community Foundation for Southeastern Michigan. **Home Addr:** 3230 Middlebury Lane, Bloomfield Hills, MI 48301.

### BROOKS, WILLIAM P.

Educator, hospital administrator. **Personal:** Born Nov 19, 1934, Newkirk, OK; son of Carl F Sr; married Sue Jean Johnson; children: Barry P, Leslie J Lykes, Terryl D Abington, William R & Virgil A. **Educ:** Friends Univ, Wichita, KS, attended 1953; Wichita Univ, attended 1967. **Career:** Hospital administrator (retired); Winfield State Hosp Training Ctr, laundry worker, 1957, voc teacher, 1961, voc training supvr, 1966, unit b, 1970, unit dir, admin officer I, 1977-87, spec asst to supt, 1987-95, supt, 1995-98. **Orgs:** Youth comt, Winfield Kiwanis Club, 1972-; pres, Winfield Quarterback Club, 1974; adv comt, Cowley City Community Col & Voc Tech Sch, 1975-; city planning comn, Winfield City, 1978-; Winfield Police Res, 1984-; bd dir, Eagle Nest Inc, currently. **Home Addr:** 1418 E 14th Ave, Winfield, KS 67156-4608, **Home Phone:** (620)221-9595. **Business Addr:** Board of Director, Eagle Nest Inc, 112 E 9th Ave, Winfield, KS 67156, **Business Phone:** (620)229-8282.

### BROOME, SHARON WESTON

President (organization), government official. **Personal:** Born Oct 1, 1956, Chicago, IL; daughter of Lucille and Willie; married Marvin Alonzo; children: David, Sarah & Daniel. **Educ:** Univ Wis, LaCrosse, BA, mass commun, 1978; Regent Univ, Va Beach, MA, commun, 1984. **Career:** Speaker, communications consultant; Arts & Humanities Coun Greater Baton Rouge, regional develop officer, 1985; Discover Mag, sales mgr, 1985; Finesse & Assocs, Baton Rouge, LA, exec dir, 1985-; Baton Rouge Opera, mkt & promotions asst, 1986; Nathan Group, dir commun, 1987-; WKG-TV, pub affairs dir, cohost, "IMPACT", Baton Rouge, 1987; Metrop Dist 7, City Baton Rouge, councilwoman, 1989, state rep, 1991; WBRZ-TV, reporter; House Rep, La, dist 29, 1992-2004, sen, La State Senate, sen dist 15, 2004-, 2007-, pres pro tempore, currently; Sharon Broome Commun Inc, pres, currently. **Orgs:** Adv, Love Outreach Faith Fel, 1985-; La Ctr Women Govt; Capital Area United Way; bd dir, Real Life Educ Found, 1989; Am Heart Asn; comt mem, La Elected Women Officials; bd mem, finance & exec comt, Ctr Women & Govt, 1991; active mem, Star Hill Church; N Baton Rouge Women's Help Ctr; bd vis, La State Univ Manship Sch; YWCA-Encore Plus; Tyrus Thomas Inc; La State Univ Manship Sch Bd Visitors; Urban Restoration Enhancement Corp; N Baton Rouge Women's Help Ctr; Quota Club Int; Baton Rouge Metro Coun. **Special Achievements:** First African-American female elected to represent District 15 in the Louisiana State Senate; First female elected as Speaker Pro Tempore of the Louisiana House of Representatives. **Home Addr:** 3352 Osceola St, Baton Rouge, LA 70805, **Home Phone:** (504)357-3111. **Business Addr:** Senator, Louisiana State Senate, PO Box 52783, Baton Rouge, LA 70892-4183, **Business Phone:** (225)359-9352.

### BROOMES, DR. LLOYD RUDY

Psychiatrist. **Personal:** Born Feb 2, 1936; married Lauvenia Alleyne; children: Lloyda & Melissa. **Educ:** Shell Technol Sch, attended 1955; Oakwood Col, BA, 1961; Loma Linda Univ, MD, 1966. **Career:** Camarillo State Hosp, staff psychiatrist, 1969-71; Meharry Alcohol Drug Abuse Prog, asst prof, 1972-89; Meharry Community Ment Health Ctr, dir clin serv; Nashville, pvt pract, 1973-86; Madison Hosp, Dept Psychiat, chief, 1978-80; Alvin C York Va Med Ctr, Psychiat Servs, chief, 1987-88; Tenn Dept MH & MR, A & DDivision, asst comnr, 1988-89; Carl Vinson Va Med Ctr, psychiat servs chief, 1989-99; pvt physician, currently. **Orgs:** Am Psychol Asn; Ga Psychiat Physicians Asn; Gov Adv Comn Alcohol & Drugs, 1972-76; Black Adventist Med Dent Asn; exec vpres, Lupus Found Am, Nashville Chap, 1986-89; Am Col Physician Execs, 1991. **Honors/Awds:** Gold Medal Award, Shell Tech Sch, 1955; Fel, Am Psychiatric Asn, 1985; Am Bd Psychiatry & Neurol, Dipl Psychiatry, 1981. **Business Addr:** Physician, 6143 Loblolly Lane, Tuscaloosa, AL 35405-7022, **Business Phone:** (205)553-4269.

### BROSSETTE, ALVIN, JR.

Educator. **Personal:** Born May 16, 1942, Montgomery, LA; married Delores Gipson; children: Derrie, Alicia & Kathy. **Educ:** Grambling State Univ, BS, elem educ, 1962; Northwestern State Univ, MEd, admin, 1970; Western Mich Univ, EdD, educ leardership, 1975; La State Univ; Southern Univ. **Career:** Winn Parish Pub Schs, Winnfield LA, teacher, 1962-67; Grant Parish Pub Schs, Colfax LA, asst prin & teacher, 1967-73; Kalamazoo Pub Schs MI, prog coordr & R&D, 1974-75; N western State Univ Los Angeles, asst prof Dept CI Col Educ, 1975-76; Prairie View A&M Univ TX, dept head Col Educ Curric & Instr, 1976-80; Wilmer-Hutchins Independent Sch Dist, gen supt; Dallas Pub Schs Syst, teacher, asst prin, prin, prin planner, mgt sch, prin; Continuing Educ N western State Univ, actg dean, dir; George L Parks Elem & Mid Sch, Prin, currently; New Enterprise Elem, St. Maurice, at J. W. Gains Elem Montgomery; Mary Graham Elem Sch, Colfax, asst prin. **Orgs:** Phi Beta Sigma, 1968-; pres, Grant Parish Educ Asn, 1972-73; Phi Delta Kappa 1975-; Nat Asn Curric Dev, 1976-; Teacher ctn adv bd Prairie View A&M Univ TX, 1979-; consult, N Forest ISD Houston, 1979-; Am Asn Sch Admin, 1980-. **Home Addr:** 7302 Bayberry Lane, Dallas, TX 75249. **Business Addr:** Principal, George L Parks Elementary & Middle School, 800 Koonce St, Natchitoches, LA 71457-3400, **Business Phone:** (318)352-2764.

### BROTHERS, AL

Manager. **Career:** Raytheon, prog mgr, currently. **Business Addr:** Program Manager, Raytheon, 1010 Prod Rd, Fort Wayne, IN 46808, **Business Phone:** (219)429-6812.

### BROTHERS, TONY

Basketball executive. **Personal:** Born Sep 14, 1964, Norfolk, VA; son of Marian Bonner. **Educ:** Old Dom Univ, BS, mgt info systs, 1986. **Career:** TB Pro-Active Basketball Officiating Sch, refree & supvr; Tidewater Consults Inc, programmer, 1986-93; Nat Basketball Asn, off, NBA referee, 1994-; Still Hope Found Inc, co-founder, 2007-. **Orgs:** Founder, A Better Way; Hampton Rds Comt 200+ Men Inc; Cent Intercollegiate Athletic Asn. **Home Addr:** PO Box 52, Smithfield, VA 23431. **Business Addr:** NBA Official, National Basketball Association (NBA), 645 5th Ave 10th Fl, New York, NY 10022-5986, **Business Phone:** (212)407-8000.

### BROUGHTON, CHRISTOPHER LEON

Magician, actor. **Personal:** Born Mar 4, 1964, Detroit, MI; son of Theo Faye McCord and Ronald Leon. **Educ:** Mercy Col, Detroit, attended 1984. **Career:** Comedian, magician, actor, Los Angeles, 1976-; Films: Amazon Women on the Moon, 1987; Action Jackson, 1988; The New Adventures Pippi Long stocking, 1988; Baby Geniuses, 1999; Playas Ball, 2003; Vegas Vampires, 2003; Tournament Dreams, composer, producer & actor, 2007; Tournament of Dreams, actor, 2007; Tvseries: "It's Show time at the Apollo", segment producer, 1987; "Hollywood Hounds", 1993; The 16th Ann Soul Train Music Awards, segment producer, 2002; The 30th Ann Am Music Awards, segment producer, 2003; The Christopher Broughton Show, performer, currently. **Orgs:** Int Brotherhood Magicians, 1984-; Mystics, 1976-89; SAG, 1984-; Am Fedn Tv & Radio Artists, 1984-; ICAP, 1988-. **Honors/Awds:** International Brotherhood of Magicians Award, 1989. **Home Addr:** 10458 Westover, Detroit, MI 48204, **Home Phone:** (313)491-8315. **Business Addr:** Magician, Comedian, The Christopher Broughton Show, 3355 Las Vegas Blvd S, Las Vegas, NV 89109, **Business Phone:** (702)414-9000.

### BROUGHTON, LUTHER RASHARD, JR.

Football player. **Personal:** Born Nov 30, 1974, Charleston, SC. **Educ:** Furman Univ. **Career:** Football player (retired); Carolina Panthers, tight end, 1998, 2001; Philadelphia Eagles, 1997, 1999-2000; Chicago Bears, 2002; Green Bay Packers, 2003. **Special Achievements:** Highest career receiving average with a minimum of five catches; First Furman football NFL draftee since 1986.

### BROUHARD, DEBORAH TALIAFERRO

Chairperson, educator. **Personal:** Born Jul 7, 1949, Springfield, MA; daughter of Ernest Carter and Julia Beatrice Addison; married John Forrest; children: Benjamin Forrest & Rebecca Julia. **Educ:** McGill Univ, Montreal, Can, 1970; Aurora Univ, Aurora, IL, BA, 1971; Ind Univ, Bloomington, IN, MSED, 1978. **Career:** Educator (retired); Aurora E High Sch, E Aurora, IL, teacher, 1971-73; Miami Univ, Oxford, OH, coordr spec serv, 1981-83; Ariz State Univ, Mesa, AZ, counr, 1985, stud recruitment & retention specialist, currently, Polytech campus Comn chair, 2009. **Orgs:** Mid-Am Asn Educ Opportunity Progs, 1981-84; Black Caucus Ariz State Univ, 1985-; bd mem, Potentials Unlimited, 1991; Comn State Women, Ariz State Univ, 1996-97. **Home Addr:** 7527 S Col Ave, Tempe, AZ 85283, **Home Phone:** (602)413-1538.

### BROUSSARD, ARNOLD ANTHONY

Administrator. **Personal:** Born Sep 26, 1947, New Orleans, LA; married Venita Lorraine Thomas; children: Danielle Lorraine & Darryl Anthony. **Educ:** Tulane Univ, BA, social anthroplogy & social psychol, 1969; Univ Pa, Wharton Sch Univ, PA, MBA, acct, opers res, 1971. **Career:** Arthur Andersen & Co, sr consult, 1971-75; J Ray McDermott & Co Inc, financial planning analyst, 1975-78; City New Orleans, exec asst to Mayor; Palm Beach Consult Group, prin, consult, currently; real estate broker, currently; Realty Group Palm Beaches, LLC, broker & owner, 2009-. **Orgs:** Co-coord Jr Achievement, 1975-77; bd dir, New Orleans Area Bayou River Health Sys Agency, 1975-78; Nat Asn Black Acct, 1976-. **Home Addr:** 7301 Edward St, New Orleans, LA 70126. **Business Addr:** Broker, Owner, Palm Beach Realty Group, 580 Village Blvd Suite 150, West Palm Beach, FL 33409, **Business Phone:** (561)594-4000.

### BROUSSARD, CHERYL DENISE

Writer, talk show host, chief executive officer. **Personal:** Born Sep 25, 1955, Phoenix, AZ; daughter of Theodore Douglas and Gwendolyn J Reid; married John B; children: J Hasan. **Educ:** Creighton Univ, attended 1975; Loyola Univ, BS, 1977. **Career:** Dean Witter Reynolds Inc, investment adv, acct exec, 1983-89; CNN Financial Network & CNN & Co, financial adv; Broussard & Douglas Inc, financial advisor, 1989-97, prin & chief investment adv, currently; Sister chief exec officer BootCamp, creator; Ms Money Millionaire Financial Boot Camp, creator; Cheryl Broussard & Co, regist investment adv, money coach, chief exec officer, currently; Mind Your Money, producer & talk show host, currently; Ebony Money Power, co-host currently; Broussard & Douglas Inc, financial dvisor prof, dir, 1989-97; Books: The Black Womans Guide To Financial Independence, 1996; Sister Chief Executive Officer: The Black Womans Guide To Starting Your Own Business, 1998; Smart Ways To Take Charge Your Money, Build Wealth & Achieve Financial Security; Whats Money Got To Do With It; Ultimate Guide How To Make Love & Money Work Your Relationship. Co-auth: Mind Your Money Syst with Cheryl Broussard; Fast Cash & Getting Back On Financial Track; The Jet Set Girls Guide To Building A Million-Dollar Online Empire; Starting Over: Fast Cash & Getting Back On Financial Track; The Jet Set Girl's Guide To Building A Million-Dollar Online Empire, 2011. **Orgs:** Nat Asn Negro Bus & Prof Women; Econ Develop Comt. **Honors/Awds:** Outstanding Business & Professional Woman Award, Iota Phi Lambda Sorority Inc, 2011; Phenomenal Woman of The Year Award, Frasernet, 2011; 2011 Women of Color Achievement Award, 2011. **Special Achievements:** Voted one of ten Woman Who Made a Difference, Minorities & Women in Business Magazine, 1992. **Home Addr:** 130 Dockside Bay, PO Box 5742, Hercules, CA 94547-5742, **Home Phone:** (510)530-7495. **Business Addr:** Chief Executive Officer, Chief Investment Advisor, Cheryl Broussard & Co, PO Box 27287, Oakland, CA 94547, **Business Phone:** (510)245-7995.

### BROUSSARD, STEVEN (STEVE NELSON BROUSSARD)

Football player, football coach. **Personal:** Born Feb 22, 1967, Los Angeles, CA; married Monique; children: Talin, Steve Jr & Kendra. **Educ:** Wash State Univ, attended 1990. **Career:** Football player (retired), football coach; Atlanta Falcons, running back, 1990-93; Cincinnati Bengals, running back, 1994; Seattle Seahawks, running back, 1995-98; Don Lugo High Sch, Chino, Calif, offensive coordr, 2000; Diamond Ranch High Sch, offensive coordr, 2001, head coach, 2002-03; Portland St vikings, wide receivers coach, 2004-06, offensive cord, 2005-07; Wash State Univ Cougars, running backs coach, 2007-09; Ariz State Sun Devils, wide receivers coach, currently. **Business Addr:** Wide Receivers Coach, Arizona State Sun Devils, 500 E Veteran's Way, Tempe, AZ 85287-2505, **Business Phone:** (480)965-3630.

### BROWDER, ANNE ELNA

Manager, executive. **Personal:** Born Jun 13, 1944, Vernon, AL; daughter of Mary E and Eddie. **Educ:** LaSalle Exten; Roosevelt Univ. **Career:** NBC News, Chicago, prod talent mgt, 1960-73; TV News Inc, off mgr, 1973-75; Tobacco Indust, nat spokesperson, 1976-86; Exec Tv Workshop, assoc, 1988-94; Inst Karmic Guid, admin asst, 1990-; Tobacco Inst, asst pres. **Orgs:** Nat Asn Advan Colored People. **Honors/Awds:** Who's Who Among Black Americans. **Special Achievements:** "Africa on My Mind: Reflections of My Second Trip", Editor, 1995. **Home Addr:** 1204 Rosedale Ct, West Hyattsville, MD 20782-2293, **Home Phone:** (301)853-2465. **Business Addr:** Administrative Assistant, The Institute of Karmic Guidance, PO Box 73025, Washington, DC 20056, **Business Phone:** (202)853-2465.

### BROWN, A. DAVID

Labor relations manager. **Personal:** Born Aug 4, 1942, Morristown, NJ; son of Arthur D Sr and Muriel Kyse; married Joan Currie. **Educ:** Monmouth Col, BS, sociol & psychol, 1965. **Career:** Bamberger NJ, personnel exec, 1968-71, admin, personnel, 1974, vpres, 1975; R H Macy & Co Inc, vpres personnel, 1981, sr vpres, human resources & labor rels, 1983-94, bd dir, 1987-92; Korn Ferry Int, vpres, consult, 1994-97; Bridge Partners LLC, founder, managing partner, 1994-2006; Selective Ins Group, lead independent dir, 1996-; Whitehead Mann Pendleton James, managing dir, 1997-2003; Zale Corp, dir, 1997-2006-; Sports Authority Inc, dir, 1998-2003; Selective Ins Group Inc, dir, 1998-2003; Hanover Direct, dir, 2003-06; Linens & Things Inc, sr vpres, human resources, 2006-09; Urban Brands Inc, exec vpres, human resources, 2009-11, exec vpres & chief admin officer, 2011-12. **Orgs:** Black Retail Action Group; bd trustee, Morristown Mem Hosp; bd trustee, Drew Univ; bd trustee, Jackie Robinson Found; trustee, Monmouth Univ; trustee, Jackie Robinson Found, 2003-11. **Business Addr:** Executive Vice President, Chief Administrative Officer, Urban Brands Inc, 100 Metro Way, Secaucus, NJ 07094, **Business Phone:** (201)319-9093.

### BROWN, A. SUE

Administrator, government official, association executive. **Personal:** Born Jun 28, 1946, Lauderdale, MN. **Educ:** Bloomfield Col, BA, 1968; Rutgers Univ Grad Sch Social Work, MSW, 1969; Univ Pa, cert mgmt, 1979; Harvard Univ Sch Pub Health, cert, 1980. **Career:** Urban League-Essex Co Newark, dir health, 1969-73; Col Med & Dent Newark, health planner, 1973-75; Newark Comprehensive Health Serv Plan, actg asst dir, 1973-75; Martland Hosp Col Med & Dent Newark, actg exec dir, 1975-77; Col Univ Hosp, Univ Med & Dent NJ, 1977-83; NJ Med Sch Newark, lectr, 1979-; Robert Wood Johnson Health Policy fel, Univ Med & Dent NJ, 1983-84; Inst Med Nat Acad Sci, fel, 1983-; DC Social Serv, dep comn, 1993-94; Comn Health Care Finance, actg comnr, 1994-96, dep dir, Dept Human Serv, 1996-97; Dept Health, Comn Social Serv, actg comnr; Dept Human Serv, Income Maintenance Admin, actg adminr, currently. **Orgs:** Comn Pub Gen Hosps, 1977; Acute Care Comn Reg Health Plan Coun, 1980-82; NJ Comprehensive Health Planning Coun; adv com Region II Health Servs Ment Health Admin Comprehensive Health Planning; Am Pub Health Asn; founding mem, Nat Asn Pub Gen Hosps; Asn C NJ; Nat Asn Advan Colored People; Nat Coun Negro Women; 100 Women Integrity Govt Baptist; Asn Am Med Cols; NIH; Am Col Hosp Adminr. **Honors/Awds:** Citizenship Award, Bloomfield College, 1968; Community Service Award, Nat Coun Negro Women, 1978; Leadership Health Service Award Leaguers, 1978; Woman Achievement Essex County Col, 1979. **Home Addr:** 4261 Nash St NE, Washington, DC 20019, **Home Phone:** (202)396-5908. **Business Addr:** Acting Administrator, Department of Human Services, 645 St NE Suite 5000, Washington, DC 20002, **Business Phone:** (202)724-5506.

**BROWN, DR. ABENA JOAN P.** See Obituaries Section.

### BROWN, ABNER BERTRAND

Educator, counselor, insurance agent. **Personal:** Born Jan 20, 1942, DeQuincy, LA; married Genevieve Mallet; children: Abner B Jr & Alvin D. **Educ:** Southern Univ, BA, 1964; TX Southern Univ, MEd, 1972, MA, 1974. **Career:** Family Serv Ctr, marriage & family counr, 1973-83; Tex Southern Univ, instr, 1975-77; State Farm Ins Co, state farm ins agt, 1983-; Fire Hon Agt; Life Hon Agt. **Orgs:** Past pres, Scenicwood Civic Club, 1975-77; Am Asn Marriage & Family Counrs, 1975-; pres, N Forest, ISD, 1983-85; Chamber Com; vol, Habitat Humanity; ambassador, Travel Qualifier. **Honors/Awds:** Bronze Tablet Qualifier. **Home Addr:** 10500 Caxton St, Houston, TX 77016-3028, **Home Phone:** (713)633-4875. **Business Addr:** State Farm Insurance Agent, State Farm Insurance Co, 2190 N Loop W Suite 402, Houston, TX 77018, **Business Phone:** (713)681-9888.

### BROWN, ADRIAN DEMOND

Baseball player. **Personal:** Born Feb 7, 1974, McComb, MS; married Lynette; children: Adrian Jr & Quartez. **Career:** Pittsburgh Pirates, outfielder, 1997-2002; Tampa Bay Devil Rays, 2002; Boston Red Sox, 2003; Kans City Royals, 2004; Tex Rangers, 2006; free agt, currently.

### BROWN, ADRIANE M.

President (organization), chief executive officer. **Personal:** Born Jan 1, 1959. **Educ:** Old Dom Univ, DHL, BS, environ health; Mass Inst Technol, Sloan fel, MBA, mgt, 1991; Old Dom Univ, PhD, 2009. **Career:** Corning Inc, shift supvr, vpres, Corning's Environ Prod Div, gen mgr, vpres, 1980-99; Honeywell Transp Systs, vpres & gen mgr, 1999-2001, pres, chief exec officer, 2005-09; Intellectual Ventures, pres & chief operating officer, 2010-. **Orgs:** Bd dir, Jobs for America's Graduates; Executive Leadership Council; dir, Harman Int Industs Inc, 2013-; bd dir, Pac Sci Ctr. **Honors/Awds:** "Automotive News," 100 Leading Women in the North American Automotive Industry, 2005;

"Fortune," Women to Watch, 2006; "Black Enterprise," The 100 Most Powerful Executives in Corporate America, 2010. **Business Addr:** President, Chief Operating Officer, Intellectual Ventures, 3150 139th Ave SE Bldg 4, Bellevue, WA 98005, **Business Phone:** (425)467-2300.

### BROWN, AGNES MARIE
College administrator. **Personal:** Born Oct 13, 1933, North Holston, VA; daughter of Frank Broady and Lonnie Johnson Broady; married Robert; children: Agnes & Robin. **Educ:** Va Union Univ, Richmond, VA, BS, 1955; Bowie State Univ, Bowie, MD, MEd, 1977. **Career:** Educator (retired); Bowie State Univ, Bowie, Md, secy pres, 1955-67, prog coordr, asst dir fed prog, 1970-78, dir fed prog, 1978-92. **Orgs:** Bowie State Univ Alumni Asn, 1978; Nat Asn Title III Admin, 1978-; Bowie State Univ Women's Asn, 1985. **Home Addr:** 11422 Deepwood Dr, Bowie, MD 20720, **Home Phone:** (301)809-0292.

### BROWN, AJA
City planner, manager, mayor. **Personal:** Born Apr 17, 1982, Altadena, CA; daughter of Brenda Jackson; married Van, Jan 1, 2003. **Educ:** Univ Southern Calif, BS, policy & planning & develop, 2004, MS, urban planning with a concentration econ develop, 2005. **Career:** City Inglewood, sr admin analyst & sr planner, 2006-09; City Pasadena, planning comnr, 2007-09; City Compton, Community Redevelop Agency, proj mgr, 2009-11; Urban Vision Community Develop Corp, prin, 2011-; City Compton, mayor, 2013-; Delta Stewardship Coun, staff. **Orgs:** Am Planning Asn, Los Angeles Chap; Int Coun Shopping Centers (ICSC); Regan's Joy Found. **Honors/Awds:** "The Root" Magazine, The Root 100 Honorees, 2013; University of Southern California 2014 Young Alumni Merit Award; Recipient of the Los Angeles Young Democrats Laurel Award; National Action Network Martin Luther King Award. **Special Achievements:** Compton's youngest mayor elected in its history. **Business Addr:** Mayor, City of Compton, 205 S Willowbrook Ave, Compton, CA 90220, **Business Phone:** (310)605-5500.

### BROWN, ALBERT JOSEPH, III. See SURE, AL B.

### BROWN, DR. ALVER HAYNES
President (organization), teacher. **Career:** Madison High Sch, guid counr, Eng teacher; auth; educ consult; Black Educr Morris County, pres, currently. **Orgs:** Founding pres, Morris County chap, Nj Asn, 1983. **Business Addr:** President, Black Educators of Morris County, 1400 Weeping Willow Dr Apt A, Lynchburg, VA 24501-3961.

### BROWN, ALVIN
Chairperson. **Personal:** Born Dec 15, 1961; married Santhea; children: Joshua & Jordan. **Educ:** Jacksonville Univ, BS, MBA, 1989. **Career:** US Secy Housing & Urban Develop Andrew Cuomo, sr advisor; Staubach Co, partner, currently. **Orgs:** Exec dir, Bush Clinton Katrina Funds Interfaith Fund; pres, Willie Gary Classic Found; chmn, Nat Black MBA Asn; sr mem, Clinton Gore Admin; co-chair, White House Task Force; exec residence, Jacksonville Univ Davis Sch Bus. **Honors/Awds:** Fredrick Douglas Award, Southern Christian Leadership Conf; Excellence Community Service Award, 100 Black Men Am; Distinguished Award, Nat Baptist Conv; Chairman's Award, Congressional Black Caucus; H Naylor Fitzhugh Award, National Black MBA Association; Nat Black MBA Asn; Honorary Doctorate, Edward Waters College in Jacksonville; Frederick Douglass Award, outhern Christian Leadership Conference. **Business Addr:** Partner, The Staubach Co, 15601 Dallas Pkwy Suite 400, Addison, TX 75001-6055, **Business Phone:** (972)361-5210.

### BROWN, DR. ALYCE DOSS
Educator. **Personal:** Born Tuscaloosa, AL; daughter of John A and Julia; married Lelton C; children: Ouida & Kimberly. **Educ:** Tuskegee Inst, BSN, 1956; Med Col GA, MSN, 1975; Nova Univ, EdD, 1993. **Career:** Mt Sinai Hosp, charge nurse, 1956-57; Colbert County Hosp, charge nurse, 1957-73; TVA, indust nurse, 1966-67; Univ N Ala, Col Nursing & Allied Health, asst prof, 1973-93, assoc prof nursing, prof, currently. **Orgs:** Am Nurses Asn; Nat League Nurses; vice chmn, Human Rights Comm Ala State Nurses Asn; pres, Muscle Shoals Chap Tuskegee Alumni Asn, 1985; dir, Christian educ N Cent Ala Conf CME Church; dir youth, WK Huntsville Dist CME Church; Univ N Ala Nursing Hon Soc; League Women Voters; bd trustee, Colbert County-NW Ala Health Care Authority; Chi Eta Phi Nursing Sorority; dir, Episcopal Dist, fifth Episcopal Dist CME Church, 1996; adv bd, Tri County Home Health Agency, 1999; trustee, Authority Bd Helen Keller & Red Bay Hosp; ambassador, Smoke-Free Alabama; neighborhood chairperson, Am Cancer Soc. **Home Addr:** 1041 Woodmont Dr, Tuscumbia, AL 35674-3940, **Home Phone:** (256)383-7663. **Business Addr:** Professor of Nursing, University of North Alabama, 236 Stevens Hall, Florence, AL 35632-0001, **Business Phone:** (256)765-4579.

### BROWN, REV. DR. AMOS CLEOPHILUS
Clergy. **Personal:** Born Feb 20, 1941, Jackson, MS; son of Charlie Daniel Sr and Louetta Bell Robinson; married Jane Evangeline Smith; children: Amos Cleophilus Jr, David Josephus & Kizzie Maria. **Educ:** Morehouse Col, AB, 1964; Crozer Theol Sem, MDiv, 1968; Univ Minn, MA, bus admin, 1975; Va Sem & Col, DD, 1984; United Theol Sem, DMin, 1990. **Career:** St Paul Baptist Church, Westchester, Pa, pastor, 1966-70; Pilgrim Baptist church, St Paul, Minn, pastor, 1970-76; Third Baptist San Francisco, Calif, pastor, sr pastor, 1976-. **Orgs:** Pres, MS Youth Coun, Nat Asn Advan Colored People, 1956-59, Hi-Y Clubs MS, 1958-59; nat chmn, Nat Asn Advan Colored People Youth Dept, 1960-62; chmn, Am Baptist Black Caucus, 1972-80, chmn, Nat Baptist Civil Rights & Human Serv Comn, 1982-; gov bd, Community Col, 1982-88; founding mem bd, Black Am Resp African Crisis, 1984; life mem, Nat Asn Advan Colored People; bd supervisors, San Francisco City County, 1996-2000; chmn bd, Community Housing Corp; St Paul Planning Comn; pres, Minn State Baptist Conv, 1971-74, nat bd dir; nat chmn, Black Caucus Am Baptist Churches; chmn, Midwestern Am Baptist Black Churchmen; nat co-chmn, Resolution Comt; Men Courage Club; chmn, Benjamin E. Mays Learning Ctr; chaplain, Minn State Senate; San Francisco Community Col; pres, San Francisco Chap Nat Asn Advan Colored People. **Honors/Awds:** Outstanding Young Man of America, Jr Chamber Commerce 1974-76; Martin Luther King Jr Ministerial Award, Colgate-Rochester Div School, 1984; Man of the Year, San Francisco Business & Professional Women Inc, 1985; Samuel D Proctor Award, Nat Rainbow & PUSH, 1997; elected, Whos Who in Black America, 1976. **Home Addr:** 434 Bright St, San Francisco, CA 94132-2802, **Home Phone:** (415)859-5853. **Business Addr:** Senior Pastor, Third Baptist Church, 1399 McAllister St, San Francisco, CA 94115, **Business Phone:** (415)346-4426.

### BROWN, ANDREA MOLETTE
Executive, association executive. **Educ:** Spelman Col, BA, polit sci, 1992; Univ Md Sch Law, JD, 1995. **Career:** Leo Burnett, media supvr, 1995-97; DDB Needham, media supvr, 1997-99; Coca-Cola N Am, dir, Strategic Media Planning, 1999-2007; DunnhumbyUSA, vice-pres media & mkt, 2008-11; Sprint Nextel, media dir, 2011-13; Stage Stores, vpres media, 2013-16. **Orgs:** Am Advert Fedn; bd dir, YMCA Greater Cincinnati, 2010-11. **Honors/Awds:** Worldwide Marketing Excellence Award, 2004, Big, Bold & Inspiring Award, Coca-Cola Marketing, 2006, North America Marketing Award, 2006-07, American Advertising Federation Award, 2007; Coca-Cola Women Of Achievement Award, YWCA of Greater Atlanta, 2005. **Business Addr:** Vice President, Stage Stores, 10201 Main St, Houston, TX 77025, **Business Phone:** (800)579-2302.

### BROWN, ANGELA LAVERNE. See STONE, ANGIE.

### BROWN, ANGELA YVETTE
Journalist. **Personal:** Born Jul 4, 1964, Sacramento, CA; daughter of Clinton Edward and Ernestine Rose Hatchette. **Educ:** Fla State Univ, Tallahassee, FL, BA, commun, 1986. **Career:** WPEC-TV, W Palm Beach, Fla, prod asst, 1987; WEVU-TV, Ft Myers, Fla, TV news reporter, 1987-89; WCBD-TV, Charleston, SC, TV news reporter, 1989-. **Orgs:** Alpha Kappa Alpha Sorority, 1985-; Nat Asn Black Journalists, 1988-; vpres, Broadcast SC Coastal Asn Black Journalists, 1989-; founding mem, SCC Asn Black Journalists, 1989; founder, SC-CAB Mentors Prog, 1989. **Home Addr:** 810-D Hideaway Dr, Mount Pleasant, SC 29464, **Home Phone:** (803)881-4034. **Business Addr:** News Reporter, WCBD-TV, 210 W Coleman Blvd, Mount Pleasant, SC 29464, **Business Phone:** (843)884-2222.

### BROWN, REV. ANNIE CARNELIA
Investment banker, clergy. **Personal:** Born Jul 19, 1928, Switchback, WV; daughter of Rufus and Rozena Manns; married Samuel Leo; children: Samuel Jr, Carnelia Ann, Susan Leona & Reginald Lee. **Educ:** Wayne State Univ, BA, 1976, Theol, dipl, 1987; Wayne County Community Col, AA, 1992. **Career:** Investor; Apostle Paul Missionary Baptist Church, co-pastor, currently. **Orgs:** Oper Get Down, 1969-72; Harambee House, 1969-72; Positive Images, 1989-; pres, Christian Women's Club. **Honors/Awds:** Ford Good Citizens Award, 1971; Recognition Award for Community Service, Wayne County Community Col, 1973; Hon DDiv, SJ Williams Sch Rel, 1991; Distinguished Clergy Award, Urban Bible Col, 1995; Gov Honor Roll Vols, 1996. **Home Addr:** 5885 Cadillac Ave, Detroit, MI 48213, **Home Phone:** (313)925-6942. **Business Addr:** Co-Pastor, Apostle Paul Missionary Baptist Church, 4400 Lillibridge, Detroit, MI 48214, **Business Phone:** (313)331-4322.

### BROWN, ANNIE GIBSON
Accountant. **Personal:** Born Aug 12, 1944, Lexington, MS; married Charles. **Educ:** Southern Ill Univ; Miss Valley State Univ, attended 1966. **Career:** Pre-sch teacher, 1966; secy, 1966-69; bk keeper, 1969-71; pub off dep, 1971-75; Holmes Co, tax assessor & collector. **Orgs:** PTSA Order E Star Daughter Elks; Assessor Collectors Asn State & Nat; vpres MS Health Serv Agency. **Special Achievements:** First African American tax assessor in Mississippi. **Home Addr:** Pennington Circle, PO Box 367, Lexington, MS 39095. **Business Phone:** (662)834-4961.

### BROWN, ANTHONY MAURICE
Counselor, executive. **Personal:** Born Dec 19, 1962, Bronx, NY; son of Alfred and Annette; children: Nicole Gooden. **Educ:** Mercy Col. **Career:** Maternity Infant Care Serv, substance abuse teen counr, 1990-92; Northern Manhattan Perinatal Partnership, Substance Abuse Outreach, 1992-95; Christopher Columbus HS, sch air counr, coach, 1995-98; Pablo Casals Mid Sch, paraprofessional, conflict resolution, 1998-; Youthwise Inc, chief exec officer, 1999-, dir. **Orgs:** Recreation leader & coach, Police Athletic League, 1999-2000. **Honors/Awds:** Phat Friends Award, All stars Talent Network, 2001. **Home Addr:** 900 Bronx Pk S Suite 5A, Bronx, NY 10460, **Home Phone:** (718)329-0642. **Business Addr:** Director, Youthwise Inc, 2007 Mapes Ave, Bronx, NY 10460, **Business Phone:** (718)583-1765.

### BROWN, ANTHONY WILLIAM. See BROWN, TONY.

### BROWN, ANTRON
Race car driver. **Personal:** Born Mar 1, 1976; married Billie Jo Brown, Feb 3, 2001; children: Arianna Celeste (b.2001), Anson (b.2004), and Alder (b.2008). **Educ:** Mercer Junior College, A.A. in Business Administration. **Career:** National Hot Rod Association, Top Fuel, Drag racer, 2008-. **Honors/Awds:** TheGrio.com, 100 Making History Today, 2012; 2012 Top Fuel National Hot Rod Association Championship; African-American Chamber of Commerce of New Jersey, Circle of Achievement Award, 2012. **Special Achievements:** First African American champion in the sport's history; first African American to win a major U.S. auto racing season championship; competed in motocross competitions at the age of 12.

### BROWN, ARNOLD E.
Lawyer, president (organization). **Personal:** Born Apr 21, 1932, Englewood, NJ; son of John Scott Jr and Hortense Melle Stubbs; married Lydia Barbara White; children: Crystal L, Beverly M Fitzhugh, Dale E Davis & Arnold E II; married Gwendolyn Wertby. **Educ:** Bowling Green State Univ, BA, 1954; Rutgers Univ Sch Law, JD, 1957. **Career:** Self-employed atty, Englewood NJ, 1957-86; Bergen County, assembly man, 1966-67; Du Bois Book Ctr, owner & pres, 1985-; pres, 1986; Brown & Assocs, pres, currently. **Orgs:** Gen Assembly, NJ, 1965-66; pres, Bergen County Urban League; Nat Asn Advan Colored People Bergen County; bd mem, Adv Comt Salvation Army Bergen County; pres, Kappa Theta Lambda Chap Alpha Phi Alpha Fraternity; forever pres, African Am Bus Enterprise Coun Northern NJ, 1986-; Bergen W Camp, Gideon Int; pres, Friends Libr; Coalition Preserv Teaneck's Indian Slave Cemetery Afro-Am Hist Soc Mus; NJ Chap Afro-Am Hist & Geneal Soc; Bergen County Hist Preserv Adv Bd. **Business Addr:** President, Du Bois Book Center, 383 Knickerbocker Rd, Englewood, CO 07631-0776, **Business Phone:** (201)567-3611.

### BROWN, ATLANTA THOMAS
Librarian. **Personal:** Born Oct 30, 1931, Bennettsville, SC; daughter of Alice Reid Thomas and Julius A; married Samuel E; children: Dale. **Educ:** SC State Univ, Orangeburg, BS, 1953; Univ Wis, Madison, MLS, 1963. **Career:** Librarian (retired); Columbia City Schs, librn, 1953-58; Richmond City Schs, librn, 1958-63; Wilmington City Schs, librn, 1963-82; Christina Sch Dist, librn, dist chair libr media, 1982-90. **Orgs:** New Castle County Libr Adv Bd, 1982-89; pres, Del Libr Asn, 1984-85; Am Libr Asn, nat libr week comt, 1984-88; charter mem, Am Asn Univ Women, Millcreek Hundred Br; Am Asn Sch Librn, legis comt, pub rels comts, 1984-86; founder & charter mem, Del Coalition Literacy, 1985-; bd dir, Ingleside Homes; Chesapeake Ctr Bd: Speer Trust Comn; pres, Del Asn Supvrn &Curric Develop, 1988-89; pres, Nat Asn Univ Women, Wilmington Br, 1994-; moderator, New Castle Presbytery, 1994-95; vol librn, Gander Hill Prison, 1994; Presby Church, gen assembly coun, 1996-2001; vol Against Adolescent Pregnancy; Delta Sigma Theta Sorority; charter mem, Nat Coun Negro Women, Wilmington Sect. **Honors/Awds:** Librarian of the Year, Wilmington City Schools, 1970; Appointee, Del Gov, State Adv Coun Libr, 1971-75 &1983-89; Wilmington Br Membership Award, Nat Asn Advan Colored People, 1979; appointee, State's White House Conf Libr, 1990; Phi Delta Kappa Int. **Special Achievements:** Tech Trends, 1986; Delaware Library Association Bulletin, Winter 1986. **Home Addr:** 4502 Pickwick Dr, Wilmington, DE 19808, **Home Phone:** (302)998-0803.

### BROWN, BARBARA ANN
Government official, photographer. **Personal:** Born Aug 17, 1949, Lynchburg, VA. **Educ:** Phillips Bus Col, AA, 1967; Cortez W Peters Bus Col, AA, 1971. **Career:** Bur Nat Affairs Inc, data entry operator, 1971; New York Inst Photog, 1983. **Orgs:** Secy, Mayfair Mansions Res Coun, 1971 6th Dist Police-Citizens Adv Coun, 1979; corresp secy, Marshall Highlights Community Develop Org Inc, 1983; Citizens Adv Com DC Bar, 1984; Prof Photogr Am Inc, 1985. **Honors/Awds:** Outstanding Community Serv ANC7A, Wash, DC, 1978-81. **Special Achievements:** For Women Only Moorland-Spingarn Res, 1983; For Black Women Photographers, Howard Univ, Wash, DC, 1984. **Home Addr:** 3770 Hayes St NE Suite 8, Washington, DC 20019.

### BROWN, BARBARA L.
Research administrator, engineer, government official. **Educ:** Fla State Univ, BS, comput sci; Univ Cent Fla, MS, eng mgt. **Career:** NASA, Kennedy Space Ctr, Artificial Intelligence Lab, systs engr, Advan Software Lab, mgr, Future Launch Systs & Advan Progs Off, X-34 proj engr, Prof Develop Prog, 1998, chief engr, chief info officer, 1998-2000, Ames Res Ctr liaison, currently; NASA, dep mgr intelligent syst human-centered comput, currently. **Honors/Awds:** NASA Exceptional Service Medal. **Home Addr:** 5543 Oak Hollow Dr, Titusville, FL 32780, **Home Phone:** (321)264-0448. **Business Addr:** Deputy Manager, Ames Research Center Liaison, Kennedy Space Center, Orlando, FL 32899-0001, **Business Phone:** (321)867-5000.

### BROWN, DR. BARBARA MAHONE
Poet, educator. **Personal:** Born Feb 27, 1944, Chicago, IL; daughter of Loniel Atticus and Anne Savage; married Rex Michael; children: Letta McBain, Aisha & Imani. **Educ:** Fisk Univ, Nashville, TN, 1965; Wash State Univ, Pullman, WA, BA, 1968; Univ Chicago, Chicago, IL, MBA, 1975; Stanford Univ, Stanford, CA, PhD, 1988. **Career:** Educator (retired), poet; Burrell Advert, Chicago, Ill, copy supvr, 1970-73; First Nat Bank, Chicago, Ill, advert mgr, 1975; Nat Broadcasting Co, New York, NY, dir planning, 1975-77; Clark Col, Atlanta, Ga, assoc prof bus admin, 1978-84; Univ Tex Austin, Austin, Tex, assoc prof commun, 1988-90; San Jose State Univ, San Jose, Calif, assoc prof mkt, prof emerita; Fielding Inst, ODE Master's Degree Prog, founding fac; Elbow Room Consult, pres. **Orgs:** Orgn Black Am Cult, OBAC, 1969-75; Steering Comt, U N Mid-Decade Women, SE Regional Conf, 1980; bd mem, Am Cancer Soc Austin, Tex Chap, 1989-90; adv task force, Atlanta City Coun Finance Comt, 1981-82; Soc Res Child Develop, 1987-; Int Commun Asn, 1987-; trustee, Hillbrook Sch, Los Gatos, CA, 1995-; bd mem, Kids Common, San Jose, CA, 1997-; Mt Madonna Sch; bd trustee, US Int Univ. **Honors/Awds:** Teacher-Scholar, San Jose State Univ, 1993-94; Author, "Advertising Influences on Youth", Journal of Communication Inquiry, 1990. **Home Addr:** 1033 Nobel Dr, Santa Cruz, CA 95060, **Home Phone:** (408)471-9432.

### BROWN, BARTRAM S.
Law enforcement officer, educator. **Educ:** Harvard Univ, BA, 1974; Columbia Univ, JD, 1977; Grad Inst Int Stud, Geneva, PhD, 1986. **Career:** Col William & Mary, asst prof govt, 1987-91; Columbia Human Rights Law Rev, managing ed; Int Criminal Tribunal, law clerk, 1995-96; Ill Inst Technol, vis scholar, Cambridge Univ; Chicago-Kent Col Law, prof law, currently, Prog Int & Comparative Law, co-dir, 1991. **Orgs:** Coun Foreign Rels; adv bd, Am Bar Asn Cent & Eastern Europ Law Initiative; legal adv, Rome Diplomatic Conf Estab Int Criminal Ct, Repub Trinidad & Tobago, 1998; pub mem, US Deleg UN Comn Human Rights, Geneva, Switz, 1999 & 2000; bd dir, Amnesty Int USA, 2000-03; Am Law Inst; vis fel Univ Cambridge, lautherpacht centre int law, int law, 2004. **Business Addr:** Professor, Co-Director, Chicago-Kent College of Law, 565 W Adams St Rm 855, Chicago, IL 60661-3691, **Business Phone:** (312)906-5046.

### BROWN, REV. DR. BEATRICE S. See Obituaries Section.

**BROWN, DR. BERTRAND JAMES**
School administrator. **Educ:** Parsons Jr Col, AA, 1953; Emporia State Univ, AB, 1957; Kans State Univ, MS, 1959; Univ Mass, EdD. **Career:** School administrator (retired); New York City Sch, teacher, sch prin, Youth & Adult Educ Ctr, dir dist prog, Cult Enrichment Prog, dir, Spec Extended Sch Prog, dir, Community Sch Dist Five, supt sch. **Orgs:** Lifetime mem, Nat Asn Advan Colored People.

**BROWN, BETTYE JEAN (BETTYE JEAN CRAWLEY)**
Manager. **Personal:** Born Jan 30, 1955, Hazlehurst, GA. **Educ:** FL State Univ, BS, 1976; GA Southwestern Col, MEd, 1983. **Career:** Jeff Davis County Bd Educ, educr, 1977-85; Southern GA Col, instr, 1983; GA Assoc Educr, united serv dir, 1985; Richmond County Asn educr, exec dir. **Orgs:** Founder & coordr, Stud Involvement Black Unity, 1978-85; coordr, Upward Bound Prog, 1981-85; pres, Jeff Davis Co Asn Educr, 1982-84; sec, Nat Asn Advan Colored People, 1984; pres, Jeff Davis County Clients Coun, 1984-88; coordr, Non-Urban Organizing Proj, 1986; vpres, Am Asn Univ Women; worthy matron Order Eastern Star; conf coordr, Nat Black Staff Network; Nat Educ Asn, Nat Coun Social Studies; vpres, Delta Sigma Theta; Negro Bus & Prof Women; Bulloch 2000 Comt; secy, State Human Rel Comt; monitor, GA Housing Coalition Comt Develop Block Grant Prog; designed & coordr progs, Am Educ Week; Miss Ebony Pageant; Jeff Davis Co Reapportionme Comn. **Honors/Awds:** Outstanding Serv Community Clients Coun, 1985; Outstanding Teacher, Y Clubs Model United Nat Club, 1985; Dedicated Serv, Nat Asn Advan Colored People, 1986; Outstanding Serv Wash Co Asn Educr, 1986; Friend Educ Award, Wash County Asn Educr, 1989. **Home Addr:** 1624 Eagles Landing Blvd Apt 84, Tallahassee, FL 32308-1557.

**BROWN, BEVERLY J.**
Consultant, chief executive officer. **Personal:** Born Oct 8, 1958, Louisville, KY; daughter of Charles Jr and Beatrice (deceased). **Educ:** Tenn State Univ, BS, 1980; Univ Louisville, MEd, 1982. **Career:** State Ky Employ Serv, sr employ counr, 1982-87; Chestnut St YMCA, Louisville, black achievers dir, 1987-95; Johnston Memorial YMCA, Charlotte, dir prog develop, 1995-96; YMCA USA, assoc dir, youth develop & nat black achievers dir, 1996-2003; BJ Brown Enterprises, chief exec officer, 2003-. **Orgs:** Alpha Kappa Alpha Sorority, 1991-; YMCA Asn Prof dir, 1996-; Nat Black Child Develop Inst, 1999-2000; Tavis Smiley Youth Leaders, 2000-; Nat Asn Advan Colored People, 2002-. **Home Addr:** 16315 Kenwood Ave, South Holland, IL 60473, **Home Phone:** (708)333-4497. **Business Addr:** Chief Executive Officer, BJ Brown Enterprises, 3318 Duvalle Dr, Louisville, KY 40211, **Business Phone:** (502)776-2222.

**BROWN, BINTA (BINTA NIAMBI BROWN)**
Human rights activist, lawyer, consultant. **Educ:** Barnard Col, BA, polit sci, 1995; Columbia Univ Sch Law, JD, 1998; Columbia Univ Sch Int & Pub Affairs, Int Econ Policy. **Career:** Wash Post Co, assoc, 1995; Cravath, Swaine & Moore LLP, assoc, 1998-2007; Gov Eliot Spitzer's Transp Policy Advisor, transition team mem, 2006; Kirkland & Ellis LLP, partner, 2007-13; Gov Andrew Cuomo's Transp Policy Advisor, transition team mem, 2010; Harvard Kennedy Sch Govt, Mossavar-Rahmani Ctr Bus & Govt, sr fel 2013-. **Orgs:** Bd mem, 2U; bd mem, Barnard Col; bd mem, Human Rights First; bd mem, Am Theatre Wing; bd mem, New York Parks Found; Coun Foreign Rels. **Honors/Awds:** "Fortune" Magazine, 40 Under 40 Business Leaders; "Crain's New York," 40 Under 40, 2011; National Organization for Women, Woman of Power and Influence, 2011; World Economic Forum, Young Global Leader, 2012; "The Root" Magazine, The Root 100 Honorees, 2013. **Special Achievements:** Has advised Hillary Clinton (informally on national security issues) as well as Governor Andrew Cuomo and members of President Barack Obama's administration. **Business Addr:** Senior Fellow, John F Kennedy School of Government, Belfer-511, Cambridge, MA 02138, **Business Phone:** (617)495-1100.

**BROWN, BOB.** See BROWN, ROBERT, JR.

**BROWN, BOBBY (ROBERT BARISFORD BROWN)**
Actor, songwriter, singer. **Personal:** Born Feb 5, 1969, Boston, MA; son of Herbert and Carol; married Whitney Houston; children: Bobbi Kristina Houston; married Alicia Etheridge; children: 2. **Career:** New Edition, mem singing group, 1980-86; solo performer, 1986-. Albums: King of Stage, 1987, Don't Be Cruel, 1988, Bobby, 1992; Forever, 1998; Ghost busters II Motion Picture Soundtrack, 1990. Films: Ghost bustersII, actor, 1989; Panther, actor, 1995; A Thin Line Between Love & Hate, actor, 1996; Two Can Play That Game, actor, 2001; Go For Broke, actor, 2002; Gang of Roses, actor, 2003; Nora's Hair Salon, actor, 2004; Nora's Hair Salon 2: A Cut Above, 2008. TV progs: "Cedric the Entertainer Presents", 2003; "Jimmy Kimmel Live", 2005; "Being Bobby Brown", exec producer, 2005; "25 Strong: The BET Silver Anniversary Spec", 2005; "Cuts", 2005; "Gone Country", 2008; "What Perez Says", 2007; "Who Ate The Soul?", 2007. **Business Addr:** Singer, MCA Records, 70 Universal City Plz, Universal City, CA 91608, **Business Phone:** (818)777-4000.

**BROWN, BOOKER T.**
Executive, labor relations manager. **Personal:** Born Aug 10, 1950, Macon, MS. **Educ:** Forest Pk Community Col, attended 1971; Boise State Univ, BSEd, 1973. **Career:** Morrison-Knudsen Int Co, dir recreation; Idaho Nat Bank, loan cr. **Orgs:** Optimist Club; Munic Credit Union Sports Softball Team; life mem, pres, Boise State Univ Alumni Asn; Boise State Univ Found; bd mem, dir, Idaho Womens Health & Fitness Educ Celebration Inc. **Honors/Awds:** Dean List Award, Boise State Univ, 1973; Todays Psychol, 1973; Outstanding Athlete of America Award, 1973. **Home Addr:** 2113 W Morning Vista Lane, Phoenix, AZ 85085-2727, **Home Phone:** (623)271-9622.

**BROWN, BRIAN A.**
Executive. **Personal:** Born Jul 7, 1952, Yonkers, NY; son of William T Sr (deceased) and Demetra A; married Lorrie L Frost. **Educ:** Boston Univ, BA, sociol, 1976; SPC, mass commun, 1977. **Career:** Black Enterprise Mag, dir prom, 1977-81; AT&T, indust consult, 1980-84; Int Bus Mach ROLM, dist sales dir, 1984-86; Wang Labs Intecom, vpres sales, 1984-86; Prom Mng Am, pres, 1986. **Orgs:** A100 Black Men, 1991-; chmn, 100 Black C Inc, 1992; bd mem, Adv Comn, NY Urban League; 1992-; exec bd, Broadway Cares Equity Fights AIDS, 1994.

**BROWN, BROADINE M.**
Government official. **Career:** US Marshals Serv, sr budget analyst mgt chief, Mgt & Budget Div, asst dir, currently. **Home Addr:** 4316 22nd Pl, TEMPLE HILLS, MD 20748, **Home Phone:** (301)423-4739. **Business Addr:** Assistant Director, US Marshals Service, 3rd Const Ave NW Rm 1103, Washington, DC 20001, **Business Phone:** (202)307-9032.

**BROWN, BYRON WILLIAM, II**
Government official, mayor. **Personal:** Born Sep 24, 1958, New York, NY; son of Byron and Clarice Kirnon; married Michelle Austin; children: Byron William III. **Educ:** Buffalo State Col, BA, jour & polit sci, 1983, MS, 1989; Harvard Univ, John F Kennedy Sch Govt, cert prog, sr exec. **Career:** City Buffalo, Coun Pres Off, exec secy coun pres, 1984-86; Erie County Legis Chmn Off, Buffalo, NY, news secy/exec asst, 1986-88; State NY Dep Speaker's Off, Buffalo, NY, dir pub rels, 1986-88; County Erie, DivEqual Employ Opportunity, Buffalo, NY, dir, 1988; 60th Dist Erie & Niagara County, sen, 2001; NY State Dem Comt, citys chief exec, mayor, 2005-. **Orgs:** Rho Lambda Chap, Alpha Phi Alpha Fraternity, 1984-; vpres, bd dir, St Augustine's Ctr, 1989-; judge, ACT-SO, Nat Asn Advan Colored People, 1989-; bd trustee, Western NY Pub Broadcasting, 1990-; asst scout leader, Boy Scouts Am, Troop 84, 1991-; mentor, Buffalo Pub Sch 38 Chamber Com, 1991-; St John Baptist Church; Erie County Dem Comt; New York State Senate; Buffalo Common Coun; Grassroots. **Home Addr:** 14 Blaine Ave, Buffalo, NY 14208-1057, **Home Phone:** (716)897-4019. **Business Addr:** Mayor, New York State Democratic Committee, 65 Niagara Sq 201 City Hall, Buffalo, NY 10010, **Business Phone:** (716)851-4841.

**BROWN, DR. CARLTON E.**
Educator, president (organization). **Personal:** Born Macon, GA; married T LaVerne Ricks; children: Kwame & Jamila. **Educ:** Univ Mass, BA, eng & Am studies, 1971, EdD, multicultural educ, 1979. **Career:** Old Dom Univ, Sch Educ, Norfolk, Va, fac, 1979-87; Hampton Univ, sr admin, Sch Educ, dean, 1987-96, Sch Lib Arts & Educ, founder, 1990-, Grad Col, vpres planning & dean, 1996-97; Savannah State Univ, pres, 1997-2006; Clark Atlanta Univ, exec vpres & provost, 2007-08, pres, 2008-. **Orgs:** Vice chmn, 2002-04, chmn, Savannah Econ Devel Authority, 2004; bd trustee, Clark Atlanta Univ. **Business Addr:** President, Clark Atlanta University, 223 James P Brawley Dr SW, Atlanta, GA 30314, **Business Phone:** (404)880-8000.

**BROWN, CAROL ANN**
Educator. **Personal:** Born Jan 25, 1952, Ann Arbor, MI; married Marcellus B; children: Brandon M, Marc A & Adam C. **Educ:** Univ Mich, BS, 1974, MS, 1975. **Career:** Ann Arbor Pub Schs, instrumental music instr, 1974-75; Joliet Pub Schs, coordr music, 1975-82; Augustana Col, asst dean stud servs, 1982. **Orgs:** Bd dir, Vis Nurse Homemaker Assoc, 1985-; pres, Delta Sigma Theta Inc Moline Davenport Alumnae, 1985-; Sounds Peace Ensemble, 1984-; Zonta Int, 1983-. **Home Addr:** 5736 S Horseshoe Pl, Boise, ID 83716-9030, **Home Phone:** (208)338-9072. **Business Addr:** IL.

**BROWN, CAROLYN M.**
Purchasing agent. **Personal:** Born Oct 12, 1948, Seattle, WA; married Jerome; children: Cesha, Channelle & Clifton. **Educ:** Anderson Col, BA, speech educ, sociol, minor educ, 1970; Baltimore State Univ, MA speech educ, Commun, 1976; Univ Berkeley. **Career:** Purchasing agent (retired); Indianapolis Publ Sch, teacher, 1970-71; Delco Remy, clerk, 1971, secy, 1971-72, supvr, 1972-75, buyer, 1975-83, sr buyer, 1983-86, gen supvr central stores, 1986. **Orgs:** Reg Minority Purchasing Coun; Nat Minority Supplier Develop Coun; Channel 49; chairperson Telesale; TV personality; Women Church God; alumni dir, Anderson Col; Baltimore State Alumni Asso; capt, Telethon Night Dr; Christian ctr, Alpha Kappa Alpha, Alpha Psi Omega; mayoral app educ comm Blue Ribbon; Madison County Fine Arts Coun, Urban League Madison County; bd dir, United Way, United Cerebral Palsy; Nat Asn Advan Colored People; Nat Republican Comn; Career Guild Assoc; Am Bus Women Am; dir, Youth Choir; Sunday Sch teacher; Kodiakanal & Woodstock Found; Smithsonian Assoc; fel sponsor Anderson Col; dr person Community Concert Ser; Black Expo Inc; sponsor Theada Club Anderson Col; judge Black Baltimore State Pageant; Jr Miss Madison County. **Honors/Awds:** Sequentennial Queen; William B Harper Award Outstanding Community Serv Madison County; Outstanding Young Woman Am; Outstanding Black Am; Outstanding Elem Teacher Am; Pres Award Urban League of Madison County; Outstanding Conf Leader-NAACP Nat Convention Anderson IN; Outstanding Lady Day AME Church Anderson IN; nom Prof Achievers Award; IN Reg Minority Supplier Develop Coun Achievement Award; Nat Supplier Year Buyer Rec Award. **Home Addr:** 7715 Harbour Isle, Indianapolis, IN 46240.

**BROWN, CAROLYN THOMPSON**
Library administrator. **Personal:** Born May 18, 1943, Brooklyn, NY; daughter of Frank and Martha Thompson; children: Christopher Leslie & Michael Arthur; married Timothy E Eastman; children: 2. **Educ:** Cornell Univ, BA, asian studies, 1965, MA, chinese lit, 1968; Am Univ, PhD, lit, 1978. **Career:** Howard Univ, asst prof, dept eng, 1978-84, assoc prof, eng dept, 1984-91, Col Lib Arts, assoc dean humanities, 1988-90; US Nat Comn Libr & Info Sci, comnr; Libr Cong, dir educ serv, 1990-92, assoc librn cult affairs, 1992-95, asst librn libr serv, Area Studies Collections, actg dir, 1995-, heads Collections & Serv Directorate, 16th div, currently, comnr, 2004-. **Orgs:** Am Libr Asn, 1990-; Asn Asian Studies; bd mem, Contemplative Mind's Soc, 1997; bd trustee, Fetzer Inst, 2002-; adv bd, Nat Foreign Lang Ctr; adv comt, Global Resources Prog, Asn Res Libr; exec comt, John W Kluge Ctr Advan Res; Asn Col & Res Libr. **Honors/Awds:** Cornell Nat Fellowship, Cornell Univ, 1961-65; Nat Defence Foreign Lang, 1965-67; Graduate Honor Fellowship, Am Univ, 1975-78; Faculty Research Grant, Howard Univ, 1980 & 1986; Rockefeller Found, grant, 2000. **Special Achievements:** Auth, Dramatic Prod "Goin Home", 1981; produced numerous articles; Article: "Paradigm of the Iron House: Shouting & Silence in Lu Hsun's Short Stories". **Business Addr:** Acting Director for Area Studies Collections, Assistant Librarian, Library of Congress, 101 Independence Ave SE, Washington, DC 20540-8000, **Business Phone:** (202)707-5000.

**BROWN, CARRIE**
Dentist, president (organization). **Personal:** Born Choppee, SC; daughter of Ervin Parker Sr and Cynthia Parker; married Thomas Brown; children: Sakita Nichelle & Shekira Jenika. **Educ:** Tuskegee Inst, BS, biol, 1971; Univ Ky Col Dent, DDS, 1980. **Career:** Professional dentist, Lexington, KY, 1983-2012. **Orgs:** Lexington Alumni Chap Delta Sigma Theta, pres, 1979-81; Delta Dent Ky, bd mem, 1994-; Nat Dent Asn, House Delegates Bd trustee, 2003-09, House Delegates, 2009-11, vice speaker House Delegates, 2010-12, vpres NDA, 2013-14, pres, 2014-; Renaissance Health Serv Corp, bd mem 2009-12; Ky Dent Asn, pres. **Special Achievements:** Delegate to the Fourth African-African American Summit, 1997; delegate to the Fifth African-African American Summit, 1999; Delegate to the Leon H. Sullivan Summit, 2008; volunteer for Black Achiever Program, the Blue Grass Dental Society, Headstart, and the Hope Center. **Business Addr:** 353 Highfield Loop, Myrtle Beach, SC 29579, **Business Phone:** (859)312-7008.

**BROWN, CARROLL ELIZABETH**
Government official, executive, vice president (organization). **Personal:** Born Aug 31, 1942, Ft. Worth, TX; married Ralph Theodore Sr; children: Ralph Jr, Erik & Shawn. **Educ:** Seattle Univ, attended 1963. **Career:** WADS Radio "Breakfast for Two", radio talk show hostess, 1976; TRW-Geom Tool, personal asst, 1978-81; Capital Temporaries Inc, placement mgr, 1980-84; Shubert Theater, grp sls assoc & community rels liaison, 1984-85; Conn Bus Inst, placement dir, 1985; Stone Acad, placement dir, 1986-90; New Haven Conv & Visitors Bur, dir visitors servs & admin, 1990-91; Legis Asst to Labor Comt, 1992-93; Spokeswoman for Chief Quiet Hawk, Paugussett Indian Tribe, temp/part-time, 1993-94. **Orgs:** Founder & pres, W Haven Black Coalition Inc, 1986-; W Haven High Parents Club, 1987-88; YWCA Ballroom Restoration Comt, 1987-89; bd dir, YWCA, 1987-89; vpres, Conn State Nat Asn Advan Colored People, 1987-91; former vpres, Greater New Haven NAACP, 1990; adv bd, Inner-City Advertiser, 1990-; Yale-New Haven Hosp Ann Appeal Comt, 1990-; bd dir, Peabody Mus, 1990-91; adv bd, Am Nat Bank, 1991-; personnel comt, Citizens Tv, bd dir, 1991-; vpres, Conn State Nat Asn Advan Colored People, 1991-; fin bd, W Haven, 1992-. **Honors/Awds:** Nominee Jefferson Award Community Servce, 1975; Outstanding Volunteer of the Year, Bridgeport Public School System, 1982-85; Mrs Connecticut Second Runner-Up, 1983; Black Family Achievement Award, West Haven High School, 1985; Nominated for Jefferson Awards, 1987; Civic/Community Service Award, Professional & Business Assn of Greater New Haven, 1988; Outstanding Member Award, Dixwell United Church of Christ, 1990; Benjamin L Hooks Outstanding Leadership Award, Connecticut State Nat Asn Advan Colored People, 1992; Community Service Award, Elm City Business & Professional Women's Assn, 1993; Local Citizen of the Year Award, 1993; District Citizen of the Year Award, 1994; Omega Psi Phi Fraternity. **Home Addr:** 56 Highview Ave, West Haven, CT 06516, **Home Phone:** (203)397-3354. **Business Addr:** Founder, President, West Haven Black Coalition Inc, 244 Fairfax St, West Haven, CT 06516, **Business Phone:** (203)933-1701.

**BROWN, CARRYE BURLEY**
Government official. **Personal:** Born Palestine, TX; daughter of Ecomet Sr and W M Burley; married Larry; children: Xavier & Xenia. **Educ:** Bright Eyed Col, Lufkin, TX; Stephen F Austin State Univ, BS, home econs, 1973; Tex Women Univ, MS, 1976. **Career:** Comt Sci & Technol, cong staffer, 1977-1994; Fed Govt, tech asst; US Fire Admin, civil servant, 1994-2001; Kingsbury Ctr, upper sch reading lab teacher, 2002-13. **Orgs:** Nat Fire Acad Alumni Asn. **Special Achievements:** First woman and the first African American to head the US Fire Administration. **Business Addr:** Administrator, US Fire Administration, 16825 S Seton Ave, Emmitsburg, MD 21727, **Business Phone:** (301)447-1018.

**BROWN, CHADWICK EVERETT**
Executive, football player. **Personal:** Born Jul 12, 1970, Altadena, CA; married Kristin; children: Amani. **Educ:** Univ Colo, mkt. **Career:** Football player (retired), owner; Pittsburgh Steelers, right inside linebacker, 1993-95, right outside linebacker, 1996, 2006; Seattle Seahawks, right linebacker, 1997-98, linebacker, 1999-2004, right outside linebacker, 1999, 2001; New Eng Patriots, linebacker, middle linebacker, 2005, 2007; Pro Exotics, owner, currently. **Honors/Awds:** Joe Greene Great Performance Award, 1993; Champion, Asian Football Confederation, 1995. **Home Addr:** 10287 Dowling Way, Highlands Ranch, CO 80126-4769, **Home Phone:** (720)479-6200. **Business Addr:** Owner, Pro Exotics, 3911 Norwood Dr Suite C, Littleton, CO 80125, **Business Phone:** (303)347-0500.

**BROWN, REP. CHARLES**
Consultant, government official, association executive. **Personal:** Born Mar 8, 1938, Williston, SC; son of Charlie Jr and Ruth A Hickson; married Angela Baker; children: Charlisa L Scott. **Educ:** Cheyney State Teachers Col, BS, 1961; Ind Univ NW, MPA, 1980. **Career:** Gary Community Sch Corp, teacher, 1961-68; Gary Youth Serv Bur, dir, 1968-82; Gen Assembly, state rep, 1983-95; City Gary, Gary, IN, affirmative action officer & risk mgr, 1968-88; Gary Comn Ment Health Ctr, chief exec officer, 1988-93; consult; Ind House Representatives, state rep, currently. **Orgs:** Bd dir, Nat Civil Rights Mus & Hall Fame; Nat Alumni Asn Hall Fame, Cheyney Univ; Coun State Health Policy Leadership; Ind Univ Sch Med Educ; Coalition Health Care Gary; Bro's Keeper Gary; trustee, St Timothy Community Church; charter mem, Nat Coun Black Child Develop; founder, Mayor Hatcher's Youth Found. **Honors/Awds:** Received numerous awards including: Mary White Ovington Award, Nat Asn Advan Colored People; Award of Merit, Ind Hosp Asn; Lake County Medical Society Award; Cheyney University National Alumni Association Award. **Special**

**Achievements:** First elected to the Indiana House of Representatives, 1982. **Home Addr:** 9439 Lake Shore Dr, Gary, IN 46403-1609, **Home Phone:** (219)938-6548. **Business Addr:** State Representative, Indiana House of Representatives, 200 W Washington St, Indianapolis, IN 46204-2786, **Business Phone:** (317)232-9600.

**BROWN, CHARLES EDWARD**
Geologist. **Personal:** Born Sep 7, 1948, Buckingham, VA; son of Warren G H and Gretchen H Jackson; married Sadie Banks; children: Karen Denise & Carla Denette. **Educ:** Va State Univ, Petersburg, VA, BS, geol, 1971; Pa State Univ, State Col, PA, MS, geol, 1974, PhD, 1976. **Career:** US Geol Surv, Reston, Va, res hydrologist & geologist, 1969-88; Chevron Oil, USA, explor geologist, 1976-78; Va State Univ, Petersburg, Va, asst prof, 1978-80; George Mason Univ, vis common wealth prof geol sci dept; Howard Univ, prof; US Dept Energy, int fossil energy specialist & sr geologist; US Geol Surv, Water Resources Div, res proj chief. **Orgs:** Soc Explor Geophysicists; Geol Soc Am; Am Geophys Union; Nat Asn Black Geologists & Geophysicists; founder, dir, Int Geohydroscience & Energy Res Inst, 2003-; Geol Soc Am; Nat Asn Black Geologists & Geophysicists; Asn Geoscientists Int Develop. **Honors/Awds:** Phi Kappa Phi Honor Society, Pa State Univ, 1974. **Home Addr:** 15094 Wetherburn Dr, Centreville, VA 20120, **Home Phone:** (703)631-5169. **Business Addr:** Exploration Geologist, American Geological Institute, 4220 King St, Alexandria, VA 22302-1502, **Business Phone:** (703)379-2480.

**BROWN, DR. CHARLES SUMNER**
Clergy, educator, association executive. **Personal:** Born Sep 18, 1937, Plant City, FL; married Joan Marie Steed; children: Charles Jr & Gene Mitchell. **Educ:** Morehouse Col, AB, 1956; United Theol Sem, MDiv, 1962; Boston Univ Sch Theol, ThD, 1973; Cent State Univ, Dhl, 1993. **Career:** Wright-Patterson Afb, mathematician fluid dynamics res br, 1956-59; Sheldon St Congregation Church Providence, pastor, 1964-66; Ebenezer Baptist Church Boston, interim pastor, 1966-67; United Theol Sem, prof church & soc, 1968-79; Yale Univ Divinity Sch, assoc prof practical theol, 1979-83; Bethel Baptist Church, pastor, 1982-. **Orgs:** Secy, The Soc Study Black Relig; vol assoc prof, Dept Med Soc Wright State Univ Med Sch; bd mem, United Way Greater Dayton; Family Serv Asn; Dayton Coun World Affairs; Dayton Art Inst; pres, Metro Churches United; Bethel Missionary Baptist Church, 1957; moderator Western Union Baptist Dist Asn; Kappa Alpha Psi Frat; Sigma Pi Phi Boule; pres, Ohio Baptist Gen Conv; Citizens Appeal Bd; Miami Valley Boy Scout Coun, exec bd; Dayton Pub Schs, Character Educ Comt. **Honors/Awds:** Protestant Fellowship Award, Fund Theol Educ, 1961-62; Presbyterian Grad Fellowship, United Presby Church, USA, 1966-67. **Home Addr:** 625 Ridgedale Rd, Dayton, OH 45406, **Home Phone:** (513)275-7828. **Business Addr:** Pastor, Bethel Baptist Church, 401 S Paul Laurence Dunbar St, Dayton, OH 45402, **Business Phone:** (937)222-4373.

**BROWN, CHERIE GREER**
Athlete, executive. **Personal:** Born Philadelphia, PA; daughter of Hal and Mayme; married Winston G; children: Capri. **Educ:** Univ Va, BS, commun, 1994. **Career:** Athlete (retired), executive; Lacrosse player; exec asst; Grant Hill the Detroit Pistons, asst; GranHco Enterprises, vpres; Hill Ventures Inc, pres; Lacrosse Mag All-Century Team, 2000; Greer Strategy Group Inc, prin, currently; Delta Realty Advisors Inc, venture partner, currently. **Home Addr:** 2632 Beacon Hill Dr Apt 204, Auburn Hills, MI 48326. **Business Addr:** Venture Partner, Delta Realty Advisors Inc, 2200 Lucien Way Suite 420, Maitland, FL 32751, **Business Phone:** (407)331-9213.

**BROWN, CHRISTINE JAMES**
Executive. **Personal:** Born Sep 9, 1952, Philadelphia, PA; daughter of Howard and Eva. **Educ:** Rutgers Univ, BA, cult anthrop, 1974; Brown Univ, PhD, anthrop. **Career:** NY City Found Sr Citizens, 1977; Planning Consult Agency Opers, 1979; dep dir admin, 1982; Allocations & Agency Rels, 1985; Fund Distrib & Community Prob-Solving, dir, 1988; United Way Southeastern Pa, pres & chief exec officer, 2004; United Way Int, pres & chief exec officer, 2004-07; Child Welfare League Am, pres & chief exec officer, 2007-; Philadelphia Chamber Com. **Orgs:** Chair, United Way Am's Nat Prof Coun; Urban League Philadelphia; bd vice chair, Community Col Philadelphia; Greater Philadelphia Chamber Com; bd, Samuel S Fels Fund; Christopher Ludwick Found; Del Valley; Pa Bar Asn Judicial Eval Comn; bd, Sch Dist Philadelphia; Community Col Philadelphia; bd, Forum Exec Women; Grantmakers; Philadelphia Urban Affairs Coalition; Pa Bar Asn Judicial Eval Comn; Red Cross vol African nation Kenya; William Penn Found; Vanguard Charitable Trusts; Eagles Youth Partnership; Ctr Effective Philanthropy; Int Eisenhower Fels Nominating Comt; Philadelphia Sch Bd. **Home Addr:** , Alexandria, VA. **Business Addr:** President, Chief Executive Officer, Child Welfare League of America, 1726 M St NW Suite 500, Washington, DC 22202, **Business Phone:** (202)688-4200.

**BROWN, HON. CHRISTOPHER C.**
Judge. **Personal:** Born Nov 20, 1938, Pontiac, MI; son of Arthur Patrick and Ardelia Christopher; married Lillian Jean Twitty; children: Alesa Bailey & Tice Christopher. **Educ:** Wayne State Univ, BA, 1962; Detroit Col Law, JD, 1966. **Career:** Pvt pract, atty, 1966-73; 50th Dist Ct City Pontiac, judge, 1972-. **Orgs:** Nat Asn Advan Colored People; Urban League; Am Bar Asn; Mich Bar Asn; Wolverine Bar Asn; Oakland Bar Asn; Nat Bar Asn; D Augustus Straker Bar Asn. **Home Addr:** 243 Cherokee, Pontiac, MI 48341. **Business Addr:** Judge, 50th Judicial District Court, 70 N Saginaw St, Pontiac, MI 48342, **Business Phone:** (248)857-8000.

**BROWN, CHUCKY (CLARENCE BROWN)**
Basketball coach, basketball player. **Personal:** Born Feb 29, 1968, New York, NY; married Melanie; children: 3. **Educ:** NC State Univ, BA, sociol, 1989. **Career:** Basketball player (retired), basketball coach; Cleveland Cavaliers, small forward, 1989-91, 2001; Los Angeles Lakers, small forward, 1991-92; NJ Nets, small forward, 1992-93; Dallas Mavericks, small forward, 1993; Panna Firenze, Italy, 1992-93; Continental Basketball Asn, Grand Rapid Hoops, 1993-94; Continental Basketball Asn, Yakima Sun Kings, 1994-95; Houston Rockets, small forward, 1994-96; Phoenix Suns, small forward, 1997; Milwaukee Bucks, small forward, 1997; Atlanta Hawks, small forward, 1997-98; Charlotte Hornets, small forward, free agt, 1999-2000; San Antonio Spurs, free agt, pt forward, 2000; Golden State Warriors, small forward, 2001; Cleveland Cavaliers, small forward, 2001; Sacramento Kings, small forward, 2002; Fayetteville Patriots, mentor; Raleigh Knights, head coach, 2004; Roanoke Dazzle, asst coach, 2004-06; Los Angeles D-Fenders, asst coach, 2006-09, head coach, 2009-10. **Special Achievements:** Championship, NBA, 1995; All-League first team, CBA, 1995. **Business Addr:** Head Coach, Los Angeles D-Fenders, Toyota Sports Ctr, El Segundo, CA 90245, **Business Phone:** (310)426-6000.

**BROWN, CINDY (CYNTHIA LOUISE BROWN)**
Basketball player. **Personal:** Born Mar 16, 1965, Portland, OR. **Educ:** Long Beach State, attended 1987. **Career:** Basketball player (retired); Sidis Ancona, Italy, forward, 1987-88; Toshiba Yana Gi Cho, Japan, 1988-92; Faenza Errieti Club, Italy, 1992-94; Elizur Holon, Israel, 1994-96; US Valenciennes Orchies, France; Detroit Shock, 1998-99; Utah Starzz, 1999. **Orgs:** Final Four All-Tournament team, 1987.

**BROWN, CLAUDELL, JR.**
Educator, government official, association executive. **Personal:** Born Jun 8, 1949, Jackson, TN; married Linda Ruth Brogden. **Educ:** Lane Col, BA. **Career:** Bur Commun & Rels, teen counr, 1969-71; Tipton Co Sch Syst, teacher, 1974; Happy C Multi-Serv Ctr, Happy C Day-Care Inc, dir; Lane Col, Eng & Fr Black Lit, tutor; Jackson City Coun, Dist 5, comnr, currently. **Orgs:** Upward Bound Proj, 1969-70; Memphis Chap, Lane Col Alumni Asn, 1971; prog rep, US Dept Health, St Louis, 1971; Chelsea Community Coord Comt, 1972; Nat Social Workers Am, 1972; bd dir, Mid-S Med Centers Coun, 1973; bd dir, Memphis-Shelby Co Legal Serv Asn, 1973; adv comt, Memphis-Shelby Co Legal Serv Asn, 1973; basileus, Theta Iota Chap Omega Psi Phi Fraternity, 1973-74; social serv coordr, dep dir Memphis-Shelby Co Comm Action Agency; Nat Asn Advan Colored People; Concert Choir; Pre-Alumni Club; Stud Christian Asn; Fr Club; Social Sci Club; Stud Tribune; Memphis Comm Singers; vpres, Shelby Co Dem Voters Coun. **Home Addr:** 41 Carlos Dr, Jackson, TN 38301-6519, **Home Phone:** (731)616-3651. **Business Addr:** Commissioner, District 5, 100 E Main St Suite 301, Jackson, TN 38301, **Business Phone:** (731)424-7004.

**BROWN, CLAUDINE K. See Obituaries Section.**

**BROWN, CLIFTON GEORGE**
Journalist. **Personal:** Born Sep 3, 1959, Philadelphia, PA; son of George Alexander and Maurita Robinson; married Carolyn Martin; children: Ashley Georgia & Alexander William; married Delores Jones. **Educ:** Howard Univ, Wash, DC, 1979; Temple Univ, Philadelphia, PA, 1981. **Career:** Boca Raton News, Boca Raton, Fla, sportswriter, 1981-83; Detroit Free Press, Detroit, Mich, sportswriter, 1983-88; NY Times, New York, NY, sportswriter, 1988-2007; Am City Bus Journals, sportswriter, 2007-13; Sporting News, NFL writer, 2007-13; Comcast Sportsnet Baltimore, ravens insider, 2013-. **Orgs:** Nat Asn Black Journalists, 1983-. **Honors/Awds:** Second Place Feature Writing, Fla Sports Writers Asn, 1983. **Home Addr:** 10 Edgewood Dr, Freehold, NJ 07728, **Home Phone:** (732)780-4961. **Business Addr:** Sports Writer, The New York Times, 229 W 43rd St 4th Fl, New York, NY 10036, **Business Phone:** (212)556-7371.

**BROWN, COLLIER, JR. See BROWN, P. J.**

**BROWN, CONELLA COULTER**
Executive, teacher. **Personal:** Born Sep 26, 1925, Kansas City, MO; daughter of Charles P and Carrie Davis; married Arnold A. **Educ:** Kans City Conserv Mus, 1949; Univ Mo, BA, 1953; Case W Res Univ, MA, 1961; Lincoln Univ; Ohio Univ; Cleveland State Univ; Bowling Green State Univ. **Career:** School superintendent, college teacher (retired), educator; Cleveland Pub Sch, Cleveland, OH, social studies teacher, 1954-63; Ford Fnd Proj, coordr area curric develop, 1963-64; Rawlings Jr. HS, asst prin, 1964-65; Off Human Rel, asst supvr, 1965-66; Supt Off Hum Rel, admin asst, 1966-72, asst supt, 1972-80; Case W Res Univ, emer bd trustee, currently. **Orgs:** Adv Com Sch dent; Delta Kappa Gamma; Am Asn Sch Admin; Nat Asn Supv & Curric Develop; bd dir, Christian C Fund; bd trustee, Free Med Clin Greater Cleveland; Delta Sigma Theta Inc; hon life mem, Cleveland Coun Parent Teacher Asn, 1974; Urban League Greater Cleveland; Phi Delta Kappa; adv bd, Accord Assocs Inc, 1980-; trustee, St. James AME Church, 1982-89; chair, founding commt, bd dir, St James AME Churches Endowment fund, 1993-; adv bd, Creative Writing Writing Workshop Proj, 2000-. **Honors/Awds:** Professional Award for Leadership in Education, Cleveland Bus & Prof women, 1973; Outstanding Achievement Award in Education, Cuyahoga Comm Col, 1973; Distinguished Educator Award, St. James AME Church; Conella Coulter Brown Day, City Cleveland, Tribute, US Rep Louis Stockes, 1989; UMKC Alumni Achievement Award, 1964. **Special Achievements:** First President to Awd Urban League of Greater Cleveland; First Woman to attain the position of Asst Supt of major OH School Dist. **Home Addr:** 13800 Fairhill Rd Suite 407, Shaker Heights, OH 44120-5510, **Home Phone:** (216)229-4242. **Business Addr:** Emeritus Trustee, Case Western Reserve University, Rm 124 Adelbert Hall 10900 Euclid Ave, Cleveland, OH 44106, **Business Phone:** (216)368-2000.

**BROWN, CONSTANCE CHARLENE**
Government official. **Personal:** Born Jun 12, 1939, Chicago, IL; daughter of Charles W Porter and Myrtle V Jones Porter-King; married Leon Paul; children: Paul Gerard, Donna Elise & Venita Charlene. **Educ:** Nat Louis Univ, Evanston, Ill, BA, 1985. **Career:** Munic Tuberculosis (Sanitarium), Chicago, clerk, 1963-65; Dept Water, Chicago, prin clerk, 1965-70; Dept Housing, Chicago, asst comnr, 1970-. **Orgs:** Nat Asn Housing & Redevelop Officials, 1985; Nat Asn Females Exec, 1990; Altrusa Club Chicago Inc, 1990; pledgee, Iota Phi Lambda Sorority, Alpha Beta Chapter, 1991. **Home Addr:** 10915 S Sangamon, Chicago, IL 60643, **Home Phone:** (312)264-2981. **Business Addr:** Assistant Commissioner, Chicago Department of Housing, 121 N La Salle St, Chicago, IL 60602, **Business Phone:** (312)744-4190.

**BROWN, CONSTANCE YOUNG**
**Personal:** Born Aug 4, 1933, Leonardtown, MD. **Educ:** Morgan State Col, BS, 1955; Univ Md, MEd, 1960 & 1973. **Career:** Bd Educ, Baltimore County, bus educ teacher, 1955-69, distrib educ teacher & coordr, 1969-71, data processing instr, 1971-74; Western Placement Serv Bd Educ, Baltimore, mgr, 1974-; Morgan St Col, trustee & senatoral scholar. **Orgs:** Pres & treas, Anne Arundel Community Br, Nat Asn Adv Colored People, 1973-76, 1977-; corresp secy, Southgate Community Asn, 1973-; vpres, Md State Conf, Nat Asn Adv Colored People, 1974-; anti-basileus, Delta Pi Omega Chap, Alpha Kappa Alpha Sorority, 1974-76; basileus, Delta Pi Omega Chap, Alpha Kappa Alpha Sorority, 1977-80; nat nom comt, Nat Asn Adv Colored People, 1980; Teachers Asn Baltimore County; Md State Teacher Asn; New Enterprise Assocs; MVA; secy & treas, MADECA. **Honors/Awds:** DAR Citizenship Award, 1950; Dr Carl Murphy Award, MD State Conf Br, Nat Asn Adv Colored People, 1974; Nat Asn Adv Colored People Award, Anne Arundel Community Br, 1977; Honoree, 1st Women's Conf, NY, Nat Asn Adv Colored People, 1980; Plaque Who's Who, Human Resources. **Home Addr:** 7938 Roxbury Dr, Glen Burnie, MD 21061.

**BROWN, CORNELL DESMOND**
Football player, football coach. **Personal:** Born Mar 15, 1975, Englewood, NJ; son of Reuben Sr and Oglessa. **Educ:** Va Polytech Inst & State Univ, grad. **Career:** Football player (retired), football coach; Baltimore Ravens, linebacker, 1997-99, 2000, 2004, left outside linebacker & right Inside linebacker, 2002, linebacker & left outside linebacker, 2003; Cologne Centurions, coach, 2005; Frankfurt Galaxy, defensive line coach, 2006-07; Va Tech Hokies, defensive line coach, 2007; Calgary Stampeders, defensive line coach, 2008; Va Tech, asst defensive line coach, 2011-; Frank Beamer's Va Tech, coaching staff. **Honors/Awds:** Super Bowl Ring, 2000; Virginia Tech Hall of Fame, 2007; Virginia Sports Hall of Fame, 2013; Super Bowl Champion. **Special Achievements:** Film: Super Bowl XXXV, 2001.

**BROWN, CORRINE**
**Personal:** Born Nov 11, 1946, Jacksonville, FL; children: Shartrel. **Educ:** Fla A&M Univ, BS, 1969, MS, 1971; Univ Fla, MA, EdS, 1974. **Career:** Fla House Reps, dist 17, state rep, 1982-92, 1994, 1996 & 1998; US House Rep, Fla third dist rep, 1993-; Fla Community Col, Jacksonville, fac, 1977-82, guid counr, 1982-92; Univ Fla, fac, 1970; Edward Waters Col, fac mem; Fla Dem Party. **Orgs:** US House Reps Comms: Transp & Infrastructure, Veterans Affairs; Sigma Gamma Rho; Phi Delta Kappa; Comt Transp & Infrastructure; Sigma Gamma Rho Sorority; Comt Veterans Affairs; VA Subcomt Health; sr mem Subcomt Coast Guard & Maritime Transp; mem, US House Representatives, Charles Bennett, 1993-2013; mem, US House Representatives, Rich Nugent, 2013-. **Home Addr:** 611 Appian Way, Jacksonville, FL 32208. **Business Addr:** Representative, US House of Representatives, 2336 Rayburn House Off Bldg, Washington, DC 20515, **Business Phone:** (202)225-0123.

**BROWN, CORWIN ALAN**
Football player, football coach. **Personal:** Born Apr 25, 1970, Chicago, IL. **Educ:** Univ Mich, BA, Eng, 1994. **Career:** Football player (retired), football coach; New England Patriots, 1994, 1996, strong safety, 1993, defensive back, 1995, defensive backs coach; Boston Univ, volunteer coach, 1996; NY Jets Patriots, 1997, defensive back, 1988; Detroit Lions, free safety, 1999, free safety, strong safety, 2000; Univ Va, coach, 2001-04; NY Jets, asst defensive backs coach, 2004; Univ Notre Dame, asst coach, currently. **Honors/Awds:** Robert P Ufer Award, 1992. **Special Achievements:** Film: 1998 AFC Championship Game, 1999. **Business Addr:** Assistant Coach, University Notre Dame, C113 Joyce Ctr, Notre Dame, IN 46556, **Business Phone:** (574)631-7196.

**BROWN, COSTELLO L.**
Educator. **Personal:** Born Oct 16, 1942, Mebane, NC; married Florida; children: Eric & Ninita. **Educ:** Hampton Inst, BS, 1963; Iowa State Univ, MS, 1966, PhD, 1968; Univ Ill, PhD, 1969. **Career:** Woodrow Wilson fel, 1963; NIH fel, 1969; Calif State Univ, from asst prof to assoc prof, 1969-77, prof chem, 1977, assoc dean, grad studies & res, actg dir fac affairs, provost, Dept Chem, prof emer; Univ Ga, vis prof, 1972-; Calif Inst Technol, vis fac assoc, 1975; NIH Marcfel, 1975; Off Advan Sci, Eng & Math Educ, dir. **Orgs:** S Calif Sect Am Chem Soc; exec comm, Sigma Xi Hon Soc; Am Chem Soc. **Home Addr:** 547 Cocopan Dr, Altadena, CA 91001, **Home Phone:** (626)676-7714. **Business Addr:** Professor Emeritus, California State University, 5151 State Univ Dr Rm 628, Los Angeles, CA 90032, **Business Phone:** (323)343-3000.

**BROWN, CYRON DEANDRE**
Football player. **Personal:** Born Jun 28, 1975, Chicago, IL. **Educ:** Univ Ill; Western Ill Univ. **Career:** Football player (retired); Denver Broncos, def end, 1998-2002; Colo Crush, def end, 2003; Tampa Bay Storm, def end, 2004; Philadelphia Soul, defe end, 2004-06; Kans City Brigade, 2006-07; Dallas Desperados, offensive lineman & defensive lineman, 2008. **Honors/Awds:** Breese Award, Univ Ill, 1997; Champion, Super Bowl, XXXIII. **Business Addr:** Defensive End, Dallas Desperados, Cowboys Ctr, Irving, TX 75063-4999, **Business Phone:** (972)556-9333.

**BROWN, D. JOAN**
Insurance executive. **Personal:** daughter of Duplain W Rhodes III and Doris M Rhodes. **Career:** Rhodes Life Ins Co La, New Orleans, La, chief exec; Nat Serv Indust Life Ins Co, chief exec; Rhodes Mutual Life Ins Co, Mobile, Ala, chief exec, currently. **Honors/Awds:** Nat Serv Indust Life Ins Co; Black Enterprise, Rhodes Life Ins Co La; Rhodes Mutual Life Ins Co Ala, 1990. **Business Addr:** Chief Executive, Rhodes Mutual Life Insurance Co, 402 Dr Martin L King Jr Ave, Mobile, AL 36603, **Business Phone:** (251)432-3665.

**BROWN, BRIGADIER GEN. DALLAS C., JR.**
Educator, military leader. **Personal:** Born Aug 21, 1932, New Orleans, LA; son of Dallas C and Rita S Taylor; married Elizabeth T; children: Dallas C III, Leonard G, Jan B, Karen L & Barbara A. **Educ:** WVa State Col, BA, hist & polit sci, Distinguished Mil Grad, 1954; Defense Lang Inst, Distinguished Grad, 1966; WVa State, BA, hist; Ind Univ, MA, govt, 1967; AUS Command & Gen Staff Col, 1968; AUS Russ Inst, 1970; US Naval War Col. **Career:** Military leader (retired); 519th Mil Intelligence Battallion, Vietnam, comdr, 1970-71; AUS Field Sta Berlin Ger, comdr, 1977-78; USA FORSCOM Atlanta, GA, dep chief staff/intelligence, 1978-80; Defense Intelligence Agency, Wash, DC, dep vice dir, 1979-80; AUS War Coll Carlisle, PA, dep commandant, 1980-84; Wva State Col, assoc prof hist, 1984-96; Bachelor Benedict Club Inc, admin. **Orgs:** Alpha Phi Alpha, 1951-; Nat Eagle Scout Asn, 1978-; Asn AUS, 1978-; chmn, Greater Atlanta Armed Forces Day, 1979; constituent, AUS War Col Found, 1981-; Am Asn Univ Prof, 1984-; Upsilon Boule Sigma Pi Phi, 1984-97; Pi Sigma Theta Nat Polit Sci Hon Soc, 1985-; Phi Alpha Theta Nat Hist Soc, 1985-; Rotary Club Int, 1987-97; Anvil Club, 1989-97; bd adv, WVa State Col, 1990-91; Wva Higher Educ Adv Bd, 1992; comdr, Sun City Veterans Asn, 1999-00; Alpha Lambda Boule, 1998-. **Honors/Awds:** Alumnus of the Year, WVa State Col, 1978; ROTC Hall of Fame, WV State Col, 1980. **Special Achievements:** First African American general officer in the field of military intelligence; Contributing author, "Soviet Views on War and Peace, " NDU, 1982; First Black American in MI to reach the rank; Received Defense Superior Service Medal. **Home Addr:** 300 Woodhaven Dr Apt 1501, Hilton Head Island, SC 29928, **Home Phone:** (843)341-3134.

**BROWN, DALTON G.**
Marketing executive. **Career:** New Detroit Real Mgt LLC, mng partner & chief operating officer. **Business Addr:** Managing Partner, Chief Operating Officer, New Detroit Real Management LLC, 14648 Ohio St, Detroit, MI 48238.

**BROWN, DEE (DECOVAN KADELL BROWN)**
Basketball player, basketball coach, executive. **Personal:** Born Nov 29, 1968, Jacksonville, FL; married Tammy; children: Alexis Kiah, Alyssa Milan, Alanni & Anakin. **Educ:** Jacksonville Univ, attended 1990. **Career:** Basketball player (retired), basketball coach, executive; Boston Celtics, guard, 1990-98; Toronto Raptors, 1998-2000; Orlando Magic, 2000-02, community ambassador; Orlando Miracle, 2000-02, head coach, 2002-04; San Antonio Silver Stars, head coach, 2003-04; Springfield Armor, head coach, 2009-11; ESPN, NBA analyst; Sirius Satellite Radio, Full Ct Press, co-host, currently; EDGE Basketball LLC, chief exec officer, pres & owner, 2005-; Deelightful Inc, chief exec officer & pres, currently; NBA All-Rookie Team; Women's Nat Basketball Asn, head coach & dir basketball opers; Detroit Pistons, asst coach, 2011-13; Sacramento Kings, asst coach & dir player develop, 2013-. **Orgs:** Women's Nat Basketball Asn. **Business Addr:** President, Chief Executive Officer, EDGE Basketball LLC, 7075 Kingspointe Pkwy Suite 4, Orlando, FL 32819, **Business Phone:** (407)996-7075.

**BROWN, DR. DELORIS ANN**
Lawyer. **Personal:** Born Los Angeles, CA; children: Nitobi. **Educ:** Calif State Univ, BA, 1964; Univ Southern Calif, MA, 1970; Peoples Col Law, JD, 1978. **Career:** Peace Corps Brazil, vol, 1964; atty-at-law. **Orgs:** State Bar Calif. **Home Addr:** 655 E Fairview Blvd, Inglewood, CA 90302, **Home Phone:** (310)672-4186.

**BROWN, DENISE J.**
Executive, lawyer. **Personal:** Born Buffalo, NY; daughter of Mary Alice; married Todd Joseph Noel; married Stephon Ray Henderson; children: Rahsaan Elijah & Tylese Geneva. **Educ:** NY Univ, BS; Brooklyn Law Sch, JD, 1986. **Career:** Lewis & Clarkson, assoc, 1986; Minter & Gaye, assoc, 1988-90; Mayer, Katz, Kaber, Leibowitz & Roberts, partner & atty; Warner Brothers Rec, black music div, sr vpres, 1995; Denise J Brown law firm, atty, pres, currently. **Orgs:** Bd Gov, Nat Acad Rec Arts & Sci; bd, Brooklyn Law Sch; Immanuel Theol Sem, BS & MS, bible, 2008. **Business Addr:** Owner, Denise Brown's Legal Direction, 327 Guthrie St, Louisville, KY 40202, **Business Phone:** (502)587-0331.

**BROWN, DENISE SHARON**
Manager. **Personal:** Born Aug 2, 1957, Manhattan, NY; daughter of James (deceased) and Geraldine (deceased). **Educ:** NC Agr & Tech State Univ, BS, 1982. **Career:** New York Admin Child Services, supvr, 1988-. **Orgs:** Ministry Catholics African Ancestry, 1983-; Nat Black Child Develop Inst, 1990-; Parish Outreach, 1995-99; Prison ministry, 1994-96; Coalition Black Trade Unionists, 1999-; NAB Social Workers, 1999. **Home Addr:** 600 Fulton Ave, Hempstead, NY 11550-7310, **Home Phone:** (516)483-6755. **Business Addr:** Supervisor, New York Administration Of Child Services, 150 William St Fl 6, New York, NY 10038, **Business Phone:** (212)676-6774.

**BROWN, DEREK DARNELL**
Football player, football coach. **Personal:** Born Apr 15, 1971, Banning, CA. **Educ:** Univ Nebr, attended 1993. **Career:** Football player (retired), coach; New Orleans Saints, 1995-96, running back, 1993-94; Bellflower High Sch, head coach, currently. **Honors/Awds:** Glenn Davis Award, 1998. **Business Addr:** Football Head Coach, Bellflower High School, 15301 S Mcnab Ave, Bellflower, CA 90706, **Business Phone:** (562)920-1801.

**BROWN, DEREK VERNON**
Football player, executive. **Personal:** Born Mar 31, 1970, Fairfax, VA; married Kristin; children: Sydney & Reece. **Educ:** Univ Notre Dame, BA, mkt, 1992. **Career:** Football player (retired), executive; New York Giants, tight end, 1992-94; Jacksonville Jaguars, tight end, 1996-97; Oakland Raiders, tight end, 1998-99; Ariz Cardinals, tight end, 1999-2000; SPD Sub Ventures IV LLC, partner, currently. **Home Addr:** , Clifton Park, NY. **Business Addr:** Partner, SPD Sub Ventures IV LLC, 1060 W Main St, Branford, CT 06405-3441, **Business Phone:** (203)481-0392.

**BROWN, DERMAL BRAM (DEE BROWN)**
Baseball player. **Personal:** Born Mar 27, 1978, Bronx, NY. **Career:** Baseball player (retired); Kans City Royals, outfielder, 1998-2004; Tampa Bay Devil Rays, outfielder, 2004-05; Ariz Diamondbacks; Tucson Sidewinders; Oakland Athletics, outfielder, 2007; Los Angeles Angels Anaheim, 2007; Los Angeles Dodgers, outfielder, 2009; Saitama Seibu Lions, 2010-11.

**BROWN, DERRICK LESLIE**
Executive. **Personal:** married Deborah; children: Linsey & Aaron. **Educ:** Eastern Mich Univ, BS, bus admin, MS, mkt, 1977; Univ Mich, Stephen M Ross Sch Bus, MBA, bus, mgt, mkt, & related support serv, 1986. **Career:** Detroit Renaissance Ctr, off leasing vpres, 1977-94; Colliers Int, dir detroit opers, 1994-2000; QC Network Int, co-owner & co-founder; Quorum Com Detroit LLC, owner, pres & chief exec officer, 2000-; Alloy Real Estate Servs, owner/pres & chief exec officer, 2000-; 5LINX Enterprises Inc, com energy consult, 2012-; Kinetic Group, co founder, 2013. **Orgs:** Commercial Real Estate, 1977; Detroit Bd Realtors, 1993; pres, Detroit Area Com Bd Realtors, 1995; dist dir, Mich Asn Realtors; Nat Asn Realtors; chmn, Realtors Polit Action comt, 2003. **Business Addr:** Owner & President, Chief Executive Officer, Quorum Commercial Detroit LLC, 422 W Cong St Suite 207, Detroit, MI 48226, **Business Phone:** (313)965-2255.

**BROWN, DIANA JOHNSON**
Police officer. **Personal:** Born Jan 25, 1951, Dania, FL; daughter of Walter Rolle and Enith Gloria Johnson Mulkey; married Sherman Leon; children: Shantel Ramsey & Laquantas. **Educ:** Broward Community Col, assoc sci, 1983; Fla Atlantic Univ, attended 1984; Barry Univ, BS, 2002. **Career:** Broward Community Col, Davie, Fla, clerk-typist, admis clerk, sect to registr, 1970-74; FAU-FIU Joint Ctr, Ft Lauderdale, Fla, clerk-typist, 1974-77; Broward County Sheriff's Off, Ft Lauderdale, Fla, corrections officer, 1977-79; City Pompano Beach, Fla, police officer, 1979-88, sgt, 1988-; Broward County Sheriff's Off, sgt, 1999, lt, 2003-10. **Orgs:** Fraternal Order Police, 1979-; pres, Broward County Law Enforcement Orgn, 1980-; secy, State Fla, 1983-85; Police Benevolent Asn, 1983-; financial secy, Southern Region, Nat Black Police Asn, 1986-; pres, Ely High Sch, Choral Parent's Asn, 1990-; steering comt mem, Preventing Crime Black Community, 4th Ann Conf; Bus & Prof Women's Asn, Pompano Beach, 1992-; pres, Nat Black Police Asn, Southern Region, 1993-99; pres, Broward County Crime Prev Asn, 1997-98; Nat Orgn Black Law Enforcement Execs. **Honors/Awds:** Officer of the Month, City Pompano Beach, 1982. **Home Addr:** 17477 88rd N, Loxahatchee, FL 33470. **Business Addr:** Lieutenant, Broward County Sheriff's Office, 2601 W Broward Blvd, Ft. Lauderdale, FL 33312, **Business Phone:** (954)831-8900.

**BROWN, DR. DIANE R.**
Administrator, executive director. **Personal:** Born Aug 11, 1944, Newark, NJ; daughter of Eugene and Mary Robinson; married George L Blair; children: Rochelle. **Educ:** Ind Univ, BA, 1966; Univ Mass, MA, 1968; Univ Md, PhD, 1984; Johns Hopkins Univ, attended 1986. **Career:** Wayne State Univ, Inst Geront, fac assoc, 1993-, Ctr Urban Studies, dir, 1995-97, CULMA Urban Health Prog, dir, 1997-2002; Karmanos Cancer Inst, Gender & Minorities, dir, 2000-02; Univ Med Dent NJ, Sch Pub Health, Inst Elimination Health Disparities, exec dir & prof, 2002-; Books: In and Out of Our Right Minds: The Mental Health of African American Women. **Orgs:** Am Sociol Asn, 1970-; Am Pub Health Asn; Asn Black Sociologists; Mich Pub Health Asn; DC Sociol Soc; N Cent Sociol Asn; Geront Soc Am; Soc Study Social Probs; Sociologists Women Soc; Southern Sociol Soc; Urban Affairs Asn; World Fedn Ment Health; Am Cancer Soc; Am Asn Cancer Res; bd mem, Am Cancer Soc Eastern Div 2003-; bd mem, Newark Community Health Ctrs, 2003-. **Home Addr:** 39 Emerson Rd, Morris Plains, NJ 07950, **Home Phone:** (973)984-2714. **Business Addr:** Executive Director, University of Medicine & Dentistry New Jersey, 65 Bergen St Suite 742 Rm 743, Newark, NJ 07107-3001, **Business Phone:** (973)972-4383.

**BROWN, DONNA DAEL THERESA ORLANDER SMITH. See ORLANDERSMITH, DAEL.**

**BROWN, DR. DORIS J. W.**
Educator. **Career:** State Wage Deviation Bd, 1995-98; Brown's Restaurant Servers Acad, pres, cheif exec officer, ambassador, 1986-. **Business Addr:** Chief Executive Officer, President, Brown's Restaurant Servers Academy, 19376 E 10 Mile Ave, Eastpointe, MI 48021-1450, **Business Phone:** (586)771-5533.

**BROWN, EDDIE C.**
Financial manager, executive. **Personal:** Born Nov 26, 1940, Apopka, FL; son of Annie M; married Sylvia Thurston; children: Tonya Yvonne & Jennifer Lynn. **Educ:** Howard Univ, BSEE, 1961; NY Univ, MSEE, 1968; Ind Univ, MBA, 1970; CFA, 1979; CIC, 1979. **Career:** Int Bus Mach, engr, 1963-68; Irwin Mgt Co, investment mgr, 1970-73; T Rowe Price Assoc Inc, investment counr, 1973-83, vpres & portfolio mgr; elec engr; chartered financial analyst; chartered investment counr; Brown Capital Mgt Inc, chmn, founder, pres & portfolio mgr, chief exec officer, 1983-. **Orgs:** Baltimore Security Analysts Soc; Financial Analysts Fed; panelist Wall St Week; bd mem, TR Baltimore Community Found; Walters' Art Gallery; MAR Econ Develop cms; E Baltimore Develop; MUNIMAE; bd dir, Open Soc Inst; ERISA Adv Coun, 1998; Md Econ Develop Comn, 1999; E Baltimore Develop Inc, 2002; bd mem, Living Classroom Found; bd mem, Walters Art Mus; bd mem, Md Inst Col Art; bd mem, Pres's Roundtable; adv bd, Univ Baltimore. **Honors/Awds:** Fellowship Grant Consortium Grad Study Mgt, 1968; Distinguished Alum, Howard Univ, 1994, 2002; Distinguished Alum, Kelley Sch Bus, 1994, 2002; Hall of Fame, Wall Street Week, 1996; Entrepreneur of the Year, Ernst & Young, 2003; Business Hall of Fame, Md Chamber Com, 2004; Marylander of Distinction Award, Md Life Mag, 2006; Business Leader of the Year, Sellinger Sch Bus, Loyola Univ, 2010; Ronald H. Brown American Journey Award, Ron Brown Scholars Prog, 2011; DHL, Johns Hopkins Univ, 2013; hon doctorate pub serv, Morgan State Univ; hon doctor bus admin, McDaniel Col; Woodrow Wilson Award, Pub Serv. **Special Achievements:** Black Enterprise Top 100 Asset Managers List, company ranked #1, 2000; Titans: 40 Most Powerful African Americans in Business. **Home Addr:** 11102 Old Carriage Rd, Glen Arm, MD 21057, **Home Phone:** (410)665-2410. **Business Addr:** President, Chief Executive Officer, Brown Capital Management Inc, 1201 N Calvert St, Baltimore, MD 21202, **Business Phone:** (800)809-3863.

**BROWN, BISHOP EDWARD LYNN**
Clergy, bishop. **Personal:** Born Apr 2, 1936, Madison County, TN; son of Willie T (deceased) and Ocie Bell (deceased); married Gladys D Stephens; children: Alonzo (deceased) & Cheronda. **Educ:** Lane Col, BS, 1960; Interdenominational Theol Ctr, Mdiv, 1963. **Career:** Bishop (retired); Christian Methodist Episcopal Church, Bishop; Dept Evangelism & Mission, bd chmn, currently. **Orgs:** Gen secy, Bd Pub Serv & Gen Educ Bd, Christian Methodist Episcopal Church; Long Range & Planning Comn, Comn Pension; rep, World Methodist Conf Evangelism, 1974; bd dir, OIC; bd dir, Memphis Nat Asn Advan Colored People; exec bd, Nat OIC; bd dir, Memphis Urban League; Int Soc Theta Phi; bd mem, Orange Mound Community Action Agency; Orange Mound Consol Civic Club; dean, S Memphis Dist Leadership Training Sch; bd mem, Memphis Community Educ Proj; bd chmn, Orange Mound & Creative Involvement Prog; Memphis & Shelby Co Welfare Comn; pres, CME Min Alliance; vpres, Memphis Ministry Asn. **Home Addr:** 3214 Dickmann, Memphis, TN 38111. **Business Addr:** Board Chairman, Evangelism & Mission, 1616 Illinois Ave, Dallas, TX 75216, **Business Phone:** (214)372-9505.

**BROWN, ELAINE M.**
Vice president (organization), writer. **Educ:** Wheaton Col, Norton, MA, BA, eng & drama; Rutgers Grad Sch Mgt, MBA, digital mkt, 2012; Univ Calif Los Angeles, Anderson Sch Mgt Exec Leadership Develop Prog; Harvard Bus Sch, CTAM & NAMIC Prof Develop Prog, bus mkt. **Career:** Home Box Off (HBO) Inc, writer-producer, vpres creative serv, 1988-94; Showtime Networks, creative dir, 1994-97; Home Box Off (HBO) Inc & Cinemax, vpres spec markets & creative serv, 1997-2009; New World Image Group LLC, brand strategy & content, 2009-; Savannah Col Art & Design, dir savannah film studios, 2015-. **Orgs:** Time Warner & HBO Multicultural Initiative, comt mem; Writers Guild Am E, mem; Women Cable & Tv; bd trustee, Wheaton Col Alumni; Wheaton Col Pres's Comn Comt; Coalition 100 Black Women; bd dir, Boys & Girls Club Bluffton, 2015. Received Numerous Awards incl: CTAM, Promax BDA, NYWFT, New York Festivals, POP, Monitor, Alpha Sorority Lit Award writing achievements, Network J, African Am Heritage & Cult Award. **Home Phone:** (201)446-0019. **Business Phone:** (201)833-8150.

**BROWN, ELLEN ROCHELLE**
Executive, television broadcaster. **Personal:** Born Mar 10, 1949, Denton, TX; daughter of John Henry and Earlene Punch. **Educ:** Southern Methodist Univ, BFA, broadcast film arts, 1971. **Career:** Columbia Univ, fel; KERA-TV, Dallas, reporter, 1971-72; NBC News, NY, news researcher, 1973-75; WROC-TV, anchor & reporter, 1975-78; KDFW-TV, Dallas, educ community affairs dir, 1978-80, multicultural affairs dir. TV series: "Insights", producer & host, 1980-86; Internet Movie Database. **Home Addr:** 2320 Daybreak Dr, Dallas, TX 75287-5805. **Business Addr:** Multicultural Affairs Director, KDFW-TV, 400 N Griffin St, Dallas, TX 75202, **Business Phone:** (214)720-4444.

**BROWN, EMERY N.**
Physician, educator. **Educ:** Harvard Col, BA, appl math, 1978; Harvard Univ, MA, stat, 1984, PhD, stat, 1988; Harvard Med Sch, MD, statist, 1987. **Career:** Mass Inst Technol, prof health sci & technol, Harvard/MIT Div Health Sci & Technol & prof computational neuro sci, Dept Brain & Cognitive Sci, currently, Inst Med Engineering & Sci, assc dir; Mass Gen Hosp, Warren M. Zapol prof anaesthesia, harvard med sch, Dept Anaesthesia & Critical Care, currently; Neuroscience Statist Res Lab, dir, currently. **Orgs:** Asn Univ Anesthesiologists, 2002; fel Am Inst Med & Biol Eng, 2006; fel Am Stat Asn, 2006; fel Am Asn Advan Sci, 2007; Nat Acad Med, 2007; Inst Med Nat Academies, 2007; fel Inst Elec & Electronics Engrs, 2008; nat adv coun Nat Insts Neurol Dis & Stroke; bd mem, Math Sci & its Applications Nat Res Coun; bd trustees, Int Anesthesia Res Soc; fel Am Acad Arts & Sci, 2012; Nat Acad Sci, 2012; adv comt Burroughs-Wellcome Fund Careers; fel, Nat Acad Inventors, 2015; Nat Acad Engineering, 2015; fel Inst Math Statist, 2016. **Honors/Awds:** NIH Director's Pioneer Award, 2007; Jerome Sacks Award, Nat Inst Statist Sci, 2011. **Special Achievements:** First African American at Massachusetts General Hospital to become a chaired professor in the 196-year history of MGH; "Construction of point process adaptive filter algorithms for neural systems using sequential Monte Carlo methods", IEEE, 2007, "Bayesian analysis of interleaved learning and response bias in behavioral experiments", 2007; "A mathematical model of network dynamics governing mouse sleep-wake behavior Journal of Neurophysiology", 2007; "General purpose filter design for neural prosthetic devices. Journal of Neurophysiology", 2007. **Home Addr:** 34 Francis St, Brookline, MD 02446-6601, **Home Phone:** (617)566-8889. **Business Addr:** Professor of Health Sciences & Technology, Professor of Computational Neuroscience, Massachusetts Institute of Technology, 77 Mass Ave E25-519, Cambridge, MA 02139, **Business Phone:** (617)726-7487.

**BROWN, EMIL QUINCY**
Baseball player. **Personal:** Born Dec 29, 1974, Chicago, IL. **Educ:** Indian River Community Col. **Career:** Baseball player (retired); Pittsburgh Pirates, outfielder, 1997-2001; San Diego Padres, outfielder, 2001; Kansas City Royals, outfielder, 2005-07; Oakland Athletics, 2008; New York Mets, outfielder, 2009. **Business Addr:** Professional Baseball Player, New York Mets, Citi Field Roosevelt Ave, Flushing, NY 11368-1699.

**BROWN, REV. EMMA JEAN MITCHELL**
Teacher, educator. **Personal:** Born Jun 1, 1939, Marshall, TX; daughter of Elvia Washington and Johnnie D; children: Charles S Jr & Gene. **Educ:** Bishop Col, BS, 1961; Univ Mass, MEd, 1966; Boston Univ, attended 1966; Howard Univ, attended 1984; Miami Univ, attended 1985; Univ Dayton, attended 1988; Bethany Sem, PhD, theol, 1997. **Career:** Educator (retired); Kans City Schs, teacher, 1961-62; Boston/

Needham Pub Schs, lang arts specialist, 1964-67; Sinclair Community Col, lectr, 1970-73; Wright State Univ, lectr, 1970-75; Univ Ibadan, Nigeria, W Africa, lectr, 1975-76; Dayton Pub Schs, teacher, 1978-86, supvr commun arts, 1986-88; int evangelist/missionary, 1989; Prayer Fel Church, Dayton, Ohio, pastor. **Orgs:** Zeta Sorority, 1958-; Miami Valley Affairs Orgn, 1975-90; Urban League Guild, 1975-85; Nat Coun Negro Women, 1975-90. **Home Addr:** 473 Marathon Ave, Dayton, OH 45406, **Home Phone:** (937)275-9133.

## BROWN, EMMETT EARL

Consultant. **Personal:** Born Jan 30, 1932, Chicago, IL; son of Joseph E and Julia H Knox; children: Paula Davis, Patricia E, Emmett E Jr, Cecilia B & Alan C. **Educ:** Pepperdine Univ, attended 1979; Calif State Univ, BS & BA, bus; Ottawa Univ, BA, bus educ. **Career:** SEIU AFL CIO Local 660, bus agt; Cent & W Basin Water Replenishment Dist, Div 1, dir, 1986; Peoples Housing Rogers Pk, dir community org; Emmett Brown & Assoc, labor consult; AFSCME Local 3190, bus agt, currently. **Orgs:** Am Fedn State, County & Munipical Employees. **Home Addr:** 4940 E Siesta Dr, Phoenix, AZ 85044, **Home Phone:** (602)414-9851.

## BROWN, ERIC JON

Football player. **Personal:** Born Mar 20, 1975, San Antonio, TX; children: Taylor. **Educ:** Miss State, grad. **Career:** Football player (retired); Denver Broncos, strong safety, 1998, free safety, 1999-2001; Houston Texans, strong safety, 2002-03, defensive back, strong safety, 2004. **Honors/Awds:** Super Bowl XXXIII. **Special Achievements:** Modeled in Texans Style Show to benefit Family Services of Greater Houston & Houston Texans Found.

## BROWN, ERNESTINE (ERNESTINE TURNER)

Art consultant, businessperson. **Personal:** Born Oct 22, 1935, Youngstown, OH; daughter of Isaac Turner and Alma Hill; married Malcolm Brown. **Educ:** Youngstown State Univ, BA, educ, 1959; Boston Univ, grad studies; Northwestern Univ, grad studies; Kent State Univ, grad studies. **Career:** Cleveland Pub Schs, bus educ teacher, 1960-66; Cuyahoga Community Col, instr bus, 1966-76; Malcolm Brown Gallery, Shaker Heights, OH, dir & co-owner, 1980-2011; pvt art dealer & consult, 1980-. **Orgs:** Adv Outreach Coun Cleveland Mus Art; Coalition 100 Black Women; Nat Asn Advan Colored People; Delta Sigma Theta. **Special Achievements:** Speaker on art-related topics.

## BROWN, ERROLL M.

Commander, military leader. **Personal:** Born Jan 1, 1950, St. Petersburg, FL; married Monica Hayes; children: Elise-Estee & Aaron. **Educ:** USGS Acad, marine eng, 1972; Univ Mich, MA, naval archit & marine eng, MA, indust & opers engrg; Rensselaer Polytech Inst, MBA, 1986; Naval War Col, MA, nat security & strategic studies, 1994. **Career:** Military leader, commander (retired); Coast Guard Icebreaker Burton Island, damage control asst & asst engr officer, 11th coast guard dists naval engrg br, type-desk mgr; USCG Cutter Jarvis, engr officer; USCG Acad, Marine Eng Dept, instr; USCG Rush, exec officer; Off Chief Staff, Progs Div, prog reviewer, Budget Div, off chief staff; Secy Transp, mil asst; Coast Guard Hq, supvr; USCG Integrated Support Command, Portsmouth, Va, comndg officer; Maintenance & Logistics Command Atlantic, Norfolk, Va, comdr; Thirteenth Coast Guard Dist, comdr, 2000-03; USCG, rear adm, Coast Guard Acad Task Force, dir. **Orgs:** Soc Naval Engrs; Soc Naval Architects & Marine Engrs; Am Soc Eng Educr; prog evaluator, Accreditation Bd Eng & Technol, currently. **Honors/Awds:** Legion of Merit; Meritorious Service Medal; Secretary's Award for Meritorious Achievement; US Coast Guard Commendation Medal; Unit Commendation; Meritorious Unit Commendation; National Defense Service Medal; Special Operations Ribbon; Bicentennial Unit Commendation Ribbon; Antarctica Service Medal; Arctic Service Medal; Sea Service Deployment Ribbon; Expert Rifleman Medal; Expert Pistol Shot Medal; Coast Guard Expert Pistol Medal; Coast Guard Expert Rifle Medal; Secretary of Transportation Outstanding Unit Award; Humanitarian Service Medal. **Special Achievements:** Co-authored a University of Michigan text entitled "Ship Replacement and Prediction of Economic Life"; First African American promoted to flag rank in the USCG; First African American Coast Guard officer to be promoted to rear admiral.

## BROWN, EVELYN

Government official. **Personal:** Born May 15, 1930, Tifton, GA; married Macon. **Career:** Cafeteria aide; Evelyn Spiritual Hour Radio Sta WRMU FM, founder & hostess, 1969; Alliance city, OH, councilwoman, 1984-85, Planning Comt, mem, Mayors Comn Aging, mem, currently. **Orgs:** Gospel Announcer's Guild Am, 1975; Dem Exec Comn, 1981; Christian Update TV, 1985; Mayor's Comn Aging, Alliance, OH. **Honors/Awds:** Nails Thounder Soc Club, 1984; Queen a Day Comm Churches, 1976; Gospel announcer, Gospel Music Workshop Am, 1978; Woman Yr, Altrusic Club, 1980; Community Service Award, 2008. **Special Achievements:** First Black Councilwoman. **Home Addr:** 1166 Sunset Dr Apt 3A, Alliance, OH 44601. **Business Addr:** Committee Member, Alliance City Council, 504 E Main St, Alliance, OH 44601.

## BROWN, EVELYN DREWERY

School administrator. **Personal:** Born Oct 29, 1935, Haddock, GA; daughter of Bennie Drewery and Ada Tatum Drewery; children: Clinton O & Toni A. **Educ:** Morris Brown Col, BS, 1957; Atlanta Univ, MA, 1969, attended 1975. **Career:** Columbia Co Bd Educ, teacher, 1957-62; Richmond Co Bd Educ, teacher, 1957-65; Atlanta Pub Sch, dept chmn & teacher, 1965-71; Econ Opportunity Atlanta, head start dir, 1965-69, prog dir, 1971-89; Mayor's Off Community Affairs, Youth Servs, adminr & coordr, currently; Zeta Phi Beta Sorority Inc, Nat Storks Nest, dir & coordr, currently; Metro Atlanta Boys & Girls Club, coordr. **Orgs:** Nat vpres, exec bd & secy, Zeta Phi Beta Sor, 1978; pres, Better Infant Birth, March Dimes, 1978-80; secy orgns & comuns, Women's Missionary Coun, 1980-; Ga Asn Educr; Nat Asn C Under Six; consult & task force mem, Parent & Child Ctrs; dir & chmn, Overseas Mission, Joint Bd Finance; pres, Women's Missionary Soc, CME Church; State bd Examiners Lic Dieticians; Holsey Temple C.M.E. Church; Morris Brown Col Nat Alumni Asn; Nat Assolciation Advan Colored People; Nat Educ Asn; Ywca. **Home Addr:** 1349 Aniwaka Ave SW, Atlanta, GA 30311-3507, **Home Phone:** (404)755-7170.

## BROWN, DR. EWART F., JR.

Physician, politician. **Personal:** Born May 17, 1946; son of Ewart A Sr and Helene A Darrell; married Wanda Henton; children: Kevin, Maurice, Ewart III & Donovan. **Educ:** Howard Univ, Wash, DC, BSc, chem, 1968, MD, 1972; Univ Calif, Los Angeles, MPH, child health, maternal family pop control & int health, 1977. **Career:** Vt-Century Med Clin, Los Angeles, Calif, med pract, med dir, 1974-93; Charles R Drew Univ Med & Sci, Dept Family Prac, asst prof, 1975-90; Marcus Garvey Sch, Los Angeles, Calif, dir, 1980-85; Bermuda Health Care Servs Ltd, Paget, Bermuda, founder, exec chmn & med dir; Brown-Darrell Clin, exec chmn; Western Pk Hosp, Calif, founder; Qual Assurance Los Angeles Doctor's Hosp, dir; Govt Bermuda, Dep Premier, minister tourism & transp, 1998-, dep premier Bermuda, 2003, premier, 2006-10; Bermuda Progressive Labour Party, party leader, currently. **Orgs:** Chmn bd, Bermuda Times, 1987-; Trustee, Charles R. Drew Univ Med & Sci, 1989-92; trustee, Howard Univ, 1990-; vpres, Union Am Physicians & Dentists; mem ed bd, Feeling Good mag; bd dir, Marina Hills Hosp, Los Angeles, CA; Nat Med Asn; Am Col Utilization Rev Physicians; Golden State Med Asn; AMA, Am Acad Family Physicians; Am Pub Health Asn; chmn bd dir; Western Pk Hosp, Calif; Caribbean Community & Common Mkt. **Home Addr:** 6726 Holt Ave, Los Angeles, CA 90056, **Home Phone:** (213)568-9277. **Business Addr:** Party Leader, Bermuda Progressive Labour Party, 16 Ct St, HamiltonHM 17, **Business Phone:** (441)292-2264.

## BROWN, FLOYD A.

Radio broadcaster. **Personal:** Born Nov 5, 1930, Dallas, TX; married Mary E Stephens; children: Floyd Keith & Diane Faye. **Educ:** Northwestern Sch Bus; Radio Inst Chicago, attended 1951. **Career:** WRMN, announcer, chief engr, prog dir & asst mgr, 1951-62; WYNR-WNUS Radio Chicago, 1962-65; NBC-WMAQ Chicago, prog mgr & announcer, 1965-71; WGN TV, staff announcer & prog host, 1971-99; Kane County Fair, mkt dir, 1994-; Floyd Brown Co, Sole proprietor, pres, currently; Selected Funds, dir, currently. **Orgs:** Bd dir, First Fed Savings & Loan; dir & bd dir, Selected Funds; co-owner, Pub Rels & Advert Firm Rotary Int; bd dir, YMCA; bd dir, Fox Valley Coun; Boy Scouts Am; Nat Asn Advan Colored People; Urban League; Elgin C C; bd dir, Larkin Home C Family Serv; chmn bd, deacons Elgin First Cong Chap; Elgin Citizens Adv Comm, Ment Health Asn; Chicago Sunday Eve TV WTTW; bd trustees, Adler Planetarium; comm man, US Golf Asn; bd gov, Chicago Dist Golf Asn; Am Fedn Tv & Radio Artists; Am Guild Variety Artists. **Honors/Awds:** D. Ray Wilson Volunteer Service Award, Judson Univ; Trailblazer Award, Quad County Urban League; Friend of Education Award, Elgin Community Col; Fox Valley Arts Hall of Fame, 2010. **Special Achievements:** First African-American hired as a network announcer; First African-American signed by a major national network, NBC. **Home Addr:** 941 Meadow Lane, PO Box 804, Elgin, IL 60123-1427, **Home Phone:** (847)888-3366. **Business Addr:** President, Brown Floyd Advertising, 51 Douglas Ave, Elgin, IL 60120, **Business Phone:** (847)888-8822.

**BROWN, FOXY.** **See MARCHAND, INGA FUNG.**

## BROWN, FRANCHOT A.

Lawyer, association executive. **Personal:** Born Jul 11, 1943, Columbia, SC; son of Rupert A and Sara D; children: Brian S. **Educ:** Howard Univ, Wash, DC, BA, 1965; Univ SC, Law Sch, Columbia, SC, JD, 1969; Univ Pa, Reginald Heber Smith Comn Lawyer, attended 1969. **Career:** Legal Aid Serv Agency, Columbia, 1969-72; pvt law pract, 1972-73; Columbia SC Magistrate, 1973-76; Franchot A Brown Law Off, lawyer, 1976-; Brown & Stanley, sr partner, 1976-90. **Orgs:** SC Blue Cross-Blue Shield; Greater Columbia Chamber Comm; Victory Savings Bank; Drug Response Op; Voc Rehab Midlands Ctr Retarded C; chmn, Citizens Adv Comm Community Develop, Columbia, SC, 1975-; Mens Resource Ctr, Columbia, SC, 1990-; chair, Community Planning Group, SC Dept Health & Environ Control. **Home Addr:** 2301 Lorick Ave, Columbia, SC 29203-7203, **Home Phone:** (803)252-5055. **Business Addr:** Lawyer, Franchot A Brown Law Offices, 1324 Calhoun St, Columbia, SC 29201, **Business Phone:** (803)779-7060.

## BROWN, DR. FRANK

Educator. **Personal:** Born May 1, 1935, Gallion, AL; son of Thomas and Ora Lomax; married Joan Drake; children: Frank G & Monica J. **Educ:** Ala State Univ, BS, 1957; Ore State Univ, MS, chem, 1962; Univ Calif, Berkeley, MA, 1969, PhD, 1970. **Career:** Ore State Univ, grad fel, 1961-62; Univ Calif, Berkeley, grad fel, 1968-70; NY State Comn Educ, assoc dir, 1970-72; Urban Inst CCNY, dir, 1971-72; State Univ New York, Buffalo, prof, 1972-83; Cora P Maloney Col, State Univ New York, Buffalo, dir, 1974-77; Buffalo Sch Desegregation Case, Fed Dist Western New York, consult & res, 1976-83; Univ NC, Chapel Hill, Sch Educ, dean, 1983-90; Inst Educ Mgt, Harvard Univ, fel, 1988; Inst Res Social Sci, Chapel Hill, NC, dir, educ res policy studies proj, 1990-; Univ NC, Cary C Boshamer prof educ, dean emer sch educ, 1990-2010; State NC, Admin. Law judge spec educ; Univ Calif, Berkeley, vis scholar, 1990-91. **Orgs:** Co-founder, State Univ New York, Buffalo, Black Fac Asn, 1972; co-founder, Western New York Black Educr Asn & Nat Urban Educ Conf, 1975-83; Pres, Rho Lambda Chapt Alpha Phi Alpha Frat, Buffalo, NY, 1977-78; bd dir, Buffalo Urban League, 1978-81; bd dir, Langston Hughes Inst-Black Cult Ctr Western New York & Buffalo, 1978-83; vpres, Div A Am Educ Res Asn, 1986-88; bd dir, Am Asn Col Teacher Educ, 1988-92; bd dir, Nat Org Legal Prob Educ, 1990-93; Nat Res Adv Bd, US Dept Educ, 1994-2001; Univ Parking Comm, Univ NC, Chapel Hill, 1996-98; chmn, Univ NC Fac Coun, 1997-99; Am Educ Res Asn; Planning Comm, Educ Law Asn, 1998-2001; Adv Comm Minority Affairs, Am Educ Res Asn, 1998-2000; Dissertation Awards Comm, Educ Law Asn, 1999-2001; chair, Adv Comm, Off Equal Opportunity, Univ NC, 2000-; Leader, Black Cult Ctr Adv Comt; Chapel Hill Boule, Sigma Phi Fraternity. **Home Addr:** 6523 Huntingridge Rd, Chapel Hill, NC 27517, **Home Phone:** (919)489-0757.

## BROWN, FRANK LEWIS

Police chief. **Personal:** Born Jul 30, 1945, Fayetteville, GA; son of Jeff and Annie; married Hazel. **Career:** Police chief (retired); E Pt Police dept, patrolman, 1967-74, sgt, 1974-79, lt, 1979-84, capt, 1984-90, maj, 1990-96, chief police, 1996-06. **Orgs:** Pres, Kiwans Club, 1995; FBI Nat Acad, 1990; Ga Chiefs Asn, 1996; Nat Orgn Black Law Enforcement Execs, 1994; Int Asn Chiefs Police, 1996. **Honors/Awds:** Officer of the Year, 1975; Man of the Year Award, TRDC, 1990. **Special Achievements:** First African American chief of police in East Point, GA, 1945. **Home Addr:** , East Point, GA 30344.

## BROWN, FREDERICK L.

Lawyer, judge. **Personal:** Born Chicago, IL. **Educ:** Harvard Col, BA (cum laude), 1954; Harvard Law Sch, LLB, 1967. **Career:** Mass Super ct, chief law clerk, 1967-69; Mass Comn Against Discrimination, legal consult, 1969-70; Owens, Dilday & Brown, pvt pract, 1969-70; State Health Facilities Appeals Bd, chmn, 1969-72; Boston Univ Law Sch, instr, 1969-72; US Dept Housing & Urban Develop, reg coun, 1970-73; Northeastern Univ Law Sch, assoc prof law, 1973-76; State Bd Higher Educ, legal consult, 1974-75; Mass Appeals Ct, judge, 1976-. **Orgs:** Lawyer's Comt Civil Rights Under Law, Boston chapt, 1969-72; dir, Boston Legal Aid Soc, 1970-75; Boston Bar Asn, 1973-76; Nat Asn Advan Colored People; visiting comt, Harvard Law Sch, 1975-80; dir, Greater Boston Legal Serv, 1976; State Mass Comt Criminal Justice, 1976-82; bd trustee, Northeastern Univ Law Sch, 1977-; Alvin Brown Fel Aspen Inst, Colo, 1977; bd dir, Lena Park Community Develop Corp, 1981-95; pres, Mass Black Judges Conf, 1983-85, 1993-95; chmn bd, Lena Park Community Develop Corp, 1985-90; chmn bd hosing div, Lena Park Community Develop Corp, 1990-95; Dana-Farber Cancer Inst; Big Brother Asn Boston; United Way Corp; trustee, Dana Farber Cancer Inst, 1995-; dir, housing div chmn, & chmn bd, Lena Pk Community Develop Corp. **Business Addr:** Judge, Massachusetts Appeals Court, John Abrams Courthouse, Boston, MA 02108, **Business Phone:** (617)557-1000.

## BROWN, GARY LEROY

Football player, football coach. **Personal:** Born Jul 1, 1969, Williamsport, PA; married Kim; children: Malena, Dorianna & Tre. **Educ:** Pa State Univ, rehab educ. **Career:** Football player (retired), football coach; Houston Oilers, running back, 1991-95; San Diego Chargers, running back, 1997; New York Giants, running back, 1998-99, coach, 2005; Williamsport Area High Sch, offensive coordr, 2000-02; Lycoming Col, running back asst coach, 2003-05; Green Bay Packers, coach, 2006; Susquehanna Univ, offensive coordr, 2006-07; Carolina Panthers, coach, 2007; Rutgers Football, running backs asst coach, 2008; Cleveland Browns, running back coach, 2009-12; Dallas Cowboys, running back coach, 2013-. **Business Addr:** Running Back Coach, Dallas Cowboys, 1 Cowboys Pkwy, Irving, OH 75063, **Business Phone:** (972)556-9900.

**BROWN, GASBY GREELY.** **See GREELY, M. GASBY.**

## BROWN, GEOFFREY FRANKLIN (GEOFF BROWN)

Journalist. **Personal:** Born Oct 30, 1952, Pittsburgh, PA; son of George F and Helen V; married Alice Clark; children: Geoffrey F Jr & Christina. **Educ:** Bowdoin Col, BA, 1974. **Career:** Pittsburgh Press, gen assignment reporter, 1974-75, 1977-78; Jet Mag, asst ed, managing ed, features ed, 1975-77, 1978-80; Pittsburgh Press, assignment reporter; Tribune, entertainment ed, n suburban bur chief, nat, foreign news ed, copy ed; Chicago Tribune, copy ed, nat-foreign news ed, suburban bur chief, entertainment ed, assoc managing ed, entertainment, assoc managing ed, lifestyle, 1980-. **Home Addr:** 1132 S Lyman Ave, Oak Park, IL 60304, **Home Phone:** (708)848-5012. **Business Addr:** Associate Managing Editor, Chicago Tribune, 435 N Mich Ave, Chicago, IL 60611, **Business Phone:** (312)222-3482.

## BROWN, GEORGE HENRY, JR.

Judge. **Personal:** Born Jul 16, 1939, Memphis, TN; son of George H; married Margaret Solomon; children: Laurita & Hank III; married Lillian Fisher Hammond. **Educ:** Fla A&M Univ, BS, polit sci, 1960; Howard Univ, Sch Law, JD, 1967. **Career:** Judge (retired); AA Latting, atty, 1967-70; Equal Employ Opport Comn, dep dir, 1969-70; Legal Serv Assoc, exec dir, 1970-73; Brown & Evans Law Firm, atty, 1973-; vice chmn, 1973 & 1978; Shelby County Circuit Ct, judge, 1983-05; Tenn Supreme Ct; Memphis Chem & Janitorial Supply Co, chief exec officer, 2000. Movie: The Firm, 1992-93. **Orgs:** Chmn, Memphis Bd Educ, 1974; Am Bar Asn; Nat Bar Asn; Memphis County Bar Asn; Shelby County Bar Asn; comnr, Memphis Bd Educ; vice-chmn, Steering Com, NSBA; trustee, Lane Col; trustee, memphis Acad Arts; bd dir, Memphis Chap, Nat Bus League; bd dir, Memphis Chap, Nat Asn Advan Colored People; vpres & bd mem, Beale St Hist Found; Vollentine & Evergreen Community Asn; coordiantor, Gov's Job Conf; chmn, Jobs Tenn Graduates. **Home Addr:** 247 Windover Grove Dr, Memphis, TN 38111, **Home Phone:** (901)324-7896.

## BROWN, REV. DR. GEORGE HOUSTON, XIX

Clergy. **Personal:** Born Oct 15, 1915, Finchburg, AL; son of A D and Annie D; married Amanda S; children: Marian Payne, LaVerne Bruce & Gwendolyn A Rothchild. **Educ:** Ala State Univ, BS, 1953, sch admin & supv, 1964, MEd, 1968; Inter Baptist Theol Sem, DD, 1967; Selma Univ, LLD, 1982. **Career:** Free Mission Dist Cong, cong dean, 1955-75; Monroe County Ment Health, bd mem, 1972-80; E Star Dist Asn, moderator. **Orgs:** Independent Order Universal Brotherhood, 1936-; Blue Lodge Masons, 1940-; Order Eastern Star, 1941-; bd mem, Coneuch-Monroe Community Action, 1950-77; Enoch Consistory No 222, 1960-; Jericho Ala, 1961-; vice-moderator, Bethlehem No 2 Dist Asn, 1963-85; pres, Monroe County-Ministerial Asn, 1965-70; cong dean, Bethlehem No 2 Cong, 1970-85; bd mem, Tom Bigbee Regional Comn, 1973-89; Monroe County Bd Educ, 1980-; United Supreme Coun, 33 Degree A & ASR, 1988. **Honors/Awds:** Moderators Award, E Star Dist, 1990; Dean Christian Educ Serv Award, Bethlehem 2 Dist Asn, 1988. **Special Achievements:** First black elected to high office in Monroe County, AL, 1980; Author of Tithing: Gods Way of Financing His Church; Gods Storehouse Robbers; The Ministries of Christs Church. **Home Addr:** 4620 Turnbull Rd, Beatrice, AL 36425,

**Home Phone:** (251)789-2195. **Business Addr:** Moderator, E Star District Association, 4620 Turnbull Rd, Beatrice, AL 36425, **Business Phone:** (251)789-2195.

### BROWN, GERALD

Basketball player, basketball coach, executive. **Personal:** Born Jul 28, 1975, Los Angeles, CA. **Educ:** Pepperdine Univ, BA, sociol, 1998. **Career:** Basketball player (retired), basketball coach, executive; Nike Desert Classic, 1998; Phoenix Suns, guard, 1998-99, free agt, 1999; Los Angeles Pro Am Summer League, 2000; La Crosse Bobcats, 2000; Rockford Lightning, 2000-01; Ind Pacers, 2000-01; Los Angeles Pro Am Summer League, 2001; Harlem Globetrotters, 2001-02; Panteras de Miranda, 2002; Gary Steelheads, 2002; Hapoel Jerusalem, 2002-03; KK Partizan, 2003-04, 2005-06; ALBA Berlin, 2004-05; CB Breogan, 2006; Baloncesto Fuenlabrada, 2006-07; Perth Wildcats, 2007-08; PBG Basket Poznan, 2008-09; Halcones UV Xalapa, 2010; Gimnasia y Esgrima, 2010-11; Ariz Scorpions, gen mgr, 2011-, asst coach, 2011-13, head coach, 2013-; Keys 2 Game LLC, founder, 2011-. **Business Addr:** Head Coach, General Manager, Arizona Scorpions, 919 N Dysart Rd Suite V, Avondale, AZ 85323, **Business Phone:** (602)710-0237.

### BROWN, GILBERT DAVID, III

Executive. **Personal:** Born Jul 22, 1949, Philadelphia, PA; son of Gilbert David Jr and Rosalie Gaynor Allen; married Edythe MacFarlane; children: Gilbert David IV & Courtney Nicole. **Educ:** Pa State Univ, BS, bus admin & mkt, 1973; Pepperdine Univ, MBA, 1983. **Career:** Gillette Co, territory sales rep, 1973-74; Inglewood Meat Co, sales mgr, 1974-79; Scott Paper Co, sr sales rep, 1979-84; Paxton Patterson, region mgr, 1984-87; McBee Looseleaf Binders Co, acct exe, 1987-88; AT&T, Gen Bus Systs, acct mgr, 1988-91, Com Markets, acct exe, 1991-92; Pac Bell, Maj BUS, acct exe, 1992-97; Consumer Mkt GRP, mgr, 1997-99; Pac Bell Serv, sales support mgr, 1999; AT&T, serv exec, 1992-2015; Kappa Alpha Psi Fraternity Inc, Prov Polemarch, 2014-. **Orgs:** Life mem, Kappa Fraternity Inc, 1969-, life mem, Pepperdine Alumni Asn, 1983-; life mem, Penn State Alumni Asn, 1985-; mentor, Young Black Scholars Prog, 1986-; Epsilon Pi Tau Fraternity, 1986; alumni recruiter, PA State Univ, 1987-95; polemarch, Los Angeles Alumni Ch, 1990-93; chr, Alliance Black TeleCommun Employees, fundraising com, 1990-91, prof networking comt, 1991; Big Ten Club Southern Calif, 1991-; adv bd mem, MAARK, 1992-; Prof Community Asn, 1992-; pres, Kappa Achievement Fund Inc, 1994; sr prov vice polemarch-western prov, Kappa Alpha Psi Fraternity Inc, 2009-. **Home Addr:** 741 W 39th St Suite 3, San Pedro, CA 90731, **Home Phone:** (310)547-0105. **Business Addr:** Province Polemarch, Kappa Alpha Psi Fraternity, inc, Philadelphia, PA 19132-4590, **Business Phone:** (215)228-7184.

### BROWN, GILBERT JESSE

Football coach, business owner, football player. **Personal:** Born Feb 22, 1971, Detroit, MI; children: Jamal, Jesse & Jada. **Educ:** Univ Kans, human develop. **Career:** Football player (retired), business owner, football coach; Green Bay Packers, 1993, defensive tackle, 1994, 2003, right defensive tackle, 1995, left defensive tackle, 1996-99, 2003, nose tackle, 1999-2003; Milwaukee Mile, co owner, currently; Continental Indoor Football League, Milwaukee Bonecrushers, head coach, 2007-08; La Crosse Spartans Indoor Football League, head coach, 2009-11; Green Bay Chill Lingerie Football League, head coach, 2011-. **Orgs:** Founder, Gilbert Brown Found; Make-a-Wish Found. **Honors/Awds:** Super Bowl champion XXXI; Green Bay Packers Hall of Fame, 2007. **Business Addr:** Founder, The Gilbert Brown Foundation, PO Box 228, Ettrick, WI 54627, **Business Phone:** (608)525-2326.

### BROWN, DR. GLENN ARTHUR (GLENN A BROWN)

Executive, executive director. **Personal:** Born Jan 27, 1953, Ft. Knox, KY. **Educ:** Harvard Univ, AB, 1975; Univ Pa, Wharton Sch, MBA, 1980, Sch Dent Med, DMD, 1982; Temple Univ, Beasley Sch Law, JD, 2003. **Career:** Ambulatory Health Care, consult, mng partner, 1980-83; About Your Smile PC, pres, dent dir, 1983-; Real World Law, PC, founder, atty, 2003-. **Orgs:** Treas, Walnut Hill Community Develop Corp, 1986-90; vpres, officer, W Philadelphia, Nat Asn Advan Colored People, 1989-91; vpres, Philadelphia Chap, Nat Black MBA Asn, 1989-90; bd mem & treas, Lutheran C & Family Serv, 1989-96; bd mem, Greater Philadelphia Health Action, 1989-92; bd mem, Chess Pa Community Health Ctr, 1993-95; bd mem, Harvard-Radcliffe Club Philadelphia; bd mem, Urban League Philadelphia Leadership Inst; bd mem, Del County Chamber Com Leadership Inst; officer, Chess-Penn Community Health Ctr; charter bd mem & treas, African Am Chamber Com, Philadelphia, 1993-; adv comt, Philadelphia Burristers Asn, 1996-97; menon bd, 1996-, treas, 1997-, A Better Chance Lowe; Acad Gen Dent; Nat Dent Asn; New Era Dent Soc; founding mem, Pa Chap, African-Am Chamber Com; Commonwealth Pa, 2003; Us Ct Appeals Third Circuit; Bar Eastern Dist Pa Ct; Nj State Bar; Dc Bar; Del State Bar; Bar US Supreme Ct. **Home Addr:** 169 Palmers Mill Rd, Media, PA 19063-1037, **Home Phone:** (610)891-9587. **Business Addr:** Attorney, Real World Law PC, 6774 Mkt St, Upper Darby, PA 19082, **Business Phone:** (610)734-0750.

### BROWN, REV. GREGGORY LEE

Clergy. **Personal:** Born Sep 14, 1953, Indianapolis, IN; son of Harold S Sr and Bettie J Palmer; married Beverly Whiteside. **Educ:** Ind Univ, Bloomington, Ind, BA, 1976; Union Theol Sem, New York, NY, Mdiv, 1980. **Career:** Jarvis Christian Col, Hawkins, Tex, assoc prof, 1979-80; St Albans Congregational Church, Queens, NY, assoc pastor, 1980-81; Springfield Garden Presby Church, Queens, NY, pastor, 1981-85; Nj Citizen Action, Hackensack, NJ, regional organizer, 1986-87; Black Tennis & Sports Found, New York, NY, exec dir, 1987-; Featherbed Lane Presby Church, Bronx, NY, interim pastor, 1988-90; Randall Memorial Presby Church, NewYork, NY, interim pastor, 1991-93. **Orgs:** Chmn, Youth March Jobs, 1977-79; pres, Black caucus, Union Theol Sem, 1978-79; chmn, St Albans Resource Ctr, 1980-81; life mem, Nat Asn Advan Colored People, 1983; vice chmn, Queens Comt, United Negro Col Fund, 1984-86. **Honors/Awds:** Merit Award, Nat Asn Advan Colored People, 1980; Coach of the Year, New York City Presbytery, 1983. **Home Addr:** 13 G Kensington Circle, Garnerville, NY 10923, **Home Phone:** (914)947-1410.

### BROWN, HANNAH M.

Association executive, airline executive, executive. **Personal:** Born Jun 23, 1939, Stamps, AR; daughter of Joseph and Eliza Gardner Junior; children: Juanita LaKay. **Educ:** Univ Nev, Las Vegas, Nev; San Mateo Col, San Mateo, Calif. **Career:** Larry's Music Bar, Las Vegas, Nev, sales assoc & mgr; Delta Air Lines, mgr, 1968-89, regional mgr; Urban Chamber Com, pres, 1999, pres emer. **Orgs:** Nat Asn Advan Colored People; YWCA; Nat Urban League; vpres, Caucus African Am Nevadans; asst sunday sch supt, Holy Trinity AME Church; bd dir, Las Vegas Clark Co; pres, Nat Coalition 100 Black Women; bd, Valley Hosp; bd, Nev State Col Found; bd mem, Workforce Connections. **Honors/Awds:** Black Women of Achievement Award, Nat Asn Advan Colored People, 1988; YWCAs Salute to Women of Achievement, 1990; 100 of the Most Promising Black Women in America, Ebony Mag, 1991; Kizzy Award; Dollars & Sense, 1991; Achievement Award, Alpha Kappa Alpha Sorority; First Annual Woman of the Year Award, Courtney Childrens Foundations; US Small Business Administration Minority Small Business Champion of the Year, State Nevada, 2006. **Home Addr:** 10056 Pt View Dr, Jonesboro, GA 30236, **Home Phone:** (404)478-4227. **Business Addr:** President, President Emeritus, Urban Chamber of Commerce, 1951 Stella Lake St Suite 26, Las Vegas, NV 89106, **Business Phone:** (702)648-6222.

### BROWN, HARDY

Publisher. **Personal:** Born Dec 8, 1942, Jones County, NC. **Educ:** Univ Redlands, Johnston Col. **Career:** Kaiser Permanente, personnel mgr; Kaiser Permanente's Fontana Hosp, Human Resources Dir; Black Voice News, chmn, co-publ, currently; Brown Publ Co, chmn, 1980-. **Orgs:** Pres, Calif Media Asn; Nat Newspaper Publishers Asn; Calif Newspaper Publishers Asn; New Calif Media; W Coast Black Publishers Asn; bd trustee, San Bernardino Unified Sch dist; past pres, San Bernardino Br, Nat Asn Advan Colored People; founder, Black Voice Found; Riverside City Coun. **Honors/Awds:** Publisher of the Year, Nat Newspaper Publishers Asn, 2000. **Business Addr:** Chairman, Co-Publisher, BPC MediaWorks, 3585 Main St Suite 201, Riverside, CA 92501, **Business Phone:** (909)682-6111.

### BROWN, HAZEL EVELYN

Association executive, executive director. **Personal:** Born Sep 3, 1940, Eden, NC; daughter of Joseph (deceased) and Mary Sue Hairston. **Educ:** Russells Bus Sch, Winston-Salem, NC, cert sec, 1960, BA, bus admin, 1982; Bab cock Ctr Wake Forest Univ, Winston-Salem, NC, cert mgt develop, 1978; NC Cent Univ, Durham, NC, cert coun & interviewing, 1982; NC Agr & Tech State Univ, Greensboro, MS, adult educ, 1985. **Career:** Winston-Salem Urban League, Winston-Salem, NC, actg dir, vpres, 1961, Bd mem, 1994-. **Orgs:** Nat Asn Advan Colored People, 1972; Mt Zion Baptist Church, 1972; Winston-Salem State Alumni Asn, 1982; Up & Coming Invest, 1986; pres, Nat Women Achievement & Clemmons Chap, 1987; Benton Conv Ctr Coliseum Comn, 1987; Delta Sigma Theta Sorority, 1988; mem bd realtors, Housing Resource, 1988; Urban Arts Arts Coun, 1988. **Honors/Awds:** Girl Friday, Urban League Guild, 1970; Service Award, NAACP, 1987; Leadership Award, Winston-Salem Urban League, 1988. **Home Addr:** 1000 Shea Ct, Winston Salem, NC 27107, **Home Phone:** (336)785-2497. **Business Addr:** Board Member, Winston-Salem Transit Authority, 100 W 5th St, Winston Salem, NC 27101, **Business Phone:** (336)748-3034.

### BROWN, HEATHER M.

Entrepreneur, educator. **Educ:** Va Polytech Inst & State Univ, BS, human resources & personal finance, 1990, higher educ admin, 1994; Old Dom Univ, PhD, instrnl design & technol, 2009. **Career:** Va. Tech, Community Asst, 1993-94; Undergrad Advising-Col Bus, dir, 1997-2001; Asynchronous Learning & Corp Develop, dir, 2001-05; Antech Systs Inc, instrnl systs designer, 2009-; Prof Consult Solutions Inc, Fee Delinq, pres, currently; Instrnl Designer-Ctr Mil & Veteran's Educ, Tidewater Community Col, 2013-. **Business Addr:** Instructional Designer-Center for Military and Veteran's Education, Tidewater Community College, 121 College Place, Norfolk, VA 23510.

### BROWN, HELEN E.

Judge. **Personal:** Born Detroit, MI. **Educ:** Wayne State Univ, BA, 1972, Sch Law, JD, 1979. **Career:** Wayne County Circuit Ct, judge; State Mich Circuit Ct, judge, currently. **Orgs:** Phi Alpha Delta; Am Bar Asn. **Business Addr:** Judge, State Mich Circuit Ct, 711 Coleman A Young Munic Ctr Suite 1107, Detroit, MI 48226, **Business Phone:** (313)224-2441.

### BROWN, HENRY H.

Chief executive officer, consultant, president (organization). **Personal:** Born Nov 17, 1930, Houston, TX; children: 4. **Educ:** Xavier Univ, New Orleans; Tex Southern Univ. **Career:** Consultant, corporate exec (retired); Howard Univ Sch Bus & Indust, adj prof; Anheuser-Busch Inc, wholesaler rep, vpres, sr vpres, mkt develop & affairs, 1964-94; HH Brown & Assocs, pres & chief exec officer, currently. **Orgs:** Develop Great Kings & Queens Africa, 1975; Anheuser-Busch's ambassador, maj leading nat orgn; chmn, Nat Bus Policy Rev; imp, Potentate Prince Hall Shriners; Pub Rels Soc Am; Am Mgt Assoc; Amer Mkt Assoc; Nat Asn Medicaid dir; St Louis Ambassador; Royal Vagabonds. **Business Addr:** President, Chief Executive Officer, HH Brown & Associates, Inc, 5215 Honey Cir, Houston, TX 77056, **Business Phone:** (713)621-9664.

### BROWN, HERBERT R.

Insurance executive. **Personal:** Born May 20, 1940, Asheville, NC; married Marcia; children: Cheryl, Adrian & Janice. **Educ:** Int Data Proc Inst, cert, 1962; Univ Cincinnati, attended 1969. **Career:** Western & Southern Fin Grp, comput systs mgt, 1964-78, personnel coordr & community affairs, 1978-87, vpres pub rels, 1987, sr vpres pub rels & corp commun, 2001, bd dir, 2008-. **Orgs:** Cincinnati Bd Educ, 1978-87; pres, Cincinnati Bd Educ; Boy Scouts Am; St Johns Social Serv Ctr; C Protective Serv; Hoffman Elem Sch, chmn, LSDMC; Asn Black Ins Professionals; bd mem, Cincinnati Br Key Bank; bd mem, Fed Res Bank Cincinnati; chmn, bd gov, Greater Cincinnati Found; pres, Community Police Partnering Ctr; bd mem, Boy Scouts Am; pres, Ohio & Nat Caucus Black Sch Bd Mem; bd dir, Good Samaritan Hosp Found. **Honors/Awds:** Jefferson Award for Public Service, Am Inst Pub Serv, 1979; Leadership Award, United Way, 1981; Ethelrie Harper Award, Cincinnati Human Rels Comn, 1990; Corporate Image Maker Award, Applause Mag, 1992; Key to the City of Cincinnati, 1993; hon doctorate, Cincinnati State & Tech Col, 1994; Silver Beaver Award, Boy Scouts Am, 1995; Joseph Hall Award, United Way & Community Chest, 1995; Reach for the Stars, Memorial Community Ctr, 1995; Bell Ringer Award, Cincinnati Union Bethel, 1995; Lifetime Achievement Award, 1996; Paul M Lund Public Service Award, 2004; DHL, Cincinnati State Tech & Community Col; Lions Award, Cincinnati Urban League; Theodore Berry Award, Nat Asn Advan Colored People. **Home Addr:** 6520 Greenfield Woods S, Cincinnati, OH 45224-2265, **Home Phone:** (513)542-8705. **Business Addr:** Board of Director, Western & Southern Financial Group, 400 Broadway, Cincinnati, OH 45202-3341, **Business Phone:** (513)629-1136.

### BROWN, HEZEKIAH

Educator. **Personal:** Born Jul 29, 1923, Monticello, MS; married Rosa L S. **Educ:** Tuskegee Inst, BS, 1950; Tenn A & I State Univ, MS, 1958; Delta State Univ, educ spec AAA cert, 1973. **Career:** Eutaula, teacher, 1950-51; Simmons High Sch, teacher, 1951-63, Carver Elem Sch, prin, 1963-70; group guide instr, 1970-96. **Orgs:** Treas, Sunflower Co Teachers Asn; Chaplain VFW Post 9732, 1955-75; vpres, Wash Teachers Asn, 1970-75; Dept Chaplain, Dept MS, 1974-75; Adv Bd CHP; bd alderman; Wash Co Solid Waste Com; VFW; Miss Teachers Asn; Miss Voc Guid Asn; Alpha Phi Alpha; Miss Munic Asn; AVA; Mil Order Cooties SS No 13. **Home Addr:** PO Box 294, Hollandale, MS 38748, **Home Phone:** (662)827-5366.

### BROWN, IMANI

Investment banker, executive director, city planner. **Educ:** Univ Md, BA, sociol & bus admin; Cornell Univ; Univ Southern Calif, PhD, 2009. **Career:** Los Angeles Metrop Transp Authority, sr contract adminr, 1990-93, Vendor Rels Dept, proj mgr & co-founder, 1993-98; U.S. House Representatives, chief dep Congresswoman Millender McDonald, 1998-2001; Calif State Univ Dominquez Hills, assoc vpres univ & govt rels, 2001-04; Univ Southern Calif, exec dir govt & civic engagement, 2011; Tom & Ethel Bradley Found, consult, 2006-13; Granite Equities LLC, managing partner, 2013-. **Orgs:** Bd dir, Gordon Brown Fel.

### BROWN, INEZ M.

Government official. **Career:** Off US Sen Don Riegle, various positions, 21 years, sr policy advr on urban affairs, 1989; US Small Bus Admin, regional advocate reg 5, currently. **Orgs:** Bd dir, Genessee County, Econ Develop Comn; Bishop Airport Authority; citizen adv bd, Univ Mich; Community Corrections State Bd; adv, Genessee Econ Revitalization Agency; adv, city clerk, Flint, MI, Mayor Woodrow Stanley, Urban Investment Plan. **Business Addr:** Regional Advocate Region 5, Senior Policy Advisor, US Senator, Off Sen, Washington, DC 20510, **Business Phone:** (312)353-6070.

### BROWN, HON. IRMA JEAN

Lawyer, superior court judge. **Personal:** Born May 17, 1948, Los Angeles, CA. **Educ:** Loyola Marymount Univ, BS, 1970; Loyola Univ Sch Law, JD, 1973. **Career:** Los Angeles Co Pub Defenders Off, law clerk, 1973; Greater Watts Justice Ctr Legal Aid Found, Los Angeles, law clerk, staff atty, 1975-77; Hudson Sandoz & Brown, law firm partner, 1978-82; Los Angeles County Munic Ct, judge, 1982-2000; State Calif Super Ct, Los Angeles County, judge, 2000-10; Inglewood Juv Ct, judge, 2010-; regist Dem, 2010. **Orgs:** Pres, Los Angeles Negro Bus & Prof Womens Club, 1965-66; vpres, So Chap Black Women Lawyers Asn, 1975-76, pres, So Chap Black Women Lawyers Asn, 1976-77; sgt arms, JM Langston Bar Asn, 1976-77; Calif Attys Criminal Justice; treas, Nat Conf Black Lawyers, 1976-77; Nat Bar Asn; Delta Sigma Theta Sorority; Urban League; Nat Asn Advan Colored People; Jordan H S Alumni Asn; Dem Club; trustee, First African Methodist Episcopal Church, Los Angeles; 100 Black Women Los Angeles, Nat Asn Women Judges; Calif Judges Asn; Calif Asn Black Lawyers; Los Angeles Co Bar Asn. **Honors/Awds:** Grant Scholar Legal Educ Opportunity, 1970-73; Delta Sigma Theta Scholar, 1970; So Calif Gas Co Scholar, 1970; publ, The Minor & The Juv Ct Legal Aid Found Los Angeles, 1975-77; Certificate of Recognition for Achievement US Congress, Calif Senate, City Compton, Carson-Lynwood, Los Angeles Co. **Home Addr:** 6151 Wooster Ave, Los Angeles, CA 90056. **Business Addr:** Judge, Inglewood Juvenile Court, 110 E Regent St, Inglewood, CA 90301, **Business Phone:** (310)419-5275.

### BROWN, DR. J. THEODORE, JR.

Chief executive officer, inventor. **Educ:** State Univ NY, Stony Brook, PhD, experimental clinical psychol, 1977. **Career:** Inventor; Georgetown Univ Schs Med; Howard Univ Schs Med; DC Gen Hosp; Dept State NY, spec consult; Mayo Clin, spec consult; US Dept Health & Human Serv, spec expert; Personal health & Hyg Inc, founder & chief exec officer; Virtual Health Systs Inc, founder, pres, chief exec officer & prin, vpres, dir clin serv, currently. **Orgs:** Am Psychol Asn. **Business Addr:** President, Chief Executive Officer, Virtual Health Service Inc, 2 E McClain Ave Suite 3, Scottsburg, IN 47170, **Business Phone:** (812)722-4858.

### BROWN, JAMES B.

Executive, football player. **Personal:** Born Jan 5, 1967, Washington, DC; married Renee; children: Leia Paris Roberts, Michael & Janee Keanna. **Educ:** Univ Md, attended. **Career:** Football player (retired); Miami Dolphins, defensive back, 1989-96; Pittsburgh Steelers, 1997; Ariz Cardinals, cornerback, 1998; Detroit Lions, cornerback, 1999-2000; Grassroots Football League, dir sports performance & training, vpres, founder; Nat Football League Northeast, coordr legend ambassador, 2013. **Business Addr:** Director of Sports Performance and Training, Vice President, Grassroots Youth Football League, Baltimore, WA.

**BROWN, JAMES G., JR.**
Executive. **Educ:** Univ Md College Park, BS, bus admin & mgt gen, 1982. **Career:** Bell Atlantic, mgr, 1982-95; CBS NFL studio; ESPN, dir-affil sales & mkt western region, sr vpres-affil sales & mkt, 1995-2012; ALFA Worldwide Ltd, co-pres, co-owner & co-founder, 2010-; REVOLT MEDIA & TV, sr vpres, head content distrib, 2014-. **Orgs:** Bd mem, Nat Asn Multi-ethnicity Commun. **Business Addr:** Senior Vice President, REVOLT MEDIA & TV, 1800 N Highland Av 6th Fl, Los Angeles, CA 90028.

**BROWN, DR. JAMES HARVEY, SR.**
Dentist, educator. **Personal:** Born Aug 30, 1924, Malcom, AL; son of Charlie Myles and Alice Woodyard Brown Ross (deceased); married Birdie Faulkner; children: Albert, Alice, Jacqueline, Renee & James Jr. **Educ:** Ala A&M Univ, Norm, AL, BS, 1946; Meharry Med Col, Nashville, TN, DDS, 1952; Tenn State Univ, Nashville, TN, MS, zool, 1961, MEd, educ admin, 1964. **Career:** Meharry Med Col Sch Dent, Nashville, TN, assoc prof, 1952-; pvt pract, 1955-; Riverside Hosp, dent staff, 1958-78; Tenn State Univ Stud HealthServ, Nashville, TN, assist dir, 1958-64, dir, 1964-69; Clover Bottom Hosp& Sch, clin supvry dent students, 1964-72; George W Hubbard HospMeharry Med Col, Nashville, TN, dent staff, 1952-, secy, treas, 1968-; Meharry-Hubbard Hosp, Dent Serv, Nashville, TN, dir, 1964-81; VeteransAdmin hosp, Nashville, TN & Murfreesboro, TN, consult, 1968-81; pvt pract, dentist, currently. **Orgs:** Alpha Phi Alpha, 1949; charter mem, Am Asn Hosp Dentists; Capital CityDent Soc; Pan Tenn Dent Asn; Nat Dent Asn; Nashville Dent Soc; Tenn StateDent Asn; Am Dent Asn; Nashville Acad Med; Davidson County Med Soc; Frontiers Inc; Tenn State Med Asn; Am Asn Dent Sch; fel, Am Acad GeneralDentistry, 1977; Am Acad Oper Dent; Am Asn Tension Control; dipl, Nat Bd Dent Examiners, 1955. **Business Addr:** Dentist, 4208 Enchanted Ct, Nashville, TN 37218-1827, **Business Phone:** (615)876-3777.

**BROWN, JAMES LAMONT**
Football player. **Personal:** Born Jan 30, 1970, Philadelphia, PA; children: Hasson & Semaj. **Educ:** Va State Univ. **Career:** Football player (retired); Dallas Cowboys, 1992; New York Jets, tackle, 1993, right tackle, 1994-95; Miami Dolphins, right tackle, 1996-99, tackle, 1999; Cleveland Browns, right tackle, 2000.

**BROWN, JAMES MARION**
Government official. **Personal:** Born Jul 30, 1952, Holdenville, OK; son of Clearnce Jr and Carrie Mae Knox; married Clarice M; children: James Jr, Tiffany & Jamie. **Educ:** E Cent Univ, Ada, BS. **Career:** McAlester High Sch, psychol teacher, 1977-; City of McAlester, coun mem, 1982; Okla Pardon & Parole Bd, chmn & gov. **Orgs:** Spec Serv Bd for State Okla Teachers, 1977-81; bd dir, State Okla Teachers Convention Comt, 1977-81; trustee, McAlester Health Authority, 1982-86; trustee, McAlester Econ Develop Serv, 1982-86; Black Elected Offs, 1982-; Okla Munic League, 1982-86; McAlester Youth Shelter, 1984; State Atty Gen Adv Comn, 1985; Gov Comt Physical Fitness; bd, Pub Works Bd, McAlester, Okla; Appointed, Okla Human Rights Comn, 1984; bd, McAlester Boy's Club, 1984-86. **Honors/Awds:** Awarded Highest Grade Point Average of Alpha Phi Alpha, 1975; Nat Asn Advan Colored People Man of the Year Award, 1988-89. **Special Achievements:** First black vice mayor, City, 1990-92. **Home Addr:** 1208 N G St, McAlester, OK 74501-3343, **Home Phone:** (918)426-1636. **Business Addr:** Chairperson, Oklahoma Pardon & Parole Board, PO Box 1814, McAlester, OK 74502-1814, **Business Phone:** (405)602-5863.

**BROWN, JAMES NATHANIEL**
Actor, founder (originator), football player. **Personal:** Born Feb 17, 1936, St. Simons Island, GA; son of Swinton and Theresa; married Sue; children: Kim, Kevin & James Jr; married Monique; children: Aris & Morgan. **Educ:** Syracuse Univ, BA, econs, 1957. **Career:** Football player (retired), actor, founder; Cleveland Browns, fullback, 1957-65, exec advisor, currently; Am-I-can, chmn & founder, 1988-. Films: Rio Conchos, 1964; The Dirty Dozen, 1967; Ice Sta Zebra, 1968; The Split, 1968; Riot, 1969; 100 Rifles, 1969; The Grasshopper, 1969; Kenner, 1969; El Condor, 1970; Tick, Tick, Tick, 1970; El Condor, 1970; Black Gunn, 1972; Slaughter, 1972; Slaughter 2: Big Rip-Off, 1973; The Slams, 1973; Three the Hard Way, 1974; I Escaped From Devil's Island, 1974; Take a Hard Ride, 1975; Kid Vengeance, 1977; Fingers, 1978; Pacific Inferno, 1978; One Down Two to Go, 1982; Black Hollywood, 1984; Lady Blue, 1985; Pac Inferno, producer, 1985; Richard Pryor Here & Now, exec producer, 1983; The Running Man, 1987; LA Heat, 1988; Crack House, 1989; Twisted Justice, 1989; Mars Attacks!, 1996; Original Gangstas, 1996; Any Given Sunday, 1999; Jim Brown: All-Am, 2002; On the Edge, 2002; She Hate Me, 2004; Dream St, 2005; Animal, 2005; Dream Street, 2010; Draft Day, 2014. TV series: "The Magnificent Magical Magnet of Santa Mesa", producer, 1977; "Healthy Wealthy & Wise", 1991; "Keeping the Music Alive", dir, 1999; "Am Roots Music", dir, 2001; "Soul Food", 2004; "Sucker Free City", 2004; "Sideliners", 2006; numerous other films & TV ser; Black Econ Union, founder. **Honors/Awds:** Pro Bowl, 1957, 1958, 1959, 1960, 1961, 1962, 1963, 1964, 1965; NFL Rushing champion, 1957, 1958, 1959, 1960, 1961, 1963, 1964, 1965; NFL MVP, 1957, 1958, 1965; UPI NFL MVP, 1958, 1963, 1965; Jim Thorpe Trophy, 1958 & 1965; Player of the Year, 1958, 1963 & 1965; Named to every All-Star Team, 1963; NFL champion, 1964; Hickoc Belt Athlete of Year, 1964; Pro Football Hall of Fame, 1971; Second on all-time rushing list; Greatest distance gained in one season; Named best football player of the 20th Century, Sports Illus; Nat Intercollegiate All-Am Football Players; Col Football Hall of Fame; Lacrosse Hall of Fame; color commentator, Ultimate Fighting Championship; greatest professional football player, Sporting News, 2002. **Special Achievements:** Author, "Off My Chest", 1964 & recent autobiography; appointed by Calif Assembly Speaker, "Willie L Brown Jr to the Comn on the Status of African American Males", 1994; In film director Spike Lee released the film "Jim Brown: All-American"; a retrospective on Brown's professional career and personal life, 2002. **Home Addr:** 6290 Sunset Blvd Suite 925, Hollywood, CA 90028. **Business Addr:** Founder, Chairman, The Amer-I-Can Foundation for Social Change, 269 S Beverly Dr Suite 1048, Los Angeles, CA 90212, **Business Phone:** (310)652-7884.

**BROWN, JAMES WILLIE, JR. See KOMUNYAKAA, YUSEF.**

**BROWN, JAMIE EARL S.**
Executive, lawyer. **Personal:** son of Josephine and Jamie Sr; married Daisy Gore; children: Michael, Mark & Martin. **Educ:** Northern Mich Univ, BS, 1970; State Univ NY, Buffalo, Sch Law, JD, 1973. **Career:** Kings County Dist Atty, law investr, asst dist atty, 1973-75; Dept Health Educ & Welfare, atty adv, 1975-83; J Earl Brown Realty Corp, pres, 1983-89; State Sen Andrew Jenkins, chief legis asst, 1989-92; J Earl Brown & Assocs, PC, law, real estate, 1992-. **Orgs:** Ancient Free & Accepted Masons, King Solomon Lodge no 5, 32nd Deg; Nat Bar Asn; Phi Alpha Delta Legal Frat; Ny Bar Asn; Omega Psi Phi Frat; Nat Asn Advan Colored People; One Hundred Black Men New York; Am Bar Asn. **Home Addr:** 431 W Chelten Ave, Philadelphia, PA 19120-4403, **Home Phone:** (215)843-9883. **Business Addr:** President, J Earl Brown Assocs Ltd, 431 W Chelten Ave, Philadelphia, PA 19144, **Business Phone:** (800)529-3275.

**BROWN, JAMIE FOSTER**
Writer, journalist. **Personal:** Born Jun 26, 1946, Chicago, IL; married Lorenzo; children: Randy & Russell. **Educ:** Univ Stockholm, Sweden, BA. **Career:** Wash Theater Group, founder; Black Entertainment TV, secy, "Video Soul", producer, "Video LP", producer; Sister 2 Sister Mag, owner & publ, 1988-; Radio show "The Sister 2 Sister Celebrity Update", founder; Books: Betty Shabazz: A Sisterfriends' Tribute in Words & Pictures. **Orgs:** Keynote speaker, Inst Polit, Harvard Univ's John F Kennedy Sch Govt; Midwest Radio & Music Asn. **Honors/Awds:** Jamie Foster Brown Day, Mayor Washington, named in honor, 1998; Anheuser-Busch Eagle Award; Martin Luther King Jr Scholarship Award for Outstanding African-American Women; Lifetime Achievement Award, Midwest Radio & Music Asn, 1998; IMPACT Super Summit Award; Lifetime Achievement Award, Golden Scissors, 2002; Shero Hall of Fame, Nat Asn Black Female Execs, 2002; Matrix Award for Professional Achievement, Asn Women Commun, 2004; Honorary Doctorate, Bennett Col, 2008; Freedom Sisters Award, Ford Motor Co, 2009. **Special Achievements:** Newsweek magazine, lauding Ms. Brown's influence, listed her among the nation's top "buzz-makers". **Home Addr:** 3127 Newton St NE, Washington, DC 20018, **Home Phone:** (202)269-1628. **Business Addr:** Owner, Publisher, Sister 2 Sister Magazine, PO Box 41148, Washington, DC 20018, **Business Phone:** (301)390-1111.

**BROWN, JAMIE SHEPARD, II**
Football player, football coach. **Personal:** Born Apr 24, 1972, Miami, FL; son of Jimmie and Jeannie Blunt. **Educ:** Fla A&M Univ, grad. **Career:** Football player (retired), football coach; Denver Broncos, tackle, 1995-97; San Francisco 49ers, left tackle, 1998; Wash Redskins, tackle, 1999; Park View High Sch, offensive line coach, security consult, 2005-06.

**BROWN, JANICE ROGERS**
Judge. **Personal:** Born May 11, 1949, Greenville, AL; daughter of Doris Holland; married Alan; children: Nathan; married Dewey Parker. **Educ:** Calif State Univ, BA, 1974; Univ Calif, Los Angeles Sch Law, JD, 1977; Univ Va Sch Law, LLM, 2004. **Career:** Calif Dept Justice, dep legis coun, 1977-79, dep atty gen, 1979-87; Calif Bus, Transp & Housing Agency, dep secy & gen coun, 1987-89; pvt pract, 1989-91; Gov Pete Wilson, legal affairs secy, 1991-94; Calif Ct Appeals, assoc justice, 1994-96; Calif Supreme Ct, assoc justice, 1996-05; US Ct Appeals DC Circuit, fed judge, 2005-. **Orgs:** Am Bar Asn; Calif State Bar Asn. **Special Achievements:** First African American woman to serve on the California Supreme Court. **Business Addr:** Federal Judge, United States Court of Appeal, 333 Const Ave NW, Washington, DC 20001, **Business Phone:** (202)216-7220.

**BROWN, JARVIS ARDEL**
Baseball player, athletic coach. **Personal:** Born Mar 26, 1967, Waukegan, IL. **Educ:** Carthage Col, grad, 2011. **Career:** Baseball player (retired), baseball coach; Minn Twins, outfielder, 1991-92; San Diego Padres, 1993; Atlanta Braves, 1994; Cincinnati Reds, 1995; Baltimore Orioles, 1995-96; Milwaukee Brewers, 1997; Minn Orgn Class A Fort Myers, coach, 1999; Class AA New Britain, coach, 2000; Twins Gulf Coast League rookie team, coach, 2001; New Haven, Northeast League, mgr, 2004; Carthage Col, asst coach, 2003, 2009; Univ Wis-Parkside, head baseball Coach, 2007-09. **Honors/Awds:** Am League Championship Series, 1991; World Champion, 1991. **Business Addr:** Assistant Baseball Coach, Carthage College, 2001 Alford Pk Dr, Kenosha, WI 53140, **Business Phone:** (262)551-8500.

**BROWN, ESQ. JASPER C., JR.**
Lawyer. **Personal:** Born Mar 27, 1946, Columbia, SC; married Sandra Cox; children: Leslie, Douglass & Jasper David. **Educ:** Hampton Inst, BS, 1969; Cath Univ, Columbus Sch Law, JD, 1974. **Career:** Gen Electric Co, prod mgr, 1969-71; Nat Labor Rels Bd Div Adv, staff atty, 1974-77; Nat Labor Rels Bd, gen coun. **Orgs:** Nat Bar Asn, 1974-; Pa Bar Asn, 1974-; NC Asn Black Lawyers, 1977-. **Home Addr:** 3110 Briarcliff Rd, Winston-Salem, NC 27106-3004, **Home Phone:** (336)631-5214. **Business Addr:** General Counsel, National Labor Relations Board, 4035 Univ Pkwy Suite 200, Winston-Salem, NC 27106-3325, **Business Phone:** (336)631-5201.

**BROWN, JEAN MARIE**
Editor. **Personal:** Born May 7, 1964, Gary, IN; daughter of Eugene and Patricia; married Tyrone Young; children: Lillian & Lucille. **Educ:** Northwestern Univ, BS, jour, 1986. **Career:** Wall St J, reporter; Post-Tribune, Gary, IN, reporter; Charlotte Observer, city govt reporter, city hall reporter, asst night city ed, night city ed, day city ed, dep features ed; Star-Telegram, city ed, 2000-03, asst mng ed 2003, mng ed & tarrant, currently. **Orgs:** Nat Asn Black Journalists; bd mem, Am Montessori Asn. **Home Addr:** 4709 Tearose Trail, Fort Worth, TX 76123, **Home Phone:** (817)370-9033. **Business Addr:** Managing Editor, Star-Telegram, PO Box 915007, Fort Worth, TX 76115, **Business Phone:** (817)685-3823.

**BROWN, REV. JEFFREY LEMONTE**
Clergy. **Personal:** Born Dec 22, 1961, Anchorage, AK; son of Jesse L and Geraldine G; married Lesley A Mosley; children: Rayna Adair. **Educ:** East Stroudsburg Univ, BA, 1982; Ind Univ, PA, MEd, 1984; Andover Newton Theol Sch, Mdiv, 1987; Harvard Divinity Sch. **Career:** Pastor (retired), Executive; Am Baptist Churches Inc, rep gen bd, 1987-91; Union Baptist Church, sr pastor, head, 1988-2009; Harvard Bus Sch, guest lectr; Twelfth Baptist Church, assoc pastor, currently. **Orgs:** Racism/sexism task force, 1986-87; Andover Newton Theol Sch; secy, United Baptist Conv Ma, RI, & NH, 1988; bd mem, Dept Church & Soc; Am Baptist Churches, MA, 1988-90; bd mem, Bd Ministry, Harvard Univ, 1989-92; bd dir, Cambridge Econ Opportunity Comn, 1990; pres, Cambridge Black Pastors Conf, 1991; co-founder, 1992, exec dir, Boston TenPoint Coalition, 2005-13; pres, managing partner, Rebuilding Every Community Around Peace, currently. **Home Addr:** 184 Raymond St, Cambridge, MA 02140. **Business Addr:** Associate Pastor, Twelfth Baptist Church, 150 Warren St, Roxbury, MA 02119, **Business Phone:** (617)442-7855.

**BROWN, JENEVER H.**
Educator, administrator, president (organization). **Personal:** Born Oct 10, 1934, Smithfield, VA; daughter of Charlie W and Caroline M Hill; married Oswald E; children: Shaun D. **Educ:** Va State Univ, BS, 1956; Hampton Univ, MA, 1975. **Career:** Educator, administrator (retired); Newport News Pub Sch, GED Prog, part-time instr, supvr, Bus Edu; Thomas Nelson Comm Col, instr; JAS Int Sys, pres; Journey Global Develop Group, sec, tres; J Group, pres; Hampton Rods, educr. **Orgs:** NEA, 1957-91; Newport News Educ Asn, 1957-91; Bus Educ Assn, 1957-91; Am Voc Assn, 1980-91; bd chair, pres, Peninsula Assn Sickle Cell Anemia, 1998-; pres, Delta Sigma Theta Sorority, Newport News Alumnae, 1998-; Nat Asn Advan Colored People, 1998-; life mem, Newport News Free Clin; pres, Jobs Va Community Develop Corp, currently. **Home Addr:** 1 Beatrice Dr, Hampton, VA 23666, **Home Phone:** (757)826-3319. **Business Addr:** President, Peninsula Association For Sickle Cell Anemia, 512 E Mercury Blvd, Hampton, VA 23663, **Business Phone:** (757)813-1021.

**BROWN, JEROME**
Educator. **Educ:** Lincoln Univ, BS, comput sci, 1996; Univ Md, MS, comput sci, 1998. **Career:** Harford Community Col, Comput & Technol Div, vis prof comput sci & math bus, 1999-; SRS Technologies, tech proj mgr, 2004-09; ManTech, sr systs analyst, 2009-13; Aquilent, proj mgr, 2013-14. **Orgs:** Fel Leadership Mgt Int, 1997-98. **Business Addr:** Visiting Professor, Harford Community College, Bel Air Hall Rm 244 401 Thomas Run Rd, Bel Air, MD 21015, **Business Phone:** (410)836-4125.

**BROWN, JIM (JAMES BROWN)**
President (organization), educator, manager. **Personal:** married Pamela Barrett Brewer. **Educ:** City Univ NY Col. **Career:** Henry Straus Productions Inc, from prod asst to prod mgr, 1963; Straus, dir, casting dir & ed; WNET Film Trng Sch, tutor; Hartford Community Film Workshop Coun, dir; 1969; Howard Univ, fac, 1971-78, dir training, 1984-96, multimedia mgr, 1998-2009; WHMM/WHUT-TV, sta mgr, 1996-98, Sch Commun, multimedia mgr; John H Johnson Sch Commun, staff & multimedia mgr, currently; 26x2 Commun, producer, 1996-, founder, pres, 2001-. **Orgs:** Bd gov, Nat Acad TV Arts & Scis, 1984-88 & 1994-98, vpres, 1998-2000; Howard Univ Sch Commun. **Home Addr:** 9139 Sligo Creek Pkwy, Silver Spring, MD 20901, **Home Phone:** (301)589-4914. **Business Addr:** President, Producer, 26x2 Communication, 1924 Kimberley Rd, Silver Spring, MD 20903, **Business Phone:** (301)439-7144.

**BROWN, JUDGE JOE**
Judge. **Personal:** Born Jul 5, 1947, Washington, DC; children: 2; married Deborah Herron. **Educ:** Univ Calif, Los Angeles, BA, polit sci, Law Sch, JD, 1973. **Career:** Pvt pract, 1978; pub serv, 1990; State Criminal Ct, Shelby Co, judge, 1990-2000; tv show, Judge Joe Brown, TV judge, 1998-2014; Judge Joe Inc, owner, currently; Shelby County, Dem primary, dist atty gen, 2014. **Orgs:** Alpha Phi Alpha fraternity. **Special Achievements:** First African-American prosecutor in the city of Memphis. **Business Addr:** Owner, Judge Joe Inc, 5900 Wilshire Blvd Suite 530, Los Angeles, CA 90036-5005, **Business Phone:** (323)549-3130.

**BROWN, JOE**
Chef, entrepreneur, business owner. **Career:** Pirates Inn, chef, 1979-89; Land Mark, exec sous chef, 1984-89; Pirates Inn, exec chef, 1989-94; Seafood Restaurant, line chef; BYOB Cajun-Ital eatery, 1995; Melange Cafe, owner & exec chef, 1995-2013; Compass Group N Am, Morrison, exec chef, 2013-14; Gensis Healthcare powerback, exec chef, 2014-15; Bethany Baptist Church, culinary dir/exec chef, currently. **Home Addr:** 18 Tanner St, Haddonfield, NJ 08033-2404, **Home Phone:** (856)354-1333. **Business Addr:** Owner, Chef, Melange Cafe, 1601 Chapel Ave, Cherry Hill, NJ 08002-2824, **Business Phone:** (856)663-7339.

**BROWN, JOHN, JR.**
Automotive executive. **Personal:** married Sylvia; children: Derwin & Ivan. **Educ:** SC State Univ. **Career:** E Tulsa Dodge Inc, pres & gen mgr; Majestic Scholar Publ Co, adminr, pres, currently. **Orgs:** Kappa Alpha Psi Fraternity Inc; bd dir, Am Red Cross; bd dir, Metrop Tulsa Chamber Com; bd dir, Metrop Tulsa Urban League. **Home Addr:** 2500 N 15th St, Broken Arrow, OK 74012, **Home Phone:** (918)355-4349. **Business Addr:** President, Majestic Scholar Publishing Co, PO Box 2892, Broken Arrow, OK 74013-2892, **Business Phone:** (918)355-4349.

**BROWN, JOHN C., JR.**
Executive, football player, administrator. **Personal:** Born Jun 9, 1939, Camden, NJ; married Gloria; children: John III & Ernie Davis. **Educ:** Univ Syracuse, BA, 1962; Univ Pittsburgh, attended 1974; Stonier Grad Sch Banking, grad degree banking, 1980. **Career:** Football player (retired), educator, executive; Cleveland Browns, prof football, 1962-66; Math & Eng, teacher & counr, 1962-63; Firestone

Tire & Rubber Co, franchise paul Warfield, 1964; Pittsburgh Steelers, prof football, 1966-71; Pittsburgh Nat Bank Oakland, credit analyst, 1970-74, comn banking off, 1974, mgr Oakland off, 1977, asst vpres, 1978, vpres, 1979, dist mgr dist X, 1980; NSD Bancorp Inc, bd dir, currently. **Orgs:** Bd dir, United Way YMCA; treas, Nat Mult Sclerosis Soc; Nat Asn Advan Colored People; Rotary Oakland; bm, Pittsburgh charitable orgn. **Home Addr:** 101 Gadshill Pl, Pittsburgh, PA 15237. **Business Addr:** Board of Director, NSD Bancorp Inc, 5004 McKnight Rd, Pittsburgh, PA 15237, **Business Phone:** (412)231-6900.

### BROWN, JOHN E.

Executive. **Personal:** Born Jul 2, 1948, Columbia, SC; son of John Jr and Naomi Burrell; married Jessie Gwendolyn Reardon; children: Michael, Roderick & Geoffrey. **Educ:** Palmer Jr Col, attended 1971; Columbia Bus Col, AA, bus admin & traffic mgt, 1979. **Career:** Richland County Sheriff's Dept, dep, 1971-72; SC Hwy Patrol, patrolman, 1972-85; Am-Pro Protective Agency, owner, pres, chief exec officer, 1982-93, chmn, 1993-97; hazard waste bus. **Orgs:** Richland County's Bus Round Table Gov's Initiative Work Force Excellence; bd dir, Am Legion; bd dir, United Way Midlands; mem steering comt, Palmetto Boys State; bd dir, Gillcreek Baptist Church; corp adv bd, Br Banking & Trust; bd dirs, SC State Mus; Columbia Urban League; Blue Ribbon Comn; United Black Fund; Community 100 Black Men; Columbia Bus Network Asn; Chamber Com Comn 100; SC Legis Black Caucus Corp Roundtable; adv comt, Palmetto Dockside Gaming Asn; bd gov, Entrepreneur Yr Judging Comt, Capital City Club; SC Chat, Entrepreneur Yr Inst. **Honors/Awds:** Gov SC, Order Palmetto, 1978; District One Highway patrolman of the Year, 1980; Minority Small Businessman of the Year Award, 1988; 8(a) Contractor of the Year, 1988; Nat Finalist Federal Sub-Contractor of the Year, 1988; Administrator's Award for Excellence, US Small Bus Admin, 1989; VC Summer Corporate Award, Columbia Urban League, 1992; Corp Award, SC Conf Branches NAACP, 1992 & 1994; Inducted to Entrepreneur of the Year Hall of Fame, 1993; SC Entrepreneur of the Year, Non-Financial Serv, 1993; Ruth Standish Baldwin, Eugene Kinckle Jones, Vol Serv Award, Nat Urban League, 1993; Outstanding Achievement Award, Hon SC Black Hall of Fame, 1994; Flour Daniel Contractor Recognition Award, 1994. **Special Achievements:** Listed 257 of the top 500 companies, 1990 & 1991; Listed 164 of top 500 companies, 1992. **Home Addr:** 209 Meadow Creek Dr, Columbia, SC 29203, **Home Phone:** (803)755-6355. **Business Addr:** Chief Executive Officer, President, Am-Pro Protective Agency, 7499 Parklane Rd Suite 136, Columbia, SC 29224.

### BROWN, GEN. JOHN MITCHELL, SR.

Executive, historian, commander. **Personal:** Born Dec 11, 1929, Vicksburg, MS; son of Ernestine Foster and Joeddie Fred; married Louise Yvonne Dorsey; children: Ronald Quinton, Jan Michelle, John Mitchell & Jay Michael. **Educ:** West Point, US Mil Acad, BS, Eng, 1955; Syracuse Univ, MBA, 1964; Univ Houston, attended 1978. **Career:** AUS, 1955-88: chief staff army, asst secy gen staff, 1970-71; 8th Inf Div, battalion comdr, 1971-73; Comptroller Army, sr exec, 1973-77; 3rd Brigade, 2nd Div, Korea, comdr, 1976-77; 2nd Inf Div, Korea, asst comdr, 1979-80; Mat Plans, Progs & Budget; Off Army Res Develop & Procurement, dep chief staff, 1980-83; Comptroller, Aus Forces Command, 1983-85; III Corps & Ft Hood Tex, dep comdr; Repub S Vietnam, combat duty; Jarvis & Kive Realty, chmn, currently; Michael Brown Analytics, pres, currently. **Orgs:** Nat Asn Advan Colored People; Vet Foreign Wars; Am Legion; Coun, 100; Chamber Com; Nat Urban League; Am Defense Preparedness Asn; Minority Develop Legal Fund; Nat Asn Minority Bus; Asn AUS; Masons. **Honors/Awds:** Three Army Commendations, 1955-; Published Defense Econ Anal Defense, Econ Anal Army, 1969; City Atlanta & State Ga Proclamation Designating June 19, "John M. Brown Day", 1985; Distinguished Serv Medal, Two Meritorious Serv Awards. **Business Addr:** President, Michael Brown Analytics Inc, 12601 Westover Ct, Upper Marlboro, MD 20772-5036, **Business Phone:** (301)599-7927.

### BROWN, JOSEPH DAVIDSON, SR.

Government official. **Personal:** Born Dec 27, 1929, St. Joseph, LA; son of Mitchell and Mary Deon; married Cleola Morris; children: Ann Marie Clayton, Mitchell George, Ollie Mae Neely, Joseph Davidson Jr, Joyce Lavel Davis & Claude Ernest. **Educ:** Eswege Germany Sch, mechanic, 1951; Tyler Barber Col, barber, 1954; Triton Col, supervision, 1978. **Career:** Government official (retired); Maywood Village, pub works, 1962, dir, dep marshal, 1992-97; Cent Area Park Dist, police officer, 1976-79, comm, 1979; Second Baptist Church, deacon, 1984; Maywood Park Dist, police officer, 1992-97. **Orgs:** Mason Pride Tensas 99, 1954-. **Honors/Awds:** Maywood Village Code Enforcement Marshal; Natural Hazards Recovery Course Inland; Emergency Mgmt Inst Emmitsburg MD; Fundamentals Water Supply Operation, Illinois Environmental Protection Agency, 1977; Fred Hampton Scholarship Image Award, 1979; Police Law Enforcement Training, Central Area Park Dist Police Dept, 1981. **Home Addr:** 223 S 12th Ave, Maywood, IL 60153, **Home Phone:** (708)681-4735. **Business Addr:** Director of Public Works, Public Works of Maywood, 1E Madison Plz, Maywood, IL 60153, **Business Phone:** (708)450-4482.

### BROWN, JOSEPH N.

Entrepreneur, lawyer. **Educ:** Hillsdale Col, BA, 1958; Univ Detroit Sch Law, LLB, 1961. **Career:** Law firm Keith, Conyers, Brown, Wahls & Baltimore, partner; Bodman, partner, currently. **Orgs:** City Detroit Civic Ctr Comn; life mem, Nat Asn Advan Colored People; bd trustee, Franklin wright Settlement; bd mem, Detroit Music Hall Ctr Performing arts; life mem, US Sixth Circuit Judicial Conf; State Bar Mich; Wolverine Bar Asn; Detroit Metrop Bar Asn. **Business Addr:** Partner, Bodman LLP, 6th Fl Ford Field 1901 St Antoine St, Detroit, MI 48226, **Business Phone:** (313)259-7777.

### BROWN, JOSEPH SAMUEL

Government official. **Personal:** Born Dec 3, 1943, New York, NY; son of Austin Samuel and Ruby Reid; married Beverly; children: Jamal Hassan, Kareem Saladin & Paul Emmanuel. **Educ:** Elizabeth City State Univ, Elizabeth City, NC, BS, 1966; NC Cent Univ, Durham, NC, MS, 1968. **Career:** NY City Bd Educ Harlem High Sch, prin, 1975-77; NYC Dept Gen Serv, New York, NY, admin staff analyst, 1977-79; NYC Dept Econ Dev Minority Bus Dev Off, New York, NY, dir, 1979-85; Darryl E Greene & Assoc, New York, NY, managing dir, 1985-88; Monroe Co, Dept Affirmative Action & HR, Rochester, NY, dir, 1988. **Orgs:** Omega Psi Phi Fraternity, 1965-; adv bd, Baden St Ctr, 1988-; Montgomery Neighborhood Ctr, 1988-; Am Civil Liberties Union Genesee Valley Chap, 1988-; adv coun, NYS Human Rights Comm, 1988-; bd dir, E House, 1988; Austin Stewart Prof Soc, 1988-; Rochester/Monroe County Coun Disabled Persons, 1991-; Rochester/Monroe County Pvt Indust, 1991-; Am Asn Affirmative Action, 1991-; Urban League Rochester; pres, local chap, vpres, Greater Rochester, Nat Asn Advan Color People; pres, Am Civil Liberties Union Nebr. **Home Addr:** 275 Lyndhurst St, Rochester, NY 14605-2612, **Home Phone:** (585)319-3303. **Business Addr:** Interim President, Greater Rochester Chapter NAACP, PO Box 31456, Rochester, NY 14608, **Business Phone:** (585)461-1120.

### BROWN, JOYCE

School administrator, association executive, executive. **Personal:** Born Aug 2, 1937, LaGrange, GA; daughter of Nellie Kate Harris Storey and Willis Storey; married Randolph F; children: Randette J, Randolph J, Ronda J & Randal J. **Educ:** Ohio State Univ, attended 1958; Sinclair Col, attended 1959. **Career:** Citibank NA, FISG Foreign Exchange, asst mgr, 1975-80, FMG Treas Serv mgr, 1980-83, NABG CSD Treas Serv Foreign Exchange, mgr, 1983-; Hempstead Pub Sch Brd pres; Citibank Citi corp, NY, asst vpres, 1983; NY Sch, Sch Brd Assn, dir brd develop, New York Community Sch Brd Improv Pro, 1989; JB Consult Serv, pres, currently, policy & governance consult, currently. **Orgs:** Chmn, Adv Com Minority Affairs NY; mem bd dir, Alliance Counr Drug &Alcohol Abuse; mem bd dir, Nat Bus & Prof Womens Clubs Inc; pres & mem, Hempstead Sch Bd, 1981-86; Nat Alliance Black Sch Educrs, 1984-; exec vpres, Nat Caucus Black Sch Bd Mems, 1986-87; chairperson, Govt Affairs, Natl Assn Black Bus & Prof Women's Clubs, 1987-; 100 Black Women Inc, 1987-; pres, Hempstead Civic Assn, 1987-88; chairperson, Hempstead Educ Comt, 1988-; life mem, Natl Assn Advan Colored People; co-chair, Nat Alliance Black Sch Educrs Policy Comn, 1991; supt search consult, NY Sch Brds Assn, 1992. **Honors/Awds:** Outstanding Service Award, 100 Black Men, 1984; Legislative Citation, Ohio State Assembly, 1984; Outstanding Service, Hempstead Sch Dist, 1986; Legislative Citation, New York State Assembly, 1989; Legislative Citation, Nassau County Elective, 1989. **Home Addr:** 254 Rhodes Ave, Hempstead, NY 11550, **Home Phone:** (516)485-8417. **Business Addr:** Policy & Governance Consultant, Policy and Governance Consultant, JB Consulting Service, 42 High St Suite 4, Medford, MA 02155-3864, **Business Phone:** (781)391-6056.

### BROWN, DR. JOYCE F.

Chief executive officer, psychologist, president (organization). **Personal:** Born Jul 7, 1947, New York, NY; daughter of Robert E and Joyce Cappie; married H Carl McCall. **Educ:** Marymount Col, BA, psychol, 1968; NY Univ, MA, psychol, 1971, PhD, psychol, 1980; Harvard Univ, Inst Educ Mgt, cert. **Career:** City Univ NY, Cent Off, univ dean, 1983-87, vice chancellor, 1987-90, prof clin psychol, 1994-98, prof emer, currently; City Univ NY, Baruch Col, actg pres, 1990; State Univ New York Syst, Fashion Inst Technol, pres, 1998-; Educ Found, Fashion Industs, chief exec officer, 1998-; Polo Ralph Lauren Corp, dir, 2001-; NY City, Pub & County Affairs, dep mayor, 1993-94; State New York, comptroller, 1993-2002; Manhattan Community College, coordr community educ proj & dir paraprofessional teacher educ prog; Bernard Baruch College, acting pres, vice chancellor. **Orgs:** Dir, Boys Harbor Inc, 1987-; Dir, NY City Outward Bound, Cent Park Conservancy; trustee, Marymont Col, 1994-2000; bd mem, Polo Ralph Lauren; bd mem, US Enrichment Corp; bd mem, Warm Up Am Found; bd mem, Linens-N-Things; bd mem, Neuberger Berman; bd mem, Paxar Corporation; trustee, Marymount College, bd mem, Links, Metropolitan Chapter. **Special Achievements:** Fashion Institute of Technology's first woman and first African-American president. **Home Addr:** 320 W St Suite 9B, New York, NY 10013, **Home Phone:** (212)724-0573. **Business Addr:** President, State University of New York, 27th St 7th Ave, New York, NY 10001-5992, **Business Phone:** (212)217-7999.

### BROWN, JULIA M.

Vice president (organization). **Educ:** McMaster Univ, Hamilton, ON, BCom. **Career:** Proctor & Gamble; Diageo, dir integration, 2001-03; Gillette, global dir, 2004-05; Clorox Co, vpres corp procurement & contract mfg, 2005-08; Kraft Foods, chief procurement officer, sr vpres procurement, 2008-12; Mondelez Int, sr vpres procurement, 2012-14, Bus Transformation Leader Latin Am, 2014-15; Carnival Corp, chief procurement officer, 2015-. **Orgs:** Bd mem, Inst Supply Mgt; bd mem, Exec Leadership Found; trustee, African Am Experience Fund. **Business Addr:** Chief Procurement Officer, Carnival Corporation, 3655 NW 87th Ave, Miami, FL 33178, **Business Phone:** (305)599-2600.

### BROWN, JULIA M.

Executive, businessperson. **Educ:** McMaster Univ, BA. **Career:** Proctor & Gamble, global purchasing, 1991-2001; Diageo, dir procurement integration, 2001-03; Gillette, dir global directs mat & strategic sourcing, 2004-05; Clorox Co, vpres global strategic sourcing, 2005-08; Kraft Foods, sr vpres, global procurement & chief procurement officer, 2008-12; Mondelez Int, sr vpres & chief procurement officer, 2012-14, bus transformation leader-Latin Am, 2014-15; Carnival Corp, chief procurement officer, 2015-. **Orgs:** Mem bd, Primo Ctr & Exec Leadership Found; trustee Nat Minority Supplier Develop Coun; African Am Experience Fund. **Honors/Awds:** Named in Top 100 Most Influential Blacks in Corporate America by Savoy Magazine; Top 100 Women to Watch by Today's Chicago Woman; Top 76 Most Powerful Women in Business by Black Enterprise. **Business Addr:** Carnival Corp, 3655 NW 87th Ave, Miami, FL 33178-2428.

### BROWN, DR. JULIUS RAY

School administrator. **Personal:** Born Feb 18, 1940, Birmingham, AL; son of Sam and Clessie; married Betty Jean; children: Laura & Kenyen. **Educ:** Wayne State Univ, BA, 1963, MEd, 1971; Univ Mich, PhD, 1973. **Career:** School administrator (retired); Proj Equality Mich, exec dir, 1969-71; Univ Mich, regional dir, 1971-76; Wayne County Community Col, regional dean, 1976-83; Community Col Allegheny County, vpres exec dean, 1983-89; Wallace Community Col, Selma, pres, 1989-2000, pres emer, 2001-. **Orgs:** Bd dir, Northside Chamber Com, 1984-; bd dir, Local Govt Acad, 1985-; bd dir, St John's Hosp, 1985-; Am Asn Community Cols; Adv Technol Environ Educ Ctr; bd mem, Southern Asn Community, Jr, & Tech Cols. **Home Addr:** 292 Deep Woods Dr, Selma, AL 36701, **Home Phone:** (205)874-6020. **Business Addr:** President Emeritus, Wallace Community College, 3000 Earl Goodwin Pkwy, Selma, AL 36702-2530, **Business Phone:** (334)876-9227.

### BROWN, JURUTHA

Government official. **Personal:** Born Apr 11, 1950, San Diego, CA; daughter of Bertha and Fred. **Educ:** Occidental Col, BS, 1972; Univ Calif, Los Angeles, CA, cert exec mgt prog, 1988; Pepperdine Univ, George L Graziadio Sch Bus & Mgt, MBA, bus, 1991. **Career:** City Los Angeles, chief police & fire selection div, 1984-87, chief workers compensation div, 1987-92, chief admin servs, 1992-95, personnel dir, 1996-97, dir pub safety employ, 1997-2001, EEO dir, chief personnel analyst, 2001-06, Los Angeles Fire Dept, EEO investr, currently; EEO & Employee Develop Div, chief, currently; Equal Opportunity & Employ Develop Div, Personal Dept, chief. **Orgs:** Treas & secy, Personnel Testing Coun So CA, 1982-84; Nat Forum Black Pub Admin, 1984-; chair, human rights comn, Int Personnel Mgt Asn, 1985; bd dir, Int Pub Mgt Asn Assessment Coun, 1984-87; pres, vpres, treas, Western Regional Inter govt Personnel Assessment Coun, 1985-87; pres, Black Alumni Occident Col; frequent speaker test devel & test rsch, Police Recruitment. **Home Addr:** 465 Oak St Apt 105, Glendale, CA 91204-3101. **Business Addr:** Chief, EEO Investigator, EEO & Employee Development Division, 700 E Temple St Rm 380, Los Angeles, CA 90012, **Business Phone:** (213)473-9311.

### BROWN, JUSTINE THOMAS

Mayor, educator. **Personal:** Born May 12, 1938, Guyton, GA; daughter of J W H Thomas Sr and Marie Easley-Gadson; married Willie; children: Rahn Andre, Willie Antjuan & Jatavia Anreka. **Educ:** Savannah State Col, BS, 1959; Ga Southern Univ, attended 1989. **Career:** Screven County Bd Educ, teacher, 1959-; City Oliver GA, mayor, 1988-. **Orgs:** Nat Asn Educrs; Nat Conf Black Mayors; Alpha Kappa Alpha Sorority; Ga Asn Educrs; life mem, Ga Municipal Asn; dir, Econ Opportunity Authority. **Home Addr:** 215 Oak St, Sylvania, GA 30467, **Home Phone:** (912)857-3163. **Business Addr:** Mayor, City Oliver, Oliver City Coun, Oliver, GA 30449-0221, **Business Phone:** (912)857-3789.

### BROWN, KAY B.

Executive. **Personal:** Born Nov 1, 1932, New York, NY; children: Clifford & Clayton. **Educ:** City Col, BFA, 1968; Howard Univ, MFA, 1986. **Career:** Medgar Evers Col, assoc prof humanities & coord art, 1972-89; Anne Arundel Community Col, asst prof, 1989-90; MLK Memorial Libr, workshop coordr, 1992-94, Wash Lifelong Learning Ctr, creative writing instr, 1998; WritersCorps, Nat Serv Network, creative writing instr, 1994-96. **Orgs:** Exec dir, Where We Black Women Artists, 1971-80; exec bd, Nat Conf Artists, 1974-78; sr writer's network, MLK Memorial Library, 1994-98. **Home Addr:** 4201 Butterworth Pl NW Suite 215, Washington, DC 20016, **Home Phone:** (202)243-3045.

### BROWN, KIMBERLY S.

College administrator, dean (education). **Educ:** Univ Richmond; Radford Univ; Va Tech, PhD. **Career:** Va Tech, Univ Acad Advising Ctr, dir, 2003-, Univ Studies, dean, interim assoc vice provost acad support serv; Div Undergrad Educ, dir acad advising; Acad support serv, assoc vpres; Radford University; Weber State University. **Orgs:** Univ Acad Advising Ctr; Ctr Acad Enrichment & Excellence Multicultural Acad Opportunities Prog; active mem, Nat Acad Advising Asn. **Home Addr:** 1255 S Franklin St, Christiansburg, VA 24073-4453, **Home Phone:** (540)382-7212. **Business Addr:** Director, Virginia Tech, 315 Burruss Hall, Blacksburg, VA 24061, **Business Phone:** (540)231-5396.

### BROWN, KWAME JAMES

Basketball player. **Personal:** Born Mar 10, 1982, Charleston, SC. **Career:** Wash Wizards, point forward, 2001-05, center, 2002-03; Los Angeles Lakers, power forward & ctr, 2005-08; Memphis Grizzlies, center, 2007-08; Detroit Pistons, center, 2008-10; Charlotte Bobcats, center, 2010-11; Golden State Warriors, center, 2011-12; Philadelphia 76ers, center, 2012-13. **Orgs:** Spokesman, Wash Chap, Nat Kidney Found. **Honors/Awds:** Mr. Georgia Basketball, 2001. **Business Addr:** Professional Basketball Player, Philadelphia 76ers, 3601 S Broad St, Philadelphia, PA 19148, **Business Phone:** (215)339-7600.

### BROWN, KWAME R.

City council member, government official. **Personal:** Born Oct 13, 1970, Washington, DC; son of Marshall and Cammie Jeffress; married Marcia; children: Lauren & Kwame II. **Educ:** Talladega Col, Morgan State Univ, BA, mkt, 1994; Darthmouth Col, Amos Tuck Bus Sch, MBEP & ABEP, 1999. **Career:** MCI, asst sales mgr, 1991-93; Walmart Corp, financial mgr, 1994-96; Citigroup, personal banker, 1996-97; First Union Nat Bank, asst vpres, 1997-99; US Dept Com, polit appointee, sr advisor, 1999; Minority Supplier Develop Coun, MD, DC, pres & chief exec officer; Coun DC, Wash, DC, councilmember at-large, 2005-11. **Orgs:** Asn Urban Bankers; founding mem, charter mem, Toastmasters Int; S Fairfax Bus Develop Ctr; Mt Vernon Chamber Com; Kappa Alpha Psi Frat Inc; Am Mkt Asn; vol, Good Samaritan Found; chmn, Coun's Comt Econ Develop, 2007; chmn, Coun Dc, 2011-12; Comt Govt Opers & Environ; Comt Libr, Parks & Recreation; Comt Finance & Revenue; Comt Pub Works & Transp; Spec Comt Statehood & Self-Determination. **Honors/Awds:** MCI, 14 time Top Salesman, 1992-93, six time Presidents Club, 1991-93; Walmart, Net Profit Award, 1995; First Union, Presidents Club, Big Board, 1998-99. **Home Addr:** 2819 Hillcrest Dr SE, Washington, DC 20020-7207, **Home Phone:** (202)584-7522. **Business Addr:** Councilmember At-Large, Council of the District of Columbia, 1350 Pa Ave NW Suite 506, Washington, DC 20004, **Business Phone:** (202)724-8174.

### BROWN, L. DON
Executive, vice president (organization). **Personal:** Born Jul 15, 1945, Horatio, AR; son of Tommie and Snowie; married Inez Wyatt; children: Daria Akilah, Ellynn Donisha & Dalila Jinelle. **Educ:** Univ Ark, Pine Bluff, BS, 1966; Univ Southwest Mo, attended 1972; Kutztown Univ, attended 1974; Univ Pa, attended 1987; Harvard Univ, attended 1987. **Career:** Howard C, instr, 1966-68; State Ark, job interviewer, 1968-69; Kraft Inc, food technologist, 1971-72; Lehigh Valley, Pa, gen supt, 1972-79; Glenview, Ill, plant mgr, 1979-85, Kraft USA, vpres prod, 1985-89; Kraft Gen Foods, White Plains, NY, vpres, mfg, 1989-91, vpres opers, Can, 1991-94, exec vpres mfg; Molson Coors Brewing Co, head & sr vpres opers & technol, 1996-, bd dir, currently. **Orgs:** Am Mgt Asn, 1972; Productivity Asn, 1975; Nat Asn Advan Colored People, 1978-84; Urban League, 1978-84; head, Indust Div, United Way, Dallas, TX, 1984; Exec Leadership Coun, 1990-; Asn 100 Black Men, 1989-93; bd dir, Alumax Inc, 1994-; bd mem, Ariz Educ Trust. **Home Addr:** 4468 Kettering, Long Grove, IL 60047, **Home Phone:** (708)821-7122. **Business Addr:** Senior Vice President Operations and Technology, Molson Coors Brewing Co, 1225 17th St Suite 3200, Denver, CO 80202, **Business Phone:** (303)927-2337.

### BROWN, LARRY, JR.
Football player, radio host. **Personal:** Born Nov 30, 1969, Miami, FL; children: 1. **Educ:** Tex Christian Univ, BA, criminal justice. **Career:** Football player (retired), co-host; Dallas Cowboys, right corner back, 1991-95, 1998; Oakland Raiders, defensive back, 1996-97; Dallas Cowboys Radio Network, co-host, currently. **Honors/Awds:** Most Valuable Player, Super Bowl XXX, 1995; Champion, Super Bowl XXVII, XXVIII, XXX. **Special Achievements:** TV SERIES: Actor, "Married with Children"; "The Gender Bowl", 2005. Film: "Super Bowl XXVII", 1993. **Business Addr:** Co-Host, SportsRadio 1310 The Ticket, 3500 Maple Ave Suite 1310, Dallas, TX 75219, **Business Phone:** (214)787-1310.

### BROWN, LARRY T.
Automotive executive. **Personal:** Born Apr 21, 1947, Inkster, MI; son of Nander and Mattie Lewis; married Angelina Caldwell. **Educ:** Wayne County Community Col, Detroit, MI, AA, 1971; Wayne State Univ, Detroit, MI, BS, 1973; Cent Mich Univ, Mt Pleasant, MI, MA, mgt & supv, 1979. **Career:** Ford Motor Co, Dearborn, Mich, dealer training prog, mkt mgr, 1969-85; Landmark Ford, Niles, Ill, pres, 1991; Ottawa Ford-Lincoln-Mercury Inc, Ottawa, Ill, pres, currently; Star Toyota, owner. **Orgs:** Bd mem, Black Ford Lincoln & Mercury Dealers Asn, 1985-; Nat Auto Dealers Asn, 1985-; Ottawa Rotary, 1986-88; Ottawa Chamber Com, 1985-90; pres, chmn, vpres, Black Ford Lincoln & Mercury Dealers Asn, 1992-93; bd dir, pres, Nat Automobile Minority Dealers Asn, Dealership Opers & Indust Rels Comts, 1993-94, & exec bd, Pub Affairs Comt; vice-chmn Region III, currently; Nat Automobile Dealers Charitable Found. **Home Addr:** 2510 Cedar Crest, Ottawa, IL 61350, **Home Phone:** (815)434-4800. **Business Addr:** President, Owner, Ottawa Ford Lincoln & Mercury Inc, Rt 23 & Ih 80, Ottawa, IL 61350-6410, **Business Phone:** (815)434-4800.

### BROWN, LAWRENCE E.
Executive. **Personal:** Born Jan 28, 1947. **Educ:** Bryant Col, BS, bus admin, 1969; Bentley Col, MS, taxation, 1979. **Career:** Peat Mawrick Mitchell & Co, supv sr acct, 1970-75; Lawrence E Brown Cert Pub Acct, owner & prin; Omni Develop Corp, vpres finance & chief financial officer, vpres, currently. **Orgs:** Dir, Opportunity Indust Ctr RI, 1970-74; pres, chmn, bd, dir, S Providence Fed Credit Union, 1971-; dir, Challenge House, 1971-74; adv bd, dir, Headstart, 1971-73; City coun, Providence, 1971-75; co-chmn, Nat Black Caucus Local Elected Officials, 1972-74; dir, Bryant Col Alumni Asn, 1974-; treas, dir, Accountants Pub Interest RI, 1975-; asst treas, Providence Dem Comn, 1975-; treas, Irreproachable Beneficial Asn, 1976-; bd dir, Bannister House, 1976-; RI Black Heritage Soc, 1976-; treas, dir, RI Minority Bus Asn, 1977-; RI Soc Cert Pub Accountants; Am Inst Cert Pub Accountants; Phi Beta Sigma; dir Comn, Workshops RI, 1974-76; Urban League RI; Nat Asn Advan Colored People; State Human Resource Investment Coun; Providence Rev Comn. **Honors/Awds:** South Providence Community Service Award, 1972. **Special Achievements:** First Black Certified Public Accountant in Rhodes Island, 1972; Second Black City Councilman in Providence. **Home Addr:** 36 Whitmarsh St, Providence, RI 02907. **Business Addr:** Vice President, Chief Financial Officer, Omni Development Corp, 810 Eddy St, Providence, RI 02905-4808, **Business Phone:** (401)461-4442.

### BROWN, DR. LAWRENCE S., JR.
Physician. **Personal:** Born Dec 4, 1949, Brooklyn, NY; son of Lawrence and Mae Rose. **Educ:** Brooklyn Col, BA, 1974; Columbia Univ, Sch Pub Health, MPH, 1979; NY Univ, Sch Med, MD, 1979. **Career:** Columbia Univ Col Physicians & Surgeons, Internship & Residency Internal Med, 1979-82, chief resident, 1982-83, Dept Med, Div Endocrinol, fel, 1983-86; Urban Resources Insititute, Addiction Res & Treat Corp, vpres res & med affairs, 1986-88, sr vpres, 1988-2008, exec sr vpres, 2008-12, interim exec dir & interim pres, 2011-12; Harlem Hosp Med Ctr & Col Physicians & Surgeons, Dept Med, Div Endocrinol, asst attend physician, 1988-98; Nat Football League, med adv, 1990-; Columbia Univ, asst clin prof med, 1986-; Cornell Univ, Weill Med Col, clin assoc prof med & healthcare policy & res, 1999-; Rockefeller Univ Hosp, assoc physician, 1999-; START Treat & Recovery Centers, chief exec officer, 2012-. **Orgs:** Am Pub Health asn, 1977-, Alcohol, Tobacco & Other Drug Sect, prog chair, 2009-11; Am Soc Internal Med, 1980-; Am Col Physicians, 1980-; Am Diabetes asn, 1989-; fel Col Probs Drug Dependency, 1990-94, bd dir, 2009-13; bd dir, Am Soc Addiction Med, 1996-2007, pres & chair, 2002-05; Ny Adv Coun; Alcoholism & Substance Abuse Serv; bd dir, US Anti-Doping Agency, 1998-2011, chair, 2010-11; bd dir, Nat Black Leadership Comn AIDS, 1999-2012; Nat Drug Abuse Treat Clin Trials Network, 2000-; Ny Off Alcoholism & Substance Abuse Serv, clin trials clin investr, 2010-13; Substance Abuse & Ment Health Serv Admin, Dept Health & Human Serv, 2010-14; Ny Dept Health, 2013-. **Special Achievements:** Over 30 peer-reviewed articles; Over 10 book chapters.; publication: Health Services for HIV & AIDS, HCV, and Sexually Transmitted Infections in Substance Abuse Treatment Programs, 2007. **Home Addr:** 301 Hanna Rd, River Vale, NJ 07675. **Business Addr:** Clinical Associate Professor of Public Health, Cornell University, 1300 York Ave, New York, NY 10021, **Business Phone:** (212)746-5454.

### BROWN, LEANDER A.
Media executive, president (organization). **Personal:** Born Jul 1, 1959, Chicago, IL; son of Leander A Jr and Joahn Weaver Nash; married Betty Catlett. **Educ:** Fisk Univ, Nashville, Tenn, BS, 1982. **Career:** City Harvey, Harvey, Ill, employ coordr, 1983-85; Tri-Assoc, Chicago, Ill, assoc, 1985-86; Payne Financial Serv, Chicago, Ill, financial consult, 1986-88; B & H Radio Co, Harvey, Ill, pres, 1988-. **Honors/Awds:** America's Best & Brightest, Dollars & Sense, 1989; Minority Business of the Month, Minority Entrepreneur, 1990; Business Profile, Chicago Defender, 1991. **Home Addr:** 17650 Springfield Ave, Country Club Hills, IL 60478, **Home Phone:** (708)534-3498. **Business Addr:** President, B & H Radio Co, 54 E 154th St, Harvey, IL 60426, **Business Phone:** (708)596-7550.

### BROWN, DR. LEE PATRICK
Business owner, government official, chairperson. **Personal:** Born Oct 4, 1937, Wewoka, OK; son of Andrew and Zelma Edwards; married Yvonne Carolyn Streets; children: Patrick, Torri, Robyn & Jenna; married Frances M Young; children: Robyn, Torri, Jenna & Patrick. **Educ:** Fresno State Univ, BS, criminol, 1960; San Jose State Univ, MS, sociol, 1964; Univ Calif, Berkeley, MS, criminol, 1968, PhD, criminol, 1970. **Career:** San Jose, Calif, police officer, 1960-68; Portland State Univ, prof, 1968-72; Howard Univ, prof, 1972-75, dir Criminal Justice progs, Inst Urban Affairs & Researc, assoc dir, 1972; Multnomah Co, sheriff, 1975-76, dir justice serv, 1976-78; Atlanta, Ga, pub safety comnr, 1978-82; African Am comnr police, Atlanta, Ga, 1978; Houston Police Dept, police chief, 1982-90; NY City Police Dept, police comnr, 1990-92; Tex Southern Univ, instr, 1992; Off Nat Drug Control Policy, dir, cabinet mem, 1993-95; White House Off Nat Drug Control Policy, dir, 1993; Rice Univ, sociol prof, 1996-97; City Houston, mayor, 1998-2004; Brown Group Int, chmn & chief exec officer, 2005-. **Orgs:** Chmn, Nat Minority Adv Coun Criminal Justice, 1976-81; founder, Nat Orgn Black Law Enforcement Exec, 1984-; Police Exec Res Forum, 1990-91; dir, Houston Rotary Club; Nat Asn Advan Colored People; bd mem, Forum Club Houston; dir, Houston Boy Scouts Am; dir, Nat Black Child Develop Inst; dir, Houston Area Urban League; Nat Adv Comn Criminal Justice Stand &Goals, Wash, DC; Nat Comn Higher Educ Police; task force mem, Nat Ctr Missing & Exploited C; adv bd, Nat Inst Against Prejudice & Violence; Alpha Phi Alpha; Greek-lett fraternity; Sigma Pi Phi. **Special Achievements:** First African American Mayor of Houston. **Business Addr:** Chairman, Chief Executive Officer, Brown Group International, 1001 McKinney Suite 1650, Houston, TX 77002, **Business Phone:** (832)366-1584.

### BROWN, LEILANI M.
Marketing executive, vice president (organization). **Educ:** Middlebury Col, BA, int studies, 1993; NY Univ, MPA, 1996. **Career:** Chubb & Son, underwriter, sr underwriter, 1993-95; NatWest Bank, asst vpres, 1995-96; AIG, mgt assoc, mkt dept mgr, 1996-99, asst vpres mkt, 2000-02, vpres & profit ctr exec, 2003-06; MetLife, vpres disability mkt, 2006-09, vpres brand mgt & mkt opers, 2009-10; CQ-Roll Call Group, sr vpres & chief mkt officer, 2010; Economist Group, consult global brand, 2011; Starr Co, vpres & chief mkt officer, 2011-. **Orgs:** Exec Leadership Coun; co-chair, Black Women's Leadership Summit; co-chair, Women Managers Symp; bd dir, Jamaica Ctr Arts & Learning, Queens, NY; bd trustee, Buckley Country Day Sch, Roslyn, NY, 2010-; bd dir, Exec Leadership Coun, 2015-; bd trustee, Middlebury, 2015-. **Business Addr:** Vice President, Chief Marketing Officer, Starr Companies, NY, **Business Phone:** (646)227-6300.

### BROWN, REV. LEO C., JR.
Association executive, clergy. **Personal:** Born Jun 17, 1942, Washington, DC; son of Leo Charles Sr and Mildred Vera; married Barbara J DeLespine; children: Debbie Jones, Fred Ross, Angela Ross, Wayne, Charles Ross, Steve Ross, Renee, Anthony, Phillip, Daniel, Jimmy & Cindy. **Educ:** Evergreen State Col, BA, pub admin, 1977; Am Baptist Sem W, MMA, 1981; Hardy Theol Inst, Seattle, Wash, DD, 1988. **Career:** Local 528 Cement Mason, cement mason, 1964-72; Progress House Assoc, exec dir, 1972-; True Vine Community Church God Christ, founder, pastor, 1975-, supt, missionary, Barbara J. Brown Manor, founder; Puget Sound Dist, supt, 1990; Church God Christ, Wash State Jurisdiction, chmn bd superintendents, 1994, jurisdictional prelate bishop, 2014; bishop tl, westbrook, dd, admin asst, 2007-. **Orgs:** Co-founder & dir, First Minority Christian Summer Camp, 1965-; founder & dir, Emmanuel Temple Prison Ministry McNeil Island, WA, 1968; vpres, Metro Develop Coun, 1973-75; chaplain, Tacoma Fire Dept, 1975-79; vpres, United Brotherhood Fel, 1977-; founder & pres, True vine Multi-Serv Ctr, 1979-; bd mem, Tacoma Urban Policy, 1979; bd mem, Family Broadcasting Sta, 1979-; founder & pres, True Vine Sr Citizen Ctr, 1980-; pres, Tacoma Ministerial Alliance, 1982-; comnr, State Wash Housing Fin Comn, 1985-; Int Halfway House Asn; Am Corrections Asn; Nat Asn Advan Colored People; Tacoma Urban League; Kiwanis Club; Prince Hall Masons; Acad Criminal Justice Soc; bd mem, United Way, Fel Reconciliation; Am Correctional Asn; Govs Pub Safety Adv Group State Wash; A L Hardy Acad Theol Doctorate Divinity. **Honors/Awds:** Service Making Award, Sertoma Club, 1978; Nominee & runner-up for Rockefeller Found Humanity Award, 1979; Distinguished Citizens Award, Tacoma Urban League, 1983; News maker of Tomorrow Award, Time Mag, 1983; Distinguished Citizen Award, Wash State Senate & Office Lt Gov, 1984; DDiv, Hardy Theo Inst Seattle, 1988. **Special Achievements:** Proclaimed Feb 6 as Dr Leo C Brown Jr Day by the Governor of Washington State, Mayor of Tacoma, & the Pierce County Executive. **Home Addr:** 4937 N Mildred St, Tacoma, WA 98407-1329, **Home Phone:** (253)564-0935. **Business Addr:** Pastor, Founder, True Vine Community Church, 5715 N 33rd St, Tacoma, WA 98407, **Business Phone:** (253)759-9059.

### BROWN, DR. LEONARD
Educator, musician. **Educ:** Wesleyan Univ, PhD; Univ Mass, Amherst, MEd, art educ, 1977. **Career:** Musician; Boston's Ann John Coltrane Memorial Concert, co-founder & prod, 1997; Am Jazz Mus, Kans City, Mo, consult; Northeastern Univ, vice provost, 2000-03, Music Dept, fac, head advisor, African Am Studies Dept, assoc prof, currently, chair. **Orgs:** Dir, Kans City Inst Jazz Performance & Hist; develop & organizer, Charlie Parker Symp; Ctr Black Music Res, Int Asn Study Popular Music; Int Asn Jazz Educrs; Soc Ethnomusicology; Sonneck Soc Am Music. **Business Addr:** Associate Professor of Music & African American Studies, Northeastern University, 360 Huntington Ave Ryder 351, Boston, MA 02115, **Business Phone:** (617)373-4128.

### BROWN, LEONARD RAY, JR. See BROWN, RAY, JR.

### BROWN, LEROY
School administrator. **Personal:** Born Dec 10, 1936, Buckner, AR; son of Odis and Pearlie; married Dorothy Jean Hughey; children: Johnny Otis, Cinini Yvette, Titian Valencia & Leviano Regatte. **Educ:** Univ Ariz, BS, chem; E Tex State Univ, MA. **Career:** School administrator (retired); Lewisville Sch Dist, Sci & Math teacher, 1960-69, asst prin & math, 1972-77, mid sch, prin, 1978; Lewisville Sch Dist, Foster HS, prin, 1970-71; City Buckner, mayor & judge, 1975-78, alderman, 1980-90, 1994-98, 2000-06, coun mem; Lewisville Sch Dist High Sch, asst prin, math, 1983-90; Lafayette Co Ar, Govt Bill Clinton, 1990; A O Smith Funeral Home, funeral dir, 1990-; App Justice Peace, Dist IV. **Orgs:** St John Bapt Church Buckner, 1948-80; AR Educ Asn, 1960-80; Nat Asn Advan Colored People Buckner Hpt, 1968-80; Nat Educ Asn, 1970-80; vpres, Lafayette Co Alumni Asn, 1977-80; sr warden, Rose Sharon Lodge, 1978-80; justice peace, 1990, fairbd mem, 1990; quorum ct mem, Lafayette County, Ark, 1990; bd mem, SW Develop coun. **Honors/Awds:** Best School Award, Red River Vo-Tech Sch, 1981-82. **Home Addr:** 617 E Myrtle St, Buckner, AR 71827, **Home Phone:** (870)533-2362. **Business Addr:** Licensed Funeral Director, A O Smith Funeral Homes Inc, 703 Thomas St, Stamps, AR 71860, **Business Phone:** (870)533-2802.

### BROWN, DR. LEROY BRADFORD, SR.
Physician. **Personal:** Born Jun 5, 1929, Detroit, MI; married Ola Augusta Watkins; children: Leroy, Rene & Rita. **Educ:** SC State Col, BS, 1954; Howard Univ Col Med, MD, 1958. **Career:** Fresno Co Gen Hosp, intern, 1958-59; City Sacramento, city physician, 1958-71; Internal Med, resident, 1959-62; Prac Med, specializing internal med, 1962-; Mercy Hosp, staff, 1962-; Med Examr, aviation, 1966-; UC Davis Med Sch, clin instr, 1977; Sr FAA Designated Aeromedical, med examr, currently; pvt pract physician, currently. **Orgs:** Am Calif & Sacramento Co Med Asn; Am Calif & Sacramento Co Socs Internal Med; dir, Sacramento Co Heart Asn; Notomas Union Sch Bd, 1971-75. **Home Addr:** 4465 Garden Hwy, Sacramento, CA 95837-9302. **Business Addr:** Physician, Private Practice, 3031 G St, Sacramento, CA 95816, **Business Phone:** (916)444-6533.

### BROWN, LES (LESLIE CALVIN BROWN)
Chief executive officer, public speaker, writer. **Personal:** Born Feb 17, 1945, Miami, FL; married Gladys Knight; children: Calvin, Patrick, Ayanna, Sumaya, Serena, & John Leslie. **Career:** Les Brown Unlimited Inc, Detroit, Mich, pres & chief exec officer; Les Brown Enterprises, chief exec officer, 1986-, prof speaker, currently; Book: Live Your Dreams; "Les Brown Show", host, 1993; It's Not Over Until You Win!, 1997; KFWB, radio host, the les brown show, 2011-. **Orgs:** Ohio House Representatives. **Home Addr:** 1547 W Birchwood Ave, Chicago, IL 60626-1703, **Home Phone:** (773)856-0061. **Business Addr:** Chief Executive Officer, Les Brown Enterprises LLC, PO Box 806217, Chicago, IL 60680, **Business Phone:** (800)733-4226.

### BROWN, LESTER J.
Government official. **Personal:** Born Aug 24, 1942, New York, NY; son of James and Earlean Price; children: Natalie Milligan, Omar A & Lesondra E. **Educ:** Lincoln Univ, BA, 1966; Fels Inst State & Local Govt, attended 1969; State Univ NY, Albany, attended 1973; Antioch Col New Eng Ctr, Med Mgt & Orgn, 1978. **Career:** Philadelphia Model Cities Prog, manpower planner, 1967-68; Philadelphia Sch Dist, teacher, 1968-70; Schenectady County Community Col, sr counr, 1970-76; Ny Div Youth, resource & reimbursement agt, 1977-79, prog mgt specialist, 1979-89; Ny Div Youth, contract compliance specialist, 1989-. **Orgs:** Consumer panel mem, NY Elec & Gas, 1991-; mem econ develop & employ comt, Broome Co Urban League; allocation panel, Broome Co United Way; life mem, Omega Psi Phi Frat Inc; Lincoln Univ Alumni Asn; pres, Price Brown Family Reunion Org; vice chmn, New York Div Youth Affirmative Action Adv Comn; Broome County Nat Asn Advan Colored People; Prince Hall Masonic; S Colonie Schs. **Home Addr:** 1 Queens Dr Apt A1, Schenectady, NY 12304-3404. **Business Addr:** Program Management Specialist, New York State for Youth, 52 Washington St, Rensselaer, NY 12144, **Business Phone:** (518)486-5164.

### BROWN, LEWIS FRANK
Lawyer, founder (originator). **Personal:** Born Aug 4, 1929, Cleveland, OH; son of Frank C and Lula Y; married Dorothy Jean Fitzgerald; children: Lewis Gene & Orville. **Educ:** San Francisco State Univ, BA, 1957; Lincoln Univ Law Sch, DJ, 1965. **Career:** Vallejo Unified Sch Dist, educr, 1957-64; Calif Greenleigh Asn, asst dir, 1964-65, dir, 1965-66; Health Educ & Welfare, pvt consult, 1966-69; Contra Costa County Off Econ, consult, 1966-70; Beeman, Bradley, Brown & Beeman, partner, 1977; Am Arbit Asn, arbit; Brown & Bradley, atty, 1978-, Lewis & Dorothy Brown Found, founder, 2011-. **Orgs:** Comt man, Solano County Demo Cent, 1959-66; Vallejo City Planning Comn, 1963-65; Vallejo City Councilman, 1965-69; vmayor, Vallejo City, 1967-69; treas, Solano County Bar Asn, 1971; golden heritage life mem, Nat Advan Asn Colored People; founder, The Lewis & Dorothy Brown Foundation, 2011. **Honors/Awds:** First Jurisdiction Service Award, Church God Christ, NC, 1982; Distinguished Record, Calif State Senate & Assembly Resolution Commending Lewis F Brown, 1982; Civic Leader Award, 1982; Legal Commendation Award, Dist Atty Solano County, City Vallejo, 1982; Resolution Commendation, Jones County, Miss Bd Supvrs, 1988; Resolution Commendation, City Coun Laurel, Miss, 1988. **Special Achievements:** Vallejo City Council named street Lewis Brown Road, July 1995; First African American in the city of Vallejo who was elected to the Planning Commission and the Democratic Central Committee; First African American elected

to an office in a general election; First African American Vice Mayor and the first African American Attorney in Solano County where he still resides. **Home Addr:** 400 Lakeside Dr, Vallejo, CA 94590-2106, **Home Phone:** (707)642-4086. **Business Addr:** Attorney, Brown & Bradley, 538 Ga St, Vallejo, CA 94590-0647, **Business Phone:** (707)643-4541.

**BROWN, DR. LILLIE RICHARD**
Nutritionist. **Personal:** Born Feb 25, 1946, Opelousas, LA; daughter of John Sr (deceased) and Hester De Jean; married Charles J; children: Jeffrey Andre. **Educ:** Southern Univ, BS, 1968; Howard Univ, MS, 1972; Command & Gen Staff Col, dipl, 1989. **Career:** DC Pub Sch, nutritionist, 1972-96; DC Nat Guard, dietitian, 1977-96; Howard Univ, asst prof nutrit scis, 1997-; State Md, Dept Corrections, dietitian, 1998-99, dietary mgr; Baltimore City Pub Sch Syst, dietitian, 1999-01. **Orgs:** Am Dietetic Asn, 1971-; Delta Sigma Theta, 1974-; Am Heart Asn, 1986-. **Special Achievements:** The Manual of Clinical Dietetics, assisted with writing, 1992. **Home Addr:** 2006 Forest Dale Dr, Silver Spring, MD 20903-1529, **Home Phone:** (301)439-3933. **Business Addr:** Dietary Manager, State of Maryland, 300 E Joppa Rd Suite 1000, Towson, MD 21286-3020, **Business Phone:** (410)540-6735.

**BROWN, LLOYD**
Social worker. **Personal:** Born Jul 5, 1938, St. Louis, MO; son of Charles W Sr and Veldia B Sproling Stinson; married Johnnie Mae Irvin; children: 4. **Educ:** Urban Develop & Black Community, Southern Ill Univ, cert, 1970; Community Organizing Parks Col, cert, 1970; Forest Pk Community Col, AA, lib arts, 1974; Northeast Miss State Univ, Kirksville, MO, BS, social sci, 1976; Webster Univ, grad work pub admin. **Career:** Manager (retired); Tandy Area Coun, youth counr, 1974-76; Wellston Sch Dist, dep gen mgr, 1976-81; Int Revenue Serv, tax rep, 1982-83; Human Develop Corp, br mgr, 1983-91; Alpha Redevelop Corp, exec mgr, 1991-94; ABC Infants Inc & Child Care, co-owner; Lucas Heights Village, exec mgr, 1994. **Orgs:** Community worker, Vols Serv Am, 1972-74; Nat Asn Housing & Redevelop, 1982-; Miss Asn Housing & Redevelop, 1982-; chmn, Wellston Housing Bd Comnr, 1982-; vpres, Wellston Bd Educ, 1983, 1986, 1989, 1992-; Miss State Sch Bd Asn, 1983; Nat Sch Bd Asn, 1983-; Wellston City Coun. **Honors/Awds:** Special Service Award, Mathew Dicky Boys Club, 1968; Student Service Award, Forest Park Col, 1972, 1973, 1974; Community Service Award, Human Develop Corp, 1972; Youth Service Award, Providence Schs, St Louis, MO, 1985, 1986, 1987; Resolution-Outstanding School Board Member, Miss State Legis, 1987. **Home Addr:** 4313 Cranford Dr, St Louis, MO 63121, **Home Phone:** (314)385-6050. **Business Addr:** Vice President, Wellston School District, 3855 Lucas & Hunt Rd Suite 203, St Louis, MO 63121, **Business Phone:** (314)290-7900.

**BROWN, LOMAS, JR.**
Football player, radio host. **Personal:** Born May 30, 1963, Miami, FL; son of Lomas Sr and Grace; married Dolores; children: Antoinette, Ashley & Adrienne. **Educ:** Univ Fla, attended 1996. **Career:** Football player (retired), broadcaster; Detroit Lions, offensive tackle & left tackle, 1985-95; Ariz Cardinals, offensive tackle & left tackle, 1996-98; Cleveland Browns, offensive tackle & left tackle & tackle, 1999; New York Giants, offensive tackle & left tackle, 2000-01; LBJB Sports, chief exec officer, 2000-; Tampa Bay Buccaneers, offensive tackle, 2002; Nat Football League Network, analyst; Entertainment & Sports Programming Network, analyst, 2004-, First Take, currently; WXYT-FM, co-host. **Orgs:** Phi Beta Sigma Fraternity; founder, Lomas Brown Found. **Honors/Awds:** Jacobs Blocking Trophy, 1984; First-team All-American, 1984; First-team All-SEC, 1984; Pro Bowl Selection, 1990-96; NFL Extra Effort Award, 1991; Super Bowl Champion; Athletic Hall of Fame, Univ Fla, 1995. **Business Addr:** Analyst, Entertainment & Sports Programming Network, ESPN Plz, Bristol, CT 06010.

**BROWN, LOUIS SYLVESTER**
Government official, association executive. **Personal:** Born Oct 11, 1930, Navassa, NC; son of Claus; married Ruby Moore; children: Yvonne, Yvette, Roderick & Valorie. **Educ:** Tyler Barber Col, Barber, 1959. **Career:** Brunswick City Hosp, bd dir, 1975-81; Town Navassa, NC, mayor, 1977-99; Sencland, bd dir, 1978-85; Apri Inst, bd dir, 1979-. **Orgs:** Masonic Pride Navassa Lodge, 1965-85; Noble Habid Temple, 1970-85; bd dir, Nat Asn Advan Colored People, 1970-; vice chmn, Recreation bd, 1975-; Navassa Community Lion Club. **Special Achievements:** Organized the first Black Men's Lion Club in North Carolina, 1989; organized the first Black Women's Lion Club in North Carolina, 1990. **Home Addr:** 220 Broadway St, Navassa, NC 28451, **Home Phone:** (910)371-3312.

**BROWN, DR. LUCILLE M.**
School administrator. **Educ:** Va Union Univ, BS, 1950; Howard Univ, hons grad; Univ Va; Univ Richmond; Va State Univ; Va Commonwealth Univ. **Career:** Supt (retired); Fluvanna County Sch, teacher; Henrico County Sch, prin; Woodbrook Elem Sch; Prin; Luther Jackson High Sch, teacher, 1954-57; Armstrong High Sch, teacher, 1957-74, prin, 1974-85; Richmond Pub Schs, Va, teacher, prin, asst supt sec educ, 1985-89, asst supt inst, 1989-91, supt, 1991-95; Albemarle County schs, chief info officer, 2006-. **Orgs:** Bd trustee, Va Union Univ; Bd Heroes Found; Black Hist Mus & Cult Ctr; James River Valley Chap Links Inc; bd dir, Educ Advan Found; Alpha Kappa Alpha Sorority Inc; Am Asn Sch Adminr; Nat Asn Sec Sch Principals; Phi Delta Kappa; Garland Ave Baptist Church; Consol Bank & Trust; Jr Achievement Va; Va Heroes Found; Black Hist Mus & Cult Arts Ctr; Richmond Urban League; Omicron Delta Kappa; Va Asn Sch Superintendents. **Home Addr:** 2600 Hawthorne Ave, Richmond, VA 23222. **Business Addr:** Board of Trustee, Virginia Union University, 1500 N Lombardy St, Richmond, VA 23220, **Business Phone:** (804)257-5600.

**BROWN, M. CHRISTOPHER, II**
College president, writer. **Educ:** SC State Univ, BS, elem educ, 1993; Univ Ky, MSEd, educ policy & eval, 1994; Pa State Univ, PhD, pub admin & polit sci, 1997. **Career:** Pa State Univ; Univ Ill at Urbana-Champaign; Univ Mo-Kans City; Univ Nev, Las Vegas, Col Educ, dean; Am Asn of Cols Teacher Educ, Progs and Admin, vpres; Res Inst of the United Negro Col Fund, exec dir & chief res scientist; Fisk Univ, Nashville, TN, exec vpres & provost, prof; Alcorn State Univ, Lorman, MS, pres, 2010-. **Orgs:** Am Asn Cols Teacher Educ, vpres Progs & admin; Social Justice & Prof Develop, Am Educ Res Asn, dir; exec dir & Chief Res Scientist, Frederick D. Patterson Res Inst United Negro Col Fund; Miss bd trustee, State Insts Higher Learning, 2010; dir, Social Justice & Prof Develop, Am Educ Res Asn; sr fel, Am Asn State Cols & Univs; AT&T Technol Fel, 2001. **Business Addr:** President, Alcorn state university, 1000 ASU Dr, Lorman, MS 39096, **Business Phone:** (601)877-6100.

**BROWN, MALCOLM MCCLEOD**
Educator, artist. **Personal:** Born Aug 19, 1931, Charlottesville, VA; son of Franklin M and Dorothy R; married Ernestine Turner; children: Malcolm, Jeffrey & Rhonda. **Educ:** Va State Col, BS, 1964; Case Western Res Univ, MA, art, 1969. **Career:** OH, internationally exhibited & acclaimed watercolorist; Shaker Hts Schs, art teacher, 1969-2000; Malcolm Brown Gallery, Shaker Heights, Ohio, co-owner, 1980-.American Watercolor Society. **Orgs:** Am Watercolor Soc; Shaker Heights bd educ Eve Fac Clev Inst Art Ohio Watercolor Soc; Nat Asn Advan Colored People; Urban League; Friends Karama; Cleveland Mus Art; Nat Conf Artists; Calif Watercolor Soc Omega Psi Phi Fraternity Inc; Omega Psi Am Watercolor Soc, 1973. **Honors/Awds:** Award Excellence, Mainstreams Int, 1970; Henry O Tanner & Award, Nat Exhib Black Artists, 1972; Purchase Award, Watercolor USA, 1974; Award in Rocky Mt Nat Water media Exhib Golden CO, 1975; Larry Quacken bush Award, 1980; Ohio Watercolor Soc Award, 1984, 1985; Board of Director's Award, Am Watercolor Soc; Distinguished Service to the Arts Award, Cleveland Arts Prize. **Home Addr:** 2681 Green Rd, Beachwood, OH 44122-2121, **Home Phone:** (216)570-1054. **Business Addr:** Co-owner, Malcolm Brown Gallery, 20100 Chagrin Blvd, Shaker Heights, OH 44122, **Business Phone:** (216)751-2955.

**BROWN, DR. MALORE INGRID**
Executive director, consultant. **Personal:** Born Sep 29, 1967, Half Way Tree; daughter of Esmie L and Mallothi. **Educ:** Marquette Univ, BA, span, 1988; Univ Wis, Milwaukee, MLIS, 1991, MA, 1991, PhD, 1996. **Career:** Milwaukee Pub Libr, community librn intern, 1990-91, librn I, 1991; Chicago Pub Libr, librn I, 1991-92, librn II, asst head, 1993; Univ Wis, Milwaukee, asst prof, 1996-2001; Rutgers Univ, vis asst prof, 2000-01; Am Libr Asn, exec dir, 2001-; US Dept Educ Title II-B Libr, career training doctoral fel; independent consult librn, currently. **Orgs:** Asn Libr Servo C, 1992-; Black Caucus Am Libr Asn, 1993-, exec bd, 1995-97; US Bd Bks Young People, 1998-; Wis Black Librns Network, 1991-2000, pres, 1995-96; Am Soc Asn Execs, 2001-. **Business Addr:** Executive Director, American Library Association, 50 E Huron St, Chicago, IL 60611-2795, **Business Phone:** (312)944-6780.

**BROWN, MARIE DUTTON**
Publisher. **Personal:** Born Oct 4, 1940, Philadelphia, PA; daughter of Benson L and Josephine; married Kenneth; children: Laini. **Educ:** Penn State Univ, BS, psychol, 1962. **Career:** Wagner High Sch, PA, teacher, 1962-65, coordr intergroup educ, 1965-67; Bronze Bks, bookstore mgr, 1970-71; Doubleday & Co, gen publ trainee, from assoc ed to ed & sr ed, 1972-81; Frederick Douglass Creative Arts Ctr, 1979-04; Elan Mag, ed-in-chief, 1981-82; Endicott Bookseller, bookseller, asst buyer, asst mgr & consult, 1982-84; Marie Brown Assoc, founder, pres & lit agt, 1984-; Allison & Busby Ltd, founder & ed dir; USA Weekend, lit agt & ed. **Orgs:** Studio Mus Harlem, 1984-2004; Coun Lit Mag & Presses, 1989-2004; Poets House, 1994-2001; Hurston Wright Found, 1999-2002; Calabash Lit Festival, 2001-; Caribbean Cult Ctr, 2003-. **Honors/Awds:** Distinguished Alumni Award, 1971; Legacy Award, Hurston Wright Found, 2005. **Business Addr:** Founder, President, Marie Brown Associates, 412 W 154th St, New York, NY 10032, **Business Phone:** (212)939-9725.

**BROWN, MARJORIE M.**
Government official, postmaster general. **Educ:** Edward Waters Col; Duke Univ; Emory Univ; Univ Va. **Career:** US Postal Serv, postmaster, Atlanta, Ga, currently. **Orgs:** Leadership Atlanta 2001; Chairperson, Fed Exec Bd, Postal Customer Coun. **Home Addr:** 381 Dollar Mill Ct SW, Atlanta, GA 30331-4412, **Home Phone:** (404)696-4379. **Business Addr:** Postmaster, US Postal Service, 3900 Crown Rd SW Rm 219, Atlanta, GA 30304-9998, **Business Phone:** (404)765-7300.

**BROWN, DR. MARSHA JEANETTE**
Physician. **Personal:** Born Oct 27, 1949, Baltimore, MD; daughter of Elwood L and Bernice C; married Ray Brodie Jr; children: Bradley Ray & Sean Elwooa. **Educ:** Howard Univ, BS, 1971; Univ Md, MD, 1975. **Career:** Mercy Hosp, internal med resident; Baltimore City Police & Fire Dept, physician; dep chief physician; pvt pract physician internal med; Mercy Health Serv, Internal Med, physician; Heartfelt Med Group LLC, physician, owner, currently. **Orgs:** Adv bd, Cent Md Community Sickle Cell Anemia; bd dir, LM Carroll Home Aged; LM Carroll Nursing Home; Girl Scouts Am Teenage Pregnancy Task Force; med consult, Glass & Assocs Ment Health; Baltimore City Police Dept; Baltimore City Civil Serv Comn, 1982-; mem bd, Eligible Internal Med, Monumental City Med Assocs; Nat Med Asn; Baltimore City Chap Links Inc; Alpha Kappa Alpha Sorority. **Honors/Awds:** Outstanding Young Women, Alpha Kappa Alpha Sorority, 1980; Citizens Service Recognition Award for Community Serv, 1986; Humanitarian Award, Nat Asn Negro Women, 1986. **Home Addr:** 1859 Wycliff Rd, Parkville, MD 21239. **Business Addr:** Physician, Heartfelt Medical Group Llc, 301 St Paul Pl McAuley Prof Off Bldg 509, Baltimore, MD 21202, **Business Phone:** (410)837-2006.

**BROWN, MARVA Y.**
School administrator, social worker, educator. **Personal:** Born Aug 25, 1936, Charleston, SC. **Educ:** SC State Col, BS, bus admin, 1958; Univ Wash, MEd, rehab couns, 1970. **Career:** Berkley Training High Sch, Monks Corner, SC, bus educ instr, 1958-59; Park City Hosp, Bridgeport, CT, asst bookkeeper, 1959-62; State Conn Welfare Dept & Health Dept, case worker & med & social worker, 1962-66; Poland Spring Job Corp Ctr, ME, sr counr, 1966-68; Servs Handicapped Studs, Edmonds Community Col, Lynwood, Wash, counr, coordr, 1971-. **Orgs:** NEA, 1971; Wash State Human Rights Comn, 1977; Gov's Comn Employ Handicapped, 1977; Nat Asn Sex Educr & Couns, 1975; Snohomish Co Alcoholic Comn, 1978. **Honors/Awds:** Del The White House Conf on Handicapped Individuals, Washington, DC, 1977. **Home Addr:** 8524 Menzel Lake Rd, PO Box 482, Granite Falls, WA 98252, **Home Phone:** (360)691-7419. **Business Addr:** Coordinator, Counselor, Edmonds Community College, 20000 68th Ave W, Lynnwood, WA 98036-5912, **Business Phone:** (425)640-1536.

**BROWN, MARY BOYKIN**
Educator, association executive. **Personal:** Born Feb 1, 1942, Sampson County, NC; married Franklin Der; children: Franklin G Jr & Franita Dawn. **Educ:** Winston-Salem State Univ, BS, nursing, 1963; Long Island Univ, Community Ment Health, MS, 1978. **Career:** Long Island Jewish Med Ctr, instr serv ed, 1966-70; Harlem Hosp Ctr NY, instr sch nursing, 1970-74; Midway Nursing Home, coord serv ed, 1974-75; Mary Gran Nursing Ctr Clinton NC, dir serv ed, 1975-76; Sampson community Col, Clinton, NC, instr, sch nursing, 1976, health progs, div chmn, 1988, nursing prog, chmn, bd mem, dir, currently. **Orgs:** Am Nurses Asn, 1964-, Nat League Nursing, 1964-, NC Nurses Asn Dist 14, 1976-; Coun Asn Degree Nursing, 1976-; teacher beginners class St Stephen Am Zion Church, 1976-84; chmn, sec Four Cty Med Ctr Bd Dirs, 1981-85; police comn, Garland Town Bd, 1983-; vpres, Browns Cleaners & Laundromat, 1985-; App Legis Comn Nursing, 1989; chmn, Sampson County Sch Bd, 1994. **Honors/Awds:** Outstanding Young Women of America, 1977; Most Outstanding 4-H Leader Sampson County, 4-H Clinton NC, 1977-78; Outstanding 4-H Volunteer NC, Gov Raleigh NC, 1980; Certificate of Appreciation Sampson County Voters League, 1981; Excellence in Teaching Award, finalist, Dept Comm Cols, 1993; Educator of the Year, Alpha Kappa Alpha Inc, Rho Omega Omega Chap, 1995. **Home Addr:** 115 E Front St, Garland, NC 28441, **Home Phone:** (910)529-5981. **Business Addr:** Board Member, Sampson Community College, 1801 Sunset Ave, Garland, NC 28441, **Business Phone:** (910)592-7176.

**BROWN, MARY KATHERINE**
Administrator, association executive. **Personal:** Born Oct 14, 1948, Vicksburg, MS; daughter of Macie Little and Elijah W. **Educ:** Tuskegee Inst, BS, social sci, 1971, MEd, stud personnel, 1972; Jackson State Univ, MPA, pub policy & admin, 1985. **Career:** MS Employ Servs, employ counr, 1972-73; Ala A&M Univ, dir new women's residence hall, 1973-74; Jackson State Univ, coordr special serv, 1974-82; Comn Housing Resources, dir 1982-84; Hinds Co Bd Supvrs, comn & econ develop specialist; Miss Bur Pollution Control, compliance officer, 1989; Miss democratic Party, chairs; founder, St. Mary's Episcopal Church, Mary Brown Environ Ctr, currently. **Orgs:** Treas, Jackson Urban League Guild, 1977-78; vpres, Jackson Urban League Guild, 1978-80; charter mem, Vicksburg Chap Delta Sigma Theta Sor, 1978; secy, MS Asn Educ Oppor Progs Personnel, 1979-80; pres, MS Caucus Conseumerism, 1979-81; treas, Asn Pub Policy & Admin, 1982-84; bd dir, Jackson Urban League, 1984-87; comn chairperson, United Negro Col Fund, 1986; chmn bd dir, Jackson Community Housing & Resources Bd, 1987-89. **Home Addr:** 530 Riley Rd, Vicksburg, MS 39183-8122, **Home Phone:** (601)619-4538. **Business Addr:** Founder, Mary Brown Environmental Center, 715 S Central Ave, Ely, MN 55731, **Business Phone:** (218)365-3364.

**BROWN, MAUREEN REILETTE.** See JACKSON, REBBIE.

**BROWN, MAXINE J. CHILDRESS**
Government official. **Personal:** Born Aug 13, 1943, Washington, DC; daughter of Herbert A and Thomasina (deceased); married James E; children: Scot, Nikki & Kimberly. **Educ:** Springfield Col, BS, 1971; Univ MA, MEd, 1973. **Career:** Univ Mass, interpreter deaf & lectr; Rochester Inst Tech, Nat Tech Inst Deaf, asst prof, 1973-74; St Col Geneseo NY, asst prof, spec ed, dir learning disabilities, 1975-78; People Helping People, exec dir, 1978-80; City Rochester, Dept Rec & Comn Servs, dir pub rel, 1980-83, councilwoman, 1999, community liaison officer; Frederick Douglass Mus & Cult Ctr, pres, currently; Health Asn, assoc exec dir; St John Fisher Col, adj prof; Women Well, vol, currently. **Orgs:** Nat cert interpreterdeaf, Am Sign Lang, 1970-85; vpres, bd dir, Puerto Rican Youth Develop, 1982-; adv bd, chmn ed comn, NY St Div Human Rights, 1984; city coun rep, adv bd Monroe County Off Aging, 1984; adv bd Ctr, Ed Develop; vpres, bd visitors, St Ag & Indust Sch Indust; bd dir, Prog Rochester Interest Stud Sci & Math; pres, Metro Women's Network; chairperson, Arts Reach Arts Greater Rochester; bd dir, Rochester Area Mult Sclerosis; Urban Ad Hoc Comn Home Econ Monroe County Coop Ext. **Honors/Awds:** Politician of the Year, Eureka Lodge Award, 1984. **Special Achievements:** Nominated by Gov Carey & Approved by State Sen for Bd of Visitors State Ag & Indust School at Indust; 12 Publ including "About Time Mag", "Improving Police/Black Comm Relations", "A Not So Ordinary Man", "A Study Skills Program for the Hearing Impared Student" Volta Review Alexander Graham Bell Journal; Author of On the Beat of Truth. **Home Addr:** 222 Chili Ave, Rochester, NY 14611-2627, **Home Phone:** (585)328-0840. **Business Addr:** President, Frederick Douglass Museum & Cultural Center, 3200 Wayman Ave, Annapolis, MD 21403, **Business Phone:** (585)546-3960.

**BROWN, MICHAEL**
Basketball coach, basketball player. **Personal:** Born Jul 19, 1963, Newark, NJ; married Esther; children: Candyce, Xavier, Chanel, Andrea & Aishah. **Educ:** George Washington Univ, attended 1985. **Career:** Basketball player (retired), basketball coach; Filanto Desio, ctr, 1985-86; Chicago Bulls, ctr, 1987-88, asst coach, 2008-; Utah Jazz, ctr, 1989-93; Minn Timberwolves, ctr, 1994-95; Teamsystem Bologna, ctr, 1995; Philadelphia 76ers, ctr, 1996; Viola Reggio Calabria, ctr, 1996-98, 1997-98; Phoenix Suns, ctr, 1997, 1998; Cantabria Lobos, 1998; Olympiacos, 1999-2000; Manresa, 2000; Ourense, 2000-01; Las Vegas Slam, coach, 2001-02; Roanoke Dazzle, D-League, 2002-04; Fayetteville Patriots, coach, 2004-06, head coach. **Business Addr:** Assistant Coach, Chicago Bulls, United Ctr 1901 W Madison St, Chicago, IL 60612-2459, **Business Phone:** (312)455-4000.

**BROWN, MICHAEL. See EALY, MICHAEL.**

**BROWN, MICHAEL DEWAYNE**
Educator. **Personal:** Born Dec 18, 1954, Franklin, VA; son of Albert L and Lola B. **Educ:** Hampton Univ, Hampton, VA, BS, 1977; George Mason Univ, Fairfax, MS, 1991; Univ Va, Charlottesville. **Career:** Principal (retired); Alexandria City Schs, teacher, 1977-93, lead teacher, 1993-94; Amideast, consult, asst prin, 1994-99; James K Polk Elem Sch, prin, 1999. **Orgs:** Supts Teacher Adv Coun, 1988-91; Strategic Planning Task Force, 1989; Kappa Delta Pi, 1990-; Phi Delta Kappa, 1990-; Educ Tech Comm, 1990-; Mid Sch Steering Comm; Va Concerned Black Men Inc NOVA; Asn Supvn & Curric Develop. **Home Addr:** 2720 S Arlington Mill Dr Suite 608, Arlington, VA 22206, **Home Phone:** (703)820-5848. **Business Addr:** Member, Phi Delta Kappa International, 1525 Wilson Blvd Suite 705, Arlington, VA 22209, **Business Phone:** (812)339-1156.

**BROWN, MICHELE COURTON**
Executive, association executive. **Personal:** children: 2. **Educ:** Boston Univ, BA, econ & urban studies, 1983; Boston Univ, MS, health commun, 2016. **Career:** Bank Boston, dir corp contrib, 1992-99; Fleet Bank, Fleet Boston Financial Found, dir, founding pres, 1999-2003; Bank Am, sr vpres, 2004-09, Charitable Mgt Servs, nat pract dir, Philanthropic Mgt Group, currently; Efficacy Inst, chief operating officer, 2009-13; Charlotte Golar Richie Mayor, sr policy advisor, 2013; Courton Brown Consult, prin, 2013-; Qual Interactions, vpres & chief operating officer & chief exec officer, 2014-. **Orgs:** Exec dir, Travelers Ins Co Found, 1988-92; Nat Found Teaching Entrepreneurship; Youth Build USA, Partnership; Chestnut Hill Sch; Ctr Women & Enterprise; Boys & Girls Clubs Boston; Mus Afro-Am Hist; Boston Symphony Orchestra Overseers; Wang Ctr Performing Arts; Treas, Kids Risk, 2000; trustee, Roxbury Community Col, 2001; dir, Judge Baker C s Ctr, 2015. **Honors/Awds:** Ten Outstanding Young Leaders Award, Greater Boston Chamber Com, 2000; Leading Woman Award, Girl Scouts Eastern Mass, 2008; Goldman Sachs 10,000 Small Business Scholar, Goldman Sachs Babson Col, 2015. **Special Achievements:** Just Money: A Critique of Contemporary American Philanthropy, 2004. **Home Addr:** 56 Lochstead Ave, Jamaica Plain, MA 02130. **Business Addr:** Chief Executive Officer, Quality Interactions Inc, 1 Broadway, Cambridge, MA 02142, **Business Phone:** (866)568-9918.

**BROWN, MICHELLE LISTENBEE**
Executive, writer. **Career:** TV Series: "Photographers", prod coordr, 1999; "The Parkers", writer, 1999-2004, exec story ed, 2000-02, co-producer, 2002-04 & 2014-15; "Don't Believe the Hype", writer, 2002; "Make a Joyful Noise", exec story ed, 2002; "Teach Me Tonight", exec story ed, 2002; "It's Showtime", exec story ed, 2002; "The Crush", exec story ed, 2002; "Road Trip", writer, 2002; "Mother's Day Blues", exec story ed, 2002; "Kimmie Has Two Moms", writer, 2003; "Judge Not a Book", writer, 2004; "Second Time Around", co-exec producer & writer, 2004-05"; "At Last", producer, 2004; "A Little Change Never Hurt Anybody", co-producer, 2004; "Could It Be You", co-producer, 2004; "Practice What You Preach", producer, 2004; A Kiss Is Still a Kiss, co-exec producer, 2004; Pilot, co-exec producer, 2004; Big Bank, Little Bank, co-exec producer, 2005; "Study Buddy", writer, 2005; "One on One", writer, 2005-06; "Fame & Older Woman", writer, 2006; "Who's Got Jokes?", segment producer, 2006; "Real Husbands of Hollywood", writer, 2013-16. Other: Real Husb co-exec producer, currently. **Business Addr:** Co-Executive Producer, United Paramount Network, 11800 Wilshire Blvd, Los Angeles, CA 90025, **Business Phone:** (310)575-7000.

**BROWN, MIKE**
Basketball coach, basketball player. **Personal:** Born Mar 5, 1970, Columbus, OH; married Carolyn; children: Elijah & Cameron. **Educ:** Univ San Diego, BA, bus finance, 1992. **Career:** Basketball player (retired), basketball coach; USD, 1990-92; Denver Nuggets, Video Coordr, Scout, 1992-97; Wash Wizards, asst coach, 1997-99; San Antonio Spurs, asst coach, 2000-03; Ind Pacers, asst coach, 2003-05; Cleveland Cavaliers, head coach, 2005-10; ESPN, studio analyst, 2010; Westlake Lee Burneson Mid Sch, asst coach; St Mary's Col, Calif, asst coach; Los Angeles Lakers, head coach, 2011-12; Cleveland Cavaliers, head coach, 2013-. **Business Addr:** Head Coach, Cleveland Cavaliers, 1 Ctr Ct, Cleveland, OH 44115-4001, **Business Phone:** (800)820-2287.

**BROWN, MILBERT ORLANDO, JR.**
Photojournalist, educator, association executive. **Personal:** Born Aug 12, 1956, Gary, IN; son of Milbert Sr and Mary Blanchard; children: Victoria Imani. **Educ:** Ball State Univ, Muncie, IN, BSJ, journ, 1978; Ohio Univ, Sch Visual Commun, Athens, OH, MA, photo jour & visual commun, 1982; Morgan State Univ, EdD, higher educ, 2010-. **Career:** Westside High Sch, Gary, Ind, dir stud publ, jour teacher, 1978-79; Dallas Times-Herald, photojournalist, 1980; Wash Post, Wash, DC, photojournalist, 1982; Veterans Admin, pub affairs writer, 1983; self-employed/freelance photogr, midwestern-based, 1983-86; Dept Army, Warren, Mich, writer, ed, 1986; Wilberforce Univ, Wilberforce, OH, instr mass media, 1986-87; Patuxent Publ Newspapers, Columbia, Md, photojournalist, 1987-89; Boston Globe, Boston, Mass, photojournalist, 1990-91; Chicago Tribune, photogr & picture ed, 1991, photojournalist, 2001, asst subj ed & photojournalist, 1991-2008; Open Shutters, instr, 1995, lectr; Brown Media Consult, managing dir, 2009-; Northern Va Community Col, adj fac arts, commun & humanities, 2011-; Wash Adventist Univ, adj fac commun & journalism, 2011-. **Orgs:** Nat Press Photogr Asn, 1974-; Omega Psi Phi Fraternity, 1976-; Nat Asn Black Journalists, 1981-; Chicago Asn Black Journalists; Am Col Personnel Asn; founder, Chicago Alliance of African Am Photogr; Foreign Correspondents Asn, Int Press; Soc for Photog Educ, life mem, Omega Psi Phi Fraternity Inc; reporting fel UN Overseas. **Honors/Awds:** Photography & Aesthetic Awareness Lecture, Morris Brown Col, 1987; Two Man Show & Lecture, Grambling State Col, 1987; Award of Excellence, Chicago Asn Black Journalists, 1992; Visual Task Force Photo Shoot-Out Award, Nat Asn Black Journalists, 1992, 1993, 1998; US Photo "Shoot Out" winner, Nat Asn Black Journalists & Coca Cola, 1992, 1993, 1998; Journalism Award, Outstanding Coverage of the Black Condition Photography, Nat Asn Black Journalists, 1992, 1994; First place winner, portrait & personality, Chicago Press Photographers Asn, 1993; Lect & Exhib, Pieces of Ebony, Photo Exhibit, Dillard Univ, 1994, Morgan State Univ, 1995; Award of Excellence, Chicago Asn Black Journalists, 1995, 1998; Pulitzer Prize, Chicago Tribune, 1995, 1998; Photographer of the Year, Chicago Press Photographers Asn, 1995; Omega Man of the Year, Omega Psi Phi, 1997; Journalism Alumnus of the Year, Ball State Univ, Dept Journ, 1997; Photographers and writers working together lecture, Nat Asn Black Jounalist Regional Conf, Minneapolis, 1998; Award of Excellence, Nat Asn Black Journalists, 1998; Living Legends of the Negro League, Art Atrium II Gallery, Portsmouth, VA, 1999; Grand Prize Winner; Langston Hughes Writing Award; Gordon Parks International Photography Award; International Graduate Omega Man of the Year, Omega Psi Phi Fraternity Inc, 2000; International Citizen of the Year, Omega Psi Phi Fraternity Inc, 2002. **Special Achievements:** First Place Sports Picture, Boston Press Photographers Asn, 1991; "Pieces of Ebony," Morgan State Univ, Baltimore, MD, 1995; "The Million Man March," Milwaukee Hist Soc, Milwaukee, WI, 1996; Soul of a New Nation-Photographs the South African Elections, Univ of IL-Chicago, 1997; "Joy- A Celebration of the Black Experience," Univ of IL-Chicago, African American Cultural Ctr, 1997; Exhibition and lecture: "Photography & Aesthetic Awareness," Morris Brown College, Atlanta, GA, Grambling State College, Grambling, LA; First Place & Best of Show for Spot News, Maryland & Delaware/DC Press Asn, 1988. **Home Addr:** 5801 W Race Ave, Chicago, IL 60644-1412, **Home Phone:** (773)626-8966. **Business Addr:** Adjunct Faculty, Northern Virginia Community College, 8333 Little River Turnpike, Annandale, VA 22003, **Business Phone:** (703)323-3425.

**BROWN, DR. MILTON F.**
President (organization), school administrator, educator. **Personal:** Born Apr 29, 1943, Rochester, NY; children: Damien. **Educ:** State Univ NY, Oswego, BS, 1965; Columbia Univ Teachers Col, MA, 1973, PhD, 1983. **Career:** Ben Franklin High Sch, teacher; Nat Inst Ed, educ policy fel, 1978-79; NY City Bd Ed, asst sup, 1979-80; NY State Educ Dept, dir 1980-82; NJ Dept Higher Ed, acad Affairs, dir, 1982-85; New York Tecnical Col, assoc provost acad affairs; Malcolm X Col, Chicago, pres, 1990-; Pasadena City Col, instr social sci. **Orgs:** Vpres, Task Force Youth Employ, 1979-80; vpres, Mondale's Task Force Youth Employ, 1979-80. **Business Addr:** President, Malcolm X College, 1900 W Van Buren St, Chicago, IL 60612, **Business Phone:** (312)850-7000.

**BROWN, MONICA DENISE. See ARNOLD, MONICA DENISE.**

**BROWN, MORSE L.**
Government official, conservationist. **Personal:** Born Oct 10, 1943, Oakland, MS; son of Stephen and Fannie J Moore; married Arma George; children: Khary Dia. **Educ:** Alcorn State Univ, Lorman, MS, BS, agr educ, pursued grad, 1965; Mich State Univ. **Career:** Conservationist (retired); US Soil Conserv Serv, Claremont, NH, soil conservationist, 1965-67, soil conservationist, 1967-71, W Br, dist conservationist, 1971-73, Muskegon, dist conservationist, 1973-82, Ann Arbor, dist conservationist, 1982-85; level GS-12 Dist Conservationist, soil conservationist, dist conservationist; Wayne County MSUE off, unty exten dir; MIFFS Multicultural Farmers Prog, proj mgr; Mich State Univ Exten Serv, Ann Arbor, co ext dir, 1985-88, co ext dir, 1988, agt, county exten dir, 2002. **Orgs:** Reg dir, Alpha Phi Alpha, Fraternity, 1975-82; reg dir, Soil Conserv Soc Am, 1983-84; mkt chair, Community to Enhance Resources Under-served Farmers; African Am Farmers Venture; Urban Consumer Groups; chmn, Brown Chapel Bldg Comt, 1986-88; pres, Alpha Phi Alpha, Fraternity Theta Zeta Lambda, 1988-90. **Honors/Awds:** Appreciation for Serv, Soil Conserv Soc, 1985; Appreciation for Serv, Washtenaw County, 1988; Resolution of Appreciation Dept Heads, Washtenaw County, 1988; Resolution of Appreciation, Washtenaw County, Bd Comnrs Washtenaw County, 1988; Dairy Herd Imp Assoc Washtenaw County, 1988; Commendation Award, 1990; Alpha Man of Year, Theta Zeta Lambda Chapter, 1991; Presidential's Cit, Mich Assoc Ext Agents, 1992; Achievement Award, Nat Asn Ext Agents, 1994; Wayne County HSCB Recognition for Health & Comn Serv Prog, 1998-99; Mich State Univ Ext Team Award, 1998; SEMCOSH Environ Justice Award, 2000. **Home Addr:** 15565 Stonehouse Circle, Livonia, MI 48154-1531, **Home Phone:** (734)432-9763.

**BROWN, DR. MORTIMER**
Clinical psychologist. **Personal:** Born Feb 20, 1924, New York, NY; married Marilyn Green; children: Frank & Mark. **Educ:** City Col NY, BS, 1949; Vanderbilt Univ, PhD, 1961. **Career:** Clinical psychologist (retired), patient advocate; Bedford Univ, distinguished prof, 1960; Ill Dept Ment Health, asst dir, 1961-69, founding dir; Fla State Univ, Tallahassee, prof, psychol, 1969-73; Fla Ment Health Inst, 1973-78; St Leo Col, adj prof psychol, 1977; Independent Prac, 1978-96; Univ Sarasota, adj prof psychol, Tampa Bay Campus, 1998; Univ S Fla's, Hons Col; Southwest Oncol Group, patient advocate; Nat Cancer Inst, Off Liaison Activ, currently. **Orgs:** Am Psychol Asn; Am Black Psychol Asn; Southeastern Psychol Asn; bd, comm mem, Fla Psychol Asn, 1980, pres, 1981; Am Cancer Soc; Colon Cancer Alliance; Colorectal Cancer Coalition; H Lee Moffitt Cancer Ctr; founding dir, Community Ment Health Ctr. **Home Addr:** 18825 Tracer Dr, Lutz, FL 33549-3822, **Home Phone:** (813)949-3202. **Business Addr:** Member, National Cancer Institute, 6116 Exec Blvd Rm 3036A, Bethesda, MD 20892-8322, **Business Phone:** (800)422-6237.

**BROWN, NA ORLANDO**
Football player. **Personal:** Born Feb 22, 1977, Reidsville, NC; son of Nathan; married Erica Devon Featherstone. **Educ:** Univ NC, grad. **Career:** Philadelphia Eagles, wide receiver, 1999-2001; Orlando Predators, 2002-03; Huntington Hammer, 2012; Sarasota Thunder, Ultimate Indoor Football League, 2013-.

**BROWN, NANCY COFIELD**
Administrator, executive director. **Personal:** Born Jul 25, 1932; married David; children: David, Stephen & Philip. **Educ:** Pratt Inst, attended 1954. **Career:** Trudy Rogers Co, asst designer, 1955-57; Family & Child Serv, coordr, 1974-77; Town Greenwich, dir community develop block grant prog, 1978-. **Orgs:** Dir, Urban League SW, Fairfield, Conn, 1970-74; dir, Conn Women's Bk, 1974-78; grants consult, Town Greenwich, 1977; consult, Affirmative Act, Town Greenwich, 1977; YMCA, 1979; Links-Fairfield, Conn, 1980; trustee, Stanford Found, 1980; Hartwick Col, trustee, 1990-; Conn Housing Fin Authority. **Honors/Awds:** Ten Outstanding Women BRAVO Award. **Home Addr:** 43 Lexington Ave, Greenwich, CT 06830. **Business Addr:** Director, Town of Greenwich, 101 Field Pt Rd, Greenwich, CT 06830-6463, **Business Phone:** (203)622-7872.

**BROWN, NORMAN E.**
Scientist, executive, government official. **Personal:** Born Feb 20, 1935, Cleveland, OH; married Mary Lee Tyus; children: Karen, Dianne, Pamela, David & Robert. **Educ:** Western Res Univ, Cleveland, OH, BA, biol, 1959; Univ Minn, Minneapolis, MS, biochem, 1970. **Career:** Western Res Univ, res assoc, 1957-64; Univ Minn, res assoc; Hoffman-LaRoche Inc, asst sci II, 1969-71, assoc sci, 1971-73, mgr equal oppor, 1973-78, asst dir equal oppor, 1978-86; Tampa Bay Regional Planning Coun, assoc housing planner. **Orgs:** Edges Inc, 1975-80; pres bd trustee, United Way Plainfield, 1978-; vpres bd trustee, United Way Union Co, 1978-; Plainfield NJ Sch Bd, 1982-85, pres, 1984-85. **Home Addr:** 4932 Ebensburg Dr, Tampa, FL 33647, **Home Phone:** (813)866-0817.

**BROWN, DR. O. GILBERT**
School administrator, educator. **Personal:** Born Jun 12, 1954, Proctor, AR; son of Mable and Zelner; children: Jacqueline & Jordan. **Educ:** Great Bend High Sch, dipl, 1972; Univ Kans, BS, 1976; Emporia State Univ, MS, counr educ, 1986; Miami Univ-Oxford, Ohio, MS, col stud personnel, 1986; Ind Univ-Bloomington, EdD, higher educ & stud affairs, 1992. **Career:** Ind Univ-Bloomington, coordr, 1986-91; Earlham Col, assoc dean, 1992-93; Ind Univ, Indianapolis, dir residence life, 1993-95, asst dean educ stud serv, dir stud serv, asst dean stud serv, 1999-2002, assoc dean, 2002-07; Purdue Univ, Sch Educ, asst dean, adj prof, 1999; Mo State Univ, assoc prof & dir stud affairs prog, 2007-. **Orgs:** Nat Asn Stud Personnel Administrators, 1984-; Kappa Alpha Psi Fraternity; Am Col Personnel Asn; fel Am Coun Educ, 2001-02. **Honors/Awds:** Experience Excellence Recognition Award, Ind Univ & Purdue Univ, 1997; Teaching Excellence Recognition Award, Ind Univ & Purdue Univ, 1998; Outstanding faculty member, Nat Asn Stud Affairs Educr Region IV-W, 2009. **Special Achievements:** Helping African-American Students Attend College, 1997; Debunking the Myth: Stories About African-American College Students. **Home Addr:** 3744 Cobble Creek Ct, Bloomington, IN 47401. **Business Addr:** Associate Professor, MS Student Affairs Program Director, Missouri State University, Col Educ, Springfield, MO 65897, **Business Phone:** (417)836-5287.

**BROWN, DR. OLA M.**
Educator. **Personal:** Born Apr 7, 1941, Albany, GA; daughter of Georgia Butler Johnson and Willie L Johnson. **Educ:** Albany State Col, BS, 1961; Univ Ga, MEd, 1972, EdS, 1973, EdD, 1974. **Career:** Thomas County Schs, Thomasville GA, teacher, 1961-67; Dougherty County Schs, Albany GA, teacher, 1967-71; Univ GA Athens, grad asst, 1972-74; Valdosta State Col GA, prof educ, 1974-91, dept head, Early Childhood & Reading Educ, 1980-90; Valdosta State Univ, dept head, prof emer, currently; Levi Strauss & Co, currently. **Orgs:** Phi Delta Kappa Educ Frat, 1975-; recording sec, Ga Coun Int Reading Asn, 1977-79; treas, Ga Asn Higher Educ, 1977-80; Am Asn Univ Prof, 1977-80; vpres, 1979-80, pres, Ga Coun Int Reading Asn, 1980-81; state coordr, Int Reading Asn, 1988-91. **Honors/Awds:** Education Instructor of the Year, Student GA Asn Educ, 1975; WH Dennis Memorial Award, Albany State Col, 1976; Ira E Aaron Reading Award, S Central GA Coun IRA, 1977. **Special Achievements:** Ola M Brown Scholarship, established in honor of Dr Ola M Brown. First African American To Head The Early Childhood And Reading Education Department in Valdosta State University. **Home Addr:** 2503 N Oak St, Valdosta, GA 31602. **Business Addr:** Professor Emeritus, Valdosta State University, 1500 N Patterson St, Valdosta, GA 31698, **Business Phone:** (229)333-5800.

**BROWN, OMAR LAMONT**
Football player. **Personal:** Born Mar 28, 1975, York, PA. **Educ:** NC State Univ. **Career:** Football player (retired); Atlanta Falcons, defensive back & safety, 1998-99; Orlando Rage, safety, 2001.

**BROWN, ESQ. OUIDA Y.**
Attorney general (U.S. federal government). **Career:** Pvt pract atty, currently. **Orgs:** Trustee, Americans United. **Business Addr:** Attorney, 600 N Wash St, Tuscumbia, AL 35674-0587, **Business Phone:** (256)383-9992.

**BROWN, P. J. (COLLIER BROWN, JR.)**
Basketball player. **Personal:** Born Oct 14, 1969, Detroit, MI; married Dee; children: Whitney, Briana, Kalani & Javani. **Educ:** La Tech Univ, attended 1992. **Career:** Basketball player (retired); Panionios (Greece), ctr, 1992-93; New Jersey Nets, ctr & power forward, 1993-96; Miami Heat, power forward, 1996-2000; Charlotte Hornets, power forward, 2000-02; New Orleans Hornets, ctr & power forward, 2002-06; NewYork Knicks, ctr, 2006; Chicago Bulls, power forward, 2006-07; Boston Celtics, power forward, 2007-08. **Honors/Awds:** J Walter Kennedy Citizenship Award, 1997; NBA All-Defensive Second Team, 1997, 1999, 2001; Louisiana Tech Athletic Hall of Fame, 1998; Sportsmanship Award, Nat Basketball Asn, 2004; NBA Nat Citizenship Award, Sports Alliance, 2005; NBA Champion, 2008. **Home Addr:** 2142 Hampshire Dr, Slidell, LA 70461-5065. **Business Addr:** MA.

**BROWN, PAULA EVIE**
Educator. **Educ:** Loyola Univ, BSBA, personnel mgt, 1973; Purdue Univ, MS, 1976; Harvard Univ, EdM, 1980; Northern Ill Univ, EdD, 1990. **Career:** Neighborhood Youth Corps, recruiter, 1973-74; Purdue Univ, instr, 1974-76; RR Donnelley & Sons, pricing estimator, 1976-79; Chicago & Northwestern Co, HRD adminr, 1981-82; Northern Ill Univ, instr, 1984-88, assoc prof, 1994-; F Webb Starks Inc, bus developer, 1989-90; Cent Mich Univ, prof, 1990. **Orgs:** Beta Gamma Sigma, 1973-; Phi Delta Kappa, 1980-; Black Alumni Coun, NIU, 1991-; Asn Bus Commun, 1991-; Nat Mich Bus Educ Asn, 1991-;

Delta Pi Epsilon, 1991-; Nat Cong Black Fac, 1992-; Res Asn Minority Profs, 1992-; Northern Univ Class II Judicial Bd, 2010-12. **Business Addr:** Associate Professor, Northern Ill University, Barsema Hall BH 245V, Dekaib, IL 60115-2897, **Business Phone:** (815)753-6187.

### BROWN, PAULETTE

Lawyer, president (organization). **Personal:** Born Apr 28, 1951, Baltimore, MD; daughter of Wilbur and Thelma; children: Dijuan. **Educ:** Howard Univ, BS, 1973; Seton Hall Univ Sch Law, JD, 1976. **Career:** National Steel Corporation, Wayne, NJ, employee; Prudential Insurance Company of America, in-house consel; Buck Consultants, in-house counsel; Brown & Childress, founding partner, 1977-93; Brown, Lofton, Childress & Wolf, foundering partner, 1993; municipal court judge, Plainfield, NJ; Duane Morris LLP, partner, 2000-05; Edwards Wildman Palmer LLP, partner and chief diversity officer, 2005-15; Locke Lord, partner and member of the Labor & Employment Practice Group, 2015-. **Orgs:** Asn Black Women Lawyers Nj, pres, 1983-86; Nj State Bar Found, mem bd trustee, treas, & second vice chair Labor & Employ sect; Nat Bar Asn, pres 1993-94; Am Bar Asn, mem House Delegates, 1997-, pres, 2015-; Am Law Inst. **Special Achievements:** First female African-American president of the American Bar Association; lecturer on labor and employment issues; certified mediator for the U.S. District Court, District of New Jersey. **Business Addr:** Locke Lord, 44 Whippany Rd Suite 280, Morristown, NJ 07960, **Business Phone:** (973)520-2365.

### BROWN, RALPH BENJAMIN

Clergy. **Personal:** Born Jul 28, 1924, Pittsburgh, PA; son of Harry H and Mary J; married Margaret L; children: Ralph B Jr & Glenn B. **Educ:** Duquesne Univ, Pittsburgh, Pa, BS & BA, 1949; Duquesne Univ Grad Sch; Howard Univ Grad Sch. **Career:** Pittsburgh Courier, asst prom mgr, res dir, 1947-54; Johnson Publ Co, field rep, 1954-56; Fodor's Mod Guides Inc, Sub Sahara Africa, rese writer, 1957-59; Ethiopian Herald, Addis Ababa, city ed, 1958-59; US Info Agency, foreign serv officer, Ghana, Malawi, Somalia, 1960-69; Howard Univ, pub rels officer, 1970-73; Rubber Manufacturers Assn, dir commun, 1973-78; AT&T, mkt acct exec, 1978-85; Wisdom Inc, pres, 1985-90; United Church of Christ, minister social outreach, currently. **Orgs:** Alpha Pi Alpha Fraternity, 1947-; sr vice comdr, Veterans Foreign Wars, Post 2562, 1946-48; Montgomery County Criminal Justice Coord Comn, 1972-89; comn minister, United Church Christ, Social Outreach, 1989-; chair, M/C, Human Rel Comn, Real Estate Panel, 1989-97; parliamentar; chair, Southern Christian Leadership Conf. **Honors/Awds:** Outstanding Service CJCC 17-years, Montgomery County Md, 1972-89; Inner Circle of Achievers, C&P Telephone Co, 1981; Award of Merit, Alpha Pi Alpha, 1987; Second annual MC Human Relations Award, 1997; Distinguished Service, VFW Post 2562, 1998; Outstanding Contribution to Human Rights, United Nations Assn, 1999; Community Service Award, 2000; Humanitarian Award, 2001; M/C chap, Alpha Phi Alpha; Inducted into M/C Human Rights Hall of Fame, 2002; Certificate of Appreciation, United Nations Association. **Special Achievements:** Helped convert weekly newspaper, Ethiopian Herald, into a daily publication, 1958-59; Attended National Sales Conference, AT&T, Acapulco, MX, as one of Top 3% in Sales, 1981. **Home Addr:** 3805 Ralph Rd, Wheaton, MD 20906-5267, **Home Phone:** (301)946-5808. **Business Addr:** Minister of Social Outreach, Lincoln Congregational Temple, 1701 11th St NW, Washington, DC 20001, **Business Phone:** (202)332-2640.

### BROWN, RANDY

Basketball player. **Personal:** Born May 22, 1968, Chicago, IL; son of Wille and Marie; married Katrina; children: Justin & Janel. **Educ:** Univ Houston, attended 1988; NMex State, BA, jour, 1991. **Career:** Basketball player (retired), coach; Sacramento Kings, pt guard, 1991-95, asst coach, currently; Chicago Bulls, pt guard, 1995-2000, dir player develop, 2009-10, spec asst, 2010-13; asst gen mgr, 2013, asst coach, 2015-; Boston Celtics, pt guard, 2000-02; Phoenix Suns, pt guard, 2002-03. **Honors/Awds:** NBA Champion, 1996, 1997, 1998. **Business Addr:** Assistant General Manager, Chicago Bulls, United Ctr 1901 W Madison St, Chicago, IL 60612, **Business Phone:** (312)455-4000.

### BROWN, RAY, JR. (LEONARD RAY BROWN, JR.)

Football player, football coach. **Personal:** Born Dec 12, 1962, Marion, AR; married Ashley; children: Lentisha, Tyler, Andrea, Miriam & Leonard. **Educ:** Ark State Univ, grad; Univ Memphis, grad. **Career:** Football player (retired); Football, coach: St Louis Cardinals, guard, 1986-88; Wash Redskins, 1989-90, 2005, left guard, 1991-95, right tackle, 2004; San Francisco 49ers, left guard, 1996-2001, guard, 1999, asst off line coach, 2010; Detroit Lions, right guard, 2002-03; Buffalo Bills, asst coach, 2008-09; Carolina Panthers, asst offensive line coach, 2011-. **Honors/Awds:** All Pro Sel, 2001; Pro Bowl sel, 2001; Super Bowl XXVI champion, Co recipient of Detroit Lions' Joe Schmidt Leadership Award, 2003. **Special Achievements:** TV Series: "NFL on FOX", 1995-2001; "NFL Monday Night Football", 1996-2001; "ESPN's Sunday Night Football", 1996-2001. Film: 1997 NFC Championship Game, 1998. **Business Addr:** Assistant Offensive Line Coach, Carolina Panthers, 800 S Mint St, Charlotte, NY 28202, **Business Phone:** (704)358-7000.

### BROWN, RAYMOND MADISON

Football player, executive. **Personal:** Born Jan 12, 1949, Ft. Worth, TX; son of Raymond E and Lutiel V Houston; married Linda; children: Derek & Christopher. **Educ:** W Tex A&M Univ, BA, bus admin & mgt, 1971. **Career:** Football player (retired), executive; Life GA, ins underwriter; Atlanta Falcons, free safety, 1971, 1975, strong safety, 1972-74, 1976-77, punt returner, 1973; New Orleans Saints, strong safety, 1978-80; real estate broker, 1980-; Brown Boy II Inc, pres & owner, 1984-; Waldo Shirt Co, New York, NY, sales rep. **Orgs:** Omega Psi Phi Frat. **Honors/Awds:** Interception Leader, Nat Football Conf, 1974; Most Valuable Player Award, Atlanta Falcons, 1974. **Special Achievements:** Author of one novel. **Business Addr:** President, Owner, Brown Boy II Inc, 4936 Lake Fjord Pass Bldg B, Marietta, GA 30068, **Business Phone:** (770)642-1316.

### BROWN, REGGIE (REGILYN DEWAYNE BROWN)

Football player. **Personal:** Born Jun 26, 1973, Highland Park, MI. **Educ:** Fresno State Univ, grad. **Career:** Football player (retired); Seattle Seahawks, running back, 1996-98 & 2000, tight end & fullback & running back Green Bay Packers, 2002. **Special Achievements:** Film: 1996 NFL Draft, 1996.

### BROWN, REGINALD DEWAYNE

Writer. **Personal:** Born Mar 14, 1952, Memphis, TN; son of Clarence and Nadolyn; married Robin Viva; children: Brian Alexander & Brittany Nicole. **Educ:** Univ Calif, Irvine, BA, drama, 1974; San Francisco State Univ, MA, film, 1979. **Career:** Reginald Brown Productions, writer, producer, dir, 1981-; Dick Clark Productions Inc, asst producer, 1985-86; Sam Riddle Productions Inc, writer, assoc producer, segment dir, 1987-91; Cent City Productions Inc, writer, clip producer, 1991-94; C's Defense Fund, Beat Odds Celebration, producer, 1996-98; "Great Women Color", dir, playwright, 1998; "An Alternative to Violence", co-exec producer, writer, dir, 2000; Runaway Bay Filmworks LLC, co-managing partner, 2007-. **Orgs:** Co-chair, Dir Guild Am, AASC, 1997-98; vice chmn, Writers Guild Am, black writers comt; dir & co-chair, AASC, currently. **Home Addr:** 13691 Gavina Ave, Sylmar, CA 91342, **Home Phone:** (818)364-1983. **Business Addr:** Director, Directors Guild of America Inc, 110 W 57th Str Suite 6, New York, NY 10019, **Business Phone:** (212)258-0800.

### BROWN, REGINALD L., JR.

Executive. **Career:** Xerox Corp, mgr govt affairs & Dir Fed Global Opers; Oracle Corp, US Solutions Sls, vpres; Cyveillance Inc, bd mem; Pres Comn Exec Exchange, Spec Asst to Secy Defense; Drone Aviation Holding Corp, head govt affairs, 2015; Brown Technol Grp, co-founder, chief exec officer, chmn bd dir, currently; Friendship Motors, prin owner, pres, chief exec officer, currently. **Orgs:** Bd trustee, Community Acad PCS; Comn Int Bus & Trade; bd dir, Agilex Technologies Inc; bd dir, Nat Infiniti Dealer Adv Bd. **Business Addr:** Chief Executive Officer, Brown Technology Group LLC, 111 Rockville Pke Suite 600, Rockville, MD 20850.

### BROWN, REGINALD ROYCE, SR.

Police officer, administrator, law enforcement officer. **Personal:** Born Mar 18, 1946, Baton Rouge, LA; son of Theresa Mae Bell; children: Reginald Jr, Tashera Patrice, D'Laniger Royce & La Toya Renee. **Educ:** Southern Univ, BA, 1965. **Career:** Administrator (retired), police service; Amendment Band 13, pub rel dir & mgr; Gov's Off Consumer Protection, prog supr, 1972-73; Southern Univ, Baton Rouge LA, centex dir, 1972-75, asst to bus mgr, 1973; Jospeh A Delpit, aide, city councilman; Reginald Brown & Assocs Inc, pres, 1972-2000; Sheriffs Off, adminr asst, 1975-2000; City Baton Rouge, city constable, 2000-; Maj Topics Weekly Radio, talk show host. **Orgs:** Bd mem, Baton Rouge YMCA; life mem, Nat Asn Advan Colored People; pres, Holiday Helpers Baton Rouge, 1987-; pres, Scotland ville Beautification Comt, 1989-; secy, Baton Rouge Detox Bd; Alcohol/Drug Detox Bd; La Bar Disciplinary Bd; bd chmn, E Baton Rouge C's Planning; chmn, Nat Constable's Asn. **Honors/Awds:** Awards for Outstanding Service, Baranco Clark YMCA, 1972; Martin Luther King Award, Shady Grove Baptist Church, 1987; Award of Distinction, Alpha Kappaha, 1989; Distinguished Officer of the Year, Blacks Law Enforcement, 1990; Outstanding Black Achiever Award, YMCA; Outstanding Humanitarian Award, Baton Rouge Human Relations Council; Outstanding Law Enforcement Officer, 1990; Outstanding Law Enforcement Officer, Pres Clinton & Atty General Janet Reno, 1994; Golden Deeds Award, Baton Rouge, La, 1997; Trailblazer Award, Southern Univ, 1998; FBI Leadership Award, 2001. **Business Addr:** Constable, Baton Rouge City Court, Rm 46 233 St Louis St Basement, Baton Rouge, LA 70802, **Business Phone:** (225)389-3004.

### BROWN, RENEE

Sports manager, basketball coach. **Educ:** Univ Nev, grad, 1978, MA, educ admin, 1981. **Career:** Univ Kans, asst coach; Stanford Univ, asst coach; San Jose State Univ, asst coach; USA Basketball Women's Nat Team, asst coach, 1995-96, Exec Comt, vpres sr women's progs, 2000-04; USA Women's Olympic Team, staff, 1996; WNBA, from dir player personnel to sr dir, 1996-99, vpres, 2000, sr vpres player personnel, 2004, chief basketball opers & player rels, currently. **Business Addr:** Chief of Basketball Operations and Player Relations, Women's National Basketball Association, 645 5th Ave, New York, NY 10022, **Business Phone:** (212)688-9622.

### BROWN, REUBEN D.

Executive. **Personal:** Born Aug 11, 1948, Detroit, MI; son of Richard and Josephine; married Maria Yuzon; children: Rochelle, E Aminata & Reuben Brandon. **Educ:** Lawrence Technol Univ, BSIM, 1982; Univ Mich, MBA, 1984. **Career:** Gen Motors Corp, construct mgr, 1973-84; Rohm & Haas Co, financial anal mgr, 1984-91; Ameriprise Financial, financial planner, sr financial advr, chartered financial consult, 1991-. **Orgs:** Corp rels chair, Black Bus Studs Orgn, 1982-84; Univ Mich Steering Comt, 1982-84; bd mem, A Better Chance, 1989-91; bd mem, financial advisor, Int Child Resource Inst, 1996-; vol, Urban League. **Home Addr:** 2101 Shorline Dr, Suite 456, Alameda, CA 94501, **Home Phone:** (510)522-5500. **Business Addr:** Financial Advisor, Business Financial Advisor, Ameriprise Financial, 533 Airport Blvd Suite 375, Burlingame, CA 94010-2018, **Business Phone:** (650)401-2280.

### BROWN, DR. RICHARD L., JR.

Chancellor (education), executive. **Personal:** married Lorraine; children: 3. **Educ:** Univ Tenn, Chattanooga, BS & MS; Univ Phoenix, MBA, finance, acct & planning; Trevecca Nazarene Univ, EdD. **Career:** Univ Tenn, Chattanooga, exec vice chancellor, finance, opers & info technol, 1984-. **Orgs:** Chattanooga Alumni Chap; pres, Leadership Chattanooga Alumni Asn; chair, Compensation Adv Bd; Chattanooga United Way; Hamilton County 911; Juv Ct Comn; Community Found Chattanooga; Enterprise Econ Develop Ctr City Chattanooga; Community Res Coun; Community Outreach Partnership Ctr; trust, Pub Land Cornerstones Southern Asn Col & Univ Bus Officers, bd dir, Siskin Rehab Hosp; bd dir, Tenn Ctr Performance Excellence; bd dir, UT Syst-wide Diversity Adv Coun. **Business Addr:** Executive Vice Chancellor, The University of Tennessee at Chattanooga, 103 Founders Hall Dept 5505, Chattanooga, TN 37403, **Business Phone:** (423)425-4393.

### BROWN, REV. RICHARD S., JR.

Clergy. **Personal:** Born Birmingham, AL; son of R S Sr (deceased); married Kirktenia; children: Christina, Jessica & Richard III. **Educ:** Univ Tenn, Knoxville, BA, polit sci & bus admin; Tenn State Univ, Nashville, Tenn. **Career:** St John Baptist Church, Knoxville, pastor; Tenn Valley Authority, Knoxville, Tenn, control analyst; Payne Ave Missionary Baptist Church, pastor, 1996-. **Orgs:** Steering comt, Alzheimer's Asn; bd dir, Knoxville Interdenominational Sch, Am Baptist Col; bd dir, Compassion Coalition; vice-moderator, Knoxville Dist Baptist Asn; asst dean, KDBA Cong Dept; pres, Knoxville Interdenominational Christian Ministerial Alliance; Knoxville leadership, CAC, 2000-01. **Business Addr:** Pastor, Payne Avenue Missionary Baptist Church, 2714 Martin Luther King Blvd, Knoxville, TN 37914, **Business Phone:** (865)524-7234.

### BROWN, ROBERT, JR. (BOB BROWN)

Consultant, government official. **Personal:** Born Mar 23, 1936, Lansing, MI; son of Robert Sr and Georgia L Dean; married Joy G Tunstall. **Educ:** Mich State Univ, BA, social work, 1958. **Career:** Mich Dept Corrections, prison counr, 1961-62, parole officer, 1962-67, dep warden, 1967-70, dep dir, 1970-84, dir, 1984-91; Fed Ct, consult; Bob Brown Enterprise, criminal justice consult, currently; Us Dist Ct, consent agreement monitor; auditor, Am Correctional Asn. **Orgs:** Alpha Phi Alpha 1955; exec bd mem, Youth Develop Corp, 1978-; pres & life mem, Mich Correctional Asn, 1984; vpres, Midwest Asn Correctional Admin, 1985-86, treas, 1986-89, pres, 1989-91; exec bd mem, Chief Okemos Coun Boy Scouts Am Exec Bd, 1986-91; exec comt mem, Am Correctional Asn, 1988-90; Sigma Pi Phi Frat; Alpha Chi Boule, 1988-; vpres, Chief Okemos Coun Boy Scouts Am Exec Bd, 1989-91; vpres, pres, Asn State Correctional Adminr, 1989-91; Trinity AME Church; Nat Asn Advan Colored People. **Home Addr:** 1912 Kuerbitz Dr, Lansing, MI 48906, **Home Phone:** (517)323-1183. **Business Addr:** Criminal Justice Consultant, Bob Brown Enterprise, 1912 Kuerbitz Dr, Lansing, MI 48906, **Business Phone:** (517)323-1183.

**BROWN, ROBERT BARISFORD.** See BROWN, BOBBY.

### BROWN, ROBERT J., III

Psychiatrist. **Personal:** Born May 31, 1919, Norfolk, VA; married Blanche Randall; children: Jeanne, Catherine & Marcia. **Educ:** Hampton Inst, BS, 1939; Howard Univ, MS, 1941, MS, MIT, MD, 1945. **Career:** Union Bay state Chem Corp, chemist, 1943-46; Howard Univ, Dept Med, asst prof, 1959-60, fel & psychiat, 1961-66, asst prof, 1966; Veterans Benefits Off, med officer, 1960-61; Howard Univ Hosp, psychiat; Reynolds Mem Hosp, internal med; Norfolk Community Hosp; Clin Opers Area B, Community Ment Health Ctr, pres, asst dir, 1972; pvt pract, psychiat, currently. **Orgs:** Am Psychiat Asn, 1966-; Med Soc Dist Columbia, 1966-; AAAS; DC Civil Serv; CTMF Med Found. **Honors/Awds:** Res Steric, Hindrance & Enolization Acetylenic Precursors Vitamin A, 1939-45. **Home Addr:** 13113 Cabinwood Dr, Silver Spring, MD 20904-3121, **Home Phone:** (202)865-6611. **Business Addr:** Psychiatry, Private Practice, 2041 Ga Ave NW, Washington, DC 20060, **Business Phone:** (202)865-6100.

### BROWN, ROBERT JOE

Administrator, chief executive officer. **Personal:** Born Feb 26, 1935, High Point, NC; married Sallie J Walker. **Educ:** Va Union Univ; NC Agr & Tech State Univ. **Career:** High Pt Police Dept, law enforcement officer, 1956-58; US Dept Treas, Fed Bur Narcotics, police officer, fed agt, 1958-60; B & C Assocs Inc, pres, 1960-68; WhiteHouse, spec asst pres, 1968-73; B & C Assocs Inc, chmn & chief exec officer, 1973-; B&C Int, chmn & chief exec officer, 1980-. **Orgs:** Bd dir, Oper PUSH Inc; bd dir, MLK Ctr Social Chg; bd dir, First Union Corp; bd dir, Sonoco; bd dir, Duke Power; So Furniture Club; Nat Asn Advan Colored People; Wisemen; Arthur W Page Soc; United Nat Bank; vice chmn, Am Cancer Soc; pres, Int BookSmart Found; bd dir, AutoNation, Inc; Blue Ridge Holdings Inc; Nat Col Athletic Asn; Duke Energy; Wachovia Corp; Wake Forest Univ Baptist Med Ctr; Sonoco Prod Co; High Pt Univ; Boston Univ; Va Union Univ; Nat Urban League; Horatio Alger Asn; Richard Nixon Found. **Honors/Awds:** Outstanding Young Man in America, Jr Chamber Com Distinguished Serv; Achievement Award, Nat Med Asn; Nat Merit Award, Alpha Phi Alpha; Nat Exec Branch Govt Award, Alpha Phi Alpha; Honorary Chief, Sioux Indian Nat; Distinguished American Award, Horatio Alger Asn; Lifetime Achievement Award, Small Bus Admin; Drum Major for Justice Award, SCLC; Tocqueville Society Award, United Way Greater High Pts, 2002; Honorary Degrees: LHD, North Carolina A & T State Univ; LHD, Tarkio Col; LHD, Clark Col; LLD, High Point Col; LLD, Daniel Payne Col; LLD, Shaw Univ; LLD, Fla Mem Col; LLD, Malcolm X Col; Citizen of the Year Award, 2005; Award for Lifetime Achievement, 2006; National Directors Legacy Award for Lifetime Achievement, 2007; Executive Networking Conference Trailblazer Award, 2010. **Home Addr:** 1129 Pennywood Dr, High Point, NC 27265. **Business Addr:** Chairman, Chief Executive Officer, B & C Associates Inc, 808 Greensboro Rd, High Point, NC 27261-2636, **Business Phone:** (336)884-0744.

### BROWN, RODGER L., JR.

Manager, executive director, association executive. **Personal:** Born Aug 15, 1955, Petersburg, VA. **Educ:** Boston Col, BA, sociol, 1977; Mass Inst Technol, 1982. **Career:** IBM, mkt rep, 1978-80; Sittler Assoc, consult, 1979-80; United S End & Lower Roxbury Develop Corp, proj mgr, 1980-83; Greater Boston Community Develop, proj mgr, 1982-83; Cruz Develop Co, develop proj mgr, 1986, vpres, 1983-89; Mintz, Levin, Cohn, Rerries Glousky & Popeo, sr prof, 1990-92; Winn Develop Co Inc, sr vpres, vpres develop, 1992-94; R. Brown & Assocs Inc, Prin, 1994-2004; Presrvation Affordable Housing, develop advisor, managing dir, 2004-. **Orgs:** MA Minority Develop Assoc; Builder Assoc Greater Boston; Intern, Boston Redeelopment Authority, 1982-83; mentor, Citizens Housing & Planning Assoc, 2014-; Urban Land Inst, 2014-; mem bd, Nat Housing & Rehab Asn, 2015-; Town Sherborn, Zoning Bd Appeal, 2016; bd trustee, Boston Archit Col, 2016-.

**Honors/Awds:** US Dept of Housing & Urban Development Minority Fellowship, 1982. **Home Addr:** 99 Prospect St, Sherborn, MA 01770-1302, **Home Phone:** (508)651-1454. **Business Addr:** Development Advisor, Managing Director, Presrvation of Affordable Housing, 40 Ct St Suite 700, Boston, MA 02108, **Business Phone:** (617)261-9898.

### BROWN, RODNEY W. (ROCK BROWN)

Executive. **Personal:** son of Sidney and Elise. **Career:** Shelly's Delaware Inc, Wilmington, Del, chief exec. **Orgs:** Minority Contractors Asn; Del Minority Bus Asn; Nat Asn Advan Colored People; United Meth Men; New Castle City Chamber Com. **Business Addr:** Chief Executive, Shelly's Of Delaware, 610 W 8th St, Wilmington, DE 19801, **Business Phone:** (302)656-3337.

### BROWN, DR. RONALD EDWARD

Educator. **Personal:** Born May 5, 1952, Springfield, IL; son of Pearl; married Lillie Sloan; children: Khari & Katura. **Educ:** Lincoln Land Community Col, Springfield, IL, AA, 1972; Southern Ill Univ, Carbondale, IL, BA, 1974; Univ Mich, Ann Arbor, MI, MA, 1984, PhD, 1985. **Career:** Univ Mich, minority grad stud fel, 1974; Eastern Michigan Univ, Ypsilanti, Mich, asst prof, 1985-89, assoc prof, 1989-92; Wayne State Univ, Col Libr Arts, assoc prof polit sci, dir, 1993-, humanities ctr fac fel, 1996. **Orgs:** Am Polit Sci Asn, 1984-; Nat Asn Black Polit Scientists, 1984-; asst supt, Sunday Sch Bethel AME Church, 1987-; Mid W Polit Sci Asn. **Home Addr:** 3731 Oak Dr, Ypsilanti, MI 48197, **Home Phone:** (734)434-9204. **Business Addr:** Associate Professor, Director, Wayne State University, 2013 F/AB, Detroit, MI 48201, **Business Phone:** (313)577-2630.

### BROWN, DR. RONALD PAUL

Educator, school administrator, consultant. **Personal:** Born Mar 19, 1938, Ravenna, OH; son of Paul L and Agnes L Ervin; married Joyce Anita Jones; children: Todd Mason, Lisa Kay & Paula Marie. **Educ:** Univ Akron, BS, 1967, MS, 1969, PhD, 1974. **Career:** Univ Akron, co-ord develop serv & stud adv, 1969-74; Cuyahoga County Bd Ment Retardation, dir habilitation serv, 1974-80; Cuyahoga County Summit, admin asst, 1981-84; Kent State Univ, asst to dean minority & women affairs, 1984-87; Kent State Univ Ashtabula Campus, asst dean & asst prof counr educ, 1987-92, asst prof Pan Africa studies & dir multi cult affairs, 1992-98; Joparo Co, owner, currently. **Orgs:** Univ Akron Alumni Coun, 1978-81; bd trustee, St Paul Am Methodist Episcopal Church, 1978-; bd dir, Alpha Homes, 1982-; bd trustee, Cuyahoga Valley Ment Health, 1982-84; Nat Cert Counr Nat Bd Cert Coun, 1984; chap secy, Nat Old Timers, 1984-87; treas, Black Alumni Asn, 1987-; vpres, Community Action Coun, Ashtabula, OH; adv bd mem, Ashtabula Salvation Army; dir, Community Resource Econ Comm, Ashtabula; bd trustee, 1990, Home Safe, 1990, adv bd, 1992; adv bd, Pvt Indust Coun, 1990; bd dir, First Merit Bank, 1990-97; pres, Jobs Ohio Graduates, 1992; bd adv, Goodwill Indust; consult & coordr, Bro to Bro Proj, 2002; E Akron Community House, 2000-; Area Aging Adv Bd, 2003; Bd Summit County, Am Cancer Control Unit; chair, Proj Blueprint Adv Comt, 2009; chair, United Way Summit County, Proj Blueprint Adv Comt. **Business Addr:** Chairperson, United Way of Summit County, 90 N Prospect St, Akron, OH 44304-1273, **Business Phone:** (330)762-7601.

### BROWN, ESQ. RONALD WELLINGTON (RON BROWN)

Entrepreneur, lawyer, consultant. **Personal:** Born Oct 17, 1945, Elizabeth, NJ; son of Leroy and Mollie; married Geraldine Reed; children: Kimberly & Michael D. **Educ:** Rutgers Univ, BA, hist, 1967; Harvard Law Sch, JD, 1971; Harvard Grad Sch Bus Admin, MBA, 1973; Columbia Univ, Parker Sch Foreign & Comparative Law. **Career:** US Dist Courts, Ct Appeals, Second Circuit; atty pract; US Supreme Ct, atty pract; bd ed & articles ed, Harvard Civil Rights-Civil Liberties Law Rev; ITT World Hq, staff coun, 1973-85; Motion Picture Asn Am, N Am & Commonwealth Opers, dir, 1985-87; NJ Transit Corp, Real Estate Develop & Property Mgt, dir, 1988; Sammy Davis Jr Nat Liver Inst Inc, exec vpres, admin, chief oper officer, 1988-91; Reed-Brown Consult Group, exec vpres & managing dir, 1990-10; BRS & W Prod, pres, chief oper officer, co-founder, 1992-94; Spooner & Burnett, Atty Law, coun, 1994-98; Nor Jean Entertainment Mgt, Bus Affairs, dir, 1996-; W Frye & Assocs PC, sr consult, spec proj mgr, 1998-; W F Golf Enterprises, chief oper officer, 1999-; Omega Golf Centers Inc, chief oper officer, 2001-. **Orgs:** Am Arbit Asn, Law Comn, Int Law Sect, 1981-; Prosperity NJ, Small Bus Comn, 1996-; chair, NJ United Minority Bus Brain Trust, 1997-; trustee & bd educ rep, Twp Montclair, Planning Bd, 1997-; bd educ rep & trustee, Dr Martin Luther King Jr Scholar Comn; Omega Psi Phi Fraternity, Eta Pi Chap; Supplier Diversity Develop Comn, Bd Pub Utilities, NJ; vice chair, Church Coun, St. Mark's United Methodist Church; Montclair Bd Educ; Montclair Twp Bd Sch Estimate; chair, Fin & Stewardship Steering Comts; pres, NJ Minority Bus Brain Trust; vpres, 100 Black Men New York; NY State Bar; Garden State Bar. **Home Addr:** 180 Union St, Montclair, NJ 07042, **Home Phone:** (973)746-1730. **Business Addr:** Executive Vice President, Managing Director, The Reed-Brown Consulting Group, 180 Union St, Montclair, NJ 07042-2125, **Business Phone:** (973)509-8243.

### BROWN, ROOSEVELT LAWAYNE

Baseball executive, business owner, baseball player. **Personal:** Born Aug 3, 1975, Vicksburg, MS; married Ronita; children: Roosevelt Jr & Rosario. **Educ:** Jackson State Univ, bus admin, 1996. **Career:** Player (retired); Coach; GCL Braves, 1993; Atlanta Braves, 1993-96, hitting instr, 2009; Idhao falls, 1994; Eugena, 1995; Fla Marlins, 1996-97; kane co, 1996-97; Iowa, 1998-2001; Chicago Cubs, outfielder, 1997-2002, 2005; Orix BlueWave, 2003-04; Atlanta Falcons, 2005; Chicago White Sox, 2005; Brown Custom Homes LLC, pres & owner, 2006-; Miss Titans, head coach, 2010-11; Brown Custom Homes LLC, pres & owner, 2006-; Miss Braves, hitting coach, currently. **Orgs:** Prof Baseball Players Am, 1993-; MLB Players Alumni, 1999-. **Honors/Awds:** PCL Post-Season All-Star, 2001. **Business Addr:** President, Owner, Brown Custom Homes LLC, 4024 E Lone Mountain Rd Cave, Creek, AZ 85331-5469, **Business Phone:** (480)488-0166.

### BROWN, DR. ROSCOE C., JR.

College administrator, television show host, executive director. **Personal:** Born Mar 9, 1922, Washington, DC; son of Roscoe Sr; children: Doris, Diane, Dennis & Donald. **Educ:** Springfield Col, MA, BS, 1943; NY Univ, MA, 1949, PhD, 1951. **Career:** New York Dept Welfare, social investr; W Va State Col, instr phys educ, 1947-48; NY Univ, prof educ, 1950-77; Bronx Community Col, pres, 1977-93; TV & Radio Prog: "Black Arts"; "Soul Reason"; "Black Lett"; "A Black Perspective"; "African Am Legends", host, currently; City Univ NY, Grad Sch & Univ Ctr, Ctr Urban Educ Policy, dir, currently. **Orgs:** Dir, Inst Afro-Am Affairs; pres, One Hundred Black Men; Boys & Girls Clubs Am; Jackie Robinson Found & Libr Future; founding mem, Am Col Sports Med; pres, 100 Black Men Am New York Chap. **Home Addr:** 4555 Henry Hudson Pkwy, Bronx, NY 10471. **Business Addr:** Director, City University of New York, 365 5th Ave Rm 4201, New York, NY 10016-4309, **Business Phone:** (212)817-7220.

### BROWN, ROSE DENISE

Banker. **Personal:** Born Chicago, IL; daughter of Willie and Maggie Williams. **Educ:** Cornell Col, BA, econs & bus, 1979. **Career:** Continental Bank, acct adminr & sect mgr, doc specialist, doc supvr, loan doc coordr, collateral analyst, job analyst, opers officer. **Orgs:** Nat Asn Urban Bankers; bd mem, Continental Bank Found; Com Fin Asn, Midwest Chap. **Business Addr:** Operations Officer, Continental Bank, 231 S LaSalle St 12th Fl, Chicago, IL 60697.

### BROWN, RUBEN PERNELL

Executive, football player. **Personal:** Born Feb 13, 1972, Lynchburg, VA; married Kenia; children: Solomon, Benjamin & Isabelle. **Educ:** Pittsburgh Univ, phys educ. **Career:** Football player (retired), broadcaster; Buffalo Bills, left guard, 1995-2003, guard, 1999; Chicago Bears, left guard, 2004-07; MSG Western New York, co-host, 2016-; Enforcers, co-host, currently; Fall Exp Football League, analyst, currently. **Orgs:** Founder & Pres, Ruben Run Found, 2001; founder & pres, Ruben Brown Found, 2001-. **Honors/Awds:** All-Big East, 1992, 1993, 1994; Pro Bowl, 1996, 1997, 1998, 1999, 2000, 2001, 2002, 2003, 2004, 2007; First-Team All-American, Am Football Coaches Asn; Honorable Mention All-American, Football News; Virginia Male Athlete-of-the-Year, 1990; All-Rookie Team, Pro Football Writers Am, 1995; Buffalo Bills 50th Anniversary Team. **Business Addr:** Founder, President, Ruben Brown Foundation, PO Box 1221, Orchard Park, NY 14127, **Business Phone:** (800)336-8260.

### BROWN, DR. RUBY EDMONIA

Psychologist. **Personal:** Born Sep 5, 1943, Pittsburgh, PA; married Ephriam Wolfolk Jr; children: Kenneth, Kevin & Keith. **Educ:** Univ Colo, BA, 1981; Univ Ore, MS, 1982, PhD, 1987. **Career:** Pikes Peak Ment Health Ctr, ment health therapist, 1976-81; Univ OR, teaching asst, instr, 1981-85; Woodburn Comn Ment Health Ctr, intern, psych, 1985; Woodburn Comn Ment Health Ctr, Psych Intern, 1986; Arlington County Behaioral Healthcare Div, proj dir, 1993-2006; RubKe Bheavioral Healthcare Consult, owner, currently. **Orgs:** Alumni & Friend Stud Yr Univ Colo, 1981; Phi Betta Kappa Hon Soc; Am Psych Asn; assoc mem, Ctr Study Women; Minority Fed Am Psychol Asn, 1981-84; Grad Teaching Fed Univ Ore, 1981-85; Res Grant Ctr Study Women Univ Ore, 1987; Jane Grant Dissertation Fed Univ Ore, 1987. **Business Addr:** Owner, RubKe Bheavioral Healthcare Consulting, Washington, DC 20002.

### BROWN, RUBYE GOLSBY

Educator, executive. **Personal:** Born Aug 20, 1923, Birmingham, AL; daughter of Clifford Golsby (deceased) and Augusta B Blalock Johnson (deceased); married Robert L; children: Harlean, Charles, Louis, Carson, Gloria, Robin & Debbie. **Educ:** Youngstown State Univ, BA, 1953, MD, 1981. **Career:** Ft Leonard-Wood, dept head, 1959-60, substitute teacher, 1960-61; Renanos' Jewelery, credit mgr, 1962-64; Mahoning Co Treas, dept treas, 1965-77; Princeton Sch, teacher, 1977; Youngstown Pub Sch, sch teacher, 1977-90; Round Rock Independent Sch Dist, high sch teacher, 1991-. **Orgs:** Youngstown Bd Educ, 1977; comt mem, State Health Bd, 1979-88; bd mem, State Health, Dept Ohio, 1980; Am Univ Women, 1981-; Red Cross; bd mem, City Cedar Park, 1999; vpres, trustee, exec bd, Internal Mgt Proj Rev; bd trustee, Educ Opportunity Youngstown; vice-chmn, Consumer Protect Agency; Nat Asn Adv Colored People; vpres, Community Action Agency; Cavelle Club; bd dirs, Negro Bus & Prof Club; Planning & Develop State Health Dept; chair, CAC; trustee, Health Syst Agency, E Ohio Valley; Nat Coun Negro Women; exec comt mem, Dem party; pres, Mahoning County Court-Watch; PoliceTask Force. **Honors/Awds:** Cert, Community Involvement & Vol Work, Jr Civic League, 1986; Appointed by Gov, State Health Bd, Columbus, OH, 1986; Only Black 19th Dist, DelPres Carter; Community Serv, Cong Carney Award. **Home Addr:** 1700 Tracy Miller Lane, Cedar Park, TX 78613-3565. **Business Addr:** Round Rock Independent School District, 1311 Round Rock Ave, Round Rock, TX 78681, **Business Phone:** (512)464-5000.

### BROWN, RUSHIA (YERUSHIA BROWN)

Executive, basketball player. **Personal:** Born May 5, 1972, Bronx, NY; daughter of Angie. **Educ:** Furman Col, BA, sociol, 1994; George Washington Univ-Sch Bus, MBA, bus, 2014. **Career:** Basketball player (retired); FIBA Europe, player, 1994-2004; Women's Nat Basketball Asn, player, 1997-2004; pres; Cleveland Rockers, forward & ctr, 1997-2002; Eastern Conf Champs, 1997; Charlotte Sting, forward, 2003; Overtime Basketball Acad, pres, 2007-; Nfinity, Basketball Brand Mgr, 2011-14; Young Black Entrepreneur, owner, 2014-. **Orgs:** Pres & chief exec officer, Women's Prof Basketball Alumni Asn, 2011-. **Home Phone:** (678)270-6316. **Business Addr:** Basketball Brand Manager, Nfinity, 1226 Spring St NW, Atlanta, GA 30309, **Business Phone:** (404)478-7873.

### BROWN, SHADEY K. TURNER

Lawyer. **Personal:** Born Jan 1, 1972. **Educ:** Hampton Univ, BS, 1994; Univ Baltimore, JD, 1999. **Career:** Judge Sheila Tillerson-Adams Circuit Ct, Prince Georges Co, MD, judicial law clerk; Fannie Mae, Off Corp Justice, legal coun, currently. **Orgs:** Fel Md State Bar Asn, 2000-. **Honors/Awds:** Young leaders of the Future Award, EBONY Mag, 2002-03. **Business Addr:** Legal Counsel, Fannie Mae, 3900 Wis Ave NW, Washington, DC 20016-2892, **Business Phone:** (202)752-7000.

### BROWN, SHANNON A.

Businessperson, executive. **Personal:** Born Jan 1, 1957?, Memphis, TN. **Educ:** Nat-Louis Univ, BA, 1978; Univ Denver, MA, 2004. **Career:** Fed Express, package handler, cargo handler, customer serv agt, vpres & gen mgr worldwide vehicle/ground support equip maintenance & air ground & freight serv southern region, FedEx Express, human resource serv mgt within Us, 1978-2005; FedEx Ground, sr vpres human resources, 2005-08; FedEx Express, sr vpres, chief human resources & diversity officer, 2008-. **Orgs:** Buckeye Technologies, Inc., 2012-; Bancorp S, Inc., 2016-; Western Gov Univ adv bd; Int Air Transp Asn Human Capital Steering Group (chmn); Univ Denver's Intermodal Transp Inst; March Dimes; Lausanne Col Sch; United Way Mid-S (chmn bd); Cent Bd Boys & Girls Club Greater Memphis; mem bd trustees, Nat-Louis Univ. **Honors/Awds:** FedEx Five Star Award; CEO Five Star Award; Distinguished Alumni Award, Nat-Louis Univ; Crystal Award, Asn Fundraising Professionals Found Philanthropy; Memphis City Schools Alumni Hall of Fame, inductee; named one of the top 50 under 50 by Black MBA magazine. **Business Addr:** FedEx, 1 Mississippi Plz, Tupelo, MS 38804.

### BROWN, SHANNON A.

Vice president (organization). **Personal:** married Beryl; children: Shanae & Cailin. **Educ:** Nat-Louis Univ, Evanston, IL, BS; Univ Denver, MS, intermodal transp, 2004. **Career:** FedEx Express, 1998-2005; FedEx Ground, sr vpres human resources, 2005-08; FedEx Express, sr vpres & chief human resources & diversity officer, 1978-; Fedex, sr vpres, human resources, 2008-. **Orgs:** Bd dir, Univ Denvers Intermodal Transp Inst; bd trustee, Nat Louis Univ; bd trustee, March Dimes; gen campaign chmn, United Way Mid-S, 2010; chair elect, United Way Mid-S, 2012-; dir, Buckeye Technologies Inc, 2012-; chair, Int Air Transp Asn. **Business Addr:** Human Resource, Senior Vice President, FedEx Express.

### BROWN, SHARON MARJORIE REVELS

Media executive, educator, consultant. **Personal:** Born Sep 26, 1938, Detroit, MI. **Educ:** Fisk Univ, attended 1957; Wayne State Univ, BA, 1960; Col Educ, post degree work, 1961; Mich Bd Pub Instrn, teaching cert, 1961; Wayne State Univ, attended 1966. **Career:** Detroit Pub Sch Hutchins Jr HS, instr, 1961-70; Hutchins Jr HS, tchr coord, 1964-65; Univ MI, educ field consult, 1969-70; Univ Mich, resources ctr coord, 1970-71; WKBD-TV, news & pub affairs sv, 1972-74; WXYZ-TV, comm rel dir, 1974. **Orgs:** Publicity com Freedom Fund Dinner Nat Asn Advan Colored People, 1977; bd dir, Nat Coun Alcholism; Homes Black C; Educ Comn New Detroit Inc; Urban Affairs Forum; Greater Detroit C C; Keep Detroit Beautiful Community; Publicity Community United Negro Col Fund; Women's Advert Club; Am Women Radio & TV; chmn, Publicity Com Afro-Am Mus Detroit; Alpha Epsilon Rho; Mich Speech Asn. **Honors/Awds:** Frat sweetheart Kappa Alpha & Psi, 1958-59; 3rd pl winner scholarship contest Miss Marracci Beauty-Talent Pageant Shriners. **Home Addr:** 20221 Grandville, Detroit, MI 48219.

### BROWN, DR. SHEILA R.

Dentist. **Educ:** Johnson C Smith Univ, BS, biol; Tex Southern Univ, MEd; Univ MI, DDS. **Career:** Assoc Dentist; SRB Dent, pvt prac, gen dentist, currently. **Orgs:** Treas, Nat Dent Asn, 2001; Seattle Study Club, 2004-. **Honors/Awds:** Received several awards & honors. **Special Achievements:** Featured on a segment of ABC7 News. **Business Addr:** General Dentist, S R B Dental P C, 850 S Wabash Ave Suite 250, Chicago, IL 60605-2182, **Business Phone:** (312)702-0734.

### BROWN, SHERMAN L.

Executive. **Personal:** Born Nov 18, 1943, Portland, OR; son of Bennie; married Mable J; children: Sherman Jr, Stephen & Stanton. **Educ:** BS, 1966; MSW, 1968. **Career:** St Elizabeth Hosp, psychiatric social worker, 1966-67; Comm Action Agency, urban planner, 1966-68; James Weldon Johnson Comm Ctr, prog dir, 1968-70; Chase Manhattan Bank, vpres, 1970-80; MCAP Group Ltd, pres, currently. **Orgs:** Bd mem, United Neighborhood Houses; bd mem, Settlement Housing Fund; founder & bd mem, Queens Youth Fedn NY; Bankers Urban Affairs Com, Kappa Alpha Psi Frat; chmn bd dir, Neighborhood Housing Serv Jamaica Inc; bd mem, S Jamaica Restoration Devel Corp; vpres bd, Bronx River Comm Ctr; bd mem, Nat Scholar Serv Fund Negro Students; Univ S Civ Rights Comm; chmn bd, Queens Urban League; bd mem, NAHRO Wash DC; bd mem, Nat Housing Conf Bd Wash DC; bd mem, United Black Men Queens Co; Nat Asn Redevelop Officials; chmn bd, Queens Co Overall Econ Devel Corp; Instr, Urban Econ Amer Inst Banking; lectr, Banks Corp Social Responsibility; lectr, Medgar Evers Col. **Honors/Awds:** Black Achiever in Industry Award, Harlem YMCA, 1973; Professional Serv Award, NY Chamber of Commerce, 1973. **Home Addr:** 1 Marlboro Rd, Westbury, NY 11590-1214. **Business Addr:** President, MCAP Group Ltd, Citibank Bldg 8950 164th St Suite 2B, Jamaica, NY 11432, **Business Phone:** (718)657-6444.

### BROWN, SIMON F.

Vice president (organization), school administrator. **Personal:** Born Sep 17, 1952, Norristown, PA; son of Albert and Lessie Forbes; married LaVerne Ransom; children: LaSia & Kevin. **Educ:** Goshen Col, BA, commun, 1974; Univ Houston, MA, higher educ admin, 1986. **Career:** Elkhart County Employ & Training Admin, Elkhart, coordr oper, 1974-77; St Joseph Hosp, mgr, AA/EEO employee rels, 1977-79; Univ Houston, asst pres affirmative action/EEO, 1979-89; Univ Med & Dent, Newark, NJ, asso cv pres, AA/EEO, 1989-95; Univ Va, Title IX coordr, Equal Opportunity Progs Officer, dir, 1995-. **Orgs:** Am Asn Affirmative Action, 1975; Exec comt mem, secy, Ensemble Theatre Co, 1989; Newark Mus Coun, 1990; Col & Univ Personnel Asn; Am Asn Higher Educ. **Home Addr:** 2960 Hannah Ave, Norristown, PA 19401-1582, **Home Phone:** (610)239-7628. **Business Addr:** Title IX Coordinator, University of Virginia, Washington Hall E Range, Charlottesville, VA 22903, **Business Phone:** (434)924-0211.

### BROWN, STANLEY DONOVAN
Government official, executive, association executive. **Personal:** Born Feb 4, 1933, Washington, DC; married Helen Hampton; children: Kevin, Kimberly & Karla. **Educ:** Southeastern Univ, BS & BA, 1962; Am Univ, attended 1968. **Career:** Dept Army, supr, comput specialist; Town Glenarden, mayor, 1983-85; Off Secy Defense, spec progs dir, 1984-. **Orgs:** Councilman, Town Glenarden, 1967-73; chmn, Glenarden Housing Authority, 1974-75; councilman, Town Glenarden, 1975-78. **Honors/Awds:** Recognition Civic Involvement, MD House Deleg, 1978; Certificate of Appreciation, Boys Scouts Am, 1980; Outstanding Loaned Exec, CFC Dept Army, 1984; Citizen of the Year, Omega Psi Phi Frat, 1984. **Home Addr:** 7916 Grant Dr, Glenarden, MD 20706-1728, **Home Phone:** (301)772-0360.

### BROWN, THOMAS EDISON, JR.
Manager, police officer, sheriff. **Personal:** Born Aug 22, 1952, Atlanta, GA; son of Thomas E Sr and Rosa B Branham; married Yolanda Smith; children: Brittany Joy & Justin Thomas. **Educ:** DeKalb Community Col, emergency med technol, 1978, fire sci technol, 1980, cert, state ga peace officer stand & training; Ga Perimeter Col, AS, Fire sci & fire-fighting, 1983; Brenau Prof Col, BS, pub admin, 1999. **Career:** Atlanta Fire Bur, dep fire chief, 1972-85; DeKalb County Pub Safety, fire chief, 1985-90, dir pub safety, 1990-, sheriff, 2001-14; Countys Police, supv; Fire, supv; Emergency Med Servs, supv; 911 Commun Ctr, supv; Animal Control Div, supv; Emergency Mgt Homeland Security, supv; T Brown Consult, 2014-. **Orgs:** Int Asn Fire Chiefs, 1983-; Nat Fire Protection Asn, 1985-; Int Asn Black Prof Firefighters, 1986-; Nat Forum Black Pub Admin, 1986-; 100 Black Men Atlanta, 1988-; S Decatur Kiwanis, 1988-; Int Asn Chiefs Police, 1990-; Nat Orgn Black Law Enforcement Execs, 1990-; DeKalb Rape Crisis Bd; Decatur Rotary Club; Alpha Phi Alpha Fraternity Inc; bd trustee, Ga Perimeter Col Found; bd dir, Nichols House; bd dir, DeKalb County Women's Resource Ctr. **Honors/Awds:** Outstanding Alumnus Award, DeKalb Community Col, 1986; Outstanding Service Award, Toney Gardens Civic Asn, 1986; Alumni of the Year, 2001; Law Enforcement Award, Nat Asn Blacks Criminal Justice; Alumni of the Year Award, Leadership DeKalb; Public Safety Officer of the Year, South DeKalb Rotary Club. **Special Achievements:** Fifth Black Fire Chief in the history of the DeKalb County; Youngest fire chief in the Georgia appointed at the age of 35, 1985. **Home Addr:** 2813 Riderwood Dr, Decatur, GA 30033, **Home Phone:** (404)982-9124. **Business Addr:** Director, DeKalb County Public Safety, 3630 Camp Circle, Atlanta, GA 30303, **Business Phone:** (404)294-2501.

### BROWN, THOMAS K. (TONY BROWN)
Executive, association executive, executive director. **Educ:** Am Int Col, Springfield, Mass, BBA, econs. **Career:** Digital Equip Corp, 1976-91; Qual mgt syst Inc, exec dir; United Technologies Automotive, vpres, supply mgt, 1997-99; Ford Motor Co, Ford Purchasing Global Strategic Planning & Process Leadership, dir, Mfg Procurement Opers, exec dir, vpres global purchasing, 2002-04, sr vpres global purchasing, 2004-08, group vpres global purchasing, 2008-13; Miniature Precision Components Inc, Sr Vpres Global Purchasing, Currently. **Orgs:** Mem & co-chmn, Procurement Coun, US Hisp Chamber Com; Mich Minority Supplier Develop Coun; bd dir, Am Red Cross; bd dir, Bus Social Responsibility; chmn, Mich Disabled Veterans Roundtable, 2013-14; bd dir, 3M US Co, 2013-. **Honors/Awds:** Keep Hope Alive Award, Rainbow & PUSH, 2006; Keeper of the Dream, Nat Action Network; 2009 Legacy in Motion Executive of the Year Award, The Michigan Chronicle, 2009. **Business Addr:** Senior Vice President, Miniature Precision Components Inc, 820 Wis St, Walworth, WI 53184, **Business Phone:** (262)275-5791.

### BROWN, TIMOTHY DONELL
Football player, radio host. **Personal:** Born Jul 22, 1966, Dallas, TX; married Sherice Weaver; children: Taylor, Timothy Jr & Tamar. **Educ:** Univ Notre Dame, sociol, 1987. **Career:** Football player (retired); Los Angeles Raiders, wide receiver & punt returner & kick returner, 1988-94; Oakland Raiders, wide receiver & punt returner, 1995-2003; Tampa Bay Buccaneers, wide receiver, 2004; Drive for Diversity prog, Nat Asn Stock Car Auto Racing; Indoor Football League Tex Revolution, Gen Mgr & Co-Owner; WRDI, radio host, Currently. **Honors/Awds:** First team All-Am, 1986-87; Heisman Trophy, 1986-87; Walter Camp Award, 1987; Sporting News Player of the Year, 1987; UPI Player of the Year, 1987; Unanimous All-American, 1987; Pro Bowl, 1988, 1991, 1993-95, 1997, 2001; College Football Hall of Fame, 2009; Alumni of the Year, Walter Camp, 2009; Silver Anniversary Award, Nat Col Athletic Asn, 2012; Bay Area Sports Hall of Fame, 2013; Pro Football Hall of Fame, 2015. **Special Achievements:** Film: Little Giants, actor, 1994; Wheel of Fortune, 2003; The Drew Pearson Show, 2013. **Home Addr:** 971 Fairway Dr, Duncanville, TX 75137, **Home Phone:** (214)224-0081.

### BROWN, TODD
Administrator, executive. **Educ:** Colgate Univ, BA, sociol, 1971; Wharton Grad Sch, MBA, mkt, 1980. **Career:** Executive (retired); Kraft Foods N Am, exec vpres, 1980-2003, e Com div, pres; Food com, bd; Advo Inc, bd; Cleveland bank, chmn; Chicago & detroit bank, chmn; Shore Bank Corp, dir, 2000-03, vchmn, 2003-09. **Orgs:** Kraft's African Am Coun; bd mem, Johnson Diversey Inc; bd mem, Colgate Univ; bd mem, Natl Charter Sch Inst; Jessie Owens Found; Shore Bank Corp mgt comt; bd dir, Horizon Blue Cross Blue Shield Nj. **Business Addr:** Vice Chairman, ShoreBank Corporation, 7054 S Jeffrey Blvd, Chicago, IL 60649, **Business Phone:** (800)669-7725.

### BROWN, TODD C.
Executive. **Personal:** Born Jun 12, 1949; married Sheryl; children: Heather. **Educ:** Colgate Univ, BA, sociol, 1971; Columbia Univ, MA, higher educ admin; Wharton Grad Sch, MBA, mkt, 1980. **Career:** Vice chairman (retired); ALANA Cult Ctr, dir; Colgate Univ, asst dean students; Gen Foods, asst prod mgr; Wharton Grad Sch, Univ Pa, dir stud servs; Kraft Foods Inc, Desserts & Snacks Div, exec vpres & gen mgr, 1996-97, Beverages & Desserts Div, vpres, 1980-2003, gen mgr, 1997-99; Diversey Inc, bd mem, 2001-11; ShoreBank Corp, vice chmn, 2003-09; Horizon Blue Cross Blue Shield Nj, bd dir, 2012-. **Orgs:** Exec Leadership Coun; bd mem, Johnson Diversey. **Business Addr:** Board of Directors, Horizon Blue Cross Blue Shield of New Jersey, 3 Penn Plz E, Newark, NJ 07105, **Business Phone:** (888)777-5075.

### BROWN, TOMMIE FLORENCE
Educator. **Personal:** Born Jun 25, 1934, Rome, GA. **Educ:** Dillard Univ, BA, 1957; Atlanta Univ, Sch Social Work, 1957; Wash Univ, St Louis, Mo, MSW, 1964; Columbia Univ, DSW, 1984, PhD, social work. **Career:** Educator (retired), Tennessee house representative; Tenn Dept Pub Welfare, child welfare worker, 1957-64, case worker, supvr & dir training, 1954-71; Univ Tenn, Chatanooga, asst prof sociol, 1971-73, dir human serv, 1977-82, SOCW & proj dir, dept head, 1977-82, assoc prof, 1982; Tenn House Representatives, Chatanooga, mem, 1992-2002; Tenn Gen Assembly, bills sponsored & co-sponsored, currently. **Orgs:** Nat AsnAdvan Colored People, Chattanooga Br, 1964-; League Women Voters, 1968-70; bd mem, Chattanooga Model Cities Prog, 1969-73; Nat sec, Nat Asn Social Workers, 1972-74; comnr, Chattanooga & Hamilton Metro Charter; steering commt, Urban Forum, 1980-81; bd mem, Chattanooga Psych Ctr, 1982-; Joint Lottery Scholar Comt Joint Select Comt Pensions & Ins House Domestic Rels Subcomt; co-founder, Chattanooga chap Nat Polit Cong Black Women; Hamilton County Dem Women's Club; Pi Omega Chap Alpha Kappa Alpha Sorority; 98th through 107th Gen Assemblies; House State & Local Govt Comt; House Finance, Ways & Means Comt; House Gen Sub-comt State & Local Govt; Joint Fiscal Rev Comt. **Honors/Awds:** Woman of the Year Award, Alpha Kappa Alpha, Pi Omega Chap, 1968-69; National Social Worker of the Year, Nat Asn Social Workers Inc, 1970; Tommie Brown Day, City of Chattanooga, 1970; Distinguished Alumni Award, Wash Univ, St Louis, 1971. **Special Achievements:** First African American Male Elected To Represent The Area In The State Legislature. **Home Addr:** 603 N Highland Park Ave, Chattanooga, TN 37404-1226, **Home Phone:** (423)622-7474. **Business Addr:** Tennessee House Representatives, Tennessee General Assembly, 301 6th Ave North, Nashville, TN 37243, **Business Phone:** (615)741-4374.

### BROWN, TONY
Columnist, television producer, educator. **Personal:** Born Apr 11, 1933, Charleston, WV; son of Royal and Catherine Davis; children: Byron Anthony. **Educ:** Wayne State Univ, BA, sociol, 1959, MA, psychiat social work, 1961; Univ Mich, LLD, 1975. **Career:** Black J Nat Educ TV, exec producer; Detroit Courier, city ed; numerous mag, pub & ed; var TV shows, host & moderator; Howard Univ Sch Commun, first dean prof & founder, 1971-2009; Howard Univ, commun Conf; Cent Wash State Univ, vis prof; Tony Brown Prods, founder & pres, 1977-; Tony Browns Jour, exec producer & host, 1978-; Tony Brown Prod Inc, founder, currently; White Girl, dir, producer, writer, 1990; Hampton Univs Scripps Howard Sch, dean, 2004. Books: Black Lies, White Lies: The Truth According to Tony Brown, 1995; Empower the People, 1999; What Mama Taught Me: The Seven Core Values of Life, 2004; The Mystical Two: Lucid Dreams, 2015. **Orgs:** Chmn bd, WHUR-FM radio, 1971-74; founder & chmn, Buy Freedom Comm, 1985; founder & pres, Video Duplication Ctr, 1986; Nat Asn Black Media Producers; Nat Asn Black TV & Film Producers; bd govs, Nat Commun Coun; adv bd, Nat Coun Black Studies; bd mem, Nat Cent Afro-Am Artists; Nat Black United Fund; Commun Comm, Nat Inst Ment Health; bd dir, Asn Study Afro-Am Life & Hist; bd dir, Nat Bus League; bd dir, Harvard Found; Nat Newspaper Pub Asn; fel Alpha Phi Alpha; Fed City Col; chairperson, Nat Orgn Black Col Alumni; bd trustee, Shaw Divinity Sch; Republican Party, 1990; Nat Acad Tv Arts & Sci Silver Circle, 2002. **Home Addr:** 444 Central Pk W Suite 19B, New York, NY 10025. **Business Addr:** Founder, Tony Brown Productions Inc, 2214 Frederick Douglass Blvd Suite 124, New York, NY 10026, **Business Phone:** (718)264-2226.

### BROWN, TONY (ANTHONY WILLIAM BROWN)
Basketball coach, executive, basketball player. **Personal:** Born Jul 29, 1960, Chicago, IL; married Exquilynn. **Educ:** Univ Ark, attended 1982. **Career:** Basketball player (retired), basketball coach, exec; Ohio Mixers, 1982-83; Ind Pacers, 1984-85; Kans City Sizzlers, 1985-86; Chicago Bulls, 1986; NJ Nets, 1986-87; Houston Rockets, 1988-89; Milwaukee Bucks, 1989-90, scout, 1994-97, asst coach, 2007; Los Angeles Lakers, 1990; Albany Patroons, 1990; Teorematur Arese, 1990;Utah Jazz, 1991; Los Angeles Clippers, 1991-92, asst coach; Seattle SuperSonics, 1992; Reggio Emilia, 1992-94; Portland Trailblazers, asst coach, 1997-2001; Exatone Inc, chief exec officer, 1999-; Detroit Pistons, asst coach, 2001-03; Toronto Raptors, asst coach, 2003-04; Boston Celtics, asst coach, 2004-07; Milwaukee Bucks, asst coach, 2007-08; Los Angeles Clippers, asst coach, 2009-10; Dallas Mavericks, asst coach, 2011-;TV series actor: "The Astronauts", 1960; "Dinner with the Family", 1959;"The Big Day", 1959. **Orgs:** Invited to Midwest Summer League. **Home Addr:** 5420 W Van Buren St, Chicago, IL 60644, **Home Phone:** (773)378-5193.

### BROWN, TONY
Executive, president (organization). **Personal:** Born Mar 1, 1961, Phoenix, AZ; married Janet; children: 2. **Educ:** Ariz State Univ, attended 1979; Northern Ariz Univ, attended 1981. **Career:** Circles Rec, asst mgr, 1981-82; KUKQ AM Radio, Tempe, Ariz, prom dir, 1982-85; Best Entertainment & Recreation, consult, 1982-92; Marshall Brown & Assocs, consult, 1982-92; Am Multi-Cinema Inc, mgr, 1985-88; Phoenix Suns Pro Basketball, community rels dir, 1990-91; Ariz Black Pages Inc, pres, 1992; Targeted Media Commun Inc, pres & creative dir, 1993-. **Orgs:** Bd mem, Vol Ctr Ariz, 1990-92; comt chair, Pub Rels Soc Am, 1991; bd mem, Black Theatre Troupe, 1991-96; bd mem, Am Heart Asn Ariz, 1991-93. **Home Addr:** PO Box 63701, Phoenix, AZ 85082, **Home Phone:** (602)706-1721. **Business Addr:** President, Creative Director, Targeted Media Communications Inc, 2601 N 3rd St Suite 102, Phoenix, AZ 85004-1144, **Business Phone:** (602)230-8161.

### BROWN, TONY K.
Vice president (organization). **Educ:** Am Int Col, Springfield, MA, BS, econs & finance. **Career:** QMS Inc, exec dir corp purchasing & transp; United Technologies Automotive, supply mgt vpres; Ford Motor Co, 1999-, Global Purchasing, group vpres, 2008. **Orgs:** Bd mem, Bus Social Responsibility; bd dir, 3M, 2013-. **Honors/Awds:** National Action Network, Keeper of the Dream, 2006; Rainbow/PUSH, Keep Hope Alive, 2008; "Black Enterprise," The 100 Most Powerful Executives in Corporate America, 2010.

### BROWN, TROY FITZGERALD
Football player. **Personal:** Born Jul 2, 1971, Barnwell, SC; married Kimberly; children: Sir'mon & SaanJay. **Educ:** Marshall Univ, comput Sci. **Career:** Football player (retired); New Eng Patriots, 1995-96, 2004, 2007, punt returner, 1993-94, 1998, wide receiver, 1997, 1999-2003, 2005-06. **Orgs:** Spokesperson, United Way; Troy Brown Fantasy Football Camp; Bartrum Brown Football Camp. **Honors/Awds:** State Championship, 1988; Staples Star of the Game, 1997; Miller Lite Player of the Game, 1997-01; All-Iron Award, 2002; Ron Burton Community Service Award, 2004; Distinguished Alumni Award, 2006; Three times Super Bowl champion (XXXVI, XXXVIII, XXXIX); College Football Hall of Fame, 2010. **Special Achievements:** Became the first Marshall University product to ever play for the Patriots; One of the best players in Patriots History; Played on the Family Guy episode "Patriot Games"; Cameo in the film "The Three Stooges", 2012.

### BROWN, TYRONE W.
Musician, composer, educator. **Personal:** Born Feb 1, 1940, Philadelphia, PA; son of Colbert and Rebecca. **Educ:** Berklee Sch Music, Boston, MA, cert arranging & compos, cert orchestration & mod harmony. **Career:** Pep's Show Bar, house bassist, 1964-69; Hist Jazz Lect & Concert Tours, staff bassist, 1968-71; Audi Prod TV Com Prod, staff bassist, 1970-72; Ill State Univ, instr jazz, 1971; Brigham Young Univ, instr jazz, 1972; Bellermine Col, instr jazz, 1975; Model Cities Cult Arts Prog, instr, 1972-74; Nat Endowment Arts, fel, 1983; 25th Anniversary Moers Ger Jazz Festival, Solo Bass Concert, 1996; Philadelphia Orchestra, guest artist, 1999; Pa Coun, Arts Artistic Excellence Jazz Compos, fel, 2001; Nirvana Music Co, owner & publ; PEW fel Arts, fel compos, 2003; Independence Found, fel compos, 2005; Univ Rochester, fel compos, 2005; Moon Falling Leaves, 2008; A Sky With More Stars; Magic Within; Between Midnight & Dawn; Suite John A Williams; Free Bird. **Orgs:** Dir, Music Dept, Model Cities Cult Arts Prog, 1974. **Home Addr:** 1510 St James Pl, Abington, PA 19001-1511, **Home Phone:** (215)657-4585.

### BROWN, DR. UZEE, JR.
Composer, educator, singer. **Personal:** Born Jan 1, 1950, Cowpens, SC. **Educ:** Morehouse Col, BA, 1972; Bowling Green State Univ, MMus, compos, 1974; Univ Mich, MMus, 1978, DMA, 1980; Berkshire Music Ctr, Tanglewood, MI; Graz Conserv, Austria; Univ Siena, Italy. **Career:** Singer, arranger, composer, instructor; Clark Atlanta Univ, Atlanta, GA, dept music chair, 1970-80; Opera singer, 1972-; Morehouse Col, Atlanta, GA, fac, 1973, Dept music, prof & chmn, 2002-; Performances: Treemonisha, Atlanta Symphony Orchestra, 1972; King Solomon, Emory Theater Productions, 1988; Jubilee, Alliance Theater, National Black Arts Festival, 1994; The Negro Speaks of Rivers, A Death Song, 1999; Zabette, Georgia State Univ, 1999; Composer: Musical prologue, 1988; O Redeemed! A Set of African-American Spirituals, Medium-High Voice, 1994; Zion, 1996; Be With Us All, Lord; Dide Ta Deo; Oh The Savior's Comin' Hallelu; Wake Me Up Lord; Zungo; This River; My God Is So High; Gonna Walk All Over God's Heaven; Keep Your Lamps Trimmed & Burning; Yes, Lord; Ain't-a That Good News!; Arranger: We Shall Overcome, 1999; Go Where I Send Thee; Rock-a My Soul; Come By Here; I'm Building Me a Home; John Was A Writer; Sweep Clean Mary. **Orgs:** Mem bd trustee, Morehouse Col, 1980-; co-founder, chair & bd dir, Onyx Opera Atlanta, 1988-; pres, Nat Asn Negro Musicians, 1996-2002; pres, dir choir, dir music, Ebenezer Baptist Church, currently; Cascade United Methodist Church, choral dir & dir music; Ben Hill United Methodist Church, choral dir & dir music; Mt Calvary Baptist Church. **Home Addr:** , Atlanta, SC. **Business Addr:** Professor, Chairman, Morehouse College, Rm 306 Brawley Hall 830 Westview Dr SW, Atlanta, GA 30314, **Business Phone:** (404)681-2800.

### BROWN, VIRGIL E., JR.
Judge, lawyer, association executive. **Personal:** son of Virgil E and Lurtissia; married Joann. **Educ:** Case Western Res Univ, BS, physics, 1968; Cleveland State Univ, JD, 1974. **Career:** Gen Elec, engr; Cleveland Growth Asn, consult; Cleveland Bus League, chmn; Shaker Heights Munic Ct, judge; Ohio Sch Dist, Dist 11, pvt pract atty, currently; Cleveland Civil Serv Comn, referee. **Orgs:** Comner Ohio's Minority Financing Bd; Ohio Bus League; Bankruptcy trustee, Chap 7; referee, Clevelands Civil Serv Comn; Bd's Resources Comt; Am Bar Asn; Cleveland Bus League; Citizens League; City Club; Bethany Baptist Church; Coun Smaller Enterprises; Am Judges Asn. **Honors/Awds:** Negro Womens Bus & Prof Asn, Businessman of the Year Award, 1992. **Home Addr:** 20896 S Woodland Rd, Shaker Heights, OH 44122. **Business Addr:** Attorney, State Board District 11, The Brown Bldg, Cleveland Heights, OH 44112, **Business Phone:** (216)851-3304.

### BROWN, VIVIAN
Television weathercaster, meteorologist. **Personal:** Born Greenville, MA; daughter of William and ReJohnna; children: 3. **Educ:** Jackson State Univ, BS Meteorol, 1986. **Career:** The Weather Channel, meteorologist & prod specialist, 1986-88, brdcst apprentice, 1988-89, on camera meteorologist, 1988-. **Orgs:** Am Meteorol Soc; Nat Weather Asn; Alpha Kappa Alpha Sorority Inc. **Honors/Awds:** The 20th-Century Pioneer in Atmospheric Science, 1999; Sports Hall of Fame, Jackson State Univ; NWA Seal of Approval; AMS Seal of Approval. **Business Addr:** On-camera Meteorologist, The Weather Channel, 300 Interstate N Pkwy, Atlanta, GA 30339, **Business Phone:** (770)226-0000.

### BROWN, DR. WALTER E.
Executive, educator, president (organization). **Personal:** Born Mar 4, 1931, St. Thomas; son of Arthur and Geraldine James; married Cheryl Ann Johnson; children: Walter E, Cheryl R & Jason Walter. **Educ:** City Col NY, BBA, 1958, MBA, 1961; NY Univ, MPA, 1972; Union Grad Sch, OH, PhD, 1978. **Career:** Shriro Inc, NY, admin asst, 1956-58; Dept Health Govt VI St Croix, admin, 1962-71; Hunter Col Sch Health Sci, City Univ New York, adj asst prof; Univ VI St Croix Campus, lectr, 1967-69; NENA Comprehensive Health Serv Ctr, 1971-87;

Univ Cincinnati Community Health Prog, 1973; Columbia Univ Sch Continuing Educ, 1973-75; New York Univ HEOP, 1980-83; Com Security Serv Ltd Inc, pres, currently. **Orgs:** Nat Asn Health Serv Exec; Am Pub Health Asn; Speaker House Del Nat Asn Neighborhood Health Ctrs, 1972-74; Comt Ambulatory Care Am Hosp Asn, 1972-74; pres, Nat Asn Neighborhood Health Ctrs, 1974-75; pres, Nat Asn Neighborhood Health Ctr, 1975-76; hon trustee, NY Infirmary Beekman Downtown Hosp NY, 1980-87; pres, Pub Health Asn NY City, 1986-87; ed consult, J Pub Health Policy. **Honors/Awds:** Morris De Castro Fellow, Govt VI St Thomas, 1970; Certificate of Appreciation for Outstanding Contribution to & Promotion of Community, Health Metro Boston Consumer Health Council Inc, 1975; Past President Award, Nat Asn Neighborhood Health Ctrs Inc, 1976; Past President Award, Pub Health Asn NY City, 1988. **Home Addr:** PO Box 6933, St. Croix00823, **Home Phone:** (340)778-9496. **Business Addr:** President, Commercial Security Services Limited Inc, 70 Sub Base, Charlotte Amalie, VA 00802-5812, **Business Phone:** (340)774-5000.

## BROWN, WARREN ALOYSIUS

Journalist. **Personal:** Born Jan 17, 1948, New Orleans, LA; married Mary Reed; children: Anthony, Binta Niambi & Kafi Drexel. **Educ:** Xavier Univ La, BA, engineering educ, 1969; Columbia Univ Grad Sch Jour, NY, MSJ, jour, 1971. **Career:** New York Times, nat news desk aide, 1969-70; Garden City, LI, intern reporter, 1969; New Orleans States Item, city reporter, 1971; Johnson Publ Co Jet Mag, assoc ed, 1972; Philadelphia Inquirer, gen assignment crime reporter, 1972-73, state corresp, 1973-76; Wash Post, fel, 1978; Duke Univ Sch Pub Policy, fel, 1978; writer 3 books; African Am Wheels, sr ed; Automotive Rhythms, sr ed; Wash Post, nat desktop writer, 1978-82, automotive writer, 1982-; Yomama Enterprises, owner, 1990-; Decisive Mag, sr ed; Warton Sch Bus, fel, 1997; WMET World Radio, 2007-. **Orgs:** Xavier Univ Alumni Asn, 1969; regular panelist, Am Black Forum, 1979. **Home Addr:** 5318 N 32nd St, Arlington, VA 22207. **Business Addr:** Business Writer, Auto Columnist, The Washington Post, 1150 15th St NW, Washington, DC 20071, **Business Phone:** (202)334-7685.

## BROWN, DR. WILLIAM, JR.

Physician, surgeon. **Personal:** Born Feb 5, 1935, New Haven, CT; son of William Sr and Viola P; married Sarah Robinson; children: Kirsten, Kecia, Kollette & Karlton. **Educ:** Univ Conn, BA, 1957; Howard Univ Col Med, Md, 1961; Am Bd Family Pract, dipl, 1971. **Career:** DC Gen Hosp, internship, 1961-62; Crownsville State Ment Hosp, resident psychiatrist, 1962-63; St Eliz Hosp, gen med officer, 1965; Howard Univ, Dept Family Pract, asst clin prof, 1972; pvt pract, physician. **Orgs:** Chi Delt Mu, 1960; nat bd mem, Nat Med Asn, 1965; DC Med Soc; Beta Sigma Gamma; Med Chirurgical Soc DC; fel Am Acad Family Physicians. **Home Addr:** 1210 Maple View Pl SE Suite 101, Washington, DC 20020-5746, **Home Phone:** (202)889-0088. **Business Addr:** Physician, Private Practice, 1210 Maple View Pl SE Suite 101, Washington, DC 20020-5743, **Business Phone:** (202)889-0088.

## BROWN, WILLIAM H., III

Lawyer. **Personal:** Born Jan 19, 1928, Philadelphia, PA; son of William H Jr and Ethel L Washington; married D June Hairston; children: Michele Denise & Jeanne Marie. **Educ:** Temple Univ, BS, 1952; Univ Pa, Law Sch, JD, 1955. **Career:** Norris, Schmidt, Green, Harris & Higginbotham, assoc, 1956-62; Norris, Green, Harris & Brown, partner, 1962-64; Norris, Brown & Hall, partner, 1964-68; EEOC, comnr, 1968-69, chmn, 1969-73; Dep Dist Atty, chief frauds, 1968; Practicing Law Inst, fac mem, 1970-85; Schnader, Harrison, Segal & Lewis, partner, atty, 1974-; Nat Inst Trial Advocacy, fac mem, 1980-; Philadelphia Spec Invest Comn, chmn, 1985-86; Ct Common Pleas, Philadelphia, judge pro tem; Schnader Harrison Segal & Lewis LLP, sr coun, currently; Equal Employ Opportunity Comn, chmn, 1969-73. **Orgs:** Regional bd dir, First Pa Banking & Trust Co, 1968-73; United Parcel Serv, 1983-; pres, bd dir, Nat Black Child Develop Inst, 1986-; bd dir, Nat Sr Citizens Law Ctr, 1988-94; co-chair & mem exec comt, Lawyers Comt Civil Rights Under Law; founding mem, World Asn Lawyers; permanent mem, Third Circuit Judicial Conf; Alpha Phi Alpha; Am Fed & Pa Bar Asn; life mem, Nat Bar Asn; Am Arbit Asn; Am Law Inst; Inter-Am Bar Asn; Comn Higher Educ, Mid States Asn Col; Nat Sr Citizen's Law Ctr bd dir, Community Legal Servs; Nat Asn Advan Colored People Legal Defense & Educ Fund; fel Am Bar Found; fel Int Acad Trial Lawyers; Philadelphia Diag & Rehab Ctr; arbitrator, Am Arbit Asn; mediator, Fed Dist Ct Eastern Dist Pa. **Honors/Awds:** Award of Recognition, Alpha Phi Alpha, 1969; Fidelity Award, Philadelphia Bar Asn, 1990; Dr Edward S Cooper Award, Am Heart Asn, 1995; Whitney M Young Jr Leadership Award, Urban League Philadelphia, 1996; The Whitney North Seymoure Award, Lawyers Comt Civil Rights Under Law, 1996; William Schnader Pro Bono Award, 1998; People Presidents Award, Philadelphia Nat Asn Advan Colored; Commission's Spirit of Partnership Award, EEOC, 2003; Honorary Member, UPS Corp Legal Dept, 2003; Lifetime Achievement Award, Lawyers Comt Civil Rights Under Law, 2004; The Best Lawyers in America for labor & employment law, 2005-10. **Special Achievements:** Author of numerous articles; Handbook Modern Personnel Admin, 1972. **Home Addr:** 513 Waldron Pk Dr, Haverford, PA 19041, **Home Phone:** (610)896-0684. **Business Addr:** Senior Counsel, Schnader Harrison Segal & Lewis LLP, 1600 Mkt St Suite 3600, Philadelphia, PA 19103-7286, **Business Phone:** (215)751-2434.

## BROWN, REV. WILLIAM ROCKY, III

Government official, clergy. **Personal:** Born Oct 10, 1955, Chester, PA; son of William Jr (deceased) and Gwendolyn Carraway; married Lorraine Baa; children: Catrina J, Robin & Janee. **Educ:** Cheyney State Univ, BA, polit sci, 1977, adult educ, pursued; Martin Luther King Jr Ctr, non-violent direct action, 1980; Eastern Baptist Theol Sem, MA, 1983; Jameson Christian Col, DDiv, 1986. **Career:** Chester-Upland Sch Dist, substitute teacher, 1978-81; Calvary Baptist Church, asst pastor, 1979-; State Pa, notary pub, 1980-; Pa Legis Dist 159, asst state rep, 1982-83; First Baptist Church Bernardtown, Coatesville, PA, pastor; City Chester, city, Law Enforcement Plng Comn, St Thomas, VI, spec asst, & city controller; Choices Inc, vpres; Brown & Assocs Ltd, pres & chief exec officer, currently; Bethany Baptist Church, pastor, currently. **Orgs:** Founder & pres, Chester Black Expo, 1979-; vpres, Pa Dept Environ Protection; Omega Psi Phi Fraternity; chmn, Grand Lodge Audio Comt; exec bd, Black Ministers Conf, 1979-; Widener Partnership Charter Sch Bd Trustees; exec bd, Chester Br Nat Asn Advan Colored People, 1979-; vpres, Chester Community Improv Proj, 1981-; pres, Bill Dandridge Art Gallery, 1982-; vpres, Environ Justice Adv Bd; exec bd, Kiwanis Club Chester, 1984-; ambassador, Philadelphia Div FBI; FBI Multi Cult Adv Committ; FBI Step Up Speak Up Prog; City Coun Chester; Gov's Drug & Crime Prev Prog, spec asst, currently; chmn, Del County Millions More Movement, currently; dep sr chaplain, Chester City Police Chaplain Corp; chaplain, Chester Twp Police & Fire Dept; chmn, Law Enforcement Chaplains Del County; PA rep, Int Conf Police Chaplains. **Honors/Awds:** Outstanding Young Man, US Jaycees, 1984; Johnson Freedom Award, Chester Br Nat Asn Advan Colored People, 1984; Outstanding Alumni, Nat Asn Equal Opportunity Higher Educ, 1985; Community service Award, Vision Christian Acad; Man of the Year Award, 1991; Negro Bus & Prof Womens Club; Humanitarian Award, Berean Presbyterian Church; Outstanding Volunteer Service Award; Employee of the Year, Crozer-Keystone Health Systs Community Hosp; Award of Excellence; The Omega Psi Phi Fraternity Community Service Award; Berean Presbyterian Church Humanitarian Award; Men Making A Difference Award, Am Cities Found. **Home Addr:** PO Box 642, St Thomas00804, **Home Phone:** (809)116-1790. **Business Addr:** Special Assistant Drug & Crime Prevention Program, City of Chester, 116 164 Subbase, St Thomas00801, **Business Phone:** (809)774-6400.

## BROWN, DR. WILLIAM T.

Scientist. **Personal:** Born Jun 11, 1947, Columbus, MS; children: Kesha. **Educ:** Dillard Univ, BS, 1969; Univ NMex, MS, PhD, 1984. **Career:** Los Alamos Sci Lab, tech staff physicist, 1969-73; Sandia Nat Lab, sr mem tech staff, tech staff physicist, 1974-92, sr scientist & group leader, 1992-. **Orgs:** Pres, bd dir, Albuquerque Montessori Soc, 1975-77; NM Acad Sci, 1975-; bd dir, Nat Consortium Black Prof Develop, 1976-79; Nat Asn Advan Colored People, 1976-; Am Phys Soc, 1977-; AAAS, 1978-; Am Phys Soc Topical Group Computational Physics; Topical Group Shock Propagation Condensed Matter; Soc Black Physicists, 1978-; bd dir, Nat Tech Asn, 1983-; Nat Black Child Develop Inst; fel African Sci Inst. **Home Addr:** 9917 Chapala Dr NE, Albuquerque, NM 87111-4861, **Home Phone:** (505)296-2496.

## BROWN, WILLIAM T.

Educator. **Personal:** Born Mar 11, 1929, Washington, DC; son of William and Henrietta; married Alfredine Parham; children: Camilla, Darrell & Kevin; married Frances Farmer. **Educ:** Howard Univ, BA, drama, 1951; Case Western Res Univ, MFA, dramatic arts, 1954. **Career:** Karamu Theatre, Cleveland, tech dir, 1951-59; Howard Univ, assoc prof drama, 1959-70, dept chmn, 1967-70; Theatre Univ, Ibadan, Nigeria, sr lectr & consult, 1963-65; Theatre Univ, Leeds, vis prof, 1975; Univ Md Baltimore County, assoc prof & chmn, 1970-75, 1982-94; Shakespeare Wheels, founder, 1985; Univ M, Baltimore County, assoc prof, emer prof, 1997-. **Orgs:** E Cent Theatre Conf; Am Theatre Higher Educ; Howard County Artistic Rev Panel, 1987-94; Md State Arts Coun, 1988-91; Shakespeare Theatre Asn Am, 1993-95; theater rev panel, Pa Coun Arts, 1993-94; bd dir, Columba Candlelight Soc; set designer & dir, Columbia Comm Players; dir, Arena Players, Set Design, 2000. **Honors/Awds:** Hines-Brooks Award of Excellence in Theatre, Howard Univ, 1961; Gold Medallion Award of Excellence in Theatre, Amoco Oil Co, 1971; Distinguished Program Award, Maryland Asn Higher Educ, 1988. **Special Achievements:** The Shakespeare on Wheels Research Scholarship Named at The University of Maryland Baltimore County. **Home Addr:** 8499 Spring Showers Way, Ellicott City, MD 21043-6058, **Home Phone:** (410)461-6197. **Business Addr:** Emeritus Professor, University of Maryland Baltimore County, 1000 Hilltop Cir, Baltimore, MD 21250, **Business Phone:** (410)455-2917.

## BROWN, WILLIE (WILLIAM FERDIE BROWN)

Football player, football coach. **Personal:** Born Dec 2, 1940, Yazoo City, MS; son of Leland Preston and Mary Ruth (Foster) B; married Yvonne; children: 3. **Educ:** Grambling Univ, BA, health & phys educ, 1962; Calif State Univ Long Beach, MS, educ. **Career:** Football player, football coach, (retired), executive; Denver Broncos, defensive back, 1963, Left cornerback, 1964-66; Oakland Raiders, defensive back, Right cornerback, 1967-77, Defensive back, 1978, defensive backfield coach, 1979-88, defensive backs asst, 1995-2009, adminr, 1995-, dir squad develop, 1999-; Calif State Univ Long Beach, head football coach, 1991; Los Angeles Jordan High Sch, coach, 1994. **Orgs:** La Sports; Grambling State Univ; Southwestern Athletic Conf; MS Sports Black Sports; Bay Area Sports Hall Fame. **Honors/Awds:** All-Star, Am Football League, 1964-69; Pro Bowl, Nat Football League, 1970-73; Pro Football Hall of Fame, 1984; Louisiana Sports Hall of Fame, 1992; Mississippi Sports Hall of Fame, 1994; African-American Ethnic Sports Hall of Fame, 2010. **Business Addr:** Director of Squad Development, Oakland Raiders, 1220 Harbor Bay Pkwy, Alameda, CA 94502, **Business Phone:** (510)864-5000.

## BROWN, WILLIE LEWIS, JR.

Government official, politician, mayor. **Personal:** Born Mar 20, 1934, Mineola, TX; son of Willie Lewis Sr and Minnie Collins Boyd; married Blanche Vitero; children: Susan, Robin & Michael. **Educ:** Calif State Univ, San Francisco, BA, polit sci, 1955; Hastings Col Law, JD, 1958. **Career:** Brown, Dearman & Smith, partner, 1959-; Calif St Assembly, St rep, 1965-95, speaker, 1980-95; City San Francisco, mayor, 1996-2004; San Francisco Air Am Radio, co-host, 2006; Wingz, lawyer & investor, 2012; Nat cable news network, commentator; Dem Party, mem, currently; Calif Pub Utilities Comn. **Orgs:** Calif rep Credentials Com Dem Conv, 1968; co-chairperson, Calif Deleg Nat Dem Conv, 1972; co-chmn, Calif Del Nat Black Polit Conv, 1972; bd dir, San Francisco-based biopharmaceutical co, 2015; Assembly Com Efficiency & Cost Control Elect & Reapportionment Govt Admin; Gov's Comn Aging; Joint Comt Master Plan Higher Educ; Legis Budget; Legis Space Needs Legis Audit; vice chmn, Select Comt Health Manpower; Select Com Deep Water Ports; bd mem, Nat Planned Parenthood Asn; fel Am Assembly; Nat Asn Advan Colored People; League Women Voters; adv bd mem, Calif & Tomorrow; hon lifetime mem, ILWU Local No 10; San Francisco Planning & Urban Renewal Asn; Sunset Parkside Educ & Action Com; Fillmore Merchants Improv Asn; Planning Asn Richmond; Hight Ashbury Neighborhood Coun; San Francisco Aid Retarded C Chinese Affirmative Action; founder, Willie Brown Inst Polit & Pub Serv. **Honors/Awds:** Outstanding Freshman Legislator Press Award, 1965; Man of the Year, Sun Reporter Newspaper, 1963; Children's Lobby Award for Outstanding Legis Efforts, 1974; Leader of the Future, Time Mag, 1974. **Special Achievements:** First African-American mayor of San Francisco 1996; First African American speaker of the California assembly; appeared in film, The Godfather Part III, 1990; Just One Night, 2000; George of the Jungle; The Princess Diaries; Hulk, 2003. **Home Addr:** 1524 Masonic, San Francisco, CA 94117. **Business Addr:** Member, Democratic Party, 430 S Capitol St SE, Washington, DC 20003, **Business Phone:** (202)863-8000.

## BROWN, WINSTON D.

Dean (education). **Educ:** Ala State Univ, BS, math; Univ Notre Dame, MS, math. **Career:** Xavier Univ La, dean admis, 1974-, admin assessment coordr, chief admis officer. **Orgs:** Nat Asn Col Admis Coun; Am Asn Col Registrars & Admis Officers; Cath Col Admis Asn & Col Bd; New Orleans City Planning Comn; New Orleans chap 100 Black Men Am; Kappa Alpha Psi Fraternity Inc; mem exec bd, Southern Asn Col Admis Coun. **Business Addr:** Dean of Admissions, Xavier University of Louisiana, 1 Drexel Dr, New Orleans, LA 70125-1098, **Business Phone:** (504)520-7388.

## BROWN, YERUSHIA. See BROWN, RUSHIA.

## BROWN, YOLANDA B.

Manager. **Career:** Dekalb County Sch Syst, coordr, sr proj mgr, currently. **Business Addr:** Coordinator, Facilities, Construction, Dekalb County School System, 1780 Montreal Rd, Tucker, GA 30084, **Business Phone:** (678)676-1375.

## BROWN, YVETTE MCGEE

Lawyer. **Personal:** daughter of Sylvia Kendrick; married Tony Brown; children: 3. **Educ:** Ohio State Univ, BS, jour, 1982, JD, 1985. **Career:** Franklin County Ct Common, Pleas, Domestic Rels & Juv div, elected lead Juv Ct judge, 1992-2001; Ctr Child & Family Advocacy at Nationwide C's Hosp, founder & founding pres, 2001; Ohio Elections Comn, elected, 2008; Supreme Ct Ohio, appointee, 2011-12; Jones Day LLP, partner & partner in-chg diversity Inclusion & advan 2013-. **Orgs:** Chair, United Way Cent Ohio; chair, Ohio State Univ Alumni Asn; chair & bd dir, YWCA Columbus; bd mem, Ohio Univ Found Award; chair, Ohio African Am Leadership Acad Bd. **Special Achievements:** Led the creation of the Family Drug Court and the SMART program as a family court judge; candidate for lieutenant governor of Ohio, 2010; first African American woman appointed to the Supreme Court of Ohio; served on the boards of Ohio University, The Ohio State University Medical Center, the National Council of the OSU Mortiz College of Law, M/I Holmes Inc., and the Fifth Third Bank of Central Ohio. **Business Addr:** Jones Day, 325 John H McConnell Blvd Suite 600, Columbus, OH 43215, **Business Phone:** (614)281-3867.

## BROWN-CHAPPELL, DR. BETTY L.

Public speaker. **Personal:** Born Nov 25, 1946, San Francisco, MI; daughter of Benjamin F and Clara Lucille; married Micheal J; children: Michael Jahi & Aisha Ebony. **Educ:** Univ Mich, BA, 1969, MSW, 1971; Univ Chicago, PhD, social policy, 1991. **Career:** City Detroit, admin, asst, 1973-77; Walter Reuther Sr Citizens Ctr, asst dir, 1977-79; Univ Ill, Chicago, vis instr, 1979-80; NE Ill Univ, assoc prof, 1980-84; Univ Chicago, asst dean, 1984-89; Univ Mich, fel, 1991-92, asst prof, 1992-96; Eastern Mich Univ, social work prof, 1996-2013, BSW Prog, dir, 2000-02, EMU McNair Scholars Prog, dir, 2008-11, emerita, 2013; NASW-MI, pres, 2002-04; JAMBE Group, consult; Author: Open Secrets: A poor person's life in higher education, journal articles. **Orgs:** Delta Sigma Theta Sorority; Nat Asn Social Work, Mich Chap, 1997-; bd mem, 13th Cong Dist, Sr Citizens Adv Coun, 1997-99; Coun Social Work Educ, Comn Racial, Ethnic, Cult Diversity, 1999-2001. **Home Addr:** 44999 Claymore Dr, Canton, MI 48187, **Home Phone:** (734)207-5035. **Business Addr:** Consultant, The JAMBE Group, Canton, MI 48187, **Business Phone:** (734)451-0063.

## BROWN-DICKERSON, TONIA

College administrator. **Career:** Savannah State Univ, interim dir comprehensive coun, asst to vpres stud affairs, currently; Southern Ill Univ, coordr. **Business Addr:** Interim Director, Savannah State University, 3219 Col St, Savannah, GA 31404, **Business Phone:** (912)356-2285.

## BROWN-ELLEN, KIMI L.

Association executive, businessperson, auditor. **Educ:** Univ Ill, Urbana-Champaign, BS, accountancy, 1992. **Career:** Deloitte & Touche LLP, auditor, 1992-94; City Col Chicago, internal auditor, 1995-97; Ace Hardware Corp, internal auditor, 1995; Benford Brown & Assocs LLC, co-founder & managing partner, 1996-; Ameritech Corp, sr internal auditor, 1997-2000; Southeast Chicago Chamber Com, pres, 2005-14. **Orgs:** Active mem, Am Inst Cert Pub Acct Inc; Ill CPA Soc; Nat Asn Black Accts; Nat Asn Female Execs; Alpha Kappa Alpha Sorority Inc; Jack & Jill Am; bd dir, Game Time Inc, currently; bd dir, Imani Pearls Community Develop Found; treas, Bingham Human Servs Inc; small pract subcomt, Ill CPA Soc, currently; pres, 87th St Stony Island Chamber Com. **Business Addr:** Managing Partner, Benford Brown & Associates LLC, 8135 S Stony Island Ave 1st Fl, Chicago, IL 60617, **Business Phone:** (773)731-1300.

## BROWN-FRANCISCO, TERESA ELAINE

Activist, state government official. **Personal:** Born Feb 25, 1960, Oklahoma City, OK; daughter of Herman and Mary McMullen; married Andre; children: Aaron Geoffrey (deceased) & Addam Michael. **Educ:** Phillips Univ, Enid, OK, 1980; Okla City Univ, Oklahoma City, OK, BA, 1983. **Career:** KOCO-TV, Okla City, OK, assoc news producer, 1984-86; Bellmon Gov, Campaign, Okla City, OK, asst press secy, 1986; Bellmon Gov, Inaugural Comn, Okla City, OK, press secy, 1986-87; Off Gov, Okla City, OK, asst gov soc servs & ethnic affairs, 1987-91; Total Concept Consults Inc, entrepreneur, 1992-; Mkt & Visual Commun, pub rels; Chevron Texaco Corp, mgr. **Orgs:** Bd dir, Urban League Greater Oklahoma City, 1987-91; bd dir, Metrop Fair Housing Coun, 1987-; Exec Leadership Inst, Nat Forum for Black Pub Adminrs, 1989-90; co-chmn, Adv Comt, Casey Family Prog, 1990-94;

bd dir, Inst Child Advocacy, 1988-91; bd dir, Oklahoma City Univ Alumni Asn, 1991-95; Jr Symphony; Econ Roundtable; Minority Bus Consortium. **Business Addr:** President, Total Concept Consults Inc, 1010 NE 14th St, Oklahoma City, OK 73117-1002, **Business Phone:** (405)272-9333.

### BROWN-GUILLORY, ELIZABETH

Writer, educator, playwright. **Personal:** Born Jun 20, 1954, Lake Charles, LA; daughter of Leo and Marjorie Savoie; married Lucius M Guillory; children: Lucia Elizabeth. **Educ:** Univ Southwestern La, BA, eng & psychol, 1975, MA, eng, 1977; Fla State Univ, PhD, eng, 1980. **Career:** Univ Southwestern La, grad teaching asst, 1976-77; Fla State Univ, res fel, grad teaching asst, 1977-79; Univ SC, Spartanburg, asst prof eng, 1980-82; Dillard Univ, asst prof eng, 1982-88; Univ Houston, african am studies fac affil, 1990-2009, Dept Eng, assoc prof eng, 1988-98; prof, 1998-2009; Tex Southern Univ, assoc provost & assoc vpres acad & fac affairs, 2009-15, distinguished prof theatre, 2009-, Thomas F Freeman Hons Col fel, 2010-, Interim Dean, 2014-. Editor: Wines in the Wilderness: Plays by African-American Women from the Harlem Renaissance to the Present, 1990; Women of Color: Mother-Daughter Relationships in 20th Century Literature, 1996; Middle Passages; Healing Place of History: Migration and Identity in Black Women's Literature, 2006. Author: Their Place on the Stage: Black Women Playwrights in America, 1988; playwright: Somebody Almost Walked off With all of My Stuff, 1982; Bayou Relics, 1983; Marry Me Again, 1984; Mam Phyllis, Snapshots of Broken Dolls, 1990; Saving Grace, 1993; Just a Little Mark, 1993; Missing Sister, 1996; La Bakair, 2001; When the Ancestors Call, 2003; The Break of Day, 2003. Plays; Bayou Relics, 1983; Snap shots of Broken Dolls, 1987; Mam phyllis, 1990; La Bakair, 2001; Break Of The Day, 2003; When the ancestors call, 2003. **Orgs:** African Lit Asn; Am Lit Asn; Asn Study Worldwide African Diaspora; Black Europ Studies in Transnational Perspectives; Caribbean Studies Asn; Col Lang Asn; Southern Conf Afro-Am Studies Inc; Col Lang Asn; pres, S Cent Mod Lang Asn; mem exec comt, Mod Lang Asn; Int Women's Writing Guild; Am Soc Theatre Res; Conf Col Teachers Eng Tex; Black Theater Network; Asn Theatre Higher Educ; founder, fac adv & mentor, Houston Suitcase Theater; Am Lit Asn; founder, Erzulie; consult, Nat endowment for Humanities; bd dir, Greater Houston Women's Chamber Com. **Home Addr:** 4390 Harvest Lane, Houston, TX 77004, **Home Phone:** (713)748-3941. **Business Addr:** Distinguished Professor of Theatre, Associate Provost & Associate Vice President for Academic and Faculty Affairs, Texas Southern University, 3100 Cleburne St, Houston, TX 77004, **Business Phone:** (713)313-1180.

### BROWN-PHILPOT, STACY

Executive. **Personal:** Born Jan 1, 1976?, Detroit, MI; children: 2. **Educ:** Univ Pa, BS, 1997; Stanford Univ Grad Sch Bus, MBA, 2002. **Career:** Price Waterhouse Coopers, sr assoc, 1997-99; Goldman Sachs, sr analyst, 1999-2000; Wily Technol, bus develop mgr, 2003; Google, dir sales finance, 2003-07, dir consumer & enterprise opers, 2007-09, sr dir online sales & opers India, 2009-10, sr dir global consumer opers, 2010-12; Google Ventures, entrepreneur residence, 2012; TaskRabbit, chief operating officer, 2013-16, chief exec officer, 2016-. **Orgs:** Delta Sigma Theta Sorority, 1996-; Trustees' Coun Penn Women, Univ Pa, 2014-; adv coun Stanford Grad Sch Bus, 2015-16; bd mem, Friends Youth, 2008-13; bd mem, Stanford Grad Sch Bus Alumni Asn Bd Dirs; bd mem, Black Girls CODE, 2015-; bd mem, HP, 2015-. **Honors/Awds:** AdColor Change Agent, Advertising Age, 2008; listed in "46 Most Important Blacks in Technology," Business Insider, 2014; listed in Fortune 2015 40 Under 40, Fortune Magazine, 2015; Henry Crown Fellowship, Aspen Inst, 2016. **Special Achievements:** Author, Vault Guide to Mastering Accounting, 1998. **Business Addr:** Task Rabbit, 425 2nd St Suite 5, San Francisco, CA 94107-1487.

### BROWN-WRIGHT, FLONZIE B.

Executive. **Personal:** Born Aug 12, 1942, Farmhaven, MS; daughter of Frank Sr and Littie P Dawson; married William Russell; children: Cynthia Verneatta Goodloe-Palmer, Edward Goodloe Jr & Lloyd Darrell Goodloe. **Educ:** Tougaloo Col; Millsaps Col. **Career:** Tougaloo Col, Fain fel; Madison County, Election Comnr; State Equal Employ Opport Officer & Training Coordr, recruiter, 1966-73; Millsaps Col, Inst Polit, vpres, 1969-73; US Equal Employ Opport Comn, investr, 1974-89; FBW & Assoc Inc, pres & chief exec officer, currently; Miami Univ, stud affairs scholar residence, 2003-. Book: Looking Back to Move Ahead, 1994. Film: Standing On My Sisters Shoulders, 1960. **Orgs:** Nat Coun Negro Women; bd dir, Nat Asn Advan Colored People, 1964-66; Southern Christian Leadership Conf; bd pres, Nat Caucus & Ctr Black Aged; founding mem & pres, Women Progress; charter mem, Bethune Day Care Ctr; founder, Vernon Dahmer Singers Freedom; pres, AFGE Local 3599 AFL-CIO; founder, Flonzie B. Wright Scholar Fund; Nat Asn Female Execs. **Home Addr:** 11942 Moses Rd, Germantown, OH 45327-8507, **Home Phone:** (937)855-2663. **Business Addr:** Student Affairs Scholar in Residence, Miami University, Middletown Campus, Middletown, OH 45042, **Business Phone:** (513)727-3200.

### BROWNE, ANUCHA CHIOGU. See SANDERS, ANUCHA BROWNE.

### BROWNE, DR. CRAIG C.

Educator. **Personal:** Born Jan 29, 1947, Philadelphia, PA; son of Carter E and Juliette; married Yvonne; children: Craig Jr, Jeffrey & Christopher. **Educ:** Cheyney Univ, BS, 1969, sec educ admin cert, 1975; Temple Univ, EdM, 1973, EdD, 1981. **Career:** Educator (retired); Philadelphia Sch Dist, math teacher, 1969-88, vice prin, 1988-90, prin, 1990-95; Newark NJ Pub Sch, Harold Wilson Mid Sch, prin, 1995-2007. **Orgs:** Chair, Christian Stronghold Baptist Church, Deacon's Ministry, 1982-; Christian Stronghold Baptist Church, Church Bible Inst, 1985-87; sch bd dir, Cheltenam Sch Dist, 1991-93; life mem, Alpha Phi Alpha Fraternity Inc; educ dir, Civil Air Patrol, Sayre Jr High Composite Sq; Orgn African Am Adminrs, 1996-. **Home Addr:** 7769 Green Valley Rd, Wyncote, PA 19095, **Home Phone:** (215)572-7865.

### BROWNE, JERRY (JEROME AUSTIN BROWNE)

Baseball player, athletic coach. **Personal:** Born Feb 13, 1966, St. Croix. **Career:** Baseball player (retired), coach; Tex Rangers, infielder, 1986-88; Cleveland Indians, infielder, 1989-91; Oakland Athletics, infielder, 1992-93; Fla Marlins, infielder, 1994-95; Toronto Blue Jays, minor league infield instr, 2002; Augusta Green Jackets, coach, 2005; Savannah Sand Gnats, hitting coach, 2006; Hagerstown Suns, 2007; Potomac Nationals, 2008-09; Syracuse Chiefs, hitting coach, 2010-11. **Special Achievements:** Flim: Kill You Twice, 1998. **Home Addr:** 2A Prince St, Christiansted, VI 00820-4801. **Business Addr:** Hitting Coach, Syracuse Chiefs, 1 Tex Simone Dr, Syracuse, NY 13208, **Business Phone:** (315)474-7833.

### BROWNE-MARSHALL, GLORIA J.

College teacher, writer, founder (originator). **Career:** Southern Poverty Law Ctr, civil rights atty; Community Legal Serv, civil rights atty; NAACP Legal Defense Fund Inc, civil rights atty; John Jay Col Criminal Justice, New York, assoc prof const law & criminal justice; syndicated columnist. **Orgs:** Founder & dir, Nat Press Club; Law & Policy Group Inc; Alpha Kappa Alpha Sorority Inc; PEN Am Ctr; Dramatists Guild; Mystery Writers Am; Nat Asn Black Journalists; Women's City Club; Nat Bar Asn. **Honors/Awds:** Award Recipient of: Nat Fedn Press Women; Del Press Asn; Asn Black Women's Attorneys; New York County Lawyers' Ida B. Wells, 2009; Wiley College's (Texas) Woman of Excellence in Law. **Special Achievements:** Author of "Race, Law, and American Society: 1607 to Present" (Routledge), "The Constitution: Major Cases and Conflicts" (Pearson Learning Solutions), and "Black Women and the Law: Salem Witches to Civil Rights Activists"; "International Crime and Justice," Contributor; first African American woman to receive credentials to cover the U.S. Supreme Court; playwright of seven plays.

### BROWNER, JOEY MATTHEW

Football player, radio host, founder (originator). **Personal:** Born May 15, 1960, Warren, OH. **Educ:** Univ Southern Calif, pub admin. **Career:** Football player (retired), radio host; Minn Vikings, defensive player & tackler, 1983-91, Tampa Bay Buccaneers, defensive player & tackler, 1992; Fox Sports, co-host; Nationwide Sports, host, currently. **Orgs:** Organizer, 1995 Native Am Games; founder, Joey Browner Found, 2009-. **Honors/Awds:** Selected first team All PAC 10; UPI All Coast; Col Pro Football Newsweekly second-team All-Am; AP third-team All-Am; USC's MVP; Indicted in the Vikings Ring of Honor, 1980; capt of team in Japan Bowl, 1983; ; Pro Bowl teams, 1985-90; African-American Hall of Fame, 2004; NFL Pro Bowl rec. **Special Achievements:** Five times NFL Hall of Fame Nominee; NFL Pro Bowl record with 3 fumble recoveries; First round draft pick out of USC for the Minnesota Vikings; Hall of Fame NFL ballot for the the last 5 years straight, 2005, 2006, 2007, 2008 & 2009. **Business Addr:** Founder, Joey Browner Foundation, PO Box 50641, Mendota, MN 55150, **Business Phone:** (651)983-5616.

### BROWNER, ROSS D.

Chief executive officer, marketing executive. **Personal:** Born Mar 22, 1954, Warren, OH; son of Jimmie Lee Sr and Julia Geraldine Cook; married Shayla Simpson; children: Rylan Ross & Max Starks IV. **Educ:** Notre Dame, BA, 1978; Southern Ohio Col. **Career:** Football player (retired), chief exec officer; Cincinnati Bengals, defensive lineman, 1978-86; Houston Gamblers, defensive lineman, 1985; Green Bay Packers, defensive lineman, 1987; Cold well Banker, Cincinnati, OH, realtor, 1989-91; Browner Productions Inc, chief exec officer, 1995-. **Orgs:** Nat Football League Players Asn; Nat Football League Alumni; Notre Dame Alumni; exec bd, Mid Tenn; Boys Scouts Am. **Home Addr:** 1135 Flamingo Dr SW, 7900 Indian Springs Dr, Atlanta, GA 30311, **Home Phone:** (615)646-7900. **Business Addr:** Chief Executive Officer, Browner Productions Inc, 7900 Indian Springs Dr, Nashville, TN 37221, **Business Phone:** (615)646-7900.

### BROWNING, REV. DR. JO ANN

Clergy. **Personal:** Born Sep 30, 1949, Nantucket, MA; daughter of James and Ruth Leonard; married Grainger; children: Grainger III & Candace. **Educ:** Boston Univ, BA, communs, 1976; Howard Univ, MDiv, 1986, DMin, 1991. **Career:** Howard Univ, grad admis counr, 1979-; Hemingway Mem AME Church, minister, 1982-86; Ebenezer African Methodist Episcopal Church, co-pastor, 1986-, pastor, currently. **Orgs:** Founder, Journey of Faith, 2006; fel Delta Sigma Theta Sorority Inc. **Honors/Awds:** Benjamin E Mays Fellow, Howard Univ; Pew Fellow, Howard Univ & Whos Who Among Am Cols & Univs, 1989-90; Honorable member, Delta Sigma Theta, 2002. **Special Achievements:** Released her first book Our Savior, Our Sisters, Ourselves: Biblical Teachings & Reflections on Women's Relationships. **Home Addr:** 606 Luxor Ct, Fort Washington, MD 20744, **Home Phone:** (301)292-4511. **Business Addr:** Co-pastor, Pastor, Ebenezer African Methodist Episcopal Church, 7707 Allentown Rd, Fort Washington, MD 20744, **Business Phone:** (301)248-8833.

### BROWNING, JOHN EDWARD

Football player. **Personal:** Born Sep 30, 1973, Miami, FL. **Educ:** Univ WVa. **Career:** Football player (retired); Kans City Chiefs, defensive tackle & right defense end & left defense end & left defense tackle & right defense tackle & Nose Tackle, 1996 & 2005; Denver Broncos, 2007. **Honors/Awds:** Rookie of the Year, 1996.

### BROWNLEE, DENNIS J.

Executive. **Personal:** son of Rufus Wesley and Helen Johnson (deceased); married Gabriella Morris. **Educ:** Princeton Univ, AB, econs, 1974; George Washington Univ; Am Univ. **Career:** US Satellite Broadcasting Co Inc, vpres, corp affairs & bd dirs, 1982-97; New Urban Entertainment Tv Inc, founder & chief exec officer, 1997-2001; Clear Channel Mkt Partnerships, mng dir, vpres, 2003-05; Advan Inc, chief exec officer; Premiere Radio Networks, vpres & mng dir urban sales & mkt, 2005-16; Connective Advisors, partner, 2016-. **Orgs:** trustee, Am Univ; trustee, Princeton Univ; chmn, Space Sta Tv LLC. **Business Addr:** Partner, Connective Advisors LLC, 519 S Maple Ave, Basking Ridge, NJ 07920.

### BROWNLEE, DENNIS JAMES

Executive. **Personal:** son of Helen Johnson (deceased) and Rufus Wesley; married Gabriella Enid Morris. **Educ:** George Washington Univ; Princeton Univ BA, econs, 1974; Am Univ Grad Studies. **Career:** New Urban Entertainment TV Inc, founder & chief exec officer; ADVAN Inc, founder & chief exec officer; US Satellite Broadcasting Co Inc, vpres; Clear Channel Mkg Partnerships, managing dir; Space Sta Tv LLC, chmn; Premiere Radio Networks, vpres & managing dir urban sales mkt, 2005-. **Orgs:** Trustee, Princeton Univ. **Business Addr:** Vice President, Managing Director, Premiere Radio Networks, 15260 Ventura Blvd, Sherman Oaks, CA 91403, **Business Phone:** (818)377-5300.

### BROWNLEE, DR. GERALDINE DANIELS

Educator. **Personal:** Born Apr 13, 1925, East Chicago, IN; daughter of Jerry and Nellie Cossey; married Brady. **Educ:** WVa State Col, BA, biol & Span, 1947; Univ Ill, attended 1950; Univ Mich, attended 1950; Univ Chicago, MST, urban educ, 1967, PhD, 1975; Ind Univ, post doctoral study. **Career:** Educator (retired); Cook County Dept Pub Welfare, 1947, caseworker, 1948-55; Univ Mich, Lions fel, 1950; Chicago Pub Sch, teacher, 1955-66; Univ Chicago, Grad Sch Educ, staff assoc & asst dir teacher training, 1967-70; Univ Ill Chicago Col Educ, asst prof, 1971-90, asst dean stud serv, 1971-74; Pk Forest ill Sch Dist, dir title VII proj, 1975-76; Am Coun Educ, fel, 1979; Univ Southern Miss, vis prof, 1990; Univ Ill, assoc prof emer, 1990; DePaul Univ, Ctr Urban Educ, consult, 1995-96. **Orgs:** Chairperson, Chicago Urban League Educ Adv Comm, 1983-90; bd dir, Chicago Urban League, 1984-90; bd dir & vpres, Young Women Christian Asn, 1991-97; comnr, Chicago United Way allocations, 1992-97; Am Educ Res Asn; Nat Soc Study Educ; Am Asn Higher Educ; Alpha Kappa Alpha; Am Asn Univ Women; Links Inc; Educ Network; int vpres, Pi Lambda Theta Hon Asn Prof Educ; Asn Supv & curric Develop; Asn Teacher Educ; Alpha Delta Sigma; Beta Kappa Chi. **Honors/Awds:** Beautiful People Award, Chicago Urban League, 1989; Fifteenth Annual Distinguished Research Award, Asn Teacher Educr; Outstanding Award, Young Women Christian Asn, 1990. **Special Achievements:** Publications: "Evaluating Nutrition Education Programs"; "Thresholds in Education", 1978; "Parent-Teacher Contacts and Students Learning, A Research Report", The Journal of Educ Research, 1981; "Characteristics of Teacher Leaders", Educational Horizons, 1979; "Teachers Who Can, Lead", 1980; "The Indentification of Teacher Education Candidates", 1985; "Research & Evaluation of Alternative Programs for High School Truants", 1988, 1989; "Minorities in Education and Unfulfilled Responsibilities", 1989; "School Improvement: It All Begins With a Vision", Catalyst, 1990; Beautiful People Award, Chicago Urban League, 1989. **Home Addr:** 6937 S Crandon Ave Apt 8E, Chicago, IL 60649-2944, **Home Phone:** (219)924-1911.

### BROWNLEE, HARVEY

President (organization), restaurateur. **Educ:** Cleveland State Univ, BA, bus, managerial econs; Northwestern Univ, MBA, 2001. **Career:** Yum! Multibrand Opers, 1987-2001; Pizza Hut Inc, vpres & head coach, 1997-2003; Yum! Brands, chief operating officer, 2003-04; Ky Fried Chicken, chief operating officer, 2004-09; Bob Evans Farms Inc, pres & chief restaurant opers officer, 2009-13; Holiday Retirement, chief operating officer, currently. **Business Addr:** Chief Operating Officer, Holiday Retirement, 5885 Meadows Rd Suite 500, Lake Oswego, OR 97035, **Business Phone:** (971)245-8396.

### BROWNLEE, JACK M.

Manager. **Personal:** Born Jul 24, 1940, St. Louis, MO; son of Johnny and Clifford; married Martha Diaz; children: Bryan, Michael & Gabriel. **Educ:** San Diego City, grad; San Diego St Col, grad. **Career:** Manager (retired); KFMB TV, dir, 1972-73, TV oper mgr, 1973-75, prod supvr, 1971-2002, prog coordr, 1995; Starburst Broadcasting, co-owner, vpres, 1990; KMOX radio, prod supvr. **Orgs:** Bd gov, Nat Asn TV Arts & Sci, 1984-85. **Honors/Awds:** Upper Level Division Scholarship Award; Emmy Award, Nat Asn TV Arts & Sci, 1983. **Special Achievements:** First black dir & First black on KFMB TV managing staff; Author: A Brand New Moon. **Home Addr:** 4773 Essington Ct, San Ysidro, CA 92173. **Business Addr:** Co-Owner, Vice President, Starburst Broadcasting Ltd, 6050 Santo Rd, San Diego, CA 92124, **Business Phone:** (858)565-7800.

### BROWNRIDGE, J. PAUL

Vice president (organization), government official. **Personal:** Born Jun 10, 1945, Macon, MS; son of James and Arna M Moore; married Rose M; children: 4. **Educ:** Univ Akron, BS, mgt/acct, 1970, JD, 1974; Ind Univ, MA, finance, 1980; Harvard Univ, John F Kennedy Sch Gov, sr execs prog, 1987. **Career:** Goodyear Tire & Rubber Co, acct, 1971-73; Container Corp Am, tax atty, 1973-78; Clark Equip Co, tax atty, 1978-80; Phillips Petrol, sr tax atty, 1980-82; Ideal Basic Industs, tax coun, 1982-84; City & County Denver, treas, dep mgr revenue, 1984-86; City Grand Rapids, treas, 1986-88; City Chicago, dir revenue, 1988; City Los Angeles, treas, 1999; LVCC Inc, dir, exec vpres, currently. **Orgs:** Bd mem, Jr Achievement, 1978-80; comnr, Denver's Comn Aging, 1984-86; chmn, Denver's Tuition Reimbursement Prog, 1984-86; mentor, Colo Alliance Bus, 1985-86; chmn, Cent Support Sub-Cabinet Mem, Exec Comn & Fin Policy Comn, City Chicago; exec bd, Govt Fin Officers Asn US & Can; bd dir, Beverly Nat Corp; Bd Overseers, Amos Tuck Sch Bus Admin at Dartmouth Col; Bd Overseers, USS Const Mus; bd dir, United Way Mass Bay; bd dir, Watts Health Charities; bd dir, Bank Am Celebrity Ser; bd dir, Nat Asn Securities Professionals; Nat Asn Corp dir; bd dir, Girls Inc Lynn, Lead Prog Bus; investment comt, Mercy Health Serv. **Home Addr:** PO Box 805091, Chicago, IL 60680-4112. **Business Addr:** Executive Vice President, Director, LVCC Inc, 151 Bradlee Ave, Swampscott, MA 01907, **Business Phone:** (978)304-1784.

### BRUCE, ADRIENE KAY

Executive. **Personal:** Born May 20, 1965, Detroit, MI; daughter of Rufus H and Rubye M. **Educ:** Howard Univ, BS, 1988; St Louis Univ, advan supply chain mgt cert, 2008. **Career:** Hecht Co, dept store mgt, 1988-89; May Co, 1988-95; Dayton Hudson Corp, dept store mgt, 1990-95; Kelly servs, Minority Owned Vendor Enterprise, prog specialist, 1996-98, prog mgr, 1998-2001; JP Morgan Chase, vpres, sr supplier, global procurement & relationship mgr, 2001-05, vpres, univ rels, 2005-06; Ameren Corp, managing exec supplier diversity, 2006-11, mgr, supplier diversity, 2011-12; United Technologies, mgr, corp responsibility & supplier diversity, 2011-12; DiversityInc Media LLC, vpres, consult, 2012-13; 180 Degrees N LLC, pres, founder & chief exec officer, 2013-15. **Orgs:** Nat Asn Advan Colored People; bd mem, Coun Supplier Diversity Profs, 1998-2005; co-chair, Mich Women's Bus Coun, 1998-2001; bd mem, Mich Minority Bus Develop Coun, 2001-05; bd mem, Forte Found, 2005-; Wall St Diversity Recruiters Group Round Table, 2005-; supplier diversity task force mem, Edison Elec Inst, 2006-11; mem bd, Regional Union Construct Ctr, St Louis, 2007-10; Fell St Louis Bus Diversity Initiative, 2008-2009; community adv bd, St Louis Regional Health Comn, 2008-10; Am Asn Blacks Energy, 2008-11; Black Repertory Theatre St. Louis, 2010-11; co-chair, Utility Indust Group, Nat Minority Supplier Develop Coun, 2010-11; bd mem, Greater New Eng Minority Supplier Develop Coun, 2011-12. **Home Addr:** 6318 Southwood Ave 3w, Clayton, MO 63105, **Home Phone:** (314)226-9410. **Business Addr:** Founder, President, 180 Degrees North LLC, PO Box 7167, Detroit, MO 48207, **Business Phone:** (313)574-7432.

### BRUCE, ARLEN
Accountant. **Home Addr:** 421 S Oak, Ottawa, KS 66067.

### BRUCE, AUNDRAY
Football player, football coach. **Personal:** Born Apr 30, 1966, Montgomery, AL. **Educ:** Auburn Univ, BA, educ, 1988. **Career:** Football player (retired), coach; Atlanta Falcons, left outside linebacker, 1988-89, linebacker, 1990-92; Los Angeles Raiders, linebacker, 1992-94; Oakland Raiders, 1995-98, line backer, 1997; Faulkner Univ Eagles, defensive line coach, currently. **Honors/Awds:** All-SEC, 1986, 1987; Most Valuable Player, Citrus Bowl, 1987; All-American, 1987. **Business Addr:** Defensive Line Coach, Faulkner University Eagles, 5345 Atlanta Hwy, Montgomery, AL 36109, **Business Phone:** (800)879-9816.

### BRUCE, CAROL PITT
Government official. **Personal:** Born Dec 25, 1941, Elkton, MD; daughter of Ralph A Pitt and Elizabeth J Sawyer; married Done Franklin; children: Donna E Bowie, Keith & Kirk. **Educ:** Morgan State Univ, BA, 1964, MBA, 1979. **Career:** Government official (retired); chief alcohol drug control officer, asst dir income maint, 1975-77; AUS 8th Inf Div ADAPCP, clin supv, 1977-79; AUS Civilian Personnel Off Ft Polk, personnel staffing spec, 1981-84; AUS Civilian Personnel Ft Geo G Meade, chief tech serv, 1984-85; AUS Chem Res Eng & Dev Ctr, Aberdeen Proving Ground, chief alcohol drug control/ea off, 1985-2006. **Orgs:** Exec bd, Baltimore Urban League, 1976-79; Nat Assoc Female Execs; Youth Program Dir, St. James AME Church 1987-; Harford County Alumnae Chap, Delta Sigma Theta Inc, 1988-. **Home Addr:** 525 Oak St, Aberdeen, MD 21001, **Home Phone:** (410)273-7940. **Business Addr:** Chief Alcohol Drug Control Officer, US Army Chemical Research Development and Engineering Center, Aberdeen, MD 21001, **Business Phone:** (410)676-3477.

### BRUCE, ISAAC ISIDORE
Football player. **Personal:** Born Nov 10, 1972, Fort Lauderdale, FL. **Educ:** W Los Angeles Jr Col; Santa Monica Col; Memphis State Univ, phys educ, 1992. **Career:** Football player (retired); St Louis Rams, wide receiver, 1994-2007; United Way, Rams spokesman, 1996; San Francisco 49ers, wide receiver, 2008-09. **Orgs:** Founder, Isaac Bruce Found, 2006-; bd dir, Childhaven; Omega Psi Phi Fraternity. **Honors/Awds:** Consensus Rookie of the Year, St. Louis Rams, 1994; Recorded 119 receptions, 1995; Most Valuable Player, St. Louis Rams, 1995-96; Pro Bowl selection, 1996, 1999-2001; All Pro selection, 1995-96, 1999; True Value Man of the Year, St. Louis Rams, 1997; Sprint Good Sport Man of the Year, St. Louis Rams, 1998; Named to play in Pro Bowl, 1999; Super Bowl XXXIV, 1999; Named to play in Pro Bowl, 2000-01; Sports Personality of the Year Award, Missouri Athletic Club, 2003; National Sportsmanship Award, 2006; St. Louis Rams 80 retired, St. Louis Rams 10th Anniversary Team. **Special Achievements:** Film: Super Bowl XXXIV, 2000. TV Series: "NFL Blast", 1997; "Super Bowl XXXVI", 2002; "Extreme Makeover: Home Edition", 2010. **Business Addr:** Founder, Isaac Bruce Foundation, 1919 Homefield Estates Dr, O'Fallon, MO 63366, **Business Phone:** (314)369-4074.

### BRUCE, DR. JAMES C.
Educator. **Personal:** Born Jul 15, 1929, Washington, DC; children: James C Jr & Jason W. **Educ:** Howard Univ, AB, 1952, MA, 1956; Univ Chicago, PhD, 1963. **Career:** SC St Col, ger instr, 1956-57; Univ Chicago, ger instr, 1961-64, from asst prof ger, to assoc prof ger, 1964-89, assoc prof emer, 1989, prof emer, currently; Soka Univ, Japan, prof engineering, 1989-2000, prof emer, currently. **Orgs:** Ill Comn Human Rel, 1971-73; secy, Am Asn Teachers Ger, 1974; Mod LangAsn Am; Midwest Mod Lang Asn; Literarische Ges Chicago; Sigma PiPhi; Kappa Alpha Psi. **Home Addr:** 1642 E 56th St, Chicago, IL 60637, **Home Phone:** (773)684-5060. **Business Addr:** Professor Emeritus, University of Chicago, 1050 E 59th St, Chicago, IL 60637, **Business Phone:** (773)702-8494.

### BRUCE, DR. PRESTON, JR.
Government official, consultant, association executive. **Personal:** Born Sep 10, 1936, Washington, DC; married Kellene Margot Underdown; children: Preston III & Kellene Elaine. **Educ:** Lyndon State Col, BS, 1958; Univ Mass, EdD, 1972. **Career:** Reads Boro Sch, prin, 1959-63; Off Econ Opport, admin asst dir, 1964-67; Head Start, dir exec asst, 1968-69; Off Child Develop, dir 4-c prog, 1969-71, dir-day care, 1974-83; Univ Mass, asst chancellor, 1971-74; USDHEW/ACYF-CB, dep dir off families; PKB & Assocs, consult, owner. **Orgs:** Lion's Club, 1958-63; Jaycees, 1969-71; vestry mem, St Mark's Church, 1971-74; bd dir, Day Care Coun Am, 1975-83; bd dir, Capitol Ballet Guild, 1978-80; bd dir, Dist Columbia O/C, 1978-82; chmn, Howard Univ, Sch S/W Vis Comt, 1979-; dir, NCCAN, ACYF-DHHS, 1983-84; exec dir, US Adv Bd, Dept Health & Human Servs, Child Abuse & Neglect. **Honors/Awds:** Professional Baseball Pitcher Pittsburgh Pirates, 1958; Horace Mannlecturer, Univ Mass, 1971-72; distinguished alumnus, Lyndon State Col, 1973; Athlete's Hall of Fame, Lyndon State Col, 1985. **Special Achievements:** First and only negro principal of white school in Vermont. **Home Addr:** 10341 Maypole Way, Columbia, MD 21044, **Home Phone:** (301)596-5706. **Business Addr:** Executive Director, US Advisory Board on Child Abuse and Neglect, 200 Independence Ave SW, Washington, DC 20201, **Business Phone:** (202)690-8137.

### BRUCE, RAYMOND L.
Judge. **Personal:** Born Jun 10, 1951, New York, NY; son of Lloyd and Jesuna; married Darlene C; children: Precious. **Educ:** New York Univ, BA, 1973; Temple Law Sch, JD, 1976. **Career:** Carver Fed Savings Bank, gen coun; NY State Atty Gen Off, asst atty gen; Bronx Criminal Ct, judge, 2002-; Supreme Ct, Bronx County, actg justice, 2004-; Civil Ct, New York, judge, 2002-11. **Home Addr:** 218 W 137th St, New York, NY 10030-2407. **Business Addr:** Judge, Bronx County Supreme Court, 265 E 161st St, Bronx, NY 10451, **Business Phone:** (718)618-3000.

### BRUMMER, CHAUNCEY EUGENE
Lawyer, educator. **Personal:** Born Nov 22, 1948, Louisville, KY; married Isabelle J Carpenter; children: Christopher & Craig. **Educ:** Howard Univ, BA, 1970; Univ Ky, JD, 1973. **Career:** Louisville & Nashville RR Co, atty & gen solicitor; Louisville Legal Aid, comm educ dir, 1973-74; Univ NC, Chapel Hill, fac, 1979-82; Univ Ark, dep chancellor, 1998-99, prof law, currently, spl asst to chancellor, interim assocv chancellor fac develop; Univ Mo-Kans City, sr admin; Louisville Legal Aid Soc, Reginald Heber Smith fel atty; fel, Am Coun Educ. **Orgs:** Ky Bar Asn; Louisville Bar Asn; Nat Bar Asn Explorer advr; Law Explorer Post, 1974-; pres, Shawnee HS Alumni Asn; Alpha Phi Omega; Am Bar Asn; bd dir, Ozark Guid Ment Health Ctr; adv bd, Salvation Army, Northwest Ark. **Home Addr:** 11901 Rockspring Dr, Louisville, KY 40223. **Business Addr:** Professor of Law, University of Arkansas, 1045 W Maple St, Fayetteville, AR 72701, **Business Phone:** (479)575-2457.

### BRUNER, VAN B., JR.
Architect, school administrator. **Personal:** Born May 22, 1931, Washington, DC; married Lillian E Almond; children: Scott V. **Educ:** Univ Mich, BS, design, 1957; Drexel Evening Col, BS, archit, 1965. **Career:** Pvt prac, archit, Pa, 1965; Spring Garden Col, dept archit, dept chmn, 1965-72, 1979-81; pvt prac, archit, NJ, 1968; Bruner Firm, archit & owner, 1968-; Nat Org Minority Archit, charter mem, 1972-; Am Inst Archit, nat vpres, 1972-74; Cornell Univ, vis lectr; Howard Univ, vis lectr; Honolulu Hawaii Univ, vis lectr; Harvard Univ, vis lectr. **Orgs:** Mem, NJ Hotel & Mult Dwelling Health & Safety Bd, 1971-; elder, Philadelphia Evangelistic Ctr; field rep, Full Gospel Bus Men's Fel Int; Sigma Pi Phi Fraternity Delta Epsilon Boule; adv bd, Sch Archit, NJ Inst Technol; fel Am Inst Architects; mem, Nat Bd dir AIA; mem, Nat AIA Nat Policy Task Force Comt; former, Nat AIA Judicial Bd; charter mem, Nat Orgn Minority Architects; LeTip. **Business Addr:** Architect, Owner, Bruner Firm, 506 W Pk Blvd, Haddonfield, NJ 08033-2961, **Business Phone:** (856)854-5258.

### BRUNSON, DAVID
Educator, manager. **Personal:** Born Aug 22, 1929, Ridgeway, SC; son of Avan and Rose Belton Peete. **Educ:** Univ Dis, AS, pub admin, corrections, 1976, BA, social rehab welfare, gerontology, 1978, MA, adult end, gerontology, 1980. **Career:** Metropolitan Police Dept, Washington, DC, patrolman officer, 1962-89. **Orgs:** Mw grand master, MW Prince Hall Grand Lodge DC Inc, 1989-90; life mem, Golden Heritage, Nat Asn Advan Colored People, 1989-; Asn Retired Policeman, DC Inc; Am Asn Adult & Continuing Educ; Int Sr Citizens Asn; US Track & Field (USATF), Potomac Valley Asn, cert official track & field; Am Asn Retired Persons; Asn Retarded Citizens DC Inc; life mem, Univ DC Alumni Asn; Univ DC, Inst Gerontology; Nat Caucus Ctr Black Aged. **Home Addr:** 1017 Decatur St NE, Washington, DC 20017, **Home Phone:** (202)526-8643.

### BRUNSON, DR. DEBORA BRADLEY
Educator. **Personal:** Born Apr 15, 1952, Orangeburg, SC; daughter of Louis and Blanche Williams; married John Edward II; children: Courtenay De'Von & Jon Emerson. **Educ:** SC State Col, Orangeburg, SC, BS, 1973, MEd, 1974, EdD, 1990. **Career:** Orangeburg City Schs, Orangeburg, SC, teacher, 1973-82, counr, 1982-86, prin apprentice, 1986-87, counr, 1987-; Elloree Elem Sch, prin, currently. **Orgs:** SC Asn Coun/Develop; Nat Asn Advan Colored People; dep registr, Orangeburg County, secy, Orangeburg County Tourism Adv Bd; Delta Sigma Theta Sorority; SC Educ Asn; Nat Educ Asn; Phi Delta Kappa; vpres, Bd Higher Educ & Campus Ministry, United Methodist Church; Asn Supv & Curric Develop; SC Asn Sch Adminrs. **Home Addr:** 1229 Dunham St, Orangeburg, SC 29118, **Home Phone:** (803)536-5278. **Business Addr:** Principal, Elloree Elem Sch, 200 Warrior Dr, Elloree, SC 29047, **Business Phone:** (803)897-2232.

**BRUNSON, ERIC DANIEL. See BRUNSON, RICK.**

### BRUNSON, FRANK
Electrical engineer. **Personal:** Born Jan 20, 1957, Cincinnati, OH; son of Robert Stokes and Arthur Lee; married Melony E White; children: Chanel D'Lynne, Frank Aaron & Jordan Tyler. **Educ:** Otterbein Col, 1976; Univ Dayton, BSEE, 1980. **Career:** Am Elec Power Co Inc, proj design engr, 1980-83, distrib engr, 1983-87, sr distrib engr, 1987-91, sr elec engr, 1991-. **Orgs:** Nat Soc Black Engrs, 1981-; Nat Soc Prof Engrs, 1982-; Young Men's Christian Asn, Black Achievers Prog, Steering Comt, 1992-. **Home Addr:** 3954 Sleaford Ave, Columbus, OH 43230, **Home Phone:** (614)475-1029. **Business Addr:** Project Design Engineer, American Electric Power Co Inc, 1 Riverside Pl Fl 1, Columbus, OH 43215-2372, **Business Phone:** (614)716-1000.

### BRUNSON, RICK (ERIC DANIEL BRUNSON)
Basketball player, basketball coach. **Personal:** Born Jun 14, 1972, Syracuse, NY; married Sandra; children: Jalen & Erica. **Educ:** Temple Univ, attended 1995. **Career:** Basketball player (retired), basketball coach; Adelaide 36ers, guard, 1995-96; Quad City Thunder, guard, 1996-97; Conn Pride, guard, 1997, 1998-99; Portland Trailblazers, guard, 1997-98 & 2001-02; NY Knicks, guard, 1999-2001; Boston Celtics, guard, 2000; Chicago Bulls, guard, 2002-04, asst coach, 2010-; Toronto Raptors, guard, 2003; Progresso Castelmaggiore, 2004; Los Angeles Clippers, guard, 2004-05; Seattle Supersonics, guard, 2005-06; Houston Rockets, guard, 2006; Philadelphia 76ers, guard, 2006; Denver Nuggets, asst player develop coach, 2007; Univ Va, Cavaliers, dir basketball opers, 2007-09; Hawks, Univ Hartford, asst coach, 2009-; Charlotte Bobcats, asst coach, 2012-13. **Orgs:** Eastern Conf championship team, 1999. **Business Addr:** Assistant Men's Basketball Coach, University of Hartford Hawks, GSU 309 200 Bloomfield Ave, West Hartford, CT 06117, **Business Phone:** (860)768-4287.

### BRUNT, SAMUEL JAY
Financial manager, educator. **Personal:** Born Jan 14, 1961, Baltimore, MD. **Educ:** Howard Univ, BA, 1979; Univ Baltimore, Yale Gordon Col Lib Arts, MPA, 1983. **Career:** Community Col Baltimore, admin asst, instr, 1983-84; Balitmore Fed Financial, new accts, invest clerk, 1984-85; MD State Legis, fiscal res, 1984, interim, 1985, leg session. **Orgs:** Nat Forum Black Pub Admin, 1984; adv, Youth Ministry Trinity Baptist Church, 1984; supt, Trinity Baptist Church Sch, 1985. **Honors/Awds:** HUD Fel, Baltimore Reg Planning Coun, 1983; Contestant, 1983; Nat Pi Alpha Alpha Manuscript competition Pub Admin Lit; Delegate 4th Nat Model OAU, Howard Univ, 1983.

### BRUTON, BERTRAM A.
Architect. **Personal:** Born May 18, 1931, Jacksonville, FL; son of George W and Lula C; married Dorothy Garcia; children: Michelle Yvette & Sabra Lee. **Educ:** Howard Univ, BArch, 1953. **Career:** Paul Rader AIA, job capt, 1956-58; James H Johnson AIA, job capt, 1958-59; Donald R Roark Denver, assoc arch, 1959-61; Bertram A Bruton & Assoc, archit & founding prin, 1961-. **Orgs:** Am Inst Architects, Nat Coun Archit Regist Bd; Nat Organ Black Arch; Mitchell Sixty-Six Assoc Develop; dir, Salvation Army; dir, Community Credit Union; CO State Bd Examiners Architects; Kappa Alpha Psi; Sigma Pi Phi. **Honors/Awds:** Award of Merit, AIA; Achievement Award, Kappa Alpha Psi; Denver Man of Year, 1974, 1984; Barney Ford Award. **Home Addr:** 2627 Adams St, Denver, CO 80205-4811, **Home Phone:** (303)322-3480. **Business Addr:** Founding Principal, BAB Associates PC, 2001 York St, Denver, CO 80205, **Business Phone:** (303)388-4314.

### BRYAN, ADELBERT M.
Government official, police officer. **Personal:** Born Aug 21, 1943, Frederiksted; son of Wilmot E and Anesta Samuel; married Jerilyn C O Ovesen; children: Lecia, Adelbert (deceased), Scheniqua, Lori, Andrea, Lyrhea & Mia. **Educ:** Col VI, AA, police sci & admin, 1975; Fed Bur Invest Acad, 1978; BS, social sci, 1988. **Career:** Government official, police officer, senator (retired); St Croix Police Dept, police officer, 1966-72, sgt, 1972-74, lt, capt, 1977-86; US VI, sen. **Orgs:** Chmn, Econ Develop & Affairs Comm 15th Legis; chmn, Educ Comn 16th Legis; Olympic Shooting Team; Deleg to Third & Fourth Const Conv. **Honors/Awds:** Medal of Honor Nat Police Award; Achievement Award Police of the Year Award; F.B.I. Firearms Award. **Home Addr:** Christiansted, PO Box D, St Croix00820.

### BRYAN, ASHLEY F.
Writer, illustrator, college teacher. **Personal:** Born Jul 13, 1923, Harlem, NY. **Educ:** Cooper Union Sch; Columbia Univ, philos. **Career:** Professor emeritus (retired); Books: The Ox of the Wonderful Horns & Other African Folktales, 1971, 1993; The Adventures of Aku, or How It Came About That We Shall Always See Okra the Cat Lying on a Velvet Cushion While Okraman the Dog Sleeps Among the Ashes, 1976; The Dancing Granny, 1977; Beat the Story-Drum, Pum-Pum, 1980; Dartmouth Col, prof art & visual studies, prof emer, 1980; The Cats Drum, 1985; Lion & Ostrich Chicks & Other African Folk Tales, 1986; Sh-Ko & His Eight Wicked Brothers, 1988; All Night, All Day, 1988; Turtle Knows Your Name, 1989; Sing to the Sun, 1992; The Story of Lightning & Thunder, 1993; Ashley Bryan's ABC of African Amer Poetry, 1997; Beautiful Blackbird, 2004; Queen's Col, painting & drawing teacher; Lafayette Col, Black Am poetry; Brooklyn Mus & Dalton Sch, teacher; freelancer, currently. **Home Addr:** Hadlock St, PO Box 283, Islesford, ME 04646, **Home Phone:** (207)244-7794. **Business Addr:** Freelancer, PO Box 283, Islesford, ME 04646.

### BRYAN, DR. CURTIS EUGENE, SR.
Executive, college president. **Personal:** Born Sep 6, 1938, Vanceboro, NC; son of Alfred H and Betty L; married bethel ellen cherry; children: Shuronia Sr, Curtis Sr, Daphne Sr & Jennifer Sr. **Educ:** Elizabeth City State Univ, BS, 1960; Temple Univ, MEd, 1968; NY Univ, PhD, 1977. **Career:** Portsmouth Va Pub Schs, asst prin, 1966-68; dir, admis Elizabeth City NC State Univ, 1968-70; Del State Col, asst acad dean & dir, 1970-78; Fayetteville State Univ, head div ed & human develop, dir teacher educ, 1978-80; Va State Univ, exec vpres, admin, 1980-82 & 1983, vpres, interim pres, 1982-83; Denmark Tech Col, pres, 1986-92. **Orgs:** Asn AUS; Nat Asn Higher Educ; AACJC Comn Small Cols; Bamberg Co Econ Develop Comn; Kappa Delta Pi Hon Soc; Phi Delta Kappa; Sigma Rho Sigma. **Special Achievements:** Author: "Quality Control in Higher Educ, " 1973; "Fac Personnel, Perspectives on Acad Freedom, " 1976.

### BRYAN, DR. FLIZE A.
Physician. **Personal:** daughter of H; children: Sylvia. **Educ:** Univ Wis, nursing, 1956; Tuskegee Inst, BSC, 1967; Pomona Col, dipl, 1968; Howard Univ Med Sch, MD, 1972. **Career:** Physician (retired); Health Dept, nurse, 1956-58; Beth Israel Hosp, New York, nurse, 1958-60; Pvt Duty, regist nurse, 1960-66; Sydenham Hosp NY, surg, 1977; Met Hosp NY Med Col, clin instr surg, 1979; Sydenham & Hosp NY, dir emergency room, 1980-99; SNFCC Harlem Hosp, surgeon, 1980; Brooklyn Hosp, staff. **Orgs:** Deleg, Doctors Coun Union, 1980-; Susan McKinley Asn, 1983; Community Bd New York, 1984-; Episcopal Women St Marks Church; St Luke's Guild; co-chmn, Health & Human servs commitee. **Honors/Awds:** Mayoral Agency (AFL-CIO). **Home Addr:** 721 E 22nd St, Brooklyn, NY 11210-1103, **Home Phone:** (718)774-5231.

**BRYAN, GLYNIS**
Executive, chief financial officer. **Educ:** York Univ, Toronto, ON, BA, psychol, 1982; Fla Int Univ, Col Bus Admin, MS, finance, 1985. **Career:** Ryder Syst Inc, asst treas, sr planning, anal mg & mgr leasing, 1984-97, vpres int, 1996-97, vpres & treas, 1997-99; chief financial officer & sr vpres, 1999-2000; APL Logistics, chief financial officer, 2001-05; Swift Transp Co Inc, exec vpres & chief financial officer, 2005-07, prin acct officer; Insight Enterprises, prin financial officer & chief financial officer, 2007-. **Orgs:** Independent dir, Pentair Inc, 2003-. **Honors/Awds:** "Black Enterprise," The 100 Most Powerful Executives in Corporate America, 2010. **Business Addr:** Chief Financial Officer, Insight Enterprises Inc, 6820 S Harl Ave, Tempe, AZ 85283, **Business Phone:** (480)333-3000.

**BRYAN, GLYNIS A.**
Chief financial officer. **Educ:** York Univ, BA, psychol, 1982; Fla Int Univ, MBA, finance, 1985. **Career:** Ryder Syst Inc, sr vpres, 1984-2000; APL Logistics, chief financial officer, 2001-05; Swift Transp Co Inc, exec vpres & chief financial officer, 2005-07; Insight Enterprises Inc, chief financial officer, 2007-. **Orgs:** Dir & chmn governance comt, Pentair Inc; Mem Compensation Comt, 2003-. **Business Addr:** Chief Financial Officer, Insight Enterprises Inc, 6820 S Harl Ave, Tempe, AZ 85283, **Business Phone:** (800)467-4448.

**BRYAN, DR. THELMA JANE**
Chancellor (education), educator. **Personal:** Born Aug 21, 1945, Scotland, MD; daughter of Joseph Webster and Mary Gertrude; married David George Preston; children: Bryan David. **Educ:** Morgan State Univ, BA, eng, MA, eng, 1974; Univ Md, College Park, PhD, eng lang & lit, 1982. **Career:** Educator (retired); Baltimore's Coppin State Col, eng fac, 1978-98, dept Chair, dean hons div & dean arts & sci, 1998; Univ Syst Md, assoc vice chancellor, 1998-2002; Pa State Syst Higher Educ, vice chancellor acad & stud affairs, 2002; Fayetteville State Univ, chief exec officer, 2003; Fayetteville State Univ, chancellor, 2003-07. **Orgs:** Baltimores Coppin State Univ, 1978-98; bd dir, Wachovia Bank; vis bd, Cent Intelligence Agency; NC Defense & Security Technol Accelerator Adv Comt; Cumberland County Workforce Devel Bd; Fayetteville Mus Art Bd. **Home Addr:** 105 Teapot Ct, Reisterstown, MD 21136-1943, **Home Phone:** (410)833-1080.

**BRYANT, ANDERSON B., JR.**
Automotive executive. **Educ:** Howard Univ, attended 1977; Temple Univ, attended 1979. **Career:** Mountain Home Ford-Mercury, gen mgr, 1994-96; Smokey Pt Buick Pontiac GMC, owner & gen mgr, 1996-2012, chief exec officer, 2002-; Ugotsta Entertainment LL, mgr; Car Pros Automotive Group, used vehicle mgr, 2013, gen mgr, 2013-14. **Orgs:** Smokey Pt Chamber Com; Wash State Auto Dealers Asn, 2010. **Business Addr:** Chief Executive Officer, Smokey Point Buick Pontiac GMC, 16632 Smokey Pt Blvd, Arlington, WA 98223, **Business Phone:** (360)659-0886.

**BRYANT, ANTHONY**
Electrical engineer, manager. **Personal:** Born Aug 27, 1963, San Francisco, CA; son of Soloman Jr and Mary A Newt. **Educ:** San Diego State Univ, BSEE, 1987. **Career:** Navy Pub Works Ctr, elec engr, 1984-87; NACME Scholar, NACME, 1986; Motorola GEG Inc, elec engr, 1987-89; Pac Gas & Elec, elec engr, 1989-93; San Francisco Energy Co, AES Corp, elec engr, 1994-97; Munic Transp Agency, Dept Pub Transp, energy analyst, 1997, Capital Planning & Construct Div, proj mgr, 1999-. **Orgs:** Vpres, treas, San Diego State Univ Nat Soc Black Engrs, 1984-86; San Diego Coun Black Engrs & Scientist, 1985-87; admin dir, Nat Soc Black Engrs, Region IV Alumni, 1991-; Ariz Coun Black Engrs & Scientist, prog dir, 1991-93. **Honors/Awds:** Serv Recognition, San Diego State NSBE, 1989. **Home Addr:** 137 Somerset St, San Francisco, CA 94134, **Home Phone:** (415)468-9160. **Business Addr:** Project Manager, Municipal Transportation Agency, 1 S Van Ness Ave 3rd Fl, San Francisco, CA 94103, **Business Phone:** (415)701-4309.

**BRYANT, ANXIOUS E.**
Educator, broker. **Personal:** Born Jan 18, 1938, Nashville, TN; married Christie Tanner; children: Karen & Karl. **Educ:** State Univ Nashville, BS, 1959; Memphis State Univ, MS, 1970. **Career:** Carver High Sch, teacher, 1959-70; Jones & Thompson Archit, archit technician, 1973; Gassner Nathan Partners, archit technician, 1977; Thompson & Miller Architects, archit technician, 1978-79; State Tech Inst Memphis, assoc prof, 1979-; Memphis One Inc Realtors, affil broker, 1980-; Rust Col, part-time lectr, 1980-; Archit Engineering Technolog, prof emer; SW Tenn Community Col, prof emer, currently. **Orgs:** Chmn exam bd, Shelby Co Plumbing Dept, 1977-. **Home Addr:** 7553 Proud Land Dr, Memphis, TN 38119-9139. **Business Addr:** Professor Emeritus, Southwest Tennessee Community College, 737 Union Ave, Memphis, TN 38103-3322, **Business Phone:** (901)333-5340.

**BRYANT, DR. BUNYAN I.**
Educator. **Personal:** Born Mar 6, 1935, Little Rock, AR; son of Christalee; married Jean Carlberg. **Educ:** Eastern Mich Univ, BS, 1958; Univ Mich, MSW, social work, 1965; Univ Manchester, PhD, 1973. **Career:** Nih, Bethesda, recreational asst & counr, 1958-59; Hawthorn Ctr, Dept Ment Health, Plymouth, child care worker, 1960; Methodist C's Village, Redford Twp, Live-Counr, 1960-61; Washtenaw County Probate Ct, ct social worker, 1961-62; Mich C's Inst, Dept Social Welfare, prog dir, 1962-66; Univ Mich, Inst Social Res, asst proj dir, 1968-79, Sch Educ, Educ Chg Team, proj dir & res assoc, 1970-72; Sch Nat Resources & Environ, asst prof, 1972-77, assoc prof, 1978-1995; Urban Technol & Environ Planning, assoc prof, 1978-90, Ctr African-Am & African Studies, assoc prof, 1982-95, Ctr African-Am & African Studies, prof, 1996-; Univ Mich, Urban Technol & Environ Planning Prog, Environ Justice Initiative, dir, 1995-, Sch Natural Resources & Environ, dir, Arthur F Thurnau prof, 1996-; Environ Justice & Philos conf, organizer, 2002; Taubman Ctr Urban Planning, prof, 2003-; Int Environ Justice Global Climate Chg Conf, 2004. Books: Environmental Advocacy: Working for Economic and Environmental Justice; Race and the Incidence of Environmental Hazards: A Time for Discourse, 1992; Environmental Justice: Issues, Policies and Solutions, 1995. **Orgs:** Bd mem, League Conserv; adv comm, USEPA Clean Air Act; Environ Justice Climate Chg Initiative, 2000-; mem, League Conserv Voters Educ Fund; protection agency, mem, Clean Air Act Adv Comt; co-prin investr, Univ Mich 1990 Detroit Area Study; Latino Environ Justice, 2002; co-organizer, Univ Mich 1990 Conf Race & Incidence Environ Hazards; EPA's Nat Environ Justice Adv Coun; lectr, Environ Justice & Orgn Advocacy. **Home Addr:** 1902 Independence, Ann Arbor, MI 48104, **Home Phone:** (734)769-4493. **Business Addr:** Professor of Natural Resources, Arthur F Thurnau Professor, University Michigan, Rm 1532 440 Church St Dana Bldg 505 S State St, Ann Arbor, MI 48109-1115, **Business Phone:** (734)763-2470.

**BRYANT, DR. CARL**
Executive, consultant. **Educ:** Univ Md Eastern Shore, BA, social sci, 1973; Univ NDak, MA, coun, 1976; Univ Md, College Park, PhD, coun, 1984. **Career:** Ctr Creative Leadership, vpres knowledge mgt, 1993-2004; Personnel Decisions Int Corp, gen mgr, 2004-08, vpres & consult dir, 2004-12; Korn Ferry Int, sr partner, 2013-14; UMES Mentors, dir, 2015; Lee Hecht Harrison, coach, 2015, assoc consult, 2015-; Independent Consult, 2014-; Dept Veterans Affairs, dir leadership develop & outreach, 2015-. **Orgs:** Nat Trustee, Boys Town, 2008-12; bd mem, Univ Md Eastern Shore, Sch Arts & Professions Exec Bd, 2014; Alpha Phi Alpha Fraternity. **Special Achievements:** First African American vice president of technolgy at Center for Creative Leadership. **Business Addr:** Director Leadership Development and Outreach, Department of Veterans Affairs, 810 Vt Ave, Washington, DC 20420, **Business Phone:** (800)827-1000.

**BRYANT, CASTELL VAUGHN**
Executive. **Personal:** Born Jasper, FL; daughter of Joseph and Bessie Mae; married Leonard Bryant Jr; children: Kathi Merdenia & Craig Leonard. **Educ:** Fla A&M Univ, BS, MS; Nova Univ, EdD. **Career:** Fla A&M Univ, 1964-74, interim pres, 2004-07, sr interim pres; Miami-Dade Community Col, dean stud servs, 1978, coordr curric/Job Placement STIP Grant, 1974-78, pres, assoc dean acad support, 1997; Dade Co Pub Sch Syst, teacher; L-C & Assocs Inc, vpres & dir; Bethune-Cookman Univ, interim vpres acad affairs, vpres acad affairs. **Orgs:** Coun Black Am Affairs; Family Christian Asn Am; Metro-Dade Art Pub Pl; Metro-Dade Addiction Bd; Delta Sigma Theta Sorority Inc. **Honors/Awds:** Unsung Heroines Award, City Miami Comn Status Women; Community Service Award, Nat Asn Negro Bus & Prof Women; Golden Rule Award, JC Penney & United Way; honoree, Florida Agricultural And Mechanical University. **Special Achievements:** Miami Metro Mags 100 Women Watch; first woman to hold interim president at the Florida A&M University. **Home Addr:** 9025 N E 4th Ave, Miami, FL 33138. **Business Addr:** Vice President-Academic Affairs, Bethune-Cookman University, Thomas White Hall 2nd Fl, Daytona Beach, FL 32114, **Business Phone:** (386)481-2000.

**BRYANT, CLARENCE W.**
Government official. **Personal:** Born May 22, 1931, Clarendon, AR; son of Clarence and Blonnell Guyden Bray; married Annie Laure Aldridge; children: Carolyn, Antonette, Sibyl & Johanna. **Educ:** City Col San Francisco, 1950, AS, elect, 1976; Calif State Univ, San Francisco, BA, design & indust, 1979, MA, 1981. **Career:** Government official (retired); Maintenance Eng Br, Los Angeles, CA, elect tech, installation, 1958-60; Western Reg, San Francisco, AF Sector Field Off, SFIA, elect tech, commun, 1960-68, Elect tech, radar, 1974, elect tech, 1974-78, elect tech regular relief, 1978-79; Fed Aviation Admin DOT, Wash, DC, supvr elect egr mgr, 1979-88, br mgr, 1988-90. **Orgs:** San Fran Black Cath Caucus, 1972; Mayors Comn Crime, 1968-71, Arch-Bishops Campaign Human Develop, 1969-72, Black Leadership Forum San Francisco; exec bd, Cath Social Serv; Top Flight Golf Club; San Francisco State Univ Alumni Asn. **Honors/Awds:** Award of Achievement, Calif State Assembly, 1968; Award, OMICA, 1968; Num Tech Award, FAA. **Home Addr:** 366 Byxbee St, San Francisco, CA 94132, **Home Phone:** (415)586-8711.

**BRYANT, CONNIE L.**
Government official, executive, labor activist. **Personal:** Born Dec 26, 1936, Brooklyn, NY; daughter of Charles (deceased) and Viola Barnes (deceased); married Alonzo Anderson; children: Bradley C Anderson. **Educ:** Empire State Labor Col, New York, NY; Cornell Univ, Exten, New York, NY. **Career:** Labor activist (retired); New York Dept Transp, 1963-83; Commun Workers Am, int vpres, 1983-89, vpres pub workers, staff rep, 1989-91. **Orgs:** Vpres, Coalition Black Trade Unionist, 1986-; chair, Labor Ad Hoc Comt Nat Coun Negro Women; bd dir, Indust Rels Coun Goals; exec bd, A Philip Randolph Inst, 1985-89. **Honors/Awds:** NY City, Dept Transportation Adminr & Trainer, 1981; Women Achievers, New York, NY, 1987; Special Womens Award, Nat Black Caucus State Legis Labor, Round Table, 1989; various other awards from local organizations. **Special Achievements:** First vice president for public workers. **Home Addr:** 17608 Gatsby Terr, Olney, MD 20832, **Home Phone:** (301)570-3772.

**BRYANT, DAMON K.**
Manager, association executive. **Personal:** son of Elmer and Dorothy. **Educ:** Univ Mo, BA, commincations, 1987; UMKC- Bloch Sch Mgt, EMBA, masters bus admin, 2012. **Career:** KSMO TV 62; KCTV TV 5, air prom mgr, 1992-94; WTVJ TV 6; WXYZ TV 7, creative serv dir, 1996-2001; WBBM CBS Chicago, dir advert & prom, 2001-02; Fox Tv Stas, vpres creative servs, 2002-07; WDAF TV Fox 4, creative servs, 2007-. **Orgs:** Pres, community trustee, Univ Mo Kans City Alumni Asn; dir, Black Community Fund, 2013; bd chair, High Asirations, 2013; Boys & Girls Clubs Greater Kans City, 2016. **Honors/Awds:** 15 Regional Emmy Awards, Nat Asn Travel Agents Singapore, 1994, 1998; Golden Peacock, NBC Universal, 1995; Defying the Odd, Univ Mo-Kans City, 2005; Four Mich Asn Broadcasters Awards; UMKC Alumni Award. **Business Addr:** Vice President of Marketing & Creative Services, WDAF-TV FOX 4, 3030 Summit St, Kansas City, MO 64108, **Business Phone:** (816)932-9133.

**BRYANT, DONNIE L.**
Secretary (organization), financial manager, administrator. **Personal:** Born Dec 20, 1942, Detroit, MI. **Educ:** Walsh Inst Acct, attended 1963; Wayne State Univ, BA, 1970; Univ Mich, Mpub Policy, 1972. **Career:** Pub Admin Staff, staff assoc, 1973-77; Neighborhood Reinvest Corp, dir finance & admin, 1977-83, secy; Govt DC, dep city admin. **Orgs:** Int City Mgt Asn, 1972-; Nat Asn Black Pub Admins, 1984-. **Honors/Awds:** Graduate Fellowship, US Dept Housing & Intl City Mgt Asn, 1971-72. **Home Addr:** 2111 Wis Ave NW, Washington, DC 20007-2226, **Home Phone:** (202)965-0988.

**BRYANT, EDWARD ETHAN, JR.** See BRYANT, JUNIOR.

**BRYANT, EDWARD JOE, III**
Military leader, manager, engineer. **Personal:** Born Sep 19, 1947, Shreveport, LA; son of Ester Lee Harper and Moses B; married Bettye Jeane Gordon; children: Lorie, Khristopher & Elizabeth. **Educ:** Air Nat Guard & Air Res Acad, grad, 1972; Baptist Col, attended 1978; Propulison Br Mgt, Chanute Ill. **Career:** USAF, jet specialist, 1965-69; Sperry-Rand Corp, maintenance engr, 1969-72; Dept Defense, aircraft powerplant specialist, 1972-; Fed Civil Serv Employee, 1972-; Palmer Col, assoc, 1975; N Charleston SC, counr, 1978-89. **Orgs:** Air res tech, 1969-86; chmn legal, Nat Asn Advan Colored People, 1975-86, State Legal Redress Comt, 1988-89, legal consult, 2008; Air Force Asn SC Personnel & Guid Asn, 1978-80; counr, Guid Sch Syst, 1978-79; legal staff, N Charleston Citizen Adv Coun, 1986-87; local chap, Air Force Asn; Partisan Defense Comt. **Honors/Awds:** Black Heritage Certificate, 1983-88; Sustained Superior Performance Award, 1983; Best Legal Activities & Staff, SC Nat Asn Advan Colored People, 1986-87; Superior Performance Award Civil Service, 1989. **Home Addr:** 5883 Mercia Lane, North Charleston, SC 29418, **Home Phone:** (843)552-2762.

**BRYANT, FAYE BEVERLY**
Educator. **Personal:** Born Mar 15, 1937, Houston, TX. **Educ:** Howard Univ, BA, 1958; Univ Houston, MEd, 1967. **Career:** Educator (retired); Houston Independent Sch Dist, teacher, 1960-67, TitleI counr, 1967-70, dep supt, personnel serv, 1988-89, dep supt, sch oper, 1989-92, dep supt, dist planning, interim supt, accountability & technol, exec dep supt, 2002; Houston Met YWCA, prog dir, 1968-69; Bellaire Sr HS, counr, 1970-75; QIE, HISD field inf co ordr, 1975; Supt Instr, prog admin, 1976; Off Supt Inst, assoc dir, 1977; Magnet Sch Prog, asst supt, 1978, dir; Magnet Sch Prog & Alternate Educ, assoc supt, 1982, asst supt enrichment progs, 1987. **Orgs:** Alpha Kappa Omega Chap Houston, 1957; South central regional dir, Alpha Kappa Alpha Sor, 1968-72; chap senator, Houston Met YWCA, 1970-74; pres, Houston Chap, 1973-74; nat past pres, Top Ladies Distinct, 1975; pres, Houston Personnel & Guidance Asn, 1975-76; vpres, Alpha Kappa Alpha Sor, 1978; 21st int nat pres, Alpha Kappa Alpha Sor, 1982-86; Nat Asn Advan Colored People, 1982-86; Houston Professional Admins & Asn Supervision Curriculum Develop; 1974 Task Force Human Concerns Tex Personnel & Guidance Asn; bd dir, Comt Admin Blue Triangle Br; Links Inc; NCNW Court Calanthe; Houston CC; bd mem, Nat Negro Col Fund; bd mem, nat chmn, Assault Illiteracy; Black Leadership Roundtable, Coalition 100 Black Women. **Honors/Awds:** Young Educator Award, Finalist, 1967; TX Personnel & Guidance Asn Outstanding Counselor Award, 1975; 1983-86; Community Service Award, TX Southern Univ's Bd Regents; Outstanding Alumni Achievement Award, Howard Univ, 1987; TX Personnel & Guidance Association Certificate of Appreciation, Recog Commitment & Serv Statewide Enchancement Counseling. **Special Achievements:** The 100 Most Influential Black Americans Ebony Mag; First African American To Serve As Deputy Superintendent For School Administration In The Houston Independent School District, 1998. **Home Addr:** 2111 Welch St, Houston, TX 77019, **Home Phone:** (713)526-8335.

**BRYANT, FRANKLYN**
Association executive. **Career:** Nat Alliance Black Salesmen & Saleswomen, pres, currently. **Home Addr:** 1420 Wood Rd Suite 3B Parkchester, Bronx, NY 10462-7222. **Business Addr:** President, National Alliance of Black Salesmen & Saleswomen, PO Box 2814, New York, NY 10027-8817, **Business Phone:** (914)668-1430.

**BRYANT, GREGORY ALEXANDER**
Educator, counselor, clergy. **Personal:** Born Dec 9, 1953, Atlanta, GA; son of Mildred and Silas Johnson; married Yvonne; children: Antoine, Shawana, Sheranda, Titus, Tiffany & Gregory Jr. **Educ:** Buelah Heights Bible Col; Atlanta Metrop Col; Christ Answer Univ, ThD; Jacksonville Theol Sem, BA, MA, 2001. **Career:** Fountain Praise Worship Ctr, pastor & founder, 1978-04; More Than Conquerors Fel Int Inc, founder & chief exec officer, 1980-04; G A Bryant Enrichment Ctr, founder & chief exec officer; G A Bryant Bible Inst, Atlanta, GA, founder & chief exec officer; Trumpet Zion Rivers Living Waters, Douglasville, GA, pastor & founder; Camp Praise Summer Camp Prog, Atlanta, GA, dir & founder; Shield Faith, founder; Fountain Praise Deliverance Ctr, sr pastor, fonder, bishop & chief exec officer, currently; bishop for more than 7 churches in Atlanta, GA, Winder, GA, Fayetteville, NC, Durham, NC. **Home Addr:** 255 Laureen Lane, Atlanta, GA 30126, **Home Phone:** (770)948-7218. **Business Addr:** Bishop, Chief Executive Officer, Fountain Of Praise Deliverance Center, 770 N Elizabeth Pl NW, Atlanta, GA 30318, **Business Phone:** (404)794-9514.

**BRYANT, HOMER HANS**
Choreographer, artistic director. **Personal:** Born St. Thomas; children: Alexandra Victoria. **Career:** Dance Theatre Harlem, prin dancer, dir; City Chicago's Gallery 37 prog, lead artist; Chicago Multi-Cultural Dance Ctr, founder & artistic dir, 1990-; US Ice Dance Medalists, guest teacher & trainer; Olympic contenders Melissa Gregory, guest teacher & trainer; Denis Petukhov, guest teacher & trainer, Can's mesmerizing Cirque Du Soleil, guest teacher & trainer; Royal Winnipeg Ballet, guest teacher & trainer. **Orgs:** Bd mem, South Loop Neighbors Assoc; asst artistic dir, Giordano Dance Chicago, currently. **Business Addr:** Founder, Artistic Director, Chicago Multi-Cultural Dance Center, Dearborn Sta bldg 47 W Polk St Lower Level, Chicago, IL 60605, **Business Phone:** (312)461-0030.

**BRYANT, HOWARD**
Journalist, broadcaster, writer. **Personal:** Born Nov 25, 1968, Boston, MA. **Educ:** Temple Univ, BS, 1991; San Francisco State Univ, MS, 1993. **Career:** Oakland Tribune, sports & technol reporter, 1991-95; "San Jose Mercury News", telecommunications & Oakland A's baseball reporter, 1995-2001; "Bergen Record", New York Yankees baseball reporter, 2001-02; "Boston Herald", columnist, 2002-05; "Washington Post", Washington Redskins reporter, 2005-07; ESPN, corresp & writer. **Honors/Awds:** New York Times, Notable Book of 2005 for "Juicing the Game"; Casey Award and "New York Times" Notable Book of 2010 for "The Last Hero". **Special Achievements:** Author of: "Shut Out: A Story of Race and Baseball" (2003); "Juicing the Game: Drugs, Power and the Fight for the Soul of Major League Baseball" (2005); "The Last Hero: A Life of Henry Aaron" (2006).

**BRYANT, HUBERT HALE**
Lawyer. **Personal:** Born Jan 4, 1931, Tulsa, OK; son of Roscoe Conkling and Curlie Beatrice Marshall; married Elnora Roberson; children: Cheryl Denise Hopkins & Tara Kay Walker. **Educ:** Fisk Univ, BA, 1952; Howard Univ Law Sch, LLB, 1956. **Career:** Pvt law pract, 1956-67, 1986-; City Tulsa, asst city prosecutor, 1961-63, city prosecutor, 1963-67; ND OK, asst US atty, 1967-77; ND OK Dept Justice, US atty, 1977-81; City Tulsa, Okla, munic ct judge, 1984-86. **Orgs:** Tulsa Urban League bd, 1962-64; trustee, First Baptist Church N Tulsa, 1970-75, 1995-2002; Sigma Pi Phi Alpha Theta Boule; exec bd, Tulsa Br, Nat Asn Advan Colored People; Alpha Kappa Alpha Sorority Inc; Nat Set Club. **Honors/Awds:** Mason of the Year, 1963; Outstanding Citizen Masons, 1978; Outstanding Alumni, Howard Univ Sch Law, 1981; Outstanding Citizen, Tulsa Br, Nat Asn Advan Colored People, 1981; Image Award Outstanding Community Service, Alpha Chi Omega Chap, 1988; Hall of Fame, Nat Bar Asn, 1997. **Home Addr:** 1818 N Boston Ave, Tulsa, OK 74106, **Home Phone:** (918)582-0484. **Business Addr:** Attorney, 2623 N Peoria Ave, Tulsa, OK 74106-2512, **Business Phone:** (918)428-6665.

**BRYANT, DR. JACQUELINE D. BROWN**
Educator, dentist. **Personal:** Born Oct 27, 1957, Nashville, TN; daughter of James H and Birdie Faulkner; married Patrick; children: Denese & Lawren. **Educ:** Brandeis Univ, Waltham, MA, BA, BS, biol, 1979; Meharry Med Col, Nashville, TN, DDS, 1983; Univ Mich, Ann Arbor, MI, MS, orthod, 1985. **Career:** Howard Univ, Dept Orthod, Washington, DC, asst prof, 1985, Sch Dent, Adv Gen Dent Prog, consult, 1986-, Gen Pract Resident Prog, attend physician, 1986-; Silver Springs, Md, pvt pract, 1986-; Howard Univ Col Dent, asst prof, 1985-06; Jacqueline Brown Bryant, owner, orthodontist, 2010-. **Orgs:** Am Asn Orthodontists, 1983-; Int Asn Dent Res, 1983-; Middle Atlantic Soc Orthodontists, 1983-; Omicron Kappa Upsilon Dent Honor Soc, 1983-; Metrop Wash Study Club, 1983-; Am Asn Women Dentists, 1987-; Am Dent Asn; Md State Dent Asn; Md State Soc Orthodontists; Mid Atlantic Soc Orthodontists; Southern Md Dent Soc. **Business Addr:** Dentist, Jacqueline D Brown Bryant, 8737 Colesville Rd Suite 301, Silver Spring, MD 20910, **Business Phone:** (301)587-8750.

**BRYANT, JAMAL HARRISON**
Televangelist, minister (clergy). **Personal:** Born May 21, 1971, Baltimore, MD; son of John Richard and Cecilia Williams; married Gizelle, Jan 1, 2002?, (divorced 2009); children: John Karston, Adore, Grace, Topaz & Angel. **Educ:** Morehouse Col, BA; Duke Univ, MDiv; Grad Theol Found, DMin, 2005. **Career:** Televangelist, 1999-; Empowerment Temple AME Church, Baltimore, MD, pastor and founder, 2000-. Television: Praise the Lord, 2006-15; The Real, 2016-. **Honors/Awds:** Chairman's Award, NAACP Image Awards, 2016. **Special Achievements:** Organizer, 2011 Power Summit; creator and host, Code Red Conference, Baltimore, MD, 2012. **Business Addr:** Jamal Bryant Ministries, 4217-4221 Primrose Ave, Baltimore, MD 21215, **Business Phone:** (443)738-0463.

**BRYANT, JAMES W., SR.**
Clergy. **Career:** Mary B Wise Memorial Baptist Church, minister. **Business Addr:** Minister, Mary B Wise Memorial Baptist Church, 1986 Stokes Blvd Apt 108, Cleveland, OH 44106-2211, **Business Phone:** (216)231-2586.

**BRYANT, JESSE A.**
Secretary (office), association executive. **Personal:** Born Aug 27, 1922, Supply, NC; married Eva Mae Fullwood; children: 4. **Career:** Int Longshoremans Asn, vice chmn, secy; Nat Asn Advan Colored People, Cedar Grove, pres. **Orgs:** Vpres, SENC Land Chap, A Phillips Randolph Inst; exec bd, Brunswick Co City Asn. **Honors/Awds:** Crowned as Mr NAACP of North Carolina. **Special Achievements:** First African American filed for county commissioner election in Cedar Grove. **Home Addr:** 1149 Morgan Rd SW, PO Box 338, Supply, NC 28462, **Home Phone:** (910)842-6670.

**BRYANT, JOHN HOPE**
Chief executive officer, association executive, entrepreneur. **Personal:** Born Feb 6, 1966, Compton, CA; son of Johnie Smith and Juanita; married Sheila Jenine Kennedy. **Educ:** San Diego City Col; Paul Quinn Col, 2004; Harvard Univ, John K Kennedy Sch Gov, exec educ prog, 2008. **Career:** Specly Lending Group, founder; Bryant Group African, staff; Global Dignity, Co-Founder, 2005-14; Press's Coun Financial Literacy, vice chmn, 2008-10, chmn, 2008-09; Bryant Group Co Inc, chmn & chief exec officer, 1990-; Univ Calif, Los Angeles, Exten, bus mgt, instr, currently; Bk:love leadership: New Way to Lead a Fear-Based World; US Press's Adv Coun Financial Capability, chmn, 2010-13; Oper Hope, chmn & chief exec officer. **Orgs:** Bd dir, Audit Comt, Southern Pac Bank; bd govs, Kravis Leadership Inst, Claremont McKenna Col; Chmn & chief exec officer, Oper Hope Inc, founder, 1992-; founder, New Leader; Banking Future; Corp Coun CEOs; bd dir, Calif African-Am Mus Found; nat bd dir, Teach Am; Global Agenda Coun World Econ Forum, 2008; bd trustee, First Am Church; exec adv bd, Renaissance Prog; founding mem, Forum Young Global Leaders, 2005-; U.S. Press's Adv Coun Financial Capability Young Americans, 2014-;U.S. Press's Adv Coun Financial Capability; 100 Black Men Atlanta; Clinton Global Initiatives; HOPE Global Forum. **Home Addr:** 7122 La Tisera, PO Box 205, Los Angeles, CA 90045, **Home Phone:** (323)860-3026. **Business Addr:** Founder, Chairman, Chief Executive Officer, Operation Hope Inc, 707 Wilshire Blvd Suite 3030, Los Angeles, CA 90017, **Business Phone:** (213)891-2900.

**BRYANT, BISHOP JOHN RICHARD**
Clergy, bishop. **Personal:** Born Jun 8, 1943, Baltimore, MD; son of Harrison James (deceased) and Edith Holland; married Cecelia Williams; children: Jamal & Thema. **Educ:** Morgan State Col, BA, 1965; Boston Univ Sch Theol, MTh, Mdiv, 1970; Colgate Rochester Div Sch, DMin, 1975. **Career:** Peace Corps, Liberia, vol, teacher, 1965-67; Var Cols & Univs, guest lectr, 1970-72; African Methodist Episcopal Church, 14th Episcopal Dist, Monrovia, Liberia, bishop, 1988-91, 10th Episcopal Dist, TX, bishop, 1991-2000, 5th Episcopal Dist, bishop, 2000-; Boston Urban League, comt organizer; St Paul AME Church, pastor; Bethel AME Church, Baltimore, MD, pastor. **Orgs:** Bd mem, Nat Community Black Churchmen; Nat Coun Churches; Black Ecumenical Comn; World Methodist Coun Evangelism; bd mem, Ecumenical Inst; bd mem, CNBC; Interdenominational Theol Sem, Atlanta, GA; Nation Church Adv Coun, Am Bible Soc; vpres, N Am Sect, World Methodist Coun; Cong Nat Black Churches; S Dallas Accents. **Home Addr:** 4000 Bedford Rd, Baltimore, MD 21207. **Business Addr:** Bishop, African Methodist Episcopal Church, 5th Episcopal Dist, Los Angeles, CA 90062, **Business Phone:** (323)296-0877.

**BRYANT, JOY (KATE HUDSON)**
Actor. **Personal:** Born Oct 19, 1976, Bronx, NY; married Dave Pope. **Educ:** Yale Univ. **Career:** Tommy Hilfiger, model; TV Series: "Carmen: A Hip Hopera", 2001; "Entourage", 2008; "Virtuality", 2009; "Love Bites", 2011; "Parenthood", 2010-14. Films: Showtime, 2002; Antwone Fisher, 2002; Kite, 2002; Baadasssss!, 2003; Honey, 2003; Spider-Man 2, 2004; Three Way, 2004; Haven, 2004; The Skeleton Key, 2005; London, 2005; Get Rich or Die Tryin, 2005; Bobby, 2006; The Hunting Party, 2007; Welcome Home Roscoe Jenkins, 2008; Hit and Run, 2012; About Last Night, 2014. **Orgs:** A Better Chance. **Honors/Awds:** Young Hollywood Award, 2003; Hollywood Film Award, 2006; Nominee, Black Reel Award, 2005, 2003; Screen Actors Guild Award, 2007. **Business Addr:** Actress, c/o Innovative Artists, 1505 10th St, Santa Monica, CA 90401, **Business Phone:** (310)656-0400.

**BRYANT, JUNIOR (EDWARD ETHAN BRYANT, JR.)**
Football player. **Personal:** Born Jan 16, 1971, Omaha, NE. **Educ:** Univ Notre Dame, BA, 1993. **Career:** San Francisco 49ers, defensive tackle, 1995-97, defensive tackle, 1998-99, defensive end, 1999-2000; Pac Global Investment Mgt Co., vpres, nat mkt & sales dir, 2011; Pac Advisors Funds, vpres, nat mkt & sales dir; Smith & Bryant Inc., co-founder, vpres & co-managing dir. **Orgs:** Founder & pres, 90 Ways. **Honors/Awds:** Rookie of the Year, 1995.

**BRYANT, KATHRYN ANN**
Banker, vice president (organization). **Personal:** Born Feb 25, 1949, Detroit, MI; daughter of Amos V and Mary Avery. **Educ:** Univ Mich, BA, polit sci, 1971; Wayne State Univ, MA, commun, 1979. **Career:** City Detroit, 1972-77, City Coun, admin asst to Councilman Kenneth Cockrel, 1978-81, Cable Comn, dep dir, 1982-88, Bd Assessors, assessor, 1988; Time Warner Cable Commun Inc, dir gov & community rels, 1988-91; Comerica Inc, vpres civic affairs, 1991-95; Comcast Cable, vpres resources & outreach, 1995-2001; AAA, vpres corp rels, 2001-03; Auto Club Group, vpres & chief pub affairs officer, 2001-08; Harrison Bryant LLC, owner & partner, 2008-. **Orgs:** Bd mem, Nat Asn Telecommunication Officers & Adv, 1986-88; bd mem, mem chair, Nat Asn Minorities Cable, 1990-91; treas, bd mem, Proj Pride, 1991-93; bd mem, Fair Housing Ctr Metro Detroit, 1991-; bd mem, Mich Metro Girl Scout Coun, 1992-96; bd mem, Arab Am Ctr Econ Soc Servs, 1992-; Delta Sigma Theta Sorority Nu Chap; Black Stud Union; CULS. **Honors/Awds:** Fair Housing Center of Metro Detroit, Distinguished Services, 1992. **Business Addr:** Owner, Partner, Harrison Bryant LLC, PO Box 201088, Ferndale, MI 48220, **Business Phone:** (313)341-6693.

**BRYANT, KIMBERLY**
Philanthropist, founder (originator), engineer. **Educ:** Vanderbilt Univ, BE, elec engineering, 1989. **Career:** Westinghouse Elec Co, sales engr, 1989-90; DuPont, plant supvr/maintenance mgr, 1990-95; Philip Morris, maintenance group supvr, 1995-98; Merck & Co., dept head, 1998-2003; Pfizer Inc, assoc dir, 2004-06; Genentech Inc, sr proj mgr, 2006-10; Inst OneWorld Health, external affairs vol, 2010-11; Black Girls Code, founder, 2011-; Life Technologies, tech proj mgr, consult, 2012-13; Novartis Vaccines & Diagnostics, tech proj mgr, consult, 2011-12; Pahara Aspen Inst, inst fel, 2015-. **Honors/Awds:** CBS Bay Area, Jefferson Award for Public Service, 2012; "The Root" Magazine, The Root 100 Honorees, 2013; White House, Champion of Change Tech Inclusion, 2013; "Business Insider," 25 Most Influential Blacks in Technology, 2013. **Business Addr:** Founder, Executive Director, Black Girls Code, PO Box 640926, San Francisco, CA 94164.

**BRYANT, KOBE BEAN**
Basketball player. **Personal:** Born Aug 23, 1978, Philadelphia, PA; son of Joe and Pam; married Vanessa Laine; children: Natalia Diamante & Gianna Maria-Onore. **Career:** Los Angeles Lakers, guard, 1996-; Kobe Basketball Acad, owner. **Orgs:** Nat basketball Asn; Make-a-Wish Found; St Jude's C's Hosp; Lawyers Comt Civil Rights; Plaza de la Raza; Vivo del Mondo; CHEIZAW. **Honors/Awds:** Naismith Prep Player of the Year, 1996; NBA Slam Dunk Contest champion, 1997; NBA All-Rookie Second Team, 1997; NBA All-Star, 1998, 2000-12; All-NBA Third Team, 1999, 2005; NBA Champion: 2000, 2001, 2002, 2009, 2010; All-NBA Second Team, 2000, 2001; NBA All-Defensive First Team, 2000, 2003, 2004, 2006, 2007, 2008, 2009, 2010, 2011; NBA All-Defensive Second Team, 2001, 2002, 2012; Most Valuable Player All-Star game, 2002, 2007, 2009, 2011; NBA Scoring Champion, 2006, 2007; Gold Medal, FIBA Americas Championship, 2007; Gold Medal, Olympic Games, 2008, 2012; NBA Most Valuable Player, 2008; NBA Finals Most Valuable Player, 2009, 2010. **Special Achievements:** Youngest player to reach 20, 000 career points; Youngest player to be named to the NBA All-Defensive Team; Youngest Slam Dunk champion (18 years, 175 days), after winning the contest at the 1997 NBA All-Star Weekend. **Business Addr:** Professional Basketball Player, Los Angeles Lakers, 555 N Nash St, El Segundo, CA 90245, **Business Phone:** (310)426-6000.

**BRYANT, LEON SERLE**
Counselor, educator, association executive. **Personal:** Born Jun 22, 1949, Akron, OH; son of Clyde H and Daisy; children: Cillicia N. **Educ:** Ariz State Univ, BA, 1974, MEd, 1991. **Career:** Dept Correction, State Ariz, correctional officer, 1974-75; Phoenix Urban League, manpower specialist, 1975-78; Ariz State Univ, career serv specialist sr, 1978-. **Orgs:** Omega Psi Phi, 1971-; bus adv comt, Phoenix Job Corp, 1988-; Nat Soc Experiential Educ, 1989-; Ariz Career Develop Asn, vpres progs, currently. **Home Addr:** 5106 S Birch St, Tempe, AZ 85282, **Home Phone:** (480)456-4292. **Business Addr:** Career Services Specialist Senior, Arizona State University, Stud Serv Bldg 329, Tempe, AZ 85287-1312, **Business Phone:** (480)965-5340.

**BRYANT, PROF. LEROY**
Educator. **Educ:** Northwestern Univ, MA, 1973. **Career:** Chicago State Univ, chair, prof hist, prof emer & chmn emer, currently. **Business Addr:** Professor Emeritus, Chairman Emeritus, Chicago State University, 9501 S King Dr, Chicago, IL 60628-1598, **Business Phone:** (773)995-2000.

**BRYANT, MARK CRAIG**
Basketball player, basketball coach. **Personal:** Born Apr 25, 1965, Glen Ridge, NJ; married Shelley; children: Taige & Poe. **Educ:** Seton Hall Univ, psychol & communs, 1988. **Career:** Basketball player (retired), basketball coach; Portland TrailBlazers, power forward-ctr, 1988-92, 1995, ctr, 1993-94; Houston Rockets, power forward-ctr, 1995-96; Phoenix Suns, power forward-ctr, 1996-97, ctr, 1998; Chicago Bulls, power forward, 1998-99; Cleveland Cavaliers, power forward, 1999-2000; Dallas Mavericks, power forward, 2000-01, asst coach, player develop staff, 2004-05; San Antonio Spurs, power forward, 2001-02; Denver Nuggets, power forward, 2002-03; Boston Celtics, power forward, 2003; Philadelphia 76ers, power forward, 2002-03; Orlando Magic, asst coach player develop, 2005-07; Seattle Supersonics, asst coach, 2007-; Okla City Thunder, asst coach, currently. **Orgs:** NBA Draft, 1988. **Honors/Awds:** Silver medal, United States squad, Summer Universiade, 1987; Haggerty Award, 1988. **Business Addr:** Assistant Coach, Oklahoma City Thunder, 208 Thunder Dr, Oklahoma, OK 73102, **Business Phone:** (405)208-4800.

**BRYANT, DR. MONA. See BRYANT-SHANKLIN, DR. MONA MAREE.**

**BRYANT, N. Z., JR.**
Insurance executive, writer, association executive. **Personal:** Born Oct 25, 1949, Jackson, MS; son of N Z Sr and Christeen M. **Educ:** Western Mich Univ, BS, 1971, MA, 1972; Univ Mich, attended 1974. **Career:** Oakland Univ, pontiac sch syst, instr, 1972-74; Detroit Col Bus, fac, acad coord, 1974-76; Pontiac Sch, teacher, 1976-79; Equitable Life Ins CPN, agt, 1980-93; Patterson Bryant Inc, pres & chief exec officer, 1982-; Mich State Univ, personal finance. **Orgs:** Greater Detroit Area Life Underwriters Asn, 1980-93; pres, Positive People Pontiac, 1982-83; charter pres, Pontiac Optimist Club, 1983-84, vpres, 1984-85; trustee, Oakland Co Br, NCP, 1984-86, treas, 1989-90; qualifying mem, Million Dollar Round Table, 1989; fin comt, Pontiac Area Urban League, 1990-91; Bd Christian Bus Network; founder, Bryant House; Western Mich Univ. **Honors/Awds:** Young Man of the Year, City Pontiac, 1985; Sales Force Agent of the Year, Equitable Life Ins CPN, 1988-89; Wall of Distinction, Western Mich Univ & Alumni Asn, 1992; Shooting Star Award; Centurion Award, Equitable Life Ins Co; Presidents Cabinet Award; Award Winner, Nat Coun Agt, Nat Leader Corp. **Special Achievements:** Author: "Investing in the 90s," 1992; Special Guest WCHB Radio Show Personal Finance Advice, 2001 & 2002; Key Note Speaker, City Pittsburgh; Listed in Who's Who in the Midwest, Outstanding Young Man of America, Outstanding Young Man of Pontiac & Success Guide 2001. **Home Addr:** 4545 W Cherry Hill Dr, West Bloomfield, MI 48323, **Home Phone:** (248)681-3160. **Business Addr:** President, Chief Executive Officer, Patterson Bryant Inc, 30600 Tel Rd 1st Fl Suite 1160, Bingham Farms, MI 48025, **Business Phone:** (248)433-1902.

**BRYANT, DR. NAPOLEON ADEBOLA, JR.**
Educator. **Personal:** Born Feb 22, 1929, Cincinnati, OH; son of Napoleon and Katie Smith; married Ernestine C; children: Karen, Derek, Brian & David. **Educ:** Univ Cincinnati, BS, 1959; Ind Univ, MAT, 1967, EdD, 1970. **Career:** Nat Defense Educ Act fel, 1968-70; Xavier Univ, sci resource teacher, prof educ, dir sec educ, 1974-79, asst vpres stud develop, 1984-86, emer prof educ, currently; Nat Sci Found, pre-col teacher develop proj, 1974-79, dir minority affairs, 1984-86; Danforth fels, 1983; Nat Sci Teachers Asn, dir multicultural sci educ, 1990-93; Cincinnati Pub Schs, teacher. **Orgs:** Basileus, Omega Psi Phi, Beta Iota Chap, 1965-; Rollman Psychist Hosp, 1976-78; co-organizer & partic, Caribbean Regional Orgn Asn Sci Educr Barbados, WI, 1979; hon life mem, Asn Sci Teachers Jamaica, 1979; ordained deacon Episcopal, 1984; Asn Supvn & Curric Develop, 1988-; charter mem, Asn Multicultural Sci Educ, 1990-; sci consult, Sci Adv Comm State Ohio; Ohio Coun Elem Sch Int; chmn, Comm Local Arrangements; life mem, Nat Asn Advan Colored People; Nat Sci Teachers Asn; consult, Elem & Sec Sci Educ Sch & Pub Firms; bd dir, Harriet Beecher Stowe Preserv Comm, William Procter Conf Ctr. **Home Addr:** 3527 Skyview Lane, Cincinnati, OH 45213-2040, **Home Phone:** (513)731-0903. **Business Addr:** Professor Emeritus, Xavier University, 3800 Victory Pkwy Dept 1, Cincinnati, OH 45207, **Business Phone:** (513)745-3000.

**BRYANT, PAMELA BRADLEY**
Public relations executive. **Personal:** Born Jun 11, 1970, Miami, FL; daughter of Matthew and Juanita; married Van K; children: Kavon & Quinn. **Educ:** Fla A&M Univ, BS, jour, 1991, MS, jour, 2000; Fla State Univ, cert pub mg, 2005. **Career:** Fla A&M Univ, Div Res, pub rels coordr & spec asst to pres commun, 2006-07; Centers Dis Control & Prev, health commun specialist, resource mgt specialist,

2007-; Fla Dept Educ, asst dir commun; Images Design LLC, pres. **Orgs:** Fla Pub Rels Asn; Nat Asn Female Execs; Fla A&M Nat Alumni Asn; Delta Sigma Theta Sorority Inc; Am Bus Women's Asn. **Honors/Awds:** Award of Appreciation, Fla A&M Univ Marching 100; Dean's Award, Fla A&M Univ Col Pharm; President's Award & Leadership Award, Fla A&M Univ Nat Alumni Asn, Leon County Chap. **Special Achievements:** Consult, DH Community Housing & Pro Player Stadium Proj, Miami, FL, 1995. **Home Addr:** 3869 Windermere Rd, Tallahassee, FL 32311-9490, **Home Phone:** (850)321-5676. **Business Addr:** Health Communication Specialist, Resource Management Specialist, Centers for Disease Control and Prevention, 1600 Clifton Rd, Atlanta, GA 30333, **Business Phone:** (800)232-4636.

### BRYANT, DR. PATRICK L.

Dentist. **Educ:** Loyola Univ; Meharry Med Col. **Career:** Howard Hosp, gen pract residency; Pvt pract dentist, currently. **Orgs:** Active Mem, Am Dent Asn; active mem, Md State Dent Asn. **Business Addr:** General Dentist, Patrick Bryant Dds PA, 3427 Fort Meade Rd, Laurel, MD 20724, **Business Phone:** (301)776-4600.

### BRYANT, PRESTON

Educator, executive. **Personal:** Born Aug 8, 1938, Chicago, IL; married Sandra; children: Carolyn & Beverly. **Educ:** Chicago Teachers Col, BEd, 1961; Roosevelt Univ, MA, 1963; Nova Univ, EdD, 1978. **Career:** Teacher, 1961-63; master teacher, 1963-67; Madison Sch, asst prin & actg prin, 1968-70; EF Dunne Elem Sch, prin, 1971-73; George Henry Corliss High Sch, prin, 1974-77; Chicago Bd Educ, supt, 1977-; Chicago Teachers Col, instr, 1975; Union Grad Sch, prof, 1979; Gov State Univ, instr, 1980; Dist ten, supt, 1977-; Shields Sch, Dept grants. **Orgs:** Samuel B Stratton Educ Asn; Ill Asn Supr & Curric Devel; Chicago Prins Asn; Nat Asn Sec Sch Prins; bd dir & vpres, George Howland Adminrs Asn; Roosevelt Univ Alumni Asn; bd mem, Roosevelt Univ Bd Govs; Roosevelt Educ Alumni Div; Citizens Schs Com; Nat Alliance Black Sch Educrs; adv coun, Olive Harvey Col Dept Nursing; Nat Asn Black Sch Educr; Nat Asn Advan Colored People; PUSH bd educ, Phi Delta Kappa; Zion Evangel Luth Ch; Forum Civic Orgn. **Honors/Awds:** School & Community Award, 1974; Outstanding Service in Education, Edward F Dunne Sch Comn, 1974; Educators Award, Operation PUSH, 1977; Outstanding Educators Award, Dr Roger's Belle Tone Ensemble, 1977. **Home Addr:** 1112 W 107th Pl, Chicago, IL 60643, **Home Phone:** (773)239-7380. **Business Addr:** Department Of Grants, Shields Schools, 4250 S Rockwell St, Chicago, IL 60632-1216, **Business Phone:** (773)535-7285.

### BRYANT, R. KELLY, JR. See Obituaries Section.

### BRYANT, DR. REGINA LYNN

Educator. **Personal:** Born Dec 1, 1950, Memphis, TN; daughter of Al C and Dorothy Scruggs. **Educ:** Tenn State Univ, BA, foreign lang, 1974; Atlanta Univ, MBA, finance, 1980; Clark Atlanta Univ, doctoral cand. **Career:** IBM, mkg rep, 1976-77; Am Telephone & Telegraph, mgt develop prog, 1980-82; Comptroller Currency, asst nat bank examiner, 1983-84; Credit Bureau Inc & Equifax Inc, finan analyst, 1984-88; Gorby Reeves, Moraitakis & Whiteman, Atlanta, Ga, legal admin, 1988-92; Atlanta Pub Schs, foreign lang instr, 1993-. **Orgs:** Alpha Kappa Alpha Sor Inc, 1971-; Nat Black MBA Assoc, second vpres acad, 1980-83; Jr Achievement Greater Atlanta, bus consult, 1983-; Atlanta Univ, Sch Bus Admin Asn, pres, 1983-85; St Anthony's Catholic Church, chair finance comm, 1984-86; Animal life Inc, asst treas, 1984-86; Merit Employment Assoc, youth motivator, 1985-; St Anthony's Night Shelter Fund Raising Comn, 1986. **Home Addr:** 1620 Tartan Lane SW, Atlanta, GA 30311, **Home Phone:** (404)629-5459. **Business Addr:** Instructor for Foreign Languages, Atlanta Public Schools, 130 Trinity Ave, Atlanta, GA 30303, **Business Phone:** (404)802-3500.

### BRYANT, RUSSELL PHILIP

Business owner, executive, printer. **Personal:** Born Dec 11, 1949, Waterloo, IA; son of Russell Sr and Selena; married Linda Allen; children: Ian, Russell III & Julian. **Educ:** Ellsworth Jr Col, AA, mkt, 1969; Grand Valley State, BS, bus adminr, 1974; Colo Univ. **Career:** Chrysler Financial Credit, sales rep, 1974-76; Petro Energy Int, pres, 1976-79; PB Steel Inc, prin, owner, 1979-82; John Phillips Printing Inc, chief exec officer, owner, 1982-. **Orgs:** Bd dir, Minority Enterprise Inc, Colo, 1992-93; bd dir, Mullen High Sch, 1992-93; Colo Asn Com & Indust, 1992-94; bd dir, Kids Against Drugs, 1992-95; bd dir, Greater Denver Chamber Com. **Honors/Awds:** Rocky Mt Regional Minorty Purchasing, Minority Supplier, 1986; Southwest Business Development, 1989; Public Service, 1990; MBE/WBE Supplier of the Year, 1990; Denver Post/Greater Denver Chamber, Minority Business, 1990-91; Music Encoding Initiative, Service Company of the Year, 1992; Entrepreneur of the Year, Ernest & Young, 1996. **Special Achievements:** Part owner of largest black-owned printing company in the Western US. **Home Addr:** 17835 E Powers Dr, Aurora, CO 80015-3092. **Business Addr:** Owner, John-Phillips Printing Inc, 3840 Forest St, Denver, CO 80207-1121, **Business Phone:** (303)333-7989.

### BRYANT, TERESENA WISE

Government official, school administrator. **Personal:** Born Jan 19, 1940, St. Petersburg, FL; daughter of Mose Gardner (deceased) and Mattie Lee Cooksey; children: Donna Kaye Drayton. **Educ:** Fla A&M Univ, BS, 1963; Howard Univ, Completion Prog Eval & Craftsmanship, cert, 1976; NY Univ, MPA, 1977; Man Col, coun psych; Fordham Univ, Urban Educ Supv & Admin, post grad studies, 1989. **Career:** Pinellas County Sch Bd, teacher; New York City, admin positions, 1974-81; State Senator, Bronx City NY, legis asst, comm liaison, 1978-83; Off of the Mayor, New York City Youth Bur, asst exec dir, 1981-83; NY State Tempy Comm to revise the SS Laws, contract mgr, sr prog analyst, 1983-; St Senator, Jos L Galiber, campaign mgr, 1978-; Off of the Mayor, New York City Youth Bur, dir planning; campaign mgr, Robert Johnson, dist atty, NY state, 1988; Bronx City Central Bd, spec asst, 1987-90; NY State Senator, Bronx, NY, legis stat & eval, 1990-92; City Affairs Liaison, admin mgr, 1992-. **Orgs:** Alpha Kappa Alpha, Tau Omega, 1975-; coordr, Comm Bronx Blacks, 1977-; under legis leadership Sen Joseph L Galiber responsible securing addn minority councilman & black assembly seat Bronx Core districting lines; chairperson & founder, Bronx Ctr Prog Serv Youth, 1981-; bd dir, PR Rep, Urban League Bronx Aux Chap, 1982-; Fla A&M Univ Alumni Asn; Am Asn Univ Women; NY City Managerial Employees Asn; Nat Asn Advan Colored People; Am Soc Pub Admin; Nat Forum Black Pub Admin; Nat Asn Female Exec; William Inst CME Church; Coun Concerned Black Exec; NY Univ Alumni NY Chap; women adv; New York Youth Bur; Women Bus Owners NY; Bronx Black Asn Educrs; Nat Coun Negro Women; Bronx Polit Women's Caucus. **Home Addr:** 950 Evergreen Ave Apt 16M, Bronx, NY 10473, **Home Phone:** (212)842-8044.

### BRYANT, ESQ. VIVIAN

Administrator. **Career:** Orlando Housing Authority, pres & chief exec officer, currently; Sanford Housing Authority, actg exec dir, 2014-. **Orgs:** Bd mem, Homeless Serv Network; bd mem, Angels Trace Found Inc. **Business Addr:** President, Chief Executive Officer, Orlando Housing Authority, 390 N Bumby Ave, Orlando, FL 32803, **Business Phone:** (407)895-3300.

### BRYANT, WAYNE R.

Lawyer, executive, association executive. **Personal:** Born Nov 7, 1947, Camden, NJ; son of Isaac R Sr and Anna Mae; children: Wayne Richard Jr. **Educ:** Howard Univ, BA, 1969; Rutgers Univ, Sch Law, JD, 1972. **Career:** Zeller & Bryant, gen partner, 1974-; Transp & Commun Comn, vice chmn, 1982-84, chmn, 1984-, majority leader, 1990-91; Independent Authorities & Commun Comn, staff, 1982-84, vice chmn, 1984-; State NJ, Dist Five, assemblyman, 1982-95; Camden Co Coun Econ Oppor, solicitor, 1980-82; Bor Somerdale, spec solicitor, 1983-; Juv Resource Ctr, solicitor, 1983-; Bor Lawnside, bond coun, 1984-, solicitor, 1984-; Camden Co Housing Auth, solicitor, 1985-97; Bor Chesilhurst, spec solicitor, 1985-; NJ State Legis, dep majority leader, 1991-, sen, 1995-2008, asst dem leader, 2002-03; Twnp Dept ford, Planning Bd, solicitor, 1996-. **Orgs:** Nat Black Caucus State Legislators; NJ Conf Minority Trans Offs; US Supreme Ct; US Ct Appeals Third Circuit Ct Appeals DC; Supreme Ct NJ; US Dist Ct Dist NJ; life mem, Nat Asn Advan Colored People; adv bd, Educ Oppor Fund Comn Rutgers Univ; Lawnside Educ Asn; chmn, Co State & Local Govts United Way Campaign Camden Co; NJ State Dem Platform Comn. **Honors/Awds:** Hon Doctorate Laws Deg, Howard Univ, 1991; Arthur Armitage Distinguished Alumni Award, Rutgers Univ Sch Law, 1992; Recognition Award, Nat Polit Cong Black Women; Distinguished Service Award, Camden Co Bd Chosen Freeholders; Distinguished Service Award, Camden Co Planning Bd; Award Merit, NJ Co Trans Asn; Legis Committment Award, Educ Improvement Ctr S Jersey Region; Outstanding Achievement Award, Lawnside Bd Educ; Award Merit, Asn Parking Authorities State NJ; Community Service Award, Gloucester Co Black Polit Caucus; Community Service Award, Grace Temple Baptist Church; Community Service Award, YMCA Camden Co; Mt Pisgah Man Year; Community Service Award, First Regular Democratic Club Lawnside; Outstanding Service to Community, Brotherhood Sheriff & Corrections Offrs; Outstanding Service Award, Good Neighbor Award, Juv Resource Ctr; Cert Appreciation, Camden City Skills Ctr; Outstanding Commitment to Human Service, Alternats Women Now Camden Co; Outstanding Service to Community Cert Appreciation Award, Camden Community Serv Ctr; Hairston Clan Community Service Award; Nat Bus League Award; Distinguished Service Award, Haddon Heights HS Afro-Am Cult Club; Citizen of the Year, Alpha Phi Alpha Frat Inc Nu Iota Chap; NJ Asn Counties Achievement Award; Cooper Hosp Med Ctr Outstanding Legislator; Outstanding achievement in the study of negotiable instruments & outstanding achievement in the study of bankruptcy and creditors rights, Am Jurisprudence Soc. **Special Achievements:** First African American elected to the General Assembly from South Jersey. **Home Addr:** 79 LaPierre Ave, Lawnside, NJ 08045. **Business Addr:** Senator, Deputy Majority Leader, New Jerrsy State Legislation, 501 Cooper St, Camden, NJ 08102-1240, **Business Phone:** (856)757-0552.

### BRYANT, DR. WILLA COWARD

Educator, president (organization). **Personal:** Born Nov 21, 1919, Durham, NC; daughter of Owen Ward Willa and Courtney King; married Harry Lee; children: Mona Maree Shanklin. **Educ:** NC Cent Univ, AB, 1951; Temple Univ, MEd, 1961; Duke Univ, EdD, 1970. **Career:** Educator (retired); Durham City Schs, teacher, 1954-61; NC Cent Univ, teacher, asst prof educ, 1961-69, adj prof educ, 1990-94; Livingstone Col, head, dir stud teaching, Div Educ & Psychol, chairwoman, 1970-83. **Orgs:** Consult, Coop Sch Improv Prog, 1964-66; fel Southern Found, 1968-70; pres, Alpha Tau Chap Kappa Delta Pi Duke Univ, 1969-70; Triangle Reading Asn, 1970-72; vpres, NC Asn Res Educ, treas; NC Asn Col Teacher Ed, 1980-81; Bd Educ Durham City Schs, 1984-92; Phi Delta Kappa Fraternity Carolina Chap, 1987. **Honors/Awds:** "Two Divergent Approaches to Teaching Reading" Am Res Asn, 1970; "Crucial Issues in Reading" Views on Elementary Reading, 1973; Phelps Stokes Scholar, 1975. **Home Addr:** 302 E Pilot St, Durham, NC 27707-3033, **Home Phone:** (919)682-7578.

### BRYANT, WILLIAM HENRY, JR.

Engineer, president (organization), chief executive officer. **Personal:** Born Feb 10, 1963, Garfield Heights, OH; son of William Henry Sr and Ruth Earle Bishop; married Myra Williams; children: Kyle J W. **Educ:** Kent State Univ, BA, aerospace flight technol, 1985; Pac-Western Univ, BS, 1987; ETI Tech Inst, prof dipl, eng design, 1989; Embry-Riddle Aeronaut Univ, MS, aeronaut sci educ, 1995. **Career:** Plain Dealer, paper carrier, 1972-78; Parker RustProofing, phosphater & gen labor, 1979-81; Kent State Libr, librn, 1981-83; Kent State Univ Airport, line serv crew, 1983-85; Campus Bus Serv, bus driver, 1983-85; AUS C Co 101 Aviation Battalion, 101st Abn Div, crew engr, 1986-88; Cleveland Rebar, cost estimator, 1989-; Veteran's Admin, rec mgr, 1989-; Aquatech Int Corp, bd drafter, 1988-90; Swagelok Toner Co, comput aided design admin, 1990-94, tool design engr, 1994-2000; Black Eagle Aviation, instr & charter pilot, 1996, chief exec officer, flight instr, prof pilot, aviation consult, 1995-; US Airways Express, 2000-01; Air Midwest Airlines, prof pilot, 2000-04; SSP Fittings, mfg engr, 2004-09; Dept Veterans Affairs, prog support clerk, 2009-10; Defense Finance & Acct Serv, DFAS garnishment DCC supvr, 2010-. **Orgs:** Secy, Am Inst Aeronaut & Astronaut, 1982-86; Aircraft Owners & Pilots Asn, 1982-; Epsilon, Epsilon Chap, 1984-85; Soc Mfg Engrs, 1984-; jr deacon, Starlight Baptist Church, 1984; Future Aviation Prof Am, 1986-88; pres, Phi Beta Sigma Fraternity, Gamma Alpha Sigma Chap, 1993; Tuskegee AirmenInc, N Coast Chap, 1993-; Asn Black Airline Pilots, 1995-; Nat Asn FlightInstrs, 1995-; F&AM Lodge Ecclesiastes, No 120, Prince Hall, Cleveland OH, 1996-; Civil Air Patrol, 1996-; vpres, Phi Beta Sigma Fraternity. **Home Addr:** 1195 Waldo Way, Twinsburg, OH 44087, **Home Phone:** (330)963-0419. **Business Addr:** Aviation Consultant, Chief Executive Officer, Black Eagle Aviation Corp, 1195 Waldo Way, Twinsburg, OH 44087, **Business Phone:** (330)963-0419.

### BRYANT, DR. WILLIAM JESSE

Dentist, educator, association executive. **Personal:** Born Apr 8, 1935, Jacksonville, FL; son of Katie Brown; married Taunya Marie Golden; children: Kiwanis Linda, William, Deron, Vincent, Michael, Kimberly, Zachary & Jessica. **Educ:** Fla A&M Univ, BA, 1960; Ariz State Univ, attended 1962; Meharry Med Col, Sch Dent, DDS, 1967; Boston Univ, cert orthod, 1970, ScD, 1971. **Career:** Fla A&M, res asst, 1961-63; Boston Univ, instr to asst prof, 1969-74; pvt pract, 1970, dentist, currently; Whittier Dent Clin, orthodontist, 1970-72; Roxbury Comprehensive Community Health Ctr, dent dir, 1971-78; Boston Univ, chmn, assoc prof, 1972; Boston Univ, assoc prof, 1974; HEW Boston, dent consult, 1974; WPFL, Stuart, FL, 1986. **Orgs:** Exec bd mem, Roxbury Med Tech Inst, 1972-74; exec bd mem, United Way, 1976; exec bd mem, Nat Asn Advan Colored People, 1976; Am Acad Craniofacial Pain, 1998; Commonwealth Dent Soc Greater Boston; Am Asn Orthodontists; NE Soc Orthodontists; Int Asn Dent Res; Am Dent Asn; Nat Dent Asn; Mass Dent Asn; Capital City Dent Soc; Nashville Dent Bd; Fla Dent Bd; Ga Dent Bd; Tenn Dent Bd; Mass Dent Bd; Am Soc Dent C; Am Anesthesiol Asn; Soc Upper 10th; Alpha Phi Alpha; Guardsmen Inc; Nat Asn Advan Colored People; exec bd mem, Health Planning Coun, Boston; Pub Health Coun; bd dir, United Way; bd mem, Big Bro Inc, Boston; bd mem, St Michael's Sch, Fla; fel Int Col Craniomandibular Orthop; pres, Martin Co Chamber Com; bd mem, Martin Co & Palm Beach Comn Found. **Honors/Awds:** Numerous awards. **Special Achievements:** Numerous publications. **Home Addr:** 4692 SW Branch Terr W, Palm City, FL 34990, **Home Phone:** (772)286-4636. **Business Addr:** Dentist, Private Practice, 204 SW Ocean Blvd, Stuart, FL 34994, **Business Phone:** (772)283-0663.

### BRYANT-ELLIS, PAULA D.

Banker, chairperson, executive. **Personal:** Born Jan 20, 1962, Youngstown, OH; daughter of James F; married Wendell R Ellis Sr; children: Wendell R Jr. **Educ:** Concordia Lutheran Col, BA, acct & bus mgt, 1992. **Career:** KOTV-6, acct, 1991-92; Bank Okla, pvt banking officer, 1992-; BOK Financial Corp, Community Develop Banking Group, currently; Tulsa Indust Authority, Chair Credit Comt; Tulsa Econ Develop Corp, pres, 2006; Tulsa Develop Authority, comnr, 2008. **Orgs:** Nat Asn Black Accountants, 1992-93; chair, Nat Asn Black Accountants, Western Region, stud conf, 1993; chair, Credit Comt, 2000; pres, Domestic Violence Intervention Serv, 2002; leader, Tulsa, 2003; pres, Tulsa Econ Develop Corp, 2006; comnr & vice chair bd, Tulsa Econ Develop Corp, currently; Fed Res Bd Consumer Adv Coun, currently; bd mem, New Markets ReDevelop, LLC, currently. **Home Addr:** 7030 E 71st Ct S, Tulsa, OK 74133, **Home Phone:** (918)492-3948. **Business Addr:** Chief Operating Officer, BOK Financial Mortgage Group, Bank Okla Tower, Tulsa, OK 74192, **Business Phone:** (918)588-6000.

### BRYANT-HOWROYD, JANICE

Chief executive officer, entrepreneur, founder (originator). **Personal:** Born Sep 1, 1952, Tarboro, NC; married Bernard; children: 2. **Educ:** NC A&T Univ, eng; Univ Md, MA; NC State Univ, PhD. **Career:** Billboard, ass dir, 1976-78; ACT 1 Personnel Servs, founder, 1978-, pres, chmn & chief exec officer, currently; Doc Scanning Systs, chief exec officer, 1996-; A-Check Am, chief exec officer, 1998; Capital Campaign, NC A&T Univ, chair; Nat Acad Sci, ed. **Orgs:** Econ Develop Corp C Los Angeles; Los Angeles Urban League; Loyola Marymount Univ, Northrop-Rice Aviation Inst Technol; bd, John F Kennedy Sch Govt, Harvard Univ; Int Womens Coun; Am Red Cross; Nat Acad Sci. **Business Addr:** Founder, Chief Executive Officer, ACT 1 Personnel Services, 18520 Hawthorne Blvd, Torrance, CA 90504, **Business Phone:** (310)371-2151.

### BRYANT-REID, JOHANNE

Executive. **Personal:** Born Mar 11, 1949, Farmington, WV; daughter of Leslie David and Jessie L Scruggs. **Educ:** WVa Univ, BS, psychol, 1971. **Career:** Executive (retired); Ran Assoc, gen mgr & placement counr, 1971-78; Merrill Lynch, exec recruitment mgr, 1978-80, corp employ mgr, 1980, vpres, 1982-88, dir human resources, 1988-95, Opers Serv, first vpres, 1995-2002; Black World Championship Rodeo, mem adv bd; Manhattan Community Col, mem adv bd. **Orgs:** Fund; bd dir, W Va Univ Found Inc; bd mem, Funk City Rec; Selection Comt, Jackie Robinson Found Scholars Prog; exec bd, Artist Space; fund raiser, United Negro Col Fund; bd mem, co-dir, Romare Beardon Found, 2000-; mem adv bd, Nat Asn Equal Opportunity Higher Educ; mem adv bd, Nat Coun Negro Women; Exec bd mem, James Robert Braxton Scholar Fund; Am Soc Personnel Adminr; Employ Managers Asn. **Home Addr:** 150 Hoover Dr, Cresskill, NJ 07626-1716, **Home Phone:** (201)894-5972. **Business Addr:** Co-Director, Romare Bearden Foundation, 350 5th Ave Suite 2820, New York, NY 10118, **Business Phone:** (212)736-6666.

### BRYANT-SHANKLIN, DR. MONA MAREE (DR. MONA BRYANT)

Educator. **Personal:** Born Mar 26, 1954, Southern Pines, NC; daughter of Harry Lee Bryant and Willa Coward Bryant; married Gerald Price Shanklin; children: Gerald Kayin Shanklin, Jamil Maree Shanklin & Tai Miquel Shanklin. **Educ:** NC Cent Univ, BA, 1976; Kans State Univ, MS, 1979; Univ NC, Chapel Hill, NC, PhD, 1996. **Career:** Kans State Govt, voc rehab coun, 1980-82; SC State Govt, educ consult & MIS/tech admin, 1982-91; Univ NC, Chapel Hill, NC, psycho educ therapist, 1991-92; Winston Salem Pub Schs & RJR, RJR res fel, 1994-95; NC Cent Univ, adj prof, ed consult, 1994-96, After Sch Prog, dir, 1995-96, educ resh consult, 1996-97; Norfolk State Univ, Dept Early Childhood, Elem & Spec Ed, assoc prof, 1997-. **Orgs:** Alpha Kappa Alpha Sorority, 1981-; gen mem & pres, Columbia SC Chap, Nat Black

Child Develop Inst, 1986-90; Nat Asn Educ Young C, 1986-; Coun Except Child, 1992-; Asn Supv & Curric Develop, 1996-2000; Int Reading Asn, 1997-2000; Am Educ Res Asn, 1997-; YMCA, 2000-; Jack & Jill Am, 2003-; Nat After Sch Asn, 2006-; Rainbows Int. **Home Addr:** 504 Wickwood Dr, Chesapeake, VA 23322-5853, **Home Phone:** (757)749-9344. **Business Addr:** Associate Professor, Norfolk State University, 700 Pk Ave, Norfolk, VA 23504-3989, **Business Phone:** (757)823-8280.

### BRYCE, DR. HERRINGTON J.

Economist, educator. **Personal:** married Beverly J Gaustad; children: Marisa Jeanine, Shauna Celestina & Herrington Simon. **Educ:** Minn State Univ, BA, 1960; Syracuse Univ, Maxwell Sch, PhD, econs, 1966; Am Col, CLU, 1985, ChFC, 1985. **Career:** Nat Planning Assoc, economist, 1966-67; Clark Univ, fac, 1967-69; Urban Inst, sr economist, 1969-70; Brookings Inst, fel, 1970-71; MIT, fac, 1972-73; Joint Ctr Polit Studies, dir res, 1973-76; Harvard Univ, Inst Polit, fel, 1978; Univ Md, Mass Inst Technol, fac; Acad State & Local Govt, vpres, 1978-80; Carlogh Corp, pres; Nat Policy Inst, pres, 1980-85; Col William & Mary, Life Va prof bus admin, 1986-; Belg, fel; Author & Editor: Washington Post; The Wall Street Journal; The New York Times; The National Employment Weekly; Financial and Strategic Management for Nonprofit Organizations; Planning Smaller Cities. **Orgs:** Nat Asn Corp Dir; Am Soc CLU & CFC; treas bd, State Va; vpres, Nat Acad State & Local Governments; fel NATO; Nat Arts Strategies. **Home Addr:** 105 Stratford Dr Apt I, Williamsburg, VA 23185-2969, **Home Phone:** (757)253-5623. **Business Addr:** Professor of Business Administration, The College of William & Mary, Tyler 226 Miller Hall 3021, Williamsburg, VA 23187-8795, **Business Phone:** (757)221-2856.

### BRYSON, PEABO (ROBERT PEABO BRYSON)

Singer. **Personal:** Born Apr 13, 1951, Greenville, SC; married Tanya Boniface; children: Linda. **Career:** Al Freeman and the Upsetters, singer, 1965; Moses Dillard and the Tex Town Display, 1968-73; Solo Albums: Peabo, 1976; Reaching for the Sky, 1978; Crosswinds, 1978; We're the Best of Friends, 1979; Paradise, 1980; Live & More, 1980; Turn the Hands of Time, 1981; I am Love, 1981; Don't Play with Fire, 1982; Born to Love, 1983; Straight from the Heart, 1984; Take No Prisoners, 1985; Quiet Storm, 1986; Positive, 1988; All My Love, 1989; Can You Stop the Rain, 1991; Through the Fire, 1994; Peace on Earth, 1997; Really Love, 1997; Family Christmas, 1998; Unconditional Love, 1999; Christmas with You, 2005; Missing You, 2007; The Essential, 2003; duet with Natalie Cole, "We're the Best of Friends; " due twith Roberta Flack, "Tonight I Celebrate My Love"; Compilation Albums: Collection, 1984; I'm So into You: The Passion of Peabo Bryson, 1997; Anthology, 2001; Beauty and the Beast-Duets+, 2002; The Very Best of Peabo Bryson, 2006; Singles: "Do It with Feeling", 1975; "It's Just a Matter of Time", 1976; "I Can Make It Better", 1977; "I'm So into You", 1978; "Gimme Some Time", 1979; "Make the World Stand Still", 1980; "Let the Feeling Flow", 1981; "We Don't Have to Talk (About Love)", 1982; "Maybe", 1983; "If Ever You're in My Arms Again", 1984; "Love Always Finds a Way", 1985; "Good Combination", 1986; "Without You", 1987; "Show and Tell", 1989; "Lover's Paradise", 1990; "Beauty and the Beast", 1991; "A Whole New World (Aladdin's Theme)", 1992; "By the Time This Night Is Over", 1993; "Why Goodbye", 1994; "Did You Ever Know", 1999; Music videos: "By the Time This Night is Over", 1993. **Honors/Awds:** Grammy Award, 1992, 1993. **Special Achievements:** Nine gold albums with songs reaching top ten lists in US and UK. **Business Addr:** Singer, Columbia Records, 51 W 52nd St, New York, NY 10019, **Business Phone:** (212)975-4321.

### BRYSON, DR. RALPH J.

Educator, executive. **Personal:** Born Sep 10, 1922, Cincinnati, OH; son of Ralph and Annie Davis. **Educ:** Univ Cincinnati, BS, elem educ, 1947, MS, educ found, 1950; Ohio State Univ, PhD, Am lit & sec educ, 1953. **Career:** Southern Univ, instr Eng, 1949; Miles Col, instr Eng, 1949-50; Ala State Univ, assoc prof Eng, 1953-62, prof & dept head, 1962-75, 2001-, chmn div humanities, 1975-77, prof Eng, 1977-92, actg chair & prof lang & lit, prof emer, currently; Univ Ala, adj prof, 1987. **Orgs:** Pres, Asn Col Eng Teachers AL; Ala Coun Teachers Eng Exec Bd; Nat Coun Teachers Eng; Mod Lang Asn; S Atlantic MLA; Col Lang Asn; Conf Col Compos & Community; advisor, Ala State Univ Chap; Phi Delta Kappa; Lectr Auth & Consult; advisor, Kappa Alpha Psi; Ed Column Bks & Such; chmn, Nat Achievement Comn; officer, Prov Bd Dir; Am Bridge Asn; chmn exec bd & sectional vpres, Montgomery Sem Arts; bd dir, Montgomery Mus Fine Arts; chmn, Black Arts Festival; bd trustee, Mus Fine Arts Asn; bd dir, Ala Writers Forum; Herman Schneider Legacy Soc. **Honors/Awds:** Bryson Endowed Scholarships Established at Univ Cinncinnati & Ohio State Univ, 1995; 56th Recipient of the Elder Watson Diggs Award, 72nd Grand Chapter elected grand historian, 73rd Grand Chapt, Kappa AlphaPsi, 1997; Dexter Ave King Memorial Baptist Church; Outstanding Journalistic Contributions & Achievement Kappa Alpha Psi; Outstanding Men of the Year & Montgomery; Cited Outstanding OH State Univ Graduate in They Came & They Conquered; Laurel Wreath Award; CECH Distinguished Alumnus. **Special Achievements:** Co-author, History of the Southern Province, Kappa Alpha Psi Fraternity, 1951-97, 1999. **Home Addr:** 3941 Cedar Ave, Montgomery, AL 36109-1605, **Home Phone:** (334)277-3503. **Business Addr:** Professor of Languages and Literature, Acting Chair, Alabama State University, 915 S Jackson St, Montgomery, AL 36104, **Business Phone:** (334)229-4323.

**BRYSON, ROBERT PEABO. See BRYSON, PEABO.**

### BRYSON, SEYMOUR L.

School administrator, educator. **Personal:** Born Sep 8, 1937, Quincy, IL; son of Claudine Jackson; married Marjorie; children: Robin, Todd & Keri. **Educ:** Southern Ill Univ, Carbondale, BA, social work, 1959, MS, rehab coun, 1961, PhD, educ psychol, 1972. **Career:** Associate chancellor(retired); St Louis State Hosp, rehab counr, 1961-65; Breckinridge Job Corps Ctr, admin, 1965-69; Southern Ill Univ, Develop Skills Prog, dir, 1969-72, Rehab Inst SIU, from asst prof to assoc prof, 1972-84, prof, 1984, Col Human Resources, assoc dean, 1977-78 & 1980-84, interim dean, 1978-80 & 1984, dean, 1984-88, Ctr Basic Skills, affirmative action, actg affirmative action officer, asst to pres, 1988-90, exec asst to chancellor & pres, 1999, dir, assoc chancellor diversity, 1999-2008. **Orgs:** Chmn, Racism Community Am Rehab Coun Asn, 1972-74; bd dir, pres, Jackson County Community 708 Ment Health Ctr, 1974-82; senate, Am Rehab Coun Asn Del Am Personnel & Guid Asn Personnel & Guid, 1976-78; bd dir, Jackson County Community Ment Health Ctr, 1980-82; gov appointee, Dept Rehab Serv Adv Coun, 1980; State Use Comn 1983-; pres, carbondale chap, Nat Asn Advan Colored People; pres, Ill Asn Non-White Concerns, 1984-85; chmn, Jackson County 708 Bd 1986-; pres, bd dir, Carbondale United Way; bd dir, Res-Care, 1989-; Am Asn Univ Admin; Asn Non-White Concerns; Am Rehab Coun Asn; interim chair, Guardianship & Advocacy Comn, 2002; African Am Family Comn, 2005. **Special Achievements:** One of three African Americans to progress from assistant professor to full professor, the first African American to serve as associate dean of a college and the second of three African American deans on the Southern Illinois University campus. **Home Addr:** 905 S Valley Rd, Carbondale, IL 62901, **Home Phone:** (618)549-0290. **Business Addr:** Associate Chancellor, Southern Illinois University Carbondale, 110 Anthony Hall 1265 Lincoln Dr, Carbondale, IL 62901, **Business Phone:** (618)453-1187.

### BUCHANAN, CALVIN D.

State government official, judge, lawyer. **Personal:** married Donna C. **Educ:** Univ Miss, BA, JD. **Career:** AUS, judge advocate, 1983-90; Northern Dist MS, asst US atty, 1990-97, US atty, 1997-2001, prosecutor, defense coun & gen civil coun; Miami-Dade Fair Musical Theatre Competition, judge, currently. **Orgs:** MS State Bar; Magnolia Bar Asn; Second MB Church Univ; bd mem, Nat Inst Law & Equity. **Home Addr:** 3010 S Lamar Blvd, Oxford, MS 38655, **Home Phone:** (662)236-9784. **Business Addr:** Board Member, Treasurer, National Institute for Law & Equity, University of Memphis, Memphis, TN 38152, **Business Phone:** (901)324-4377.

### BUCHANAN, DARRYL E.

City council member. **Personal:** Born Jan 1, 1954?. **Career:** Flint City Coun, obudsman, 1989, 1994-96, coun mem, 2001-07, adminr, 2007-09, mayor, coun pres, currently; Baker Col, adj instr. **Orgs:** Exec bd mem, Flint Area Chamber Com; bd mem, Mass Transp Authority. **Home Addr:** 6501 Karen Dr, Flint, MI 48504-3602, **Home Phone:** (810)789-3150. **Business Addr:** Council President of Ward 1, Flint City Council, 1101 S Saginaw St, Flint, MI 48502, **Business Phone:** (810)766-7418.

### BUCHANAN, RAYMOND LOUIS

Football player, artist, broadcaster. **Personal:** Born Sep 29, 1971, Chicago, IL; married Sheree; children: Destinee, Ray Jr & Baylen. **Educ:** Univ Louisville, grad. **Career:** Indianapolis Colts, free safety, 1993-94, left defensive back, 1994-96, punt returner, 1995; Atlanta Falcons, left defensive back, 1997-2003, cornerback, 1999; Oakland Raiders, free safety, 2004; Plasticity, art dir, 2011; Fox Sports, host, currently; rap artist, album: "Favor", 1998; "Roll With Me", 1999; Films: 1991 Sunkist Fiesta Bowl, 1991; 1995 AFC Championship Game, 1996; 1998 NFC Championship Game, 1999; Super Bowl XXXIII, 1999. TV Series: "ESPN's Sunday Night Football", 1993-2004; "TNT Sunday Night Football", 1997; "The Daily Show with Jon Stewart", 1999; "NFL Monday Night Football", 1999-2003; "NFL on FOX", 2001; "ESPN SportsCentury", 2003; "The NFL on CBS", 2004; "Quite Frankly with Stephen A. Smith", 2006; "Breakfast", 2008-10. **Orgs:** Ray Buchanan Found, Make A Wish. **Honors/Awds:** American Football Conference Defensive Player of the Week, 1994; Pro Bowl National Football Conference, 1998. **Special Achievements:** Starter in the Pro Bowl for the National Football Conference in 1998; Created Christian rap music album in 2002. **Business Addr:** Co Host, Fox Sports Radio, 1203 Troy Schenectady Rd, Latham, NY 12110, **Business Phone:** (518)452-4800.

### BUCHANAN, SAM H., JR.

Lawyer. **Personal:** married Tabitha; children: 2. **Educ:** Jackson State Univ, BA, polit sci, 1979; Univ Iowa Sch Law, JD, 1982. **Career:** Hattiesburg Pub Sch Dist, pres, chmn & Trustee; Miss Ctr Legal Serv, exec dir admin, currently. **Orgs:** Miss Bar Asn; Miss Vol Lawyers Proj. **Business Addr:** Attorney, Executive Director, Mississippi Center for Legal Services, 111 E Front St, Hattiesburg, MS 39401-3463, **Business Phone:** (601)545-2950.

### BUCHANAN, SHAWN D.

Executive, baseball player. **Personal:** Born Feb 2, 1970, Gay, IN; married Kelli; children: 2. **Educ:** Univ Nebr-Lincoln, BA, psychol, 1991. **Career:** Chicago White Sox, outfielder, 1991-96; Nebr Beef, 1995; All Am Meats Inc, founder, pres & chief exec officer, 1995-. **Orgs:** Am Logistics Asn; Nat Minority Supplier; Better Bus Bur; Nat Meat Asn; Nebr Alumni Asn; Omaha Sports Comn. **Business Addr:** President, Chief Executive Officer, All American Meats Inc, 2505 N 24th St Suite 503, Omaha, NE 68110, **Business Phone:** (402)453-0200.

### BUCHANAN, SHONDA T. (NYESHA KHALFANI)

Editor, college teacher, educator. **Personal:** Born Jan 1, 1968, Kalamazoo, MI. **Educ:** Loyola Marymount Univ, BA, MA, eng, 2003; Antioch Univ, MFA, creative writing, poetry, 2010. **Career:** Turning Pt, assoc ed, Managing Ed & asst ed, 1997-2002; Marketplace Radio, commentator; Loyola Marymount Univ, Teaching fel, 2002-04; Hampton Univ, prof eng, poet, novelist, essayist & asst prof, 2004-; Ed: Voices from Leimert Park: A.Poetry Anthology; Libr Va Ann Lit Awards, judge, poetry contest, 2014-; Salvation Army, workshop leader sch prog, 2015-. **Orgs:** Fel, Sundance Inst Writing; AWP, MLA, LMU Alumni Asn; adv bd mem; exec bd mem, Poetry Socs Va, 2010-. **Home Addr:** , Los Angeles, CA 90046. **Business Addr:** Associate Professor, Hampton University, Hampton, VA 23668, **Business Phone:** (757)728-6525.

### BUCK, IVORY M., JR.

School administrator. **Personal:** Born Dec 25, 1928, Woodbury, NJ; married Ernestine Holmes; children: L Tanya Ivy & Ivory M III. **Educ:** William Paterson Bus Inst, cert bus ad, 1956; Glassboro State Col, BA, 1960, MA, 1968. **Career:** School administrator (retired); Pub Schs Deptford NJ, teacher, 1958-64; Johnstone Training Res Ctr, teacher, 1960-62; Jr High Sch Deptford, dirguid, 1964-68; Glassboro State Col, asst registr, 1968-71, Adv Ctr, asst dir; Gloucester Co Col, counr, 1969-72. **Orgs:** White House Conf Libr Serv, 1978; alumni treas, Glassboro State Col, 1979; Evaluation Team Sec Educ, 1980; secy gen, Prince Hall Scottish Rite Masons 33 Degrees, 1983; secy bd dir, Fitzwater Housing Project, 1985; nat elected officer, Prince Hall Shriners, 1980-; past imp potentate, Desert Nj, 1996-98; bd dir, Camden Co YMCA; Berlin bd, Jr Chamber Com; chairperson Inclusion, Black Studies Monroe Twp Pub Schs; imp potentate AEAO, Nobles Mystic Shrine; Nat Asn Advan Colroed People, Elks; Phi Delta Kappa Frat; co-chmn, Kappa Alpha Psi; chmn, Grand Encampment Knights Templar. **Honors/Awds:** The Chapel of Four Chaplains Award, Philadelphia, Pa, 1964, 1984; Leadership Award, Marabash Museum New Egypt NJ, 1978; Legion of Honor Award for Leadership & Service Shriners, 1980; Distinguished Alumni Award, Glassboro State Col, 1981; Honorary Police Captain, Capitol Heights Maryland, Commissioned Ky Colonel, Recipient Seagram Vanguard Award; Mayor City, Valdosta, Ga, proclaimed March 27, 1993, Ivory M Buck Jr Day. **Home Addr:** 29823 Dustin Ave, Easton, MD 21601, **Home Phone:** (410)822-0249. **Business Addr:** Co-Chairman, Kappa Alpha Psi Fraternity Inc, 28 Harrell Ave, Williamstown, NJ 08094, **Business Phone:** (609)728-0788.

### BUCK, DR. JUDITH BROOKS

Educator. **Personal:** Born Mar 3, 1949, Norfolk, VA; daughter of George A Sr; married Henry Jr; children: Kimberly & Michael Henry. **Educ:** Bennett Col, Greensboro NC, BA, spec educ & psychol, 1971; Univ Va, MEd, admin & supv, 1986, PhD, educ policy & leadership, 2001. **Career:** Coun Except C, info spec, 1972; Fairfax County, bd educ, learning disabilities teacher, 1972-74; Harford County, bd educ, crisis resource teacher, 1974-76; Norfolk Pub Schs, child develop spec, 1976-77, learning disabilities teacher, 1980-81; USAF, child care ctr, pre sch dir, 1978-80, spec educ teacher, 1983-86; Huntsville Pub Sch, alternative prog coord, 1981-83; Va State Univ, Grad Prof Educ Prog Educ Admin & Supv, IRB, comt mem, assoc prof, prof, currently; Huntsville City Sch, spec educ area specialist, prin; Challenger Mid Sch, prin; Hampton Univ, dept educ, asst prof. **Orgs:** Shiloh Baptist Church, 1959; Delta Sigma Theta, 1968; Nat Va Educ Assoc, 1976; Fed Women's Clubs Am, 1984-85; Nat Asn Sec Sch Prin, 1986; First Baptist Church, 1986; Nat Asn Elem Sch Prin, 1988; sec, bd dir, Huntsville & Madison County Daycare Asn, 1991-; comnr, Housing Authority; exec dir, OPE VI Family Self Sufficiency Prog; educ consult, Am Coun Educ. **Honors/Awds:** Freedom Fund Award, Nat Asn Advan Colored People; Most Notable Women in America for the Year, 2003. **Special Achievements:** Dr.Brooks Buck is listed in Whos Who Among Black Americans; Whos Who in American Education; Whos Who Among Executives and Professionals. **Home Addr:** 104 Blue Jay Ct, Huntsville, AL 35824, **Home Phone:** (205)464-9762. **Business Addr:** Professor, Virginia State University, 1 Hayden Dr, Petersburg, VA 23806, **Business Phone:** (804)524-5445.

### BUCKHALTER, DR. EMERSON R.

Physician. **Personal:** Born Nov 10, 1954, El Monte, CA; married Veretta Boyd; children: Monica C. **Educ:** Univ Calif Los Angeles, BA, 1976; Howard Univ Col Med, MD, 1980. **Career:** Univ Southern Calif, resident & internship, 1980-83; Hawthorne Comm Med Group, physician, 1983-86; Los Angeles Co-Usc Med Ctr, resident internal med; St Francis Care Med Group, physician, 1986-; Regal Med Group, sr physician, currently. **Orgs:** Am Med Asn. **Honors/Awds:** Alpha Omega Alpha Honor Med Soc, 1979; Nat Med Fel; Henry J Kaiser Found Merit Scholar, 1980. **Home Addr:** 5936 S Croft Ave, Los Angeles, CA 90056-1611, **Home Phone:** (323)294-3087. **Business Addr:** Physician, St Francis Primary Care Medical Group, 3628 E Imperial Hwy Suite 202, Lynwood, CA 90262-2600, **Business Phone:** (310)631-5000.

### BUCKHANAN, DOROTHY WILSON

Marketing executive, association executive, executive. **Personal:** Born Jul 12, 1958, Sumter, SC; daughter of Ida Gregg; married Walt A. **Educ:** Benedict Col Columbia SC, BS, bus, 1980; Atlanta Univ Grad Sch Bus, MBA, 1982. **Career:** Xerox Corp, mkt asst, 1982-84; SC Johnson & Son Inc, prod mgr, 1984-91; Pvt Indust Coun Milwaukee, exec dir-milwaukee job ctr network, 1997-2000; Top Ladies Distinction Inc, vpres; Goodwill Industs Southeastern Wis Incorporation, vpres mission svcs, 2000-15; Employ Solutions Inc, exec dir, 2000-01; Alpha Kappa Alpha Sorority Inc, nat 1st vpres, 2010-14; cent regional dir, 2002-06; Int Secy, 2006-10; int vpres, 2014-. **Orgs:** Am Mkt Asn, 1980; Toastmaster's Int, 1980-82; Nat Black MBA Asn, 1984; vpres, fundraising chmn & corresp secy, Alpha Kappa Alpha, 1984-87; vpres, Top Ladies of Distinction Inc, 1985-88; Greater Milwaukee Comt, exec dir, 1992-1996. **Honors/Awds:** Outstanding Undergrad Award, Alpha Kappa Alpha, 1979; Nat Deans List Atlanta Univ, 1980-82; Exec Scholar Fel, Atlanta Univ, 1982-84; Employee Recognition Award, Xerox Corp, 1983; Distinguished Alumni Award, Benedict Col, 1987; Serv Award, Alpha Kappa Alpha, 1988; Outstanding Speaker Award, Dale Carnegie Inst, 1989; 100 Most Influential Business Leaders, Milwaukee Community J, 1998; Lifetime Achievement Award, Milwaukee Community J, 1999; Community Achiever Award, Fox 6 TV, 2006; Goodwill Leading Change Award, Goodwill Industries, 2007; Black Excellence in Business Award, WISN ABC 2007; Carey B. Preston Leadership Award, Alpha Kappa Alpha Sorority Inc, 2014; Founders Graduate Service Award, Alpha Kappa Alpha Sorority Inc. **Special Achievements:** National First Vice President. **Home Addr:** PO Box 250841, Milwaukee, WI 53225-6514. **Business Addr:** International Vice President, Alpha Kappa Alpha Sorority Inc, 5656 S Stony Island Ave, Chicago, IL 60637, **Business Phone:** (773)684-1282.

### BUCKHANAN, REV. SHAWN L.

Clergy, educator. **Personal:** Born Feb 22, 1962, Albuquerque, NM; son of George Kenneth and C Jacquelyn; married Rosalind G Chelf; children: Shawn L II & Solomon L. **Educ:** Univ NMex, acad scholar Bus Mgt; Phoenix Univ, BS, bus admin, 1996. **Career:** Chase Bank Ariz, asst br mgr, 1983-91; US W Commun, operator, 1991-93; Ctr Acad Success High Sch, prin, 1996-2002; Laymen's & Youth Dept, instr; St Paul Missionary Baptist Church, pastor, sr pastor, currently. **Orgs:** Omega Psi Phi, Baslieus, 1980-83; educr, Nat Baptist Conv, USA Inc, 1981-; Nat Asn Advan Colored People, Youth Servs Ministers Div, 1995-; pres, Phoenix Citywide Youth Ministerial Asn, 1998-2001; moderator, Southern Ariz Missionary Baptist Dist Asn, 1998-2006; pres, Sierra Vista Ministerial Asn, 1998-2001; Paradise Baptist State Conv, HMB liaison, 2000-; rep, Nat Baptist Conv Home Mission Bd; treas & financial secy, Home Mission Bd, currently; active polit cand, City Sierra Vista City Coun. **Honors/Awds:** Chapter of the Year, Omega Psi Phi, 1981; Parent of the Year, Phoenix Pub Sch, 1991; Youth Division Image Award, Nat Asn Advan Colored People, 1992; numerous others. **Home Addr:** 5273 Highland Shadows Dr, Sierra Vista, AZ 85635-8239, **Home Phone:** (520)452-8597. **Business Addr:** Senior Pastor, St Paul Missionary Baptist Church, 227 N Carmichael Ave, Sierra Vista, AZ 85635, **Business Phone:** (520)458-5809.

**BUCKLEY, DOUGLAS TERELL. See BUCKLEY, TERRELL.**

**BUCKLEY, GAIL LUMET (GAIL HORNE JONES)**
Writer, journalist. **Personal:** Born Dec 21, 1937, Pittsburgh, PA; daughter of Louis Jones and Lena Horne Hagton; married Kevin; children: Amy & Jenny; married Sidney Lumet; children: 2. **Educ:** Radcliff Col, BA, 1959. **Career:** Journalist, writer; Marie-Claire Mag, journalist, 1959-63; Nat Scholar Serv & Fund Negro Studs, stud counr, 1961-62; Life Mag, journalist, 1962-63; contributor to periodicals, 1980; writer, currently; Books: The Hornes: An American Family, 1986; American Patriots: The Story of Blacks in the Military from the Revolutionto Desert Storm, 2001; Co-authored: Hirschfeld's Harlem / Al Hirschfeld, 2004; Black American families for PBS, 2002. **Honors/Awds:** DHL, Univ Southern Ind, 1987. **Special Achievements:** Television Appearance: "American Masters", 1996. **Home Addr:** 21 E 90th St, New York, NY 10128. **Business Addr:** Author, c/o Lynn Nesbit, 40 West 57th St, New York, NY 10128, **Business Phone:** (212)556-5600.

**BUCKLEY, MARCUS WAYNE**
Executive, football player. **Personal:** Born Feb 3, 1971, Ft. Worth, TX. **Educ:** Tex A&M Univ, attended 1992. **Career:** Football player (retired), executive; New York Giants, linebacker & right linebacker, 1993-99; Atlanta Falcons, line backer, 2000; NB Homes, Ltd, founder, 2001-, pres, currently. **Honors/Awds:** Consensus All-American, 1992. **Business Addr:** Founder, President, NB Homes Ltd, 1550 Eastchase Pkwy, Ft Worth, TX 76120.

**BUCKLEY, TERRELL (DOUGLAS TERELL BUCKLEY)**
Football player, football coach. **Personal:** Born Jun 7, 1971, Pascagoula, MS; son of Eddie Sr and Laura; married Denise; children: Sherrell, Brianna & Britney. **Educ:** Fla State Univ, attended 2007. **Career:** Football player (retired), coach; Green Bay Packers, defensive back, 1992-94; Miami Dolphins, 1995-99, 2003; Denver Broncos, 2000; New Eng Patriots, 2001-02; NY Jets, 2004; NY Giants, 2005: Fla State Univ, coach, 2007-11; Univ Akron, corner back coach, 2012-13; Univ Louisville, corner back coach, 2014-15; Miss State Univ, safeties coach, 2016-. **Honors/Awds:** Concensus All-American, NCAA, 1991; Jim Thorpe Award winner, 1991; Jack Tatum Trophy, 1991; Super Bowl XXXVI champion; Consensus All-Am, 1991; Fifth pick 1992 NFL Draft, Green Bay; Hall of Fame, Fla state Univ, 2003. **Special Achievements:** Film: 1992 NFL Draft , 1992; TV Series: "2001 AFC Championship Game", 2002; "17th Annual American Century Championship", 2006; "Rome Is Burning", 2007, 2009. **Business Addr:** Safeties Coach, Mississippi State University, 175 Pres Circle, Mississippi State, MS 39762, **Business Phone:** (662)325-7400.

**BUCKNER, BRENTSON ANDRE**
Football coach, broadcaster, football player. **Personal:** Born Sep 30, 1971, Columbus, GA; married Denise. **Educ:** Clemson Univ, grad. **Career:** Football player (retired), football coach; Pittsburgh Steelers, right defensive end, 1994, left defensive end, 1995-96, nose tackle, 1995; Cincinnati Bengals, nose tackle, 1997; San Francisco 49ers, 1998, right defensive tackle, 1999-2000, defensive tackle, 1999; Carolina Panthers, left defensive tackles, 2001-05, defensive tackle, 2002; Ariz Cardinals, asst coach, defensive line coach, 2015-; WFNZ, host; NFL network, NFL analyst, currently; ESPN, NFL analyst, currently; N side Christian Acad high sch, head coach, currently; Faith Before Fame Clothing LLC, owner. **Orgs:** Pittsburg Steelers orgn. **Honors/Awds:** Peach Bowl Defensive MVP. **Business Addr:** Head Coach, Northside Christian Acad High Sch Football, 333 Jeremiah Blvd, Charlotte, NC 28262.

**BUCKNER, FLOYD**
Publisher, city council member. **Career:** Community Times Dispatch, publ, currently; Colleton County, councilman, currently. **Special Achievements:** First African American descent to have a government building named after him in Colleton County. **Business Addr:** Publisher, Councilmen, Community Times Dispatch, 202 Bailey St, Walterboro, SC 29488, **Business Phone:** (843)549-1754.

**BUCKNER, DR. JAMES LOWELL**
Executive, dentist. **Personal:** Born Jul 29, 1934, Vicksburg, MS; son of Florice Williams and Clarence E; children: JaSaun, Jordan & Justina. **Educ:** Univ Ill, BSD, 1957, DDS, 1959. **Career:** Pvt pract dentist, 1959-; Chicago Econ Develop Corp, vice chmn, 1972-75; Seaway Commun Inc, vpres, 1977-85, chmn, 1985-97. **Orgs:** Founder, bd dir, Seaway Nat Bank, 1965-86; pres, Lincoln Dent Soc, 1965-66; secy, bd dir, Nat Dent Asn, 1966-67; bd dir, Chicago Econ Develop Corp, 1966-81; bd adv, Supreme Life Ins Co, 1970-; trustee, WTTW, Channel 11, 1970-74; bd dir, City Col Chicago, 1971-76; chmn, Chicago Dent Soc Comn Pub Aid, 1971-80; pres, Coun Minority Bus Enterprise, 1972-75; Gov Walkers Pub Health Transition Task Force, 1972-73; bd adv, Midwest Sickle Cell Anaemia Inc, 1972-; trustee, Univ Ill Dent Alumni Asn, 1973-75; co-chmn, Chicago United, 1973-75; pres & dir, Chicago Urban League, 1973-76; chmn, Chicago Fin Develop Corp, 1973-76; chmn, Coun Nat Urban League, 1975-76; pres, Trains & Boats & Planes Inc, 1978-92; pres, Food basket Inc, 1980, 1988-; Am Soc Travel Agents; chmn, Push Found, 1987-; vice chmn, Ill Serv Fed Savings & Loan, 1988-; Ill Dent Soc; Am Dent Soc; Ill Dent Serv Corp; Ill Dept Pub Aid Dent Adv Comt; chmn, Chicago Finance Develop Corp. **Honors/Awds:** Ten Outstanding Young Men Award, South End Jaycees, 1965; Certificate Achievement, Am Inst Banking, 1965; Certificate Achievement, Nat Dent Asn, 1966; Certificate of Appreciation, Chicago Area Coun Boy Scouts, 1970; Community Service Award, Big Buddies Youth Serv Inc, 1971; Man of the Year Award, Chicago Urban League, 1972; Certificate of Appreciation, Commonwealth Church, 1972; Certificate of Recognition, Coun Nat Urban League Pres, 1977; Outstanding Achievement Award, Women's Div, Chicago Urban League, 1985. **Home Addr:** 6954 N Sheridan Rd, Chicago, IL 60626, **Home Phone:** (773)856-6334. **Business Addr:** Chairman, Seaway Communications Inc, 371 Target Indust Circle, Bangor, ME 04401, **Business Phone:** (207)945-6457.

**BUCKNER, QUINN (WILLIAM QUINN BUCKNER)**
Basketball player, basketball coach, basketball executive. **Personal:** Born Aug 20, 1954, Phoenix, IL; married Rhonda; children: Jason, Cory, Lauren & Alexsandra. **Educ:** Ind Univ, BS, bus, 1976. **Career:** Basketball player, coach (retired), basketball executive; Milwaukee Bucks, point guard, 1976-82; Boston Celtics, point guard, 1982-85; Ind Pacers, point guard, 1985-86; NBC TV, NBA telecasts, analyst, 1993; Dallas Mavericks, head coach, 1993-94; Cleveland Cavaliers, analyst; Pacers Sports & Entertainment, vpres commun, 2004-; ESPN, broadcaster; FSN Midwest, Ind Pacers, color analyst & barker, currently. **Orgs:** Pacers Found; Spec Olympics Ind; Community Health Found; Indianapolis Zool Soc; Ind Youth Inst; YMCA; Alpha Phi Alpha. **Honors/Awds:** Bronze Medal, FIBA World Championship, 1974; Gold Medal, Pan American Games, 1975; Gold Medal, Olympic games, 1976; Championship, Nat Col Athletic Asn, 1976; All-Defensive Team, Nat Basketball Asn, 1978, 1980, 1981, 1982; Championship, Nat Basketball Asn, 1984. **Business Addr:** Color Analyst, FSN Midwest, The Annex Bldg, St. Louis, MO 63103, **Business Phone:** (314)206-7000.

**BUCKNER, WILLIAM QUINN. See BUCKNER, QUINN.**

**BUCKSON, TONI YVONNE (TONI BYRD)**
Transportation consultant, association executive. **Personal:** Born Jun 5, 1949, Baltimore, MD; married Robert Byrd Sr. **Educ:** Coppin State Col, BS, 1971; Univ Baltimore, MS, 1978; Northeastern Univ, cert, 1985; Atlanta Univ, cert, 1985. **Career:** Mayor & City Coun Baltimore, CATV task force mgr, 1979-81; Nat Aquarium Baltimore, grp events coordr, 1981-82; Mass Transit Admin, ride sharing dir, 1982-86; Md Transp Authority, asst admin bridges, 1986; Wash Metrop Area Transit Authority, customer Serv Info Off, supvr, coordr, prog mgr, 1992-. **Orgs:** Curric adv, Goucher Col, 1975-78; bd mem, Jr League Md, 1978-80; trainer, Nat Info Ctr Vol, 1979-81; bd mem, Md Food Bank, 1979-81; bd mem, Future Homemakers Am, 1980-81; bd mem, Girl Scouts Cent Md, 1982-84. **Honors/Awds:** Service Award, Girl Scouts Cent Am, 1984; Affirmative Action Award, Md Dept Transp, 1984; Outstanding Young Women in America, 1985; presidential citation, Nat Asn Equal Opportunity Higher Educ, 1986. **Home Addr:** 6 Tallow Ct, Baltimore, MD 21244-2517. **Business Addr:** Coordinator, Program Manager, Washington Metropolitan Area Transit Authority, 600 5th St NW, Washington, DC 20001, **Business Phone:** (202)962-1234.

**BUFORD, DAMON JACKSON**
Baseball player. **Personal:** Born Jun 12, 1970, Baltimore, MD; son of Don. **Educ:** Univ Southern Calif. **Career:** Baseball player (retired); Australian Baseball League, 1992; Baltimore Orioles, outfielder, 1993-95; NY Mets, 1995; Tex Rangers, 1996-97; Boston Red Sox, 1998-99; Chicago Cubs, 2000-01; Wash Nat, outfielder, 2004.

**BUFORD, HOWARD**
Chief executive officer. **Educ:** Harvard Univ, AB, psychol, 1979; Harvard Bus Sch, MBA, 1983. **Career:** Procter & Gamble, brand mgt, 1979-81; Young & Rubicam, asst acct exec, 1983-84, acct exec, 1984-86; Young & Rubicam advert, vp, 1985-88; Young & Rubicam Group, Vice Pres/Client Serv Mgr, Burson-Marsteller, 1988-89; UniWorld Group, group acct dir, 1989-93; Prime Access Inc, pres & chief exec officer, 1990-2014; Quorum Consult, managing dir, pres & chief exec officer, 2015-. **Business Addr:** President, Chief Executive Officer, Quorum Consulting, 180 Sansome St 10th fl, San Francisco, CA 94104, **Business Phone:** (415)835-0190.

**BUFORD, JAMES A.**
Administrator. **Educ:** Tenn State Univ, BS, biol, 1957; William Jewell Col, NSF, 1959; Kans State Univ, NSF, 1960; Cent Mo State Univ, MS, educ admin, 1965; Univ Mich, MPH, med care orgn & admin, 1972; Harvard Univ, planning regulation, 1977. **Career:** State Mo, sci teacher; Kings Co Hosp, NY City, exec dir; Urban Community Serv Dept, Kans City, dir; DC Dept Human Serv, agency dir, proj mgr, dir, 1980-83; Buford & Assocs Inc, pres, 1983-85; Dept Urban Community Serv, MO, dir, 1985-86; NY Health & Hosp Corp, 1986-92; Kings County Hosp Ctr, exec dir, 1988-91; Div Hosp Opers, NY, exec dir, 1991-92; Human Resources Admin, NY, mgt consult, 1992-94; Univ Res Corp, mgt consult, 1994-99; Dept Health & Welfare, Newark, dir; Detroit Health Dept, staff, 1999-2002, dir, 1999-; Govt DC, Dept Health, chief operating officer, 2002, interim dir, 2002, actg dir, 2002, dir, currently. **Orgs:** Am Pub Health Asn; Nat Asn Health Serv Exec; Am Magt Asn; Nat Pub Hosp Asn. **Home Addr:** 1800 Campau Farms Cir, Detroit, MI 48207, **Home Phone:** (313)259-2191. **Business Addr:** Director, District of Columbia, 825 N Capitol St NE, Washington, DC 20002, **Business Phone:** (202)671-5000.

**BUFORD, JAMES HENRY**
Association executive, chief executive officer. **Personal:** Born Jun 2, 1944, St. Louis, MO; son of James and Myrtle Margaret Brown; married Susan; children: 2; married Helen Joyce Freeman; children: James H Jr Jason. **Educ:** Forest Park Community Col, AA, bus admin; Elizabeth town Col, Elizabeth town, PA, BA human serv admin. **Career:** Smith, Kline & French, St Louis, Mo, regional mkt rep, 1972-75; St Louis Community Col, St Louis, Mo, prog coordr, 1975-76; Harris Stowe Community Col, emer staff; 70001 Ltd, St Louis, Mo, vpres, 1976-80; Int Mgt & Develop Group LTD, Washington, DC, sr vpres, 1980-81, St Louis, Mo, exec vpres, 1981-85; Urban League Metrop, St Louis, pres & cheif exec officer, 1985-; Urban League, partner, 2001; YWCA, partner, 2001. **Orgs:** Nat Asn Advan Colored People; bd mem, Leadership St Louis, 1985-88; exec comt mem, Blue Cross/Blue Shield, 1986-; exec bd, Boy Scouts, 1986-; bd dir, St Louis Community Col Bldg Corp, 1986-; chmn, bd regents, Harris Stowe State Col, 1989; chair nominating comt, Sigma Pi Phi, 1988; Personnel Adv Comt Pres George Bush, 1989; chmn, St. Louis Community Col Bldg Corp; chmn, St. Louis Connectcare; chair emer, Harris Stowe State Univ; vice chmn, Heat Up St. Louis & Cool Down St. Louis; exec bd mem, St. Louis Coun Boy Scouts Am; bd mem, Downtown St. Louis Partnership; bd mem, Fair St. Louis; bd mem, St. Louis Sci Ctr; bd mem, Chancellor's Coun Univ Mo-St. Louis; bd mem, US Bank; bd mem, Forest Pk Hosp; bd mem, St. Louis Muny Opera; bd mem, Jobs Ams Graduates; bd mem, Metrop Sewer Dist. **Honors/Awds:** Brotherhood & Sisterhood Award, Nat Conf Community & Justice; Humanitarian Award, Kappa Alpha Psi-St Louis, 1984; Professionalism Award, Kappa Alpha Psi-St Louis, 1986; Lamp Lighter Award, Pub Rels Soc Am, 1993; DHL, Harris Stowe Col, 1993; DHL, Univ Mo, 1995; Distinguished Alumni Award, St Louis Community Col, 1995; Lifetime Achievement Award, St Louis Gateway Classic, 1997; Whitney M. Young Award, Boy Scouts, 1999; DHL, Webdster Univ, 2000; Mentor St Louis Award, 2005; DHL, Eden Theol Sem, 2006; Hon Dr, Humane Lett Degrees, Harris Stowe State Col, 1993, Univ Mo St Louis, 1995, Webster Univ, 2000, Eden Theol Sem, 2006. **Special Achievements:** Order of the First State, Governor of Delaware, 1981. **Home Addr:** 1 Kingsbury Pl, St. Louis, MO 63112, **Home Phone:** (314)361-8565. **Business Addr:** President, Chief Executive Officer, Urban League Metropolitan St Louis, 3701 Grandel Sq, St. Louis, MO 63108, **Business Phone:** (314)615-3600.

**BUFORD, WESLEY R.**
Executive. **Personal:** Born Feb 17, 1949, Oakland, CA; children: Kyshanna Thompson. **Career:** Sarah Lee Corp, ProBall Food & Beverage Affil, pres & chief exec officer; Urban TV Network, chief exec officer & exec producer; Montel Williams Show, co creator, co owner, co exec producer; Freedom Card Inc, founder, chmn, pres & chief exec officer. **Orgs:** Co developer, NFL Youth Edu Town; chair, State Ill, Minority & Small Bus Comt; founding co chair, City Los Angeles Task Force African Am Affairs; bd dir, Boys Choir Harlem; Oper Hope Banking Ctr; bd dir, Kappa Alpha Psi; dipl, Int Cir World Affairs Coun; bd mem, Nat Bankers Asn.

**BUFORD, WILLIAM KEN M., III**
Executive, president (government). **Educ:** St Louis Univ, attended; Northwestern Univ, MBA. **Career:** Reliant Indust Inc, chmn & chief exec officer. **Home Addr:** 120 Sycamore Dr, Bolingbrook, IL 60490, **Home Phone:** (630)759-5821.

**BUGG, DR. GEORGE WENDELL, SR.**
Physician. **Personal:** Born Jun 17, 1935, Nashville, TN; children: George Jr, Michael Stanley, Kevin Gregory & Kisha Monique. **Educ:** Tenn State Univ, BS, 1958; Meharry Med Col, MD, 1962. **Career:** Homer G Phillips Hosp, intern, 1962-63, resident, 1963-64; St Louis Connect Care, resident, 1964-66; G W Hubbard Hosp, Meharry Col, resident, 1966-67; Pvt pract gen surgeon; Dept Social Serv, med consult, 1989-. **Orgs:** Chmn, Cecil C Hinton Comm Ctr, 1969-72; chmn, W Fresno Fed Neighborhood Ctr, 1972; chmn, Comm Serv Am Heart asn, 1972; pres, Daniel H Williams Med Forum, 1974-77; AMA; Can Med Asn; Nat Med Asn; Surveyors; Joint Comn Accreditation Hosps; Alpha Phi Alpha Inc; Fresno-Madera Med Found; Comm Coun Black Educ Affairs. **Honors/Awds:** Physicians Recognition Award, AMA, 1969; ACE Award, 1993. **Home Addr:** 4696 N Crestmoor Ave, Clovis, CA 93619-4612, **Home Phone:** (559)440-5352.

**BUGG, MAYME CAROL**
Social worker, lawyer. **Personal:** Born Apr 18, 1945, Portsmouth, VA; daughter of George W and Mayme P. **Educ:** Fisk Univ, BA, sociol, 1966; George W Brown Sch Soc Work Wash Univ, MSW, 1968; Cleveland State Univ, JD, 1977. **Career:** Oberlin Col, educ prog dir, 1969-70; Cleveland City Hall, city planner, 1970-71; Cuyahoga Community Col, asst to dept head, 1971-74; Comt Action Against Addiction, ct liaison, 1976-77; United Labor Agency, proj dir, 1977-79; Cuyahoga Co Juv Ct, referee, 1979. **Orgs:** League Pk Neighborhood Ctr, 1979-84; bd mem, Citizens League Greater Cleveland, 1980-84; Drop-Out Prev Comt, Cleveland Bd Educ, 1981-; vis comt, Case Western Res Univ Law Sch, 1986-; adv comt, Fenn Educ Fund, 1987-94; Serv Black Families, 1989-92; bd mem emer, Proj Friendship Big Sister Prog, 1991; Harambee Serv Black Families; Fisk Univ Cleveland Alumni Club; Cuyahoga Co Bar Asn; Proj Friendship; Asn Blacks Juv Justice Syst; Leadership Cleveland; Alpha Kappa Alpha Sorority; United Way Serv Leadership Develop Prog; African-Am Family Cong; Norman S Minor Bar Asn; bd mem & first vpres, Harambee; Nat Asn Advan Colored People. **Honors/Awds:** Office of Economic Opportunity Scholar, Wash Univ, 1967; Tots & Teens Leadership Award, Cleveland Chap, 1986; Certificate of Recognition, Nat Asn Black Social Workers. **Home Addr:** 4421 Granada Blvd, Cleveland, OH 44128, **Home Phone:** (216)475-6499. **Business Addr:** Referee, Cuyahoga County Juvenile Court, 2163 E 22nd St, Cleveland, OH 44115, **Business Phone:** (216)443-8400.

**BUGG, ROBERT L.**
Government official, educator. **Personal:** Born Jun 3, 1941, Topeka, KS; son of Walter and Mattie; married Jacqueline Shope; children: Glen, Chris & Anton. **Educ:** Washburn Univ, Topeka, BA, corrections, 1974; Kans Univ, Lawrence, MA, pub admin, 1976. **Career:** Government official (retired), executive; State Kans, Topeka, correctional officer, 1962-66; City Topeka, Topeka, police officer, chief admin officer 1966-68, field rephuman rels, 1968-69; E Topeka Methodist Church, Topeka, dir coun, 1969-70; Big Bros & Big Sisters, Topeka, KS, dir vehicles, 1982-87; State Kans, Topeka, dir vehicles, 1982-87; City Topeka, Topeka, personnel dir & laborrels, interim dir, 1987-; City Topeka, spec asst to Mayor & chief admin officer, 1997-2000, interim dir, Human Rels Comn, currently; Robert Bugg & Assocs, owner, currently. **Orgs:** Chmn, Black Dem Caucus Kans, 1982-89; chair, founder, Martin Luther King Birthday Celebration, 1986-; exec

bd mem, Nat Asn Advan Colored People; chair, Topeka Housing Authority; founder, Living Dream; chairperson, Topeka Human Rels Comn; Gov's Comt Criminal Justice. **Home Addr:** 3721 SE Evans Dr, Topeka, KS 66609-1408, **Home Phone:** (913)267-2347. **Business Addr:** Owner, Robert Bugg & Associates, 700 SW Jackson St, Topeka, KS 66603, **Business Phone:** (785)232-4565.

## BUGGAGE, CYNTHIA MARIE

Government official. **Personal:** Born Oct 26, 1958, Donaldsonville, LA; daughter of Wilfred Joseph Sr and Yvonne Stewart. **Educ:** Grambling State Univ, LA, BS, 1979; Tex Southern Univ, Houston, TX, MPA, 1988. **Career:** City Houston Parks & Rec, Houston, TX, grants adminr, 1980, supvr; Univ Houston, Houston, TX, adj prof, 1986-89; US House Representatives Congresswoman Sheila Jackson Lee, dist dir & chief staff; Am Red Cross, sr assoc govtrels; Tex Southern Univ, Houston, TX, asst athletic dir & bus mgr; Am Red Cross, sr assoc hurricane recovery prog; Southern Univ Law Ctr, Baton Rouge, LA, dir develop, currently. **Orgs:** Regional dir, Nat Asn Advan Colored People, 1979-; Grambling Univ Nat Alumni Asn, 1980-; bd dir, Polit Activ League, 1986-87; Nat Forum Black Pub Adminrs, 1987-89; Nat Asn Female Exec, 1991; Alpha Kappa Alpha Sorority. **Honors/Awds:** Human Enrichment of Life Prog, Black Achiever Houston, Tex Award, 1994. **Home Addr:** 745 Int Blvd Suite 745, Houston, TX 77024, **Home Phone:** (713)686-9614. **Business Addr:** Director Office of Development, Southern University Law Center, PO Box 9294, Baton Rouge, LA 70813, **Business Phone:** (225)771-5044.

## BUGGS, JAMES FERDINAND

Insurance executive, real estate executive. **Personal:** Born Apr 27, 1925, Summerfield, LA; son of Clifton (deceased) and Lucille Franklin; married Johnye Allen; children: James F & Bruce J. **Educ:** Spauling Bus Col. **Career:** Ins exec & real estate salesman, 1973-; Caddo Parish, Shreveport, LA, dep tax assessor, 1982-2003; Primerica Fin Serv, life ins exec. **Orgs:** Pres, Shreveport Negro Chamber Com, 1972-73; chmn trustee, Am Legion 525, 1973-78; deacon, Galilee Baptist Church; worshipful master, Fred D Lee Lodge Prince Hall affil. **Honors/Awds:** Prince Hall Masonic Lodge, Certificate for 50 years membership, 1996. **Business Addr:** Life Insurance Executive, Independent/Individual Sales, 2839 Round Grove Lane, Shreveport, LA 71107-5950, **Business Phone:** (318)425-1824.

## BUIE, PASTOR SAMPSON, JR.

School administrator, clergy. **Personal:** Born Sep 18, 1929, Fairmont, NC; married Catherine O; children: Debra, Janice & Velma. **Educ:** NC Agr & Tech State Univ, BS, 1952; Univ NC, Greensboro, MEd, 1973, EdD, 1982. **Career:** School administrator (retired); Boy Scouts Am, asst scout exec, 1954-70; NC Agr & Tech State Univ, dir community relations, 1970-82, dir off alumni affairs, 1982-93; State NC, Dept Admin, dep secy progs; Roberts Chapel Missionary Baptist Church, Goldston, NC, sr pastor, currently. **Orgs:** Bd dir Greensboro Rotary Club, 1969-; mem bd visitors, Shaw Univ Div Sch, 1981-; NC Comn Develop Comn, 1982-; trustee, Gen Baptist State Conv NC, 1982-; Col & Grad Comt, Chamber Com, Greensboro United Fund; vpres, Gen Greene Coun BSA; NC A&T State Univ Nat Alumni Asn; Phi Beta Sigma; Greensboro Citizens Asn; Nat Univ Ext Asn; Guilford City Recreation Comn; Greensboro-Guilford City Pulpit Forum; Drug Action Coun Personnel Search Comn; NC State Adv Comn on Recruitment Minorities State Criminal Justice Syst; Nat Coun BSA; consult, Monitoring & Tech Asst Training USHUD; NC Comn Volunteerism & Community Serv, 2003; comnr, monitoring prm NC comn, 2005-. **Honors/Awds:** Nathaniel Greene Award City of Greensboro, 1969; Achievement Award NC A&T State Univ Alumni Asn, 1969; United Negro Col Fund Award, Bennett Col, 1972; Silver Beaver Award, BSA, 1978; Minister of the Year, Deep River Baptist Asn, 1983. **Special Achievements:** Numerous professional papers including "Andragogy Pedagogy, Characteristics of Adults That Impact on Adult Learning & Dev" 1983; "Lifelong Learning, A Necessity & Not a Luxury" 1983. **Home Addr:** 2111 Belcrest Dr, Greensboro, NC 27406, **Home Phone:** (336)273-3729. **Business Addr:** Senior Pastor, Roberts Chapel Missionary Baptist Church, 439 Roberts Chapel Church Rd, Goldston, NC 27252, **Business Phone:** (919)898-4822.

## BULLARD, EDWARD A., JR.

Educator, accountant, systems analyst. **Personal:** Born Apr 2, 1947, Syracuse, NY; married Terrlyon D; children: Lan R, Edward III & Terron D. **Educ:** Southern Univ, BS, 1969; Syracuse Univ, MBA, 1972; Univ Detroit Law Sch, JD, 1978. **Career:** Carrier Corp, analyst, 1969; Ernst & Young, acct, 1969-72; Univ MI, Flint, prof, 1972-93; GMI, assoc prof actg, 1972-93; Detroit Col Bus-Flint, prof; Tax Info Tech, consult. **Orgs:** Bd mem, Urban League Flint, 1984, Flint Comn Develop Corp, 1984; Am Actg Asn; adv, Flint City Schs Bus Prog, 1985; City Flint Cable TV Adv Panel; Small bus consult & urban analyst; Am Bus Law Asn; bd, Urban League Flint; bd, Flint Community Develop Coord; legal regress comn, exe comt, Nat Asn Advan Colored People, Flint; adv panel, Flint Cable TV; consult, Jr Achievement, Beecher High Sch; Cong Black Caucus-Flint; treas, ACLY Greater Flint; numerous others. **Home Addr:** 3026 Concord St, Flint, MI 48504, **Home Phone:** (810)233-3057.

## BULLARD, KEITH

Automotive executive. **Career:** Chrysler Corp, Chrysler Plymouth, dealer, 1978-84; Airport Lincoln Mercury, owner, currently; Keith Bullard Used Car Super Inc, owner, 2002-. **Orgs:** Pres, Chrysler Black Dealer Asn, 1985-86. **Business Addr:** Owner, Keith Bullard Used Car Super Inc, 1466 Beers Sch Rd, Coraopolis, PA 15108-2543, **Business Phone:** (412)299-0400.

## BULLARD, ROBERT DOYLE

Sociologist, dean (education), activist. **Personal:** Born Dec 21, 1946, Elba, AL; son of Nehemiah and Myrtle Brundidge. **Educ:** Ala A&M Univ, BA, hist & govt, 1968; Atlanta Univ, MA, sociol, 1972; Iowa State Univ, PhD, sociol, 1976. **Career:** City Des Moines, IA, urban planner, 191-74; Polk County, Des Moines, IA, res coordr, 1975-76; Tex Southern Univ, asst prof, 1976-80, dir res Urban Res Ctr, 1976-78, assoc prof, 1980-87; Univ Tenn, assoc prof, 1987-88; Univ Calif Berkeley, vis scholar/assoc prof, 1988-89; Univ Calif, Riverside, assoc prof, 1989-90, prof, 1990-94; Univ Calif Los Angeles, vis prof & dir res, 1993-94; Clark Atlanta Univ, prof & dir Environ Justice Res Ctr, 1994-2011; Tex Southern Univ's Barbara Jordan-Mickey Leland Sch Pub Affairs, dean, 2011-. **Orgs:** Chair Health & Res Subcomt, Nat Environ Justice Adv Coun; Am Sociol Asn; Am Pub Health Asn; Environ Justice Leadership Forum Climate Chg; Environ Justice Climate Chg; Nat Black Environ Justice Network. **Special Achievements:** Known as the father of environmental justice; member of President Clinton's transition team, 1990; author of books on environmental issues, including "Dumping in Dixie: Race, Class and Environmental Quality" (Westview Press, 2000) and "Just Sustainabilities: Development in an Unequal World" (MIT Press, 2003), and "The Black Metropolis in the Twenty-First Century: Race, Power and the Politics of Place" (Rowman & Littlefield, 2007). **Business Addr:** Barbara Jordan-Mickey Leland School of Public Affairs, 3100 Cleburne Ave, Houston, TX 77004, **Business Phone:** (713)313-6840.

## BULLETT, VICTORIA ANDREA (VICKY BULLETT)

Basketball player, basketball coach. **Personal:** Born Oct 4, 1967, Martinsburg, WV. **Educ:** Univ Md, BA, gen studies, 2001. **Career:** Basketball player (retired), basketball coach; Us Team, 1988, 1992; Us Olympic Teams, 1998, 1992; Bari, 1990-93; Cesena, 1993-97; Charlotte Sting, ctr, 1997-99; Wash Mystics, 2000-02; asst coach & mgr, 2009; Hagerstown Community Col, asst coach, 2009-12; head coach, 2012-. **Home Addr:** 218 Vicky Bullett St, Martinsburg, WV 25404-4511, **Home Phone:** (304)263-4832. **Business Addr:** Head Coach, Hagerstown Community College, 11400 Robinwood Dr, Hagerstown, MD 21742, **Business Phone:** (240)500-2000.

## BULLINS, ED

Playwright, television producer, educator. **Personal:** Born Jul 2, 1935, Philadelphia, PA; son of Edward and Bertha Marie Queen; married Trixie; children: Eddie Jr, Donald, Ronald, Darlene,Patsy, Diane, Sun Ra, Ameena & Catherine Room. **Educ:** Los Angeles City Col, attended 1963; San Francisco State Col; NY Sch Visual Arts; William Pa Bus Inst, gen bus cert; Antioch Univ, BA, 1989; San Francisco State Univ, MFA, 1994. **Career:** Black Arts/W, founder, producer, 1966-67; New Lafayette Theatre Harlem, playwright, assoc dir, 1967-73; Black Theatre Mag, ed, 1968-73; New York Shakespeare Festival, writers unit coordr/press assst, 1975-82; New York Univ, Sch Continuing Educ, instr, 1979, dramatic writing instr, 1981; Berkeley Black Repertory, pub rels dir, 1982; Magic Theatre, prom dir pro tem, 1982-83; Julian Theatre, group sales coordr, 1983; City Col San Francisco, drama instr, 1984-88; Antioch Univ, San Francisco, playwriting instr, admin asst, pub info & recruitment, 1986-87; Bullins Memorial Theatre, producer/playwright, 1988; Northeastern Univ, prof theater, distinguished artist residence, 1995-2000; playwright, currently. **Orgs:** Dramatists Guild; mentor, Act Roxbury Playwrights Unit, 1999-2003; mentor; Cherry Land Theatre, Playwrights, 2002-03. **Home Addr:** 37 Vine St Suite 1, Roxbury, MA 02119-3354. **Business Addr:** Playwright, c/o The Farber Literary Agency, 14 E 75th St, New York, NY 10021, **Business Phone:** (212)861-7075.

## BULLOCK, ALICE GRESHAM

Lawyer, educator, association executive. **Personal:** children: 2. **Educ:** Howard Univ, BA, 1972; Howard Univ Sch Law, JD, 1975; Georgetown Law Ctr, post grad study, taxation. **Career:** Georgetown Law Ctr, fel; Off Chief Coun, IRS, trial atty, 1975-79; Howard Univ Sch Law, from asst prof to assoc prof, 1979-87, prof, 1987-, assoc dean, 1988-92, actg dean, 1990, interim dean, 1996-97, dean, 1997-2002; Hart Carroll & Chavers, coun, 1983-86. **Orgs:** Am Law Inst; ABA Comt Teaching Taxation; bd dir, Coun Legal Educ Opportunity; bd visitors, Brigham Young Univ Law Sch; bd trustees, InstIndependent Educ; US Supreme Ct; DC Bar; Soc Am Law Teachers; Am Asn Higher Educ Adv Comt; Am Bar Asn; Nat Bar Asn; Wash Bar Asn; fel Am Bar Found; dep dir, Asn Am Law Schs, 1992-94; Nat Adv Bd Nat Underground Freedom Ctr; independent dir, Bd Dirs Calvert Group; bd trustee, N Country Sch; Leadership Wash; vice chair, Montgomery County; vice chair, Md Charter Rev Comn. **Honors/Awds:** Outstanding Service Award, Nat Bar Asn, 1980; Meritorious Service Award, Howard Univ, 1996; President's Distinguished Service Award, Nat Asn Equal Opportunity, 1997; Outstanding Service Award, Student Bar Asn, 1997; Hon Doctor Laws Degree, Suffolk Univ, 1999; Outstanding Dean Award, Mid Atlantic Fac Color, 2000; NBA Gertrude B Rush Award, 2004. **Special Achievements:** Article: "Taxes, Social Policy and Philanthropy: The Untapped Potential of Middle and Lower-Income Taxpayers"; One of the Most Powerful Women in Washington by Washingtonian Magazine, 2001. **Business Addr:** Professor of Law, Howard University School of Law, 414 Houston Hall, Washington, DC 20008, **Business Phone:** (202)806-8049.

**BULLOCK, ANNA MAE.** See TURNER, TINA.

## BULLOCK, BYRON F.

Special education teacher. **Personal:** son of Gloria and Willie; married Antoinette L; children: Melanie & Aaron. **Educ:** Lincoln Univ, BA, 1977; James Madison Univ, MEd, 1989. **Career:** Univ Del, asst dir; James Madison Univ, assoc vice pres stud affairs, 1985-99; St Augustines Col, dean enrollment mgt; Univ Mass, Amhers, vice chancellor stud affairs, vice pres stud affairs, 1999-2006; Univ Mass Amherst, assoc vice chancellor stud affairs & campus life, 2006-11; Am Univ Nigeria, dean, 2011-. **Orgs:** Nat Asn Stud Personnel Adminr; Rotary Int Yola; Alpha Phi Alpha Fraternity. **Home Addr:** 4909 Goosedown Ct, Raleigh, NC 27604, **Home Phone:** (919)255-9109. **Business Addr:** Dean, American University of Nigeria, Lamido Zubairu Way, Yola640001.

## BULLOCK, J. JEROME

Executive, legal consultant. **Personal:** Born Jan 3, 1948, Hogansville, GA; son of Jerry L and Vivian Baker. **Educ:** Tuskegee Univ, BS, polit sci, 1969; Howard Univ Sch Law, JD, 1975. **Career:** US Marshals Serv, assoc legal coun, 1975-77, 1982-84, US Ma US Marshals Serv, assoc legal coun, 1975-77, 1982-84, US Marshal, 1977-82, chief cong & pub affairs, 1984-85; Air Security Corp, vpres, 1983-85; Off Internal Security, chief, 1985-89; US Dept Justice, asst inspector gen Invest, 1989-94, assoc legal coun; Australian govt, consult, 1992-95; Decision Strategies Inst, managing dir, 1994-97; Price Waterhouse, LLP, managing dir, 1997-; Bullock & Assocs Inc, prin officer, Currently. **Orgs:** Nat Asn Flight Instrs, 1984-; Iowa State Bar Asn; Phi Alpha Delta Law Fraternity; Int Asn Chiefs Police; Kappa Alpha Psi Am Region; 352nd Civilian Affairs Command. **Honors/Awds:** Special Achievement Award, US Marshals Serv, 1976; Meritorious Service Award, US Marshals Serv, 1978; Tuskegee Alumni Award, Tuskegee Inst, 1979; Distinguished Service Award, US Marshals Serv, 1987. **Business Addr:** Principal Officer, Bullock & Associates Inc, 5335 Wisconsin Ave NW Suite 440, Washington, DC 20015-2034, **Business Phone:** (202)966-5006.

## BULLOCK, JAMES N.

Educator, lawyer. **Personal:** Born Aug 22, 1926, Charleston, MS; married Lois W; children: Joseph. **Educ:** Tex Southern Univ, BA, 1967; Thurgood Marshall Sch Law, JD, 1970. **Career:** US Postal Serv, supvr; Tex Southern Univ, assoc prof law, currently. **Orgs:** Justice Greener Chap Phi Alpha Delta Legal Frat; TX Black Caucus; Am BarAsn; Nat Bar Asn; St Bar TX; Houston Bar Asn; Houston Lawyers Asn; PhiAlpha Delta Legal Frat; S & Cent YMCA; Nat Asn Advan Colored People; Harris Co Orgn; TX Asn Col Teachers. **Home Addr:** 3704 S MacGregor Way, Houston, TX 77021, **Home Phone:** (713)748-1538. **Business Addr:** Associate Professor of Law, Texas Southern University, 3100 Cleburne St, Houston, TX 77004, **Business Phone:** (713)313-7395.

## BULLOCK, THURMAN RUTHE

Municipal government official, association executive. **Personal:** Born Oct 6, 1947, Richmond, VA; son of Warren and Dorothy Hargrove; married Anne Leshner; children: Thurman Martin. **Educ:** Franklin & Marshall Col, Lancaster, PA, BA, 1970; Temple Univ, Philadelphia, PA, MS, 1979. **Career:** Comptroller Currency, Philadelphia, Pa, asst nat bank examr, 1970-75; Deloitte Haskins & Sells, Philadelphia, Pa, auditor, 1977-80; Bell Pa, Philadelphia, Pa, internal auditor, 1980-82; City Pa Off Controller, Pa, deputy city controller, 1982-; Philadelphia FIGHT, treas, currently. **Orgs:** Nat Asn Black Accountants, 1979; Am Inst Cert Pub Accountants, 1980-; secy, Pa Inst Cert Pub Accountants, treas, 1980-89, pres, 1989-; Govt Fin Officers Asn, 1981; pres, mem, Philadelphia Fedn Black Bus & Prof Orgn, 1981-; bd mem, Coun Int Progs, 1981-; Int Prof Exchange, 1981-; Opportunities Acad Mgt Training Inc, 1981-; bus adv bd, House Umoja, 1986-; Philadelphia Clearinghouse, 1989; vpres, adv bd mem, Community Accountants; Acct Res Asn, 1989; Am Soc Pub Admin, 1989; Asn Local Govt Auditors, 1989; fin adv, Lesbian & Gay Task Force, currently; Nat Jr Tennis League; Zion Nonprofit Trust; NGA Inc; E Mt Airy Neighbors; Fund Future Philadelphia; bd dir, Philadelphia FIGHT, currently. **Business Addr:** Treasurer, Philadelphia FIGHT, 1233 Locust St 5th Fl, Philadelphia, PA 19107, **Business Phone:** (215)985-4448.

## BULLS, HERMAN

President (organization), executive, founder (originator). **Educ:** US Mil Acad, W Pt, BS, engineering, 1978; Harvard Bus Sch, MBA, finance, 1985. **Career:** LaSalle Partners, 1989-98; Jones Lang LaSalle, managing dir, 1998-2000, chief exec officer pub insts, 2011-, int dir & vice chmn; Green Pk Financial, chief operating officer & exec vpres, 2000-01; Fannie Mae Delegated Underwriting & Servicing (DUS), exec vpres & chief operating officer, 2000-01; Comfort Systs USA, dir, 2001-; Bulls Adv Group, chief exec officer & pres, 2001-; Bulls Capital Partners, co-founder, pres & chief exec officer, 2004-10; Rasmussen Inc, dir, 2009-; Tyco Int, dir, 2014-. **Orgs:** Bd dir, 1996-, vice chair bd dir, 2010-13, W Pt Asn Graduates; pres, African Am Real Estate Professionals; Real Estate Adv Comt, Ny Teachers' Retirement Syst, 2000-; chmn, Exec Leadership Coun, 2004-06; bd dir, USAA, 2010-; Mil Bowl presented by Northrop Grumman, 2010-; dir, Found Independent Higher Educ; dir, United Serv Automobile Asn, 2010-; bd dir, ITT Exelis, 2011-15; US Dept Veterans Affairs, 2015-; Nat Asn Col & Univ Bus Officers. **Business Addr:** International Director, Vice Chairman, Jones Lang LaSalle Inc, 200 E Randolph Dr, Chicago, IL 60601.

## BULLS, HERMAN E.

Real estate executive, president (organization). **Personal:** Born Feb 4, 1956, Florence, AL; son of William George and Lucy; married Iris; children: Herman Jr, Nathaniel & Jonathan. **Educ:** US Mil Acad, Westpoint, BS, engineering, 1978; Harvard Univ, MBA, finance, 1985. **Career:** Jones Lang La Salle, managing dir, 1989-2000, founder & chief exec officer, currently; Green Pk Financial, exec vpres & chief exec officer, 2000-01; Fannie Mae Delegated Underwriting & Servicing apt lenders, chief operating officer, 2000-01; Bulls Adv Group, pres & chief exec officer, 2001-; Bulls Capital Partners, pres & chief exec officer, 2004-10. **Orgs:** Chmn, Exec Leadership Coun, 1995-; bd mem, Kennedy Ctr Community & Friends, 1995-2003; bd trustees, W Pt, 1996; Adv bd Asset Mgt Sun Trust Bank; bd dir, Comfort Systs, USA NYSE, 2001-; Real Estate Exec Coun, 2003-; NY State Teachers' Retirement Syst Real Esate Adv Coun, 2003-; chair, Exec Leadership Found, 2005-; mem bd dirs, Rasmussen Inc, Deltak, 2009-; mem bd dirs, USAA, 2010-; mem bd dirs, Exelis, 2011-15; MyVA Adv Comt, US Dept Veterans Affairs, 2015-; mem bd dirs, Comput Sci Corp, 2015-; Lambda Alpha Int; Leadership Wash; Nat Black MBA Asn; Real Estate Group Wash, DC; founder, African Am Real Estate Profs; Nat Asn Col & Univ Bus Officers; bd dir, Found Independent Higher Educ; bd dir, Comfort Systs, USA; Nat Asn Col Univ Bus Officers; bd dir, Found Independent Higher Educ; APPA Leadership Inst; John F Kennedy Ctr; chmn, Pub Insts. **Honors/Awds:** Passing the Torch, honoree, African Am Real Estate Prof, 2007; Minority Executive of the Year, Commercial Property News, 2007; Honored by the Global Diversity Summit, 2008; Trail Blazer Award, Global Real Estate Diversity Conf, Atlanta, GA, 2008; Minority Business Leader Award, Wash Bus J, 2009; APEX Award, Morgan State Univ Earl Graves Sch Bus & Mgt, 2015. **Business Addr:** President, Chief Executive Officer, Bulls Advisory Group, 9610 Crosspointe Dr, Fairfax Station, VA 22039, **Business Phone:** (202)256-1814.

## BULLY-CUMMINGS, DR. ELLA MAE

Lawyer, police chief. **Personal:** Born Jan 1, 1958, Kanagawa Prefecture; daughter of Daniel Lee Bully; married William; married

Warren C Evans. **Educ:** Madonna Univ, BA, pub admin, 1993; Mich State Uinv, Detroit Col Law, JD, 1998. **Career:** Police chief (retired); Detroit Police Dept, police officer, 1977-87, sgt, 1987-93, lt, 1993-95, inspector, 1995-98; comdr, 1998-99, asst chief, 2002-03, chief police, 2003-08; Foley & Lardner, assoc atty, 1992-2002; Miller, Canfield, Paddock & Stone PLC, assoc atty; Detroit Free Press, receptionist, secy & admin asst. **Orgs:** State Bar Mich, 1998; Nat Bar Asn; Wolverine Bar Asn; Int Asn Chiefs Police; Nat Org Black Law Enforcement Execs; Mcih Asn Chiefs Police. **Honors/Awds:** History Maker in the Making, Gen Motors & Black Entertainment Tv's, 2005; Lifetime Achievement Award, Nat Ctr Women & Policing. **Special Achievements:** First woman to serve as chief of police in Detroit, 2002. **Business Addr:** Chief of Police, Detroit Police Department, 1300 Beaubien St, Detroit, MI 48226.

### BUMPHUS, DR. WALTER GAYLE
Administrator, educator. **Personal:** Born Mar 19, 1948, Princeton, KY; married Aileen Thompson; children: Michael, Brian & Fran. **Educ:** Murray State Univ, BS, speech commun, 1971, MA, guid & coun, 1974; Univ Tex, Austin, PhD, higher educ admin, 1985. **Career:** Murray State Univ, counr & dormetry asst, 1970-72, dir minority affairs, 1972-74; E Ark Community Col, dean, 1974-78; Howard Community Col, dean stud, vpres, 1987-91; Univ Tex, Austin, Richardson fel, 1983; Regional Univ, admin; Brookhaven Col, pres, 1991-97, Dallas County Community Col Dist, pres; Voyager Expanded Learning, Higher Educ Div, pres1997-2000; Brookhaven Col, pres; Baton Rouge Community Col, chancellor, 2000-01; La Community & Tech Col Syst, pres, 2001-07, pres emer, 2007-; Univ Tex, Austin, prof & chair, 2007-10; Am Asn Community Cols, pres & chief exec officer. **Orgs:** Consult, Off Educ Title IV, 1986; chairperson, Mid Stated Accredited Asn Team, 1986; pres, Nat Asn Stud Develop; chmn, Am Asn Community Cols, 1996-; bd dir, Am Coun Educ. **Home Addr:** 9535 Caboose Ct, Columbia, MD 21045. **Business Addr:** Department Chair, Professor, College of Education University of Texas, SZB 348 1 Univ Sta D5400, Austin, TX 78712, **Business Phone:** (512)471-7545.

### BUNCH, LONNIE G., III
Executive, educator, historian. **Personal:** Born Nov 18, 1952, Newark, NJ; married Maria Marable; children: Sarah & Katie. **Educ:** Am Univ, Wash, DC, BA, 1974, MA, 1976, PhD, Am hist & African hist. **Career:** Nat Air & Space Mus, educ specialist, 1978-79; Am Univ, Wash, DC, adj lectr, 1978-79; Univ Mass, Dartmouth, MA, Am & Afro-Am hist, asst prof, 1979-81; Packer Col Inst, Brooklyn, NY, teacher & historian, 1981-83; Calif African Am Mus, Los Angeles, CA, founding cur hist & prog mgr, 1983-89; George Wash Univ, Wash, DC, adj prof mus studies, 1989-2000; Am Hist Mus, supvr cur, 1989-92, asst dir cur hist, 1992-94; Smithsonian's Nat Mus African Am Hist & Cult, assc dir, 1994-2000, founding dir, 2005-; Univ Md, prof; Chicago Hist Soc, pres, 2001-05. **Orgs:** Trustee, Am Asn State & Local Hist; Orgn Am Historians; Am Antiqn Soc. **Business Addr:** Founding Director, Museum of African American History & Culture, SI Bldg Rm 153 MRC 010, Washington, DC 20013-7012, **Business Phone:** (202)633-4300.

### BUNCHE, CURTIS J.
Automotive executive, football player. **Personal:** Born Aug 4, 1955, Crystal River, FL; son of Ruth; married Melinda; children: Mykisha, Cetera & Malcolm. **Educ:** Albany State Col, 1979. **Career:** Philadelphia Eagles, defensive end, 1979-80; Tampa Bay Bandits, defensive end, 1983-84; C&C Assocs, pres, 1981-87; Mon-Valley Lincoln-Mercury, pres, 1987-93; Riverview Ford Lincoln Mercury, pres, 1994-. **Orgs:** Rotary, 1988-; premier mem, Nat Asn Minority Automobile Dealers. **Home Addr:** 5 Sugarloaf Lane, Wilmington, DE 19808. **Business Addr:** President, Owner, Riverview Ford Lincoln Mercury, 200 S Broadway, Pennsville, NJ 08070, **Business Phone:** (856)678-3111.

### BUNDLES, A'LELIA
Writer, executive. **Personal:** Born Jun 7, 1952, Chicago, IL; daughter of S Henry Jr and A Lelia Mae Perry. **Educ:** Harvard Univ, Radcliffe Col, AB, 1974; Columbia Univ Grad Sch Jour, MSJ, 1976. **Career:** Madam Walker, pres, 1970-; Summit Labs, 1971; Newsweek Chicago Bur, intern, 1973; Harvard Univ, Kennedy Inst Polit, summer res fel, 1973; WTLC-FM, Indianapolis, Ind, anchor & reporter, 1974; Du Pont Co, Wilmington, Del, staff asst, 1974-75; Columbia Sch Jour, NBC & RCA fel, 1975-76; NBC News, NY, Houston & Atlanta burs, field producer, 1976-85; NBC News Wash, DC, producer, 1985-89; ABC News, Wash DC, World News Tonight, producer, 1989-96, dep bur chief, 1996-99, dir talent develop, 2000-06, consult, 2000-01; freelance writer, currently; Pub Affairs Dept, asst.Book: On Her Own Ground, The Life and Times of Madam C.J. Walker; Spark Camp, Camper, 2014. **Orgs:** Chairperson, Nat Asn Black Journalists, 1980-; trustee, pres, Radcliffe Col, 1985-89; adv bd, Schlesinger Libr Hist Women, 1986-94; dir, Harvard Alumni Asn, 1989-91; Alpha Kappa Alpha; Links Inc; bd, Harvard Club, Wash, DC, 1995-99; adv bd, Radcliffe Quart; bd mem, vice chairperson, Madam Walker Theatre Ctr, 1996-12; pres, Radcliffe Col Alumnae Asn, 1999-2001; co-chair, NABJ Authors Showcase; dean's coun, Radcliffe Inst Advan Story, Harvard Univ, 2003-; Alpha Iota Chap, Phi Beta Kappa Harvard Col; trustee, Colombia Univ; bd mem, Woodlawn Conservancy, 2006-; trustee & vice chair, Columbia Univ, 2006-; chair & pres, Found Nat Arch, 2006-; Friends Woodlawn Cemetery; adv coun mem, Schlesinger Libr at Radcliffe Inst at Harvard, 2011-; adv bd, Schlesinger Libr, Radcliffe Inst Advan Study; Yaddo, fel, 2012; chair, Columbia Univ Grad Sch Journalisms alumni adv comt; Auth's Guild, 2014. **Home Addr:** 4109 Garrison St NW, Washington, DC 20016, **Home Phone:** (202)363-4191.

### BUNDY, KISSETTE L.
Writer, broadcaster, educator. **Educ:** Boston Univ, BS, broadcasting & film; Columbia Univ, MS, print & broadcast, 1987. **Career:** Keystone Foods Corp, corp commun coordr, 1985-86; WNET-TV Educ Broadcasting Corp, supv producer, 1988-96; Columbia Univ, post-grad fel broadcast journalist instr, 1987-88; WBIS+ Dow Jones Tv, daytime programming unit mgr, 1996-97; Col New Rochelle, media instr; KLB Productions, Prin, 1994-2004; Frederick Douglass Creative Arts Ctr (New York), educ supvr, 1998-2004; Hampton Univ, Scripps Howard Sch Journalism, asst prof, 2005-10; Passaic County Community Col, adj fac, 2012-. **Honors/Awds:** National Newspaper Publishers Association Merit Award, Winner as Editor for "The Philadelphia Tribune"; Capital Cities/Columbia University David Jayne Fellow; John Patterson Broadcast Award, recipient; Emmy as Producer and Series Development at WNET-13 (New York) for "The Kids Are Not All Right". **Special Achievements:** Articles have published in "Essence" magazine. **Business Addr:** Adjunct Faculty, Passaic County Community College, 1 College Blvd, Paterson, NJ 07505, **Business Phone:** (973)684-6868.

### BUNKLEY, ANITA RICHMOND
Writer. **Personal:** Born Columbus, OH; children: 2; married Crawford. **Educ:** Mt Union Col, BA, span & fr; Ohio State Univ, advan work, fr studies. **Career:** Mid sch lang teacher; adult educ teacher; auth & pub speaker, currently; Marcil-OFarrell Literary LLC, rep. Author: Emily: The Yellow Rose, 1989; Black Gold, 1994; Wild Embers, 1995; Starlight Passage, 1996; Balancing Act, 1997; Steppin' Out With Attitude: Sister, Sell Your Dream!, 1998; Mirrored Life, 2002; Silent Wager, 2006. **Orgs:** Tex Inst Letts; Circle-Let's Inc; Between Lines Bk Club; dir, Social Security Admin; dir, Am Red Cross; dir, Youth Understanding; inductee, Who's Who Black Houston. **Home Addr:** 3554 Ashfield Dr, PO Box 821248, Houston, TX 77282-1248, **Home Phone:** (281)531-0566. **Business Addr:** Writer, Kensington Books, 850 3rd Ave, New York, NY 10022, **Business Phone:** (877)422-3665.

### BUNKLEY, LONNIE R.
Real estate developer, executive, business owner. **Personal:** Born Aug 12, 1932, Denison, TX; son of Ruth Smith and C B; married Charlene Marie Simpson; children: Karen Annette & Natalie Anitra. **Educ:** Prairie View Univ, BA, 1952; CA State Univ LA, MS, 1964; Univ So CA, grad studies, 1965. **Career:** LA Neighborhood Youth Corps Econ & Youth Oppor Agency, dir, 1968; E LA Col & Compton Col, col instr, 1970-78; LA Co Probation Dept, div chief, 1982; Pac Properties, real estate develop, pres & broker; Com Devel Corp, pres; Bunkley Investment Mgt Co, owner, currently. **Orgs:** Pres, Los Angeles Alumni, Prairie View Univ, 1960; Mem exec comt, Southside LA Jr C C, 1966; SE Welfare Planning Coun, 1973; bd dir, Compton Sickle Cell Anemia Educ & Detection Ctr; CA Probation & Parole Asn; Black Probation Officers Asn; bd dir, Nat Black United Fund; bd trustees, Los Angeles Brotherhood Crusade; Omega Psi Phi Frat; ruling elder, St Paul's Presby Church; bd dir, Black Support Group, Calif State Univ; S Cent Diabeties Assoc; founder, Burkley Found. **Honors/Awds:** Commendation Southside Jr Chamber Com, 1962; Cert, Prairie View Univ Alumni Award, 1970; Outstanding Serv Award, Brotherhood Crusade, 1972; Cert Ctr for Health Urban Educ & Res, 1982; Commendatory Resolution City of Compton, 1982; Compton Sickle Cell Educ & Detection Ctr, 1982; Cert of Appreciation, US Cong, 1983; Award, LA Co Bd Supvr, 1984; Commendation, State of Calif, 1990; Citizen of the Year, Omega Psi Phi, Lambda Omicrom Chap, 1997. **Home Addr:** 6711 Bedford Ave, Los Angeles, CA 90056-2105, **Home Phone:** (714)994-8426. **Business Addr:** Owner, Bunkley Investment Management Co, 880 Apollo St Suite 231, El Segundo, CA 90245-4726, **Business Phone:** (310)648-0214.

### BUNTE, DORIS
Administrator. **Personal:** Born Jul 2, 1933, New York, NY; children: Yvette, Harold & Allen. **Educ:** Boston Univ, Metro Col; Univ Mass, Boston, doctoral prog; Suffolk Univ, attended 1973; Harvard Univ, BA & MA, educ, cert, Advan Environ Studies. **Career:** Boston Housing Authority, bd comnr, 1969-75; Southern End Neighbourhood Action Prog & Boston, dir housing, 1969-70, Boston housing authority, chief exec officer, 1984-92; Southern End Neighbourhood Action Prog Boston, dir personnel, 1970-72; Seventh Suffolk Dist, state rep, 1973-85; Northeastern Univ, Ctr Study Sport Soc, consult, dir community rels & human resource coordr, 1993-2010; consult & mediator, housing & community develop issues, currently. **Orgs:** Dem Nat Conventions, 1972-76; Loeb Fel Harvard Grad Sch Design, 1975-76; MALEG Black Caucus; Third World Jobs Clearing Hse; Mass Asn Paraplegics; Combined Black Phi-lanthropies; Mass Legis Women's Caucus; Nat Asn Advan Colored People; Nat Order Women Leglis; Black Polit Task Force; Mass Conf Human Rights; Citizen's Housing & Planning Asn; Solomon Carter Fuller Ment Health Ctr; Rosbury Multi-Serv Ctr Declaration; Urban Outreach Coun; chairwomen, Fed Fin Assistance; Critical Minority Affairs Comt; Nat Asn Housing & Redevelop; Nat Tenants Orgn; Citizens Housing & Planning Asn. **Honors/Awds:** Citizen of the Year, Omega Psi Frat Inc, Iota Chi Chap, 1978; Citizen of the Year Award, Nat Asn Social Workers, 1980; Notary Pub, Commonwealth Mass; appointee, Nat Rent Adv Bd Phase II Econ Stabilization Act; Award Black Housing Task Force; Award Roxbury Action Prog; Guest Lectr to numerous Cols incl Boston Col, Boston Univ, John F Kennedy Sch, Simmons Col, Suffolk Univ, Southern Univ & Univ Mass. **Special Achievements:** First African-American woman elected to the Massachusetts Legislature; Publ, Address to City Missionary, 1973; "Child Advocacy" a dependency cycle is not a goal, 1977; "Our & Third World Comm Revitalization Through Access By Mandte Example & Monitoring"; First woman to be appointed to a position in the House leadership in 48 years. **Home Addr:** 7 Ocean View Dr Suite 610, Dorchester, MA 02125, **Home Phone:** (617)288-0120. **Business Addr:** Director Community Relations, Northeastern University, 716 Columbus Ave Suite 161 CP, Boston, MA 02115-5000, **Business Phone:** (617)373-4861.

### BUNTING, THEO H., JR.
Public utility executive, president (organization). **Personal:** married Beverly; children: Ryan & Trey. **Educ:** US Naval Acad; Hendrix Col, Conway, AR, BA, econs & bus, 1981, cert pub acct, 1983. **Career:** Arthur Andersen & Co, pub acct, 1981; Entergy Ark, Entergy Gulf States, Entergy La, Entergy Miss & Entergy New Orleans, vpres & chief financial officer, 2002-04, Syst Entergy Inc, sr vpres, chief acct officer, 2007-; Entergy Corp, sr vpres, chief acct officer, 2007-12, group pres utility opers, 2012-. **Orgs:** Am Inst Cert Pub Accountants; Am Asn Blacks Energy; Nat Asn Black Accountants; bd trustee, Hendrix Col, 2006-; chmn, Robert J. Taylor Scholar Found; dir, Imation Corp, 2012-; dir & chmn, Nuclear Elec Ins Ltd; Found for Mid S; Unum Group; Exec Leadership Coun. **Business Addr:** Group President of Utility Operations, Entergy Corp, 639 Loyola Ave, New Orleans, LA 70113, **Business Phone:** (504)576-4000.

### BUNYON, RONALD S.
Executive, school administrator. **Personal:** Born Mar 13, 1935, Philadelphia, PA; son of Ulysses and Mamie; married Josephine; children: Ronald Jr, Judith, Joann S Herbert, Joyce & Jodetta. **Educ:** Mitchell Col, ASE, 1965; Univ New Haven, CT, BS, 1969; Southern Conn State Univ, MS, urban studies; Rensselaer Polytech Inst, MS, urban environ, 1992. **Career:** Gen Dynamics Nuclear Ship Bldg, sr designer, 1958; Nat Prog asst Econ Devel, reg dir, 1972; Zion Investments Philadelphia, bus mgr, 1973; Opportunities Ind Ctr Int, mgt spec, 1976; Drexel Univ Philadelphia, asst vpres, 1979; Bus Ventures Int Inc, pres, 1979-2013. **Orgs:** Alpha Ki Alpha Hon Soc, 1967; Bd Educ, leadership comt, Philadelphia, 1978; US Dept Comn, Export Coun, 1979; World Trade Asn, Philadelphia, 1979; Nat Teachers Asn, 1986; asst vpres, Community Affairs & Govt Rels. **Home Addr:** 4265 Terrace Ave, Pennsauken, NJ 08109-1627. **Business Addr:** .

### BURCHELL, DR. CHARLES R. (CHARLES RUFFIN BURCHELL)
Physiologist, broadcaster, radio host. **Personal:** Born Nov 24, 1946, New Orleans, LA; married Paulette Martinez. **Educ:** Tulane Univ, attended 1966; Southern Univ, attended 1968; La State Univ, BA, 1968, MA, 1971, PhD, 1977; Soc Police & Criminal Psychol, dipl. **Career:** WXOK Radio Baton Rouge, radio announcer, 1966-72; WJBO; WFMF; WGSO; LA State Univ, Dept Psychol, instr, 1971-; WRBT-TV, TV news & reporter, 1972-74, 1976; WWOZ, host, 2004; New Orleans Police Dept, psychologist, currently. **Orgs:** Psi Chi, 1968; AFTRA, 1970; Southern Psychol Asn, 1974-75; Int Asn Chiefs Police; Soc Police & Criminal Psychol. **Honors/Awds:** Welfare Rights Orgn Service Award, 1973. **Home Addr:** 347 S 20th St, Baton Rouge, LA 70806. **Business Addr:** Psychologist, New Orleans Police Department, 715 S Broad St Rm 527 5th Fl, New Orleans, LA 70803, **Business Phone:** (504)658-5858.

### BURD, STEVEN A.
Executive. **Personal:** Born Jan 1, 1949, Valley City, ND; married Chris; children: 2. **Educ:** Carrol Col, BS, econs, 1971; Univ Wis, MA, econs, 1973. **Career:** Southern pac transp Co, marketer, 1974-82; Arthur D Little, mgt consult, 1982-87; Safeway, consult, 1986-87, 1991, pres, 1992-2013, chief exec officer, 1993-2013, chmn bd, 1998-2013; self employed, mgt consult, 1987-91; Stop & Shop, consult, 1988-89; Fred Meyer, consult, 1989-90. **Orgs:** Prostate Cancer Found; Republican Party; dir, Physiotherapy Assocs Inc; dir, Vons Co Inc, 1993-; bd dir, Kohls, 2001-; dir, Blackhawk Network Holdings Inc, 2007-. **Home Addr:** , CA. **Business Addr:** Chairman, President, Chief Executive Officer, Safeway Inc, 5918 Stoneridge Mall Rd, Pleasanton, CA 94588-3229, **Business Phone:** (925)467-3000.

**BURDEN, DR. WILLIE JAMES.** **See Obituaries Section.**

### BURDETTE, DR. LAVERE ELAINE
Psychologist. **Personal:** Born Chicago, IL; daughter of Leonard Charles Dixon and Dorothy Earl. **Educ:** Kent State Univ, BS, 1969; Wayne State Univ, MSW, 1972; Union Grad Sch, MA, psychol, 1982, PhD, 1985. **Career:** Cigna Ins Co, employee assistance specialist; Blue Cross & Blue Shield Mich, adv bd, 1990-; Burdette & Doss Psychol Serv, exec dir, pres. **Orgs:** Am Asn Black Psychologists; Mich Psychol Asn; Am Psychol Asn. **Special Achievements:** Author: The Self in Search of Unity Through Confrontation, 1985, Stress Mgt Workbook, 1987, Handling Conflict: Fighting for Happiness, 1991. **Business Addr:** Executive Director, President, Burdette & Doss Psychological Services, 17352 W 12 Mile Rd Suite 100, Southfield, MI 48076, **Business Phone:** (248)559-0730.

### BURESS, HANNIBAL
Actor, television producer, comedian. **Personal:** Born Feb 4, 1983, Chicago, IL; son of John and Margaret. **Educ:** Southern Ill Univ, Carbondale, attended 2004. **Career:** Stand-up comedian, 2002-; actor, 2009-; television writer, 2009-; television producer, 2012-. Television: The Very Funny Show, 2009; Saturday Night Live, NBC, 2009-10; Louie, 2010; Delocated, 2010; 30 Rock NBC, 2010-12; Promos, 2012; The Mindy Project, 2013; The Kroll Show, 2013; High Maintenance, 2013; Bob's Burgers, 2013; China, IL, 2013-15; Chozen, 2014; Lucas Bros Moving Co, 2014-15; Broad City, Comedy Central, 2014-16; The Jim Gaffigan Show, 2015; Children's Hospital, 2016; Adventure Time, 2016; Easy, 2016; High Maintenance, 2016. Film: The Kings of Summer, 2013; Neighbors, 2014; Are Your Joking?, 2014; Band of Robbers, 2015; Daddy's Home, 2015; Nerdland, 2016; Neighbors 2: Sorority Rising, 2016; The Angry Birds Movie, 2016; The Nice Guys, 2016; Flock of Dudes, 2016; The Secret Life of Pets, 2016. Television writer: Saturday Night Live, NBC, 2009-10; 30 Rock, NBC, 2011; Funny as Hell, 2011-13; Hannibal Buress: Animal Furnace, 2012; Mash Up, 2012; The Eric Andre Show, 2012-15; Why? With Hannibal Buress, 2015; Hannibal Buress: Comedy Camisado, 2016. Executive television producer: Hannibal Buress: Animal Furnace, 2012; Why? With Hannibal Buress, 2015; Unemployable, 2015; Hannibal Buress: Comedy Camisado (special), 2016; Hannibal Takes Edinburgh, 2016. Television producer: The Eric Andre Show, 2014-16. **Honors/Awds:** Alumnus of the Year, Chicago Debate League, 2014. **Special Achievements:** Albums: My Name is Hannibal, 2010. **Business Addr:** 3 Arts Entertainment, 9460 Wilshire Blvd 7th Fl, Beverly Hills, CA 90212.

### BURGES, JOYCE M.
Association executive. **Personal:** married Eric D; children: Eric Jr, Lawrence, Candace L, Candra E & Victoria. **Career:** Nat Black Home Educr Resource Asn, co-founder, 2000-; Lectr; adv. **Special Achievements:** Guest on BET Tonight, national broadcast hosted by Queen Latifah on August 15, 2001; featured in several periodicals such as Newsweek Magazine, Essence Magazine Sept, 2002, Jet Magazine Sep, 2003. **Home Addr:** 2707 McHugh Rd, Baker, LA 70714-2458, **Home Phone:** (504)778-0169. **Business Addr:** Co-Founder, The National Black Home Educators Resource Association, 13434 Plank Rd, Baker, LA 70714, **Business Phone:** (225)778-0169.

**BURGES, MELVIN E.**
Executive. **Personal:** Born Oct 15, 1951, Chicago, IL; son of Ruth N and Malcolm M Sr; children: Necco L McKinley. **Educ:** Loyola Univ, BA, acct, 1982; DePaul Univ, MBA, finance, 1984. **Career:** Ceco Corp, reg controller, 1972-90; Winter Construct Co, corp controller, 1990-92; Sanderson Industs Inc, vpres fin admin, 1992-93; Syst Software Assoc, fin appln consul, 1994; Thomas Howell McLarens Toplis Inc, nat fin mgr, 1995-97; Harcon Inc, chief financial officer, 1997-. **Orgs:** Pres, Construct Fin MGT ASN, 1989-; dr corp affairs, Nat Black MBA Asn, 1990-; Nat Asn Black Accountants, 1990-; AMR IST Cert Pub Accountants, 1990-; IBT Capital Grp Investment Club, 1991-; trustee, chmn outside properties, Ebenezer Baptist Church, 1992-; Being Single Mag Pinnacle Club, 1992. **Special Achievements:** US Tennis Association Tennis Official, Rookie of the Year. **Home Addr:** 3092 Meadow Mere W, Atlanta, GA 30341, **Home Phone:** (770)451-1625. **Business Addr:** Chief Financial Officier, Harcon Inc, 1121 Alderman Dr, Alpharetta, GA 30005, **Business Phone:** (678)636-3676.

**BURGESS, CHAKA**
Biotechnologist. **Educ:** Howard Univ, attended 1998. **Career:** Amgen Inc, dir global govt affairs. **Orgs:** Cong Black Caucus Found Inc. **Business Addr:** Director Global Government Affairs, Amgen Inc, 1 Amgen Ctr Dr, Thousand Oaks, CA 91320-1799, **Business Phone:** (805)447-1000.

**BURGESS, JAMES PAUL**
Football player. **Personal:** Born Mar 31, 1974, Miami, FL; son of James Sr. **Educ:** Miami Univ, Fla, grad. **Career:** Football player (retired); Kans City Chiefs, 1997; Dallas Cowboys, 1997; San Diego Chargers, line backer, 1997, 1998; Orlando Rage, 2001; Calgary Stampeders, line backer, 2002; Oakland Raiders, line backer, free agent.

**BURGESS, LINDA GAIL**
Basketball coach, basketball player. **Personal:** Born Jul 27, 1969, Madison, AL; daughter of Charles. **Educ:** Univ Ala, BS, phys educ, 1993. **Career:** Basketball player (retired), basketball coach; Belinzona, Switz, forward, 1992-93; Ramat HaSharon, Israel, 1993-94, 1996-97; Beni-Yeuda, Israel, 1994-95; SPO Rouen, France, 1995-96; Los Angeles Sparks, 1997; Sacramento Monarchs, 1998-2000; Univ W Ala, asst coach; Stillman Col, head coach, 2002-03.

**BURGESS, LORD.** See BURGIE, IRVING LOUIS.

**BURGESS, MELVIN THOMAS, SR.**
Government official, police officer. **Personal:** Born May 23, 1938, Memphis, TN; son of Eddie and Katherine S; married Johanna Sandridge; children: Melvin Thomas II & Pamela Camille. **Educ:** Memphis State Univ, BA, police admin, 1981; Grambling Col. **Career:** Police officer (retired); City Memphis, patrol officer, 1962-66, detective sgt, 1966-79, lt, 1979-81, capt, 1981-85, inspector, 1985-86, chief inspector, 1986-88, dir police serv, 1991-94; Lin-Cris Inc. **Orgs:** NEI Maj Cities Chief Police, 1992; vpres, Kappa Alpha Psi; Nat Asn Advan Colored People; Int Asn Chiefs Police; Comn Future Tn Judicial Syst. **Home Addr:** 1888 S Pkwy E, Memphis, TN 38114-1911, **Home Phone:** (901)278-1346.

**BURGESS, DR. NORMA J.**
Educator. **Personal:** Born May 24, 1954, Stanton, TN; daughter of John A and Athis M Bond; married Charlie; children: Wesley & Shenon. **Educ:** Univ Tenn Martin, BA, polit sci, 1975; NC State Univ, MPA, 1980, PhD, sociol, 1986. **Career:** Miss State Univ, prof, 1986-93; Nat Sci Found, res fel, 1990-93; Syracuse Univ, Dept Child & Family Studies, assoc prof, 1993-2007, chmn & sociologist, prog adminr, 2007; Lipscomb Univ, Col Arts & Sci, dean, currently. **Orgs:** Southern Sociol Soc, 1985-; Southeastern Coun Family Rels, 1986-93; Nat Coun Family Rel, 1986-; chair, Am Asn Higher Educ, Women's Caucus, 2000-02. **Home Addr:** PO Box 278, Syracuse, NY 13210. **Business Addr:** Dean, Lipscomb University, 1 Univ Pk Dr, Nashville, TN 37204-3951, **Business Phone:** (615)966-6146.

**BURGESS, ROBERT E., SR.**
Executive. **Personal:** Born Oct 13, 1937, Lake City, SC; married Mary Elizabeth; children: W Michael Tiagwad, Tamara Tiagwad Wagner & Robert E Jr. **Educ:** J M Wright Tech Sch, Electrical, 1957; Norwalk Comn Col Cert City Housing Planning & Develop, 1973; IBM Mgt Develop Prog Community Execs, 1983. **Career:** Self-employed, band leader, 1958-63; Norden Aircraft, inspector, 1963-66; self-employed, restaurant owner, 1966-69; Comt Training & Employment, admin asst, 1966-71; Norwalk Econ Opportunity Now Inc, exec dir. **Orgs:** Chmn & organizer, Fairfield Cty Black Bus Assoc, 1969; organizer, Norwalk Conn Fed Credit Union, 1970; S Norwalk Comm Ctr Bd, 1970; admin asst, Norwalk Econ Opportunity Now Inc, 1970-72, exec dir, 1972-; State Manpower Training Coun Gov Meskill, 1972; bd dir, Springwood Health Unit, 1973; New Eng Comn Action Prog Dir Assoc, 1973; chmn & org dir Assoc, Nat Comn Action, 1973; State Employ Training Coun Gov Grasso, 1978; pres, CT Assoc Community Action, 1978-84; State Energy Adv Comm Gov Grasso, 1979; State Negotiated Invest Strategy Team Gov O'Neill, 1983; Dist Heating Comn, 1984; Rev Team ACVS Headstart, 1984; mem Exec Comn, vpres, Action Housing, 1989; Adv Comn Housing Finance Authority, 1989; CT Employ & Training Comn, 1989; CT Comn Study Mgt State Govt, 1989; chmn, SW Region CT Housing Coalition Gov Weicker, 1991; Mayor's Blue Ribbon Comt Race Rel, 1993; Negotiating Team, Police Community Rels, 1993; bd dir, Norwalk Community Health Ctr, 1995; CT Employ & Training Comn, 1996; Norwalk Hosp Inst Rev Bd, 1996; Citizens Fair Housing, 1997; Work Force Develop Performance Measurement Comt, 1998; Welfare Reform Implementation Comt, 1998; sec, CT Employ & Training Comn, 1998; Norwalk Tribal Coun, 1998; Nat Asn Advan Colored People Negotiating Team Fair Housing Suit, 2002-03; chmn, Norwalk Br Capitol Region, 2003; Black Chamber Com; vchmn, Capitol Region Black Chamber Com, 2003; Capitol Region Chamber Com; First Congregational Church; United Church Christ; chmn, Norwalk Comn Develop Citizens Partic Comn Mayor Irwin; Nat Asn Advan Colored People Exec Comm; legis chmn, CT Assoc Comn Action; United Way Commnity Prob Solving Task Force; Gen Asst Task Force; UCONN Downstate Initiative Adv Comt; bd dir, Community Econ Develop Fund. **Honors/Awds:** Citizen of the Year, Alpha Nu Chap Omega Psi Phi, 1981; Award for Outstanding Service to Norwalk Corinthian Lodge, 16 F&AM PHA, 1982; Roy Wilkins Civil Rights Award, CT State NAACP, 1984; Arthur L Green Human Rights Award, CT State NAACP, 2003; Roodner Court Tenants Award, 2003. **Home Addr:** 37 Brooklawn Ave S, South Norwalk, CT 06854-2147.

**BURGESS, TITUSS**
Singer, actor. **Personal:** Born Feb 21, 1979, Athens, GA; son of Sandra Burgess Morse. **Educ:** Univ Ga, BA, 2001. **Career:** Walt Disney World, performer; actor, 2000-. Stage: Abelard and Heloise, 2003; Good Vibrations, 2004; Jersey Boys, 2004; Good Vibrations, 2005; Jersey Boys, 2006; The Wiz, 2006; The Little Mermaid, 2008; Guys and Dolls, 2009. Television: The Battery's Down, 2009; 30 Rock, 2011-12; Blue Bloods, 2012; Royal Pains, 2013; Unbreakable Kimmy Schmidt, 2015-; Elena of Avalor, 2016. Film: Are You Joking?, 2014; The Angry Birds Movie, 2016; Catfight, 2016. **Honors/Awds:** Webby Award, 2015; Golden Derby TV Award, 2015, 2016. **Special Achievements:** Albums: Here's to You, 2006; Comfortable.

**BURGEST, REV. DR. DAVID RAYMOND**
Educator, baptist clergy, consultant. **Personal:** Born Dec 10, 1943, Sylvania, GA; son of Rufus Sr and Marie Cooper; married Loretta Jean Black; children: Juanita Marie, Angela Lynore, David Raymond II & Paul Reginald. **Educ:** Paine Col, BA, 1965; Wayne State Univ, MSW, 1968; Syracuse Univ, PhD, 1974; Univ Chicago Sch Divinity, postdoctoral studies, 1985. **Career:** Clergy, consultant, prof (retired); Cent State Hosp, Milledgeville, GA, social work aide, 1965-66, chief social worker, 1968-69; Syracuse Univ, asst prof 1969-72; State Univ New York, Upstate Med Col, Syracuse, assoc prof psychol, 1971-72; Univ Nairobi, Kenya, vis prof sociol 1980-81; Atlanta Univ, Sch Social Work, social work consult, 1986-87; Gov State Univ, prof, 1972-80, prof social work, 1981-98; Roosevelt Univ, Chicago, IL, part-time prof, African-Amer studies, 1989-90; Univ W Indies, Vis Prof Social Work, 1993; Atlanta Univ, Sch Social Work, lectr; New Faith Baptist Church, ministry God, Pk Forest, Ill, co-founder & assoc minister; Greater Faith Baptist Church, assoc minister; St James AME Church, Chicago, Ill, assoc minister; Metrop AME Church, Trinidad, W Indies, assoc minister; Providence Missionary Baptist Church, Atlanta, Ga, assoc minister, currently. **Orgs:** Founder & pres, Cir Human Learning & Develop Specialists Inc, 1975-; lic gospel minister 1976; ed bd, Black Caucus Jour Nat Asn Black Social Workers 1979-80; prison ministry, Stateville Prison Joliet Ill & other facil Ill 1982-; consult, Suburban Nat Asn Advan Colored People, 1984-; ed bd Jour Pan-Africans Studies, 1986-; Univ Pk Libr Bd, 1987-91; pres, Lower N Youth Centers/Chicago, 1989-91; WGCI-AM, ment health youth serv advr, 1988-90; pres, Abyssinia Repetory Theatre, 1990-; pres, Self Taught Publishers, 1989-; Consult, var local, nat & int social serv orgn Am, Europe, Can & Africa such Dept Family Svcs, Alcoholism Couns, United Charities, & voc Rehabilation. **Home Addr:** 2692 Lafeville Cir Apt 1, Cincinnati, OH 45211, **Home Phone:** (513)534-0859. **Business Addr:** Associate Minister, Providence Missionary Baptist Church, 2295 Benjamin E Mays Dr, Atlanta, GA 30311, **Business Phone:** (404)752-6869.

**BURGETT, DR. PAUL JOSEPH**
Executive, school administrator. **Personal:** son of Arthur C and Ruth Garizio; married Catherine G Valentine. **Educ:** Univ Rochester, Eastman Sch Music, Rochester, NY, BM, 1968, MA, 1972, PhD, 1976. **Career:** Black Music Res Columbia Col; Hochstein Mem Music Sch, exec dir, 1970-72; Greece Cent Sch Dist, music teacher, 1973-77; GreeceNazareth Col, Rochester, NY, lectr, 1976-77, asst prof music, 1977-81; Univ Rochester, Eastman Sch Music, dean students, 1981-88, vpres & dean students, 1988-2001, vpres & gen secy, 2001-, adj prof music & sr adv pres, currently; Nazareth Col of Rochester, asst prof. **Orgs:** Chair & vice chair, Zoning Bd Appeals, 1981-86; bd dir, Gov Bd Hochstein Mem Music Sch, 1982-88; bd dir, Corp Bd YMCA Rochester & Monroe Co, 1983-91; Nat Adv Bd, Ctr Black Music Res, 1985-; dir, bd trustee & chmn, Margaret Woodbury Strong Mus, 1987-2000; bd dir, Urban League, Rochester, 1987-94; bd dir, Am Automobile Asn, Rochester, 1995; bd dir, Genesee Co Village & Mus, 2000-; bd dir, Hillside Family Agencies, 2001; Rotary Club, 2001; bd dir, Arts & Cult Coun Rochester; bd dir, United Way; adv bd, Mt. Hope Family Ctr; bd dir, Young Audiences Inc.; bd dir, Int Mus Photog, currently. **Home Addr:** 7 Corn Hill Ter, Rochester, NY 14608-2255, **Home Phone:** (716)423-0719. **Business Addr:** Vice President, General Secretary, University of Rochester, 236 Wallis Hall, Rochester, NY 14627, **Business Phone:** (585)273-2284.

**BURGIE, IRVING LOUIS (LORD BURGESS)**
Publisher, composer, songwriter. **Personal:** Born Jul 28, 1924, Brooklyn, NY; married Page Turner; children: Irving Jr & Andrew. **Educ:** Juilliard Sch Music, attended 1948; Univ Ariz, attended 1949; Univ Southern Calif, attended 1950. **Career:** Self-employed composer & lyricist; Harry Belafonte Albums, composer, 1955-60; Songs: "Jamaica Farewell"; "Island In the Sun"; "Day O"; Am Guild Authors & Composers, 1956; Ballad Bimshire, composer & writer, 1963; Barbados Nat Anthem, Barbados, composer, 1966; "Banana Boat Song". **Orgs:** Am Soc Composers, Authors & Publishers, 1956; Local no 802 Am Fedn Musicians; pres & publ, Caribe Music Corp; life mem, Nat Asn Advan Colored People; Harlem Writers Guild; United Black Men Queens; hon chmn, Camp Minisink; United Black Men Queens County Fedn. **Honors/Awds:** Numerous awards & citations including Silver Crown Merit, Barbados Govt, 1987; DHL, Univ Wis, 1989; Lord Burgess Caribbean Day, Assembly Prog Publ, named in honor. **Special Achievements:** Belafonte's Calypso Album, first album sold one million copies; Book In Plenty & Time Need, 1966. **Business Addr:** Composer, Lyricist, 11215 177th St, Jamaica, NY 11433, **Business Phone:** (718)297-9080.

**BURGIN, BRUCE L.**
Banker. **Personal:** Born Oct 22, 1947, Cincinnati, OH; married Ollie Keeton. **Educ:** NC Cent Univ, BS, com, 1970. **Career:** Freedom Savings Bank, br mgr, 1973-85; Empire Am Fed Savings Bank, br mgr, 1986-88; Life Savings Bank, br mgr, 1988-89; Fortune Bank, br mgr, 1989. **Orgs:** Tampa Alumni Chap, KAP, 1986-; Tampa Bay Urban Bankers, 1986-89. **Honors/Awds:** Polemarch Award, Tampa Alumni Chap, KAP, 1991. **Home Addr:** 10674 Grand Riviere Dr, Tampa, FL 33647-3330.

**BURKE, ALFREDA**
Teacher, opera singer. **Personal:** Born Jun 17, 1961, Chicago, IL; daughter of John H Jr and Mamie; married Rodrick Dixon. **Educ:** Roosevelt Univ, Chicago Col Music, BMus, 1984, M Mus, 1987. **Career:** Dr. Martin Luther King Jr. Experimental Laboratory Schools, general music and choral teacher, 1985-96; opera performer, 1995-; Chicago Symphony Orchestra Musicians Residency/South Shore Cultural Center, voice instructor, 1996-98; Wheaton College Conservatory, guest lecturer, 1997-2009; DiBurke Inc, co-owner, 2002-; "Too Hot to Handel" Education Outreach, Detroit Opera House, 2002-, Auditorium Theatre 2006-; Carl Sandburg High School, voice teacher, 2004-07; Chicago State University, faculty member, 2007-08; Wright State University Music & Medicine Symposium, performer, present, clinician, 2009-13; Young Musicians Choral Orchestra (YMCO), artist residency, 2009-; master class teacher. Opera performances include: "Elektra", Carnegie Hall, Orchestra Hall, 1995; performed with the Chicago Symphony at Ravinia, 1998, Detroit Symphony Orchestra and Rackham Symphony Choir, 2002, Milwaukee Symphony Orchestra, 2003, Lancaster Festival, 2003, Chorus Angelorum, 2003, 2010, Chicagoland Pops Orchestra, 2004, Millennium Park Gala, 2008, Prague Philharmonic, 2010, Cincinnati Pops Symphony Orchestra, 2011; also performed at Auditorium Theatre, 1995, Chicago Symphony Center, 1997, Kennedy Center, 1998, TodiMusicFest, 2007, Umbria Music Festival, Italy, 2007, Miss World, China, 2012, NATO Chicago Summit, 2012. **Orgs:** Roosevelt Univ Chicago Col Performing Arts, adv bd mem; Chicago Olympic 2016 Bid Comt Arts & Cult Adv Coun. **Special Achievements:** Solo recording artist, "From the Heart", 2002; "I Will Stand", 2008; recording appearances, "Hallelujah Broadway", EMI/Manhattan Records, 2010.

**BURKE, BRIAN**
Government official. **Personal:** Born Apr 19, 1958, Milwaukee, WI. **Educ:** Marquette Univ, BA, hist, lit, 1978; Georgetown Univ, JD, 1981. **Career:** Us Dept Justice, trial atty; Domestic Policy Coun, sr policy analyst; sr coun, DC off Holland & Knight, LLP; Sen John Kerry's Presidential campaign, policy dir; sr dir, State Govt Affairs Microsoft Corp; State Wis, senate chmn, 2002, State Senate 3rd dist, 2002, joint comt finance, co-chmn, 2002; asst state pub defender, Wis State Pub Defender, currently. **Orgs:** Bd dir, Mass Broadband Inst, 2014; counr, Secy Energy. **Business Addr:** Assistant State Public Defender, Wisconsin State Public Defender's Office, 315 N Henry St 2nd Fl, Madison, WI 53703-3018.

**BURKE, DONNA M.**
Executive, vice president (organization). **Personal:** married Greg; children: Devan & Kellian. **Educ:** Calif State Univ, BA, jour. **Career:** Capital Pub Radio; SBC Ameritech Mich, dir external affairs, vpres external affairs, community rels 2003-, chairperson; AT&T, regional vpres constituency rels, 2007-, exec dir external affairs, currently. **Orgs:** Metrop Affairs Coalition; Nat Newspaper Publishers Asn; Calif Nat Asn; Calif Small Bus Roundtable; Asian Resources Inc; bd mem, Automation Alley co, Sacramento Black Chamber Com Found.. **Business Addr:** Vice President, External Affairs, SBC Ameritech Michigan, 444 Mich Ave Suite 1700, Detroit, MI 48226, **Business Phone:** (313)223-6688.

**BURKE, GARY LAMONT**
Executive. **Personal:** Born Oct 4, 1955, Baltimore, MD; son of William A (deceased) and Gwendolyn I; married Nina J Abbott; children: Brandon L, Christopher J, Jonathan D, Amanda J & Rachel N. **Educ:** Babson Col, BA, acct, 1977; cert, 1990. **Career:** Coopers & Lybrand, staff acct, 1977-79, sr acct, 1979-81; Rouse CPN, internal auditor, 1981-82, sr auditor, 1982-83, acquisitions mgt, mgr, 1983-87; US F&G Realty Inc, investment officer, 1987-89, asst vip, 1989-90, US F&G Corp, chief staff, 1990-91, vpres, 1991-94; F&G Life Ins Co, vpres bus develop, 1994-95, vpres spec mkt, 1995-97, sr vpres, 1999-2001; CMO Atlanta Life Ins Co, vpres, 1998; TSA Sales, sr vpres, Brokerage & Agency Develop, 2000; CNA Life Ins, vpres, 2002-04; Structured Financial Assoc Inc, pres & coo, 2004-06; JLM Risk Mgt, consult, chief operating officer & broker, 2006-07; ING US Financial Serv, dir mkt, 2007-08; Union Labor Life Ins Co, actg pres, 2008, pres 2008-2011; New York Life Ins Co, agt, 2011-12; Prudential Ins Co Am, agt, currently; Burke & Assocs, pres, 2012-2015; 5Star Ins Co, Consult, currently. **Orgs:** Past pres, Nat Asn Black Accts, 1982; Nat Tax Sheltered Accts Asn; Nat Structured Settlements Trade Asn. **Home Addr:** 12902 Woodmore N Blvd, Bowie, MD 20720, **Home Phone:** (301)464-3566. **Business Addr:** Consultant, 5Star Insurance Co, 909 N Wash St, Alexandria, VA 22314, **Business Phone:** (703)706-5975.

**BURKE, KIRKLAND R.**
Manager, basketball coach. **Personal:** Born Jan 4, 1948, Chicago, IL; son of Alonzo Waymond and Johnnie Irene. **Educ:** Chicago Tech Col, BA, 1966; Chicago State Univ, BA, 1986. **Career:** Asst M & M instr, 1970; Holy Angels Roman Cath Sch, teacher, 1973-74; Reliable Prom, prom mgr, 1974-75; Warner, Elektra, Atlantic Corp, prom mgr, 1975-78; Warner Bros Rec, midwest prom mgr; Ind Univ, Whitney Young Magnet High Sch, Girl's Basketball, asst coach; Am Coaching Effectiveness Prog, cert coach; MBS Broadcasting Network, co-owner, 2002-; KCAT-AM, co-owner, currently; WJIW-FM, co-owner, currently; Harold Wash Col, teacher, currently. **Orgs:** Nat Assoc TV & Radio Announcers, 1972-77; youth div asst chmn, Oper PUSH, 1972-75, Nat Choir, 1972-75; asst coach, Near N High Sch Chicago, Ill Girls Basketball, 1986-87; bd dir, RALD Inst, Chicago, 1994-97; Speaker, Chicago Pub Sch Youth Motivation Prog; Black Music Assoc; nat adv bd, Nat Arch African Am Music & Cult; Chicago Pub League Basketball Coaches Hall Fame. **Honors/Awds:** Fifty four gold & platinum records, Warner Bros Records; Am Legion Nat Chmpnshp Chicago Cavaliers D & B Corps, 1969; VFW & Am Legion IL St Championship Chi Cavaliers, 1969; Cert Merit, Chicago Bd Educ, Special Arts Festival, 1980; Cert Merit, Mesetrey Sch, 1982; Cert Merit, James Madison Sch, 1985; Representative of the Year, Warner Bros Records Promotiom, 1994; Legacy Award, Warner-Elektra-Atlantic Corp, 1996. **Special Achievements:** Album: "I Got a Feeling", Exec Prod, 1986.

**Home Addr:** 742 Pk Dr, Flossmoor, IL 60422-1119, **Home Phone:** (708)799-2380. **Business Addr:** Co-Owner, KCAT-AM Christian Gospel Radio, 1207 W 6th Ave, Pine Bluff, AR 71601-3927, **Business Phone:** (870)534-5001.

## BURKE, OLGA PICKERING
Business owner, accountant, executive. **Personal:** Born Jan 6, 1946, Charleston, SC; daughter of Dr L Irving and Esther Robinson; married Philip C Sr; children: Philip C Jr & Brian. **Educ:** Johnson C Smith Univ, AB, Econ & Acct, 1968; Nat Rural Develop Leaders Sch, cert, 1976; Life Investors Inc Co, ins lic, 1981. **Career:** HA Decosta Co, acct, 1969-70; Allied Chem Corp, lost acct, 1970-72; Charleston Area Minority Assoc, fiscal officer, 1972-75; Minority Develop & Mgt Assoc, exec dir, 1975-79; Affiliated Mgt Serv Inc, pres, owner, 1979-. **Orgs:** Martin Luther King Comm YWCA Charleston, 1977-79; organizer SC Rural Am, 1979; econ adv coun, Clemson Univ, 1978-81; vpres, Regional Minority Purchasing Coun, 1981; policy comm YWCA Charleston, 1981; Nat Assoc Minority Contr; Charleston Bus & Prof Asn, 1980-83; treas, SC Sea Island Small Farmers Co-op, 1981-83; Columbia Adv, Coun US Small Bus Admin, 1981-83; MBE Gov's Comm State SC, 1982; Bus Develop, Sub-Comt City Charleston, 1982; Am Soc Prof Consult, 1983; chmn bus comm, Charleston Trident Chamber Comm, 1984; bd trustee, treas, Philip Simmons Found. **Home Addr:** 1216 Ravenel Dr, Charleston, SC 29407, **Home Phone:** (843)556-2265. **Business Addr:** Owner, Affiliated Management Service, 5651 Broadmoor St, Shawnee Mission, KS 66202-2407, **Business Phone:** (913)677-9470.

## BURKE, ROSETTA Y.
Military leader. **Personal:** children: Tirlon. **Educ:** Adelphi Univ, Harlem Hosp Sch Nursing; Long Island Univ, CW Post Ctr, masters degree. **Career:** Military Leader (retired); USAR, Army Nurse Corps, lt gen duty nurse, 1962-66, capt & nurse instr, 1966-74, maj, 1974-78, lt col, 1978-83, col, 1983-89, Nat Guard, col & chief nurse, 1993-94, adj asst gen, 1994-95, brig gen, 1995-97, maj gen, 1997; 74th Field Hosp, Bronx, New York, chief nurse, 1974; 815th Sta Hosp, chief nurse, 1978-89; 365th Gen Hosp, chief nurse, 1978-89; NY State Dept Correctional Servs, coordr & dir nurses, 1983-89, Summit Shock Incarceration Correctional Facil, supt, 1989-92; St Joseph's Sch Nursing, nurse instr; Bronx State Hosp, nurse supvr; Develop Disabilities Prog, specialist & community res coordr; NY Selective Serv Syst, state dir, 2002. **Orgs:** Reserved Officers Asn; Retired Officers Asn; Nat Guard Asn; Asn Mil Surgeons US; Nat Black Nurses Asn; Harlem Hosp Sch Nursing Alumni; hon mem, Alpha Kappa Alpha Sorority; pres, Nat Asn Black Mil Women, 2002; pres, BMW Found. **Special Achievements:** First female General Officer in the 220 year history of the New York Army National Guard; First female Assistant Adjutant General in New York State and of the Army National Guard; First female to receive the brevet promotion to Major General in the history of the New York Army National Guard and in the Army National Guard; First female to be appointed as the State Director for Selective Service System for the State of New York. **Home Addr:** 37 Nelson Ave, Latham, NY 12110, **Home Phone:** (518)783-7299. **Business Addr:** President, National Association of Black Military Women, 5695 Pine Meadows Ct, Morrow, GA 30261-1053, **Business Phone:** (404)675-0195.

## BURKE, STERLING
Vice president (organization), naval officer, administrator. **Educ:** Northwestern Univ, BS, math, 1969. **Career:** IBM, bus unit exec, 1969-2001; City Cols Chicago, Vice Chancellor CIO, 2001; Foster Group, sr partner, 2003; USN, aviation officer; DeltaHawk Engines Inc, vpres, mkt & sales, 2008-. **Business Addr:** Vice President, DeltaHawk Engines Inc, 2903 Golf Ave, Racine, WI 53404.

## BURKE, VIVIAN H.
Government official, educator. **Personal:** Born Charlotte, NC; married Logan; children: Todd. **Educ:** Elizabeth City State Univ, BS; NC Agr & Tech State Univ, MS; Univ Va, cert; Ind Univ; Livingstone Col, DHL, 2002; Winston-Salem State Univ, DHL, 2004; Elizabeth City State Univ, DHL, 2011. **Career:** Educator (retired), government official; Forsyth County Sch Syst, Winston-Salem, sch guid counr & Indust Educ Coord; NC Dept Environ & Natural Resources, field officer mgr; Winston-Salem State Univ, prog coord; City Winston-Salem, NC, NE Ward, coun mem, mayor pro tempore, 1977-, alderman, 2004; Liberty St E Redevelop Inc, adv; Guid Coun Admin & Curric Instrnl Specialist. **Orgs:** Bd dir, Piedmont Health Syst Agency; minority interest group, NC Sch Sci & math; Trans Adv Coun; chmn, Am's Four Hundredth Anniversary Comt; mem bd trustees, Elizabeth City State Univ; organizer, Flora Buffs Garden Club; Nat Women Achievement; past pres, PTA E Forsyth Sr High Sch; PTA Adv Coun; Forsyth Health Coun; admin coun Patterson Ave, YWCA; Recreation & Parks Comn; basileus Alpha Kappa Alpha Sorority; Nat memship chmn, Alpha Kappa Alpha Sorority, currently; chmn, Carver Precinct; co-chair, 5th Coun Dist elect Jimmy Carter; deleg, local State Dem Conv; life mem, bd dir, Nat Asn Advan Colored People; Meridian Chap Eastern Star; Alpha Kappa Alpha Sor; Forsyth Asn Classroom Teachers; NC Asn Educr; Top Ladies Distinction Inc; 5th Dist Black Leadership Caucus; vice chair, Finance Admin Intergovt Rel Comt; League Women Voters; app State Dem Affirmative Action Comt, 1983; chmn, Mondale Pres Forsyth Co, 1983; bd dir, 1983, mem-at-large, 1984; League Munic; Mayor Pro Tempore; Chair, pub Safety Comt; Finance Comt; trustee, Winston-Salem State Univ; founding mem, NC Black Elected Munic Officials; NC Ment Health Bd; Nat AsnEqual OpportunityHigher Educ; Black Polit Awareness League; Meridian ChapEastern Star; trustee Grace Presby Church, currently; exec bd, Piedmont Triad Res Pk; bd dir, Exp Self Reliance; United Negro Col Fund. **Honors/Awds:** Outstanding Political & Community Serv, NAACP; Outstanding Woman of the Year, Pres of the Year, Grad Leadership Award, Most Distinguished Political Award, AKA Soc; Outstanding Volunteer ESR; Outstanding Volunteer Heart Fund; Gen Alumni Outstanding Political Award, Elizabeth City State Univ; Gov's Order of Long Leaf Pine; Outstanding Political & Community Service Award, Black Polit Action League; Outstanding Serv Polit & Community Northeast Ward; Dedicated Service Award, 5th Dist Black Leadership Caucus Banquet; Service Award, Forsyth County Health Coun; Distinguished Citizen Award, Sophisticated Gents; Outstanding Women's Achievers Award, Prof Business League; DHL, Livingstone Col, 2002; DHL, Winston-Salem State Univ, 2004. First Annual Kwanzaa Award for Outstanding Community Contributions; McDonald's Rhythm of Triumph Award, 2008; President's Volunteer Service Award, 2010; Human Relations Award, 2010; Community Visionary Award, 2011. **Special Achievements:** First woman and first black appointed to the public safety chairmanship City of Winson-Salem; one of first two women appointed to Public Works Commission; Written numerous books. **Business Addr:** Council Member, Mayor Pro Tempore, City Council City of Winston-Salem, 3410 Cumberland Rd, Winston-Salem, NC 27105, **Business Phone:** (336)661-6460.

## BURKE, DR. WILLIAM ARTHUR
Association executive, air force officer. **Personal:** Born May 13, 1939, Zanesville, OH; son of Leonard and Hazel Norris; married Yvonne Brathwaite; children: Christine & Autumn. **Educ:** Miami Univ, BS, 1961; Boston Univ, attended 1964; Harvard Univ, attended 1964; Univ Mass, EdD, 1977; Lane Col & Mt Ida Col, DCL, 1991. **Career:** S Coast Air Qual Mgt Dist, chmn, vicechmn, currently, speaker; Tennis Commr XXIII Olympiad; State of Calif Fish & Game Comn, State CA, pres; Wildlife Conserv Bd, pres, CA; Genesis Int, bd chmn; World Mining Devel Co Inc, pres; Los Angeles City Counman, dep, 1966-69; Radio & TV, CA State Legis, dir legis; Batik Wine & Spirits, pres; Gen Repub Mali, hon consult; City Los Angeles Marathon, pres & founder. **Orgs:** Founder & pres, Am Health Care Delivery Corp; bd mem, State Calif Air Resources Bd, 2000; Fire Comn, Los Angeles, 2000; Calif Coastal Comn, 2002; Alpha Epsilon Rho. **Business Addr:** President, Founder, Los Angeles Marathon Inc, 11110 W Ohio Ave Suite 100, Los Angeles, CA 90025, **Business Phone:** (310)444-5544.

## BURKE, YVONNE WATSON BRATHWAITE (PERLE YVONNE WATSON)
Government official, executive, lawyer. **Personal:** Born Oct 5, 1932, Los Angeles, CA; daughter of James A Watson and Lola Moore Watson; married William A; children: Autumn Roxanne & Christine; married Louis Brathwaite. **Educ:** Univ Calif, AA, 1951; Univ Calif, Los Angeles, BA, 1953; Univ Southern Calif Law Sch, JD, 1956. **Career:** CA State Assembly, mem, 1966-72; US House Rep 28th dist, mem, 1973-79; Los Angeles County 4th dist, supvr, 1979-80; Kutak Rock & Huie, partner, 1981-83; MGM & UA Home Entertainment, mem & bd dir; Burke Robinson & Pearman, partner, 1984-87; Jones, Day, Reavis & Pogue, Los Angeles & Cleveland, partner; Los Angeles Country 2nd Dist, supvr, 1992-2008, chair bd supvr, 1993-94, 1997-98, 2002-03, 2007-08; Calif Transp Comn, Comn mem, 2013-17. **Orgs:** Trustee, Urban League, Women's Lawyer's Asn; Nat Coalition 100 Black Women; vice chmn, Univ Calif Bd Regents; bd mem, Educ Testing Serv; dir & chair, Los Angeles Br Fed Res Bank San Francisco; Ford Found Bd Trustee; fel Inst Polit J F Kennedy Sch Govt, Harvard, 1971-71; chmn, Cong Black Caucus, 1976; vice chmn, US Olympics Organizing Comt, 1984; chmn, Founders Savings & Loan. **Honors/Awds:** Loren Miller Award NAACP; Professional Achievement Award, UCLA, 1974, 1984; Future Leader of America, Time Mag, 1974; Outstanding Alumni Award, Univ Southern Calif, 1994; Alumni of the Year, Univ Calif, Los Angeles, 1996; Enterprise Person of The Year, Metrop News, 2003. **Special Achievements:** First African American woman from California to be elected to US House of Rep, 1972; She became the first member of Congress to give birth while in office. **Home Addr:** PO Box 25665, Los Angeles, CA 90025-0665. **Business Addr:** Commission Member, California Transportation Commission, 1120 N St, Sacramento, CA 95814, **Business Phone:** (916)654-4245.

## BURKEEN, ERNEST WISDOM
Government official. **Personal:** Born Aug 28, 1948, Chattanooga, TN; son of Mildred J and Ernest W; married Margaret; children: Jeannee M & Ernest W III; married Margaret. **Educ:** Mich State Univ, BS, 1975, MA, 1976. **Career:** Mich State Univ, Grad asst, 1975-76; Univ Mich, asst dir, 1976-77; City Detroit, recreation instr, 1977-80; Huron-Clinton Metro Parks, from asst supt to supt, 1980-94; Family Life Ministry, Creighton Univ, 1990-; Detroit Parks & Recreation, dir, 1994; City Ft Lauderdale, Parks & Recreation Dept, dir, 2002; City Miami Parks & Recreation, dir; Baltimore Dept Recreation & Parks, dir, currently. **Orgs:** Prog comt, Nat Recreation Parks Asn; pres, Kiwanis Club; bd mem, EthnicMinority Soc; youth servs bd, Spectrum Human Servs; recreation adv comt, Eastern Mich Univ; pres, Mich Recreation & Parks Asn; pres, Nat Recreation Ethnic Minority Soc. **Honors/Awds:** Fellowship Award, Md Recreation & Parks Asn, 1988; Innovated ProgramAward, 1988; Appreciation Award, Detroit Metro Youth Fitness, 1993; Outstanding Service Award, Nat Recreation & Park Ethnic Minority Soc, 1994; Am AcadPark & Recreation Admin. **Special Achievements:** Author: "Crossroads for Recreation," "Selective Law Enforcement," "WattNow," Michigan Leisure; "Handicapped Usage of Recreational Facilities, "NIRSA Journal; "Affirmative Action as Charades," NIRSA Newsletter. **Home Addr:** 500 River Pl Suite 5209, Detroit, MI 48207, **Home Phone:** (313)259-6818. **Business Addr:** Director, Baltimore City Department of Recreation and Parks, 2600 Madison Ave, Baltimore, MD 21217, **Business Phone:** (410)396-7931.

## BURKETT, GALE E.
Chairperson, chief executive officer, executive director. **Personal:** children: Ivan. **Career:** Texas Aerospace Comn, commnr; Horizon Capital Bank, dir; GB Tech Inc, pres, chief exec officer & chmn, 1985-. **Orgs:** Bd mem, Houston Technol Ctr; exec comt, Bay Area Houston, 2007. **Honors/Awds:** NASA Public Service Medal, 2004; Boeing Performance Excellence Award, The Boeing Company, 2009. **Special Achievements:** Named to the list of "Fifty Influential Minorities in Business" by Minority Business & Professionals Network Inc. **Business Addr:** Chairman, Chief Executive Officer, GB Tech Inc, 2200 Space Pk Dr Suite 400, Houston, TX 77058, **Business Phone:** (281)333-3703.

## BURKETTE, DR. TYRONE L.
College president, columnist. **Personal:** married Dorothy Chambers; children: Michelle & Gordon. **Educ:** Livingstone Col, BS, sociol; Interdenominational Theol Ctr, MDiv; United Theol Sem, DMin. **Career:** Barber-Scotia Col, pres, 1988-89; NC Synod Presby Church, prof, assoc exec; Presby News, auth & columnist.

## BURKS, DARRELL
Executive, founder (originator). **Personal:** Born Sep 3, 1956, Indianapolis, IN; married Suzanne F Shank. **Educ:** Ind Univ, BS, acct, 1978. **Career:** Executive (retired); Coopers Lybrand, Ind, staff, 1978-86, Detroit, mgr, 1986-89; Detroit Pub Schs, dep supt, 1989-91; Price Waterhouse Coopers LLP, Detroit, dir, 1991-92, partner, 1992, treas. **Orgs:** New Detroits Community Fund & Tech Asst Team; housing chmn, Kappa Alpha Psi; treas, Urban Educ Alliance; bd dir, treas, Health Educ Advocacy League; bd dir, treas, Homes Black C; bd dir, Easter Seals; bd dir, treas, personnel & fin comt chmn, Mich Metro Girl Scouts; bd dir, treas, Police Athletic League; bd dir, treas, Am Inst Cert Pub Accts; Mich Ohio Conn & Ind Asn Cert Pub Accts; adv comt, Md Asn Cert Pub Accts; Greater Detroit Chamber Com Bus Educ Alliance; Leadership Detroit; Adv Comn Mich Dept Treas Comn Govt Acct Auditing; bd mem, Wilberforce Univ; Detroit African Am Mus; Coleman A Young Found; Future Detroit Found; Govt Finance Officers Asn; bd mem, Univ Detroit Jesuit; Metrop Affairs Coalition; bd trustee, Charles H Wright Mus African Am Hist; bd dir, Blue Cross Blue Shield Mich, 2012-; bd dir, Col Creative Studies, 2012-; bd dir, Greektown Casino-Hotel, 2012-; bd dir, M1-Rail, 2013-. **Home Addr:** 5363 Wayfind Lane, Bloomfield, MI 48302-2955, **Home Phone:** (248)646-6334.

## BURLESON, DR. HELEN L.
Real estate agent, poet, consultant. **Personal:** Born Dec 8, 1929, Chicago, IL; daughter of Blaine Major and Beatrice Hurley; children: Earl Fredrick III & Erica Elyce Fredrick. **Educ:** Cent State Univ, BS, 1950; Northwestern Univ, MA, 1954; Nova S Eastern Univ, DPA, 1983. **Career:** High Sch Eng teacher, 1951-56, 1958-61; Bd Educ, Flossmoor, Ill, 1972-75, 1975-78, re-elected, 1978-81; Nurturing Experiences Enterprises, pres & founder, 1987-; Century 21 Dabbs & Assocs, realtor, currently, doctor admin & lives. **Orgs:** Alpha Kappa Alpha, 1948; Nat Asn Advan Colored People, 1950-; vpres & bd mem, SD 161, Flossmoor, Ill, 1972-81; proposal reader, Ill Humanities Coun, 1976-83; Ill St Bd Educ, 1981-83; Gov Task Force Study Med Malpractice, 1982; founder, Enhancement Orgn Olympia Fields, 1994. **Honors/Awds:** Alumni of the Year, Cent State Univ, 1973; Centurion Awards, Century 21 Int, 1991-95; Masters Hall of Fame, Century 21 Int, 1995; Centurion Hall of Fame, Century 21 Int, 1997; Humanitarian Awards, Dr Charles Gavin Found, St Matthews AME Church. **Home Addr:** 56 Graymoor Lane, Olympia Fields, IL 60461-1218, **Home Phone:** (708)747-0919. **Business Addr:** Realtor, Century 21 Dabbs & Associates Inc, 905 W 175th St Suite 301, Homewood, IL 60430, **Business Phone:** (708)957-7070.

## BURLESON, JANE GENEVA
Government official, administrator, association executive. **Personal:** Born May 22, 1928, Ft. Dodge, IA; daughter of William Kelly Jones and Octavia Bivens Jones Dukes; married Walter; children: Charles (deceased). **Career:** George A Hormel & Co, 1948-81; Ft Dodge Sch Syst, para prof, 1982-; Ft Dodge City Coun, councilwoman, 1984, dean coun. **Orgs:** Rec sec P-31 United Food & Comm Workers, 1974-75; League Women Voters, Mayors Adv Comm, 1980; pres A Philip Randolph Inst Ft Dodge Chap; Superintendents Adv Comm, 1984; bd mem, Jazz Festival, 1984-85; Nat Camp Fire, 1985-86; IA Tomorrow Comm, 1985-; City Fin Comt, Govr Brand stad, 1986-94; nominating bd mem, Girl Scouts, 1990; bd mem, ICCC Illiteracy, 1989-; bd mem, County Magistrate, 1990-. **Honors/Awds:** Comm Status Women Cert State IA, 1979; Cert Apprec IA Devel Comm, 1983, 1984; First African American Woman Elected Ft Dodge City Coun. **Special Achievements:** First woman and First African-American city councilor. **Home Addr:** 207 Cent Ave, Ft Dodge, IA 50501-3750, **Home Phone:** (515)955-3014.

## BURLEW, ANN KATHLEEN
Psychologist, educator. **Personal:** Born Dec 10, 1948, Cincinnati, OH; married John Howard. **Educ:** Univ Mich, Ann Arbor, MI, BA, 1970, MA, 1972, PhD, social psychol, 1974. **Career:** Social Tech Syst, sr partner, 1974-80; Univ Cincinnati, McMicken Col Arts & Sci, Dept Psychol, asst prof, 1972-78, prof, 1978-; Nat Inst Drug Abuse, Prin Investr, currently; Crossroads Ctr, psychol supvr; J Black Psychol, ed, 1987-2001, assoc ed, 2013-. **Orgs:** Chair, Eval Com & YWCA Shelter Battered Women, 1977-79; vip, Cincinnati Asn, Black Psychol, 1979-80; CETA Adv Com United Appeal, 1979-80; Cot Develop Adv Com, 1980; bd mem, United Appeal/Cot Chest Planning Bd, 1980; vip, United Black Asn Fac & Staff, 1980; Asn Black Psychologists, 2010-; Ohio Psychol Asn, 2010-; Am Psychol Asn, 2011-. **Honors/Awds:** Summer fac res grant, Univ Cincinnati, 1977, 1980; Career Women of Achievement, Young Women Christian Asn, 1988; Distinguished Psychologist Award, 1995; Faculty Achievement Award, 1996; University Excellence in Mentoring Award, 2007; Edith C. Alexander Distinguished Teaching Award, 2007; Kenneth and Mamie Clark Award, Am Psychol Asn, 2011; Outstanding Faculty Mentoring Award, Psychol Grad Stud Asn, 2012; Hewett Award, 2014. **Special Achievements:** Co-author, "Minority Issues in Mental Health"; co-author, "Reflections on Black Psychology"; Published numerous articles. **Home Addr:** 6353 Iris Ave, Cincinnati, OH 45213-1507. **Business Addr:** Professor, University of Cincinnati McMicken College of Arts & Sciences, 4130D Edwards 1 Edwards Ctr 2600 Clifton Ave, Cincinnati, OH 45221-0002, **Business Phone:** (513)556-5541.

## BURLEY, DALE S.
Engineer, journalist, executive. **Personal:** Born Aug 6, 1961, New York, NY; son of Lloyd C and Anne L Thompson. **Educ:** Morgan State Univ, Baltimore, BS, 1983. **Career:** WEAA-FM, Baltimore, Md, newswriter/reporter, 1982-84; WLIB-AM, New York, NY, newswriter/asst ed, 1983, 1984; WINS-AM, New York, NY, prod engr, 1984-86; WNYE-FM, Brooklyn, NY, prod engr, 1986-, asst producer, producer, currently; The Daily Challenge, Brooklyn, NY, reporter, 1993-. **Orgs:** Nat Asn Advan Colored People, 1980-; Omega Psi Phi Fraternity, 1985-; Abyssinian Baptist Church, 1988-; Nat Asn Black Journalists, 1988-. **Home Addr:** 100 Lane Salle St Suite 13H, New York, NY 10027, **Home Phone:** (212)932-1322. **Business Addr:** Production Engineer, Producer, WNYE-FM, 112 Tillary St Master Control, Brooklyn, NY 11201, **Business Phone:** (718)250-5800.

## BURLEY, JACK L., SR.

President (organization), executive, chairperson. **Personal:** Born Apr 26, 1942, Pittsburgh, PA; son of Andrew C and Lynda; married Joanne E; children: Diana Gant & Jack L Jr. **Educ:** Pa State Univ, BS, 1965; Univ Pittsburgh, MBA, 1974. **Career:** Fed Power Comn, acct, 1965-66; Gen Foods, financial analyst, 1968-70; HJ Heinz, mgr financial planning, 1970-80; Heinz USA, controller, 1983-85, vpres finance & admin, 1985-89, vpres logistics & admin, 1989-91, vpres opers & logistics, 1991-93; Heinz Serv Co, pres, 1993; Manchester Bidwell Corp, bd vice chmn, currently. **Orgs:** Exec bd dir, Leadership Coun; bd dir, Urban League Pittsburgh; bd dir, Forbes Health Syst; Omega Psi Phi Fraternity; Sigma Pi Phi Fraternity; Bethesda Presby Church; life mem, Manchester Bidwell Corp. **Home Addr:** 320 Shalimar Ct, Monroeville, PA 15146, **Home Phone:** (412)856-5479. **Business Addr:** Vice chairman, Life Member, Manchester Bidwell Corp, 1815 Metrop St, Pittsburgh, PA 15233, **Business Phone:** (412)323-4000.

## BURNETT, ARTHUR LOUIS, SR.

Judge. **Personal:** Born Mar 15, 1935, Spotsylvania County, VA; son of Robert Louis and Lena Bumbry; married Frisbieann Lloyd; children: Darnellena Christalyn, Arthur Louis II, Darryl Lawford, Darlisa Ann & Dionne. **Educ:** Howard Univ, BA (cum laude), polit sci, econ, 1957; NY Univ Sch Law, LLB, 1958. **Career:** Dept Justice, Adv Criminal Div, atty, 1958-65, asst US atty DC, 1965-68; Metrop Police Dept, legal advisor, 1968-69; Dist Columbia, US Magistrate, judge, 1969-75 & 1980-87; Civil Serv Syst, legal advisor, 1975; US Civil Serv Comn, Legal Div, asst gen coun, 1975-78; Off Personnel Mgt, assoc gen coun, 1979-80; Super Ct Dist Columbia, Magistrate Judge, 1980-87, pres, judge, 1987-98, sr judge, 1998-; Cath Univ Columbus Sch Law, adj prof, 1997; Howard Univ Sch Law, adj prof, 1998-; Nat African Am Drug Policy Coalition, nat exec dir, 2004-. **Orgs:** Chmn, Conf Spec Ct Judges, Am Bar Asn, 1974-75; chmn, Criminal Law & Juv Justice Comm, Admin Law & Regulatory Pract Sect, 1983-85; vice chair, Criminal Rules & Evidence Comt, Criminal Justice Sect, 1985-92; asst secy, Admin Law & Regulatory Pract Sect, 1990-93; chair, 1992-97, secy, 1993-95, Criminal Justice Mag Ed Bd, Criminal Justice Sect, chair, 1996-99; Steering Comt Unmet Needs C, 2003-04; chmn, Nat Com Utilization US Magistrates Fed Cts, Fed Bar Asn, 1980-; chmn, Fed Litigation Sect Admin Justice, 1983-85; pres, Nat Coun US Magistrates, 1983-84; pres, DC Chap, 1984-85; Coun Admin Law & Regulatory Pract Sect, Am Bar Asn, 1987-90; Juv Justice Comt, 1987-; admin conf US, 1990-94; chair, Audit Comt, Nat Fed Bar Asn, 1999-; coun & spec asst to pres, Nat Bar Asn, 2003-04; DC Bar Asn; Wash Bar Asn; Am Judges Asn; Am Judicature Soc; chmn, Nat Criminal Law Com; chair, Nat Bar Asn Juv Justice Task Force; bd dir, Nat Asn C Alcoholics; mem dist, Columbia Fel Christian Athletes Inc. **Special Achievements:** First General Counsel of the Metropolitan Police Department, 1968; First African-American to hold the position of United States Magistrate Judge, 1969. **Home Addr:** 6229 32nd Pl NW, Washington, DC 20015, **Home Phone:** (202)362-6210. **Business Addr:** Adjunct Professor, Howard University, 2900 Van Ness St NW, Washington, DC 20008, **Business Phone:** (202)806-8000.

## BURNETT, REV. BESCYE P.

Librarian, educator. **Personal:** Born Apr 29, 1950, Roseboro, NC; daughter of Casey and Selena Boone; married Charles; children: Denise & Shawn. **Educ:** Winston-Salem State Univ, NC, BS, elem educ, 1972; Univ NC, Greensboro, NC, MLS, 1977; Los Angeles County Pub Libr, supv cert, 1986; Miami Univ, Oxford, OH, cert mgt, 1990; Cleveland State Univ, master, psychol diversity, 1999; United Theol Sem Twin Cities, Mdiv, 2008. **Career:** Startown Elem Sch, Newton, NC, teacher, 1972-73; Winston Salem & Forsyth Sch, Winston-Salem, NC, teacher & librn, 1973-79; State NC, Raleigh, NC, media consult, 1979-80; Univ Ill-Champ, Urbana, Ill, vis prof, 1980-81; Fashion Inst, Los Angeles, Calif, librn, 1981-82; County Los Angeles Pub Libr, Downey, Calif, literacy librn, 1982-87; Johnson County Libr, Shawnee, KS, vol coordr adult servs, 1988-89; Cleveland Heights-Univ Heights, depdir, beginning, 1989; Great River Regional Libr, dir, 2001-05; United Methodist Church, teacher, 2005-. **Orgs:** Nat Asn Advan Colored People, 1980-; ALA, 1987-; PLA, 1987-; bd mem, Proj Learn, 1989-96; BCALA Strategic Planning Comt, 1991-; tutor, bd mem, literacy orgn; pres community adv counci, St. Cloud State Univ; United Way Bd; Create CommUNITY; United Ministry Higher Educ; Community Found Womens Fund; ServeMinnesota Bd; Minn State Univ Diversity Coun; MN Ann Conf Relig; Race Action Team; Election Nominating Comt, 1994. **Home Addr:** 3378 Hartwood, Cleveland, OH 44112, **Home Phone:** (216)451-0550. **Business Addr:** Director, Great River Regional Library, 405 W St Germain, St. Cloud, MN 56301-3697, **Business Phone:** (320)251-7282.

## BURNETT, DR. CALVIN W.

School administrator. **Personal:** Born Mar 16, 1932, Brinkley, AR; son of Elmer Clay and Vera Rayford Payne; married Martha Alma Ware; children: Vera, Susan & David; married Gretta L Gordy; children: Tywana. **Educ:** St Louis Univ, BA, biol & polit sci, 1959, PhD, sociol psychol, 1963. **Career:** St Louis State Hosp, res social psychologist, 1961-63; Health & Welfare Coun Metro St Louis, res dir spec proj, 1963-66; Cath Univ Am, assoc prof, 1966-69; Upward Bound Prog, US Off Educ, consult, 1966-70; Nat Planning Orgn Wash, consult, 1967-68; Urban Syst Corp Wash, consult, 1967-69; Southern Ill Univ, assoc prof, 1969-70; Coppin State Col MD, pres, 1970-2002; Md Higher Educ Comn, actg secy higher educ, 2004, secy higher educ, 2004-07; Cath Univ Am, fac mem; Southern Ill Univ, fac mem. **Orgs:** Am Asn State Col & Univ, 1970-74; Correctional Training Comn, 1977-2003; State Scholar Bd, 1983-89; chmn bd, YMCA Greater Baltimore, 1984-86; bd dir, Nat Asn Equal Opportunity Higher Educ, 1985-; bd dir, Empowerment Baltimore Mgt Corp, 1996-97; chair, State Planning Comt Higher Educ, 2004-; Segmental Adv Coun, 2004-; Gov's Exec Coun, 2004-; Gov's Subcabinet Int Affairs, 2004-; Smart Growth Subcabinet, 2004-; Bd, Col Savings Plans Md, 2004-; Gov's Comn Serv & Volunteerism, 2004-; Southern Regional Educ Bd, 2004-; Gov's Workforce Investment Bd, 2004-; Coord Coun Juv Serv Educ Progs, 2004-; Educ Coord Comt, 2004-; Educ Coord Coun Correctional Insts, 2004-; Md Heritage Areas Authority, 2004-; Md K-16 Partnership Leadership Coun, 2004-; Md Adv Comn Mfg Competitiveness, 2004-; Interdepartmental Adv Comt Minority Affairs, 2004-; Md Educ Coun, 2005-; Gov's Comn Qual Educ Md, 2004-05; Statewide Comn Crisis Nursing, 2004-05; co-chair, Community Col Students with Disabilities Task Force, 2005; Task Force to Convene a Summit Civic Literacy Md, 2006-; Statewide Comn Shortage Health Care Workforce, 2006-; dir res, Health & Welfare Coun, St Louis; pres, Baltimore Area Coun; pres, Boy Scouts Am; pres, Black-Jewish Forum Md; bd mem, Baltimore Urban League; bd mem, Gilman Sch; bd mem, McDonogh Sch; Md Civil Rights Comn. **Home Addr:** 1490 Bollinger Rd, Westminster, MD 21157-7211, **Home Phone:** (410)840-0132. **Business Addr:** Secretary of Higher Education, Maryland Higher Education Commission, 839 Bestgate Rd Suite 400, Annapolis, MD 21401, **Business Phone:** (410)260-4516.

## BURNETT, DAVID LAWRENCE

Journalist, television news anchorperson, consultant. **Personal:** Born Apr 6, 1956, Indianapolis, IN; son of Boyd Jr and Mary Ogburn; married Lauren Jefferson; children: David Jr & Janet Elaine. **Educ:** Ball State Univ, Muncie, IN, BS, commun, 1978. **Career:** WTLC-FM, Indianapolis, Ind, reporter & anchor, 1979; WTTG-TV, reporter & anchor, reporter-training prog, developer & coordr; WTVW-TV, Evansville, Ind, reporter & anchor, 1979-82; Dayton, Ohio, reporter & anchor, 1982-86, Wash, DC, reporter & training prog, developer & coordr, reporter & anchor, 1986-99; Hill & Knowlton Pub Rels, Wash, mgr dir; Pincus Group Inc, vpres & sr trainer, currently. **Orgs:** Alpha Phi Alpha Fraternity, 1975-; vpres, Dayton Asn Black Journalists, 1984-85; pres, Wash Asn Black Journalists, 1989-90; Alzheimer's Asn; Am Heart Asn; Concerned Black Men; United Negro Col Fund; Ball State Univ Human Rels Comt; pres, Wash DC Chap Nat Asn Black Journalists. **Home Addr:** 130 Chanel Terr Suite 204, Falls Church, VA 22046, **Home Phone:** (703)237-2409. **Business Addr:** Vice President, Senior Trainer, The Pincus Group Inc, 309 Reserve Gate Terr, Silver Spring, MD 20016, **Business Phone:** (301)938-6990.

## BURNETT, DR. MYRA N.

College administrator, clinical psychologist, college teacher. **Personal:** Born Ft. Worth, TX. **Educ:** Harvard Univ, BA, psychol, 1977; Stanford Univ, MA, social psychol, 1980; Duke Univ, PhD, clin psychol, 1987. **Career:** Spelman Col, prof, 1985-2004, vice provost acad affairs & assoc prof psychol, 2004-, interim provost & vpres acad affairs, 2014-; Peachtree Psychol Serv, psychologist, currently; Spelman Col, Off Instnl Res Assessment & Planning, dir. **Orgs:** Fac Resource Network; Am Psychol Asn; Asn Black Psychologists, 1982-2009; Nat Inst Gen Med Sci; adv bd, Southern Asn Cols & Schs Comn; Howard Hughes Med Inst. **Home Addr:** , Atlanta, GA. **Business Addr:** Associate Professor, Vice Provost, Spelman College, Rockefeller Hall Rm 112, Atlanta, GA 30314-4399, **Business Phone:** (404)270-5027.

## BURNETT, ROBERT BARRY

Broadcaster, football player. **Personal:** Born Aug 27, 1967, East Orange, NJ. **Educ:** Syracuse Univ, econ, 1990. **Career:** Football player (retired), commentator; Cleveland Browns, left defensive end, 1990-95; Baltimore Ravens, left defensive end, 1996-98, defensive back, 1999-2001; Miami Dolphins, 2002-03; WBAL, commentator, 2006; real estate investment co owner. **Orgs:** Toys Tots; United Way; Police Athletic League; Make A Wish Found; founder, Facing Our C's Urban Situation. **Honors/Awds:** Pro Bowl, 1994; Champion, Super Bowl, XXXV.

## BURNETT, ZARON WALTER, JR.

Writer, artist. **Personal:** Born Dec 16, 1950, Danville, VA; son of Zaron W Sr and Johnsie Broadway; married Pearl M Cleage; children: Zaron W III, Deignan Cleage-Lomax & Meghan V. **Educ:** Hampton Inst, attended 1969; Pa State Univ, 1974; Ga State Univ, Atlanta, GA, BS, 1977. **Career:** Harrisburg Free Clin, dir pub outreach, 1972-74; CDC-VD Contrib Prog, health prog rep, 1978; N Cent Ga Health Syst Agency, proj rev analyst, 1979-80; Atlanta Southside Community Health Ctr, dir res, 1980; Fulton County Gov, exec aide chair & bd commissioners, 1980-83; Just Us Theater Co, exec producer, 1989-, co-owner & dir, 1994-; Bks: We Speak Your Names, 2006; Carthaginian Hon Soc. **Orgs:** Mayor's fel arts, Atlanta Mayor's Off, 1990. **Home Addr:** 1665 Havilon Dr SW, Atlanta, GA 30311, **Home Phone:** (404)755-9655. **Business Addr:** Producing Director, Founder, Just Us Theater Co, 1665 Havilon Dr SW, Atlanta, GA 30311-0271, **Business Phone:** (404)753-2399.

## BURNETTE, DR. ADA PURYEAR

Educator. **Personal:** Born Darlington, SC; married Paul Puryear Sr; children: Paul Puryear Jr & Paula Puryear; married Thomas. **Educ:** Talladega Col, BA, 1953; Univ Chicago, reading, MA, 1958; Fla State Univ, PhD, 1986, cert pub supvr & cert pub mgr training; Tex Southern Univ; Chicago State Univ; Fla A&M Univ; Fla State Univ, cert pub supvr, 1989; Chicago Teachers Col, elem educ courses; Tex Southern Univ, Houston, TX, early childhood training & cert; Tuskegee Univ, Tuskegee, AL, comput programming; Leon Co Pub Schs Dist, prin training sessions. **Career:** Winston Salem NC Pub Schs, high sch math teacher, 1953-54; Chicago Pub Schs, elem sch teacher, 1954-58; Norfolk State Col, asst prof, founder, dir reading clin, 1958-61; Univ Chicago, Reading Clin, teacher, 1958; Tuskegee Inst, adminr & teacher, asst prof reading founder, dir reading clin, 1961-66; Fisk Univ, asst prof math, 1966-70; Fla DOE, adminr, 1973-88; Bethune-Cookman Col, adminr & teacher, 1988-90; Fla A&M Univ, Develop Res Sch Dist, supt & dir, 1990-93, dept chair, prof, PhD dir, 1993-98, Robert H Anderson Educ Leadership Libr, dir, fac senate pres, prof emer, 2003, adj fac, 2003-07, prof, chair dept educ leadership & human serv, 2007-; Col Ed Off-Campus coordr, 2005-07; Valdosta State Univ, assoc prof reading & coordr off-campus progs, 2005-07. **Orgs:** Secy & treas, Afro-Am Res Asn, 1968-73; bd dir, Christian Sch Performing Arts; deacon, Trinity Presby Church; parliamentarian undergrad adv, treas & secy, Alpha Kappa Alpha; pres, historian, reporter & vpres, Drifters Tallahassee; pres, publicity chmn & initiation chmn, Phi KappaPhi, Fla State Univ; Phi Delta Kappa, Pi Lambda ta; nat mem chmn, Drifters Inc; Fla Elem & Mid Schs; comnr, Sourn Asn Col & Schs, 1978-88; Leon Dem Exec Bd, 1982-88; pres teen sponsor, Jack & Jill AmTallahassee, 1984-85; pres, Int Read Asn Affil Concerned Educ Black Students, 1984-86; Fla Coun Elem Educ; DOE liaison; secy & co-organizer, Societas Docta Inc, 1987-; Fla Asn Supv & Curric Develop Bd, 1988-; pres, Les Beau Monde, 1989-90; Fla Asn Sch-Adm; Am Asn Sch-Adm; Fla Elem & Mid Sch Principals; Nat Asn Elem Sch Principals; Nat Asn Sec Sch Prin; Links; pres, Ladies Art & Social Club; Nat Asn Female Execs; Friends Black Arch; SE Asn Prof Ed Lead; pres & nat financial secy, Holidays Tallahassee, 1993-97; Asn Supv & Curric Develop; Fla Coun Educ Mgt, 1994-99; nat vpres, Holidays Tallahassee, 1997-2001; pres, Holidays Tallahassee, 2001-; bd trustee, Fla A&M Univ, 2002-03; bd mem, FSCPM; Societas Docta Inc; secy, Links Int Trends; pres, Big Bend Homeless Coalition; co-chair, HOPE Homeless Facil Adv Bd; Big Bros Big Sisters Bd S Ga; Kappa Delta Pi Hon Socs; Gadsden Co Declamation Judge; Miracle Hill Nursing Home, Libr Estab Comt; secy & chair, United Way Big Bend Allocation Panel; United Negro Col Fund Telethon; Voter Registr; Emergency Health Care Orgn; Links Exec Comt; chair, Links Pub Rels; Links Hope Homeless Community Liaison; co-chair, Links Int Comt; co-pres, AAUW; AKA Handbk Comt; pres, Refuge House Fund Raiser Lead Person; Community Child Care Coord Coun Bd; Terrell House Volunteer. **Home Addr:** PO Box 38543, Tallahassee, FL 32315-8543, **Home Phone:** (850)575-8585. **Business Addr:** Department Chair, Professor, Florida A & M University, 310 Perry Paige Bldg S, Tallahassee, FL 32315-8543, **Business Phone:** (850)561-2268.

## BURNEY, BILL. See BURNEY, WILLIAM D, JR.

## BURNEY, WILLIAM D., JR. (BILL BURNEY)

Government official. **Personal:** Born Apr 23, 1951, Augusta, ME; son of William D Sr and Helen Nicholas; married Lynne Godfrey. **Educ:** Boston Univ, Boston, MA, BS, pub commun, 1973; Univ Maine Sch Law, Portland, ME, JD, 1977. **Career:** Maine State Housing Authority, Augusta, ME, asst develop dir, 1981; City Augusta, ME, mayor, 1988-97; US Dept Housing & Urban Develop, field off dir, 2001-. **Orgs:** Augusta City Coun, 1982-88; Transp & Commun Steering Comt, Nat League Cities, 1990; chmn, Maine Conf Mayors, 1993; bd dir, Holocaust Human Rights Ctr Maine; bd dir, Am Baptist Churches Maine; nominating comt, Kennebec Girl Scout Coun Maine; bd dir, Yankee Healthcare, Augusta, ME; chair, Augusta Bd Educ, currently. **Home Addr:** 44 Wilson Pl, Augusta, ME 04332-5215, **Home Phone:** (207)622-1241. **Business Addr:** Field Office Director, US Department of Housing & Urban Development, 1 Merchants Plz Suite 601, Bangor, ME 04401-8302, **Business Phone:** (207)945-0467.

## BURNHAM, MARGARET ANN

Judge, lawyer. **Personal:** Born Dec 28, 1944, Birmingham, AL. **Educ:** Tougaloo Col, BA, hist, 1966; Univ Pa, Law Sch, LLB, 1969. **Career:** Roxbury Defenders, Boston, MA, staff atty, 1972-74; Burnham, Stern & Shapiro, founding partner, 1974-77; Trial Ct Massachusetts, Munic Ct Dept, assoc judge, 1977-83; Boston Munic Ct, justice, Boston, 1977-82; Radcliffes Bunting Inst, fel, 1985; Harvards DuBois Inst, fel; Law Off of Margaret Burnham, Solo Practr, 1987-89; Mass Inst Technol, Dept Polit Sci, lectr polit sci & Prog Womens Studies, lectr, 1989-2002; Burnham & Hines, partner, 1989-2002; Northeastern Univ, Law Sch, assoc prof law, 2002-06, prof law, 2006-; Wellesley Col, Newhouse Ctr for the Humanities Fel, 2008; Univ Leiden, Grotius Inst, fel, 2009. **Orgs:** Atty, Nat Asn Advan Colored People, Legal Defense & Educ Fund Inc, NY, 1969-72; exec dir, Nat Conf Black Lawyers, 1983-85, chief coun, 1983-85; chmn, bd dir, Nat Ctr Afro-Am Artists, 1992-; bd trustee, Old S Meeting House, 1993-; fel, WEB DuBois Inst; Int Adv Bd, Grenada Educ & Develop Prog, 1996-; bd dir, Algebra Proj, 1997-; bd dir, S Africa Partners, 1997-98; nat adv bd, Radcliffes Bunting Inst, 1999-2002; advisor, Cold Case Proj. **Home Addr:** 255 Clinton Rd, Brookline, MA 02445-4225. **Business Addr:** Professor of Law, Northeastern University School of Law, 81 Cargill Hall 400 Huntington Ave, Boston, MA 02115, **Business Phone:** (617)373-8857.

## BURNIM, MELLONEE VICTORIA

Educator, association executive, musician. **Personal:** Born Sep 27, 1950, Teague, TX; married C Jason Dotson; children: Jamel Arzo. **Educ:** Northern Tex State Univ, BM, music educ, 1971; Univ Wis Madison, MM, African Music, ethnomusicology, 1976; Ind Univ, PhD, ethnomusicology, 1980. **Career:** Delay Mid Sch, dir, choral music, 1971-73; Univ wis, res asst, 1973, acad adv, 1973; Opera Theater, choral dir, 1976-80; Ind Univ, Bloomington, Afro-Am Choral Ensemble, dir, 1976-82, Dept Afro-Am Studies, assoc prof, Arch african am music & cult, dir, Dept Folklore & Ethnomusicology, adj prof, prof, currently. **Orgs:** Alpha Lambda Delta, 1968; Sigma Alpha Iota, NTSU, 1969; chap vpres, Mortar Bd, NTSU, 1970-71; Pi Kappa Lambda, 1971. **Honors/Awds:** Full Music Scholar, NTSU, 1969-71; Nat Defense Foreign Language Fellow, Arabic, Univ Wisconsin, 1973-74; fellow, Nat Fel Fund, Univ Wisconsin & Ind Univ, 1973-78; Eli Lilly Postdoctoral Teaching Fellow, 1984; alternate, National Research Council Postdoctoral Fellow, Wash, DC, 1984; Institute for Advanced Study and CAHI Grant, 2010-11. **Special Achievements:** Musical dir, video tapes2-30 minutes, "Life & Works Undine S Moore", Afro-Am Arts Inst, Ind Univ, 1979; musical dir, WTUI Bloomington, "Contemporary Black Gospel Music", 1979. **Home Addr:** 3628 S Sowders Sq, Bloomington, IN 47401-8758, **Home Phone:** (812)339-4906. **Business Addr:** Professor, Indiana University, 504 N Fess 203, Bloomington, IN 47408, **Business Phone:** (812)855-4258.

## BURNIM, DR. MICKEY L.

Educator. **Personal:** Born Jan 19, 1949, Teague, TX; son of Arzo and Ruby; married LaVera Levels; children: Cinnamon & Adrian. **Educ:** N Tex State Univ, BA, econ, 1970, MA, econ, 1972; Univ Wis-Madison, PhD, econ, 1977; Univ NC, Chapel Hill, attended 1983; Harvard Univ, attended 1991. **Career:** Fla State Univ, asst prof econs, 1976-82; Univ NC, asst vpres acad affairs, 1982-86, adj asst prof econs to adj assoc prof econs, 1983-86; Univ Ga, asst vpres acad affairs, 1982-86; Trans century Corp, consult, 1986; NC Cent Univ, vice chancellor acad affairs & prof econs, 1986-95, provost & vice chancellor, 1990-95; Elizabeth City State Univ, interim chancellor, 1995-96, chancellor, 1996-2006; Bowie State Univ, pres, 2006-. **Orgs:** Chmn, Educ Comn, Nat Asn Advan Colored People, 1979-80; mem & bd dir, Tallahassee Urban League, 1979-80; Brookings Econ Policy fel Brookings Inst, 1980-81; Am Econs Asn; Nat Econs Asn; Durham Chamber Com; bd dir, bd trustee, CAEL; Wachovia Adv Bd; Salvation Army; Elizabeth City Chamber Com; Southern Asn Col & Sch; Elizabeth City Rotary Club; Minority Adv Coun Wachovia Bank; N eastern NC Sch masters Club; bd dir, Nat Asn Equal Opportunity Educ; bd dir, Cent Intercollegiate Athletic Asn, chair, 2003-05; presidents coun, Nat Col Athletic Asn; Bowie Rotary Club; bd visitors, Bowie State Univ, 2006-; Col Success Task Force, P-20 Leadership Coun Md, 2009-10; chair, Univ Syst Md, 2011-; bd dir, Am Asn State Cols & Univs, 2011-; Clean Energy Prog Task Force, 2013-14; Nat Col Athletic Asn, Div II, presidents coun. **Special Achievements:** Publ:1.) "The Impact of the Brown Decision on Public HBCUs: A North Carolina Case Study" in Brown v. Board of Education: Its Impact on Public Education, 1954-2004; 2) "The Changing Status of Economic Minorities: 1948-77" (with David Rasmussen) in The Review of Black Political Economy; 3) "Benefits and Costs of a Public Service Employment Program: A Case Study in Florida" (with J.H. Cobbs) in Growth and Change; 4) "The Earnings Effect of Black Matriculation in Predominantly White Colleges" in Industrial and Labor Relations Review; 5) "Investments in College Education for Black Males" in Proceedings of the American Statistical Association; 6) A Survey of Minority Business in Florida; 7) An Evaluation of the Public Service Employment Projects in Florida Created Under Title VI of the Comprehensive Employment and Training Act of 1973; and 8) three invited presentations-"Equality in Education and Employment?" (Oliver Cromwell Cox Lecture Series of the Kennedy School of Government at Harvard University); "Black Employment, Unemployment, and Labor Force Participation During the 1980's" (Washington-Based Black Economists Organization); and "The Black Labor Force in the 1980's (Williams College, Williamstown, MA). **Home Addr:** 840 Drifting Sands Dr, Corolla, NC 27927. **Business Addr:** President, Bowie State University, 14000 Jericho Park Rd, Bowie, MD 20715-9465, **Business Phone:** (301)860-3555.

## BURNLEY, DR. LAWRENCE A. Q. (REV. DR. LARRY BURNLEY)
College administrator, college teacher, educator. **Personal:** Born OH; married Naima Quarles; children: Thulani Rashad (deceased). **Educ:** Univ Cincinnati, BA, African Am studies, 1979; Christian Theol Sem, Mdiv, 1990; Univ Pa, PhD, 2006. **Career:** Global Ministries Christian Church, ordained minister; Off Racial Ethnic Rels, exec; United Church Christ, exec; Messiah Col, assoc dean multicultural progs & spec asst provost, currently; Whitworth Univ, asst vpres diversity & intercultural rels & asst prof hist, 2010-. **Orgs:** Nat Campus Ministry Asn, 1990-96; Asn Christian Church Educr, 1990-; Asn United Christian Educr, 1997-; Nat Benevolent Asn. **Home Addr:** 652 Pk Ridge Dr, Mechanicsburg, PA 17055. **Business Addr:** Assistant Vice President for Diversity & Intercultural Relations, Assistant Professor of History, Whitworth University, McEachran Hall 220 300 W Hawthorne Rd, Spokane, WA 99251, **Business Phone:** (509)777-4215.

## BURNS, BENJAMIN O.
Lawyer. **Career:** Burns, Colbert, Mose & Beaner LLC, atty, currently. **Orgs:** La State Bar Asn. **Business Addr:** Attorney, Burns, Colbert, Mose & Beaner LLC, 224 St Landry St Suite 2D, Lafayette, LA 70506-3578, **Business Phone:** (337)232-7239.

## BURNS, CALVIN LOUIS
Clergy, journalist. **Personal:** Born Mar 16, 1952, Memphis, TN; son of Andrew and Freddie McClinton; married Regina Whiting. **Educ:** Memphis State Univ, Memphis, TN, BA, 1974, grad sch, attended 1983; Charles Harrison Mason Bible Col, assocs, 1979. **Career:** Memphis Press Scimitar, journalist, 1974-83; Interstate Transp, mgr comm, 1985-88; Church God Christ, Memphis, Tenn, assoc news dir; Tri-State Defender, Memphis, Tenn, managing ed, 1988-. **Orgs:** Exec dir, Bethesda Outreach, 1984-; commun dir, Memphis region, Nat Asn Black Journalists, 1990-; bd mem, Memphis State Univ Journalist Alumni, 1991. **Honors/Awds:** Outstanding citizen Award, Congressman Harold Ford, 1983; Citizen Achievement Award, Shelby County Sheriffs Dept, 1989; Ten Outstanding Achievement Award, Gov Tenn, 1990; Professional Achievement Award, Gospel Acad, Memphis, 1991. **Home Addr:** 5015 McKallar Woods Suite 8, Memphis, TN 38116, **Home Phone:** (901)398-9334. **Business Addr:** Managing Editor News/Editorial, Tri-State Defender Newspaper, 124 E Calhoun Ave, Memphis, TN 38101, **Business Phone:** (901)523-1818.

## BURNS, DIANN
Actor, journalist. **Personal:** Born Sep 29, 1956; married Marc Watts; children: Ryan. **Educ:** Cleveland State Univ, polit & mass Commun; Columbia Univ NY Grad Sch Jour. **Career:** Cleveland Plain Dealer, gen assignment reporter, 1979-80; WPIX Tv, 1981-84; WCMH, reporter, 1984-85; Cleveland Call & Post, ed, photogr & reporter; Independent Network News, field producer & reporter; WLS-TV, co-anchor, 1985-2003; Anchor; Films: Richie Rich, 1994; Primal Fear, 1996; The Negotiator, 1998; WBBM, CBS2Chicago, co-anchor, 2003-08; Next TV, host, 2010. **Orgs:** Spokesperson, Pediatric AIDS Chicago; Ronald McDonald House; Northern Ill Chap Mult Sclerosis Soc, & Support Group; Nat Asn Black Journalists; Nat Asn TV Arts & Sci; active in several civic & charitable orgns. **Honors/Awds:** Local Emmy Awards; Outstanding Individual Excellence; Silver Dome Award, ill Broadcasters Asn, 2005. **Special Achievements:** The First African-American woman to serve as lead anchor of a 10:00 PM news broadcast in Chicago, and remains the only woman of color serving in that role today. **Home Addr:** , IL. **Business Addr:** Co Anchor, CBS 2 Chicago, 630 N McClurg Ct, Chicago, IL 60607, **Business Phone:** (312)202-2222.

## BURNS, FELTON V.
Social worker, lecturer. **Personal:** Born Mar 12, 1936, Tillar, AR; married Verlene Dean; children: Gregory L & Pamele E. **Educ:** Fresno St, BA, 1962; Calif State Univ, Fresno, MA, 1972; Univ Southern Calif, EdD, 1977. **Career:** Calif, Fresno, social worker, 1962-65; Econ Opportunities Comn, asst dir, 1965-68; Calif State Univ, Fresno, asst dean stud, 1968-71, staff coun, 1971, prof emer, 2000-; Foster Parent Training Proj, dir, 1994-99; Calif State Univ, Counr, counr emer Health & Psychol Serv, currently. **Orgs:** Pres, Spectrum Asn, 1977-85; dir, Advan Res Tech, 1978-83; Am Asn Coun & Develop, 1985; Calif Black Fac & Staff Asn. **Honors/Awds:** Troy Award, Educ Fresno Comt Serv, 1975; Albright Endowed Chair Excellence, Calif State Univ, Fresno, Stud Affairs Div, 1984-85; Rosa Parks Award, 1998; Fresno Foster Parents, 1999; Fresno State EOP Leadership Award, 1999. **Home Addr:** 6378 N 8th St, Fresno, CA 93710-5703. **Business Addr:** Counselor Emeritus, California State University, 5241 N Maple Ave, Fresno, CA 93740, **Business Phone:** (559)278-2795.

## BURNS, JANICE ROBINSON
Executive, executive director, educator. **Educ:** Wesleyan Univ, BA, psychol, 1986; NY Univ, MPA, 1995; Univ Mich, Advan Human Resources Exec Prog, grad. **Career:** New York Pub Schs, teacher, 1986-87; Chem Bank, asst vpres, 1987-92; DDi Corp, sr consult, mgr, pdm serv; MasterCard Worldwide, mgr us enhancement serv, 1992-93, dir pt-of-sale serv qual, 1993-94, sr dir customer satisfaction, 1994-97, vpres regional stand & customer support, 1997-98, vpres diversity & worklife, 1998-2001, sr vpres cent resources, 2001-05, sr vpres human resources-global prod, 2005-08, chief diversity officer, 2007-10, group head human resources global prod & solutions, 2008-12, group head global talent develop & orgn effectiveness global human resources, chief learning officer, 2012-. **Honors/Awds:** National Salute to Black Achievers in Industry Award, Harlem YMCA. **Special Achievements:** Top Influential Women in Corporate America, Savoy, 2012. **Business Addr:** Chief Learning Officer, MasterCard, 2000 Purchase, St Purchase, NY 10577, **Business Phone:** (914)249-2000.

## BURNS, JEFF, JR.
Executive. **Personal:** Born Varnville, SC; son of Jeff Sr and Genevieve. **Educ:** Howard Univ, BBA, 1972; Livingstone Col, DHL. **Career:** Howard Univ, MPA Mag publ Procedures Sem, lectr; Johnson Publ Co, dir, vpres, 1984-93, sr vpres, Assoc Publ, 1997-2007, Ebony mag, assoc publ, 1997-2007; Howard Univ, bd visitors, vice chmn, 2005-; Soul S Tv Network, exec vpres, chief mkt officer, 2011-. **Orgs:** PUSH Int; bd dir, Trade Bur; Caribbean Tourism Orgn; Howard Univ Alumni Asn NY; bd dir, NY Urban League, African Am Mkt Asn; bd adv, Arthur Ashe Athletic Asn; Madison Ave Initiative; vice chmn, John H Johnson Sch Commun, Howard Univ; bd visitors, Howard Univ Sch Commun; bd visitors, Johnson C Smith Univ; Five Towns Community Ctr; Greater Harlem Chamber Com. **Home Addr:** 91 Bayview Ave, Inwood, NY 11096. **Business Addr:** Chief Marketing Officer, Executive Vice President, Soul of the South Television Network, Little Rock, AR.

## BURNS, JESSE L., JR.
School administrator, college president. **Educ:** Stetson Univ, BS, 1973, MBA; Univ S Fla, PhD. **Career:** Edward Waters Col, interim pres, pres, 1994-96; African Methodist Episcopal Church, episcopal supvr, dean; Connectional Lay Orgn, pres, 2005-2009. **Orgs:** African Methodist Episcopal Church, 2003-09; pres & treas, Connectional Lay Orgn, 2005-09; Resume Liars Club.

## BURNS, KEITH BERNARD
Football coach, football player. **Personal:** Born May 16, 1972, Greeleyville, SC; son of Tracy; married Michelle; children: Keith, Danielle & Rachel. **Educ:** Navarro Jr Col, AA; Okla State Univ. **Career:** Football player (retired), football player coach; Denver Broncos, linebacker & mid linebacker, 1994-98, 2000-03, 2005-06, asst coach, 2007-12; Chicago Bears, 1999; Tampa Bay Buccaneers, linebacker, 2004; Washington Redskins, special teams coordinator, 2013. **Honors/Awds:** Super Bow Champion Twice XXXII, XXXIII. **Home Addr:** , Alexandria, VA. **Business Addr:** Assistant Coach, Denver Broncos, 13655 Broncos Pkwy, Englewood, CO 80112, **Business Phone:** (303)649-9000.

## BURNS, KHEPHRA
Writer, editor. **Personal:** Born Oct 2, 1950, Los Angeles, CA; son of Isham A Rusty and Treneta C; married Susan L Taylor; children: Shana-Nequai Taylor. **Educ:** MoorPark Community Col, AA, lib arts, 1970; Univ Calif, BA, Eng, 1972. **Career:** Golden State Mutual Life Ins, salesman, 1974-76; Var Bands, musician, 1976-78; PBS tv affil, assoc producer, 1978; WNET-13, writer, assoc producer, 1978-80; RTP Inc, speech writer, publicist, 1980-81; Self-Employed, freelance writer, ed, 1981-; co-producer & writer: Black Champions (WNET-13), 1986; Black Stars in Orbit (WNET-13), 1989; Images & Realities: African Am (NBC), 1992-94; Black Stars in Orbit, (Harcourt Brace), 1995; The Essence Awards (CBS, Fox), 1993-99; The Power of One (ABC), 1997; Books: Confirmation: The Spiritual Wisdom That Has Shaped Our Lives, 1997; Black Stars in Orbit; Mansa Musa; African Odyssey, 1997; Tall Horse, 1997. **Orgs:** Writers Guild Am, E Inc, 1993; The Auth Guild Am, 1995; One Hundred Black Men, 1995; Sigma Pi Phi Fraternity, Alpha Sigma Blvd, 1995; Grand Graptor, Sigma Pi Psi; Guardsmen. **Honors/Awds:** Award of Excellence, Communications Excellence to Black Audiences; Empire State Award; 1993 Essence Awards, 1993; The Essence Awards, 1994; 1996 Essence Awards, 1996; 10th Anniversary Essence Awards, 1997; 2000 Essence Awards, 2000. **Special Achievements:** Burns articles have appeared publ Essence, Swing Journal (Japan), Omni & Art & Auction. **Home Addr:** 220 Riverside Blvd Suite 3A, New York, NY 10023.

## BURNS, LAMONT ANTONIO
Football player. **Personal:** Born Mar 16, 1974, Greensboro, NC; children: Dyion. **Educ:** E Carolina Univ, BA, commun. **Career:** Football player (retired); New York Jets, guard, 1997; Philadelphia Eagles, 1998; Wash Redskins, guard, 1998; Xtreme Football League, Las Vegas Outlaws, offensive guard, 2000; Oakland Raiders, 2001. **Orgs:** Nat Hon Soc.

## BURNS, REGINA LYNN
Publicist. **Personal:** Born Feb 19, 1961, Memphis, TN; daughter of Prince Whiting Jr and Rowena Hooks Whiting; married Calvin L. **Educ:** Abilene Christian Univ, Abilene, TX, BA, 1983; State Tech Inst, Memphis, TN, attended 1989; Memphis State Univ, Memphis, TN, mag writing, 1990. **Career:** KRBC-TV, Abilene, TX, reporter & photogr, 1982-83; WSLI Radio, Jackson, MS, anchor & reporter, 1984; WMKW, Memphis, TN, anchor, 1984; WLOK-AM, Memphis, TN, news dir, 1984-85; WGKX-KIX 106, Memphis, TN, dir, news & pub affairs, 1985-; Tri-State Defender, Memphis, TN, freelance writer, 1986-; Univ Tex, Arlington, Dept Commun, lectr; Harvest Reapers Commun, owner, 2003-. **Orgs:** Pres, Tenn Assoc Broadcasters Asn, 1990-91; pres, Memphis Asn Black Journalists, 1990-; Radio-TV News Dirs Asn; Nat Asn Black Journalists. **Honors/Awds:** Journalist of the Year, Tenn Asn Press Broadcasters Asn, 1989; International Radio Festival of New York Award, 1990; American Women in Radio & Television Award, 1991; Award, Radio-TV News Dir Asn, 1992; National Association of Black Journalists Award; Ten Outstanding Young Americans, United States Jr Chamber Com, 1993. **Special Achievements:** First African American woman and the first Memphis journalist to win the Broadcaster of the Year award from the Tennessee Associated Press Broadcasters Association. **Home Addr:** 5015 McKellar Woods Dr Suite 8, Memphis, TN 38116, **Home Phone:** (901)398-9334. **Business Addr:** Owner, Harvest Reapers Communications, 1227 Pin Oak Dr Apt J5, Flowood, MS 39232-9725, **Business Phone:** (214)726-0978.

## BURNS, RONALD MELVIN
Artist, painter (artist), printmaker. **Personal:** Born Feb 2, 1942, New York, NY; married Edith Bergmann; children: Elizabeth & Alexi. **Educ:** High Sch Music & Art, New York, 1959, Sch Visual Arts, NY, 1960. **Career:** Collections: Mus Mod Art, Stockholm, Sweden; Lincoln Ctr; Art Working Pl, Copenhaggen, Denmark; Kaptensgarden-Borstahusen-Landskrona-Sweden; Exhibs, Provinceton Gallery-Paul Kessler-USA, 1962; Gallery Sari Robinson, Pa, 1964; Passepartout-Charlotteborg, 1966; Passepartout-Bergen, 1969; Landskrona Konsthall, 1969-70 & 1980; Galleri Heland-Stockholm, 1970; Galerie Migros-Lausanne, 1970; Teatergalleriet-Malmo, 1970; Graphikbienale-Wien, 1972; Corcoran Gallery Art, Wash, DC, 1975; Gallerie Unicorn, 1975; Fundacion Rodriquez-Acosta-Granada, 1977; Galleria II Traghetto-Venice, 1977-80; Galerie Schindler Bern, 1978; Hvidovre Bibliotek, 1980; numerous others USA, Denmark, Sweden, & Switz; Spelman Col, retrospective exhib, Dept Art, artist, 1994. **Orgs:** Artist's Exhib Group AZ-Venice Italy, Spain, Ger; Artist's Exhib Group-Gallery 2016 Switz; Artist's Exhib Group, Gronningen-Denmark-Gallery, Terry Dintenfass, NY; Peg Alston Fine Arts, NY, 2003; Galerie Eichenwand, Dusseldorf, Ger, 2003; Tempra Mus Contemp Arts, Mgarr, Malta; Wignacourt Mus, Rabat, Malta; Aghia Trias Permanent Collection, Greece; Royal Danish Acad Fine Art. **Honors/Awds:** First Prize Drawing & Fourth Prize Painting, Second Int Biennale, Malta, 1997; American Women's Club-Exhibition Achievement Award-FAWCO-Denmark, 2006. **Home Addr:** HC Orsteds Vej 71, Copenhagen1879-V. **Business Addr:** Painter, Gammel Kongvej 136, Copenhagen1967-09-20.

## BURNS, TOMMIE, JR.
Executive, president (organization). **Personal:** Born Jul 5, 1933, MS; son of Tommie Sr and Rosetta; married Barbara; children: 4. **Career:** Mercantile Bank, Louisville; Burns Packaging Inc, owner; Burns Rigging, owner; Burns Chem Co, owner; Bus Support Serv Inc; T&WA Inc, majority owner, chmn & chief exec officer, 1992; Burns Enterprises Inc, Ky, owner, chief exec officer & pres, currently. **Orgs:** Kentuckiana Minority Supplier Develop Coun; Boys Girls Clubs Am; Boy Scouts Am; March Dimes; Chestnut St YMCA; Third Christian Church; Big Bros & Big Sisters Kentuckiana; Ky Ctr Arts; active mem, Greater Louisville Inc; Ky Ctr Arts; African-Am Venture Capital Fund, dir, currently. **Home Addr:** 3616 Foxglove Lane, Louisville, KY 40241-2634, **Home Phone:** (502)394-0787. **Business Addr:** Chief Executive Officer, President, Burns Enterprises Inc, 1631 W Hill St, Louisville, KY 40210, **Business Phone:** (502)585-4548.

## BURNS, URSULA M.
Chief executive officer. **Personal:** Born Sep 20, 1958, New York, NY; married Lloyd Bean; children: Malcolm & Melissa. **Educ:** Polytech Inst NY, BS, 1980; Columbia Univ, MS, mech engineering, 1981. **Career:** Xerox Corp, prod develop & planning, 1980-2000, vice pres & gen mgr departmental bus unit, 1997-99, vice pres worldwide mfg, 1999-2000, sr vpres strategic serv, 2000-01, sr vpres & pres doc systs & solutions, 2001-02, sr vpres & pres bus group opers, 2002-07, pres, 2007-09, bd mem, 2007-, chief exec officer, 2009, chmn, 2010-. **Orgs:** Am Express; CASA (Natl Ctr Addiction & Substance Abuse at Columbia Univ); FIRST (For Inspiration & Recognition Sci & Technol); Nat Acad Found; bd dir, Nat Asn Manufacturers; MIT Corp; U.S. Olympic Comt; trustee, Univ Rochester; Friends Hillary; Hillary Clinton Pres; Obama Am; bd mem, PQ Corp; bd mem, Boston Sci, 2002-; bd mem, Am Express, 2004-; vice chair, Pres Export Coun, 2010; bd mem, Exxon Mobil, 2012-. **Business Addr:** Former President, Chairman, Xerox Corp, 45 Glover Ave, Norwalk, CT 06856-4505, **Business Phone:** (203)968-3000.

## BURNS-COOPER, ANN
Editor. **Personal:** Born Charleston, SC; daughter of Walter Burns and Janie Williams Burns. **Educ:** SC State Col, BA, 1969; NY Univ, cert, 1978. **Career:** RR Bowker Co, booklister, 1970-73, ed asst, 1974-78, asst ed, 1979-81, ed coordr, 1982-87; Cahners Bus Info, staff ed, 1987-98; Reed Bus Info, Libr Jour, assoc ed, 1998-. **Home Addr:** 1725 Purdy St Suite Apt 6C, Bronx, NY 10462-6350, **Home Phone:** (718)863-3472.

## BUROSE, RENEE (RENEE BUROSE SQUIRES)
Television journalist. **Personal:** Born May 17, 1962, Memphis, TN; daughter of Aron and Beatrice Lewis. **Educ:** Memphis State Univ, Memphis, TN, BA, 1984; Old Dom Univ, Spec Educ, 2011. **Career:** WLOK-AM, Memphis, Tenn, anchor & producer, 1983-86; WHBQ-TV, Memphis, Tenn, prod asst & admin asst, 1985-88; WJTV-TV, Jackson, Miss, assoc producer, 1989; WJW-TV 8, Cleveland, Ohio, producer, 1989-93; WKYC TV, exec producer, 1993-96; WGXA TV, interim news dir & producer, 1997-98; WGNX TV, exec producer, 1999; WDIV TV, writer, 1999; WXYZ TV, Weekend morning news producer, 1999-2001; Homewood Pub Schs, substitute teacher, 2001-02; WLS TV ABC 7 Chicago, writer, 2001-04; Hampton City Schs, instrnl asst, 2007-12; Charlotte Mecklenburg Schs, tutor, 2012-. **Orgs:** Nat Asn Black Journalists, 1989-. **Honors/Awds:** Best Newscast, Assoc Press, 1989. **Home Addr:** 3813 Faversham Rd, Cleveland, OH 44114.

## BURRAS, ALISA MARZATTE
Basketball player. **Personal:** Born Jun 23, 1975, Chicago, IL; daughter of Phil and Nancy. **Educ:** La Tech, BA, 1998. **Career:** Basketball player(retired); Lady Techsters, 1996-98; Colo Xplosion, ctr, 1998; Cleveland Rockers, 1999; Portland Fire, ctr, 2000-02; Seattle Storm, ctr, 2003; Birmingham Power, 2004.

### BURRELL, BARBARA

Advertising executive, business owner, real estate agent. **Personal:** Born Mar 19, 1941, Chicago, IL; daughter of Wiley Jones; children: Bonita, Aldridge, Alexandra & Jason. **Educ:** Northern Ill Univ, BS, educ, 1963. **Career:** Chicago Brd Educ, teacher, 1963-65, 1966-67; Needham, Harper, Steers, Chicago, media estimator, 1965-66; Continental Bank, Chicago, personnel counr, 1973-74; Burrell Commun Group, pres & managing broker, sr vpres, finance & admin, 1973-90; Burrell Advert, Chicago, sr vpres, sec-treas, 1974, vice chmn, currently; Hyde Pk Fed Savings, Chicago, dir, 1979-82; S Shore Bank, Chicago, dir, 1982-; Burrell Realty, managing broker, pres & chief exec officer, 1997-; Ariel Capital Mgt LLC, dir, currently. **Orgs:** Aux bd, Hyde Pk Art Ctr, Chicago; Hyde Pk-Kenwood Dev Corp, Chicago; SE Chicago Comn; adv comm, DuSable Mus African Am Hist, 1983-; Vol, Chicago Pub Sch; educ fund, Inst Psychoanalysis, 1983-; Alpha Gamma Pi; gen chairperson, Blackbook's Natl Bus & Prof Awards, 1989; pres, Proj Match Families Transition; bd dir & vice chmn, Chicago Sister Cities Int; bd mem, Sarah's Circle; bd mem, Ariel Investments LLC. **Home Addr:** 3750 N Lake Shore Dr Apt 14D, Chicago, IL 60613-4234, **Home Phone:** (773)661-9782. **Business Addr:** President, Chief Executive Officer, Burrell Realty, 35 E Wacker Dr Suite 3400, Chicago, IL 60601, **Business Phone:** (312)925-1204.

### BURRELL, GARLAND, JR. (GARLAND ELLIS BURRELL, JR.)

Judge. **Personal:** Born Jul 4, 1947, Los Angeles, CA. **Educ:** Calif State Univ, BA, sociol, 1972; George Warren Brown Sch Soc Work, Wash Univ, MSW, 1976; Calif Western Sch Law, JD, 1976. **Career:** Off Sacramento Dist Atty, Criminal Div, dep dist atty, 1976-78; Off Sacramento City Atty, dep city atty, 1978-79, sr dep atty, 1986-90; Off US Atty, Civil Div Chief, Eastern Dist Calif, Sacramento, asst US Atty, 1979-85, 1990-92; Pvt bus litigation law firm, 1985-86; US Attorneys Off, Chief Atty, 1990-92; US Dist Ct, Sacramento, Calif, judge, 1992; US Dist Ct, Eastern Calif, chief dist judge, 2007-08; Us Dist Ct, Eastern Dist Calif, fed judge, currently. **Orgs:** Calif Bar Asn, 1976. **Special Achievements:** Presided over the "Unabomber" trial, the First African American judge to hear a high-profile murder case; First African-American federal judge in Sacramento; Publ: Mental Privacy: An International Safeguard to Governmental Intrusions Into the Mental Processes, 6 California Western Law Journal 613, 1975; Collective Bargaining Statutes And Their Effect On The Home Rule Of Municipalities, 39 National Institute of Municipal Law Officers Municipal Law Review No. 11, 1976. **Business Addr:** Federal Judge, United States District Court, US Courthouse, Sacramento, CA 95814, **Business Phone:** (916)930-4000.

### BURRELL, GEORGE REED, JR.

Lawyer, government official. **Personal:** Born Jan 4, 1948, Camden, NJ; married Doris; children: Stephen, Leslie & Wesley. **Educ:** Univ Pa, Wharton Sch, BS, 1969; Univ Pa Law Sch, JD, 1974. **Career:** Empire Sports Inc, Denver Broncos, defensive back, 1969; Goodis Greenfield, Henry & Edelstein, 1974-77; Wolf Block Schorr & Solis-Cohen, atty; Colonial Penn Ins Co, asst gen coun, 1978-80; City Philadelphia, dep mayor, 1980-84, secy external affairs, 2001-06; Philadelphia City Coun, At-Large mem, 1988-91; Mayor John F. St, 1995-2000; PRWT Serv, exec vpres & gen coun; Philadelphia regional econ develop agency, chief exec officer; Secy External Affair; Sturdivant & Co, pres; Kappa Alpha Psi Fraternity, mem; Univ Pa, young alumni trustee; Pa Conv Ctr Authority; Kleinbard LLC, Bus & Finance Dept, atty & partner, 2011-; Innovation Philadelphia Inc, pres & chief exec officer; Univ Pa, mentor to african am students; Penn Black Alumni Soc, pres emer; Pa Conv Ctr; Philadelphia Conv & Visitors Bur. **Orgs:** Vpres, Nat Bar Asn; reg dir, bd dir, Philadelphia Baristers Asn; Am Judictre Soc; Am Bar Asn; Philadelphia Bar Asn; bd dir, World Affairs Coun; bd mgr, Friends Hosp; bd dir, Kimmel Ctr Regional Performing Arts; bd mem, African-Am Mus; Philadelphia Theatre Co; Pa Conv Ctr; pres, Pa Black Alumni Soc; bd dir, Visitors Bur & Ctr City; bd chmn, Urban League Philadelphia; bd trustee, Bright Hope Baptist Churc; Econ League Greater Philadelphia; Ctr City Dist; Barristers Asn Philadelphia; African Am Mus; Philadelphia Theatre Co; Nat Liberty Mus. **Honors/Awds:** William F. Hall Award, Barristers' Asn Philadelphia; Judge Learned Hand Award, Am Jewish Comt; Judge for Ernst & Young's Entrepreneur of the Year Awards. **Home Addr:** 2043 Walnut St, Philadelphia, PA 19103, **Home Phone:** (215)972-8001. **Business Addr:** Attorney, Partner, Kleinbard LLC, 1 Liberty Pl 46th Fl 1650 Mkt St, Philadelphia, PA 19103, **Business Phone:** (215)496-7231.

### BURRELL, DR. JOEL BRION

Physician. **Personal:** Born Nov 27, 1959, Orange, NJ; son of Robert and Barbara. **Educ:** Rutgers Univ, BS, 1982; Temple Univ Sch Med, MD, 1987. **Career:** Abington Memorial Hosp, internal med resident, 1987-88; Mt Sinai Med Ctr, neurol resident, 1988-91; Cleveland Clin, neuroimmunology fel, 1991-93; Med Col OH, asst clin prof neurol, 1993-98; pvt pract neurologist & neuroimmunologist, 1993-. **Orgs:** Am Acad Clin Neurophysiology; Am Acad Neurol, 1990-98; Am Med Asn, 1990-00; Nat Ohio Med Asn, 1991-98; fel Am Heart Asn, 1995-; life mem, Nat Asn Advan Colored People, 1995-. **Honors/Awds:** Names one of Top 8 Young Physicians, Ohio Med Asn, 1995; African American Business of the Year, Cleveland Black Pages, 1997. **Home Addr:** 1454 W River Rd, Elyria, OH 44035. **Business Addr:** Physician, 1466 Oak Harbor Rd, Fremont, OH 43420, **Business Phone:** (419)355-0013.

### BURRELL, JUDITH ANN

Executive. **Personal:** Born Dec 28, 1952, Boston, MA; daughter of Bernice C and Wilbur C Sr; married Charles C Stephenson Jr; children: Zora Ayesha Stephenson. **Educ:** Brown Univ, BA, 1974; Columbia Univ, Grad Sch, MS, jour, 1976. **Career:** Muscular Dystrophy Asn, staff writer, 1976-77; Medgar Evers Col, CUNY, dir inst advan, 1977-80; US Dept Com, sr comn mgr, 1980-83; New York Off Mayor, asst press sec, asst legis rep, 1983-89; US Conf Mayors, asst exec dir energy, environ, transp & commun, 1989-92; US Dept Transp, Off Sec, dir exec secretariat, 1992-96; Newspaper Asn Am, asst exec dir, 1996-, sr vpres commun & diversity, 2003; Presstime, publ, 1996-; ACS Govt Syst Inc, cmo; Pareto Energy Ltd, exec vpres, vpres bus develop, 2005-; McKinney & Assocs PR, sr commun assoc, currently; Smith Dawson & Andrews, sr assoc, Burrell Proj Consult LLC, prin, owner, 2005-. **Orgs:** Womens Transp Sem, 1987-96; YWCA DC, 1988-97; DC Taxicab Comn, 1995-97; Morris G Johnson Scholarsip Golf Classic, host, 1996-98; Ed Koch; vpres, Nat Coun Pub-Pvt Partnership; Wash InCharities Found. **Home Addr:** 9527 Brookchase Dr, Raleigh, NC 27617, **Home Phone:** (202)299-7576. **Business Addr:** Owner, Burrell Project Consult LLC, 9527 Brookchase Dr, Raleigh, NC 27617, **Business Phone:** (202)299-7576.

### BURRELL, KENNETH EARL

Musician, educator. **Personal:** Born Jul 31, 1931, Detroit, MI. **Educ:** Wayne State Univ, BMus, 1955. **Career:** Introducing Kenny Burrell, 1956; Kenny Burrell Volume 2, 1956; Swingin, 1956; All Night Long, 1956; Two Guitars, 1957; All Day Long, 1957; Earthy, 1957; Kenny Burrell, 1957; K.B. Blues, 1957; Kenny Burrell and John Coltrane, 1958; Blue Lights Volume 1, 1958; Blue Lights Volume 2, 1958; On View at the Five Spot Cafe, 1959; A Night at the Vanguard, 1959; Weaver of Dreams, 1960; Bluesin' Around, 1961; Bluesy Burrell, 1962; Blue Bash, 1963; Midnight Blue, 1963; Freedom, 1963; Soul Call, 1964; Guitar Forms, 1965; The Tender Gender, 1966; Have Yourself a Soulful Little Christmas, 1967; Blues-the Common Ground, 1968; Asphalt Canyon Suite, 1969; God Bless the Child, 1971; Round Midnight, 1972; Ellington Is Forever, 1975-77; Moon and Sand, 1979; Listen at Dawn, Muse, 1980; Generation, 1986; Pieces of Blue and the Blues, 1988; Guiding Spirit, 1989; Sunup to Sundown, 1991; Collaboration, 1994; Lotus Blossom, 1995; Primal Blue, 1995; Love is the Answer, featuring The Boys Choir of Harlem, 1998; 12-15-78, 1999; Lucky So and So, 2001; Blue Muse, 2003; 75th Birthday Bash Live!, 2007; Be Yourself: Live at Dizzy's, 2010; The Road to Love, 2015; Univ Calif, Dept Music & Ethnomusicology, distinguished prof, dir Jazz Studies, currently. **Orgs:** Kappa Alpha Psi; Phi Mu Alpha; founder, Jazz Heritage Found. **Honors/Awds:** Inter Nat Jazz Critics Awards, 1957, 1960, 1965, 1969-73; Winner of Down Beat critics and readers polls, 1968-70; Jazz Educator of the Year Award, DownBeat mag, 2004; Jazz Master, Nat Endowment Arts, 2005; Honorary Doctorate, William Patterson Univ. **Business Addr:** Director of Jazz Studies Program, Professor, University of California, 2539 Schoenberg Music Bldg, Los Angeles, CA 90095-1657, **Business Phone:** (310)206-3033.

### BURRELL, LEROY RUSSELL

Athletic coach, athlete, entrepreneur. **Personal:** Born Feb 21, 1967, Philadelphia, PA; son of Leroy Brown and Delores; married Michelle Finn; children: Cameron, Joshua & Jaden. **Educ:** Univ Houston, BA, radio & tv commun. **Career:** Olympic athlete, 1992; Modern Men Inc, partner, currently; Univ Houston, head coach, track & field, 1998-. **Home Addr:** 3918 Indian Pt, Missouri City, TX 77459-6357, **Home Phone:** (281)431-8509. **Business Addr:** Head Coach, University of Houston, 3100 Cullen Blvd, Houston, TX 77204-6742, **Business Phone:** (713)743-2255.

### BURRELL, SCOTT DAVID

Basketball player, basketball coach. **Personal:** Born Jan 12, 1971, New Haven, CT. **Educ:** Univ Conn, commun sci, 1993, BA gen studies, 2010. **Career:** Basketball player (retired), basketball coach; Charlotte Hornets, forward-guard, shooting forward, 1993-97; Golden State Warriors, 1996-97; Chicago Bulls, 1997-98; NJ Nets, shooting forward, 1999-2000; Charlotte Hornets, shooting forward, 2000-01; Quinnipiac Univ, asst coach, 2007-15; Southern Conn State univ, coach, 2015-. **Honors/Awds:** NBA Draft, First round pick, 1993; NBA Champion, Chicago Bulls, 1998; Most Improved Player Award, Nat Basketball Asn. **Special Achievements:** The first American athlete to be a first round draft-pick of two major sporting organizations (the NBA and MLB). **Business Addr:** Coach, Southern Connecticut State University, 501 Crescent St, New Haven, CT 06515, **Business Phone:** (203)392-7278.

### BURRELL, STANLEY KIRK. See HAMMER, M. C.

### BURRELL, THOMAS J., JR.

Association executive, executive, founder (originator). **Personal:** Born Mar 18, 1939, Chicago, IL; son of Thomas and Evelyn; married Barbara Aldridge; children: Alexandra & Jason; married Joli Owens. **Educ:** Roosevelt Univ, Chicago, IL, BA, Eng, 1961. **Career:** Wade Advert Agency, mail room clerk, copy trainee, copywriter, 1960-64; Leo Burnett Co, Chicago, copywriter, 1964-67; Foote Cone & Belding London, 1967-68; Needham Harper & Steers, copy suprv, 1968-71; Burrell McBain Advert, co-owner, 1971-74; Ad Coun Inc, dir-at-large; Burrell Commun Group, founder & chief exec officer, 1971-2004, chmn emer & consult, 2004-. **Orgs:** Standing comt, Am Advert Fedn Found; Exec Comt, Chicago United; Chicago Urban League; bd govs, Chicago Lighthouse Blind; Press Adv Coun Roosevelt Univ; Adv Coun Howard Univ Sch Commun; Execs Club Chicago; Econ Club; Nat Advert Rev Bd; chmn, Chicago Coun, Am Asn Advert Agencies, 1991-92; Alpha Phi Alpha fraternity. **Honors/Awds:** Clio Awards, Coca Cola, 1978; Advertising Person of the Year Award, Chicago Advert Club, 1985; Albert Lasker Award for Lifetime Achievement in Advertising, 1986; Honors Medal for Distinguished Service, Sch of Jour, Univ Mo, 1990; Lifetime Achievement Award, Chicago Lighthouse Blind, 1998; Living Legend Award, Rainbow & PUSH Coalition, 2003; Lifetime Achievement Award, Publicity Club Chicago, 2007. **Special Achievements:** Profiled on the PBS show "Bridgebuilders, " 1998; Advertising Hall of Fame, American Advertising Federation, 2005. **Home Addr:** 11416 S Mich Ave, Chicago, IL 60628, **Home Phone:** (773)821-7436. **Business Addr:** Chairman Emeritus, Consultant, Burrell Communication Group, 233 N Mich Ave 29th Fl, Chicago, IL 60602, **Business Phone:** (312)297-9600.

### BURRIS, BERTRAM RAY

Entrepreneur, athletic coach, baseball player. **Personal:** Born Aug 22, 1950, Idabel, OK; son of Cornelius and Clara Mae; married Debra Marie Foots; children: Djemal Jermaine, Ramon Jerome, Damon Jevon, Deneen Janice & Bobby J. **Educ:** Southwestern Okla State Univ, BA, 1972. **Career:** Baseball player (retired), athletic coach, entrepreneur; Chicago Cubs, 1973-79; NY Yankees, 1979; NY Mets, 1979-80; Montreal Expos, 1981-83; Burris-Neiman & Assocs Inc, Can, pres, 1983-; Oakland Athletics, 1984; Milwaukee Brewers, 1985, 1987; Am League; Burris-Neiman & Assocs Inc, US, bd dir, 1985, pres, 1985-; St. Louis Cardinals, 1986; Baseball Network, exec vpres, 1987-; Milwaukee Brewers, admin asst, instr, 1987-; Circle Life Sports Agency, vpres, 1988; Burbrook Investments, founder, 1988; Sr Prof Baseball Asn, W Palm Beach Tropics, 1989; St Louis Cardinals, pitching instr, 2001-02; Oneonta Tigers, pitching coach, 2006; W Mich Whitecaps, pitching coach, 2006-07; Erie SeaWolves, pitching coach, 2008-12; Ray Burris Acad, owner & instr, currently; Detroit Tigers, pitching coach, currently; Philadelphia Phillies, Lehigh Valley IronPigs, pitching coach, 2013-15. **Orgs:** Bd dir, Friendship Pentacostal Holiness Church; Citizen Adv Bd, United Cancer Coun; chmn, Athletic Adv Coun; bd dir, Baseball Network, BNA-Can; chmn, Fund Raising Comt, Baseball Network; bd dir, Mt Olive Baptist Church; adv bd, Child Abuse Prev Fund, 1990-. **Honors/Awds:** Player of the Month, Nat League, 1976; Athletic Hall of Fame, Southwestern Okla State Univ, 1985; Jackson County Oklahoma Hall of Fame, 1985; NAIA Hall of Fame, 1994. **Business Addr:** Coach, Detroit Tigers, 2100 Woodward Ave, Detroit, MI 48201, **Business Phone:** (248)258-4437.

### BURRIS, JEFFREY LAMAR

Football coach, executive, football player. **Personal:** Born Jun 7, 1972, Rock Hill, SC; married Lisa A; children: Sienna & Jaden. **Educ:** Univ Notre Dame, bus mgt. **Career:** Football player (retired), coach; Buffalo Bills, punt returner, 1994, left defensive back & punt returner, 1995-97; Indianapolis Colts, left cornerback, 1998-99, defensive back & left cornerback, 2000, left cornerback, 2001; Cincinnati Bengals, left cornerback, 2002-03; Sienna Amore, owner; Fishers High Sch, coach, 2007; Warren Cent High Sch, defensive back coach; Sacramento Mountain Lions, defensive back coach, 2011; UMass Minutemen, cornerback coach, 2012; Miami Dolphins, cornerback coach & defensive qual control, 2013-16, asst defensive backs coach, 2015-16; Univ Notre Dame, defensive analyst, 2016-. **Honors/Awds:** Most valuable Player, 1993; South Carolina Player of the Year. **Home Addr:** 718 Creekgarden Ct, Atlanta, GA 30339-2994. **Business Addr:** Defensive Analyst, University of Notre Dame, Notre Dame, IN 46556, **Business Phone:** (574)631-5000.

### BURRIS, ROLAND W.

Government official, legal consultant. **Personal:** Born Aug 3, 1937, Centralia, IL; married Berlean Miller; children: Rolanda Sue & Roland Wallace II. **Educ:** Southern Ill Univ, BA, polit sci, 1959; Univ Hamburg, Ger, Int Law, 1960; Howard Univ, JD, 1963. **Career:** US Treas Dept, comptroller & nat bank examr, 1963-64; Continental Ill Nat Bank & Trust, tax acct, com banking officer & second vpres, 1964-73; State Ill Dept Gen Serv, cabinet appointee & dir, 1973-77; Oper PUSH, nat exec dir & chief operating officer, 1977-78; State Ill, comptroller, 1979-91, 39th atty gen, 1991-95; Jones, Ware & Grenard, managing partner; Buford & Peters, coun, 1999-2002; Southern Ill Univ, adj prof, 1995-98; Burris & Lebed Consult LLC, mgr & chief exec officer, 2002; State Ill, us sen, 2009-10. **Orgs:** Am Bar Asn; Cook County Bar Asn; Am Inst Banking; Independent Voters Ill; Nat Asn Advan Colored People; Cosmopolitan Chamber Com; Nat Bus League; Chicago So End Jaycees; Assembly Black State Execs; Alpha Phi Alpha; vice chair, Dem Nat Comt; Nat Asn State Auditors Comptrollers & Treass; pres & chmn, Inter governental rels comt, Nat Asn Attys Gen; life mem, Nat Asn Advan Colored People; life mem, Alpha Phi Alpha Fraternity; life mem, Southern Ill Alumni Asn; trustee, Financial Acct Found, 1991-94; bd mem, Nat Ctr Responsible Gaming, 1996-2005; Ment Health Asn Greater Chicago; US Jaycees; Southern Ill Univ Found; bd mem, Auditorium Theater Chicago, 2001-06; bd dir, Ill CPA Soc, 2000-02; bd mem, Better Bus Bur, 2008; bd dir, Inland Real Estate Corp, 2008; Sigma Pi Phi Fraternity. **Honors/Awds:** Distinguished Service Award, Chicago South End Jaycees, 1968; Jr Chamber Int Scholar, 1971; Cook County Bar Public Service Award, 1974-75; 100 Most Influential Black Americans, Ebony Magazine, 1979-95; Outstanding Alumnus Award, Howard Univ Law Sch Alumni Asn, 1980; Award of Financial Reporting Achievement, Govt Finance Officers Asn US & Canada, 1985; President Award, Nat Asn; State Auditors, Comptrollers, & Treasurers Service Award, Govt Finance Officers Asn, 1990; One of the Top Three Government Financial Officers in the Nation, City and State Magazine, 1989; Alumnus of the Year Award, Howard Univ Alumni Asn, 1989; Distinguished Public Service Award, Anti-Defamation League B'nai B'rith, 1988; Peace & Justice Award, Kappa Alpha Psi, 1991; Distinguished Accomplishments in the Field of Law, National Bar Association, 1993; Wall of Fame, Southern Illinois University Carbondale, 1997; Honorary Doctors of Laws Degree, National Louis University; Honorary Doctors of Laws Degree, Tougaloo College; Centralia High School Alumni Association Award, 2008. **Special Achievements:** First African American to examine banks in the US; featured in the film: The Fugitive; first African-American elected to statewide office in Illinois. **Home Addr:** 8358 S Indiana Ave, Chicago, IL 60619. **Business Addr:** Senator, State of Illinois, 230 S Dearborn Suite 3900 Kluczynski Fed Bldg, Chicago, IL 60604, **Business Phone:** (312)886-3506.

### BURRIS-FLOYD, PEARL

County commissioner, state government official. **Personal:** children: Jessica. **Educ:** Univ NC, BA, biol, 1978, Sch Med Cytol Sch, Chapel Hill, MHA; Pfeiffer Univ, MA, health admin. **Career:** Cent Piedmont Community Col, adj fac, 1992-; UNC Sch, Cytotechnology, guest lectr, pres, 2000-04; Gaston County Comn, Dallas Twp, comnr, 2001-08, vice chair, 2006-08; Rowan Regional Med Ctr, Salisbury, NC, cancer screener, sect chief, 2005-09; NC Gen Assembly, 110 House Dist rep, 2008-10; NC Dept Health & Human Serv, sr adv secy, 2013-14; Greensboro Partnership, vpres govt affairs, 2014-15; Gaston Regional Chamber Com, chief operating officer, 2015-. **Orgs:** Piedmont Chap Links; Alpha Kappa Alpha Sorority; vpres, pres, Carr Eleme Sch PTA; bd dir, Gaston County Health Dept; trustee, Schiele Mus, 2001-03; trustee, Gaston Mus Hist, 2004-; Aging, Health, Appropriations Comt; Ment Health Reform Comt, Educ Comt, Campaign Finance Reform Comt, Joint Health Oversight Comt; Nc Inst Med Task Force on Elderly & Medically Fragile Comt; Gaston County Republican Exec Comt; Cleveland County Republican Exec Comt; First Baptist Church, Dallas; chairwoman, First Baptist Church Bd trustee; Nat Asn Counties; mem, bd trustee, NC Ins Pool; bd mem, Partnership C Gaston & Lincoln Counties; mem state bd dir, Partnership C; bd dir, NC Inst Polit Leadership, 2013-; bd dir, CaroMont Health, 2015-. **Home Addr:** 518 E Main St, Dallas, NC 28034, **Home Phone:** (704)922-2970. **Business Addr:** Representative 110 House District,

North Carolina General Assembly, Rm 1319 Legis Bldg 16 W Jones St, Raleigh, NC 27601, **Business Phone:** (919)715-2002.

**BURROUGHS, HUGH CHARLES**
Executive. **Personal:** Born Feb 6, 1940; son of Vernon and Evalina; married Linda D Kendrix; children: Kwame & Dawn; married Henrietta E Johnson. **Educ:** Columbia Univ, BA, econs, 1966, MA, econs, 1969; Harvard Univ, Non-profit Mgt Inst, cert prog, attended 1973. **Career:** Columbia Univ, asst dean, 1967-69; Martin Luther King Jr. Fel Prog Woodrow Wilson Nat Fel Found, assoc dir, 1969-71; John Hay Whitney Found, exec dir, exec staff mem, 1971-77; William & Flora Hewlett Found, prog officer, 1977-87; Henry J. Kaiser Family Found, vpres, 1987-93; Packard Found, prog dir, 1993-2001; David & Lucile Packard Found, dir external affairs & philanthropy grantmaking, 1995-2001; Berry Gordy Family Found, pres & chief exec officer, 2001-03; Johnson Ctr Philanthropy, pres, chief exec officer, 2003-, instr, currently; part time mgt consult. **Orgs:** Chmn, bd vis, Clark Col; bd overseer, Morehouse Sch Med; chmn, bd dir, Asn Black Found Exec, 1973-77; bd dir, Women Philanthropy, 1977-80; bd dir, Coun Found, 1987-93; Northern Calif Grantmakers; Nat Charities Inform Bur; trustee, Peninsula Community Found; Hispanics Philanthropy; Grantmaking Sch Adv Bd; CIVICUS; bd trustee, Found Ctr. **Honors/Awds:** James A. Joseph Lecture, 1999. **Special Achievements:** Co edited "More Minorities in Health" and contributed to "Perspectives on Collaborative Funding". **Home Addr:** 4 Portofino Ct, San Carlos, CA 94070-3512, **Home Phone:** (650)591-3077. **Business Addr:** President & Instructor, Chief Executive Officer, Johnson Center for Philanthropy, 201 Front Ave SW, Grand Rapids, MI 49504, **Business Phone:** (616)331-7585.

**BURROUGHS, DR. JOAN HAMBY**
Educator. **Educ:** Tuskegee Univ, BS, health & phys educ; Ind Univ, Bloomington, MS, phys educ; NY Univ, PhD, anthrop dance, 2000. **Career:** New York Univ, New York Pub Sch Syst, adj prof dance; Fla A&M Univ, dir, Orchesis Contemp Dance Theatre, 2004, chair, dept Health phys educ & recreation, vis asst prof, currently. **Orgs:** Am Anthrop Asn; bd mem, Fla A&M Univ, Orchesis Contemp Dance Theatre. **Business Addr:** Visiting Assistant Professor, Florida A&M University, 221 Gaither Off Complex, Tallahassee, FL 32307, **Business Phone:** (850)599-8678.

**BURROUGHS, JOHN ANDREW, JR. See Obituaries Section.**

**BURROUGHS, JORDAN (JORDAN ERNEST BURROUGHS)**
Athlete. **Personal:** Born Jul 8, 1988, Camden, NJ; son of Leroy and Janice; married Lauren Mariacher, Jan 1, 2013?; children: Beacon. **Educ:** Univ Nebr-Lincoln, BA, 2011. **Career:** Competitive wrestler, 2005-; Univ Nebr, Lincoln, asst coach, 2014-15. **Honors/Awds:** High school state title, 135 lbs., 2006; University of Nebraska Most Outstanding Wrestler, 2008, 2009, 2011; NCAA champion, 157 lb, 2009; Dan Gable Most Outstanding Wrestler Award (Midlands Championship), 2011; InterMat Wrestler of the Year, 2011; NCAA champion, 165 lb, 2011; U.S. Open champion, 74 kg, 2011; World Championship titles, 2011, 2013; Hodge Trophy, 2011; Summer Olympics, gold medal, 74 kg, 2012; World Championships, bronze medal, 2014. **Special Achievements:** SPA Former number one ranked wrestler in his weight class; fourth wrestler ever to win an NCAA championship and a world championship in the same year; had a 69 match win streak through 2014; member of 2016 US Summer Olympic team. **Business Addr:** William Morris Endeavor, 9601 Wilshire Blvd 3rd Fl, Beverly Hills, CA 90210.

**BURROUGHS, ROBERT A.**
Lawyer. **Personal:** Born Mar 30, 1948, Durham, NC; son of Lottie Edwards and Leslie; married Laverne Davis; children: James, Christina & Whitney. **Educ:** NC Cent Univ, BA, psychol, 1971; Emory Univ, Atlanta, Ga, JD, 1978. **Career:** State NC, magistrate, 1970-71; Law Firm Robert A. Burroughs, PC, 1979-82, 1985-90, 1992-2000; USMC, defense coun; McCalla, Raymer, Padrick, Cobb, Nichols & Clark, partner, 1982-85, 1990-92; Burroughs & Keene, LLC, 2001-07; Burroughs Johnson Hopewell, LLC, 2007-12; Burroughs Keene Paulk & Von Schuch, currently. **Orgs:** State Bar Asn Ga, 1978; pres, De Kalb Lawyers Asn, 1985; Gate City Bar Asn; Gen Coun Nat Asn, Real Estate Brokers, 1985-; Spec Asst Atty, GenState Ga Law Dept; chair, DeKalb County Bd Tax Assessors; bd mem, Grady Hosp; adv bd, DeKalb County Develop; bd mem, DeKalb County Planning Comn; Greater Travelers Rest Baptist Church; 100 Black Men Am, Inc; exec comt, Real Property Law Sect State Bar Ga; Am Bar Asn; Empire Real Estate Bd. **Home Addr:** 1460 Doe Valley Dr, Lithonia, GA 30058-6202, **Home Phone:** (770)482-9602. **Business Addr:** Attorney, Burroughs Keene Paulk & Von Schuch, 2900 Paces Ferry Rd SE Bldg C 2000, Atlanta, GA 30339-5702, **Business Phone:** (770)432-2100.

**BURROUGHS, SARAH G.**
Advertising executive, president (government), executive. **Personal:** Born Oct 19, 1943, Nashville, TN; daughter of Herman Griffith and Celestine Long Wilson; children: Rachael Ann. **Educ:** Lincoln Univ, Jefferson City, Mo, BA, 1964; Northwestern Univ, Chicago, IL, 1967. **Career:** Executive (retired); Foote Cone & Belding, Chicago, Ill, assoc res dir, vpres, 1964-74; Burrell Commun Group, Chicago, Ill, gen mgr, sr vpres, 1974-94, vice chmn, pres & chief operating officer, 1991-96, chief mkt & commun, 2001. **Orgs:** Nat Asn Advan Colored People; Urban League; Bryn Mawr Community Church. **Honors/Awds:** Outstanding Women in Business, Dollars & Sense Mag; Kizzy Award, Kizzy Found. **Home Addr:** 5830 S Stony Island, Chicago, IL 60637.

**BURROUGHS, TIM (TIMOTHY BURROUGHS)**
Executive, basketball player. **Personal:** Born Oct 14, 1969, Hopkins, SC. **Educ:** Independence Community Col, attended 1989; Delgado Community Col, attended 1990; Jacksonville Univ, BS, bus admin & mgt, 1992. **Career:** Basketball player (retired), executive; Minn Timberwolves, 1992; Wash Bullets, 1994; Washington Wizards, 2000-01; Titan Brick, Dir Bus Develop, 2011-. **Business Addr:** Director, Titan Brick, Inc, 100 NW Loop 410 Suite 700-107, San Antonio, TX 78213, **Business Phone:** (800)515-2080.

**BURROUGHS, DR. TODD STEVEN**
Journalist, writer. **Personal:** Born Feb 17, 1968, Newark, NJ; son of Doris. **Educ:** Seton Hall Univ, S Orange, NJ, BA, mass commun, 1989; Univ Md, MA, jour, 1994, PhD, mass commun, 2001. **Career:** Nj Afro-Am, freelance reporter, 1985-88; Star-Ledger, NJ, gen assignment reporter, 1989-92; Seton Hall Univ, S Orange, NJ, adj prof, 1990-93, 1997; Knight-Ridder Minority Pub Affairs, fel, 1992-93; Writing & Res Consult, self employed, 1992-; Univ Md, Philip Merrill Col Journalism, adj prof, 1998; Changing Media, Univ Md Tv, assoc producer, 2005-07; Howard Univ, John H. Johnson Sch Commun, adj prof, 2005-06; Morgan State Univ, Dept Commun Studies, lectr, 2007-. **Orgs:** News mgt & reporter, NNPA, 1992-2002; writer-researcher, Nat National Association for the Advancement of Colored People, 1993-94; researcher, researcher, Nat Coun Churches, New York, 1996. **Honors/Awds:** Scholarship, Martin Luther King, 1985-89; Internship Recipient, 1988; Grant Recipient, UMCP Committee On Africa And The Americas, 2000; Nat Asn Black Journalists; Hon Mention, American Journalism Historians Assn Doctoral Dissertation Prize Competition, 2002; Scholar, Martin Luther King, four-year renewable, 1985-89; Cand, Fulbright Sr Specialist Prog, 2002-. **Business Addr:** Lecturer, Morgan State University, 1700 E Cold Spring Lane, Baltimore, MD 21251, **Business Phone:** (301)706-3736.

**BURROWS, CHELSYE J.**
Executive. **Educ:** Am Univ, BA, broadcast jour & span, MA, pub rels. **Career:** Film Life Inc, dir, currently; Western Regional Instrumentation Ctr, promotions mgr; WRIC TV, prom mgr, 1987-88; Burson-Marsteller, sr assoc, media rels, 1989-92; Home Box Off, mgr affil pub rels, 1992-97, dir, 1996-97; Uniworld Group Inc, dir pub rels, 1998-99; Starz Entertainment Group LLC, dir multicultural commun, 1999-2003, exec dir corp commun, 2003-06, vpres programming publicity, 2006-11; UP Entertainment LLC, vpres pub rels, 2011-. **Orgs:** Dir, bd dir, comt mem, Asn Cable Communicators; Cable Tv Pub Affairs Asn; former pres, Nat Asn Multi-ethnicity Commun; Acad Tv Arts & Sci; Pub Rels Soc Am, 2016. **Business Addr:** Vice President Public Relations, UP Entertainment LLC, 1514 E Cleveland Ave Suite 240, East Point, GA 30344, **Business Phone:** (770)969-7936.

**BURROWS, CLARE**
Health services administrator. **Personal:** Born Sep 29, 1938, Kansas City, MO; married William L; children: James Michael Pickens, Joye Nunn Hill, Carla Nunn, Anita Nunn Orme & Maurice Nunn. **Educ:** Col St Mary Omaha, BS, 1962; Univ Calif, Los Angeles, Calif, MPH, 1972. **Career:** Stanford Univ Palo Alto, compliance auditor, 1975-78; Community Hosp Santa Rosa Calif, dir med rec, 1978-80; Univ Calif San Francisco, dir patient serv, 1980-82; Calif Med Rev San Francisco, monitor, 1982-86; Beverly Enterprises Inc, dir bus admin. **Orgs:** Tutor Urban League, 1980-82; consult, Med Rec Assoc, 1980-84. **Honors/Awds:** Outstanding Church Work Mt Hermon AME Church, 1984. **Home Addr:** 160 N Pantano Rd, Tucson, AZ 85710, **Home Phone:** (602)886-5508. **Business Addr:** Director, Beverly Enterprises Inc, 2900 E Ajo Way, Tucson, AZ 85713, **Business Phone:** (602)294-0005.

**BURROWS, STEPHEN**
Fashion designer. **Personal:** Born Sep 15, 1943, Newark, NJ. **Educ:** Philadelphia Mus Col Art, 1962; Fashion Inst Technol, New York, attended 1966. **Career:** Weber Originals, New York, fashion designer, 1966-67; Allen & Cole, designer, 1967-68; O boutique, proprietor, cofounder, 1968; Henri Bendel Stores, in-house designer, 1968-73, designer, 1977-82, 1993-; Burrows Inc, New York, founder & dir, 1973-82; Ready-to-wear Design, designer, 1989; Custom Design, designer, 1990; Tony Lambert Co, designer, 1991. **Honors/Awds:** Winnie Award, Community Am Fashion Critics, 1973, 1974, 1977; Special Award, 1974; Critics Award, Coun Am Fashion, 1975; Crystal Ball Award, Knitted Textile Assocs, 1975; Coty-Award winning designer. **Special Achievements:** Authored two books; one of the most audacious and auspicious talents in contemporary fashion, Contemporary Fashion; First African Americans to become famous as a fashion designer. **Business Addr:** Managing Director, SBX Holdings LLC, c/o John Robert Miller, New York, NY 10018, **Business Phone:** (212)391-9411.

**BURRUS, WILLIAM HENRY, JR.**
Executive. **Personal:** Born Dec 13, 1936, Wheeling, WV; son of William and Gertude; married Ethelda I; children: Valerie, Doni, Kimberly, Kristy & Stepson Antwon. **Educ:** WVa State Univ, attended 1957. **Career:** Ohio Postal Union, dir res & educ, 1971, pres, 1974-80; Am Postal Workers Union, dir, bus agt, 1978-80, nat exec vpres, 1980-2000, nat pres, 2002-10. **Orgs:** Labor del, Cleveland Fed, AFL-CIO, 1977, vpres, Exec Coun, 2001, chmn, Civil & Human Rights Comt, 2005; vpres, Black Trade Labor Union, 1977; Ohio Adv Bd Civil Rights Comn, 1979-81; vpres, Philip Randolph Inst, 1982-. **Honors/Awds:** Ohio House of Representative, 1981; Frederick O'Neal Award, 1981; Philip Randolph Achievement Award, 1982; num union awards & recognition; Distinguished Service Award, Martin Luther King Ctr, 1989. **Special Achievements:** First African American to be directly elected president of a national union. **Home Addr:** 10806 Brooks Reserve Rd, Upper Marlboro, MD 20772-6631, **Home Phone:** (301)574-2677.

**BURSE, DR. LUTHER, SR.**
President (organization), association executive, educator. **Personal:** Born Jan 3, 1937, Hopkinsville, KY; son of Monroe Perry and Ernestine Perry; married Mamie Joyce Malbon; children: Luther Jr & Elizabeth N. **Educ:** Ky State Univ, BS, 1958; Univ Ind, MEd, 1960; Univ Md, EdD, 1969. **Career:** Educator, executive (retired); Chicago Pub Sch, teacher, 1958-59; Elizabeth City State Univ, instr, 1960-66; Univ Md, res asst, 1966-69; Cheyney St Col, prof, 1969-81, actg pres, 1981-82; Chester Pub Sch, consult, Philadelphia Bd Exam; Ft Valley State Col, pres, 1983-89; US Forest Serv, spec asst to chief, dir civil rights; Nat Asn State Univ Land Grant Col, vpres spec proj, dir urban progs & diversity; Ky State Univ, pres; Elizabeth City State in Nc & Cheyney State Col, Pa; Shell Oil, Exxon Mobil & U. S. Dept of Energy, founder. **Orgs:** Am Coun Indust Techer Educ; Pa State Educ Asn; Am Asn State Cols & Univs; pres, Indust Arts Asn Pa; pres, Pa Asn Voc & Practical Arts Educ; Higher Educ Caucus; Black Caucus; Women's Caucus; Voc Caucus; NEA; Alpha Kappa Mu Hon Soc; Omega Psi Phi Frat; Iota Lamda Sigma Frat; life mem, Nat Asn Advan Colored People; Am Coun Educ Leadership; bd dir, Ga Asn Minority Entrepreneurs; Sigma Pi Phi Fraternity; Ga Asn Cols; Nat Asn State Univs; Land Grant Cols; pres, Ky State Univ Nat Alumni Asn; dir, Urban Progs; dir, Diversity Nat Asn State Univs & Land Grant Cols; dir, U.S. Forest Serv; U.S. Dept Energy. **Home Addr:** 2020 Brooks Dr Suite 729, Forestville, MD 20747. **Business Addr:** Member, President, Kentucky State University, 1306 Whistling Duck Dr, Upper Marlboro, MD 20774, **Business Phone:** (202)478-6026.

**BURSE, RAYMOND MALCOLM**
Executive, lawyer. **Personal:** Born Jun 8, 1951, Hopkinsville, KY; son of Joe and Lena Belle; married Kim M, May 17, 1980; children: Raymond M Jr, Justin Malcolm & Eric M. **Educ:** Ctr Col Danville, Ky, BS, chem & math, 1973; Oxford Univ, org chem, 1975; Harvard Law Sch, JD, 1978. **Career:** Wyatt, Tarrant & Combs, assoc, 1978-82, partner, 1989-95; Ky State Univ, pres, 1982-89, interim pres, 2014-; GE Appliances, sr coun, 1995-2002; GE Consumer Prod, gen coun, 2002-05; GE Consumer & Indust, vpres & gen coun, 2005-12. **Orgs:** Bd chmn, Louisville Fed Res, 1987 & 1990; Am Bar Asn; Ky Bar Asn; Nat Bar Asn; bd mem, State YMCA; chair, Louisville Free Pub Libr Advy Comn; bd mem, Greater Louisville Chestnut St YMCA; vice chair, Louisville Community Found. **Honors/Awds:** Featured Speaker For Centre College's celebration of Martin Luther King Jr Day, 2007; Rhodes Scholar; Fred M Vinson Hon Grad, Centre Col; John W Davis Award, NAACP Legal Defense & Educ Fund. **Special Achievements:** First African American to earn three "Blues," one in rugby. **Home Addr:** 7010 New Bern Ct, Prospect, KY 40059-9668, **Home Phone:** (502)228-0841. **Business Addr:** Interim President, Kentucky State University, 400 E Main St, Frankfort, KY 40601, **Business Phone:** (502)597-6000.

**BURT, CARL DOUGLAS**
Government official, police chief. **Personal:** Born Mar 20, 1952, Newport News, VA; son of Will and Ella; married Helen; children: Carl II & Michelle. **Educ:** Thomas Nelson Community Col, AAS, police sci, 1976; Christopher Newport Univ, BS, govt admin, 1979; FBI Nat Acad, dipl, 1991; Sr Mgt Inst Police, dipl, 1997; Police Exec Leadership Inst, dipl, 1999; Univ Richmond, police exec leadership sch. **Career:** Newport News Police Dept, sergeant, 1984-88, lt, 1988-95, capt, 1995-98, asst chief police, 1998, interim chief, 2004, dep chief police, 2005-06; Abbitt Realty Co LLC; Norfolk State Univ, chief police. **Orgs:** Fraternal Order Police, 1974-; Kappa Alpha Psi, 1986-; chair deacons, Zion Baptist Church, 1988-99; chap vpres, Nat Org Black Law Enforcement Execs; pres, PTA, Moton Elem Sch; bd dir, vice chair, Peninsula Reads, 1996-99; bd trustee, vpres, Scott Ctr HOPE, 1999-2000; bd mem, trustee, Newport City News Retirement Bd, 1999-; pres, Kiwanis Monitor Club, 2001-02; bd mem, Scott Ctr Hope, chmn; Am Red Cross, 2002; trustee, Zion Baptist Church, chmn, 2002; bd mem, Hampton Roads Chap; bd mem, Hampton Roads Criminal Justice Training Acad. **Business Addr:** Chief of Police, Norfolk State University, 700 Pk Ave, Norfolk, VA 23504, **Business Phone:** (757)823-8600.

**BURTON, BARBARA ANN**
Executive. **Personal:** Born Dec 27, 1941, Houston, TX; daughter of Isiah and Alice; married James Henderson. **Educ:** TEX Southern Univ, BS, 1966, MS, 1972, MEd, 1974. **Career:** City Houston, cot develop mgr, 1966-70, City Coun, exec asst, 1980-83; Model Cities, prog mgr; TEX Southern Univ, cot develop, Soc Ins, dir, 1975-80; State TEX, prog mgr, cot develop, 1983-87; Austin Metrop BUS Resource CTR, pres, chief exec officer, 1987-, exec dir. **Orgs:** Pres, NCW, 1986-; chmn bd, Capital Metro, 1987-; comt chair, Capital Area Workforce Alliance, 1990-; Women's COC, 1990-; chair, Precinct 141, 1991-; pres, CNF MNY Transp Officials, 1991-; pres, TEX Asn Minority BUS Enterprises, 1991-; exec dir, Tex Minority Bus Opportunity Comt, 2001. **Home Addr:** 1833 Coronado Hills Dr, Austin, TX 78751, **Home Phone:** (512)322-0177.

**BURTON, BRENT F.**
Government official, president (organization). **Personal:** Born Nov 16, 1965, Los Angeles, CA; son of Adam and Marian; married Jeanetta S; children: Andre, Shani & Adam III. **Educ:** Dillard Univ, Exec Develop Inst, cert completion. **Career:** Los Angeles County Fire Dept, cert paramedic, capt, 1985; Carl Holmes Exec Develop Inst, Clark-Atlanta Univ Atlanta, Ga, instr, currently. **Orgs:** Los Angeles County Fire Dept Firefighter Olympic Basketball team, Charity Football Team, 1993-95; staff supv, primary instr, James Shern Fire Fighter Acad, 1994; exec vpres, Los Angeles County Black Fire Fighters Asn, 1997-; vpres, 1997, pres, African-Am Fire Fighter Musm; asst regional dir, Southwest Region Int Asn Black Prof Fire Fighters, 1999-; pres, Stentorians LosAngeles County Inc, 2000-10; dir, Jr Firefighter Youth Found; LA County Fire Dept Recruitment Cadre; co-chair, IABPFF Conv Los Angeles, 2004; 100 Black Men Los Angeles Mentor Comt. **Honors/Awds:** Community Protector Award, Los Angeles County Bd Supvr, 1989; Outstanding Dedication, Stentorians, 1997; Outstanding Service Award, IABPFF, Southwest Region, 1998, President's award; Burton lect, hist of African Americans, Fire Serv; Employee of the Month award, County Los Angeles, 2000; Overachiever Award, L.A. County Fire Dept, 2002; Public Administrator of the year Award, Nat Forum Black Pub Adminr, 2005; Community Safety award, City Inglewood; President's award, Millennium Momentum Found; Community Leader award, Bank Am Black Prof Group. **Home Addr:** 3467 S Sycamore Ave, Los Angeles, CA 90016-5263, **Home Phone:** (323)936-7571. **Business Addr:** President, The African American Fire Fighter Museum, 1401 S Cent Ave, Los Angeles, CA 90021, **Business Phone:** (213)744-1730.

**BURTON, DR. CHARLES HOWARD, JR.**
Gynecologist, obstetrician. **Personal:** Born Sep 21, 1945, Richmond, VA; married Adline Mildred Johnson; children: Stuart Howard, Stacee Michelle & Stephanie Brouke. **Educ:** VA State Col, BS, 1968; Meharry

Med Col, MD, 1975. **Career:** Brooke Army Med Ctr, intern, obstet & gynec; AUS, chief obstet & gynec; pvt pract, currently. **Orgs:** Fel Am Col Obstet & Gynec, 1983; Am Col Surgeons, 1984; Omega Psi Phi Frat; 32 Degree Mason, Shriner. **Honors/Awds:** Army Commendation Medal, AUS, 1978. **Home Addr:** 3852 High Green Dr, Marietta, GA 30068-2573, **Home Phone:** (770)565-9148. **Business Addr:** Chief Obstetrics & Gynecology, Nova Obstetrics & Gynecology Pc, 2550 Windy Hill Rd SE Suite 312, Marietta, GA 30067, **Business Phone:** (770)994-6806.

### BURTON, CHERYL

Television news anchorperson. **Personal:** Born Dec 25, 1962, Chicago, IL; married Jim Rose. **Educ:** Univ Ill, Champaign-Urbana, BS, psychol & biol. **Career:** Chicago Honey Bears, cheerleader, 1983-86; WGN-TV, co-anchor, 1989-90; WMBD-TV, gen assignment reporter, 1990-; KWCH-TV, Wichita, Kan, weeknight anchor, 1990-92; ABC 7 News, weekend co-anchor, news anchor & reporter, 1992-; WLS-TV, co-anchor, 1992-. **Orgs:** Chicago Asn Black Journalists; Nat Asn Black Journalists; vol, Boys & Girls Club Am; motivational speaker, Chicago Pub Schs; bd mem, Life Lupus Guild; Soc Prof Journalists; Asn Black Journalists; Delta Sigma Theta Sorority. **Honors/Awds:** Phenomenal Woman Award, Today's Black Woman, 1997; Kizzy Image and Achievement Award, 1998; Russ Ewing Award, Chicago Asn Black Journalists, 1995, 2003, 2004; Thurgood Marshall Award, 2004, 2005; Sisters in the Spirit Award, 2005; Procter & Gamble Award, 2009; Emmy award; Chicago's Robert Lindblom High School, hall of fame, 2007; Salute to Excellence International, National Association of Black Journalist, 2008. **Special Achievements:** Was the first recipient of the 2005 "Sisters in the Spirit" Award, given by Chicago area gospel singers to persons who exemplify a faith-based life. **Business Addr:** News Anchor, Reporter, WLS-TV, 190 N State St, Chicago, IL 60601, **Business Phone:** (312)750-7777.

### BURTON, DAVID LLOYD

Accountant. **Personal:** Born Aug 1, 1956, Detroit, MI; son of C Lutressie Johnson and Freddie George Sr; children: David Malik. **Educ:** Wayne State Univ, BS, 1977, MBA, acct, 1980. **Career:** Arthur Young & Co CPA, auditor, 1980-81; Barrow Aldridge & Co CPA, semi-sr auditor, 1981-84; Ford Motor Co, internal auditor, opers rep, 1985-88; Reeves & Assocs, Griffin, Ga, controller, 1988-90; US Securities & Exchange Comn, Wash, DC, staff acct, 1991-. **Orgs:** Nat Asn Black Acct, 1979; Nat Black MBA Asn, 1981; Cascade United Methodist Church, 1986; Urban Round Table, 2001. **Home Addr:** 6197 Old Brentford Ct, Alexandria, VA 22310-4348, **Home Phone:** (703)719-9312. **Business Addr:** Staff Accountant, United States Securities & Exchange Commission, 450 5th St NW, Washington, DC 20001, **Business Phone:** (202)942-8088.

### BURTON, DONALD C.

Law enforcement officer, consultant. **Personal:** Born Apr 21, 1938, Lawnside, NJ; son of William E Sr and Josephine B; married Marcia E Campbell; children: Donald Jr, Barry D, Jay S, Robert T, Christopher & Matthew. **Educ:** Camden County Col, AS, 1974; Rutger State Univ, BA, 1977. **Career:** Correction consult, pvt bus, 1973-; Cherry Hill Police Dept, Detective Sergeant, polygraph oper, 1973-, lt; Camden Co Sheriff's Dept, under sheriff, 1984-88; Bergen Co Sheriff's Dept, under sheriff, 1988-89; Mark Correctional Systs Inc, correctional consult, 1989-93; City Lawnside, dir pub safety, 1992-96; Donald C Burton & Assoc, consult, owner. **Orgs:** Pres, Cherry Hill 176 Policemens Benevolent Asn, 1969-71; deleg, NJ State Policemens Benevolent Asn, 1970-72; pres, NJ Chap NOBLE, 1983-88; regional vpres, NOBLE, 1987-88; trustee, HOPE Ex-Offenders. **Home Addr:** 22 Ashland Ave, Blackwood, NJ 08012, **Home Phone:** (856)384-6080. **Business Addr:** Owner, Donald C Burton & Assoc Inc, 44 Cooper st 110, Woodbury, NJ 08096, **Business Phone:** (856)853-5566.

### BURTON, KENDRICK DURAN

Football player. **Personal:** Born Sep 7, 1973, Decatur, AL. **Educ:** Univ Ala, grad. **Career:** Football player (retired); Houston Oilers, defensive end, 1996-97; Barcelona Dragons, NFLE, 1999; Seattle Seahawks, 2000.

### BURTON, LANA DOREEN

Educator, school principal. **Personal:** Born Mar 25, 1953, Evansville, IN; daughter of William Dulin and Gloria Wickware Beckner; married Rickey; children: Alexander Richard. **Educ:** Ind State Univ, Terre Haute, IN, BS, 1975; Univ Evansville, Evansville, IN, MA, elem educ, 1979, admin cert, 1990. **Career:** Breckinridge Job Corp Ctr, Morganfield, KY, teacher, 1975-76; Evansville-Vanderburgh Sch Corp, Evansville, Ind, educr, 1976-92, adminr, 1992-; John M Culver Elem Sch, prin; Harper Elem Sch, prin, currently. **Orgs:** Pres, Evansville Chap, 1985-90; Jr League Evansville, 1986-; Evansville Youth Coalition, 1989-93; vpres, Coalition African-Am Women, 1990-94; bd mem & pres, YWCA, 1990-; teacher, supt, Sunday Sch, Zion Missionary Baptist Church, 1991-94, 1998-; Evansville Port Authority, 2005; bd dir Evansville African Am Mus. **Home Addr:** 1424 Brookside Dr, Evansville, IN 47714, **Home Phone:** (812)401-4449. **Business Addr:** Principal, Harper Elementary School, 21 S Alvord Blvd, Evansville, IN 47714-1291, **Business Phone:** (812)476-1308.

### BURTON, LEVAR, JR. (LEVARDIS ROBERT MARTYN BURTON, JR.)

Television director, artistic director, actor. **Personal:** Born Feb 16, 1957, Landstuhl; son of Levardis Robert and Erma Jean Christian; married Stephanie C Cozart; children: Michaela & Eian. **Educ:** Univ Southern Calif. **Career:** Films: Almos' a Man, 1976; Looking for Mr Goodbar, 1977; Dummy, 1979; The Hunter, 1980; The Acorn People, 1981; Grambling's White Tiger, 1981; Emergency Room, 1983; The Jesse Owens Story, 1984; Booker, 1984; And the Children Shall Lead, 1985; The Midnight Hour, 1985; The Supernaturals, 1987; Firestorm: 72 Hours In Oakland, 1993; Parallel Lives, 1994; Star Trek Generations, 1994; Star Trek: First Contact, 1996; Yesterday's Target, 1996; Trekkies, 1997; The Tiger Woods Story, dir, 1998; Star Trek: Insurrection, 1998; Our Friend, Martin, actor & dir, 1999; Dancing in September, 2000; Ali, 2001; Star Trek: Nemesis, actor & dir, 2002; Blizzard, actor, 2003; Reach For Me, actor & dir, 2008; Taken In Broad Daylight, 2009; Superman/Batman Public Enemies, 2009. TV series: "Roots", 1977; "Reading Rainbow", series host, 1983-; "Star Trek: The Next Generation", 1987-88; "Murder, She Wrote", 1987; "Houston Knights", 1987; "A Spec Friendship", 1987; "A Roots Gift", 1988; "Captain Planet & the Planeteers", 1990-93; "Christy", 1995; "Nightingale", dir, 2000; "Star Trek: Voyager", dir, 2001; "Homestead", dir, 2001; "Q2", dir, 2001; "JAG", dir, 2003; "Similitude", dir, 2003; "Extinction", dir, 2003; "Pulse Rate", dir, 2003; "Boomtown", actor, 2003; "TheAugments", dir, 2004; "The Forgotten", dir, 2004; "Family Guy", 2005; "Miracle's Boys", dir, 2005; "Vaya Con Leos", dir, 2005; "Battle of the Hexes", dir, 2005; "Extreme Makeover WorldEdition", dir, 2005; "Enterprise", dir, 2005; Demons, dir, 2005; "Charmed", dir, 2006; "Las Vegas", 2006; "The Torn Identity", dir, 2006; "The Super Hero Squad Show", 2009; "The Jensen Project", 2010; "The Big Bang Theory", 2011-12; "Community", 2011; "Transformers: Rescue Bots", 2011-14; "Perception", 2012-14; "Rise of the Zombies", 2012; "Adventure Time", 2013. **Honors/Awds:** ImageAward, Nat Asn Advan Colored People, 1980, 1995, 1996, 2002 & 2003; Star on the Hollywood Walk of Fame, 1990; Daytime Emmy Award, 1990, 1993, 2001-03, 2005 & 2007; Peabody Award, 1993; Best of the Fest, Chicago Int C's Film Festival, 2004; Anniversary Award, TV Land Awards, 2007. **Home Addr:** 13251 Stoneridge Pl, Sherman Oaks, CA 91413-4933. **Business Addr:** Actor, Marion Rosenberg Prods, 8428 Melrose Pl Suite B, Los Angeles, CA 90069-5308, **Business Phone:** (323)822-2793.

### BURTON, PATRICIA LEWIS

Vice president (organization). **Personal:** children: Justin Harrison. **Educ:** Univ Bridgeport, mgt, 1984. **Career:** EI DuPont de Nemours & Co, sr mgt human resources, mfg opers & mat mgt, 1989-2000; US Surg Corp; Nat Semiconductor Corp; IBM, Global Technol Serv, vpres human resources, 2000-11; Lockheed Martin Corp, vpres human resources, 2011-15, sr vpres human resource, 2014-. **Orgs:** IBMs Multicultural Womens Comt; Soc Human Resource Mgt; Nat Asn Female Execs. **Business Addr:** Vice President, IBM, 294 NY-100, Somers, NY 10589, **Business Phone:** (914)766-1900.

### BURTON, RONALD J.

Executive. **Personal:** Born Jun 12, 1947, Montclair, NJ; son of Joseph and Ruth Jackson; married Carolyn Ievers; children: Christopher & Alison. **Educ:** Colgate Univ, Hamilton, NY, BA, hist, econs, 1969; Wharton Sch, Philadelphia, PA, grad courses. **Career:** Dallas Cowboys, Dallas, Tex, prof athlete, 1969; EI Dupont, Wilmington, mkt mgr, 1969-74; RH Donnelley, NY, mgr, 1975-87, vpres, 1988; Dun & Bradstreet Corp, vpres, exec dir, 2000-; vpres bus develop, consult; Jackie Robinson Found, sr vpres; Alliance Mezzanine Investors, partner & advisor, currently. **Orgs:** Bd mem & vpres, Colate Alumni Club, 1975-80, chmn; bd mem, George Jr Repub Asn, Ithaca, NY, 1979-85; Montclair Pub Schs, 1985-87; Mountainside Hosp, Montclair, NJ, 1987-; bd trustee, Colgate Univ; trustee, Athletic, Develop, Admis & Stud Affairs comt; comnr, Jersey Sports & Expos Authority, treas; bd trustee, Jackie Robinson Found; independent trustee, THL credit sr loan fund. **Home Addr:** 197 Midland Ave, Montclair, NJ 07042-3035, **Home Phone:** (973)744-3467. **Business Addr:** Executive Director, Dun & Bradstreet Corp, 103 JFK Pkwy, Short Hills, NJ 07078, **Business Phone:** (973)921-5500.

### BURTON, VALORIE

Executive, columnist, writer. **Personal:** married Jeff. **Educ:** Fla State Univ, BA; Fla A&M Univ, MA, jour; Univ Pa, MS, appl positive psychol; Coach Univ, prof coach training. **Career:** CPA firm, Dallas, mkt dir; Burton Agency, founder; Gov Comn Women, 2001-03; Inspire Inc, coach, colmnist & speaker, currently; Coaching & Positive Psychol Inst, founder, currently; Author: Listen to Your Life; What's Really Holding You Back?; Rich Minds, Rich Rewards & Why Not You?; 28 Days to Authentic Confidence; How Did I Get So Busy? The 28-Day Plan to Free Your Time, Reclaim Your Schedule & Reconnect with What Matters Most. **Orgs:** Int Coach Fed; Nat Speakers Asn; Victory World Church. **Honors/Awds:** Miss Black Tex USA; named one of the nations 30 rising stars in public relations, PR Week Magazine, 2000. **Home Addr:** , Atlanta, GA. **Business Addr:** Coach, Columnist, Inspire Inc, 1009 Bay Ridge Ave Suite 150, Annapolis, MD 21403, **Business Phone:** (410)561-6041.

### BURTON, WILLIAM A.

President (organization), chief executive officer. **Educ:** Loyola Univ Chicago, BA, bus admin & technol, 1985; Northwestern Univ, Kellogg Sch Mgt, entrepreneurship, entrepreneurial studies, 2010. **Career:** Xerox, systs engr, 1984-95; Prof Systs Inc, pres & chief exec officer, 1995-. **Orgs:** Alpha Phi Alpha Fraternity, 2004-12; bd trustee, DuSable Mus; Chicago Urban League; NextOne Bus Accelerator Alumni; Northwester Univ-Kellogg; S Cent Community Serv; Toastmasters Int. **Business Addr:** President, Chief Executive Officer, Professional Systems Inc, 14108 S Ind Ave, Riverdale, IL 60827, **Business Phone:** (708)849-7000.

### BURTON-LYLES, BLANCHE

Musician, educator, teacher. **Personal:** Born Mar 2, 1933, Philadelphia, PA; daughter of Anthony H (deceased) and Ida Blanche Taylor (deceased); married Thurman W; children: Thedric (deceased). **Educ:** Curtis Inst Music, MusB, 1954; Temple Univ, Philadelphia, BMusEd, 1971, MusM, 1975. **Career:** Educator (retired); Musician; Soc Orch LeRoy Bostic's Mellowaires, pianist; concert pianist, US, 1939; Philadelphia Bd Educ, teacher, 1960-93; Marian Anderson Hist Soc Inc, founder & pres, 1993-. **Orgs:** Delta Sigma Theta Sor, 1954; Pro Arts Soc; Music Ed Nat Conf, 1970-; Russell Johnson-Negro Asn Musicians, 1990-; founder, Marian Anderson Hist Soc; Union Baptist Church. **Honors/Awds:** Music Specialist, 25 Years, Women in Education, 1991; Shirley Chisholm Philadelphia Political Congress of Black Women Award, 1994; Black Music Caucus Award, 1995; Coalition Award of 100 Black Women; Mary McLeod Bethune Award, NatCoun Negro Women, 2000; All-Star Award, Philadelphia 76ers' Community Service, 2004; Sadie T. Alexander Award, Delta Sigma Theta Sorority, 2005; Edythe Ingram Award, Alpha Kappa Alpha Sorority, 2006; Martin Luther King Jr Drum Major Cultural Award, 2007; Unsung Hero Award, Nat Asn Negro Bus & Prof Women, 2007. **Special Achievements:** The first African Am female pianist to play at Carnegie Hall with the New York Philharmonic Orchestra in 1947; First African-Am woman pianist to grad and receive a bachelors degree from Curtis Inst; first black woman pianist to grad from Curtis Inst of Music Philadelphia 1953. **Home Addr:** 1118 S 19th St, Philadelphia, PA 19146-1822, **Home Phone:** (215)732-6723. **Business Addr:** Founder, President, The Marian Anderson Historical Society Inc, 762 Marian Anderson Way, Philadelphia, PA 19146-1822, **Business Phone:** (215)732-9505.

### BURTON-SHANNON, DR. CLARINDA

Obstetrician, gynecologist. **Personal:** Born Jan 16, 1959, Philadelphia, PA; daughter of James and Gracie; married Charles Langford Sr; children: Michael Joshua. **Educ:** Cheyney State Col, BA, 1980; Meharry Med Col, MD, 1984. **Career:** G W Hubbard Hosp-Meharry Col, training obstet & gynec; Univ Med Ctr, physician, currently; Lebanon Womens Clin, obstetrician & gynecologist; Women's Wellness Lebanon, obstetrician & gynecologist, currently. **Home Addr:** 2107 Putnam Lane, Mount Juliet, TN 37122-3655, **Home Phone:** (615)758-5490. **Business Addr:** Obstetrician, Gynecologist, Women's Wellness of Lebanon, 1420 Baddour Pkwy, Suite 230, Lebanon, TN 37087, **Business Phone:** (615)547-5400.

### BURTS, EZUNIAL

President (organization), executive director, government official. **Career:** Port Los Angeles, exec dir, 1984-97; Los Angeles Area Chamber Com, pres, 1996-2001. **Business Addr:** President, Los Angeles Area Chamber of Commerce, 350 S Bixel St, Los Angeles, CA 90017.

### BURWELL, BRYAN ELLIS

Broadcaster. **Personal:** Born Aug 4, 1955, Washington, DC; son of Harold H and Ursula Tomas; married Dawnn Turner; children: Victoria Renee. **Educ:** Va State Univ, Petersburg, VA, BA, eng lit, 1977. **Career:** Baltimore Sun, Baltimore, Md, sports reporter, 1977-79; Wash Star, Wash, DC, sports reporter, 1979-80; NY Newsday, New York, NBA writer, 1980-83; NY Daily News, New York, NY, NFL columnist, 1983-89; Detroit News, Detroit, Mich, sports columnist, 1989-; HBD Sports, New York, NY, Inside NFL reporter, 1990-02; USA Today, sports columnist, 1992-96; Sporting News, columnist, 1996-97; St Louis Post-Dispatch, sports columnist, currently. **Orgs:** Kappa Alpha Psi, 1975-; Pro Football Writers Am; Nat Asn Black Journalists. **Honors/Awds:** Number 5 Feature Writer in Country, APSE, 1988; Number 4 Columnist in Country, 1989; Michigan's Top Sports Columnist, UPI, 1989. **Home Addr:** 4357 McNay Ct, West Bloomfield, MI 48323, **Home Phone:** (313)932-0898. **Business Addr:** Sports Columnist, St Louis Post-Dispatch, 900 N Tucker Blvd, St Louis, MO 63101, **Business Phone:** (314)340-8000.

### BUSBY, DELIA BLISS ARMSTRONG

Educator, educational consultant. **Personal:** Born Nov 28, 1945, Los Angeles, CA; daughter of Willard and Zeltee; married Ronald; children: Aaron & Preston Shelton. **Educ:** CA State Univ, Los Angeles, CA, BA, 1967; Univ Colo Springs, MA, admin & leadership, attended 1977; Harvard Univ, John F. Kennedy Sch Govt, cert, governance, leadership & governance, 2016. **Career:** Colo Springs Pub Schs, educr, 1970-94; Ctr Qual Schs, consult, 1995-97; Denver Pub Schs, consult, 1997-99; Delia Bliss Armstrong Busby Consult, pres, 1999-2010; Adventures Learning k-12, pres & founder, 1999-; Mitchell High Sch, prin; Milwaukee Pub Schs, consult, 2001; Alliance Qual Pub Sch, founder; Absence Addiction Achievement Serv, staff; Women's Workplace & Educ Initiative, consult. **Orgs:** Bd mem, vp, Urban League, 1990-98; Colo Springs D 11, 1999-2000; bd, D-11, 2001; bd vp, Pikes Peak Commnunity Col; Nat Asn Advan Colored People; Boys & Girls Club; Girl Scouts; Tutmuse Acad; Harvard fel Kennedy Sch Govt; Am Petrol Inst; Harvard Kennedy Sch; Adventures Learning Career Academies Inc; Alpha Kappa Alpha Sorority. **Honors/Awds:** Milken Award For National Education Leadership, Milken Found, 1990; State Colo, Educ Cert, 1990-93; Drug Free Communities, Educ cert, 1990; SW Regional Drug Free Schs, 1993. **Special Achievements:** Absence Addiction Work Book, 1995; first African American female elected to the board of education in Colorado Springs largest school district; first African American female selected to a high school principalship, Colorado. **Business Addr:** Founder, President, Adventures In Learning K-12 Inc, 2236 Monteagle Ave, Colorado Springs, CO 80909, **Business Phone:** (719)578-5373.

### BUSBY, EVERETT C.

Educator, social worker. **Personal:** Born Muskogee, OK. **Educ:** Langston Univ, BA, sociol, 1950; Univ Norman, cert, social work, 1951; Univ Tex, Austin, MSW, 1953. **Career:** AUS, Med Serv Corps, psychiat social worker, 1953-55; Kings Col, Psychiat Hosp, NY, psychiat social worker, 1956-59; Seton Hall Col Med & Dent, Jersey City NJ, instr & dept psychiat, 1959-61; Fordham Univ, Grad Sch Social Serv, assoc prof, 1961, assoc prof emer, currently; NIAAA HEW, Wash DC, consult, 1970-72; Pvt Pract, supv psychotherapist, trianer & assoc, 1971-80. **Orgs:** Coun Soc Workers Educ, 1985; Am Asn Univ Prof, 1985; Nat Asn Black Soc Workers, 1985; Nat Conf Soc Welfare, 1985; Nat Conf Soc Welfare, 1985; Consult training ed, Bedford-Stuyvesant Youth Act, Brooklyn; consult training ed, Haryou-Act NYC; educ & training bd mem, Nat Coun Alcohol, NT; Am Civil Liberties Union; Alpha Phi Alpha Fraternity. **Honors/Awds:** Bene Merenti Award, Fordham University, 1961. **Home Addr:** 311 W 95th St Apt 6b, New York, NY 10025-6106, **Home Phone:** (212)749-4597. **Business Addr:** Associate Professor Emeritus, Fordham University, Grad Sch Soc Serv Lincoln Center Campus, New York, NY 10023, **Business Phone:** (212)636-6000.

### BUSH, DEVIN MARQUESE

Football player. **Personal:** Born Jul 3, 1973, Miami, FL; married Kesha; children: Jazmin, Deja & Devin Jr. **Educ:** Fla State Univ. **Career:** Football player (retired); Atlanta Falcons, defensive back & safety, 1995-98; St Louis Rams, safety, 1999-2000; Cleveland Browns, defensive back, 2001-02; football coach, currently. **Orgs:** Rookie Yr, 1995. **Home Addr:** 10278 Laurel Rd, Davie, FL 33328-1356, **Home Phone:** (954)476-5040. **Business Addr:** Football Coach, Charles W Flanagan High School, 12800 Taft St, Pembroke Pines, FL 33028, **Business Phone:** (754)323-0650.

**BUSH, DWIGHT L., SR.**
Ambassador, businessperson. **Personal:** Born Feb 4, 1957, East St. Louis, MO; son of Charlie Bush and Jessie Bush; married Antoinette Cook Bush; children: Dwight Jr & Jacqueline. **Educ:** Cornell Univ, BA, govt & econ, 1979. **Career:** Chase Manhattan Bank, int & corp banking, corp finance & proj finance, 1979-94; Sallie Mae Corp, vpres corp develop, 1994-97; SatoTravel Holdings, vpres & chief financial officer, 1997-2002; D.L. Bush & Assocs, founder, 2002-; Stuart Mill Capital LLC, prin, 2002-06; Enhanced Capital Partners LLC, vice chmn, 2004-05; EntreMed Inc., dir, 2004-, vice chmn, 2010-; Urban Trust Bank, founding chief exec officer & pres & pres Urban Trust Bank Educ Finance LLC, 2006-08; US Ambassador to Kingdom Morocco, 2014-. **Orgs:** Bd mem, Cornell Univ, Xavier Univ, GAVI Alliance, Joint Centers Social & Econ Studies, & Nat Symphony Orchestra. **Special Achievements:** First African-American managing director for Chase Manhattan Bank. **Business Addr:** Embassy of the United States of America, Km 5 7, Souissi, Rabat10170.

**BUSH, ESTHER L.**
Chief executive officer. **Personal:** Born Oct 26, 1951, Pittsburgh, PA; daughter of Willie C and Ola Mae. **Educ:** Morgan State Univ, BA, educ; Johns Hopkins Univ, MS, guid & coun; Univ Hartford, JD, 1997; Carlow Col, PhD, 2004; Allegheny Col, DHL, 2009. **Career:** Baltimore Pub Sch, teacher, 1973-77; Coppin State Col, Career Planning & Placement Ctr, asst dir, 1977-80; Nat Urban League, New York, Labor Educ Advan Prog, from asst dir to dir, manhattan br dir, 1980-81; Donchian Mgt Servs, assoc consult, 1982; Staten Island Urban League, dir, 1982-86; Manhattan Urban League, dir, 1986-89; Urban League Greater Hartford, pres & chief exec officer, 1989-94; WAMO AM 860, talk show host; Urban League Greater Pittsburgh, pres & chief exec officer, 1994-; Pa State Bd Educ, PA comn, Crime & Delinq, law enforcement & community rels task force, gov's comn acad stand & voting modernization task force. **Orgs:** State Bd Educ; Urban League Pittsburgh Charter Sch; August Wilson Ctr African Am Cult; Carnegie Mellon Univ; trustee, Int Womens Forum Bd dir; Judicial Eval Comn, Pa Bar Asn; Pa Comn Crime & Delinq; Pittsburgh Cult Trust; adj fac mem, Univ Pittsburgh Med Ctr Health Syst; exec comt, Nat Urban League Asn; chmn, Urban League Greater Pittsburgh Charter Sch Bd trustee; bd UPMC; United Way; bd mem, Duquesne Univ; adj fac mem, Sch Social Work; adj fac mem, Univ Pittsburgh. **Special Achievements:** She is the first female to serve as assistant director, director, chief executive officer and president in the Urban League movement. **Home Addr:** 1304 Sheridan Ave, Pittsburgh, PA 15206, **Home Phone:** (412)362-4412. **Business Addr:** President, Chief Executive Officer, Urban League of Greater Pittsburgh, 610 Wood St, Pittsburgh, PA 15222-2222, **Business Phone:** (412)227-4802.

**BUSH, EVELYN**
Police officer, government official. **Personal:** Born Jan 8, 1953, Danbury, CT; daughter of Ruben and Annette; children: Maghan Kadijah. **Educ:** Univ Conn, Storrs, BA, 1975, MS. **Career:** Conn State Dept Corrections, affirmative action officer, 1976-77, personnel officer, 1977-79, Hartford Correctional Ctr, dep warden, 1979-84, Hartell DWI Unit Windsor Locks, warden, 1984-92, 1994-2001; Correctional Servs, dir, dep comnr, 1992-94. **Orgs:** Bd mem, House Bread, 1982-83; vpres, bd Families Crisis, 1982-; vol counr, YWCA Sexual Assault Crisis, 1982-90; comnr, City Hartford Drug/Alcohol, 1986-90; Manch Bd Educ, 1995-98; Tenn Mentor, 1996-; Conn Criminal Justice Asn; Am Correctional Asn; Mid Atlantic States Correctional Asn. **Honors/Awds:** Connecticut Zeta of the Year, Zeta Phi Beta Sorority, 1978; Community Service Award, Phoenix Soc Firefighters, 1985; Community Service Award, Hope SDA Church & Metro AME, 1985; Goverment Service Recognition, YWCA, 1985; Outstanding Working Women Glamour Magazine, 1985; Outstanding Connecticut Women, Conn United Nations Asn, 1987. **Special Achievements:** First African American woman warden. **Business Addr:** Warden, Connecticut State Department Corrections, 251 Middle Tpke, Mansfield, CT 06268, **Business Phone:** (860)487-2712.

**BUSH, HOMER GILES**
Narrator. **Personal:** Born Nov 12, 1972, East St. Louis, IL; married Monica. **Career:** Baseball player (retired); Fla Marlins, player, 2002; Az Pdres, player, 1991; Charleston Rainbows, player, 1992; Waterloo Diamonds, player, 1993; Ranca Cucamongo Quakes, player, 1994; Wichita Wrangles, player, 1994; Memphis chicks, player, 1995; Las Vegas Stars, player, 1996-97; Columbus Clippers, player, 1997, 2004; New York Yankees, infielder, 1997-98, 2004; Toronto Blue Jays, infielder, 1999-2002; Dunedin Blue Jays, player, 1999-2001; Syracuse Skychiefs, player, 2001; Fla Marlins, player, 2002.

**BUSH, JAMES, III**
Politician. **Personal:** Born Feb 13, 1955, Panama City, FL; married Bernadine; children: James IV & Joshua D. **Educ:** Bishop Col, Undergrad Studies, Music & Relig, 1976; Bethune-Cookman Col, BS, phys educ, 1979; Nova Southeastern Univ, MS, educ admin & supv, 1984, PhD, educ leadership, 2003; Smith Chapel Bible Col, Dr, ministry Christian educ, 2004. **Career:** Fla House Rep, dem exec committeeman, 1984-92; Fla House Rep, Dist 109, rep, 1992-2000; Elected House, 2008. **Orgs:** Bd mem, Community Action Agency Bd; chair, Fla Martin Luther King Jr Inst Nonviolence; United Teachers Dade; bd mem, Opportunity Industrialization Ctr; United Teachers Dade; Exec Committeeman, Miami Dade Dem Party, 1984-92; Dade County Pub Schs, 1986-88; Chair Voter Regist, Fla Dem Party, 1989-90; bd mem, Juv Justice Coun; assoc minister, Antioch Missionary Baptist Church Brownsville, 1990-92; Chair Affirmative Action, Fla Dem Party, 1990-91; fel Nat Conf Black State Legislators, 1992-2000; mem, Nat Conf Black State Legislators, 1992-2000; chmn, bd chmn emer, Fla Martin Luther King Jr Inst Nonviolence Bd, 1992-2000; Govt Accountability Act Coun; Health Care Regulation Policy Comt; Joint Comt Pub Coun Oversight; First Vpres, People United Lead Struggle Equality, 1999-2006; Nat bd mem, Southern Christian Leadership Conf, 2003-; Econ Develop Policy Comt; Elder & Family Serv Policy Comt; Health & Family Serv Policy Coun; Health Care Regulation Policy Comt. **Home Addr:** 3015 NW 49th St, Miami, FL 33142, **Home Phone:** (305)250-1763. **Business Addr:** Representative, Florida House of Representative, 513 The Capitol, Tallahassee, FL 32399-1300, **Business Phone:** (850)488-1157.

**BUSH, HON. MARY K.**
Banker. **Personal:** Born Apr 9, 1948, Birmingham, AL. **Educ:** Fisk Univ, BA, econ, 1969; Univ Chicago, MBA, fin, 1971. **Career:** Chase Manhattan Bank NA, credit analyst, 1971-73; Citibank NA, acct officer, 1973-76; Bankers Trust Co, vp, world corp dept, team leader, 1976-82; US Treas Dept, exec asst dep secy, 1982-84; Int Monetary Fund, us alt ed, 1984-88; Fed Nat Mortgage Asn, Head Int Finance, 1988-89; Fed Home Loan Bank Syst, Managing Dir-Fed Housing Finance Bd, 1989-91; Bush Int, pres, chmn, founder, 1991-; Reynolds Am Inc, dir, 1999-; Brock Capital Group LLC, sr managing dir, 2010-. **Orgs:** Vice chair, treas Women's World Banking, NY, 1983-; Exec Women Gov, 1984-; Univ Chicago Bus Sch, 1979-; bd trustee, YMCA, Wash, DC, 1985-; bd, Texaco Inc; bd, Nat Bank Trust Co; US Govt's rep, Int Monetary Fund Bd; head, Fed Home Loan Bank Syst; bd mem, Sallie Mae; bd; Discover Financial Serv; bd, ManTech Int; bd, Marriott Int Inc; Kennedy Ctr Community Adv Bd; bd gov, Investment Co Inst; gov coun, Independent Dirs Coun; chmn, audit comt, Mortgage Guaranty Ins Corp; Brady Corp; chmn, policy admin comt, Pioneer Family of Mutual Funds; US Adv Bd, Global Leadership Found; chmn, HELP Comn; dir, Briggs & Stratton, 2004-09; head, Int Finance Dept, Fannie Mae. **Honors/Awds:** Scott Paper Co Leadership Award; Who's Who in Finance & Indust; Outstanding Young Women Am; Who's Who Am Col & Univ. **Home Addr:** 4201 Cathedral Ave NW, Washington, DC 20016, **Home Phone:** (202)364-8585. **Business Addr:** Director, Reynolds Am Inc, 401 N Main St, Winston-Salem, NC 27102, **Business Phone:** (336)741-5500.

**BUSH, NATHANIEL**
Association executive, lawyer. **Personal:** Born Jan 19, 1949, Washington, DC; son of Thelmen and Elouise Graves; married Marsha Diane Jackson; children: Traci, Nathan & Matthew. **Educ:** Ripon Col, BA, 1973; Cleveland Marshall Col Law, JD, 1977; Wharton Sch Bus, cert, 1984. **Career:** Cambridge Univ, distinguished vis prof law, grad asst, 1976-77; Bur ATF Dept, treas, atty, 1979-81; Univ Dist Columbia, adj prof criminol, 1982-84; DC State Campaign Jesse Jackson, pres, gen coun, 1983-84; DC Bd Educ, vpres; Ward VII rep; Pvt Pract, lawyer, currently. **Orgs:** Bd dir, Southeast Neighbors Citizens Asn; bd dir, Far E Comm Serv Inc; chmn, bd dir, Concerned Citizens Alcohol & Drug Abuse; Bar State, OH, 1977; State Bar Asn, 1979-; DC Bar, 1979-; Moot Ct Bd Govs, Cleveland Marshall Col Law. **Honors/Awds:** First Place, Third Annual Douglas Moot Ct Competition, 1975; Outstanding Young Men America, 1984. **Home Addr:** 1119 44th Pl SE, Washington, DC 20019, **Home Phone:** (202)360-8446. **Business Addr:** Lawyer, 1000 Conn Ave NW, Washington, DC 20036, **Business Phone:** (202)584-0007.

**BUSH, PATRICIA R.**
Executive. **Personal:** Born Cambridge, MA. **Educ:** Mt Holyoke Col, BA, math; Univ Va, Darden Grad Sch Bus Admin, MBA. **Career:** Polaroid Corp, Channel Opers & Develop, dir; consult; Palladium Group, vpres; Balanced Scorecard Collab, vpres govt solution, prin & pub sector pract leader, currently; Bush Mcfee Group, managing partner, currently. **Orgs:** Co-chairperson, Polaroid Sr Black Mgrs; founder, Nat Coalition 100 Black Women, Boston Chap; bd dir, Urban League Eastern Mass. **Business Addr:** Managing Partner, Bush Mcafee Group LLC, 13800 Aston Manor Dr Unit 1, Silver Spring, MD 20904, **Business Phone:** (202)679-1957.

**BUSH, THOMAS W.**
Law enforcement officer. **Personal:** son of Thomas J and Wanda L. **Educ:** Morehouse Col, Atlanta Ga, 1964; Univ Ga, mgt develop; US Dept Justice, human rel, 1982; Southern Police Inst Ga Police Acad, Admin Officers Training, 1984. **Career:** Dekalb Cty Dept Pub Safety, patrolman, 1974-79, master patrolman, 1979-80, sgt, 1980-82, lt, 1982-90, capt, 1990; DeKalb Co Police Dept, Comdr Spec Oper, currently. **Business Addr:** Commander Special Operator, Dekalb County Government - Police & Fire Rescue Services, 3630 Camp Cir, Decatur, GA 30032, **Business Phone:** (404)294-2693.

**BUSIA, AKOSUA CYAMAMA**
Actor, writer. **Personal:** Born Dec 30, 1966; daughter of Kofi Abrefa; married John Singleton; children: Hadar. **Educ:** Oxford Univ, Oxforshire, Eng, UK. **Career:** Films: Ashanti, 1979; The Final Terror, 1983; The Color Purple, 1985; Crossroads, 1986; Low Blow, 1986; Native Son, 1986; Saxo, 1987; The Seventh Sign, 1988; NewJack City, 1991; Rosewood, 1997; Mad City, 1997; Ill Gotten Gains, 1997; Beloved, writer, 1998; Tears of the Sun, 2003; A Collaboration of Spirits Casting and Acting The Color Purple, 2003; Journey to Safety Making Tears of the Sun, 2003; Ascension Day, 2007; TV appearances: "Warp speed", 1981; "Knight Rider", 1983; "Louisiana", 1984; "Late Starter", 1985; "A.D.", 1985; "Badge of the Assassin", 1985; "Simon & Simon", 1985; "The George McKenna Story", 1986; "Babies Having Babies", 1986; "The Twilight Zone", 1986; "St. Elsewhere", 1986; "A Special Friendship", 1987; "Highway to Heaven", 1987; "A Different World", 1989; "Brother Future", 1991; "Dead Man's Walk", 1996; "ER", 1999; Book: The Seasons of Beento Blackbird: A Novel, 1997. **Orgs:** Royal Family Wenchi. **Honors/Awds:** Michael Landon Award, 1987; Princess, Ghana, Africa; Best Actress, 2003. **Special Achievements:** Nominated for Oscar award in 1985; nominated for an Academy award, Golden Satellite Award and Black Film Award. **Business Addr:** Actress, Author, c/o Greater Talent Network Inc, 437 5th Ave, New York, NY 10016.

**BUSKEY, JAMES E.**
Educator, state government official. **Personal:** Born Apr 10, 1937; married Virginia. **Educ:** Ala State Univ, BS, sec educ; Univ NC, Chapel Hill, MAT, math; Univ Colo, Boulder, EdS. **Career:** LeFlore High Sch, asst prin; Williamson High Sch, asst prin; E.S. Chestang Mid Sch, prin; Commonwealth Nat Bank, founder & dir, currently; Franklin Primary Health Ctr, founder& dir; Franklin Memorial Clin, prin, currently; Community Convalescent Ctr, founder & dir; Mobile Co House Legis Deleg, chmn; Ala State House Rep, 99th Dist, rep, 1976-. **Orgs:** Ala Dem Conf; AL State Dem Exec Comt; Omega Psi Phi; SOMI; Aimwell Baptist Church; Nat Educ Asn; Ala State Educ Asn; Ala Dem Conf. **Home Addr:** 2207 Barretts Lane, Mobile, AL 36617-2734, **Home Phone:** (251)457-7928. **Business Addr:** State Representative, House of Representatives of Alabama, 104 S Lawrence St, Mobile, AL 36617, **Business Phone:** (251)208-5480.

**BUSTAMANTE, J. W. ANDRE**
Publisher. **Personal:** Born Jun 18, 1961, Cleveland, OH; son of John Henry and Frances Joy Simmons; children: Auschayla Quinae Brown. **Educ:** Boston Univ, Boston, BS, 1986; Entrepreneurial Acad, dipl, basic & advan curric, 2006. **Career:** Wang Labs Inc, Lowell, MA, auditor, 1982; Trustees Health & Hosps City Boston, Inc, acct, budget controller, 1983; Commonwealth Mass Dept Revenue, Boston, MA, tax examr, 1983-84, 1985-87; Harvard St Health Ctr, Boston, MA, bus mgr, 1985; First Bank Nat Asn, Cleveland, OH, exec asst chmn, 1987-88; Call & Post Newspapers, Cleveland, OH, pres/gen mgr, 1988-95; Bottom Line Productions Inc, vpres, 1987-; PW Publ Co Inc, pres & gen mgr, 1988-89; Augrid Corp, vpres, 1995-99, exec asst comnr; R A Energy Int Inc, pres, 1998-, vpres, sales & mkt, 2002-; Cuyahaoga County, exec asst, 1999-2002; Entrepreneurial Acad, mgr, 2006-07; RA Repair & Improv, owner, 2003-10. **Orgs:** Urban League, Cleveland Chap; Nat Asn Black Acct, Cleveland Chap; Am Entrepreneurs Asn; bd dir, Job Corps Community Rels Comt; Cleveland Schs Summit CNL; bd & nominating comt, UNIV Circle Inc; Ohio Citizens; Adv Coun; Nat MNY Golf Asn Bd; co-chmn Ohio Bush-Quayle 92; Repub Nat Comt; Nat Rifle Asn; NCP, Cleveland Chap; adv, African Solar Village Proj; vol; Clergy United Juv Justice; vol, Peace in Hood; asst dir, Spirit a Rainbow; edial bd, SE J Ed, TN State Univ; chair, Youth Develop Coun; bd dir, WAS Nat Bank. **Honors/Awds:** Certificate of Appreciation, CARE, 1987; Certificate of Appreciation, Republican Nat Committee, 1988, 1989; Certificate of Appreciation, United Negro Col Fund, 1990; Certificate of Recognition, Republican Senatorial Inner Circle, 1990; Senatorial Commission, 1991; Presidential Task Force Honor Roll, 1991; Order of Merit, 1991; Presidential Commission, 1992; Presidential Advisory Committee Commission, 1992; Citation of Leadership, Republican Inner Circle, 1996; US Senatorial Commission, 1996; Outstanding Young Americans, 1997. **Home Addr:** PO Box 1892, Cleveland, OH 44106, **Home Phone:** (216)791-3467. **Business Addr:** President, Vice President, RA Energy Int Inc, 6802 Carnegie Ave Suite 4, Cleveland, OH 44103-4634, **Business Phone:** (216)431-0200.

**BUSTAMANTE, Z SONALI. See WILSON, SONALI BUSTAMANTE.**

**BUSUMBRU, LISA OPOKU**
Executive. **Personal:** married Bernard; children: Jordan. **Educ:** Univ Minn, BA, sociol, 1993; Harvard Law Sch, JD, 1996. **Career:** Richards, Spears, Kibbe & Orbe, partner, 2004; Goldman Sachs Co, Asia Securities Div, managing dir & chief operating officer, 2004-. **Orgs:** Bd mem, Loan Syndications & Trading Asn; fundraiser, Found Orthop & Complex Spine; fundraiser, Women's Comn Refugee Women & C; mentor, Stud Sponsor Prog. **Business Addr:** Chief Operating Officer, Managing Director, Goldman Sachs & Co, 200 W St, New York, NY 10282, **Business Phone:** (212)902-1000.

**BUTCHER, CHARLES PHILIP. See BUTCHER, DR. PHILIP.**

**BUTCHER, DR. PHILIP (CHARLES PHILIP BUTCHER)**
Educator, writer. **Personal:** Born Sep 28, 1918, Washington, DC; son of James W (deceased) and Jennie Rosa Lawrence Jones; married Ruth; children: Wendy & Laurel; married Margaret Just Wormley; married Vada Easter; children: Grace Toni. **Educ:** Howard Univ, BA, 1942, MA, 1947; Columbia Univ, PhD, 1956. **Career:** Opportunity, Journ Negro Life, 1947-48; Morgan State Col, eng teacher, 1947-49, from asst to assoc prof, 1949-59; SC State Col, vis prof, 1958; Morgan State Univ, prof, 1959-79, dean grad sch, 1972-75, prof emer, 1979-; Howard Univ, staff, 1934-76, prof, 1909-94. **Orgs:** Col Lang Asn; Mod Lang Asn; Soc Study So Lit. **Honors/Awds:** General Education Board & John Hay Whitney Fellowship; Creative Scholarship Award, Col Language Asn, 1964; many research grants; many citations, reference works; many books & articles published. **Home Addr:** 9326 Mellenbrook Rd, Columbia, MD 21045, **Home Phone:** (301)596-4579. **Business Addr:** Professor Emeritus, Morgan State University, 1700 E Cold Spring Lane, Baltimore, MD 21251, **Business Phone:** (443)885-3333.

**BUTLER, ANNETTE GARNER**
Lawyer. **Personal:** Born Jun 23, 1944, Cleveland, OH; daughter of Rudolph Garner and Minnie Garner; children: Christopher & Kimberley. **Educ:** Case Western Res Univ, BA, sociol & psychol, 1966; Cleveland State & Cleveland Marshall Law, JD, 1977. **Career:** Civil rights specist, D & HEW Off Civil Rights, 1970-74; Guren, Merritt, Sogg & Cohen, assoc atty, 1974-81; dir legal affairs, Off Sch Monitoring, 1981-82; Us Attorneys Off, asst Us atty, 1982-2006; Academic court reporting & Butler Law Firm, atty & instr paralegal studies prog, 2006-11; Cuyahoga County Board of Revision, hearing officer, judge, 2011-12, hearing officer, 2011; Butler Law Firm, atty, 2013-. **Orgs:** Trustee, vpres grievance comm, Cleveland Bar Asn; founder, past pres, Black Women Lawyers Asn; bar admiss Ohio 6th Circuit Ct Appeals; Supreme Ct US; trustee, treas, vice-chmn, Cleveland State Univ; past pres, Cleveland City Club; past pres, Cleveland Heights Univ Libr Bd; bd trustee, Shaker Heights Recreation Bd; pres, bd trustee, Shaker Heights Libr Bd; vpres, trustee, Citizens League Res Inst; past pres, Fed Bar Asn, Northern Dist Ohio Chap; Golden Key Nat Hon Soc. **Honors/Awds:** Distinguished Serv, Cleveland Jaycees; Outstanding Achievement Narrator, Cleveland Chap Nat Acad Arts & Scis; Woman Year, Negro Bus & Prof Club; Outstanding Achievement, Cuyahoga County Bar Asn; Distinguished Alumnus Award, Cleveland State Univ. **Home Addr:** 1503 Wash Heights Blvd, Ann Arbor, OH 48109, **Home Phone:** (216)851-3259. **Business Addr:** Attorney, Butler Law Firm, 1007 Mumma Rd, Lemoyne, PA 17043, **Business Phone:** (717)236-1485.

**BUTLER, B JANELLE. See PHIFER, B. JANELLE BUTLER.**

### BUTLER, DR. CHARLES H.
Physician. **Personal:** Born Feb 12, 1925, Wilmington, DE; children: Yvonne, Kathy, Charla & Leslie. **Educ:** Ind Univ; Univ Pa; Meharry Med Col, MD, 1953. **Career:** Pvt pract physician; Coatesville Hosp, staff. **Orgs:** Nat Med Asn; Am Acad Family Physicians; Pa Med Soc; med adv, Loacl Draft Bd Pres Pa St Conf Nat Asn Advan Colored People; pres, Coatesville Br Nat Asn Advan Colored People, 1968; vpres, Unite Polit Act Comt; Chester Co; past pres, Chester Co Rep Club; former exec comn, 32 deg Mason; Charles E Gordon Consistory no 65; IBPOE, Wilmington; treas, past pres, Pan-hellenic Assembly, Chester County Wilmington Alumni Chap Kappa Alpha Psi. **Honors/Awds:** Mason & Year, 1967; Citation Optimist Club Coatesville, 1972; Life member Humanitarian Award, Chester County Bus & Prof Women's Culb Inc, 1973; Community Achievement Award, Lily Valley Lodge no 59, 1973. **Home Addr:** 31 Prout Dr, Coatesville, PA 19320, **Home Phone:** (610)384-4254.

### BUTLER, CLARY KENT
Clergy, broadcaster. **Personal:** Born Jul 5, 1948, Charleston, SC; son of Carl Dallas and Mary Capers; married Patsy Swint; children: Tammy R, Clary K Jr & Cora L. **Educ:** SC State Col, Orangeburg, SC, BA, 1970; Webster Univ, Charleston, AFB, 1987. **Career:** House God Church, pastor, 1980-89; Berkeley Broadcasting Corp, WMCJ Radio, Monicks Corner SC, pres, 1984-. **Orgs:** Omega Psi Phi; bd mem, Am Cancer Soc, Charleston County Br, 1985; Berkeley County Chamber Com, 1989; dir large, SC Broadcasters Asn, 1989. **Home Addr:** 1339 Kiki Way, Charleston, SC 29407-5154, **Home Phone:** (803)571-2566. **Business Addr:** President, Berkeley Broadcasting Corp, 314 Rembert Dennis Blvd, Moncks Corner, SC 29461, **Business Phone:** (803)761-9625.

### BUTLER, DON
Automotive executive, vice president (organization). **Educ:** Kettering Univ, Flint, MI, Gen Motors Inst, BS, elec engineering, 1986; Harvard Bus Sch, MBA, 1990. **Career:** Corvette Elec Systs Group, design engr; Detroit Zone, zone mgr; Grand Am, mkt planner, brand planning mgr; Aztek, brand mgr; Gen Motors, Planning & Bus Develop, vpres, 2001-05; Gen Motors, Egypt, managing dir, 2005-07; Gen Motors, Truck Mkt Chevrolet Div, exec dir, 2007-08; OnStar, Global & OEM Bus, vpres, 2008-10; Inrix, Mkt & Prod Planning, vpres, 2010; Cadillac, US mkt vpres, 2010-; Ford Motor Co, exec dir, 2014. **Orgs:** Bd dir, CureDuchenne. **Business Addr:** Executive director, Ford Motor Company, Dearborn, MI.

### BUTLER, DOUTHARD ROOSEVELT
Educator. **Personal:** Born Oct 7, 1934, Waxahachie, TX; son of Corine McKinney and Lonnie; married Jo Jewell Ray; children: Douthard Jr, Carolyn, Barbara & Katherine. **Educ:** Prairie View A&M Univ, BS, 1955; Cent Mich Univ, MA, 1976; George Mason Univ, Fairfax, VA, DPA, 1993. **Career:** George Mason Univ, Fairfax, VA, grad teaching asst, 1986-88, acad coordr, 1990-95, assoc athletic dir, acad resources, 1995-2003, assoc athletic dir community rels, 2002-; Fairfax Co Pub Sch Syst, VA, math teacher, 1989-90; Pa State Univ, scholar-in-residence, 1989; Rotary Dist 7610, dist gov, 1993-94. **Orgs:** Pres, DC Metro Chap, Prairie View A&M Univ Alumni Asn, 1978-81; pres, Prairie View A&M Univ Nat Alumni Asn, 1981-83; pres, Rotary Club, Mt Vernon, Va, 1987-88, 2005-06; pres, Nat Pan Hellenic Coun, Northern Va Chap, 1989-91; gov, Rotary Dist, 1993-94; bd mem, Cold War Museum. **Home Addr:** 6909 Lamp Post Lane, Alexandria, VA 22306-1324, **Home Phone:** (703)768-2093. **Business Addr:** Associate Athletic Director for Community Relation, George Mason University, 10515 Patriot Sq, Fairfax, VA 22030, **Business Phone:** (703)993-3251.

### BUTLER, DUANE
Executive, football player. **Personal:** Born Nov 9, 1973, Trotwood, OH. **Educ:** Ill State Univ, BS, comput info systs, 1997. **Career:** Football player (retired), executive; Int Bus Mach Corp, intern, 1991-92; Minn Vikings, defensive back, 1997-98; NFL Europe, London Monarchs, 1998-99; Nail Haiven, silent investor, 1998-2001; Cleveland Browns, 1999-2000; Berlin Thunder, NFL Europe, defensive back, 2000-01; Birmingham Thunderbolts, 2001; Tiger-Cats, defensive back, 2001-03; Hamilton Tiger-Cats, 2002; Montreal alouettes, line back, 2003-07; Duane Butler Football Acad, founder & chief exec officer, 2010-. **Business Addr:** Founder, Chief Executive Officer, Duane Butler Football Academy, Toronto, ON, **Business Phone:** (905)536-9594.

### BUTLER, ERIC L.
Vice president (organization), manager. **Educ:** Carnegie Mellon Univ, BS, mech engineering, 1981 & MSIA, 1986. **Career:** Union Pac Rr Co, rr, 1986-, vpres supply, vpres planning & anal & dir corp compensation, vpres & gen mgr automotive, vpres & gen mgr indust prod, 2005-, exec vpres mkt & sales & chief mkt officer, 2012-. **Honors/Awds:** "Black Enterprise," The 100 Most Powerful Executives in Corporate America, 2010. **Business Addr:** Executive Vice President, Union Pacific Railroad, 1400 Douglas St, Omaha, NE 68179, **Business Phone:** (402)544-5000.

### BUTLER, EULA M.
Educator, executive. **Personal:** Born Oct 15, 1927, Houston, TX; married Henry C. **Educ:** Tex Southern Univ, BS, 1954, MEd, 1958; Mt Hope Bible Col, DM, 1984; Univ Tex, grad study; Prairie View Univ, educ & psychol, coun & guid; Tex Southern Univ, spec educ. **Career:** TX Southern Univ, pub rels, community, 1985-87; Region IV Educ Serv Ctr, TX Educ Agency, classroom teacher, vis teacher, counr, first teacher cert, Head Start Prog, writing demonstr, workshop presenter; Sch After Sch Inc, founder, dir & educ mgr. **Orgs:** 21st pres, Houston Alumnae, 1969-71, dir, 1972-76, 15th regional dir; bd dir, ARC mem Harris Co Grand Jury, 1974-; bd mem, Nat Delta Res & Educ Found Inc, 1985-88; coordr, First State Rehab & Prog Fed Female Offenders; Delta Sigma Theta Sor; comn coun, Parents & Students; Young Women Christian Asn Nat Coun Negro Women Top Ladies Distin; Am Judicature Soc; bd dir, Harris Co; bd dir, Girl Scout; Task Force Qual Integrate Educ Houston Independent Sch Dist; dir, SW Region Delta Sigma Theta; past pres, Houston Chap Delta Sigma Theta; Am PGA NEA TSTA Guid & coun Asn; Vis Nurses Asn, Light House Houston, Nat Housing & Properties, Delta Sigma Theta, Houston Network Family Life Edu; Houston Enrichment Life Prog Inc; bd mem, Metro Teacher Educ Ctr, Vols Pub Sch, Houston Independent Sch Dist. **Honors/Awds:** Teacher Year Award, 1969; Christian Service Award, Beth Baptist Church, 1985; Community Service Award, Mt Corinth Baptist Church, 1985; School After School Award, Sch After Sch Faculty & Staff, 1985; Recognition Excellence Achievement Award, Phillis Wheatley High Sch, 1985; Black History Making Award, 1986; Community Leadership Award; Delta Sigma Theta Cert Appreciation; Leadership Award, United Negro Col Fund; Golden Life Member, Delta Sigma Theta Sor. **Home Addr:** 4706 Providence St, Houston, TX 77020-6408, **Home Phone:** (713)672-1837. **Business Addr:** Director, Houston Alumnae Chapter, 1 Delta Plz 3333 Old Span Trl, Houston, TX 77021, **Business Phone:** (713)747-8175.

### BUTLER, ESQ. FREDERICK DOUGLAS (FRED D BUTLER)
Lawyer, executive director. **Personal:** Born Nov 5, 1942, Philadelphia, PA; married Sara Vitori; children: Frederick Douglas II. **Educ:** Rutgers Univ, BA, 1974; NY Univ, MA, pub admin, 1977; Univ Calif, Hastings Col Law, JD, 1986. **Career:** Newark Housing Authority, dir family & community serv, 1973-80; White Plains Housing Authority, exec dir, 1980-81; Govt Trinidad & Tobago Nat Housing Authority, consult, 1984-85; Carroll Burdick & Mc Donough, atty, 1986-88; Petitt & Martin, atty, 1988-89; State Calif, atty, sr coun, 1989-2004; arbitrator, Mediator & Neutral, 1995-; Univ Calif, Hastings Col Law, adj prof, 2003-; San Francisco Off Citizen Complaints, hearing officer; ADR Serv Inc, arbitrator & mediator, currently.; Ctr Negotiation & Dispute Resolution, adj prof, currently. **Orgs:** World Affairs Coun; Am Soc Pub Admin; Inst Real Estate Mgt; Nat Asn Housing Officials; Afro-Am Hist Soc; former pres, United Community Corp, Newark NJ, Newark Citizen's Adv Bd; Soul-House Drug Abuse Prog; NJ Col Med & Dent; pres, bd trustee, Mediation Soc; San Francisco Bar Asn; Am Bar Asn; Indust Res Rels Asn; Am Arbit Asn; Asn Conflict Resolution; Equal Employ Opportunity Comn; Dept Justice ADA-Weybridge Found; Nat Ctr Employ Dispute Resolution; co-chair, Bar Asn SF Arbit Comt; pres, Northern Calif Mediation Asn; Calif State Bar ADR Comt; pres, Community Boards SF; pres, Hastings Col Law Alumni Asn. **Honors/Awds:** Community Service Awards, Newark Tenants Coun, Serv Employees Int Union, Newark Cent Ward Little League, Frontiers Int; American Jurisprudence Award. **Home Addr:** 17 Berkeley Way, San Francisco, CA 94131-2517, **Home Phone:** (415)826-5629. **Business Addr:** Mediator, Arbitrator, ADR Services Inc, 915 Wilshire Blvd Suite 1900, Los Angeles, CA 90017, **Business Phone:** (415)772-0900.

### BUTLER, DR. GRACE L.
College teacher. **Educ:** Xavier Univ, BS; Northwestern Univ, MM, music educ, 1963; NY Univ, PhD, educ admin, 1976. **Career:** Univ Houston, Dept Educ Leadership & Cult Studies, prof & assoc vpres fac affairs, 1989-99, prof emer, 1999-; Hope Through Grace Inc, founder & chief exec officer, 2002-. **Orgs:** Pub mem, Exec Coun Phys Ther & Occup Ther Examiners; Nat Cancer Inst Consumer Advocates in Res & Related Activ; Cancer Ther Eval Prog; founding mem, Camp All Found; Adv Bd, Tex C's Cancer Ctr; MD Anderson Cancer Ctr, Univ Tex; Hope Through Grace Inc; Pres, Bush's panel nat health leaders, White House. **Business Addr:** Founder & Chief Executive Officer, President, Hope Through Grace Inc, 4660 Beechnut St Suite 102, Houston, TX 77096, **Business Phone:** (713)668-4673.

### BUTLER, GWENDOLYN L.
President (organization), executive. **Personal:** Born Detroit, MI. **Educ:** Univ Mich, BA, econs, 1977; JL Kellogg Grad Sch Bus Northwestern Univ, MBA, finance & econs, 1984. **Career:** Continental Ill Natl Bank & Trust Co, corp finance banker, sr dir, 1977-92; SEI, sr capital advisor, 1992-94; Bear Stearns Asset Mgt, managing dir, 1994-2001; UBS Global Asset Mgt, exec dir, 2001-07; Capri Capital Partners LLC, vice chairwoman, 2007-, chief mkt officer, 2007-08, pres & chief operating officer, 2008-, partner, currently. **Orgs:** Chair, Natl Asn Securities Professionals; bd dir, pres, YWCA Metrop Chicago, 2010-14; bd Investment comt, Capri Investment Group, LLC; Global Mgt Bd; bd mem, Seaway Bank & Trust Co, 2014-; Econ Club Chicago; Community Develop Comn; Real Estate Exec Coun. **Business Addr:** President, Chief Executive Officer, Capri Capital Partners LLC, John Hancock Ctr 875 N Mich Ave Suite 3430, Chicago, IL 60611, **Business Phone:** (312)573-5300.

### BUTLER, DR. J. RAY
Clergy. **Personal:** Born Aug 5, 1923, Roseboro, NC; son of Amos Delonzo and Mary Francis Cooper; married Marion Lucas; children: Charles Ervin, Ellis Ray, Larry Davis & Vincent Recardo. **Educ:** Friendship Col, DDiv, 1966; Southeastern Theol Sem, attended 1967; Southeastern Theol Sem, DTh, 1969; Shaw Univ, BA, BDiv, MDiv, 1974, DDiv; McKinley Theol Sem, Doctor Laws, 1976; Tri County Col & Sem, Maxton, DMin, 1999. **Career:** Ebenezer Baptist Church Wilmington, pastor, 1954-70; First Baptist Church Creedmoor, pastor; Mt Olive Baptist Church, Fayetteville, pastor; New Christian Chapel Baptist Church RoseHill, pastor; Shiloh Baptist Church Winston Salem, pastor, 1970-90; United Cornerstone Baptist Church, pres, founder, pastor. **Orgs:** Past pres, Interdenominational Ministerial All; past pres, Interracial Minister Asn; past pres, Wilmington Civic League; past pres, PTA; life mem & vpres, Nat Asn Advan Colored People; bd dir, ARC; Man Power Delvelop; Citizens Coalition Bd; pres, large Gen Baptist State Conv; pres, Baptist Ministers Conf & Assoc; Forsyth Clergy Asn; chmn, Gen Baptist St Conv NC Inc; exten teaching staff, Shaw Univ; exec bd, Lott Carey Baptist Foreign Missions & Conv; app bd, lic gen contractors Gov Jim Hunt NC; founder, Shilohian & St Peters Day Care; moderator, Rowan Baptist Missionary Asn, 1988-92; life mem, Alpha Phi Alphi Fraternity. **Honors/Awds:** Various tours foreign countries; Pastor of the Year Award, Midwestern Baptist Laymen's Fellowship Chicago, 1975, 1976; elected, Content Writer Nat Baptist Sunday Sch Pub Bd; author, The Christian Commun Related Jewish Passover & Monetary Commitment, 1985; From Playtime Pulpit Serv; "The Chronicles Lifetime Achievers", 1998. **Home Addr:** 2745 Patria St, Winston-Salem, NC 27127-4043, **Home Phone:** (336)785-1268. **Business Addr:** Pastor, United Cornerstone Baptist Church, 9 JW Thomas Way, Thomasville, NC 27360, **Business Phone:** (336)476-7218.

### BUTLER, JEROME M.
Lawyer. **Personal:** Born Jul 15, 1944, Chicago, IL; married Jean Brothers. **Educ:** Fisk Univ, BA, bus admin, 1966; Columbia Univ, JD, 1969. **Career:** Tucker Watson Butler & Todd, atty; Chicago Housing Auth Gen, Coun Off, atty, 1996-99; Chicago Transit Auth, assoc gen coun; Sengstacke Enterprises, vpres, gen coun & chief exec officer, 2000-03; State Bd Elections, treas; Ill Dept Human Serv, chief fiscal officer, chief operating officer, 2003-, asst secy, currently. **Orgs:** Cook County Chicago Bar Asn. **Home Addr:** 5446 S Cornell Ave, Chicago, IL 60615, **Home Phone:** (312)241-5082. **Business Addr:** Assistant Secretary, Illinois Department of Human Services, 100 S Grand Ave E, Springfield, IL 62762, **Business Phone:** (217)785-3887.

### BUTLER, JERRY
County commissioner, singer. **Personal:** Born Dec 8, 1939, Sunflower, MS; son of Jerry Sr and Arvelia Agnew; married Annette Smith; children: Randall Allen & Anthony Ali. **Educ:** Gov State Univ, BS, polit sci, MA, criminal justice studies. **Career:** Albums: For Your Precious Love, 1958; Come Back My Love, 1958; Lost, 1959; A Lonely Soldier, 1960; He Will Break Your Heart, 1960; Find Another Girl, 1961; I'm a Telling You, 1961; Moon River, 1961; Aware of Love, 1961; Make It Easy On Yourself, 1962; You Can Run, 1962; Theme from Taras Bulba, 1962; Whatever You Want, 1963; Need To Belong, 1963; Giving Up On Love, 1964; I Stand Accused, 1964; I Don't Want To Hear It Anymore, 1964; Let It Be Me, 1964; Ain't That Loving You Baby, 1964; Smile, 1964; Good Times, 1965; I Can't Stand To See You Cry, 1965; Just For You, 1965; For Your Precious Love, 1966; Love, 1966; I Dig You Baby, 1967; Mr Dream Merchant, 1967; Lost, 1967; Never Give You Up, 1968; Hey, Western Union Man, 1968; Are You Happy, 1968; Only the Strong Survive, 1969; Moody Woman, 1969; What's the Use of Breaking Up, 1969; A Brand New Me, 1969; Don't Let Love Hang You Up, 1969; Got To See If I Can Get Mommy, 1970; I Could Write a Book, 1970; Where Are You Going, 1970; Special Memory, 1970; You Just Can't Win, 1971; Ten and Two, 1971; If It's Real What I Feel, 1971; Ain't Understanding Mellow, 1971; How Did We Lose It Baby, 1971; Walk Easy My Son, 1971; I Only Have Eyes For You, 1972; Close To You, 1972; One Night Affair, 1972; Can't Understand It, 1973; The Love We Had Stays On My Mind, 1973; The Power of Love, Mercury, 1973; Sweet Sixteen, Mercury, 1974; That's How Heartaches Are Made, 1974; Take the Time To Tell Her, 1974; Playing On You, 1974; Love's on the Menu, Motown, 1976; The Devil In Mrs Jones, 1976; Suite for the Single Girl, Motown, 1977; I Wanna Do It To You, 1977; Chalk It Up, 1977; It's a Lifetime Thing, 1977; Cooling Out, 1978; Nothing Says I Love You Like I Love You, Philadelphia International, 1979; Best Love I Ever Had, Philadelphia Int, 1980; Don't Be An Island, 1980; Ice 'n' Hot, Fountain, 1982; No Love Without Changes, 1982; In My Life, 1983; The Best of Jerry Butler, Rhino, 1987; Iceman: The Mercury Years, Mercury, 1992; Time & Faith, Ichiban, 1993; Jerry Butler Prod, Chicago, IL, owner, 1960-; Iceman Beverage Co, Chicago, IL, chief exec officer, 1984-89; Cook County, IL, comnr, 1985-; Chicago City, alderman. **Orgs:** Chicago Chap, Nat Asn Advan Colored People; N Star Lodge No 1 FAM PHA 33 degree; Groove Phi Groove Fel; bd dir, Firman Comm Serv; vpres, Northern Ill Planning Comn, 1990; Alpha Phi Alpha; Rhythm & Blues Found; grand lectr, MWPHGL, State Ill & Jurisdiction, 1997; pres, Northeastern Ill Planning Comn, 1997. **Honors/Awds:** Musical Composition Citation Achievement, Broadcast Music, 1960, 1970; 3 Grammy Nominations; Song of the Yer, 1969; Clio Award Advert, 1972; Ceba Award Advert, 1983; Mason of the Year Award, Prince Hall Grand Lodge Ill, 1989; Valuable Research Award, Chicago Pub Schs; Elected Rock Hall of Fame, 1991. **Home Addr:** 627 E 33rd Pl, Chicago, IL 60616-4143, **Home Phone:** (773)925-4944. **Business Addr:** City Commissioner, Cook County, 118 N Clark St Rm 567, Chicago, IL 60602, **Business Phone:** (312)603-6391.

### BUTLER, JOHN O.
Executive. **Personal:** Born Nov 28, 1926, Bristol, TN; son of Pinkney and Olivia J; married Marjorie M Jackson; children: Deborah, David, Brian & Bruce. **Educ:** Howard Univ, BS, mech engineering, 1950. **Career:** GE Co, design engr, 1950-57; Raytheon Co, mgr indus engr, 1958-64; GTE Sylvania Inc, dir value engr, 1965-68; Deerfield Corp, founder & pres, 1963-. **Orgs:** Regist prof engr, MA; MA Bus Asn; Tau Beta Pi Engrg Hon Soc, 1952; cooperator, Framingham Union Hosp; Rotary Int; Twn Repub Com; Nat Soc Prof Engrs; comnr, MA Gov's Exec Coun Value Anal, 1966-72; comnr, Framingham Housing Auth; dir, Framingham Regional YMCA, 1971-75. **Business Addr:** Founder, President, Deerfield Corp, 6 Doyle Cir, Framingham, MA 01701-2824, **Business Phone:** (508)877-0143.

### BUTLER, DR. JOHN SIBLEY
Educator. **Personal:** Born Jul 19, 1947, New Orleans, LA; son of Johnnie Mae Sibley and Thojest Jefferson; married Rosemary Griffey; children: John Sibley. **Educ:** La State Univ, Baton Rouge, LA, BA, 1969; Northwestern Univ, Evanston, IL, MA, 1971, PhD, orgn behav & methods & statist, 1974. **Career:** Univ Tex, Dep Sociol, social prof, 1974, grad adv, 1978-81, African & Afro-Am Res Ctr, interim dir, 1990-91, 1992, Centennial Prof Sociol, 1990-99, Arthur James Douglass Centennial Prof Entrepreneurship, 1991-, Sam Barshop Centennial Fel, 1992-, Dept Sociol, chair, 1992-96, Dept Mgt, chair, 1999-, Gale Chair Small Bus & Entrepreneurship, 1999-, Herb Kelleher Ctr Entrepreneurship Growth & Renewal, dir, IC2 Inst, dir, 2002-13; Nat Ctr Neighborhood Enterprise, res fel, 1989-; State Farm Ins, Southwest, mgt consult, 1990; Nissan N Am Lectr, 1995; Aoyama Gakuin Univ, vis distinguished prof, 1996-99; Univ Texas, Austin, prof. **Orgs:** Fel Northwestern Univ, 1971-74; vis res fel, Human Sci Res, 1974; vis lectr, Am Sociol Asn, 1980; IC2 Univ Tex at Austin,, 1980-; pres, Am Asn Black Sociologists, 1980-81; Sigma Pi Phi; Kappa Alpha Psi; Omicron Nu; Phi Delta Kappa; US Asn Small Bus & Entrepreneurship; Southwestern Sociol Asn; Inter Univ Sem Armed Forces & Soc; Pres, La St Univ, Alumni Asn, Austin, 1988-91; Southern Sociol Asn; exec bd, Inter-Univ Sem Armed Forces & Socs, 1989-; bd dir, Glofish, 2003-. **Home Addr:** 5301 Musket Ridge, Austin, TX 78759, **Home Phone:** (512)345-6570. **Business Addr:** IC2 Research Fellow, University Texas, A0300 1 Univ Sta Stop B6300, Austin, TX 78712, **Business Phone:** (512)471-4788.

**BUTLER, DR. JOHNNELLA E.**
Educator. **Personal:** Born Feb 28, 1947, Roanoke, VA. **Educ:** Col Our Lady Elms, BA, 1968; Johns Hopkins Univ, MA, 1969; Univ Mass Amherst, EdD, 1979. **Career:** Johns Hopkins Univ, ford found fel, 1968-69; Towson State Univ, instr eng & black studies, 1970-74; Smith Col, instr, 1974-79, asst prof, 1979-81, assoc prof tenure, Dept Afro-Am Studies, instr, 1974-76, asst to dean, 1976-77, dept chair, 1977-79; Mt Holyoke Col, Womens Studies Dept, vis lectr, 1984; Univ Wash Seattle, Dept Afro-Am Studies, Grad Sch, prof, assoc dean & assoc vice provost am ethnic studies, 1989-2005; Spelman Col, chief adv, provost & vpres acad affairs, 2005-14, Dept Comparative Womens Studies, prof, 2005-; Berkeley Exec Leadership Acad, fac, currently. Book: The Matrix of American Ethnic Studies, ed, 2015. **Orgs:** Chair, 5 Col Black Studies Exec Comt, Towson State Univ, 1978-79; brd trustee, Col Our Lady Elms, 1984-89; consult, Womens Studies Prog, UnivIll Champagne-Urbana, 1984; Racism & Sexism, Patterson Col, 1984; Black Women Am Lit, Univ Ill, DeKalb, 1984; Black Studies & Womens Studies, Carleton Col, 1984; Wellesley Ctr Res Women, 1984; 21st Century Coun Cong Black Caucus Inst; Drew Univ, Fac Develop Workshop, 1984; fac, Higher Educ Resources Serv, currently; Adv Bd Nat Inst Technol Lib Educ; bd dir, Asn Am Cols & Univs. **Special Achievements:** First black woman to be tenured at Smith College. **Home Addr:** 35 S St 304, Northampton, MA 01060. **Business Addr:** Professor, Spelman College, Rm 112 Rockefeller Hall 350 Spelman Lane SW, Atlanta, GA 30314-4399, **Business Phone:** (404)270-6068.

**BUTLER, JOYCE M.**
Marketing executive. **Personal:** Born Jun 12, 1941, Gary, IN; daughter of Robert W Porter and Dorothy Paige Porter; married Mitchell; children: Stephanie Lynn & Adam Mitchell. **Educ:** Wright Col, Chicago, Ill, AA, 1963; DePaul Univ, Chicago, Ill, BA, urban planning, 1976, MS, mgt pub servs, 1980. **Career:** Loop Col, Chicago, Ill, admin asst, 1963-78; City Chicago, Dept Planning, Chicago, Ill, city planner, 1978-83, Mayor's Off Inquiry & Info, Chicago, Ill, prog mgr, 1983-88, dir prog serv, 1988-89; Michel Mkt, vpres, 1989-, City Col Chicago, Kennedy King Col, stud serv advisor & Acad Advisors, scholar Advisor, currently. **Orgs:** Oper PUSH, 1972-; Nat Forum Black Pub Adminr, 1985-; Soc Govt Meeting Planners, 1988-; Nat Asn Female Exec, 1989; Publicity Club Chicago, 1989. **Honors/Awds:** Paul Cornell Award, Hyde Pk Hist Soc, 1986. **Home Addr:** 11206 S Eggleston Ave, Chicago, IL 60628-4738, **Home Phone:** (773)520-1794. **Business Addr:** Student Services Advisor, Kennedy-King College, Rm W-110 6301 S Halsted St, Chicago, IL 60621, **Business Phone:** (773)602-5037.

**BUTLER, KATHLEEN JEAN**
Librarian. **Personal:** Born Aug 8, 1967, Philadelphia, PA; daughter of William Deloatch and Elizabeth; married Tracey J Hunter Hayes; children: Jalaal A Hayes & Makkah I Hayes. **Educ:** Lincoln Univ, Pa, BA, 1989; Cheyney Univ, Pa, MEd, 1991; Univ Pittsburgh, MLS, 1992. **Career:** Sch Dist Philadelphia, teacher, 1989-91, sch librn, 1996-; Ky State Univ, Curric Instrnl Media Ctr, head, 1993-95; Southern IL Univ, asst prof educ, psychol librn, 1995. **Orgs:** Am Libr Asn, 1991-; Black Caucus Am Libr Asn, 1991-; Kappa Delta Pi Int Hon Soc, 1991-; Ky Asn Blacks Higher Educ, 1994-97; chair, Bookfair Comt, 1996-; Asn Pub Sch Libr, 1996-; Bldg Comt, Sch Dist Philadelphia, 1999-; pres, Parent Coun, Sch Dist Philadelphia, 1999-; Asn Philadelphia Sch Librarians; life mem, Lincoln Univ; Philadelphia Chap Baptist Ministers Wives & Ministers Widows Union; bd trustee, Lincoln Univ, 2008-10. **Honors/Awds:** National Honor Society Award, Kappa Delta Pi, 1991; Lincoln University Founder Day Award, 2005; Association of Philadelphia School Librarians Irene Garson Librarian of the Year Service Award, 2006. **Special Achievements:** Publication: "A View of the Academic Curriculum and Instructional Media Library Center in Educating Future Elementary School Teachers: An Analysis and Bibliography", Multicultural Review, 3 (4), Dec 1994; The Annual Fall Teachers Conference, workshop presenter, Oct 1994. **Home Addr:** 1129 W Thompson St, Philadelphia, PA 19122-4140, **Home Phone:** (215)232-4262. **Business Addr:** Librarian, The School District of Philadelphia, 440 N Broad St, Philadelphia, PA 19130, **Business Phone:** (215)400-4000.

**BUTLER, KEITH ANDRE**
Government official, clergy. **Personal:** Born Nov 22, 1955, Detroit, MI; son of Robert L and Ida L Jackson; married Deborah Lorraine Bell; children: Keith Andre II, Michelle Andrea & Kristina Maria Jenkins (Joel). **Educ:** Oakland Community Col, attended 1974; Rhema Bible Training Ctr, pastoral studies, 1978; Eastern Mich Univ, Ypsilanti, MI, attended 1985; Univ Mich, Dearborn, MI, attended 1987; Univ London, NW, DDiv, 1988; Can Christian Col, dipl. **Career:** Word Faith Int Christian Ctr, Detroit, MI, founder & pastor, 1979-, bishop, currently; Faith Christian Ctr, founder & pastor; Faith4Life Dallas, pastor; Keith Butler Ministries, founder & pres; Faith Harvest Church, founder; Faith Life Church, founder; church & ministry sch, 2008. **Orgs:** Detroit Econ Develop Plan; adv bd, Henry Ford Hosp Care Prog, 1987; corp bd, Holy Cross Hosp; bd trustees, Metrop Youth Found; Alliance Against Casino Gambling Detroit; bd dirs, Mich Cancer Found, 1992; bd dirs, Teach Mich, 1992; Vision Faith Christian Acad; city coun mem, City Detroit, Detroit, Mich; Republican Nat Comt; exec bd, Christians United Israel. **Honors/Awds:** Five Outstanding Young People Mich, 1988; Ten Outstanding Americans Award, 1989. **Home Addr:** 19160 Bretton, Detroit, MI 48223, **Home Phone:** (313)531-6583. **Business Addr:** Founder, Word of Faith International Christian Center, 20000 W 9 Mile Rd, Southfield, MI 48075, **Business Phone:** (248)353-3476.

**BUTLER, LEROY, III**
Founder (originator), football player. **Personal:** Born Jul 19, 1968, Jacksonville, FL; son of Eunice; children: Sharon, L'Oreal & Gabrielle. **Educ:** Fla State Univ. **Career:** Football player (retired); Green Bay Packers, 1990, right cornerback, 1991, strong safety, 1992-2001; LeRoy Butler Ford, owner, 2012; LeRoy Butler Inc, founder, currently. **Orgs:** Founder, LeRoy Butler Cancer Found. **Honors/Awds:** Prep All-America, 1985; Rookie of the Year, 1990; NFL All-Decade Team, 1990s, Pro Football Hall of Fame; AP and UPI All-America, Florida St Univ, 1989; Pro Bowl Selection, 1993, 1996, 1997, 1998; All-Pro Selection, 1993, 1996, 1997, 1998; Super Bowl Champion (XXXI); Green Bay Packers Hall of Fame, 2007. **Home Addr:** 7632 Las Palmas Way, Jacksonville, FL 32256. **Business Addr:** Founder, LeRoy Butler Inc, 11800 W Grange Ave, Hales Corners, WI 53130.

**BUTLER, MELBA**
Executive. **Personal:** Born Apr 18, 1954, New York, NY; daughter of Martin and Juanita Jones; children: Thomas Martin & Sean David Hamilton. **Educ:** Long Island Univ, New York, NY, BA, psychol, 1975; Columbia Univ, New York, NY, MS, social work, 1979; City Univ NY, PhD, social welfare; Univ State New York, cert social worker. **Career:** St Joseph C Servs, caseworker, 1975; Queens Family Ct, Jamaica, NY, probation intern, 1977-78; Woodside sr asst Ctr, Woodside, NY, from asst to dir, 1978-79; Madison Sq Boys Club, New York, NY, from asst to dir, 1978-79; Sr Counr State Communities Aid, proj dir, 1979-82; New York Bd Educ, New York, NY, sch social worker, 1983-84; Brooklyn Col Women's Ctr, Brooklyn, NY, vol supvr, 1983-84; Pub Mgt Systs Inc, New York, NY, consult & trainer, 1984-86; Enter Inc, consult & supvr, 1989-90; Harlem Dowling-Westside Ctr C & Family Servs, New York, NY, exec dir, 1990-2006; Black Agency Execs, Admin Consult; Forestdale Inc, Admin Dir; Hunter Col, Adj Lectr; Black Equity Alliance, sr prog consult, Prog & Admin Consult, pres & chief exec officer; Butler Consult, pres & chief exec officer, 2006-. **Orgs:** Vice chmn, adv comt, Urban Womens Shelter, 1986-88; Nat Asn Social Workers; Nat Black Child Develop Inst, 1986-; Black Agency Execs, 1992-2009; bd dir, Coun Family & Child Caring Agencies; bd pres, Harlem Community Inc. **Business Addr:** President, Chief Executive Officer, Butler Consulting, PO Box 49713, Colorado Springs, CO 80949.

**BUTLER, MICHAEL E. (ME BUTLER)**
Editor. **Personal:** Born Jul 14, 1950, New York, NY; son of Bernard E Jr and Myrtle Martin; married Eileen Payne. **Educ:** Pace Univ, NY, BBA, 1972; Univ Calif, Berkeley, MPH, 1974. **Career:** NY City Health & Hosps Corp, asso exec dir, 1975-80; NYS Comt Health Educ & Illness Prvention, exec dir, 1980-81; Comt Family Planning Coun, exec dir, 1981-82; NY State Div Youth, regional dir, NY City Health & Hosps Corp, asso exec dir, 1975-80; NYS Comt Health Educ & Illness Prev, exec dir, 1980-81; Comt Family Planning Coun, exec dir, 1981-82; NY State Div Youth, regional dir, NYC; Exec Health Group, vpres; Lowe McAdams Healthcare, ed, 1991-97; Harrison & Star, mgr ed serv, 1997-2000; Falk Healthcare, dired serv, 2000-01; exec dir, Hutton Settlement; Butler Kane Inc, chief exec officer. **Orgs:** Am Health Asn, Blue Cross Asn, 1974-75; 100 Black Men, 1977-85; bd dir, Pace Univ, Alumni Asn, 1983-86; Pace Univ, Bd Educ Plcs Comn, 1984-86; Fairfield County Found. **Home Addr:** 624 E 20th St Apt 4C, New York, NY 10009-1421, **Home Phone:** (212)533-0197.

**BUTLER, MICHAEL KEITH**
Chief executive officer, surgeon, college teacher. **Personal:** Born Aug 29, 1955, Baton Rouge, LA; son of Felton Earl and Mildred Alexander; married Marian Thompson; children: Ebony Bolden & Yashica Bolden. **Educ:** Amherst Col, BA, 1976; Tulane Univ, Sch Med, MD, 1980, Sch Pub Health & Trop Med, MHA, 1990. **Career:** S La Med Assocs, gen surgeon, 1986-95, chief exec officer; Leonard J Chabert Med Ctr, chief surg pract, 1987-95, dir med staff qual mgt, 1988-95; LSU Sch Med, chief admin officer, 1995-96; Med Ctr LA, New Orleans, chief operating officer & med dir, 1995-97; La Health Care Authority, med dir, 1997-2001; LSU Health Care Servs Div, cheif med officer, 1999-2007, exec dir; LSU Hosp, La Healt Care Serv Div, interim chief exec officer & prof surg, 2007-09; Jackson Health Syst, exec vpres & chief med officer, 2010-. **Orgs:** Fel Am Col Surgeons, 1989; Am Col Physician Exec, 1990; Am Bd Quality Assurance Utilization Rev Physicians, 1994; Am Bd Med Mgt; Am Soc Gen Surgeons; La Surg Asn; Nat Med Asn; Nat Asn Health Serv Exec; Fel Am Col Physician Exec, 2008. **Home Addr:** 1990 Indust Blvd, Houma, LA 70364, **Home Phone:** (985)873-1265. **Business Addr:** Executive Vice President, Chief Medical Officer, Jackson Health System, 1611 NW 12th Ave, Miami, FL 33136-1096, **Business Phone:** (305)585-8007.

**BUTLER, MITCHELL LEON**
Executive, basketball player. **Personal:** Born Dec 15, 1970, Los Angeles, CA. **Educ:** Univ Calif, Los Angeles, commun, 1993. **Career:** Basketball player (retired), exec; Wash Bullets, shooting guard, 1993-96; Portland Trail Blazers, shooting guard, 1996-97, 2001-02; Cleveland Cavaliers, shooting guard, 1998-99; Zalgiris Kaunas, 1999-2000; San Diego Wildfire, 2000-01; Yakima Sun Kings, 2002-03; Wash Wizards, shooting guard, 2003-04; Denver Nuggets, guard, 2004-05; Lagardere Unlimited, NBA sport agt; Rival Sports Group, pres; sports agt, currently. **Orgs:** Mitchell Butler Found; co chair, Fannie Mae Found. **Honors/Awds:** McDonalds All American, 1989; CBA title, 2003. **Special Achievements:** Film appearances: Blue Chips, 1994; Rebound: The Legend of Earl 'The Goat' Manigault, 1996. **Business Addr:** President, Rival Sports Group, 9464 Wilshire Blvd, Beverly Hills, CA 90212, **Business Phone:** (800)549-9711.

**BUTLER, OLIVER RICHARD**
Executive, vice president (organization), executive director. **Personal:** Born Jul 3, 1941, New Orleans, LA; son of Richard M and Rose M Desvignes; married Naurine M Jackson; children: Janee, Eric & Shann. **Educ:** Xavier Univ La, BS, pharm, 1962; Univ Ill Polk, St Campus, Grad Course Org, chem, 1968; Univ New Orleans, grad bus courses, 1977. **Career:** Walgreen Co, Chicago, store mgr & pharmacist, 1962-69; Bruxelles Pharm, store owner, 1970-73; Ayerst Labs, sales positions, 1974-78, dist mgr, 1978-83, asst field sales mgr, 1983-84, dir sales opers, 1984-88; Wyeth-Ayerst Labs, sales admin, exec dir, 1988-91, asst vpres, 1991-. **Orgs:** New Orleans Comm/Human Rels, 1970; exec comt, LA High Blood Pressure Prog, 1978; guest lectr, Xavier Univ Med Tech Dept, 1978-81; adv bd, Food/Drug Admin, 1979; vpres, Ursuline Acad, 1979-80; treas, Acro I Gymnastic Club, 1981-82; pharm dean search comt, Xavier Univ Col & Pharm, 1981-82; adv comt, Xavier Univ Col Pharm 1982-; Apothecary bd visitor, Fla A&M Col Pharm, 1990-93; Ad Hoc Comt Sampling, pharmaceut Mfr Asn, 1990-93; Philadelphia Credit Alliance Drug Educ, 1992. **Home Addr:** 201 Hilloch Dr, West Chester, PA 19380. **Business Addr:** Assistant Vice President, Wyeth-Ayerst Labs, 555 E Lancaster Ave, Radnor, PA 19087, **Business Phone:** (610)971-5552.

**BUTLER, PATRICK HAMPTON**
Lawyer. **Personal:** Born Jul 24, 1933, Gonzales, TX; married Barbara; children: Daphne & Ann Marie. **Educ:** Colo Col, BA, 1956; Univ Colo Sch Law, JD, 1961. **Career:** Fed Trade & Comn, 1961-62; US Dept Justice, trial atty, 1962-65; US Dept Labor, spec asst, 1965-66; Ind Univ, asst prof, law, 1966-68; Eli Lilly & Co, asst coun; Dist Judge. **Orgs:** Bd govs, Indianapolis Bar Asn, 1972-74. **Home Addr:** 858 W 56th St, Indianapolis, IN 46228, **Home Phone:** (317)276-3487.

**BUTLER, PINKNEY L.**
Government official, city manager, founder (originator). **Personal:** Born May 3, 1948, Greensboro, NC; son of James and Louise Alexander Thompson; married Mary Green; children: Monecia, Patrick & Prentice. **Educ:** Southwestern Christian, Terrell, AA, 1969; Pepperdine Univ, Los Angeles, BA, 1971; Corpus Christi State Univ, MA, 1980. **Career:** Government official (retired), founder; City Victoria, Tex, exec dir & dep community affairs, 1974-77; Nueces County Adult Probation, Corpus Christi, Tex, adult probation officer, 1977-78; City Corpus Christi, Tex, admin asst, 1978-83; City Tyler, Tex, asst city mgr, 1983-97, city mgr, 1997; Better World Sounds, founder, 1992-. **Orgs:** Officer, E Tex City Mgr Asn, 1983-; Int City Mgr Asn, 1983-; Nat Forum Black Pub Admin, 1986; comt person, Tex City Mgr Asn, 1987-. **Home Addr:** 6704 Fleta Ct, Tyler, TX 75703-4606, **Home Phone:** (903)581-7109. **Business Addr:** Founder, Principal, Better World Sounds, 6704 Fleta Ct, Tyler, TX 75711, **Business Phone:** (903)372-1415.

**BUTLER, ESQ. REX LAMONT**
Lawyer. **Personal:** Born Mar 24, 1951, New Brunswick, NJ. **Educ:** Fla Jr Col, AA, 1975; Univ N Fla, BA, jour, 1977; Howard Univ Sch Law, Wash, DC, JD, 1983. **Career:** Howard Univ Sch Law, teaching asst, 1981-83; Md-Nat Capital Pk & Planning Comn, law clerk, 1982-83; M Ashley Dickerson Inc, assoc, 1983; State Alaska, Atty Gen's Off, legis asst, 1984, asst atty gen, 1984-85; Anchorage Community Col, adj prof, 1985; Rex Lamont Butler & Assocs Inc, atty, 1985-; Univ Alaska Anchorage, adj prof, 1990-2006, atty & counr law; Juno, alaska personal injury lawyer, car accident lawyer; Justice Ctr, atty & counr law, adj prof; Rex Lamont Butler & Assocs Inc PC, pres, chair, owner; Rights Advocacy Proj Inc, litigation atty, atty & counr law. **Orgs:** Bd Mem, Anchorage Bar Asn, 1983-; Alaska Acad Trial Lawyers, 1983-; Jesse Jackson Pres Comt, 1984; Asn Trial Lawyers Am, 1984-; life mem, Omega Psi Phi, 1985-; Am Bar Asn, 1985-; Fed Bar Asn, 1985-86; Anchorage Tel Utility Comn, 1985-86; Akeela House Bd Dirs, 1985-; Nat Bar Asn, 1986-; Ctr Drug Probs, 1986-88; Nat Asn Criminal Defense Lawyers, 1986-; Mt. KcKinley Lion's Int, 1989-; Eagle River Missionary Baptist Church, 1997-; life mem, Nat Asn Advan Colored People, trustee bd, 1990-, Alaska Chap, dir; Phi Alpha Delta; Phi Theta Kappa; bd mem, Rav Inc; pres & chmn, Univ Alaska Anchorage; Alaska Bar Asn; Mayors Anti-Gang & Youth Violence Policy Team; dir, Brotherhood Inc. **Honors/Awds:** Who's Who Among Students in American Cols and Universities, 1978; Outstanding Young Men of America, 1984; Featured in Black Enterprise Mag, 1984; Certificate of Appreciation, Anchorage Equal Rights Comn, 1987; Public Service Award, Major Tony Knowles, 1987; Martin Luther King, Jr.Community Service Award, 1987; Peer selected, Best Lawyers in America, 2007. **Business Addr:** Attorney, Rex Lamont Butler & Associates Inc, 745 W 4th Ave Suite 300, Anchorage, AK 99501-2136, **Business Phone:** (907)272-1497.

**BUTLER, ROSALIND MARIE**
School administrator. **Personal:** Born Feb 19, 1955, Detroit, MI; daughter of Booker Dennis and Marion Riddick; married Charles W; children: Keith M Curry. **Educ:** Eastern Mich Univ, BS, 1976; Wayne State Univ, MEd, 1993. **Career:** Detroit Pub Schs, teacher, 1976-86, Title 1 Reading Support, 1986-97, staff coordr, 1997, ast prin; Rose Elem Sch, prin, currently. **Orgs:** Asn Supv & Curric Develop; Int Reading Asn; Metrop Reading Asn; Black Female Adminr Network, 1997; Detroit Orgn Sch Adminr & Supv. **Home Addr:** 3517 Iroquois St, Detroit, MI 48214-1886, **Home Phone:** (313)925-0120. **Business Addr:** Principal, Detroit Public School, 5830 Field St, Detroit, MI 48213, **Business Phone:** (313)245-3673.

**BUTLER, ROY**
Engineer, manager. **Personal:** Born Jun 24, 1949, Tyler, TX; son of Roy and Gertha McClendon; children: Stephen & Shannon. **Educ:** Univ Colo, Boulder, Colo, BSCE, 1975. **Career:** Western Slope Gas Co, Denver, Colo, eng tech, 1970-74, spec proj engr, 1974-76; Sun Pipe Line Co, Tulsa, Okla, sr pipeline engr, 1976-78, Seminole, Okla, mgr field eng, 1978-80, gen foreman maintenance & opers, 1980-83, Drumright, Okla, gen foreman maintenance & opers, 1980-83, Tulsa, Okla, mgr bus opers, 1987-. **Home Addr:** 1909 N 24th W Ave, Tulsa, OK 74127-2252, **Home Phone:** (918)582-2846. **Business Addr:** Manager, Sun Pipe Line Co, Rm 1119 907 S Detroit St, Tulsa, OK 74120, **Business Phone:** (918)586-6943.

**BUTLER, TONIA PAULETTE**
Educator, nurse. **Personal:** Born Jun 5, 1970, Florence, AL; daughter of Paul Frank Hamilton and Madgie Lee Hill; married James Spencer; children: Kesley & Kayla. **Educ:** Northwest Shoals Community Col, LPN, 1991, AAS, 1993, ADN, 1995; Univ N Ala, BSN, 1995; Univ Ala, MSN, nursing admin, 1998, post MSN nurse practr, 1999. **Career:** Glenwood Nursing Home, 1992-97; EMC Hosp, intensive care unit, regist nurse, 1997-98; Sunrise Muscle Shoals, asst dir nursing, 1998, dir nursing, 1998-99; Huntsville Hosp, regist nurse, critical care, 1999-2000, nurse practr; Calhoun Community Col, nursing instr, 2000-. **Home Addr:** 507 Springwood Ct, Florence, AL 35634, **Home Phone:** (256)757-5558. **Business Addr:** Nursing Instructor, Calhoun Community College, PO Box 2216, Decatur, AL 35609, **Business Phone:** (256)306-2500.

**BUTLER-BUSH, TONIA**
Government official. **Career:** White House, Off Commun, Stud Correspondence, dep dir, staff asst dir. **Business Addr:** Staff Assistant Director, The White House, 1600 Pa Ave NW, Washington, DC 20500, **Business Phone:** (202)456-1111.

**BUTLER-SMITH, LYNN. See WHITFIELD, LYNN C.**

**BUTTERFIELD, GEORGE KENNETH, JR.**
Judge. **Personal:** Born Apr 27, 1947, Wilson, NC; son of George and Addie Lourine; married Jean Farmer; children: Valeisha, Tunya & Lenai. **Educ:** NC Cent Univ, BA, 1971; NC Cent Univ, polit sci & sociol, Sch Law, JD, 1974. **Career:** Lawyer; Nc, rep; Nc Resident Super Ct, judge, 1989-2001; Nc state supreme ct, justice, 2001-02; Nc spec super ct, judge, 2002-04; Nc's 1st Cong Dist, U.S house rep, 2004-. **Orgs:** Energy & Com Comt, Subcomt Environ & Econ, 2011-12; life mem, Jackson Chapel First Missionary Baptist Church; dem, One Hundred Eighth Cong; Comt Energy & Com, 2013-14; Subcomt on Health, 2015-16; Cong Motorcycle Safety Caucus; Int Conserv Caucus; Cong Black Caucus; Subcomt Com, Mfg &Trade; House Armed Serv Comt; House Agr Comt; House Dem Steering and Policy Comt; Affordable Health Care Act. **Home Addr:** 5314 Ward Blvd, Wilson, NC 27893-4368. **Business Addr:** Congressman, 1 District of North Carolina, 216 NE Nash St Suite A, Wilson, NC 27893, **Business Phone:** (252)237-9816.

**BUTTERFIELD, ESQ. TORRIS JERREL**
Lawyer. **Personal:** Born Nov 14, 1971, Miami, FL; son of Thomas and Margaret Cason; married Kimley; children: Nadia & Jared. **Educ:** Ft Valley State Col, BA, Eng, 1993; Mercer Univ, Walter F George Sch Law, JD, 1997. **Career:** Fulton County Pub Defender's Off, sr staff atty, 1997-2004; Torris J Butterfield & Assoc PC, pres, chief exec officer, owner, currently; TJB Recovery Syst LLC, pres & chief exec officer, currently. **Orgs:** Ga Asn Criminal Defense Lawyers, 1997-; juv law comt, 1999-, criminal law comt, 2000-, mem, State Bar Ga; Gerry Spence Trial Lawyers Col; Ga Supreme Ct; Ct Appeals State Ga; Ga Super Ct; Am Bar Asn; Nat Asn Criminal Defense Lawyers; US Dist Ct Northern Dist Ga; US Dist Ct Mid Dist Ga; US Ct Appeals Eleventh Circuit; life mem, Alpha Phi Alpha Fraternity Inc. **Honors/Awds:** Blue Tip All-American Scholar Award, 1992; Young Positive Men, Certificate of Appreciation, 2001; Rising Star, Super Lawyers Mag. **Home Addr:** 1341 Pebble Beach Lane, Hampton, GA 30228-6146, **Home Phone:** (770)210-4861. **Business Addr:** President, Chief Executive Officer, Torris J Butterfield and Associates PC, Hurt Bldg 50 Hurt Plz SE Suite 1120, Atlanta, GA 30303, **Business Phone:** (404)522-5056.

**BUTTS, CALVIN OTIS, III**
Clergy, educator. **Personal:** Born Jul 19, 1949, Bridgeport, CT; married Patricia; children: 3. **Educ:** Morehouse Col, BA, philos, 1971; Union Theol Sem, MDiv, 1975; Drew Theol Sch, DMin, church & pub policy, 1982. **Career:** City Col New York, adj prof African Studies dept; Fordham Univ, Black Church Hist; African Studies Dept NY City Col, adj prof; Abyssinian Baptist Church, asst minister, pastor, 1972-77, exec minister, 1977-89, head pastor, 1989-; NY Col, Old Westbury, pres, 1999-. **Orgs:** Pres, Coun Churches City NY; chmn, founder, Abyssinian Develop Corp, 1989; vice chmn bd dir, United Way New York, 1999; mem bd dir, The September 11th Fund; chmn, Nat Affil Develop Initiative Nat Black Leadership Comn AIDS, 1999; bd trustee, N Gen Hosp Harlem; mem bd, Am Baptist Col, Nashville, TN; pres, Africare; chmn bd, The Harlem YMCA; Kappa Alpha Psi Fraternity; Prince Hall Masons; New York Bd Educ; Nat Black Leadership Comn; bd, New York Blood Ctr; Kappa Alpha Psi Fraternity; bd dir, United Way; chmn, N Gen Hosp; Presidential Adv Coun HIV/AID; New Visions Pub Schs. **Honors/Awds:** Shirley Chisholm Community Service Award; The Morehouse College Candle Award; The William M Moss Distinguished Brotherhood Award; Louise Fisher Morris Humanitarian Award; Man of the Year, Morehouse Col Alumni Asn; Louise Fisher Morris Humanitarian Award, Utility Club New York; Community Against Social Injustice Award, Am Corp; Candle Award, Morehouse Col; William M Moss Distinguished Brotherhood Award; hon degree, The City Col New York; hon degree, Tuskegee Univ, Alabama; hon degree, Claflin Col, Orangeburg, SC; hon degree, Dillard Univ, New Orleans; hon degree, Muhlenberg Col, Allentown, PA; hon degree, Trinity Col, Hartford, Conn; Recognized as Living Treasure, New York Chamber Com & Indust. **Home Addr:** 2331 100th St, East Elmhurst, NY 11369-1319, **Home Phone:** (718)426-5569. **Business Addr:** Pastor, The Abyssinian Baptist Church, 132 Odell Clark Pl, New York, NY 10030, **Business Phone:** (212)862-7474.

**BUTTS, CARLYLE A.**
Executive. **Personal:** Born Nov 10, 1935, Richmond, VA; son of Thomas A and Coral P; married Omeria A Roberts; children: Brian E & Gregory. **Educ:** Howard Univ, BSEE, 1963; USC, MBA, 1969; Univ Calif, Los Angeles, Exec Mgt Prog, 1988. **Career:** Executive (retired); Howard Univ, electronic lab instr asst, 1958-63; Hughes Aircraft Co, electronics test engr, 1963-64, var positions mat dept, 1964-69, head prod control, 1969-70, head facil planning, 1972-76, proj mgr, 1970-72, proj mgr, 1977, dept mgr radar systs group, 1978, prod opers mgr, 1987, asst div mgr, ground systs group, 1988-90, qual dir, electro-optical & data systs group, 1990-92, aerospace & defense sector, 1992-94, qual dir, staff vp qual, 1994-96; Ladera Career Paths, chmn & bd dir, 1993-97. **Orgs:** Am Mkg Asn; Nat Contracts Mgt Asn; Intercollegiate Coun Black Col; Bus Mgt Consult; Hughes Mgt Club; pres, Howard Univ Alumni Club So CA, 1971-73, 1980; past pres, bd trustees, Crenshaw Ch Relig Sci, 1974-77; den leader Webelos Pack 162c Holman Meth Chl, 1978; Basileus Omega Psi Phi Fraternity, LA chap, 1993-94, 1996-98; Founding mem, Mended Hearts Inc; vpres, 1998-2000, Pres, bd dir, Am Diabetes Asn, afa Chap Los Angeles, Calif. **Honors/Awds:** Howard Hughes Fellowship, 1967; Los Angeles City Resolution for Service to Youth Community, 1983; Omega Man of the Year, Lambda Omicron, 1992, 1994, 1998; Omega Psi Phi Fraternity; BLK Engineer of the Year, Hughes Aircraft Co, 1989; Distinguished Alumni, Mentor Award Recipient, Howard Univ, 1998; Alumni Asn Southern CA, 1998. **Home Addr:** 4906 Maymont Dr, Los Angeles, CA 90043-2032, **Home Phone:** (323)295-2758.

**BUTTS, DR. HUGH FLORENZ**
Psychiatrist, psychoanalyst, physician. **Personal:** Born Dec 2, 1926, New York, NY; son of Lucius Cornelius and Edith Eliza Higgins; married June Dobbs; children: Lucia Irene, Florence & Eric Hugh; married Clementine; children: Sydney Clementine, Samantha Florenz & Heather Marguerita. **Educ:** City Col NY, BS, 1949; Meharry Med Col, MD, 1953. **Career:** Morrisania City Hosp, intern, 1955; Bronx VA Hosp, resident, 1958; St Lukes Hosp, staff physician, 1958-74; Hillcrest Ctr C, staff psych, 1959-61; pvt prac, psych, 1959-74; Wiltwyck Sch Boys, clin dir, 1961-63, chief, in-patient psych serv, 1962-69; Gracie Sq Hosp, staff physician, 1961-66; Montefiore Hosp, resident, staff physician, 1961-65; Columbia Univ Psychoanal Clin, Cert Psychoanal Med, 1962; Beth-Israel Hosp, staff physician, 1962-63; Harlem Hosp Ctr, assoc prof & dir psych, 1962-69; pvt prac, psycho analyst, 1962-74; Vanderbilt Clin Presby Hosp, staff physician, 1963-65; New York Dept Voc Rehab, staff physician, 1963-69; Columbia Univ Col Phys & Surgeons, asst clin prof psych, 1967-74; NY St Dept Ment Hyg, staff physician, 1974-76; Bronx State Hosp, dir, staff physician, 1974-79; Albert Einstein Col Med, prof psychiat, 1974-81; New Hope Guild, Brooklyn NY, psychiat consult, 1980-96; Lit Mind Asn, pres, 1986-; Clementine Publ Co, Leeds NY, pres & founder, 1989-; Episcopal Diocese NY, psychiat consult, 1989-; Columbia Law Sch-Fair Housing Clin, psychiat consult, 1993; New York Col Podiatric Med, Dept Primary Podiatric Med Sci, adj prof, 1995; Open Housing Ctr, psychiat consult, 1996-; St. Vincent's Ment Health Serv, psychiat, 1996-. **Orgs:** Vet Affairs Med Ctr, resident Psychiat; Consult, Neuro psychiat Ctr, NY, 1957; psych consult, Jewish Bd Guardians, 1962; NY Psych Inst, 1962-74; supvr training analyst, Columbia Univ Psychoanal Clin Training & Res, 1968-81; Asn Psychoanal Med, 1968-71; Am Psych Asn, 1970, Am Ortho Psychiat Asn, 1970-73; psych consult, Fieldston-Ethical Cult Sch, 1970-74; US Fed Ct, 1970-75; staff psych, Manida Juv Detention Ctr, 1972-74; supvr psych, Bronx State Hosp, 1973-79; NY City Police Dept Psychol Clin, 1974-76; psych consult, Allegheny City Ment Health & Ment Retardation Asn, 1974-75; traininganaly, supvr analyst Post-Grad Ctr Ment Health, 1975-; actg dir residence training, Bronx State Hosp, 1977-79; Nat Med Asn, AMA, NY Med Soc, Alumni Asn Psychoan Clin Training & Res; fel NY Acad; Med Adv Bd; chmn, Med Herald, 1990-; distinguished life fel Am Psychiat Asn. **Honors/Awds:** Spec Merit Award, Asn Psychoanalytic Med, 1967; Nat Med Asn Award, 2005; Annual Dr Eugene F Williams Sr Scholar of Distinction Award, Nat Med Asn, 2006. **Special Achievements:** New York State Department of Mental Hygiene, first deputy commissioner, 1975. **Home Addr:** 350 Central Pk W Apt 131-A, New York, NY 10025-0019, **Home Phone:** (212)864-6191. **Business Addr:** Adjunct Professor, New York College of Podiatric Medicine, 1800 Pk Ave, New York, NY 10035, **Business Phone:** (212)410-8000.

**BUTTS, JANIE PRESSLEY**
Educator. **Personal:** Born Aug 25, 1936, Nesmith, SC; daughter of Ollie Epps and Lillie D; married Thomas A Jr; children: Derrick, Steven & Karlton. **Educ:** S Calif State Col, BBA, 1958; Eastern Conn State Col, elem cert, 1973. **Career:** Educator (retired); Groton Bd Educ, sixth grade teacher, 1968-69; E Lyme Bd Educ, Flanders Elem Sch, fifth grade teacher, 1969-90; E Lyme Libr Found. **Orgs:** Nat Edu Asn; NCW Inc; NCP; Shiloh Baptist Church; Conn Coop Mentor Teaching Prog. **Home Addr:** 15 Parker Dr, East Lyme, CT 06333, **Home Phone:** (860)739-9272.

**BUTTS, MARION STEVENSON, JR.**
Football player. **Personal:** Born Aug 1, 1966, Sylvester, GA. **Educ:** Northeastern Okla A&M Univ; Fla State Univ. **Career:** Football player (retired); San Diego Chargers, running back, 1989-93; New Eng Patriots, running back, 1994; Houston Oilers, running back, 1995. **Honors/Awds:** Pro Bowl, 1990, 1991.

**BUTTS, DR. SAMANTHA F.**
Educator, physician. **Educ:** Harvard Univ, Cambridge, MA, BA, hist & sci-cum laude, 1994; Harvard Univ Sch Med, MD, Boston, MA, 1998; Univ Pa Sch Med, Philadelphia PA, MSCE, 2006. **Career:** Univ Pa Health Syst, Hosp Univ Pa, intern, resident, fel, Dept Obstet & Gynec, asst prof obstet & gynec, currently, Ctr Res on Reproduction & Women's Health, fac, currently. **Orgs:** Health Disparities Spec Interest Group, 2009-; Environ & Reproduction Spec Interest Group, 2010-; Poster Prize Award Comt Am Soc Reproductive Med, 2011, 2013; Nutrit Spec Interest Group, 2012-; Soc Assisted Reproductive Technologies-Clin Outcomes Reporting Syst Res Comt, 2012-; advocacy & pub outreach core comt, Endocrine Soc, 2014-; fel & chair, Gynec Pract Subcomt Reproductive Endocrinol, Am Col Obstetricians & Gynecologists, 2014-; Am Soc Reproductive Med Pract Comt, 2014-; Pac Coast Reproductive Soc; Soc Reproductive Endocrinol & Infertility. **Home Addr:** 225 S 18th St Apt 14 21, Philadelphia, PA 19103, **Home Phone:** (215)875-9659. **Business Addr:** Assistant Professor, University of Pennsylvania Health System, 3701 Market St 8th Fl, Philadelphia, PA 19104, **Business Phone:** (215)662-2975.

**BYARS, KEITH ALLAN**
Football coach, football player, television sportscaster. **Personal:** Born Oct 14, 1963, Dayton, OH; married Margaret Bell; children: Taylor Renae & Keith Allan II. **Educ:** Ohio State Univ, attended 1985. **Career:** Football player (retired), coach, TV sportscaster; Philadelphia Eagles, runningback, 1986-90, Fullback, 1991, Fullback & Tight end, 1992; Miami Dolphins, Fullback, 1993-96; New Eng Patriots, Fullback, 1996-97; New YorkJets, Fullback, 1998; Ohio State Univ, pres & post-game radio analyst; Yankees Entertainment & Sports Network LLC, "New York Football Weekly" & "This Week in Football", TV analyst, currently; Boca Raton High Sch, coach, 2009-11. **Orgs:** Founder, Keith Byars PRO Found. **Honors/Awds:** Humanitarian of the Year, Philadelphia Sports Writers Asn, 1991; Community Service Award, Big Bros Big Sisters Philadelphia, 1991; Pro Bowl, 1993. **Business Addr:** TV Analyst, Yankees Entertainment & Sports Network LLC, The Chrysler Bldg, New York, NY 10174-3699, **Business Phone:** (646)487-3600.

**BYARS, DR. LAURETTA F.**
College administrator. **Personal:** Born Jan 1, 1949. **Educ:** Morehead State Univ, BA; Univ Ky, MSW, social work, 1972, EdD, educ, 1982. **Career:** Univ Ky, vice chancellor minority affairs, dir, undergraduate program, asst dean, stud affairs; Social Servs Coun, chair; Prairie View A&M Univ, vpres, stud affairs & instnl rels, currently, asst dean stud affairs, currently. **Orgs:** Bd, KY Hist Soc; Delta sigma Theta sorority. **Business Addr:** Vice President for Institutional Relations & Public Services, Prairie View A&M University, Al Thomas Suite 102, Prairie View, TX 77446-0519, **Business Phone:** (936)261-2130.

**BYEARS, LATASHA NASHAY**
Basketball player. **Personal:** Born Aug 12, 1973, Memphis, TN. **Educ:** DePaul Univ, phys educ, attended 1996. **Career:** Basketball player (retired); Sacramento Monarchs, guard, 1997-2000; Los Angeles Sparks, forward, 2001-03; Wash Mystics, 2006; CSKA Sofia, Bulgareia, 2006; Houston Comets, guard forward, 2007, free agt, 2007-08. **Orgs:** Meals on Wheels. **Business Addr:** Professional Basketball Player, Houston Comets, 1730 Jefferson St Suite 127, Houston, TX 77003, **Business Phone:** (713)627-9622.

**BYERS, SUSAN M. (SUE BYERS)**
Executive director. **Educ:** Univ Wash, sociol, 1983; Evergreen State Col, BA, 1987; Pac Oaks Col, MA, 1996. **Career:** Seattle Pub Sch, dir spec proj, 1972-2004; Mid Col, co founder, 1990; Pac Oaks Col, adj fac, 1998-2002; IslandWood, sr proj officer, co-dir, 2014-. **Orgs:** Steering comt; Eliminating Achievement Gap Action Comt; chief acad officer, Col Success Found, 2004-14; bd dir, Chices Educ Group, currently. **Business Addr:** Board of Director, CHOICES Education Group, 1818 Westlake Ave N Suite 317, Seattle, WA 98109, **Business Phone:** (206)246-4237.

**BYNAM, SAWYER LEE, III**
Construction worker, founder (originator). **Personal:** Born Sep 15, 1933, Houston, TX; married Betty Ann; children: Keith Wayne. **Educ:** Tex Southern Univ, BS, cert, construct planning & estimating. **Career:** Gen & Sub-Contractors Asn, contract develop; Africa AIDS Fund, co-founder & pres. **Business Addr:** Co-Founder, President, Africa AIDS Fund, 457 Arnold Str NE, Atlanta, GA 30308, **Business Phone:** (404)659-9900.

**BYNER, EARNEST ALEXANDER**
Football coach, football player. **Personal:** Born Sep 15, 1962, Milledgeville, GA; married Tina M; children: Semeria S, Adrian Monique, Brandi S & Kyara. **Educ:** E Carolina Univ, phys educ. **Career:** Football player (reitred), coach; Cleveland Browns, running back & kick returner, 1984-88, 1994-95; Wash Redskins, fullback & running back, 1989-93, coach, 2004-07; Baltimore Ravens, running back, 1996-97, dir player develop, 1998-2003; Tenn Titans, running backs coach, 2008-09; Jacksonville Jaguars, running back coach, 2010-11; Tampa Bay Buccaneers, 2012-13. **Orgs:** Kappa Alpha Psi Fraternity. **Honors/Awds:** AFC Championship Game, 1986 & 1987; Pro Bowl, 1990 & 1991; Ed Block Courage Award, 1986; NFL Extra Effort Award, 1986; NFL PA Unsung Hero Award, 1997; True Value NFL Man of the Year Award, 1997; East Carolina Hall of Fame, 1998; 70 Greatest Redskins. **Special Achievements:** Film: Masters of the Gridiron, 1985. **Home Addr:** 1016 Sattui Ct, Franklin, TN 37064-7909, **Home Phone:** (615)595-6133. **Business Addr:** Runningbacks Coach, Tennessee Titans, 460 Great Circle Rd, Nashville, TN 37228, **Business Phone:** (615)565-4000.

**BYNES, DR. FRANK HOWARD, JR.**
Physician. **Personal:** Born Dec 3, 1950, Savannah, GA; son of Frank and Frenchye Mason; married Janice Ann Ratta; children: Patricia F & Frenchye D. **Educ:** Savanna St Col, BS, 1972; Meharry Med Col, MD, 1977. **Career:** New York Univ Downtown Hosp, residency, internal med, 1983-86; Staten Island Univ Hosp, residency, 1978-81; USAF, internist, 1986-87; self-employed, internist, 1987-; Americall Corp Savannah Inc, chief exec officer. **Orgs:** Alpha Phi Alpha Fraternity, 1969-; Am Med Asn, 1973-; New York Acad Scis, 1983-; AAAS, 1984-; Am Col Physicians, 1985-; Air Force Asn, 1987-; Asn Mil Surgeons US, 1987-; Mem chmn, Hilton Head Island Kennel Club. **Business Addr:** Physician, 2 Roberts St, Savannah, GA 31408, **Business Phone:** (912)527-1100.

**BYNES, GLENN KENNETH**
Auditor. **Personal:** Born Jan 17, 1946, Orlando, FL; son of Arthur; married Norma; children: Glenn K III & Ingrid N. **Educ:** Hampton Jr Col, AS, 1966; Tenn State Univ, BS, 1971. **Career:** McDonnell Douglas, aircraft maintenance engr, 1971-73; EI DuPontde Nemours, prod supvr, 1973-74; Martin Marietta Info group, mr, auditor operations, 1974-. **Orgs:** Registr, Accreditation Bd; regist lead auditor, 1993-. **Home Addr:** PO Box 770502, Orlando, FL 32877. **Business Addr:** Manager, Martin Marietta Information Group, 12506 Lake Underhill Rd, Orlando, FL 32825, **Business Phone:** (407)826-1707.

**BYNOE, DR. PETER CHARLES BERNARD**
Executive. **Personal:** Born Mar 20, 1951, Boston, MA; son of Victor C and Ethel M Stewart; married Linda Walker. **Educ:** Harvard Col, Cambridge, MA, BA, 1972; Harvard Bus Sch, Boston, MA, MBA, finance & mkt, 1976; Harvard Law Sch, Cambridge, MA, JD, 1976. **Career:** Citibank, exec intern, 1976-77; James H Lowry & Assocs, exec vpres, 1977-82; Telemat Ltd, chmn, 1982-; Ill Sports Facil Authority, exec dir, 1988-92; Denver Nuggets, gen partner, 1989-92; DLA Piper Rudnick Gray Cary US LLP, sr coun, partner, 1995-; Uniroyal Technol Corp, dir; Jacor Commun, dir; J&G Industs, dir; Huffman-Koos Inc, dir; River Valley Savings Bank, dir; Equity Group Investments, managing dir. **Orgs:** Chmn, Chicago Landmarks Comn, 1986-97; dir, chmn, life trustee, Goodman Theatre, 1987-; trustee, Rush Univ Med Ctr; dir, Uniroyal Technol Corp; overseer, Harvard Univ, 1992-2001; dir, Ill Sports Facil Authority, 1993-2002; dir, Dine Rewards Network Inc; pres, United Ctr Community Econ Develop Fund; consult, Atlanta Comt Organize Olympic Games, 1996; dir, Covanta Holding Corp, 2004-; trustee & dir, Ctr Prev, Care & Res Infectious Dis CORE; consult, Atlanta Fulton County Recreation Authority; Ill State Bar Asn; Chicago Bar Asn; Ill Sports Facil Authority; Chicago Art Inst Alliance; Harvard Club Chicago; dir, Frontier Commun, 2007-; dir, Citizens Commun, 2007; dir, Real Indust Inc; dir, Covanta Energy Corp. **Business Addr:** Senior Counsel, Partner, DLA Piper US LLP, 203 N LaSalle St Suite 1900, Chicago, IL 60601-1293, **Business Phone:** (312)368-4090.

**BYNUM, DR. JUANITA, II (JUANITA BYNUM WEEKS)**
Writer, public speaker. **Personal:** Born Jan 16, 1959, Chicago, IL; married Bishop Thomas Weeks III. **Educ:** PhD, theol. **Career:** Juanita Bynum Ministries, founder & pres, currently; Juanita Bynum enterprises, founder & pres, chief exec officer, currently; Trinity Broadcasting Network, Worldwide Flagship Prog, host; Recorded videos include: No More Sheets; Are You Planted for the Kingdom; I'm Too Fat For the Yoke; Limp of the Lord; Now That's Dominion; The Refiner's Fire; My Delivery; The Spirit of Isaac; The Umpire of my Soul; Tied to the Altar; Books: No More Sheets; Don't Get off the Train; Author: The Threshing Floor; The Matters of the Heart; Albums: Morning Glory, 1999; Morning Glory, Volume 2: Behind The Veil, 2000; A Piece of My Passion, 2005; Gospel Goes Classical, 2006; Christmas at Home with Juanita, 2006; Pour My Love On You, 2008; More Passion, 2010; The Diary of Juanita Bynum, 2010. **Home Addr:** 15 Astor Ct, Hempstead, NY 11550, **Home Phone:** (912)287-0032. **Business Addr:** President, Founder, Juanita Bynum Ministries, 415 N Crawford St, Waycross, GA 31503, **Business Phone:** (912)287-0032.

**BYNUM, KENNETH BERNARD (KENNY BYNUM)**
Football player. **Personal:** Born May 29, 1974, Gainesville, FL. **Educ:** SC State Univ, bus admin. **Career:** Football player (retired); San Diego Chargers, kick returner, 1997-98, running back, 1999, 2000. **Home Addr:** 613 SW 2nd Terr, Gainesville, FL 32601.

**BYNUM, DR. RALEIGH WESLEY, II**
Optometrist. **Personal:** Born May 27, 1936, Jacksonville, FL; son of John T and Corene Brown; married Thelmetia Argrett; children: Raleigh, Monjya & Zerrick. **Educ:** Fla A&M Univ, attended 1956; Ill Col Optom, BS & OD, 1960; Univ SC, MPH, 1975; Command & Gen Staff Col AUS, cert, 1976. **Career:** Am Opt Asn Retirement Fund, trustee, var comt, 1978; Nat Optom Asn, pres, bd chmn, 1979; Am Acad Optom, vpres, NC chap, 1980-85; Nat Optom Found, chmn bd, 1980-88; RMZ assoc, pres; pvt ratice, optometrist, currently. **Orgs:** Regional dir, NOA Minority Recruitment Proj, 1971-77; pres & bd dir, Charlotte Bethlehem Ctr, 1973; Nat HBP Coord Comt, 1976-84; gen partner, Westside Prof Assoc, 1972-; pilot-instr, Rated Single Engine Land Airplane, 1975-; vice chmn & bd dir, McCrorey Br YMCA, 1983-91; vice chmn & bd dir, Charlotte Mint Mus, 1983-87. **Honors/Awds:** Optometrist of the Year, Nat Opt Asn, 1980; Deacon, Friendship Baptist Church, 1978-; President Medal of Honor, Ill Col Optom, 1999. **Home Addr:** 8910 Frank Grier Rd, Charlotte, NC 28215-9426, **Home Phone:** (704)563-7404. **Business Addr:** Optometrist, Private Practice, 107 W Morehead, Charlotte, NC 28204, **Business Phone:** (704)375-3935.

**BYNUM, VALERIE COLLYMORE**
Musician. **Personal:** Born Mar 9, 1942, Bronx, NY; married Louis S Jr; children: Adam & Tanisha. **Educ:** Ithaca Col Sch Music, BS, 1963; Sch Arts, NY. **Career:** Radio City Music Hall Orchestra, New York, violinist; Freelance musician, 1965; Jr High Sch, teacher, 1965-67. **Orgs:** Radio City Music Hall Symphony, 1963-66; Symphony New World, 1965-72. **Home Addr:** 11 Trotting Dr, Chester, NY 10918-1137, **Home Phone:** (845)469-4507.

**BYRD, ALBERT ALEXANDER**
Educator. **Personal:** Born Nov 6, 1927, Baltimore, MD; married Alice Muriel Poe; children: Karen Leslie Forgy-Hicks. **Educ:** Howard Univ, BA, 1949; Temple Univ, MFA, 1959; Univ Nat Autonoma Mex, attended 1959; State Inst Arts Porto Romano, Florence, Italy, attended 1962. **Career:** Educator (retired); Baltimore Pub Sch Dist, art teacher, 1949-63; Sacramento City Col, Humanitites & Fine Arts, prof, 1963-91. **Orgs:** Am Fed Teachers; Fac, Asn Calif Community Col; Kappa Alpha Psi; Howard Univ Alumni Asn. **Home Addr:** 1165 Derick Way, Sacramento, CA 95822, **Home Phone:** (916)441-0563.

**BYRD, ALICE TURNER**
President (organization), administrator. **Career:** CIGNA Corp; Turning Training Inst, owner & pres, 2003-. **Business Addr:** Owner, President, Turning Training Institute, 11 Mountain Ave Suite 205, Bloomfield, CT 06002, **Business Phone:** (860)243-3900.

**BYRD, ARTHUR W., JR.**
Social worker. **Personal:** Born Dec 24, 1943, Washington, DC; son of Arthur W and Doris Littlejohn; married Inez Marie Coleman; children: Arthur III William, Ashley Wendall & Allyn Winthrop. **Educ:** Livingstone Col, BA, sociol, 1965; Univ NC, MSW, community orgn & advocacy, 1972; Univ Ky; Univ Chicago. **Career:** Univ VA, Clinch Valley Col, fac, 1972; Longwood Col, Farmville, VA, fac, 1972; Livingstone Col, Salisbury, 1974; Va Asn Community Serv Bd, community contracting adminr, currently; Va Community Col Syst, asst prof human serv, 1975-. **Orgs:** Nat Asn Advan Colored People, 1964; dir, Neighborhood Youth Sch & out Sch Progs, Salisbury, NC, 1968-70; NC Neighborhood Workers Asn, 1969; NASW, 1970; CSWE, 1970; dir, Outreach to Teenage Fathers, Durham, NC, 1970; comm contact Rep, Youth Serv Bur, Winston Salem, NC, 1971; Rowan Co, Civic League, 1973; S Asn Undergrad SW Educ, 1973; Salisbury & Statesville, NC; state dir, Res Facil Mently Retarded; Adj J Sargent, Reynolds Comm Col, 1975. **Honors/Awds:** Babcock Fel, 1970-72; Distinguished Serv Award, Salisbury Rowan Com Serv Coun; POP Award, Coop Sch Girls Durham, NC; estab Social Work Action Group, SWAG Livingstone Col, 1973-74. **Special Achievements:** Estab first Afro-Am Student Org Longwood Col, 1972-73. **Home Addr:** 6801 West Rd, Chesterfield, VA 23832-8346, **Home Phone:** (804)276-9183. **Business Addr:** Community Contracting Administrator, Virginia Association of Community Service Board, 10128 B W Broad St, Glen Allen, VA 23060, **Business Phone:** (804)786-7594.

**BYRD, BUTCH.** **See BYRD, GEORGE EDWARD, JR.**

**BYRD, CAMOLIA ALCORN**
Educator. **Personal:** Born Baton Rouge, LA; married Lionel Patrick; children: Cheryl P, Lionel P Jr, Judith I, Roderick J & Janell M. **Educ:** Southern Univ Baton Rouge, BA, 1944; Cent State Univ, MA, 1964. **Career:** Okla City Pub Schs, teacher, 1959-70, consult, 1970-76, asst coordr, 1976-80, coordr, 1980-86; I Can Learning Ctr Inc, dir, 1988-. **Orgs:** Assault on Illiteracy, NTU Art Asn, 1986; campaign mgr, Sen Vicki Lynn Miles La Grange, Okla City, 1986; Asn Supv & Curric Develop; Int Reading Asn & Okal Reading Asn; Teachers Eng Speaker Other Lang & Okla TESOL; Nat& Local Black Educrs Asn; Nat Coun Negro Women; Fed Col Womens Club; Phi Delta Kappa Inc; African Art Mus; Jack & Jill Inc; Okla E Side Cult Club; Alpha Kappa Alpha Sor. **Home Addr:** 4125 Woodnoll St, Oklahoma City, OK 73121, **Home Phone:** (405)424-7300. **Business Addr:** Director, I Can Learning Center Inc, 2613 NE 22nd St, Oklahoma City, OK 73111, **Business Phone:** (405)424-0651.

**BYRD, CAROLYN H.**
President (organization), founder (originator). **Personal:** Born Jan 1, 1949?. **Educ:** Fisk University (Nashville, TN), Bachelor's in Economics and Business Administration, 1970; The University of Chicago, Booth School of Business, Master's in Finance and Business Administration, 1972. **Career:** Citibank, Acct. Officer and Sr. Acct. Officer, 1972-77; Coca-Cola, various positions including Sr. Financial Analyst, Treasury Specialist, Mgr. of Corporate and U.S. Treasury Services, Asst. Treasurer, and Mgr. of Latin American Treasury Services, 1977-93, VP, 1993-97; The Coca-Cola Financial Corporation, President, 1997-00; GlobalTech Financial LLC, Chairman, CEO, and Founder, 2000-. **Orgs:** Popeyes Louisiana Kitchen, Director, Member of Audit Committee, Member of People Services Compensation Committee; St. Paul Companies, Inc., Board of Directors (former); Reliastar Financial, Board of Directors (former); ING Americas, Board of Directors (former); RARE Hospitality, Inc., Board of Directors (former); Fisk University, Board of Trustees, 1999-; Executive Leadership Foundation, Board of Directors, 1999-05; AFC Enterprises Inc., Director, 2001-; Travelers Property Casualty, 2001-04; Circuit City Stores, Inc., Board of Directors, 2001-09; The Travelers Companies Inc., Director, 2004-05; Federal Home Loan Mortgage Corporation, Board of Directors, 2008-; Regions Financial Corporation, Board of Directors, 2010-. **Honors/Awds:** Atlanta's Top 100 Women of Influence, Recipient; "Black Enterprise" Magazine, 21 Women of Achievement, 1991; 100 Black Men of Atlanta, Atlantan on the Move, Recipient, 1992; "Women Looking Ahead" Magazine, Woman of the Year, 1999; "Business-to-Business" Magazine, Diva, 2002; Governors Mentor Protege, Participant, 2004.

**BYRD, DONNA**
Publisher. **Personal:** Born Apr 26, 1970, Fort Lee, VA. **Educ:** Univ Virginia, BA, Am govt, 1992; Duke Univ, MBA, 1996; Univ Cape Town, grad bus studies, 1995. **Career:** Procter & Gamble, asst sales mgr, 1992-94; Coca-Cola, brand mgr, 1996-99; EzGov.com, vpres mkt, 1999-2000; Black Am Web, chief exec officer, 2001-03; Kickoff Mkt, co-founder & managing partner, 2003-08; Wash Post, publ TheRoot.Com, 2008-. **Orgs:** Member, Aspen Global Leadership Network. **Business Addr:** The Root, 1350 Connecticut Ave NW, Washington, DC 20036, **Business Phone:** (646)495-4018.

**BYRD, DORIS M.**
Police officer. **Educ:** Chicago State Univ. **Career:** Police officer, Detective (retired); Chicago Police Dept, 22nd Dist, patrol officer, sergeant, 1977-04. **Orgs:** Coalition Law Enforcement Officers, 1985-98; regional pres, Nat Black Police Asn, 1998-00; chmn, Nat Black Police Asn, 2000-02. **Honors/Awds:** Chicago Police Dept, Dept Commendation, 1980, Unit Meritorious Award, 1983; Community Serv, NBPA Midwest Region, 1997. **Home Addr:** 601 E 90th St, Chicago, IL 60619, **Home Phone:** (773)783-5475. **Business Addr:** Sergeant, Chicago Police Department, 1718 S State St, Chicago, IL 60616, **Business Phone:** (312)745-4290.

**BYRD, EDWIN R.**
Educator. **Personal:** Born Feb 23, 1920, Kansas City, KS; married Dorothy Wordlow; children: Terri E. **Educ:** Kans State Teachers Col, BS; Univ Kans, ME, 1950. **Career:** Educator (retired); Mo Sch Dist, 1946-81, from elem sch to jr high sch teacher, 1946-56, counr jr & sr high sch, 1956-60; Yates Elem Sch, prin, 1960-61; Dunbar Sch, prin, 1961-63; Richardson Sch, prin, 1963-68; Martin Luther King Jr High Sch, prin, 1968-75; Nowlin Jr High Sch, prin. **Orgs:** KC Sch Admin Assoc; NEA; Mo State Teachers Assoc; prin, Mo Assoc Sch; prin, Nat Assoc Sch Prin; Phi Delta Kappa; PTA; Am Legion 149; Nat Advan Asn Colored People; YMCA; Kiwanis Club; inst rep Boy Scouts; elder Swope Pkwy United Christian Ch; Alpha Phi Alpha; Res Acad KC, Selective Serv Bd; adv comn, Jr Red Cross; pres, Inter-City Kiwanis Club, 1983-84; Am Assoc Retired Persons. **Honors/Awds:** Service Award, YMCA, 1962; Service Award, ParentTeacher Asn, 1968; Athletic Service Award, 1973; Outstanding Sec Educator Am, Sigma Pi Phi, 1974; Kin Community Service Award, 1975; Outstanding Member Award, Beta Lambda Chap Alpha Phi Alpha, 1979; Super Quota Buster Award, YMCA, 1984. **Home Addr:** 2533 W Paseo Blvd, Kansas City, MO 64108-2960, **Home Phone:** (816)474-6241. **Business Addr:** MO.

**BYRD, GEORGE EDWARD, JR. (BUTCH BYRD)**
Loan officer, football player. **Personal:** Born Sep 20, 1941, Watervliet, NY; son of George Sr and Louise Collins; married Alice Hill; children: Sharon Collins, George III, Michael & Christopher. **Educ:** Boston Univ, BS, 1964; Univ Mich, exec mgt prog, 1980. **Career:** Buffalo Bills, right cornerback, punt returner, 1964-70; Denver Broncos, cornerback, 1970-72; Chrysler/Plymouth Corp, sales mgr, New Haven, CT, opers mgr, 1973-81; Polariod Corp, regional mkt mgr/regional oper mgr, 1981-86, mkt mgr, 1986-87, gen mgr; Primary Residential Mortgage Co, sr loan officer. **Honors/Awds:** Thomas Gastall Award, 1963; Am Football League All-Star, 1964, 1965, 1966, 1967, 1969; All-Pro, NFL, Buffalo Bills, 1965, 1966, 1968, 1969; Man of the Year, African Meeting Houses, 1989; Boston Univ Hall of Fame, 1980; Greater Buffalo Sports Hall of Fame, 2008; Kent Hull Hard Working Man Award, Hanes Supply Inc, 2010. **Home Addr:** 23 Wayside Rd, Westborough, MA 01581, **Home Phone:** (508)870-1807. **Business Addr:** Senior Loan Officer, Primary Residential Mortgage Co, Westboro, MA 01581.

**BYRD, HARRIETT ELIZABETH.** **See Obituaries Section.**

**BYRD, DR. HELEN P. BESSENT**
Clergy, educator. **Personal:** Born Feb 27, 1943, Waynesboro, GA; daughter of Oscar S Bessent and Josie C Bessent; married Shedrick B; children: Shedrick Tyrone. **Educ:** Warren Wilson Col, AA, 1961; Berea Col, BA, 1963; Temple Univ, MEd, 1965; Univ Conn, PhD, 1972; Columbia Univ, Teachers Col, postdoctoral study, 1973, 1976, Long Island Post Campus, attended 1987; Univ Ga, attended. **Career:** Educator (retired); Sch Dist Philadelphia, teacher, 1963-65; Atlanta Pub Sch Syst, teacher, 1966-68; Atlanta State Univ, vis prof, 1968; Savannah GA State Col, vis prof, 1971; Norfolk State Univ, spec educ dept, prof, head, 1977-80, coordr, Spec Educ Grad Progs. **Orgs:** Fel BEH-USOE Ment Retardation, 1965-66; fel Soc Fel Fund, 1970-72; Comn Minority Groups; bd trustee, Boggs Acad, 1976-83; prog agency bd, United Presby Church, USA, 1977-83, bd mem, 1976-79, vice chmn, 1979-80; bd mem, Norfolk Comm Improv Educ; bd mem, Hope House Found, 1977-83; Presby Comn Minority Educ, 1982-88, sec, 1985, mem, 1983-88, vice chmn, 1988; Va Interagency Coord Coun, 1987-2003; Norfolk Comm Serv Bd; bd mem, Cult Experiences Unlimited; bd, Norfolk Pub Libr, 1992-97; Coun Presbytery Eastern Va, 1998-2002; pastor, Covenant Presby Church, currently. **Home Addr:** 7112 Hunters Chase, Norfolk, VA 23518, **Home Phone:** (757)853-6553. **Business Addr:** Pastor, Covenant Presbyterian Church, 913 Covenant St, Norfolk, VA 23504, **Business Phone:** (757)623-1875.

**BYRD, HERBERT LAWRENCE, JR.**
Electrical engineer, chief executive officer. **Personal:** Born Oct 12, 1943, Hampton, VA; son of Henry Singleton and Pearline Singleton; married Beverly Ann Ramsuer; children: David H II. **Educ:** Am Inst Engineering & Technol, BSEE, 1966; Syracuse Univ, L. C. Smith Col Engineering & Comput Sci, MSEE, 1975. **Career:** IBM Corp, proj mgr, 1966-78; Sycom Inc, pres & chief exec officer, 1978-; MOJA Inc, chmn, gen mgr, prog mgr & chief exec officer & pres, 1995-. **Orgs:** Armed Forces Commun & Electronic Asn. **Home Addr:** 2821 Ingram Dr, Haymarket, VA 20169, **Home Phone:** (703)754-2802. **Business Addr:** Owner, President, Chief Executive Officer, General Manager & Program, MOJA Inc, 7010 Inf Ridge Rd, Manassas, VA 20109-2316, **Business Phone:** (703)369-4339.

**BYRD, HON. ISAAC, JR.**
Judge, entrepreneur. **Personal:** Born Jan 1, 1952; children: Isaac III & Caron. **Educ:** Tougaloo Col, 1973; Northwestern Univ Law Sch, Chicago, 1976. **Career:** Miss Bd Corrections, vice chmn; State Miss, chancery judge, 1989; Byrd & Assoc, Managing Partner, founder, currently. **Orgs:** Presidential Club mem, Asn Trial Lawyers Am; bd mem, Miss Trial Lawyers Asn; Nat Asn Advan Colored People; fel Miss State Bar; Nat Am Civil Liberties Union; treas, Miss Ctr for Justice. **Honors/Awds:** Vernon Dahmer Award, Nat Asn Advan Colored People, 1985; Goodman Chaney Schwerner Award, Nat Asn Advan Colored People, 1998; Trial Lawyer of the Year Award, 2002; African American Donor's Award, Kresge Found, Southern Educ Found & The Coca-Cola Co, 2002; Hall of Fame, Tougaloo Col Nat Alumni Asn, 2002; Stanford Young Lifetime Achievement Award, Bd Miss Trial Lawyers Asn, 2006. **Special Achievements:** In 2003 Black Enterprise Magazine recognized him as one of the top black lawyers in the country; First African-American chancery judge to preside in a Mississippi courtroom; First major donor to the Mississippi Center for Justice. **Business Addr:** Managing Partner, Founder, Byrd & Associates PLLC, 427 E Fortification St, Jackson, MS 39201, **Business Phone:** (601)354-1210.

**BYRD, ISAAC, III**
Football player, executive. **Personal:** Born Nov 16, 1974, St. Louis, MO. **Educ:** Kans Univ, BA, commun, broadcasting, 1997. **Career:** Football player (retired), executive; Tennessee Oilers, wide receiver, 1997-99; Tennessee Titans, wide receiver, 1997-99; Carolina Panthers, wide receiver, 2000-02; Elite Ment Training, owner, founder, 2009-. **Orgs:** partner, Mathews-Dickey Boys & Girls Club, 2011-; partner, Sports Int Football Camps, 2011-; partner, Herbert Hoover Boys & Girls Club. **Honors/Awds:** Missouri Player of the Year. **Special Achievements:** Films: "1999 AFC Championship Game", 2000; "Super Bowl XXXIV", 2000. Books: "How To: Think Like a Pro, Act Like a Pro & Play Like a Pro", 2011. **Business Addr:** Founder, Owner, Elite Mental Training.

**BYRD, JERRY STEWART**
Lawyer, judge. **Personal:** Born Dec 11, 1935, Greenville, SC; son of Elliott and Ethel; married Paula Deborah Aughtry; children: Jerry Jr. **Educ:** Fisk Univ, AB, 1961; Howard Univ, JD, 1964; Southeastern Univ, AS, bus admin, 1975. **Career:** Magistrate judge, associate judge (retried); Nat Labor Rels Bd, Regional Adv Br, atty, 1964-65; Neighborhood Legal Serv Prog, Managing Atty & Dep Dir, 1965-72; Howard Univ, polit sci instr, 1971-72; Thompson, Evans & Dolphin, pvt pract lawyer, 1971; United Planning Orgn Model Cities Consumer Protection Prog, supv atty, 1972-73; Mayor Wash, D.C. Consumer Repair Bd, 1974-77; Super Ct, DC, hearing comnr, 1981-97; Soc Security Admin Super Ct, magistrate Judge, 1998-2002; DC Super Ct Judges (51), Dept Justice, assoc judge, 2003-09. **Orgs:** Fed Admin Law Judges Conf; Spec Judges Div, Am Bar Asn; Wash Bar Asn; Nat Bar Asn; gen secy & vpres, Wash Buddhist Vihara Soc Inc; bd dir, Hospitality Comn, Fed Credit Union; Neighborhood Legal Serv, managing atty, 1965-69 & 1974-81, dep dir, 1970-71; DC Consumer Goods Repair Bd, 1974-77; Hearing Comn, Bd Prof Responsibility, 1982-85; Beta Kappa Chi Sci Soc; pres, Omega Psi Phi Social Fraternity; Howard Law J; Nat Child Support Enforcement Asn; Sigma Delta Tau Legal Fraternity, mem bd dir, Hospitality Community Fed Credit Union; vpres, Buddhist Vihara Soc Inc. **Honors/Awds:** Black Belt, Jhoon Rhee Inst Tae Kwon Do, 1982; Federal Adminstrative Law Judge Certificate, 1997. **Special Achievements:** Publ: "Parental Immunity in Negligence Actions Abolished, 9 How L J 183", 1963; "Courts, Slums and Feasibility of Adopting the Warranty of Fitness The DC Housing Research Comm Report", 1967; "Important Cases, Thompson v Mazo 421 F 2d 1156, 137 US App DC 221", 1970; rev 245 A2d 122 (DC App1968); Durmu v Gill 227 A2d 104 (DC App 1970); Coleman v District of Columbia 250 A2d 555 (DC App 1968); Nix vs Watson, RS-650-80R; 18 Family Law Reporter (Nov 12, 1991). **Home Addr:** 2110 T St SE, Washington, DC 20020, **Home Phone:** (202)889-1392. **Busi-**

ness Addr: Associate Judge, DC Superior Court Judges 51, 500 Ind Ave NW, Washington, DC 20001, **Business Phone:** (202)879-4797.

### BYRD, JOAN EDA (JOAN EDA)

Librarian. **Personal:** Born May 12, 1942, Washington, DC; daughter of Robert and Edna; married Leonard; children: Kai-Mariama. **Educ:** Howard Univ, BFA, 1965; Cath Univ Am, MLS, 1976; New Sch Social Res, MA, 1978. **Career:** DC Pub Libr, ref librn, 1965-76; John Jay Col, mgr, librn, 1979-81; Brooklyn Publ Libr, ref librn, 1983-86, asst div chief, 1986-88; Donnell Media Ctr, NY Pub Libr, supv librn film/video & programmer, 1996-2001, asst librn, librn, currently. **Orgs:** NY Film/Video Coun, 1988-; pres & bd trustee, Black Maria Film/Video Festival. **Honors/Awds:** Purchase Award for Photography, Perkins Ctr Arts, 1988. **Special Achievements:** Cover art for 10th anniversary publication of The Color Purple (Alice Walker), 1992; photography-in-performance piece: Friends and Friends II, by Blondell Cummings, 1980; numerous photography exhibitions. **Home Addr:** 136 Spring St, Leonia, NJ 07605, **Home Phone:** (201)944-3881. **Business Addr:** Librarian, Donnell Media Center, Donnell Libr Ctr Lower Level 20 W 53rd St, New York, NY 10019-6185, **Business Phone:** (212)621-0618.

### BYRD, JOSEPH KEYS

School administrator. **Personal:** Born Oct 3, 1953, Meadville, MS. **Educ:** William Carey Col, BS, 1975, MEd, 1980. **Career:** William Carey Col, counr & instr, 1980-82; Univ New Orleans, develop specialist counr, 1981-82; Xavier Univ, New Orleans, LA, gen counr, 1982-83, asst dean stud serv, 1986-, vpres stud serv, currently; Univ New Orleans, asst dir dev ed, 1983-86. **Orgs:** Counr, tutor & coordr, William Carey Col, 1975-80; adv, Omicron Delta Kappa, 1978, Chi Beta Phi 1980; vpres, pres, La Conf, Alpha Phi Alpha Fraternity Inc, 1982-; exec secy, Sigma Lambda Chap; Nat Asn Advan Colored People New Orleans LA, 1984; pres, Greater New Orleans Chap Nat Pan-Hellenic Coun Inc, 1989; steering comm, Greater New Orleans Found; bd dir, Human Serv Cable. **Home Addr:** 5414 Music St, New Orleans, LA 70122, **Home Phone:** (504)283-5330. **Business Addr:** Vice President- Student Services, Xavier University of Louisiana, 1 Drexel Dr, New Orleans, LA 70125, **Business Phone:** (504)520-7357.

### BYRD, DR. KATIE W.

Manager. **Personal:** Born Mobile, AL; children: Marcus Dalton & Taynetta Joi. **Educ:** Ala A&M Univ, BS, MS; PA State Univ, PhD. **Career:** Teacher educ specialist; counr; equal opportunity officer; supvry mgt analyst; Univ Ala A & M, prof. **Orgs:** Womens Equity Action League; Nat Asn Black Psychologists; Nat Asn Adminr Counrs & Deans; Pi Lambda Theta; Nat Asn Advan Colored People; Phi Beta Kappa; Md Asn Univ Women; chairperson, pres, Social Action-Delta Sigma Theta Sorority Inc; Womens Polit Caucus; state recorder, vpres, Huntsville Chap AL New S Coalition; pres, Delta Sigma Theta Sorority, 2005-07; vice pres, HHC Found Bd; gov bd dir, bd chmn, civic leader, Harris Home C & Community Action Agency. **Honors/Awds:** Equal Employment Opportunity Award; Outstanding Young Women Am; Outstanding Black Human Service; Good Govt Award, Huntsville Jaycees; Outstanding Leadership Award; Outstanding Committee Service Award; Class Achievement Award. **Home Addr:** 6029 Norm Heights Cir NW, Huntsville, AL 35810, **Home Phone:** (256)852-4709. **Business Addr:** Civic Leader, Harris Home for Children & Community Action Agency, 1210 Church St NW, Huntsville, AL 35801-5916, **Business Phone:** (256)837-0332.

### BYRD, LEWIS E.

Entrepreneur. **Educ:** Harvard Col, BA, econ; Harvard Bus Sch, MBA, gen mgt. **Career:** Talco Metals, Philadelphia, Pa, plant mgr; Meridian Pt Partners, managing dir, currently; First Boston Corp; PaineWebber Inc; Opportunity Capital Partners, gen partner, 1990-; Harvard Bus Sch Alumni Asn, dir; Keystone Community Ventures, dir. **Orgs:** Mem bd dir, Argon Industs; mem bd dir, BioGenex Labs; mem bd dir, NetAbacus; mem bd dir, Satisfusion; chair, bd trustee, SFJAZZ, currently; trustee, St. Paul's Episcopal Sch; dir mem exec comt, Harvard Bus Sch Alumni Asn Bd; adv bd, TPW Investments; bd dir, Tri-City Homeless Coalition. **Business Addr:** General Partner, Opportunity Capital Partners, 2201 Walnut Ave Suite 210, Fremont, CA 94538, **Business Phone:** (510)795-7000.

### BYRD, LUMUS, JR.

Executive. **Personal:** Born Apr 25, 1942, Clinton, SC; son of Lumus Sr and Mary J. **Educ:** SC State Col, BS, bio, 1963, MS, bio, 1969. **Career:** Charleston, SC Sch Dist 20, educ, 1965-70; Jos Schlitz Brewing Co, dist mgr, 1970-74; Greyhound Lines Inc, dir Sales, 1974-78; Willie Davis Distributing Co, vpres & gen mgr, 1958-88; Greyhound Corp, mgr mkt develop, 1978-82; T & T Iron Works, pres, 1989; Byrd Enterprises Inc, pres, chmn, chief exec officer & owner; sc state univ, Acad Affairs & Fac Liaison Comt, vice chair, currently. **Orgs:** Vpres Nat Asn Mkt Develop, 1980; treas, Am Mkt Asn, 1982; vpres, Phoenix Advert Club, 1984; dir, bd Valley Leadership Inc, 1984; vpres, Alpha Hi Alpha Frat, 1985; adv bd, YMCA, 1985; chmn bd, Presby Col; bd dir, Assoc Marine Inst; bd dir, aurens County Community Found; bd dir, US Selective Serv Syst; bd comnr, Clinton Mus; bd visitor, chmn, Presby Col; bd mem, Clinton Econ Develop Corp; bd dir, Clinton YMCA; bd dir, Laurens County Community Found; bd dir, Rotary Club Clinton; adv bd, Carolina First Bank. **Honors/Awds:** Distinguished Alumni, SC State Col, 1984; Man of the Year, Alpha Phi Alpha Frat, 1983; Outstanding Toastmasters, 1984; Outstanding Freshman Trustee of the Year Award; Martha A Green Award. **Home Addr:** 105 Shellcreek Ct, Clinton, SC 29325-5200, **Home Phone:** (864)833-2700. **Business Addr:** Vice Chair, South Carolina State University, 300 College St NE, Orangeburg, SC 29117, **Business Phone:** (803)536-7000.

### BYRD, MANFORD, JR.

School administrator. **Personal:** Born May 29, 1928, Brewton, AL; son of Manford and Evelyn Patton; married Cheribelle; children: Carl, Bradley & Donald. **Educ:** Iowa Cent Col, BA, 1949; Atlanta Univ, MA, 1954; Northwestern Univ, PhD, 1978. **Career:** School administrator (retired); Quincy, teacher, 1949-54; Chicago Pub Schs, teacher & asst prin, elem & high sch prin, asst gen supt, 1954-67, dep supt, 1968, dep supt instr & dep supt pupil serv, gen supt, 1985-90, consult, 1990-. **Orgs:** Bd dir, Chicago State Univ; Joint Negro Appeal; Chicago State Univ Found, Mid-Am Chap; Am Red Cross; Sigma Pi Phi, Beta Boule; Nat Treas, Sigma Phi Fraternity, 1980; Nat Alliance Black Sch Educrs; chmn, Christian Educ, Trinity United Church; Large Unit Dist Asn; bd dir, Coun Great City Schs; Found Excellence Teaching; Nat Asn Advan Colored People; United Church Bd World Ministries; trustee, Cent Col; trustee, Adler Planetarium Chicago, trustee, Pella Iowa. **Honors/Awds:** Recipient of more than 100 awards and commendations for excellence in teaching and academic administration, including honorary doctorates from Central College, Hope College and the National College of Education. **Home Addr:** 9515 Parnell Ave, Chicago, IL 60628, **Home Phone:** (773)779-8910.

### BYRD, DR. MARQUITA L.

Educator. **Personal:** Born Mar 24, 1950, Atlanta, GA; daughter of Robert and Wilhelmina; married Henry Neal Wilbanks III; children: Marquis Lawrence. **Educ:** Cent Mo State Univ, BS, speech & dramatic arts, 1972; Southern Ill Univ, Edwardsville, MA, commun, 1975; Univ Mo, Columbia, PhD, 1979. **Career:** Univ Southern MS, asst prof, 1977-81; Univ Houston-Downtown, asst prof, 1981-83; Southeast MO St Univ, asst prof, 1983-87; Cent MO St Univ, asst prof, 1987-91; San Jose St Univ, assoc prof, commun studies, 1991-. **Orgs:** Nat Commun Asn, 1977-; Phi Beta Kappa, 1989; Am Acad Relig, 1999. **Home Addr:** 2151 Oakland Rd Suite 507, San Jose, CA 95101, **Home Phone:** (408)428-9551. **Business Addr:** Associate Professor, Department of Communication, San Jose State University, 1 Wash Sq, San Jose, CA 95192-0112, **Business Phone:** (408)924-5385.

### BYRD, DR. TAYLOR, JR.

Educator, college teacher. **Personal:** Born Nov 2, 1940, Greene County, AL; married Katie W; children: Marcus Dalton & Taynetta Joy. **Educ:** Ala A&M Univ, BS, 1963; Tuskegee Inst, MEd, 1969; Pa State Univ, PhD, 1972. **Career:** Educator (retired); TN Valley High Sch, instr, 1963-64; Woodson High Sch, Andalusia, AL, instr, asst coach, 1964-66; TN Valley High Sch, instr, asst prin, 1966-70; PA State Univ, grad res asst, 1970-72;AL Agr & Mech Univ, NASA tech, Agr Bus Educ Dept, chmn, 1972-, dir & prof agr bus educ, res prof, distance learning prof, assoc prof & chmn dept agribusiness Educ, currently. **Orgs:** Proj dir, Cross-Cult Skills & Interpersonal Effect Urban Environ, 1972; Evaluator, So Reg Agr Educ Conf Mobile, Al, 1973; chmn, Greater Huntsville 100 Black Men Am; Nat Educ Asn; Am Eval Asn; dir, Tenn Valley Authority; regional mgr, Minority econ develop, Community Diversity Develop; dir, Distance Learning Develop; dir, Recruitment & Retention; res prof, Dept Agribusiness, Col Agr, Life & Biol Sci. **Home Addr:** 5204 Steger St NW, Huntsville, AL 35810. **Business Addr:** Professor, Alabama Agricultural & Mechanical University, 225 Dawson Bldg Meridian St, Normal, AL 35762, **Business Phone:** (256)858-4968.

**BYRD, TONI. See BUCKSON, TONI YVONNE.**

# C

### CABBELL, EDWARD JOSEPH

Educator. **Personal:** Born Jun 26, 1946, Eckman, WV; son of John Marshall and Cassie Haley King; married Madeline Harrell; children: Melissa Yvette & Winnia Denise. **Educ:** Concord Col, BS, educ, 1970; Appalachian State Univ, MA, 1983. **Career:** Upward Bound & Spec Serv Disadvantaged Stud, dir, 1969-75; Creativity Appalachian Minorities Prog, coordr, 1975; John Henry Folk Fest, dir, 1975-; John Henry Rec, producer, 1978-; Black Diamonds Mag, ed, 1978-; John Henry Blues Socs, coord, 1988-; Appalachian doc, dir; Appalachian St Univ, financial aid asst, 1993, John Henry Ctr Cult & Hist Exchange, cur, currently, John Henry Festival & Conf, dir, currently; Book: Blacks in Appalachia; Black blues: notes of black experience. **Orgs:** Photog Proj, 1977-; adv comm, Folklife Festival, 1982; Worlds Fair, 1982; bd Coun, Sourn Mountains, 1984; gov appointee bd mem, WV Martin Lur King Jr State Holiday Comm, 1986-97; WEB DuBois fel WVa Univ, 1987-89; Birthplace Country Music Alliance & Smithsonian Cult Comt, 2001; founder & dir, John Henry Mem Found Inc. **Home Addr:** 352 Demain Ave, PO Box 1172, Morgantown, WV 26501, **Home Phone:** (304)292-8016. **Business Addr:** Curator, Appalachian University, 247 Beechurst Ave Suite 1-A, Morgantown, WV 26507, **Business Phone:** (304)292-0767.

### CABBIL, LILA

Manager, president (organization), association executive. **Personal:** Born Detroit, MI. **Educ:** Wayne State Univ, BS, MS, human develop & resources. **Career:** Univ Mich Hosp, Occup therapist; Asn Educ & Rehab, Rehab teacher; Upshaw Inst Blind, Detroit, Mich, supvr occup info & c's servs, 2003; LMC Diversified Consult, pres; Rosa & Raymond Parks Inst, pres, pres emer; Race Rels Initiative, lead consult; Wayne State Univ, Urban Labor & Metropolian Affairs, Multicultural Experience Leadership Develop Prog, dir, 2003-, Ctr Peace Conflict Studies, prog dir. **Orgs:** Proj dir, High Vision Games; Multicultural Curric Develop Master Teachers Visually Impaired, Univ Colo; bd mem, Am Found Blind; Vis Nurse Asn; Mr Bus & Youth Club; Child Care Coord Coun; Ethnic Coun; Detroit Asn Black Orgns, & Mich Coalition Human Rights. **Honors/Awds:** Migel Medal Award, 2001. **Home Addr:** 1946 Pine Ridge Lane, Bloomfield Hills, MI 48302, **Home Phone:** (248)851-1218. **Business Addr:** Project Director, Wayne State University, 656 W Kirby St, Detroit, MI 48202, **Business Phone:** (313)577-2210.

### CABELL, ENOS MILTON, JR.

Baseball manager, executive, baseball player. **Personal:** Born Oct 8, 1949, Ft. Riley, KS; son of Enos Sr; married Kathy M; children: Marcus E, Stephen & Cordell. **Educ:** Harbor Jr Col. **Career:** Baseball player (retired), baseball manager, executive; Baltimore Orioles, third baseman, first baseman & outfielder & Designated hitter & second baseman & right fielder & left fielder, 1972-74; Houston Astros, first baseman, 1975-80; San Francisco Giants, 1981; Detroit Tigers, 1982-83; Houston Astros, 1984-85, consult baseball opers, spec asst gen mgr, 2004-; Los Angeles Dodgers, ctr fielder & third baseman & right fielder & left fielder & shortstop, 1985-86; HSE Telecasts, analyst, 1991-94; KCOH Radio, host weekly call-show, 1991-96; Enos Cabell Chevrolet & Buick, car dealership owner, 1992-95; Cabell Motors Inc, chief exec officer, 1999; Tex Southern Univ, interim athletic dir, 2000. **Orgs:** Am Cancer Socs; United Negro Col Fund; Houston Citizens Chamber Com; Kiwanis Int; Tex Southern Univ Bd Regents, 1995-01; bd dir, Joe Niekro Found; bd chmn, Superstar Found. **Honors/Awds:** Houston Astros Hall of Fame, 1993. **Home Addr:** 4103 Frost Lake Ct, Missouri City, TX 77459, **Home Phone:** (281)261-2764. **Business Addr:** Special Assistant to the General Manager, Houston Astros, Enron Field, Houston, TX 77002, **Business Phone:** (713)259-8000.

### CABRERA-WHITE, ELOISE J.

Educator. **Personal:** Born Dec 9, 1932, Evinston, FL; daughter of Zebbie Johnson (deceased) and Maude S Johnson (deceased); married Marion Charles; children: Yolanda Alicia & Liggins Yolanda; married Charles J. **Educ:** Fla A&M Univ, BS, educ, 1954; Ind Univ, MS, educ, 1963; Nova Univ, educ leadership, EdD, 1985; Mich State Univ, community educ; Univ S Fla, adult educ. **Career:** Teacher (retired); Broward County Sch Syst, elem teacher, 1954-56; Elem Dept Sch, US Dependent Sch Baum holder, Ger, teacher, 1956-57; Howard WBlack, High Sch teacher, 1958-63, counr, 1963-66; Neighborhood Youth Corp, Fed Prog, counr, 1966-77, asst proj dir, 1966-69; Hills City Pub Sch, supvr comm educ prog, 1969-77, Williams Elem, prin, 1977. **Orgs:** Nat Community Educ Asn; Am Asn Univ Women; Fla Asn Community Educ; Tampa Urban League; Fla Adult Educ Asn; Nat Asn Advan Colored People, Nat Coun Negro Women; Tampa Alumnae Chap Delta Sigma Theta Sorority, May Week & Awards Day, Golden Life chair, Corr Sec; Orgn Concerned Parents; Eastern Seal Adv Bd; bd dir, Girl Scouts; bd dir, Hillsborough Community Col-Found; St Peter Claver Cath Church; Hillsborough Alliance Black Sch Educr, Retired Educr Ambassador. **Home Addr:** 5167 Puritan Cir, Tampa, FL 33617-8371, **Home Phone:** (813)988-9291.

### CADDELL, PHYLLIS

Entrepreneur. **Personal:** Born Los Angeles, CA. **Educ:** MA, orgn communs. **Career:** Pc Pub Rels & Mgt Inc, chief exec officer, owner, 1996-; PC2 Media, chief exec officer, 2003-; Lithobit Publ, owner, auth & publ, 2006-. **Special Achievements:** Author, Put Your Best Foot Forward; featured in the 2001 issue of Essence Magazine; Publisher, Do-It-Yourself Publicity: For Those Too Cheap or Too Broke To Hire A Publicist. **Business Addr:** Chief Executive Officer, Founder, Owner, Pc Public Relations & Management Inc, 1680 N Vine St Suite 716, Los Angeles, CA 90028, **Business Phone:** (323)993-0773.

### CADE, BRIGADIER GEN. ALFRED JACKAL

Executive, military leader. **Personal:** Born Feb 4, 1931, Fayetteville, NC; married Florence; children: 5. **Educ:** Va State Col, BS, gen psychol; Syracuse Univ, MBA, 1965; Artil Sch; Qm Sch; AUS Field Artil Sch; AUS Command & Gen Staff Col; Indust Col Armed Forces; St. Peter's Col, hon degree. **Career:** Retired, AUS, budget action officer, comptroller, financial mgt, 2nd Lt, 1952-54, brig gen, 1954-78; asst sector adv, 1966-67; Phu Yen Prov Vietnam, sector adv, 1967; US Milit Command Vietnam, dep sr prov adv, 1967; Pac-Vietnam, comdr 1st Battalion 92nd Arty, 1967-68; budget opers officer, 1968-69; Dir Army Budget Wash, exec officer, 1970-72; Mat Command Wash, DC, asst comptroller budget, 1972; 210th Field Arty Group Europe, comdr, 1973-74; AUS, brig gen, 1978; Caesars Atlantic City, sr vpres, govt rels, 1979-96; Fleet Bank NJ, off chmn, spec adv. **Orgs:** NJ Comn Higher Educ, 1994, Chmn, 1999; bd trustee, Rowan Univ & Atlantic Cape Community Col; past pres, secy, Vietnam Veterans Memorial Found; chmn emer, Atlantic County Conf Community & Justice; chmn, NJ State Chamber Com; Syracuse Univ, Sch Mgt, Corp Adv Bd; bd mem, Va State Univ; chmn emer, Atlantic County Conf Christians & Jews; chmn, Greater Atlantic City Chamber Com. **Honors/Awds:** Hon degree, St. Peter's Col.

### CADE, HAROLD EDWARD

School administrator, football coach. **Personal:** Born Aug 25, 1929, Bon Ami, LA; married Josephine Lockhart; children: Deryl Vernon. **Educ:** Prairie View A&M Univ, BA, 1955, BS, 1958; Univ Colo, MA, 1960; N Tex State Univ, MEd, 1967. **Career:** VISD Gross HS, teacher, biol & chem, 1955-66, football coach, 1960; VISD Victoria/Stroman HS, counr, 1965-; TSTA Dist 3, pres, 1975; VISD Patti Welder Jr High, prin, 1975-85; Stroman Mid Sch, asst prin, 1992. **Orgs:** Football coach, Lockhart Pub Schs, 1953; football coach, FW Gross, 1955-66; counr, Victoria HS, 1965-67; asst prin, Stroman HS, 1967; pres, Victoria Kiwanis Club, 1975; lt govr, Div 25 Tex/Okla Dist, 1977; pres, Victoria TSTA, 1978; Honored, African Am Chamber Com. **Honors/Awds:** Tex State Teacher Asn, 1967; supt, Palestine Baptist Church SS, 1979-85; Young Men's Christian Asn Victoria, 1980-85. **Home Addr:** 2909 Mayfair Dr, Victoria, TX 77901, **Home Phone:** (361)573-2581. **Business Addr:** Victoria, TX 77901.

### CADE, WALTER, III

Artist, painter (artist), musician. **Personal:** Born Jan 1, 1936, New York, NY; son of Walter and Helen Henderson Brehon. **Educ:** Inst Modern Art NY; Lee Strasberg Sch Dramatic Arts; Muse Drama Workshop. **Career:** Musician; Painter, currently. **Honors/Awds:** Best Show, Whitney Mus, NY, 1978; Best Show, Mus Modern Art, NY, 1979; Award of Distinction, Nat Endowment Arts Mus Prog, 1979; Best Show, Metro Mus Art, NY, 1980; Best Show, Nat Gallery Art, Washington, DC, 1980; Award of Distinction, Guggenbeim Mus, NY, 1981; Best Show, Smithsonian Inst, Washington, DC, 1981; Best Show, Bruce Mus, CT, 1994; Award of Merit, Mus Modern Art, NY, 1986. **Special Achievements:** Numerous exhibitions. **Home Addr:** 17203 119th Ave, Jamaica, NY 11434-2261, **Home Phone:** (718)527-5634.

### CADET, RON

Executive. **Educ:** Rensselaer Polytech Inst, BS, comput & syst engineering, 1986. **Career:** Systs Programming Analyst, Westinghouse; Wild 107 & KSOL-FM, San Francisco, Calif, asst prog dir, 1987-91;

XHRM-FM, San Diego, Calif, prog dir, 1992-93; KBLX-FM, San Francisco, Calif, music dir, 1994-98; Imhotech, co-founder, pres & chief technol officer, 1998-2001; MTV Interactive, Online Radio, music dir, 1998-2005; BayView Systs, co-founder, 2001-03; comput & systs eng; radio prog dir; MusicNet, NY, dir tech partnerships, 2003-06; Imhotech Inc, co-founder, chmn, pres & chief technol officer; Sawyer Law Group, tech specialist digital media, currently; Tedac Digital, founder, 2006-; AdPassage Inc, Technol & Prod Develop, vpres, 2009-10; jamble.fm, co-Founder & chief exec officer, 2010-12; Dhingana, Mobile Web, Lead UI Engr, 2012-14; View, prin UI/UX architect, 2014-. **Business Addr:** Founder, Tedac Digital, 857 Crompton Rd Suite A, Redwood City, CA 94061.

### CADOGAN, MARJORIE A.
Lawyer, executive. **Personal:** Born Dec 11, 1960, New York, NY; daughter of George and Doreen Leacock. **Educ:** Fordham Univ, BA, Eng & Span, 1982, JD, 1985. **Career:** NY City Law Dept, asst corp coun, 1985-90; NY City Loft Bd, coun, 1990-91; NY City Dept Parks & Recreation, gen coun, 1990-95; Primary Care Dev Corp, dir opers & external affairs, 1995-2002; Citywide Health Ins Access, Human Resource Admins Off, exec dir, exec dep comnr, 2002-. **Orgs:** Am Bar Asn, 1985-; treasr, Asn Black Women Attys, 1991-93, vpres, 1993, pres, 1998-2004; bd dir, New York Women's Found, 1996-2002; Herman Biggs Socs; New York Acad Med's Sect Health Care; Ny Health Found; NYS Health Found's Community Adv Comt. **Honors/Awds:** Robert B McKay Advocacy Award, 1985; Outstanding Asst Corp Coun, NY City Bar Asn, 1990; Fordham Univ Sch Law. **Home Addr:** 3000 Valentine Ave Apt 5B, Bronx, NY 10458-1675. **Business Addr:** Executive Deputy Commissioner, Citywide Health Insurance Access, 22 Cortlandt St, New York, NY 10007, **Business Phone:** (212)693-1850.

### CADORIA, BRIGADIER GEN. SHERIAN GRACE
Executive, manager, military leader. **Personal:** Born Jan 26, 1943, Marksville, LA; daughter of Joseph and Bernice McGlory. **Educ:** Southern Univ, BS, bus educ, 1961; AUS, Command & Gen Staff Col, dipl, 1971; Univ Okla, MA, human rels, 1974; AUS, War Col, dipl, 1979; Nat Defense Univ, Inst Higher Defense Studies, 1985. **Career:** Military (retired), consultant; Women's Army Corps Sch & Ctr, instr, human rels officer, 1971-73; Women's Army Corps Br, AUS Mil Personnel Ctr, exec officer/personnel officer, 1973-75; Law Enforcement Div Officer, dep chief staff, Personnel Hq Dept Army, personnel staff officer, 1975-76; Mil Police Stud Battalion, battalion comdr, 1977-78; Phys Security Div AUS Europe & 7th Army, div chief, 1979-82; 1st Region Criminal Invest Command, brigade comdr, 1982-84; Dept Army, chief, Off Army Law Enforcement, 1984-85; Pentagon Orgn Joint Chiefs Staff, dir manpower & personnel, 1985-87; US Total Army Personnel Command, dep comdr, dir mobilization & oper, 1987-90; AUS, brig gen; Cadoria Speaker & Consult Serv, pres, 1990-2004; CLECO Corp, Compensation Comn, dir, 1993-2012; Cleco Power LLC, mgr, 1993-. **Orgs:** Hon mem, La Asn Develop Educ; WAC Vet Asn, 1980-; Vet Foreign Wars, 2000; Order Holy Sepulchre Jerusalem, 2000; Horatio Alger Asn, 2003; vol prin, Marksville Cath Sch; Audit Comt; Nominating & Governance Comt; Qualified Legal Compliance Comt; dir, Christus St Frances Cabrini Hosp, Alexandria, LA. **Honors/Awds:** George Olmstead Scholar, Freedom Found, Valley Forge, PA, 1972; Social Aide to the Pres USS, 1975-76; Distinguished Alumni Award, Southern Univ, 1984; Distinguished Serv Medal, Hofstra Univ, 1986; Int Black Woman of the Year, Los Angeles Sentinel, 1987; Roy Wilkens Meritorious Serv Award, Nat Asn Advan Colored People, 1989; Hall of Fame, LA Black Hist, 1992; DHL, OHI Dominican Univ, 1992, Benedictine Univ, 1993; YMCA Spirit of Giving, 1999; Strong Men & Women Excellence in Leadership, 1999; Regional Hall of Fame, AUS Military Police, 2000; LA Vet Hall of Honor, 2002; Horatio Alger Distinguished Am, 2003. **Special Achievements:** First woman to command an all-male battalion; first woman to lead a criminal investigation brigade; First African-American woman to be admitted to Command and General Staff College and the US Army War College; First African-American woman director for the Joint Chiefs of Staff. One of Ams Top 100 Black Bus & Professional Women 1985; One of 75 Black Women who helped change history in the I Dream A World photo exhibit in Corcoran Gallery, USA West/Life Mag, 1989. **Home Addr:** 322 Azalea Lane, Pineville, LA 71360. **Business Addr:** President, Cadoria Speaker & Consultancy Service, 107 Lancelot Dr, Mansura, LA 71350-3900, **Business Phone:** (318)253-9121.

### CADWELL, REV. HAROLD H., JR.
Clergy. **Personal:** Born Apr 7, 1968, Detroit, MI; son of Harold Sr and Faye; married Angela; children: Charles, Dominique, Ericka, Dwight, Stephen, Harold III & Terrance. **Educ:** Morehouse Col, Atlanta, Ga; Wayne State Univ, Detroit, Mich. **Career:** New Providence Baptist Church, pastor's armor bearers, 1991-99; Mt Olive Baptist Church, Detroit, Mich, admin asst, pastor, 1999-. **Orgs:** Black Preaching Network. **Business Addr:** Pastor, Mt Olive Baptist Church, 9760 Woodward Ave, Detroit, MI 48202, **Business Phone:** (313)871-5854.

### CAESAR, DR. LAEL O.
Educator. **Personal:** son of Riley and Lucy; married Lena; children: Lloyd & La Vonne. **Educ:** Caribbean Union Col, BS, 1973; Andrews Univ, MA, relig, 1986; Univ Wis-Madison, Hebrew & Semitic Studies, MA, 1988, PhD, Hebrew, 1991. **Career:** Univ Montemorelos, Montemorelos, NL, Mex, assoc prof, 1993-96; Andrews Univ MA Relig exten prog Montemorelos Univ, Universite Adventiste dHaiti, Zaokski Theol Sem, Russia, Cernica, Ilfov, Romania, adj prof OT, 1994-; Andrews Univ, assoc prof, relig, 1996-2003, res prof, Currently; Adventist Rev & Adventist World mag, assoc ed, currently; Solusi Univ, Zimbabwe, vis prof, 1999; Loyola Univ, assoc prof & coordr, Speech Lang Path. **Orgs:** Gen Conf Bibl Res Inst Adv Comt. **Home Addr:** 10867 Ridgewood, Berrien Springs, MI 49103, **Home Phone:** (616)471-9139. **Business Addr:** Professor of Research, Andrews University, 10867 S Ridgewood, Berrien Springs, MI 49103-9724, **Business Phone:** (269)471-3184.

### CAESAR, SHIRLEY ANN
Songwriter, singer, evangelist. **Personal:** Born Oct 13, 1938, Durham, NC; daughter of James and Hannah; married Bishop Harold I Williams. **Educ:** Shaw Univ, BS, bus admin, 1984; Divinity Sch Duke Univ. **Career:** Singer, songwriter & rec artist; Songs: "I'd rather have Jesus", 1951; Caravan Singers, singer, 1958; "No Charge", 1987;-; "Hold My Mule", 2001; "I Remember Mama", "He'll Do It Again", 2005; Mt Calvary Holy Church Winston-Salem, pastor, 1990; The Shirley Caesar Outreach Ministries Inc, pres, currently;The Caesar Singers, singer;The Caravans, singer. Albums: Live in Chicago, 1988; I Remember Mama I, Mama II, Mama III, 1992; He's Working It Out For You, 1993; Stand Still, 1994; Live He Will Come, 1995; Just A Word, 1996; Miracle In Harlem, 1997; You're Next in Line, 1997; Christmas with Shirley Caesar, 1998; Hymns, 2001; He Will Come to You, 2002; Shirley Caesar & Friends, 2003; The Passion of Jesus, 2004; The Gospel Legends, 2005; I Know the Truth, 2005; Church Is in Mourning, 2006; This Is Gospel: King & Queen, 2007; Still Sweeping Through The City After 40 Yrs, 2009; A City Called Heaven, 2009. **Orgs:** Shirley Caesar Outreach Ministries, NC; bd dir, Divinity Sch Shaw Univ, 1984; spokeswoman, McDonald's Salute to Gospel Music, 1987; fel Delta Sigma Theta Sorority Inc. **Business Addr:** President, The Shirley Caesar Outreach Ministries Inc, PO Box 3336, Durham, NC 27702, **Business Phone:** (919)683-1161.

### CAFFEY, JASON ANDRE
Basketball player. **Personal:** Born Jun 12, 1973, Mobile, AL; son of Thomas and Rose. **Educ:** Univ Ala, attended 1995. **Career:** Basketball player (retired), basketball coach; Chicago Bulls, power forward, 1995-98; Golden StateWarriors, power forward, 1998-2000; Milwaukee Bucks, power forward, 2000-03; Mobile Bay Hurricanes, Am Basketball Asn, head coach. **Honors/Awds:** NBA Championship, 1996, 1997.

### CAFRITZ, PEGGY COOPER
Executive, school administrator, founder (originator). **Personal:** Born Apr 7, 1947, Mobile, AL; daughter of Gladys Mouton and Algernon Johnson; married Conrad; children: Zachary & Cooper. **Educ:** George Washington Univ, BA, 1968, JD, law, 1971. **Career:** Executive (retired); Workshops Careers Arts, Wash, DC, co-founder, 1968; Duke Ellington High Sch Fine & Performing Arts, Wash, DC, founder, vpres, fundraiser & developer, 1968-; DC Arts Comn, exec comt chmn, 1969-74; Post-Newsweek Stas Inc, spec asst pres, 1970; St People Study Plan Redevelop Pub Spaces Downtown Wash, Wash proj dir; Trustee Am Film Inst, independent consult, 1970-73; Woodrow Wilson Int Ctr Scholars, fel, 1972; Minority Cult Proj, exec dir, 1977-79; WETA, Channel 26, Wash, DC, arts critic, 1986-; Wash DC Bd Educ, pres, 2000-06; WTOP-TV, doc producer, 1974-77. **Orgs:** DC Bar, 1972; exec comt, DC Bd Higher Educ, 1972-76; Arts Educ & Am Nat Panel, 1975-; Nat Assembly State Art Agencies, 1979-, exec bd, 1980-86, plng comt, 1986-; chair, DC Comn Arts & Humanities, 1979-87; bd trustee, Atlanta Univ, 1983-86; Wash Performing Arts Soc, 1983; bd dir, PEN Faulkner Found, 1985-88; Nat Jazz Serv Orgn, 1985-; bd trustee, Kennedy Ctr Performing Arts, 1987; bd mem, Womens Campaign Fund, 1987; co-chair, Smithsonian Cult Equity Subcomt, 1988-; chair, Smithsonian Cult Educ Comt, 1989-; co-founder, Duke Ellington Sch Arts; vice chairperson, Pres's Comt, Arts & Humanities, 1993; pres, Clintons Comt Arts & Humanities, 1994; New Yorks Whitney Mus; adv bd, WEB DuBois Inst; fel, Woodrow Wilson Ctr Scholars. **Home Addr:** 2002 Mass Ave NW, Washington, DC 20036-1020, **Home Phone:** (202)537-7040.

### CAGE, ATHENA
Singer. **Personal:** Born Russellville, KY. **Educ:** Western Ky Univ. **Career:** Country star Amy Grant; R&B giants; Isley Brothers; Sweat's Elektra; KutKlose; chorus accolades police & fire personnel; Wash Redskins; Priority Rec, solo recording artist; Singles: "Nobody", 1996; "Hey Hey", 2001; "Until You Come Back To Me", 2001; "All Or Nothing", 2002. Album: The Art Of A Woman, 2001; Kut Klose, mem. **Orgs:** Athena Cage Scholarship Fund, Western Kentucky Univ. **Honors/Awds:** Pop Song of the Year, BMI; Screaming Eagles Award; the Second Street in Russellville was renamed to "Athena Cage Way", 2004. **Special Achievements:** Hey Hey, premiered in Billboard Rhythmic Top 40. **Home Addr:** 304 Pk Ave S Suite 3, New York, NY 10010-4301. **Business Addr:** Recording Artist, c/o Priority Records, 32 W 18th St Fl 12, New York, NY 10011, **Business Phone:** (212)627-8000.

### CAGE, MICHAEL JEROME, SR. (JOHN SHAFT)
Basketball player, television broadcaster. **Personal:** Born Jan 28, 1962, West Memphis, AR; married Jodi; children: Alexis, Michael Jr & Sydney. **Educ:** San Diego State Univ, speech commun, 1984. **Career:** Basketball player (retired), basketball coach, business man, television broadcast analyst; Pan Am Games, United State Men's Basketball Team, 1983; Los Angeles Clippers, 1984-88; Seattle Supersonics, 1988-94; Cleveland Cavaliers, 1994-96; Philadelphia 76ers, 1996-97; Nj Nets, 1997-2000; Memphis Grizzlies, basketball analyst, commentator, 2004-06; Foxs Sports W, basketball analyst, 2004-; Michael Cage Found, founder & pres, 2009-; Westwood One Dial Global, basketball analyst, 2010-; Mater Dei High Sch, asst coach, 2012-; Fox Sports San Diego, col basketball analyst, 2012-. **Orgs:** Pres, Fel Christian Athletes Los Angeles Clippers. **Home Addr:** 826 Orange Ave Suite 501, Coronado, CA 92118. **Business Addr:** Founder, President, Michael Cage Found, 826 Orange Ave Suite 501, Coronado, CA 92118.

### CAGE, PATRICK B.
Lawyer, executive. **Personal:** Born Aug 11, 1958, Chicago, IL; son of Thomas and Gwendolyn Monroe. **Educ:** Ill State Univ, BS, psychol & criminal justice, 1981; Ohio Northern Univ, JD, health care, 1984. **Career:** Lima State Hosp, patient advocate Criminally Insane; State Farm Ins Cos, arbitrator; Cook County Ct, arbitrator; City Chicago, sr atty, corp coun, 1985-88; Fr, Kezelis & Kominiarek, sr assoc, 1988-; O'Hagan Smith & Amundsen LLC, atty & partner; Chicago State Univ, vpres labor & legal affairs & gen coun, 2009-. **Orgs:** Alpha Phi Alpha, 1978-; Cook County Bar Asn, 1984-; bd trustee, Anixter Ctr; Am Bar Asn, 1984-; Ill State Bar Asn, 1984-; Chicago Bar Asn, 1984-; Nat Asn Col & Univ Attorneys, 1984-. **Honors/Awds:** Broker of Year Award, Alpha Phi Alpha, 1979. **Home Addr:** 345 W Fullerton Pky, Chicago, IL 60614, **Home Phone:** (773)883-3489. **Business Addr:** Vice President of Labor & Legal Affairs, General Counsel, Chicago State University, 9501 S King Dr, Chicago, IL 60628, **Business Phone:** (773)995-2000.

### CAGE-BIBBS, PATRICIA. See BIBBS, PATRICIA.

### CAGGINS, DR. RUTH PORTER
Educator. **Personal:** Born Jul 11, 1945, Natchez, MS; daughter of Corinne Baines Porter and Henry Chapelle Porter; married Don Randolph; children: Elva Rene, Don Randolph Jr & Myles Chapelle. **Educ:** Dillard Univ, BS, nursing, 1967; NY Univ, MA, psychiat ment health nursing, 1973; Tex Woman's Univ, PhD, nursing res, 1992; Emory Univ, PhD. **Career:** Montefiore Hosp & Med Ctr, staff & head nurse, 1968-71; Lincoln Comm Ment HTH Ctr, staff nurse & therapist, 1972-73; Metrop Hosp & Med Ctr, nurse clin & clin adm sup, 1973-76; Univ Southwestern la, asst prof, 1976-78; Prairie View A&M Univ, teacher, assoc prof, tenured, 1979-2010, flc dir, 2001, Nurse Educr, 2010-; AMR Nurses Asn, Minority Fel, 1989-92. **Orgs:** Sigma Theta Tau, 1973-93; A K Rice IST, assoc mem, Cent States Ctr, 1992-93, gen mem, Tex Ctr, 1992-93; Asn Black Nursing Fac, prog chair, 1993 Spring Regional; Prairie View A&M Univ Col Nursing, LIFT Ctr proj dir, 1994; Nat Black Nurses Asn; AMR Nurses Asn; Nat League Nursing; Houston Asn Psychiat Nurses. **Home Addr:** 5602 Goettee Cir, Houston, TX 77091, **Home Phone:** (713)682-1264. **Business Addr:** Associate Professor, Prairie View A&M University, 6436 Fannin St 9th Fl, Houston, TX 77030, **Business Phone:** (713)797-7058.

### CAILLIER, JAMES ALLEN
School administrator, executive, vice president (organization). **Personal:** Born Sep 24, 1940, Lafayette, LA; married Geraldine Elizabeth Raphael; children: Jennifer, Gerard & Sylvia. **Educ:** Univ Southwestern La, BS, 1964; Southern Univ, MS, 1968; La State Univ, PhD, EdD, 1978. **Career:** Pub Schs, supvr, 1967-69, teacher, 1964-67; Univ Southwestern La, dean & prof jr div, 1975, dir & prof, 1970, vpres admin affairs, 1984; US Off Educ, nat field reader, 1972-77, nat consult, 1974; Comnr Lafayette Harbor Term & Indust, 1975; Delgado & Nunez Community Col, pres; La State Col & Univs, pres, bd trustee; Univ La Syst, pres, pres emer, currently; Taylor Energy Co LLC, spokesman, dir & vpres external affairs, 1997-. **Orgs:** Bd dir, Lafayette Chamber Com, 1975-; bd dir, Taylor Energy Co LLC; exec dir, spokesman, Patrick Taylor Found, currently. **Home Addr:** 140 Nickerson Pkwy, Lafayette, LA 70501, **Home Phone:** (337)261-5965. **Business Addr:** Vice President of External Affairs, Taylor Energy Co LLC, 1 Lee Cir, New Orleans, LA 70112, **Business Phone:** (504)581-5491.

### CAIN, FRANK
Government official. **Personal:** Born Sep 30, 1930, Mocksville, NC; son of Arthur Reece and Ella Florence Eaton; children: Dishon Franklin. **Educ:** A&T State Univ, BS, 1956, MS, 1967; NC State Univ; Univ Okla. **Career:** Government official (retired); NC Agr Ext Serv, asst co-agt, 1957-62; Us Dept Agr Fm HA, asst co-supvr, 1962-66, co supvr, 1966-85. **Orgs:** Black & Minority Employee Orgn; NC Asn Co Supvr; chmn, trustee bd, Bldg Fund Chinquepin Grove Baptist Church; Prince Hall Grand Lodge F&A Masons NC; pres, Alamance County Chap; A&T State Univ Alumni. **Home Addr:** 857 Dewitt Dr, Mebane, NC 27302-9455, **Home Phone:** (336)578-1277.

### CAIN, FRANK EDWARD, JR.
Lawyer. **Personal:** Born Feb 1, 1924, Blenheim, SC; married Dollie M Covington; children: Cherryetta & Anthony. **Educ:** SC State Col, BA, LLB, 1951. **Career:** Kollock Elem Sch, Wallace, SC, teacher, 1653-55; Bennettsville, SC, atty pvt practice, currently. **Orgs:** SC Bar Asn; SC State Bar; SC Black Lawyers Caucus; Marlboro Co Bar; past & Pole march Cheraw Alumni Chapt; Kappa Alpha Psi Fraternity; Sr Warden Sawmill Masonic Lodge 375; vpres, Marlboro Co Br, Nat Advan Asn Colored People; comn, Am Legion Post 213; US Dist Ct Dist SC; US Ct Appeals; pres, W Bennettsvl Precinct Dem Party. **Honors/Awds:** Cert Dist Educ, SC Dept Educ, 1966; Certificate of Achievement, Kappa Alpha Psi Fraternity, 1966. **Home Addr:** 99 Ellison Ct, Bennettsville, SC 29512, **Home Phone:** (843)479-2894. **Business Addr:** 225 W Mkt St, Bennettsville, SC 29512, **Business Phone:** (843)479-2552.

### CAIN, HERMAN
Executive. **Personal:** Born Dec 13, 1945, Memphis, TN; son of Luther Jr and Lenora Davis; married Gloria Etchison; children: Melanie & Vincent. **Educ:** Morehouse Col, BS, math, 1967; Purdue Univ, MS, comput sci, 1971. **Career:** Pillsbury Co, vpres & corp, syst & servs, 1977-82; Burger King Corp, regional vpres, 1982-86; Godfather's Pizza Inc, pres, 1986-96, chief exec officer, 1988-96, chmn bd, 1996; Nat Restaurant Asn, chief exec officer & pres, 1996-99; Bob Dole presidential campaign, sr econ adv, 1996; Dept Navy, mathematician; Coca-Cola Co, bus analyst; Fox News, commentator, 2013; N Star Writers Group, syndicated columnist; New Voice Inc, pres & chief exec officer, currently. **Orgs:** Bd mem, Creighton Univ, 1989-95; bd mem, Super Valu Inc, 1990-99; bd mem, Utilicorp United Inc, 1992; bd mem, Whirlpool Corp, 1992; chmn, Fed Res Bank Kans City, 1989-96; pres & chmn bd, Nat Restaurant Asn, 1994-95; bd mem, Nabisco Inc, 1995-2000; bd mem, Hallmark Cards, 2001; bd mem, Reader's Dig, 2001; founder, New Voice Found; chmn & pres, Tax Leadership Coun, pub educ component Am Fair Taxation; bd dir, AGCO Inc; bd dir, Aquila Inc; bd dir, Ga Chamber Com; bd dir, Morehouse Col, Atlanta, Ga. **Business Addr:** President, Chief Executive Officer, THE New Voice Inc, 825 Fairways Ct Suite 303, Stockbridge, GA 30281, **Business Phone:** (678)565-5335.

### CAIN, JOSEPH HARRISON, JR.
Football player. **Personal:** Born Jun 11, 1965, Los Angeles, CA; children: Ayana & Joseph III. **Educ:** Stanford Univ, grad; Ore Inst Technol, grad. **Career:** Football player (retired); Minnesota Vikings, 1988; Seattle Seahawks, linebacker, 1989-92, right linebacker, 1990, left linebacker, 1992, 1997; Chicago Bears, left linebacker, 1993-94, 1996, middle linebacker, 1995; Stanford Univ, asst linebackers coach, head coach. **Special Achievements:** Film: 1988 NFL Draft, 1988.

### CAIN, NATHANIEL Z., JR.
President (organization), chief executive officer, automotive executive. **Personal:** Born Feb 1, 1946, Gary, IN; son of Nathaniel Sr and Evelyn Carr (deceased); married Jacqueline Weaver; children: Fredrick, Jeffrey & Natalie. **Educ:** Purdue Northwest, attended 1970. **Ca-**

reer: Ford dealership, Gary, 1969; Mad Hatter Rest & Show Lounge, owner, 1976-81; Bart Allen Buick, gen mgr, 1982-85; Chuck White Buick, gen mgr, 1985-86; Tyson Motor Corp, vpres, 1986-; Tyson Lincoln Mercury, dealer-prin, pres & gen mgr, 1989-, chief exec officer, 1996-; Melrose Lincoln Mercury Inc, co-owner & vpres, 1997-; Tyson Ford, Pres & dealer-prin; Highland Lincoln Mercury Inc, chief exec officer, pres, currently. **Orgs:** Chrysler-Plymouth Minority Dealers Asn, 1986; Nat Automobile Dealers Asn, 1986; Ind COC, 1989; Highland COC, 1989; Northwest Ind Auto Dealers Asn, 1989; Ford Lincoln Mercury Minority Dealers Asn, 1989; Nat Asn Minority Auto Dealers, 1990; bd dir, Boys Girls Clubs Am; bd trustee, Gary YWCA; bd dir, NW Ind Urban League; bd dir, Gary Men Health Asn; bd, Girls Clubs Northwest Ind. **Home Addr:** 3367 Ga St, Gary, IN 46409-1136, **Home Phone:** (219)884-1953. **Business Addr:** President, Chief Executive Officer, Highland Lincoln Mercury Inc, 2440 45th St, Highland, IN 46322, **Business Phone:** (219)924-5500.

### CAIN, DR. ROBERT R., JR.
President (organization). **Personal:** Born Mar 2, 1944, Chicago, IL; married Azucena Becerril; children: Azucena II, Lisa, Carla & Paula. **Educ:** Univ Nebr, BS, 1977; Northern Colo, MA, 1978; Nat Univ, MBA, 1986, JD, 1995, PhD, 1999. **Career:** US Govt Serv, 1962-82; Super Care Inc, clin dir, 1982-86; Northeast Clin Care Serv, chief exec officer, 1986-88. **Orgs:** Scottish Rite Mason Shriner 32 degree Mason, 1976-86; Alpha Phi Alpha, 1982. **Home Addr:** 111 Water Bluff Lane, Richmond, TX 77406.

### CAIN, RUBY
Administrator, executive. **Educ:** Wayne State Univ, BA, sociol; Univ Phoenix, MA, orgn mgt; Ball State Univ, EdD, adult & community educ, 2009. **Career:** United Way Allen Co, adminr diversity & inclusiveness; Creative Training Excellence Inc, pres & chief exec officer, 1994-; Ind Tech, adj fac, 2010; Ball State Univ, dir, asst prof, acad advisor, adult & community educ, 2010-; NE Ind Area Health Educ Ctr, dir, currently. **Orgs:** Ft Wayne African Am Cancer Alliance; founding mem, Health Disparity Coalition; pres, Pi Lambda Theta; publicity chair, Links Inc, Ft Wayne Chap; diversity chair, Am Asn Univ Women; bd mem, YWCA; bd mem, United Way Allen County; bd mem, Ind Pub Health Asn; bd mem, HealthVisions Midwest; Delta Sigma Theta Sorority Inc; commun chair, Ft Wayne Alumnae Cha; lifetime mem, adv bd pres, Ft Wayne African Am Cancer Alliance; planning comt mem, Nat Black Geneal Summit; Allen County Health Disparity Coalition, 2003; Int Soc Educ Biog; Am Asn Adult & Continuing Educ, 2012; fel Scholar Teaching & Learning, 2012; Asn Non-Traditional Students Higher Educ, 2015. **Business Addr:** Director, Northeast Indiana Area Health Education Center, 2700 S Lafayette St Suite 100, Ft. Wayne, IN 46806, **Business Phone:** (260)744-1188.

### CAIN, DR. RUDOLPH ALEXANDER KOFI
Educator, college administrator. **Personal:** Born Sep 13, 1940, Richmond, VA; son of William and Mary. **Educ:** Hampton Inst, BA, 1962; NY Univ, MA, 1968; Columbia Univ Teachers Col, MA, 1976, EdD, 1977. **Career:** Cath Home Bur Dependent C, case aide, 1962-65; City Courts NY, probation officer, 1965-68; Manpower Develop Training Prog, New York Bd Educ, supv counr, 1968-69; Pace Univ, Mgt Career Prog Disadvantaged Stud, asst dir, 1969-73; City Univ New York, Medgar Evers Col, SEEK acad counr, 1973-74; State Univ NY, Empire State Col, prof & dir, 1974, Bedford-Stuyvesant Unit, fac mentor & unit coordr, dir. **Orgs:** Omega Psi Phi Fraternity; Health Task Force, NY African Am Inst, 1984; chair, Educ Taks Force, Bedford-Stuyvesant Community Conf, 1986-91; trustee, Soc Preserv Weeksville & Bedford-Stuyvesant Hist, 1988-90; community bd, Parks & Recreation Comt, 1994-96. **Home Addr:** 1360 Fulton St, Brooklyn, NY 11216, **Home Phone:** (718)852-0888.

### CAIN, SIMON LAWRENCE
Lawyer. **Personal:** Born Dec 19, 1927, Augusta, GA; married Ada Spence. **Educ:** Howard Univ, BA, 1949, LLB, 1957. **Career:** Estate Planning & Admin Real Estate; Pvt pract atty, currently. **Orgs:** Wash Bar Asn; Am Bar Asn; Nat Bar Asn; DC Bar Asn; pres, Lamond-Riggs Citizen Asn, 1968-70; pres DC Fedn Civic Asn, 1969-71; chmn, highways & transp Palisades Citizens Asn, 1974. **Honors/Awds:** Recipient Korean/UN 3 Battle Stars, USAF, 1950. **Home Phone:** (202)362-3093. **Business Addr:** Attorney, 4901 Klingle St NW, Washington, DC 20016-2651, **Business Phone:** (202)244-1081.

### CAINES, BRUCE STUART
Photographer. **Personal:** Born Jan 7, 1959, Jamaica, NY; son of David and Inez; married Lisa Bernad; children: 2. **Educ:** Sch Visual Arts, NY, BFA, photog, 1981. **Career:** Nickelodeon's Blue's Clues, dir; Bruce Caines Photog, photogr & dir, currently; Wacky Dog Imageworks, producer, dir, 2005-; Film: Turn Right by Yellow Dog; A Corner Paradise. **Orgs:** NY Cares, vol, 1990-94; Black Women in Publ, 1994-96; Film Video Arts, NY; Asn Independent Video & Filmmakers. **Honors/Awds:** Emmy nomination for Outstanding Directing. **Special Achievements:** Our Common Ground, Portraits of Blacks Changing the Face of America, Crown Publ, 1994; Our Common Ground, Nat Photography Exhibit, Art Inst Chicago, 1994-95; Contributing Photogr For Jazziz Mag, La Style, Essence, Emerge, Newsweek, Philadelphia Inquirer, Sunday Mag; Dir, Music Videos; Producer & Dir, Short Film, "Breaking Up", 2001; Contributing Ed, Archetype Mag; Emmy nomination for Outstanding Directing in a Children's Series, 2003. **Home Addr:** 2 Adrian Ave Suite 2A, New York, NY 10463. **Business Addr:** Photographer, Director, Bruce Caines Photography, 2 Adrian Ave Suite 2A, New York, NY 10463, **Business Phone:** (718)295-0950.

### CAISON-SOREY, DR. THELMA JANN
Physician. **Personal:** Born Apr 26, 1950, Brooklyn, NY. **Educ:** Winston Salem State Univ, BS, biol, 1972; State Univ NY, Buffalo Sch Med, MD, 1977; Cent Mich Univ, MSA, 1993; Managed Care Col, attended 1997; Wayne State Univ, attended 2001. **Career:** Bd Educ New York, biol teacher, 1972-73; Harlem Hosp Med Ctr, medi externship trauma surg & surg ICU, NY, 1974, medi externship obstet & gyn, 1975; Downstate Med Ctr Kings Co Hosp Ctr, summer med externship inter nalmed, NY, 1976; Montefiore Hosp Med Ctr, resident, 1977-79; N Cent Bronx Hosp, resident Pediat, physician, 1977-83; Henry Ford Hosp Dept Pediat & Div Adolescent Med, div head, 1983-; Primary Care Pediat & Adolescent Med, div head, 1985-2000; Sch Based & Community Health Care Prog, NY, 1991-; Clin & Managed Care Serv, assoc med dir, 1997-2000; Kids Care Mich, qual dir, 1998-2000; NIH Res Grant, clin adv bd, 2001-08; Blue Cross Blue Shield Mich, sr med dir, 2001-; Univ Mich, Sch Pub Health, adj prof, 2006-. **Orgs:** AMA, 1970-80; Nat Med Asn, 1979-80; Comt Residents & Interns, 1979-80; State Univ NY Buffalo & Sch Med Alumni Asn; Delta Sigma Theta Nat Sor; Am Bd Pediat, 1988-; Winston Salem Univ Alumni Asn; fel Am Acad Pediat, 1991-; Mich State Med Soc; Wayne Co Med Soc; bd advisor, Detroit Sci Ctr, 2005-; Am Col Physician Execs, currently; Soc Adolescent Med, currently. **Honors/Awds:** Medical Scholastic Honor, State Univ NY Buffalo Sch Med, 1973-77; Pride in Heritage Award, field med Phi Delta Kappa Nat Sor, 1978; guest speaker, seminar hypertension & nutrition Phi Delta Kappa Sor, 1979; Senior Staff Award, Univ Mich, 1994; Senior Staff Award, Henry Ford Health Syst, 1995; Physician Recognition Award, AMA, 1999; Spirit of Detroit Award, Detroit City Coun, 2001; Certificate of Achievement, by Detroit Mayor, 2001; NCQA Certificate, Blue Cross Blue Shield Mich, 2005; Leadership Recognition Award, Soc Adolescent Med, 2008; Ludwig Award, Mich Health & Hosp Asn, 2008; Founder of Adolescent Health Award, AAP Nat Conf, 2008. **Home Addr:** 2799 W Grand Blvd, Detroit, MI 48202, **Home Phone:** (313)916-2600. **Business Addr:** Adjunct Professor, University of Michigan, 1415 Washington Heights, Ann Arbor, MI 48109-2029, **Business Phone:** (248)448-8366.

### CALAWAY, TONIT M.
Vice president (organization). **Personal:** daughter of George. **Educ:** Univ Wis, Milwaukee, WI, BS, polit sci; Univ Chicago, Law Sch, JD, 1992. **Career:** Davis & Kuelthau SC; Godfrey & Kahn SC; Harley-Davidson Inc, atty, 1998, assoc gen coun, 2004-07, asst gen coun, chief compliance coun, 2008-10, asst secy, vpres human resources, 2010-. **Orgs:** Pres, Harley-Davidson Found, 1998-; bd dir, Meta House, 2007-; bd dir, Univ Wis-Milwaukee Found; bd dir, Boys & Girls Club Greater Milwaukee, currently. **Business Addr:** Vice President of Human Resources, Assistant Secretary, Harley-Davidson Inc, 3700 W Juneau Ave, Milwaukee, WI 53208, **Business Phone:** (414)342-4680.

### CALBERT, DR. ROOSEVELT
Government official. **Personal:** Born Nov 13, 1931, Philadelphia, MS; son of Jim and Ann; married Thelma Nichols; children: Debra C Brown, Jacquelyn C Smith, Rosalyn C Groce & Lori A. **Educ:** Jackson State Univ, BS, sci, 1954; Univ Mich, MA, sci, 1960; Univ Kans, MS, physics, 1969, PhD, plasma physics, 1971. **Career:** Alcorn State Univ, physics prof, 1960-63; AL State Univ, math & physics coordr, 1963-68; Univ Kans, res asst, 1969-71; Inst Servs Educ, coop acad planning, dir, 1971-75; Nat Sci Found, prog dir, div dir, currently. **Orgs:** Phi Beta Sigma Frat, 1951-; Alpha Kappa Mu Nat Hon Soc, 1952-; founder, Heritage Fel Church, 1978; bd chmn, Community Investors Corp, 1982-; AAAS, 1984-. **Home Addr:** 11331 French Horn Lane, Reston, VA 20191, **Home Phone:** (703)758-9777. **Business Addr:** Deputy Division Director, Program Director, National Science Foundation, 4201 Wilson Blvd, Arlington, VA 22230, **Business Phone:** (703)292-5111.

### CALBERT, REV. WILLIAM EDWARD, SR.
Clergy, military leader. **Personal:** Born Jun 11, 1918, Lemoore, CA; son of William Riley (deceased) and Sadie Emma Hackett (deceased); married Katie Rose Baker; children: William E (deceased), Rose M Findley, Muriel L, Katherine E Jackson & Yvonne A DeSena; married Madlyn G Williams; children: William E Jr. **Educ:** SF State Col, CA, AB, 1949; Am Baptist Sem W, Berkeley, M Div, 1952; Teachers Col, Columbia Univ, MA, 1963; Am Univ, Wash DC, Post Grad Study, 1971. **Career:** US, Far E, Ger, unit & org chaplain, 1952-62; AUS Chaplain Sch, Brooklyn, NY, staff & fac, 1963-67; Concord Baptist Church Brooklyn, NY, Pastoral Assoc & dir christian educ part-time, 1964-67; AUS, Vietnam, staff chaplain, dep Staff, 1967-68; Hq first AUS, Ft Meade MD, asst army chaplain, Lt Col, 1968-69; Far E Comm Serv Anti-Poverty Agency, DC, asst dir, exec dir, 1970-73; St Elizabeths Hosp, DC, staff chaplain, 1973-81; Shiloh Baptist Church, Minister educ Wash, DC, 1981-85; Chaplaincy & Pastoral Coun Serv, Am Baptist Churches, USA, Valley Forge, PA, interim dir, 1986-87; Shiloh Baptist Church, Wash, DC, pulpit assoc, 1987, minister, 2004-. **Orgs:** Phi Delta Kappa; Nat Asn Advan Colored People; Urban League; Asn study Afro-Am Life & Hist; Afro-Am Hist & Geneal Soc; Alpha Phi Alpha; past pres, DC Grad chp; Retired Officer Asn; Nat Geneal Soc; Asn Prof Chaplains; Nineth & Tenth Calvary Asn; Wash DC Vote Coalition; bd mem, Housing Develop Corp, 1972-76; DC Mayor's Health Planning Adv Comt, 1972-77; pres, Am Baptist Sem W, 1989-93, int pres, 1990-92, sem trustee, 1990-92; memship comt, Asn Ment Health Clergy, 1988-90; State Adv Coun Adult Educ, Wash, DC, 1990-93; past pres, Wash DC Chap; Nat Trustee Bd, 1996-99; adv bd, Comm Ment Health Ctr, No 2 Wash, DC; Wash, DC Hist Rec Adv Bd, 2002-05; Hist Comn, DC Baptist Conv; trustee & exec comt mem, Nat Mil Chaplains Asn. **Honors/Awds:** Certificate of Apppreciation, DC Govt, 1973; Superior Performance Award, St Elizabeth's Hosp, Wash, DC, 1981; Cert Commendation, Am Baptist Churches, 1987; Am Baptist Seminary of the West, Alumnus of the Year, 1996; Mary McLeod Bethune Service Award, Asn Study Afro-Am Life & History, 2002. **Home Addr:** 1261 Kearney St NE, Washington, DC 20017-4022, **Home Phone:** (202)832-7305. **Business Addr:** Minister, Shiloh Baptist Church, 1500 9th St N W, Washington, DC 20001, **Business Phone:** (202)232-4288.

### CALDWELL, ADRIAN BERNARD
Basketball player. **Personal:** Born Jul 4, 1966, Falls County, TX. **Educ:** Navarro Col, Corsicana, TX, attended 1984; Southern Methodist Univ, Dallas, TX, attended 1986; Lamar Univ, Beaumont, TX, attended 1987. **Career:** Basketball player (retired); Houston Rockets, 1989-91, 1994-95; Shamp Clear Cantu, Italy, 1991-93; Sioux Falls Sky force, 1993-95; Houston Rockets, 1994-95; Indiana Pacers, 1995-96; NJ Nets, 1997; Philadelphia 76ers, 1996-97; Cleveland Cavaliers, 1997; Dallas Mavericks, 1997-98. **Home Addr:** 2419 Leffingwel St, Houston, TX 77026.

### CALDWELL, ARDIS
Executive. **Personal:** Born Jun 14, 1953, Ypsilanti, MI; children: Jason & Lyndsi. **Educ:** Wayne State Univ, BS, 1977; Leading Strategic Chg, cert, 2002. **Career:** Bank One, teller, 1976-78, mgt trainee, 1978-79, sr asst mgr, 1980-85, br mgr, 1985-92, call ctr site mgr, 1993-. **Orgs:** Vpres, Justice Unity Generosity & Serv; steering comm, African Am Network; African Am Mus. **Home Phone:** (248)885-2096. **Business Addr:** Senior Vice President, Bank One, 1235 E Big Beaver Rd, Troy, MI 48083, **Business Phone:** (248)680-2750.

### CALDWELL, BARRY H.
Vice president (government), executive. **Educ:** Dartmouth Col, BA, hist, 1982; Georgetown Univ Law Ctr, JD, 1985. **Career:** Kutak Rock & Campbell, 1985-89; Cole Corette & Abrutyn, 1989-91; US Sen Arlen Specter, coun & chief staff, 1991-96; Pharmaceut Res & Manufacturers Am, vpres, Fed Affairs, 1996-2000; CIGNA Corp, vpres govt rels, 2000-02; Waste Mgt Inc, sr vpres govt affairs & corp communs, 2002-14, sr vpres corp affairs & chief legal officer, 2014-. **Orgs:** Vpres, Fed Affairs Pharmaceut Res & Manufacturers Am, 1996-2000; Nat Solid Wastes Mgt Asn; bd dir & bd chmn, Keep Am Beautiful; bd, Environ Industs Asn; bd dir, Discovery Green Conservancy; bd dir, Arthur W. Page Soc; bd dir, Nat Asn Manufacturers; bd trustee, Nat Waste & Recycling Asn. **Business Addr:** Senior Vice President, Waste Management Inc, 1001 Fannin St Suite 4000, Houston, TX 77002, **Business Phone:** (713)512-6200.

### CALDWELL, BENJAMIN
Playwright. **Personal:** Born Sep 24, 1937, New York, NY. **Career:** Plays: Mission Accomplished, 1967; Four plays, 1968; Prayer Meeting or The First Militant Minister, 1968; Hypnotism, Afro-Arts Anthology, 1969; The King of Soul, Family Portrait, New plays From the Black Theatre, 1969: An Anthology, 1969; The Job, Black Identity, 1970; All White Caste, Black Drama Anthology, 1971; An Obscene Play, 1971; The Wall, Scripts, 1972; What Is Going On, 1973; The World of Ben Caldwell, 1982; The Solutions to All the World's Problems, 2004: An Evening of Short Works for the stage. **Orgs:** Black Arts Movement, 1960-. **Honors/Awds:** Guggenheim fellowship for playwriting, 1970. **Business Addr:** PO Box 656, New York, NY 10026.

### CALDWELL, DR. CLEOPATRA HOWARD
Educator. **Educ:** NC A&T State Univ, BS, psychol, 1973; Wayne State Univ, MA, human develop, 1975; Univ Mich, AM, psychol, 1983, PhD, social psychol, 1986. **Career:** Merrill-Palmer Inst, res asst, 1973-74; Howard Univ, Ment Health Res & Develop Ctr, res asst, 1975-81; Univ Mich Sch Pub Health, Dept Psychol, Prog Res Black Americans, res asst II, 1981-86, Predoctoral Fel, 1982-85, African Am Ment Health Res Ctr, res investr, 1991-96, Health Behav & Health Ed, fac, Inst social Res, staff, asst prof, 1996-2004, Res Ctr Group Dyn, staff, Sch Pub Health, staff, Health Behav & Health Ed, assoc prof, 2004-, Prog Res Black Am, co assoc dir, 1995-2010, Ctr Res Ethnicity, Cult & Health, Sch Pub Health, dir, 2011-; Capital Hill US Congressman J Roy Rowland, health policy analyst, 1986-88; US Congressman Sander Levin, fel, 1986-87; Univ Md, study dir & instr, 1989-91. **Orgs:** Am Pub Health Asn; Soc Res Adolescents; Soc Res Child Develop; dir, Nat Acad Sci, 1988-89; fel US Congressman Sander Levin. **Home Addr:** 305 Burr Oak Dr, Ann Arbor, MI 48103-2079, **Home Phone:** (734)668-8509. **Business Addr:** Associate Professor, Co-Associate Director, University Mich School Pub Health, 1415 Wash Heights 2858 SPH I, Ann Arbor, MI 48109-2029, **Business Phone:** (734)647-3176.

### CALDWELL, ELETA J.
School principal. **Career:** Art High Sch, Newark, NJ, prin, 1992-2003.

### CALDWELL, DR. ESLY SAMUEL
Physician. **Personal:** Born Sep 25, 1938, Lancaster, SC; married Judith Mary Slining; children: Esly III, Christina C & Robert S. **Educ:** Howard Univ, Col Lib Arts, BS, 1960, Col Med, MD, 1964; Univ Mich Sch Pub Health, MPH, 1979. **Career:** Henry Ford Hosp, resident internal med, 1967-70, intern, 1970-71; Univ Mich Hosps & Health Ctr, resident internal med, 1971-72; Ann Arbor Veterans Affairs Med Ctr, med genetics, 1972; Michael Reese Hosp Med Ctr, resident; Daugherty Med Group, physician; intern physician, pvt pract, currently. **Orgs:** Phi Beta Kappa; pres, Cincinnati Med Asn. **Honors/Awds:** Fel Royal Col Physician Can; fel Am Acad Family Physicians; fel Am Col Physicians. **Business Addr:** Physician, 2230 Auburn Ave, Cincinnati, OH 45219-2975, **Business Phone:** (513)861-6610.

### CALDWELL, GEORGE THERON, SR.
Government official. **Personal:** Born Jun 5, 1939, Mississippi County, AR; son of Harry Larnell and Mary Alice Warren; married Jacqueline Romaine Hinch; children: Darri Alice, Jacqueline Michelle, George T II, Robert L, Richard D, Marilynn Kitt, Felecia, Terry, Delores S, Pamela & Shelly Murphy. **Educ:** Univ Minn, Gen Col, AA, 1972; Univ Minn, Col Lib Arts, Hons Div, BA, 1976. **Career:** Affirmative Action Dept, County Hennepin, res analyst, 1973-76, asst dir, 1976-80; Dept Civil Rights, City Minneapolis, exec dir, 1980-84, Pub Schs, dep dir, 1997-2003, Human Resources Dept, dir employ servs, 2004-; Minn Valley Transp Co Inc SW, owner, 1984-86; Univ Minn, asst dir EO & AA, 1986-91, human resources adr, 1991-97. **Orgs:** Bd dir, Minneapolis Br Nat Asn Advan Colored People, 1976-77; bd dir, Benjamin E Mays Fundamental Sch, 1977-81; trustee, Mt Olivet Baptist Church, 1978-80; chmn, Inter govt Compliance Inst, 1978-81; pres, MN State Affirmative Action Assoc, 1979-80; founder & directorate, MN Soc Open Community, 1983. **Home Addr:** 2421 Germain St, St. Paul, MN 55109, **Home Phone:** (651)770-4149. **Business Addr:** Director of Employment Services, City of Minneapolis, Pub Serv Ctr, Minneapolis, MN 55415, **Business Phone:** (612)673-2282.

### CALDWELL, ISIAH MICHAEL, JR. See CALDWELL, MIKE ISAIAH, JR.

**CALDWELL, JAMES E.**
Lawyer, executive. **Personal:** Born May 22, 1930, Louisville, KY; son of George and Emmie Lou; married Dolores Robinson; children: Janelle, James & Randall. **Educ:** Univ Pittsburgh, BA, 1952; Res Officers' Training Corps Univ Pittsburgh, grad, 1952; Howard Univ, Sch Law, JD, 1958; Univ Chicago, MBA, 1973. **Career:** Gen Coun, US Treas Dept, Hon Law Grad Prog, 1959; Internal Revenue Serv off Chief Coun, sr trial atty, 1959-70; Amoco Oil Co, tax atty, 1970-71; Stand Oil Co, sr tax atty, 1971-84; James E Caldwell & Assocs, managing partner, 1984-; Chicago Bd Appeals, vice chmn, 2006-; Caldwell & Hubbard, partner. **Orgs:** Joint bd trustee, bd pres, St Anne's & St Elizabeth Hosp; pres, Roseland Econ Develop Corp; bd, mgrs treas, Chicago Bar Asn, 1973-75; Chicago Bar Asn, 1975-77; Cook County Bar Asn; Nat Bar Asn; Ill Bar Asn; Supreme Ct; US Bar Asn; bd dir, Univ Chicago Club XP Prog; alumni, Grad Sch Busi, Univ Chicago; bd trustee, CBA Pension Fund; bd dirs, CAM Health Trust; Comnr, Supreme Ct, Ill; pres, Coun Legal Edu Opport. **Home Addr:** 9217 S Wabash Ave, Chicago, IL 60619, **Home Phone:** (773)785-4813. **Business Addr:** Managing Partner, James E Caldwell & Associates, 69 W Washington Suite 1420, Chicago, IL 60602, **Business Phone:** (312)368-1788.

**CALDWELL, JAMES L.**
Football coach. **Personal:** Born Jan 16, 1955, Beloit, WI; son of Willie and Mary Evelyn; married Cheryl Lynn Johnson; children: Jimmy, Jermaine, Jared & Natalie. **Educ:** Univ Iowa, BA, Eng, 1977. **Career:** Univ Iowa, grad asst, 1977; Southern Ill Univ, football coach, defensive backs, defensive coordr, wide receivers coach, 1978-80; Northwestern Univ, football coach, defensive backs, 1981-82, offensive asst, 1981; Univ Colo, wide receivers coach, football coach, outside linebackers, quarterbacks, 1982-84; Univ Louisville, football coach, defensive backs, 1985; PA State Univ, football coach, quarterbacks coach, 1986-92; Wake Forest Univ, head football coach, 1993-2000; Tampa Bay Buccaneers, quarterback coach, 2001; Indianapolis Colts, asst head coach & quarterbacks coach, 2002-08, head coach, 2009-11; Baltimore Ravens, quarterbacks coach & offensive coordr, 2012-13; Detroit Lions, head coach, 2014-. **Orgs:** Kappa Alpha Psi Fraternity Inc; Omicron Delta Kappa; founder, Caldwell Found, 2009; Am Football Coaches Asn; Am Football Coaches Asn Bd Trustees; Col Hall Fame Selection Comt; Kappa Alpha Psi fraternity. **Honors/Awds:** Super Bowl Champion (XLI, XLVII); AFC Championship, 2006, 2009, 2012; Beloit Daily News Headliner Award, 2010; Johnnie L. Cochran, Jr. Salute to Excellence Award, 2009, 2010; NFL Rookie Head Coach. **Business Addr:** Head Coach, Detroit Lions, 222 Republic Dr, Allen Park, MI 48101, **Business Phone:** (313)216-4000.

**CALDWELL, JOHN EDWARD**
Insurance executive, chief executive officer. **Personal:** Born Feb 10, 1937, Newberry, SC; son of George (deceased) and Elmira; married Patricia Henderson; children: Sean. **Educ:** Benedict Col, Columbia, BS, chem & mathematics, 1965. **Career:** Insurance executive (retired), chief executive officer, school teacher; Independent Life & Accident Ins Co, staff sales mgr, 1965-96; JE Caldwell Properties, owner & chief exec officer, currently. **Orgs:** Trustee, 1970-80, chmn trustee bd, 1980-82, Newberry Co Mem Hosp; bd mem, Newberry Co Task Force Educ, 1982-87; bd mem, United Way Midlands, 1983-86; bd mem, Cent Midlands Human Resources, 1983-87; Newberry Co Coord United Negro Col Fund, 1983-87; bd mem, Newberry Co Voc Educ, 1984-87; bd mem, Piedmont Area Occup Training; coordr, State Community Block Grant Bd; mem bd comnr, GLEAMNS Human Resources Comn; Overall Econ Develop Bd; Bethlehem Baptist Ch; chmn & treas, Deacon Bd; pres, chmn, Newberry Co Coun, 1997-2002; bd mem, Nat Asn Counties, 2000; Newberry Co Coun, Counman; bd dir, SC Asn Counties, 2004-08; shriner; 32nd degree Mason Bethlehem Baptist Church, chmn, treas, Deacon Bd; pres, County Govt Asn; S Carolina Asn Counties. **Honors/Awds:** Civic Award Outstanding Services, 1984; Outstanding Alumni, Newberry Co Alumni Club, 1985; Recognized in Who's Who Among Black Leaders, 1988; National Sales Award, Independent Life & Accident Co Inc. **Special Achievements:** First African American Staff Sales Manager in the State of South Carolina; First Black elected to Newberry Co Coun, 1983; First & only black staff mgr for Independent Life & Accident Ins Co; First blacks elected to Newberry County Memorial Hospital Board of Trustees. **Home Addr:** 711 McSwain St, Newberry, SC 29108-3753, **Home Phone:** (803)276-5328. **Business Addr:** Owner, Chief Executive Officer, J E Caldwell Properties, 621 Drayton St, Newberry, SC 29108-4215, **Business Phone:** (803)276-5477.

**CALDWELL, KIRBYJON**
Writer, minister (clergy). **Personal:** Born Jan 1, 1953?, TX; son of Booker T and Jean; married Patrice Johnson; married Suzette Turner; children: 2. **Educ:** Carleton Col, BA, 1975; Univ Pa Sch Bus, MBA, 1977; Perkins Sch Theol, MA, 1981. **Career:** First Boston, New York, investment banker, 1970s; Hibbard, O'Conner & Weeks, 1975-78; United Methodist minister, 1981-; St. Mary's United Methodist Church, asst pastor, 1981-82; Windsor Village United Church, sr pastor, 1982-; Houston Texans NFL franchise, ltd partner. **Orgs:** Chair Governance Nominating Comt, NRG Energy; bd mem, Bridgeway Capital Mgt, Greater Houston Partnership Exec Comt, Southern Methodist Univ, & M.D. Anderson-Univ Cancer Found. **Honors/Awds:** Doctor of Law, Huston-Tillotson College; Doctor of Law, Carleton College; named of Newsweek's "Century Club". **Special Achievements:** Co-author, The Gospel of Good Success: A Road Map to Spiritual, Emotional, and Financial Wholeness, 1999; Entrepreneurial Faith: Launching Bold Initiatives to Expand God's Kingdom, Waterbrook Press, 2004. **Business Addr:** Windsor Village United Methodist Church, 6011 W Orem Dr, Houston, TX 77085, **Business Phone:** (713)723-8187.

**CALDWELL, LISA JEFFRIES**
Lawyer. **Personal:** Born Jan 14, 1961, Burlington, VT; daughter of Roy and Pauline; married Alan Lorenzo; children: Tyler Alan & Lauren Brianna. **Educ:** Univ NC, Chapel Hill, BS, bus admin, 1983; Wake Forest Univ, Sch Law, JD, 1986. **Career:** Womble Carlyle Sandridge & Rice, atty, 1986-90; W & Banks, atty, 1990-91; Reynolds Am Inc, mgr, employ practs, 1991-93, personnel mgr, Manuf Opers, 1993-94, personnel mgr, eng environ & support, distrib, logistics, 1994-96, dir human resources eng, distrib & logistics & leaf opers, 1996-2000, dir, human resources strategic planning, 2000-02, vpres, human resources, 2002-06, sr vpres & human resources, 2006-08, exec vpres & chief HR officer, 2008-. **Orgs:** Life mem, Delta Sigma Theta Sorority, 1988-; const comt co-chair, corresp secy, Moles, 1991-93, rec secy, 1996-98, vpres, 1998-00; bd mem, Univ NC Gen Alumni Asn, 1990-93; Forsyth Co Morehead Scholar Selection Comt, 1988-93; bd mem, Goodwill, 1995-; W Cent Region, Morehead selection comt, 1994-; bd mem, Reynolds Fed Credit Union, 1995-; bd dirs, Safe Passage Group, 1997-; bd dirs, Hospice, 1998-2000; bd dirs, CERTL, 1997-2000; bd dirs, Piedmont Triad Partnership Found, 2000; United Metrop Missionary Baptist Church; bd trustee, Winston-Salem State Univ Found, currently; Moles Inc; Links Inc; Wake Forest Univ Sch Bus. **Honors/Awds:** Morehead Scholarship, Morehead Found, 1979-83; National Achievement Scholarship, 1979-83; Wake Forest Law Scholarship, Wake Forest Univ, 1983-86. **Home Addr:** 1370 Kerner Rd, Kernersville, NC 27284, **Home Phone:** (910)992-1003. **Business Addr:** Chief Human Resources Officer, Executive Vice President, Reynolds American Inc, 401 N Main St, Winston Salem, NC 27101, **Business Phone:** (910)741-5000.

**CALDWELL, MARION MILFORD, JR.**
Educator. **Personal:** Born Mar 11, 1952, San Antonio, TX; son of Marion Milford (deceased) and Mazie Hammond (deceased); married Priscilla Robertson; children: Priscilla & Marina. **Educ:** Del State Col, BS, 1978; Univ DC, MBA, 1983; Howard Univ, doctoral stud. **Career:** Del Tech Community Col, instr bus, 1984; Del State Col, prof mkt, 1984-91; Anthony & Lee Realtors LLC, real estate agt. **Orgs:** Omega Psi Phi; Prince Hall Mason Prudence Lodge No 6; Am Mkt Assoc; Nat Black MBA Assoc; MBA Exec; Nat Advan Asn Colored People; rep, Fac Senate; Int Platform Asn; Prudence Lodge No 6 F & AM, PHA; Nat Community Asn, 1995. **Home Addr:** 106 Bertrand Dr, Dover, DE 19904-3410, **Home Phone:** (302)674-1061. **Business Addr:** Real Estate Agent, Anthony & Lee Realtors LLC, Dover, DE 19904-6901, **Business Phone:** (302)346-5000.

**CALDWELL, MIKE ISAIAH, JR. (ISIAH MICHAEL CALDWELL, JR.)**
Football player, football coach. **Personal:** Born Aug 31, 1971, Oak Ridge, TN; son of Bobbie; married Sue; children: Sydnei, Saniah & Simeon. **Educ:** Mid Tenn State Univ, BS, bus admin, 1996. **Career:** Football player (retired), football coach; Cleveland Browns, line backer, 1993-94, right line backer, 1995; Baltimore Ravens, right line backer, 1996; Ariz Cardinals, 1997; Philadelphia Eagles, 2000, left line backer, 1998, line backer, 1999, 2001, defensive qual control coach, 2008-09, asst linebackers coach, 2010, linebackers coach, 2011-12; Chicago Bears, line backer, 2002; Carolina Panthers, 2003; Ariz Cardinals, linebackers coach, 2013-; New York Jets, Asst head coach & inside linebackers coach, 2015. **Business Addr:** Defensive Quality Control Coach, Philadelphia Eagles, 1 NovaCare Way, Philadelphia, PA 19145, **Business Phone:** (215)463-2500.

**CALDWELL, DR. SANDRA ISHMAEL**
Dentist. **Personal:** Born Aug 23, 1948, Ft. Knox, KY; children: Rhonda. **Educ:** Howard Univ, BS, microbiol, 1971, Col Dent, DDS, dent, 1981. **Career:** Food & Drug Admin, microbiologist, 1971-77; Ton Ron Productions, vpres; pvt pract, dentist, 1991-; Full Circle Dent, dentist, 1981-2011, owner, 1991-2011. **Orgs:** Nat Dent Assoc; Acad Gen Dent; Beta Kappa Chi Hon Soc; Prince George's Soc Health Profls, Sigma Xi Sci Res Soc; co-chmn, secy, Robert T Freeman Dent Soc, 1982-; co-chmn, Delta Sigma Theta Sor Inc; dent alumni recruiter, Howard Univ; Internet Dent Alliance; Minority Women Sci; Prince Georges Co Md Chamber Com, 2005-. **Honors/Awds:** Outstanding Young Women of America, 1980; Who's Who Among Stud, Am Univ & Cols, 1981. **Home Addr:** 101 Prospect Dr, Upper Marlboro, MD 20774, **Home Phone:** (301)390-4372. **Business Addr:** General Dentist, Full Circle Dentistry, 6495 NH Ave Suite 108, Hyattsville, MD 20783, **Business Phone:** (301)270-5100.

**CALHOUN, CINDY BOLDEN**
Manager, executive director, association executive. **Educ:** MA. **Career:** Community Health Awareness Group, exec dir & chief financial officer, HIV prev coordinatoor, currently. **Home Addr:** 3824 Sturtevant St, Detroit, MI 48206, **Home Phone:** (313)834-5415. **Business Addr:** Executive Director, Chief Financial Officer, Community Health Awareness Group, 1300 W Ft St, Detroit, MI 48226, **Business Phone:** (313)963-3434.

**CALHOUN, DOROTHY EUNICE**
Administrator, teacher. **Personal:** Born Jul 16, 1936, Salitpa, AL; daughter of Joshua and Maggie Cunningham; married Roosevelt; children: Michael W Moore & Daryl T Moore. **Educ:** Ala State Univ, BS, 1957; Atlanta Univ, MLS, 1972; Auburn Univ, attended 1973. **Career:** Administrator (retired); Clarke Co Bd Educ, teacher, 1957-59; Montgomery Co Bd Educ, teacher & librn, 1959-70; Maxwell AFB, Ala, librn, 1970-94. **Orgs:** NEA, 1959-70; Am Libr Asn, 1970-85; Ala Libr Asn, 1979-83; Delta Sigma Theta Sor; Spec Libr Asn, 1986. **Honors/Awds:** Teacher of the Year, Clarke Co Bd Educ, 1958; Twenty Years Cert Serv, 1970-90; Theses, A Study of the Jr High Sch Libr Fac & Serv, Atlanta Univ, 1972; Librarian of the Year, ATC Comdr, 1980. **Home Addr:** 9006 Brixham Ct, Montgomery, AL 36117-8882, **Home Phone:** (334)215-9973.

**CALHOUN, ERIC A.**
Government official, real estate agent. **Personal:** Born Nov 20, 1950, Gary, IN; son of William and Lillian B; married Delores Brown; children: Asha D. **Educ:** Wilberforce Univ, Wilberforce, OH, BS, acct, 1974; Ky State Univ, Frankfort, KY, MPA, 1982; Miles Law Sch, Fairfield, AL, JD, 1989. **Career:** Cent State Univ, Wilberforce, Ohio, adminr, 1972-78; Wendy's Int, Dayton, Ohio, store co-mgr, 1978-79; Ky State Univ, Frankfort, KY, adminr, 1979-83; Miles Coll, Fairfield, AL, adminr, 1983-85; City Birmingham, Birmingham, AL, admin analyst, 1985-87; Mayor's Off, Birmingham, AL, admin asst, 1987-98; White & Assocs Realty, realtor, 1996-; Birmingham Parking Authority, asst dir, 1998-. **Orgs:** Drug Abuse Task Force, Bethel Baptist Church, 1989-; UAB Special Studies Adv Comt Black Professionals, 1989-. **Business Addr:** Realtor, White & Associates Realty, 813 3rd Ave N, Birmingham, AL 35203, **Business Phone:** (205)326-3000.

**CALHOUN, ESSIE LEE**
Executive, executive director. **Personal:** daughter of James Arthur; married Lee Arthur; children: Kwame Mandulo. **Educ:** Univ Toledo, BEd, social sci; Bowie State Univ, MS, admin & supv. **Career:** S Bend Skills Ctr, instr, 1970-71; Washtenaw Intermediate Sch Dist, consult, spec progs, 1971-73; Prince George's City Schs, teacher & adminr, 1973-81; Eastman Kodak Co, Copy Prod Div, sales rep, 1982, mkt specialist, sales mgr, Community & Pub Affairs Div, dir pub affairs planning, 1988, dir community rels, 1989, dir community rels & contrib, 1994, vpres, 1999-2000, corp vpres, 2000, dir multicultural mkt, 2002-, chief diversity officer & dir, 2003-11, vpres community affairs, currently; Rochester Inst Technol, Minett prof, 2001-02. **Orgs:** Vice chair, Greater Rochester Health Found; bd mem, Roberts Wesleyan Col; bd mem, Rochester Inst Technol; Muhammad Ali Ctr; bd mem, United Way Greater Rochester; founder var orgn incl: exec comt, United Way Greater Rochester, 1989; African Am Leadership Develop Prog, 1991-94; corp adv coun, Cong Black Caucus Found, 1992; chair, Urban League Rochester, 1993; African Am Leadership Roundtable; Kodak Youth Leadership Acad; pres, Eastman Kodak Charitable Trust; corp assoc United Way Am, 1994; human rels comt Monroe County, Rochester, 1994; Pub Rels Socs Am; Nat Corp Women's Network; Bus Policy Rev Coun; Kodak Women's Mgt Forum. **Business Addr:** Vice President, Eastman Kodak Co, 343 State St, Rochester, NY 14650-0517, **Business Phone:** (716)724-1980.

**CALHOUN, FRED STEVERSON**
Educator. **Personal:** Born Mar 20, 1947, McDonough, GA; son of Mattie W and Willie M (deceased); married M Janice Wright; children: Roshunda. **Educ:** Fullerton Col, attended 1966; Cypress Col, AA, 1971; Univ Calif, Irvine, BA, social ecol, 1973; Calif State Univ, Long Beach, MA, psychol, 1977; Nova Univ, EdD, 1989. **Career:** Educator (retired); Cypress Col, Stud Educ Devel Ctr, work study jobs & recruitment coord, 1968-71; UC Irvine, Social Ecol Dept, res asst, 1971-73; Corbin Ctr, asst coord, 1973; Cypress Col, Stud Educ Devel Ctr, asst dir, 1973-79, dir 1979. **Orgs:** Bd trustee, N Orange County Community Col, 1988; N Orange County Community Col Affirmative Action Task Force; Cypress Col Affirmative Action Comn, N Orange County Community Col Dist; Mgt Group, N Orange County Community Col Dist; EOPS Adv Comn, Cypress Col; Extended Opportunities Prog & Serv Asn. **Home Addr:** 6525 Mount Whitney Dr, Buena Park, CA 90620.

**CALHOUN, GREGORY BERNARD**
Entrepreneur, president (organization). **Personal:** Born Sep 10, 1952, Detroit, MI; son of Thomas and Coretta; married Verlyn Pressley; children: Malcolm, Shakenya & Gregory. **Educ:** Trenholm Jr Col, attended 1973; Cornell Univ, attended 1979. **Career:** Hudson & Thompson Supermarkets, package clerk, 1970-71, stock clerk, 1972-73, asst mgr, 1973-75, co-mgr, 1975-79, mgr, 1979-82, pub rels dir, 1982-84; Calhoun Commun; Super Brokerage, Montgomery, Ala; Access Commun; Calhoun Enterprises Inc, pres & chief exec officer, currently; Calhoun & Assocs Network, consult & owner, currently; Calhoun Commun, 1998; Calhoun Foods Distrib Ctr Inc, 2004-; Calhoun Financial Group LLC, 2004-; Calhoun Enterprises, founder, chief exec officer, currently. **Orgs:** Bd mem, Sterling Bank, 1990-; Us Dept Com Wash, 1990; bd mem, Food Mkt Inst, 1994-; minority diversity consult, Albertson's Inc, 1994-; minority diversity consult, Coca Cola Co, 1995-; minority diversity consult, NASCAR, 1996-; bd mem, Montgomery Area Chamber Com; bd mem, Tuskegee Savings & Loan; Montgomery Area Lions Club; bd mem, Hot 105 Radio; exec roundtable, IGA Inc; pres & bd dir, Sickle Cell Anemia Found; bd mem, Montgomery Area Comt 100; Young Men's Christian Asn; bd mem, Nat Asn Adv Coloured People; nat bd mem, Rainbow Push Coalition; bd mem, Coca-Cola Retail Coun; lifetime bd mem, Southern Christian Leadership Conf; lifetime mem, Omega Psi Phi Fraternity; Cosmopolitan Club, Montgomery, AL; vice chmn bd dir, Pub Affairs Comt. **Honors/Awds:** Entrepreneur Dreamer Award, MLK Found, 1988; Progressive Junior Collegian, SCLC, 1989; Annual Leadership Award, 1987; National Minority Retail Firm of the Year, US Dept Com, 1990, Regional Minority Retailer of the Year, 1990; Governor of Alabama, Mar 24, "Greg Calhoun Day", Honoree, 1992. **Special Achievements:** Black Enterprise's Top 100 Industrial/Service companies, ranked No 28, 1999, No 23, 2000; First African-American Board Member of The Coca-Cola Retail Council; First African-American of Food Marketing Institute. **Home Addr:** 3800 Llyde, Montgomery, AL 36106, **Home Phone:** (205)260-0858. **Business Addr:** President, Chief Executive Officer, Calhoun Enterprises Inc, 4155 Lomac St Suite G, Montgomery, AL 36106-2864, **Business Phone:** (334)272-4400.

**CALHOUN, DR. JOSHUA WESLEY**
Psychiatrist. **Personal:** Born Mar 21, 1956, Macon, GA; son of E M (deceased) and Harriett Hixon Williams; married Deloris Davis; children: Joshua W II, Amanda Joy, Adrianna Jade & Austin Judge. **Educ:** Yale Univ, BA, 1978; Univ Cincinnati Col Med, MD, 1982. **Career:** Cincinnati Gen Hosp, med internship, 1982-83; MA Ment Health Ctr, fel, resident psychiat, 1983-87, chief resident, child psychiat, 1986-87; Harvard Med Sch, clin fel psychiat; St Louis Univ Med Sch, asst clin prof; pvt pract, psychiatrist, 1990-; Our Lady Residential Home C, med dir, 1997-. **Orgs:** Nat Inst Ment Health, 1983-86; ed bd, Jefferson J Psychiat, 1985-87; Adolescent Task Force, 1986-87; consult, C Ctr Behav Develop, 1987-90; consult, Annie Malone C Home, 1988-90; Am Psychiat Asn; Am Acad Child Psychiat; Black Psychiatrists Am; Am Med Asn; adv bd, Health Link Inc, 1996; bd mem, Nat Alliance Ment Ill, St Louis, 1998; bd mem, Gateway Adv Bd Develop Disabilities, 1998; fel Am Psychiat Asn. **Honors/Awds:** Honor Roll, Healthgrades. **Home Addr:** 239 Westgate Ave, St. Louis, MO 63130-4709, **Home Phone:** (314)726-4564. **Business Addr:** Psychiatrist, Pediatric Psychiatrist, Private Practice, 1504 S Grand Blvd, St. Louis, MO 63104, **Business Phone:** (314)531-1770.

**CALHOUN, KEVIN**
Engineer, administrator. **Educ:** NC State Univ, BS, mech engineering, 1990. **Career:** Corning Cable Systs, mgr customer qual, 2000-03, dir global qual & training, 2003-07, exec dir global qual & environ

mgt, 2007-10, dir global voice customer prog, 2011-12; Qyest Forum, bd mem, 2007-13; New Freedom Ventures IV LLC, vpres, 2012-13; Axis Teknologies, chief operating officer, 2013-. **Orgs:** Manufactures Alliance/Productivity Inst; Am Soc Qual; Six Sigma Forum; proj dir, 2004, bd alt, 2005-08, leadership coun, 2005, vice chair, 2009, exec bd chair, 2010, exec bd chair emer, 2011, exec bd mem, 2012, exec bd contribr, 2013, Quest Forum; bd mem, Global VOC; NC Awards Excellence. **Business Addr:** Chief Executive Officer, Axis Teknologies LLC, 8800 Roswell Rd Bldg A Suite 265, Sandy Springs, GA 30350, **Business Phone:** (678)441-0260.

## CALHOUN, MONICA

Actor. **Personal:** Born Jul 29, 1971, Philadelphia, PA; daughter of Lorraine; children: 1. **Educ:** Los Angeles County High Sch Arts. **Career:** Acad Players Dir, actress, 1987-; Universal Pictures, actress, 2013-. Films: Sister Act 2: Back in the Habit, 1993; Jack the Bear, 1993; What About Your Friends, 1995; Sprung, 1997; The Players Club, 1998; Park Day, 1998; The Best Man, 1999; Love & Basketball, 2000; Faux Pas, 2001; Final Breakdown, 2002; Civil Brand, 2002; Pandora's Box, 2002; Guns & Roses, 2003; Gang of Roses, 2003; Love Chronicles, 2003; From the Outside Looking In, 2003; Justice, 2004; The Salon, 2005; The Best Man Holiday, 2013. TV movies: "She Stood Alone", 1991; "Jacksons: An American Dream", 1992; "The Ernest Green Story", 1993; "Rebound", 1996; "The Ditchdigger's Daughters", 1997; "Intimate Betrayal", 1999; "Nature Boy", 2000; "Grey's Anatomy", 2006; "Cold Case", 2008; "Diary of a Single Mom", 2009-11. TV guest appearances: "A Different World", 1987; "The Wayans Brothers", 1996; "The Jamie Foxx Show", 1998; "Malcolm & Eddie", 2000; "NYPD Blue", 2003; "Coming Clean", 2003; "Strong Medicine", 2003; "Break on Through", 2006; "Everybody Hates Chris", 2006; "Everybody Hates Funerals", 2006; "Dirt", 2007. **Honors/Awds:** Best Performance by an Actress, Am Black Film Festival, 2002; Indie Series Award, 2011; Hollywood Award, Acapulco Black Film Festival, 2014. **Business Addr:** Actress, Abrams Artists & Associates, 9200 Sunset Blvd Suite 1130, Los Angeles, CA 90069, **Business Phone:** (310)859-0625.

## CALHOUN, DR. NOAH ROBERT

Oral surgeon. **Personal:** Born Mar 23, 1921, Clarendon, AR; son of Noah and Della; married Cecelia C; children: Stephen M & Cecelia N. **Educ:** Dent Sch Howard Univ, DDS, 1948; Tufts Med & Dent Col, MSD, 1955. **Career:** Med Ctr, Tuskegee, AL, Va, oral surgeon, 1950-64; Med Ctr Va, asst oral surg, 1964-72, asst chief dent, 1972-75, chief dent surg, 1975-82, coordr dent res; Georgetown Dent, prof & lectr, 1970-; Va & Atena Ins Co, consult, 1982-; Dent Sch Howard Univ, prof, oralmaxillofacial surg, 1982-92, prof emer, 1992-. **Orgs:** Fel Am Col Dent; dir, Red Cross, Tuskegee Inst, 1962-64; fel Int Col Dent Inst Med, 1982; dir & vpres, Credit Union, Va, 1982; adv comn, Am Bd Oral Surg Inst Med; ed & ed bd, Int Oral & Maxillofacial Surg; St Michael's Church Fin Comt; Inst Med Acad Sci; pres, Bridge Masters, ABC Bridge Asn. **Honors/Awds:** Dental Alumni Award, Howard Univ, 1972. **Home Addr:** 1413 Leegate Rd NW, Washington, DC 20012-1211, **Home Phone:** (202)882-1846. **Business Addr:** Professor Emeritus, Howard University, 600 W St NW, Washington, DC 20059, **Business Phone:** (202)806-0440.

## CALHOUN, DR. THOMAS

Educator. **Personal:** Born Oct 6, 1932, Marianna, FL; son of Thomas Pittman and Sylvia Barnes Thompson; married Shirley Kathryn Jones; children: Thomas Jr, Christine, Kathyne Y & Maria. **Educ:** Fla A&M Univ, BS, 1954; Fisk Univ, grad sch; Meharry Med Col, MD, 1963; Am Bd Surg, dipl, 1971; Howard Univ Hosp, training. **Career:** Fisk Univ, instr, 1957-58; Tennis Circuit, amateur traveller, 1958; US Postal WA, employee, 1958-59; Howard Univ, clin assoc prof surg; Delmarva Med Found, assoc med dir, 2002; DC Med Res Corp, med dir, 2004-. **Orgs:** Life mem, Am Tennis Asn; Am Med Tennis Asn; life mem, US Tennis Asn; Dist Columbia Med Soc; Bd, Surgeons Police Fire Dept; St Thomas Apostle Cath Church; fel Am Col Surgeons, 1972; fel Am Asn Abdominal Surgeons, 1977; med adv, Care-Plus, Delmarva reg med dir; fel Am Col Nutrit; pres, Med-Dent Staff, Providence Hosp, Wash DC; Am Col Physician Execs; Sung Care Assoc. **Home Addr:** 4010 Argyle Terr NW, Washington, DC 20011-5301, **Home Phone:** (202)291-2327. **Business Addr:** Medical Director, DC Medical Reserve Corp, 1620 L St NW Suite 1275, Washington, DC 20036, **Business Phone:** (202)293-9650.

## CALHOUN, PROF. THOMAS C.

Educator, school administrator. **Personal:** Born Aug 31, 1946, Crystal Springs, MS; son of Walter and Ernestine Abney. **Educ:** Tex Wesleyan Col, BA, sociol, 1970; Tex Tech Univ, MA, sociol, 1971; Univ Ky, PhD, sociol, 1988. **Career:** Mt Union Col, Dept Sociol & Anthrop, Instr, 1971-75; Stark County Coun Drug Abuse, Canton, Ohio, Adult Addictive Treat Facil, adminr, 1973-74; Old Dom Univ, Dept Sociol & Anthrop, Instr, 1975-77; Univ Ky, Dept Sociol, teaching asst, 1981-84; Western Ky Univ, instr, 1984-88; 8th Judicial Dist, Admin Off Courts, pretrial serv officer, 1985-88; Ohio Univ, asst prof sociol, 1988-96; Univ Nebr, Lincoln, Nebr, from asst to assoc prof sociol, African Am studies, 1996-2001, Inst Ethnic Studies, dir, 1998-2000, interim assoc vice chancellor acad affairs, 2000-01; Southern Ill Univ, prof sociol, 2001, prof emer, currently; Jackson State Univ, Jackson, Miss, chair social dept, 2003-, assoc vpres provost acad affairs, currently, Col Lib Arts, interim dean, 2012-. **Orgs:** Pres, N Cent Sociol Asn, 1997; pres, Mid-S Sociol Asn, 1997; chair, Asn Black Sociologists, 1998-2000; pres, Asn Social & Behav Scientists, 2000-; ed-in-chief, J Educ Rev Adv Bd. **Home Addr:** 100 Thomas Cir, Crystal Springs, MS 39059, **Home Phone:** (769)232-8223. **Business Addr:** Interim Dean, Jackson State University, PO Box 18019, Jackson, MS 39217-0619, **Business Phone:** (601)979-2246.

## CALLAWAY, LOUIS MARSHALL, JR.

Manager, executive, association executive. **Personal:** Born Jan 22, 1939, Chicago, IL; married Duryea Dickson. **Educ:** Drake Univ, BA, 1961. **Career:** Ford Motor Co, asst plant mgr to plant mgr, 1976-80; Ford Truck plant, Wayne, MI, asst plant mgr, qual control mgr; Ford's Chicago, plant mgr; Ford Dearborn Assembly Plant, mgr; Adv Mat Processing Corp, exec vpres & chief operating officer. **Orgs:** Chicago SCC; dir, Chicago Asn Com & Indust; corp mem, Blue Cross Blue Shield; trustee, New Help Source. **Home Addr:** 4562 Cross Creek Dr, Ann Arbor, MI 48108, **Home Phone:** (734)747-9048.

## CALLENDER, HON. CARL O.

Commissioner, lawyer, judge. **Personal:** Born Nov 16, 1936, New York, NY; married Leola Rhames. **Educ:** Brooklyn Community Col, Brooklyn NY, AB, BA, econ, polit econ, 1961; Hunter Col, Bronx NY, AB, 1964; Howard Univ Sch Law, Wash DC, JD. **Career:** Judge (retired); Hunter Col, New York, asst libr aide, 1966; Palystreet New York, dir, 1967; Harlem Assertion Rights Inc, staff atty, 1968-70; Prentice-Hall's Fed Tax Serv Bulletins NJ, legal edit, 1968; Regin Ald Heber Smith fell Harlem Assertion Rights, 1969-70; CALS Reginald Heber Smith Fell Prog, New York, coordr, 1970-71; US Dist Ct Southern Dist New York, 1970; Comn Law Offices, dep dir, 1971-72; US Ct Appeals 2nd Circuit, 1972; benezer Gospel Tabernacle, ordained minister, 1972; Comn Law Off Prog, dir, 1972-75; Housing Litigation Bur, dir, 1975-76; New York Civil Ct Kings County, judge; Queens Legal Serv Corp, exec dir. **Orgs:** Chmn & pres, Nat Young People's Christian Asn; chmn & pres, Christian Leaders United; elec comn, Stud Bar, Asn admin asst; Housing Res Com; Phi Alpha Delta Legal Fraternity. **Honors/Awds:** American Jurisprudence Award, 1967. **Business Addr:** Project Director, Queens Legal Services Corp, 8900 Sutphin Bvld Fl 2nd, Jamaica, NY 11435-3700, **Business Phone:** (718)657-8611.

## CALLENDER, DR. CLIVE ORVILLE

Educator, physician. **Personal:** Born Nov 16, 1936, New York, NY; son of Joseph and Ida; married Fern Irene Marshall; children: Joseph, Ealena & Arianne N. **Educ:** Hunter Col, AB, 1959; Meharry Med Col, MD, 1963; Univ Minn, transplant surg training, 1973; Univ Pittsburgh, 1987. **Career:** Univ Cincinnati, internship, 1963-64; Harlem Hosp, asst resident, 1964-65; Howard Univ & Freedmen's Hosp, asst resident, 1965-66, chief resident, 1968-69, instr, 1969-70; Hosp Cancer & Allied Dis, asst resident, 1966-67; DC Gen Hosp, med officer, 1970-71; Port Harcourt Gen Hosp Nigeria, consult, 1970-71; Univ Minn, spec post-doctoral res & clin transplant fel, 1971-73; Howard Univ Med Col, asst prof, 1973-76, assoc prof, 1976-80, prof, 1980-; Howard Univ, prof, vice chmn dept surg, 1982-95, transplant ctr, dir, 1973-, Howard Univ Col, LaSalle D Leffall Jr Prof Surg, prof surg & chmn, Dept Surg, HUH, 1996-. **Orgs:** Pres, Alpha Phi Omega Frat, 1959; fel Am Cancer Soc, 1965-66; DC Med Soc; Soc Acad Surg; Transplant Soc; Am Soc Transplant Surg; ed adv bd, New Directions; bd dir, Kidney Found Nat Capital Area; dip, Am Bd Surg, 1970; fel Am Col Surg, 1975; pres, Nat Kidney Found Nat Capital Area, 1979-; chmn & mem comt, Am Soc Transplant Surgeons; pres, Med Dent Staff Howard Univ Hosp, 1980; pres, Alpha Omega Alpha; Alpha Phi Alpha; liver transplant fel, Univ Pittsburgh, 1987-88; adv comt secy health, End Stage Renal Dis Data, 1990-; founder & prin investr, MOTTEP-Nat Minority Orgn, tissue transplant educ prog; bd gov, NMA Gov ACS, 1991; Am Surg Asn, 1991; Southern Surg Asn, 1996; bd trustee, Hunter Col Found, 1999; vpres, pres, Soc Black Acad Surgeons, 1999-. **Home Addr:** 509 Kimblewick Dr, Silver Spring, MD 20904-6341, **Home Phone:** (301)622-4560. **Business Addr:** Founder, Chairman, National MOTTEP, Ambulatory Care Ctr, Washington, DC 20060, **Business Phone:** (202)865-3785.

## CALLENDER, LEROY N.

Engineer, founder (originator). **Personal:** Born Feb 29, 1932, New York, NY; children: Eric. **Educ:** City Col City NY, BCE, 1958. **Career:** Leroy Callender PC Consult Engrs, founder, pres & struct mgr, 1969-. **Orgs:** Distinguished Jury, Pier 40 Design Competition, 1998. **Honors/Awds:** Black Engr of the Year Award, 1992. **Home Addr:** 242 W 27th St Suite 4a, New York, NY 10001, **Home Phone:** (212)989-2900. **Business Addr:** Founder, President, Leroy Callender PC, 236 W 26 St Suite 7, New York, NY 10001-6736, **Business Phone:** (212)989-2900.

## CALLENDER, LUCINDA R.

Educator. **Personal:** Born Oct 26, 1957, Xenia, OH; daughter of Richard E Sr and Isabel Long. **Educ:** Ohio State Univ, Columbus, OH, BA, 1979, MA, 1981, PhD, 1985. **Career:** Ohio Wesleyan Univ Upward Bound Proj, Del, Ohio, teacher & actg assoc dir, 1977-84; Ohio State Univ, Columbus, Ohio, grad teaching assoc, 1980-85; Univ Mo-Columbia, Columbia, Mo, asst prof, 1985-88; San Diego State Univ, San Diego, Calif, asst prof polit sci, 1988-95. **Orgs:** Western Polit Sci Asn, 1990-; Midwest Polit Sci Asn, 1983-89; Southern Polit Sci Asn, 1989-90; Am Polit Sci Asn, 1985-90; Nat Conf Black Polit Scientists. **Home Addr:** 482 Wilson Dr, Xenia, OH 45385-1812, **Home Phone:** (937)372-4296.

## CALLENDER, WILFRED A.

Educator, lawyer. **Personal:** Born Mar 23, 1929, Colon; son of Newton N (deceased) and Isaline Brathwaite (deceased); married Beth Robinson; children: Neil & Melissa. **Educ:** Brooklyn Col, BA, 1954, MA, 1963; Brooklyn Law Sch, JD, 1969. **Career:** Boys High Sch Brooklyn, educator, 1957-69; Dept Real Estate Com Labor Indust Corp Kings, asst dir, 1969-70; Wade & Callender, atty, 1972-; Hostos County Col, prof, 1970-91; Wade & Callender ESQS Pract Law. **Orgs:** Brooklyn Bar Asn; Bedford Stuyvesant Lawyers Asn; Nat Conf Black Lawyers; bd Trustee, Encampment Citizenship, 1971-; pres, Black Caucus Hostos, 1972-; bd trustee, Social Serv; bd, NY Soc Ethical Culture. **Home Addr:** 14477 41st Ave Apt 112, Flushing, NY 11355. **Business Addr:** Lawyer, 2809 Church Ave, Brooklyn, NY 11226-4168, **Business Phone:** (718)284-5406.

## CALLOWAY, CHRISTOPHER FITZPATRICK (CAB CALLOWAY)

Executive, football player. **Personal:** Born Mar 29, 1968, Chicago, IL. **Educ:** Univ Mich, commun & film. **Career:** Football player (retired), executive; Pittsburgh Steelers, wide receiver, 1990, 1991; NY Giants, wide receiver, 1992-98; MTV Live, production asst, 1998; Atlanta Falcons, wide receiver, 1999; New England Patriots, wide receiver, 2000; Assoc Global Serv, info technol recruiter, 2009. **Honors/Awds:** Meyer Morton Award, 1989; Robert P. Ufer Award, 1989. **Business Addr:** Recruiter, Associated Global Services, 73 Southwoods Pkwy Suite 130, Atlanta, GA 30354, **Business Phone:** (404)675-8900.

## CALLOWAY, LAVERNE FANT

Librarian. **Personal:** Born Mar 6, 1950, Byhalia, MS; daughter of Ralph and Alanza Saulsberry; married Otis. **Educ:** Wayne State Univ, BS, bus admin, 1993, MLIS, 1996. **Career:** Schroeder Info Servs Gen Motors Media Arch, indexer, 1996-98; McGregor Pub Libr, dir, 1998-01; Univ Detroit Mercy, Outer Dr Campus Libr, dir, 2001-. **Orgs:** Wayne State Univ Alumni Asn, 1996-; Mich Libr Asn, 1998-; Lions Club Highland Park, 2000-; McGregor Pub Libr Comn, 2002-. **Honors/Awds:** Beta Phi Mu. **Home Addr:** 99 McLean, Highland Park, MI 48203, **Home Phone:** (313)868-2877. **Business Addr:** Director, University of Detroit Mercy, 8200 W Outer Dr, Detroit, MI 48219-0900, **Business Phone:** (313)993-6228.

## CALLOWAY, VANESSA BELL

Actor. **Personal:** Born Mar 20, 1957, Cleveland, OH; married Anthony; children: Ashley & Alexandra. **Educ:** Ohio Univ, BA. **Career:** Actress & dancer; Broadway Prodn dream girls, dancer: TV: "All My Children", 1985; "Days of Our Lives", 1985; "The Colbys", 1986; Simon & simon", 1986; "227", 1987; "In The Heat Of the Night", 1989; "Polly", 1989; "China Beach", 1990; "Piece of Cake", 1990; "Father Dowling Mysteries", 1991; "Memphis", 1992; "Stompin' at the Savoy", 1992; "Rhythm & Blues", 1992; "The Sinbad Show", 1993; "Touched by an Angel", 1995; "The Cherokee Kid", 1996; "Under One Roof"; "Sparks", 1997; "Prey", 1998; "Orleans"; "Moesha", 1998; "The Temptations", 1998; "Malcolm & Eddie", 1999; "The Division", 2001; "One on One", 2002; "The Parkers", 2002; 10-8: Officers on Duty, 2003-04; CSI: Miami, 2004; Strong Medicine, 2004; Joan of Arcadia, 2005; "Oh Drama!"; "Black in the 80s", 2005; The Closer, 2006; "Stompin", 2007; "Vanessa Bell Callowy: In The Company Of Friends", TV One, 2007; CSI, 2009; Cold Case, 2009; Hawthorne, 2010, Shameless, 2011; Ringer, Rizzoli & Isles, Go On, 2012; Between Sisters, 2013; Films: Coming to America, 1988; Bebe's Kids, 1992; What's Love Got to Do With It, 1993; The Inkwell, 1994; Crimson Tide, 1995; Daylight, 1996; Archibald the Rain bow Painter, 1998; When It Clicks, 1998; The Brothers, 2001; All About You, 2001; Dawg, 2002; Biker Boyz, 2003; If You Were My Girl, 2003; Cheaper by the Dozen, 2003; Love Don't Cost a Thing, 2003; Lakeview Terrace, 2008; Killing of Wendy, 2009; The Obama Effect, 2010; The Last Fall, 2012. **Orgs:** Mem, Alpha Kappa Alpha Sorority Inc. **Honors/Awds:** Image Award, Nat Assn Advan Coloured People; Greek Alumni Hall of Fame, Ohio Univ. **Home Addr:** , Los Angeles, CA 90001. **Business Addr:** Actor, Los Angeles, CA 90001, **Business Phone:** (310)289-1088.

## CALLOWAY-MOORE, DORIS

Administrator, scout. **Personal:** Born Jan 1, 1953?. **Educ:** Boston Univ, BS, pub rels, 1975. **Career:** Administrator (retired); Franklin County C Serv, spokeswoman, assoc dir community rels, recruitment dir, 1976-11, commun dir, 2011; Doris Calloway Moore Consult, commun prof.

## CALLUM, AGNES KANE

Genealogist, historian, writer. **Personal:** Born Feb 24, 1925, Baltimore, MD; daughter of Philip Moten and Mary Priscilla Gough; married Solomon Melvin; children: Paul A Foster, Agnes H Lightfoot, Arthur M, Martin J & Martina P. **Educ:** Morgan State Univ, BA, 1973; Univ Ghana, W Africa, 1973; Morgan State Univ, MS, 1975. **Career:** Baltimore City Eve Sch, teacher; Beauty Queen Co, sales mgr, 1954-58; NC Mutual Life Ins Co, 1958-62; Rosewood State Hosp, Ownings Md, practical nurse, 1962-66; US Postal Serv, rev clk, 1966-86; Douglass High Eve Sch, teacher, 1977-80; Coppin State Col, teacher, 1978; Forest Black Geneal Journ, founder & ed, 1982-; Auth: Kane-Butler Family Geneal Hist a Black Family, 1978; Kane Family News Notes, founder & ed, 1979; publ, Flower the Forest Black Geneal J, founder, ed, 1982-; auth, Inscriptions From The Tomb Stones at Mt Calvary Cemetery, 1926-82, 1985; Black Genealogical Journal, 1982-98; Colored Vols Md, 7th Regt Us Colored Troops, 1990; Black Marriages St Mary's County, 1991; Black Marriages Anne Arundel County, Md, 1950-86, 1994. **Orgs:** Nat Asn Advan Colored People; Asn Study Afro-Am Life & Hist; Baltimore City Hosp; Md Geneal Soc; Afro-Am Hist & Geneal Soc; historian, Nat Alliance Postal & Fed Employees Local; historian, St Francis Xavier Cath Church, 1988; Adv Comt Md State Arch, 1989; Archive Comt Md Comn Afro-Am Life & Cult; trustee, Satterly Plantation Mansion, Hollywood, MD, 1991; comnr, Md Civil War Heritage Comn, 1993-95; trustee, Sotterley Found. **Honors/Awds:** City Baltimore Mayor's Citation, Citizenship, 1967; Senate of Maryland Award Outstanding Community Worker, 1986; City Coun Baltimore Retirement, 1986; Citizen Citation of Baltimore Leadership, 1986; US Postal Service 20 year Service Award, 1986; Nat Coun Negro Women Historian Award, 1988. **Home Addr:** 822 Bonaparte Ave, Baltimore, MD 21218, **Home Phone:** (410)235-6697. **Business Addr:** Trustee, Sotterley, 44300 Sotterley Lane Rte 245, Hollywood, MD 20636, **Business Phone:** (301)373-2280.

## CALVERT, DR. WILMA JEAN

Educator. **Personal:** Born St. Louis, MO; daughter of John Phillip and Amanda Bond. **Educ:** Oral Roberts Univ, BSN, 1981; Univ Okla, MSN, 1986; Univ Mo, St Louis, MO, PhD, 2002; Wash Univ, MPE. **Career:** Deaconess Hosp, staff nurse, 1981-82; St John Med Ctr, staff nurse, 1982-84, 1991-92; City Faith, Tulsa, OK, staff nurse, 1984-87; Oral Roberts Univ, instr, 1987-82; Hillcrest Med Ctr, staff nurse, 1989-91; Barnes Col, asst prof, 1992-; Univ Mo, St Louis, MO, Barnes Col Nursing & Health Studies, clin assoc prof, 1994-2013, fac, 1994-, Nat Inst Drug Abuse Training Prog Drug Abuse, post doctoral fel. Books: Integrated literature review on effects of exposure to violence upon adolescents, 1999; Neighborhood disorder, individual protective factors and the risk of adolescent delinquency, 2002; Adolescent risky behaviors and alcohol use, 2008; African American males motivations for participation in health education activities, ed, 2010; Early drinking and its association with adolescents participation in health compromising behaviors, 2010; Health-related quality of life and health-seeking behaviors in Black men, 2012; Motivators and barriers to participating in health promotion behaviors in Black men, 2013. **Orgs:** Asn Black Nursing Fac, 1990-; Mu Iota Chap, Sigma Theta Tau, NAACOG, 1989-; Soc Sci Study Relig; Res Soc Alcoholism; Nat Ctr Fac Develop & Diversity; chair, Midwest Nursing Res Soc; Am Pub Health Asn. **Home Addr:** 4875 Cote Brilliante Ave, St Louis, MO 63113-1816, **Home Phone:** (314)531-3713. **Business Addr:** Assistant

Professor, University of Missouri, 222 Nursing Admin Bldg 1 Univ Blvd, St. Louis, MO 63121-4400, **Business Phone:** (314)516-7073.

## CALVIN, DR. VIRGINIA BROWN

School administrator, educator. **Personal:** Born Jun 16, 1945, Lake Providence, LA; daughter of Arthur Brown and Vera Brown; married Richmond E; children: Brent Tremayne & Shannon D. **Educ:** Alcorn State Univ, BS, 1966; NMex Highlands Univ, MA, 1970; Tex Women's Univ, EdD, 1973; N Tex State Univ, attended 1970; Ind Univ, South Bend, attended 1979. **Career:** Teacher, 1967-71; S Bend Community Sch Corp, counr, 1972-76, adminr, 1977-2000, Muessel Elem Sch, prin, actg exec dir, Div Instr & Curric, 1991-93, supt S Bend sch, 1993-2000; Ivy Tech State Col, chancellor, 2000-. **Orgs:** Chairperson, Validation-Head Start, 1979; secy, Delta Kappa Gamma Hon Soc, 1984; bd mem, Leadership Chamber Com, 1985-93; bd dir, Jr LeagueS Bend, 1984, Art Ctr, 1985; bd mem, Broadway Theatre League, 1986-; bd mem, St Joseph County Parks Bd, 1990-; pres, Alpha Kappa Alpha Sorority, 1991-93; bd mem, United Way St Joseph County, 1991-92; bd mem, St Joseph County C's Ctr, 1992-; bd mem, Firefly Festival, 1992-; bd mem, Healthy Comm Initiative, 1992-; bd mem, Jr Achievement; bd dir, Am Red Cross; bd dir, Michiana Inc; S Bend Community Revitalization Dist; St Joseph County Minority Health Coalition; St Joseph Parks; Urban League, St Joseph County; bd, Festival & Broadway Theatre League; India Comn Women; Nat Adv Comt, New Venture Philanthrophy; Workforce Invest Bd; S BendRotary Club. **Honors/Awds:** Women of the Year, Plano, TX, 1971; Women of the Year, SBCSC YWCA, 1984; Educator of the Year, Executive Journal, 1991; Bond Award, AKA, 1976, 1991; Nat Blue Ribbon School Award, Muessel Elem Sch, 1992; Redbook Magazine's America's Best Elementary School Award, Muessel Elem Sch, 1993; Educator of the Year, Comm Educ Roundtable, 1991; Indiana State Superintendent of the Year, 1996; Lifetime Achievement Award, Fest Inc, 1996; Lifetime Achievement Award, Women Fest Inc, 1997; Distinguished Service Award, S Bend Asn Pub Sch Adminr, 1999; Named Sagamore of the Wabash, Governor Frank OBannon, 2000; Outstanding Science, Technology or Engineering Educator in Indiana, Hi Tech Inc, 2002; Distinguished Alumna, Alcorn State Univ, 2003; Age of Excellence Honoree, REAL Services Inc; Vision Award, St Joseph County Health Initiatives; Community Service Visionary Award, Urban League South Bend; Distinguished Leadership Award, Chamber of Commerce. **Special Achievements:** First African-American and the first female chief executive South Bend School Corporation, 1993. **Home Addr:** 17530 Bending Oaks, Granger, IN 46530. **Business Addr:** Chancellor, Ivy Tech Community College, 220 Dean Johnson Blvd, South Bend, IN 46601, **Business Phone:** (574)289-7001.

## CAMBOSOS, BRUCE MICHAEL

Psychiatrist. **Personal:** Born Jul 20, 1941, New Haven, CT; married Syleatha Hughes; children: Shanay. **Educ:** George Wash Univ, attended 1961; Howard Univ, BS, 1964, MD, 1969. **Career:** Va Hosp, staff psychiatrist, 1973-75; Ugast Treat Ctr, WA, staff psychiatrist, 1976-; Howard Univ Col Med, instr, 1976-83; pvt pract, currently. **Orgs:** Am Psychiat Asn; Wash Psychiat Asn; St George Soc; Capital Med Soc Trustee. **Honors/Awds:** Scholarship, George Wash Univ, 1959; Tutorial Scholarship, Howard Univ, 1965; Williams Award, Howard Univ, 1969. **Home Addr:** 6511 7th St NW, Washington, DC 20012, **Home Phone:** (202)722-2995. **Business Addr:** Private Practice, 2700 Martin Luther King Ave SE, Washington, DC 20032, **Business Phone:** (202)645-8788.

## CAMBRIDGE, DEXTER RYAN

Basketball player. **Personal:** Born Jan 29, 1970, Eleuthra. **Educ:** Lon Morris Jr Col, Jacksonville, TX, attended 1990; Univ Tex, Austin, attended 1992. **Career:** Dallas Mavericks, forward & small forward, 1992-93, free agt, 1992; Pallacanestro Petrarca Padova, Italy, 1993-96; Gigantes de Carolina, Pr, 1996-97; Dinamica Grizia, Italy, 1996-98; Fabriano Basket, 1998-99; Regatas San Nicolas, Arg, 1999-2000; Panteras de Miranda, Venezuela; Obras Sanitarias, Arg, 2000-01. **Business Addr:** Free Agent, Dallas Mavericks, 2909 Taylor St, Dallas, TX 75226, **Business Phone:** (214)651-1446.

## CAMBY, MARCUS D.

Basketball player. **Personal:** Born Mar 22, 1974, Hartford, CT; married Eva; children: Milan & Maya. **Educ:** Univ Mass, Amherst, Massachusetts, attended 1997. **Career:** Basketball (retired); Toronto Raptors, ctr forward, 1996-98; NY Knicks, ctr forward, 1998-2002, power forward, 2012-13; Denver Nuggets, ctr forward, 2002-08; Los Angeles Clippers, ctr forward, 2008-10; Portland Trail Blazers, ctr forward, 2010-12; Houston Rockets, ctr forward, 2012; free agt, currently. **Orgs:** Founder, Cambyland Found, 1996; NBA All-Defensive Team. **Honors/Awds:** Atlantic 10 Freshman of the Year, 1993-94; East Regional Most Outstanding Player, Nat Col Athletic Asn, 1995-96; Oscar Robertson Trophy, 1995-96; Player of the Year Award, Naismith Col, 1995-96; John R. Wooden Award, 1995-96; Athlete of the Year, NY Mag, 1999; Metlife Community Assist of the Month Award, 2001; Chopper Travaglini Award, 2004; Defensive Player of the Year Award, Nat basketball Asn, 2006-07; Hall of Fame, UMass Athletic, 2010; The Sporting News College Player of the Year. **Home Addr:** , Pearland, TX. **Business Addr:** Professional Basketball Player, Los Angeles Clippers, 1111 S Figueroa St Suite 1100, Los Angeles, CA 90015, **Business Phone:** (888)895-8662.

## CAMERON, REV. JOHN EARL, SR.

Clergy. **Personal:** Born Jun 11, 1932, Hattiesburg, MS; son of AC and Courtney; married Lenora Woods; children: Jonetta & John Earl Jr. **Educ:** Alcorn A&M Col; Am Baptist Theo Sem, BTh, 1956; Rust Col, BS, 1957. **Career:** First Baptist Church, Oxford, Miss; Hattiesburg Ministers Proj, dir, 1954-65; Star Inc, Natchez, ctr dir, 1966-68; Star Inc, Jackson, coach, 1968-71; Greater Mt Calvary Baptist Church, pastor, 1970-, sr pastor; Div Youth Affairs Gov's Jackson, coordr, 1972; Mt Calvary Baptist Church, minister; Mt Calvary Community Develop Agency Inc, coordr, 1974. **Orgs:** Pres, Nat Baptist Stud Union, 1954; ambassador, Cent Am, 1954; cand, US Cong fifth Cong Dist MS, 1964; job Develop Specialist Star Inc, 1969-71; sponsor, Boy Scouts; Mason; historian Progressive Nat Bapt Conv; comnr, Criminal Justice Syst State, MS; comnr, LEAA; bd dir, pearl River Valley Redevelop Basin Hinds Co. **Honors/Awds:** Cited, Who's Who in Black America, Notable Americans in the Bicentennial Era & Outstanding Community Leader. **Home Addr:** 311 Overlook Cir, Jackson, MS 39213, **Home Phone:** (601)366-2417. **Business Addr:** Senior Pastor, Greater Mount Calvary Baptist Church, 1400 Robinson St, Jackson, MS 39209, **Business Phone:** (601)352-8585.

## CAMERON, DR. JOSEPH A.

Educator, association executive. **Personal:** Born Apr 25, 1942, Fairfield, AL; son of Arthur and Searcie; married Mary E Stiles; children: Joseph Jr, Jozetta, Cecelia & Juanita. **Educ:** Tenn State Univ, BS, biol, 1963; Tex So Univ, MS, exp biol, 1965; Mich State Univ, PhD, endocrinol, 1973. **Career:** Tex Southern Univ, grad teaching asst, 1965; Grambling State Univ, Dept Biol Sci, instr, 1965-66, asst prof, 1967-69; high sch sci teacher, consult, 1967-69; Mich State Univ, Equal Opportunity Pro, tutor, 1969-71, Dept Natural Sci, instr, 1969-73, asst prof, 1973-74, Nat Sci Lab Manual, contrib auth, 1971; Jackson State Univ, Dept Biol, asst prof, 1974-78, coordr, grad progs, 1976-85, prof, 1978-, Baccalaureate Degree Prog, dir; Nat Sci Found, consult & reviewer, 1978-91; Nat Inst Health, consult & proposal reviewer, 1978-95, biomed sci prog, dir, 1980-84; Univ Miss Med Ctr/Jackson State Univ, Sch Sci & Technol, actg dean, 1984, health careers opportunity prog, fac, 1985, dir minority instnl restraining prog, 1986; Bridges Baccalaureate Degree Prog, dir, 1993-95; Ind Univ, Bridges Doctorate Degree Prog, coordr, currently; Purdue Univ Indianapolis, currently. **Orgs:** Tri Beta Biol Hon Soc; Am Soc Zool; Am Asn Univ Prof; Tissue Cult Asn; Soc Sigma XI; AAAS; Miss Acad Sci, Alpha Phi Alpha Frat Inc; Am Heart Asn; Endocrine Soc; Phi Delta Kappa; pres, Phi Kappa Phi, 1990; Outstanding Contrib to Sci Mississippi Award, Miss Acad Sci, 2004. **Honors/Awds:** Academic Tuition Scholarship, Univ Iowa, 1966-67; Soc Sigma XI Award, Meritorious Res, Mich State Univ, 1973; apptd Fair field Ind HS Hall Fame, 1973; King/Chavez/Parks Vis Prof, Mich State Univ, 1992. **Special Achievements:** Published numerous journal articles. **Home Addr:** 2735 Hemingway Cir, Jackson, MS 39209-7004, **Home Phone:** (601)969-7890. **Business Addr:** Professor, Jackson State University, Rm 402 JAP Sci Bldg 1400 Lynch St, Jackson, MS 39217, **Business Phone:** (601)979-2470.

## CAMERON, KRYSTOL

Founder (originator), chief executive officer, executive. **Personal:** Born Mar 14, 1967, Brooklyn, NY; son of John and Jean Clark; married Deidre DeRiggs. **Educ:** Mass Inst Technol, comput engineering, 1980. **Career:** Int Bus Mach, sr design engr, 1984-85; ComputerLand; BusinessLand; Comput Factory Entre Comput; Cameron Systs Inc, pres, 1987-; Chase Rec Inc, vpres, prod, 1990-; Facile Mgt, vpres, commun, 1990-; ATC Music, pres, publ, 1992-; Hudson Delta Group, founder; Digital Frames Inc, founder; MTV; Golan Entertainment; Kingsborough Community Col; BMG Entertainment; Epic Rec; MJJ/Sony; Arista Rec; EMI Rec; James Brown W; Jean Denoyer Melba Moore; LaFace Rec; Uptown Rec; Brentwood Cult Ctr; Spikes Joint; Ashton Film Inc, pres, 1992-; Odyssey Pictures Corp; Sun Microsystems Inner Circle; SimplyTV, founder, chief exec officer, 1996-2000; Nb Develop Corp, panel speaker, 1996; Career Commun Group, speaker, educr, 1997; Medgar Evers Col City Univ New York, speaker, educr, 1997; Seton Hall Univ, supporter, speaker, 1997; Hollywood E, panelist, 1997; Streaming Media, speaker, panelist, 1998; Home Theater Now, presenter, panelist, 1999; Simply ME TV, owner, 2000-07; Global Entertainment & Media Summit, speaker, panelist, 2003; Hollywood Reporter, judge, 2005-; Simply ME, owner, 2007-; World Lock Rec, chief exec officer, currently; Gerson Lehrman Group, Worldwide Telecom & Media Consult, 2007-; Advert Age, panel mem, 2007-; Digital Hollywood Spring, speaker; Economist Intelligence Unit, panel mem, 2012-. **Orgs:** Patron, Black Filmmaker Found, 1988-; Nat Tech Asn; Nat Christina Found; Nat Asn Mkt Developers; Caribbean-Am Chamber Com; USA Chamber Com; Orgn Black Designers Comput Technol; Indust Asn; Hollywood E Found; Nat Asn Tv Arts & Scis; UN / IMSCO; Lotus Develop Asn; Video Software Dealers; Asn Website Adv Coun; Visionary Network Asn; Who's Who Entertainment; Internet Developers Asn; Black Data Processing Asn; CMP Channel Adv Coun; Who's Who Info Technol; Int Soc Internet Prof; Asn Interactive Media; bd engrs, Socs Motion Picture Tv Engrs; develop sector mem, Int Telecommunications Union; fel Int Radio TV Socs; Int Socs Internet Professionals; Sun Microsystems; adv bd mem, Berean Inst, 1997-; Christopher Wallace Memorial Found, 1998-2000; Int Radio & TV Soc, supporter, 1999-; Int Acad Tv Arts & Sci, 1998-2003; speaker, Nat Asn Broadcasters, 1998-; supporter, Mus Mod Art, 1998; judge, TEC Found, 1999; Int Telecommunications Union, 1999-2004; Int Engineering Consortium; MIT Enterprise Forum; supporter, Kids Int Deportees, 2013-; nat media sponsor, Team Vick Found, 2014-. **Business Addr:** Owner, SimplyME, 90 Danbury Rd, New Milford, CT 06776, **Business Phone:** (800)240-1197.

## CAMERON, MARY EVELYN

Educator, college teacher. **Personal:** Born Sep 8, 1944, Memphis, TN; married Joseph Alexander; children: Jozetta Louise, Joseph Alexander Jr, Cecelia Denise & Juanita Evette. **Educ:** Marian Col, Indianapolis, IN, BA, 1966; Univ Iowa, Med Ctr, ADA cert, 1967; Jackson State Univ, MS, 1979. **Career:** State Miss, nutritionist, mem surv team, 1967-68; Grambling State Univ, admin dietitian, 1968-69; Sparrow Hosp, clin dietitian, 1969-74; Hinds Gen Hosp, clin dietitian, 1974-79; Va Med Ctr, clin dietitian, 1979; Univ Miss Med Ctr, asst prof, 1979-, res nutritionist, 1980-84; Belhaven Col, adj prof biol, currently. **Orgs:** Pre Cent Dist Dietetic Asn, 1978-79; Tri Beta Biol Hon Soc, 1979-; pres, Nutritionists Nursing Educ, 1981-82; Miss Heart Asn, Prof Educ Comn, 1982-84; chmn, Nutrit Subcomt, Prof Educ Comn, 1982-85; Diocesan Sch Bd, 1982-86; nutrit consult, Oper Head start Prog, 1982-; Miss Heart Asn Nutrit Comn, 1983-; pres, Miss Dietetic Asn, 1983-84; bd dir, Miss Dietetic Asn, 1985-; pres, Health Adv Comn Hinds Co Proj Head start, 1987; Am Cancer Soc, 1987-; Am Heart Asn, 1991-; PTSA pres, Forest Hill HS, 1991-; Bd CUP, Univ S Miss; Phi Delta Kappa Hon Soc. **Special Achievements:** Reviewed numerous articles for professional journal, 1982-84; Presented res abstract at Reg Hypertension Mtg, 1983; Reviewed a major nutrition text Mosby Publ, 1984; Published article in professional refereed journal, 1985. **Home Addr:** 2735 Hemingway Cir, Jackson, MS 39209-7004, **Home Phone:** (601)942-0090. **Business Addr:** Adjunct Professor, Belhaven College, 1500 Peachtree St, Jackson, MS 39202, **Business Phone:** (800)960-5940.

## CAMERON, MICHAEL TERRANCE

Executive, baseball player. **Personal:** Born Jan 8, 1973, LaGrange, GA; married JaBreka; children: Taja, Dazmon & Mekhi. **Career:** Baseball player (retired); Chicago White Sox, outfielder, 1995-98; Cincinnati Reds, 1999; Seattle Mariners, 2000-03; First State Golf Tournament Inner City Kids, host, 2002; NY Mets, 2004-05; San Diego Padres, ctr fielder, 2006-07; Milwaukee Brewers, 2008-09; Boston Red Sox, 2010-11; Fla Marlins, 2011; Wash Nationals, 2011-12. **Orgs:** Make-A-Wish Found; Starlight Found; founder, Cam4Kids Found. **Special Achievements:** Together with Greg Brown and Robin Roberts, Cameron wrote a book titled "It Takes a Team: Mike Cameron", published in 2002 by Triumph Books.

## CAMERON, RANDOLPH W.

Marketing executive. **Personal:** Born Jersey City, NJ; son of Randolph W; married Martha; children: Randolph Jr & Michele. **Educ:** Del State Col, BS, bus admin, 1958; New Sch Social Res, MA, commun, 1985. **Career:** D Parke Gibson Assoc Inc, vpres, mkt & pub affairs, 1962-72; Avon Prod Inc, div sls mgr, 1972-73, dir field sls support, dir mkt commun, 1978-85, dir mktg comm; Medgar Evers Col Sch Bus, prof; Grey Advert; Ford Found; United Way NY; Inst Church Admin & Mgt; United Methodist church; Cameron Enterprises, founder, pres, currently. **Orgs:** Bd mem, Am Cancer Soc; Econ Adv Comn; New York Bus Soc; adv comt, New York Jobs Youth; C's Aid Soc; New York Mission Soc. **Honors/Awds:** Athletic Hall of Fame, Delaware State Univ, 1989. **Special Achievements:** Black Achievers Indust; Author: "The Minority Executives' Handbook", Warner Books, 1989; The Minority Executives' Handbook, revised, Amistad Press, 1998; Minority Manager, 2004. **Home Addr:** 100 W 94th St, New York, NY 10025, **Home Phone:** (212)662-7177. **Business Addr:** President, Founder, Cameron Enterprises, 11877 Goldring Rd, Arcadia, CA 91006, **Business Phone:** (626)358-6130.

## CAMERON, DR. WILBURN MACIO, JR.

Dentist. **Personal:** Born Richmond, VA; married Jacqueline Amelia; children: Wilburn Macin III & Charles Anderson. **Educ:** Va State Col, BS, 1950; Howard Univ Grad Sch; Meharry Med Col, attended 1956. **Career:** Pvt pract dent, currently. **Orgs:** Peter B Ramsey Dent Soc; Old Dom Dent Soc; Va Acad Gen Dent; Chi Delta Mu Frat; YMCA; Kappa Alpha Psi Fraternity; Va Acad Gen Dent, fel Int Acad Gen Dent. **Honors/Awds:** President Award, Old Dominion Dentist Soc, 1977, 1978; Meharry's President Award. **Business Addr:** Dentist, 12 W Marshall St, Richmond, VA 23220-3928, **Business Phone:** (804)644-0228.

## CAMMACK, CHARLES LEE, JR.

Manager, vice president (organization), journalist. **Personal:** Born Oct 8, 1954, Ft. Wayne, IN; son of Charles Lee Sr and Sarah Elizabeth Jackson; married Michelle Lynn Duncan. **Educ:** Purdue Univ, BA, commun, 1977; Univ Wis, Madison, MA, commun, 1978. **Career:** WKJG-TV, Ft Wayne, reporter, anchor, broadcast journalist, 1978-87; Ft Wayne Newspapers, mgt trainee, 1987-89, benefits & systs mgr, 1989-, mgr employ safety & security, 1992-, mgr human resources; PNI, dir, 1998; Philadelphia Daily News, vpres human resources; Philadelphia Inquirer; Knight Ridder Inc, vpres human resources; Post-Tribune, dir human resource; Ft Wayne Community Schs, human resources dir, 2008-10, chief opers officer, 2010-. **Orgs:** Youth Resources, 1988-; bd diversity comt, Newspaper Asn Am; chmn, Workplace Issues Comt Newspaper Asn Am; co-chmn, Youth Leadership, Ft Wayne; bd mem, Leadership Ft Wayne; fel McCormick Tribune, 1998; PA Newspaper Asn; Nat Asn Minority Media Execs; bd dir, NAA bd diversity comt, YMCA's Ann. **Honors/Awds:** First Place News Documentary, Ind Assoc Press, 1980; First Place News Feature, Ind Assoc Press, 1981; Community Service Award, Union Baptist Church, 1982; Second Place News Documentary, Ind Press Photographers Asn, 1982. **Home Addr:** 1024 Southview Ave, Fort Wayne, IN 46806-5167, **Home Phone:** (260)745-1661. **Business Addr:** Chief Operations Officer, Fort Wayne Community School, 1200 S Clinton St, Fort Wayne, IN 46802, **Business Phone:** (260)467-2010.

## CAMP, KIMBERLY

Artist, arts administrator. **Personal:** Born Sep 11, 1956, Camden, NJ; daughter of Hubert E and Marie Dimery. **Educ:** Am Univ, Wash, DC, 1974; Univ Pittsburgh, Pittsburgh, PA, BA, studio arts & art hist, 1978; Drexel Univ, Philadelphia, PA, MS, arts admin, 1986. **Career:** Kellogg Nat Leadership Prog, fel XVI; City Camden, NJ, visual arts dir, 1983-86; Nat Endowment F&T Arts, arts mgt fel, 1986; Commonwealth Pa, Coun Arts Harrisburg, Pa, dir, artist educ & minority arts serv, 1986-89, prog dir; Smithsonian Inst, Wash, DC, Exp Gallery, dir, 1989-93; Charles H Wright Mus African Am Hist, exec dir & pres, 1989-94, chief exec officer, 1994-98; Barnes Found, chief exec officer & exec dir, 1998-, pres; Richland Pub Facil Dist, chief exec officer, 2007-11; Kimberly Camp Studios, founder & consult, auth, currently; Galerie Marie, owner, 2013-; The Lincoln Univ, Sr Lectr, 2015-. **Orgs:** Chairperson, Asn Am Cult, 1984-89; Nat Endowment Arts fel, 1986; dir, Pa Coun for Arts, 1986-89; bd mem, Intercult Advan Inst Gettysburg Col, 1988-89; nat adv comn mem, Nat Asn Artists Orgns, 1989-90; Links Inc, 1990-94; vice bd mem, Arlington Art Ctr, 1990-94; Detroit Chap, 1994-98, Arlington Va Chap; bd mem, Bus Vols Arts, 1994-97; adv bd, Jr League, 1994-97; bd mem, Am Asn Mus, 1995-97; bd mem, Empowerment Zone Develop Corp, 1996-97; W.K. Kellogg Found fel, 1997-2000. **Home Addr:** PO Box 216, Merion, PA 19066. **Business Addr:** Founder, Kimberly Camp Studios, 4101 S Ledbetter St, Kennewick, WA 99337, **Business Phone:** (509)586-0968.

## CAMP, ESQ. MARVA JO

Lawyer, businessperson. **Personal:** Born Sep 17, 1961, Washington, DC; daughter of Fab Jr and Ernestine Alford. **Educ:** Univ Va, Charlottesville, BA, 1983; Univ Va, Sch Law, Charlottesville, JD, 1986. **Career:** Gartrell & Alexander Law Firm, Silver Spring, Md, atty, assoc, 1986-87; Congressman Harold E Ford, Wash, DC, legis dir, tax coun, 1987-88; Cong Task Force Minority Bus, Wash, DC, dir, legal coun, 1987-; Congressman Mervyn M Dymally, Wash, DC, adv, 1988-; Crenshaw Int Corp, Wash, DC, pres, chief exec officer; Bowie State Univ, dir govt & community outreach, currently; Marva Jo Camp & Assocs, atty, currently. **Orgs:** Vpres & bd dir, Edward C Mazique Parent Child Ctr, 1986; legal coun, Inst Sci, Space & Technol, 1987-;

consult, Minority & Small Bus, 1987; adv, Dem Nat Comn, 1988; legal coun, Carribean Am Res Inst, 1988; pres, bd dir, Young Black Prof, 1988-; co-chair, treas, African-Am Polit Fund, 1988; bd dir, 14th & U Coalition, 1988; adv pres, Cong Black Asn, 1988; comt mem, Md State Bar Asn, 1998-; Soc Outstanding Young Am; lobbyist, Prince George's County Coun; Pro Bono Coun; trustee, Md Citizens Arts & Panel Mem Arts Pub Places; pres, Prince George's Arts & Humanities Coun; Prince George's Tennis & Educ Found; Dem Cent Comt; chmn, Leadership Prince George's; vchair, Prince George's Econ Develop Corp; treas, Md Citizens Arts Inc; Alpha Kappa Alpha Sorority Inc; Links Inc; Jack & Jill Prince George's County; Dc Bar Asn; J Franklyn Bourne Bar Asn; Nat Asn Health Serv Execs; Supreme Ct Bar. **Honors/Awds:** Congressional Certificate of Recognition. **Special Achievements:** Author: Federal Compliance with Minority Set-Asides, 1988, Future of African-Amer, 1988. **Home Addr:** 1301 Sea Pines Terr, Mitchellville, MD 20721-3109, **Home Phone:** (301)499-8429. **Business Addr:** Treasurer, Maryland Citizens for the Arts, 120 W N Ave Suite 302, Baltimore, MD 21201, **Business Phone:** (410)467-6700.

### CAMPBELL, ALMA PORTER
Elementary school teacher, educator. **Personal:** Born Jan 5, 1948, Savannah, GA; daughter of William Porter and Gladys B Porter. **Educ:** Savannah State Univ, BS, 1969; State Univ NY Col, Brockport, NY, MS, 1971, CAS, 1988. **Career:** Educator (retired); Rochester City Sch, Rochester, NY, third grade teacher, 1974-87, chp one reading teacher, 1987, basic skills cadre, 1988-90, lead teacher mentor, 1991-92; Theodore Roosevelt Sch No 43, vice prin, 1993-94, prin, 1992-2003. **Orgs:** Chmn, Nominating Comt, Alpha Kappa Alpha, 1988-90; Phi Delta Kappa Hon Fraternity Educ, 1989-; bd dir, Hamm House, 1990-91; bd dir, Jefferson Ave Early Childhood Ctr, 1990-91; bd Christian Ed, Memorial AME Zion Church, 1986-; Alpha Kappa Alpha, Ivy Leaf reporter; African-Am Leadership Develop Prog, steering-comt; chairperson, Climate Comt, No 43 Sch, Introduced twenty four staff mems Peer-Mediation Training Module; chairperson, Artist Residence Progs; teacher trainer, Coop Learning; Leadership Group, Local Statewide Systemic Initiative, R&D Schs; LARC-Lyell Ave Revitalization Comt; RCEL, Rochester Coun Elem Adm; Internal Reading Leadership Asn; Rochester Teaching Ctr & Steering Comn; treas, Phi Delta Kappa Hon Educ Fraternity; speaker, African Am CriticalIssues Network, 1998; Rochester Teachers Policy Bd. **Home Addr:** 40 Menlo Pl, Rochester, NY 14620, **Home Phone:** (716)256-1679.

### CAMPBELL, ANN-MARIE
President (organization). **Personal:** Born Jan 1, 1965?; married Christopher; children: 2. **Educ:** Ga State Univ, BS, philos, MBA. **Career:** Home Depot, cashier, store mgr, dist mgr, 1985-, vpres opers, 2001-02, regional vpres, 2002-04, vpres merchandising & spec orders, 2004-05, vpres retail mkt & sales, 2005-06, vpres vendor sales, 2006-09, pres southern div, 2009-. **Orgs:** Beta Gamma Sigma; Nat Scholars Hon Soc; adv bd, Atlanta Union Mission; Atlanta Women's Network; adv bd, Ga State Univ's Robinson Col Bus & Catalyst; bd dir, Potbelly Corp; independent dir, Barnes & Noble. **Business Addr:** President, Home Depot, 2450 Cumberland Pkwy, Atlanta, GA 30339, **Business Phone:** (770)432-9930.

### CAMPBELL, ANTHONY. See CAMPBELL, TONY.

### CAMPBELL, DR. ARTHUR REE
Nurse, educator. **Personal:** Born Feb 20, 1943, Bessemer, AL; son of Levi Williams Sr and Menyarn Miller Williams; married Shadrach; children: Korey Lanier, Kareem Damohn & Kheela Delores. **Educ:** Tuskegee Univ, Tuskegee, AL, BSN, 1965; Univ Md, Baltimore, MD, MSN, 1967; Univ Ala, Tuscaloosa, AL, EdD, 1984. **Career:** Univ Ala Hosp, Birmingham, AL, charge nurse, 1965; Jefferson County Dept Health, Birmingham, AL, psychiatric nurse, 1967-75; Univ Ala, Sch Nursing, Birmingham, AL, assoc prof, 1975-. **Orgs:** Pres, Ment Health Asn Cent Ala; treas & vpres, Family & Child Serv; YWCA; Am Red Cross. **Home Addr:** 7308 Earlwood Rd, Fairfield, AL 35064-2403, **Home Phone:** (205)923-8016. **Business Addr:** Associate Professor, University of Alabama, 1530 3rd Ave S, Birmingham, AL 35294-1210, **Business Phone:** (205)934-3485.

### CAMPBELL, BLANCH
Executive. **Personal:** Born Dec 4, 1941, Biscoe, AR; daughter of Oscar Louderdale and Louella Calbert Louderdale; children: Tanja Marie Smith. **Educ:** Webster Col, St Louis, MO, BA, 1981. **Career:** Executive (retired); Southwestern Bell Tel, St Louis, Mo, serv asst, 1966-68, group chief operator, 1968-72, supvr bus serv, 1972-74, supvr course develop, 1974-75, staff mgr training, 1975-78, dist mgr, 1978-91; Trip With Me Travelers Inc, founder, chief exec officer, pres. **Orgs:** Pres, Jr Kindergarten Bd, 1981-87; pres, Proj Energy Care Bd, 1984; loan exec, United Way, 1984-85; pres elect, 1985-86, pres, 1986-88, bd dir, City N Y's Men Club; Monsanto YMCA, 1989; chairperson, placement educ info comt, Greater Mt Carmel Baptist Church; Women Leadership, 1984-; consult, Emprise Designs, 1988-89; regional dir elect, 1990-91, regional dir, 1991-92, Y's Men Intl; nat first vpres, pres, Continental Soc Inc, St Louis Chap, 1989-97, 1999, 2013-; admin coun, 1993-97; Phyllis Wheatley YWCA, 1991; regional dir Continental Soc Inc Midwest-Western Region, 1997-99; bd mem, new Mid-Co Chamber. **Home Addr:** 4107 Fireside Dr, Florissant, MO 63033-4308, **Home Phone:** (314)831-1830. **Business Addr:** Chief Executive Officer, Trip With ME Travelers, 4107 Fireside Dr, Florissant, MO 63033-4308, **Business Phone:** (314)831-1116.

### CAMPBELL, BOBBY LAMAR
Manager, research scientist. **Personal:** Born Sep 30, 1949, Fairmont, NC. **Educ:** Brooklyn Col, BA, 1979; Howard Univ, MCP, 1982; Nat Inst Power Engrs, attended 1984. **Career:** US HUD, prog analyst, 1980-81; Howard Univ, researcher, 1981-82; Polinger Mgt Co, resident mgr, 1983-85; DC Mutual Housing Asn Inc, property mgr, 1985-. **Orgs:** Vet counr, Brooklyn Col, 1975-79; ANC comt, 4D Adv Neighborhood Comn, 1980-84; stud rep, Am Planning Asn, 1981-82; site coordr, Nat Capitol Health Fair Proj, 1982; steering comt mem, DC Off Planning, 1983-84; pres, Upper Northwest Civic Group, 1984. **Honors/Awds:** Outstanding Community Serv, DC Recreation Dept, 1983; Contrib Auth, Wash Foot NCAC APA/Smithsonian Press, 1983; Outstanding Community Serv, 4D Adv Neighborhood Comn, 1984. **Home Addr:** 236 Hamilton St NW, Washington, DC 20011. **Business Addr:** Property Manager, DC Mutual Housing Association Inc, 1436 Independence Ave SE, Washington, DC 20003.

### CAMPBELL, CARLOS, SR.
Manager, president (organization). **Personal:** Born Dec 23, 1946, Warrenton, VA; son of Albert and Martha; married Ethel Douglas; children: Carlos II. **Educ:** AUS, Air Defense Sch, cert, opers & intelligence, 1967; North Ala Col Com, cert, bus admin & acct, 1972; Ala A&M Univ, BS, 1975; Ala A&M Univ, MBA. **Career:** AL A&M Univ, univ recruiter, 1975-76, dir veterans affairs, 1975-76; Chesebrough Ponds Inc Prince Matchabelli Div, prod scheduler, 1976-78, sr prod planner, 1978-80, supvr warehousing & inventory control, 1980-86, senior prod supvr, 1986-87; Consolidated Industries, prod control mgr, 1989-. **Orgs:** Mem Madison Co Dem Exec Comn, exec bd, Madison Co Nat Asn Advan Colored People; vice chmn, AL Dem Conf Exec Bd; chmn, Univ & Indust Cluster AL A&M Univ; chmn bd mgr, N W YMCA; chmn, athletic exec bd, AL A&M Univ; prof, Black Exec Exchange Prog Nat Urban League; Youth Motivation Task Force Nat Alliance Bus; Alpha Phi Alpha Frat, Govt Rel Comn AL A&M Univ; bd dir, N Ala Regional Hosp; life mem, 1814 Color Guard US Army Air Defense Command; exec bd, Police Athletic Asn; pres, JD Johnson High Sch PTA; pres, Sch Bd Parents Asn. **Home Addr:** 6726 Hollow Rd NW, Huntsville, AL 35810, **Home Phone:** (205)852-8876. **Business Addr:** Production Control Manager, Consolidated Industries, 4015 Pulaski Pke NW, Huntsville, AL 35810, **Business Phone:** (205)859-6890.

### CAMPBELL, CARLOS CARDOZO
Banker, association executive. **Personal:** Born Jul 19, 1937, Harlem, NY; married Sammie Marye Day; children: Kimberly & Scott. **Educ:** MI State Univ, BS, 1959; US Naval Post Grad Sch, dipl engr sci, 1965; Cath Univ Am, MA city & regional planning, 1968. **Career:** VA Polytech Inst & State Univ, adj prof summer, 1974; Am Revolution Bicentennial Admin, dep asst admin, 1974-76; Carlos C Campbell & Assoc, prin & owner, 1976-81; US Dept Comt, asst secy econ develop, 1981-84; Inter Am Develop Bank, alt exec dir designee; CC Campbell & Co, mgt consult & pres, 1985-2011; Cataray Inc, bd dir, 1985-89; Graphic Scanning Inc, 1987-89; Dom Bank, Tysons, 1988-92; Comput Dynamics Inc, 1992-96; Resource Am Inc, dir, 1992-; Fidelity Leasing Inc, 1996-; Pico Holdings Inc, dir, 1998-; NetWolves Corp, dir, 2003-; Herley Industs Inc, dir, 2005-11; Global 21 LLC, pres, 2011-; Initiative Films LLC, pres, 2011-. **Orgs:** Sr systs analyst Ctrl Data Corp, 1968-69; spec asst, US Dept Housing & Urban Develop, 1969-72; Screen Actors Guild, 1972-; vpres, Corp Comt Develop, 1973-74; bd dir, Am Soc Planing Officials, 1973-74; bd dir, McLean Savings & Loan Asn, 1975-77; vpres, Am Coun Int Sports, 1978-81; comnr, Northern VA Reg Planing Dist Comt, 1980-82; US Dept Treas Task Force Debt Mgt; Aircraft Owners & Pilots Asn; Nat Asn Corp Dirs, leadership fel. **Honors/Awds:** Grant Nat Endowment Arts, 1972; Ford Found, 1973; Author New Towns, Another Way Live, 1976; Book Month Club Alternate Selection, 1976. **Special Achievements:** Author: New Towns; Another Way to Live, 1976. **Home Addr:** 11577 Lake Newport Rd, Reston, VA 20194-1211. **Business Addr:** Director, NetWolves Corp, 4805 Independence Pkwy Suite 101, Tampa, FL 33634-7527, **Business Phone:** (813)286-8644.

### CAMPBELL, DR. CHARLES EVERETT
Dentist. **Personal:** Born Aug 13, 1933, Statesboro, GA; son of Fred and Ernestine; married Phyllis; children: Charles, Jacqueline & Andrea. **Educ:** Oakwood Col, attended 1959; Meharry Med Col, attended 1968; Univ NC, attended 1974. **Career:** Dentist (retired); Mt Sinai Hosp, 1959-60; Va Hosp, med tech, 1960-64; Hubbard Hosp & Va Hosp, dent intern, 1968-69; Neighborhood Health Ctr, staff dentist, 1969-73; Orange Chatham Comprehensive Health Serv Inc, Carrboro, NC, dent dir, 1974-94. **Orgs:** Old N State Dent Soc; Durham Acad Med; Nat Dent Asn; Black Adventist Med Dent Asn; treas, Oakwood Col Nat Alumni Asn; Meharry Med Col Alumni Asn; Immanuel Temple Seventh-day Adventist Church, Durham, NC; pres, Chap Oakwood Col Alumni Asn, Durham, NC. **Honors/Awds:** Nashville Dental Prize; John Bluford Award; College Alumni Association Award, Cumberland Chap Oakwood, 1973; Oakwood College National Alumni Award, 1993; Alumni Award, Meharry Med Col, 1993; Outstanding Alumanus Oakwood Col, 2001. **Home Addr:** 343 Warren Way Ct, Chapel Hill, NC 27516, **Home Phone:** (919)967-4655.

### CAMPBELL, ESQ. CHRISTOPHER LUNDY
Lawyer, athlete. **Personal:** Born Sep 9, 1954, Westfield, NJ; son of Howard Thomas and Marjorie Lee; married Laura Sue Beving; children: Christopher Lundy, Auasa Ebony & Jonathan Edward. **Educ:** Univ Iowa, BS, sociol, 1979; Iowa State Univ, Iowa City IA, attended 1983; Cornell Law Sch, JD, 1987. **Career:** Iowa State Univ, asst wrestling coach, 1979-84; Cornell Univ, asst wrestling coach, 1985-87; United Technologies CRP, staff atty, 1987-88; Carrier CRP, coun, atty, 1988, Human Resources Dept, civil litigation, 2000-; Ct Arbit Sport, arbitrator, 1993-; Olympic Games, Ad Hoc Div, 1996; Kenney & Markowitz LLP, atty, 2000-04; Chapman & Intrieri LLP, atty, 2006-; Carlton Di Sante & Freudenberger, atty; pvt pract, currently; Law Off Christopher L Campbell, owner, currently. **Orgs:** Chair educ comt, Black Law Stud Asn, 1986; mem exec comt, USA Wrestling, 1992; Athletes adv bd, US Olympic Comt, 1992; bd dir, US Olympic Comt, 1993; bd dir, Vegetarian Times, 1993; chmn, Am Arbit Asn; Ct Arbit Sport; Nat Col Athletic Asn. **Honors/Awds:** Olympic Trials Champion, 1980, 1992; National Freestyle Champion, 1980, 1983, 1990-91; Sullivan Award, 1981; Gold Medal, World Wrestling Championship, 1981; World Champion, selected as the "world's most technically prepared wrestler", First American to receive Award, 1981; World Cup Champion, 1981, 1983-84, 1991; World Silver Medalist, 1990; Tbilisi champion, 1991; Bronze Medal Winner, US Olympic Team, 1992; Distinguished Member, Nat Wrestling Hall Fame. **Home Addr:** 248 Chaffinch Island Rd, Guilford, CT 06437-3207. **Business Addr:** Attorney, Law Office of Christopher L Campbell, 515 Oak Manor Dr, Fairfax, CA 94930, **Business Phone:** (415)459-3481.

### CAMPBELL, CLEMENTINA DINAH. See LAINE, DAME CLEO.

### CAMPBELL, DIANE
College administrator. **Educ:** Morgan State Univ, Baltimore, MD, BS; Trenton State Col, MEd; Col NJ, MS; Rutgers Univ, EdD. **Career:** Inner workings Inst, consult; Mercer County Community Col, exec dean stud affairs, dean enrollment & stud serv, currently; Kellogg fel; Virtual Campus, asst dean & dir; Virtual Consortium, assoc prof, psychol. **Orgs:** Pres, vice chairperson, Virtual Community Col Consortium; dir, Virtual Community, Montgomery County Community Col; liaison, Distance Learning Adv Bd JEdge Steering Comt; Trenton Sch Bd; bd trustee, United Way Greater Mercer County; bd mem, Shiloh Community Develop Corp; bd mem, Nj Planning Coalition; bd mem, Shiloh Baptist Church, currently; bd mem, Trenton Ecumenical Area Ministry; adv bd, Trenton Area Campus Ministry. **Business Addr:** Dean for Enrollment & Student Services, Mercer County Community College, 1200 Old Trenton Rd, West Windsor, NJ 08550-3407, **Business Phone:** (609)570-3222.

### CAMPBELL, EDNA
Basketball player, real estate agent. **Personal:** Born Nov 26, 1968, Philadelphia, PA; children: David. **Educ:** Univ Md, College Park; Univ Tex, attended 1991. **Career:** Basketball player (retired); Hungary, 1995-96; Colo Xplosion, guard, 1996-98; Phoenix Mercury, guard, 1999; Seattle Storm, guard, 2000; Sacramento monarchs, guard, 2001-04; San Antonio Silver Stars, free agt, 2005, guard, 2005-06; WNBA, TV commentator, 2006, spokesperson; realtor & loan consult, currently. **Orgs:** Nat spokesperson, Breast Cancer Found.

### CAMPBELL, ELDEN JEROME
Basketball coach, basketball player. **Personal:** Born Jul 23, 1968, Los Angeles, CA. **Educ:** Clemson Univ, attended 1990. **Career:** Basketball player (retired), coach; Los Angeles Lakers, power forward, 1990, 1992-99, ctr, 1991; Charlotte Hornets, ctr, 1998-99, power forward, 2000-01; New Orleans Hornets, ctr, 2002-03; Seattle Supersonics, 2003; Detroit Pistons, ctr, 2003-05; NJ Nets, ctr, 2005; Okla City Hornets, head coach, 2005. **Honors/Awds:** Champion, Nat Basketball Asn, 2004.

### CAMPBELL, DR. EMMETT EARLE
Educator, physician. **Personal:** Born Dec 22, 1927, Dayton, OH; married Geneva Sydney; children: Michael, Heather, Kimberly & Laura. **Educ:** Univ Dayton, pre-med, 1948; Univ Cincinnati Col Med, MD, 1953. **Career:** Mercy Med Ctr, Rockville Ctr, New York, med staff, chief otol; State Univ New York, Brooklyn, staff; Temporal Bone Lab, staff; New York Eye & Ear Infirmary, asst dir, resident; State Univ New York Health Sci Ctr, Brooklyn, internship; Long Island Jewish Hosp, staff surgeon; Nassau Co Med Ctr, staff; Cleft Palate Clin, N Shore Univ Hosp, consult; Otolaryngologist, 2000; Winthrop Univ Hosp, staff; New York Med Col, prof otolaryngol; State Univ New York Health Sci Ctr, Brooklyn, prof; New York Eye & Ear Infirmary, physician. **Orgs:** Fel Am Col Surgeons; diplomat, Am Bd Otolaryngol, 1966; fel Nassau Acad Med, Continuing Med Educ Comt; pres, Nassau Surg Soc, coun mem, chmn; AMA; Nassau Otolaryngol Soc; NY St Soc Surgeons; Empire Med Polit Action Comt; Nassau Physicians Guild; Am Coun Otolaryngol; Nassau Co Peer Rev Comt; Continuing Med Educ Comt; fel Nassau Acad Med; fel Am Acad Otolaryngol; fel Am Col Surgeons. **Business Addr:** Otolaryngologist, 520 Franklin Ave Suite L9, Garden City, NY 11530, **Business Phone:** (516)742-0220.

### CAMPBELL, EMORY SHAW
Executive, executive director, health services administrator. **Personal:** Born Oct 11, 1941, Hilton Head Island, SC; son of Reginald and Sarah; married Emma Joffrion; children: Ochieng & Ayoka. **Educ:** Savannah State Col, BS, biol, 1965; Tufts Univ, MS, 1971. **Career:** Harvard Sch Pub Health, Boston, res asst, 1965-68; Process Res Cambridge, Boston, biologist, 1968-70; Bramley Health Comm Ctr, Boston MA, asst dir, 1971; Beaufort Jasper Comprehensive Health, dir comm serv, 1971-80; Pa Ctr, dir, 1980, hon paramount chief, 1989, exec dir emer, 2002; Gullah Heritage Consult Servs, founder & dir, pres, currently. **Orgs:** Hilton Head Rural Water, 1980; bd dir, Beaufort Jasper Water Admin, 1978-82; Planning comm, Beaufort Co Planning Comm, 1982; Bible Transl Comt; chmn, Gullah-Geechee Cult Heritage Corridor Comn. **Honors/Awds:** South Carolina Black Hall of Fame, 1999; Governor's Award, 1999; DHL, Bank Street Col, 2000; Carter G. Woodson Memorial Award, National Education Association, 2005. **Special Achievements:** Author: Gullah Cultural Legacies, 2003; published numerous publications. **Home Addr:** 208 Spanish Wells Rd, Hilton Head Island, SC 29926, **Home Phone:** (843)681-5836. **Business Addr:** President, Founder, Gullah Heritage Consulting Services, 70 Honey Horn Rd, Hilton Head, SC 29925, **Business Phone:** (843)681-7066.

### CAMPBELL, ESTELLE ALEXANDER
Clergy. **Personal:** Born Jan 31, 1927, Montego Bay; married Estelle Jones; children: Alexis, Paula, Edwin & Susan. **Educ:** Cornwall Col, Jamaica, 1944; Va Union Univ, BA, 1952; Va Union Theol Sem, Mdiv, 1955; Hartford Sem Found, MA, 1957; McCormick Theol Sem, DMin, 1975. **Career:** Clergy (retired); Churches-in-Transition, proj dir, prog developer; Urban Church Strategy IN-KY Conf UCC; Ind-Ky Conf United Church Christ, pastor. **Orgs:** Dorm dir, counr men, Va Union Univ, 1954-55; assoc conf minister, RI Conf United Church Christ, 1962-72; area chmn, NE Comn Church Leadersn 1971-72; dir, host Church & Comm TV Prog RI; chairperson, Oak River Forest HS Human Rels Comn; pres, Christian Educ Coun United Church Christ; vpres, Greater Hartford Coun Church; vpres, NE Comm United Ministry Higher Educ; bd dir, United Church Bd World Ministries; dir, Black Church Empowerment Prog; vpres, Barrington Prog Action; bd mem, RI People Against Poverty; bd mem, Ed Comm RI Childrens Ctr; bd dir, Oak Park Housing Ctr; Negro Hist & Cult; Apha Phi Alpha, Urban League; pres, Louisville Interdenomi Nat Ministerial Alliance; bd mem, Nat Asn Advan Colored People. **Home Addr:** 1411 Sylvan Way, Louisville, KY 40205-2476, **Home Phone:** (502)459-4178.

**CAMPBELL, DR. EVERETT O.**
Physician. **Personal:** Born Nov 15, 1934, Chicago, IL; married Anne Big Ford. **Educ:** Univ Mich, Med Sch, MD, 1958; Univ Calif, Los Angles, Med Sch. **Career:** Univ Calif, Los Angles, asst clin prof; Chas Drew Post Grad Med Sch, asst prof; Martin Luther King Hosp; pvt pract, physician, currently. **Orgs:** AMA; Calif Med Asn; Los Angeles Co Med Asn; Appl Health Res. **Special Achievements:** Author of paper on cancer; Organizing dept of Sexual studies at Martin Luther King Hosp. **Business Addr:** Physician, Private Practice, 1141 W Redondo Beach Blvd Suite 40, Gardena, CA 90247, **Business Phone:** (310)538-9045.

**CAMPBELL, FRANKLYN D.**
Airplane pilot. **Personal:** Born Feb 11, 1947, Washington, DC. **Educ:** Embry-Riddle Aeronaut Univ, pilot training; BS, 1971. **Career:** Dept Recreation, neighborhood youth corps, coordr, 1969; Page Airways Inc, lineman, 1970; Embry Riddle Aero Univ, stud flight dispatcher, teacher, 1970-71; Saturn Airways Inc, aircraft planner, 1971-72; Flying Tiger Line Inc, Airline Pilot, 1974; Garrett Air Res Aviation Co, test pilot, 1974. **Orgs:** Nat Col Flight Safety Coun; Nat Asn Advan Colored People; Brotherhood Crusade; Airline Pilot Asn; Negro Airman Int Inc. **Honors/Awds:** Outstanding Flight Student, 1970. **Home Addr:** 2945 Steeplechase Lane, Diamond Bar, CA 91765-3632. **Business Addr:** Airline Pilot, Flying Tigers Inc, 7401 World Way W, Los Angeles, CA 90009.

**CAMPBELL, GARY LLOYD**
Educator, football coach. **Personal:** Born Feb 15, 1951, Ennis, TX; married Alola McKinney; children: Phyllis, Traci & Bryan (deceased). **Educ:** Univ Calif Los Angeles, BA, sociol, 1973. **Career:** Univ Calif Los Angeles, grad asst, 1976-78; Southern Univ, asst coach, running backs football, 1979-80; Howard Univ, running backs football asst coach, 1981; Pacific Univ, running backs football asst coach, 1982; Univ OR, running backs football asst coach, running back football coach, 1983-. **Orgs:** Am Football Coaches Assoc, 1978-; Am Cong on Real Estate, 1984-. **Home Addr:** 3318 Lakeside Dr, Eugene, OR 97401-1592, **Home Phone:** (541)346-5463. **Business Addr:** Football Coach, University of Oregon, 1098 E 13th Ave 5210 Univ Oregon, Eugene, OR 97401-8833, **Business Phone:** (541)346-1000.

**CAMPBELL, DR. GEORGE, JR.**
Association executive, president (organization). **Personal:** Born Dec 2, 1945, Richmond, VA; son of George and Lillian Britt (deceased); married Mary Schmidt; children: Garikai, Sekou & Britt. **Educ:** Drexel Univ, Philadelphia, PA, BS, physics, 1968; Syracuse Univ, NY, PhD, 1977; Yale Univ, New Haven, CT, Exec Mgt Prog, 1988. **Career:** Nkumbi Col, Kabwe, Zambia, sr fac, 1969-71; AT&T Bell Lab, Holmdel, NJ, tech staff mem, 1977-83, third level mgr, 1983-88; NACME Inc, New York, NY, pres, 1989-2000; Cooper Union Advan Sci & Art, pres, 2000-11; Edison Inc, bd dirs, currently; Barnes & Noble Inc, bd dirs, currently. **Orgs:** Emer mem, Secy Energy Adv Bd, 1989-; AAAS Comt Sci Eng & Pub Policy, 1990-; Am Phys Soc, 1968-; pres, Coun NY Acad Sci, 1984-; Nat Soc Black Physicists, 1977-; chmn, Nat Adv Comt, NSF Comprehensive Regional Ctr Minorities, 1989-91; bd trustee, Rens selaer Poly tech Inst, 1992-; bd trustee, Crossroads Theater Co, 1991-; adv Coun NY State Off Sci, Technol & Acad Res; bd trustee, MITRE Corp; bd trustee, Montefiore Med Ctr; bd trustee, Josiah Macy Found. **Home Addr:** 457 W 144th St, New York, NY 10031, **Home Phone:** (212)690-2977. **Business Addr:** President, Barnes & Noble Inc, PO Box 111, Lyndhurst, NJ 07071, **Business Phone:** (800)962-6177.

**CAMPBELL, GERTRUDE M.**
Association executive, manager. **Personal:** Born Aug 3, 1923, Dallas, TX; married Quintell O; children: Patricia. **Educ:** Prairie View Col, BS, 1943; Univ Southern Calif, attended 1968. **Career:** US Energy Res & Dev Adminstrn, dir officer mgt serv, 1975; US employ disadv Adults, Oakland Adult Minor Proj, br mgr; Berkeley Human Resource Develop Ctr, ctr mgr. **Orgs:** Life mem, Past Western Dist Govern; E Bay Area Nat Asn Negro Bus & Prof Womens Clubs; life mem, Nat Coun Negro Women; Zeta Phi Beta; Past Matron Order Eastern Star; secy El Cerrito Br Nat Asn Advan Colored People; Golden State Bus League; Prairie View Alumnae Asn; Bay Area Personnel Women; N CA Ind rel coun Who's Who Am Women, 1971; comn mem, Govern Commn Status Women. **Honors/Awds:** Service Awards, Zeta Phi Beta; Community Service Award, Order Eastern Star; Employer Awards, Nat Asn Negro Bus & Prof Women. **Special Achievements:** First female To serve in US Energy Research and development administration; First female centre manager in Berkeley Human Resource Development Center; First president in Past Western District Government. **Home Addr:** 6487 Conlon Ave, El Cerrito, CA 94530. **Business Addr:** 1333 Broadway, Oakland, CA 94612-1917.

**CAMPBELL, GERTRUDE SIMS**
Government official, postmaster general. **Personal:** Born May 13, 1942, Greenville, MS; daughter of Eugene Sims and Beatrice Parker Smith; married Willie James; children: Kimberly Jamille. **Educ:** Wm F Bolger Acad, Supvr Skills Training, Memphis, Tenn, 1990. **Career:** US Postal Serv, clerk positions, 1966-90, supvr customer serv, 1990, postmaster, 1998-. **Orgs:** Afro Am United Success Postal Serv, 1990-93; League Postmasters, 1992; Nat Asn Postal Supvr, 1993; Nat Asn Postmasters Us, 1997. **Honors/Awds:** Special Achievement Award, US Postal Service, 1973, 1987; Diversity Peace setters Award, 1996. **Home Addr:** PO Box 2212, Starkville, MS 39760-2212. **Business Addr:** MS.

**CAMPBELL, DR. HELEN**
Educator. **Educ:** Ala State Univ, BS; Univ Ala, MA, PhD. **Career:** Bishop State Community Col, instr & directress choir, currently, music dept, prof. **Home Addr:** 260 S Cedar St, Mobile, AL 36602, **Home Phone:** (251)438-1922. **Business Addr:** Instructor & Directress of Choir, Bishop State Community College, 351 N Broad St, Mobile, AL 36603-5833, **Business Phone:** (251)405-7000.

**CAMPBELL, REV. JAMES W. (BISHOP WILLIE JAMES CAMPBELL)**
Clergy. **Personal:** Born Mar 17, 1945, Chicago, IL; son of Jessie (deceased); married Lady Lori; children: James, Jesse, Jared & Bridgett. **Educ:** Wilson Jr Col; Moody Bible Inst. **Career:** St James Church God Christ, ministry, 1966, supt State, 1977; dist supt, 1972; 5th Jurisdiction Ill, secy, 1973; St. James Ministries Church God, pastor, currently; WJYS Channel 62, speaker. **Orgs:** Resolution Comn Nat & Elders Coun, 1975-77; Westside br Nat Asn Advan Colored People; Nat Petrolman's Asn; Nat Asn Child Develop; Int bd Minister's; Int Asn Pastor's; Nat Elders Coun; Gospel Music Worship Am Announcers Guild; Ministers Alliance; Oper PUSH; Area Asns Relig Comm; Chicago Urban League; Nat Const Comt; Am Asn Respiratory Care; Nat Evangelism Dept, pres dept Evangelism, Church GodChrist inc, 2009-. **Honors/Awds:** COGIC special citation, City Chicago; Pastor of the Year Award, Christian Guild Soc, 1979; Award for Dedicated & Faithful Services, State Sunday Sch Supt Sunday Sch Dept Ill, 1980. **Home Addr:** 718 S 2nd Ave, Maywood, IL 60153. **Business Addr:** Pastor, St James Church Of God In Christ, 11750 S Lowe Ave, Chicago, IL 60628, **Business Phone:** (773)291-0200.

**CAMPBELL, LAMAR**
Radio host, executive, football player. **Personal:** Born Aug 29, 1976, Chester, PA. **Educ:** Univ Wis, Madison, BA, educ, 1998; Univ Pa, Wharton Sch, Bus Mgt, 2008; Bowling Green Univ, Nat Football League Sports Jour & Commun Bootcamp, 2013. **Career:** Football player (retired), exec, host; Detroit Lions, defensive back, 1998-2005; Solid Source Realty, com & residential sales rep, 2005-13; VoiceAmerica Talk Radio WTR LLC, radio host, life after game, 2011-13; Univ Wis-Madison, stud-athlete develop seasonal coordr & assoc stud serv coordr, 2014-; Univ Wis, Whitewater, warhawk roundtable, 2016; Good Karma Broadcasting LLC, col gameday pre & postgame, 2014-; Life After Game Consult, owner, 2011-; Edgewood Col, adj prof-bus capstone, 2016-. **Honors/Awds:** Rookie of the Year, 1998. **Special Achievements:** Publications: For retired NFL players, most challenging 'season' just beginning, 2011, Living and Thriving after the NFL, 2012, Put Pride aside and ask for help, 2012, Pro Athletes ignore backlash, show true political colors, 2012, Why I am donating my brain, 2013, for Cable News Network. **Business Addr:** Adjunct Professor-Business Capstone, Edgewood College, 1000 Edgewood College Dr, Madison, WI 53711, **Business Phone:** (800)444-4861.

**CAMPBELL, LLOYD E.**
Executive. **Personal:** Born Jan 1, 1958?. **Educ:** Georgetown Univ, BS, bus admin; Univ Pa, Wharton Sch, MBA. **Career:** Teachers Ins, staff, 1980-; Credit Suisse First Boston, Pvt Fin Grp, mng dir & head, 1985-2001; Rothschild Inc, global pvt placement grp, mng dir & head, 2001-; Spencer Stuarts, consult, currently; Aurora Mgt Partners, spec adv, currently; Spartech Plastics LLC, dir, 2002-. **Orgs:** Bd mem & bd dir, Spartech Corp, 2002-; Rothschild Inc firms Investment Banking Comm; bd dir, mem compensation comt & mem nominating & corp governance comt, Alderwoods Grp, LLC, 2002-; dir, Mem Audit & Risk Comt, Mem Investment Comt, Guardian Life, 2006-; bd trustee, Georgetown Univ; chmn & founder, Pride First Corp; dir & chair, nominating & governance comt; bd mem, Argyle Security Inc, 2008-2009; pres, Gephardt; Hillary Rodham Clinton US Senate Comt; Obama Am; sr advisor, Rothschilds merchant banking activ; Annuity Asn. **Home Addr:** , NY. **Business Addr:** Consultant, Spencer Stuat, 277 Pk Ave 32nd Fl, New York, NY 10172, **Business Phone:** (212)336-0200.

**CAMPBELL, MAIA**
Actor, chairperson. **Personal:** Born Nov 26, 1976, Takoma Park, MD; daughter of Tiko and Bebe Moore. **Educ:** Spelman Col, Atlanta, GA, theatre. **Career:** MCC Inc, owner, producer, writer, head chmn & chief exec officer, 1994-. TV series: "Thea", 1993; "South Central", 1994; "In The House", 1995-99; "Moesha", 1997; "Sister, Sister", 1998; "Seventeen Again", 2000; Films: Poetic Justice, 1993; Kinfolks, 1998; Trippin', 1999; The Luau, 2001; The Trial, 2002; With or Without You, 2003; Sweet Potato Pie, 2004; Envy, 2005; Sorority Sister Slaughter, 2007; The Rimshop, 2008. **Special Achievements:** Nominee, Young Artist Award, 1996. **Business Addr:** Owner, Chief Executive Officer, MCC Incorporation, 3607 S Main St, Blacksburg, VA 24060, **Business Phone:** (540)951-8202.

**CAMPBELL, DR. MARGIE**
Educator, association executive. **Personal:** Born Jun 17, 1954, Musella, GA; daughter of Margret Smith; children: MeQuanta. **Educ:** Gordon Col, AS, 1991; Mercer Univ, BS, 1995. **Career:** Monroe Co Bd Educ, sch secy, 1978-; Mary Persons High Sch, teacher, currently. **Orgs:** Vol, Fire Fighter, 1977-; Parker Chapel AME Church; GA Munic Asn, 1984; Gov Proj Steering Comt, 1984; vpres, Band Booster, 1990-; vpres, Basketball Tip-Off Club, 1991. **Honors/Awds:** Comm Leader Award, Gov's Proj Competition Atlanta, 1982; Teacher of the Year, Monroe Achievement Ctr. **Special Achievements:** Selected as one of the 50 most influential Black women in GA-GA Informer 1983. **Home Addr:** PO Box 13, Culloden, GA 31016-0013, **Home Phone:** (478)885-2444. **Business Addr:** Teacher, Mary Persons High School, 25-A Brooklyn Ave, Forsyth, GA 31029-1308, **Business Phone:** (478)994-7072.

**CAMPBELL, MARY ALLISON**
City council member, educator, teacher. **Personal:** Born Feb 18, 1937, Shelby, NC; daughter of A C Allison; married Fred N Sr; children: Alison Winifred & Fred N Jr. **Educ:** Benedict Col, BS, 1960; Winthrop Col, attended 1973. **Career:** Educator (retired); Harold Fagges Assoc, NY, clerk, 1963-68; Clover Town County, coun mem; Clover Sch Dist, teacher, 1968-98. **Orgs:** Pres, The Progressive Women's Club, 1970-75; assoc matron, Magnolia Chap OES 144, 1982-84; pres, YCEA, 1988-89. **Honors/Awds:** School Yearbook Dedication, Roosevelt Sch, 1970; Appreciation Award, United Men's Club, 1980; Outstanding Black Citizen of Clover Community, 1989; Citizen of the Year, Clover County, 1993. **Home Addr:** 104 Wilson St, Clover, SC 29710-1059, **Home Phone:** (803)222-4671.

**CAMPBELL, MARY DELOIS**
Administrator. **Personal:** Born Jul 21, 1940, Greenville, TX; married David; children: Keith Devlin. **Educ:** Jarvis Christian Col Hawkins, TX, BS, bus admin, 1962; Bishop Col, Dallas, 1963. **Career:** Bishop Col Dallas Co Community Action, clerical, 1962-68; Dallas Co Comn Action Inc, Neighborhood Ctr coordr, 1968-69; City Dallas, asst youth coordr, 1969-71; N Cent TX Coun T, manpower planner, 1971-76, human serv & planner, 1976-77; Housing Auth City Dallas, asst dir soc serv, 1979-80; Housing Auth City Dallas, asst dir res selection, 1980. **Orgs:** Bd dir, Dallas Urban League, 1974-77; Dallas Comn C & Youth, 1975; pres bd dir, Dallas Urban League, 1977-78; bd dir, Goals Dallas, 1977-79. **Home Addr:** 1404 Crosspointe St, Duncanville, TX 75137-2013, **Home Phone:** (972)298-6300.

**CAMPBELL, DR. MARY SCHMIDT**
Dean (education), college administrator, artist. **Personal:** Born Oct 21, 1947, Philadelphia, PA; daughter of Harvey N Schmidt and Elaine Harris Schmidt; married George Jr; children: Garikai, Sekou & Britt Jackson. **Educ:** Swarthmore Col, BA, eng lit, 1969; Syracuse Univ, MA, art hist, 1973, PhD, humanities, 1982. **Career:** Syracuse Univ, Syracuse, NY, lectr; Nkumbi Int Col, Kabwe, Zambia, instr, 1969-71; Syracuse New Times, Contribr,, art ed, 1974-77; Ford Found, fel, 1973-75; Nat Fel Fund, dissertation yr fel, 1976-77; Everson Mus, cur, guest cur, 1974-76; Studio Mus Harlem, exec dir, 1977-87; Rockefeller Found, fel, 1985; New York Dept Cult Affairs, comnr cult affairs, 1987-91; Swarthmore Col, bd mgr, 1988-2000; New York Univ, Inst Humanities, fel, 1989-, assoc provost arts, 2005-07; Tisch Sch Arts, dean, 1991-2014, Dept Art & Pub Policy, chair, 2000-, assoc provost, 2004-07, Art & Pub Policy, prof, 2014-, dean emer, 2014-; NY Coun Arts, chair, 2007-09; Pres Emeritius Cooper Union Advan Sci & Art; Spelman Col, pres, 2015-. Books : Harlem Renaissance: Art Black Am, co-auth; Romare Bearden, author, 1994; Artistic Citizenship: A Pub Voice Arts, co-ed, 2006. Film: Sembene: A Biography, producer. **Orgs:** Co-founder, Community Folk Art Gallery Syracuse Univ, New York, 1971-77; Film Forum, 1980-86; Asn Art Mus dir, 1984-87; fine arts vis comt, Harvard Univ, 1986-88; bd trustee, Col Art Asn, 1987-89chair, Stud Life Comt, Swarthmore Col Bd Mgrs, 1988-2000; chair, Adv Comt African Am Instnl Study, Smithsonian Inst, 1989-91; chair & adv comt, African Am Instnl Study, Smithsonian Inst, 1990-91; Barnes Found, 1991-; VisCom Fine Arts, Harvard Col Bd Overseers, 1991-93; bd trustee, Jazz at Lincoln Ctr, 1993-99; Mayors Adv Comn Film & Tv, NYC, 1995-2001; fel Am Acad Arts & Sci; adv bd, Romare Bearden Found, 1997-; bd trustee, Am Acad Rome, 1997-2009; bd trustee, Brooklyn Mus Art, 1998-2002; adv bd, Figure Skating Harlem, 2000-; bd trustee, Thomas S Kenan Inst Arts, 2000-02; fel Am Acad Arts & Sci, 2001-; bd trustee, Un Int Sch, 2001-07; chmn bd, NYU Tisch Sch Arts Asia, 2007-14; vice chair, Pres Comt Arts & Humanities, 2009-; bd trustee, Alfred P. Sloan Found, 2009-; bd trustee, Pub Theater/New York Shakespeare Festival, 2009-14; bd trustee, 1996-2000, bd dir, 2010-13, Harlem Sch Arts; Tony Awards Nominating Comt, 1996-2002, 2012-. **Home Addr:** 457 W 144th St, New York, NY 10031, **Home Phone:** (212)690-2977. **Business Addr:** President, Spelman College, 350 Spelman Lane SW, Atlanta, GA 30314-4399, **Business Phone:** (404)681-3643.

**CAMPBELL, MELANIE L.**
Chief executive officer, association executive, executive director. **Personal:** Born Titusville, FL; daughter of Isaac Campell Sr and Janet. **Educ:** Clark Atlanta Univ, BA, bus admin & finance, 1983. **Career:** City Atlanta, Off Educ, asst dir, 1990-92; Mayor's Off Youth Servs, dir, 1992-94; self-employed polit strategist, 1994-95; Nat Coalition Black Civic Participation, dep dir, 1995-97, int dir, 1997-98, exec dir, pres & chief exec officer, 1998-; Harvard Univ, John F. Kennedy Sch of Govt's Inst of Polit, resident, 2003. **Orgs:** Delta Sigma Theta Sorority; Nat Coun Negro Women; Nat Asn Advan Colored People; Rainbow & PUSH Coalition; Nat Asn Female Exec; Nat Polit Cong Black Women; SCLC Women; bd dir, Nat Coalition Black Civic Participation. **Business Addr:** Executive Director, President & Chief Executive Officer, National Coalition on Black Civic Participation Inc, 1050 Conn Ave 10th Fl Suite 1000, Washington, DC 20036, **Business Phone:** (202)659-4929.

**CAMPBELL, MELVIN DARNELL, JR. See MUHAMMAD, MUHSIN, II.**

**CAMPBELL, MICHELLE**
Basketball player. **Personal:** Born Feb 20, 1974, Carson, CA. **Educ:** Univ Southern Calif. **Career:** Basketball player (retired); Philadelphia Rage, ctr, 1997; Utah Starzz, 1999; Wash Mystics, 2000.

**CAMPBELL, DR. OTIS, JR.**
Physician, educator. **Personal:** Born Sep 9, 1951, Tampa, FL; son of Otis Sr and Georgia Mae; married Carol Y Clarke; children: Davin, Desmond, Donovon & Danyel. **Educ:** Fla A&M Univ, BS, biol, 1973; Meharry Med Col, PhD, pharmacol, 1982, MD, 1986; Am Bd Internal Med, dipl. **Career:** Spec Med Prog Meharry Med Col, instr, 1982-84; Biomed Sci Prog Meharry Med Col, instr, 1982-84; UNCF Fisk Univ Pre Med Inst, 1982-84; Vanderbilt Univ, summers, post doctoral res fel, 1982-85; Tenn State Univ Weekend Col, prof, 1982-86; Meharry Med Col, Dept Pharmacol, Nashville, TN, prof, 1986-; McMinnville, TN, pvt pract, internal med, 1990-. **Orgs:** Mid Tenn Neuroscience Soc; Am Med Asn. **Honors/Awds:** Alpha Omega Alpha Medical Honor Soc, 1986; Hall of Natural Scientists, Fla A&M Univ, 1987. **Home Addr:** 3723 Stevens Lane, Nashville, TN 37218, **Home Phone:** (615)876-7207. **Business Addr:** Physician, 3109 John A Merritt Blvd, Nashville, TN 37209, **Business Phone:** (615)320-0338.

**CAMPBELL, ROGERS EDWARD, III**
Executive. **Personal:** Born Jul 14, 1951, Jersey City, NJ; son of Rogers E Jr and Anne Mae Powell. **Educ:** St Peter's Col, BS, 1973; Rutgers Univ, MBA, 1974. **Career:** Marketcorp Int, pres; Nabisco Foods Group, sr dir mkt; Gen Mills Inc, asst prod mgr 1978-81; Mattel Electronics, prod mgr, 1982-83; Schering-Plough Corp, dir mkt, 1983-88; Marketcare Consumer HTH, svp, managing dir, 1988-; Overseas Mil Sales Corp, vpres & chief mkt officer, 2004-08; DeCA E Region, dir, currently. **Orgs:** Admis liaison officer, US Mil Acad; chmn, pub rels

comm Rutgers Grad Sch Bus; IOTA Phi Theta Fraternity; Clinton Hill Develop Corp. **Home Addr:** 66 Highland Ave, Maplewood, NJ 07040, **Home Phone:** (973)762-4224. **Business Addr:** Director, Public Affairs Officer, Defense Commissary Agency Eastern Region, 1300 E Ave, Fort Lee, VA 23831-1800, **Business Phone:** (804)734-8000.

## CAMPBELL, SANDRA
Library administrator. **Career:** Univ Ark, Libr Media Specialist, 1982; Southeast Ark Regional Libr, Libr Specialist, 1982-83; Univ Ark, Monticello Libr, dir, currently. **Business Addr:** Director, University of Arkansas, 514 Univ Dr, Monticello, AK 71656, **Business Phone:** (870)460-1080.

## CAMPBELL, SANDRA DUPREE. See DUPREE, SANDRA KAY.

## CAMPBELL, SANDRA PACE
Government official, consultant. **Personal:** Born Aug 24, 1955, Detroit, MI; daughter of Willie and Laura Pace; married John F Jr; children: Domonique, John III, Scott & Clarissa. **Educ:** Wayne State Univ, BBA, 1985; Univ Detroit, MBA, 1991. **Career:** Alan C Young & Assoc, sr acct, 1985-87, acct supvr, 1987-93; Eastern Mich Univ, asst controller, 1993-95; City Detroit, mgr rev collections, 1995-2002; Pacemaker Acct Pc, chief financial officer, 2002-. **Orgs:** Dir, Univ Mich Credit Union, 1993-; dir, secy, Booker T Wash Bus, 1992-96; audit chair, Elliottorians Bus women, 1991-; vpres, Nat Assoc Black Acct, 1984-85; mem co-chair, Nat Assoc Black MBAs, 1996-97; Jr Achievement, bus trainer vol, 1982-96; mentor, WADE McCree Incentive Scholar Prog, 1988-97; dir, Detroit Black Chamber Com, 2001; dir, Black United Fund, 2002-; dir, Travelers AID Soc, 2003-; treas, Delta Sigma Theta Sorority Inc, Detroit Alumnae Chap, 2003-05; bd dir, Black United Fund, Mich. **Home Addr:** 18314 Warrington Dr, Detroit, MI 48221-3722, **Home Phone:** (313)345-7977. **Business Addr:** Chief Financial Officer, Pacemaker Accounting PC, 10641 W McNichols Rd, Detroit, MI 48221, **Business Phone:** (313)927-9100.

## CAMPBELL, DR. SYLVAN LLOYD
Physician. **Personal:** Born Oct 8, 1931, Boston, MA; son of Vera and Silvanis; children: Steven. **Educ:** Boston Col, AB, 1953; Howard Univ, MD, 1961. **Career:** Philadelphia Gen Hosp, intern, 1961-62, res, 1962-65; Boston, Practicemed, specializing ob & gynecol, 1965-2000; Beth Israel Hosp, Boston, Mass, obstet-gynecol, 1965-2000; Harvard Univ, obstet asst clin prof emer, 1975; Dimock Comm Hlth Ctr, currently. **Orgs:** Hon Staff Beth Israel Hosp; Am Bd Obstet-Gynecol Boston Obstet Soc; Mass Med Soc, 1966-; Am Col Obstetricians & Gynecologists, 1969-2000. **Home Addr:** 29 Converse Ave, Newton, MA 02458-2503, **Home Phone:** (617)244-3830. **Business Addr:** Dimock Community Health Center, 55 Dimock St, Roxbury, MA 02119, **Business Phone:** (617)442-8800.

## CAMPBELL, TEVIN JERMOD
Singer, actor. **Personal:** Born Nov 12, 1976, Dallas, TX; son of Rhonda Byrd. **Career:** As Featured Performer: "I Know That My Redeemer Liveth", 1991; Albums: TEVIN, 1991; I'm Ready, 1993; Back To The World, 1996; Tevin Campbell, 1999; The Best of Tevin Campbell, 2001; Qwest & Warner Bros, singer, currently; Films: Graffiti Bridge, 1990; A Goofy Movie, 1995; TV series: Wally & the Valentines, 1989; "Saturday Night Live", 1990; "The Fresh Prince of Bel-Air", 1991; The Parent 'Hood, 1997; "Moesha", 1999. Singles: "Tomorrow (A Better You, ABetter Me) With Quincy Jones", 1989; "Round & Round", 1990; "Just Ask Me To", 1991; "Tell Me What You Want Me to Do", 1991; "Goodbye", 1992; "Strawberry Letter 23", 1992; "Alone With You", 1992; "Confused", 1993; "One Song", 1993; "Can We Talk", 1993; "I'm Ready", 1994; "Always In My Heart", 1994; "Don't Say Goodbye Girl", 1995; "Back To The World", 1996; "I Got It Bad", 1996; "You Don't Have to Worry", 1997; "Could You Learn To Love", 1997; "Another Way", 1998; "For Your Love", 1999; "Losing All Control", 1999. **Honors/Awds:** Young Artist Award, 1990; Soul Train Music Award, 1994. **Special Achievements:** Nominated for many Grammy awards & Am Music Awards, 1992-98. **Business Addr:** Singer, Qwest & Warner Brothers, 3300 Warner Blvd, Burbank, CA 91505, **Business Phone:** (818)846-9090.

## CAMPBELL, THOMAS W.
Musician. **Personal:** Born Feb 14, 1957, Norristown, PA. **Educ:** Berklee Col Music. **Career:** Webster Lewis, drummer, 1978; MarLena Shaw/Gap Mangione, drummer, 1979; Berklee Performance Ctr, concert, 1979; Baird Hersey & Year of the Ear, drummer; Own Group "TCB", Boston, drummer; Dizzy Gillespie Band, prof jazz drummer, 1985; First Music Group; The Mandells; Music: Elizabeth Catlett: Sculpting the Truth, ed, 1999; Richard Mayhew: Spiritual Landscapes, ed, 2000; School's Out: Self-taught Artists, ed, 2002; Rooftop Serenade, dir, writer, producer & ed, 2002; Chuck Close: Close Up, ed, 2004; Pulling, ed, 2004; Buying Wine (or How Not To), dir, co-producer & ed, 2004; West Side Demise, dir, writer & ed, 2005; I Can Fly: Kids and Creativity, ed, 2006; Red Grooms: Sculptopictoramatist, ed, 2008; Birth of the Sun, dir, writer & exec producer, 2009; Athena, ed, 2009; Saint Vitus Dance, ed & assoc producer, 2011; Better Love, actor, ed, writer & co-producer, 2014. Films: Pulling, ed, 2004. **Orgs:** Big Brother Activities. **Home Addr:** 21 Barrett Rd, Marlborough, MA 01752-1364. **Business Addr:** Musician, Sutton Artists Corp, 119 W 57 Suite 818, New York, NY 10019.

## CAMPBELL, TONY (ANTHONY CAMPBELL)
Athletic director, basketball player, basketball coach. **Personal:** Born May 7, 1962, Teaneck, NJ. **Educ:** Ohio State Univ, Columbus, OH, commun, 1984; Fairleigh Dickinson Univ, BA, film & broadcasting, 1999; Univ Phoenix, MEd, leadership & supv, 2014. **Career:** Basketball player (retired), basketball coach, athletic dir; Detroit Pistons, 1984-87; Nj Jammers, 1987; Albany Patroons, 1987-88; Los Angeles Lakers, 1987-89; Minn Timberwolves, 1989-92; New York Knicks, 1992-94; Dallas Mavericks, 1994; Cleveland Cavaliers, 1994-95; AEK Athens, Greece, 1995; Fla Beachdogs, 1996-97; Paramus Cath High Sch, athletic dir & boy's basketball head coach, 2002-07; Bay Ridge Prep Sch, athletic dir, 2007-. **Special Achievements:** First player to earn an NBA ring (1987-1988 Lakers) and CBA ring (Albany Patroons) in the same season. **Business Addr:** Director of Athletics, Bay Ridge Preparatory School, 7420 4th Ave, Brooklyn, NY 11209, **Business Phone:** (718)833-5839.

## CAMPBELL, TRECINA EVETTE. See ATKINS, TINA.

## CAMPBELL, WILLIAM
Government official, politician, attorney general (U.S. federal government). **Personal:** Born Jan 1, 1953, Raleigh, NC; married Sharon; children: Billy & Christina. **Educ:** Vanderbilt Univ, BA; Duke Univ, JD, law. **Career:** Politician (retired) Dem Party, mem; Atlanta City Coun, 12 yrs; City Atlanta, mayor, 1994-2002; pvt pract atty. **Orgs:** Omega Psi Phi Fraternity. **Home Addr:** 940 Waverly Way NE, Atlanta, GA 30307.

## CAMPBELL, WILLIAM EARL
Government official. **Personal:** Born Aug 26, 1965, Dermott, AR; son of Eddie Sr and Alice Allen. **Educ:** Univ Ark-Monticello. **Career:** City Reed, Ark, mayor, 1990-98; Ariz Employ Security Dept, prog supvr, off mgr, 1992-. **Orgs:** Gen secy, bd dir, New Hope Baptist Church, 1985-91; Southeast Ark Literacy Coun; bd dir, Nat Conf Black Mayors; pres, Ariz Conf Black Mayors; TEA Coalition; Monticello Econ Develop Comn; adv bd, Workforce Training Ctr; Sch bd, McGehee Spec Sch Dist; Develop Info Net Ark. **Home Addr:** 204 S Church St, PO Box 223, Tillar, AR 71670, **Home Phone:** (870)392-7738. **Business Addr:** Office Manager, Program Service Advisor, Arkansas Employment Security Department, 1001 S Tenn St, Pine Bluff, AR 71601-5032, **Business Phone:** (870)534-1920.

## CAMPBELL, BISHOP WILLIE JAMES. See CAMPBELL, REV. JAMES W.

## CAMPBELL, DR. ZERRIE D.
Educator, school administrator. **Personal:** Born Feb 9, 1951, Chicago, IL; daughter of Robert Rice and Lorraince Rice; children: Sydney Adams. **Educ:** Northern Ill Univ, BA, eng, 1972, MS, sec prof educ, 1974; Chicago State Univ, MA, eng, 1978. **Career:** Northern Ill Univ, grad asst, 1972-73, asst dormitory dir, 1973-74; Malcolm X Col, dir, asst dean stud supportive serv, 1974-77, instr, 1977-82, vpres, acad affairs, 1989-92, pres, 1992-; Harold Wash Col, asst prof, 1983-87; City Col Chicago, actg assoc, Lib Arts & Scis, vice chancellor, 1987-89. **Orgs:** Pres, Alpha Kappa Alpha, Xi Nu Omega Chap; pres, Monarch Awards Found; Langston Hughes Lit Asn; NIU Black Alumni Coun; Mod Lang Asn; Ill Comt Black Concerns Higher Educ; Nat Coun Instrnl Adminr; Am Coun Educ & Nat ID Prog AWHE; Am Asn Women Community Cols; Am Asn Univ Women; Nat Asn Female Execs; bd mem, Am Asn Community Col; adv coun, Nat Inst Leadership Develop; Chicago Network; N Cent Asn Cols & Schs Consult Evaluator Corps; Econ Club Chicago; bd dir, Habilitative Systs Inc; bd dir, Chicago Multi-Cult Dance Ctr; bd mem, United Ctr Community Econ Develop Fund, bd mem; Ill Comt Black Concerns Higher Educ; Networking Group Minority Exec; adv bd, Community Bank Lawndale, adv bd. **Home Addr:** 1220 S Fed St Suite C, Chicago, IL 60605-3385, **Home Phone:** (312)341-9912. **Business Addr:** President, Malcolm X College, 1900 W Van Buren Rm 1100, Chicago, IL 60612-3197, **Business Phone:** (312)850-7037.

## CAMPBELL-MARTIN, TISHA MICHELLE
Actor, movie director, television comedy writer. **Personal:** Born Oct 13, 1968, Oklahoma City, OK; daughter of Clifton Campbell and Mona; married Duane; children: Xen & Ezekiel. **Career:** Films: Little Shop of Horrors, 1986; Sch Daze, 1988; Rooftops, 1989; House Party, 1990; Another 48 Hours, 1990; House Party 2, 1991; Boomerang, 1992; House Party 3, 1994; Snitch, 1996; Homeward Bound II: Lost in San Francisco, 1996; Sprung, 1997; Get Up Stand Up Comedy, dir, 2001; The Last Place On Earth, 2002; The Seat Filler, writer, 2004; Angels Can't Help But Laugh, 2007; Zack and Miri Make a Porno, 2008; Pastor Brown, 2009. TV series: "Gina on Martin", 1992-97; "Linc's", 1998; "TheSweetest Gift", 1998; "Sabrina, the Teenage Witch", 2000; "The HalloweenScene", 2000; "The Victoria's Secret Fashion Show", 2001; "My Wife & Kids", dir, 2001-05; "The Last Place On Earth", 2002; "Calvin Goes to Work", 2004; "A Family Affair", 2004; "The Proposal", 2004; "The Maid", 2004; "All of Us", 2004-06; "The 'V' Story", 2005; "Silence Is Golden", 2005; "My Wife & Kids", dir, 2005; "My Two Dads", 2006; "The Courtship of Robert's Father", 2006; "Carmen's Karma", 2006; "Trying to Love Two", 2006; "All of Us", 2006-07; "Wright vs. Wrong", 2010; "Lemonade Mouth", 2011; "The Protector", 2011; "Robot Chicken", 2011; "Private Practice", 2012; "Malibu Country", 2013; "LA Live the Show", 2013. **Orgs:** Am Film Inst. **Honors/Awds:** Image Award for Outstanding Actress in a Comedy Series, Nat Asn Advan Colored People, 2003; BET Comedy Award, 2004; Independent Spirit Award. **Special Achievements:** Nominated 5 times for Image Awards. **Business Addr:** Actress, The Kohner Agency, 9300 Wilshire Blvd, Beverly Hills, CA 90212, **Business Phone:** (310)550-1060.

## CAMPER, DIANE G.
Journalist, editor. **Personal:** Born Feb 27, 1948, New York, NY; daughter of Roosevelt P and Clinice Coleman. **Educ:** Syracuse Univ, Syracuse, NY, BA, 1968; Yale Univ, New Haven, CT, MSt, law, 1977. **Career:** Newsweek, ed asst, 1968-72, Wash Bur corresp, 1972-83; New York Times, ed writer, 1983-97; Baltimore Sun Ed Bd, asst ed page ed, 2004-. **Orgs:** Women Commun Inc, 1968-; Delta Sigma Theta Sorority, 1974-; Nat Assoc Black Journalists, 1985; Annie E Casey, sr fel, pub affairs mgr, 1997-04; Pub Welfare Found, commun officer, 2008-. **Honors/Awds:** Page One Award, New York Newspaper Guild, 1977; Chancellor's Citation, 1986, Syracuse Univ; Publisher's Awards, New York Times, 1988, 1990; George Arents Pioneer Medal, 1990. **Home Addr:** 370 Cent Pk W Suite 311, New York, NY 10025, **Home Phone:** (212)316-3623. **Business Addr:** Communications Officer, Public Welfare Foundation, 1200 U St NW, Washington, DC 20009-4443, **Business Phone:** (202)965-1800.

## CAMPHOR, MICHAEL GERARD
Health services administrator. **Personal:** son of James and Lillie. **Educ:** Morgan State Univ, BA, 1978; Univ Baltimore, MPA, health serv admin 1984; Naval Health Sci Educ & Training Command, cert financial & supply mgt, 1986. **Career:** Columbia Res Syst, res asst, 1976-77; N Cent Baltimore Health Corp, ctr adminr, 1980-84; Dept Housing & Community Develop, proj mgr, 1983-84; Cent Md Health Systs Agency, health implementor & liaison, 1984-85; US Naval Hosp, Philadelphia, Pa, comptroller/hosp adminr, 1985-; US Naval Hosp, Mat Mgt & Contracting, Yokosuku, Japan, head officer; Dept Housing & Urban Develop, Grad Studies fel. **Orgs:** E Baltimore Community Orgn, 1978-83, Waverly Human Serv Coord Coun, 1980-83; site coord, Nat Health Screening Coun Vol Orgn, 1980-83; Dallas F Nicholas Elem Sch Adv Bd, 1981-84; Johns Hopkins Hosp Community Develop Adv Bd, 1983-84; Nat Naval Officers Asn. **Honors/Awds:** MJ Naylor Award, Highest Dept Average Morgan State Univ, 1978; Admin of the Year, N Cent Baltimore Health Corp, 1981; Outstanding Young Men of America Jaycees, 1983. **Home Addr:** , Seattle, WA 98104. **Business Addr:** Manager, US Navy Hospital.

## CANADA, REV. DR. ARTHUR W.
Presbyterian clergy. **Educ:** PhD. **Career:** Grandale Presby Church Master, presbyter; 212th Gen Assembly, Detroit, vice moderator, comnr, currently; McClintock Presby Church, pastor, currently. **Orgs:** Bd dir, Montreat Conf Ctr, currently. **Business Addr:** Pastor, McClintock Presbyterian Church, 14008 Erwin Rd, Charlotte, NC 28273, **Business Phone:** (704)588-2733.

## CANADA, GEOFFREY
Chief executive officer. **Personal:** Born Jan 13, 1952, South Bronx, NY; son of McAlister and Mary Elizabeth; married Yvonne Grant; children: 4; married Joyce Henderson; children: 1. **Educ:** Bowdoin Col, Brunswick, ME, BA, psychol & sociol, 1974; Harvard Grad Sch Educ, MA, educ, 1975. **Career:** Camp Freedom Ctr Ossipe, Nh, supvr, 1974-75; Robert White Sch, fac, 1975-76, asssoc dir, 1976-77, dir, 1977-81; Marion Wright Edelman & C's Defense Fund, partner; Rheedlen Insts Truancy Prev Prog, prog dir, 1983-90; Chang Moo Kwan Martial Arts Sch, found, dir, chief instr, 1983-; Harlem C's Zone, chief exec officer, 1990-2014, pres, 1990-; Black Community Crusade C, E Coast reg coordr, 1991-. Books: Fist Stick Knife Gun: A Personal History of Violence in America, 1995; Reaching Up For Manhood: Transforming the Lives of Boys in America, 1998; New York Gov's Coun Econ & Fiscal Advisor, 2011. **Orgs:** Bd trustee, City Proj, 1990-; bd trustee, Black Child Develop Inst, 1992-; bd dir, Fund City NY & Found Ctr, 1995-; bd trustee, Harlem C's Zone, currently; New York Mayor Michael Bloomberg, co-chair, 2006. **Business Addr:** President, Chief Executive Officer, Harlem Children's Zone, 103 W 107th St, New York, NY 10025, **Business Phone:** (212)866-5579.

## CANADY, DR. ALEXA IRENE
Physician, educator. **Personal:** Born Nov 7, 1950, Lansing, MI; daughter of Clinton Jr and Hortense Golden; married George Davis. **Educ:** Univ Mich, Ann Arbor MI, BS, zool, 1971, MD (cum laude), 1975. **Career:** Chief Pediat Neurosurg (retired); Univ Minn, training neurosurg, 1976-81; Univ Pa, instr neurosurg, 1981-82; Henry Ford Hosp, Detroit, Mich, instr neurosurg, 1982-83; Wayne St Univ, Sch Med, Detroit, Mich, clin instr, 1985, clin assoc prof, 1987-90, assoc; C's Hosp Mich, Chief Neurosurg, 1987-2001; C's Hosp Detroit, dir neurosurg. **Orgs:** Am Col Surgeons; Am Asn Neurol Surgeons; Cong Neurol Surgeons; AMA; Nat Med Asn; Am Soc Pediat Neurosurg; Mich St Med Soc; Alpha Omega Alpha Socs; Delta Sigma Theta Sorority. **Home Addr:** 6064 Forest Green Rd, Pensacola, FL 32505, **Home Phone:** (850)477-7091.

## CANADY, BLANTON THANDREUS
Executive. **Personal:** Born Nov 25, 1948, West Point, GA; son of William Jr and Grace Warrick; married Yvonne; children: Andre Reynolds & Blanton T II. **Educ:** Univ Ill, BA, finance, mkt, 1970; Univ Chicago, Booth Sch Bus, MBA, finance & gen, 1976. **Career:** Ill Bell Tel, Chicago, commun consult, 1970-73; Xerox Corp, telecomm mgr, 1973-76; Am Hosp Supply Corp, fin serv mgr, 1976-81; Great Lakes Div, pres, 1981; McDonald's Corp, pres, exec vpres & chief oper officer, owner, 1981-2010; BTII Inc, pres, 1981-; Canady Enterprises, pres-. **Orgs:** Pres, Black McDonald's Owners Asn, Chicago, 1986-88; vpres, McDonald's Owners Chicagoland & NW, Ind, 1988-90, pres, 1990-92; exec comn, S Side Planning Bd, 1990-; bd mem, Midwest Asn Sickle Cell Anemia, 1990-; Near S Planning Bd; Northern Trust Bank Adv Bd. **Home Addr:** 4901 S Greenwood, Chicago, IL 60615, **Home Phone:** (312)624-1544. **Business Addr:** President, BTII Inc, 1700 E 56th St, Chicago, IL 60637, **Business Phone:** (773)493-7660.

## CANADY, HON. HERMAN G., JR.
Judge. **Personal:** Born Kanawha County, WV; married Barbara L; children: 3. **Educ:** Northwestern Univ, BA; WVa Univ Col Law, JD. **Career:** Judge (retired); Kanawha County, asst prosecuting atty; Circuit Ct, Charleston, WVa, judge, 1982, 1984, 1992, 2000-02; Wva Supreme Ct Appeals, spec Justice. **Orgs:** Sigma Pi Phi Fraternity; vpres, secy, treas, pres, Wva Judicial Asn; life mem, Nat Asn Advan colored people; Wva Socs Blind Severely Disabled; bd dir, Opportunities Industrialization Ctr; pres, Wva Trial Lawyers Asn, secy, treas; Legal Aid Soc. **Honors/Awds:** Fairest Judge Award, Wva Trial Lawyers Asn, 1985-86. **Special Achievements:** First and only African-American student at Charleston High School; Second African-American to graduate from the WVU College of Law; First African-American to serve as Judge in Kanawha County; First African-American Lawyer to be employed in The Legal Aid Society. **Home Addr:** 212 Oakwood Rd, Charleston, WV 25314, **Home Phone:** (304)346-1207.

## CANADY-LASTER, RENA DELORIS
Executive. **Personal:** Born Jul 29, 1953, Effingham County, GA; daughter of Johnnie B (deceased) and Rena Elizabeth (deceased); married Willie L; children: Hawa Shahlette, Sherri Latrice Wiley, Elizabeth Renae & Omega Lynn Wiley. **Educ:** Ga Southwestern State Univ, BS, psychol, 1975; Augusta State Univ, MS, clin psychol, 1977. **Career:** Sumter Cty Taylor Cty Ment Retard Ctr, behav spec, 1977-78; Taylor Cty Ment Retard Ctr, actg dir, 1978; Mid Flint Behav

Healthcare, equal employ oppty rep, dir, child adolescent outpatient servs, 1978-, part time employ area PhD Psychol; Child & Adolescent Prog, dir, 1978-97; Child & Adolescent Intake worker, counr, supvr, 1997-2002; Canady Memorial Life Builders, ordained minister, 1997-; Cent Ga Life Builders, life chg & bus coach, 2003-; New Hope Int, minister, 2006-11; US Fed Govt, fed grant reviewer, 2007; Ga Mil Col, adj prof, 2009-; Cent Ga Tech Col, instr, 2012-; JBRE Kids, publ & auth, 2013-; Westgate Travel Partner, assoc, 2014-. **Orgs:** Life mem, Delta Sigma Theta, 1973-; sch bd mem, Am City Bd Ed, 1980-93; vice chmn, Americus City Bd Ed, 1980-93; secy, Early Bird Civitan Club, 1983-84; jr hs group facilitator, Taylor Cty Pregnancy Prev Prog, 1984-; pres, Sumter Cty Ment Health Asn, 1984-85; bd dir, GA Ment Health Asn, 1984-85; bd mem, Visions Sumter, 1984-, pres, 1995-96; group facilitator, Arrive Alive GA, 1985; pres, elect Early Bird Civitan Club, 1985, pres, 1986-; Dist 8 Infant Mortality Task Force, 1986-; Consult area agencies sch; City Zoning Appeals Bd, 1996-; pres, Visions Sumter, 2002; bd mem, Am Red Cross, 2014; Sumter 2000 Comt; family selection comt, Habitat Humanity; provider area workshops, Child Sexual Abuse Child Abuse, other c's issues; Cent Ga Red Cross Chap. **Honors/Awds:** Blue Key Nat Honor Frat GA Southwestern Col, 1981; Outstanding Service Award, Sumter County Mental Health Assoc, 1982; Employee of the Year, C A Program, 1997; Outstanding Service, AFA Drum Majors, Americus Sumter Cty, 1997; Outstanding COT Service, 1998. **Special Achievements:** First Female on Americus City Board of Education 1980-1992. Author children's coloring books & stories. **Home Addr:** 300 Northfield Dr, Warner Robins, GA 31093-1649, **Home Phone:** (478)929-4658. **Business Addr:** Instructor, Central Georgia Technical College, 3300 Macon Tech Dr, Macon, GA 31206, **Business Phone:** (478)757-3400.

### CANE, KATHRYN T. SINGLETON

Educator, executive. **Personal:** Born May 15, 1951, Orange, TX; daughter of Gertie M and Lester B Sr (deceased); married Lonnie M. **Educ:** Univ Incarnate Word, BS, health info mgt, 1973; State Univ NY, MS, health sci eval & educ, 1978. **Career:** Highsmith Rainey Memorial Hosp, dir, Med Rec Dept, 1973-76; Henry Ford Hosp, asst dir, Med Rec Dept, 1978-79; Univ Wis, asst prof, 1978-80; Holy Cross Hosp, adr, Med Rec Dept, 1980-82; Tascon Inc, pres, chief exec officer, 1986-2008; Health RSI, 2008-13; DeVry Univ, prof, 2013-. **Orgs:** Am Med Rec Asn; exec bd mem, DIS Med Rec Asn; chmn, Hosp Coun Med Rec DRR's Div, NAT Capitol Area; MAR DRR's Div; fac senate mem, Univ Wis; Alpha Kappa Alpha Sorority; chmn, Metrop Baptist Church, New Mem Orientation Prog. **Honors/Awds:** Young Comunity Leadership Award, 1989-91. **Special Achievements:** New Technologies Affecting Medical Records, J Am Med Rec Asn, 1987; Portable Information Technology, J Am Med Rec Asn, 1987. **Business Addr:** Professor, DeVry University, 3005 Highland Pkwy, Downers Grove, IL 60515, **Business Phone:** (630)515-3000.

### CANE, RUDOLPH C.

Engineer, government official, executive. **Personal:** Born May 23, 1934, Somerset County, MD; married Louella Fitchett; children: Rudolph Jr & Renee Cane McCoy; children: 2. **Educ:** Md State Col, attended 1957; Coppin State Col, attended 1968. **Career:** Canes Rentals, vpres, 1955-; State Hwy Admin, Bur Mat & Res, eval engr, 1957-68; Eval Engr, Bur Mat & Res, 1957-68; Eastern Regional Lab, dir admin, 1968-84; Shore Up Inc, bd dirs, 1978-83, adminr community & housing develop, 1984-; Housing & Community Develop, adminr; Md House Delegates, Dist 37A, deleg, 1999-. **Orgs:** Md Asn Engrs, 1963-84; coordr, Spec Proj, 1968; vpres, Nat Asn Advan Colored People, 1969, Md State Conf Br, co-ordr spec proj, 1968; U.S. Comn Civil Rights, 1970-02; vpres, Westside Schs, 1970-71; Coop Area Manpower Planning Syst, 1975-77; Citizen's Adv Bd Holly Ctr, 1976-98; chair, New Directions Polit & Social Chg, 1977; pres, Mardela Mid & High Schs, 1977-78; Univ Md Eastern Shore, 1977-80; Delmarva Adv Coun, 1980-98; Wicomico County Zoning Bd Appeals, 1980-90; Md Rural Develop Corp, 1987-98; Wicomico County, Dist 1, 1990-94; House Delegates, 1999-2015; Lower Eastern Camp Comt; deleg, Dem Party Nat Conv, 2000; Queen City Lodge 1051, Elks; Lamech Lodge 30; Prince Hall Affiliated Free & Ancient Masons; Am Legion Post 145; Veterans Foreign Wars Post 10159; Ebenezer United Methodist Church; chairperson, Md legis Black Caucus, 2005-06; chmn, Legis Black Caucus Md. **Home Addr:** 27249 Ocean Gateway, Hebron, MD 21830, **Home Phone:** (410)376-0444. **Business Addr:** Delegate District 37A, Maryland House of Delegates, House Off Bldg Rm 364, Annapolis, MD 21401, **Business Phone:** (410)841-3427.

### CANEDY, DANA

Writer, journalist. **Personal:** children: Jordon. **Educ:** Univ Ky, BS, jour. **Career:** Times, reporter; New York Times, reporter & sr ed, 1996-. Book: A Journal for Jordan. **Honors/Awds:** Pulitzer Prize, 2001. **Business Addr:** Senior Editor, New York Times, 229 W 43rd St, New York, NY 10036, **Business Phone:** (212)556-1234.

### CANNIDA, JAMES THOMAS, II

Football coach, football player. **Personal:** Born Jan 3, 1975, Savannah, GA; married Ieesha; children: Jameson. **Educ:** Univ Nev, Reno, BA, broadcast jour. **Career:** Football player (retired); Tampa Bay Buccaneers, defensive tackle & nose tackle, 1998-2001; Indianapolis Colts, right defensive tackle, 2002; Wash Redskins, 2003; Dallas Desperado, 2005-07; Scoggins Mid Sch, head football coach. **Business Addr:** 7070 Stacy Rd, McKinney, TX 75070, **Business Phone:** (469)633-5150.

### CANNON, CALVIN CURTIS

Executive, manager. **Personal:** Born Mar 2, 1952, Lenoir, NC; married Anna Laura Copney; children: Calvin IV. **Educ:** Univ Mich Grad Sch Bus, BBA, 1974; Wayne State Univ Sch Engineering; Howard Univ Sch Divinity. **Career:** Proctor & Gamble Co, client rep, 1974-76; Vitro Labs, sect leader, 1977-79; Planning Res Corp, unit mgr, 1979-81; Gen Elec Info Serv Co, proj coordr, 1981-83; Comp-U-Staff, staff mgr, 1983-84; Exec Off Pres, Wash, DC, mgr OMB info serv, 1984-87; Automated Info Mgt Inc, Lanham, MD, dir ADP, 1987-89; Roy F Weston Inc, prin mgr, 1989-94; M-Cubed Info Systs Inc, prog mgr, 1995-96; DC Govt, Wash, DC, actg dir, 1997-98; Ultra Technologies Inc, prog mgr, 1998-2000, bus develop mgr, 2002-03; Gen Serv Admin/FEDSIM, proj mgr, 2000-02; Montgomery County Pub Schs, substitute teacher, 2004-05; New Light Technologies, prog mgr, 2005-08, consult, 2006-08; Tower Technologies Inc, consult, 2005-06; Ofori & Assocs, consult, 2008-09; DC Pub Schs, instrnl aide, 2009-. **Orgs:** African Methodist Episcopal Zion Church. **Home Addr:** 8709 Shryrock Mill Rd, Thurmont, MD 21788-2632, **Home Phone:** (301)898-8250. **Business Addr:** Manager OMB Information Systems, Executive Office Of The President, 726 Jackson Pl NW, Washington, DC 20503.

### CANNON, DR. CHARLES EARL

Educator, chemist. **Personal:** Born Jan 30, 1946, Sylacauga, AL; son of Eugene and Carrie. **Educ:** Ala A&M Univ, BS, chem, 1968; Univ Wis-Milwaukee, PhD, phys org chem, 1974. **Career:** Amoco Res Ctr, res chemist, 1974-85; Elmhurst Col, adj fac, 1984-87; W Aurora Sch Dist, educr 1985-86; Ill Math & Sci Acad, pioneer fac, 1986-92; Columbia Col, Sci & Math Dept, chmn, prof distinction chem, 1992-. **Orgs:** Am Chem Soc Chicago, 1974-; fel Am Inst Chemists, 1979-92; Exec Interested Polit, 1982-88; Nat Alumni Asn Ala A & M Univ, pres, 1982-84, 2000-04; bd dir, regional vpres, Nat Asn Negro Musicians, 1984-2011; Apostolic Church God, Chicago; Great Lakes Regional ACS Meeting Planning Comm, 1986-87, at-large, 1987-88; Nat Asn Advan Black Chemists & Chem Eng; Ill Asn Chem Teachers, pres, 1998-99; Am Asn Univ Professors; Nat Orgn Advan Black Chemists & Chem Engrs; Nat Sci Teachers Asn; life mem, Nat Asn Advan Colored People; secy, Col Chicago Coun; chair, Budget & Priorities; Gen Educ Adv Committe; chair, Sabbatical & Fac Develop Awards Comt; Retirement Plan Admin Comt; chair, Fac Develop Comt; fel Am Chem Soc, 2013; Chatham Pk Pl Homeowners Asn. **Home Addr:** 8120 S Prairie Pk Pl, Chicago, IL 60619-4800, **Home Phone:** (773)651-4588. **Business Addr:** Professor of Distinction in Chemistry, Columbia College, 623 S Wabash Rm 500, Chicago, IL 60605-1996, **Business Phone:** (312)369-7396.

### CANNON, DAVITA LOUISE BURGESS

Editor. **Personal:** Born Mar 17, 1949, Jersey City, NJ; daughter of James (deceased) and Bernice. **Educ:** St Peters Col, BS, mkt mgt, 1973; New York Univ Grad Sch Bus, advan mgt prog, 1983; Am Computa, 1988. **Career:** JM Fields, dicta sec, 1978-79; Off Force Inc, exec secy & admin asst, 1979-83; NJ Afro Am, columnist, 1980; Cannon Clues, publ, chmn, 1981-, owner, 1988-. **Orgs:** Bd dir, Bayonne Youth Ctr, 1974-92; pres chair, New York Metro Area Chap Am Asn Blacks Energy, 1983-84; chmn, US Rep Parren J Mitchell Brain Trust, 1984; Nat Bd Adv, Am Biol Inst, 1985; prin officer, NJ Coalition 100 Black Women, 1986-91; pres chair, Concerned Comn Women JC Inc, 1986-92; Gov's Planning Comn, 1986-87; comnr, NJ Develop Authority Small Minority & Women's Bus, 1987-92; reappointed coun mem, Gov Adv Coun Minority Bus Develop, 1987-92; chair, charter mem, Republican Presidential Task Force, 1989-; Chandeliers Un, 1992-; comnr, Presidential Comn Am Agenda; 100 African Peoples Nation, 1998; chair bd, Ford Found, 2000-; vice chmn, Coun HOS. **Honors/Awds:** Distinguished Service Award, Pavonia Girl Scout Coun, 1981; Mary McLeod Bethune Award, Com-Bin-Nations, Jersey City, 1984; VIP Award, Concerned Comn Women Jersey City Inc, 1984; Small Business Award, Roselle Br Nat Asn Advan Colored People, 1984; Woman of Achievement, 1986; Black Leadership Reception 100 Black Men NJ, 1988; Outstanding Am Award, Outstanding Young Am. **Home Addr:** 528 Ave A-5, Bayonne, NJ 07002. **Business Addr:** Principal Owner, Cannon Clues, 528 Ave A5, Bayonne, NJ 07002-1627.

### CANNON, DR. DONNIE E.

Business owner. **Personal:** Born Magnolia, AR; married Chapman R Jr; children: Donald Chatman. **Educ:** MME C J Walker Beauty Col, Grad; Eugene Hair styling Acad, Paris, France; Myriam Carriages Inst De Beaute, Paris, France; Ophelia De Voores Modeling & Charm Sch, Grad; Bethune-Cookman Col, PhD. **Career:** Am Beauty Prod Co Inc, co-owner & treas, 1966-; Johnson Prods, natl rep; LaRoberts & Gray's Beauty Sch, NY. **Orgs:** Alpha-Chi Pi Omega organized First chap, Hempstead; Tulsa Urban League Guild; Greenwood C C; Tulsa Community Develop Ctr; Okla Beauty Culturist League; Tulsa Urban League Inc; hon mem, YWCA; Nat Beauty Culturist League; bd trustee, Bethune-Cookman Col; Tulsa C C; Nat Asn Advan Colored People. **Honors/Awds:** Bus & Indust Award, 1973; Service Awd, Greenwood C C, 1974; Basilleus Tulsa Chap Alpha Chi Pi Omega; Top 100 Black Bus & Professional Women in America, 1985; Hon Deg Dr Law, 1984; Outstanding Women Indust, YWCA, 1977; Outstanding Achievement Award, Nat Beauty Culturists League, 1982; Outstanding Achievement Award, Black Hair Olympics, 1982; Mfr of the Year Award, Black Hair Olympics, 1983; Hon Alumnus Award, Langston Univ. **Special Achievements:** Co-author, autobiography, How We Made Millions and Never Left the Ghetto, 1983; Co-publisher, Beauty Classic Magazine, 1984-87; Co-founder New York Beauty Classic Rolls Royce Competition. **Home Addr:** 3605 N Louisville, Tulsa, OK 74115. **Business Addr:** Co-Owner, American Beauty Manufacturing Inc, 1623 E Apache St, Tulsa, OK 74106, **Business Phone:** (918)425-4241.

### CANNON, EDITH H.

Educator, association executive, administrator. **Personal:** Born Aug 8, 1940, Tougaloo, MS; married Dan Jr; children: Audra Charmaine & Portia Camille. **Educ:** Tougaloo Col, BS, 1961; Boston State Col, grad studies, 1976; Bridge water State Col, grad studies, 1983; Eastern nazarene Col, MEd, 1984. **Career:** Greenville MS Pub Schs, elem teacher, 1961-65; Boston Head Start, educ dir, 1969-73; Randolph Pub Schs, elem teacher, 1973-81; N Jr High Sch, diag prescriptive teacher reading, 1981-, prin, currently. **Orgs:** Randolph Fair Practices, 1973-, past vice chmn, 1980-81; conf presenter, Mass Teachers Asn, 1982-84; chair, minority affairs comt, Mass Teachers Asn, 1982-; Gov's Task Force Educ Reform, 1983-84; black caucus secy, NEA; bd mem, S Shore Coun C, 1983-85; bd dir, Norfolk County Teachers Asn, 1983-; commun, Mass Teachers Asn, 1984-. **Honors/Awds:** Outstanding Service, Randolph Teachers Asn, 1980-82; Citation for Service, Gov Michael Dukakis, 1983; Delta Kappa Gamma Soc, Int Honor Soc Women Educrs, 1985. **Home Addr:** 38 Sunset Dr, Randolph, MA 02368, **Home Phone:** (781)986-4160. **Business Addr:** Principal, North Jr High School, 225 High St, Randolph, MA 02368, **Business Phone:** (781)961-6243.

### CANNON, DR. JOSEPH NEVEL

Chemical engineer, educator. **Personal:** Born May 2, 1942, Weldon, AR; son of Joseph Henry and Elmer Lewis; married Carmen Bianchi; children: Devi, Arville, Bianca, Changa & Erin. **Educ:** Univ Wis, Madison, Wis, BS, chem engineering, 1964; Univ Colo, Boulder, Colo, MS, chem engineering, 1966, PhD, chem engineering, 1971. **Career:** Dow Chem Co, Midland, Mich, process engr, 1964; Procter & Gamble, Cincinnati, OH, res chem engr, 1965-68, Miami Valley Labs, research staff; Howard Univ, Wash, DC, Sch Engineering & Comput Sci, Dept Chem Engineering, faculty, asst prof, assoc prof, 1971-79, chair, 1974-94, interim asst dean, 1998, prof, 1979-; acad consult, HUSEM prog, currently; Nat Insts Health, Bethesda, Md, Biomed Engineering & Instrumentation Br, res chem engr, 1972-78; DC, regist prof engr. **Orgs:** Am Inst Chem Engrs, 1970-; Sigma Xi Sci Res Soc, 1980-; Am Asn Advan Sci, 1978-; Tau Beta Pi Nat Hon Soc, 1980-; Nat Org Black Chemists & Chem Engrs; Kappa Alpha Psi. **Honors/Awds:** Outstanding Faculty, Chem Engr Stud Soc, 1977, 1979, 1981, 1986; Outstanding Professor Award, Nat Org Black Chemists & Chem Engrs, 1983; Distinguished Engineering Alumnus, Univ Colo, Sch Engineering, 1989; Centennial Medal, Univ Colo, Col Engineering & Appl Sci, 1994; Lifetime Achievement Award, Howard Univ; Percy Julian Medal, Nat Org Black Chemists & Chem Engrs. **Home Addr:** 415 Ridgepoint Pl, Gaithersburg, MD 20878, **Home Phone:** (301)721-9534. **Business Addr:** Professor, Academic Consultant, HUSEM Program, Howard University, Rm 1016 2300 6th St NW, Washington, DC 20059, **Business Phone:** (202)806-6669.

### CANNON, REV. DR. KATIE GENEVA

Theologian, educator. **Personal:** Born Jan 3, 1950, Concord, NC; daughter of Esau Lytle and Corine Lytle. **Educ:** Barber-Scotia Col, BS, 1971; Johnson C Smith Sem, Atlanta, MDiv, 1974; Union Theol Sem, New York, MPhil, 1983, PhD, Christian ethics, 1983. **Career:** Rockfeller Prostestant Fel Fund Theol Educ, 1972-76; Episcopal Divinity Sch, asst prof; New York Theol Sem, admin fac, 1977-80; Ascension Presby Church, pastor, 1975-77; Roothbert fel, 1981-83; Yale Divinity Sch, vis lectr, 1987; Harvard Divinity Sch, vis scholar & woman res assoc, 1983-84; Wellesley Col, vis prof, 1991; Temple Univ, Dept Relig, from assoc prof ethics to prof ethics & theol, 1993-2001; Union Theol Sem & Presby Sch Christian Educ, Annie Scales Rogers prof christian ethics, 2001-. **Orgs:** Ecumenical dialogue, Third World theologians, 1976-80; Mid E Travel Guide, NY Theol Sem, 1978-80; Am Acad Relig, 1983-; Asn Black Women Higher Educ, 1984-; bd dir, Women's Theol Ctr, 1984-; mem bd dir, Soc Christian Ethics, 1986-90; pres, Soc Study Black Relig, 1986-; World Alliance Reformed Churches Presby & Congregational, 1986-91. **Honors/Awds:** Isaac R Clark Preaching Award, Interdenominal Nat Theol Ctr, 1973; woman res assoc-Ethics, Harvard Divinity Sch, 1983-84; Episcopal Church's Conant Grant, 1987-88; Association of Theology School Young Scholar Award, 1987-88; Radcliffe Col Bunting Inst, 1987-88; Excellence in Teaching Award, Am Acad Relig, 2011; Distinguished Professor Award, Spelman Col. **Special Achievements:** The first African-American woman ordained in the United Presbyterian Church USA; First African American Woman to Earn Phd Degree From Union Theological Seminary In NYC; co-ed, God's Fierce Whimsy, 1985; Inheriting Our Mothers' Garden, Westminster Press, 1988; Author, Black Womanist Ethics, Scholars Press, 1988; Interpretation for Liberation, 1989; Katie's Canon: Womanism & the Soul of the Black Community, 1995. **Home Addr:** 3901 Conshohoken Ave Suite 3304, Philadelphia, PA 19131. **Business Addr:** Annie Scales Rogers Professor of Christian Ethics, Union Theological Seminary & Presbyterian School of Christian Education, 3401 Brook Rd, Richmond, VA 23227, **Business Phone:** (804)278-4331.

### CANNON, NICK (NICHOLAS SCOTT CANNON)

Actor, writer, rap musician. **Personal:** Born Oct 8, 1980, San Diego, CA; son of James and Beth Gardner; married Mariah Carey; children: Monroe & Moroccan. **Career:** TV series: "Kenan & Kel", 1996; "Cousin Skeeter", 1998; "All That", 1998-2000; "The Parkers", 2000; "Taina", 2001; "The Nick Cannon Show", producer, 2002; "Nick Cannon Presents: Wild 'N Out", sketch dir, 2005, composer & exec producer, 2005-07; "Nick Cannon Presents: Short Circuitz", dir, exec producer, 2007; "TeenNick Halo Awards", exec producer, 2009, 2011; "A Very School Gyrls Holla-Day", dir, 2010; "Hatin' on '09", producer, 2010; "Top 100 Number Ones", 2011; "Up All Night", 2011; "Nick Cannon: Mr. Show Biz", exec producer, 2011; "Rags", exec producer, 2012; "30 Rock", 2012; "Incredible Crew", exec producer, composer, 2012-13; "Nick Cannon's Big Surprise", exec producer, 2013; "Wild 'n Out: Wildest Moments", exec producer, 2013; "F#Ck Nick Cannon", exec producer, 2013; "Real Husbands of Hollywood", 2014; "Drumline: A New Beat", producer, 2014. Films: Whatever It Takes, 2000; Men In Black II, 2002; Drumline, 2002; Love Don't Cost a Thing, 2003; Garfield, 2004; Shall We Dance, 2004; Underclassman, exec producer, 2005; Roll Bounce, 2005; The Beltway, exec producer, 2005; Even Money, 2006; The Adventures of Brer Rabbit, 2006; Weapons, 2006; Monster House, 2006; Bobby, 2006; Goal II: Living the Dream, 2007; American Son, 2008; Day of the Dead, 2008; Ball Don't Lie, 2008; The Killing Room, 2009; School Gyrls, dir, exec producer, 2009; School Dance, dir, 2014. Mr. Renaissance, owner, currently. **Honors/Awds:** Blimp Award, 2002; Hollywood Film Award, Hollywood Film Festival, 2006; Chopard Trophy, Cannes Film Festival, 2007; Image Award, Nat Asn Advan Colored People, 2012. **Business Addr:** Actor, c/o Nickelodeon, 231 W Olive St, Burbank, CA 91502.

### CANNON, PAUL L., JR.

Chemist. **Personal:** Born Nov 21, 1934, Harrisburg, PA; son of Paul L and Mildred A Mercer. **Educ:** Lincoln Univ, BA, 1956. **Career:** Harrisburg Hosp, clin chem, 1956-58; PA Dept Highways, chemist, 1958; Dept Army, res chem, 1958, AUS Edgewood Res Dev Eng Command, res chemist. **Orgs:** Omega Psi Phi Frat; Sigma Xi. **Honors/Awds:** Electrochemistry Patents US. **Special Achievements:** Published articles on electrochemistry and analytical chemistry. **Home Addr:** 21 N 15th St, Harrisburg, PA 17103, **Home Phone:** (717)238-7639. **Business Addr:** Research Chemist, US Army, AMSRD-EBC-RT-AE, Aberdeen Proving Ground, MD 21010-5424, **Business Phone:** (410)436-7639.

### CANNON, REUBEN

Executive, television producer. **Personal:** Born Feb 11, 1946, Chicago, IL; married Linda Elsenhout; children: Tonya, Reuben Jr, Christopher & Sydney. **Educ:** Southeast City Col. **Career:** Univ Studios, mail room clerk, 1970-72, sec casting dept, 1972-74, casting dir, 1974-78; Warner Bros, head TV casting, 1977-78; Reuben Cannon & Assoc, Los Angeles, CA, pres, 1979-; Cast: The Rockford Files; Roots II; The Next Generation; A Soldiers Story; The Color Purple; The A Team; Hunter; Riptide; Moonlighting; Amen; Amerika; Ironside; Under One Roof, Touched By An Angel; Eddie Whats Love Got to Do With It; American Heart; Who Framed Roger Rabbitt; The Women of Brewster Place; TV series: "Hunter: The Princess & the Marine", 2001; "My Wife & Kids", 2001-03; "Hunter: Return to Justice", 2002; "Johnson Family Vacation", 2004; "30 Days Until Im Famous", 2004; "Night of Terror", 2005; "Bernie Mac Show", 2005-06; "Fumes of Detente", 2006; "Bernies Angels", 2006; "Tom Sarah & Usher", 2007; "Thank You for Not Snitching", 2007; "Stinkmeaner Strikes Back", 2007; "The Story of Thugnificent", 2007; "Attack of the Killer Kung Fu Wolf Bitch", 2007; "The Boondocks", 2007; "Conditional Love", 2008; Producer: Down on the Delta, Get on the Bus, Dancing; Diary of a Mad Black Woman, 2005; Madea's Family Reunion, 2006; Daddy's Little Girls, 2007; House of Payne, 2007; Why Did I Get Married?, 2007; Meet the Browns, 2008. **Orgs:** Bd dir, Los Angeles Urban League; Casting Socs Am; Motion Picture Acad Am. **Home Addr:** 849 S Keniston, Los Angeles, CA 90005. **Business Addr:** President, Reuben Cannon & Associates, 5225 Wilshire Blvd Suite 526, Los Angeles, CA 90036, **Business Phone:** (323)939-3190.

### CANNON, TYRONE HEATH

Dean (education), library administrator. **Personal:** Born Jan 16, 1949, Hartford, CT; son of Laura R Cohens and Jesse Heath. **Educ:** Univ Conn, BS, 1973, MSW, 1975; Univ Pittsburgh, MLS, 1981. **Career:** Hartford Pub Schs, sch soc worker, 1975-77; Child & Family Serv Inc, clin soc worker, 1977-80; Univ Tex, Arlington, soc sci librn, 1981-83; Columbia Univ, soc work librn, 1984-88; Okla St Univ, Soc Sci Div, head, 1988-89; Boston Col, head res, 1989-91, sr assoc univ librn, 1991-95; Univ San Francisco, dean univ libr, 1995-. **Orgs:** Title IIB Fel Univ Pittsburgh, 1980; counr, ACRL Div, Am Libr Asn; Asn Col & Res Libr; Black Caucus Am Libr Asn; Am Asn Higher Educ. **Business Addr:** Dean, University San Francisco, 2130 Fulton St Gleeson 307, San Francisco, CA 94117, **Business Phone:** (415)422-6167.

### CANSON, FANNIE JOANNA

Educator, administrator. **Personal:** Born Apr 26, 1926, Bainbridge, GA; married Robert L. **Educ:** Spelman Col Tuskegee Inst, BS, 1945; Univ Ore, MS, 1967, PhD, 1967. **Career:** Calif St Univ, Sacramento, assoc prof; high sch teacher; Corrections Proj, teacher corps, univ admin dir; Nat Coun Chap, teacher; lic marriage & family counr. **Special Achievements:** First African American school teacher for the City Schools. **Home Addr:** 2178 Morley Way, Sacramento, CA 95864, **Home Phone:** (916)489-2469. **Business Addr:** Educator, California State University, 6000 J St, Sacramento, CA 95819, **Business Phone:** (916)278-6011.

### CANTARELLA, DR. MARCIA ELAINE YOUNG

Educator, association executive. **Personal:** Born Oct 31, 1946, Minneapolis, MN; daughter of Whitney M Young Jr and Margaret Buckner Young; married Francesco; children: Mark Boles, Michele & Maratea. **Educ:** Bryn Mawr Col, Pa, BA, polit sci, 1968; Univ Iowa Law Sch, attended 1968; Simmons Col, Boston, Mass, MA, mid mgt prog, 1979; NY Univ, Mass, MA, Am studies, 1992, PhD, Am studies, 1996. **Career:** Medicare Health Care Qual Improv, dir; Sen Robert F Kennedy's Wash Off, summer intern, 1967; Rabat Am Sch, Rabat Morocco, social studies teacher grades 6-8, 1970-71; Zebra Assoc, NY, advert, 1971-72; Avon Prod Inc, NY, mgr, 1972-76, dir pub affairs, 1976-80, dir spec markets, 1980-82, dir proj commun, 1982-85; Mom's Amazing, NY, pres, 1985-88; Nat Coalition Women's Enterprise, NY, exec dir; New York Univ Stern Sch Bus, mgt consult, 1988-89, Col Arts & Sci, Acad Enhancement, dir, 1992-99, Off Dean Col Arts & Sci, dir, 1995-99, Gallatin Sch Individualized Study, fac, 1995-2000; Princeton Univ, asst dean & lectr, 1999-2002; Metrop Col New York, vpres stud affairs, 2002-05; Hunter Col, Sch Arts & Sci, actg assoc dean, assoc dean stud opportunities, 2005-08; Hunter Col BMI, consult, 2008-; Cantarella Consult, owner, consult, 2008-; Col Countdown, 2012-; Chg Create Transform, subj matter expert, 2015-. **Orgs:** Bd dir, Fedn Protestant Welfare Agencies, 1973-80; Women & Founds Group, 1974-80; Asn Black Found Execs, 1974-80; bd dir, Blue Cross & Blue Shield Greater New York, 1974-80; founding bd mem, New York Regional Asn Grant Makers, 1975-80; dir, C's Mus Manhattan, 1986-91; Vaseline Baby Care Coun, 1987-88; bd dir, New York Police Found, 1988-91; bd dir, Equity Inst, 1990-93; planning comt, Support Ctr NY, 1992-; trustee, Trickle-Up Prog; bd mem, Women's Leadership Exchange Cong Ital Am Orgn; Mellon Found Task Force Mentoring; chair, bd adv, Eagle Acad Found, 2001-. **Honors/Awds:** Woman of the Year, Nat Coun Negro Women, 1976; Listed in Who's Who. **Special Achievements:** Published articles in Working Mother, McCalls, Essence, Working Parent, Boardroom Reports, Lears. **Home Addr:** 144 W 86th St, New York, NY 10024-4028, **Home Phone:** (212)580-1495. **Business Addr:** Consultant, Hunter College, Rm 803 E 695 Pk Ave, New York, NY 10021, **Business Phone:** (212)772-4000.

### CANTRELL, BLU (TIFFANY COBB)

Singer. **Personal:** Born Oct 1, 1976, Providence, RI; daughter of Susi Franco. **Career:** Albums: So Blu, 2001; Bittersweet, 2003; TBA, 2014. Songs: "Hit 'em Up Style (Oops!)", 2001; "Round Up", 2002; "Breathe", 2003; "Make Me Wanna Scream", 2004; Film: Drumline, 2002; TV series: "Soul Food", 2001; "Soul Train", 2002-03; "Celebrity Circus", 2008. **Special Achievements:** Included in top ten of Billboard 200 and Billboard Top R&B/Hip-Hop Albums Charts for So Blu, 2001; "Hit 'Em Up Style (Oops!)" #1 song on Billboard's Top 40 Mainstream and Top 40 Tracks Charts, 2001. **Business Addr:** Recording Artist, c/o Arista Records, 6 W 57th St, New York, NY 10019, **Business Phone:** (212)489-7400.

### CANTRELL, FORREST DANIEL

Executive. **Personal:** Born Dec 30, 1938, Atlanta, GA; married Cheryl Francis; children: John. **Educ:** San Francisco State Univ, BA, 1968; Univ CA, MBA, 1970; Harvard Bus Sch, AMP, 1977. **Career:** Mile Sq Health Ctr Inc, pres, proj dir, adminr; San Francisco Police Dept, police, officer; Vallejo Police Dept, patrolman; Dept Corrections, corr officer. **Orgs:** Pres, Nat Asn Neighborhood Health Ctr Inc; pres bd dir, Miles Sq Serv Corp; commr, Chicago Health Planning & Resources Develop Comn; bd dir, Chica United Black Appeal Fund.

### CANTY, CHRIS (CHRISTOPHER SHAWN PATRICK CANTY)

Football player. **Personal:** Born Mar 30, 1976, Long Beach, CA. **Educ:** Kans State Univ. **Career:** Football player (retired); New Eng Patriots, defensive back, 1997-98; Seattle Seahawks, right cornerback, 1999-2000; New Orleans Saints, right cornerback, 2000; Las Vegas Gladiators, 2005; Rio Grande Valley Dorados, defensive back, 2006-08. **Honors/Awds:** Jack Tatum Award, 1996. **Special Achievements:** First round pick, No 29, NFL Draft, 1997.

### CANTY, GEORGE

Chemist, executive. **Personal:** Born Dec 7, 1931, Manning, SC; married Mabel Lucille Scott; children: Andria G & Alison D. **Educ:** Univ Pittsburgh, BS, chem, 1954; Am Univ, MS, physics & chem, 1966. **Career:** NIH Bethesda MD, chemist, 1958-63; Nat Bur Stand, Wash DC, chemist, 1961-63; Gillete & Res Inst, Wash DC, res & develp, 1965-67; Celanese Res Co, Summit, NJ, sr res chemist, 1967-73; 3m Ctr, St Paul, MN, supr prod devel, 1973. **Orgs:** Mem & basileus, NJ Chap Omega Psi Phi Fraterity, 1953-; Am Chem Soc, 1960-; Minn Chem Soc, 1973-; guest lectr, Black Exec Exchange Prog, Nat Urban League, 1974. **Honors/Awds:** Catalyst Club Award, 3m Co Film & Allied Prod Div, 1977; patented Photosensitive Composite Sheet Material, 1979; Publisher of articles and books. **Home Addr:** 2117 Cameron Dr, St. Paul, MN 55125, **Home Phone:** (651)731-2990.

### CANTY, DR. RALPH WALDO, SR.

Clergy, executive. **Personal:** Born Oct 9, 1945, Sumter, SC; son of Benjamin F Sr (deceased) and Rena Smith (deceased); married Jacqueline Wright; children: Bryant, Ralph Jr & Serena; married Toye Jane Richburg; children: Christina Jackson & Richburg Williston. **Educ:** Morris Col, BA, 1967, BD, 1970, DD, 1981; Benedict Col, LLD. **Career:** Savannah Grove Baptist Church, pastor, funeral dir, 1969-; Morris Col, pub rel dir, 1970-75; BF Goodrich, asst personnel dir, 1975-78; Progressive Nat Baptist Conv, pres. **Orgs:** Pres, chmn, Bd Job's Mortuary, 1970-; pres, Brenca, 1976-; pres, S C Baptist Cong Christian Educ, 1978-82; bd mem, Nat Coun Churches, 1980-84; bd mem, Baptist World Alliance, 1980; pres, Progressive Nat Baptist Conv, USA, 1981-82; Baptist World Alliance, 1981-83; bd mem, Morris Col, 1982; pres, Black Concerned Clergy Asn; trustee, Morris Col, 1984-93; moderator, Pee Dee Baptist Asn; moderator, Black Concerned Clergy Asn, 1988-91; pres, S C Morticians Asn, 1991-94; Omega Psi Phi Frat Inc; pres, bd dir, Cong Nat Black Churches, 1999-; life mem, Nat Asn Advan Colored People; local adv bd, Salvation Army; Goodfellows Social Club; Omega Psi Phi Fraternity Inc; pres, Sc Morticians Asn; legislator, Legis Black Caucus; Joint Judicial Screening Comn; Gen Coun World; Nat Coun Churches Christ; Baptist World Alliance; Community Immediate Care Facil. **Special Achievements:** Listed l00 Most Influential African Americans, Ebony Magazine, 1981-82. **Home Addr:** 104 S Salem Ave, Sumter, SC 29150-5606, **Home Phone:** (803)775-2263. **Business Addr:** Pastor/ Funeral Director, Savannah Grove Baptist Church, 2620 Alligator Rd, Effingham, SC 29541-4313, **Business Phone:** (843)662-7851.

### CAPEL, FELTON JEFF, II (JEFF CAPEL, II)

Basketball coach. **Personal:** Born Jan 6, 1953, NC; son of Felton Jeffrey and Jean; married Jerry; children: Jeff III & Jason. **Educ:** Univ Hampton Inst; Fayetteville State Univ, 1971, 1977. **Career:** Pinecrest High Sch, coach, 1980-86; Wake Forest Univ, asst coach, 1986-89; Fayetteville State Univ, head coach, 1989-93; NC A&T State Univ, head coach, 1993-94; Old Dom, head coach, 1994-2001; Fayetteville Patriots, head coach, 2001-04; Charlotte Bobcats, asst coach, 2004-11; Philadelphia 76ers, asst coach, 2011-13. **Home Addr:** , Charlotte, NC.

### CAPEL, FELTON JEFFREY, SR.

Executive. **Personal:** Born Feb 26, 1927, Richmond County, NC; son of Acie and Elnora Leak; married Jean Walden; children: Felton Jeffrey Jr, Mitchell Gregory & Kenneth Oriel. **Educ:** Hampton Univ, BS, 1951. **Career:** Century Metal Craft Corp, salesman, 1958-61, sales mgr, 1958-61, reg sales mgr, 1965-77; southeastern area sales dir; Presto Pride Cookware, dir sales, dist mgr & area sales dir; Century Asn NC, pres, chief exec officer, 1977-; First Savings Bank, Moore County, dir, 1990-98; First Bank, Troy NC, dir, 1999-; Century Metalcraft Corp, sales rep firms cookware; Century Asn NC, pres & chmn, owner, currently. **Orgs:** City Counman, Southern Pines, 1959-68; dir, Carolina P & L Co, 1972-; bd dir, Southern Nat Bank, 1974-85, First Fed Savings & Loan, 1978-85, NC Asn Minority Bus; Durham Corp, 1988-; Durham Life Ins, 1988-; NC Citizens Bus & Ind, Raleigh, NC, 1988-; Wachovia Corp, Winston-Salem, NC, 1989; Wachovia Bank & Trust Co, NA Winston-Salem, NC, 1989; city treas & chmn, Moore County, Bd Elections, 1980-86; dist gov, Rotary Int; chmn, Moore Co United Way; chmn, Moore County Chap Am Red Cross; NC Comn Educ, 1989; chmn, bd trustee, Fayetteville State Univ, 1978-87; Dist 7690 Rotary Int, gov; bd dir, NC Found; bd dir, GTP; bd dir, Boys & Girls Club Sandhills; bd dir, First Tee Sandhills; vice chmn, Fayetteville State Univ Found; bd mem, dir, United Way NC; chmn, Moore County Am Red Cross; bd dir, Global Trans Pk Found; bd dir, First Bank; bd dir, NC Zool Soc; bd dir, Kate B Reynolds Health Care Found; bd dir, Kate B Reynolds Health Care Trust; charter bd mem, NC Outward Bound Sch; vice chmn, NC Asn Minority Bus; pres, club mem, cookware sales, Southern Pines Rotary Club; founder, Century Assocs Inc; NC Citizens Bus & Indust; bd dir, Carolina Power & Light Co; bd mem, First Savings Bancorp Inc; chmn, pres, Laymen's League Pee Dee Baptist Asn; chmn & pres, Harrington Chapel Men's Club, Sunday Sch Leader; life bd mem & chmn, Nat Asn Advan Colored People; chmn, Moore County Citizens Input Priorities Minorities; chmn, Stadium Comt Construct Pinecrest High Sch Stadium; chmn & pres, W Southern Pines Civic Club; chmn, Am Red Cross; bd dir, N Carolina Citizens Bus & Indust. **Honors/Awds:** Int Mgr Sales Award Century Metalcrft, 1962; Bd Mem of Year, NC Dept Conservation & Devel, 1971; chmn of the year, Sandhills Area Chamber Com, 1977; Delta Mu Delta Nat Hon Bus, FSU; Fayetteville State Univ, Basketball Arena Named Felton J Capel Arena; Rotary Int, Distinguished Service Award, 1981-82; Meritoriuos Service Award, 1984-87; Sandhills Kiwanis Club's Builders Cup, 1997; Inducted into the NC Bus Hall of Fame, 1998; University Award, Bd Govs, Univ NC, 2000; United Way of Moore County Cornerstone Award; Silver Spoon Award, Methodist Col, 2006. **Home Addr:** 1165 W Iowa Ave, Southern Pines, NC 28387-4415, **Home Phone:** (910)692-3784. **Business Addr:** Chairman & Chief Executive Officer, President, Century Associates of North Carolina, 1800 S Walnut St, Pinebluff, NC 28373-0037, **Business Phone:** (910)281-3194.

### CAPEL, JEFF, II. See CAPEL, FELTON JEFF, II.

### CAPEL, DR. WALLACE

Physician. **Personal:** Born Nov 12, 1915, Andalusia, AL; son of Henry and Callie; married Carrie Ford; children: Carolyn Harrison, Jacqueline D, Denise L & Wallace Jr. **Educ:** Howard Univ, BS, 1940, MD, 1944; Baylor Univ, MHA, 1970. **Career:** Physician (retired); Tuskgee Va Hosp, dir & chief med serv; Tuskegee Va Med Ctr, chief staff, 1993. **Orgs:** Am & Nat Med Asn, 1970; Macon County Med Soc, 1973; Am Red Cross; bd trustees, Wash Chapel AME Church; grand med registr, Masonic Temples. **Honors/Awds:** Executive of the Year, Prof Secretaries Int, 1979. **Home Addr:** Franklin Rd, PO Box 2608, Tuskegee, AL 36083, **Home Phone:** (334)727-5270. **Business Addr:** Physician, 525 Al Hwy 49, Tuskegee, AL 36083.

### CAPERS, JAMES, JR.

Basketball executive. **Personal:** Born Nov 8, 1961, Chicago, IL; son of James Sr. **Educ:** Northern Ill Univ, attended 1984. **Career:** James Capers Found, founder; James Capers Bk Scholar, founder; Goodcall Referee Sch, founder; corp sales, Xerox, Colgate-Palmolive & Bristol-Myers; Squibb Nat Basketball Asn, referee, currently. **Home Addr:** 454 E 105th St, New York, NY 10029, **Home Phone:** (212)369-9234. **Business Addr:** Referee, National Basketball Association, 645 5th Ave 10th Fl, New York, NY 10022-5986, **Business Phone:** (212)407-8000.

### CARADINE, TRACY

Executive. **Personal:** Born Jan 1, 1969?. **Career:** Jarvis Christian Col, dir libr serv, 2003. **Business Addr:** Director, Jarvis Christian College, 1470 Hwy 80, Hawkins, TX 75765, **Business Phone:** (903)769-5820.

### CARAWAY, YOLANDA H.

Public relations executive, manager. **Personal:** Born Sep 1, 1950, Rochester, NY; daughter of Earl and Cecile Carr; children: Theron Tucker Jr. **Career:** State Rep Wendell Phillips, admin asst, 1976-80; Congresswoman Barbara Mikulski, legis aide, 1980-81; Dem Nat Comn, dir educ & trng, 1981-85, spec asst chmn & staff dir, Fairness Comn, 1985, chmn Paul G Kirk, Jr, dep chmn, 1988-89; Mondale & Ferraro Gen Election Campaign, dep asst polit dir, 1984; Nat Rainbow Coalition, chief staff, 1985-86; Citizenship Educ Fund, exec dir, 1986-87; Caraway Grp Inc, pres & chief exec officer, 1987-; Jesse Jackson Pre, chief staff, 1987-88; Pres Inaugural Comn, off chmn, dir, 1992-93; Microsoft Corp; Mgm Mirage; Bristol Myers Squibb; MCI; Mitsubishi & Texaco; 2000 Site Adv Comt, vice chmn, 1998; Democracy Live 2000, exec producer, 2000. **Orgs:** Dep chair, chmn, at-large mem, Dem Nat Comt, 1988-2009; bd dir, Am Univ Campaign Mgt Inst; mem bd dir, Am Dem Action Educ Fund; Am Coun Young Polit Leaders; steering comt, Ronald H Brown Found; vice chmn, Dem Nat Conv, Site Adv Comn, 2000; bd dir, Ellington Fund; bd dir, Naval; Cong Black Caucus Found; Cong Hisp Caucus Inst; U.S. Dept. Com; Ctr Am Progress; NATO 50th Anniversary Summit; Martin Luther King Jr. Nat Memorial Found; nat coordr, First Mayor's Urban Summit, 1990; Coun Am Polit, 2009. **Home Addr:** 713 Fitzhugh Way, Alexandria, VA 22314. **Business Addr:** President, Chief Executive Officer, The Caraway Group Inc, 1010 Wis Ave NW Suite 550, Washington, DC 20007, **Business Phone:** (202)965-2810.

### CARBY, HAZEL V.

Educator. **Personal:** Born Jan 15, 1948, Oakhampton Devon; daughter of Carl Colin and Iris Muriel; married Michael Denning; children: Nicholas Denning. **Educ:** Portsmouth Polytech, BA, eng, 1970; London Univ, Inst Educ, PGCE, 1972; Birmingham Univ, Ctr Contemp Cult Studies, MA, eng, 1979, PhD, 1984. **Career:** London bor Newham, high sch teacher, 1972-79; Yale Univ, Eng Dept, lectr, 1981-82, Am & African Am studies, dir, 1989-90, prof eng, 1989-94, Am studies & African Am studies, prof, 1994-, African Am studies, chair, 1996-; Charles C & Dorothea S Dilley, prof african am studies, currently, dir initiative race gender & globalization, currently; Wesleyan Univ, Eng Dept, fac, instr, 1982-84, asst prof, 1985-88, assoc prof, 1988-89; Books: Cultures in Babylon: Black Britain and African America; Race Men; Reconstructing Womanhood: The Emergence of the Afro-American Woman Novelist; What is This Black in Irish Popular Culture?; The Magazine Novels of Pauline Hopkins, ed; The Empire Strikes Back: Race and Racism in Seventies Britain, co-ed. **Orgs:** Ed bd, Yale J Criticism; ed bd, Callaloo & Diaspora: A J Transnational Studies; chair, African Am Studies Prog, 2000. **Business Addr:** Charles C & Dorathea S Dilley Professor African American Studies, Chair, Yale University, 493 College 303, New Haven, CT 06511, **Business Phone:** (203)432-9059.

### CARD, LARRY D.

Judge. **Personal:** Born Oct 23, 1947, Liberal, KS; married Mini E; children: Larry II, Krista & Kenneth. **Educ:** Wichita State Univ, Wichita, KS, BA, polit sci, 1969; Kans Univ Law, Lawrence, KS, JD, 1976. **Career:** Judge (retired); pvt & pub law pract, 1976-93; asst US atty, 1989-91; State Alaska, Super Ct, Third Judicial Dist, judge, 1993-2005; Univ Alaska, adj prof. **Orgs:** Inns Ct; Am Bar Asn; Alaska Bar Asn; Anchorage Bar Asn; Am Trial Lawyers Asn; bd mem, Boys & Girls Club Alaska. **Home Addr:** 825 W 4th Ave Suite 638, Anchorage, AK 99501.

**CAREY, DR. ADDISON, JR.**
Educator, president (organization). **Personal:** Born Mar 10, 1933, Crescent City, FL; son of Addison Sr and Laura Dowdell; married Clara Lee Parker; children: Leon, Alphonso, Pamela, Katrenia, Addison III, Michael & Douglas. **Educ:** Fla A & M Univ, BS, 1958; Ohio State Univ, MA, 1960; Tulane Univ, PhD, 1971. **Career:** Southern Univ, New Orleans, prof polit sci, 1960; dir vis scholars lectseries, 1972-78; admin asst to chancellor, 1983-85. **Orgs:** Bd mem, YMCA, 1978-; pres, Retired Mil Asn New Orleans, 1980-89; pres, Econ Devel Unit, 1984-94; Civil Serv Comn, City New Orleans, LA, 1987-93; pres, LA Polit Sci Asn; Nat Conf Black Polit Scientists; Pi Sigma Alpha Hon Soc; African Am Heritage Asn. **Home Addr:** 4844 Mendez St, New Orleans, LA 70126-2331, **Home Phone:** (504)288-5400. **Business Addr:** New Orleans, LA 70126, **Business Phone:** (504)286-5368.

**CAREY, AUDREY L.**
Government official, nurse. **Personal:** Born Nov 28, 1937, Newburgh, NY; children: Davina Henry, Dana & David C Jr. **Educ:** St Luke's Hosp Sch Nursing, reg prof nurse, 1961; NY State Dept Educ, cert sch nurse teacher, 1971; NY Univ Grad Sch Educ, advan deg admin & super, 1976; State Univ NY, Up State Med Col, pediat nurse practr cert, 1980; State Univ Col, One Onta, BS, educ nursing. **Career:** St Luke's Hosp, asst head nurse, 1963-69; Head start & N Jr HS, sch nurse teacher, 1966-69; Newburgh Sch Dist, drug educ coord, 1969-74; Newburgh Free Acad, sch nurse teacher, 1975-80; Newburgh Free Acad HS, pediat nurse practr, 1980-; City Newburgh, Newburgh, councilwoman & mayor, 1991-96; Newburgh Enlarged City Sch Dist, health serv coordr, dir Nursing & Health, 2009. **Orgs:** Bd dir, Orange Co Dept Ment Health, 1971-73; Inst Black Studies Mt St Mary's Col, 1973-74; assoc coord, Non-Credit Progs St Mary's Col, 1973-74; panelist, NYS Bd Regents Conf, 1973-74; bd trustee, Orange Co Comn Col, 1973-82; bd dir, YWCA, 1975-76; Newburgh City Counwoman, 1977-; panelist, Robert Wood Johnson Found Sch Health Conf, 1980-81; chmn, Newburgh Comn Action Head Start Policy Adv Coun, 1983-84; bd dir, Newburgh Performing Arts Acad. **Honors/Awds:** Prof Achievement Award, Omega Psi Phi Frat Upsilon Tau Chap, 1961; Distinguished Service Award, Jaycees, 1973; Outstanding Community Service Award, Nimrod Lodge 82 AF & AM, 1977; Continuous Service Award, Black Commonwealth of Newburgh, 1979; Distinguished Service Award, NAACP, 1981; Outstanding Comn Serv HVOIC Mary C Christian Award, 1982; Achievement Award Newburgh Comn Action Head Start, 1984; Comn Achievement Award, Black History Month, 1985; Recognition Award, Newburgh Optimist Club, 1985. **Special Achievements:** First African-Am woman ever elected mayor in the State of NY; Publication "Adolescence, Feeling Good, Looking Fine, Acting Fit" Natl Sch Health Digest, 1981. **Home Addr:** 285 Powell Ave, Newburgh, NY 12550, **Home Phone:** (845)562-0632. **Business Addr:** Director, Newburgh Enlarged City School District, 124 Grand St, Newburgh, NY 12550, **Business Phone:** (845)563-3400.

**CAREY, CARNICE L.**
Executive director, government official. **Personal:** Born Dec 17, 1945, Chicago, IL; daughter of Joe Stephen and Ora Gardner Stephen; married Lloyd L; children: Patrice Carey-Houston & Leslie R. **Educ:** Loop Jr Col, Chicago, IL; Northeastern Ill Univ, Chicago, IL. **Career:** City Chicago, Ill, contract compliance coord, 1972-75; Regiona lTransportation Authority, Chicago, Ill, eeo officer, 1975-84; City Chicago, Ill, contract compliance coord, 1985-94, dir contact monitoring & compliance, 1994-2002, City Chicago, Dept Procurement Serv, dep procurement officer, 2002-; Cosmopolitan Chamber of Com, exec dir. **Orgs:** Admin bd, Redeemer Methodist Church, 1970; Wesley Methodist Church, 1980-; Seventh Ward Dem Org, 1988-; exec dir, Cosmopolitan Chamber Com; adv comt, Consumers Organized Reliable Elec. **Home Addr:** 9017 S Crandon Ave, Chicago, IL 60617-3808, **Home Phone:** (773)221-9743. **Business Addr:** Executive Director, Cosmopolitan Chamber Of Commerce, 1455 S Michigan Ave 240, Chicago, IL 60605, **Business Phone:** (312)499-0611.

**CAREY, CLAIRE LAMAR**
Executive, manager, association executive. **Personal:** Born Aug 11, 1943, Augusta, GA; daughter of Peter W and Serena James; married Harmon Roderick; children: Roderick Lamar. **Educ:** Fisk Univ, BS, chem, 1964; Ohio Univ, attended 1965; Univ Del, mgt cert, 1975. **Career:** Hercules Inc, personnel supvr, 1974-76, corp recruiter, 1976-79, training specialist, 1979-80, mgr educ & training, 1980-89, mgr prof develop, 1989-91, mgr col rels & staffing, 1991-93, dir workforce diversity, 1993-. **Orgs:** Pres, Alpha Kappa Alpha Sorority Zeta Omega, 1962-; Sigma Xi Sci Hon Soc, 1969-; Am Chem Soc Educ Comn, 1974-; adv bd, Del Tech Comn Col, 1974-76; secy, Govt Comn Magistrates Screening; vpres & bd dir, YWCA; bd dir, NCCJ; pres & bd dir, YWCA, 1987-89; bd dir, Boy Scouts Am; bd dir, Nat YWCA, 1990. **Honors/Awds:** Committee Service Award, United Way Del, 1975; Minority Achiever in Industry Award, Wilmington Br, YMCA, 1976; Leadership Award, Alpha Kappa Alpha, N Atlantic Region, 1979; Outstanding Achiever in Industry, Brandywine Prof Asn, 1985; inducted Del Womens Hall of Fame, 1992; NCCJ Award, 1996; Girls Inc Award, 1996. **Home Addr:** 2018 Silverside Rd, Wilmington, DE 19810-4350, **Home Phone:** (302)475-8928. **Business Addr:** Director Workforce Diversity, Hercules Inc, Hercules Plz 1313 N Market St, Wilmington, DE 19894-0001, **Business Phone:** (302)594-6030.

**CAREY, HARMON RODERICK**
Real estate executive, executive, businessperson. **Personal:** Born Jul 7, 1936, Wilmington, DE; married Claire D Lamar; children: Roderick. **Educ:** Cent State Univ, BA, 1957; Univ PA, MSW, 1962, post grad; Temple Univ Law Sch, 1965; Univ Del, MA, 1977; Univ Del, attended 1996. **Career:** Dept Pub Welfare Wilmington, caseworker, 1958-60; Family Ct, supr, 1960-65; Asn Greater Wilmington Neighborhood Ctrs, exec dir, 1970-74; Pine Beverage Inc, pres; Bar-B-Que Pit Windsor Mkt & Deli, owner & operator; Haral Realty, pres; Human Resources Consult, founder & pres. **Orgs:** Dir youth lounge, YMCA, 1959-64; prog dir exec dir, Peoples Settlement Asn, 1965-70; conf coord, Nat Fed Settlements, 1971; Nat Asn Soc Workers, Acad Cert Soc Workers; Nat Asn Advan Colored People; Black Alliance; Kappa Alpha Psi; Alpha Kappa Mu; Equity DE Monday Club; numerous publ; founder, Minority Bus Asn DE; pres, Carey Enterprises Unlimited; founder & pres, African-Am Heritage Coalition; founder, African-Am Family Reunion Festival; founder, African-Am Heritage Day DE; co-founder, Slave Ship Replica Proj; pres, African-Am Heritage Tours DE; exec asst, African-Am Heritage, Dep Hist & Cult Affairs, State DE; Bd dir, Equity Farm Trust; instr, Univ DE Exten Div; founder, King Collection; vpres, Commun graphics Inc; founder, Afro-Am Hist Soc DE, pres, exec asst, exec dir. **Special Achievements:** First African-American art gallery in Delaware. **Home Addr:** 2018 Silverside Rd, Wilmington, DE 19810, **Home Phone:** (302)478-5591. **Business Addr:** President, Executive Director, Afro-American Historical Society of Delaware, 512 East 4th St, Wilmington, DE 19801, **Business Phone:** (302)571-1699.

**CAREY, JENNIFER DAVIS**
Educator, secretary general. **Personal:** Born Oct 2, 1956, Brooklyn, NY; daughter of Phillippa Stoute and Reuben K; married Robert J Jr; children: Michael, Christopher & Helena. **Educ:** Harvard & Radcliffe Col, AB, psychol, 1978; Harvard Grad Sch Educ, EdM, psychol, 1979, PhD, admin & planning. **Career:** Ohio Univ, asst dean, asst dir stud prog, 1979-81; Harvard & Radcliffe Col, sr admissions & financial aid officer, dir minority recruitment prog, 1982-92; Vista Group, partner, 1986; Bancroft Sch, Worecester, dir colcouns, 1992-98; Off Gov, spec asst to gov, 1998-99; Mass Exec Off Elder Affairs, state aging disaster officer, dir consumer affairs, 1999-2003, secy elder affairs, 2003-07; Commonwealth Med, sr dir training & educ, 2007-09. **Orgs:** Bd dir, Albert Oliver Prog, 1983-; Asn Afro-Am Mus, 1986; Visions Found, 1986; Nat Asn Advan Colored People; exec dir, Worcester Educ Collab. **Home Addr:** 21 Circuit Ave E, Worcester, MA 01603, **Home Phone:** (508)752-7891.

**CAREY, MARIAH**
Singer, songwriter, actor. **Personal:** Born Mar 27, 1970, Huntington, NY; daughter of Alfred Roy and Patricia; married Tommy Mottola; married Nick Cannon; children: Moroccan & Monroe. **Career:** Vocalist, songwriter, rec producer, 1987-; albums incl: Mariah Carey, 1990; Emotions, 1991; Daydream, 1995; Butterfly, 1997; Rainbow, 1999; Glitter, 2001; Charm bracelet, 2002; Songs: "All I Want Christmas You", 2003; "I Know What You Want", 2004; "Fly Like a Bird", 2005; We Belong Together/Fly Like a Bird", 2006; actress, 1999-; films incl: Bachelor, 1999; Glitter, 2001; Wise girls, 2002; Death a Dynasty, 2003; State Property two, 2005; Sweet Sci, 2005, State Property 2, 2005; Tenn, 2008; Precious, 2009; producer: Lovers & Haters, 2007. **Business Addr:** Actress, Singer, Tommy Mottola, 550 Madison Ave 32nd Fl, New York, NY 10022, **Business Phone:** (212)833-8000.

**CAREY, PROF. PATRICIA M.**
School administrator. **Personal:** Born Chicago, IL; daughter of Ezekiel J Morris Jr and Mildred Fowler Morris; married Robert B; children: Meredith Brooke & Jason Morris. **Educ:** Mich State Univ, BA, psychol, 1962, MA, psychol, 1963; NY Univ, New York, NY, PhD, educ psychol, 1982. **Career:** Mkt Res, New York, NY, psychologist, 1968-69; New York Univ, New York, NY, counr, 1970-76, dir, coun servs, 1976-79, dean stud affairs, 1979, adj prof, asst provost, assoc vice provost, Diversity Progs & assoc dean stud servs & pub affairs, currently; Univ Buffalo, gen educ prog adminr, asst vice provost fac affairs. **Orgs:** NY City Comn Status Women, 1986-; Am Asn Univ Women, Am Psychol Asn, Asn Black Women Higher Educ Inc; trustee, Bennett Col, 1987-; Nat Asn Women Higher Educ; bd mem, Arts Connection, 1989-; Manhattan Country Sch Bd, 1991-; bd mem, Cathedral St John Divine; bd mem, vpres, United Neighborhood Houses. **Home Addr:** 120 E 101st St, New York, NY 10029-6106, **Home Phone:** (212)534-8834. **Business Addr:** Adjunct Professor & Associate Vice Provost, Associate Dean, New York University, Pless Hall 82 Wash Sq E 2nd Fl, New York, NY 10003-6680, **Business Phone:** (212)998-5065.

**CAREY, DR. PHILLIP**
Educator. **Personal:** Born Mar 3, 1942, Andros; son of Gerald and Edna Smith Lewis; married Jean Harvey; children: Phillipa, Phillip Jr & Peter. **Educ:** Okla State Univ, Stillwater, OK, BSc, gen psychol, 1969, MSc, social & indust psychol, 1970, PhD, sociol & higher educ admin, 1975. **Career:** Univ Md, Dept psychol, lect, 1975-76; Am Sociol Asn, Wash, DC, dir, fel prog, 1975-76; Ark State, Jonesboro, assoc prof, 1976-77, chair, 1976-79; Univ Minn, Minneapolis, MN, assoc prof, 1977-79; Morgan State Univ, Baltimore, MD, assoc prof, 1979-81; Oakland Col, vis prof, 1986-87; Austin Peay State, Clarksville, MD, asst to pres & assoc prof, 1989-90; Amway Corp, mkt consult & dir, 1981-88; Laser Int Freight Transp Co, mkt mgt consult, 1982-86; Langston Univ, Langston, Okla, dean & dir, 1990-91, assoc prof, 1990-94; Col Bahamas, Nassau, prof sociol, 1994-95; Col St Benedict/St Johns Univ, Nassau, Bahamas, prof sociol, 1994-95; Bahamas Commonwealth Col, pres & prof sociol & psychol, 1995-97; Southeastern Credit Bur/Pk Dansan Gastonia, NC, dir educ & training, 1997; NC Agri & Tech State Univ, Col Arts & Sci, dean, 2000-02, prof sociol, dir, undergrad social work prog, currently, coordr sociol, currently, dir, bachelors sociol prog & prof sociol, currently. **Orgs:** Coordr, Okla State Univ, 1970-71; dir, Illinova Corp, Leadership Inst; chmn, Am Health & Home-Care LLC; dir, Am Sociol Asn, Wash, DC, 1975-76; founder & dir, Univ Minn, 1977-79; founder & dir, Inst Urban Res, Morgan State Univ, 1979-81; chair, Acad Policies & Curric Comt, Langston Univ, 1990-; chair, Acad Retention Task Force Comt, Langston Univ, 1990; chair, Presidential Spec Comt, Langston Univ, 1990-; Okla Acad State Goals, State Okla, 1990-; Asn Higher Educ, 1990-; Atlantic Coun USA, 1991-94; Am Soc Training & Develop; Am Acad Polit & Social Sci; Am Sociol Asn; Southern Sociol Asn; Southwestern Sociol Asn; Psi Chi Hon Soc; AKD Hon Soc; Tri-City Christian Acad, 2007-. **Home Addr:** 3837 Falling Leaf Lane, Orlando, FL 32810-2269, **Home Phone:** (407)282-1608. **Business Addr:** Director, Professor, North Carolina Agri & Tech State University, Gibbs Hall Suite 206 Off G, Greensboro, NC 27411, **Business Phone:** (336)285-2295.

**CAREY, TANISHA MONET.** See MONET, JERZEE.

**CAREY, VINCE**
Broker. **Educ:** BS, physics; MS, elec engineering; MBA, currently. **Career:** IBM Corp, engr; Coldwell Banker Corp, broker assoc; Howard Perry & Walston, broker, currently. **Orgs:** Pres, Int Focus Inc; pres election, Raleigh Regional Asn Realtors; Cary & Garner Chambers Com. **Business Addr:** Broker, Howard Perry & Walston, 1130 Kildaire Farm Rd Suite 100, Cary, NC 27511, **Business Phone:** (919)380-8585.

**CAREY, WAYNE E.**
Executive. **Personal:** Born Feb 8, 1945, Norwalk, CT; son of Edward E and Etta J; married Olivia Thompson. **Educ:** Howard Univ, Col Lib Arts, BA, 1968, Sch Law, JD, 1971. **Career:** Bendix Corp, contracts mgr, prog develop mgr, Affirmative Action Affairs, creative dir, social responsibility; Mich Nat Corp, creative dir, staffing-staff rels; Abbott Labs, dir, corp staffing; Lee Hecht Harrison, sr vpres & hub pract leader, currently. **Orgs:** Soc Human Resources Mgt; Employ Mgt Asn; SPP Fraternity. **Home Addr:** 7351 E 6th Ave, Denver, CO 80230-7205, **Home Phone:** (303)364-2257. **Business Addr:** Senior Vice President, Hub Practice Leader, Lee Hecht Harrison, 50 Tice Blvd, Woodcliff Lake, NJ 07677-8429, **Business Phone:** (201)930-9333.

**CAREY, WILHEMINA COLE**
Consultant, business owner, government official. **Personal:** daughter of Estell Swinton Nesmithchildren: Gilbert Flemin Jr & Tyrone Sr. **Educ:** Univ Md, AA, BS, MBA, PhD; St Elizabeths Hosp, post grad course psychiat, 1960; exec housekeeper cert, 1967. **Career:** Exec housekeeper, 1951-58; St Elizabeths Hosp, lpn, supvr, 1960-65, from asst hosp housekeeping officer to hosp housekeeping officer, 1965-89; fed govt employee, 1960-87, city govt employee, 1987-91; Logistics Mgt Br, dep chief, 1984-91; Carey & Hester Inc, consult, pres, owner, 1992-; St Elizabeths hosp Mus, founder, cur mgr; Arlington Pub Sch, teacher, mkt, currently. **Orgs:** Coordr, Upper Rm Baptist Church, 1991; bd mem, Int Exec Housekeepers Asn; life mem, Veterans Foreign Wars. **Honors/Awds:** The Wilhemina C. Carey Retirement Resolution, named in honor for 30 years of Outstanding Public & Dedicated Service, St Elizabeths Hosp, DC Govt, 1992. **Special Achievements:** Author: The Housekeeping Manual, 1979; "Hospital Housekeeping Education and Training, A Case Study", 1971; Designed and established a library which is affiliated with the DC Library; developed and implemented a nine month Housekeeping Training Prog for two Liberian students under the auspices of the Agency for International Development, US Dept State; First woman to be Supreme Master of the National Ideal Benefit Society; Developed and implemented programs of lesser training for others under similar housekeeping programs for US Dept State. **Business Addr:** Consultant, Owner, Carey & Hester Inc, 33 54th St SE, Washington, DC 20019-6560, **Business Phone:** (202)584-7010.

**CARGILE, WILLIAM, III**
Founder (originator), president (organization). **Personal:** married Novella; children: Carol & William IV. **Career:** William Cargile Contractor Inc, Cincinnati, OH, founder, chief exec & pres; William Cargile Construct II Inc, pres, currently; AlCargile Construct Servs Ltd, managing dir, currently. **Orgs:** Pres, United Minority Contractors Asn; fel Union Baptist Church. **Honors/Awds:** Ohio Contractors Association award; Applause Magazine Imagemakers Award; Building America Award; YMCA Black Achievers Award, 1981; Cincinnati Chamber of Commerce Board of Trustees Award; Spirit of Construction Foundation Lifetime Achievement Award, 2006; CEG President Award, 2013. **Business Addr:** President, William Cargile Construction II Inc, 1418 Cent Pkwy Suite 205B, Cincinnati, OH 45202, **Business Phone:** (513)381-2442.

**CARGILL, SANDRA MORRIS**
Executive. **Personal:** Born May 8, 1953, Boston, MA; daughter of Richard B Morris and Ida R Morris; married Ronald Glanville. **Educ:** Univ bedlands, BS, bus admin, 1984. **Career:** Am Acquisitions Inc, admin asst, 1976-77; Mode O Day Co, asst buyer, secy, 1977-78; Loral Xerox Electro Optical Syst, sr contract admin, 1978-85; Calif Inst Tech Jet Propulsion Lab, contract specialist, 1985-91; Cargill Planning & Predevelopment Serv, pres, 1990-; Urbcap Ventures Inc. **Orgs:** Pres, Prin Developer Xerox Electro Optical Systs Tutorial Prog, 1980-83; Black Womens Forum, 1980-83; Youth Motivation Task Force, 1981-83; Loral EOS Mgt Club, 1983-85; gen mem, Jr Achievement Prog, 1983-85, bd dir logistics, 1986-87, exec adv, 1984-85; Nat Contract Mgt Asn, San Gabriel Valley, 1983-; Caltech Mgt Club, Calif Inst Tech, 1985-. **Honors/Awds:** Outstanding Achievement in Contract, Admin Xerox Electro Optical Systs, 1981; Group Achievement Award, NASA, 1989; Outstanding Achievement Award, General W Harmon, 1990; Outstanding Achievement Award, NCMA, 1990; Clinton's National Service Prog Award, Los Angeles Pilot, 1993. **Home Addr:** 7924 Woodman Ave Suite 75, Van Nuys, CA 91402, **Home Phone:** (818)780-9510. **Business Addr:** President, Cargill Planning & Predevelopment Services, 6442 Coldwater Canyon, Panorama City, CA 91606, **Business Phone:** (818)760-0289.

**CARLISLE, JAMES EDWARD, JR.**
Educator, lawyer. **Personal:** Born May 30, 1944, Acmar, AL; son of James E Sr and Juanita; married Deborah Ann Carter; children: Constance Isabelle & Phillip Joseph. **Educ:** Youngstown State Univ, BA, 1967; Bowling Green State Univ, MEd, 1978; Univ Toledo Col Law, JD, 1985. **Career:** Perkins Bd Educ, staff, 1967-69; Toledo Bd Educ, staff, 1969-; Waite High Sch, educr; atty, currently. **Orgs:** Pres, Youngstown Univ Chap, Nat Asn Advan Colored People, 1966-67; Am Fed Teachers, 1969-; Big Brothers Am, 1970-73; Homeless Awareness Proj, 1988-; Nat Bar Asn, Ren Daniels Pres, campaign organizer, 1992; reading coordr, Nubia; Toledo Alliance Black Educr; Toledo Bar Asn; Am Bar Asn; Ohio Bar Asn; Wood Co Bar Asn. **Home Addr:** 110 Harmony Lane, Toledo, OH 43615, **Home Phone:** (419)720-1717. **Business Addr:** Educator, Waite High School, 301 Morrison Dr, Toledo, OH 43605, **Business Phone:** (419)671-7000.

**CARLO, NELSON**
Executive, marketing executive. **Personal:** Born Jan 1, 1938, Boqueron, PR. **Educ:** Career Automotive Trade Sch, voc course, 1961; Amos Tuck Bus Sch, bus mgt, 1972. **Career:** Abbott Prod Inc, Chicago, Ill, pres & chief exec officer, 1970-92; Carlo Steel Corp, owner, pres & chief operating officer, 1989-2011; Amberleaf Cabinetry, sales

& mkt rep, 2011-; Altra Steel Co, mgt consult/sales rep, 2011-; Tri-zee Countertops, sales & mkt rep, 2012-; L-M Welding Co, Sales Rep & Bus Consult, 2014-. **Home Phone:** (773)777-0665. **Business Addr:** Management Consultant, Altra Steel Co, 650 Cent Ave, University Park, IL 60484, **Business Phone:** (708)534-2100.

## CARLOTTI, VALENTINO D.

Executive. **Educ:** Yale Univ, BA; Harvard Grad Sch Bus, MBA. **Career:** Goldman Sachs Brazil Bank, San Paolo, Brazil, pres, 2007-12; Goldman Sachs, head securities div instnl client group, sr partner, 2012-. **Orgs:** vpres, trustee, Boys Club New York; Exec Leadership Coun; adv coun, Albert G. Oliver Prog; Lincoln Ctr Corp Fund; bd mem, Am Ballet Theatre; Pa Acad Fine Arts; Guild Hall; Carter Burden Ctr Aging. **Special Achievements:** Top 100 Most Influential Blacks in Corporate America, Savoy, 2012. **Business Addr:** Senior Partner, Goldman Sachs & Co, 200 W St 29th Fl, New York, NY 10282, **Business Phone:** (212)902-0300.

## CARLTON, BARBARA

Librarian. **Career:** George Hall Elem Sch, librn, currently. **Business Addr:** Librarian, George Hall Elementary School, 1108 Autwerp St, Mobile, AL 36605, **Business Phone:** (251)476-3299.

## CARLTON, PAMELA GEAN

Banker. **Personal:** Born Oct 17, 1954, Cleveland, OH; daughter of Alphonso A and Mildred Myers; married Charles Jordan Hamilton Jr; children: Charles III & Samuel Aaron. **Educ:** Williams Col, BA, polit econ, 1976; Yale Sch Mgt, MPPM, bus, 1980; Yale Law Sch, JD, 1980. **Career:** Cleary Gottlieb Stein & Hamilton, assoc coun, 1980-82; Morgan Stanley Co Inc, assoc investment banking, 1982-85, vpres investment banking, 1985, prin finance dept; JP Morgan Chase, managing dir, 2003; Spelman Col, Ctr Leadership & Civic Engagement, co exec dir, 2003-; Springboard Partners, pres & founder, currently; Tri-Continental Corp, dir, 2008-. **Orgs:** NY State Bar; bd mem, Studio Mus, Harlem, 1982-87; Westchester Bd Planned Parenthood; Grad Sch City Univ NY; bd mem, World Resources Inst, 1991-94; JP Morgan Chase Corp Diversity Coun; adv bd, Yale Sch Mgt; trustee, Williams Col; adv bd, Yale Sch Mgt; Yale Law Sch Alumni Exec Comt; Grad Sch, City Univ, New York; bd, New York Presby Hosp; River-Source Mutual Funds; trustee, fund complex Columbia Funds, 2007-; independent dir, Columbia Frontier Fund Inc, 2007-. **Home Addr:** 11 Salem Dr, Scarsdale, NY 10583. **Business Addr:** President, Founder, Springboard - Partners in Cross Cultural Leadership, 817 Broadway 10th Fl, New York, NY 10003, **Business Phone:** (212)777-0406.

## CARLYLE, SHANNIA W.

Administrator. **Career:** Patent & Trademark Off, trademark atty. **Business Addr:** Trademark Attorney, Patent & Trademark Office, Rm 7D05 S Tower 2900 Crystal Dr, Arlington, VA 22202, **Business Phone:** (703)308-9110.

## CARMAN, EDWIN G.

Government official. **Personal:** Born Feb 13, 1951, New Brunswick, NJ; married Pamela M Vaughan. **Educ:** Rutgers Univ, BA, journalism & political sci, 1974. **Career:** Mid sex County Col Found, bd mem, 1980-; Middlesex County Econ Opportuniy Corp, bd mem, 1975-, chmn, 1981-84; City NB, councilman, 1975, coun pres, 1987; Dept Educ; Dept Transp; Motor Vehicle Comn; NJ Sch Bd Asn, Govt Rels Dept, sr lobbyist; Nj Dept Community Affairs chief staff, 2007-. **Orgs:** Am Coun Young Polit Leaders; bd mem, NJ Foster Grandparents, 1986 Transp Task Force, 2006. **Honors/Awds:** Political Action Award, New Brunswick Area, Nat Asn Advan Colored People, 1983. **Home Addr:** 137 Commercial Ave, New Brunswick, NJ 08901. **Business Addr:** Chief of Staff, New Jersey Department of Community Affairs, 101 S Broad St, Trenton, NJ 08625-0800, **Business Phone:** (609)292-6055.

## CARMICHAEL, BENJAMIN G.

Educator. **Personal:** Born Jul 7, 1938, Atlanta, GA; married Dorothy; children: Christopher & Jennifer. **Educ:** San Francisco St Col, BA, 1963; Univ Calif, MA, 1968, Dcrim, 1971. **Career:** US Comm Porno, prin invest; Transit Robby Study, Univ CA, asst proj dir, 1968-70; Univ San Francisco, lectr, 1968-69; Hunters Pt Comm Devel Proj, proj dir, 1966-68; CA State Univ, prof, 1969-2004, chmn, dept criminal justice admin, 2004, prof emer, 2004-. **Orgs:** Consult Law Enforce Asst Admin; adv bd mem, Admin Just Prog, Ohlone Jr Col, Alpha Phi Alpha; Nat Urban League; Hunters Pt Riot, Pol Frust, Issues in Crime, Vol 4 1969; Nat Coun Cr & Delinq Youth Cr Urban Comm, St Hustlers & Their Crimes, Crime & Delinq Vol 21, 1975. **Home Addr:** 6500 Pinehaven Rd, Oakland, CA 94611-1247. **Business Addr:** Chairman, Professor Emeritus, California State University, 25800 Carlos Bee Blvd E Bay, Hayward, CA 94542-3095, **Business Phone:** (510)885-3590.

## CARMICHAEL, CAROLE A.

Journalist, editor, teacher. **Personal:** Born Jul 9, 1950, Brooklyn, NY. **Educ:** NY Univ, BA, 1972; Roosevelt Univ, Chicago, MS, mgt & mkt; Columbia Univ, Grad Sch Jour, Nat Arts Jour Prog, 2003; Northwestern Univ Kellogg Sch Mgt, Media Exec Leadership Prog, 2008. **Career:** Stephen Decatur Jr High Sch, eng teacher 1972-73; Chicago Tribune, careers ed; UPI Omaha & NY, news reporter 1973-76; Fairchild Publ Inc, NY, news reporter 1976; Working Women Mag, contrib writer, 1977-; Clmb Col Chicago, instr journalism 1978-79; Essence Mag, contrib writer, 1979; Philadelphia Inquirer & Daily News, news reporter; Philadelphia Newspapers Inc, exec mgt asst to publ, 1988-91; Seattle Times, asst news managing ed, 1991-98, asst features managing ed, 1998-2011, asst managing ed community engagement, 2011-; Chicago Tribune, bus reporter, currently; Daily News, bus ed, exec asst, bus develop mgr, currently. **Orgs:** Advan study fel econs journalists, Brookings Inst, Wash, DC, 1978; pres, Chicago Asn Black Journalists, 1978-80; bd dir, YWCA Metro Chicago, 1978-79; bd dir, Assoc Press Managing Ed Asn; Freedom Forum fel, 1993; fel, Nat Arts Journalism Prog, Columbia Univ, New York, 2002-03. **Business Addr:** Assistant Managing Editor, Seattle Times, 1120 John St, Seattle, WA 98109, **Business Phone:** (206)464-3116.

## CARMICHAEL, RICHARD O.

Executive. **Career:** Summit Bank, Capital Markets Treas Serv Div, exec vpres & sr mng dir; FleetBoston Fin Corp, Global Serv Div, exec vpres & head cash mgt; Neil Cerbone Assocs, managing dir. **Business Addr:** Head Cash Management, FleetBoston Financial Corp, 100 Fed St, Boston, MA 02110, **Business Phone:** (617)434-2200.

## CARNELL, LOUGENIA LITTLEJOHN

Executive, manager. **Personal:** Born Mar 12, 1947, Memphis, TN; children: Gizele Montrece. **Educ:** Dept Agr Grad Sch; Cath Univ; Univ DC Chester. **Career:** MEECN Systs Eng Off Def Commun Agency, div sec steno, 1971-73; Staff Chaplain Mil Dist, Wash, admin sec steno, 1973-75; Inter agency Coun Minority Bus Enterprise Dept Com, personal asst exec dir, 1975-76. **Orgs:** Med asst, vol ARC Alexandria Chap, 1973-76; Fed Women's Prof; chmn, Dept Energy Task Force Concerns Minority Women, 1979-80; Nat Coun Career Women; nat mem, Smithsonian Assocs. **Honors/Awds:** Key to City, New Orleans, 1975; Recital WTOP-TV Wash DC, 1975; Cert pin ARC Alexandria Chap, 1976; People on the Move, Black Enterprise Mag, 1979; Women in Energy, Newsletter, 1979; Cert participation, Ill Off Minority Bus Enterprise Statewide Annual Conf, 1979; Observance black history month Prog Adv Dept Energy. **Special Achievements:** First female in 108 yrs to be mem of bd of trustees, Mt Olive Bapt Ch Arlington, 1977; First chmn, Dept Energy Task Force, Minority Women Wash DC, 1979. **Home Addr:** PO Box 4356, Arlington, VA 22204-0356.

## CARNEY, LLOYD A.

President (organization), chief executive officer. **Personal:** Born Feb 13, 1962, Kingston; children: 2. **Educ:** Wentworth Inst, BS, elec engineering technol; Lesley Univ, MS, appl bus mgt. **Career:** Wellfleet Commun, dir tech opers, 1990, vpres, 1993; Bay Networks; Nortel Networks, exec vpres; Juniper Networks, chief operating officer & exec vpres, 2002; Micromuse Inc, chmn & chief exec officer, 2003; Cypress Semiconductor Corp, dir, audit & compensation comts, 2005-; Int Bus Mach, Net Cool Div, genmgr, 2006; Big Band Networks, bd dir; Xsigo Systems, chief exec officer, 2008; Carney Global Ventures LLC, chmn & chief exec officer; Wentworth Inst Technol, speaker, 2013; Brocade Communications Systems, chief exec officer, 2013. **Orgs:** Pres, adv coun; dir, Boys & Girls Club Peninsula; bd dir, Xsigo Systems, 2008; bd dir, Brocade Communications Systems, 2013; bd dir & chmn, technol comt, Technicolor; contributer, Silicon Valley Start-up Common. **Business Addr:** Chairman, Cypress Semiconductor Corp, 198 Champion Ct, San Jose, CA 95134, **Business Phone:** (408)943-2600.

## CARO, RALPH M.

Executive. **Personal:** Born Jun 8, 1948, Kansas City, MO; son of Ralph and Lena; married Carolyn W Cameron. **Educ:** Univ Kans, BA, zool, 1969; Univ Miss, Kans City, MBA, 1998. **Career:** Xerox Corp, high vol mkt exec, 1978-97; Swope Pkwy Health Ctr, adminr & chief exec officer, pres, 1997-2004; Lincoln Univ, bd curators, vpres; Samuel U Rodgers Health Ctr, chief operating officer, 2008-; Univ of Mo-Kans, adj prof. **Orgs:** Pres, Spoilers Golf Club, 1994-; chapt pres, Alpha Phi Alphi Fraternity, 1994-97; Nat job fair chmn, Alpha Phi Alpha Fraternity, 1996-99; bd mem, Full Employ Coun, 1998-; alumni bd, Univ Miss, Kans City, 1998; pres, Beta Lambda Educ Inst, 1998-; adv bd, Capper Found, 1999-; bd adv, Kans Univ Mini-Med Sch, 1999-2000; Prime Health Found Nat Asn Advan Colored People; Theta Boule; Sigma Pi Phi Fraternity; United Inner Cities Serv. **Home Addr:** 16950 Max Ct, Belton, MO 64012, **Home Phone:** (816)318-4053. **Business Addr:** Chief Operating Officer, Samuel U Rodgers Health Center, 825 Euclid Ave, Kansas City, MO 64124, **Business Phone:** (816)474-4920.

## CAROLINE, JAMES C.

Football coach, football player, educator. **Personal:** Born Jan 17, 1933, Warrenton, GA; married Laverne Dillon; children: Jayna & Jolynn. **Educ:** Fla A&M Univ, BS, phys educ, 1956; Ill Univ, BS, 1967. **Career:** Football player, football coach (retired), teacher; Montreal Allouetts, 1955-56; Chicago Bears, defensive back, 1956-65; Univ Ill Athletics Asn, Fighting Illini, asst football coach, 1967-76; Urbana High Sch, head football coach, teacher phys educ, currently. **Orgs:** Bd dir, Don Moyers Boys Club. **Honors/Awds:** All-Am Football, 1953; All Prof, 1956; College Football Hall of Fame, 1980. **Home Addr:** 2501 Stanford Dr, Champaign, IL 61820. **Business Addr:** Physical Education Teacher, Urbana High School, 1002 S Race St, Urbana, IL 61801, **Business Phone:** (217)384-3505.

## CARPENTER, DR. BARBARA WEST

Association executive, educator. **Personal:** Born Baton Rouge, LA; daughter of Patrick and Erin; married Dana. **Educ:** Southern Univ, Baton Rouge, LA, BS, voc educ & sec sci, MEd, sec educ; Kans State Univ, PhD, adult & occup educ. **Career:** Ohio Univ, Colo Col, post-doctoral fel; Southern Univ, prof, admin, 1980, Div Distance Educ, dir, Div Continuing Educ & Ctr Serv Learning, dir, currently, dean int educ, currently, Univ Agency Int Develop, proj dir. **Orgs:** Pres, Zeta Phi Beta Sorority Inc, Baton Rouge, 1996-2002; March Dimes; Phi Delta Kappa Educ Fraternity; Rotary Int Baton Rouge; Phi Upsilon Omicron Hon Soc; bd comnr, Baton Rouge Housing Authority. **Home Addr:** 1734 New Hampshire Ave NW, Washington, DC 20009. **Business Addr:** Dean of International Education, Director of Continuing Education & Center for Service Learning, Southern University, 1100 Harris Hall, Baton Rouge, LA 70813, **Business Phone:** (225)771-2613.

## CARPENTER, DR. CARL ANTHONY

School administrator, dean (education), vice president (organization). **Personal:** Born Feb 29, 1944, Gaffney, SC; son of John H and Teacora; married Parthelia Davis; children: Carla P Adams & Carl A II. **Educ:** SC State Univ, BS, 1966, MEd, 1970; Univ SC, PhD, 1973. **Career:** Educator(retired), consult; Sumter, SC Sch Dist 17, teacher, 1966-70; Sc State Dept Educ, 1972; SC State Univ, from asst prof to assoc prof, 1972-75, asst vpres acad affairs, 1975-80, vpres acad affairs, 1980-86, prof, 1986-92, interim pres, 1992-93, prof educ, 1993-94, Div Acad Affairs, interim vpres, 2007-; Consol Consultative Serv, pres, 1994-96; Voorhees Col, exec vpres & acad dean, 1996; Claflin Univ, prof. **Orgs:** NAFEO; MEAC Coun Pres; Nat Asn Advan Colored People; Omega Psi Phi Fraternity Inc; Phi Delta Kappa Educ Fraternity; Alpha Kappa Mu; bd trustee, Presby Col & Rabun Gap Nacoochee Sch; bd dir, Presby Church Found; bd dir, Heritage Corridor Partnership. **Home Addr:** 150 Kinard St, Orangeburg, SC 29117, **Home Phone:** (803)536-1793. **Business Addr:** Interim Vice President, South Carolina State University, 300 Col St NE, Orangeburg, SC 29117, **Business Phone:** (803)536-7000.

## CARPENTER, CLARENCE ELMORE, JR.

Real estate agent, executive, manager. **Personal:** Born Feb 5, 1941, Nashville, TN; son of Clarence E Sr and Mary Carney; married Faye Powell; children: Brenda Thomas, Yvonne Campbell, Gail, Clarence E III, Tiffany & Bryanna. **Educ:** Southwestern Christian Col, Terrell, TX, AA, 1961; Northeastern Ill Univ, Chicago, IL, BA, 1988. **Career:** Mother of Savior Seminar, Blackwood, NJ, mgr, admin, 1962-65; Chem Co, Pavisboro, NJ, shipping mgr, 1965-68; Kraft, Philadelphia, PA, acct exec, 1968-71; Kraft, NY, Wash, DC, supvr, zone mgr, 1971-76; Kraft, Albany, NY, Rochester, NY, dist mgr, area mgr, 1976-82; Kraft, Chicago, Ill, region grocery mgr, region vpres, 1982-89; Kraft Gen Foods, Glenview, Ill, vpres retail opers, 1989, vpres E sales, region mgr, Charlotte, NC. **Orgs:** Vis prof, exec, Urban League, 1988-. **Home Addr:** 14107 Wilford Ct, Charlotte, NC 28277-2497, **Home Phone:** (704)341-2026. **Business Addr:** Region Manager, Kraft General Foods, 1338 A Hundred Oaks Dr, Charlotte, NC 28217, **Business Phone:** (704)565-5608.

## CARPENTER, LEWIS I.

Government official. **Personal:** Born Feb 1, 1928, Brantley, AL; son of H D and Bessie; married Myrtice Bryant. **Educ:** Covington Cty Training Sch, AA, 1956; LBW Jr Col, acct, 1982. **Career:** Government official (retired); Covington County Bank, custodian, 1959, banker; City Andalusia, councilman, 1984. **Orgs:** Masonic Rose Sharon Lodge, 1965-, Adv Comm LBW Jr Col, 1970-; Covington County Sheriff Res, 1970-; adv, Local Draft Bd, 1980-; adv, OCAP Comm, 1982-. **Honors/Awds:** First black City Councilman in Andalusia City Councilman, 1984. **Home Addr:** 210 Lowe Ave, Andalusia, AL 36420-5423, **Home Phone:** (334)222-5939.

## CARPENTER, RAYMOND PRINCE

Lawyer. **Personal:** Born Apr 2, 1944, Little Rock, AR; son of Reuben and Ellen; married Barbara Pearson; children: Raymond Prince Jr. **Educ:** Philander Smith Col, attended 1963; Univ Ark, BA, 1966; Emory Univ Sch Law, JD, 1975; Harvard Bus Sch, MBA. **Career:** Lockheed Ga Co, assoc atty, 1975-76; City Atlanta-Solicitor's Off, asst solicitor, 1976-78; Sears Roebuck & Co, sr atty, 1978-86; Price Waterhouse LLP, managing dir, 1986-92; Huey, Guilday & Tucker, managing partner, 1992-94; Holland & Knight, partner, 1994-, sr partner, dirs comn, firmwide diversity partner, 1999-2002. **Orgs:** Chair, taxation sect, State Bar Ga, 1995-97; secy-treas, chair, Atlanta Bar Asn, 1996-; bd mem, Nat Inst State Taxation, 1990-; state tax sect bd, Am Bar Asn, 1990-; bd pres, Child Welfare League Am Inc; Nat Asn State Bar Asn; bd mem, Families First; bd mem, Atlanta Legal Diversity Consortium Inc. **Honors/Awds:** Outstanding Public Achievement, Fulton County Ga, 1990; Georgia Super lawyers, Law & Politics magazine, 2004-09. **Special Achievements:** Tax Executive Institute, National Mtg, 1989; Journal of State Taxation, Florida Svc Taxes, 1986; Georgia Bar Journal, State Tax Issues, 1989. **Home Addr:** 8665 Sentinae Chase Dr, Roswell, GA 30076-4469, **Home Phone:** (770)992-5311. **Business Addr:** Attorney, Holland & Knight LLP, 1201 W Peachtree St NE Suite 2000, Atlanta, GA 30309, **Business Phone:** (404)817-8500.

## CARPENTER, RONALD, JR.

Football coach, football player. **Personal:** Born Jan 20, 1970, Cincinnati, OH; married Tamara; children: Kamron & Aidan. **Educ:** Miami Univ, Oxford, Ohio, BA, urban & regional planning, 1993. **Career:** Football player (retired), coach; Cincinnati Bengals, defensive back & free safety, 1993; Minn Vikings, safety, 1993; New York Jets, safety, 1995-96; Amsterdam Admirals, World League, 1995, 1997; St Louis Rams, 1998-99; New York Hawks, 1998; Las Vegas Outlaws, 2000; Nashville Kats, 2000-01; Los Angeles Xtreme, 2001; Ga Force, 2002; Detroit Fury, 2003-04; Las Vegas Outlaws, defensive back; Cent State Univ, defensive backs & spec teams coordr, 2009-11; Ind Univ, col football coach, 2011-12; Miami Univ, defensive backs coach, 2012-14; Univ Cent Ark, safeties coach, 2014-. **Home Addr:** , Cincinnati, OH. **Business Addr:** Safeties Coach, University of Central Arkansas, 201 Donaghey Ave, Conway, NV 72035, **Business Phone:** (501)450-5000.

## CARPENTER, DR. VIVIAN L. (VIVIAN CARPENTER STRATHER)

Educator. **Personal:** Born Nov 3, 1952, Detroit, MI; daughter of Doyal Wilson Thomas (deceased) and Jennie Pettway; married Aldan J; children: Andrea Nicole Strather & Carmen Lavern Strather; married Aldan J. **Educ:** Univ Mich, Ann Arbor, BSE, indust & opers res, 1973, MBA, 1975, PhD, bus admin, 1985. **Career:** Ford Motor Co, Dearborn, Mich, res engr, 1972-73; Arthur Andersen & Co, Detroit, Mich, sr consult, 1975-77; Mich Dept Treas, Lansing, dep state treas, 1979-81; Univ Mich, Ann Arbor, vis prof indust & opers res, 1990-91; Wayne State Univ, Detroit, Mich, asst prof act, 1984-92; Fla A&M Univ, assoc prof, dir acad progs, 1992-95, asst dean; Sch Bus & Indust, asst dean, 1995-2001; Atwater Entertainment Assocs LLC, pres & founder, 2002-05; Motor City Casino, chair mgt & audit, Detroit, Mich, currently. **Orgs:** Am Inst CPAs, 1979-; Mich Asn CPA's, 1979-; Govt Fin Officers Asn, 1978-84, 1990-93; Nat Asn Black Accts, 1979-90, 1994-; Am Acct Asn, 1984-; dir, Atwater Entertainment Assocs; dir, Detroit Com Bank; dir, Motor City Casino; dir, Atwater Found; dir, Detroit Inst Arts; chairperson bd, Detroit Black Chamber Com; bd mem, Mich Front Page newspaper; bd mem, Univ Mich Sch Bus Alumni Asn; Govt Acct Stand Bd; Ford Found; Nsf; Fulbright Int Bus Admin. **Home Addr:** 200 Riverfront Dr, Detroit, MI 48226, **Home Phone:** (313)259-0148. **Business Addr:** Chair, MotorCity Casino, 2901 Grand River Ave, Detroit, MI 48201, **Business Phone:** (313)237-7711.

**CARPENTER, WILLIAM ARTHUR**
Writer, editor. **Personal:** Born Fayetteville, NC; son of William A Sr and Via Maria Randall. **Educ:** Univ Dijon, France, cert, 1985; Am Univ, BA, 1991. **Career:** Smithsonian-Nat Mus Am Hist, exhib writer, 1987; Vietnam Veterans Am, Wash, DC, press asst, 1987; Gospel Highlights Newsletter, ed, 1987-89; Bush & Quayle Campaign, Wash, DC, campaign worker, 1988-89, 1992; J Gospel Music, Mitchellville, MD, ed, 1990-92; Wash New Observer, staff writer, 1990-93; Carp Shank Entertainment, sr publicist, 1992-95; All-Music Guide, Miller-Freeman, gospel ed, 1992; EMI Music, publicist, 1993-95; March Wash, 1993; Capital Entertainment, co-founder, sr publicist, 1996-; Music Jam, radio host, currently; Freelance articles: Am Gospel, Destiny, Goldmine, Living Blues, YSB, Players, People Mag, Rejoice, Wash Post; Time Life, consult, 2007-12. **Orgs:** Nat Asn Black Journalists; Gospel Music Prof Network. **Business Addr:** Co-Founder, Senior Publicist, Capital Entertainment, 217 Seaton Pl NE, Washington, DC 20002, **Business Phone:** (202)636-7028.

**CARPER, GLORIA G.**
Educator, social worker. **Personal:** Born Aug 10, 1930, Montclair, NJ; children: Gladyce & Terri. **Educ:** Morgan State Col, BS, 1950; WVa Univ, MA, 1971. **Career:** Educator, social worker (retired); WVa Dept Welfare, social worker, 1961-64; WVa Dept Ment Health, welfare supvr, 1964-67; WVa Dept Ment Health, admin asst med div, 1967-72; Day Care Ctr, Ment Retarded C, Dept Ment Health, dir, 1972-73; WVa State Col, acting dir guid & placement, foreign stud adv & counr devel serv, 1982-98. **Orgs:** Nat Asn Retarded C Inc; Kanawha Asn Retarded C Inc; pres, Charleston Inst; Delta Sigma Theta; bd mem, Charleston Oppty Indust Ctr Inc; organist, First Baptist Church.

**CARR, CHRIS DEAN**
Basketball coach, basketball player. **Personal:** Born Mar 12, 1974, Ironton, MO. **Educ:** Southern Ill Univ, attended 1995. **Career:** Basketball player (retired), basketball coach, executive; Phoenix Suns, guard, shooting guard, 1995-96; Minn Timberwolves, shooting guard, 1996-99; NJ Nets, shooting guard, 1998-99; Golden State Warriors, shooting guard, 1999-2000; Chicago Bulls, small forward, 1999-2000; Boston Celtics, shooting guard, 2000-01; AEK Athens, 2001-02; KK Lavovi 063, 2002-03; Cleveland Cavaliers; 43 Hoops Basketball Acad, founder, owner & coach, 2003-. **Honors/Awds:** Mo Valley Conf MVP; Mo Conf Tournament MVP; Missouri Valley Conference Player of the Year, 1995. **Business Addr:** Owner, Coach, 43 Hoops Basketball Academy, 1002 Second St NE, Hopkins, MN 55343, **Business Phone:** (952)294-4667.

**CARR, CORY JERMAINE**
Basketball player. **Personal:** Born Dec 5, 1975, Fordyce, AR. **Educ:** Tex Tech Univ, attended 1998. **Career:** Tex Tech Raiders, 1994-98; Atlanta Hawk, 1998; Chicago Bulls; 1998-99; Quad City Thunder, 1999; New Mex Slam Slam, 1999-2000; Pau-Orthez, France, 2000; Maccabi Raanana, Israel, 2000-02; SLUC Nancy, France, 2002; Hapoel Galil Elyon, Israel, 2003; Hapoel Haifa, Israel, 2003-04; Maccabi Giv'at Shmuel, Israel, 2004, 2008-09; Elitzur Ashkelon, Israel, 2004-05; Ironi Nahariya, 2005-06; RB Montecatini Terme, Italy, 2006-07; Ironi Ashkelon, Israel, 2007-08, 2009-10, 2011; Pizza Express Primetel Apollon, 2010-11; Hapoel Tel Aviv, Israel, 2011-12; Maccabi Haifa, Israel, 2012-13; Ironi Nes Ziona, Israel, 2013-. **Business Addr:** Player, Ironi Nes Ziona, Israel.

**CARR, GWENN L.**
Executive. **Educ:** Mich State Univ Col Law; Mich State Univ, BS, social sci. **Career:** Univ Del, mem Adv Bd Corp Governance Inst; IRRC Adv Bd, mem; Lawyers Alliance New York, dir; ITT Corp, sr coun, 1988, vpres, secy & assoc gen coun, 1990; MetLife Life & Annuity Co Conn, secy; MetLife Inc, secy, 1999-2009, exec vpres, chief staff, 2007, off chmn, 2009, vpres, currently; Am Natural, vpres & secy; Eastern Dist Mich, asst Us atty. **Orgs:** Chmn, MetLife Found; law depts AT&T; pres, Stockholder Rels Socs New York; chmn, Am Socs Corp Secretaries; dir, United Way New York; adv bd, IRRC; dir, YWCA City New York; chmn, Investor Responsibility Res Ctr; mem bd dir, Girl Scouts Coun Greater New York; adv bd, Univ Del, Corp Governance Inst. **Home Addr:** 150 E 69th St, New York, NY 10021-5704, **Home Phone:** (212)794-9779. **Business Addr:** Vice President, Chairman & Chief Executive Officer, METLIFE Inc, 200 Pk Ave, New York, NY 10166-0188, **Business Phone:** (212)578-2211.

**CARR, GWENN L.**
Vice president (organization). **Educ:** Mich State Univ, BS, social sci; Mich State Univ Col Law. **Career:** Eastern Dist Mich, asst US atty; Am Natural Resources, chief securities & exchange comn officer, vpres & Secy; ITT Corp, vpres, secy, assoc gen coun, 1990-99; MetLife Inc, corp secy, 1999-2009, chief staff, 2007-, exec vpres, off chmn, currently. **Orgs:** Dir, Lawyers Alliance New York; mem law depts, AT&T; Am Natural Resources; mem bd dir, Girl Scouts Coun Greater New York; mem bd dir, New Sch Pub Engagement; adv bd corp governance inst, Univ Del; chmn, Am Soc Corp Secretaries; chm, Investor Responsibility Res Ctr; pres, Stockholder Rels Soc NY; dir, YWCA City NY; dir, United Way NY. **Business Addr:** Executive Vice President, Office of the Chairman, MetLife Inc, 200 Pk Ave, New York, NY 10166, **Business Phone:** (212)578-6000.

**CARR, KENNETH ALAN**
Basketball player. **Personal:** Born Aug 15, 1955, Washington, DC; married Adrianna; children: Cameron, Devon & Alyx. **Educ:** NC State Univ, attended 1977. **Career:** Baskeball player (retired); Los Angeles Lakers, forward, 1977-79; Cleveland Cavaliers, forward, 1979-82; Detroit Pistons, forward, 1982; Portland Trail Blazers, forward, 1982-87. **Home Addr:** 1210 W Adams Blvd Apt 106, Los Angeles, CA 90007-7700.

**CARR, KURT**
Gospel singer, music director. **Personal:** Born Oct 12, 1964, Hartford, CT. **Educ:** Univ Conn, BA, fine arts. **Career:** James Cleveland, pianist & musical dir, 1980-91; Andrae Crouch, musical dir, 1991-94; Kurt Carr Singers, founder, 1991, rec artist, 1991-, producer, 2003-; W Angeles Church God In Christ, musical dir, minister music, 1990-2001, creative dir, currently; Albums: Together, Serious About it, 1994; No One Else, 1997; Awesome Wonder, 2000; One Church, 2004; Come Let us Worship, 2005; Just Beginning, 2008; Bless This House, 2012. **Orgs:** Phi Beta Sigma fraternity. **Honors/Awds:** Stellar Award Song of the Year, for "In The Sanctuary, " 2002; Stellar Award Song of the Year, for "The Presence of the Lord Is Here", 2005. **Business Addr:** Creative Director, West Angels Church God Christ, 3045 Crenshaw Blvd, Los Angeles, CA 90016, **Business Phone:** (323)733-8300.

**CARR, LENFORD**
Government official, business owner. **Personal:** Born Sep 21, 1938, Haywood County, TN; married Ella R Porter; children: Vincent Louis & Bridgett Genese. **Educ:** Knoxville Col, attended 1958. **Career:** Milan Arsenal; Humboldt City Pk Comn Bd, mem, 1977-85; Humbol dt City Sch Bd, mem & secy, 1979-88, bd mem, currently; Carr's Catering Serv, owner, currently; Humbol dt Dist 4, County Comnr, 2005-. **Orgs:** City Schs-Transp-Bldg & Calendar Comn; Morning Star Baptist Church; Nat Asn Advan Colored People Humboldt Chap; pres, Humbol dt Dem Concerned Citizens Club; Gibson County Dem Exec; comt mem, Stigall Ethnic Libr Hist Mus. **Honors/Awds:** Plant Manager Award, Martin Marietta Aluminum Sales, 1970; Culinary serv, Morning Star Baptist Church, 1977; Community serv, NAACP-, IBPOWELK, 1980-83; educ boardsmanship, Humbol dt City Schs Bd, 1983; Outstanding Citizen Polit Involvement AKA Sorority, 1983. **Home Addr:** 94 Maple St, Humboldt, TN 38343, **Home Phone:** (731)855-7613. **Business Addr:** Mayor, County Commissioner, Gibson County, 94 Maple St, Trenton, TN 38343.

**CARR, MICHAEL LEON**
President (organization), basketball player. **Personal:** Born Jan 9, 1951, Wallace, NC; married Sylvia. **Educ:** Guilford Col, BA, hist, 1973. **Career:** Basketball player (retired), pres; Israel Sabers, 1974-75; Spirits St. Louis, 1975-76; Detroit Pistons, 1976-79; Boston Celtics, forward, 1979-85, scout, 1985-91, dir community rels, 1991-94, sr exec vpres & dir basketball group, gen mgr, 1994-97, head coach, 1995-97; M L Carr Enterprises, pres; WARM2Kids Inc, pres & chief exec officer, currently; Charlotte Bobcats, minority owner, 2004; CodeOne Technologies Inc, pres, currently. **Orgs:** Founder, ML Carr Scholar Found, Guilford Col, 1987; founder, JohnHenry Carr Alzheimer & Aging Found. **Business Addr:** President, Chief Executive Officer, WARM2kids Inc, 61 N Beacon St, Allston, MA 02134, **Business Phone:** (617)254-9276.

**CARR, PERCY L.**
Basketball coach. **Personal:** Born Nov 19, 1941, Longview, TX; married Helen; children: Kacy. **Educ:** Calif State Univ, Fresno State, BS, phys educ, 1968, MA, phys educ, 1972. **Career:** Tulare Union High Sch, teacher & coach, 1968-70, Edison High Sch, teacher, asst vice prin & dean boys, coach, 1970-74; basketball camps & clins, 1971-74; Stanford Univ, asst basketball coach, 1974-75; San Jose City Col, Jaguars, head basketball coach, currently. **Orgs:** Masonic Lodge; Alpha Phi Alpha. **Honors/Awds:** All Metro Coach of the Year, 1971; Coach of the Year, Cent Calif Basketball Coaches Asn, 1974; All Metro Coach of the Year Fresno Bee, 1974; Coach of the Year, 1976; Outstanding Teacher-Coach Award, 1988; Santa Clara County Coach of the Year, 1989; Coach of the Year, Sacramento Kings Northern Calif, 1994; Coast Conference Coach of the Year, 1996-97; Basketball Hall of Fame, Calif Community Col, 1998; Educator of the Year, 100 Black Men of the Silicon Valley Orgn, 2000. **Special Achievements:** An academic program that involves all the student athletes Creative Athletic Retention Response (C.A.R.R); Ranked 6th JC coach in the USA, Basketball Times, August 1998. **Home Addr:** 4441 Albert St, Oakland, CA 94619-2720. **Business Addr:** Basketball Head Coach, San Jose City College, Rm 301 2100 Moorpark Ave, San Jose, CA 95128, **Business Phone:** (408)288-3739.

**CARR, RODERICH MARION (RICK CARR)**
Investment banker, executive. **Personal:** Born Nov 5, 1956, Birmingham, AL; son of Edgar A; married Charlotte Bland; children: Hamilton Taylor & Chesleigh Marie. **Educ:** Johns Hopkins Univ, BSEE, 1978; Univ Chicago, Grad Sch Bus, MBA, fin & mkt, 1980. **Career:** Citigroup, dir, 1980-2005; Wachovia Securities, managing dir & exec search consult, 2005-09; MKP Capital Mgt LLC, managing dir instnl mkt & managing dir client develop, 2009-10; BlueBay Asset Mgt, dir sales, 2010-13; Deutsche Bank, managing dir corp finance, 2013-14; CastleOak Securities LP, sr managing dir, co-head sales & trading, 2015-; Corp & Investment Bank, managing dir & exec search consult; Salomon Smith Barney, dir; Johns Hopkins Univ, Whiting Sch Engineering, adv mem & trustee; Salomon Bros Inc, vpres sales; Citigroup, Global Trans Serv, dir & sales mgr, prod mgr asset mgt, dir instnl client serv; Wells Fargo Corp, investment banking div. **Orgs:** Vpres, Nat Black MBA Asn, 1978-80; bd dir, Jobs Youth, 1986-; Socs Engineering Alumni Coun, 1994; Univ Alumni Coun, 2001; trustee, pres alumni coun, Johns Hopkins Univ, 2002-06, 2004-06; fel Nat Adv Coun; pres & vpres, Johns Hopkins Alumni Asn; fel Johns Hopkins Univ, bd trustee. **Honors/Awds:** Heritage Award. **Home Addr:** 2437 N Janssen Ave, Chicago, IL 60614, **Home Phone:** (312)404-1749. **Business Addr:** Senior Managing Director, Co-Head of Fixed Income Sales & Trading, CastleOak Securities LP, 110 E 59th St 2nd Fl, New York, NY 10022, **Business Phone:** (646)521-6700.

**CARR, WILLIAM**
Football coach, football player. **Personal:** Born Jan 13, 1975, Dallas, TX. **Educ:** Univ Mich, attended. **Career:** Football palyer (retired), coach; Carolina Panthers, defensive tackle, 1997; Orlando Predators, defensive back, 1999, 2005; Barcelona Dragons, 2000; Ga force, defensive back, 2003-04; Grand Rapids Rampage, 2005; Mich football camp, coach; Ariz Western Col, defensive line coach, 2012-13.

**CARR-WILLIAMS, GAIL. See WILLIAMS, GAIL.**

**CARREATHERS, DR. KEVIN R.**
Educator. **Personal:** Born Feb 26, 1957, Denison, TX; son of Raymond E and Ernestine T. **Educ:** Univ N Tex, BA, psychol, 1979; Prairie View Agr & Mech Univ, MEd, guid & coun, 1980. **Career:** Depauw Univ, asst dean students, 1980-82; E Tex State Univ, head resident advisor, 1982-83; Tex Agri & Mech Univ, stud develop specialist, 1983-88, multicultural servs coordr, 1988-, dept multicultural servs, dir, 1989-, asst pres, 1994; Univ Memphis, assoc dean students, 1998; Salisbury Univ, asst to vpres acad affairs, asst to provost & dir instnl diversity, currently; Carreathers Consult, consult, 2009-. **Orgs:** Life mem, Alpha Phi Alpha, 1976-; personnel admin, Tex Asn Univ & Col Stud, 1982-; Tex Asn Black Personnel Higher Educ, 1982-; coord bd, Minority recruitment & retention comn, Tex Col & Univ Syst, 1985-88; adv bd, TAMU Nat Youth Sports Prog; adv bd, Minority Leadership Develop; Statewide Retention Comm; founder, Multicultural Affairs Inst; co-founder, Diversity Educ Inst. **Home Addr:** 314 Mill Pond Lane Suite 620, Salisbury, MD 21804. **Business Addr:** Assistant to the Provost, Director of Institutional Diversity, Salisbury University, 159 Holloway Hall, Salisbury, MD 21801, **Business Phone:** (410)543-6426.

**CARREKER, WILLIAM, JR.**
Educator. **Personal:** Born Oct 17, 1936, Detroit, MI. **Educ:** City Col San Francisco, AA, 1964; Univ Calif, BA, 1966, MSW, 1968, MPH, 1971. **Career:** Columbia Univ Sch Social Work, asst dir admis, financial aid off; Alameda County Welfare Dept, child welfare worker, 1968-70; Tufts-Delta Health Ctr, intern, 1971; Univ Calif Med Ctr, staff assoc, 1971-72; Golden State Med Asn, proj dir, 1972-73. **Orgs:** Vol coun Jr Leadership Prog, 1968; Calif State Sch Deaf & Blind, 1971; Offenders Aid & Restoration, 1974-75; Nat Asn Black Soc Workers, 1974-77. **Home Addr:** 315 W 61st St Apt 11Q, New York, NY 10023-1107, **Home Phone:** (212)245-0787. **Business Addr:** 622 W 113th St, New York, NY 10025.

**CARRIER, CLARA L. DEGAY**
Educator, association executive, administrator. **Personal:** Born Jan 15, 1939, Weeks Island, LA; daughter of Georgianne Henry DeRoven and Clarence; children: Glenda, Melvin T, Marcus W, Robby Bethel, Clarence (deceased), Patrick R & Dawn Nicole. **Educ:** Dillard Univ, attended 1957; Southwestern Univ, attended 1980. **Career:** JHH Sch Stud Body, pres, 1955-56; JB Livingston Elem PTC, secy, 1961-67; Les Aimu Civic & Social Club, secy, 1974-; Iberia Parish Sch Bd, exec mem, 1979-82, vpres, 1985-, sch bd vice mem, pres; Smile, CAA, teacher; City New Iberia Parks & Recreations, supvr. **Orgs:** Nat Asn Advan Colored People, 1963-65; teacher's aide, Acadiana Nursery Head Start, 1965; teacher's aide, SMILE CAA Head Start, 1970-76; social worker, SMILE CAA, 1976-79; bd mem, La Caucus Black Sch, 1980-85; bd dir, Bayou Girls Scout Coun, 1983-84; Nat Sch Bd Asn; bd dir, La Sch Bd Asn, 1993; bd mem, Greater Iberia Chamber Com; bd mem, La Sch Bd Asn, Iberia Parish Sch Bd, 2010-. **Honors/Awds:** USL Honor Soc, Psi Beta Honr Soc, 1978; Service Youth Award, Park Elem, 1982-84; The President's Award, Park Elem, 1982-84; Certificate of Recognition Contribution, Comm Zeta Phi Beta Sor, 1983; Omega's Citizen of the Year, Omega Rho Omicron Chap, 1983; Martin Luther King Jr Award, 1995. **Special Achievements:** First African American woman to be elected president in the Iberia Parish School System, 1992. **Home Addr:** 717 Elizabeth St, New Iberia, LA 70560-5211, **Home Phone:** (337)364-2049. **Business Addr:** Board Member, Iberia Parish School Board, 1500 Jane St, New Iberia, LA 70560, **Business Phone:** (337)365-2341.

**CARRIER, MARK ANTHONY, III**
Football player, football coach, television broadcaster. **Personal:** Born Apr 28, 1968, Lake Charles, LA; married Andrea; children: Mark Anthony & Lexi. **Educ:** Univ Southern Calif, BA, commun, 1989. **Career:** Football player (retired), football coach, host; Chicago Bears, free safety, 1990-96; Detroit Lions, free safety, safety, strong safety, 1997-99; Wash Redskins, free safety, 2000; WGN, Chicago, sports commentator; WKBD-TV, co-host sunday night sports telecasts; ESPN XTRA 910, sports commentator; Brophy Prep, Phoenix, sec coach, 2001-03; Sun Devils, Ariz State Univ, sec coach, 2004-05; Baltimore Ravens, sec coach, defensive backs coach, 2006-09; New York Jets, defensive linr coach, 2010-11; Cincinnati Bengals, defensive backs coach, 2012-15. **Orgs:** Founder, MacKids Found. **Honors/Awds:** Jim Thorpe Award, 1989; Named National Football Conference Pro Bowl Team, Nat Football League, 1990-93, 1999; Pro Bowl, 1990, 1991, 1993; Defensive Rookie of the Year, Associated Press, 1990; Defensive Rookie of the Year, Football News, 1990; National Football League Top Free Safety, Sports Illus, 1998; Joe Schmidt Leadership Award winner, 1998, 1999; USC Athletic Hall of Fame, 2006. **Business Addr:** Defensive Line Coach, New York Jets, 437 Madison Ave Suite 1A3, New York, NY 10022-7002, **Business Phone:** (212)355-4040.

**CARRINGTON, DR. CHRISTINE H.**
Psychologist. **Personal:** Born Jun 7, 1941, Palatka, FL; children: Michael, David & Lisa. **Educ:** Howard Univ, BS, 1962, MS, 1965; Univ MD, PhD, coun psychol, 1979. **Career:** Psychologist (retired); DC Pub Schs, sch psychol, 1966-70, consult sch psychol, 1971-72; Bowie State Col, instr, 1970-74; Fed City Col, asst prof, 1972; Bowie State Col, res consult, 1974-75; Howard Univ Hosp, Psychiat Inst Wash, PsychiatricInst Mont Co, consult psychol privileges; Dept Human Res Wash, DC, consult psychol; Howard Univ, Couns Serv, couns psychol, asst prof psychiat, chief psychol; Georgetown Univ, adj assoc prof, psychiat. **Orgs:** Couns therapist Family Life Ctr Columbia MD; psychol Res Team Howard Univ Med Sch; Am Psychol Asn; Am Asn Psychol Pvt Pract; DC Psychol Asn, 1969; Nat Asn Black Psychol, 1970-; Nat Asn Sch Psychol, 1970-79; liaison bd APA; DC Asn Black Psychol, 1972-; Am Asn Univ Profs, 1972-; Asn Coun Ctr Training Dirs, 1981-; bd dir, Asn Psychol Internship Ctrs; Nat Depression Screening Day Site, dir; founding fel Acad Cognitive Ther Assn. **Home Addr:** 10632 Little Patuxent Pkwy, Columbia, MD 21044, **Home Phone:** (301)596-2558.

**CARRINGTON, LEON T., JR.**
Athletic coach. **Career:** St Augustine's Col, assoc athletic dir compliance & coach, head women's tennis coach, currently. **Orgs:** Cent Intercollegiate Athletic Asn. **Business Addr:** Head Coach, Associate Athletic Director, St Augustine College, 1315 Oakwood Ave, Raleigh, NC 27610-2298, **Business Phone:** (919)516-4236.

### CARRINGTON, MARIAN H.

Business owner. **Educ:** Univ Ill Urbana-Champaign. **Career:** Allstate Ins Co, sr div mgr, 1978-89, human resource exec; Carrington & Carrington Ltd, prin & co-owner, 1991-. **Orgs:** Fel Leadership Greater Chicago; exec mem, Chicago United; pres, 100 Black Women Chicago; exec bd mem & secy, Athena Int; bd mem, YWCA Chicago; bd mem, Asn Exec Search Consults; bd mem, Howard Brown Health Ctr. **Business Addr:** Principal, Co-Owner, Carrington & Carrington Ltd, 39 S LaSalle St Suite 400, Chicago, IL 60603-1557, **Business Phone:** (312)606-0015.

### CARRINGTON, TERRI LYNE

Musician, songwriter, singer. **Personal:** Born Aug 4, 1965, Medford, MA; daughter of Solomon Mathew and Judith Ann Sherwood. **Educ:** Berklee Col Music, Boston, MA, 1983, hon doctorate, 2003. **Career:** Clark Terry, New York, NY, drummer, 1984; David Sanborn, New York, NY, drummer, 1986-; Wayne Shorter, Los Angeles, Calif, drummer, 1986-; Stan Getz, Los Angeles, Calif, drummer, 1988, 1990; Arsenio Hall Show, Los Angeles, Calif, drummer, 1989; Polygram Recs, New York, NY, rec artist, singer, songwriter & drummer, 1988-; Al Jarreau, Los Angeles, Calif, drummer, 1991-94; Herbie Hancock, LA, drummer, 1994; Dianne Reeves, Los Angeles, Calif, drummer, 1996-97, producer, 1997; Vibe TV show, house drummer, 1997; Jazz Is A Spirit, 2002; Structure, 2004; More to Say, 2009; Mosaic Project, 2011; Money Jungle: Provocative in Blue, 2013; The Mosaic Project: Love and Soul, 2015. Univ Southern Calif, prof, currently; Berklee BeanTown Jazz Festival, artistic dir, currently. **Orgs:** NARAS. **Honors/Awds:** Youth Achiever Award, NAJE, 1981; Boston Music Awards, 1988, 1989; Nominee, Grammy, NARAS, 1990; Nominee, Image Award, National Association Advancement Colored People, 1990; Dr Martin Luther King Music Achiever Award, City Boston, 1991; Distinguished Alumna Award, Berklee Col Music; Eubie Blake Award; IAJE Award, Outstanding Serv to Jazz Educ; National Association of Jazz Educators Young Talent Award. **Home Addr:** 10524 Arnwood Dr, Lake View Terrace, CA 91342-6801. **Business Addr:** Professor, University of Southern California, Univ Pk Campus, Los Angeles, CA 90074, **Business Phone:** (213)740-2311.

### CARROLL, BEVERLY A.

Clergy. **Personal:** Born Oct 23, 1946, Baltimore, MD; daughter of James E and Lillian N Mercer; children: Rudolph Weeks II. **Educ:** Univ Md, College Park, MD, BA, admin, 1981; Towson State Univ, Towson, MD, MA, lib arts, 1987. **Career:** Archdiocese Baltimore, Baltimore, Md, exec dir, assoc dir, clerk typist, 1967-87; Baltimores Urban Affairs Off, dir; US Conf Cath Bishops, Secretariat African Am Catholics, Wash, DC, exec dir, 1988-, founding dir, currently. **Orgs:** Pres, Fr Charles A Hall Sch Bd, 1970-75; secy, Nat Asn Black Cath Adminr, 1985-87; Mayor's Comt Alt Use Firehouses, 1988-; adv comt, Inst Black Cath Studies; bd mem, Secours Health Syst, MD; trustee, Siena Col; bd mem, Nat Black Cath Cong; Holy Name Prov Franciscans' African Am Comt; bd mem, Bon Secours Health Syst Md; trustee, Siena Col; Franciscans African Am Comt; Initial Formation Comt; Bon Secours Health Syst Md. **Honors/Awds:** Woman of the Year Award, Zeta Phi Beta Sorority Inc, 1998; Martin Luther King Award; Honorary Doctorate of Human Letters, Siena Col, 1999. **Home Addr:** 611 Cumberland St, Baltimore, MD 21217-1719, **Home Phone:** (410)523-9476. **Business Addr:** Executive Director, US Conference of Catholic Bishops' Secretariat, 3211 4th St NE, Washington, DC 20017-1194, **Business Phone:** (202)541-3177.

### CARROLL, CHARLENE O.

Business owner, executive. **Personal:** Born Apr 17, 1950, Boston, MA; married Ronald E; children: Kiet, Robyn & Ronald. **Educ:** La Newton Beauty Rama, dipl, 1971. **Career:** Charlene's Hair Salon Inc, pres & owner, 2004-; consult. **Orgs:** Mass Cosmetologists; Nat Cosmetologists; Hair Am; pres, Black Hair Olympics, 1984. **Special Achievements:** Featured in numerous publications including: Black Hair; Shoptalk; Black Enterprise; Essence; Milany Standard Text Book, co-author with Floyd Kenyatta, 1998; Consulted for major companies including Revlon, American Beauty Products, Soft Sheen. **Home Addr:** 10 Tilden Commons Dr, Quincy, MA 02171-3116, **Home Phone:** (617)689-0963. **Business Addr:** Owner, President, Charlenes Hair Salon Inc, 53 Humboldt Ave, Roxbury, MA 02119-1644, **Business Phone:** (617)427-7718.

### CARROLL, DR. CONSTANCE MARIE

School administrator. **Personal:** Born Sep 12, 1945, Baltimore, MD. **Educ:** Duquesne Univ, BA, humanities, 1966; Knubly Univ, Athens, Greece, cert, 1967; Univ Pittsburg, MA, classics, 1969, PhD; Harvard Univ, Grad Sch Educ, Inst Educ Mgt; Knubly Univ, cert hellenic studies. **Career:** John Hay Whitney Scholar Marshall fel Classics, 1968; Univ Pittsburgh, Col Arts & Sci Advising Ctr, asst dir, 1970-71, dir freshman advising, 1971-72; Univ Maine, Portand-Gorham, Col Arts & Sci, from asst dean to assoc dean, from asst prof classics to assoc prof classics, 1972-77; Indian Valley Col, pres, 1977-83; Marin Community Col Dist, interim chancellor, 1979-80; Saddleback Col, pres, 1983-93; San Diego Mesa Col, pres, 1993-2004; San Diego Community Col Dist, chancellor, 2004-. **Orgs:** Maine Humanities Coun, 1973-75; Panel Mus & Hist Soc, Nat Endowment Humanities, 1973-75; co-chair, Comn Higher Educ, Nat Coun Negro Women, 1973-75; Calif Coun Humanities; adv bd, Inst Leadership Develop; adv bd, Policy Anal Calif Educ; Nat Humanities Fac; Calif Post sec Educ Community Task Force Women & Minorities; evaluator, Western Asn Schs & Cols; Am Philol Asn; Class Asn New Eng; Vergilian Soc Am; Nat Asn Black Prof Women Higher Educ; Coun Cols Arts & Sci; Community Concerns Women New Eng Cols & Univ; bd mem, Film Study Ctr Portland; Commonwealth Club Calif; Community Concerns Women CA Cols & Univ; Coun Black Am Affairs Western Region; Asn Calif Community Col Adminr; Nat Adv Coun Continuing Educ, 1980-81; adv bd, Ms. Mag & Found Educ, 1980-83; bd dir, Am Asn Community Col, 1986-89; bd dir, Nat Inst Leadership Develop, 1985-, chair, 1987-89; Calif Coun Humanities, 1985-89, chair, 1987-89; chair, Am Asn Community Cols Comn New Technologies, 1988; Delta Sigma Theta Sorority Inc, 1988-; bd dir, Community Col Humanities Asn, 1989-; chair, 1996-98, Western Asn Schs & Cols Accrediting Comn Community & Jr Cols, 1990-99; Am Coun Educ Comn Women Higher Educ, 1991-93; adv bd, Automobile Club Southern Calif, 1992-98; bd dir, Installation Gallery, 1993-95; Am Asn Community Cols Comn Int & Intercultural Serv, 1997-2000; San Diego Dialogue, 1998-2001; ational Conf Community & Justice, 1998-2004; bd dir, San Diego Youth & Community Serv, 1998-; mem & founding chair, Community Col Leadership Develop Initiatives & Found, 1999-2010; Coun Higher Educ Comn Recognition & Comt Transfer & Pub Interest, 1999-2001; Coun Higher Educ, 1999-201; Calif Dept Educ Prof Develop Task Force, 2000-02; Calif Joint Legis Comt, 2000-02; Town Adv Bd, Nat Football League Youth Educ, 2001-, chair, 2002-04; Super Bowl XXXVII Host Comt, 2001-03; bd dir, Catfish Club, 2001-; Diocesan High Sch Planning Comn, 2002-; bd dir, San Diego Opera, 2002-10; bd dir, San Diego Urban League, 2004-10; bd dir, Am Coun Educ, 2005-08; bd trustee, Univ San Diego, 2010-; bd gov, San Diego Found, 2010-; Nat Coun Humanities, 2011; bd trustee, San Diego Mus Man, 2013-. **Business Addr:** Chancellor, San Diego Community College, 10440 Black Mountain Rd, San Diego, CA 92126, **Business Phone:** (858)536-7800.

### CARROLL, DIAHANN (CAROL DIAHANN JOHNSON)

Actor, singer. **Personal:** Born Jul 17, 1935, Bronx, NY; daughter of John Johnson and Mabel Faulk; married Vic Damone, Jan 1, 1987, (divorced 1996); children: Suzanne Ottilie Kay Bamford; married Robert DeLeon, Jan 1, 1975; married Fred Glusman, Jan 1, 1973, (divorced 1973). **Educ:** NY Univ, sociol; Manhattan's Sch Performing Arts. **Career:** Films: Carmen Jones, 1954; Porgy & Bess, 1959; Goodbye Again, 1961; Paris Blues, 1961; Hurry Sundown, 1967; The split, 1968; Claudine, 1974; Sister, Sister, 1982; The Five Heartbeats, 1991; Eve's Bayou, 1997; Jackie's Back, 1999; Over The River...Life of Lydia Maria Child, Abolitionist for Freedom, 2008; Tyler Perry Presents Peeples, 2013; The Masked Saint, 2014. TV Series: "The Man in the Moon", 1960; "Death Scream", 1975; "I Know Why the Caged Bird Sings", 1979; "Julia", 1984-87; The Sweetest Gift, 1998; "Having Our Say: The Delany Sisters First 100 Years", 1999; "The Courage to Love", 2000; "Sally Hemings: An American Scandal", 2000; "The Natalie Cole Story", 2000; "The Ct", 2002; "Half & Half", 2002; "The Court Justice De-Sett:", 2002; Strong Med", 2003; "Soul Food", 2003-04; "Whoopi", 2004; "Soul Food", 2004; "Grey's Anatomy", 2006-07; "Hug & Tell", 2008; "Back To You", 2008; "White Collar", 2009; "Diahann Carroll: The Lady, The Music, The Legend", 2010. **Orgs:** AEA; AFTRA; SAG; hon mem, Alpha Kappa Alpha Sorority Inc. **Honors/Awds:** Tony Award, 1962; Golden Globe, 1969; Oscar Nomination for "Claudine", 1974; Image Award, Nat Asn Advan Colored People, 1975; Walk of Fame, 1990; Crystal Award, Women in Film, 1992; Lucy Award, 1998; Black Reel Award, 2001; Groundbreaking Show, 2003; Hall Fame, Television Academy, 2011; Ten Int Best Dressed List; Patron Performer John F Kennedy Ctr; Two Emmy Nominations; Entertainer of the Year, Cue Mag; Won first prize on TV's "Chance Of A Lifetime"; Star on the Hollywood Walk of Fame. **Special Achievements:** Author: "Diahann: An Autobiography", 1986; "Own Designer Label of Clothes", 1998; First African American actress to star in her own television series. **Home Addr:** PO Box 57593, Sherman Oaks, CA 91403. **Business Addr:** Actress, Jeffrey Lane & Associates Inc, 6363 Wilshire Blvd, Los Angeles, CA 90048, **Business Phone:** (323)852-0492.

### CARROLL, GEORGE D.

Judge. **Personal:** Born Jan 6, 1923, Brooklyn, NY; son of John T and Maude V; married Janie Mabry. **Educ:** Brooklyn Col, BA (cum laude), 1943; Brooklyn Law Sch, JD (cum laude), 1950. **Career:** Judge (retired); Dist Atty Kings County, 1946-51; atty, NY, 1951-52; Richmond City Coun, coun mem, 1961-65; City Ricmond, mayor, 1964-65; Gov Edmund G Brown, judge, 1965; Bay Munic Ct, judge, 1970, 1976, 1982, 1985. **Orgs:** NY Bar Asn, 1950; CA Bar Asn, 1953; judicial coun, Nat Bar Asn; CA Judge Asn; jud admin sect, Am Bar Asn; pres, Richmond Bar Asn; life mem, Nat Asn Advan Colored People; Charles Houston Bar Asn; Am Judicature Socs; Sigma Pi Phi; Omega Phi Fraternities. **Special Achievements:** First African-American on the Richmond City Council; First African-American mayor of Richmond; First African-American judge in Contra Costa Count. **Home Addr:** 280 Washington Ct, Richmond, CA 94801.

### CARROLL, DR. JAMES S.

Lawyer. **Personal:** Born Sep 17, 1945, Brooklyn, NY; son of James S and Mabel G Duncan; married Celia Antonia; children: Jason Sean, Jamaal Samuel, Khadijah & Jameson. **Educ:** NY Univ, BA, 1966; Howard Law Sch, JD, 1970. **Career:** Nat Conf Black Lawyers, atty, 1970-72; Com Develop Harlem Assertion Rights, dir, 1972-73; pvt pract atty, 1973-79; VI, asst US atty, 1979-92, sr litigation coun, 1992-95, civil chief, 1995-98, 2001-; US Atty's Off, Chief Civil Div, first asst US atty, 1998-2001, civil chief, child exploitation & possessing child pornography, currently. **Orgs:** Nat Bar Asn; Am Bar Asn; Nat Asn Asst US Attys; Nat Black Prosecutors Asn. **Honors/Awds:** Root-Tilden Scholar; Reginald Heber Smith Fel, 1970-72; Dirs Award, Atty Gen US, 1990; Spec Achievement Award, US Dept Justice, 1992, Spec Commendation, 1995. **Home Addr:** PO Box 9811, St Thomas00801. **Business Addr:** Civil Chief, US Attorney Office, Rm 260 5500 Veterans Dr, St. Thomas00802-6424, **Business Phone:** (340)774-5757.

### CARROLL, JASON

Journalist, broadcaster. **Personal:** Born Westlake Village, CA. **Educ:** Univ Southern Calif, BA, iterature & creative writing. **Career:** 60 Minutes, intern; KAKE (ABC affil Wichita, KS), gen assignment reporter; WPIX-TV (New York), gen assignment reporter; CBS 2 News (Los Angeles), gen assignment reporter; CNN, nat corresp & co-host "Ahead of the Curve," 2001-. **Honors/Awds:** Daytime Emmy Award for Outstanding Morning Program, nominated; Edward R. Murrow Award for breaking news, 2011.

### CARROLL, JOE BARRY

Painter (artist), basketball player, businessperson. **Personal:** Born Jul 24, 1958, Pine Bluff, AR. **Educ:** Purdue Univ, BA, econs, 1980. **Career:** Basketball player (retired), businessperson; Golden State Warriors, ctr, 1980-83, 1985-87; Simac Milano, 1984-85; Houston Rockets, 1987-88; NJ Nets, 1988-90; Denver Nuggets, 1990-91; Phoenix Suns, 1991; investment advisor & businessperson, currently. **Orgs:** Broad-View Found. **Special Achievements:** Growing Up . . . In Words and Images, 2014. **Home Addr:** , Atlanta, GA.

### CARROLL, LAWRENCE WILLIAM, III

Television journalist. **Personal:** Born Dec 11, 1950, Chicago, IL; son of Lawrence William Jr and Annie Lee Goode; married Roman Abebe Wolder; children: Yenea Lucille & Lawrence William IV. **Educ:** Pomona Col, Claremont, Calif, BA, econs, 1973. **Career:** KABC-TV, Los Angeles, Calif, reporter & anchor, 1973-89; KCAL-TV, Los Angeles, Calif, news anchor, 1989-; KFWB News 980, news anchor, 2001-; KSPC-FM, news dir & prog dir; KHJ-TV Channel 9, asst producer; One Origin Inc, exec vice chmn & co-founder. **Orgs:** Acad TV Arts & Sci, 1989-; Radio TV News Asn, 1989-; African Rim Inst & Hosanna Broadcasting. **Honors/Awds:** Numerous honors including an Emmy award, Image Award nomination, 6 Emmy nominations, 7 Golden Mike Awards, an Associated Press Award and Grand award; 20th Anniversary Award, Congressional Black Caucus. **Home Phone:** (818)368-1281. **Business Addr:** News Anchor, KFWB News 980, 6230 Yucca St, Los Angeles, CA 90028, **Business Phone:** (323)871-4633.

### CARROLL, DR. NATALIE L.

Physician, president (organization). **Personal:** Born Jan 26, 1950, Nashville, TN; daughter of Carl Mark and Ruth; married Warren Dailey; children: 2. **Educ:** Lake Forest Col, BA, psychol, 1971; Meharry Med Col, MD, 1974. **Career:** Wash Hosp Ctr, Washington, DC, surg intern, 1974-75, ob gyn resident, 1975-78; Darnell Army Hosp, chair, supvr, 1978-80; Hermann Memorial Hosp, assoc clin instr, 1980-, staff physician, 1980-, qual assurance sub-comt, 1980-; St Elizabeths Hosp, chair, 1983-85; Howard Univ Col Med, externship; Baylor Col Med, externship; pvt pract obstetrician & gynecologist, currently. **Orgs:** Alpha Kappa Alpha Sorority Inc; Meharry Alumni Asn; Am Col Obstet & Gynec; fel Inst Advan Multicultural & Minority Health Care; Depelchin C's Ctr; Harris County C's Protective Serv; Tex Dept Health Adv Bd Comn; pres, Lone Star State Med Asn; officer, Houston Med Forum; bd chair, Riverside Nat Bank; Alpha Omega Alpha Med Hon Soc; Links Inc; fel Am Col Obstet & Gynec; Am Diabetes Asn; Agency Healthcare Res & Qual's; Tex Med Asn; Houston Gynec Soc; pres, Nat Med Asn, 2002. **Special Achievements:** First woman to complete a surgery internship at the Washington Hospital Center in Washington, DC, 1975; First African American woman to complete an obstetrics/gynecology residency at the same facility, 1978. **Business Addr:** President, National Medical Association, 1012 10th St NW, Washington, DC 20001, **Business Phone:** (202)347-1895.

### CARROLL, ROBERT F.

Chief executive officer, executive. **Personal:** Born Jun 18, 1931, Bartow, FL; son of Robert F Sr (deceased) and Emma H (deceased); married Gwendolyn Jackson; children: Tosca, Denise & Robert III. **Educ:** Fla A&M Univ, BA, 1960; Univ Conn, attended 1961; Columbia Univ, MA, 1963; Yale Univ, attended 1964. **Career:** NY City Dept Social Serv, dep comt, 1967-71; NY City Human Resources Admin, dep admin, 1971-74; City Col NY, vpres, 1974-78, asst adminr & dir; Cong Chas B Rangel, chief staff, 1978-81; R F Carroll & Co, chmn & chief exec officer. **Orgs:** Am Asn Pub Admin, 1973-; Bd mem, WNET TV, 1982-85; Pub Rels Soc Am; Am Asn Polit Sci; Alpha Phi Alpha Fraternity; bd gov, Mill River Country Club; bd mem, exec comt, Metrop Golf Asn. **Honors/Awds:** Educator of Year, Asn Black Educrs, 1975; Distinguished Service Award, Univ Taiwan, 1979; Public Service Award, US Dept HEW, 1970. **Home Addr:** 37 Reynolds Rd, Glen Cove, NY 11542-1438, **Home Phone:** (516)671-8322. **Business Addr:** Chief Executive Officer, Owner, R F Carroll & CO, 37 Reynolds Rd, Glen Cove, NY 11542-1438, **Business Phone:** (516)671-8322.

### CARROLL, ROCKY (ROSCOE FULTON CARROLL)

Actor. **Personal:** Born Jul 8, 1963, Cincinnati, OH; married Gabrielle Bullock; children: Elissa. **Educ:** Sch Creative & Performing Arts, attended 1981; Webster Univ, BFA. **Career:** Films: Born on the Fourth of July, 1989; Prelude to a Kiss, 1992; Fathers& Sons, 1992; The Chase, 1994; Crimson Tide, 1995; The Great White Hype, 1996; Best Laid Plans, 1999; The Ladies Man, 2000; Spider-Man 2, 2004; Prisoner, 2007; Yes Man, 2008. TV series: "Roc", 1991-94; "Chicago Hope", 1996-2000; "The Agency", 2001; TV movie: "Five Desperate Hours", 1997; TV guest appearances: "Law & Order", 1990; "Gargoyles", 1994-96; "Early Edition", 1998; "Welcome to New York", 2000; "The West Wing", 2001; "Family Law", 2001; "The Agency", 2002; "Boston Legal", 2004; "Am Dreams", 2005; "Invasion", 2006; "The Game", 2006; "Haunt You Every Day", 2007; "Grey's Anatomy", 2007; "Yes Man", 2008; "NCIS", 2008-14; "NCIS: Los Angeles", 2009-14. **Business Addr:** Actor, Starstruck Films, c/o Shelley Browning, Universal City, CA 91608, **Business Phone:** (818)777-2868.

### CARROLL, RODNEY J.

Association executive, executive. **Personal:** Born Philadelphia, PA. **Career:** United Parcel Serv, part-time loader, 1978, Willow Grove Facil, hub mgr, 1983, Phila Air Hub, opers div mgr, vpres, chief exec officer, pres; Welfare Work Partnership, pres & chief exec officer; Bus Interface LLC, vpres bus outreach, 1998-2000, pres & chief exec officer, 2000-; Works Partnership, pres & chief exec officer. **Honors/Awds:** Mickey Leland Humanitarian Award, Cong Black Caucus, 2000, 2003; Martin Luther King Jr Humanitarian Award, Univ Ga Perimeter Col, 2003. **Special Achievements:** Author: No Free Lunch, 2002; Featured on TV programs such as The Paula Zahn Show on Fox News, the Diane Rehm Show and NBC Today Show. **Business Addr:** Chief Executive Officer, President, Business Interface LLC, 1129 20th St NW Suite 800, Washington, DC 20036, **Business Phone:** (301)883-8701.

### CARROLL, SALLY G.

President (organization), association executive. **Personal:** Born Roanoke, VA. **Educ:** Essex Jr Col. **Career:** Executive (retired); Newark Police Dept, 1949-51, pres, 1968; Essex Co Sheriff's Off, attend, 1951. **Orgs:** Trustee, Bd Gr Newark Urban Coalition; Newark Mus; Milt Campbell Youth Ctr; chmn, Newark Nat Asn Advan Colored People Day Care Bd; pres, Batons Inc Nat Asn Negro Bus & Prof Women's Club; adv bd, Proj, COED; Hich Impact Anti-Crime Bd; Affirmative

Action Rev Coun; Citizens Adv Bd Mayor's Policy & Develop Off; life mem, former secy, treas, pres, Newark Br Nat Asn Advan Colored People; nat bd mem, Nat Asn Advan Colored People. **Honors/Awds:** Woman of the Year Award, Frontiers Internat; Sojourner Truth Award, Bus & Prof Women; Outstanding Negro Woman, Imperial Ct Isis PHA; 1st woman NJ appointed, NJ St Parole Bd six yr term. **Special Achievements:** First African American female police officer in Newark. **Home Addr:** 138 S 13th St, Newark, NJ 07107-1012, **Home Phone:** (973)485-6493.

### CARRUTHERS, DR. GEORGE ROBERT

Physicist, scientist. **Personal:** Born Oct 1, 1939, Cincinnati, OH; son of George and Sophia. **Educ:** Univ Ill, BS, aeronaut eng, 1961, MS, nuclear eng, 1962, PhD, aeronaut & astron eng, 1964. **Career:** Nat Sci Found, fel, 1964; US Naval Res Lab, rocket astron res physicist, 1964-82, head ultraviolet measurements br, 1980-82, Ultraviolet Measurements Grp, Space Sci Div, sr astrophysicist head, 1982-. **Orgs:** Am Asn Advan Sci; Am Astron Soc; Am Geophys Union; Am Inst Aeronaut & Astronaut; chmn edit & rev comt edit j, Nat Tech Asn, 1983-; Soc Photo-optical Instrumentation Engrs; vpres, SMART Inc, 1995-; coun mem, Smithsonian Inst, 1995-; Chicago Rocket Soc; fel NSF. **Honors/Awds:** Arthur S Flemming Award, Wash Jaycees, 1970; Exceptional Achievement Scientific Award Medal, Nat Aeronaut & Space Admin, 1972; Alumni Award, University of Illinois, 1975; Samuel Cheevers Award, Nat Tech Asn, 1977; Black Engineer of the Year, 1987; Warner Prize, Am Astron Soc; Honorary Doctor Engineering, Mich Technol Univ; NIS Outstanding Scientist Award, 2000; National Inventors Hall of Fame, 2003; Distinguished Lecturer, Office of Naval Research, 2009; National Medal of Technology and Innovation, 2012. **Special Achievements:** First Recipient of NIS Outstanding Scientist Award, 2000. **Home Addr:** 337 O St SW, Washington, DC 20024-2901. **Business Addr:** Astrophysicist, US Naval Research Laboratory, 4555 Overlook Ave SW, Washington, DC 20375-5320, **Business Phone:** (202)767-3200.

### CARRY, REV. HELEN WARD

School administrator, executive. **Personal:** Born Chicago, IL; daughter of Anderson and Minnie; children: Ronald & Julius J III. **Educ:** Xavier Univ, New Orleans, La, BA, Eng & Fr, 1946; Loyola Univ, Chicago, MEd, 1963; Calif Coastal Univ, EdD, 2000. **Career:** Chicago Pub Schs, teacher, 1952, adjust counr, 1962; Chicago Pub Schs Head Start, coord, 1965-69; Webster Sch, Chicago Pub Schs, asst prin, 1965, prin, 1970; Christ Universal Temple, asst minister, 1990, fel minister, exec minister, dir, currently; Johnnie Colemon Acad, dir & prin, 1999; Johnnie Colemon Inst, dir. **Orgs:** Consult, David Cook Publishing; Delta Sigma Theta Sor. **Honors/Awds:** Outstanding Prin, Dist 8 Chicago Pub Schs; Black Rose Award, League BlackWomen, 1987; Lifetime Career Achievement Award, Nat Pub, 1990; Positive Image Award, Westside Ctr Truth, 1990; Tubman & Truth Woman Yr Award, 1992; Recipient, Dollars & Senses Lifetime Career Achievement Award, 2008; VIP of the Year, Worldwide Branding, 2013; NRelig Award, NDIGO Found; Inductee, Worldwide Lifetime Achievement; Recipient, Achiever in Religion Award, NDigo Found; Recipient Black Rose Award; Recipient, Positive Image Award; Recipient, National Association of University Women Award. **Special Achievements:** Featured, Americas Top 100 Black Business and Professional Women. **Home Addr:** 8600 S Mich Ave, Chicago, IL 60619-5626, **Home Phone:** (773)651-1230. **Business Addr:** Executive Minister, Christ Universal Temple, 11901 S Ashland Ave, Chicago, IL 60643-5434, **Business Phone:** (773)568-2282.

### CARSON, ANDRE

Law enforcement officer. **Personal:** Born Oct 16, 1974, Indianapolis, IN; married Mariama Shaheed; children: Salimah. **Educ:** Concordia Univ-Wis, BA, criminal justice mgt; Ind Wesleyan Univ, MA, 2005. **Career:** Ind State Excise Police Dept, investigative officer; Ind Dept Homeland Security; Dept Homeland Security's Intelligence Fusion Ctr, 2006; House Dem Caucus, sr whip; Indianapolis City-County Coun, law enforcement officer. **Orgs:** Bd mem, Indy Parks Kennedy-King Park Advisory Bd; Citizens Neighborhood Coalition; House Financial Serv Comt; House Transp & Infrastructure Comt; House Permanent Select Comt Intelligence; 113th Cong; Cong Black Caucus Exec Leadership Team; Indianapolis City-County Coun, mem, 2007-2008; US House Representatives, mem, 2008-; Progressive Caucus; New Dem Coalition; Chair & Founder, Higher Ed Caucus. **Business Addr:** United States Congressman, US House of Representatives - Indiana's 7th Congressional District, 300 E Fall Creek Pkwy N Dr Suite 300, Indianapolis, IN 46205, **Business Phone:** (317)283-6516.

### CARSON, DR. BENJAMIN SOLOMON, SR. (BEN CARSON)

Physician, neurosurgeon. **Personal:** Born Sep 18, 1951, Detroit, MI; son of Robert Solomon and Sonya Copeland; married Lucena Rustin; children: Murray Nedlands, Benjamin Jr & Rhoeyce Harrington. **Educ:** Yale Univ, New Haven, CT, BA, psychol, 1973; Univ Mich, Ann Arbor MI, MD, 1977; Gettysburg Col, hon doctor sci, 1988. **Career:** Johns Hopkins Univ, Baltimore MD, chief resident neuro surg, 1982-83, asst prof, neuro surg, 1984, asst prof, oncol, 1984, asst prof, pediat, 1987, dir pediat neuro surg, 1984-91, assoc prof, 1991-99, co-dir, 1991-, dir, prof pediat, plastic surg, oncol & neurol surg, 1999-2013; Queen Elizabeth II Med Ctr, Perth, Australia, sr registr neuro surg, 1983-84; Books: Gifted Hands, author, 1990; Think Big, author, 1996; The Big Picture, author, 2000; Take The Risk, author, 2008. **Orgs:** AAAS, 1982-; Nat Pediat Oncol Group, 1985-; Nat Med Asn, 1986-; hon chmn, Regional Red Cross Cabinet, 1987-; med adv bd, C Cancer Found, 1987-; life mem, Md Cong Parents & Teachers, 1988-; Am Asn Neurol Surgeons, 1989-; Cong Neurol Surgeons, 1989-; dir, Kellogg Co, Costco Whole sale Corp; trustee, Yale Univ; pres co-founder, Carson Scholars Fund. **Honors/Awds:** Citations for Excellence, Detroit City Coun, 1987, Philadelphia City Coun, 1987, Mich State Senate, 1987, PA House of Representatives, 1989, Detroit Medical Society, 1987; American Black Achievement Award, Bus & Prof, Ebony & Johnson Publs, 1988; Clinical Practitioner of the Year, Nat Med Asn Region II, 1988; Certificate of Honor for Outstanding Achievement in the Field of Medicine, Nat Medical Fellowship Inc, 1988; Candle Award for Science and Technology, Morehouse Col, 1989; Black book Humanitarian Award, Black book Publ, 1991; Excellence in Leadership Award, Center for New Black Leadership, 2000; Healthcare Humanitarian Award, 2004; Spingarn Medal, NAACP, 2006; Presidential Medal of Freedom, 2008; medical superstar, Ebony mag; Civilian Award; received more than 60 honorary doctorate degrees & Numerous Awards. **Special Achievements:** Numerous natl network television appearances (med & social issues), 1985-; performed first intrauterine shunting procedure for a hydrocephalic twin, 1986, first successful separation of occipital craniopagus Siamese twins, 1987; Author of Numerous Books. **Home Addr:** 15117 Old Hanover Rd, Upperco, MD 21155, **Home Phone:** (410)955-7888.

### CARSON, CLAYBORNE

College teacher, historian. **Personal:** Born Jun 15, 1944, Buffalo, NY; married Susan Ann Carson; children: Malcolm & Tamera. **Educ:** Univ Calif, Los Angeles, BA, 1967, MA, 1971, PhD, Am hist, 1975. **Career:** Audience Studios Inc., Los Angeles, CA 1965-66; Los Angeles Free Press, staff writer, 1966; UCLA Surv Res Ctr (Inst Social Res), comput programmer, 1968-71; UCLA, actg asst prof, 1971-74; Stanford Univ, asst prof, 1974-81, assoc prof, 1981-90, Martin Luther King, Jr., Papers Proj, ed & dir, 1985-, prof, 1990-, Martin Luther King, Jr., Centennial Prof, 2014-; Martin Luther King Jr. Res & Educ Inst at Stanford Univ, dir & founder, 2005-; Emory Univ, distinguished prof, 1996-97; Morehouse Col, Martin Luther King Jr. Distinguished Prof, 2008-09. **Orgs:** Soc Am Historians. **Special Achievements:** Oversaw production of seven volumes of "The Papers of Martin Luther King, Jr."; author "In Struggle: SNCC and the Black Awakening of the 1960s" (1981), "Malcolm X: The FBI File" (1991), and "Martin's Dream: My Journey and the Legacy of Martin Luther King, Jr." (2013); coauthor "African American Lives: The Struggle for Freedom" (2005); playwright "Passage of Martin Luther King" (1993); senior advisor on television series "Eyes on the Prize", 1986, 1990; numerous national television and radio show appearances. **Business Addr:** King Institute, Cypress Hall D, Stanford, CA 94305-4146, **Business Phone:** (650)723-2092.

### CARSON, DR. EMMETT D.

Chief executive officer, educator, association executive. **Personal:** Born Oct 6, 1959, Chicago, IL; son of Emmett and Mary; married Jacqueline Copeland. **Educ:** Morehouse Col, BA, econs, 1980; Princeton Univ, MA, pub admin pub & int affairs, 1983, PhD, pub admin pub & int affairs, 1985. **Career:** Libr Cong, social legis anal, 1985-86; Joint Ctr Polit & Econ Studies, proj dir, 1986-89; Univ Md, Col Pk, adj lectr, 1987-89; Ford Found, Rights & Social Justice Prog, prog officer, 1989-92; Governance & Pub Policy Prog, prog officer, 1989-92; Minneapolis Found, pres & chief exec officer, 1994-2006; Silicon Valley Community Found, pres & founding chief exec officer, 2006-. **Orgs:** Bd dir, Nat Econs Asn, 1993-95; chair, bd dir, Asn Black Found Exec, 1994-95; bd chair, Coun Found, Blue Cross Blue Shield Minn, Southern Educ Found; Univ Minn Humphrey Inst Pub Policy; joint venture bd mem, Silicon Valley Community Found. **Honors/Awds:** Phi Beta Kappa, 1981; Grad Fel, Princeton Univ, 1981-85; E B Williams Econs & Bus Award, Morehouse Col, 1981; Dissertation Award, Nat Econ Asn, 1985; Super Performance Award, Joint Ctr Polit & Econ Studies, 1988; hon degrees, ndiana Univ, Morehouse Col, National Hispanic Univ. **Special Achievements:** Designed & directed the first Nat comparative study of the charitable giving and volunteer behavior of Black and White Am; Internationally recognized as a catalyst for progressive social change. **Home Addr:** 5230 Green Farms Rd, Edina, MN 55436, **Home Phone:** (952)988-9070. **Business Addr:** President, Chief Executive Officer, Silicon Valley Community Foundation, 1300 S El Camino Real Suite 100, San Mateo, CA 94402-3049, **Business Phone:** (650)458-2660.

### CARSON, IRMA

Counselor, executive director. **Personal:** Born Jun 24, 1935, Monroe, LA; children: Sharon(Deceased), Karen & Camille. **Educ:** Bakersfield Col, AA; Calif State Col, BA; Kern Co Law Enforcement Acad; Univ CA, Santa Barbara, cert criminal justice; Univ CA, Los Angeles, teaching credential; CA, teaching credential. **Career:** Bakersfield City Sch Dist, bd mem; Bakersfield City Police, police sgt; Bakersfield City Schs, pres bd educ; Ebony Coun Ctr, dir, exec dir, currently; Legis & Litigation Comt; Personnel Comt; Water Resources Comt; Bakersfield City Coun, vice mayor, 1999-2000; Kern County Network C; Work Force Investment Act Bd; Proposition Ten Tech Adv Comt; City Bakersfield, coun mem, currently. **Orgs:** Am Bus Women's Asn; Kern Co Child Sex Abuse Treat Comt; Black Hist Comn; BAPAC; Nat Asn Advan Colored People; CFBL; Cain Mem AME Church; co-auth "The Handbk for Battered Women"; Rape Prev Workshop; Parent's Rights & Responsibilities Workshop; Nat Polit Inst Workshop, 1984; NSBA Urban Bd Educ Coun; State Supt, Ethic Adv Coun; Dem Nominee State Assembly, 1992; trustee, Bakersfield City Sch Dt Bd Educ; co-chair, Joint City-County Standing Comt Combat Gang Violence. **Honors/Awds:** Officer of the Year, 1974; Nat Asn Advan Colored People Comm Serv Award, 1979; People's Baptist Church Community Serv Award, 1980; Black Hist Parade Grant Marshal, 1980; The Golden West Leadership Award, 1981; Elks Lodge Community Serv Award, 1981; Calif Alliance of Black Educators Distinguish Serv Award, 1982; Comm Appreciation Reception, 1982; Black Hist Parade Grand Marshal, 1983. **Special Achievements:** First African-American woman elected to the council, 1994; the first African-American to work in City Hall; first black woman officer, Bakersfield Police Department; first black woman on the city council. **Home Addr:** 4300 Garnsey Lane, Bakersfield, CA 93309, **Home Phone:** (661)325-4327. **Business Addr:** Council Member, Ward 1, City of Bakersfield, 1600 Truxtun Ave, Bakersfield, CA 93301-5141, **Business Phone:** (661)326-3767.

### CARSON, ESQ. JOHN HAROLD, JR.

Lawyer. **Educ:** John Carroll Univ, BS; Kent State Univ, BA; Cleveland-Marshall Col Law, JD. **Career:** Pvt prac atty, currently. **Orgs:** Ohio State Bar Asn. **Business Addr:** Attorney, 614 W Superior Ave Suite 1300, Cleveland, OH 44113-1338, **Business Phone:** (216)344-9220.

### CARSON, JOHNNIE

Diplomat, ambassador, government official. **Personal:** Born Apr 7, 1943, Chicago, IL; son of Dupree and Aretha Rhodes; married Anne Diemer; children: Elizabeth Diemer, Michael Dupree & Katherine Anne. **Educ:** Drake Univ, BA, hist & polit sci, 1965; Univ London, Sch Orient & Afr Studies, MA, int rels, 1975. **Career:** Am Embassy Lagos, Nigeria, consular & polit officer, 1969-71; Namibia Bur Intelligence & Res, 1971-74; State's bur intelligence & res, desk officer Africa, 1971-74; Am Embassy, Maputo, Mozambique, dep chief, 1975-78; Secy State, staff officer, 1978-79; US House Rep, staff dir, Africa Subcomt, 1979-82; Dept State, desk officer, Angola, Mozambique; Am Embassy Gaborone, Botswana, dep chief, 1986-90; Repub Uganda, US ambassador, 1991-94; Repub Zimbabwe, US ambassador, 1995-97; Am Embassy, Harare, Zimbabwe, ambassador, 1995-97; US Dept State, Africa Bur, prin dept asst secy, 1997-99; Am Embassy, Nairobi, Kenya, ambassador, 1999-2003; Nat Defense Univ, sr vpres, 2003-06; US Dept State, Bur African Affairs, asst secy state, 2009-. **Orgs:** Nat intelligence officer Africa, Nat Intelligence Coun; peace corps vol, Tanzania, 1965-68. **Honors/Awds:** Superior Honor Award, Dept State, 1997; Presidential Service Award, White House, 1998; Doctor of Public Affairs, Drake Univ, 1998; Champion of Prevention Award, Ctrs for Disease Control, 2003; Meritorious Service Award, Secretary of State Madeleine Albright. **Home Addr:** 11427 Tanbark Dr, Reston, VA 20191-4103, **Home Phone:** (703)390-0424. **Business Addr:** Assistant Secretary, US Department of State, 2201 C St NW, Washington, DC 20520.

### CARSON, LISA NICOLE

Actor. **Personal:** Born Jul 12, 1969, Brooklyn, NY; daughter of Lester and Fannie. **Career:** TV series: "ER", recurring role, 1996-2001; "Ally McBeal", 1997-2002; "Getting Personal", 1998; "Damon", 1998; "Ally", 1999-2000; "Aftershock: Earthquake in New York", 1999; "Harrys Law", 2012; TV Movie, Aftershock: Earthquake in NY, 1999; Film roles: Jason's Lyric, 1994; Devilin a Blue Dress, 1995; Divas, 1995; Love Jones, 1997; White Lies, 1997; Eve's Bayou, 1997; Life, 1999. **Honors/Awds:** Nominee for Q Award, 1998; Nominee for Image Award, 1998-99, 2000, 2002; Nominee for Actor Guild Award, 1998, 2000-01; Actor Guild Award, 1999; Voted to "10 Sexiest Women of the Year", Black Men Mag, 2000.

### CARSON, LOIS MONTGOMERY

Administrator. **Personal:** Born Jul 3, 1931, Memphis, TN; married Harry L; children: Harry Jr, William, Patricia, John, Brian & Felicia. **Educ:** Wilberforce Univ; Calif State Col, BA, 1967; Univ Calif, MA, 1974; Calif State, Sec Teaching Credential, 1970. **Career:** Freewalk Gazette, 1963-64; San Bernardino County Probation Dept, counr, 1964-68; precinct reporter, 1964-69; San Bernardino County Sch, teacher, 1968-72; Am News, staff, 1969; Univ Calif, dir proj Upward Bound, 1973-76; Calif State Univ, prof eng & educ, 1977-78; Comm Serv Dept, dep dir, 1978-80; Community Action Partnership Riverside Co, exec dir, 2010, retired. **Orgs:** Calif Teachers Asn, 1968-73; Calif Conf Black Elected officials, 1973-74; Mil Acad Bd 38th Cong Dist, 1973-74; pres bd, San Bernardino Comm Col Dist, 1973; state vice chairperson, Calif Adv Health Coun, 1976-; Nat Bd Asn Comm Col trustee, 1978; Delta Kappa Gamma Int Soc; Alpha Kappa Alpha Sorority; Calif OEO Adv Bd; secy, Nat Bd Nat Coun Negro Women; bd dir, Nat Asn Clean Air Agencies; Asn Community Col; Empire chapNat Coun Negro Women. **Honors/Awds:** Distinguished Achievement Award, 1969; Calif State Assembly Public Service Award, 1973; Woman of the Year, Inland Empire Sect Nat Coun of Negro Women, 1973; Black Woman of the Year, San Bernardino, 1974; Women of Achievement, San Bernardino, 1975; Good Citizenship Award, Alpha Kappa Alpha, 1976; Outstanding Achievement Award, Far Western Region, 1979, 1984; Public Administrator of the Year, 1980; Calif State Distinguished Alumnus, 1980; Woman of the Year, State of California, 2007; Distinguished Alumna, Calif State Univ. **Home Addr:** 745 N Dallas, San Bernardino, CA 92410, **Home Phone:** (909)885-1708. **Business Addr:** Executive Director, Community Action Partnership, 2038 Iowa Ave Suite B102, Riverside, CA 92507, **Business Phone:** (909)955-4900.

### CARSON, DR. REGINA M. E.

Educator. **Personal:** Born Washington, DC. **Educ:** Howard Univ Col Pharm, BS, 1973; Loyola Col, Baltimore, MD, MBA, mkt, 1987, health servs admin, 1987. **Career:** Provident Hosp, Baltimore, Md, dir, pharm servs, 1979-86; Ridgeway Manor, Catonsville, Md, mgr, pharm servs, 1986-87; Univ MD, Sch Pharm, asst prof, 1987-88; Howard Univ, Col Pharm & Pharmaceut Scis, coordr prof pract prog, asst prof, 1988-95; Off Educ, consult, 1990-; Marrell Consult, consult, 1995-; Sunrise Towson Retirement Homes, admin, 1997-; Cent Carolina Tech Col, Acad Affairs & Health Sci, pharm technician & acad prog mgr, currently; Randallstown Med Ctr & Hilton Ct Partnership Pharmacies, vpres. **Orgs:** Chair, Bus & Econ Develop Comn, 1991-92; Nat Black MBAs, DC Chap; bd mem, Auxiliary, Northwest Hosp Ctr; steering comt, Home Health Care Comn, 1990-92; NARD; life mem, Nat Pharmacist Asn; Nat Asn Health Serv Exec; fel Am Soc Consult Pharmacists; bd trustee, Community Col Baltimore Co; bd dir, Alzheimers Asn. **Home Addr:** 3827 Janbrook Rd, Randallstown, MD 21133, **Home Phone:** (410)521-5734. **Business Addr:** Program Manager, Pharmacy Technician, Central Carolina Technical College, H111 506 N Guignard Dr, Sumter, SC 29150, **Business Phone:** (803)778-6621.

### CARSON, DR. WARREN JASON, JR.

Educator. **Personal:** Born Feb 12, 1953, Tryon, NC; son of Warren J and Esther Maybrey. **Educ:** Univ NC, AB, 1974; Atlanta Univ, MA, Afro-Am studies, 1975; Univ SC, Columbia, SC, PhD, 1990. **Career:** Isothermal Community Col, instr, 1975-76; Piedmont OIC, head career prep div, 1975-80; Rutledge Col, dean acad affairs, 1980-84; Univ SC, Spartanburg, prog dir, Dept Eng, prof, 1984-2004, chmn, currently, Col Arts & Sci, asst dean; Roseland Community Ctr, pres, interim dean, currently; Univ SC, Upstate, Col Arts & Sci, Upstate, SC, prof eng, 2004-, Dept Lang Lit & Compos, chair, 2004-, chief diversity officer, 2008-; Univ SC, Greenville, SC, interim vice chancellor, currently; Col Lang Asn J, pres & managing ed. **Orgs:** Pres, Nat Asn Advan Colored People, Polk Co, 1976-96; chmn, Mayor's Adv Task Force, 1980-83; pres, Tryon Schs, PTA, 1980-81; Polk Co (NC), Bd County Comners, 1986-88; Polk Co, Dept Soc Serv, 1986-94; City Coun, Tryon, NC, 1989-; Polk County Child Protection Team, 1993-; trustee, Isothermal Comm Col, 1997-. **Honors/Awds:** Outstanding Teacher Award, Piedmont OIC, 1980; Outstanding Teacher Award, Rutledge Col, 1982-83; Church & Comm Award, 1984; Teacher of the Year,

Univ SC, Spartan burg, 1989; Amoco Outstanding Teacher Award, Univ SC, 1989; Governor's Distinguished Professor Award, SC Comn Higher Educ, Governor's Office, 1989, 2002, 2003; Carson Scholarship Program established, 1998; Distinguished Service Award, Univ Sc Upstate, 2014. **Home Addr:** 631 E Howard St, PO Box 595, Tryon, NC 28782, **Home Phone:** (828)859-6793. **Business Addr:** Professor, Chairman, University South Carolina Upstate, Smith 215C 800 Univ Way, Spartanburg, SC 29303, **Business Phone:** (864)503-5634.

## CARSWELL, DWAYNE A.

Football player. **Personal:** Born Jan 18, 1972, Jacksonville, FL; married Tamara; children: Ashley & Aaron. **Educ:** Liberty Univ, grad. **Career:** Football player (retired); Denver Broncos, 1994, tight end & fullback, 1995-2004, 2005; Orlando Predators, 2007. **Honors/Awds:** Two Super Bowl rings, Broncos, 1998, 1999; Named Second-team All-State; All-Conf, All-Dist & All-County Honors; Named Top 100 Athletes of Jacksonville, 1999; Pro Bowl, 2001; Ed Block Courage Award, 2005.

## CARSWELL, GLORIA NADINE SHERMAN

Certified public accountant. **Personal:** Born Dec 27, 1951, Cairo, GA; daughter of Eugene Martin and Mary Martin; married Willie F Carswell Jr; children: Mercedes Elaine & John Garfield. **Educ:** Mercer Univ, Macon, Ga, BS, 1972; Fla State Univ, MA, 1976. **Career:** Grady Cty Bd Ed, math instr, 1972-74; Deloitte Haskins & Sells, sr acct, 1976-81; Charter Oil Co, plng analyst, 1981-82; Charter Co, sr internal auditor, 1982-83, mgr internal finance reporting, 1983-86; AT & T Am Transtech, mgr ESOP rec keeping, 1986-94; JEA, mgr, 1994-. **Orgs:** Fla Inst CPA's, Am Inst CPA's; Jacksonville Women Network; Jr League Jacksonville; Community Connectors Inc; Nat Coun Negro Women. **Home Addr:** 1634 Dunsford Rd, Jacksonville, FL 32207-4234, **Home Phone:** (904)399-1523. **Business Addr:** Manager, JEA, 21 W Church St, Jacksonville, FL 32202, **Business Phone:** (904)632-6257.

## CARTER, DR. ALLEN C.

Psychologist. **Educ:** Morehouse Col, BA; Columbia Univ, PhD, clin psychol. **Career:** Univ Calif Sch Med, internship; Morehouse Col, Wellness Resource Ctr, clin psychologist, dir clin serv, 2004; Atlanta, Ga, pvt pract, psychologist, currently; WSB-TV, Channel 2, consult; WAGA, Channel 5, consult; Jet Mag, consult; Cable News Network, consult; Ebony Mag, consult; Atlanta Tribune & Atlanta Daily World, writer; Who/What Am I Inc, psychologist, currently. **Orgs:** Comt Advan Prof Pract Am Psychol Asn; pres, Ga State Bd Examiners Psychologists; pres, Ga Psychol Asn; Bd Prof Affairs; Comt Urban Initiative; Comt Recruitment, Training & Retention Minority Psychologists; CAPP Liaison State Leadership Organizing Comt; bd dir, CAPP Coordr Comt; Sub comt Implementations Integration Diverse Pract Agenda; consult, Govt Rels Pract Directorate; Personnel Sub comt Pract Directorate; Bd Conven Affairs. **Honors/Awds:** Karl F Heiser Presidential Award, Am Psychol Asn, 2000. **Special Achievements:** The first African American elected President of state leaders for the American Psychological Association; One of the highest elected African Americans in the American Psychological Association. Author: "What is This Thing Called I". **Business Addr:** Clinical Psychologist, Who/What Am I Inc, 600 W Peachtree St NW Suite 1570, Atlanta, GA 30308, **Business Phone:** (404)874-9207.

## CARTER, ALPHONSE HALEY

School administrator, association executive, executive. **Personal:** Born Oct 3, 1928, Baton Rouge, LA; son of Elvinna Pritchard Yarborough (deceased) and Haley (deceased); married Carolyn McCraw; children: Cynthia Susan. **Educ:** Albany St Col, attended 1957; Duquesne Univ, BS, 1961; Univ Cincinnati, PhD, 1975. **Career:** School administrator (retired); R Housing Authority City Pittsburgh, interviewer, 1961-62, asst mgr, 1962; Kroger Co, mgt trainee, 1962-63, store mgt, 1963-65, div indust engineering, 1965-66, div personnel mgt, 1966-68, corp personnel coord, 1968-72; Carter Carter & Assoc Inc, mgt consult pres; 1972-76, dir, human resources, 1976-81; Westinghouse Elec Corp, Pittsburgh, Pa, mgr, Corp Qual training, 1981-86; Grambling St Univ, Grambling, La, assoc prof, mgt, 1986-88; Hampton Univ, Hampton, Va, dean, sch bus, 1988-99. **Orgs:** Nat Asn Advan Colored People, 1946-; Soc Advan Mgt, 1958-; Urban League, 1958-; BOAZF & AM, 1960-; Personnel Asn, 1966-; bd mem, Cit Com Youth, 1969; Nat Alliance Businessmen Col Cluster, 1969-72; bd mem, Opportunities Industrialization Ctr, 1969-72; block club pres, Homewood-Brushton Improv Asn, 1958-61; bd mem, Victory Neighborhood Serv Agency, 1969-72; Community Chest, 1970-72; Nat Urban League, 1970-71; met dir, Nat Alliance Businessmen, 1971; trustee, Funds Self Enterprise, 1972-; Task Force Com Univ Cincinnati Sch Educ, 1972; adv com, Retired Sr Vol Prog, 1972-73; Alpha Mu Sigma Prof Fraternity Mgt Devel, 1974; pres, Churchill Area Kiwanis, 1978-79; lt gov Kiwanis Div 6-A, 1980-81; bd mem, Allegheny Trails Boy Scout Coun, 1979; bd mem, Hampt Parking Authority, 1990-; bd mem, Va Peninsula Chamber Com, 1991-; bd mem, Penninsula Chap, Nat Conf Christians & Jews, 1990; Delta Beta Lambda Chap; Alpha Phi Alpha Fraternity, 1995. **Honors/Awds:** Alpha Mu Sigma Award for Excellence Scholarship Achievement Management, 1975. **Home Addr:** 15 Pine Ridge Rd, Arlington, MA 02476-7501.

## CARTER, ANTHONY JEROME

Manager, programmer analyst. **Personal:** Born Jun 28, 1956, Tuscaloosa, AL; son of George Jr and Hazel; married Anna; children: Anthony Jerrard. **Educ:** Barry Univ, BS, comput sci, 1988. **Career:** SystOne, sr syst analyst/team leader, 1978-89; Burger King Corp, sr programmer analyst, dist mgr, 1989-. **Orgs:** Cub master, Boy Scouts Am, 1991-; Leadership Miami, 1992-; Burger King Reach Adv Comt; Cre Acad Cities Schs/Burger King Acad Prog; Kids Power Work Prog; adv, Jr Achievement. **Honors/Awds:** Americas Best & Brightest, Dollars and Sense Magazine, 1992. **Home Addr:** 18162 27th St, Miramar, FL 33029, **Home Phone:** (954)432-0450. **Business Addr:** Senior Programmer Analyst, Burger King Corp, 17777 Old Cutler Rd, Miami, FL 33157, **Business Phone:** (305)378-3112.

**CARTER, ANTONIO MARCUS.** **See CARTER, TONY A.**

## CARTER, ARLINGTON W., JR.

Executive. **Personal:** Born Mar 13, 1933, Chicago, IL; son of Arlington Sr and Martha; married Constance E Hardiman. **Educ:** IL Inst Tech, BSEE, 1961. **Career:** Boeing Co, Seattle Housing Develop, exec dir, 1971-73, prog mgr, 1973-77, gen mgr, 1977-81, prog mgr, 1981-85, gen mgr space syst, 1985-88, Defense Syst Div, vpres, 1988-89, Missile Syst Div, vpres & gen mgr, 1989-90, CQ 1, vpres, 1990-93, Facil & Capital Investments, vpres, 1993-98; Assoc Mem Inst Engrs, co-chm exec bd. **Orgs:** chmn, Western Region Nat Asn Advan Colored People, 1966; chmn, King County Personnel Bd, 1970-77; exec bd mem, United Way, 1978-82; Nat Space Club, 1981-85; pres, Boeing Mgt Asn, 1982-84; exec bd mem, Seattle Comt Col Found, 1982-85; Am Defense Prepared Assoc; exec bd mem, Metrop YMCA; Seattle Urban League; exec bd mem, Seattle Hearing & Speech Ctr; secy & treas, Northwest Chap Ill Inst Alumni Asn; NC A&T Bd Visitors; Am Inst Aeronaut & Astronaut; Ill Inst Tech Pres's Coun; Nat Adv Comt Nat Engg Educ Coaltion; bd dir, Seattle Alliance Educ; bd dir, Seattle Pub Libr Found; bd dirs, Sand Pt Country Club; co-chmn, exec adv comt, Advan Minority Interest Engg. **Honors/Awds:** Black Engineer of the Year, 1990; Professional Achievement Award, Ill Inst Tech, 1991. **Home Addr:** 722 35th Ave, Seattle, WA 98122-5204, **Home Phone:** (206)324-9995.

## CARTER, DR. BARBARA LILLIAN

Educator. **Personal:** Born Jun 20, 1942, Mexia, TX. **Educ:** Fisk Univ, AB, 1963; Brandeis Univ, MA, 1967, PhD, 1972; Harvard Univ, Inst Educ Mgt, attended 1984. **Career:** Fed City Col, asst prof 1969-72, from assoc provost to assoc prof, 1972-77; Univ Dist Columbia, assoc vpres & prof, 1977-80, vpres acad affairs 1980-81; Spelman Col, provost, vpres acad affairs & dean 1981-, actg pres, 1986-87, prof sociol & Anthrop, currently; Fel Aspen Inst Humanistic Studies, 1981; Fel Woodrow Wilson, 1963. **Orgs:** Phi Beta Kappa, 1963; Fel Nat Inst Ment Health, 1964-67; Am Sociol Asn, 1969-; bd dir YWCA Atlanta, 1982-; bd dir, United WayAtlanta 1985-, Pub Brdcst Asn, 1985-; bd trustee, Atlanta Col Art, 1986-; bd trustee, Chatham Col. **Home Addr:** 1301 DeFoors Mill Dr, Atlanta, GA 30318. **Business Addr:** Professor, Spelman College, Gills Hall Rm 319 350 Spelman Lane SW Suite 325, Atlanta, GA 30314-4399, **Business Phone:** (404)681-3642.

## CARTER, BILLY L.

Lawyer. **Personal:** Born Montgomery, AL; married Brenda T. **Educ:** Tuskegee Inst, BS, 1967; Howard Payne Univ Law Sch, JD, 1970; Univ Va, attended 1971. **Career:** Gray Seay & Langford, atty, 1970-71; Gray Seay & Langford, assoc atty, 1974-; Recorder's Ct City Tuskegee, prosecutor atty, 1974-; AUS, Ft Meade, Md, chief defence coun; Carter & Knight Law Offices, atty, currently. **Orgs:** Am Bar Asn; Nat Bar Asn; Am Trial Lawyers Asn; Ala Bar Asn; Ala Black Lawyers Asn; DC Bar Asn; Kappa Alpha Psi. **Honors/Awds:** Distinguished Military Graduate, 1967. **Home Addr:** 1120 S Ct St, Montgomery, AL 36104-4900, **Home Phone:** (334)262-2723. **Business Addr:** Attorney, Carter & Knight Law Offices, 1120 S Ct St, Montgomery, AL 36104-4900, **Business Phone:** (334)262-2723.

## CARTER, BUTCH (CLARENCE EUGENE CARTER, JR.)

Basketball executive, basketball coach, basketball player. **Personal:** Born Jun 11, 1958, Springfield, OH; married Jill; children: Brandon, Blake & Baron. **Educ:** Ind Univ, BA, mkt, attended 1980. **Career:** Basketball player, basketball coach (retired), exec; Los Angeles Lakers, small forward, 1980-81; Ind Pacers, shooting guard, 1981-84; New York Knicks, shooting guard, 1984-85; Philadelphia 76ers, 1985; Cincinnati Slammers, 1985-86; Mid town Ohio High Sch, coach, 1986-88; Long Beach State Univ, asst basketball coach, 1989; Univ Dayton, asst coach, 1990-91; Milwaukee Bucks, asst coach, 1991-96; Toronto Raptors, asst coach, 1997-98, head coach, 1998-2001; Carter Group Can, 2001-11; Toyota Bastrop, motivational speaker, 2001-13; Carter Group Inc, group chief exec ofiicer, 2001-13; Can Basketball League LP, gen partner, 2013-. **Orgs:** Big Bros, Big Sisters, 1977-80; founder, Energy Loonie, 2013. **Honors/Awds:** NBA draft, 1980; Ohio Coach of the Year, AP, 1988; Athletic Hall of Fame, 1998; Supplier of Year, Delphi Automotive Group, 2002; Toyota President Award, 2009. **Business Addr:** General Partner, Canadian Basketball League LP, 120 Eglinton Ave E 8th Fl, Toronto, ON M4P 1E2, **Business Phone:** (416)322-5188.

## CARTER, CECILIA K.

Association executive, executive director. **Educ:** Northwestern Univ, BA, psychol, 1980; Kellogg Grad Sch Mgt, MBA, mkt & finance, 1985; Univ Nh, hon degree. **Career:** Starbucks Corp, vpresof global diversity, policy & advocacy, 2011-13; Starbucks Found, gen mgr; UBS Found, head community affairs & exec dir, 2006-10; AstraZeneca; Pfizer; JP Morgan Chase; ABB Inc; Am Express, mgr-corp card, 1987-89; AT&T; GE Small Bus Solutions, sr vpres commun, 1989-2002; Burson-Marstellar's dir, 2004-06; PepsiCo, vpres human resource commun, 2014-16; Strategy Chick, owner, 2015-; Workplace Success Group LLC, consult & coach, 2016-; AIIR Consult, exec coach, 2016-. **Orgs:** Asn Nat Advertisers, chmn emerita bus-to-bus comt; Nat Black MBA Assoc; HandsOn Network's Corp Coun; Urban League Southern Conn, bd mem; GE's Corp Mkt Coun; exec dir, Rhythm & Blues Found, 2003-04. **Honors/Awds:** Dr, humane letters, Univ New Haven, 2010. **Business Addr:** Executive Director, Rhythm & Blues Foundation, PO Box 22438, Philadelphia, PA 19101, **Business Phone:** (215)985-4822.

## CARTER, CHARLES MICHAEL

Lawyer, executive, association executive. **Personal:** Born Apr 18, 1943, Boston, MA; son of Charles and Florence; children: Brandon H, Chad F, Courtney C & Candice A. **Educ:** Univ Calif, Berkley, BS, 1967; George Washington Univ Sch Law, JD, 1973. **Career:** Lawyer; Winthrop, Stimson, Putnam & Roberts, assoc, 1973-81; Singer Comp, div coun & finance staff & investment coun, 1981-83; RJR Nabisco Inc, sr corp coun, 1983-87; Concurrent Comput Corp, vpres, gen coun & secy Corp Develop, 1987; Dole Food Co Inc, bd dir, 2013, exec vpres & gen coun, currently; Securitas Security Serv USA Inc, exec vpres, gen goun & corp secy, Currently. **Orgs:** Am Bar Asn; Nat Bar Asn; trustee, George Wash Univ; dir, HCE Corp. **Home Addr:** 542 W Farms Rd, Howell, NJ 07731, **Home Phone:** (908)938-5307. **Business Addr:** Executive Vice President, General Counsel, Securitas Security Services USA Inc, 2 Campus Dr, Parsippany, NJ 07054-4400, **Business Phone:** (973)267-5300.

**CARTER, CHESTER C.** **See Obituaries Section.**

## CARTER, CHRIS (CHRISTOPHER GARY CARTER)

Football player. **Personal:** Born Sep 27, 1974, Tyler, TX. **Educ:** Univ Tex. **Career:** Football player (retired); New Eng Patriots, defensive back & free safety, 1997-99; Cincinnati Bengals, defensive back & strong safety & free safety, 2000-01; Houston Texans, defensive back, 2002.

## CARTER, CHRISTOPHER ANTHONY

Police officer. **Personal:** Born Jul 23, 1963, Columbus, GA; son of Jeff Fred and Artha Dean; married Gwendolyn Denise Martin; children: Precious Gwendolyn. **Educ:** Columbus Col, attended 1983; Columbus Area Voc Sch, attended 1984. **Career:** Blue Cross & Blue Shield, electronic data processor, 1980-81; Manpower Temp Serv, data entry operator, 1983-84; Columbus Police Dept, patrolman, 1984; Ga State Patrol, trooper, currently. **Orgs:** Family Law Bar Asn, 1981; Voice Tibet, 1981; YMCA, 1984; master guide, Pathfinders, 1990; Prof Bowlers Asn; FOP. **Honors/Awds:** Officer of the Year, Columbus Exchange Club, 1992; Officer of the Year, Optimist Club, 1992; Officer of the Year, Am Legion No 35, 1992; Officer of the Year, Columbus Police Dept, 1992; GEO's Officer of the Year, Am Legion 40/8, 1992. **Special Achievements:** Poems published by the Columbus Times, Columbus Ledger/Enquirer, and various other sources, 1987-; Most commentated officer in the history of the Columbus Police DPT, 1992; third place winner for Officer of the Year for the United States, 1992; first black officer to be Officer of the Year for Columbus, 1992; Published: From My Heart To You. **Home Addr:** 120 Cosby Rd, Junction City, GA 31812-4202, **Home Phone:** (706)269-2707. **Business Addr:** Trooper, GA State Patrol, 7800 Scenic Heights, Manchester, GA 31816, **Business Phone:** (706)846-3106.

**CARTER, CLARENCE EUGENE, JR.** **See CARTER, BUTCH.**

## CARTER, CRIS (GRADUEL CHRISTOPHER DARIN CARTER)

Football player, television broadcaster, football coach. **Personal:** Born Nov 25, 1965, Troy, OH; son of Duron; married Melanie Morgan; children: Duron Christopher & Monterae. **Educ:** Ohio State Univ, grad. **Career:** Football player (retired), analyst; Philadelphia Eagles, wide receiver, 1987-89; Minn Vikings, wide receiver, 1990-2001; Miami Dolphins, wide receiver, 2002; St. Thomas Aquinas High Sch, asst coach, offensive advisor, 2005; Entertainment & Sports Programming Network, sunday nat football league countdown analyst, monday night countdown analyst; Eltekon Mgt Group, co-founder; HBO, inside nat football league host, currently; Yahoo Sports, nat football league analyst, currently; ordained minister. **Honors/Awds:** Pro Bowl, 1993-2000; National Football League Extra Effort Award, 1994; First-team All-Pro selection, 1994, 99; Bart Starr Award, Athletes in Action, 1994; Citizen Athlete Award, Midwest Sports Channel, 1995; Byron "Whizzer" White Award, Nat Football League Players Asn, 1998; Walter Payton Man of the Year, 1999; Minnesota Vikings Ring of Honor; Alumni Wide Receiver of the Year, Nat Football League, 2000; Ohio State Univ Men's Varsity "O" Hall Fame, 2003; Pro Football Hall of Fame, 2013. **Special Achievements:** Two Year Total of 244 Catches was the Most In National Football League History. **Business Addr:** Host, HBO, 1100 Avenue of the Americas, New York, NY 10036, **Business Phone:** (212)512-1000.

## CARTER, DAISY

Government official. **Personal:** Born Oct 17, 1931, Stuart, FL; daughter of Robert C and Lottie Thompson Simmons; children: Marilyn D Jewett. **Educ:** St Joseph's Col, social work, 1972; Temple Univ, BS, recreation admin, 1980. **Career:** Government Offical (retired); Philadelphia Dept Recreation, ctr recreation leader, asst day camp dir, drama specialist, dist coordr retarded prog, 1968-71; Zion Church, ctr supvr, 1969-70, sr citizen's community worker, 1971-72; E Ger town Recreation Ctr, day camp dir, 1972-78, sr citizen's prog supvr, 1972-81; Penrose Playground, ctr supvr, 1981-88; Juniata Pk Older Adult Ctr, prog dir, 1989-91, therapeut recreation prog dir, 1989-91; City Philadelphia, Dept Recreation, ctr supvr, 1991-99, grant coordr, 1996-99. **Orgs:** Penn Pk & Recreation Soc; Penn Therapeut Recreation Soc; Black Social Workers Asn; Nat Pk & Recreation Asn; Nat Therapeut Recreation Asn; Nat Recreation & Parks Asn Ethnic Minority Soc; Philadelphia Young Women Christian Asn; Nat Asn Advan Colored People; Philadelphia People Fund; W Mt Airy Neighbors; chairperson, PA Pk & Recreation Soc Minority & Women Comm; comm chairperson, State Rep David P Richardson Jr, Sr Citizens & Recreation Progs; pres & bd dir, Temple Univ Health, Phys Educ, Recreation, & Dance Alumni Comm Chmn; bd dir, HPERD Alumni Temple's Gen Alumni Bd; bd dir & vpres, Temple Alumni; bd mem, Pa Chap; Nat Coalition 100 Black Women, 1986; life mem, Nat Coun Negro Women, Philadelphia Coun, 1986-; Temple Univ Alumni Athletic Comt, 1987-99; bd mem, Quantum Leap Publ I, 1990-; pres, Temple Univ Col HPERD Alumni Asn; bd mem, historian, Ethnic Minority Soc, Nat Recreation & Parks; adv comm, Intercolgiate Athletics, Temple Univ, 1998, steering comm; bd dir, Hist Lyric Theater, 1999-; Recreation Adivsory Bd, City Stuart, 2000-; second vpres & exec comm, Martin County Dem Party, 2001-. **Home Addr:** 1352 SE Madison Ave Sarita Hts, Stuart, FL 34996, **Home Phone:** (772)219-7363.

## CARTER, DALE LAVELLE

Football player, executive. **Personal:** Born Nov 28, 1969, Covington, GA; children: Nigel Warrior. **Educ:** Univ Tenn, grad. **Career:** Football player (retired), exec; Kans City Chiefs, punt returner, right cornerback, 1992-93, right cornerback, 1994, left cornerback, 1995-98; Denver Broncos, cornerback, right cornerback, 1999-2000; Minn

Vikings, left cornerback, 2001; New Orleans Saints, left cornerback, right cornerback, 2002-03; Baltimore Ravens, defensive back, left cornerback, strong safety, 2003-05; Olivia Carter Found, owner. **Honors/Awds:** National Football League Rookie of the Year, Pro Football Writers, 1992; Bert Bell Trophy, 1992; Rookie of the Year, UPI AFL-AFC, 1992; Four Times Pro Bowler, 1992-97; Pro Bowl, 1994-97.

### CARTER, DARLINE LOURETHA
Library administrator. **Personal:** Born Dec 7, 1933, Pinola, MS; daughter of Cora Lee and Gennie. **Educ:** Tougaloo Col, BS, elem educ, 1955; Syracuse Univ, NY, MLS, 1960. **Career:** Library administrator (retired); Cleveland Miss, sch librn, 1955-59; Syracuse Univ, asst librn, 1959-60; Tougaloo Col Miss, circulation librn, 1960-62; W Islip Pub Libr, NY, c's librn, 1962-66, asst dir, 1966-69, libr dir, 1969-2000. **Orgs:** Exhibs Comn, Mem Comn, NY Libr Asn, 1962-85; Am Libr Week Comn; HW Wilson Awards Jury; Mem Comn, Am Libr Asn, 1969-85; vpres rec sect & chmn, Pub Libr Dir Asn, 1969-85; 6th Ann Libr Admin Devel Prog, Univ Md, 1972; hon life mem, W Islip PTA, 1971; exec bd, Suffolk Co Libr Asn, 1973-85; reaccreditation comn, Palmer Sch Libr & Info Sci, Long Island Univ, CW Post Ctr, 1983; pres, Suffolk Libr Consortium Inc, 1986-92; pres, Spring Inst. **Home Addr:** 57 Mortimer Ave, Babylon, NY 11702.

### CARTER, DR. DAVID G., SR.
School administrator, educator, scholar. **Personal:** Born Oct 25, 1942, Dayton, OH; son of Richard and Esther Dunn; married Sandra C Holley; children: Ehrika Carter Gladden, David Holley, David George Jr & Jessica. **Educ:** Cent State Univ, BS, 1965; Miami Univ, MEd, 1968; Ohio State Univ, PhD, 1971. **Career:** Dayton City Schs, 6th grade teacher, 1965-68, asst prin, 1968-69, elem prin, 1969-70, unit facilitator, 1970-71; Dayton Pub Sch, serv unit dir, 1971-73; Wright State Univ, adj prof, 1972; Booz-Allen & Hamilton Inc, consult, 1972-73; Pa Dept Educ, consult, 1973-77; So Ea Delco Sch Dist, consult, 1973-83; Penn State Univ, Dept Educ Admin, from asst prof to assoc prof, 1973-77; Syracuse Univ Res Corp, consult, 1976; Univ Conn, Dept Educ Admin, assoc prof, 1977-79, prof, 1980-, Sch Educ, assoc dean, 1977-82, assoc vpres acad affairs, 1982-; Pressional Develop Assoc, consult, 1979-80; Jour Eduquity & Leadership, ed bd, 1980; Milwaukee Pub Sch, consult, 1980; Windham I Comm Hosp, corporator, 1982, trustee, 1984; Univ Conn, Storrs, CT, assoc vpres acad affairs & assoc dean 1982-88; Windham Healthcare Sys Inc, dir, 1984; Eastern Conn State Univ, Willimantic, pres, 1988-06; Conn State Univ Syst, chancellor, 2006-11. **Orgs:** Good Samaritan Ment Health Adv, 1968-73; bd trustee, Dayton Mus Nat Hist, 1973; Ctr County Ment Health & Ment Retardation Adv Bd, 1974-76; Adv Coun Bd Ment Health Prog Dev, 1977-80; Gov's Task Force Jail & Prison Overcrowding, 1980; bd dir, Nat Organiz Legal Prob Educ, 1980-83; bd dir, New Eng Reg Exchange, 1981-; Conn State chmn, 1990-94; Urban League Greater Hartford, bd dir, 1994-97; Millennium Leadership Initiative, founding mem 1996, co chair, 1996-99; IAUP/UN Comm Disarmament Educ, Conflict Resolution & Peace, 1997-; Marine Corps Univ, 1998-; Am Coun Educ, 1999-2001; bd visitor, 2001, chair, 2003-, Comm Div III NCAA, chair, Am Asn State Col & Univ, 2003-; Phi Delta Kappa; Am Educ Res Asn; Nat Asn Advan Colored People; Pi Lambda Theta; Phi Kappa Phi; Int Union Univ Pres; Hartford Club; Am Asn State Cols & Univs; bd dir, Am Coun Educ; fel Nat Col Athletic Asn Div III Presidents Coun; bd dir, Coun Higher Educ Accreditation; secy, Nat Asn Syst Heads; bd, New Eng Bd Higher Educ; bd trustee, Eastern States Expos; Exec Comt Conn Ctr Sci & Explor; Steering Comt. **Home Addr:** 9 Charles Rd, Storrs, CT 06268. **Business Addr:** Chancellor, Connecticut State University System, 39 Woodland St, Hartford, CT 06105, **Business Phone:** (860)493-0000.

### CARTER, EDWARD EARL
Executive, mayor. **Personal:** Born Oct 9, 1939, Havelock, NC; son of Nettie Morris and Leander; married Evelyn Jean; children: Regina Yvette, Tonya Denise & Jacquelyn. **Educ:** Va State Univ, Petersburg, VA, BS, 1963; Pitt Community Col, Greenville, NC, AAS, 1979. **Career:** Columbia Univ, Hudson Labs, NY, res physicist, 1962-63; Burroughs Wellcome Co, Greenville, NC, Admin Servs Dept, head & executive scientist, 1971-95; City Greenville, NC, mayor, 1987-89. **Orgs:** Life mem, Alpha Phi Alpha Fraternity, 1960-; Pitt County Mayors Asn, 1987-89; Black Nat Conf Mayors, 1987-89; Transp Policy Commun Safety Comn, NC League Cities, 1988-89; Nat Asn Advan Colored People; bd dir, Govs Crime Comn NC, 1988-; bd dir, Pitt-Greenville Chamber Com, 1988-89; bd dir, Proj Parenting, 1988-; charter mem & bd dir, Milennia Community Bank, 2001-. **Special Achievements:** Second African American, inducted, group honorary compatriots during Saturdays ceremony. **Home Addr:** 104 Fireside Rd, Greenville, NC 27834-1107, **Home Phone:** (252)757-3521.

### CARTER, ESTHER YOUNG
Educator. **Personal:** Born Feb 8, 1930, NC; daughter of Johnny Argro Young and Bertha Perry; married Robert; children: Gwendolyn C Adamson, Johnny Jerome & Robert Gilbert. **Educ:** NC Cent Univ, BS, 1953; Johnson C Smith Univ, elem educ cert; NC A&T State Univ, MS, 1975. **Career:** Carver Col, secy & teacher, 1954-59; Douglas Aircraft Co, secy, 1959-66; Greensboro Pub Schs, teacher, 1966-92. **Orgs:** Nat Educ Asn, 1966-92; Greensboro Alumnae Chap, 1976; corresp secy, 1986-90, pres, 1990-94, Delta Sigma Theta Sorority Inc; life mem, NC Cent Alumni Asn; Black Child Develop Inst, 1988-; Metrop Coun Negro Women, 1989-; Pinochle Bugs Social & Civic Club Inc, Greensboro Chap, pres, 1991-; NEA-R, 1993-. **Home Addr:** 908 Highgrove Ave, Greensboro, NC 27405-5502, **Home Phone:** (919)375-3447.

### CARTER, ETTA F.
Educator. **Personal:** Born Warren, OH; daughter of Edward and Mamie Wilborn; married William T; children: Carla F & William T Jr. **Career:** Chicago Bd Educ, elem teacher & reading spec, 1966-79; New York Bd Educ, coordr stud serv, 1986-88; Pub Sch 220, interim prin, 1987-89; Pub Sch 80, asst prin, 1989-93; Pub Sch 50, prin, 1993-96; Dist 16, dep supt, 1996-98; Bd Educ City NY, dep supt, 1998-. **Orgs:** Pres, Beta Omicron Chap, 1989-; bd dir, Beta Omicron Early Childhood Ctr, 1991-; ASCD, 1993-; bd dir, Big Sister Ctr, 1996-; Phi Delta Kappa, 1998-; conf co-chairperson, Nat Sorority Phi Delta Kappa Inc, 1999-. **Business Addr:** Deputy Superintendent, Board of Education City New York, 109-59 Inwood St, Jamaica, NY 11435, **Business Phone:** (718)526-5523.

### CARTER, FREDRICK JAMES
Basketball player, basketball coach, business owner. **Personal:** Born Feb 14, 1945, Philadelphia, PA; married Jacqueline; children: Stephanie, Mia, Christopher, Amee, Jason & Aaron. **Educ:** Mt St Mary's Univ, Emmitsburg, MD, eng, 1969. **Career:** Basketball player, basketball coach (retired), executive; Baltimore Bullets, 1969-71; Philadelphia 76ers, 1971-76, asst coach, 1987-89, head coach, 1992-94; Wash Bullets, 1974; Milwaukee Bucks, 1976-77; Atlanta Hawks, asst coach, 1981-83; Chicago Bulls, asst coach, 1983-85; Wash Bullets, asst coach, asst coach, 1985-87; TNT, studio analyst; Entertainment & Sports Programming Network, basketball analyst, Nat Basketball Asn TV, analyst, currently; SAMJAC Indust Inc, owner & pres, currently. **Orgs:** Instrumental devt & instr mayor Wash's inner-city basketball Clinics; Little City Found. **Business Addr:** Owner, President, Samjac Industries Inc, 5070 Parkside Ave, Philadelphia, PA 19131, **Business Phone:** (215)877-9513.

### CARTER, DR. GENE RAYMOND
Chief executive officer, school administrator. **Personal:** Born Apr 10, 1939, Staunton, VA; married Lillian Young; children: Gene Raymond Jr & Scott Robert. **Educ:** Va State Univ, Petersburg, BA, hist, 1960; Boston Univ, MA, educ admin, 1967; Teachers Col Columbia Univ, NY, EdD, instrnl & curricular pract, 1973. **Career:** St Emma Mil Acad & Norfolk Pub Sch, teacher, 1960-69; Campostella Jr High Sch, educ develop spec, intern prin, 1969-70; Maury High Sch, Norfolk VA, asst prin instr, 1970-71; Englewood Pub Sch NJ, admin asst res & planning, 1972-73; Norfolk Pub Sch, supvr curric resources, 1973-74; Sch Educ Old Dom Univ, Norfolk VA, adj assoc prof 1974; Norfolk Pub Schs, reg asst supt, 1979-83, supt sch 1983. **Orgs:** Bd mem, Tidewater Juv Detention Home Adv Bd, 1978-80; bd mem, Comm Mgt Serv YMCA Norfolk, 1978-80; pres, exec bd mem Sunrise, Optimist Club Norfolk, Va, 1979-80; pres, Gene R Carter & Assoc, Chesapeake VA, 1979; bd mem, St Marys Infant Home Norfolk, 1980; bd trustee, Va Wesleyan Col, Educ Comt States Adv Bd; bd dir, Norfolk Southern Corp; bd dir, Am Bar Asn Adv Comn Pub Educ; bd dir, Am-Israel Friendship League Educ Adv Comt; bd dir, Educ Comn States Adv Bd; bd dir, Nat Comn Serv Learning; bd dir, Nat Comn Asia Schs; bd dir, Longview Found; exec dir & chief exec officer, 1992-2014, emer exec dir, 2014-, Asn Supvr & Curriculam Develop. **Home Addr:** 1570 Spring Gate Dr Suite 7206, Mc Lean, VA 22102-3430. **Business Addr:** Emeritus Executive Director, Association for Supervision & Curriculum Development, 1703 N Beauregard St, Alexandria, VA 22311-1714, **Business Phone:** (703)578-9600.

### CARTER, HON. GEOFFREY NORTON
Commissioner, judge. **Personal:** Born Jan 28, 1944, St. Louis, MO; son of Robert and Daphne Louise Tyus. **Educ:** St Louis Univ Sch Arts & Sci, BA (cum laude), span, 1966; St Louis Univ Law Sch, JD, 1969. **Career:** Legal Aid Soc St Louis, staff atty, 1969-70; USAF, judge advocate, 1970-74; atty pvt pract, 1975-88; New Motor Vehicle Bd, Calif, admin law judge, 1982-88; Alameda County, cert rev hearing officer, 1984-88; Citizens Complaint Bd, Oakland, comnr, 1980-82; Oakland Munic Ct, Oakland, CA, comnr, 1988-98; Alameda City Super Ct, comnr, 1998-. **Orgs:** Asn Black Collegians, 1967-69; Alameda County Bar Asn, 1975-; bd dir, 1976-77, secy, 1979-, vpres, 1980-, Charles Houston Bar Asn; Nat Lawyers Guild, 1976-87; Calif Attorneys Criminal Justice, 1976-86; Criminal Courts Bar Asn, 1976; treas, 1978-89, bd dir, 1977, Calif Asn Black Lawyers; Nat Bar Asn, 1979-80; Calif Pub Defenders Asn, 1980-88; cmnr, City Oakland Citizens' Complaint Bd, 1980; pres, Alameda County Dem Lawyers Club, 1984; mem bd, Heritage Trails Fund, 1987-97; Calif Judges Asn, 1989-; bd dir, Bay Area Ridge Trail Coun, 1994-; bd dir, vpres, Metrop Equestrian Preserv Soc; pres, E Bay Area Trails Coun; pres, Eden Saddle Club; vpres, Oakland City Stables; Bay Area Ridge Trail Coun; Metrop Horsemen's Asn; San Ramon Valley Horsemen's Asn. **Home Addr:** 11136 Sun Valley Dr, Oakland, CA 94605, **Home Phone:** (510)568-5812. **Business Addr:** Commissioner, Alameda County Superior Court, 600 Washington St, Oakland, CA 94607, **Business Phone:** (510)268-7606.

### CARTER, GRADUEL CHRISTOPHER DARIN. See CARTER, CRIS.

### CARTER, GWENDOLYN BURNS
Educator. **Personal:** Born Nov 21, 1932, Lufkin, TX; daughter of Robert and Tressie Stokes; married Purvis Melvin; children: Purvis Melvin III, Frederick Earl & Burnest Denise. **Educ:** Univ Denver; Univ Colo; Univ Southern Ill; Univ Tex; Huston Tilloston Col, BS, 1954; Prairie View A&M Univ, MEd, 1960. **Career:** Educator (retired); Hempstead Elem Sch, resource teacher. **Orgs:** Pres, Jack & Jill Am Inc, 1980-82; pres, Waller Co Teachers Assoc, 1983-84; career treas, Top Ladies Distinction Inc, 1985-87; Coun Except C; Nat Educ Asn; adv coun, Except C, 1986-; youth develop comn, Mt Corinth Baptist Church, 1986-; pres, Top Ladies Distinction, 1988-; vpres, Delta Sigma Theta Sorority, 1988-. **Home Addr:** PO Box 2243, Prairie View, TX 77446, **Home Phone:** (936)857-3522.

### CARTER, HARRIET LASHUN
Executive, executive director. **Personal:** Born Feb 16, 1963, Muskegon, MI; daughter of John Edward and LuLa Fae Williams. **Educ:** Mich State Univ, E Lansing, BA, int rels, 1985; Cert Meeting Planner & Cert Hospitality Sales Prof. **Career:** Detroit Metro CVB, 1989; Bur's conv sales dept, acct exec; Muskegon Harbour Hilton, Muskegon, Mich, supvr, night auditor, 1986-88; Radisson Resort Hotel, Ypsilanti, Mich, sales mgr, 1987-89; Metro Detroit Conv & Visitors Bur, Detroit, Mich, acct exec, 1989, dir bur serv, currently. **Orgs:** Alpha Kappa Alpha Sorority Inc; Nat Coalition Black Meeting Planners; Relig Conf Mgt Asn; Int Soc Hisp Meeting Planners. **Home Addr:** 200 Riverfront Dr, Detroit, MI 48226-4594, **Home Phone:** (313)393-5316. **Business Addr:** Director Bureau Services, Detroit Metro Convention & Visitors Bureau, 211 W Ft St Suite 1000, Detroit, MI 48226, **Business Phone:** (313)202-1981.

### CARTER, J. B., JR.
Educator, manager. **Personal:** Born Oct 5, 1937, Pascagoula, MS; married Mary Mallard; children: J B III, Joy Bonita & Janelle Betrice. **Educ:** Tougaloo Col, BA, 1960. **Career:** Manager (retired); Pub Sch Miss, teacher coordr; Litton Industs, labr rels, pers mgr, EEO coor mgr; Keesler AFB, mgt specialist; Miss State Employ Security Comn, employ interviewer; Jackson Co Neighborhood Youth Corps, dir; Jackson Co Justice Ct, ct adminr, 1994-2003; Gulf Coast Safety Soc, secy, 1975-2005. **Orgs:** Jackson Co Civic Action Com, 1969; decon, First Christian Church; Omega Psi Phi Frat; chmn Pas-pt Handicap Comt, 1972; co-chmn, Bi-racial Com, Moss Pt Sch Syst, 1972; pres, Jackson Co Task Force; secy & bd trustee, Moss Pt Munic Separate Sch Dist, 1975; adv bd, Jackson Co Salvation Armys Bldg Fund Dr, 1975; bd trustee, Asbury Chapel African Methodist Episcopal Zion Church; mem adv bd, Gulf Coast Community Col. **Honors/Awds:** Omega Man of Year, 1967; Distinguished Service Award, Pas Point Jaycees, 1972; Outstanding Citizen, Jackson County Non-partisan Voters League, 1974. **Special Achievements:** First Black Employment Interviewer in Mississippi Employment Security Commission Office 1966. **Home Addr:** 10404 Twin Knoll Way, Upper Marlboro, MD 20772, **Home Phone:** (301)780-3383. **Business Addr:** Board of Trustee, Asbury Chapel African Methodist Episcopal Zion Church, 1109 Convent Ave, Pascagoula, MS 39567, **Business Phone:** (228)769-3899.

### CARTER, JACKIE
Vice president (organization), publisher. **Educ:** Hampton Univ, early childhood educ, 1975. **Career:** Teacher; Marvel Comics, vpres Marvel Kids, 1997-99; Sesame St Mag, assoc ed; Disney Publ Worldwide, ed dir, 2000-05; Scholastic Inc, vpres, publ, currently. **Honors/Awds:** 25 Influential Black Women in Business, "The Network Journal: Black Professionals & Small Business Magazine", 2010. **Business Addr:** Vice President, Publisher, Scholastic Inc, 557 Broadway, New York, NY 10012, **Business Phone:** (212)343-6100.

### CARTER, HON. JAMES
Educator, mayor, businessperson. **Personal:** Born Jul 6, 1944, Woodland, GA; son of Jimmie L and Mae Bell; children: Willie B, Isabell Huff, Millie Blount & Laura Taylo. **Educ:** Albany St Col, Albany, Ga, BS, bus, PE; Ga State Univ, Atlanta, Ga, 1968; Univ Ga, Athens, Ga, Finance, 1992. **Career:** Ctrl HS Talbotton, Ga, teacher, 1966; City Woodland, Woodland, Ga, mayor, 1982-; Self-employed, small bus mgr; Home S, Greenville, Ga, contract writer, 1988. **Orgs:** Baptist Stud Union; Nat Conf Black Mayors; Joint Ctr Polit Studies-SBCC; Nat Towns & Townships-GRWA; Small Towns; Ga Conf Black Mayors; Master Mason; Ga Asn Black Elected Officials; bd mem, Rural Develop Ctr; chair, Mayor's Motorcade; GMA, Munic & Finance Comt. **Honors/Awds:** Teacher of the Year, Cent High Sch, 1979; Named Man of the Century, Citizens Woodland, 1984; Man of the Century Award, Concerned Citizens, 1988; Special Alumni Award, Albany St Col, Albany, Ga, 1989; GMA Community Leadership Award, 1993; Community Leader Award, Nat Advan Asn Colored People, 1993; Man of the Year Award, Nat Advan Asn Colored People, 1994; Montel Williams Award, 1994; Outstanding Service Award, Rural Develp Ctr, 1997; Outstanding Citizen Award, Farm City, 1997; Children Research Award, St Judge Cancer, 1997; Community Service Award, St Judge C Hosp, 2000; Community Service Award, Delta Sigma Soroity, 2000; Outstanding Community Service Award, Nat Advan Asn Colored People, 2000. **Special Achievements:** First African Am mayor and judge of Woodland, GA. **Home Addr:** 8th Ave Martin L King Jr Dr, PO Box 148, Woodland, GA 31836-0148, **Home Phone:** (706)674-2386. **Business Addr:** Mayor, City of Woodland, 220 W South Ave, Woodland, GA 31863, **Business Phone:** (706)674-2700.

### CARTER, DR. JAMES EARL, JR.
Physician, surgeon. **Personal:** Born Oct 13, 1943, Kansas City, KS; son of James E Sr and Anna Sneed; married Nina Sharon Escoe; children: Chisty & Kimberly. **Educ:** Univ Mo, BS, 1965; Univ Mo, Md, 1969. **Career:** Walter Reed Hosp, internal med, 1969-70; Ventura County Med Ctr, resident, 1972-73; Wayne Miner Health Ctr, family physician, 1973-75; Family practr, 1975; Family physician & pres, 1975-; James E Carter Md PC, pres, currently. **Orgs:** Am Heart Asn, Kans City Chap; life mem, Nat Asn Advan Colored People; life mem, Africare; Metrop Med Soc. **Honors/Awds:** Fellowship Award, Am Acad Family Pract, 1975. **Home Addr:** 4307 W 125th Ter, Leawood, KS 66209-2203, **Home Phone:** (913)663-2365. **Business Addr:** Physician, President, James E Carter MD PC, 7800 Paseo Blvd, Kansas City, MO 64131-1859, **Business Phone:** (816)523-3055.

### CARTER, DR. JAMES EDWARD, III
School administrator. **Personal:** Born Sep 3, 1938, Columbia, SC; son of James E Jr and Lakesha Hudgens; married Judy Luchey; children: James E IV & Mason Johnson III. **Educ:** Howard Univ, attended 1958; Paine Col, BS, 1960; SC State Col, Med, 1973; Faith Col, LHD, 1978. **Career:** School administrator (retired); Richmond County Bd Educ, teacher, counr, prin, 1960-73; AUS, AUSR, instr med corps, 1963-67; Franklin LifeInsurance Co, agt, financial consult, 1969-72; Med Col Ga, recruiter, counr, assoc dean, stud affairs, 1973-97, Dept Pediat, prof emer. **Orgs:** Pres, Belair Hills Asn, 1973-75; vice dist rep, 7th Dist, Omega Psi Phi, 1974-77; chair, Black Heritage Community, 1975-; pres, Alpha Mu Boule; Sigma Pi Phi, 1979-81; appointee, Gov's Adv Coun Energy, 1980-82; pres, Nat Asn Med Minority Educ, 1983-85; pres, Nat Asn Stud Affairs Professionals, 1987-88; bd dir, Health Cent, 1988-91; appointee, Govenor's Intercultural Speakers Bur, Human Rels Comn, State Ga, 1990; appointee, Richmond County Comn Hist Preser, 1990; exec bd, Boy Scouts Am, 1993-; exec bd, Augusta Housing Authority, 1994-99; trustee, Hist Augusta; 1997-; Augusta African Am Hist Community, 1999-; comnr, Downtown DevelopAuthority, 1999-; chair, 1-cent sales tax community, 1999-2000; trustee, Augusta Mus Hist, 2002-. **Honors/Awds:** Distinguished Achievement Awards, United Negro Col Found, 1977-83; President Alumni Award, Paine Col, 1979 & 1997; Presidential Citation, Nat Asn Med Minority Educr, 1982, 1984, 1985, 1987, 1990 & 1996; Distinguished AlumniAward, Lucy C Laney High Sch, 1983; Arkansas Governor's Award, 1984; Presidential Award, Nat Asn Personnel Workers, 1985, 1989, 1991 & 1996; Nat Humanitarian Award, Chi Eta Phi, 1997. **Special Achievements:** Article, "The Need for Minorities in the Health Professions in the 80's:The National Crisis and the Plan for Action,"

1986; Augusta's black history guru. **Home Addr:** 1-7th St Suite 1001, Augusta, GA 30901-1364. **Business Addr:** Professor Emeritus, Medical College of Georgia, 1120 15th St, Augusta, GA 30912, **Business Phone:** (706)721-0211.

## CARTER, CDR JAMES HARVEY, JR. (JAY CARTER)

Neurosurgeon, educator. **Personal:** Born Jan 17, 1960, Raleigh, NC; son of James Harvey Sr and Jettie Lucille Strayhorn; married Brigit Maria. **Educ:** Morehouse Col, BA, psychol, 1981; Duke Univ, BHS, physician asst, 1986, MHS, physician asst, 1994. **Career:** Southeastern Emergency Med Serv, emergency med technician, dispatcher, 1980-81; Fulton County Alcoholism Treat Ctr, emergency med technician, 1980-81; Tom Higgs Serv, emergency med technician, 1981-82; NES Govt Serv Inc, physician asst, 1995-98; Duke Univ Med Ctr, physician asst, 1986-88, Div Neurosurg, Dept Surg, asst prof, 1986-, sr physician asst, 1988-96, clin assoc, 1996-2002, asst clin prof, 2002-. **Orgs:** Am Legion, Post No, 1981, 1995-; Triangle Area Phys Assts, vpres, 1988-91, pres, 1991-96; bd mem, chair, minority affairs comt, N Carolina Acad Physician Assts;, 1990-96 Compassionate Tabernacle Faith Missionary Baptist Church, 1992-, Finance Comt, 1994-97; trustee, NCAPA Endowment, 1992-98, bd dir, 1993-96, Conf Planning Comt, 1993-96; Alumni Steering Comt, 2001-, pres, 2006-; pres, NOSC Raleigh Wardroom, 2006; Asn Mil Surgeons US; Am Asn Surg Phys Asst; Naval Asn Phys Asst; Res Officers Asn US; US Naval Inst; Am Acad Physician Asst; Asn Neurol Phys Asst; Duke Univ Phys Asst Soc; Asn Med Serv Corps Officers USN; NC Med Soc; Nat Asn Emer Med Technician; Am Asn Neurol Surgeons; Southern Med Asn; Nat Asn Advan Colored People; pres & chair, Triangle Area Physician Assts, Community Serv Comt; health care adv bd ctr employ training, Southern High Sch Voc Adv Bd. **Honors/Awds:** Cert Merit, 1993; Cert Appreciation, Am Heart Asn, 1994; Cert Appreciation, Am Acad Phys Assts, 1994; Cert Appreciation, NC Acad Physician Assts, 1994; Cert Recognition, Church God Propey Youth Dept, 1995. **Special Achievements:** USNR, direct comn officer, 1988, comdr, 1989-, Camp Lejeune during Oper Desert Storm, 1990-91, Navy Oper Support Ctr, officer chg, 2007, Naval Res Oper Hosp Support Unit, med officer, 2009; Navy & Marine Corps Achievement Medal Gold Star; Armed Forces Res Medal Bronze Star; Expert Rifle Medal; Cert Appreciation; Lett Appreciation; Cert Commendation; Lett commendation; Sharpshooter Pistol Ribbon; Nat Defense Serv Medal Bronze Star. **Home Addr:** 1403 Ainsworth Blvd, Hillsborough, NC 27710, **Home Phone:** (919)732-6370. **Business Addr:** Assistant Professor of Surgery, Duke University Medical Center, 4518 Busse Bldg, Durham, NC 27710, **Business Phone:** (919)681-6421.

## CARTER, DR. JAMES P.

Chairperson, educator, pediatrician. **Personal:** Born Chicago, IL. **Educ:** Northwestern Univ, BS; Columbia Univ Sch Pub Health, MS, PhD. **Career:** Tulane Univ Sch Pub Health & Trop Med, Dept Nutrit & Nursing, prof, head & chmn; Ibadan Univ, chmn; Egypt, staff pediatrician. **Honors/Awds:** Numerous publ. **Business Addr:** Professor, Head & Chairman, Tulane University, Sch Pub Health & Trop Med, New Orleans, LA 70112, **Business Phone:** (504)988-5187.

## CARTER, JANDRA D.

Government official. **Personal:** Born May 11, 1948, St. Louis, MO; daughter of Larry Spinks and Mamie France Spinks; married Alvin; children: Brian, Traci Evans & Chaun. **Educ:** Univ Mo, Columbia, MO, BS, 1979; Cent Mo State Univ, Warrensburg, MO, MS, 1984. **Career:** Mo Div Youth Serv, Jefferson City, Mo, training officer, delinq prevspec, facil mgr, group leader, youth spec, 1971-81; Mo Dept Ment Health, Jefferson City, staff develop, 1981-84, dir invest, 1989-92, prog coordr, 1992-95, dir caring communities, 1995; Mo Dept Corrections, Jefferson City, dir training, 1984, Bd Probation & Parole, 1997-2002, Western Zone, asst div dir, 2002-06; Off Mo Gov Jay Nixon, Jefferson City, Mo, Citizens Adv Comt Corrections, 2010. **Orgs:** Nat Asn Blacks Criminal Justice, 1979-; State Training Adv Bd State Mo, 1984-89; pres, Mo Chap NABCJ, 1985-87; Self Eval Task Force Girl Scouts, 1990-; chair, adv bd, William Woods Col Sch Social Work, 1991-92; Mo State Employees Retirement Syst, currently. **Home Addr:** 12703 Rte B, St. Thomas, MO 65076-2133, **Home Phone:** (660)477-3640. **Business Addr:** Member, Missouri State Employees' Retirement System, 907 Wildwood Dr, Jefferson City, MO 65109, **Business Phone:** (573)632-6100.

## CARTER, JIMMY (J C CARTER)

Government official. **Personal:** Born Jun 12, 1947, Memphis, TN; married Sharon Singleton; children: Sherrie, Torrie & Denise. **Educ:** Univ Louisville, BS, mgt, 1974, MIM, 1978. **Career:** Jefferson Co Police Dept, 1972-80; US Dept of Justice, FBI asst dir, sr exec serv, 1995, FBI Acad, prog mgr & instr, supvr applicant, Atlanta FBI Off, admin asst spec agt. **Orgs:** Chief exec officer, Nat Orgn Black Law Enforcement; Int Asn Chiefs Police; FBI Nat Acad asn; Blacks Govt; Nat Exec Inst, 1999-. **Honors/Awds:** Presidential Rank Award, 2000. **Home Addr:** 2748 Pembaly Dr, Vienna, VA 22181.

## CARTER, JOANNE WILLIAMS

Educator, artist, community activist. **Personal:** Born Mar 19, 1935, Brooklyn, NY; daughter of Edgar T and Elnora Bing Morris; married Robert L; children: Anthony Tyrone, Tiffany Lucille & Janine Lynn Chevalier; married Bob. **Educ:** Brooklyn Col, City Univ NY, Brooklyn, NY, BA, 1976, MA, 1986. **Career:** High Sch Telecommunication Arts & Technol, registr; Citibank; Chase; New York, bd educ, 1974-94; prof artist, 1980-. **Orgs:** Patron, Studio Mus Harlem; adv coun, Brooklyn Mus Art; pres, Soc Preserv Weeksville & Bedford & Stuyvesant Hist; charter mem, Schomberg Soc Schomberg Libr NY; charter mem, Nat Mus Women Arts; patron & panelist, Nat Endowment Arts, Wash, DC, 1994; Delta Rho Chap, Alpha Kappa Alpha Sorority; mem, Brooklyn Chap, LINKS Inc; founding mem, Emily Pickens Club; pres, Eastville Hist Soc Sag Harbor; Artists Alliance E Hampton, NY; trustee, Sag Harbor, Whaling & Hist Mus; Warden, Vestry Christ Episcopal Church, Sag Harbor; Choral Soc Hamptons; rec secy, pres, Eastville Community Hist Soc, treas, currently. **Home Addr:** 153 Hampton St, Sag Harbor, NY 11963-4213, **Home Phone:** (631)725-3713.

## CARTER, DR. JOHN H.

Executive. **Personal:** Born Sep 26, 1948, Thomaston, GA; son of Augustus Jr and Rosa Mathews; married Susan Gibson; children: Gregory L & Candace M. **Educ:** Robert E Lee Inst, dipl, 1966; Morris Brown Col, BA, social studies, 1970; Univ Utah, MS, hr mgt, 1979; Univ Southern Calif, MS, mgt, 1989; Calif Coast Univ, DBA, bus, 2001. **Career:** Cambridge Sch Syst, instr, 1970; Southern Bell Tel & Tel Co, Atlanta, mgt asst, 1972-73, bus off mgr, 1973-74, 1976-77, personnel supr, 1974-76; dist mgr personnel admin, 1979-80, dist mgr copr plg, 1982-87, opers mgr supplier rels, dir pur, 1987-88, gen mgr, property & serv, 1989-91, asst vpres, procurement, property & serv mgt, 1991-92; Am Tel & Tel Co, Basking Ridge, NJ, dist mgr eeo goals anal & vpres, 1977-99, Atlanta, GA, dist mgr assessment, 1980-81; BellSouth Fel, vpres cop support, 1972-99, Univ Southern Calif, 1988-89, Operator Serv, pres, 1993-95, Corp Resources, pres, 1995-99; Wash D. C. MLK Memorial Found Inc, initial proj mgr, 1996-2000; City Atlanta, Mayor's Off, loan exec, 1992; Fleet & Serv, asst vpres, 1992-93; Carter & Carter LLC, managing partner, exec coach & owner, 2001-; Strayer Univ, adj prof bus, 2006-16. **Orgs:** Life mem, Alpha Phi Alpha Fraternity, 1967-, pres, 1969-70; pres, Mt Olive Jaycees NJ, 1977-78; chmn admin bd, SuccaSunna United Meth Chap, 1978-79; bd dir, Atlanta Met Fair Housing, 1983-84; loan exec, Fulton Co Comn, GA, 1981-82; pres, Huntington Comt Asn Atlanta, 1981-82; vpres, Clark Col Allied Health Comn Atlanta, 1981-; vpres, Fulton Co Zoning Orgin Rev Comt, 1982-; vpres, Seaborn Lee Sch PTA Atlanta, 1983-84; Econ Develop Adv Bd, 1985-; chmn, Douglas HS Bus Adv Coun, 1985-92; BellSouth Fel Columbia Univ, 1986; Adult Sch Super Ben Hill United Meth Church, 1986-87; bd dir, Renaisssance Capital Corp, 1987; bd dirs, Opportunities Industrialization Ctr, 1989-92; bd dir, Bobby Dodd Ctr, 1989-92; bd dir, Am Lung Asn, 1990-94; dir educ, Alpha Phi Alpha Fraternity, Ga Dis, 1991-98; bd dirs, Am Red Cross, 1992-97; proj mgr, MLK Memorial Proj; Worldwide Asn Bus Coaches; Int Asn Facilitators; Bd Ctr African-Am Male Res, Success & Leadership, Univ W Ga; adv, Strayer Univ Cobb Campus Bus Club; Am Lung Asn; Scottish Rite C's Med Ctr; Renaissance Capital Corp. **Honors/Awds:** New Jersey Jaycee of Year, 1978; Outstanding Young Man in America, 1978; AT&T Community Achievement Award, 1978; Who's Who in Black America, 1981; Loaned Executive, Fulton County Comn, 1981; Who's Who in the South and Southeast, 1984; Businessman of Year, Douglass High Sch, 1987; Leadership South Fulton, 1987; Alumni of Year, Morris Brown Col, 1988; Who's Who in America, 1988; Nat Black Col Hall of Fame, 1989; Leadership Atlanta, 1990, 1991; Success Guide, 1991; Metro Atlanta, 1991; Nat Alpha Phi Alpha "Man of the Year", 1992; Loaned Executive, Mayor of Atlanta, 1992; BellSouth Quality Champion of the Year, 1994; Certification of Appreciation, Alpha Kappa Alpha Sorority Inc; Distinguished Leadership Award, United Negro Col Fund, 1999; President's Distinguished Alumnus Award, Morris Brown Col, 1999; Executive Sponsor Award, Morris Brown Col Advan Degree Prog, 1999; Executive Sponsor Award, BellSouth Network African-Am Telecommunications Prof, 1999; Distinguish Service Award, Alpha Phi Alpha Fraternity; Distinguished Alumnus Award, Morris Brown Coll; BellSouth Quality Champion of the Year; Southern Region Alpha Phi Alpha Man of the Year; Georgia Alpha Phi Alpha Man of the Year; AT&T Community Achievement Award; New Jersey Jaycee of Year. **Special Achievements:** Initial Project Manager for the Washington DC Martin Luther King Jr Memorial Project Foundation, Inc. **Home Addr:** 3465 Somerset Trl SW, Atlanta, GA 30331, **Home Phone:** (404)349-4333. **Business Addr:** Executive Coach, Owner, Carter & Carter LLC, 3465 Somerset Trl, Atlanta, GA 30331, **Business Phone:** (404)349-4332.

## CARTER, JOHN R.

Executive, mayor, government official. **Personal:** Born Sep 2, 1941, Laurens, SC; married Carrie; children: Anthony, Wadis & Kris. **Career:** Laborer, 1960-69; Laurens Co Dept Soc Serv, human serv specialist; TownGray Ct, mayor, currently. **Orgs:** Pres, SC Conf Black Mayors; pres, Laurens Chap, St Employees Asn; Deacon Pleasant View Baptist Church; Opportunity Off & Assocs; past-pres, Laurens County Chap Nat Asn Advan Colored People; worship fel minister, Red Cross Masonic Lodge FMPHA; pres, SC Equal Opportunity Assocs Laurens County Select Serv Bd Town Coun Gray Ct SC; Nat Conf Black Mayors Inc. **Special Achievements:** Numerous achievements including First African-American to serve on Gray Court Council. **Home Addr:** 214 Willis St, PO Box 274, Gray Court, SC 29645-0274, **Home Phone:** (864)876-3775. **Business Addr:** Mayor, Town of Gray Court, 329 W Main St, Gray Court, SC 29645, **Business Phone:** (864)876-2581.

## CARTER, JOSEPH CHRISTOPHER (JOE CARTER)

Baseball player, broadcaster. **Personal:** Born Mar 7, 1960, Oklahoma City, OK; son of Joseph and Athelene; married Diana; children: Kia Kionne, Ebony Shante & Jordan Alexander. **Educ:** Wichita State Univ. **Career:** Baseball player (retired), broadcaster; Chicago Cubs, outfielder, 1981-83; Cleveland Indians, right fielder, 1984-89; San Diego Padres, right fielder, 1990; Toronto Blue Jays, right fielder, 1991-97; Baltimore Orioles, 1998; San Francisco Giants, 1998; CTV Sports Net, Toronto Blue Jays, announcer, 1999-2000; WGN-TV, Chicago Cubs, color commentator, 2001-02. **Home Addr:** 1800 NE 51st, Oklahoma City, OK 73111.

## CARTER, DR. JOYE MAUREEN

Consultant, pathologist, writer. **Personal:** Born Jun 3, 1957, Wellsville, OH; daughter of Russell and Marjorie Hart. **Educ:** Wittenberg Univ, Springfield, BA, 1979; Howard Univ, MD, 1983. **Career:** Booth Memorial Hosp, NY City, NY, intern, 1983-84; Howard Univ, resident, 1984-88, chief resident pathol, 1988-89; Dade County, forensic pathol fel, 1988-89; George Washington Univ, assoc prof, 1989, Armed Forces Intitution Pathol, dir forensic sci master's prog, 1989-92, dep chief med examr, 1991-92, asst clin prof, 1992; Howard Univ, asst clin prof, 1991; Wash, DC, chief med examr, 1992-96; Harris County, Tex, chief med examr, 1996-2002; Auth, 2001-; J&M Forensic Consult, independent forensic consult, 2002-; Bibl Dogs Inc, owner, currently. **Orgs:** DC Med Soc, 1992-96; secy pathol sect, NMA, 1992-94; Nat Asn Advan ColoredPeople; Nat Asn Med Examiners; Am Acad Forensic Sci; Aerospace Med Asn; founder, Save Our Kids, 2000-; Healthy People 2000 Anti-Violence Campaign; chair, sci adv comt, Bd Life; pres, Houston Med Forum; Asn St & Territorial Health Officials; chief med examr, Harris County, 1996-2002. **Honors/Awds:** Honoree, Metro's Annual Black History Month Celebration, 2002; Contemporary Black History Maker, Houston Community Col, 2002; Lou Holtz Upper OH Valley Hall of Fame, 2002. **Special Achievements:** First African American chief medical examiner in Houston (Harris County), 1992; first woman chief medical examiner in Houston, first woman chief medical examiner in Washington, DC; Author: My Strength Comes From Within, 2001; I Speak for the Dead, 2003; Let Me Give You a Peace of My Mind: Don't Rent Space in Your Head, Evict Negativity, 2013; First female & First African American to be appointed Chief Forensic Pathologist in the history of the State of Indiana; First Graduate of Howard University to achieve board certification in Forensic Pathology. **Home Addr:** 3598 N Pa St, Indianapolis, IN 46205, **Home Phone:** (317)920-0483. **Business Addr:** Owner, Biblical Dogs Inc, 303 High St, Petersburg, VA 23803, **Business Phone:** (804)722-8267.

## CARTER, DR. JUDY L.

Educator. **Personal:** Born Jun 7, 1942, McCormick, SC; married James III; children: Mason III. **Educ:** Paine Col, Augusta, GA, BS, 1967; Augusta Col, Augusta, GA, MEd, 1976; Univ SC, EdD, curric & instr, 1981; Bryn Mawr Col; Harvard Univs Sch Educ. **Career:** Richmond County, Bd Educ, Augusta, GA, teacher, 1967-76; Paine Col, Augusta, GA, instr, 1976-80, assoc vpres & vpres, acad affairs, chmn, educ dept, 1984-; Univ SC, Aiken, SC, dir stud teaching, 1980-84; Dillard Univ, New Orleans, LA, chmn dept educ, 1993-98; Voorhees Col, Denmark, SC, assoc vpres acad affairs; Livingstone Col, asst pres instnl & educ improv; Benedict Col, Columbia, SC, Dept Educ Child & Family Studies, porf educ, chmn educ, consult; Ft Valley State Univ, Col Educ, dean, 2006-; Ga Regents Univ, Col Educ, interim Chair, dept teacher educ. **Orgs:** Vpres, Alpha Kappa Alpha Sorority Inc, 1985-87; Ga Asn Col Teacher Educ, 1985-; pres, Augusta Chap Links Inc, 1986-89; chmn, Ga Adv Coun, 1988-89; dir, Bush Fac Develop Prog, 1988-; site coordr, Ford Teacher-Scholar Prog, 1990-; bd dir, Child Enrichment; health care bd, Univ Hosp; bd dir, Girls Club; Prep Acad Adv Comt; educ consult, Build teacher educ progs, 2011-. **Home Addr:** 1 7th St Suite 1001, Augusta, GA 30901-1364, **Home Phone:** (706)823-1080. **Business Addr:** Professor, Chairman of Department of Education, Paine College, 1235 Fifteenth St, Augusta, GA 30901, **Business Phone:** (706)432-0725.

## CARTER, JUDY SHARON

Teacher, executive, labor relations manager. **Personal:** Born Dec 22, 1951, Miami, FL; daughter of James and Ola. **Educ:** Fisk Univ, BS, 1973; Univ Mich, MA, 1974, Col Financial Planning, AFP. **Career:** Dade Cty Sch, Miami FL, teacher, 1974-75; City Miami, FL, admin asst, 1975-77, personnel officer, 1977-78, sr personnel officer, 1978-79, exec dir, civil serv bd, 1979; Assoc Financial Planning; Vondon Enterprises Inc, treas. **Orgs:** Bd trustee, City Miami Pension Bd, 1980; pres, Nat Assoc Civil Serv Comn, 1983; Leadership Miami Alumni Assoc; nat Forum Black Pub Admin, Intl Personnel Mgt Assoc, FL Pub Personnel Assoc, Fed Selective Serv Syst Be, Nat Assoc Female Exec; Delta Sigma Theta Inc; secy, Miami-Fisk Alumni Club; Young Adult Choir & New Way Fel Baptist; Nat Assoc Negro & Prof Womens Club, Credit Union Loan Comt, Carver Young Mens Christian Assoc, Greater Miami Urban League, Am Assoc Individual Investors, Intl Assoc Financial Planners; YWCA; coordr, Women's Growth Inst, New Way Fel Baptist; Nat Asn Advan Colored People; Inst Cert Financial Planners; dir & vpres, S Fla Black Tennis Asn Inc. **Honors/Awds:** Grad Class Leadership Miami, Greater Miami Chamber Com, 1980; article & pub, Carter, Judy S & Timmons, Wm M "Conflicting Roles in Personal Bds, Adjudications vs Policy Making" Pub Personnel Mgt, Vol 14, 2, 1985. **Special Achievements:** First black trustee in City Miami Pension Bd. **Home Addr:** 3150 NW 49th St, PO Box 20071, Miami, FL 33142.

## CARTER, DR. KEITH D.

Educator, ophthalmologist. **Personal:** Born Apr 19, 1955, Indianapolis, IN; son of James O and Pearlie G; married Cheryl; children: Evan & Erin. **Educ:** Purdue Univ, BS, pharm; Ind Univ, MD, 1983. **Career:** Methodist Hosp, Ind, intern, 1983-84; Univ Mich, W K Kellogg Eye Ctr, resident, 1984-87; Univ IA, Dept Opthamology, Oculoplastics & Orbital Surg fel, 1987-88; Univ Iowa Hosps & Clins fel, Col Med, Dept Ophthal, from asst prof to assoc prof, 1988-2001, clin med dir, currently, prof ophthal & visual sci, prof otolaryngol, 2001-, Lillian C O'Brien & Dr C S O'Brien chair & head, 2006-; Veterans Admin Hosp, Iowa City, IA, Oculoplastics Surg Serv, staff physician, 1998-. **Orgs:** Prog dir resident educ, Resident selection comm, 1990-2006; fel CIC Acad Leadership Prog, 1995; treas, Am Soc Ophthal Plastic & Reconstructive Surg, 1998-2000; off provost, Univ Iowa; secy, Am Eye Study Club, 2002-06; bd trustee, Am Acad Ophthamol, 2006-; Am Col Surgeons; AMA; fel Am Acad Facial Plastic & Reconstructive Surg; Asn Res Vision & Ophthal; Iowa Eye Asn; Asn Univ Prof Ophthamol; Iowa State Med Soc. **Home Addr:** 32 Hummingbird Lane, Iowa City, IA 52245-9258, **Home Phone:** (319)337-3214. **Business Addr:** Professor, Head, University of Iowa, 11136F-PFP, Iowa City, IA 52242, **Business Phone:** (319)356-2867.

## CARTER, KELLY ELIZABETH

Writer. **Personal:** Born Nov 27, 1962, Los Angeles, CA; daughter of Lucille Turner and Ernest. **Educ:** Univ Southern Calif, Los Angeles, CA, AB, jour, 1985. **Career:** Iowa City Press-Citizen, Iowa City, IA, sportswriter, 1986-87; Pittsburgh Press, Pittsburgh, PA, sportswriter, 1987-89; Dallas Morning News, Dallas, TX, sportswriter, 1990-; Am, writer, currently; Jet Set Pets, founder & pres, currently. **Orgs:** Delta Sigma Theta Sorority, 1982-; regional coordr, Asn Women Sports Media, 1986-; Nat Asn Black Journalists, 1986-; Dallas-Ft Worth Asn Black Communicators. **Honors/Awds:** Golden Quill Award, Pittsburgh Press Club, 1989. **Special Achievements:** First Female Beat Writer to Cover Los Angeles Lakers. **Business Addr:** Founder, President, The Jet Set Pets, 6709 La Tijera Blvd Suite 361, Los Angeles, CA 90045, **Business Phone:** (310)295-9396.

## CARTER, KENNETH GREGORY

Executive. **Personal:** Born Aug 12, 1959, Louisville, KY; son of Garland K and Laura L Grant; married Ellen Melissa Pullen; children: Kenneth Jr & Brandon G. **Educ:** Univ Louisville, BSC, 1981; Ohio State Univ, MBA, 1983. **Career:** Int Bus Mach, Ky, sales, 1980-90; D&D Consult Serv Inc, adv coun; Brown-Forman Corp, Ky, nat sr brand mgr, 1990, vpres, dir ethnic mkt, div bus mgr, currently. **Orgs:** Bd dir, Urban league, 1990; Nat Asn Advan Colored People; Adv Coun. **Home Addr:** 122 Northwestern Pkwy, Louisville, KY 40212, **Home Phone:** (502)775-4056. **Business Addr:** Vice President, Division Business Manager, Brown-Forman Corp, 850 Dixie Hwy, Louisville, KY 40210, **Business Phone:** (502)585-1100.

## CARTER, KENNETH WAYNE

Advertising executive, business owner. **Personal:** Born Sep 8, 1954, Muskogee, OK; son of Ira and Doris; children: Burch Merrick. **Educ:** Southern Univ & Agr & Mech Col, BA, jour, 1976. **Career:** KALO Radio, sports dir, 1976-77; Am Heart Asn Inc, dir pub rel, 1977-81; Focus Commun Inc, exec vpres, 1981-87, pres, 1981-, chief exec officer, 1988-; Dallas Weekly, co-owner. **Orgs:** PRSA, Multicultural Affairs Comt, 1982-; bd mem, Dallas Ft Worth Minority Bus Develop Div Coun, 1983-86; City Dallas, Pub Info Task Force, 1990; Dallas Citizens Coun, 1994-95; bd mem, Dallas Urban League, 1994-98, vchmn; bd mem, Dallas Conv & Vis Bur, 1996-98; bd mem, DFW Regional Sports Comn; Tex Pub Rels Asn; Int Asn Bus Communicators; Dallas Advert League; chmn, Nat Minority Supplier Develop Coun; Dallas Regional Minority Purchasing Coun; Ft Worth Minority Supplier Develop Coun; Black Nurses Asn; Thelma Boston Found; Dallas Black Chamber Com. **Honors/Awds:** Target Impact Award Tex, Affiliate Am Heart Asn, 1980; Man of the Year, Nat Asn Negro Bus & Prof Women's Club, Dallas Metrop Chap, 1986; Quest for Success Award, Dallas Morning News & Dallas Black Chamber Com, 1987. **Special Achievements:** First Black mem, bd dir, Pub Rel Soc Am, North Tex Chap, serv two terms, one as scy; Only Black mem, Pub Info Task Force, City Dallas, also serv Steering Comt. **Home Addr:** 4909 Haverwood Lane Suite 2106, Dallas, TX 75287-4434, **Home Phone:** (214)485-6543. **Business Addr:** President, Chief Executive Officer, Focus Communications Inc, 1412 Main St Suite 1000, Dallas, TX 75202, **Business Phone:** (214)744-1428.

## CARTER, KEVIN ANTONY

Executive, executive director, vice president (organization). **Personal:** Born May 23, 1960, Cleveland, OH; son of John and Lavenia. **Educ:** Vanderbilt Univ, BA, philos, 1982; Case Western Res Univ, Weatherhead Sch Mgt, MBA, finance, 1987. **Career:** Ernst & Young, sr consult strategic planning, 1986-89; LTV Steel Co, sr analyst strategic planning, 1989-93; McDonald Co Investment, Diversity Bus Develop, vpres & dir, 1993-2006; Nat City Corp, Work Force Diversity, vpres & dir, 2006-. **Orgs:** Exec comt mem, Nat Asn Advan Colored People, Cleveland Br, 1992-94; chairperson, African Am Bus Consortium, 1992-; telethon chairperson, United Negro Col Fund, Cleveland/Canton/Akron, 1993-; adv bd chairperson, Kaleidoscope Mag, 1994-; bd chair, City Cleveland Community Rels, Youth Subcomt, 1994-; City Cleveland Investment Oversight Comt, 1994-; nat bd mem, Nat Black MBA Asn; pres, Cleveland Chap, 1994-; bd mem, Securities Indust Asn; Greater Cleveland Growth Asn;Nat Asn Advan Colored People; chmn, E Ninth St Proj; Cleveland Conv Ctr; Ctr Contemp Art. **Home Addr:** 1701 E 12th St Suite 19CW, Cleveland, OH 44114. **Business Addr:** Director, Vice President, National City Corp, Nat City Ctr 1900 E 9th St, Cleveland, OH 44114-3484, **Business Phone:** (216)222-2000.

## CARTER, KEVIN LOUIS

Football player, executive. **Personal:** Born Sep 21, 1973, Miami, FL; married Shima. **Educ:** Univ Fla, BS, zool, 1995. **Career:** Football player (retired), executive; St Louis Rams, defensive end, 1995-2000; Univ Fla, Kevin Carter Football Endowment, founder, 1998-; Tenn Titans, defensive tackle, 2001-04; Miami Dolphins, 2005-06; Tampa Bay Buccaneers, 2007-08; Entertainment & Sports Programming Network, commentator & col football studio analyst, 2012-. **Orgs:** Founder, Kevin Carter Found, 2002-; exec comm mem, Nat Football League Players Asn. **Honors/Awds:** Championship, Southeastern Conf, 1991.1993, 1994; Carroll Rosenbloom Memorial Award; St Louis Rams Rookie of the Year, 1995; Most Valuable Player, St Louis Rams, 1998; Hall of Fame "Gator Great", 1998; Sacks Leader, Nat Football League, 1999; All-Pro, 1999; Pro Bowl, 1999, 2002; Tennessee Titans Community Man of the Year, 2002; University of Florida Athletic Hall of Fame; Florida-Georgia Hall of Fame; Champion, Super Bowl, XXXIV. **Business Addr:** Founder, The Kevin Carter Foundation, 1601 Dodd Trl, Murfreesboro, TN 37128-7647, **Business Phone:** (813)870-2700.

## CARTER, KI-JANA (KENNETH LEONARD CARTER)

Football player, executive. **Personal:** Born Sep 12, 1973, Westerville, OH. **Educ:** Pa State Univ, bus mkt. **Career:** Football player (retired); Cincinnati Bengals, running back, 1995-99; Wash Redskins, 2001; New Orleans Saints, running back, 2003-04; OPENSports.com, sports blogger; Byoglobe, chief exec officer, 2008-; Sunrise, chief exec officer. **Orgs:** Big Bros Big Sisters. **Honors/Awds:** All-American, 1994; Rose Bowl MVP, 1995; Ed Block Courage Award, 1998. **Special Achievements:** Films: 1995 Rose Bowl, 1995; 1995 NFL Draft, 1995; Jerry Maguire, 1996. **Home Addr:** , Miami, FL. **Business Addr:** Chief Executive Officer, ByoGlobe Inc, 4960 Southwest 52nd St, Davie, FL 33314, **Business Phone:** (754)208-1496.

## CARTER, DR. LAMORE JOSEPH

School administrator, psychologist. **Personal:** Born Apr 18, 1925, Carthage, TX; married Lena Mae Jones; children: Greta Lisa & Kris-Lana. **Educ:** Wiley Col, attended 1947; Fisk Univ, AB, zool, 1950; Univ Wis, MS, educ psychol & sci methods, 1952; Univ Chicago, postgrad, 1954; State Univ Iowa, PhD, psychol, 1958; Univ Tex, attended 1966; Am Bd Prof Psychol. **Career:** Grambling Col, instr, 1952-54, dir & psychologist, asst prof, coordr, 1961-66; State Univ Iowa, res asst, 1956-58; Inst Res, admin, 1966-68; Southern Asn Cols & Schs, res fel, 1969-70; Morehouse Col, vis distinguished prof psychol, 1970; Tex Southern Univ Houston, dean faculties, 1970-71; Grambling State Univ, assoc dean admin, 1971-76; Peace Corps W Africa, consult, 1971-76; Southern Asn Cols & Schs, consult, 1971-82; Am Coun Educ, fel acad admin, 1976-77; Grambling State Univ, provost & vpres acad affairs, 1977-91; Wiley Col, pres, 1993-96. **Orgs:** Chap pres, Am Asn Univ Profs, 1960-63; consult, Headstart Prog, 1968-76; founder & pres, Lions Club Int, 1981-84; Am Educ Res Asn; Am Southwestern; La Psychol Asn; Am Asn Higher Educ; Am Asn Ment Deficiency; Nat Soc Study Educ; La Asn Ment Health; Nat Educ Asn; Phi Delta Kappa; Phi Beta Sigma; Dem; Meth; Am Psychol Asn; bd dir, United Campus Ministry; Am Coun fel Am Asn Ment Deficiency; bd trustee, Wiley Col. **Honors/Awds:** Dr Kara Vaughn Jackson Education Award, 2013; Mason 33rd degree; Diplomate, Am Bd Prof Psychol; Licensed School Psychologist, La Bd Examiners Psychologists; Bronze Star, AUS. **Special Achievements:** Contributed articles to professional journals, books & monographs. **Home Addr:** 101 Richmond Dr, Grambling, LA 71245-3019, **Home Phone:** (318)247-6286.

## CARTER, LAVONYA QUINTELLE. See CARTER, QUINCY.

## CARTER, DR. LAWRENCE

President (organization), college administrator, educator. **Personal:** Born Oct 4, 1942, Valdosta, GA; son of Isabell Beady; married Marva L Moore; children: Mauri D & Laurent L. **Educ:** Ft Valley State Col, GA, BS, agr educ, 1968; Tuskegee Inst, AL, MS, agr educ, 1969; Fla State Univ, Tallahassee, FL, EdS, 1973, PhD, adult educ, 1976. **Career:** Goldkist Indust, Atlanta GA, mgr trainee, 1969-71; Tuskegee Inst, Tuskegee, AL, asst prof adult educ, 1973-74; Fla A&M Univ, Tallahassee, Fla, exten rural develop specialist, 1974-80, actg dir agr res, 1980-87, dir coop exten, 1980, assoc dean, dir & prof, currently, dir spec outreach activ coop exten adminr, prin investr, adminr. **Orgs:** Ft Valley State Col Alumni Asn, 1968; Tuskegee Alumni Asn, 1969; Adult Educ Asn Am, 1973, Fla A&M Univ Alumni Asn, 1974; consult, Univ Fla Int Prog, 1980; dir, Steering Comt, Bethel Baptist Church, 1982-84; mem bd dir, Southern Rural Develop Ctr, 1987; pres, Phi Beta Sigma, Local Chap, 1987; consult, Kellog Proj, NC A&T Univ, 1988; Policy Comm, Exten Serv, USDA, 1989; Rural Am Virtual Community Ctr; Nat 4 H Agents Asn; Phi Delta Kappa; Southern Asn Hort Scientists; Am Asn Agr Engrs; Exten Adminr Asn; Agr Administrs Asn; exec bd mem, Phi Beta Sigma Fraternity Inc. **Home Addr:** 8124 Hugh Lane, Tallahassee, FL 32308-9424, **Home Phone:** (850)668-0181. **Business Addr:** Professor, Associate Dean, Florida A&M University, Perry-Paige Bldg Rm 215 S, Tallahassee, FL 32307, **Business Phone:** (850)599-3546.

## CARTER, DR. LAWRENCE EDWARD, SR.

Clergy, dean (education), college teacher. **Personal:** Born Sep 23, 1941, Dawson, GA; son of John Henry III and Bernice; married Marva Lois Griffin; children: Lawrence Edward Jr. **Educ:** Va Univ, Lynchburg, BA, soc studies & psychol, 1964; Boston Univ, Mdiv, theol, 1968, STM Pastoral Care, attended 1970, PhD, pastoral care & coun, 1978; Andover Newton Theol Sch; Ohio State Univ; NY Univ; Harvard Univ; Ga State Univ; Univ Wis; George Washington Univ; Lewis Univ; Brown Univ; Multi-Disciplinary Clin Training, cert; cert, clin pastoral educ. **Career:** Roxbury United Presby Church, minister youth, 1965-67; Boston Pub Schs, sub teacher, 1966-77; Twelfth Baptists Church, minister coun, 1968-71; Boston Univ Warren Residence Hall, resident coun & asst dir, 1968-71; Boston Univ MLK Jr African-Am Cult Ctr, dir, 1971-73; People's Baptist Church, assoc minister, 1971-78; Harvard Univ, Div Sch, clergy teaching adv, 1976-77; Marsh Chapel Boston Univ, assoc dean, 1978-79; Morehouse Col, prof philol & relig, 1979-, Martin Luther King Jr Int Chapel, dean, 1979-, col cur, 1979-; archivist & cur, 1982-97; Fulbright Scholar, Brazil, 1994; vis prof, Bates Col, 1996-2000; assoc dean, Daniel L. Marsh Chapel; Ga State Univ, assoc prof, music hist & lit, currently. **Orgs:** Coordr, Afro Am Studies Prog, Simmons Col, 1977-78; Am Acad Relig, 1979; bd dir, Nat Coun Churches Christ, 1983-90; Soc Study Black Relig, Class Leadership Atlanta, 1986; Nat Endowment Humanities, 1993, 1996; bd visitors, Mercer Univ Sch Theol, 2001-03; Nat Asn Col & Univ Chaplains; ACLU; Am Acad Relig; Asn Black Prof Relig; Ministries Blacks Higher Ed; Nat Asn Adv Colored People; Atlanta UN Asn; fel Nat Endowment Humanities; bd trustee, Soka Univ Am; fel Omega Psi Phi Fraternity Inc. **Home Addr:** 3708 Cherry Ridge Blvd, Decatur, GA 30034, **Home Phone:** (404)244-0073. **Business Addr:** Senior Dean, Professor, Morehouse College, 830 Westview Dr SW, Atlanta, GA 30314, **Business Phone:** (404)681-2800.

## CARTER, LINDA

Writer, educator, editor. **Educ:** Morgan State Col, BA, MA; Univ Md, PhD. **Career:** Morgan State Univ, assoc prof Eng. **Special Achievements:** Has written over 100 articles on African American literature and culture; co-editor of "James Baldwin: In Memoriam" (1982); "Images of the Black Male in Literature and Film: Essays in Criticism" (1994); "Humanities in the Ancient and Pre-Modern World: An Africana Emphasis" (1999); "Humanities in the Modern World: An Africana Emphasis" (2001).

## CARTER, MARGARET LOUISE

Educator, government official. **Personal:** Born Dec 29, 1935, Shreveport, LA; daughter of Hilton and Emma; children: 5; married Elvis. **Educ:** Portland State Univ, BS, educ, 1972; Ore State Univ, MEd, psychol, 1973; Wash State Univ, post-grad studies. **Career:** Albina Youth Opportunity Sch, instr, 1971-73; Portland Community Col, counr, 1973; bus woman, 1975; Ore House, 1984; Conf Comt Martin Luther King Jr State Holiday, co-chair, 1985; Joint House-Senate Comt Trade & Econ Develop, 1985; Spec Joint Comt Health Care, mem, 1986; Ore House Human Resources Comt, vice chair, 1987; Ore State, Dist 22, sen, 2000-09, pres pro tempore senate, 2005; Ore Dept Human Serv, Human Serv Progs, dep dir, 2009-12; Ore Hist Soc, bd dir, 2012-. **Orgs:** Ore Alliance Black Sch Educ; vice-chair, Ways & Means; Ore State Hosp Patient Care Comt; Health & Human Serv; Portland Teachers Asn; Ore Assembly Black Affairs; Am Fedn Teachers; Spec Comn Parole Bd Matrix Syst; Nat Asn Advan Colored People; Ore Polit Women's Caucus; Alpha Kappa Alpha Sorority; House Educ Comt, 1985-; co-founder, Black Leadership Conf, 1986; gov appointee, Ore Task Force Drug Abuse, 1986-; Gen Adv Comt Victims Rights, 1986-; pres, Urban League Portland, 1999-2002. **Honors/Awds:** Zeta Phi Beta Sorority Award; Musical Director of the Joyful Sound, Piedmont Church Christ, Portland; Jeanette Rankin First Woman Award, Ore Women's Polit Caucus, 1985; Jefferson Image Award, 1985; Elliott Human Rights Award; Legislator of the Year Award, Nat Black Caucus State Legislators. **Special Achievements:** First African-American female in history to be elected to Oregon Legislative Assembly; First African-American woman in the United States to serve as President Pro-Tempore of a State Senate. **Home Addr:** 2948 NE 10th, Portland, OR 97212, **Home Phone:** (503)280-6003. **Business Addr:** Board Director, Oregon State Senate, 1200 SW Park Ave, Portland, OR 97205, **Business Phone:** (503)222-1741.

## CARTER, DR. MARION ELIZABETH LOUISE JACKSON

Executive, educator. **Personal:** Born Washington, DC; daughter of James Martin and Marion Jackson. **Educ:** Wellesley Col; Howard Univ, MA; Middlebury Col, MA; Georgetown Univ, MS; Cath Univ, romance lang, PhD; Georgetown Univ, Ling, PhD. **Career:** World Univ, trustee; Wellesley Col, vis prof; Gordon Col, prof; Teachers Col, prof; Howard Univ, instr; Barber Scotia Col, assoc prof; Wiley Col, assoc prof; Univ La Gaguna, lectr; Univ Andes, Meridan, Venezuela, lectr; Am Lang Inst Georgetown Univ, teacher; St Mary Univ, Ns, lectr. **Orgs:** Nat Asn Foreign Stud Affairs; Le Droit Park Civic Asn; Smithsonian Inst; past sec, Am Asn Teachers Spanish & Portuguese; Am Asn Univ Professors; Am Asn Univ Women; trustee, World Univ; elected mem, Order Int Fel. **Honors/Awds:** Buena Aires Conv Award; Agnes Meyer Award; American Association of Teachers of Spanish and Portuguese Award, Spain; Directory of Am Scholars; Fulbright Award, Spain; plaque, Lifetime Bd Gov, Am Biog Inst; Int Hall of Leaders, Great Minds of the 21st Century; IBC Book of Dedications; ABI Int Peace Prize. **Special Achievements:** Book: "Skyward or E Pluribus Unum", 2004. **Home Addr:** 402 U St NW, Washington, DC 20001-2333, **Home Phone:** (202)387-8139.

## CARTER, MARTIN JOSEPH

Clergy. **Personal:** Born Jul 31, 1930, High Point, NC. **Educ:** Emerson Col, BA, 1956; Cornell Univ, BA, 1956, MEd, 1960. **Career:** Harvard Univ, consult, 1970-74; St Joseph Comm Parochial Sch, teacher, coor dr, facilitator, 1970-75; Dissemination Prog, partic, 1971-72; Univ Ill Curric Studies Math, model teacher; St Francis De Sales Church, 1975-76; Archdiocese Kingston, pastor, 1976-; Our Lady Victory Church, pastor. **Orgs:** Nat Black Cath Clergy Caucus, 1968-77; Caribbean Ecumenical ConstDevel, 1976-77; exec, Jamaica Coun Churches, 1976-77. **Honors/Awds:** Publ: "Teen-Age Marriage", 1974; "Homiletic & Pastoral Rev - Diocesan Policy on Teenage Marriages", 1975; "Dignitatis Humanae Declaration on Religious Freedom"; The New Cath Encycl, 1979. **Special Achievements:** First African-American to serve as pastor at Our Lady of Victory Church. **Home Addr:** Lot 307 Goodman Ave Gregory Pk, Bridge Port33345. **Business Addr:** Church of Reconciliation, Bridge Port33345.

## CARTER, MARTY LAVINCENT

Football player. **Personal:** Born Dec 17, 1969, LaGrange, GA. **Educ:** Middle Tenn State Univ. **Career:** Football player (retired); Tampa Bay Buccaneers, Nat Football League, defensive back, free safety, 1991, strong safety, 1992-94; Chicago Bears, Nat Football League, strong safety, 1995-98; Atlanta Falcons, Nat Football League, safety, 1999; strong safety, 1999-2001; Detroit Lions, strong safety, 2001. **Special Achievements:** TV Series: NFL Monday Night Football, 1970; ESPN's Sunday Night Football, 1987; NFL on FOX, 1994. A Broken Code, 2012.

## CARTER, MARVA GRIFFIN

Dean (education), educator. **Personal:** Born Jun 4, 1947, Cleveland, OH; daughter of Marvin C; married Lawrence E Sr; children: Lawrence E Jr. **Educ:** Boston Conserv Music, BM, 1968; New Eng Conserv Music, MM, 1970; Boston Univ, MA, musicol, 1975; Univ ill, Urbana, IL, PhD, musicol, 1988. **Career:** Boston Univ, admin asst, Afro-Am Studies Prog, 1970-71, coordr freshman & sophomore seminars, 1972-73; Simmons Col, coordr Afro-Amstudies prog, 1973-77; Univ Ill, fel, 1977; Morehouse Col, dean, 1979; Clark Atlanta Univ, adj assoc prof music, 1988-89; Ebenezer Baptist Church, organist & music coordr, 1982-92; Morris Brown Col, coordr music, 1988-93; Ga State Univ, asst dir, Sch Music, 1993-95, asst prof music hist & lit, assoc prof music hist & lit, 1993-. **Orgs:** Am Musicol Soc, cult diversity & comt publ Am Music, 1973-77, 1993-; Sonneck Soc Am Music, nominating comt, educ comt & cult diversity comt, 1973-77, 1993-; assoc mem, Ctr Black Music Res, 1993-; Soc Ethnomusicology, 1973-77, 1993-; bd mem, ed comn, Young Audiences Atlanta, 1992-94; Atlanta Symphony Action Comt Black Audience Develop, 1992-94. **Special Achievements:** First African American to be awarded a PhD in musicology from the University of Illinois. **Home Addr:** 265 Ross Rd, Tallahassee, FL 32305-3429. **Business Addr:** Associate Professor, Georgia State University, 712 Haas Howell, Atlanta, GA 30302-4097, **Business Phone:** (404)413-5932.

## CARTER, MARY LOUISE

Government official, mayor. **Personal:** Born Jun 27, 1937, Clarksdale, MS; daughter of Julia M Turner; married Everett L; children: Danny C & Eric L. **Educ:** Coahoma Jr Col, AA, 1959; Alcorn Col, 1960; Fontbonne Col, attended 1977. **Career:** Sears Credit Cent, credit analyst, 1969; City Pagedale, alderperson, 1981-92, actg mayor, 1984-85, mayor, 1992, 2008-; Mo Div Families Servs, caseworker, 1995. **Orgs:** Bd mem, Normandy Munic Coun, 1981-88; bd mem, Adult Basic Educ, 1981-86; actg pres bd, City Pagedale, 1984-86; chair, Pub Awareness Adult Basic Educ, 1984-85; Black Elected Offs St Louis Co, 1990; Nat Conf Black Mayors; bd dir, St Louis County Econ Coun's. **Honors/Awds:** Positive Imate; Award for Services, Scout Troop, 1995. **Special Achievements:** Outstanding Contrib in Adult Literacy, 1994. **Home Addr:** 1284 Kingsland Ave, Pagedale, MO 63133. **Business Addr:** Mayor, City of Pagedale, 1420 Ferguson Ave, Pagedale, MO 63133-1720, **Business Phone:** (314)726-1200.

## CARTER, MATT

Chief executive officer, president (organization). **Educ:** Northwestern Univ, BS; Harvard Bus Sch, MBA. **Career:** Leap Wireless, chief mkt officer, 2001-03; PNC Financial Serv, sr vpres mkt; Sprint, Base Mgt, sr vpres, 2006-08; Boost Mobile, pres, 2008-10; Sprint, 4G, pres, Global Wholesale & Emerging Solutions, pres, 2010-; Inteliquent Inc, chief exec officer, pres, 2015-. **Orgs:** Bd dir, USG Corp, Apollo Educ Group, 2012; bd trustee, Bishop's Sch, 2013-; Boys & Girls Clubs Am.

**Home Addr:** 4022 N Clarendon Ave, Chicago, IL 60613-3120, **Home Phone:** (256)536-9073. **Business Addr:** Chief Executive Officer, President, Inteliquent Inc, 550 W Adams St Suite 900, Chicago, IL 60661, **Business Phone:** (866)388-7258.

## CARTER, NANETTE CAROLYN

Painter (artist), educator, association executive. **Personal:** Born Jan 30, 1954, Columbus, OH; daughter of Matthew Gameliel and Frances Hill. **Educ:** L'Accademia di Belle Arti, Perugia Italy, 1975; Oberlin Col, OH, BA, 1976; Pratt Inst Art, Brooklyn, NY, MFA, 1978. **Career:** Dwight-Englewood Sch, Englewood NJ, teacher printmaking & drawing, 1978-87; New York State Coun Arts, artist in resident, 1984; self-employed artist & painter, 1987-; City Col New York, adj prof, 1992-93; Pratt Inst Art, vis asst prof fine arts, 2001, adj assoc prof fine arts & undergrad coordr drawing, currently; Art Works: Yale Gallery Art, New Haven CT; Mus Art, Rhode Island Sch Design, RI; ARCO, Philadelphia, Pa; Studio Mus in Harlem, NY; Merck Pharmaceut Co, Pa; Motown Corp, CA; MCI Telecommunication IL; IBM, CT; Pepsi-Cola, NY; Gen Electric, Fairfied, CT; Salomon Bros, NY; Schomburg Libr, NY; Reader's Digest, Pleasantville, NY; Morgan Guaranty, NY; The Libr Cong, WA, DC; Planned Parenthood, NY; Bristol-Meyers Squibble Co, Princeton, NJ; Merch Pharmaceut Co, Phildelphia, Pa; Nextel Corp; Los Angeles, CA; Magic Johnson Enterprises, Los Angeles, CA; AT&T, NJ; Collections: Mudd Libr, Oberlin Col; Rutgers Grad Sch Mgt; Cochran Found, Am Express, Minneapolis, MN; Solo Groups: June Kelly Gallery, NYC, NY, 2000; Sante Webster Gallery, Philadelphia, Pa, 2001; Conkling Gallery, MN State Univ, MN, 2001; GR N-Nanti Gallery, Chicago, Ill, 2002; GR N'Nanti Gallery, Detroit, Mich, 2002; O.G.T. Gallery, NYC, NY, 2002; Sante Webster Gallery, Philadelphia, Pa, 2003; Group Shows: Rhode Island Sch Design, Providence, RI, 2000; Jack Tilton & Anna Kustera Gallery, NYC, NY, 2000; Pa Acad Fine Arts, Philadelphia, Pa, 2000; Cover for "The Intl Review of African-Am Art, "Hampton Univ, Va, Vol 18 No 4, 2003; Collections: Columbus Mus Art, Ohio; Newark Mus, NJ; The Pa Acad Arts, Pa; Schomburg Ctr for Res, Black Culture, NY; AT&T, NJ; Nat Steel Corp, Pittsburg, Pa. **Orgs:** Bd mem, Harlem Sch Arts; fel Bob Blackburn's Printmaking Workshop, 1989; fel Brandywine Workshop, Phila, PA; fel Lower Eastside Printshop, 1997; fel Brandywine Workshop, 1999. **Honors/Awds:** Jerome Found Grant, 1981; Nat Endowment for the Arts Grant, 1981; New Jersey State Coun Grant, New Jersey State Coun Arts, 1985; New York Found for the Arts Grant, 1990; Pollock-Krasner Found Inc Grant, 1994-; The Wheeler Found Grant, 1996; Pratt Faculty Development Grant, Pratt Inst Art, Brooklyn, NY, 2009. **Home Addr:** 788 Riverside Dr Apt 3C, New York, NY 10032, **Home Phone:** (212)690-7512. **Business Addr:** Adjunct Associate Professor, Pratt Institute of Art, Brooklyn Campus S Hall 1 200 Willoughby Ave, Brooklyn, NY 11205, **Business Phone:** (718)636-3634.

## CARTER, NIGEA

Football coach, football player. **Personal:** Born Sep 1, 1974, Coconut Creek, FL; children: 2. **Educ:** Mich State Univ, attended 1996. **Career:** Football player (retired); Tampa Bay Buccaneers, wide receiver, 1997; Mid Sch Football Team, coach. **Honors/Awds:** Player of the Year, Spartans Orgn, 1996.

## CARTER, NORMAN L.

Executive, manager. **Personal:** Born Jun 16, 1949, Pittsburgh, PA; married Zelia; children: Norman IV. **Educ:** Ind Univ, PA, BA, 1971; Johns Hopkins Univ, MS, mkt, 2000. **Career:** Brown & Root Inc, Houston, Tex, sr auditor; Ernst & Young, sr auditor; Westinghouse Elec Corp, internal auditor; Ft Wash Hosp, mem & bd dir; Potomac Elec Power Co, prin, bus process consult, mgr, Prince Georges County Affairs, mgr econ develop, div mgr, econ minority bus develop, sr auditor; mgr econ develop, 1981-, Process Mgt Initiative, prin bus process consult, currently; Utility Econ Develop Asn Inc, pres. **Orgs:** Am Inst Cert Pub Acct; founder & pres, Nat Asn Black Acct; bd dir & pres, Prince Georges Chamber Com; chmn, Utility Network Community Based Develop; pres, Utility Econ Develop Asn; bd dir, Wash Cathedral Choral Soc; vpres, Md & DC Minority Supplier Develop Coun; bd dir, Downtown Bus Improv Dist; vpres, Md Indust Develop Asn; Int Develop Res Coun; Am Econ Develop Corp; Coun Urban Econ Develop; Ft Wash Hosp; Int Develop Res Coun; Gateway Ga Ave Revitalization Corp; bd dir, Am Red Cross Nat Capital Area; Am Inst Cert Pub Accountants; pres, Pittsburgh chap, Nat Asn Black Accountants, founder; pres, Pa chap, Nat Asn Black Accountants, founder; bd mem, Jr Achievement Inc; bd dir, Md Indust Develop Asn. **Home Addr:** 203 Blackpowder Lane, Fort Washington, MD 20744, **Home Phone:** (301)292-1972. **Business Addr:** Manager of Economic Development, Potomac Electric Power Co, 1900 Pa Ave NW, Washington, DC 20068, **Business Phone:** (202)872-3357.

## CARTER, ORA WILLIAMS

Educator, association executive, painter (artist). **Personal:** Born Aug 25, 1925, Ferndale, MI; daughter of Samuel and Emma Kinney; married Walter H. **Educ:** Clark Col, AB, 1947; Wayne State Univ, MEd, 1963. **Career:** Black Mountain Col, Rosenwald fel, 1946; Detroit Bd Educ, teacher, 1953-67; Harvard Univ, Rosenwald fel, 1965; Commun Skills Ctr, instr & diagnostician, 1967-72; Bow Elem Sch, instr, 1972-76; Roosevelt Elem Sch, precision teacher, 1976-81; Ora's Studio, artist, 1978-. **Orgs:** Nat Conf Artists, Metrop Detroit Reading Coun, 1965-81; bd dirs, Delta Home Girls, 1968-78; bd mgt, YWCA, 1972-79 & 1980-84; pres, Detroit Alumnae Chap Delta Sigma Theta Sorority, 1973-75; bd dirs, Fedn Girls homes, 1975-78; chairperson bd mission, Educ & Social Action, 1976-80; Detroit Arts Comt, 1982-89; vpres, Top Ladies Distinction, 1987-88; vice moderator, Church Coun, 1991-92; Mayflower Congregational United Church Christ; Div Mission Detroit Metro Asn United Church Christ; Clark Atlanta Univ Alumni Asn; Mich Asn Calligraphers; Detroit Fedn Teachers; charter mem, Fred Hart Williams Gen Soc; Founders Soc & Friends African Art; life mem, Nat Asn Advan Colored People; Charles H Wright Mus African Am Hist. **Honors/Awds:** Artist of the Month, Afro-Am Mus Detroit, 1975; first vice president, Top Ladies of Distinction, 1987-88; Community Service Award, 1993. **Home Addr:** 19501 Hubbell St, Detroit, MI 48235, **Home Phone:** (313)342-8246.

## CARTER, DR. PAMELA LYNN

State government official, vice president (organization). **Personal:** Born Aug 20, 1949, South Haven, MI; daughter of Dorothy Elizabeth Hadley Fanning and Roscoe Hollis Fanning Dorothy Elizabeth Hadley Fanning; married Michael Anthony; children: Michael Anthony Jr & Marcya Alicia. **Educ:** Univ Detroit, BA (cum laude), 1971; Univ Mich, MSW, 1973; Ind Univ, JD, 1984. **Career:** Univ Mich, Sch Pub Health, res analyst, treat dir, UAW, Detroit, 1973-75; Ment Health Ctr for Women 7 C, exec dir, 1975-77; UAW-Gen Motors Legal Servs, Indpolis, consumer litigation atty, 1983-87; Secy State, Ind, securities atty, 1987-89; Gov Ind, exec asst for health & human servs, 1989; State Ind, atty gen, 1993-97; Cummins Inc, vpres, gen coun & corp secy, 1998-2005; Fleetguard Inc, pres, 2005-06; Cummins Filtration, pres, 2005-07; Cummins Distrib, pres, 2006-. **Orgs:** Ind Bar Asn, 1984-; Cath Social Servs; Jr League; Nat Bar Asn; Coalition 100 Black Women; bd dir, dir, Spectra Energy Corp, 2007-; dir, mem governance comt & mem opers & pub affairs comt, CSX Corp, 2010-; bd mem, Meijer Inc; Sub Saharan Africa Adv Coun Export Import Bank US. **Home Addr:** 2710 Pomona Ct, Indianapolis, IN 46268, **Home Phone:** (317)875-5323. **Business Addr:** President, Cummins Filtration, 500 Jackson St, Columbus, IN 47202-3005, **Business Phone:** (812)377-5000.

## CARTER, PAMELA LYNN

President (organization), lawyer, government official. **Personal:** Born Aug 20, 1949. **Educ:** Univ Detroit, AB; Univ Mich, MSW; Ind Univ Sch Law, JD. **Career:** United Auto Workers Litigation atty, 1984-87; Ind State Off, securities enforcement atty, 1987, dep chief staff & exec asst health policy, 1988-92; Baker & Daniels, 1992-93; pvt legal pract & Atty Gen Ind, 1993-97; Ind State House Representatives, 1997; Johnson, Smith, Pence, Densborn, Wright & Heath, partner, 1997; Cummins Inc, vpres & gen coun, 1997-99, vpres Europe, Mid E, Africa, 1999-2001, gen mgr, vpres global sales & mkt, Fleetguard, 2001-04, Filtration unit, exec vpres & pres, 2005-07, Distrib Unit, pres & exec vpres, 2007-15; Aspen Inst fel. **Orgs:** Dir, Spectra Energy Corp, 2007-; dir, CSX Corp,2010-; independent dir, Hewlett Packard Enterprise Co, 2015-; bd mem, Meijer Inc; Ind State Bar Asn; US Supreme Ct Bar. **Honors/Awds:** "Black Enterprise," The 100 Most Powerful Executives in Corporate America, 2010. **Special Achievements:** First African-American woman in the country to be elected as attorney general for the state of Indiana. **Business Addr:** Retired President, Cummins Inc, 500 Jackson St, Columbus, IN 47202, **Business Phone:** (812)377-5000.

## CARTER, PAT (WENDELL PATRICK CARTER)

Football player, football coach. **Personal:** Born Aug 1, 1966, Sarasota, FL; married Charlene; children: Jamelle & Alec. **Educ:** Fla State Univ. **Career:** Football player (retired), coach; Detroit Lions, tight end, 1988, tight ends coach, 2006-; Los Angeles Rams, tight end, 1989-93; Houston Oilers, tight end, 1994; St Louis Rams, tight end, 1995, coaching intern, offensive asst, 2004-05; Ariz Cardinals, tight end, 1996-97. **Honors/Awds:** First Team All-America honors, Sporting News; Hall of Fame, 2015. **Business Addr:** Tight Ends Coach, Detroit Lions, 222 Repub Dr, Allen Park, MI 48101, **Business Phone:** (313)216-4056.

## CARTER, PATRICK HENRY, JR. (PAT CARTER)

Executive, association executive, naval officer. **Personal:** Born Jan 8, 1939, Memphis, TN; son of Patrick and Annie; married Mattie Pearl Bland; children: Kimberly & Patrick H III. **Educ:** Miss Valley State Univ; LeMoyne Col; Gen Motors Inst. **Career:** Exxon Mobil Corp, instr, 1972; Gen Motors Co; Pat Carter Pontiac Inc, pres; Super Serv, partner, 1990-; Memphis Rockets Basketball Team, owner; Olympic Staffing Inc, owner & pres, 1993-. **Orgs:** Deacon, Mid Baptist Church, 1970-; exec bd, Liberty Bowl, 1982-; bd mem, Boy Scouts Am, 1986; bd mem, Pub Bldg Authority, 1988-94; bd mem, Sr Citizens, 1990-95; Chamber Com, 1992-94; pres, Whitehaven Community Develop Corp, 1994-97; Memphis Sports Authority; chmn & bd dir, Lifeblood. **Honors/Awds:** Achiever, Pontiac Motor Div, 1984-86; Top 100 Black Businesses, Black Enterprise Mag, 1984, 1985, 1986 & 1987; Small Business of the Year, Memphis Business Jour, 1988. **Home Addr:** 708 W Brentwood Cir, Memphis, TN 38111, **Home Phone:** (901)789-2855. **Business Addr:** Board of Director, Chairman, Lifeblood, 1040 Madison Ave, Memphis, TN 38104-2198, **Business Phone:** (901)529-6300.

## CARTER, PERRY LYNN

Football player, football coach. **Personal:** Born Aug 15, 1971, McComb, MS; children: 1. **Educ:** Southern Miss Univ, grad. **Career:** Football player (retired), football coach; Kans City Chiefs, defensive back, 1995-96; Oakland Raiders, right cornerback, 1997-98; Edmonton Eskimos, 2000-01; Montreal Alouettes, 2002; BC Lions, 2003; Detroit Lions; Hamburg Sea Devils, asst defensive backs coach, 2006; Houston Texans, defensive asst, 2006-09, asst defensive backs coach, 2010-13. **Business Addr:** Asst Defensive Backs Coach, Houston Texans, 2 Reliant Pk, Houston, TX 77054, **Business Phone:** (832)667-2002.

## CARTER, PHILIP W., JR.

School administrator, educator. **Personal:** Born Feb 1, 1941, Widen, WV; married Beverly Thomas; children: Philippa, Stacey & Frederick. **Educ:** Marshall Univ, BA, polit sci, 1964; Univ Pittsburgh, MSW, 1970. **Career:** Cong Racial Equality, Cleveland, dir, 1967-68; Univ Pittsburgh, Grad Sch Pub Int Affairs, instr, 1970-78; Comn Action Reg Training, dir, 1972-73; Univ Pittsburgh, asst provost, 1979; DIGIT Inc, pres, 1967-; Ford Found, fel, 1968; Univ Pittsburgh, Intercultural House, consult, 1969-70; Clarion Univ Pa, consult, 1973, 1976, 1980-81 & 1983-85; Marshall Univ, dir social work prog, bd mem, prof & chmn soc work, currently. **Orgs:** Chmn, Western Pa Black Polit Assembly, 1974-; campaign mgr, Mel King Mayor Boston, 1979; bd mem, Schuman Juv Ctr, 1979-81; Black Polit Action Comt; bd mem, Human Rels Comn, 1982-; bd mem, Barnett Day Care Ctr, Huntington, WVa, 1982-84; campaign mgr, Doris Smith Judge Spring, 1985; pres, Huntington Br, Nat Asn Advan Colored People, 1988-92, 1996-00. **Home Addr:** PO Box 510, Huntington, WV 25710. **Business Addr:** Professor, Chairman of Social Work, Marshall University, Rm 207 Old Main 1 John Marshall Dr, Huntington, WV 25755, **Business Phone:** (304)696-2790.

## CARTER, QUINCY (LAVONYA QUINTELLE CARTER)

Football player, football executive. **Personal:** Born Oct 13, 1977, Decatur, GA; son of Lavonya Sr. **Educ:** Univ Ga, attended 2000. **Career:** Football player (retired), executive; Dallas Cowboys, quarterback, 2001-03; New York Jets, quarterback, 2004-05; Montreal Alouettes, 2006; Bossier-Shreveport Battle Wings, quarterback, 2007; Kans City Brigade, 2008; Abilene Ruff Riders, quarterback, 2009; Corpus Christi Fury, 2016; free agt, currently. **Honors/Awds:** Freshman of the Year, Southeastern Conf, 1998. **Business Addr:** Player, Abilene Ruff Riders, 301 Cypress, Abilene, TX 79601, **Business Phone:** (325)677-7277.

## CARTER, DR. RAYMOND GENE, SR.

Executive, educator. **Personal:** Born Nov 12, 1936, Youngstown, OH; married Virginia Averhart; children: Raymond, John Amos & Dewayne Dwight. **Educ:** Youngstown State Univ, BA, 1959, MEd, 1975; Univ Pittsburgh, PhD. **Career:** McGuffey Ctr Inc, admin dir, 1976-86; Youngstown State Univ, ltd serv fac, 1976-; Model City, dep dir; Curbstone Coaches, bd dir; Youngstown State Univ, ltd serv fac polit & social dept; Park view Coun Ctr, sr therapist, currently. **Orgs:** Minority rep Stub Canal pvt Sector; chmn, Welf Adv Bd; Social Serv; bd dir, Assoc Neighborhood Ctr; vpres, bd dir, Meth Comn Ctr; Eval Com Area Health; bd dir, C C; Kiwanis Club; Big Bros; bd dir, Eastern Ment Health High Sch; Selective Svc; foreman Mahoning County Jury, 1981. **Honors/Awds:** Leadership & Citizenship Award; Col Most Valuable Athlete; Curbstone Coaches Hall of Fame Youngstown; Athletic Achievement Award, Service Award, Youngstown City Mayor; Community Service Award, Black Knight Police Assoc; Choffin Career Center Award, 1988; Youngstown State Univ Football Hall of Fame, 1997. **Home Addr:** 47 Eliot Lane, Youngstown, OH 44505-4817, **Home Phone:** (216)747-8242. **Business Addr:** Senior Therapist, Parkview Coun Center, 611 Belmont Ave, Youngstown, OH 44502-1095, **Business Phone:** (330)744-2991.

## CARTER, REGINA

Jazz musician. **Personal:** Born Aug 6, 1966, Detroit, MI; daughter of Grace; married Alvester Garnett. **Educ:** Oakland Univ, Rochester, BA; New Eng Conservatory Music, Boston. **Career:** Berklee Col Music, instr; Albums: Regina Carter, 1995; Something For Grace, 1997; Rhythms of the Heart, 1998; Motor City Moments, 2000; Free fall, 2001; Paganini: After a Dream, 2003; I'll Be Seeing You: A Sentimental Journey, 2006; MacArthur fel, 2006; Reverse Thread, 2010; Southern Comfort, 2014. **Honors/Awds:** LHD, Albion Col, MI, 2006; MacArthur Fellows Program grant, Award, 2006. **Special Achievements:** Nominated for Grammy Award, 2002; Distinguished Artist Award, Int Soc for Performing Artists, 2007. **Business Addr:** Jazz Violinist, Unlimited Myles Inc, New York, NY 10104, **Business Phone:** (732)566-2881.

## CARTER, DR. RICARDO T.D.

Physician. **Educ:** Univ Xochicalco Sch Med, MD. **Career:** Lutheran Med Ctr, Brooklyn, NY, internship internal med & resident; Boston VA Med Ctr & Boston Univ, fel; Geisinger-Lewistown Hosp, med dir, internal med, physician, currently; Pa State Milton Hershey Med Ctr, med staff; Penn State Milton Hershey Med Ctr, staff mem, clin assoc prof; Premier Oncol Hemat Mgt Soc, assoc; Pa State Sch Med, clin assoc prof. **Orgs:** Chmn, Cent Pa Oncol Group; chmn & mem, bd dir, Lewistown Hosp Inc; bd dir, Pa Hemat & Oncol Soc; bd dir, Premier Oncol Hemat Mgt Soc. **Business Addr:** Physician, Geisinger-Lewistown Hospital, Elec Ave Med Ctr 310 Electric Ave Suite 231, Lewistown, PA 17044, **Business Phone:** (717)242-3760.

## CARTER, ROBERT LOUIS, JR.

Educator, school administrator. **Personal:** Born Nov 11, 1937, Loganville, GA; son of Robert Louis and Elizabeth; married Cathleen Jane Cole; children: Robert Louis, William Stephen, Joyce Elizabeth & Valerie Denise. **Educ:** Beloit Col, BA, classics, 1962; Northwestern Univ, MA, 1964, PhD, 1980. **Career:** Northwestern Univ Fel, 1962-65; Univ Ill, classics instr; Beloit Col, classics instr, dir High Potential Progr, exec dir, Beloit Improv Coalition, 1971-73, spl asst provost, 1969-73; Assoc Col Midwest, dir, Educ Develop Prog, 1973-83; exec bd, Wis Higher Educ Aids Bd, 1982-84; Wayne State Univ, dir, Univ Studies, Weekend Col Prog, 1984-86, assoc dean, Adult Degree Progs, 1986-87, dean, Col Life long Learning, 1988; Univ Pittsburgh, Pitts Col Gen Studies, dean, 1996. **Orgs:** Bd dir, Nat Coun Educ Opportunity Asns, 1980-82; Mid-Am Asn Educ Opportunity Prog Personnel, pres, 1981-82, exec secy, 1984; Nat Univ Continuing Educ Asn, 1987-; Asn Continuing Higher Educ; chair, Coord Coun Continuing Higher Educ, 1991-. **Home Addr:** 27200 Franklin Suite 524, Southfield, MI 48034, **Home Phone:** (313)357-2988. **Business Addr:** MI.

## CARTER, ROBERT T.

Executive. **Personal:** Born Mar 21, 1938, Cleveland, OH; married Virginia; children: Robert John. **Educ:** Baldwin Wallace Col, BA, 1959; Pepperdine Grad Sch Bus. **Career:** Cleveland, teacher, 1959-64; Shell Oil Co Long Beach, sales rep, 1964-66; Hoffman LaRoche, sales & hosp rep, 1966-68; KFI Radio Inc, acct exec, 1968-. **Orgs:** Nat Asn Mkt Develop; Radio Salesman La; Southern Calif Broadcasters; La Brotherhood Crusade; New Frontier Dem Club; United Crusade Fund Raising Comt, 1974-75; Leukemia Soc Am; Southern Calif Striders Track Club. **Home Addr:** 15556 High Knoll Rd, Encino, CA 91316.

## CARTER, ROBERT THOMPSON

School administrator, executive director. **Personal:** Born Mar 16, 1937, Cleveland, OH; son of Robert (deceased) and Evelyn (deceased); married Tessa Rosemary Felton; children: Robert & Jacqueline. **Educ:** Dartmouth Col, BA, 1959. **Career:** Joseph T Ryerson & Son Inc, supvr personnel admin, 1967-68, mgr, comm rels 1968-70; N Lawndale Econ Develop Corp, asst gen mgr, 1970-72; Inland Steel Develop Corp, asst reg mgr & proj mgr, 1972-77; Inland Steel-Ryerson Found, exec dir, sec, 1981-86; Dearborn Pk Corp, vpres, corp commun & corp sec, 1977-81; Nat Merit Scholar Corp, exec dir, 1987-88, vpres, 1988-; Chicago Bridges Work demonstration, proj dir; Music Theatre Workshop, dir; Suburban Job-Link Corp, dir, currently, Pub/Pvt Ventures, dir, currently. **Orgs:** Co-founder, Black Contractors

United, 1979; bd chairperson, Just Jobs Inc, 1982-86; dir, Performance Comm, 1982-86; vpres, Asn Black Found Execs, 1984-86; founding mem, dir, Ind Donors Alliance, 1984-86; corp adv bd, Independent Col Funds Am, 1984-86; vpres, Music Theatre Workshop, 1986-; dir, Brass Found Inc, 1987; dir, Blacks Develop, 1987-; trustee, Gaylord & Dorothy Donnelley Found, 1988-; Horizon Hospice, dir, 1992-; Garfield Coun Ctr. **Home Addr:** 6301 N Sheridan Rd Suite 3M, Chicago, IL 60660, **Home Phone:** (312)743-8459. **Business Addr:** Director, Public/Private Ventures, 2000 Market St Suite 600, Philadelphia, PA 19103, **Business Phone:** (215)557-4400.

### CARTER, RODA WARD

Executive, cosmetics executive. **Educ:** Fashion Inst Technol, NY, AS, fashion design, 1987; Conn Inst Hair Design, AAS, cosmetology, 1994; Rollins Col, MBA, bus admin & mgt, 2011. **Career:** Ann Taylor & Coach, counter mgr; Model: Disney, Weight Watchers, Tupperware, Nicole Miller, Nordstrom, Saks Fifth Ave; Beauty Enterprises, distribr; Naomi Sims Cosmetics, vpres prod develop, 1987-92; Universal Colors Cosmetics, owner, pres & chief exec officer, 1999-2006; Carter Health, vpres, 2007-2013; Carter-Health Disposables LLC, pres & chief exec officer, 2009-. **Orgs:** NAFE; Boys & Girls Club; contribr, United Way; Teaching Tolerance. **Business Addr:** President, Chief Executive officer, Carter-Health LLC, 4370 LB McLeod Rd, Orlando, FL 32835, **Business Phone:** (407)296-6689.

### CARTER, ROLAND M.

Composer, educator, association executive. **Educ:** Hampton Univ, BS, music educ, piano; NY Univ, MS, music educ, choral. **Career:** Univ Tenn, Chattanooga, UC Found, distinguished composer-arranger & conductor, prof music, currently, Cadek Dept Music, Ruth S Holmberg Prof music; MAR-VEL, founder & chief exec officer; "The Choral Music of Roland M. Carter, Volume I", 2009. **Orgs:** Nat Asn Negro Musicians; life mem, Nat Asn Negro Musicians, bd dir, chair comt Choral Stand; life mem, Am Choral Dir Asn; Music Educrs Nat Conf; Music Teachers Nat Asn; Phi Mu Alpha Sinfonia; Kappa Alpha Psi Fraternity; co-chair, NEA; Chattanooga African Am Mus; Chattanooga Symphony & Opera Asn; dir, Choral Soc Preserv African Am Songs; hon mem, Morehouse Glee Club, 2004; Tenn Arts Comn; Southern Arta Found; Nat Assembly State Arts Agencies, Allied Arts Greater Chattanooga. **Honors/Awds:** Received numerous awards & honors; hon doctorate music degree, shaw Univ; Tennessee Governor Arts Award, 2003. **Business Addr:** Professor, University of Tennessee, 308 Fine Arts Dept 1451 615 McCallie Ave, Chattanooga, TN 37403, **Business Phone:** (423)425-4601.

### CARTER, RUTH E. (RUTHE CARTER)

Costume designer. **Personal:** Born MA. **Educ:** Hampton Univ, fine & performing arts. **Career:** Assoc prod, The Family Man, 1979; costume designer: School Daze, 1988; I'm Gonna Git You Sucka, 1988; Do the Right Thing, 1989; Mo' Better Blues, 1990; The Five Heartbeats, 1991; Jungle Fever, 1991; House Party 2, 1991; Malcolm X, 1992; What's Love Got to Do with It, 1993; The Meteor Man, 1993; Surviving the Game, 1994; Crooklyn, 1994; Cobb, 1994; Money Train, 1995; Clockers, 1995; Rosewood, 1996; The Great White Hype, 1996; How Stella Got Her Groove Back; Sunchaser, 1996; Amistad, 1997; B*a*p*s, 1997; Rosewood, 1997; Summer of Sam, 1999; Bamboozled, 2000; Price of Glory, 2000; Shaft, 2000; Love & Basketball, 2000; Dr. Dolittle 2, 2001; Baby Boy, 2001; Dr. Dolittle 2, 2001; I Spy, 2002; Daddy Day Care, 2003; Against the Ropes, 2004; Four Brothers, 2005; Serenity, 2005; Faceless, 2006; "Thief ", 2006; "Shark", 2006-07; Meet Dave, 2008; Spread, 2009; Frankie & Alice, 2009; Spread, 2009; Black Dynamite, 2009; Imagine That, 2009; Bring It On: Fight to the Finish, 2009; "Miami Med", 2010; Teen Beach Movie, 2011; Sparkle, 2012. **Honors/Awds:** Am Black Film Festival Career Achievement Award for Women, 2002. **Special Achievements:** Academy Award, nominated.

### CARTER, SHAWN COREY

Rap musician, actor, entrepreneur. **Personal:** Born Dec 4, 1969, Brooklyn, NY; son of Adnis Reeves and Gloria; married Beyonce Knowles; children: Blue Ivy. **Career:** Roc-A-Fella Records, co-founder, vocalist, 1997; Albums: Reasonable Doubt, 1996; In My Lifetime, 1997; Hard Knock Life, 1998; (with various artists) Streets Is Watching, 1998; The Life & Times of Shawn Carter, 1999; "Saturday Night Live", 2000-10; TheDynasty: Roc la Familia, 2000; The Blueprint, 2001; Jay-Z: Unplugged, 2001; Chapter One: Greatest Hits, 2002; (with R. Kelly) The Best of Both Worlds, 2002; The Blueprint 2: The Gift & the Curse, 2002; Bring It On: The Best of Jay-Z, 2003; The Blueprint 2.1, 2003; The Black album, 2003; (with R. Kelly) Unfinished Business, 2004; (with Linkin Park) Collision Course, 2004; "20 to 1", 2006-10; Kingdom Come, 2006; American Gangster, 2007; The Blueprint 3, 2008; Watch the Throne, 2011; Magna Carta Holy Grail, 2013. Singles: "Criminal Minds", 2008; "Dancing on Ice", 2009; The Taking of Pelham 1 2 3, 2009; "The Jay Leno Show", 2009; "WWF Raw", 2009; "Arthur and the Revenge of Maltazard", 2009; "The Paul O'Grady Show", 2009; "EastEnders: E20", 2009; "Dancing on Ice", 2009-10; "Dancing with the Stars", 2009-10; "Live from Studio Five", 2009-10; "Brit Awards 2010", 2010; "Isle of Wight Festival 2010: Live", 2010; Films: Streets Is Watching, 1998; Hard Knock Life, 2000; State Property, 2002; Paper Soldiers, 2002; Paid in Full, producer, 2002; Fade to Black, 2004; I Will Not Lose, 2004; Diary of Jay-Z: Water for Life, 2006; Hope for Haiti Now: A Global Benefit for Earthquake Relief, 2010; The Great Gatsby, exec producer, 2013; Top Five, co-producer, 2014; Annie, producer, 2014. TV series: "Robins", 2006-10; "Sandra Lee's Taverns, Lounges & Clubs", 2012 Def Jam Recordings, pres & chief exec officer, 2005; The 40/40 Club, co-owner, currently; New Jersey Nets, co-owner, currently. **Orgs:** Shawn Carter Scholarship Fund. **Honors/Awds:** Grammy Award, 2004-06, 2008-14, American Music, MTV Music Video, Soul Train and Billboard Awards; Blimp Award, 2010. **Special Achievements:** First Hip-Hop artist to be featured on the news program; First non-athleteto have a signature sneaker line; The S. Carter is the fastest selling sneaker in Reebok history; One Of The 10 Most Fascinating People of 2006. **Business Addr:** Owner, The 40/40 Club, Six W 25th St, New York, NY 10010, **Business Phone:** (212)832-4040.

### CARTER, DR. STEPHEN L.

Educator, novelist. **Personal:** Born Oct 26, 1954, Washington, DC; son of Lisle and Emily; married Enola Aird; children: 2. **Educ:** Stanford Univ, BA, hist, 1976; Yale Univ Law Sch, JD, 1979. **Career:** Writer, Educator; US Ct Appeals, DC Circuit, Judge Spottswood W. Robinson, III, law clerk; US Supreme Ct, Justice Thurgood Marshall, clerk; Yale Law Sch, from asst prof to prof, 1982-91, William Nelson Cromwell prof law, 1991-; Books: Reflections of an Affirmative Action Baby; God's Name in Vain, 2000; The Culture of Disbelief: How American Law & Politics Trivialize Religious Devotion, 1993; Confirmation Mess: Cleaning up the Federal Appointments Process, 1994; Integrity, 1996; Dissent of the Governed: A Meditation on Law, Religion & Loyalty, 1998; Civility: Manners, Morals & the Etiquette of Democracy, 1998; God's Name in Vain: The Wrongs & Rights of Religion in Politics, 2000; The Emperor of Ocean Park, 2002; New England White, 2007; Palace Council, 2008; Jericho's Fall, 2009; The Violence of Peace: America's Wars in the Age of Obama, 2011; The Impeachment of Abraham Lincoln, 2012; Back Channel, 2010. **Orgs:** Bd trustee, Aspen Inst. **Business Addr:** William Nelson Cromwell Professor of Law, Yale Law School, 127 Wall St, New Haven, CT 06511, **Business Phone:** (203)432-2364.

### CARTER, THOMAS, III

Executive, football player. **Personal:** Born Sep 5, 1972, Saint Petersburg, FL; married Renee; children: Cameron (deceased), Peyton, Madison & Alex. **Educ:** Notre Dame Univ. **Career:** Football player (retired), executive; Wash Redskins, left cornerback, 1993-96; Chicago Bears, left cornerback, 1997, defensive back, 1998, right cornerback, 1999; Cincinnati Bengals, left cornerback, 1999-2000, cornerback, 2000, 2001; Nat Football League Players Asn, regional dir, currently; WVIR-TV NBC29, news reporter, currently. **Business Addr:** Regional Director, National Football League Players Association, 1133 20th St NW Suite 600, Washington, DC 20036, **Business Phone:** (202)463-2200.

### CARTER, THOMAS, III

Dean (education). **Educ:** Henderson State Univ, BS. **Career:** Univ Ark, Stud Serv & Stud Affairs, asst dean, currently. **Orgs:** Adv, Nat Soc Black Engrs; Northwest Riders; adv, Am Indian Sci & Engineering Soc; NAMEPA. **Business Addr:** Assistant Dean of Student Services & Student Affairs, Office of the Dean, University Arkansas, 4183 Bell Engineering Ctr, Fayetteville, AR 72701, **Business Phone:** (479)575-5009.

### CARTER, THOMAS ALLEN

Consultant. **Personal:** Born Jul 12, 1935, Cincinnati, OH; son of Fernando Albert and Mary Gladys Gover; married Janet Tucker; children: Barry E, Duane A & Sarita A. **Educ:** Jones Col, AB, 1980, BBA, 1982. **Career:** Consultant (retired); Red Lobster Restaurant Const Dept, contract adminr, 1976-78; JH Dunlap Roofing Co, consult cost estimating, 1978-84; Harcar Inc, pres, 1978-80; Blacando Develop Corp, exec secy, dir, 1980-84; Solomon A Williams Inc, proj engr, 1984-2002, chief engr, 2002. **Orgs:** Robinson's Custom Homes, 1980-84; Bluejackets Choir USN; Bluejackets Octet USN; Fleet Res Asn; treas, Rafman Club Inc. **Honors/Awds:** Sailor of the Year, 9th Naval Dist, 1960; SeaBee of the Month Argentia Newfoundland Canada, 1965. **Home Addr:** 4128 Arajo Ct, Orlando, FL 32812, **Home Phone:** (407)859-9948.

### CARTER, THOMAS J., II

Lawyer, educator. **Personal:** Born Feb 27, 1953, St. Louis, MO; son of Thomas and Everline; married Dorothy L, Sep 25, 1972; children: LaDon D. **Educ:** Univ Md, BS, bus admin & minor acct, 1980; St Louis Univ Sch Law, JD, 1983. **Career:** City St. Louis, Housing Ct, hearing officer, 1966-; Law Officers Bussey & Jordan, law clerk, 1981-93, assoc, 1993-94; Off Atty Gen, asst atty gen, 1984-85; Moser & Marsalek, PC assoc, 1985-92, shareholder, 1992-95; St Louis Univ, adj prof civil pract, 1988-; Collier, Dorsey, Carter, Williams, partner, 1995; Pvt pract, atty, currently. **Orgs:** Am Bar Asn; Mo Bar Asn; Bar Asn Metrop, St Louis; Mo Orgn Defense Lawyers; Asn Defense Coun St Louis; Nat Bar Asn; Ill State Bar Asn; Mound City Bar Asn, pres, 1991-92; Asn Defense Coun. **Honors/Awds:** State MO, License, 1984; US Dist Ct Eastern MO, Admis, 1985; US Dist Ct Western MO, Admis, 1985; State Ill, License, 1986; US Ct Appeals, 8thCircuit, Admis, 1987. **Special Achievements:** Lawyers Role Polit Empowerment: the Struggle Continues Minorities & Women, St Louis Daily Records, May 1, 1990. **Home Addr:** 5447 Claxton Ave, St. Louis, MO 63120-2524, **Home Phone:** (314)389-5470. **Business Addr:** Adjunct Professor, Saint Louis University School of Law, 100 N Tucker Blvd Suite 986, St. Louis, MO 63101-1930, **Business Phone:** (314)977-2800.

### CARTER, TONY A. (ANTONIO MARCUS CARTER)

Football player. **Personal:** Born Aug 23, 1972, Columbus, OH. **Educ:** Univ Minn, grad. **Career:** Football player(retired); Chicago Bears, running back & fullback, 1994-97; New England Patriots, fullback, 1998-2000; Denver Broncos, 2001; Green Bay Packers, right back, 2002.

### CARTER, TRACY L.

Health services administrator. **Personal:** Born Oct 9, 1970, Akron, OH; daughter of Bennie and Tanya; married Stanley Johnson; children: Jaylen. **Educ:** Ohio Univ Col Bus, BBA, 1993; Univ Mich Sch Pub, masters, health admin, 1995. **Career:** Ohio Univ, stud ctr mgr, 1992-93; Henry Ford Health Syst, mkt & outreach intern, 1994; WK Kellog Found, community based pub health liaison, 1994-95; Summa Health Syst, admis fel, 1995-96, dir, corp projs, 1996-99, dir, corp projs, community serv, 1999, Advocacy & Health Policy, syst dir govt affairs & health policy, currently. **Orgs:** Bd chair, Healthy Connections Network, 1996-; Leadership Akron, 1998-; vpres, YWCA bd, 1999-; personnel chair, Summa Cty C Servs Bd, 2000-; personnel chair, Caring Communities Summit Community, 2001-; EJ Thomas Hall/ Akron Civic Theatre, multicultural prog comn, 2002-; adv comn, United Way, Proj Blueprint, 2002-; Area Helath Educ Ctr Bd, 2002-. **Home Addr:** 979 Amelia Ave, Akron, OH 44302, **Home Phone:** (330)869-9157. **Business Addr:** Director of Government Affairs & Health Policy, Summa Health System, 525 E Market St Suite 2D, Akron, OH 44304, **Business Phone:** (330)375-7566.

### CARTER, TROY A.

Government official, educator, vice president (organization). **Personal:** Born Oct 26, 1963, New Orleans, LA; son of Theodore R and Eartha F; married Melanie Sanders; children: Troy II & Joshua. **Educ:** Xavier Univ, BA, polit sci & bus admin, 1986; Carnegie-Mellon Sch Urban & Pub Affairs, MPA; New Orleans Regional Leadership Inst, grad, 2001. **Career:** New Orleans, exec aide to mayor Sidney J Barthelemy, 1988-91; La State, rep, 1992, City Coun, rep Dist C, 1994; WD Scott Group Inc, Environ Eng Consult, vpres; Planning & Mgt Consult Firm, pres & managing partner; Xavier Univ, polit sci instr, currently; Policy & Planning Partners LLC, managing partner, chief exec officer, currently; Commonwealth Properties, L.L.C, pres, currently. **Orgs:** Bd dir, Big Bros & Big Sisters; bd dir, Nat Youth Sport Found; chmn dist C, Orleans Parish Dem Exec Comt; charter mem, 100 Black Men New Orleans; Green Found fel Harvard Univ; Nat Asn Advan Colored People; Nat Orgn Black Pub Admin; life mem, Kappa Alpha Psi Fraternity Inc; Nat Forum Black Pub Adminr; chmn, Opers Comt, Controversial Opers Comt, Sewerage & Water Bd. **Home Addr:** 92 Eng Turn Dr, New Orleans, LA 70131, **Home Phone:** (504)392-6213. **Business Addr:** Chief Executive Officer, Managing Partner, Policy & Planning Partners LLC, 650 Poydras St Suite 2417, New Orleans, LA 70130, **Business Phone:** (504)299-3293.

### CARTER, VINCE (VINCENT LAMAR CARTER)

Basketball player. **Personal:** Born Jan 26, 1977, Daytona Beach, FL; married Ellen Rucker; children: Kai Michelle. **Educ:** Univ NC, attended 1998. **Career:** Toronto Raptors, forward, 1998-2004; Olympics, Sydney, Australia, US men's basketball team, 2000-04; NJ Nets, guard & forward, 2004-09; Orlando Magic, 2009-10; Visions InFlight Inc, pres, 2010; Phoenix Suns, 2010-11; Dallas Mavericks, 2011-14; Memphis Grizzlies, 2014-; videogame series: NBA Inside Drive, 2002; NBA Live, 2004; films: Like Mike, 2002; "This Is My Party", 2002; "Back for More", 2003; TV series: Mis-Directed Study, 1999. **Orgs:** Founder, Embassy Hope Found; goodwill ambassador, Big Bros Big Sisters Am; Omega Psi Phi. **Business Addr:** Professional Basketball Player, Dallas Mavericks, 2500 Victory Ave, Dallas, TX 75219, **Business Phone:** (214)747-6287.

### CARTER, VINCENT G.

Manager, interior designer. **Personal:** Born Feb 22, 1956, Milwaukee, WI; son of Walter A Sr and Lessie M. **Educ:** Univ Wis-Milwaukee, BS, gen studies, pre med emphasis, 1977; Univ Wis-Madison, MS, interior design, 1983. **Career:** Visual Graphics Created, designer, 1980-95; World Bank, client rep, 1983-95; Howard Univ, asst prof, 1984-2000; Vincent G Carter Assocs Inc, owner, vice chmn, prin, 1994-, sr prog mgr, 1995-; Karn Charuhas Chapman Twohey Architects, sr interior designer, 1997-99; McKissack & McKissack, sr interior designer, 1999-2003; DIA, sr architect, 2003-09; Louis Berger Group, sr interior designer, 2003-05; Dept Defense, sr space planner, 2005-09; US Dept Homeland Security, sr prog mgr, 2009-; Bodley Head Ltd, dean. **Orgs:** Bd dir, Am Soc Interior Designers, 1980-; Facil Mgt Asn, 1988-; Interior Design Educr Coun, 1990-; Int Interior Design Asn, 1991-; Nat Coun Interior Design Qualifications, 1991-; Nat Legis Coalition Interior Design, 1992-; int chmn, Wash DC Bd Interior Designers, 1993-97; site visitor, Coun Interior Design Accreditation, Accreditation Comn, etc, 1996-2009; Woodlawn Plantation & Pope-Leighey House Coun, 1997-2000; vice chmn, Int Codes Coun, 2001-; Alpha Phi Alpha Fraternity Inc. **Honors/Awds:** America's Best & Brightest Young Bus Professionals, 1990; Howard Univ Teaching Award, 1994; Wash Metro ASID Design Humanity, 1998; Medalist Award, Am Socs Interior Designers, 2000; Fasid Community Ser Award, Sheri K Lake, 2002. **Special Achievements:** Admission to the College of Fellows, ASID, 2009. **Home Addr:** PO Box 31197, Washington, MD 20030-1197, **Home Phone:** (202)255-8384. **Business Addr:** Principal, Owner, Vincent G Carter Associates Inc, 2711 Centerville Rd Suite 400, Wilmington, DE 19808.

### CARTER, DR. WARRICK L.

Educator, executive. **Personal:** Born May 6, 1942, Charlottesville, VA; son of Charles M and Evelyn Jones; married Laurel; children: Keisha. **Educ:** Tenn State Univ, Blair Acad Music, BS, advan percussion, 1965; Mich State Univ, MM, 1966, PhD, music, 1970; Univ Chicago, cert fund raising, 1978. **Career:** Univ Md, dept Music, asst prof, 1966-71, dir bands; Mich State Univ, dir dept urbanmusic, 1970-71; Gov State Univ, coordr, fine & performing div, 1971-84, coord music prog, 1976-79, chmn div Fine & Performing Arts, prof music, 1979-84; Sch Music Univ Sao Paulo Brazil, guest lectr, 1976; Northwestern Univ, guest prof Afro-Am Studies, 1977-84; Univ Santa Cantarina Floriano polis Brazil, guest lectr dept music, 1980; Berklee Col Music, dean fac, 1984-95, provost & vip acad affairs, 1984-96; Walt Disney Entertainment, dir entertainment arts, 1996-2000; Columbia Col, pres, 2000-13; Calif State Univ LA, vis prof, Music Dept. **Orgs:** Exec dir, Nat Black Music Caucus, 1974-78; bd mem, Found Advan Music, 1982; IAJE, 1982-; past pres, NAJE, 1982-84; bd mem, Nat Jazz Cable Network, 1982-84; chmn, Jazz Panel Nat Endow Arts, 1982-85; co-chair, Music Policy Panel Nat Endowment, 1983-84; bd dir, Int House Blues Found, 1993-; ASCAP; bd dir, Rotary Int; Adv Boards Interlochen; Lincoln Libr; New City Bank; bd dir, New Orleans Ctr Creative Arts; adv bd, Music Fest USA & EPCOT Inst Entertainment Arts; int advisor, Jikei Group. **Honors/Awds:** Fac Mem of the Year, Univ Md, 1967-68; Grad Fel Ctr Urban Affairs Mich State Univ, 1969-70; Best Drummer Award, Collegiante Jazz Festival, Notre Dame Univ, 1970; Distinguished Teacher Award, Gov's State Univ, 1974; "The Whistle" comn Nat Endowment Arts, 1982-83; International Jazz Educators Hall of Fame, 1997; National Black Music Caucus Achievement Award. **Special Achievements:** First African American pres of Columbia Col Chicago, named as one of ten Outstanding Music Educr Sch Musician, 1983. Who's Who in Black America. **Home Addr:** 17 E Scott, Chicago, IL 60610, **Home Phone:** (312)397-1329. **Business Addr:** President, Columbia College Chicago, Rm 505 600 S Mich Ave, Chicago, IL 60605, **Business Phone:** (312)663-1600.

**CARTER, WENDELL PATRICK.** See CARTER, PAT.

## CARTER, DR. WESLEY BYRD

Psychiatrist, physician. **Personal:** Born Apr 22, 1942, Richmond, VA; son of Wesley T; married Norma Archer. **Educ:** Va Union Univ, BS, 1964; Va Commonwealth Univ Med Col Va, Sch Med, MD, 1968. **Career:** Med Col Va, pediat internship, 1969; Med Col Va, Gen Psychiat Resident, 1971-72, intern; Va Commonwealth Univ Sch Med, resident, intern; Va Treat Ctr C, child psychiat fel, 1973; Child Psychiat Ltd, child psychiat, 1975-83; Psychiat Med Col Va, asst clin prof, 1976-; Psychiat Inst Richmond C Unit, med chief, 1983-87; Psychiat Inst Richmond, actg med dir, 1986; Horizons Inc, pres, 1986-93; Charter Westbrook Hosp, clin dir adult serv, 1987, clin dir RTP, 1989-92, actg med dir, 1990; Show Whats Your Mind, WANI Richmond, radio host; Memorial Child Guid Clin, psychiatist, 2004; Richmond Pub Schs, psychiat consult; Caroline County Pub Schs, psychiat consult; Friends Asn Richmond, psychiat consult; Real Sch Richmond Pub Schs, spec consult; St Mary's Hosp, hosp staff; Richmond Mem, Richmond Community Hosp, hosp staff; Richmond Metro Hosp, hosp staff; Westbrook Hosp, hosp staff; Psychiat Inst Richmond, hosp staff; Med Col Va, hosp staff; Chippenham Hosp, hosp staff; Memorial Child Guid Clin, pvt practr, currently. **Orgs:** Bd dir, Ment Health Asn Va, 1991; Youth Serv Comn Richmond; Spec Educ Adv Comt; Richmond Pub Schs; Med Col Va Med Curric Comt; Richmond Acad Med; pres, Richmond Med Soc; pres, Va Coun Child Psychiat; pres psychiat, Soc Va; Va Soc Adolescent Psychiat; Med Soc Va; fel Am Psychiat Asn; Am Acad Child Psychiat; Black Psychiat Am; Asn Air Force Psychiat; Chi Delta Mu; fel Alpha Phi Alpha; Thebans Richmond; Old Dom Med Soc; Nat Med Asn; AMA; State Human Rights Comt Va, Dept Ment Health, Ment Retardation & Substance Abuse Serv; Am Acad Child & Adolescent Psychiat; fel Beta Kappa Chi; Cent Tex Med Found. **Honors/Awds:** Practitioner Of The Year, Old Dom Med Soc, 1999; Distinguished Life Fel, Am Psychiat Asn, 2005; Walter Lester Henry Award, Richmond Med Soc, 2009. **Home Addr:** 1407 Wentbridge Rd, Richmond, VA 23227, **Home Phone:** (804)353-8006. **Business Addr:** Child Psychiatrist, Memorial Child Guidance Clinic, 2319 E Broad St, Richmond, VA 23223, **Business Phone:** (757)888-0400.

## CARTER, WILL J.

Executive. **Career:** Carter Indust Serv Inc & Carter Express Inc, Anderson, Ind, chief exec officer, 1992-. **Orgs:** GAAFU Pres, New York Fisk Alumni Asn; Nat Asn Advan Colored People. **Home Addr:** , Anderson, IN 46012, **Home Phone:** (765)642-8533. **Business Addr:** Chief Executive Officer, Carter Industrial Service Inc, 2403 Raible Ave, Anderson, IN 46014-4147, **Business Phone:** (317)644-6601.

## CARTER, WILLIAM BEVERLY, III

Executive. **Personal:** Born Feb 22, 1947, Philadelphia, PA; son of W Beverly Jr and Rosalie A Terry; married Kay Sebekos; children: Terence S. **Educ:** Univ Col Nairobi, Kenya, African polit & African hist, 1966; Univ de Paris Sorbonne, cert, Fr lang & lit, 1966; Howard Univ, BA, hist & govt, 1971; Johns Hopkins Univ Sch Adv Int Studies, MA, foreign policy towards southern Africa, 1973. **Career:** Executive (retired); Rockefeller-Luce Fel, 1971-73; US Community Orgn Govt Conduct Foreign Policy, staff mem, 1973-75; US Dept State, escort interpreter, 1972-75; Comn Orgn Govt Conduct Foreign Policy, staff asst, 1973-75; Brookings Inst, res asst, 1974-75; US Dept Energy, sr foreign affairs officer, 1976-81; Amazing Grace, Corolla, NC, resort real estate developer, 1982-2013; Inst Int Educ, Prof Exchange Progs, prog officer, assoc dir, interim dir, 1984-2005. **Orgs:** Nat Gen Soc, 1974-; bd dir, Lupus Found Greater Wash DC, 1984-93; adv bd, Lupus Found Greater Wash, 1993-; chmn, Nat Adv Comt Diversity, NCIV, 1993-96; bd dir, Nat Coun Int Visitors, NCIV, 1993-99; bd dir, Int Asn Black Prof Int Affairs, 1999-2002; chair, Calif Univ Pa, Jennie Adams Carter Scholar Fund. **Honors/Awds:** William C Foster Award, JH Univ Sch Advan Int Studies, 1972-73. **Home Addr:** 8009 Ashboro Ct, Chevy Chase, MD 20815-3052, **Home Phone:** (301)589-4647.

## CARTER, DR. WILLIAM THOMAS, JR.

Physician. **Personal:** Born Apr 27, 1944, Norfolk, VA; married Juatina M Redd; children: William III, Dominique Michelle & Tiasha Malitha. **Educ:** Fisk Univ, AB, 1967; Tenn A&I State Univ, MS, 1969; Meharry Med Col, Md, 1973. **Career:** USN, dir emergency med; Southern Md Hosp, emergency med doctor, currently. **Orgs:** Kappa Alpha Psi Fraternity, 1963-; Assoc Mil Surgeons US, 1981-; ATLS instr, Am Col Surgeons, 1982-; Pigskin Club Inc, 1984-; Nat Asn Advan Colored People, 1987-; Nat Med Asn, 1987-; Am Col Emergency Physicians, 1987-. **Honors/Awds:** Publication: "Gunshot Wounds to the Penis", NY Acad Urol, 1979. **Home Addr:** 4411 Marquis Pl, Woodbridge, VA 22192. **Business Addr:** Director of Emergency Medicine, US Navy, 7503 Surratts Rd, Clinton, MD 20735, **Business Phone:** (301)870-7001.

## CARTER, YVONNE PICKERING

Educator, artist, association executive. **Personal:** Born Feb 6, 1939, Washington, DC; daughter of Lorenzo Irving Pickering and Esther Robinson; married Joseph Payne; children: Cornelia Malisia. **Educ:** Traphagen Sch Design, NY, cert interior design, 1959; Howard Univ, BA, 1962, MFA, 1968. **Career:** Dist Display Wash, DC, display coordr, 1962-63; Howard Univ, libr asst, 1963-68, asst librn, 1968-71; Fed City Col, asst prof art; Univ DC, Art Dept, prof art, Dept Mass Media Visual & Performing Art Prof, dept chairperson, prof emer, currently; Gallery Cornelia, owner & cur, currently. **Orgs:** Am Soc African Cult, 1966; Col Art Asn, 1971-; Nat Asn Study Negro Life & Hist, 1971-72; Am Asn Univ Prof, 1974-; Women's Caucus Art, 1976-; Col Art Asn, 1976-; Artists Equity, 1987-89; Women ColorArt, 1996-97; Mus Contemp Art, 1996-97. **Honors/Awds:** Publ imprints by Am Negro artists, 1962, 1965; Exhibitor, Howard Univ JA Porter Gallery, one-woman show, 1973; Visual Artist Grant, DC Comn of the Arts & Humanities, 1981, 1982, 1995; Corrine Matchell Award (WCA/DC); Commonwealth George Mason U. 1990-92; Mobile Oil Grant, Artisis in Kazakstan; Paintings WA Gallery Wash DC, two-woman show; Smith-Mason Gallery Nat Exhbn Black Artist Wash DC; selected group shows & performances: NJ State Mus black artist show; Howard Univ Art Gallery; Franz Bader Gallery Wash DC; Corcoran Gallery of Art; Miami-Dade Pub Libr; Los Angeles African-Amer Mus; Kenkelaba House, New York, NY; Baltimore Mus; Fendrick Gallery; Walters Art Gallery, MD; CA Afro-Am Mus; Anacostia Mus Kenkeleba Gallery; NY, Bronx Mus of Arts; Natl Mus of Women in the Arts; Gumbo Yayya: Anthology of Contemp African Am Women Artists, 1989. **Home Addr:** 526 29th Ave NE, Washington, DC 20002-4818. **Business Addr:** Owner, Gallery Cornelia, 90 Cannon St, Charleston, SC 29403, **Business Phone:** (843)805-8444.

## CARTER, ESQ. ZACHARY WARREN

Lawyer. **Personal:** Born Mar 19, 1950, Washington, DC; son of Joseph W and Margaret G (deceased); married Rosalind Clay; children: Chandler Clay. **Educ:** Cornell Univ, BA, 1972; NY Univ Sch Law, JD, 1975. **Career:** EDNY Dep Chief, Crim Div, asst US atty, 1975-80; Patterson, Belknap, Webb & Tyler, gen litigation, 1980-81; DA Kings County DA's Off, exec asst, 1982-87; NYC Courts, from asst to dep chief admin, 1987; Criminal Ct, City NY-Queens, County, judge, 1987-91; EDNY, US magistrate judge, 1991-93; US Dept Justice, US atty-EDNY, 1993-99; Dorsey & Whitney LLP, partner, head trial group, co-chair, 1999-; Marsh & McLennan Co Inc, dir, 2004-14; Cable vision New York Group Inc, dir, 2006-14; New York City, Corp Coun, 2014-. **Orgs:** Exec comt mem, Criminal Law Sect, NY State Bar Asn; assoc bar, Comn Encourage Judicial Serv; bd trustees, Fed Bar Coun; bd trustees, NYU Law Found; past vice chair, bd dir, Community Action Legal Serv; past vpres, Nat Black Prosecutors Asn; bd dir, Hale House; bd trustees, New York Univ Sch Law; bd dir, VERA Inst Justice; chmn, New York Mayor Comt, 2002-13. **Honors/Awds:** Public Interest Law & Society Award, NYLPI, 2006; New York Super Lawyer, 2009. **Business Addr:** Partner, Co-Chair, Dorsey & Whitney LLP, 250 Pk Ave, New York, NY 10177, **Business Phone:** (212)415-9345.

## CARTHAN, EDDIE JAMES

Government official. **Personal:** Born Oct 18, 1949, Tchula, MS; married Shirley Unger; children: Cissye, Neketa & Jowina. **Educ:** Miss Valley State Univ, BS, 1971; Jackson State Univ, MS, 1977; Univ Miss. **Career:** St Col, instr, 1972; US Dept Comn Off Minority Bus Enterprise, bus develop; Lexington Bus Serv Inc, bus specislist, 1973; Sch Durant Attendance Ctr, teacher; Saints Col Lexington, teacher; Carthan's Convenience Store, owner & mgr; Carthan's Pkg Store; Crystal Resturant; Tchula, mayor, 1979; Good Samaritan Ecumenical Church, minister & pastor; Miss Family Farmers Asn, pres. **Orgs:** Bd dir, Delta Found; Gov Midas Comn; King David Mason Lodge 112; Holmes Co Bd Educ; Holmes Co Elks, chair, Nat Juneteenth Black Farmers Comn; pres, Holmes Co Bd & Educ, 1973. **Honors/Awds:** The Sacco-Vanzetti Memorial Award, 1983. **Special Achievements:** Book: The Last Hired & First Fired; Success & Hard Work; editor, If Things CouldTalk; We've Come A Long Way Baby; Bus Ruralite. **Home Addr:** PO Box 29, Tchula, MS 39169, **Home Phone:** (662)998-2840.

## CARTHEN, JOHN, JR.

Automotive executive. **Career:** River View Ford Mercury Inc, owner, 1988-; Lakeland Ford Lincoln Mercury Inc, owner. **Business Addr:** Owner, River View Ford Mercury Inc, 600 Columbia Ctr, Columbia, IL 62236-2542, **Business Phone:** (618)281-5106.

## CARTLIDGE, DR. ARTHUR J., SR.

Teacher, educator, school superintendent. **Personal:** Born Jun 28, 1942, Rolling Fork, MS; married Helen Rose King; children: Byron Darnell, Arthur J Jr & Kirsten Jamille. **Educ:** Miss Valley State Univ, BS, 1965; Delta State Univ, MS, 1972, spec degree admin, attended 1977. **Career:** T L Weston High Sch, chem & math teacher, football & track coach, 1965-70; H W Solomon Jr High Sch, math teacher, 1970-72, asst prin, 1972-79, prin, 1979-81; Coleman Jr High Sch, prin, 1981-85; Greenville Pub Schs Dist, dir, 1985-86, supt, 1999-2005; Helena-W Helena, dep supt, 1987-90; Delta State Univ, off-campus instr, 1988-93; N Bolivar Sch Dist, supt educ, 1990-93; Yazoo City Sch Dist, supt, 1993-99, head. **Orgs:** Bd mem, Miss Valley State Univ, 1964-65; Math Teacher Asn; Greenville Teacher Asn; Dist Teacher Asn; Miss Teacher Asn; Nat Educ Asn; Nat Coun Sect Prin; Uniserve Bd; Jr Warden Lake Vista Masonic Lodge; Mt Horeb Bapt Church; Southern Asn Col & Schs Coun Accreditation & Sch Improv; bd mem, Greenville Area Chamber Com; Asn Supv & Curric; Phi Delta Kappa; Delta Area Asn; MVSU & Delta Supt's Partnership; Miss Asn Sch Superintendents; United Way Wash; 100 Black Men Miss Delta;Rotary Club; Mid-Delta Work Force Alliance; Advent Heights Weed & Seed Prog; Nat Asn Sch Superintendents; Our House Domestic Violence Task Force; Team City Greenville. **Home Addr:** 244 Wiley St, Greenville, MS 38703, **Home Phone:** (662)335-9494. **Business Addr:** Superintendent, Greenville Public Schools District, PO Box 1619, Greenville, MS 38702-1619, **Business Phone:** (662)334-7000.

## CARTWRIGHT, BILL (JAMES WILLIAM CARTWRIGHT)

Basketball player, basketball coach, executive. **Personal:** Born Jul 30, 1957, Lodi, CA; married Sheri Johnson; children: Justin William, Jason James Allen & Kristen. **Educ:** Univ San Francisco, BA, sociol, 1979, MA, orgn develop, 1994. **Career:** Basketball player (retired); basketball coach, executive; NY Knicks, 1979-88; Chicago Bulls, 1988-94, asst coach, 1996-2001, coach, 2001-03; Seattle Supersonics, 1994-95; W Coast consult; Nj Nets, head coach, 2004-08; Phoenix Suns, asst coach, 2008-12; CartwrightDownes Inc, chmn bd, 2008-; Osaka Evessa, Japan, 2013-. **Orgs:** Charity work Easter Seals; Boys Hope, Chicago. **Home Addr:** 689 E Ill Rd, Lake Forest, FL 60045-2401. **Business Addr:** Chairman of the Board, CartwrightDownes Inc, 950 Lee St Suite 110, Des Plaines, IL 60016, **Business Phone:** (800)323-2049.

## CARTWRIGHT, BRENDA YVONNE

Educator. **Personal:** Born Aug 30, 1950, Richmond, VA; daughter of Louise Haynie. **Educ:** Mt Providence Jr Col, AA, span, 1970; McDaniel Col, BA, span, spec educ, 1972; Univ Mich, MA, guid & coun, 1979; George Washington Univ, EdD, rehab coun leadership, 1996. **Career:** Mich Sch Deaf, spec educ teacher, 1972-76; Bur Rehab, voc rehab counr, 1976-79; Rehab Serv Admin, voc rehab spec, 1979-98; Gallaudet Univ, Dept Coun, lect, 1996; George Wash Univ, vis prof, 1997-98; Coppin State Univ, asst prof, 1998-2001; Bowie State Univ, Dept Coun, lectr, 2000; Univ Dist Columbia, Dept Psychol & Coun, lectr, 2000; Univ Hawaii, Manoa, HI, asst prof counr educ, 2001, assoc prof counr educ, currently, dept chair, currently; Univ Hawaii, Honolulu, HI, Dept Counr Educ, assoc prof, 2005-07, chair, 2007-08, assoc prof, 2008-11, prof, 2011-13; Kyungpook Nat Univ, vis scholar, 2006; Leeward Community Col, Waianae, Hi, lectr, 2010-; Winston-Salem State Univ, Nc, prof rehab coun, 2012-. **Orgs:** Ed rev bd, J Coun & Develop, 1995-05; chair, 1999-, bd mem, 2000-, Nat Asn Multicultural Rehab Concerns; Am Coun Asn; scholar chair, Delta Sigma Theta Inc, Hawaii Alumnae Chap, 2002-; bd mem, Hawaii Rehab Coun Asn, 2003, treas, 2007-; mem comt, Nat Rehab Asn, 2003-; bd dir, Lanakila Pac; sec & bd dir, Rehab Asn Hawaii, 2003-04; Nat Rehab Asn, 2003-04; co chair, Nat Coun Rehab Educ, 2007-; comnr, Rehab Educ Comn Stand & Accreditation, Representing Nat Asn Multicultural Rehab Concerns Coun, 2003-11; Region IV Rep, Bd dir Nat Coun Rehab Educ; Comn Rehab Counr Cert. **Home Addr:** 3029 Lowrey Ave J-3207, Honolulu, HI 96822, **Home Phone:** (808)988-8593. **Business Addr:** Professor, Winston-Salem State University, 601 S Martin Luther King Jr Dr, Winston-Salem, NC 27110, **Business Phone:** (336)750-2379.

## CARTWRIGHT, DAVID G.

Real estate executive. **Career:** Riverpointe Walker & Assocs, realtor, currently. **Business Addr:** Realtor, Riverpointe Walker & Assocs, 21711 W 10 Mile Rd Suite 201, Southfield, MI 48075, **Business Phone:** (248)354-1500.

## CARTWRIGHT, JAMES WILLIAM. See CARTWRIGHT, BILL.

## CARTWRIGHT, HON. JOAN S.

Judge. **Personal:** married Lawrence R Neblett. **Educ:** Mich State Univ, BA, 1965; Univ Iowa, Col Law, JD, 1976. **Career:** State Calif, Munic Ct Judge, 1991-96, Alameda County Super Ct, judge, 1996-. **Orgs:** Calif Bar Asn, 1979-. **Honors/Awds:** Charles Houston Bar Association Award, 1983; Minority Bar Coalition Unity Awards, 2003; CHBA Judicial Excellence Awards, 2009. **Business Addr:** Judge, Alameda County Superior Court, 1225 Fallon St Rm 209, Oakland, CA 94612-4293, **Business Phone:** (510)891-6048.

## CARTWRIGHT, JONATHAN, SR.

Executive. **Career:** Wayne Co Community Col, exec dist dir, govt rels & community affairs, currently. **Special Achievements:** Jonathan Cartwright hosted the Education First radio show with Dr. Hattie Johnson-Norris concerning the Performing Arts and Theater program and upcoming productions. **Business Addr:** Director of Government Relations & Community Affairs, Wayne County Community College, 801 W Ft St, Detroit, MI 48226, **Business Phone:** (313)496-2731.

## CARUTHERS, DR. PATRICIA WAYNE

Educator, school administrator. **Personal:** Born Aug 28, 1939, Kansas City, KS; daughter of Bertram Sr and Evelyn W. **Educ:** Emporia State Univ, BS, 1962; Univ Mo, 1965, PhD, 1975. **Career:** US Dist No 500, teacher, 1962-69; Kans City Community Col, part-time instr, teacher, 1969-72, asst dean cont educ, 1972-76, asst to pres, 1978-92; Instnl & Stud Serv, vpres, 1992-94; Donnelly Col, part-time instr, 1997; Penn Valley Comn Col, part-time instr, 1997; Kans City Bd Pub Utilities, Ethics Comn, comn mem, 2006-. **Orgs:** Comn Kans City Kans Planning & Zoning Bd, 1975-; govt intern, Off Educ HEW, 1976-78; chmn, Kans City Kans Econ Devel Comn, 1980-; pres, Alpha Kappa Alpha Sorority Inc, 1981-83; regent, Kans Bd Regents, 1982-86; treas, Links Inc, 1984-86; Kans City Zoning Appeals Bd; Kans City Consensus, 1990-94; Youth Empowerment Task Force, 1994; Empowerment Zone Comn, 1994; comnr, Kans City Area Transp Authority, 1994-; bd dir, Friends Union Sta, 1994; bd mem, Cancer Action Inc; chair, Wyandotte Co Overall Econ Develop/SIA Bd. **Home Addr:** 3235 N 37th St, Kansas City, KS 66104. **Business Addr:** Member, Kansas City Board of Public Utilities, 540 Minnesota Ave, Kansas City, KS 66101-2930, **Business Phone:** (913)573-9000.

## CARVER, DR. JOANNE Y.

College administrator, administrator. **Educ:** EdD. **Career:** Hampton Univ, Sch Libr Arts & Educ, asst dean, currently; Va Dept Educ, dir teacher educ & teacher qual enhancement commonwealth, currently. **Orgs:** Adv Bd Teacher Educ & Licensure. **Home Addr:** , VA. **Business Addr:** Director of Teacher Education, Virginia Department of Education, James Monroe Bldg 101 N 14th St 24th Fl, Richmond, VA 23219-3684, **Business Phone:** (804)371-2475.

## CARVER, SHANTE EBONY

Football coach, football player. **Personal:** Born Feb 12, 1971, Stockton, CA. **Educ:** Ariz State Univ, BS, sociol, 1994. **Career:** Football player (retired), football coach; Dallas Cowboys, 1994, defensive end, 1995, right defensive end, 1996-97; B.C. Lions, 2000; Memphis Maniax, 2001; Dallas Desperados, defense, 2002-04; RDR Prod Builders, safety mgr, 2003-05; Scottsdale Community Col, defensive line coach, 2005-08; Westside Monsoon, head coach, 2009-; Moon Valley High School, defensive line coach, 2011. **Honors/Awds:** Two time All-America selection, 1992, 1993; Super Bowl Champion, XXX. **Business Addr:** Head Coach, Westside Monsoon, Phoenix, AZ.

## CARWELL, HATTIE V.

Physicist. **Personal:** Born Jul 17, 1948, Brooklyn, NY; daughter of George and Fannie Tunstall. **Educ:** Bennett Col, BS, chem & biol, 1970; Rutgers Univ, MS, health physics, 1971; UC Berkeley, post grad work, PhD. **Career:** Physicist (retired); US Dept Energy, San Francisco Oper Off, health physicist, 1973-80, sr health physicist, 1985-90, high energy & nuclear sci prog mgr, 1990-92, Berkeley Site Off, sr fac ops mgr, 1992, Lawrence Berkeley Nat Lab, opers lead, 1994; Atomic Energy Agency, Vienna, nuclear safeguards inspector & grp leader, 1980-85; Thomas Jefferson Univ, res asst; Mus African Am Technol Sci Village, exec dir, 2009-. **Orgs:** Nat Health Physicist Soc, 1971-; Nat Soc Black Physicists, 1975-; Nat Tech Asn, 1975-80; Western Reg Coun Engrs & Scientists, 1977-79; Develop Fund for Black Students in Sci & Technol, chairperson, 1983-2011; Nat Asn Advan Colored People, 1986-; pres, Northern Calif, Coun Black Prof Engr, 1986-87, 1994-95, 2000-02; chairperson, 1983-, int comm chair, 1990-, Develop Fund Black Students Sci & Technol, bd mem, 2000-09; Nat Coun

Black Engrs & Scientists, 1994-; bd mem, Collaborating Agencies Responding Disasters, 2007-09; immediate past pres, Nat Tech Asn, 2011-12; exec dir, Mus African Am Technol Sci Village. **Honors/Awds:** Special Mgr's Recognition, US Dept Energy, 1977-; Fed Community Service Award, 1977; North Calif Coun Black Prof Engrs, Prof Service Award, 1981; Elijal McCoy Award, 1989; Nat Black Col Hall of Fame, 1991; Bennett Col, hon doctorate, 1993; James C Jones Humanitarian Award, 2000; Inspiring Scientist Award, Oakland Junior Arts & Science Ctr, 2002. **Special Achievements:** Published numerous articles in tech publications, 1974-; Book, Blacks in Science: Astrophysicist to Zoologist, 1977; Booklet, In Pursuit of Excellence (Dr Warren Henry: World Class Scientist), 1998; co-founded the Develop Fund Black Students Sci & Technol, 1983; co-founded Museum African Am TechSci Village, 2000. **Business Addr:** Executive Director, Museum of African American Technology (MAAT) Science Village, 4622 Meldon Ave, Oakland, CA 94619, **Business Phone:** (510)893-6426.

## CARY, LORENE

Writer. **Personal:** Born Nov 29, 1956, Philadelphia, PA; daughter of John W and Carole J; married Robert C Smith; children: Geoffrey Smith, Laura & Zoe Smith. **Educ:** Univ Pa, BA, MA, 1979; Sussex Univ, MA, Victorian lit, 1980. **Career:** Time, intern writer, 1980; TV Guide, assoc ed, 1980-82; St Paul's Sch, teacher, 1982-83; Antioch Univ, Phila campus, lectr, 1983-84; Phila Univ Arts, lectr, 1984-86; Essence, AMR Visions, Philadelphia Inquirer Sunday Mag, Philadelphia TV Guide, freelance writer, 1985-88; Newsweek, contrib ed, 1991-93; Univ Pa, eng, lectr, 1995-, sr lectr creative writing, cur. Art Sanctuary's, founder & exec dir, currently. Author: Black Ice, 1981, 1991, Price A Child, 1995, Pride, 1998; The Price of A Child; Pride; Free! Great Escapes from Slavery on the Underground Railroad. **Orgs:** Author's Guild, 1991-; Pew Fellowship Arts; Art Sanctuary, 1998; Philadelphia's Sch Reform Comn, 2011-13. **Honors/Awds:** Hon Doctorate, Letters, Colby Col, 1992; Notable Books Citation, Black Ice, Am Library Asn, 1992; Bronze Star Award, Nat Hook-up Black Women, 1992; Hon Doctorate, Keene State Col, New Hampshire, 1997; Hon Doctorate, Chestnut Hill Col, 1997; Provost's Award for Distinguished Teaching, 1998; The Philadelphia Award; Rising Star Award, American Red Cross, 2000; Women's Way Agent of Change Award, 2002; Price of A Child Named "One Book, One Philadelphia", Choice, 2002; The Philadelphia Award, 2003. **Special Achievements:** Cary's essays have appeared in publications including Newsweek, Time, Essence, & O Magazine. **Home Addr:** 2033 Bainbridge St, Philadelphia, PA 19146-1308, **Home Phone:** (215)893-0308. **Business Addr:** Author, Senior Lecturer - Creative Writing, University Pennsylvania, 3451 Walnut St, Philadelphia, PA 19121, **Business Phone:** (215)898-5000.

## CARY, REBY

Legislator, city council member, broker. **Personal:** Born Sep 9, 1920, Cary, TX; daughter of Smith; married Nadine S; children: Faith Annette. **Educ:** Prairie View A&M Univ, BA, hist & polit sci, 1941, MS, hist & polit sci, 1948; Tex Christian Univ, attended 1953; N Tex State Univ, attended 1971. **Career:** McDonald Col Indust Arts, dir/teacher, 1946-49; Tarrant Co/Johnson Co Voc Sch, lead teacher, 1954-64; Dunbar High Sch, counr, 1953-64, asst prof, 1964-67; Tarrant Co Jr Col, asst prof, 1966-69; Univ Tex, Arlington, assoc dean stud life, adminr, asst prof hist, 1969-78, dir minority affairs, 1975-78; Tex House Rep, Dist 32-B State Legis, state rep, 1978-82; Cary's Real Estate, real estate broker, 1980; Tex State Rep, Dist 95, state legislator, 1979-85; Ft Worth Transp Authority, bd dir, currently. **Orgs:** Nat Educ Found Bd; Alpha Phi Frat, 1974-75; reg educ dir, 1972-75; sec Ft Worth Independent Sch Bd, 1974-75; trustee, choir dir New Rising Star Baptist Church; bd dirs, Boy Scouts Am; Am Legion; bd, Tarrant Co United Way; community dev bd, City Ft Worth; Tex Coun Black Republicans; Ft Worth City Coun. **Honors/Awds:** Man of the Year, Omega Psi Phi, 1974; Outstanding Citizen Award, St James AME, 1975. **Special Achievements:** First African-American elected at-large to the Fort Worth independent School District School Board; author: A Magnified Princes Shall Come Out of Egypt, Texas, & Fort Worth; Intercultural History: The Negro; First African-American administrator and assistant professor at the University of Texas; First African-American state legislators from Tarrant County; I. M. Terrell High School, the first black school in Fort Worth. **Business Addr:** Real Estate Broker, Cary's Real Estate, 1804 Bunche Dr, Ft. Worth, TX 76112, **Business Phone:** (817)429-0679.

## CARY, REV. WILLIAM STERLING

Executive, clergy. **Personal:** Born Aug 10, 1927, Plainfield, NJ; son of Andrew and Sadie; married Marie B Phillips; children: Yvonne, Denise, Sterling & Patricia. **Educ:** Morehouse Col, BA, 1949; Union Theol Sem, MDiv, 1952; Elmhurst Col, DDiv. **Career:** Baptist Church, ordained, 1948; Butler Memorial Pres by Church, pastor, 1953-55; Int Church Open Door, Brooklyn, pastor, 1955-58; Grace Congregation Church, pastor, 1958-68; Metro & Suffolk Asss NY Conf United Church Christ, area minister, 1968-75; Ill Conf United Church Christ, conf minister, 1974-94, emer minister, 2001-. **Orgs:** Pres, Nat Coun Churches, 1972-75; UCC Coun Ecumenism, 1977; chair, Comn Racial Justice; mem gov bodies, Coun Christian Soc Action & Off Commun; Task Force Vietnamese Refugee Relocation; UCC rep, Church Union; Nat Ministerial Adv Coun; Chicago Theol Sem Bd; Comt Denominational Exec Ill Conf Churches; Exec Coun United Church Christ; Church World Serv Comn; chair, Coun Relig Leaders Metrop Chicago, 1986-92; chmn, Coun Relig Leaders; Nat Coun Churches; Union United Church Christ. **Honors/Awds:** LLD, Bishop Col, Dallas, 1973; DD, Elm hurst Col, Ill, 1973; DD, More house Col, 1973; honorary doctorate, Alen Univ, 1975; DHL, Ill Col, 1988. **Special Achievements:** First African American President of the National Council of Churches, 1972. **Home Addr:** 206 LeMoyne Pkwy, Oak Park, IL 60302, **Home Phone:** (708)261-8378. **Business Addr:** Emeritus Minister, Illinois Conference United Church of Christ, 1840 Wchester Blvd Suite 200, Westchester, IL 60154, **Business Phone:** (708)344-4470.

## CASANOVA, DR. GISELE M. (GISELE CASANOVA OATES)

Clinical psychologist, educator. **Personal:** Born Apr 27, 1960, Chicago, IL; daughter of Isidro and Marguerite Boudreaux; children: Tatiyana Noelle. **Educ:** Ill Wesleyan Univ, BA, psychol, 1982; Northern Ill Univ, MA, clin psychol, 1986, PhD, clin psychol, 1989. **Career:** Inst Stress Mgt, clin assoc, 1989-90, consult, 1990-95; Purdue Univ, Calumet, asst prof psychol, 1990-94, Ethnic Studies Prog, coordr, 1994-2000, assoc prof psychol, 1995-. **Orgs:** Cent Regional Dir, Alpha Kappa Alpha; Xi Nu Omega Chapt, 1981-; pres, Xi Nu Omega Chap, 1995-96; Midwest Asn African Americans Higher Educ; Asn Black Psychologists; Top Ladies Distinction Inc; chmn, Chi Omega Omega Chap. **Home Addr:** 17139 S Dobson Ave, South Holland, IL 60473, **Home Phone:** (708)333-7646. **Business Addr:** Associate Professor of Psychology, Purdue University Calumet, 2200 169th St Port Hall 218A, Hammond, IN 46323-2094, **Business Phone:** (219)989-2781.

## CASE, DR. ARTHUR M.

Dentist. **Personal:** Born May 18, 1950, Philadelphia, PA. **Educ:** Temple Univ, DDS, 1979. **Career:** Pvt pract dentist; JFK Memorial Hosp, staff. **Orgs:** Alpha Omega Fraternity; New Era Dent Soc; Oral Surg Hon Soc; Peridontal Hon Soc. **Home Addr:** 528 Westview St, Philadelphia, PA 19119, **Home Phone:** (215)843-3642. **Business Addr:** Dentist, 1640 W Cheltenham Ave, Philadelphia, PA 19019, **Business Phone:** (215)924-7744.

## CASEY, CAREY

Association executive, president (organization), chief executive officer. **Personal:** married Melanie; children: 4. **Educ:** Univ NC, Chapel Hill, BA. **Career:** Summer Olympic Games Seoul, S Korea, chaplain, 1988; Kans City Chiefs, chaplain; Nat Ctr Fathering, Kans City, chief exec officer, 2006-; Inner-City Church, Ill Community, pastor; Fel Christian Athletes, found pres; Lawndale Community Church, co-pastor; World Cong Sports & Sr Bowl, lectr; OneWay2Play prog, exec dir; First-ever Nat Urban, dir. **Orgs:** Mem exec comt, Nat Fatherhood Leaders Group; chaplain, Dallas Cowboys, 1983-88; chaplain, Summer Olympic Games, Seoul, 1988; chaplain, NFL Team; chaplain, Kans City Chiefs; pres, FCA Found. **Special Achievements:** He is author of the book Championship Fathering: How to Win at Being a Dad in 2009 and general editor of The 21-Day Dad's Challenge in 2011. **Home Addr:** 519 SE Granada, Lees Summit, MO 64063. **Business Addr:** Chief Executive Officer, National Center for Fathering, PO Box 413888, Kansas City, MO 64141, **Business Phone:** (913)378-1047.

## CASEY, REV. CAREY WALDEN, SR.

Clergy, chief executive officer, football player. **Personal:** Born Oct 12, 1955, Radford, VA; son of Ralph Waldo Jr and Sarah Adline Coles; married Melanie Little; children: Christie, Patrice, Marcellus & Chance. **Educ:** Northeastern Okla, Miami, Okla, phys educ, 1976; Univ NC, Chapel Hill, BA, relig, 1979; Gordon-Conwell Theol Sem, S Hamilton MA, MDiv, 1981; Sch Theol Va Union Univ, Richmond, Va, MDiv, 1984. **Career:** Northeastern Univ, stud athletes counr, 1980-81; Total Action Against Poverty, Roanoke, Va, youth employ coordr, 1981; First Baptist Church, residence minister, 1982-83; Christian Athletes Fel, Dallas, Tex, urban dir, 1983-88; Mt Hebron Baptist Church, interim pastor, 1984-85; Dallas Cowboys Football Club Training Camp, counr, 1986-87; Christian Athletes Fel, Kans City, Mo, nat urban dir & Dallas Cowboys, Chaplain, 1988-92; Olympic Protestant Chaplain, 1988; Lawndale Community Church, pastor, 1992; Nat Ctr Fathering, chief exec officer, 2006-; Miss Univ, Kans City, Mo, Guest lectr. **Orgs:** Martin Luther King Ctr, 1984-88; speaker, Athletes Action, 1984-; Boys & Girls Clubs Am, 1986-; Nat Asn Advan Colored People, 1986-; nat consult, Salvation Army, 1988-; bd consult, Int Sports Coalition, 1988-; steering comt, Kans City Star Times, 1989-; bd mem, Mich Asn Leadership Develop Inc, 1989-; bd mem, sports Outreach USA, 1990-; bd mem, Urban Life Outreach, 1990-; exec & sr vpres, Nat Bd Fel Christian Athletes, 1992-; mem exec comt, Nat Fatherhood Leaders Group, exec dir, OneWay2Play prog; Nat Urban dir & pres, FCA Found. **Honors/Awds:** Outstanding Young Men Am, US Jaycees, 1980-83; NFL, Maj League Baseball Chapel Speaker USA, 1980; Juanita Craft Contrib to Sports in Community, Nat Asn Advan Colored People, 1984; Alumni of the Year, Northeastern Okla A&M, 1991; Dollar & Sense Magazine Award, 1991; Whos Who in Black Am, 1991-97; Salem Alumni Hall of Fame, Salem Educ Found & Alumni Asn; Billy Graham Scholarship; Presidents Medallion, Midwestern Baptist Sem, Kansas City. **Special Achievements:** Proclamation Carey Casey Day, December 5, 1988; First ever National Urban Director for the Fellowship of Christian Athletes; Books: Championship Fathering: How to Win at Being a Dad, 2009; The 21-Day Dad's Challenge, gen ed, 2011. **Home Addr:** , Lees Summit, MO. **Business Addr:** Chief Executive Officer, National Center for Fathering, 10200 W 75th St Suite 267, Shawnee Mission, AR 66204, **Business Phone:** (913)384-4661.

## CASEY, FRANK LESLIE

Journalist, television journalist, social worker. **Personal:** Born Jan 29, 1935, Stotesbury, WV; son of Conston and Mary; married Lenore Thompson; children: Zauditu, Tamarat, Bakaffa & Charles Arnold. **Educ:** WVa State Col, BS, 1962. **Career:** Repub Aviation, tech illusr, 1963; New York Dept Welfare, social worker, 1969; WPIX-TV, New York, tv reporter. **Orgs:** Nat Asn Advan Colored People. **Honors/Awds:** Good Conduct Medal; New York Area Tv Acad Award, Nat Acad TV Arts & Sci, 1976-77; Uniformed Firefighters Asn Award for excellence in T.V. coverage for fire fighting, 1971; Humorous Writing Award, Soc Silurians, New York, 1986; Hon Mem for Fair & Impartial Reporting for Police Stories, Retired Detectives Police Dept city New York Inc, 1984. **Home Addr:** 3636 Huyton Ct, Charlotte, NC 28215.

## CASH, DR. JAMES IRELAND, JR.

Educator, dean (education). **Personal:** Born Oct 25, 1947, Ft. Worth, TX; married Clemmie L; children: Tari & Derek. **Educ:** Tex Christian Univ, BS, math & comput sci, 1969; Purdue Univ, MS, comput sci, 1974, PhD, mgt info syst & acct, 1976. **Career:** Tex Christian Univ Comput Ctr, syst programmer, 1969; Langston Univ, dir comput ctr, 1969-72, instr & asst prof vo-tech prog, 1969-72; Arth Drug Stores Inc, syst analyst & programmer consult, 1973-76; Inst Educ Mgt, exec educ course, MIS instr, 1977-79; Harvard Grad Sch Bus Admin, asst prof, 1976-2003, instr exec educ course, MBA Prog, chmn, 1992-95, James E. Robison prof bus admin, James E. Robison prof bus admin emer, currently; HBS Publ, sr assoc dean & chmn; IBM Syst Res Inst, adj prof, 1980; Gen Catalyst Partners, spec advisor, currently; Cambridge Technol Partners, dir; Chubb Corp, dir, 1996-; Gen Elec Co, independent dir, 1997-; Verne Global, dir; Banner 17 LLC, partner & dir, 2002-; Babson Col, adminr, 2003-; Veracode Inc, dir, 2009-; Virtual Instruments, dir, 2013-; Highland Capital Partners, spec advisor; Boston Celtics, partner. **Orgs:** Bd adv, Am Acct Asn; Asn Comput Mach; Qual Assurance Inst; adv bd, Soc Info Mgt; Strategic Mgt Soc; US Dept State Adv Comn Trans Nat Enterprises, 1976-83; bd mem, HBS Publ, 1976-2003; Index Syst Inc, 1978-; bd trustee, Pk Sch, 1983-; adv bd, BOSCOM, 1983-; ed bd, Harvard Bus Rev, 1983-; MA Gov's Adv Comn Info Processing, 1983-88; trustee, Bert King Found; Mass Gen Hosp; Partners Healthcare; Nat Asn Basketball Coaches Found; bd dir, Knight-Ridder Inc; mem adv bd, State St Bank; mem adv bd, Trust Co; AP Capital Partners; adv bd, Met Fund; trustee, Harlem C's Zone; trustee, Newton-Wellesley Hosp; Overseer Boston Mus Sci; bd mem, Knight-Ridder, 1995-2006; mem bd dir, Chubb Corp, 1996-; dir, Winstar Commun Inc, 1997-; Alcon Inc; trustee, Markle Found; mem bd dir, Gen Elec, 1997-; chair, HBS Publ 1998-2003; mem bd dir, Microsoft Corp, 2001-; dir, Sci-Atlanta Inc, 2001-; bd mem, Sci-Atlanta, 2001-06; bd mem, Microsoft, 2001-09; mem bd dir, Phase Forward Inc, 2003-; Trustee, Babson Col, 2003-; bd mem, Phase Forward, 2003-09; mem bd dir, Walmart Bd dir, 2006; bd mem, Veracode, 2009-; mem bd dir, Gen Elec & Chubb Corp, 2012; mem bd dir, Veracode; mem bd dir, Boston Celtics ownership group; coun mem, Smithsonian Mus African-Am Hist & Cult; co-founder, Bert King Found; develop comt mem, Am Acad Arts & Sci; Grain Commun Group; bd mem, ITM Software; bd mem, State St Bank & Trust, Tandy; bd mem, Winstar Commun; trustee, Boston Mus Sci, Massachusetts Gen Hosp, Partners HealthCare Syst, Newton-Wellesley Hosp. **Home Addr:** 71 Maugus Ave, Wellesley Hills, MA 02481. **Business Addr:** Special Advisor, General Catalyst Partners, 20 Univ Rd 4th Fl, Cambridge, MA 02138, **Business Phone:** (617)234-7000.

## CASH, LISA

Executive. **Personal:** daughter of Tommy. **Educ:** Howard Univ, commun; Fr Culinary Inst. **Career:** Sheraton Hotel Restaurant; B Smiths Restaurant, 1988; Shark Bar, fl mgr, 1989, vpres opers, 1999, owner; Soul Food Concepts, vpres opers, 2003.

## CASH, PAMELA J.

Librarian. **Personal:** Born Oct 26, 1948, Cleburne, TX; daughter of James and Juanita Beatty; married Gervis A Menzies Sr; children: Gervis A Jr. **Educ:** Univ Okla, BA, 1970; Univ Ill, MLS, 1972; Fisk Univ . **Career:** Univ Ill, asst Afro-Am bibliogr, 1970-71, librn Afro-Am studies, 1971-72; Univ Tex, humanities librn, 1972-73; Johnson Publ Co, libr, vpres multiMedia resources, 2003; Dallas Pub Libr, br manage; P J Cash Resources LLC, consult. **Orgs:** Black Caucus Am Libr Asn; Spec Libr Asn; Asn Black Librarians Chicago. **Home Addr:** 4800 S Lake Pk Ave Apt 2202, Chicago, IL 60615-2071, **Home Phone:** (773)924-8301. **Business Addr:** Librarian, Johnson Public Co, 820 S Michigan Ave, Chicago, IL 60605, **Business Phone:** (312)322-9200.

## CASH, SWINTAYLA MARIE (SWIN CASH)

Basketball player. **Personal:** Born Sep 22, 1979, Pittsburgh, PA; daughter of Cynthia; children: 2. **Educ:** Univ Conn, commun sci, 2002. **Career:** Detroit Shock, forward, 2002-07; Swincash Enterprises, founder, 2002; Seattle Storm, 2008-11; Chicago Sky, 2012-. **Orgs:** Founder, CashKids, 2005. **Business Addr:** Professional Basketball Player, Chicago Sky, 5500 W Howard, Skokie, IL 60077, **Business Phone:** (312)828-9550.

## CASH-RHODES, WINIFRED E.

Educator, executive director. **Personal:** Born Savannah, GA; daughter of William L Cash Sr and Clifford Brown Cash; married Augustus H; children: Eva Carol, Lydia Ann & Victoria Elizabeth. **Educ:** Fisk Univ, AB, 1934; Univ Southern Calif, MS, 1959. **Career:** Educator (retired); Teacher Sec Math, 1935-40, 1945-52, dept chairperson, math, 1957-65; Univ Calif, Berkley, fel, 1960; Los Angeles Unified Sch, supvr sec Math teachers, 1966-68, specialist res & develop, 1968-78; NY Univ, fel, 1970. **Orgs:** Sec Baldwin Hills Home owners Assoc, 1976-82; dir, 13th Far Western Regional Dir Alpha Kappa Alpha Sorority Inc, 1970-74; Exec Coun United Church Christrepresenting So, Calif & NV, 1981-87; chmn, Nominating Comn, Southern Calif Ecumenical Coun, 1987-92; Southern Calif Interfaith Coalition Aging Bd, 1989-94; Am Asn Univ Women, 1989-; Calif Retired Teachers Asn, 1992-. **Honors/Awds:** Named honor: Award Given from entrant name as The Winifred Cash Rhodes Undergraduate Award. **Special Achievements:** Article "What Jesus Means to Me", United Church of Christ, New York, 1982. **Home Addr:** 4554 Don Felipe Dr, Los Angeles, CA 90008-2826, **Home Phone:** (323)291-7847.

## CASHIN, SHERYLL D.

Government official, educator. **Personal:** Born Huntsville, AL; son of John and Joan; married Marque Chambliss; children: Logan & Langston. **Educ:** Vanderbilt Univ, BE, elec engineering, 1984; Oxford Univ, MA, Eng law, 1986; Harvard Univ, JD, 1989. **Career:** Off Vpres, Community Empowerment Bd, staff dir; Off Transition Coun, assoc coun; Sirote & Permutt PC, assoc; US Ct Appeals, Dist Columbia Circuit, law clerk, 1989-90; US Supreme Ct Justice Thurgood Marshall, law clerk, 1990-91; Clinton White House, adv urban & econ policy, dir community develop, 1993-96; Georgetown Univ Law Ctr, prof law, 1996-. **Orgs:** Harvard Law Rev; Poverty & Race Res Action Coun. **Honors/Awds:** Walter R. Murray Jr. Distinguished Alumnus Award, Asn Vanderbilt Black Alumni, 2000. **Special Achievements:** Author: The Failures of Integration: How Race & Class are Undermining the Am Dream, 2004, The Agitator's Daughter: A Memoir of Four Generations of One Extraordinary African-American Family, 2008, Place Not Race: A New Vision of Opportunity in America, 2014; Appeared on NPR All Things Considered, The Diane Rehm Show, The Tavis Smiley Show, The Newshour With Jim Leher, CNN, BET & ABC News. **Business Addr:** Professor of Law, Georgetown University Law Center, 600 NJ Ave NW, Washington, DC 20001, **Business Phone:** (202)662-9461.

## CASON, MARILYNN JEAN

Lawyer, executive. **Personal:** Born May 18, 1943, Denver, CO; daughter of Evelyn L Clark and Eugene M; married P Wesley Kriebel. **Educ:** Stanford Univ, BA, polit sci, 1965; Univ Mich Law Sch, JD, 1969; Roosevelt Univ, MBA, 1977. **Career:** Executive (retired); Dawson Nagel Sherman & Howard, assoc atty, 1969-73; Kraft Inc, atty, 1973-75; Johnson Prods Co Inc, vpres, managing dir, 1979-83, vpres & corp coun, 1975-86, vpres int, 1986-88; DeVry Inc, vpres & gen coun, 1989-96, sr vpres, secy & gen coun, 1996. **Orgs:** dir, 1979-, chairman, 1991-2003, Arthritis Found, Ill Chap; Ill Humanities Coun, 1987-96; Int Trade Club & Comt Foreign Affairs; Chicago Coun Foreign Rel. Trustee, Arthritis Found, Atlanta, 1993-96; Chicago Symphony Orchestra, 1997-2003; bd dirs, Int House, 1986-92; bd dirs, 1997-, chmn, 2002-, Lit All US; Am Bar Asn; Nat Bar Asn; pres community law proj, Cook County Bar Asn, 1986-88. **Home Addr:** 3108 Colfax St, Evanston, IL 60201, **Home Phone:** (847)866-6421.

## CASON, UDELL, JR.

School administrator, educator. **Personal:** Born Jul 30, 1940, Glasgow, MO; married Emma R Bothwell; children: Carmen Q & Udell Q. **Educ:** Drake Univ, BS, 1965, MS, 1970. **Career:** Educator, school administrator (retired); City Des Moines, admin asst, 1965-68; Des Moines Pub Sch, teacher, 1968-70, prin, 1972-, coordr, 1970-72, Capitol View, interim prin; Moore Elem Sch, prin. **Orgs:** Chmn, vice chmn & trustee bd, Union Bapt Chap, 1965-; pres, United Black Fedn, 1967-69; pres, Kappa Alpha Psi Fraternity, 1980-81; bd dir, Des Moines Young Men's Christian Asn, 1982-89; chmn, bd dir, Iowa C & Family Serv, 1984-89; metrop bd dir, Young Men's Christian Asn, 1993-97; bd dir, Cent Iowa AIDS, 1997-99; amp bd, Young Men's Christian Asn, 1998-; sec chmn prin, Des Moines Pub Sch. **Honors/Awds:** Task Force Award State Of Iowa, 1968; Mayor Task Force Award, City Des Moines, 1968; Outstanding Achievement, Kappa Alpha Psi, 1975; Double D Award, Drake Univ, 1979; Service to Youth Award, YMCA, 1988; Tae Kwon Do Instructor, Young Men Christian Asn, 1979-; One of Des Moines Finest Citizens, 1999. **Home Addr:** 3816 Patricia Dr, Urbandale, IA 50322, **Home Phone:** (515)278-4567.

## CASSELBERRY, JAMES ARTHUR

Executive, consultant, executive director. **Educ:** Tex Christian Univ, attended 1979; Univ Ill, BS, econs, 1986; Univ Chicago Grad Sch Bus, MBA, finance, 2001. **Career:** First Nat Bank Chicago, portfolio mgr, 1986-91; Wedgewood Capital Mgmt, chief operating officer & portfolio mgr, 1995-96; Millennium Income Trust, chmn, chief exec officer & portfolio mgr; Trias Capital Mgt Inc, founder, chief exec officer & chmn, 1996-2004; Ennis Knupp Assoc, prin, 2004-06; Dearborn Pk Group LLC, founder & managing partner, 2006-11; Morrill & Assocs PC, consult, currently; Alternative Asset Advisor Group, prin; NexGen Capital Partners LLC, sr consult prin, 2011-12; NexGen Holdings LLC, sr managing dir, 2011-; Valparaiso Univ, adj prof, 2012-; NexTier Capital Solutions LLC, sr managing dir, 2012-. **Orgs:** Dir, John D & Catherine T MacArthur Found, 1991-95. **Business Addr:** Financial Industries Consultant, Morrill & Associates PC, 300 N LaSalle St 40th Fl, Chicago, IL 60654, **Business Phone:** (312)546-4622.

## CASSELL, SAMUEL JAMES, SR. (SAM CASSELL)

Basketball player, entrepreneur, basketball coach. **Personal:** Born Nov 18, 1969, Baltimore, MD; son of Donna; children: Sam Jr. **Educ:** San Jacinto Col, attended 1991; Fla State, attended 1993. **Career:** Basketball player (retired), basketball coach; Houston Rockets, guard, 1993-96; Dallas Mavericks, player, 1996-97; Phoenix Suns, player, 1996; New Jersey Nets, player, 1997-99; Milwaukee Bucks, player, 1999-2003; Minnesota Timberwolves, player, 2003-05; Boston Celtics, player, 2008; Washington Wizards, asst coach, 2009-14; Los Angeles Clippers, guard, 2005-08, asst coach, 2014-; We R One, co-founder, currently. TV Series: "Rome Is Burning", 2003. Film Producer: Chain Letter, 2009; Poet Pride, 2009. **Home Addr:** , TX. **Business Addr:** Assistant Coach, Los Angeles Clippers, 1111 S Figueroa St Suite 1100, Los Angeles, CA 90015, **Business Phone:** (213)742-7500.

## CASSIS, GLENN ALBERT

Vice president (organization), school administrator, executive director. **Personal:** Born Nov 11, 1951, Jamaica, NY; married Glynis R; children: Glenn Jr. **Educ:** Univ Con, BA, polit sci, 1973, MFA, arts admin, 1974. **Career:** Jorgensen Auditorium, Univ Conn, Storrs, admin asst, 1973-74; Oakland Ctr, Oakland Univ, Rochester, asst dir 1976-78, asst dir stud acct, 1974-76; N Adams State Col, dir campus ctr, 1978; Assoc Col Union-Int, region 1 comp coord, 1979-; Conn Pre-Eng Prog, exec dir, currently. **Orgs:** Bd dir, Nat Entertainment & Campus Act Asn, 1972-74; co-founder, minority affairs, comm Nat Entertainment & Campus Act Asn, 1973; adv bd, Salvation Army, 1980-; Min Coun Comm Concerns, 1980-; Conn TRAC currently; Nat Soc Black Engr; African-Am Cult Ctr; trustee, Union Baptist Church; bd mem, Bloomfield Raiders Youth Football; vpres, Conn Coun Philanthropy; Conn Acad Educ Bd dir; reviewer, Nat Sci Found, NASA & State Dept Higher Educ. **Business Addr:** Executive Director, Connecticut Pre Engineering Program Inc, 950 Trout Brook Dr, West Hartford, CT 06119, **Business Phone:** (860)769-5283.

## CASTENELL, DR. LOUIS ANTHONY

School administrator, educator. **Personal:** Born Oct 2, 1947, New York, NY; son of Louis and Marguerite; married Mae E Beckett; children: Louis C & Elizabeth M. **Educ:** Xavier Univ LA, BA, educ, 1968; Univ Wis, Milwaukee, MS, educ psychol, 1973; Univ Ill, PhD, 1980. **Career:** Univ Wis-Milwaukee, coordr, acad adv & bus mgr, 1971-74; Xavier Univ, dir alumni affairs, 1975-77, assoc prof, 1980-88, dean grad sch, 1981-89; Univ Ill, fel, 1977-78; Nat Inst Ment Health, fel, 1978-80; Univ Cincinnati, dean, col educ, 1990-99; Univ Ga, Col Educ, dean, 1999-2008, founding interim assoc provost, 2001-02, prof, 2008-. **Orgs:** Ed Bds, J Curric Theorizing, 1990-95; reviewer, J Teacher Educ; reviewer, J Educ Founds, Educ Task Force Urban League, 1984; chair, Human Rights & Acad Freedom AERA, 1985-86; consult Sch Educ, 1980-; bd mem, Learning First Alliance; bd mem, Ronald McDonald House La, 1987; bd mem, Nat Asn Advan Colored People; bd mem, C Mus Cincinnati; bd mem, Nat Bd Prof Teaching Stand; bd mem, Nat Bd Examiners & Am Coun Educ; bd chair, Am Asn Cols Teacher Educ; Kappa Delta Epilson; Am Educ Studies Asn; Asn Multicultural Coun & Develop; Am Educ Res Asn; Am Asn Col Teachers Educ; Nat Hon Soc Psychol; bd mem, Ga Partnership Excellence Educ; bd mem, Mod Red Schoolhouse Inst Ga Coun Econ Educ. **Honors/Awds:** Craig Rice Scholarship, Xavier Univ, 1968; over 15 published works on aspects of educ; Critic's Choice Awards, Am Educational Studies Asn, 1993; Presidential Award, Networking Together Inc, 1996; Action Agency Award, Cincinnati-Hamilton County, 1996; Outstanding Faculty, Kappa Delta Epsilon, 2000; Distinguished Alumnus in Higher Education Award, Univ Illinois, 2002; Chairman Award, Am Asn Cols Teacher Educ, 2002; Board Service Award, Am Coun Educ, 2003; Pedro Zamora Horizons Award, Univ Ga, 2003; Leadership Service Award, 2006. **Special Achievements:** First African-American dean of a college at University of Georgia. **Home Addr:** 1320 Beverly Dr, Athens, GA 30606, **Home Phone:** (706)316-3949. **Business Addr:** Professor, University Of Georgia College of Education, G-3 Aderhold Hall, Athens, GA 30602, **Business Phone:** (706)542-6446.

## CASTLE, KEITH L.

Marketing executive, marketing executive, executive. **Career:** Phase One Off Prods Inc, Cambridge, MA, pres & chief exec officer, 1978-96; Corp Express, dir mkt develop, 1996-2000; Green Castle Bus Solutions LLC, pres & chief exec officer, 2009-. **Orgs:** New Eng Minority Purchasing Coun; Cambridge Chamber Com. **Business Addr:** President, Chief Executive Officer, Green Castle Business Solutions LLC, PO Box 160, Boston, MA 02131, **Business Phone:** (617)307-4461.

## CASTLEMAN, ELISE MARIE

Social worker. **Personal:** Born May 30, 1925, Duquesne, PA; daughter of Guy L Tucker (deceased) and Fannie M Ridley (deceased); children: John II. **Educ:** Howard Univ, BA, 1947; Univ Pittsburgh, attended 1949. **Career:** Fel grad study social work, Family Serv Asn, 1947-49; Family & Childrens Agency, social worker, 1949-53; DC Gen Hosp, social worker, 1953-58; Wayne County Gen Hosp & Consult Ctr, social worker, 1958-59; United Cerebral Palsy, social worker, 1960-66; Ment Hyg Clin Veterans Admin, social worker, 1967-; Defense Construct Supply Ctr, mgt analyst, 1982-85. **Orgs:** Columbus Bd Educ, 1971-79; exec adv comn, Off Minority Affairs, Ohio State Univ, 1972-73; adv bd, Martin Luther King Serv Ctr, 1963-67; Howard Univ Womens Club, 1953-58; Ohio Sch Bd Asn, 1972-; bd mem, Columbus Civil Rights Coun, 1973-; Nat Asn Advan Colored People, Black Womens Leadership, 1973-76; exec comn, Ohio Sch Bds Asn; bd mem, Young Women's Christian Asn, 1974-76. **Honors/Awds:** Public Service Award, 1979; Public Service Award, Inner City Sertoma Club, 1978; Public Service Award, Nat Asn Advan Colored People, Columbus Chap, 1980; Certificate of Appreciation for Service & Leadership in the Field of Public Education, Ky State Univ, 1980; Award for Distinguished Community Service, Ohio House Rep, 1981. **Home Addr:** 384 Noe Bixby Rd, Columbus, OH 43213.

## CASTRO, GEORGE A.

State government official, association executive. **Personal:** Born Dec 27, 1936, Providence, RI; married Avis L; children: Regina, Terri & Brian Dave. **Educ:** Duke Univ, Providence Col. **Career:** Ri Gen Assembly, state rep, dist 20; Vol Ctr RI, Blacks Interested Commun, pres & exec dir, currently. **Orgs:** Chmn, Martin Luther King Jr State Holiday Comn; bd mem, RI Black Heritage Soc; Int Inst; bd mem, Cranston Gen Hosp Corp; Nat Asn Advan Colored People, Newport Chap; chmn, Comn Boxing & Wrestling RI; Gov Adv Comn Sr Citizens; Urban Educ Ctr; adv comn mem, Radio & TV; Minority Adv Comn; Pep Mgt Adv Comn, Boxing, Wrestling, Kickboxing; Ri Black Heritage Soc. **Home Addr:** 57 Carolina Ave, Providence, RI 02905, **Home Phone:** (401)941-1660. **Business Addr:** Director, President, Volunteer Center of Rhode Island, 1468 Broad St, Providence, RI 02905, **Business Phone:** (401)941-9370.

## CASTRO, OCTAVIO ANTONIO FERNANDEZ. See FERNANDEZ, TONY.

## CASWELL, ROSELL R.

Executive, counselor. **Educ:** Fla A&M Univ, BA, bus educ, MA, guid & coun. **Career:** Fla A&M Univ, Ctr Human Develop, coordr stud affairs, dir stud affairs, coun serv, res coordr, 1964. **Orgs:** Nat Asn Stud Personnel Administr; pres, Nat Asn Stud Affairs Professionals. **Business Addr:** Research Coordinator, Florida A&M University, 101 Sunshine Manor, Tallahassee, FL 32307, **Business Phone:** (850)599-3145.

## CATCHING-KYLES, SHARRON FAYE

Police officer. **Personal:** Born Jan 3, 1950, Jackson, MS; daughter of Willie Lee and Bennie Lee Lewis; married James Tyrone; children: Darrell Augustues & La Keista Renee. **Educ:** Jackson State Col, Jackson, Miss, 1969; Jackson Police Training Acad, Jackson, Miss, 1975. **Career:** Jackson Police Dept, patrol sgt, 1978-95, lt, 1995-98, dep chief police, 1998-; Juv Detention Ctr, dir. **Orgs:** Pres, Smith Chapel Freewill Baptist Church Choir, 1975-85; pres, Jackson Concerned Officers Progress, 1980-88; Community Admin, YWCA, 1984-94; Nat Black Police Asn, 1986-92; New Mt Zion Inspirational Choir; Nat Asn Advan Colored People; Miss Mass Choir Live Gospel Rec, 1988; Anderson United Methodist Church; Nat Orgn Black Law Enforcement Exec. **Honors/Awds:** Outstanding Heroic Performance Award, Lanier Class, 1965 & 1985; Outstanding Bravery, N Jackson Kiwanis Club, 1983; Lawman of the Year, La & Miss & W Tenn Dist Kiwanis, 1983-84; Distinguished Service Award, Jackson Police Dept, 1984; Police Officer of the Month, Jackson Asn Life Underwriters, 1984; J-Cop Silver Shield for Community Service, Jackson Concerned Officers Progress, 1985. **Home Addr:** 486 Hanging Moss Circle, Jackson, MS 39206, **Home Phone:** (601)366-5060. **Business Addr:** Deputy Chief, Jackson Police Department, 327 E Pascagoula St, Jackson, MS 39205, **Business Phone:** (601)960-1365.

## CATCHINGS, HOWARD DOUGLAS

Insurance agent. **Personal:** Born Jun 19, 1939, Copiah County, MS; son of Corean and H D; married Danella Brownridge; children: Sebrena, Douglas, James & Daniel. **Educ:** Jackson State Univ, BEd, 1963, MEd, 1973. **Career:** Jackson Pub Sch, teacher, 1963-80; United Founders Ins Co, rep, 1967-68; Trans-Am Life, gen agt; Transamerica Life Ins Agency, gen agt, 2003; Catchings Ins Agency, gen agt, currently. **Orgs:** Vpres, 1098-88, pres, 1993-94, Jackson State Univ; pres, Miss Asn Life, 1985-89 & 1993-94; comt mem, Million Dollar Round Table; pres, Jackson GAMA, 1986-87; bd dirs, Jr Achievement; State Job Training Coord Coun; coun mem, Bus, Indust, Educ Regional Coun; past chmn bd, Jackson Chamber Com; regional officer, GAMC; nat bd mem, Pub Educ Forum; past pres, Miss Asn Life Underwriters; chmn, Jr Achievement Miss; bd mem, past pres, Rotary Club Jackson; Metrop Crime Comn; First Am Bank; St Dominic Health Serv; Hancock Group Incl Jackson Gen Agents Mgr Asn Ct Table; adv bd, Top Table; adv bd, TransAm Life Ins Co; adv bd, Stand & Poor's Rating Co; First Am Bank; Miss Econ coun; pres, Jackson State Univ Nat Alumni Asn; Jackson State Univ Develop Found; St Dominic Health Serv; Univs Ctr; Metrop Crime Comn; founder, Greater Jackson Chamber Partnership Bd Dirs; chmn, Bd Metro Jackson Chamber Com; gen agt's adv bd, Transamerica Life ins Co; adv Coun, Stand & Poor's Rating Co. **Honors/Awds:** One of top ten agents, Nat Old Line Ins Co, 1971-94; Outstanding Teacher in Human Relations, Jackson Pub Schs, 1972; Outstanding Achievement Award, Jackson State Univ Nat Alumni Asn; No 1 Salesman, 1986 & 1993-94; Citizen of the Year, March Dimes; Hall of Fame, Jackson Asn Life Underwriters; Hall of Fame, Miss Asn Life Underwriters; Nat Sales Rep, 1993-97; Mississippi's Citizen of the Year; Volunteer of the Year; Mississippi Insurance Hall of Fame; Jackson Insurance Hall of Fame; Mississippi Business Hall of Fame; Firm of the Year. **Home Addr:** 6027 Woodlea Rd, Jackson, MS 39206, **Home Phone:** (601)946-1120. **Business Addr:** General Agent, Catchings Insurance Agency, 945 N State St, Jackson, MS 39202-2627, **Business Phone:** (601)355-7489.

## CATCHINGS, DR. YVONNE PARKS

Painter (artist), educator. **Personal:** Born Jan 1, 1935, Atlanta, GA; daughter of Andrew Walter and Hattie Marie Brookins; married James Albert A; children: Andrea Hunt Warner, Wanda Hunt McLean & James A A Jr. **Educ:** Spelman Col, AB, 1955; Teachers Col Columbia, MA, 1958; Univ Mich, MMP, 1971, PhD, 1981. **Career:** Detroit Mich pub sch syst, art teacher, 1955; Spelman Col, instr, 1956-57; Marygrove Col, instr, 1970-72; Specialist; Detroit Bd Educ, instr, 1959-; Valdosta State Col, asst prof art, 1987-88; Detroit Bd Educ, specialist, 1988-. **Orgs:** Nat Art Educ Asn, 1956-; prog chr bd, Detroit Soc Genelogical Res, 1965-; nat treas, Smart Set, 1976-78; archivist pub rel, Mich Art Ther Asn, 1981-; reg art therapist, Am Art Ther, 1981-; chmn, Heritage Arch Delta Sigma Theta Sorority, 1983-; bd chr, peace Am Asn Univ Women, 1981-; art chr, Links, 1981-; comt mem, Fred Hart Williams Geneal Soc. **Home Addr:** 1306 Joliet Pl, Detroit, MI 48207, **Home Phone:** (313)393-9521.

## CATES, HON. SIDNEY HAYWARD, IV

Judge. **Personal:** Born Mar 10, 1931, New Orleans, LA; married Betty; children: Sidney IV & Kim. **Educ:** Loyola Univ, BA, 1975, Sch Law, JD, 1976. **Career:** Govt off, atty; Housing Authority New Orleans, exec dir; La Dept Justice, atty gen; GSS Inc, vpres gen mgr; Hibernia Nat Bank, mkg officer; Law Enforce Asn Admin, consult; City New Orleans, asst chief admin officer; New Orleans Police Dept, judge; Civil Dist Ct Parish Orleans, Div C, Sect 10, judge, 2004-. **Orgs:** Bd dir, Loyola Univ; Red Cross; Boy Scouts Am; United Way; Goodwill; St.Claude Gen Hosp; Mid Winter Sports Asn; Knights St Peter Claver; Equestrian Knights Holy Sepulchre; pres, Studs Club; Chamber Com; vice chmn, Bicentennial Comt; C Bur City New Orleans; La State Bar Asn; New Orleans Bar Asn, 1976-; Tex State Bar Asn; pres bd dir, New Orleans Legal Assistance Corp; chmn, Civil Serv Comn, City New Orleans; Alpha Sigma Nu; Nat Jesuit Hon Soc; Delta Epsilon Sigma; New Orleans Alcoholic Beverage Control Bd; New Orleans City Coun; bd gov, La Trial Lawyer's Asn; Louis A Martinet Legal Soc; law vis comt, Loyola Univ; Am Judges Asn; New Orleans Bar Asn Inn Ct; Bar Asn Fifth Fed Circuit; Nat Bar Asn. **Honors/Awds:** Alfred E Clay Award; Honor, Charles E Dunbar; Career Civil Service Award; Papal Honor, Knights of the Holy Sepulcher. **Home Addr:** 8 Duckhook Dr, New Orleans, LA 70118-2668. **Business Addr:** Judge, Civil District Court for the Parish of Orleans, Rm 306 421 Loyola Ave, New Orleans, LA 70112-1109, **Business Phone:** (504)407-0220.

## CATHEY, LEON DENNISON

Lecturer. **Personal:** Born Oct 11, 1932, San Diego, CA; son of Joseph and Barbara Dennison. **Educ:** San Francisco State Col, BA, geog, 1958, MA, biol, 1972; Int Grad Sch Stockholm, grad dipl social studies, 1979; San Francisco State Univ, MA, 1972, MA, ethnic studies, 1990. **Career:** San Francisco Unified Sch Dist, sci instr, 1960-88; San Francisco State Univ, lectr ethnic studies, 1995-. **Special Achievements:** Man & Land: One Man, Whose Land, 1983; Philippine News SF, LA, NY, 1983. **Business Addr:** Lecturer, San Francisco State University, 1600 Holloway Ave, San Francisco, CA 94132, **Business Phone:** (415)338-1111.

## CATO, KELVIN T.

Basketball player. **Personal:** Born Aug 26, 1974, Atlanta, GA; son of Donald and Carolyn; children: Parrish, Xavier & Kealand. **Educ:** Univ S Ala, attended 1993; Iowa State Univ, attended 1997. **Career:** Basketball player (retired), agt; Portland Trail Blazers, ctr, 1997-99; Houston Rockets, ctr, 1999-2004; Orlando Magic, ctr, 2004-06; Detroit Pistons, ctr, 2006; New York Knicks, 2006-07, free agt, 2006-10.

## CATOR, JOHNNY

Executive. **Personal:** married Stephanie. **Career:** Microsoft Inc, sr acct exec; Vietnam Express, founder, 1990-; Network Plus; Compu-Tel, founder; City Soft, vpres opers, sr vpres opers, vice chmn; WebcTel Inc, founder, pres & chief exec officer, 2000-. **Orgs:** Haitian Am Health Asn; Urban League; Adopt a Community in Haiti. **Business Addr:** Founder & President, Chief Executive Officer, WebcTel Inc, 162 2nd St, Cambridge, MA 02142, **Business Phone:** (617)573-5225.

## CAUDLE, ANTHONY L., SR.

Banker. **Personal:** Born May 20, 1965, Indianapolis, IN; son of Harvey and Ann; married Nina Simone; children: Anthony L II & Krysten Simone. **Educ:** Purdue Univ, BS, elec engineering, 1987; Howard Univ, MS; Univ Chicago, Grad Sch Bus, MBA, 1994. **Career:** Kraft Gen Foods, sr corp elec engr, 1989-93; Merrill Lynch, assoc, investment banking, 1994-95; Ford Motor Co, sr financial analyst, treas, 1996-99; Delphi Automotive, mgr capital markets treas, 1999-2001;

Comerica Securities Inc, bus develop officer, Corp Finance, vpres investment banking, managing dir & head investment banking, 2001-. **Orgs:** Alpha Phi Alpha, 1985-; assoc minister, Tabernacle Missionary Baptist Church, 1996-; 100 Black Men Detroit, 2003-; trustee, Henry Ford Health Systs, 2003-; bd mem, Detroit Rescue Mission Ministries; MDiv, Howard Univ Sch Divinty, 2005; bd dir, Detroit Rescue Mission Ministries. **Special Achievements:** Started Comerica Bank's Cooperate Investment Banking Pract. **Home Addr:** 6983 Hawkwoods Ct, West Bloomfield, MI 48322-4568, **Home Phone:** (248)865-1187. **Business Addr:** Managing Director, Head of Investment Banking, Comerica Securities Inc, 25 Mich Ave W, Battle Creek, MI 49017-3610, **Business Phone:** (313)964-5068.

**CAULKER, FERNE YANGYEITIE**
Dance director. **Personal:** Born Aug 9, 1947; children: Yetunde Bronson. **Educ:** Univ Ghana, Am Forum African Studies, cert, 1969; Univ Wis, BS, 1972. **Career:** Ko-Thi Dance Co, founder & artistic exec dir, 1969-, prog asst, tutor, 1971-72; Creative Dance Workshop, dir, 1975-77; Fulbright res fel, 1994-95; Nat Endowment Arts 2000 Dance panel; Univ Wis-Milwaukee, lectr, 1971-77, asst prof, 1977-88, dept dance, prof, 1989-. **Orgs:** Nat Endowment Arts, 2000; Wis Arts Bd, 1974; Wis Acad Sci, Fel, 1990; lect, Univ Dar es Salaam; Arusha United African Am Cult Ctrassisted, UWASA cult group; Blue Ribbon Comn Arts; bd dir, Wis Arts Bd. **Honors/Awds:** Governor's Special Award, Wis Gov, 1984; Woman of the Year, Woman Woman Conf, 1989; Outstanding Contribution in Arts, Black Women's Network, 1994; Women's History Month Award, US Postal Serv, 1999; Outstanding Artist Award, City Milwaukee, Milwaukee Arts Bd, 2000; Distinguished Alumna Award in the Field of Arts & Humanities, Univ Wis Milwaukee, 2006. **Special Achievements:** Presentation, "Religious Dance In the Black American Experience," WI Dance Coun Conf, 1977; "Benito Cerno," guest choreographer, Milwaukee Repertory Theater, 1996; author, "Saving Children Through the Arts," WI Sch News, 2000. **Business Addr:** Founder, Executive Director, Ko-Thi Dance Co, 342 N Water St 7th Fl, Milwaukee, WI 53202, **Business Phone:** (414)273-0676.

**CAUSEY-KONATE, TAMMIE M.**
Educator. **Educ:** Univ New Orleans, BA, sec educ, 1986, MEd, curric & instr, 1996, PhD, K-12 educ admin, 2000; Univ Innsbruck, Austria; La State Univ; Southern Univ. **Career:** Dillard Univ, Div Educ & Psychol Studies, asst dean; Univ New Orleans, Grad Coord K-12 Educ Leadership, assoc prof, currently. **Orgs:** Ed Bd, J Negro Educ; Nat Coun Accreditation Teacher Educ; NASSP Bull. **Business Addr:** Associate Professor, Graduate Coordinator, Univ New Orleans, Bicentennial Education Bldg ED 174 Rm 240-242, New Orleans, LA 70148-2515, **Business Phone:** (504)280-6451.

**CAUSWELL, DUANE**
Actor, basketball player. **Personal:** Born May 31, 1968, Queens Village, NY; married Leslie; children: Kaelyn Alana, Dylan & Jalen. **Educ:** Temple Univ, attended 1990. **Career:** Basketball player (retired), TV series; Sacramento Kings, ctr, 1990-97; Miami Heat, 1997-2001; San Antonio Spurs, 2000, free agt, currently. TV Series: "Eddie", 1996. **Business Addr:** Basketball Player, San Antonio Spurs, 1 AT&T Ctr Pkwy, San Antonio, TX 78219, **Business Phone:** (210)444-5000.

**CAUTHEN-BOND, DR. CHERYL G.**
Ophthalmologist. **Personal:** Born Nov 13, 1957, Flint, MI; daughter of Joseph Jr; married William; children: William II, Robert & Jeannette. **Educ:** Howard Univ, attended 1977; Howard Univ Col Med, MD, 1981. **Career:** DC Gen Hosp, intern-med, 1981-82; Howard Univ Hosp, resident ophthal, 1982-85; Howard Univ Col Med, instr dept surg ophthal div, 1985-86; Norfolk Eye Physicians & Surgeons, physician, 1986-; Eastern Va Med Sch, asst prof ophthal, asst prof, currently. **Orgs:** Am Acad Ophthal; Nat Med Asn; Am Med Asn; Norfolk Med Soc; Norfolk Acad Med; Old Dom Med Soc; Med Soc Va; med adv, House Eastern Ministries Inc; bd dir, d'ART Ctr; bd dir, House Esther Ministries; Friends Hampton Roads, currently. **Business Addr:** Assistant Professor of Ophthalmology, Eastern Virginia Medical School, 604 Fairfax Ave, Norfolk, VA 23501-1980, **Business Phone:** (757)446-9236.

**CAVE, DR. ALFRED EARL**
Physician, surgeon. **Personal:** Born Jan 23, 1940, Brooklyn, NY; son of Alfred Sr and Theodora; married Jeanne Byrnes; children: Christine. **Educ:** Columbia Col, BA, 1961; State Univ NY, Downstate Med Ctr, MD, 1965. **Career:** State Univ New York, Health Sci Ctr, internship, 1965-66, resident, gen surg, 1966-71, ownstate Med Ctr, instr, 1971, asst prof surg, 1971-77; Kings County Hosp Brooklyn, attend physician, 1971-77; Long Beach Memorial Hosp, attend surgeon, 1976-79; Lydia Hall Hosp, attend surgeon, 1977-78; Nassau Co Med Ctr, attend surgeon, 1978-2002; Syosset Community Hosp, attend surgeon, 1978-2002; pvt pract, currently. **Orgs:** Sigma Pi Phi Frat. **Honors/Awds:** National Medical Fellowship Award, 1961; New York State Medical Scholarship, 1961. **Business Addr:** Physician, 1 Hutch Ct, Dix Hills, NY 11746, **Business Phone:** (631)499-3997.

**CAVE, PERSTEIN RONALD**
President (organization), school administrator, government official. **Personal:** Born Sep 24, 1947, Brooklyn, NY; son of Perstein and Dorothy; children: Christopher, Joscelyn & Jeralyn. **Educ:** Kingsborough Community Col, AA, 1967; City Col NY, BA, 1970; Univ Hartford, MBA, 1981; CGFM. **Career:** Aetna Life & Casualty Ins Co, expense coordr, 1977-80; ESPN & ABC TV, spec proj consult, 1980-85; Asn untuck Comm Col, bus mgr & assoc dean, 1985; Twins Community Col, bus mgr, 1988-89; State CT, asst financial dir, 1989, fiscal admin mgr, currently. **Orgs:** Ministerial servant, Windsor CT Congregation Jehovah's Witnesses, 1980-; Nat Asn Acct, 1980-; Nat Black MBA Asn, 1982-; Asnuntuck Community Col; Affirmative Action Comt, 1985-; Asn Govt Accts; Inst Internal Auditors; pres, AGA Boston Chap. **Home Addr:** 4 Vinlen Dr, Windsor, CT 06095-3854, **Home Phone:** (860)242-0068. **Business Addr:** Fiscal Administrative Manager, State of Connecticut, 250 Const Plz, Hartford, CT 06103, **Business Phone:** (860)757-9040.

**CAVINESS, REV. EMMITT THEOPHILUS**
Clergy, president (organization). **Personal:** Born May 23, 1928, Marshall, TX; son of Lula Page and Will Stone; married James Pitts; children: Theophilus James & Theodosia Jacqueline. **Educ:** Bishop Col, BA; Eden Theol Sem, BDiv. **Career:** Greater Abyssinia Bapt Church, pastor, sr pastor, 1961-; Greater Abyssinia Bapt Church Fed Credit Union, pres, 1979-83; St Mark's Baptist Church; Mt Nebo Baptist Church; St Paul Baptist Church; Southern Christian Leadership Conf, pres, currently. **Orgs:** Historian & bd dir, Nat Bapt Conv USA; pres, Ohio Bapt State Conv; pres, Bapt Min Conf; exec asst, Mayor Cleveland Off; bd dir, Nat Asn Advan Colored People; bd dir, Cong Racial Equality; bd dir, Ohio Civil Rights Comn; Baptist Minister's Conf Cleveland; bd dir, Blacktie Cleaveland; Ohio Baptist Gen Conv; Nat Baptist Conv USA Inc; exec bd, Greater Cleveland Growth Asn; City Cleveland, Bd Zoning Appeals. **Honors/Awds:** DDiv, Virginia Sem and Col; hon doctorate law, Cent State Univ. **Special Achievements:** First clergy member of Cleveland council. **Home Addr:** 123 Hampton Ct, Cleveland, OH 44108-1186. **Business Addr:** Senior Pastor, Greater Abyssinia Baptist Church, 1161 E 105 St, Cleveland, OH 44108, **Business Phone:** (216)795-1842.

**CAVINESS, LORRAINE F.**
Educator. **Personal:** Born Apr 8, 1914, Atlanta, GA; married Clyde E; children: Muriel E. **Educ:** Spelman Col, BA, 1936; Atlanta Univ, attended 1948; Am Univ, attended 1952; DC Teachers Col, attended 1960. **Career:** Winston-Salem Teachers Col, asst teacher, 1936-37; Voc High Sch, teacher, 1937-38; US Govt Dept Labor, res asst, 1942-44, Dept Army, 1947-51; Wash DC Pub Sch, 1946, 1963-64. **Orgs:** Treas, Brightwood Community Asn, 1968-70; Chmn, Educ Comt, 1969; Spelman Col Alumnae Asn; Century Club Spelman Col, 1977; DC Nat Retired Teachers Asn; Wash Urban League; Fedn Civic Asn; Adv Neighborhood Coun. **Home Addr:** 6653 13th St NW, Washington, DC 20012, **Home Phone:** (202)829-9513.

**CAYOU, NONTSIZI KIRTON**
Educator. **Personal:** Born May 19, 1937, New Orleans, LA; married William. **Educ:** San Francisco State Univ, AB, dance ethnol, 1962, MA, 1973. **Career:** Educator (retired); San Francisco Unified Sch Dist & Woodrow Wilson HS, 1955; San Francisco Unified Sch Dist & Woodrow Wilson High Sch, 1963; San Francisco State Univ, teacher dance prog, 1963, 1965-67, chair, 1995, Dept Dance, head, prof, coordr dance prog; Univ San Francisco, 1972-73, teacher guest artist, 1969-70; Stanford Univ, 1976-77. **Orgs:** Chmn, Oakland Dance Asn, 1966-68; dir founder, Wajumbe Cultural Ensemble, 1969; chmn, Comn Black Dance, 1969; host chair, Fifth world Congress, Int Cong Orisa Tradition & Culture, 1997, dep secy, 1997-99; Ctr African & African Am Art & Cult; Calif Dance Educrs Asn; Nat Dance Asn. **Honors/Awds:** Hall of Fame, San Francisco State Univ, 1999. **Special Achievements:** Griot Soc Publ, "The Dance is People", New African article, 1965; Black Scholar, 1970; books: "Modern Jazz Dance", 1973. articles: "Origins of Jazz Dance". **Home Addr:** 238 Geneva Ave, San Francisco, CA 94112.

**CAZENAVE, PROF. NOEL ANTHONY**
Educator. **Personal:** Born Oct 25, 1948, Washington, DC; son of Herman Joseph and Mildred Depland; married Anita Washington; children: Anika Tene. **Educ:** Dillard Univ, BA (magna cum laude), psychol, 1970; Univ Mich, MA, psychol, 1971; Tulane Univ, PhD, sociol, 1977; Univ NH, attended 1978; Univ Pa, PhD, 1989. **Career:** Temple Univ, asst prof, 1978-84, assoc prof, 1984-91; Univ Conn, prof sociol, currently. **Orgs:** Am Sociol Asn; Asn Black Sociologists. **Home Addr:** 6 Atwood St Unit B, Hartford, CT 06105-1801, **Home Phone:** (860)548-9799. **Business Addr:** Professor of Sociology, University of Connecticut, 123 Manchester Hall, Storrs, CT 06269-2068, **Business Phone:** (860)486-4190.

**CEBALLOS, CEDRIC Z.**
Basketball player, basketball coach, executive. **Personal:** Born Aug 2, 1969, Maui, HI; married Sherlynn Cook; children: 2. **Educ:** Ventura Col, Ventura, CA, attended 1988; Calif State Univ, Fullerton, CA, attended 1990. **Career:** Basketball player (retired), basketball coach, exec; Phoenix Suns, forward, 1990-94, 1997-98; Los Angeles Lakers, 1994-97; Dallas Mavericks, 1997-2000; Detroit Pistons, 2000-01; Miami Heat, 2000-01; Handle Your Bus, founder, 2000; Hapoel Tel Aviv, 2002; Lokomotiv Mineralnye Vody, 2002-2003; Sioux Falls Skyforce, 2003; San Miguel Beermen, 2003-04; Phoenix Mercury, spec asst coach, 2004; Los Angeles Stars, 2004-05; Maywood Buzz, 2005-07; Phoenix Flame, 2007; Alik Entertainment, owner, currently; Phoenix Suns, emcee, currently; Nothing but Net, host, currently; Phoenix Flame, coach, currently; Am Basketball Asn, part owner, currently. **Orgs:** Cystic Fibrosis Found. **Business Addr:** Assistant Coach, Phoenix Flame, 111 W Monroe, Phoenix, AZ 85003, **Business Phone:** (602)258-0175.

**CEDENO, CESAR ENCARNACION**
Baseball player, baseball executive. **Personal:** Born Feb 25, 1951, Santo Domingo; son of Diogene; married Cora Lefevre; children: Cesar Jr, Cesar Roberto & Cesar Richard. **Career:** Baseball player (retired), coach, baseball executive; Houston Astros, amateur free agt, 1967, outfielder, 1970-81; Cincinnati Reds, outfielder, 1982-85; St Louis Cardinals, outfielder, 1985-86; Los Angeles Dodgers, outfielder, 1986; Toronto Blue Jays, free agt, 1986; Dominican & Venezuelan Winter Leagues, fielding & hitting coach; Wash Nationals, coach; The Greenville Astros, hitting coach, currently. **Home Addr:** 9919 Sagedowne Lane, Houston, TX 77089-4309, **Home Phone:** (407)201-5043. **Business Addr:** Coach, The Greenville Astros, 135 Shiloh Rd, Greeneville, TN 37743, **Business Phone:** (423)638-0411.

**CELESTINE, VON C.**
Association executive, vice president (organization). **Educ:** Southern Univ & Agr & Mech Col, BS, acct, 1987; Univ Tex, Austin, MBA, 1992. **Career:** United Healthcare, finance mgr; Prudential Health Care, compliance mgr; Arthur Andersen, acct mgr; Exxon, acct mgr; Smith, Graham & Co Investment Advisors LP, sr vpres & dir finance & admin, 2000-06; Bridgeway Capital Mgt, partner, 2006-. **Orgs:** Adv bd, Southern Univ; adv bd, River Pointe Church. **Business Addr:** Partner, Bridgeway Capital Management Inc, 5615 Kirby Dr Suite 518, Houston, TX 77005.

**CENTERS, LARRY EUGENE**
Football player. **Personal:** Born Jun 1, 1968, Tatum, TX; son of Don and Margie; married Vanesse Lampkin; children: 5. **Educ:** Stephen F Austin State Univ. **Career:** Football player (retired); Phoenix Cardinals, running back & fullback & kick returner, 1990-93; Ariz Cardinals, fullback, 1994-98; Wash Redskins, running back & fullback, 1999-2000; Buffalo Bills, fullback, 2001-02; New Eng Patriots, fullback, 2003. **Honors/Awds:** Pro Bowl, 1995, 1996, 2001; All-Pro, 1996; Champion, Super Bowl, XXXVIII. **Home Addr:** PO Box 2505, Longview, TX 75606-2505. **Business Addr:** 6101 Long Prairie Rd, Flower Mound, TX 75028.

**CHAFFERS, JAMES ALVIN**
Educator. **Personal:** Born Nov 30, 1941, Ruston, LA; married Geraldine; children: Pedra & Michael. **Educ:** Southern Univ, Baton Rouge, BArch (cum laude), 1964; Univ Mich, MArch, 1969, DArch, 1971; Stanford Univ, post doctoral, design mgt, 1981. **Career:** La State Univ, Dept Psychol, educ prog consult, 1970; Wastenaw Co, comnr, 1970-71; Southern Univ, Col Eng, assoc prof archit, 1971-73; State La, Off Gov, environ design consult, 1971; Nathan Johnson & Assoc, arch; Univ Mich, Alfred Taubman Col Archit & Urban Planning, from asst prof to assoc prof, 1973-75, prof archit, 1979-208, chair doctoral prog, 1991-94, prof emer, currently; Stanford Univ, fel, 1980-81; Villa Corsi-Salviati Design Studio, Italy, dir, 1995; Martin Luther King Jr Nat Mem Proj, design consult, 1997-; Taubman Col W African Studio, dir, 2000-08; J Chaffers Archit, pres & design prin. **Orgs:** Chmn, Southern Univ Dept Archit; dir, Community based Design Workshops N Cent Ann Arbor & SW Detroit; Am Inst Architects; Mich Soc Architects; Asn Col Sch Archit; Mich Acad Sci, Arts & Lett; Mich Soc Architect; Asn Col Sch Architect; Mich Acad Sci, Arts & Lett; founder, Detroit Ann Arbor Workshop, 1973-98; Nat Coun Archit Regist Bd; Nat Housing Ctr Elderly Housing Policy, Health & Human Serv; Am Inst Archit; Bd dir, design prog & educ consult, Milo Thompson Archit & African Cult Arts Ctr, 1976-77; Wayne Co Rd Comn, 1982-85. **Home Addr:** 1415 Normandy Rd, Ann Arbor, MI 48103-5940, **Home Phone:** (734)769-9016. **Business Addr:** Professor Emeritus, University of Michigan, 2000 Bonisteel Blvd, Ann Arbor, MI 48109-2069, **Business Phone:** (734)936-0213.

**CHALLENOR, HERSCHELLE SULLIVAN**
School administrator. **Personal:** Born Oct 5, 1938, Atlanta, GA. **Educ:** Spelman Col, BA, 1959; Univ Grenoble; Columbia Univ, PhD, 1966; Sorbonne Univ; Johns Hopkins, MA, 1973. **Career:** Polit Sci Dept Brooklyn Col, asst prof, 1969-72; Am Polit Sci Assoc, cong fel, 1972-73; Div Ed & Res Ford Found, prog officer, 1973-75; Un Educ Sci & Cult Orgn Wash Liaison Off, founding dir, 1978-93; Clark Atlanta Univ, Sch Pub & Int Affairs, dean, 1993-2002, prof int rels & african affairs, 2002; USAID, team leader, 2004-06, Bur Africa, sr advisor, asst adminr, currently. **Orgs:** Consult, Sub-com Africa; UN Asn Coun Foreign Rel, Am Polit Sci Asn, Natl Conf Black Polit Sci, Brd Oper Crossroads Africa; Intl Block United Fund; Spelman l Scholar; chair, bd dir, Nat Summit Africa; dir, US House Representatives Subcomt; USAID AAAS diplomacy fel AA/AFR. **Business Addr:** Senior Advisor, Consultant, US Agency for International Development, Ronald Reagan Bldg, Washington, GA 20523, **Business Phone:** (202)712-1562.

**CHALMERS, THELMA FAYE**
Executive director, manager. **Personal:** Born Feb 21, 1947, Shreveport, LA; daughter of Leonard Hampton and Ivy Williams Hampton; married Jimmy L; children: Troy, Douglas & Celeste. **Educ:** Chandler Col, assoc degree, 1966; Southern Ill Univ, Edwardsville Sch Bus, assertive mgt cert, 1985; Bus Women's Training Inst, image & commun skills cert, 1986. **Career:** St Clair Co Intergovernmental Grants Dept, Community Action Agency, prog monitor, 1979-81, prog planner, 1981-83, equal employ opportunity officer, 1982-, spec assignment supvr, 1983-86, div mgr, 1988-90, exec dir, 1990-. **Orgs:** Staff liaison, Serv Delivery Area 24 Pvt Indust Coun, 1984-; Ill Employ & Training Asn, 1985; Ill Employ & Training Partnership, 1988-91; bd mem, Ill Employ & Training Asn, 1989-90; IETP Prof Develop Comt, 1989-90; vice chair, Adv Coun Prog Serv Older Persons. **Home Addr:** 1517 Oak Meadow Dr, O Fallon, IL 62269-3025, **Home Phone:** (618)632-4698. **Business Addr:** Executive Director, St Clair County Intergovernmental Grants Department, 19 Public Sq Suite 200 1220 Ctrville Ave, Belleville, IL 62220-1624, **Business Phone:** (618)277-6790.

**CHAMBERLAIN, BYRON DANIEL**
Football player, foundation executive. **Personal:** Born Oct 17, 1971, Honolulu, HI; married Robyn. **Educ:** Univ Mo; Wayne State Univ, BS, commun, 2008. **Career:** Football player (retired); Denver Broncos, tight end, 1995-2000, 2004; Minn Vikings, tight end, 2001-02; Wash Redskins, tight end, 2003. **Orgs:** Founder, Byron Chamberlain Found, 2000. **Honors/Awds:** Harlon Hill Trophy finalist; Pro bowl, 2001; Super Bowl champion XXXII, XXXIII. **Special Achievements:** Films: 1998 AFC Championship Game, 1999. TV series: "ESPN SportsCentury", 2002. **Business Addr:** Founder, The Byron Chamberlain Foundation, 1804 Garnet Ave Suite 234, San Diego, CA 92109.

**CHAMBERLAIN, WESLEY POLK**
Chief executive officer, baseball player. **Personal:** Born Apr 13, 1966, Chicago, IL; son of Bettie L; children: Wesley Polk II. **Educ:** Simeon Career Acad, sheet metal technol & sheetworking, 1984; Jackson State Univ, BBA, 1987. **Career:** Baseball player (retired), cheif executive officer; Pittsburgh Pirates, 1987-90, free agt, 1997; Philadelphia Phillies, outfielder & right fielder & left fielder, 1990-94; Boston Red Sox, right fielder & left fielder & outfielder & Designated hitter, 1994-95; Japan Chiba Lotte Marines, 1996, 2006; Winnipeg Goldeyes, 2000; Schaumburg Flyers, 2001-02; Newark Bears, 2002; Northern League, Gary S Shore Rail Cats, 2003; Theweschamberlain.com, chief exec officer, 2003-. **Orgs:** SAA. **Honors/Awds:** Most Valuable Player, Eastern League, 1989; Minor League Player of the Year, 1989; Topps All-Star, 1989; Eastern League All-Star, 1989; Player of the Month, 1989; Topps

Player of the Month, 1989; Player of the Week, Nat League, 1991. **Business Addr:** PO Box 1358, Homewood, IL 60430.

### CHAMBERS, CAROLINE E.

Executive, president (organization). **Personal:** Born Mar 30, 1964, Detroit, MI; daughter of DeMarr and Blanche Solomon; married Anthony; children: Eve. **Educ:** Univ Ga, BA, jour & mass commun, 1986; Univ Mich, MPA, pub admin, 1994. **Career:** ICMA Retirement Corp, midwest mkt mgr, 1987-92; Mich Metro Girl Scout Coun, develop dir, 1992-94; Mich Health Care Corp, pub affairs dir, 1994-97; Comerica Charitable Found, Comerica Bank, corp contrib mgr, pres, vpres & nat dir corp contrib, 1997-2011, vpres & nat dir diversity initiatives, 2011-. **Orgs:** Bd chair, Core City Neighborhoods Non Profit Housing Corp, 1998-2000; bd treas, Elder Law Mich, 1999-; bd mem, Communities Schs, 2000-; bd mem, Detroit Discovery Mus, 2001-. **Business Addr:** Vice President, National Director of Diversity Initiatives, Comerica Bank, 500 Woodward Ave, Detroit, MI 48226-3390, **Business Phone:** (313)222-7356.

### CHAMBERS, CHRIS

Executive. **Educ:** NY Univ, BS, jour, commun, 1991. **Career:** Acct exec, 1990-92; Mercury Rec, mgr, dept dir, 1992-95; EMI Rec, sr dir publicity, 1995-97; Interscope Rec, sr dir publicity, 1997-2000; Arista Rec, vpres publicity, 2001-05; SONY BMG Music Entertainment, sr vpres publicity & artist develop, 2004-06; Chamber Grp, chief exec officer, founder & pres, 2006-. **Business Addr:** Founder, President & Chief Executive Officer, The Chamber Group, 416 W 13th St Suite 105, New York, NY 10004, **Business Phone:** (212)366-5801.

### CHAMBERS, CHRISTOPHER J.

Football player, executive. **Personal:** Born Aug 12, 1978, Cleveland, OH; son of Linda; married Stacey Bernice Saunders; children: 2. **Educ:** Univ Wis, BS, sociol & law, 1997; USA Weightlifting, cert, sports performance coach, 2012. **Career:** Football player (retired), executive, owner; Miami Dolphins, wide receiver, 2001-07, tight end, 2004; King Ape Entertainment, exec producer, 2006-09; San Diego Chargers, wide receiver, 2007-09, tight end, 2008; Kans City Chiefs, wide receiver, 2009-11; Chamber Fitness, owner, 2012-. **Orgs:** Pres & chief exec officer, founder, CATCH 84 Found, 2005-; spokesperson, Big Bros Big Sisters, 2013. **Honors/Awds:** Honorable mention All-Big Ten, 1999; Football Most Valuable Player, Univ Wis, 2000; Miami Dolphins Rookie of the Year, 2001; Receiving Touchdowns Leader, Am Football Conf, 2003; Dolphin team Most Valuable Player, Nat Football League, 2006; Pro Bowl, 2006; Man of the Year Award, 2006. **Business Addr:** Founder, President, C.A.T.C.H. 84 Foundation, PO Box 440296, St. Louis, MO 63144, **Business Phone:** (954)873-1332.

### CHAMBERS, DR. DONALD CLIVE

Physician. **Personal:** Born May 17, 1936; married Jacqueline; children: Christopher, Kimberly & Bradley. **Educ:** NY Univ, BA, 1957; Howard Univ, Col Med, MD, 1961. **Career:** Kings Co Hosp Ctr, res training, 1961-66; St Univ NY, asst prof, 1964-66; Baltimore, pvt pract physician, 1968-; Sinai Hosp, physician; Provident Hosp, physician; Lutheran Hosp, physician; Northwest Hosp, physician gynec, currently; New Horizons Womens Care, obstetrician & gynecologist, currently. **Orgs:** Pan Am Med Soc; Am Soc Abdominal Surgeons; Am Bd Obstet & Gynec; Nat Asn Advan Colored People; Monumental City Med Soc; Health Care Stand Comt; Md Found Health Care; Wash Policy & Asn Mgt; fel Am Col Obstet & Gynec, 1969; fel Am Col Surgeons, 1973; fel Royal Soc Health. **Special Achievements:** Contributing author for Urban Health Magazine. **Home Addr:** 5400 Old Ct Rd Ste 302, Randallstown, MD 21133-5127, **Home Phone:** (410)521-3636. **Business Addr:** Physician, Private Practice, 2300 Garrison Blvd Suite 200, Baltimore, MD 21216, **Business Phone:** (410)947-5100.

### CHAMBERS, HARRY, JR.

Educator, consultant. **Personal:** Born Jul 4, 1956, Birmingham, AL; son of Harry A Sr and Bessie L; married Linda Giles; children: Hali Alexandria, Harry Alonso III & Kayla Melissa. **Educ:** Ala State Univ, BS, bus admin/acct, 1989; Samford Univ, MBA, 1985; Dale Carnegie, Human Rel & Leadership Training; Univ Ala, Birmingham, MA, acct, 1990; Capella Univ, PhD, acct, 2015. **Career:** US Gen Acct Off, co-op stud, 1976-77; Bank Am NT & SA, int auditor Europe, 1979-80; Amsouth Bank NA, div acct officer opers, 1980-86; US Treas, IR Sgt, 1987-88; Chambers Consult Ltd, financial partner & owner, 1987-; Birmingham Southern Col, adj prof, 1988-; Drake Beam Morin, consult, 1996-98, UnitedHealth Group, expense planning mgr, 1998-99; facilitator outplacement serv, 2005-08; Bham Water Works Board, consult strategic plan, 2006-08; Alternative Bd-Tab, Facilitator, 1999; Osborne Enterprises Inc, managing partner, currently; Samford Univ, MADD, vpres, 2001; Better Business Better Communities Research Inc, vpres bus develop, 2011-; Team National, Independent mkt dir, 2011-. **Orgs:** Life mem, Kappa Alpha Psi, 1978-; life mem, Nat Black MBA Asn Birmingham Chap, 1985-; sunday sch teacher, Sixth Ave Baptist Church, 1985-; deacon, Sixth Ave Bapt Church, 1986-; treas & bd mem, Acad Fine Arts Inc, Birmingham Ala, 1988-. **Home Addr:** 1040 50th St Ensley, Birmingham, AL 35208-2420, **Home Phone:** (205)780-0141. **Business Addr:** Managing Partner, Chambers Consulting Ltd, 800 25th St Ensley, Birmingham, AL 35218-1936, **Business Phone:** (205)780-7903.

**CHAMBERS, JOHN CURRY, JR. See Obituaries Section.**

### CHAMBERS, JUANITA CLAY

Educator, executive. **Personal:** married Wilson. **Educ:** Wayne State Univ, BS, sci educ, MS, sci educ, PhD, educ admin. **Career:** Educator (retired); Hopewell City Schs, bd dir, vice chmn, 1989-2011; Detroit Pub Sch, teacher, supvr, div dir, chief acad officer, Div Educ Serv, assoc supt, Dwight D. Eisenhower Prog, proj dir, Detroit Urban Syst Initiative, proj dir, Ctr Learning Technol Urban Sch, proj dir, Math & Sci Ctr Prog, proj dir, Dept Curric Develop & Related Progs, chief, currently. **Orgs:** Appomattox Regional Gov's Sch, Petersburg. **Business Addr:** Associate Superintendent, Detroit Public Schools, 3011 W Grand Blvd, Detroit, MI 48202, **Business Phone:** (313)873-7094.

### CHAMBERS, MADRITH BENNETT

Government official. **Personal:** Born Oct 23, 1935, Beckley, WV; married Robert E; children: Stephanie M Rosario, Gregory B, Patrick M, Jennifer E & Sharri L. **Educ:** Bluefield State Col, AS, law enforcement, BS, criminal justice admin, 1985. **Career:** Social Security Admin, contact rep. **Orgs:** Councilwoman City Pax, 1972-74; vpres, Am Legion Women's Aux, 1982-84; chairperson, City Beckley Human Rights Comn, 1978-; pres, Beckley Chap Bluefield St Col Alumni Asn, 1983-; Alpha Kappa Alpha; bd dir, Community Health Syst; bd dir, Heart god Ministries; vpres, Nat Asn Advan Colored People Raleigh. **Home Addr:** PO Box 625, Beckley, WV 25802. **Business Addr:** Contact Representative, Social Security Administration, 214 N Kanawna St, Beckley, WV 25801.

### CHAMBERS, OLIVIA MARIE

Government official. **Personal:** Born Sep 27, 1942, Denver, CO; married Bill D; children: Maria. **Educ:** Dale Carnegie Ctrs Human Rel, cert, 1977; Univ Denver, Mgt Cert Prog, 1983; Colo Univ Ext Ctr & Community Col. **Career:** State Colo, Interstate Dept Employ & Training Unit, mgr, 1976-77, chief benefits, 1977-84, Dept Labor & Employ, Tax Dept, chief, 1984-. **Orgs:** IAPES; bd mem, Community Homemaker Suc, 1981-83. **Honors/Awds:** Distinguished State Service Award, Denver Fed Exec Bd, 1981. **Home Addr:** 4311 Cathay St, Denver, CO 80249-6593, **Home Phone:** (303)375-6713. **Business Addr:** Chief, Colorado Department of Labor & Employment, 1515 Arapahoe Tower 2 Suite 400, Denver, CO 80202-2117, **Business Phone:** (303)603-8235.

### CHAMBERS, PAMELA S.

Police officer. **Personal:** Born Nov 5, 1961, Gadsden, AL; daughter of Hurley S and Mildred L Douglas; children: Carlon. **Educ:** Ferris State Col, Big Rapids, MI, AA, pre-law, 1982. **Career:** Not Just Nails, a nail salon, owner & pres, 1989; City Pontiac Mich, police cadet, 1982, police officer, 1982, police sergeant, 1988, police capt, currently, Admin Serv Div, div comdr, currently; Univ DC, dep chief pub safety. **Orgs:** Secy, Soc Afro-Am Police; bd mem, Nat Black Police Asn; assoc mem, Nat Org Black Law Exec (NOBLE), officer leader. **Honors/Awds:** Distinction of being the first black woman promoted to police sergeant in the history of the city of Pontiac. **Special Achievements:** First Black Female Lt of the Pontiac Police Dept, 1998; First Black Female Captain of the Pontiac Police Dept, 1999; First Female Black Dir for City of Pontiac Homeland Security, 2003; youngest person ever to be promoted to sergeant in the city of Pontiac. **Home Addr:** 2711 Oak View Ct, Rochester Hills, MI 48307-5901. **Business Addr:** Police Captain, Division Commander, City of Pontiac, 110 E Pke St, Pontiac, MI 48342, **Business Phone:** (248)758-3400.

### CHAMBLISS, ESQ. ALVIN ODELL, JR.

Lawyer. **Personal:** Born Jan 22, 1944, Vicksburg, MS; son of Alvin O Sr and Ledorsha A; married Josephine Johnson, Dec 31, 1973; children: Sadarie, Alvin O III & Alvenia. **Educ:** Jackson State Univ, BA, 1967; Howard Univ Sch Law, JD, 1969; Univ Calif, Berkeley, CA, LLM, const law, 1971. **Career:** Cohon, Jones & Fazande Law Firm, 1972-74; N Miss Rural Legal Serv, sr atty, 1975-93; Tex Southern Univ Thurgood Marshall Sch Law, lectr, 1994-2002; Univ Ind, vis prof, 2004-07; NC Cent Sch Law, vis prof, 2006; Univ Ind Bloomington, vis prof, 2004-07; Atty Law WW Wright Educ 4260, atty, currently. **Orgs:** Vice chair, Nat Black Media Coalition; gen coun, Black Mississippian Coun Higher Educ; pres, Oxford-Lafayette County Br Nat Asn Advan Colored People; chmn, Nat Conf Black Mayors; ct watch chair, Magnolia Bar Asn; affil adv, Miss Asn Educr; community liaison, Methodist Men Burns; Nat Conf Black Lawyers; Oper PUSH; Legal Aid Soc Alameda County; New Orleans Legal Assistance. **Honors/Awds:** Ming Award Lawyer of the Year, Nat Asn Advan Coloured People, 1992; SCLC Chauncy Estridge Distinguished Barrister of Law, 1992; Lawyer of the Year, Miss Educ Asn, 1993; Lawyer of the Year, Miss Legis Black Caucus, 1993; Man of the Year, Masonic Orders, PHA North Miss, 1993; Chaucey Ethridge Award, 1993; NCBL Freedom Fighter Lawyer of Year, 1994; Most Significant Blacks in the Last 100 Years, 2000; TLPJ Layers of Year, Trial Lawyers Pub Justice, 2002; TX NAACP ALEX Award, Lawyer of Year, 2003; Mississippi Man of the Year Award, 2004. **Special Achievements:** Voting Rights & Citizen Participation Manual, 1986; Ayers Brown III The New Frontier in Higher Education, 1989; Trends in the Eighties, Mississippi State Practice, 1989; Nat Nat Asn Advan Coloured People Summit on Higher Education, Higher Education Desegregation Advancing African-Americans Towards Equality, 1992; Ayers v Fordice, "Where Do We GoFrom Here in Higher Education Desegration", 1993; Ayers v Fordice, Reversing the Trend in Higher Education Desegration From Closure to Parity for HBCUs, 1993; "Black Colleges Under Fire", Emerge, 1993. **Home Addr:** 3022 S Lamar Blvd, Oxford, MS 38655-5364, **Home Phone:** (662)259-2784. **Business Addr:** Attorney, Law WW Wright Education 4260, 201 N Rose Ave, Bloomington, IN 47405, **Business Phone:** (812)856-8587.

### CHAMBLISS, DR. PRINCE C., JR.

Lawyer. **Personal:** Born Oct 3, 1948, Birmingham, AL; son of Rev Prince C Sr; married Patricia Toney; children: Patience Bradyn. **Educ:** Wesleyan Univ, attended 1968; Univ Ala, Birmingham, BA, polit sci & sociol, 1971; Harvard Univ, Sch Law, JD, 1974. **Career:** Univ Ala, Birmingham, spec asst to pres, 1974-75; Judge Sam C Pointer Jr, law clerk, 1975-76; Armstrong Allen, et al, assoc atty, 1976-2001; Stokes Bartholomew, Evens & Petree PC, partner & atty, 2001-11; atty & auth, Prince Chambliss, 2011-12; Law Div, City Memphis, asst Atty, 2012-. **Orgs:** Bd dir, Memphis Mid-S Chap; bd dir, Am Red Cross, 1987-; vpres, Tenn Bd Law Examiners, 1988-; secy, Tenn Bar Asn, 1994-97; bd dirs, Memphis Bar Asn, 1994-; pres, Memphis Bar Asn, 1997-98; chmn, Ben F Jones Chap Nat Bar Asn, judicial recommendations comt; Grant Info Ctr Inc; ACCTM, 1999-; fel Am Col Civil Trial Mediators, fel Am Bar Found, fel Tenn Bar Found, fel Memphis Bar Found; bd mem, Girls Club Memphis; trustee, Miles Col Sch Law; founding bd mem, Grant Ctr; trustee, LeMoyne-Owen Col. **Honors/Awds:** Judicial Conference Community Service Award, Nat Bar Asn, 1986; Boss of the Year, Memphis Legal Secretaries Asn, 1983; America's Top Black Lawyers, Black Enterprise Mag, 2003; Best Lawyers in America for Commercial Litigation, listed, 2006. **Special Achievements:** Legal Ethics for Trial Lawyers, The Litigator; "Inconsistent Verdicts: How to Recognize & Cope With", The Litigator; First black president of the Memphis Bar Association in 1997; First black member of the Tennessee Board of Law Examiners. **Home Addr:** 1917 Miller Farms Rd Suite 700, Germantown, TN 38138-2752, **Home Phone:** (901)525-6781. **Business Addr:** Partner, Attorney, Evans & Petree PC, 1000 Ridgeway Loop Rd Suite 200, Memphis, TN 38120, **Business Phone:** (901)525-6781.

### CHAMP-YERBY, TAMI

Executive. **Career:** City Petersburg Blandford, dir park & leisure servs, parks & recreation dir, currently. **Business Addr:** Director Parks, Leisure Services, City Petersburg Blandford, 1937 Johnson Rd, Petersburg, VA 23805, **Business Phone:** (804)733-2394.

### CHAMPION, JAMES A.

President (organization), executive. **Personal:** Born May 9, 1947, Bronx, NY; son of James William and Jean Simmons; married Victoria Lindsey; children: Nicole, Jayson, Christopher & Lindsey. **Educ:** Ala A&M Univ, Huntsville, BS, educ, 1970; Rutgers Uni, NB, credits labor rels & human resource mgt, 1976; Univ Miami, MS, lib arts, 2007. **Career:** Chase Manhattan Bank, asst mgr, 1970-72; US Dept Labor Recruitment & Trng Prog, exec dir, 1972-79; Merrill Lynch & Co, asst vpres, human resource, 1979-85; Ryder Truck Rental Inc, div dir employee rels, 1985-89, dir human resource, 1989-93, corp dir diversity & employee affairs, 1993-95; Champion Serv Grp Inc, pres & chief exec officer, 1995-; Ryder Systs Inc, exec dir. **Orgs:** Kappa Alpha Psi Fraternity; pres, Asn Affirmative Action Prof, Miami; chmn adv grp, Focal Pt Elderly; bd mem, Miami & Dade Chamber Com; bd mem, Jobs Progress, Miami; bd mem, Epilepsy Found Miami; bd mem, Jackson Mem Found; bd mem, Fla Reg Minority Bus Coun; bd mem, Exec Comn, Greater Miami Chamber Com; bd mem, Exec Comn, Greater Miami Tennis Found; bd mem, Black Exec Forum; bd mem, New World Sch Arts; S Fal Indust - Off Fed Contract Compliance Prog Liaison Grp; Black Hr Network; Soc Hr Mgt; United Way Dade Co Ctr Excellence; One Hundred Black Men NY; former bd mem, Mus Sci; former bd mem, Vis Indust Coun; former bd mem, Urban League Greater Miami; former bd mem, Miami Cares Kids; founder & former nat pres, Ryder Black Employees Network; Miami Dade Chamber Com; bd dir, Jackson Memorial Found; Greater Miami Tennis Found; Fla Memorial Univ Scholar Comt; founder, Champion Serv Grp Inc; bd mem, Fla Reg Minority Bus Coun; bd dir, First Serve Miami; Human Resources Mgt; Equal Employ Adv Coun; Asn Cert Fraud Examiners; Soc Human Resources Mgt. **Honors/Awds:** Black Achiever, Harlem YMCA, 1982; Black Achiever, Family Christian Asn Am, 1986; Prof Achiever, Dollars & Sense Publ, 1987; Community Achiever, NC A&T Alumni, 1990; Community Achiever, Comn Total Employ, 1990; Humanitarian Award, 1990; Service Award, 1990; Community Achiever, Alpha Kappa Alpha, 1991; Achiever, Nat Asn Equal Opportunity Higher Educ, 1993; Small Business of the Year, Miami-Dade Chamber Com, 1998; Emerging Black Business of the Year, Greater Miami Chamber Com, 1998; Minority Business Year Runner Up, Small Bus Admin, 2000; President Award, Fl Regional Minority Bus Coun, 2002. **Home Addr:** 9026 SW 97th Ave Apt 1, Miami, FL 33176-1952, **Home Phone:** (305)238-0743. **Business Addr:** President, Chief Executive Officer, The Champion Services Group Inc, 6501 NW 36th St Suite 300, Miami, FL 33166, **Business Phone:** (305)871-4866.

### CHANCE, DR. KENNETH BERNARD, SR.

Dentist, educator, administrator. **Personal:** Born Dec 8, 1953, New York, NY; son of George Edward and Janie Bolles; married Sharon L Lewis; children: Kenneth B II, Dana Marie, Christopher Weldon & Jacquelyne Lee. **Educ:** Fordham Univ, BS, 1975; Case Western Res Univ Dent Sch, DDS, 1979; NJ Dent Sch, cert endodontics, 1982; PEW Nat Dent Educ Prog, cert, 1986. **Career:** Jamaica Hosp GP, Resident, 1980; Harlem Hosp, attend 1981-90; N Cent Bronx Med Ctr, asst attend, 1982-92; Jamaica Hosp, asst attend, 1982-86; Kings Co Med Ctr, chief endodontics, 1983-91; Kings brook Jewish Med Ctr, asst attend, 1985-89; NJ Dent Sch, dir external affairs, 1985-89; assoc prof endodontics, 1987-97; Univ Med & Dent Nj, asst dean external affairs & urban resource develop, 1989-97, head dept endodontics, univ fed rels advisor; Comnr health, Dept Health, consult, NJ, 1991-97; Health Policy Prog, Joint Ctr Polit & Econs Studies, dir, 1992-93; US Sen Frank Lautenberg (D-NJ), health policy advr, 1992-94; Meharry Med Col, Sch Dent, dean, prof, 1997-2000, Univ Ky Col, Dent, chief, prof endodontics, 2000-. **Orgs:** Am Asn Endodontists, 1980-86, Nat Dent Asn, 1980-; minister, music & srorganist Sharon Bapt Ch, 1983-94; Int Asn Dent Res, 1984-86-; pres, Greater Metro Dent Soc NY, 1985-86; consult, Commonwealth Dent Soc, NJ, 1985-97; Am Asn Dent Schs, 1990-; Am Polit Sci Asn, 1992-99; fel Omicron Kappa Upsilon Hon Dent Soc, Omega Omega Chap, 1992; Am Dent Asn, 1993-; fel Acad Polit Sci, 1995; Admin Bd Coun Deans Am Dent Educ Asn, 1999; Ky Asn Endodontists, 2000-; Bluegrass Dent Soc, 2000-; bd trustee, Case Western Res Univ, 2005-; chmn, Am Dent Educ Asn; chmn, Govs Oral Health Policy 2000 Adv Comt. **Home Addr:** 2140 Mangrove Dr, Lexington, KY 40513, **Home Phone:** (859)389-7951. **Business Addr:** Chief, Professor of Endodontics, University of Kentucky School of Dentistry, 800 Rose St D-446, Lexington, KY 40536-0297, **Business Phone:** (859)323-5891.

### CHANCEY, ROBERT DEWAYNE

Football player. **Personal:** Born Sep 7, 1972, Macon, AL; children: Ja Myra Jackson. **Career:** Football player (retired); San Diego Chargers, fullback, 1997, running back, 2000; Chicago Bears, running back & fullback, 1998; Dallas Cowboys, running back, 1999.

### CHANDLER, ALLEN EUGENE

Physician, military leader. **Personal:** Born Sep 16, 1935, Hagerstown, MD; married Barbara Hardiman; children: Allen (deceased), Rodney & Roderick. **Educ:** Morgan State Col, Baltimore, Md, BS, chem, 1957; Jefferson Med Col, Philadelphia, Pa, attended 1961. **Career:** Gen Leonard Wood Army Hosp, Ft Leonard Wood, Miss, chief pediat dept, 1964-66; Pa Army Nat Guard, 108th Combat Support Hosp, chief med servs, 1976-83, state surgeon, Hq State Area Command, 1983, advr Nat Guard Bur Surgeon, 1984, asst adj gen, State Area Command, 1987-; Army Nat Guard Alliance Health Care Professionals, pres; Jefferson Med Col, fac; pvt med pract, Philadelphia, PA, currently; Philadelphia Health Dept, sr pediatrician, med dir & sr physician, currently. **Orgs:** Nat Med Asn; Am Acad Pediat; US Mil Acad Selection Comt Cong man & House Majority Whip William H Gray; Nat Guard Asn Pa; Nat Guard Asn US; Asn Mil Surgeons; bd trustee, Thomas Jefferson Univ, 2000; bd dir, Philadelphia Diag & Rehab Ctr, currently; med co chmn, United Negro Col Fund. **Special Achievements:** Highest ranking African-American physician in the Department of Defense. **Home Addr:** 901 W Mt Airy Ave, Philadelphia, PA 19119-3332, **Home Phone:** (215)248-6262. **Business Addr:** Physician, Private Practice, 901 W Mt Airy Ave, Philadelphia, PA 19119.

### CHANDLER, ALTON H.
Publisher. **Personal:** Born Oct 4, 1942, Philadelphia, PA; son of Herman A and Frances Houston Leysath. **Educ:** Pa State Univ, Univ Pk, PA, BA, 1964; Cooper Sch Art, Cleveland, OH, Design & Ad Art, 1965; Philadelphia Col Textiles & Sci, Textile Design, 1967; Philadelphia Col Art, Advert Art, 1969. **Career:** AT&T, Wayne, PA, Newark, NJ, art dir, 1964-68; Compo Inc, managing dir, 1971-75; Am Baptist Churches, Valley Forge, PA, art dir, 1975-76; Directional Concepts Inc, Abington, PA, proprietor, 1975-77; Perkasie Industs Corp, Perkasie, PA, advert & mkt dir, 1976-80; Econ Inc, advert & mkt dir, 1980-84; ShopTalk Mag, Chicago, IL, creative dir, 1984-85; Chandler White Publ Co Inc, Chicago, IL, founder & pres, 1985-. **Home Addr:** 30 E Huron St Suite 5602, Chicago, IL 60611, **Home Phone:** (215)438-6775. **Business Addr:** President, Chandler White Publishing Co Inc, 30 E Huron St Suite 4403, Chicago, IL 60611, **Business Phone:** (312)280-9451.

### CHANDLER, DEBORAH
Executive, business owner, legal consultant. **Career:** Mortuary Transp Serv, owner; Cert Pub Notary. **Home Phone:** (202)494-7421. **Business Addr:** Owner, Mortuary Transportation Services, 3900 16th St NW Apt 224, Washington, DC 20011, **Business Phone:** (202)882-1490.

### CHANDLER, EVERETT A.
Lawyer. **Personal:** Born Sep 21, 1926, Columbus, OH; son of Everett P and Mary C (Turner); married Mittie Rene Olion; children: Wayne B, Brian E, Rhette V & Mae Evette; children: Wayne B, Brian E, V Rhette & Mae Evette. **Educ:** Ohio State Univ, BSc, 1955; Howard Univ Law Sch, JD, 1958. **Career:** Juv Ct Cuyahoga County, referee, 1959; City Cleveland, housing inspector, 1960; Cuyahoga County Welfare Dept, legal investr, 1960-64; Cuyahoga County, asst city prosecutor, 1968-71; City Cleveland, chief police prosecutor, 1971-75; Prin Everett A Chandler, atty, 1975-. **Orgs:** Mt Olive Missionary Baptist Church, 1958-; bd mem, Cedar Br, YMCA, 1965; Comt Action Against Addiction, 1975-80, bd chmn, 1980-87; polemarch & bd chmn, Cleveland Alumni Chap, Kappa Alpha Psi Inc, 1976, 1980-83; bd mem, Legal Aid Soc Cleveland, 1982-84; Nat Asn Advan Colored People; Urban League; bd mem & bd pres, CIT Ment Health; Excelsior Lodge 11 F&AM; Norman S Minor Bar Asn. **Honors/Awds:** Meritorious Service Award, Cleveland Bar Asn, 1972. **Special Achievements:** Book review, Vol 21 #2 Cleveland State Law School Law Review 1974. **Home Addr:** 12450 Shaker Blvd Suite 306, Cleveland, OH 44120, **Home Phone:** (216)295-9478. **Business Addr:** Attorney, PO Box 28459, Cleveland, OH 44128-0459, **Business Phone:** (216)283-1677.

### CHANDLER, JAMES PHILLIP, III
Educator, lawyer. **Personal:** Born Aug 15, 1938, Bakersfield, CA; son of Isaac and Lillie Mae; married Elizabeth Thompson; children: Elizabeth Lynne, James Phillip Jr, Isaac, Dennis Augustine, Ruth Rebekah, Aaron Daniel Pushkin & David Martin Thompson. **Educ:** Univ Calif, Berkeley, AB, 1962; Univ Calif, Davis, JD, 1970; Harvard Univ, LLM, 1971; La Academia Mexicana de Derecho Internacional, LLD, 1988. **Career:** US Dept Defense, electronic comput programmer, 1961-65; Univ Calif, res asst, 1968-69, instr, 1969-70; Harvard Univ, grad fel, 1970, vis scholar, 1984; Boston Univ, instr, 1970-71; Univ MD, assoc prof, 1971-74; Stanford Univ, Engineering Dept, fac fel, 1972-75; US Gen Acct Off Govt Contracting & Related Labor, 1973-82; Howard County, Md, Spec Coun, 1973-75; Md Ct Appeals Admin Off, 1974-76; Wash Univ, assoc prof, law, 1975-77; Univ Miss Sch Law, distinguished vis prof law, 1976; Univ Colo, vis prof, law, 1977; George Wash Univ, Nat Law Ctr, Law Sch, prof law & Dir, Comput Law Inst, 1977-94, prof emer, 1994-; US Dept Energy, 1989-91; Nat Intellectual Property Law Inst, pres & prof, 1993-; Chandler Law Firm Chartered, chmn, 1994-; prof arbitrator. **Orgs:** Alpha Phi Alpha Frat, 1961-; DC Bar; Pa Bar, Am Soc Int Law, 1969-; Am Asn Univ Profs, 1971-; Fel, Acad Engrg Nat Acad Scis, 1971; Md Bar Asn, 1971-75; Am Soc Law Profs, 1972-75; Comput Law Asn, 1972-81; sect coun mem, Am Bar Asn, 1974-98; Am Arbit Asn, 1974-; Asn Teaching & Res Intellectual Property, 1975-; bd dir, Ch God Eve Light Saints, 1992-97; vice chmn, Int Intellectual Property Rights Comt; Nat Security Adv Comt; Nat Infrastructure Assurance Coun, 1999. **Home Addr:** 10813 Tara Rd, Potomac, MD 20854-1341, **Home Phone:** (202)296-8484. **Business Addr:** President, National Intellectual Property Law Institute, 2020 Pennsylvania Ave NW Suite 185, Washington, DC 20006, **Business Phone:** (202)789-0234.

### CHANDLER, KERRY D.
Chief executive officer, basketball executive, vice president (organization). **Educ:** Lincoln Univ, BPA; Wash Univ, MS, human resources mgt; McGill Univ, MS, mgt. **Career:** McDonnell Douglas Corp, employee-rels & col-rels rep; Exxon Chem Co, human resources analyst; Motorola Inc; IBM Global Serv, dir human resources strategy; ESPN Inc, sr vpres human resources; Hong Kong Disneyland, sr vpres human resources; Walt Disney Co, sr vpres corp responsibility; Nat Basketball Asn, exec vpres human resources, 2007-, chief human resources officer, Under Armour, currently. **Orgs:** Human Resources Policy Inst; Exec Leadership Coun; adv bd mem, espnW; New York Urban League; bd mem, Nat Asn Multi-ethnicity Commun; bd mem, InMotion; bd mem, Cable & Telecommunications Human Resources Asn; bd mem, Sr Human Resources Forum Am Chamber Com Hong Kong; bd mem, Univ Exeter, Ctr Leadership Studies UK; bd mem, Asia Pac Human Resources Coun Conf Bd. **Business Addr:** Chief Human Resources Officer, Under Armour Inc, 1020 Hull St, Baltimore, MD 21230, **Business Phone:** (410)454-6428.

### CHANDLER, DR. MITTIE OLION
Educator, consultant, research scientist. **Personal:** Born Jul 25, 1949, Detroit, MI; daughter of Lurie Mae and Johnson Davis; children: Mae Evette. **Educ:** Mich State Univ, Lansing, MI, BA, social sci, 1971; Wayne State Univ, Detroit, MI, MUP, 1979, PhD, polit sci, 1985. **Career:** Detroit Housing Dept, pub housing mgr, 1972-77; Detroit Community & Econ Develop Dept, city planner, 1977-81; New Detroit Inc, Detroit, Mich, dir, neighborhood stabilization & housing div, 1981-85; Cleveland State Univ, Cleveland, OH, asst prof, 1985-91, assoc prof, 1991-, Master Urban Planning, Design & Dev Prog, dir, 1993-99, Master Sci Urban Studies Prog, dir, 1995-99, asst dean stud serv, 1999-2001, Maxine Goodman Levin Col Urban Affairs, Urban Child Res Ctr, dir, 2002-. **Orgs:** Alpha Kappa Alpha Sorority, 1969-; Living in Cleveland Ctr, 1986-92; Garden Valley Neighborhood House, 1987-93; Nat Conf Black Polit Scientists, 1990-; bd trustee, Prof Housing Serv, 1990-92; pres, Living In Cleveland Ctr, 1990-92; pres, Garden Valley Neighborhood House, 1991-93; Empowerment Ctr Greater Cleveland, 1997-; N Coast Community Homes, 1997-2001; Help Found, 1999-2001; Nat Asn Advan Colored People; vpres, Empowerment Ctr Greater Cleveland, 2000-; Renaissance Develop Corp, 2002-; trustee, Policy Bridge, 2005-; trustee, Kids Health 2020, 2005-; Preschool literacy progs; Community Learning Ctr. **Special Achievements:** Book: Urban Homesteading: Programs and Policies. **Home Addr:** 2635 Ramsay Rd, Beachwood, OH 44122, **Home Phone:** (216)464-1829. **Business Addr:** Director Urban Child Research Center, Associate Professor, Cleveland State University, 2121 Euclid Ave UR 208, Cleveland, OH 44115, **Business Phone:** (216)687-3861.

### CHANDLER, TYSON
Basketball player. **Personal:** Born Oct 2, 1982, Hanford, CA; son of Frank and Vernie Threadgill; married Kimberly; children: Sacha Marie, Tyson II & Sayge Jozzelle. **Career:** Chicago Bulls, power forward, 2001-06; New Orleans Hornets, ctr, 2006-09; Okla City Thunder, 2009; Charlotte Bobcats, 2009-10; Dallas Mavericks, 2010-11, 2014-15; New York Knicks, 2011-14; Phoenix Suns, 2015-. **Orgs:** Bulls All-Star Reading Team, NBA's All-Star Reading Team. **Business Addr:** Professional Basketball Player, Phoenix Suns, 201 E Jefferson St, Phoneix, AZ 85004, **Business Phone:** (602)379-7900.

### CHANDLER-STAGGERS, ROBIN. See STAGGERS, ROBIN L.

### CHANEY, ALPHONSE (AL CHANEY)
Salesperson, manager, insurance agent. **Personal:** Born Jul 24, 1944, Detroit, MI; son of Norman and Gussie; married Clara Hinton; children: Kristina, Stacy Sanders & Jason. **Educ:** Western Mich Univ, BS, 1967; Univ Mich, attended 1970; Wayne State Univ. **Career:** DC Heath & Co, sales rep, 1973-87; Oak Pk Bus, agt; State Farm Ins Co, agt, 1987-, agency mgr. **Orgs:** Nat Asn Life Underwriters; Who's Who Among Am Bus People, 1994-95; Alliance Asn Mentor Nat Conv; Chamber Com Mich Life & Charter. **Honors/Awds:** National Sales Achievement Award, DC Heath & Co, 1985; Charter Member Health Hall of Fame, 1987; Michigan Life Hall of Fame, State Farm Ins, 1987, 1988-91, 1993; Legion of Honor; National Convention Qualifier. **Business Addr:** Agent, Agency Manager, State Farm Insurance Companies, 1460 Walton Blvd Suite 108, Rochester Hills, MI 48309-1753, **Business Phone:** (248)652-6636.

### CHANEY, DONALD RAY (DON CHANEY)
Basketball coach, basketball player. **Personal:** Born Mar 22, 1946, Baton Rouge, LA; married Jackie; children: Michael, Donna & Kara. **Educ:** Univ Houston, attended 1968. **Career:** Basketball player (retired), basketball coach; NBA, Boston Celtics, prof basketball player, 1968-75, 1978-80; ABA, St Louis Spirits, 1975-76; NBA, Los Angeles Lakers, 1976-77; Detroit Pistons, asst coach, 1980-83, 1992-93, head coach, 1993-95; Los Angeles Clippers, from asst coach to head coach, 1983-87; Atlanta Hawks, asst coach, 1987-88; Houston Rockets, head coach, 1988-92; NY Knicks, asst coach, 1995-2002, head coach, 2001-04.TV series: "The Fish That Saved Pittsburgh", 1979. **Home Addr:** 20711 Pk Pine Dr, Katy, TX 77450-2811, **Home Phone:** (281)647-8250.

### CHANEY, JOHN
Basketball coach. **Personal:** Born Jan 21, 1932, Jacksonville, FL; married Jeanne; children: Pamela, John & Darryl. **Educ:** Bethune-Cookman Col Univ, BS, educ, 1955; Antioch Col, MA. **Career:** Basketball coach (retired); Simon Gratz HS, basketball coach, 1966-72; Cheyney State Univ, basketball head coach, 1972-82; Temple Univ, basketball coach, 1982-2006. **Home Addr:** 1 Liaccuras Ctr 1776 N Broad, Philadelphia, PA 19121.

### CHANEY, MATTHEW
School administrator. **Personal:** Born Flint, MI. **Educ:** Ferris State Univ, BS, 1993, MS, career & tech educ, 2000. **Career:** Ferris State Univ, asst dir minority stud affairs, interim dir, Multicultural Stud Serv, dir, currently. **Business Addr:** Director, Multicultural Student Services, Ferris State University, 1010 Campus Dr Suite 159, Big Rapids, MI 49307, **Business Phone:** (231)591-2617.

### CHANEY, REGMON A.
Association executive, manager. **Educ:** La State Univ, BA, polit Sci, 1966, MA, pub admin, higher educ & workforce develop, 2005. **Career:** Phyllis Perron & Assocs, govt rels intern, 1995-96; La State Univ, minority recruitment, asst dir, 2000-05; Entergy, mgr inclusion initiatives, 2006-08, mgr benefits educ, 2008-12, mgr learning & develop, 2012-15, HR Bus Partner, mgr, 2015-. **Orgs:** Pres, Black Fac & Staff Caucus, La State Univ; community rel & diversity mgr, Blue Cross Blue Sheild, 2005-06. **Business Addr:** Manager - HR Business Partner, Entergy Services Inc, 639 Loyola Ave, New Orleans, LA 70113-3125, **Business Phone:** (504)576-6116.

### CHANNELL, EULA L.
Secretary (office). **Personal:** Born Jan 29, 1928, Greenville, SC; daughter of Caesar and Ruby Davenport. **Educ:** Benedict Col; Greenville Tech Col, AA, 1974. **Career:** Recreation Dept City Greenville, supvr, 1955-65; Allen Music Co, sheet music dept, mgr; Phillis Wheatley Asn Greenville, girls worker, 1965-69; SC Comt Aging Greenville, off worker, 1972. **Orgs:** Greenville Urban League; Nat Asn Advan Colored People; ARC; Bethel Church God; Blue Triangle Garden Club; Lend-A-Hand Federated Club; Greenville Dem Women; SC Literacy Asn; YWCA; Adv Housing Comn; Girl Scout Leader; Greenville Chap Human Servs; SC Fed Women & Girls Club; pres, Lend-A-Hand Fed Club; PTA; deleg state conv Guille County Dems; charter mem, secy, Greenville Chap Top Ladies Distinction; Camp Pregnant Girls; Girl Scouts; Boy Scouts; Cancer Soc; Arthritis Found; March Dimes; United Fund. **Honors/Awds:** Honored, serv rendered Family Planning Asn; Citizen of week, Focus Newspaper; letter of congratulations, US Senator James R Mann; First runner up, Woman of Yr Greenville Chap NAACP; hon, Mayor of City vol Serv creation; record of award vol services, exec dir Phyllis Wheatley Asn; part in City wide voter registration project, Political Action Comn. **Home Addr:** 144 Catlin Cir Hyde Pk, Greenville, SC 29607. **Business Addr:** Para Professional, School District of Greenville County, 301 E Camperdown Way, Greenville, SC 29601, **Business Phone:** (864)355-3100.

### CHANNER, COLIN
Writer, educator, journalist. **Personal:** Born Oct 13, 1963, Kingston; son of Charles and Phyllis; children: Addis & Makonnen. **Educ:** City Univ NY, Hunter Col, BA, media commun. **Career:** Squad, owner, 1962; Essence, asst ed; freelance writer & copy ed; Eziba, co-creative dir, 2001; Medgar Evans Col, NY, asst prof eng, currently; **Books:** Soul fires: Young Black Men Love & Violence, 1996; Got to Be Real: Four Original Love Stories, 2000; Satisfy My Soul, 2002; Iron Balloons, 2006, So Much Things to Say, 2010, Kingston Noir, 2012, Providential, 2015; How to Beat a Child Right & Proper Way; Novels: I'm Still Waiting; Waiting Vain, 1998; Satisfy My Soul, 2002; Passing Through, One World Ballantine, 2004; Girl With Golden Shoes, 2007; Lovers Rock, 2008; Medgar Evers Col, asst prof eng & coord BA creative writing prog; City Univ NY, Medgar Evers Col, asst prof Eng & coordr, B.A. creative writing prog; Wellesley Col, vis prof, Creative Writing. **Orgs:** Pres, Jamaican Ctr Int PEN; mem int steering comt, World Festival Black Arts; bd mem, Brooklyn Lit Coun; bd mem, Up S Int Bk Festival; founder & artistic dir, Calabash Inter Nat Lit Festival Trust, 2001-. **Honors/Awds:** Critic's Choice Award, Wash Post for Waiting in Vain, 1998; Silver Musgrave Medal in Literature, Jamaican Govt, 2010; Honor Fellowship in Poetry and Fiction, Ri State Coun Arts, 2014 & 2015. **Special Achievements:** Bass player in the reggae band Pipecock Jaxxon; One of the most significant literature in the Caribbean. **Home Addr:** 158 S Oxford St, Brooklyn, NY 11217, **Home Phone:** (718)399-6305. **Business Addr:** Author, c/o 1 World/Ballantine Bks, New York, NY 10019.

### CHAPLIN, C. EDWARD (CHUCK CHAPLIN)
President (organization), chief financial officer. **Educ:** Univ Wis-Madison, BBA, acct & finance; Rutgers Col, BS, BA; Harvard Univ, MA, city & regional planning. **Career:** Prudential Financial Inc, assoc investment mgr, 1983-93, managing dir & asst treas, 1993-95, treas, 1995-2000, sr vpres, 2000-06; MBIA Inc, pres, chief admin officer & chief financial officer, 2006-; MBIA Ins Corp, vice chmn & chief financial officer, 2006-; Am Skandia Life Assurance Corp, chief financial officer & vice chmn; Optinuity Alliance Resources Corp, pres, chief admin officer & chief financial officer. **Orgs:** Bd trustee, Newark Sch Arts; Rutgers Univ, Bd Overseers; bd mem & treas, Exec Leadership Coun; Hampton Univ, Pres's Adv Coun; chmn, Financial Controls Coun; bd dir, MBIA Inc, 2002-; dir, MBIA Ins Corp, 2003-06; Prudentials Disclosure Comt; bd dir, MGIC Investment Corp, 2014-; bd dir, Mortgage Guaranty Ins Corp, 2014-; bd dir, Am Skandia Life Assurance Corp; bd dir, Pruco Life Ins Co. **Business Addr:** President, Chief Financial Officer, Chief Administrative Officer, MBIA Inc, 1 Manhattanville Rd Suite 301, Purchase, NY 10577, **Business Phone:** (914)273-4545.

### CHAPMAN, DR. AUDREY BRIDGEFORTH
Physician. **Personal:** Born Aug 30, 1941, Yonkers, NY; daughter of Leon Charles and Alice Lee Bridgeforth. **Educ:** Goddard Col, Plain field, VT, BA, 1974; Univ Bridgeport, Bridgeport, CT, MA, 1976; Fielding Inst, Santa Barbara, CA, pre-doctorate psychol cand, currently. **Career:** Hamden Ment Health Serv, ment health therapist, 1976-78; Ctr Syst & Prog Develop, staff develop, trainer, 1979-80; Howard Univ, Inst Urban Affairs & Develop, dir community action prog, 1980-81, Coun Serv, family marriage counr & trainer, 1981-; A B Chapman Assocs, pres human rels training & staff mgt, 1988-, family therapist, currently; auth trainer & relationship expert, currently. **Orgs:** Nat Bd Cert Counselors, 1983-; Counselors Asn, 1983-. **Honors/Awds:** APA Minority Fel Social Res, 1983; Certification of Appreciation, Howard Univ, Div Student Affairs, 1988. **Special Achievements:** Author: Mansharing: Black Men and Women: Battle For Love and Power; "Black Men Do Feel About Love", article; WHUR-FM, "All About Love",hostess, 1981-; Entitled to Good Loving: Black Men and Women and the Battle for Love and Power, Henry Holt, 1994; Books: Getting Good Loving: Seven Ways to Find Love and Make It Last; Seven Attitude Adjustments for Finding a Loving Man; WHUR 96.3 FM, "The Audrey Chapman Show", host. Appeared on dozens of national and television programs. **Business Addr:** Family Therapist, A B Chapman Assocs Inc, 1101 Pennsylvania Ave NW 6th Fl, Washington, DC 20004, **Business Phone:** (202)756-5042.

### CHAPMAN, CLEVELAND M.
Executive. **Career:** Englewood Construct Co, Chicago, Ill, chief exec officer, currently. **Business Addr:** Chief Executive Officer, Englewood Construction Co, PO Box 439183, Chicago, IL 60643-9183, **Business Phone:** (312)264-2700.

### CHAPMAN, ESQ. DAVID ANTHONY
Lawyer, government official. **Personal:** Born Nov 6, 1949, Akron, OH; married Sharon Gail McGee; children: Brandon. **Educ:** Univ Akron, BA, 1972; Univ Cincinnati Col Law, JD, 1975. **Career:** City Cincinnati Law Dept, asst city solicitor, 1975-82; Civil Pract Cincinnati, atty gen, 1975; Cincinnati Inst Career Alternatives, interim dir, 1982-85; City Atlanta, Ga, dep chief procurement officer, currently; pvt pract atty, currently. **Orgs:** Mayor's Task Force Minority Bus En-

terprise, staff writer, 1978; Ohio State Bar Asn, 1975; Cincinnati Bar Asn, 1975; Black Lawyers Asn Cincinnati, 1975. **Home Addr:** 1110 Cheyenne Dr, Cincinnati, OH 45216, **Home Phone:** (513)641-1500. **Business Addr:** Deputy Chief Procurement Officer, City of Atlanta, 55 Trinity Ave Suite 1900, Atlanta, GA 30303, **Business Phone:** (404)330-6204.

### CHAPMAN, DIANA CECELIA
Detective, secretary (organization). **Personal:** Born Sep 3, 1954, Mobile, AL; daughter of John Williams and Cleo Miller Williams; married Nathan; children: Miquel. **Educ:** Jarvis Christian Col, Hawkins, TX, BS, sociol, 1977. **Career:** Mobile County Youth Ctr, Mobile, AL, house-parent, 1982-83; Mobile Police Dept, Mobile, AL, detective, instr, 1983-2013. **Orgs:** Vpres, Mobile Police Benevolent Asn, 1990; secy, S Region Nat Black Police Asn, 1990-94; Semper Fidelis Federated Club, 1990; vpres, Mobile Police Benevolent Asn, 1990-93; Zeta Phi Beta Sorority, 1973; organist, Azalza City Elks, 1992-93; treas, Mobile Police Benevelent Asn, 1993; bd, Nat Black Police Asn, 1996; Bd dir, Vol Mobile Inc; Nat Black Police Asn. **Honors/Awds:** Wille "WD" Camron Leadership Award, 1991. **Home Addr:** 5928 Heatherwood Ct, Mobile, AL 36618, **Home Phone:** (205)344-2082.

### CHAPMAN, DR. GEORGE WALLACE, JR.
Educator. **Personal:** Born May 14, 1940, Somerville, TX; son of George W and Angelona Goin; children: Craig, Kevin & Jennifer. **Educ:** Prairie View A&M Univ, BS, 1957; Howard Univ, MD, 1966. **Career:** Univ Iowa, asst prof, 1981-83; Boston Univ, asst prof, 1983-85; La State Univ, asst prof, 1985-89; Univ Calif, Irvine, Calif, asst prof, 1988; NJ Med Sch, assoc prof, 1989-92; Howard Univ Hosp, assoc prof; Brooke Army Med Ctr, staff; Kaiser Permanente Med Ctr, staff. **Home Addr:** 2051 Westchester Dr, Silver Spring, MD 20902.

### CHAPMAN, DR. GILBERT BRYANT, II
Manager, automotive executive. **Personal:** Born Jul 8, 1935, Uniontown, AL; son of Gilbert Bryant and Annie Lillie Stallworth; married Loretta Woodard; children: Annie L, Bernice M, Gilbert B III, Cedric N, David O, Ernest P & Frances Q H; married Betty J Ellis Carithers; children: Michael, Lorri & Marc. **Educ:** Baldwin Wallace Col, BS, 1968; Cleveland State Univ, MS, 1973; Mich State Univ, MBA, advan mgt, 1990; Univ Windsor, PhD, 2007. **Career:** NACA Lewis Res Ctr, propulsion test tech, 1953-58; NASA Lewis Res Ctr, mat characterization engr, 1961-77; Ford Motor Co Res, proj engr leader, 1977-86; DaimlerChrysler Corp Eng, advan mat testing specialist, 1986-89, advan mats specialist, 1989-91, advan prod specialist, 1991-94, sr mgr advan mat, 1992-2003; advan mats consult, 1994-98; Advan Transp Tech, consult, advan automotive mat & processes, 2003-; Wayne State Univ, MLK prof physics, 2001. **Orgs:** Vice chmn, Cleveland Sect, Soc Appl Spectros, 1977, prog chmn; lay leader, Metrop SDA Church, Southfield SDA Church & Farmington; chmn, Chair-Detroit Sect Am Soc Nondestructive Testing, 1985-86; bd mem, Mt Vernon Acad; adv bd, Soc Mfg Engrs & CMA, 1996, chmn; Int Symp Automotive Technol & Automation, matls conf, 1996; Automotive Composites Consortium, 1996, 1999; Am Assoc Adv Sci; Am Chem Soc; Am Phys Soc; Am Soc Cinematographers; Am Soc Microbiol; Am Soc Nondestructive Testing; ASTM; Engrng Soc Detroit; Nat Tech Asn; Soc Automotive Engrs; Inst Elec & Electronics Engrs; SPIE, Sigma Pi Sigma; Nat Physics Hon Soc; Am Soc Nondestructive Testing; indust adv bd mem, Iowa State Univ, 1990; Univ Tex Pan Am; Cent State Univ, Wayne State Univ; Lay Leader, Metrop Seventh-day Adventist Church; Farmington SDA Church; Socs Automotive Engrs; Socs Mfg Engrs; Soc Plastic Engrs. **Home Addr:** 38671 Greenbrook Ct, Farmington Hills, MI 48331-2979, **Home Phone:** (248)324-5037. **Business Addr:** Consultant Advanced Automotive Materials and Processes, Advanced Transportation Technologies, 38671 Greenbrook Ct, Farmington Hills, MI 48331-2979, **Business Phone:** (248)324-5037.

### CHAPMAN, DR. JOSEPH CONRAD, JR.
Physician. **Personal:** Born Nov 18, 1937, Poplar Bluff, MO; son of Joseph and Louise; married Myrna Loy; children: Joseph & Christopher. **Educ:** Howard Univ, BS, 1959, MD, 1963. **Career:** Georgetown Univ Hosp, residency, 1968; pvt pract otolaryngologist, 2004; Howard Univ, asst clin prof. **Orgs:** Medico Chururgical Soc DC, Med Soc DC, Nat Med Asn, Am Acad Otolaryngol, Am Coun Otolaryngol; Alpha Phi Alpha; fel Am Bd Otolaryngol, 1970. **Home Addr:** 12th Allison Sts N, Washington, DC 20001. **Business Addr:** Otolaryngologist, 1160 Varnum St NE Suite 10, Washington, DC 20017, **Business Phone:** (202)529-2626.

### CHAPMAN, KELLY
Executive, singer, writer. **Personal:** daughter of Wilma. **Educ:** Case Western Res Univ, BA, commun sci; Northwestern Univ, JL Kellogg Grad Sch Mgt, MBA, 2000. **Career:** AT&T, EA to SVP Com Markets, 1989-94; Ameritech, gen mgr, 1994-2000, nat sales mgr, 1998-99; Lightwood Enterprises LLC, founder, managing dir/exec recruiter, 2000-; Eaton Corp, head internal exec search pract, 2005-06; A Technol Corp, dir diversity recruiting, 2006-11; Microsoft, dir diversity recruiting, 2006-11; RLJ Co, sr vpres; Macolicious, Owner. **Orgs:** Adv bd mem, Salvation Army; SHRM Diversity Stand Taskforce; founder, Cleveland Found, Wilma A Chapman Scholar Fund; New Song Church. **Business Addr:** Owner, Macolicious, 5217 Laurel Canyon Blvd, Valley Village, CA 91607, **Business Phone:** (818)824-3802.

### CHAPMAN, LEE MANUEL
Insurance executive, business owner, manager. **Personal:** Born Aug 4, 1932, Chesterfield, SC; son of Jesse and Marie M; married Emily Bernice; children: Victoria Lenice & Leander M. **Educ:** SC State Col, Orangeburg, BA, 1954; Bibl Sch Theol, Hatfield, attended 1958; Temple Univ, Philadelphia, attended 1958. **Career:** NC Mutual, spec ordinary agt, 1957-60; Equitable Life Assurance Soc, agency mgr, 1960-81; Lee Chapman & Assocs, fin planner, owner, 1981-. **Orgs:** Christian Bus Men Int, 1982-; camp pres & reg dir, Gideon Int, 1986-; pres, Int Asn Stewardship, 1990-. **Honors/Awds:** Young Man of the Year, Jaycees Awards, 1967; Developers Award, Nat Asn Mkt, 1967; National Citation Award, Equitable Life Assurance Soc, 1967, 1968 & 1980. **Home Phone:** (215)844-3054. **Business Addr:** Financial Planner, Lee Chapman & Associates, 6850 Anderson St, Philadelphia, PA 19119-1422, **Business Phone:** (215)848-6955.

### CHAPMAN, DR. MELVIN. See Obituaries Section.

### CHAPMAN, NATHAN A., JR.
Banker. **Personal:** Born Sep 3, 1957, Baltimore, MD; married Valerie; children: Taylor, Jordan & Jillian. **Educ:** Univ Md, BS, 1979. **Career:** Chapman Co, founder, chief exec officer, 1986-, pres & chmn bd dir; eChapman Inc, founder; Chapman Capital Mgt Inc, founder. **Orgs:** Bd regents, Univ Md Syst.

### CHAPMAN, ROSLYN C.
Executive, association executive, manager. **Personal:** Born Mar 10, 1956, Richmond, VA; daughter of Howard and Bertha. **Educ:** Hampton Univ, BA, psychol, 1978. **Career:** Johnson Prod Co, sales rep, 1979-80, key acct mgr, 1980-81, dist mgr, 1981-83, regional mgr, 1983-84, natl accts mgr, 1984-85; Alberto Culver Co, natl accts mgr, 1985-90, nat sales mgr, 1990-94, dir retail sales, 1994-2000, dir nat accounts, 1985-2000; Chapman Edge, pres, 2000-. **Orgs:** Cabrini Green Tutorial Bd; Midwest Women's Ctr Bd; Delta Sigma Theta Sor, Nat Black MBA; bd mem, Boys & Girls Clubs Chicago, 2008-11. **Home Addr:** , Chicago, IL. **Business Addr:** President, The Chapman Edge, 4170 N Marine Dr Suite 21K, Chicago, IL 60613, **Business Phone:** (773)244-6457.

### CHAPMAN, SAMUEL OTHA, JR.
Chief executive officer. **Personal:** Born Jan 1, 1945?; son of Samuel O Sr; married Carolyn Belle. **Career:** Shop Rite of West Haven, chief exec officer, 1998-. **Business Addr:** Chief Executive Officer, Shop Rite of West Haven, 1131 Campbell Ave, West Haven, CT 06516-2004, **Business Phone:** (203)934-5660.

### CHAPMAN, SHARON JEANETTE
Marketing executive. **Personal:** Born Oct 25, 1949, St. Louis, MO; children: Leslie Michelle Lee. **Educ:** Southern Ill Univ, BS, 1970; Col St Thomas, MBA, bus mgt, 1981. **Career:** Famous Barr Dept Store, asst buyer, 1971-72; Donaldson's Dept Store, dept mgr, 1972-75; IBM, systs engr, 1976-83, mkt rep, 1983-86; League Women Voters Minneapolis, admin mgr, 2008-10; Job Trak Systs Inc, dir mkt & sls, 1986-. **Orgs:** Second vpres, 1983-85, pres, bd mem, 1985-87, Twin Cities Chap Black MBA's; trustee, Pilgrim Bapt Church, 1984-87; bd dir, Survival Skills Inst, 1985-; chap pres, 1987-; Minneapolis Urban League, St Paul Nat Asn Adv Colored People. **Home Addr:** 1435 Hampshire Ave S Apt 215, St Louis Park, MN 55426-2165, **Home Phone:** (952)738-9389. **Business Addr:** Director Marketing, Operations, Jobtrack Systems Inc, 7269 Flying Cloud Dr, Eden Prairie, MN 55344, **Business Phone:** (612)829-0337.

### CHAPMAN, SUSAN (SUSAN E CHAPMAN-HUGHES)
Administrator, businessperson. **Educ:** Vanderbilt Univ, BS, engineering; Univ Wis-Madison, MBA, real estate finance & urban land econs, 1998; Univ Mass, MS, regional planning. **Career:** Security Capital Group, investment banking mgr, 1998-2000; Level 3 Commun Inc, Global Real Estate & Procurement, dir, 2000-04; Citi Realty Serv, chief strategy officer, chief admin officer, global head opers, 2004-10; Am Express, sr vpres, global real estate & workplace enablement, 2010-13, sr vpres, US-Acct Develop, Global Corp Payments-Americas, 2013-, sr vpres, US Large Mkt, Global Corp Payments, 2014-; Potbelly Sandwich Works, dir, 2014-. **Orgs:** Citigroup Realty, 2005; bd mem, Brotherhood Sister Sol; Exec Leadership Found; Core Net Global, NY Univ Adv bd; Urban Land Inst; Wis Real Estate Alumni Assoc; sr vpres, Ctr Urban Land Econs Res Bd. **Special Achievements:** Named on the "Hot List: Best and Brightest Under 40", by Black Enterprises in 2003, 2005, and 2007; distinguished Young Alumni Award, Univ of Wisconsin Foundation, 2007. **Business Addr:** Global Head of Operations, Citigroup Center, 153 E 53rd St, New York, NY 10022, **Business Phone:** (212)559-9124.

### CHAPMAN, TRACY
Singer, songwriter, musician. **Personal:** Born Mar 30, 1964, Cleveland, OH; daughter of George and Hazel Winters. **Educ:** Tufts Univ, BA, anthrop, 1986; Am Conserv Theater, MA, fine arts, 2009. **Career:** Singer-songwriter; Elektra rec, 1987; Song: "Talkin' about Revolution", 1988; "Telling Stories", 2000; "It's OK", 2000; "Wedding Song", 2000; "Baby Can I Hold You", 2001; "You're The One", 2002; "Another Sun", 2003; "Change", 2005; "America", 2006; "Fast Car"; "Baby Can I Hold You". Albums: Tracy Chapman, 1988; Crossroads, 1989; Matters of the Heart, 1992; New Beginning, 1995; Telling Stories, 2000; Collections, 2001; Let It Rain, 2002; Where You Live, 2005; Our Bright Future, 2008. **Honors/Awds:** Billboard Music Award, 1988; Best Selling Album by a Female Artist, Nat Asn Rec Merchandisers, 1988; Grammy Award, Best Female Pop Vocal Performance, 1989; Grammy Award, Best New Artist, 1989; Grammy Award, Best Contemporary Folk Recording, 1989; Best Int Female Artist, The Brits, 1989; American Music Award, 1989; Brit Award, 1989; Grammy Award, Best Rock Song,1997; IFPI Platinum Europe Music Award, 2002; SXSWi, 2009; Best Selling Album by a New Artist; Best Int Newcomer. **Special Achievements:** Plays the ukulele, organ, clarinet, & guitar; played at Wembley Stadium, Eng, Nelson Mandela Birthday Tribute. **Home Addr:** 506 Santa Monica Blvd Suite 400, Santa Monica, CA 90401, **Home Phone:** (213)394-2944. **Business Addr:** Recording Artist, Elektra Entertainment, 75 Rockefeller Plz, New York, NY 10019-6908, **Business Phone:** (212)275-4490.

### CHAPMAN, DR. WILLIAM TALBERT
Neurologist. **Personal:** Born Oct 15, 1944, Camden, NJ; married Ingrid; children: William Jr, Marcus, Blaire & Leigh. **Educ:** Rutgers Univ, BA, 1966; Howard Univ, Col Med, MD, 1971. **Career:** Columbia Presby Affil Hosp, intern, 1972; Cook County Hosp, resident, 1973; Ninty Seventh Gen Hosp, asst chief neurol, 1976-78; Silas B Hayes Hosp, chief neurol, 1978-79; pvt pract neurologist, 1979-. **Orgs:** Nat Med Asn, 1971, Am Bd Neurol, 1977, Am Bd EEG, 1985, AMA, 1987; Epilepsy Found San Diego County. **Honors/Awds:** Alpha Omega Alpha Med Hon Soc; Army Commendation Medal, AUS, 1979. **Home Addr:** 3951 The Hill Rd, Bonita, CA 91902, **Home Phone:** (619)479-8751. **Business Addr:** Neurologist, Private Practice, 2340 E 8th St Suite G, National City, CA 91950, **Business Phone:** (619)475-3870.

### CHAPMAN, WILLIE R.
Research scientist. **Personal:** Born Sep 2, 1942, Memphis, TN; married Marion N Evans; children: William Eric & Lamont Everett. **Educ:** LeMoyne Owen Col, BS, chem, 1964; Memphis State Univ, MAT, chem, 1975. **Career:** Schering-Plough Inc, sr res chemist, 1965-77; Chattem Inc, mgr, res & develop, 1977-87; Chattanooga State Tech Community Col, instr chem. **Orgs:** Soc Cosmetic Chemists; conduct & ethics comn, chap affairs comn, 1982, chmn prof rels & status, 1983, area dir, 1984-86, chmn educ comn, 1986-; Alpha Phi Alpha, 1985-87, social chmn, 1985-86, chair educ comn, 1986-87; Phi Delta Kappa, 1987; Sigma Phi Fraternity; Nat Asn Advan Colored People; Explorer Prog/BSA; Urban League. **Special Achievements:** Author: "Cosmetic Creams and Lotions for Dark Tone Skins", 1980; Cosmetics and Toiletries; "The Development of Skin Lighteners", Cosmetics and Toiletries, 1983. **Home Addr:** 707 Stone Crest Cir, Chattanooga, TN 37421, **Home Phone:** (615)892-6685.

### CHAPMAN-HUGHES, SUSAN E. See CHAPMAN, SUSAN.

### CHAPMAN-HUGHES, SUSAN E.
Real estate executive, investment banker, vice president (organization). **Personal:** Born Jan 1, 1969?; daughter of Semue P Chapman Sr and Issie R Chapman; married Christopher, May 11, 2013. **Educ:** Vanderbilt Univ, BS, engineering; Univ Wis-Madison, MBA, real estate finance & urban land econs; Univ Mass, Amherst, MA, regional planning. **Career:** Security Capital Group, investment banking mgr, 1998-2000; Level 3 Commun, dir global real estate & procurement, 2000-04; Citigroup Inc, CAO Citi Realty, 2004-10; Am Express, sr vpres global real estate & workplace enablement, 2010-13, Global Corp Payments-Americas, sr vpres US acct develop, 2013-; Potbelly Sandwich Works, dir, 2014-. **Orgs:** Am Express Exec Women's Network, Mem; World Monuments Fund Watch List, Adv Comt Mem; Nat Trust Hist Preserv, Audit Comt Chair; Regional Plan Asn (RPA), Bd Mem; Leadership Educ & Develop (LEAD), Bd Mem; A Better Chance, Bd Mem; Girls Inc., Bd Mem; NYU Schack Inst Real Estate, Adv Bd; Exec Leadership Coun, Mem. **Honors/Awds:** TheGrio.com, 100 Making History Today, 2012; "Savoy," Most Influential Women in Corporate America, 2012; "Fast Company," 100 Most Creative People in Business, 2013. **Business Addr:** Senior Vice President, American Express Co, 200 Vesey St, New York, NY 10285-3106, **Business Phone:** (212)640-2000.

### CHAPMAN-HUGHES, SUSAN EVELYN
Vice president (organization). **Educ:** Vanderbilt Univ, BS, engineering; Univ Mass, Amherst, MS, regional planning; Univ Wis, Madison, MBA, real estate & urban land econs. **Career:** Security Capital Group, investment banking mgr, 1998-2000; Level 3 Commun, dir global real estate & procurement, 2000-04; Citigroup Inc, Citi Realty Serv, chief admin officer, 2004-10; Am Express Co, Global Real Estate & Workplace Enablement, sr vpres, 2010-13, US-Acct Develop, Global Corp Payments-Americas, sr vpres, 2013-14, US Large Mkt, Global Corp Payments, sr vpres, 2014-. **Orgs:** Am Express Exec Women's Network; adv comt mem, World Monuments Fund Watch List; bd mem, Nat Trust Hist Preserv; bd mem, Leadership Educ & Develop (LEAD); bd mem, Girls Inc, currently; Urban Land Inst; Exec Leadership Coun; Univ Wis, Sch Bus, Real Estate Alumni Asn; bd mem, Nat Trust Hist Preserv, currently; audit comt chair, Regional Plan Asn, currently; bd mem, A Better Chance, currently. **Home Addr:** , New York, NY. **Business Addr:** Senior Vice President, American Express Company, 200 Vesey St, New York, NY 10285.

### CHAPMAN-MINUTELLO, ALICE MARIAH
Executive, executive director. **Personal:** Born Dec 31, 1947, New York, NY; daughter of Elijah Sr and Elizabeth Brooks (deceased); married Frank Minutello. **Educ:** City Univ NY, lib arts, 1969; NY Univ, bus admin, 1974. **Career:** RKO Gen Inc, corp equal employ compliance mgr, 1976-78, corp dir equal employ opportunity, 1983-87; WOR Radio, dir pub serv & community affairs, 1978-80; Waxy Radio, dir pub affairs & community rels, 1980-83; City NY, dep city personnel dir-equal employ opportunity, 1987-89; NY Health & Hosp Corp, Affirmative Action, actg vpres, 1989-92; Darryl E Greene & Assocs, chief exec officer, 1992-94; NY Unified Ct Syst, Workforce Diversity Off, Div Human Resources, adminr, dep dir human resource, dir, 1994-2009, spec asst to dep chief admin, 2009-. **Orgs:** Bd dir, Raritan Valley Chap, Links Inc; Jr League Greater Princeton; Women Bar Asn. **Home Addr:** 4023 Symes Dr, Belle Mead, NJ 07931, **Home Phone:** (085)02-4207. **Business Addr:** Special Assistant to the Deputy Chief Administrative Judge, New York State Unified Court System, 25 Beaver St Rm 1009, New York, NY 10004, **Business Phone:** (212)428-2540.

### CHAPPELL, EMMA CAROLYN
Banker. **Personal:** Born Feb 18, 1941, Philadelphia, PA; daughter of George Bayton Sr and Emma Lewis (deceased); married Verdayne; children: Tracey & Verdaynea. **Educ:** Temple Univ, Berean Bus Inst, 1967. **Career:** Continental Bank Philadelphia, staff, clerk-photogr & vpres, community bus loan & develop dep, 1959-201; raised money black-owned bank startup, 1987-92; United Bank Philadelphia, founder, chair, chief exec officer & pres, 1992-; Altroy Int, pres & chief exec officer. **Orgs:** Am Bankers Asn; Nat Bankers Asn; Robert Morris Asn; Nat bd mem & dir, Push; adv bd dir, Girl Scouts Greater Philadelphia Inc; vpres, admin & treas, Nat Rainbow Coalition; founder & chair, Womens Network Good Govt; bd mem, Temple Univ, Col Arts & Scis; Chestnut Hill Col Pres Coun, Cheyney Univ Found, United Way Southeastern Pa; United Negro Col Fund, Philadelphia Chap, PA; Econ Develop Partnership; bd, March Dimes, Del Valley Chap; vice chmn, African Develop Found; bd mem, United Bank Philadelphia; treas, Jesse Jackson Presidential campaign; Black Patriots Found. **Special Achievements:** First Women Vice President of Continental Bank, 1977; First Black Female Banker of Philadelphia. **Home Addr:**

PO Box 43581, Philadelphia, PA 19106. **Business Addr:** Founder, Chief Executive Officer, United Bank of Philadelphia, 30 S 15th St, Philadelphia, PA 19102, **Business Phone:** (215)829-2265.

**CHAPPELL, KEVIN**
Editor. **Educ:** Howard Univ, BA, commun & jour, 1991; Am Univ, MA, pub affairs, commun & interactive jour, 2012. **Career:** Johnson Publ Co Inc, sr ed; New York Times, campus stringer, 1988-91; Hilltop, ed chief, 1991-91; Wash Post, jr reporter, 1991-92; Chicago Tribune Media Group, intern, 1992; Charlotte Observer, educ reporter, 1992-93; Charlotte Observer, youth affairs reporter, 1993-95; Ebony Mag, assoc ed, 1995-97, sr ed, 1997-2000, White House Corresp, sr ed, 2000-12; Enova Int, pub rels consult, 2012-13; Nat PTA, sr ed mgr, 2013-15; Us Postal Serv, sr speechwriter, 2015-. **Orgs:** White House Correspondents Asn; Nat Asn Black Journalists; Nat Press Club. **Business Addr:** Senior Speechwriter, United States Postal Service, 475 L'Enfant Plz SW Rm 2P530, Washington, DC 20260-0546, **Business Phone:** (202)268-3251.

**CHAPPELL, MICHAEL JAMES**
Government official, educator. **Personal:** Born Dec 27, 1946, Ann Arbor, MI; son of Willie and Dorothy Freemen; married Betty Brown; children: Michael Jahi & Aisha Ebony. **Educ:** Eastern Mich Univ, BS, 1970; Keller Grad Sch Mgt, MBA, 1982. **Career:** Government official (retired), educator; Social Security Admin, dist mgr, 1971; Admin Law judge, 2000. **Orgs:** Regional dir Citation, Dept Health & Human Serv, 1988; vpres, Chicago Region Social Security Mgt Asn, 1988-90; adv & mentor, Black Affairs Adv Coun; pres, Chicago Social Security Mgt; chair, adv coun alt bd mem, sr Alliance, Area Agency Aging; vice chmn, bd dir, Wayne Metrop Community Serv Agency; chair, Local Fed Coord Comt; Combined Fed Campaign Local Fed Coord Comm; exec bd, Detroit Fed. **Home Addr:** 44999 Claymore Dr, Canton, MI 48187. **Business Addr:** Local Federal Coordinating Committee Member, Combined Federal Campaign, 44999 Claymore Dr, Canton, MI 48124, **Business Phone:** (734)451-0063.

**CHAPPELLE, DAVE (DAVID KHARI WEBBER CHAPPELLE)**
Comedian, television producer. **Personal:** Born Aug 24, 1973, Washington, DC; son of William David III and Yvonne K Reed; married Elaine Mendoza Erfe; children: Sulayman, Ibrahim & Sonal. **Educ:** Wash's Duke Ellington Sch Arts, theatre arts, 1991. **Career:** Films: Undercover Blues, 1993; Robin Hood: Men in Tights, 1993; Getting In, 1994; The Nutty Professor, 1996; Joes Apartment, 1996; Damn Whitey, screenwriter, 1997; Bowl of Pork, 1997; The Real Blonde, 1997; Con Air, 1997; Half Baked, screenwriter, 1998; Woo, 1998; You've Got Mail, 1998; 200 Cigarettes, 1999; Blue Streak, 1999; Screwed, 2000; Undercover Brother, 2002; Dave Chappelle's Block Party, 2005; TV Series: "Russell Simmons' Def Comedy Jam", 1992; "Buddies", 1995; "Dave Chappelle: Killin' Them Softly", screenwriter, 2000; "Dave Chappelle: For What It's Worth", screenwriter, 2004; "Chappelle's Show", screenwriter, 2003-06; "All Star Def Comedy Jam", host; Screenwriter: The Dana Carvey Show, 1996; The Dave Chappelle Project, 1997. **Special Achievements:** Is Number 43 on Comedy Centrals 100 Greatest Standups of All Time & is the youngest person to make the list; Nominated for Emmy Awards & Image Awards. **Business Addr:** Actor, ML Management Associates Inc, 1740 Broadway 15th Fl, New York, NY 10019, **Business Phone:** (212)333-5500.

**CHAPPELLE, DR. EDWARD H., JR.**
Dentist. **Personal:** Born Sep 15, 1954, Washington, DC; son of Edward Sr and Nelli Mitchell; married Sherra H; children: Edward H III & April Nicole. **Educ:** Rutgers Col, Rutgers Univ, BA, mathematics, 1975; Meharry Med Col, DDS, 1979. **Career:** Eastman Dent Ctr, gen pract residency, 1980; Gennessee Hosp, gen pract residency, 1981; Family Dent Care, dentist, 1981-83; pvt pract, 1983-; Aesthet Dent Care Inc, owner & pres, 1983-. **Orgs:** Pres, Robert T Freeman Dent Soc, 1999; treasr, Nat Dent Asn; fel Groove Phi Groove Social; Omega Psi Phi Frat; Holmehurst S Civic Asn; Am Acad Cosmetic Dent; adv panel, Am Dent Asn; fel Acad Gen Dent, 1996; Southern Md Dent Soc. **Home Addr:** 4406 Holmehurst Way, Bowie, MD 20720-3452, **Home Phone:** (301)464-9488. **Business Addr:** President, Owner, Aesthetic Dental Care Inc, 3060 Mitchellville Rd Suite 107, Bowie, MD 20716, **Business Phone:** (301)390-9185.

**CHAPPELLE, JOSEPH C.**
Executive. **Personal:** Born Nov 24, 1969, Jacksonville, FL; son of Dennis and Juanita; married Nicole; children: Jade & Joseph II. **Educ:** Fla State Univ. **Career:** Executive (retired); Premier Holdings Group Inc, consult, chmn, founder, pres & chief exec officer. **Orgs:** Chmn, Eastside Historical Community Found. **Business Addr:** Chairman, Chief Executive Officer, Premier Holdings Group, 112 W Adam St Suite 816, Jacksonville, FL 32202, **Business Phone:** (904)355-8381.

**CHARBONNET, LOUIS, III**
Funeral director, president (organization). **Personal:** Born Mar 12, 1939, New Orleans, LA; son of Louis Jr (deceased) and Myrtle Labat (deceased); married Simone Monette; children: Kim Marie. **Educ:** Commonwealth Col Sci, BS, mortuary sci, 1961. **Career:** State La, state rep; Total Community Action Agency, pres, 1973-; Cresent City Funeral Home, dir; Cooper-Glapion Funeral Home, owner; Charbonnet Labat Funeral Home, owner, currently. **Orgs:** Cresent City Funeral Dir Asn; bd dir, Treme Child & Enrichment Ctr; bd mem, Criminal Justice State La; vice chmn, Bd Appropriations State LA; bd dir, La State Mus Bd; New Orleans Embalmers Asn; St. Peter Claver Cath Church. **Home Addr:** 1607 St Phillip St, New Orleans, LA 70116, **Home Phone:** (504)581-3521. **Business Addr:** Owner, Charbonnet Labat Funeral Home, 1615 St Phillip St, New Orleans, LA 70116-2936, **Business Phone:** (504)581-4411.

**CHARGOIS, JAMES M.**
Automotive executive. **Personal:** Born Houston, TX. **Career:** Pavillion Lincoln Mercury Inc, pres, 1988; Northwood Lincoln Mercury, owner & pres, 1996-; San Marcos Toyota, owner & pres, 2000-; JMC Auto Group LLC, owner, currently; Triangle Restaurant Group, head, currently. **Orgs:** United Negro Col Fund; Boys & Girls Club Austin. **Business Addr:** Owner, President, Northwood Lincoln-Mercury Inc, 20440 Interstate 45, Spring, TX 77373, **Business Phone:** (284)539-4900.

**CHARIS (SHARON DIANA JONES)**
Clergy. **Personal:** Born Nov 14, 1948, Ft. Riley, KS; daughter of Theodore D and Agnes D Burrus. **Educ:** Mo Valley Col, Marshall, Mo, BA, 1970; Ga State Univ, Atlanta, Ga, MA, 1974; Univ Calif, Santa Barbara, Santa Barbara, Calif, 1988. **Career:** Muscogee Co Sch Dist, Colubmus, Ga, math teacher, 1970-78; Sisterhood Holy Nativity, Fond Du Lac, Wis, relig sister, 1978-. **Orgs:** Gamma Sigma Sigma Sorority, 1968-70; Union Black Episcopalians, 1988-. **Honors/Awds:** Numerous religious awards, 1979-. **Business Addr:** Religious Sister, Church of the Advent, 338 Acad St, Madison, GA 30650, **Business Phone:** (706)342-4787.

**CHARITY, LAWRENCE EVERETT**
Executive. **Personal:** Born Jun 21, 1935, Washington, DC; married Suzanne G Leach; children: Alexander P L & Danika E N. **Educ:** Rhode Island Sch Design, BFA & Int Arch Des, 1957; Cranbrook Acad Art, MFA & Design, 1958. **Career:** Skidmore Owings & Merrill, designer, 1958-68; Sewell & Charity Ltd Designers, prin, 1968-74; RI Sch Design, adj asst prof & design, 1972-73; Interior Concepts Inc, prin, 1974-86; Lawrence Charity Design, prin & designer, 1986-. **Orgs:** Indust Designers Soc Am, 1974-. **Honors/Awds:** Best of Competition Award for design, 1992; Retail Design Award for design, Am Soc Interior Designers, 1992. **Home Addr:** 30 Brown Rd, Kent, CT 06785-1203, **Home Phone:** (860)927-4147. **Business Addr:** Principal, Designer, Lawrence Charity Design, 8 Gracie Sq, New York, NY 10028, **Business Phone:** (212)737-9793.

**CHARLES, BERNARD L.**
Educator, executive, association executive. **Personal:** Born Feb 27, 1927, New York, NY; married Eleanor; children: Bernard II, Dominique & Bridgette. **Educ:** Fisk Univ, BS, psychol, 1952; Yeshiva Univ, MS, spec educ, 1965; Rutgers Univ Grad Sch Educ; Marymount Col, DHL. **Career:** Teacher, Pub Sch 613, Brooklin Pub Sch 614, Bronx, 1955-62; Jr Guid Classed Prog, NY City Bd Educ, asst dir, 1962-66; Life Skills Educ Training Resources Youth, dir, 1965-66; NY St Coun Black Elected Dem, treas, 1965-77; Off Civil Rights Region II, NY, dep dir, 1966-68; TownRamapo, co man & dep supvr, 1966-74; Human Resources Admin, dir spec proj, 1968; Off Master Plan Bd Higher Educ City, Univ NY, coordr, 1968-70; Livingston Col Rutgers Univ, dept urban educ, prof & chmn, 1970-; Rockland Co Legis, vice chmn, 1975-77; Dem Nat Comn, NY State Voter Reg Dr, dir, 1976; Qual Educ Minorities, sr vpres qual educ; McKenzie Group, sr exec; Carnegie Corp, sr programmer, NY; Univ Cape Town, Safrica; Univ Cape Coast, Ghana; Livingston Col Rutgers Univ, dept urban educ, dean; Univ Summer Workshop Teachers, co-dir; Nsf, tech asst consult. **Orgs:** Asn Teacher Educ; Am Asn Higher Educ; Am Asn Univ Profs; Am Asn Sch Adminr; Nat Adv Coun; Nat Adv Health Coun; treas, Inst Mediation & Conflict Resolution; pres, Broadjump Inc; dir, Action Priorities Inc; Rockland Community Action Coun; bd dir, World Rehab Fund; st clubworker, NY City Youth Bd, 1954-55; Bulova Watchmaking Sch, St Cordr, Gov Samuels paign, 1974; chmn, NY St Govr's Adv Comn Black Affairs; nat adv bd, res & training ctr, Howard Univ. **Home Addr:** 109 Old Nyack Tpke, Spring Valley, NY 10977, **Home Phone:** (845)356-3664. **Business Addr:** Senior Executive, The McKenzie Group, 555 13th St NW, Washington, DC 20004, **Business Phone:** (202)393-0010.

**CHARLES, DAEDRA JANEL (DAEDRA CHARLES-FURLOW)**
Basketball player, basketball coach. **Personal:** Born Nov 22, 1968, Detroit, MI; daughter of Helen; married Anthony Furlow; children: Anthonee. **Educ:** Tenn State Univ, BS, child & family studies, 1991. **Career:** Basketball player, basketball coach (retired); USA Natl Teams, 1989, 1992, 1994; City Detroit, Don Bosco Hall, supvr; Como, Italy, ctr, 1991-92; DKB, Japan, 1992-93; US Women's Olympic Basketball team, 1992; Sireg, Italy, 1993-94; Tarbes, France, 1994-95; Galatasaray, Turkey, 1995-96; Sopron, Hungary, 1996-97; Los Angeles Sparks, 1997; DePorres High Sch, coaching staff, 2001-02; Univ Detroit Mercy, asst coach, 2003-06; Detroit Titan, grad asst coach, 2003-04, asst coach, 2004-08; Auburn Tigers, asst coach; Univ Tenn, asst coach; dir character develop, 2010-11; United States Olympic Team. **Orgs:** US Basketball Writers' Asn; Basketball Weekly's All-Am Teams. **Home Addr:** Los Angeles Sparks 26730 Joy Rd Apt 3, Redford, MI 48239-1939. **Business Addr:** Assistant Coach, Lady Vols, Univ Tenn, Knoxville, TN 37996, **Business Phone:** (865)974-4275.

**CHARLES, JOSEPH C.**
Law enforcement officer. **Personal:** Born Jan 12, 1941, Lake Charles, LA; married Doris J; children: Caron Scott. **Educ:** BA, AA, 1969. **Career:** Mitchell Pac Devel Corp, pres; San Diego Co Probation Dept, dep probation officer II; Webchar Construct Corp, pres. **Orgs:** Black Bus Asn; Black Investors; secy, Res Officers Asn; charter mem, Black Stud Union San Diego St Col; San Diego Co Employ Asn; Calif St Corrections Asn. **Home Addr:** 6006 Egret St, San Diego, CA 92114, **Home Phone:** (619)266-2025.

**CHARLES, LEWIS**
Welder. **Personal:** Born Aug 24, 1945, Jackins County, GA; married Rosetta W; children: Tracy C. **Educ:** Atlana Univ. **Career:** Fulghum Indust Mgt Co, demonstr; Hudson Mortuary Wadley, GA, asst mgr; city councilman, 1970. **Orgs:** GA State Fireman Wadley, GA No 2217; Dem Party GA, 1972; Free & Accepted Mason; Brinson Hill Baptist Church; life mem, Ga Munic Asn; Wadley & Borlow City League; Nat Pilots Asn. **Honors/Awds:** Award Wadley & Borlow City League, 1972; Spec Award, Brinson Hill Baptist Church, 1973. **Home Addr:** PO Box 577, Wadley, GA 30477. **Business Addr:** Demonstrator, Fulghum Indust Management Co, Wadley, GA 30477.

**CHARLES, DR. RODERICK EDWARD**
Psychiatrist. **Personal:** Born Sep 4, 1927, Baltimore, MD; married Mamie Rose Debnam; children: Kimberly Anne & Roderick Todd. **Educ:** Howard Univ, BS, 1951; Univ MD, MD, 1955. **Career:** Mil City Gen Hosp, internship, 1955-56; Meyer Memorial Hosp, psychiatrist resident, 1956-59; NYS, 1959-60; Erie County Med Ctr, att psychiat, 1960-66; State Univ NY, Brooklyn Sch Med, asst clin prof, 1966-96; pvt pract psychiat, 1966-; Univ Buffalo, fac. **Orgs:** Build Acad H Prog, 1971-75; state coun, Met H Plan, 1977-81; pres, WNY Psych Asn, 1967-68; Fedn Citizens Coun Human Rel, 1964; Am Psych Asn; Black Psychiatrists Am; Nat Med Asn; adv SMNA Univ Buffalo, 1975; consult, Gowando State Hosp, 1982-87. **Special Achievements:** First African American medical student at the University of Maryland. **Home Addr:** 316 Rivermist Dr, Buffalo, NY 14202, **Home Phone:** (716)852-5582. **Business Addr:** President, NMA Buffalo Chapter, 142 N Pearl St, Buffalo, NY 14202-1108, **Business Phone:** (716)883-2782.

**CHARLES, RUPAUL ANDRE**
Entertainer. **Personal:** Born Nov 17, 1960, San Diego, CA; son of Irving and Ernestine. **Career:** Entertainer (actor, singer, talk-show host, dancer), 1981-; Albums: Sex Freak, 1985; RuPaul is Starbooty, soundtrack, 1986; Supermodel of the World, 1993; Foxy Lady, 1996; Ho, Ho, Ho, 1997; Arrested Soul, 2002; The Lizzie McGuire Movie, writer, 2003; Party Monster, writer, 2003; Red Hot, 2004; Beauty Shop, writer, 2005; Whitepaddy, 2006; ReWorked, 2006; Zombie Prom, 2006; Bachelor Party Vegas, soundtrack, 2006; Champion, 2009. TV series: "Saturday Night Live", 1993; "Sister, Sister", 1994; "In the House", 1995; "The RuPaul Show", 1996-98; "Nash Bridges", 1996-98; "The Truth About Jane", 2000; "V.I.P.", 2001; "The Groovenians", voice, 2002; "Son of the Beach", 2002; "The Biggest Loser", composer, 2004; "Rick & Steve the Happiest Gay Couple in All the World", 2009; "Ugly Betty", 2010; "RuPaul's Drag Race: Untucked!", exec producer, 2010-14, acctress, 2014; "Happy Endings", 2013; "Hey Qween ", 2014; "Mystery Girls", 2014. Films: RuPaul Is: Starbooty!, 1987; Crooklyn, 1994; The Brady Bunch Movie, 1995; Blue in the Face, 1995; To Wong Foo, Thanks for Everything! Julie Newmar, 1995; Red Ribbon Blues, 1995; A Mother's Prayer, 1995; A Very Brady Sequel, 1996; Fled, 1996; EDtv, 1999; But I'm a Cheerleader, 1999; The Truth About Jane, 2000; The Eyes of Tammy Faye, 2000; Who is Cletis Tout?, 2001; Michael Lucas Dangerous Liaisons, dir & writer, 2005; Starr booty, actress & producer, 2007; Another Gay Sequel: Gays Gone Wild, 2008; "RuPaul's Drag Race", television show hoster, 2008-10; "Glamazon", 2011-13; "Born Naked", 2014; "Realness", 2015; "Gay for Play and Butch Queen", 2016; Hurricane Bianca, 2016. **Orgs:** Co-chair, MAC AIDS Fund, 1995-; spokes model, MAC cosmetics, 1995-; spokes model, Bailey's Irish Cream, 1995. **Honors/Awds:** Vito Russo Award, 1999. **Special Achievements:** Letting It All Hang Out, autobiography, 1994. **Business Addr:** Entertainer, c/o Tommy Boy Entertainment, 32 W 18th St, New York, NY 10011-4612.

**CHARLES-FURLOW, DAEDRA.** **See CHARLES, DAEDRA JANEL.**

**CHARLESTON, DR. GOMEZ, JR.**
Educator, cardiologist. **Personal:** Born Mar 19, 1950, Chicago, IL; son of Gomez and Margie Williams; married Robin Prince. **Educ:** Univ Chicago, BA, 1971, MD, 1975. **Career:** Michael Reese Hosp Med Ctr, Chicago, internship, resident cardiovasc dis, 1975-78, fel, 1978-80, attend physician cardiol, 1980-, cardiac catheterization lab, dir, 1987-88; Stony Island Med Asn Ltd, Chicago IL, partner, 1980-; Pritzker Sch Med, Univ Chicago, asst clin prof med, 1980-; Northwestern Memorial Hosp; Presence St Joseph Hosp; Presence Resurrection Med Ctr; Unite Here Health; Northwestern Univ Feinberg Sch Med, Clin Med-Gen Internal Med & Geriatrics, asst prof, currently. **Orgs:** Am Med Asn; Ill Med Soc; Chicago Cardiol Group; fel Am Col Cardiol, 1982. **Honors/Awds:** Sigmund E. Edelstone fel cardiol, Michael Reese Hosp & Med Ctr, 1980. **Home Addr:** 9000 S Stony Island Ave, Chicago, IL 60637-1717, **Home Phone:** (773)731-0670. **Business Addr:** Assistant Professor, Northwestern University Feinberg School of Medicine, Rubloff Bldg 750 N Lake Shore 10th Fl, Chicago, IL 60611, **Business Phone:** (312)503-6400.

**CHARLTON, REV. CHARLES HAYES**
Educator, clergy. **Personal:** Born Dec 22, 1940, Radford, VA; son of Lawrence and Ollie; married Janet Lee Lewis; children: Charles. **Educ:** Christiansburg Inst, attended 1959; Va Sem; E Tenn State Univ, BS, philos, 1982, MEd, literacy studies, 1984; Emmaus Bible Inst Sem, Elizabeth, Tenn, ThD, 1986; Cornerstone Univ, PhD, clin Christian coun, 1995. **Career:** Radford City Sch Bd, staff, 1972-74; Radford City, Va, mayor, 1974-76; Friendship Bapt Church, pastor; Emmaus Bible Inst & Sem, Elizabethton, TN, dean educ, 1984-89; CASA Northeast, Johnson City, TN, coordr, 1987-; CASA, staff, 1987-92; Johnson City, planning comn, 1990-; ETSU, Johnson City, TN, career counr, 1991-92; Northeast State Tech Community Col, instr, 1992, counr & advisor, 1994, asst prof study skills, assoc prof reading & learning strat, currently; Johnson City, bd dir; Big Hill Baptist Church, Salem, VA, pastor; First Baptist Church, Elliston, VA, pastor; First Baptist Church, Blacksburg, VA, pastor; Southern Baptist Conv, Black Psychol & Marriage & Family Dynamics, lectr. **Orgs:** Moderator Schaetter Mem Asn SW Va, 1974-77; moderator, Bethel Dist Asn Tenn, 1982-; dean ed, Emmaus Bible Inst & Sem, Elizabethton, TN, 1984-; dir, Pastors Conf TN BM&E Conv, 1984-; pres, Black Ministers Alliance, 1990-91; zone chmn, Wash Co Dem Party, 1994-, bd educ, 1996-, comn, 2001-; treas, Bethel Dist Asn; vpres, Radford Jaycees; moderator, Schaeffer Memorial Baptist Asn; moderator, Bethel Dist Baptist Missionary & Educ Asn; dir pastor, Baptist Missionary & Educ Asn. **Honors/Awds:** Radfords Outstanding Young Men, Radford Jaycees, 1973; Honored for Contributions, State Va & Va Hist Soc. **Special Achievements:** Published "Agony & Ecstasy of the Ministry, Making The Fundamentals Fun", 1993; "Love is the Key, To Love And Be Loved, How To Really Love Your Pastor, This We Believe, Meditations on Love", 1994; Author of Religious Columns Published in Radford News Journal & Johnson City Press; First African-American Board of Education member in Radford, VA; First African-American Mayor in Southwest, VA. **Home Addr:** 511 Rose Ave, Johnson City, TN 37601-2152, **Home Phone:** (423)929-1575. **Business Addr:** Associate Professor, Northeast State Technical Community Col-

lege, 2425 Tenn 75, Blountville, TN 37617-0246, **Business Phone:** (423)323-3191.

**CHARNA, DANIEL A.**
Entrepreneur, executive. **Educ:** Rochester Inst Technol, BS, food admin, 1977; Ashland Univ, MBA, exec, 1985. **Career:** Ashland Univ, assoc prof bus admin, 1982-85; Hospitality Specialist Inc, gen partner & mgr, 1985-89; William F. Williams Co, vpres opers, 1987-90; Glory Foods Inc, co founder, partner, vpres opers, chief operating officer, founding partner, 1989-2013; Mid Ohio Food Bank, food aquisition comt mem, 2013-; Charna Strategic Consult, chief exec officer, 2013-; Ohio Wesleyan Univ, asst prof econs, 2013-. **Orgs:** Vol, LifeCare Alliance, 2000-; adv comt, Columbus Health Dept, 2012-; Feeding Am; Nat Jewish Health; Am Heart Asn; Am Cancer Soc; US Power Squadrons; United Way Cent Ohio; United Way Cent Ohio Nutrit & Fitness Results Comt; United Way Cent Ohio Tax Prep Vol Columbus Pub Health Food Protection Adv Comt. **Business Addr:** Assistant Professor of Economics, Ohio Wesleyan University, 61 S Sandusky St RW Corns Bldg Suite 210, Delaware, OH 43015, **Business Phone:** (740)368-3588.

**CHASE, ANTHONY R.**
Executive, founder (originator), educator. **Educ:** Harvard Col, BA, 1977; Harvard Bus Sch, MBA, 1981; Harvard Law Sch, JD, 1981. **Career:** Telecom Oppurtunity Inst, co-founder, 1998; Chase Com LP, chmn & cheif exec officer, currently; ChaseSource Real Estate Serv L.P, chmn; ChaseSource L.P, chmn; SBC Commun Inc, co founder & chmn, currently; Fed Res Bank Dallas, dir, vchmn, currently; Leap Wireless Int Inc, dir, currently; Cornell Co Inc, dir, currently; AT&T Corp; Anadarko, dir; Tex Med Ctr, dir; Sarepta Therapeut, dir; Chase Radio Partners, chmn & cheif exec officer, currently; Faith Broadcasting, L.P, pres & chief exec officer, 2007; Univ Houston Law Ctr, assoc prof, currently; Western Gas Partners, dir. **Orgs:** Chmn, Houston Zoo Develop Bd; Coun Foreign Rels; bd dir, United Way Tex Gulf Coast & Houston Parks; bd mem, 2011, vice chmn & chmn, 2012-, Greater Houston Partnership Bd; Eagle Scout. **Business Addr:** Associate Professor of Law, University of Houston Law Center, 4604 Calhoun Rd, Houston, TX 77204-6060, **Business Phone:** (713)743-2100.

**CHASE, ANTHONY RAY.** **See CHASE, TONY.**

**CHASE, ARNETT C.**
Executive, army officer. **Personal:** Born Apr 5, 1940, Green Cove Springs, FL; son of Leo (deceased); married Dianne J Thomas; children: Avis Chiquita & Arnett Cameron. **Educ:** Am Acad Funeral Serv, 1963; Univ Fla, cert ophthal, 1972. **Career:** Apprentice embalmer & funeral dir, 1965, mgr, 1970; Leo C Chase & Son Funeral Home, funeral dir, currently. **Honors/Awds:** Certificate of Apppreciation, St Paul AME Church, 1973; Fla Morticians Service Award, 1974. **Home Addr:** 817 W 2nd St, St. Augustine, FL 32095-3911, **Home Phone:** (904)829-8152. **Business Addr:** Funeral Director, Owner, Leo C Chase & Son Funeral Home, 262 W King St, St. Augustine, FL 32084, **Business Phone:** (904)824-2865.

**CHASE, DEBRA MARTIN**
Lawyer, executive, television producer. **Personal:** Born Oct 11, 1956, Greater Lakes, IL; daughter of Robert Douglas and Beverly M Barber; married Anthony. **Educ:** Mt Holyoke Col, BA, 1977; Harvard Law Sch, JD, 1981. **Career:** Butler & Binion, assoc, 1981-82; Mayor, Day & Caldwell, assoc, 1982-83; Tenneco Inc, atty, 1984-85; Columbia Pictures, motion picture dept, atty; Mundy Lane Entertainment, sr vpres, 1992-95; Brown House Productions, exec vpres, producing partner, 1995-2000; Martin Chase Productions, 2000-. TV Series: Cinderella, 1997; The Cheetah Girls, 2003; "1-800-Missing", 2006; The Cheetah Girls 2, 2006; The Cheetah Girls: One World, 2008; Lemonade Mouth, 2011; Lovestruck: The Musical, 2013; Saige Paints the Sky, 2013; Aaliyah: The Princess of R&B, 2014. Films: Hank Aaron: Chasing the Dream, 1995; Courage Under Fire, 1996; The Preacher's Wife, 1996; Cinderella, 1997; The Princess Diaries, 2001; The Princess Diaries 2: Royal Engagement, 2004; The Sisterhood of the Traveling Pants, 2005; The Sisterhood of the Traveling Pants 2, 2008; Just Wright, 2010; McKenna Shoots For the Stars, 2012; Sparkle, 2012; Dirty Dancing Remake, 2013; Isabelle Dances Into the Spotlight, 2014; Grace Stirs Up Success, 2015. **Business Addr:** Producer and Executive, Martin Chase Productions, 500 S Buena Vista St Animation 2E 6, Burbank, CA 91521-1757, **Business Phone:** (323)650-2670.

**CHASE, DEBRA MARTIN**
Television producer, lawyer, movie producer. **Personal:** Born Oct 11, 1956, Great Lakes, IL; daughter of Robert Douglas Martin and Barbara M Barber Martin; married Anthony. **Educ:** Mt Holyoke Col, AB, 1977; Harvard Law Sch, JD, 1981. **Career:** Butler & Binion, Houston, TX, 1981-82; Mayor, Day & Caldwell, Houston, assoc, 1982-83; Tenneco Inc, atty, 1984-85; Stroock, Stroock & Lavan, 1985-87; Avon Prod, in-house coun, 1988; Michael Dukakis presidential campaign & David Dinkins campaign, mem, 1988; Columbia Pictures, motion picture dept, exec asst & atty, 1989-92; film & tv producer, 1992-; Mundy Lane Entertainment, producer, 1992-95; Brown House Productions, producer, 1995-2000; Martin Chase Productions, founder & pres, 2000-; ABC Studios, producer, 2012-. Film producer: Hank Aaron: Chasing Dream, 1995; Courage Under Fire, 1996; Preacher's Wife, 1996; Princess Diaries, 2001; Princess Diaries 2: Royal Engagement, 2004; Sisterhood Traveling Pants, 2005; Sisterhood Traveling Pants 2, 2008; Just Wright, 2010; McKenna Shoots Stars, 2012; Sparkle, 2012; Isabelle Dances into Spotlight, 2014; Am Girl: Isabelle's Dance Jam, 2014; Grace Stirs Up Success, 2014; Lea to Rescue, 2016. Tv producer: Cinderella, 1997; Cheetah Girls, 2003; 1-800-MISSING, 2003-06; Cheetah Girls 2, 2006; Cheetah Girls: One World, 2008; Lemonade Mouth, 2011; Lovestruck: Musical, 2013; Saige Paints Sky, 2013; Aaliyah: Princess R&B, 2014; Zoe Ever After, 2016. **Orgs:** Television Arts and Sciences; Producers Guild of America; Second Stage Theatre; New York City Ballet; Mount Holyoke College Board of Trustees; Columbia College. **Honors/Awds:** Named of the 150 Most Influential African Americans in America, Ebony Magazine, 2007, 2008, 2009; Top Ten Most Bankable African American Movie Producers in Hollywood, Black Enterprise Magazine, 2012; Entertainment Award, Trumpet Awards Foundation, 2013; Ashley Boone Award, 2014. **Business Addr:** Martin Chase Productions, 500 S Buena Vista St, Burbank, CA 91521, **Business Phone:** (818)560-3952.

**CHASE, DOOKY (EDGAR DOOKY CHASE, JR.)**
Entrepreneur, chef. **Personal:** married Leah Lange; children: 4. **Career:** Dooky Chase Restaurant, owner, currently; New Orleans Tourist Comn, vpres, 1978-83. **Orgs:** Nat Asn Advan Colored People; Jazz & Heritage Festival. **Business Addr:** Owner, Chef & Manager, Dooky Chase Restaurant, 2301 Orleans Ave, New Orleans, LA 70119, **Business Phone:** (504)821-0535.

**CHASE, SONIA LYNN**
Basketball player, basketball coach, executive. **Personal:** Born Mar 9, 1976, Baltimore, MD. **Educ:** Univ Md, BA, eng & lit, 1998, cert acad hon. **Career:** Basketball player (retired), basketball coach, executive; Charlotte Sting, forward, beginning, 1998-99; Chase Your Dreams Inc, pres & chief exec officer, 2001-; Minn Lynx, guard, 2003; Baltimore City Pub Schs, eng teacher, 2005-06; Birmingham Power, guard; GlaxoSmithKline, sr pharmaceut sales rep, 2006-08; Forest Pharmaceut, specialty sales mgr, 2008-10; Lady Eagles Girls Basketball Team, asst coach, currently; Chase Your Dreams Acad, founder & pres, 2009-; Chase Your drams Inc, pres & ceo, 2009-; ILC Network/ Reebok Team, dir & spokesperson grassroots progs, 2012-. **Orgs:** Founder & exec dir, Chase Your Dreams Acad, 2009-. **Business Addr:** Founder, Executive Director, Chase Your Dreams Academy, PO Box 4921, Upper Marlboro, MD 20775, **Business Phone:** (410)812-7670.

**CHASE, TONY (ANTHONY RAY CHASE)**
Educator, chairperson, chief executive officer. **Personal:** Born Mar 17, 1955, Houston, TX. **Educ:** Harvard Col, BA, econs & govt, 1977; Harvard Bus Sch, MBA, 1981; Harvard Law Sch, JD, 1981. **Career:** Univ Houston, Bauer Col Bus, assoc prof law, 1990-; Crest Investment Corp, prin, 1993-; Faith Broadcasting LP, chief exec officer, pres, 1993-; SBC Communs Inc, Telecom Opportunity Inst, chmn & co-founder, 1998-; ChaseCom LP & Chase Radio Partners, chmn & chief exec officer, 1998-2007; Fed Res Bank, Dallas, chmn pro tem, dep chmn, vice chmn, 2006-08; Leap Wireless Int Inc & Cornell Cos Inc, bd dir, 2008-10; ChaseSource LP, chief exec officer & chmn, 2007-; Western Gas Partners LP, 2008-; AVI BioPharma, dir, 2010-; Sarepta Therapeut Inc, dir, 2010-; Chase Telecommunications, founder; Plaza Group Ltd, dir, 2012-. **Orgs:** Vice chmn, Fed Res Bank; chmn, Houston Zoo Develop Bd; chmn, Technol Opportunity Inst; bd mem, Fisk Univ; United Way; Greater Houston Partnership; Coun Foreign Rels; Am Bar Asn; State Bar Tex; bd, Fed's Houston; dir, Northern Trust Bank Tex; fel Coun Foreign Rels; fel Eagle Scout; dir, Tex Med Ctr; dir, Western Gas Resources. **Business Addr:** Chairman, Chief Executive Officer, ChaseSource LP, 3311 W Ala, Houston, TX 77098, **Business Phone:** (713)874-5800.

**CHASE-RIBOUD, DR. BARBARA DEWAYNE**
Sculptor, writer. **Personal:** Born Jun 26, 1939, Philadelphia, PA; daughter of Charles Edward and Vivian May Braithwaite West; married Marc Eugene; children: David & Alexis; married Sergio G Tosi. **Educ:** Temple Univ, BFA, 1957; Yale Univ, MFA, 1960. **Career:** Sculptor, poet, novelist, writer; One-Woman Shows: The Univ Mus, Berkeley, CA; The Mus Mod Art, Paris, France; The Kunstmuseum, Dusseldorf, Ger; The Detroit Art Inst, Detroit, MI; The Indianapolis Art Mus, Ind, IN; The Mus Mod Art, New York, NY; From Memphis & Peking: poetry, Random House, 1974; The Kunstmuseum, Freilburg, W Ger, 1976; The Musee Reattu, Arles, France, 1976; Europ Drawings, Berlin, W Ger, 1980; five-mus tour, Australia, 1980-81; Studio Mus, 1996; Milwaukee Art Mus, 1997; Chicago Cult Ctr, 1997; Mus SC, 1997; Mint Mus, 1997; Los Angeles Mus Contemp Art, 1997; Smithsonian, 1998; The Metrop Mus Art, NY, 1999; Metrop Mus Art, NY; The Studio Mus, NY 2000; The Walters Mus Art, Baltimore, 2000; The Brit Mus, London, 2001; The Philadelphia Mus, 2002-03; Selected Group Exhibs: Documenta 77"Kessel, W Ger, 1977; Mus Contemp Crafts, NY, 1977; Smithsonian Inst Renwick Gallery, 1977; Sally Hemings: A Novel, 1979; The Whitney Mus Noeuds et Ligatures Fond Nationale des Arts, 1983; Calif Mus Afro-Amer Art, 1985; Celopatra, The Brit Mus London, 2001; Selected Pub Collections: Mus Art New Orleans; The Philadelphia Art Mus; The Philadelphia Art Alliance; The Scnburg Collection New York; NY State Coun on the Arts; St John's Univ, Harlem State Off Bldg, The Metrop Mus Art, NY; The Nat Collections, France; Mus Mod Art, Berkley Mus, Los Angeles; The Brit Mus, London; Monuments: "Africa Rising", Foley Sq, NY. Auth: Sally Hemings, Viking, 1979; Albin Michel, 1981; Valide: A Novel of the Harem, 1986; Portrait of a Nude Woman as Cleopatra, William Morrow, 1987; Echo of Lions, William Morrow, 1989; The Pres's Daughter, Crown Publishers, 1994; Egypt's Nights, Ed Felln, Paris, 1994; Monogr: Barbara Chase-Riboud, Sculptor, A Jansen & P Selz, 1999; By Herself: Collected poems; under press, Sally Hemings, New Rev, Little Brown, UK, 2001; Hottentot Venus: novel, Doubleday, 2003; Hottentot Venus, Doubleday, NY, 2004; Bk: Black Writers, first ed, 1989; St. James Guide to Black Artists, 1997; Barbara Chose-Riboud: Sculptor. Harry N. Abrams, 1999; Sculptor, Mao's Organ, 2008. **Orgs:** PEN; PEN Am Ctr; Century Asn; Yale Alumni Asn; Alpha Kappa Alpha; John Hay Whitney Found Fel, 1957-58. **Home Addr:** 3 Rue Auguste-Comte, Paris75006. **Business Addr:** Author, Palazzo Ricci, Rome00186.

**CHASTANG, MARK J.**
Hospital administrator, executive director, vice president (organization). **Educ:** Fisk Univ, BA, 1974; Univ Kans, MPA, 1976; Ga State Univ, MBA, 1984. **Career:** DC Gen Hosp, exec dir, chief exec, 1990-94; E Orange NJ Gen Hosp, pres & chief exec officer, 1995-2004, admin; Grady Health Syst, exec vpres & chief operating officer; Med Col Ohio Hosp, vpres & exec dir, 2004-; Essex Valley Healthcare Inc, pres; Emory Univ Hosp, asst dir; Univ Chicago Med Ctr, vpres opers; Cathedral Healthcare Syst Inc, vpres; Fulton DeKalb Hospita, chief operating officer; Univ Toledo Med Ctr, vpres & exec dir, chief exec officer, currently; independent consult. **Orgs:** Hosp Coun Nortwest Ohio; fel Am col of Healthcare execs. **Business Addr:** Chief Executive Officer, The University of Toledo, 2801 W Bancroft, Toledo, OH 43606-3390, **Business Phone:** (800)586-5336.

**CHASTINE, ROBERT**
President (organization). **Educ:** Embry Riddle Univ, BS, aeronaut mgt, 1977; Ala A&M Univ, int logistics, 1989. **Career:** Mgt Technol Assoc, vpres, mkt bus develop, 1988-90, chief exec officer & pres, 1990-. **Orgs:** Soc Am Mil Engrs; past pres, N Huntsville Chap; life mem, AUS Black Aviation Asn; Huntsville Asn; Huntsville Econ Diversity Coun; advisor, Huntsville Chief Police Minority Recruitment. **Honors/Awds:** Hixon Fellowship Award; Received numerous awards. **Business Addr:** Chief Executive Officer, President, Management Technology Association, 688 Discovery Dr, Huntsville, AL 35806-2802, **Business Phone:** (256)922-1110.

**CHATMAN, ALEX**
Educator, magistrate, county commissioner. **Personal:** Born Oct 6, 1943, Greeleyville, SC; son of Alex Oscar (deceased) and Alma Montgomery; married Mariah Williams. **Educ:** Williamsburg County Training Sch, attended 1962; Benedict Col, dipl, 1965; SC State Col, BS, 1973; Univ RI, ME, 1966; Univ SC, attended 1970. **Career:** Greeleyville, teacher, 1965-; magistrate, 1973-81; Williamsburg Co Coun, supvr, chmn, 1996. **Orgs:** Pres, Greeleyville Br Nat Bus Leauge, 1970-; Credential Com State Dem Conv, 1971 & 1974; pres, Williamsburg County Educ Asn, 1974-75; chmn, sixth Cong Dist Polit Action Com Educ, 1974; Nat Asn Advan Colored People; United Teaching Prof; Nat Bus League; mem off, Black Caucus Nat Educ Asn; SC Magistrate's Asn; SC Asn Co, 1982-; Governor's Coun Rural Devel, 1982-86; SC Pvt Indus Co, 1984-87. **Home Addr:** 10656 Us Hwy 521, Greeleyville, SC 29056, **Home Phone:** (843)426-2768. **Business Addr:** County Supervisor, Williamsburg County, 147 W Main St, Kingstree, SC 29556, **Business Phone:** (803)354-9321.

**CHATMAN, DR. DONALD LEVERITT**
Physician. **Personal:** Born Dec 27, 1934, New Orleans, LA; married Eleanor; children: Lynn Ann, Eleanor Louise & Eric Leveritt. **Educ:** Harvard Univ, AB, 1956; Meharry Med Col, MD, 1960. **Career:** Cooper Hosp NJ, rotating internship, 1960-61; Michael Reese Hosp Med Ctr, resident obstet & gynec; Lake Charles LA, gen pract, 1961-63; Chicago, pvt pract ob-gyn, 1969-; Michael Reese Hosp & Med Ctr, Dept Obstet & Gynec, asst attend, 1969-74; Univ Chicago-Pritzker Sch Diamine Oxidase Pregnancy, Dept Obstet & Gynec, clin instr; Northwestern Univ Feinberg Sch Med, assoc prof; Michael Reese Med Asn, pvt pract physician, Michael Reese Hosp & Med Ctr, obstetrician & gynecologist, currently. **Orgs:** Chicago Med Soc; pres, Chicago Med Soc S Chicago Br, 1969-70; Am Asn Gynec Laparoscopists; Ill State Med Soc; Am Med Soc; Nat Med Asn; Am Col Obstet & Gynec; Am Bd Obstet & Gynec, 1972; Endometriosis Asn; Am Cong Obstetricians & Gynecologists. **Business Addr:** Physician, Obstetrician & Gynecologist, Michael Reese Medical Associates, 111 N Wabash Ave Suite 1017, Chicago, IL 60602, **Business Phone:** (312)220-9255.

**CHATMAN, DR. JACOB L.**
Clergy. **Personal:** Born Aug 5, 1938, Patterson, GA; married Etty; children: Mario. **Educ:** Fla Memorial Col, BS, 1963; Eastern Theol Sem, MDiv, 1968; Univ Massachusetts, PhD, 1974. **Career:** Second Baptist Church, Coatesville, Pa, pastor; St John Missionary Baptist Church, pastor; Drop-outs, Drugs, Planned Parenthood, Family Coun, couns; day care organizer; Eastern Col, St. Davids, Pa, Ctr Coun & Acad Support Serv, dir, Stud Affairs & Long Range Curric Planning, consult; Pinn Memorial Baptist Church, pastor, sr pastor, currently. **Orgs:** Dir, Pinn; chmn, Ctr Pa Title I Coatesville Sch Dist; Am Asn Univ Profs; Coatesville Area Clergy; Kappa Alpha Psi Frat; trustee, Cheyney State Teachers Col; pres, Comn Disadvantaged Eastern Sem; bd mgrs, exec bd, Pa DEChurched Am Baptist Conv; Task Force Foreign Mission; Black Churchmen Am Baptist Conv; vpres, Coatesville Opportuinity Coun; chmn, Non profit Housing Corp Sec Baptist Church; chmn, Comn Support Day Care; vice chmn, Coatesville Task Force World Hunger; rotary mem, Am Baptist Conv; pres, Interfaith Ministerium; Chester County Health & Welfare Coun; Coatesville Rotary Club; trustee, YMCA, Coatesville; trustee, Coatesville Hosp; ctr dir & consult, Eastern Col; bd gov, Palmer Theol Sem; bd gov, Eastern Univ. **Honors/Awds:** Recipient, citizenship YMCA, 1955; Eagle Scout, 1955; Chapel Four Chaplains Award, 1969; Citation, Coatesville Record Outstanding Service, 1970-74; Cititation Award, Mt Labanon HRAM PA, 1972; Outsanding Service Award, Fla Memorial Col, 1972; The Most Outstanding Young Man of America Award, 1972; Humanitarian Award, 1973. **Business Addr:** Senior Pastor, Pinn Memorial Baptist Church, 2251 N 54th St, Philadelphia, PA 19131, **Business Phone:** (215)878-2742.

**CHATMAN, MELVIN E., SR.**
Educator. **Personal:** Born Feb 9, 1933, Springfield, TN; married Velma R; children: Vera, Melvin Jr, Carol, Bobby, Jeff & Karl. **Educ:** Lane Col, BS, 1955; Fisk Univ, MA, 1963; Univ Tenn, EdS, 1975; Am Baptist Col, ThB, 1996. **Career:** R Bransford High Sch, teacher, coach, 1957-68; Springfield High Sch, teacher, 1968-70, asst prin, 1970-73, supvr spec educ, 1973-95. **Orgs:** Nat Educ Asn; Robertson City Teacher Asn; Coun Except C; Tenn Asn Suprv & Curric Develop; Mid-Cumberland Coun Gov; Ment Health Harriett City; Tenn Voter Coun, City Ctr, 1972-74; Alpha Phi Alpha; Beard Chapel Baptist Church. **Home Addr:** 4940 Hwy 41 N, Springfield, TN 37172, **Home Phone:** (615)384-3268.

**CHATMAN, RONALD DEAN**
School administrator, college administrator. **Personal:** Born Nov 28, 1946, Mobile, AL; son of John A and Bessie Mae Gholston; children: Ronald Dean II. **Educ:** Ala State Univ, BA, 1965; Calif State Univ, Los Angeles, CA, MA, 1972. **Career:** Compton Community Col, dean develop & continuing edu, 1979-81, dean spec proj, 1981-82, dir develop, 1982-85, exec dir instnl develop, 1985-96, vpres instnl develop & external affairs, 1996-98, dep supt & exec vpres; St. Timothy's Episcopal Day Sch, headmaster. **Orgs:** Nat Asn Advan Colored People, 1971-; Asn Calif Community Col Adminrs, 1983-; Vestry Bd, St Timothy's Episcopal Church, 1990-; 100 Black Men Los Angeles, 1992-; Fac Asn Calif Community Col, 1993-; bd dir, Inner City Theater, 2001-; Los Angeles County Beach Comn, 2001-; exec dir, St Timothy's Tower & Manor Inc, currently. **Home Addr:** 1172 E Cartagena Dr, Long Beach, CA 90807-2426, **Home Phone:** (562)424-7849. **Busi-**

**ness Addr:** Headmaster, St Timothy's Episcopal Day School, 312 S Oleander Ave, Compton, CA 90220, **Business Phone:** (310)638-6319.

### CHATMAN, TYRONE
Association executive, executive director. **Personal:** Born Jan 1, 1952. **Educ:** Highland Park Community Col, social work. **Career:** Salesman; Mich Automobile Indust, staff, 1972-72; Neighborhood Serv Orgn, intern; Mich Veteran's Found, Detroit Vet Ctr, Detroit, Mich, assoc exec dir, exec dir, chief exec officer, currently. **Orgs:** Detroit City Coun Pres's Shelter Ordinance & Lic Task Force; State Mich Target Cities Adv Comt; community health leader, Robert Wood Johnson Found, 1999; bd mem, Cass Community Social Serv. **Business Addr:** Executive Director, Chief Executive officer, Michigan Veterans Foundation, 2770 Pk Ave, Detroit, MI 48201-3012, **Business Phone:** (313)831-5500.

### CHATMAN-DRIVER, PATRICIA ANN
Software developer. **Personal:** Born Jul 19, 1956, Batesburg, SC; daughter of Mamie Chatman; married Allen Jerome; children: Jamiyl, Allen Jr & Amanda. **Educ:** SC State Col, BS, math, 1979. **Career:** Vitro Labs, mathematician, 1979-82; Sperry & UNISYS, mem eng staff, 1982-87; self-employed, 1987-88; Mystech Assocs Inc, sr software engr, 1988-. **Home Addr:** 20004 Manor View Terr, Laytonsville, MD 20882, **Home Phone:** (301)987-1304. **Business Addr:** Senior Software Engineer, Mystech Associates Inc, 5205 Leesburg Pke Suite 1200, Falls Church, VA 22041, **Business Phone:** (703)671-8680.

### CHATMON, LINDA CAROL
Educator, consultant. **Personal:** Born Nov 13, 1951, Louisville, KY; daughter of L C Fox and Betty A Savage; children: Dana Marie. **Educ:** Univ Louisville, BA, 1980, MSSW, 1982, PHD, social work. **Career:** Creative Employ Proj, counr, 1982-84; Univ Louisville, coord coop educ, 1984, instr & counr 1984-89; GYSG Corp, consult, 1986-88; Univ Louisville, Kent Sch Social Work, dir admis & stud serv, adj asst prof; First Neighborhood Pl, Thomas Jefferson Mid Sch, adminr. **Orgs:** Community chair, Urban League, 1982-88; Youth Performing Arts Sch, 1983-87; secy bd, Seven Counties Ment Health Serv. **Home Addr:** 10009 Hydrangea Way Bldg 7, Louisville, KY 40241. **Business Addr:** Administrator, First Neighborhood Place, 1503 Rangeland Rd, Louisville, KY 40219, **Business Phone:** (502)962-3160.

### CHATTERJEE, LOIS JORDAN
Banker. **Personal:** Born Aug 4, 1940, Nashville, TN; married Suchindran S. **Educ:** Tenn State Univ, BS, 1962; Univ Tenn, attended 1963. **Career:** Juv City Davidson Co, legal secy, 1962-66; St Dept Corrections, counr youthful offenders, 1966-70; Model Cities Prog, evaluator, 1971; Com Union Bank, bank officer bus develop, 1972-; Essence Mag, Publ, 1974. **Orgs:** Metrop Coun, 1971-; Negro Bus & Prof Womens League; Mid Tenn Bus Asn; Nat Bus League; secy, SE Nashville Civic League; charter mem, Dudley Pk Day Care Ctr; bd dir, Goodwill Indust; House Between; Nashville County C; League Women Voters; YWCA; Nat Coun Crime & Delinq; Nat League Citizens. **Home Addr:** 4025 Buena Vista Pke, Nashville, TN 37218-2019. **Business Addr:** Educator, Metropolitan School System, 2601 Bradford Ave, Nashville, TN 37204.

### CHAUNCEY, MINION KENNETH. See MORRISON, DR. K. C.

### CHAVARRIA, DR. JILL BARGONETTI. See BARGONETTI, JILL.

### CHAVIS, BENJAMIN FRANKLIN, JR. See MUHAMMAD, BENJAMIN CHAVIS.

### CHAVIS, OMEGA ROCHELLE
Banker. **Personal:** Born Jan 1, 1951, TN; daughter of Eddie H and Estella M. **Educ:** Wayne State Univ, BA, 1970. **Career:** Security Pac Nat Bank, asst vpres, 1973-86; Fox Film Corp, assoc dir, 1986-87; Glendale Fed Bank, sr vpres, 1987-. **Orgs:** Bd dir, Savings Asn Mortgage Co Inc; exec bd, Los Angeles Home Loan Coun Ctr; United Negro Col Fund; Nat Asn Female Execs; Los Angeles Urban Bankers; Cs Defense Fund; Alpha Kappa Alpha Sorority Inc; First AME Church; Co founder, Calif State EDD Adv Coun. **Honors/Awds:** State of California Health & Welfare Agency Public Service Award. **Special Achievements:** LDF Black Woman of Achievement. **Home Addr:** 5159 Village Green, Los Angeles, CA 90016-5205, **Home Phone:** (323)497-3303. **Business Addr:** Senior Vice President, Glendale Federal Bank, 401 N Brand Blvd Suite 200, Glendale, CA 91203, **Business Phone:** (818)500-2155.

### CHAVOUS, BARNEY LEWIS
Executive, football player. **Personal:** Born Mar 22, 1951, Aiken, SC; married Odessa; children: Shedric, Jasmine & Nikeya Monique. **Educ:** SC State Univ, Phys Ed. **Career:** Football player (retired), coach, executive; Denver Broncos, right defensive tackle, 1973, left defensive end, 1974-85; Minority Arts & Educ Found, chmn; TW Josey High Sch, Augusta, GA, teacher, head football coach; Tutt Mid Sch, team sports coach, currently. **Honors/Awds:** Defensive Rookie Year Hon, Nat Football League Players Asn, 1973; Defensive Lineman Year, Pittsburgh Courier's NFL, 1978; All-Conf & defensive Most Valuable Player at SC State; All-Am by AP; collegiate Defensive Lineman Year; North-South Game; The Senior Bowl; Coaches' All-Am Game. **Business Addr:** Head Football Coach, T W Josey Comprehensive High School, 1701 15th St, Augusta, GA 30901, **Business Phone:** (706)737-7360.

### CHAVOUS, COREY LAMONTE
Football player. **Personal:** Born Jan 5, 1976, Aiken, SC. **Educ:** Vanderbilt Univ, human & orgn develop. **Career:** Football player (retired); Ariz Cardinals, right cornerback, 1998-2001, cornerback, 2001; Minn Vikings, strong safety, 2002-05, left cornerback, 2002, free safety, 2005; St Louis Rams, strong safety, 2006-08, free safety, 2008; DraftNasty.com, founder, 2009-; CBS Sports, nfl draft analyst, currently. **Orgs:** Vol, Minneapolis Pub Sch; vol, Shriners Hosp; United Negro Col Fund. **Honors/Awds:** Pro Bowl selection, 2003; Defensive Player of the Week, Natl Football League, 2003; Ed Block Courage Award; Carl Ekern Spirit of the Game Award, 2008. **Special Achievements:** TV Series: "2 Live Stews", 2006. Featured On Various Sports Programs As An Analyst Of College Football Talent. **Business Addr:** NFL Draft Analyst, CBS Sports, 51 W 52nd St, New York, NY 10019-6188, **Business Phone:** (212)975-4321.

### CHAVOUS, MILDRED L.
School administrator, executive director, counselor. **Personal:** Born Columbia, AL; daughter of William H Lynn and Juanita Jackson; married Jarret C. **Educ:** Franklin Univ, BS, 1946. **Career:** Executive director (retired); Ohio State Univ Grad Sch, counr, 1964-77, acad counr, 1977-84, acad counr & staff asst, 1984-86, assoc, 1986-90, dir grad serv, 1990-97. **Orgs:** Bd dir, chairperson, League Women Voters, Educ Comn, 1965-; CMS Pub Sch Personnel Policies Ohio, 1971-73; exec comt mem, Ohio Humanities Coun, 1974-80; trustee, Franklin Co Bd Ment Retardation & Develop Disabilities, 1974-77; founding mem, Metrop Human Serv Comn, 1977-90; State Libr Ohio, Adv Comn, Fed Libr Prog, 1984-87; trustee & chairperson, Players Theatre Columbus, Outreach Comt, 1989-95; Europ Womens Mgt Network, 1992-; Coun Acad Excellence Women, 1994-; trustee, Thurber House, Thurber Nat Award Am Humor Comn, 1995-; trustee, Scioto Valley Health Systs Agency, 1996-; bd gov, Ohio State Univ Critical Difference Women, Int Coun, 1996-; adv bd, Jefferson Fel, 1996; nat pres, Circle-Lets Inc, 1997-; Links Inc; Asn Fac & Prof Women; treas, Crichton Club; fel Univ Senate Select Comt Minorities & Women; steering comt Critical Difference Women Campaign; co-chair Ohio States United Way Campaign; mayor Columbus; Columbus City Coun; Ohio House Representatives. **Honors/Awds:** Commendation, Ohio House Rep 110th Gen Assembly, 1971; Distinguished Serv Award, United Negro Col Fund, 1981; Mayors Cert Recognition, City Columbus, 1982; Commendation, Ohio House Rep 116th Gen Assembly, 1983; Distinguished Staff Award, Ohio State Univ, 1986; Cert of Appreciation, Health Plan Rev, 1988-95; Coalition, 100 Black Women Honoree, 1992; Black Women Courage Honoree, 1995; Commendation, Coun City Columbus, 1996; Commendation, Recognition of Accomplishments, Ohio House Rep, 121 Gen Assembly, 1995; Distinguished Vol Serv, Columbus Cancer Clinic, 2001. **Special Achievements:** Women's editor, Columbus Call and Post, 1970-85; First African American & woman co-chair, Ohio State University, United Way Annual Campaign, 1981; First woman general chair, United Negro College Fund Annual Telethon, Central Ohio, 1982; co-editor, "Graduate School News," The Ohio State University, 1990-97; First African American President, board of directors, Columbus Cancer Clinic, 1993-2001; First African American president Promusica Sustaining Board. **Home Addr:** 1939 Haverhill Dr, Columbus, OH 45406-4635, **Home Phone:** (614)237-5227. **Business Addr:** Enarson Hall 154 W 12th Ave, Columbus, OH 43210.

### CHEADLE, DONALD FRANK, JR.
Actor. **Personal:** Born Nov 29, 1964, Kansas City, MO; son of Donald Sr and Bettye; married Bridgid Coulter; children: 2. **Educ:** Calif Inst Arts, BA, actg. **Career:** TV series: "Fame", "L.A. Law", 1986; "Hill Street Blues", "The Bronx Zoo", 1987; "Night Court", "Hooper man", 1988; "Booker", 1989; "China Beach", "The Fresh Prince of Bel-Air", 1990; "The Golden Palace", 1992; "Hang in' With Mr. Cooper", 1992-93; "Picket Fences", 1993-95; Animated Tales of the World, The Simpsons, 2000; The Bernie Mac Show, ER, 2002; MADtv, 2003; "The Colbert Report", 2006; "The Henry Rollins Show", 2007; "Drunk History", 2010; "30 Rock", 2012; "House of Lies", 2012-14. Films: Moving Violations, 1985; Hamburger Hill, 1987; Colors, 1988; Roadside Prophets, 1992; The Meteor Man, Lush Life, 1993; Things to Do in Denver When You're Dead, Devil in a Blue Dress, 1995; Volcano, Rosewood, Boogie Nights, 1997; Out of Sight, The Rat Pack, Bulworth, 1998; Traffic, Mission to Mars, The Family Man, 2000; Things Behind the Sun, Manic, Swordfish, Rush Hour 2, Ocean's Eleven, 2001; Abby Singer, 2003; The United States of Leland, 2003; Ocean's Twelve, The Cookout, After the Sunset, The Assassination of Richard Nixon, Hotel Rwanda, 2004; Crash, 2005; The Dog Problem, Make Your Own Superbowl Ad, 2006; Reign Over Me, 2007; Talk to Me, 2007; Ocean's Thirteen, 2007; Darfur Now, 2007; Traitor, Producer, 2008; Hotel for Dogs, 2008; Brooklyn's Finest, 2009; Iron Man 2, 2010; The Guard, 2011; Flight, 2012; Iron Man 3, 2013. **Honors/Awds:** LAFCA Award for Best Supporting Actor, 1995; LAFCA Award, Los Angeles Film Critics Asn, 1995; NSFC Award, Nat Soc Film Critics, 1996; FFCC Award, Fla Film Critics Circle, 1998; OFTA Television Award, Online Film & Tv Asn, 1999; Golden Globe Award, 1999, 2013; Black Reel Award, 2000, 2001, 2006 & 2012; Screen Actors Guild Award, 2001, 2006; Special Award, San Diego Film Critics Soc, 2004; Gotham Award, 2004, 2007; Black Movie Award, 2005; Golden Satellite Award, 2005; Hollywood Film Award, 2005; Independent Spirit Award, 2006; Critics Choice Award, Broadcast Film Critics Asn, 2006; AAFCA Award, African-Am Film Critics Asn, 2007; BET Award, 2007; ShoWest Award, 2007; Humanitarian Award, BAFTA/LA Britannia Awards, 2008; Joel Siegel Award, Broadcast Film Critics Asn, 2008; Image Award, Nat Asn Advan Colored People, 2013; NAMIC Vision Award, 2013. **Special Achievements:** Co-author of the book Not On Our Watch: The Mission to End Genocide in Darfur and Beyond, 2007; Nominated for Oscar and 18 other awards. **Business Addr:** Actor, United Talent Agency, 9560 Wilshire Blvd 5th Fl, Beverly Hills, CA 90212, **Business Phone:** (310)273-6700.

### CHEANEY, CALBERT NATHANIEL
Basketball player, basketball coach. **Personal:** Born Jul 17, 1971, Evansville, IN; married Yvette; children: Julian & Sydney. **Educ:** Ind Univ, attended 1993. **Career:** Basketball player (retired), basketball coach; Wash Wizards, guard-forward, 1993; Wash Bullets, 1994-99; Boston Celtics, 1999-2000; Denver Nuggets, 2001-02; Utah Jazz, 2003; Golden State Warriors, guard-forward, 2003-06, spec asst coach, 2009-11; Ind Univ, dir basketball opers, 2011-13, dir internal & external player develop, 2012-13; St Louis Univ, asst coach, 2013-16. **Honors/Awds:** All-Am, 1991-93; All-Big Ten, 1991-93; Player of the Year, Naismith Col, 1993; John R. Wooden Award, 1993; Big Ten Conference Most Valuable Player, 1993; Player of the Year, Us Basketball Writers Asn, 1993; Adolph Rupp Trophy, 1993; Player of the Year, Nat Asn Basketball Coaches, 1993; USBWA College Player of the Year, 1993; AP College Player of the Year, 1993; UPI College Player of the Year, 1993; Sporting News College Player of the Year, 1993; Big Ten Conference Player of the Year, 1993; Big Ten's All Time Scoring Leader; Indiana Universities All-Time leading scorer; Four time IU team Most Valuable Player; Selected to Indiana University's All-Century First Team; inducted, Indiana University Sports Hall of Fame, 2003. **Special Achievements:** NBA Draft, first round, sixth pick, 1993. Film: Blue Chips, 1994. **Business Addr:** Assistant Coach, Saint Louis University, 3330 Laclede Ave, St. Louis, MO 63103, **Business Phone:** (314)977-3178.

### CHEATHAM, BETTY L.
Government official, manager. **Personal:** Born Dec 5, 1940, SC. **Educ:** Benedict Col, BS, bus admin, 1962. **Career:** Int City Mgt Asn, prog mgr, 1974-80, minority prog dir, 1980-83; DC Water & Sewer Authority, chief, asst gen mgr. **Orgs:** Coalition, Black Pub Admins, 1982-85; Int City Mgt Asn, 1983-85; Black Pub Admins Forum, 1984-85. **Home Addr:** 859 Venable Pl NW, Washington, DC 20012-2611. **Business Addr:** DC.

### CHEATHAM, HENRY BOLES
Television director, educator. **Personal:** Born Oct 5, 1943, Bentonia, MS; son of Thomas and Maude; married Helen M Hughes; children: Tonita R & Jomo K. **Educ:** Columbia Col, BA, radio & tv, 1973; Univ Ill, Chicago, MA, mass commun, 1980. **Career:** Ford Motor Co, utility man, 1965-73; WISH-TV Indianapolis, producer, 1973-2008; WSNS-TV, Chicago, producer, dir, writer & cameraman, 1973-; Yoton Commun Inc, pres, founder & owner, 1980-; Richard J Daley City Col, Chicago, instr, 1997-. **Orgs:** Exec bd, Union steward NABET, 1980-; Chicago Area Broadcast Pub Affairs Asn, 1980-83; Nat Black United Front, 1983-; Oper PUSH, 1983-; vpres & bd dir, Order Kush, currently. **Home Addr:** 10847 S Prospect Ave, Chicago, IL 60643-3403, **Home Phone:** (773)881-0426. **Business Addr:** Instructor, Richard J Daley City College, 7500 S Pulaski, Chicago, IL 60652, **Business Phone:** (773)838-7500.

### CHEATHAM, LINDA MOYE
Government official, executive. **Personal:** Born Nov 2, 1948, Richmond, VA; married Harold D Jr; children: Michelle, Maxanne & Harold III. **Educ:** Wheaton Col, BA, 1970; Harvard Univ; Va Commonwealth Univ. **Career:** City Norfolk, planner, 1970-72; City Richmond, planner, 1972-75, opers mgr, 1975-79, sr budget analyst, 1979-84, dir gen serv, 1984-87, budget dir, 1987-91; City Richmond, Fed Credit Union, bd dir, 1984; John B Cary Elem Sch, Parent Teacher Asn, treas, 1985-88; US Dept Comn, Int Trade Admin, chief financial officer & dir admin, currently; Va Dept Transp, Procurement Div, div adminr, currently. **Orgs:** Int City Mgt Asn, 1980-; bd govs, William Byrd Community House, 1983-; Conf Minority Pub Admin, 1983-; chap coun, VA Chap, Am Soc Pub Admin, 1984-. **Home Addr:** 7592 Triana Ct, Myrtle Beach, SC 29572. **Business Addr:** Division Administrator, Virginia Department of Transportation, 1401 E Broad St, Richmond, VA 23219, **Business Phone:** (804)371-6716.

### CHEATHAM, DR. ROY E.
Educator. **Personal:** Born Sep 14, 1941, Memphis, TN; married Gertie Brenell Wilson; children: Roy III & Gina Rochele. **Educ:** Lincoln Univ, BA, eng & jour, 1965; St Louis Univ, MA, 1969, PhD, 1975. **Career:** Human Dev Corp, adult & educ cord, 1966-67; adult educ curric specialist, 1969; Metrop Col, dean; St Louis Univ, Col Arts & Sci, asst dean, 1969-70, dir spec acad prog, dir col asst prog & upward bound, 1970-73, Educ leadership & higher educ, asst prof. **Orgs:** Educ Enrichment Prog, 1972-75; Basic Educ Opportunity Grant Planning Comn, 1972; Am Col Pesonnel Asn Comn XIV, 1973-76; pres, Roy Cheatham & Assoc; Financial Aid Panel, 1973; vice chmn brd dir, Inroads Inc, 1973-76; brd educ, Univ City Pub Sch Dist, 1974-77; Reg VII off Higher Educ pres, 1976-77; comnr, Mark Twain Boy Scout Dist; brd dir, Comm Learning Ctr; brd dir, Sophia House; bd mem & pres, Lincoln Univ Found, currently. **Home Addr:** 12173 Royal Valley Dr, St. Louis, MO 63141-6620, **Home Phone:** (314)576-6059. **Business Addr:** Board Member, President, Lincoln University Foundation, 820 Chestnut St, Jefferson City, MO 65101, **Business Phone:** (573)681-5000.

### CHECKER, CHUBBY. See EVANS, ERNEST.

### CHECOLE, PROF. KASSAHUN
Publisher. **Personal:** Born Jan 22, 1947, Asmara; married Nevolia E Ogletree; children: MuluBirhan & Senait. **Educ:** Haile Selassie Univ, attended; State Univ NY, Binghamton, BA, social & polit econ, 1974, MA, sociol, 1976. **Career:** Rutgers Univ, instr, 1979-85; Af Res & Publ Proj, dir, 1979-; El Colegio De Mex, res prof, 1982-; The Red Sea Press Inc, founder, pres & publ, 1982-; Wash Sch Inst Policy Studies, lect; Af World Press Inc, founder, pres & publ, currently. **Orgs:** Vice chmn, Eritrean Relief Comn Inc, 1983-85; ed bd, Saga Race Rels Abstracts, Horn Africa; active mem, Asn Eritrean Students N Am; Pan-Africanism, human rights & relief orgn. **Home Addr:** 556 Bellevue Ave, Trenton, NJ 08618, **Home Phone:** (609)695-3402. **Business Addr:** President, Publisher, Africa World Press Inc, 541 W Ingham Ave Suite B, Trenton, NJ 08638, **Business Phone:** (609)695-3200.

### CHEEK, DONALD KATO
Educator. **Personal:** Born Mar 24, 1930, New York, NY; married Calista Patricia Duff; children: Don Jr, Gary, Alan, Stephan & Donna; married Patti Dorothy Walker. **Educ:** Seton Hall Univ, S Orange, NJ, BS, 1953; Fordham Sch Soc Serv, NY, MSW, 1955; Univ Southern Calif, doctoral curric, 1959; Temple Univ, PhD, 1971. **Career:** Nat Inst Ment Health, grad fel, 1965-69; Lincoln Univ, PA, vpres stud affairs, dean, lectr, 1967-69; Claremont Col, Claremont, CA, dir black studies, Human Resources Inst, vpres, lectr social psychol, 1969-73; Calif Polytech St Univ, San Luis Obispo, counr & prof social psychol, 1973-77, prof education, 1973-99, prof emer, currently, rehab counr, 1984-, ordained minister, 1987-; Nat Bd Officer, Prison fel, 1989-; Calif St Univ, Col Soc Sci, Fresno, part-time lectr, 2003-. **Orgs:** NIMH Grad Fel, 1965-69; prin trainer & consult, Pa Gov's Conf Race Rels,

1970-72; founding chmn, State-Wide Minority Task Force Univ Counors, 1974-77; admin consult, Paso Robles Boys Sch, Calif Youth Authority, 1977-82; coun consult & facilitator, Fed Correctional Inst, Lompoc, CA, 1980-85; presenter, Int Consult Coun & Ethnic Minorities, Univ Utrecht Neth, 1985; consult speaker & workshop facilitator, Milwaukee; Ment Health Ctr, Orangeburg, SC; Ann Guid Conf, NY Salomon Bros, Las Vegas, NV; Am Personnel & Guid Asn Conv, New Orleans; La Asn Black Soc Works; Drug Educ Prev & Treat, Daytona Beach, FL; Bethune Cookman Col; Emporia Kans St Univ; Omaha NE Crighton Univ; nat bd officer, Prison Fel, USA 1989-; Sanford Fl Seminole Comm Col; Xenia Ohio Co Ment Health; Evansville Ind Human Rel Comn; Univ Cinn Col Nursing; Cleveland Urban Minority Alcoholism Outreach Proj, SC Sch Alcohol & Drug Studies, City Portland, OR; Univ ND, LA Black Prof Engrs. **Home Addr:** PO Box 1476, Atascadero, CA 93423. **Business Addr:** Part-Time Lecturer, California State University, 2225 E San Ramon M/S SB 69, Fresno, CA 93740-8029, **Business Phone:** (559)278-2832.

## CHEEK, DONNA MARIE

Horse trainer. **Personal:** Born Dec 5, 1963, Philadelphia, PA. **Career:** Equestrian; Exhib Equestrian, coordr; Seven Star Farms, Hunter & Jumper Training Facil Horses & Riders, owner & operator; KCBX, Pub Radio Animal Issues & Ideas, host. **Orgs:** Corp sponsorship Univox Calif Inc, Pro-Line Corp, Quincy Jones Prod, Ed Laras Westside Distr; spokesperson Involvement Young Achievers Inc, 1982; Avon Found NY, 1983. **Honors/Awds:** Financial Grant Black Equestrian Sports Talent, 1980-; Image Award, Nat Asn Advan Colored People; Bronze Halo Award, Southern Calif Motion Picture Coun; Medal Champion, Am Horses Shows Asn; F.B. Hart Perpetual Trophy. **Special Achievements:** Pub "Going for the Gold-The Story of Black Women in Sports, " 1983; "One More Hurdle" Autobiography NBC TV, starred in one hour drama 1984; "Profiles in Pride" NBC TV, starred 1985; "Ebony/Jet Showcase", 1986; first equestrienne inductee, Womens Sports Hall of Fame, 1990; first African American on US Equestrian Team.

## CHEEK, KING VIRGIL, JR.

Educator, vice president (organization), writer. **Personal:** Born May 26, 1937, Weldon, NC; son of King Virgil and Lee Ella Williams; married Annette Walker; children: King Virgil III, Kahlil, Antoinette & Antoine. **Educ:** Bates Col, Lewiston, Maine, BA, econ, 1959; Univ Chicago, MA, 1967; Univ Chicago, JD, 1969. **Career:** Midwest Inter-Libr Loan Ctr, Chicago, 1959-64; Shaw Univ, Raleigh, NC, asst prof econs, 1964-65, from actg dean to dean, 1965-67, vpres acad affiars, dean, 1967-69, Citizenship Lab, from lectr to pres, 1968-71; Morgan State Col, Baltimore, pres, 1971-74; Univ Experimenting Cols & Univ, form vpres to pres planning develop, 1974-78; Baltimore Contractors, bd dir, 1974; NY Instnl Technican, Wash Ctr, exec dir, 1978-85, Inst Econ Develop, bd dir, 1978, dir sr exec develop prog, Govt Bermuda, 1983-85, vpres dean grad studies, 1985-90, sr vp Instnl advan, 1990-92, vp acad affairs, 1992-96; BCI Contractors, Baltimore, vp mkt sales pub rel, 1996-97; ew York Col Health Professionals, chancellor, 2001-03; Col Integrated Med, founder, 2005-; New York Inst Technol, prof, dean grad studies. **Orgs:** Bd dir, Baltimore Contractors, 1974; bd dir, Inst Econ Develop, 1978; Martin Ctr Col; bd trustee, Shaw Col, Detroit; bd visitor, Univ Chicago Law Sch; bd trustee, Warnborough col, Oxford, Eng. **Honors/Awds:** Grand Commander Order of Star Africa, 1971; Hon Doctoratre, Univ Md, Bates Col, 1972. **Special Achievements:** American Academy change magazine awarded as Top young leader award in 1978; Author, 'The Quadrasoul', four novels that explore four dimensions of the human spirit; Author Of Numerous Books. **Home Addr:** 14009 Broomall Lane, Silver Spring, MD 20906, **Home Phone:** (301)460-7784.

## CHEEKS, DR. CARL L.

Dentist. **Personal:** Born Jul 7, 1937, Poplar Bluff, MO; married Shirley K Magness; children: Darryl & Shalonda. **Educ:** Fisk Univ, BA, 1960; Meharry Med Sch, DDS, 1965. **Career:** Pvt pract dentist, 1967-. **Orgs:** Am Dent Asn; Nat Dent Asn; N Shore Dent Asn; Lincoln Dent Soc; Am Acad Gen Dent; Rel Analgesia Seminars; Chicago Dent Soc; Nat Asn Advan Colored People; Kappa Alpha Psi Frat; United Community Serv Evanston; Martin Luther King Lab Sch PTA; Black Bus & Prof Asn; Evanston Sch Bd; Fisk Jubilee Singers; Black Male Stud Naval Acad. **Honors/Awds:** Cert merit, Minority Youth Motivation, 1968-74; Chessman Club Award, Aiding Civic Prog. **Business Addr:** Dentist, 1626 Darrow Ave, Evanston, IL 60201-3418, **Business Phone:** (847)869-9708.

## CHEEKS, DARRYL LAMONT

Auditor, executive, association executive. **Personal:** Born Apr 7, 1968, Evanston, IL; son of Carl and Beaulah Brittain. **Educ:** Univ Ill, Urbana-Champaign, BS, acct, 1990; Harvard Summer Venture Mgt Prog. **Career:** Dent asst, 1978-86; Golden Touch Cleaners, owner & mgr, 1987-88; Krispy Kits Karmel Korn, owner & mgr, 1988; Southwestern Christian Col, chmn bd; Arthur Andersen & Co, auditor, 1989-93; Abbott Labs, financial & oper consult, 1993-95; Soul Food Prison Ministries, founder & exec dir, 1993-; Hoyt Fastener Co, controller, 1995-; Chicagoland Barbecue Inc, founder, pres & chief exec officer, 1996-; Taylor Cheeks & Assoc, co-managing partner, 1998-. Black Rhino Financial Group, chief exec officer & managing partner, 2006-; Monroe St Church Christ, asst pastor; AXS Solutions, chief financial officer. **Orgs:** Dir educ, asst minister, jail ministry dir, trustee, Monroe St Church Christ, 1989-; Nat Asn Black Accountants, 1991-; Ill CPA Soc, 1992-; bd dir, treas, Reba Pl Day Nursery, 1992-; bd dir, treas, Jan Erkert & Dancers, 1994-; Univ Ill Deans Bus Coun. **Honors/Awds:** President's Scholarship Award, Univ Ill, 1986-90; Fred G Carpenter Award, Business, Evanston Township, Miss, 1986; Outstanding College Students of America, 1987-90; Mom's Day Scholastic Award, Univ Ill, 1987, 1988, 1990; High Honor Roll, Dean's List, Univ Ill, 1987; Ebony Mag, 1990. **Special Achievements:** youngest person to be hired by Abbott Laboratories as a Financial and Operational Consultant. **Home Addr:** 325 N 8th Ave, Des Plaines, IL 60016-2103. **Business Addr:** Managing Partner, Black Rhino Financial Group Inc, 1480 Renaissance Dr Suite 410, Park Ridge, IL 60068, **Business Phone:** (847)268-8440.

## CHEEKS, MAURICE EDWARD (MO CHEEKS)

Basketball player, basketball coach. **Personal:** Born Sep 8, 1956, Chicago, IL; children: 2. **Educ:** W Tex State Univ, attended 1978. **Career:** Basketball player (retired), basketball coach; Philadelphia 76er's, guard, 1978-89, asst coach, 1994-2001, coach, 2005-08; San Antonio Spurs, guard, 1989-90; New York Knicks, 1990-91; Atlanta Hawks, guard, 1991-92, Nj Nets, 1992-93, guard, 1993; CBA, Quad City Thunder, asst coach; Portland Trail Blazers, head coach, 2001-05; Okla City Thunder, asst coach, 2009-13, 2015-; Continental Basketball Asn, coach; Detroit Pistons, head coach, 2013-14. **Business Addr:** Head Coach, Detroit Pistons, Palace Auburn Hills 6 Championship Dr, Auburn Hills, MI 48326-1752, **Business Phone:** (248)377-0100.

## CHELSI, CHELSI (CHELSI MARIAM PEARL SMITH)

Fashion model, actor. **Personal:** Born Aug 23, 1973, Deerpark, TX; daughter of Craig and Denise Trimble; married Kelly Blair. **Career:** Actress & fashion model, currently; Films: Playas Ball, 2003; One Flight Stand, 2003; Miss Teen USA 2006 pageant, judge; Host: "Beyonce: Family & Friends Tour", co host; TV series: "Due South", 1996; The Sweetest Thing, sound track, 2002. **Honors/Awds:** Miss Galveston County USA, 1994; Miss Congeniality, 1994; Miss USA, 1995; Miss Universe, 1995. **Special Achievements:** First American woman of biracial origin to win the Miss Texas USA, Miss USA, and Miss Universe titles, was the sixth Miss USA to be crowned Miss Universe, and the seventh woman from Seventh Texas Woman to be crowned Miss USA; the first & only Miss USA to win Miss Congeniality in the Miss USA competition; Co-wrote & recorded her first single,"Dom Da Da". **Business Addr:** Actress, Fashion Model, c/o William Morris Agency, 151 El Camino Dr, Beverly Hills, CA 90212, **Business Phone:** (310)859-4000.

## CHENAULT, JOHN

Playwright, poet, labor activist. **Personal:** Born Jan 3, 1952, Cincinnati, OH; married Gwendline Harper. **Educ:** Union Inst, BFA, 1977; Univ Cincinnati, Beacon Col, libr & info sci & pan african studies & african am studies; Univ Ky, MLIS, libr & info sci, 2006; Univ Louisville, MA, pan african studies, 2007, PhD, pan african studies, 2011-. **Career:** Librettist; poet; educator; librarian; playwright; theatrical producer; Poetry: Blue Blackness, 1969; The Invisible Man, 1992; Plays: Blood Ritual, 1971; Warren is Backin the World, 1993; The Buckwheat Book of the Dead, 1995; The X-periment, 1996; Stolen Moments, 1997; Librettos: Ode to A Giant, 1993; Ghost in Machine, 1995; The Buckwheat Book of the Dead, 1995; The X-periment, 1996; Stolen Moments, 1997; Mingus-Live in the Underworld, 1997; More Than Miles, 1997; Yesterday's News, 1999; The Fools of Time, 2000; My Name is Citizen Soldier, 2000; New Theatre/Free Theatre Cincinnati, actor, playwright, producer, stage tech & playwright, 1967-; Black Arts Ensemble, performer, 1968-70; author, 1969-; Univ Cincinnati, instr African & African-Am studies, 1972; Sunship percussion group, founder & performer, 1973; Zamani Band, Washington, DC, founder & performer, 1977; Beacon Col, instr African & African-Am studies, 1977; Wash Int Col, exec dean, 1978-82; Sickle Cell Awareness Group, exec dir, 1986-94; Applause, columnist, 1991-93; Artrage, columnist, 1992-93; WAIF Radio, writer & co-producer, 1993; librettist, 1993-; TV series: "Young Men Grow Older"; Trane: Beyond the Blues, music designer, 2002; Univ Louisville, Kornhauser Health Sci Libr, asst prof, 2004-, Pan African Studies Dept, lectr; Artrage Mag, columnist & sect ed. **Honors/Awds:** Brotherhood Award, Nat Conf Christians & Jews, 1972; nominee, Emmy Award, 1972. **Home Addr:** 1370 S 6th St Suite 1, Louisville, KY 40208. **Business Addr:** Assistant Professor, University of Louisville, 2301 S 3rd St, Louisville, KY 40292, **Business Phone:** (502)852-5555.

## CHENAULT, KENNETH IRVINE

Chief executive officer, lawyer, consultant. **Personal:** Born Jun 2, 1951, Long Island, NY; son of Hortenius and Anne Quick; married Kathryn Cassell; children: Kevin & Kenneth Jr. **Educ:** Bowdoin Col, BA, hist, 1973; Harvard Law Sch, JD, 1976. **Career:** Firm Rogers & Wells, atty, 1977-79; Bain & Co, mgt consult, 1979-81; Am Express Co, div head green cards, 1981-89, Consumer Card Group US, pres, 1989, vice chmn, 1995-97, pres & chief operating officer, 1997-2001, chief exec officer & chmn, 2001-, Travel Related Serv, US Div, pres, 1993-95, chief exec officer, 1997-, chmn, 2001-; New York Inc, co chmn; Am Express Bank Ltd, dir; Int Bus Mach Corp, dir, 1998-; Procter & Gamble Co, dir, 2008-. **Orgs:** Bd mem, Int Bus Mach; Coun Nat Mus African Am Hist & Cult; Deans Adv Bd Harvard Law Sch & Coun Foreign Rels; dir, Phoenix House Found Inc; dir, Nat September 11 Memorial & Mus, World Trade Ctr Found Inc; dir, Nat Ctr Addiction & Substance Abuse; trustee, Mt Sinai NYU Med Ctr & Health Syst; vice chmn, Nat Acad Found; Westchester Country Club, 1990-. **Home Addr:** 65 Overlook Cir, New Rochelle, NY 10804-4501. **Business Addr:** Chief Executive Officer, Chairman, American Express Co, 200 Vesey St, New York, NY 10285-5104, **Business Phone:** (212)640-2000.

## CHENEVERT-BRAGG, IRMA J.

Judge. **Personal:** Born Nov 17, 1951, Detroit, MI; daughter of Arthur and Ruth Green; married Sidney Sr; children: Arica Chenevert & Arianna Powers. **Educ:** Eastern Mich Univ, BS, 1973; Detroit Col Law, JD, 1982. **Career:** US Dist Ct, Eastern Dist MI, law clerk, 1982-84; Wayne County Prosecutor's Off, asst prosecuting atty, 1984-85; Joselyn Rowe Etal, atty, 1985-86; Detroit Bd Police, spec proj asst, 1986-87; self-employed, atty, 1986-89; State Mich, law judge, 1986-89; 36th Dist Ct, magistrate. **Orgs:** State Bar Mich. **Honors/Awds:** HIP Award, Handgun Intervention Prog, 1996; Wolverine Student Bar Association, Special Alumni Award, 1985. **Home Addr:** 17500 Muirland, Detroit, MI 48221, **Home Phone:** (313)342-9434.

## CHENNAULT, DR. MADELYN

Educator, educator. **Personal:** Born Jul 15, 1934, Atlanta, GA; daughter of Benjamin Q and Othello Ann Jones; married Thomas Mark. **Educ:** Morris Brown Col, BS, 1957; Univ Mich, MA, 1961; Ind Univ, PhD, 1973. **Career:** Pub Schs Ga CA, Mich, educr, 1957-62; Albany State Col, asst prof Psychol, 1962-64; Ind Univ, res asst, 1964-66; Atlanta Univ, asst prof educ, 1966-67; Ft Valley State Col, assoc prof educ to prof educ, 1967-72; Counsult, Coun Except C Regional Meeting; consul, Atlanta, Ga, 1967; spl educ consult, Grambling Col, 1968; educ psych consult, Univ Conn, 1969; elem educ consult, Ala A & M Univ, 1969; ment retardation consul, Ga State Dept Educ, 1969-71; sch integration consul, Americus Ga Pub Schs, 1970; Head Start consul, Heart Ga Proj, 1970-71; spec educ, vis scholar NC Cent Univ, 1971; Nat Sci Found Visit Scientist Ala State Univ, 1971; spec serv proj consult, Ft Valley State Col, 1971-72; Nat Sci Found Vis Scientist Talledega Col, 1972; main speaker, Alpha Kappa Alpha Sor Founders Day Prog, 1972; spec educ consult & psychometrist, Peach Co Pub Sch, 1972; So Regional Rep Asn Black Psychologists, 1972-74; exec adv comn, Comn-Clin Psych Proj So Reg Educ Bd Atlanta, 1972-75; Community Hypertension Intervention Prog, prof educ & clin dir, 1972-89; Jackson Hinds Comn Ment Health Ctr, cont psych, 1973; psych consult, Miss State Univ, 1973; Chennault Enterprise, pres, 1974-; Univ Ga, post doctoral study clin psychol; Univ Miss Med Ctr, post doctoral internship. **Orgs:** Asn Adv, Behav Ther; Am Asn Ment Def; Am Asn Univ Profs; Am Psych Asn; Am Res Asn; Ga Psych Asn; Nat Educ Asn; Alpha Kappa Alpha Sor Links Inc. **Special Achievements:** Published numerous articles. **Home Addr:** 215 Piedmont Ave NE Suite 1006, Atlanta, GA 30308, **Home Phone:** (404)223-6874.

## CHEROT, ESQ. NICHOLAS MAURICE

Lawyer, secretary general. **Personal:** Born Jun 30, 1947, Ann Arbor, MI; son of Romeo Augustus and Flora L. **Educ:** Univ Mich, BA, 1969; NY Univ Sch Law, JD, 1972. **Career:** Autumn Indust Inc, secy, treas, 1977-; Autumn-Everseal Mfg Co Inc, secy, treas, 1979-; Powell Blvd Holding Co Inc, dir & partner; Cherot & Michael PC, atty, currently. **Orgs:** Powell Blvd Asn, 1979-; Harlem Lawyers Asn, NY; New York County Lawyers Asn; Nat Bar Asn, 1973; Black Allied Law Students Asn. **Business Addr:** Attorney, Cherot & Michael PC, 305 Broadway Suite 600, New York, NY 10007-1136, **Business Phone:** (212)962-6442.

## CHERRY, DR. CASSANDRA BRABBLE

Administrator. **Personal:** Born May 29, 1947, Norfolk, VA; married Maurice L. **Educ:** Bennett Col, BA, 1969; Va State Univ, MEd, 1974; Richard Bland Col; Col Wilson & Mary, mgt dipl, 1975; Nova Univ, EdD, 1980. **Career:** AUS Qm Sch, educ specialist, 1974; AUS Logistics Ctr, educ specialist, 1974-78; AUs Training Support Ctr, educ specialist, 1978-79; Naval Supply Ctr, employee develop specialist, 1979; Defense Activ Non-Traditional Educ Support, mgr instrnl delivery prog, 1980-03. **Orgs:** Phi Delta Kappa; bd dir, Minorities-Media, 1982-83; Federally Employed Women; publicity chmn Equal Employ Opportunity Coun Pensacola Naval Complex, 1985, 86; Am Inst Mortgage Brokers; Nat Asn Advan Colored People. **Home Addr:** 1444 Watkins Trl, Pensacola, FL 32506, **Home Phone:** (850)456-6855. **Business Addr:** Pensacola, FL 32509.

## CHERRY, DERON LEIGH

Football player. **Personal:** Born Sep 12, 1959, Palmyra, NJ; son of George and Lillian; married Faith; children: 2. **Educ:** Rutgers Univ, BS, 1980. **Career:** Football player (retired), executive; Kans City Chiefs, safety, 1981-82, free safety, 1983-91; United Beverage, owner, 1992-; Deron Cherry's All Pro Ford, owner, 1990s; Jacksonville Jaguars, partner, 1994-; United Beverage Co, managing gen partner. **Orgs:** Bd dir, Kans City Sports Comn; bd mem, Jackson County Sports Complex Authority, 2006-. **Honors/Awds:** Defensive Player of the Year, Am Football Club, 1986; Byron White Humanitarian Award, NFL Players Asn, 1988; inducted, Chiefs Hall of Fame, 1995; Sports Hall of Fame of New Jersey, 1996; Missouri Sports Hall of Fame, 2002; Kansas City Chiefs Hall of Fame. **Special Achievements:** Second African Am toattain part ownership in an NFL franchise, 1993. **Home Phone:** (816)537-4469. **Business Addr:** Board Member, Jackson County Sports Complex Authority, No 4 Arrowhead Dr, Kansas City, MT 64129, **Business Phone:** (816)921-3600.

## CHERRY, EDWARD EARL, SR.

Educator, executive. **Personal:** Born Dec 4, 1926, Greenville, NC; son of Jasper and Velma Smith; married Mary Jean Jordan; children: Edward Jr & Todd J (deceased); married Tarah Stanton. **Educ:** Howard Univ, BArch, 1953. **Career:** Edward Cherry Architect, pres, 1963; Yale Univ Sch Archit, asst prof, 1971, vis critic, 1972-81; Edward E Cherry & Assocs, pres, currently. **Orgs:** Basileus, Chi Omicron Chap, Omega Psi Phi Fraternity, 1957-; corp mem, Conn Soc Architects, AIA, 1960-; founder, bd dir, pres, Greater New Haven Bus Prof Asn, 1964-; worshipful master, Orient Lodge No 6, F&AM PHA, 1966-68; New Haven Consistory No 7, AASR PHA, 1968-; pres, Heritage Hall Develop Corp, 1980; State Hist Preserv Rev Bd, Conn Hist Comt, 1980-; grand inspector gen, AASR, PHA, Northern Jurisdiction, 1986; archon, Beta Tau Boule, Sigma Pi Phi, 1986; bd dir, Found New Haven Green, 1986-89. **Honors/Awds:** Man of the Year, New Eng States, First Dist, Omega Psi Phi Fraternity, 1979; Grand Basileus Service Award, Omega Psi Phi, 1979; AIA Design Award, Conn Soc Archit, AIA. **Home Addr:** 22 Pine Ridge Rd, Woodbridge, CT 06525, **Home Phone:** (203)397-1975. **Business Addr:** President, Edward E Cherry & Associates, 60 Connolly Pkwy Bldg 15A, Hamden, CT 06514-2593, **Business Phone:** (203)281-1300.

## CHERRY, JE'ROD L.

Football player, radio host. **Personal:** Born May 30, 1973, Charlotte, NC; married Lisa; children: Jay Martin. **Educ:** Univ Calif, Berkeley, polit sci, 1995, MEd, 2000. **Career:** Football player (retired); New Orleans Saints, defensive back & corner back & safety, 1996-99; Oakland Raiders, 2000; Philadelphia Eagles, defensive back, 2000; New Eng Patriots, corner back & safety, 2001-04; WKNR AM 850, sports talk show host & NFL analyst, currently. **Business Addr:** Sports Talk Show Host, NFL Analyst, WKNR AM 850, 1301 E 9th St Suite 252, Cleveland, OH 44114, **Business Phone:** (216)583-9901.

## CHERRY, LEE OTIS

Chief executive officer, research administrator. **Personal:** Born Nov 20, 1944, Oakland, CA; son of Knorvel and Lucy; married Lauran Michelle Waters; children: Aminah L & Jamilah L. **Educ:** Merritt Community Col, AA, 1965; San Jose State Univ, BSEE, electronic engineering, 1968; Hazardous Mat Mgt, Univ Calif, cert, 1995; Site Assessment

& Remediation, regist environ assessor, CA, 1997. **Career:** African Sci Inst, bd mem, pres & chief exec officer, 1967-; Int Bus Mach, systs analyst, 1968-69; Pac Gas & Elec Co, elec engr, 1969-79, Dept Defense, proj mgr, 1979-92, Dept Defense, environ mgr, 1992-2000; US Trade Rep, Indonesia Country, currently; landmine clearing, tech adv, currently; Int Inst Engineering, exec dir; Northern Calif Coun Black Prof Engr, co-founder, pres, 2006. **Orgs:** Proprietor, L&L & Assocs Network Mkt, 1980-; Linkages Int, 1993-; co-founder, African Sci Inst; co-founder, Ghanaian-Am Chamber Com, bd mem, ASI Fel; Hollywood, Our Town Inc, co-founder, bd dir, 2001-. **Business Addr:** President, Chief Executive Officer, African Scientific Institute, PO Box 20810, Piedmont, CA 94620, **Business Phone:** (510)653-7027.

## CHERRY, ROBERT LEE

School administrator, executive director, executive. **Personal:** Born Feb 17, 1941, Barrackville, WV; son of William Elmo and Elizabeth McNair; married Ann Theresa Luckett; children: Norma Jean, Mary Elizabeth, Robert Lee & Ebon Michael. **Educ:** Wittenberg Univ, EdB, 1964; Wright State Univ, EdM, 1973. **Career:** Educator (retired); Int Harvester Co, supvr, 1964; Wittenberg Univ, Upward Bound Prog, prog dir, 1968; Clark Tech Col, admis officer, 1973; Springfield Ohio, city commnr, 1974; DMVC-EDNL Opportunity Ctr, exec dir, 1975; Clark Tech Col, dir student serv, 1975. **Orgs:** Past mem & pres, Ohio Asn Upward Bound Dir, 1970; bd mem, OpportunitiesIndustrialization Ctr, 1974; cert com mem, Ohio Asn Student Financial AidAdminstr, 1974; Ohio Asn Student Serv Dir, 1977; chmn, Clark Co 648 MentalHealth & Retardation Bd, 1975; bd mem, Clark State Community Col, 2007-08. **Honors/Awds:** Community Merit Award, Springfield Frontiers Int, 1962; Outstanding YoungMen, Am OYMA, 1970; Community Service Award, St John Baptist Church, 1980. **Home Addr:** 303 W Perrin Ave, Springfield, OH 45506, **Home Phone:** (937)323-3525.

## CHESS, EVA L.

Executive. **Personal:** Born Feb 6, 1960, High Point, NC; daughter of Hon and Sammie Jr. **Educ:** Univ NC, Chapel Hill, BA, 1982; Univ Va, JD, 1985. **Career:** JP Morgan & Co Inc, pvt banker, 1985-91; Sara Lee Corp, sr mgr, pub responsibility; RR Donnelley Found, vpres external affairs, currently; RR Donnelley & Sons Co, sr dir, dir commun bus process redesign proj. **Orgs:** Bd dir, United Way Stamford, CT; officer, bd dir, Coalition 100 Black Women Lower Fairfield County; Bus Policy Rev Coun; Urban Bankers Coalition; Am & Va Bar Asns; bd dir, Chicago Cosmopolitan Chamber Com; Deacon, Chicago United; corp adv comt., Ctr Women Policy Studies; corp adv coun, League Women Voters; bd dir, Am Asn Univ Women Educ Found; bd dir, Midwest Women's Ctr; bd mem, YWCA Metrop Chicago; Jackie Robinson Found, adv bd, Leadership Ill; Int Asn Bus Communicators; Int Women Forum; Women Fund Greater Milwaukee & Milwaukee Film Festival. **Honors/Awds:** America's Best & Brightest, Dollars & Sense Mag, 1993. **Business Addr:** Vice President, RR Donnelley Foundation, 111 S Wacker Dr 36th Fl, Chicago, IL 60606-4301, **Business Phone:** (312)326-8000.

## CHESTANG, DR. LEON WILBERT

Educator, dean (education), social worker, dean (education), social worker. **Personal:** Born May 16, 1937, Mobile, AL; son of Joseph James and Emmie; married Aurelia C Taylor; children: Nicole & Yvette. **Educ:** Blackburn Col, BA, 1959; Wash Univ, MSW, soc work, 1961; Univ Chicago, PhD, soc serv admin, 1977. **Career:** Ill Dept Pub Welfare, social worker, 1961-63; Ill Dept C & Family Serv, supvr 1963-65; Ill Dept Pub Aid, social casework instr, welfare exec, 1966-69; Family Care Chicago, dir casework serv, 1967-71; Univ Chicago, asst prof, mem fac, 1971-78; Univ Ala, prof, 1978-80, spec asst to pres, 1979-80; Wayne State Univ, dean prof, dean social work, mem fac, 1981-99, distinguished prof, 2000-04, prof emer, 2004-; VA Univ Commonwealth, distinguished commonwealth prof, 1984-86; Smith Col, distinguished Lydia Rapport prof, 1985; pvt practr, consult; Co-editor: The Diverse Society. **Orgs:** Community assoc, Chicago Asn Retarded C, 1965-66; bd mem, C's Aid Soc Detroit, 1983-; bd mem, Detroit Urban League, 1985-; bd mem, Nat Asn Social Workers, 1985-88; fel Am Coun Educ. **Home Addr:** 682 Pallister St, Detroit, MI 48202, **Home Phone:** (313)872-4438. **Business Addr:** Professor Emeritus, Wayne State University, 4756 Cass Ave, Detroit, MI 48202, **Business Phone:** (313)577-4409.

## CHESTER, LARRY TRAVIS

Football player. **Personal:** Born Oct 17, 1975, Hammond, LA; married Nicole; children: Jadore Larya. **Educ:** Temple Univ. **Career:** Football player (retired); Indianapolis Colts, defensive tackle, 1998, left defensive tackle & right cornerback, 1999, 2000; Carolina Panthers, right defensive tackle, 2001; Miami Dolphins, right defensive tackle, 2002-04.

## CHESTNUT, DR. DENNIS EARL

Educator, psychologist. **Personal:** Born May 17, 1947, Green Sea, SC. **Educ:** E Carolina Univ, BA, psychol & soc, 1969, MA, clin psychol, 1971; Univ Utah, Doc Prog, clin psychol, 1974; NY Univ, PhD, commun psychol, 1982. **Career:** Univ Utah, NIMH fel, 1971-74; Camden Co MH Ctr, psychol consult, 1974-75; E Carolina Univ, asst prof psychol, 1974, prof, asst prof emer, prof emer; Neuse Ment Health Ctr, qual assurance consult, 1975-77; NY Univ, NIMH fel, 1978; Univ Medgar Evers Col City NY, instr psychol, 1979-81. **Orgs:** Reg rep, NC Grp Behav Soc, 1981-; vice bishop, United Pentecostal Holiness Churches Am, 1981-; pres, Young People's Holiness Asn, United Pentecostal Holiness Churches AmInc; Alpha Phi Alpha Frat; nat treas, Asn Black Psychologists, 1983-84; original liaison, Asn Humanistic Psychol, 1983-84; s reg rep, Asn Black Psychologists, 1984-85; bd dir mem, Asn Humanistic Psychol, 1984-85; pastor, Mt Olive Holiness Church Tabor City NC, 1984-; treas, NC Asn Black Psychologists; Pitt Ment Health Asn; pres, NC Chap Asn Black Psychologists, 1986-87; dir, Minority Affairs Asn Humanistic Psychol, 1986-; co-chmn, Nat Black Family Task Force Asn Black Psychologists; Lifelong resident Ward 7; Neighborhood/Environ activist. **Home Addr:** 1801 E 5th St, Greenville, NC 27858-2903, **Home Phone:** (252)757-1531. **Business Addr:** Professor Emeritus, East Carolina University, Rawl 239, Greenville, NC 27858-4353, **Business Phone:** (252)328-6308.

## CHESTNUT, MORRIS L.

Actor. **Personal:** Born Jan 1, 1969, Cerritos, CA; married Pamela Byse; children: 2. **Educ:** Univ Calif, Northridge, finance & drama. **Career:** Films: Boyz 'N the Hood, 1991; The Last Boy Scout, 1991; The Inkwell, 1994; Under Seige 2, 1995; Higher Learning, 1995; GI Jane, 1997; The Best Man, 1999; The Brothers, 2001; Two Can Play That Game, 2001; Scenes of a Crime, 2001; Like Mike, 2002; Half Past Dead, 2002; Confidence, 2003; Ladder 49, 2004; Breakin' All the Rules, 2004; Anacondas: The Hunt for the Blood Orchid, 2004; The Cave, 2005; The Game Plan, 2007; The Perfect Holiday, 2007; The Prince of Motor City, 2008; Prince of Pistols, 2008; Not Easily Broken, actor & exec producer, 2009; Castle, 2009; Takers, exec producer, 2010; Think Like a Man, 2012; Identity Thief, 2013; The Call, 2013; Kick-Ass 2, 2013; The Best Man Holiday, 2013; TV series: In the Line of Duty: Street War, 1992, The Ernest Green Story, 1992; Out All Night, 1992; Firehouse, 1997; The Killing Yard, 2001; "Dante", 2005; "Bones", 2005; "Stage Black", exec producer, 2007; "The Prince of Motor City", 2008; "V", 2009-11; "American Horror Story", 2011; "American Dad!", 2013; "Nurse Jackie", 2013-14. **Honors/Awds:** Annual Madden Bowl, 1998; Hollywood Award, Acapulco Black Film Festival, 2014; Image Award, Nat Asn Advan Colored People, 2014. **Business Addr:** Actor, Creative Artists Agency, c o Michael Nilon, Beverly Hills, CA 90212-1825, **Business Phone:** (310)288-4545.

## CHEW, BETTYE L.

College administrator. **Personal:** Born Dec 10, 1940; children: Gordon W, Cheryl L & Donna V. **Educ:** Rosenwald Community Jr Col, attended 1959; Cortez W Peters Bus Sch, attended 1964; Bowie St Col. **Career:** Annapolis Urban Renewal & Prog, secy, 1967-69; Univ Md Coop Exten Serv, secy, 1969-72; Bowie St Col, Bowie Md, Off Dean, secy, 1972-. **Orgs:** Sunday sch teacher, First Baptist Church, 1964-; Nat Asn Advan Colored People; reg rep, Annapolis Sr HS Citizens Adv Comt, 1974-; leader Girl Scout Troop 43, 1974; proj coordr, Am Issues Forum Prog, Bowie St Col, 1976; Offender Aid & Restoration Counr, Anne Arundel Co Detention Ctr; chmn, Citizen Adv Comt, Annapolis Sr HS, 1976-77; Human Rel Comt Annapolis Sr HS, 1977; co-founder, Donna Y. Chew Breeden Memorial Fund, 2010. **Home Addr:** 110 M F Bowen Rd, Huntingtown, MD 20639-9128, **Home Phone:** (410)535-0184. **Business Addr:** College Administrator, Bowie State College, 14000 Jerico Pk Rd, Bowie, MD 20715-6943, **Business Phone:** (877)772-6943.

## CHEW, CHERYL

Executive. **Orgs:** Dir, mgr, corp partner, Nat Black MBA Asn Inc. **Home Addr:** , Chicago, IL. **Business Addr:** Director, Manager, Corporate Partner, National Black MBA Association Inc, 1 E Wacker, Chicago, IL 60601, **Business Phone:** (312)236-2622.

## CHEW, RAY

Music director, musician. **Personal:** Born Dec 23, 1958?, New York, NY; son of Henry Chew and Elaine Chew; married Vivan Scott; children: Bianca & Loren. **Career:** Toured with Melba Moore, 1974; produced music for Nick Ashford & Valerie Simpson, 1975 and arranged music seven of their albums; Chew Entertainment, co-founder, 1988; Power to Inspire, co-founder; "The Gilded Six Bits", score composer, 2001; Democratic National Convention, band leader, 2008; Neighborhood Inaugural Ball, director, 2009. Music director, 2010-. Music director: "Saturday Night Live Band", 1980; Showtime at the Apollo, 1992; BET Awards, 2010, 2011, 2012; "American Idol", 2011; A Message of Peace: Making of the UN Day Concert 2012, 2013; 65th Emmy Awards, 2013; Miss Universe, 2013, 2014; "Dancing with the Stars", ABC/BBC, music dir, 2014; "Rising Star", 2014; Macy's Thanksgiving Day Parade, NBC broadcast, 2014; Grammy Awards Premiere Ceremony, 2015; the 44th Annual NAACP Image Awards; "Sunday Best", BET. **Orgs:** Apollo Theater Found, music dir; Nat Asn Rec Arts & Sci, nat trustee. **Special Achievements:** Music arranger and instrumentalist with musicians such as Gladys Knight, Quincy Jones, Diana Ross, Aretha Franklin, Alicia Keys, and Rihanna; curated "A Night of Inspiration", Carnegie Hall, 2015. **Business Addr:** Chew Entertainment, 460 Queen Anne Rd, Teaneck, NJ 07666, **Business Phone:** (201)928-1696.

## CHEW, VIVIAN SCOTT

Executive, founder (originator). **Personal:** Born May 14, 1958, Queens, NY; daughter of William Scott and Mamie Murphy; married Ray Leighton; children: Loren & Bianca. **Educ:** Georgetown Univ, attended 1977. **Career:** Kashif, personal asst; Louise C W Esq, exec asst; Polygram Rec, dir artist & repertoire, 1987-90; Sony Music Entertainment, dir artist & repertoire, Epic Rec, 1990; Epic Rec, vpres artist & repertoire, 1991-97; Urban Music Dept, Epic Rec, vpres, 1994-96, head, 550 Music & Sony, Epic Rec, head artist repertoire & urban music, 1994-97; Time Zone Intl, owner, prin & founder, 1997-. **Orgs:** Co-founder, Juv Diabetes Found Music Indust Dinner; pres, Am Soc Composers, Authors & Publishers, 1985-87; bd mem, Black Rock Coalition; bd mem, Winston Prepatory Sch; co-founder, Chew Entertainment; fel Opus 118. **Business Addr:** Founder, Principal, Time Zone International, PO Box 331, Bogota, NJ 07666, **Business Phone:** (201)928-1999.

## CHICOYE, ETZER

Research administrator. **Personal:** Born Nov 4, 1926, Jacmel; son of Appoline Briffault and Rigaud; married Dolores Bruce; children: Lorena & Rigaud. **Educ:** Univ Haiti Port Au Prince, BS, 1948; Univ Wis Madison, MS, 1954, PhD, 1968. **Career:** Research administrator (retired); Chicago Pharmacol, chemist qual control, 1955-57; Julian Labs, prod chemist, 1957-62, chemist res & develop, 1962-64; Miller Brewing Co, chem res supvr, 1968-72, mgr res, 1972-77, dir res & develop, 1977-92. **Orgs:** YMCA; Am Chem Soc; Am Soc Brewing Chemists. **Home Addr:** 1259 SW 172nd Terr, Pembroke Pines, FL 33029-4821, **Home Phone:** (414)464-5673.

## CHIDEYA, FARAI

Writer, journalist. **Personal:** Born Jul 27, 1969, Baltimore, MD; daughter of Lucas and Cynthia. **Educ:** Harvard Univ, BA, 1990. **Career:** Newsweek, researcher & reporter, 1990-93; Wash bur, reporter, 1993-94; MTV News, assignment ed, 1994-96; Freedom Forum Media Studies Ctr, fel, 1996; CNN, polit analyst, 1996-97; ABC News, corresp, 1997-99; "Pure Oxygen, " Oxygen Media, host, 1999-; Los Angeles Times Syndicate, syndicated columnist, 2000-; Knight Fel Stanford Univ, 2001-02; PopandPolitics.com, founder, pres; NPR's News & Notes, host, 2006-09; Author: Don't Believe the Hype, Plume/Penguin, 1995; The Color of Our Future, William Morrow, 1999; Trust, Soft Skull Press, 2004; Kiss the Sky, 2009. **Orgs:** Nat Asn Black Journalists, 1992-; bd mem, Pop & Polit; Jour Adv Comn, Knight Found; fel, Harvard Inst Polit. **Honors/Awds:** Nat Education Reporting Award, 1992; Ed Press Award, 1992; NABJ Unity Award, 1994; Glaad Media Award, GLAAD, 1994; WIN Young Women of Achievement Award; Named as Dream Team, 1996; Named to Newsweek's Century Club, 1997; MOBE IT Innovator Award; Young Lion Award, Black Entertainment & Telecommunications Asn, 2004; Special Award, Lesbian & Gay Journalists assoc, 2008; Enterprise reporting award, Nat assoc of Black Journalists, 2007; North Star Award, covering communities of color, 2006. **Special Achievements:** Named one of Alternet's New Media Heroes; Ranked in PoliticsOnline.com's worldwide survey of 25 Who Are Changing the World of Internet and Politics; Published articles in newspapers and magazines including The New York Times, The Los Angeles Times Magazine, Time, Spin, Vibe, O, The California Journal, Mademoiselle, and Essence. **Home Addr:** PO Box 1374, Culver City, CA 90232, **Home Phone:** (310)815-4382. **Business Addr:** Host, NPR, News and Notes, PO Box 1374, Culver City, CA 90232.

## CHIGBU, GIBSON CHUKS

President (organization), executive, chief executive officer. **Personal:** Born Sep 21, 1956, Aba; son of Jason N and Rhoda N Amadi; married Florence Ihekwoaba; children: Gibson Jr, Krystal, Jasmine & Michael. **Educ:** Southern Univ & A&M Col, Baton Rouge, LA, BS, archit, 1981, MS, arts, 1982. **Career:** Hunt-Thurman & Assocs, Baton Rouge, La, draftman, 1979-81; Barber & Johnson Engrs, Baton Rouge, La, designer, 1981-82; Hewitt-Wash Archits, New Orleans, La, proj archit, 1982-85; Gee Cee Grp Inc, New Orleans, La, owner & pres, 1985-, chief exec officer. **Orgs:** Pres, Asn Nigerians New Orleans, 1985, 1986; provost, Orgn Nigerian Profs-USA, 1986-87; chmn, Construct Comt, Black Econ Develop Coun, 1991; nat pres, Orgn Nigerian Profs, USA Inc, 1992-; nat bd dir, Nat Bus League, 1996-; nat pres, Nkwerre Aborigine's Union, USA, elected Dallas, TX, 1996; bd mem, Urban League Greater New Orleans; pres, La Contractors Asn; bd mem, Specialty Bus & Indust Develop Corp; pres bd, New Orleans Tech Initiative Contractor Emergence. **Honors/Awds:** Certificate of Recognition, US Dept Com, 1989-90; Best of Black Business-New Orleans, 1994. **Home Addr:** 7001 Lake Barrington Dr, New Orleans, LA 70128-2220, **Home Phone:** (504)248-5577. **Business Addr:** President, Owner, The Gee Cee Company of LA Inc, 5552 Grand Bayou Dr, New Orleans, LA 70189, **Business Phone:** (504)254-1212.

## CHILDRESS, RANDOLPH

Basketball player. **Personal:** Born Sep 21, 1972, Washington, DC; married Jen-Ai; children: Brandon & Devin. **Educ:** Wake Forest Univ, attended 1995. **Career:** Basketball player (retired), basketball coach, executive; Portland Trailblazers, 1995-96; Detroit Pistons, 1996-97; Tofas Bursa, Turkey, 1997-98; Kombassan Konya, Turquie, 1998-99; Cholet Basket, France, 1999; Rec Napoli, Italy, 2000-01; Sydney Kings, Australia, 2001; Rida Scafati, Italy, 2001-03; SLUC Nancy, France, 2003-04; Premiata Montegranaro, Italy, 2004-07; Pepsi Caserta, Italy, 2007-08; Cimberio Varese, Italy, 2008-10; Dinamo Sassari, Italy, 2010; Mazzeo San Severo, Italy, 2010-11; Pallacanestro Varese, Italy, currently; Wake Forest Univ, dir player develop, asst coach, 2013-. **Business Addr:** Assistant Coach, Wake Forest University, 1834 Wake Forest Rd, Winston-Salem, NC 27106, **Business Phone:** (336)758-5000.

## CHILDS, CHRIS

Basketball player. **Personal:** Born Nov 20, 1967, Bakersfield, CA; son of James; married Maisha McGee; children: Crystal; married Karla; children: Jesse, Jenne & Jade. **Educ:** Boise State Univ, attended 1989. **Career:** Basketball player (retired); Columbus Horizon, Continental Basketball Asn, 1989-90, 1990-91; Rapid City Thrillers, Continental Basketball Asn, 1989-90; LaCrosse Catbirds, Continental Basketball Asn, 1990-91; Rockford Lightning, Continental Basketball Asn, 1990-91, 1991-92; Bakersfield Jammers, Continental Basketball Asn, 1991-92; Quad City Thunder, Continental Basketball Asn, 1992-93, 1993-94; Miami Tropics, US Basketball League, 1993, 1994; NJ Nets, pt guard, 1994-96, 2002-03; NY Knicks, pt guard, 1996-2001; Toronto Raptors, pt guard, 2000-02. **Honors/Awds:** Player of the Year, Big Sky Conf, 1989; Championship, Continental Basketball Asn, 1994; Most Valuable Player, Continental Basketball Asn, 1994; MetLife Community Assist Award, 1998, 2000; Eastern Conference Championship, Nat Basketball Asn, 1999; Good Guy Award, NY Press Photographers Asn, 2000.

## CHILDS, DR. FRANCINE C.

Educator. **Personal:** Born Wellington, TX; children: Jimmy Fenley. **Educ:** Paul Quinn Col, BS, biol, 1962; E Tex State Univ, MEd, sociol, guid & coun, 1970, EdD, 1975; Jacksonville Theol Sem & Hocking Valley Sch Bible, PhD, 1996. **Career:** Wiley Col, dean studs, 1970-72; E Tex State Univ, proj dir spec servs, 1972-74; Ohio Univ, prof afro-am studies, 1974-85, 1985-2007, chmn, afro-am studies, 1974-96, dir summer prog, 1975-78, chairperson, 1984-89, prof emer dept afro-am studies, 2007-; Fannie Lou Hamer Statue proj. **Orgs:** Local pres & adv, Ohio Univ Chap Nat Asn Advan Colored People, 1971-; League Women Voters, 1977-; educ chair, Ohio Conf Br Nat Asn Advan Colored People, 1978-; nat coord, Booker T Wash Alumni Asn, 1982-; prayer coord, Athens Christian Women Club, 1984-86; workshop leader, Ohio Bapt Women Auxillary Conv, 1985-; local conf host & prog comm, Nat Coun Black Studies, 1987; Nat Alliance Black Sch Educ; assoc pastor, Mt Zion Baptist Ch, currently; Black Alumni Reunion; Human Rels Couns; Nat Prof Asns; Educ Comns rep, Nat Black Family Conf; White House Task Force Educ. **Home Addr:** 25 Elliott St, Athens, OH 45701-2608, **Home Phone:** (740)593-7093. **Business Addr:** Professor Emeritus, Ohio University, 314 Lindley Hall, Athens, OH 45701, **Business Phone:** (740)593-1307.

### CHILDS, JOSIE L.

Government official. **Personal:** Born Oct 13, 1926, Clarksdale, MS; daughter of Charles Washington and Julia Brown; married James M Sr. **Educ:** LeMoyne Owen Col; Northwestern Univ. **Career:** Metrop Sch Tailoring, adminr; City Chicago, dir planning, 1989-, Dept Cult Affairs, 1983-90; Harold Wash Tribute Comt, founder, 2013. **Orgs:** Bd mem, Friend Chicago Pub Libr; bd mem, Know Your Chicago; Univ Chicago; Vivian Harsh Soc, 2003; Duke Ellington Soc, Joint Negro Appeal; Know Your Chicago. **Honors/Awds:** Pride Award, outstanding contributions to Image & Pride Black Womanhood, 1985; Unsung Hero Award, Congional Black Caucus, 2002; Vivian Harsh Society Award, Outstanding contributions to African-Amn Music, 2003; Georgia Palmer Award, Congressman Danny K Davis, 2013. **Home Addr:** 6935 S Crandon Ave Apt 2D, Chicago, IL 60649-1741, **Home Phone:** (773)643-4828. **Business Addr:** Director, City of Chicago, 78 E Wash St, Chicago, IL 60602-4801, **Business Phone:** (312)744-6630.

### CHILDS, JOY B.

Lawyer, executive, consultant. **Personal:** Born Apr 10, 1951, Wilmington, NC; daughter of Joseph and Mable. **Educ:** Univ Calif, Los Angeles, BA, 1973, MA, 1975; Georgetown Univ Law Ctr, JD, 1981. **Career:** Screen Actors Guild, contract admin, 1981-83; Atlantic Richfield Co Legal Dept, paralegal, 1983-84; Peace Officers Res Asn CA, labor rels rep, 1984-86; CA St Univ, employee rels admin, 1986-90; Hughes Aircraft Co, sr labor rels consult, 1990-94; Warner Bros, Employee Rels, mgr; Dunn-Edwards Corp, dir human resources, human resources dir, currently. **Orgs:** KCET Comm Adv Bd, 1984-, Univ Calif, Los Angeles, Black Alumni Asn, 1985-, Black Labor Attys LA, 1985-, Black Entertainment & Sports Lawyers Asn, 1986-; Women Color, 1987-; chair, Donor Recruitment Devel Comt, mem executive comt, Dunn-Edwards Corp; Am Red Cross Serv. **Home Addr:** 620 W Hyde Pk Blvd Suite 121, Inglewood, CA 90302. **Business Addr:** Chair of Donor Resources Development Committee, Dunn-Edwards Corp, 4885 E 52nd Pl, Los Angeles, CA 90058, **Business Phone:** (888)337-2468.

### CHILDS, OLIVER BERNARD

Association executive, educator. **Personal:** Born Jan 15, 1933, Philadelphia, PA; son of Edmond A Sr and Ogetta Faust; married Dorothy Collins; children: Renee Olivia, Oliver Jr & Sean Vincent. **Educ:** Cheyney State Teachers Col, Cheyney, PA, BS, 1958; Univ Utah, Salt Lake City, UT, MS, 1980. **Career:** Philadelphia Bd Educ, Philadelphia, Pa, teacher, 1958-65; Opportunities Industrialization Ctrs, Philadelphia, Pa, dir training, 1965-66, LosAngeles, Calif, exec dir, 1966-68; OIC Inst, Philadelphia, Pa, asst dir ext serv, 1968-71; OIC Am, Dallas TX, regional dir, 1971-74, dir fund develop, 1974-83; OIC Int, Philadelphia, Pa, dir resource develop, 1984-; Univ Md, Eastern Shore, asst prof, 1990-94, Hotel & Restaurant Mgt, asst prof, actg chmn, interim dir, currently; Richard A Henson Conf Ctr, dir, currently. **Orgs:** Kappa Alpha Psi Fraternity, 1956-, Nat Soc Fund Raising Exec, 1976-; Nat Asn Advan Colored People, 1978-; chmn, Troop Comt, Boy Scouts Am, 1980-; bd mem, Independent Charities Am, 1989-; Minority Adv Comt, Philadelphia Visitors & Conv Bur, 1989-; pres & bd dir, Nat Coalition Black Mgt Planners, 1989. **Home Addr:** 706 Parker Rd, Salisbury, MD 21804-1934, **Home Phone:** (410)548-9047. **Business Addr:** Interim Director, Acting Chair, University Maryland Eastern Shore, Henson Ctr, Princess Anne, MD 21853, **Business Phone:** (410)651-2200.

### CHISHOLM, DR. JOSEPH CARREL, JR.

Physician. **Personal:** Born May 16, 1935, Detroit, MI; son of Joseph and Maizie Jones; married Maurita; children: John, Lynn, Kim & Kelly. **Educ:** Univ Chicago, BS, 1958, MS, 1960; Meharry Med Col, MD, 1962. **Career:** Univ Il Hosp & Clin, resident internal med; Va Hosp, Wash, DC, consult, 1968-77; US Dept State, consult, 1970-; DC Soc Internal Med, mem exec bd, 1972-80; DC VNA, mem exec bd, 1982-; Am Col Physicians, Wash, DC, gov's bd, 1984-; pvt pract physician, 1984-. **Orgs:** Alpha Phi Alpha, 1957; Alpha Omega Alpha Hon Soc, 1960-; Am Lung Asn, 1970-; Am Heart Asn, 1970; DC Soc Internal Med, 1970; fel Am Col Physicians, 1970-; NY Acad Sci, 1975-; Nat Asn Advan Colored People, 1978-; Southern Med Soc, 1980-; Nat Med Asn; DC Thoracic Soc; DC Heart Asn; DC Med Soc; Sigma Pi Phi Frat, 1986-; Viceroys, 1990-; Am Bd Internal Med. **Honors/Awds:** Order of the C Univ Chicago, 1954-; Rockefeller Research School Allergy Immunology, 1959-61; Pulmonary Research School, Nat Insts Health, 1965-66; Pig skinners of Washington DC, 1980-. **Business Addr:** Physician, Private Practice, 2000 N Twr 106 Irving St NW Suite 2000, Washington, DC 20010, **Business Phone:** (202)723-3250.

### CHISHOLM, DR. JUNE E.

Clinical psychologist, educator. **Personal:** Born Apr 29, 1949, New York, NY; daughter of Wallace and Luretta Brawley. **Educ:** Syracuse Univ, BA, psychol, 1971; Univ Mass, MS, psychol, 1974, PhD, psychol, 1978. **Career:** New York Univ Med Ctr, intern psychol, 1975-77, Dept Psychiat, adj prof, 1984-; Manhattan, pvt pract, 1980; Harlem Hosp, sr psychologist, 1982-; Pace Univ, asst prof, 1986, prof, currently. **Orgs:** New York Asn Black Psychol, 1977-; Am Psychol Asn, 1979-; New york Soc Clin Psychologists, 1980-; Ny Psycholl Asn, 1980; EPA, 1988-. **Honors/Awds:** Teaching fellow, NY Univ Med Ctr, 1976-77; Dr. Hilda A. Davis Distinguished Educator Award, Nat Asn Univ Women, 2010; Certificate of Achievement and Appreciation, Univ State New York, Dept Educ, 2012. **Home Addr:** 260 W 72nd St Apt 1b, New York, NY 10023-2820, **Home Phone:** (212)873-3034. **Business Addr:** Professor, Pace University Dyson College of Arts and Sciences, 13th Fl 41 Park Row, New York, NY 10038, **Business Phone:** (212)346-1438.

### CHISHOLM, DR. REGINALD CONSTANTINE

Educator, physician, executive director. **Personal:** Born Oct 13, 1934; married Cecilin Coy. **Educ:** Howard Univ, BS, 1962, MD, 1966. **Career:** Freedmens Hosp, intern, 1966-67, residency internal med, 1967-70; Shaw Comm Health clin, internist, 1970-71; Howard Univ, chief med oncol; Nat Cancer Inst-Va, Oncol Serv, WA, fel clin assoc, 1971-73; Cancer Screening & Detection clin, chief, 1977; Howard Univ, assoc dir, 1977; Howard Univ Cancer Ctr, physician, currently. **Orgs:** Post-grad fel, 1971-73; DC Med Soc; Wash Soc Oncol; Nat Cancer Inst; Nat Med Asn. **Honors/Awds:** Recommended for Student Teaching Award, 1990; H.U Oncology Fellows Teaching Award, 2005. **Special Achievements:** Books: "Hypercalcitonemig Cancer of the Breast", Nat Med Asn, 1975. **Home Addr:** 1317 Canyon Rd, Silver Spring, MD 20904, **Home Phone:** (301)384-4206. **Business Addr:** Physician, Howard University Cancer Center, 2041 Georgia Ave NW Suite 5100, Washington, DC 20060, **Business Phone:** (202)806-7697.

### CHISHOLM, SAMUEL JACKSON

Advertising executive. **Personal:** Born May 15, 1942, Philadelphia, PA; son of Thomas J and May L Jackson; married Thelester McGinns; children: Heather & Jason. **Educ:** Va State Univ, Petersburg, VA, BS, bus admin & acct, 1965; NY Univ, grad studies. **Career:** Corn Prod Corp, New York, NY, claims adjuster, 1965-66; Phelps Dodge, NY, jr acct, 1967; Benton & Bowles, NY, media planner, 1967-69; Jack Tinker & Partner, NY, asst media dir, 1969; Continental Can Co, NY, adv dir, 1969-74, mkt exec; Malk Co & Uniworld Group Inc, NY, acct supv, 1974-80; Chisholm-Mingo Group Inc, NY, vpres & mgt supvr, 1980-84, sr vpres & dir clients, 1984-86, exec vpres & gen mgr, 1986-88, pres, 1988-90, chief exec officer & chmn, 1990-, Head, 2000-. **Orgs:** Advert Coun, Kappa Alpha Psi Fraternity; bd mem, Conn Comn Regional Planning Asn; Traffic Audit Bur; NY Bd Govs 4/a's; Worldwide Partners; Ad Hall Fame Coun Judges; Urban League 4/a's SW Conn; Am Advert Fedn Found; Madison Ave Initiative. **Honors/Awds:** National Business & Professional Men & Women, Dollars & Sense, 1990; Kappa Alpha Psi Community Award, 1990; Outstanding Minority Business Award, Nat Minority Bus Coun Inc, 2000; Entrepreneur of the Year, Ernst & Young, 2001. **Business Addr:** Chief Executive Officer, Chairman, The Chisholm-Mingo Group Inc, 228 E 45th St, New York, NY 10017-3303, **Business Phone:** (212)697-4515.

### CHISM, HAROLYN B.

Financial manager, government official. **Personal:** Born Jan 4, 1941, Columbia, SC; children: John Patrick & Sharon Elizabeth. **Educ:** Benedict Col, BS, 1967. **Career:** Gen Acct Off, clk typist, 1962-63; Fed Power Comn, clk typist, 1963-64; IRS, sec, 1964-65; US Dept Agr-Off Mgt Serv, budget analyst, 1967-72; US Dept Agr-Animal & Plant Health Insptn Serv & Food Safety & Qual Serv, supr budget analyst, 1972-78; US Dept Comm Minority Bus Develop Agency, budget officer, 1978. **Orgs:** Am Asn Budget & Prog Analyst, 1980; secy, Boy Scouts Am, T351, 1973-75; EEO counr, USDA APHIS & FSQS, 1974-78; bd mem, US Dept Agr Credit Union, 1977-78. **Honors/Awds:** Incentive Award, Fed Power Comn, 1964; cert of merit, USDA & APHIS, 1975; cert merit, USDA & FSQS, 1978. **Home Addr:** 512 Peacock Dr, Landover, MD 20785.

### CHISUM, DR. GLORIA TWINE

Psychologist. **Personal:** Born May 17, 1930, Muskogee, OK; daughter of Chauncey Depew (deceased) and Nadine (deceased); married Melvin Jackson. **Educ:** Howard Univ, BS, psychol, 1951, MS, psychol, 1953; Univ Pa, PhD, psychol, 1960. **Career:** Univ Pa, fel, 1958, lectr psychol, 1958-68; Naval Air Develop Ctr, res psychologist, 1960-65, Vision Lab, dir, head, 1965-80, Environ Physiol Res Team, head, 1980-90; Free Lib Philadelphia, emer, currently. **Orgs:** Trustee, Univ PA, 1974-2000, vice chair, 1990-2000; bd mem, Arthritis Found E PA, 1972-80; bd mem, World Affairs Coun Philadelphia, 1977-80; trustee, Philadelphia Saving Fund Soc, 1977-85; dir, Fischer & Porter Co, 1978-94; Philadelphia Orchestra Asn, 1979-85; bd mem, Meritor Fin Group, 1979-93, dir, Meritor Fin Group, 1985-92; chairwoman, Free Libr Philadelphia; chmn, bd trustee, Meritor Fin Group, 1990-93. **Honors/Awds:** Raymond F Longacre Award, Aerospace Med Asn, 1979; Distinguished Daughter Pennsylvania, 1983; Okla Hall of Fame, 1984; George Washington Carver Scientific Achievement Award; Ralph S Barnaby Award, Naval Civilian Admin Asn. **Special Achievements:** First African-American woman to join the Board of Trustees of the University of Pennsylvania; Published more than 70 scientific papers & reports on sensation & perception, vision and psycho-physics; holds two patents & is a frequent presenter at scientific & professional meetings. **Home Addr:** 4120 Apalogen Rd, Philadelphia, PA 19129-5504, **Home Phone:** (215)849-0714. **Business Addr:** Emeritus, Free Library of Philadelphia, 1901 Vine St, Philadelphia, PA 19103, **Business Phone:** (215)686-5322.

### CHIVERS, GWENDOLYN ANN

Pharmacist, educator. **Personal:** Born Jun 30, 1946, Sturgis, KY; daughter of Herman and Lillian McGee; married Richard. **Educ:** Kellogg Community Col, assoc degree, 1968; Univ Mich, BS, 1972; Century Univ, MBA, health care mgt, 1993. **Career:** Univ Mich, pharmacist, 1972-76, asst chief pharmacist, 1976-83, chief pharmacist & adj clin instr, 1983-, Catherine Mc Auley Hosp, pharmacist, 1983-85; Perry Drugs, pharmacist, 1988-89; INterium admin Lead PT, x-ray, lab, 2001-02. **Orgs:** Univ MI Health Serv, admin comn, 1994-; bd dir, Am Soc Pharm Law, 1994-96; State MI Health Occupations Coun, 1991-93; Univ MI Pharm Alumni Bd Gov, 1992-94; Am Pharmaceut Asn, 1985-; MI Pharmacists Asn, 1993-; Am Col Health Asn; bd dir, Am Soc Pharm Law. **Home Addr:** 5647 Dexter Ann Arbor Rd, Dexter, MI 48130-9504, **Home Phone:** (734)995-2043. **Business Addr:** Adjunct Clinical Instructor, Chief Pharmacist, University Michigan, 428 Church St, Ann Arbor, MI 48109-1065, **Business Phone:** (734)764-7312.

### CHONG, RAE DAWN

Actor. **Personal:** Born Feb 28, 1961, Edmonton, AB; daughter of Tommy and Maxine Sneed; married Owen Baylis, Jan 1, 1982?; children: Morgan; married C Thomas Howell, Jul 11, 1989, (divorced 1990); married Nathan Ulrich, Jan 1, 2011. **Career:** Cursed Part 3, dir, writer & producer, 2000; Films: Stony Island, 1978; Quest for Fire, 1982; Beat Street, 1984; The Corsican Brothers, 1984; Choose Me, 1984; Fear City, 1984; American Flyers, 1985; City Limits, 1985; The Color Purple, 1985; Commando, 1985; Running Out of Luck, 1986; Soul Man, 1986; The Squeeze, 1987; The Principal, 1987; Walking After Midnight, 1988; Far Out, Man!, 1990; Tales from the Dark side: the Movie, 1990; Denial: the Dark Side of Passion, 1991; Loon; Chaindance; In Exile; The Borrower, 1991; Amazon, 1992; When the Party's Over, 1992; Time Runner, 1993; Boca, 1994; Boulevard, 1994; Crying Freedom, 1994; Power of Attorney, 1995; The Break, 1995; Mask of Death, 1996; Starlight, 1996; Goodbye America, 1997; Highball, 1997; Small Time, 1998; Dangerous Attraction, 2000; The Visit, 2000; Constellation, 2005; Solitaire, 2006; Max Havoc: Ring of Fire, 2006; Cyrus, 2010; Jeff, Who Lives at Home, 2011; Shiver, 2012; Knock 'em Dead, 2014. TV movies: The Whiz Kid and the Mystery at Riverton, 1974; Top of the Hill, 1980; Badge of the Assassian, 1985; Curiosity Kills, 1990; Prison Stories: Women on the Inside, 1991; Broadway credits: Oh Kay!, 1991; Father & Son: Dangerous Relations, 1993; For Hope, 1996; Valentine's Day, 1998; Pegasus Vs. Chimera, 2012. TV series: "Disneyland", 1974; "Lou Grant", 1980; "St. Elsewhere", 1983-85; "Tall Tales and Legends", 1986; "The Hitchhiker", 1991; "Nitecap", 1992; "Melrose Place", 1992-93; "Lonesome Dove: The Series", 1994; "Crazy Love", 1995; "The Outer Limits", 1995; "Highlander", 1996; "Poltergeist: The Legacy", 1997; "Mysterious Ways", 2000-02; "Judging Amy", 2002; "Wild Card", 2003-04; Greasy Rider, 2006; "That's So Raven", 2007. **Orgs:** Screen Actors Guild; Am Fed TV Recreation Arts & Radio Artists. **Honors/Awds:** Genie Award, 1983; Clarence Muse Award, Black Filmmakers Hall of Fame, 1986. **Special Achievements:** Sex, Drugs & AIDS, educ documentary, narrator, book, contributor, 1987. **Business Addr:** Actor, Metropolitan Talent Agency, 4526 Wilshire Blvd, Los Angeles, CA 90010.

### CHRETIEN, GLADYS M.

Executive. **Personal:** Born TX; children: Joseph P III & Perry Duncan. **Educ:** Prairie View Col; Wiley Col. **Career:** Salesman, 1961; broker, 1962; Gladys M Chretien Realty Co, real estate broker, realtor & realtist; Consol Realty Bd, pres; Mult Listing, chmn; Wash Escrow Co, part owner & vpres; Wall St Enterprises & Wash Reconveyance Corp, part owner & stock holder; Century 21 Chretien Realty, owner. **Orgs:** Church Christ; La County Tax Appeals Bd Found. **Honors/Awds:** La County Tax Appeals Bd Founders Achievement Award, Consolidated Realty Bd, 1969-70; Top Ten Contributers, Consolidated Realty; many sales awards. **Home Addr:** 1144 S Citrus Ave, Los Angeles, CA 90019, **Home Phone:** (323)857-0450.

### CHRICHLOW, LIVINGSTON L.

Administrator, executive director. **Personal:** Born May 13, 1925, Brooklyn, NY; son of Alfred and Viola; married Mary Atkinson; children: Gordon H. **Educ:** City Univ NY, Queens Col, BA, 1975; Baruch Col, MPA, 1979. **Career:** Administrator (retired); Dept Defense, contract adminr, 1951-80; Lutheran Immigration & Refugee Serv, coordr, 1980-82; Lutheran Church Am, asst dir urban ministry, 1982-87. **Orgs:** Better Comt Civic Asn, 1955-57; vpres, Comn Sch Bd, 1965-70; chmn, Fin Comt New Hope Church, 1975-89; Sec Asn Black Lutherans, 1979-88; mem chmn, Minority Concerns Comt, NY Synod, 1979-87; dir, Proj Equality, NY, 1980-87; secy, Boy Scouts Am Alumni, 1980-; pres, Parkhurst Civic Asn, 1984-96; vol, Income Tax asst, 1989-2003; treas, New Hope Church, 1990-93, vpres, 1994-97; stewardship comt, Metro NY Synod, Lutheran Church Am, 1990-93. **Honors/Awds:** Distinguished discipleship, Metro NY Synod, Lutheran Church Am, 1970; Distinguished Citizen, Springfield Gardens Sr Citizens, 1980; Community Service Award, Elmont Youth Outreach, 1994; Black History Month Award, ECAP, 2005. **Home Addr:** 2232 Leighton Rd, Elmont, NY 11003-3515, **Home Phone:** (516)352-6074.

### CHRISS, HENRY THOMAS

Consultant, executive. **Personal:** Born Nov 24, 1964, Cleveland, OH; son of Frank James and Mary Glynn; married Sandra Renee; children: Henry II, Jasmine & Tiffany. **Educ:** Bowling Green State Univ, BA, bus admin & mgt, 1985; Akron Univ, polymer sci, 1986; Kent State Univ, bus admin, 1990; Colo Tech Univ, BSBA, int bus, 2014-; Case Western Res Univ, Weatherhead Sch Mgt, bus admin & mgt. **Career:** Polychem Dispersions, prod & lab mgr, 1985-87; Duramax Johnson Rubber, prod supvr, 1987-88, prod technician, 1988-89, qual control chem lab supvr, 1989-91; NIKE Inc, chem R&D lab mgr, 1991-93, environ affairs dir, 1993-94, dir strategic acct logistics, 1994-96, gen mgr footwear distrib, 1997-2000; Aramark, vpres supply chain mgt, 2000-03; Clariante Growth Solutions Inc, chief exec officer, pres & founder, 2003-14; Henry Thomas Designs LLC DBA Old Skool Cycle Werks, chief exec officer & partner, 2005-. **Orgs:** Am Chem Soc, 1991-; Am Black Sporting Goods Prof, 1992-. **Honors/Awds:** State Qualifier Wrestling, Ohio High Sch Athletic Asn, 1983; 2nd Team All Nation, US Semi-Pro Football League, 1987. **Special Achievements:** Congressional nomination to West Point, 1982; US Patent, Recycling Polymer Technology, 1994. **Home Addr:** 5193 NW 171st Pl, Portland, OR 97229, **Home Phone:** (503)531-9020. **Business Addr:** President, Founder, Clariante Growth Solutions Inc, 1913 E Bearss Ave Suite 2061, Tampa, FL 33613, **Business Phone:** (813)789-1717.

### CHRISTBURG, SHEYANN WEBB

School administrator, speaker of the house of representatives (U.S. federal government), executive. **Personal:** Born Feb 17, 1956, Selma, AL; daughter of John Webb and Betty; married Andre. **Educ:** Tuskegee Inst, BS, social work, 1979; Ala State Univ. **Career:** Ala State Univ, Stud Activ Ctr, coordr; KEEP Prod Youth Develop Prog, dir, owner & pres, founder, currently; Selma, Lord, Selma: Girlhood Memories of the Civil Rights Days, co-auth; Sheyann Webb Group, chief exec officer, currently; Sheyann Webb Found, chief exec office, currently. **Orgs:** Chair, Martin Luther King B'Day Celebration, 1993-; bd mem, State SCLC, 1996-; chair, Lyceum Comt, 1997-98; advisor, Miss Ala State Univcoordr, ASU Trust Fund. **Home Addr:** 2847 Jan Dr, Montgomery, AL 36116, **Home Phone:** (334)288-2188. **Business Addr:** Chief Executive Officer, Sheyann Webb Group, 600 S Ct St, Montgomery, AL 36104, **Business Phone:** (334)221-6787.

### CHRISTIAN, DR. CORA LEETHEL

Physician. **Personal:** Born Sep 11, 1947, St. Thomas; daughter of Ruth Brown and Alphonso; married Simon B Jones Hendrikson; children: Marcus Benjamin & Nesha Rosita. **Educ:** Marquette Univ, BS, 1967; Jefferson Med Col, MD, 1971; Johns Hopkins Univ, MPH, 1975. **Career:** John Hay Whitney Found, John Hay Whitney Fel, 1969; Howard Univ Family Pract, admin chief resident, 1973-74, intern, 1974-75; Nat Urban Coalition Found, nat urban coalition fel, 1974; Ingeborg Nesbitt Clin Dept Health, physician in-chg, 1975-77; VI Med Inst, founder, 1977, exec dir, 1977-94, med dir, 1994-; Col Vi, med coordr, 1977-78; Vi Chap, actg dir, 1978-; VI Dept Health, asst comnr, 1978-81, asst comnr ambulatory care serv, 1981-87; Vi Med Inst Prof Serv Rev Orgn (PSRO) Inc, exec dir, med dir, 1981-; asst comnr prev health prom & protection, 1987-92; Thomas Jeffer Univ, lect, 1990-; Hovensa, cheif med consult, med dir, 1992-; Pan Am Health Orgn (PAHO), consult; HOPE, consult; Hess Oil VI Corp, med dir, currently. **Orgs:** Deleg, Am Pub Health Asn; pres, secy, treas, VI Med Soc, 1976-77, 1980-81 & 1983-84; chmn, PSRO Comt, 1977-; vpres, Charles Harwood Memorial Hosp Med Staff, 1977-79; chmn, Midwinter Clin Conf, 1978; proj dir, Frederiksted Health Ctr, 1978-80; pres, Charles Harwood Memorial Hosp & Ingeborg Clin, 1978-79; League Women Voters VI, 1979; bd mem, Interfaith Coalition St Croix; dir, Family Planning VI Dept Health, 1979-; chief staff, actg dir, MCH, 1982-; pres, Am Acad Family Physicians Comn Gov & legis affairs, 1978-; vpres, Vi Med Soc, 1984; pres, VI Med Soc, 1985-; vice territory chief, Caribbean Territory Soka Gakkau Int; exec secy & treas, VI Med Soc, 1997-2002; exec secy & treas, VI Med Soc, 1997-2002; VIMS, 1997; VI Olympic Comt physician, 1998-; pres, Caribbean Studies Asn, 2001; pres, VI Chap; AARP Nat Bd, 2004; AMA; Nat Med Asn; chair, Univ VI Found; Paul Harris Fel Rotary Int; chmn, Judiciary Comt Dept Family Pract. **Honors/Awds:** Edward Wilmot Blyden Scholarship in 1960; Wilmont Blyden Scholarship VI, 1963; Outstanding Woman, AKA, 1997; Best Doctors of America, 1999; Trail-Blazer Award, Women's Bus Ctr St Croix, 2000; Physician Award, Community Serv; Physician of the Year, VI Med Soc, 2003. **Special Achievements:** First Native female of the U.S. Virgin Islands to become a medical doctor; One of the primary spokespersons on health-related issues for the AARP Virgin Islands Speakers Bureau. **Home Addr:** 40 Eg La Grange Frederiksted, PO Box 1338, St Croix, VI 00841-1338, **Home Phone:** (340)772-3665. **Business Addr:** Medical Director, Virgin Islands Medical Institute Incorporation, 1AD Diamond Ruby Sunny Isle, Christiansted00823-5989, **Business Phone:** (340)712-2400.

### CHRISTIAN, DOLLY LEWIS

Executive, manager, vice president (organization). **Personal:** Born New York, NY; daughter of Daniel and Adeline Walton. **Educ:** Manhattan Community Col. **Career:** IBM Corp, prog mgr affirmative action prog; The Sperry & Hutchison Co, personnel mgr, supvr, spec proj & rec, employ specialist, dir civic affairs, currently. **Orgs:** Chmn, bd NY Urban League, 1977-85; Panel Arbitrators Am Arbit Asn, 1978; comnr, New York, Comn Human Rights, 1987-90; bd mem, Coalition 100 Black Women, 1979; vpres, Edges Group Inc; Coun Concerned Black Exec; Nat Urban Affairs Coun Off; Mgt Assistance Comm Greater NY Fund. **Business Addr:** Civic Affairs Director, Sperry & Hutchinson Co, 330 Madison Ave, New York, NY 10017, **Business Phone:** (212)983-7962.

### CHRISTIAN, ERIC OLIVER, JR.

Consultant. **Personal:** Born Jan 1, 1951, Tortola; son of Eric O Sr and Ethel Trotman Thomas; married Shelia; children: Eric O III & Cosine. **Educ:** Tenn State Univ, BSed, 1973. **Career:** Gov Virgin Islands, teacher, 1973-85, consult, 1990-; Am Bankers Life, mgr, 1975-89; Black Bus Coun, pres, 1988-; Gov St Kitts, West Indies, consult, 1989-90; Caribbean Small Bus Asn, consult, 1989-. **Orgs:** Exec coun, Am Fed Teachers, 1973-85; Tony Browns Buy Freedom Movement, 1989-; exec mem, Nat Asn Black Chambers; Status CMS, VI, 1989-; Black Meeting Planners, 1990-. **Honors/Awds:** Manager of the Year, Am Bankers Life, 1990; Musician & Choral DRR of the Year, AT&T, 1991. **Home Addr:** 39 L Lindberg Bay, St Thomas00801, **Home Phone:** (809)776-4433. **Business Addr:** President, Black Business Chamber of Commerce, PO Box 8033, St. Thomas00801, **Business Phone:** (809)774-8784.

### CHRISTIAN, JOHN L.

President (organization), executive. **Personal:** Born Jan 27, 1940, Winton, NC; son of John Albert and Addie Beatrice Weaver; married Lesley Evans; children: Andrea Lenore & John A II. **Educ:** Hampton Univ, Hampton, Va, BS, 1961; Wharton Sch, Philadelphia, Pa, cert, 1978; Harvard Sch Pub Health, Boston, MA, cert, 1988. **Career:** Leasco Systs & Res Corp, Bethesda, Md, div mgr, 1964-69; Polaroid Corp, Cambridge, MA, div mgr, 1969-74; Trustees of Health & Hosps, Boston, MA, vpres, 1974-92; Enterprise Group Ltd, exec vpres, treas, pres, owner & cheif exec officer, currently. **Orgs:** Bd chmn, Crispus Attucks C's Ctr, 1972-; pres, Nat Guardsmen Inc, 1978-79; allocations rev comt, United Way Mass Bay, 1980-91; pres, Sigma Pi Phi-Beta Beta, 1981-82; Pres, Int Soc Res Adminr, 1988-89; bd, Brookline Community Fund, 1988-; Urban League Eastern Mass. **Honors/Awds:** Outstanding Citizen, Nat Asn Advan Colored People, 1982; Hartford-Nicholson Service Award, Soc Res Adminr, 1985. **Home Addr:** 129 St Paul St, Brookline, MA 02446-5247, **Home Phone:** (617)232-9790. **Business Addr:** Owner, President, Enterprise Group Ltd, PO Box 925, Brookline, MA 02446-0007, **Business Phone:** (617)232-9790.

### CHRISTIAN, HON. MARY T.

State government official, politician, educator. **Personal:** Born Jul 9, 1924, Hampton, VA; married Wilbur B; children: 3. **Educ:** Hampton Inst, BS, 1955; Columbia Univ, MA, speech & drama, 1960; Mich State Univ, PhD, 1967. **Career:** State govt off (retired), politician, educr; Aberdeen Elem Sch, teacher, 1955-60; Mich State Univ, 1966; Hampton Univ, Sch Educ, prof emer, dean; Va House Reps, state rep, 1986-03. **Orgs:** First Baptist Church; bd mem, Peninsula Asn Sickle Cell Anemia; Am Asn Univ Women; Nat Asn Advan Colored People; chmn, Groups Representing Org United Progress; Hampton Crusade Voters; Coalition 100 Black Women; Am Lung Asn; adv bd mem, Sovran Bank; Jr League Hampton Rds; VA Adv Bd Gifted Educ; chair, Va Legis Black Caucus; Hon bd mem, Nat Patient Advocate Found; Gen Assembly; Va House Representatives; ardent supporter, healthcare legis; House Delegates; Women's Auxiliary; Chair, Const Adv Comt; Gen Govt, Natural Resources, Compensation & Retirement; chair, Conserv & Natural Resources Subcomt, Educ Subcomt, Labor & Com Subcomt; Sunrise Caucus; Va Interagency Coord Coun; State Adv Bd Gifted Educ; Inst Govt, Univ Va; Comn Future Higher Educ; pres, Coalition Community Pride & Progress; life mem, Nat Asn Advan Colored People; N Phoebus Adv Bd; Peninsula Asn Sickle Cell Anemia; bd dir, Sarah Bonwell Hudgins Found; Exec Bd, Y. H. Thomas Community Ctr; bd dir; Patient Advocate Found; mem, Gov's Comn Environ Stewardship; Hampton Pub Sch Bd; mem, bd trustee, Cornell Univ; mem, bd dir, Am Asn Cols Teacher Educ; mem, Publ & Ed Adv Bd; mem, bd dir, Peninsula Nations Bank. **Home Addr:** 1104 W Ave, Hampton, VA 23669-2729, **Home Phone:** (757)723-2673.

### CHRISTIAN, SPENCER

Meteorologist, television show host, writer. **Personal:** Born Jul 23, 1947, Newport News, VA; son of Spencer and Lucy Greene; married Diane Chambers; children: Jason & Jessica. **Educ:** Hampton Univ, Hampton, VA, BA, Eng, 1970. **Career:** Stony Brook Prep Sch, Long Island, teacher, 1970; WWBT-TV, Richmond, Va, news reporter, 1971, weatherman, 1972-75; WBAL-TV, Baltimore, weatherman, 1975-77; WABC-TV, weatherman, 1977-86; Good Morning Am, weatherman, co-host & interviewer, 1986-98; BET, "Triple Threat", Game Show, host, 1992-93; HGTV, Spencer Christian's Wine Cellar, host, 1995-99; TV Food Network, staff; ABC7 News team, KGO-TV, weather forecaster, 1999-; ABC7's daily, View from Bay, co-host, 2006-10. **Orgs:** March Dimes; Spec Olympics; Cystic Fibrosis Found; Am Cancer Soc; Big Bros; Boy Scouts & Girl Scouts Am; Tomorrow's C; United Negro Col Fund; Up With People; Daytop Village; Make-A-Wish Found; Iota Phi Theta Fraternity Inc. **Honors/Awds:** Better Life Award; Emmy Award; Whitney M Young Jr Service Award, Greater New York Coun, Boy Scouts Am, 1990; Honorary Chairman, NJ Chap, March Dimes, 1979; Virginia Communications Hall of Fame, 1993; Virginian of the Year, Va Press Asn, 1993. **Special Achievements:** Author of Spencer Christian's Weather Book, Spencer Christian's Geography Book, & Electing Our Government; Spencer Christian's World of Wonders." The first four books are titled: "Can It Really Rain Frogs?," "Shake, Rattle, & Roll," "What Makes the Grand Canyon Grand?," & "Is There a Dinosaur in Your Backyard?"; WABC, serving first as weatherman. **Business Addr:** Weather Forecaster, ABC7/KGO-TV/DT, 900 Front St, San Francisco, CA 94111-1450, **Business Phone:** (415)954-7777.

### CHRISTIAN, WILLIAM LEONARD

Actor. **Personal:** Born Sep 30, 1955, Washington, DC; son of William L and Evelyn M Shaw; married Gail; children: 1. **Educ:** Cath Univ, AME, BA, 1976; Am Univ, MA, 1980. **Career:** Films: The January Man, 1989; Love & Orgasms, 2003; Nine Lives, 2004; Contradictions of the Heart, Three Takes, 2009; The Au Pairs, 2010; TV Series: Another World, 1964; "The Cosby Show", 1985; Tattingers, 1988; Another World, 1990; All My Children, 1990-2005; "Law & Order", 1997-2001; Spin City", 1999; "Malcolm in the Middle", "Without a Trace", 2003; ER, Moonlight, "Prison Break", "Hannah Montana", "Desperate Housewives", 2008; "Monk", 2009; "I'm in the Band", 2009. **Honors/Awds:** Nominee, Daytime Emmy Award for Best Supporting Actor in Drama "All My Children" (1970), 1991. **Home Addr:** 1499 La Loma Rd, Pasadena, CA 91105-2194. **Business Addr:** Actor, c/o William Morris Agency, 151 El Camino Dr, Beverly Hills, CA 90212, **Business Phone:** (310)859-4000.

### CHRISTIAN-CHRISTENSEN, DONNA-MARIE

Politician. **Personal:** Born Sep 19, 1945, Teaneck, NJ; daughter of Almeric Leander (deceased) and Virginia Sterling; married Chris; children: Rabiah Layla Green, Karida Yasmeen Green, Bryan, David, Lisa & Esther. **Educ:** St Mary's Col, Notre Dame, IN, BA, 1966; George Washington Univ, Wash, DC, MD, 1970. **Career:** Family Physician; Vi Dept Health, St Croix, Vi, var positions, 1975-80; F'sted Health Ctr, St Croix, Vi, med dir, 1980-85; Dir Mch & Family Planning, St Croix, Vi, med dir, 1985-87; St Croix Hosp, St Croix, Vi, med dir, 1987-88; Vi Dept Health, St Croix, Vi, asst comnr, 1988-94, comr, 1994-95; Television journalist, 1992-96; US House Reps, congresswoman, 1997-2015. **Orgs:** Dem Nat Women Comt, 1984-; Dem Territorial Comt, 1980-; Vi Bd Educ, 1984-86; pres, Vi Med Soc, 1990-91; Christiansted chair, Friedenstal Moravian Church, 1988-; chair, Cong Black Caucus Health Brain trust; Nat Med Asn; Caribbean Studies Asn; Vi Med Soc; Caribbean Youth Orgn; hon bd advisors, Nat Stud Leadership Conf.

### CHRISTIE, ANGELLA

Saxophonist, gospel musician. **Personal:** Born Los Angeles, CA; daughter of Girvin and Catherine. **Educ:** Houston Baptist Univ, BSW, BA, music, 1984. **Career:** Saxophonist; Angella Christie Sound Ministries, founder & chief exec officer, 1985-; Sisters In The Spirit Tour, artist, 2000; Albums: Because He Lives, 1985; Rejoice, 1986; It Is Well, 1987; Eternity, 1996; Hymn & I, 1998; Draw the Line, 2003; The Breathe of Life, composer & co-producer, 2008. **Orgs:** Dir, Angella Christie Found. **Honors/Awds:** Award of Excellence, Gospel Music Workshop Am, 1999; Instrumental Gospel of the Year, Nat Black Progammers Coalition, 1999; Stellar Award, Instrumental CD of the Year-The Breath of Life, 2009. **Special Achievements:** Stellar Award Nominee, 1997, 1999, 2006; performed for former US President Bill Clinton, Bishop T D Jakes's Woman Thou Art Loosed Conference, NBAAll-Star Weekend & National Association of Black Journalists. **Business Addr:** Founder, Chief Executive Officer, Angella Christie Sound Ministries, PO Box 361888, Decatur, GA 30036, **Business Phone:** (770)498-0404.

### CHRISTIE, DOUGLAS DALE

Basketball player. **Personal:** Born May 9, 1970, Seattle, WA; son of John Malone and Norma; married Jackie; children: Douglas Jr & Chantel. **Educ:** Pepperdine Univ, BA, sociol, 1992. **Career:** Basketball player (retired); Seattle Supersonics, guard-forward, 1992-93; Los Angeles Lakers, shooting guard, 1993-94; New York Knicks, shooting guard, 1994-96; Toronto Raptors, small forward, 1996, shooting guard, 1996-2000; Sacramento Kings, shooting guard, 2000-05; Orlando Magic, shooting guard, 2005; Dallas Mavericks, shooting guard, 2005-06; Los Angeles Clippers, shooting guard, 2006-07. **Orgs:** Toronto community. **Honors/Awds:** Player of the Year, West Coast Conference, 1991, 1992; Tournament Most Valuable Player, West Coast Conference, 1992; Toronto Raptors all-time Leader in Steals. **Special Achievements:** NBA Draft, First round pick, 1992.

### CHRISTIE, JAMES ALBERT, JR.

Veterinarian, commissioner, government official. **Personal:** Born Nov 2, 1939, Stuart, FL; son of James Sr and Minnie; married Helen L; children: Gary, Donald, Tracy, Lanier & James A III. **Educ:** Stuart Training Sch. **Career:** Stuart Animal Hosp, sr head tech, 1977; City Stuart, mayor, 1986, 1992; Stuart City Comn, Stuart Community Redevelop Agency, bd mem, city comnr, currently. **Orgs:** Fla Black Caucus Asn Elected Off, 1984-94; second vpres, Martin County Black Heritage Asn, 1985; Martin County Dem Asn; Martin County Nat Asn Advan Colored People; Fla League Cities; pres, Concerned Citizens E Stuart/Martin County Inc, 2001. **Honors/Awds:** Martin County Black Image Award; Martin County Politician of the Year; Achievement Award, E Stuart Civil Asn. **Home Addr:** 915 SE Hall St, Stuart, FL 34994-5613, **Home Phone:** (772)287-6371. **Business Addr:** City Commissioner, City of Stuart, 121 SW Flagler Ave, Stuart, FL 34994, **Business Phone:** (772)288-5312.

### CHRISTOPHE, CLEVELAND A.

Capitalist or financier. **Personal:** Born Jan 1, 1946?, Savannah, GA; son of Cleveland and Lucy; married Cheryl S; children: Jean-Paul & Kimberly D. **Educ:** Howard Univ, BA, 1966; Univ Mich, Grad Sch Bus, MBA, 1967. **Career:** First Nat City Bank, securities analyst, 1967-69, venture capital analyst, 1971-72, investment analyst team head, 1972-75, Paris, county opers head, 1975-79, San Francisco, corp banking team head, 1980-83, Jamaica, country head, 1983-85, Columbia, country head, 1985-87; Kenton Corp, asst to chmn, 1969; Soul Stop Inc, pres, chief exec off, chmn, 1970; TLC Group, sr vpres, 1987-88; Christophe Corp, pres, 1988-89; Equico Capital Corp, vpres, 1990-92; TSG Ventures, prin, 1992-95; TSG Capital Group, LLC, managing partner, 1994-08; US&S, Inc, pres, 2009-; Builders FirstSource, Inc, dir, currently. **Orgs:** Bd dir, Nat Conf Comm & Justice; RF Toigo Found; Stamford Health Syst SACIA; Nat Asn Investment Co. **Honors/Awds:** Chartered Financial Analyst, Inst Chartered Financial Analysts, 1975; Walter H Wheeler Jr Leadership Award, 2004. **Special Achievements:** Author of Competition in Financial Services, Citicorp, 1973; Only Black among the Schools 800 MBA students; First National City Banks (FNCB) youngest officers ever. **Home Addr:** 543 Wire Mill Rd, Stamford, CT 06903, **Home Phone:** (203)595-9766. **Business Addr:** President, US&S Inc, 50 Grand Ave, Greenville, SC 29607, **Business Phone:** (864)233-8035.

### CHRISTOPHER, JOHN A.

Microbiologist, immunologist, college teacher. **Personal:** Born Aug 19, 1941, Shreveport, LA. **Educ:** Tex State Univ, attended 1963; Bishop Col, BS, 1964; Baylor Univ, MS, 1967; Iowa State Univ, PhD, 1971. **Career:** Univ Tex S western Med Ctr, res tech, 1964-65; Inst Baylor Univ, grad res fel, 1965-67; Iowa State Univ, grad res/teaching asst, 1967-71; Univ Minn Med Sch, post doctoral res fel, 1971-73; Southern Univ, prof dept chem. **Orgs:** AAAS; Soc Sigma Xi; S Cent Br Am Soc Microbiol; YWCA; Nat Asn Advan Colored People; Community Coun Inc; Nat Fund March Dimes. **Home Addr:** 3417 Bellaire Ave, Shreveport, LA 71109-1701, **Home Phone:** (318)631-4774. **Business Addr:** Professor, Southern University, 3050 Martin Luther King Jr Dr, Shreveport, LA 71107, **Business Phone:** (318)670-6000.

### CHURCHWELL, ANDRE L.

Dean (education), administrator, physician. **Personal:** married Dorothea Henderson; children: Crystal A & Andre L Jr. **Educ:** Vanderbilt Univ Sch Engineering, BA, 1975; Harvard Med Sch, MD, 1979. **Career:** Emory Univ Sch Med & affiliated hosps, intern, resident & cardiol fel, 1979-86; Emory Univ Sch Med, asst prof & instr, 1986-91; Vanderbilt Univ Sch Med, adjust instr, 1991-94, asst clin prof med, 1994-2006, asst prof med, 2006-08, assoc prof med, 2008-13; assoc dean diversity grad med educ & fac affairs, 2007-14, prof med, prof radiol & radiol sci, prof biomed engineering, 2013-, sr assoc dean diversity affairs, 2014-; Cardiovasc Engineering & Technol: A J Biomed Engineering Soc, ed bd mem, 2011-; Vanderbilt Univ Med Ctr, chief diversity officer, 2016-. **Orgs:** Cheekwood Bot Gardens & Mus Art Bd Trustees, 2011-; Cumberland Univ Bd Trustees, 2015-. **Honors/Awds:** Biomedical Engineering Student Program Award, 1975; Robert Wood Johnson Foundation Minority Medical Faculty Development Award, 1986; J. Willis Hurst Award, 1991; Emory University School of Medicine Resident Distinguished Achievement Award, 2004; Walter R. Murray, Jr., Distinguished Alumnus, Association of Vanderbilt Black Alumni, 2005; Distinguished Alumnus Award, Vanderbilt University School of Engineering, 2010; Trumpet Award for Medicine, 2011; Distinguished Faculty Award, Vanderbilt University Organization of Black Graduate and Professional Students, 2012, 2013; named one of the Top 15 Most Influential African-American Health Educators, Black Health Magazine. **Special Achievements:** First African American chief medical resident at Grady Memorial Hospital, Atlanta, GA, 1984-85; co-founder and first president, The Hurst-Logue-Wenger Cardiovascular Fellows Society of Emory University School of Medicine, 2013. **Business Addr:** Vanderbilt University Office for Diversity Affairs, 319 Light Hall, Nashville, TN 37232-0190, **Business Phone:** (615)322-7498.

### CHURCHWELL, DR. CAESAR ALFRED

Dentist. **Personal:** Born Nov 26, 1932, Newton, GA; married Ruth; children: Caesar Jr, Gabrielle, Eric & Jonathan. **Educ:** Mt Union Col, BS, 1956; Howard Univ Col Dent, DDS, 1967. **Career:** Pvt pract dentist, currently. **Orgs:** Nat Advan Asn Colored People; personnel comn mem, bd dir, Nat Advan Asn Colored People Urban League, 1971-72; adv bd, Fulcrum Saving & Loan, 1973; Black Leadership Forum; Men Tomorrow; Black Unity Coun; pres, W Twin Peaks Lions Club, 1973; activ chmn, BSA, 1974; vpres, San Francisco Black Chamber Com; pres, San Francisco Black Leadership Forum; adv bd, SE Community Col; SF Dent Forum; Acad Gen Dent; No Chap Med; Dent & Pharm Asn; pres, NCNDA, 1974; ADA; SFDS; CDS; Western Peridontal Soc; SF Dent Found, 1975; Bicentennial Comn So SF, 1975-76; Co San Mateo, 1975-76; vpres, San Francisco African Am Chamber Com. **Home Addr:** 2309 Wexford Ave, South San Francisco, CA 94080-5514, **Home Phone:** (650)588-1143. **Business Addr:** Dentist, Private Practice, 933 Geneva Ave, San Francisco, CA 94112, **Business Phone:** (415)586-3696.

### CHURCHWELL, CHARLES DARRETT

School administrator, educator. **Personal:** Born Nov 7, 1926, Dunnellon, FL; son of John Dozier and Lee Annah De Laughter; married Yvonne Ransom; children: Linda & Cynthia. **Educ:** Morehouse Col, BS, 1952; Atlanta Univ, MS, 1953; Univ, Ill, PhD, libr sci, 1966; City Col; Hunter Col; NY Univ, attended 1961. **Career:** Educator, school administrator (retired); Prairie View A & M Col, instr, 1954-57; Univ Houston, assoc dir libr, 1966; Miami Univ, prof, dir libr, 1970-72, prof, assoc provost acad serv, 1972-74; Univ Mich, vis lectr, 1972, 1976; Brown Univ, libr, 1974-78; Wash Univ, dean libr serv, 1978-87; Wayne State Univ, vis prof, libr sci, 1987, prof, 1988-90; Clark Atlanta Univ, Sch Libr & Info Studies, dean, 1990-99, interim provost, vpres acad affairs, 1990-91; Atlanta Univ Ctr, Robert W Woodruff Libr, dir, 1990-99; New York Pub Libr, ref librn; Univ Ill, librn. **Orgs:** Life mem, Am Libr Asn, 1968-; life mem, Nat Asn Advan Colored People; Ga Libr Asn; vice chmn, bd dir, Coun Libr Resources; Southern Asn Cols & Univs. **Honors/Awds:** Acad Admin Fel, Am Coun Educ, 1971-72; Outstanding Alumni Award, Atlanta Univ, Sch Libr & Info Studies, 1986. **Special Achievements:** First African American male to earn a Ph.D. from the Univ of Illinois; First African American to work for the university. **Home Addr:** 5621 Waterman Blvd Suite 1, St Louis, MO 63112.

### CICCOLO, ANGELA
Executive, lawyer. **Personal:** Born Indianapolis, IN; married Christopher; children: Christopher, Nicholas & Danielle. **Educ:** Georgetown Univ, BS, foreign serv, 1983, Law Ctr, JD, 1992. **Career:** Ashcraft & Gerel, atty; Spec Olympics, chief legal officer & secy, 2010-. **Orgs:** Interim Gen Coun & Secy, Nat Asn Advan Colored People, 2008-10; bd governors, DC Trial Lawyers Asn; DC Bar, 1992-; MD Bar; United States Supreme Court Bar; dir bd, Am Judicature Soc. **Business Addr:** Chief Legal Officer, Secretary, Special Olympics North America, 3712 Benson Dr Suite 102, Raleigh, NC 27609, **Business Phone:** (919)785-0699.

### CISSOKO, DR. ALIOUNE BADARA
School administrator, psychotherapist, artist. **Personal:** Born Jun 15, 1952, Kolda Casamance; son of Fatoumata Mara and Moussa Balla; married Sonia H; children: Moussa Balla, Fatoumata & Djibril Kalif. **Educ:** Univ Dakar Inst Arts, BA, 1975; RI Sch Design, MFA, 1979; Univ RI, cert arts mgt, 1982; Northeastern Univ, MA, 1984, PhD; cert case mgr. **Career:** Int House RI, prog asst, 1978-80; Soc Cons, arts consult, 1979-; Am Sociol Asn, mem, 1983-; Am Anthrop Asn, mem, 1983-; Northern RI Community Ment Health Ctr Psychiat Counr Crisis Beds, psycholsocial counr & therapist; Southeastern MA Univ, pub rel prof arts, 1985-; Brown Univ, Dept Police & Security, mgr spec servs, 1993, counr, mem bd dir, dir training, currently. **Orgs:** Fine artist Performing Arts RI, 1977-; RI Black Heritage Soc, 1979-; Int House RI, 1979-; folk artist artist educ RI State Coun Arts, 1980-; listed Talent Bank NEA Wash DC, 1983-; Nat Coun Creative Educ Ther; co-founder, Black Artists RI. **Honors/Awds:** Founder, Douguoto Ngnagnya Af Drums & Dance Ensemble, 1982-; Citation, State RI & Providence Plantations, 1984; RI State Council Award, Creative Educ Therapy. **Home Addr:** 108 Miller Ave, Providence, RI 02905, **Home Phone:** (401)781-7884. **Business Addr:** Counselor & Director of Training, Member Board of Director, Brown University Police Department, 54 Doyle Ave, Providence, RI 02906-0227, **Business Phone:** (401)863-2542.

### CLACK, FLOYD
State government official, educator. **Personal:** Born Dec 21, 1940, Houston, TX; married Brenda J Jones; children: Michael & Mia. **Educ:** Tex Southern Univ, BS, 1965, Sch Law, 1966; Eastern Mich Univ, MA, 1972, educ leadership, 1985. **Career:** Old Fisher Body Plant, factory worker; Houston Pub Sch, teacher; Fed Govt Job Corps Ctr, teacher, 1967-68; Flint Community Sch Syst, teacher, 1968-82, guid counr; Flint City Coun, mem, 1979-82; Mich House Reps, state rep, 1982-96; Genesee County Bd Commrs Dist2, councilman, 1996-2004; Genesee Co Metrop Planning Comn, bd comnr, comnr, 1997; Eastern Mich Univ, Flint Community Sch, bd regents, 2005-, 2007-. **Orgs:** Kappa Alpha Psi Fraternity; Nat Conf State Legiss; Nat Conf Black Legis; Mich Alternative Educ Asn; Nat Alternative Educ Asn; Urban League Flint; bd dir, Genesee Co Boy Scouts Am; Coun State Govts; Acad Criminal Justice; Am Corrections Asn; Mich Corrections Asn; Flint Inner City Lions Club; Ky Colonels; Genesee Co Community Action Agency; Metrop Chamber Com; Mich Polit Hist Soc; Nat Dem Party; Dem Leadership Conf; Dem Black Caucus; Mich State Alumni Asn; Eastern Mich Alumni Asn; Buckham Alley Theater; Nat Civic League; Am Legis Exchange Coun; CARE Adv Bd; founder, Youth Leadership Inst Flint; founder, Floyd Clack Thanks giving Dinner Citizens, 1983; Floyd Clack Comt Proj; charter mem, Flint Inner City Lions Club; pres, Flint Nat Asn Advan Colored People; Genesee County Bd Commrs Dist2; vice chair, Stud Affairs comt; vice chair, Athletic Affairs comt; secy, Eagle Admin Serv Bd. **Home Addr:** 3120 Helber St, Flint, MI 48504, **Home Phone:** (810)232-7007. **Business Addr:** Board of Regents, Eastern Mich University, 900 Oakwood St, Ypsilanti, MI 48197, **Business Phone:** (734)487-1849.

### CLAIBORNE, CHRIS (CHRISTOPHER ASHONE CLAIBORNE)
Football player, football coach. **Personal:** Born Jul 26, 1978, San Diego, CA. **Educ:** Univ Southern Calif, pub policy & mgt, 1999. **Career:** Football player (retired), coach; Detroit Lions, linebacker, 1999-2000, mid linebacker, 2001-02, right outside linebacker, 2001; Minn Vikings, linebacker, 2003-04; St Louis Rams, mid linebacker, 2005-06; New York Giants, 2006; Jacksonville Jaguars, 2007; Frat boyz, mentor & coach, 2012-; Oaks Christian High Sch, coach, 2013-. **Honors/Awds:** Nat Defensive Player of the Year, The Sports Network & Football News; Pac - 10 Defensive Player of the Year; Glenn Davis Award, 1995; Dick Butkus Award, 1998; Lions Mel Farr Rookie of the Year, 1999; Lions Lem Barney Devensive Most Valuable Player, 2002. **Business Addr:** Coach, Oaks Christian School, 31749 La Tienda Rd, Westlake Village, CA 91362, **Business Phone:** (818)575-9900.

### CLAIBORNE, LORETTA
Athlete, public speaker. **Personal:** Born Jan 1, 1953, York, PA; daughter of Rita (deceased). **Educ:** Quinnipiac Univ, PhD, 1995; Villanova Univ, PhD, 2003. **Career:** Spec Olympics athlete. **Orgs:** Bd dir, Pa Spec Olympics, 1982; Spec Olympics Int, 1991; Proj GOLD Comm, US Olympics, 1996; Walt Disney co. **Home Addr:** 440 E King St Apt 182, York, PA 17403, **Home Phone:** (877)885-3091.

### CLANCY, SAM, JR.
Basketball player. **Personal:** Born May 4, 1980, Pittsburgh, PA; son of Sam Sr. **Educ:** Univ Southern Calif, sociol, 2002. **Career:** Philadelphia 76ers, forward, beginning, 2002; Fayetteville Patriots, 2003; Yakima Sun Kings, 2003-04; Cocodrilos de Caracas, 2004; Forum Filatelico Valladolid Spain, Continental Basketball Asn, basketball player; Idaho Stampede, Continental Basketball Asn, 2004-05; Portland Trail Blazers, 2005; Mankato Mallards, 2005; Valladolid, 2005; UNICS Kazan, 2006; Vive Menorca, Span pro basketball league, 2006; Menorca Basquet, 2006-07; Incheon ET L & Black Slamer, 2007; Venezuelan LBP; Le Mans Sarthe Basket, 2007-08; Krasnie Krilya Samara, Russia, 2007-08; Ural Great Perm; CSK VVS Samara, 2008-09; Bnei HaSharon, 2009-10; Hapoel Jerusalem, 2010-11; Gallitos de Isabela, 2011; Grupo Capitol Valladolid; Southeast Hoopstars, 2011; Atenas de Cordoba, 2011-12; 9 de Julio de Rio Tercero, 2012; Ciclista Olimpico, 2012-13; Marinos de Anzoategui, 2013; Gimnasia Indalo, 2013-; free agt, currently. **Business Addr:** Player, Gimnasia Indalo, Roque Saenz Pena Comodoro Rivadavia, Chubut700-798, **Business Phone:** (959)603-6035.

### CLANSY, DR. CHERYL D.
Executive, educational consultant, educator. **Personal:** Born Oct 8, 1961, Los Angeles, CA; daughter of Sidney D and Beverly Jones. **Educ:** Northeast La Univ, Monroe, BM, vocal performance, 1984; Midwestern State Univ, MM, vocal performance, 1986; Grambling State Univ, EdD, stud develop & personnel serv, 1997. **Career:** Educator (retired), executive; Southern Univ, chmn vocal music & dir choral activities, 1987-89; Grambling State Univ, coordr vocal music, 1989-98; Wiley Col, dean enrollment mgt, 1998-2000; Jarvis Christian Col, assoc vpres academic affairs & choir dir, 2000; Charis Psychol Assocs, ADR specialist, therapist, coach, notary, parenting coordr & educ consult, currently. Houston, teaches, currently. **Orgs:** Tex Music Educr Asn; Delta Sigma Theta Sorority Inc; life mem, Delta Omicron; Top Ladies Distinction Inc; Phi Delta Gamma; Phi Kappa Lambda. **Home Addr:** 2611 S SE Loop 323 Suite 134, Tyler, TX 75701. **Business Addr:** ADR Specialist, Charis Psychological Associates, 8303 SW Fwy, Houston, TX 77074, **Business Phone:** (713)777-8633.

### CLANTON, DR. LEMUEL JACQUE
Physician. **Personal:** Born Mar 11, 1931, New Orleans, LA; married Barbara Guy; children: Mark, Lynn, Justine, Lemuel J Jr & Leslie. **Educ:** Howard Univ, BS, 1952; Meharry Med Col, MD, 1956. **Career:** Med Asn, physician; Hg Phillips Hosp, internship, 1957, resident, 1962; Alegent Health Immanuel Med Ctr, pvt pract physician, currently. **Orgs:** Bd Cert Surgeon; Am Bd Surg; AMA; Nat Med Asn; bd mem, Lafon Home Aged, 1975. **Home Addr:** 200 S Broad St 100B, New Orleans, LA 70126, **Home Phone:** (504)821-4222. **Business Addr:** Physician, Alegent Health Immanuel Medical Center, 6901 N 72nd St, Omaha, NE 68122, **Business Phone:** (402)572-2295.

### CLARDY, WILLIAM J.
Educator, executive, manager. **Personal:** Born May 1, 1935, Newalla, OK; married Patricia Ann Lomax; children: D Vincent, Terri Lynette & William Gerald. **Educ:** Okla State Univ, attended 1960; USN Community Tech Class A Sch; Iowa State Univ, attended 1972. **Career:** Lennox Ind Inc, Pac Div, terr mgr htg & air cond equip, instr; LA Unified Sch Dist, instr; Lincoln Job Corp, Ctr Northern Sys Co, sr instr htg & air cond; Utah Sheet Metal Con Asn, 1971; Cal-Poly Workshop, 1972; Ann Ed Con CARSES, 1974. **Orgs:** Bd dir, Marshall town Chap Jaycees; bd dir, Marshall town Chap Am Field Serv; bd dir, YMCA Omaha; Optimist Club Int, Marshall town, IA. **Home Addr:** 15612 Bechard Ave, Norwalk, CA 90650, **Home Phone:** (213)819-0168.

### CLARK, ANTHONY CHRISTOPHER. See CLARK, TONY.

### CLARK, DR. AUGUSTA ALEXANDER. See Obituaries Section.

### CLARK, DR. BERTHA SMITH
Educator. **Personal:** Born Sep 26, 1943, Nashville, TN; daughter of James Robert and Louise; married Phillip Hickman; children: Phillipa Jayne, Margaret Ann & Sheryll Clark Nelson. **Educ:** Tenn State Univ, BS, speech correction, 1964; George Peabody Col Teachers, MA, deaf educ emphasis, 1965; Vanderbilt Univ, PhD, early childhood educ, 1982. **Career:** Bill Wilkerson Hearing & Speech Ctr, head teacher OE 1 proj, 1965-70, speech pathologist, 1965-78, 1980-87; Tenn State Univ, Area Speech Lang path, Instr, 1969-78, asst Prof, 1982-87; Mama Lere Parent Infant Home, Bill Wilkerson Hearing & Speech Ctr, parent-infant trainer, 1982-87; Vanderbilt Univ, Div Hearing & Speech Scis, from instr to asst prof, 1970-87, supvr aural rehab, adj asst prof, 1987-98; Mid Tenn State Univ, Dept Speech & Theatre, asst prof, 1987-90, assoc prof, 1990-96, prof commun dis, 1996-. **Orgs:** Delta Sigma Theta Sorority Inc, 1962-; bd dir, League Hearing Impaired, 1973-87; Childrens House, 1984-86; adv comt, Early Develop & Assistance Proj Kennedy Ctr, 1984-88; co-chmn, YWCA, 1985; admin comm, vpres educ TN Speech & Hearing Asn, 1985-87; chmn, Cochlear Implant Scholar Comm, 1985-86; Compton Scholar Community Vanderbilt Univ, 1985-86; bd dir, Peabody Alumni, 1986-89; bd dir, Bill Wilkerson Ctr, 1990-95; bd dir, Effective Advocacy Citizens Handicaps, 1991-92; bd dir, CFAW, Mid Tenn State Univ, 1991-95; Founding Chair, Tenn Asn Audiologists & Speech Lang Pathologists, 2001-02; bd dir, Tenn Asn Audiologists & Speech, 2002-06; pres, Nat Asn Pre prof Progs, 2006-07. **Home Addr:** 2626 Forest View Dr, Antioch, TN 37013-1336, **Home Phone:** (615)361-5531. **Business Addr:** Professor, Middle Tennessee State University, 1301 E Main St BDA 206, Murfreesboro, TN 37132-0001, **Business Phone:** (615)898-2272.

### CLARK, BEVERLY GAIL
Writer. **Personal:** Born Jul 23, 1947, Oklahoma City, OK; daughter of James and Isabella; married Alvin; children: Catana Hughes, Alvin Jr, Dayna, Ericca & Gloria. **Educ:** Lawrence Technol Univ, genre fiction writing. **Career:** Bk Nook, bookseller, 1992-; Walden Bks, bookseller, 1996-98; Bk Stop, bookseller, 1998-; Novels: Yesterday Is Gone, 1997; A Love to Cherish, 1998; The Price of Love, 1999; Echoes of Yesterday, 2005; Bound by Love, 2006; A Perfect Frame, 2007; The Fires Within, 2007; Cherish The Flame, 2007; Beyond Rapture, 2008; A Twist Of Fate, 2009. **Orgs:** Romance Writer Am, 1990-; Friends Lib, 1991-. **Honors/Awds:** Publ Writer-Fiction, Romance Writer Am, 1996. **Home Addr:** 1501 Arnica Lane, Lancaster, CA 93535-4441, **Home Phone:** (661)948-9522.

### CLARK, CLAUDE LOCKHART
Artist, educator, businessperson. **Personal:** Born Mar 28, 1945, Philadelphia, PA; son of Claude and Daima Mary Lockhart. **Educ:** Calif Col Arts & Crafts, BA, applied arts, 1968; Univ Calif, Berkeley, MA, sculpture, 1972. **Career:** Oakland High Sch, instr, 1969-70; Calif Col Arts & Crafts, instr, 1970-80; Alameda Col, instr, 1971-72; San Jose State Univ Afro-Am Studies Dept, instr crafts course, 1974-80; Univ Calif, Berkeley, Afro-Am Studies Dept, 1974, 1977, SOS upward bound prog, 1974-80; House Vai African Imports, owner, 1977-; craftsman; photographer; painter; Calif Acad Scis, consult, 1982-92; African Metropolis, co founder, 1997-; African Metropolis Profiles, founder, 1998-; Frick Mid Sch, staff, 1998-2000; W Contra Sch Dist, teacher, 2000-. **Orgs:** Music Pub Am, 1947; Tuesday Club Picture Rental Servive Sacramento, 1972; Acts Art Gallery, NY, 1973; San Francisco Mus Art, 1974; W Coast, 1974; Black Image, Eb Crocker Art Gallery, 1974-75; Ill Afro-Am art, Dept Art, Fisk Univ, 1975-76; San Francisco Art Inst, 1976; Am Fedn Arts, 1976; partic, Nat African-Am Crafts World Print Coun, 1979; Conf & Jubilee, Memphis, 1979; Contemp African-Am Crafts Exhib Brooks Memorial Art Gallery, Memphis, 1979; Smithsonian Inst, 1980; Meml Union-Art Gallery, Univ Calif, Davis CA. **Honors/Awds:** Third Prize, Nat Ford Indus Arts Contest; First Prize, Oakland Art Mus's Exhib Pub Schs; Elected Citizen of the Day, KABL Radio San Francisco; Scholarship CA Col Arts & Crafts, 1963. **Special Achievements:** Co-Author: "A Black Art Perspective: A Black Teacher's Guide To A Black Art Curriculum", 1970; Author: "The Complete Annotated Resource Guide to Black America Art", 1978. **Home Addr:** 788 Santa Ray, Oakland, CA 94610, **Home Phone:** (510)652-8615. **Business Addr:** Owner, House of Vai, PO Box 8172, Oakland, CA 94662, **Business Phone:** (510)435-2628.

### CLARK, DAVID EARL (DAVE CLARK)
Baseball player, manager. **Personal:** Born Sep 3, 1962, Tupelo, MS; married Vivian; children: Meki & Kiki. **Educ:** Jackson State Univ, attended. **Career:** Baseball player, manager (retired); Cleveland Indians, outfielder, 1986-89; Chicago Cubs, 1990 & 1997; Kans City Royals, 1991; Pittsburgh Pirates, 1992-96, coach, 2001-02; Los Angeles Dodgers, 1996; Houston Astros, mgr, 1998, interim mgr, 2009, coach, 2009-13; Corpus Christi Hooks, 2005-07; Round Rock Express, mgr; Los Tigres del Licey, mgr, 2010; Detroit Tigers, coach, 2014-. **Business Addr:** Coach, Detroit Tigers, Comerica Pk 2100 Woodward Ave, Detroit, MI 48201, **Business Phone:** (313)471-2000.

### CLARK, DELLA L.
Executive. **Personal:** Born Jul 20, 1953, Tyler, TX; married Alfonso; children: Alorie & Allee. **Educ:** Am Univ, Kogod Sch Bus, BS, 1975. **Career:** Martin Marietta Aluminum, acct; Delark Indust Inc, owner; Enterprise Ctr, exec dir, pres, 1992-; Ohio Univ, George V. Voinovich Ctr Leadership & Pub Affairs, sr policy fel, 1998-2000. **Orgs:** Bd mem, United Way Southeastern Pa; small bus adv bd, Fed Res Bank Pa; bd mem, Univ Pa Mus Archael & Anthrop; bd Philadelphia Conv & Visitors Bur; bd mem, Forum Exec Women; bd mem, Nat Bus Incubation Asn; sr policy fel, George V Voinovich Ctr Leadership & Pub Affairs, Ohio Univ, 1998-2000; bd mem, St Christopher Found. **Business Addr:** President, The Enterprise Center, 4548 Mkt St, Philadelphia, PA 19139, **Business Phone:** (215)895-4005.

### CLARK, DORINDA GRACE. See COLE, DORINDA CLARK.

### CLARK, DOUGLAS L.
Educator. **Personal:** Born May 2, 1935, Swedesboro, NJ; married Ellen; children: Douglas Jr & Dana Lynn. **Educ:** Glassboro State Teachers Col, BS, 1956, MA, 1970; Laurence Univ, PhD, 1975. **Career:** Real Estate, lic salesman, 1963; Jr high sch NJ, inst, 1956-67; NJ Rural Manpower Prog, educ specialist, 1967-68; Glassboro State Col, asst dir, 1968-70, dir educ opportunity prog, 1970-; Glassboro State Col, dir educ programme, currently. **Orgs:** Mt Calvary Baptist Church; Businessman Asn, 1975; NJ dir Asn EOF; Nat Asn Advan Colored People; bd dir, UYA. **Home Addr:** 232 Hunter St, Woodbury, NJ 08096. **Business Addr:** Director of Education Programme, Glassboro State College, La Spata House, Glassboro, NJ 08028.

### CLARK, EDWARD
Executive, artist, painter (artist). **Personal:** Born May 6, 1926, New Orleans, LA; son of Edward Sr and Merion. **Educ:** Art Inst Chicago, attended 1951; L'Academie de la Grande Paris, attended 1952. **Career:** Univ Del, vis artist, 1969-78; Univ Ore, vis artist, 1969-78; Art Inst Chicago, vis artist, 1969-78; Showkegan Sch Painting & Sculpture, vis artist, 1969-78; Ohio State Univ, vis artist, 1969-78; La State Univ, vis artist, 1969-78; Syracuse Univ, 1985; artist, currently. **Orgs:** Bd dir, Orgn Independent Artists, NY; adv bd, Cinque Gallery NY; charter mem, Brata Gallery NY. **Honors/Awds:** Adolph Gottlieb Award, 1981; National Endowment Grant, 1982; Congressional Achievement Award, 1994; Joan Mitchell Awards, 1998; "art for life"Honored Artist, Rush Philanthropic Arts Found, 2000. **Special Achievements:** Numerous exhibits & one-man shows at Cont Arts Center New Orleans, NC A & T Univ, Randall Gallery NYC, Museum of Solidarity Titograd Yugoslavia, Art Salon NYC, LA State Univ, "Contemp Black Art" FL Intl Univ, Sullivant Gallery OH State Univ, James Yu Gallery NYC, Acad of Arts & Letters NYC, Whitney Mus NYC, Lehman College NYC, Afro-Amer Exhib Mus of Fine Arts Boston, Morgan State Coll, Mod Mus Tokyo, Stockholm, Nova Gall Boston,Amer Ctr Artists, Amer Embassy Paris, Gall Creuze Paris, Salon d'Automne Paris, and numerous others, 1952-. **Home Addr:** 4 W 22nd St, New York, NY 10010.

### CLARK, DR. ELIGAH DANE, JR.
Government official. **Personal:** Born Apr 20, 1943, Aliceville, AL; son of Elijah and Lula. **Educ:** Stillman Col, Tuscaloosa, AL, BS, 1963; Emporia State Univ, KS, MS, 1968; Univ Miss, JD, 1977. **Career:** Judge (retired); Alcorn State Univ, French instr, 1972-74; Navy-Marine Corps, judge advocate, 1974-87, Trial Judiciary, judge, 1987-94, Ct Criminal Appeals, judge, 1994-98; Dept Vet Affairs, chmn bd vet appeals, 1998-2004; Clerk, US Bankruptcy Ct, 2005-. **Orgs:** Omega Psi Phi; MS State Bar; Nat Naval Officers Asn; Ct Appeals Armed Forces Bar; Fed Bar Asn; US Supreme Ct Bar; Nat Bar Asn; Am Judges

Asn; bd trustee, Stillman Col. **Home Addr:** 9403 Caldran Dr, Clinton, MD 20735, **Home Phone:** (301)856-0544. **Business Addr:** Clerk, US Bankruptcy Court, 1800 5th Ave N, Birmingham, AL 35203, **Business Phone:** (205)714-4000.

### CLARK, FRANK M.
Chairperson, chief executive officer, association executive. **Personal:** Born Jan 1, 1946; married Vera; children: Frank III & Steve. **Educ:** DePaul Univ, BA & JD, 2004. **Career:** Unicom Corp, sr vpres; ComEd (Exelon), 1966, pres, 2001-05, sr vpres, 2001-04, exec vpres, chief staff, 2004-05, chmn & chief exec officer, 2005-12. **Orgs:** Dir, Waste Mgt Inc; bd dir, ComEd; bd trustee, Mus Sci & Indust; bd trustee, Adler Planetarium & Astron Mus; bd trustee, DePaul Univ; bd trustee, Chicago Symphony Orchestra; bd trustee, Univ Chicago Med Ctr; bd dir, Metrop Family Serv; bd dir, Ill Manufacturers Asn; bd dir, Big Shoulders Fund; bd dir, United Way Metrop Chicago; bd dir, Abraham Lincoln Presidential Libr Found; exec comt mem, Chicago Community Trust; gov bd mem, Econ Ill; Chicago Bar Asn; Econ Club Chicago; Com Club Chicago; Execs' Club Chicago; Mus Sci & Indust; co-founder, Rowe-Clark Math & Sci Acad Chicago's W side; bd dir, Harris Financial Corp; dir & chmn, BMO Financial Corp, 2005-; Dir, Aetna Inc, 2006-; dir, PECO Energy Co; dir, ShoreBank Corp. **Honors/Awds:** "Fortune," 50 Most Powerful Black Executives in America, 2002; "U.S. Black Engineer & Information Technology," 100 Most Important Blacks in Technology, 2008; "Black Enterprise," The 100 Most Powerful Executives in Corporate America, 2010; Hon doctor, humane lett, Gov State Univ, 2005; Hon doctor, Law, DePaul Univ; HistoryMakers Award; National Humanitarian Award, Nat Conf Community & Justice. **Business Addr:** Chairman of the Board, Exelon Corp, 10 S Dearborn St, Chicago, IL 60680, **Business Phone:** (312)394-7398.

### CLARK, DR. FRED ALLEN
Psychologist, business owner. **Personal:** Born Jul 8, 1929, Toledo, OH; son of Idus and Rose; children: Kevin & Kim. **Educ:** San Francisco State Col, BA, 1967, MA, 1968; Wright Inst, PhD, social-clin psychol, 1971. **Career:** Coun Clins Inc, exec dir, 1972-81; Calif Youth Authority, staff psychologist, 1982-89; pvt pract psychologist, 1989-; Nat Univ, instr; Clarco Enterprises, owner & chief exec officer, currently. **Orgs:** Am Psychol Asn; Calif Asn Marriage Counrs. **Special Achievements:** Author: All for Nothing, 1989; Teenage Gangs, 1993; articles: "Series on Teenage Gangs", Ebony Magazine, Sep 1992; Observer Newspaper, 1992; lecturer, "Teenage Gangs",Sierra Vista Hospital, 1991-92; Author, Teenage Street Gangs, 1996. **Business Addr:** Psychologist, Clarco Enterprises, 6748 Calvine Rd, Sacramento, CA 95823, **Business Phone:** (916)688-0801.

### CLARK, GARY C., JR.
Football player, executive. **Personal:** Born May 1, 1962, Radford, VA. **Educ:** James Madison Univ, grad. **Career:** Football player (retired), executive; Us Football League, Jacksonville Bulls, 1984-85; Wash Redskins, wide receiver, 1985-92; Phoenix Cardinals, wide receiver, 1993-94; Ariz Cardinals, wide receiver, 1994; Miami Dolphins, wide receiver, 1995; Am Mortgage Bank, financial serv provider; S Beach Restaurant & Martini Bar, owner; Gridiron Legacy, founder, 2010-. **Orgs:** Owner, Nat Football League Players Asn. **Honors/Awds:** Pro Bowl, 1986, 1987, 1990 & 1991; College Offensive Player of the Year, James Madison Univ, 1983, Athletic Hall of Fame, James Madison Univ, 1994; Redskins Offensive Player of the Game, 1985; Virginia Sports Hall of Fame, 2007; Redskins Ring of Honor, 2007; Super Bowls Champion; James Brown Awards, Nat Football League Players Asn. **Special Achievements:** Guest, The Darrell Green Show; First Receiver In National Football League History To Catch At Least 50 Passes In His First Ten National Football League Seasons; First Person In James Madison History To Have His Jersey Retired. **Home Addr:** , Seattle, WA.

### CLARK, DR. GRANVILLE E., SR.
Physician, pediatrician. **Personal:** Born Jun 14, 1927, Santiago; married Mary E; children: Granville Jr, Robert, Joseph & James. **Educ:** Inst Sup De Cien Med De La Habana, Santiago, BS, 1947; Univ Havana, MD, 1954. **Career:** Provident Hosp, intern, 1954-55; Norfolk Community Hosp, physician, 1955-57; Resd Gen Hosp, physician, 1957-59; pvt pract physician, 1959; KCMC Day Care Ctr, pediatrician consult; Truman Med Ctr-W, pediat; pvt prac, currently; S Towne Pediat Asn, prac. **Orgs:** SW Pediat & Soc; KC Med Soc; Pan-MO State Med Soc; NMA; Jackson Co Med Soc; Mo Med Asn; Coun Selection Med Sch; bd mem, Lead Poison Prog; KCSickle Cell Anemia; Mid-Am Comprehensive Health Planning Agency; chmn, Med Exec Comt, Martin Luther King Hosp; adv bd, Douglas State Bank; pres, Metro-Metic Clin; Nat Asn Advan Colored People; YMCA; Greater Ky Boys Club; Cent Tex Med Found. **Honors/Awds:** Numerous awards & recognitions. **Home Addr:** 5227 Norton Ave, Kansas City, MO 64130-3041. **Business Addr:** Pediatrician, South Towne Pediatric Association, 6025 Prospect Ave Suite 206, Kansas City, MO 64130, **Business Phone:** (816)333-3112.

### CLARK, DR. HARRY WESTLEY
Physician, educator, executive director. **Personal:** Born Sep 6, 1946, Detroit, MI. **Educ:** Wayne State Univ, BA, chem, 1969; Univ Mich, MD, 1973, MPH, 1974; Harvard Univ, JD. **Career:** Univ Mich Hosp, resident; San Francisco VA Med Ctr, fel; Nat Inst Ment Health, exec asst; pvt pract, psychiatrist, currently; US Dept Veterans Affairs Med Ctr, chief assoc substance abuse progs; Univ Calif, San Francisco, Dept Psychiat, assoc clin prof; Robert Wood Johnson, Substance Abuse Policy Prog, sr prog consult; Nat Inst Drug Abuse Funded Res Grants, co-investr; Substance Abuse & Ment Health Serv Admin, US Dept Health & Human Serv, dir ctr substance abuse treat, currently. **Orgs:** Am Bd Psychiat & Neurol; Wash DC Bar Asn. **Honors/Awds:** Vernelle Fox Award, Calif Soc Addiction Med, 2000; Meritorious Executive Award, Pres US Am Rank, 2003; Distinguished Executive Award, Pres US Rank, 2008; Secretary's Award; John P. McGovern Award, Am Soc Addiction Med, 2008. **Home Addr:** PO Box 141, Ann Arbor, MI 48107. **Business Addr:** Director of the Center for Substance Abuse Treatment, Substance Abuse & Mental Health Services Administration, Rm 1020 1 Choke Cherry Rd Suite 5, Rockville, MD 20857, **Business Phone:** (240)276-1660.

### CLARK, DR. IRVIN R.
College administrator, executive, football coach. **Educ:** Fla A&M Univ, BS, polit sci, 1991; Savannah State Univ, MS, pub admin, 1999; Fielding Grad Univ, Santa Barbara, CA, EdD, educ leadership, 2003. **Career:** Football player (retired), executive; Tampa Bay Buccaneers, DL, 1991; Savannah State Univ, football asst coach & residence hall dir, 1992-97, Ctr Residential Serv & Progs, dir, interim athletics dir, Off Stud Affairs, asst vpres, vpres, 2009-13; Radford Univ, assoc vpres & dean students, 2013-. **Orgs:** Chair, self study steering comt, Savannah State Univ; NCAA Athletics Cert Steering Comt; Ga Exec Leadership Inst; Savannah Leadership Prog; pres, Nat Asn for Stud Affairs Professionals; Am Col Personnel Asn; adv comt, Sr Stud Affairs Officer. **Business Addr:** Associate Vice President, Dean of Students, Radford University, 801 E Main St, Radford, VA 24142, **Business Phone:** (540)831-5000.

### CLARK, JAMES E.
Executive, college president. **Personal:** Born Jan 1, 1952?, Quincy, FL; son of Edmond and Annie. **Educ:** Mass Inst Technol, BS; Mass Inst Technol Sloan Sch Mgt, MS. **Career:** Gould Inc, Gen Elec, Gillette & Exxon Int, employee; AT&T, vpres; Bell Labs, exec dir; NCR Corp, chief technol officer; BANG! Technologies, a prin & founder; S Carolina State Univ, pres, 2016-. **Orgs:** Exp Aircraft Asn (former pres chap 242 & mem bd dirs); Benedict Col bd trustees; S Carolina State Univ bd trustees (former); S Carolina Res Found (chmn three terms). **Special Achievements:** Chairman of a special 60th anniversary reunion of the Tuskegee Airmen; airshow performer. **Business Addr:** South Carolina State University, 300 College St NE, Orangeburg, SC 29117, **Business Phone:** (803)536-7013.

### CLARK, PASTOR JAMES IRVING, JR.
Manager, clergy. **Personal:** Born Apr 18, 1936, Paterson, NJ; son of James I Sr and Rachel; married Shirley Lorraine Matthews; children: James I III, Renee Therese & Rhonda Ellise. **Educ:** Am Divinity Sch, BTH, 1966; Union Theol Sem, MA, divinity; Baruch Col, attended 1968; Columbia Univ, MBA, 1973, D Ed; Cong Nat Black Churches, Nat Fel; Auburn Theol Sem, Bennett Fel. **Career:** Slant/Fin Corp, asst rels mgr, 1962-69; New Era Learning Corp, exec vpres, 1969-71; Christ Temple Church, pastor, 1969; Church Christ Bible Inst, actg dean, 1971; Columbia Univ, COGME fel, 1971, Grad Sch Bus, pres, 1971-73; Pfizer Diagnostics, personnel rels mgr, 1973-75, mgr prof placement, 1975-78, mgr training & develop, 1978; Church Our Lord Jesus Christ Apostolic Faith Inc, apostle, 2001-07; Greater Refuge Temple, asst pastor; Westchester Diocese, bishop; Foreign Missions Caribbean, bishop. **Orgs:** bB chair, COOLJC; Corp Adv Coun Childrens Aid Soc. **Honors/Awds:** Business Service Award, Columbia Univ, Grad Sch Bus, 1973; Black Achiever Award, Pfizer Inc & YMCA, NY, 1974; Hudnut Award, Union Theol Sem. **Home Addr:** 111 20 174th St, Jamaica, NY 11433. **Business Addr:** Apostle, Church Of Our Lord Jesus Christ of the Apostolic Faith Inc, 2081 Adam Clayton Powell Jr Blvd, New York, NY 10029, **Business Phone:** (212)926-0426.

### CLARK, DR. JAMES N.
Dentist, consultant. **Personal:** Born Sep 16, 1934, Brooklyn, NY; son of Luther and Augusta Neale; married Patricia; children: Melissa, Holly & James II. **Educ:** City Col NY, BS, 1956; Columbia Univ, Col Dent Med, DDS, 1964; Acad Gen Dent, FAGD, 1974; Am Col Dentists, FACD, 1980. **Career:** ITT, dent dir, 1965-69; Pvt Prac, dent; World Wide ITT, dent consult, 1969-90. **Orgs:** Nat Asn Advan Colored People, Omega Psi Phi, 1955-; consult staff, Newark Beth Israel, 1969-; secy, Commonwealth Dent Asn, 1969; Newark Beth Israel Hosp Attend, 1969; Civil Defense, 1972-79; pres, Am Asn Indust Dentists, 1973; co-chmn, United Way, 1973; secy, Cent Pkwy Asn, 1974; 100 Black Men, 1975; Life mem, Omega Psi Phi, 1976; pres, Ad Hoc Community Orange Cent Young Men's Christian Asn, 1976-80; secy, 100 Black Men, 1980; fel Am Col Dentists, 1980-; bd trustees, Rampo Col, 1982-93; pres, Univ Med & Dent NJ, Dent Assisting Adv Bd, 1986-90; treas, Columbia Univ Alumni Asn, 1986-92; chmn, bd trustees, Ramapo Col, 1988-; vpres, external affair, 100 Black Men, 1988-94; Dent asn attend, Hosp Ctr Orange, 1988-96; bdgovrs, Ramapo Col, 1993-; Essex County Vincinage Comt, Minority Concerns Judicial, 1994-; adv coun, NJ Corrections Dept, 1994. **Honors/Awds:** Smith & Noyes Scholar, 1960, 1964; John Hay Whitney Fel, 1963; Gold Foil Award First Prize, Dent Stud Exhibit; Superstar Award, Young Men's Christian Asn, 1979; Centennial Community of Orange Award, 1989; Minority Achievement Award, Ramapo Col, 1990. **Business Addr:** Dentist, 185 Cent Ave Suite 301, East Orange, NJ 07018-3318, **Business Phone:** (973)672-1717.

### CLARK, JESSE B., III
Administrator. **Personal:** Born Feb 12, 1925, Philadelphia, PA; married Lucille Field; children: Bruce, Kevin, Blair & Cynthia. **Educ:** Pa State Univ, BA, 1950; Univ Pa, attended 1952. **Career:** Urban League, dir vocaliors, 1954-59; Campbell Soct Co, personnel spec, 1959-62; Abbotts Dairies, dir pub rels, 1962-64; Pa Cath Archdiocese, Cardinal Comn, Econ Opportunity, exec dir; Pa Crime Comn, dir. **Orgs:** Pres & bd chmn, St Edmonds Home Children, 1983-; trustee, St Charles Seminary Archdiocece Philadelphia, 1984, Mercy Catholic Medical Ctr, 1974-; past pres, Serra Club Philadelphia, 1972; treas, Catholic Soc Serv Bd, 1974-; trustee, Villanora Univ Villanora Pa, 1974-84; comnr, Charter Revision Comn Philadelphia, 1976; bd mem, Nat Catholic Stwrdshp Coun, 1983-; bd mem Inst Mentally Retarded, 1985-; sec Nat Adv Comt US Conference Bishops, 1987; pres, Sierra Club Pa. **Honors/Awds:** Knight of the Order Saint Gregory the Great, 1977; Commandor Knight of the Order Saint Gregory the Great, 1986. **Home Addr:** 6382 Woodbine Ave, Philadelphia, PA 19151-2526.

### CLARK, JOE LOUIS
School administrator, educator, public speaker. **Personal:** Born May 8, 1939, Rochelle, GA; son of Maggie Majors and Rhomie; children: Joetta, Joe Jr & Hazel. **Educ:** William Paterson Col, BA, elem educ, 1960; Seton Hall Univ, MA, 1974; Rutgers Univ. **Career:** Educator, army drill instructor (retired), speaker; Eastside High Sch, Paterson NJ, teacher, 1960-74, coordr lang arts, 1976-79, elem sch prin, 1979-82, sec sch prin, 1983-90; Keppler Assoc, lectr, ed reformer; Essex Co Juv Detention house, Newark, NJ, dir, div youth serv, 1995-; motivational speaker, currently; Book: Laying Down The Law, auth, 1989. **Orgs:** Nat Asn Sec Sch Prin; Nat Asn Advan Colored People; NJ Prins & Adminrs Asn; Paterson Prins Asn. **Home Addr:** 51 Beverly Rd, West Orange, NJ 07052, **Home Phone:** (201)325-3081.

### CLARK, JOHN JOSEPH
Executive. **Personal:** Born Jun 26, 1954, Pittsburgh, PA; son of John L and Anna Bluett; married C Lynne. **Educ:** Northeastern Univ, Boston, BS & BA, bus, econs & comput courses, 1977; Univ Chicago, MBA, 1985. **Career:** Basktball Player (retired); Boston Celtics, 1976; Arthur Andersen & Co, auditor, 1977-80; Bell & Howell, sr auditor, 1980-81; Baxter Travenol Labs (Large Hosp Supply firm), mkt mgr, 1981-86; Community Col Allegheny Co, prof, 1992-97; John J. Clark & Assocs, pres, 1986-. **Orgs:** Sch coordr, Chicago Asn Com & Ind Youth Motivation Prog, 1977-; Nat Asn Black Accts, 1978-86, treas, 1980; Nat Black MBA Asn, 1985-96; bd mem, Hollywood Tower Condo Asn, 1986-88; Greater Pittsburgh Chamber Com, 1987, Pittsburgh Reg Minority Pur Coun, 1996; Alumni Assocs, Chicago Coun Foreign Rels; comn mem, PACE, 1990-93; co-chmn, Allegheny County MBE Adv Comt, 1990-92, bd dir, Garfield Jubilee Asn, 1991-95, bd dir, E Liberty Develop Inc, 1993-95; vpres communs, Am Mkt Asn, Pittsburgh Chap; Pittsburgh Chap, Inst Community Leadership Educ, 2000-01. **Business Addr:** President, Clark & Associates, 16 Niagara Rd Suite 2B, Pittsburgh, PA 15221, **Business Phone:** (412)973-9285.

### CLARK, KAREN
Gospel singer. **Personal:** Born Nov 15, 1960, Detroit, MI; daughter of Elbert and Mattie Moss-Clark; married Rev John Drew Sheard; children: Keirra & John Drew Sheard II. **Career:** Gospel vocalist; The Clark Sisters; Island Inspirational All Stars, vocalist, 1996; Island Black Records, solo artist, 1997-; Broadway play, Mr. Right Now, vocalist, 1999. IInd Chance, vocalist, currently; Albums: Finally Karen, 1992; 2nd Chance, 2002; The Heavens Are Telling, 2003; It's Not Over, 2006; All in One, 2010. Singles: "Prayed Up", 2010; "He Knows", 2010; "Sunday A.M.", 2014. Film: Blessed & Cursed, 2010; TV series: "The Sheards", 2013; "BET HONORS", 2014. **Orgs:** Found & chief exec officer, KCS Ministries. **Honors/Awds:** Stellar Awards, Female Vocalist of the Year, 1999; Music Video of the Year; Contemporary Female Vocalist of the Year; nominated, Grammy Award; Lady Of Soul Award. **Special Achievements:** Member of the Clark Sisters; has appeared on the albums of several other artists. **Business Addr:** Gospel Vocalist, Care of Elektra records, 75 rockefeller plz, New York, NY 10019, **Business Phone:** (212)275-4000.

### CLARK, KEON ARIAN
Basketball player. **Personal:** Born Apr 16, 1975, Danville, IL. **Educ:** Irvine Valley Col, attended 1995; Dixie State Col Utah, attended 1996; Univ Nev, Las Vegas, NV, criminal justice, 1998. **Career:** Basketball player (retired); Orlando Magic, 1998-99; Denver Nuggets, ctr, 1998-2000, power forward, 2000-01; Toronto Raptors, power forward, 2001, ctr, 2001-02; Sacremento Kings, ctr, 2002-03; Utah Jazz, power forward, 2003-04; Phoenix Suns, 2004. **Orgs:** Nat Basketball Asn.

### CLARK, LARON JEFFERSON, JR.
School administrator, librarian. **Personal:** Born Dec 6, 1938, Atlanta, GA; son of Laron Jefferson Sr and Doshia Mary Alice Blasingame; married Mary Ellen Smith; children: Laron III, Jeremy & Allison. **Educ:** Morehouse Col, BA, 1961; Atlanta Univ, MS, 1965; Univ Tulsa, attended 1968. **Career:** Brooklyn Pub Libr, adult serv librn, 1961-63; Queensborough Pub Libr, suprv, br librn, 1963-66; Langston Univ, chief librn, Libr Sci Dept chmn, assoc prof, 1966-68; Langton Univ, dir develop, 1968-71; Atlanta Univ, exec dir, univ rels & develop, 1971-75; Hampton Univ, vpres develop, 1975-; Morehouse Col, vpres inst advan, res & planning, 1998. **Orgs:** Trustee, Hampton Rd Acad, 1978-; Kiwanis Club, 1979-, Tidewater Longshoremen Scholar Comt, 1982-, Soc Fund Raisers, 1980-; mem bd dir, Cult Alliance Greater Hampton Roads, 1985-; secy & bd dir, Cult Alliance Greater Hampton Roads; Fund Raising Comt, Va Air Space Ctr Mus; treas, Cult Alliance Greater Hampton Roads, 1990-; bd dir, Yorktown Found. **Home Addr:** 1733 Golfcrest Ct, Stone Mountain, GA 30088. **Business Addr:** Vice President for Development, Hampton University, 100 E Queen St, Hampton, VA 23668, **Business Phone:** (757)727-5356.

### CLARK, LEON STANLEY
Educator, government official. **Personal:** Born Mar 31, 1913, Bunkie, LA; son of Daniel and Leola Dodson; married Ernestine Mack; children: Mary D & Leon S Clark Jr. **Educ:** Southern Univ, Baton Rouge, BS, 1959, MEd, 1966, cert, supv & admin, 1970. **Career:** Educator (retired), supervisor; Avoyelles Parish Sch, Marksville, teacher, 1959-69; Avoyelles Parish Sch, Alexendria, LA, teacher, 1969-70; Saginaw Schs, Saginaw, teacher, 1970-83; Saginaw County Juven, Sagniaw, unit supvr, 1970-74; Buena Vista Charter Twp, supvr, currently; Trustee, Board Of Education; Buena Vista School District. **Orgs:** Bethel African Methodist Episcopal Ch; Kappa Alpha Fraternity. **Home Addr:** 2809 S Outer Dr, Saginaw, MI 48601, **Home Phone:** (989)752-3684. **Business Addr:** Supervisor, Buena Vista Charter Township, 1160 S Outer Dr, Saginaw, MI 48601, **Business Phone:** (517)754-6536.

### CLARK, PROF. LINDA DAY
Artist, educator. **Educ:** Howard Community Col, AA; Md Inst Col Art, BFA; Univ Del, MFA. **Career:** Baltimore Mus Art, educr; Coppin State Univ, assoc prof, 1998, prof, currently; visual artist, currently; TV Series: "Woman of Triumph"; "Winners: Linda Day Clark"; "Simple & stunningly beautiful"; "What art is all about."; "Winners!". **Home Addr:** 2068 Linden Ave, Baltimore, MD 21217-4429, **Home Phone:** (410)523-5602. **Business Addr:** Professor of Art, Coppin State University, Rm 516 2500 W N Ave 5th Fl, Baltimore, MD 21216-3698, **Business Phone:** (410)951-3365.

### CLARK, MARIO SEAN
Executive, football coach, football player. **Personal:** Born Mar 29, 1954, Pasadena, CA; son of Oscar and Lois Prince; married Lisa Clark Adkins; children: Taylor Alexander. **Educ:** Univ Ore, interior design, 1984. **Career:** Football player, football coach (retired), executive; Buffalo Bills, left central back, defensive back, 1976-83; San Francisco

49ers, defensive back, 1983-84; John Muir High Sch, Sec Coach, C.I.F. Go-Champions, 1988-89; Pasadena City Col, Sec Coach, Pony Bowl Champions, 1989-90; Elegant Pillow Upholstery, owner; Rose Bowl Operating Co, community outreach coord, community outreach dir, currently. **Orgs:** Bd mem, George Steuart Memory Football Camp, 1985; consult, Boys Club Pasadena, 1985. **Honors/Awds:** Super Bowl Winner, San Francisco 49ers, 1985; Pasadena High Sch Hall of Fame, 1996; Cert of Appreciation, Pasadena Police Dept. **Special Achievements:** All-rookie team Buffalo Bills, 1976. **Business Addr:** Community Outreach Director, Rose Bowl Operating Co, 1001 Rosebowl Dr, Pasadena, CA 91103, **Business Phone:** (626)577-3100.

### CLARK, MILDRED E.

Executive, educator, association executive. **Personal:** Born Dec 16, 1936, Columbus, GA; married Henry L; children: Henry L & Kenneth. **Educ:** Lane Col, Jackson, Tenn, lib arts, 1957; Wayne State Univ, Detroit, adult educ training, 1958; Univ Toledo, BA, 1963, MA, 1982; Davis Bus Col, comput prog, 1981. **Career:** Toledo, legal secy, 1958-59; Realty Co, secy, 1960-61; Rossford Ordinance, clerk typist, 1961-63; Eli B Williams Sch, educr, 1963-65; Anna Pickett Elem Sch, educ; Toledo Pub Sch Syst, 1963-93, adult educ classes, 1982, grad assist, 1965-67, adult night classes, instr; Martin Luther King Jr Elem Sch, 1983; WNGT-TV, channel 48, co-owner; Step Up Toledo Inc, owner, exec producer & dir, 1993-; Ghana's Academies & Cul Arts Acad, founder & admin, 1997; Ghanashia Bed & Breakfast Haven, owner, currently. **Orgs:** Founder, Ghanited Neighborhood Orgn, 1970-; chmn, Human Rels Bd, Toledo Educ Asn, 1966-67, 1973; Toledo Fed Teachers, 1973; Black Caucus Toledo Teachers; Frederick Douglass Community Asn Nat Adv Asn Colored People; Black African Peoples Asn; Black Hist Soc; secy, PTA; founder & chief exec officer, Ghanaian Found, 1982-; bldg rep, Toledo Fedn Teachers, 1983; founder, Hon Soc hon Dr Martin Luther King Jr. **Honors/Awds:** Outstanding service Doer's Award, Toledo Educ Assoc; Media Achievement Award, 2002. **Special Achievements:** Developed career unit for students' enrichment; produced and directed TV program for elem students, "The Beat Goes On", channel 30, WGTE-TV, 1970; initiated, produced, First Annual Black History Quiz Bowl for elem students, Toledo, channel 13, WTVG-TV, 1977; Off Minority Affairs, organized, prepared job opportunity announcements Collegiate newspaper, Univ Toledo, 1982; organized city-wide "King's Oratorical" contest: a celebration of Dr King's birthday and holiday, 1984-; Ex Producer & Dir:Step Up Toledo, tv program, 1996; appointed by governor to serve as MLK Jr Ohio Comnr. **Home Addr:** 7959 Hill Ave, Holland, OH 43528, **Home Phone:** (419)865-6306. **Business Addr:** Owner, Ghanashia Bed & Breakfast Haven, 11 S Centennial Rd, Holland, OH 43528-9702, **Business Phone:** (419)868-8396.

### CLARK, DR. MORRIS SHANDELL

Surgeon. **Personal:** Born Nov 27, 1945, Princeton, WV; son of Willie R Sr and Clarie; children: Gregory Morris & Angela Maureen. **Educ:** WVa State Col, BS, zool, 1967; Univ Calif, San Francisco, CA, BDS, 1973, DDS, 1973; Columbia Univ, Oral & Maxillofacial Surg Cert. **Career:** Columbia Univ, internship residency oral & maillofacial surg, 1976; Univ Med & Dent NJ, asst prof oral & maillofacial surg, 1976-81; Univ Colo Sch Dent, Sch Med, prof oral & maxillofacial surg, currently, dir anesthesia, 1982; Rose Hosp, Dept Oral & Maxillofacial surg, chief; Nationwide Parking, owner, currently. **Orgs:** Am Asn Oral & Maxillofacial Surgeons; bd dir, Am Dent Soc Anesthesia; Am Dent Soc; bd dir, Make-A-Wish Found; fel Am Col Dent; Am Dent Asn Coun Sci Affairs; Am Dent Asn Coun Dent Therapeut. **Honors/Awds:** Excellence Teaching Award, 1981; Chancellor's Diversity Award, Univ Colo Denver & Health Sci Ctr, 2003; Kappa Man of the Year; Chancellor's Diversity Award. **Special Achievements:** Author: The Handbook of Nitrous Oxide and Oxygen Sedation 3rd Edition; Co-Auth: Sedation a guide to patient management 5th Edition; Co-Author: Surgery of the Oral Cavity, Yearbook; Over 50 publications in medical & dental literature; 15 major research projects; spoken & lectured throughout the world. **Business Addr:** Professor of Oral & Maxillofacial Surgery, Director of Anesthesia, University of Colorado Denver School of Dental Medicine, 13065 E 17th Ave Rm 130, Aurora, CO 80045, **Business Phone:** (303)724-6975.

### CLARK, PATRICIA ANN

Research librarian. **Personal:** Born May 12, 1951, Philadelphia, PA; daughter of George and Rosalie Maynor. **Educ:** Barnard Col, BA, 1972; Columbia Univ, Sch Libr Serv, MLS, 1974. **Career:** Columbia Univ, ref librn, 1974-76; Time Warner Inc, res librn, 1976-92, Res Ctr, Time Inc, mgr cent res group, 1992-; Univ at Buffalo, libr clerk, currently. **Orgs:** Special Libraries Asn, 1990-. **Business Addr:** Library Clerk, University at Buffalo Libraries, N Campus 134 Lockwood Libr Bldg, Buffalo, NY 14260-2210, **Business Phone:** (716)645-8572.

### CLARK, RALPH A.

Executive, chief executive officer. **Educ:** Univ Pac, BS, econs, 1981; Harvard Bus Sch, MBA, bus admin & mgt, 1993. **Career:** IBM, mkt rep, 1981-87, staff mkt, 1987-88, mkt mgr, 1988-90, investment banker; Boeing Co, dir mkt & sales, 1990-91; Lotus Develop, consult, 1992-93; Goldman Sachs, assoc, 1993-95, investment banker; Merrill Lynch, assoc, 1995-96, investment banker; Evolve, vpres finance & bus develop, 1996-98; Inqusit, pres, chief exec officer, 1997-98; Direct Med Knowledge, pres, chief exec officer, 1998-99; Blue Makoi, founder & chief exec officer, 1999-2000; Ascend Venture Group LLC, venture partner, 2001-03; Snap Appliance, chief financial officer, 2003-04; Adaptec, vpres, fin, 2004-05; GuardianEdge Technologies Inc, pres, chief operating officer, 2005-10; SST Inc, dir, chief exec officer & pres, currently; ShotSpotter Inc, chief exec officer & pres, 2010-; TSG Solutions Inc, bd dir; Tactical Surv Group Inc, dir, currently. **Orgs:** Bd dir, chmn, Oakland Boys & Girls Club, 2000-05; guest fac mem, Pac Community Ventures, 2000-; mem bd dir, PrintRoom, 2007-; trustee, bd dir, Oakland Mus Calif, 2007-; Silicon Valley Community Ventures; Mus Childrens Art; bd trustee, Practicing Law Inst. **Business Addr:** President, Chief Executive Officer, SST Inc, 7979 Gateway Blvd Suite 210, Newark, CA 94560-1156, **Business Phone:** (510)794-3144.

### CLARK, RANDOLPH A.

Architect. **Personal:** Born Nov 25, 1939, Marshall, TX; married Mae A Wesley; children: Dawn & Randalyn. **Educ:** Prairie View A&M Univ, BS, 1961. **Career:** Gen Serv Admin, archit, 1963-73; Randolph A Clark & Assoc Archit, owner, 1973-; Hex Learning Ctr Urban Six Partnership, owner; Urban League, dir vocaliors, 1954-59; Campbell Soct Co, personnel spec, 1959-62; Abbotts Dairies, dir pub rels, 1962-64. **Orgs:** Am Inst Archit; Nat Orgn Minority Archit; Rotary Int; Alpha Phi Alpha; bd dir, Hex Learning Ctr. **Home Addr:** 2222 Parkhill Dr, Arlington, TX 76012, **Home Phone:** (817)460-3938. **Business Addr:** 3113 S Univ Dr, Ft. Worth, TX 76109.

### CLARK, ROBERT G., JR.

Teacher, state government official, executive. **Personal:** Born Oct 3, 1928, Ebenezer, MS; son of Robert Fletcher and Julian Williams; married Essie B Austin; children: Robert George III & Bryant Wandrick. **Educ:** Jackson St Col, BS, 1953; Miss Valley St; Mich State Univ, MA, admin & educ serv, 1959; Fla A&M Univ, attended 1960; Western Mich Univ, attended 1965. **Career:** Lexington High Sch, teacher & coach; St Miss, Holmes & Vazoo Counties, Dist 49, rep, 1968; Miss House Representatives, chmn, 1977; House Clark Furniture Store, owner, currently. **Orgs:** Founder & bd mem, Cent MS Inc Comt Action Progs; Int Bd Basketball Officials; pres, Cent MS Bd Athletic Officials; pres, Holmes CoTeachers Asn, 1969; fel Inst Polit John F Kennedy Sch Govt Harvard Univ, 1979; dem party nominee, Cong Seat, 1982, 1984; pres, Fine Housing Enterprises; chmn, Ed Comt House Reps; appropriations comm, House Reps; sec rules comm, House Reps; pres & bd trustee, C Ctr Lexington; Nat Coalition Advocates Studs; Dem Nat Comt Voter Participation Task Force; co-chmn, MS Del So Reg Coun. **Honors/Awds:** Alumnus of the Year, Jackson St Col, 1968; Outstanding Service & Inspiration to Humanity Award; Distinguished Alumni, Nat Asn Equal Opportunity Higher Educ, 1982. **Special Achievements:** First African-American to be elected to a Mississippi House of Representatives; First African-American committee chairman in the Mississippi House of Representatives; first African American to have a Mississippi state building named after him; His biography was published in a book named, Robert G Clark's Journey To The House: A Black Politician's Story, 2003; first African American elected since Reconstruction. **Business Addr:** Owner, House Clark Furniture Store, Lexington, MS 39095.

### CLARK, ROSALIND K.

Dancer. **Personal:** Born Nov 16, 1943, Dallas, TX. **Educ:** Tex Southern Univ, BMus, 1965. **Career:** Las Vegas Hilton, nightclub performer; Playboy Club, nightclub performer; Jackson's Penthouse, nightclub performer; After Dark, nightclub performer; Studio One, nightclub Performer; The Tonight Show, guest; Merv Griffin, guest; Dinah, guest. **Orgs:** Vpres, Celebration Soc, 1970-74; Alpha Kappa Alpha Sor. **Honors/Awds:** Entertainment Hall of Fame Awards. **Business Addr:** Actor, c/o Actors Equity, 165 W 46th St, New York, NY 10036.

### CLARK, DR. SANZA BARBARA

Educator. **Personal:** Born Jul 3, 1940, Cleveland, OH; daughter of Dewell Davis and Gladys Sanders Davis; children: Msia. **Educ:** Ky State Univ, BA, 1967; Duquesne Univ, MA, 1970; Howard Univ, CAS, 1980; Univ Ill, PhD, 1985. **Career:** Univ Pittsburgh, Swahili instr, 1969-72; Tanzanian Min Nat Educ, educ officer, IIA, 1972-78; Univ Ill, statist consult, 1980-83; Ohio State Univ, Swahili instr, 1983-84; Cleveland State Univ, assoc prof educ & res, 1985, Dept Curric & Found, Social Founds Search Comt, chmn, currently, Assoc Prof Emer, dir mali yetu prog, currently. **Orgs:** Pres, Orchard Family Housing Coun, 1981-83; Guide-Formulas-Hypothesis Testing Univ Ill, 1982; pres, Parents Qual Educ, 1986-87; chmn, Mali Yetu Alternative Educ Sch, 1988-; trustee, Ctr Human Servs, 1989-91; Phi Delta Kappa Prof Soc; Phi Kappa Phi Hon Soc. **Home Addr:** 2 Brandywine Sq, Euclid, OH 44143. **Business Addr:** Associate Professor Emeritus, Cleveland State University, 2121 Euclid Ave RT 1437, Cleveland, OH 44115, **Business Phone:** (216)687-5437.

### CLARK, SAVANNA M. VAUGHN

Vice president (organization), educator, lecturer. **Personal:** Born Hutchinson, KS; daughter of Charles Theola and Helen Vermal Grice; married Charles Warfield. **Educ:** Prairie View A&M Univ, TX, BS, 1949; Univ Okla, Norman, MEd; Okla State Univ, Stillwater, post grad & doctoral studies. **Career:** Educator (retired); Southern Univ, Baton Rouge LA, instr; Ponca City Pub Schs, Ponca City OK, instr; NC Cent Univ, Durham, NC, instr; Langston Univ, OK, asst prof; Univ DC, asst prof, 1974. **Orgs:** Am Pub HTH Asn; Am Alliance Health, Phys Educ, Recreation & Dance; Nat Educ Asn; Am Med Auxiliary Asn Inc; founding mem, Phi Delta Kappa, Univ DC Chap; Delta Sigma Theta Sorority; founding mem, Kennedy Ctr Friends & Vols; vpres, Women's Comm, Wash Ballet; patron, Mus African Art; donor, founding mem, Mus Women Arts, WA DC; exec bd mem, YMCA, WA DC area, 1974; founder, 1979, pres, 1981, Capital City Links Inc, WA DC; chairperson, Northwest Quadrant, Am Cancer Soc, 1984; chairperson, Fund-Raiser Arts, C's Mus, 1988; bd mem, Peoples Bank & Trust Co Inc; comnr, Southern Asn Cols & Schls; Pres Round table; bd mem, Innovation Cte. **Home Addr:** 2922 Ellicott Terr NW, Washington, DC 20008, **Home Phone:** (202)726-6550.

### CLARK, SHEILA WHEATLEY

Accountant, association executive, executive. **Personal:** Born Sep 4, 1948, Houston, TX; daughter of Reuben and Helen. **Educ:** Univ N Tex, BBA, acct, 1969, MBA, acct, 1972. **Career:** Shell Oil Co, gas acct, 1969-70; Peat, Marwick, Mitchell & Co, audit partner, 1972-. **Orgs:** Am Inst Cert Pub Accountants; Nat Asn Black Accountants; Am Women's Soc CPA; Comn Tech Stand TX State Bd pub Accountancy; TX Soc CPA; TASBO; N TX State Univ Dept Accouting; Delta Sigma Theta Sor Inc; Houston Bus Forum; Bold Black Organ Leadership Develop; Nat Asn Advan Colored People; Houston Chamber Com; United Way Houston; YWCA; Prof Christian Women Asn; Nat Coalition 100 Black Women; INROADS; acct instr, TX Southern Univ, 1977-78; teaching fel N TX State Univ; instr, TX Soc CPA Continuing Prof Educ seminars; auditing instr, Miller CPA Rev Courses, 1980-82; guest lectr, AICPA summer sem, 1978 & 1983; bd regents, TX State Univ Syst; Chmn Bd, Inroads Houston. **Honors/Awds:** National Accounting Achievement Award, NABA; Accountingtg Achievement Award, NABA Houston Chapt; Cert appreciation, NABA Annual Convention, 1981; Alumni of the Year, Phillis Wheatley Sr HS, 1982; NABA Achievement Award, NY Chap, 1982; Outstanding Alumni Award, N TX State Univ, 1987; Women on the Move Houston Post, Texas Exec Women, 1986; Eagle within Award, Inroads, 1986. **Home Addr:** 7802 Candle Lane, Houston, TX 77071, **Home Phone:** (713)776-0368. **Business Addr:** Partner, Peat Marwick Main & Co, 700 Louisiana, Houston, TX 77210.

### CLARK, SHIRLEY LORRAINE

Executive. **Personal:** Born Oct 26, 1936, Boston, MA; married James I Jr; children: James I III, Renee T & Rhonda E. **Educ:** Am Divinity Col, BRE, 1961, ThM; CPCU Col Ins, 1978; Am Inst Prop & Liability Underwriters, 1978. **Career:** Executive (retired); EG Bowman Co Inc, staff, 1969, supr, 1974, mgr, 1975, asst vpres, 1978, vpres, 1980-86. **Orgs:** Dir & missionary pres, Christian educ Christ Temple Apostolic Faith, 1975-80; NY Chap Soc Chartered Pro & Casualty Underwriters, 1979-80; Notary Pub, 1980; fel Am asn christian counrs; Christ Temple Village Harlem. **Special Achievements:** First black woman in US to receive Chartered Property Casualty Underwriter Designation 1978. **Home Addr:** 11120 174th St, Jamaica, NY 11433, **Home Phone:** (718)658-8229. **Business Addr:** Christ Temple In The Village of Harlem, 17 W 128th St, New York, NY 10027, **Business Phone:** (212)534-4200.

### CLARK, HON. TAMA MYERS

Judge. **Educ:** Morgan State Univ, BS, 1968; Univ Pa Law Sch, JD, 1972; Univ Pa Grad Sch, MA, city planning, 1972. **Career:** Judge (retired); Off Dist Atty for the City & City Philadelphia, asst dist atty, 1973-80; Human Serv Div City Philadelphia Law Dept, dep city solicitor, 1980-83; Resource Ctr Human Serv, vpres; Ct Common Please Criminal Trial Div, judge, 1984-2010. **Orgs:** Pa State Conf of Trial Judges; bd dir, Community Serv Planning Coun; bd dir, New Directions Women, Prisoners Family Welfare Assn; Youth Serv; Child Support Proj; Family Welfare Asn; The Links Inc; Coalition of 100 Black Women; Women & Girl Offenders Task Force; Mayor's Comn Women. **Honors/Awds:** Woman of the Yr, Nat Sports Found, 1984; Distinguished Alumni Yr, Morgan State Univ; Nat Asn Equal Opportunity Higher Educ, 1984; Outstanding Woman, Community Bright Hope Baptist Church Women's Comn, 1984; Distinguished Alumnus, Philadelphia Chap Morgan State Univ Alumni Asn, 1984. **Home Addr:** 3028 S 72nd St, Philadelphia, PA 19153, **Home Phone:** (215)686-9133.

### CLARK, TEMPY M. HOSKINS

Educator. **Personal:** Born Oct 25, 1938, Hazen, AK; married Wilber L Hoskins; children: Jamele, Monroe & Brian McKissic. **Educ:** Philander Smith Col, BA, 1963; Western Mich Univ, MA, 1971. **Career:** Grand Rapids Bd Educ, elem prin; McKinley Upper Grade Ctr, Chicago IL, vocal music teacher; S Mid Sch Grand Rapids MI, vocal music teacher, chmn. **Orgs:** Minister, mus True Light Bapt Ch Grand Rapids; bd dir, Blue Lake Fine Arts Camp; pres, Negro Bus & Prof Club Inc; Delta Sigma Theta Sor; pres, local chap, Delta Sigma Theta; travel abroad summer, 1972; hs students Belg Holland Eng & France. **Home Addr:** 4491 Buckingham Cir, Decatur, GA 30035-2109, **Home Phone:** (770)593-4535.

### CLARK, DR. THEOTIS, JR.

Scientist, scholar, educator. **Personal:** Born Sep 15, 1961, Akron, OH; son of Theotis Sr and Alberta June Norman; married K S Madsen. **Educ:** Marion Tech Col, AS, mech engineering technol, 1983, AS, indust engineering technol, 1985, AS, elec & electronics engineering, 1987; Wright State Univ, BS, chem, 1990; Iowa State Univ, MS, chem, 1995; Univ Wyo, PhD, anal chem, 1998. **Career:** Quaker Oats Comp, chem clerk, 1982-87; Los Alamos Nat Lab, res scientist; Univ Calif, prof, 1998-2000; Truman State Univ, Div Sci, asst prof, currently. **Orgs:** Am Chem Soc, 1990-; Electro Chem Soc, 1990-; Div Anal Chem, 1991-; Younger Chemist Comt, 1992-; Microscope Soc Am, 1996-; Mat Res Soc, 1999-; President's Postdoctoral Fellowship Recipients, 1998-99. **Home Addr:** PO Box 425, Los Alamos, NM 87544, **Home Phone:** (505)660-0252. **Business Addr:** Assistant Professor, Truman State University, 100 E Normal, Kirksville, MO 63501, **Business Phone:** (660)785-4000.

### CLARK, TONY (ANTHONY CHRISTOPHER CLARK)

Baseball player, executive director. **Personal:** Born Jun 15, 1972, Newton, KS; married Frances; children: Kiara,Jazzin & Aeneas. **Educ:** San Diego State Univ; Univ Ariz. **Career:** Baseball player (retired), executive director; Detroit Tigers, infielder, 1995-2001; Boston Red Sox, 2002; NY Mets, 2003; NY Yankees, 2004; Ariz Diamondbacks, first baseman, 2005-07, 2008-09; San Diego Padres, 2008; Free agt, currently; MLB Network, studio analyst, currently, dir player rels, 2010, exec dir, currently. **Orgs:** Detroit Tigers. **Business Addr:** Executive Director, MLB Networks, 1 MLB Network Plz, Secaucus, NJ 07094, **Business Phone:** (201)520-6400.

### CLARK, VINCENT W.

Government official, vice president (organization). **Personal:** Born Apr 11, 1950, Bronx, NY; son of Vincent and Gladys Young; married LaVerne McBride; children: Derrick & Noelle. **Educ:** LaGuardia Community Col, AS, 1979; York Col, BA, polit sci, 1983; NY Univ, MPA, 1987. **Career:** NY City Bd Educ, 1980-90; NY Univ, mayors scholar, 1985-86; NY City Emergency Med Serv, assoc exec dir, 1990; NY City Health & Hosp Corp, sr asst vpres; NY City Bd Educ, asst dir, mgt analyst, bus mgr, budget dir & sr chief exec; Lehman Col, vpres admin & finance, 2010-; Community Learning Support Orgn, chief exec officer, currently. **Orgs:** Am Soc Pub Admin, 1982-; Asn Sch Bus Officials. **Home Addr:** 93 E Sanford St, Yonkers, NY 10704, **Home Phone:** (914)237-9278. **Business Addr:** Vice President, Lehman College, 250 Bedford Pk Blvd W, Bronx, NY 10468, **Business Phone:** (718)960-8000.

### CLARK, WALTER H.

Consultant, administrator. **Personal:** Born Jun 5, 1928, Athens, GA; son of John and Beulah; married Juanita E Dillard; children: Hilton P & Jaunine C. **Educ:** Southern Ill Univ, BBA, 1951; DePaul Univ, MBA, 1958; Harvard Univ, post grad, 1971. **Career:** Ill Fed Savings & Loan Asn, acct, 1952, 1954-55; First Fed Savings & Loan Assoc Chicago, staff, 1955-73, exec vpres & chief financial officer, 1973-; Citicorp, 1983-86; Harold Wash's Finance Comt, chmn, 1983; Chicago Transit Authority, chmn, 1986-88; Bear Stearns Co Inc, vpres, 1986-91; financial consult, 1991; Wheat First Securities Inc, sr financial analyst & broker; Clark Consult Co, owner, 1991; Chicago Bd Educ, finance authourity; Peer Group, chrmn; Hyde Park-Madison Corporation, prin. **Orgs:** Travelers Aid Soc Serv League, 1967; Invest Comt, YMCA Metro Chicago; bd dir, Better Govt Asn; bd dir, adv coun, Col Bus Admin, Univ Ill; bd dir, Univ Southern Ill, bd dirs; Nat Soc Controllers & Fin Officers; Fin Exec Inst Econ Club; Alpha Phi Alpha; Union League Club; bd dir, Harvard Bus Sch, Snakes Soc Club; trustee, Park Manor Congregational Church; First Fed Savings & Loan Assoc Chicago. **Honors/Awds:** Black Achievers of Industry Recognition Award, YMCA, 1974; Business School Hall of Fame, Southern Ill Univ, 1986. **Business Addr:** Principal, Hyde Park-Madison Corp, 1235 E Madison Pk, Chicago, IL 60615, **Business Phone:** (773)285-2286.

## CLARK, WALTER L.

Executive. **Personal:** Born Dec 5, 1963, Baltimore, MD; married Mikki; children: Aaron. **Educ:** RETS Electronic Engineering, AA, 1985; Howard Co Community Col, AA, 1995; Johns Hopkins Univ, BS, finance, 1996. **Career:** Wheat First Securities, investment officer, 1988-92, vpres Wealth Mgt, 1990-95, vpres & investment officer, 1992-95; Clark Capital Wealth Mgt, pres & chief exec officer, 1989-, portfolio mgr, 1993; Gruntal & Co LLC, vpres investment, 1995-96, pres, 1996-, vp wealth advisor, 1995-99; Clark Capital Financial LLC, founder, pres & chief exec officer, 1999-; Newbridge Mortgage Corp; Howard County, leadership; Westrock Advisors, regist rep & investment advisor rep. **Orgs:** Wheat First's Exec Club, 1990-95; vis, Nurse Asn Found; Howard County Pension Oversight Commn; BE's Million Dollar Round Table; adv, Wash Women's Investment Club. **Business Addr:** President, Chief Executive Officer, Clark Capital Financial LLC, 6851 Oak Hall lane Suite 118, Columbia, MD 21045, **Business Phone:** (410)381-9500.

## CLARK, WILLIE CALVIN, JR.

Educator, football player. **Personal:** Born Jan 6, 1972, New Haven, CT; children: Tre. **Educ:** Univ Notre Dame. **Career:** Football player (retired), educator; San Diego Chargers, defensive back, 1994-96, 1998; Philadelphia Eagles, defensive back, 1997; San Diego Chargers, 1998; Palmetto High Sch, prin, currently. **Business Addr:** Principal, Palmetto High School, 1200 17th St W, Palmetto, FL 34221, **Business Phone:** (941)723-4848.

## CLARK-COLEMAN, IRMA

School administrator, government official. **Personal:** Born Apr 14, 1937, GA; married Ron D Sr; children: 2. **Educ:** Wayne State Univ, BA, commun, MA, commun. **Career:** Stenographer; Wayne County Rd Comn, asst dir, 1967; Wayne County Human Rels Div, dir; Wayne County Exec, media rels dir; Detroit Bd Educ, pres, vpres, 1996-98; Mich State Senate; Mich Senate Dem Caucus, Mich 3rd Dist, sen, 2003-10. **Orgs:** Mich House Representatives, Dist 11, mem, 1999-2002; Life mem, Nat Asn Advan Colored People; vpres bd dir, God Land Unity Church; Mich Dem Party; bd dir, Travelers Aid Soc; March Dimes; Detroit Goodfellows Dr; Civic Ctr Optimist Club; TULC; United Way Community Servs; vice co chair, Detroit Pub Schs; bd dir, Nat Sch Bd Asn; bd dir, Mich Asn Sch Bds; Nat Alliance Black Sch Educrs; life mem, Trade Union Leadership Coun; 14th Cong Dist Precinct Deleg; Alpha Rho Chap Alpha Kappa Sorority Inc; bd dir, Detroit Works Partnership; bd dir, Nat Asn Black County Officials; bd dir, Civic Ctr Optimists Club; Detroit Bd Educ. **Home Addr:** 2688 Oakman Blvd, Detroit, MI 48238, **Home Phone:** (517)373-0990.

## CLARK-HUDSON, VERONICA L.

Administrator, educator, executive director. **Personal:** Born Aug 22, 1946, Baltimore, MA; daughter of Harold A Clark and Flozella R; married Arturio M; children: Kristin Jordan. **Educ:** Albright Col, attended 1963; Howard Univ, BA, eng, 1967; Univ Pa Sch Law, attended 1972; Gemological Inst Am, GG, AJP, CG, 1985. **Career:** Int Bus Mach Corp, instr, analyst, 1967-70; Sperry Rand Corp, Univac Div, instr, mkt, 1971-72; Hong Kong Int Sch, instr upper div, 1974-78; Summer Olympics, microcomputer analyst, 1981-84; ABC TV, staff, 1984; Hospity Lane Flowers, owner, 1984-87; Best Jewelry, asst store mgr, 1987-89; Gemological Inst Am Inc, exten instr, 1990-92, sales mgr, 1992-97, dir Los Angeles educ, 1997-. **Orgs:** GIA Alumni Asn, 1986-; Am Gem Soc, 1990-; prog chmn, Women's Jewelry Asn, 1997-. **Business Addr:** Director of Los Angeles Education, Gemological Institute of America Inc, 5345 Armada Dr, Carlsbad, CA 90013-2407, **Business Phone:** (760)603-4000.

## CLARK-TAYLOR, KRISTIN

Executive, poet laureate, columnist. **Personal:** Born Jan 1, 1959, Detroit, MI; daughter of James Clark and Elizabeth Clark; married Lonnie; children: Lonnie Paul & Mary Elizabeth. **Educ:** Mich State Univ, BA, 1982. **Career:** Detroit Free Press, internship, 1982; USA Today, columnist, news writer, ed bd, 1982-87; White House, sr adv, corp pub rels exec & journalist, secy, dir media rels, 1987-90; Bell S Corp, dir commun, 1990-94; Sallie Mae, vpres external affairs; Author: The First to Speak: A Woman of Color Inside the White House, Doubleday, 1993; Black Mothers: Songs of Praise and Cellebration, 2000; Black Fathers: A Call for Healing, 2003; Black Mothers, 2007; The Forever Box, 2011; Stud Loan Mkt Asn, vpres external affairs; Auth, lectr & consult, currently. **Special Achievements:** First African-American woman to serve as White House Director of Media Relations. **Home Addr:** , Great Falls, VA. **Business Addr:** Author, c/o Random House Inc, 1745 Broadway 3rd Fl, New York, NY 10019, **Business Phone:** (212)572-6066.

## CLARK-THOMAS, ELEANOR M. (ELEANOR M THOMAS)

Educator, consultant. **Personal:** Born Sep 18, 1938, Houston, TX; daughter of George Jr (deceased) and Alberta Palmer Henderson; married Bob; children: Natalie, Brandon & Shannon. **Educ:** Kent State Univ, BS, 1960; Calif State Univ, MA, 1973; ASHA, cert clin competence speech path, cert clin competence audiol; Univ Southern Calif, EdD. **Career:** Educator (retired); Stockton Unified Sch Dist, speech & hearing therapist, 1960-61; Ella Sch Dist & Olive hurst, speech & hearing therapist, 1961-63; Sacramento City Unified Sch Dist, speech & hearing specialist, 1963-76; St Dept Educ, consult, educ commun handicapped, 1976; Calif St Univ N ridge, assoc prof, 1985; Folsom Cordova Sch Dist, speech therapist; Sacramento Co Schs, speech therapist C, admin asst spec educ, Calif Dept educ, compliance unit mgr. **Orgs:** Delta Kappa Gamma, 1977; Calif Speech & Hearing Asn, 1986-87; bd dir, Sacramento Hearing Soc; Am Speech & Hearing Asn; treas, coordr, coun, Sacramento Area Speech & Hearing Asn; NAUW, NBLSHA, NASDSE; pres, La S Bay Alumnae Chap, Delta Sigma Theta, 1989-91. **Honors/Awds:** Sustained Superior Accomplishment Award, State Dept Educ, 1983-85. **Home Addr:** 8340 MediTeranean Way, Sacramento, CA 95826-1658, **Home Phone:** (916)388-1668.

## CLARKE, ALYCE GRIFFIN

State government official, educator, nutritionist. **Personal:** Born Jul 3, 1939, Yazoo City, MS; daughter of Henry Griffin and Fannie Merriweather Griffin; married Lee William Jr; children: DeMarquis. **Educ:** Alcorn State Univ, BS, 1961; Tuskegee Univ, Tuskegee, AL, MS, 1965; Miss Col, Clinton, MS, 1979; Jackson State, Jackson, MS, 1982. **Career:** Nutritionist, consultant, politician; Wash County Pub Schs, Leland, Miss, teacher, 1961-68; Miss Action Progress, Jackson MS, nutritionist, 1969-71; Jackson Hinds Health Ctr, Jackson MS, nutritionist, dir, 1971-87; Nutritionist, currently; Miss State House Representatives, state rep, 1984-; B-Free Drug & Alcohol Treat Ctr pregnant women, founder. **Orgs:** Alcorn State Univ Alumni, 1961-89; Miss Asn Community Health Centers, 1971-89, Nat Soc Nutrit, 1980-89, Mayor's Adv Comn, 1980-89; bd mem, Miss Mult Sclerosis Nat Soc, 1984-89; Miss Food Network, 1985-89; NatWomen's Polit Caucus, 1985-89; bd mem, United Way, 1986-89, Southeastern Educ Improv Lab, 1986-89; chmn, Jackson Crime Prev Comn, 1988; Alpha Kappa Alpha; Jack & Jill Am; Miss Pub Health Asn; Regional Asn Drug Free Schs & Communities; State Parent Teacher Asn; chair, House Comt Ethics; Alcorn Alumni; Dem party. **Home Addr:** 1053 Arbor Vista Blvd, Jackson, MS 39209, **Home Phone:** (662)354-5453. **Business Addr:** State Representative, Mississippi State House of Representatives, 400 High St Rm 204 D, Jackson, MS 39215-1018, **Business Phone:** (601)359-9465.

## CLARKE, HON. ANNE-MARIE

Lawyer, commissioner. **Personal:** Born St. Louis, MO; daughter of Thomas Phillip (deceased) and Mary Ann Vincent; married Richard K Gaines. **Educ:** Forest Pk Community Col, attended 1968; Northwest Mo State Univ, BA, polit sci, 1970; St Louis Univ Sch Law, JD, 1973. **Career:** Arthur D Little Inc, researcher, 1974-94; Northeast Utilities, asst corp sec, 1974-77; Bi-State Develop Agency, staff coun, 1977-79; Self Employed, pvt pract law, 1980-92; Mound City Bar Asn, pres, 1981-83; 22nd Judicial Circuit Ct Mo, juv div hearing officer, 1986, family ct, comnr, 1998-, atty; Domestic Rels div, 2005. **Orgs:** Bd gov, Mo Bar, 1986-90, 1991-95; dir, Bar Plan Mutual Ins CPN, 1986-; treas, City St Louis Bd Police Commissioners, 1993-98, pres, 1994-98; chair prev juv crime task force, Confluence St Louis, 1993; Nat Bar Asn Judicial Coun, 2004; Judicial Coun's Exec Bd, 2005; diamond life mem, Delta Sigma Theta Sorority; St Louis Metrop Alumnae Chap; St Alphonsus "Rock" Cath Church; exec comt, Nat Bar Asn; exec comt, NBA Judicial Coun. **Honors/Awds:** Achievement Award, Nat Coun Negro Women Bertha Black Rhoda Sect, 1990; Achievement Award, Nat Orgn Blacks Law Enforcement, 1993; Jordan-McNeal Award, Mo Legis Black Caucus, 1994. **Special Achievements:** The History of the Black Bar", St Louis bar Journal, 1984; First Black member of the Board of Governors for The Missouri Bar, 1986; First African American woman to serve on the St. Louis Board of Police Commissioners, 1993. **Home Addr:** 3439 Longfellow Blvd, St. Louis, MO 63104-1630. **Business Addr:** Commissioner, City of St Louis, Rm 2 Div 30 Ct, St. Louis, MO 63108, **Business Phone:** (314)552-2025.

## CLARKE, BENJAMIN LOUIS

Labor relations manager. **Personal:** Born Mar 5, 1944, Springfield, OH; married Janet; children: Bryan & Darryl. **Educ:** Lincoln Univ, BS, soc sci, 1966; Xavier Univ, Med Coun, 1972; Univ Cincinnati, MA, indust rels, 1984. **Career:** Manager (retired); Ford Motor Co, supvr personnel, mgr personnel serv, hr mgr. **Orgs:** Just Us Individual Investment Club, 1985-; unit comt, Detroit Boy Scout Leader, 1985-; Hartford Optimist Club; bd mem, Lincoln Univ Found; Xavier Univ Alumni Asn; Univ Cincinnati Alumni Asn; NACIREMA Club, 1998; Ford African-Am Network; pres, Detroit Chap, Lincoln Univ Alumni. **Home Addr:** 25124 Friar Lane, Southfield, MI 48033-5818, **Home Phone:** (248)356-1583.

## CLARKE, BRYAN CHRISTOPHER

Engineer. **Personal:** Born May 23, 1971, Cincinnati, OH; son of Benjamin L and Janet E. **Educ:** Mich State Univ, BS, elec engineering, 1998. **Career:** Ford Motor Co, assembly technician, 1996; Dept Com & Indust, Financial Inst Bur, info systs analyst, 1997-98; Silicon Graphics Inc, syst support engr, 1998-; Digital Takeover Inc, secy, treas. **Orgs:** Nat Soc Black Engrs, 1990-. **Honors/Awds:** NSBE, Pepsi-Cola Scholar Award. **Home Addr:** 630 Venice Way Apt Suite 111, Inglewood, CA 90302-2845, **Home Phone:** (310)677-0527. **Business Addr:** System Support Engineer, Silicon-Graphics Inc, 1500 Crittenden Lane, Mountain View, CA 94043, **Business Phone:** (650)960-1980.

## CLARKE, CHARLOTTE

Engineer, golfer. **Educ:** Eastern Mich Univ, BS, 1987; Purdue Univ. **Career:** Digital Equip, mfg engr, 1988-92; Pitney Bowes, mfg engr, 1992-96, process engr; Craigowan Golf & Country Club, golf player, currently. **Orgs:** Nat Soc Black Engrs; Nat Black MBA Asn. **Business Addr:** Golf Player, Craigowan Golf & Country Club, 595838 Hwy 59 N RR 6, Woodstock, ON N4S 7W1, **Business Phone:** (519)462-2743.

## CLARKE, CHERYL L.

College administrator, poet, executive director. **Personal:** Born May 16, 1947, Washington, DC; daughter of James and Edna. **Educ:** Howard Univ, BA, eng, 1969; Rutgers Univ, MA, 1974, MSW, 1980, PhD. **Career:** Conditions, ed, 1981-90; Ctr Gay & Lesbian Studies, City Univ New York Grad Ctr, co-chair bd, 1990-92; Rutgers Univ, Off Diverse Community Affairs & Lesbian Gay Concerns, dir, 1992-2009, dean students, 2009-13. Film Appearance: Water melon Woman, 1997; Corridors Nostalgia, 2006. Poetry collection: Living a Lesbian, 1986; Humid Pitch, 1989; Exp Love, 1993; Theorizing Back Feminisms; Long Shot Mag; Gay Community News; African-Am Rev; Advocate; Blue Stones & Salt Hay: An Anthology Nj Poets; Radical Am; Callaloo; Dangerous Liaisons: Blacks & Gays Fighting Oppression; Black Like Us: A Century Black Gay, Lesbian, Bisexual Fiction. Bloom: A J Writing by Lesbian & Gay Writers. **Orgs:** NY Women Against Rape, 1985-88; grad fac, Women & Gender Studies; steering comt mem, NJ Women & Aids Network; Ctr Lesbian & Gay Studies, CUNY Grad Ctr; Astraea Lesbian Found Justice; bd dir, Newark Pride Alliance. **Business Addr:** Dean of Students, Rutgers University, 57 US Hwy 1, New Brunswick, NJ 08901-8554, **Business Phone:** (732)932-1711.

## CLARKE, DR. DONALD DUDLEY

Scientist, educator. **Personal:** Born Mar 20, 1930, Kingston; son of I Dudley and Ivy Burrowes; married Marie B Burrowes; children: Carol, Stephen, Paula, David, Ian, Sylvia & Peter. **Educ:** Fordham Univ, BS (cum laude), 1950, MS, 1955, PhD, 1955. **Career:** NY Psychiat Inst, res assoc, 1957-62; Columbia Univ Med Sch, sr res scientist, 1960-62; Fordham Univ, assoc prof, 1962-70, prof chem 1970-, Currently; Dept Neurol Mt Sinai Sch Med, vis prof, 1993-94. **Orgs:** Consult Nat Inst Ment Health, 1972-76, chmn, Counlor NY secy Am Chem Soc, 1976-; chmn, chem dept Fordham Univ, 1978-84; co-chmn, Kingsbridge Manor Neighborhood Asn, 1980-84; Nat Inst Health, 1981-85. **Home Addr:** 2528 Grand Ave, Bronx, NY 10468, **Home Phone:** (718)733-3638. **Business Addr:** Professor, Fordham University, 441 E Fordham Rd, Bronx, NY 10458, **Business Phone:** (718)817-4444.

## CLARKE, EVEREE JIMERSON

Writer, educator. **Personal:** Born Jul 6, 1926, Merritt Island, FL; married Vospher; children: Renee(deceased) & Frances Yvette. **Educ:** Lincoln Univ, attended 1948; Juilliard Sch Music, 1954; Nova Univ, attended 1982. **Career:** Everee Clarke Sch Charm & Dance Inc, pres, 1960-; Nat Bus League, nat sec, 1972-76; asst regional, vpres, 1986-, pres & ceo; Tri Co Chap Nat Bus League, pres; Elegante Int.Book: Pleasant City West Palm Beach, auth. **Orgs:** Frances Bright Women's Club Debutante Cotillion, C Hour early childhood develop prog, Palm Beach Co Cities Schs prog, 1985-86; Broward Co Republican Exec Comm, 1985-88; Serv Tri-Co Chap, Nat Bus League, founder, 1986; City W Palm Beach Human & Community Develop Educ Comm, 1987; Broward Co Coun Black Econ Develop; founder & pres, Pleasant City Family Reunion Comm Inc & Heritage Gallery; consult, Prof Beauty & talent pageant; Urban League; Nat Asn Advan Colored People; Voters League. **Home Addr:** 4290 NW 19th St, Ft. Lauderdale, FL 33313, **Home Phone:** (305)485-4363. **Business Addr:** Founder, President, Pleasant City Family Reunion Committee Inc, 2117 N Dixie Hwy, West Palm Beach, FL 33407-0816, **Business Phone:** (561)832-9799.

## CLARKE, DR. GRETA FIELDS

Health services administrator, dermatologist. **Personal:** Born Detroit, MI; daughter of George Fields and Willa Fields; children: Richard. **Educ:** Univ Mich, BS, 1962; Univ Mich, grad study, biochem; Howard Univ, MD, 1967; Am Bd Dermat, dipl. **Career:** Spectrum Cosmetics, med dir; Harlem Hosp NY, internship, 1967-68, residency internal med, 1968-69; NY Univ Med Ctr, residency dermat, 1969-72; pvt pract dermatologist, 1972-. **Orgs:** Fel Am Acad Dermat; trustee, chair, Nat Med Asn; San Francisco Dermat Soc; Links Inc; Reg VI Nat Med Asn, 1986-90; Comt Women Med, Calif Med Asn, 1986-90; Oakland Chapter Carrousels Inc; Women's Dermat Asn; Soc Cosmetic Chemists; Dermat Asn; Soc Cosmetic Chemists; Am Soc Clin Hypn; Alta Bates Summit Med Ctr; San Francisco Dermtological Soc. **Business Addr:** Dermatologist, Private Practitioner, 3300 Webster St Suite 1106, Oakland, CA 94609, **Business Phone:** (510)763-2662.

## CLARKE, JUDGE HUGH BARRINGTON, JR.

Lawyer. **Personal:** Born Jul 14, 1954, Detroit, MI; son of Hugh Barrington Sr and Gwendolyn; married Judith Brown; children: Hugh Barrington IV. **Educ:** Oakland Community Col, assoc arts, 1973; Wayne State Univ, BS, criminal justice, 1975; Thomas M Cooley Law Sch, JD, 1979. **Career:** Mich State Senate, Senate Judiciary Comt, senate spec consult, 1977-79; State Mich & State Senate, assoc gen coun, 1979-81; self-employed, atty, 1981-; Rosenbaum, Holland, Clarke & Foster, pract atty, 1981; Hugh B Clarke Jr & Assocs, founder, 1989-; 54-A Judicial Dist Ct, dist ct judge, 2010-; Hugh Clarke & Assocs, founder; Black Law Stud Asn, founder & pres. **Orgs:** Equality justice comt, State Bar Mich, 1999-2001, stand criminal jury instructions comt, 2000-; Lansing Black Lawyers Asn, 2003; pres, vpres, Lansing Bd Educ, 2003-10; pres, Lansing Black Lawyers Asn, 2007; bd mem, Ingham County Bar Asn - Young Lawyers Sect, 2016-; Phi Alpha Delta Fraternity; Davis-Dunnings Bar Asn; Asn Black Judges Mich; Am Judges Asn; treas, Mich Dist Judges Asn; St. Paul's Episcopal Church. **Honors/Awds:** Alumni of the Year, TM Cooley Black Law Student Asn, 2000; Distinguished Citizen of the Year Award, Cent Mich Heritage Enterprise; Community Hero Award, Eastside Community Action Ctr; Community Champion Award, Tabernacle David Worship Ctr; E Patterson Community Award, United Auto Workers Loca 652. **Home Addr:** 3800 Colchester Rd, Lansing, MI 48906-3420, **Home Phone:** (517)327-8482. **Business Addr:** District Court Judge, 54-A Judicial District Court, 124 W Mich Ave 6th Fl, Lansing, MI 48933, **Business Phone:** (517)483-4441.

## CLARKE, JOSEPH LANCE

Manager, executive. **Personal:** Born Apr 6, 1941, New York, NY; married Marion Joyce Herron; children: Bernadette, Leslie & Lancelot. **Educ:** Southern Ill Univ, Carbondale, attended 1963; City Col NY, BA, 1967; NY Univ, attended 1968. **Career:** Livingston Inst, mgr, 1966-67; Supreme Beauty Prod, dir sales, 1971-73; Fashion Fair Cosmetics, dir sales, 1973-74, exec vpres, 1974-; Johnson publ co, merchandising rep. **Orgs:** Vpres, Alpha Phi Alpha Frat Beta Eta Chap, 1962-63; vpres, Young Dem Mt Vernon, NY, 1966-68. **Honors/Awds:** Business Award, Supreme Beauty Prod, 1970.

### CLARKE, JOY ADELE LONG
Writer, elementary school teacher. **Personal:** married Ronald Eugene; children: Dylan Terence, Kelcey Lamar & Darcy Marie. **Educ:** Cent State Univ, Wilberforce, OH, BS, elem educ, 1960; Univ Northern Colo, Greeley, CO, MA, 1978. **Career:** Aims Community Col, Greeley Colo, teacher multicultural diversity; Springfield Pub Schs, Springfield, Ohio, teacher, 1960-62; Pershing Elem Sch, Ft Leonard Wood, Mo, 1962-63; Boulder Valley Schs, Boulder, Colo, teacher, 1972-83; Creekside Elem Sch, phys educ teacher, currently; Tucson Pub Schs, Tucson, AZ, libr media specialist, 1978-81; Denver Pub Schs, Denver, Colo, 1985-92; Libr Media Specialist, Lngmnt, Co, St Vrain Valley Schs, libr media specialist, 1992-93. Bks: African Am Activ, 1997, 2002; Spiritual Nourishment Selected Bible Verses Arranged from A to Z, 2002. **Orgs:** Am Sch Librns; Alpha Kappa Alpha Sorority; Alpha Delta Kappa Teacher's Sorority; Nat Asn Advan Colored People; Am Libr Asn; Asn Black Caucus Am Libr Asn. **Business Addr:** Physical Education Teacher, Creekside Elementary School, 5321 Ephesus Church Rd, Durham, NC 27707, **Business Phone:** (919)560-3919.

### CLARKE, KENTON
Executive, president (organization), chief executive officer. **Personal:** Born Nov 17, 1951, Bridgeport, CT; son of Haywood and Ruth. **Educ:** Norwalk State Tech Col, assoc degree, comput sci, 1972; Univ New Haven, BA, opers mgt, 1979; Northwestern Univ, JL Kellogg exec mgt prog. **Career:** Comput Consult Assocs Int Inc, pres, chief exec officer & founder, 1980-09; Div2000.com, founder, 1980-; DiversityBusiness.com, founder, chief exec officer, 1999-. **Orgs:** Dir, Nor tech Found, 1989-; bd dir, Conn Minority Purchasing Coun; bd dir, Norwalk Community Tech Col; United Fund; Gov's Coun on Econ Competitiveness & Technol; bd mem, Univ New Haven; adv bd, Grad Sch Mgt Sacred Heart Univ. **Home Addr:** 30 Jelliff Lane, Southport, CT 06490. **Business Addr:** Chief Executive Officer & Founder, President, DiversityBusiness.com, 200 Pequot Ave, Southport, CT 06890, **Business Phone:** (203)255-8966.

### CLARKE, LEON EDISON
Consultant, surgeon, health services administrator. **Personal:** Born Nov 17, 1949, Monrovia, CA; married Fatu; children: Tanya, Nina & Lee Ann. **Educ:** George Washington Univ, MD, 1975; Am Bd Surg, gen cert. **Career:** Med Col Pa, fel surg oncol; Hosp Univ PA, surg resident, 1977; Med Col PA, intern, 1977-80, attend surgeon, 1981, instr surg, 1982-85, med dir surg procedure unit, 1985-, asst prof surg; Veterans Admin Hosp, Philadelphia PA, consult, 1981-; Mercy Cath Med Ctr, dir surg, 1988-; Thomas Jefferson Univ Hosp, clin assoc prof surg, currently; Misericordia Hosp, dir surg, currently. **Orgs:** Am Cancer Soc; Am Col Physician Execs; Soc Black Acad Surgeons; fel Am Col Surg. **Home Addr:** 964 Clyde Lane, Philadelphia, PA 19128. **Business Addr:** Director of Surgery, Mercy Hospital of Philadelphia, 501 S 54th St, Philadelphia, PA 19143, **Business Phone:** (215)748-9000.

### CLARKE, LEROY P.
Artist, poet, painter (artist). **Personal:** Born Nov 7, 1938, Port-of-Spain; married Vera Mitchell; children: Kappel & Ra-nkosane; married Aileen Goddard. **Career:** St Phillip's E.C. Sch, teacher, 1959-67; prof painter, 1969-; Studio Mus, prog coordr & artist resident, 1971-74; Portfolios Drawings: a Quiet Way, 1971; Fragments a Spiritual, 1972; Studio Mus Harlem, artist-in-residence, 1972-75. Books: Taste of Endless Fruit, 1974; Douens, 1976; De Word Love Poems for Ettylene, 2004; The El Tucuche Poems, 1984-2007; Secret Insect of a Bird Deep in Me, Wanting to Fly, 2008. **Orgs:** Art Soc Trinidad & Tobago; hon fel University of Trinidad and Tobago; The Trinidad Theatre Workshop, 1962-67. **Honors/Awds:** Achievement of Excellence Award, Nat Asn Empowerment African People; Folk Arts Award, Trinidad & Tobago Folk Arts Inst, 2005; Honorary Doctor of Letters, Univ Trinidad & Tobago, 2008; Sunshine Award, 2008. **Home Addr:** 2 Hermitage Rd, Port-of-Spain3410.

### CLARKE, PRISCILLA
Public relations executive, business owner, publicist. **Personal:** Born Aug 3, 1960, Swindon; daughter of Gilbert Lee and Dorothy Sharples; children: Huda, Ilyas & Qasim. **Educ:** Western New Eng Col; Columbia Union Col; NY Inst Photog. **Career:** Eat To Live Health Food Store, owner, 1988-92; Channel 10 Fairfax County, TV producer; NEB Security, pres & owner, 1992-97; NEB Entertainment, pres, 1995-2000, publicist, currently; Clarke & Assocs LLC & Clarke PR, exec, pres & chief exec officer, 1995-; Black Belt Chinese Kenpo Karate, martial arts instr; N Am Sch Firearms, Pa, gun prof; Rouse Sch Spec Detective Training, pvt invest; Cong Black Caucus Found Inc, sr pub rels & entertainment consult, 2002-11; Music World Entertainment, publicist, 2004-13. **Orgs:** Gov bd, Rec Acad, Wash, D.C. Chap; bd mem, Duke Ellington Sch Arts; bd mem, KISS Found; Nat Asn Female Execs, 1986-; officer, Nat Asn Exec Bodyguards Inc, 1990-; mar state rep, US Karate Asn, 1990-93; Rouse Detective Asn; Nat Coun Negro Women; Parent Teachers Assn; Better Bus Bur; vol, Conn State Black Caucus. **Special Achievements:** Nominated as an African-American History Maker; Named one of Fifty Influential Minorities in Business. **Home Addr:** 402 Careybrook Lane, Oxon Hill, MD 20745. **Business Addr:** President, Chief Executive Officer, Clarke & Associates LLC, 2020 Pa Ave NW Suite 271, Washington, DC 20006, **Business Phone:** (202)723-2200.

### CLARKE, RAYMOND R.
President (organization). **Personal:** Born Aug 2, 1950, Cincinnati, OH; son of William and Genie Johnson; married Debra; children: Terri & Paul S. **Educ:** Univ Ariz, Tucson, AZ, BS, 1973, MS, 1978. **Career:** Univ Ariz, counr youth, 1971, 1972; Pima County Juv Ct Ctr, dep dir probation, 1973-84; Univ Ariz, consults stud athletes, 1980-81; Gov Bruce Babbitt, exec dir health coun, 1984-86; Tucson Urban League Inc, pres & chief exec officer, 1986-06; Las Vegas Clark County Urban League, pres & chief exec officer, currently. **Orgs:** Pi Lambda Theta, 1977-; Co-Founder, Tucson Chap Nat Asn Black Soc, 1978; pres, Tucson Chap Nat Asn Black Social Workers, 1978-79; Ariz Small Bus Asn, 1979; Mayor's Task Force, Econ Develop, 1988-89; Gov's Task Force Welfare Reform, 1988-89; Regents Ad-Hoc Comt, Minority Access & Retention, 1988-; State Supreme Ct Taskforce, 1989; Tucson Community Found Grants Comt, 1988-; US Selective Serv Syst, 1981-; Citizens-Police Adv Comt, City Tucson, 1984; vpres western regional coun exec, Nat Urban League, 1991; Tucson Local Develop Corp, City Tuscson, 1987; Tucson Civil Rights Coalition, Tucson Community, 1990; bd pres, Dragonfly Village; southwest regional vpres, Amity found. **Home Addr:** 3441 W Quail Haven Cir, Tucson, AZ 85745-5006, **Home Phone:** (602)792-3594. **Business Addr:** President, Chief Executive Officer, Las Vegas Clark County Urban League, 1058 W Owens Ave, Las Vegas, NV 89106-2516, **Business Phone:** (702)636-3949.

### CLARKE, SHIRLEY. See FRANKLIN, SHIRLEY CLARKE.

### CLARKE, STANLEY MARVIN
Composer, musician. **Personal:** Born Jun 30, 1951, Philadelphia, PA; son of Marvin and Blanche Bundy; married Carolyn Helene Reese; children: Christopher Ivanhoe; married Sofia Sara Espinoza Woters. **Educ:** Philadelphia Music Acad, 1971. **Career:** Horace Silver Band, mem, 1970; Joe Henderson Band, 1971; Stan Getz Band, 1971-72; Return to Forever, 1972-76; Stanley Clarke Group, leader, 1976-; Composer, Life is Just a Game, Stanley Clarke Songbook, 1977; I Wanna Play for You Songbook, 1979; New Barbarians tour group, 1979; Clark & Duke Proj, 1980-; Albums: Clarke Duke Proj II, 1983; Find Out, 1985; Modern Man, 1985; Midnight Magic; Hideaway, 1986; If This Bass Could Only Talk, 1988; The Toys of Men, 2007; Jazz in the Garden, 2009; The Stanley Clarke Band, 2010; Song: "Sweet Baby", 1981; Film: Higher Learning, 1995; Eddie, 1996; Sprung, 1997; Down in the Delta, 1998; The Best Man, 1999; Dangerous Ground, 1999; Romeo Must Die, 2000; Undercover Brother, 2002; Undisputed, 2002; The Transporter, 2002; Roll Bounce, 2005; Into the Sun, 2005; Like Mike 2:Streetball, 2006; TV: Knightwatch, 1988; A Man Called Hawk, 1989; Hull High, 1990; Tales from the Crypt, 1990; Soul Food, 2000; Lincoln Heights, 2006; The Best Man Holiday, 2013. **Orgs:** Musicians Local 802 Union; Nat Acad Rec Arts & Sci; Am Fedn Tv & Radio Artists; Screen Actors Guild; Hubbard Asn Scientologists Int. **Business Addr:** Musician, c/o Universal Music Publishing Group, Los Angeles, CA 90064-1712, **Business Phone:** (310)752-6066.

### CLARKE, REP. YVETTE DIANE
City council member. **Personal:** Born Nov 21, 1964, Brooklyn, NY; daughter of Una S T. **Educ:** Oberlin Col; Medgar Evers Col. **Career:** Bronx Overall Econ Develop Corp, dir bus develop; New York, Coun, Dist 40, coun mem, 2002-04, US House Representatives, NY 11 Dist, congresswomen, 2007-; US House Homeland Security Subcomt Emerging Threats, Cybersecurity, Sci & Technol, chair. **Honors/Awds:** Honorary Doctorate Law Degree, St Francis Col. **Business Addr:** Congresswoman, New York City Council, 123 Linden Blvd 4th Fl, Brooklyn, NY 11226, **Business Phone:** (718)287-1142.

### CLASH, KEVIN
Actor, television producer, movie producer. **Personal:** Born Sep 17, 1960, Baltimore, MD; son of George and Gladys; married Genia; children: Shannon Elise. **Career:** Films: Muppet Monster Adventure, 2000; Elmo's Letter Adventure, 2001; Elmo's World: The Wild Wild West, 2001; Sesame Street: Computer Caper, 2002; Elmo Visits the Fire House, 2002; Zoe's Dance Moves, 2003; Sesame Street: 4-D Movie Magic, 2003; Muppets Party Cruise, 2003; Sesame Street: Happy Healthy Monsters, 2004; What's the Name of That Song, 2004; Sesame Street: Friends to the Rescue, 2005; Sesame Street: All-Star Alphabet, 2005; Elmo Visits the Doctor, 2005; Elmo's World: Reach for the Sky, 2006; Guess That Shape & Color, 2006; Sesame Beginnings: Beginning Together, 2006; Sesame Beginnings: Make Music Together, 2006; Elmo's World: Pets!, 2006; Elmo's Potty Time, 2006; A Sesame Street Christmas Carol, 2006; Sesame Beginnings: Exploring Together, 2006; Kids Favorite Country Songs, 2007; Sesame Beginnings: Moving Together, 2007; Elmo's World: What Makes You Happy?, 2007; Ready for school, 2007; Being Green, 2009; Elmo and the Bookaneers, 2009; Elmo and Abby's Birthday Fun, 2009. Families Stand Together, 2009; Elmo's Animal Adventures, 2009; Sesame Street: Elmo Loves You, 2010; Sesame Street: Elmo's Alphabet Challenge, 2012; Sesame Street: Fairy Tale Fun!, producer, 2013; TV Series: "Sesame Street", 1982-2014; "Learn Along with Sesame", 1996-2011; "Elmo's Musical Adventure", 2000; "Rove Live", 2001-09; "Deadline", 2001; "Oobi", 2003; "The West Wing", 2004; Sesame Street Presents: The Street We Live On, 2004; The Muppets' Wizard of Oz, 2005; A Capitol Fourth, 2006; Elmo's Christmas Countdown, 2007; "Sesame Street", 2008; Macy's Thanks giving Day Parade, 2008; "Scrubs", 2009; "The Game", 2009; "Coming Home: Military Families Cope with Change", actor & producer, 2009; "Late Night with Jimmy Fallon", 2009-12; "Dinner: Impossible", 2009; "Live from the Red Carpet", 2009; "Families Stand Together: Feeling Secure in Tough Times", dir & producer, 2009; "The 7PM Project", 2010; "The Wendy Williams Show", 2010-12; "When Families Grieve", 2010; "Growing Hope Against Hunger", actor & producer, 2011; "Conan", 2011; "Macy's Thanksgiving Day Parade", 2011; "Coming Home", 2012; "Little Children, Big Challenges", actor & co-executive producer, 2012-13; "Michael Buble: Home for the Holidays", 2012; "Sesame Street Mexico", 2013; "Math Bites", dir, 2014. **Honors/Awds:** Daytime Emmy Award, Nat Acad Tv Arts & Sci, 1990, 2001-14; Primetime Emmy Award, 2012; PGA Award, 2013. **Home Addr:** The Muppets, PO Box 20726, New York, NY 10023. **Business Addr:** Principal Muppeteer, Jim Henson Productions, 117 E 69th St, New York, NY 10021, **Business Phone:** (212)794-2400.

### CLAXTON, MELVIN L.
Journalist. **Personal:** Born Jan 1, 1958?. **Career:** Vi Daily News, managing ed, part time reporter & writer, 1983-85, reporter, 1985, frelancer, reporter, 1994-97; Probe Mag, founding ed, 1987; Chicago Tribune Media Group, investigative reporter, 1997-98; Detroit News, reporter, 1998, sr investigative reporter, 1998-2005; Tennessean Nashville, sr investigative reporter, 2005-07; Premier 3D Animation, sr managing partner, 2010-13; Epic 4D LLC, chief exec officer, 2013-. **Home Addr:** , TN. **Business Addr:** Chief Executive Officer, Epic 4D LLC.

### CLAY, BILL, SR. See CLAY, WILLIAM LACY, SR.

### CLAY, DR. CAMILLE ALFREDA
School administrator, mental health counselor. **Personal:** Born Aug 21, 1946, Washington, DC; daughter of James and Doris Coates. **Educ:** Hampton Inst, BA, 1968; Univ DC, MA, coun, 1974; George Washington Univ, EdD, 1984. **Career:** DC Comn Ment Health Dept, ment health specialist, 1971-72; SW Interagency Training Ctr, manpower develop specialist, 1972-74; pvt pract, group therapist 1973-79; City Bowie Md Youth Serv Bur, asst dir, 1974-76; Towson State Univ, sr counr, 1977-85, asst vpres diversity, 1986-04; pvt pract, ment health & career counr, 1983-; Univ Dc, adj prof. **Orgs:** Nat Advan Asn Colored People; Phi Delta Kappa; Alpha Kappa Alpha; bd dir, Alfred Adler Inst DC; pres, DC Ment Health Counr Asn, 1987-88, 2005-06; treas, DCMHCA, 2006-; Am Coun Asn, DCCA; Asn Multi-Cult Coun & Develop; Am Ment Health Counrs Asn; Asn Black Psychologists; pres, DC Ment Health Counr Asn; sr counr, Towson Univ, 1978-86; Omicron Delta Kappa Hon Leadership Soc, 1988; chair Bd, prof Counr; chmn, Licensure DCACD; Am Asn Health Educ, NAWDAC; chmn, D.C. Prof Coun Licensure Bd, 1993-06. **Home Addr:** 4618 New Hampshire Ave NW, Washington, DC 20011, **Home Phone:** (202)882-7849. **Business Addr:** Mental Health Counselor, Private Practitioner, 4014 Georgia Ave, Washington, DC 20011, **Business Phone:** (202)882-1400.

### CLAY, CASSIUS MARCELLUS, JR. See ALI, MUHAMMAD.

### CLAY, CLIFF
Artist, publisher. **Personal:** Born Greenwood, MS. **Educ:** Cleveland Inst Art; Cooper Art Sch. **Career:** Self employed painter; Drums Along Ohio, publ, founder & ed; Cleveland Inst Art, affil. **Orgs:** Karamu House; Nat Asn Advan Colored People; Urban League Hon Am Indian PowWow, 1969; hon mem, 101 Ranch Ponca & City OK; bd mem, 101 Ranch Restoration Found, Ponca City, OK; bd mem, Afro Am Hist & Cult Mus, Cleveland, OH; scout, Red Carpet County; founder, Inventors Connection Greater Cleveland. **Honors/Awds:** Honorary Official deputy sheriff, Kay Co, OK; patent for the process of painting on the fur side of animal hides that has been described as second oldest art form recorded. **Home Addr:** 11215 Itasca Ave, Cleveland, OH 44106-1350, **Home Phone:** (216)721-9938. **Business Addr:** Painter, 10605 Chester Ave, Cleveland, OH 44106, **Business Phone:** (216)721-9938.

### CLAY, ERIC LEE
Judge, lawyer. **Personal:** Born Jan 18, 1948, Durham, NC; son of Austin Burnett and Betty Allen (deceased); married Kathleen McCree Lewis. **Educ:** Univ NC, BA, 1969; Yale Univ Law Sch, JD, 1972. **Career:** Chambers Stein Ferguson & Lanning, law clerk, 1970; US Dist Ct Eastern Dist Mich, law clerk, 1972-73; U.S. Ct Appeals Sixth Circuit, judge; Detroit, Mi, pvt prac, 1973-97; Lewis White & Clay PC, partner & co-founder, chmn, shareholder, dir, atty, 1973-97; State Mich, spec asst atty gen, 1974-75; US Dist Ct Eastern Dist Mich, 1992-95; Clinton-Gore finance comt Mich, exec bd, 1992; Ct Appeals US 6th Circuit Judges, circuit judge, 1997-; Carolina Polit Union, chmn. **Orgs:** State Bar Mich, 1972-; Wolverine Bar Asn, 1973-; Am Bar Asn, 1973-; bd dir, Detroit Bar Asn, 1973, chmn, 1988-90; special asst atty gen, State Mich, 1974-75; Arbitrator Am Arbit Asn, 1976-; Nat Asn Rr Trial Coun, 1977-78; Nat Asn Railroad Trial Coun, 1978-77; Mich Soc Hosp Attorneys, 1978-97; Am Arbit Asn, 1978-82; Mich Soc Hosp Atty, 1978-; 6th Circuit Judge Conf, 1979; Merit Selection Panel US Magistrates, 1980-81; Phi Beta Kappa; Nat Bar Asn; life mem, Nat Advan Asn Colored People; State Bar Mich Ins Law Comn, 1984-86; trustee, Detroit Bar Asn Found, 1985-88; Hearing Panelist, Atty Discipline Bd State Mich, 1985-97; Merit Selection Panel Bankruptcy Judge ships, 1986-87; 6th Circuit Comt Bicentennial Const, 1986-; co-chmn, Pub Adv Comt Detroit Bar Asn, 1988-90; exec comt, Yale Law Sch Asn, 1989-; bd dir, Detroit Bar Asn, 1990-; Mediator, Mediation Tribunal Asn, Third Judicial Circuit Mich, 1993-97; DC Bar Asn, 1994-; Bar Dist Columbia Ct Appeals, 1997-; pres, Philanthropic Soc; life mem, Nat Asn Advan Colored People; Mus African Am Hist Detroit. **Honors/Awds:** John Hay Whitney Opportunity Fellow, Yale Univ. **Business Addr:** Judge, US Court of Appeals, 231 W Lafayette Blvd 5th Fl, Detroit, MI 48226, **Business Phone:** (313)234-5005.

### CLAY, ERNEST H.
Architect, college teacher, chief executive officer. **Personal:** Born Feb 17, 1972, Chicago, IL; son of Ernest and Beatrice. **Educ:** Univ Ill, Urbana-Champaign, BAr, 1969, MAr, 1970; State Ill, lic pract archit, 1973. **Career:** Nat Aeronaut & Space Admin, res fel, 1978-79; Nat Orgn Minority Archit Students, co-founder, 1978; Univ Ill, Sch Archit, prof emer, 1991-99; Hardwick & Clay Architects, partner; Hardwick, Clay, Voelker & Petterson Architects, owner, partner; Univ Ill, Sch Archit, Urbana, Ill, assoc prof, 1999 retired; E H Edric Clay & Assocs, chief exec officer, currently. **Orgs:** Exam rev mem, Nat Coun Archit Regist Bd, 1979; AIA; founding mem, Nat Orgn Minority Architects, Ill Chap. **Honors/Awds:** Execellence in Architecture, Soc Gargoyle, 1971; Ill Pub Serv Award, Excellence Design, City Champaign, 1979-82; Cert Recognition Archit, Ill House Representatives, 1991. **Special Achievements:** Appointed a NASA Res Fel in 1978, 1979 to begin preliminary design work on Space Station Freedom. **Home Addr:** 2217 Ave B, PO Box 278, Bradenton Beach, FL 34217-2256, **Home Phone:** (941)779-1586.

### CLAY, REV. JULIUS C.
Clergy. **Personal:** married Denise M Cummings; children: Kimberly. **Educ:** Lane Col, Jackson, Tenn, BS; Univ Mo, St Louis, Mo, MEd; Eden Theol Sem, St Louis, Mo, MDiv; United Theol Sem, Dayton, Ohio, Doctor Ministry. **Career:** Greater Cleaves Christian Methodist Episcopal Church, paster; Williams Instnl Christian Methodist Episcopal Church, pastor, currently, Southeast Mo-Ill-Wis Region, Former Asst Secy; Israel Metrop CME Church, Gary, Ind, Leader bldg a church edifice; CME Gen Conferences, Deleg, 1986, Nairobi, Kenya, 1986, 1990, 1994, Rio de Janeiro, Brazil, 1996, 1998, World Methodist Conferences Brighton, Eng, 2001, 2002, & 2006, rep, Nat Coun Churches, Cong Nat Black Churches; CME Church Leadership Schs, Okla City (Okla), Gary (Ind), & Milwaukee (Wis), Former Dean; Former Adj Prof, Wimberly Sch Relig & Grad Theol Ctr Okla City Univ, Okla City, Okla. **Orgs:** Vpres, pres, Interfaith Clergy Coun, 1992-94;

vpres, Police Chaplaincy; vpres, Nat Advan Asn Colored People, Milwaukee Chap; nat chmn, Friends Phillips Sch Theol; Omega Psi Phi Faternity; bd mem, Tri-State Law Enforcement; Found; bd mem, Nat Inst Human Develop, Inc; chaplain, founder, first pres, Lane Col Alumni Asn, Gary, Ind; chaplain, Detroit Chap LCAA; vpres, Methodist Ministers Alliance Okla City; Okla Coun Churches; Concerned Clergy Spiritual Renewal; adv bd, Lincoln Nat Bank; pres, Interfaith Clergy Coun Gary, Ind; vpres, Gary Community Sch Corp; Bank One Adv Bd Merrillville, Ind; adv bd, Steele City Hall Fame; adv bd, Sheriff's Chaplaincy Lake County, Ind; founder & first chmn, Milwaukee United Better Housing Prog; pres, Milwaukee Ministerial Housing Coun. **Honors/Awds:** Distinguished Man of the Milwaukee, Top Ladies Distinction Inc; Student Christian Association Award, Lane Col. **Special Achievements:** Author, Leadership Skills Required to Renew a Declining Church in a Decaying Community. **Home Addr:** 2337 Wash St, Gary, IN 46407, **Home Phone:** (219)883-3859. **Business Addr:** Pastor, Williams Institutional Christian Methodist Episcopal (CME) Church, 151 W 136th St, New York, NY 10030, **Business Phone:** (212)283-6959.

### CLAY, LACY. See CLAY, WILLIAM LACY, JR.

### CLAY, DR. REUBEN ANDERSON, JR.
Physician. **Personal:** Born Feb 8, 1938, Richmond, VA; son of Reuben A and Sue Clarke; married Ardelia Brown; children: Raymond Alan & Adrienne Beth. **Educ:** Amherst Col, BA, 1960; Univ Rochester, MD, Obstet & Gynec, 1964. **Career:** San Francisco Gen Hosp, internship, 1964-65; Cornell Univ Med Ctr, resident, 1967-68; Univ Cailf, resd obstet-gynec, 1968-71; pvt prac, physician; Univ Calif, assoc clin prof, 1981; Ralph K Davies Med Ctr, chief gynec, 1982-86; Pac Gynec Ctr, gynec, 2004-; pvt pract gynec, currently. **Orgs:** San Francisco City Med Soc, 1971-; Nat Med Asn; AMA; Am Fert Soc; dipl, Am Bd Obstet Gynec, 1973; fel Am Col Obstet Gynec, 1974; asst clin prof, Univ Calif San Francisco, 1974-; San Francisco Gynec Soc; pres, Parnassus Hosps Obstet Gynec Med Group Inc, 1979-89; secy, Dist IX Am Col Obstet Gynec, 1981-88; fel Am Cong Obstetricians & Gynecologists. **Home Addr:** 53 Presidio Dr, Novato, CA 94949-6160, **Home Phone:** (415)234-6316. **Business Addr:** Physician, Pacific Gynecology & Obstetric Medical Group, 2100 Webster St Suite 319, San Fransisco, CA 94115, **Business Phone:** (415)923-3123.

### CLAY, ROSS COLLINS
Educator. **Personal:** Born Dec 15, 1908, Conehatta, MS; married Ollie Dolores Billingslea; children: Ross Jr. **Educ:** Jackson State Univ, attended 1934; Fisk Univ, MA, 1940; N Western Univ, MUSM, Educ, 1953; Ind Univ, attended 1962; Miss Southern Univ, Workshop, 1970. **Career:** Dir Music Educ Tutorial Teacher, composer ch music, piano, organ, instruments, voices; Corinth High Sch, dir music, 1934-35; Humphries Co Tr Sch, music educ, 1935-36; AR Baptist Col, music educ, 1936-38; Geeter High Sch, music educ, 1940-43; Friendship Jr Col, dir music defense worker, 1943-46; Philander Smith Col, dir music, 1946-48; Lane Col, dir music, 1948-53; Jackson State Univ, dir music educ, tutorial teacher, 1953-74. **Orgs:** Music Educators Nat Con; Nat Educ Asn; MTA; Am Asn Univ Profs; Nat Coun Sr Cits; AARP. **Honors/Awds:** NART Cert Merit, JSU, 1974; Honorary Doctorate of Divinity, Mc Kinley Theological Seminary, 1981. **Home Addr:** 1750 Topp Ave, Jackson, MS 39204, **Home Phone:** (601)352-4371.

### CLAY, STANLEY BENNETT
Actor, writer, television producer. **Personal:** Born Mar 18, 1950, Chicago, IL; son of Raymond Leon Fleming and Bertha Florence Fleming. **Career:** Argo Reportory Co, artistic dir, 1971-74; One Flight Up Theatre Co, resident dir playwright, 1974-80; Preceptor Commun, producer, dir, playwright; Sepia mag, entertainment ed, 1981; London's Blues & Soul mag, am corresp, 1984-87; Los Angeles Theatre Rev, theatre critic, 1989-91; Why Do Fools Fall In Love, music dir; SBC Mag, auth, ed-in-chief/publ; TV Series: "Room 222", 1970-71; Sanford and Son, 1972; Marcus Welby MD, 1973; Police Story, 1974; Good Times, 1975; Harry O, 1976; Serpico, 1977; Police Woman, 1978; Annihilator, 1986; Cheers, 1990-91; Ritual, writer & dir, 2000; In Search of Pretty Young Black Men, auth, 2001; "The Wanda Sykes Show", 2009; Films: Private Duty Nurses, 1971; Cleopatra Jones, 1973; Man Friday, 1975; Cannonball, 1976; All the President's Men, 1976; The Strange Thing About the Johnsons, 2011. **Orgs:** Exec comt, Nat Asn Advan Colored People, Beverly Hills, 1977-80; bd dirs, Int Friendship Network; vpres, bd dirs, Los Angeles Black Theatre, 1989-92; Los Angeles Black Playwrights, 1988-; vpres, bd dir, Minority AIDS Proj, 1990-97. **Honors/Awds:** Three Drama Logue Awards; NAACP Image Award; 2 NAACP Theatre Awards; Outstanding Cultural Achievement Award, African Am Gay & Lesbian Cultural Alliance, 1990; 2 Drama-Logue Awards, Jonin, Drama-Logue Mag, 1989; Lifeguard/Role Model Award, Genre Magazine, 1993; Pan African Film Festival Jury Award; Int Edna Crutch field Founders Literary Achievement Award, Black Writers & Artists, 1997. **Special Achievements:** Novels: Diva, In Search Of Pretty Young Men; Looker, 2007. Co-author: Visible Lives. **Home Addr:** 19309 Hillford Ave, Carson, CA 90746. **Business Addr:** Author Publisher and Editor, SBC Magazine, 1155 4th Ave, Los Angeles, CA 90019, **Business Phone:** (323)733-5661.

### CLAY, TIMOTHY BYRON
Manager. **Personal:** Born Sep 22, 1955, Louisville, KY; son of Bernard H and Louise Middleton; married Phyllis Wells; children: Jacqueline Simone & Arielle Christine. **Educ:** Univ Louisville, bus admin, 1974; Morehouse Col, bus admin, 1975; Oakwood Col, Huntsville AL, BS, bus admin, 1978; Univ Ala, Birmingham, AL, MBA, acct & mgt, 1982; Dartmouth, Grad Tuck, MBA, acct & data processing, 2006. **Career:** BellSouth Servs, staff analyst, 1978-86; Acct & Bus Consults Inc, co-owner & pres, 1984-; creator, writer & sem producer, 1985-; Protective Indust Ins Co, comptroller, controller, 1986-87; Miles Col, instr, 1986-89; Birmingham Minority Bus Develop Ctr, exec dir, 1987-94; Porter White Yardley Capital Inc, Birmingham, AL, proj dir, 1987; Maui Writers Conf, atendee, 2006. **Orgs:** Writer Birmingham Times; Big Bros/Big Sisters; Birmingham Asn Urban Bankers, 1988-; bd dir, Nat Alliance Tax Bus Owners, 2003-. **Honors/Awds:** Leadership Award, Birmingham, AL, 1989. **Home Addr:** 1812 Carson Rd Apt A, Birmingham, AL 35215-9304, **Home Phone:** (205)202-4686. **Business Addr:** President, Co-owner, Accounting & Business Consultants Inc, 4120 2nd Ave S, Birmingham, AL 35222, **Business Phone:** (205)425-9000.

### CLAY, WILLIAM LACY, SR. (BILL CLAY, SR.)
Politician, social worker, army officer. **Personal:** Born Apr 30, 1931, St. Louis, MO; son of Irving and Luella Hyatt; married Carol Ann Johnson; children: Vicki Flynn, William Lacy Jr & Michelle Katherine. **Educ:** St Louis Univ, BS, hist & polit sci, 1953. **Career:** Congressperson (reitred); Real estate broker, St Louis, Mo, 1955-59; Indust Life Ins Co, mgr, 1959-61; 26th Ward, St Louis, Mo, dem alderman, 1959-64; St Co & Munic Employees Union, bus rep, 1961-64; Steamfitters Union, Local 562 Educ, rep, 1966-67; 26th Ward, demcommitteeman, 1964-85; Comt Post Off & Civil Serv, chmn, 1991-95; US House Rep, Dist one, congressman, 1969-2001. **Orgs:** Nat Asn Advan Colored People; CORE; St Louis Jr Chamber Com; founder, William L Clay Scholar & Res Fund, 1985-; hon bd adv, Nat Stud Leadership Conf; mem bd, Perdue Farms, 2001-; co-founder, Cong Black Caucus, 2007; founder, William L. Clay Scholarship and Research Fund. **Honors/Awds:** Distinguished Citizens Award, Alpha Kappa Alpha, 1969; Argus Award, St. Louis Argus Newspaper, 1969; St. Louis Walk of Fame; named honor, Poplar Street Bridge renamed Congressman William L. Clay Sr. Bridge, 2013; St. Louis Walk of Fame. **Special Achievements:** Book: "To Kill or Not to Kill: Thoughts on Capital Punishment", 1990; "Just Permanent Interests: Black Americans in Congress, 1870-1991", 1992; "Racism in the White House: A Common Practice of Most United States Presidents", 2002; "Bill Clay: A Political Voice at the Grass Roots", 2004. **Home Addr:** 8021 W Florissant Ave, St Louis, MO 63136-1449. **Business Addr:** Founder, William L Clay Scholarship and Research Fund, PO Box 4693, St Louis, MO 63108, **Business Phone:** (314)721-0091.

### CLAY, WILLIAM LACY, JR. (LACY CLAY)
Government official, politician. **Personal:** Born Jul 27, 1956, St. Louis, MO; son of William L and Carol Ann Johnson; married Ivie Lewellen; children: Carol & William III. **Educ:** Univ Md, BS, polit sci, 1983, cert paralegal studies, 1982; Harvard Univ, John F Kennedy Sch Govt, attended 1993. **Career:** US House Rep, asst door keeper, 1976-83, Mo State, house rep, 1983-90; W.A. Thomas Realty, real estate agt, 1986-2000; paralegal; Mo Gen Assembly, sen, 1991-2001; US House Reps, first dist MO rep, 2001-. **Orgs:** Bd dir, Cong Black Caucus Found & William L Clay Scholar & Res Fund, 1989-; Mo Legis Black Caucus; Dem Nat Comt; Cong Black Caucus; Cong Progressive Caucus; Kappa Alpha Psi fraternity; Int Conserv Caucus; House Oversight & Govt Reform Comt; House Financial Serv Comt; chair, House Info Policy Subcomt. **Honors/Awds:** Legislator of the Year, Mo Asn Social Welfare; Political Leadership Award, Young Democrats City St Louis. **Home Addr:** 6023 Waterman, St Louis, MO 63112, **Home Phone:** (314)721-8582. **Business Addr:** Representative, United States House of Representatives, 625 N Euclid St Suite 326, St. Louis, MO 63108, **Business Phone:** (314)367-1970.

### CLAY, WILLIE JAMES
Football player. **Personal:** Born Sep 5, 1970, Pittsburgh, PA; son of Marsha. **Educ:** Ga Inst Technol. **Career:** Football player (retired); Detroit Lions, 1992, defensive back, 1993, strong safety, 1994-95; New Eng Patriots, free safety, 1996-98; New Orleans Saints, free safety, 1999.

### CLAYBORN, RAYMOND DEWAYNE
Football player, executive. **Personal:** Born Jan 2, 1955, Ft. Worth, TX; son of Jessie Wilson and Adell; married Cindy Cavazos; children: Lindsey Marie. **Educ:** Univ Tex, Austin, BS, commun, 1977. **Career:** Football player (retired), representative; New Eng Patriots, left cornerback & right cornerback & kick Returner & 1977-89; Cleveland Browns, right cornerback & defensive back, 1990-91; Houston Texans, Nat Football League Uniform Prog, rep, currently. **Honors/Awds:** Pro Bowl, 1983, 1985, 1986; National Foundation & Hall of Fame. **Special Achievements:** Pro Football Weeklys All-AFC & All-Pro squads as a kick of freturner; set 5 Patriot kick off return records as a rookie; Second Team All-AFC by UPI; Second Team All-Pro by Col & Pro Football News weekly; Second Team All-NFL by NEA. **Business Addr:** Uniform Program Representative, Houston Texans, 2 Reliant Pk, Houston, TX 77054, **Business Phone:** (832)667-2002.

### CLAYBORNE, ONEAL N.
Government official. **Personal:** Born Dec 17, 1940, De Kalb, MS; married Deborah Roberts; children: Michelle & Shaneal. **Career:** Policeman (retired); Pct no 48 E St Louis, pct committeeman, 1979-87; City E St Louis, alderman, 1979-89; Aldermanic Pub Safety Comn, chmn, 1981-85; St Clair Co, spec dep sheriff, 1989-99. **Orgs:** Chmn, Proj ONEAL Citizen Patrol Neighborhood Watch, 1982-85. **Honors/Awds:** Special Achievement Award, Nat Coalition Ban Handguns, 1982. **Home Addr:** 840 N 79th St, East St. Louis, IL 62203-1816, **Home Phone:** (618)398-7507.

### CLAYBROOKS, JOHN, JR.
Executive, vice president (organization). **Personal:** Born Jan 21, 1968, Nashville, TN; son of John Sr and Gwendolyn; married Yolanda; children: Morgan Isabella. **Educ:** Univ Tenn, Knoxville, BS, mkt, 1990; Emory Univ Law Sch, JD, 1995; Vanderbilt Univ, MBA, 1997; Harvard Bus Sch, Exec Educ, IBM premier prog acct execs, 1999. **Career:** Procter & Gamble, mkt intern, 1988-89, sales rep, 1988-92; Gen Elec, MBA intern, 1996; IBM, global client mgr, 1997-99, e-bus mktg mgr, 1999-2000; LeasePlan, vpres bus integration, 2000-01, sr vpres sales & chief mkt officer, 2001-03; Home Depot Inc, dir brand mkt, 2003-08; Dow Chem, dir, corp brand mgt & advert, 2008-13; CSX Corp, global dir, brand, digital media & mkt commun, 2013-. **Orgs:** INROADS Inc, 1984-; Gov, Tenn Am Legion Boys State, 1985; Alpha Phi Alpha, 1987-; Univ Tenn Nat Alumni Asn, Bd Gov, 1989-90; Phi Delta Phi Int Law Fraternity, 1994-; IBM Atlanta Metrop Area Diversity Coun, 1999-2000; Metro Atlanta Chamber Com, bd advisor, 2001-03; Habitat Humanity, Home Depot Vol, 2003-08; Asn Nat Advertisers, Brand Develop Comt, 2004-; bd dir, Communities Schs Atlanta, 2006-08; Int Asn Bus Communicators, 2013-. **Home Addr:** 713 Peteywood Dr, Austell, GA 30106, **Home Phone:** (770)434-9957. **Business Addr:** Senior Vice President, Chief Marketing Officer, LeasePlan USA, 2030 Dow Ctr, Midland, MI 48674, **Business Phone:** (989)636-1792.

### CLAYE, CHARLENE MARETTE
Art historian. **Personal:** Born Apr 6, 1945, Chicago, IL; daughter of Anne and Clifton. **Educ:** Univ Bridgeport, BA, 1966; Univ Paris, cert, 1968; Howard Univ, MA, 1970. **Career:** Univ DC, instr, 1970, 1973; Howard Univ Wash, instr, 1970, 1973; Spelman Col, Atlanta, instr, 1971-72; Clayton Jr Col, instr, 1972-; New Muse, exec dir, 1974-78; Calif African Am Mus, exec dir, 1982-83; Claye Inst, exec dir, currently. **Orgs:** Assoc dir, African Cult Serv, 1970; pres, Nat Conf Artists, 1976-78; Am Soc Aesthetics; Nat Educ Asn. **Honors/Awds:** Pubished curator "The Black Artist in the WPA", 1933-43, Grants, Travel Museum Professional Nat Museum Act, 1976; Aid, Special Exhibitions Nat Endowment Art, 1976 & 1977, Planning Grant, Nat Endowment Humanities, 1976. **Special Achievements:** Article on symbolism of African Textiles Contemporary Weavers Asn of Texas, cover design for Logic for Black Undergrad, Curator permanent exhibit on "The Black Contrib to Devel of Brooklyn 1660-1960". **Home Addr:** 3209 Ewing St, Houston, TX 77004. **Business Addr:** Executive Director, The Claye Institute, Rt 1, Fordyce, AR 71742-8781.

### CLAYTON, DR. ALFRED BANNERMAN
Neurologist. **Personal:** married Mary. **Educ:** Univ Edinburgh, BS, 1963, MD, 1966. **Career:** Professor (retired), physician; Columbia Univ Col Physicians & Surgens, prof; Jamaica Hosp Med Ctr, neurologist; Muhlenberg Regional Med Ctr, internship, 1966-67; Marcy Psychiat Ctr, residency, neurol, 1967-68; Metrop Hosp Ctr, residency, neurol, 1968-69; New York Med Col, Metrop Hosp Ctr, residency, neurol, 1969-72; New York Presby Hosp, physician; neurologist, pvt pract, currently. **Orgs:** Am Bd Psychiat & Neurol. **Home Addr:** 180 Salem Rd, Westbury, NY 11590, **Home Phone:** (505)368-6401. **Business Addr:** Neurologist, Private Practitioner, 8906 135th St S, Jamaica, NY 11430, **Business Phone:** (718)658-2430.

### CLAYTON, DR. CONSTANCE ELAINE
Educator, school administrator. **Personal:** Born Jan 1, 1937?, Philadelphia, PA; daughter of Levi and Willabell Harris. **Educ:** Temple Univ, BA, elem educ, MA, elem sch admin, 1955; Univ Pa, PhD, 1974, EdD, 1981. **Career:** Educator(retired); Philadelphia Pub Sch Syst, William H. Harrison Sch, fourth grade teacher, 1955-64, social studies curric designer, 1964-69, African & Afro-Am studies prog, head, 1969-71; US Dept Labor, Women's Bur, dir, Mid Atlantic States, 1971-72, Early Childhood Develop Prog, dir, 1973-83, assoc supt, supt, 1982-93; Harvard Grad Sch Educ, first supt-in-residence, 1994; MCP Hahnemann Sch Med, Sch Pub Health, assoc dean, 1995; Drexel Univ, Ctr Community Health & Prev, prof & assoc dean community affairs. **Orgs:** Nat Asn Advan Colored People; chmn, Delta Sigma Theta; St Paul's Baptist Church; Nat Asn Advan Colored People; fel Rockefeller Found; Asn Schs Pub Health.

### CLAYTON, HON. EVA M.
Consultant, politician. **Personal:** Born Sep 16, 1934, Savannah, GA; married Theaoseus; children: Joanne, Theaoseus Jr, Martin & Reuben. **Educ:** Johnson C Smith Univ, Charlotte, BS, 1955; NC Cent Univ, MS, 1962. **Career:** NC State Dept Natural Resources & Community Develop, asst secy, 1977-81; Warren County Comn, chairperson, 1982-90, comnr, 1990-92; US House Rep, congresswoman, 1993-2003; UN Food & Agr Orgn, Rome, Italy, spec adv asst dir gen; Int Alliance against Hunger, secy; World Food Summit, spec adv; Eva Clayton Assocs Int, founder, consult, currently. **Orgs:** Co-chair, Rural Caucus; Chair, Cong Black Caucus Found; pres, freshmen class; Cotton Memorial Presby Church; Alpha Kappa Alpha Sorority; Ranking Dem mem, Agr Comt opers, oversight, nutrit. **Home Addr:** 59 River Rd, Littleton, NC 27850. **Business Addr:** Founder, Eva Clayton Associates Intl, 3100 Smoketree Ct Suite 420, Raleigh, NC 27604, **Business Phone:** (919)877-9229.

### CLAYTON, JANET THERESA
Journalist, editor. **Personal:** Born May 10, 1955, Los Angeles, CA; daughter of Pronzell B and Pinkie B Hodges; married Michael D Johnson; children: Jocelyn Michelle & Aaron. **Educ:** Univ Southern Calif, Los Angeles, CA, BA, jour, 1977; Cambridge Univ, study prog. **Career:** The Times; Los Angeles Times, staff writer, 1977-87, ed writer, 1990, asst ed, ed page, 1990-95, ed, ed pages, 1995-04, vpres, 1997-, asst managing ed, 2004-07; ThinkCure, pres, 2008-11; Edison Int/Southern Calif Edison, sr vpres, 2011-. **Orgs:** Black Journalists Asn Southern Calif, 1980-; Nat Asn Black Journalists, reporting team, 1986-; Am Soc Newspaper Eds; Phi Beta Kappa; fel, Brit-Am Conf; fel, Williamsburg Conf, Hong Kong; pres, Marysville Pub Schs. **Honors/Awds:** Reporting Team Award, Nat Asn Black Journalists, 1983; Black Woman of Achievement, Nat Asn Advan Colored People Legal Defense Fund. **Business Addr:** Assistant Managing Editor, Senior Vice President, Los Angeles Times, 202 W 1st St, Los Angeles, CA 90012.

### CLAYTON, LLOYD E.
Association executive, businessperson. **Personal:** Born Jul 8, 1921, Mobile, AL; son of William H and Ruby Roberts; married Lela Maxwell; children: Kenneth R, Robert L & Carole M. **Educ:** Howard Univ, BS, 1955. **Career:** Walter Reed Army Inst Res, res chemist, 1951-68; Task Force Health Care Disadvantaged, dep chmn, 1968-71; Status Health Black Community, proj officer, 1971; Status Dent Health Black Community, proj officer, 1972; Minority Physician Recruitment Nat Health Serv Corps, proj officer, 1973; Sickle Cell DisProg, proj officer, 1976; Black Cong Health & Law, proj officer, 1980, staff consult, 1980-88; Health Pact Inc, exec dir, pres & chief exec officer, 1993-; Carson Co, health scientist adminr, 2000-. **Orgs:** Asn Sports Int Track Club, 1967; off timer, Nat Invitational Track Meet, 1967-68. **Honors/Awds:** Appreciation and Gratitude Award for Outstanding Leadership in the Field of Sickle Cell Anemia San Juan PR, 1978; Superior Service Award, Nat Black Health Planners Asn Wintergreen VA, 1986; Meeting Planner of the Year, Nat Coalition Black Meeting Planners, 1989; Community Service Award, Am Diabetes Asn, 2000. **Business Addr:** President, Chief Executive Officer, Health Pact Inc, 4821 Blagden Ave NW, Washington, DC 20011-3715, **Business Phone:** (202)726-7510.

### CLAYTON, MATTHEW D.
Lawyer, executive. **Personal:** Born Mar 5, 1941, Philadelphia, PA; married Ramona Carter; children: Rebecca, Janice & Matthew D III. **Educ:** Univ Md, attended 1961; Univ Minn, attended 1963; PA State Univ, BA, 1966; Howard Univ Sch Law, JD, 1969. **Career:** Philadelphia Prisons Syst, correctional officer, 1963; Philadelphia Crime Presention Asn, staff, 1966; Small Bus Admin, legal asst, 1968; US Dept Labor, regional trial atty, 1969-72; Coun Corp Law, 1972-74; Smith Kline Corp, corp employee rels & litigation coun; pvt pract atty; Clayton & Assoc, atty, owner. currently. **Orgs:** Nat Bar Asn; Am Bar Asn; Fed Bar Asn; PA Bar Asn; Philadelphia Bar Asn; Indust Rel Res Asn; sect labor study young prof, US Dept Labor, 1970-72; coord, US Dept Labor; Nat Urban League; Nat Panel Arbitrators; Am Arbit Asn; Am Mgt Asn; Am Trial Lawyers Asn; Barristers Club; fund mem, World Lawyers Asn. **Honors/Awds:** Outstanding Academic Achievement America Jurisprudence Award; Outstanding Legal Service, Small Bus Admin. **Business Addr:** Attorney, Owner, Clayton & Associates, 865 Belmont Ave Suite 1, Philadelphia, PA 19104, **Business Phone:** (215)477-4400.

### CLAYTON, MINNIE H.
Librarian. **Personal:** married Robert L; children: Robert J III & Myrna A. **Educ:** Ala State Univ, BS, 1954; Atlanta Univ, MLS, 1970. **Career:** Dev & Book Col Porton, all ages, consult; Martin Luther King Ctr Social Change, libr archivist, 1969-78; Atlanta Univ Ctr, Southern Regional Coun Archives Proj, Dept Arch & Rec Mgt, proj archivist, 1978-80; Robert W Woodruff Libr, Div Arch & Spec Collections, dir, 1982-88, processing archivist, 1988-. **Orgs:** Am Libr Asn; Ga Library Asn; Metro-Atlanta Libr Asn; Nat Hist Soc; Soc Am Archivists; Am Asn Univ Professors; African Am Family Hist Asn; Ga Archivists; adv bd, State Hist Record Ga. **Home Addr:** 668 Waterford Rd NW, Atlanta, GA 30318-7147, **Home Phone:** (678)886-5318.

### CLAYTON, ROBERT L.
Labor relations manager, association executive. **Personal:** Born Dec 6, 1938, Morris Station, GA; son of Henry and Willie Mae Mercer; married Sharon Cage; children: Robert & Angela. **Educ:** Cent State Univ, Wilberforce, BS, bus admin, 1962; Akron Univ, Akron, postgrad studies, 1966. **Career:** Executive (retired), owner; Co-op Supermarkets, Akron, comptroller, 1965-73; Fiberbd, San Francisco, Calif, sr financial analyst, 1973-79; CH2M Hill, vpres diversity, 1979; BOBBY C's Lounge & Grille, owner, currently. **Orgs:** Soc Human Resources, 1980-; Nat Asn Minority Eng Prog Admin, 1983-; Nat Forum Black Pub Admin, 1984-; adv bd, Univ Calif, Los Angeles, 1986-93, indust tech adv bd, Statewide MESA, 1986-93, minority eng bd, Univ Calif Fullerton, 1988-93; Kappa Alpha Psi Fraternity; 32nd Degree, Mason Shrine; Owl Club Denver, 1994-. **Home Addr:** 2109 E Leo Pl, Chandler, AZ 85249. **Business Addr:** Owner, Principal, Bobby C's Lounge and Grille, 1140 E Wash St, Phoenix, AZ 85034-1051, **Business Phone:** (602)252-2273.

### CLAYTON, ROYCE SPENCER
Baseball player. **Personal:** Born Jan 2, 1970, Burbank, CA; married Samantha Davies; children: Royce Jr, Imani, Niya & Elijah. **Career:** Baseball player (retired); San Francisco Giants, shortstop, 1991-95; St Louis Cardinals, 1996-98; Tex Rangers, 1998-2000; Chicago White Sox, 2001-02; Milwaukee Brewers, 2003; Colo Rockies, 2004; Ariz Diamondbacks, 2005; Wash Nationals, 2006; Cincinnati Reds, 2006; Toronto Blue Jays, 2007; Boston Red Sox, 2007. **Orgs:** Founder, Royce Clayton Family Found, 1997-; vpres external affairs, Nat Alliance African Am Athletes. **Special Achievements:** Actor and producer, known for Sunday Night Baseball (1990), Moneyball (2011) and Macy's 4th of July Fireworks Spectacular (2015). **Home Addr:** 5924 Paseo Canyon Dr, Malibu, CA 90265-3130, **Home Phone:** (310)589-8834.

### CLAYTON, THEAOSEUS T., SR.
Lawyer. **Personal:** Born Oct 2, 1930, Roxboro, NC; married Eva McPherson; children: 4. **Educ:** Johnson C Smith Univ, AB, 1955; NC Cent Univ, Sch Law, JS & JD, 1958. **Career:** McKissick & Berry Durham, NC, atty, 1961; Gilliland & Clayton, jr partner, 1961-66; Theaoseus T Clayton PA Inc, sole propietorship, 1963-66, pres, atty law, 1979-, sr atty; Clayton & Ballance, sr partner, 1966-78; Dist Ct, law pract; Super Ct, law pract; Ct Appeals, law pract; NC Supreme Ct, law pract; Fed Dist Ct, law pract; US Supreme Ct, law pract. **Orgs:** Nat Bar Asn; Am Bar Asn; NC State Bar; NC Bar Asn; NC Trial Lawyers Asn; NC Asn Black Lawyers; Nat Conf Black Lawyers; secy & treas, ninth Jud Dist Bar Asn; pres, Charles Williamson Bar Asn; chief coun, Floyd B McKissick & Floyd B McKissick Enterprises Inc; life mem & state vpres, Nat Asn Advan Colored People; Warren County Dem Party; Warren County Polit Action Coun; second Cong Dist Black Caucus; vice chmn, NC Bd Youth Develop. **Special Achievements:** First lawyer to practice in Warren County. **Home Addr:** 177 Northside Dr, Littleton, NC 27850-8314, **Home Phone:** (252)586-4865. **Business Addr:** Attorney at Law, Theaoseus T Clayton PA Inc, 3100 Smoketree Ct Suite 420, Raleigh, NC 27629-1403, **Business Phone:** (919)981-0400.

### CLAYTON, XERNONA
Executive, executive director, association executive. **Personal:** Born Aug 30, 1930, Muskogee, OK; daughter of James Brewster and Lillie; married Edward; married Paul L Brady; children: Laura & Paul L Jr. **Educ:** Tenn State Univ, BA, 1952; Univ Chicago, MA, 1957. **Career:** Urban League, Chicago, IL, undercover agt, 1952; vol sch dropout prog Los Angeles, CA, 1960; WAGA-TV, hostess, 1968-75; Atlanta Voice, newspaper columnist; Chicago & LA, teacher pub schs; photog & fashion modeling; Turner Broadcasting Syst Inc, consult & asst corp vpres-urban affairs & coordr minority affairs & dir, 1988-. **Orgs:** Atlanta Womens C C; Doctors Comt Implementation, 1966; State & Manpower Adv Comt GA Dept Labor; Nat Asn Mkt Develop; Arts Alliance Guild; Am Women Radio & TV; pres, Nat Asn Media Women, 1982-90; bd dir, Nat Asn Press Women; Atlanta Chap Sigma Delta Chi; Atlanta Broadcast Exec Club; founder, Atlanta Chap Media Women; Nat Acad TV Arts & Sci; Ebenezer Bapt Ch; Alpha Kappa Alpha Sorority; bd dir, Greater Atlanta Mult Sclerosis Soc; hon assoc, So Ballet; founder, Trumpet Awards; Nat Acad Tv Arts & Sci; Southern Christian Leadership Conf; Grand Dragon Ku Klux Klan; founder, pres & chief exec Officer, Trumpet Awards Found Inc, currently. **Honors/Awds:** Outstanding Leadership Award; winner, Nat Asn Mkt Develop, 1968; Bronze Woman of Yr; Human Rels Award, Phi Delta Kappa Sorority, 1969; Press Award, GA Assoc, 1969-71; Mother of Yr, Future Homemakers Am Douglas HS, 1969; Excellence in TV Programming Award, LA Chap Negro Bus & Prof Women, 1970; Flying Orchid Award, Delta Airline; named Atlanta's Five Best Dressed Brentwood Models, 1971; named Atlanta's Ten Best Dressed Women Women's C C, 1972; Xernona Clayton Scholar, Am Intercultural Stud Exchange, named in hon, 1987; Emmy Award, 1987; Media Woman of the Yr, 1989; Distinguished Leadership Award, Nat Asn Equal Opportunity Higher Educ, 1996, Corp Award, 2003; Local Community Serv Award, 2004; Leadership & Dedication in Civil Rights Award, 2004; Xernona Clayton Scholar, Atlanta Asn of Black Journalists, named in hon; Mickey Leland Award, Nat Asn Minorities Cable; Coretta Scott King Award, SCLC; Madam C. J. Walker Award, EBONYS Outstanding Women Mkt & Commun; Outstanding Corp Prof Award, PowerNetworking Family; Hon DHL, Tenn State Univ; Justice Award, Southern Christian Leadership Conf, 2004. **Special Achievements:** South First Black person to have her own tv show; appointed by Gov of GA to Motion Picture & TV Commn for4-yr term, 1972-76; She is one of the ten top black women, BlackVoice.com, 2002; first African American appointed as a Federal Administrative Law judge. **Home Addr:** 1185 Niskey Lake Rd SW, Atlanta, GA 30331. **Business Addr:** President, Chief Executive Officer, Trumpet Awards Foundation Inc, Centennial Twr, Atlanta, GA 30303, **Business Phone:** (404)878-6738.

### CLAYTOR, CHARLES E.
Association executive. **Personal:** Born Jun 2, 1936, Hotcoal, WV; son of Harvey and Fairy Hickman; married Annette Broadnax; children: Dreama, Charles Jr & Brien. **Educ:** NY City Col. **Career:** United Brotherhood Carpenters, New York, pres, 1967. **Home Addr:** 21 Autumn Lane, Amityville, NY 11701, **Home Phone:** (631)842-8023.

### CLEAGE, PEARL MICHELLE (PEARL LOMAX)
Writer, novelist, journalist. **Personal:** Born Dec 7, 1948, Springfield, MA; daughter of Albert B Jr and Doris Graham; married Zaron W Burnett Jr; married Michael Lomax; children: Deignan. **Educ:** Howard Univ, attended 1969; Spelman Col, BA, 1971. **Career:** Catalyst Mag, founding ed, 1986-96; Mayor Maynard Jackson, press secy; Atlanta Tribune, columnist, 1988-; Spelman Col, playwright-in-residence, instr drama, 1991-93; Smith Col, playwright-in-residence, 1994; City Atlanta, commun dir; productions Puppetplay, playwriting, 1980; Univ Mass, Amherst, Bateman scholar-in-residence, 1996; Agnes Scott Col, Laney prof-in-residence, 1997; writer, currently; plays: Flyin' West, 1992; Blues for An Alabama Sky, 1995; Bourbon at the Border; essays: Mad at Miles & Deals with the Devil: A Black Woman's Guide to Truth, 1990; Good Brother Blues; Deals with the Devil; novels: What Looks Like Crazy on An Ordinary Day, Avon Books, 1997; I Wish I Had a Red Dress, Morrow/Avon, 2001; Some Things I Never Thought I'd Do, 2003; poems: Broadside Press, 1971; We Don't Need No Music; Spelman Col, playwright, currently; Just Us Theater Co, artistic dir, currently. **Honors/Awds:** Bronze Jubilee Award, 1983; Outstanding Columnist Award, Atlanta Asn Black Journalists, 1991; Onstage Award, Outstanding New Play, AT&T, 1992; Outstanding Columnist Award, Atlanta Asn Media Women, 1993; Award, Asn Southern Writers, 1994; 2 Audellco Awards, Hon off Broadway Achievements, Best Play & Best Playwright. **Business Addr:** Writer, Novelist, Just Us Theater Co, PO Box 42271, Atlanta, GA 30311-0271.

### CLEAMONS, JAMES MITCHELL (JIM CLEAMONS)
Basketball coach, basketball player. **Personal:** Born Sep 13, 1949, Lincolnton, NC. **Educ:** Ohio State Univ, attended 1971. **Career:** Basketball player (retired), basketball coach; Los Angeles Lakers, 1971-72; Cleveland Cavaliers, 1972-77; New York Knicks, 1977-79; Wash Bullets, 1979-80; Furman Univ, asst coach, 1982-83; Ohio State Univ, asst coach, 1983-87; Youngstown State Penguins, head coach, 1987-89; Chicago Bulls, asst coach, 1989-96; Dallas Mavericks, head coach, 1996-97; Chicago Condors, 1998-99; Los Angeles Lakers, asst coach, 1999-2004; New Orleans Hornets, asst coach, 2004-06; Okla City Hornets, 2006; Los Angeles Lakers, asst coach, 2006-11; Zhejiang Guangsha, China, 2011-12; Milwaukee Bucks, asst coach, 2013-; New York Knicks, asst, 2014-. **Business Addr:** Assistant Coach, Milwaukee Bucks, 3501 S Lake Dr, Milwaukee, WI 53207, **Business Phone:** (414)489-2100.

### CLEAVER, EMANUEL, II
Government official, mayor, clergy. **Personal:** Born Oct 26, 1944, Waxahachie, TX; married Dianne; children: Evan Donaldson, Emanuel III, Emiel Davenport & Marissa Dianne. **Educ:** Prairie View A&M Col, BS; St Paul Sch Theol, Kansas City, MDiv; St Paul Sch Theol, DSE. **Career:** St James-Paseo United Methodist Church, pastor, 1972-2009, sr pastor; Kans City, City Coun, councilman, 1979-91; City Kans City, mayor, 1991-93; KCUR-FM, host; US House Rep, Mo 5th Cong Dist, 2005-. **Orgs:** Bd dir, De La Salle Ed Ctr; mid-cent reg vpres, Southern Christian Leadership Conf; pres, bd trustee, Leon Jordan Scholar Fund; bd trustee, St Paul Sch Theol; coun finance, United Methodist Conf; bd dir, chmn bd, Freedom; Alpha Phi Alpha; Nat Asn Advan Colored People; chair, Cong Black Caucus, 2010; founder, Southern Christian Leadership Conf; Alpha Phi Alpha; Dem Nat Comt. **Honors/Awds:** Achievements & honors, 41; Man of the Year, Alpha Phi Alpha, 1968; Community Leaders Am, 1971; Builder of Boys Award, Boys Club Am, 1976; White House Guest, Pres Jimmy Carter, 1977; Recognition of Thanks, Woodland Elem Sch, 1983; Apprec Award, Nat Asn Advan Colored People, 1984; Black History Award, Univ MO-Kans City, 1984; Distint Service Award, Exceptional Leadership & Devoted Serv Civil Rights, Alpha Phi Alpha, 1984; Award for Outstanding Service, Freedom Inc, 1984; Citizen of the Year, Omega Psi Phi; Harold L Holliday Sr Civil Rights Award, Drum Maj Justice Award, 1991; Nat Asn Advan Colored People, 1992; Distinguished Graduate Award, St Paul Sch Theol, 1993; Kansas City Anti-Apartheid Award, 1993; James C. Kirkpatrick Excellence for Government Award, 1993; Distinguished Citizen of the Midwest Award, Nat Conf Christians & Jews, 1993; Highest Distinction Award, Alpha Alpha Chapter, 1999; LLD, Ottawa Univ, 1999; Conspicuous Service Medal, Mo Governor Mel Carnahan, 1999; A road in Kansas City consisting Brush Creek Blvd, was renamed Emanuel Cleaver II Boulevard, 2000; Fannie Lu Hamer Award, Nat Conf Black Mayors, 2001. **Special Achievements:** First African-American elected mayor to Kansas City. **Home Addr:** 8217 E Gregory Blvd, Kansas City, MO 64133-6325. **Business Addr:** Representative, US House Representatives, 400 E 9th St Suite 9350, Kansas City, MO 64106, **Business Phone:** (816)842-4545.

### CLEGG, DR. LEGRAND H., II
Lawyer. **Personal:** Born Jun 29, 1944, Los Angeles, CA; son of LeGrand (deceased) and Genell. **Educ:** Univ Calif, Los Angeles, BA, 1966; Howard Univ, Sch Law, JD, 1969; Compton Community Col, AA. **Career:** Attorney (retired); Compton Community Col, instr; Robert Edelen Law Offices, atty, 1975-; Compton, Calif, admin asst, 1970-72; Dept Justice, legal intern, 1968-69; pvt law practr, 1974-; Compton Unified Sch Dist, co-counr, 1976-77; Vassar Col, 1978-79; City Compton, Calif, dep city atty, 1977, chief dep city atty, 1981-93, city atty, 2009. **Orgs:** LA Bar asn; Calif Lawyers Criminal Justice; Langston Law Club; Nat Conf Black Lawyers; Compton Cult Commn; Asn Black Psychol; Pilgrim Missionary Bapt Ch. **Honors/Awds:** Pubs La Times, 1974; Current bibliography on African Affairs, 1969, 1972. **Special Achievements:** Editor & Publisher: "The Vanishing Evidence Of Classical African Civilizations Part 1: The Temple Evidence", 1997. **Home Addr:** 2001 N Nestor Ave, Compton, CA 90222, **Home Phone:** (310)631-8367.

### CLEMENDOR, DR. ANTHONY ARNOLD
Physician, educator, dean (education). **Personal:** Born Nov 8, 1933; son of Anthony and Beatrice Stewart Thompson; married Elaine C Browne; children: Anthony A & David A; married Janat Jenkins. **Educ:** NY Univ, BA, 1959; Howard Univ Col Med, MD, 1963. **Career:** NY Med Col, clin prof, OB-GYN, dir off minority affairs, assoc dean; pvt pract gynec, currently. **Orgs:** Pres, Stud Am Med Asn Chap, Howard Univ, 1961-62; dir, Off Minority Affairs, NY Med Col, 1974-97; pres, NY Gynec Soc, 1988; bd dirs, Caribbean Am Ctr, 1988; pres, NY County Med Soc, 1992; Nat Urban League; Nat Asn Advan Colored People; 100 Black Men; NY Urban League; bd mem, Elmcor; fel Am Col OB-Gyn; Am Pub Health Asn; co-chair, Med Soc State NY, Health Care Disparity. **Honors/Awds:** SNMA Award, Univ Buffalo Chap, 1984; T & T Alliance Award, Trinidad & Tobago Alliance NA, 1984; Trinidad & Tobago Nurses Asn Am Inc Award, 1988; Nat Award, Nat Asn Med Minority Educr, 1989; Physician of the Year Award, Manhattan Cent Med Soc, 1989. **Special Achievements:** Publications: "Achalasia & Nutritional Deficiency During Pregnancy", 1969; "Transient Asymptomatic Hydrothorax in Pregnancy", 1976. **Home Addr:** 125 E 80th St, New York, NY 10075, **Home Phone:** (212)249-4501. **Business Addr:** Physician, Private Practice, 100 East 77 St, New York, NY 10075, **Business Phone:** (212)628-1210.

### CLEMENT, ANTHONY GEORGE
Football player. **Personal:** Born Apr 10, 1976, Lafayette, LA; married Fatima; children: Ebony, Langhsten, Anthony Jr & Caleb. **Educ:** Univ La, Lafayette, attended. **Career:** Ariz Cardinals, 1998, 2002, right tackle, 1999-2001, 2003-04, tackle, 1999; San Francisco 49ers, left tackle, 2005; New York Jets, right tackle, 2006-07; New Eng Patriots, 2008; free agt, currently. **Honors/Awds:** All-District 6A; All-Louisiana Class AAA. **Special Achievements:** Only Cardinals Offensive Liner to start all 16 games. **Business Addr:** Professional Football Player, New England Patriots, 1 Patriot Pl, Foxborough, MA 02035-1388, **Business Phone:** (508)543-8200.

### CLEMENT, WILLIAM A., JR.
Chief executive officer, computer executive. **Personal:** Born Jan 22, 1943, Atlanta, GA; married Ressie Guy; children: Anika P & Leanetta Spencer. **Educ:** Morehouse Col, BA, bus admin & mathematics, 1964; Univ Mich Sch Bus, comput sci, 1965; Univ Pa, Wharton Sch Finance, PA, MBA, ins & finance, 1967; London Sch Econs & Polit Sci, attended 2004. **Career:** Bank Am, com loan officer, 1967-69; Prudential-Bache Securities Inc, stockbroker, 1969-71; Robinson Humphrey Co, rep & stockbroker, 1971-73; Citizens Trust Bank Atlanta, vpres & loan officer, 1973-77; US Small Bus Admin, assoc adminr, 1977-81; Dobbs Ram & Co, chmn & chief exec officer, 1981-2008; Atlanta Life Ins Co, dir, 1992, 2001; Radiant Systs Inc, outside corp dir, 2005-11; Atlanta Life Financial Group Inc, pres & chief exec officer, 2008-11, TRX Inc, independent dir, 2008-12; BSR Trust LLC, independent dir, 2009-12; NC Mutual Life Ins Co, life ins agt, exec vpres; Robinson Humphrey & Am Express Inc, stockbroker; Bache & Co, rep; NC Nat Bank, credit analyst & com loan officer; Citizens Trust Bank, vpres & sr loan officer; Nat Bank Wash; Natl Consumer Coop Bank, bd dir; NCNB Corp, com loan officer; Dobbs Bus Serv, pres & chief exec officer, chmn, currently. **Orgs:** Former chmn bd, Clement Ins Group Inc, 1993-98; bd dir, Bus League, Atlanta Urban League; bd dir, Big Bros Atlanta; bd chm, chief vol officer, Atlanta Bus League; bd dir, Atlanta Chamber Com; bd dir, Metrop Atlanta Community Found; bd dir, Leadership Atlanta; bd dir, Atlanta Conv & Visitors Bur; bd mem, Res Atlanta, Atlanta Exchange, Alliance Theatre Co; Atlanta Coalition 100 Black Men; Soc Int Bus Fels; Int Bus fel London Bus Sch; chmn bd, Atlanta Bus League; vice chmn, Atlanta Downtown Improv Dist; Zeil Millers Future Communities Comn; vice chmn, Opportunity Funding Corp; bd dir, Radiant Systs; co-chmn, Atlanta Action Forum; trustee, Maynard Jackson Youth Found; fel Antioch Urban Ministries; fel Carter Ctr Bd Counors; chmn bd dirs, USEP Inc; life mem, Alpha Phi Alpha; life mem, Morehouse Col Nat Alumni Asn; bd mem, Nat Coop Bank. **Honors/Awds:** Chartered Life Underwriter, American College Chartered Life Underwriters, 1972; Entrepreneur of the Year, NABMBA, 1990; Small Bus Person of the Year, Atlanta Chamber Com, 1990; Entrepreneur of the Year, Crim High Sch, 1992; Bus Owner of the Year, Atlanta Tribune, 1992; Entrepreneur of the Year, SuccessGuide, 1992. **Home Addr:** 402 Castle Rock, McDonough, GA 30253-4295, **Home Phone:** (404)378-5364. **Business Addr:** Chairman, Chief Executive Officer, Dobbs Business Services, 2 Midtown Plz 1349 W Peachtree St NE Suite 1550, Atlanta, GA 30308, **Business Phone:** (404)897-1033.

### CLEMENTS, FR. GEORGE HAROLD
Priest, founder (originator), activist. **Personal:** Born Jan 26, 1932, Chicago, IL; son of Samuel and Aldonia Peters. **Educ:** Chicago Quigley Acad Sem, attended 1945; St Mary Lake Sem, BA, sacred

theol, MA, philos, 1957. **Career:** Pastor (retired), executive; Quigley Sem, first black grad ordained, 1945; Archdiocese Chicago, ordained priest, 1957; Holy Angels Roman Cath Church, pastor, 1969-85; One Church-One Child, founder, 1980, pres; One Church-One Addict, founder, 1994; One Church-One Inmate founder, 1999. **Orgs:** Chaplain, Afro-Am Patrolmen's League; Afro-Am Firemen's League; Postal Workers' League; bd, SCLC's Oper Breadbasket; Nat Asn Advan Colored People; Urban League; Better Boys Found; Black Panther Party Malcolm XCol; organizer, Black Clergy Caucus. **Honors/Awds:** Priest of the Year, Asn Chicago Priests, 1977; North American Council on Adoptable Children Award, 1982; Family Spirit Award, 1998; Trumpet Awards; Has been honored by numerous organizations, including the Kentucky State Senate, which issued are solution praising his deeds. **Special Achievements:** First African American graduate of Quigley Academy Seminary in 1945; First African American pastor of Holy Angels Catholic Church on the South Side of Chicago in 1969; First Catholic priest in the Chicago area to adopt a child, 1981; A film starring Lou Gossett, Jr., The Father Clements Story, was produced and broadcast by NBC, 1987. **Business Addr:** Founder, One Church One Child, PO Box 370, Union City, GA 30290.

### CLEMMONS, CLIFFORD R.

Law enforcement officer. **Personal:** Born Kansas City, MO; son of H B and Constance Alice Sargent; married Jimmie E Hill; children: Jennifer M Johnson-Barnett & C Robert Jr. **Educ:** Oakwood Jr Col, Huntsville, AL, dipl, 1939; Cent State Univ, Wilberforce, OH, BS, social work, 1948; Ohio State Univ, MS, social admin, 1950; NY Univ; Columbia Univ, criminal justice. **Career:** Law enforcement officer (retired); Greenpoint Hosp, med social worker, 1950; Probation Dept New York, probation officer, 1951-66, supvr probation officer, 1966-82; City NY, Dept Probation, br chief, 1982-87. **Orgs:** Pres, Counrs, Probation & Parole Officers, 1964-68; pres, bd dir, United Veterans Mutual Housing Co, 1967-70; chmn, bd dir, Fedn Negro Serv Orgn Inc, 1968-77; vpres, dd dir, Munic Credit Union, 1971-77; state dir, Alpha Phi Alpha Fraternity Inc, 1971-87; chmn emer, dd dir, Sickle Cell DisFound, 1972-87; pres, Consumer Groups Greater New York, 1973-75. **Home Addr:** 4345 Senna Dr, Las Cruces, NM 88011-7636, **Home Phone:** (505)521-1508.

### CLEMMONS, PROF. JACKSON JOSHUA WALTER

Pathologist, educator. **Personal:** Born Mar 24, 1923, Beloit, WI; son of Ora Bell and Henry; married Lydia Monroe; children: Jackson, Lydia, Laura, Jocelyn & Naomi. **Educ:** Univ Wis, BS, biochem, 1947, MS, biochem, 1949, PhD, biochem & exp path, 1955; Western Res Univ, MD, 1959. **Career:** Professor (retired), professor emeritus; Univ Wis Madison, res asst, biochem, 1942-43, res assoc, biochem & experpath, 1947-52; Karolinska Inst biophys & Cell Res Stockholm, Sweden, resfel, 1950; Sloan Kettering Inst Cancer Res NY, spec res fel, 1953; Univ Wis Madison, Wis, proj assoc exper path, 1953-55; Am Cancer Soc Inst Path, Western Res Univ, Cleveland, Ohio, postdoctoral fel, 1956-57, fel path, 1957-61, Helen Hay Whitney fel, 1961-64; Univ Vt Col Med, Burlington Vt, asst prof, 1962-64, prof emer path, currently. **Orgs:** Am Bd Path Anat Path, 1964; sch dir, Champlaign Vlly Union HS, 1967-74, vice chmn, Gov Adv Comm Coun Aging, 1970-72; Univ VT Radioisotope Comn, 1968-; exec comt, Grad Sch Fac, 1969-71; deleg, VT White House Conf C & Youth, 1971; path trainicomm Nat Inst Gen Med Sci, 1971-73; vpres, Univ Vt Chap Sigma Xi, 1971-72, pres, 1971-72; Univ Vt Admin Policy Comt, 1971-76; admiss comt, Univ Vt Col Med, stud affairs comt, 1974-; Nat Adv Coun Health Prof Educ, 1975-78; admiss comn, Univ Vt, 1977-, exec comt, 1977-; AMA; Am Asn Path & Bacteriologists; VT State Med Soc; Chittenden Co Med Soc; New Eng Rheumatism Soc; Sigma Xi; Phi Lambda Upsilon; Gamma Alpha; Am Soc Exp Path; Int Acad Path; Am Soc Clinal Chem; NY Acad Sci; AmSoc Clin Pathologists. **Home Addr:** 2158 Greenbush Rd, Charlotte, VT 05445, **Home Phone:** (802)425-3125. **Business Addr:** Professor Emeritus, University of Vermont, 85 S Prospect St, Burlington, VT 05405-0068, **Business Phone:** (802)656-3131.

### CLEMMONS, MAJOR GEN. REGINALD G.

Educator, military leader. **Personal:** Born Wilmington, NC; married Sylvia; children: Regina & Adrienne. **Educ:** NC A & T, BS, math, 1960; SC State Col, ME, educ, 1970; Field Officer Basic & Advan courses, 1972; Armed Forces Staff Col, attended 1984; AUS War Col, attended 1990. **Career:** Military leader (retired), educator; AUS, commissioned field artillary second lt, 1968, Seventh Battalion, from forward observer to liaison officer, 1968-69; Fort Carson, Fifth battalion, comdr, 1969-70, 1st Battalion, Fourth Inf Div, comdr, 1970-71; Third Battalion, AUS Europe & Seventh Army, asst s-3, 1972, 1974, comdr, 1972-74, liaison officer, 1974-75; SC State Univ, AUS Res Officers Training Corps Instr Group, asst prof military scI, 1975-79; First Battalion, Eighth AUS, from asst fire support coordr to exec officer, 1979-80; AUS Logistics Ctr, from opers res analyst to logistics assessment officer, 1980-84; Ft Bragg, 18th Airborne Corps & 82nd Airborn Div, dep asst fire support coordr, exec officer & comdr, 1984-89, 1991-92; Aus Joint Readiness Training Ctr, sr observer, 1989-90; Schofield Barracks, 25th Infantry Div, comdr, 1992-94; Ft Sill, AUS Field Artil Ctr, Fire Support & Combined Ops Directorate, dir, 1994-95; Allied Land Forces Cent Europe, asst chief staff Opers, 1995-96; AUS Europe & Seventh Army & Task Force Able Sentry, asst div comdr, 1996-97; Allied Land Forces Southeastern Europe, dep comndg gen, 1997-99; AUS Europe & Seventh Army, dep comndg gen, 1999-2000; Nat War Col & Nat Defense Univ, commandant, 2000-03; Grantham Univ, Acad Adv Bd, bd mem, currently. **Business Addr:** Board Member, Grantham University, 7200 NW 86th St, Kansas City, MO 64153, **Business Phone:** (816)595-5759.

### CLEMMONS, DR. SONYA SUMMEROUR

Executive, association executive. **Personal:** Born Aug 10, 1971, Gainesville, GA; daughter of Leroy and Alice M. **Educ:** Spelman Col, BS, physics, 1993; Ga Inst Technol, BS, mech engineering & bioengineering, 1994; Univ Calif, San Diego, CA, MS, bioengineering, 1994, PhD, bioengineering, 1999, Anderson Sch Mgt, MBA, corp strategy & mkt, 2005. **Career:** Univ Calif, Cardiac Tissue Engineering, grad res fel, 1994-99; Univ Pa Sch Med, postdoctoral res fel, 2000; SSC Enterprises, prin consult, pres & chief exec officer & dir, 2000-; VitaGen Inc, prin res bioengineer, 2000-02; MediVas, dir bus develop, 2004-06; Biotech Vendor Serv Inc, vpres strategic mkt & corp develop, 2006-08; After Sch Progs Inc, strategic mkt & bus develop mgr, 2009-12; Marietta City Schs, STEM Teacher, 2015-. **Orgs:** Asn Women Sci Bd Dirs; Licensing Exec Socs; Nat Black MBA Asn; San Diego Venture Grp; Ga Inst Technonology / Emory Parker H. Petit Inst Bioscience & Biomed Engrg External Adv Bd; External Adv Bd Drug Delivery Technol Mag; Biomed Engrg Socs Bd Dirs, 2001-04; Biotechnology Indust Orgn; biosciences comt mem, Athena Forum Exec Women; Corp Dirs Forum; Nat Socs Black Engrs Alumni Exten publ; Next Generation Network; assisted teacher, Powder Springs Elem, 2009-; teacher & mentor, Marietta City Schs, 2015-. **Honors/Awds:** Inducted, Prestigious Georgia Tech Oustanding Young Engineering Alumni, 2004; San Diego Science & Engineering Trailblazer of the Year, 2004; Top Forty Under 40, San Diego Metropolitan Mag, 2004; Top Forty Under 40 Leaders, Black Enterprise Mag, 2003 & 2005; GA Mission Preservation & Restoration Society Award, 2005; Women Who Mean Business, San Diego Bus Jour, 2006. **Special Achievements:** Featured in Black Enterprise Magazine (May & Dec 2003); Featured in book commissioned by the White House entitled "Extraordinary Female Engineers"; First African American to earn a Ph.D. in Bioengineering from the University of CA, San Diego; First Group of UNCF-Merck Fellowship recipients; Nominated for induction into American Institute Medical & Biological Engineering, 2005; Nominee for Executive Women Pinnacle Award, UCSD Athena Forum, 2005; Diversity Star Minority Scientist Role Model, Scientist Magazine, 2006& 2007. **Business Addr:** President, Chief Executive Officer, SSC Enterprises, 5068 Hartford Pl, Flowery Branch, GA 30542, **Business Phone:** (619)823-7418.

### CLEMON, U. W.

Judge. **Personal:** Born Apr 9, 1943, Fairfield, AL; son of Mose and Addie Bush; married Barbara Lang; children: Herman Isaac & Addine Michelle. **Educ:** Morehouse Col, Atlanta, Ga, 1961; Miles Col, Birmingham, Ala, BA, 1965; Columbia Univ Sch Law, NY, JD, 1968. **Career:** Federal judge (retired); Nat Asn Advan Colored People, Legal Defense Fund, New York, NY, law clerk, 1966-69; Adams, Burg & Baker, Birmingham, Ala, assoc, 1969-70; Adams, Baker & Clemon, Birmingham, Ala, partner, 1970-77; Adams & Clemon, Birmingham, Ala, partner, 1977-80; State Ala, Montgomery, Ala, senator, 1974-80; US Courts, Birmingham, Ala, dist judge, 1980; US Dist Court Northern Dist Ala, chief judge, 1999; White Arnold & Dowd P.C, Shareholder, currently. **Orgs:** Earl Warren Fel, NAACP Legal Defense Fund, 1968-70; Ala Women's Comn, 1975-77; Ala Permanent Judicial Study Comn, 1976-80; pres, co-founder Ala Black Lawyers Asn, 1976-78; coun mem, Sect Individual Rights, 1976-79; legal coun, AL Chap, Southern Christian Leadership Conf, 1974-80; chmn, Rules Comt; chmn, Judiciary Comt; Alpha Phi Alpha Fraternity; coun, individual rights & responsibilities, Am Bar Asn; Ala Bar Asn; Birmingham Bar Asn; Nat Bar Asn; judicial coun, Eleventh Circuit; Leadership, Birmingham Bd, 1986-88; bd mem, Oper New Birmingham, 1992-; bd mem, Birmingham Civil Rights Inst, 1993-98; bd mem, Glenwood, Inc, 2000-. **Honors/Awds:** Honorary Doctorate of Humane Letters, Miles Col, 1976; Drum Major Award, Southern Christian Leadership Conf, 1980; Law & Justice Award, Southern Christian Leadership Conf, 1980; C Francis Stradford Award, Nat Bar Asn, 1986; William H Hastie Award, Judicial Coun, Nat Bar Asn, 1987; Judicial Award of Merit, Ala Bar Asn's; Howell T Heflin Award, Ala Trial Lawyer's Asn; Distinguished Jurist Award, Miss State Univ, 1992; Brotherhood Award, Nat Conf Christians & Jews, 1996; UW Clemon Pre-Law Scholarship, Honorary Doctor of Humanities, Birmingham-Southern Col, 2002, 2003; Honorary Fel, Col Labor & Employ Lawyers Inc, 2002; Distinguished Visiting Professor, Univ Ala Law Sch, 2002. **Special Achievements:** Alabama's First black federal judge; First two blacks elected to the Alabama Senate since Reconstruction. **Home Addr:** 5202 Mountain Ridge Pkwy, Birmingham, AL 35222-4143. **Business Addr:** Shareholder, White Arnold & Dowd PC, 2025 Third Ave N Suite 500, Birmingham, AL 35203, **Business Phone:** (205)323-1888.

### CLEMONS, ALOIS RICARDO

Public relations executive, president (organization), executive director. **Personal:** Born Jan 19, 1956, Durham, NC; son of Theodore Quick and Mary Alice; married Gail Melinda Shaw; children: Jason Alois & Perry Ricardo. **Educ:** Univ Mar, BS, jour, 1977, pursuing MA, jour. **Career:** Howard Univ, from asst sports info dir to sports info dir, 1980-85, asst atheletic dir, 1989-91; Miller Brewing Co, mkt commun, 1985-88; ARC & Assoc, pres, 1988-91; Maj League Baseball, mgr, pub rels, 1991; Nat League Prof Baseball Clubs, vpres pub rels & mkt develop, exec dir pub rels, 1994-. **Orgs:** Pres, Kappa Alpha Psi Fraternity, Theta Theta Chap, 1977-78; NABJ, 1989. **Honors/Awds:** Tough-Minded Businessman, Salesmanship Award, The Southwestern Co, 1979; Outstanding Alumni Award, 1988; Journalism Grant, 1989. **Special Achievements:** Produced more than 50 media guides for Howard Univ Athletic Dept, 1980-85; Venue press chief for Olympics, 1984; Facilities for Journalists, Vol 1 & 2, Los Angeles Olympic Comt, 1984; Press liaison, USOC, 1985; Howard Univ Spring Media Guides, second place, Col & Sports Info, dir am, 1985; The Olympian, US Olympic Comt, 1985; Track & field interview room mgr, Olympics, 1996. **Home Addr:** 30 Waterside Plz Suite 18F, New York, NY 10010.

### CLEMONS, CHARLIE FITZGERALD

### CLEMONS, DUANE ANTHONY

Football player, executive, football coach. **Personal:** Born May 23, 1974, Riverside, CA; married Rana; children: Brea & Butch. **Educ:** Univ Calif, Berkeley, BA, ethnic studies, 1996; MidAmerica Nazarene Univ, BS, bus mgt & human resources, 2013. **Career:** Football player (retired), executive, coach; Minn Vikings, defensive end, 1996-99, defensive tackle, 1999; Kans City Chiefs, defensive end, 2000-02; Cincinnati Bengals, defensive end, 2003-05, right defensive tackle, 2004; Can Football League, pract roster, 2008; Toronto Argonauts, 2008; Kane Able Inc, human resource & prod supvr, 2009-; Unicept, co-owner; Client Serv Body Regeneration Ctr, dir, currently; MidAmerica Nazarene Univ Pioneers, coach, currently. **Orgs:** Active Mem, Kans City Chiefs Ambassadors, 2012; bd mem, Evergreen Living inst Johnson Couty KS, 2014. **Special Achievements:** Film: 1996 NFL Draft, 1996. TV Series: "ESPN's Sunday Night Football", 2001; "The NFL on CBS", 2002-04. **Home Addr:** 30181 W 231st St, Spring Hill, KS 66083. **Business Addr:** Coach, MidAmerica Nazarene University Pioneers, 2030 E College Way, Olathe, KS 66062, **Business Phone:** (913)782-3750.

### CLEMONS, REV. EARLIE, JR.

Clergy. **Personal:** Born Oct 9, 1946, Austin, TX; son of Earlie Sr and Velma Piper; married Carolyn Hickman; children: Rodney L & Roland E. **Educ:** Tex Southern Univ, BS, 1969; Episcopal Theol Sem, MDiv, 1982. **Career:** Walgreen's Drugs, chief pharmacist, 1971-76; Medi Save Pharm, pharmacist, mgr, 1976-79; Paul Quinn Col, asst prof, 1983-85; St James Church, vicar, 1987-90; Chaplain Prairie View, chaplain, 1990-; St Francis Church, rector, vicar, 1990; Upper Manhattan Day Care & Child Develop Ctr Inc, dir, 2003-. **Orgs:** Chi Delta Mu Prof Fraternity, 1968; Alpha Phi Alpha Fraternity, 1972; Episcopal Coalition Human Needs, 1990; Prairie View-Waller Ministerial Alliance, 1990; bd mem, Waller Closet & Pantry, 1990; vice chmn, Episcopal Comn Black Ministry, 1990; chmn, Diocesan Comn Black Ministry, 1991; steering comt, Episcopal Soc Ministry Higher Educ, 1991. **Honors/Awds:** Merit Award, Black Cult Workshop, 1985. **Home Addr:** 13927 Wickersham Lane, Houston, TX 77077-5321. **Business Addr:** Director, Upper Manhattan Day Care & Child Develop Center Inc, 207 W 133rd St, New York, NY 10030, **Business Phone:** (212)368-3500.

### CLEMONS, JAMES ALBERT, III

Journalist. **Personal:** Born Nov 10, 1953, Lake Charles, LA; son of James A Jr and Rupert Florence Richardson (deceased); married Linda E Lewis; children: Anitra Jornell, Jasmine Angelle & James A IV. **Educ:** Univ Southwestern La, attended 1973; McNeese State Univ, attended 1982; Ga State Univ; Master's Divinity Sch, 2001. **Career:** Hughes Tool Co, assembly line worker, 1975-76; La Dept Corrections, prison guard, 1977; Cities Servs Oil Co, operating engr, 1977-83; Lake Charles, La, Am Press, sports writer, 1979-81; Lake Charles, La, Recorder, owner & publ, 1980-82; Monroe, La, News Star World, sports writer, 1983-84; Courier-Jour, Louisville, Ky, sports writer, 1984-89; Atlanta Jour Consitution, night sports ed, 1989-97, sports ed & columnist, 1999; Montgomery Advertiser, sports ed, 1997-99. **Orgs:** Nat Asn Black Journalists, 1984-; Atlanta Asn Black Journalists, 1996-; Assoc Press Sports Ed, 1996-; Soc Prof Journalists, 1996-; Atlanta Press Club, 1996-; Nat Asn Advan Colored People; Laborers Intl Union N Am, Local 706. **Honors/Awds:** Second Place, LA Sportswriters Asn Contest, 1984; First Place Editing, Georgia Sports Writers Asn, 1991; Man of the Year, Gumbeaux Magazine, 1996; Salute, Nat Asn Women's Basketball Coaches, 1996; Column writing, 2nd place, Ala Sports Writers Asn, 1998. **Home Addr:** 6436 Valerie Bluff, Lithonia, GA 30058, **Home Phone:** (770)484-8464. **Business Addr:** Assistant Sports Editor, Columnist, Atlanta Journal Constitution, 72 Marietta St 8th Fl, Atlanta, GA 30302, **Business Phone:** (404)526-5334.

### CLEMONS, JOHN GREGORY

Public relations executive. **Personal:** Born Mar 24, 1954, Newark, NJ; son of John and Laura Christine Adams; married Corine Kendrick; children: Diarra Joi. **Educ:** Seton Hall Univ, S Orange, NJ, 1973; Syracuse Univ, Syracuse, NY, BS, news journ, 1976; Syracuse Univ, MS, commun mgt, 2011. **Career:** Star-Ledger, Newark, NJ, reporter, 1976-79; Black Enterprise Mag, New York, NY, assoc ed, 1979-81; AT&T, Basking Ridge, NJ & Atlanta, Ga, pub rels spec, 1981-87; Contel Corp, Atlanta, Ga, mgr-internal commun, 1987-88; GTE, Tampa, Fla, dir commun, 1987-92; Joint Ctr Polit & Econ Studies, vp commun, 1992-95; Marriott Int, vpres, 1995-98; SBC Commun, dir internal commun, 1998-2000; Nextel Commun Inc, vpres internal commun, 2000-02; Clemons Commun, founder & prin, 2002-03, 2012; Am Online, commun consult, 2003; Raytheon Tech Serv Co LLC, dir commun, 2003-10; AOL, commun consult, 2003; Raytheon, corp dir community rels, 2010-12; Int Asn Bus Communicators, interim exec dir, 2012; Walmart, dir global assoc commun, 2012-14, sr mgr, commmunications & training, 2014-15, sr mgr ii, commun, Global Off Cult, Diversity & Inclusion, 2015-16; Newell Brands, dir Global Employee Commun, 2016-. **Orgs:** Pub Rels Soc Am, 1987; Tampa Chamber Com, 1989-92; Tampa Bay Male Club, 1990-92; dir, exec bd, Int Asn Bus Communicators, 1990-92; bd dir, PRSA Nat Capital Chap, 1994; Capital Press Club; Black Pub Rels Soc; chmn & chief vol officer, Int Asn Bus Communicators, 2001-02; River Creek Homeowners Asn Commun Comt; Kappa Alpha Psi Fraternity; Syracuse Univ Alumni Network; SI Newhouse Sch Pub Commun Alumni Group. **Honors/Awds:** Newsletter Award-First Place, Int Asn Bus Communicators/Atlanta, 1987; Golden Flame, Int Asn Bus Communicators/Atlanta, 1988; Media Professionals Worldwide; Communicator of the Year, IABC Wash, 1997; Silver Inkwell Awards, 1997 & 2003; Gold Quill Award, 1997; Thoth Award, PRSA, 2004; IABC Gold Quill Awards, 2007-08; EXCEL Award, 2010; Compliance Customer Service Award, Walmart US, 2015; Hall of Fame Career Achievement Award, IABC Southern Region, 2016. **Special Achievements:** Hearst vis Prof, Univ Fla, Col Journ & Commun, 1995. **Home Addr:** 18411 Inverrary Cir, Leesburg, VA 20176-3954, **Home Phone:** (813)910-2909. **Business Addr:** Director of Global Associate Communications, Walmart, 950 Edwards Ferry Rd NE, Leesburg, VA 20176, **Business Phone:** (703)779-0102.

### CLEMONS, LINDA K.

Founder (originator), association executive. **Personal:** Born Dec 26, 1957, Cleveland, OH. **Educ:** Ball State Univ, BA. **Career:** Christ My Life Found, founder; Living Legends Black, founder; Women Rainbow, Award Excelience, nat founder; Sisterpreneur Inc, founder, pres, sales trainer speaker, body lang expert, 2000-, chief exec officer, 2002-, sole proprietor, currently; Nat Asn African Am Entrepreneurs, founder. **Honors/Awds:** Minorities & Women Bus, Role Model of Year, 1992; listed in the Congressional Record of United States, 1992, proclamation from governor of Ind, 1992; Sagamore Of The Wabash Award, Ind State. **Special Achievements:** Artistic director/writer, two plays: When God Calls A Woman, Lord I Wanna Dance. **Home Addr:** 9489 Colony Pointe E Dr, Indianapolis, IN 46250-3465, **Home Phone:** (317)479-1178. **Business Addr:** Chief Executive Officer, Founder, Sisterpreneur Inc, PO Box 1191, Indianapolis, IN 46250-3465, **Business Phone:** (866)557-3199.

### CLEMONS, DR. MICHAEL L.
College teacher, school administrator. **Personal:** Born Jul 18, 1955, Worth, WV; son of Delores S and Lawrence D; married Sharon D Brown; children: Miisha Michelle, Nyasha Denise & Nia Sabree. **Educ:** Univ Md, College Park, MD, BA, govt & polit, 1976, MA, urban studies, 1979; Atlanta Univ, Atlanta, GA, PhD, polit sci, 1985. **Career:** Honeywell Info Syst, McLean, Va, assoc syst analyst, 1977-79; Univ Md Urban Studies, grand fe, 1977-78; Atlanta Univ, Dept Polit Sci, Nat Sci Found Fel, 1979-82 Gen Elec Info Serv, Atlanta, Ga, programmer, analyst, 1979-80; Atlanta Jr Col, Atlanta, Ga, res assoc syst analyst, 1981-84; State Univ New York, Oswego, NY, dir, instnl res & MIS, 1984-87; Old Dom Univ, Norfolk, Va, Univ Planning & Instnl Res, dir, 1987-, assoc prof polit sci, currently; Univ Press New Eng, publ; Fel Humanities Teaching Develop. **Orgs:** Omicron Delta Kappa Nat Hon & Leadership Soc, 1977; Nat Conf Black Polit Scientists, 1982-; Am Polit Sci Assoc, 1986-; Soc Col & Univ Planners, 1986-; Asn Instnl Res; Va Asn Mgt & Planning, 1987-; Southern Asn Instnl Res, 1987-; Va Mgt Inst, 1989; dir, Univ Planning & Instnl Res; chair, Interdisciplinary Studies Prog; dir, Inst for Study Race & Ethnicity; dir, African Am & African Studies. **Home Addr:** 1636 Castlefield Rd, Virginia Beach, VA 23456, **Home Phone:** (804)471-0976. **Business Addr:** Director, Associate Professor of Political Science, Old Dominion University, 350 W 21st St Batten Arts Lett Bldg 700, Norfolk, VA 23529, **Business Phone:** (757)683-3858.

### CLEMONS, SANDRA L.
Government official. **Personal:** Born Dec 12, 1945, Detroit, MI; daughter of George and Inez; married Lloyd F; children: Theresa Calhoun & Karen A Russell. **Educ:** Madonna Univ, BS, 1986; Univ Mich-Dearborn, MPA, 1993. **Career:** Detroit Police Dept, Police Communs, asst, 1966-79; Detroit Election Comn, Ballot Tabulation, supvr, 1979-84; Focus Hope, admin asst, 1987-89; City Detroit, Water & Sewage Dept, gov analyst, 1989-92, Detroit Recreation Dept, human resources officer, 1992-95, Human Resources, training dir, 1995-97; Detroit Pub Libr, Admin Serv, assoc dir, 1997-99, dep dir, 1999-2001; Right Mgt, career mgt consult, 2002-09. **Orgs:** Nat Asn Advan Colored People, 1980-; Univ Miami Alumni Asn, 1992-; Asn Qual & Participation, 1995-; bd mem, League Women Voters-Detroit, 1995-98; bd mem, Int Personnel Mgt Asn, 1997-98; Am Libr Asn, 1997-; Mich Libr Asn, 1997-; chair, Pub TV WTVS Comt Adv Panel, 1999; gov bd, retirement community. **Home Addr:** 2340 Oakman Blvd, Detroit, MI 48238, **Home Phone:** (313)931-4230. **Business Addr:** MI.

### CLEMONS, TANYA C.
Vice president (organization). **Educ:** Univ New Orleans, BA, psychol; La State Univ, PhD, indust & orgn psychol. **Career:** Anheuser Busch, dir, 1989-94; Ga Pac Corp, dir, exec develop & orgn planning, 1993-95; IBM, vpres global exec & orgn capability, 1995-2002; Microsoft Corp, corp vpres, people & orgn capability, 2002-07; Pfizer Inc, sr vpres & chief talent officer, worldwide res & develop, 2007-; Int Consortium for Exec Develop Res. **Orgs:** Pfizer Leadership Team; exec bd mem, Pfizer Sr Leadership Coun; bd mem, Nat Urban League Inc; exec bd mem, Conf Bd & Best Pract Inst. **Business Addr:** Senior Vice President, Chief Talent Officer, Pfizer Inc, 235 E 42Nd St, New York, NY 10017.

### CLEMONS, THOMASINA W.
College administrator. **Personal:** Born Nov 23, 1938, Charleston, WV; daughter of Charles Henry and Fannie Estelle Hairston Coles; married Otis William Wade. **Educ:** Univ Hartford, W Hartford, CT, BA, 1964; Univ Conn, Storrs, CT, MBA, 1982. **Career:** CT Comn Human Rights & Opportunities, New London, Conn, investr, regional mgr, 1967-75; Univ Conn, Storrs, Conn, dir, affirmative action, 1975-95; Employ Task Force, Conn Dept Higher Educ, chair, 1983-85; Harvard Univ, Mgt Develop Prog, fac, 1990; Vernon Town Coun, 1991-94; Conn State House Representatives, rep, 1994-2000; Vernon Arts Comn, assoc comnr, currently. **Orgs:** Past state coordr, Community Coun, Am Asn Affirmative Action, 1978-; Nat Coalition 100 Black Women, Vernon Dem Town Comt, 1980-83, 1986; bd dir, pres & vpres, Hockanum Valley Community Coun, 1990, 1993 & 1994; pres, Northeastern Conn Chap, 1990; pres & founding mem, Vernon Chap Habitat Humanity steering comt; Vernon Hist Soc. **Home Addr:** 655 Talcottville Rd Apt 7, Vernon, CT 06066, **Home Phone:** (860)871-2443. **Business Addr:** Associate Commissioner, Vernon Arts Commission, Town Vernon Memorial Bldg, Vernon, CT 06066, **Business Phone:** (860)870-3599.

### CLERMONT, DR. VOLNA
Health services administrator, physician, pediatrician. **Personal:** Born Sep 15, 1924, Jeremie; married Hazel Baggett; children: Karen, Kimberly & Christopher. **Educ:** Lycee Petion, Port-au-Prince Haiti, BA, 1943; Ecole Nationale de Medecineet de Pharmacie Univ d'Haiti Port-au-Prince Haiti, MD, 1949. **Career:** Mt Sinai Hosp, resident; St Joseph Hosp, resident; Childrens Hosp Mich, pathologist, 1960-69; Comprehensive Neighborhood Health Ctr, chief pediat, 1969-72; SW Detroit Hosp, chief staff; DMIC-PLRESCAD, med dir, 1972-; pvt pract, pediat, currently; Assoc Health Care Ctr, pediat; MiSinai Grace Hosp. **Orgs:** Detroit Med Soc; life mem, Nat Asn Advan Colored People; Nat Med Asn; Detroit Pediat Soc; Dipl Bd Pediat, Wayne County Med Soc; Mich State Med Soc; Med staff Hutzel Hosp C's Hosp; Sinai-Grace Hosp; Urban League; Founders Soc; African Art Gallery; Int African Mus Soc; Alpha Phi Alpha Frat. **Business Addr:** Physician, Private Practice, 2814 Oakman Blvd, Detroit, MI 48238, **Business Phone:** (313)834-7061.

### CLEVELAND, GRANVILLE E., SR.
Librarian. **Personal:** Born Nov 25, 1937, Springfield, OH; married Juanita; children: Granville & Tivonnia. **Educ:** Tougaloo Col, attended 1957; Cent State Col, BS, 1960; Wittenberg Univ, attended 1963. **Career:** Univ Notre Dame Law Sch, asst law lib & fac mem, 1969; Springfield Bar & Law Libr Asn, lib & exec sec, 1963-68; basketball referee; Univ Notre Dame Law Sch, emer asst law librn, currently. **Orgs:** Am Asn Law Libr; Ohio Reg Asn Law Libr; Univ Notre Dame; Community Welfare Coun; Housing & Jobs Human Rels Comt; adult adv Springfield Youth Club; Legal Aid Soc; United Appeal Fund; City Rec Dept; Planned Parenthood; YMCA; Black Stud Affairs Comt; asst dir, Civil Rights Ctr. **Home Addr:** 3710 Eastmont Dr, South Bend, IN 46628. **Business Addr:** Assistant Law Librarian Emeritus, Notre Dame Law School, Notre Dame, IN 46556.

### CLEVERT, HON. CHARLES NELSON, JR.
Judge. **Personal:** Born Oct 11, 1947, Richmond, VA. **Educ:** Davis & Elkins Col, Elkins, BA, 1969; Georgetown Univ Law Ctr, WA, JD, 1972. **Career:** Milwaukee Co Dist Attys Off, asst dist atty, 1972-75; US Atty Off, Eastern Dist WI, asst US atty, 1975-77; US Att Northern Dist Ill, spec asst, 1977; US Bankruptcy Ct, Eastern Dist WI, US bankruptcy judge, 1977-95, chief bankruptcy judge, 1986-95; Univ Wis Law Sch, lectr, 1989-90; US Dist Ct, Eastern Dist Wis, Judge, 1996-2012, chief dist judge, 2009-12, sr judge, 2012-. **Orgs:** WI Bar Asn; Milwaukee Bar Asn; WI Asn Minority Attys; 7th Circuit Bar Asn; Alpha Phi Alpha; Judicial Coun NBA; African Methodist Episcopal Church; vice chair, Natl Conf Fed Trial Judges; bd mem, Am Bankruptcy Inst; bd mem, Am Judicature Socs; immediate pres, Thomas Fairchild Am Inn Ct; bd mem, Men Tomorrow; bd mem, Anvil Housing Corp; comt budget, Judicial Conf US; Sigma Pi Phi; Am Jury Proj Adv Comt; chair, Nat Conf Fed Trial Judges, 1998-99; Fed Judicial Ctr Dist Judges Educ Comt, 2001-; bd, Am Judicature Socs Anvil Housing Corp; fel Am Col Bankruptcy. **Home Addr:** 7230 N Redwood, Glendale, WI 53209, **Home Phone:** (414)351-1575. **Business Addr:** Senior District Judge, The United States District Court, Rm 208 US Courthouse, Milwaukee, WI 53202, **Business Phone:** (414)297-1585.

### CLIFF, MICHELLE
Writer. **Personal:** Born Nov 2, 1946, Kingston; married Adrienne Rich. **Educ:** Wagner Col, BA, 1969; Warburg Inst, London, MPhil, 1974. **Career:** Life, reporter & researcher, 1969-70; WW Nortont & Co, prod supvr Norton Libr, 1970-71, copyeditor, 1974-75, manuscript & prod ed, 1975-79; They Taught Me To Despise, Persephone Press, 1980; Sinister Wisdom, co-publ & ed, 1981-83; Norwich Univ, cycle fac, adult degree prog, 1983-84; Martin Luther King Jr Pub Libr, teacher, creative writing & hist; Auth: Claiming Identity They Taught Me to Despise, 1980; Land Look Behind: Prose & Poetry, 1985; No Tel to Heaven, 1987; Bodies Water, 1990; Abeng, Penguin Bks, 1991; Free Enterprise, 1993; Bodies of water, Penguin Group, 1995; Store a Million Items: Stories, 1998; Free Enterprise: A Novel Mary Ellen Pleasant, 2004. **Orgs:** Fel McDowell Col, 1982; fel Nuclear Energy Agency, 1982; fel MA Artists Found, 1984.

### CLIFFORD, CHARLES H.
Government official. **Personal:** Born Sep 8, 1933, Sacramento, CA; married Claudean Akers; children: Carla, Carolyn & Caren. **Educ:** Sacramento Jr Col, AA, 1958; Sacramento St Col, BA, 1965. **Career:** Dept Corr St CA, human rel consult, 1964. **Orgs:** Area pres, Black Corr Coalition; pres, Calif corrections officers, 1969-72; Urban League; Black Caucus; Nat Asn Advan Colored People; Calif Young Dems. **Home Addr:** 4213 Roosevelt Ave, Sacramento, CA 95820.

### CLIFFORD, THOMAS E.
Military leader, business owner. **Personal:** Born Mar 9, 1929, Washington, DC; married Edith Sanders; children: Maria, Edwin, Larry & Mark. **Educ:** Howard Univ, BA, 1949; George Washington Univ, MBA, 1963. **Career:** Military leader, bussiness owner (retired); AUS, supply officer, 1949-50; USAF, Tyndall AFB, Fl, pilot, 1950-52, McGuire AFB, NJ, pilot, 1952-53, Ladd AFB, Fairbanks, AK, flight cmdr, 1953-56, Oxnard AFB, Calif, flight cmdr, 1956, Air Div Jet Instrument Sch, first chief, 1956-58, George AFB, Calif, flight cmdr, 1959-62; USAFE, Lindsey Air Sta, Wiesbaden, Ger, chief prog anal div, 1962-62, Da Nang AFB, dep comdr, 1971-73, Sembach AFB, Ger, vice comdr, 1973-74; Nortan AFB, Calif, dir inspect, 1974-76, Luke AFB, Ariz, cmdr, 1976-78; Pentagon, dir aerospace prog, dep chief, 1966-67; Off Asst Secy Defense Admin, mil asst, 1967-69; Gen Motors Corp, plant mgr, 1979-86; Clifford Motors, owner, 1987-93; Howard univ, maj gen, 1977. **Orgs:** VFW; Am Legion; AFA; Nat Asn Advan Colored People; Daedalians; comt mem, SCOPED. **Honors/Awds:** Legion of Merit with two oak leaf clusters, Distinguished Flying Cross, Air Medal with four oak leaf clusters, the Air Force Commendation Medal with oak leaf cluster, the Air Force Outstanding Unit Award ribbon and the Republic of Vietnam Gallantry Cross with palm. **Home Addr:** 11940 W 14th Ave, Blythe, CA 92225.

### CLIFT, DR. JOSEPH WILLIAM
Physician. **Personal:** Born Apr 24, 1938, Patoka, IN; son of Cecil William and Mary Esther Lucas; married Ulyssine Gibson; children: Kory Grant & Nathalie Louise; married Ulyssine Gibson. **Educ:** Tex Sothern Univ, BS, 1959; Univ Tex Med Br, MD, 1965. **Career:** Alameda Co Med Ctr, resident internal med; self emploted physician, 2003. **Orgs:** Pres, Delta Theta Chap Alpha Phi Alpha Fraternity, 1959; pres, Alameda Contra Costa Co Diabetes asn, 1975 bd dir, Samuel Merritt Hosp, 1976-79; dipl, Am Bd Internal Med, 1978; pres med staff, Highland Gen Hosp, 1983-84; pres, E Bay Soc Internal Med, 1984- Nat Med asn; AMA; Calif Med asn counr, pres Alameda-Contra-Costa Medasn, 1992-; Calif Soc Internal Med, 1991-92; Sigma Pi Phi Fraternity, Alpha Gamma Boule, Oakland-Berkeley, Calif, 1987. **Honors/Awds:** Resident of the Year, Highland General Hosp, 1971. **Home Addr:** 8211 Skyline Circle, Oakland, CA 94605-4231, **Home Phone:** (510)562-6154. **Business Addr:** Physician, 3300 Webster St Suite 702, Oakland, CA 94609, **Business Phone:** (510)832-0147.

### CLIFTON, DR. IVERY DWIGHT
Educator. **Personal:** Born Apr 6, 1943, Statesboro, GA; son of B J and Rosetta B; married Patricia A Davis; children: Kalisa & Kelli. **Educ:** Tuskegee Inst, BS, 1965, MS, 1967; Univ Ill, PhD, 1976. **Career:** Educator (retired), emeritus; TVA AL, agr econ 1967; AUs, AUs officer, 1967-70; US Dept Agr, DC, agr econ, 1970-76;Clifton Farms Inc, pres, 1985; Univ GA, prof & vpres, Acad Affairs, Col Agr & Environ Sci, 1988-, assoc dean, 1988, sr assoc dean, int head dept; Univ Ga, dean, 1994-95, assoc dean & sr assoc exec dean, 1995-2003; Univ Ga, prof Emer, Col of Agr & Environ Sci, 2003-. **Orgs:** Secy, Alpha Phi Alpha, 1975; Chi Gamma Iota Univ Ill Chap Urbana, 1975; spec asst to vpres acad affairs, Univ GA, 1977-78; Phi Kappa Phi Univ GA, Chap Athens, 1979; consult, Resources Future, 1979; Gamma Sigma Delta, Univ GA Chap Athens, 1980; pres, Steward Bd First Am Church, 1979-80. **Special Achievements:** First African American Dean at the University of Georgia. **Home Addr:** 162 Doubles Bridges Xing, Winterville, GA 30683-4808, **Home Phone:** (706)549-7390.

### CLIFTON, ROSALIND MARIA
Chief executive officer. **Personal:** Born Oct 23, 1950, St. Louis, MO; son of Houston Gant and Lois; married Pierce T. **Career:** Internal Revenue Serv, agt; Claims Overload Syst, bus mgr, 1986-89; Black log Ltd, owner, pres, chief exec officer, 1989-. **Business Addr:** President, Chief Executive Officer, Backlog Ltd, 20 E Jackson Blvd Suite 1250, Chicago, IL 60604, **Business Phone:** (312)554-8800.

### CLINE, DR. EILEEN TATE
School administrator. **Personal:** Born Jun 25, 1935, Chicago, IL; daughter of Herman and Inez Duke; married A W Phinney III; children: Jon Christopher & Joy Michele; married William P. **Educ:** Geneva C Robinson Chicago Musical Col, priv piano study, 1952; Univ Chicago, lib arts, 1952; Curtis Chicago Musical Col, class piano course, 1950; Rudolph Ganz scholar stud, priv piano study, 1958; Oberlin Conserv Music, B Mus Educ, 1956, B Mus piano perf, 1956; Univ Colo, Boulder, M Mus piano perf, 1960; independent piano studio, 1975; Ind Univ Sch Music, Doctor Mus Educ, 1985; Harvard Inst Educ Mgt, 1986. **Career:** School administrator (retired); Univ Colo, co ordr cont educ piano, 1965-75; Neighbourhood Mus Sch, New Haven, Conn, exec dir, 1980-82; Peabody Conserv Mus, Johns Hopkins Univ, assoc dean, 1982-83, dean, 1983-95; Inst Policy Studies, Johns Hopkins Univ, sr fel, 1998, Peabody Conserv, dean emer, currently. **Orgs:** Founder & dir, Boulder C's Choir, 1972-75; stud activ chmn, Colo State Music Teachers' Asn, stud activ chmn, exec bd; prog chmn, Boulder Area Music Teachers' Asn; Music Prog Prof Training Panel, Nat Endowment Arts, 1980-; pres, Young Musicians Boulder; alumni-elected trustee, Oberlin Col, 1981-88; bd trustee, Hopkins Sch, 1981-82; bd mem, Nat Guild Community Schs Arts, 1982-88; nat Keyboard Community Music Educs; Nat Conf; adv bd, Young Women's Christian Asn, Univ Colo; Music Community Colo Coun Arts & Humanities; Col Bd, Theory AP Test Develop Comn, ETS, 1983-; Eval Team Mid States Accredit Asn, 1983-; MTNA, MENC, Col Music Soc, Nat Guild Piano Teachers, Soc Values Higher Educ, bd mem, Am Symphony Orchestra League, 1989-; Baltimore Symphony Orchestra Community Outreach Comt, Educ Outreach, 1989-95, music comn, 1993-; bd mem, Nat Guild Community Schs Arts, 1982-88; bd mem, Kenan Inst Arts; advy bd mem, Harvard Univ Kennedy Sch Prog Non-Profit Leadership; Md State Dept Educ, arts advy panel, 1995-; bd mem, Marlboro Music; advy bd, El Paso Pro Musica; advy bd, Van Cliburn Int Piano Competition; advy bd, Am Bach Soc. **Honors/Awds:** Research grants, Ind Univ Found, Ind Univ Office Res & Grad Develop; Oberlin Col Alumni Res Grant; Acad scholars & hons, Univ Colo, 1958-60, Oberlin Col, 1953-56; Danforth Found Fel, 1975-; lectures, performance competitions; Outstanding Woman Awd Natl Exec Club, 1984; Outstanding Alumni Awd Univ of Colorado College of Music 19 Peabody Faculty and Administration Award for Outstanding Contribution to the Peabody Community, 1986; Article of the Year Award for "Anyone Can Winel3, " at wo-part article in American Music Teachers, 1990; Keynote speaker ASOL/Unv of Chicago/Chicago Symphony Orchestra 100th Anniversary Symposium: "The Training of Orchestral Musicians"; Torch Bearer Award for distinguished service, Coalition of 100 Black Women, 1991; Panelist: NJ State Arts Council; Massachusetts Cultural Council; Keynote Speaker, Coll Music Society Annual Mtg, 1995; My Father Never Told Me, or, A View From this Bridge; NASM Task Force Report: Minority Access to Music Study, Nov, 1994. **Special Achievements:** Published, "Reflections of Cultural Synthesis and Social Reality as Seenin George Walker's Sonata No 2" Soc for Values in Higher Education Conf Dickinson Col, 1979; "The Competition Explosion, Impact on Higher Education" MTNA Natl Convention 1980; "Education Relationships to Professional Training and Career Entry" NASM Conv Dallas, TX 1981; "The Competition Explosion, Impact on Education" The American Music Teacher Parts I-III Jan-March, 1982; First black dean Peabody Conserv. **Home Addr:** 12837 Stone Eagle Rd, Phoenix, MD 21131, **Home Phone:** (410)252-2887. **Business Addr:** Dean Emeritus, Johns Hopkins University, 1 E Mt Vernon Pl, Baltimore, MD 21202, **Business Phone:** (410)659-8100.

### CLINGMAN, KEVIN LOREN
Executive. **Personal:** Born Oct 9, 1961, Detroit, MI; son of Simeon and Gloria; married Sherry Bryant; children: Kameron. **Educ:** Morehouse Col, BA, econs, 1985. **Career:** Owens Corning Fiberglass, buyer & mat supvr, 1985-88; Union Pac Rr, prod mgr, 1988-92; Norwest Bank Nebr, Omaha Small Bus Network, pres, 1993-96; N Omaha Bus Develop Corp, 1993-96; LCBD Enterprise Group, pres, 1996-97; Small Bus Loan Source, vpres bus develop, 1998-2003; Repub Bank, Ohio, com loan officer, vpres com real estate lending, 2003-06; One Ga Bank, vpres, mgr govt guaranteed lending, 2006-11; Embassy Nat Bank, sr vpres, 2011-12; Citizens Savings Bank & Trust, group vpres, 2013-; Community Bank Pickens County, sr sba mgr, 2014-. **Orgs:** Finance comn, Salem Baptist Church, 1989-96; bd dir, Ctr Stage Theatre, 1989-94; bd dir, Omaha Small Bus Network, 1992-96; bd dir, N Omaha Bus Developt Corp, 1992-96; pres, Black Employee Network Union Pac Rr, 1992; bd dir, Nat Bus Incubation asn, 1996; bd dir, One Church One Child Louisville, 1996; bd dir, Canaan Community Develop Corp, 1997; bd dir, Ga Cert Develop Corp, 2011; loan comt, Invest Atlanta, 2012; Kappa Alpha Psi Fraternity Inc, 2013; exec leadership prog alumni, Leadership Memphis, 2014. **Honors/Awds:** Special Commendation, Union Pac Rr, 1989. Microenterprise Incubator of the Year, Nat Bus Incubation Asn, 1996. **Home Addr:** 7004 Ridge Run Cir, Prospect, KY 40059, **Home Phone:** (502)228-3488. **Business Addr:** Senior SBA Manager, Community Bank of Pickens County, Camp Rd 15 Sammy Mcghee Blvd, Jasper, GA 30143, **Business Phone:** (706)253-9600.

### CLINKSCALES, DR. JERRY A.
Educator. **Personal:** Born Sep 25, 1933, Abbeville, SC; married Jerrolyn Holtzclaw; children: Mary, Jerry, David E & Stephen. **Educ:** SC State Col, BSA, 1956; Tuskegee Inst, DVM, 1960; Univ Ill, advan training, 1972; Univ Tex, advan training, 1981. **Career:** Educator, admission director (retired); Tuskegee Inst, instr, 1960, 1967, asst prof, dir vet admis, 1994-2001; US Dept Agr, poultry insp div, 1966; small animal clin, 1968; vet serv, Macon County Racing Comn, Shorter. **Orgs:** Am Vet Med Asn; Am Asn Vet Clinicans; Am Animal Hosp Asn; Tus-

kegee Area CC; Omega Psi Phi Frat; Phi Zeta Hon Vet Frat; adv, City Recreation Dept; City Canine Control Ctr. **Honors/Awds:** Outstanding Teacher of the Year Award Norden's, 1972-73. **Home Addr:** PO Box 742, Tuskegee, AL 36087-0742, **Home Phone:** (334)727-1488.

**CLINKSCALES, KEITH**
Executive. **Personal:** Born Jan 7, 1964, Bridgeport, CT. **Educ:** Fla A&M Univ, BA, acct & finance, 1986; Harvard Bus Sch, MBA, 1990. **Career:** Urban Profile, Publ & Ed Chief, 1988-92; VIBE Mag, pres & chief exec officer, 1993-99; Vanguarde Media Inc, chmn & chief exec officer, 1999-2003; ESPN Publ, sr vpres, content develop & enterprises, 2007-, gen mgr, 2005-; Shadow League Digital, chief exec officer, 2011; ESPN ABC Sport, consult; KTC Ventures, pres, currently. **Orgs:** Tres, Apollo Theater Found Bd trustee; Pepsicos Multicultural Adv Bd; Adv Bd, UrbanWorld Media Inc; Acad Dir, Stanford Prof Publ Course; Young Presidents Orgn; bd dir, Fla A&M Univ (FAMU) Found, 2012-; bd Visitors Howard Univs Sch Commun; Pres, Kappa Alpha Psi fraternity. **Special Achievements:** First African American named as a president at Time, Inc. **Business Addr:** President, KTC Ventures.

**CLINKSCALES, DR. MARCIA J.**
College teacher. **Educ:** Univ Northern Colo, BA; Emory Univ, Mdiv; Univ Denver, PhD, 1975. **Career:** Nat Commun Asn Organ Commun Pre-Conf, facilitator, 2002; Howard Univ, Dept Human Commun Studies, asst prof, 2003-; Nehemiah Consult Group, founder & prin consult. **Orgs:** Founder & pres, Ctr You; itinerant elder, African Methodist Episcopal Church; ministerial team, Payne Memorial AME Church, Baltimore, MD. **Home Phone:** (202)806-7924. **Business Addr:** Assistant Professor, Howard University, 2400 6th St NW, Washington, DC 20059, **Business Phone:** (202)806-6100.

**CLIPPER, MILTON CLIFTON, JR.**
Chief executive officer, teacher, executive. **Personal:** Born Feb 3, 1948, Washington, DC; son of Milton Sr and Gladys Robertson; married Paulette Parker; children: Faith Ann & Jaime Marie. **Educ:** Montgomery Col; Corcoran Sch Art, visual commun. **Career:** Wash Post, graphic designer; Corcoran Sch Art, art teacher; WTOP-TV, artist, 1970-73; WJXT-TV, art dir, 1974-76; WDVM TV 9 Wash, DC, asst prom mgr, 1985; Pub Broadcasting Atlanta, Atlanta Educ Telecommunications Collab Inc, pres & chief exec officer, 1995-. **Orgs:** Ed bd, WJXT-TV, 1975-76; Metro Art Dirs & Club WA; guest lectr, TV & Newspaper Graphics; Black Ski; Wash Urban League; Am Film Inst; adv bd mem, Big Bros Nat Capital area; bd trustee, Oglethorpe Univ; bd mem, Atlanta Conv; bd mem, Visitors Bur; bd mem, Consumer Credit Coun; bd mem, Midtown Alliance; bd trustee, Atlanta Col Art; bd mem, Atlanta Jr Golf Asn; bd mem, Outreach Inc; bd dir, Leadership Atlanta; Women Prof Billiards Asn. **Honors/Awds:** Second pl Metro Art Dirs Club, 1972; Exhib Abstr Art, 1973; Gold Award, Broadcast Designers Asn, 1984; Finalist Inst Film Fest, 1984. **Home Addr:** 725 13th St NE, Washington, DC 20002, **Home Phone:** (202)388-3818. **Business Addr:** President, Chief Executive Officer, Public Broadcasting Atlanta, 740 Bismark Rd NE, Atlanta, GA 30324, **Business Phone:** (678)686-0321.

**CLOSE, BILLY RAY**
Educator. **Personal:** Born Jan 1, 1965?, Donaldsonville, GA; son of Frank Sr and Daisy; married Fran T; children: Nia SeKayi, Nataki Adia & Nyla Imani. **Educ:** Fla State Univ, BS, criminol & psychol, 1988, MS, criminol, 1992, PhD, criminol & criminal justice, 1997. **Career:** Gov's Coun Phys Fitness & Sports, admin asst, 1988; Lincoln High Sch, head men's track & field coach, 1988-89; Fla State Univ, Black Studies Prog, grad res, 1988-94, Supreme Ct State Fla Racial & Ethnic Bias Study Comn, res consult, 1989-91, Summer Black Grad Orientation Prog, prog dir, 1989-2004, Black Studies Prog, asst dir, 1994-98, African-Am Studies Prog, fac assoc, 1994-, actg dir, 1995-96, Bro Pride, dir, 1992-2007, Sch Criminol & Criminal Justice, asst prof, 1997-, Ctr Acad Retention & Enhancement, summer fac mem, 2003-; Paradigm Consult & Assocs Inc, pres, 2001-; Fla Agr & Mech Univ, adj prof, 2004; Beyond Athlete Inc, pres & founder, 2005-. **Orgs:** Founder & exec dir, Beyond Athlete; pres, Paradigm Consults & Assoc; Fla State Univ Athletic Bd Comt, 1986-88, 2009-; McKnight Achievers Soc, 1990-; Acad Criminal Justice Sci, 1997-; Nat Asn Blacks Criminal Justice, 1997-; vpres & bd dir, Lincoln High Sch Alumni Asn, 2002-; Am Soc Criminol; community consult, Steele-Brooks Inst, Tallahassee, Fla, 2003-; bd mem, life mem, Fla State Univ Varsity Club, 2003-; bd mem, Tallahassee Marine Inst Inc, 2004-; Leon County Sch Found Inc, 2007-; Nat Orgn Black Law Enforcement Exec; dir, grad stud summer orientation prog, Fla State Univ; Bit Hits Found, 2008; Col Reach-Out Prog Adv Coun, Fla Dept Educ, 2009-; Fla State Univ Int Progs Asn, 2012-. **Business Addr:** Assistant Professor, The Florida State University, Epps Hall 145 Convocation Way, Tallahassee, FL 32306-1273, **Business Phone:** (850)644-5344.

**CLOSE, FRAN T.**
Educator. **Personal:** married Billy; children: Nia & Nataki. **Educ:** Fla State Univ, BS, biol sci, 1989; Fla A&M Univ, PhD, pharmacol & toxicol, 1994. **Career:** Fla State Univ, Postdoctoral Res Assoc, biol sci, 1994-98; Fla A&M Univ, Col Pharm & Pharmaceut Studies, Inst Pub Health, assoc prof, 2003-, interim asst dean stud serv. **Orgs:** Pres & bd dir, Capital Area Healthy Start Coalition; Ctr Healthy Options & Innovative Community Empowerment; Healthy Start Redesign Subjects Matter Experts Comt, currently. **Business Addr:** Associate Professor, Interim Dean, Florida A&M University, 209C Frederick S Humphries Sci Res Ctr, Tallahassee, FL 32307-3800, **Business Phone:** (850)599-3053.

**CLOSS, KEITH MITCHELL, JR.**
Basketball player. **Personal:** Born Apr 3, 1976, Hartford, CT; son of Keith Sr and Tia Jamerson; married Aracely. **Educ:** Cent Conn State Univ, attended 1996. **Career:** Los Angeles Clippers, 1997-2000; Pa Valley Dawgs, 2003; Rockford Lightning, forward; Buffalo Silverbacks, ctr, 2007-08; Yunnan Bulls, 2008-. **Business Addr:** Professional Basketball Player, Yunnan Bulls.

**CLOUD, WILLIAM ERIC**
Lawyer. **Personal:** Born Feb 26, 1946, Cleveland, OH; son of William Walter and Alfreda Ruth; married Carole Anne Henderson; children: Andre Deron & Sharrief. **Educ:** Morris Brown Col, BA, 1973; Antioch Sch Law, JD, 1977; George Washington Univ Law Sch, LLM, int & comparative law, 1980. **Career:** Dag Hammarskjold Col, fel, 1974; US Dept Labor, spec asst int tax couns, 1976-78; US Dept Treas, consult, 1979-80; atty, 1982-; HMM Inc, construct mgr, 2004-09; cloudlaw, 2006-; Wash Afro-Am Newspaper, corresp; Morris Brown Col, adj prof int relations, 2015-; Pvt pract atty int law. **Orgs:** Am Bar Asn, 1977; Nat Bar Asn; Morris Brown Col Alumni Asn; Dc Bar. **Honors/Awds:** Good Samaritan of the Year, Mayor Carl Stokes, 1968; Award for Best Article, 1990. **Special Achievements:** Book: "Tax Treaties the Need for the US to Extend its Treaty Network to Developing Countries in Light of the New International Economic and Political Realities"; "Four Walls/Eight Window", 1990. **Home Addr:** 10605 Woodlawn Blvd, Largo, FL 20774-2349, **Home Phone:** (301)336-3181. **Business Addr:** Lawyer, 1003 K St NW, Washington, DC 20001-4425, **Business Phone:** (202)347-5724.

**CLOUDEN, LAVERNE C.**
Music director, educator. **Personal:** Born Dec 6, 1933, Cleveland, OH; married Aubrey B; children: Norman, Karen & Nathan. **Educ:** Case Western Res Univ, BS, 1966, MA, 1970. **Career:** Cleveland music instructor; Buckeye State Band, dir, 1958-; F D Roosevelt Jr High Sch, instr & dir, 1966-72; Music Dept Nathan Hale Jr High Sch, chmn, 1972-74; John F Kennedy High Sch, dir instrumental music, band dir, 1974-85; E High Sch, fine arts dept chmn & instr, dir & vocal dir, 1985-. **Orgs:** Mt Pleasant Symphony Orchestra Parma Symphony; Cleveland Womens Symphony; Buckeye State Band; Mt Pleasant Musicians Guild; dir, Musicians Union 4; Music Educrs Nat Conf Ohio Music Educrs Asn; Women Band dir Nat Asn; Nat Band Asn; Int Platform Asn; Nat Asn Music Ther; Mu Phi Epsilon; dir, Nat Bd Am Youth Symphony & Chorus europ good will concert, 1980. **Special Achievements:** City's first female high school marching band and orchestra director. **Home Addr:** 3851 E 151 St, Cleveland, OH 44128, **Home Phone:** (216)751-5558. **Business Addr:** Chairman, Director, East High School, 1349 E 79th St, Cleveland, OH 44103, **Business Phone:** (216)431-5361.

**CLOWNEY, AUDREY E.**
Consultant, manager. **Personal:** Born Aug 29, 1961, Pittsburgh, PA; daughter of Gordon W and Helen A. **Educ:** Univ Mich, BS, engineering, indust engineering, 1983; Columbia Univ, Columbia Bus Sch, MBA, mkt, 1985; Birkman Int, cert. **Career:** Quaker Oats Co, brand mgr, 1985-92; Coca-Cola Co, mkt, 1992-2000; PwCES, consult, 2001-02; SkyLab Inc, chief exec officer, exec coach & mgt consult, 2000-; ASTD Atlanta, Leadership Acad, co-chair, 2011. **Orgs:** Youth Guidance, 1988-89; Nat Black MBA Asn-Chicago Chapter, 1990-; Arts Forum, 1990-. **Honors/Awds:** One of "The 100 Most Promising Black Women in Corporate America", Ebony Magazine, 1991; Judge of the Executive Coaching Corporate Awards, PRISM, 2009. **Home Addr:** 1405 Wickenby Ct, Atlanta, GA 30338, **Home Phone:** (770)668-0702. **Business Addr:** Chief Executive Officer, SkyLab Inc, 4780 Ashford Dunwoody Rd Suite A 453, Atlanta, GA 30338, **Business Phone:** (404)259-7586.

**CLYBURN, JAMES EMOS (JIM CLYBURN)**
**Personal:** Born Jul 21, 1940, Sumter, SC; son of Enos Lloyd and Almeta; married Emily E; children: Mignon L, Jennifer(Walter Reed) & Angela(Cecil Hannibal). **Educ:** SC State Col, BS, hist, 1961; Univ SC Law Sch, 1974. **Career:** Teacher & politician; High sch, hist teacher, 1962-65; SC Employee Sec Commn, couns, 1965-66; Neighborhood Youth Corps, dir, 1966-68; SC Commn Farm Workers Inc, exec dir, 1968-71; Gov John C W SC, spec asst human resource develop, 1971-74; SC Human Affairs Comn, comnr, 1974-92; CBC, head, 1998-2000; US House Rep, 6th Dist SC, congressman, 1993-; 111th Cong, House majority whip; House Dem's Faith Working Group, leader. **Orgs:** Pres, Nat Asn Advan Colored People; US House Rep; numerous polit & civic orgns; Omega Psi Phi fraternity. **Home Addr:** 501 Juniper St, Columbia, SC 29203, **Home Phone:** (803)786-1402. **Business Addr:** Congressman, US House Representative, 242 Cannon House Off Bldg, Washington, DC 20515-4006, **Business Phone:** (202)225-3315.

**CLYBURN, JOHN B.**
Executive. **Personal:** Born Oct 22, 1942, Sumter, SC; married Vivian Hilton; children: Jeffrey, Erica & Kimberly. **Educ:** SC State Col, BS, 1964; Northeastern Univ, MEd, 1968; Univ WI, PhD, urban ed. **Career:** ESC, nat coord, 1969-70, proj dir, 1970-71, vpres, 1971-72, exec vpres, 1972-73; Decision Info Systs Corp, chmn; Precise Solutions Inc, chmn & chief exec officer; Wiltwyck Sch Boys Inc, sr counr; New Eng Home, weekend supvr; Hayden Goodwill Inn Sch Boys, exec asst; SC Voc Rehab Dept, voc rehab counr; Repub Sq Ltd, staff, currently. **Orgs:** Nat Asn Mkt Develops; Am Mgt Asn; Child Care Proj Adv Comn; Nat Rehab Asn; Day Care & Child Develop Corp Am; Nat Asn Educ Young C; Delta Psi Omega; lectr, Nat Head Start Conf; Nat Asn Black Soc Workers; Nat Conf Inst Serv. **Home Addr:** 2711 Unicorn Lane NW, Washington, DC 20015, **Home Phone:** (202)966-2699. **Business Addr:** Staff, Republic Square Ltd, 1280 Maryland Ave SW Suite 280, Washington, DC 20024, **Business Phone:** (202)863-0300.

**CLYNE, JOHN RENNEL**
Lawyer, consultant. **Personal:** Born Feb 25, 1926, New York, NY; son of Reginald and Urielle Linard; married Jessie MacFarlane; children: Diana, Reginald & Robert Marcel. **Educ:** St Johns Univ Sch Law, LLB, 1958, JD, 1968. **Career:** US & W Indies, engr, 1958; pvt practice lawyer, NY, 1958-62; New York City Transit Auth, atty, 1963-65; US Agency Intl Develop Nigeria, Brazil, Nicaragua, Honduras, regional legal advisor, 1965-83; US Agency Intl Develop, asst gen coun, 1983-85; self-employ, econ develop consult, currently. **Honors/Awds:** Nominated, Fed Exec Sr Sem, 1977; Senior Foreign Service Award, 1984; Secy State's Tribute Appreciation Distinguished Serv Foreign Disaster Asst, 1985. **Home Addr:** 2200 Eugenia Ct, Oviedo, FL 32765, **Home Phone:** (407)677-4215. **Business Addr:** Self, Clyne & Self PA, 324 Datura St Suite 235, West Palm Beach, FL 33401, **Business Phone:** (561)832-7080.

**COAKLEY, H. M.**
Entrepreneur, executive, movie producer. **Personal:** Born Jan 1, 1971, St. Thomas, VI; married Camille C Irons. **Educ:** Howard Univ, BS, physics; Columbia Univ, MS, fine arts film making; Univ Calif, Los Angeles, PhD, physics. **Career:** Producer, dir, writer, music supvr, dir photog; Film Independent, head programming; Cal State Univ-Fullerton, Columbia Col Hollywood, adj prof; USC Sch Cinema, guest lectr; Rockstone Pictures Inc, chmn, chief exec officer, co founder & exec dir, currently; The UAFW, co-founder & exec dir; Urban-Am Filmmakers Workshop, co-founder & exec dir; Producer: Ten Benny, 1995; Restaurant, 1998; Playboy: Queen of Clubs, 2004; Up Against the 8 Ball, 2004; Speed-Dating, 2010; Holla II, 2013. Director: Holla, 2006; Writer: Holla, 2006; Editor: Holla, 2006; Music Supervisor: Holla, 2006. **Orgs:** Nat Asn Latino Independent Producers. **Business Addr:** Chairman, Chief Executive Officer, Executive Director, Rockstone Pictures Inc, 1800 Century Pk E Suite 600, Los Angeles, CA 90067, **Business Phone:** (310)260-2587.

**COAKLEY, WILLIAM DEXTER**
Executive, football player, football coach. **Personal:** Born Oct 20, 1972, Charleston, SC. **Educ:** Appalachian State Univ, BA, commun & advert, 1997. **Career:** Football player (retired), coach; Dallas Cowboys, right linebacker, 1997-98, linebacker, 1999-2004; St Louis Rams, linebacker, 2005-06, 2007; Sanchez & Assocs, land develop, 2008-11; Spine-X, DME sales prof, 2012-; Oakridge Sch, linebackers coach, softball coach, currently. **Honors/Awds:** Southern Conference Freshman of the Year, 1993; Southern Conference Defensive Player of the Year, 1994, 1995, 1996; Southern Conference Male Athlete of the Year, 1995, 1996; Buck Buchanan Award Winner, 1995, 1996; All-Iron Award, 1999; Pro Bowl, 1999, 2001, 2003; College Football Hall of Fame, 2011; Southern Conference Hall of Fame, 2011; Most Valuable Player. **Business Addr:** Linebackers Coach, Softball Coach, The Oakridge School, 5900 W Pioneer Pkwy, Arlington, TX 76013, **Business Phone:** (817)451-4994.

**COAR, DAVID H.**
Federal court judge. **Personal:** Born Aug 11, 1943, Birmingham, AL. **Educ:** Syracuse Univ, BA, 1964; Loyola Univ Chicago Law Sch, JD, 1969; Harvard Univ, LLM, 1970. **Career:** Judge (retired); Nat Asn Advan Colored People Legal Defense & Educ Fund, NY, Legal intern, 1970-71; Pvt pract, Ala, 1971-72, Birmingham, 1974; Crawford & Cooper, Mobile, Ala, atty, 1971; Adams, Baker & Clemon, Birmingham, Ala, atty, 1972-74; DePaul Univ, instr, assoc prof, 1974-79, assoc dean, 1982-86; Northern Dist Ill, Dept Justice, trustee, 1979-82; Col William & Mary, Marshall Wythe Law Sch, vis prof, 1985; US Dist Ct, Northern Dist Ill, bankruptcy judge, 1986-94, dist ct judge, 1994-; sr, 2009-10. **Orgs:** Fed Bar Asn; Nat Conf Bankruptcy Judges; Ala Bar Asn; Chicago Bar Asn; bd dir, Boys & Girls Clubs Chicago; Am Bankruptcy Inst; Nat Bankruptcy Conf; Bankruptcy Judges Educ Comt, Fed Judicial Ctr; Bur Nat Affairs; Am Bar Asn; Legal Club Chicago; Chicago Inn Ct; Chicago Bar Asn. **Business Addr:** Judge, US Dist Ct, Everett McKinley Dirksen Bldg, Chicago, IL 60604, **Business Phone:** (312)435-5648.

**COASTON, SHIRLEY ANN DUMAS**
Educator, president (organization). **Personal:** Born Nov 27, 1939, New Orleans, LA; daughter of Cornelius and Pearl Bailey; married George Ellis Sr; children: Debra Ford, George E Jr & Angela R. **Educ:** Dillard Univ, New Orleans, LA, BA, 1962; Univ Calif, Berkeley, CA, MLS, 1970. **Career:** Univ Calif, San Francisco, Calif, libr asst, 1966-69; Peralta Community Col Dist, Oakland, Calif, eve ref librn & head librn, dir, 1970-87, head librn, 1988-2011; Contra Costa Community Col Dist, Richmond, Calif, ref librn, 1987-88; Laney Col, head librn, currently, fac sen pres, 2006-07. **Orgs:** Treas, Calif Librns Black Caucus N, 1980-; secy & bd dir, Salem Lutheran Home, 1986-91; chairperson, Prof Develop Comt, Laney Col, 1989-91; Aid Asn Lutherans, 1989-; secy, Bay Net, 1990-92; vpres, Peralta Fed Teachers, 1991-; asst secy, San Francisco Bay Area Panhellenic Coun, 1992-; ann conv planning comt mem, Calif Libr Asn, 1993; Am Libr Asn; am libr asn Black Caucus; Delta Sigma Theta Sorority; Nat Asn Advan Colored People; Nat Coun Negro Women. **Home Addr:** 3226 Hood St, Oakland, CA 94605, **Home Phone:** (510)632-0702. **Business Addr:** Head Librarian, Laney College, 900 Fallon St, Oakland, CA 94607, **Business Phone:** (510)986-6947.

**COATES, BEN TERRENCE**
Football player, football coach. **Personal:** Born Aug 16, 1969, Greenwood, SC; married Yvette; children: Lauren, Brianna & Destiny. **Educ:** Livingstone Col, BS, sports mgt, 1991. **Career:** Football player (retired), football coach, advisor; New Eng Patriots, tight end, 1991-99; Baltimore Ravens, tight end, 2000; Livingstone Col, offensive coordr, asst football coach, 2001-04; NFL Europe, head coach, coach; Carolina Sharks Atlantic Indoor Football League, coach & gen mgr, 2004; Cleveland Browns, tight ends coach, 2005-07; Cent State Univ, asst head coach & offensive coordr, 2009-12; St Augustine's Col, asst football coach, 2013-14; Signature Consults, develop advisor, 2014-. **Honors/Awds:** Livingstone's Most Valuable Player Award, 1987, 1988 & 1990; National Football League 1990s All-Decade Team; Won Baxter Holman Mem Award freshman; S W Lancaster Award; Offensive Player of the Year, 1993; Associated Press First-team All-Pro selection, 1994-95; Pro Bowl selection, 1994-98; Baltimore Ravens Super Bowl XXXV Champions; New England Patriots Hall of Fame, 2008. **Special Achievements:** Ranked seventh among the Patriots' all-time leading scorers with 290 career points; Owns franchise records for most receptions in a season (96). **Business Addr:** Develop Advisor, 200 S College St Suite 1400, Charlotte, NC 28202, **Business Phone:** (704)334-0119.

**COATES, DR. JANICE EULA**
Optometrist. **Personal:** Born Aug 27, 1942, Zanesville, OH; daughter of Bessie Kennedy Mayle and Urschel Mayle; children: Stephanie, Stephlynn, Melissa & Tischa. **Educ:** Wright State Univ, BS, comprehensive sci, BS, sec educ, 1974; Ind Univ, MD, optom, 1979. **Career:** Dr Frederick Grigsby, urologist asst, 1963-65; Sanders Stone Ins Agency, ins rater, 1965-66; Montgomery Co Welfare Dept, welfare worker, 1967-69; Dayton Bd Educ, substitute teacher, 1969-74, sci teacher, 1974-75; Capital Univ, educ, 1980-82; pvt pract optometrist, 1980-.

**Orgs:** Ohio Optom Asn, 1980-; Minority recuirt, Am Optom Asn; liasion, state rep Miami Valley Soc Optometrists, 1981-; prog coordr, 1982-83, treas, 1983-84, Am Bus Womens Asn; Gem City Med Soc, 1982-; trustee, Nat Optom Asn, 1983-, exec bd, 1983-89, secy, 1985-87; Nat Asn Advan Colored People, 1983-; exec bd, Youth Engaged Success, 1985-97. **Honors/Awds:** One of Dayton's Top Ten African American Women. **Home Addr:** 4387 Pkwy Dr, Dayton, OH 45416-1638, **Home Phone:** (937)278-7391. **Business Addr:** Optometrist, 4387 Pkwy Dr, Dayton, OH 45416-1638, **Business Phone:** (937)278-7391.

## COATES, TA-NEHISI
Writer, periodical editor. **Personal:** Born Jan 1, 1975?, Baltimore, MD; daughter of William Paul Coates and Cheryl Coates; married Kenyatta Coates; children: Son. **Educ:** Baltimore Polytechnic Institute, Attended; Howard University, Attended. **Career:** "Philadelphia Weekly," Writer; "The Village Voice," Writer; "Washington City Paper," Writer; "Time" Magazine, Writer; "The Washington Post," Writer; "Washington Monthly," Writer; "O" Magazine, Writer; "The Atlantic," Senior Editor and Blogger; "The New York Times," Guest Columnist; Massachusetts Institute of Technology, Visiting Professor, 2012-13. **Honors/Awds:** "Time" Magazine, 25 Best Blogs of 2011; The Sidney Hillman Foundation, Hillman Prize for Opinion & Analysis Journalism, 2012; "The Root" Magazine, The Root 100 Honorees, 2013. **Special Achievements:** Autobiography, "The Beautiful Struggle: A Father, Two Sons, and an Unlikely Road to Manhood," Spiegel & Grau, 2008.

## COATIE, ROBERT MASON
Teacher, educator, association executive. **Personal:** Born May 19, 1945, Mound City, IL; son of Dixon C and Georgia B Mason; married Birdeen Golden; children: Dionne & Robert M II. **Educ:** Ball State Univ, BS, 1968, MA, 1972. **Career:** Muncie Comm Sch Corp, teacher, 1967-68; Ind Civil Rights Comn, proj dir, 1968-69; Ball State Univ, asst dir minority stud develop, 1969-84; Univ Louisville, Ctr Acad Achievement, dir, 1984-92; Fla Int Univ, Multicultural Progs & Servs, dir, sr dir, 2002-. **Orgs:** Kappa Alpha Psi Fraternity, 1964-; chmn, treas, Area VI Coun Aging, 1974-84; bd mem, Hoosiers Excellence, 1983-85; Nat Asn Develop Educ, 1985-; vpres, Cent High Sch Parent Teachers Asn, 1985-89; Southeastern Asn Educ Prog Personnel, 1986-90; YMCA Black Achiever's Parent Adv Comt, 1986-89; Am Asn Coun & Develop, 1987-90; Nat Asn Stud Personnel Admin, 1987-; Asn Supv & Curric Develop, 1987-90; secy, Brown Sch Parent Teachers Asn, 1986-89; Am Asn Univ Adminr, 1989-92; Am Asn Higher Educ. **Honors/Awds:** Observer White House Conf on Aging, 1981; Black Achiever, Muncie, Ind, 1988; Athletic Hall of Fame, Del County, Ind, 1988; Retention Excellence Award, Noel & Levitz, 1991; Outstanding Black Alumni, Ball State Univ Alumni Asn, 1998. **Home Addr:** 8360 NW 166th Terr, Hialeah, FL 33016, **Home Phone:** (305)826-3100. **Business Addr:** Senior Director, Florida International University, 11200 SW 8th St, Miami, FL 33199, **Business Phone:** (305)348-2436.

## COAXUM, HARRY LEE
Executive, vice president (organization), manager. **Personal:** Born Sep 25, 1953, Awendaw, SC; son of Henry Sr and Myrtle W; married Donna Bunch; children: Todriq, Nia & Maya. **Educ:** Talladega Col, BA, econs, 1975. **Career:** McDonalds Corp, Philadelphia Region, multi dept head, 1986-89, dir field trng, 1989-90, dir minority opers, 1990-94, dept dir western zone, 1994-96, asst vpres, franchising, 1996; McDonald's Corp, corp vpres, 1996-2003, Pac Sierra Region, regional vpres, 2003-06, Philadelphia Region, regional vpres & gen mgr, 2006-08, Atlanta Region, regional vpres & gen mgr, 2008-12.Dartmouth Col Amos Tuck Sch Bus, exec develop, 1995-; Northwestern Univ Kellogg Sch Mgt, exec develop, 2012-. **Orgs:** Omega Psi Phi Fraternity, 1972; Urban League Leadership Inst Philadelphia charter, 1988; Trinity United Church Christ, 1993; 100 Black Men Am, Chicago, 1996; Nat Asn Guardsmen, 2002; Sigma Pi Phi, 2002; Nat Asn Black Accountants; Quad County Urban League; chair, trustee bd, Talladega Col. **Home Addr:** 2246 Lotus Ct, Naperville, IL 60565, **Home Phone:** (708)420-7480. **Business Addr:** Vice President, General Manager, McDonald Corp, 2111 McDonald, Oak Brook, IL 60523, **Business Phone:** (630)623-3000.

## COAXUM, HENRY L., JR.
Executive. **Personal:** Born Jan 27, 1951, Charleston, SC; son of Henry Sr and Myrtle Weston; married Karen Nabonne. **Educ:** Talladega Col, BA, Am hist, 1973; Ind Univ Bloomington, MPA, pub & environ affairs, 1975. **Career:** City Chicago, planning analyst, 1975-79; DuSable Mus African-Am Hist, develop officer, 1979-81; Southtown Planning Assoc, exec dir, 1981-83; Amistad Res Ctr, dir develop, 1982-84; McDonalds Corp, mgr trainee, asst vpres, vpres, gen mgr, owner & operator, Atlanta Region, 1984-2002; Coaxum Enterprises Inc, pres, 2002-. **Orgs:** Pres, Chicago Talladega Col Alumni Club, 1977-81; dir, United Bank & Trust New Orleans, 1995-; 100 Black Men Metro New Orleans, 1995-; dir, Grambling State Univ Athletic Found, 2000-; bd trustee, dir, United Way Greater New Orleans, 2002-; dir, New Orleans E Businessmens Asn, 2004; chmn, NOLA Bus Alliance; bd mem, Greater Philadelphia Chamber Com; Omega Psi Phi Fraternity; bd commissioners city Hosp Serv Dist Bd. **Honors/Awds:** Successful Setting Restaurant Award, Nation Restaurant News, 2003; Success Guide's Minority Achievers Award, City Bus Mag, 2003; McDonald's Great Southern Region Rookie of the Year, 2003; Howie Technology Award, 2003; National Black McDonald's Operator Association Award, 2003; C Ray Nagin Minority Entrepreneurship Award, 2004; Nation's Restaurant News Franchisee Star Award, 2007; Entrepreneur of the Year Award, Nat Black Chamber Com, 2007; Phoenix Award, 2008; Leadership Award; Greater New Orleans Area Alexis de Tocqueville Award, United Way; The Ronald Award, McDonald's Corp; Laureate of the Junior Achievement Business Hall of Fame, 2012; McDonald's 365Black Award, 2014; Doctor of Humane Letters, Talladega Col, 2016. **Special Achievements:** Honorary Ambassador, La Dept Econ Develop, 2004; First couple to be honored as Young Leadership Council Role Models. **Home Addr:** 13328 Hayne Blvd, New Orleans, LA 70128-1511, **Home Phone:** (504)309-7621. **Business Addr:** President, Coaxum Enterprises Inc, 231 Harbor Circle Ct, New Orleans, LA 70126, **Business Phone:** (504)241-6942.

## COBB, CYNTHIA JOAN
Manager, president (organization). **Personal:** Born Sep 22, 1959, Indianapolis, IN; daughter of Marcella Jean Collins Taylor and Henry Marshall Taylor; married Arthur Jr. **Educ:** Purdue Univ, West Lafayette, BSE, biomed engineering & engineering mgt, 1981; Ind Univ, Bloomington, MBA, human resources & opers mgt, 1985. **Career:** Corning Med, Medfield, Mass, process eng, 1981-83; Eli Lilly, Indianapolis, summer intern, 1984; Baxter Healthcare Corp, Deerfield, compensation analyst, 1985, sr compensation analyst, 1986, assoc, col rels, 1986-88, supvr, col rels, 1988, staffing mgr, 1988-91; hr mgr, 1991-92, dir staffing & develop, 1992-95, dir strategic staffing, 1995-96, dir human resource; Exec Coaching Connections, coach, currently; 3C-Cynthia Cobb Consult, LLC, pres & prin, 2004-; Tastefully Simple, sr consult, current; Monument Consult Group, LLC, managing partner, currently. **Orgs:** Chmn, pharmaceut, HC employers, Midwest Col Placement Asn, 1987-89, vpres-employer, 1990-91, vice chmn, ed adv bd, 1989-90, assembly, 1989-90; bd dir, YWCA Lake County, 1994-95, secy, 1998, pres, 1999-2002; sec, pres, Womens Bus Exchange; Lifetime Mem Girl Scouts; bd dir, Ctr Co; Bernie's Bk Bank. **Honors/Awds:** YMCA of Metro Chicago Leadership Award, 1989; 100 Most Promising Black Women in Corporate Am, Ebony/Johnson Publishing, 1991; Eagle Award, Most Influential AFA Lake County, 2001. **Home Addr:** 760 Ravinia Dr, Gurnee, IL 60031, **Home Phone:** (847)548-4548. **Business Addr:** Coach, Executive Coaching Connections LLC, 1000 Skokie Blvd Suite 340, Wilmette, IL 60091, **Business Phone:** (847)548-4548.

## COBB, DELMARIE L.
Consultant, journalist, president (organization). **Personal:** Born Chicago, IL; daughter of James A Wells and Johnnie Mae. **Educ:** Univ Cincinnati; Northwestern Univ. **Career:** WSBT-TV, CBS, gen assignment reporter, 1981-83; WVEC-TV, ABC, gen assignment reporter, 1983-85; WTHR-TV, NBC, gen assignment reporter, 1985-87; Jackson Pres, nat traveling press secy, 1988; WVON-AM, talk show host, 1988-90; Congressman Jesse Jackson, dir commun & press secy; Dem Nat Conv Comt, press secy, 1996; Publicity Works, pres, chief exec officer, owner, 1990-; Deleco Commun Inc, owner & pres, 1990-. **Orgs:** Women & media proj adv bd em, Fairness & Accuracy Reporting, 1995-; bd mem, Chicago Asn Black Journalist, 1996-97; vice chmn, Gamaliel Found Bd. **Home Addr:** 3533 S Martin Luther King Dr, Chicago, IL 60653, **Home Phone:** (773)924-7678. **Business Addr:** President, Owner, The Publicity Works, 3533 S King Dr, Chicago, IL 60653, **Business Phone:** (773)373-3860.

**COBB, ETHEL WASHINGTON.** **See Obituaries Section.**

## COBB, REV. HAROLD
Clergy, government official, business owner. **Personal:** Born Jul 20, 1941, Covington, GA; son of Toy Quintella and Mary Alice; married Reta Jean Davis; children: Sheila, Shermekia & Harrell. **Educ:** Atlanta Area Tech Sch, attended 1970; Marsh-Drangron Bus Col, attended 1972; Oxford Col, Emory Univ, attended 1978; DeKalb Community Col, attended 1981; Emory Univ, ministerial course, 1989. **Career:** Cobb's Printing, founder & owner, 1971-80; Cousins Mid Sch PTO, pres, 1973-75; City Covington, lab analyst water treat, 1974-78; Newton City Ment Health, bd dir, 1974-76; Ford Motor Co, lab analyst water treat, 1978-; C&C Rental, founder & owner, 1984-; City Covington, comnr; E FlatRock United Methodist Church, minister; Grace Episcopal Church, pastor, rector. **Orgs:** Masonic Lodge Friendship No 20 F&AM, 1969-; pres & founder, Newton City Voter League, 1970-77; Wash State Community Ctr, 1980-83; bd mem, Newton City Pub Defenders, 1980-; co-founder, Newton Co King Scholar Prog, Emory Univ, Oxford Col, 1986-. **Honors/Awds:** Inkind Contrib Headstart, 1977; Outstanding Progress, Newton City, 1978; Appreciation Awards, Recreation Dept Supporter, 1981-84; Outstanding Serv, 1981; Gaithers Chapel United Methodist Church Appreciation, 1983; Support Indust Growth, Newton City Chamber Com, 1984; I Have A Dream Award, Martin Luther King Scholar Fund, 1988; Outstanding Serv, Toney Gardens Civic Asn, 1989; Appreciation Award, Union Grove Church, 1990. **Home Addr:** 15 Harvey Ave, Covington, GA 30016, **Home Phone:** (770)786-4423. **Business Addr:** Rector, Grace Church, 1400 E Brambleton Ave, Norfolk, VA 23504, **Business Phone:** (757)625-2868.

## COBB, REV. HAROLD JAMES, JR.
Clergy. **Personal:** Born Jun 10, 1958, Burlington, NC; son of Harold James Sr and Armadia Goodson; married Sheliah Jeffries; children: Caryn. **Educ:** Univ NC, Chapel Hill, BA, 1982; Episcopal Theol Sem, MDiv, 1990. **Career:** Good Samaritan Church, pastor & founder, 1980-87; Saint Stephens Church, rector, 1990; Grace Church, rector, currently. **Orgs:** Comnr, NC Gov's Comn Family, 1985-88; alumni exec comt, Episcopal Sem, 1990-91; bd higher educ, Diocese NC, 1990-; Youth Comn, 1990-; NC Episcopal Clergy Asn, 1990-; Alpha Pi Alpha; The Order Cross; The Royal Order Soc, St George. **Honors/Awds:** Harold J Cobb Jr Day, 1989; Hon Doctor Divinity, St Paul's Col; Humanitarian Award, Va Ctr Inclusive Communities, 2013. **Special Achievements:** Author: The Organization of Black Episcopal Seminarians, Seminary Jour, 1987. **Home Addr:** 2748 Knob Hill Dr, Clemmons, NC 27012, **Home Phone:** (757)855-0003. **Business Addr:** Rector, Grace Church, 1400 E Brambleton Ave, Norfolk, VA 23504, **Business Phone:** (757)625-2868.

## COBB, DR. JEWEL PLUMMER
Cancer researcher, college administrator, educator. **Personal:** Born Jan 17, 1924, Chicago, IL; daughter of Frank V and Carriebel Cole; married Roy; children: Jonathan. **Educ:** Talladega Col, Talladega, AL, BA, biol, 1945; NY Univ, New York, NY, MS, 1947, PhD, cell physiology, 1950. **Career:** Professor (retired); Woods Hole Marine Biol Lab, independent investr, 1949; New York Univ, NY, instr, 1955-56, asst prof, 1956-60; Hunter Col, vis lect, 1956-57; Sarah Lawrence Col, Bronxville, NY, biol prof, 1960-69; Conn Col, New London, Conn, zool prof, dean, 1969-76; Rutgers Univ, Douglass Col, Nb, NJ, biol prof, dean, 1976-81; Calif State Univ, Fullerton, Calif, pres, 1981-90, pres emer, 1990-, fullerton & trustee prof, Los Angeles, currently; Access Ctr, princ dir, 1991-, princ investr, currently; Ascend Proj, Sci Tech Eng Prog Up Youth, 2001-. **Orgs:** Tissue Cult Asn Educ Comt, 1972-74; Nat Sci Bd, 1974-80; bd trustee, Inst Educ Mgt, 1973-; developer & dir, Fifth Yr Post Bacc Pre-Med Prog; bd dir, Am Coun Educ, 1973-76; bd dir, Educ Policy Ctr, NY City; Nat Acad Scis, Human Resources Comn, 1974-; bd dir, Nat Sci Found, 1974-; bd dir, Travelers Ins Co, 1974-; bd dir, 21st Century Found; trustee, Nat Fund Minority Eng Studs, 1978-; bd dir, Califs Prev Violence, 1983-; bd dir, First Interstate Bancorp, 1985-; bd dir, Am Assembly Barbard Col, 1986-; bd mem, Newport Harbor Mus; Alpha Kappa Alpha; bd dr, Allied Corp. **Honors/Awds:** Res grant, Am Cancer Soc, 1969-74, 1971-73, 1974-77; hon doctorates, Wheaton Col, 1971, Lowell Tech Inst, 1972, Pa Med Col, 1975, City Col City, Univ NY, St Lawrence Univ, Col New Rochelle, Tuskegee Univ, Fairleigh Dickinson Univ; Lifetime Achievement Award, Nat Acad Sci, 1993; Ronald Wilson Award, Am Coun Educ, 2001; Reginald Wilson Award; Hon doctorates, Med Col Pa; Hon doctorates, Northern Univ; Hon doctorates, Rensselaer Polytech Inst; Hon doctorates, Rutgers Univ; Hon doctorates, Tuskegee Univ. **Special Achievements:** Author: "Filters for Women in Science", Annals of the New York Academy of Sciences, 1979; "Breaking Down Barriers to Women Entering Science", 1979, "Issues and Problems: A Debate", 1979. **Home Addr:** , NJ.

## COBB, KEITH HAMILTON (TYR ANASAZI)
Actor. **Personal:** Born Jan 28, 1962, North Tarrytown, NY; son of James and Mary Lane. **Educ:** Westchester Community Col; NY Univ, Tisch Sch Arts, attended 1987. **Career:** Youth Theatre Interactions Inc, theatrical consult; TV series: "All My Children", 1994-96; "Beastmaster", 1999; "Gene Roddenberry's Andromeda", 2000; "Soap Talk", 2003; "The Young and the Restless", 2003-05; "Noah's Arc", 2006; "CSI: Miami", 2007. Films: Cold Light of Day, 1989; Astonished, 1990; Eyes Beyond Seeing, 1995. **Honors/Awds:** Soap Opera Digest Award, 1995, 1996; Nominated for Image Award, 2005. **Special Achievements:** Emmy nominee, Award for Outstanding Younger Actor in a Drama Series, 1995; nominated four times for Image Award; named one of 50 Most BeautifulPeople in the World, People mag, 1996. **Business Addr:** Actor, The Young & the Restless, 7800 Beverly Blvd, Los Angeles, CA 90036.

## COBB, REGINALD JOHN
Football player, scout. **Personal:** Born Jul 7, 1968, Knoxville, TN; married Stephanie; children: DeMarcus. **Educ:** Univ Tenn. **Career:** Football player (retired), scout; Tampa Bay Buccaneers, running back & fullback, 1990-93; scouting interns; Green Bay Packers, running back, 1994; Jacksonville Jaguars, running back, 1995; New York Jets, running back, 1996; Oakland Raiders, scout; Washington Redskins, admin scout, 2001; San Francisco 49ers, col scout, 2009-11. **Honors/Awds:** Most Valuable Player, Peach Bowl, 1987; Greater Knoxville Sports Hall of Fame, 2011. **Business Addr:** College Scout, San Francisco 49ers, Rm 400 490 Jamestown Ave, San Francisco, CA 94124, **Business Phone:** (415)464-9377.

**COBB, TIFFANY.** **See CANTRELL, BLU.**

## COBBIN, W. FRANK, JR.
Executive, executive director. **Personal:** Born Jul 2, 1947, Youngstown, OH; married Deborah Walk; children: Kevin M Jr & Kimberly N. **Educ:** Cleveland State Univ, BA, psychol & Eng, 1971; Univ Exec Pgm, prof mgr & bus functions, 1981. **Career:** OH Bell Tel Co, mgr bus off, 1973-77, mgr installation, 1977-78, dist mgr installation, 1978-79, mkt mgr, 1979, dist mgr, 1979-82; AT&T Am Transtech, dir tel response ctr, 1982-83, exec dir mkt serv, vpres direct mkt serv, 1987-. **Orgs:** Direct Mkt Assoc; Telemarketing Assoc; Mayors Econ Develop Coun; Jax Urban League Bd; Basileus Omega Psi Phi Frat Inc; United Way, Univ N FL Bus Adv Coun, Jacksonville Univ Career Beginnings Prog. **Special Achievements:** Author, SIM 1989 Jury Award Paper. **Home Addr:** 4430 Glen Kernan Pkwy E, Jacksonville, FL 32224-5626, **Home Phone:** (904)642-8422. **Business Addr:** Vice President, AT&T American Transtech, 8000 Baymeadows Way, Jacksonville, FL 32256-7520, **Business Phone:** (904)636-1000.

## COBBINS, LYRON DURYEA
Football player. **Personal:** Born Sep 17, 1974, Kansas City, KS. **Educ:** Univ Notre Dame, grad. **Career:** Football player (retired); Ariz Cardinals, linebacker, 1997; Barcelona Dragons, linebacker, 1999.

## COBBS, HARVEY, JR.
Counselor. **Personal:** Born Mar 19, 1952, Twist, AR; son of Harvey and Paralee Jackson; married Willie Mae Lewis; children: Harvey III, Carolyn, Davina & Yvonne. **Educ:** Bakersfield Col, AA, 1976; CA State Univ, Bakersfield, BA, criminal justice, 1980. **Career:** Counselor (retired); USY, mil policeman, sentry dog handler, 1972; Calif Correctional Inst, Dept Corrections, correctional officer, 1979-82, Junipero Serra-Work Furlough, inmate supvr, counr, 1987. **Orgs:** Life & golden heritage, NCP, 1990; AM Correctional officers ASN, 1989; life mem, Nat Asn Black Veterans; Nat Asn Blacks Criminal Justice, 1998; life mem, Col Allensworth Hist Black Pk; life mem, Ninth-Tenth Cavalry Asn. **Honors/Awds:** Golden Heritage Award, NCP, 1990; Certificate & Badge, CA Corrections Officers Asn, 1987; Recognition Plaque, AM Criminal Justice Asn, 1990; Intl Asn Correctional Officers, Certificate; Nat Asn Black Veterans, 1971; CA State Senator. **Home Addr:** 213 Northrup St, Bakersfield, CA 93307, **Home Phone:** (661)323-1887.

## COBBS, DR. PRICE MASHAW
Executive, psychiatrist. **Personal:** Born Nov 2, 1928, Los Angeles, CA; son of Peter Price and Rose Mashaw; married Evadne Priester; children: Price Priester & Marion Renata; married Frederica Maxwell. **Educ:** Univ Calif, Berkeley, CA, BA, 1954; Meharry Med Col, MD, psychiat med, 1958. **Career:** San Francisco Gen Hosp, intern, 1958-59; Mendocino State Hosp, psychiat res, 1959-61; Langley Porter Neuropsychiat Inst, psychol resident, 1961-62; psychiat pvt pract, 1962-; Univ Calif, San Francisco, asst clin prof psychiat, 1963-; Pac Mgt Syst, founder, pres, 1967-, chief exec officer, currently; Cobbs Inc, chief exec officer. **Orgs:** Nat Med Asn; Nat Asn Advan Colored People; consult many Fortune 500 co, govt agencies & community groups; charter mem, Nat Urban League; chair, First Nat Diversity Conf; co-founder/pres, Renaissance Bks; adv bd, Black Scholar; bd dir, Found Nat Progress; fel Am Psychiat Asn; Nat Acad Sci; Inst Med Nat Acad Sci; Black

Behav Scientists; Univ Cali Black Caucus; founding mem, Diversity Collegium. **Honors/Awds:** Outstanding Psychiatrist, Black Enterprise, 1988; Pathfinder Award, Asn Humanistic Psychol, 1993; Rollo May Award, Saybrook Grad Sch & Res Ct; Harvey Russell Award, PepsiCo; Al Martins Heritage Award, Exec Leadership Coun. **Special Achievements:** Co Author: "Black Rage, The Jesus Bag & My American Life From Rage to Entitlemen". **Business Addr:** President, Chief Executive Officer, Pacific Management Systems, 3528 Sacramento St, San Francisco, CA 94118-1847, **Business Phone:** (415)922-1017.

## COBBS, DR. WINSTON H. B.

Physician. **Personal:** Born May 7, 1955, Flushing, NY; married Valerie Crouch; children: Noelle Bianca & Paige Alfreda. **Educ:** Boston Univ, BA, biol, 1976; Meharry Med Col, MD, 1980. **Career:** Long Island Jewish Med Ctr, resident internal med, internship internal med, 1980-81; Nassau Co Med Ctr, residence internal med, 1983-85; Montefiore M C-H & l Moses Div, resident Radiol; Franklin Hosp & Med Ctr, secy med staff; Booth Memorial Med Ctr, pulmonary med, 1986-88; pvt pract, 1988-. **Orgs:** Am Soc Int Med; Am Thoracic Soc; assoc mem, Am Col Physicians, Am Col Chest Physicians; fel Am Col Chest Physicians. **Honors/Awds:** Martin Luther King Scholarship Award. **Special Achievements:** Publications: "The Effects of Phospho-Diesterase on Insulin Metabolism", A Research Study The Diabetes and Endocrinology Ctr Nashville 1972; "The Spirometric Standards for Healthy Black Adults", A Research Study Meharry Medical Coll Nashville, The Journal of the Natl Medical Assoc 1981. **Business Addr:** Physician, 1800 Dutch Broadway, Elmont, NY 11003-4246, **Business Phone:** (516)775-2184.

## COCHRAN, DANIEL CHESTER

Executive. **Personal:** Born Nov 14, 1946, Chicago, IL; son of Jacqueline and Conrad. **Educ:** Amherst Col, BA, 1968; Princeton Univ, MPA, 1974. **Career:** US State Dept, foreign serv officer, 1969-73; Exxon Corp, asst treas, 1974-89; Corp & Instnl Client Group, chief financial officer; Int Pvt Client Group, chief operating officer; Global Markets & Invet Banking, chief acct officer; Merrill Lynch & Co, chief financial officer, dep treas finance, Global Pvt Client, sr vpres & chief operating officer, dir, 2000-05, sr vpres, 2001-, chief admin officer, 2005, off pres, currently; ML Bank & Trust Cayman, dir, 2006; Merrill Lynch Portfolio Managers Ltd, dir. **Orgs:** Trustee, Winthrop H Smith Mem Found, 2001-; sr advr, ML LGBT Prof Network, 2002-; ML Diversity Employee Adv Coun, 2003-06; dir, Human Rights Campaign, 2007-; dir & bd mem, Lambda Legal, 2007-; fel Exec Leadership Coun; Mark DeGarmo Dance; Amherst Trustee Nominating Comt. **Honors/Awds:** Black Achievers Award, YMCA, 1992. **Special Achievements:** First African Americans to Hold a Position of Senior Vice President and Chief Operating Officer on Wall Street. **Home Addr:** 252 7th Ave Apt 16-I, New York, NY 10001-7326, **Home Phone:** (646)314-4121. **Business Addr:** Senior Vice President, Office of the President & Head of Administration, Merrill Lynch & Co Inc, 4 World Fin Ctr 34th Fl, New York, NY 10080, **Business Phone:** (212)449-1000.

## COCHRAN, EDWARD G.

Manager. **Personal:** Born Jun 16, 1953, Chicago, IL; married Barbara Porter; children: Rashida & Marcus. **Educ:** Lake Forest Col, BA, 1975; DePaul Univ, MBA, 1985. **Career:** Allstate Ins; First Data Corp; Sears Commun, telecomm mgr; Consult Telecommun; Mundelein Col, undegrad, adj fac; Univ Chicago, Loyola, adj fac; DePaul Univ, grad, adj fac; Cochran Group LLC, pres, currently; Continental Bank, opers analyst, 1975-77; IBM, systs engr, 1977-81; Sitel, sr vpres & gen mgr, 1994-2000; Greater Omaha Chamber, N Omaha Develop Proj, exec dir, 2008-11; Creighton Univ, dir philanthropy, dir maj gifts, 2006-10; Exponential Results LLC, partner, 2011-; Hansen-Mueller Co, dir, 2014-; Univ Nebr Omaha, Col Bus Admin, instr. **Orgs:** Pres & chief exec officer, Urban League Nebr Inc; Nebr C Home Soc. **Honors/Awds:** Forester Athletic Hall of Fame, 1990; Several articles and papers published on Telecommunications; One Enterprise Award, American Express. **Special Achievements:** First person to graduate from Lake Forest College with a triple major. **Business Addr:** Instructor, University of Nebraska Omaha, Mammel Hall Suite 300, Omaha, NE 68182, **Business Phone:** (402)554-2335.

## COCHRAN, DR. JAMES DAVID, JR.

Pediatrician. **Personal:** Born Oct 24, 1951, Muskegon, MI. **Educ:** Univ MI, BS, 1973; Howard Univ, MD, 1977. **Career:** Howard Univ Hosp, internship, 1977-78, resident, 1978-80; Nat Health Serv Corps, med officer, 1980-83; Collier Health Serv, staff physician, 1983-84, med dir; HealthPark Med Ctr; Gulf Coast Med Ctr; Pediat Centers Lee County, physician, currently. **Orgs:** Local vpole march, Kappa Alpha Psi Frat; Am Nat Med Assocs; Collier County Med Soc; counr, Collier County Youth Guid; Big Bros Collier County; Hope House Aids Refuge Coun. **Special Achievements:** Publication "Study of Sickle Cell in an Animal Model", J of NMA, 1980. **Home Addr:** 6474 Royal Woods Dr, Ft. Myers, FL 33908. **Business Addr:** Physician, Pediatric Centers of Lee County, 4048 Evans Ave Suite 209, Ft. Myers, FL 33901, **Business Phone:** (239)278-9983.

## COCKBURN, DR. ALDEN GEORGE, JR.

Surgeon. **Personal:** Born Mar 8, 1947, Ancon; son of Alden G Sr and Edith E Gittens; children: Alexis & Justin. **Educ:** City Col NY; Tufts Univ, MD, 1974. **Career:** Tufts New Eng Med Ctr Hosp, Boston, surg intern, 1974-75, surg asst resident, 1975-76; Lahey Clin Found Hosp, Burlington, Mass, urol resident, 1976-79; Lahey Clin, Boston, Mass, asst attend urologist, 1979-80; Memorial-Sloan Kettering Cancer Ctr, NY, NY, urol-oncol fel, 1980-81; Harlem Hosp Med Ctr, NY, dir, div urol, 1981-85; Columbia Univ Sch Med, NY, asst prof urol, 1981-85; Clin Asst Prof Urol, Univ S Fla; self-employed surgeon, Tampa, Fla, 1986-; Vasectomy Reversal Ctr, urologist, surgeon, 1986-; Tampa Gen Hosp, vice chief surg; Taos Surg Specialties, urologist, surgeon, currently. **Orgs:** Pres, Bay Area Med Asn; Sigma Pi Phi; bd trustee, Tampa Gen Hosp. **Business Addr:** Vice Chief of Surgery, Vasectomy Reversal Center, 4700 N Habana Ave Suite 500, Tampa, FL 33614, **Business Phone:** (813)875-8080.

## COCKERHAM, HAVEN EARL

Business owner, chief executive officer, manager. **Personal:** Born Aug 13, 1947, Winston-Salem, NC; married Terry Ward; children: Haven Earl Jr & Audra. **Educ:** NC Agr & Tech State Univ, BS, econ, 1969; Mich State Univ, Eli Broad Grad Sch Mgt, MBA, 1979. **Career:** GMC, hr dir, 1969-89, personnel admin exec comp, 1978-79, admin personnel, 1979-80, sr human resources exec; Fisher Body, gen off gen admin, 1980-82; Pgh plant, dir personnel, 1982-83; Gen Motors, world hq dir personnel, 1983-84, gen dir personnel; Chevrolet Dealership S Carolin, owner & operator, 1989-92; Bankmont Financial Corp, bd mem; Bank Montreal, prin; McCain & Assocs, pres, 1991-94; DTE Energy, chief & vpres human res, 1994-98; Stellar Retail Shops LLC, partner; R R Donnelley & Sons Co, sr vpres human resources, 1998, chief human resources officer, 1998-2004; Bartech Group Inc, bd dir, mem, currently; Metrop Family Serv, dir, currently; Harris Financial Corp, dir, currently; Cockerham & Assocs LLC, founder, pres & chief exec officer, 2004-. **Orgs:** Pres, Detroit Chap, Nat Black MBA Asn, 1981; bd mem, Nat Black MBA Asn, 1981; Mon Yough Chamber Com Pgh, 1982-83; leadership mem, Leadership Detroit Chamber Comt; bd mem, Detroit S Macomb Hosp; chmn, ea cent sec Detroit Area Coun Boy Scouts Am; Leadership Detroit VI; Hope United Methodist Church. **Honors/Awds:** Outstanding Leadership Award, Detroit Chap Nat Black MBA Assoc, 1982; Outstanding Service Award, Detroit Area Boy Scouts. **Home Addr:** 28346 Harwich, Farmington Hills, MI 48334. **Business Addr:** President, Chief Executive Officer, Cockerham & Associates LLC, 875 N Mich Ave Suite 3100, Chicago, IL 60611, **Business Phone:** (312)253-4037.

## COCKERHAM, KIMBERLY CLARICE AIKEN. See AIKEN, KIMBERLY CLARICE.

## COCKERHAM, PEGGY

Automotive executive, business owner. **Personal:** married John Ali; children: Pam & Anwar. **Educ:** Greensboro Col, BS, acct; Clark Atlanta Univ, MBA, finance, 1983. **Career:** Nations Bank, Charlotte, NC, vpres, com banker & lender; Southlake Buick & Imports, pres & owner, 1992-2000; Franklin Pontiac Buick GMC, founder, owner, pres, 2001-11. **Orgs:** Secy, Nat Asn Minority Automobile Dealers. **Business Addr:** Owner, President, Southlake Buick Volvo Subaru, 1345 Southlake Pkwy, Morrow, GA 30260, **Business Phone:** (770)968-3610.

## COCKRELL, MECHERA ANN

Insurance agent. **Personal:** Born Jul 8, 1953, Brookshire, TX; married Thomas; children: Twanna Nicole Randle. **Educ:** TX Southern Univ, BS, 1975, MA, 1978; Espanola's Beauty Col, Licensed Cosmetologist, 1978; Leonard's Sch Ins, Group II license, 1986. **Career:** Cockrell Ins, gen agent. **Orgs:** Teachers Educ Assoc; adv, Jack & Jill Am; teacher, 4H Prairie View Chap; Home Econ Educrs Amer. **Home Addr:** PO Box 25, Simonton, TX 77476. **Business Addr:** General Agent, Cockrell Insurance, 33405 Reynolds Rd, Simonton, TX 77476, **Business Phone:** (713)346-1302.

## COFER, MICHAEL LYNN

Football player. **Personal:** Born Apr 7, 1960, Knoxville, TN; married Reba M; children: Michael Isaiah & Philip. **Educ:** Univ Tenn. **Career:** Football player (retired); Detroit Lions, linebacker & right defensive end, 1983, left defensive end, 1984, right outside linebacker, 1985-90, 1992, linebacker, 1991. **Honors/Awds:** Pro Bowl, 1988. **Home Addr:** 110 Bridgestone Cv, Fayetteville, GA 30215-8159, **Home Phone:** (678)586-5075.

## COFFEE, AJ JEMISON. See JEMISON, AJ D.

## COFFEE, DR. LAWRENCE WINSTON

Dentist. **Personal:** Born Apr 29, 1929, Detroit, MI; married Drexell R; children: Lawrence Jr, Roderic & LaJuan. **Educ:** Wayne State Univ, BS, 1957; Meharry Med Col, DDS, 1961. **Career:** Dentist (retired); Chrysler Corp, mach operator, 1949-51; Detroit First Aid Co, drug shipper, 1953-55; C's Hosp Mich, med tech, 1955-57; pvt pract dent surgeon. **Orgs:** Mich Dent Asn; Am Dent Asn; Nat Dent Asn; Wolverine Dent Soc; Detroit Dist Dent Soc; trustee, St Stephen AME Church; BSA; dist comnr, Chi Health & Safety, 1968-77; bd mgt, Meharry Med Col Alumni Asn; past pres, Meharry Med Col Alumni Asn. **Honors/Awds:** Trophies BSA, 1966-67; Dentist of the Year, Meharry Detroit Chap, 1972. **Home Addr:** 7640 Tireman, Detroit, MI 48204, **Home Phone:** (313)272-3304.

## COFFEY, DR. BARBARA JORDAN

Educator. **Personal:** Born Nov 24, 1931, Omaha, NE; daughter of Earl L Sr and Eva Williams-Cooper; children: William Jai III. **Educ:** Univ Nebr, BA, 1951, PhD, 1976; Fisk Univ, MA, 1953. **Career:** Educator (retired); US Dept Comn, Chicago Regional Off, surv statist, 1963-65; United Comn Serv Omaha, planning assoc, 1965-67; Greater Omaha Comn Action Inc, dep dir, 1967-70; Univ Nebr, Omaha, assoc dean stud & instr sociol, 1970-71; US Dept HEW, consult region VII, 1971; Univ Nebr Syst, from asst to pres, equal opportunity coord, 1971-78; Northwestern Bell Tel Co, supvr mgt training, 1978-81; Metro Community Col, scampus mgr, 1981-84, dir mkt, 1984-95, Barbara M Angelillo, exec dir. **Orgs:** Bd dir, United Comn Serv, 1972-74; bd dir, United Way Midlands, 1988-96; vpres & founding dir, NE Civil Liberties Union; Omaha Metro Nat Asn Advan Colored People Hon Soc; Nat Asn Women Deans Admin & Couns; chairperson, NE Equal Opportunity Comt; Alpha Kappa Delta; Alpha Lambda Delta; Phi Delta Kappa; pres, Omaha Chap Links Inc; charter, Omaha Chap Jack & JillInc; Delta Sigma Theta Sorority; United Methodist Comn Ctr; All Saints Episcopal Church; bd dir, Omaha Head Start Child Develop Corp; Conf Inclusive Commun, 2008. **Home Addr:** 6940 Burt St, Omaha, NE 68132-2644, **Home Phone:** (402)558-1138.

## COFFEY, DR. GILBERT HAVEN, JR.

Physicist, government official. **Personal:** Born Nov 27, 1926, Lackawanna, NY; married Madelyn Elizabeth Brewer; children: Denise E. **Educ:** Univ Buffalo, BA, 1952; cert physio ther, 1955; Meharry Med Col, MD, 1963; Am Bd Phys Med & Rehab, dipl. **Career:** Wayne Co Gen Hosp Eloise MI, physio therapist, 1956-59; Am Acad Phs Med & Rehab Comnr Parks & Recreation Instr, MI, 1958-59; internship, 1963; Va Hosp Buffalo, resident, 1964-67, asst chief phys med & rehab serv, 1967-69, chief phys med & rehab serv, 1969-70; Cent Off, VA, Wash, prog develop policy, chief phys med & rehab, 1970; Univ Buffalo Med Sch, prof, 1968-70; Howard Univ Med Sch, Wash, 1971; George Wash, Univ Med Sch, asst dir prof, 1971-. **Orgs:** Alpha Phi Alpha; Montgomery County Stroke Asn; Mason 32nd degree; Nat Med Asn; Am Cong Rehab. **Home Addr:** 1500 Billman Lane, Silver Spring, MD 20902-1416, **Home Phone:** (301)933-0367. **Business Addr:** Physician, Howard University Hospital, 2041 Georgia Ave NW, Washington, DC 20060, **Business Phone:** (202)865-6100.

## COFFEY, RICHARD LEE

Basketball player, basketball coach, administrator. **Personal:** Born Sep 2, 1965, Aurora, NC; children: 3. **Educ:** Univ Minn, BAS, sociol, 1980. **Career:** Basketball player (retired), basketball coach, administrator; Minn Timber wolves, 1990-91; Reel Experts, host & exec producer; Minneapolis Select Basketball, co-founder, currently; Alete Cleaning Serv, owner, 2009-; Richard Coffey Unlimited, owner, 2013-. **Business Addr:** Owner, Richard Coffey Unlimited, 1002 Main St Suite 203, Hopkins, MN 55434, **Business Phone:** (952)345-0692.

## COFIELD, JAMES E., JR.

Executive, association executive. **Personal:** Born May 16, 1945, Norfolk, VA; son of James E and Elizabeth B; married Carolyn W; children: Nicole. **Educ:** Univ NC, BS, 1967; Stanford Univ, Grad Sch Bus, MBA, 1970; Howard Univ, Law Sch. **Career:** Roxse Homes Inc, chmn, 1971-92; Babson Col, mem bd overseer; Arthur D Little Inc, consult; Malmart Mortgage Co Inc, pres & chief exec officer; Cofield Properties Inc, Brookline, MA, pres, currently; Stanford Univ, actg instr elec engineering dept; Black Polit Task Force, atty; Us Petrol Corp, pres. **Orgs:** MAS Black Legis Caucus; trustee & chmn, Audit Comt, WGBH Educ Found; bd dir, Roxse Homes Inc; dir & vpres, Exec Comt Greater Boston Chamber Com; pres & mem bd gov, Mass Mortgage Bankers Asn; treas, Black Polit Task Force. **Honors/Awds:** Outstanding Committee Service Annual Award, Comt Boston, 1979; Business Award, 1991. **Special Achievements:** Ten Outstanding Young Leaders Boston Jaycees 1980. **Home Addr:** PO Box 470827, Brookline Village, MA 02447-0827, **Home Phone:** (617)524-2131. **Business Addr:** President, Cofield Properties Inc, 10 Malcolm Rd, Boston, MA 02130, **Business Phone:** (617)524-9090.

## COFIELD, MARVIS

Chief executive officer. **Career:** Kettering High Sch, substitute teacher, 1980-90; County Wayne, Mich, Dept C & Family Serv, pres; Alkebu-lan Village, founder & chief exec officer, currently. **Orgs:** Detroit Bd Educ, 1999-2006; Detroit Pub Sch; Nat Asn Advan Colored People; chmn, African Centered Ed Sub Comt, currently; City Detroit, Acad Arts; Skillman Found. **Business Addr:** Chief Executive Officer, Founder, Alkebu-Lan Village, 7701 Harper Ave, Detroit, MI 48213, **Business Phone:** (313)921-1616.

## COGDELL, D. PARTHENIA

School administrator, association executive. **Personal:** Born Sep 12, 1938, Wayne County, NC; daughter of Nathaniel (deceased) and Geneva Herring (deceased); children: Samuel George Sanders III. **Educ:** Fayetteville State Univ, NC, BS, 1959; Trenton State, NJ, MA, 1971; Glassboro State, NJ, 1974; Hunter Col, NY, 1982. **Career:** School administrator (retired); Burlington Co Spec Serv, prin, 1974-76, prog dir, 1976-79; NJ Dept Educ, admin asst, 1979-81, bur dir, 1981-92; Camden City Schs, Off Personnel Serv, 1992-98; Rowan Univ, adj prof. **Orgs:** Reader, US Dept Educ & Spec Educ Off, 1974-79; chairperson, NJ State Adv Coun Handicap, 1974-76; pres, Int Coun Except C, 1978-79; proj dir, Low Incidence Handicap Proj, 1979-80; Phi Delta Kappa; pres, Rancocas Valley, Delta Sigma Theta Sor, 1988-92; pres, Found Except C, 1989-91; pres, NJ State Coun Delta Sigma Theta Sor, 1999-2002, corresp secy. **Honors/Awds:** Dan Ringeheim Award of Excellence, NJ State Fedn; Outstanding Special Educator, Int Coun Except C, 1998; Woman of the Year, Zeta Phi Beta Sorority. **Home Addr:** 117 Harrington Cir, Willingboro, NJ 08046, **Home Phone:** (609)877-9516. **Business Addr:** Corresponding Secretary, Delta Sigma Theta Sorority Inc, Rancocas Valley Alumnae Chap, Rancocas, NJ 08073.

## COGGS, DR. GRANVILLE COLERIDGE

Physician. **Personal:** Born Jul 30, 1925, Pine Bluff, AR; son of Tandy and Nannie; married Maud Currie; children: Currie, Anita & Carolyn Anne. **Educ:** Univ Nebr, BS, 1949; Harvard Med Sch, MD, 1953. **Career:** Murphy Army Hosp, 1953-54; Letterman Gen Hosp, intern, 1954; Univ Calif, resident, 1955-58; Permanente Med Group Northern Calif, partner, 1958-71; Univ Calif Sch Med, asst chief, 1969-71, assoc clin prof, 1971-75; Univ Tex Health Sci Ctr, prof radiol dept, 1975-89; Bexar County Hospital, staff radiologist; Audie Murphy VA Hospital, staff radiologist, 1975-81; Otto Kaiser Memorial Hosp, radiol, 1994-2003; Gonzaba Med Group, staff radiologist, 1998-2004; Brook Army Med Ctr, Civil Serv radiologist, 2004-08. **Orgs:** Phi Beta Kappa, 1949; Am Col Radiol, 1959-; Harvard Med Sch Alumni Surv Comn, 1973-78; assoc mem, Sigma Xi; fel ACR, 1972; Am Inst Ultrasound Med, 1972-82; Am Thermographic Soc, 1972-80; fel Am Col Radiol. **Honors/Awds:** Scientist of the Year, San Antonio Alumni Chapter of Kappa Alpha Psi Fraternity; Recipient of National Dunbar Alumni Association Dunbar Legacy Award, 1999; Gold medal, men's 75-79 400 meter dash, Florida State Senior Games Championships; Gold Medal, Mens 75-79 age group, Texas State Senior Games. **Special Achievements:** First African American Physician, member of the staff of the Kaiser Foundation Hospital. **Home Addr:** 4219 Laurel Trl, PO Box 690647, San Antonio, TX 78240, **Home Phone:** (210)699-6824.

## COGHILL, GEORGE

Football coach, football player. **Personal:** Born Mar 30, 1970, Fredericksburg, VA; married Velisa; children: Paul, Tre & Mikayla. **Educ:** Wake Forest Univ, BA, sociol, 1993. **Career:** Football player (retired), coach; Scottish Claymores, 1995-97; Denver Broncos, defensive back,

1998-2001; Denver Broncos Acad, player spokesperson; coach, James Monroe High Sch, 2004-09; Lake Brantley High sch, 2009-12; head coach; Mountain View High Sch, head coach, cuurently. **Honors/Awds:** Third-Team All-Am Wake Forest, 1992; All World League selection, 1996; Scottish Claymores Hall of Fame, 1999. **Business Addr:** Head Coach, Mountain View High School, 3535 Truman Ave, Mountain View, CA 94040, **Business Phone:** (650)940-4600.

### COGSVILLE, DONALD J.

Chief executive officer, chairperson, executive. **Personal:** Born May 16, 1937, New York, NY; son of Johnny and Frances; married Carol Atherton; children: Rachel & Donald Paul. **Educ:** Mt Union Col, BA, 1963. **Career:** Off Econ Opportunity, dep dir, 1968-71; Clark-Phipps-Clark & Harris Consults Firm, affirmative action advisor; NY State Urban Develop Corp, affirmative action officer; Harlem Urban Devel Corp, gen mgr, chmn, pres & chief exec officer. **Orgs:** Nat Task Force Educ & Training Minority Bus; pres, NY Urban League Trenton, NJ. **Home Addr:** 914 Carteret Ave, Trenton, NJ 08618, **Home Phone:** (609)393-7483.

### COHEA, FR. VICTOR

Clergy. **Educ:** John Carroll Univ, BA, sociol; Oakvale, MS; Notre Dame Sem, MDiv, old test; Xavier Univ, MTh, hist theol; Union, PhD. **Career:** St John Prep Sem, teacher, 1982-85; Community Faith Econ Empowerment, vice chair, currently; St Maria Goretti Parish, chaplain; St Francis De Sales Church, Pan African Roman Cath Clergy Conf, pres; St Francis De Sales Cath Church, pastor, currently. **Business Addr:** Pastor, St Francis De Sales Church, 2203 2nd St, New Orleans, LA 70113-2545, **Business Phone:** (504)895-7749.

### COHEN, GWEN A.

Executive. **Personal:** Born Eufaula, AL; daughter of Johnie and Clementine Morris Gilbert; married Paul M. **Educ:** Tuskegee Univ, BS, bus admin/mkt; Northwestern Univ, Kellogg Grad Sch Mgt, MBA, 1982. **Career:** BM, mkt, mfg, 1974-80; Quaker Oats, brand mgt, 1982-84; Morgan Stanley Dean Witter, wealth advisor, acct exec, assoc vpres, vpres invest, 1986-, wealth advisor, currently. **Orgs:** Chair, C's Hosp, child life, 1976-80; exec comt, Nat Black MBA, Chicago, 1984-89; exec comt, 1990-, pres, Leadership Ill, 1992-94; judge, Hugh O'Brian Youth Found, 1993-; co-chair, ETA Cult Arts, Gala, 1994-; judge, Am Jr Miss, Ill, judge, 1994-; judge, Miss Am, Chicago, 1995-; Leadership Am, 2004; bd mem, Chicago Col Performing Arts; bd mem, Chicago Found Women, 1991-2013; bd mem, Leadership Ill; Womens Networking Community; S Side Community Arts Ctr; DuSable Mus; bd mem, Kellogg Sch Mgt, 2009-13; Girl Scouts, 2009-13; bd mem, Roosevelt Univ:Col Performing Arts, 2006-; Vision 2020; Securities Investor Protection Corp; adv bd mem, POWER Women's Networking, 2009-; bd mem, WTTW Planned Giving Adv Comt, 2009-; bd mem, Morgan Stanley's Diversity Coun. **Home Phone:** (312)443-6527. **Business Addr:** Vice President Investments, Wealth Advisor, Morgan Stanley Dean Witter, 70 W Madison St, Chicago, IL 60602, **Business Phone:** (312)443-6527.

### COHEN, JANET LANGHART (JANET FLOYD)

Television show host, television journalist. **Personal:** Born Dec 22, 1941, Indianapolis, IN; daughter of Sewell Bridges and Floyd Stamps; married Melvin Anthony Langhart, Jan 1, 1968, (divorced 1968); married Robert Kistner, Jan 1, 1978, (divorced 1989); married William S, Feb 14, 1996. **Educ:** Butler Univ, attended 1962; Ind Univ. **Career:** WBBM-TV, Chicago, tv weathercaster, 1960; WCVB TV, Boston, MA, co-host, 1974-78; New Eng's Good Day, ABC Affil, talk show host, 1981-85; Nationally syndicated You Asked It, overseas corresp, 1985-86; Boston Herald, columnist, 1986-88; Home Show, ABC, guest host, 1990; Entertainment Tonight, corresp, 1990; Black Entertainment TV, commentator; Nationally Syndicated Am Black Forum, co-host, 1991-96; Personal Diary with Janet Langhart, host, 1993-94; Capitol Hill with Janet Langhart, host, 1995-96; Media-Wise, gen partner, 1995-; Invest Am, creator, developer, 1996-; Langhart Commun, pres & chief exec officer, 1996-; Spec Assignment, host, 1997-2001; US News & World Repor, spokesperson; Avon Cosmetics, spokeswoman. **Orgs:** US News & World Report; Digital Equip Corp; US Senate Spouses; judge, New Eng White House Fel; judge, Miss Am Pageant; bd mem, United Negro Col Fund; bd mem, US Nat Arboretum; founder, Citizen Patriot Orgn, 1990. **Honors/Awds:** Outstanding Young Leader Award, Boston's Junior; Israel Cultural Award; The Casper Award, City of Indianapolis; One of Boston's Brights, Glamour Magazine; Miss Chicagoland, Ebony Fashion Fair. **Special Achievements:** Featured in Francesco Scavullo's, Scavullo Women; Portrayed self in the movie adaptation of John Dean's "Blind Ambition," CBS-TV; Acted in Haskell Wexler's movie, "Medium Cool"; Author of My Life in Two Americas & From Rage to Reason, Love in Black and White; Emmy Nomination for writing, producing & hosting "Janets Special People"; First black Weathergirl for WBBM-TV. **Business Addr:** President, Chief Executive Officer, Langhart Communications, 5335 Wis Ave NW Suite 440, Washington, DC 20015, **Business Phone:** (202)393-5158.

### COKER, DR. ADENIYI ADETOKUNBO, JR.

Educator. **Personal:** Born Sep 27, 1962; son of Modupe and Adeniyi; married Angela Denise Johnson; children: Kikelomo, Morenike & Modupeola. **Educ:** Univ Ife, Nigeria, BA, 1983; City Univ NY, Brooklyn Col, MFA, 1987; Temple Univ, PhD, African Am studies, 1991. **Career:** William Paterson Col, NJ, asst prof, 1987-91; Univ Colo, assoc prof, 1991-92; Univ WY, dir & assoc prof; Eastern Ill Univ, dir & assoc prof, currently; Univ Ala, Dept Theatre, dir & assoc prof, currently. **Orgs:** Ed bd, Jour Black Studies, 1993-; exec bd mem, Nat Coun Black Studies, 1994-; dir, UABs African-Am Studies Prog. **Special Achievements:** First Person to receive doctorate in African American Studies from Temple University. **Home Addr:** 1506 Woodlawn Dr, Charleston, IL 61920-4248. **Business Addr:** Associate Professor, Director African American Studies, University of Alabama, 1530 3rd Ave S 1055 Bldg, Birmingham, AL 35294-2060, **Business Phone:** (205)975-9652.

### COLBERT, BENJAMIN JAMES

Educator. **Personal:** Born Jun 2, 1942, Savannah, GA; son of Jack B and Anna Chaplin; married Deborah Raikes; children: Edwin M, Kenneth & Jonathan R. **Educ:** Savannah State Col, BS, 1963; Univ Ga, MFA, 1971. **Career:** Metro Atlanta Talent Search Prog, dir; Univ Ga, admissions counr, instr; Savannah Bd Educ, teacher, assoc prog dir admissions testing prog; fel Health & Human Serv, 1980-81; Educ Testing Serv, assoc dir, prog adminr, 1981. **Orgs:** Consult, Col Entrance Exam Bd & US Off Educ Trio Prog; adv bd, Southern Educ Found; Human Rels Comn; Nat Asn Col Admis Counrs; Nat Scholar Serv & Fund Negro Studs; Nat Asn Advan Colored People; Am Pub Gardens Asn; Alpha Phi Alpha; Witherspoon Presby Church. **Home Addr:** 137 Lawrenceville Pennington Rd, Lawrenceville, NJ 08648-1414, **Home Phone:** (609)896-2303.

### COLBERT, GEORGE CLIFFORD

School administrator, association executive, marine corps officer. **Personal:** Born Mar 22, 1949, Cedar Rapids, IA; son of Louis Charles and Betty Mae; married Marion Patricia Clark; children: Bridget Lynette Clark & Donta Kami. **Educ:** Kirkwood Community Col, AA, 1972; Mt Mercy Col, BA, 1974; Northern Ariz Univ, MEd, 1993. **Career:** IA State Men's Reformatory, correctional officer II, 1975-76; Rock well Int, security guard, 1976-78; Kirkwood Community Col, chmn, 1986-87, coordr, outreach worker & employer, sch prog, 1978-89; Cent Ariz Col, dir, community educ & stud serv, 1989-95, stud serv assoc, 1995-. **Orgs:** Chmn, Gen Mills, FMC Minority Scholar Prog, 1978; vpres, Nat Advan Asn Colored People, 1978-80; founder & chmn, Higher Educ Minority Scholar Prog, 1979; Nat Coun Instr Adminr; Nat Coun Community Serv & Continuing Educ; life mem, AMVETS Post 15. **Honors/Awds:** Certificate Volume Service Award, Jane Boyd Comn House, 1974; Humanities Award, Nat Advan Asn Colored People Freedom Fund Banquet, 1979; Appreciation Recognition Service Student Affairs, Kirkwood Community Col, 1979; Several awards for service, Apache Junction Community Sch System. **Home Addr:** 6228 Covina St, Mesa, AZ 85205-7515, **Home Phone:** (480)396-5394. **Business Addr:** Student Service Associate, Central Arizona College, 8470 N Overfield Rd, Coolidge, AZ 85128, **Business Phone:** (800)237-9814.

### COLBERT, VIRGIS W.

Executive, vice president (organization), association executive. **Personal:** Born Oct 13, 1939, Jackson, MS; son of Quillie and Eddie Mae; married Angela Johnson; children: Jillian, Alyssa & V William II. **Educ:** Cent Mich Univ, BS; Earlham Col Exec Inst. **Career:** Chrysler Corp, 1966-68, foreman, 1968-70, gen foreman, 1970-73, mfg supt, 1973-77, gen mfg supt, 1977-79; Miller Brewing Co, asst to plant mgr, 1979-80, prod mgr, 1980-81, plant mgr, 1981-87, asst dir can mfg, 1987-88, dir can mfg, 1988-89, vpres mat mfg, 1989-90, vpres plant opers, 1990-93, sr vpres opers, 1993-95, sr vpres worldwide opers, 1995-97, exec vpres worldwide opers, 1997-2005; Delphi Corp, bd dir, 1999-2006; Manitowoc Co, bd mem, 2001-; Merrill Lynch & Co Inc, bd dir, 2006-; Stanley Works, dir, 2003-; Sara Lee Corp, dir, 2006-. **Orgs:** RBDM, OIC, Fisk Univ; Omega Psi Phi; Prince Hall Masons; Shriners; life mem, Nat Asn Advan Colored People; NUL Black Exec Exchange Prog; Exec Adv Coun, Sigma Pi Phi; Wey co Group Inc; Delphi Automotive Syst; trustee, Fisk Univ; chmn emer, Thurgood Marshall Scholar Fund; bd dir, Bradley Ctr, 1998-2009; Weyco Group, bd mem, 2000-05; chair, Prod Stamping Inc, 2004-07; bd mem, Lorillard Tobacco, 2008-; bd trustee, Milwaukee Sch Engineering; Boy Scouts Milwaukee City Coun Bd. **Honors/Awds:** Black Achiever Milwaukee YMCA; Role Model Nat Alliance Bus; Silver Ring Merit Award, Philip Morris Co Inc; Role Model, Several Black Cols; Trumpet Award, Turner Broadcasting. **Special Achievements:** One of the Top 40 Black Exec in Am, Ebony Mag; One of the Top 24 Black Exec in Am, Black Enterprise Mag; Top 50 African-Am in Corp Am Fortune Mag. **Home Addr:** 706 Eastwyn Bay Dr, Mequon, WI 53092. **Business Addr:** Executive Vice President, Miller Brewing Co, 3939 W Highland Blvd, Milwaukee, WI 53208-2816.

### COLE, ANDREA M.

Executive director, chief executive officer. **Educ:** Wayne State Univ, BA, finance, 1991; Wayne State Univ, MBA, 1995. **Career:** Skillman Found, asst vpres & controller, treas, dir finance, chief financial officer, 1987-07; Ethel & James Flinn Found, exec dir & chief exec officer, 2008-. **Orgs:** Bd mem & treas, Coun Mich Foundations, 2007-2014; visitors mem, Wayne State Sch Med Bd. **Business Addr:** Executive Director, Chief Executive Officer, Ethel & James Flinn Foundation, 333 W Ft St Suite 1950, Detroit, MI 48226-3134, **Business Phone:** (313)309-3436.

### COLE, DR. ARTHUR

Educator. **Personal:** Born Nov 6, 1942, Buffalo, NY; married Alice Bailey; children: Arthur & Brandon. **Educ:** State Univ NY, Buffalo, NY, BS, educ, 1964, MS, rehab coun, 1968, PhD, found educ, 1974. **Career:** State Univ Col Buffalo, counr, 1967-68, res asst, 1968-70, personnel dir libr, 1973-75; Dept HEW, fel, 1975; US Off Educ, educ prog specialist, 1975-79; White House, asst to dep asst to pres, 1979-80; Earmark Inc, vpres, 1979-; US Dept Educ, dep dir Horace Mann Learning Ctr, Sch Improv Off, dir sch improv progs, 2000; Univ Okla, Pub Serv Inst, exec prog adv, sr advisor, 2003-; Teachers Corp, analyst; Off Civil Rights, analyst; White House, Off Hisp Affairs, analyst; Peace Corps mission, country dir. **Orgs:** Chap secy, Omega Psi Phi, 1967-69; Phi delta Kappa, 1967-; Am Lib Asn, 1973-. **Home Addr:** 10806 Meadowhill Rd, Silver Spring, MD 20901. **Business Addr:** Senior Advisor, University of Oklahoma, 1156 15th St NW Suite 1005, Washington, DC 20005, **Business Phone:** (202)862-8514.

### COLE, BARBARA DOWE

Auditor, executive, association executive. **Personal:** Born Jun 1, 1943, Washington, DC; daughter of Roy and Edith Dowe; children: Maurice E. **Educ:** Roosevelt Univ, BSBA, bus admin, finance, gen, 1979. **Career:** Executive (retired); United Planning Org, vol coordr, 1964-70; Johnson Publ, bookkeeper, 1978-79; Continental Bank, auditor, 1979-80; Lucent Technol, tech writer & instrnl designer, systs analyst, 1980-2001. **Orgs:** Bd mem, Proniso Area United Way, 1983-, pres, 1987-97; Soc Tech Commun, 1988-; Maywood Better Gov Commun, 1989-90; comnr, Maywood Civic Ctr Authority, 1989-; Loyola Healthy Teens Proj, 1994-; bd mem, founder & dir, Maywood Youth Mentoring Prog, 1994-; Girl Scouts, Strategic Planning Comn, 1996-97; pres, Proviso Area United Way, 1997-2000; Maywood Alliance Better Gov, 1999-; secy, Maywood Alliance Better Govt, 2000-; adv, Univ Ill 4-H Leadership Club, 2000-. **Honors/Awds:** Community Serv Award, Maywood Chamber Comn, 1992; I Care Award, Girl Scouts, 1995; Community Spirit Award, Maywood Park Dist, 1997; Community Service Award, Jeptha Lodge 90, 1997; Peace Leader Award, Ill Dept Violence Prev, 1997. **Special Achievements:** Published: Just-In-Time, AT&T APEX Conference Proceedings, 1995. **Home Addr:** 1412 S 21st Ave, Maywood, IL 60153-1737, **Home Phone:** (708)344-3577. **Business Addr:** Director, Founder, Maywood Youth Mentoring Program Inc, PO Box 65, Maywood, IL 60153, **Business Phone:** (708)344-3577.

### COLE, CAROL THOMPSON. See THOMPSON, CAROL BELITA.

### COLE, CHARLES ZHIVAGA

Association executive. **Personal:** Born Oct 7, 1957, Birmingham, AL; son of Howard Hover and Louise. **Educ:** McNeese State Univ. **Career:** CBC Organ & Mc Neese, mr calendar, 1978; John G Lewis Consistory, Thirty Second degree, mason nat, 1981-85; S Bapt Conv, travels local state & nat ambassador goodwill, speaks lectr & teaches, nat vol consult. **Orgs:** ROTC, 1976-78; N Lake Charles Kiwanis, 1977; Mc Neese State Lions Club, 1978; assoc secy, Nat Asn Advan Colored People, 1978-85, nat youth ambassador, 1980-84, civil rights activist, 1984-; nat ambassador speaker, Christian Educ Spec Sci Olympic, 1984-; musician dir, Music Ministry, Tarsus Bible Baptist Church & Curry Chapel CME, Local State & Nat, 1985; Star Bethlehem Baptist Ctr; Macedonia Baptist, Cameron, LA. **Honors/Awds:** All Star Drum Major, 1973-74; Mr Calendar, Mc Neese State, 1978; Louisiana State Senatorial Award, Hon State Sen Clifford L Newman, 1986; Distinguished American Citizens, Emory Univ, 1993-94; Governors Award; Outstanding Leadership Award for Service to Community. **Special Achievements:** Author of books and articles. **Home Addr:** 2817 1/2 Fitz/M L King, Lake Charles, LA 70615.

### COLE, DR. DEBORAH A.

Chief executive officer, president (organization). **Educ:** Tenn State Univ, BS, MBA; DDiv, theocentric bus & ethics; La State Univ, Grad Sch Banking S; Univ Notre Dame, Cannon Financial Inst; Gemological Inst Am. **Career:** Citizens Savings Bank & Trust Co, internal auditor, pres & chief exec officer, currently. **Orgs:** Chair, Nat Bankers Asn; bd mem, Tenn Bankers Asn, 2005-06. **Business Addr:** President, Chief Executive Officer, Citizens Savings Bank & Trust Co, 2013 Jefferson St, Nashville, TN 37208, **Business Phone:** (615)327-9787.

### COLE, DORINDA CLARK (DORINDA GRACE CLARK)

Singer. **Personal:** Born Oct 19, 1957, Detroit, MI; daughter of Mattie Moss. **Career:** Clark Conserv Music, Detroit, adminr & instr, currently; Greater EmmanuelInstnl Church God Christ, adminr, currently; Lifeline Prod Inc, founder & chief exec officer, 1999-; Albums: Dorinda Clark-Cole, 2002; Live From Houston: The Rose of Gospel, 2005; Take It Back, 2008; In The Face Of Change (EP), 2009; I Survived, 2011; Songs: "No Not One", "I'm Coming Out", "Still Here", 2002; "Great IsThe Lord", "So Many Times", 2005; "Take It Back", 2008; "Change", "This Is It", 2009; "Back to You", "He Brought Me", "God Will Take of You", "For My Good", 2011; "Thank You", "You Are", 2014; "Bless This House", 2014. **Orgs:** Pres, First Ecclesiastical Southwest Jurisdictional No. 1, Church God Christ; vpres, Church God Christ Int Music Dept; Greater Emmanuel Instnl Church. **Honors/Awds:** Honorary "Doctorate of Divinity", Mt. Carmel Theol Sem Fresno, CA. **Business Addr:** Singer, Cole Enterprises, Haith Johnson & Cymantha Channey, PO Box 3936, Southfield, MI 48034, **Business Phone:** (866)744-7664.

### COLE, DR. EDYTH BRYANT

School administrator. **Personal:** Born Detroit, MI; children: Charles R, Constance A & Leslie B. **Educ:** Eastern Mich Univ, BA, 1945, MA, 1952; Univ Mich, EdD, 1972; Univ Toledo. **Career:** Ypsilanti Mich Pub Sch, teacher, 1945-66; Wayne Co Mich Intermediate Sch Dist, educ consult rede segregation, 1966-69; Wayne Co Intermediate Sch Dist, shared learning experiences prog, 1967-69; Highland Pk Mich Pub Sch, admin ast curric, 1969-71; Nat Resolutions Comn, asn supv & curric develop, 1971-74; Elizabeth City State Univ, chmn dept educ & psychol, 1972-, dir summer sessions, 1973-80; NC St Univ. **Orgs:** Nat Defense Educ Act Grant Univ Toledo, 1965; chmn teacher educ, Elizabeth City St Univ, 1972-78; chap basileus, Alpha Kappa Alpha Sorority, 1976-78; pres, L'Esprit Club; bd dir, Mus Albermarle, 1977-79. **Special Achievements:** Pub article re curriculum changes "Curriculum Trends" Croft Pub Co, 1974. **Home Addr:** 700 7th St SW, Washington, DC 20024, **Home Phone:** (202)554-3370. **Business Addr:** Director, Elizabeth City State University, 1704 Weeksville Rd, Elizabeth City, NC 27909, **Business Phone:** (919)335-3400.

### COLE, HARRIETTE

President (organization), writer. **Personal:** Born Mar 14, 1961, Baltimore, MD; daughter of Harry A and Doris Freeland; married George Chinsee; children: Carrie Emmanuelle Chinsee. **Educ:** Howard Univ, attended 1983. **Career:** Model; Essence Mag, lifestyle asst ed & fashion dir; Harriette Cole Prods (formerly Profundities, Inc.), pres & creative dir, 1995-; Uptown, ed dir; Ebony mag, creative dir, ed chief. Bks: Vows; Coming Together; Choosing Truth: Living an Authentic Life; Jumping Broom: African-Am Wedding Planner, 1993; Jumping Broom Wedding Workbook; Sense & Sensitivity; How to Be: Contemp Etiquette African Americans; Entitled Vows(simon&schuster), 2004. **Orgs:** Secy, Capital Hill; Adv bd mem, Knot.com; Nat Comn Arts & Lett; Delta Sigma Theta Sorority; Phi Beta Kappa. **Special Achievements:** Has appeared on numerous TV shows such as "Perfect Match New York" "The Oprah Winfrey Show", "The View"; Has appeared in mag such as O, In Style, Brides & more; Host: XM Satellite radio; Magazines: American Legacy Woman; Savoy; Uptown. **Home Addr:** , New York, NY. **Business Addr:** President, Creative Director,

Harriette Cole Productions, 10 W 15th St Suite 526, New York, NY 10011, **Business Phone:** (212)645-3005.

## COLE, JAMES O.
Lawyer. **Personal:** Born Feb 6, 1941, Florence, AL; married Ada; children: Barry. **Educ:** Talladega Col, BA, 1962; Harvard Univ, Law Sch, JD, banking, corp, finance & securities law, 1971. **Career:** Clorox Co, assoc gen coun, 1973-93, vpres, corp affairs, 1993-97; Kirkland & Ellis Chicago, 1971-73; Auto Nation Inc, sr vpres, gen coun & corp secy, legal dept, 1997-2001; Ruden McClosky Smith Schuster & Russell PA, corp, mem real estate & landuse pract groups; Cole Holdings, chief exec officer & chmn. **Orgs:** Ill Bar Asn; Calif Bar Asn; Am Bar Asn; Alpha Phi Alpha; Urban League; pres, Nat Bar Asn; pres, Calif Asn Black Lawyers; pres, Charles Houston Bar Asn; chair, State Bar's Judicial Nominations Evaluations Comn; bd dir, Black Filmmakers Hall Fame; Nat Asn Advan Colored People; Legal Defense & Educ Fund; African Am Experience Fund; Calif Asn Black Lawyers; Charles Houston Bar Asn; bd mem, Joe Dimaggio & Memorial Hosp Found; Fla bar asn; Harvard Law Sch Black Alumni Asn; Vpres, Fla Chap Nat Asn Guardsmen, 2007-; Nat Vpres, Nat Asn Guardsmen, 2013; grand sire archon, Sigma Pi Phi Fraternity, 2014-2016. **Honors/Awds:** Program Award for Volunteer Legal Service; Hall of Fame, Charles Houston Bar Asn; C. Francis Stradford Award, Nat Bar Asn. **Special Achievements:** Publication: "Diversity News", 2009; Listed as one of South Florida top 100 individuals in law and health professions. **Home Addr:** 10 Nurmi Dr, Ft. Lauderdale, FL 33301, **Home Phone:** (954)467-9092. **Business Addr:** Member of Corporate Real Estate & Land Use Practice Groups, Ruden McClosky Smith Schuster & Russell PA, 200 E Broward Blvd St 1500, Ft. Lauderdale, FL 33301, **Business Phone:** (954)527-6229.

## COLE, DR. JOHNNETTA BETSCH
School administrator, manager. **Personal:** Born Oct 19, 1936, Jacksonville, FL; daughter of John Sr and Mary Frances; married Arthur J Robinson Jr; married James D Staton Jr; married Robert; children: David, Aaron & Che. **Educ:** Oberlin Col, BA, sociol, 1957; Northwestern Univ, MA, 1959, PhD, anthrop, 1967. **Career:** WA State Univ, asst prof & instr anthrop, dir black studies, 1964-70; Univ MA, fac anthrop, Afro-Am studies, 1970-84; Hunter Col, Russell Sage vis prof anthrop, 1983-84, prof anthrop, 1984; Spelman Col, Atlanta, pres, 1987-97, pres emer, currently; Emory Univ, prof emer anthrop, Womens Studies & African Am studies, currently; Bennett Col Women, pres, 2002-07; Smithsonian Inst, dir, currently; Bennett Col Women, chmn, pres, 2002-07; Smithsonian Nat Mus African Art, dir, 2009-. **Orgs:** Fel Am Anthrop Asn, 1970-; Coalition 100 Black Women; contrib & adv ed, Black Scholar, 1979-; pres, Asn Black Anthropologists, 1980; merck bd dir, 1994-; bd chair, United Way Am, 2004-06; bd trustee, Bennett Col Women; Delta Sigma Theta sorority; Am Acad Arts & Sci. **Special Achievements:** First African-American female president of Spelman College; First African American chair of the board of United Way of America; First woman to serve on the board of Coca-Cola Enterprises. **Home Addr:** 1360 Beechwood Hills Ct NW, Atlanta, GA 30327. **Business Addr:** Director, National Museum of African Art, 950 Independence Ave SW, Washington, DC 20560, **Business Phone:** (202)633-4600.

## COLE, JOYCE BOWMAN
Educator. **Personal:** Born Sep 18, 1936, Racine, WI; daughter of Fred and Eunice; children: Michelle Lynn Lusk, Michael Timothy Bland & Monique Tori Roberson. **Educ:** Del Mar Col, assoc, 1969; Tex A & I, BA, 1975; A&M Univ, master, 1976. **Career:** Crossroads Bus Training Sch; Clear Creek Independent Sch Dist; Corpus Christie Independent Sch Dist; El Paso Pub Libr. **Orgs:** Coordr & dir, ASPIRE, 1987-88; coordr & dir, COLORS, 1989-93; counr &teammate, Bill Glass Prison Ministries, 1997-. **Home Addr:** 2823 Salt River Ct, Missouri City, TX 77459, **Home Phone:** (281)438-8696. **Business Addr:** English Teacher, Clear Creek Independent School District, PO Box 799, League City, TX 77574, **Business Phone:** (281)488-3255.

## COLE, LYDIA
Executive. **Personal:** married Reginald; children: Iman & Maya. **Educ:** Howard Univ, BA, tv & film prod, MBA mkt, 1986; Georgetown Univ, MS, pub rels & corp commun/digital commun concentration, 2015-. **Career:** WTOP-TV/WDVM-TV, Asst Dir, 1975-78; WUSA-TV Channel 9, On-Air Prom Coordr, 1978-80; WDVM-TV, PM Mag Producer, 1980-81; WTOP News Radio-Bonneville Int, Prom Dir, 1981-82; WJLA-TV, actg dir, Advert & Prom, 1983-84; actg dir, mgr, WHUT-TV, Mgr, Creative Serv, 1983-87; Black Entertainment Tv, dir, advert, Prom & Entertainment Programming, 1987-93, VP, Programming, Advert & Prom, 1993-98; BET Cable Network & BET Jazz, vpres prog, 1997-; Lydia Cole Commun Consult, owner, 1998-2005; Lockheed Martin Aeronaut, Commun Sr Mgr, employee & exec commun, employee engagement team lead, f-35 prog commun, 2006-15. **Orgs:** Howard Univ Stud Asn; Juv Diabetes Found; Nat Cable Acad. **Special Achievements:** Nomination for Cable Ace Award, National Cable Academy, 1991, 1993 & 1995. **Business Addr:** Vice President Programming, BET Cable Network, 1 BET Plz, Washington, DC 20018-1211, **Business Phone:** (202)608-2901.

## COLE, MARK T.
Administrator, business owner. **Career:** Inner City Fishing Inst, prin, founder & chief exec officer, 2003-. **Orgs:** Human Dimensions Recreational Fisheries AFS Comt. **Business Addr:** Founder, Chief Executive Officer & Principal, Inner City Fishing Institute, 2301 Prfmce Dr Apt 303, Richardson, TX 75082, **Business Phone:** (972)442-2126.

**COLE, NATALIE.** See Obituaries Section.

## COLE, DR. OLEN, JR.
College administrator, educator. **Educ:** Calif State Univ, Fresno, BA, 1972, MA, 1976; Univ NC, Chapel Hill, PhD, 1987. **Career:** Smithsonian Inst, Woodrow Wilson Int Ctr Scholars, res assoc, 1974-77; Nat Arch, arch technician, 1977; N Carolina Agr & Tech State Univ, instr hist, 1977-87, asst prof hist, 1987-92; assoc prof hist, 1992-99, prof hist & chairperson, 2000-13, prof hist, 2013-; Purdue Univ, post-doctoral fel, 1990; Author: The African-American Experience in the Civilian Conservation Corps, 1999. **Orgs:** Advisor, Asn African Students, 2004-05; Asn Study African Am Life & Hist; Orgn Am Historians; Phi Delta Kappa Prof Educ Fraternity; Asn Historians N Carolina. **Business Addr:** Professor, Chairperson of the History Department, North Carolina Agricultural & Technical State University, 1601 E Mkt St, Greensboro, NC 27411, **Business Phone:** (336)285-2326.

## COLE, PATRICIA A.
Activist, consultant, executive. **Personal:** Born Oct 25, 1940, Detroit, MI; daughter of Thomas Aaron Allen and C Marie Johnson Wilson; children: B Derek & Jason A. **Educ:** Univ Detroit Mercy, Detroit, MI, BA, bus acct, 1980. **Career:** Cert instr, cert prof consult, cert prof mgr, regist prof mgr & community activist; City Detroit, govt analyst, 1971-83; Client Focused Solutions or Cole Financial Serv Inc, Detroit, Mich, treas, chief exec officer, owner, pres & founder, 1983-. **Orgs:** Gen chairperson, Am Asn Prof Consults, SE Conf, 1987-; nat adv bd, Black Career Women, Exec Circle, 1989-; Nat Asn Woman Consults, 1990-; counr & presentor, Score, SBA Chap 48, 1990-; co-chairperson, Metro Atlanta Coalition 100 Black Women, 1990-; Womens Informal Network; Vols Am; Civic Searchlight; Jewish Voc Serv & Community Workshops. **Honors/Awds:** Outstanding Volunteerism, Optimist Club NW Detroit, 1987; Black Career Women, Nat Adv Bd, 1989; Certified Professional Manager, Prof Servs Mgt Inst, 1990; Registered Professional Consultant, Am Asn Prof Consults; Women Who Make a Difference, Minorities & Women Bus; Sojourner Truth Award, NANBPWC; Best Business Entrepreneur, Black Women Contracting Asn, 2005; Leadership Coach, 2007. **Business Addr:** President, Owner, Cole Financial Services Inc, 3170 E Lafayette Blvd, Detroit, MI 48207, **Business Phone:** (313)570-7516.

## COLE, RANSEY GUY, JR.
Executive director, lawyer, judge. **Personal:** Born May 23, 1951, Birmingham, AL; son of Ransey G Sr and Sarah Nell Coker; married Kathleine Kelley; children: Justin Robert Jefferson, Jordan Paul & Alexandra Sarah. **Educ:** Tufts Univ, BA, 1972; Yale Law Sch, JD, law, 1975. **Career:** Varys, Sater, Seymour & Pease Law Firm, assoc, 1975-78, 1980-82, partner, 1983-86, 1993-95; Civil Div Com Litigation Br, Dept Justice, trial atty, 1978-80; Civil Serv Comn, comnr, 1986; US Bankruptcy Ct, judge, 1987-93; US Ct Appeals Sixth Circuit, judge, 1995-, chief judge, 2014-. **Orgs:** Nat Conf Bankruptcy Judges, 1983-95; bd trustee, Nationwide Investing Found, 1984-86; bd trustee, Columbus YMCA, 1984-86; bd trustee, Neighborhood House, 1985-88; bd trustee, Cent Ohio March Dimes, 1985-86; bd trustee, Columbus Area Int Prog, 1986-94; trustee, C Hosp, 1990-; bd govs, Columbus Bar Asn, 1990-94; bd trustee, Childrens Hosp, 1990-2002l; trustee, Univ Club, 1992-; Am Bankruptcy Inst, 1993-95; dir, Am Bankruptcy Bd Cert, 1993-95; dir, Bankrupty Arbit & Mediation Servs, 1993-95; trustee, US Health Corp, Community Health & Wellness; trustee, I Know I Can; Ohio Bar Asn; Nat Bar Asn; Sigma Phi Fraternity; Alpha Phi Alpha Fraternity; Judicial Conf US, exec comt mem, Sixth Circuit Judicial Coun, 1996-; Am Bar Asn. **Honors/Awds:** Founders Day Award, Alpha Phi Alpha Fraternity; Professionalism Award, Alpha Phi Alpha Fraternity, 1994. **Special Achievements:** Second African American to work Law firm of Vorys, Sater, Senour and Pease, Columbus, OH, 1975; First African American partner at the firm, 1983; One of Ten, Emerging Leaders for Columbus, The Columbus Dispatch, 1985. **Home Addr:** 170 Cameron Ridge Dr, Columbus, OH 43235-6479, **Home Phone:** (614)431-0134. **Business Addr:** Chief Judge, US Court Appeals Sixth Circuit, 532 Potter Stewart US Courthouse 100 E 5th St, Cincinnati, OH 45202-3988, **Business Phone:** (513)564-7000.

## COLE, DR. THOMAS WINSTON, JR.
Educator, president (organization), school administrator. **Personal:** Born Jan 11, 1941, Vernon, TX; son of Thomas W Sr and Eva Mae (Sharp) C; married Brenda S Hill; children: Kelley, Susan & Thomas Winston III. **Educ:** Wiley Col, Marshall, TX, BS, 1961; Univ Chicago, PhD, org chem, 1966. **Career:** Woodrow Wilson, fel, 1961-62; Atlanta Univ, asst prof, 1966-82, Fuller EC allaway prof, 1969-79, chmn dept chem, 1970-79, proj dir resource ctr sci & eng, 1978-82, univ provost, vpres acad affairs, 1979-82; Miami Valley Lab, Procter & Gamble Co, summer chemist, 1967; Univ Ill, vis prof, 1972; Mass Inst Technol, vis prof, 1973-74; Celanese Corp, Charlotte, NC, chemist, 1974; UNCF, lectr, 1975-84; Wva State Col, pres, 1982-88; WVa Bd Regents, chancellor, 1986-88; Clark Col, pres, 1988-89; Clark Atlanta Univ, Atlanta, Ga, pres, 1989-2002, pres emer, 2002-; Great Schs, pres & chief exec officer, 2004-06; Univ Massachusetts, interim chancellor, 2007-08. **Orgs:** Allied Chem fel, 1963; bd mem, Fernbank Mus, 1989-; Am Chem Soc; AAAS; NatInst Sci; Nat Orgn Prof Advan Black Chemists & Chem Engrs; Sigma Xi Sci Res Soc; Sigma Pi Phi; Alpha Phi Alpha Fraternity; bd mem, Qual Educ Minorities; trustee, Knoxville Col; trustee, Univ Charleston; trustee, Africa Univ; trustee, Andrews Col; Westvaco, 1994-2002; MeadWestvaco Corp, 2002-; chmn, Qual Educ Minorities Network. **Special Achievements:** First President of Clark Atlanta University, 1989. **Home Addr:** 4825 Regency Trce SW, Atlanta, GA 30331-6844, **Home Phone:** (404)344-9101. **Business Addr:** President Emeritus, Clark Atlanta University, 223 James P Brawley Dr SW, Atlanta, GA 30314, **Business Phone:** (404)880-8000.

**COLE-MCFADDEN, CORA.** See MCFADDEN, CORA.

## COLEMAN, ANDREW LEE
Public relations executive, parole officer, football player. **Personal:** Born Jan 30, 1960, Humboldt, TN; son of Lonnie Lee (deceased) and Mae Doris Scott Lovelady. **Educ:** Vanderbilt Univ, BS Polit Sci, sociol, 1982; Dyersburg Community Col, attended 1990; Jackson State Community Col, parole training, 1987. **Career:** Humboldt City Parks, asst supvr summer, 1977; Jones Mfg Co, laborer, 1978-79; Vanderbilt Athletic Dept, letterman, 1978-81; Foster & Creighton Const Co, laborer, 1981; Denver Broncos, football player, 1982; New Orleans Saints, football player, 1982; Classic I Kitchenware Inc, sales distribr, 1983; Humboldt Sch, sub teacher, 1983; City Humboldt, alderman, 1983; Gibson City Vote Coordr, coordr, 1984; Jesse Jackson Pres, coordr, 1984; Drew Enterprise, owner, pres, 1985; Jonah Inc, organizer/off mgr, 1985; Al Williams Inc, sales rep, 1986; TN Bd Paroles, parole officer/counr, 1986; Morgan & Assocs Realtors, affil broker, 1987; Jackson State Community Col, 1993. **Orgs:** TN Black Elected Officials; TN Voters Coun; Gibson City Voters Coun; Am Probation & Paroles; Decatur County Community Corrections; patron, Order Eastern Star; Gibson County Fraternal Order Police; co-chmn, Humboldt Strawberry Patch, 1988; Lane Col Alumni Asn, 1989; Brownstown Alumni Club Memphis, 1990; TN State Troopers Asn; TN Correctional Asn; Am Correctional Asn; Just Organized Neighborhood Area Hq; Steward, Lane Chapel CME Church; TN Sheriff Asn; Nat Asn Advan Colored People; Golden Heritage; 100 Black MenW Tenn; Beta Upsilon Lambda Chap; Alpha Phi Alpha; Vanderbilt Alumni Asn; Miracle Develop Acad Lane Chapel CME Church; Nat Asn Blacks Criminal Justice; TN Sch Bd Asn; TN Legis Network. **Honors/Awds:** Most Valuable Player, Vanderbilt Football, 1980; voted Most Athletic Class of 1982; All Am Mid Linebacker, Vanderbilt Univ, 1982; Am Outstanding Names & Faces Nat Org, 1982; Community Service Award, Humboldt Nat Asn Advan Colored People, 1988; Community Service Award, Phi Delta Kappa, 1992; Community Service Award, Phi Delta Kappa, 2001; Community Service Award, Comm Action Dream Keepers, 2003; Jackson Sun Player of the Week; Exchange Club Player of the Week. **Business Addr:** President, Owner, The Drew Enterprise, 1610 Osborne St, Humboldt, TN 38343, **Business Phone:** (731)784-5774.

## COLEMAN, APRIL HOWARD
School administrator, lawyer. **Personal:** married Donald Sr; children: Rebekah & Donald Jr. **Educ:** Univ Mich, BA; Tex Southern Univ, JD; Thurgood Marshall Sch Law. **Career:** Univ Detroit Mercy, adj prof; Wayne State Univ, adj prof; Swanson, Torgow & Lyons, PC, atty; pvt prac atty, currently. **Orgs:** Founder, Detroit Teen Anti-Violence Prog; charter mem, Detroit City Coun's Youth Adv Comt; chair, Youth Task Force Citizens Comt, Wayne County; founder, Detroit St Law Proj; chair, Community Confidence Comt, Detroit Sch Bd, 1989, 1991 & 1992; pres, Detroit Bd Educ. **Business Addr:** Attorney, April Howard Coleman, 9488 Lakepointe St, Detroit, MI 48224-2809, **Business Phone:** (313)494-1270.

## COLEMAN, ASHLEY
Fashion model. **Personal:** Born Jan 1, 1981, Camden, DE; children: 2. **Educ:** Del State Univ, educ. **Career:** Tommy Hilfiger; Rite Aid; Johnson & Johnson; Seventeen; Teen People; Fashion model, currently. **Honors/Awds:** Miss Delaware Teen USA, 1998; Miss Teen USA, Shreveport, LA, 1999; Third Runner-up, Miss California USA 2006 pageant. **Special Achievements:** First delegate from Delaware to win the national title.

## COLEMAN, AUDREY RACHELLE
School administrator, association executive. **Personal:** Born Aug 26, 1934, Duquesne, PA; daughter of Dave and Ola Dixon; married Bill; children: Bill Jr. **Educ:** Youngstown Univ, BMus; Boston St Col, MEd, advan admin. **Career:** Youngstown Ohio Pub Schs, teacher; Boston Pub Schs, teacher, asst prin, admin, dir comprehensive sch planning, currently. **Orgs:** Nat First Anti-Basileus Lambda Kappa Mu; conductor Nat Workshops Lambda Kappa Mu; conductor City wide Workshops Boston Pub Schs; Mass St Rev Team Chap I Prog, 1978; grand basileus Lambda Kappa Mu, 1981-85; bd dir, Nat Coalition-Black Meeting Planners, 1984-86; nat bd mem, Lambda Kappa Mu (past nat pres); nat vpres, Am Fed Sch Admin; bd mem, Boston Conv & Visitor's Bur; pres Middlesex County Chap Links Inc; Nat nominating comt, 1992, Nat protocol comt, found bdm-at-large, Links Inc; New Col Fla, bd trustee, 2011-. **Honors/Awds:** Certificate of Achievement & Leadership Urban League, 1979; 'Mary MBethune Award', Nat Coun Negro Women, 1982; Distinguished Serv Key Award Lambda Kappa Mu, 1983; Featured on front cover of Black Monitor Magazine, 1984; Dollars & Sense Magazine Award to Outstanding Afro-American Women, 1989; Mayor of Boston Award for Leadership, 1988; Humanitarian Award, South Shore United Methodist Church, Chicago, Ill, 1987; Nat Freedom's Found Award; Bd mem, Mass Lodging Asn Educ Found; Links Inc. Assembly, General chmn, 1998; Girls Inc the Community Found Sarasota; Womens Resource Ctr. **Special Achievements:** She was selected as one of the "ten most influential" African American women to meet with President Reagan at the White House in 1985. **Home Addr:** 35 Colgate Rd, Needham, MA 02492, **Home Phone:** (718)444-1891. **Business Addr:** Board of Trustee, New College of Florida, 5800 Bay Shore Rd, Sarasota, FL 34243, **Business Phone:** (941)487-5000.

## COLEMAN, AVANT PATRICK
Educator, government official. **Personal:** Born Jun 16, 1936, Rocky Mount, NC; son of Edward William and Bessie D Phillips; married Willa Jean Monroe; children: Jacqueline, Elliotte & Wanda. **Educ:** NC Agr & Tech State Univ, BS, agr & biol, 1960; NC State Univ, MS, adult educ, 1978; Exten Exec Develop Inst, 1984. **Career:** Government Officer (retired): Lenoir City Bd Ed, teacher, voc agr, 1960-61; Greene City Bd Ed, teacher, voc agr, 1961-62; NC Agr Exten Svc, exten agt 4-H, 1962-; Wilosn City Coun, Coun Dist 1, NC, coun mem, pres, 1976-77; Wilosn County, Coop Exten Agt. **Orgs:** Bd trustee, NC Local Govt Employees Retirement Syst; Bd dir United Way, 1985-2004; Small Cities Coun, Nat League Cities, 1988-1995; chmn, Red Cross Chap, 1988-89; pres, NC League Munic, 1991-92; founder & bd mem, Cornerstone Bank, Wilson, NC, 1999-2002; chmn, Region L Coun Governments, 1990-92, 2006-07. **Home Addr:** 2406 Belair Ave SE, Wilson, NC 27893-4185, **Home Phone:** (252)237-3284. **Business Addr:** Councilmember, Wilosn City Council, 112 N Goldsboro St, Wilson, NC 27893, **Business Phone:** (252)243-5656.

## COLEMAN, BARBARA SIMS
Executive, consultant, social worker. **Personal:** Born Mar 5, 1932, Wichita, KS; daughter of Hugh Napoleon and Rossa Velma Whitehead; married Julian D Jr; children: Julian, Hugh & Mark. **Educ:** Howard Univ, BS, 1953; Univ Wis, MS, 1956. **Career:** Social worker (retired); Larue Carter Memorial Hosp, asst dir soc work, 1957-73, supvr, 1957-73, psychiat soc worker, 1957-73; Ind Univ Sch Med, asst prof soc work & psychiat; Riley Pediat Hosp, Child Guid Clin, chief psychiat social worker, 1973-93. **Orgs:** Mem bd pres, Raines Couns Cent, 1968-84; consult supvr, Christian Theol Sem Pastoral Couns Prog, 1972-; mem bd, Planned Parenthood Cent IN, 1980-89; Nat Asn Social Workers & Acad Cert Social Workers; bd, C Bur Indianpolis

Inc, 1993-2000; adv coun, Buchanan Coun Ctr, 1994-2000; Greater Indianapolis Lit League, 1995-99. **Honors/Awds:** Social Worker of the Year, Region 7, Ind, Nat Asn Social Workers, 1989. **Home Addr:** 4370 Knollton Rd, Indianapolis, IN 46228-3346, **Home Phone:** (317)299-2900.

## COLEMAN, BONNIE WATSON

Legislator (U.S. state government), legislator. **Personal:** Born Feb 6, 1945, Camden, NJ; daughter of John S Watson and Marie Watson; married William; children: William, Troy & Jared. **Educ:** Thomas Edison State Col, BA, 1985. **Career:** New Jersey General Assembly, member, 1998-2014; New Jersey State Assembly, majority leader, 2006-09; New Jersey State Democratic Committee, member, 2002-06; U.S. House of Representatives, member representing New Jersey's 12 Congressional District, 2015-. **Orgs:** Alpha Kappa Alpha; Congressional Black Caucus; Congressional Progressive Caucus; Congressional Caucus for Women's Issues; Congressional LGBT Equality Caucus; House Committee on Oversight and Government Reform; House Committee on Homeland Security. **Special Achievements:** First African-American woman to serve as majority leader of the New Jersey General Assembly; first African-American woman to serve as the chair of the New Jersey Democratic State Committee; first African-American woman to represent New Jersey in Congress. **Business Addr:** 126 Cannon House Off Bldg, Washington, DC 20515, **Business Phone:** (202)225-5801.

## COLEMAN, CECIL R.

Manager, executive, association executive. **Personal:** Born May 15, 1934, Centralia, IL; married Betti Thomas; children: Karla M & Mark C. **Educ:** Northwestern Univ, Kellogg Grad Sch Mgt, BBA, 1970. **Career:** Mammoth Life Ins Co, sales rep asst mgr & mgr, 1954-65; Harris Trust & Savings Bank, asst mgr, 1965, vpres, 1978-80; dir. **Orgs:** Chicago Chap AIB Bd Regents; TAP Cons; Alpha Delta Sigma; Chicago Stud Symp; Sci & Math Conf, 1973; bd dir, Chatham YMCA; Community Fund Rev Panel; Old Town Boys Club; chmn, CHASI; C Home & Aid Soc Ill, chmn, gov trustee, currently. **Honors/Awds:** Chicago Merit, Employee Week, 1967; Jaycee Month, Chicago Chap, 1969; WGRT Radio Great Guy Award, 1973; Chicago Black Achiever, 1974. **Special Achievements:** The First African American named as chairman of the board of trustees at Children's Home & Aid Society of Illinois in the 115-year history of the Organization. Numerous National Institute Association awards & sales achievements. **Home Addr:** 9441 S Hoyne Ave, Chicago, IL 60643-6316, **Home Phone:** (773)233-9148. **Business Addr:** Governing Trustee, Children's Home & Aid Society of Illinois, 125 S Wacker Dr 14th Fl, Chicago, IL 60606, **Business Phone:** (312)424-0200.

## COLEMAN, CHRISENA ANNE

Journalist, writer. **Personal:** Born Mar 20, 1963, Hackensack, NJ; daughter of Wilbert and Dorothy; children: Jordan & Justin. **Educ:** Northeastern Univ, BA, 1968; Emerson Col, attended 1982. **Career:** Hackensack Bd Educ, counr family literacy prog; Rec, staff writer, journalist, currently; New York Daily News, staff writer, freelancer, currently; Black Enterprise, freelancer, currently; Thegrio.com, freelancer, currently; Author: Mama Knows Best; Just Between Girlfriends. **Orgs:** Vpres, Garden State Asn Black Journalists; Nat Asn Black Journalists; Alpha Kappa Alpha Sorority. **Honors/Awds:** Black Woman of Inspiration, Alpha Kappa Alpha, Bergen Chap, 1992; Black Hist Honoree, NAACP, Passaic Chap; Featured: E! Television "Fatal Honeymoons". **Special Achievements:** Film: Paying The Price, producer; Say It Loud, producer. **Home Addr:** 212 Prospect Ave Apt 2C, Hackensack, NJ 07601-2466, **Home Phone:** (201)343-6150. **Business Addr:** Journalist, The Record, 150 River St, Hackensack, NJ 07601-7172, **Business Phone:** (201)646-4100.

## COLEMAN, HON. CLAUDE M.

Police officer, executive, judge. **Personal:** Born Oct 26, 1940, Newberry, SC; son of Willie and Roberta Spearman; married Barbara Saunders; married Barbara Bell. **Educ:** Rutgers Univ, Newark, NJ, BS, 1974; Rutgers Law Sch, Newark, NJ, JD, 1977; Fed Bur Invest Nat Acad, VA, 1978; Nat Fire Acad, MD, 1987. **Career:** Judge, police (retired); City Newark, NJ, police officer, 1964-80, atty pvt pract, 1977-91, police legal adv, 1980-86, fire dir, 1986-88; police dir, munic judge; Newark Munic Ct, judge, 1991-2002; NJ Vicinage 5, State NJ Super Ct, judge, 2002-10. **Orgs:** Pres, Bronze Shields Inc, chmn, 1964-; 100 Black Men NJ; Nat Orgn Black Law Enforcement Execs; IACP; chmn, Law Enforcement Exec Forum. **Home Addr:** 649 Lake St Suite 653, Newark, NJ 07104, **Home Phone:** (973)268-2709. **Business Addr:** Judge, State of New Jersey Superior Court, Wilentz Justice Complex 212 Wash St 10th Fl, Newark, NJ 07102, **Business Phone:** (973)693-6642.

## COLEMAN, COLUMBUS E., JR.

Executive, banker. **Personal:** Born Jul 13, 1948, Wharton, TX. **Educ:** Univ Tex, BS, 1970; Univ NC, MBA, 1975; Univ San Francisco, Law Courses, 1979. **Career:** Gulf & Oil Co, Port Arthur Refinery, elec engr, 1970-71; First Nat Bank Dallas, corp banking officer, 1975-77; Wells Fargo Bank, asst vpres, 1977-79; Wells Fargo Securities Clearance Corp, exec vpres, gen mgr, 1979-. **Orgs:** Pres, Alpha Phi Alpha Epsilon Iota Chap, 1970-71; Adv capt Am Cancer Asn Dr, 1977; Small Bus Asn; adv, Jr Achievement, 1978; Partic Big Bros Asn; Nat Asn Advan Colored People. **Home Addr:** 308 92nd St, New York, NY 10025, **Home Phone:** (212)877-9298. **Business Addr:** Executive Vice President, General Manager, Wells Fargo Securities Clearance Corp, 45 Broad St, New York, NY 10004.

## COLEMAN, DEBORAH STEWART

President (organization), chief executive officer. **Personal:** Born Jan 1, 1953?; children: 2. **Educ:** Southern Ill Univ, BA, psychol; Wash Univ, St Louis, MO, MA, psychol, 1977; Baker Col, MBA, int bus. **Career:** Ford Motors, 1977-2007, Ford Southern Africa, chief exec officer & group managing dir, 2001-04, Americas Region, vpres global qual, 2004-07; Nat Urban League, exec vpres & chief opers officer, 2007-08; Int Bus Solutions, pres & chief exec officer, 2008-. **Orgs:** NiSource Inc, 2007-. **Business Addr:** Member, 801 E 86th Ave, Merrillville, IN 46410, **Business Phone:** (219)647-5200.

## COLEMAN, REV. DR. DEEDEE M.

Clergy. **Personal:** Born New Orleans, LA. **Educ:** William Tyndale Col, BA, bus admin; Marygrove Col, MA, pastoral ministry; United Theol Sem, PhD, inter cult commun. **Career:** Ecumenical Theol Sem, adj prof; Russell St Missionary Baptist Church, pastor, currently. **Orgs:** Co-chair, Progressive Nat Baptist Convs Comn Social Justice Prison Ministry; secy, Coun Baptist Pastors Detroit Vicinit; fel Delta Sigma Theta Sorority Alumni Chap; dir, Detroit Area Apprenticeship Trades Asn. **Honors/Awds:** Edwin T Dalhberg Peace Award, 2007; Dahlberg Peace Award, Am Baptist Churches, USA. **Special Achievements:** First female pastor to hold the office of Secretary of the Council of Baptist Pastors of Detroit & Vicinity. **Business Addr:** Pastor, Russell St Missionary Baptist Church, 8700 Chrysler Dr, Detroit, MI 48211-1249, **Business Phone:** (313)875-1615.

## COLEMAN, DENNIS

Writer, entrepreneur. **Personal:** Born Dec 31, 1951, North Chicago, IL; son of J C Sr and Eupha Lee; married Cheryl Diane Jarnigan; children: Dennis II, Felicia Marie & Steven Anton. **Educ:** Knoxville Col, BS, bus, 1974. **Career:** Burger King Corp, crew supvr, 1970-74, restaurant mgr, 1974-77, dist mgr, 1977-81; Coleman Enterprises, pres, 1981-90; Five Star Inc, DBA Rally's Hamburgers, pres; Variety Foodservices Inc, prod mgr, 2005-. **Orgs:** Phi Beta Sigma, 1971-; Big Fellas Asn; Minority Franchise Asn. **Honors/Awds:** Minority Franchisee of the Year, Michigan Dept Com, 1992. **Special Achievements:** First minority to own a Rally's Franchise in the country, 1992; highest award received at Whopper College, 1974; Top Ten Graduates at Burger King University. **Home Addr:** 18840 Capitol Dr, Southfield, MI 48075, **Home Phone:** (248)569-0543. **Business Phone:** (586)864-8548.

## COLEMAN, DERRICK D.

Basketball player, business owner. **Personal:** Born Jun 21, 1967, Mobile, AL; married Gina Cook. **Educ:** Syracuse Univ, Syracuse, NY, attended 1990. **Career:** Basketball player (retired), bus owner; NJ Nets, forward, 1990-95; Philadelphia 76ers, 1995-99, 2001-04; Charlotte Hornets, 1999-2001; Detroit Pistons, forward, 2004-05; SNYX Sneaker Studio, owner, currently. **Home Addr:** 15474 Lindsay St, Detroit, MI 48227. **Business Addr:** Owner, SNYX Sneaker Studio, 8961 Linwood Ave, Detroit, MI 48206.

## COLEMAN, DR. DON EDWIN

Educator, football player, football coach. **Personal:** Born May 4, 1928, Ponca City, OK; son of George and Nancy; married Geraldine J Johnson; children: Stephanie Lynn. **Educ:** Mich State Univ, BS, 1952, MS, 1956, MA, 1958, PhD, 1971. **Career:** Educator, football player (retired); Mich State Spartans, tackle, 1949-51; Flint Mich Sch, teacher, 1954-67, dean students; Doyle Community Sch, prin, 1966-68; Mich State Univ, teacher, coach, 1968-69; Col Osteop Med, prof community health sci, 1978-92, dean, grad sch, prof emer; Duffy Daugherty's, asst coach. **Orgs:** Pres, Mich Health Coun, 1980; Am Pub Health Asn; Am Col Pers Asn; Nat Asn Stud Pers Admin; Nat Comm Sch Dir Asn, 1963-67; Mich Elem Prin Asn, 1967-68; Phi Delta Kappa; Alpha Phi Alpha Frat; Epsilon Upsilon Lambda; Kappa Delta Lambda; Red Feather United Fund, 1964-68; BS Am; Prince Hall Masonic Order; Elks Genesee Temple; Nat Asn Advan Colored People; Urban League; exec comt, Planned Parenthood, 1952-60; Flint Jr Chamber Comm; bd mem, Listening Ear, 1970-73; Air Pollution Bd; Tri-Co Plannig Comt; Mich State Univ Athletic Coun; Alpha Phi Alpha Frat; exec dir, Black Child & Family Inst, 1986; chmn, Ingham Co, Bd Health, 1987; bd trustees, Mich Capital Med Ctr, 1988. **Honors/Awds:** The 10 Year Award Big Brothers Am, 1955-68; Blue Key Nat Scholastic Honor; Unanimous All-Am Tackle, 1950-51; Outstanding Lineman, 1951 1952; Col All Star game, 1952; Outstanding Lineman Hula Bowl Silver Anniversary, 1971; Nat Football Found & Hall Fame, 1975; Nat Col Athletic Asn Silver Anniversary Award, 1976; Greater Flint Area Sports Hall Fame, 1980; Greater Flint African-American Hall of Fame, 1988; Mich State Univ (MSU) Athletic Hall of Fame, 1992; Michigan Sports Hall of Fame, 1997; Governor of Michigan Award; all-time interior lineman in Michigan State. **Special Achievements:** First Spartan football player ever to have his jersey retired, 1952; First African-American All-American football player at Michigan State; First black swimmer to enter Royal Oak's pool; First African-American teacher at Flint Central; First African-American to serve on the coaching staff at Michigan State. **Home Addr:** 424 McPherson Ave, Lansing, MI 48915-1158, **Home Phone:** (517)372-3204.

## COLEMAN, DONALD

Business owner, baseball executive, police officer. **Personal:** Born Aug 18, 1953, Marion, AL; son of Elijah (deceased) and Alma; married Constance Lin; children: Benjamin Ashley & Christopher Andrew. **Educ:** New Hampshire Col, BS, bus mgt, 1976. **Career:** Barney McCosky Baseball League, little league coach, 1986-93; City Detroit, police sgt, police officer, 1987-; Flowers Miss Marion, co-owner, currently. **Orgs:** Kappa Sigma Int Fraternity, 1974. **Honors/Awds:** Fraternity Brother of the Year, 1975; 8th Precinct, Police Officer of the Year, 1993; Police Officer of the Month, 3 times; Performance Award, 6 times. **Home Addr:** 8190 Esper St, Detroit, MI 48204-3153, **Home Phone:** (313)934-1860. **Business Addr:** Police Officer, City of Detroit, 14655 Dexter Ave, Detroit, MI 48238, **Business Phone:** (313)596-2660.

## COLEMAN, DONALD ALVIN

Administrator, chief executive officer, president (organization). **Personal:** Born Jan 11, 1952, Toledo, OH; son of Augustus and Dorothy O Bowers; married Jo Moore; children: Kelli. **Educ:** Univ Mich, BA, jour, 1974; Hofstra Univ, MBA, mkt, 1976. **Career:** Professional Football Player (retired), Executive; New Orleans Saints, 1974-75; New York Jets, 1976-77; Campbell-Ewald Advert, vpres, 1980, sr vpres; Burrell Advert, sr vpres; Don Coleman Advert, founder, 1988; New Am Strategies Group, pres & chief exec officer; Nat Action Network, vice chmn; PrivateBank, dir; Talmer Bancorp Inc, dir, 2010-; First Michiganbank, dir; Global Hue, gen mgr, 2010-, pres & chief exec officer, chmn, currently. **Orgs:** Bd Control, Univ Mich Athletic Dept; Nat Football League Players Asn; bd, C's Ctr Mich; bd dir, Ad Coun; chmn, Am Advert Fedn Found; Adcraft Club Detroit; co-chair, Charles H. Wright Mus African Am Hist's Capital Campaign; hon dir, Advert Coun Inc; Louis Carr Internship Found; Coleman Educ Found. **Business Addr:** Chairman, Chief Executive Officer, Globalhue, 4000 Town Ctr Suite 1600, Southfield, MI 48075, **Business Phone:** (248)223-8900.

## COLEMAN, REV. DONALD LEROY, SR.

Broadcaster, association executive, executive. **Personal:** Born Oct 25, 1937, Greenfield, OH; son of Charles and Susie (Jackson); married Ann; children: Donna Coker, Robin Jackson, Donald Jr, John & Timothy. **Educ:** Doane Col, Lincoln, NE, BA, 1995. **Career:** Iowa Army Nat Guard, state career counr, 1980-84; Radio KOJC, sta mgr, 1981-84; Lincoln Pub Schs, security, 1992-94; Lincoln Police Dept, youth aid, 1992-2001; MAD Dads Lincoln Inc, pres, 1993-; KBMT-FM, gospel announcer, 1994; KLIN-AM, talk show host, 1997; KZUM-FM, talk show host, 1998-. **Orgs:** Chaplain, sr chaplain, Lincoln Police & Fire Chaplain Corps, 1987, 1993-96; chaplain, Vietnam Veterans Am, 1990-; Kiwanis Int, 1997-; vpres, Optimist Int, 1998-01; Lincoln Rotary 14 Int, 1998-; Urban League, Lincoln, 1998-; Nat Asn Advan Colored People, Lincoln Chap, 1999-; life mem, Disabled Am Vet; Parent's Day Coun. **Honors/Awds:** Gospel Announcer of the Yr, Savoy Record Co, 1978; Volunteer of the Yr, United Way, 1993; received gold key, City of Lincoln, 1993-94, 2000; Senior Award, Doane Col Alumni, 1995; Serv to Mankind Award, Sertoma Int, 1995; Community Hero Torch Bearer, 1996; hon asst applied sci, Lincoln Sch Com, 1996; Lincoln Interfaith Leadership Award, 1997; Forensic Speaker of the Yr, Univ Nebr, 1997; Friend of Youth Award, Optimist Int, 1999; Nebr Parents of the Yr, 1999; Nat Parents of the Yr, 2000; Steven G Gil baugh Vietnam VFW Post 10617 Award, 2001; hon asst bus admin, Lincoln Sch Com, 2001; Bus Resource Award, Lincoln Independent Bus Asn, 2001; Hall of Famer Buck O'Neil Legacy Seat Recipient, 2009-10; Dr. Marin Luther King Jr. Humanitarian of the Year for Nebraska, 2011; Hazel G. Scott Midle School wall of honor, 2011; Dr. Martin Luther King Jr. humanitarian of the year, 21st Century Lions Club Lincoln, 2012. **Home Addr:** 3257 S St, Lincoln, NE 68503, **Home Phone:** (402)474-3352. **Business Addr:** President, MAD Dads Lincoln Inc, 5610 Seward Ave, Lincoln, NE 68507, **Business Phone:** (402)742-0224.

## COLEMAN, DR. EDWIN LEON, II

Educator. **Personal:** Born Mar 17, 1932, El Dorado, AR; son of Mae Otis and Edwin; married Charmaine Joyce Thompson; children: Edwin III & Callan. **Educ:** City Col San Francisco, AA, Bus Admin, 1955; San Francisco State Univ, BA, theatre arts, 1961, MA, theatre arts, 1962; Univ Ore, PhD, 1971. **Career:** Melodyland Theatre, technician, 1963; San Francisco State Univ, Instr, 1962-63; Chico State Univ, Speech Dept, asst prof, 1963-66; Speech Dept, Instr, 1966-69; Off Acad Advising, instr, 1969-70; Univ Ore, Dept Eng, prof, 1988-98, from asst prof to assoc prof, 1971-87, dir, 1985-91, prof emer, currently, Folklore Ethnic Prog, assc dir, 1981-85; Communicative Arts Prog, dir, 1966; prof musician. **Orgs:** Bd Campus Interfaith Ministry, 1975-; bd Sponsors Inc, 1980-; bd Clergy & Laity Concerned, 1980-; bd OR Arts Found, 1981-84; pres, OR Folklore Soc, 1983-84; consult, Nat Endowment Arts, 1983-; Nat Humanities, fac; Am Folklore Soc; Nat Asn Advan Colored People; Kappa Alpha Psi; Ore Track Club; bd, Western States Arts Found; African Am Community Coalition; Am Fedn Musicians; Am Civil Liberties Union; Philol AsnPac Coast; Am Fedn Teachers, Black Evaluators Nat Comt; Human Rels Comt. **Honors/Awds:** Ford Fellow, Educ Grant, 1970; Danforth Assoc, 1977-; Distinguished Black Faculty, 1978; Distinguished Faculty Award, National Campus Magazine, 1982; Outstanding Faculty, Nat Mgt OR Art Comn, 1982; Frederick Douglass Scholarship Award, Nat Coun Black Studies, 1986; Charles S.Johnson Service Award, UNIV Oregon; Lifetime Achievement Award, NAACP; outstanding achievement in the area of racial justice from the City Eugene, 1990; Dr.Edwin Coleman Speaker Series Award, Univ Oregon, 1998; Honorary Member, Golden Key National Honor Society, 1990; Achievement Award Racial Justice, Ba-hai Faith, Lane County, 1991.Outstanding Faculty Award, University Oregon, 1991; Martin Luther King, Jr. Lifetime Achievement Award, 1991. **Special Achievements:** Published numerous books & articles. **Home Addr:** 1895 Fillmore St, Eugene, OR 97405, **Home Phone:** (541)485-8103. **Business Addr:** Professor Emeritus, University of Oregon, 1286, Eugene, OR 97403-1286, **Business Phone:** (541)346-3967.

## COLEMAN, ELIZABETH SHEPPARD

Executive, secretary (organization), manager. **Personal:** children: Nedra, Andre, Jelinda, Angela & Aretha. **Educ:** Muskegon Comm Col, assoc, 1973; Grand Valley State Col, BS, 1975, masters gen & urban educ, 1979. **Career:** Adv Coun Muskegon Heights Police, 1975-77; Muskegon Heights Bd Educ, trustee, secy, 1975-81; Muskegon County Repertory Ctr, dir, 1976-85. **Orgs:** Muskegon County Coun Black Org, 1975-77; Muskegon County Human Res Comt, 1977-79; secy, Muskegon Co Black Org, 1977-79; Muskegon Co Human Resource, 1979; Muskegon County Nat Asn Advan Colored People. **Home Addr:** 706 Overbrook Dr, Muskegon, MI 49444-3134, **Home Phone:** (231)563-6562.

## COLEMAN, ERIC DEAN

Lawyer, government official. **Personal:** Born May 26, 1951, New Haven, CT; son of Julius and Rebecca Ann Simmons; married Pamela Lynette Greene; children: Trevonn, Lamar, Erica, Brittany, Jessica & Margarita. **Educ:** Columbia Univ, BA, polit sci, 1973; Univ Conn Sch Law, JD, 1977. **Career:** Hartford Neighborhood Legal Serv, atty, 1977-78; Conn Div Pub Defense Serv, atty, 1978-81; Aetna Life & Casualty, consult, 1981-86; Conn Gen Assembly, state rep, 1983-95, state sen, 1995-; pvt pract atty, 1986-; Conn State House Representatives, majority whip, 1991, rep, 1993; Judiciary Comt, chair, 2001; Planning & Develop Comt, chairmanship, currently; Conn State Senate, dep pres pro tempore, currently. **Orgs:** Greater Hartford Urban League, 1974-; Greater Hartford Nat Asn Adv Coloured People, 1974-; AmBar Asn, 1978; Conn Bar Asn, 1978-; George W Crawford Law Asn, 1978; Charter Oak Lodge Elks, 1982-; Action Plan Infant Health, 1984-2000; Omega Psi Phi Fraternity; Bloomfield Dem Town Comt, 1984-2002; Metro AME Zion Church; pres, Bloomfield Black Dem Club, 1998-; bd dir, Greater Hartford Legal Assistance Asn Inc, 1998-; Ciritan Club, 2000-; bd dir, Bloomfield Educ Found; bd dir, Caldwell McCoy Scholar Found; Hartford County Bar Asn; bd dir, Humanidad Inc; Missoula Hartford County Bar Asn; vice chmn, Pub

Safety & Security Comt; vice chmn, Human Serv Comt Conn Gen Assembly; co-chair, Judiciary Comt, Conn Gen Assembly; Finance, Revenue & Bonding; Prog Rev & Invests. **Special Achievements:** First African-American to serve as Chair of the Judiciary Committee. **Home Addr:** 77 Wintonbury Ave, Bloomfield, CT 06002-2529, **Home Phone:** (860)243-8118. **Business Addr:** State Senator, Second District, Connecticut General Assembly, Legislative Office Bldg Rm 2100, Hartford, CT 06106-1591, **Business Phone:** (860)240-5302.

## COLEMAN, DR. FAYE

President (organization), chief executive officer, administrator. **Educ:** Simmons Col, BS, sociol, 1968; Univ Mass, MEd, early childhood educ, 1973; Univ Md, PhD, educ & human develop, 1981. **Career:** Tech & mgt consult firms, WA, prog mgr & proj dir; Ctr Systs & Prog Develop, prog mgr, 1977-80; Creative Assocs Int Inc, group leader, 1980-83; Southeastern Univ, bd dirs; USAF, contracted proj; Westover Consults Inc, Silver Spring, Md, pres & chief exec officer, 1984-2015; Westover Health Inst Inc, founder, chief exec officer, 2010-. **Orgs:** Bd dir, Wash C Develop Coun; Delta Sigma Theta Sorority, 1966; bd chair, prog chair, Leadership Greater Wash, 1993; Simmons Leadership Coun, 2003-; bd dir, Quantum Leaps Inc, 2008-; Enterprising Women Adv Bd, 2005-; chair, bd dir, Women Dream Inc, 2013-; Women Impacting Pub Policy, 2014-; dir, Nat Womens Bus Ctr Inc, currently; Nat Asn Female Execs; Women's Bus Enterprise Nat Coun; Womens Leadership Exchange. **Business Addr:** Director, National Womens Business Center Inc, 1001 Connecticut Ave NW, Washington, DC 20036, **Business Phone:** (202)785-4922.

## COLEMAN, FRANKIE LYNN

Manager. **Personal:** Born Aug 21, 1950, Columbus, OH; daughter of Franklin L R Young and Mary A Young; married Micheal Bennett; children: Kimberly, Justin & John-David. **Educ:** Mt Union Col, BA, psychol & sociol, 1972; Cent Mich Univ, MPA, urban planning & community leadership, 1974. **Career:** City Columbus, lead planner, 1974-83; State Ohio Bur Employ Serv, Job Training Partnership, dir, 1983-88; Pvt Indust Coun Columbus & Franklin Co Inc, exe dir & chief exec officer; Ohio state community affairs, dir community affairs, 2001, asst mgr work force affairs, 2006-07. **Orgs:** Employ comt chair, Gov Black Male Comn, 1990; exec bd, Ohio Job Trng Partnership, 1992; fund-raising co-chair, Jack & Jill, Columbus Chapt, 1993-94; Links Inc, Columbus Chap; Nat Asn Pvt Indust; chair, Commun Comt; Columbus Rotary Club; bd mem, Columbus One-Step Governace; Fel Black mem dem comts; bd dir, Nat Asn Workforce, prog & conf comt; bd mem, Columbus Coalition; bd mem, Komen Race Cure Comt; founder & chair, Mayor Campaign Breast Cancer Awareness. **Honors/Awds:** Excellence in Community Service Award, WCKX, 1990; Woman of the Year, YMCA, 1991; Mayor's Excellence in Business Award, 1991; EEO Award, Columbus Urban League, 1992; YWCA Woman of Achievement, 1994. **Special Achievements:** Co-Author, The State of Black Males in Ohio, 1991; Induction into the Columbus Public Schools' Hall of Fame. **Home Addr:** 136 Brassic Way, Columbus, OH 43213, **Home Phone:** (614)231-7081.

## COLEMAN, GEORGE EDWARD

Bandleader, saxophonist. **Personal:** Born Mar 8, 1935, Memphis, TN; son of George and Indiana Lyle; married Gloria Bell; children: George & Gloria; married Carol Hollister. **Career:** BB King Band, mem, 1952, 1955; Walter Perkins group, saxophonist, 1956-58; music shows, writer & arranger; Lenox MA Jazz Sch Music, consult, 1958; Max Roach Quintet, 1958-59; Miles Davis Quartet, 1963-64; Lionel Hampton Orchestra, 1965-66; Lee Morgan Quintet, 1969; Elvin Jones Quartet, 1970; George Coleman Quartet & George Coleman Octet, 1974-; Film appearances: Sweet Love Bitter, 1967, Freejack, 1992; Preachers Wife, 1996. Albums: Revival, 1976; Amsterdam After Dark, 1976; Dynamic Duo, 1977; Playing Changes, 1979; Manhattan Panorama, 1985; Convergence, 1990; My Horns of Plenty, 1991; At Yoshis, 1992; Seven Steps to Heaven; My Funny Valentine; Four & Miles Davis in Europe; Blues Inside Out, 1996; The Music of Richard Rodgers, 1998; Danger High Voltage, 2000; Four Generations of Miles: A Live Tribute to Miles, 2002; Charles Mingus Orchestra; Betty Carter Orchestra; Chet Baker Orchestra; Shirley Scott Orchestra; Charles McPherson Orchestra; Cedar Walton Orchestra. private teaching jazz educ; New Sch Univ, consult & teacher; New Sch Soc Res, consult & teacher; Long Island Univ, consult & teacher; New York Univ, Mannes Sch Music, consult & teacher; Tenor alto & soprano, saxophonist, currently. **Honors/Awds:** Numerous honors & awards including International Jazz Critics Polls, 1958; Artist of the Year, Rec World Mag, 1969; Knight of Mark Twain, 1971; Grantee National Endowment of the Arts, 1975 & 1985; Beale St Musical Festival Award, 1977; Tip of the Derby Award, 1979, 1980; New York Jazz Award, 1979; Gold Note Jazz Award, 1982; Key to the City of Memphis, 1992; Life Achievement Award, Jazz Found Am, 1997; Concertband Jazz Award, Netherlands, 2002. **Home Addr:** 63 E 9th St, New York, NY 10003, **Home Phone:** (212)982-4154. **Business Addr:** Musician, Maurice Montoya Music Agency, 1133 Broadway Suite 1605, New York, NY 10010, **Business Phone:** (212)229-9160.

## COLEMAN, DR. HARRY THEODORE, JR.

Dentist. **Personal:** Born Jul 6, 1943, Somerville, TN; married Olivia Jackson; children: Brian & Chandra. **Educ:** Johnson C Smith Univ, BS, 1965; Meharry Med Col, DDS, 1969. **Career:** Hubbard Hosp, internship, 1970-71; pvt pract, dentist, currently. **Orgs:** Nat Dent Asn; Shelby Co Dent Soc; Pan Tenn Dent Asn; Am Dent Asn; Memphis Jr C C; Kappa Alpha & Psi frat; Nat Asn Advan Colored people; YMCA. **Home Addr:** 2221 Thornwood Lane, Memphis, TN 38119-6718, **Home Phone:** (901)756-8686. **Business Addr:** Dentist, Private Practice, 3087 Pk Ave, Memphis, TN 38111-3019, **Business Phone:** (901)327-4200.

## COLEMAN, HURLEY J., JR.

Government official, executive director, commissioner. **Personal:** Born Apr 14, 1953, Saginaw, MI; son of Hurley J Sr (deceased) and Martha Chatman (deceased); married Sandra Morris; children: Natoya Dinise, Hurley J III & Tasha Noel. **Educ:** Eastern Mich Univ, BA, com recreation admin, 1977. **Career:** Washtenaw County Parks & Recreation Dept, Ann Arbor, Mich, prog specialist & com recreation planner, 1977-78; Saginaw County Parks & Recreation Comn, Saginaw, Mich, recreation prog coordr, 1979-85, recreational supt; City Saginaw Recreation Div, Saginaw, Mich, recreation supt, 1985-89; Wayne County parks, dir, 1989, strategic plng & prog develop, asst co exec, 2001; MRPA fel, 1994; Greater Coleman Temple Church, pastor, 2001; City Detroit, Dir recreation, 2001; Liberty Dist, supt; Bishop Samuel L Duncan, Prelate Southwest 3rd Jurisdiction, admin asst; Nat Adjutancy Core Churches God Christ, Inc; Dept Natural Resources, comnr, currently. **Orgs:** Mich State Univ, Natural Resources/Pub Policy, 1986-88; pres, Ethnic Minority Soc, Nat Rec & Pk Asn, 1987-96; exec bd mem, Saginaw County Leadership Saginaw Prog, 1987-88; chmn, Gov's Recreation Adv Comn, 1988-; pres, Mich Recreation & Pk Asn, 1988; Mich State Univ, Mich Outdoor Recreation Task Force, 1988; comt mem, Nat Recreation & Pk Asn; Nat Forum Black Pub Admin, United Way Saginaw County, Kappa Alpha Psi Fraternity; Saginaw Human Rels Comn; Optimist Club; Lions Club; Exec mem, Mich Recreation & Pk Asn; chmn, Jurisdictional AIM Conv; Col Musicians; Secy Elders Coun. **Honors/Awds:** Ten Outstanding Young People Mich, Jaycees, 1986; Distinguished Alumni, Eastern Mich Univ, 1988; Community Serv Award, Phillip Randolph Inst, 1988; Serv Award, Nat Parks & Recreation Asn, 1991; Presidential Award, Nat Parks & Recreation Asn, 1995; NRPA EMS Young Professor Award, 1993; Employee Yr, 1996; Hon Doctorate Degree, Divinity from St Thomas Christian Col & Theol Sem Jacksonville, 2011. **Special Achievements:** Second African-American male president of the association, 1990. **Home Addr:** 22144 Roxford, Detroit, MI 48219, **Home Phone:** (313)534-3631. **Business Addr:** Commissioner, Department of Natural Resources, 2405 Bay Rd, Saginaw, MI 48602, **Business Phone:** (989)752-7957.

## COLEMAN, JAMES WILLIAM

Research scientist. **Personal:** Born Mar 29, 1935, Mound Bayou, MS; son of Harriet B and Gus C Sr; married Lois Bradley; children: Bradley C. **Educ:** Tougaloo Col, BS, biol, 1957; Tuskegee Univ, MS, bact, 1964; Univ Louisville, Sch Med, PhD, microbiol, 1972. **Career:** Tuskegee Univ, instr, 1964; Joseph E Seagram & Sons Inc, sr res scientist, 1969-85; USAF, Epidemiol Lab, epidemiologist; Univ Louisville, Sch Med, Sch Med, assoc prof, 1974-79; Coleman Builders, builder, currently; Cancer Res Ctr Am, pres, chief exec officer, 1990-. **Orgs:** Beta Kappa Chi Sci Soc, 1958-; Am Soc Microbiol, 1958-85; first vpres, Louisville Br, NCP, 1972-74, 1990-92. **Home Addr:** 8622 Blackpool Dr, Louisville, KY 40222, **Home Phone:** (502)426-5815. **Business Addr:** President, Chief Executive Officer, Cancer Research Center of America Inc, 8622 Blackpool Dr, Louisville, KY 40222, **Business Phone:** (502)339-1282.

## COLEMAN, JOHN H.

Government official, building inspector. **Personal:** Born Jul 29, 1928, Memphis, TN; married Willa Nicholson; children: Patrice, Sylvia, John jr, Elissia & Tracey. **Educ:** Ind Univ, BS, phys educ, 1951; Ill Univ. **Career:** Steel mills post off, 1955-59; caseworker, 1959; off mgr, 1969; admin asst, 1972; Quad Co IL Dept Pub Aid, bldg oper supvr, 1974-. **Orgs:** Planning comn, Ill Welfare Asn; bd mem, Strong Ctr; Maple Pk United Methodist Church; prog chmn, Maple Pk Methodist Men's Club; vpres, 116 Ada St Block Club; Maple Pk Home owners Asn. **Home Addr:** 11620 S Ada St, Chicago, IL 60643, **Home Phone:** (773)264-2821. **Business Addr:** 624 S Michigan, Chicago, IL 60605.

## COLEMAN, KENNETH L. (KEN COLEMAN)

Computer executive, founder (originator), chief executive officer. **Personal:** Born Dec 1, 1942, Centralia, IL; son of Louis Boyd and Katie Owens; married Caretha; children: Kennetha, Karen, Kimberly, Kristen & Kenneth. **Educ:** Ohio State Univ, BS, indust mgt, 1965, MBA, 1972. **Career:** Hewlett-Packard Co, corp staffing mgr div personnel, mgr northern Europ personnel, mgr, 1972-82; Activision Inc, Prod Develop, vpres human resources, vpres, 1982; Silicon Graphics Inc, Global Sales, Serv & Mkt, exec vpres, sales, sr vpres global serv, sr vpres admin & bus develop, 1987-98; Graphics Properties Holdings Inc, exec vpres global sales, serv & mkt, 2001; ITM Software, founder, chmn & chief exec officer, 2001-07; Accelrys Inc, lead independent dir, dir, 2003-, chmn, 2006-, currently. **Orgs:** Past pres, Peninsula Assoc Black Person Admin, 1975-; State Calif, MESA Bd, 1984-85; bd mem, Bay Area Black United Fund, 1984-85; Univ Santa Clara, Indus Adv Comn, 1984-85; Ohio State Bus Adv Bd, 1984-85; bd dir, chmn community reinvestment act comt, mem compensation, nominating & governance comt, City Nat Bank, 2003-; dir & mem nominating comt, Classmates Media Corp, 2007-; dir, CSAA Ins Exchange, 2008-; adv group, Pvt Sector Adv Group, 2010; spec advisor, Andreessen Horowitz, 2013-; bd mem, Univ Calif; bd dir, Mich PS Technologies; bd dir, United Online; indust adv, Bay Area Black MBA Asn; bd mem, San Francisco Exploratorium; Ohio State Univ Col Bus Dean's Adv Coun; bd mem, C Health Coun; bd mem, Community Found Santa Clara County; Tech Mus Innovation; chmn, Saama Technologies Inc; Strategic Adv Bd Corefino Serv LLC; spec advisor, Carrick Capital Partners LLC. **Honors/Awds:** Award for Excellence, Community Serv, 1981; Named one of the ten most influential African Americans in the San Francisco Bay Area, 1999; Top 25 Black executives in technology, Black Enterprise Mag, 2001; Mkt Opportunities in Bus & Entertainment Award, 2001; The Ohio State Univ Distinguished Service Award; Living Legend Award, National Alliance of Black School Educators Living Legend Award; The American Leadership Forum of Silicon Valley Exemplary Leader Award; The One Hundred Black Men of Silicon Valley Lifetime Achievement Award; The Silicon Valley Jr Achievement Bus Hall of Fame. **Home Addr:** 26855 Ortega Dr, Los Altos Hills, CA 94022. **Business Addr:** Chairman, Accelrys Inc, 10188 Telesis Ct Suite 100, San Diego, CA 92121, **Business Phone:** (858)799-5000.

## COLEMAN, LEONARD S., JR.

Baseball executive, executive. **Personal:** Born Feb 17, 1949, Newark, NJ; married Gabriella Morris. **Educ:** Princeton Univ, BA, hist, 1971; Harvard Univ, MA, pub admin & MA, educ & social policy; John F Kennedy Sch Govt, MPA. **Career:** Protestant Episcopal Church US, consult, 1976-80; NJ Dept Community Affairs, Dept Energy, comnr, 1982-88; Beneficial Co LLC, dir, 1990-; Maj League Baseball, Mkt Develop, dir, 1992, pres, 1994-99, sr advisor, 1999-2005; Omnicom Group, bd dir, 1993-; NJ Resources Corp, dir, 1995-; Cendant Corp, db dir, 1997-2006; H J Heinz Co, dir, 1998-; Aramark, bd dir, 2000-; Electronic Arts, bd dir, 2001-; Churchill Downs, dir, 2001-14; State Comn Ethical Stand, vice chmn; NJ Housing & Mortgage Finance Agency, chmn; Hackensack Meadowlands Develop Comn, chmn; Kidder, Peabody & Co, munic finance banker; Radio Unica Corp, dir. **Orgs:** Bd Mem, Omnicom Group, 1993-; pres, Maj League Baseball Nat League, 1994-99; hon chmn, Jackie Robinson Found, 1996-; bd mem, Owens Corning, 1996-; bd mem, Cendant, 1997-06; bd mem, H J Heinz, 1998-; bd mem, NJ Resources; bd mem, Electronic Arts, 2001-; Urban Enterprise Zone Authority; Econ Develop Authority; Urban Develop Authority; pres, State Planning Comn; pres, NJ Pub Tv Comn; bd dir, Cs Defense Fund; dir, Metrop Opera; dir, Schumann Fund; dir, Little League Baseball; chmn, Jackie Robinson Found; pres, Nat League Prof Baseball Clubs; US chmn, Bishop Tutu Scholar Fund; pres, Greater Newark Urban Coalition; Metrop Opera; chair, Presiding Bishop's Fund; nat trustee, Urban League; bd mem, Churchill Downs; bd mem, Avis Budget Group, 2006-; vp munic finance, Kidder Peabody; trustee, Seton Hall Univ; trustee, New York Metrop Opera. **Special Achievements:** One of the highest ranking African-American executives in the sports world; Only the second African-American to assume the role of president of the National League. **Business Addr:** Board Director, H J Heinz Co, 600 Grant St, Pittsburgh, PA 15219, **Business Phone:** (412)456-5700.

## COLEMAN, MARCO DARNELL

Football player, football coach, broadcaster. **Personal:** Born Dec 18, 1969, Dayton, OH; married Katrina; children: Kenneth, Kabrione & Kennedy. **Educ:** Ga Inst Technol, mgt. **Career:** Football player (retired), coach, radio analyst; Miami Dolphins, right defensive end & left outside linebacker, 1992-95; San Diego Chargers, right defensive end, 1996-98; Wash Redskins, defensive end, 1999-2001; Jacksonville Jaguars, defensive end, 2002; Philadelphia Eagles, 2003; Denver Broncos, defensive end, 2004-05; Allen D Nease High Sch, coach, currently; radio analyst, currently. **Orgs:** Alpha Phi Alpha Fraternity. **Honors/Awds:** Nat Football League Rookie of the Year, Sports Illus, 1992; Defensive Rookie of the Year, Football News, 1992; Pro Bowl, 2000. **Special Achievements:** Film: Ace Ventura: Pet Detective, 1994. **Home Addr:** 12882 Oxford Crossing Dr, Jacksonville, FL 32224-1668, **Home Phone:** (904)829-0579. **Business Addr:** Allen D Nease High School, 10550 Ray Rd, Ponte Vedra Beach, FL 32081, **Business Phone:** (904)547-8300.

## COLEMAN, MARCUS LE'SHA

Football player, executive, business owner. **Personal:** Born May 24, 1974, Dallas, TX. **Educ:** Tex Tech Univ, activ & socs, 1996. **Career:** Football player (retired); NY Jets, defensive back, 1996-97, 1998, right cornerback, 1999-2001, cornerback, 2000; Houston Texans, right cornerback, 20002-03, free safety, 2004-05; Dallas Cowboys, free agt, 2006; Wilman Energy, founder & analyst, 2008-09; KGOW 1560 AM, On-air personality, 2009-10; Black Barrel Energy, LP, broker W Power & Natural Gas Derivatives, 2010-11; KCOH 1430 AM, air personality, 2011-12; MLC Holdings LLC, owner, 2003-; Vigour Inc, owner, 2007-. **Orgs:** Spokesperson, Texans Blood Dr; Marcus Coleman Found, founder & Bd chair, 2002-. **Honors/Awds:** All-conf hons; AFC Defensive Player of the Week, 1999; NFL Play of the Week, Direc TV, 2000; AFC Defensive Player of the Month, 2003; Texas Tech Athletics Hall of Fame. **Business Addr:** Owner, Vigour Inc, Houston, TX.

## COLEMAN, MARIAN M.

Educator. **Personal:** Born Aug 7, 1948, Laurens, SC. **Educ:** Friendship Jr Col, AA, 1967; Claflin Col, BS, 1969. **Career:** Palmetto High Sch, instr, 1969-70; Benning Terr Recreation Ctr, recreational specialist, 1970; Pamplico Mid Sch, instr, 1970-72; Laurens Community Action Inc, social worker, 1973-74; Comprehensive Employ Training Act, couns; Gleams Community Action Inc, counr, 1974-. **Orgs:** SC Educ Asn, 1969-73; asst secy, Usher Bd White Plain Baptist Church, 1973-75; adv, Youth Chap Nat Asn Advan Colored People, 1974; asst secy, April Shower Chap 184 OES, 1974-75; SC Head Start Asn, 1975. **Home Addr:** 304 Jersey St, Laurens, SC 29360. **Business Addr:** Counsellor, Gleams Community Action Inc, PO Box 1326, Greenwood, SC 29646.

## COLEMAN, DR. MELVIN D.

Psychologist, commissioner. **Personal:** Born Oct 9, 1948, Cleveland, OH; son of James and Neda. **Educ:** Univ Wis, BS, 1969, MS, psychol & clin psychologist, 1974; Univ Minn, cert, behav anal, 1978. **Career:** Youth Employ Orgn, youth counr summers, 1967-68; Cuyahoga County Welfare, social worker, 1969-70; Ohio Youth Comn, parole officer, 1970; Univ Wis, Stout, teaching asst, 1970-71; State Minn, med disability adj, 1971-72, voc rehab, 1972-79; Harley Clin, MN, psychologist, 1978-92; Inst Black Chem Abuse, consult, 1990-91; pvt pract, psychologist; Minn Dept Health, comnr, currently. **Orgs:** Minn Behav Anal Asn, 1978-87; consult, Pilgrim Baptist Church, 1984-90; Bryn Mawr & Queen Nursing Homes, 1985-90; Gestalt Family Preserv Consult Serv, 1990; State Bd Psychol. **Honors/Awds:** Basketball Hall Fame, Univ Wis, Stout, 1978; Black Gestalt, 1987; Reclaiming Black Child, 1989; Parenting Skills Training Cert, Prog Mothers Attempting Reunite Infant C, 1996-; BC & Phoenicia, 1998. **Special Achievements:** First Team National Association Inter College Athelete, Basketball All Am, 1969; 3rd Round Draft Choice, Carolina Cougars Basketball ABA, 1969; 6th Round Draft Choice, Cincinnati Royals Basketball NBA, 1969; Florence Meets Africa: A Jazz Concerto, 1988; author: Parenting Fundamentals 101, 2000; Black Fatherhood: A Call From the Heart, 2002; established Gestalt Publications as distribution outlet for positive black literature. **Home Addr:** 3828 Clinton Ave, Minneapolis, MN 55409, **Home Phone:** (612)822-4419. **Business Addr:** Commissioner, Minnesota Department of Health, 625 N Robert St, St. Paul, MN 55164-0975, **Business Phone:** (651)201-5000.

## COLEMAN, MICHAEL BENNETT

Government official, lawyer, mayor. **Personal:** Born Nov 18, 1954, Indianapolis, IN; son of John and Joan; married Frankie L; children: Kimberly, Justin & John David. **Educ:** Univ Cincinnati, BS, polit sci, 1977; Univ Dayton Sch Law, JD, 1980. **Career:** Schottenstein, Zox & Dunn, partner, atty, 1984-99; City Columbus, councilman, 1992-99, Columbus City Coun, pres, 1997-99; City Coun's Finance & Zoning Comt, chair; Coun Utilities's Safety & Judiciary, develop, rules & ref comt; City Columbus, mayor, 2000-. **Orgs:** Nat Conf Black Lawyers,

1980-; Columbus Conv Ctr Citizens Adv Group, 1986; Downtown Develop Corp's Retailer's Task Force, 1987; vpres, Robert BElliot Law Club, 1989; Union Grove Baptist Church; OH State Bar Asn, 1990-; Am Bar Asn, Minority Coun Demonstration Prog, 1990-; Comt Housing Network; CMACAO; Columbus Youth Corps; Rosemont Ctr; Veterans Memorial Conv Ctr; Black Family Adoption; Cent OH Transit Authority; Kappa Alpha Psi; Prince Hall Freemason. **Special Achievements:** First African-American mayor of Ohio's capital. **Home Addr:** 271 E State St, Columbus, OH 43215, **Home Phone:** (614)221-6563. **Business Addr:** Mayor, City of Columbus, City Hall 2nd Fl 90 W Broad St, Columbus, OH 43215, **Business Phone:** (614)645-7671.

## COLEMAN, MICHAEL VICTOR

Government official, lawyer. **Personal:** Born Oct 12, 1953, Detroit, MI; son of Osborn V and Mary Elizabeth; married Andrea Arceneaux; children: Lauren, Ashley, Christopher, Jonathan, Justin & Jordan. **Educ:** Univ Evansville, BS, 1976; Vanderbilt Univ, Sch Law, JD, 1979. **Career:** Manson, Jackson & Assoc, law clerk, 1977-78; Tenn State Atty Gen Off, law clerk, 1978-79; Securities Div, Tenn Dept Ins, staff atty, 1979-80; Hon Horace T Ward, law clerk, 1981-82; Wildman, Harrold, Allen, Dixon & Br, assoc, 1982-84; Trotter, Smith & Jacobs, assoc, 1984-88, shareholder, 1988-90; City Atlanta, city atty, 1990-93; Troutman Sanders LLP, partner, 1994; Lord Bissell & Brook LLP, atty, 2004-, partner, 2006-; Turner Broadcasting Syst. **Orgs:** Grady Hosp Bd Visitors, 1983-; chmn, Gate City Bar Asson, CLE comt, 1984, exec comt, 1984-88; Butler St YMCA, 1986; Am Civil Liberties Union Ga, 1986-88; Nat Asn Securities Prof, 1989-; Am Bar Asn; Gate City Bar Asn; Atlanta Bar Asn; Vanderbilt Law Sch Alumni Bd, 1993-96; bd dir, Atlanta Cont Olympic Games, 1994-99; trustee, Univ Ga Found, 1995-98; bd mem, Metrop YMCA, 1996-98; Nat Bar Asn; bd mem, Res Atlanta, 1997-2000; Firm Corp Serv pract. **Home Addr:** 165 Milano Dr SW, Atlanta, GA 30331-8379, **Home Phone:** (404)505-0043. **Business Addr:** Managing Partner, Attorney, Lord Bissell & Brook LLP, Proscenium Suite 1900, Atlanta, GA 30309, **Business Phone:** (404)870-4612.

## COLEMAN, MONTE LEON

Football player, football coach. **Personal:** Born Nov 4, 1957, Pine Bluff, AR; married Yvette M; children: Jasmine D, Kyndall & Kyle. **Educ:** Cent Ark Univ. **Career:** Football player (retired), football coach; Cent Ark, 1975-78; Wash Redskins, 1983, 1990, 1992, 1994, linebacker, 1979, right linebacker, 1980, 1984, 1987, right linebacker & left linebacker, 1981, left linebacker, 1988, linebacker, 1982, 1985-86, 1989, 1991, 1993; Data Distrib Serv, vpres pub rels & sales; Univ Ark, linebacker coach & team chaplain, head football coach, 2007-. **Orgs:** Co-chair, Majors City Character Bd; Ark Sports Hall Fame; hon chmn, Make-A-Wish Found; hon chmn, United Way; Boys & Girls Club Wash DC. **Honors/Awds:** Post-season play: NFC Championship Game, 1982-83, 1986-87, NFL Championship Game, 1982-83, 1987; Redskin Ring Stars; All Madden Team, 1993; Washingtonian of the Year Award, 1996; Athletic Hall of Fame, Univ Cent Ark, 1998; Redskins 70th Greatest Players, Univ Central Ark, 2003; Elijah Pitts Award, 2007; Distinguished Alumnus Award, Univ Cent Ark. **Special Achievements:** Co-hosted his own weekly TV show on Home Team Sports "National Defense", a celebrity guest on ESPN-Talk2, BET, PSA Commercials & numerous featured guest spots on television and radio; played more games & years than any other Redskin in history, 216; helped Redskins win three Super Bowls. **Home Addr:** 4700 S Beech St, Pine Bluf, AR 71603-7327, **Home Phone:** (870)534-0322. **Business Addr:** Head Football Coach, University of Arkansas, 1200 North Univ Dr, Pine Bluff, AR 71601, **Business Phone:** (870)575-8000.

## COLEMAN, QUINCY

Football player. **Personal:** Born May 23, 1975, Macon, MS. **Educ:** Jackson State Univ. **Career:** Football player (retired); Chicago Bears, defensive back; Can Football League, Edmonton Eskimos, 2001-05; Can Football League, Ottawa Renegades, 2005. **Honors/Awds:** Grey Cup, Edmonton Eskimos, 2003.

## COLEMAN, ROBERT A.

Government official, activist, editor. **Personal:** Born Feb 8, 1932, Hopkinsville, KY; children: Dominic Joseph. **Educ:** Paducah Community Col. **Career:** US Postal Serv, postal carrier; Paducah, Ky, city comnr, 1973-, mayor pro tem; Masonic Herald, ed. **Orgs:** Pres, Nat Asn Lett Carriers, Paducah Br 383, 1971, 1973; chmn exec bd, Ky State, 1974; bd dir, Paducah McCracken County Red Cross Chap; bd dir, Boys Club Paducah; adv bd, Paducah Community Col; bd dir, Opportunity Industrialization Ctr; bd dir, Family "Y" Paducah mem, Ky Crime Comn; life mem, Nat Asn Advan Colored People. **Honors/Awds:** Hall of Fame, Ky Comn Human Rights, 2005. Blackburn Park in Paducah, KY was renamed the Robert Coleman Park. **Special Achievements:** First African American director of personnel and director of solid wastes; First black director of building maintenance and 911 emergency communications; First African American to serve as president of the Paducah Local of the National Association of Letter Carriers Union; First to serve as chairman of the executive board of the Kentucky State Association of the National Association of Letter Carriers. **Home Addr:** 639 N 23rd St, Paducah, KY 42001-3707, **Home Phone:** (270)442-1502.

## COLEMAN, ROBERT EARL, JR.

Journalist. **Personal:** Born Jan 27, 1961, St. Louis, MO; son of Robert E Sr and Fredonia West. **Educ:** St Louis Univ, St Louis, MO, BA, 1987. **Career:** KMOX-AM, St Louis, MO, writer, ed, 1982-83; Church God Christ, St Louis, MO, dir pub rels, 1984-90; KTVI-TV, St Louis, MO, video tape ed, 1983-. **Orgs:** Nat Asn Black Journalists, 1987-; Greater St Louis Asn Black Journalists, 1987-; Nat Acad TV Arts & Scis, 1987-; Nat Asn Advan Colored People, 1988-; Church God Christ Inc; bd mem, AbideInChrist. **Home Addr:** 3205 Los Feliz Blvd Suite 8 324, Los Angeles, CA 90039, **Home Phone:** (213)661-1819. **Business Addr:** Editor, KCAL-TV, 5515 Melrose St, Los Angeles, CA 90039, **Business Phone:** (213)960-3840.

## COLEMAN, ROBERT L.

Executive. **Personal:** married Carolyn; children: 1. **Educ:** Univ Mo-Rolla, BS, physics; Stanford Univ, MBA. **Career:** Composite Holdings LLC, chmn; Booz, Allen & Hamilton, consult; Prepac Inc, pres, chief exec officer, gen mgr, 1978-84; Minority Bus Develop Ctr, exec dir, 1985; Seven-Up Bottling Co, pres, chmn, chief exec officer, 1987; Worldwide Technol, owner, 1995; Wittnauer Int, chmn, chief exec officer, 1996; Alert Staffing, chief restructuring officer, 2001; Composite Resources LLC, managing mem, currently; Chi Rho Group LLC, managing dir, 2007-09; Emerson Group & Emerson Health Care, manage sales. **Business Addr:** Managing Member, Composite Resources LLC, 12033 Avery Lane, Bridgeton, MO 63044-3008, **Business Phone:** (314)283-0445.

## COLEMAN, RODNEY ALBERT

Executive, vice president (organization). **Personal:** Born Oct 12, 1938, Newburgh, NY; son of Samuel C and Reba Belden; children: Terri Lynne & Stephen A. **Educ:** Howard Univ, Wash, DC, BArch, 1963; Univ Mich, Ann Arbor, MI, exec mgt prog, 1988. **Career:** White House, White House Fel, 1970-71; Dist Columbia City Coun, exec asst chmn, 1973-79; Pa Ave Develop Corp, design consult, 1978-80; Gen Motors Corp, dir Govt rels, 1980-85, exec dir urban & Munic affairs, 1980-94, dir munic govt affairs, 1985-90; USAF, Dept Air Force, asst secy, 1994-98; ICF Kaiser Int, exec vpres, 1998-99; Alcalde E Fay, partner, 1999-; Govt Procurement & Mkt Assocs, sr adv defense, currently. **Orgs:** White House FelsAsn, 1971-; bd dir, Nat Coun Urban Econ Develop, 1986-93; corp rep, Nat League Cities, 1986-94, US Conf Mayors, 1986-94; Gen Motors rep bd, New Detroit Inc, 1986-94, Detroit Econ Growth Corp, 1986-94; Urban Affairs Comm, Greater Detroit, Chamber Com, 1986-94; corp rep, Nat Forum Black Pub Admin, 1987-94; Exec Leadership Coun, 1991-; chmn, bd adv, Mus Aviation, 1999-; trustee, Air Force Aid Soc, 1998-2004; bd dir, Wash Hosp Ctr, 2003-05; bd adv, i2Telecom, 2007-. **Home Addr:** 17519 Edinburgh Dr, Tampa, FL 33647, **Home Phone:** (813)929-7370. **Business Addr:** Partner, Alcalde & Fay, 2111 Wilson Blvd 8th Fl, Arlington, VA 22201, **Business Phone:** (703)841-0626.

## COLEMAN, DR. RONALD GERALD

Educator, association executive. **Personal:** Born Apr 3, 1944, San Francisco, CA; son of Gertrude Hughes and Jesse; children: Danielle D, Joron S & Cori D. **Educ:** Univ Utah, BS, sociol, 1966, PhD, hist, 1980; Calif State Univ, MA, soc sci, 1973. **Career:** Gen Mills Inc, grocery sales rep, 1966-67; San Francisco Unified Sch Dist, fac teacher social studies phys ed, 1968-70; Sacramento City Col, fac instr social sci, 1970-73; Univ Utah, Dept Hist, instr, 1973-80, asst prof, 1980-91, dir african-am studies, 1981-91, assoc prof hist & ethnic studies, coordr ethnic studies prog, 1984-91, assoc vpres diversity & fac devel, 1989-99, Dept Hist, prof, 1991; Calif State Univ, Hayward, vis lectr, 1981; Univ Vt, educ consult; Calif State Univ, educ consult; Utah Transit Authority, educ consult; Fed Bur Invest, educ consult; Nat Trust Hist Preserv, educ consult. **Orgs:** Consult, Utah State Cult Awareness Training Prog, 1974-76; Phi Kappa Phi, 1979; consult, Utah State Hist Soc, 1981; consult, Utah State Bd Educ, 1981; Utah Endowment Humanities, 1982-88; comnr, Salt Lake City Civil Serv Comn, 1983-93; chairperson, Salt Lake City Br, Nat Asn Advan Colored People Educ Comn, 1984-85, life mem; Utah Chap, Am Civil Liberties Union, 1989-; Salt Lake Sports Adv Bd, 1990-; Utah Bd State Hist, currently; Cottonwood Heights Hist Comt; life mem, co-chair, Alta Henry Educ Found Bd; bd dir, Utah Chap Nat Conf Community & Justice; Salt Lake County Sports Adv Bd; Afro Am Hist & Geneal Asn; Univ Utah Senate; Utah Hist Soc; Asn Study African-Am Life & Hist; Western Hist Asn. **Honors/Awds:** Merit Society for Distinguished Alumni, George Wash High Sch, 1987; Calvin S & JeNeal Hatch Award, Univ Utah, 1990; Albert B Fitz Civil Rights Worker of the Year, Nat Asn Advan Colored People, Salt Lake Br, 1991; Olaudah Equiano Award of Excellence, Univ Utah, 1993; Utah Minority Bar Association Award, 1995; Governor's Award, Utah Humanities Coun, 2000; Utah Humanities Council's Governors Award, 2000; Crimson Club Athletic Hall of Fame, Univ Utah, 2001; Merit Award, Utah Acad Sci, Arts & Letters, 2002; Diversity Award, Univ Utah, 2004; Honors Program Teaching Award, Univ Utah, 2006. **Special Achievements:** Published numerous articles. **Home Addr:** 1979 Forest Creek Lane, Salt Lake City, UT 84121-5050, **Home Phone:** (801)944-4311. **Business Addr:** Associate Professor of History, Coordinator of African American Studies, University of Utah, Carolyn Tanner Irish Humanities Bldg, Salt Lake City, UT 84112, **Business Phone:** (801)581-6990.

## COLEMAN, RONNALD DEAN

Bodybuilder, police officer. **Personal:** Born May 13, 1964, Bastrop, LA; son of Jessie Benton; married Rouaida Christine Achkar; children: Jamilleah & Valencia Daniel. **Educ:** Grambling State Univ, BS, acct, 1986. **Career:** Bodybuilder, police officer (retired); Arlington Police Dept, res police officer, 1989-2003; prof bodybuilder. **Honors/Awds:** Mr Texas, 1990; World Amateur Championships, 1991; Mr Universe, 1991; Canada Pro Cup, 1995 & 1996; Grand Prix Russia, 1997, 2003 & 2004; Night of Champions, 1998; Toronto Pro Invitational, 1998; Mr Olympia, 1998-2005; Grand Prix Finland, 1998; Grand Prix Germany, 1998; World Pro Championships, 1999; Grand Prix England, 1999, 2000 & 2004; Mr Brody Langley, 2000; World Pro Championships, 2000; New Zealand Grand Prix, 2001; Admiral in the Texas Navy Certificate Award, 2001; Arnold Schwarzenegger Classic, 2001; Grand Prix Holland, 2002, 2004, 2006; Scott W. Emmerson Long Dong memorial, 2003; Grand Prix Austria, 2006; Grand Prix Romania, 2006; Olympia, 2006, 2007. **Special Achievements:** Featured in various magazines. **Home Addr:** 706 Gentry Dr, Arlington, TX 76018-2350, **Home Phone:** (817)465-3676. **Business Addr:** Reserve Police Officer, Arlington Police Dept, 620 W Div St, Arlington, TX 76011, **Business Phone:** (817)459-5600.

## COLEMAN, HON. RUDY B.

Judge. **Personal:** Born Jan 1, 1947, Tams, WV; married Marguerite; children: Matthew. **Educ:** Marshall Univ, BA, 1968; State Univ NY, Sch Law, JD, 1974. **Career:** Carpenter, Bennett & Morissey law firm, atty, partner; US Dist Ct Dist NJ, 1974; US Ct Appeals 3rd Circuit, 1976; US Ct Fed Claims, 1978; Richard J Hughes Am Inn Ct, Master & treas, 1991-; Super Ct, NJ, judge, 1995-03, Appellate Div, judge, 2002-, Criminal Div, Union County, judge, 2003-. **Orgs:** Comn Rules Prof Conduct, Supreme Ct, NJ; Comn Prof Law, Supreme Ct, NJ; Vicinage Adv Comt Minority Concerns; NJ Bar Asn; Am Arbit Asn; co chmn, Comt Prods Liability, Am Bar Assn; subcomt, Automobile Prod Liability; Kappa Alpha Psi; Kappa Delta Pi; bd trustee, Essex County Bar Asn, 1987-90; secy, Essex County Bar Asn, 1990-91; treas, Essex County Bar Asn, 1991-92; pres, Essex County Bar Asn, 1992-94. **Business Addr:** Judge, State of NJ Super Court Appellate Division, LeRoy F Smith Jr Pub Safety Bldg 60 Nelson Pl, Newark, NJ 07102-1501, **Business Phone:** (973)792-5840.

## COLEMAN, DR. SINCLAIR B.

Consultant, economist, statistician. **Personal:** Born Feb 17, 1946, Halifax, VA; son of N Wyatt and Bessie Bowman. **Educ:** Hampton Inst, BA, 1967; Univ Chicago, MS, 1970; Rand Grad Sch, PhD, 1975. **Career:** US Cong Budget Off, anal staff, 1976-78; Rand Corp, res staff, consult, 1968-76 & 1978-. **Honors/Awds:** Woodrow Wilson Fel, Univ Chicago, 1967-68. **Special Achievements:** Published numerous articles, reports & reviews; sem & briefings univs, rsch inst, govt agencies, confs, & prof meetings; attended Seventh international Atlantic Economic conference. **Home Addr:** 510 Village Unit 401, Manhattan Beach, CA 90277-2757. **Business Addr:** Research Staff, Consultant, Rand Corp, 1776 Main St, Santa Monica, CA 90401-3208, **Business Phone:** (310)393-0411.

## COLEMAN, TREVOR W.

Journalist. **Personal:** Born Jan 12, 1960, Hudson, NY; son of Leonard Gresham and Mary C; married Karl Elaine; children: Sydnie Lianne & Trevor W II. **Educ:** Ohio State Univ, BA, commun, 1986. **Career:** Author & reporter: Satin Mag, reporter, 1985-86; The Times-Leader, reporter, 1987; The Hartford Courant, reporter, 1987-90; The Detroit News, reporter, 1990-93; Detroit Free Press, ed writer & columnist, 1996-2003; The Cincinnati Enquirer, ed writer, 1993-96; Emerge Mag, contrib ed, 1993-99; The Hartford Courant, columnist & reporter, 1994-96; Knight Ctr Specialized Jour, Univ Md, fel, 1996; The Detroit Free Press, ed writer, 1996-03, replacement worker, 1996-2003; Off Gov, chief speech writer, 2003-04; Mich Dept Civil Rights, dir commun, 2004-09; McConnell Commun Inc, exec commun consult, 2009-; Thornhill Commun, exec commun consult, 2009-; Citizens Alliance Prisons & Pub Spending, commun consult & dir, 2013-. Articles: Cover Story Emerge Mag: Clarence Thomas, 1993; Cover Story Emerge Mag: Clarence Thomas, 1996; "Friend of a Friend", 1996; Affirm Action Wars, 1998. **Orgs:** The Nat Asn Black Journalist, 1987-; vice chair, The Nat Conf Ed Writers, Mny Concerns Com, 1994-; The Detroit Press Club, 1992-; Alpha Phi Alpha Fraternity Inc, 1982-; Detroit Chap Nat Asn Black Journalist, 1990-; The Ohio State Univ Black Alumni Soc, 1990-. **Honors/Awds:** Distinguished Alumni Award, Kappa Chap & Alpha Phi Alpha, 1992; Award News Reporting, Detroit Press Club, 1992; Unity Award, Lincoln Univ, 1st Place Coverage Minority Affairs & Soc Issues, 1992; Best Gannet Award, Pub Serv Reporting, 1992; Award for Distinguished Jour, Columbia County, Nat Asn Advan Colored People, 1992; Pulitzer Prize, Pub Serv Reporting, 1992; Detroit Press Club, 1998; Pulitzer Prize for Ed Writing, 1999; MI Press Asn Award for column writing, 1999; Lincoln University Award for Magazine writing, 2000; Nat Asn of Black Journalists Award for commentary, 2000; American Diabetes Asn Award, 2000. **Special Achievements:** Hudson NY High School, Commencement Speaker, 1994. **Home Addr:** 620 Sheffield Rd, Auburn Hills, MI 48326, **Home Phone:** (248)745-5653. **Business Addr:** Editorial Writer, Free Press, 100 Main St, Northampton, MA 01061, **Business Phone:** (413)585-1533.

## COLEMAN, HON. VERONICA F.

Government official, advocate. **Personal:** daughter of Robert and Mary Freeman. **Educ:** Howard Univ, BA, sociol, 1966; Memphis State Univ, JD, 1975. **Career:** Fed Express Corp, sr litigation atty; Memphis State Univ, legal coun, pres, adj instr; dist atty; gen pub defender; Western Dist Tenn, US atty, 1993-2001; Nat Inst Law & Equity, NILE, pres & chief exec officer, 2001-; Mothers of the NILE inc, pres & chief exec officer. **Orgs:** Asst Tenn Comn Criminal Rules Procedures; Law bd examiners; adv bd, Univ Tenn Health Sci Ctr; bd dir, Bank Bartlett; Ben F Jones chap Nat Bar Asn, pres; Fed Bar Asn; Nat Bar Asn Women Attorneys; Memphis Bar Asn; Tenn Asns Women Lawyers; Blues City Cult Ctr; founding pres, Memphis Chap Coalition 100 Black Women; pres, Ben F. Jones chap Nat Bar Asn; Goals Memphis; Urban League; Sentencing Proj; regional adv bd, Memphis & Shelby County Dept Regional Serv Metrop Planning Organ. **Business Addr:** Advisory Board Member, University of Tennessee Health Science Center, 66 N Pauline Ave Suite 463, Memphis, TN 38163, **Business Phone:** (901)448-1298.

## COLEMAN, WILLIAM T., JR. (WILLIAM THADDEUS COLEMAN)

Lawyer, executive. **Personal:** Born Jul 7, 1920, Germantown, PA; son of William Sr and Laura Beatrice; married Lovida Hardin; children: William T III, Louida Jr & Hardin L. **Educ:** Univ Pa, AB, 1941; Harvard Bus Sch; Harvard Law Sch, LLB, 1946; Bates Col, LLD, 1975. **Career:** Harvard Law Rev, ed; Judge Herbert F Goodrich US Ct Appeals 3rd Circuit, law clerk, 1947-48; Justice Felix Frankfurter Assoc, Judge Supreme Ct, law clerk, 1948-49; Paul Weiss Rif kind Wharton & Garrison NY, assoc, 1949-52; City Philadelphia, spec coun transit matters, 1952-63; Dilworth Paxson Kalish Levy & Coleman, partner law firm, 1956-75; US Arms Control & Disarmament Agency, consult, 1963-75; Pres's Comn Assassination Pres, sr consult & asst coun, 1964; S Eastern PA Transp Authority, spec coun, 1968-; US Dept Transp, secy, 1975-77; dir, Pan Am World Airways Inc; dir, IBM; dir, Pepsi Co; dir, Chase Manhattan Corp; dir, Amax Inc; dir, CIGNA Corp; O'Melveny & Meyer, sr partner & sr counr, 1977-; Dilworth, Paxson, Kalish, Levy & Coleman, sr partner; US Ct Mil Comn Rev, 2004-09. **Orgs:** Vpres, Philadelphia Mus Art; chmn bd, Nat Asn Advan Colored People Legal Defense & Educ Fund; trustee, Rand Corp; trustee, Brookings Inst; fel Am Col Trial Lawyers; fel Am Col Appellate Lawyers; Trilateral Commun Coun Foreign Rels; officer, Fr Legion Hon; coun, Am Law Inst; Am Bar Asn; Am Bar Asn Task Force Judicial Admin; Philadelphia Bar Asn; DC Bar Asn; Am Arbit Asn; bd trustee, Carnegie Inst Wash; Brookings Inst; vpres, Philadelphia Mus Art; New York Ballet, Inc; bd dir, Nat Symphony Orchestra; Trustee Coun, Nat Gallery Art; Nat Comn Productivity, 1971-72. **Honors/Awds:** Pres Medal Freedom; Thurgood Marshall Lifetime Achievement Award, Nat Asn Advan

Colored People Legal Defense & Educ Fund; Hon Degree, Gettysburg Col, 2011. **Special Achievements:** Author, co-author contributor numerous legal writings; First African American to serve as a Supreme Court law clerk. **Home Addr:** 1286 Ballantrae Farm Dr, McLean, VA 22101-3026. **Business Addr:** Senior Partner, Senior Counselor, O'Melveny & Myers LLP, 1625 Eye St NW, Washington, DC 20006, **Business Phone:** (202)383-5300.

### COLEMAN-BURNS, DR. PATRICIA WENDOLYN
Educator. **Personal:** Born Nov 23, 1947, Detroit, MI; daughter of Jessie Mae Ray and Dandie; married John II; children: Robert Burns. **Educ:** Wayne State Univ, Detroit, MI, BA, 1969, MA, 1976, PhD, commun & rhet criticism, 1987. **Career:** Motown Rec, Detroit, Mich, admin asst, 1969-72; Inst Labor Studies, Detroit, Mich, part time fac, 1972-87; Wayne State Univ Detroit, Mich, speech comt, grad asst, 1972-76, Africana studies, grad asst, 1976-78, part-time fac, Africana studies, lectr, 1978-91; Univ Mich, Off Multicultural Affairs, asst prof & dir, 1991-, spec advisor to dean multicultural affairs. **Orgs:** Chairperson, WSU Pres Comn Status Women, 1985-89; Pres CounNon-Discrimination, Affirmative Action, 1986-90; pres, bd dir, Women's Justice Ctr, 1990-; Co-owner, Ctr Prof Develop & Mentoring (CPDM); planning comt, Univ Mich, Cent Campus & Health Sci, 1991-; curric comt, Sch Nursing, 1991; Subcomt maj rev LEO lectr, 2006-10; Senate Assembly Comt a Multicultural Univ, 2006-09; dean rep, Greater Detroit Area Health Coun, Regional Action Network Nursing, 2008-; Subcomt, Univ Mich Health Syst, 2009-10. **Home Addr:** 1825 Woodbury, Ann Arbor, MI 48104. **Business Addr:** Assistant Professor, Director, University of Michigan School of Nursing, Rm 2306 400 N Ingalls Bldg, Ann Arbor, MI 48109-0482, **Business Phone:** (734)763-5964.

### COLES, BIMBO (VERNELL EUFAYE COLES)
Basketball player, radio host, basketball coach. **Personal:** Born Apr 22, 1968, Covington, VA; married Weslea; children: Ryan, Brielle, Bella & Bailee. **Educ:** Va Polytech Inst & State Univ, Blacksburg, VA, attended 1990. **Career:** Basketball player (retired), basketball executive, broadcaster; Miami Heat, guard, 1990-96, 2003-04, asst coach & advan scout, 2005-; Golden State Warriors, 1996-99; US Olympic team, 1998; Atlanta Hawks, 1999-2000; Cleveland Cavaliers, 2000-03; Boston Celtics, 2003; 560 WQAM Sports Radio, "Opening Tip with Bimbo Coles", host, 2006-; Country Roads CrossFit, co-owner & head coach, 2009-. **Business Addr:** Co-Owner, Head Coach, Country Roads CrossFit, 113 Davis Stuart Rd, Ronceverte, WV 24970, **Business Phone:** (304)520-2011.

### COLES, DARNELL
Baseball player, sports manager. **Personal:** Born Jun 2, 1962, San Bernardino, CA; married Shari; children: Deanna, Darnell Jr & Jared. **Educ:** Orange Coast Col, Costa Mesa, CA. **Career:** Baseball player (retired), coach, sports manager; Seattle Mariners, infielder, 1983-85; Detroit Tigers, infielder, 1986-87, infielder & outfielder, 1990, asst hitting coach, currently; Pittsburgh Pirates, infielder & outfielder, 1987-88; Seattle Mariners, infielder & outfielder, 1988-90; San Francisco Giants, 1991; Cincinnati Reds, 1992; Toronto Blue Jays, 1993-94; St Louis Cardinals, 1995; Chunichi Dragons, 1996; Colo Rockies, 1997; Hanshin Tigers, 1997; Countryside High Sch, coach; Vt Lake Monsters, mgr, 2007; Nationals' Triple-A affil, hitting coach, 2008; Syracuse Chiefs, batting coach, currently; Milwaukee Brewers, hitting coordr, 2010-11, hitting coach, 2014-; Huntsville Stars, mgr, 2012-13. **Home Addr:** 1813 Stonebrook Lane, Safety Harbor, FL 34695-5425. **Business Addr:** Assistant Hitting Coach, Detroit Tigers, Comerica Pk 2100 Woodward Ave, Detroit, MI 48201, **Business Phone:** (313)471-2000.

### COLES, JOHN EDWARD, SR.
Chief executive officer. **Personal:** Born Jul 18, 1951, Roanoke, VA; son of George (deceased) and Louise (deceased); married Jerelena Perdue; children: Caron N, Jonlyn E, John E Jr & Christin N. **Educ:** Tenn State Univ, attended 1970; Hampton Univ, BS, bus mgt, 1973. **Career:** Citizens Budget Adv Comt, 1980-81; Consumer Credit Counsling Peninsula, mem, 1982; Hampton City Educ Bd, Va, mem, 1982-83; A Builders Va, dir, 1983; People Savings & Loan Asn, exec secy & chief managing officer, pres. **Orgs:** Keeper fin, Omega Psi Phi Frat Zeta Omicron, 1977-80; Va Peninsula Econ Develop Coun, 1982-; treas, Peninsula Asn Ment Retardation, 1982-84; pres, Citizen's Boys Club, Hampton, 1982-84; life mem, Nat Asn Advan Colored People; Omega Psi Phi Fraternity. **Home Addr:** 4 Shaughanassee Ct, Hampton, VA 23666-4573, **Home Phone:** (757)838-3590.

### COLES, KIMBERLEY
Actor, writer, television producer. **Personal:** Born Jan 11, 1966, Brooklyn, NY. **Career:** Lane Bryant clothing stores, spokesperson; The Single Life According to Kim Coles, 1997; Kids in America, 2005; Wig, 2009; TV series: "In Living Color", actress & writer, 1990; "Bigger Brother", 1990; "Strictly Business ", 1991; "Martin", 1993; "Living Single", actress & writer, 1993-98; "The Crew", 1995; "Deandra and Them", 1996; "Forgive Us Our Trespasses", 1997; "New Attitudes", 1999; "Frasier", 2000; "The Geena Davis Show", actress & writer, 2000-01; "Mary Christmas", 2000; "Follow That Car", 2004; Real Gay, 2005; Hell on Earth, 2007; Living Single: The Reunion Show, 2008; "10 Items or Less", 2009; "Pay It Off", 2009; "Love That Girl!", 2011; "Let's Stay Together", 2012; "The Soul Man", 2012; "Wendell and Vinnie", 2013; "Baby Daddy", 2014; "Quick Draw", 2014. **Orgs:** Delta Sigma Theta Sorority. **Honors/Awds:** Nominated for 3 NAACP Image Awards as Best Actress in a Comedy for herwork on "Living Single, " 1996-98; nominated as Best Supporting Actress for a guest appearance on "Frasier, " 2001. **Special Achievements:** Appeared in commercials for BurgerKing and Sears; performed "Homework", HERE Theater in NYC; Book: I'm Free, But It'll Cost You. **Business Addr:** Actress, c/o Kimmicat Inc, 4929 Wilshire Blvd Suite 920, Los Angeles, CA 90010, **Business Phone:** (213)965-7327.

### COLES, ROBERT TRAYNHAM
Architect. **Personal:** Born Aug 24, 1929, Buffalo, NY; son of George Edward and Helena Vesta; married Sylvia Rose Meyn; children: Marion Brigette & Darcy Eliot. **Educ:** Hampton Univ, Hampton Inst, attended 1949, Univ Minn, BA, 1951, BArch, 1953; Mass Inst Technol, MArch, 1955. **Career:** Perry Shaw Hepburn & Dean, 1955-57; Shepley Bulfinch Richardson & Abbot, 1957-58; Carl Koch & Assoc, designer, 1958-59; Boston Archit Ctr, 1957-59; Adv Planning Assoc, assoc, 1959-60; Techbuilt Inc, design mgr, 1959-60; Deleuw Cather & Brill Engrs, coord architect, 1960-63; Robert Traynham Coles Architect PC, pres, 1963-; Saul Alinsky, owner, 1964; NY State Univ Col, 1967, Hampton Inst, 1968-70, Univ Kans, teacher, 1969; Am Inst Architects, dep vpres minority affairs, 1974-75; Univ Kans, pro archit & urban studies; Carnegie Mellon Univ, Pittsburgh, PA, assoc prof, 1990-95. **Orgs:** Consult, Union Carbide Corp, 1963; owner, Indust Area Found, 1964; treas, 1975-77, vpres, 1977-79, Nat Orgn Minority Architects; trustee, secy, bd dir, Preserv League Ny Inc, 1976-; Am Inst Architects, Comt Planning Assistance Ctr; Assoc Comn Design Develop Ctr; NY State Assoc Architects; mayors adv comn, Buffalo Urban Caucus, BANC; Cit Adv Coun; Goals Met Buffalo; comt, Urban Univ; E Side Comn Org; Ellicott Talbert Study Comt; NY State Sub-Comn US Comt Civil Rights; Comt Community Improv; Friendship House Study Comt; vpres, Buffalo Arch Guidebook Corp, 1979-82; pres, Am Arch Mus & Resource Ctr, 1980-82; trustee, Western New York Pub Broadcasting Assoc, 1981-; fel Am Inst Architects, 1981, exec comt, 1990-95, chancellor, 1995; NY State Bd Archit, 1984-; comnr, Erie County Horizons Waterfront Comn, 1989-94; chair, NY State Bd Archi, 1990-91; Alpha Kappa Mu; Arts Am; coun mem, Burchfield Art Ctr. **Honors/Awds:** Outstanding Professor Achievement, Urban League, 1961; Centennial Medal, Honorary Doctor of Letter, Medaille Col, 1975; Whitney E Young Award, AIA, 1981; Langston Hughes Distinguished Professor of Architecture & Urban Design, Univ Kans, 1989; Sam Gibbons Chair Nominee, Univ S Fla, Tampa, FL, 1990; Citizen of Distinction, City Buffalo, 1997; Alumni Achievement Award, Univ Minn Col Archit & Landscape Archit, 1997. **Home Addr:** 321 Humboldt Pky, Buffalo, NY 14208-1023, **Home Phone:** (716)884-7969. **Business Addr:** President, Robert Traynham Coles Architect PC, 730 Ellicott Sq, Buffalo, NY 14203-1102, **Business Phone:** (716)842-2280.

### COLES, VERNELL EUFAYE. See COLES, BIMBO.

### COLEY, DENISE
Executive director, manager. **Educ:** George Washington Univ, speech path & audiol; Univ Pac, master, speech path; Univ Phoenix, MBA. **Career:** Cisco Systs Inc, sr mgr & supplier diversity, 2000-05, dir global supplier diversity bus develop, 2005-11, dir global supplier diversity bus develop commun & chg mgt coe, 2011-14. Articles: "Mentoring Two by Two", 1996; "Cisco's Denise Coley Promotes Supplier Diversity", 2014; "Train the Trainer/Vol 3: Training Programs"; "Minority Supplier Development in China-SDSupplier Diversity at Cisco". **Orgs:** Bd mem, chairperson bd develop comt & secy, Leadership Am; secy, Leadership Calif; alumni Bd, Community Leadership San Jose; bd mem, Northern Calif Supplier Develop Coun; bd mem, Rocky Mountain Minority Supplier Develop Coun; bd mem, Nat Minority Supplier Develop Coun; co-chair, Conf Bd Supplier Diversity Leadership Coun; bd mem, Europ Supplier Diversity Bus Coun; NAWBO Silicon Valley Educ Group Adv Comt; co-chair, WeConnect Int Bd; bd mem, Minority Supplier Develop UK Coun. **Business Addr:** Director, Global Supplier Diversity Business Development, Cisco Systems Inc, 170 W Tasman Dr, San Jose, CA 95134, **Business Phone:** (408)526-4000.

### COLEY, MALCOMB
Executive, accountant, businessperson. **Personal:** Born Goldsboro, NC. **Educ:** Univ NC, Wilmington, BS, 1986, MBA, 1989; Northwestern Univ, exec leadership prog, 2007; Harvard Univ, exec leadership prog. **Career:** Ernst & Young (EY), employee, 1992-2003, partner and assurance partner, 2003-13, office managing partner, 2013-. **Orgs:** AICPA, Nat Asn Black Accountants (founding mem, Res Triangle Pk chap), 100 Black Men Atlanta, & Alpha Phi Alpha; Ernst & Young Inclusiveness Steering Comt & Ethnicity leader Southeast Region; Charlotte Chamber Com bd dirs; United Way Cent Carolinas bd dirs; First Tee Greater Charlotte bd dirs; UNCC Belk Col Bus bd advisors; Cameron Sch Bus Exec Adv Bd UNC-Wilmington; UNC Wilmington Bd Visitors; Rehab Ther Found Inc. (pres). **Special Achievements:** Licensed CPA in North Carolina, Florida, and Georgia. **Business Addr:** Ernst & Young, 100 N Tryon St Suite 3800, Charlotte, NC 28202, **Business Phone:** (704)372-6300.

### COLIN, KATHLEEN
Executive. **Career:** Prudential Securities Inc, vpres investments, 1998-; Intercapital Securities Harbourside Fin, NJ, rep, currently. **Orgs:** Pres Detroit Chap, Nat Asn Securities Professionals, first vpres, 2008, bd dir, 2010-. **Business Addr:** Representative, Intercapital Securities Harbourside Financial, 1100 Plz 5 12th Fl, Jersey City, NJ 07311, **Business Phone:** (212)341-9780.

### COLLETON, KATRINA YVETTE
Basketball player, basketball coach. **Personal:** Born Mar 17, 1971, Tampa, FL; daughter of Pamela. **Educ:** Univ Md, BS, criminal justice & criminol, 1993; Barry Univ, MS, marriage & family ther, 2004. **Career:** Basketball player (retired), basketball coach, executive; Ranana, Israel, pro basketball player, 1995-96; Los Angeles Sparks, forward, 1997-98; Miami Sol, forward, 2000-01; Barry Univ, asst coach, 2001-02; Women's Nat Basketball Asn, guard; Colleton Family Wellness Therapies LLC, clin prof counr & clin marriage & family therapist, currently; Inst Family Centered Serv, lic therapist, 2005-; I Believe, founder & pres, 2009-, dir opers & prog develop; Found Sch Montgomery County, lic therapist, 2009-. **Business Addr:** Clinical Professional Counselor, Clinical Marriage & Family Therapist, Colleton Family Wellness Therapies LLC, 927 Russell Ave, Gaithersburg, MD 20879, **Business Phone:** (240)257-0916.

### COLLEY, NATHANIEL S., JR.
Playwright. **Personal:** Born Jun 8, 1956, Sacramento, CA; son of Nathaniel S Sr (deceased) and Jerlean J; married Toni Denise Conner; children: Jasmine Nicole, Aishah Simone & Mazuri Francis. **Educ:** Univ Mich, polit sci & psychol, 1977, Law Sch, JD, 1979; Univ Calif, Davis, grad study, anthropol. **Career:** Sextus Prod, partner, 1974-; WCBN-FM Radio Sta, disc jockey, 1974-76, talk show host, 1976-78, prog dir, 1978, gen mgr, 1979; Colley-Lindsey & Colley, partner, 1980, atty, 1980-2003; Tiny Tickets, owner, 2003-07; Thomson W, westlaw trainer, 2006-07; Thomson Reuters, competitive mkt, 2008; Nat Colley Law Off, atty, 2008-; Sacramento law firm Colley, Lindsey & Colley, partner; McGeorge Law Sch, adj prof; Semantic Law, owber, 2013-. Playwright: Shoebox; A Sensitive Man; Doctor Rome; Moving Arts; Films: Abortion Mary Williams, writer & dir; Acting Alone at Elephant Asylum, writer & producer. **Orgs:** Nat bd dir, Nat Asn Advan Colored People, 1972-75; Am Legion Boy's State, CA, 1973; Calif Youth Senate, 1973; vpres, Sacramento Nat Asn Advan Colored People Youth Coun, 1973-74; Univ Mich Asn Black Communicators, 1974; Black Music Asn, 1979-; rep, Calif Bar Asn, 1987. **Honors/Awds:** National Merit Scholarship Finalist, 1974; Finalist, Showtime's Black Filmmaker Prog, premiered on Showtime, 1998; Dramalogue Award. **Business Addr:** Attorney, The Law Office of National Colley, PO Box 741825, Los Angeles, CA 90004, **Business Phone:** (323)769-5753.

### COLLIE, KELSEY E.
Educator, administrator, talent agent. **Personal:** Born Feb 21, 1935, Miami, FL; son of James George and Elizabeth Malinda Moxey; married Joyce Jenkins Brown; children: Kim Denyse & Vaughn Hayse. **Educ:** Hampton Inst, AB, 1957; George Washington Univ, MFA, 1970; Howard Univ, PhD, 1979. **Career:** Libr Cong, accessioner & doc librn, 1960-70; Howard Univ, C's Theatre, founder, 1973-91; Howard Univ, prof drama, 1973-95, consult, prof emer, currently; Col Fine Arts Drama Dept, prof & asst dean, 1976-79; Kelsey E Collie Playmakers Repertory Co, artistic dir, 1976-; Diva Productions, artistic dir, 1986-87; playwright; Color Me Human Players Inc, currently; Kelsey E Collie Talent Assoc, talent mgr, 1991-; Kelsey E Collie C Theatre Experience, artistic dir & owner, currently; Kuumba Learning Ctr, eng & drama teacher, 2013-; Nellie Mc Caslin's Theater Young Audiences, contrib; Plays: "Black Images! Black Reflections", 1977; "Bro, Bro, Bro Mine", 1979. **Orgs:** Bd dir, Pierce Warwick Adoption Serv, 1973-89; Am Community Theatre Asn, 1977-87; Theatre Arts Prods Inc, 1980-87; Artist-in-Educ Panel DC Comn Arts, 1983-85; Am Coun Arts, 1985-86; Black Theatre Network, 1986-; artistic dir & bd mem, Color Me Human Players, 1986-; pres, OPM Prods, 1991-93; exec dir, Nat African Am C's Theater; founder, Howard Univ C's Theater; moderator, Helen Hayes Theatre Legacy Proj. **Home Addr:** 1924 Shepherd St NE, Washington, DC 20018-3230, **Home Phone:** (202)269-9441. **Business Addr:** Owner, Kelsey E Collie C Theatre Experience, 207 Unicorn Pl, Capitol Heights, MD 20743, **Business Phone:** (202)479-4357.

### COLLIER, BETTYE MARIE. See COLLIER-THOMAS, DR. BETTYE.

### COLLIER, CLARENCE MARIE
Educator, association executive, administrator. **Personal:** Born St. Francisville, LA; son of Thomas and Sarah Asbell; children: Chandler III & Brandon I; married Caroline Dees. **Educ:** Southern Univ, BS; Tuskegee Inst, MS; La State Univ, MS; Grambling State Univ; NY Univ Syst. **Career:** Southern Univ, vpres, stud affairs & community serv; Teacher Corps Prog, admin; Parish Sch Syst, elemprin, supvr educ. **Orgs:** Asn Supvr & Curric Develop; Phi Delta Kappa; Na Educ Asn; La Educ Asn; Nat Alliance Black Sch Educr; Am Coun Educ; adminr, & counselor, Nat Asn Women Deans; SW Asn Stud Personnel; admin co-chmn, La Comn Observance Int Women's Yr; Delta Sigma Theta; State & Nat Women's Polit Caucus; Leauge Women Voters; Women Polit; Nat Coun Negro Women; Comn Asn Welfare Schc; bd dir & past pres, YWCA, 1974-75. **Honors/Awds:** Operation Upgrade Advancement of Women Award, Nat Orgn for Women; Arts & Letters Award, Delta Sigma Theta Inc; Certificate of Merit, Gov La; Certificate of Recognition, E Baton Rouge City Parish Coun; Citation of outstanding contribution to educ Prince Hall Masons. **Home Addr:** 2878 78th Ave, Baton Rouge, LA 70807, **Home Phone:** (225)357-4900.

### COLLIER, DR. EUGENIA W.
Educator. **Personal:** Born Apr 6, 1928, Baltimore, MD; daughter of Harry Maceo and Eugenia Jackson; married Charles S; children: Charles Maceo, Robert Nelson & Philip Gilles. **Educ:** Howard Univ, BA, 1948; Columbia Univ, MA, 1950; Univ Md, PhD, eng, 1976. **Career:** Educator (retired); Balt Dept Pub Welfare, case worker, 1950-55; Morgan State Univ, from asst instr to asst prof, 1955-66, Dept Eng, chair; Comm Col Baltimore, from asst prof to prof, 1966-74; Workshop Ctr African & Afro-Am Studies, consult, 1969; Pine Manor Jr Col, fac, 1970; S Ill Univ, vis prof, 1970; Atlanta Univ, vis prof, 1974; Univ MD, assoc prof, 1974-77; Howard Univ, assoc prof, 1977-87; Coppin State Col, prof, 1987-92; Morgan State Univ, prof eng, 1992-96; Author: Marigolds, 1969; A Bridge to Saying It Well, 1970; Sweet Potato Pie, 1972; Langston Hughes: Black Genius, 1971; Afro-Am Writing: An Anthology of Prose & Poetry, 1972; Mod Black Poets: A Collection of Critical Essays, 1973; Ricky, 1976; Spread My Wings, 1992; Breeder & Other Stories, 1993; Impressions in Asphalt: Images of Urban Am, 1999. **Orgs:** Nat Conf African-Am Theater; Nat Coun Teachers Eng; Mid Alantic Writers Asn; Col Lang Asn; African-Am Writers Guild; Arena Players; Col Lang Asn; Asn Study Negro Life & Hist; Mid Atlantic Writers Asn; African Am Writers Guild. **Home Addr:** 2608 Chelsea Terr, Baltimore, MD 21216, **Home Phone:** (410)242-6574.

### COLLIER, JULIA MARIE
School administrator, educator. **Personal:** Born Aug 23, 1949, Athens, AL; daughter of John Robert Sr and Louise Benford. **Educ:** Berea Col, BA, 1971; Temple Univ, MEd, 1973; Eastern Kent Univ, MA, 1979. **Career:** Ministry Educ, Nassau, Bahamas, fac, 1973-76; Manchester Col, fac, 1978-79; Franklin Wright Settlement, admin coordr, 1979-80; Aldine Independent Sch Dist, counr, 1980-83; Kenne saw Assoc, assoc dir admis; Nat Abbr Leader, Independent Rep, Am Comm Network, currently; Carter, Reddy & Assocs Inc, regional dir, regist agt, currently. **Orgs:** Comt mem, Southern Assoc Col Regist & Admis Offices 1985; conf presenter Southern Assoc Col Regist & Admis Offices 1986-87; workshop presenter, ELS Lang Ctr, 1986; comt mem, Ga Educ Articulation Comt, 1987-89; exec comt, Ga Asn Colegiate Registrars & Admis Officers, 1988-95; chmn, Ga Asn Foreign Stud Affairs, 1989-90; bd mem, ELS Lang Ctr; Nat Adv Bd Comt, ELS,

Lang Ctrs; regional dir, N Huntsville Civic Asn Educ Comt. **Business Addr:** Regional Director, Registered Agent, Carter, Reddy & Associates Inc, 24123 Greenfield Rd Suite 307, Southfield, MI 48075, **Business Phone:** (866)903-7323.

## COLLIER, LOUIS KEITH (LOU COLLIER)

Baseball player. **Personal:** Born Aug 21, 1973, Chicago, IL. **Educ:** Triton Community Col. **Career:** Baseball player (retired); Pittsburgh Pirates, infielder, 1997-98; Milwaukee Brewers, 1999-2001; Montreal Expos, 2002; Boston Red Sox, 2003; Philadelphia Phillies, left fielder, 2004; Korean Baseball Org, Lucky Goldstar Twins, 2005-06; Hanwha Eagles, 2006; Ottawa Lynx, 2007. **Orgs:** Founder, Lou Collier Baseball Asn Inc, 1992. **Home Addr:** 14227 S Md, Dolton, IL 60419.

## COLLIER, DR. MILLARD JAMES, JR.

Physician. **Personal:** Born Nov 8, 1957, Atlanta, GA; son of Millard James Sr and Catherine Walker; married Dolores Maire Perez; children: Millard J III. **Educ:** Morehouse Col, BS; Ga's Health Scs Univ, Med Col Ga, MD, 1984; dipl, Am Bd Family Pract, 1988; dipl, Am Acad Occup Med, 1991. **Career:** Southwest Comm Hosp & M C, resident Family Med; Atlanta W Health Care Primary Care Asns, med dir, 1990-; pvt pract, currently; WYZE 1480 AM, "Your Health Important" talk show, host. **Orgs:** Am Med Asn; Atlanta Med Asn; Nat Med Asn; Am Acad Family Physicians; vpres, Ga Acad Family Physicians; Ga State Med Asn; pres, 100 Black Men Am, S Metro chap; Alpha Phi Alpha Fraternity Inc; Am Acad Family Pract; Med Asn Ga; Southern Med Asn; Am Col Occup & Environ Med. **Honors/Awds:** Young Physician of the Year, Atlanta Med Asn, 1996; 100 Black Men, Member of the Year, 1996; AAFP, Teaching Recognition Award, 1996. **Business Addr:** Physician, Medical Director, Atlanta West Healthcare, 939 Thornton Rd, Lithia Springs, GA 30122-2676, **Business Phone:** (770)948-5400.

## COLLIER, DR. TROY L.

Educator, association executive, dean (education). **Personal:** Born Apr 18, 1941, Nacogdoches, TX; married Claudette Liggns. **Educ:** Phoenix Col, AA, bus admin, 1962; Utah State Univ, BS, social work, 1964; SMeth Univ, MLA, 1971; Nova Univ, PhD. **Career:** Dean (retired); Harlem Globetrotters Basketball Team, prof basketball player, 1964-67; City Phoenix AZ, youth progs coordr & neighborhood organizer, supvr, 1967-68; Youth Progs Coordr & Neighborhood, organizer supvr, 1968-69; Univ Southern Fla, asst vpres, sudent affairs; Clearfield Job Corps Ctr, res life counr, 1969-71; Univ S Fla, Off Adult & Transfer Stud Servs, assoc dean, dean. **Orgs:** Bd dir, DACCO; Citizens Adv Com, Hillsborough Co Sch Bd; Am Civil Liberties Union, State Bd & Tampa Chap; bd mem, Nat Asn Human Rights Workers; Soc Asn Black Adminr; Am Asn Affirmative Action; Tampa Urban League; Nat Asn Advan Colored People; Tampa-Hillsborough Manpower Coun; Phi Theta Kappa Hon Soc Zeta Fla Alumni Asn; bd dir, Carl T Boles Baseball 4 Kids Found Inc. **Home Addr:** 6101 E 112th Ave, Tampa, FL 33617-3131, **Home Phone:** (813)987-2063. **Business Addr:** Board of Director, Carl T Boles Baseball 4 Kids Foundation Inc, PO Box 340251, Tampa, FL 33694.

## COLLIER, WILLYE

Educator. **Personal:** Born Sep 26, 1922, Hattiesburg, MS; son of Eugene M and Effie A; married Cisero; married Petros B Mdodana. **Educ:** Tuskegee Inst, BS, 1943; Univ Wis, MS, 1946. **Career:** SC Public Schs, home econs teacher, 1946-49; Southern Univ, dir dietetics, 1949-56; Los Angeles Paso Robles & San Luis Obispo, consult diet, 1956-57; San Luis Obispo City Schs, teacher, 1960-64; Bakersfield Col, prof food & nutrition, 1964. **Orgs:** Chmn, Home Econ Dept Benedict Col; Liasion Rep, Home Con Asn Calif Teachers Asn & NEA; Am Dietetic Asn; Am Pub Health Asn; Am Home Econ Asn; Basileus, Gamma Alpha Sigma Chap Sigma Gamma Rho Inc, 1976-78; Int Fed Home Econ; chmn, bd Kern County Health Asn; chmn, Nut Comn KC Heart Asn, 1970-76; mem bd, Kern Co Ment Health Asn, 1974-80, organizer, pres, 1977-79; chmn bd, Kem Co Ment Health Asn, 1980-81; Links Bakersfield, 1977; Nat Advan Asn Colored People. **Honors/Awds:** Outstanding Contributor, Kern County Heart Asn, 1974; Sigma of the Year, Sigma Gamma Rho Sor, 1975; Who Award. Calif Higher Educ, 1976. **Home Addr:** 422 9th, Bakersfield, CA 93304. **Business Addr:** Professor, Bakersfield College, 1801 Panorama Dr, Bakersfield, CA 93305, **Business Phone:** (661)395-4011.

## COLLIER-MILLS, CHERYL

Educator. **Career:** Univ Md Eastern Shore, Princess Anne, MD, Dept Rehab Coun, dir admis, regist & recruitment, asst vpres, Div Stud Affairs, chair & asst vpres stud affairs & enrollment mgt, currently. **Business Addr:** Assistant Vice President, Chair, University Maryland Eastern Shore, Stud Serv Ctr Suite 2169, Princess Anne, MD 21853-1299, **Business Phone:** (410)651-6687.

## COLLIER-THOMAS, DR. BETTYE (BETTYE MARIE COLLIER)

Educator, administrator. **Personal:** Born Feb 18, 1941, Macon, GA; daughter of Joseph and Katherine Bishop; married Charles John. **Educ:** Allen Univ, BA, Am hist, 1963; Atlanta Univ, MA, Am hist, 1966; George Washington Univ, PhD, Am hist, 1974. **Career:** Ford Found Fel; Wash Perry Jr High Sch, Columbia, SC, instr, 1963-65; Howard Univ, instr, 1966-69, Col Lib Arts, dir hons prog, adminr, 1969-71, prof, 1969-76; Wash Tech Inst, asst prof, 1969-71; William & Mary Col, assoc prof, 1969-70; Univ Md, Baltimore County, lectr, hist dept, 1971-74, asst prof, 1974-76; Nat Endowment for the Humanities, consult, 1977-81; Mary McLeod Bethune Memorial Mus & Nat Arch Black Women's Hist, exec dir & founder, 1977-89; Temple Univ, fac, assoc prof hist, Ctr African-Am Hist & Cult, dir, 1989-97, prof hist, 1997-2010. Books: The Impact of Black Women in Education, auth, 1982; Towards Black Feminism: The Creation of the Bethune Museum-Archives, auth, 1985; Race, Class and Color: The African American Discourse on Identity, co auth & co-ed, 1994; African American Women and the Vote, auth, 1997; Daughters of Thunder: Black Women Preachers and Their Sermons, auth, 1998; My Soul is a Witness: A Chronology of the Civil Rights Era, co auth & co-ed, 2000; African American Women in the Civil Rights-Black Power Movement, co auth & co-ed, 2001; Biography, Race Vindication and African American Intellectuals, co auth & co-ed, 2002; John Hope Franklin: Mentor and Confidante, auth, 2009; Jesus, Jobs and Justice, auth, 2010. **Orgs:** Am Asn Univ Profs; Nat Educ Asn; Asn Study Afro-Am Life & Hist; Alpha Kappa Alpha; Orgn Am Historians; Am Hist Asn; Rockefeller Found Fel, Nat Humanities Ctr, 2001-02; fel, Woodrow Wilson Ctr Int Scholars, 2008-2009. **Business Addr:** Professor, Director of Center for African-American History, Temple University, 1115 W Polett Walk 908 Gladfelter Hall, Philadelphia, PA 19122, **Business Phone:** (215)204-1750.

## COLLIER-WILSON, WANDA

President (organization), chief executive officer. **Personal:** children: 2. **Educ:** Miss State Univ, polit sci. **Career:** Jackson Conv & Visitors Bur, pres & chief exec officer, 1998-. **Orgs:** Pres, Missi Tourism Asn, 2008; Destination Mkt Asn Int; Metro Jackson Attractions Asn; Travel & Tourism Res Asn; Southeast Tourism Soc; adv bd, Downtown Jackson Partners; standing comt, Jackson Conv & Vis Bur, currently. **Business Addr:** President, Chief Executive Officer, Jackson Convention & Visitors Bureau, 111 E Capitol St Suite 102, Jackson, MS 39201, **Business Phone:** (601)960-1891.

## COLLINET, GEORGES ANDRE

Television broadcaster, television producer. **Personal:** Born Dec 16, 1940, Sangmelima; son of Raymond Maurice and Myriam Nyangono K'Pwan; married Louise Wilma Lutkefedder; children: Georges Alexandre William Zuom. **Educ:** Univ de Caen, France, BA. **Career:** Voice Am, producer, 1965-88; Soul Music Mag, founder, ed, 1975-79; USIA TV, talent coordr, 1976-; GC Prods, pres, 1979-; "Afropop Worldwide", host, 1980-; "Kora All Africa Music", host; Georges Collinet Productions, owner, currently. **Orgs:** Founding mem, Marracas dOr, 1975-78; Prix de la Jeune Chanson Francaise, 1976-78; Sharon Pratt Kelly, Art steering community. **Honors/Awds:** Gold Award for Best Series; Silver Award for Best Prog; Corp for Pub Broadcasting. **Home Addr:** 1622 Allison St NW, Washington, DC 20011, **Home Phone:** (202)722-1886. **Business Addr:** Host, Afropop Worldwide, 220 36th St Unit B626, Brooklyn, NY 11232, **Business Phone:** (718)398-2733.

## COLLINS, ANDRE PIERRE

Football player, football executive. **Personal:** Born May 4, 1968, Riverside, NJ; married Ericka; children: 3. **Educ:** Pa State Univ, BS, health policy & admin, 1991. **Career:** Football player (retired), exec; Penn State Univ, linebacker, 1989; Wash Redskins, left linebacker, 1990-94; Cincinnati Bengals, right linebacker, 1995-97; Chicago Bears, left linebacker, 1998; Detroit Lions, linebacker, 1999; NFL Players Asn, dir retired players, Prof Athletes Found, exec dir, currently; Full Fitness Union, founding partner. **Honors/Awds:** First-team All-Am selection, Football Writers Asn, 1989. **Special Achievements:** A Butkus Award finalist, Pa State Univ, 1989. **Business Addr:** Executive Director, National Football League Players Association, 1133 20th St NW, Washington, DC 20036, **Business Phone:** (202)463-2200.

## COLLINS, ANNAZETTE

Government official. **Personal:** Born Apr 28, 1962, Chicago, IL; married Keith Langston; children: Angelique Nicole & Taylor Kourtnie. **Educ:** Northern Ill Univ, BA, sociol; Chicago State Univ, MS, criminal justice. **Career:** Chicago Sch Bd, admin; Ill House Representatives, Ill Dept C & Family Serv, pub serv adminr; Cook County Social Serv, Probation Dept; Bur Prisons, correctional officer; 10th Dist, rep, 2001-. **Orgs:** Ill State Senate; Alpha Kappa Alpha Sorority Inc. **Special Achievements:** First elected to the House of Representative, 2000. **Home Addr:** , Chicago, IL 60624. **Business Addr:** State Representative, 10th District, 259 N Pulaski Rd, Chicago, IL 60624, **Business Phone:** (773)533-0010.

## COLLINS, AUDREY B.

Judge. **Personal:** Born Jun 12, 1945, Chester, PA; daughter of Furman Brodie Jr and Audrey Moseley Brodie; married Tim Collins, Dec 19, 1967?; children: 2. **Educ:** Howard Univ, BA, polit sci, 1967; American Univ, MPA, 1969; Univ Calif, Los Angeles, JD, 1977. **Career:** Norman Topping Stud Aid Fund at Univ Southern Calif, dir, 1972-74; Legal Aid Found, Los Angeles, asst atty, 1977-78; Los Angeles County Dist Atty, dep dist atty, 1978-87, head dep Torrance Br, 1987-88, asst dir Bureaus Cent & Spec Opers, 1988-92, asst dist atty, 1992-94, dep gen coun Off Spec Advisor, 1992-94; Dist Ct Cent Dist Calif, judge, 1994-2009, chief judge, 2009-12; Calif 2nd Dist Ct Appeal, assoc justice Div Four, 2014-. **Orgs:** Pres, Asn Dep Dist Attorneys, 1984; mem, Phi Beta Kappa, Nat Bar Asn, Los Angeles County Bar Asn, Black Women Lawyers Los Angeles County, John M. Langston Bar Asn, Women Lawyers Los Angeles, Nat Asn Women Judges. **Special Achievements:** First African-American woman head deputy, Los Angeles County District Attorney, 1987; chair, LACBA Task Force on the State Criminal Justice System, 2002-03. **Business Addr:** California 2nd District Court of Appeals, Ronald Reagan State Bldg, Los Angeles, CA 90013.

## COLLINS, BARBARA-ROSE

Politician. **Personal:** Born Apr 13, 1939, Detroit, MI; daughter of Lamar Richardson and Lou Versa Richardson; married Virgil Gary; children: Cynthia & Christopher. **Educ:** Wayne State Univ, anthrop & polit sci. **Career:** Wayne State Univ, bus mgr, physics dept, 9 yrs, off asst equal opportunity off, neighbhorhood rels; Region I Pub Sch Bd, 1971-73; Mich House Rep, 21st Dist Detroit, state rep, 1975-81 & 1991-97. **Orgs:** Detroit Sch Region I, bd mem, 1971-73; Mich State House Representatives, 1975-81; Detroit City Coun, coun mem, 1982-91 & 2002-; Regional co ord Mich, Ohio Nat Black Caucus Local Elected Officials, 1985; trustee, Mich Munic League, 1985; bd mem, Comprehensive Health Planning Coun S eastern Mich, 1985; trustee, Int Afro-Am Mus; chair, Region I Polit Action Comm; City-Wide Citizens Action Coun Dem Party; ACLU; League Women Voters; Am Dem Action, Kenyatta Home owners & Tenants asn; Black Teachers Caucus; Black Parents Qual Educ; Inner-City Parents Coun; Nat Order Women Legislators; bd mem, Detroit Black United Fund; Spec Comm Affirmative Action; Shrine Black Madonna Church; I WY State Coord Comm Nat Int Womens Yr Comm; Mich Deleg IWY Conv; chair, Const Rev & Women's Rights Comm; prin sponsor bills which were later passed Incl Food Dating Bill, Sex Educ Bill, Pregnancy Ins Bill; mem, Detroit Human Rights Comm; regional dir, Nat Black Caucus Local Elected Officials; Cong Black Caucus; Cong Womens Caucus; Cong Automotive Caucus; Cong Arts Caucus; Cong Human Rights Caucus; Steel Caucus; Cong Travel & Tourism Caucus. **Home Addr:** PO Box 07167, Detroit, MI 48207.

## COLLINS, BERNICE ELAINE

Dancer, manager. **Personal:** Born Oct 24, 1957, Kansas City, KS; daughter of William H and Wanda J Coby. **Educ:** Ringling Bros Barnum Bailey Clown Col, dipl, 1977; Transworld Travel Col, Kansas City, dipl, 1985. **Career:** Doctor Off, receptionist, 1975-77; Ringling Bros Barnum Bailey Circus, clown, 1978-79, dancer & showgirl, 1980-84, apprentice tiger trainer, 1983; Trans World Airlines, int flight attend, 1985-86; Kans City Riverboat, entertainer & asst mgr, 1986-87; Ringling Bros Barnum & Bailey Circus, dancer & showgirl, 1988-90, horse act, 1992-93, admin asst, 1994-96; Big Apple Circus, co mgr, 1996-2000; Alvin Ailey Am Dance Theater, co mgr. **Honors/Awds:** HS Art Award; Gold Key Awards, 1974-75. **Special Achievements:** First African-Am woman clown Ringling Bros Barnum & Bailey Circus, 1978; First African-Am woman tiger trainer, 1983. **Home Addr:** 1213 Douglas Dr, Las Vegas, NV 89102-1815, **Home Phone:** (913)621-3849.

## COLLINS, BERT

Insurance executive, executive, association executive. **Personal:** Born Nov 9, 1934, Austin, TX; son of James K (deceased) and Marie (deceased); married Carolyn Porter; children: Suane, Brandy Suggs & Bert E. **Educ:** Hoston-Tillotson Col, BBA, 1955; Univ Detroit, MBA, 1959; NC Cent Univ Law Sch, JD, 1970; Univ NC-Chapel Hill, young exec prog. **Career:** Sidney A Sumby Memorial Hosp, chief acct, 1956-61; Austin Wash & Davenport CPA's, sr staff acct, 1962-67; NC Mutual Life Ins Co, admin asst, 1967, asst vpres, off staff, 1970, vp, controller, 1974, bd dir, exec comt, 1978, fin comt, 1979, sr vpres, controller, 1982, sr vpres, admin, 1983, chmn securities comt, 1983, chmn field comn, 1986, exec vpres, chief operating officer, 1987-90, pres & chief exec officer, 1990-. **Orgs:** Kappa Alpha Psi; Sigma Pi Phi Boule'; First Church Christ Scientist; Mich Asn CPA's; NC Asn CPA's; Am Inst CPA's; Am Bar Asn; NC State Bar; George White Bar Asn; bd visitors, NC A&T State Univ; Durham Comn Affairs Black People; Durham Bus & Prof Chain; Durham Chamber Com; bd dir, treas, former pres, State Easter Seal Soc; vice chair, exec comn, bd, Mutual Savings Bank; coun mgt, bd dir, NC Amateur Sportsmem, Africa News; app Bd Arts & Humanities (NC); Nat Bd Boys & Girls Clubs Am; NC Bus Coun Mgt & Develop; bd gov, Univ NC, Chapel Hill, 1998-99; Nat Ins Asn, pres emer. **Honors/Awds:** Doctor of Humane Letters, Barber Scotia Col; CC Spaulding Award, Nat Bus League. **Special Achievements:** Black Enterprise's list of Top Insurance Companies, ranked No 1, 1999-2000. **Home Addr:** 2404 Vintage Hill Dr, Durham, NC 27712, **Home Phone:** (919)471-1611. **Business Addr:** President, Chief Executive Officer, NC Mutual Life Insurance Co, 411 W Chapel Hill St, Durham, NC 27701, **Business Phone:** (919)682-9201.

## COLLINS, DR. BOBBY L.

Dentist. **Educ:** Univ Iowa, Col Dent, grad, 1975. **Career:** Pvt pract, dentist, currently; SmartPract Dent Consult LLC, founder, 2004-; Univ Tenn Sch Dent, fac mem. **Orgs:** Pres, Tenn Bd Dent, 1988, 1993; Am Dent Asn; Acad Gen Dent; pres, Tenn Dent Asn. **Honors/Awds:** Fel Award for Distinguished Service, Tenn Dent Asn. **Special Achievements:** First African-American president, second African-American appointed mem, Tennessee Board of Dentistry. **Home Addr:** 4466 Elvis Presley Blvd, Memphis, TN 38116, **Home Phone:** (901)396-7097. **Business Addr:** Founder, SmartPractice Dental Consulting LLC, Peabody Pl 119 S Main St Suite 500, Memphis, TN 38103, **Business Phone:** (901)322-4430.

## COLLINS, BOOTSY (WILLIAM EARL COLLINS)

Singer, songwriter, bass guitarist. **Personal:** Born Oct 26, 1951, Cincinnati, OH. **Career:** Albums: Stretchin Out, 1976; Ahh The Name is Bootsy, Baby, 1977; Bootsy? Player of the Yr, 1978; Ultra Wave, 1980; The One Giveth & the Count Taketh Away, 1982; What's Bootsy Doin?, 1988; Jungle Bass, 1990; Back in the Day: The Best of Bootsy, 1994; Fresh Outta "P" Univ, 1997; Glory B da Funks on Me, 2001; Play With Bootsy-A Tribute To The Funk, 2002; Live In Concert 1998, 2006; Christmas Is 4 ever, 2006; Science Faxtion, 2008; Funk For Your Ass, 2008; The Greasy Beat, 2009; Tha Funk Capital of the World, 2011; Bootzilla Productions Inc, owner, currently. Songs: "Vanish In Our Sleep"; "Stretchin' Out", 1976; "What's a Telephone Bill", "Munchies For Your Love", 1977; "You Got Me Wide Open", 1995. **Business Addr:** Artist, Bootzilla Productions Inc, 813 Barg Salt Run Rd, Cincinnati, OH 45244-1105, **Business Phone:** (513)528-3404.

## COLLINS, CALVIN LEWIS

Software developer, football player. **Personal:** Born Jan 5, 1974, Beaumont, TX. **Educ:** Tex A&M Univ, BA, bus admin; SetFocus LLC, C masters prog cert. **Career:** Football player (retired), software developer; Atlanta Falcons, ctr, 1997, 2000, left guard, 1998, 2000, guard & right guard, 1999; Minn Vikings, left guard, 2001; Houston Texans, 2002; Pittsburgh Steelers, 2003; Denver Broncos, guard, 2004; CFC Capital Group LLC, owner & pres, 2001-05; Set Focus LLC, software developer, 2005-. **Orgs:** Nat Hon Soc; W Brook Powerlifting. **Honors/Awds:** NFL All-Rookie Team, 1997. **Business Addr:** Software Developer, SetFocus LLC, 4 Century Dr, Parsippany, NJ 07054, **Business Phone:** (973)889-0211.

## COLLINS, CARL

Executive. **Career:** Charity Motors Car Donation, mgr, pres & chief exec officer, currently. **Business Addr:** President, Manager, Chief Executive Officer, Charity Motors Car Donation, 10431 Grand River Ave, Detroit, MI 48204, **Business Phone:** (313)255-1000.

## COLLINS, CHARLES MILLER

Real estate executive. **Personal:** Born Nov 22, 1947, San Francisco, CA; son of Daniel A and DeReath Curtis James; married Paula Robinson; children: Sara & Julia. **Educ:** Williams Col, BA, 1969; Athens

Ctr Ekistics, Athens, Greece, cert, Urban Planning & Develop, 1971; Mass Inst Technol, MCP, Urban Studies & Planning, 1973; Harvard Law Sch, JD, 1976. **Career:** Pvt law pract, atty, 1976-79; State Calif, Dep Sec Bus, Transp & Housing, 1980-82; Western Develop Group Inc, prin, 1982-87; WDG Ventures Inc, chmn & pres, 1987-; WDG Ventures Ltd, managing gen partner, 1987-; Family Serv Agency San Francisco, pres, 2002-04; Venture Philanthropy Partners Inc, patner, currently. **Orgs:** Trustee, Howard Thurman Educ Trust, 1976-97; Alpha Phi Alpha; Sigma Pi Phi; trustee, Nat Urban League, 1989-; trustee, Clark Art Inst; trustee, San Francisco Mus Mod Art; chmn, Spec Awards Comn, San Francisco Found; dir, San Francisco Jazz Orgn; social policy adv comt, Bank Am; pres, chief exec officer, YMCA San Francisco, 2004-; sr vice chmn, bd trustee, Nat Urban League, 2003. **Honors/Awds:** Fel, Thomas J Watson Found, 1969-71; Bicentennial Award, Williams Col, 2003. **Special Achievements:** Editor: The African Americans A Celebration of Achievement, Viking Studio Books, 1993; A Day Life Africa, 2002. **Home Addr:** 24 6th Ave, San Francisco, CA 94118-1324, **Home Phone:** (415)221-7712. **Business Addr:** Chairman, President, WDG Ventures Inc, 109 Stevenson St 5th Fl, San Francisco, CA 94105, **Business Phone:** (415)896-2300.

### COLLINS, CLIFFORD JACOB

Executive director, association executive. **Personal:** Born Mar 6, 1947, Jamaica, NY; son of Clifford Jr and Mamie Hale; married Electra Bazemore; children: Makina & Ahmed. **Educ:** Roger Williams Col, AA, 1970; Shaw Univ, BA, 1975; Ga State Univ, MEd, 1977. **Career:** Goodwill Industs, Atlanta, Ga, dir, indust serv, 1983-84; Atlanta Regional Comm, Atlanta, Ga, chief planner, 1985-86, prin planner, 1986-87; Nat Asn Advan Colored People Baltimore, Md, asst dir, back, sch stay sch, 1987-88, prom dir, back sch stay sch, 1988, 1992; dir, voter educ, 1989; Second Cong Dist, deleg; Job Opportunities Task Force, exec dir. **Orgs:** Bd dir, Nat Coalition Black Voter Participation, 1990-; Minority Educ Coord Coun Baltimore County Pub Schs, 1990-; Citizens Adv Comm Gifted & Talented Prog, Baltimore Co Pub Schs, 1990-; NW Adv Coun, 2003; Nat Asn Secretaries State; 2000 Census Adv Comn, US Census Bur; Nat Comn Renewal Am Democracy; Decennial Census Adv Comn; Nat Asn Advan Colored People; chair, Northwest Adv Coun. **Honors/Awds:** Award Outstanding Coop Advancing Pub Understanding, Census, 1990; US Dept Com Bureau Census, 1991; Co-auth, Nat Asn Advan Colored People Redistricting Proj Handbook, Nat Asn Advan Colored People, 1991; Certificateof Recognition Outstanding Volunteer Serv, Old Court Middle Sch. **Special Achievements:** Publications: Personal Care Homes: A Local Govt Perspective, res study personal care homes Atlanta, GA, Atlanta Regional Comn. **Home Addr:** 8917 Greens Lane, Randallstown, MD 21133-4240, **Home Phone:** (410)629-6281. **Business Addr:** Executive Director, Job Opportunities Task Force, 2 E Read St 6th Fl, Baltimore, MD 21202, **Business Phone:** (410)234-8045.

### COLLINS, CORENE

Government official, administrator. **Personal:** Born Apr 20, 1948; married Tony; children: Craig & Kisten. **Educ:** Fla A&M Univ, BA, sociol & criminol, 1970; Rutgers Univ, MA, criminal justice admin. **Career:** Youth Serv Bur, E Orange, NJ, dir, 1974-78; United Way Community Planning & Develop, Newark, NJ, dir, 1978-80; Black Spectrum TV Show, producer & host volunteer, 1978-79; Div Community Serv, Tampa, Fla, dep dir, 1981-85; Div Cult Serv, Hillsborough County, dir; Univ S Fla, Sch Social Work, asst dir, Fl Kinship Ctr, currently. **Orgs:** Exec dir & volunteer, Oper PUSH, 1977-79; pub rels coordr & newsletter co-ed, Tampa Orgn Black Affairs, 1980-84; pres, Tampa Bay Investment Club, 1982-85; Nat Forum Black Pub Admin; Tampa Chamber Com, Govt Comn; bd mem, Am Cancer Soc; N Am Coun Adoptable C; statewide coord, Hillsborough County, Fl; Summit Planning Comt, C's Bd Hillsborough County, currently. **Home Addr:** 5209 Gorham Ct, Tampa, FL 33624, **Home Phone:** (813)961-3985. **Business Addr:** Assistant Director, University of South Florida, 4202 E Fowler Ave, Tampa, FL 33620, **Business Phone:** (813)974-4946.

### COLLINS, CORNELL

Fashion designer. **Personal:** Born Nov 2, 1974, Trenton, NC. **Educ:** Brooks Col, grad; Los Angeles Fashion Inst Design & Merchandising. **Career:** Fashion designer, currently. **Honors/Awds:** Award for the Best Avant Garde Collection at Graduation Show, 1996. **Special Achievements:** Collections featured in numerous magazines & fashion shows.

### COLLINS, DAISY G.

Judge. **Personal:** Born Feb 5, 1937, Butler, AL; daughter of Booker T Sr (deceased) and Luevinia Mitchell. **Educ:** Ohio State Univ, acct, 1958, BS, bus admin, 1958; Howard Univ Sch Law, JD, 1970. **Career:** Judge (retired); Commonwealth Edison Co, Chicago, mgt trainee, 1958-60; City Detroit, acct, 1960-64; Gen Foods Corp, White Plains, cost & budget analyst, 1964-66; US State Dept, African Affairs, Stud asst legal adv, 1969; N MS Rural Legal Serv Greenwood, staff atty, 1970-71; Ohio Turnpike Comn, asst gen coun & staff lawyer, 1973-74; Northern Dist Ohio, asst US atty, 1975-77; Capital Univ Law Sch, vis assoc prof law, 1981-82; Equal Opportunity Comn, Cleveland Dist Off, admin judge, 1986-90; Off Hearings & Appeals, admin law judge, Social Security Admin, 1990-94; Bus Law & Acct, Cleveland State Univ & Cuy CC, part-time instr. **Orgs:** Life mem, Nat Advan Asn Colored People, exec secy, Cleveland Br, 1979-80; Alpha Kappa Alpha Sorority. **Honors/Awds:** Appreciation Award, Law J Notes Ed, 1970; Meritorious Service Awards, Cleveland Bar Asn, 1972-73; Hon Mention, Cleveland Fed Exec Bd Community Serv, 1976; Six American Jurisprudence Awards; Most Outstanding Grad Woman Col C & Admin, Phi Chi Theta Scholar Key; Inducted, Berea High Sch Distinguished Alumni Hall of Fame, 2002. **Special Achievements:** Articles published in Howard Law J & Crnt Bibliography African Affairs; HLJ Notes Ed. **Home Addr:** 12501 Brooklawn Ave, PO Box 110051, Cleveland, OH 44111-5025, **Home Phone:** (216)671-6542.

### COLLINS, DOROTHY (DOROTHY BOWERS)

College administrator, basketball coach, basketball player. **Personal:** married David; children: Doriyon & David. **Educ:** Youngstown State Univ, BS, educ, 1990, MS, educ, 1994; Capella Univ, PhD. **Career:** Penguins, basketball player, 1984-88; Calvary Christian Acad, asst coach, 1996-98; Pro-Star Basketball Camp, camp coach, 1996-98; Youngstown YMCA, vol head coach, 1997-; Youngstown State Univ, campus supvr, 1999-2002, coordr multicultural stud serv, 2000-02, asst women's basketball coach; Mahoning & Columbiana Trng Asn, career consult; Jefferson Community Col, TRiO stud support servs, coordr, dir, currently. **Home Addr:** 4211 Chester Dr, Boardman, OH 44512. **Business Addr:** Director, Jefferson Community College, 109 E Broadway Suite 300, Louisville, OH 40202, **Business Phone:** (740)266-9663.

### COLLINS, DOROTHY LEE

Educator, association executive. **Personal:** Born Jan 19, 1932, Nacogdoches, TX; married Samuel M Prin. **Educ:** Tex Southern Univ, BS, elem educ, 1952; Our Lady Lake Univ, MEd, 1973; Trinity Univ, MA, 1977. **Career:** Lincoln Elem Sch, teacher, 1957-63; Winston Elem Sch, teacher, 1963-71; E.T. Wrenn Jr High Sch, counr & vice prin, 1971-73; Johnson Elem Sch, prin; Perales Elem Sch, prin; Las Palmas Elem Sch, prin, 1973-95. **Orgs:** Bd dir, Young & Women Christian Asn, 1966-69; Tex Cong Parents &Teachers, 1969; Ella Austine Community Ctr, 1969-77; pres, Edgewood Classroom Teachers Asn, 1969-71; ambassador, Good Will State Tex, 1970; Nat Educ Asn, 1970-75; exec comn, United Negro Col Fund Inc; adv bd, Edgewood ISD, 1970-75; Gary Job Corp Ctr, Voc Adv Coun, 1970-73; exec comn, Tex State Teachers Asn, 1971-77; Tex State Teachers Asn & Nat Educ Asn; treas, Tex Elem Principals & Supervisors Asn; vpres, San Antonio Leag Bus & Prof Women Inc, 1971-76; Nat Educ Asn Task Force Testing, 1972-75; bd dir, Tex Classroom Teachers, 1972-1975; rep, proj area comn San Antonio Develop Agency, 1973-78; State Bd Exam Teacher Educ, 1975-77; adv bd, educ dept Our Lady Lake Univ, 1976-77; pres, Edgewood Admin & ServsPersonnel Asn, 1976-77; chairperson, Hardin-Simmons Univ, Abilene, TX, 1978-79; life mem, Nat Coun Negro Women Inc, 1979; vpres, San Antonio Chap Our Lady Lake Univ Alumni Asn, 1979-80; chmn, Tex Educ Agency Teacher Educ Eval Team Visit, 1979; mem adv bd educ dept, Our Lady Lake Univ, 1980-81; treas, Dist XX Tex ElemPrin & Supr Asn, 1980-81; bd dir, Bexar Co Opportunity Indst Ctr; lifemem, Nat Advan Asn Colored People; spec state mem, comn Tex State Teachers Asn. **Honors/Awds:** Hon roll cert Tex, Southern Univ, 1951; Citation-Historical Achievement Among Negroes San Antonio Smart Set Club, 1965; citation, Woman's Pavilion Hemisfair 68 Vol Guide, 1968; Past President Award, Edgewood Classroom Teachers Asn, 1971; Distinguished Education Service Award, Prince & Princess Soc & Civic Club Inc, 1971; Outstanding Education Award, Zeta Phi Beta Sorority, 1973; Tex Classroom Teachers Association Service Award, 1973; Distinguished Service Award, Task Force Testing Nat Educ Asn, 1976; Miss Black San Antonio Board of Director Model Community Leadership Award, 1976; Service Award, Tex State Teachers Asn, 1977; Cert Apprec, Tex State Teachers Asn, 1977; Boss of the Year, Mission City Chap Am Bus Women's Asn, 1978; Educ Adminstrator of the Year, Delta Rho Lambda Ch Alpha Phi Alpha Frat, 1978; Cert Apprec, Edgewood Inde Sch Dist, 1978. **Special Achievements:** First African American to Integrate Teaching Profession, Edgewood ISD, 1963; first-grade teacher at Winston Elementary School, 1963; First Black President of Tex State Teachers Assn Affiliate, 1969-71; First black mem, Tex Classroom Teachers Asn Bd Dirs Rep Dist, 1973-73. **Home Addr:** 1217 Delaware St, San Antonio, TX 78210, **Home Phone:** (210)532-4497. **Business Addr:** Principal, Edgewood ISD, 5358 W Commerce St, San Antonio, TX 78237, **Business Phone:** (210)444-4500.

### COLLINS, DR. ELLIOTT

Educator, dean (education), president (organization). **Personal:** Born Mar 18, 1943, Eastman, GA; son of Johnnie C and Elvin W; married Carol Jones; children: Kimberly L. **Educ:** Univ Del, BA, polit sci, 1966; NY Univ, MPA, pub admin, 1971, PhD, Am studies, 2000; Drew Univ, Madison, NJ, MA, polit sci, 1983. **Career:** City E Orange NJ, asst city planner, 1969; Drew Univ, Upsala Col, Educ Opportunity Fund Prog, dir & coordr, 1970-76, lectr polit sci, 1974-79, affirmative action off, 1974-77, coordr sci enrichment prog, 1976-77, asst dean acad coun, 1976-77; Passaic Co Community Col, Paterson, NJ, Dept Hist, dean students, 1979-86, dean acad servs, 1986-89, vpres, 1989-90, prof hist, 1990-, interim pres, 1990-91, pres, 1991-96; Gilbert Residence Hall Complex, resident adv. **Orgs:** Vpres, United Way & Community Serv Coun, 1971-75; vpres & bd dir, Rotary Club E Orange, NJ, 1971-72; bd trustee, Family Servs & Child Guid Ctr, 1975-76; bd dir, Paterson YMCA, 1983-87; bd dir, Opportunities Industrialization Ctr, 1987-95; bd trustee, Passaic-Clifton YMCA, 1989-93; NJ Regional Chamber Comm, 1991-95; secy, bd trustee, Passaic Co Community Col, 1991-96; bd dir, United Way Passaic Valley, 1992-95; bd trustee, Inner City Christian Action Housing Inc, 1992-96; exec bd mem, Passaic Valley Coun Boy Scouts Am, 1992-95; bd trustee, Passaic Co Hist Soc, 1993-98. **Home Addr:** 92 Greenwood Dr, Millburn, NJ 07041. **Business Addr:** Professor of History, Passaic County Community College, 1 Col Blvd, Paterson, NJ 07505, **Business Phone:** (973)684-6868.

### COLLINS, ELSIE

Educator, teacher. **Personal:** Born Durham, NC; children: Leslie Jean & Kimberly Ruth. **Educ:** Del State Col, BA, 1945; Columbia Univ, MA, 1952; Union Grad Sch, PhD, 1977. **Career:** Booker T. Wash Jr High Sch, teacher, social studies; Dover DE Jr & Sr High Schs, teacher, 1945-59; Beth Jacob Jewish High Sch, New York, teacher, 1960-61; Core Curr Jr High Sch, Trenton NJ, teacher, 1961-62, 1964-68, demonstration teacher, 1965-68; Trenton State Col, NJ, supvr summer semester teachers, 1965-75, asst prof & asst dir Corp; emer educ, currently; Consult Serv & In-serv Workshops, Trenton; NJ State Dept Higher Educ, teacher educ, 1967-72; Nat Teachers Corp, Trenton NJ, team leader, 1968-71; Afro-AmStudies, 1969-76; Urban Educ Curric Spec, 1972-. **Orgs:** Am Asn Univ Women, 1954-60; Community Leaders & Noteworthy Am, 1979; Doctorate Asn NY Educrs, 1980; NJ Hist Soc Am Asn Negro Mus; Nat Asn Adv Colored People; Urban League Coun Soc Studies Nat Educ Asn; New Jersey Educ Asn; Poverty Law Ctr AKA Asn; Supvr & Curric Develop. **Home Addr:** 583 Arena Dr Apt B, Trenton, NJ 08610, **Home Phone:** (609)888-2624. **Business Addr:** Emeritus of Education, Trenton State College, 2000 Pennington Rd, Ewing, NJ 08628-0718, **Business Phone:** (609)771-1855.

### COLLINS, JAMES (JAMES EDGAR COLLINS)

Basketball player, basketball coach. **Personal:** Born Nov 5, 1973, Jacksonville, FL. **Educ:** Fla State Univ, attended 1997. **Career:** Basketball player (retired), head coach; Los Angeles Clippers, shooting guard, 1997-98; US Basketball League, Jacksonville Barracudas, 1998; Continental Basketball Asn, LaCrosse Bobcats, 1998-99; Continental Basketball Asn, Quad City Thunder, 1999; Strasbourg IG, France, 1999; Joventut Badalona, Spain, 2000; Pinturas Bruguer, 2000; Continental Basketball Asn, Grand Rapids Hoops, 2000-02; Guaiqueries de Margarita, Venezuela, 2002; Air Avellino, Italy, 2002-03; Eurorida Scafati, Italy, 2003-04; Cimberio Novara, Italy, 2004-05; Vertical Vision Cantu, Italy, 2006; Indesit Fabriano, Italy, 2006-07; Andrew Jackson Sr High Sch, Jacksonville, Fla, head boys basketball coach, currently. **Business Addr:** Head Coach, Andrew Jackson High School, 3816 N Main St, Jacksonville, FL 32206-1450, **Business Phone:** (904)630-6950.

### COLLINS, JAMES DOUGLAS

Educator, radiologist. **Personal:** Born Dec 11, 1931, Los Angeles, CA; son of James and Edna Alice O'Bryant; married Cecila Edith Lyons; children: Keith, Jelana Carnes & Jenine. **Educ:** Univ Calif, BA, 1957, MA, 1959; Meharry Med Col, Nashville, MD, 1963. **Career:** Los Angeles City Gen Hosp intern, 1963-64; Univ Calif, LA, resident radiol, 1964-68; Martin Luther King Jr Hosp, attend physician, 1969-; Vet Admin (Wadworth/Spelveda), attend radiologist, 1972-; Martin Luther King Jr Gen Hosp Los Angeles, attend radiologist, 1973-; Olive View Mid-Valley Hosp Van Nuys, attend radiologist, 1976-; Univ Calif, Los Angeles, assoc prof radiol, 1976-96, prof, 1996-. **Orgs:** Am Bd Radiol, 1968; search comt chmn, Radiol Dept, Martin Luther King Jr Gen Hosp, 1969-70; Radiol Soc N Am, 1969-; Asn Univ Radiologist, 1971-; Am Asn Clin Anatomists, 1993-; Am Asn Anatomists, 1996-; Brit Asn Clin Anatomists; Alpha Omega Alpha Hon Med Soc; vol, Venice Community Health Ctr; Los Angeles County Radiol Soc; Nat Med Asn. **Honors/Awds:** Josiah Macey Fellow, 1959-63; William Allan Jr, MD, Memorial Lectr, Ninety eighth NMA, 1993. **Home Addr:** 4119 Fairway Blvd, Los Angeles, CA 90043. **Business Addr:** Professor, University of California Los Angeles, 757 Westwood Plz, Los Angeles, CA 90095-8358, **Business Phone:** (310)301-6800.

### COLLINS, JAMES H.

Executive director. **Personal:** Born Feb 1, 1946, Moline, IL; son of Alphonso and Mattie Pennington; married Karen J Raebel; children: James Jr, Kimberly, Candace, Anthony & Kevin. **Educ:** St Ambrose Col, BA, sociol, 1969. **Career:** John Deere 1968-71; Proj Now Comt Action Agency, exec dir, 1968-71; John Deere, indust rels rep, 1971-74, EEO, coordr, 1974-75, mgr prsnl, 1975-83; Iowa Civil Rights Comn, comnr, 1989-92; E Moline, gen laborer; Parts Distrib Ctr, personnel mgr; Deere & Co, dir community rels, currently; St Ambrose Univ, proj diversity, fundraising & stud enrichment activites, currently; Ill QC Chamber Com, pres, 1995-96; Corp Citizenship Ctr Excellence, dir; John Deere Found, pres, currently. **Orgs:** Quad Cities Merit Employ Coun; Iowa Human Rights Comn; Quad Cities United Way; Quad Cities Coun Crime & Delinq; Human Rights & Employ Practices Comm; Bus Adv Coun, Ill Dept Rehab Serv; Iowa Civil Rights Com; Pres, John Deere Found; St Ambrose Univ; Genesis Med Ctr; educ task force mem, QC Vision Future, 1988; Diversity Work Group; pres, Serv Automation Unit Alumni Asn, 1991-95; QC Econ Develop Group, 2000-07; Community Found Great River Bend; bd mem, bus consult classroom, Jr Achievement Heartland; educ comt & exec comt mem, Quad Cities Br Nat Asn Advan Colored People. **Home Addr:** 2706 E 28 Ct, Davenport, IA 52803. **Business Addr:** Director, St Ambrose University, 518 W Locust St, Davenport, IA 52803, **Business Phone:** (563)333-6000.

### COLLINS, JEFFREY G.

Judge. **Educ:** Northwestern Univ, BA, 1981; Howard Univ Sch Law, JD, 1984. **Career:** Bell & Hudson, Detroit, law clerk, 1984, assoc, 1984-87; Law Offices Jeffrey G Collins, Detroit, atty, 1987-92; Detroit Recorders Ct, judge, 1994-98; Wayne State Law Sch, adj prof, 1995-2000; Wayne County Circuit Ct, judge, 1998, Mich Ct Appeals, judge, 1998-2001; Eastern Dist Mich, us atty, 2001-04; Foley & Lardner LLP, Detroit, partner, 2004-07; White Collar Criminal Defense Pract, head, currently; Phifer & White PC, Detroit, shareholder, currently; Collins & Collins PC, Detroit, partner, 2008-. **Orgs:** Bd dir, Neighborhood Serv Orgn; Mentor, Man to Man Prog Paul Robeson Acad; Past Pres, Asn Black Judges Mich; Am Bar Asn Lectr; Wayne County Chap Mich Leadership Develop; deacon, Plymouth United Church Christ; chmn, Wayne Co Criminal Advocacy Prog. **Honors/Awds:** Mich Lawyer of the Year, Mich Lawyers Weekly, 2003; Damon J Keith Community Spirit Award, Wolverine Bar Found, 2003; Founder's Award Outstanding Achievement, Nat Black Prosecutors Asn, 2004; Named a Michigan "Super Lawyer", Law & Politics Media Inc, 2006, 2007; D Augustus Straker Bar Asn Trailblazer Award, 2006. **Special Achievements:** One of the nation's top African-Am attys, Black Enterprise Mag, 2003; Published, Congress Passes Internet Gambling Legislation Aimed at the Banks; Coordination is Essential. **Business Addr:** Head, Shareholder, Phifer & White PC, 1274 Libr Suite 500, Detroit, MI 48226.

### COLLINS, DR. JOANN RUTH

School administrator. **Personal:** Born Nashville, TN; married John H; children: John K & Guy R. **Educ:** Mich State Univ, BS, psychol, 1971, MA, educ psychol, 1973, PhD, admin higher educ. **Career:** Lansing Community Col, adj prof, 2002-; Dept Civil Serv, State Mich, women's training officer; Mich State Univ, coord col work study prog; Breckinridge Job Corps Ctr KY, dir, family servs, dir & nursery & kindergarten; Collins & Assocs Inc, pres. **Orgs:** Black Fac & Admin, Mich State Univ, 1973; women's steering com, Mich State Univ, 1973; bd dir, Lansing Sr Citizens Inc, 1974-76; adv com bus & off Educ Clubs, Mich HS, 1974-; pres, Nat Asn Fin Assistance Minority Stud, 1974-; Nat Task Force Stud Aid Probs. **Home Addr:** 4109 Lowcroft, Lansing, MI 48910.

### COLLINS, JOANNE MARCELLA

Banker, activist. **Personal:** Born Aug 29, 1935, Kansas City, MO; daughter of William and Mary Frances Porter; married Robert Lawrence; children: Jerri Ann & Francis Damont; married Robert Lawrence. **Educ:** Kans Univ, attended 1955; Stephens Col, BA, 1988; Baker Univ, MS, 1990; St Louis Univ, cert; Weaver Sch Real Estate, sales & property mgt. **Career:** Univ Kans Med Ctr, Clendenning Med Libr, libr clerk, 1955-58; Robert Hughes & Co Real Estate, agt, 1958-62; US Post Off, postal clerk, 1960-63; Wheatley Provident Hosp, Greater Kans City Baptist & Community Hosp Asn, admin asst, 1964-72; US Dept Com, Metrop Kanssa City, supvr dicennial census, 1970-71; Kans City, Mo, city coun woman, 1974-; Halls Crown Ctr, Retail Sales Div, 1973-75; Conn Mutual Life Ins Co, assoc, 1977-79; United Mo Bank Kans, NA, vpres; US Dept Housing & Urban Develop, community builder fel. **Orgs:** Salvation Army, Greater Kans City Chap, Adult Rehab Ctr; life mem, Nat Asn Advan Colored People; Delta Sigma Theta; Urban League Greater Kans City; St Paul AME Zion Church; Womens Pub Serv Network; adv bd & pres, Emily Taylors Women Resource; bd dir, Liberty Memorial Asn; Miss Capital Punishment Resource Ctr; adv bd, United Minority Media Asn; Urban Youth Corps; Womens Leadership Fountain Comt; Womens Pub Serv Network; Fifth Cong Dist Republican Club; Soroptimist Int Inc; Financial Women Int; Ethnic Enrichment Comn; Avila Col Sch Nursing; Stephens Col Alumnae Asn; chairperson, Mo Adv Comt; bd dir, Goodwill Industs; bd dir, March Dimes; bd dir, Salvation Army; bd dir, Truman Med Ctr; bd dir, Vis Nurses Asn-Kans City Chap; Mo Fedn Republican Women; adv trustee, St Josephs Hosp; Nat Coun Negro Women; Mo State Adv Comn US Comn Civil Rights; bd dir, Women Munic Govt; chair, United Way Wyandotte County Inc, currently. **Home Addr:** 4030 Bellefontaine Ave, Kansas City, MO 64130, **Home Phone:** (816)861-6604. **Business Addr:** Chair, United Way of Wyandotte County Inc, 434 Minnesota Ave, Kansas City, MO 66117, **Business Phone:** (913)371-3674.

### COLLINS, KENNETH L.
Lawyer, executive. **Personal:** Born Aug 23, 1933, El Centro, CA; married Beverly Jean Sherman; children: Kevin & Leslie. **Educ:** Univ Calif, Los Angeles, BA, 1959; Univ Calif, Los Angeles, JD, 1971. **Career:** Fed Pub Defenders Off, dep pub defender, 1972-75; San Fernando Valley Juv Hall, actg dir; La Co, probation officer, 1957-68; RK Law Group, lawyer, currently. **Orgs:** Langston Law Club; Calif Attys Criminal Justice; Calif State Bar; chmn bd dir, Black Law J; past pres, Kappa Alpha Psi Upsion, 1957-58; co-founder, Black Law J; BarDc Ct Appeals. **Honors/Awds:** Chancellors Award, Univ Calif, Los Angeles, Calif, 1971. **Home Addr:** 125 S Vt Ave, Los Angeles, CA 90004, **Home Phone:** (213)387-7300. **Business Addr:** Lawyer, RK Law Group, 1710 N La Brea Ave 2nd Fl, Los Angeles, CA 90046, **Business Phone:** (213)995-2222.

### COLLINS, LAVERNE VINES
Government official. **Personal:** Born Feb 3, 1947, Livorno; daughter of Thomas Fulton Vines (deceased) and Myrtle Elizabeth Coy Vines (deceased); married Alfred; children: Alfred (deceased), Anthony & McAllister. **Educ:** Univ Mich, Ann Arbor, MI, 1966; Western Mich Univ, Kalamazoo, MI, BA, 1968, MA, 1971. **Career:** Western Mich Univ, Kalamazoo, Mich, dean students staff, 1969-71; US Census Bureau, Suitland, Md, statistician, 1971-72; Off Mgt & Budget, Washington, DC, statistician, 1972-82; US Census Bur, Atlanta, Ga, survey statistician, 1982-83, Los Angeles, Calif, asst regional dir, 1983-85, Philadelphia, Pa, regional dir, 1985-91, Washington, DC, supervisory social sci analyst, 1992-94, chief pub info off, 1994-99, asst to the assoc dir commun, 1999. **Orgs:** Alpha Kappa Alpha Sorority, 1965-; bd dir, Budget Fed Credit Union, 1980-82; Am Statist Asn, 1973-83; Am Pop Asn, 1985-86; bd dir, United Way Southeastern PA, 1987-90; Coalition 100 Black Women Southern Nj, 1989-90. **Home Addr:** 208 Weymouth St, Upper Marlboro, MD 20774, **Home Phone:** (301)249-3490. **Business Addr:** DC.

### COLLINS, DR. LENORA W.
Consultant, special education teacher. **Personal:** Born Feb 25, 1925, Fayette, MS; married Joe H. **Educ:** Xavier Univ, BS, 1946; Gov State Univ, MA, 1974; Univ Sarasota, EdD, 1977; DePaul Univ, advan study. **Career:** Chicago Bd Educ, home econs teacher, 1948-54; Supvr Caseworker, 1959-61; Supvr Home Econs, 1962-63; Bur Home Econs Cook County Dept Pub Aid, asst chief, 1964-73; Dept Pub Aid St Ill, econs consult; Lorman Community Develop Orgn, Lorman, Miss, exec dir. **Orgs:** Chmn, Health & Welfare Sect Ill Home Econ Asn, 1968-69; pres, Chicago Home Econ Asn, 1970-71; secy, Jefferson Co Hosp, 1979-80; life mem, Am Home Econs Asn; life mem, Ill Home Econs Asn; vice chmn, Human Serv Sect; Chicago Nutrit Asn; Am Pub Welfare Asn; bd mem, Chicago Met Housing Coun Tenant Proj; trustee, Jefferson Co Hosp; Nat Negro Bus & Prof Women's Club; Delta Sigma Theta; Wacker Neighborhood Asn Chicago Urban League; Nat Asn Advan Colored People; bd mem, jefferson Co Sch Dist. **Honors/Awds:** Recipient Finer Womanhood Award, Zeta Phi Beta, 1967; Silver Jubilee & Alumnus Award, Xavier Univ, 1971; Listed in Chicago Almanac & Ref Book, 1973. **Home Addr:** PO Box 308, Lorman, MS 39096.

### COLLINS, LEROY ANTHONY, JR.
Government official, president (organization). **Personal:** Born Jan 13, 1950, Norfolk, VA; son of Leroy and Thelma Taylor; children: Kisten & Lyndsey. **Educ:** Howard Univ, attended 1970; Rutgers Univ, BS, 1973; Temple Univ Sch Bus, attended 1981. **Career:** City Newark, NJ, asst budget dir, 1974-78; City Miami, Fla, asst city mgr, 1978-80; Pa Mutual Life Ins Co, sr investment analyst, 1980-83; City Tampa, Fla, mgr econ develop, 1983-86; City St Peters burg, Fla, dir econ develop; Promethens Innovations Inc, pres. **Orgs:** Chmn, Black Bus Investment Bd, 1988-; bd mem, Oper PAR; bd mem, Suncoasters; Fla Export Fin Authority; Tampa Bay Defense Transition Task Force; Enterprise Fla Capital Devt Bd; bd dir, Bennett Bank Pinellas County; Enterprise Fla Int Trade & Econ Develop Bd; bd mem, vice chair mkt comn, Tampa Bay Partnership. **Home Addr:** 11460 7th St E, Treasure Island, FL 33706. **Business Addr:** President, Prometheus Innovations Inc, 11295 Gulf Blvd, St. Petersburg, FL 33706.

### COLLINS, MARK ANTHONY
Football player, football coach, executive. **Personal:** Born Jan 16, 1964, San Bernardino, MO. **Educ:** Calif State Univ Fullerton, BA, mass commun & media studies, 1986. **Career:** Football player (retired), coach, executive; New York Giants, defensive back, left corner back, 1986-93; Kans City Chiefs, left corner back, 1994, free safety, 1995-96; Green Bay Packers, 1997; Seattle Seahawks, 1998; 2XChamp Sports LLC, pres & chief exec officer, 2008-; MidAmerica Nazarene Univ, Sec Coach, 2011. **Honors/Awds:** Defensive Player of the Year, 1985; All-NFL Team, Sports Illustrated, 1993; Super Bowl champion. **Business Addr:** Football Coach, MidAmerica Nazarene University, 2030 E Col Way, Olathe, KS 66062, **Business Phone:** (913)782-3750.

**COLLINS, MO.** **See Obituaries Section.**

### COLLINS, DR. PATRICIA HILL
Educator. **Personal:** Born May 1, 1948, Philadelphia, PA; married Roger L; children: Valerie. **Educ:** Brandeis Univ, AB, 1969, PhD, 1984; Harvard Univ, MAT, 1970. **Career:** Harvard Univ, Teacher, 1970-72; Harvard U TTT Prog, teacher, curric spec, 1970-73; Design Progs Inc, Educ Consult, 1972-73; St Joseph Community Sch, curric specialist, 1973-76; Tufts Univ, dir African Am Ctr 1976-80; Univ Cincinnati, from asst prof to assoc prof African-Am Studies, 1982-94, assoc prof social, 1988, prof, 1994-2005, Charles Phelps Taft Distinguished prof, 1996-2005, Taft prof social, 2003, Dept African Am Stud, chmn, 2003, head dept african am studies; PHC Educ Serv Inc, pres, 2002-; Charles Phelps Taft Distinguished Emer, 2005-; Univ Md, Col Pk, Wilson Elkins prof, sociol, 2005-06, Distinguished Univ Prof, 2006-. **Orgs:** Chmn, Minority Fel Prog Comm, 1986-89; vpres, Great Rivers Girl Scouts Coun, 1992-94; Pres, Am Sociol Asn, 2008-2009. **Special Achievements:** Hon doctorate of humane letters from Arcadia C. John Jay C. of Criminal Justice, Duquesne U. C. of Wooster. **Home Addr:** , OH. **Business Addr:** Distinguished University Professor, University of Maryland, 3834 Campus Dr, College Park, MD 20742, **Business Phone:** (301)405-7707.

### COLLINS, PAUL
Artist. **Personal:** Born Dec 11, 1936, Muskegon, MI. **Career:** Paintings, drawings & book: Black Portrait African Journey, 1969-71; Paintings C Harlem, 1976-78; Great Beautiful Black Women, 1976-78; Joseph P Kennedy Found, spec olympics drawings & paintings, 1976-79; Famous Moments Black Am Hist, mural, 1978-80; paintings Working Americans, 1980-83; mural & book: Gerald R Ford, A Man in Perspective, 1976; Paintings: Voices of Israel, 1986-89; The National Physical Fitness Poster for the Carter administration and the NASA space shuttle emblem; 40th Anniversary of Israel Mural, pres Ford Mural; Collins Fine Art, artist & painter, currently. **Orgs:** Bd trustee, Robeson Players, 1972-80; Am Indian Movement, 1972-84; adv bd, John F Kennedy Ctr Performance Arts, 1976-80; co-chmn, Western Mich United Negro Col Fund, 1989-90; Martin Luther King Jr. Non-Violence Ctr; Arts Coun Grand Rapids, Mich. **Honors/Awds:** Mead Book Award, 1972; People's Choice Award, Am Painters Paris, 1976; Arts Council Award, Grand Rapids Arts Coun, 1979; Black Achievement Award, 1979; Tadlow Fine Art Award; Golden Centaur of Italy Ceba Award of Excellence; Peoples Choice Award. **Special Achievements:** Featured in 20 Outstanding Figure Painters & How They Work, 1979; designer of the Martin Luther King Peace Prize Medal, 1979-80; First artist from the United States invited to participate in the International Arts Festival in Sarajevo in 1998. **Home Addr:** , MI. **Business Addr:** Artist, Figure & Cultural Painter, Paul Collins Fine Art, 146 Monroe Center Suite 146, Grand Rapids, MI 49503, **Business Phone:** (616)742-2000.

### COLLINS, REV. DR. PAUL L.
Clergy, executive director. **Personal:** Born Apr 19, 1931, Shreveport, LA; son of Paul (deceased) and Willie Mae Adams (deceased); married Shirley Alexander; children: Paula & Darryl. **Educ:** Southern Univ, BA & MEd, hist & sociol, 1958; George Wash Univ, EdD, col stud coun & personnel serv, 1976. **Career:** Carver Jr High Sch, 1958-59; BTW High Sch, prof mil Sci, 1959-62; Wash Jr High Sch, teacher, 1962-65; Roosevelt High Sch, dir guid, 1965-68; Off Human Rights, asso exec int rels, govt res policy & anal-regist lobbyist Prof Devel Prog; Non White Concerns, dir; Wash Tech Inst, asso prof, 1968-71; Am Asn Coun & Devel, assoc exec, 1970-83; prof counr, 1978-; Nazarene Outpost Ministries, founder, exec dir, pres & chief exec officer, 1987-; CE Int, owner, 2011-. **Orgs:** Pres, Asn SpecialistsGroup Work, 1985-86; pres, Capitol Hill Kiwanis Club, 1981-82; chmn bd, Prepare Our Youth, 1987-; dean, Mt Bethel Baptist Educnl Cong, Nat Baptist Conv, 1984-92; assoc pastor, New Order Christia N Fel, 1987-90; community adv bd dir, Wash CTRAging Servs, 1988-; pres, DC Ment Health Counsrs Asn, 1992-93; asst to chief prot chaplin, DC Gen Hosp, 1989-92; cert crisis intervener, ABECI, 1990; Am Evangelistic Asn, 1992-; field missionary, Mt Bethel Baptist Asn, 1994-. **Honors/Awds:** Outstanding Teacher Award, 1960; Outstanding Leadership Award, 1962; Outstanding Leadership Voc Guidance, 1970; Christian Leadership, 1967; United Nations USA Award, 1971-72; Nat Counr Cert, Nat Bd Cert Counr, 1983-88; Certificate Excellence Spiritual Aims, 1988, Outstanding Club Leadership Award, 1982, Capitol Hill Kiwanis Club; Clin Pastoral Edu Cert, 1990. **Home Addr:** , DC. **Business Addr:** President, Chief Executive Officer, Nazarene Outpost Ministries, 111 Rhode Island Ave NW, Washington, DC 20001, **Business Phone:** (202)832-6174.

### COLLINS, ROBERT FREDERICK
Judge. **Personal:** Born Jan 27, 1931, New Orleans, LA; son of Frederick and Irma Anderson; married Aloha M; children: Francesca McManus, Lisa Ann, Nanette C & Robert A. **Educ:** Dillard Univ, BA, 1951; La State Univ Law Sch, LLB, 1954; La State Univ, JD; Univ Nev Nat Judge Col, 1973. **Career:** Augustine Collins Smith & Warren New Orleans, partner, 1956-59; Southern Univ Law Sch, Baton Rouge, La, instr, 1959-61, 1981-90; Collins Douglas & Elie New Orleans, sr partner, 1960-72; New Orleans Police Dept, asst city atty, legal adv, 1967-69; Traffic Ct New Orleans, judge ad-hoc, 1969-72; State La, asst bar examr, 1970-78; Housing Authority New Orleans, atty, 1971-72; Criminal Dist Ct Orleans Parish, La, judge magistrate sect, 1972-78; US Dist Ct, Eastern Dist La, judge, 1978-93. **Orgs:** Trustee, Loyola Univ, 1977-83; La Bar Asn; Am Bar Asn; Alpha Phi Alpha; Sigma Pi Phi; Phi Alpha Delta; pres, Louis A Martinet Legal Soc, 1959-60; reg dir, Nat Bar Asn, 1964-65; Am Judicature Soc; 5th Circuit Dist Judges Asn. **Honors/Awds:** Honor Soc, Alpha Kappa Mu, 1950; Passed Bar, La, 1954; LLD, Dillard Univ, 1979. **Home Addr:** 4840 St Bernard Ave, New Orleans, LA 70122, **Home Phone:** (504)283-9601. **Business Addr:** Judge, US District Court, Rm C-151 500 Poydras St, New Orleans, LA 70130, **Business Phone:** (504)589-7600.

### COLLINS, RODNEY
Manager. **Career:** Seligman Growth & Income Team, investment assoc, 1992; Seligman Income Fund, co-portfolio mgr, 1996; J & W Seligman & Co Inc, co-portfolio mgr, 2001, sr vpres, vpres, investment mgr, currently. **Business Addr:** Senior Vice President, Vice President, J & W Seligman & Co Inc, 100 Pk Ave, New York, NY 10017-5510, **Business Phone:** (212)850-1864.

### COLLINS, ROSECRAIN
Dentist. **Personal:** Born Feb 14, 1929, Nashville, TN; married Elizabeth Ann Terry; children: Michelle & Adrienne. **Educ:** Tenn State Univ, BS, 1952; Meharry Med Col, DDS, 1958. **Career:** Martin Luther King Health Ctr, dentist, 1971-74; Kennedy Ryan & Monigal Realtors Asn, 1973-; Chicago Child Care Soc, dentist, 1976-; Chicago Dept Pub Aid, dent consult, 1977-; pvt pract, currently. **Orgs:** Lincoln Dent Soc, 1959-; Ill Dent Soc, 1959-; Am Dent Soc, 1959-; Nat Dent Soc, 1959-; Dent Health Screening Chicago Pub Sch, 1961-63; Treas, Great Western Investment Ltd, 1969-; treas, Chicago Dent Soc, 1970-74; dir, Int Sporting Club, 1974; Acad Gen Dent, 1974-; partner, Forestry Recycling Mill, 1975-. **Honors/Awds:** Citation, pub serv City Chicago, 1962-63. **Home Addr:** 6722 S Euclid Ave, Chicago, IL 60649, **Home Phone:** (773)684-2873. **Business Addr:** Dentist, 1525 E 53rd St Suite 904, Chicago, IL 60615-4572, **Business Phone:** (773)752-2300.

### COLLINS, TESSIL JOHN
Manager, television producer. **Personal:** Born Aug 29, 1952, Boston, MA; son of Tessil A and Evelyn A Gill; children: Dionna. **Educ:** Boston Latin Sch, attended 1971; Tufts Univ, BA, Eng, 1975; Boston Univ, exec prog cert, small bus develop prog, 1985; Nat Asn Broadcasters Educ Foundations, broadcast leadership training prog, 2008. **Career:** Boston Pub Sch, sr coordr, support/career & tech educ; Madison Pk Tech Voc High Sch, instr, commun arts & tv prod, 1984-; Beantown Music, nat dir promotions & mkt; RCA & A&M & Arista Rec, field merchandiser, 1981-83; WILD Radio, Boston, acct exec, 1975, 1980-81; Rep Melvin H King, campaign mgr, 1978-79; WBCN Radio, acct exec, 1978-80; WBZ Radio, dir pub serv, producer, 1973-78; Sun-Music, producer; Spectrum Broadcasting Corp, owner, 1984-, pres & chief exec officer, currently; Internet Radio Sta, Sun Music.net, exec producer, currently; Spec Collections & Arch, res assoc, Healy Libr UMass Boston, Roxbury Hist Blog. Videos: "I'm Different, You're Different, We're All Okay", Tufts Univ, 1985; "Mrs Black Boston Pageant", 1986; "It's Christmastime Again", recorded by TSOC, 1994; "Beat, "A St Smarts Collab Video Proj, Boston Police Dept, 1995; "Voice", WBPS-AM, Boston; one six Greater Boston "Unsung Heroes", Tribune Broadcasting, WB56 Boston & BlackVoices.com, 2002; "My Roxbury"; Atlantic Rec, northeast prom mgr; Boston Pub High Sch, sr coordr, Dorchester Acad, dir univ & bus partnerships, extended learning & grant mgt. **Orgs:** Prince Hall Grand Lodge F & AM; bd mem, Dimock COT HTH CTR, Proj Africa; bd mem, Berklee Col Music Community Adv Comt; bd mem, vpres, Ford Hall Forum; pres, trustee, Roxbury Crossing Hist Trust, currently. **Honors/Awds:** Certificate Media Technology, MA Dept Educ Div Occup Educ, 1985; position at Beantown, Black Enterp May & Feb, 1984; Grand Prize, Fla Citrus Comn Music Video Competition, 1987. **Home Addr:** 1575 Tremont St Suite 1202, Boston, MA 02120, **Home Phone:** (617)739-3552. **Business Addr:** President, Chief Executive Officer, Spectrum Broadcasting Corp, PO Box 201045, Boston, MA 02120, **Business Phone:** (617)287-8770.

### COLLINS, REV. DR. WILLIAM, JR.
Clergy. **Personal:** Born Jul 3, 1924, St. Louis, MO; married Margaret Elizabeth Brown; children: Sylvia, Deirdre, William & III. **Educ:** St Louis Univ, BS, 1956, PhD, 1973; Colgate Rochester Div Sch, BD, 1960, MDiv, 1972; Univ Rochester, MEd, 1960; Eastern Nebr Christian Col, DD, 1972. **Career:** Mo Dept Welfare St Louis, caseworker, 1948-51; US Postal, employee, 1951-56; Second Baptist Church Leroy NY, stud pastor, 1959-60; Antioch Baptist Church St Louis, minister christian educ, 1960-61, pastor, 1961-2010, pastor emer, currently; Blue field State Col, dir pub rel & asst registr, 1961. **Orgs:** Eagle Scout, 1939; Alpha Phi Alpha Frat, 1947; Preaching Mission Am Baptist El Salvador & Nicaragua Latin Am, 1966; bd, Health & Hosp St Louis, 1968-; Landmark & Urban Design Comn St Louis, 1968-72; bd mem, Annie Malone C Home St Louis, 1970-; bd, St Louis Munic Nurses, 1970-; Adult Welfare Comns St Louis, 1970-; Am Baptist Conv; Task Force; Int Ministries Africa, 1971-; Missionary Involvement Tour; Am Baptist W Africa, 1972; bd trustee, St Louis Jr Col Dist elected six yr term, 1975. **Business Addr:** Pastor Emeritus, The Antioch Baptist Church, 4213 W North Market, St. Louis, MO 63113, **Business Phone:** (314)535-1110.

**COLLINS, WILLIAM EARL.** **See COLLINS, BOOTSY.**

### COLLINS-EAGLIN, DR. JAN THERESA (JAN COLLINS-EAGLIN)
Counselor, psychologist. **Personal:** Born Dec 2, 1950, New York, NY; daughter of John E and Naomi Fraser; married Fulton; children: Christopher, Jennifer & Jessica. **Educ:** Calif State Univ, Dominguez Hills, BA, 1977; Univ Mich, Ann Arbor, MA, MS, 1980, EdS, 1980, PhD, 1983. **Career:** Univ Mich, Ann Arbor, Mich, lectr, 1983-85; Eastern Mich Univ, Ypsilanti, Mich, psychologist, 1985-87, coordr, 1987-90, prof, 1990-; Wayne State Univ, dir coun servs, dir stud affairs; Mich State Univ, Dept Multi Ethnic Coun Ctr Alliance, dir, currently. **Orgs:** Alpha Kappa Alpha Sorority, 1975-; Am Psychol Asn, 1983-; Coun Ctr, Mich State Univ; Acad Success Ctr; Educ Accessibility Serv; Mich Col Personnel Asn, 1987-; Links, 1988-; regional found Offr, Jack & Jill Am, 1988-. **Honors/Awds:** Nat Inst Ment Health Fel, 1977-81; Am Psychol Asn Fel, 1978-82; Res & grants col retention black studs: Select Stud Support Servs, State Mich, 1987-90; Summer Incentive Prog, Dept Labor, 1987-90. **Home Addr:** 2610 Arbor Rd, Ann Arbor, MI 48197, **Home Phone:** (313)485-6819. **Business Addr:** Director, Michigan State University, 207 Stud Serv Bldg, East Lansing, MI 48824, **Business Phone:** (517)355-8270.

**COLLINS-GRANT, EARLEAN**
State government official. **Personal:** Born Sep 4, 1937, Rolling Fork, MS; married John; children: Dwarrye. **Educ:** Univ Ill, Chicago, BS, soc, childhood develop; Crane Jr Col, real estate, lib arts. **Career:** Collins Realty & Ins Agency, self employed, 1969-72; State IL, Dept C & Family Servs, soc serv admin, 1972-76; State IL Gen Assembly, state sen, 1976-98; Cook Co, Dist I, comnr, 1998-. **Orgs:** Westside Bus Asn; Nat Asn Soc Workers; Nat Conf State Leg; Conf Women Leg; Intergovernmental Coop Coun; comt chair, Bus & Econ Develop; Pub Health; Family Ct & Juv Detention Ctr; bd mem, Forest Preserve Dist; vice chairperson, Labor & Com Comt; Dem Leader Exec Comt. **Special Achievements:** First African American female to be elected to the Illinois Senate, 1976. **Home Addr:** 5939 W Race Ave, Chicago, IL 60644, **Home Phone:** (312)287-7197. **Business Addr:** Commissioner, Cook County, 118 N Clark St Rm 567, Chicago, IL 60602-1304, **Business Phone:** (312)603-4566.

**COLLONS, FERRIC JASON**
Football player. **Personal:** Born Dec 4, 1969, Belleville, IL. **Educ:** Univ Calif, criminal justice. **Career:** Football player (retired); New Eng Patriots, defensive end, 1995, left defensive end, 1996-98, 1999. **Special Achievements:** Films: 1996 AFC Championship Game, 1997; Super Bowl XXXI, 1997.

**COLLYMORE, DR. EDWARD L.**
Educator. **Personal:** Born Jan 5, 1938, Cambridge, MA; son of Eulah M Johnson and Percival E; married Marcia L Burnett; children: Sandra Coleman & Edward Jr. **Educ:** Villanova Univ, BS, econ, 1959, MA, coun, 1971; Univ Pa, EdD, admin, 1984. **Career:** Educator (retired); Villanova Univ, Off Soc Action Prog, staff, 1960, Off Multicultural Affairs, exec dir, 2005; Cambridge Pub Sch, substitute teacher, 1963; Liberty Mutual Ins Co, casualty underwriter, 1963-66; Third Dist Ct Cambridge; juv probation officer, 1966-69. **Orgs:** Comt Action Agency Del, CO. **Home Addr:** 715 Polo Rd, Bryn Mawr, PA 19010, **Home Phone:** (610)525-7577.

**COLON, HARRY LEE**
Football player, football coach. **Personal:** Born Feb 14, 1969, Kansas City, KS. **Educ:** Univ Mo, grad; Stanford Grad Sch Bus, BS, sociol, MS, sports mgt. **Career:** Football player (retired), coach, trainer; New Eng Patriots, strong safety, 1991; Detroit Lions, free safety, 1992-94, defensive back, 1997; Jacksonville Jaguars, strong safety, 1995; John H. Reagan High Sch, athletics dept, head football coach & athletic dir, currently; Positive Coaching Alliance, lead trainer, currently. **Honors/Awds:** Most Valuable Player. **Business Addr:** Lead Trainer, Positive Coaching Alliance, 1001 N Rengstorff Ave Suite 100, Mountain View, CA 94043, **Business Phone:** (866)725-0024.

**COLSTON, DR. FREDDIE C.**
Executive, educator, association executive. **Personal:** Born Mar 28, 1936, Gretna, FL; son of Henry Bill and Willie Mae; married Doris Marie; children: Deirdre & Charisse. **Educ:** More house Col, BA, political science, 1959; Atlanta Univ, MA, 1966; OH State Univ, PhD, 1972. **Career:** Educator (retired); OH State Univ, Dept Polit Sci, teaching assoc, 1968-71; Southern Univ, Baton Rouge, LA, fel, 1971-72, assoc prof, polit sci, 1972-73; Univ Detroit, MI, assoc prof, polit sci, 1973-76; Dillard Univ, New Orleans, LA, chmn, div soc sci, 1976-78; Delta Col, Univ Cent Mich, asst prof, polit sci, 1978-80; Exec Sem Ctr, US Off Personal Mgt, assoc dir, 1980-87; TN State Univ, prof & cood grad studies, 1987-88; NC Cent Univ, prof & cood grad studies, 1988-89; NC Cent Univ, dir pub admin prog, 1989-91; GA Southwestern State Univ, Dept Hist & Polit Sci, GA, prof, 1992-97; Ft Valley State univ, polit sci fac. **Orgs:** Omega Psi Phi Frat, 1956; Pi Sigma Alpha Nat Pol Sci Hon Soc, 1958-; Alpha Phi Gamma Nat Hon Soc, 1958-; Am Polit Sci Asn, 1968-; Ctr Study Presidency, 1976-; Am Soc Publ Admin, 1983-; bd mgmt, YMCA Metrop, Detroit, 1976; Govt Subcmt Task Force 2000, Midland, Mich, 1979; Nat Forum Black Publ Admin, 1984-; Am Asn Higher Educ, 1987-; Am Mgt Asn, 1988; Oak Ridge Conv & Visitors Bur bd. **Honors/Awds:** Mr. Psi, Psi Chap, Omega Psi Phi, 1959; hon fel, John F. Kennedy Presidential Library, 1986; Outstanding Fac Award, Kappa Delta Sor, 1995; Superior Service Award, 1996 & 1997; Outstanding Fac Award, South western State Univ, 1997. **Special Achievements:** Author of numerous books. **Home Addr:** 116 Downing Dr, Oak Ridge, TN 37830, **Home Phone:** (865)482-4152.

**COLSTON, DR. WANDA M.**
Administrator, executive. **Educ:** Shaw Univ, BS; Univ DC, MS; Howard Univ, PhD. **Career:** Norfolk State Univ, assoc vpres acad affairs; Univ Md Eastern Shore, Off Pres, proj dir, exec vpres & sr vpres, currently. **Orgs:** Chair, Univ Strategic Planning Comt, Univ Md Eastern Shore. **Business Addr:** Executive Vice President, Senior Vice President, University Of Maryland Eastern Shore, 1 Backbone Rd, Princess Anne, MD 21853, **Business Phone:** (410)651-6410.

**COLTER, MIKE (MIKE RANDAL COLTER)**
Actor. **Personal:** Born Aug 26, 1976, Columbia, NC; son of Eddie Lee Sr; married Iva; children: 1. **Educ:** Univ SC, BA; Rutgers Univ Mason Gross Sch Arts, MFA, 2001; Benedict Col. **Career:** Actor, 2001-. Film: Million Dollar Baby, 2004; Brooklyn Lobster, 2005; And Then Came Love, 2007; Salt, 2010; Men in Black 3, 2012; Zero Dark Thirty, 2012; America Is Still the Place, 2015. Stage: A Soldier's Play, Second Stage Theater, New York City, 2005; Drunken City, Playwrights Horizon, 2008. Television: Silver Bells, 2005; Solving Charlie, 2009; Taking Chance, 2009; Ringer, 2011-12; The Surgeon General, 2013; American Horror Series, 2013-14; Halo: Nightfall, 2014; The Following, 2013-15; The Good Wife, CBS, 2010-15; Jessica Jones, 2015; Agent X, 2015; Luke Cage, 2016-.

**COLVIN, ALEX, II**
Educator. **Personal:** Born Nov 17, 1946, Birmingham, AL; son of Alex and Novella; children: Atiba, Jawanza, Kimba, Alex III, Marc & Taylor. **Educ:** Univ Calif, Los Angeles, 1974; Univ DC, 1978. **Career:** DC Gov, chief boiler inspector, 1972-. **Orgs:** Instr, Nat Asn Power Engrs, 1974-; Am Soc Mech Engrs, 1981-; nat bd, Boiler & Pressure Vessel Inspectors, 1993-; rec secy, Nat Asn Black Scuba Divers, 1999; pres, UAS, 2003. **Home Addr:** 1183 Neal St NE, Washington, DC 20002-3821, **Home Phone:** (202)388-8137. **Business Addr:** Chief Boiler Inspector, District of Columbia Government, 941 N Capitol St NE, Washington, DC 20002, **Business Phone:** (202)442-4695.

**COLVIN, ALONZA JAMES**
Government official, publishing executive. **Personal:** Born Jul 8, 1931, Union Springs, AL; married Billie J Williams; children: Judy Webb, James E, Jimmie, Chris (Deceased), Maxwell Barrington, Mark & Elizabeth Buckley. **Educ:** GED only. **Career:** Gen Motors, gen labor, 1950-75; Saginaw Model Cities Inc, chmn, 1967-71; Valley Star News, ed-publ, 1967-73; Buena Vista Charter Twp, trustee, 1980. **Orgs:** Nat Newspaper Publ Asn, 1967-73; producer & dir, Autumn Leaves Pageant, 1967-73; bd dir, Police-Comn Rels Comn, 1970-83; vpres, Miss Saginaw County Pageant, 1970-; bd dir, Saginaw Econ Develop Corp, 1971-72; bd dir, Big Bros Saginaw, 1972-76. **Home Addr:** 2926 S Outer Dr, Saginaw, MI 48601-6988, **Home Phone:** (989)754-2905. **Business Addr:** Trustee, Buena Vista Charter Township, 1160 S Outer Dr, Saginaw, MI 48601, **Business Phone:** (989)754-6536.

**COLVIN, CEDRIC B.**
Government official, lawyer. **Personal:** Born Dec 1, 1962, Tuscaloosa, AL; son of Isaac and Mary. **Educ:** Univ Akron, BS/AAS, polit sci & govt, 1990; Univ Ala, JD, 1993. **Career:** Summit Co Presecutor's Off, atty, 1991; Ala Atty Gen Off, asst atty gen, 1993; Legal & Gen, atty, 1993-; Al St House, Off Atty Gen, atty, currently. **Orgs:** Proj Plus Adult Reading Prog, 1992-93; Partner's Educ, 1993-94; Boy Scouts, 1993; AL Bar Asn, Access to Legal Servs Comt, 1996-98, Task force Minority Participation, 1997-2000. **Home Addr:** 4001 Pickfair St, Montgomery, AL 36116. **Business Addr:** Attorney, Alabama State House, 501 Wash Ave, Montgomery, AL 36130-0152, **Business Phone:** (334)242-7300.

**COLVIN, DR. ERNEST J.**
Dentist. **Personal:** Born Jan 20, 1935, Chester, SC; son of Alex and Alberta Moffett; married Shirley Beard; children: Ernest J II. **Educ:** Morgan State Col, BS, biol, 1956; Howard Univ Sch Dent, DDS, 1968. **Career:** Dentist (retired); Howard Univ Sch Dent, adj fac, 1968-71; Colvin Ernest J Dr & Assocs, pvt pract, dentist. **Orgs:** Bd dir, Horseman's Benevolent Protective Asn, WV; Chi Delta Mu Frat; Am Dent Asn; financial secy, Md State Dent Asn; Baltimore City Dent Soc; Am Indodontic Soc; Am Dent Soc Anesthesiol; Am Soc Gen Dent; Kappa Alpha Psi Frat; Columbia Chap Jack & Jill Am Inc; Columbia Nat Asn Advan Colored People; Am Cancer Soc; Com Health Coun Baltimore City; Md State Racing Comn; bd dir, NW Baltimore Community Health Care; St Johns Evangelist Roman Cath Church; comn chmn, Md Racing Comn. **Home Addr:** 3700 Shady Lane, Glenwood, MD 21738-9539.

**COLVIN, DR. WILLIAM E.**
Educator, school administrator. **Personal:** Born May 27, 1930, Birmingham, AL; son of Lucius Will and Lucille White; married Regina A Bahner; children: Felicia Imre & Gracita Dawn. **Educ:** Ala State Univ, BA, 1951; Ind Univ, MA, 1960; Ill State Univ, PhD, 1971. **Career:** Stillman Col, Dept Art, prof & chair, 1958-69, chair, 2003-; Ill State Univ, dir ethnic studies, 1974-78, prof art, 1971-91; Eastern Ill Univ, prof art, 1987-, chair Afro studies, 1991-, dir afro am studies, 1991. **Orgs:** Rockefeller fel, 1973-74; Elected rep, US & Brazilian Mod Art Soc, 1981-; dir career prog, Ill Comn Black Concerns Higher Educ, 1983-; Nat Conf Artists; Nat Art Educ Asn; Phi Delta Kappa Hon Soc Educ. **Home Addr:** 507 N Grove St, Normal, IL 61761, **Home Phone:** (309)452-6849. **Business Addr:** Professor, Chairman, Stillman College, 3601 Stillman Blvd, Tuscaloosa, AL 35403, **Business Phone:** (205)349-4240.

**COLYER, DR. SHERYL LYNN**
Labor relations manager, labor activist. **Personal:** Born Dec 20, 1959, Portsmouth, VA; daughter of Joshua (deceased) and Lubertha Alexander. **Educ:** Howard Univ, Wash, DC, BS, psychol, 1981; Columbia Univ, NY, MA, orgn psychol, 1983; George Washington Univ, PhD, 1996. **Career:** Internal Revenue, Wash, DC, pers psychologist, 1983-84; Technol Appls Inc, Falls Church, Va, consult, 1984-85; Gen Motors, Ft Wayne, Ind, 1985-88, human resource specialist; Fed Home Loan Mortgage Corp, training & devel consult, 1988-90; Pepsico, KFC, Hanover, Md, div mgr, 1990-92; Hechinger Co, dir, 1992-95; George Washington Univ, mgt consult & adjunt instr, 1992-97; Independent mgt consult, 1995-97; US Retail & HNW; Citigroup Global Markets, managing dir & head admin, 1997-2008; Citigroup Asset Mgt, dir global human resources, 2006-08; Pfizer Pharmaceut, human resource leader, currently. **Orgs:** Pres, Alpha Chap, Delta Sigma Theta, 1980-81; Am Psychol Asn; Am Soc Training & Devel; Soc Indust & Orgn Psychol Inc; Am SocPersonnel Admin; Nat Asn Securities Dealers. **Honors/Awds:** Outstanding Young Women of Am, Ebony Magazine. **Special Achievements:** Listed among 100 Most Promising Black Women in Corp America, 1991. **Home Addr:** 135 W 70th St Suite 8H, New York, NY 10023, **Home Phone:** (212)291-3860. **Business Addr:** Human Resource Leader, Pfizer Pharmaceuticals, 235 E 42nd St, New York, NY 10017-5703, **Business Phone:** (914)690-6000.

**COMBS, DR. JULIUS V.**
President (organization), executive. **Personal:** Born Aug 6, 1931, Detroit, MI; son of Everlee Dennis and Julius; married Alice Ann Gaston; children: Kimberly A & Julius G. **Educ:** Wayne State Univ, BS, 1953, MD, 1958, Affilated Hosp, 1964; Am Bd Obstet-Gynec, dipl, 1967. **Career:** Executive (retired): Vincent & Combs Bldg Corp, pres; Wayne State Univ, Sch Med, clin asst, 1976; Omni Care Health Plan, dir, 1973, chmn emer; chmn bd, 1980-92, exec comt; Assoc Med Develop Corp, vpres, 1979-81; United Am Health Corp, chmn, chief exec officer; obstet & gynec pract; asst clin prof, 1996; Nat Healthcare Scholars Found, chmn (retired) & pres, currently. **Orgs:** Kappa Alpha Psi Fraternity; House Del NMA, 1967-; Detroit Med Soc; chmn, Region IV NMA, 1975-77; Am Fertil Soc; NMA; Detroit Med Soc; Mich State Med Soc; Wayne Co Med Soc; Am Asn Gyn Laparoscopists; Am Col Obstet-Gynec; Detroit Inst Arts comnr; Nat Asn Advan Colored People; bd mem, Music Hall Ctr Performing Arts; bd mem, Oakland Univ; bd mem, United Way Southeastern Mich; fel AGOG. **Home Addr:** 200 Riverfront Dr Apt 17k, Detroit, MI 48226, **Home Phone:** (313)393-5477. **Business Addr:** Managing Director, President, National Healthcare Scholars Foundation, 300 River Pl Suite 4950, Detroit, MI 48207, **Business Phone:** (313)393-4549.

**COMBS, SAMUEL, III (SAM COMBS)**
Executive. **Personal:** married Rita; children: 3. **Educ:** Okla State Univ, BS, indust engineering, 1980; Univ Mich Bus Sch, exec prog, 1999; Harvard Univ. **Career:** Okla Nat Gas Co, vpres, 1996, Western Region, vpres, 1998, pres & chief operating officer, 2001; Co Okla City Dist, 1996-99, vpres Western Reg, 1999-2001, pres & chief operating officer, 2001-05; ONEOK Distrib Co, pres, 2005-09; ONEOK Inc, pres-. **Orgs:** Govs Coun Workforce, Econ Develop & bds Okla State Univ Found; bd chmn, Urban League Greater Okla City; Okla Judicial Nominating Comn; Nat Asn Corp Dir; dir, First Fidelity Bank; dir, i2E Inc; dir, Southern Gas Asn; dir, SSM Health Care Okla; Exec Leadership Coun; pres, chmn, bd advisor, Leadership Okla; dir, United Way Cent Oklahmoma, currently. **Business Addr:** Director, United Way of Central Oklahoma, 1444 NW 28th St, Oklahoma City, OK 73106, **Business Phone:** (405)236-8441.

**COMBS, SAMUEL, III**
President (organization), business owner. **Personal:** married Rita Combs. **Educ:** Okla State Univ, BS, indust engineering, 1980; Univ Mich Bus Sch, exec prog, 1999; Northwestern Univ Kellogg Sch Mgt, minority dir develop prog, 2004. **Career:** Okla Natural Gas Co, pres & chief operating officer, 1984-2005; Oneok Distrib Cos., pres, 2005-09; GiANT Partners, exec partners, 2009-; Women's Nat Basketball Asn (WNBA) Tulsa Shock, minority owner, 2010-. **Orgs:** Dir, Southern Gas Asn; dir, SSM Health Care Okla; Gov's Coun Workforce & Econ Develop; bd mem, Okla State Univ Found; bd mem, Okla State Chamber; Exec Leadership Coun. **Honors/Awds:** Oklahoma Governor Brad Henry and the Department of Commerce, "Oklahoma Star," May, 2003; "Black Enterprise," 75 Most Powerful African Americans in Corporate America," January, 2005; "Black Enterprise," The 100 Most Powerful Executives in Corporate America, 2010.

**COMBS, SEAN JOHN**
Executive, rap musician. **Personal:** Born Nov 4, 1969, Harlem, NY; son of Melvin Earl (deceased) and Janice; children: Justin Dior, Christian Casey, D'Lila Star, Jessie James & Chance. **Educ:** Howard Univ, bus admin, attended 1990. **Career:** Directed & Produced: Jodeci, Mary J Blige, Craig Mack, the Notorious BIG, Faith Evan; Albums: Puff Daddy & The Family, No Way Out, 1997-98; Forever, 1999; The Saga Continues, 2001; Press Play, 2006; Dirty Money & acting, 2010-13; Money Making Mitch, No Way Out 2, 2014-; Songs: "I'll Be Missing You"; "with Faith Evans & group 112, 1997"; Films: Made, 2001; Monster's Ball, 2001; Death of a Dynasty, 2003; Seamless, 2005; Getting Up: Contents Under Pressure, 2005; Carlito's Way: Rise to Power, 2005; A Raisin in the Sun, 2008; Get Him to the Greek, 2010; Draft Day, 2014; Muppets Most Wanted, 2014; TV: "CSI: Miami", 2009; "Entourage", 2010; "Hawaii Five-0", 2011; "It's Always Sunny in Philadelphia", 2012; "Black-ish", 2015; Writer: "Run's House", 2005-08; Uptown Records, intern; Uptown Entertainment, vpres A&R, 1990-91; Justin's Bar & Restaurant, Manhattan, owner, 1997; Daddy's House Rec Studios, owner; Notorious Mag, founder; Sean John clothing line, owner; Bad Boy Entertainment, chief exec officer, founder, currently. **Orgs:** Am Fedn Musicians, 1993-; Am Fedn Tv & Radio Artists, 1994-; Daddy's HouseProgs; founder, Sean "Puffy" Combs & Janice Combs Endowed Scholar Fund. **Business Addr:** Founder, Bad Boy Entertainment Inc, 8-10 W 19th St 9th Fl, New York, NY 10011, **Business Phone:** (212)381-1540.

**COMEGYS, DAPHNE D.** **See HARRISON, DR. DAPHNE DUVAL.**

**COMER, DR. JAMES PIERPONT**
Psychiatrist, educator, school administrator. **Personal:** Born Sep 25, 1934, East Chicago, IN; son of Hugh and Maggie Nichols; married Shirley Ann Arnold; children: Brian Jay & Dawn Renee. **Educ:** Ind Univ, BA, 1956; Howard Univ Col Med, MD, 1960; Univ Mich, Sch Pub Health, MPH, 1964. **Career:** St Catherine Hosp, E Chicago, intern, 1960-61; US Pub Health Serv DC, intern, 1961-63; Yale Univ Sch Med, psychiat fel, 1964-66, psychiat residency, 1964-74, assoc dean, 1969-, Child Study Ctr, fel, 1966-67, asst prof, 1968-70, co-dir, Baldwin-King Prog, 1968-73, assoc prof, 1970-75, dir, Sch Develop Prog, 1973-, prof psychiat, 1975-, Maurice Falk Prof Child Psychiat, 1976-; Hillcrest C's Ctr, Wash, DC, psychiat fel. Nat Inst Ment Health, staff mem, 1967-68; Parent's Mag, columnist, 1978-; Sch Develop Prog, Yale Univ Sch Med Child Study Ctr, founder & chmn, currently.Books: Beyond Black and White, 1972; Black Child Care, 1975; Raising Black Children, 1992; The Life and Times of a Black Family, 1988; Leave No Child Behind: Preparing Today's Youth for Tomorrow's World, 2004; What I Learned in School: Reflections on Race, Child Development and School Reform, 2009. **Orgs:** Dir, Conn Energy Corp, 1976-; trustee, Conn Savings Bank, 1971-91; dir, Field Found, 1981-88; trustee, Hazen Found, 1974-78; trustee, Wesleyan Univ, 1978-84; trustee, Albertus Magnus Col, 1989-; trustee, Carnegie Corp NY, 1990-; trustee, Conn State Univ, 1991-94; co-founder, 1968, vpres, 1969-72, pres, Black Psychiats Am, 1973-75; Am Psych Asn, 1970-; Ad Hoc Com Black Psychiatrists APA, 1970-71; Nat Med Asn, 1967-; Am Ortho psychiat Asn, 1968-; chmn, Coun Probs Minority Group Youth, 1969-71; chmn, Adolescent Comt, 1973-77; Inst Med Nat Acad Sci, 1993; Nat Acad Educ, 1993; Laureate Chap, Kappa Delta Pi, 1993; fel Am Acad Arts & Sci, 1994; redlich fel Ctr Advan Study Behav Sci, 1994; bd mem, Nellie Mae Educ Found, 2003-; Nat Asn Advan Colored People; Am Med Asn; Nat Orthopsychiatric Asn; Am Acad Child Psychiat; Nat Asn Ment Health; Soc Health & Human Values; Assocs Renewal Educ, Nat Asn Advan Colored People. **Home Addr:** PO Box 6557, Hamden, CT 06517-0557. **Business Addr:** Maurice Falk Professor of Child Psychiatry, Associate Dean for Student Affairs School of Medic, Yale University Child Study Center, 230 S Frontage Rd NIHB 102, New Haven, CT 06520-7900, **Business Phone:** (203)737-4000.

**COMER, JONATHAN**
Government official, president (organization), executive director. **Personal:** Born Mar 21, 1921, Eufaula, AL; son of Jesse and Beatrice Sanders; married Emma Mount; children: William, Joseph & Kathy. **Career:** LTV Steel, East Chicago, Ind, first helper, 1948-69; Local Union 1011, USWA, E Chicago, Ind, pres, 1967-68; United Steelworkers Am, Pittsburgh, Pa, asst dir, civil rights dept, 1969-83; Gary Human Rels Comn, Gary, exec dir, comnr, 1989. **Orgs:** Steering comt/chairperson, A Philip Randolph Inst, 1977-79; chmn labor & industry, 1965-70, exec secy, Ind conf br, 1983-89; State Nat Asn Advan Colored People; Gary Human Rels Comn; chmn bd, Friendship Baptist Church E Chicago. **Home Addr:** 2575 W 19th Ave, Gary, IN 46404-2601, **Home Phone:** (219)944-8492. **Business Addr:** IN.

**COMER, DR. NORMAN DAVID, SR.**
Dean (education), school administrator, educator. **Personal:** Born Dec 8, 1935, East Chicago, IN; married Marilyn Gaines; children: Norman Jr & Karen. **Educ:** Northwestern Univ, BS, 1958; Ind Univ, MS, 1965; Loyola Univ, Chicago, IL, EdD, 1974. **Career:** Educator, school administrator (retired); Loyola Univ, adj fac; E Chicago Pub Sch, eng teacher, 1960-66, asst prin, 1966-70, asst supt, 1970-93, supt, 1988-94; Ivy Tech Community Col Ind, exec dean, 1996-2006. **Orgs:** Alpha Phi Alpha, 1958; Phi Delta Kappa, 1972; Asn Supv & Curric Develop, 1972; evaluator, Princeton Desegregation Plan, Jackson Mich Bd Educ, 1973; chmn, N Cent Asn Evaluations, Gage Pk & Hirsch High Sch, Chicago, 1973-74; consult, Chicago Pub Sch, Yr Round Sch Study, 1974; Rockefeller Eval Task Force, E Chicago Pub Sch; E Chicago Chamber Com; Nat Alliance Black Sch Educr; Northwest Ind Coalition Educ; Educ Res Found. **Home Addr:** 2209 Purdue Dr, East Chicago, IN 46312.

**COMPTON, CHARLETTA ROGERS**
Administrator. **Educ:** Mountain View Col, AA; Dallas Baptist Univ, BBA; Cert, contract compliance adminr. **Career:** Dallas County Community Col Dist, bd audit comt, 2000-01, chmn, 2004, bd trustee, currently, audit comt, 2004-; Rogers & Assocs, Creative Productions, pres, 2004. **Orgs:** Adv bd, Martin Luther King Jr. Ctr; dir, Shakespeare Festival Dallas; sdv bd, Young Audiences Dallas; asn community col trustee, Pub Policy Comt; Mgt rev comt, Intel Corp; bd mem, N Cent Tex Regional Cert Agency; Dallas Conv & Visitors Bur; Dallas Together Forum; DFW Minority Bus Develop Coun; bd dir, Arts Dist Friends; bd dir, Partnership Art Cult & Educ; Dallas County Hist Comn; Dallas County Col Fac Asn; Conv & Tourism adv comt mem, Dallas Black Chamber Com; pres, Kimball United Neighborhood Asn; parliamentarian, Southwest Dallas Neighborhood Asn; bd dir, Dallas County Heritage Soc; diversity comt, Asn Community Col trustee; trustee, Dist #7, 2014-. **Business Addr:** Board Trustee, Dallas County Community College District, 701 Elm St, Dallas, TX 75202, **Business Phone:** (214)378-1824.

**COMPTON, JAMES W.**
Executive director, association executive. **Personal:** Born Apr 7, 1939, Aurora, IL; children: Janice H & James Jr. **Educ:** Morehouse Col, BA, polit sci, 1961; Univ Grenoble, France, attended 1961. **Career:** Chicago Urban League, on-the-job training rep, 1965-67, exec dir; W Side Off Employ Guid Dept Chicago Urban League, pecialist-in-charge, 1967-69; WSide Proj Urban League, dir, 1968-69; Comt Serv Dept Chicago Urban League, dir, 1968-69; Broome Co Urban League Binghamton NY, exec dir, 1969-70; Opportunities Broome Broome Co Urban League & Bingham, NY, interim exec dir, 1970; Urban League, pres & chief exec officer, 1978-2006; Chicago Urban League Develop Corp, pres & chief exec officer, 1983-2005; Unicom Corp, dir, 1994-; Seaway Nat Bank Chicago, bd dir, 2004-; Wabash Global Group LLC, sr advr, currently; Commonwealth Edison Co, dir, 2006-. **Orgs:** Dir, ComEd, 1989-; teacher, Upper Grade Social Studies, Chicago Bd Educ; dir, Chicago Com Urban Opportunities; dir, Chicago Regional Purchasing Coun; dir, Comt Fund Chicago; dir, Leadership Coun Metro Open Comt; dir, Roosevelt Univ Col Educ; dir, Union Nat Bank Chicago Chicago & Alliance Collab Effort, Steering Comt; Chicago Manpower Area Planning Coun; adv bd, WNUS AM/FM; dean, adv bd, Col Educ Roosevelt Univ; Chicago Press Club; Chicago Forum; Citizens Com Employ; Citizens Com Greater Chicago Inc; Com Foreign & Domestic Affairs; Mayor's Comn Sch Bd Nominations; Concerned Citizens Police Reform; Cong Blue Ribbon Panel; Nat Conf Social Welfare; NE Ill Planning Comn; WBEE Radio Comt Needs Comt; WGN Cinental Broadcasting Co; DePaul Univ; bd trustee, Ariel Mutual Funds; Com Ed; life trustee, Field Mus Natural Hist; Northwestern Univ Bd Community Assocs; ETA Creative Arts Found; Big Shoulders Fund; Morehouse Res Inst; Seaway Bank; bd pres, Chicago Pub Librar & Chicago Bd Educ. **Honors/Awds:** Merrill Scholar, 1959-61; S End Jaycees Certificate of Appreciation, 1972. **Special Achievements:** Ten Outstanding Young Men Award, Chicago Jr Asn Com & Indust, 1972; Ten Outstanding Young Men Award, S End Jaycees Chicago. **Home Addr:** 1427 W Harrison St, Chicago, IL 60607. **Business Addr:** Board of Director, Seaway National Bank Chicago, 645 E 87th St, Chicago, IL 60619, **Business Phone:** (773)487-4800.

**COMVALIUS, DR. NADIA HORTENSE**
Obstetrician. **Personal:** Born Jan 21, 1926, Paramaribo; daughter of Rudolf Bernard W and Martha M James. **Educ:** Univ Utrecht, MD, 1949; Bd Cert Obstet Gynec, 1970. **Career:** Obstetrician (retired); Jewish Meml Hosp, dir gynec; Lenox Hills Hosp & Beth Israel Hosp, attend obstet-gynec; Harlem Hosp, resident, 1955-56; Mt. Sinai Hosp, resident, 1956-57; Hahnemann Med Col, cancer researcher, 1959-61; Wyckoff Heights Hosp, resident, 1961-62; Grand Cent Hosp, intern, 1962-63; Mont Sinai Med Ctr, intern; Planned Parenthood Westchester, med dir, 1970-72; Petromin Med Ctr Yeddah K Saudi Arabia, consult obstet, gynec; White Mountain Community Hosp, dir obstet, gynec, 1994. **Orgs:** Mt Sinai Alumni ASN; Ariz Med Bd; Planned Parenthood, 1966-71; dir, Jewish Memorial Hosp, 1978-83; dir, White Mountain Hosp, 1991-93; bd dir, White Mountain Regional Med Ctr. **Home Addr:** PO Box 325, Springville, AZ 85938-0325.

**CONAWAY, MARY WARD PINDLE**
Government official. **Personal:** Born Jan 26, 1943, Wilson, NC; married Frank M; children: Frank M Jr, Belinda & Monica. **Educ:** NC Cent Univ, BA, 1970; Juilliard Sch Music, 1966; Coppin State Col, MEd, 1975; Univ Md, College Park, clin psychol 1978; Wesley Theol Sem, Wash, DC, MDiv. **Career:** Yonkers Bd Ed, music teacher, 1970-71; Martin Luther King Jr Parent & Child Ctr, cord, 1971-72; Baltimore City Schs, music teacher, 1972-74, spec teacher, 1974-81; prof singer: John Wesley Waterbury United Meth Church, pastor; Baltimore City, regist wills, 1982-. **Orgs:** Deleg, Dem Party Natl Conv, 1988, 1992; Baltimore City Dem Cent Comt, 1990-94; Recognition, Negro Nat Col Fund; Stalwarts & Achievers, Nat Assn Advan Colored People; Alpha Kappa Alpha Sorority; Regist Wills Asn; life mem, Nc Univ Alumni; BCCC Technol Adv Bd; Annapolis Dist Clergy; United Methodist Ebony Clergy Women; NAACP; Nc Univ Alumni Life; Interdenominational Ministerial Alliance. **Honors/Awds:** Women of the Month, Ebeneezer Baptist Church Wilson, NC; Spec Achiev Award, Baltimore City Coun; Award of Merit; Award for Demonstrating Outstanding Courage, HUB Inc; Humanitarian Serv Award, United Cerebral Palsy; Honoree, Natl United Affiliated Beverage Assn Conv Baltimore City; Maryland's Top 100 Women Award, 2008; Shirley Chisholm Award, 2009; Afro-American Outstanding Educator's Award; Volunteer Service Award; The Governor's Most Valuable Citizen Award, 2008; National Congress of Black Women Shirley Chisholm Award, 2009. **Special Achievements:** First Black & Female, an Ordained Elder for the Baltimore Washington Conference of the United Methodist Church, & Pastor of Cecil Memorial United Methodist Church in Annapolis. **Home Addr:** 3210 Liberty Heights Ave, Baltimore, MD 21215. **Business Addr:** Register of Wills, Baltimore City, 111 N Calvert St Suite 311, Baltimore, MD 21202, **Business Phone:** (410)752-5131.

**CONAWAY, SAMUEL L. (SAM CONAWAY)**
Executive. **Educ:** Am Univ; Univ Phoenix. **Career:** Cardiovasc technologist; Mallinckrodt Med, sales exec; Abbott Vascular, DVI Med, sales rep, 1989-94, sales rep, 1994-97, regional sales mgr, 1997-2000, CRM Div, dir sales, 2000-04, vpres, human resources & training, 2003-04, vpres sales corenary, 2004-10, us vpres sales endovascular & coronary, 2010-12; SentreHEART Inc, us vpres sales, training & med educ, 2012-; Boston Sci Corp, IC Sales & Strategic Accoounts, vpres, 2013-, vpres interventional cardiol & struct heart, chmn close gap, 2014-. **Orgs:** Nat Sales Network; Asn Black Cardiologist. **Business Addr:** Vice President, Boston Scientific Corp, 300 Boston Sci Way, Marlborough, MA 01752-1234, **Business Phone:** (508)683-4000.

**CONCHOLAR, DAN R.**
Executive director. **Career:** Art Info Ctr Inc, exec dir, consult, 1991-. **Orgs:** Panelist, Gallery Syst, 1994. **Business Addr:** Executive Director, Art Information Center, 55 Mercer St, New York, NY 10012, **Business Phone:** (212)966-3443.

**CONDE, SANTOS ALOMAR, SR. See ALOMAR, SANDY, SR.**

**CONE, DR. CECIL WAYNE. See Obituaries Section.**

**CONE, DR. JAMES H.**
Educator. **Personal:** Born Aug 5, 1938, Fordyce, AR; son of Charlie and Lucille. **Educ:** Philander Smith Col, BA, 1958, LLD, 1981; Garrett Theol Sem, BD, 1961; Northwestern Univ, MA, 1963, PhD, syst theol, 1965. **Career:** Philander Smith Col, asst prof theol & relig, 1964-66; Adrian Col, Adrian, Mich, asst prof, 1966-69; Union Theol Sem, Dept Theol, from asst prof to prof, 1970-77, Charles A Briggs, chair 1977-87, Charles A Briggs Distinguished Prof, 1987-. Books: Black Theology and Black Power, 1969; A Black Theology of Liberation, 1970; For My People: Black Theology and the Black Church, 1984; Martin & Malcolm & America: A Dream or Nightmare, 1992; Speaking the Truth: Ecumenism, Liberation and Black Theology, 1999; The Cross and the Lynching Tree, 2012. **Orgs:** Soc Study Black Relig; Am Acad Relig; ordained minister, African Methodist Episcopal Church; Ecumenical Asn Third World Theologians, Philippines. **Home Addr:** 99 Claremont Ave Apt 302, New York, NY 10027, **Home Phone:** (212)662-9402. **Business Addr:** Charles A Briggs Distinguished Professor, Union Theological Seminary in the City of New York, 3041 Broadway 121st St, New York, NY 10027, **Business Phone:** (212)280-1369.

**CONE, DR. JUANITA FLETCHER**
Physician. **Personal:** Born Nov 13, 1947, Jacksonville, FL; married Cecil Wayne. **Educ:** Howard Univ, BS, 1968, MD, 1974; Morehouse Sch Med, MPH, 2003. **Career:** Bridgeport Hosp, resident, 1974-77; Morehouse Sch Med, resident internal Med, 2001-03; pvt pract med doctor; Crescent Med Ctr, Kaiser Permanente facil, Southeast Permanente Med Group Inc, adult internist, currently. **Orgs:** Am Col Physicians; Jacksonville Med Dent & Phar Asn; Nat Med Asn; Jacksonville Chamber Com; Nat Coun Negro Women; Jacksonville Chap Links Inc. **Honors/Awds:** Dipl, Am Bd Internal Med, 1979. **Home Addr:** 580 W Eigth St Suite 610, Jacksonville, FL 32209-6553. **Business Addr:** Internist, Kaiser Permanente Crescent Medical Centre, 200 Cres Ctr Pkwy, Tucker, GA 30084, **Business Phone:** (770)496-3625.

**CONEY, LORAINE CHAPELL**
Educator, association executive, musician. **Personal:** Born Feb 8, 1935, Eustis, FL; son of Francis (deceased) and Julia M Graham; married Bettye Jean Stevens; children: Gessner & Melodi. **Educ:** Fla A&M Univ, BS, 1958. **Career:** Streep Music Co, sales rep, 1964-69; Omega Psi Phi, bas Gamma Tau, 1965-67; Sumter Co Music Teachers, chmn, 1973-77; Sumter Co Bd Pub Instr, band & choral dir. **Orgs:** Chmn, Music Educ Nat Conf, 1958-77; chmn, Fla Band Dirs, 1963-67; guest woodwind tutor, LCIE Univ Fla, 1971, 1974; Sumter Co Educ Asn Nat Asn Advan Colored People; Omega Psi Phi; Masonic Lodge. **Honors/Awds:** Sch Band Man Sumter Co, 1959-77; Organized Band & Prod Super Performers; Fla Bandmasters Asn Adjudicator, 1986. **Special Achievements:** First Award Winning Co Band Dir, 1959; First Black Instrument Salesman, Fla, 1964-69. **Home Addr:** 33605 Co Rd 468, PO Box 1058, Leesburg, FL 34748, **Home Phone:** (352)787-5667. **Business Addr:** PO Box 67, Bushnell, FL 33513.

**CONGREAVES, ANDREA FIONA**
Basketball player, basketball coach. **Personal:** Born Jun 3, 1970, Epsom, SR; daughter of Oscar (deceased) and Thelma. **Educ:** Mercer Univ, BA, 1993. **Career:** Basketball Player (retired), basketball coach; Viterbo, Italy, 1993-94; Vivo Vicenza, Italy, 1994-95; Dorna Codella, Spain, 1995-96; Como, Italy, 1996-97; Charlotte Sting, forward-ctr, 1997-98; Pool Comense, 1997-98; Orlando Miracle, 1999; Fennerbache, 1998-99; Fenerbahce S.K, 1998-99; Bourges, 1999-2000; Priolo, 2000-01; C.R. Canarias, 2001-02; Kumho Falcons, 2002; Barcellona, 2002-04; U.B. Barca, 2003-04; Alessandria, 2004-05; Rhondda Rebels, 2005-09; Barking Abbey, 2008-09; Perfumerias; Gran Canaria; Nottingham, 2010-11; Nottingham Wildcats, 2010-11; Univ Nottingham, women's head basketball coach, 2013-; Mansfield Giants, women's head coach, 2013-. **Business Addr:** Head Coach, Mansfield Giants, NottinghamshireNG183RT, **Business Phone:** (016)2365-077.

**CONLEY, JAMES SYLVESTER, JR.**
Executive. **Personal:** Born Jun 7, 1942, Tacoma, WA; son of James S and Vera F Dixon; married Eileen Louise Marrinan; children: Kimberly, Kelli, James III, Ward James W Martin Jr, Erin & Matthew. **Educ:** Univ Puget Sound, Tacoma, WA, BS, jour, 1961; US Mil Acad W Pt, NY, BS, eng, 1965; NY Univ, GBA, MBA, finance, 1981. **Career:** Capital Formation, NY, exec dir, 1970-72; CEDC Inc, Hempstead, NY, vpres, 1972-74; Avon Prod, NY, dir sales coord, 1981-82; Delco Moraine, Dayton, OH, plant mgr, 1985-88, dir tech serv, 1988-89, dir mkt & planning, 1989-90; Gen Motors Corp, Detroit, Mich, n am truck planning dept, 1990-92, automotive components group, technol & planning, 1992, dir minority supplier develop, 1992-95, dir raw mat group, worldwide purchasing, 1995-98. Main CHB Inc, pres & chief exec officer, 2005-; Nat Life Group, reid assocs, 2010-11; Simplified Wealth Strategies, partner, 2012; Conley Financial Servies LLC, partner, pres, 2012-. **Orgs:** Bd dir, Nat Devel Coun, 1973-80; trustee, bd dir & emer, Asn Graduates, US Mil Acad, 1975-; lifetime mem, W Pt Soc NY; Soc Automotive Engrs, 1986-. **Business Addr:** Partner, Conley Financial Servies LLC, 566 Pilgrim Ave, Birmingham, MI 48009-1211, **Business Phone:** (248)645-5454.

**CONLEY, MARTHA RICHARDS**
Executive, lawyer. **Personal:** Born Jan 12, 1947, Pittsburgh, PA; married Charles D; children: David & Daniel. **Educ:** Waynesburg Col, BA, 1968; Univ Pittsburgh Sch Law, JD, 1971. **Career:** Attorney (retired), executive; Sch Dist Pittsburgh, asst solicitor, 1972-73; Brown & Cotton, atty, 1973-74; US Steel Corp, asst mgr labor rel, arbit, asst mgr compliance, 1984-85, compliance mgr, 1985-87, atty, 1987-93, gen atty, 1993, sr gen atty; Film: Tango Macbeth, asst dir; doc Lost Hype about intersection race & sport Pittsburgh, assoc producer. **Orgs:** Admitted pract, Bar Supreme Ct Pa, 1972; bd dir, Louise Child Care Ctr, 1973-77; comn, Prog Aid Citizen Enterprise, 1973-78; admitted pract, Supreme Ct US, 1977; bd dir, Health & Welfare Planning Assoc, 1978-84; mem, Int Toastmistress Club Inc; pres, Aurora Reading Club Pittsburgh, 1984-85; Nat Asn Advan Colored Peopel; Homer S Brown Law Assoc; Allegheny City Bar Assoc; life mem, NBA; Am Bar Assoc; Alpha Kappa Alpha. es, Aurora Reading Club Pittsburgh, 1984-85; Nat Asn Advan Colored Peopel, 2005-; Homer S Brown Law Assoc; Allegheny City Bar Assoc; life mem, NBA; Am Bar Assoc; Alpha Kappa Alpha; Good Schs Pa. **Special Achievements:** First African-American female graduate of the University of Pittsburgh, School of Law. **Home Addr:** 6439 Navarro St, Pittsburgh, PA 15206-1876, **Home Phone:** (412)361-7872.

**CONLEY, MIKE, SR. (MICHAEL ALEX CONLEY, SR.)**
Athlete, executive. **Personal:** Born Oct 5, 1962, Chicago, IL; married Rene Corbin; children: Mike Jr, Jordan, Sydney & Jon. **Educ:** Univ Ark, attended 1985; Ind Wesleyan, BS, bus admin, 2004. **Career:** Athlete (retired), executive; Olympic Athlete, triple jump, 1984, 1992; USA Track & Field, Elite Athlete Progs, exec dir; World Sport Chicago, pres, bd dir, currently; NBA, agt, currently; Prof Athletic Asn, chief exec officer, founder, currently; BDA Sports Mgt, vpres player representation, currently; MMG Sports Mgt Group, chief exec officer; HTWO, chief exec officer. **Orgs:** Chmn, High Performance Comt, USATF, currently. **Honors/Awds:** Bronze Medal, Third Place Long Jump, Silver Medal, Fourth Place Triple Jump, Bronze Medal, Triple Jump, Gold Medal, Triple Jump, World Championships, 1983, 1987, 1991, 1993; Triple Jump Second Place, World Univ Games, 1983; Silver Medal Triple Jump, Olympic Games, 1984; USA Indoor Championships, 1985, 1986, 1987 & 1992; Jim Thorpe Award, USATF, 1986; Gold Medal, Pan Am Games, 1987; Gold Medal, World Indoor Championships, 1987, 1989; Top field events athlete, 1992; Gold Medal Triple Jump, Olympic Games, 1992; inductee, USA Track & Field Federation Hall of Fame, 2004; Master of the Game Award, Nat Sports Law Inst. **Business Addr:** Director, World Sport Chicago, 200 E Randolph St 20th Fl, Chicago, IL 60601, **Business Phone:** (312)861-4850.

**CONNALLY, C. ELLEN (CECELIA ELLEN CONNALLY)**
Judge. **Personal:** Born Jan 26, 1945, Cleveland, OH; daughter of George L and Gwendolyn J; children: Seth George. **Educ:** Bowling Green State Univ, BS, social studies teacher educ, 1967; Cleveland State Univ, MS, am hist, JD, 1970; Cleveland State Univ, MA, 1997; Univ Akron, PhD, am hist. **Career:** Judge (retired); 8th Dist Ct Appeal, law clerk, OH, 1971-72; Cuyahoga County Probate Ct, trial referee, 1972-80; Cleveland Munic Ct, judge, 1980-2004; City Cleveland, spec prosecutor, 2006; Univ Akron Col Law, vis & adj prof law, 2006-08; Cuyahoga County Coun, coun pres, currently. **Orgs:** Northern OH Munic Judges Asn, pres, sec, treas; Task Force Violent Crime, Youth Violence Comm, chmn; Mayor's Adv Comm Gang Violence, chair; Bowling Green State Univ Black Alumni Asn, founding mem, pres; Greater Cleveland Safety, CNL, Traffic Safety, vpres; Cleveland Pub Theater, bd trustees; Am Judges Asn; Cuyahoga County Ct Col, Women's Ctr & Women's Studies Adv Comm; Cleveland Cath Diocese, Church City Proj; Ch Savior UMC. **Home Addr:** 13507 Cormere Ave, Cleveland, OH 44120-1523, **Home Phone:** (216)932-3871. **Business Addr:** Adjunct Professor, University of Akron, 302 Buchtel Common, Akron, OH 44325.

**CONNELL, ALBERT GENE ANTHONY**
Football player. **Personal:** Born May 13, 1974, Fort Lauderdale, FL. **Educ:** Tex A & M Univ. **Career:** Football player (retired); Wash Redskins, wide receiver, 1997-2000; New Orleans Saints, wide receiver, 2001; Calgary Stampeders, CFL, 2003-04, free agt.

**CONNER, GAIL PATRICIA**
Law enforcement officer, government official. **Personal:** Born Mar 20, 1948, Detroit, MI; daughter of George and Alice. **Educ:** Exchange stud Bates Col, attended 1967; Wilberforce Univ, BA, 1969; Antioch Col, MA, 1970. **Career:** Detroit Pub Schs, teacher, 1971-73; State Mich, state probation/parole officer, 1973-77; US Courts-Detroit, sr US probation/parole officer, 1977-. **Orgs:** Greater Quinn AME Church, 1948-; Nat Asn Advan Colored People, 1971-; Fed Probation Officers Asn, 1977-; Erma Henderson re-election steering comt, 1978; vpres, Wilber force Alumni Asn, 1978-82; bd mem, YWCA Detroit, 1983-; nat dir educ, 1983-87, nat dir memship, 1987-92, Nat Asn Negro Bus & Prof Womens Club Inc, 1983-; Nat Asn Black Alumni Steering Comt; parliamentarian, Alpha Kappa Alpha Sorority Inc, 1990-. **Honors/Awds:** Spirit Detroit City Detroit, 1981; Scroll Distinction Negro Bus & Prof, 1982; Appreciation Detroit Pub Schs Award Jr Achievement, 1982; NANBPW Yellow Rose Award Nat, 1982; NANBPW Club Woman of the Year, 1982; Appreciation Award, Mott Community Col, 1983; Nat Black Monitor Hall of Fame, 1985; Mich Women Resource Guide; Wilberforce Univ Dist Alumni Service Award, 1985; AOIP Hall of Fame, 1985; Outstanding Alumni of Wis Univ, 1985. **Home Addr:** 2082 Hyde Pk Dr, Detroit, MI 48207, **Home Phone:** (313)393-1311. **Business Addr:** Probation/Parole Officer, US Justice Department, 415 Federal Bldg, Detroit, MI 48226, **Business Phone:** (313)234-5436.

**CONNER, DR. LABAN CALVIN**
Librarian. **Personal:** Born Feb 18, 1936, Ocala, FL; son of Dorothy Helen Todd and Laban Calvin. **Educ:** Univ Nebr-Omaha, Omaha, Nebr, B Gen Ed, 1959; Emporia State Univ, Emporia, Kans, MSLS, 1964; Nova Univ, Ft Lauderdale, Fla, EdS, 1979; Pac Western Univ, Los Angeles, Calif, PhD, 1980. **Career:** Librarian (retired); Dade County Pub Schs, Miami, Fla, teacher, 1959-63, librn, 1963-68, cord libr serv, 1968-70, teacher, librn, 1973-81; Miami Dade Community Col, Miami, Fla, asst prof, libr sci, 1970-73; Fla Memorial Col, Miami, Fla, libr dir, 1981-98. **Orgs:** Am Libr asn, 1965-; Fla Libr asn, 1963-; Dade County Libr asn, 1963-; African Methodist Episcopal Ch, 1936-; bd dir, Coop Col Libr Ctr. **Honors/Awds:** Kappa Delta Phi (Phi Eta Chapter), 1995. **Home Addr:** 18601 NW 39th Ave, Opa Locka, FL 33055, **Home Phone:** (305)624-7982.

**CONNER, LESTER ALLEN**
Basketball player, basketball coach. **Personal:** Born Sep 17, 1959, Memphis, TN; married Stacy; children: Simone & Alana. **Educ:** Los Medanos Col, attended 1979; Chabot Col, attended 1980; Ore State Univ, attended 1982. **Career:** Basketball player (retired), basketball coach; Golden State Warriors, 1982-86; Rapid City Thrillers, 1986-87, 1993-94; Houston Rockets, 1987-88; NJ Nets, 1988-91; Milwaukee Bucks, 1991-92, asst coach, 2005-07; Los Angeles Clippers, 1993-94; Ind Pacers, 1994, asst coach, 2007-10; Los Angeles Lakers, 1995; Fla Beach Dogs, 1996-97; Boston Celtics, asst coach, 1998; Philadelphia 76ers, assoc head coach, 2004-05; Atlanta Hawks, asst coach, 2010-13; Denver Nuggets, asst coach, 2013-. **Business Addr:** Assistant Coach, Denver Nuggets, Pepsi Ctr 1000 Chopper Cir, Denver, CO 80204, **Business Phone:** (303)405-1100.

**CONNER, MARCIA LYNNE**
City manager. **Personal:** Born Feb 26, 1958, Columbia, SC; daughter of Edward Eugene and Joan Delly. **Educ:** Talladega Col, Talladega, Al, BA, 1980; Univ Cincinnati, Cincinnati, Ohio, MCP, urban planning & orgn mgt, 1982. **Career:** Metrop Dade County Miami, Fla, mgt intern, 1982-83, budget analayst, 1983-85; City Opa-Locka, Opa-Locka, Fla, asst city mgr, 1985-87, city mgr, 1987; Austin City, asst city mgr, 1995-2001; City Durham, city mgr, 2001-04; MLC Consuting, pres, 2004-. **Orgs:** Am Soc Pub Adminrs, 1982; Int City Mgr's Asn, 1982; Leadership Miami, 1986; secy, Greater Miami YWCA, 1987; Big Bros & Sisters Miami, 1987; bd mem, Nat Forum Black Pub Adminrs, 1999-2001. **Honors/Awds:** Outstanding Young Professional, S Fla Am Soc Pub Admin, 1982; Up & Comers Award, S Fla Bus Jour, 1989. **Special Achievements:** One to Watch in 88, S Fla Mag, 1988. **Home Addr:** 4970 NW 102 Ave Suite 206, Miami, FL 33178, **Home Phone:** (305)477-6405.

**CONNER, STEVE**
Advertising executive. **Educ:** Syracuse Univ, Mkt. **Career:** Grey; Warwick; Campbell Mithun Esty; Lockhart & Pettus; Drossman; Lehman; Merino; Radio One Inc, managing partner & chief creative officer; UniWorld; STEVE/STORM, chief exec officer & chief creative officer, 1995-2004; Steve Agency, founder, 1998-; Fluid Inc, owner, 2007-; Burrell Commun Group LLC, chief creative officer, managing partner, 2005-07; Draftfcb, EVP group creative dir, 2008-10; Tugcontent, owner, 2013-. **Orgs:** Mkt commitee, Oak Pk River Forest Community Found; Founder, Chicago 3D meetup; founder, nPlay foundation, 2008-; founder and chief exec officer, Hehp Foundation, 2014-. **Honors/Awds:** Judge, Nat ADDY Awards, 2005; Judge, Multicultural Advert. **Special Achievements:** Director and part of the creative team that brought forth the award-winning "Whassup!" campaign for Budweiser in 2000. **Business Addr:** Owner, Fluid Inc, 1611 Telegraph Ave, Oakland, CA 94612, **Business Phone:** (877)343-3240.

**CONNOR, DOLORES LILLIE**
Entrepreneur. **Personal:** Born Sep 15, 1950, Mineral Wells, TX; daughter of Walter Malone and Alpearl Sadberry. **Educ:** Univ Tex, Arlington, Tex, BS, 1975; Amber Univ, Garland, Tex, MS, 1989. **Career:** Vought Systems Div LTV, Dallas, Tex, material control analyst, 1969-76; Recognition Equipment, Irving, Tex, buyer, 1975-77; Tex Instruments, Dallas, Tex, buyer, 1977-78, small & minority bus liaison officer, 1978-87, int officer, 1978-80, small bus prog, mgr, 1987-89, small bus prog mgr, 1985-89, mgr, corporate minority procurement, 1989-91; A Piece Mine Corp, pres, currently. **Orgs:** Zeta Phi Eta Honor Fraternity & Commun, 1975; Ft Worth Negro Bus & Prof Women's Club, 1975-77; bd mem, Dallas Urban League, 1979-80; Richardson Bus & Prof Women's Club, 1979-86; Leadership Dallas; bd chmn, D & FW Minority Purchasing Coun, 1980-83; Tex Governor's Comt Employ Disabled, 1981; bd mem, Mayor's Comt Employ Disabled, 1981-85; exec dir, Loan-D & FW Minority Purchasing Coun, 1983; capt, Neighborhood Watch, Richardson, Tex, 1983-87; Delta Sigma Theta Sorority Inc; Leadership Tex Alumni, 1991-92. **Honors/Awds:** Outstanding Business woman of the Year, Iota Phi Lambda Sorority, 1995; Quest for Success Winner, Dallas Black C C, 1996-97; Busines of the Year, St Luke COT United Methodist Ch, 1997; Young Careerest, Richardson Bus & Prof Women's Club, 1980; Youth Motivator, Nat Alliance Bus, 1983; Supporter Entrepreneurs, Venture Magazine & Arthur Young, 1987; Entrepreneurs Hall of Fame, 1988. **Special Achievements:** Published article "Winning Ways for Women Managers" in Hispanic Engineer and US Black Enterprise, 1990. **Home Addr:** PO Box 8863, Fort Worth, TX 76124, **Home Phone:** (214)492-0596. **Business Addr:** President, A Piece of Mine Corp, PO Box 201338, Arlington, TX 76006-1338, **Business Phone:** (972)606-7478.

**CONNOR, HERMAN P.**
Executive. **Personal:** Born Aug 27, 1932, Garfield, GA; son of George and Melvina; children: Sharon, Gregory, Stephanie, Leigh & Donna. **Career:** Consoar Corp, pres. **Business Addr:** President, Consoar Corp, 49 Cedar Ave, Montclair, NJ 07042, **Business Phone:** (973)783-0666.

**CONNORS, NELDA J.**
President (organization), chief executive officer. **Educ:** Univ Dayton, BS & MS, mech engineering; Univ Tokyo, ME, int finance & econs. **Career:** Monsanto Corp, engr; Ford Motor Comp; Chrysler; Mogami Denki; Toyota Motor Co, Japan, mfg engr supvr; Chrysler Corp; Eaton Corp, Clutch Div Truck Group, vpres & gen mgr, 2002-08, dir, 2006-; Allied Holdings US Inc, chief exec officer, 2008-, pres, currently; Tyco Elec & Metal Prod, pres, 2008-10; Boston Sci Corp, independent dir, 2009-; Atkore Int Inc, pres & chief exec officer, 2010-11; FocalPoint Partners LLC, indust coverage leader; Blount Int Inc, dir, 2012-; Echo Global Logistics Inc, dir, 2013-; Vesuvius plc, non-exec dir, 2013-; Pine Grove Holdings LLC, chair, founder & chief exec officer, currently. **Orgs:** Trustee, Peggy Notebaert Nature Mus; trustee, Mus Contemp Art Chicago; Atkore Int; Fed Res Bank Chicago. **Business Addr:** Director, Boston Scientific Corp, 300 Boston Scientific Way, Marlborough, MA 01752-1234, **Business Phone:** (508)683-4000.

**CONRAD, DR. CECILIA ANN**
Foundation executive. **Personal:** Born Jan 4, 1955, St. Louis, MO; daughter of Emmett J and Eleanor N; married Llewellyn Miller; children: Conrad Jr. **Educ:** Wellesley Col, BA, 1976; Stanford Univ, MA, 1978, PhD, 1982. **Career:** Bell Labs Coop, res fel, 1976-81; Fed Trade Comn, economist, 1978-79; Duke Univ, asst prof, 1981-85; Hunter Col, vis asst prof, 1984-85; Barnard Col, assoc prof, 1985; Pfizer Inc, consult, 1992-, Rev Black Polit Econ, ed; Black Enterprise Mag, bd economists, 1993-; Feminist Econs, assoc ed; Pomona Col, Dept Econ, fac, 1997-, assoc dean, 2004-07, Vice Pres Acad Affairs, 2009-12, Actg Pres, 2012, Stedman-Sumner prof, emer; Scripps Col, Vice Pres Acad Affairs, 2007-09; MacArthur Found, managing dir, 2013-. **Orgs:** Chmn & pres, Nat Econ Asn, Col Bd; Test Develop Comt, Advan placement exam econ; pat bd mem, Comn Status Women Econ Prof, Phi Beta Kappa, 1976; comt bd mem, Status Women Econs Profession. **Home Addr:** 140 S Dearborn St60611, **Home Phone:** (312)643-1044. **Business Addr:** Managing Director, MacArthur Fellows, Awards and Exploratory Philanthropy, MacArthur Foundation, 140 S Dearborn St, Claremont, NY 60603, **Business Phone:** (312)917-0444.

**CONTEE, DR. CAROLYN ANN (CAROLYN CONTEE-LASSITER)**
Dentist. **Personal:** Born Feb 14, 1945, Washington, DC; married Dr James E Lassiter Jr; children: Lisa C Butler. **Educ:** Howard Univ, BA, 1969, MEd, 1973, DDS, 1981; MPH. **Career:** DC Pub Schs, elem teacher, 1969-77; pvt dent pract, dentist, 1981-86; Upper Cardozo Community Health Ctr, staff dentist, 1982-86; Shaw Community Health Ctr, staff dentist, 1982-86; Fairleigh Dickenson Col Dent, asst prof, 1987; Airport Dent Ctr, asst dir, 1986-; Eric B. Chandler Health Ctr, dent dir, currently; pvt pract dentist, currently. **Orgs:** Dir continuing educ exec bd, Robert Freeman Dent Soc, 1982-84; house delegates, Nat Dent Asn, 1982-86, exec comt, 1986, asst treas, 1986; bd trustee, Nat Dent Asn Found, 1983-; Potomac Chap Links, 1984-. **Honors/Awds:** Outstanding Service, Robert T Freeman Dent Soc, 1984; Outstanding Service Capital Head start Certificate, 1985. **Home Addr:** 140 Hill Hollow Rd, Watchung, NJ 07069, **Home Phone:** (908)668-1787. **Business Addr:** Dental Director, Eric B Chandler Health Center, 277 George St, New Brunswick, NJ 08901, **Business Phone:** (732)235-6700.

**CONTEE-LASSITER, CAROLYN.** **See CONTEE, DR. CAROLYN ANN.**

**CONWAY, CURTIS LAMONT**
Football player, television broadcaster. **Personal:** Born Mar 13, 1971, Los Angeles, CA; married Laila Ali; children: Curtis Mohammad Jr & Sydney; married Leoria Sanamu; children: Cameron, Kelton & Leilani. **Educ:** Univ Southern Calif, pub admin. **Career:** Football player (retired), television actor, analyst; Chicago Bears, kick returner, wide receiver, 1993, wide receiver, 1994-99; San Diego Chargers, wide receiver, 2001-02; New York Jets, wide receiver, 2003; San Fransisco 49ers, wide receiver, 2004; Compass Media Networks, color analyst, 2009; TV: "Damn Bundys, 1997; "Married with children", 1997; "ESPN's Sunday Night Football", 1993-2000; "NFL's Monday Night Football", 1994-2003; "Rome is Burning", 2005-06; "Dancing with the Stars", 2007; "Entertainment Tonight", 2007; "11-04-04: The Day of Change", 2009; "Total Access", co host, currently; Pac-12 Network, studio analyst, currently; Nat Football Network, co-host, currently. **Honors/Awds:** Trojans Offensive Player-of-the-Year, 1992; First Team All American. **Home Addr:** . **Business Addr:** Television Actor, Starz Entertainment LLC, 8900 Liberty Circle, Eaglewood, CO 80112, **Business Phone:** (720)852-7700.

**CONWILL, GILES**
Clergy, educator. **Personal:** Born Dec 17, 1944, Louisville, KY. **Educ:** Univ San Diego, BA, philos, 1967; Athenaeum OH, Mdiv, 1973; Emory Univ, PhD, cult studies, 1986. **Career:** Barona & Santa Ysabel Missions, relig educ instr, 1965-67; Miramar Naval Air Sta, chaplains asst, 1966-67; St Henrys Sch, elem sch teacher, 1967-68; Verona Fathers Sem, choir dir, asst organist, 1968-69; Diocese San Diego, Roman Cath Priest, 1973; St Rita's Church, assoc pastor, 1973-76; San Diego Relig Vocations Off, diocesan coordr, pre-marriage instr, 1975; Nat Off Black Catholics, Dept Church Vocations, dir, 1976-80; St Anthony's Church, Atlanta, assoc pastor, 1980-85; St Joseph's Cathedral, San Diego, assoc pastor, 1985-86; Morehouse Col, Dept Hist, assoc prof hist, 1987-, chmn, currently; Xavier Univ, Inst Black Cath Studies, New Orleans, assoc prof, 1990; Emory Col, assoc prof, currently; Upper Room Publ Co. **Orgs:** Vpres, Southeast San Diego Interdenomi Nat Ministerial Alliance, 1975; Black Cath Clergy Caucus, 1975; Asn Study African Am Life & Hist, 1987-; Southern Conf African Am Studies Inc, 1987-; Black Cath Theol Symp, 1990; Asn Southern Historians, 1992-; Ga Asn Historians, 1992; Am Anthrop Asn, 1994. **Home Addr:** PO Box 10506, Atlanta, GA 30310, **Home Phone:** (404)608-1887. **Business Addr:** Professor History, Chairman, Morehouse College, Rm 202 Brawley Hall 830 Westview Dr SW, Atlanta, GA 30314, **Business Phone:** (404)215-2620.

**CONWILL, DR. HOUSTON EUGENE**
Sculptor. **Personal:** Born Apr 2, 1947, Louisville, KY; married Kinshasha Holman. **Educ:** Howard Univ, attended 1973; Univ Southern Calif, 1976. **Career:** Self-employed artist, 1987-. **Honors/Awds:** John Simon Guggenheim Fellowship, 1983; Fellowship, Prix De Rome, 1984; Louis Comfort Tiffany Foundation Award, 1987; Niagara Univ, Hon Doctorate, 1991. **Special Achievements:** Public Art Monuments in cities throughout the nation and some international. **Business Addr:** 290 Broadway Ted Weiss Fed Bldg, New York, NY 10023.

**CONWILL, KINSHASHA (KINSHASHA HOLMAN CONWILL)**
Museum director. **Personal:** Born Atlanta, GA. **Educ:** Howard Univ, BA, fine arts; Univ Calif, MA, bus admin. **Career:** Frank Lloyd Wright Hollyhock House, coordr, 1976-78; Mus Am Indian New York, asst exhib coordr, 1979; Studio Mus, New York, dir; Studio Mus Harlem, dir, exec dir, 1988-99, dir emer, currently; Smithsonians Nat Mus African Am Hist & Cult, dep dir; A Cult Blueprint New York, proj dir. **Orgs:** Sr policy advisor, Mus & Community Initiative Am Asn Mus, 2002-03; fel Mus Loan Network; fel Times Sq Alliance; fel Ctr Black Music Res; fel New York Arts Coalition; fel New York Found Arts; fel New York Times Co Found; fel Pan Asian Repertory Theatre; fel Riverside Church; chmn, Nat Mus Serv Bd; mem bd, Munic Art Soc New York & Urban Assembly; mem adv bd, Donor Res Proj Ctr Study Philanthropy Grad Sch; steering comt, 21st Century Learner Initiative Inst Mus & Libr Serv. **Honors/Awds:** National schievement scholar, Mount Holyoke Col. **Business Addr:** Director Emeritus, Studio Museum Harlem, 144 W 125th St, New York, NY 10027, **Business Phone:** (212)864-4500.

**CONWILL, DR. WILLIAM LOUIS**
Psychologist, educator, consultant. **Personal:** Born Jan 5, 1946, Louisville, KY; son of Adolph Giles (deceased) and Mary Luella Herndon; married Faye Venetia Harrison; children: Giles Burgess, Leonart Mondlane & Justin Neal. **Educ:** Univ San Diego, BA, philos, 1968; St Patrick's Sch Grad Theol, attended 1969; Calif State Univ, San Jose, MA, exp psychol, 1973; Stanford Univ, PhD, coun psychol, 1980. **Career:** Santa Clara County, Juv Probation Dept, group counr I, group counr II, sr training counr, 1969-72; Cities Richmond & San Francisco, Police Dept, trainer & res asst, 1972-73; Univ Calif, Santa Cruz, coun psychologist II, 1974-77; Stanford Univ, lectr, 1977; Nairobi Col, instr, 1978; Calif State Univ, guest lectr, 1978; Ment Health Dept, County San Mateo, Calif, coordr, chief consult & educ, 1980-82; Univ Louisville, Dept Psychiat, asst prof, lectr, 1983-88; Spalding Univ, lectr, 1987; City Louisville, Dept Human Servs, res assoc, 1988-90; Family Stress Inst Inc, pres & founder, 1988-97; City Louisville Off Mayor, Off Human Servs, community statist res assoc, 1988-90; mem police admin adv comt, 1989; Jefferson County Ky Bd Educ, instr adult educ, 1989; Lakeshore Ment Health Inst, Tenn, Dept Ment Health, Ment Retardation, psychologist, chief psychol, C & Youth Servs, 1990-97; Child & Family Ther Ctr, psychologist, 1990; Univ Tenn, Coun, fac; Family Stress Inst, pres, founder, 1997; Minority Male Consortium, prev specialist; Am Psychol Asn, trainer; HIV Off Psychol Ed, HOPE Prog; Univ Tenn, Dept Educ Psychol & Coun, asst prof, 1999-2004; Implementation Sci Int Inc, consult, 2002-; Univ Fla, Counr Educ & African Am Studies, affil fac, Coun Educ & Ctr African Studies, asst prof, 2004-11; Univ Ill, assoc prof, 2015-. **Orgs:** Am Psychol Asn; Am Pain Soc; Asn Black Psychologists; Tenn Psychol Asn; Ky Soc Psychologists; NCP; Behav Med Soc; Knoxville Area Psychol Asn; Asn Behav Sci & Med Educ; Am Group Psychother Asn; Assoc Multicultural Coun & Develop, 2005; chief consult, Harrison Conwill Assocs, 2010-; Nat Asn Prof Martial Artists; Social Justice Tenn Psychol Asn; Am Psychol Asn; Asn Black Psychologists; Nat Regist Health Serv Providers. **Home Addr:** 1709 Dunraven Dr, Knoxville, TN 37922-6237. **Business Addr:** Chief Consultant, Harrison Conwill Associates, 901 Prof Ctr 901 NW 8th Ave Suite C-8, Gainesville, FL 32601.

**CONYERS, CHARLES L.**
School administrator, educator. **Personal:** Born Sep 8, 1927, Cyrene, GA; son of Luther H Sr and Ella Brown; married Mary Foster; children: Charles C, Andrei B & Brian K. **Educ:** Savannah State Col, BS, 1949; Va State Col, BS, MS, 1958; Univ Ill, grad study; Univ Va. **Career:** School administrator (retired); G W Carver High Sch, Culpeper, Va, teacher, 1949-51; Mary N Smith High Sch, 1952; AG Richardson High Sch, Louisa, teacher, 1952-61; Cent Acad Sch, Fincastle, prin, 1961-63; John J Wright Sch, Snell, prin, 1963-66; State Dept Educ, Richmond, asst super title one, 1966, supvr, title I & migrant educ, 1972, assoc dir, title one, 1979, dir, div compensatory educ, 1981, dir, div spec & compensatory progs, 1987, educ lead specialist, grants admin, 1992. **Orgs:** Nat Educ Asn; Va Educ Asn; life mem, Iota Sigma Chap; Phi Delta Kappa; first pres, Nat Asn State Dirs Migrant Educ; pres, Nat Asn State Dirs Chap one; Nat Adv Coun Neglected or Delinq Progs; Phi Beta Sigma Fraternity. **Honors/Awds:** Outstand-

ing Educator Award, Phi Delta Kappa, 1976; State Superintendent's Award, 1989; Literacy Award, International Reading Asn, 1989; Distinguished Alumni Award, Nat Asn Equal Opportunity Higher Educ, 1990. **Home Addr:** 3213 Griffin Ave, Richmond, VA 23222, **Home Phone:** (804)329-8303.

### CONYERS, DR. JAMES ERNEST, SR.

Educator. **Personal:** Born Mar 6, 1932, Sumter, SC; son of Crenella and Emmett; married Joan Farris; children: Judy, Jimmy & Jennifer. **Educ:** Morehouse Col, BA, 1954; Atlanta Univ, MA, 1956; Wash State Univ, PhD, social sci, 1962. **Career:** LeMoyne Col, Memphis, instr, 1955-56; Wash State Univ, Pullman, teaching fel, 1958-62; Ind State Univ, Terre Haute, asst prof sociol, 1962-64; Atlanta Ga Univ, assoc prof sociol, 1964-68; Ind State Univ, Terre Haute, prof sociol, 1968, prof emer sociol, currently; Asn Black Sociologists, pres. **Orgs:** Young Men Civic Club, Terre Haute, 1970-; pres, Asn Social & Behav Scientists, 1970-71; comn chmn, Participation & Status Racial & Ethnic Minorities; prof, Amer Sociol Asn, 1971-72; chmn, Caucus Black Sociologists Am, 1973-74; Selection Comt Nat Fel Fund Grad Fel Black Am, 1973-78; Adv Panel Sociol, NSF, 1975-77; Coun N Cent Sociol Asn, 1991-93; life mem, Nat Asn Advan Colored People. **Honors/Awds:** WEB Dubois Award, Asn Social & Behav Scientists, 1962; Distinguished Scholar Award, Asn Black Sociologists, 1994. **Special Achievements:** Various articles published in Sociology & Social Research; Co-editor, Sociology for the Seventies, 1972; Co-author, Black Elected Officials, 1976; First African American professor at Indiana State Teachers College. **Home Addr:** 5862 E Cougar Dr, Terre Haute, IN 47802-8535. **Business Addr:** Professor Emeritus, Indiana State University, 200 N 7th St, Terre Haute, IN 47809-9989, **Business Phone:** (812)237-3535.

### CONYERS, JEAN LOUISE

Association executive, chief executive officer. **Personal:** Born Nov 10, 1932, Memphis, TN; daughter of Marshall D and Jeffie Ledbetter Farris; married James E; children: Judith, James Jr & Jennifer; married Dr James E; children: Judith, James Jr & Jennifer. **Educ:** Lemoyne Owen Col, BA, 1956; Univ Tenn Sch Social Work, attended 1959; Atlanta Univ, Sch Bus, MBA, 1967. **Career:** Administrator (retired); Wash State Univ, Dept Zool, exec secy; Atlanta Univ Sch Bus, pullman, 1958-62, 1965-68; Vigo County Community Action, planner, 1968-78, exec dir, 1978-79; United Way Genessee & Lapeer Counties, sr assoc exec, 1980-82; GFOTC, prog coordr, 1982-86; Metrop Chamber Com, pres & chief exec officer, 1980, 1986; Conyers & Assocs, pres, chief exec officer, 1982-86; Ultimate Learning Systs Inc, pres, chief exec officer, 1990-; USDOT LOSP Small Bus Off, regional dir. **Orgs:** Bd dir, Urban Coalition, 1988-; Life Mem, Alpha Kappa Alpha Basileus, 1992-; pres, Opportunity Network, 1997; pres, Metrop Chamber Com; life mem, Nat Asn Advan Colored People; life mem, Strathmores Whos Who; prog chair, Quinn Chapel African Methodist Episcopal Church; Kiwanis; Zonta Club Flint II. **Honors/Awds:** Meritorious Service Award, Nat Asn Negro Bus & Prof Women, 1994; Partner in Community Service, Black Caucus Found Mich, 1994; Community Activist Award, Community Coalition, 1996; Community Service Award, Boy Scouts Am, 1996. **Special Achievements:** Designed Special Entrepreneurial Curriculum and had it licensed by the Michigan Department of Education; Developed Kidpreneur Training Prog for 5th & 6th Graders; Initiated Community Business Partnership Project; First African American Chamber of Commerce in the state of Mich. **Home Addr:** 3118 Begole St, Flint, MI 48504, **Home Phone:** (810)232-7907. **Business Addr:** President, Chief Executive Officer, Metropolitan Chamber of Commerce, 400 N Saginaw St Suite 101A, Flint, MI 48502, **Business Phone:** (810)235-5514.

### CONYERS, JOHN JAMES, JR.

State government official, association executive. **Personal:** Born May 16, 1929, Detroit, MI; son of John and Lucille Simpson; married Monica Ann Esters; children: John III & Carl Edward. **Educ:** Wayne State Univ, BA, 1957, JD, 1958; Wilberforce Univ, LLD, 1969. **Career:** Congressman John Dingell, legis asst, 1958-61; Conyers Bell, Carl Edward & Townsend, sr partner, 1959-61; Mich Workman's Compensation Dept, referee, 1961-63; US House Representatives, Mich 1st Dist, rep, 1965-93, Mich 14th Dist, rep, 1993-2013, Mich 13th Dist, rep, 2013-. **Orgs:** Nat Bd Am Dem Action; exec bd mem, Detroit Br Nat Asn Advan Colored People, 1963-; Nat Adv Bd Am Civil Liberties Union, 1964-; Wolverine Bar Asn; Tabernacle Baptist Church; Kappa Alpha Psi Fraternity; Pub Field; chmn, House Comn Govt Opers, 1988-94; orginal co-founder, Cong Black Caucus, 1969-; chmn, Comt Oversight & Govt Reform, 1989-95; ranking mem, House Comn Judiciary, 1994-; hon bd advisor, Nat Stud Leadership Conf. **Honors/Awds:** Rosa Parks Award, 1967; Southern Christian Leadership Conference Award; honorary degrees from colleges and universities throughout the nation. **Special Achievements:** First African-American to hold the distinction as Dean of Congress. **Business Addr:** Representative, Congressman, US House of Representatives, 2426 Rayburn Bldg, Washington, DC 20515, **Business Phone:** (202)225-5126.

### CONYERS, NATHAN

Publisher. **Career:** Milwaukee Times, publ & founder, currently. **Home Addr:** 2183 N Sherman Blvd, Milwaukee, WI 53208-1212, **Home Phone:** (414)871-7632. **Business Addr:** Founder, Publisher, Milwaukee Times Printing & Publishing Co, 1936 N Doctor Martin Luther King Dr, Milwaukee, WI 53212, **Business Phone:** (414)263-5088.

### CONYERS, NATHAN G.

Automotive executive, president (organization). **Personal:** Born Jul 3, 1932, Detroit, MI; son of John Sr and Lucille Simpson; married Diana Callie Howze; children: Nancy, Steven, Susan, Ellen & Peter. **Educ:** Wayne State Univ, Detroit, MI, LLB, 1959. **Career:** Atty pvt pract, 1959-69; Keith, Conyers, Anderson, Brown & Wahls, sr partner, 1960; Small Bus Admin, closing atty, 1963-64; Veteran's Admin, closing atty, 1964-65; pvt pract, atty, 1965-69; State Mich, Atty Gen Off, spec asst, 1967-70; Conyers Riverside Ford Inc, Detroit, Mich & Supreme Ford Inc, Mason, Mich, founder & pres, 1970-; Supreme Ford, pres, 1991-93; Jaguar Novi, pres, 2001-. **Orgs:** Life mem, Nat Asn Advan Colored People; Asn Computational Ling; Young Men's Christian Asn; bd mem, Greater Detroit COC; bd mem, Blue Cross & Blue Shield MIC; bd mem, tre, Diversitech; Wolverine Bar Asn; NAT Lawyers Guild; bd mem, State Canvassers, 1968-74; pres, Nat Black Dealers Asn, 1970; Greater Detroit Area Hosp CNL, 1972-73; Univ N Fla, 1972-75; adv bd, United FND, 1973-75; bd mem, Black Ford Lincoln & Mercury Dealers Asn, 1979-; adv coun, State Mich, Com DEPT, minority bus, 1986-; Detroit Bd Police CMSers, 1987-89; bd dir, PUSH Intl Trade Bur; Rivertown Auto Dealers Asn; Conyers longest serv African Am car dealer country; Nat Minority Dealership Asn. **Business Addr:** President, Jaguar of Novi, 24295 Haggerty Rd, Novi, MI 48375, **Business Phone:** (248)478-1111.

### COOGLER, RYAN

Screenwriter, movie director. **Personal:** Born May 23, 1986, Oakland, CA; son of Ira Coogler and Joselyn Thomas Coogler. **Educ:** Saint Mary's College of California, Attended; Sacramento State, Attended; University of Southern California, School of Cinematic Arts, Graduate. **Career:** San Francisco Juvenile Hall, Counselor; Short-film director of "Locks," "Gap," and "Fig"; Director of feature film "Fruitvale Station," 2013. **Honors/Awds:** Tribeca Film Festival short film award and Dana and Albert Broccoli Award for Filmmaking Excellence for "Locks"; Jack Nicholson Award for Achievement in Directing for "Gap"; HBO Short Filmmaking Award and DGA Student Filmmaker Award for "Fig"; Sundance Film Festival, Grand Jury Prize and Audience Award for "Fruitvale Station," 2013; Cannes Film Festival, Best First Film for "Fruitvale Station," 2013; "Time" Magazine, 30 Under 30: World Changers (with actor Michael B. Jordan), 2013; "The Root" Magazine, The Root 100 Honorees, 2013; "Filmmaker" Magazine, 25 New Faces of Independent Film, 2013.

### COOK, ALICIA AUGELLO. See KEYS, ALICIA.

### COOK, ANTHONY ANDREW

Football player. **Personal:** Born May 30, 1972, Bennettsville, SC. **Educ:** SC State Univ, attended 1999. **Career:** Football player (retired); Houston Oilers, defensive end, 1995, left defensive back, 1996; Tenn Oilers, left defensive end, 1997, defensive back, 1998; Wash Redskins, defensive end, 1999; New York jets, defensive end, 2000.

### COOK, CHARLES A.

Educator, physician, executive. **Personal:** Born Jun 19, 1946, Biloxi, MS; son of Norman Sr and Eleanor Posey Shelby; married Shirley A Bridges; children: Timothy, Tamotha & Torryhe. **Educ:** Tougaloo Col, Tougaloo, BA, MS, 1971; Tufts Univ, Sch Med, Boston, nephrology, MA, MD, 1975; Harvard Univ, Sch Pub Health, Boston, MA, MPH, 1975; Univ NC, Chapel Hill NC, cert, 1982. **Career:** Boston Univ, hypertension fel; State MA, Boston, spec asst, ment health, 1974-75; State Miss, Jackson, asst chief, discontrol, 1979-80; Univ Miss Med Ctr, asst prof med, 1979-80; State NC, Raleigh NC, chief adult health, 1980-85, med dir; Univ NC, Chapel Hill, Sch Pub Health, adj assoc prof, 1987-; Assoc Resources Consult Group, pres, currently. **Orgs:** Bd mem, Am Heart Asn, NC, 1980-89; bd mem, Am Cancer Soc, NC, 1980-85; NC Ins Comn, 1988-89. **Honors/Awds:** Airman of the Month, US Air Force, 1965; Doctor of the Year, Hinds County Med Soc, 1979; Tarheel of the Week, Raleigh News & Observer, 1983; Honored Volunteer, NC Diabetes Asn, 1983; Volunteer of the Year, State Baptist Convention, 1984. **Special Achievements:** Has Published various articles. **Home Addr:** 3414 6 Forks Rd, Raleigh, NC 27609-7234, **Home Phone:** (919)783-0200. **Business Addr:** President, Association Resources Consulting Group, 3414 6 Forks Rd, Raleigh, NC 27609, **Business Phone:** (919)783-0200.

### COOK, ELIZABETH G.

Newspaper editor. **Personal:** Born Jun 30, 1960, Lexington, KY; daughter of Roy L Lillard and Betty L Lillard; married Robert B; children: Casey A. **Educ:** Univ NC, BA, jour, 1977; Ohio State Univ, Columbus, OH, attended 1983. **Career:** Columbus Call & Post Newspaper, Columbus, OH, sports writer, 1986-88; State Ohio, Columbus, OH, pub info officer, 1983-88; Ohio State Univ, asst dir sports info, 1988; Salisbury Post, reporter, lifestyles ed, managing ed, 1978-93, ed, 1993-. **Orgs:** Col Sports Info Dirs Am, 1988-; Am Soc Newspaper Ed; former, pres, NC Press Asn. **Honors/Awds:** State Career Women of the Year, Bus & Prof Women, 1995. **Home Addr:** 1360 Picard Rd, Columbus, OH 43227, **Home Phone:** (614)237-8907. **Business Addr:** Editor, Salisbury Post, 131 W Innes St, Salisbury, NC 28144, **Business Phone:** (704)797-4244.

### COOK, FRANK ROBERT, JR.

Business owner, lawyer, accountant. **Personal:** Born Aug 19, 1923. **Educ:** BS, 1945; JD, 1949; PhD, 1951; LLM, 1955; BCS, 1963; MCS, 1964; DD, 1967. **Career:** Integrity Adjust Co, owner, 1944-49; RE Broker, bus chance broker, 1945-; Frank R Cook Jr, atty pub acct & mgt consult, real property appraiser, 1950; C Church Christ, minister, 1966-. **Orgs:** Wash Bar Asn; Nat Soc Pub Acct; Adm Planned Parenthood & Sex & Marriage Coun Prog, 1967. **Business Addr:** 1715 11th St NW, Washington, DC 20001, **Business Phone:** (202)332-8108.

### COOK, FREDERICK NORMAN

Banker. **Personal:** Born Feb 19, 1968, Tupelo, MS; son of Richard Jr; married Gwendolyn Woodard; children: Jamie Mariah & Reagan Michelle. **Educ:** Mo Valley Col, BS, 1992; MS Sch Banking, 1999; TN Consumer Lending Sch, 2001. **Career:** Fleet Finance, asst mgr, 1993-94; Money Tree Finance, asst mgr, 1995-97; Peoples Bank & Trust Com, lending officer, asst vpres, 1997-. **Orgs:** St Joseph Masonic Lodge #131 Verona, MS, sr warden, 1993; Traveling Consistory #20 Tupelo, MS 32, 1997; Neighborhood asn, pres, 2000; Boys & Girls Club North MS, bd mem, 2000; Black Bus asn, dir, 2001-; Family First, bd mem, 2001-. **Home Addr:** 3093 Monterey Dr, Tupelo, MS 38801, **Home Phone:** (662)566-1217. **Business Addr:** Loan Officer, Peoples Bank & Trust Co, 209 Troy St, Tupelo, MS 38802, **Business Phone:** (662)680-1221.

### COOK, DR. HENRY LEE, SR.

Dentist. **Personal:** Born Sep 7, 1939, Macon, GA; married Mamie R Richmond; children: Cathy L & Henry L II. **Educ:** Tuskegee Univ, BS biol, 1962; Meharry Medical Col, DDS, 1969. **Career:** Pvt pract, dentist, currently. **Orgs:** Chmn, Minority Asst Corp, 1977-87; mem Col Bd Health, 1978-87; pres, Alpha Phi Sigma, Phi Beta Sigma, 1980-87, L & L Sports Unlimited, 1980-87; vice chmn bd, YMCA, 1982-87; treas, Ga Dent Soc, 1983-87; nat vpres, Tuskegee Nat Alumni, 1985-87; nat trustee Nat Dent Assoc, 1986-87; Am Col Dent; Pierre Fauchard Acad; Nat Dent Asn; Ga Dent Asn; Western Dist Dent Soc; former chmn, bd Columbus Tech Found; chmn, Minority Assistance Corp; Columbus Bus Develop Ctr; Supvry Bd Personal Rev. **Honors/Awds:** Outstanding Young Man of America; Civil Rights Award, Natl Dental Assoc; Governor, Statewide Health Coord Coun; Dr. J.E. Carter Award, Nat Dent Asn; Civil Rights Award, Nat Dent Asn; Georgia Dental Society. **Home Addr:** 2051 Piedmont Lake Rd, Pine Mountain, GA 31822-3598, **Home Phone:** (706)663-9088. **Business Addr:** Dentist, 1190 Martin Luther King Jr Blvd, Columbus, GA 31906, **Business Phone:** (706)322-3218.

### COOK, HON. JULIAN ABELE, JR.

Judge. **Personal:** Born Jun 22, 1930, Washington, DC; son of Julian Abele Sr (deceased) and Ruth Elizabeth McNeill; married Carol Annette Dibble; children: Julian Abele III, Peter Dibble & Susan Annette. **Educ:** Pa State Univ, BA, 1952; Georgetown Univ, JD, 1957; Univ Va, LLM, 1988. **Career:** Judge Arthur E Moore, law clerk, 1957-58; pvt pract atty, 1958-78; State MI, spec asst & atty gen, 1968-78; Univ Detroit-Mercy, adj prof law, 1970-74; Eastern Dist MI, US Courthouse, Detroit, US Dist judge, 1978-89, chief judge, 1989-96, sr judge, 1996-; Harvardn Univ, Trial Advocacy Workshop, instr, 1988-; US Dept Justice's Trial Advocacy Prog, instr, 1989-; Univ Detroit Sch Law, adj prof. **Orgs:** Chair & bd dir, Oakland Univ Proj Twenty Comt, 1966-68; pres, Pontiac Area Urban League, 1967-68; chair, Mich Civil Rights Comt, 1968-71; bd dir, Todd Phillips C's Home, 1968-78; bd dir, Am Civil Liberties Union, 1976-78; founder, master bench, chap XI, Am Inn Ct, 1994-96; Cont Legal Educ Comt, Oakland County Bar Asn, 1968-69, judicial liaison, Dist Ct Comt, vice chair, 1977; Cont Legal Educ Comt, 1977; Unauthorized Prac Law, 1977; MI Supreme Ct Defense Serv Comt, 1977; exec bd dir, 1968-89, pres, 1975-76, Child & Family Serv Mich; chmn, Sixth Circuit Comt Stand Jury Instr, 1986-; bd dir, Am Heart Asn Mich; fel Am Bar Asn, 1981-; bd dir, Detroit Urban League, 1983-85; Brighton Health Srev Corp, 1985-92; chmn, Comt Financial Disclosure, Judicial Conf US, 1990-93; Harvard Univ, trial advocacy workshop, instr, 1988-; lifemem, Nat Asn Advan Colored People; Pa State Univ Alumni Asn, alumni coun, 1986-92; bd dir, Hutzel Hosp, 1984-95; bd visitor, Georgetown Univ, 1992-; NY Univ Root Tilden Snow Scholar Prog, screening panel, 1991-99; Mediation Tribunal Asn; bd dir, Third Judicial Circuit Mich, 1992-; Am Law Inst, 1996-; Judicial Coun Sixth Circuit, sr judge personnel comt, 1996-97; fel Mich Bar Found, 1987-, chair, 1993-; co-chair, Nat Exec Comm, Arch Labor & Urban Affairs Wayne State Univ, 1988-; Am Bar Asn; Nat Bar Asn; State Bar Mi; Wolverine Bar Asn Am Bar Found; co-chmn, Prof Develop Task Force, Mich Bar Asn; Mich Asn Black Judges; Fed Bar Asn; Georgetown Univ Alumni Asn. **Honors/Awds:** Distinguished Citizen of the Year, Nat Asn Advan Colored People, 1970; Citation of Merit, Pontiac, MI Area Urban League, 1971; chmn, Civil Rights Commn, achieved resolution, State of MI, House of Representatives, 1971; Boss of the Year, Legal Secretary Asn, 1973-74; Pathfinders Award, Oakland Univ, 1977; Service Award, Todd-Phillips Home Inc, 1978; Focus & Impact Award Oakland Univ, 1985; Distinguished Alumnus Award, Pa State Univ, 1985; Distinguished Alumnus Award & John Carroll Award, Georgetown Univ, 1989; Augustus Straker Award, 1988; Absalom Jones Award, Union Black Episcopalians, Detroit Chap, 1988; Bench-Bar Award, Wolverine, Detroit Bar Asn, 1987; Presidential Award, North Oakland Co, Nat Asn Advan Colored People, 1987; Honor Soc, Univ Detroit Sch Law, 1981; B nai B rith Barrister, 1980; Fed Bar Asn, 1978; Doctor of Law, Honoris Causa, Georgetown Univ, 1992; Brotherhood Award, Jewish Law Veterans of the US, 1994; Champion of Justice Award, MI State Bar, 1994; Doctor of Laws, Honoris Causa, Univ Detroit-Mercy, 1996; Wayne State Univ, Doctor of Laws, Honoris Causa, 1997; Paul R Dean Award, Georgetown Univ, 1997; Michigan State University, Doctor of Laws, Honoris Causa, 2005; First Annual Trailblazers Award, D. Augustus Straker Bar Asn; Humanitarian Award, City Wide Choir Union; named one of the Most Respected Judges in Michigan. **Special Achievements:** Published: Jurisprudence of Original Intention, co-author, 1986; A Quest for Justice, 1983; Some Current Problems of Human Administration, co-author, 1971; The Changing Role of the Probation Officer in the Federal Court, article, Federal Sentencing Reporter, vol 4, no 2, p 112, 1991; An Overview of the US District Court for the Eastern District of Michigan, article, Inter Alia, vol 28, no 1, winter 1990; Rule 11: A Judicial Approach to an Effective Administration of Justice in the US Courts, 15Ohio N U L 397, 1988; ADR in the United States District Court for Eastern District of Michigan, Michigan Pleading and Practice ADR, Section62A-405-62A-415, 1994; Thur good Marshall and Clarence Thomas: A Glance at Their Philosophies, Michigan Bar Journal, March 1994, Vol 73, No 3, p298; George A Googasian-58th President of the State Bar of Michigan, Michigan Bar Journal, Oct 1992, vol 71, No 10; "Family Responsibility, Federal Sentencing Reporter," 1995; Federal Civil Procedure Before Trial: Sixth Circuit, 1996; "Dream Makers: Black Judges on Justice," Univ of MI Law Review, 1996; "Death Penalty," co-author Cooley Law Review, 1996; "Closing Their Eyes to the Constitution: The Declining Role of the Supreme Court in the Protection of Civil Rights," co-author, Detroit Col of Law, 1996;"Professionalism: An Order of the Court," Michigan Bar Journal, August1998, No 8, p 848; voted one of the "Most Respected Judges in Michigan" by the subscribers to Michigan Lawyers Weekly, 5 Michigan Law Weekly, 666, April 29, 1991; MI Lawyers Weekly, voted 1 of 25 Most Respected Judges in MI, 1990, 1991; Detroit Monthly, voted 1 of the best Judges in the Metro Detroit area, 1991; First African-American law clerk to an Oakland County, Michigan judge. **Home Addr:** 13000 Burton, Oak Park, MI 48237. **Business Addr:** Senior Judge, United States District Court, 231 W Lafayette Blvd Fl 5, Detroit, MI 48226, **Business Phone:** (313)234-5100.

### COOK, KEITH LYNN

Banker. **Personal:** Born May 24, 1963, Chicago, IL; married Tia. **Educ:** Roosevelt Univ, attended 1992. **Career:** Citibank ISB, mortgage acct exec, 1986-92; Harris Trust & Savings Bank, residential mortgage specialist, 1992-95, asst mgr, 1995-, mgr, bus develop, currently. **Orgs:** Nat Asn Black Accts, 1990; affil mem, S & Southwest Bd Realtors, 1992; Dearborn Real Estate Bd, 1994; Chicago Real

Estate Fund, 1994; Urban Bankers Chicago, 1996-; Network Black Real Estate Profs, 1993; Cosmopolitan Coun, 1996-. **Honors/Awds:** Reinvestment Act Award, Harris Bank, 1992, 1993. **Home Addr:** 901 E 47th St, Chicago, IL 60615. **Business Addr:** Manager Business Development, Harris Trust & Savings Bank, 111 W Monroe, Chicago, IL 60603-4096, **Business Phone:** (312)461-5798.

**COOK, LEVI, JR.**
Executive, president (organization), chief executive officer. **Career:** Advantage Enterprises Inc, dir, secy, pres, treas, pres & chief exec officer, 1980-. **Business Addr:** President, Chief Executive Officer, Advantage Enterprises Inc, 5030-T Advantage Dr, Toledo, OH 43612, **Business Phone:** (419)727-0027.

**COOK, DR. NATHAN HOWARD**
Educator. **Personal:** Born Apr 26, 1939, Winston-Salem, NC; married Thelma Vernelle Upperman; children: Carlene Y & Erika Y. **Educ:** NC Cent Univ, BS, 1961, MA, 1963; Univ NC, Greensboro, 1964; NC State Univ, grad credit, 1965; Okla State Univ, PhD, 1972. **Career:** Barber-Scotia Col, asst prof biol, 1962-68; Wica Chem Inc, fac intern, 1968; Okla State Univ, grad teaching asst, 1968-69; Lincoln Univ, Dept Biol, vpres acad affairs, prof emer, head, currently. **Orgs:** Fel Ford Found, 1969-71; chmn, Sickle Cell Adv Comm Mo Div Health, 1972-79; eval, panelist Nat Sci Found, 1976; bd dir, Am Cancer Soc Cole Unit 1981-85; consult, rev panelist, Nat Inst Health/div Res Resources, 1982; Environ Qual Comm, 1981-; pres elect, Mo Acad Sci, 1984-85; pres, Sunrise Optimist Club Jefferson City, 1984-85. **Home Addr:** 2908 Sue Dr, Jefferson City, MO 65101. **Business Addr:** Professor Emeritus, Vice President, Lincoln University, 820 Chestnut St, Jefferson City, MO 65101, **Business Phone:** (573)681-5000.

**COOK, RALPH D.**
Lawyer. **Personal:** Born Apr 29, 1944, Birmingham, AL; son of Joe and Nannie; married Charlsie Davis; children: Kimberly, Nakela & Ralph Jr. **Educ:** Tenn State Univ, BS, 1964; Howard Univ Sch Law, JD, 1967; Univ Nashville. **Career:** Legal Asst Found, 1971-72; City Berkeley, Calif, 1972-73; Miles Col, prof; Bessemer, asst dist atty, 1974-76; Miles Law Sch, dean, 1975-90; Miles Law Sch, prof law, 1975-99, dean, 1976-90; San Jose State, prof, 1975-99; Cabrillo Col, prof; Frequent CLE speaker; Family Ct Jefferson County, dist judge, 1977-81; 10th Circuit, Circuit Judge, 1981-93; Supreme Ct Ala, assoc judge, 1993-2000, Family Ct Jefferson County, Bessemer Div, dist judge & Bessemer Div Tenth Judicial Circuit, circuit judge, 1981-84; Kiwanis Int, lt gov, 1991-92; Hare, Wynn, Newell & Newton LLP, atty, 2001-. **Orgs:** Birmingham Bar Asn; Calif State Bar Asn; Ala State Bar Asn; Am Bar Asn; pres, Ala Trial Lawyers Asn, 1992-93; Bessemer Bar Asn; Am Law Inst; Nat Bar Asn; pres, Ala Law Asn, 1992-93; charter pres & mem bd dir, W Jefferson Kiwanis Club; chmn & bd trustee, Bethel African Methodist Episcopal Zion Church; fel Am Col Trial Lawyers; bd dir, Ala Power Co; bd dir, Birmingham Civil Rights Inst; bd dir, Ala Civil Justice Found; bd dir, Community Found, Greater Birmingham; bd mem, Kiwanis Club Birmingham; bd dir, St Vincents Found; pres, Ala Asn Justice, 2006-07; Salvation Army; Bessemer Hall Hist & Bessemer YMCA; chmn bd trustee, Birmingham Mus Art, 2011. **Business Addr:** Attorney, Hare, Wynn, Newell & Newton LLP, Historic Massey Bldg, Birmingham, AL 35203-3378, **Business Phone:** (205)328-5330.

**COOK, RASHARD**
Football player, real estate executive. **Personal:** Born Apr 18, 1977, San Diego, CA; married Joy Scott; children: 5. **Educ:** Univ Southern Calif, BA, sociol, 1998. **Career:** Football player (retired); Philadelphia Eagles, defensive back, 1999-2004; Home team Mortgage & Realty & Intero Real Estate Serv, owner, agt, currently. **Business Addr:** Owner, Agent, Hometeam Mortgage & Realty, 2127 Olympic Pkwy Suite 242, Chula Vista, CA 91915, **Business Phone:** (619)746-4331.

**COOK, ROBERT A.**
Administrator, executive. **Educ:** Del State Univ, BS, mkt bus admin. **Career:** Atlanta Neighborhood Develop Partnership; Ga Housing and Finance Authority; Augusta's Planning Comn, legis appointee; Augusta Neighborhood Improv Corp, pres & chief exec officer, exec dir, 2000-. **Business Addr:** President, Chief Executive Officer, Augusta Neighborhood Improvement Corp, 925 Laney Walker Blvd 3rd fl, Augusta, GA 30901-2959, **Business Phone:** (706)724-5565.

**COOK, RONALD R.**
Association executive. **Educ:** Univ Detroit Mercy Law Sch, mentors. **Career:** Health Alliance Plan, Detroit, sr coun, dir legis affairs & vpres, assoc atty, 2000-; Howard & Howard Attorneys, staff; Henry Ford Health Syst, staff; Mich House Representatives, staff. **Orgs:** Assoc coun & chair, Legis Comt, Mich Asn Health Plans; Detroit Regional Chamber; chmn, City Detroit Bd Ethics. **Honors/Awds:** Named in 100 Emerging Business Leaders, Detroit Reg Chamber. **Special Achievements:** One of the YMCAs Minority Achievers for 2002-03. **Business Addr:** Associate Attorney, Vice President, Health Alliance Plan, 2850 W Grand Blvd, Detroit, MI 48202, **Business Phone:** (800)422-4641.

**COOK, RUFUS (RUFUS LYNWOOD COOK)**
Lawyer, executive. **Personal:** Born Nov 22, 1936, Birmingham, AL; children: Bruce. **Educ:** Talladega Col, BA, 1956; Univ Chicago, PhD, 1959. **Career:** Judge Luther M Swygert US Dist CT, law clerk, 1959-60; pvt pract lawyer, 1963; Cook & Revak Ltd, pres, currently. **Orgs:** Pres & bd chmn, Continental Inst Tech Inc; pres, Phoenix Realty Inc; partner, Cook Apts Assocs; pres, Pinnacle & Graphics Corp; Nat Moot Ct Team Univ Chicago, 1958-59; chmn bd, Hyde Park -Kenwood Community Conf, 1966-68; bd mem, Chicago Fedn Settlements, 1967-69; Daniel Hale Williams Univ. **Honors/Awds:** Prize, Univ Chicago, 1958. **Home Addr:** 7330 S Ridgeland Ave, Chicago, IL 60615, **Home Phone:** (773)947-9777. **Business Addr:** President, Owner, Cook & Revak Ltd, 7411 S Stony Island Ave, Chicago, IL 60649-3613, **Business Phone:** (773)752-2000.

**COOK, DR. SAMUEL DUBOIS**
College administrator, college president. **Personal:** Born Nov 21, 1928, Griffin, GA; son of Manuel and Mary Beatrice Daniel; married Sylvia Merelene Fields; children: Samuel Jr & Karen Jarcelyn. **Educ:** Morehouse Col, AB, hist, 1948; Ohio State Univ, MA, polit sci, 1950, PhD, 1954. **Career:** Educator (retired); Southern Univ, prof, 1955-56; Atlanta Univ, chmn, 1956-66; Univ Ill, vis prof, 1962-63; Univ Calif, vis prof; Duke Univ, prof, 1966-74; Ford Found, prog officer, 1969-71; Dillard Univ, pres, 1975-97. **Orgs:** Bd trustee, Martin Luther King Ctr Soc Chg, 1969-; ed bd, Am Polit Sci Rev; ed bd, Jour Polit; ed bd, Jour Negro Hist; bd dir, Southern Christian Leadership Conf; bd dir, Am Coun Libr Resources; bd trustee, Coun Relig Int Affairs; pres, Southern Polit Sci Asn; Mayor's Charter Rev Comt; bd dir, Inst Serv Educ; Exec Coun, Am Polit Sci Asn; vpres, Am Polit Asn; Phi Beta Kappa; Pi Sigma Alpha; Nat Coun Humanities, Omicron Delta Phi; Omega Psi Phi; Sigma Pi Phi; chmn, United Negro Col Fund; trustee emer, Duke Univ. **Special Achievements:** First African American professor at Duke University. **Home Addr:** 2601 Gentilly Blvd, New Orleans, LA 70122.

**COOK, DR. SUZAN DENISE JOHNSON**
Clergy, educator. **Personal:** Born Jan 28, 1957, New York, NY; daughter of Wilbert T and Dorothy C; married Ronald; children: Samuel David & Christopher. **Educ:** Emerson Col, BS, speech, 1976; Columbia Univ Teachers Col, MA, 1978; Union Theol Sem, Mdiv, 1983; United Theol Sem, Doctor Ministry, 1990; Dartmouth Col. **Career:** WBZ-Boston, WPLG-Miami & WJLA-Wash, DC, tv producer, 1977-80; NBC, tv producer; Austrilian Broadcasitng Corp, tv producer; CBS, tv producer; Bronx-Lebanon Hosp Ctr, Bronx, NY, pub rels officer, 1980-81; Mariners' Temple Baptist Church, sr pastor, 1983-96; Multi Ethnic Ctr, exec dir & founder, 1985-; New York Theol Sem, adj prof, 1988; NY Police Dept, chaplain; Harvard Univ, Divinity Sch, vis prof, dean; White House, Domestic Policy Coun, 1993-94; Faith Initiatives, HUD secy, 1994-97; Bronx Christian Fel, sr pastor & chief exec officer, 1996-; JONCO Productions Inc, co founder, chief exec officer, currently; United State Dept, us ambassador-at-large int relig freedom, 2011-13. **Orgs:** Vpres, NY Coalition 100 Black Women, 1996-97; Am Baptist Churches; adv bd mem, Pres's Initiative On Race & Reconciliation, 1997-98; Delta Sigma Theta sorority, 2013. **Honors/Awds:** Essence Woman, Essence Magazine, 1983; YWCA Award, 1986; Young Achievers, Nat Coun Negro Women, 1988; Woman of Conscience Award, Nat Coun Women, United Nations, 1989; Martin Luther King Award, CBS TV, 1995; Visionary Leaders Award, SOBRO, 1997. **Special Achievements:** Book: "Wise Women Bearing Gifts, Judson: Valley Forge", ed, 1988; "Preaching In Two Voices, Judson: Valley Forge", 1992; "Sister to Sister", 1995; "Too Blessed to be Stressed Words of Wisdom for Women on the Move", 1998; "Sister Strength", 1998; First African American woman to be elected to an American Baptist Church; One of top 15 Women in Ministry, Ebony, November, 1997; First African American woman & first women to be elected to Ambassador-at-Large for International Religious Freedom, 2011; First female senior pastor in the 200-year history of the American Baptist Churches; First black woman to earn a doctorate from Union Seminary; First woman elected president of the Hampton University Ministers, 2002. **Home Addr:** 1020 Grand Concourse Suite 6F, Bronx, NY 10451, **Home Phone:** (212)538-2169. **Business Addr:** Pastor, Jonco Productions, PO Box 226, New York, NY 10272-0226, **Business Phone:** (212)289-4374.

**COOK, TOI FITZGERALD**
Football player, executive. **Personal:** Born Dec 3, 1964, Chicago, IL; married Kristine; children: Connor, Carson & Caitlyn. **Educ:** Stanford Univ, commun, 1987. **Career:** Football player (retired), consult, executive; New Orleans Saints, defensive back, 1987-93; Stanford Univ, outfielder, 1987; San Francisco 49ers, 1994-95; Carolina Panthers, 1996-97; Stanford Athletic, bd dir, currently; Broadband Sports, consult, 1999-2002; Gersh Agency, Bus Develop Sports Div, exec vpres, 2004-06; Toi Cook Mgt Group LLC, owner, 2007-; A2 Holdings, consult, 2008; Dreier Sports, 2008; Dreier Stein Kahan Browne Woods George LLP, Sports Group, consult, 2008; Empire Film Group, pres, 2012. **Orgs:** NFL Alumni Asn Southern Calif, 1987-2002; bd advisor, Amarantus BioSciences Inc, 2012-. **Honors/Awds:** Stanford Athletic Hall of Fame, 2014. **Business Addr:** Board of Advisor, Amarantus BioSciences Inc, 953 Ind St, San Francisco, CA 94107, **Business Phone:** (408)737-2734.

**COOK, TONYA DENISE**
School administrator. **Personal:** Born Feb 4, 1968, Atlanta, GA; daughter of Robert Stinson Jr and Mary. **Educ:** Ga State Univ, BBA, mkt, 1994; Andrew Young Sch Policy Studies, MS, human resource develop, 2005. **Career:** Women Hold Up Half Sky Total Dance Co, dancer/actress, 1989-98; Nat Black Arts Festival, Dance With Total Dance Co, 1994 & 1996; Fox Theatre, usher, 1994-2008; Ga State Univ, Off African Am Stud Serv & Prog, spec events coordr, 1996-99, Off Diversity Educ Prog, admin coordr, 1999, Off Stud Life & Leadership Inter cult Rels, Multicultural Ctr, 1999-, prog specialist, 1999-, front line supvr, 2002, interim greek advisor, 2005, leadership acad women, 2005-06, interim prog advisor, 2006-07; Stork's Nest Blitz, event producer, 1998-. **Orgs:** Zeta Phi Beta Sorority Inc, 1989-; vol, Atlanta Conv & Visitor's Bur, 1994-2002; chair, African Am Heritage Awards, 1994, 1997, 1998 & 1999; World Union African People, 1998-; Atlanta Asn Black Journalists, 1999-; Nat Asn Exec Secretaries & Admin Assts, 1999-; adv bd, Event Planning Mag, 1999-; Vol Steering Comt, Jomandi Prod, 1999-; Enlighten Cir, 2000-; Nat Black Arts Festival's Contemp Circle; Atlanta Women Found's Destiny Fund, 2008; Nat Asn Prof Women; Arts Leader Metro Atlanta Leadership Class, 2013; Dance Africa Atlanta Planning Comt, 2013; Women Looking Ahead. **Home Addr:** 270 Martin St Suite 91, Atlanta, GA 30312, **Home Phone:** (404)584-7706. **Business Addr:** Program Specialist, Georgia State University, 44 Courtland St, Atlanta, GA 30303-3965, **Business Phone:** (404)413-1850.

**COOK, VICTOR TRENT**
Singer, actor. **Personal:** Born Aug 19, 1967, New York, NY. **Career:** TV Series: "The Days & Nights of Molly Dodd", 1991; "Smokey Joe's Cafe: The Songs of Leiber & Stoller", 2000; "My Favorite Broadway: The Love Songs", 2001; "Three Mo' Tenors", 2001; "Cook, Dixon & Young: In Concert", 2005; "Tavis Smiley", 2006. **Honors/Awds:** Nominee, Tony Award, 1995; $100, 000 Male Vocal Champion!, Star Search, 1998. **Business Addr:** Singer, c/o Tradwick Artist Management, 250 W 57th St Suite 901, New York, NY 10107, **Business Phone:** (212)581-6181.

**COOK, WALLACE JEFFERY**
Clergy, dentist. **Personal:** Born Jul 14, 1932, El Reno, OK; married Martha Louise Charles; children: Cheryl, Jeffery & Jeryl. **Educ:** Ariz State Univ, BA, 1954; Howard Univ, DDS, 1957; Colgate Rochester Crozer Divinity Sch, MDiv, 1964; Va Union Univ, DDiv, 1973; Union Theol Sem, Richmond, DMin, 1978. **Career:** USAF, Dentist, 1957-61; First Baptist Church Yardley PA, pastor, 1963-64; Ebenezer Baptist Church Providence RI, pastor, 1964-94; Joseph Samuels Dent Clin, dentist, 1969; Providence Pub Sch, dentist dept health, 1970; Ebenezer Baptist Church, pastor emer, currently; Guildfield Baptist Church, interim co-pastor, currently. **Orgs:** Urban League, 1970; Urban Coalition, 1970; Richmond Comm Sr Ctr, 1975; Richmond Opportunity Indus Ctrs, 1976. **Home Addr:** 3700 Moss Side Ave, Richmond, VA 23222-1820, **Home Phone:** (804)321-2210. **Business Addr:** Pastor Emeritus, Ebenezer Baptist Church, 216 W Leigh St, Richmond, VA 23220, **Business Phone:** (804)643-3366.

**COOK, PROF. WILLIAM WILBURT**
Educator. **Personal:** Born Aug 4, 1933, Trenton, NJ; son of Frances Carter and Cleve. **Educ:** Trenton State Col, BS, valedictorian, 1954; Univ Chicago, MA, 1976. **Career:** Trenton Pub Sch, teacher Eng & social studies, 1954-61; Princeton Regional Sch, Eng Dept, teacher Eng, chair, 1961-73; Dartmouth Col, assoc prof Eng, prof Eng, 1973, dir African & Afro-Am studies, 1977-84, 1985-90; Dartmouth Col, Israel Evans Prof Oratory & Belles Lettres, 1991-, Dept Eng & chair, 1994, prof Eng, prof emer, currently. **Orgs:** Humanities consult, Nat Fac Arts & Sci, 1976-; Danforth Asn, 1979-85; bd dir, Am Folk Theater, 1982-; patron & dir, N Country Theater, 1983-; chair & adv comn minority affairs, Conf Col Comp & Commun, 1983-85; cmedia consult, Nat Endowment Humanities, 1984-; adv bd, Nat Civil Rights Mus, 1986-88; asst chair 1990-91, prog chair, 1991 & chair, 1992, Conv Col Comp & Commun. **Home Addr:** 13 Dresden Rd, Hanover, NH 03755, **Home Phone:** (603)643-2054. **Business Addr:** Professor Emeritus, Dartmouth College, 6032 Sanborn House, Hanover, NH 03755, **Business Phone:** (603)646-2316.

**COOKE, ANNA L.**
Librarian. **Personal:** Born Jackson, TN; daughter of Thurston Lee and Effie Cage Lee; married James A; children: Elsie Holmes. **Educ:** Lane Col, BA, 1944; Atlanta Univ, MLS, 1955. **Career:** Librn (retired); Douglas Jr High Sch Haywood County, Tenn, prin, 1944-46; Jackson City Sch, teacher, 1947-51, librn, 1951-63; Lane Col, catalog librn, 1963-67, PR & Alumni dir, 1966-69, head librn, 1967-88; Metro Forum, Jackson Sun, freelance writer, 1990-; Links, Inc, charter mem. **Orgs:** Am Libr Asn, 1964-; bd dir, Am Cancer Soc, 1967-73; sec bd dir, Jackson Arts Coun, 1974-76; bd dir, Reelfoot Girl Scout Coun, 1974-86, First vpres, 1983-86; bd trustee, Jackson Madison Co Libr, 1984-93; Tenn Libr Asn; W Tenn Libr Asn; Am Libr Asn; Delta Sigma Theta Sorority Inc; Links Inc; NAACP; bd dir, Jackson Vol Ctr, 1988-90; chmn, women's adv bd, HCA Reg Hosp Jackson, 1990-96; Jackson/Madison County Hist Zoning Comm, 1993-96. **Honors/Awds:** Library Sci Lane Col, 1966; Hon Fellow Philosophical Soc Eng, 1969; Serv Plaque City of Jackson, 1972; Alumni Plaque Lane Col, 1975; Action Award, Radio Station WJAK, 1982; Girl Scout Friendmaker Award, 1985; Serv Plaque Delta Sigma Theta Sor; Distinguished Service Award, State Tenn, 1988; Diamond Jubilee Service Award, Delta Sigma Theta Sorority, 1988; Certificate of Merit, Lane Col, 1988; Presidential Citation, National Asn Equal Opportunity Higher Educ, 1989; Metro Forum Service Award, 1991-97; Distinguished Service Award, City of Jackson, 1992; Jackson/Madison County Library Board Service Award, 1993; Hon DHL, Atlanta Univ, 1993; Distinguished Service Plaques, Delta Sigma Theta Sorority, 1994-95; Hall of Fame, Alpha Kappa Alpha Community Affairs, 1995; Service Award, Delta Sigma Theta, 1995; Service Award, Housing Historic Zoning CMS, 1996; Treasure Award, Jackson City Community, 1997; Metro Forum Publisher's Award, 1997; Recognition Award, City of Jackson, 2001; Meritorious Sevice Award, NAACP, Jackson-Madison Cty Branch, 2002; Griat Literary Award, 2003. **Special Achievements:** Author "History of Lane College", 1987; Published poem God's Love in Dark Side of the Moon: The Natl Library of Poetry, 1994. **Home Addr:** 120 Hale St, Jackson, TN 38301, **Home Phone:** (731)427-7995.

**COOKE, CLARA SYLVIA. See MARTIN, SYLVIA COOKE.**

**COOKE, LEONARD G**
Law enforcement officer, president (organization), police officer. **Personal:** Born Weldon, NC. **Educ:** FBI Nat Acad, cert graduation, 1989; Linfield Col, BA, lib arts, 1996; Univ Va, Sorensen Inst Polit Leadership, cert graduation, 2004; Va Common Health Univ, Va Exec Inst, 2003, Grace E Harris Leadership Inst, 2004; Va Polytech Univ, MPA, 206. **Career:** Metrop Police Dept, City Wash, DC, police officer, 1970-92; Int Asn Chiefs Police, fel, 1988; Eugene Police Dept, City Eugene, Ore, chief police, 1992-98; Portsmouth Va Police Dept, City Portsmouth, Va, chief police, 1998-2002; Commonwealth Va, Dept Criminal Justice Serv, dir, 2002-10; White House, exec off pres & chief security officer, 2010-11; INL/State Dept, int police advisor, 2012-13. **Orgs:** FBI Nat Acad; nat pres, Nat Orgn Black Law Enforcement Exec; Off Comnr Pub Appointments; Int Asn Chiefs Police, Civil Rights Comn; Va Asn Chiefs Police; Nat Asn Advan Colored People; pres, Va Asn Chiefs Police. **Home Addr:** 8 N Point Dr, Portsmouth, VA 23703-3644, **Home Phone:** (804)261-3780. **Business Addr:** Director, Commonwealth of Virginia, 202 N 9th St 10th Fl, Richmond, VA 23219-3694, **Business Phone:** (804)786-8718.

**COOKE, MELL. See COOKE, NELLIE.**

## COOKE, NELLIE (MELL COOKE)

Educator. **Personal:** Born Dec 17, 1948, Brighton, AL; daughter of Loudelia Freed and Prentis; married Robert Jefferson; children: Derek Vincent. **Educ:** DC Teachers Col, Wash, DC, BA, 1973; VPI-Va Tech, Blacksburg, VA, masters degree, 1988. **Career:** Shaw Jr High Sch, Wash, DC, teacher & dean stud, 1974; Bertie Backus Mid Sch, asst prin. **Orgs:** Chmn, Nat Jr Red Cross; adv comn, WHMM-TV, Washington, DC, currently; adv bd, Young Writers Contest Found. **Home Addr:** 10835 Lockwood Dr Suite 3, Silver Spring, MD 20901, **Home Phone:** (301)681-0655. **Business Addr:** Assistant Principal, Bertie Backus Mid Sch, 5171 S Dakota Ave NE, Washington, DC 20017, **Business Phone:** (202)576-6110.

## COOKE, HON. THOMAS H., JR.

Executive. **Personal:** Born Oct 13, 1929, Camden, SC; married Audrey E Wilson; children: Bonnye A Jefferson, Julie L & Michael W Thomas III. **Educ:** NY Univ, BS, 1954; Montclair State Col, MA, 1974. **Career:** US Veterans Admin Hosp, corrective therapist, 1957-58; Newark Bd Educ, Victoria plan coordr, 1958-77; City E Orange, mayor, 1978-85; McLaughlin PivenVogel Inc, sr govt bond specialist, 1986-87; Maintenance Mgt Specialists Inc, pres. **Orgs:** Bd dir, vpres, Nat Conf Black Mayors, 1978-85; govt rels comn, Nat United Way, 1979-; bd dir, exec comt, US Conf Mayors, 1981-85; bd dir, finance comt, Nat League Cities, 1981-85; comnr, NJ Martin L King Commemorative Comn, 1983-; comnr, NJ Drug Adv Comn, 1983-; bd dir, NJ Multi Housing Indust, 1987-; life mem, Nat Asn Advan Colored People; Nat Coun Negro Women; Nat Coun Jewish Women. **Home Addr:** 74 Hawthorne Ave, East Orange, NJ 07018, **Home Phone:** (201)674-3745.

## COOKE, WILCE L.

Mayor, government official. **Personal:** Born Jun 18, 1939, Benton Harbor, MI; son of Elizabeth Walker; married Beverly. **Educ:** Oakland Community Col Sch, prac nursing, 1968; Inst Adult Educ, 1970; Lake Mich Col, AA, 1975; Western Mich Univ, BS, 1976, MA, 1985. **Career:** City Benton Harbor, mayor. **Orgs:** Adv brd, Tri-Can; suprv comn, Ppl Comm Fed Credit Union; bd dir, org Self Help Co-Op; charter rev comn, Benton Harbor Charter Comn; treas, mercy Hosp Staff Coun, 1977-82; Phi Theta Kappa; Benton Two Black Coalition; bd dir, Berrien County Heart Unit, Mich Heart Asn; trustee bd, asst sunday sch supt, Bethlehem Temple Pentecostal Church; Alpha Kappa Delta. **Honors/Awds:** Scholarship Compet, Natl Upper Div, 1976; Outstanding Service Award, Benton Harbor Concerned Citizens; Spearheading drive in retaining Open Heart Surgical Unit at Mercy Hosp in Southwestern Michigan, Berrien County Med Soc, 1978. **Home Addr:** 1130 Salem Ave, Benton Harbor, MI 49022-5633, **Home Phone:** (269)925-2358. **Business Addr:** Mayor, City of Benton Harbor, 200 E Wall St Benton Harbor City Hall, Benton Harbor, MI 49022, **Business Phone:** (269)927-8400.

## COOLEY, KEITH WINSTON

Consultant, executive, government official. **Personal:** Born Oct 7, 1945, Ann Arbor, MI; son of Roy Van and Hyacinth Holmes; married Yvonne A Smiley; children: Brett Winston, Todd Lloyd, Ross Allyn & Erin Blair. **Educ:** Univ Mich, BSE, engineering physics, 1967, MSE, nuclear engineering, 1972. **Career:** Gen Elec Corp, Knolls Atomic Power Lab, exp physicist, 1968-69, res engr, 1972-73, Environ Activ Staff, staff proj engr, 1973-78, Cadilac Motor Car, staff proj engr, 1978-83, prog mgr, future car line, 1983-86, engineering dept head, 1986-94, dir strategic planning & issues mgr, 1994-96; Univ Mich, dir, 1969-72; Gen Motors, proj engr, 1972, prog mgr & engineering dir, 1985; GM Corp Communs, dir strategic bus planning, 1994; Principia Inc, bus consult, pres, 1997; Motorola Corp, dir; Telematics Int Sales, GM acct, 2001; Focus: HOPE, chief operating officer, 2002-06, chief exec officer, 2006-; Dept Labor & Econ Growth, Mich, dir, 2007-; Adv Firm, chief exec officer; NextEnergy, pres & chief exec officer; Principia LLC, pres & chief exec officer, 2010-. **Orgs:** Founder, Minority Engineering Programs Office, Engineering Soc Detroit, 1980-; Detroit Inst Ophthal; Workforce Innovation Regional Econ Develop; life mem, Nat Black MBA Asn; Tau Beta Pi Engineering Hon Soc; Tenn Squire Asn; Univ Mich Alumni Soc; bd dir, Univ Mich Engineering Alumni Asn, 1991-93; founder, Principia Inc, 1997; Univ Mich Engineering Adv Coun; Mich Environ Coun; Mich Strategic Econ Investment & Commercialization Bd; Pub Sch Academies Detroit. **Home Addr:** , MI. **Business Addr:** President, Chief Executive Officer, Principia, LLC, **Business Phone:** (313)909-3034.

## COOLEY, HON. WENDY C.

Television show host, judge, television producer. **Personal:** Born Jan 1, 1952, Birmingham, AL; daughter of Louise Cargill and Bessie Crenshaw. **Educ:** Eastern Mich Univ, educ, 1968; Univ Mich, higher educ, 1972; Univ Detroit, JD, 1980. **Career:** Judge (retired), host, producer, spec educ Consult, community col instr.; 36th Dist Ct, judge, 1984; "Winning Ways", TV & Radio show, host & producer, 1990; Supreme Ct Mich, 1997. **Orgs:** Mich Dist Judges Asn; Asn Black Judges; Mich State Bar Asn; Nat Bar Asn; Nat Asn Negro Bus & Prof Women's Club Inc; Coalition 100 Black Women; Delta Sigma Theta; Gamma Phi Delta; Mich Martin Luther King Jr Holiday Comn; Nat Speakers Asn; Delta Sigma Theta; founder, pres, Women Who Win. **Home Addr:** 9811 W Charleston Blvd Apt 2-307, Las Vegas, NV 89117-7528, **Home Phone:** (702)363-4771.

## COOMBS, FLETCHER

Executive. **Personal:** Born Jul 8, 1924, Atlanta, GA; son of Fletcher and Pearl Magnolia Floyd; married Helen Grimes; children: Toni & Kei. **Educ:** Morehouse Col, AB; Atlanta Univ Sch Bus Admin, MBA; Ind Univ Bloomington, IN, Grad Sch Savings & Loan, cert, 1971. **Career:** Executive (retired); Mutual Fed Savings & Loan Assn, var positions, 1953-73, pres, 1973-90, vice chmn, bd dir, 1990-97. **Orgs:** Ga AAA Adv Bd, AAA S; fin chmn, bd mem, Sadie G Mays Nursing Home. **Home Addr:** 380 Waterford Rd NW, Atlanta, GA 30318-7247, **Home Phone:** (404)691-8366.

## COOMBS, HARRY JAMES

Executive, manager. **Personal:** Born Sep 19, 1935, Washington, DC; married Barbara Ann Parrish. **Career:** Schwartz Bros Whis Rec Dist, local prom mgr, 1965-67; Ramsel Prods, dir, 1968-68; CBS Recs Inc, E coast reg prom rep, 1969-69; Capitol Rec Dist Corp, E coast reg prom rep, 1969-70; Tangerine Recs Corp, nat field rep, 1970-71; R&B Prom, Easter Region, mgr; Philadelphia Int Rec, exec vpres, 1971, mgr, currently; Gamble-Huff Rec Inc, vpres promos. **Orgs:** Mem exec coun, Black Music Asn, 1978. **Home Addr:** 4905 Parkside Ave, Philadelphia, PA 19131, **Home Phone:** (215)877-6753. **Business Addr:** Manager, Philadelphia International Records, 309 S Broad St, Philadelphia, PA 19107, **Business Phone:** (215)877-6753.

## COOPER, ALBERT, SR.

Executive. **Personal:** Born Sep 22, 1934, Americus, GA; son of Anderson; married Josephine Wiggins; children: Albert Jr, Booker Alphonse & Jerel Boyd. **Educ:** Sumter Co Sch, dipl, gen educ, 1986; Ga Southwestern Col, Americus, GA, 1987. **Career:** Cooper's Const Co, owner, 1970-85; Cooper's Groc & Mkt, 1979-83; Kiwanis Club; Dist 1 City Coun. **Orgs:** Zoning bd, City Americus, 1978-85; Councilman, Americus, Ga, 1979-91; Early Bird Ctr, 1980; bd gov, Chamber Com, 1981; elected mayor, protem, 1982, 1985; chmn, Americus Housing Authority; chmn, Sumter Co Bd Health. **Home Addr:** 306 Southerfield Rd, Americus, GA 31719, **Home Phone:** (229)924-7611.

## COOPER, ESQ. ALMETA E.

Lawyer. **Personal:** Born Dec 27, 1950, Durham, NC; daughter of Patricia Carter and Horton; children: Elise Adele Nelson. **Educ:** Wells Col, BA, 1972; Northwestern Univ, Sch Law, JD, 1975. **Career:** Joint Community Accreditation Hosps, lectr; Am Col Hosp Adminrs, lectr; New Eng Hosp Assembly, lectr; Vedder Price Kaufman & Kammholz, assoc, 1975-77; Am Med Asn, asst dir health law div, 1977-82; Tuggle Hasbrouck & Robinson, partner, 1980-82; Meharry, Med Col, corp secy & gen coun, 1982-88; St Thomas Hosp, Nashville, TN, gen coun, 1988-91; Allegheny Health, Educ & Res Found, sr coun & vpres, 1992-98; Col St Francis, Nashville, TN, adj fac; MCP-Habemann Univ, sr coun, 1988-99; Ohio State Med Asn, gen coun, 1999-2008; Ohio State Univ Wexner Med Ctr, assoc vpres & assoc gen coun, 2008-13, exec dir advocacy, regulatory & qual improv progs, 2013-14; Morehouse Sch Med, sr vpres, gen coun & corp secy, 2014-. **Orgs:** Am Soc Hosp Attys; bd dir, Minority Legal Educ Resources; alt mem, Hines Veterans Admin Coop Studies Prog Human Rights Comn; pres & bd dir, Ill Family Planning Coun; Renaissance Women; Nashville Pvt Ind Coun; financial comnr, League Women Voters Nashville; Am Acad Health Attys, 1980-97; Leadership Nashville, 1986-87; Music City Chap Links; Tenn Bar Asn; Napier-Looby Bar Asn; Am Bar Asn, 1991-; pres, Am Health Lawyers Asn, 2004-05, fel 2012; Women Bus Leaders, 2002-13; Ohio State Univ Med Ctr Clin Professionalism Comt, 2004-08; US Healthcare Indust Found. **Honors/Awds:** Outstanding Alumna, Spelman Col; Outstanding Volunteer, Chicago Urban League; National Finalist for White House Fellowship, 1982; Woman of Achievement, Central Ohio YWCA, 2009; Inaugural Top Corporate Counsel Award, Bus First, Columbus, OH, 2011; David J. Greenburg Service Award, Am Health Lawyers Asn, 2012. **Special Achievements:** Publs, J Am Med Asn & St Louis Univ Law J. **Home Addr:** 381 Northview Dr, PO Box 2163, Columbus, OH 43209-1048, **Home Phone:** (614)372-1929. **Business Addr:** General Counsel, Senior Vice President, Morehouse School of Medicine, 720 Westview Dr SW, Atlanta, GA 30310, **Business Phone:** (404)752-1500.

## COOPER, ANTOINETTE (TONI COOPER)

Executive director. **Personal:** children: 2. **Educ:** Princeton Univ, AB, eng, 1982; Univ NC, Keenan-Flagler Bus Sch, Wachovia exec leadership prog; Kaplan Col. **Career:** Chase Bank; Fleet Bank; Citibank; Manufacturers Hanover Trust; Wachovia Wealth Mgt, Atlantic Region, managing dir, 1994-. **Orgs:** Diversity Coun Wealth Mgt; Corp Womens Adv Coun; Princeton Alumni Schs Comt; bd dir, Louise Wise Adoption Agency. **Business Addr:** Managing Director, Wachovia Wealth Management, 299 Morris Ave, Summit, NJ 07901, **Business Phone:** (908)522-5425.

## COOPER, BARBARA J.

Federal government official, security guard, teacher. **Personal:** Born NC; daughter of Jasper and Ezola Cooper Britt. **Educ:** Hampton Univ, BS; Mich State Univ, MBA; Stanford Univ, grad cert. **Career:** Federal government official, security guard (retired); Portsmouth VA Sch Syst, teacher; Cent Intelligence Agency, spec asst dep dir, dep dir personnel; dep inspector gen invests, dep dir financial mgt, dir financial mgt; security officer III. **Orgs:** Alpha Kappa Alpha Sorority; Nat Hampton Alumni Asn; vpres, Northern Va Chap, Nat Hampton Alumni Asn, 1984-86; adv coun, Howard Univ Sch Bus; adv bd, Omniplex World Servs Corp; pub affairs fel Stanford Univ. **Home Addr:** 1641 Morrill Ct, McLean, VA 22101.

## COOPER, BARRY MICHAEL

Screenwriter, journalist. **Career:** Journalist; Village Voice, investigative reporter, 1980-89; William Morris Agency LLC, screenwriter, currently; Films: New Jack City, screenplay, 1991; Sugar Hill, writer, 1993; Above Rim, screenplay, 1994; Blood Wall, screenplay, exec producer, dir & ed, 2005; Ser: "Pvt Times", 1991; "Am Gangster", producer, 2006; "Bloomberg Game Changers", 2010. **Business Addr:** Screenwriter, William Morris Agency LLC, 151 El Camino Dr, Beverly Hills, CA 90212, **Business Phone:** (310)274-7451.

## COOPER, BARRY MICHAEL

Entrepreneur, editor. **Personal:** Born Jan 1, 1956. **Educ:** Univ SC, Columbia, SC, BA, jour. **Career:** Orlando Sentinal Online, mgr, ed, managing ed; Blackvoices.com, founder, creator, chief exec officer. **Orgs:** Nat Asn Black Journalists; YMCA Black Achievers; Boy Scouts of Am; Nat Asn Advan Colored People. **Honors/Awds:** Pulitzer Prize nomination, 1983; MOBE IT Award, 1999, 2000. **Business Addr:** Managing Editor, Orlando magazine, 801 N Magnolia Ave Suite 201, Orlando, FL 32803.

## COOPER, DR. BOBBY G.

Educator, association executive, college administrator. **Personal:** Born Nov 3, 1938, Bolton, MS; married Della M Larkin; children: Christopher, Demetria Miles & LaCarole. **Educ:** Tougaloo Col Tougaloo, BS, 1961; Univ Ill, Urbana-Champaign, MS, 1970; Univ Colo, Boulder, EdS, 1971, EdD, 1977. **Career:** E T Hawkins High Sch, Forest MS, music tech, 1961-68; Camp Tree Tops, Lake Placid NY, counr, 1968-69; Spec Educ Opportunity Univ Ill Urbana, counr, 1969-70; Utica Community Col, chmn, 1972-, Humanities Div chair, music instr, currently, opera S, chorus master, 1980-81; Jubilee Singers, dir, currently; Hinds Community Col, choral dir, currently, chmn. **Orgs:** Am Choral Dir Asn; Music Comt Meth Church, 1976; Phi Delta Kappa; organist Asbury United Meth Church, Bolton, 1961-; trustee, Asbury United Meth Church Bolton, 1975-; dir, Wesley Found. **Honors/Awds:** Music scholarship Tougaloo Col, 1958; leadership develop grant, FordFound, 1968; inducted into Tougaloo Col Nat Alumni Hall of Fame; Instructor of The Year, Hinds Community Col; Hinds Community College Distinguished Instructor, 1998; Higher Education Appreciation Day Working for Academic Excellence Teacher of the Year Award, 1999; 3-E Award, Hinds Community Col, 2000; Distinguished Alumni Award, 2003; Southern Region Faculty Member Award, Asn Community Col Trustees, 2004; Tougaloo College Hall of Fame, 2005; Humanities Teacher of the Year Award, 2007. **Home Addr:** 270 Somerset Dr, Jackson, MS 39206, **Home Phone:** (601)981-1296. **Business Addr:** Choral Director, Hinds Community College, 3925 Sunset Dr, Jackson, MS 39213, **Business Phone:** (601)366-1405.

## COOPER, BRIDGETT LOUISE

Opera singer, singer. **Personal:** Born Jan 24, 1968, Washington, DC; daughter of Clement; children: Darby. **Educ:** E Carolina Univ, BM, opera performance, 1990; Am Inst Musical Studies, Opera Prog, opera & recital performance, 1993. **Career:** Wa Opera; Lyric Opera Chicago; Livent, Showboat; Living Arts Intl Tour; Aspen Opera Theater; Isreal Music Festival; USO Entertainer Tour Roster; Diaspera Opera Co; opera singer; Bridgette Cooper, Mezzo Soprano, Class Singer,1990-. **Orgs:** Alpha Kappa Alpha Sorority; Am Guild Musical Artists; Music Educators; Opera Am; Actor's Equity; SAG; AFTRA. **Honors/Awds:** Distinguished Alumni Award East, Carolina Univ Sch Music, 2013; Paul Robeson National Vocal Competition; Marjorie Lawrence International Vocal Competition; Outstanding College Students of America; YWCA Studio Club Competition; Meistersinger Competition; Who's Who of International Business & Professional Women; Ms District of Columbia Achievement; Bel Canto Competition Chicago, Semi Finalist, 1998; Voices of the New Millenium, Carnegie Hall, 2000; Black Archives of Southern Florida, 2001; Marjorie Lawrence Intl Vocal Comp, Semi Finalist, 2001; 1st place, Paul Robeson Nat Vocal Competition, 2001; Ms American Achievement of Washington DC. **Special Achievements:** AIMS, Graz Austria, 1993; Washington Opera, 1999; Bicentenial Celebration Recital, Christ Episcapal Church, 2002. **Home Addr:** 728 Dahlia St NW, Washington, DC 20012. **Business Addr:** Opera Singer, 244 5th Ave Suite B246, New York, NY 10001.

## COOPER, HON. CANDACE D.

Judge, lawyer. **Personal:** Born Nov 23, 1948, Los Angeles, CA; daughter of Eunice and Cornelius. **Educ:** Univ Southern Calif, BA, 1970, Univ Southern Calif Law Ctr, JD, 1973. **Career:** Judge (retired); Omelveny & Myers, summer assoc, 1972; Gibson Dunn & Crutcher, atty, 1974-80; Los Angeles Munic Ct, judge, 1980-87; Occidental Petrol Oil Co, law clerk, 1971; Los Angeles Super Ct, judge, 1987-99; Calif Ct Appeal, Second Appellate Dist, Div 2, assoc justice, 1999-2001; Calif Ct Appeal, Second Appellate Dist, Div 8, presiding justice, 2001-08. **Orgs:** Calif Asn Black Lawyers, 1975-87, Black Woman Lawyers Los Angeles, 1975-87; Nat Asn Women Judges, 1980-87; life mem, Nat Bar Asn; Nat Asn Advan Colored People; bd dir, Watts/Willowbrook Boys & Girls Club, 1982-87; Except C Found, 1982-87; Munic Ct Judges Asn, Planning & Res Adv Comt, 1984-87; Marshals Comt, 1982; chairperson, Ann Meetings Sem Comt, 1986; pres, Calif Judges Asn, 1988-89; Judicial Coun Adv Comt Pvt Judges, 1989-90; Judicial Coun Adv Comt Racial & Ethnic Bias Courts, 1991-97; State Bar Calif, 1992-95; Judicial Coun Select Comt Judicial Retirement, 1993; bd councilors, Univ Southern Calif Law Ctr, 1997-. **Honors/Awds:** Outstanding Alumni Ebonics, Univ S Calif, 1982; Woman of Achievement, Bus & Prof Women Los Angeles Sunset Chap, 1985; Bernard S Jefferson Judge Of the year Award, 1986, 2002; Beta Pi Sigma Sor Inc Alpha Chap Outstanding Black Achievement Award, 1986; A Los Angeles Ernestine Stalhut Award, Women lawyers, 1990; Judge Of the year, Los Angeles County Bar Asn, Criminal Justice Section, 1990, 1992; Criminal Judge Of the year, Century City Bar Asn, 1992; Silver Achievement Award, Los Angeles YWCA, 1991; Jurist Of the year Award, Los Angeles County Bar Asn, 1992, 1993; Achievement Award, YWCA, 1991; Alumni Merit Award, Univ Southern Calif Gen Alumni Asn, 1994; Outstanding Achievement in the Legal Profession Award, Univ Southern Calif Asn Black Law Alumni, 1996; Justice Joan Dempsey Klein Distinguished Judge Award, Calif Women Lawyers, 1997; Crystal Heart Award, Loved Ones Homicide Victims, 2000; Roger J. Traynor Memorial Award, Appellate Justice of the Year, Consumer Attorneys Asn Los Angeles, 2003; Power of One" Award, Black Women Lawyers Asn Los Angeles Found, 2006; Honoree, Nat Bar Asn Hall Fame, 2015.

## COOPER, CARDELL

Government official. **Personal:** married Sandy; children: Tiffane & Dana. **Educ:** Montclair State Univ, BS, polit sci, 1974; Rutgers Univ, MA, pub admin, 1978. **Career:** City E Orange, NJ, mayor, 1989-95; Essex, NJ, county adminr, 1989-90; US Dept Housing & Urban Develop, asst secy community planning & develop, 1998-; Cooper Assocs, pres, 2001-; Nat Community Develop Asn, Wash, exec dir, 2006-. **Orgs:** Advy bd, Conf Mayors; chair, Health & Human Servs Comt & Task Force Immigration; Sister Cities Int; bd mem Nat Housing Inst. **Business Addr:** Executive Director, National Community Development Association, 522 21st St NW Suite 120, Washington, DC 20006, **Business Phone:** (202)293-7587.

## COOPER, CECIL CELESTER

Baseball player, manager. **Personal:** Born Dec 20, 1949, Brenham, TX; son of Roy and Ocie; married Octavia; children: Kelly, Brittany & Tori Camille. **Educ:** Prairie View A&M Univ. **Career:** Baseball player (retired), manager; Boston Red Sox, infielder, 1971-76; Milwaukee Brewers, infielder, 1977-87, drr player dev, 1996-99; spec asst, 1999; CSMG Int, player agt, 1996; Brewers, scout, farm dir; Dugout, bench coach; Triple-A Indianapolis Indians, 2003-04; Houston Astros, bench coach, 2005; Coord Sports MGT Co Inc, vp, sports opers, owner; Houston Astros, mgr, 2007-09. **Orgs:** Milwaukee Brewers Baseball Club. **Home Addr:** 1431 Misty Bend, Katy, TX 77450, **Home Phone:** (281)392-3269.

### COOPER, DR. CHARLES W.
Physician. **Personal:** Born Jun 13, 1929, Hayti, MO; son of Roy Sr and Louise Black; married Bobbye Jean Hollins; children: Terri Lyn, Janis Kaye, Karyl Jean, Daryl Dean & Alan Jeffrey. **Educ:** Lincoln Univ, MO, BS, 1951; Univ Wichita, attended 1956; Meharry Med Col, MD, 1964. **Career:** Advocate Ill Masonic Med Ctr, intern, 1965; Wesley Med Ctr, resident, 1967; pvt pract, physician, 1989-. **Orgs:** Trustee, Quinn Chapel Am Methodist Episcopal Church, 1967-; pres, Lincoln Univ Found, 1972-73; Am Hereford Asn; fel Am Acad Family Phys. **Honors/Awds:** Nat Methodist Scholar, Meth Church, 1962-63; Mead Johnson Award, Mead Johnson Pharm Co, 1966; dipl, 1973. **Home Phone:** (573)896-9312. **Business Addr:** Physician, Private Practice, 12410 Cooper Rd, Holts Summit, MO 65043-2080, **Business Phone:** (573)896-5783.

### COOPER, CLARENCE
Lawyer, judge. **Personal:** Born May 5, 1942, Decatur, GA; married Shirley; children: Jennae Marie & Corey. **Educ:** Howard Univ Sch Law; Clark Col, BA, 1964; Emory Univ Sch Law, JD, 1967; Harvard Univ, John F Kennedy Sch Govt Pub Admin, MPA, 1978. **Career:** Atlanta Legal Serv Prog, atty, 1967-68; Fulton Co Ga, asst dist atty, 1968-76; City Atlanta Munic Ct, judge, 1975-80; Atlant Munic Ct, assoc judge, 1976; Fulton Co Super Ct, judge, 1980-90; Ga Ct Appeals, 1990-94; Harvard Univ, pub admin; US Dist Ct, Northern Dist Ga, judge, 1994-2009, fed judge & sr judge, 2009-. **Orgs:** Nat Bar asn, Gate City Bar asn; Nat Conf Black Lawyers, State Bar Ga, Atlanta Bar asn; Atlanta Legal Aid Socs; Atlanta Br Nat Asn Advan Colored People; Friendship Force Inc, 1986; Nat Urban League; bd dir, Amistrad Prod, EOAs Drug Prog; MIT Comm fel Prog, fel 1977; Atlanta Judicial Comn. **Special Achievements:** First African-American appointed to a full-time judgeship on the Atlanta Municipal Court. **Home Addr:** 3203 Kingsdale Dr SW, Atlanta, GA 30311-3635, **Home Phone:** (404)699-1468. **Business Addr:** Senior Judge, US District Courthouse, 1701 Richard B Russell Fed Bldg & US Courthouse, Atlanta, GA 30303-3309, **Business Phone:** (404)215-1390.

### COOPER, CONSTANCE M.
Educator. **Personal:** Born Lorain, OH; married Hewitt J; children: Candace, Adrienne & Hewitt Jr. **Educ:** Univ Mich, BBA, acct & finance, 1975, MBA, acct & finance, 1977. **Career:** Univ Cincinnati, Dept Bus & Com assoc prof & head, prof, currently, Carl H. Lindner Col Bus, dir diversity pathway, currently. **Orgs:** Treas, SUMA, 1999; Col Eve & Continuing Educ, Univ Cincinnati, Teaching Fel, 1999-2001; secy & bd dir, Coun Aging, 2001; treas, Victory Neighborhood Serv Agency, 2003; Teaching Comt, 2010-12. **Business Addr:** Professor, Director, University of Cincinnati, 302 Carl H Lindner Hall, Cincinnati, OH 45206-2839, **Business Phone:** (513)556-0871.

### COOPER, DANEEN RAVENELL
Engineer, manager, executive. **Personal:** Born Oct 27, 1958, St. Albans, NY; daughter of James and Carrie; married Maurice N; children: Elana Simone & Kellen Marsalis. **Educ:** Columbia Univ Sch Engrg & Appl Sci, BSEE, 1980. **Career:** Bell Labs, sr tech assoc, 1976-79; NJ Bell, engr, 1980-86; United Parcel Serv, Wireless Date Dept, mgr, 1986-. **Orgs:** Bell Labs Engrg Scholar Prog, 1976-80; counr, Sponsors Educ Opportunity, 1982-84; pres, Coun Action Minority Prof, 1983-87; pres, Coun Action Minority Prof, 1984-85; Consortium Telecom Execs, 1985-86; 100 Black Women, 1985-; Black Dp Asn, 1989-; Inst Elec & Electronics Engrs, 1989-; Maplewood So Orange, Parents Adv Coun, 1993-; pres, YMCA, Jaguar Track Club Parents Asn. **Honors/Awds:** Honored Dorson Community Found. **Home Addr:** 25 Highland Ave, Maplewood, NJ 07040-1815, **Home Phone:** (973)763-0617. **Business Addr:** Wireless Communications Manager, United Parcel Services, 340 MacArthur Blvd, Mahwah, NJ 07430.

### COOPER, DRUCILLA HAWKINS
Police officer. **Personal:** Born Dec 27, 1950, Riverside, CA; daughter of Alton and Thelma Anthony Williams; married Aubery J; children: Alton C Strickland & Crusetta A. **Educ:** City Col, San Francisco, CA, 1970; Los Med Amos Col, Pittsburg, basic law cert, 1970; Contra Costa Col, San Pablo, AA, 1982. **Career:** Police officer (retired); Plaza Hotel, San Francisco, maid, 1966; Sutter Hotel, San Francisco, maid, 1969-70; Blue Shield Ins Co, San Francisco, claims examr, 1973-78; Contra Costa County, Martinez, dep sheriff, 1978; Dr C Stephens, Richmond, billing clerk, 1979-80; City Berkeley, police officer. **Orgs:** Berkeley Black Police Officers Asn, 1981-; nat deleg, Nat Black Police Officers Asn, 1984-; Women's Peace Officers Asn, 1989-; star pt, Order Eastern Star, 1990-. **Honors/Awds:** Basic Intermediate & Advance Certificate, State Calif Dept Justice, 1981, 1985, 1989; Three Certificate of Completion, Juvenile Law & Procedures, Univ Southern Calif, 1985-86; Certificate of Training, Sexual Assaults Warrants, Dom Viol, Leandro Police Dept, 1985-85; Six Certificates, Criminal Justice Admin, NBPA, 1985-90. **Home Addr:** 5067 Hartnett Ave, Richmond, CA 94804, **Home Phone:** (510)233-9914.

### COOPER, DUANE (SAMUEL DUANE COOPER)
Basketball player, basketball coach. **Personal:** Born Jun 25, 1969, Benton Harbor, MI. **Educ:** Univ Southern Calif, pub admin, 1992; Argosy Univ Los Angeles, attended 2011. **Career:** Basketball player (retired), coach, speaker; Los Angeles Lakers, pt guard, 1992-93; Phoenix Suns, pt guard, 1993-94; Omaha Racers, Continental Basketball Asn, 1994-95; Charlotte Hornets, 1995; Okla City Cavalry, Continental Basketball Asn, 1995; Ft Wayne Fury, Continental Basketball Asn, 1995-96; Toronto Raptors, 1996; Yakima Sun Kings, Continental Basketball Asn, 1996-97, 1999-2000; Pogon Ruda slaska, Poland, 1997-98, 2000-01; Panionios, Greece, 1998-99; Asseco Prokom Gdynia, Poland, 1999; Znicz Pruszkow, Poland, 2001-02; Polonia Warsaw, Poland, 2002-03; Compton Dominguez High Sch, interim boys basketball coach, 2008-09; AUHSD, teacher, 2009-; Motivational Speaker, 2011-. **Honors/Awds:** NBA draft, 1992.

### COOPER, EARL
Management consultant, executive director. **Personal:** Born Feb 4, 1944, Oakland, CA; son of Martha and Earl. **Educ:** Merritt Col Oakland, AA, 1968; Golden Gate Col, San Francisco, BA, 1970; Univ Southern Calif, MBA, 1973. **Career:** IMPAC, bus anal, 1972-74; Jim Dandy Fast Foods Inc, mkt rep, 1974; Los Angeles Econ Develop Corp, exec dep dir, 1974-83; EC II & Assocs, pres, 1979-; White House Conf Small Bus, deleg, 1980; Counman Gilbert W Lindsay, Los Angeles, spec consult, 1983-86. **Orgs:** Nat Black MBA Asn, LA Chap, 1974-; US Small Bus Admin, Region Adv Comm, 1978-; pres, Black Bus Asn, Los Angeles, 1979-; Los Angeles Co Pvt Indust Coun, 1979-84; Mayor's Off Small Bus Assistance, 1980-; comnr Housing Auth Los Angeles, 1984-86; vpres, Nat Asn Advan Colored People, Los Angeles Br, 1986-88; pres, African Am Develop Consortium; nat bd mem, Minority Bus Enterprise Legal Defense & Educ Fund Inc; bd advisors, Oper HOPE Inc; bd advocates, Consumer Equity Inc; adv comt mem, African Am Tobacco Educ Network; Nat Bd Mem Educ Fund Inc; bd dirs, Nat Black Bus Coun; Southern Calif Gas Co Community Adv Comt; pres, Calif Coun Black Chambers. **Honors/Awds:** Nat Education for Business Development Award, 1983; Nat Award Excellence, SBA, 1983; Minority Business Advocate Year for State Calif, US Small Bus Admin, 1985; Outstanding Service Award, Federation Minority Business Association; Outstanding Volunteer Service, Human Relations Commission. **Home Addr:** 3949 Don Tomaso Dr, Los Angeles, CA 90008, **Home Phone:** (323)754-3116. **Business Addr:** President, EC II & Associates, 727 S Ardmore Ave Suite 602, Los Angeles, CA 90005.

### COOPER, EDITH W.
Executive. **Educ:** Harvard Univ, BA, 1983; Northwestern Univ, Kellogg Sch Mgt, MBA, 1986. **Career:** First Chicago Bank, first scholar, 1983-86; Bankers Trust, vpres, 1986-91; Morgan Stanley, prin, 1991-96; Goldman Sachs, sales mgt, managing dir, 1998-2000, partner, global head human capital mgt, 1996-, exec vpres, 2011-. **Orgs:** Bd Trustee, Teach Am's Fairfield Chap; vice chmn, Partnership Comt; Mgt Comt; adv bd, Kellogg Sch Mgt Global; bd dir, Brown Univ Sports Found; bd trustee, Northwestern Univ; bd trustee, Mus Mod Art; Boards Dirs Horizons. **Honors/Awds:** "Black Enterprise," 75 Most Powerful Blacks on Wall Street, 2011. **Business Addr:** Executive Vice President, Global Head of Human Capital Management, Goldman Sachs, 200 W St 29th Fl, New York, NY 10282, **Business Phone:** (212)902-1000.

### COOPER, DR. EDWARD SAWYER
Educator, physician. **Personal:** Born Dec 11, 1926, Columbia, SC; son of H H Sr (deceased) and Ada Sawyer (deceased); married Jean Marie Wilder; children: Lisa Hudgins, Edward S Jr (deceased), Jan Jones & Charles W. **Educ:** Lincoln Univ Pa, AB, 1946; Meharry Med Col, MD, 1949; Univ Pa, MA, 1973. **Career:** Philadelphia Gen Hosp, internship med res, 1949-54, staff physician, fel cardiol, 1956-57, co dir, Stroke Res Ctr 1968-74, pres med staff, 1969-71, chief med serv, 1972-76; Nat Heart Inst, fel, 1956-57; Univ Pa Sch Med, fac, 1958; Univ Pa, prof med, 1973-95, prof emer med, 1996-. **Orgs:** Cert & recertified Am Bd Internal Med, 1957-74; chmn talent recruitment coun & mem ed bd, J Nat Med Asn, 1959-77; Master Am Col Physicians, 1960; co-dir, Stroke Res Ctr Philadelphia Gen Hosp, 1968-74; mem coun, Col Physicians Philadelphia, 1970-84, 1994-98; bd dir, Blue Cross Greater Philadelphia, 1975-; bd dir, Am Found Negro Affairs, 1977-; chmn & mem exec comt, Stroke Coun Am Heart Asn, 1982-84; pres, Am Heart Asn, 1992-93; Am Col Physicians; bd trustee, Rockefeller Univ; Hosp Univ PA; Col Physicians Philadelphia; chmn exec comt; Am Health Educ African Develop; bd dir, Independence Blue Cross. **Special Achievements:** First African-American National President, American Heart Association and Tenured Professor, University of Pennsylvania School of Medicine. **Home Addr:** 6710 Lincoln Dr, Philadelphia, PA 19119-3155, **Home Phone:** (215)849-8234. **Business Addr:** Professor Emeritus, University of Pennsylvania School of Medicine, 3601 Mkt St, Philadelphia, PA 19104-2646, **Business Phone:** (215)662-4000.

### COOPER, ERNEST, JR.
City planner, educator, executive. **Personal:** Born Jun 19, 1941, Toone, TN; son of Ernest and Pauline Anderson; married Marva Harper; children: Jeanine, Ernest III & Keita. **Educ:** Lincoln Univ, BS, 1963; Howard Univ, MA, 1970; Univ PA, ABD. **Career:** Nia Group, pres; Adult & Voc Sch Cairo Ill, math instr, 1965-68; Wash Tech Inst, asst prof, math, 1968-70; ML King Jr Study Grant Woodrow Wilson Found, 1969-70, 1971-72; Wash Tech Inst Conceptualized Urban Plnng Tech Prog, train para-prof; Urban Inst, consult eval staff, 1971; Univ DC, Dept Urban & Reg Planning, chmn. **Orgs:** Am Planning Asn; Nat Asn Planners; Am Asn Univ Prof; Metrop Wash Planning & Housing Asn. **Home Addr:** 4122 18 St NW, Washington, DC 20011-5307, **Home Phone:** (202)291-6581. **Business Addr:** Chairman, University DC, 4200 Conn Ave NW, Washington, DC 20008, **Business Phone:** (202)282-3821.

### COOPER, EVELYN KAYE
Judge. **Personal:** Born Jun 23, 1941, Detroit, MI. **Educ:** Univ Detroit, BBA, 1968; Wayne State Univ, postgrad math; Wayne State Univ Law Sch, JD, 1973. **Career:** Detroit Jr High Sch, bd educ, 1966-70; Self-employed, atty law off, 1974-77; Detroit Traffic Ct, traffic ct referee, 1977-78; Recorder's Ct, judge, 1978. **Orgs:** Nat Asn Women Judges; Mich State Bar Asn; Mich Judges Asn; Womens Lawyers Asn; Women's Conf Concerns; Nat Asn Advan Colored People; March Dimes; Delta Sigma Theta Sorority; Nat Bar Asn; Wolverine Bar Asn. **Home Addr:** 1981 Thornhill Pl, Detroit, MI 48207-3824, **Home Phone:** (313)393-1994.

### COOPER, FRANK, III
Marketing executive, association executive. **Personal:** married Nina; children: 2. **Educ:** Univ Calif, Berkeley, Calif, BS, bus admin, 1986; Harvard Law Sch, JD, const law, 1990. **Career:** Motown Rec, sr bus affairs exec; Def Jam Recordings, sr bus affairs exec, 1993-96; Tommy Boy Music, sr exec, 1996-98; Urban Box Off Networks, co-founder, 1998-2001; Am Online Inc, vpres interactive mkt, 2001-03; PepsiCo, vpres mkt, 2003-05, chief mkt officer sparkling beverages, 2005-10, chief mkt officer global consumer engagement, 2010-; Pepsi-Cola N Am, vpres multicultural mkt & strategic initiatives, 2003, chief mkt officer sparkling beverages, 2008-10, vpres promotions & interactive mkt; Cornerstone Agency, 2010; BuzzFeed, chief mkt officer & chief creative officer, 2015-. **Orgs:** Chmn, Am Advert Fedn, 2009-11; bd dir, Bus Diplomatic Action. **Honors/Awds:** Video Gaming Partner of the Year, MI6, 2006; Industry Career Achievement, Am Advert Fedn, 2008; Recipient, ADCOLOR, 2010. **Special Achievements:** 100 Most Creative People in Business, Fast Company, 2010; The 100 Most Powerful Executives in Corporate America, Black Enterprise, 2012. **Business Addr:** Chief Marketing Officer, Chief Creative Officer, BuzzFeed, 7323 Beverly Blvd, Los Angeles, CA 90036, **Business Phone:** (323)930-1100.

### COOPER, DR. GARY T.
Physician. **Educ:** Marquette Univ, BS, 1970; Howard Univ Col Med, MD, 1975; Loyola Col Md, MBA, 1996. **Career:** Planned Parenthood Wash, med dir, 1979-80; pvt pract physician obstet & gynec, 1979-92; Grady Memorial Hosp, resident obstet & gynec; Providence Hosp, resident obstet & gynec; Howard Univ Hosp, resident coordr, 1980-87; instr, 1980-86; asst prof, 1986-87; Prudential Health Care Mid Atlantic Region, med dir. **Orgs:** Am Col Ob & Gyn, 1978; Med Soc Dist Columbia, 1979; Dipl, Am Bd Ob & Gyn, 1983; Wash Gynec Soc, 1981; Kappa Alpha Psi Fraternity; Southern Med Asn. **Home Addr:** 15213 Middlegate Rd, Silver Spring, MD 20905.

### COOPER, GEORGE E.
Education reformer, college president. **Educ:** Florida A&M University, B.S. in Animal Husbandry; Tuskegee University, M.S. in Animal Science; University of Illinois-Urbana, Ph.D. in Animal Science. **Career:** Winrock Int Livestock Res & Training Ctr (AR), scientist; Ala A&M Univ, vpres acad affairs & prof animal sci; Tuskegee Univ, admin & fac; U.S. Dept Agr's Nat Inst Food & Agr; S Carolina State Univ, pres, 2008-12; Am Asn State Cols & Univs, sr fel; White House Initiative Historically Black Cols & Univs (HBCUs), exec dir, 2013-. **Orgs:** Orangeburg Chamber of Commerce in South Carolina, Board Member; National Collegiate Athletic Association, Board Member; HBCU and Limited Resource Institution, Academic Advisory Group Member; Association of Public and Land Grant Universities, Board Member; USDA/1980 Task Force Board Member; Collaborative Brain Trust, University Consulting, Consultant; Kellogg Food System Leadership Development Program, Advisor; Joint Experiment Station Committee on Organization and Policy, Advisory Committee Member; Organization Policy Leadership Development Program, Academic Committee Member. **Special Achievements:** Appointed by President Barack Obama to the post of Executive Director of the White House Initiative on HBCUs in 2013.

### COOPER, GORDON R., II
Lawyer. **Personal:** Born Mar 22, 1941, Wallisville, TX; married Barbara Ellison; children: Gordon R III. **Educ:** Tex Southern Univ, BA, 1965, JD, 1970. **Career:** Humble Oil Co, Labor Rels Dept; Inst Underwriter, pvt pract; State Bar Tex; Cooper & Cooper, lawyer, currently. **Orgs:** Tex Am Houston Jr Bar Asn; regional dir, Nat Bar Asn; Alpha Phi Alpha Fraternity; Phi Alpha Delta Legal Fraternity; Harris County Criminal Lawyers Asn. **Home Addr:** 3722 Rio Vista, Houston, TX 77021. **Business Addr:** Lawyer, Cooper & Cooper, 3620 S Mac Gregor Way, Houston, TX 77021-1504, **Business Phone:** (713)747-1446.

### COOPER, HELENE
Writer. **Personal:** Born Apr 22, 1966, Monrovia. **Educ:** Univ NC, Chapel Hill, BA. **Career:** Wall St J, foreign corresp, reporter & ed, 1992-2004; New York Times, asst ed page ed, 2004-06, diplomatic corresp, 2006-09, White House corresp, 2009-, Pentagon corresp. **Honors/Awds:** Raymond Clapper Award, 2000; National Association of Black Journalists Award, 2004; George Polk Award, 2015; Overseas Press Club Award, 2015; Pulitzer Prize for international reporting (co-winner), 2015. **Special Achievements:** Author: "The House at Sugar Beach: In Search of a Lost African Childhood", 2008; "Madame President; The Extraordinary Story of Ellen Johnson Sirleaf", 2017; Editor, "Daniel Pearl: At Home in the World", 2002. **Business Addr:** New York Times, 620 Eighth Ave, New York, NY 10018.

### COOPER, IRIS N.
Educator. **Personal:** Born Oct 30, 1942, Ahoskie, NC. **Educ:** NC Cent Univ, BA, 1964. **Career:** Portsmouth Sch Syst, instr; Palmer Memorial Inst, instr, 1964; Norfolk State Eve Coll, instr, 1968-69; Proj Upward Bound, Norfolk St Col, instr, 1968-71; Church land High Sch, Dept foreign lang, head. **Orgs:** Northeastern Avicult Socs; Va Educ Asn; Portsmouth Educ Asn; Va Asn Classroom Teachers; Portsmouth Asn Classroom Teachers; Am Asn Women; Tidewater Alliance Black Sch Educs; Am Asn Teachers Span & Port; Ebenezer Bapt Chap; Nc Cent Univ Alumni Asn; Norfolk Players Guild; Portsmouth Chap Delicados Inc; Gamma Delta Omega Chap; Alpha Kappa Alpha. **Home Addr:** 5033 Reese Dr N, Portsmouth, VA 23703-4608, **Home Phone:** (757)483-4424.

### COOPER, IRMGARD M.
Executive. **Personal:** Born Jun 29, 1946, Teisendorf; daughter of Senator Richard A and Ruth St Ville. **Educ:** DePaul Univ, Chicago, IL, BS, bus teacher educ, 1968; Northern Ill Univ, DeKalb, IL, MS, adult & continuing educ & teaching, 1977. **Career:** Grad fel, Northern Ill Univ, DeKalb, Ill, 1976-77; Jones Metrop High Sch, Chicago, Ill, teacher/coordr, 1970-82; IMC Automation Inc, Chicago, Ill, pres, 1985-2005; IMC Prod Inc, Muskegon, Mich, founder & pres, 1990-; IMC CONNECT INC, owner-operator, 1995-. **Orgs:** Founding bd mem & secy, Streeterville Chamber Com, Chicago, 1991, pres, 1996-98; exec club, 1998-, edu comt; Panelist, W Mich Supplier Diversity Conf, 2001; bd mem, Muskegon Area Chamber Com, 2001-06; luncheon co-chair, W Mich Supplier Diversity Conf, 2002; bd mem, MMBDC W Mich Roundtable, 2003-06; vol, Womans Pl, 2003-; co-presenter, W Mich Alliance Women Entrepreneurs, 2004-07; Panelist, Muskegon Community Col, "Growing Entrepreneurship Mich", 2005; Entrepreneurship Video Contribr, Muskegon Career Technol Ctr, 2005; Panelist, Alliance Women Entrepreneurs Women Bus Owners, 2005; Panel Facilitator, Muskegon Chamber Com Bus Diversity Showcase, 2005; Presenter, Muskegon Community Col, "Secrets to Success"

Noon Hour Col Ser Working Women, 2005; founding mem & secy, Muskegon Inventors Network, 2005-2011; Hills Chamber Com; DePaul Univ Alumni Asn; Bus & Prof Womens Network N Mich Ave BPW; Top 100 Diversity Owned Businesses, State Ill; secy & treas, Chicago Exec Network. **Home Addr:** 600 N McClurg, Chicago, IL 60611, **Home Phone:** (312)664-0624. **Business Addr:** Owner-Operator, IMC Connect Inc, 1751-D W Howard St Suite 234, Chicago, IL 60626, **Business Phone:** (312)656-1053.

## COOPER, JEROME GARY

Marine corps officer. **Personal:** Born Oct 2, 1936, Lafayette, LA; son of Algernon Johnson (deceased) and Gladys Catherine Morton (deceased); married Beverly; children: Patrick C, Joli & Gladys Shawn. **Educ:** Univ Notre Dame, BA, 1958; George Washington Univ, grad study; Harvard Sch Bus, attended 1979. **Career:** Army official (retired), bus exec; State Ala Dept Human Resources, Montgomery, Ala, comnr, 1974-78; David Volkert & Assocs, Mobile, Ala, vpres, 1981-89, sr vpres, 1992-94; USMC, Wash, DC, dir personnel procurement, 1988; US Dept Defense, Wash, DC, asst secy air force, 1989-92; Hq Marine Corps, dir, personnel, 1988-89 Commonwealth Nat Bank, chmn & chief exec officer, currently. **Orgs:** AFCOMAP, 1990-; Air Force Asn, 1990-; Nat Image, 1991-; life mem, Res Officers Asn; life mem, Montford Pt Marine Asn; Marine Corps Res Asn; fel, Ala State House Representatives, 1974-78; bd mem, US Steel; bd dir, Gencorp; bd dir, bd dir, protective life; bd dir, PNC Financial Serv. **Honors/Awds:** Man of Year, Nonpartisan Voters League, 1977; Highest Award, 1978; MO Beale Scroll of Merit for Good Citizenship, Mobile Asn, 1979; John J Cavanaugh Award, Alumni Asn Univ Notre Dame, 1987; Roy Wilkins Meritorious Service Award, Nat Asn Advan Colored People, 1989; Benjamin Hooks Meritorious Service Award, 1990; Distinguished Service Medal, 1991; Hon LLD, Troy State Univ, 1990; Navy Distinguished Service Medal; Bronze Star Medal; Purple Hearts; Republic of Vietnam Gallantry Crosses. **Special Achievements:** First Black to lead infantry into combat USMC, 1967; Second African-American General in the Marine Corps; United States Ambassador to Jamaica, 1994-97; only Black to be promoted to general while in the Corps reserves; First African American to ever command a Marine Corps infantry company. **Home Addr:** 2400 41st St NW Suite 202, Washington, DC 20007, **Home Phone:** (202)625-2752. **Business Addr:** Chairman, Chief Executive Officer, Commonwealth National Bank, 2214 St Stephens Rd, Mobile, AL 36601, **Business Phone:** (334)476-5938.

## COOPER, JOLI C.

Founder (originator). **Educ:** Univ Notre Dame, BBA, finance, 1981; Univ Pa Wharton Sch, MBA, mkt & finance; Duke Univ. **Career:** Vitality Beverages Inc, sr vpres & chief mkt officer; Nestle USA, assoc brand mgr; Pasco Brands Inc, pres & chief operating officer; Cooper Nelson & Assocs Inc, pres & chief exec officer; Cordova Smart & Williams LLC, indust partner, 2003-. **Orgs:** Bd mem, Berkshire Blanket; bd mem, Sqwincher Corp; bd mem, Eateries Inc; bd mem, Greater Tampa Chamber Com; bd mem, United Way Tampa Bay Inc; bd mem, C's Home Inc; bd mem, Jr Achievement; bd mem, Notre Dame Club Greater Tampa; bd mem, Univ Pa's Wharton Sch Alumnae Bd. **Honors/Awds:** Woman of the Year, Girls Inc, 1996; Wharton Alumnae of the Year, 2002; "The Network Journal: Black Professionals and Small Business Magazine", 25 Influential Black Women in Business, 2007. **Business Addr:** Industry Partner, Cordova Smart & Williams LLC, 60 Madison Ave Suite 1115, New York, NY 10010, **Business Phone:** (212)920-3704.

## COOPER, JOSEPH

Lawyer, educator, association executive. **Personal:** Born Dec 20, 1937, Hemingway, SC; son of Harmon and Mary; children: Kenneth. **Educ:** Calif State Univ, Sacramento City Col, BA, 1965; Univ Pac, McGeorge Law Sch, JD, 1969. **Career:** First Capital Real Estate, pres; atty gen pract, 1969-; Northwestern Calif Univ, prof law & dean acad affairs; Joseph Cooper Law Corp, pres & atty, 1970-; Sacramento Super Ct, Settlement Conf, judge proterm, currently. **Orgs:** Bd dir, Calif Trial Lawyers Asn; Am Trial Lawyers Asn; founder & pres, Success Inst Am Inc; Am Back Soc; Sacramento Consumer Atty Asn; Calif St Bar; Am Bar Asn; bd reagents mem, Northwestern Calif Univ; Am Asn Justice; bd dir, Consumer Attorneys Calif. **Honors/Awds:** Distinguished Service Award, City of Sacramento. **Home Addr:** 23 Sail Ct, Sacramento, CA 95831. **Business Addr:** Founder, Owner, Joseph Cooper Law Corp, 1310 H St, Sacramento, CA 95814, **Business Phone:** (916)441-5300.

## COOPER, JOSEPHINE H.

Educator. **Personal:** Born Apr 7, 1936, Salinas, CA. **Educ:** Houston Tillotson Col, Austin, TX, BA; San Francisco State Univ, San Francisco, CA, MA. **Career:** Educ Serv Inst, asst dir; Progs Mentally Handicapped, head teacher; Meritt Col, GED prog, 1968; Low Income Housing Prog Voc Coun; Laney Col, counr, currently. **Orgs:** Calif Teachers Asn; Nat Asn Advan Colored People; United Taxpayers & Voter's Union Calif; Alameda Co Contra Costa Co Community Equal Opportunity Apprenticeship Training; Berkeley Dem Club; Nat Coun Negro Women Inc; Peralta Col Dist, bd trustee. **Home Addr:** 1530 Summit Rd, Berkeley, CA 94708. **Business Addr:** Counselor, Laney College, 900 Fallon St, Oakland, CA 94607, **Business Phone:** (510)464-3152.

## COOPER, JULIUS, JR.

Law enforcement officer. **Personal:** Born Jan 8, 1944, Sarasota, FL; son of Julius Sr and Johnnie Mae Jones Ramey; married Barbara Irene Campbell; children: Julius, Julian, Adrienne, Tara, Taheim & Wanda. **Educ:** Essex Co Col, attended 1977; Nat Crime Prev Inst, attended 1983; Security Mgt & Admin Inst, attended 1984; Rutgers Univ, BS, 1985; Seton Hall Univ, MS, 1990. **Career:** Law enforcement officer (retired); Essex Co Police Dept, breathaly zeroper, affirmative action officer, supvr, 1983-84, instr, 1983-85, crime prev coordr, 1983-86, sgt; Newark, NJ Bd Educ, substitute teacher, 1991; Rutgers Univ, guest prof, 1991; Essex Co Col, prof, 1992; Zion Missionary Baptist Church, deacon, 1996-97; Zion Bapt Church, deacon, 1997, minister, 2001, assoc minister, 2002. **Orgs:** Vpres, Ebony Six Coop; life mem, Nat Asn Advan Colored People; PBA. **Honors/Awds:** Certificate Award, US Dept Health & Human Serv, 1985; Achievement Award, Essex Co PBA Conf, 1985; Achievement Award, 1986; Valor Award, 1987; Essex Co Bd Freeholders.

## COOPER, KENNETH JOSEPH

Writer, journalist. **Personal:** Born Dec 11, 1955, Denver, CO; son of George Howard Jr and Maxine Marie; married Lucilda Loretta Dassardo. **Educ:** Wash Univ, BA, eng, 1977. **Career:** St Louis Am, assoc ed, 1977; St Louis Post Dispatch, reporter, staff writer, 1977-80; Boston Globe, reporter, staff writer, 1980-86; Knight Ridder Inc, nat reporter, 1986-89; Wash Post, nat reporter, 1989-95, S Asia bur chief, 1996-99, nat reporter, 1999-2000; Bay State Banner, contrib writer, 2006-; independent journalist, 2006-; Maynard Inst, dir, editing prog, 2007; Boston Globe, nat ed; Univ Mass-Boston, ed, 2008-; freelance writer, currently. **Orgs:** Nat Asn Black Journalists, 1978-; Omega Psi Phi Fraternity, 1983-; fel Inst Polit, Harvard's Kennedy Sch Govt; fair health journalism fel Joint Ctr Polit & Econ Studies; fulbright scholar, US Fulbright Comn. **Honors/Awds:** Public Service Award, 1984; Pulitzer Prize, Spec Local Reporting, Columbia Univ, 1984; Distinguished Alumni, Wash Univ, 1989; SAJA Journalism Award, 1998; Pulitzer Prize winner. **Home Addr:** 2003 Chillum Rd, Hyattsville, MD 20782. **Business Addr:** Freelance Writer, 14814 Reddington, Maple Heights, OH 44137, **Business Phone:** (216)663-9984.

## COOPER, DR. LAMOYNE MASON

Educator. **Personal:** Born Aug 8, 1931, Emporia, VA; son of Edgar and Theresa; married William Franklin; children: Derrick Matthews, Yvette Matthews & Kevin Matthews. **Educ:** Morgan State Univ, AB, 1951; Howard Univ, MSW, 1961; Univ Md, PhD, 1976. **Career:** Educator (retired); Morgan State Univ, prof social work, 1969-82; Foreign Serv, US Dept State, 1987-91. **Orgs:** Life mem, Delta Sigma Theta, 1950-; Baltimore Mus Art; Baltimore Zoo; Chesapeake Audubon Soc; Tucson Desert Mus. **Honors/Awds:** Education to Africa Study Grant, 1974; 100 Outstanding Baltimore Women, Delta Sigma Theta, 1974; Award, Baltimore County Bd Educ, 1979-84. **Home Addr:** 2150 N Sarnoff Dr, Tucson, AZ 85715, **Home Phone:** (520)290-2354.

## COOPER, LARRY B.

Manager, teacher, consultant. **Personal:** Born Jul 25, 1946, Fordyce, AR; son of Charles and Brucella; children: Sherri Jean. **Educ:** Univ Ark, Pine Bluff, BS, 1969; Southern Methodist Univ, MBA, 1996. **Career:** Kans City Sch Dist, teacher & coach, 1969-72; Southwestern Bell Tele Co, mgt trainee, 1972-73, engr, 1973-74, sr engr, 1974-77, mgt dev supvr, 1977-79, dist staff mgr-pers & budgets, 1979-81, staff mgr mgt develop, 1981-83, dist staff mgr res serv, 1983-85, dist mgr res serv, 1985-87, dist mg bus serv, 1987-89, div mgr educ & econ develop, St Louis, Mo, gen mgr, operator servs, dir, Local Provider Acct Team, 2002, sr vpres, Local Provider Acct Team, exec dir; consult, currently. **Orgs:** Kappa Alpha Psi Alumni Asn; pres, Tall Timber Home Owners, 1978-79; United Way Planning & Allocation Comt, 1982-84; bd dir, Southwest City Civitan, 1985-; exec bd dir, Boy Scouts Am, 1985-; comnr, Tall Timber Imp Dist, 1986; adv bd, Voc Tech Educ, 1989-92; chmn, Ark Regional Minority Purchasing Coun, 1986-92; Ark Advocate Family & C, 1990-; Ark State Coun Econ Educ, 1991-92; Dallas Downtown Improv Dist; chmn, Pine Bluff Found Bd, Univ Ark, currently. **Honors/Awds:** Distinguished Achievement Award, Kappa Alpha Psi, 1985; Distinguished Alumni Award, NAFEO, 1986; Bernard De La Harde Award for Community Leadership, Little Rock Chamber Com, 1989-91; Black Corp Execs Award, Nat Am Advan Colored People, 1991. **Home Addr:** 10108 Andre Dr, Irving, TX 75063. **Business Addr:** Chairman, University of Arkansas, 700 W Research Ctr Blvd, Fayetteville, AR 72701.

## COOPER, LINDA G.

Entrepreneur, president (organization). **Personal:** Born Jun 1, 1954, Jacksonville, FL; daughter of Benjamin H and Freddie Lang. **Educ:** Fla State Univ, BS, 1974; Ind Univ, MBA, 1977; Nat Multicultural Inst, cert, diversity training. **Career:** Hallmark Cards Inc, budget analyst, 1977-81, mktg budget mgr, 1981-85, dir minority affairs, 1985-92; LGC & Assocs Inc, pres & owner, 1992-. **Orgs:** Alpha Kappa Alpha Sorority, 1972-; Defense Adv Comn Women Serv, 1984-87; pres & bd trustee, Greater KC Black Econ Union, 1984-92; Nat Asn Mkt Developers, 1985-91; bd mem, YMCA, 1987-90; Greater KC Chamber Com; pres, Cent Exchange; Nat Black MBA Asn; bd gov, Urban League GKC. **Home Addr:** 730 Val Verde Cir E, Litchfield Park, AZ 85340-4517, **Home Phone:** (623)935-9204. **Business Addr:** Owner, President, LGC & Associates Inc, 1601 E 18th St Suite 120, Kansas City, MO 64105, **Business Phone:** (816)842-0542.

## COOPER, LOIS

Vice president (organization). **Personal:** daughter of Lula Dupree; married Joseph. **Educ:** Am Univ, BA, sociol & commun; Baruch Col, MBA, human resources mgt/personnel admin. **Career:** Young & Rubicam, equal employ opportunity officer, recruiter & human resources asst; John Alden Life Ins Co, human resources supvr; Chase Bank, asst vpres & workforce diversity specialist; MTV Networks, human resources dir; Adecco Group, vpres employee rels & diversity, 1998-2010, vpres corp social responsibility & inclusion, 2010-14; Lee Hecht Harrison Strategies Inc, consult & pract leader human capital solutions, 2015-. **Orgs:** Adecco Group Womens Leadership. **Business Addr:** Vice President, Adecco, 551 5th Ave, New York, NY 11747, **Business Phone:** (212)391-7000.

**COOPER, LOIS LOUISE.** See Obituaries Section.

## COOPER, MAUDINE R.

Association executive, chief executive officer. **Personal:** Born Sep 30, 1941, Benoit, MS; children: Maria Teresa. **Educ:** Howard Univ, BA, bus admin, 1964, Sch Law, JD, 1971. **Career:** President, chief executive officer (retired); Fed Progs, asst dir, 1973; Nat Urban League, asst dir, 1973-76, dep dir, 1976-79, asst vpres pub policy, 1979, vpres Wash Oper, 1980-83; DC Off Human Rights, dir, 1983-89; DC OHR & Minority Bus Opportunity Comn, exec dir & head, 1987-89; staff dir, Off Mayor, 1989-90; Mayor Marion Barry, chief staff, 1989-90; Greater Wash Urban League, chief exec officer & pres, 1990; Emergency Transition Ed Bd, Washington, DC, chair. **Orgs:** Bd dir, Nat Bar Asn, 1979-80; bd dir, Centennial One Inc, 1982-87; vpres legis affairs Black Women's Agenda, 1983-; legal adv, MCAC & Delta Sigma Theta Sor, 1985-88; treas, Wash Chap Nat Asn Human Rights Workers, 1986-87; several bar Asns; bd dir, Doug Williams Found; bd dir, DC Pvt Indus Coun, 1993; bd dir, Bell Atlantic, Wash, DC, 1994-96; Howard Univ Hosp, 1995-96; Eastern High Sch Choral Soc, 1995-99; chair, Emergency Transitional Bd dir DC Pub Schs, 1997-99; DC Bar Asn; Nat Asn Advan Colored People; life mem, Greater Wash Urban League; bd dir, Women Wash; United Way Nat Capital Area; Acad Fellows; DC Agenda Proj; Leadership Wash. **Home Addr:** 1705 Irving St NW, Washington, DC 20010, **Home Phone:** (202)387-7856. **Business Addr:** President, Chief Executive Officer, Greater Wash Urban League, Headquarters Bldg, Washington, DC 20009, **Business Phone:** (202)265-8200.

## COOPER, MERRILL PITTMAN

Executive. **Personal:** Born Feb 9, 1921, Charlestown, WV. **Educ:** Storer Col, attended 1938. **Career:** Transp Workers Union, int exec bd, 1965-68, int vpres, Local 234, secy, treas & vpres, 1968-77, pres. **Orgs:** Vpres, Philadelphia AFL CIO, 1977-; int vpres, Transp Workers Union, 1977-; Urban League; Negro Trade Union Leadership Coun; Nat Asn Advan Colored People. **Home Addr:** PO Box 861375, Ft Myers, FL 33906.

## COOPER, MICHAEL GARY

State government official. **Personal:** Born Jan 11, 1954, Cleveland, OH; son of Fletcher Lee Bailey; married Corrinne Crockett; children: Stacy, Michael Fletcher & Malik. **Educ:** Univ Pittsburgh, BA, 1975; Atlanta Univ, MA, hist, 1979, MSW, 1979. **Career:** Young Men's Christian Asn, asst dir, 1975-76; City Atlanta, field coordr, 1979; DeKalb Co Comn Off, affirmative action officer, 1979-88; Fulton Co Govt, dir contract compliance & eeo, 1988-98; GA Dept Transp, div dir contract compliance & equal employ opportunity, 1998-. **Orgs:** Am Asn Affirmative Action, 1982-; Southern Civil Rights Transp Asn, 1998-; Am Asn State & Hwy Transp Officials, Sub-Comt Civil Rights, 1999-; vpres, Stone Mountain Youth Soccer Asn; Boy Scouts Am. **Home Addr:** 3122 Northchester Pl, Lithonia, GA 30038-2292, **Home Phone:** (770)808-6677. **Business Addr:** Division Director, Georgia Department of Transportation, 1 GA Ctr 600 W Peachtree St N W 7th Fl, Atlanta, GA 30308, **Business Phone:** (404)631-1990.

## COOPER, MICHAEL JEROME

Basketball player, administrator, athletic coach. **Personal:** Born Apr 15, 1956, Los Angeles, CA; married Wanda; children: Michael Jr, Simone, Miles & Nils. **Educ:** Pasadena City Col, attended 1976; Univ NMex, 1978. **Career:** Basketball player (retired), basketball coach; Los Angeles Lakers, prof basketball player, 1978-90, asst coach, 1994-98; Virtus Roma, prof basketball player, 1990-91; Los Angeles Sparks, head coach, 1999-2004, 2007-; Denver Nuggets, asst coach, 2004-05; Albuquerque Thunderbirds, head coach, 2006-07; Univ Southern Calif, Women Troy Basketball Team, head coach, 2009-; Nat Basketball Asn, player. **Orgs:** Jr Blind Founf; state spokesperson, NM Red Ribbon Campaign Nationwide; Hollywood Senior Citizen Center. **Home Addr:** PO Box 67581, Los Angeles, CA 90067, **Home Phone:** (310)277-9711. **Business Addr:** Head Coach, Los Angeles Sparks, 888 S Figueroa St Suite 2010, Los Angeles, CA 90017, **Business Phone:** (213)929-1300.

## COOPER, ROBERT N.

Manager, executive. **Personal:** married Marcia; children: Robin & David. **Educ:** Oakland Univ, BA; Mich State Univ, MBA. **Career:** Mich Bell, technician, 1973-89; Ameritech, Mich, sr dir distrib serv, 1989-93, pres, dir mkt & bus develop; Ameritech Cellular, vpres human resources, 1993-96; SBC, Mich, pres; Amcor N Am, mgr controls engineering, 2003-. **Orgs:** Bd dir, Greater Detroit Chamber Com; bd dir, Detroit Symphony Orchestra; bd dir, Detroit Renaissance; bd dir, United Way Community Serv. **Business Addr:** Manager of Controls Engineering, Amcor Ltd, 935 Technol Dr Suite 100, Ann Arbor, MI 48108-8919, **Business Phone:** (734)428-9741.

## COOPER, RONALD

Football coach, football player. **Personal:** Born Feb 11, 1962, Huntsville, AL; son of Wilbert H and Martha B; married Kim; married Djuna; children: Tyler, Tristan & Ronald Jr. **Educ:** Jacksonville State Univ, BS, educ, 1983; Appalachian State Univ, MA, 1986. **Career:** Football player (retired), football coach; Jacksonville State Univ, football player, 1979-82; Appalachian State Univ, coach, 1983; Univ Minn, asst coach, 1984; Austin Peay State Univ, asst coach, 1985-86, recruiting crd, linebackers; Murray State Univ, coach, 1987-88, defensive crd, defensive backs; E Carolina Univ, asst coach, 1989, linebackers; Univ Nev Las Vegas, defensive coordr, linebackers, 1990; Univ Notre Dame, asst head coach, defensive backs, 1991-92; Eastern Mich Univ, head football coach, 1993-94; Univ Louisville, head football coach, 1995-97; Ala A&M Univ, coach, 1998-2001; Univ Wis, coach, 2002; Miss State Univ, coach, 2003; Univ SC, asst head coach, 2004-08; La State Univ, defensive backs coach, 2009-11, Tampa Bay Buccaneers, defensive back coach, 2012; S Fla, athletic coach, 2013-14; Fla Int Univ, defensive back coach, 2015, Defender Centre coach & linebacker, 2016. **Orgs:** Fel Christian Athletes, 1980-; KAP Fraternity Inc, 1982-; Masonic Order, 1983-; AMR Football Coaches Asn, 1983-; Black Coaches, 1989-. **Honors/Awds:** Sugar Bowl, Notre Dame vs FLA, 1992; Cotton Bowl, Notre Dame vs TEX A&M, 1993. **Special Achievements:** Teaching films: Deep Coverage, 2 vols; Coverage, 3 vols; Punt-Block; drill film: UNLV Defensive Team and Position Drills; manual: Techniques of Defensive Backs. **Business Addr:** Defensive Backs Coach, Florida International University, 3000 NE 151st St, North Miami, FL 33181, **Business Phone:** (305)919-5500.

**COOPER, SAMUEL DUANE.** See COOPER, DUANE.

## COOPER, HON. SAMUEL H., JR.

Government official. **Personal:** Born Feb 2, 1955, Nassawadox, VA; son of Samuel H Sr and Margaret C; married Sandra; children: Cedrick & Shenae. **Educ:** Norfolk State Col, attended 1975; John Tyler Col, AAS, 1977. **Career:** Cooper & Humbles Funeral Co Inc, owner;

Accomack Circuit Ct, 2nd Judicial Circuit Va, clerk, currently. **Orgs:** Macedonia AME Church; bd dir, BB&T; pres, Va Ct Clerks Asn; bd dir, Tidewater AAA. **Home Addr:** 20168 Nandua Heights, Onancock, VA 23417. **Business Addr:** Clerk, Accomack Circuit Court, 23316 Courthouse Ave, Accomac, VA 23301-0126, **Business Phone:** (757)787-5776.

### COOPER, SHAN
Manager, vice president (organization). **Personal:** married Eddie; children: 1. **Educ:** Emory Univ, Roberto C Goizueta Bus Sch, MBA; Rutgers Univ, Sch Mgt & Labor Rels, Global Exec Masters Human Resource Leadership Prog, grad. **Career:** Lucent Technologies; Lockheed Martin Info Systs & Global Solutions (IS&GS), vpres human resources; Lockheed Martin Aeronaut Co, vpres & dep human resources; Lockheed Martin, sr mgr diversity workforce mgt, 2002, vpres diversity & equal opportunity progs, 2004, vpres & gen mgr, 2011-. **Orgs:** Bd mem, Boy Scouts Am Atlanta Area Coun; bd mem, Cobb County Chamber Com; bd mem, Metro Atlanta Chamber Com; bd mem, Ga Mil Affairs Coord Comt; Exec Leadership Coun; bd mem, Carter Ctr; Marietta Kiwanis Club; bd trustee, Woodruff Arts Ctr; bd trustee, WellStar Found; bd mem, Emory Univ; chmn, Ga Partnership Excellence Educ; Atlanta Rotary Club; Ga Mil Affairs Coord Comt; Girls Inc; Girl Scouts; YWCA. **Business Addr:** Vice President, General Manager, Lockheed Martin Aeronautics Company, 2859 Paces Ferry Rd SE, Atlanta, GA 30339, **Business Phone:** (866)562-2363.

### COOPER, TONI. See COOPER, ANTOINETTE.

### COOPER, WALTER, SR.
Research scientist, chemist. **Personal:** Born Jul 18, 1928, Clairton, PA; son of Alonzo and Lula; married Helen E Claytor; children: Robert B & Brian P. **Educ:** Wash & Jefferson Col, BA, 1951; Univ Rochester, PhD, phys chem, 1956; Wash & Jefferson Col, ScD, 1987. **Career:** research scientist, chemist (retired); Eastman Kodak Co, res chemist, 1956, sr res chemist, 1964, res assoc, 1965, res assoc, 1969, mgr, Off Tech Comun, 1984-86; Action Better Community, assoc dir, 1964-65; res assoc, 1966; NY State Adv Comn, US Civil Rights Commn 1966; US Small Bus & Admin, spec consult admin, 1968-69; Univ State New York, regent emer, currently. **Orgs:** Celanese Corp Am fel, 1952-54; NSF fel, 1955-56; Sigma Xi, 1956; Am Chem Soc, 1959; AAAS, 1960; bd mem, Dartnell Enterprises Inc; Am Phys soc; Nat Asn Advan Colored People, 1960-65; founder, Urban League Rochester, 1965-71; bd gov, Genesee Hosp, 1966; Urban Suburban Pupil Transfer Prog, 1973; Genesee Reg Health Plng Coun, 1974; chmn, Bamako Mali Sister City Comt; bd trustee, Wash & Jefferson Col, 1975; bd dir, Rochester Area Found, 1975; NY State Bd Regents, 1988-97; bd mem, Baden St Settlement. **Honors/Awds:** Leroy E Snyder Award, Rochester Jr Chamber Com, 1966; Outstanding Achievement Award & Rochester Club Nat Negro Prof & Bus Women Inc, 1966; Rochester Chamber of Commerce Development Award, 1966; Distinguished Alumni Award, Wash & Jefferson Col, 1968; Achievement Award, Int Org Eastern Stars, 1974; Knight Nat Order Repub Mali, 1982; International Relations Award, Rochester Chamber Com; Hutchinson Medal, Univ Rochester, 1994; Hon degree, Doctor of Humane Letters, State Univ NY, 2005; Frederick Douglass award, University of Rochester, 2008. **Special Achievements:** First African American to earn the PhD in Physical Chemistry from the University of Rochester; 3 patents in Photographic Science & Technology; 25 scientific & technical publications. **Home Addr:** 68 Skyview Lane, Rochester, NY 14625, **Home Phone:** (585)381-9528.

### COOPER, WARREN
Executive, founder (originator), president (organization). **Career:** Fed Aviation Admin, air traffic control specialist, 1980-93; Merrill C Meigs Field; Midway & O'Hare Int Airports; Chicago City Cols, 1988; Cook Co Sheriff's Dept; solicitor Gen of the US; Johnson & Johnson Corp; Methadone clins, bd dir; pro-bono consults, social sector agencies; Accu-Lab Med Testing Inc, founder & pres, 1991-. **Orgs:** Am Ass Clin Chemist; Regional Purchasing Coun Chicago Urban League; Cosmopolitan Chamber Com. **Special Achievements:** First African-American to work in that capacity assigned to O'Hare International Airport in Chicago. **Business Addr:** Founder, President, AccuLab Medical Testing Inc, 2600 S Mich Ave, Chicago, IL 60616, **Business Phone:** (312)939-3535.

### COOPER, WILLIAM B.
Executive, association executive. **Personal:** Born Sep 5, 1956, Washington, DC; married Sandra F Burrus. **Educ:** Control Data Inst, 1976; Univ Md, 1980. **Career:** Data Control Corp, operating syst developer, systs analyst, 1974-79; TYMSHARE Inc, applications consult, 1979-80; CGA Comput Assoc Inc, sr software developer, 1980-84; Cray Res Inc, acct exec, pre-sales analyst, 1984-92; Fed Data Corp, dir technol, 1992-97; FedHunters Inc, pres, 1997-2004; Iron Bow Technologies, capture mgr, dir tech sales, 2005-16. **Orgs:** Chmn, Montgomery County Republican Party, 1979-80; Assoc Comput Mach, 1979; Nat Panel Consumer Arbitrators, 1980-; Deacon Plymouth Congregational UCC, 1981-; cub master, Cub Scout Pack 340, 1981; pres, Cooper & Assocs, 1982. **Honors/Awds:** Comnr Adv Neighborhood Comn, 1982-85; delegate DC Statehood Const Conv, 1982-85; Outstanding Young Men Am, 1983. **Home Addr:** 300 50th St SE, Washington, DC 20019. **Business Addr:** Director of Technical Sales, Capture Manager, Iron Bow Technologies, 4800 Westfields Blvd Suite 300, Chantilly, VA 20151, **Business Phone:** (703)279-3000.

### COOPER, WINSTON LAWRENCE
Advertising executive, executive. **Personal:** Born Oct 27, 1946, Port-of-Spain; married Jeanne A Cox; children: Zara. **Educ:** Trinity Col WI, GCE, 1963; Univ WI, BA, 1967. **Career:** Ogilvy & Mather Inc, acct suprv, 1970-77; Case & McGrath Adv Inc, mgt suprv, 1977-79; Uni world Group Inc, vpres mgt suprv, 1982-85. **Home Addr:** 510 E 86th St, New York, NY 10028, **Home Phone:** (212)628-6642.

### COOPER-DYKE, CYNTHIA (CYNTHIA LYNNE COOPER-DYKE)
Basketball player, basketball coach. **Personal:** Born Apr 14, 1963, Chicago, IL; daughter of Kenny and Mary Cobbs; married Anthony Stewart; married Brian; children: Brian Jr & Cyan. **Educ:** Univ Southern Calif, attended 1986. **Career:** Basketball player (retired), basketball coach; Samoa Betera, Spain, 1986-87; Parma team, Italy, 1987-94, 1996-97; Alcamo team, Italy, 1994-96; Houston Comets, WNBA, guard, 1997-2000, 2003-04; Phoenix Mercury, head coach, 2000-02; Houston Rockets, TV analyst & halftime reporter, 2004-05; Prairie View A&M Univ, head women's basketball coach, 2005-10; Univ NC, Wilmington, head coach, 2010-12; Tex Southern Univ, head coach, 2012-13; Univ Southern Calif, head coach, 2013-. **Honors/Awds:** Champion, Nat Collegiate Athletic Asn, 1983, 1984; Gold Medal, FIBA World Championship, 1986, 1990; Most Valuable Player, Europ League, All-Star Game, 1987; Gold Medal, Pan American Games, 1987; Gold Medal, Olympic Games, 1988, 1992; All-Star, Women's Nat Basketball Asn, 1999, 2000, 2003; Scoring Champion, Women's Nat Basketball Asn, 1997, 1998, 1999; Champion, Women's Nat Basketball Asn, 1997, 1998, 1999, 2000; Most Valuable Player, Women's Nat Basketball Asn, 1997, 1998, 1999, 2000; City Championship, 300 Hurdles; Gold Medal, FIBA Under-19 World Championship, 2007; Hall of Fame, Women's Nat Basketball Asn, 2009; Women's Basketball Hall of Fame, 2009; Basketball Hall of Fame, 2010; CAA Coach of the Year, 2010. **Special Achievements:** General Motors, spokeswoman, 1997; author, autobiography, She Got Game: My Personal Odyssey, 2000. **Business Addr:** Head Coach, University of Southern California, Univ Pk, Los Angeles, CA 90089, **Business Phone:** (213)740-2311.

### COOPER-FARROW, VALERIE
Executive. **Personal:** Born Oct 18, 1961, Stamford, CT. **Educ:** Morgan State Univ, BS, mental health admin, comput sci, 1983; Columbia Univ Grad Sch Bus, MBA, 1987. **Career:** Travelers Co, comput programmer, 1983-85; Goldman Sachs & Co, vpres info technol. **Orgs:** Alpha Kappa Alpha Sor Inc, 1980-; Nat Black MBA Asn, 1985-; Network Inc, 1986-; life mem, Morgan State Univ Alumni Asn. **Home Addr:** 84 Courtland Ave, Stamford, CT 06902, **Home Phone:** (203)348-9797. **Business Addr:** Vice President, Goldman Sachs & Co, 200 W St, New York, NY 10282, **Business Phone:** (212)902-1000.

### COOPER-GILSTRAP, JOCELYN ANDREA
Executive. **Personal:** Born Jun 29, 1964; daughter of Andrew and Jocelyn Cooper. **Educ:** Hampton Univ, BA, commun, 1986. **Career:** Polygram Rec, tracking airplay new releases & promoting co urban music; Warner Chappell Music Inc, creative mgr; Mercury Rec, 1992; Midnight Songs, co-founder & pres, currently; Universal Music Group, sr vpres & spec asst to chmn, head, 1995-2002; Hitco Music Publ, managing dir; Jocelyn A Cooper LLC, consult, 2002-05; Hitco Music Publ, managing dir, 2006-08; AFROPUNK, partner, 2008-. **Orgs:** Bd mem, RUSH Philanthropic Arts Found; bd mem, City Sun Publ; Nat Asn Rec Arts & Sci Inc, 1991-, bd gov, 1999-; bd mem, Prospect Pk Alliance. **Home Addr:** 350 Grand Ave, Brooklyn, NY 11238. **Business Addr:** Senior Vice President, Special Assistant to the Chairman, Universal Music Group, 1755 Broadway 7th Fl, New York, NY 10019, **Business Phone:** (212)373-0731.

### COOPER-LEWTER, REV. DR. NICHOLAS CHARLES
Clergy, writer, educator. **Personal:** Born Jun 25, 1948, Washington, DC. **Educ:** Ashland Col, BA, sociol, 1970; Ecumenical Ctr, African-Am church studies, adv studies, DMin prog, 1978; Univ Minn, MSW, 1978; Calif Coast Univ, PhD, psychol, 1988; Am Baptist Sem W, Mdiv, audited, divinity/ministry. **Career:** Auth; motivational speaker, 1972-; Univ Minn, Ctr Youth Develop Res, res specialist, 1972-73, teaching asst, 1974-75, Sch Social Work, deans grad fel, 1974; Sports Performance consult, personal success coach, 1976-; Pastoral Care & Coun, clergy consult, soul ther, 1976-; Greater Bethel Missionary Baptist Church, San Bernardino, Calif, ordained clergyman, 1977; Cooper Lewter Hypn Ctr, NB CA, dir owner, 1978-83; Cooper-Lewter Consult LLC, owner, pres & chief exec officer, 1978-; US Jr Olympic Team NRA, 1983-90; Calif State Fullerton Football Prog, 1983-84; Univ Calif, Los Angeles, Basketball Prog, 1984-85; New Garden Gethsemane, sr pastor, 1985-90; Kung Ling Kung Fu Temple, grandmaster, 1988-; Bethel Col & Sem, prof social work, Cross Cult Coun, vis instr, 1990-95; Cooper-Lewter Rites Passage Inc, founder, 1995-; Metrop State Univ, psychol & social work fac, 1996-2000; Benedict Col, prof, chair social work, 2000-03; Univ SC, vis prof social work, 2003-05, lectr social work, 2005-; Capp Inst, CTI, 2012. **Orgs:** Chap founder, First basileus, Xi Theta Chap, Omega Psi Phi Fraternity, Ashland Univ, 1966-70; bd dir, Am Acad Med Hypnoanalysts, 1977-83; bd mem & dir, Hmong Golden Village Cult Ctr, 1997-2000; Big Bros & Big Sisters Greater Columbia, 2002-04; Nat African Am Drug Policy Coalition; VI Basketball Fedn, 2004-; Nat Asn Social Workers; ACSW; Nat Asn Black Social Workers; Minn Bus Prof Am; TDVP; Nat Asn Advan Colored People; Nat Urban League; bd mem, TURN Leadership Found; Minn Black Psychologists Asn; Baccalaureate Prog Dirs Asn; adv bd mem, Salvation Army, St Paul, Minn; bd mem, Adoptive Families Am Inc; bd mem, Minn Coun Social Work Educ; charter mem, Rotary Int, Fountain Valley. **Honors/Awds:** Presidential Grant/Award for Student Leadership, Ashland Col, Ashland, Ohio, 1969-70; Outstanding Management, Standard Oil Company, Cleve, Ohio, 1970; Journal of the SMH Outstanding Contributing Author Award, 1976; Outstanding Young Men of America, 1983; Distinguished Faculty Service Award, Bethel Col Seminary, 1992; SE Hall Community Service Award, St Paul Urban League, 1992; Nominee Excellence in Teaching Award, Metropolitan State Univ, Minn, 1999; Inductee, Phi Alpha Social Work Honor Society, 2007; Teaching Excellence Award, USC, 2007; Educator of the Year, Graduating Class Col Social Work, 2009; Pyramid Award, Nat Asn Black Social Workers, 2012; Best-Selling Authors Award, Nat Acad Best-Selling Authors, 2015. **Special Achievements:** Co-author: Soul Theology: The Heart of American Black Culture, 1986, 1991; Black Grief and Soul Therapy, Univ of Richmond, Tubman Press, 1999 (4th Printing); "Keep On Rollin' Along: The Temptations and Soul Therapy," The Journal of Black Sacred Music, vol 6, num 1, Spring 1992; "My Jesus was Jim Crowed!" Colors Magazine Vol 3 Issue 3 May/June 1994; "Soul Therapy: A Call to Resilience" in Mental Health in the African American Community, In Press; "The Initial Environmental Experience: A Powerful Took for Psychotherapy &Hypnotherapy," Journal of Medical Hypnoanalysts, 1981, "Sports Hypnotherapy: Contenderosis & Self Hate," Journal of Med Hypnoanalysts, 1980; "Concerns of Working Youth," People Human Svs MN, 1974, "Working Youth: Selected Findings from Exploratory Study," Journal Youth & Adolescence, 1974. **Home Addr:** 120 Wildewood Pk Dr Suite A, Cola, SC 29223, **Home Phone:** (803)917-0862. **Business Addr:** Lecturer in Social Work, University of South Carolina, 335 DeSaussure, Columbia, SC 29223, **Business Phone:** (803)777-1382.

### COPAGE, MARC DIEGO
Entertainer, actor, singer. **Personal:** Born Jun 21, 1962, Los Angeles, CA; son of John and Alibe. **Career:** Actor, singer & comedian; Nat Broadcasting Corp, child artist, 1967-70; Metro media Rec, rec artist; Avco Rec & Sussex Rec, rec artist, currently; Films: Twisted Nightmare, 1987; The Kid, 2000; TV series: "Julia", 1968-71; Honeymoon Game?, 1971; "Young Dr. Kildare", 1972; "Temperatures Rising", 1973; "Sanford & Son", 1975; Best of Times, 1981; "CBS Afternoon Playhouse", 1981; "ABC After sch Specials", 1981; "The Wave", 1981; "Diff'rent Strokes", 1985; "CBS Summer Playhouse", 1987; "Cop Rock", 1990; "TV Land Confidential", 2005; "Changing Times and Trends 2005", 2005. **Orgs:** Screen Actors Guild; Am Fedn Tv & Radio Artists. **Honors/Awds:** Numerous honors & awards including Human Rights Award, NEA, 1970; Nominee Best Actor, Nat Asn Advan Colored People Image Awards, 1971; Community Award, Calif Teachers Asn. **Home Addr:** PO Box 461677, West Hollywood, CA 90046. **Business Addr:** Actor, c/o William Morris Agency, 151 El Camino Dr, Beverly Hills, CA 90212, **Business Phone:** (310)859-4000.

### COPELAND, BARRY B.
Manager, government official, association executive. **Personal:** Born Aug 1, 1957, Paterson, NJ; son of Albert and Levonia; married Canary Gasaway; children: Eric, Antoine, Elise L, Timothy & Malcolm J. **Educ:** Prairie View Agr & Mech Univ, BBA, acct, 1979. **Career:** Internal Revenue Serv, IRS agt, 1979; AUS, acct, 1980-82; AUS, Corpus Christi Army Depot, auditor, 1982-85; Beeco Acct Serv, owner & acct, 1985-; Defense Contract Audit Agency, sr auditor, 1985-88, opers auditor, 1988-91, supvry auditor, 1991-2000, procurement liaison auditor, 2000-02; Barry B Copeland, cert pub acct, owner, 1988-; NASA Johnson Space Ctr, prog & financial analyst, 2002-12; City Houston, asst city auditor III, 2012-. **Orgs:** Alpha Phi Omega, 1977-, Nat Asn Advan Colored People, 1986-; Asn Govt Acct, 1988. **Honors/Awds:** Exceptional Performance Award, Corpus Christi Army Depot, 1985; Exceptional Performance Awards, Defense Contract Audit Agency, 1988, 1990, 1994, 1996, 1999, 2000; Exceptional Performance Award, NASA, 2003, Group Achievement Award, 2007. **Home Addr:** 26803 Cascade Woods Lane, Cypress, TX 77433-3539, **Home Phone:** (281)304-0161. **Business Addr:** Assistant City Auditor, City of Houston, 901 Bagby St, Houston, TX 77002, **Business Phone:** (713)837-0311.

### COPELAND, DR. ELAINE JOHNSON
Educator, administrator. **Personal:** Born Mar 11, 1943, Catawba, SC; daughter of Aaron J Johnson and Lucille Hawkins Johnson; married Robert M; children: Robert M Jr. **Educ:** Livingstone Col, BS, biol, 1964; Winthrop Univ, MAT, psychol, 1971; Ore State Univ, PhD, coun, 1974; Univ Ill, Urbana-Champaign, MBA, 1987. **Career:** Wilson Jr High Sch, biol teacher, 1964-65; Jefferson High Sch, biol teacher, 1966-70; Ore State Univ, counr & instr, 1970-74; Livingstone Col, vpres acad affairs & dean; Univ Ill, Urbana-Champaign, Grad Col, assoc dean, assoc prof emer educ psychol, 1975-, assoc vice chancellor acad affairs; Harvard Univ, instr educ mgt, 2001; Clinton Col, psychol, bus dept, head, pres, 2002-. **Orgs:** Pres, Girls Club Champaign County, 1977; pres, Univ Ill YWCA, 1979; pres, Univ Ill Chap Hon Soc, Phi Kappa Phi, 1982; pres, Champaign-Urbana Alumnae Chap, Kappa Phi Chap Delta Sigma Theta Sorority, 1984-86; affirmative action rep, Div E coun & Develop, Am Educ Res Assoc, 1984-86; Assoc Rels Nat Assoc Women Deans Adminrs & Counr, vpres, 1985-87, adminr & counr, 1988-89; Chamber Com Bd, 2004-05; Rock Hill Rotary, 2004-06; Am Asn Univ Women; Am Psychol Asn; Am Educ & Res Asn; life mem, Delta Sigma Theta Inc; Am Coun Educ; Comn Advan Racial & Ethic Equity; Upper Palmetto Bd, Rock Hill YMCA, 2004-07; United Way Board; Catawba Regional Coun; bd mem, Rock Hill Develop Corp. Book: How Black Colleges Empower Black Students, 2006. **Home Addr:** 503 Birmingam Ct, Rock Hill, SC 29732, **Home Phone:** (803)329-6944. **Business Addr:** President, Clinton Junior College, 1029 Crawford Rd, Rock Hill, SC 29730, **Business Phone:** (803)327-7402.

### COPELAND, HORACE NATHANIEL
Football player. **Personal:** Born Jan 2, 1971, Orlando, FL; married Tangela; children: 4. **Educ:** Univ Miami, grad. **Career:** Football player (retired); Tampa Bay Buccaneers, wide receiver, 1993-97, 1998; Miami dolphins, 1998; Oakland Raiders, 1999-2000. **Home Addr:** 9 7th Ave, Mount Vernon, NY 10550, **Home Phone:** (914)668-3751.

### COPELAND, JOHN (JOHN ANTHONY COPELAND)
Football player. **Personal:** Born Sep 20, 1970, Lanett, AL. **Educ:** Univ Ala. **Career:** Football player (retired), coach; Cincinnati Bengals, left defensive end, 1993-97, defensive end, 1999, right defensive tackle, defensive end, 2000; Tuscaloosa Acad, defensive coordr, off-season strength & conditioning coach, currently. **Honors/Awds:** All-American, 1992; National Championship, 1992. **Business Addr:** Football Player, Tuscaloosa Academy, 420 Rice Valley Rd N, Tuscaloosa, AL 35406, **Business Phone:** (205)758-4462.

### COPELAND, KEVON
Financial manager. **Personal:** Born Mar 29, 1953, Pittsburgh, PA; son of Edward S Jr and Mary Jo Boxley; married Valire Renaye Carr. **Educ:** Conn Col, BA, hist, asian studies, 1976; Univ Pittsburgh Sch Law, int law, 1979; Univ Pittsburgh Sch Bus, MBA, int finance, 1980. **Career:** PNC Bank, PNC Financial, asst vpres, 1980-97, Asia, acct officer, 1981-90, asst vpres, foreign direct investment, 1987-91, vpres, credit policy div, 1991-93, asst vpres, Affil Nat Banking, 1993-; Urban Redevelop Authority Pittsburgh, sr bus develop specialist, 1986-. **Orgs:** Pres, vpres & secy, Nat Black MBA Asn Pittsburgh Chap;

founding mem, 100 Black Men Western PA; Alumni Comt, Conn Col, 1987-96, bd trustee, 1991-96; exec bd mem, Alumni Asn Conn Col, 1987-96; bd trustee, Sewickley Acad, 1991-95; pres bd, Fund Advan Minorities Through Educ, 1992-97; adv bd & founding mem, Summer bridge Pittsburgh, 1992-96; trustees, Conn Col, finance comt, chair, 2013-. **Honors/Awds:** Robert L Hampton Award, Unity Alumni Council Conn Col. **Home Addr:** 5700 Callowhill St, PO Box 23031, Pittsburgh, PA 15206, **Home Phone:** (412)441-1208. **Business Addr:** Senior Business Development Specialist, Urban Redevelopment Authority Pittsburgh, Civic Bldg 200 Ross St Suite 6, Pittsburgh, PA 15219-2016, **Business Phone:** (412)255-6546.

## COPELAND, DR. LEON L., SR.

Educator. **Personal:** Born Sep 14, 1945, Portsmouth, VA; married Mary B; children: Leon Jr. **Educ:** Norfolk St Col, BS, indust educ, 1968; Va St Univ, MEd, indust educ, 1974; Va Polytech Inst & State Univ, EdD, educ admin, 1977. **Career:** Smith High Sch, Chesapeake, Va, teacher, 1968-75; Univ Md, asst prof; VZ Tech, co-op counr, 1975-77; Univ Md Eastern Shore, Dept Technol, asst prof, 1977-89, assoc prof & chmn, 1990-99, prof & chair, 1983-, dir, currently; Technol Educ Regional Prof Develop Md State Dept Educ, projdir, 1998-2000; Enterpreneuiral Develop Inst, co-proj coordr; NSF, Technol Educ Leadership Proj, proj investr. **Orgs:** Kappa Alpha Psi Fraternity, 1968-; Ind Arts Asn, 1973-; Phi Delta Kappa, 1977-79; Am Voc Asn, 1977-; Emergency Sch Aid Adv Comn, 1978-79; Salisbury Housing Rehab Com, 1980; Am Coun Construct Educ; Int Technol Educ Asn; Md Technol Educ Asn; Am Soc Eng Educ; Assoc Schs Construct. **Honors/Awds:** Recipient Outstanding Young Men of America Award; US Jaycees, 1979; Dept Instructor of the Year, Univ Md, 1979; One of Ten Nat Leaders, Ind Arts Va Tech, 1979; Board of Faculty Regents Award, Univ Syst Md, 1998; Leadership Award, Technol Educ Asn Md, 1998; Distinguished Service Award, Nat Asn State Dir Career Technol Educ, 2001. **Business Addr:** Professor, Chairman & Director of Technology, University of Maryland Eastern Shore, MD-21853, Princess Anne, MD 21853-1299, **Business Phone:** (410)651-6468.

## COPELAND, MARGOT JAMES

Executive, businessperson. **Personal:** Born Dec 4, 1951, Richmond, VA; daughter of Reverend William Lloyd Garrison James and Thelma Taylor James; children: Kimberley, Garrison & Michael. **Educ:** Hampton Univ, BS, physics; Ohio State Univ, MA, educ res & statist. **Career:** Xerox Corp, employee; Polaroid, employee; Picker Int, employee; Leadership Cleveland, exec dir, 1992-99; Greater Cleveland Roundtable, pres & chief exec officer, 1999-2001; KeyCorp, vpres-dir corp diversity & philanthropy, exec coun mem, 2001-; KeyBank Found, chair & chief exec officer. **Orgs:** Pres, Links Inc., 2010-15; pres, Jr League Cleveland Inc.; mem, Delta Sigma Theta sorority, Girl Friends Inc. **Special Achievements:** Former board member, Kent State University; member Business School Advisory board, Hampton University; delegate, White House Conference on America's Future. **Business Addr:** KeyBank, 127 Public Sq, Cleveland, OH 44114.

## COPELAND, MISTY

Ballet dancer. **Personal:** Born Sep 10, 1982, Kansas City, MO; daughter of Sylvia DelaCerna. **Educ:** San Pedro Dance Ctr, ballet studies; Lauridsen Ballet Ctr; San Francisco Ballet Sch. **Career:** ABT's Studio Co, 2000; Am Ballet Theatre, mem corps de ballet, 2001-, soloist, 2007-; Dance Performances: Don Quixote; Sugar Plum Fairy; Nutcracker; La Bayadre; Swan Lake; Sechs Tnze; Within You Without You: A Tribute to George Harrison; Amazed Burning Dreams; Gong & Hereafter. **Orgs:** Boys & Girls Club; Am Ballet Theatre. **Honors/Awds:** Los Angeles Music Center Spotlight Award, 1998; American Ballet Theatre National Coca Cola Scholar, 2000; Leonore Annenberg Fellowship in the Arts, 2008; Council's Breakthrough Leadership Award, Coun Urban Professionals, 2012. **Special Achievements:** First African-American female soloist for the American Ballet Theatre, 2008. **Business Addr:** Ballerina, Soloist, American Ballet Theatre, 890 Broadway, New York, NY 10003, **Business Phone:** (212)477-3030.

## COPELAND, RICHARD ALLEN

Executive, chief executive officer. **Personal:** Born Aug 5, 1955, Minneapolis, MN; son of John and Laura; children: Leo, Laura & Derick. **Educ:** Univ Minn, BS. **Career:** Mr Rib, mgr; Lincoln Deli, cook; Flyers Bar & Deli, owner; Copeland Cartage, vpres; Thor Construct, founder, pres & chief exec officer, 1983-; Copeland Truc-King Inc, chief exec officer, 1985-; Milestone Growth Fund, dir. **Orgs:** Pacesetters, 1985-90; pres, Nat Asn Minority Contractors, 1990-92; Minneapolis Minority Purchasing Coun; Minority Bus Enterprises Input Comm; Rotary, 1992; bd mem & co-founder, African-Am Chamber Com. **Business Addr:** Chief Executive Officer, Copeland Truc-King Inc, 5400 NE Main St Suite 201, Minneapolis, MN 55421-1132, **Business Phone:** (763)572-0505.

## COPELAND, ROBERT S.

Secretary (office), college administrator, vice president (organization). **Educ:** Walsh Univ, BA, acct & finance. **Career:** Wilberforce Univ, dir develop; Univ Dayton, asst vpres; Wright State Univ, Sch Med, sr develop officer, asst vpres develop & dir advan, currently; Boonshoft Sch Med, chief fundraising officer, 1999-2006; Univ's Tomorrow Takes Flight campaign, principle architects; Int Rett Syndrome Found, chief develop officer, 2014. **Orgs:** Bd mem, OVR; coun, Advan & Support Educ CASE Mem, Wright State Univ; bd, African Am Community Fund; staff, Wright State's develop, 1998; dir, mkt & commun med sch, 2007; dir, WSU Advan & exec dir commun & mkt Wright State. **Home Addr:** 546 Conroy St, Cincinnati, OH 45214-1911. **Business Addr:** Assistant Vice President of Advancement, Director of Development, Wright State University, 108 Allyn Hall, Dayton, OH 45435-0001, **Business Phone:** (937)775-2972.

## COPELAND, DR. RONALD LOUIS

Physician, surgeon. **Personal:** Born Jul 5, 1951, Rochester, NY; son of Claude and Sarah; married Vicki; children: Airrion, Jamon & Nia. **Educ:** Dartmouth Col, BA, biol & psychol, 1973; Univ Cincinnati Med Col, MD, 1977. **Career:** State Univ New York Upstate Med Univ, surg residency, 1977-82; Ohio Permanente Med Group, chief surg, 1989-91, regional dir, surg servs, 1991-93, assoc med dir, 1993-96, vpres & assoc med dir, 1996-97, pres & med dir, 1998-2013; Kaiser Foundation Health Plan, sr vpres diversity & inclusion strategy & policy, chief diversity officer, 2013-. **Orgs:** Co-chair, Health & Safety Servs, Am Red Cross, 1995-; Liaison Coun Cert Surg Tech, 1995-; Cleveland Acad Med, 1998-; Adv Bd, UNCF, 1998; adv bd, Minority Organ Tissue Transplant Ed Prog, 1999-; Kaiser Permanente Nat Diversity Coun; Kaiser Permanente Care Experience Coun, 1999-; bd dirs, Kaiser Permanente Care Mgt Inst, 1999-; Kaiser Permanente Partnership Group, 2000-; Permanente Fed Exec Comn, 2000-; adv bd, Cuyahoga Comn Col Surg Tech, 2001-; trustee, Am Heart Asn Inc; Permanente Fedn; fel Weatherhead Sch Mgt Soc; fel Am Col Surgeons. **Honors/Awds:** Upstate Medical Center Outstanding Teaching, State Univ NY, Dept Surg, 1982; Mayor's Certificate of Recognition, 1986; Physician Recognition Award, Am Med Asn, 1986-89; Outstanding Physician Award, Asn Surg Technologist, 1995-97; Alumni of the Year Award, James Madison High, 2000. **Special Achievements:** Author of numerous articles. **Home Addr:** 1189 Yellowstone Rd, Cleveland Heights, OH 44121, **Home Phone:** (216)691-6978. **Business Addr:** Senior Vice President, Chief Diversity Officer, Kaiser Permanente, Kaiser Plz 19th Fl, Oakland, CA 94612, **Business Phone:** (510)271-5953.

## COPELAND, TERRILYN DENISE

Medical researcher. **Personal:** Born Toledo, OH. **Educ:** Kent State Univ, BS, speech & hearing, 1976; Bowling Green State Univ, MA, commun dis, 1980; Univ Toledo, MS, pub health, 1999. **Career:** Lucas Co Bd Ment Retardation, instr & speech pathologist, 1978-81; contract home health speech pathologist, 1981-86; St Francis Rehab Hosp, staff speech pathologist, 1986-88; Flower Mem Healthplex, staff speech pathologist, 1988-89; St Francis Rehab Hosp, dir speech path & audiol, 1989-93; Rehab Am, rehab coordr, 1993-94; St Charles Mercy Hosp, patient coordr, 1994-2002; Med Col OH, speech pathologist; Sylvania Pub Schs, speech pathologist, 2002-04, 2006-07, 2008-11; Progressus Ther, prog mgr, 2011-12; Univ Toledo Med Ctr, speech lang pathologist, 2002-; Lima City Schs, speech lang pathologist, 2012-; Ther Partners, speech lang pathologist, 2012-. **Orgs:** Delta Sigma Theta Sor; Am Speech & Hearing Asn; area rep, legis rep, Aphasiology Asn OH, 1987-92; Am Asn Univ Women, 1986-89, 2002; League Women Voters, 1986-01; bd dirs, 1986-94; OH Speech & Hearing Asn, 1980-93; Am Bus Womens Asn, 1989-93; Nat Head Injury Found, 1986-90; Jr League; bd dirs, Toledo Hearing & Speech Ctr, 2000-02. **Home Addr:** 5136 Greyln Dr, Toledo, OH 43615. **Business Addr:** Speech Pathologist, Lima City Schools, 755 St Johns Ave, Lima, OH 45804, **Business Phone:** (419)996-3400.

## COPELIN, SHERMAN NATHANIEL, JR.

Businessperson, legislator. **Personal:** Born Sep 21, 1943, New Orleans, LA; son of Sherman N Sr and Marie Armant; married Donna Sorapuru; children: Sherman Nathaniel III, Michon Jarel, Shane Nathan & Courtney Marie. **Educ:** Dillard Univ, BA, 1965; Loyola Univ, New Orleans, advan study psychol, 1966, advan study real estate investment, 1978. **Career:** Aide, 1968; Pro Tempore, speaker, 1992-96; Superdome Serv Inc, pres & chief exec officer, 1973-80; Mkt Serv Inc, pres & chief exec officer, 1978-; State La, state rep, 1986-99; Health Corp S, chmn, 1989-; 107 Group Inc, pres, currently; Gateway S Travel Agency, secy & treas, currently. **Orgs:** Pres, Nat Bus League, 1977; vice chmn bd, 1984-92, pres, 1992-; co-chmn, La Coun Policy Rev, 1985-; chair, La Bus League; chair, Nat Coun Policy Rev; treas, chair, La Legis Black Caucus; exec comt, Nat Black Caucus State Legislators; exec comn, Southern Legis Conf; Nat Dem Comt man; State Cent Comt man; US Chamber Com, Small Bus Coun; pres, New Orleans E Bus Asn, head; chair bd, EST Inc; Nat Conf State Legislators. **Special Achievements:** First African-American woman to serve in the Louisiana House of Representatives. Author: How Can the US & Local Chamber Encourage and Support the Emerging Minority-Owned Business?; US Chamber of Commerce Small Bus Council Task Force on Emerging Business, 1992. **Home Addr:** 101 Pinehurst Ct, New Orleans, LA 70128, **Home Phone:** (504)242-7996.

## COPES, RONALD ADRIAN

Insurance executive, executive director. **Personal:** Born Dec 1, 1941, Hartford, CT; son of Aelix and Mamie Weaver Bailey; married Melva Washington; children: Ronald A II & Rodney A. **Educ:** Lincoln Univ, Jefferson City, Mo, BS, acct, 1963; Atlanta Univ, Atlanta, Ga, MBA, 1974. **Career:** Mass Mutual Life Ins Co, vpres disability income, 1990-2008, vpres community rels, exec dir MassMutual Found; Massachusetts Mutual Life Insurance Co, vpres; United way pioneer valley, interim pres, 2008-10; Copes consult group, pres, 2008-. **Orgs:** Vice Basileus, Omega Psi Phi Fraternity, 1989-90. **Honors/Awds:** Hon Soc, Delta Mu Delta, 1971-73. **Home Addr:** 54 Blueberry Ridge, Westfield, MA 01085, **Home Phone:** (413)572-4759. **Business Addr:** President, Copes Consulting Group, Springfield, MA.

## CORAM, WILLIE MAE

School administrator, government official, association executive. **Personal:** Born Apr 20, 1934, Fayetteville, NC; daughter of Willie Clayton and Mary Helen Council; children: Lynn D Allen & Bruce Allan Sr. **Educ:** Boston Univ, BA, 1955; Univ Med & Dent NJ, PhD, 1983. **Career:** School administrator (retired); Grassland Hosp, res technician, lab supvr, 1955-63; Montefiore Hosp, lab supvr, 1963-64; GEIGY Chem Corp, res scientist, supvr autonomic pharmacol group, 1964-71; CIBA-GEIGY Corp, numerous positions, 1971-89; Univ Med & Dent NJ, asst dean stud & alumni affairs, 1989-2000. **Orgs:** Nat Asn Grad Admis Profs; Sigma Xi; AAAS; NY Acad Scis; Mid States Asn Col Registr & Officers Admis; Am Asn Col Registr & Admis Officers; bd dir, Carlisle Commonwealth Community Asn. **Honors/Awds:** Achievement Award, Nat Asn Negro Bus & Prof Women's Clubs Inc, 1985; Certificate of Recognition, Nat Urban League, 1986; CIBA-GEIGY TWIN Award, 1986; Outstanding Leaders in Business, Education & Industry, Jersey City State Col, 1988; Special Service Award, Rutgers, State Univ NJ, 2001. **Special Achievements:** Restoration of Normal Tissue K+ Levels in Heart, Aorta and Skeletal Muscle of Furosemide-Treated Rats on Mg++-Deficient Diet, 1988; Effects of CGS10078B on Catecholamine Content of Brain, Heart, Uterus and Plasma in Conscious Rats, 1986; numerous others. **Home Addr:** 4074 Armswood Pl, Stone Mountain, GA 30083, **Home Phone:** (404)299-3184.

## CORBETT, DR. ALEXANDER E., III

Administrator, buyer. **Personal:** Born Feb 13, 1944, Portsmouth, VA; son of Alexander Jr (deceased); married Barbara W; children: Aric. **Educ:** Kennedy-Western Univ, BS, bus admin, 1989; St Pauls Col, LHD, 2001. **Career:** Joslyn Mfg & Supply Co, clerk & expeditor, 1971-74; AMF-World Tobacco Group, buyer, 1974-76; Dom Va Power, sr supply chain specialist, 1976-2000; Town Belmont, clerk. **Orgs:** Am Asn Blacks Energy, 1993-95; Va Mus Fine Arts Multicultural Coun, 1994; bd trustee, comt co-chair, St Pauls Col, 1996-2000, 2001; Asn Gov Bds, cols & univs, 1996-2000; Jamestown-Yorktown Found Partnership Group, 1999-; acute care bd dir, Bon Secours Health Syst, 2003. **Home Addr:** 501 Clauson Rd, Richmond, VA 23227-1203, **Home Phone:** (804)264-1256.

## CORBETT, DR. DORIS R.

Editor, educator, chairperson. **Personal:** Born Jun 9, 1947, Elizabethtown, NC; daughter of Henry Edward and Isadora Beatty White; married William Johnson. **Educ:** NC Cent Univ, Durham, NC, BS, 1969, MS, 1972; Univ Md, College Park, MD, PhD, 1981. **Career:** Camp Curtin Jr High Sch, Harrisburg, PA, high sch teacher, 1969-70; John Harris Sr High Sch, Harrisburg, PA, high sch teacher, 1970-71; Emporia State Univ, distinguished univ prof; Howard Univ, WA, DC, Dept Phys Educ & Recreation, assoc prof, 1972-, dir grad studies, prof sport sociol, Dept Health, Human Performance & Leisure Studies, chairperson, prof emer sport studies, currently, dept head; US Capitol Hist Soc, fel; US Mil Acad, distinguished prof & consult; Emporia State Univ, prof; Nanyang Technol Univ, prof; Univ Northern Iowa, Sch Health, Phys Educ & Leisure Serv, dir, currently; Editor: Unique Games and Sports Around the World: A Reference Guide, 2001. **Orgs:** Pres, Nat Asn Girls & Women Sports, 1980-81; pres, Eastern Dist Asn, 1987-88; pres, Am Alliance Health, Phys Educ, Recreation & Dance, 1990-91, chmn bd gov, 1990-91; int pres, Int Coun Health, Phys Educ & Recreation, 1991-99; pres, DC Asn; Int Olympic Commit Sport; adv bd, Inst Int Sport, Univ RI; adv bd, Northeastern Univ Ctr; adv bd, Women Sports Found; adv bd, Pres's Coun Phys Fitness & Sport Sci Bd; j reviewer, Palestinian J Sport Sci, currently. **Home Addr:** 10604 Cannonview Ct, Fort Washington, MD 20744, **Home Phone:** (301)292-7253. **Business Addr:** Professor of Sport Sociology, Chairperson & Director, Howard University, 6th st & Girard St NW, Washington, DC 20059, **Business Phone:** (202)806-7186.

## CORBI, LANA E.

Executive. **Personal:** Born Jan 1, 1955, Los Angeles, CA; daughter of Carl King and Elizabeth; married Al; children: 2. **Educ:** Univ Southern Calif, BA, jour, 1979; Calif State Univ, grad studies, tv & film, 1980. **Career:** Fox Broadcasting, vpres, 1991, sr vpres, 1994-95, pres, network distrib, 1995-96; Blackstar, pres & chief operating officer, 1995-96, exec vpres, 1996-97; Odyssey Holdings, chief operating officer, 1999-; Crown Media Holdings, exec vpres & chief operating officer, 2000-01; Crown Media US LLC, chief operating officer, 1999-2000, pres, chief exec officer, 2001-02; Corbico, pres, chief exec officer, 2002-. **Orgs:** Bd mem, Monte Carlo Festival Hon Comt; bd mem, Entertainment Industs Coun; bd mem, Int Acad TV, Arts & Sci; bd mem, Nat Asn Minorities Commun; Women Cable Telecommun; Am Women Radio & TV. **Business Addr:** President, Chief Executive Officer, Corbico Ltd, 47 Dartford Rd, San Diego, CA 92128, **Business Phone:** (760)519-5761.

## CORBIN, DR. ANGELA LENORE

Physician. **Personal:** Born Nov 19, 1958, Washington, DC; daughter of Maurice C and Ruby. **Educ:** Howard Univ, BS, 1980; Meharry Med Col, MD, 1984. **Career:** Univ Md Hosp, resident & intern, 1984-87, Med Syst, nephrology fel, 1987-89; Med Syst, pvt pract physician, currently. **Orgs:** Am Col Physicians; Am Med Asn; Alpha Omega Alpha Med Honor Soc, 1984; Nat Med Asn; bd mem, Internal Med. **Home Addr:** 11304 Class Lane, Silver Spring, MD 20901, **Home Phone:** (301)593-6772. **Business Addr:** Physician, Private Practice Section of Nephrology, 2101 E Jefferson Blvd, Rockville, MD 20849, **Business Phone:** (301)816-2424.

## CORBIN, SEAN

Basketball executive. **Personal:** Born Jan 1, 1920. **Career:** Nat Basketball Asn, referee, currently. **Business Addr:** Official, National Basketball Association, 645 5th Ave 10th Fl, New York, NY 10022-5986, **Business Phone:** (212)826-7000.

## CORBIN, STAMPP W.

Chief executive officer, executive. **Educ:** Stanford Univ, BA, econ, 1982; Harvard Univ, MBA, gen, 1986. **Career:** Bull HN, dir mkt develop, 1987-91; Centerline Software Inc, regional sales dir, 1991-92; Resource One Comput Systs Inc, pres & chief exec officer, 1992-2009; RetroBox LLC, owner, founder & chief exec officer, 1996-2006; Intechra LLC, chief strategic officer, currently; MedLOCK, chief exec officer, 2009-; San Diego LGBT Weekly, publ, 2010-. **Orgs:** Treas, Asn Ohio Recyclers, 2002-; bd dir, Easter Seals, currently; vpres Bd dir, Columbus AIDS Task Force, currently; vpres bd trustee, Mt Carmel Health Syst, 2006-; co-chair Obama Nat LGBT Leadership Team, Nat LGBT Polit, 2007-2009; bd trustee, Columbus Col Art & Design; pledging mem, Basel Action Network; bd dir, Nat Recycling Coalition, 2008-; chmn, San Diego Citizens Equal Opportunity Comn, 2009-; Greater San Diego Bus Asn Charitable Found; Human Rights Campaign. **Business Addr:** Chief Executive Officer, Resource One Computer Systems Inc, 1159 Dublin Rd, Columbus, OH 43215, **Business Phone:** (614)485-4800.

## CORBIN, TYRONE KENNEDY

Basketball player, basketball coach, basketball executive. **Personal:** Born Dec 31, 1962, Columbia, SC; married Dante; children: Tyjha & Tyrell. **Educ:** DePaul Univ, BS, comput sci, 1985. **Career:** Basketball player (retired), basketball coach, exec; San Antonio Spurs, forward, 1985-87; Cleveland Cavaliers, 1987-88; Phoenix Suns, 1988-89; Minn Timberwolves, 1989-91; Utah Jazz, 1991-94, asst coach, 2004-11, head coach, 2011-14; Atlanta Hawks, 1994-95, 1996-99; Sacramento Kings, 1995-96, 1999-2000, asst coach, 2014, interim coach, 2014-15, advisor, 2015-; Miami Heat, 1996; Toronto Raptors, 2000-01; Charleston Lowgators, player mentor; New York Knicks, from gen mgr to mgr,

2003-04. **Business Addr:** Advisor, Sacramento Kings, 1 Sports Pkwy, Sacramento, CA 95834.

### CORBITT, DR. JOHN H.

Clergy. **Personal:** Born Aug 24, 1941, Salley, SC; son of John and Thelma; married Betty Starks; children: Bruce & Terry. **Educ:** SC State Univ, BA, 1962; Interdenominational Theol Ctr, MDiv, 1966; Vanderbilt Univ; Yale Div Univ; McCormick Theol Sem, DMin, 1979; Morris Col, Ddiv, 2001. **Career:** Bells Chapel Baptist Church, pastor, 1966-67; Owen Col, col minister & prof bible & relig, 1966-67; Mt Pleasant Baptist Church, pastor, 1967-74; Ark Baptist Career, interim dean relig; Philander Smith Col, col chaplain & prof relig & philos, 1970-74; Nat Baptist Stud Union Retreat, nat dir, 1973-96; Springfield Baptist Church, pastor, 1974-2011, minister; Nat Baptist Cong Christian Educ, dean, 1984-99; SC Baptist Cong Christian Educ, pres, 1986-90; Monks Grove Baptist Church, interim pastor, currently. **Orgs:** Foreign Mission Bd Nat Baptist Conv USA Inc, 1968-74; consult, Nat Stud Ministries So Bapt Conv, 1969-87; Gov's Comn First Offenders State Ark, 1969; Nat Asn Col & Univ Chaplains; Ministries Blacks Higher Educ; pres, Interdenomi Nat Ministerial Alliance, Greater Little Rock; App by Gov Dale Bumpers Bd Pardons & Parole, State Ark, 1971; nat dir, Nat Baptist Stud Union Retreat, 1973-96; nat dir, NH Baptist Stud Union Retreat, 1973-96; life mem, Nat Asn Advan Colored People; pres, Enoree River Cong Christian Educ, 1975-79; Preaching Teams, 1979; pres, Greater Greenville Ministerial Asn, 1980-81; dean, Nat Baptist Cong Christian Educ, 1984-99; bd adv, Little Rock Urban League; App by Gov James B Edwards to Greenville Area Bd Ment Health; pres, SC State Cong Christian Educ, 1986-90; Soviet Union, 1988; former pres, Greater Greenville Ministerial Asn; chap pres, Phi Beta Sigma Fraternity; exec bd, Nat Baptist Conventional; pres, Baptist Ministers Fel Greenville Vicinity; vice chair, Acad Affairs & Fac Liaison Comt; Res, Econ Develop; 1890 Prog Comt; fac mem, Baptist World Youth Cong; Comn Evangelism & Educ, Baptist World Alliance; vice chmn, SC State Bd Trustees; Religions Educ Asn US & Can; bd trustee, SC State Univ, 2001-; Asn Gov Boards Univs & Cols; trustee, Morris Col; pres, SC Baptist Cong Christian Educ. **Honors/Awds:** The Order of the Palmetto, 1988; Order of the Palmetto, Gov SC, 1988; Alumnus of the Year, McCormick Theol Sem, 1991; Honored, Morehouse Col, 1992; Arkansas Traveler Award, 1992; Named to Martin Luther King, Morehouse Col, 1992. **Special Achievements:** Author: Black Churches Reaching Coll Students, 1995. **Home Addr:** 202 Dove Tree Rd, Greenville, SC 29615-4428. **Business Addr:** Board of Trustee, South Carolina State University, 300 Col St NE, Orangeburg, SC 29117, **Business Phone:** (803)536-7000.

### CORDELL, LADORIS HAZZARD

Judge. **Personal:** Born Nov 19, 1949, Bryn Mawr, PA; children: Cheran & Starr. **Educ:** Antioch Col, BA, 1971; Stanford Law Sch, JD, 1974. **Career:** Nat Asn Advan Colored People Legal Defense & Educ Fund, staff atty, 1974-75; atty, pvt pract, 1975-82; Stanford Law Sch, asst dean, 1978-82; State Ct Appeal Sixth Dist, justice pro tem, 1986-87; Munic Ct Santa Clara Co, judge, 1982-88; Supr Ct Santa Clara Co, judge, 1988-2001; Palo Alto City Coun, mem; Stanford Univ, vice provost & spec counr, pres, campus rels, 2001-; CBS 5, Legal Analyst, currently. **Orgs:** Nat Bar Asn; Am Bar Asn; Nat Asn Advan Colored People; Boards United Way Santa Clara County; Nat Conf Community & Justice; Lucile Packard Found C; Asian Law Alliance, & Mills Col; Calif Judges Asn; Calif Women Lawyers; chmn, bd dir, Manhattan Playhouse, E Palo Alto, 1980; bd dir & steering comt, Nat Conf Women & Law, 1980, 1984-85; policy bd, Ctr Res Women Stanford Univ, 1980-82; chairperson, bd dir, E Palo Alto Community Law Proj, 1984-87; bd trustee, United Way Santa Clara County, 1987-; bd dir, Police Activ League, San Jose Chap, 1987-89, Nat Conf Christians & Jews Inc, Santa Clara County, 1988-; bd trustee, Mills Col, Oakland, Calif, 1996-; bd dir, Lucile Packard Found C, Stanford, Calif, 1997-; Silicon Valley Forum Coun, Commonwealth Club Calif, 1997-; bd dir, Asian Law Alliance, San Jose, Calif, 1997, Adv bd, Healthy Alternatives African Am Babies, San Jose, Calif, 1994-; Am Law Inst, 1996-. **Honors/Awds:** Black History Award, Tulip Jones Womens Club, 1977; Community Involvement Award, E Palo Alto Chamber Com, 1982, 1983; Public Service Award, Delta Sigma Theta, 1982; Public Service Awards, Nat Coun Negro Women, 1982; Outstanding Mid-Peninsula Black Woman Award, Mid-Peninsula, YWCA, 1983; Political Achievement Award, Calif Black Women's Coalition & the Black Concerns Asn, 1982; Featured in Ebony Mag, 1980, 1984; Implemented a minority recruitment prog, Stanford Law School asst dean; Elected presiding judge Municipal Court, 1985-86 term; Achievement Award, Western Ctr Domestic Violence, 1986; Santa Clara County Woman of Achievement Award, 1985; Recipient of first Juliette Gordon Lowe Award for Community Serv, 1987; Distinguished Citizen Award, Exchange Club, 1989; Don Peters Outstanding Volunteer Award, United Way Santa Clara County, 1991; Baha'I Community Service Award, 1992; Special Recognition Award, Human Relations Comn, Santa Clara County, 1994; Youth Service Award, Legal Advocates Children & Youth, 1996; Unsung Heroes Award, Minority Access Comt, Santa Clara County Bar Asn, 1996; Social Justice award, San Franscisco Women's Ctr, 1996; Legal Impact Award, Asian Law Alliance, 1996; Advocate for Justice Award, Legal Aid Soc, Santa Clara County, 1996; Martin Luther King, Junior Award, The San Jose Peace Ctr, 1998; Josephine & Frank Dulveneck Humanitarian Award, 1998; Jacqueline Kennedy Award, John F Kennedy Univ, 1999; Rosa Parks Ordinary People Award, San Jose, Nat Asn Advan Colored People, 1999; Women's Equality Award, Comn Status Women, 2000. **Special Achievements:** First Black Woman Judge in Northern Calif; First black woman on Superior Court in Northern California, 1988-; East Palo Alto, CA; First lawyer to open a private law practice in Mex Am community; Author: "Before Brown v Bd of Educ--Was It All Worth It?", Howard Law J Vol 23 No 1, 1980; Co-author: "The Appearance of Justice: Judges' Verbal and Nonverbal Behavior in Criminal Jury Trials", Stanford Law Review Vol 38, No 1, 1985; "Black Immigration, Disavowing the Stereotype of the Shiftless Negro", Judges' J Spring, 1986; First African American woman to sit on the Superior Court in northern California, "Musings of a Trial Court Judge", Indiana Law J, vol 68, No 4, 1993; First African American Superior Court Judge in US. **Business Addr:** Legal Analyst, CBS 5.

### CORLETTE, EDITH PARKER

Lawyer, secretary general. **Personal:** Born Oct 19, 1942, Oklahoma City, OK; daughter of Stephen Parker and Gwendolyn Parker. **Educ:** Hampton Inst, BS, 1964; Northwestern Univ Sch Law, JD, 1974; Univ Calif, MS, 1975. **Career:** Woodrow Wilson fel, 1964; NW Urban fel, 1973-74; self-employed atty. **Orgs:** Delta Sigma Theta Sorority, 1962; Alpha Kappa Mu Hon Soc, 1963-64; Langston Law Club, 1974; SW Bar Asn, 1974; La Co Bar Asn, 1975; Nat Conf Black Lawyers, 1975; Calif State Bar Asn, 1975-; secy, Black Women Lawyer S CA, 1975; Nat Bus Asn, 1976; Beverly Hills Law Asn, 1977; bd dir, Nat Asn Advan Colored People, Hollywood Br; bd dir, Proj heavy; pres, Womens Div NBA; secy, Calif Asn Black Lawerys; Nat Bar Asn. **Honors/Awds:** Outstanding Young Women America, 1966. **Home Addr:** 4619 6th Ave, Los Angeles, CA 90043. **Business Addr:** Attorney, PO Box 8504, Los Angeles, CA 90008-0692, **Business Phone:** (323)298-7223.

### CORLEY, DR. CHARLES J.

President (organization), chairperson, educator. **Personal:** married Karen Ann; children: Lauren Celeste, LaRae, Jamie L & Charles James III. **Educ:** Hampton Inst, BA, sociol/social work, 1981; Bowling Green State Univ, MA, criminol, 1984, PhD, social psychol family, 1986. **Career:** Less Secure Detention Facil, Hampton, juv supv, 1980-81; Bowling Green State Univ, teaching fel, 1981-85, grad asst, 1986; Lucas County Ct Intake officer, Toledo, 1982-84; Lucas County Criminal Justice Training Acad, Toledo, tech asst, 1982; Winthrop Col, asst prof sociol, 1986-89; Mich Judicial Inst, adj fac, 1990-; Mich State Univ, Sch Criminal Justice, asst prof, assoc prof, 1990, Lilly Endowment teaching fel, 1992, prof, currently, rev comt, 1994-95; Calif Corrections Leadership Inst, adj fac, 1996-2000; Books: The media: crime rates and race, Police Traffic Enforcement Actions on a Midwestern University Campus: A Case Study in Challenging American Police: A Reader for the 21st Century, Juvenile justice: muticultural issues, "Conceptions of family and juvenile court processes: a qualitative assessment, "Race and criminal justice: employment of minorities in the criminal justice system, Socioeconomic, Sociodemographic and Attitudinal Correlates of the Tempo of Divorce, Recognizing the truth about Black families: An introspective evaluation. **Orgs:** Am Socs Criminol, 1994; Inst Educ Leadership; pres, bd dir, chairperson; Treas, Sankofa Cult Asn; bd mem Statewide Adv Coun Mich Neighborhood Builders Alliance; Acad Criminal Justice Sci; Southern Demog Asn; N Cent Sociol Asn; Nat Asn Advan Colored People; Rock Hill, Cent City Optimist Club; bd dir, Highfields, 2005-06; Midwest Criminal Justice Asn; Highfields, bd dir; Inst Educ Leadership; Midwest Criminal Justice Asn; chairperson, bd dir, Sankofa Shule; treas, Sankofa Cult Asn; bd mem, Statewide Adv Coun Mich Neighborhood Builders Alliance; Acad Criminal Justice Sci; Southern Demog Asn; Am Soc Criminol; N Cent Sociol Asn; Nat Asn Advan Colored People; Rock Hill, Cent City Optimist Club. **Home Addr:** 3400 Colchester, Lansing, MI 48906, **Home Phone:** (517)327-6101. **Business Addr:** Associate Professor, Michigan State University, Baker Hall 655 Auditorium Rd Rm 516, East Lansing, MI 48824, **Business Phone:** (517)432-4236.

### CORLEY, EDDIE B., SR.

Automotive executive. **Personal:** married Gladys Mae; children: 8. **Educ:** Prairie View Col. **Career:** Humble Oil Serv Sta; Clothing Store, owner; Grocery Store, owner; Fast Food Restaurant, owner; Ed Corley Automotive Group, Ed Corley Ford Lincoln Mercury Inc, chief exec officer & dealer, 1982; Ed Corley Nissan, 1996; Ed Corley Chrysler Jeep Dodge, NMex, 1997, pres, currently. **Business Addr:** Chief Executive Officer, Ed Corley Chrysler Dodge Jeep, 1870 W Santa Fe Ave, Grants, NM 87020, **Business Phone:** (888)447-1779.

### CORLEY, LESLIE M.

Investment banker, chief executive officer. **Personal:** Born , 1946, Chicago, IL; son of Lorena Turner and Leslie T. **Educ:** Univ Ill, BS, aeronaut & astronaut engineering, 1969; Harvard Grad Sch Bus Admin, MBA, 1971. **Career:** Exxon Inc, fin analyst, 1969-71; Fidelity Investments, investment analyst, 1972-77; Norton Simon Inc, mgr acquisitions strategic planning, 1977-81; Kelso & Co, gen partner, chair, partner, 1981-88; LM Capital Corp, Pres & chief exec officer, 1988-; LM Capital Securities Inc, founder, 1993-; Convenience Corp Am Inc, chmn, 1995-96. **Orgs:** Urban League Palm Beach County, dir, 1996-97; d'essence Designer Fragrances, LLC, dir, 1996-97; Tri-W Inc, dir, 1986-88; Am Sterilizer Inc, dir, 1984-86; Manhattan Community Bd 9, treas, 1991-92; treas & dir, Aaron DavisHall, 1986-95; Personal Luxury Prod Int Inc, dir, 1998-; bd mem, bd dir, Enterprise Fla Inc; chair, Fla Atlantic Univ Found bd; Bus Develop Brd Palm Beach County; Econ Coun Palm Beach County; vice chmn, Criminal Justice Comn Palm Beach County; bd mem, Econ Coun Palm Beach County. **Home Addr:** 260 Clarke Ave, Palm Beach, FL 33480, **Home Phone:** (561)837-6576. **Business Addr:** President, Chief Executive Officer, LM Capital Securities Inc, 610 Clematis St Suite 132, West Palm Beach, FL 33401, **Business Phone:** (561)623-1700.

### CORLEY, TODD

Entrepreneur, executive. **Educ:** Le Moyne Col, BS, 1991; Georgetown Univ, McDonough Sch Bus, MBA, 1997. **Career:** Towers Perrin, sr consult global diversity & chg mgt; Starwood Hotels & Resorts Worldwide, creator inclusion strategy; Abercrombie & Fitch, vpre diversity & inclusion, 2004-08, sr vpres & global chief diversity officer, 2008-14; TAPO Inst, founder, creator & catalyst, 2014-. **Orgs:** Columbus Jazz Arts Group bd; Columbus Urban League bd; Salvation Army Greater Columbus bd; Georgetown Univ Chief Diversity Officer Consortium, chair, 2007-14; Exec Leadership Coun (New Cand Selection comt, 2010-; No Bully adv bd, 2014-; Nat Soc High Sch Scholars Found Bd, chair, 2012-; Le Moyne Col, bd regents, 2016-. **Honors/Awds:** Claes Nobel World Betterment Prize, 2013. Listed in "30 Under 30," Ebony Magazine; "100 Most Influential in Business," SAVOY Magazine. **Special Achievements:** Author: "FITCH PATH: A Cautionary Tale about a Moose, Millenials, Leadership and Transparency", 2015. **Business Addr:** Tapo Institute, 175 South Third St Suite 200, Columbus, OH 43215, **Business Phone:** (614)721-1993.

### CORLEY, TODD L.

Vice president (organization). **Personal:** Born Jan 20, 1969, Glen Cove, NY; son of Luther and Lillian Mitchell. **Educ:** Le Moyne Col, BA, finance, 1991; Georgetown Univ, MBA, orgn develop & chg mgt, 1997. **Career:** Towers Perrin's Global Diversity & Chg Mgmt Pract, sr consult & area leader, 1997-2003; Starwood Hotels & Resorts-Worldwide, sr mgr, diversity & inclusion, 2003-04; Georgetown Univ, chair, Georgetown Univ chief diversity officer consortium, 2007-14; Abercrombie & Fitch, diversity & inclusion, vpres, 2004-08, sr vpres & global chief diversity officer, 2008-14; TAPO Inst, creator & catalyst, 2014-. **Orgs:** Nat INROADS Alumni Asn, 1991-; dir, Alhpa Phi Alpha, 1992-; lifetime mem, Nat Black MBA Asn, 1997-; 100 Black Men, 1999-; mem adv bd, Le Moyne Coll, 1999-; mem bd, UNCF Columbus; bd mem, Cornell Univ, Chief Diversity Officer Roundtable; Exec Leadership Coun, mem & comt mem, new cand selection, 2010-; No Bully, mem adv bd, 2014-. **Home Addr:** 30 Fawn Ridge, Millwood, NY 10546. **Business Addr:** Creator & Catalyst, The TAPO Institute.

### CORLEY-BLANEY, JANICE

Broker. **Personal:** children: 4. **Educ:** Tex Southern Univ, BA, finance, 1979. **Career:** Gen Motors Corp, Finance Dept; C21 Stanmeyer; Coldwell Banker Stanmeyer; Coldwell Banker NRT, asst reg mgr; Elite Residential Serv, owner, 2000-; Remax Exclusive Properties, chief exec officer, 2000-04, 2011-, chmn, 2011-; Sudler Sothebys Int Realty, founder & managing broker, 2004-11. **Honors/Awds:** Top Recruiter Award, 2004; Best Office Award. **Business Addr:** Chairman, Chief Executive Officer, Remax Exclusive Properties, 2951 N Lincoln Ave, Chicago, IL 60657, **Business Phone:** (312)337-3629.

### CORLEY-SAUNDERS, ANGELA ROSE

Government official. **Personal:** Born Jun 9, 1947, Washington, DC. **Educ:** Howard Univ, BA, 1975; Sch Divinty. **Career:** White House, spec asst, 1977-77; US Dept Agri Off, Asst Secy Rural Develop, spec asst, 1977-79; US Dept Agri Farmers Home Admin, mgt analyst, 1979-; Equal Opportunity Specialists, 1986-; US Dept Agri Rural Econ & Community Develop, civil rights staff & equal employ specialist, 1987-. **Orgs:** Nat Coun Negro Women, 1978-; bd mem, Unity Wash, DC, 1983-; lic unity teacher, Asn Unity Churches, 1996-. **Home Addr:** 1338 Shepherd St NE, Washington, DC 20017-2343, **Home Phone:** (202)269-4373. **Business Addr:** Equal Employment Specialist, United States Department of Agriculture, 1400 Independence Ave SW Suite 2077, Washington, DC 20250, **Business Phone:** (202)720-6633.

### CORMIER, LAWRENCE J.

Executive. **Personal:** Born Sep 26, 1927, San Benito, TX; married Helen Jones; children: Patricia Watkins, Janet & Lawrence. **Educ:** Pace Univ, acct, 1970. **Career:** US Merchant Marine, third officer, 1950-55; Ebony Oil Corp, bd chmn & chief exec officer, 1955-88; Cormier Ebony Trucking Inc, bd chmn & chief exec officer, 1964-87; Inner City Mgt Co, chief exec officer & bd chmn, 1977-85; Cormier Group Ltd, Jamaica, NY, owner, chief exec officer & bd chmn, 1990-. **Orgs:** Charter mem, bd mem, Assoc Minority Bus Enterprise NY; bd mem, vpres, Gr Jamaica Chamber Com; pres, Int Kiwanis, Jamaica Club; pres, bd mem, charter mem, United Black Men Queens City; br pres, Jamaica Nat Asn Advan Colored People, Saint Albans, NY; pres, dir emer, Greater Jamaica Develop Corp. **Home Addr:** 880 State Rte 3, PO Box 310840, Plattsburgh, NY 12901, **Home Phone:** (518)562-3456. **Business Addr:** Chief Executive Officer, Owner, Cormier Group Ltd, 90 25 161 St Suite 510, Jamaica, NY 11431, **Business Phone:** (718)298-9010.

### CORMIER, DR. RUFUS P., JR.

Lawyer. **Personal:** Born Mar 2, 1948, Beaumont, TX; married Yvonne Clement; children: Michelle, Geoffrey & Claire. **Educ:** Southern Methodist Univ, BA, anthrop, 1970; Yale Univ, JD, 1973. **Career:** Paul Weiss Rifkind Wharton & Garrison, atty, 1973-74; US House Reps Judiciary Comm, spec asst coun, 1974; Baker & Botts, atty & partner, 1974, partner, 1983-; Tex Southern Univ, chmn bd regents; Yale Law Sch Asn, mem exec comt; Houston City Planning Comn, comnr. **Orgs:** Am Bar Asn; Am Bar Found; Houston Bar Asn; Houston Lawyers Asn; vice chmn bd dir, Houston Bar Found; State Bar Tex; Tex Bar Found; vice chmn bd dir, Am Red Cross; bd mem, Houston Zoo Inc; bd mem, Ctr Houston; Mem Exec Bd, Southern Methodist Univ; bd trustees, St. Johns Sch; adv bd mem, William A. Lawson Inst Peace & Prosperity; bd mem, Tex Equal Access; United Way Tex Gulf Coast Leadership Coun; Gulf Coast Legal Found. **Honors/Awds:** Avella Winn Hay Achievement Award, 1970; Outstanding Young Texans, Tex Jaycees, 1981; Karen H Susman Jurisprudence Award, 2004; Texas Super Lawyers, Tex Monthly & Law & Politics, 2006; Leon Jaworski Award, Houston Bar Asn; Silver Anniversary Mustang Award, SMU Lettermen's Asn. **Special Achievements:** First African American lawyer to make partner in Baker & Botts LLP. **Home Addr:** 1507 Kirby Dr, Houston, TX 77019-3301. **Business Addr:** Partner, Baker & Botts LLP, 1 Shell Plz 910 La St, Houston, TX 77002-4995, **Business Phone:** (713)229-1544.

### CORNELIUS, CHARLES HENRY

Insurance executive, president (organization), chief executive officer. **Personal:** Born Nov 13, 1955, Bronx, NY; son of Melvin and Dolores; married Sheila Harris; children: Charles Jr & Michael. **Educ:** Univ Hartford, BA, polit sci, 1977; Univ Va, exec prog. **Career:** Allstate Ins Co, mgr, 1977-84; Chubb Grp Ins Co, br mgr & vpres, 1984-96; Atlanta Life Fin Grp Inc, pres & chief exec officer, 1996-2005; Inroads Inc, pres & chief exec officer, 2005-. **Orgs:** Atlanta Action Forum, 1996-; dir, Nat Ins Asn, 1997-; 100 Black Men Atlanta, 1996-; Nat Asn Advan Colored People, 1997-; dir, Albany Inst Art & Hist, 1993-96; dir, Urban League NE NY, 1994-96; bd visitor, Metrop Atlanta Chamber Com, 1998-; dir, Atlanta Asn Ins Profs, 1998-2000; dir, Butler St YMCA, 1998-2002; dir, Zoo Atlanta, 1998-2002; dir, High Mus Art, 1998-2000; bd visitor, Emory Univ, 1998-01; bd visitor, Grady Health Syst, 1998-; dir, Altanta Comn Pub Educ, 1998-; Aid Atlanta, 1998-; dir, Atlanta Urban League, 1999-2001; bd trustee, Leadership Atlanta, 1999-2001; adv coun, Cool Girls Ins; adv coun, Rotary Club Atlanta; bd coun, Carter Ctr, 2002-. **Honors/Awds:** Black Achievers Industries, YMCA Harlem Br, 1991; Honoree, Nat Ins Ind Asn, 1996. **Special Achievements:** Black Enterprise's list of Top Insurance Companies, ranked 2, 1999, 2000. **Home Addr:** 115 Foalgarth Way, Alpharetta, GA 30097-1452, **Home Phone:** (770)582-0711. **Business Addr:** President, Chief Executive Officer, Inroads Inc, 10 S Broadway Suite 300, St Louis, MO 63102, **Business Phone:** (314)241-7488.

### CORNELIUS, REV. ULYSSES S., SR.

Clergy. **Personal:** Born Dec 12, 1913, Waskom, TX; married Willie Hicks; children: Ulysses Sidney Jr. **Educ:** Bishop Col, BA, 1947, MEd, 1952, DD, 1975; Miami Univ; Va Univ. **Career:** Mt Sinai Baptist Church, Dallas, pastor; TX, pastor; LA, pastor; Waskom, TX, instr pub schs; Interracial Baptist Inst, Dallas, instr; Bishop Col, instr. **Orgs:** Vpres, Nat Baptist SS & Baptist Training Union-Cong Inc; pres, BM & E St SS & BTU Cong TX; secy & treas, LK Williams Ministers Inst; Inter dnmntnl Ministerial All Dallas; trustee bd, BM & E Conv TX; bd dir, Interracial Baptist Inst Dallas; 32 Deg Prince Hall Masons; bd trustee, Bishop Col; bd dir, Black C C, Dallas; bd dir, Tex Fed Garden Clubs. **Honors/Awds:** Alumni Citation Award, Bishop Col, 1968; Cert of Appreciation, Advan Bishop Col, 1969-75; Service Award, Bethlehem Baptist Church, Bonham, TX, 1971; Service Award, Mt Sinai Baptist Church, Dallas, 1973; Service Award, NW Dist Baptist Asn, 1974; Big Boss Leadership Award, YMCA. **Home Addr:** 5620 Trailwood Dr, Dallas, TX 75241, **Home Phone:** (214)374-6327. **Business Addr:** Clergy, Apostolic Assembly, 1106 Pemberton Hill Rd, Dallas, TX 75217-5214, **Business Phone:** (214)398-5610.

### CORNELL, BOB

Executive. **Personal:** Born Jersey City, NJ; son of Frank and Sylvia; married Janice; children: Patricia, Valerie, Robert, Andrew & David. **Educ:** Arapahoe Community Col, AAS, 1975; Metrop State Col, attended 1979; Colo Sales Training Inst, cert. **Career:** Maiden Form Bra Co; Colo Sls Trng Inst, consult; US Fed Protective Serv, trng officer; Littleton Police Dept, police officer; People Skills Inst, pres, chief exec officer & founder, 1978-; MasterStream, facilitator, trainer & consult, 1978; cert instr, Human Synergistics Inc; Develop Dimensions Int, instr; Human Synergistics Inc, instr; Fred Pryor/CareerTrack, instr. **Orgs:** Bd mem, Colo Chap, Inst Mgt Consults; Bd Advisors; sr assoc dir, exec adv bd, Nat Bur Cert Consults, Colo chap; Am Soc Training & Develop; founder, People Skills Inst; sr assoc dir, Nat Bur Cert Consults; Chambers Com. **Home Addr:** PO Box 101148, Denver, CO 80250-1148, **Home Phone:** (303)756-6771. **Business Addr:** Founder, President & Chief Executive Officer, People Skills Institute, 4225 E Mex Ave Apt 508, Denver, CO 80222-4109, **Business Phone:** (303)756-6771.

### CORNISH, AUDIE

Talk show host, journalist, radio host. **Personal:** Born Oct 9, 1979; married Theo Emery. **Educ:** University of Massachusetts Amherst, Bachelor's. **Career:** NPR station WBUR, Reporter; Associated Press (Boston), Reporter; National Public Radio (NPR), "Weekend Edition Sunday," 2011-12, co-host "All Things Considered," 2012-. **Orgs:** National Association of Black Journalists, Member. **Honors/Awds:** National Awards for Education Writing, First Prize (shared) for "Reading, Writing, and Race," 2005; Grady College of Journalism and Mass Communication at the University of Georgia, George Foster Peabody Award, 2011; Columbia University Awards Center, Alfred I. duPont, 2012; "The Root" Magazine, The Root 100 Honorees, 2013.

### CORNISH, BETTY W.

School administrator, educator, consultant. **Personal:** Born Jul 10, 1936, New York, NY; daughter of John A and Edna Charles; married Edward H. **Educ:** Boston Univ, BFA, 1958; Univ Hartford, MEd, 1962, MAEd, 1980. **Career:** Hartford Neighborhood Ctrs, youth group leader, 1959-63; Bloomfield Pub Schs, teacher, 1958-68; Cent Conn State Col, asst prof, art ed, 1966-83; Gemini User Group Inc, exec dir, 1983-91, educ consult, 1991-92; St Joseph Col, dir, inter cult affairs, 1992-2001. **Orgs:** Conn Educ Assoc, 1960-74; coord, Afro-Am Studies Prog, 1969-73; pres & exec bd, Conn Art Educ Asn, 1975; Am Asn Univ Profs, 1976-; exec bd, New Eng Art Educ Conf, 1977-79; pres, affirm action comn, Cent Conn State Univ, 1978-80, co-chair; Pres Comn Race Rels; Soc Conn Craftsmen, Hartford Reading Fundamental Comn; presentations civic sch & adult groups; Afro-Am Studies Prog, CCSC, chmn stud fac comn; Coun Unitarian Soc Hartford; Literacy Vols Am; Conn Col Personnel Asn. **Honors/Awds:** Delta Sigma Theta Scholarship Award, 1954-55; Boston Univ Full-Tuition Scholarship Award, 1954-58; Outstanding Art Education in Connecticut Award, 1979; Black Alumni CCSU Service Award. **Home Addr:** 163 Thomaston St, Hartford, CT 06112, **Home Phone:** (860)278-6487.

### CORNISH, JEANNETTE CARTER

Lawyer. **Personal:** Born Sep 17, 1946, Steelton, PA; daughter of Ellis Pollard and Anna Elizabeth Stannard; married Harry L; children: Lee Jason & Geoffrey Charles. **Educ:** Howard Univ, BA, govt & econs, 1968; Howard Univ Law Sch, JD, 1973. **Career:** Off Gen Coun USDA, law clerk, 1968-71; Newark-Essex Jt Law Reform Proj, atty, 1971-72; Equal Employ Opportunity Comn, atty, 1972-73; Inmont Corp, atty asst sec, 1974-82, sr atty asst sec, 1982-85; United Technologies, sr atty, 1979-85; BASF Corp, sr coun, 1985-99; Axiom Law, atty, 2004-08; J C Cornish Law & Mediation, atty, 2008-; Single Stop USA Inc, legal advisor, 2014-. **Orgs:** Am Bar Asn; Nat Bar Asn; Am Corp Coun Asn; bd mem, Paterson YWCA; bd mem, Lenni-Lenape Girl Scout Coun; trustee, Barnert Hosp, Paterson; NJ Equal Employ Opportunity Adv Comn; Girl Scouts Northern NJ; Nat Asn Women Lawyers. **Home Addr:** 614 11th Ave, Paterson, NJ 07514. **Business Addr:** Legal Advisor, Single Stop USA, 1825 Pk Ave Suite 503, New York, NY 10035, **Business Phone:** (212)480-2870.

### CORNWALL, DR. SHIRLEY M.

Dentist. **Personal:** Born Dec 8, 1918, Panama City; married Jerlene G; children: Howard Alphonse, Caral S, Cedric, Rupert M, Vicount Patrick & Francis Wilhelm. **Educ:** BS, biology, 1946; MS, 1947; DDS, 1952; NC Col, Durham, MA. **Career:** Charlotte NC, intern & residency, 1952; DDS, pvt pract, 1955; real estate bus, 1960. **Orgs:** N MS Med Dent Pharm & Nurses Soc; Kappa Alpha Psi Fraternity; St &Francis Cath Church. **Special Achievements:** First African-American to receive MA from NC Col Durham NC. **Home Addr:** 205 Walthall ST, Greenwood, MS 38930. **Business Addr:** 125 W Johnson St, Greenwood, MS 38930.

### CORNWELL, DR. JOANNE

Educator. **Personal:** Born Dec 17, 1948, Detroit, MI; daughter of Joseph and Dora Lee Smith Jenkins. **Educ:** Univ Calif, Irvine, PhD, fr African lit, 1981. **Career:** San Diego St Univ, asst prof, 1984-92, assoc prof, Fr & AfricanStudies, 1992-; Sisterlocks, founder & owner, 1993-. **Orgs:** African Studies Asn, 1990-; founder & co-dir, African Ctr Cult Literacy &Res, SDSU, 2000; hq dir, African Lit Asn, 2000-; founding mem, African Am Alumni Chap, SDSU, 2001; Am Hairbraiders & Natural Haircare Asn. **Home Addr:** 4912 Mt Bigelow Dr, San Diego, CA 92111, **Home Phone:** (858)569-6922. **Business Addr:** Founder, Owner, Sisterlocks, 2043 El Cajon Blvd, San Diego, CA 92104, **Business Phone:** (619)291-5116.

### CORNWELL, W. DON

Executive. **Personal:** Born Jan 17, 1948, Cushing, OK; son of Felton and Lelia; married Saundra Williams; children: Don & Samantha. **Educ:** Occidental Col, AB, polit sci, 1969; Harvard Bus Sch, MBA, gen & finance, 1971. **Career:** Corp Finance, vpres; Hartford Comn Capital Corp, Hartford Nat Corp, mgr, 1970; Goldman Sachs, 1971-88, Invest Banking Div, vpres, 1976-88, Finance Dept, chief operating officer, 1980-88; CVS Caremark Corp, dir, 1994-2007; Telecommunications Develop Fund, Chmn, 1997-2007; Granite Broadcasting Corp, co foundr, chmn & chief exec officer, 1988-2009. **Orgs:** Bd trustee, Nat Urban League; bd trustee, Big Bros Big Sisters NY; Zeta Boule; bd dir, Pfizer Inc, 1997-; chmn bd, Telecommun Develop Fund, 1997-2006; bd dir, Hershey Trust; bd dir, Milton Hershey Sch; bd dir, Wallace Found; bd dir, Nat Asn Broadcasters; New York Univ Med Ctr; trustee, Occidental Col; trustee, Citizens Budget Comn, 2001-05; bd dir, Am Int Group Inc; bd dir, Avon Prod, 2003; Nat Asn Corp dir, 2005-13; bd dir, AIG Ins, 2011-; Comcast Corp; trustee, Edna McConnell Clark Found, 2015-.

### CORPREW, CHARLES SUMNER, JR.

Educator, president (organization). **Personal:** Born Feb 14, 1929, Norfolk, VA; married Bertha Delois Bryant; children: Jovandra Stacey Sanderlin & Charles Sumner III. **Educ:** WVa State Col Inst, AB, 1951; NY Univ, MA, 1963; Kent State Univ; Old Dominion Univ. **Career:** Educator (retired); Norfolk City Sch bd, adv coun vice chmn, 1965, elemprin, 1967-69; Educ Asn Norfolk, pres, 1969-70; Norfolk City Sch, asst prin admin, 1969-71, prin sec, 1971-93, personnel coordr, 1993-94. **Orgs:** Keeper recs & seals, Omega Psi Phi Fraternity, 1954-55; Classroom teacher sstate pres, Norfolk City Sch, 1960; eastern reg dir, Nat Coun Urban Educ Asn, Nat Educ Asn, 1964-67; educ com chmn, Chamber Com, Norfolk, 1969; Phi Delta Kappa Educ Fraternity, 1970; pres, Norfolk Teachers Asn, Fed Credit Union, 1978-; music dept chmn, First Baptist Church, Norfolk, 1978-80; trustee, finance comm, First Baptist Church, Norfolk, 1990-; Optimist Club, Norfolk Chap, 1992; Retired Teachers Asn-Dist L; life mem, Nat Ed Asn; life mem, Omega Psi Phi Fraternity; chmn, Norfolk teachers asn; chmn, Norfolk fed Teachers Credit Union, currently. **Honors/Awds:** Outstanding Contribution Field Educ Award, Omega Psi Phi Frat Norfolk, VALambda Omega Chap, 1971; Outstanding Contrib Field Education Award, VA Educ Asn Minority Caucus, 1977; NAACP, Thurgood Marshall Service Award, partic "In The Trenches" Civil Rights Struggle, 1994. **Special Achievements:** First African American president of the Education Association of Norfolk. **Home Addr:** 1204 Gladiola Cres, Virginia Beach, VA 23453, **Home Phone:** (757)427-3407. **Business Addr:** Chairman, Norfolk Teachers Association Federal Credit Union, 1701 Church St, Norfolk, VA 23504, **Business Phone:** (757)627-0845.

### CORPREW, WILBERT E.

College teacher. **Educ:** Va Union Univ, BA, 1964; Crozier Theol Sem, attended 1965; Rutgers Univ, attended 1972; State Univ NY, Binghamton, MA, 1990. **Career:** J J Newberry, asst mgr, 1965-68; Rutgers Univ, asst registr, 1968-73; State Univ NY, Binghamton, assoc registr, 1974-94; Broome Community Col, registr, 1994-2004, adj hist instr, currently; State Univ NY, NY, vpres regist & rec mgt. **Orgs:** Am Asn Registr & Admis Officers, 1968-; Am Fed Teachers, 1974-; NY United Teachers, 1974-; pres, United Univ Prof, 1974-94; from vpres to pres, State Univ NY Registrars Asn; vpres, 1992-94, pres elect, 1996-97, pres, 1997-98, Mid States Asn, Col Registrars & Officers Admis; Alpha Phi Alpha Fraternity; vpres prof develop & publ, Am Asn Col Registrars & Admis Officers, 2000-03; bd dir, Boys & Girls Club Western Broome. **Home Addr:** 402 Beckwith Ave, Endwell, NY 13760, **Home Phone:** (607)754-6643. **Business Addr:** Adjunct Instructor, Broome Community College, 907 Front St Suite 1 T-202, Binghamton, NY 13902, **Business Phone:** (607)778-5000.

### CORROTHERS, GARRY JAMES

Lawyer. **Personal:** Born May 4, 1956, Warren, MI; son of Charles and Billie; married Donna; children: Garry Jr. **Educ:** Univ Cent Ark, BMusEd, 1979, MmusEd, 1981; Univ Ark Little Rock, William H Bowen Sch Law, JD, 1988. **Career:** State Ark, admin hearing officer, 1998-90; Cross, Kearney & McKissic, atty, 1990-91; Corrothers Law Off, atty, 1991-; sole practr, currently. **Orgs:** Ark Bar Asn, 1989-; W Harold Flowers Law Soc, 1989-; Ark Asn Criminal Defense Lawyers. **Home Addr:** 9801 Grapevine Dr, Little Rock, AR 72210-5636, **Home Phone:** (501)455-5306. **Business Addr:** Attorney, Corrothers Law Office, 221 W 2nd St Suite 617, Little Rock, AR 72201, **Business Phone:** (501)376-0812.

### CORTADA, DR. RAFAEL LEON

School administrator. **Personal:** Born Feb 12, 1934, New York, NY; son of Rafael and Yvonne; married Sloanie Head; children: Celia, Natalia & Rafael. **Educ:** Fordham Col, BA, philos, 1955, PhD, 1967; Columbia Univ, MA, sec educ, 1958; Fordham Univ, Latin Am & mod Europ hist, 1967; Harvard Grad Sch Bus, cert, 1974. **Career:** New Rochelle High Sch, New York, teacher, hist, 1957-64; Univ Dayton, Ohio, asst prof, 1964-66; State Dept, foreign serv off, 1966-69; Fed City Col, Wash DC, Smith Col, Mass; Howard Univ; Medgar Evers Col; Hostos Community Col, New York; Metrop Community Col, Minneapolis, Minn, pres, 1974-77; Black Studies, auth, 1974; Community Col, Baltimore, pres, 1977-82; El Camino Col, Torrance, Calif, pres, 1982-87; Univ DC, pres, 1987-90; Wayne County Community Col, Detroit, Mich, 1987-90; Cent Ohio Tech Col, Newark, OH, pres, 1994-99; Ohio State Univ, Newark, hist, dean & dir, 1999-2001, assoc proff emer, 2001-. **Orgs:** Vpres, Wash Task Force On African Affrs, 1969; Overseas Liaison Comt, 1970; bd gov, Univ Guyana, 1971-; Nat Adv Comm Danforth Found; E Harlem Exp Col, 1971-75; consult, Media Sys Corp, 1976; adv, KTCA TV Minneapolis, 1976; visitor, Mid States Asn; ed bd "Current Biblio on African Affrs" 1973; Am Coun Educ Comm Minorities Higher Educ, 1982-. **Honors/Awds:** Pub 88 articles & reviews In Caribbean, Afro-Amer, Latin Amer; History publ "Black Studies, An Urban & Comparative Curriculum", 1974. **Home Addr:** 2912 Constellation Way, Finksburg, MD 21048, **Home Phone:** (410)857-7696. **Business Addr:** Associate Professor Emeritus, Department of Educational Studies, Ohio State University, 121 Ramseyer Hall Bldg 090 29 W Woodruff Ave, Columbus, OH 43210, **Business Phone:** (614)292-5181.

### CORTOR, ELDZIER

Artist, printmaker, teacher. **Personal:** Born Jan 10, 1916, Tidewater, VA; son of John and Ophelia Twisdale; married Sophia Schmidt; children: Michael, Mercedes, Stephen & Miriam. **Educ:** Art Inst Chicago, attended 1936; Inst Design, Columbia Univ. **Career:** Works Progress Admin, Fed Arts Proj, S Side Community Art Ctr, co-founder, 1941; Rosenwald Fel, 1944-45; Guggenheim Fel, 1949; Ctr D'Art, Port-au-Prince, Haiti, teacher, 1949-51; Kenkeleba Gallery, exhibitor, 1988; Fed Art Proj; Southern Gate, exhibitor, 2002; Studio Mus Harlem, Mus Nat Ctr Afro-Am Artist, currently. **Orgs:** Soc Am Graphic Artists; Asn Am Artists; Founding mem, S side Community Art ctr, Chicago; Asn Am Artists. **Honors/Awds:** Carnegie Award; Bertha Aberle Florsheim Award; William H Bartels Award; Am Negro Expos Award. **Special Achievements:** One of the first African-American artists to make African-American women his major theme. **Business Addr:** Artist, The Studio Museum, 144 W 125th St, New York, NY 10027, **Business Phone:** (212)864-4500.

### CORYATT, QUENTIN JOHN

Football coach, football player. **Personal:** Born Aug 1, 1970, St. Croix, VI. **Educ:** Tex A&M Univ. **Career:** Football player (retired), football coach; Indianapolis Colts, left inside linebacker, 1992, mid linebacker, 1993, right linebacker, 1994-97; Dallas Cowboys, line back, 1999; Football Univ, linebackers coach, currently. **Honors/Awds:** Rookie of the Year, 1992; Hall of Fame, Tex A&M Univ, 2009. **Business Addr:** Linebackers Coach, Football University, 175 N Main St, Wharton, NJ 07885, **Business Phone:** (973)366-5027.

### COSBY, CAMILLE OLIVIA HANKS (CAMILLE HANKS)

Philanthropist, actor, television producer. **Personal:** Born Mar 20, 1944, Washington, DC; daughter of Guy A Sr and Catherine C; married William Henry; children: Erika, Erinn, Ennis (deceased), Ensa & Evin. **Educ:** Univ Mass, Amherst, MA, 1980, EdD, educ, 1992; Univ Md, psychol. **Career:** Speaker, educator; Plays: "Bill Cosby: Mr Sapolsky, with Love", co-exec producer, 1996; Ennis Gift, exec producer, 2000; Fat Albert, exec producer, 2004; TV series: "The Cosby Show", actress, 1986; "No Dreams Deferred", exec producer, 1994; "Having Our Say: The Delany Sisters First 100 Years", actress & producer, 1999; "Sylvia's Path", exec producer, 2002; "Obkb", exec producer, 2010-12; "Extra", 2014; "CNN Newsroom", 2014; "OMG Insider", 2014. **Orgs:** Commencement speaker, Howard Univ, 1987; commencement speaker, Spelman Col, 1989; hon mem, Delta Sigma Theta Sorority. **Honors/Awds:** Hon degree, Spellmen Col, 1989; Candace Award, Nat Coalition 100 Black Women, 1992; Tony Award Nomination, Having Our Say: The Delany Sisters' First 100 Years. **Special Achievements:** Camille Olivia Hanks Cosby Academy Center Constructed in Honor; appeared on PBS-TV's MacNeil-Lehrer News Hour. **Business Addr:** Philanthropist, c/o The Cosby Show, 34 12 36th St, Astoria, NY 11106.

### COSBY, MARCUS D.

Religious leader. **Personal:** son of Rogers and Bobbie J; married Audrey Marie; children: Adrienne Marie, Ashley Marie, Aliyah Marie, Marcus D II & Matthew D. **Educ:** Fisk Univ, Nashville, Tenn, BA, relig & Eng; Morehouse Sch Relig at Interdenominational Theol Ctr, Atlanta, GA, MDiv, homiletics & Christian educ. **Career:** Wheeler Ave Baptist Church (Houston, TX), assoc pastor, 1998-2004, sr pastor, 2004-; Houston Grad Sch Homiletics, adj prof. **Orgs:** Bd mem, Samuel Dewitt Proctor Conf; bd mem, Home Mission Bd Nat Baptist Conv; bd mem, USA Inc; bd mem, Fisk Univ Bd Trustees & Gen Alumni Asn Fisk Univ Inc; bd dirs mem, African Am Pulpit; bd dirs mem, Houston Area Urban League; bd dirs mem, Interfaith Ministries Greater Houston; bd dirs mem, Tex Comn Community Serv & Volunteerism; adv bd mem, Gardner C Taylor Preaching Arch & Listening Room (Atlanta, GA); Alpha Phi Alpha Fraternity Inc; Sigma Pi Phi Fraternity; life mem, NAACP. **Honors/Awds:** Recognized as: "Outstanding Young Men of America" and "Isaac R. Clark Preaching Award"; "African American Pulpit", Twenty to Watch List, 2001; Martin Luther King Jr. Board of Preachers at Morehouse College (Atlanta, GA), inductee.

### COSBY, DR. WILLIAM HENRY

Entertainer, comedian, actor. **Personal:** Born Jul 12, 1937, Germantown, PA; son of William Henry Sr and Anna Pearl C; married Camille O; children: Erika, Erinn, Ennis (deceased), Ensa & Evin. **Educ:** Temple Univ, BA, 1971; Univ MA, MA, 1973, EdD, 1976, PhD, 1977. **Career:** Comedian, appearing in numerous night clubs; guest appearances on TV shows: "I Spy", 1965-68; "The Electric Co", 1972; "Capt Kangaroo"; "The Bill Cosby Show", 1969, 1972-73; recs: Revenge, To Russell, My Brother, With Whom I Slept, Top Secret, 200 MPH, Why Is There Air?, Wonderfulness, It's True, Bill Cosby Is a Very Funny Fel, Right, 1963, I Started Out as a Child, 1964 & numerous others; has appeared on several TV commercials. Films: Hickey & Boggs, Man & Boy, 1972; Uptown Saturday Night, 1974; Let's Do It Again, 1975; Mother Jugs & Speed, 1976; Aesop's Fables, A Piece of the Action, 1977; Calif Suite, 1978; Devil & Max Devlin, 1979; Leonard Part VI, 1987; Ghost Dad, 1990; star & producer, The Cosby Show, 1984-92; You Bet Your Life, 1992; The Cosby Mysteries, 1995; Jack, 1996; Kids Say The Darnedest Things, 1997; NJ Nets, part-owner; Fat Albert, 2004; 500 Years Later, 2005; The Pact, 2006; A Table in Heaven, 2007; Bill Cosby 77, 2014. TV Movies: "The Oprah

Winfrey Show", 1989-2008; "Late Show with David Letterman", 1995-2008; "Touched by an Angel:, 1997; "Little Bill", 1999; "Becker", 1999; "Larry King Live", 2003-07; "Hey Hey Hey: Behind the Scenes of Fat Albert", 2004; "An Evening of Stars: Tribute to Quincy Jones", 2004; "The Tonight Show with Jay Leno", 2004-07; "Cosby 90", 1996-2000; "Dr. Phil", 2005; "The Harlem Globe trotters: The Team That Changed the World", 2005; "ABC News Nightline", 2005; "The Electric Company's Greatest Hits & Bits", 2006; "Buffy Sainte-Marie: A Multimedia Life", 2006; "Good Morning America", 2007; "Obkb", 2010-11; "Stand Up Planet Comedy Showcase", 2014. Music Albums: Disco Bill, 1977; Where You Lay Your Head, 1990; "The New Mixes Vol. 1", 2004; State of Emergency, 2009. Comedy Albums: I Started Out as a Child, 1964; Revenge, 1967; To Russell, My Brother, Whom I Slept With, 1968; 8:15 12:15, 1969; Fat Albert, 1973; My Father Confused Me... What Must I Do? What Must I Do?, 1977; Bill's Best Friend, 1978; Those of You With or Without Children, You'll Understand, 1986; OH Baby, 1991. **Orgs:** Pres, Rhythm & Blues Hall Fame, 1968-; bd dirs & nat chmn, Sickle Cell Found; United Negro Col Fund; life mem, Nat Asn Advan Colored People; Oper PUSH; Omega Psi Phi Fraternity. **Honors/Awds:** Grammy Awards, 1965-72, 1987; Golden Apple Awards, 1966, 1985; Man of the Year, Harvard Univ, 1969; Daytime Emmy Awards, 1981, 2002, 2004; Afton bladet TV Prize, 1986-90; BMI Film & TV Awards, 1987-98; Kennedy Center Honors, 1998; Vision Awards, TV's Man of the Year, 1999; Presidential Medal of Freedom, 2002; Emmy, Bob Hope Humanitarian Award, 2003; Ford Freedom Award, 2004; Mark Twain Award, Am Humor, 2009; Lone Sailor Award, Usn Memorial, 2010; Hollywood Walk of Fame; Four Emmy Awards; NAACP Image Award. **Special Achievements:** Author of "The Wit & the Wisdom of Fat Albert", 1973; "Fatherhood", 1986; "Time Flies", 1987; "Love & Marriage", 1989; "Childhood", 1991; Acad of TV, Arts & Scis, Hall of Fame, 1992; "Little Bill Books for Beginning Readers", 1997; "Kids Say the Darndest Things", 1998; "Congratulations! Now What?: A Book for Graduates", 1999; "American Schools: The $100 Billion Challenge. New York", 2000; "Cosbyology: Essays and Observations from the Doctor of Comedy", 2001; "Friends of a Feather: One of Life's Little Fables", 2003; "I Am What I Ate And I'm Frightened", 2003; "Bill Cosby's Personal Guide to Power Tennis; Come on, People: On the Path from Victims to Victors", 2007; "I Didn't Ask to Be Born (But I'm Glad I Was)", 2011. **Business Addr:** Comedian, Richard De La Font Agency Inc, 4845 S Sheridan Rd, Tulsa, OK 74145, **Business Phone:** (918)665-6200.

## COSE, ELLIS

Writer, journalist, columnist. **Personal:** Born Feb 20, 1951, Chicago, IL; married Lee Llambelis; children: Elisa Maria. **Educ:** Univ Ill, Chicago, BA, psychol, 1972; George Washington Univ, MA, sci, technol & pub policy, 1978. **Career:** Chicago Sun-Times, columnist & reporter & ed, 1970-77; Joint Ctr Polit Studies, sr fel & dir energy policy studies, 1977-79; Detroit Free Press, ed, writer & columnist, 1979-81; Nat Acad Sci, res fel, 1981-82; USA Today, spec writer, 1982-83; Inst Journalism Educ, pres, 1983-86; Columbia Univ, Ctr Media Studies, 1987; Gannett Time Mag, contrib ed, essayist, 1989-90; New York Daily News, edit bd chmn, 1991-93; Newsweek Mag, author, contrib ed & columnist, 1993-; Books: The End of Anger: A New Generation's Take On Race and Rage; Disintegration: The Splintering of Black America; Energy & Equity, Some Social Concerns, 1978; Energy & the Urban Crises, 1978; The Rebirth of Community Power, 1983; The Press, 1988; A Nation of Strangers, 1992; Decentralizing Energy Decisions: The Rage of a Privileged Class, 1993; The Rage of a Privileged Class, 1994; A Man's World, 1995; Color-Blind: Seeing Beyond Race in a Race-Obsessed World, 1997; The Best Defense, 1999; The Envy of the World, 2002; Bone to Pick: On Forgiveness, Reconciliation, Reparation & Revenge, 2004; Beyond Brown v. Board: The Final Battle for Excellence in American Education, 2004. **Orgs:** Nat Asn Black Journalists; Env Adv Comn, Dept Energy, 1978-79; Nat Urban League Energy Proj, 1979-80; fel Gannett Ctr for Media Studies at Columbia Univ; fel The Ford Found; fel Andrew Mellon Found; fel Rockerfeller Found Grant; fel Aspen Inst Humanistic Studies. **Honors/Awds:** Named Outstanding Young Citizen of Chicago Jaycees, 1977; News Writing Award, United Press Int, 1973; Stick-o-Type Award, Chicago Newspaper, Guild, 1975; Best Polit Reporting, Lincoln Univ Nat Unity Award, 1975, 1977; Myers Center Award, Human Rights N Am; numerous others; Vision Award, Maynard Inst Jour Educ. **Special Achievements:** First place 2003 awards for commentary and magazine features. **Business Addr:** Contributing Editor, Essayist, Newsweek Mag, 251 W 57th St, New York, NY 10019, **Business Phone:** (212)445-4000.

## COSHBURN, HENRY S., JR.

Executive. **Personal:** Born Mar 15, 1936, New York, NY; son of Henry (deceased) and Dorothy; married Veanna G Ferguson; children: Williams S. **Educ:** Univ Pa, BS, 1957; Columbia Univ, MS, 1964. **Career:** AUS Signal Corps, chem engr, 1958-60; Yardney Elec Corp, sls engr, 1960-63; Mobil Oil, sr engr, 1964-68; Esso Eastern, mkt analyst, 1968-71; Exxon Intl Co, acct exec, 1973-82; First Nat Crude Oil, vpres; Southern Univ Bethune Cookman Col, vis prof mkt; Wilberforce Univ, vis prof mkt; Miles Col, vis prof; Norfolk St Col, vis prof mkt. **Orgs:** Alpha Phi Alpha; Alpha Chi Sigma; Am Inst Engrs; Am Electrochem Soc; Am Chem Soc; Am Soc Lub Engrs; Princeton Club; NY Admis Rep Univ PA; instr, ICBO Mkt mem Harlem Hosp Bd; pres, Harlem Civ Imp Coun; vpres, Penn & Princeton Club NYC; bd dir, Univ PA Alumni Asn. **Home Addr:** 2600 Netherland Ave, Bronx, NY 10463.

## COSTA, ANNIE BELL HARRIS

Journalist. **Personal:** Born Oct 24, 1943, New Madrid, MO; married Ernest Antone; children: Kara Ann & Todd Bernard. **Educ:** Mich State Univ, BA, jour, 1978; Univ Calif, Berkeley & Inst Jour Educ Minority Reporting Prog, 1985, MA, Christian Educ, Union Theol Sem & Presby Sch Christian Educ, Richmond, Va, 2003. **Career:** Mich Dept Corrections, pub info specialist, 1978-80; Mich Employ Security Comn, ed, 1980-85, 1987-91; Lansing State J, staff writer & reporter, 1985-87; Mich Off Community Corrections, pub info officer, 1991; pub rels consult & freelance writer. **Orgs:** Inst Jour Educ Alumni Asn; Detroit Black Writers Guild. **Honors/Awds:** Award of Merit for Spec Publ, Torch Dr United Fund, 1981; Selected for the Univ Calif, Jour Educ Minority Reporting Prog, Berkeley, 1985; hon mention Ninth Annual Paul Lawrence Dunbar Poetry Contest, Detroit Black Writers Guild, 1995; hon mention Thumb Area Writers Conf, Winter Writing Contest, 1995; hon mention External Newslettter, Intl Assn of Bus Communicators, Detroit Chap, 1990; Mich Woman Courage Certificateof Recognition, Women of Color Health Conf, 1997. **Special Achievements:** Torch Dr United Fund, Award of Merit Spec Publ, 1981; Univ Calif, Berkeley, Summer Prog Minority Journalists, 1985; Intl Assn of Bus Communicators, Detroit chap, External Newsletter, Hon Mention, 1990. **Home Addr:** 3438 Capland Ave, Clermont, FL 34711, **Home Phone:** (352)241-9255.

## COSTEN, DR. MELVA WILSON

Theologian. **Personal:** Born May 29, 1933, Due West, SC; daughter of John Theodore Wilson Sr and Azzie Lee Ellis Wilson; married James Hutten; children: James Jr, Craig Lamont & Cheryl Clay. **Educ:** Harbison Jr Col, Irmo SC, 1950; Johnson C Smith Univ, Charlotte, NC, BA, educ 1952; Univ NC, Chapel Hill, NC, MA, music, 1964; Ga State Univ, Atlanta, GA, PhD, curric & instr music, 1978; Univ NC, MATM. **Career:** Professor (retired): Mecklenburg County Sch, Charlotte NC, elem teacher, 1952-55; Edgecombe Co, Rocky Mt, Nashville, NC, elem teacher, 1956-57; Nash Co, Nashville, NC, elem & music teacher, 1959-65; Atlanta Pub Schs, Atlanta, Ga, itinerant music teacher, 1965-73; Interdenominational Theol Ctr, Dept Music, Atlanta Ga, Helmar Emil Nielsen prof worship & music, 2005; Yale Divinity Sch, Inst Sacred Music, vis prof liturgical studies, currently. **Orgs:** Regional dir, Nat Asn Negro Musicians, 1973-75; co-chair, Choral Div, Dist V Ga Music Educr Asn, 1981-82; bd mem, Presby Asn Musicians, 1982-86; chairperson & elder, Presbyn Church Hymnal Comt, 1984-90; bd mem, Liturgical Conf, 1985-91; bd mem, Mid-Atlanta Unit, Cancer Soc Am, 1985-87; chairperson, Presby Hymnal Comt, 1985-90; artistic dir, Atlanta Olympics, 1996-99; Atlanta Univ Ctr Choruses, 1996; Adv Comt, African Am Heritage Hymnal; African Am Worship Traditions, dir prog; Johnson C Smith Interdenominational Theol Ctr, Atlanta, Ga, chair. **Honors/Awds:** Teacher of the Year, Slater Sch, Atlanta, Ga, 1973; Teacher of the Year, InterdenomiNat Theological Ctr, 1975; Golden Dove Award, Kappa Omega Chap, Alpha Kappa Alpha Sorority, 1981; Conducted 800-voice adult choir, Reuniting Assembly of Presbyterian Church, 1983; Two Doctor of Humane Letters, Erskine Col, Due West SC, 1987; Two Doctor of Humane Letters, Wilson Col, Chambersburg, Pa. **Special Achievements:** Published book African-American Christian Worship, Nashville, Abingdon press, 1993. **Home Addr:** 225 E Ct Dr SW, Atlanta, GA 30331, **Home Phone:** (404)696-5900. **Business Addr:** Visiting Professor of Liturgical Studies, Yale Institute of Sacred Music, 409 Prospect St, New Haven, CT 06511, **Business Phone:** (203)432-5180.

## COTHORN, JOHN A.

Lawyer. **Personal:** Born Dec 12, 1939, Des Moines, IA; son of John L and Marguerite E; married Connie C; children: Jeffrey A & Judith A. **Educ:** Univ Mich, BS, maths, BS, aeronaut engineering, 1961, JD, 1980. **Career:** US Govt, exec officer, 1966-88; Washtenaw County, MI Prosecutor's Off, asst prosecutor, 1981-83; Kitch, Drutchas, Wagner & Kenney, PC, partner, 1983-93; Meganck & Cothorn, PC, partner, 1994-96; Meganck, Cothorn & Stanczyk PC, managing partner, 1996-98; Cothorn & Stanczyk PC, managing partner, 1998-; Cothorn & Assocs PC, managing partner, 2000-. **Orgs:** Phi Alpha Delta Law Fraternity, 1982; Nat Asn Advan Colored People; Am Bar Asn; Nat Bar Asn; State Bar MI; Detroit Bar Asn; Soc Automotive Engrs; Kappa Alpha Psi Fraternity; contribr, Inst Continuing Legal Educ; Mich State Bar; Fed Bar Asn; State Bar Mich. **Home Addr:** 48211 Bayshore Dr, Belleville, MI 48111-4603, **Home Phone:** (734)697-1323. **Business Addr:** Managing Partner, Cothorn & Associates PC, 535 Griswold St Suite 530, Detroit, MI 48226-3602, **Business Phone:** (313)964-7600.

## COTMAN, DR. HENRY EARL

Physician. **Personal:** Born Apr 13, 1943, Archer, FL; married Jacqueline Nickson. **Educ:** Fla A&M Univ, BS, 1965; Univ Fla; Harvard Peter Bent Brigham Hosp, externships; MD, 1970. **Career:** Union Memorial Hosp, med internship, 1970-71; Univ Minn, resident, 1971-74; Univ Ariz Health Div Sci Ctr Div Radiation Oncol, asst prof, 1975-77; Women Beaumont Army Hosp Med Ctr Div Radiation Oncol, chief, 1975; Mich St Univ, asso clin prof; Bayfront Med Ctr, radiation oncologist, 2004; Union Memorial Hosp, Vet Affairs Med Ctr, Fairview-Univ Med Ctr, resident; Gulf Coast Oncol Ctr, pvt prac, currently. **Orgs:** Am Col Radiol; Am Soc Therapeut Radiol; Nat Med Asn; Ingham Co Med Soc; Alpha Phi Alpha Frat Inc; fel Am Cancer Soc, 1971-74; cheif resident, Radiation Oncol, 1974; Oncol Comt; Res & Rev Comt. **Special Achievements:** First African-American to graduates College of Medicine Schools, 1970; The Usage The Bipedal Lymphogram As A Guide During Laparotomy in Hodgkin's & Non-Hodgkin's Lymphomas ACTA Radiol; Combination Radiotherapy & Surger in the Mgmt of Squamous Carcinoma of the Head & Neck" Radiology Soc meeting 1976. **Business Addr:** Physician, Gulf Coast Oncology Center, 701 6th St S, St. Petersburg, FL 33731, **Business Phone:** (727)893-6103.

## COTMAN, DR. IVAN LOUIS

State government official. **Personal:** Born Apr 4, 1940, Detroit, MI; son of Louis Richard and Marguerite Kaine; married Jeanetta Hawkins; children: Ivan Louis Jr, Arthur Robert & Amir Charles. **Educ:** Ky State Univ, BA, eng soc sci, 1962; Atlanta Univ, MA, social Work, 1964; Univ Mich, Sch Pub Health Med Care Orgn, 1970; Univ Manchester, cert, new town planning, 1972; Wayne State Univ, EdD, curric & admin, 1975; Univ Okla, advan studies, 1983; Harvard Univ JFK Sch Govt. **Career:** Detroit Bd Educ, sch social worker, 1964-69; United Co Serv Detroit, agcyprog consul assist budget dir, 1969-72; Detroit Bd Educ, electee, 1971-73; New Detroit Inc, dir employ, 1972-73; Mich Dept Ed Disability Deter Serv, area admin, 1973-79; Mich Dept Educ, assoc supt, 1979, intern, regtlobbyist, 1989-, direct servs, dep supt, 1992-97; Davenport Univ, dir, off enrichment & community serv, 1992-94; Cotman & Assocs, chief exec officer, 1997-, lead consult, currently; Wayne State Univ, Planned Giving Comt, mem, currently. **Orgs:** Bd, Mountain Retreat & Learning Ctr, 1999-2002; bd, Davenport Ed Found, 2000-; Acad Certif Social Workers; Nat Assoc Disability Exams; Nat Asn Social Workers; Nat Rehab Asn; Mich Civil Serv Oral Appraisal Bd; Mich Occup Info Statutory Comm; nat vpres, Alpha Phi Alpha Frat Inc, pres, 1976-78; bd mem, United Neighborhood Ctr Am; Nat Asn Advan Colored People; adj prof, Mich State Univ; State Credit Union Supvr Comt; bd Govs, Univ Chicago, Meadville, Lombard Theol Sch. **Honors/Awds:** Resolution of Tribute Mich Senate, 1973; Distinguished Alumni, Ky State Univ, 1975; Dist Citizen Mich House of Rep, 1977-80; Regional Commissioner's Citation Social Sec Administration, 1979; Order of Kentucky Colonels; Distinguished Alumni Award, Ky State Univ, Nat Asn Equal Oppor Higher Educ; Cited for Leadership, US Sec Educ; 6 week exec placement in Washington based Commn on Excellence, US Dept of Education; Articles on Leadership published in Mich Sch Bd Journal, Waterloo Press, Detroit News, Michigan Chronicle, Congressional Record; Board of Governors, Meadville Lombard Theology School; Resolution of Merit, Mich House, 1989; Israel Study Mission, 1994; Davenport University Education Foundation, 2000; US Taxpayers Advocacy Panel, 2002-. **Home Addr:** 20141 McIntyre, Detroit, MI 48219. **Business Addr:** Chief Executive Officer, Lead Consultant, Cotman & Associates, 4605 Cass Ave, Detroit, MI 48201, **Business Phone:** (313)833-1181.

## COTTLE, CHRISTOPHER

Educator. **Educ:** Kean Col NJ, BA, elem educ, 1979, MA, prog guid & coun, 1981; Montclair State Univ, MA, family & child studies, 2011. **Career:** Essex Co Col, Clara E Dasher Ctr, asst dean stud life & activ, 1986-2004; Montclair State Univ, dept advisor, family & child studies, currently. **Business Addr:** Department Advisor, Family and Child Studies, Montclair State University, Univ Hall 4147 1 Norm Ave, Montclair, NJ 07043, **Business Phone:** (973)655-3387.

## COTTON, GARNER

Civil engineer. **Personal:** Born Nov 10, 1923, Chicago, IL; son of Deleon (deceased) and Pearl Little; children: Garner T & Atry S. **Educ:** Lincoln Univ, BS, bldg engineering, 1943; Drexel Univ, civil engineering, 1951; Edison Tech Sch, basic electronics, 1960; Temple Univ, naval archit & metall, 1961. **Career:** Gen Indust Eng, struct designer, checker, 1947-54; City Philadelphia, Water Dept, struct designer, checker, 1954-56; United Eng & Construct Co, 1956-58; Frederick Massiah Concrete Contractor, asst construct supt, 1958-59; Boeing Aircraft Co, facil, struct engr, 1959-60; United Engrs & Construct Co, 1960-62; NY Shipbuilding Corp, Sci Group, struct engr, 1962-65; Allstate Engr & Develop Co, struct engr, 1965-67; Sch Dist Philadelphia, staff construct engr, struct designer, 1967-88; State NJ, regist prof engr, regist prof planner; Prof Engineering Socs S Jersey, pres; G Cotton Eng Assocs Inc, founder, coun pres, partner, 1976-. **Orgs:** Pres, Lawnside (Nj) Munic Govt Bor Coun, 1961-75; pres, Prof Engineering Soc Southern Nj, 1983-84; fel Am Soc Civil Engrs; Nat Soc Prof Engrs; Asn Sch Adminrs; Am Arbit Asn; Lincoln Univ Found. **Honors/Awds:** Citizen Award, Lawnside Democratic Club, 1970; Citizen Award of the Year, NJ Soc Prof Engrs, 1977; Registered Prof Civil Engr NJ; Registered Prof Planner NJ; Prof Civil Engr; DHL, Lincoln Univ, 1997; Distinguished Engr, Am Soc Civil Engrs, 2000; Specialty Award, Drexel Univ Evening Col Alumni Asn, 2000; Drexels Alumni Service Community Award. **Home Addr:** 505 N Warwick Rd, Lawnside, NJ 08045, **Home Phone:** (856)546-8363. **Business Addr:** Owner, Partner, G Cotton Eng Assocs Inc, 505 N Warwick Rd, Lawnside, NJ 08045, **Business Phone:** (856)546-8363.

## COTTON, JAMES WESLEY

Basketball player. **Personal:** Born Dec 14, 1975, Los Angeles, CA. **Educ:** Calif State Univ, Long Beach, CA. **Career:** Basketball player (retired); Long Beach State, shooting guard, 1993-97; Denver Nuggets, 1997; Seattle SuperSonics, guard, 1997-99; Chicago Bulls, 1999; W Sydney Razorbacks, Australian Nat Basketball League.

## COTTON, JOSEPH CRAIG

Executive, administrator. **Personal:** Born Nov 3, 1954, Greensboro, NC; son of Harold C and Mary B; married Cynthia. **Educ:** NC A&T State Univ, BA, eng-mass commun, 1979; Temple Univ, MEd, sport mgt, 1993. **Career:** Univ Md Eastern Shore, sports info dir, 1981-88; Temple Univ, assoc sports infodir, 1988-92; Del State Univ, sports info dir mkt, 1992-97, pub rels dir, 1999; Olympic Festival, St Louis, Mo, press officer, 1993; Pan Am Games, US media rep, 1994; Summer Olympics, press opers mgr, 1996; Howard Univ, mkt mgr, 2000-01; Assoc Athletic Dir & Exec Dir NSU Athletics Found, assoc athletics dir external affairs, 2001-, Athletics Found, asst to exec dir, exec dir, currently. **Orgs:** Col Sports Info dir Asn, 1981-; Kappa Alpha Psi Fraternity, 1985-; Nat Asn Black Journalist; Pub Rels Soc Am, 1998-. **Home Addr:** 804 Woodcrest Dr, Dover, DE 19904, **Home Phone:** (302)677-0218. **Business Addr:** Associate Athletics Director, Executive Director of Athletics Foundation, Norfolk State University, 331 Harrison B Wilson Hall 700 Pk Ave, Norfolk, VA 23504, **Business Phone:** (757)823-2667.

## COTTON, THOMASENIA GREEN

Executive. **Educ:** NC Cent Univ, BA, sociol, 1963; Univ Utah, MS, human resource mgt; Temple Univ, PhD, urban educ. **Career:** Opportunities Industrialization Centers Am Inc, chief staff officer, proj officer, supvr, chief protocol & mgr, field specialist, dir off field serv coordn, pres & chief operating off, chief exec officer, 2003; IBM Community Exec Prog, Tarrytown, NY; Philadelphia Employ Develop Corp, supvr; Career & Acad Develop Inst, pres, chief operating officer; Cemci, chief exec officer. **Orgs:** Prog dir, YWCA, SW Belmont; Am mgt asn; bd mem, Women's Empowerment Initiative; bd dir, AmeriDream Inc. **Business Addr:** President, Chief Operating Officer, Opportunities Industrialization Centers of America Inc, Leon H Sullivan Human Serv Ctr, Philadelphia, PA 19122-3323, **Business Phone:** (215)236-4500.

## COTTROL, ROBERT JAMES

Educator. **Personal:** Born Jan 18, 1949, New York, NY; son of Robert W and Jewel Gassaway; married Susan Lemmerbrock; children: John Marshall II. **Educ:** Yale Univ, BA, 1971, AM, hist, 1973, PhD, Am studies, 1978; Georgetown Univ Law Ctr, JD, 1984. **Career:** Yale Univ, Sociol Dept, teaching fel, 1973, Hist Dept, teaching fel, 1974; Conn Col, vis instr, 1974-77; Emory Univ, asst prof, 1977-79; Georgetown Univ, asst dean, 1979-82, lectr, 1979-84; Boston Col Law Sch, from asst prof to assoc prof law, 1984-95; Univ Va Sch Law, vis assoc prof, 1988-89; Rutgers Sch Law, Camden, NJ, from assoc prof to prof, 1990-96; George Wash Univ Law Sch, vis prof law & legal hist, 1995-96, prof law, hist & Sociol, 1995-, Harold Paul Green res, prof law, currently. Books: The Afro-Yankees: Providence's Black Community in the Antebellum Era, 1982; Gun Control and the Constitution: Sources and Explorations on the Second Amendment, 1993; Yankee: Narratives of Slavery and Freedom in Antebellum New England, 1998; The Long, Lingering Shadow: Slavery, Race and Law in the American Hemisphere, 2013. **Orgs:** Am Hist Assn, 1974-; Consult, Ga Commn Humanities, 1978-79; Am Soc Legal Hist, 1982-; Am Bar Assn, 1985-; Law & Socs Asn, 1985-. **Home Addr:** 3424 Sharon Chapel Rd, Alexandria, VA 22310-2311, **Home Phone:** (703)329-2973. **Business Addr:** Professor of Law, The George Washington University Law School, 2000 H St NW, Washington, DC 20052, **Business Phone:** (202)994-5023.

## COULON, BURNEL ELTON, II
Educator, manager. **Personal:** Born Jul 6, 1929, New Orleans, LA; married Sylvia; children: Michele, Angela, Burnel II & Sylvia II. **Educ:** Tuskegee Inst, BS, 1953; NC Agr & Tech State Univ, MS, 1960. **Career:** Educator, dean (retired), director; MS Valley State Univ, dir pub rels, 1953-60; Louisville Pub Schs, instr graphic arts, 1961-64; Shortridge Press & Indianapolis Pub Schs, instr & mgr, 1964-76; Paramount Graphics, pres, 1970, chmn indust arts, 1976-79; Indianapolis Pub Schs, dean stud; Ind Univ-Purdue Univ Indianapolis, Div Stud Affairs, asst dir, currently. **Orgs:** Vpres, Iota Omicron; bd dir, MS State Negro Fair, 1957-59; secy, Marion Co Graphic Arts Asn, 1968-70; pres, Indianapolis Fedn Teachers, 1973-76; secy, Indianapolis Chap Phi Delta Kappa, 1978-79; pres grand basileus, Omega Psi Phi Fraternity, 1978-79, 1979-82, co-chair; Grand Marshal, Omega's Nat Conv, 2000; bd dir, Omega Life Mem Found, 2001-04. **Honors/Awds:** Outstanding Graduate Alumnus, NC A&T, 1975; Omega Man of the Year, 10th Dist Omega Psi Phi Fraternity, 1976; Certificate of Merit, Mayor New Orleans, 1980. **Home Addr:** 3173 W 48th St, Indianapolis, IN 46208-2101, **Home Phone:** (317)293-9919. **Business Addr:** Assistant Director, Indiana University-Purdue University Indianapolis, 420 Univ Blvd Suite 217, Indianapolis, IN 46202, **Business Phone:** (317)278-8511.

## COULTER, PHYLLIS A.
Association executive. **Personal:** Born May 5, 1962, Newark, NJ; daughter of Arthur and Maxine; married Craig. **Educ:** Purdue Univ, Krannert Sch Mgt, BS, acct, 1984; Univ Minn, Carlson Sch Mgt, MBA, mgt, 1990; Travel Inst, cert, travel assoc. **Career:** Pillsbury Co, supvr, 1984-86; Am Express Financial Advisors, mgr, 1986-93; St Davids Sch, controller, 1993-96; Metro Detroit Conv & Visitors Bur, finance & admin, vpres, 1996-99; Deloitte Consult, dir admin, 1999-2000; Destinations Unlimited Travel, owner & travel consult, 2000-05; Liberty Travel, travel consult, 2005-06, team leader, mgr, 2008-11, area acct, 2011-13; AXA Assistance USA, mgr travel & concierge, 2006-08; Corp Traveler USA, travel mgr, 2013; BCD Travel, sr corp travel consult, 2013-15; Jacobson Group, admin & travel serv mgr, 2015-. **Orgs:** Alpha Kappa Alpha Sorority; Black MBA Asn; consult, Jr Achievement; Int Asn Conv & Visitor Bureaus. **Home Addr:** 611 Highlands Dr, Canton, MI 48188, **Home Phone:** (734)981-8141. **Business Addr:** Accountant, Liberty Travel, 5 Woodfield Mall, Schaumburg, IL 60173-5012, **Business Phone:** (847)517-9235.

## COUNCIL, LAVERNE H.
Vice president (organization), executive, chief executive officer. **Educ:** Western Ill Univ, BS, bus, 1983; Ill State Univ, MBA, opers mgt, 1986; Drexel Univ, DBA, bus admin, 2010. **Career:** CAPGEMINI, partner; Dell Inc, Global Bus Solutions & Develop Serv, global vpres info technol, 2000-06; Johnson & Johnson, corp vpres, chief info officer, 2006-11; Coun Adv Serv LLC, chief exec officer, 2012-15; Info & Technol, Dept Veterans Affairs, asst secy, 2015-. **Orgs:** Bd trustee & chmn, March Dimes, 2010-; chair bd, Liberty Sci Ctr; Res Bd; CIO Exec Bd; Exec Leadership Coun; Workforce Outsource Serv; Corp Global Operating Comt. **Home Addr:** 330 Lafayette St, Rahway, NJ 07065-5106, **Home Phone:** (732)388-9881. **Business Addr:** Corporate Vice President, Chief Information Officer, Johnson & Johnson Services Inc, 1 Johnson & Johnson Plz, New Brunswick, NJ 08933, **Business Phone:** (732)524-0400.

## COUNTS, ALLEN W.
Executive, chairperson. **Educ:** Howard Univ, BS, JD; Univ Pa, Wharton Sch, MBA. **Career:** Lic atty; Citibank World Corp, head shipping group, 1973-80, vpres; Pryor, McClendon, Counts & Co, co-founder & pres; Citibank NA, vpres; Doley Securities, chmn, 2005-. **Orgs:** Gen Securities Prin, Financial & Oper Prin, Regist Rep, NASD. **Business Addr:** Chairman, Doley Securities Inc, 616 Baronne St 3rd Fl, New Orleans, LA 70113, **Business Phone:** (504)561-1128.

## COUNTS, DR. GEORGE W.
Physician, educator. **Personal:** Born Jun 14, 1935, Idabel, OK; children: George IV, David & Philip. **Educ:** Univ Okla, BS, 1957, MS, 1960; Ohio State Univ, MD, 1965. **Career:** Educator (retired), physician; Leopold Schepp Found Scholar, 1961-65; Ohio State Univ Hosp, internal residence, 1965-68; Univ Wash, fel, Infectious Dis, 1968-70, from assoc prof to prof, 1975-89; Univ Miami, asst prof med, 1970-75, Sch Med, asst prof pathol, 1972-75; Jackson Mem Hosp, dir clin microbiol secy, 1972-75, dir infection control dept, 1972-75; Harbor view Med Ctr, chief div infectious dis, 1975-84; CRMB, Div AIDS, chief, 1989-94; NIH, assoc dir Clin Res Activ, Div Microbiol & Infectious Disease, dir, Off Res Minority & Women's Health, Nat Inst Allergy & Infectious Dis, 1994-2004. **Orgs:** Fel Nat Med, 1961-65; Soc Hosp Epidemiol Am; Am Fed Clin Res; fel Am Col Physicians, 1971; fel Infectious Dis Soc Am, 1974; bd dir, Asn Practitioners Infection Control, 1977-85; fel Am Acad Microbiol, 1997; bd mem, Pub Health Seattle & King County, currently; Fred Hutchinson Cancer Res Ctr. **Honors/Awds:** Leinfelder Award, Univ Iowa, 1965; Alpha Omega Alpha, 1965; diplomate Am Bd Internal Med, 1970; Service Award, 1992; Career Achievement Award; Distinguished Service Award, Am Soc Microbiol, 2006. **Special Achievements:** Co-authored an article on "Provision of treatment in HIV-1 vaccine trials in developing countries", 2003; Co-authored ten other articles. **Home Addr:** 2627 Warren Ave Suite 200, Seattle, WA 98109, **Home Phone:** (301)469-6761. **Business Addr:** Board Member, Public Health Seattle & King County, 401 5th Ave Suite 1300, Seattle, WA 98104, **Business Phone:** (206)296-4600.

## COUSIN, ERTHARIN
Executive, vice president (organization). **Personal:** Born May 12, 1957, Chicago, IL; daughter of Julius and Anne; children: Maurice. **Educ:** Univ Ill, Chicago, BA, 1979; Univ Ga, JD, 1982. **Career:** AT&T, dir; Chicago Ethics Bd; Ill atty Gen off, asst atty gen & western regional off dir, 1987-89; Dem Nat Comt, dep chief staff, 1993-97; US Dept State, white house liaison, admin, 1994; Clinton admin, 1994; Olympic Games, sr advisor, 1996; Clinton-Gore presidential campaign, 1996; Albertson's Inc, vpres, sr vpres pub affairs, pres, chair, spokesperson; Govt & Community Affairs Jewel Food stores, vice-pres; bd int Food & agr develop, 1997; Obama Am, sr advisor, 2007-08; Polk St Group, a nat pub affairs firm, pres, 2006-09; Us Mission to UN Agencies Rome, chief; Am Second Harvest, exec vpres & chief operating officer, currently; US Rep to Un Agencies Food & Agr, ambassador, 2009-12; World Food Programme, exec dir, 2012-. **Orgs:** Dep dir, Chicago Ethics Bd; exec vpres & chief operating officer, Am's Second Harvest, 2004. **Home Addr:** 1640 E 50th, Chicago, IL 60615, **Home Phone:** (773)955-8083. **Business Addr:** Senior Vice President, Chief Operating Officer, America's Second Harvest, 35 E Wacker Dr Suite 2000, Chicago, IL 60601, **Business Phone:** (312)263-2303.

## COUSIN, REV. PHILIP R.
Clergy. **Personal:** Born Mar 26, 1933, Pittston, PA; married Margaret Joan Grier; children: Philip Jr, Steven, David, Michael & Joseph. **Educ:** Cent State Univ, BA; Boston Univ, Mdiv; ThM; Colgate Rochester Divin Sch, PhD. **Career:** Pastored churches NC, VA & FL; Kittrell Col, pres, 1960-65; AME Church, bishop, AL; Edward Waters Col, pres; African Methodist Episcopal Church, bishop 11th episcopal dist, bishop, 4th episcopal dist, sr bishop, currently; Philip R Cousin African Methodist Episcopal Church, owner & pastor; Kittrel Col, pres. **Orgs:** Chmn bd, Edward Waters Col; nat bd, SCLC; trustee Lincoln Hosp, Durham, 1966-72; chmn, Polit Comm Durham Comm Affairs Black People, 1966-; chmn, Human Rels Comn, Durham, 1968-69; chmn, NC Voter Educ Proj, 1968-; Durham County Bd Soc Serv, 1970-; trustee, Fayetteville State Univ, 1972-; Durham County Bd Educ, 1972-; pres, bd govs, Nat Coun Churches Christ, 1983-88; pres, Nat Coun churches, AME Church; Nat Asn Advan Colored People; chmn, Church World Serv Unit Comt NCCC. **Honors/Awds:** Kellogg Fellow, 1965; Martin Luther King Fellow, Black Church Studies, 1972; Honoree of the Religious Award Achievements, 1985; Leadership Bishop. **Special Achievements:** Conducted Days Dialogue Ger AUS Europ, 1973; First black from a predominantly black denomination to preside over the National Council of Churches. **Business Addr:** Pastor, Philip R Cousin African Methodist Episcopal Church, 110 S Wash St, Naperville, IL 60540, **Business Phone:** (630)742-1102.

## COUSINS, ALTHEA L.
Educator. **Personal:** Born Nov 5, 1932, New York, NY; married Carl M; children: Kimberly & Karen. **Educ:** Fisk Univ, BA, 1953; Columbia Univ, MA, 1955; Temple Univ, MA, 1957; Walden Univ, doctoral prog, 1976. **Career:** Barratt Jr High Sch, teacher, 1953-54; Sartain Elem Sch, teacher, 1954-57, coun teacher, 1957-66; Friends Neighborhood Day Camp, supvr, 1958-59; Gideon Summer Sch, teacher, 1960; Wagner Jr High Sch, asst prin, 1966-67; Miller Sch, outreach counr, 1966, head start coun summer, 1966, elem sch prin, admin asst dist supt, 1967-70; Compers Elem Sch, prin, 1970-71, 1972-73; Sch Dist Philadelphia, Div Pupil Personnel & Coun, dir. **Orgs:** Exec bd, Ithan Elem Sch, 1969-71; Golden Circle Women 32 degree Masons, 1975; Nat Asn Pupil Personnel Adminr; Nat Educ Asn; Am Personnel & Guid Asn; Am Sch Counors Asn; Pa Sch Counors Asn; Nat Asn Col Admiss Counors; Philadelphia Asn Sch Adminr; Women Educ; bd dir, MainLine Day Care Ctr; Rotary Ann's Group; Mt Hebron Friends & Neighbors Comn Group; Women's Aux; Am Vet Med Asn; Links Inc; Delta Sigma Theta Sor; Zion Baptist Church; Women's Aux; Alpha Phi Alpha Fraternity; League Women Voters. **Home Addr:** 517 W Lancaster Ave, Haverford, PA 19041-1413, **Home Phone:** (215)871-4442.

## COUSINS, FRANK G., JR.
Sheriff, government official. **Personal:** Born May 7, 1958, Boston, MA; married Nicole; children: Gardner William. **Educ:** Springfield Col, BA, human serv, MS, criminal justice. **Career:** Newburyport City, coun, 1989-93; MA State Legis, state rep, 1992-96; Mass House rep, 1993-96; Mass Black Legis Caucus, chmn, 1996-; Essex Co, sheriff, 1996, 1998, 2004 & 2010; Mass Sheriffs Asn, pres, 2006-. **Orgs:** Bd dir, Provident Bank, 2003-. **Honors/Awds:** Flemming Fellowship Award, 1995. **Special Achievements:** First elected African American sheriff in Massachusetts. **Home Addr:** 65 Bromfield St, Newburyport, MA 01950. **Business Addr:** Sheriff, Essex County, 20 Manning Ave, Middleton, MA 01949-2807, **Business Phone:** (978)750-1900.

## COUSINS, WILLIAM, JR.
Government official, lawyer. **Personal:** Born Oct 6, 1927, Swiftown, MS; son of William and Drusilla Harris; married Hiroko Ogawa; children: Cheryl, Noel, Yul & Gail. **Educ:** Univ Ill, BA, polit sci, 1948; Harvard Univ, LLB, 1951. **Career:** Lawyer (retired), government official; Chicago Title & Trust Co, atty, 1953-57; Cook Co, asst state's atty, 1957-61; Turner, Cousins, Gavin & Watt firm, pvt pract law, 1961-76; 8th Ward Chicago, alderman, 1967-76; DePaul Law Sch, lectr, 1981-84; Circuit Ct Cook Co, judge, 1976-92; Ill Appellate Ct, justice, 1992-2002. **Orgs:** Asst moderator, United Church Christ, 1981; US Dist, Fed Ct Appeals & US Supreme Ct; exec comt, Ill Supreme Ct; Ill Judicial Conf, 1984-2002; chmn, Ill Judicial Coun, 1987-88; chmn, Ill Judicial Conf, 1989-90; Am Bar Asn; Chicago Bar Asn; Ill Bar Asn; Nat Bar Asn; Cook Co Bar Asn; Delta Sigma Rho; Kappa Alpha Psi; Sigma Pi Phi Fraternity; judicial coun, Nat Bar Asn, 1995-96; bd mem & chair, Nat Ctr State Courts, 1996-2002; bd mem, Judicial Coun NBA, 1997-2002; trustee, Lincoln Memorial United Church Christ; pres, Chatham Avalon Pk Comm Coun; vpres, Independent Voters Ill; bd mem, PUSH; bd mem, Chicago Chap, Nat Asn Advan Colored People; bd mem, Planned Parenthood Asn; Parkway Comm House; Am Dem Action. **Home Addr:** 1745 E 83 Pl, Chicago, IL 60617, **Home Phone:** (773)375-5449.

## COVIN, DR. DAVID L.
Educator, writer. **Personal:** Born Oct 3, 1940, Chicago, IL; son of David and Lela Jane Clements; married Judy Bentinck Smith; children: Wendy & Holly. **Educ:** Univ Ill, BA, 1962; Colo Univ, MA, 1966; Wash State Univ, PhD, 1970. **Career:** Calif State Univ, Sacramento, Govt & Ethnic Studies, asst prof, 1970-74, assoc dean gen studies, 1972-74, from assoc prof govt & ethnic studies to prof govt & ethnic studies, 1975-05; Union Grad Sch, adj prof, 1979-; Pan African Studies, Ethnic Studies Dept, dir, prof, 1990-2004, s, Ethnic Studies Dept, dir, prof, 1990-2004, emer prof govt & pan African studies, Calif State Univ, Sacramento, currently; Sate CA, consult, 1979; Race & Dem Am, founding proj, co-dir, 1998-2005. Founder Blue Nile Press, 2011. **Orgs:** Sacramento Citizens Comn Police Practices, 1972-73; contrib ed, Rumble, 1973-80; comnr, CA Educ Eval & Mgt Comn, 1977-81; Cong Black Caucus Criminal Justice Brain Trust, 1977-90; vice-chmn, Sacramento Area Black Caucus, 1978-83; consult, Sacramento City United Sch Dist, 1980; pres, Party New Black Polit, 1980-81; Nat Fac, 1988-; co-convener, NBIPP, 1980-81; actg chair, Nat Ed Rev Bd, NBIPP, 1982-84; co-chair, Sacramento local organizing Comt NBIPP, 1981-85; Sacramento Chap, Nat Rainbow Coalition Org Comt; deleg, Nat Party Cong, Nat Black Independent Polit Party, Nat Party Cong, 1981; pres, World Peace Asn, 1985-86; educ co-chair, Black Community Activist Comt, 1985-86; act chair, Save Our C Task Force Against Drugs & Gangs, 1987-88; act chair, Black Sci Resource Ctr, 1987-2005; exec bd, Women's Civic Improv Club, 1987; Sacramento City Police Dept Task Force Black Youth Gangs & Drugs, 1987-92; steering comt, Cooper-Woodson Col, 1988-; chair, SABC, 1988-90, 1995-96; partic, Am Assembly, 1990; ed, SABC Newsletter, 1990-96, chair, SABC Polit Comt, 1997-2006; co-chair, Man March Comt, Sacramento, 1995-96; Calif State Supt Educ African Am Adv Comt, 1998-2000; Ed Brd, 1999-2005, exec coun, 2001, pres, 2003-05, organizer, Nat Conf Black Polit Scientists; Sacramento Cong African Peoples, 2002-; Nat Black Conv Planning Comt, Nat Black Conv, 2004; second vpres, WCIC, 2005-; founder, Black Group, 2005; Sacramento Black Parallel Sch Bd Exec Coun, 2006-. **Home Addr:** 4131 44th St, Sacramento, CA 95820, **Home Phone:** (916)456-4981. **Business Addr:** Emeritus Professor, Publisher & Editor In-Chief, Blue Nile Press, Pan African Studies, 6000 J St, Sacramento, CA 95819-6013, **Business Phone:** (916)288-3060.

## COVINGTON, KIM ANN
Journalist. **Personal:** Born Mar 30, 1964, Centerville, IL; daughter of Wendell Sr and Delores Collins; married Derrick Grant; children: Jordan & Camille. **Educ:** Univ Mo, Columbia, MO, BJ, jour, 1986. **Career:** KYTV, Springfield, Mo, news reporter, 1986-88; KPLR-TV 11, St Louis, Mo, dir pub affairs, 1988-89, gen assignment reporter, 1989-96; KSDK-TV 5, anchor/reporter, 1996-98; WZZM TV 13, co anchor, 1998-2006; KPNX-12 News, anchor, 2006-. **Orgs:** Delta Sigma Theta Sorority Inc, 1984-; Nat Asn Black Journalists, 1986-; Commun comt, Urban League Greater St Louis, 1987-90; Multiracial Asn Professionals; Legion Black Collegiates. **Honors/Awds:** Unity Award, Lincoln Univ, 1988; Arkansas Asniated Press Award, Investigative Reporting, 1988; Investigative Reporting, Mo Asniated Press Award, 1988; Investigative Reporting, Nat Asn Press Honorable Mention; Distinguished Service Award, Sigma Delta Chi, Reporting, 1988; Horace Mann Award, PSA, 1989; Won Local Emmy, Spot News Coverage; Rocky Mountain Southwest Chapter Emmy Award, 2007; Arizona School Public Relations Association Award, 2008; ASBA Media Award for Excellence in Public Education Reporting, 2008. **Home Addr:** 906 Hanna Oaks Ct, Manchester, MO 63021. **Business Addr:** Anchor, KPNX 12 News, 1101 N Cent Ave, Phoenix, AZ 85004, **Business Phone:** (602)257-1212.

## COVINGTON, TARRIEL LAMONT
Executive. **Personal:** Born Jun 20, 1957; son of Wally and Gloria Smith; married Paralea Payne; children: Tari Jenelle, Ahmane Shay, Tian Latrell & Eric Jerome. **Educ:** Univ Mo, attended 1980; BS, jour, radio TV prod. **Career:** Proj Video, owner & exec producer, 1999-; Emory Univ, Atlanta, GA, supvry, media specialist & prod coordr. **Orgs:** Independent Nat Producers Asn; Image Film & Video; GA Lawyers Arts; actg pres, Avondale Bus Asn; bd chmn, Youth VIBE Inc; fel Leadership DeKalb; pres, Atlanta Black Newcomers Network; First Mt Bethel Church. **Honors/Awds:** Outstanding Radio Reporting Award, United Press Int, 1984; Nat Communicator's Award, 2002. **Business Addr:** Owner, Executive Producer, Project Video, 120 N Avondale Rd Suite F, Avondale Estates, GA 30002, **Business Phone:** (404)299-0299.

## COWAN, LARINE YVONNE
Administrator. **Personal:** Born Mar 25, 1949, Kensett, AR; daughter of William and Ola Mae; children: Alexander Milton Omar & Christopher Alvin Lamar. **Educ:** Univ Ark, Pine Bluff, BA, 1971; Univ Ark, Little Rock, MSW, 1973. **Career:** University Chancellor (retired); City Champaign, Community Rels Dept, dir, 1974-79; Univ Ill, Urbana-Champaign, Affirmative Action Nonacad Off, equal opportunity officer, 1982-85, dir, 1984-91, Off Vice Chancellor, affirmative action dir, asst vice chancellor, 1991-92, asst chancellor, assoc dir, 1992-94, asst to chancellor & dir, 1994-96. **Orgs:** State coord, Ill State Coun Opportunities Industrialization Ctrs Am Inc (OIC), 1983-87; campus coord, Nat Coalition Bldg Inst (NCBI), Prejudice Reduction Team, 1987-93; co-chair, Conf Comm, 1989-90; Savoy Rotary Club, 1990-92; Univ Ill Black Fac & Prof Staff Caucus & Adv Comn, 1991-93; Nat Asn Female Execs, 1993; Am Asn Affirmative Action; Am Asn Higher Educ; Am Asn Univ Women, Champaign-Urbana Chap; bd dir, Champaign County Urban League; Exec Women's Club-Champaign County; co-chair, Ill Affirmative Action Officers Asn, Educal Initiative Comm, Ill Comm Black Concerns Higher Educ; Nat Asn Advan Colored People; Pvt Indust Coun-Champaign, Ford, Iroquois & Piatt Counties, Prog Servs Comm; State Ill Job Serv, Employ Comm; Southern Poverty Law Ctr & Klanwatch Proj. **Home Addr:** 1906 Golfview Dr, Urbana, IL 61801, **Home Phone:** (217)328-2294. **Business Addr:** Assistant Chancellor, Director, University of Illinois at Urbana-Champaign, 100 Swanlund Admin Bldg MC-304, Champaign, IL 61820-5796, **Business Phone:** (217)333-0885.

**COWANS, ALVIN JEFFREY**
Executive. **Personal:** Born Jun 15, 1955, Alexandria, VA; son of Willie L and Jessie M; married Shirley Mae Smith; children: Alvin Jeffrey II & Marcus Adrian. **Educ:** Univ Fla, BS, jour, 1977; Inst Financial Educ, supvry training cert, 1979; Fla Credit Union Mgt Inst, attended 1988; CUNA's Advan Mgt Inst, cert credit union exec, 1989. **Career:** Univ Fla Fighting Gator Football Team, 1973-76, co-capt, 1976-78; Pittsburgh Steelers, draft choice, 1977; Jim Walter Corp, pipe salesman, 1977-78; Pioneer Fed Savings Loan, asst vpres, off mgr, admin asst, 1978-83; McCoy Fed Credit Union, sr vpres, pres, 1983-85, chief exec officer, 1986-; Sarasota Coastal Credit Union, pres & chief exec officer, 1990-2009; Orlando Fed Credit Union, pres & chief exec officer, 1990-. **Orgs:** Pres, Credit Union Serv Corp, 1985; regional dir, Nat Asn Fed Credit Unions, 1993; Fed Res's Consumer Adv Coun; former dir, Southeast Fed Credit Union, 1994-97; bd mem, Univ FL Found, dir, 1998; adv bd, Payment Systs Financial Serv, 2003-; dir, Univ Cent Fla Golden Knights Club, 2006; bd dir, CU24 Inc, 2006; Cent Fla Amateur Athletic Union; Orange Co Schs Partners Educ; mem bd govs, African Am Chamber Com Cent Fla; Greater Orlando Chamber Com; Rotary Club Orlando; Cent Fla Urban Bankers Asn; secy, Mt Pleasant Missionary Baptist Church; bd dir, Fla Credit Union League Serv Group; dir, Univ Fla Found; Fed Reserves Consumer Adv Counc; Credit Union Exec Soc; past pres, Univ Fla Lettermens Asn; dir, Gator Booster Bd; dir, Orange County Minority Bus Enterprise; former bd mem, Cent Fla Kidney Found; bd dir & chmn bd, Credit Union 24. **Honors/Awds:** Graduate of the Chamber of Commerce Leadership Orlando Program, 1980; Outstanding Young Men in America, 1981; Citizen of the Year, Chi Tau Chap, Omega Psi Phi Fraternity; Hall of Fame, Univ Fla Gator, 2003. **Home Addr:** 8042 Citron Ct, Orlando, FL 32819, **Home Phone:** (407)299-3096. **Business Addr:** President, Chief Executive Officer, McCoy Federal Credit Union, PO Box 593806, Orlando, FL 32859-3806, **Business Phone:** (407)855-5452.

**COWARD, ONIDA LAVONEIA (ONIDA COWARD MAYERS)**
Educator. **Personal:** Born Sep 26, 1964, Panama City; daughter of Ricardo E and Marcia E Pitter; married Gregorio Mayers. **Educ:** Buffalo State Col, NY, BA, commun, 1986; Zicklin Sch Bus Baruch Col, MBA, 2000. **Career:** Paragon Cable Manhattan, NY, pub & leased mgr, 1987-89; Brooklyn Community Access TV, Brooklyn, NY, founding dir, 1989-2003; New York Voter Assistance Comn, exec dir & coordr, 2004-2010; NYC Campaign Finance Bd, dir voter assistance, 2011-. **Orgs:** Nat Asn Minorities Cable, 1987; Nat Asn Black Jour, 1988; One Hundred Black Women, 1988; bd mem, Am Cancer Soc, Harlem Unit, 1991; bd mem, Harlem YMCA 100 Yrs Basketball, 1991; Jack & Jill Am, Brooklyn chap, 2000-; vpres, Nat Asn Advan Colored People, Brooklyn, 2013-. **Home Addr:** 5810 Beverly Rd, Brooklyn, NY 11203. **Business Addr:** Director, New York City Campaign Finance Board, 100 Church St 12th Fl, New York, NY 10007, **Business Phone:** (212)409-1800.

**COWART, SAM (SAMUEL COWART, III)**
Football player, business owner, insurance agent. **Personal:** Born Feb 26, 1975, Jacksonville, FL; married Karkeisha; children: Deja & Samuel IV. **Educ:** Fla State Univ, polit sci, 1998; Harvard Bus Sch, exec educ prog, 2005; Kellogg Sch Mgt, entrepreneurial studies, 2006. **Career:** Football player (retired), executive, business owner, insurance agent; Buffalo Bills, linebacker, 1998-2001; New York Jets, 2002-04; Minn Vikings, 2005; Houston Texans, 2006; Northwestern Mutual Financial Network, fin rep; 56 Fashion Inc, owner, 2006-. **Orgs:** Ronald McDonald House; United Way. **Business Addr:** Owner, 56 Fashion Inc, 5430 Soutel Dr, Jacksonville, FL 32219, **Business Phone:** (904)766-7142.

**COWDEN, MICHAEL E.**
Educator, actor, poet. **Personal:** Born Jul 17, 1951, Louisville, KY; son of Alberta Fields. **Educ:** Shoreline Commun Col, AA, 1971; Univ Wash, BA, Am ethnic studies. **Career:** Louisville Pub Sch, martial arts instr, chinese boxing, 1975-; poet; playwright. Film: Abby, 1974. **Honors/Awds:** US Achievement Academy's All Am Scholar, 1993-94. **Home Addr:** 1734 S 23rd St, Louisville, KY 40210-2152.

**COWELL, DR. CATHERINE**
Nutritionist, consultant. **Personal:** Born Nov 13, 1921, Norfolk, VA. **Educ:** Hampton Inst, BS, 1945; Univ Conn, MS, 1947; NY Univ, PhD, 1983. **Career:** Univ CT, grad asst nutrit, 1945-47; Metab Clin Mt Sinai Hosp, NYC, lab tech, 1947-49, pub health nutrionalist, 1969; Bur Nutrit, actg dir, 1971; NY Med Col Flower Fifth Ave Hosp, asst clin instr preventavemed pub health indust & hyg, 1953-55; Albert Einstein Sch Med Yeshiva Univ, instr nutrit environ med, 1962-69; NY Univ, vis lectr; Montclair State Tchr; Col Rep NY Nutrit Coun, 1963; Nutrit Bur Dept Health, NY, dir, 2002; Mailman Sch Pub Health, clin prof pop & family health. **Orgs:** Manhattan Br; Nat Coun Negro Women; fel Am Pub Health Asn; Am Home Econ Asn; NY State Home Econ Asn; chmn, Health & Welfare Sect, 1961-62, pres, 1971-; St George Asn New York Health Dept; Royal Soc Health; Hampton Alumni Asn; nat pres, Lambda Kappa Kappa Mu, 1961-65; White House Conf Food Nutrit & Health, 1969; adv coun, Ch Human Ecol, Cornell Univ, 1970-72; Order Eastern Star Club; New York Acad med; bd dir, New York Zero-To-Three Network. **Honors/Awds:** Nutritional Award, New York Pub Health Asn, 1960; JF Goodwin Scholarship, Reading PA; Public Health Nutrition Award named in honor, Am Pub Health Asn; Honored by Nat Asn 100 Black Men Am Inc, 1999. **Special Achievements:** Author: "Nutrit Assessment A Comprehensive Guide for Planning Intervention"; contributor of articles to journals. **Home Addr:** 730 Riverside Dr Apt 3B, New York, NY 10031, **Home Phone:** (212)234-5416. **Business Addr:** Clinical Professor, Columbia University, Allan Rosenfield Bldg 722 W 168th St Suite 14, New York, NY 10032, **Business Phone:** (212)305-3927.

**COX, DR. ARTHUR JAMES, SR.**
Educator. **Personal:** Born Jun 15, 1943, Avon Park, FL; married Deloris Murray; children: Arthur Jr, Travis J & David I. **Educ:** Howard Univ, AB, 1965, MSW, 1970; Columbia Univ, DSW, 1978. **Career:** NIMH fel; doctoral study, 1973-74; Fla State Univ, asst prof, 1975-78; E Tenn State Univ, chmn & assoc prof, 1978-83; Southern Ill Univ, dir & assoc prof, 1983-86; Salem State Col, dean & prof, 1986-. **Orgs:** Fel ACE, 1979; chmn, Human Serv Goals Directions 2000 Prog, 1980-83; secy & treas, Inst C Resources, 1980-82; steering comn mem, Southeast Child Welfare Training Resource Ctr, Univ Tenn Sch Social Work, 1981-82; treas, Asn Baccalaureate Prog dir, 1981-83; pres, Tenn Chap, Nat Asn Social Workers, 1981-82; Publ Comn Coun Social Work Educ, 1981-84; Alcohol Treat Serv Adv Bd Jackson Co Comn Ment Health Ctr, Carbondale, IL, 1984-; mem ed rev bd, Jour Social Serv Res GWB Sch Social Work, Wash Univ, St Louis, 1985-88; Nat Asn Black Social Workers; Nat Asn Social Workers; Coun Social Work Educ; Nat Conf Social Welfare; elected deleg, Tenn Gov's State Conf Families, White House Conf Famili Minneapolis; pres & chief exec officer, Mid Fla Ctr Ment Health & Substance Abuse Serv Inc, currently. **Home Addr:** 1282 Lake Lotela Dr, Avon Park, FL 33825-9737. **Business Addr:** President, Chief Executive Officer, Mid-Florida Center for Mental Health & Substance Abuse Services Inc, PO Box 33, Avon Park, FL 33826-0033, **Business Phone:** (863)533-2321.

**COX, BRYAN KEITH**
Football player, football coach. **Personal:** Born Feb 17, 1968, East St. Louis, IL; married Kim; children: Lavonda, Brittani, Chiquita, Kelli & Bryan Jr. **Educ:** Western Ill Univ, BS, mass commun. **Career:** Football player (retired), football coach; Miami Dolphins, right outside linebacker & right linebacker & middle linebacker, 1991-95, pass rush coach, 2011-; Chicago Bears, middle linebacker, 1996-97; New York Jets, right linebacker & left inner linebacker, 1998-2000, asst defensive line coach, 2006-08; New Eng Patriots, linebacker & middle linebacker, 2001; New Orleans Saints, middle linebacker, 2002; TVG Network, analyst, 2004-05; Cleveland Browns, defensive line coach, 2009-11; Miami Dolphins, pass rush coach, 2011; Tampa Bay Buccaneers, defensive asst, 2012; Atlanta Falcons, defensive line coach, 2014-. **Honors/Awds:** Pro Bowl, 1992, 1994, 1995; Extra Effort Award, Nat Football League, 1994; All-Pro selection, 1992, 1994, 1995; Super Bowl Champion, XXXVI. **Business Addr:** Defensive Line Coach, Atlanta Falcons, Sun Life Stadium, Flowery Branch, FL 30542, **Business Phone:** (770)965-3115.

**COX, CORINE G.**
Editor. **Personal:** Born May 31, 1944, Mansfield, LA; married Doyl; children: Dwayne E. **Educ:** Tex Southern Univ, attended 1963; Univ Bus Col, cert sec training, 1964. **Career:** Soc & Women's Ed Forward Times Pub Co, compositer, supvr, news writer soc ed, 1964-. **Orgs:** Adv bd, Ct Calanthe; Eta Phi Beta; Mt Rose Missionary Baptist Church; secy, Prairie View A&M Univ. **Home Addr:** 4406 Kelley St, Houston, TX 77026-1632, **Home Phone:** (713)491-0027. **Business Addr:** Editor, 4411 Almeda Rd, Houston, TX 77004.

**COX, COURTLAND**
Federal government official. **Career:** City Wash, DC, Minority Opport Comn, dir, 1980-83, Off Int Bus, dir, 1983-85, spec asst to mayor; US Dept Com, Off Civil Rights, dir, Minority Bus Develop Agency, dep secy, dir, 2001; pvt bus advisor & consult; Off Civil Rights, agency dir & Int Trade Admin, spec asst; DC Sports & Entertainment Comn, bus enterprise develop, LSDBE Develop, dir, currently; Drum & Spear bookstore, co owner & mgr; Drum & Spear Press, co owner & mgr. **Orgs:** Stud Non Violent Coord Comt; Emergency Fund S Africa; Ctr Nat Security Studies; secy gen, Sixth Pan-African Cong, 1973; secy gen, Int meeting African people Tanzania, 1973. **Special Achievements:** Developed in-depth expertise on Africa, and promoted awareness of economic development, technology advancement, advanced cultural and racial issues to increase cooperation and communication between US and foreign nations. **Business Addr:** Director, DC Sports & Entertainment Commission, 2400 E Capitol St SE, Washington, DC 20003, **Business Phone:** (202)547-9077.

**COX, DR. GEORGETTA MANNING**
Educator. **Personal:** Born Sep 16, 1947, Washington, DC; married Walter Bishop Jr; children: Malakia Iman. **Educ:** Hampton Inst, BA, biol, 1970; Howard Univ Col Dent, DDS, 1976; Johns Hopkins Univ, MPH, health care admin, 1979. **Career:** Howard Univ, Sch Dent, prog coordr, 1977-78, asst prof, 1979-86, chmn & assoc prof, 1980-; Howard Univ Col Dent, assoc prof & Dir, div community dent, 1977-; pvt practise, prin, 1976-. **Orgs:** Consult, United Planning Org Health Adv Comt, 1982-; managing ed, NDAJ Nat Dent Asn, 1983-, vpres, 1984, pres, 1985; vpres, Howard Univ Dent Alumna Asn, 1985; presentor & mem, Int Asn Dent Res; Sigma Xi Res Soc, Am Pub Health Asn; Omicron Kappa Upsilon Nat Dent Honor Soc. **Home Addr:** 1301 Mass Ave NW Apt 100, Washington, DC 20005, **Home Phone:** (202)249-1429. **Business Addr:** Associate Professor, Chairman, Howard University, 600 W St NE, Washington, DC 20059, **Business Phone:** (202)806-0084.

**COX, J. LINLOY**
Accountant. **Educ:** Howard Univ, BBA, summa cum laude, 1987; Univ Md, College Park, MBA, 1992. **Career:** Deloitte & Touche, pub acct profession. **Orgs:** Chief financial officer, Nat Asn Advan Colored People, 1999-. **Business Addr:** Chief Financial Officer, NAACP National Headquarters, 4805 Mt Hope Dr, Baltimore, MD 21215, **Business Phone:** (410)580-5777.

**COX, FR. JESSE**
Church historian, preacher. **Educ:** Loyola Univ, BA, theol & eng; Dominican Novitiate, 1981; Aquinas Inst Theol, MDiv, 1987; Xavier Univ, ThM, MA, black cath studies. **Career:** Hales Franciscan High Sch, teacher, 1987-91; Dominican Fathers, 1987; Dominican Friars, voc dir, 1991-97; Archdiocese Detroit, dir, 1997-; St. Dominic Church, dir Nat Evangelization, currently; Marygrove Col, dir campus ministry, 2010-. **Orgs:** Coordr, Nat Joint Conf, 1998; Black Dominicans Conf, currently; advisor, new fraternity, Marygrovea; bd, St Dominic Outreach Ctr & Intercultural Consult Serv. **Special Achievements:** Preached & lectured in US, India, Africa & Europe. **Business Addr:** Director, Marygrove College, 8425 W McNichols, Detroit, MI 48221, **Business Phone:** (313)927-1200.

**COX, JOSEPH MASON ANDREW**
Writer, poet, educator. **Personal:** Born Jul 12, 1930, Boston, MA; son of Hiram and Edith Henderson. **Educ:** Columbia Univ, BA, 1945, LLB, 1953; World Univ, Hong Kong, PhD, art psychol, 1972. **Career:** New York Age, reporter & writer, 1955; NY Post, New York, NY, reporter & feature writer, 1958-60; Afro-Asian Pur Comn, New York NY, pres, 1961-68; New York Bd Educ, Brooklyn NY, consult, 1969-71; Manhattan Community Col City Univ New York, NY, lectr, 1972-73; Medgar Evers Col City Univ NY, Brooklyn NY, asst prof Eng, 1973-74; Cox & Hopewell Publ Inc, NY NY, pres, 1974; poet & writer; prof City Univ NY, Manhattan Community Col, Bronx Community Col, Medgar Evers Col, New York Univ Res Ctr, 1975-83; Fed Govt Crime Ins, 1983-88; Poems: The Collected Poetry of Joseph Mason Andrew Cox, 1970; Shore Dimly Seen, 1974; New & Selected Poems, 1979; Unfolding Orchid, 1993; Novels: The Search, 1963; Ode to Dr Martin Luther King, Jr, 1970; Indestructible Monument, 1974; Great Black Men of Masonry: Qual Black Achievers Who Were Freemasons, 1982; Blue Diamond Press, 1982. **Orgs:** Int Poetry Soc; Int Poets Shrine; United Poets Laureate Int; World Lit Acad; Auth League Am; Poetry Soc Am; Phylaxis Soc; NAACP; Int Acad Arts, Sci & Letters. **Honors/Awds:** Internaltional Essay Award, Daniel S Mead Agency, 1964; Great Society Writer's Award, Pres Lyndon B Johnson, 1965; Master Poets Award, Am Poet Fel Soc, 1970; World Poets Award, World Poetry Fel Soc, 1972; PEN grant, 1972; Humanitarian Award & Gold Medal for poetry, Int Poets Shrine, 1973; United Poet Laureate, Int Gold Crown, 1976; Am Book Award nomination, 1979, for New & Selected Poems; NCP Medal of Distinction, Asbury Park Neptune, 1984; "Statue of Victory" World Culture Prize, Accademia Italia, 1985; Science & Letters Bronze Statue, Int Acad Arts, 1985; Gold Medal, Am Biog Asn, 1987; Gold Medal, Am Biog Asn, 1988. **Home Addr:** 801 Tilden St Apt 21B, Bronx, NY 10467, **Home Phone:** (212)882-8160.

**COX, KEITH**
Chief executive officer, manager, president (organization). **Personal:** Born St. Vincent. **Educ:** Brooklyn Col, BA; Stony Brook Univ, health sci. **Career:** Cox Nissan Inc, owner & chief exec officer, gen mgr & pres, 2000-08; Cox Preowned Cars Inc, owner, currently; Cox Autos Getty Serv Sta, owner, currently. **Orgs:** New York Automobile Dealers Asn. **Business Addr:** General Manager, President & Chief Executive Officer, Cox Nissan Inc, 3700 Boston Rd, Bronx, NY 10460, **Business Phone:** (718)515-7300.

**COX, KEVIN C.**
State government official. **Personal:** Born Dec 1, 1949, Oklahoma City, OK; son of Frank and Martina; married Carlise Ann Washington; children: Kenny. **Educ:** Fla A&M Univ, BS, polit sci, 1972; Univ Ga, MPA, pub admin, 1974. **Career:** State OK, field monitor, 1974-77; Energy Conserv & Housing Found, minority bus develop, 1977-80; State OK, Dist 97, state rep, 1980-2004. **Orgs:** Fla A&M Alumni Asn; bd dir, E side YMCA; Kappa Alpha Psi Frat Inc; Nat Asn Advan Colored People; mem bd dir, Urban League; chmn, Ins Comm; 33 Degree Prince Hall Mason; Prince Hall Shriner; United Native Am, rep; Langston Univ Alumni Asn. **Home Addr:** 5300 N Lottie, Oklahoma City, OK 73111, **Home Phone:** (405)557-7367.

**COX, LAVERNE**
Actor, television producer, activist. **Personal:** Born Mobile, AL. **Educ:** Marymount Manhattan Col. **Career:** Reality TV series "I Want to Work for Diddy", partic, 2008; VH1 reality TV show "TRANSform Me", co-host & producer; Movie "Musical Chairs", actress, 2011; Movie "The Exhibitionists", actress, 2012; Netflix TV series "Orange is the New Black", actress, 2013-14; Documentary "Laverne Cox Presents: The T Word", exec producer & narrator, 2014. **Honors/Awds:** Anti-Violence Project, Courage Award honoree, 2013; "Out Magazine", OUT10 Gala, 100 Most Compelling People of the Year, Reader's Choice Award, 2013; Massachusetts Independent Film Festival, Best Supporting Actress for movie "Musical Chairs", 2013; "Glamour" magazine, Woman of the Year, 2014; "Root 100", Listee; "The Guardian", World Pride Power List, 2014; Gay & Lesbian Alliance Against Defamation (GLAAD), Stephen F. Kolzak Award recipient, April 2014; "The Huffington Post", Country's Top 50 Trans Icons, Listee; "Metro Source" magazine, 55 People We Love, listee. **Special Achievements:** First openly transgender person to: receive an Emmy nomination in an acting category and appear on the cover of "Time" magazine; first African American transgender person to produce and star in her own TV show.

**COX, M. MAURICE**
Executive, vice president (organization), journalist. **Personal:** Born Dec 20, 1951, Dover, NC; son of Nicy Chatmon and Earl E; married Earlene Hardie; children: Michelle Hardie & Michael M. **Educ:** Univ NC, Greensboro, NC, BA, econ, 1974. **Career:** Greensboro News Co, Greensboro NC, journalist, 1973-74; Assoc Builders & Contractors, Wash, DC, ed, 1975-78, asst dir commun & speechwriter, 1979-81; Pepsi-Cola Co, Somers, NY, sr mgr, fed & state affairs, 1981-85, dir fed, state affairs & consumer rels, 1986-90, vice pres diversity & corp develop--pepsi-cola compaby, 1991-2006; vpres, diversity & inclusion developmment, 2007-12; 3MC Mgt Strategies LLC, managing dir, 2012-. **Orgs:** Black Mgrs Asn, 1986; mentor, White Plains Youth Coun, 1988-; Food Patch, Exec Leadership Coun. **Business Addr:** Managing Director, 3MC Management Strategies, LLC, 4 Sunrise Pl, Armonk, NY 10504, **Business Phone:** (914)273-8356.

**COX, OTIS GRAHAM, JR.**
Government official. **Personal:** Born Oct 29, 1941, Winston-Salem, NC; son of Otis (deceased) and Geraldine Cox (deceased); married Wanda Woodlon; children: Wendi, Kevin & Keith. **Educ:** Savannah State Col, GA, BSIA, 1963; FBI Acad Quantico, VA, law enforce cert, 1969; Suffolk Univ, Boston, MPA, 1980. **Career:** Baltimore Co, sch teacher, 1963-67; Westinghouse Elec Corp, engr writer, 1967-69; FBI, spec agt investr, 1969; FBI, Boston, supr civil rights, 1977; FBI, admin-str pub, 1979; spec agt supr pub, asst sect chief; St WV, cabinet Sec, pub safety, 1997-2001; Nat Hwy Traffic Safety Admin, Dept Transp's, dep adminr, 2003-; Wva Univ, pub safety coordr; Marshall Univ, Grad Col, asst prof. **Orgs:** Alpha Phi Alpha Fraternity; Nat Police Asn; MA Assoc Afro Am Policemen; Am Soc Pub Admin; NOBLE; Urban League; Black Exec Exchange Prog; Int Asn Chief Police Inc; Deacon

Peace Mind Baptist Church; Rotarian; bd dir, United Hosp Ctr; exec bd, Boy Scouts Am; Social Justice Vis Comt, 2011. **Honors/Awds:** Toland Collier Memorial Award, Savannah State Col, 1961; A A Leadership Award, Alpha Phi Frat Delta Eta, 1963; Cert of Bravery, MA Asn Afro Am Policemen, 1975; Cert Accomplishment, Assessment & Designs Inc, 1975; Achievement Award, Order Eastern Star, 1992; Except Accomplishment Award, The Mountain State Bar Asn, 1992; Exec of the Year, Fraternal Order of Police, 1992; Sigma Pi Phi Frat; Int Speakers Bur. **Home Addr:** 118K Oak Dr, Dunbar, WV 25064. **Business Addr:** Deputy Administrator, West Virginia Highway Safety Program, Capitol Complex, Charleston, WV 25301, **Business Phone:** (304)558-1515.

## COX, RONALD EUGENE, SR.

Football coach, football player. **Personal:** Born Mar 29, 1968, Fresno, CA; married Michelle; children: Cailin, Kelsey & Ron Jr. **Educ:** Fresno State Univ, BS, bus mgt. **Career:** Football player (retired), coach; Chicago Bears, 1990-91, linebacker, 1992-94, right linebacker, 1995, left linebacker, 1997; Green Bay Packers, linebacker, 1996; Land Dev & construct Co, Cent Calif, gen mgr; Calif State Univ, football coach; Lake Forest Col, linebacker coach, Div III, asst defensive coordr. **Honors/Awds:** Most Valuable player, 1989; Poor Man's Guide, Nat Football League; Defensive Player of the Year, 1989; Fresno Athletic Hall of Fame, 2001; Super Bowl champion. **Home Addr:** 2601b N Chapel Hill Rd, PO Box 523, McHenry, IL 60051-3632. **Business Addr:** Football Coach, Lake Forest Col, 555 N Sheridan Rd, Lake Forest, IL 60045.

## COX, DR. SANDRA

Executive director. **Personal:** daughter of Odessa. **Educ:** Calif State Univ, Los Angeles, CA, BA; Univ Southern Calif, MA, educ psychol; Claremont Grad Univ, PhD, educ. **Career:** SouthCentral RTEC, Los Angeles Anger Mgt Teacher; Palm Springs Life, couns & therapist; Coalition Ment Health Profs, exec dir & co founder, 2003-. **Orgs:** Past pres, Asn Black Psychol. **Business Addr:** Executive Director, Co Founder, Coalition Mental Health Professionals, 9130 S Figueroa St Suite 100, Los Angeles, CA 90003, **Business Phone:** (323)777-3120.

## COX, DR. SANDRA HICKS

Lawyer, executive. **Personal:** Born Apr 28, 1939, Baton Rouge, LA; daughter of Henry Beecher Sr and Eleanor Victorine Frazier; married Ronald Virgil; children: Michelle Louella & Damien Monroe. **Educ:** Howard Univ, BA, polit sci, 1959; OH State Univ Col Law, JD, 1962. **Career:** Donald P McCullum, Oakland, Calif, coun, 1965; Dixon & White & William CDixon & Assocs, Oakland, Calif, coun, 1965-67; San Francisco Neighborhood Legal Assistance Found, domestic rels coun, 1967-69; San Francisco Legal Assist Found, chief domestic rels dept, 1969-72; State CA Pub Utilities Comn, legal asst pub utilities comnr, 1972-73; Kaiser Found Health Plan Inc, coun, 1973-84; Kaiser Found Hosp & Kaiser Found Health Plan Inc, vpres & regional coun, sr legal & regulatory compliance officer, 1984-98; Art Odyssey, owner & vpres, 1999-; Cox Firm, sr partner, 2009-. **Orgs:** OH State Bar, 1963-; CA State Bar, 1964-; Agency Rels Coun United Way Inc, 1985-86; Nat Bar Asn; Los Angeles County Bar Asn; Jack & Jill Am Inc, 1990-93. **Honors/Awds:** Parliamentarian, Delta Sigma Theta Sorority Inc, 1986-87, 1991; Black Women Achievement Award, Nat Asn Advan Colored People Legal Defense & Educ Fund Inc, 1987; House Counsel Year, John M Langston Bar Asn, 1990; President's Compass Award, Nat Bar Asn, 1990, Sr Advisor to President, Langston Bar Asn, 1994. **Home Addr:** 1566 Meadowbrook Rd, Altadena, CA 91001-3227, **Home Phone:** (626)797-7376. **Business Addr:** Owner, Vice President, Art Odyssey, **Business Phone:** (626)818-1451.

## COX, TAYLOR H., SR.

Accountant. **Personal:** Born Feb 28, 1926, Clarksburg, WV; son of Wade (deceased) and Matilda (deceased); married Betty Leftridge; children: Taylor Jr, Patricia Elam & Nancy Phillips; married Edith Burroughs; children: Annette Austin & Lamont Seals. **Educ:** WVa Wesleyan Col Buckhannon, BS, bus econ, 1953; Ind Univ, Bloomington, MBA, 1954. **Career:** Accountant (retired); Home Fed Savings & Loan Assoc, Detroit, gen mgr, 1954-59; Mich Chronicle, columnist, 1955-79; Detroit Coca-Cola Bottling Co, asst to sales mgr, 1959-64; Motown Rec Detroit, dept head-artist mgt, 1964-72; Invictus Rec Detroit, vpres artist mgt, 1972-73; New Detroit Inc, proj mgr, 1978-79; Mich Bell Tel Co, dist mgr minority econ develop. **Orgs:** Nat Asn Advan Colored People; Urban League Detroit; Nat Bus League; Am Bridge Asn, 1979-80; Detroit Asn Bus Econ. **Honors/Awds:** Numerous Certificates of Appreciation & Plaques Nat Asn Advan Colored People, Urban League, New Detroit Inc, United Comm Serv. **Special Achievements:** First African-American manager, Detroit Coca-Cola Bottling Co; listed Nat Top 50 List Am Bridge Asn, 1979-80. **Home Addr:** 26836 Summerdale Dr, Southfield, MI 48034-2233, **Home Phone:** (248)352-1074.

## COX, TYRONE YAMANI (TY COX)

Government official, accountant. **Educ:** NC Cent Univ, BBA, acct, 1994. **Career:** Durham City Coun, coun mem; NC Off State Auditor; Ty Cox Acct & Bus ServInc, pres & chief exec officer; Leonard & Cox PLLC; Cox Gibbs & Thomas, partner; CPAs PLLC, founding partner, managing partner; Alpha Mgt Community Serv Inc, bus mgr & chief financial officer, currently; Ty Cox & Co CPAs PLLC, bus mgr, chief financial officer & founding partner, managing sr partner, currently. **Orgs:** Bd mem, NC Pub Allies; nat bd mem, Nat Asn Black Accts Inc; Triangle Transit; bus mgr & chief financial officer, Alpha Mgt Community Serv Inc; Nc State Bd Cert Pub Acct Examiners, 2005; bd mem, Nc State Bd CPA; bd mem, Nc State Bd Transp; mem bd trustee, Triangle Transit Authority; bd mem & city councilman, Transp; State Bd Transp. **Home Addr:** 2115 Alpine Rd, Durham, NC 27707. **Business Addr:** Managing Senior Partner, Ty Cox & Co CPAs PLLC, 4419 Sun Valley Dr, Durham, NC 27707-5689, **Business Phone:** (919)493-9897.

## COX, WARREN E.

Lawyer, government official. **Personal:** Born Apr 26, 1936, Brookhaven, MS; son of Pinkie; married Alpha Whiting, Apr 20, 1957; children: Diethra D & Reggie R. **Educ:** Alcorn A&M Col, BSEd, 1957; Southern Ill Univ, MEd, 1966; Univ Miss, JD, 1969. **Career:** Gentry High Sch, teacher band dir, 1957-64; Lincoln's Attendance Ctr, teacher band dir, 1964-69; Univ Law Sch, res asst, 1966-69; Holly Springs, staff atty, 1969-72; Equal Employ Opportunity Comn, sr investr, 1973; US DOL & OFCCP, asst dist dir, 1987-91; US Equel Employ Opp Comn, dist coun; Cox Mediation Serv, owner; pvt pract atty, currently. **Orgs:** Nat Advan Asn Colored People; Miss Dem Pary; Miss Bar Asn; Nat Bar Asn; AmBar Asn; Magnolia Bar Asn; Miss Lawyers Asn; Fed Bar Asn; Am Judicate Soc; Miss State Bar. **Home Addr:** 5238 Cloverdale Dr, Jackson, MS 39272, **Home Phone:** (601)373-1161. **Business Addr:** Owner, Cox Mediation Services, 5238 Cloverdale Dr, Jackson, MS 39272, **Business Phone:** (601)373-1161.

## COY, JOHN T.

Private investigator, business owner, police officer. **Personal:** Born Oct 5, 1939, Princeton, NJ; son of John I and Alice Jeanette Douglas; married Faithe Suzanne Parago; children: Barrie A (deceased), Wendy D, David S, Dhana P & Dawn C. **Educ:** Trenton State Col, Ewing Twp NJ, attended 1974; Mercer County Community Col, W Windsor NJ, attended 1986; Atlanta Univ, Criminal Justice Inst, attended 1988. **Career:** Trenton Police Dept, Trenton NJ, patrolman, 1964-70, detective, 1970-78, sgt, 1978-82, detective sgt, 1982-93; John T Coy & Assoc, founder & pvt investr, pres, chief exec officer & owner, 1993; J T Coy Security Inc, owner, 1996-; City Tours Inc, owner, 2004-. **Orgs:** Pres, Bro Officers Law Enforcement Soc, 1968-; Trenton Super Officers Asn, 1978-; Mayor's Adv Comt Affirmative Action, 1981-; bd dir, Carver Youth & Family Ctr, 1983-; Roga Golf Club, 1983; deleg, Nat Black Police Asn, 1983-; pres, Carver Century Club, 1984-; info officer, Nj Coun, Nat Black Police, 1985-; Nat Asn Advan Colored People, 1985-; info officer, Northeast Region, Nat Black Police Asn, 1987-; mem bd dir, Nat Black Police Asn, 1987-96; founder & exec dir, NJ Security Officer's Asn; bd dir, Trenton Downtown Asn, 2004-, exec comt, currently. **Honors/Awds:** Valor Award, Trenton Police Div, 1980; founder & current pres, Carver Century Club, 1984; founder & current editor, Vanguard ANJ Publication for Black Police Officers, 1984; superior office of the year, City of Trenton, 1985; founder & current editor, Northeast Regional News, Nat Black Police Asn, 1985; member of the year, Nat Black Police Asn Northeast Region, 1986. **Special Achievements:** Author of article on police/community relations in The Police Chief, 1974; author of Police Officer's Handbook for the Trenton Police Division 1980, 1986. **Home Addr:** 513 Eggerts Crossing Rd, Ewing, NJ 08638-1805, **Home Phone:** (609)883-1749. **Business Addr:** President, Owner, John T Coy & Associates, 40 W Lafayette St, Trenton, NJ 08608-2011, **Business Phone:** (609)393-8900.

## CRAFT, DR. GUY CALVIN

Librarian. **Personal:** Born Oct 19, 1929, Atlanta, GA; son of Josie Hubert Glass and Guy; married Martha Broadwater; children: Guy Jr, Audrey, Anthony, Gayle & Scott. **Educ:** Morehouse Col, Atlanta, Ga, AB, 1951; Atlanta Univ, Atlanta, Ga, MSLS, 1962; Southern Ill Univ, Carbondale, Ill, PhD, 1976. **Career:** Acad Libr; Fla Mem Col, St Augustine, Fla, head librn & VP Pub Rels, 1957-62; Phi Kappa Phi, Kappa Delta Phi, Phi Delta Kappa, Carnegie Fel, 1957; Elizabeth City State Univ, Elizabeth City, NC, chief cataloger, 1962-65; Albany State Col, Albany, Ga, head librn, 1965-85; Develop Leaders Fel, 1974; Atlanta Univ Ctr/Robert W Woodruff Libr, Atlanta, Ga, libr dir, 1985-; Clark Atlanta Univ, intern dean, 1989. **Orgs:** Pres, Community Rels Coun, 1976-78; chmn, Chehaw Coun Boy Scouts, 1976-80; bd dir, CCLC, 1977-; Metrop Atlanta Red Cross, 1986-87; Kiwanis Club, 1987-; Phi Kappa Phi, Kappa Delta Pi; Phi Delta; Am Libr Asn; Am Asn Higher Educ; Am Asn Col Teacher Educ; Asn Col & Res Libr, Ga Libr Asn; Soc Ethnic & Spec Studies; Southeastern Libr Asn Kappa. **Honors/Awds:** Hon Cert, Morehouse Col, 1976; Hon Cert, Job Corps, 1977; Hon Cert & Plaque, Boy Scouts, 1978; Resolution Commendation, Ga House Representatives, 1986; Boss of the Year, ABWA, 1988. **Home Addr:** 3002 Parc Lorraine Cir, Lithonia, GA 30038. **Business Addr:** Director, Robert W Woodruff Library, 111 James P Brawley Dr SW, Atlanta, GA 30314, **Business Phone:** (404)522-8980.

## CRAFT, SALLY-ANN ROBERTS (SALLY-ANN ROBERTS)

Journalist. **Personal:** Born Feb 14, 1953, Chandler, AZ; married Willie Jerome; children: Judith, Kelly & Jeremiah. **Educ:** Univ Southern Miss, BA, 1976, MS, 1977. **Career:** WXXX Radio Sta Hattiesburg, radio announcer, Miss, 1976; WDAM TV Sta Hattiesburg, weathercaster, reporter, weekend anchor, Miss, 1977; WUSM, reporter, announcer & anchor; Community Rels, dir; Miss radio sta, announcer & news reporter; Going Live, auth, 1998; WWL-TV New Orleans, reporter, 1977-, co-anchor, currently. **Orgs:** MS Press Women, 1977; Am Fed TV & Radio Artists; big sister Big Sisters Greater New Orleans; prog; com mem, St Mark's United Methodlic Church; found, Each One Save One prog, New Orleans. **Honors/Awds:** First place Gen Reporting MS Press Women, 1977; Second place Gen Reporting Nat Asn Press Women, 1977; Gaines Baston Member Award, Am Fed TV & Radio Artists, 1978; TV journalist yr Physically Ltd Asn More Construct Environ, 1979. **Special Achievements:** Author of Going Live: An Anchorwoman Reports Good News; First person to use the term cyber missionary. **Home Addr:** 5831 Kensington Blvd, New Orleans, LA 70127-2808. **Business Addr:** Co-Anchor, WWL-TV, 1024 N Rampart St, New Orleans, LA 70116-2487, **Business Phone:** (504)529-6275.

## CRAFT, DR. THOMAS J., SR.

Educator, administrator, biologist. **Personal:** Born Dec 27, 1924, Monticello, KY; son of Thomas Marion and Wonnie Travis; married Joan Ruth Hunter; children: Thomas J Jr & Yvonne Diane. **Educ:** Cent State Univ, BS, 1948; Ky State Univ, MA, 1950; Ohio State Univ, PhD, 1963. **Career:** Cent State Univ, Instr, 1950-51, from asst prof to assoc prof, 1951-63, prof, 1963-79; Wright State Univ, Med Sch, adj prof, 1973-79; Cent State Univ, emer prof biol, 1979-; Fla Memorial Col, Dept Energy Grant, prog dir, 1980, Natural Scis & Math Div, dir, 1981, instnl planning dir, 1982, dean fac, 1984-87. **Orgs:** Consult, Nat Sci Found, Gujurat Univ, Ahmedebad, India, 1967; Osmania Univ, Hyderabad, India, 1968; NSF NIH Ohio State Dept Health ad hoc consult; investr Res Projs, 1970-77; Exec Comm Ohio Acad Sci, 1975-77; chmn, Res Resources (NIH) Group Minority Bio Med Res, 1976-77; chmn, WSU & Med Sch Anat Fac Search Comm, 1976-77; health sci admin, HEW NIH Div Res Resources, Bethesda, MD, 1977-79; fel Ohio Acad Sci; mem Adv Panel, Educ Devel Ctr, Newton, Mass, 1984-87; bd dir, c servs bd, Greene County, Ohio, 1989-93; fel Aaas; health subcomt, Gov's Comn Disadvantaged Black Male, 1990; bd dir, educ comt; Xenia, Ohio Area Chamber Com; chmn, Wilbert Force Planning & Develop Coun, 1990-; bd dir, Greene Oaks Health Ctr, Xenia, OH, 1993-; chmn, Greene Oaks Health Ctr, 2001-; Sigma Pi Phi Boule. **Home Addr:** 1280 Wenofred Dr, PO Box 252, Xenia, OH 45384, **Home Phone:** (937)372-5006.

## CRAIG, CARL

Musician. **Personal:** Born May 22, 1969, Detroit, MI; married Hannah Sawtell; children: 1. **Career:** Retro Active Label, co-founder, 1990; Planet E Commun, founder, 1991-; Detroit Electronic Music Festival & Ford Focus, artistic dir, 2000-01; Albums: Psyche; Paper Clip People; 69; Designer Music and Inner zone Orchestra; Bug in a Bassbin, 1992; Land cruising, 1995; 69: The Sound of Music, 1995; Paper clip People: The Secret Tapes of Doctor Eich, 1996; More Songs about Food and Revolutionary Art, 1997; Innerzone Orchestra: Programmed, 1999; Designer Music: The Remixes, 2000; Onsumothasheeat, 2001; The Workout, 2002; The Album Formerly Known As, 2005; "Paris Live", 2007; Sessions, 2008; ReComposed, 2008; BBC Radio 1 Essential Mix, 2011. Singles: "No More Words", 1991; "69: 4 Jazz Funk Greats", 1991; "Throw", 1994; "Science Fiction", 1995; "The Climax", 1995; "Floor", 1996; "A Wonderful Life", 2002; "Just Another Day", 2004; "Sparkle / Home Entertainment", 2005; "Darkness/Angel", 2006; "Paris Live", 2007. **Honors/Awds:** Best Label Award for Planet E, Musik Und Maschine Awards, 2001. **Business Addr:** Musician, Planet E Communications, 4221 Cass Ave Apt 900, Detroit, MI 48201, **Business Phone:** (313)831-8771.

## CRAIG, DAMEYUNE VASHON

Football player, football coach. **Personal:** Born Apr 19, 1974, Mobile, AL; married Neke; children: Devin Chanse & Drake Christian. **Educ:** Auburn Col, grad. **Career:** Fotball player (retired), football coach; Auburn Tigers Football, 1994-97; Carolina Panthers, quarterback, 1998-2001; Scottish Claymores, 1999; Arena Football League, 2002; Ind Firebirds, 2002; Wash Redskins, 2002; Ottawa Renegades, 2002; Blount HS, coach, 2003; La State Univ Nick Sabanocos staff, grad asst, 2004; Miami Dolphins, asst coach, 2005; Tuskegee Univ, quarterbacks coach, 2006-07; Univ S Ala, wide receivers coach, 2008-09; Fla State Univ, quarterbacks coach & recruiting coordr, 2010-12; Auburn Univ, co-offensive coordr & wide receivers coach, 2013-; La State Univ, wide reveivers coach, 2016-. **Business Addr:** Wide Receivers Coach, Louisiana State University, 112 Thomas Boyd, Baton Rouge, LA 70803, **Business Phone:** (225)578-1686.

## CRAIG, DR. FREDERICK A.

Oral surgeon. **Personal:** Born Apr 28, 1933, Selma, AL; married Leslie J Cyrusd. **Educ:** Fisk Univ, BS, 1954; MS, 1958; Meharry Med Col, DDS, 1963. **Career:** Fisk Univ, instr, 1956-58; US Post Off, 1958; pvt dent pract, 1966-67; Chicago Bd Health, oral surg, 1967-70; Daniel Hale Williams Neighborhood Health Ctr, dent dir. **Orgs:** Bd dir, Daniel Hale Williams Heighorhood Health Ctr; Dent Subcom Chicago Heart Asn; Ill Soc Oral Surg; Chicago Soc Oral Surg; Am Ill Chicago Dent Socs; Alpha Phi Alpha Frat. **Home Addr:** 7601 S Chappel Ave, Chicago, IL 60649-4128, **Home Phone:** (773)374-2970.

## CRAIG, RHONDA PATRICIA

Judge. **Personal:** Born Nov 27, 1953, Gary, IN; daughter of William and Myrtle Glover; married Fulton Smith Jr; children: Andaiye Spencer & Fulton Douglass. **Educ:** Valparaiso Univ, BA, 1975, Sch Law, JD, 1978. **Career:** Wayne Co Neighborhood Legal Servs, staff atty, 1978-79; Legal Aide & Defender's Off, pub defender, 1979-80; Wayne Co Corp Coun, asst corp coun, 1981; State Mich, admin law examiners, admin law judge, 1982-2011. **Orgs:** Legal Coun Soc Engrs & Appl Scientists, 1982-; Wolverine Bar Asn, 1982-; Asn Black Judges Mich, 1983-; bd dir, Legal Aide & Defender's Asn, 1987; Augusta D Straker Bar Asn. **Honors/Awds:** Spec Achievement Award, SEAS, 1984. **Home Addr:** 17522 Alta Vista Dr, Southfield, MI 48075, **Home Phone:** (248)569-4095. **Business Addr:** Administrative Law Judge, State of Michigan, Mich Plz 1200 6th St Suite 540, Detroit, MI 48226-2418, **Business Phone:** (313)256-2063.

## CRAIG, STARLETT RUSSELL

Educator, lecturer. **Personal:** Born Aug 17, 1947, Asheville, NC; daughter of Robert; children: Kemi & Karma. **Educ:** Spelman Col, BA, social sci, 1969; Bryn Mawr Grad Sch Social Work & Social Res, MSS, 1971; Clemson Univ; Univ NC, Chapel Hill. **Career:** Univ NC, Asheville, dir off aging, 1978-80; Western Carolina Univ, foreign stud adv, asst to vice chancellor stud develop, 1981-89; Clemson Univ, lectr & dir acad progs, currently. **Orgs:** Mem res comn, NC Asn Women Deans, Counors & Admin, 1982-85; grad adv, Alpha Kappa Alpha Sorority, 1984-85; asn int educr, Nat Asn Foreign Stud Affairs; Jackson Co Coun Status Women; mem nat bd, Bardoli Global Inc; mem Diversity Scholar Rev Comt, Am Inst Foreign Study; online mentor, Proj Learning Abroad, Training & Outreach, Loyola Marymount Univ; Citizens World Proj, Clemson Univ. **Home Addr:** RR 04, PO Box 210, Central, SC 29630. **Business Addr:** Lecturer, Director of Academic Excellence, Clemson University, Tillman Hall G11, Clemson, SC 29634-5128, **Business Phone:** (864)656-0676.

## CRAIG-RUDD, JOAN

Government official, manager. **Personal:** Born Oct 5, 1931, Flushing, NY; children: Carolyn Hopkins, Michael & Reginald. **Educ:** Immanuel Lutheran Col, attended 1949; NC Cent Univ, attended 1950; AUS Logistics Mgt Ctr, attended 1969; Nat Contract Mgrs Assoc, sem, 1978. **Career:** USAF Brooklyn, expeditor, 1958-64; AUS NY City, purchasing agt contract negotiator, 1967-71; Otis Afb, procurement specialist, 1971-72; NY City Off Track Betting Corp, contract adminr, contracts compliance officer, mgr contracts, 1975. **Orgs:** Credit union loan comn Off Track Betting Corp, 1976-; Nat Contract Mgrs Assoc, 1976-81; OTBC rep NY City Prevailing Wage Coun, 1981-; OTBC Informal Hearing Officer, 1983-; life mem, Nat Asn Advan Colored People, 1985; peer counr, NY Chap Nat Mult Sclerosis Soc, 1985-

. **Home Addr:** 16842 127th Ave Apt 2A, Jamaica, NY 11434-3125, **Home Phone:** (718)481-9374.

### CRANFORD, DR. SHARON HILL

Executive director, writer. **Personal:** Born Feb 8, 1946, Joaquin, TX; daughter of Garfield (deceased) and Eulalia; married Evies; children: Charlton F & Corey M. **Educ:** Tex Woman's Univ, BA, 1966; Clark Atlanta Univ, MA, educ coun, 1970; Kans State Univ, PhD, adult educ & family coun, 1981. **Career:** Educator (retired), historian, consultant; Tex State Dept Hr, coord vol serv, 1976-77; Jarvis Christian Col, dir stud union, 1977-79; Residential Homes Boys, dir, 1983-84; Wichita State Univ, asst prof, 1984-85; Storyteller with ARISE, Arts Partner with USD 259, historian, 1988-; Cranford Adult Living-Learning Ctrs Inc, exec dir; Hesston Col, diversity dir & instr, 2002-07; self employed consult, 2007-; auth. **Orgs:** Soprano & soloist, Calvary Baptist Ch & Choir, 1984-; corres secy, Links Inc, 1985-87; pub rels chair, Alpha Kappa Alpha Sor Inc, 1985-87; vpres, City Wichita Pub Libr Bd dir, 1985-; Coalition Ment Health; pres, Residential Area Providers Handicapped Serv; Kans State Dept Social Serv Bd, 1987-89; Kans Para Transit Coun; grad adv, Alpha Kappa Alpha Sor Inc. **Home Addr:** 2420 N Dellrose St, Wichita, KS 67220-2903, **Home Phone:** (316)685-0452. **Business Addr:** Diversity Director, Hesston College, 325 S Col Dr, Hesston, KS 67062, **Business Phone:** (620)327-4221.

### CRAVEN, JUDITH B.

Educator, public health official, administrator. **Personal:** Born Jan 1, 1944?, Cleveland, OH; children: 2. **Educ:** Bowling Green State Univ, BS, 1966; Baylor Col Med, MD, 1974; Univ Tex Sch Pub Health, MPH, 1981. **Career:** City Houston Health Dept, chief family health serv, 1978-83; Univ Tex Sch, Allied Health Sci, Houston, Tex, dean, 1983-92; Univ Tex Health Sci Ctr, Houston, vpres, 1987-92; United Way Tex Gulf Coast, pres, 1992-98; Riverside Gen Hosp, chief anesthesia; Boulder Growth & Income Fund Inc, 1998-; Baylor Col Med, clin asst prof community med; Shanghai Med Univ, vis prof pub health; JAE & Assocs LLC, pres, 2002-. **Orgs:** Bd dir, Belo Corp, 1992-; bd dir, bd dir, Sysco Corp, 1996-; bd dir, Luby's Inc, 1998-; Am Pub Health Asn; AMA; bd mem, Variable Annuity Life Ins Co; Compaq Comput Corp; Univ Tex Syst, Austin, Tx, bd regents, 2001-07. **Business Addr:** Board Director, Belo Corp, 400 S Rec St, Dallas, TX 75202-4841, **Business Phone:** (214)977-6606.

### CRAVER, AARON LERENZE

Football player, football coach. **Personal:** Born Dec 18, 1968, Los Angeles, CA; married Dawn; children: Jalen, Kyndol, Maia & Bryce. **Educ:** El Camino Jr Col, grad; Fresno State Univ, grad. **Career:** Football player (retired), football coach; Miami Dolphins, running back & kick returner, 1991-94; Denver Broncos, fullback, 1995-96; San Diego Chargers, fullback, 1997; New Orleans Saints, fullback & tailback, 1998-99; Artesia High Sch, football head coach, currently. **Honors/Awds:** Ed Block Courage Award, 1998. **Special Achievements:** Film: 1992 AFC Championship Game, 1993. **Business Addr:** Football Head Coach, Artesia High School, 12108 Del Amo Blvd, Lakewood, CA 90715, **Business Phone:** (562)926-5566.

### CRAWFORD, BETTY MARILYN

Manager, receptionist. **Personal:** Born Sep 25, 1948, Philadelphia, PA; daughter of James and Dolores Fuller. **Educ:** DC Bible Inst, 1987; Gayles Theol Sem, DC, 1988. **Career:** Univ Pa, receptionist; Internal Revenue Serv, Wash, DC, temp clerk & typist acct dept, acct maintenance clocker, comput systs analyst, 1977-83, prog analyst, 1983-. **Orgs:** Asn Improv Minorities-Internal Revenue Serv, 1972-; Guildfield Baptist Church, Wash, DC, 1983-; dir, Dist Fed Young People DC & Vicinity, 1987-; chmn, Black Employ Prog Mgrs-Internal Revenue Serv, 1988-. **Honors/Awds:** Honored Outstanding Adopt-A-School Volunteer, 1988; Employee of the year, Internal Revenue Serv, 1989. **Special Achievements:** Profiled in Black Enterprise magazine for career accomplishments in 1987. **Home Addr:** 1039 Mich Ave NE, Washington, DC 20017, **Home Phone:** (202)526-8430. **Business Addr:** Program Analyst, Internal Revenue Service Department Of Treasury, 550 Main St, Cincinnati, OH 45202, **Business Phone:** (202)622-8001.

### CRAWFORD, BRENITA

Hospital administrator, educator, president (organization). **Personal:** Born Amory, MS. **Educ:** Jackson State Univ, BS, biol & chem, 1973; Univ Ala, MS, hosp & health admin, 1978; Med Univ, SC, DHA, 2011. **Career:** Professor (retired); Univ Miss; Univ NC, joint res team, data collection; LeBonhuer Med Ctr, admis adminr; Henry Ford Hosp, group vpres, 1986-98, assoc adminr, 1987-91; Mercy Hosp, pres & chief exec officer, 1991-98; Methodist Health Ctr, exec vpres, 1998-2002; Reg Med Ctr, exec asst position, vpres, chief operating officer, 2002-06; Amara Mgt Resources, pres, chief exec officer, 2006-07; Univ Memphis, Div Health Admin, asst prof, 2007-12. **Orgs:** Warren Conner Develop asn; Cancer Found; Greater Detroit Area Health Coun; Healthy Detroit; Am Col Health Care Exec; Am Acad Med Adminrs; m Hosp asn; Nat Ctr Health Leadership; adv bd, Sch Health Related Professions; Univ Ala, Birmingham; Tenn Hosp Asn Coun Diversity; bd, Church Health Ctr; Lifeblood Found bd; Delta Sigma Theta; Am Hosp Asn; adv bd, Sch Health Related Professions. **Home Addr:** 16849 Chandler Pk Dr, Detroit, MI 48224. **Business Addr:** Assistant Professor, University of Memphis, 3720 Alumni Ave, Memphis, TN 38152, **Business Phone:** (901)678-2000.

### CRAWFORD, DR. CARL M.

School administrator, consultant. **Personal:** Born Nov 14, 1932, Tallahassee, FL; married Pearlie Wilson; children: LeVaughn Harrison. **Educ:** Fla A&M Univ, Tallahassee, BA, 1954; Boston Univ, MA, MEd, 1965; Univ Miami Sch Educ, Coral Gables, EdD, 1971. **Career:** Battery D 95th Anti-Aircraft Artil Battalion, Mannheim Ger, exec officer, 1954-56; Dillard Elem Sch Grades 1-6, Ft Lauderdale FL, art, 1956-60, grade 6 1960-61, grade 5, 1961-62, art grades, 1-6, 1962-65; S Fla Sch Desegregation Consult Ctr, Sch Educ, Univ Miami, asst consult, 1965-66, assoc consult, 1966-67; Art Ctr Title III ESEA Proj Broward Co Bd Pub Instr, coordr, comt, 1967-70; Miami-Dade Community Col S Campus, Miami FL, Psychol & Educ Dept, chmn, 1970-73, chmn, self-study steering comt, 1972-73; N Campus Broward Comm Col, dean, 1974-75. **Orgs:** Nat & S Regional Coun Black Am Affairs; Nat Asn Black Sch Educrs; Phi Delta Kappa; Fla Asn Community Col; Am Asn Community & Jr Col; Nat Asn Advan Colored People; Urban League; consult, Ann Fest Arts Nat YMCA Week NW Br YMCA Ft Lauderdale, Fla, 1963-66; consult, World Work Conf Dept Attendance & Equal Educ Oppor, Palm Beach, Fla, 1966; speaker African Art Spring Fest Music/Drama & Art Dillard Comp HS Ft Lauderdale, Fla, 1966; consult, Pinellas Co Teachers Asn Human Rel Coun Conf Integration Sch Fac Chinsegut Hill Univ S Fla, 1968; speaker African Art Cult Enrichment Ser Allapattah Jr HS Miami, Fla, 1968; consult, African ArtIntro to Afro-Am Studies Palm Beach Jr Coll Palm Beach, Fla, 1969; consult, Miami Springs Jr HS HumanizingFac & Studs, 1971; chmn Curric Com S Vis ComEval St Thomas HS Ft Lauderdale, Fla, 1971; reactor SynergyMed Serv sponsored by SAA at Dupont Plaza Hotel Miami, Fla, 1971; secy, Fla Arts Coun, 1980; Samuels Campus, provost. **Honors/Awds:** Distinguished Service Award, Prof Educ Broward Co Teachers Asn, 1967; Outstand Achievement & Serv in the Field of Educ Award Piney Grove 1stBapt Ch, 1971; Award for Appreciation Symbolic of Friends of Educ Mrs Susie H Womack Principal, Sunland Park Elem Sch, 1972; Cert of Recog for Serv as a Resource Bank Vol for Enriching the Classroom Exper of Studs in Broward Co Sch, 1974-75; Appreciation for Outstand Contrib in Fostering Better Comm Rel in Broward Co Award Broward Co Off of Comm Rel, 1975; Outstand Educators of Am in Admin Published by a Div of Fuller & Dees Wash, DC, 1975; Cert of Appreciation for Educ Achievement, The Links Inc, 1975; The Johnnie Ruth Clarke Award for Excell in Comm & Jr Coll Serv S Regional Coun Black Am Affairs Richmond, Va, 1982; Biography in "Black Pioneers of Broward Co" "A acy Revealed" published by The Links Inc The Ft Lauderdale Chap, 1976. **Home Addr:** 2737 NW 24th Ave, Oakland Park, FL 33311-2129, **Home Phone:** (954)731-0270.

### CRAWFORD, CRANFORD L., JR.

Executive. **Personal:** Born Jan 12, 1940, Marshall, TX; married Jennie Henry; married Brenda. **Educ:** Tex S Univ, BA, 1963. **Career:** Reynolds Elec & Engineering Co, sr clerk; Zion Univ Meth Church, black comt developer; Juv Ctr, probation officer, 1970-73; Prot Serv & Juv Prob, supr intake units, 1973-76; Clark City Juv Ctr Servs, prog dir, 1976-87, div supr detention, 1987-. **Orgs:** Vpres, Nat Asn Advan Colored People, 1973-77; life mem, Alpha Phi Alpha NV Chap; Nat Asn Black Soc Workers; Prince Hall Mason; Clark City Comn Christian Social Concerns; Westside Athletic Asn; Alpha Kappa Alpha; grand master, Most Worshipful Prince Hall; MWPH Grand Lodge NV, F&AM, 1985-; Scottish Rite Masson 33 degree; hon mem, imp adv Ophir Temple; AEAONMS; Las Vegas Juv Justice Serv; bd mem, financial secy & house mgr, Las Vegas Black Gospel Theatre, 1990-, treas; Univ United Methodist Church. **Home Addr:** 2215 Matheson St, North Las Vegas, NV 89030-4043, **Home Phone:** (702)642-5291. **Business Addr:** Board Member, House Manager, Las Vegas Black Gospel Theatre, 2215 Matheson St, Las Vegas, NV 89126-3103, **Business Phone:** (702)678-0484.

### CRAWFORD, CURTIS J.

Executive, president (organization), chief executive officer. **Personal:** Born Jan 1, 1947, IL. **Educ:** Joliet Jr Col, AAS; Gov State Univ, BA, bus admin & comput sci, 1972, MA, bus admin & mkt, 1974; DePaul Univ, Charles H Kellstadt Grad Sch Bus, MBA, 1977; Capella Univ, PhD, org & mgt, 2000. **Career:** Int Bus Mach Corp, systs engr, 1973, vpres mkt, 1973-88; AT&T Comput Systs, vpres sls, 1988-91; AT&T Microelectronics, vpres & co-chief exec officer, 1991-93, pres, 1993-95; Lucent Technologies, Micro electronics Grp, pres, 1995-97, grp pres & chief exec officer, 1997-98, Intellectual Property Div, pres, 1997-98; Intellectual Property Div, pres, 1997; DuPont, cor bd mem, 1998-; ZiLOG Inc, chmn, pres & chief exec officer, 1998-2001, chmn bd dirs, 1999-2001; Onix Microsystems Inc, pres & chief exec officer, 2002-03; XCEO Inc, founder, pres & chief exec officer, 2013-. **Orgs:** Bd dir, Lyondell Petrochemical Co; chmn & bd dir, I-Stat Corp; Semiconductor Indust Asn; Nat Action Coun Minority Engrs; bd mem, 1995-96, chairman, 1996-99, iStat Corp; bd dir, ITT Indust Inc, 1996-; Xylem Inc, 1996-; bd trustee, DePaul Univ; bd dir, Agilysys Inc; bd dir, EI du Pont de Nemours Co; bd dir, ON Semiconductor Corp, 1999-; vice chmn, bd dir, ZiLOG Inc; EI DuPont de Nemours & Co. **Business Addr:** Founder, President & Chief Executive Officer, XCEO Inc, 4800 Great America Pky Suite 307, Santa Clara, CA 95054, **Business Phone:** (408)855-0000.

### CRAWFORD, DAN (DANNY CRAWFORD)

Basketball executive. **Personal:** Born Nov 23, 1953, Chicago, IL; married Claudia; children: Drew & Lia. **Educ:** Northeastern Ill Univ, attended 1976. **Career:** Nat Jr Col Nationals, off, 1983-84; Chicagoland Col Athletic Conf, off; Mo Valley Conf, off; Nat Basketball Asn, basketball referee, 1984-85, off, currently; Japan Games, off, 1992; NBA All-Star Games, off, 1994, 2001. **Business Addr:** Official, National Basketball Association, 645 5th Ave, New York, NY 10022, **Business Phone:** (212)407-8000.

### CRAWFORD, DAVID

Administrator, manager, vice president (organization). **Personal:** Born Mar 12, 1941, Charlotte, NC; son of Columbus and Margaret Adams; married Joan McGill; children: Davaree & Darlisa. **Educ:** Johnson C Smith Univ, Charlotte, NC, BS, 1963; Univ Liverpool, Eng, 1964; Univ NC, Chapel Hill, MA, 1966; Rensselaer Polytech Inst, Hartford, CT, MS, 1983. **Career:** Administrator (retired); UTC Pratt & Whitney, E Hartford, CT, mgr, sr controls engr, manpower planning & devel, 1972-75, divisonal supt, mach shop, 1975-78, exec asst to pres, 1978-80, N Haven, CT, prod mgr, 1980-84, Southington, CT, plant mgr, 1984-91, N Haven, CT, plant mgr, 1991-93; Advan Mfg UTC, Pratt & Whitney, plant mgr, dir, 1993-97; consult, 1997. **Orgs:** Bd dir, Conn Pre-Eng Prog, 1990-; vpres, Cheshire Lion Club, 1981-. **Home Addr:** 381 Crestwood Dr, Cheshire, CT 06410-3202, **Home Phone:** (203)272-3703.

### CRAWFORD, DEBORAH COLLINS

Educator, artist, founder (originator). **Personal:** Born Oct 6, 1947, San Antonio, TX; children: Candice Aundrea. **Educ:** Prairie View A&M Col, BS, health, phys educ & fitness, 1969; Our Lady Lake Univ, MEd, sch admin, 1982. **Career:** Educator (retired), exec; St Philips Col, dance instr; Union Carbide, accts recv clk, 1970; Valhalla Sch Dist, pe instr, 1970-71; Summer Camp, White Plains, Pe instr, 1971; Debbie's Darlings Inc, Dance Troupe, dir, 1976-; Alamo Community Col Dist Mgt Workshop, coord insvc, comput literacy instr, 1987; City San Antonio Human Resources, presenter "Why Man Creates"; San Antonio Independent Sch Dist, asst prin; Except Women, Founder; Kingdom Hearts Found, founder & pres; Carver Sch Visual & Performing Arts, coordr, 2006-07. **Orgs:** Am Women Radio & TV, coord, YWCA Sem; lectr, Our Lady Lake Univ Black Hist Activ; Bus & Prof Womens Club; co-emcee, Miss PV Pageant; res person, Nat Asn Advan Colored People State Conv; Links Inc; AKA Sor; Miss Black SAP agt & Choreographer, 1977; Ella Austin Comm Ctrs Bd; St Philips Col Rest Mgt Prog; E side Boys Club; Pine St & Ctr YWCA; Girl Scouts Publicity Com; Nat Asn Advan Colored People publicity com; Youth Philharmonic; Black Expressions Art League; City Fine Arts Comn; Tex State Teachers Asn; Dance Educr Am; Jack & Jill Am; Prairie View A & M Alumni, Nat Conv, publicity chair, 1999; Heights Baptist Church. **Honors/Awds:** Distinguished Public Service Award, Prairie View A&M, 1974; Award Cause Human Dignity Nat Asn Advan Colored People, 1975; nominee Outstanding Young Woman Am, 1976; Service Award, Sr Opportunity Serv Ctr, 1975-76; Model Comn Leaders Award, Miss Black SA Bd, 1976; Community Service Award Walker-Ford Gospel Singers; mayoral appointment Martin Luther King Jr mem Comn City San Antonio Media Chairperson, 1987; city coun appointment arts & cult adv bd; citation Mayor Cisneros & Councilman Webb, Pub Serv, 1989. **Home Addr:** 5641 Galewind Dr, San Antonio, TX 78239-1910, **Home Phone:** (210)599-4227. **Business Addr:** Owner, Dance With A Flair and Creative Services LLC, 5641 Galewind Dr, San Antonio, TX 78239.

### CRAWFORD, H. R.

Housing developer. **Personal:** Born Jan 18, 1939, Winston-Salem, NC; married Eleanora Braxton; children: Leslie, Hazle, George, Gregory & Lynne. **Educ:** Howard Univ, attended 1963; DC Teachers Col, attended 1965; Am Univ, attended 1968; Chicago State Univ, polit sci, BA; NC Archit & Training Univ, hon LLD, 1975. **Career:** Dept Defense, comdr navy yard, 1969-73; Kate Maramont, Rep Victor Degrozia, Chicago, Ill, consult, 1969-73; Nat Asn Home Builders Successful Housing Mgt, lectr, 1969-73; Univ Mich, Taught Successful Housing Mgt, assoc prof, 1969-73; Howard Univ, Sch Archit, assoc prof, 1969-73; Crawford Corp, pres, 1969-73; Kaufman & Broad, vpres & asst mgr, 1971-73; Pollinger & Crawford, vpres & sr mgr, 1972-73; US Dept Housing & Urban Develop, asst secy, 1973-76; Nat Capitol Housing Authority Monteria Ivey, dept dir; Nat Corp Housing Partnership & George DeFranceaux, consult, pres, 1976-79; Mid City Deveop & Eugene Ford, pres, 1976-79; Crawford Edgewood Mgrs Inc, chief exec officer, 1979-, pres, currently; DC Councilman, Ward 7, 1980-92. **Orgs:** Accredited Resident Mgr, Inst Real Estate Mgt; Builders Owners & Mgrs Asn; Nat Asn Housing & Redevel Off; Prof Property Mgrs Asn; Wash Bd Realtors; Wash Planning & Housing Asn; regist apt mgr, Nat Asn Home Builders; Resident Mgrs Asn; dir, Bonabond Inc; Wash DC Adv Bd Recreation; Anacostia Econ Develop Corp; Frederick Douglass Community Ctr; Cong Heights Asn Serv & Educ; Am Cancer Soc; Jr Citizens Corp Inc; pres, Nat Asn Real Estate Brokers, Wash, DC Chap, 1994-96; chmn, DC Real Estate Comn, 1995-; vpres, Nat Asn Advan Colored People, Wash DC Chap, 1995-97; Kiwanis Club; bd dir, Metro Wash Airport Authority; Mayors Comn Veterans Affairs; vpres; Nat Asn Advan Colored People; chmn, pres, Metrop Wash Coun Governments; City Coun; chmn, Eleventh Police Precinct Citizens Adv Coun; chmn, Dc Neighborhood Planning Councils; chmn, Sixth Dist Police Citizens Adv Coun. **Honors/Awds:** IREM Manager of the Year Award, 1973; Distinguished Serv Award, Nat Real Estate Brokers & Omega Tau Rho; Cherokee Indians Goodwill Award. **Special Achievements:** First Minority in Region to Receive CPM Designation, Second in US to Receive CPM Designation. **Home Addr:** 3195 Westover Dr SE, Washington, DC 20020, **Home Phone:** (202)583-7777. **Business Addr:** Chief Executive Officer, President, Crawford Edgewood Managers Inc, 916 Pa Ave SE, Washington, DC 20003, **Business Phone:** (202)547-4300.

### CRAWFORD, JAYNE SUZANNE

Executive director, association executive. **Personal:** Born May 11, 1958, Hartford, CT; daughter of Odell and Beatrice. **Educ:** Lincoln Univ, BA, 1980. **Career:** Inquirer Newspaper Grp, reporter, 1980-82; Focus Mag, assoc ed, 1981-83; Crawford Johnson Assoc, partner, 1981-; Comm Renewal Team, indus organizer, 1983-84, asst, exec dir, vpres direct serv, currently. **Orgs:** Pres, gen chaiman, Urban League Guild Greater Hartford, 1982-85; bd dir, Urban League Greater Hartford, 1982-85; co-chmn, Young Execs, 1983; exec chairperson, New Eng Urban League Guild Network, 1986-87; Key Issues Leadership Forum, Hartford Conrant, 1989-; Leadership Greater Hartford Inc. **Special Achievements:** Co-editor "Beyond Ourselves", Community Renewal Team, 1982. **Home Addr:** 117 Town Colony Dr, Middletown, CT 06457-5901.

### CRAWFORD, KEITH (KEITH LECHARLES CRAWFORD)

Football player. **Personal:** Born Nov 21, 1970, Palestine, TX. **Educ:** Howard Payne Univ. **Career:** Football player (retired); New York Giants, wide receiver, 1993; Green Bay Packers, 1995; St Louis Rams, wide receiver, 1996-97; Kans City Chiefs, 1998; Atlanta Falcons, 1998; Green Bay Packers, wide receiver & safety, 1999.

### CRAWFORD, KERMIT R.

President (organization). **Educ:** Univ Va, MA, res clin & community psychol, 1980; Tex Southern Univ, Pharm Sch, Houston, TX, BS, pharm, 1983. **Career:** Walgreens, pharm intern, 1983, store mgr, dist mgr, 1989, vpres store opers, 2000-04; Walgreens Health Serv, sr vpres, 2005-09; Walgreen Co, pres pharm, health & wellness, 2010-; Health & Wellness Walgreen Co, sr vpres pharm serv, 2007-11, drug-store chain, 2011-, exec vpres & dir, pres pharm, 2013. **Orgs:** Dir, Ctr Mutlicultural Training Psychol, 1998-; dir, Ctr Multicultural Training Psychol, 1998-; dir, Ctr Multicultural Training Psychol, 1998-; dir, Ctr Multicultural Ment Health, Boston Med Ctr, 1999-; dir, Am Diabetes Asn Inc; dir, Nat Asn Chain Drug Stores (NACDS), 2009-; bd counr, Univ Southern Calif, Sch Pharm; bd advisor, Fla A&M Univ, Col Pharm & Pharmaceut Sci Apothecary; Am Pharmaceut Asn; dir,

Northwestern Lake Forest Hosp, 2012-; bd mem, Allstate Corp, 2013. **Business Addr:** Director, Ctr for Multicultural Mental Health, Boston Medical Center, 1 Boston Med Ctr Pl, Boston, MA 02118, **Business Phone:** (617)638-8000.

### CRAWFORD, DR. LAWRENCE DOUGLAS

Mayor, dentist. **Personal:** Born Jun 13, 1949, Saginaw, MI; married Winnie Hill; children: Lawrence D Jr & Alan A. **Educ:** Univ Mich, polit sci, 1970, Dent Sch, DDS, 1974. **Career:** Dentist, 1974-; Town Saginaw, city councilman, mayor, 1981-, secy, currently; DBM Technologies, pres & chief exec officer, currently; Vitec Llc, dir, currently. **Orgs:** Saginaw County Dent Soc; Saginaw Valley Dent Soc; Mich State Dent Asn; Nat Dent Asn; Am Dent Asn; Mid-State Study Club; consult, Univ Mich, Dent Admis Hattie M Strong Found; bd dir, first Ward Community Ctr; commis, ECent Mich Planning Commis; pres, RCA View Develop Corp; Frontier's Int, Black Businessmen's Asn Saginaw; Alpha Phi Alpha Fraternity; E Side Lions Club; Bethel African Methodist Episcopal Church; chair bd dir & chmn, Delta Dent Mich; vice chair, Delta Dent Found; Nat Asn Black Automotive Suppliers; Delta Dent Plan Mich; Delta Dent Bd Dirs, 1989-; bd dir, Minority Bus RoundTable, currently. **Honors/Awds:** Nat Merit Semifinalist; Honor Award, 1967; Frontier's Businessman of the Year, Frontier's Int, Saginaw, 1980; Family Members United Meritorious Service Award, 1980; Professional Achievement Award, Zeta Phi Zeta Sorority, 1981. **Home Addr:** 8590 Hornbeam, Saginaw, MI 48603, **Home Phone:** (989)793-0495. **Business Addr:** Board of Director, Minority Business RoundTable, 1629 K St NW Suite 300, Washington, DC 20006, **Business Phone:** (202)289-8881.

### CRAWFORD, MARGARET WARD

Government official. **Personal:** Born Apr 18, 1937, Pontiac, MI; married Samuel Kenneth Sr; children: Cheryl, Samuel Jr, Gary, Sara Elizabeth & Adrienne Irene. **Educ:** Wayne State Univ, BS. **Career:** Mich Dept Social Serv, social worker, 1960-73; Free Lance Vol, counr, facilitator, polit, soc activist, 1973-; Schrock Adult Care Homes, admin, asst dir, 1980-; Lincoln Consult Schs, pres brd educ. **Orgs:** Mich Assn Sch Brds, 1974-; trustee, Lincoln Schs Brd Edn, 1974-; Nat Assn Sch Brds, 1975-; instr, Mich Dist Cong Christian Educ, 1979-; Speaker &consult, Studs Rights, Spec Educ, Sch Bds manship, Youth Advocacy, State& Fed Legis Impacting Youth, Womens Issues, 1979-; pres, Lincoln SchsBd Educ, 1981-; Sumpter Housing Rehab Coun, 1981-; bd dir, Corner Health Ctr, 1981-82; Legis Comn, 1982-84, Wash tenaw County Black Elected Officials, 1983-; designated friend, Corner Health Ctr, 1983-; Sumpter Twp Polit Action Comn, 1984-; trustee, church clerk, Mt Hermon Missionary Baptist Church, 1984-; Resolutions Comn, 1985-; ex-officio mem, Sumpter Young Women's Assn, 1985-; Sumpter Nat Assn Advan Colored People; Gifted &Talented Spec Educ Child Advoc; mem deleg, Wash tenaw County Sch Off Assn. **Honors/Awds:** Key Award, Mich Asn Sch Bds, 1984; Certificate, Twp School Dist & NatBlack Child Develop Coun. **Home Addr:** 49372 Arkona Rd, Belleville, MI 48111-9687, **Home Phone:** (734)461-9704.

### CRAWFORD, MURIEL C.

Executive. **Educ:** Hampton Univ, BS, 1956; Cuyahoga Comn Col, refresher course architdrawing, 1978; Univ WI Sch Engineering & Sci, attended 1979; Case Western Res Univ Weatherhead Sch Mgt, course bus planning, 1986. **Career:** York Rd Jr HS, art instr, 1956-57; Cleveland Bd Educ, art instr, 1957-69; Charles Eliot Jr HS, chmn art dept, 1967-69; Self-employed, interior designer, 1969-75; The Halle Bros Co, interior designer, 1975-78; Edith Miller Interiors, interior design, 1978-84; Mgt Off Design Inc, pres, 1982-. **Orgs:** Am Soc Interior Designers; Interior Design Educ Tour Eng Am Soc Interior Designers, 1978; designer, Dining Rm Hope House Am Cancer Soc Am Soc Interior Designers Benefit, 1979; vignette designer, March Dimes Gourmet Gala & ASID Benefit, 1984; speaker, Nat Endowment Arts Recognition Women Design Prof, 1985; juror, Nat Coun Interior Design Qualification Qualifying Exam for Interior Design Prof, 1986. **Home Addr:** 1214 Lonewood Dr, El Paso, TX 79925, **Home Phone:** (915)321-4574. **Business Addr:** President, Management of Office Designers Inc, 16611 Chagrin Lee Plz Suite 202, Shaker Heights, OH 44120, **Business Phone:** (216)991-0498.

### CRAWFORD, ODEL

Salesperson, government official, manager. **Personal:** Born Apr 23, 1952, Brownwood, TX; son of Charles Williams and Jewel Crawford Danner; married Catherine Goodwin; children: Vanessa Yvonne, Ashanti Monque & Pharren Rene. **Educ:** Abilene Christian Univ, BS, bus admin & mgt & gen, 1974; Howard Payne Univ, bus law, 1975. **Career:** Mutual Omaha, sales agt, 1976; KMART Corp, asst mgr, 1976-78; Tex Employ Comn, area mgr, 1978-2003; Tex Workforce Comn, prog admin & area mgr, currently; Carver Heights Church Christ, minister, 2004-. **Orgs:** Bd mem, Greater Odessa Chamber Com, 1988-; bd secy, Tex Asn Black Chambers Com, 1988-; bd mem, Odessa Boys & Girls Club, 1988-97; bd mem, Permian Basin Pvt Indust Coun, 1989-92; classroom consult, bd mem, Jr Achievement, Odessa, 1990-96; bd dir, pres, W Tex Adult Literacy Coun, 1991-95; chmn, bd mem, Bus Devel Bd & Enterprise Zone Comt, 1991-96; bd dir, pres, chief exec officer, Black Chamber Com, Permian Basin, 1994-2012; chmn, Tex Asn African Am Chambers Com, 2008-10. **Honors/Awds:** Ebony Bar Award, Black Chamber Com, 1986; Dean K Phillips Award, Nat Vet Training Inst, 1988. **Special Achievements:** Publications: Minorities are Huge Force in Workplace, 1989; Helps to Employers on Hiring and Firing, 1989; Government Provides Many Services to Local and National Small Businesses, 1989. **Home Addr:** 303 Carver Ave, Odessa, TX 79761, **Home Phone:** (915)580-4423. **Business Addr:** Program Administrator, Area Manager, Texas Workforce Commission, 2626 JB Sheppard Pkwy, Odessa, TX 79761-1957, **Business Phone:** (432)367-3332.

### CRAWFORD, PAM SCOTT (PAMELA D CRAWFORD)

Executive. **Personal:** Born Sep 17, 1969, Nyack, NY; daughter of Wilton and Mary; married Vinson. **Educ:** Pa State Univ, BS, polit sci, 1991; Georgetown Univ, JD, 1995. **Career:** US Dist Ct, clerk, 1995-96; Tex Senate, atty, legis aide, 1997-99; Tex Coun Admin Spec Educ, asst dir, 1999-2000, exec dir & gen coun, 2000-; Tex Asn Sch Bd, asst dir; KB Home, dir govt affairs, 2002-05; Real Estate Co, owner, 2004-; Centex Homes, dir govt affairs, 2005-06; Crawford Consult, prin, 2006-09; Pasadena Independent Sch Dist, educr, 2010-. **Orgs:** Sigma Gamma Rho, 1988-91; bd mem, Breast Cancer Resource Ctr, 1999-. **Home Addr:** 11907 Tobler Trail, Austin, TX 78753, **Home Phone:** (512)491-7308. **Business Addr:** Educator, Pasadena ISD Administration, 1515 Cherrybrook Lane, Pasadena, TX 77502, **Business Phone:** (713)740-0000.

### CRAWFORD, RAINEY JAMES

Basketball player, executive. **Personal:** Born Jan 1, 1940?, St. Louis, IL; married Thelma J Fields; children: Sharon Marie (Calvin Butler). **Educ:** Southern Ill Univ, BS, educ, MS, educ; Mich State Univ, MBA, advan mgt. **Career:** Baseball player (retired); Webster Univ, adj prof; Mo Nat Guard, officer; St Louis Cardinals Baseball Asn; Kans City Athletics Baseball Asn; Ford Motor Co, labor rels mgr, chief labor contract negotiator & dir reg govt affairs, 1994-2001; Off Chief Army Res, army res ambassador, currently; First Watch Environ Recycling & Consults, pres & chief exec officer, currently; TCG Consults, owner & pres, currently, Crawford Group Unlimited LLC, chmn & chief exec officer, currently. **Orgs:** Corp Round Table; bd mem, Citizenship Sports Alliance; bd mem, Mo Chamber Com; bd mem, Ark State Chamber Com. **Business Addr:** Director, Ford Motor Co, PO Box 6248, Dearborn, MI 48126.

### CRAWFORD, VANESSA REESE

Executive, administrator. **Personal:** Born Dec 30, 1952, Petersburg, VA; daughter of Richard A Reese Jr and Esther Elizabeth Taylor Reese (deseased); married Leon; children: Latricia, Richard, Roderick, Cornell II, Leon Jr & Courtney. **Educ:** Va Commonwealth Univ, Richmond, VA, BS, 1974. **Career:** Cent State Hosp, Petersburg, Va, social worker, 1974-78; Chesterfield Correctional Unit, Chesterfield, Va, counr, 1978-85, asst supt, 1985-87; Dinwiddie Correctional Unit, Church Rd, Va, asst supt, 1987-89; New Kent Correctional Unit, Barhamsville, Va, supt, 1989-91; Pocahontas Correctional Unit, Chesterfield County, Va, supt, 1991-99; Va Dept Corrections, Res & Mgt Servs, lead analyst, 2000-03; City Petersburg, sheriff, currently. **Orgs:** Bethany Baptist Ch, 1961; Nat Asn Blacks Criminal Justice, 1980; Am Bus Women's Asn, 1987; Petersburgh Chap 33 Order Eastern Star, 1989; secy, Parent & Dist Adv Coun, Petersburg Sch, 1990; Nat Asn Female Execs, 1990-; Dist 19 Community Serv Bd, Petersburg, Va, 1993; chair, Camelot Neighborhood Watch Asn; Petersberg Symphony Orchestra Women's Comt; mentor, Va Commonwealth Univ; pres, Petersburg High Sch Boosters Club; bd dir, Town & Country Nursery Sch Found; bd dir, Burger King, Communities Sch; parent adv coun, Petersburg High Sch; teenage pregnancy coun-Southside Regional Med Ctr; Petersburg Pub Sch, Character Educ Task Force; Nat Asn Negro Bus & Prof Women's Club, Petersburg chp, financial secy; Appomatox Reg Gov Sch, bd mem; Petersburg Task Force Domestic Violence; Am Cancer Bd, Petersburg chap; Petersburg Police Athletic League; trustee, Good Shepherd Baptist Church; Civilian Rev Bd; vpres, Petersburg Kiwanis Lunch Club; Women's Comt Petersburg Symphony Orchestra; bd dir, Va Sheriff's Asn; pres, Petersburg-Dinwiddie Crime Solvers. **Home Addr:** 1616 Kings Rd, Petersburg, VA 23805, **Home Phone:** (804)732-6344. **Business Addr:** Sheriff, The Petersburg Sheriff's Office, 8 Courthouse Ave, Petersburg, VA 23803, **Business Phone:** (804)733-2369.

### CRAWFORD, VERNON DEAN, JR.

Football player, football coach. **Personal:** Born Jun 25, 1974, Texas City, TX. **Educ:** Fla State Univ, criminol. **Career:** Football player (retired), coach; New Eng Patriots, linebacker, 1997-99; Green Bay Packers, 2000; New York/NJ Hitmen, 2001; Manchester Wolves, 2004; Curry Col, defensive coordr, coach; Randolph High Sch, defensive coordr, coach; Walpole Sch Dist, defensive coordr; Randolph Community Mid Sch, RRR room, currently; Seekonk High Sch, head football coach, 2012-. **Business Addr:** Head Football Coach, Seekonk High School, 261 Arcade Ave, Seekonk, MA 02771, **Business Phone:** (508)336-7272.

### CRAWFORD, VICTOR L.

President (organization), manager. **Educ:** Boston Col, BS, acct, 1983. **Career:** Pepsi-Cola Bottling Co, finance, sales & gen mgr, 1990; Marriott Int, sr vpres, 2000-05, exec vpres & gen mgr, 2001-03, Eastern div chief operating officer, 2002-05; PBG's Mid-Atlantic Bus Unit, sr vpres & gen mgr, 2005-06; Pepsi Bottling Group, sr vpres & gen mgr, 2005-07, worldwide opers sr vpres, 2006-08, Field Opers, pres, 2006-, Global Opers & Syst Transformation, sr vpres, 2008-10; Pepsi Beverages Co, exec vpres supply chain & syst transformation, 2010-11; PepsiCo, pres N Am field opers, 2010-12; ARAMARK Healthcare, group pres & chief operating officer, 2012-15, group pres & chief operating officer healthcare, educ & facil, 2015-. **Orgs:** Bd trustee, Nat Urban League; bd mem, Exec Leadership Coun; bd mem, Pepsi Bottling Group Found; bd mem, Int Foodservice Distribr Assoc; bd mem, Greater Chicago Chamber Com; chairperson, Chicago Coun Urban Affairs; Col Fund Telethon. **Honors/Awds:** "Black Enterprise," The 100 Most Powerful Executives in Corporate America, 2010.

### CRAWFORD-MAJOR, TONI

Executive director. **Educ:** Colo Univ, BA, jour, 1977. **Career:** Philadelphia Tribune, dir commun, 1991-93; Common Wealth Pa, Dept Community & Econ Develop, Southeast regional dir, currently; Gov Ctr Local Govt Serv, exec dir, currently. **Orgs:** Mem serv mgr, Philadelphia Conv & Visitors Bur, 1993-96. **Business Addr:** Southeast Regional Director, Common Wealth of Pa, 801 Mkt St Suite 6106, Philadelphia, PA 19107, **Business Phone:** (215)560-2083.

### CRAWLEY, BETTYE JEAN. See BROWN, BETTYE JEAN.

### CRAWLEY, DARLINE H.

Government official. **Personal:** Born Sep 3, 1941, St. Louis, MO; married Lou E. **Career:** Real estate entrepreneur; City Pagedale, MO, alderwoman ward 3. **Orgs:** Women Leadership; deaconess, Fifth Baptist Church. **Home Addr:** 1835 Ferguson Ave, St Louis, MO 63133-1815, **Home Phone:** (314)721-1708. **Business Addr:** Alderwoman, City of Pagedale, 1404 Ferguson Ave, St Louis, MO 63133, **Business Phone:** (314)726-1200.

### CRAWLEY, GEORGE CLAUDIUS

Government official. **Personal:** Born Mar 19, 1934, Newport News, VA; married Cynthia Hewitt; children: Judith Johnson & Jason. **Educ:** Va State Univ, BA, econs, 1956. **Career:** Government official (retired); Newport News Redevelop & Housing Authority, mgr-trainee, 1956-57, housing mgr, 1963; Southeastern Tidewater Oppor Proj, assoc exec dir to exec dir, 1966-73; City Norfolk, div social serv dir, 1973-76, dept human resources dir, 1976-83, city mgrs off asst city mgr, 1983-96; Norfolk Pub Schs Found Inc, city mgr. **Orgs:** Dir, Legal Serv Corp VA, United Way Tidewater, Athletic Found Norfolk State Univ; Darden Sch Bus, Univ VA Inst Mgt, Southeastern Tide water Manpower Auth; Norfolk Investment Corp; founder, Southeastern Tidewater Opportunity Proj Organ; chmn, Hampton Roads Alumni Group Va State Univ; dir, Va State Univ Alumni, adv bd; dir, Girls & Boys Club Hampton Rds VA, St John AME Church; secy, Elizabeth City State Univ; United Way S Hampton Roads Found; bd trustee mem, United Way Found; bd mem, SHARE Mid-Atlantic; bd mem, Norfolk Pub Schs Found Inc; charter mem bd trustee, Norfolk Cosmopolitan Found. **Home Addr:** 1466 Holly Point Rd, Norfolk, VA 23509-1213, **Home Phone:** (757)627-1466.

### CRAWLEY, DR. OSCAR LEWIS, SR. See Obituaries Section.

### CRAWLEY, SYLVIA

Basketball coach, basketball player. **Personal:** Born Sep 27, 1972, Steubenville, OH; daughter of James and Marie. **Educ:** Univ NC, BA, commun & radio, tv & motion pictures, 1994; Aenon Bible Col, ministerial lic. **Career:** Int teams: Rouen, France; Vigo, Spain; Reggio, Italy; Lugo, Spain; Pro Europ League, 1994-96, 1999-2000; World Univ Games, 1995; Jones cup, 1996; Colo Explosion, 1996-99; Portland Power, forward, 1996-99; Pan Am Games, 1999; Am Basketball League, Portland Fire, forward, 2000-02; Univ NC, asst coach, 2000-02; San Antonio Silver Stars, 2003; San Antonio Spurs & Stars, mgt; Fordham Univ, top asst; Korea, player, 2005; Fordham rams, interim head coach, 2006; Ohio Bobcats, Ohio Univ, head coach, 2006-08; Monarch Mag, co-founder & publ; Boston Coll Eagles, head coach, 2008-12. **Orgs:** Nat Collegiate Athletic Asn, 1994; Atlantic Coast Conf, 1994. **Home Addr:** 3016 SW 153rd Dr, Beaverton, OR 97006. **Business Addr:** Head Coach, Ohio University, Convocation Ctr, Athens, OH 45701, **Business Phone:** (740)593-1193.

### CRAY, ROBERT

Guitarist, singer, actor. **Personal:** Born Aug 1, 1953, Columbus, GA; son of Henry and Maggie; married Susan Turner. **Career:** The Robert Cray Band, leader, 1974-. Albums: Who's Been Talkin', 1980; Bad Influence, 1983; False Accusations, 1985; Strong Persuader, 1986; "Smoking Gun", 1986; "I Guessed I Showed Her", 1987; "Right Next Door", 1987; "Nothin' But A Woman", 1987; "Don't Be Afraid of the Dark", 1988; "Night Patrol", 1988; Don't Be Afraid Of The Dark, 1988; "Acting This Way", 1989; "Consequences", 1990; "The Forecast (Calls for Pain)", 1990; Midnight Stroll, 1990; "Just a Loser", 1992; I Was Warned, 1992; Shame+ A Sin, 1993; "1040 Blues", 1993; Some Rainy Morning, 1995; "Baby Lee", 1996; Sweet Potato Pie, 1997; Take Your Shoes Off, 1999; Should a Been Home, 2001; Time Will Tell, 2003; Twenty, 2005; Live From Across The Pond, 2006; Live At The BBC, 2008; This Time, 2009; Cookin' In Mobile, 2010; "You Move Me", 2014. Home video appearances include: Hail! Hail! Rock 'n' Roll, tribute to Chuck Berry, 1988; Break Every Rule, HBO spec with Tina Turner, 1987; 24 Nights, concert video with Eric Clapton, 1991; The Robert Cray Collection, music, videos, live performances, interviews, 1991; Hoodoo U Voodoo live pay per view concert, with the Rolling Stones, 1994; MTV Unplugged: Ballads, 2000; Through Riley's Eyes, 2000; John Lee Hooker: That's My Story, 2001; Lightning in a Bottle, 2004; "Biography", 2004; "The Late Late Show with Craig Ferguson", 2005; "Crossroads Guitar Festival", with Eric Clapton, 2007. Film: Animal House, actor, 1978; Otis Day & the Knights, actor. TV series: "The Tonight Show with Jay Leno", 1995; "Robert Cray: Cookin' in Mobile", 2010; "Nothin But Love", 2012; "In My Soul", 2014; "4 Nights Of 40 Years Live", 2015. **Honors/Awds:** Rolling Stone critics, Best R&B Artist; five Grammy Awards, six additional Grammy nominations; San Francisco Bay Area Music Awards, BAMMIE; numerous awards by Northwest Area Music Asn; numerous W C Handy Awards; Blues Hall of Fame, Showdown!, 1989; platinum & gold status albums worldwide. **Business Addr:** Musician, c/o Grabow & Associates, 4219 Creekmeadow Dr, Dallas, TX 75287-6806, **Business Phone:** (972)250-1162.

### CRAYTON, DR. JAMES EDWARD

Administrator, library administrator. **Personal:** Born Dec 18, 1943, Thomasville, AL; son of Bennie and Ernestine. **Educ:** Ala State Univ, BS, 1964; Atlanta Univ, MLS, 1968; Calif State Univ, Long Beach, MA, 1975; Claremont Grad Sch, PhD, higher educ admin, 1980. **Career:** Educator (retired); Milton, Fla Sch Dist, 1964-65; Cobb Co Bd Educ Austell Ga, 1965-67; Anaheim Pub Lib, 1968-70; Los Angeles County Pub Lib, 1970-72; Pasadena City Col, libr, 1972-78, teacher & coordr, acquisitions librn, 1972-80, dir occup educ, 1980, Community Educ Ctr, div dean. **Orgs:** Mem coun, Calif Lib Asn; minority adv, 1973-74; chmn, Black Caucus Leg Comm; Nat AsnAdvan Colored People LA Urban League. **Home Addr:** 5440 Weatherford Dr, Los Angeles, CA 90008. **Business Addr:** Division Dean, Community Education Centers, 35 Fairfield Pl, West Caldwell, NJ 07006, **Business Phone:** (973)226-2900.

### CREARY, LUDLOW BARRINGTON

Physician, educator. **Personal:** Born Nov 17, 1930, Kingston; son of Creary; married Lou Jene. **Educ:** Long Island Univ, BS, 1956; Howard Univ, MD, 1960; Univ Calif, Los Angeles, MPH, 1972. **Career:** Educator (retired); Wayne Co Hosp Detroit, internship, 1960-61; Ventura Co Hosp CA, resident family pract, 1961-63; Broadway Hosp, chief med, 1969-72; Martin Luther King Jr Hosp, 1970; W Adams Community Hosp, chief med staff, 1971-72; Charles R Drew Postgrad Med Sch; Drew Med Ctr, chmn, prof, 1981-2000; Univ Calif Los Angeles, Univ Med & Sci, prof & chmn, Dept Family Med, chief serv, prof, 1972-2001; pvt pract, currently; VALA, owner, med dir, 2001-. **Orgs:** Am Acad Family physicians; Los Angeles County Med Asn; bd trustee, Calif Acad family physicians found; Nat Med Asn; Golden State Med Asn; Charles R. Drew Med Soc & Imp Partners. **Honors/Awds:** General Practitioner of the Year, Nat Med Asn, 1976; Physician Award as Active Teachers in Family Medicine, Am Acad Family Physicians, 1977; Outstanding Service Award, Bd Dirs, Calif Blue Shield, 1977-86; Meritorious Service Award, Western Pk Hosp Med Ctr, 1984; Distinguished Physician Award, Minority Health Inst, 1996. **Home Addr:** 1315 Carla Lane, Beverly Hills, CA 90210.

**CREFT, BRENDA K.**
Medical researcher. **Educ:** Northwestern State Univ. **Career:** Travis AFB, David Grant USAF Med Ctr, col, chief nurse, dir nursing, currently. **Business Addr:** Director of Nursing, Travis Air Force Base, 101 Boden Cir, Travis Air Force Base, CA 94535, **Business Phone:** (707)423-7720.

**CREIGHTON, LORENZO DAVID**
Executive, businessperson. **Personal:** Born Jan 5, 1953, Waterloo, IA; son of David and Lucille Fox; married Lisa; children: 5. **Educ:** Luther Col, BA, polit sci, 1975; Drake Univ Law Sch, JD, 1988. **Career:** Iowa Department of Corrections, interviewer for Pre-Trial Release Project; National Bank of Waterloo, marketing director, 1978-85; Iowa Department of Personnel, labor contract negotiator and consultant, 1988-89; Iowa Racing and Gaming Commission, deputy director, 1989; Mississippi Gaming Commission, executive director; Lady Luck, Natchez, MS, general manager; President Casinos, St. Louis, MO, general manager; Bally's Casino, New Orleans, LA, vice president of operations, 1995-2001; Flamingo Hilton, Las Vegas, pres, 2002-05; New York New York Hotel and Casino, Las Vegas, president and COO, 2005; MGM Grand Detroit, president and COO; Gateway Casinos, Vancouver, Canada, chief exec officer, 2010-12; MGM National Harbor, president and COO, 2012-. **Special Achievements:** First African-American property president on the Las Vegas strip, and president of a major Las Vegas casino resort, 2002. **Business Addr:** MGM National Harbor, 120 Waterfront St Suite 500B, National Harbor, MD 20745.

**CREIGHTON-ZOLLAR, DR. ANN**
Educator. **Personal:** Born Sep 16, 1946, Thomasville, AL; daughter of Thomas E and Jimmie A Gordon; children: James A & Nicai Q. **Educ:** Univ Ill Chicago, BA, sociol, 1973, MA, sociol, 1976, PhD, sociol, 1980. **Career:** Garfield Pk Comprehenisve Comm Health Ctr, supvr res & eval, 1979-80; VaCommonwealth Univ, asst prof sociol, 1981-88, Afro-Am Studies Prog, actg coordr, 1984-85, Dept Sociol & Anthrop, assoc prof, 1988-2010, African Am Studies Prog, from interim dir to dir, 1993-98, prof emerita, 2010-. Books: A Member of the Family: Strategies for Black Family Continuity, 1985; Adolescent Pregnancy and Parenthood: An Annotated Guide, 1990; The Social Correlates of Infant and Reproductive Mortality in the U.S: A Reference Guide, 1993. **Orgs:** Phi Kappa Phi Nat Hon Soc, 1973. **Business Addr:** Professor Emerita, Virginia Commonwealth University, Rm 224 Hibbs Bldg 900 Pk Ave, Richmond, VA 23284-2547, **Business Phone:** (804)827-1349.

**CRENSHAW, DR. REGINALD ANTHONY**
Research scientist, college administrator. **Personal:** Born Sep 29, 1956, Mobile, AL; son of Johnnie Mae; married Portia LaVerne Johnson; children: Dante, ReginaldJr & Whitney. **Educ:** Morehouse Col, BA, econs, 1978; Univ S Ala, MPA, pub admin, 1984; Univ Southern Miss, PhD, higher educ admin. **Career:** Mattie T Blount HS, high sch instr, 1978-79; City Prichard, councilman & pres, 1980-88; Bishop State Community Col, res analyst, instr & dir stud servs, 1980-; Ala State Dist, pres; Dist 3 Comnr, 2008-; Ala State Univ, adj instr. **Orgs:** Adv bd, Commonwealth Nat Bank, 1982-; bd dir, Mobile Co Urban League, 1983-; vpres bd dir, Deaborn St Com Ctr, 1984-; vpres, Beta Omicran Lambda Chap Alpha Phi Alpha Fraternity; pres, Nat Leadership Develop Comt; Highpoint Baptist Church; founder & chmn, Highpoint Educ & Community Enrichment Found Bd; comnr, Mobile County Sch Bd, 2009; pres, Mobile Alumni Chap; dir, Title III Progs, currently dir, Off Instnl Res & Develop. **Honors/Awds:** Man of the Year Award, Alpha Phi Alpha Frat, 1980; UNCF Distinguished Leadership Award, 1982 & 1983; Mobilian of the Year Award, Mobile Chap Phi Beta Sigma Frat, 1983; Community Leadership Award, Ladies Auxiliary knights Peter Claver, 1984. **Home Addr:** 1021 Sample St, Prichard, AL 36610. **Business Addr:** Commissioner, District 3, Mobile County Public Schools, 1 Magnum Pass, Mobile, AL 36618, **Business Phone:** (251)221-4387.

**CRENSHAW, WAVERLY DAVID, JR.**
Lawyer, administrator. **Personal:** Born Dec 17, 1956, Nashville, TN; son of Waverly D Sr and Corinne Smith. **Educ:** Vanderbilt Univ, BA, Law Sch, 1978, JD, 1981. **Career:** Chancery Ct, legal coun chancellors, 1981-82; US Dist Judge John T Nixon, law clerk, 1982-84; State Tenn, asst atty gen, 1984-87; pvt law pract, 1987-; Law firm Passino, Delaney & Hildebrand, assoc, 1987-90; Waller Lansden Dortch & Davis, assoc, 1990-, atty & partner, 1994-; Vanderbilt Univ Sch Law, adj law fac, 1994; Us Dist Ct Mid Dist Tenn, Us Dist Judge, 2015. **Orgs:** Civil Justice Reform Act Adv Group, Us Dist Ct, Mid Dist Tenn; comt mem, Bd Prof Responsibility Supreme Ct Tenn; staff mem & Ed bd mem, Vanderbilt J Transnational Law, 1979-81; Panel Selection US Magistrate, 1984; pres, Napier-Looby Bar Asn, 1986-87; bd mem, Nashville Bar Asn Young Lawyers Div, 1986; bd mem, Mid Tenn, Am Civil Liberties Union, 1986-88; bd mem, Nashville Urban League, 1986-90; Chancellors Comt Women & Minorities, Vanderbilt Univ, 1987; bd mem, Tenn Capital Case Resource Ctr, 1988-92; Charter mem, Harry Phillips Am Inst Ct; Am Bar Asn; Nashville Elec Servs Ethics & Audit Comn, 1992-; bd govs, Nashville Area Chamber Com, 1994-97, legal coun, 1995-96; secy, treas, Gen Coun & dir, Nashville Bar Asn, 1994-97; legal coun, 100 Black Men Tenn Inc; legal coun, Nashville Area Chamber Com, 1996; chmn, Merit Selection Panel US Magistrate, US Dist Ct, Mid Dist Tenn, 1997-98; chmn, Tenn Supreme Ct's Adv Comt, 2004; life mem, Conf Sixth Judicial Circuit Us; bd mem, chmn, Labor & Employ Sect, Tenn Bar Asn, 2005; bd dir, Boys & Girls Clubs Mid Tenn Inc; mayoral appointment, Hosp Authoritys bd dir Nashville; bd dir, Mid Tenn Workforce Develop Bd; adj instr pressional ethics, Vanderbilt Univ Sch Law Pressional Licenses; fel Nashville Bar Found; fel Tenn Bar Found; mem & bd chair, Metropolitian Nashville Hosp Authority Bd trustee, 2008; bd mem, Tenn Independent Cols & Univs Asn; Nat Asn Col & Univ Attorneys; Leadership Nashville, 2009. **Home Addr:** 895 Oak Valley Lane, Nashville, TN 37220-1123, **Home Phone:** (615)269-8867. **Business Addr:** Attorney, Waller Lansden Dortch & Davis, 511 Union St Suite 2700, Nashville, TN 37219, **Business Phone:** (615)850-8909.

**CREUZOT, CHERYL D.**
Financial manager. **Personal:** Born May 9, 1959, Washington, DC; daughter of David and Gloria Williams; married Percy P III; children: Percy P IV, Coline M & Philippe P. **Educ:** Univ Houston, BS, bus technol, 1981; Col Financial Planning, cert, financial planner, 1985-; Col Financial Planning, attended 1985; Univ Houston Law Ctr, JD, taxation, 1992, LLM, taxation law, 1999, C.T. Bauer Col Bus, MBA, 2012; Univ Calif, Berkeley, cert, financial statement anal. **Career:** AFP Group, financial planner, 1983-99, pres & chief operating officer, 1999-2001; Wealth Develop Strategies LLC, pres & chief exec officer, 2001-, managing partner, currently. **Orgs:** Financial Planning Asn, 1985-; Million Dollar Round Table, 1989-; bd dir & finance comm, Proj Row Houses, 1991-; State Bar Tex, 1992-; Tex Pub Finance Authority Bd, 1993-99, vice chairwomen, 1995-97; state co-chairperson, Dem Nat Comms Women Leadership Forum, 1996-; bd dir, African Am Arts Mus, 2000-; bd dir, Ensemble Theatre, 2000-; chair, Univ Houston Alumni Orgn; chair, Mus Fine Arts 5A Gala, 2004; chair, United Negro Col Fund Black Tie Gala, 2005; Nat Coalition 100 Black Women; chair, Tex Women's Empowerment Found; regist player financial advisor, Nat Football League; vice chair, Houston Mus African Am Cult; bd, Unity Nat Bank; mem bd, Proj Row Houses; mem bd, Menil Collection; trustee, Univ Houston Found; bd dir, MD Anderson Univ Cancer Found. **Honors/Awds:** Financial Planner Month, Mutual Funds Mag, 2000; Super Achiever Award, Greater Houston YMCA, 2001; March of Dimes, 2002, 2004, 2006; Leadership Empowerment Award, National Black MBA, Houston Chapter, 2004; Corporate Sector Achievement Award, Univ Houston Law Alumni Asn, 2008; Woman of Distinction, Houston Crohn's & Colitis Found, 2008. **Special Achievements:** One of the Top 100 Advisors in the country, Mutual Funds Magazine, 2001 & 2002. **Home Addr:** 3701 S MacGregor Way, Houston, TX 77021, **Home Phone:** (713)748-8464. **Business Addr:** Managing Partner, President, Chief Executive Officer, Wealth Development Strategies LP, 4203 Montrose Blvd 5th Fl, Houston, TX 77006, **Business Phone:** (713)561-8100.

**CREW, DR. RUDOLPH FRANKLIN (RUDY CREW)**
School administrator. **Personal:** Born Sep 10, 1950, Poughkeepsie, NY; son of Eugene. **Educ:** Babson Col, Wellesley, MA, BA, mgt, 1972; Univ Mass, Amherst, MEd, urban educ, 1972, DEd, educ admin, 1974. **Career:** Boston Pub Schs, dep supt curric & instr, 1985-87; Sacramento City Unified Sch Dist, supt, 1988-93; Tacoma Pub Schs, supt, 1993-95; Calif State Univ, Sacramento, adj asst Prof urban educ, 1995-97; San Antonio High Sch, Claremont, Calif, adminr; New York Bd Educ, chancellor, 1996-2000; Univ Wash's Inst K-12 Leadership, exec dir, 2000-02; Stupski Found, exec, 2001-03; Harvard Grad Sch Educ, assoc educ; Calif State Univ, adj asst prof; Lesley Col, adj prof; Wash, Tacoma Schs, supt; Miami-Dade County Pub Schs, supt, 2004-08; Presidents Educ Policy Coun, Advisor, 2009-; Univ Southern Calif's Rossier Sch Educ, prof Clin Educ, 2009-; Ore state, chief educ officer, 2012-; Medgar Evers Col, pres, 2013-. **Orgs:** Lincoln Ctr Performing Arts; New York Philharmonic; Wash Asn Black Sch Educr; bd mem, Fred Hutchinson Cancer Res Ctr, 2000-; bd mem, Ctr Arts Educ. **Business Addr:** Professor, USC Rossier School of Education, Waite Phillips Hall, Los Angeles, CA 90089, **Business Phone:** (213)740-2833.

**CREW, SPENCER R.**
Curator, president (organization), chief executive officer. **Personal:** Born Jan 7, 1949, Poughkeepsie, NY; son of R Spencer and Ada L Scott; married Sandra Lorraine Prioleau; children: Alika L & Adorn S. **Educ:** Brown Univ, Providence, RI, AB, 1971; Rutgers Univ, Nb, NJ, MA, 1973, PhD, hist, 1979. **Career:** Univ Md, Baltimore Co, asst prof, 1978-81; Smithsonian Inst, Natl Mus Am Hist, historian, 1981-87; Nat Mus Am Hist, historian, 1981, Div Community, cur, 1987-89, chair, Dept Social & Cult Hist, 1989-91, dep dir, 1991-92, actg dir, 1991-92; dir, 1994-2001; Nat Underground Rr Freedom Ctr, exec dir, pres & chief exec officer, 2001-. **Orgs:** Prog chair, 1985-86, exec bd mem, 1986-90, Oral HistMid-Atlantic Region; mem Oral Hist Asn, 1988-; 2nd vpres African Am Mus Asn, 1988-91; prog co-chair, Oral Hist Asn, 1988; comnr & bd mem, Banneker-Douglass Mus, 1989-93; ed bd mem, J Am Hist, 1989-93; prog chair, African Am Mus Asn, 1989; sr youth group coordr, St John Baptist Church, 1989, co-ed, Newsletter Am Hist Asn, 1990-; trustee, Brown Univ, 1995-; bd mem Am Asn Mus, 1995-98; chair, Nat Coun Hist Educ; bd mem, Nat Trust Hist Preserv, currently. **Honors/Awds:** Osceola Award, Delta Sigma Theta Sorority, 1988; Cert Award, Smithsonian Inst, 1989-92; Robert A. Brooks Award, Smithsonian Inst, 1994; Service Award, Asn Study African Am Life & Hist, 1994; Hall of Distinguished Alumni Inductee, Rutgers Univ, 2003; McMickmen Col Distinguished Leadership Award, Univ Cincinnati, 2004. **Special Achievements:** Author: Field to Factory: Afro-American Migration 1915-40, 1987; Co-cur: "Go Forth and Serve: Black Land Grant Colleges Enter a Second Century", 1990, "African American Images in Postal Service Stamps", 1992; Black Life in Secondary Cities: A Comparative Analysis of the Black Communities of Camden and Elizabeth, NJ, 1860-20, 1993; Published extensively in the areas of African Am Hist & Pub Hist; co-auth, "The American Presidency: A Glorious Burden", 2002; Inducted to the Rutgers Hall of Distinguished Alumni, 2003; Youngest & the First African-American Director of a Major Smithsonian Museum. **Home Addr:** 2914 Fairfield Ave, Cincinnati, OH 45206, **Home Phone:** (513)961-0723. **Business Addr:** President, Chief Executive Officer, National Underground Railroad Freedom Center, 50 E Freedom Way, Cincinnati, OH 45202, **Business Phone:** (513)333-7500.

**CREWS, DONALD**
Writer, illustrator. **Personal:** Born Aug 30, 1938, Newark, NJ; son of Marshanna White and Asa H; married Ann Jonas; children: Nina Melissa & Amy Marshanna. **Educ:** Cooper Union Advan Sci & Art, New York, NY, cert completion, 1959. **Career:** Dance Mag, NY, asst art dir, 1959-61; Will Burton Studios, NY, staff designer, 1961-62; freelance designer for various employers, auth & illusr, 1979; Books: We Read: Ten Black Dots, 1968; Freight Train, 1978; Caldecott Honor, 1979; Truck, 1980; Caldecott Honor, 1981; Carosel, 1982; School Bus, 1984; A to Z, 1984; Bicycle Race, 1985; Flying, 1986; Harbor, 1987; Bigmamas, 1991; Each Orange Had 8 Slices, illusr, 1992; Shortcut, 1992; Sail Away, 1995; Night at the Fair, 1998; Tomorrow's Alphabet, illusr, 1999; Cloudy Day Sunny Day, 1999; This is the Sunflower, illusr, 2000; Inside Freight Train, 2001; Video: Parade, 1983; Fair, 1998; HarperCollins C's Books, auth, currently. **Honors/Awds:** Caldecott Honorable Award, Freight Train, 1979, Truck, 1980, Am Library Asn; NYT, Ten Best Illustrated Books for Flying, 1986. **Home Addr:** 263 Northern Blvd, PO Box 279, Germantown, NY 12526-0279, **Home Phone:** (518)537-4676. **Business Addr:** Author, HarperCollins Childrens Books, 1350 Avenue of the Americas, New York, NY 10019-4703, **Business Phone:** (212)261-6644.

**CREWS, VICTORIA WILDER**
State government official, counselor. **Personal:** Born Sep 18, 1946, Brownsville, TN; daughter of Calvin C Sr and Eutropia B; children: Christine, Charles & Kara. **Educ:** Franklin Univ, bus admin, 1985; Ohio Dominican Col, attended 1987. **Career:** Govt off (retired); Ohio Dept Health, ade asst, 1969-87; Ohio Dept Alcohol & Drug Addiction Servs, crd women's progs, 1987-90, mgr, prevservs unit, 1990, chief div prev serv, 2000. **Orgs:** Gov Nat Educ Goals, 1991-92; Gov Head Start Collab, 1991-92; adv bd, Ohio Prev & Educ Resource Ctr, 1990-92; Gov Drug-Exposed Infants Task Force, 1989-91; Nat Drug Prev Network Rep Ohio, 1990-92; Ohio Credentialing Bd Chem Dependency Profs, 1990-92; Nat Coun Negro Women; bd mem, Ohio Chem Dependency Prof Bd, 2006; First Church God. **Home Addr:** 2761 Mellowbrook St, Columbus, OH 43232, **Home Phone:** (614)575-1120.

**CREWS, REV. WILLIAM HUNTER**
Educator, clergy, executive director. **Personal:** Born Mar 18, 1932, Winston-Salem, NC; married June; children: William H. **Educ:** Va Union Univ; NY Univ, MEd; Union Theol Sem NY; George Col Downers Grove Ill. **Career:** Executive director, clergy (retired); YMCA, Highland Park Br, Detroit, exec dir, dir, assoc prof; Shiloh Baptist Church, pastor, 1969-2002. **Orgs:** Bd dir, Rotary Int Baptist & Pastors Coun Detoit; bd dir, Mich Ment Health Soc; Omega Psi Phi. **Honors/Awds:** Community Service Award, First Baptist Church, 1970; Outstanding Community Service Award, St Mich, 1973. **Home Addr:** 18964 Wildemere St, Detroit, MI 48221, **Home Phone:** (313)863-6105.

**CREWS, WILLIAM SYLVESTER**
Vice president (organization), executive. **Personal:** Born Mar 5, 1947, Advance, NC; married Belinda Harden; children: David, Angela & William Jr. **Educ:** Winston Salem State Univ, BA, 1969. **Career:** Wachovia Bank Trust, audit control trainee, 1969-70, asst local auditor, 1970-73, retail credit analyst, 1973-75, mgr, bond opers, 1975-80, vpres, sr vpres, currently. **Orgs:** Bankersednl Soc, 1978; Nat Bankers Asn, 1978; Omega Psi Phi Frat, 1967; treas, Nat Sci Ctr, 1979. **Home Addr:** 3615 Willow Ridge Lane, Winston-Salem, NC 27105-6959, **Home Phone:** (336)748-8443. **Business Addr:** Senior Vice President, Wachovia Bank & Trust NA, PO Box 3099, Winston-Salem, NC 27102, **Business Phone:** (919)748-5770.

**CRIBB, JUANITA SANDERS**
Government official, consultant, personal trainer. **Personal:** Born Nov 18, 1950, Winston-Salem, NC; married Kenneth; children: Darrell, Dawn & Kenya. **Educ:** Carolina Sch Broadcasting & Jour, AAS, 1977; Univ Sedona, commun; Univ Ariz, psychol, 2005; Beulah Heights Univ, MA, 2013. **Career:** Albany Local Develop Corp, Ga, exec dir, 1986-88; Crystal Commun Corp, Albany, Ga, prin, consult & trainer, 1988-07; Les Brown Unlimited, prof speaking coach, 1990-2000; JSC Commun, prin, 1998-2000, inspirational speaker; Sanders Commun Co, speaker & coach, 2007-. **Orgs:** Leadership Albany, 1988-89; secy, Black County Comnr Ga, 1988-; Gov Adv Coun Ga Clean & Beautiful, 1989-; dir-at-large, Nat Asn Black County Officials, 1989-; bd dir, Southwest Ga Community Action Coun, 1989-; Pathways Family Worship Ctr. **Home Addr:** PO Box 3267, Atlanta, GA 31706, **Home Phone:** (229)446-1778. **Business Addr:** Speaker, Coach, Sanders Communications Co, 1375 Adams Dr SW, Atlanta, GA 30311-3619, **Business Phone:** (404)699-9708.

**CRIDER, EDWARD S., III**
Judge. **Personal:** Born Feb 7, 1921, Kimball, WV; married Verdelle Vincson. **Educ:** WVa State Col, BS, 1941; Columbia Univ, attended 1949; Brooklyn Law Sch, JD, 1953; Mod Mgt Tech Long Island Univ, cert, 1970. **Career:** Administrative law judge (retired); Sr pub health sanitarian, 1947-67; part time practr law, 1955-; NY City Dept Health, regional dir, 1967-77, spec asst to dir pest control, 1974-77, admin law judge. **Orgs:** Pres, Brooklyn Alumni Chap, Kappa Alpha Psi, 1957-59; fel Food & Drug LawInst, NY Univ Law Sch, 1959; pres, NY Chap, WV Col Alumni Asn, 1975; Y'sMen; secy, Westbury Br, Nat Asn Advan Colored People; Urban League; YMCA; Kimball HS Alumni NY Chap; NY State Trial Lawyers Asn; Nassau Co Bar Asn; NY State Sanitarians Conf. **Home Addr:** 431 Upland St, Westbury, NY 11590-2461, **Home Phone:** (516)997-7468. **Business Addr:** Director of Pest Control, The New York State Department of Health, 65 Worth St, New York, NY 10013.

**CRIGHT, LOTESS PRIESTLEY**
School administrator. **Personal:** Born Dec 3, 1931, Asheville, NC; married George Edward; children: Shaun, Shaniqua, Shannon, George & Wilson. **Educ:** Johnson C Smith Univ, BA, 1953; Brooklyn Col, MS, 1971. **Career:** School administrator (retired); Pub Sch, teacher, 1953-69; City Univ New York, NY Tech Col, reading instr, 1969-71, coordr coun, 1971-77, dir spec serv, 1977; Brooklyn Col,

dir stud support serv, 1994, lectr educ servs; Amistad Child Care & Family Ctr, admin dir, 1995. **Home Addr:** 16834 127th Ave Apt 6A, Jamaica, NY 11434-3108, **Home Phone:** (718)712-2646.

## CRIM, RODNEY

Executive. **Personal:** Born Jun 29, 1957, Chicago, IL; son of Katie Brown and Elisha; married Cynthia; children: 2. **Educ:** Univ Minn, Minneapolis, MN, BSB, acct & bus/mgt, 1980; St Thomas Univ, Minneapolis, MN, MBA, 1991; Harvard Univ, Kennedy Sch Govt, sr exec leadership prog, 2007. **Career:** CPA; Pillsbury, Minneapolis, Minn, internal auditor, 1980-81; Musicland Group, Minneapolis, Minn, financial analyst, 1981-82; Am Express Financial Servs, Minneapolis, Minn, gen acct supvr, 1982-83, human resources staffing assoc, 1983-84, mgr financial reporting, 1984-87, asst controller, 1987-88, dir controller, 1988-91, dir oper audit, 1991-92; Microtron Inc, Minneapolis, Minn, chief financial officer, 1992-96; Shore Bank, pres & chief exec officer, 1997-2001; St. Louis Develop Corp, from exec dir to pres, 2002-13; St. Louis Econ Develop Partnership, pres, 2013-. **Orgs:** Pres, Alpha Phi Alpha, Minneapolis MN, 1977-78; allocation panel mem, United Way, 1985; pres, Nat Asn Black Acct, MN, 1985-87; Leadership Minneapolis Prog, 1987; bd mem, YMCA Bd, Minneapolis MN, 1988-89; Minneapolis Community Col Adv Bd, 1991; Nat Asn Black MBAs; Nat Asn Black Accts. **Home Addr:** 3756 Calif Ave, St. Louis, MO 63118-3839, **Home Phone:** (314)772-4038. **Business Addr:** President, St Louis Development Corp, 1015 Locust St Suite 1200, St. Louis, MO 63101, **Business Phone:** (314)622-3400.

## CRIPPENS, DAVID L.

Media executive. **Personal:** Born Sep 23, 1942, Nashville, TN; son of Nathaniel and Dorothy; married Eloise; children: Gerald. **Educ:** Antioch Col, Yellow Springs, OH, BA, polit sci, 1964; San Diego State Univ, San Diego, Calif, MA, social work, 1968. **Career:** San Diego State Univ, assoc dir, 1968-69; KPBS-TV, producer, 1969-71; WQED-TV, freelance writer, journalist, staff producer & newsperson, 1971-73; KCET, Channel 28, LA CA, dir educ servs, 1973-77, vpres, educ serv, 1977-90, vpres & stage mgr, 1980-83; KCET Pub Television-Educ Enterprises, vpres, nat productions, 1983-85, Educ Enterprises, sr vpres, 1985-. **Orgs:** Bd trustee, Calif Fedn Employ & Disability, Black Black Crime, Antioch Col; pres, chief exec officer, DLC & Assoc, currently; dir, Nsf; Antioch Univ Adv Comt; Nat Black Programming Consortium; Ctr Occup Res & Develop; Community Coalition Substance Abuse Prev & Treat. **Honors/Awds:** Corp for Public Broadcasting fels, 1969; Distinguished alumni, Graduate Sch Social Work, San Diego State Univ, 1973; Most influential blacks, Pittsburgh Post Gazette, 1973; Service to Media Award, San Diego chapter Nat Asn Advan Colored People, 1975; Minority Telecommunications Award, Nat Assoc Educ Broadcasters, 1978; Commendation, California State Legislature for Voices of Our People, 1983; Outstanding Service Award, Young Advocates, 1986; Honored by Nat Assoc Media Women, 1986; Euclan Award, Sch Educ, UCLA, 1990; National Citation Award, National Sorority of Phi Delta Kappa, 1992; Positive Image Award, Frank D Parent PTA, 1992; Outstanding Educational Leadership Award, National Sorority of Phi Delta Kappa, 1992; Principals Organ Award, Senior Highschools, 1991; Excellence in Educational Commun Award, Cal Poly, 1991; John Swett Award, California Teachers Association; Distinguished Service to Health Education Award, Association Advancement Health Education, 1997. **Home Addr:** 5252 W 64th St, Inglewood, CA 90302-1016, **Home Phone:** (310)215-9646. **Business Addr:** Senior Vice President, KCET Pub Television-Educ Enterprises, 4401 Sunset Blvd, Los Angeles, CA 90027, **Business Phone:** (323)666-6500.

## CRISP, DR. ROBERT CARL, JR.

Educator. **Personal:** Born Apr 17, 1947, Sanger, TX; son of Robert and Martella Turner (deceased); married Carolyn M Tyler; children: April Nichole & Adria Camille. **Educ:** Langston Univ, Langston, OK, BA, 1969; Univ Mich, Ann Arbor, MI, MA, 1971, PhD, 1976. **Career:** Music director (retired); Detroit Pub Schs, Detroit, Mich, band dir, 1969-84, dept head, 1979-84, music supvr, 1984-94, Off Music Educ, dir, 1994. **Orgs:** Bd trustee, Messiah Baptist Church, 1979-; Class Roots Steering Comt; Detroit Symphony, Orchestra, 1985-88; bd trustee, Detroit Chamber Winds, 1987-; bd trustee, Community Treat Ctr, 1989-; nat talent co-chmn, Omega Psi Phi Fraternity, 1990-; bd dir, Blue Lake Fine Arts Camp, bd dir; Community Treat Ctr; bd dir, Mich Performing Arts Youth Theater; bd dir, Neighborhood Serv Orgn. **Home Addr:** 17596 Oak Dr, Detroit, MI 48221-2747, **Home Phone:** (313)863-8341. **Business Addr:** MI.

## CRISP, SYDNEY A.

Executive. **Career:** Bank Am, exec vpres, global serv, Dir Customer Support Serv; Fleet Nat Bank, Dir Customer Support Serv; FleetBoston Financial, Dir Customer Support Serv; Robertson Stephens Inc, exec vpres, global serv, 2013-.

## CRISWELL, ARTHURINE DENTON

President (organization), administrator. **Personal:** Born Jan 30, 1953, Memphis, TN; daughter of Arthur and Celia Hambrick; married Gordon Maxwell; children: Joshua Michael. **Educ:** Park Col, BA, 1973; Univ KS, MSW, 1981. **Career:** Kans Dept Social & Rehab Serv Income maintenance worker, 1976-79, grad intern, 1980-81 Income maintenance supvr, 1981-84, area dir, 1984-89, lawrence area off, dir, 2004; KS City Serv League, social work intern, 1979-80; Univ Kans, grad res asst, 1979-81; Univ Kans Med Ctr, proj dir, 1989. **Orgs:** Nat Asn Social Workers 1979-; Nat Asn Couples Marriage Enrichment, 1983-; bd mem, Pvt Indust Coun, 1984-85; bd dir, Wyandotte County United Way, 1988; pres, Jr League Wyandotte & Johnson Counties, 1995; Nat Forum Black Pub Adminr. **Home Addr:** PO Box 12611, Kansas City, KS 66112, **Home Phone:** (913)207-4362. **Business Addr:** Director, American Family Insurance, Social & Rehab Services, PO Box 590, Lawrence, KS 66046.

## CRITTENDEN, RAYMOND C., IV

Football player, executive. **Personal:** Born Mar 1, 1970, Washington, DC. **Educ:** Va Polytech Inst & State Univ, BS, 1992; Barry Univ, MS, biomed sci, 2007. **Career:** Football player (retired), clin res assoc; New Eng Patriots, wide receiver, kick returner, 1993-94, free agt, 1994-96; San Diego Chargers, wide receiver, 1997; Horizon Inst Clin Res, clin res coordr, 2005-07; Univ Miami, Miller Sch Med Sylvester Comprehensive Cancer Ctr, supvr qual assurance, 2007-12; MEDNAX, clin res assoc, 2012-. **Honors/Awds:** Most valuable offensive player of the Metro Invitational Tournament; All-South Atlantic Region honors; Ranked fifth in the American Football Conference Kick-off Returns as a Rookie; Hall of Fame, Va Tech Univ, 2006. **Business Addr:** Clinical Research Coordinator, Horizon Institute for Clinical Research, 3990 Sheridan St Suite 210, Hollywood, FL 33021, **Business Phone:** (954)964-6881.

## CROCKER, WAYNE MARCUS

Library administrator. **Personal:** Born May 26, 1956, Petersburg, VA; son of George and Nancy Cooley; married Sabrina Tucker; children: Shannon Nicole & Courtney Lynn. **Educ:** Va State Col, Petersburg, VA, BS, 1978; Atlanta Univ, Atlanta, GA, MSLS, 1979. **Career:** Petersburg Pub Libr, Petersburg, Va, page & libr aide, 1973-78; Atlanta Pub Libr, Atlanta, Ga, libr asst & libr, 1978-80; Petersburg Pub Libr, Petersburg, Va, secy, Libr Serv, dir, 1980-. **Orgs:** Am Libr Asn, 1980-; Va Libr Asn, 1980-; Alpha Phi Alpha Fraternity, 1985-; pres & bd dir, Petersburg City Employees Fed Credit Union, 1987; State Networking Users Adv, 1989-. **Honors/Awds:** Louise Giles Minority Scholar, Am Libr Asn, 1978. **Home Addr:** 101 S Plains Dr, Petersburg, VA 23805-9105, **Home Phone:** (804)862-3198. **Business Addr:** Director of Library Services, Secretary, Petersburg Public Library, 137 S Sycamore St, Petersburg, VA 23803, **Business Phone:** (804)733-2387.

## CROCKETT, DELORES LORAINE

Government official. **Personal:** Born Jun 18, 1947, Daytona Beach, FL; children: Ayanna T. **Educ:** Spelman Col, BA, psychol, 1969; Atlanta Univ, MA, guid & couns, 1972. **Career:** Government official (retired); Minority Women's Employ Prog, proj dir, 1974-77; Avon Prod Inc, employ & commun suprv, 1977-79; Nat Alliance Bus, metro dir, 1979; US Dept Labor, reg dir, Women's Bur, reg adminr, actg dep dir. **Orgs:** Selected Leadership Atlanta, 1977, Leadership Ga, 1978; bd trustee, Leadership Atlanta, 1981; bd dir, Am Red Cross, 1982-; bd dir, Big Bros & Big Sisters, 1985-; AH Task Force Nat Conf Black Mayors, 1985. **Honors/Awds:** Woman of Achievement, Bus & Prof Women's Clubs Inc, 1977, 1979; One of the Ten Outstanding Young People of Atlanta, 1979; one of two reps to serve on Panel III studying Intl Training Prog to Eliminate Sex Imbalances in the Work Place, Paris, France, Labor Dept, 1983, 1984; Cit Outstanding Comm Serv, Atlanta Women Bus, 1984; Outstanding Alumnae Award, Spelman Col Class of 1969, 1984. **Home Addr:** 4017 Pinehurst Valley Dr, Decatur, GA 30034. **Business Addr:** Acting Deputy Director, US Department of Labor, 200 Constitution Ave NW Rm S-3002, Washington, DC 20210, **Business Phone:** (202)693-6710.

## CROCKETT, GEORGE W., III

Judge, government official. **Personal:** Born Dec 23, 1938, Fairmont, WV; son of George William Jr (deceased) and Emily Ethelene Jones; married Mireya A Carvajal; children: Enrique Raul III. **Educ:** Morehouse Col, BA, 1961; Wayne State Univ, attended 1959; Detroit Col Law, JD, 1964. **Career:** Judge (retired); pvt pract, 1964-67; Wayne Co Neighborhood Legal Serv Ctr, supv atty, 1967-70, asst corp coun, 1967; Defenders Off Detroit, dep defender, 1970-77; Third Judicial Circuit Ct, judge, 2003. **Orgs:** Nal Bar Asn; Mich State Bar; Wolverine Bar Asn; Asn Black Judges Mich; Nat Asn Advan Colored People. **Home Addr:** 5463 Crystal Anne Dr, West Palm Beach, FL 33417, **Home Phone:** (561)444-8693.

## CROCKETT, HENRI

Executive, football player. **Personal:** Born Oct 28, 1974, Pompano Beach, FL. **Educ:** Fla State Univ, BS, criminol. **Career:** Football player (retired), executive; Atlanta Falcons, right linebacker, 1997-98, linebacker, 1999-2001; Denver Broncos, 2001; Minn Vikings, linebacker, 2002-03; S Fla Develop & Investment Co, pres & chief exec officer; Guaranteed Enterprise Trucking Serv, pres & chief exec officer; Vanity Salon, owner & operator. **Orgs:** Founder, Team 94; founder & pres, Crockett Found; Omega Psi Phi Fraternity. **Honors/Awds:** Man of the Year, Boys & Girls Club; Fla State Univ. **Special Achievements:** Film:1998 NFC Championship Game, 1999. **Home Addr:** , Pembroke Pines, FL. **Business Addr:** Founder, President, The Crockett Foundation, PO Box 3774, Hallandale Beach, FL 33008, **Business Phone:** (954)200-1924.

## CROCKETT, PHYLLIS. See CROCKETT-NTONGA, NOLUTHANDO.

## CROCKETT, RAY

Football player. **Personal:** Born Jan 5, 1967, Dallas, TX; married April; children: Joi, Ray Jr & Darryl. **Educ:** Baylor, BA, comput sci, 1992. **Career:** Football player (retired), actor, executive; Detroit Lions, 1989, Detroit Lions, left central back, 1990-93; Denver Broncos, left corner back, 1994-2000, right corner back, 1994, corner back & left corner back, 1999; Kans City Chiefs, left corner back & corner back, 2001-03; mem, Fox Sports Net; TV series: "Bound for Glory", 2005; "Identity", 2006; TV & Radio host: "Count down to Kick off"; "Little Big Man"; "30 Days", Nite Tales The Movie, The Hustle, 2008; "Nite Tales: The Series", 2009; Real estate developer, currently. **Orgs:** United Way; Crock 39 Found. **Honors/Awds:** Mackey Award,1991; NFC Interception Leader,1991. **Special Achievements:** Two-time Super Bowl champion. **Business Addr:** Member, Fox Sports Net, 10000 Santa Monica Blvd, Los Angeles, CA 90067, **Business Phone:** (310)284-2362.

## CROCKETT, TRACEE HALL. See HALL, TRACEE K.

## CROCKETT, ZACK THEOPOLIS

Football player, scout. **Personal:** Born Dec 2, 1972, Pompano Beach, FL. **Educ:** Fla State Univ, criminol. **Career:** Football player (retired), scout; Indianapolis Colts, 1995, fullback, 1996-98; Jacksonville Jaguars, fullback, 1998; Oakland Raiders, running back, 1999, fullback & running back, 2000, 2003-06, 2001-02, tight end, 2006, scout, 2009-; Tampa Bay Buccaneers, 2007; Dallas Cowboys, 2007. **Orgs:** Omega Psi Phi Fraternity. **Special Achievements:** Film: 1995 NFL Draft, 1995; 1995 AFC Championship Game, 1996; Super Bowl XXXVII, 2003. TV Series: "Mike & Mike", 2013. **Home Addr:** 5491 Gate Lake Rd, Tamarac, FL 33319. **Business Addr:** Scout, Oakland Raiders, 1220 Harbor Bay Pkwy, Alameda, CA 94502, **Business Phone:** (510)864-5000.

## CROCKETT-NTONGA, NOLUTHANDO (PHYLLIS CROCKETT)

Journalist. **Personal:** Born Jul 14, 1950, Chicago, IL; daughter of Leo Crockett and Mae Corbin Williams; children: Adina Gittens. **Educ:** Univ Ill, Chicago, BA, 1972; Northwestern Univ, Medill Sch Journ, MA, 1979; Stanford Univ, Palo Alto, CA, Knight Fel, 1991. **Career:** WSOC News Radio, producer, reporter, anchor, 1978-79; AP/UPI, Raleigh & Durham, NC, freelance reporter, 1978-80; WFNC & WQSM, producer, reporter, anchor, 1979-80; Johnson C Smith Univ, vis instr, 1979; Am's Black Forum, panelist, 1980-83; Fayetteville State Univ, vis instr, 1980; Sheridan Broadcasting Network, exec ed & spec corresp, 1980-81; Howard Univ, panelist & guest lectr; Univ DC, panelist & guest lectr; Stanford Univ, panelist & guest lectr; DC Pub Schs, Fairfax County Pub Schs, 1980-; WTTG-TV, news writer, 1981-82; Nat Pub Radio, reporter, 1981-89, White House corresp, 1989-91, sr corresp, 1992-; Pac News Serv, freelance reporter, 1984, CNN analyst, 1992-; Black Entertainment Tv, analyst, 1987-; C-SPAN Cable TV Network, WHHM-TV, analyst, 1987-. **Orgs:** Nat Asn Black Journalists, 1978-; Sigma Delta Chi, 1979 -; Smithsonian Inst, African Am Adv Comt, 1989-; commun dir, Corp Coun Africa, currently; Nat Newspaper Publ Asn; founding mem, Wash Asn Black Journalists. **Honors/Awds:** Frederick Douglass Award, Nat Asn Black Journalists, 1984; NEA Award, 1988; Robert F Kennedy Award, 1990; Nat Asn Black Journalists Award. **Business Addr:** Communications Director, The Corporate Council on Africa, 1100 17th St NW Suite 1100, Washington, DC 20036, **Business Phone:** (202)263-3515.

## CROEL, MICHAEL

Football player, graphic artist. **Personal:** Born Jun 6, 1969, Detroit, MI; children: 2. **Educ:** Univ Nebr, grad. **Career:** Football player (retired), graphic artist; Denver Broncos, right linebacker & right inside linebacker, 1991, left outside linebacker, 1992-93, left linebacker, 1994; New York Giants, left linebacker, 1995; Baltimore Ravens, left outside linebacker, 1996; Seattle Seahawks, line backer, 1998; Los Angeles Xtreme, 2001; football coach & graphic designer, currently. **Honors/Awds:** Defensive Rookie of the Year, Nat Football League, 1991; Rookie of the Year, Am Football Conf, United Press Int, 1991; Univ Nebr, Football Hall of fame, 2003.

## CROFT, WARDELL C.

Chief executive officer, insurance executive, consultant. **Personal:** Born Gadsden, AL; son of Thomas and Minnie; married Theora Cunniggham; children: Bobbie. **Educ:** Stillman Col; Alexander Hamilton Inst Bus; Univ Mich, Detroit. **Career:** Wright Mutual Ins Co, agency dir, genl mgr, exec vpres, pres, chmn, 1950, chief exec officer, 1962-97, chmn emer & consult, 2007-. **Orgs:** Bd dir, Physician Drug Ctr, Detroit Renaissance, 1970; Exec comt, United Negro Col Fund, vice chair, 1991-92; vice chmn, UNCF Exec Comt Mich, 1991-92; vice chmn bd dir, First Independence Nat Bank One Founders; bd trustee, New Detroit Inc; bd trustee, Stillman Col; bd dir & chair, Life Ins Asn Mich; chmn, Detroit Inst Com; bd dir, Inner-City Coun Alumni UNCF; adv bd mem, Metrop Detroit; Boy Scouts Am; life mem, Nat Asn Advan Colored People Golden Heritage; Detroit Coun Ins Execs; bd trustees, Citizen Res Mich; Econ Club Detroit; Metrop Growth & Develop Corp; adv bd mem, YMCA Metrop Detroit; fel Life Mgt Inst; chmn, Trustee Bd Second Baptist Church; pres, Booker T Wash Bus Asn; Nat Ins Asn; Life Ins Asn Mich. **Honors/Awds:** Citizen Res Mich; Michigan Citizen of the Year, Mich Chronicle; S Award, Stillman Col; Citizen Award, Phi Beta Sigma Frat; Silver Beaver Award, Boy Scouts of Am; CC Spaulding Award, Nat Bus League; Mich Ins Hall of Fame. **Business Addr:** Chairman Emeritus, Consultant, Wright Mutual Insurance Co, 2995 E Grand Blvd, Detroit, MI 48202, **Business Phone:** (313)871-2112.

## CROMARTIE, ERNEST W., III

Lawyer. **Personal:** Born Waverly, SC; son of Ernest William and Charlie Mae Harrison; married Raynette White; children: Ernest W & Antionette. **Educ:** Mich State Univ, BA, mkt & bus admin, 1968; George Washington Univ, JD, 1971. **Career:** Cureton & Cromartie, atty, 1974-76; Law Off Ernest W Cromartie III LLC, atty, 1975-; EW Cromartie II, atty, 1976-; City Columbia Dist II, councilman, 1983; SC Supreme Ct, pract; US Dist Ct, pract; US Ct Appeals 4th Circuit, pract; Midlands Tech Col, adj prof; Charles R Drew Wellness Ctr, chmn, currently; U.S Securities & Exchange Comn, fel; U.S. Overseas Pvt Investment Corp (OPIC), fel; U.S. Dept Treas, fel. **Orgs:** Zoning Bd Adjustments & Appeals, Mayor City Columbia, 1976-80, 1980-85; chmn, Eau Claire Task Force Community Ctr, 1980-81; nat deleg, SC Dem Nat Conv, 1986, 1996; Nat Asn Advan Colored People; Optimist Club; E Columbia Jaycees; bd trustees, United Way; 32nd Degree Mason; Shriners, Midlands Elks; Townmen Club; Columbia Chamber Com; Housing Comn Greater Columbia, Chamber Com; United Way Gov Bd, Kiwanis Club; Bishop Memorial AME Church; pres usher bd, sunday sch teacher, bd trustee, chmn bldg fund, Men's Day Activ; SC Bar Asn; Richland City Bar Asn; Am Bar Asn; SC Trial Lawyers Asn; Am Trial Lawyers Asn; bd, SC Youth Serv; Midlands Tech Col Found Bd; Alpha Phi Alpha Fraternity Inc; Richland Kiwanis Club; charter mem, 100 Black Men SC; City Columbia Planning Comn; chmn, City Columbia Bd Zoning Appeals; Midlands Fatherhood Coalition; S Carolina Bar Asn. **Honors/Awds:** Attorney of the Year, 1979; Distinguished Service Award, Nat Black Caucus; Outstanding Service Award, SC Chap, Nat Asn Real Estate Brokers; Living Legacy Award, Nat Coun Negro Women; Order of the Palmetto. **Special Achievements:** First African American to win seat on Columbia City Council, 1983. **Business Addr:** Attorney, Law Office of Ernest W Cromartie III LLC, 1607 Harden St E W Cromartie Bldg, Columbia, SC 29204-1012, **Business Phone:** (803)256-3462.

**CROMARTIE, EUGENE RUFUS**
Executive director, association executive. **Personal:** Born Oct 3, 1936, Wabasso, FL; son of Ulysses and Hannah; married Joyce Bell Mims; children: Eugene II, Leonardo, Marcus & Eliseo. **Educ:** Fla Agr & Mech Univ, BS, 1957; Univ Dayton, MS, 1968; AUS Command & Gen Staff Col, attended 1970; Nat War Col, attended 1977. **Career:** Int Asn Chiefs Police, Arlington, Va, dep exec dir & chief staff, 1990-; Univ Dayton, Ohio, asst prof mil sci; AUS Mil Police Sch, staff fac mem; Command & Gen Staff Col, staff fac mem; 82nd Airborne Div, provost marshal; Wash, DC, assignment officer personnel directorate; AUS Criminal Invest Command, spec asst to comndg gen; AUS Criminal Invest Command Ft Meade, Md, comdr first reg; AUS Europe & Seventh Army, dep provost marshal, provost marshal; AUS Mil Community Comdr Mannheim, Ger; AUS Criminal Invest Command, comndg gen. **Orgs:** Alpha Phi Alpha Fraternity, 1954-; Int Fedn Sr Police Officers, 1981-; Nat Coun Law Enforcement Explorer Boy Scouts Am, 1983-; Nat Orgn Black Law Enforcement Exec, 1984-; nat chmn, Law Enforcement Exploring Comm Boy Scouts Am, 1986-; Mil Police Regt Asn. **Honors/Awds:** Meritorious Achievement Award, Fla Agr & Mech Univ, 1982; Outstanding Floridian, Fla State Resolution, 1982; Key to Tallahassee City, 1982; First inductee into Fla Agr & Mech Univ Hall of Fame, 1986; Centennial Medallion for Distinguished Service Award, Fla Agr & Mech Univ, 1987; Meritorious Service Award, Nat Asn Advan Colored People, 1989; Public Service Award, Nat Asn Fed Investr, 1989; President's Award, National Sheriffs Asn, 1989; Honorary Doctor of Laws, Fla Agr & Mech Univ, 1990; bd dir, Dasie Bridgewater Hope Center. **Special Achievements:** City of Tallahassee & Leon Co declared May 1, 1982 as Brigadier Gen Eugene R Cromartie Day. **Home Addr:** 909 Sero Estates Dr, Ft. Washington, MD 20744-6082, **Home Phone:** (301)292-9892.

**CROMBAUGH, REV. HALLIE**
Media executive. **Personal:** Born Sep 9, 1949, Indianapolis, IN; married Dennis; children: Trenna & Kendra. **Educ:** Porter Col, 1974; Ind Central Col; St Mary Woods Col. **Career:** Col & U Corp, auditor, gen acctg dept, 1974-75; WISH-TV, asst dir, comn affairs, 1975-76, dir, comn affairs; Ind Today & Comm, dir, comm affairs, exec producer & host; Am Fletcher Nat Bank, IBM & opr; Ind Nat Bank, NCR opr. **Orgs:** Chmn by-laws comt, Nat Broadcast Asn Comn Affairs; bd dir, Comn Serv Coun Greater Independent; chmn, Family Violence Task Force; chmn bd dir, Wishard Mem Hosp Midtown Comm Ment Health Ctr; adv bd, Indianapolis Jr League; vchmn, Queens Selection & Coronation Comt Indianapolis 500 Fest Asn bd dir, Indianapolis 500 Asn Inc; Gamma Phi Delta Int Sor Inc; asso min St Paul Am Chap IN; Conf 4th Episcopal Dist; ordained deacon Am Chap; chmn adv bd, Auntie Mames CDC. **Honors/Awds:** Outstanding Service Award, United Award, 1975-79; Media Year Award, Marion Co Heart Asn, 1975-76; Outstanding Service Award, Indianapolis Pre-Sch Inc, 1975-79; Outstanding Service Award, Indianapolis Pub Sch Operation Catch-up, 1977; Outstanding Service Award, Indy Trade Asn, 1977; Outstanding Mental Health Service Award, 1978-79; Golden Heart Award, Am Heart Asn, 1979. **Home Addr:** 1926 Alvee Cir, Indianapolis, IN 46239, **Home Phone:** (317)353-6106.

**CROMER, RONNIE E., JR.**
Lawyer. **Educ:** Univ Detroit, BS, polit sci & int econs, 1990; Univ Detroit Mercy Sch Law, JD, law, 1999. **Career:** Law Offices Ronnie E Cromer Jr, atty, 2000-07; Diallo Cromer Toussaint Posey & Polk PLLC, sr partner, 2007-10; Cromer Law Group PLLC, founding partner, 2010-. **Orgs:** Mich Asn Justice; State Bar Mich Employ Law; Am Bar Asn; Nat Police Accountability Proj (NPAP); Fed Defenders Panel; Wolverine Bar Asn; Straker Bar Asn. **Business Addr:** Founding Partner, The Cromer Law Group PLLC, 24901 Northwestern Hwy Suite 612, Southfield, MI 48226, **Business Phone:** (248)809-6790.

**CROMWELL, ADELAIDE MCGUINN**
Educator. **Personal:** Born Nov 27, 1919, Washington, DC; daughter of John W Jr and Yetta M; children: Anthony C Hill. **Educ:** Smith Col, BA, sociol, 1940; Univ PA, MA, sociol, 1941; Bryn Mawr, cert soc work, 1943; Radcliffe Col, PhD, sociol, 1952. **Career:** Educator (retired); Hunter Col, mem fac, 1942-44; Smith Col, mem fac, 1945-46; Boston Univ, prof sociol, 1951-85, dir, 1969, Afro-Amer studies, 1953, prof emer sociol. **Orgs:** Adv comt, Corrections Commonwealth, MA, 1955-68; adv comm, Vol AID, 1964-80; dir, African Studies Asn, 1966-68 Nat Order Ivory Coast, 1967; Nat Endowment Humanities, 1968-70; adv comm dir, IRS; Nat Ctr Afro-Am Artists, 1970-80; African Scholars Coun, 1971-80; bd mem, Wheelock Col, 1971-72; Commonwealth Inst Higher Educ, 1973-74; Nat Fel Fund, 1974-75; Bd Sci & Technol Int Develop, 1984-86; African Studies Asn; Am Social Asn; Asn Study African Am Life & Hist; Acad Arts & Sci; Coun Foreign Rels; Mass Hist Comn, 1993-; Mass Hist Soc, 1997-; exec coun, Am Soc African Cult; Am Negro Leadership Conf; adv coun, Vol Foreign Aid; pres, Heritage Guild Inc; Phi Beta Kappa; Am Sociol Asn. **Honors/Awds:** Alumnae Medal Smith Col, 1971; LHD, Univ Southwestern Mass, 1971; Trans Africa Freedom Award, 1983; Honorary Doctor Humanities, George Washington University, 1989; Honorary Doctor of Humane Letters, Boston Univ, 1995; Distinguished Service & Leadership Award, Black Women in the Acad, 1999; Life Achievement Award, Smithsonian Nat Mus Am Hist, 1999; Citation from the Nat Order of Cote d'Ivoire; Carter G. Woodson Medal, Asn Study African Am Life & Hist. **Special Achievements:** Convened the first conf W African social workers in Ghana, 1960; conf African and African Am scholars & policymakers, 1983; authored : Apropos of Africa: Sentiments of Negro American Leaders Towards Africa from the1800s to 1950s, 1969; The Fulbright Program in Africa, 1946-86, 1986; An Afro-Victorian Feminist: Adelaide Smith Casely Hayford, 1868-1960, 1962; First African-American faculty member. **Home Addr:** 51 Addington Rd, Brookline, MA 02445-4519, **Home Phone:** (617)731-4391. **Business Addr:** Professor Emeritus, Boston University, 705 Commonwealth Ave, Boston, MA 02215, **Business Phone:** (617)353-2696.

**CROOM, SYLVESTER, JR.**
Football coach, football player. **Personal:** Born Sep 25, 1954, Tuscaloosa, AL; son of Sylvester Sr. **Educ:** Univ Ala, BS, 1975, MA, 1977. **Career:** Football player (retired); football coach; Univ Ala, player, 1972-74, centers coach & grad asst coach, 1976, inside linebackers coach, 1977-81, 1984-86, outside linebackers coach, 1982-83; New Orleans Saints, 1975; Tampa Bay Buccaneers, running backs coach, 1987-90; Indianapolis Colts, running backs coach, 1991; San Diego Chargers, running backs coach, 1992-96; Detroit Lions, offensive coordr, 1997-2000; Green Bay Packers, running backs coach, 2001-03; Miss State Univ, head coach, 2004-08; Running Backs Coach, St. Louis Rams, 2009-11; Jacksonville Jaguars, running backs coach, 2012; Tenn Titans, running backs coach, 2013-. **Honors/Awds:** Named Kodak all-America, sr capt, 1974; SEC Coach of the Year, 2007; Liberty Mutual Fan Coach of the Year, 2007. **Special Achievements:** First African American head football coach in the Southeastern Conference. **Business Addr:** Running Backs Coach, Tennessee Titans, 460 Great Cir Rd, Nashville, TN 37228, **Business Phone:** (615)565-4000.

**CROPP, DR. DWIGHT SHEFFERY**
School administrator, educator. **Personal:** Born Aug 5, 1939, Washington, DC; married Linda Washington; children: Allison & Christopher. **Educ:** Howard Univ, BA, MA, 1965; Am Univ, MPA, George Washington Univ, EdD. **Career:** US Dept St, res analyst, 1964; DC Pub Schs, educ, 1965; DC City Coun, spec asst chmn, 1971; DC Pub Schs, exec asst to supt, 1971; DC Bd Educ, exec sec; DC Off Intergovernmental Rels, dir; George Washington Univ, assoc prof, Pub Policy & Pub Admin, currently. **Orgs:** Am Asn Sch Admin; Urban League. **Home Addr:** 4001 18 St NW, Washington, DC 20011, **Home Phone:** (202)726-0505. **Business Addr:** Associate Professor, George Washington University, MPA Bldg 601F 805 21st St NW, Washington, DC 20052, **Business Phone:** (202)994-5191.

**CROSBIE, IVAN**
Educator. **Educ:** Los Angeles Trade Tech Col, AA; Calif State Univ, Los Angeles, BA, jour, Dominguez Hills, MA, lit. **Career:** Los Angeles Trade Tech Col, prof eng & mass commun; Webster Career Col, eng instr; Los Angeles Col Spec Educ, eng instr; Compton Community Col, chmn, eng dept, vpres acad senate, dir, pub rels dir, pres, asst prof, 1992-. **Orgs:** Marco Antonio Firebaugh; Assemblyman Mervyn Dymally; Congresswoman Linda Sanchez; Congresswoman Lucille Roybal-Allard; Hermandad Mexicana Nat; Lynwood Unified Sch Dist; Los Angeles Unified Sch Dist; Wonder Reading Found; Agape Music Inst; San Emigdius High Sch; Hermandad Mexicana Nat; Adelante; Plaza Mex; Tweedy Mile Asn; Huntington Pk Chamber Com; Lynwood Chamber Com; Compton Chamber Com; Salvadorian Chamber Com. **Business Addr:** Assistant Professor, Compton Community College, Rm F-41 1111 E Artesia Blvd, Compton, CA 90221, **Business Phone:** (310)900-1600.

**CROSBY, DR. EDWARD WARREN**
School administrator, vice president (organization), educator. **Personal:** Born Nov 4, 1932, Cleveland, OH; son of Frederick Douglass and Marion Grace Naylor; married Shirley G Redding; children: Kofi M Khemet, Darryl M L & Elliott Malcolm. **Educ:** Kent State Univ, BA, Ger & Span, 1957, MA, Ger & Span, 1959; Univ Kans, PhD, medieval Ger lang & lit & medieval hist, 1965. **Career:** Educator (retired); Kent State, 1957; Hiram Col Hiram, Ohio, chmn, 1958; Tuskegee Inst, 1962; Greater Akron Community Action Coun, Ohio's Summit County, vol, assoc dir, 1966; Southern Ill Univ, Exp Higher Educ, dir educ, 1966-69; Educ Resources Inst Inc E St Louis, vpres prog devel, 1968; Inst African Am Affairs, Kent State Univ, founder, dir, 1969-76; Kent State Univ, assoc prof, 1969-94, chmn, dept pan-african studies, 1976-94; Univ Wash, dir black studiesprog, 1976-78; Network Educ Devel & Enrichment, Kent Ohio, vpres, 1988; Kent Univ, emer chmn & prof pan-african studies & Ger & slavic lang & lit, 1994. **Orgs:** Fac, Inst Black World, 1970-72; consult, Peat Marwick Mitchell & Co, 1971-72; pres, NE Ohio Black Studies Consortium, 1974; pres, Ohio Consortium Black Studies, 1980-; bd mem, Harriet Tubman, African Am Mus, 1985-; resident consult, Regional Coun Int Educ. **Honors/Awds:** Hon Leadership Award, Omicron Delta Kappa, 1976; Hon mem, Alpha Kappa Mu. **Special Achievements:** Published many books including, "The Black Experience, An Anthology", 1976; "Chronology of Notable Dates in the Hist Africans in the America & Elsewhere", 1976; "The Education of Black Folk, An Historical Perspective, The Western Journal of Black Studies", 1977; "The African Experience in Community Devel", Two Vols 1980; "Your History, A Chronology of Notable Events", 1988; First and second African American educational ventures. **Home Addr:** 437 Silver Meadows Blvd, Kent, OH 44240-1913, **Home Phone:** (330)673-9271. **Business Addr:** Educator, Kent State University, Rm 117 Ctr Pan-African Cult, Kent, OH 44242, **Business Phone:** (216)672-2300.

**CROSBY, FRED CHARLES.** See Obituaries Section.

**CROSBY, FRED MCCLELLEN**
Executive. **Personal:** Born May 17, 1928, Cleveland, OH; son of Fred Douglas and Marion Grace Naylor; married Phendalyne Tazewell; children: Fred C, James R & Llionicia L. **Career:** Crosby Furniture Co Inc, pres, chief exec officer, chmn. **Orgs:** Vpres, Nat Asn Advan Colored People, Cleveland Br, 1971-72; Cuyahoga Co Community Improv Corp; trea, Urban League, 1973-74; bd dir, First Bank Nat, 1974-90; Appointee USA, Adv Coun, SBA, 1978-80; gov appointee, State Boxing Comn, 1984-94; CBL Econ Develop Corp; Buckeye Exec Club State OH; ex bd trustee, Greater Cleveland Growth Asn; Auto Club, Ohio Retail Merchants Asn; bd trustee, Pub TV; Better Bus Bur; Cleveland Cuyahoga Co Port Authority, 1986-90; vice-chair, Ohio Coun Retail Merchants Asn, 1988-91, chmn, 1994-95; chmn, First Inter-City Banc Corp, 1988; bd mem, Cuyahoga Co Loan Rev Comn; bd trustee, United Black Fund; bd trustee, Am Auto Asn, 1993-98. **Home Addr:** 20676 Southgate Pk Blvd Suite 103, Maple Heights, OH 44137-2954, **Home Phone:** (216)752-5678.

**CROSBY, JAMES R.**
Chief executive officer, publisher. **Educ:** Banking, Corp, finance & securities law, 1982; Kent State Univ, BBA, 1985; Univ Akron, MBA, finance, 1990. **Career:** First Bank, mortgage loan opers, 1984-90; Amertrust Bank, com loan officer, 1990-92; City Cleveland, minority bus develop, dir, 1992-94; Life Publ, pres & publ, 1994-98; Village Tv, co-founder & vpres, 2003-07; TransOhio Mortgage & Loan Inc, chmn & chief exec officer, 2001-09; MyCity Transp, chief exec officer, 1994-; CityNews Newspaper Group, chief exec officer & publ, 1994-. **Business Addr:** Chief Executive Officer, Publisher, CityNews Newspaper Group, 1419 E 40th St, Cleveland, OH 44103, **Business Phone:** (216)881-0799.

**CROSBY, LORETTA**
President (organization), editor, administrator. **Personal:** Born Sep 14, 1957, Clover, SC. **Educ:** Lander Col, Greenwood, SC, BS, psychol, 1979; Winthrop Col. **Career:** SC Dept Social Servs, generalist & analyst, 1982-86; Richmond County Dept Family & C Servs, county eligibility consult, 1986; Emory Univ, personnel generalist, 1986; Greenville News-Piedmont Co, exec secy, 1986-87; Ardyss Int; Core Health Prod; Max Int; RobKeller OGF; Legal Shield; SheaButterCenter, ed; RecallingHealth, founder, ed-N-chief; SC Develop Disabilities Counc, exec dir, 1987-; JusLo & Assocs, gen mgr, pres & owner, 1993-; BWC, secy asst, 1995-97, ed asst, 1997-99; One Pupil Publ, ed & publ, 2011-. **Orgs:** Vpres & pres, Lambda Lambda Chap, Alpha Kappa Alpha, 1977-78; treas, Pamoja Club African-Am; Psychol Club Greek Coun; Entertainment Coun rev Mag staff; partic, Poetry People Workshop, 1981. **Home Addr:** 206A Willowbrook Dr Suite A, Morganton, NC 28655, **Home Phone:** (704)798-6117. **Business Addr:** President, Owner, JusLo & Associates, PO Box 99838, Raleigh, NC 27624-9838, **Business Phone:** (919)771-7959.

**CROSBY, DR. MARGAREE SEAWRIGHT**
Educator. **Personal:** Born Nov 21, 1941, Greenville, SC; daughter of Josie Williams Seawright and Mark Seawright; married Willis H Jr; children: Anthony Bernard, Anedra Michelle & Erich Garrett. **Educ:** SC State Univ, BS, 1963; Clemson Univ, MEd, 1973; Univ Mass, EdD, 1976. **Career:** Sch Dist Greenville County, elem teacher, 1964-68, headstart teacher, 1965-66, reading resource teacher, 1968-74; Univ Mass, teaching asst, CUETEP coord, 1974-76; Univ SC, Spartanburg, asst prof, 1976-77; ClemsonUniv, assoc prof, 1977, prof emer, currently. **Orgs:** Govr Blue Ribbon Com Job Training, 1985; Clemson Univ, Univ self studycom, 1986; Affirmative Action Com; Sunbelt Human Advan Resources, Projrise adv bd, 1988-; Nat Asn Black Reading & Lang Arts Educrs; chap, nominating com, Greenville Hosp Syst Bd trustee, 1991-97; Nat Asn Black Educrs, 1991-; Elem Curric Com, dept head search com, 1985, Fac search com, chmn, 1988, 1992; bd, chap, conf pro comn, SC Coun Int Reading Asn, 1992. **Home Addr:** 516 Edwards Mill Rd, PO Box 1273, Greenville, SC 29602-1273, **Home Phone:** (864)907-7413. **Business Addr:** Professor Emeritus, Clemson University, 105 Sikes Hall, Clemson, SC 29634-5124, **Business Phone:** (864)656-3311.

**CROSBY, MARY LYNNE R.**
Chief executive officer. **Personal:** married Keith E. **Educ:** Univ Mich-Ann Arbor, BS, elec engineering, MBA. **Career:** Andersen Consulting; Daimler Chrysler, qual mgr & specialist; Univ Mich; Fruitful Works Inc, chief exec officer, founder, pres, 2002-; Ford Motor Co; Tree Life Bible Fel Church, teacher. **Orgs:** Detroit Regional Chamber. **Business Addr:** Chief Executive Officer, President, FruitfulWorks Inc, 18701 Grand River Suite 134, Detroit, MI 48223, **Business Phone:** (313)833-3555.

**CROSBY, DR. WILLIS HERMAN, JR.**
Administrator, executive. **Personal:** Born Jul 31, 1941, Anderson, SC; son of Willis H (deceased) and Alwille Hardy; married Margaree S; children: Anthony, Anedra & Erich. **Educ:** SC State Univ, BA, 1963; Furman Univ, MA, 1972; Univ Mass, Amherst, EdD, 1977. **Career:** Spartanburg Sch Dist 7, social studies teacher, 1963-66; Sch Dist Greenville County, social studies teacher, 1966-70, ombudsman, 1970-73; Ford Found Leadership Develop Prog fel, 1973-74; Univ Mass, res asst, 1974-76; Tri-County Tech Col, div chmn, 1976-79; Sunbelt Human Advan Resources Inc, exec dir, 1979-94, pres & chief exec officer, 1994-; Willmar Group Inc, chief exec officer; S Carolina Pub Schs Inc, vice chmn. **Orgs:** Pres, SC Social Welfare Forum, 1983-85; pres, SC Asn Community Action Agencies, 1986-88; bd mem, Southeastern Asn Community Action Agencies, 1986-; bd mem, SC Educ Resource Ctr Missing & Exploited C, 1990-94; pres, Greater Greenville Pan Hellenic Coun, 1990-92; pres, SC Asn Human Serv Agencies, 1991-93; bd mem, Greater Greenville Chamber Com, 1991-94; voc comt chmn, Greenville Breakfast Rotary Club, 1992-93; exec dir, Aiken/Barnwell Counties Community Action Comn Inc; bd mem, Sunbelt Human Advan Resources Inc; Gov's Interagency Adv Coun; Basic Skills Adv Comn; Greenville BrNat Asn Advan Colored People Educ Comt; Greenville Asn dir Health & Social Serv Agencies; Greenville County United Way Bd dir; exec coordr, Sunbelt Econ Opportunity Conf; exec comt, Omega Psi Phi Fraternity Inc; coord consult, Omega Teens Enrichment Proj. **Home Addr:** 514 Edwards Mill Rd, PO Box 1273, Taylors, SC 29687, **Home Phone:** (864)244-3576. **Business Addr:** President, Chief Executive Officer, Sunbelt Human Advancement Resources Inc, 1200 Pendleton St, Greenville, SC 29611-4832, **Business Phone:** (864)269-0700.

**CROSS, JUDGE DENISE L.**
Lawyer, judge. **Personal:** Born May 16, 1953, Cincinnati, OH; daughter of Paul and Julia Martin; married Edward H IV; children: Vashon, Danielle & Hewitt. **Educ:** Wilberforce Univ, BA, 1975; Univ Akron Law Sch, JD, 1978. **Career:** Erie County Pa, asst pub defender, 1979-87; Montgomery County Prosecutors Off, asst prosecuting atty, 1988-90; Montgomery Cty Juv Ct, chief magistrate, legal dir, 1990-2001; Montgomery County Common Rels Ct, admin judge, currently; Pvt practr; Legal Aid Soc Dayton, domestic rels supv atty. **Orgs:** Child Protection Task Force Montgomery County; Delta Sigma Theta Sorority Inc, Dayton Alumnae chap; Thurgood Marshall Law Soc; Ohio Bar Asn; Ohio Asn Magistrates; Girl Scout Leader Troop 69, Buckeye Trails Girl Scout Coun; Supreme Ct Ohio Adv Comt C; Families & Ct; Nat Bar Asn; Nat Asn Ct Mgt; Dayton Bar Asn Ethics Comt; Nat Asn Women Judges; Nat Asn Ct Mgt; Dayton Bar Asn; Dayton Bar Asn Ethics Comt; Ohio State Bar Asn; Queens Finance; Carrousels Inc Dayton Chap; lifetime mem, Nat Asn Adv Coloured People; Stan Greenberg Family Law Forum. **Honors/Awds:** Girl Scouts of Western Ohio Women of Leadership Hall of Fame, 2010. **Home Addr:** 6801 Peters Pk, Dayton, OH 45414-2113, **Home Phone:** (937)454-0443. **Business Addr:** Administrative Judge, Dayton Montgomery County Courts, 301 W 3rd St 2nd Fl, Dayton, OH 45422-2160, **Business Phone:** (937)225-4063.

**CROSS, DR. DOLORES E.**
School administrator. **Personal:** Born Aug 29, 1938, Newark, NJ; daughter of Charles Tucker and Ozie Johnson; children: Thomas Edwin Jr & Jane Ellen. **Educ:** Seton Hall Univ, BS, educ, 1963; Hofstra Univ, MS, educ, 1968; Univ Mich, PhD, 1971. **Career:** Northwestern Univ, asst prof educ & dir MA teaching, 1970-74; Claremont Grad Sch, assoc prof educ & dir teacher educ, 1974-78; City Univ New York, vice chancellor stud affairs & spec prog, 1978-81; New York State Higher Educ Serv Corp, pres, 1981-88; Univ Minn, assoc provost & assoc vpres acad affairs, 1988-90; Chicago State Univ, pres, 1990-97; Morris Brown Col, pres, 1998-2002; Claremont Grad Univ, prof & univ adminr, currently. **Orgs:** Women Exec State Govt; adv bd mem, Asn Black Women Higher Educ; Nat Asn Advan Colored People; Am Educ Res Asn, 1990; vice chmn, Am Asn Higher Educ; vice chair, Campus Compact, sr consult, S Africa Proj; bd mem, Inst Int Educ, Nat Ctr Pub Policy, Field Mus; bd trustee, Adelphi Univ, 2002; Am Coun Educ & Inst Int Educ; chairperson, Am Asn Higher Educ. **Home Addr:** 10400 Longwood Dr, Chicago, IL 60643. **Business Addr:** Professor, University Administrator, Claremont Grad University, 150 E 10th St, Claremont, CA 91711, **Business Phone:** (909)621-8000.

**CROSS, REV. HAMAN**
Clergy. **Personal:** Born Jan 28, 1949, Detroit, MI; son of Haman Sr and Malettor Gause; married Roberta Alexander; children: Haman III, Gilvonna Corine & Sharryl Lanise. **Educ:** Nyack Missionary Col, Nyack, NY, attended 1968; William Tyndale Col, BA, 1971. **Career:** Detroit Afro Am Mission, Detroit, Mich, dir youth guid, 1971-82; William Tyndale Col, Farmington, Mich, varsity basketball coach, 1973-79; Rosedale Pk Baptist Church, founder & sr pastor, 1982-; Publications: Sanctified Sex, 1991; Let's Talk About Sex, 1992. **Orgs:** Bd mem, Carver Foreign Missions; bd mem, Christian Res & Develop; bd mem, Here's Life Black Am; bd dir, Joy Jesus, 1983; Victory Christian Sch, 1984; consult, Taylor Univ, 1985; consult, World Christian Ctr, 1985; consult, Cedine Bible Mission, 1986; bd dir, C's Ctr, Detroit, Mich, 1986; consult, Justice Fel, 1987; bd dir, Ctr Black Church, 1987; bd dir, Black Am Response African Crisis; bd dir, Carver Foreign Missions; bd dir, Detroit Afro-Am Mission; speaker, Campus Christ. **Home Addr:** 14017 Robson, Detroit, MI 48227, **Home Phone:** (313)837-4813. **Business Addr:** Founder, Senior Pastor, Rosedale Park Baptist Church, 14179 Evergreen Rd, Detroit, MI 48223, **Business Phone:** (313)538-1180.

**CROSS, HOWARD EDWARD, JR.**
Football player, broadcaster, executive. **Personal:** Born Aug 8, 1967, Huntsville, AL; married Pia; children: Isabella & Howard. **Educ:** Univ Ala, BA, bus & BA, finance, 1988. **Career:** Football player (retired), executive; NY Giants, tight end, 1989-2001; YES Network, broadcaster, 2002-10, co-host & color commentator, currently; New York Giants, radio reporter; Colliers Int, sr managing dir, 2008-12; Cresa, real estate broker, sr vpres, 2012-. **Orgs:** Mem, Fel Christian Athletes. **Honors/Awds:** Super Bowl, 1990; True Value Man of the Year, NY Giants, 1995. **Home Addr:** , NJ. **Business Addr:** Senior Vice President, Cresa, 450 Lexington Ave 32nd Fl, New York, NY 10017, **Business Phone:** (212)758-3131.

**CROSS, JUNE VICTORIA**
Journalist, educator. **Personal:** Born Jan 5, 1954, New York, NY; daughter of James and Norma Catherine Storch; married Larry Storch; married Waldon Ricks. **Educ:** Harvard-Radcliffe Col, BA, 1975. **Career:** The Boston Globe, Boston, Mass, corresp, 1975-76; WGBH-TV, PBS, Boston, Mass, asst dir, 1976-78; WGBH-TV, PBS, Boston, Mass, prod mgr, 1977-78; Nac Neil & Lehrer News Hour, reporter urban reg affairs, 1978-80, reporter def & nat secy, 1980-84, reporter polit, 1984-85, producer & corresp, 1985-, producer CBS News, 1987-91; Frontline WGBH-TV CFR, producer, sr producer, 2001-; Columbia Univ, Grad Sch Jour, assoc prof, prof, 2006-; Doc: "This Far By Faith"; "The Old Man & The Show"; "Ashes of the Cold War; Showdown in Haiti; The Confessions of RosaLee"; "A Kid Kills", "Wilheminas War". **Orgs:** Trans Africa, 1979-; founding bd mem, Harvard-Radcliff Black Alumni Assn, NY, 1980, Wash, 1983; judge, Electron Jour Awards Robt F Kennedy Memorial, 1983; Judge, Electron Journalism Awards Nat Urban Coalition, 1984; coun, foreign rels, Nat Press Club; Nat Acad TV Arts & Sci; Nat Assn Black Journalists, 1988; fel WEB DuBois Inst Afro-Am Studies, Harvard Univ; fel Carnegie-Mellon Univ Sch Urban & Pub Affairs. **Honors/Awds:** Emmy Award Outstanding Coverage of Breaking News Story, Nat Acad TV Arts & Scis, 1983 & 1997; Emmy nominee Outstanding Series, 1985; Defense Debate, 1986; Joan S Barone Award, Outstanding Reporting Defense Debate; DuPont-Columbia jounalism Award, Excellence in Broadcast Jour, 1995; DHL, Knox Col, 2015. **Special Achievements:** Author Of "Secret Daughter A Mixed Race Daughter and the Mother Who Gave Her Away", 1996. **Home Addr:** 2611 Frederick Douglass B, New York, NY 10030, **Home Phone:** (212)926-0105. **Business Addr:** Associate Professor, Columbia University, 2950 Broadway, New York, NY 10027, **Business Phone:** (212)854-7221.

**CROSS, FR. WILLIAM HOWARD**
Clergy, librarian, teacher. **Personal:** Born Oct 19, 1946, Cincinnati, OH. **Educ:** Univ Cincinnati; St Gregory's Sem, PhB; St Mary's Sem, MDiv. **Career:** Mt St Mary's Sem, stud librn, 1972-73; St James Cathedral Sch, Dayton, Ohio, relig educ, 1973-74; Theol McNicholas High Sch, teacher, 1980; St Andrew Church, Cincinnati, Ohio, pastor, 1988; St Joseph Church & Archdiocese Cincinnati, assoc pastor; St Joseph Cathedral Sch, rel educ coordr; St Margaret Mary Church, Cincinnati, Ohio, assoc pastor; Social Justice & New Testament Guardian Angels Church, assoc pastor. **Orgs:** Archdiocesan Soc Action Comn; First degree Knights Columbus; Cincinnati W End Task Force; Nat Off Black Catholics; Nat Black Cath Clergy Caucus; bd dir, Jobs People; bd dir, Nat Asn Advan Colored People; Cincinnati chap. **Special Achievements:** First African-American Archdiocesan priest to be appointed a pastor at St Andrew Church in 1988. **Home Addr:** 609 Maple Ave, Cincinnati, OH 45229.

**CROSS-BATTLE, TARA**
Volleyball player. **Personal:** Born Sep 16, 1968, Houston, TX; daughter of Leo O Cross Jr and Ruthie M Tate; married Spencer. **Educ:** Calif State Univ, Long Beach, attended 1989. **Career:** Vollyball player (retired); Ital Volleyball League, spiker, 1993; Women's Natl & Olympic Volleyball Team, 1990-2004; Pallavolo Ancona, 1992-95; Leites Nestle, 1996-99; Parana Volei Clube, 1999-2000; Flamengo, 2000-01; Volley Bergamo, 2001-02; Reggio Emilia, 2002-03; Tex Pride VBC, head coaching, 2011; Houston Juniors Volleyball Club, head coach, currently. **Honors/Awds:** Player of the Year, NCAA, 1988, 1989; Amateur Women's Sports Day, Player of the Year (all sports), 1989; Honda, Honda Award, 1990; Silver Medal, NORCECA, 1991; US Women's National Team, Coach's Award, 1991-92; Olympics, Bronze Olympic Medal, 1992; Bronze Medal, FIVB Super Four, 1992; Most Valuable Player & Best Scorer, FIVB World Grand Prix, 1995; Silver Medal, Pan American Games, 1995; Most Valuable Player, NORCECA Championships, 2001; World Grand Prix, Gold Medal, 2001; Silver Medal, Women's Volleyball World Championships, 2002; Gold Medal, Pan American Games, 2003; Bronze Medal, 2003; Bronze Medal, World Cup, 2003. **Home Addr:** PO Box 2064, Seaside, CA 93955-2064. **Business Addr:** Head Coach, Houston Juniors Volleyball Club, 15400 Hempstead Rd, Houston, TX 77040, **Business Phone:** (832)678-4670.

**CROSS-MCCLAM, DELORIS NMI**
Automotive executive. **Personal:** Born Aug 5, 1952, Lake City, SC; daughter of Louis J and Pauline; children: LaTarcha D. **Educ:** Prince George's Community Col, AA, 1987; Columbia Union Col, BS, bus admin, 1991; Mercer Univ, MBA, 1997. **Career:** AVCO Financial Serv Spring Lake, NC, admin asst, 1972, asst mgr, 1978; Ford Motor Credit Co, clerical position, 1979; Ford's Rental Distrib & Bus Oper, mkt & sales mgr. **Orgs:** Nat Asn Advan Colored People, 1978-; Howard Univ Scholar Comt, 1986-; Nat Black MBA Asn, 1996. **Honors/Awds:** Hall of Fame, Co Sch Dis, Florence, SC, 1997; SC African American Women's Conference Award, 1994. **Home Addr:** 1400 Martinique Ct SW, Atlanta, GA 30331, **Home Phone:** (404)349-5631.

**CROSS-WHITE, AGNES**
Publisher. **Personal:** children: Sherman R Jr. **Educ:** Howard Univ, BA, hist, 1967. **Career:** Charlottesville/Abermale Tribune, publ & ed, 1991-; We People Online, Publ, 2011-; Goldie's Organics, owner, 2012-13. **Orgs:** Assoc, African-Am leadership orgn Proj 21a. **Business Addr:** Publisher, Charlottesville/Abermale Tribune, 250 W Main St Suite 402, Charlottesville, VA 22902-5070, **Business Phone:** (804)979-0373.

**CROSSE, REV. ST GEORGE IDRIS BRYON, III**
Government official, clergy. **Personal:** Born Sep 16, 1939, St. Georges; son of Winston C and Iris Ernest Thomas; married Delois Bowman; children: Karin Vanessa & Liris Jewel Christina. **Educ:** Univ Md Eastern Shore, BS, 1964; Coppin State Col, MEd, 1975; Wesley Theol Sem, Mdiv, 1980; Univ Baltimore Sch Law, JD, 1970. **Career:** Calvary United Methodist Church, sr pastor, 1975-78; Lewin United Methodist Church, sr pastor, 1978-80; Crosse-Henson & Assoc, pres & ceo, 1979-83; St Matthew's United Methodist Church, sr pastor, 1980; US Dept Housing & Urban Devel, spec adv minority affairs, regional mgr Md, 1987-89; Morgan State Univ, Baltimore, Md, asst to pres, 1989-; Fallston Fed Hill Charge, United Methodist Church, sr pastor, 1989. **Orgs:** Staff atty, Md Human Rels Comt; founder & pres, Soc Advan Families Everywhere, 1979-85, Baltimore Coalition Against Crime, 1980; nat deleg, Nat Repub Conv, 1980; founder, Md Coalition Against Crime, 1981; Md State Cent Community, 1982; Baltimore Wash Conf United Methodist Church; Md Housing Policy Coun; Regional Planning Coun. **Home Addr:** 3509 Kings Point Rd, Randallstown, MD 21133-1605, **Home Phone:** (410)655-0174.

**CROSSLAND, PAULA**
Sales manager. **Career:** Citicorp, sales training mgr. **Business Addr:** Sales Training Manager, Citicorp, 14700 Citicorp Dr Bldg 2 Fl 2, Hagerstown, MD 21742, **Business Phone:** (301)714-5832.

**CROSSLEY, DR. FRANK ALPHONSO**
Engineer, manager. **Personal:** Born Feb 19, 1925, Chicago, IL; son of Joseph Buddie and Rosa Lee Brefford; married Elaine J Sherman; children: Desne Adrienne. **Educ:** Ill Inst Tech, BS, chem engineering, 1945, MS, PhD, MetE, 1947, 1950. **Career:** Engineer (retired); Tenn A&I State Univ, instr, 1948-49, prof foundry engineering & dept head, 1950-52; IIT Res Inst, sr scientist, 1952-66; Lockheed Palo Alto Res Lbtry, sr mem, 1966-74; Lockheed Missiles & Space Co, dept mgr, 1974-79, mgr dept missile body mech engineering, 1978-79, cnltg engr, 1979-86; Aerojet Propulsion Res Inst, res dir propulsion mat, 1986-87; Gen Corp Aerojet Tech Syst, dir mat applns, 1987-90, Propulsion Div, tech prin, 1990-91; Mus Fine Arts, position, develop. **Orgs:** Minerals, Metals & Mat Soc; Am Inst Mining, 1946-; Sigma Xi, 1947-; Nat Mat Adv Bd Ad Hoc Comt Welding High Strength Struct, 1972-74; chmn, Titanium Comt Metall Soc-Am Inst Motion Engrs, 1974-75; fel fel ASM Int, 1978-; Mat Comt Am Inst Aero & Astro, 1979-81; fel African Sci Inst, 2006; Am Inst Aeronaut & Astronaut. **Honors/Awds:** Gen Corp Aerojet R B Young Technical Innovation Award in quality & manufacturing, 1990; Trailblazer Award, The Northern CA Coun Black Prof Engrs & Nat Soc Black Engrs-Alumni Ext, Silicon Valley Chap, 1994; Leadership Award for Community Service, S Middlesex Men's Club, 2006. **Special Achievements:** One of fewer than forty African American integrated USN officers during WW II in an experiment which proved that white military personnel would take orders from black officers; Published in various technical journals and symposia, 1951-90; Patents 7 issued, 1957-83; Author: Physical Metallurgy Basis for Achieving 300-KSI Strength in Transage Titanium Alloys, 1973; Correlation of Microstructures with Fracture Toughness Properties in Metals, 1973; Articles 58 service Northern CA Council of Black Professional Engineers 1978; First African-American to receive a doctorate degree in Metal Engineering. **Home Addr:** 44 Goodnow Lane, Framingham, MA 01702-5505, **Home Phone:** (508)620-9353.

**CROUCH, PASTOR ANDRAE EDWARD.** **See Obituaries Section.**

**CROUCH, ROBERT ALLEN**
Government official. **Personal:** Born Aug 9, 1955, St. Joseph, MO; son of Robert A Sr and Arvilla Hughes. **Educ:** Southwest Mo State Univ, Springfield, MO, BS, psychol, 1978; William Woods Univ, MBA, bus mgt, 2000; Capella Univ, PhD, mgt. **Career:** Mo Dept Pub Safety, Jefferson City, Mo, prog specist, 1979-81; Mo Dept Labor & Ind Rel, Jefferson City, Mo, asst dir, 1981, dir admin, 1994-2005; Mo Div Workers Compensation, dep dir, 1992-94; Village of Matteson, Matteson, IL, dir human resources, 2005-07; Ill State Treas, dir human resources, 2007-11; UC San Diego, asst vice chancellor human resources, 2015-. **Orgs:** Chmn, Black Christian Single Adult Task Force, 1984-; Nat Asn Advan Colored People, Urban League, 1981, Nat Forum Black Pub Adminrs, 1987; Alpha Phi Alpha Fraternity; Soc Human Resources Professionals; Nat Asn African Americans Human Resources; Col & Univ Prof Asn Human Resources. **Home Addr:** 1415 Summity View Dr, Holts Summit, MO 65043. **Business Addr:** Assistant Vice Chancellor, UC San Diego, University of California, La Jolla, CA 92093-0005, **Business Phone:** (858)534-3135.

**CROUTHER, DR. BETTY JEAN**
Educator. **Personal:** Born Mar 2, 1950, Carthage, MS; daughter of Eugene Garner and Lee M; children: Velsie Dione Pate. **Educ:** Jackson State Univ, BS, art educ, 1972; Univ Miss, MFA, art, 1975; Univ Mo, Columbia, PhD, art hist, 1985. **Career:** Lincoln Univ, asst prof art, 1978-80; Jackson State Univ, asst prof art, 1980-83; Univ Miss, assoc prof art hist, 1983-; Stanford Univ, J Paul Getty postdoctoral fel, 1986. **Orgs:** Col Art Asn; Southeastern Col Art Conf; Nat Art Educ Asn; Miss Art Educ Asn; Phi Kappa Phi Hon Soc; Kappa Pi Int Hon Art Fraternity; Pi Delta Phi Hon Fraternity; acad freedom & fac responsibility, Univ Standing Comt; chair & co-chair, Southeastern Col Art Asn & Col Art Asn conferences; fel, Kress Found, Ford Found; bd trustee, Miss Pub Univs. **Home Addr:** PO Box 2805, University, MS 38677. **Business Addr:** Associate Professor of Art History, University of Mississippi, 263 Meek Hall, University, MS 38677, **Business Phone:** (662)915-7647.

**CROUTHER, BETTY M.**
Educator, elementary school teacher, association executive. **Personal:** Born Jun 5, 1931, St. Joseph, MO; married Melvin S Jr; children: Lou-Ann. **Educ:** Lincoln Univ, BA, 1952; NY Univ, MA, 1953. **Career:** Stephens Sch, Asheville, 1953-54; Newport Sch, 1954; AR Baptist Col, Little Rock, AR, 1954-56; Blewett Sch, St Louis, 1956-61; Garfield Sch, Columbus, OH, 1961-63; Moses Cleveland Sch, teacher, 1963-77; Cleveland Bd Educ, 5th grade enrichment teacher, 1985. **Orgs:** Chmnvars comm, life mem & past pres, Nat Asn Negro Bus & Prof Women's Clubs; pres, Nat Coun Negro Women; Delta Sigma Theta; Nat Bus League; NOWCuyahoga Co Coalition; Alpha Wives. **Honors/Awds:** Woman of the Year, Baptist Ch, 1972; Ollie C Porter Leadership Award, 1973; Outstanding Elementary Teacher of Am, 1974; Appreciation Award, Cleveland Sr Club, 1976. **Home Addr:** 3719 Concord Dr, Beachwood, OH 44122, **Home Phone:** (216)464-8269. **Business Addr:** Teacher, Moses Cleveland School, 4092 E 146 St, Cleveland, OH 44128, **Business Phone:** (216)295-3508.

**CROWELL, DR. BERNARD GENE**
Educator, executive. **Personal:** Born Nov 3, 1930, Chickasha, OK; married Virginia M; children: Bernard Jr & Christopher L. **Educ:** Langston Univ, BS, 1953; Univ Ore, MS, 1958; Okla State Univ, DEd, 1970. **Career:** Educator, executive (retired); Langston Univ, exec asst to pres, 1970-75; dir inst rsch, 1973-75, inst rsch consortium, 1973-75, dirinter discip prog coord col & univ, 1973-74; dir admis & rec, 1973-75; Tenn State Univ, vpres acad affairs, 1975-84, exec admin intl affairs, 1984, resolution fac senate, 1984. **Orgs:** Pres, Coun Tenn State Univ, 1975-; chmn, Satisfactory Progress Comt Tenn State Univ, 1985-; fac athletics rep, Tenn State Univ, 1986-; pres, Optimist Club, 1986-; Nat Col Athletic Asn. **Honors/Awds:** Boss of the Year, Tenn State Univ Secretaries Asn, 1977; Phi Beta Lambda Award, 1981; Distinguished Service Award, Tenn State Univ, 1984. **Home Addr:** 4800 Traceway Dr, Nashville, TN 37221-4079, **Home Phone:** (615)646-0141. **Business Addr:** TN.

**CROWELL, GERMANE L.**
Football coach, football player. **Personal:** Born Sep 13, 1976, Winston-Salem, NC; son of Napolean and Patricia. **Educ:** Univ Va, attended 1994. **Career:** Football player (retired), coach; Detroit Lions, 2001, wide receiver, 1998, 2000, 2002, tight end, wide receiver, 1999; Burning Flame Christian Church, pastor, currently; N Forsyth High Sch, teacher's asst, currently; Carver High Sch, Winston-Salem, NC, head varsity football coach, 2013-. **Business Addr:** Head Varsity Football Coach, Carver High School, 3545 Carver Sch Rd, Winston-Salem, NC 27105, **Business Phone:** (336)727-2987.

**CRUDUP, GWENDOLYN M.**
Television producer. **Personal:** Born Aug 14, 1961, Lebanon, TN. **Educ:** Univ Tenn, Knoxville, TN, BS, commun, 1983; Univ Mo, Columbia, MA, jour, 1987. **Career:** WAND-TV, Decatur, producer, 1987-88; WTEN-TV, Albany, producer, 1988-90; WPVI-TV, Philadelphia, assoc producer, 1990-. **Orgs:** Soc Prof Journalists, 1987-88; Nat Asn Black Journalists, 1987-; Philadelphia Asn Black Journalists, 1990-92, 1994-95; Nat Asn Female Execs, 1991-92. **Honors/Awds:** Grad & Prof Scholar Recipient, 1985-87. **Home Addr:** 3900 City Ave D807, Philadelphia, PA 19131-2905. **Business Addr:** Associate Producer, WPVI-TV6/Capital Cities, 4100 City Ave, Philadelphia, PA 19131, **Business Phone:** (215)878-9700.

**CRUISE, ESQ. WARREN MICHAEL**
Lawyer, government official. **Personal:** Born Jun 3, 1939, Baltimore, MD; children: Enid & Wesley. **Educ:** Morgan State Univ, BA, 1963; Howard Univ, Sch Law, JD, 1970, MA, phil, 1996. **Career:** DC Govt, Off Employee Appeals, admin judge, exec dir, 1980; Nat Ed Asn, legal coun, 1985; Neighborhood Legal Serv Prog, staff atty. **Orgs:** Vpres, bd dir, NEA Credit Union; Retirement Bd, NEA Kappa Alpha Psi Frat; Phi Alpha; Delta Law Frat; Nat Asn Advan Colored People; Nat Bar Asn; Conf Black Lawyers; Am Bar Asn; asst sec, Kirkwood Ski Educ Found, 2008. **Honors/Awds:** MJ Naylor Memorial Award. **Home Addr:** 415 12th St NW Rm 303, Washington, DC 20004-1905. **Busi-**

**ness Addr:** Executive Director, DC Govt, 1100 4th St SW (E Bldg) Suite 620E, Washington, DC 20024, **Business Phone:** (202)727-0004.

### CRUM, DR. ALBERT B.

Physician, psychiatrist. **Personal:** Born Nov 17, 1931. **Educ:** Univ Redlands, BS, 1953; Harvard Med Sch, MD, 1957; NY Univ, MS, neuroanatomy & neurosciences, 1987. **Career:** Columbia Univ Div, Bellevue Hosp, internship, 1957-58, psychiat resident, 1963; Psychiat Inst Columbia Presby Med Ctr, residency; Am Inst Addictive Dis, chief psychiat; Human Behav Found, med dir, gen ed, chmn; New York Univ, clin prof behavioural sci, mgt sci & adj prof base sci, 1987-2002; ProImmune Co, pres & founder, 2000-; StressWatchers Inc, pres & founder, 2000-. **Orgs:** AMA; Kings County Med Soc; Delta Alpha Hon Soc; NY St Med Soc; World Med Asn; chmn, Duke Hall Camp Harvard Med Soc; Harvard Club NY; Acad Med Studies, MENSA; Kappa Alpha Psi; bd dir, Univ Redlands Sci Asn, Hon DSc, Redlands Calif, 1974; Phi Beta Kappa; Sigma Xi; Mensa; fel Royal Col physicians & surg, 1984; life mem, Sci Res Soc; life mem & life fel Am col Forensic Examiners, 1998. **Honors/Awds:** Diplomat Nat Bd Med Exam, 1958; Brooklyn Young Man of the Year, 1966; Pope John XXIII Gold Medallion, 1974; Bicentennial Award, Nat Jogging Asn, 1976; Diplomat Am Bd Forensic Examr, 1998; Diplomat Pan Am Med Asn; Hall of Fame, 2005; Outstanding Achievement Award; Harvard Medical Student Research Fellowship; Jubilee Medallion Award Recipient, Univ Redlands; Outstanding Young Man of the Year Award, Brooklyn Jr Chamber Com; Citizen of the Year Award, Brooklyn Philharmonic; Who's Who in America; Who's Who in the World; Who's Who in Medicine and Health Care; Who's Who in Finance and Industry; Who's Who in Science and Engineering. **Home Phone:** (845)876-6135. **Business Addr:** President, Founder, The ProImmune Company LLC, 64 E Mkt St, Rhinebeck, NY 12572, **Business Phone:** (845)876-3222.

### CRUMP, DR. ARTHEL EUGENE (GENE)

Lawyer, executive director. **Personal:** Born Oct 19, 1947, New York, NY; son of Walter Eugene and Mary Yeates; married Linda Rose Cooke; children: Kathryn Rose & Eric Eugene. **Educ:** Nebr Wesleyan Univ, attended 1967; Univ Nebr, Lincoln, BA, sociol, 1973; Univ Nebr Col Law, JD, 1976. **Career:** Legal Serv Southeast Nebr, atty, 1976-82; Nebr Gov Robert Kerrey, legal coun, 1983-85; Nebr Dept Justice, dep atty gen, 1985-91, gen coun, chief dep tax comnr, 1991; Nebr Wesleyan Univ, Criminal Justice Dept, vis instr, 1992, 1995 & 1998; Univ Nebr, assoc gen coun, 2001-; Cent Interstate Low-Level Radio active Waste Comn, exec gen coun, exec dir. **Orgs:** Nebr State Bar Asn; Nat Asn Atty Gen; Nat Gov's Asn; bd dir, Univ Nebr Gymnastic Booster Club; bd dir, Family Serv Asn Lincoln; bd dir, United Way Lincoln & Lancaster County; bd dir, Theater Arts Youth; bd dir, Malone Community Ctr; bd dir, Lincoln Community Playhouse; panel mem, Nebr Arts Coun; Touring Artists Progs; Nat Asn Advan Colored People; Nebr Civil Liberties Union; Coalition Black Men; Univ Nebr Booster Club Womens Athletics; bd trustee, Nebr Wesleyan Univ; adv comt, Lincoln Pub Schs Gifted C; adv comt, Lancaster County Child Care; Malone Area Citizens Coun; Lincoln Pub Schs Eval Stud Health Educ Proj; bd dir, Pinewood Bowl Asn; bd dir, Leadership Lincoln; Nebr Supreme Ct Judicial Nomination Comn; Lincoln Bar Asn; Midwest Bar Asn; Nat Low-Level Waste Forum Comn Rep; Lincoln Interfaith Coun; Cornhusker Coun BSA; Crucible Club; Troop 49 Boy Scouts Am, Arborland Dist; Nebr Urban League; bd dir, Found Educ Funding; d dir, Nebr Wesleyan Univ; Newman United Methodist Church; Bd Higher Educ& Campus Ministry; Nebr United Methodist Church; Community Leaders Am; Found Eucational Serv; Nat Stud Loan Prog; Woods Charitable Fund; Ctr PeopleNeed; Nebr Dem State Cent Comt; Phi Delta Phi. **Honors/Awds:** Nebr Law Col Scholarship; Kelso Morgan Scholarship; Alumni Achievement Award, Nebr Wesleyan Univ; Silver Key Award, Law Student Div, Am Bar Asn; Lincoln Alumni Achievement Award, Univ Nebr; Leonore Lettcher Community Service Award, Nat Asn Advan Colored People. **Home Addr:** 3260 S 31st St, Lincoln, NE 68502-5207, **Home Phone:** (402)423-8406. **Business Addr:** Associate General Counsel, University of Nebraska, 241 Varner Hall 3835 Holdrege St, Lincoln, NE 68583, **Business Phone:** (402)472-7138.

### CRUMP, BENJAMIN L.

President (organization), lawyer. **Personal:** Born Oct 10, 1969, Lumberton, NC; son of Helen; married Genae Angelique. **Educ:** Fla State Univ, Sch Law, BA, law, 1992, JD, 1995. **Career:** Parks & Crump LLC, pres, partner & prin, currently. **Orgs:** Virgil Hawkins Fla Chap; Nat Bar Asn; Tallahassee Barrister's Asn; Am Bar Asn; Acad Fla Trial Lawyers, Civil Trial Lawyers Div; Small Firms & Solo Practitioners Div; bd dir, N Fla Legal Servs; Bethel baptist church; Am Asn Justice; Am Bd Trial Lawyers; Am Inns Ct; Boy Scouts Am N Fla Coun; Omega Psi Phi Fraternity; Nat Black Alumni Asn Fla State Univ; Fed Bar Asn; Fla Justice Asn; Nat Asn Advan Color People; N Fla Ctr Equal Justice Inc; bd chmn, Fla's Big Bend Fair Housing Ctr Inc. **Business Addr:** Partner, Principal & President, Parks & Crump LLC, 240 N Magnolia Dr, Tallahassee, FL 32301, **Business Phone:** (850)222-3333.

### CRUMP, JANICE RENAE

Manager, executive director. **Personal:** Born Aug 9, 1947, Dragerton, UT; daughter of Jerry Andrew Green Sr and Johnnie Lee Roney Lewis; married Maurice Malone Sr; children: Maurice Jr, Jason Bernard & Toiya Danielle. **Educ:** Tuskegee Inst, Tuskegee, Ala, BS, fashion design & illus, 1969; NC Cent Univ, Durham, NC, BA, media jour, 1988; Simmons Grad Sch Mgt, cert, 1989. **Career:** AT&T Southern Bell, Atlanta, Ga, 1970; Ga Power Co, Atlanta, Ga, customer serv, 1970-72; Delta Airlines, Atlanta, Ga, reservationist, 1972-74; Soul City Co, Soul City, NC, pub rels, 1975-80; WTVD II/Cap Cities ABC, Durham, NC, community affairs dir; US Cong, Housing & Urban Develop, 1992-94; Hon Eva M Clayton, press secy, 1993-94; US, dep asst secy, 1994-98; Cong Black Caucus Found Inc, nat dir, 1998-2001, dir media rels & commun, 1999-2006, media consult, 2004-06; Comt House Admin, US House Representatives, sr dir spec proj, 1998-2006, dir commun, 2007-09; JRC Commun, pres, 2011-. **Orgs:** Chmn, Warren Co Bd Elections, 1975-82; pres, Northside & Norlina & Warren High PTA's; 1976-88; Gov Small Bus Adv Coun, 1979-81; pres, Warren Co Dem Women, 1982-83; vice chair, Z Smith Reynolds Found, 1988-91. **Honors/Awds:** Volunteer Award, Am Cancer Soc Co; Community Service Award, WTVDII Adv Comm; Parent of the Year Award, Soul City Interfaith Coun, The Silver Bell Award, Ad Coun, Total Sta; Project Award, NBACA; Women of Achievement Silver Medallion Award, Women of Achievement Organization, 1991; Exceptional Service Award, HUD Secretary Andrew Cuomo, 1998; Chief Architect Award, Brown Vs Board of Education National Essay Contest, 2004; Award for Community Service, community & the public service organization, Delta Sigma Theta Sorority, Inc, 2005. **Home Addr:** PO Box 27, Soul City, NC 27553, **Home Phone:** (919)456-2180. **Business Addr:** President, JRC Communications, 1200 Braddock Pl, Alexandria, VA 22314, **Business Phone:** (703)618-5090.

### CRUMP, NATHANIEL L., SR.

Engineer. **Personal:** Born Jul 18, 1920, Little Rock, AR; married Ruby M Chappell; children: N Lloyd Jr. **Educ:** Lincoln Univ, BS, chem, 1948. **Career:** Engineer (retired); Du Good Micro-anal Lab, micro-analyst, 1948-52; Universal Match R & D Arma Div, lab asst, proj eng, 1952-59; Hanley Ind & Pyrotechnics & Explo Chem, proj eng, 1959-61; St Louis Child's Hosp, Cardiol Sec, res asst, 1961-62; Mercury, Gemini, Apollo, Sky Lab Shuttle Progs, unit chief, 1962; McDonnell Douglas Aerospace Co, space eng, 1987. **Orgs:** Am Chem Soc; Soc Aerospace Mat & Process Eng; Am Asn Contam Cont Kappa Alpha Psi Frat; bd mem, Coalition Environ; vpres, St L Co Chap, Civil Int Civic Org; adv comt to vpres Humphrey, Youth Motivation, 1965-68; bd mem, Human Rel Univ City, MO, 1972-78; loaned exec, Greater St Louis United Way Dr, 1987-94; loaned exec, Arts & Educ Coun Dr, 1988-93; bd mem, Tower Village Nursing Home, 1992-93; adv bd mem, Mid E Area Agency Aging Found, 1992-94, bd mem, 1995; bd mem, ABHF, 1993. **Honors/Awds:** Inducted in Greater St Louis Area Amateur Baseball Hall of Fame, 1992; Distinguished Alumnus Award, Harris Stowe State Col, 1993. **Special Achievements:** Author papers on "Organic Micro analysis, Analytical Chemistry", "Space System Contam Continent", "Aircraft Hydralic System Clean Control". **Home Addr:** 950 Shandel Dr, St Louis, MO 63132, **Home Phone:** (314)727-1399.

### CRUMP-CAINE, LYNN

Executive. **Personal:** Born Jan 1, 1957?; married John B Caine; children: Mikelle & John. **Career:** McDonald's, 1975-99, sr vpres U.S, 1998-2000, exec vpres, US restaurant systs, 1999-2001, exec vpres worldwide systs & opers, 2001-04; McDonald's Innovation Ctr, Romeoville, Ill, 2004; OutsideIn Consult, founder & chief exec officer, 2004-; Krispy Kreme Donuts, dir, 2007-; G&K Serv Inc, dir, 2008-. **Orgs:** Nat Asn Female Exec; NAWBO; vice chmn, Advocate Health Care; Women Looking Ahead news mag; Goodman Theatre; Nominating & Corp Governance Comts. **Business Addr:** Founder, Chief Executive Officer, OutsideIn Consulting, Concourse Ctr 5 Concourse Pkwy Suite 3000, Atlanta, GA 30328, **Business Phone:** (770)392-3304.

### CRUMPLER, CARLESTER T., JR.

Executive, football player. **Personal:** Born Sep 5, 1971, Greenville, NC; son of Carlester; married Kimberly; children: 2. **Educ:** E Carolina Univ, BA, finance, 1993, MBA, 2004. **Career:** Football player (retired), executive, analyst; Seattle Seahawks, tight end, 1994-98; Minn Vikings, tight end, 1999; 24 Hour Fitness, corp sales liaison, fitness counr, 2001-02; Pirate Radio 1250AM, col football analyst, 2003-04; Bank Am, officer, credit prod analyst, 2005-06, asst vpres, sr client mgr analyst, 2006-10, client mgr, sr vpres & sr relationship mgr, 2010-. **Orgs:** Trustee, E Carolina Univ Found Bd; bd trustee, Vidant Med Ctr, 2014-; N Pt Ministries, Buckhead Church; Healthcare Financial Mgt Asn; NFL Retired Players Asn; Toastmasters Int; Radical Mentoring. **Business Addr:** Assistant Vice President, Bank of America Corp, 100 N Tryon St Suite 170, Charlotte, NC 28202, **Business Phone:** (980)335-3561.

### CRUMPTON, DR. LESIA (DR. LESIA L CRUMPTON-YOUNG)

Educator, college administrator, chief executive officer. **Personal:** married Reginald; children: Mattlyn & Ashlee. **Educ:** Tex A&M Univ, BS, indust engineering, 1988, MS, human factors engineering & ergonomics, safety engineering, 1991, PhD, human factors engineering & ergonomics, safety engineering, 1993. **Career:** Tex A&M Univ, minority engineering prog, 1987-88, dean engineering & instr, 1990-91, assoc provost undergrad studies, 2011; Bryan Independent Sch dist, substitute teacher, 1989; Miss State Univ, assoc dean engineering res & outreach, 1999-2002, assoc prof indust engineering, 1993-99, developer, Ergonomics & Human Performance Res Ctr, dir, 1994-2002; Univ Cent Fla, Dept Indust eng & Mgt syst, chmn & prof, 2002-06, Inst Advan Syst Engineering, prof, currently; ergonomic consult; Ctr Engineering Leadership & Learning, founding dir, 2005-07; Powerful Educ Technologies LLC, founder, prof engineering, pres & chief exec officer, 2007-13; Ctr Advancing Fac Excellence, 2008-. Co-author: Advancing Your Faculty Career. **Orgs:** Nat Action Coun Minorities Engineering; sr mem, Inst Indust Engrs; newsletter ed, Indust Ergonomics Tech Group Human Factors & Ergonomic Soc; founder, Power Promise Orgn; Alpha Pi Mu; Nat Sci Found Indust, 2003-; Sigma Xi; Engineering Adv Comt NSF, AUS Sci Bd; adv bd, Nat Acad Engineering; prog dir, Nat Sci Found, 2007-2009. **Special Achievements:** First African-American female to receive a PhD in engineering from Texas A&M University; First female to serve as a Department Head within the College of Engineering; First female to serve as Associate Dean of Engineering; First female to receive the Hearin-Hess Professor of Engineering Award. **Home Addr:** , FL. **Business Addr:** Founding Director, Center for Advancing Faculty Excellence, 12201 Research Pkwy Suite 221, Orlando, FL 32826.

### CRUMPTON-YOUNG, DR. LESIA L. See CRUMPTON, DR. LESIA.

### CRUSOE-INGRAM, CHARLENE

Executive, vice president (organization). **Personal:** Born New Albany, MS; daughter of Robert and Virginia Simmons; married Earnest. **Educ:** Bradley Univ, BA, sociol fr, 1972, MA, personnel serv, 1975. **Career:** Am Hosp Supply Corp, safety mgr & sr personnel specialist, 1980-82; Abbott Labs, div personnel mgr & corp recruiter, 1983-86; Enterprise Systs Inc, vpres human resources, 1986-88; Coca-Cola Co, human resources mgr, 1988-91, dir human resources, 1991-94, dir client serv, 1994-95, vpres, client serv, 1995-96, sr vpres orgn & people strategy, 1996-2001, Diversity Strategy & Cult, vpres, 2001-03; NDCHealth, exec vpres human resources, 2004-06; Interim Chro, Prin Strategist & Exec Coach, Crusoe-Ingram consulting LLC, 2004-. Atlanta Housing Authority, sr vpres human resources & chief human resources officer, 2011-14. **Orgs:** Bd mem, Inroads, 1995-; Womens Food Serv Forum, 1995-; bd dir, Nexus Contemp Arts Ctr, 1996-; vol, Literacy Coun, 1994-95; bd trustee, Knoxville Col, 1998; bd dir, Atlanta Women's Found. **Business Addr:** Interim CHRO, Principal Strategist, Executive Coach, Crusoe-Ingram Consulting, LLC.

### CRUSTO, MITCHELL FERDINAND

Real estate developer, educator, lawyer. **Personal:** Born Apr 22, 1953, New Orleans, LA; married Lisa Jupiter; children: Eve Michelle, Mia Elizabeth & Theresa Byles. **Educ:** Yale Univ, New Haven, CT, BA, hist, 1975, PhD, 1977, JD, 1981; Oxford Univ, Oxford, Eng, BA, jurisp, 1980, MA, jurisp, 1985. **Career:** Donovan, Leisure, Newton & Irvine, New York, NY, 1981; Hon John M Wisdom, US Ct Appeals, New Orleans, La Fifth Circuit, advisor, judicial law clerk, 1981-82; Jones, Walker, Waechter, Pointevent, Carrere & Denegre, New Orleans, La, atty, 1982-84; Stipend fel, Nicolaus & Co Inc, St Louis, Mo, sr vpres & gen coun, 1984-88; Wash Univ Bus Sch, St Louis, Mo, instr, 1985-89, vis prof law, 2006-; Webster Univ, St Louis, Mo, instr, 1986; St Louis Univ Law Sch, St Louis, Mo, adj prof, 1987-88; Crusto Capital Resources Inc, St Louis, Mo, pres & chief exec officer, 1988-89; US Small Bus Admin, Wash, DC, assoc dep adminr finance, investment & procurement, 1989-91; Monsanto Co, dir, corp environ policy, 1991-93; Arthur Andersen & Co, sr mgr, environ serv, 1993-95; Environ Law Inst, lectr, 1993; US Small Bus Admin; Stifel, Nicholas & Co; Jones Walker, Cravath, Swaine & Moore, New York, NY; Vt Law Sch, vis prof, 2000-03; Loyola Univ, Col Law, New Orleans, La, prof law, 2005-; Univ Miami, Fla, vis prof; Vt Law Sch, vis prof, 2007-08; Articles: Enslaved Constitution; Unconscious Classism; Obama's Moral Capitalism. **Orgs:** Vpres, Mo Mutual Funds Asn, 1985-87; dir, Big Bros & Big Sisters, 1985-89; Securities Indus Asn, Compliance & Legal Div, 1986-88; dir, St Louis Econ Develop Corp, 1987-89; arbitrator, Nat Asn Securities Dealers, 1988-; Am Bar Asn; Fed Bar Asn; Am Corp Coun Asn; Ill Bar Asn; La Bar Asn; Mo Bar Asn; Hon Soc Mid Temple Brit Barrister Asn; President Bill Clinton's Transition Team, 1992. **Business Addr:** Professor, Loyola University New Orleans, 7214 St Charles Ave, New Orleans, LA 70118, **Business Phone:** (504)861-5743.

### CRUTCHER, DR. RONALD ANDREW

School administrator, president (organization). **Personal:** Born Feb 27, 1947, Cincinnati, OH; son of Andrew and Burdella; married Betty Joy Neal; children: Sara Elizabeth. **Educ:** Miami Univ, BA, BM, music performance & music hist, 1969; Yale Univ, MMA, music performance & lit, 1972, DMA, music performance & lit, 1979; State Acad Music, Frankfurt, W Ger, dipl, 1976. **Career:** Bonn Sch Music, W Ger, cello instr, 1976-79; Wittenberg Univ, asst prof, 1977-79; UNC Greensboro, asst prof, 1979-83, assoc prof & cordr string area, 1983-88, assoc vchancellor acad affairs, 1988-90; Cleveland Inst Music, vpres acad affairs, dean conserv, 1990-94; Univ Tex, Sch Music, Austin, TX, dir, 1994-99; Miami Univ, Oxford, OH, provost, exec vpres acad affairs & prof music, 1999-2004; Wheaton Col, pres, 2004-14, pres emer, 2014-; Univ Richmond, pres & prof music, currently. **Orgs:** Consul NC Arts Coun, 1981-88; bd dir, Am Cello Community Coun, 1982-88; founder & pres, Carolina Cello Club, 1983-88; consult, Nat Endowment Arts, 1986-; bd dir, Greensboro Cerebral Palsy Asn, 1986-88; pres, NC Am String Teachers Asn, 1986-88; bd dir, Eastern Music Festival, 1988; bd dir, United Arts Coun Greensboro, 1988; univ coun mem, Case Western Res Univ, 1990-; adv comt mem, Northeast Ohio Jazz Soc, 1990-; Community Music Proj, 1991-; Klemperer Trio; founding mem, Chanticleer Sting Quartet; vice chair, Asn Am Cols & Univs; bd mem, Fulbright Asn; founder, Ctr Am & World Cultures; bd trustee, Berklee Col Music, 2004; Phi Beta Kappa; Delta Phi Alpha; Pi Kappa Lambda; Omicron Delta Kappa; YMCA; founding co-chair, Lib Educ & Am's Promise; Am Coun Educ; Cincinnati Symphony Orchestra; Richmond Symphony. **Home Addr:** 3624 Glenwood Rd, Cleveland Heights, OH 44121-1604, **Home Phone:** (216)381-0511. **Business Addr:** President, Wheaton College, 26 E Main St, Norton, MA 02766-2322, **Business Phone:** (508)286-8200.

### CRUTCHER, SIHON HEATH

Engineer. **Personal:** Born Mar 30, 1970, Huntsville, AL; son of James and Catherine; married Deborah. **Educ:** Tuskegee Univ, BS, math & physics, 1972; Kent State Univ, MS, physics, 1994; Univ Ala-Huntsville, MS, math, 1999; PhD. **Career:** Univ Ala, Huntsville, reaching asst; Nichols Res, syst analyst; Qual Res, sr software engr; Raytheon, group mgr & sr syst engr; AUs, comput engr. **Orgs:** House Raphe; Eagle Wings Ministries; Am Asn Physics Teachers. **Honors/Awds:** Commendation, Dept of the Army, 2000. **Home Addr:** 2300 Hammonds Ave, Huntsville, AL 35816, **Home Phone:** (256)489-9200.

### CRUTCHFIELD, JAMES N.

Newspaper publisher, executive, 001172. **Personal:** Born Dec 7, 1947, McKeesport, PA; son of Charles and Nancy Viola Summers Hill; married Becky J Hoover; children: 5. **Educ:** Duquesne Univ, BA, commun, 1992; Cleveland State Univ; Oakland Univ. **Career:** Publisher (retired), director; Pittsburgh Press, reporter, 1968-71; Pittsburgh Press, reporter, 1968; Pittsburgh Post-Gazette, reporter, Knight Ridder newspapers, reporter, 1976, Free Press, dep managing ed; Beacon J, managing ed; Press-Telegram, Long Beach, Calif, sr vpres & exec ed; Publ Philadelphia Inquirer, asst; Philadelphia Daily News; Philly.com; Beacon J, gen mgr, 2000-01; Akron Beacon J, (Knight newspaper) & Ohio.com, pres & publ; publ to newspaper's sale, Akron, 2001-06; Cronkite Sch Journalism & Mass Commun; Ariz State Univ, Cronkite Sch Journalism, mass commun fac, 2007-12; Duquesne Univ Pittsburgh, Dept Journalism & Multimedia Arts, fac; Weil Family Prof, currently. **Orgs:** Nat Asn Black Journals, 1983-; Alpha Phi Alpha Fraternity, 1966-; pres, Soc Prof Journals, 1991-93; Akron Art Mus; Weathervane Community Playhouse diversity comt; Summit Educ Initiative; Asian Am Journals Asn, 1998-; Nat Asn Hisp Journals, 1998-; Am Soc Newspaper Eds, 1993-; Nat Asn Minority Media Execs; Ohio Newspaper Asn; E Akron Community House's, 2001-02; fundraising campaign; chair, United Way Summit Co campaign, 2004; press secy, US Sen Carl Levin Mich, 1979-81; chair, Akron Community Adv Comt, 2002-04; trustee, Knight Found,

2004; Prog Comt; Akron community; bd mem, Akron Community Found, Greater Akron Chamber, Summit Educ Initiative & United Way Summit County; chair, local United Way's, 2004 fund-raising campaign; bd mem, Duquesne; Am Soc Newspaper Ed; Nat Asn Black Journalists; Nat Asn Minority Media Execs & Asian Am Journalists Asn; bd mem, Duquesne Univ, currently; bd mem, trustee, John S & James L Knight Found; 2004-; United Way Exec Comt; Greater Akron Chamber's Exec Comt; Am Socs Newspapers. **Home Addr:** 3900 Yellow Creek W Rd, Akron, OH 44333, **Home Phone:** (330)666-7710. **Business Addr:** Director Student Media, Weil Family Professor of Journalism, Walter Cronkite School of Journalism and Mass Communication, Stauffer Hall A 231, Tempe, OH 85287-1305, **Business Phone:** (480)727-6884.

### CRUTCHFIELD, LISA
Executive, vice president (organization). **Personal:** Born Mar 21, 1963, Philadelphia, PA; daughter of Johnnie and Ann. **Educ:** Yale Univ, BA, econs & polit sci, 1985; Harvard Bus Sch, MBA, finance, 1990. **Career:** Philadelphia Nat Bank, com lending officer, 1985-88; Bankers Trust Co, assoc & corp finance, 1990-92; City Philadelphia, dep finance dir, 1992-93; Pa pub Utility comn, vchmn, 1993-97, vpres; Duke Energy Corp, vpres, 1997-2000; TIAA-CREF Southern Serv Ctr, vpres & gen mgr, 2000-03; PECO Energy, Sr vpres regulatory & external affairs, 2003-08; Nat Grid, Exec vpres, 2008-11; Highview Capital Partners, Managing Dir, 2012-. **Orgs:** Bd mem, Mus New S; investment comm, United Way Cent Carolinas Inc, 1998-; bd trustee, Independent Col Fund NC, 1998-; Nat Coalition 100 Black Women Greater Charlotte; bd dir, TransLink Develop Corp; bd dir, Univ NC; bd dir, Carolinas HealthCare Syst; Charlotte Chamber Com; bd dir, NC Dept Transp; bd dir, Urban League Philadelphia; Am Asn Blacks energy; bd mem, bd dir, Unitil Corp, 2012-; Mem Bd dir, Fulton Financial Corp, 2014-. **Business Addr:** Managing Director, Highview Capital Partners, 25 Braintree Hill Off Pk Suite 301, Braintree, MD 02184, **Business Phone:** (781)353-6429.

### CRUTCHFIELD-BAKER, VERDENIA (VERDENIA C BAKER)
Executive, government official. **Personal:** Born Jul 27, 1958, Sylvester, GA; married Joe Thomas. **Educ:** Fla State Univ, BS, 1979, MSPA, 1982. **Career:** Health & Rehabilitative Serv, counr; Sch Bd St Lucie Co, teacher, 1980; Dept Labor Employ Security, interviewer, 1982; Broward City Budget Off, budget analyst; Palm Beach Co, dep co adminr, administrator, currently. **Orgs:** Nat Asn Advan Colored People, 1977-79; Delta Sigma Theta, 1977; Am Soc Pub Admin, 1981; Nat Forum Black Pub Admin, 1983. **Home Addr:** 2231 Ridgewood Cir, Royal Palm Beach, FL 33411-6155, **Home Phone:** (561)204-2976. **Business Addr:** Deputy County Administrator, Palm Beach County, 301 N Olive Ave, West Palm Beach, FL 33401, **Business Phone:** (561)355-6726.

### CRUTHIRD, J. ROBERT LEE
Educator, cook. **Personal:** Born Dec 10, 1944, Leflore County, MS; son of Harvie and Mary Florence Black; married Jeannett M Williams; children: Robert Lee Jr. **Educ:** Univ Ill, BA, sociol, 1973, MA, sociol, 1976; Chicago State Univ, attended 1982; Critical Thinking & Acculturation Inst, Univ Chicago, attended 1986; Univ Wis, attended 1983; Heed Univ, PhD, sociol, 1994. **Career:** IL Dept Corrections, correctional, counr, 1977-78; Kennedy-King Col, dirinstnl res, 1982, asst prof sociol, assoc prof sociol, Dept Soc Sci, chmn, 1996-, distinguished prof, 2003-04, emer prof, 2004-; Crime & Delinq Res Training, fel, 1976; Nat Endowment Humanities, fel, 1983; KKC, Title III basic skills develop, 1985-86; City Cols Chicago, Mayor's Summer Youth Employ Prog, site coordr, 1984-86; Acad Support Serv, coordr, 1986-87, Col Advisement Proj, coordr, 1987, asst prof social, 1987; MSYEP, asst dir, 1987-; Phi Theta Kappa, advisor. **Orgs:** Am Sociol Asn; Asn Inst Res; Asn Study Life & Hist Afro-Am; consult, Educ Mgmt Assocs, 1981-82; sponsor, Phi Theta Kappa, 1982-; life mem, Univ Ill Chicago Alumni Asn; Nat Asn Develop Educ; Alpha Phi Alpha Fraternity Inc. **Honors/Awds:** Vis scholar, Univ Wis, 1983; Hall Honors IL, Phi Theta Kappa, 1984, 1986, 1988-91; "Black Rural-Urban Migration", ERIC, 1984; "Remedial & Developmental Instructions", ERIC, 1986; honors scholar 23rdInst, NY, 1990; honors scholar 24th Institute, Minneapolis, 1991; Monarch Award in Education, Alpha Kappa Alpha, 1999. **Home Addr:** 259 E 107th St, Chicago, IL 60628, **Home Phone:** (773)568-8951. **Business Addr:** Professor Emeritus, Kennedy-King College, 6800 S Wentworth Ave, Chicago, IL 60621, **Business Phone:** (773)602-5174.

### CRUZ, DR. ILUMINADO ANGELES
School administrator, physician. **Personal:** Born Nov 20, 1936, Navotas; son of Iluminado S Sr and Flora Angeles; married Aurora Bunda; children: Danny, Eliza & Loralei. **Educ:** Univ Philippines, MD, 1962. **Career:** Howard Univ Col Med, instr, 1968-69, asst prof, 1971-76, assoc prof, 1976-92, Hemodialysis Ctr, med dir, 1976-92, prof, 1992-; Manila-Us Mail, columnist, 1992; Univ Cent Fla, Col Med, assoc prof, currently. **Orgs:** Dir, Hemodialysis Unit Howard Univ; fel Am Col Physicians; Am Soc Nephrology; Int Soc Nephrol; Nat Med Asn; Med Chirurogical Soc DC; DC Med Soc; Am Heart Asn; Nat Capital Med Found; Am Bd Nephrology; dipl, Am Bd Internal Med; Philippine Med Asn; Dc Med Soc; Int Soc Nephrology; fel Am Col Physicians; Nat Kidney Found, 1986-91; advisor, Filipino Am Republican Coun, 1990-93. **Home Addr:** 6103 Goldtree Way, Bethesda, MD 20817, **Home Phone:** (301)320-2670. **Business Addr:** Professor, Univ Central Florida College of Medicine, 6850 Lake Nona Blvd, Orlando, FL 32827, **Business Phone:** (407)266-1000.

### CRUZ, PATRICIA
Executive director. **Personal:** married Emilio. **Career:** Harlem Stage, exec dir, 1998-; Studio Mus Harlem, deputy dir; Aaron Davis Hall Inc, exec dir, 1998-. **Orgs:** Past bd mem, Andy Warhol Found; pres, New York Found Arts; CalArts Bd Overseers; bd dir, Harlem Stage. **Business Addr:** Executive Director, Harlem Stage, 150 Convent Ave W 135th St, New York, NY 10031, **Business Phone:** (212)650-6900.

### CRUZAT, DR. GWENDOLYN S.
Association executive, educator, consultant. **Personal:** Born Chicago, IL. **Educ:** Fisk Univ, BS, mathematics & physics, 1951; Atlanta Univ, MLS, 1954; Wayne State Univ, PhD, 1976. **Career:** Fisk Univ, asst librn, 1954-60; Harper Hosp, Detroit, asst librn, 1960-64; Wayne State Univ, Med Sch Libr, res librn; Univ Western Ont, vis lectr, 1970; Univ Mich, Sch Info, from lectr to prof, 1970-93, prof emer, 1993-; Univ Hawaii Grad Sch Libr & Info Studies, vis assoc prof, 1977; Univ Am Sch Libr & Info Studies, vis lectr, 1978; Nat Libr Med, regent, 1981-84; Dept Educ, Div Libr Prog, consult, 1987; consult, 1987. **Orgs:** Med Libr Asn, 1969-73; Am Libr Asn, 1971-90; Univ Mich Stud Group, adv, 1973-90; Comn Collective Bargaining, chair, 1976-80; Ala Comn Accreditation, 1984-86; Univ Mich Alumni Asn, dir-at-large, 1986-89; fel Med Lib Asn, 1993; Fisk Univ, bd trustees, 1996-2005; Am Soc Info Sci; Am Asn Univ Prof; Spl Libr Asn; Metro Detroit Med Libr Group; Asn Col & Univ Res Libr; Asn Libr & Info Sci Educ. **Honors/Awds:** Gabriel Award Scholarship, Fisk Univ; Beta Phi Mu Honor Soc, 1954-; Distinguished Service Award Univ MI, 1977; Janet Doe Lectr Med Lib Asn, 1978-79; Alumna Award, Atlanta Univ's Sch Info & Libr Studies, 1989; Honorary Doctor of Humane Letters from Fisk University, 2006. **Special Achievements:** School's first minority tenure-track faculty member, 1971. **Business Addr:** Professor Emeritus, University of Michigan, 304 W Hall, Ann Arbor, MI 48109-1092, **Business Phone:** (734)763-2285.

### CRYER, DR. LINKSTON T., JR.
Dentist. **Personal:** Born Jul 10, 1933, Mt. Hermon, LA; married Elizabeth J. **Educ:** Southern Univ, BS, 1945; Meharry Med Col, DDS, 1961; Dade Co Res Clin, endodontics, oral surg, minor tooth movement, periodont surg. **Career:** Fla State Dent Health Dept, 1961-62; pvt pract dent surgeon, 1962-; Variety C Hosp, staff. **Orgs:** Dade Co Dent Soc, 1961-; pres, S Dade Polit Action League, 1965-80; pres, Richmond Enterprises Inc, 1965-; vpres, Dunbar Med Arts Inc, 1971-; pres, Iota Pi Lambda Chap Alpha Phi Alpha, 1972-; Dade Co Dent Res Clin, 1980-; Acad Gen Dent, 1980-; pres, Dade Co Dent Soc, 1985-87; Am & Nat Dent Asn, Am Inst Hypn. **Home Addr:** 14200 SW 72nd Ave, Palmetto Bay, FL 33158-1361, **Home Phone:** (305)233-3513. **Business Addr:** Dentist, Private Practice, 3311 Gentian Blvd, Columbus, GA 31907-5626, **Business Phone:** (706)563-0327.

### CUDJOE, DR. SELWYN REGINALD
Educator, writer. **Personal:** Born Dec 1, 1943, Tacarigua; son of Lionel Reginald and Carmen Rose; married Gwendolyn M Long; children: Frances Louise & Kwamena. **Educ:** Fordham Univ, BA, Eng, 1969, MA, Am lit, 1972; Cornell Univ, PhD, Am lit, 1976. **Career:** Fordham Univ, instr Afro-Am studies, 1970-72; Ithaca Col, asst prof Afro-Am studies, 1973-74; Ohio Univ, assoc prof Afro-Am studies, 1975-76; Harvard Univ, asst prof Afro-Am studies, 1976-81, WEB DuBois Inst AFA Res, vis fel, 1991, vis scholar African Am studies, 1992-94; Cornell Univ, Soc Humanities, sr lectr, 1980, assoc prof Africana studies, 1981-82, sr fel, 1992; Wellesley Col, prof african studies, 1986-, Marion Butler McLean prof & chmn hist ideas, 1995-99, Margaret E Deffenbaugh & LeRoy T Carlson prof comparative lit, currently; NEH, fel, 1991-92 & 1997-98; Am Coun Learned Soc, fel, 1991-92; Harvard Univ, Afro-Am studies Dept, vis fel, 1991; Brandeis Univ, teacher; Auburn State Prison, Auburn, NY, speaker; Bedford-Stuyvesant Youth-in-Action, teacher; Calaloux Res Assocs, pres; Trinidad & Tobago TV, interviewer; Books: Resistance & Caribbean Literature, 1980; Movement the People, 1983; Grenada: Two Essays, 1983; Ajust & Moral Socs, 1984; VS Naipaul: A Materialist Reading, 1988; Caribbean Women Writers: Essays from the First International Conference, ed, 1990; Eric E Willliams Speaks: Essays on Colonialism & Independence, ed, 1993; Tacarigua: A Village in Trinidad, ed, 1995; CLR James: His Intellectual Legacies, ed, 1995; Maxwell Philip, Emmanuel Appadocca, or, Blighted Life: A Tale of the Boucaneers, ed, 1997; Beyond Boundaries: The Intellectual Tradition of Trinidad & Tobago in the Nineteenth Century, 2002; Caribbean Visionary: A. R. F. Webber & the Making of the Guyanese Nation, 2008; Narratives of Amerindians in Trinidad and Tobago or Becoming Trinbagonian, ed, 2016; Author & editor of Numerous Books. **Orgs:** Fel Nat Endowment Humanities, 1991-92 & 1994-98; bd dir, Cent Bank Trinidad & Tobago; pres, Nat Asn Empowerment African People; Cabinet - App Round Table Discussion Race Rels. **Honors/Awds:** Endowment for the Humanities Award, 1995-97. **Home Addr:** 22 Belair Rd, Wellesley, MA 02482-6915, **Home Phone:** (617)237-2230. **Business Addr:** Professor, Wellesley College, 106 Cent St, Wellesley, MA 02481, **Business Phone:** (781)283-2568.

### CUFF, GEORGE WAYNE
Clergy, executive, naval officer. **Personal:** Born Sep 3, 1923, Chester, PA; son of Theodore and Lydia; married Mary Elizabeth; children: Henry Earl Tucker Jr & Selena Simpson. **Educ:** Lincoln Univ, BA, 1951; Crozer Theol Sem, MDiv, 1955. **Career:** Clergy (retired); pastor, 1955-69; Dover Dist Peninsula Conf, supt, 1969-73; Wilmington Dist Peninsula Conf, supt, 1973-75; Hillcrest Bellefonte, United Methodist Church, pastor, 1975-79; Bd Global Ministries, United Methodist Church, 1979-87; Off Finance & Field Serv, field rep. **Orgs:** Bd trustee, Wesley Col, 1970-92; bd gov, Wesley Theol Sem, 1973-80; bd dir, Wilmington Good Will Indust, 1973-79; gen bd mem, Global Ministries United Methodist Church. **Honors/Awds:** Plaque of Appreciation, Methodist Action Prog, Wilmington Dist, 1975; Good Conduct Medal; WWII Medal; Sharp Shooters Medal. **Home Addr:** 21 John Collins Cir, Dover, DE 19901-5426, **Home Phone:** (302)674-4511.

### CULBREATH-MANLY, TONGILA M.
Executive. **Personal:** Born Jun 9, 1959, Atlanta, GA. **Educ:** Univ Colo, Boulder, BA, commun, 1981; Atlanta Univ, MBA, mkt, 1987; Walden Univ, DBA, int bus, 2015. **Career:** Educ Media Ctr, media tech, 1977-81; H Harper's Design Studios, asst mgr, 1981-82; Sandusky Broadcasting KNUS-AM, tech producer, 1982-84; New City Comn WYAY-FM, acct exec, 1984-88; Summit Commun, WVEE/WAOK, acct exec, 1988-89; WEDR Inc, WEDR-FM, sales mgr, 1989-90; WRIC-TV, acct exec, 1991-; Manly Group, owner, 1994-2009; TMG Solutions Pty Ltd, chief exec officer, owner, 1996-; TMG Solutions, owner, 1996-; Enterprise Fla, managing dir, 2001-12; Bafikile Bus Serv, managing dir, 2003-07. **Orgs:** Nat Black MBA Asn, 1986-87; Exec Women Int; Am Mgt Asn; Int Bus Innovation Asn, 2015-; bd mem, Jacksonville Sister City Asn, 2015-. **Home Addr:** 9240 Tuckerbrook Lane, Alpharetta, GA 30022, **Home Phone:** (706)739-6031. **Business Addr:** Chief Executive Officer, Owner, TMG Solutions USA, LLC, 6 S Roscoe Blvd, Ponte Vedra Beach, GA 32082, **Business Phone:** (904)305-8466.

### CULLORS, DERRICK SHANE
Football player. **Personal:** Born Dec 26, 1972, Dallas, TX. **Educ:** Murray State Univ; Tex Christian Univ. **Career:** Football player (retired); New Eng Patriots, running back, kickoff returner, 1997-99.

### CULPEPPER, BETTY M.
Librarian. **Personal:** Born Jan 15, 1941, Lynchburg, VA; daughter of Roosevelt and Agnes Head Witcher. **Educ:** Howard Univ, BA, 1963; Kent State Univ, MA, 1966; Cath Univ, MS, 1969; Howard Univ, MPA, 1981. **Career:** Wash DC Pub Libr, reader's adv, 1964-67; Prince George's County Memorial Libr, br librn, 1967-72; Washingtoniana Div DC Pub Libr, chief, 1972-77; Moorland-Spingarn Res Ctr, Howard Univ, bibliogr & head ref, 1977-86, asst chief librn, tech serv & auto, 1986-90; Libr Cong, Wash, DC, asst head, 1990-. **Orgs:** Am Libr Asn; Afro-Am Hist & Gen Soc; Nat Asn Advan Colored People; Asn Study Afro-Am Life & Hist; ALA Caucus Black Librarians; Alpha Kappa Alpha; Hist Soc Wash. **Honors/Awds:** Awarded Scholarship Howard Univ; Fel, Kent State Univ; Scholarship Md Libr Assn. **Special Achievements:** Book: Hughes & Head Black Studies Books, 2005. **Home Addr:** 9770 Basket Ring Rd, Columbia, MD 21045, **Home Phone:** (410)730-1484. **Business Addr:** Assistant Head, Library of Congress, 101 Independence Ave SE, Washington, DC 20001, **Business Phone:** (202)707-5000.

### CULPEPPER, DAUNTE RACHARD
Football player. **Personal:** Born Jan 28, 1977, Ocala, FL; son of Barbara Henderson; married Kimberly Rah. **Educ:** Cent Fla Univ. **Career:** Football player (retired); Minn Vikings, quarterback, 1999-2005; Miami Dolphins, quarterback, 2006; Oakland Raiders, quarterback, 2007; Detroit Lions, quarterback, 2008-09; Sacramento Mountain Lions, 2010; African Am Adoption Agency. **Orgs:** Speaker, United Way Reason To Be Thankful. **Honors/Awds:** Mr. Football Award, Athletic Coaches Association, 1994; Sammy Baugh Natl Passer of the Year Award, 1998; ESPN Award, ESPN, 2000; NFC Pro Bowl selection, 2000 & 2003-04; All-Pro, USA Today, 2000; NFL Quarterback of the Year, Natl Quarter back Club, 2000; All-NFC, Pro Football Weekly, 2000; NFL passing touchdowns leader, 2000; Ed Block Courage Award, Minnesota Vikings, 2001; Best Breakthrough Athlete ESPY Award, 2001; NFL's Extra Effort Award, 2003; Korey Stringer Good Guy Award, 2003, 2004; NFL passing yards Leader, 2004. **Special Achievements:** Drafted by NY Yankees, 1995; Culpepper appeared in an episode of George Lopez, along with Donovan McNabb; Culpepper also appeard in the movie " 50 First Dates". **Home Addr:** Berkshire Ct, Southwest Ranches, FL 33331-1331. **Business Addr:** Professional Football Player, Detroit Lions, 222 Republic Dr, Allen Park, MI 48101, **Business Phone:** (313)262-2002.

### CULPEPPER, DELLIE L.
Manager. **Personal:** Born Mar 24, 1941, Talbotton, GA; daughter of Willie and Daisy. **Educ:** Dimery's Bus Col, Atlanta, GA, assoc bus admin, 1963; Atlanta Law Sch, Atlanta, GA, LLB, legal professions & studies, 1979. **Career:** Southwest Coun Atlanta Chamber Com, mem exec comt, 1978; City Ct Atlanta, ct dir, 1978-97; Traffic Ct, Atlanta, GA, ct admin & dir; GetAway Travelers, independent travel agt, 1997-2012. **Orgs:** Nat Asn Advan Colored People, 1980; Ida Prather YWCA, 1980; vpres, Cruisers Fund Raising, 1984; Black Pub Adminr, 1984; Nat Asn Trial Ct Adminr, 1984; Atlanta Chap COMPA, 1985; bd dir, Nat Asn Ct Mgt. **Home Addr:** 120 Culpepper Rd, Waverly Hall, GA 31831. **Business Addr:** Director, City Court of Atlanta, 104 Trinity Ave SW, Atlanta, GA 30335, **Business Phone:** (404)658-6959.

### CULPEPPER, LOUIS S.
Chief executive officer, president (organization), founder (originator). **Personal:** Born Tampa, FL. **Educ:** Univ Md, BS, 1977; Cent Mich Univ, MBA, 1979; Univ Phoenix, PhD; Eastern Ky Univ, dipl, police admin & training; FBI Nat Acad, Quantico, VA, grad. **Career:** Culpepper & Assocs Security Serv, chmn, pres, chief exec officer, founder, owner, 1992-. **Orgs:** Int Asn Chiefs Police; USAF Security Police Asn; Sigma Pi Phi Fraternity, Delta Upsilon Boule; Omega Psi Phi Fraternity; 100 Black Men Atlanta Inc; found bd mem, Atlanta Tech Col; ASIS Int; Nat Orgn Black Law Enforcement Execs; Int Orgn Black Security Execs; Nat Black MBA Asn; FBI Nat Acad Assocs; Atlanta Bus League; Nat Classification Mgt Soc. **Home Addr:** , GA. **Business Addr:** President, Chief Executive Officer, Culpepper & Associates Security Services Inc, 1810 Water Pl Suite 180, Atlanta, GA 30339, **Business Phone:** (770)916-0060.

### CULPEPPER, DR. LUCY NELL
Educator, physician. **Personal:** Born Jun 11, 1951, Awin, AL; daughter of L C and Lucy Lee Davis; married Joseph Williams. **Educ:** Ala A&M Univ, BS, 1973; Meharry Med Col, MD, 1977. **Career:** Ala A&M Univ, prof; Martin Luther King Jr Gen Hosp, intern, resident, 1977-80; Nat Health Serv Corps, pediatrician med dir, 1980-82; pvt pract pediatrician, 1982-88; Maude Whatley Health Ctr, pediatrician, 1988-, med dir, health serv dir, 1989-99. **Orgs:** Bd dir, Tuscaloosa Dept Human Resources; Tuscaloosa Family Coun Serv; Zeta Phi Beta Sor Inc, 1972-; active staff mem, Dept Health Res Regional Med Ctr, 1980-; Tuscaloosa Co Med Soc, 1982-; Med Asn State Ala, 1982-; youth dir, First Baptist Church, 1984-90; W Ala Pediat Soc, 1984-, W Ala Med Asn, 1985-, Ala State Med Asn, 1985-; bd dir, W Ala Chap Sickle Cell Dis Asn, 2000-; bd dir, Family Coun Serv, 2002-; bd dir, Dept Health Res, 2000-; exec dir, Tuscaloosa chap Sickle Cell Dis Asn Am. **Honors/Awds:** Outstanding Black Woman of the Year, Christian Study Ctr, Alabama, 1983; Outstanding Young Women of America. **Home Addr:** 4415 Maple Lane, Northport, AL 35473, **Home Phone:** (205)339-8935. **Business Addr:** Medical Director, Health Services Director, Maude Whatley Health Ctr, 2731 Martin Luther King Jr Blvd, Tuscaloosa, AL 35403, **Business Phone:** (205)758-6647.

**CULPEPPER, PAMELA**
Vice president (organization). **Personal:** married Clifton; children: Jordan. **Educ:** Univ Ark, Little Rock, AR, BA, psychol, 1988; Calif State Univ, Hayward, CA, MS, orgn chg, 1994. **Career:** McKesson-HBOC Inc, dir human resources, 1997-2000; Clorox; Wells Fargo; Quaker Foods & Snacks, vpres human resources; Frito-Lay N Am, dir human resources-nat sales, 2000-02; Quaker, Tropicana & Gatorade (QTG), vpres talent mgt & diversity, dir orgn capability & inclusion; PepsiCo Beverages & Foods, vpres, talent mgt & inclusion, 2005-07; PepsiCo Americas Beverages Supply Chain, vpres human resources, 2007-10; PepsiCo, Quaker Foods & Snacks, vpres & chief petty officer human resources, 2010-11; PepsiCo, sr vpres global diversity & inclusion officer, 2011-; Golin, chief people officer, human resources exec 2014. **Orgs:** Bd mem, VSO Int, UK, 2011-; adv bd mem, Nat Black MBA Asn. **Business Addr:** Chief People Officer, Human Resources Executive, Golin, PepsiCo Inc, 875 N Michigan Ave, Chicago, IL 60611, **Business Phone:** (312)729-4000.

**CULVER, RHONDA**
Accountant, lecturer. **Personal:** Born Phoenix, AZ; daughter of Roscoe and Rose. **Educ:** Ariz State Univ, BS, bus admin, 1981, MBA, acct emphasis, 1986. **Career:** Honeywell, bus mgr & acct mgr, 1983-99; Searle Consumer Prod Div, asst cost acct, 1983-84; Garrett Airline Serv Div, sr acct, 1984-86, acct supvr, 1986-; Am Express, dir finance, 1999-2006; Super Qual Realty / HomeMart, broker & sales agt, 2007-Sales & Property Mgt, realtor, 2009-; Mesa Community Col, adj prof, 2013-. **Orgs:** Bd dirs & treas, Nat Asn Accountants, Phoenix, 1983-; Asn MBA Execs, 1984; Mayor's Citizen Tax Fairness Comt, 1986; comm chmn, United Negro Col Fund, Phoenix, 1986-87; finance comn, Alpha Kappa Alpha Sor, 1985-87; tech commun coord, Focus Software Users Group. **Honors/Awds:** Black Bd of Dirs Honoree Phoenix, 1986; Outstanding Woman, 1987; CFO Premier Award, Am Express, 2004. **Home Addr:** 15410 S 42nd St, PO Box 27786, Phoenix, AZ 85044, **Home Phone:** (480)706-7051. **Business Addr:** Adjunct Professor, Mesa Community College, 1833 W Southern Ave, Mesa, AZ 85202, **Business Phone:** (480)628-9595.

**CUMBER, VICTORIA LILLIAN**
Columnist, talent agent. **Personal:** Born Feb 5, 1920, San Antonio, TX; daughter of David H Johnson and Lora L. **Educ:** Phillips Bus Sch, attended 1936; Metro Bus Sch, attended 1938. **Career:** Sepia Hollywood Mag, publ, 1941-45; Herald Attractions Agency, mgr, 1949-55; Lil Cumber Attractions Agency, theatrical agt, 1956-; SW Wave Newspaper, columnist, 1967-86; Scoop Newspaper, 1986-. **Orgs:** Life mem, Nat Asn Advan Colored People Hollywood Beverly Hills Br, 1937-; secy, Community Actions Comn, 1958-60. **Honors/Awds:** Plaque Bus & Prof Womens Club, 1967; Black Filmmakers Hall of Fame, 1974; honoree, S Calif Motion Picture Coun, 1987; Special Pioneer Award, Afro American Humor Awards, 1990; Beverly Hills Hollywood 4th ann Theater Trailblazer Award, 1991; Golden Star Halo Award, Motion Picture Coun, 1994; honoree, African Am Short Film Market Place Short Film Festival, 1998; Sojourner Truth Award, Pan African Film & Arts Festival, 2002. **Special Achievements:** Coorganized the first Com Casting Dirs Indust Awards saluting honorees who have been voted as an awardee by their peers, 1982; Beverly Hills Hollywood Image Awards, co organizer, 1967; First Black Woman Agentin Los Angeles; Am Artists Entertainment Group. **Home Addr:** 1629 S Van Ness Suite 3, Los Angeles, CA 90019. **Business Addr:** Consultant, Lil Cumber Attractions Agency, 6363 Sunset Blvd Suite 807, Hollywood, CA 90028, **Business Phone:** (213)469-1919.

**CUMMINGS, AEON L.**
Banker. **Personal:** Born Jul 5, 1963, Annotto Bay; son of Wilmore and Gladys; married Shawn Lawson. **Educ:** Hamilton Col, AB, econ & govt, 1985; Brooklyn Col, MA, econ, 1988; Univ Va, Darden Sch Bus, MBA, finance, 1991. **Career:** NYC Bd Educ, eng teacher, 1985-88; NYC Housing Preserv & Develop, analyst, 1989-90; Citibank, NA, vpres, prod mgr; GE Consumer Finance, vpres, currently. **Orgs:** Hamilton Col, alumni recruiting & fund raising, 1985-; Univ Va, Darden Bus Sch, pres, 1990-91; UNCF Citicorp Mentors, mentor, 1991-93; Nat Black MBA, 1993-. **Honors/Awds:** Outstanding Student in Economics, Brooklyn Col, 1988; one of 10 Nat fellows, Citicorp & Citibank Fel, 1990-91; Achievement Award, Fairfield County NBMBAA, 1994. **Special Achievements:** Master Thesis, "The Determinants of Housing Prices in Brooklyn NY", 1988; selected as one of the MBAs of the future by Minority MBA Mag. **Home Addr:** 477 E 24th St, Brooklyn, NY 11210-1129, **Home Phone:** (718)434-5726. **Business Addr:** Vice President, GE Consumer Finance, 6610 W Broad St, Richmond, VA 23230.

**CUMMINGS, ALEXANDER B., JR. (ALEX B CUMMINGS, JR.)**
Executive, vice president (organization). **Personal:** Born Jan 1, 1956?. **Educ:** Northern Ill Univ, BS, finance & econs; Atlanta Univ, MBA, finance. **Career:** Pillsbury Co, vpres finance & chief financial officer; SC Johnson & Son Inc, bd mem; Coca-Cola Co, dep region mgr Nigeria, 1997-98, managing dir, region mgr Nigeria, 1998-2000, pres N & W Africa Div Morocco, 2000-01, pres Africa Group, 2001-08, exec vpres & chief admin officer, 2008-; Chevron Corp, bd dir, 2014-. **Orgs:** African Presidential Arch & Res Ctr; bd mem, Ctr Global Develop's Comn U.S. Policy toward Low-Income Poorly Performing States (LIPPS); bd mem, C.A.R.E.; bd mem, Clark Atlanta Univ; bd mem, Coca-Cola Bottling Co; Exec Leadership Coun; Corp Coun Africa; Africare; African-Am Inst; bd dir, Heartt Inc. **Business Addr:** Executive Vice President, Chief Administrative Officer, Coca-Cola Company, PO Box 1734, Atlanta, GA 30301, **Business Phone:** (800)438-2653.

**CUMMINGS, ANNETTE MERRITT (ANNETTE MERRITT JONES)**
Marketing executive, public relations executive, advertising executive. **Personal:** Born May 14, 1946, Grady, AL; daughter of Henry W and Virgie Mathews Dowdell; married Iran; children: Michael O & Angela J. **Educ:** Cuyahoga Community Col, AA, 1975; Cleveland State Univ, BA, 1977; Univ Detroit, MBA, finance, 1993. **Career:** Occidental Petrol, Madison Heights, Mich, sr sales rep, 1979-81; Publs Rep, Detroit, Mich, independent contractor, 1981-82; NW Ayer Inc, sr acct exec, 1982-88; Nat Bd Prof Teaching, dir commun & mkt, 1988-92; Campbell & Co, vp, 1992-94; Paul Werth Assocs, vpres, 1996; Bernard Hodes Group, Diversity & Inclusion Solutions, vpres & nat dir, 1998-2010; Cummings & Co, LLC, founder & managing partner, 2010-; Courier-Jour Newspaper, mkt communs mgr; Independent Commun Practr, consults; EI DuPont de Numours, Wilmington, Del. **Orgs:** Adcraft Club Detroit, 1985-; Literacy Vols Am, 1986-; Women's Econ Club Detroit, 1987-; Nat Soc Fund-Raising Execs, 1988-; Detroit Rotary Club Int, 1989-; Nat Black MBA Asn, 1992; Pub Rels Soc Am; bd mem, Strategies Against Violence Everywhere; vis comt, Cleveland State Univ's Col Lib Arts & Sci; Nat Asn African Americans HR; Design Grants & Policy Panel Nat Endowment Arts; Pub Rels Soc Am; Nat Trust Hist Preserv; Americans Arts. **Honors/Awds:** PRSA, Bronze Anvil, 1992. **Special Achievements:** Contributing Author: "The Census 2000 Toolkit"; "Black Professionals and for Black Enterprise". **Home Addr:** 209 Mallet Hill Rd, Columbia, SC 29223-3203, **Home Phone:** (803)462-9417. **Business Addr:** Founder, Managing Partner, Cummings & Co LLC, 382 Springfield Ave Suite 203, Summit, NJ 07901, **Business Phone:** (908)522-8311.

**CUMMINGS, DR. CARY, III**
Executive, physician. **Personal:** Born Jul 13, 1949, Monticello, FL; children: Lindsey. **Educ:** State Univ NY Binghamton, BS, 1972; Meharry Med Col, MD, 1976. **Career:** Univ Rochester, intern, 1976-77; US Pub Health Serv, lt commander, 1977-79; Harrisburg Hosp, residency; Hershey Emergency Med Prog, asst profdept internal med, 1981-83; Memorial Sloan-Kettering Cornell Univ, felcritical care med, 1983-84; Harrisburg Hosp, asst prof dept internal med, 1984-86; Hershey Med Ctr, asst prof emergency med & trauma, 1985-86; pvt pract physician, 1985-; Univ Calif San Francisco, fel, 1990-92, 1992-93; Dialysis Care 2000 Inc, founder & owner, developer; Cummings Assocs PC, owner; Physicians Renal Care Inc, pres, chmn bd & chief med officer, currently. **Orgs:** Dauphin Co Med Soc; PA Med Soc; Am Med Asn; Pa Med Soc; Dauphin County Med Soc; Am Soc Internal Med; Int Soc Nephrology. **Home Addr:** 1617 N Front St, Harrisburg, PA 17102, **Home Phone:** (717)236-4682. **Business Addr:** Chairman, Chief Medical Director, Physicians Renal Care Inc, 3405 N Front St, Harrisburg, PA 17110, **Business Phone:** (717)236-1825.

**CUMMINGS, ELIJAH EUGENE**
**Personal:** Born Jan 18, 1951, Baltimore, MD; married Maya Rockeymoore. **Educ:** Howard Univ, BS, polit sci, 1973; Univ Md Sch Law, JD, 1976. **Career:** Atty; Md House Delegates, 39th Dist, 1983-96; Speaker Pro Tempore, 1995-96; US House Rep, Md 7th Dist, congressman, 1996-; House Transp & Infrastructure Comt, Coast Guard & Maritime Transp, chmn. **Orgs:** Chair, MD Govs Comn Black Males, 1990-96; founder, MD Bootcamp Aftercare Prog, 1991-; Md Comprehensive Transit Plan Transit Adv Panel, 1998-99; Juv Offender Aftercare Assessment Team, 1999-2000; New Psalmist Baptist Church; first vicechair, chmn, Cong Black Caucus, 2003-; bd Visitor, US Naval Acad, 2005-; bd Regents, trustee, Morgan State Univ, 1999-; trustee, Baltimore Aquarium; bd dir, Baltimore Area Coun Boy Scouts Am; Md State Bar Asn; Phi Beta Kappa; pres, Bancroft Lit Soc; bd trustee, Baltimore City Hist Soc, 2002-; Nat Aquarium; exec bd, Dunbar-Hopkins Health Partnership; bd advisor, Univ Md Sch Med, Inst Human Virol; chmn, Legis Black Caucus Md. **Special Achievements:** First African American in Maryland history to be named Speaker pro Tempore. **Business Addr:** Congressman, United States House of Representative, 2235 Rayburn House Off Bldg, Washington, DC 20515-2007, **Business Phone:** (202)225-4741.

**CUMMINGS, FRANCES MCARTHUR**
School administrator. **Personal:** Born Feb 2, 1941, Lumberton, NC; children: Isaiah T. **Educ:** Livingstone Col, BS, 1961; NC Cent Univ, MS, 1974; Univ NC, Greensboro, Bus & Off Voc Cert, 1976. **Career:** Educator (retired); NC Asn Classroom Teachers, 1978-79; SE Reg Asn Classroom Teachers, pres, 1980; Nat Educ Asn, dir, 1980-87; NC Asn Educ, pres, 1983-84; Lumberton Sr High Sch, teacher; NC Asn Educr, exec dir, 1987-89; House Dist 87, elected NC House Rep, 1993-97. **Orgs:** Hilly Br Baptist Church, 1970-85; chartered mem, Alpha Kappa Alpha, 1974; Robeson City Dem Women, 1979-85; NC Coun Status Women, 1980-85; bd dir, NC Ctr Pub Policy Res, 1983-86; bd dir, NC Math & Sci Alliance; chair, Women & Minority Panel, Gov Appt, 1990; Pvt Indus Coun Lumber River comnrs, 1990; pres, NC Retired Sch Person, 2013-. **Special Achievements:** Book: The Girl Who Never Quit, 2005. **Home Addr:** 1708 Maryland St, Lumberton, NC 28358, **Home Phone:** (910)739-0094. **Business Addr:** President, North Carolina Retired School Personnel, 700 S Salisbury St, Raleigh, NC 27611, **Business Phone:** (800)662-7924.

**CUMMINGS, JAMES C., JR.**
Executive. **Personal:** Born Sep 22, 1929, Indianapolis, IN; married Norma Lewis; children: Cynthia, James III, Cecilia, Ronald & Claudia. **Educ:** Ind Cent Univ, BS, 1962. **Career:** Village Mgt Corp, proj mgr, 1960-66; Bd Fundamental Educ, dir opers, 1966-70; Oxford Develop Co, asst vpres, 1970-71; Urban Advance, pres; US Dept of Housing Urban Develop, regional adminr. **Orgs:** Chmn, Nat Black Rep Coun, exec comt Rep Nat Comn; chmn, Ind Black Rep Coun; exec asst chmn, Ind Rep State Comt; del Rep, Nat Convocation Fed, 1976; pres, Ind Black Expo, 1971-73; vice chmn, Inst Industrialized Bldg Oppurtinuty; Pub Works IN; bd mem, Zoning Appeals IN; mem bd, Nat Asn Advan Colored People. **Home Addr:** 4224 Manning Rd, Indianapolis, IN 46208.

**CUMMINGS, DR. JAY R.**
Educator, president (organization), administrator. **Personal:** Born Jan 6, 1942, Jenkins, KY; married Victoria Gerald; children: Darryl, Toi, Jabari, Brandi, Jordan & Trent. **Educ:** Cent State Univ, BS, 1963; Cleveland State Univ, MEd, 1971; Ohio State Univ, PhD, educ leadership, 1974; Tex Women's Univ, post doctoral, 1981. **Career:** Ohio St Univ, Ford Found fel, Urban Educ Lead, 1973; Dallas Independent Sch Dist, cent adr, 1976-86; Tex Educ Agency, asst comnr, 1986-89, dep comnr, 1989-91, exec dep comnr, 1992-95, assoc comnr, 1995-97, asst to Tex comnr, 1997-99; St Edward's Univ, adj prof, 1987-90; Career & Technol Educ syst, state dir; Univ NTex, Col Educ, prof, 1999-2001; Tex Southern Univ, Col Educ, dean, 2001-, prof, Educ Admin, interim dept chair, currently. **Orgs:** Bd mem, Tex Lead, Educ & Governance, 1987-91; community adv, Austin Jr League, 1987-88; founder & charter mem, Tex Alliance Black Sch Educr, 1989-; community adv, KLRU (Pub TV), 1989-95; exec bd dir, Nat Asn St dir Voc Educ Consortium, 1994-98; chair, Nat Alliance Black Sch Educr, Demonstration Sch Inst, 1994-97; Nat CMS African Am Educ, 1998-; chair, voc tech inst comm, CMS Sec Sch, 1998-; bd mem, Comt Accreditation & Sch Improv, Southern Asn Cols & Schs; founding bd mem, Advanced. **Home Addr:** 10831 Kitty Brook Dr, 6301 Almeda Rd Suite 1023, Houston, TX 77071-1705, **Home Phone:** (713)777-7434. **Business Addr:** Dean, Interim Department Chair, Professor, Texas Southern University, 241 Paige Educ Bldg Rm 200 3100 Cleburne St, Houston, TX 77004, **Business Phone:** (713)313-7087.

**CUMMINGS, MIDRE ALMERIC**
Baseball player. **Personal:** Born Oct 14, 1971, St. Croix, VI; son of Neville and Carmen Bastian; married Annette Lewis; children: Mijon & Mikel. **Career:** Baseball player (retired); Pittsburgh Pirates, outfielder, 1993-97; Philadelphia Phillies, 1997; Boston Red Sox, 1998, 2000; Minnesota Twins, 1999-2000; Arizona Diamondbacks, 2001; Tampa Bay Devil Rays, outfielder, 2004; Baltimore Orioles, 2005; La New Bears, 2006.

**CUMMINGS, PAT**
Writer. **Personal:** Born Nov 9, 1950, Chicago, IL; daughter of Arthur and Christine Taylor; married Chuku Lee. **Educ:** Pratt Inst, BFA, 1974. **Career:** Free-lance auth, illusr, 1974-; HarperCollins Publ Inc, auth, illusr, currently; Parsons Sch Design, Manhattan, C bk illus, instr; Books: My Mama Needs Me, illusr; My Aunt Came Back, auth & illusr; Angel Baby, auth & illusr; Clean Your Room Harvey Moon, auth & illusr; I Need a Lunch Box, illusr; Just Us Women, illusr; Pickin' Peas, illusr; C Is for City, illusr; Petey Moroni's Camp Runamok Diary, illusr. **Orgs:** Graphic Artists Guild; Soc C Book Writers & Illusr; Auth Guild; Writers Guild Am. **Honors/Awds:** Coretta Scott King Award, 1983; Black Women in Publ Illusr Award, 1988; Orbis Pictus, NAACP Image Award Horn Book Award, Boston Globe, 1992. **Home Addr:** 28 Tiffany Pl, Brooklyn, NY 11231-2991, **Home Phone:** (718)834-8584. **Business Addr:** Author, c/o Harper Collins Publ Inc, New York, NY 10022, **Business Phone:** (212)207-7791.

**CUMMINGS, ROBERT TERRELL.** **See CUMMINGS, TERRY.**

**CUMMINGS, TERRY (ROBERT TERRELL CUMMINGS)**
Basketball player, president (organization). **Personal:** Born Mar 15, 1961, Chicago, IL; son of John L and Verda; children: Robert Terrell Jr, Sean & Antonio. **Educ:** DePaul Univ, attended 1982. **Career:** Basketball player (retired), exec; Church God Christ, ordained pentecostal minister; San Diego Clippers, forward, 1982-84; Cummings Entertainment Group, pres, 1984-; Milwaukee Bucks, 1984-89, 1995-96; San Antonio Spurs, 1989-95; Seattle Supersonics, 1997; NY Knicks, 1997-98; Philadelphia 76ers, 1997-98; Golden State Warriors, forward, 1999-2000. **Business Addr:** President, Cummings Entertainment Group, 10004 Wurzbach Rd Suite 367, San Antonio, TX 78230, **Business Phone:** (210)696-4667.

**CUMMINGS, THERESA FAITH**
State government official, business owner. **Personal:** Born Springfield, IL; daughter of Nelson Mark and Mary Jeanette Irvine. **Educ:** Winston-Salem State Univ, BS, educ; Southern Ill Univ, MS, Per, Sch Med, fel, 1979. **Career:** St Louis Pub Sch Syst, teacher, 1957-67; Multi-purpose Neighborhood Serv Ctr Syst Springfield, Sangamon Co Comm Action Agency, proj dir, 1967-69, exec dir, 1969-85; Aband Mine Hands Reclam Coun, asst dir; Ill Dept Natural Resources, chief exec officer, equal employ opportunity officer; Cummings Assocs, chief exec officer & owner, currently. **Orgs:** Counr & guid chairperson, Human Develop Corp, 1965-67; planner & counr, Mr.Achievers Summer Inst Banneker Dist St Louis Pub Sch, 1966-67; League Women Voters; Am Asn Univ Women; Nat Coun Negro Women; bd dir, Sangamon CoMarch Dimes; St Paul AME Church; life mem, Nat Asn Advan Colored People; licensing bd, Ill Ambulatory Surg Treat Ctr; vice chairperson, chairperson & state treas, Nat Woman Polit Caucus; adv coun, Fed Res Consumer; Bus & Prof Women's Club; treas, pres, dist dir & vpres, State Pres Fed BPW, Women Govt; Women Mgt; pres, Nat Assoc Bus Women Owners; Am Bus Women Club; chairperson, Imp Credit Union; Iota Phi Lambda Sorority Inc; pres, Ill Fedn Bus &Prof Women; tres, Ill Affirmative Action officers Asn; bd dir, Sr Serv Cent ill; Am Soc Pub Adminr; Nat Asn Women; State Hist Soc; Ill Women Govt. **Honors/Awds:** Citation, Gr Lakes Regional Off Econ Opportunity Serv; citation, Springfield Ministerial Alliance Dedication & Devotion Duty; certified for service & contribution to Proj Mainstream Together Inc; cert Consumer Credit Counseling Serv Bd of Dirs; cert Contrib to Comm Develop OH Chapter of NACD; runner-up plaque, Lola M Parker Achievement Award; Medallion, Serv March Dimes; Woman of the Year, Zeta Phi Beta Sorority, 1982; Elizabeth Cady Stanton Awardee, Springfield Women Polit Caucus; Charlotte Danton Award for Government, Women Mgt; Fredda Witherspoon Award; Business Woman of the Year, Iota Phi Lambda Alpha Zeta. **Home Addr:** 2636 W Lawrence Ave, Springfield, IL 62704.

**CUNNINGHAM, COURTNEY**
President (organization), chief executive officer, government official. **Personal:** Born Feb 17, 1962, Ocala, FL; son of James Charles Sr and Juanita Perry. **Educ:** Univ Fla, Gainesville, FL, BA, polit sci & govt, 1983; Univ Fla Col Law, Gainesville, FL, JD, 1986. **Career:** Fisher, Rushmer, Orlando, Fla, assoc, 1986-87; Rumberger, Kirk, Orlando, Fla, assoc, 1987-89; Republican Nat Community, Wash, DC, dep chief coun, 1989-90; Interstate Com Comn, Wa, DC, atty & adv, 1990-91; Off Cong & Intergovernmental Affairs, Dept Labor, sr legis officer, 1991-93; Am Trucking Asn, sr legis rep, Wash, DC, 1993; Top Wall St firm, officer & investment banker; Miami-Dade County & Miami-Dade County Housing Finance Authority, sr invest banker; Ryder Syst Inc, dir, govt rels, Miami, Fla, 1994-96; Miami-Dade County Comn, Off Chairperson, chief staff, 1996-98; Barreto Cunningham

May Dudley Maloy, partner, currently; Cunningham Group, pres, founder, 1998-; SWAY Pub Rels Pub Affairs, chief exec officer; Commonground, MGS, founder, managing partner, 2014-. **Orgs:** Fla Blue Key Fraternity, 1983-86; vice chmn, Justice Campbell Thornal Moot Ct Bd, 1986; Fla Bar Asn, 1987; Fla Bd Osteop Med Examr, 1988; Am Judicature Soc, 1988; dep chief coun, Republican Nat Comt, 1989-91; Consult, Nat Republican Inst Intl Affairs, 1990; Fla bar; bd trustee, bd dir, Univ Fl, 2005; bd dir, Big Bros Big Sisters Greater Miami, 2013-. **Home Addr:** 14723 Breckness PL, Miami Lakes, FL 33016, **Home Phone:** (305)556-3598. **Business Addr:** Partner, Barreto Cunningham May Dudley Maloy, 235 Catalonia Ave, Coral Gables, FL 33134-6704, **Business Phone:** (305)444-4648.

### CUNNINGHAM, DAVID S., JR.

Government official, educator, mayor. **Personal:** Born Jun 24, 1935, Chicago, IL; son of David S Sr and Eulah Mae Lawson; married Mary; children: David Srumier III, Leslie Leslie & Robyn Elaine. **Educ:** Univ Riverside, BA, polit sci & econs, 1962; CORO Found Internship Pub Affairs, cert completion, pub policy anal, 1963; Occidental Col, MA, urban studies, 1972; Univ Calif, Riverside, attended 1972. **Career:** Calif State Assembly, admin aide assemblyman charles warren, 1963-64; DuKane Corp, W Africa regional mgr, 1964-67; Hughes Aircraft Co, Community Rels, mgr, 1967-68; Cunningham Short Berryman & Asn Inc, founder & owner, 1968-73, consults partner, vpres; Los Angeles City Coun, 1973-87, mayor, 1973; Dem Nat Comt, state chmn, 1976-86; Univ Southern Calif, vis lectr, 1977-78; Cranston/Prescott Investment Banker, sr vpres, 1986-88; Dave Cunningham & Assoc, owner, 1988-; Community Housing Equity Corp, sr vpres, 1988-91. **Orgs:** Chmn, LA Brotherhood Crusade, 1971-72; coun mem, Los Angeles City Coun, 1973-86; state chmn & calif deleg, Dem Nat Conv, 1976; S Calif Asn Govts Comn & Econ Develop Comn, 1978-79; bd dir, Nat League Cities, 1981-83; nat pres, 1984-85, bd dir, Nat Black United Fund; pres, bd dir, UCRiverside Alumni Asn, 2010-11; chmn, Grants Housing & Community Develop; vice chmn, Finance & Revenue Comn; Police Fire & Pub Safety Comn; authored or co-authored many laws among incl establish Mayor's Off Small Bus Ast; reduction minimum age fore firefighters 21 to 18 yrs; pioneered use fed block grants local govt use; created city's dept aging; created Vista Montoya Los Angele's first subsidized condo proj low & median income families; initiated organ Mid Town Chamber Com & Pico Union Chamber Com; charter mem, Calif Minority Employ Coun; Los Angeles Black Agenda; Bd Interracial Coun Bus Affairs; Urban League; bd dirs, Los Angeles Co Sanit Dist No 1; chmn, Nat Black United Fund; past pres, CORlumni Asn; life mem, Omega Psi Phi FratInc; life mem, Nat Asn Advan Colored People; life mem, Nat Coun Negro Women; col Calif Guard; World Affairs Coun; bd dir, 100 Black Men Los Angeles; bd dir, Miles Col; chmn, bd trustee; bd dir, Except C Found Los Angeles; bd dir, Los Angeles Econ Develop Corp; C's Hosp Los Angeles; pres, Riverside Alumni Asn; pres, bd dir, Delta Sigma Theta Life Develop Ctr. **Honors/Awds:** Man of Tomorrow, Omega Psi Phi, 1973; Los Angeles Brotherhood Crusade, 1973, 1976; Honorary Mayor, Baton Rouge LA, 1974; Mid City Chamber Commerce, 1974; Delta Sigma Theta, 1982-84; Dept Navy, 1984; Boy Scouts Am; South CA Fair Housing Congress, 1984; Alex Haley Heritage Award, 1984. **Business Addr:** Owner, Dave Cunningham & Associates, 4871 Dockweiler St, Los Angeles, CA 90019-1729.

### CUNNINGHAM, DON

Business owner, entrepreneur, executive. **Personal:** Born Dec 13, 1965; son of Don Sr and Valerie; married Laura; children: 3. **Educ:** Shippensburg Univ, BA, commun, jour, & related progs, 1987; Villanova Univ, MA, polit sci, 1991. **Career:** Philadelphia Inquirer, suburban corresp; Bethlehem Globe Times, reporter, 1988-92; Moravian Col, Bethlehem, media rels dir; Pa Power & Light Co, Allentown, sr info specialist; Bethlehem City Coun, 1995-97.City Bethlehem, PA, mayor, 1997-2003; Commonwealth Pa, Dept Gen Serv, secy, 2003-05; OEM Erie Inc, owner; Lehigh County, chief exec, 2006-12; Valley Econ Develop Corp, pres & chief exec officer, 2012-. **Orgs:** Int Econ Develop Coun, 2012-; pres, Pa League Cities; Bethlehem City Coun. **Special Achievements:** First elected to the City Council at 28 and became the Bethlehem's youngest mayor in history at 31. **Business Addr:** President, Chief Executive Officer, Valley Economic Development Corp, 2158 Ave C Suite 200, Bethlehem, PA 18017, **Business Phone:** (610)266-7565.

### CUNNINGHAM, E. BRICE

Lawyer. **Personal:** Born Feb 17, 1931, Buffalo, TX; son of Hattie and Tessie Roblow; married Rosie Nell Portis (Deceased), Mar 6, 1964; children: Ledner Vernard, Michele Denise & Elana Brice. **Educ:** Howard Univ Sch Law, BA, ID, LLB, 1960. **Career:** E Brice Cunningham, atty, counr law & munic ct judge, 1971-72; City Dallas, appeals judge; licences minister; atty law, currently. **Orgs:** State Bar Tex, 1960; Planning Comn city Dallas, 1973-76; State Bar Com Coord with Other & Groups; State Bar Pub Affairs Com; State Bar Sub-Com Grievance Com; Dallas Bar Asn; Spec Cts Com; Fee Disputes Com Dallas Bar Asn; Courthouse Com; State Bd Code Criminal Pruc Study Com; regional dir, Nat Bar Asn Inc, Region VI; AmJudicature Soc; S Dallas Br YMCA; Grand Atty, United Supreme coun; Past Grand legal Adv, Most Worshipful Prince Hall Grand Lodge F&AM Tex; bd dir, C Aid Soc; Alpha Phi Alpha Fraternity; Elks; Nat Asn Advan Colored People; Dallas City Planning Comn. **Honors/Awds:** Recipient Award, Law Com 100, 1973; Award for Legal Services, Dallas Tex Nat Asn Advan Colored People, 1977; A. Maceo Smith Community Service Award, 1979; Cert of Merit, Legislative Black Caucus State Tex, 1981; S Cent Bus & Prof Women's Club, Man of the Year Award, 1986; Six Bar Asn Dallas, Dr Martin Luther King Jr Justice Award, 1995; Tex Nat Asn Advan Colored People, Tex Heroes Award, 1997; Black Hist Achievement Award, Aldersgate United Methodist Church; Cert Merit, J L Turner Legal Asn. **Home Addr:** 2210 Van Cleave Dr, Dallas, TX 75216, **Home Phone:** (214)946-3486. **Business Addr:** Attorney, 777 S RL Thornton Freeway Suite 121, Dallas, TX 75203-2951, **Business Phone:** (214)946-1153.

### CUNNINGHAM, DR. JAMES J.

Educator, dean (education). **Personal:** Born Apr 19, 1938, Pittsburgh, PA; son of Steve and Roberta; married Lois Vines; children: Lita Denise & James Jr. **Educ:** Va State Univ, BS, elem educ, 1964; George Washington Univ, MA, guid & coun, 1967, Edsp, 1969, EdD, educ admin higher educ, 1971. **Career:** Elem sch teacher, 1964-66; Wash DC, coun & prin, 1966-68; Fed City Col, WADC, 1968-71; assoc Cont Res & Anal Inc, WA DC, consult, 1969; Fed City Col, dir admis, 1971; HEW & DE, WA DC, consult, 1971; Moton Consortium Admin & Financial Aid, co-dir, 1971-72; Tex Southern Univ, dean studs, prof higher educ, 1972-74, Houston, Dept Educ Admin & Foundations, spec asst pres, 1986, vpres instadvan, assoc dean stud affairs, prof educ, Ctr Strategic Advances Educ, co dir, currently; Mankato State Col, Mankato, MN, vpres stud servs, prof educ, 1974; Am Coun Educ & NASPA Inst, ACE fel, 1975; Col Continuing Educ, interim assoc dean & prof; Publications: "The Evaluation of Reading Readiness in the Head Start Program", 1965; "The New Breed-Black Activist", 1971; "An Analysis of the Open Door Admissions Policy at Federal City: 1968-1971", 1971; A Handbook of University Governance, 1978; Sources of Finance for Higher Education, 1980; Collective Bargaining and Governance in Higher Education, 1984. **Orgs:** Nat Asn Higher Educ; Personnel Guid Asn; Asn Col Admin Coun; DC Coun Asn; Elem Classroom Teachers Asn; Nat Teachers Asn; Tex Personnel Serv Adminrs; Minn State Col Stud Asn; Minn Stud Serv Adminr; Nat Asn Advan Colored People; Tex Asn Col Teachers; Am Asn Univ Professors; Nat Educ Asn; Nat Asn Stud Personnel Adminr; Phi Delta Kappa; NCAA cert comt; Univ Convocation Commitee; Univ Charter Day Comt; Asn Higher Educ; Tex conf Cols & Univ; Tex Asn Cols-Univ Fac. **Home Addr:** 15307 Paladora Dr, Houston, TX 77083, **Home Phone:** (281)495-0747. **Business Addr:** Professor of Education, Texas Southern University, 245 Paige Educ Bldg, Houston, TX 77004, **Business Phone:** (713)313-7256.

### CUNNINGHAM, JOY VIRGINIA

Judge. **Personal:** children: 1. **Educ:** City Univ NY, BS, nursing, 1975; John Marshall Law Sch, JD, 1982. **Career:** Fr Rogers Kezelis & Kominiarek, atty; Cook County Circuit Ct, Ill, judge, 1997-2000; Northwestern Memorial Syst, sr vpres, gen coun & corp secy, 2000; Ill Appellate Ct, asst ill atty gen & judicial law clerk; First Dist, 3rd Div, appellate judge, 2006-. **Orgs:** Nat Asn Advan Colored People; Urban League; Am Bar Asn; Am Health Lawyers Asn; Cook County Bar Asn; Black Women Lawyers Asn; Ill State Bar Asn; Women's Bar Asn Ill; Econ Club Chicago; assoc gen coun, Loyola Univ Chicago & Loyola Univ Health Syst, 1989-97; sr vpres, gen coun, corp secy, Northwestern Memorial Syst, 2000; pres, Chicago Bar Asn, 2004-05; dir bd, Chicago Bar Found; dir bd, Ctr Conflict Resolution; dir bd, Ctr Disability & Elder Law; dir bd, Chicago Legal Clin. **Business Addr:** Appellate Judge, Illinois Court, 160 N LaSalle St, Chicago, IL 60601, **Business Phone:** (312)793-5484.

### CUNNINGHAM, MALENA ANN

Journalist, television journalist. **Personal:** Born Oct 27, 1958, Laurens, SC; daughter of O'Dell (deceased) and Betty Brummell. **Educ:** Univ Ga, ABJ, pub rels & jour, 1980. **Career:** Atlanta Gas Light Co, pub rels assoc, 1980-82; Cable News Network, writer & producer, 1982-86; WTVQ-TV, reporter, 1986-87; WHTM-TV, reporter, 1987-88; WSAV-TV, anchor, 1988-91; WVTM-TV, anchor & reporter, 1992; Strategic Media Rels, owner, pres & chief exec officer, 2004-. **Orgs:** Nat Asn Black Journalists, 1992-; Birmingham Asn Black Journalists, vpres, broadcasting, 1992-; Delta Sigma Theta, 1977-; Jr bd mem, YWCA, 1992-; Birmingham Asn Black Journalists, pres, 1994; co-chmn, The Cool Community task force; adv bd, Womens Fund, 2006-. **Honors/Awds:** United Press Intl, First Place, Spot News Reporting, 1988; Second Place, Assoc Press, Spot News Reporting, 1988; Best Newscast, Assoc Press, 1990; Emmy Award, Academy Television Arts & Sciences, 1992; Emmy Award, Academy Television Arts & Sciences, 1995; Emmy Award, Academy Television Arts & Sciences, 1996; Edward R. Murrow Award, 2004; National Association of Black Journalists Award of Excellence. **Home Addr:** 526 Highland Pk Cir, Birmingham, AL 35242, **Home Phone:** (205)980-2154. **Business Addr:** Owner, President, Strategic Media Relations, PO Box 380846, Birmingham, AL 35238, **Business Phone:** (205)746-9942.

### CUNNINGHAM, PATRICK DANTE ROSS. See CUNNINGHAM, RICK.

### CUNNINGHAM, DR. PAUL RAYMOND GOLDWYN

Surgeon, educator. **Personal:** Born Jul 28, 1949, Mandeville; son of Winston P and Sylvia F Marsh; married Sydney Keniston; children: Shawn, Rachel, Lucinda & Tifanie. **Educ:** Univ Wis, Jamaica, MD, 1972. **Career:** Mt Sinai Med Ctr, New York, surg intern, 1974-75, surg resident, 1975-79; Jt Dis N Gen Hosp, New York NY, asst dir surg, 1979-81; Bertie Memorial Hosp, Windsor NC, attend physician, 1981-84; E Carolina Univ, Broody Sch Med, Div Surg, physician, 1984-94, interim dir, prof & chief, 1994-2002, dean, 2008-, Med Affairs, sr assoc & vice chancellor; Pitt County Memorial Hosp, Greenville, NC, attend surgeon, 1984-02, chief med staff, 1991-92; State Univ New York, Upstate Med Univ, Dept Surg, prof & chair, 2002-08; Am Col Surgeons, gov, currently. **Orgs:** AMA, 1979-; Nat Med Asn, 1983-; Asn Acad Surg, 1985-; Am Col Surgeons, Am Coun Transplantation, Sigma Xi, Sci Res Socs, 1986-; Pan Am Trauma Socs, 1988-; Socs Critical Care Med, Socs Phi Kappa Phi, Acad Surg Res, 1989-; Asn Surg Educ, 1990-; pres, Eastern Asn Surg Trauma, 2000; Southern Surg Asn; Transplantation Soc; fel Am Col Surgeons; founding mem, Am Soc Minority Health & Transplant Prof; Soc Black Acad Surgeons. **Home Addr:** 327 River Bank Lane, Greenville, NC 27834, **Home Phone:** (252)355-0906. **Business Addr:** Dean, East Carolina University, 600 Moye Blvd, Greenville, NC 27834, **Business Phone:** (252)744-1020.

### CUNNINGHAM, RANDALL

Business owner, football player, clergy. **Personal:** Born Mar 27, 1963, Santa Barbara, CA; son of Samuel and Mabel; married Felicity de Jagar; children: Randall II, Vashti & Grace. **Educ:** Univ Nev, Las Vegas, BA, film. **Career:** Football player, business owner (retired), pastor; Philadelphia Eagles, quarterback, 1985-95, 2002; TNT Network, TV studio analyst, 1996; Minn Vikings, 1997-99; Dallas Cowboys, 2000; TNT, football analyst, 1999-2000; Baltimore Ravens, 2001; marble & granite bus owner; rec studio & musical group, producer; Remnant Ministries, founder, 2004; pastor & founder, Cupbearer, Las Vegas, 2004-; Silverado High Sch, offensive coordr, 2009. Films; Minister of Defense: The Reggie White Story, 2006; E True Hollywood Story, 2006; Tazon Latino II, 2008; iGames, 2010; Town of the Living Dead, 2011. **Home Addr:** 5020 Span Heights Dr, Las Vegas, NV 89118. **Business Addr:** Pastor, Founder, The Cupbearer, 325 E Windmill Rd, Las Vegas, NV 89123, **Business Phone:** (702)269-7803.

### CUNNINGHAM, RICK (PATRICK DANTE ROSS CUNNINGHAM)

Football player. **Personal:** Born Jan 4, 1967, Los Angeles, CA. **Educ:** Tex A&M Univ, Eng, 1989. **Career:** Football player (retired); Indianapolis Colts, tackle, 1990; Phoneix Thunder, 1992-93; Ariz Cardinals, right tackle, 1994; Minn Vikings, tackle, 1995; Oakland Raiders, 1996-98; Montreal Alouettes, 2000 & 2002; Edmonton Eskimos, 2001-02; Las Vegas Gladiators, 2003-05.

### CUNNINGHAM, ROBERT SHANNON, JR.

Executive. **Personal:** Born Jan 17, 1958, Columbia, SC; son of Robert Shannon Sr and Dorothy Mae Bell; married Shenita Gilmore. **Educ:** Johnson C Smith Univ, Charlotte, NC, BS, 1980. **Career:** Union Carbide, Simpsonville, SC, prod supvr, 1980; IBM Corp, Charlotte, NC, financial analyst, 1980-89; IBM Corp, Res Triangle Pk, NC, bus planner, 1989-91, develop prog mgr, 1991-98, sr prof develop mgr, 1998; IBM, sr prog mgr, 1980-2011; IBM Global Bus Serv, sr prog mgr 2008-. **Orgs:** Vice chmn, Mecklenburg Co Personnel Comn Bd, 1982-88; City Charlotte Cert Develop Bd, 1989; secy, Focus Leadership Bd, 1987; United Way Community Resource Bd, 1981; Urban League, 1985-; numerous positions, Omega Psi Phi Fraternity, 1977. **Home Addr:** 1008 Sunny Brae Ct, Apex, NC 27502, **Home Phone:** (919)387-4750. **Business Addr:** Senior Manager, IBM Corp, 600 Pk Rd Bldg 660 Hwy 54, Research Triangle Park, NC 27709, **Business Phone:** (919)543-0515.

### CUNNINGHAM, T. J., SR.

Lawyer. **Personal:** Born Feb 6, 1930, Plant City, FL; son of Garrison S and Janette Rome; children: Belinda C Palmore, Tequesta C Alston, Yolanda Griffin, Kimberly & T J Jr. **Educ:** Fla A&M Univ, BS, sociol, 1952; Howard Univ Law Sch, JD, 1957. **Career:** Cunningham & Cunningham, owner, 1960-. **Orgs:** Fla Bar; DC Bar Asn; Am Bar Asn; US Ct Appeals; US Supreme Ct; Palm Beach County Bar Asn; Nat Bar Asn; Fla Acad Trial Lawyers; founder & mem, F.Malcolm Cunningham, Sr Bar Asn; Fla Bar Grievance Comt, Palm Beach County; World Peace through Law; Nat Bar Asn; Fla Chap, Nat Bar Asn; Nat Asn Advan Colored People; Alpha Phi Alpha; Fla Chap Nat Guardsmen Asn; Forum Club Palm Beaches; Fla State Action Coun; Nat Urban League; advcoun, Fla A & M Univ; Cunningham Bar. **Honors/Awds:** Chairman Convention Award, Nat Bar Asn, 1972; President's Award, 1975; F Malcolm Cunningham Senior Bar Achievement Award, 1981; President's Service Award, Fla Chapter NBA, 1981; Fla A&M Univ Alumni Leadership Award, Palm Beach County; Leadership Award, 1986. **Home Addr:** 900 Bear Island Cir, West Palm Beach, FL 33409-3508. **Business Addr:** Attorney, Cunningham & Cunningham PA, 1897 Palm Beach Lakes Blvd, West Palm Beach, FL 33409-3507, **Business Phone:** (561)683-2900.

### CUNNINGHAM, DR. VERNESSA SMALLS-BRANTLEY

Physician. **Personal:** Born Aug 4, 1949, Charleston, SC; married Herman. **Educ:** Spelman Col, BS, 1971; Meharry Med Col, MD, 1975. **Career:** Martland Hosp Newark NJ, resident, 1975-76; Monmouth Med Ctr, Long Br, NJ, resident, 1976-77, fel, 1977-79; Perth Amboy Gen Hosp, dir nurseries, 1980-83; pvt pract pediatrician, 1983-85; Pt Pleasant Hosp, dir nursery, 1985-86; Kaiser-Permanente, pediatrician & neonatologist. **Orgs:** Am Acad Pediat, 1983-85; Nat Asn Black Bus & Prof Women, 1985-; Atlanta Med Soc, 1987. **Honors/Awds:** Achievement Award, Nat Coun Negro Women, N Shore Area, 1985. **Home Addr:** 5024 Klondike Rd, Lithonia, GA 30038-4245, **Home Phone:** (770)593-4234. **Business Addr:** Pediatrician, Neonatologist, Kaiser-Permanente, 1525 Clifton Rd NE, Atlanta, GA 30322, **Business Phone:** (770)469-9026.

### CUNNINGHAM, WILLIAM (WILL CUNNINGHAM)

Basketball player. **Personal:** Born Mar 25, 1974, Augusta, GA. **Educ:** Temple Univ. **Career:** Continental Basketball Asn, Ft Wayne Fury, prof basketball player; Philadelphia 76ers, ctr, 1998; Utah Jazz, 1998; Toronto Raptors, 1999; NJ Nets, 1999; Atletico Arenas, Uruguay, 2006.

### CUNNINGHAM, DR. WILLIAM DEAN

Educator. **Personal:** Born Aug 9, 1937, Kansas City, MO; children: Crystal. **Educ:** Univ Kans, BA, 1954; Univ Tex, MLS, 1962; Univ Md, PhD, 1972. **Career:** Educator (retired); Fed Aviation Agency, chief libr serv, 1965-67; Topeka Pub Libr, head adult serv, 1967-68; US Dept Educ, prog officer, 1968-71; Howard Univ, dir univ libr, 1970-73; Univ Md, Col Libr & Info Servs, asst prof, 1973. **Orgs:** Am Libr Asn, 1970, Asn Study Afro-Am Life & Hist, 1974; bd dir, Soul Journey Enterprises, 1974; Nat Black Heritage Coun, 1984. **Home Addr:** 1201 Fairlakes Pl, Bowie, MD 20721, **Home Phone:** (301)336-7643.

### CUNNINGHAM, WILLIAM L.

Government official, economist. **Personal:** Born Aug 28, 1939, Little Rock, AR; married Annette; children: Karm Joy. **Educ:** Univ Ark, Pine Bluff, BS, 1961; St Vincent Med Ctr, assoc, 1964; US Dept Agr, Salt Lake City, mgt cert, 1967; Univ Utah, attended 1972. **Career:** State Utah Anti-discrimination Div, investigator, conciliator & pres; Univ Ark Med Ctr, biochemist, 1964-65; Univ Utah Med Ctr, researcher, 1965-66; US Dept Agr, field adv, 1965-68, agr engr, 1966-68; Univ Wash Med Center, med consult, 1968-69, lab supvr, 1968-70; State Utah, liberal economist, 1970-72, economist adv, 1971-73. **Orgs:** Bd mem, Nat Asn Advan Colored People, 1957-61, vpres, 1996, first vpres, 1997-; officer, 1965-68, Elks, bd mem, 1966-67. **Honors/Awds:** Hon mem cert Am Basketball Asn, 1973; Special Service Award, 1975, Exalted Ruler Award, 1977, Outstanding Citizen Award, 1979, Elks; Earnest Turner Day Award, Beehive Elks Lodge, 1991; President Award, Nat Asn Advan Colored People, 1997. **Home Addr:** 955 E Essex Way Suite 4, Midvale, UT 84047, **Home Phone:** (801)532-4541. **Business Addr:** Senior Investigator, Conciliator, State Utah, 160 E 300 S, Salt Lake City, UT 84114-6640, **Business Phone:** (801)530-6918.

**CUNNINGHAM, WILLIAM MICHAEL**
Executive, chief executive officer. **Personal:** Born Jul 16, 1958, Washington, DC. **Educ:** Howard Univ, BA, econ, 1978; Univ Chicago, MBA, finance, 1983, MA, econ, 1983. **Career:** Data Resources Inc, mktg rep, 1977-83; Conn Mutual Life, invest anal, 1983-85; Merrill Lynch, instnl sales, 1985-87, acct exec; Fed Home Loan Mkt Corp, instnl sales, 1987-88; Creative Investment Res Inc, social investment adv, 1989-, chief exec officer, owner, currently; US Securities & Exchange Comn, regist investment adv, 1990-; DC Pub Serv Comn, investment adv, 1994; Evangel Lutheran Church, mgr social purpose investing; Nat Crowdfunding Serv, managing partner; Georgetown Univ, stud advisor. **Orgs:** Am Friends Serv Comt, fin comn; Social Investment Forum; Asn Investment Mgt & Res; Twin Cities Soc Security Analysts; CFA Inst; CFA Soc; Social Investment Forum. **Home Addr:** 3540 Hennepin Ave, Minneapolis, MN 55408, **Home Phone:** (612)822-9605. **Business Addr:** Chief Executive Officer & Owner, Creative Investment Research Inc, PO Box 55793, Minneapolis, MN 55458-0725, **Business Phone:** (866)867-3795.

**CURBEAM, ROBERT LEE, JR.**
Astronaut, naval officer. **Personal:** Born Mar 5, 1962, Baltimore, MD; married Julie Dawn Lein; children: 2. **Educ:** US Naval Acad, BS, aerospace engineering, 1984; Naval Postgrad Sch, MS, aeronaut engineering, 1990, aeronaut & astronaut engineering, 1991. **Career:** Astronaut (retired); US Naval Acad, naval flight officer, 1984, capt, Weapons & Systs Eng Dept, instr, 1994; Strike Aircraft Test Directorate, F-14A/B Air-to-Ground Weapons Separation Prog, proj officer; Astronaut Off, Comput Support Br; NASA, CAPCOM, spacecraft communicator, 1994, br chief, Safety & Mission Assurance, dep assoc adminr, 2002, dir Safety, Reliability & Qual Assurance, dep dir Flight Crew Opers, 2007; ARES Corp, Aerospace & Defense Div, pres; Raytheon, vpres mission assurance, currently. **Orgs:** US Naval Acad Alumni Asn; Asn Old Crows. **Honors/Awds:** Fighter Wing One Radar Intercept Officer of the Year, 1989; US Naval Test Pilot School Best Developmental Thesis (DT-II) Award. **Special Achievements:** Mission specialist on STS-85 assignment, shuttle Discovery, 1997; First person to perform four spacewalks on a single mission. **Business Addr:** Vice President, Raytheon Co, 50 Apple Hill Dr, Tewksbury, MA 01876, **Business Phone:** (978)858-5000.

**CURETON, EARL**
Basketball player, basketball coach. **Personal:** Born Sep 3, 1957, Detroit, MI. **Educ:** Robert Morris Col, attended 1976; Univ Detroit, attended 1979. **Career:** Basketball player, (retired), head coach; Philadelphia 76ers, ctr & pt forward, 1980-83; Olimpia Milano, 1983, 1989-90; Detroit Pistons, ctr & pt forward, 1983-86; Chicago Bulls, ctr, 1986-87; Los Angeles Clippers, ctr & pt forward, 1987-88; Charlotte Hornets, pt forward & ctr, 1988-89, 1991; New Haven Skyhawks, 1991; Tours Joue Basket, France, 1991-92; Sioux Falls Skyforce, 1993-94; Houston Rockets, ctr & pt forward, 1994-96; Toronto Raptors, ctr, 1996-97; Camden Power, coach, 1998; Long Beach Jam, coach, 2003-04; Orange County Crush, head coach, 2004-05. **Honors/Awds:** Championship, Nat Basketball Asn, 1983, 1994. **Business Addr:** Head Coach, Orange County Crush, CA 90001, **Business Phone:** (562)861-6089.

**CURETON, JOHN PORTER**
Manager, consultant. **Personal:** Born Oct 4, 1936, Oxford, NC; son of John and Marie; married Carolyn Bethea; children: Tonya Yvette & John Porter. **Educ:** Johnson C Smith Univ, BS, psychol, 1960; Adelphia Univ, postgrad, 1961; Univ Pa, attended 1963; Univ Hartford, attended 1980. **Career:** NY Dept Ment Hyg, psychiat social worker, 1960-62; Inter-State Staffing Inc, mgt consult, 1962-66; Philco Ford Corp, sr employ rep, 1966-68; Tanatex Div, Sybron Corp, indust rels mgr, 1968-73; US Postal Servs, reg labor rels exec, 1973-75; Heublein Inc Groc Prod Group, mgr employee rels, 1975-78; US Tobacco Co, Indust & Sales Rels, asst, dir presonnel, 1978-98. **Orgs:** Nat Asn Mkt Developers; Employ Mgt Assoc; Inst Rels & Res; Inst Collective Bargaining & Group Rels; Soc Human Resources Mgt; Am Soc Training & Develop; bd mem, Vol Action Ctr; Ct UNCF Comn; Kappa Alpha Psi; Nat Urban League; Nat Asn Advan Colored People; Western NE Org Develop Network. **Honors/Awds:** Various awards from UNCF, UL, BNA-Personnel Policies Forum, Kappa Alpha Psi, YMCA. **Home Addr:** 802 Walcott Way, Cary, NC 27519-9536, **Home Phone:** (919)469-2884.

**CURETON, MICHAEL**
Police officer, government official. **Personal:** Born Nov 15, 1955, Cincinnati, OH; son of James A Sr and Dolores J Thomas Rowland; married Jennifer L Horton; children: Shana, Mike Jr, Christopher, Angela & Brandon. **Educ:** Xavier Univ, BS; Univ Cincinnati, AS, 1976. **Career:** City Cincinnati, police cadet, 1973-76; Procter & Gamble Co, security, 1976-78, sales rep, 1978-80; City Cincinnati, dist two comdr, asst chief police, 1976-2011, police officer, 1980; Univ Cincinnati, dir pub safety & chief police, patrol officer to asst police chief, 2011-13; Brighter Day Consult, prin consult, 2014-. **Orgs:** Pres, Sentinel Police Asn, 1986-; steering comt, Dr Martin Luther King Coalition, 1988-; hairperson ways & means, Nat Black Police Asn Eastern Reg, 1989-; vol chair site security, Nat Coun Negro Women Black Family Reunion, Cincinnati Site, 1989-; First Baptist Church Kennedy Heights; bd mem, YMCA, 2010; Alpha Phi Sigma Hon Soc. **Home Addr:** 7942 Glen Orchard Dr, Cincinnati, OH 45237, **Home Phone:** (513)948-1995. **Business Addr:** Assistant Chief of Police, Director of Public Safety, Cincinnati Police Division, 3295 Erie Ave, Cincinnati, OH 45208, **Business Phone:** (513)556-4951.

**CURRIE, BETTY (BETTY GRACE WILLIAMS)**
Presidential aide, secretary (organization), government official. **Personal:** Born Nov 10, 1939, Edwards, MS; daughter of Theodore R and Vivian U Williams; married Bob; children: 1. **Educ:** Waukegan Twp High Sch's bus course, 1957. **Career:** Government official, presidential aide (retired); Navy Dept, staff; Postal Serv, staff; US Agency Int Develop, staff; Peace Corps & Dept Health & Human Servs, staff; White House, Off Pres, personal secy, 1993-2001. **Orgs:** Bd dir, Nat Peace Corps Asn, 2006; Bd mem, Alcohol Beverage Bd St. Mary's County, 2008-. **Home Addr:** , MD.

**CURRY, CLARENCE F.**
Lecturer, management consultant. **Personal:** Born Aug 15, 1943, Hampton, VA; married Agnes A Mason; children: Clarence III & Candace. **Educ:** Lafayette Col, BS, met engineering, 1965; Univ Pittsburgh, col bus admin, MBA, 1971; Carnegie Mellon Univ, MS, IA, 1973. **Career:** Sports & Exhib Authority, sr diversity coordr, 2007-; Westinghouse Elec Corp, engr; Univ Pittsburgh Sch Bus, dir Small Bus Devel Ctr, asst vice chancellor; Pittsburgh Gaming Task Force Mem, Pittsburgh Penguins; CFC-3 Mgt Serv, prin consult, currently. **Orgs:** Panelist, Am Arbit Asn; Minority Bus Opportunity Comm; Int Coun Small Bus; USAS BC; Small Bus Inst Dir Asn. **Honors/Awds:** Pa Minority Bus Advocate, SBA, 1983. **Special Achievements:** International consultant on business development in Brazil, Peru, Poland and Czech Republic and Slovakia; Several consulting projects for 500 firms. **Home Addr:** 200 Richland Lane, Pittsburgh, PA 15208, **Home Phone:** (412)243-2084. **Business Addr:** Senior Diversity Coordinator, Sports & Exhibition Authority, 171 10th St 2nd Fl, Pittsburgh, PA 15222, **Business Phone:** (412)393-7102.

**CURRY, DELL (WARDELL STEPHEN CURRY)**
Executive, basketball player, basketball coach. **Personal:** Born Jun 25, 1964, Harrisonburg, VA; son of Stephen; married Sonya; children: Stefan, Seth & Sydell. **Educ:** Va Polytech Inst & State Univ, Blacksburg, VA, 1986. **Career:** Basketball player (retired), exec; Utah Jazz, 1986-87; Nat Basketball Asn, 1986-2002; Cleveland Cavaliers, 1987-88; Charlotte Hornets, 1988-98; Milwaukee Bucks, 1998-99; Toronto Raptors, 1999-2002; Charlotte Bobcats, dir player progs, 2003-, asst coach, 2007. **Orgs:** Founder, Dell Curry Found, 1998. **Business Addr:** Director of Player Programs, Charlotte Bobcats, 333 E Trade St, Charlotte, NC 28202, **Business Phone:** (704)688-8600.

**CURRY, EDDY ANTHONY, JR.**
Basketball player. **Personal:** Born Dec 5, 1982, Harvey, IL; son of Eddy Sr; married Patrice; children: Noah, Brandi, Eddy III, Ava (deceased), Reidan, Reiganna, Reign & Reigan. **Educ:** DePaul Univ. **Career:** Chicago Bulls, ctr, 2001-05; NY Knicks, ctr & forward, 2005-10; Miami Heat, ctr, 2011-12; Dallas Mavericks, ctr, 2012-13; Zhejiang Golden Bulls, China, 2012-13; free agt, currently. **Orgs:** Co-chair, Bulls Holiday Heroes Prog. **Honors/Awds:** Full Athletic Scholar, DePaul Univ; Most Valuable Player, McDonalds All-Am Game, 2001; Illinois Mr Basketball, 2001; NBA Champion, 2012. **Business Addr:** NY.

**CURRY, ERIC FELECE**
Football player. **Personal:** Born Feb 3, 1970, Thomasville, GA. **Educ:** Univ Ala, grad. **Career:** Football player (retired); Tampa Bay Buccaneers, right defensive end & defensive end, 1993-97; Jacksonville Jaguars, defensive end, 1998-99. **Orgs:** Theta Delta Chapter Phi Beta Sigma Fraternity Inc. **Honors/Awds:** All-American, 1992. **Home Addr:** , Jacksonville, FL.

**CURRY, GLADYS J. See WASHINGTON, GLADYS J.**

**CURRY, DR. JAMES H.**
Educator. **Personal:** Born Jan 1, 1948?, Oakland, CA. **Educ:** Univ Calif, Berkeley, BS, 1970, MS, 1971, PhD, math, 1976. **Career:** Howard Univ, fac; Nat Ctr Atmospheric Res, Boulder, Colo, postdoctoral fel; Massachusetts Inst Technol, postdoctoral assoc, 1978-80; Univ Minn, 1981; CRAY High Performance Comput Syst, 1981; Univ Colo, prof appl math, 1989-, assoc dir, dept appl mathematics, dept chair, 2003-12; NAM Claytor, Lecture, 1995; Nsf, proj officer; pres's teaching scholar, 1993; J. R. Woodhull/Logicon, teaching prof, 1999-2012; David Blackwell, lecture, 2003; Univ Mich, marjorie lee brown lecture, 2012. **Orgs:** Bd trustee, Colo Univ Found; Sect on Mathematics, 1995-98; Vietnam Educ Grad Selection Comt, 2005 & 2007; ed bd, MAA Math; Educ Comt Socs Indust & Appl Mathematics; Comt Exemplary MathDepts; Morgan Prize Comt Outstanding Undergrad Res; Comt Profession Am Math Socs; Electorate Nominating Comt; SIAM Mem Comt; Colo Ctr Chaos & Complexity; fel, Nat Ctr Atmospheric Res; prog dir, NSF Div Math Sci, 2012-14; proj officer, Nsf. **Business Addr:** Professor, Department Chair, University of Colorado, PO Box 526, Boulder, CO 80309-0526, **Business Phone:** (303)492-6901.

**CURRY, JASON R.**
Religious leader, educator. **Personal:** married Angela; children: John, Nia & Samuel. **Educ:** Morehouse Col, BA, philos & relig, 1992; Harvard Divinity Sch, MDiv, 1996; Vanderbilt Univ, PhD, 2005. **Career:** St. Matthews AMEC Midway, Ky, sr pastor; Hist St. Peter African Methodist Episcopal Church (AMEC) Harrodsburg, Ky, sr pastor; dir, Ky State Univ, 2001-03; Fisk Univ, assoc vpres, dir; Fisk Memorial Chapel, dean chapel, 2003-. **Orgs:** Agape African Methodist Episcopal Church (AMEC), Itinerant Elder; Fisk Memorial Chapel Assistants, Founder, 2003; Leaders of the Interfaith Fellowship Team (L.I.F.T.), Founder. **Honors/Awds:** Fund for Theological Education as a Benjamin E. Mays Scholar, 1994-96; Vanderbilt University, Graduate Fellow, 1997-99; Outstanding Young Americans, 1998; Vanderbilt University, Dissertation Fellow (2003). **Special Achievements:** Published: the forward in "Now They Call Me Reverend" by Sidney F. Bryant (2006); "The Essence of Holy Communion" in the "Journal of Christian Education" (African Methodist Episcopal Church Sunday School Union, 2006); "An Inquiry Concerning the Validity of the Religious Association Scale and the Validity of Self-Reports Among Substance Abusers" in "The A.M.E. Church Review" (September 2003); presented a paper titled "Institutional Research and the Wider Community: The Importance of Collaborative Efforts" at the Conference on Institutional Research in Historically Black Colleges and Universities hosted by Spelman College (2003). **Business Addr:** Dean of the Chapel, Fisk University, 1000 17th Ave N, Nashville, TN 37208, **Business Phone:** (615)329-8582.

**CURRY, MAJOR GEN. JERRY RALPH**
Administrator. **Personal:** Born Sep 7, 1932, McKeesport, PA; son of Mercer and Jesse; married Charlene; children: Charlein, Jerry, Toni & Natasha. **Educ:** Univ Nebr, BA, 1960; Command & Gen Staff Col, attended 1967; Boston Univ, MA, int rels, 1970; Luther Rice Univ, dr ministry, 1978; AUS War Col, grad. **Career:** Army (retired), consultant, singer; AUS, pvt to maj gen, Test & Eval Command, comndg gen; Carter Admin, mil dep asst secy defense; Reagan Admin, Secy Defense, press secy; US Cong, cand, 1988; Nat Hwy Traffic Safety Admin, adminr, 1989-92; Nat Res Coun Transp Res bd, mem; opera singer & bus consult, currently. **Orgs:** Bd mem, Greater Wash, DC, Bd Trade; bd mem, Am Red Cross; fed trustee, Fed City Coun; Delta Phi Alpha; Nat Hon Ger Soc; Phi Alpha Theta; Int Hon Soc Hist; Nat Eagle Scout Asn; chmn Black Revolutionary War Patriots Found; fel Oxford Socs Scholars; Asn Advan Automotive Med; Soc Automotive Engrs; advisor, S Vietnamese inf regt. **Honors/Awds:** Distinguished Alumni, Univ Nebr, 1979; Washingtonian of the Year, Washingtonian Mag, 1982; The Secret Service Honor Award; Order of Orange-Nassau, Queen Beatrix of the Netherlands; received several military & government awards. **Special Achievements:** Author of book: From Private to General: An African-American Rises Through The Ranks; CD, Generally Singing. **Business Addr:** Business Consultant, Chateau Antioch, Haymarket, VA 20168-0407, **Business Phone:** (703)753-2615.

**CURRY, LEVY HENRY**
Administrator, vice president (organization), executive. **Personal:** Born Feb 3, 1949, Buffalo, NY; son of Levi and Cora Marie; married Dianne; children: Tasha. **Educ:** Morehouse Col, BA, polit Sci, 1972; Atlanta Law Sch, JD, 1975; Univ Mich & Southern Methodist Univ. **Career:** EEOC, Atlanta, Ga, staff atty; Consol Mfg Co, plant mgr, 1970-71; Int Harvester, sales mgr, 1971-74; Equal & Employ Opportunity Comn, legal res anal, 1974; Steak & Ale Restaurants Am, dir personnel, 1975-87, dir affirmative action, 1975; Nat Urban League Beep Prog, vis prof, 1977; Hospitality Indust Inc, bd dir, 1978; Am Fed Bank, sr vpres; Pillsbury Restaurant Group, vpres human resources; PageNet, vpres human resources, 1988-98; Deloitte's Human Capital Adv Servs, sr dir & mgt consult, 1998-2001; 7-Eleven Inc, dir Compensation, Benefits & Employee Rel, 2001-04; Kaiser Found Health Plan Mid-Atlantic States, vpres human resources, 2004-07; HR Search Firm, managing dir, 2007-. **Orgs:** Morris Brown Col Sch Restaurant & Instrumental Mgt, 1977; Dallas Personnel Asn, 1977; Am Soc Personnel, 1977; bd dir, Chain Restaurant Compensation Asn, 1978; consult, Jr Achievement Proj Bus, 1979; Morehouse Col Alumni Asn; bd trustee, African Mus Life & Cult; Jr Black Acad Arts & Lett; bd mem, Aquinas Fund, 2005; bd mem, SW Med Sch Found; Univ Tex, adv bd; African Am Mus, adv bd. **Honors/Awds:** Mary C Miller Scholar, Nat Urban League, 1967. **Business Addr:** Vice President of Human Resources, Kaiser Foundation Health Plan of the Mid-Atlantic States Inc, 2101 E Jefferson St, Rockville, MD 20852, **Business Phone:** (301)816-2424.

**CURRY, MARK G.**
Actor. **Personal:** Born Jun 1, 1961, Oakland, CA. **Educ:** Calif State Univ, Hayward. **Career:** TV series: "Hangin' With Mr Cooper", 1992-97; "ABC Mark Curry & Delta Burke Back Lot Special", 1994; "Motocrossed", 2001; "The Poof Point", 2011; "Hold This", 2005; "Fat Actress", 2005; "Poolboy: Drowning Out the Fury", 2011; "The Secret Life of the American Teenager", 2011-12; "See Dad Run", 2012-14; "One Love", 2014; TV guest appearances: "Show time at the Apollo", host; "The Arsenio Hall Show"; "Sinbad and Friends"; "HBO One Night Stand", 1989; "The Jamie Foxx Show", 1997, 1998; "The Drew Carey Show", 2000; "For Your Love", 2000; Films: Talkin' Dirty After Dark, 1991; Martin, 1992; Living Single, 1993; Panther, 1995; Switchback, 1997; Armageddon, 1998; A Man Is Mostly Water, 1999; Bad Boy, 2002; Poolboy: Drowning Out the Fury, 2011; Writer: "Def Comedy Jam", 2006; "Comedy Central Presents", 2006; Laffapalooza!, 2008.

**CURRY, REV. MICHAEL BRUCE**
Clergy, bishop. **Personal:** Born Mar 13, 1953, Chicago, IL; son of Kenneth S L and Dorothy A Strayhorne; married Sharon Clement; children: Rachel & Elizabeth. **Educ:** Hobart Col, BA, 1975; Yale Univ Divinity Sch, MDiv, 1978; Col Preachers; Princeton Theol Sem; Wake Forest Univ; Ecumenical Inst; St Mary's Sem; Inst Christian Jewish Studies. **Career:** St Stephen's Episcopal Church, deacon-in-charge, 1978-82, rector, 1979-82; Diocese Southern Ohio, racism staff, 1982-87; St Simon Cyrena Church, rector & pastor, 1982-88; Bethany Sch, chaplain, 1983-88; St James Episcopal Church, rector & pastor, 1988-2000; Episcopal Diocese, NC, bishop, 2000-. **Orgs:** NCP; Union Black Episcopalians; Col Preachers Bd. **Honors/Awds:** Hon degree, Sewanne univ; Hon degree, Yale univ; 11th Bishop Episcopal Diocese NC, February 11, 2000. **Special Achievements:** Power in the Word, Sermons that Work II; Servant Woman, Sermons that Work II; First African American elected Episcopal bishop in the South; The First African American bishop to lead a southern diocese of the Episcopal Church; First African-American Episcopal Bishop of North Carolina. **Home Addr:** 2914 W Strathmore Ave, Baltimore, MD 21209, **Home Phone:** (410)358-3540. **Business Addr:** Minister, St James Episcopal Church, 1020 W Lafayette Ave, Baltimore, MD 21217, **Business Phone:** (410)523-4588.

**CURRY, MICHAEL EDWARD**
Basketball executive, basketball player, basketball coach. **Personal:** Born Aug 22, 1968, Anniston, AL; married Katrina; children: Xavier Michael Jr Crysten & Deon. **Educ:** Ga Southern, BA, 1990; Va Commonwealth Univ, MA, 2001. **Career:** Basketball player (retired), basketball coach; Steiner Bayreuth, forward, 1990-91; Continental Basketball Asn, Capital Region, guard, 1992-93; SClear, guard, 1993-94; Philadelphia 76ers, guard & shooting guard, 1993-94; Clear Cantu, Italy, 1994; Valvi Girona, guard, Spain, 1994-95; Continental Basketball Asn, Omaha Racers, guard, 1995-96; Wash Bullets, guard & shooting guard, 1996; Detroit Pistons, guard & shooting guard, 1996-97, 1999-2001, small forward, 2002-03; Milwaukee Bucks, guard & small forward, 1997-99; Toronto Raptors, guard, 2003-04; Ind Pacers, guard & small forward, 2004-05; NBA Develop League, vpres player develop, 2005-06; Nat Basketball Asn, vpres basketballopers, 2006-07; Detroit Pistons, asst coach, vpres, 2007-08, head coach, 2008-09; Philadelphia 76ers, assoc head coach, 2010-13; Fla Atlantic Univ, head coach, 2014-. **Orgs:** pres, BA Players Asn. **Honors/Awds:** Community Asst Award, Nat Basketball Asn, 2003. **Business Addr:** Head Coach, Florida Atlantic University, 777 Glades Rd, Boca Raton, FL 33431, **Business Phone:** (561)297-3000.

### CURRY, REV. DR. MITCHELL L.
Psychotherapist, clergy. **Personal:** Born Feb 5, 1935, Augusta, GA; son of Walter Lee and Ernestine; married Carolyn D; children: Rachel M & Michele L; children: Sonja & Reuben. **Educ:** Morris Brown Col, Atlanta, Ga, BA, 1960; Andover Newton Theol Sch Newton Ctr, MA, MDiv, 1964; Univ Louisville, KY, MSW, 1972; Reed Christ Col Angeles, DHL, 1976; Sch Theol, Claremont, CA, PhD, 1979. **Career:** Miles Memorial CME Church, pastor, 1968-69; Nat Urban League-Western Region, asst reg dir, 1972-75; Lewis Metro Meth Church, LA, minister, 1974-76; Florence Ave Presby Church, LA, minister, 1976-80; La Co Dept Ment Health, psychotherapist, 1976-86; Allen Am Church San Bernardino, pastor, 1985-90; pvt pract psychotherapist, currently; Hollywood Bethany Christian Church, Pac Southwest Region, minister, currently. **Orgs:** Alpha Phi Alpha Fraternity, 1959; consult, Nat Inst Ment Health, 1972-79; Acad Cert Social Workers, NA SW, 1974-; LC SW State Calif, 1975; fel Am Asn Pastoral Counr, 1979-; bd gov, Nat Coun Church, 1980; lic clin social worker, dipl clin social work, DC SW, 1984; Bd Cert dipl. **Honors/Awds:** Scholarship Grant, Am Missionary Asn, 1960-64; Scholarship Grant, Lilly Found, 1961; Scholarship Grant, Nat Inst Ment Health, 1970-72. **Home Addr:** 5177 W 20th St, Los Angeles, CA 90016-1338. **Business Addr:** Minister, Hollywood Bethany Christian Church, 1745 N Gramercy Pl, Los Angeles, CA 90028, **Business Phone:** (323)467-3121.

### CURRY, SADYE BEATRYCE
Educator, physician, association executive. **Personal:** Born Jan 1, 1941, Reidsville, NC; daughter of Charlie Will and Limmmer P. **Educ:** Johnson C Smith Univ, BS, 1963; Howard Univ Col Med, MD, 1967. **Career:** Duke Univ Med Ctr, internship, 1967-68, gastroenterol fel, 1969-72, med instr, 1969-72; VA Hosp, Wash, DC, internal med residency, 1968-69; Howard Univ, asst prof med, 1972-77; Lincoln Hosp, Durham, NC, med consult; Howard Univ Svc, Wash DC Gen Hosp, asst chief med off, 1973-74; Howard Univ Col Med, asst chief med, 1974-78, assoc prof med, 1978-. **Orgs:** chair gastroenterol, Nat Med Asn, 1973-01, co chair, 1994-2009, bd trustee, chair educ affairs comt, currently; AMA; Medico-chirurgical Soc DC; DC Med Soc; Nat Inst Arthritis Metab & Digestive Dis Training Grants Com Gastroenterol & Nutrit, NIH, 1972-73; Am Digestive Dis Soc; Gastrointestinal Drug Adv Comn, FDA, 1975-76; Alpha Kappa Alpha; Beta Kappa Chi; Alpha Kappa Mu; US Friendship Force Ambassador W Berlin, 1980; past pres, Leonidas Berry Soc Digestive Dis; bd trustees, Lake Land Or Property Owners Asn, Ladysmith VA; Am Soc Internal Med; Leonidas Berry Soc Digestive Dis. **Honors/Awds:** Student Council Faculty Award, Howard Univ Col Med, 1975; Kaiser-Permanente Award, Howard Univ Col Med, 1978; Woman of the Year Award, Howard Univ Col Med Stud Am Med Women's Asn, 1990; Kaiser Permanente Faculty Award, Student Council Faculty Award, Howard Univ. **Special Achievements:** First African American woman postgraduate trainee at Duke University Medical Center in 1969; First African American woman to become a gastroenterologist in the United States in 1972; Only African American to train in the gastroenterology fellowship program at Duke University. **Home Addr:** 11016 Balantre Lane, Potomac, MD 20854-1322, **Home Phone:** (301)469-7456. **Business Addr:** Associate Professor, Howard University College of Medicine, 2225 Georgia Ave NW, Washington, DC 20059, **Business Phone:** (202)238-2330.

### CURRY, STEPHEN (WARDELL STEPHEN CURRY, II)
Basketball player. **Personal:** Born Mar 14, 1988, Akron, OH; son of Dell and Sonya; married Ayesha Curry; children: Riley & Ryan Carson. **Educ:** Davidson Col, 2009. **Career:** Basketball player; Davidson College, 2006-09; Golden State Warriors, guard, 2009-; USA Men's Basketball Senior National Team, guard, 2010. **Special Achievements:** NCAA Division I scoring leader, 2009; drafted in with the 7th pick in the first round of 2009 NBA Draft; Taco Bell Skills Challenge at NBA All-Star Game, winner, 2011; set NBA single season record for three-pointers, 2012-13 season; won NBA Championship, 2013-14 season; United Nations Nothing But Nets campaign, supporter; Curry Celebrity Classic Golf Tournament, Charlotte, NC, host; American Century Championship celebrity golf tournament, South Lake Tahoe, NV, player. **Business Addr:** Golden State Warriors, 1101 Broadway, Oakland, CA 94607.

### CURRY, THOMAS LEE, SR.
Executive. **Personal:** Born May 20, 1952, Jackson, NC; son of Edward and Mary; married Linda; children: Tomara, Thomas Jr, Reila & Tailyn. **Educ:** Seton Hall Univ, BS, 1974; Fairleigh Dickinson Univ, MPA, 1986. **Career:** Calvary Baptist Community Ctr Inc, administer, 1975-80, Health Ctr, exec dir, 1980-90, Community Ctr, exec dir, 1990. **Orgs:** Bd dir, Paterson YMCA, vip, 1975-84; pres, Mayor's Coun Youth, 1976-78; Passaic Valley United Way, Allocation Comt, 1984-86; vip, NJ Asn Community Health Ctrs, 1983-90; chair, Paterson Housing Authority, 1990-99. **Home Addr:** 26 Ellison St, Paterson, NJ 07501, **Home Phone:** (973)225-1065.

### CURRY, REV. VICTOR TYRONE
Radio broadcaster, clergy. **Personal:** Born Mar 8, 1960, Carver Ranches, FL; married Cynthia D Baskin; children: Victoria, Veronica & Victory. **Educ:** Fla Bible Col, Hollywood, FL, theol, 1981; Fla Mem Col, Miami, FL, BS, community-clin psychol, 1986; Jacksonville Baptist Theol Sem, MMin, Dmin; St Thomas Christian Col, DDiv. **Career:** Mt Carmel Missionary Baptist Church, Miami, Fla, pastor & adminr, 1984-91; Dade Co Sch Bd, Miami, Fla, classroom teacher, 1987-89; Margolis Broadcasting Co, Miami Beach, Fla, radio announcer, talk show host, 1989; WMBM AM Radio AM, 1990, radio host, currently; St. Ruth Missionary Baptist Church, pastor, 2009. **Orgs:** Pres, Miami Christian Improv Asn, 1986; exec comt mem, Nat Asn Advan Colored People Miami Dade Br, 1988-; Omega Psi Phi Fraternity, Sigma Alpha Chap, Miami, Fla, 1989-; vice moderator, Fla E Coast Missionary Baptist Asn; Progressive Race Inspired & Dedicated to Empower; bd trustee, Fla Memorial Univ; active mem, Alpha Phi Alpha Fraternity Inc. **Honors/Awds:** Numerous honors & awards including Citizen of the Year; Pastor of The Year; Future Leader of America; Humanitarian of The Year; Image Award, Nat Asn Advan Colored People; JM Family African American Achiever Award for Business & Entrepreneurism, 2003; Kools Achievers Award; Black Achievers Award & DDiv, St Thomas Christian Col, 2004; hon Doctorate, DDiv, Saint Thomas Christian College; hon Doctorate, Humane Lett Degree, Fla Memorial Univ; He is honored by Florida State Senate is the remaining of NW 135 Street between NW 7 th and NW 27 th Avenue to Bishop Victor Tyrone Curry Boulevard. **Special Achievements:** Books: The Stewardship Test; The Stewardship Task Workbook; Where Your Treasure Is; It Takes a Fool to Lose Twice; How Can I Trust Them with My Soul. **Home Addr:** 3940 SW 25th St, Hollywood, FL 33023, **Home Phone:** (305)949-7840. **Business Addr:** Senior Pastor, Teacher, New Birth Baptist Church Cathedral of Faith International, 2300 NW 135th St Suite 8207, Miami, FL 33167, **Business Phone:** (305)685-3700.

### CURRY, WARDELL STEPHEN. See CURRY, DELL.

### CURRY, WARDELL STEPHEN, II. See CURRY, STEPHEN.

### CURRY, DR. WILLIAM THOMAS
Physician, surgeon, college teacher. **Personal:** Born Jan 4, 1943, Great Neck, NY; married Katherine E Lum; children: William Jr & Christian. **Educ:** NY Univ, BS, 1964; Howard Univ Col Med, Md, 1968; Am Bd Surg, dipl, 1974. **Career:** George Wash Hosp, surg intern, 1968-69; NY Hosp Cornell Med Ctr, surg resident, 1969-72, chief resident surgeon, 1972-73; Cornell Univ Med Col, asst prof; NY Hosp, attend surgeon, fel surg, 1969-72, instr surg, 1972-76; Cornell Univ Med Col, clin asst prof surg, 1976-, asst attend surgeon. **Orgs:** Fel Am Col Surgeons, 1976; Kappa Alpha Psi Fraternity; Reveille Club NY; bd dir, Music Westchester Symphony Orchestra; Mt Kisco Country Club; chmn, Comt Ins Rev, NY County Med Soc, 1988-; Shinnecock Hills Golf Club. **Honors/Awds:** Teaching Award, Cornell Univ Med College, 2003. **Special Achievements:** Cornell Medical Students, Senior List. **Business Addr:** Surgeon, Clinical Assistant Professor, Cornell University Medical College, Day Hall Lobby, Ithaca, NY 14853, **Business Phone:** (212)628-1681.

### CURTIN, HON. JOHN T.
Judge, naval officer, lawyer. **Personal:** Born Aug 24, 1921, Buffalo, NY; son of John J and Ellen Quigley; married Jane R Good; children: Ann Elizabeth, John James, Patricia Marie, Eileen Jane, Mary Ellen, MarkAndrew & William Joseph. **Educ:** Canisius Col, BS, 1946; Buffalo Univ, LLB, 1949. **Career:** Pvt pract, atty, 1949-61; US Atty's Off, Western Dist NY, US atty, 1961-67; US Dist Ct, Western Dist NY, law clerk, sr dist judge, 1967-, chief judge, 1974-89, sr judge, 1989-. **Orgs:** NY State Bar Asn; Am Bar Asn; Erie Co Bar Asn. **Home Addr:** 774 US Courthouse, 2 Niagara Sq, Buffalo, NY 14202. **Business Addr:** Senior District Judge, United States District Court Western New York, US Courthouse, Buffalo, NY 14202-3405, **Business Phone:** (716)551-4221.

### CURTIS, CHRISTOPHER PAUL
Writer, government official, automotive industry worker. **Personal:** Born May 10, 1953, Flint, MI; son of Herman and Leslie; married Habon Aden; children: Ayaan Leslie & Ebyaan Hothan. **Educ:** Univ Mich, Flint, BS, 1999; Univ Windsor, PhD, 2009. **Career:** Fisher Body Plant, Flint, Mich, assembly line, 1972-85; asst to Senator Don Riegle, Lansing, Mich; Automatic Data Processing, Allen park, Mich; Books: The Watsons Go to Birmingham, 1963; Bud, Not Buddy, 1999; Bucking the Sarge; Mr Chickee's Funny Money, 2007; Elijah of Buxton, 2007; Mr Chickee's Messy Mission, 2008; The Mighty Miss Malone, 2012. **Honors/Awds:** Newberry Medal, Univ Mich; Hopwood prize for rough draft, Publishers Weekly, Best Books, 1995; Best Books, New York Times, 1995; Newbery honor, Am Libr Asn, 1996; Best Books for Young Adults, 1996; Coretta Scott King Text honor, 1996; Newbery Medal, 2000; Coretta Scott King Award for African American Authors, Am Libr Asn, 2000; Scott O'Dell Historical Fiction Award; Anne V Zarrow Award. **Special Achievements:** His second novel, Bud, Not Buddy, is the first book ever to receive both the Newbery Medal and the Coretta Scott King Author Award. **Business Addr:** Author, Delacorte Press, 1540 Broadway, New York, NY 10036-4094, **Business Phone:** (212)354-6500.

### CURTIS, JAMES
Lawyer, television show host. **Personal:** Born Los Angeles, CA; children: 3. **Educ:** Univ Calif, San Diego, BA; Calif Western Sch Law, San Diego, JD; Thurgood Marshall Col, span lit. **Career:** State Senate & Govs Off, Calif, 1980-84; Riverside County, Dist Atty's Off, prosecutor, 1989-99; Justice Project Inc, consult, 1999-2001; King World/CBS, New York, NY, 2000-01; KUCR Radio, host; James Curtis & Assoc law firm, owner, 2005-; TV Show: Court TV, "Closing Arguments", co-anchor, "Curtis Court", host, 2000-01, anchor & commentator, 2001-05; FOX News, "The O'Reilly Factor", commentator; ESPN2, "Cold Pizza", commentator; "Michael Jackson Trial", E Entertainment, host & correspondent, 2005; "Dateline NBC", "ABC's World News Tonight", "CNBC", "Rivera Live", "World News Tonight", "The Early Show", "Dateline", "Weekend Today Show", "The Oreilly Factor", "Hannity & Colmes", "At Large with Geraldo Rivera", "Cold Pizza", "The Big Idea with Donny Deustch", "Hardball with Chris Matthews", "The News with Brian Williams", "Larry King Live", "Nick News Special". **Orgs:** Bd mem, Criminal Law Sect, Calif State Bar Asn; pres, Black Students Union. **Honors/Awds:** Prosecutor of the Year Award & Bull Dog Award, 1997; Beacon Award, 2004; Recognition for Lifetime Commitment to human and civil rights, NAACP, NY. **Business Addr:** Owner, James Curtis & Associates, 7121 Magnolia Ave, Riverside, CA 92504-3805, **Business Phone:** (951)200-4155.

### CURTIS, DR. JAMES L.
Physician. **Personal:** Born Apr 27, 1922, Jeffersonville, GA; son of Will and Frances; married Vivian A Rawls; children: Lawrence & Paul. **Educ:** Albion Col, BA, 1943; Univ Mich, MD, 1946; MI State Med Lic, 2015; Am Bd Psychiat & Neurol, psychiat, cert. **Career:** Westland Med Ctr, intern, 1947, resident, psychiat, 1948; VA Med Ctr, resident, 1949-50; State Univ NY, instr, asst prof, 1954-67; Cornell Univ, Med Col, assoc prof, 1968-81; Columbia Univ, Col Physicians & Surgeons, clin prof psychiat, 1982-2000, emer prof psychiat, 2000; Harlem Hosp Ctr, dir psychiat. **Orgs:** Fel Am Psychiat Asn; Am Orthopsychiatric Asn; NY Acad Med; Am Acad Psychoanalysis; AMA; Nat Med Asn; Am Acad Addiction Psychiatrists; Cert Group Psychotherapists. **Special Achievements:** Published: 'Blacks Medical School & Society', 'Affirmative Action in Medicine' & many other publications. **Home Addr:** 17816 Murdock Ave, Jamaica, NY 11434, **Home Phone:** (718)657-9224. **Business Addr:** Clinical Professor Emeritus, Columbia University, 180 Ft Wash Ave, New York, NY 10032, **Business Phone:** (212)305-6001.

### CURTIS, JEAN TRAWICK
Library administrator. **Personal:** Born Washington, DC; daughter of Ivory Wilson (deceased) and Dannie May; children: Karen Elizabeth & Jeffrey Lynn. **Educ:** Howard Univ, Wash, DC, BA, libr sci, 1958; Univ Md, Col Park, Md, MLS, 1971, Libr Adminrs Develop Prog, 1977. **Career:** Library administrator (retired); DC Pub Libr, Wash, DC, C's librn, 1958-65, reader's advr, 1965-69; Univ Md, Col Park, Md, res asst, 1969-71; Enoch Pratt Free Libr, Baltimore, Md, young adult field worker, 1971-75, regional librn, 1975-78, chief extension div, 1978-85; Detroit Pub Libr, dep dir, 1986-87, dir, 1987. **Orgs:** Am Libr Asn; Mich Libr Asn; dir, Univ Cultural Ctr Asn, 1987-; dir, New Detroit Inc, 1987-; Southeastern Mich League Libvs, 1987-; Libr Mich, Libr Servs & Construction Act Adv Commt, Task Force Libr Interdependency & Funding, 1987-90; bd pres, Detroit Assoc Librs Network, 1988-90; Xonta Int, Detroit Chap, 1988-90; Mayor's Trouble Shooting Task Force, 1985. **Honors/Awds:** Michigan Women's Hall of Fame, Hist Honors Comt; Operated campaign to secure community and political endorsements in favor of increase millage to support schools and libraries; Reorganized Detroit Public Library administration; speaker at several university seminars on library science; consultant to Information Access Company on strategic planning, 1990. **Home Addr:** 555 Brush St, Detroit, MI 48226.

### CURTIS, DR. MARVIN VERNELL
Educator, musician. **Personal:** Born Feb 12, 1951, Chicago, IL; son of John W Jr and Dorothy Marva; married Sharon Curry. **Educ:** N Park Univ, Chicago, BMus, 1972; Presby Sch Christian Educ, Stockton, CA, MA, 1974; Westminister Choir Col, attended 1978; Juilliard Sch Music, attended 1982; Univ Pac, EdD, 1990; Univ Ghana. **Career:** Graham Sch, music teacher, 1975-80; Riverside Church, dir church sch music, 1978-80; Emmanuel Baptist Church, minister music, 1980-84; San Diego State Univ, dir gospel choir, 1984-86; Morse High Sch, chmn music dept, 1985-86; Calif State Univ, Stanislaus, asst prof music educ, 1988-91; Va Union Univ, dir choral activ, 1991-94; Fayetteville State Univ, choral dir & prof, currently; Conductor: Emmanuel Baptist Church Concert, 1983, Va Union Univ Concert Choir, 1992, Alice Tully Hall-Lincoln Ctr; Richmond Sym, guest conductor & musical adv, currently. **Orgs:** Fac sen, Calif State Univ, Stanislaus, 1989-91; pres, San Joaquin Co Arts Coun, 1989-91; grants panel mem, Calif Arts Coun, 1990-; asst treas, Nat Asn Negro Musicians Inc, 1991-; nat chairperson ethnic & minority concerns, Am Choral dir Asn, 1992-94; Cent Va Fac Consortium, 1992-; Music Educrs Nat Conf. **Home Addr:** 1600 Leeland Pl, Richmond, VA 23231, **Home Phone:** (804)226-6188. **Business Addr:** Choral Director, Assistant Dean, Fayetteville State University, 1200 Murchison Rd, Fayetteville, NC 28301, **Business Phone:** (910)672-1111.

### CURTIS, MARY C.
Columnist, editor. **Personal:** Born Jan 1, 1950?, Baltimore, MD; daughter of Thomas E and Evelyn C Thomas; married Martin F Olsen; children: Zane A Olsen. **Educ:** Fordham Univ, NY, BA, communs; Harvard Univ, jour, 2006. **Career:** Assoc Press, NY & Hartford, Conn, ed & writer, freelance newspaper & mag reporter, 1977-81; Travelers Ins Co, mkt servs coord, 1977-81; Ariz Daily Star, Tucson, Ariz, copy ed, 1981-83; Baltimore Sun, Md, travel ed, asst features ed, 1983-85, arts & entertainment ed, 1984-85; New York Times, copy ed, Cult Dept, 1985-94, from dep ed to ed, 1988-91, Living Arts Sec, ed, Home Sec, 1991-93, educ life ed, 1993-94; McClatchy-Tribune News Serv, columnist, 1994-2008; Charlotte Observer, Dance writer/critic, columnist, 1994-2008, exec features ed & columnist, currently; AOLs PoliticsDaily.com, nat corresp, 2009-11; Ariz Daily Star; Harvard Univ, Nieman fel, 2005-06; Columns: "The lots may be bare, but I'll be tree-shopping today", 2006, "Merry Christmas, baby--now, go fix your face", 2006; "Christmas past: Shorter lists & wondrous gifts", 2006; Fox Tv, weekly commentator; Creative Loafing, contribr, 2008-; Root.com, contribr, 2008-; WCCB Charlotte, commentator, 2009-; Wash Post, contribr, 2011-; TheGrio.com, contribr, 2012-; OpEd Proj, facilitator, 2013-. **Orgs:** Soc Prof Journalists, 1972-; Nat Asn Black Journalists, 1984-; Am Asn Sunday & Feature Eds, 1994-; Nat Socs Newspaper Columnists; Trotter Grp African Am columnists; Am Asn Sunday & Feature Ed; exec bd mem, Soc Prof Journalists, 1972-; Maynard Inst, 1981-10; Nat Asn Black Journalists, 1984-; Am Asn Sunday & Feature Eds, 1994-; Nat Socs Newspaper Columnists; Trotter Grp African Am columnists; exec bd mem, Charlotte-Mecklenburg Schs; Fel Harvard Univ, 2006; commentator, Nat Pub Radio, 2007-; columist, Women's Inter-cult Exchange 2008-2009, St Gabriel Cath Church, 2008-; bd, Actors Theatre Charlotte. **Home Addr:** 2835 Colony Rd, Charlotte, NC 28211. **Business Addr:** Executive Features Editor, Columnist, Charlotte Observer, 600 S Tryon St, Charlotte, NC 28202, **Business Phone:** (704)358-5000.

### CURTIS, REV. DR. WILLIAM H.
Clergy. **Personal:** Born Baltimore, MD; married Christine Y Richardson; children: Houston. **Educ:** Morgan State Univ, BA, relig studies & philos; Howard Univ Sch Divinity, Mdiv; United Theol Sem, Dayton, OH, DMdiv. **Career:** Mt Ararat Baptist Church, Pittsburgh, Pa, sr pastor, currently. **Orgs:** Bd mem, Urban League Pittsburgh; African Am Leadership Comt; pres, Hampton Univs Ministers Conf; founder, William H Curtis Ministries, 2001. **Special Achievements:** Participation in a nation "think-tank" with former President Clinton, inclusion in a book title "Outstanding Black Sermons, Volume Four"; Featured on WAMO 860 AM. **Business Addr:** Senior Pastor, Mount Ararat Baptist Church, 271 Paulson Ave, Pittsburgh, PA 15206, **Business Phone:** (412)441-1800.

### CURTIS-BAUER, M. BENAY (BENAY CURTIS)
Stockbroker. **Personal:** Born Aug 12, 1948, Berkeley, CA; daughter of Emory C and Dorothy A Curtis; married Jon K Bauer. **Educ:** Univ

Calif, Berkeley, BA. **Career:** Morgan Stanley, regist rep, 1991; Alamo Capital, vpres, investment counsr, currently. **Orgs:** St Dominic's Church, Finance Coun. **Home Addr:** 1723 Blake St, Berkeley, CA 94703. **Business Addr:** Vice President, Alamo Capital, 201 N Civic Dr Suite 360, Walnut Creek, CA 94596, **Business Phone:** (800)645-5560.

### CURTIS-HALL, VONDIE
Actor. **Personal:** Born Sep 30, 1956, Detroit, MI; son of Curtis and Angeline; married Kasi Lemmons; children: Henry & Zora. **Educ:** Richmond Col, London. **Career:** Films: Shakedown, 1988; Coming to Am, 1988; Mystery Train, 1989; Black Rain, 1989; Die Hard 2, 1990; One Good Cop, 1991; The Mambo Kings, 1992; Passion Fish, 1992; Falling Down, 1993; Sugar Hill, 1994; Crook lyn, 1994; Clear & Present Danger, 1994; Drop Squad, 1994; Tuesday Morning Ride, 1995; Broken Arrow, 1996; Heaven's Prisoners, 1996; Romeo & Juliet, 1996; Gridlock'd, 1997; Eve's Bayou, 1997; Dr. Hugo, 1998; Turn It Up, 2000; Glitter, dir, 2001; Waist Deep, dir & writer, 2006; Talk to Me, 2007; Honeydripper, 2007; Life Is Hot in Cracktown, 2009; Port of Call New Orleans, 2009; Cymbeline, 2014; TV series: "CopRock", 1990; "Heat Wave", 1990; "And Then She Was Gone", 1991; "What She Doesn't Know", 1992; "Murder Without Motive: The Edmund Perry Story", 1992; "There Wasa Little Boy", 1993; "Dead Man's Revenge", 1994; "Chicago Hope", 1994; "Keys", 1994; "Zooman", 1995; "Don King: Only in America", 1997; "Sirens", 1999; "Ali: An Am Hero", 2000; "Freedom Song", 2000; "ER", 2001; "Fastlane", 2001; "The Sopranos", 2002; "1-800-Missing", 2003; "Soul Food", 2004; "Deceit", 2004; "Dense", 2004; "LAX", 2005; "Insurgents", 2005; "Law & Order", 2006; "Sleeper Cell", dir, 2006; "Second Opinion", 2007; "Boston Legal", dir, 2008; "The Starter Wife", dir, 2008; "Gossip Girl", dir, 2008; "Fear Itself", 2009; "Criminal Minds", 2009; "Chance", 2009; "Life Is Hot in Cracktown", 2010; "Taking on Different Hats", 2010; "A Gifted Man", 2011' "NYC 22", 2012; "Reparations", 2011; "Abducted: The Carlina White Story", dir, 2012; "Tin Man", 2014; "Chasing Life", 2014. **Orgs:** Black Filmmaker Found. **Honors/Awds:** Audelco Award, 1987; Golden Satellite Award, 1998; Black Reel Award, 2005, 2013; Gotham Award, 2007. **Special Achievements:** Nominated for Emmy Award in 1995. **Business Addr:** Actor, Director, The Gersh Agency, 232 N Canon Dr, Beverly Hills, CA 90210, **Business Phone:** (310)274-6611.

### CURTIS-RIVERS, SUSAN YVONNE (SUSAN MANGO CURTIS)
Journalist. **Personal:** Born Jun 27, 1958, Savannah, GA; daughter of William and Lillain; married James Socrates; children: Jasmine DuBignon. **Educ:** Va Commonwealth Univ, BFA design, 1981. **Career:** Nat Rifle Assn, art dir, 1981-84; NUS Corp, graphic supvr, 1984-86; Phillips Publ Inc, art dir, 1986-87; Wash Post Mag, asst art dir, 1987-88; Theimes J Newspaper, Springfield, designer, 1988-90; Akron Beacon J, asst managing ed, 1990; Northwestern Univ, Medill Sch Jour, asst prof, currently. **Orgs:** Nat Asn Black Journalists; comt co-chair, Visual Task Force, 1993, co-chmn Visual Task Force, 1995; bd dirs representing Region 4, 1999, pres, treas, secy, 2001, vpres, 2002-04, Soc Newspaper Design, 1990-95; Nat Asn Minority Media, 1991-94; comt co-chair, Visual Task Force, 1993; chair, Visual Task Force, 1994, co-chair, 1995; Nat Asn Hisp Journalist; Fla A&M Univ Sch Journalism & Graphic Arts, bd visitors, 1996; Assoc Press Soc; Unity Visual Task Force, 2004. **Honors/Awds:** Knight-Ridder Entrepreneurial Excellence Award, 1990; The Asniated Press soc of Ohio Award, 1991; Soc Newspaper Design: The Beacon Journal Art Dept Staff won 2 Silver Awards, 1 Bronze Award, & 4 Awards of Excellence, 1992; The Cleveland Press Club Excellence in Journalism, 1993; The Pulitzer Prize Gold Medal for Public Service, 1994; Nat Headliner Award, 1995; Soc Newspaper Design, Staff won 2 Awards of Excellence, 1996; Garth C Reeves Sr Chair, Fla A&M Univ, Sch Journalism & Graphic Arts, 1996; Award of Excellence in Photojournalism, Nat Asn Black Journalists Visual Task Force, 2000; Leadership Team, Nat Asn Black Journalists Visual Task Force, 2003. **Home Addr:** 16 Harbour View Dr, Akron, OH 44319, **Home Phone:** (330)645-1408. **Business Addr:** Assistant Professor, Northwestern University, MTC 2-113, Evanston, IL 60208-2101, **Business Phone:** (847)467-2999.

### CURWOOD, STEPHEN THOMAS
Writer, television producer, journalist. **Personal:** Born Dec 11, 1947, Roxbury, MA; son of James L and Sarah Ethel Thomas; children: Anastasia & James. **Educ:** Westtown Sch, Westtownn Pa, 1965; AB Harvard Col, Cambridge, Hons concentration probs develop soc, 1969. **Career:** Bay State Banner, managing ed, 1971-72; Boston Globe, writer & investigative reporter, 1972-76, writer/columnist, 1982-89; WGBH TV, producer/reporter, 1976-79; National Pub Radio, reporter & host, 1979-, sr host, "World of Opera, " 1990-, exec producer & host, "Living on Earth, " currently. **Orgs:** PRS, World Media Foundation; Harvard Univ, lectr; Socs of Environ Journalists; Westtown Sch; Haverford Col, trustee. **Honors/Awds:** Pulitzer Prize for public service, part of Boston Globe team, 1975; Edward R Murrow Award for radio documentary, 1995; New England Environmental Leadership Award, for work on promoting environmental awareness, 1992; New England Environmental Leadership Award, Tufts University, 1992; David A Brower Award, excellence in environmental reporting, Sierra Club, 1993; Global Green Award, Media Design, 2003. **Business Addr:** Executive Producer, Host, Nat Public Radio, 8 Story St, Cambridge, MA 02138-0639, **Business Phone:** (617)520-6851.

### CUSHINGBERRY, GEORGE, JR.
Government official, clergy, lawyer. **Personal:** Born Jan 6, 1953, Detroit, MI; son of George Sr and Edna Louise; married Maria Hazel Drew; children: George III & Brandon Drew. **Educ:** Wayne State Univ, BA, 1983, MA, polit sci, urban polit, policy & admin, 1988, PhD, 2006-; Univ Detroit, JD, 1991. **Career:** Mich House, Lansing Off, 4th House Dist, adminr, 1974-82, 8th Dist, rep, 2004-10; Am Pub Affairs Consult/Capitol House, lobbyist, 1983-95; Wayne Co Bd Comnrs, 1986-2002; Pro-Tempore City Coun, pres, 2014, Budget, Finance & Audit Comt, chmn; Wayne State Univ, Southend News, ed; Asn Black Students, vice-chmn; New Starlight Baptist Church, asst pastor; Prospector Reveals TV Show, host; State Mich, state rep; WDRJ 1440 AM, host; ordained minister, currently. **Orgs:** Life mem, Nat Asn Advan Colored People; Founders Soc, Detroit Inst Arts; Mich Ethnic Heritage Ctr; bd trustee, Mus African Am Hist; Mich Humanities Coun; coun mem, Detroit City Coun; Wayne County Bd Commissioners. **Honors/Awds:** Superior Cadet Award, Cass Tech High, 1971; Young Man of The Year, Jaycees, 1975; Community Service Award, EBONI Women, 1975; Young Democratic Award, First Cong Dist, 1975; Community Service Award, Together Bros & Sisters, 1975; Man of The Year, Mich Chronicle Newspaper, 1977. **Special Achievements:** Youngest person ever elected to the Michigan House of Representatives (age 21), 1975-82. **Home Addr:** 8625 Marygrove, Detroit, MI 48221. **Business Addr:** Council Member, Detroit City Council, 2 Woodward Ave Suite 1340, Detroit, MI 48226, **Business Phone:** (313)224-4535.

### CUSTIS, ACE (ADRIAN CUSTIS)
Basketball player, basketball coach. **Personal:** Born May 24, 1974, Nassawadox, VA; married Denedra; children: Charles Mapp, Adrian Custis II & Evan. **Educ:** Va Tech, attended 1997. **Career:** Dallas Mavericks, forward, 1993-97; Va Tech, NCAA, 1993-97; Portsmouth Invitational Tournament, 1997; Nike Desert Classic, 1997; Dallas Mavericks, 1997-98; Pa Valley Dawgs, 1999 & 2000; Dallas Mavericks, 1999; Grand Rapids Hoops, 1999-2000; Dallas Mavericks, Nat Basketball Asn, 2000-01; ASPAC Texmaco Jakarta, 2001; Blu Summer League, Treviso, 2001; Rocky Mountain Summer League, 2001; Sporting Al Ryadi, 2001-03; Sporting Al Ryadi Beirut, 2003-04; OSG Phoenix, 2004-05; San Miguel Beer, 2005-06; Matsushita Elec Panasonic Kangaroos, Japan, 2006-07; Panasonic Trians, Japan, 2007-11; Univ Md Eastern Shore; asst coach; 2014-. **Home Addr:** , Fruitland, MD. **Business Addr:** Assistant Coach, University of Maryland Eastern Shore, 30665 Stud Serv Ctr, Princess Anne, MD 21853, **Business Phone:** (410)651-7747.

### CUSTIS, ANDREA L.
Administrator, vice president (organization), president (organization). **Educ:** Morgan State Univ, BS, psychol; Univ Pa, MS, coun psychol. **Career:** Verizon, vpres, 1977-2011; Verizon Enterprise Solutions, vpres, 2001-03, Verizon Ave, pres & chief operating officer, 2003-; Verizon Commun Nj region, vpres, currently. **Orgs:** Bd dir, Better Bus Bur NY; bd gov, Acad Appl Elec Sci; Verizon's Consortium Info & Telecommunication Exec; Hisp Support Orgn employee groups; Nat Asn Advan Colored Peoplel; Del Valley Childcare Coun; bd advisors, Express Fed Incs; bd dir, League Philadelphia, Del Valley Child Care Coun, Inroads, Philadelphia Chamber Com & New York Chamber Com; chmn bd, Capitol VOIP Solutions, 2013-; bd dir, Redda Group, 2013-; bd trustee, Lincoln Univ. **Business Addr:** President, Chief Operating Officer, Verizon Avenue, 1880 Campus Commons Dr 2nd Fl, Reston, VA 20191, **Business Phone:** (703)295-4830.

### CUTLER, DONALD
Educator. **Personal:** Born Oct 20, 1943, Tampa, FL; married Rosemary N. **Educ:** Albany State Col, Albany, GA, BS, 1971; Ga State Univ. **Career:** WAYX Radio, Waycross, GA, radio announcer, 1965-66; Waycross Jour Herald, Waycross, GA, news corresp, 1965-66; WJIZ Radio, Albany, GA, disc jockey, 1969-70; Goodwill Ind, Albany, GA, dir work adj training, 1971-72; Dougherty Co Pub Sch, educr, 1972; WALB-TV, Albany, GA, sports announcer, weekend anchor, 1973-77; Dougherty Co Albany, co comn bd commrs, 1978-. **Orgs:** Vpres Cong Black Orgn Albany, 1977-; spokesman, Albany Black Caucas, 1979-; NEA/GAE/DCAE/ Nat Asn Advan Colored People; Ga Easter Seal Soc, 1976; exec comt, SW Ga APDC. **Home Addr:** 709 Don Cutler Sr Dr, Albany, GA 31705, **Home Phone:** (229)903-9197. **Business Addr:** Pine Ave, Albany, GA 31701.

### CUYJET, DR. ALOYSIUS BAXTER
Educator, administrator. **Personal:** Born May 20, 1947, Jersey City, NJ; son of Aloysius and Barbara Baxter; married Beverly M Granger. **Educ:** Brandeis Univ, BA, biol, 1968; NY Univ Sch Med, MD, 1972; Columbia Univ, Mailman Sch Pub Health, MPH, 1998. **Career:** Harlem Hosp Ctr, intern & resident, 1972-75, cardiol fel, 1975-77; Columbia Univ Col Physicians & Surgeons, asst instr, 1975-77; United Hosps Med Ctr, dir, 1980-97, adult critical care med, assoc chief med, sect chief, 1997-2005; Nassau Univ Med Ctr, chair dept med & vpres clin effectiveness & minority health initiatives, sr vpres, chief health equity officer, 2005-11, chmn & prog dir, 2006, Inst Healthcare Disparities, founder, currently; Stony Brook Sch Med, clin prof; Univ Med & Dent, NJ, Dept Med, asst prof med, assoc prof; HealthCare Partners, regional med dir, 2012-. **Orgs:** Bd mem, Asn Black Cardiologists; bd dir, Am Heart Asn, bd mem; Soc Critical Care Med; Am Col Cardiol, 1988; bd mem, United Health Care Syst; bd mem, NJ Blood Ctr; 100 Black Men Am; bd mem, Nat Boxing Safety Ctr; co-chiar, Nassau County Minority Health Task Force. **Home Addr:** 90 Walnut Rd, Glen Cove, NY 11542, **Home Phone:** (516)676-7153. **Business Addr:** Senior Vice President, Chairman, Nassau University Medical Center, 2201 Hempstead Turnpike, East Meadow, NY 11554, **Business Phone:** (516)572-0123.

### CUYJET, CYNTHIA K.
Executive, consultant, educator. **Personal:** Born May 16, 1948, Philadelphia, PA; daughter of Esther King and C Jerome. **Educ:** Marymount Col, BA, 1970; Marymount Col, Fordham Univ, BA; Jersey City St Col, MA, 1974. **Career:** Marymount Col, Tarrytown, New York, admis counr, 1970-71; Prudential Ins Co, adult educ instr, 1971-72; Jersey City State Col, asst admis dir, 1972-76; Supermarkets Gen Corp, Selection & Placement mgr, 1976-77; Avon Prod Inc, supvr mgt develop, 1977-84, mgr, job opportunity, corp mgr mgt develop & training, 1978-80, div sales mgr, 1980-84; Coca-Cola USA, sr proj mgr, mgr mgt training, 1984-87; Cuyjet Mgt Consults Inc, managing dir, 1987-99, 2010-; Heller Int, asst vpres employee develop & training, 1993-96; ABN AMRO / LaSalle Bank Corp, vice pres leadership & prof develop, 1999-2002; Univ Chicago, Grad Sch Bus, sr assoc dir; LaSalle Bank Corp, vpres, 2003-2005; Health Care Serv Corp, orgn effectiveness lead, 2006-10. **Orgs:** Co-chairperson, Women Bus Comt, Atlanta Bus League; Atlanta Womens Network; Am Soc Training/Develop; chair, employ comt, Coalition 100 Black Women; exec bd mem, Coun Concerned Black Execs, 1976-80; exec bd mem, Nj Asn Sickle Cell Anemia; Black Merit Acad, E St Louis, Ill; Black Exec Exchange Prog, Nat Urban League; Am Soc Training & Develop; YWCA Metrop Chicago, vpres & exec bd. **Business Addr:** President, Consultant, Cuyjet Management Consultants Inc, 980 N Mich Ave Suite 1400, Chicago, IL 60611-7500, **Business Phone:** (312)266-3388.

### CWIKLINSKI, CHERYL A.
Executive. **Educ:** Roosevelt Univ; DePaul Univ. **Career:** Technomic Res Assoc, mgr; Telemedia Inc; Blue Cross & Blue Shield; Nat Controls Corp; Xerox Corp; Comprehensive Computerized Bus Serv Inc, Staffing & Training Specialist, chief exec officer & founder, 1982-; Cwik's Different by Design, prin, chief exec officer, 1982-, pres, assoc, 1990-; CwikGallo & Assocs, chief exec officer, pres, 1998-2004; Staffing Partners Int, prin, currently. **Orgs:** Adv bd, Col Com, DePaul Univ; adv bd, Heartland Alliance; Asn Info Syst Professionals; Chicago Asn Com & Indust; Chicago Bus Educ Asn; Hoffman Estates Chamber Com; Mayor's Off Employ & Training; Nat Asn Female Execs Inc; Nat Asn Temp Serv; Nat Asn Women Bus Owners; Women's Coun REALTORS; Accredited Staging Professionals; Int Asn Home Staging Professionals; Lifetime mem, Inst Am Entrepreneurs, 1991; vol info serv area, St. Alexius Med Ctr, 2009-. **Business Addr:** Principal, Chief Executive Officer, Cwik's Different by Design, 1633 Pebble Beach Dr, Hoffman Estates, IL 60169, **Business Phone:** (847)464-1099.

### CYRUS-ALBRITTON, SYLVIA
Executive director, association executive. **Educ:** Hampton Univ, BS, human ecol, retail mkt, 1977. **Career:** JC Penney, asst buyer, 1977-88; Comprehensive Supplies, gen mgr, 1989-2000; NJ Pub Schs, off mgr-bus off, 2000-02, asst bus adminr, 2002-03; Asn Study African Am Life & Hist, exec dir, 2003-; Hist Inc, exec dir. **Orgs:** Bd mem, Asn Study African Am Life & Hist; Beta Alpha Omega Chap; Silver Star & Life Mem; Alpha Kappa Alpha. **Business Addr:** Executive Director, Association for the Study of African American Life & History, CB Powell Bldg, Washington, DC 20059, **Business Phone:** (202)865-0053.

# D

### DABBS, HENRY ERVEN
Executive, arts administrator. **Personal:** Born Oct 15, 1932, Clover, VA; son of Charles and Gertrude; married Loretta D Young; children: Lisa DeLane. **Educ:** Pratt Inst, BFA, 1955. **Career:** Berton Wink Inc, bk designer, 1958-62; Afro-Amer Hist Highlights, auth, 1968; Eng town, publ, 1968. Fitzgerald Sample NYC, art dir, producer, dancer; USN John F Small Adv Agency, creative dir minority adv, 1975-78; Henry Dabbs Prod Eng town NJ, pres, 1977; Cinema & Graphic Design Jersey City St Col, instr, 1977; Films: Joshua, producer, dir, 1979. **Orgs:** Nat Asn Advan Colored People; First MultiMedia, audio visual prog Black Am. **Home Addr:** 2706 Carrickton Cir, Orlando, FL 32824-4230, **Home Phone:** (407)850-0767.

**DADDY, BIG. See BOWE, RIDDICK LAMONT.**

### DAGGS, LEON, JR.
Automotive executive, manager, president (organization). **Personal:** Born Feb 12, 1941, St. Louis, MO; son of Leon and Dorothy Echols; married Saundra Stills; children: Christopher. **Educ:** Pensacolas Naval Air Sta; Harris Teachers Col, St Louis, MO, BA, 1964; St Louis Univ, St Louis, MO, MBA, 1971. **Career:** St Louis Bd Educ, St Louis, Mo, teacher, 1963-64; Procter-Gamble, St Louis, Mo, sales, 1968-70; McDonnel Aircraft, St Louis, Mo, mgr, 1970-71; Ford Motor Co, Dearborn, Mich, parts & serv mgr & supvr, 1971-85; Hub City Ford-Mercury, Crestview, pres, 1986; Walton Co Ford-Mercury, Defuniak Springs, pres, 1996; Panhandle Automotive Inc, pres, 2002. **Orgs:** Kappa Alpha Psi Fraternity, 1961-; bd mem, bd dir, Nat Asn Advan Colored People, 1973-77; dir, Chamber Com, Crestview, 1986-; bd mem, Pvt Indust Coun, 1986-; charter mem, Crestview Rotary Club, 1988-; spec dep, Okaloosa City Sheriff Dept, 1988-; bd dir, Ford Lincoln-Mercury Minority Dealers Asn, 1994-. **Home Addr:** 326 Timberline Dr, Crestview, FL 32539-8330, **Home Phone:** (850)682-4747. **Business Addr:** President, Panhandle Auto Inc, 4404 Blountstown Hwy, Tallahassee, FL 32304, **Business Phone:** (850)576-8298.

### DAILEY, LENORA SHELL
Basketball coach. **Personal:** Born Aug 24, 1963, Fayetteville, NC; daughter of Walter and Faye Bollin; married Eric; children: Eric L Jr. **Educ:** Univ Tex, BS, advert & mkt, 1986. **Career:** Univ Tex, Womens Basketball Team, capt; Tex Christian Univ, asst coach, 1992, head coach, 1993-96; Tex A&M, asst coach, 1997-98, Recruiting Coordr; Am Basketball League, Nashville Noise, asst coach, 1998; Univ Sc Gamecocks, asst coach, 1999-2003, Recruiting Coordr; WNBA, San Antonio Silver Stars, asst coach, interim head coach, 2003-04; Univ Fla womens basketball, asst coach, 2007, IMG Acad, dir womens basketball, head coach, 2012-. **Orgs:** Delta Sigma Theta; Women Basketball Coaches Asn. **Special Achievements:** First African American coach in the History of School, TX. **Home Addr:** 1 Lake Mist Ct, Columbia, SC 29229, **Home Phone:** (803)419-2378. **Business Addr:** Director of Women's Basketball, Head Coach, IMG Academy, 5500 34th St W, Bradenton, FL 34210, **Business Phone:** (941)755-1000.

### DAILEY, THELMA
Association executive, publisher. **Personal:** Born Baltimore, MD; married Guilbert. **Educ:** Bowie State Univ Md, BS; NY Univ, MA, coun & personnel admin; George Washington Univ, EdD, coun. **Career:** Ethnic Woman Int, publ, 1969-; Trade Union Women African Heritage Inc, pres, founder; N Cent Western Md Col, vis prof; Univ Wis, vis prof; Harvard Univ, vis prof; Baltimore County Bd Educ, coordr guid. **Orgs:** Nat treas, 1963-67, nat vpres, 1971-75, nat pres, Delta Sigma Theta Sorority Inc; nat pres, Am Sch Coun Asn, 1971-72; pres, Am Personnel & Guid Asn, 1975-78; Veteran feminists Am, 1992-; bd mem, vice chmn, Nat Coun Negro Women; Women's Forum Inc; coordr, Bronx Chap Un Asn; Multi-Ethnic Woman Workshop, Fashion

Inst Tech; coordr, Inst Polit Educ Black Women; IWY Tribune; assoc, Women's Inst Freedom Press; nat dir Women, NAACP; bd dir, Nat Testing Serv. **Special Achievements:** The First woman to chair the National Advisory Council on Career Education; Who's Who Among Black Americans. **Home Addr:** 3730 Laconia Ave, Bronx, NY 10469. **Business Addr:** Publisher, The Ethnic Woman International, PO Box 1033, New York, NY 10003, **Business Phone:** (718)655-1657.

## DAILY, BYRON
Executive. **Career:** Three BM! Internet Syst LLC, Lithonia, Ga, prin, currently. **Business Addr:** Principal, 3BM Internet Systems, 6246 Phillips Lake Way, Lithonia, GA 30058, **Business Phone:** (770)484-9141.

## DAILY, LORI BEARD
Sales manager, advertising executive, public relations executive. **Educ:** Spelman Col, BA, Eng, 1984. **Career:** Delta Air Lines, facilitator & trainer, 1990-93, mkt mgr, 1995-96, advert mgr, 1996-98, advert dir, 1998-2008; LBD Advert Assoc Inc, chief exec officer, 1998-; BeardDaily Inc, mkt commun consult, 2002-12; Cox Media Group, digital mkt, 2012-13; EY, commun consult, 2014; Cancer Treat Centers Am, commun consult, 2015; Arbys & Hilton Airport, acct team. **Orgs:** Governance Coun, Chamblee CHarter High Sch; bd mem, Jack & Jill Am Inc; Community Advisor, Jr League Dekalb Co. **Honors/Awds:** Women of Wonder Award, 2015; Pulitzer Prize. **Business Addr:** Digital Marketing, Cox Media Group, 6205 Peachtree Dunwoody Rd, Atlanta, GA 30328, **Business Phone:** (678)645-0000.

## DAIS, LARRY
Administrator, association executive. **Personal:** Born Nov 3, 1945, Columbia, SC; son of Wade and Mamie Jeffcoat; married Olga Carter; children: Landon & Larik. **Educ:** Baruch Col, BS, 1974; Columbia Univ Grad Sch Bus, MS, 1976; Cornell NYSSILR & Hofstra Univ Sch Law, cert, 1986. **Career:** Educator (retired), consultant; Grumman Engineering, admin, 1964-68; State Univ Farmingdale, admin, 1968; Leadership Inst Hofstra Univ, asst dir, 1968-69; Columbia Univ, Columbia Col, Double Discovery Ctr, dir, 1969-81, asst vpres govt rels & dir govt & community affairs, 1981-2007, Athletics Dept, Community Outreach Prog, consult, currently; Abyssinian Develop Corp, past-chair; Columbia Univ, labor arbitrator, vpres, currently. **Orgs:** Nat Urban Leagues Comn Stand & Attributes Urban Affil; bd dir, NY Urban League; chmn, Whitney M Young Football Classic; bd dir, Harlem USA, LDC, Harlem Commonwealth Coun; bd dir, Harlem Congregations Community Improvements, New York, NY; bd dir, Greater Harlem Chamber Comm, New York, NY; vpres, 100 Black Men Inc, New York, NY Am Arbit Asn; chmn & bd mgr, Harlem YMCA; chmn, St Marys Rehab Ctr C, Ossining, NY; pres & founder, Nat Coun Educ Opportunity Asn, Wash, DC; chmn, TRIO Adv Bd NJ; pres, chmn & bd dir, Asn Equality & Excellence Educ; pres, Coun Bd; chairpersons, Nat Urban League Affil; vice chmn, Harlem Community Develop Corp, New York, NY. **Honors/Awds:** Samuel D Proctor Phoenix Award, Columbia Univ, 1997; Distinguished Trustee Award, United Hosp Fund NY, 1998; Arthuro A Schomburg Distinguished Service Award; CBS Martin Luther King Living The Dream Award; Presidential Service Award, Coun Bd Chair, Nat Urban League Affiliates; Community Service Award, Harlem Athletic Asn; Vision Award, Harlem Congregations Community Improvement; Appreciation Award, Harlem Inst Fashion; Leo B Marsh Leadership Award, Harlem YMCA; Appreciation Award, Greater Harlem Chamber Comm; Educational Award, Greater Harlem Chamber Comm; Founders Award, Nat Coun Educ Opportunity Asn; Presidents Award, Nat Coun Educ Opportunity Asn; Black Accountants Community Service Award, NY Chapter; Distinguished Service Award, NY Urban League; Martin Luther King Humanitarian Award, NY State; Samuel E Proctor Phoenix Award, Abyssinian Develop Corp; Man of the Year Award, YMCA, Greater NY; Educational Service Award, Marquette Univ; President's Award, Nat Coun Educ Asn; Award of Excellence, Asn Equality & Excellence Educ; Outstanding Leadership Award, Leadership Inst, Hofstra Univ. **Home Addr:** 268 W 117th St, New York City, NY 10026, **Home Phone:** (917)991-5696. **Business Addr:** Arbitrator, Dais Associates, 268 W 117th St, New York City, NY 10026.

## DALE, BRYANT
Founder (originator). **Educ:** Univ Bridgeport, BS, acct, 1988; Pace Univ, Lubin Grad Sch Bus, MBA, investment mgt, 1996. **Career:** Reich & Teng LP, staff, 1989; Dean Witter Morgan Stanley, Mutual Fund Div, 1989-93; Lehman Bros, Pvt Client Serv, investment assoc, 1993-96; Bryant Group Inc, portfolio mgr, founder, pres, 1996-. **Orgs:** Contribr, Black Enterprise; contribr, KIP Bus Report. **Honors/Awds:** The 40 Under 40 Award, Network J; Caribbean Am Chamber of Com & Indust Visionary Award. **Special Achievements:** Has been interviewed on CNNfn, BET.com. **Business Addr:** Founder, President, The Bryant Group Inc, 305 Broadway 9th Fl, New York, NY 10007-1158, **Business Phone:** (212)822-1468.

## DALE, CLAMMA CHURITA
Opera singer. **Personal:** Born Jul 4, 1953, Chester, PA; daughter of Granvaul and Clara Robinson; married Terry C Shirk. **Educ:** Settlement Mus Sch Philadelphia; Juilliard Sch, New York, BA, voice studies, 1970, MS, 1975. **Career:** New York Opera Co, 1975; Houston Opera Co, singer, 1976; Bronx Opera Co, performer; Brooklyn Opera Theatre, performer; Metrop Opera's Mini-Met; Houston Grand Opera Co, 1976-77; Manhattan Theatre Club, 1977; Paris Opera, performer; Berlin Opera, performer; New York Opera, performer; Opera Co Philadelphia, performer; DAL Prod Ltd, pres, 1989-. TV appearances: Liberty Weekend, 1986; "Great Performances", 1987. **Honors/Awds:** Cue Golden Apple, 1976; Tony Award, leading actress-musical, 1977; 2Naumburg Awards. **Special Achievements:** Recitals at Avery Fischer Hall & Lincoln Center. **Business Addr:** President, DAL Productions Ltd, PO Box 898 Ansonia Sta, New York, NY 10023, **Business Phone:** (212)496-7677.

## DALE, DR. LOUIS, SR.
Dean (education). **Personal:** Born Nov 24, 1935, Birmingham, AL; son of Anne Mae Boykins and Finley; married Gladiola Watts; children: Louis Jr, Valerie Louise, Annice Jeanette & Jonathan David. **Educ:** Miles Col, Birmingham, AL, BS, math, 1960; Atlanta Univ, Atlanta, GA, MS, math, 1964; Univ Ala, Tuscaloosa, AL, PhD, math, 1973. **Career:** Wayne State Univ, grad asst, 1960-68; Atlanta Univ, Atlanta, Ga, instr, asst prof mathematics, 1964-66; Miles Col, Birmingham, Ala, chmn, Div Natural Sci, 1968-70; Sch Natural Sci & Math, acting dean, 1970-71; Interim Dean, 1970-71; Univ Ala, Birmingham, Ala, asst prof mathematics, 1973-77, affirmative action officer, Sch Natural Sci & Mathematics, 1975-81, asst prof mathematics, 1977-80, prof mathematics, 1980-, interim chair, Dept Math, 1982-84, assoc dean, Sch Natural Sci & Mathematics, 1987-91, dir, Alliance for Minority Participation Proj, 1991-, Minority & Spec Prog, assoc vpres, Acad Affairs, 1991-95, assoc vpres, Minority & Spec Progs, 1995-97, assoc provost, Minority & Spec Progs, 1997-, vpres, Equity & Diversity, 2003-; Review Panelist for National Science Foundation Proposals, 1988-. **Orgs:** Chmn, Comt Recruitment & Retention, 1983-; Am Math Soc, 1975-; bd dir, Nat Asn Mamaticians, 1977-79; bd dir, Am Math Soc, 1977-79; bd dir, Nat Asn Mamaticians, 1977-79; Search Comt vpres Univ Col, 1978; chmn, Pres's Adv Comt Minority Grad Studies, 1978-80; Univ Ala at Birmingham Athletics Comt, 1978-; Search Comt Chmn Dept Mamatics, 1978; Fac Senate, 1980-85; Adv Comt Chancellor Search Univ Ala Syst, 1981; Search Comt Dean Sch Natural Sci & Mamatics, 1981; Search Comt Sr vpres Univ Col, 1983; pres, 1984-88, mem, 1978-88, Birmingham Bd Educ; chmn, Sch Natural Sci & MathFac Affairs Comt, 1984-88 & 1985-86; Fac Grievance Comt, 1986; Search Comt, 1987; rev panelist, Nat Sci Found Proposals, 1988-; Comprehensive Minority Fac Develop Prog Comt, 1988-96; Univ Col Stud Retention Comt, 1988-89; dir, Ala Alliance Minority Participation Proj, 1991-; bd dir, Ala Asn Sch Bd; Nat Asn Math; Minority Stud & Fac Affairs Comt, 1996-. **Home Addr:** 663 Dublin Ave, Birmingham, AL 35212-3431, **Home Phone:** (205)595-3151. **Business Addr:** Vice President, Equity & Diversity, University of Alabama, 452 Campbell Hall, Birmingham, AL 35294-1170, **Business Phone:** (205)934-8762.

## DALE, ROBERT J.
Advertising executive, executive, association executive. **Personal:** Born May 2, 1943, Chicago, IL; son of Charles McDearmon and Jessie M; married Shirley J White; children: Kondo, Yusef & Kareem; married Ottie Andre Bryant. **Educ:** Ariz State Univ, BS, bus, 1971; Stanford Univ, Calif, MBA, bus & mkt, 1973. **Career:** Kaiser Broadcasting, Chicago, Ill, acct exec, 1973-74; Kaiser Spot TV Sales, nat acct exec, 1974-75; R J Dale & Assocs, consult, 1976-78; Small Bus Admin, mgt consult, 1978-79; Chicago State Univ, asst prof, 1979-84; R J Dale Advert & Pub Rels Inc, co-founder, pres & chief exec officer, 1979-. **Orgs:** Am Mkt Asn, 1977-, PUSH Int Trade Bur, 1984-, Nat Black United Front-Chicago, 1984-, Am Asn Advert Agencies, 1986-; co-chair, Chicago State Univ Col Bus Hall Fame Bd, 1987-; adv bd mem, Black Pub Rels Soc Chicago, 1988-; bd mem, March Dimes Birth Defects Found, 1989-; pres, IST Positive Educ, 1989; chair, Black Ensemble Theatre CRP, 1990; speaker, 24th Ann Black Bus Students Asn Conf, Stanford Univs Grad Sch Bus; Asn Bus Leaders & Entrepreneurs. **Honors/Awds:** Outstanding Black Businessman Award, Nat Black United Front, 1986; Pinnacle Award, Being Single Mag, 1989; Col Bus Hall of Fame, Chicago State Univ, 2003. **Special Achievements:** Black Enterprise's list of Top Advertising Agencies, ranked 9th, 1999, 10th, 2000. **Home Addr:** 8755 S Merrill Ave, Chicago, IL 60617, **Home Phone:** (312)731-5655. **Business Addr:** President, Chief Executive Officer, R J Dale Advertising & Public Relations Inc, 211 E Ont St Suite 200, Chicago, IL 60611-3284.

## DALEY, THELMA THOMAS
Educator. **Personal:** Born Annapolis, MD; married Guilbert A. **Educ:** Bowie St Col, BS; NY Univ, MA, coun & personnel admin; George Washington Univ, EdD, coun. **Career:** Baltimore County Bd Educ, coordr guid & coun serv; NC Cent Western Md Col, vis prof; Univ Wisc, vprof; Harvard Univ, vprof. **Orgs:** Nat treas, Delta Sigma Theta, 1963-67, nat vpres, 1971, pres, 1975-79; Nat Asn Advan Colored People; Nat Proj Chmn, 1967-71; Black Adoption Prog, 1968-73; Natpres, Am Sch Counr Asn, 1971-72; pres, Am Personnel & Guid Asn, 1975-76; chair, WomenCommunity Serv; United Negro Col Fund; Women NAACP, nat dir; bd dir, Nat Testing Serv. **Honors/Awds:** Md Personnel & Guidance Achievement Award, 1972; Life Mem Award, Nat Asn Advan Colored People, 1973. **Special Achievements:** First woman to chair the National Advisory Council on Career Education. **Home Addr:** 4417 Elderon Ave, Baltimore, MD 21215-4206, **Home Phone:** (410)542-0176.

## DALEY, TREVOR
Hockey player. **Personal:** Born Oct 9, 1983, Toronto, ON; son of Trevor Sr and Trudy; married Kristy West, Jan 1, 2008?. **Career:** Hockey player, 1998-, Vaughan Vipers (Junior A), 1998-99, OHL, Sault Ste. Marie Greyhounds, 1999-2002, AHL Utah Grizzlies, 2003-04, NHL Dallas Stars, 2003-15, AHL Hamilton Bulldogs, 2004-05, Team Canada, 2005-06, NHL Chicago Blackhawks, 2015, NHL Pittsburgh Penguins, 2015-. **Honors/Awds:** Stanley Cup, 2016. **Special Achievements:** Drafted NHL Dallas Stars, 2nd round, 2002. **Business Addr:** c/o Pittsburgh Penguins, 1001 Fifth Ave, Pittsburgh, PA 15219.

## DALEY-MELESCHI, VALRINE
Manager. **Educ:** Univ Wash, BA, polit sci & econs; Columbia Univ's Teachers Col, BA, adult learning; Harvard Univ, Sch Law; Ctr Creative Leadership, cert; Achieve Global Group, cert; Zenger Miller Global, Leadership Prog, cert. **Career:** Montclair Newark Jr League, prof develop & trng chair, 2005-06; Cornell Univ, Sch Indust & Labor Rels, adj fac; City Univ, New York, adj fac; Citigroup, pract mgr orgn develop & internal coaching; consult pract; Kesslin Assocs Inc, consult, training chair, currently; Corp Investment Bank, pract mgr orgn develop & internal coaching; Columbia Univ, staff; Clear Peak Commun, pract mgr, currently. **Orgs:** Cornell Univ Sch Indust & labor Rels; City Univ NY; speaker & facilitator: Ford Motor Co; Financial Women's Asn; Citigroup; YMCA. **Home Addr:** 415 Claremont Ave, Montclair, NJ 07042-1849, **Home Phone:** (973)746-2901. **Business Addr:** Kesslin, Clear Peak Communications, 167 W 21st 3rd Fl, New York, NY 10011, **Business Phone:** (646)336-7566.

## DALFERES, EDWARD R., JR.
Medical researcher, educator. **Personal:** Born Nov 4, 1931, New Orleans, LA; son of Edward Sr and Ray; married Anita Yvonne Bush; children: Edward Rene & Anthony Renard. **Educ:** Xavier Univ, BS, biol, 1956. **Career:** St John Parish Sch Bd, sci teacher, 1956-57; La State Univ Sch Med, med res, 1957-75, instr; Tulane Univ, Tulane Ctr Cardiovasc Health, instr & res biochem, 1992-2000. **Orgs:** La Heart Asn; AAAS; Southern Connective Tissue Soc; Soc Complex Carbohydrates; Sigma Xi. **Home Addr:** 2259 Leon C Simon Dr, New Orleans, LA 70122-4323, **Home Phone:** (504)286-9562. **Business Addr:** Instructor, Research Biochemist, Tulane Center Cardiovasc Health, 1440 Canal St 18th Fl, New Orleans, LA 70112, **Business Phone:** (504)988-5388.

## DALLAS, H. JAMES
Vice president (organization). **Educ:** Univ SC-Aiken, BS, acct; Emory Univ, MBA. **Career:** Ga Pac Corp, acct, 1984, group dir bldg prod & distrib info resources, 1998-2000, Lumber Div, pres, 2001-02, vpres bldg prod distrib sales & logistics, 2000-01, vpres & chief info officer maj pub corp, 2002-05; Medtronic, chief info officer, Qual & Opers, 2006-08, sr vpres qual & opers, 2008-13. **Orgs:** Bd mem, KeyCorp, dir, 2005-; bd mem, YMCA-Greater St. Paul & Metrop Minneapolis; Cool Girls; City Atlanta's Dept Info Technol cabinet; Eaton Corp, Eaton-Aeroquip Inc; Eaton Hydraul; Eaton Elec; Eaton Yale Co; El DuPont de Nemours & Co; Greater Cleveland Partnership; United Way Greater Cleveland; Elec Manufacturers Club; Musical Arts Asn. **Honors/Awds:** "Black Enterprise," The 100 Most Powerful Executives in Corporate America, 2010. **Business Addr:** Senior Vice President of Quality & Operations, Medtronic, 710 Medtronic Pkwy, Minneapolis, MN 55432, **Business Phone:** (763)514-4000.

## DALLEY, GEORGE ALBERT
Lawyer, government official, executive. **Personal:** Born Aug 25, 1941, Havana; son of Cleveland Ernest and Constance Joyce; married Pearl Elizabeth Love, Aug 1, 1970; children: Jason Christopher & Benjamin Christian. **Educ:** Columbus Col, BA, econ, 1963; Columbia Univ Sch Law, JD, 1966; Columbia Univ Grad Sch & Bus, MBA, 1966. **Career:** Metrop Appl Res Ctr, asst pres, 1967-69; Stroock & Stroock & Lavan, assoc couns, 1970-71; US House Reps Comt Judiciary, asst coun, 1971-72; US Dept State, dep asst secy state, 1977-79; Africare, Transafrica DC Support Group, chmn, bd dir, 1980-; US Civil Aero Bd, mem, 1980-82; Am Univ Sch Law, adj prof, 1981-85; Mondale Pres, dep camp mgr, 1983-84; Cong Charles Rangel, counr & staff dir, 1985-89; Neill & Co Inc, sr vpres, 1989-93; Neill & Shaw, partner, 1989-93; Holland & Knight, partner, 1994-2001; Congressman Charles B. Rangel, chief staff, 2001-09; Rep Charles B Rangel, chief staff; Apollo Theater Found Inc, asst secy, currently, chmn real estate comt, currently. **Orgs:** Am Bar Asn; Urban League, 1974-; Int Law Comt, Nat Bar Asn Fed Bar Asn, 1976-; Transafrica, Nat Asn Advan Colored People; Crestwood Community Asn, 1986-; Apollo Theatre Found; consult, UN Develop Prog, 1989-; Coun Foreign Rels; Am Bar Found; DC Judicial Nominating Comn. **Special Achievements:** Published "Art Federal Drug Abuse Enforcement", 1974; "Speeches Dem Corp Select Process", 1976; "Various Mags Articles", 1977; First black Member Of Civil Aeronautics Board, 1980. **Home Addr:** 2099 Pa Ave NW Suite 100, Washington, DC 20006. **Business Addr:** Assistant Secretary, Apollo Theater Found Inc, 253 W 125th St, New York, NY 10027, **Business Phone:** (212)531-5300.

## DALTON, DR. DAVID
Chief executive officer. **Educ:** WVa Univ, BS, pharm, 1971, PhD, pharm, 1974. **Career:** Rite Aid Corp, corp vpres, 1971-89; Sherman Mgt Group & Med Ser Agency, chmn, pres & cheif exec officer, 1989-94; MEDNET, exec vpres; Managed Care Rx; Health Resources Inc, founder, pres & chief exec officer; Health Resources Inc, owner, currently; Univec Inc, dir, pres & chief exec officer, currently; Pharmacy Serv Inc, owner, currently. **Orgs:** Essences Nature Asn; Salford Royal NHS Found; Blue Shield Pa; United Way; Nat Health Asn; Nat Asn Chain Drug Stores; bd dir, Nat Coun Prescription Drug Prog. **Business Addr:** President & Chairman, Chief Executive Officer, Health Resources Inc, 10 E Baltimore St Suite 1404, Baltimore, MD 21202, **Business Phone:** (410)347-1540.

## DALTON, RAYMOND ANDREW
School administrator, artist, association executive. **Personal:** Born Jan 15, 1942, Chicago, IL; son of Ernest Mitchell and Dorothy Mitchell Hunter; married Alfonsa Vicente; children: Carlos, Julio & Solange. **Educ:** Ill State Univ, BS, 1964, MS, 1966; Univ San Francisco, doctoral study, 1978; Purdue Univ, PhD, 1990. **Career:** Antelope Valley High Sch, instr, 1965-67; Lake Hughes, instr, 1967; Drew Jr High Sch, instr, 1967-68; Univ Ill, asst dean, asst prof, 1971-84; Purdue fel, 1987-89; Cornell Univ, Ithaca, NY, Minority Educ Affairs & Cosep, dir, 1989-, sr lectr art, 1989-94, exec dir, 1994-2009, visual artist, 2004-; Alpha Phi Alpha Fraternity Inc, pres, Iota Iota Lambda Chap, 2007-12. **Orgs:** Adv, Black Stud Organ Archit & Art, 1972-75; Art Comm, 1972; consult, Park Forest Pub Sch Black Art Workshop, 1973; co-adv, Orgn Int Stud, 1975; Prof Orgn Acad Affairs Admin Midwest; Nat Conf Artists; Union Black Artists; Col Art Asn; Nat Art Educ Asn; Nat Conf Art Admin; Asn Col Registrars & Counrs; Nat Orgn Minority Architects; grad asst, Ill State Univ, 1964-65, Purdue Univ, 1984-85; sab lv, Univ Pr, 1977; sab lv, Nigeria, 1982; Gamma Delta Iota Fraternity, 1986-; Omicron Delta Kappa Soc, 1989-; Purdue Circle, 1989-; chair, Minority Stud Affairs Coun; bd Trustee & found bd Dir, TC3. **Honors/Awds:** Edwards Medal, Ill State Speech Contest, 1965; William H Myers Multicultural Professional Service Award, 2008. **Home Addr:** 405 Lake St Suite A21, Ithaca, NY 14850, **Home Phone:** (607)272-5059. **Business Addr:** Visual Artist, Cornell University, 100 Barnes Hall, Ithaca, NY 14853, **Business Phone:** (607)255-7000.

## DALY, DR. FREDERICA Y. (FREDDY DALY)
Psychologist, educator. **Personal:** Born Feb 14, 1925, Washington, DC; daughter of Samuel P Young and Geneva A Sharper Young; married Michael E. **Educ:** Howard Univ, BS, 1947, MS, 1949; Cornell Univ, PhD, 1956. **Career:** Psychologist (retired); Howard Univ, instr, 1950; Cornell Univ, teaching asst, 1953-55; Cornell Univ, Cora Smith Fel, 1953-54, Grantfel, 1954-55; George Jr Repub, clin psychol, 1955-72, social serv dir; State Univ NY, Empire State Col, assoc prof,

1972-80; Univ NMex, asst prof, 1979, Ment Health Prog, clin psychol, 1980-81, Dept Veteran's Affairs, Alcohol Dependence Prog, coordr, 1981-88. **Orgs:** Bd mem, Family Serv Agency, 1958-60; Gov's task force mem, State NMex, 1984; NMex Bead Soc; Am Psychol Asn; Inst Noetic Scis; Soc Layerists Multi-media. **Honors/Awds:** Work appeared in several publications including Freedomways. **Special Achievements:** Perspectives Native Am Women's Racism & Sexism Experiences, paper presented Am Asn Advan Sci, 1990; Poetry pub & one poem to be published in a Russian J; Feminist Press, City Univ NY, Challenging Racism & Sexism. **Home Addr:** 526 Hermosa NE, Albuquerque, NM 87108-1030, **Home Phone:** (505)265-2425.

## DALY, RONALD EDWIN

Executive. **Personal:** Born Feb 23, 1947, Chicago, IL; son of Edwin W and Ella McCreary Brown; married Dolores; children: Dawn, Ronald Jr & Erin. **Educ:** Gov State Univ, Univ Park, IL, BA, bus admin, 1977; Loyola Univ, Chicago, IL, MBA, finance, 1980. **Career:** R R Donnelley & Sons, Chicago, Ill, supvr, 1972-79, mgr, 1980-84, Telecommunications Bus Unit, pres, 1995-2001, Print Solutions, pres, 2001-02; Cherry Hill NJ, gen mgr, 1984-87, Lancaster, Pa, gen mgr, 1987-88, Chicago, Ill, div dir; RR Donnelley Norwest Inc, sr vp; Portland, Ore, 1991-94; Americas Global Software Servs, sr vpres opers, 1994; OCE USA Holding Inc, pres & chief exec officer, 2002-; Supervalu, dir, 2003-. **Orgs:** Trustee, Chicago Symphony; vice chmn, bd pres, Environ Law & Policy Ctr; pres, bd mem, Leadership Greater Chicago; adv bd, Loyola Sch Bus; bd dir, mem bd, Supervalu, 2003-; mem bd, US Cellular, 2004-; Nat Black MBA Asn; Bill Bradley President; trustee, Chicago Symphony Orchestra; coun operating execs, Conf Bd; Obama Am; Obama Ill. **Home Addr:** 40 E 9th St Apt 313, Chicago, IL 60605-2140, **Home Phone:** (312)945-0511. **Business Addr:** Director, Supervalu, 7075 Flying Cloud Dr, Eden Prairie, MN 55344, **Business Phone:** (952)828-4000.

## DAMES, DR. KATHY W.

Executive. **Personal:** Born Jan 22, 1963, Chicago, IL; daughter of Sellers Williams Jr and Katie C Williams. **Educ:** Western Ill Univ, BA, 1984, MA, 1991; Roosevelt Univ, PhD; Harold Wash Col, EdD, 1997. **Career:** Ill State Comptrollers Off, asst legis liaison, 1986-88, chief legis liaison, 1988-90; Bd Gov Univs, lobbyist, 1990-; Chicago State Univ, dir alumni rels, 1993-95; Harold Wash Col, asst to pres, 1995; Roosevelt Univ, dir alumni develop, currently. **Orgs:** Chicago Women Gov; Ill Women Gov; Ill Women Adrs; Women's Legislative Network; Asn Black Women Higher Educ Inc; Illinois Comt Black Concerns Higher Educ; Delta Sigma Theta Inc. **Home Addr:** 10601 S Union Ave, Chicago, IL 60628, **Home Phone:** (773)821-6217. **Business Addr:** Director of Annual Giving, Alumni Relations, Roosevelt University, 430 S Mich Ave Rm 124, Chicago, IL 60605, **Business Phone:** (312)341-3725.

## DAMES, SABRINA A. (SABRINA DAMES CRUTCHFIELD)

Television journalist, writer, journalist. **Personal:** Born Nov 9, 1957, Washington, DC; daughter of Anita Mae Wilson and Harold Alexander Sr; married Curtis A Crutchfield; children: Ayana. **Educ:** Howard Univ, Wash, DC, BA, 1979; Columbia Univ, New York, NY, MS jour, 1981. **Career:** Huntington Advertiser newspaper, reporter; WTOP Radio, Wash, DC, news writer, 1981-84; WJLA-TV, Wash, DC, news writer, 1984-86; CBS News Nightwatch, Wash, DC, news writer, 1984-85; DC bur, package producer; CNN, package producer; Black Entertainment TV, Wash, DC, reporter, anchor, freelance producer, 1986-; McCollum & Assocs LLC, painting artist, 1995-. **Orgs:** Nat Asn Black Journalists, currently; AFTRA, 1981-84; Alpha Kappa Alpha Sorority, 1983-; Nat Tv & Radio Correspondents Asn, 1986-. **Honors/Awds:** Central Eastern Business Association Award; Cable Ace Award Nominee, News Special "Beyond The End", 1995. **Business Addr:** Reporter, Producer, Black Entertainment TV, 1235 W St NE, Washington, DC 20018-1211, **Business Phone:** (202)608-2000.

## DAMPER, RONALD EUGENE

Executive, chief executive officer, president (organization). **Personal:** Born Sep 18, 1946, Birmingham, AL; son of Willie and Ruby; married Patricia Dianne Ward; children: Ronald Sean & Shevonn Denise. **Educ:** Knoxville Col, BS, math, 1967; NY Univ, attended 1970; Univ Conn, Bridgeport, MBA, 1977. **Career:** GEEC, mkt mgr, 1973-77; Greyhound Leasing, dist mgr, 1977-79; Bankers Trust, vpres, 1979-81; Citi corp, vpres, 1981-84; Visions Entertainment, Blockbuster Video, prin, 1990-; Damron Corp, founder, 1984, pres & chief exec officer, 1985-, gen mgr, 2001. **Orgs:** Bd trustee, Tea Asn US, 1987; bd dir, Demico Youth Servs, 1988-; bd mem, Community Serv Develop Comt, 1989-93; bd mem, Ill Dept Community Affairs, 1990-; chmn & bd trustee, Monday Col, 1990-; Alliance Bus Leaders & Entrepreneurs, 1992-; leadership mem, Boy Scouts Am, 1992; chmn, McDonald's Diversity Supplier Coun, 1993-96. **Home Addr:** 8120 Woodside Lane, Burr Ridge, IL 60527-8055, **Home Phone:** (520)378-4158. **Business Addr:** President, Chief Executive officer, Damron Corp, 4433 W Ohio St, Chicago, IL 60624, **Business Phone:** (773)826-6000.

## DAMPIER, ERICK TREVEZ

Basketball player. **Personal:** Born Jul 14, 1975, Jackson, MS; son of Kenneth and Mary. **Educ:** Miss State Univ, attended 1996. **Career:** Ind Pacers, ctr, 1996-97; Golden State Warriors, ctr, 1998-2004; Dallas Mavericks, ctr, 2004-10; Miami Heat, ctr, 2010-11; Atlanta Hawks, ctr, 2012; free agt, currently. **Orgs:** Kappa Alpha Psi; founder, Erick Dampier Found. **Special Achievements:** NBA Draft, First round pick, No 10, 1996. **Home Addr:** Wainsborough Lane, Dallas, TX 75287-5525. **Business Addr:** GA.

## DANCE, DR. DARYL CUMBER

Educator. **Personal:** Born Jan 17, 1938, Richmond, VA; daughter of Allen W Cumber and Veronica Bell Cumber; married Warren C; children: Warren C Jr, Allen C & Daryl Lynn. **Educ:** Va State Col, AB, 1957, MA, 1963; Univ Va, PhD, 1971. **Career:** Va State Col, asst prof eng, 1962-72; Va Commonwealth Univ, from asst prof eng to prof eng, 1972-92; Jour W Indian Lit, ed adv, 1986-; Univ Calif, Santa Barbara, vis prof, african-am studies, 1986-87; Univ Richmond, Dept Eng, prof, 1992-; Ford Foundation Fel; Peepal Tree Press. **Orgs:** Ford Found Fel Asian Studies, 1964; Danforth Asn, 1964-; adv ed, African Am Rev, 1978-, MaComere, 1998-, Callaloo, 2000-; Va Endowment Humanities Resident Fel, 1997; Va Writers Club; ed advisor, J W Indian Lit; Va Festival; Behav Sci Fel, 1989-99. **Business Addr:** Professor, University of Richmond, 28 Westhampton Way, Richmond, VA 23173, **Business Phone:** (804)289-8295.

## DANCE, HON. ROSALYN R. (ROZ DANCE)

Nurse, mayor. **Personal:** Born Feb 10, 1948, Chesterfield, VA; married Nathaniel A Jr; children: Nathaniel A III & Tanya Kelly. **Educ:** John Tyler Community Col, AD, nursing, 1975; Va State Univ, BS, nursing, 1986; Va Commonwealth Univ, MPA, 1994; Gen educ develop, dipl. **Career:** Nurse (retired), Mayor; City Petersburg, mayor, 1992-; Va House Deleg, mem, 2005, deleg, 2007; S side Va Training Ctr, nurse's aide, head nurse, supt nursing, actg prog dir, dep dir residential serv; Va St Univ, fac; Va House Delegates, del, currently; Manhattans Restaurant, Richmond, owner, currently. **Orgs:** Hon mem, Petersburg Chamber Com, 1995; Nat Conf Black Mayors; Sub-Comt, Com Agr & Natural Resources; Sub-Comt, Gen Govt & Technol; Baptist Church; bd dir, John Tyler Community Col Found; chmn, bd managers, Southside Va YMCA; chmn, bd mem, United Way, Southside Opers; Phi Kappa Phi; Petersburg Dem Comt; Petersburg Links Inc; pres, Petersburg Breakfast Rotary; Petersburg Alumnae Chap, Delta Sigma Theta; hon mem, Tri-City Univ Womens Club. **Honors/Awds:** Certificate of Appreciation, Va Asn Neighborhoods, 1992; Certificate of Appreciation, Am Bus Women's Asn, Appomattox Chap, 1992; Golden Apple Award, Petersburg Pub Schs, 1992; Citizen of the Year, Omega Psi Phi Fraternity Inc, Delta Omega Chap, 1993; Certificate of Merit, Va State Univ, 1993; Certificate of Achievement, Woodstock Job Corps, 1993; Martin Luther King Jr Legacy Award for Extraordinary Contributions in Citizenship, Alpha Phi Alpha Fraternity Inc, 1994; Honorary Life Membership Award, Petersburg Chamber Com, 1995; Outstanding Woman in Government, YWCA, 1996; Certificate of Appreciation, 24th Quartermaster Battalion, 1998; Distinguished Alumni, Va Commonwealth Univ, 2003; Inductee, Hall of Fame, Va Community Col, 2003. **Business Addr:** Delegate 63rd District, Virginia House of Delegates, PO Box 2584, Petersburg, VA 23804, **Business Phone:** (804)862-2922.

## DANCY, REV. WILLIAM F.

Clergy. **Personal:** Born Nov 6, 1924, Greenville, MS; son of William Pearl and Belle Washington; married Darnell E Pruitt; children: Antonia M, William F Jr, Winnona D, Darryl B & Kimberly E. **Educ:** Roosevelt Univ; Cent Baptist Theol Sem KCKS. **Career:** KC-Topeka Dist, presiding elder; African Methodist Episcopal Church, assoc pastor, pastor, 1996-98. **Orgs:** Third Degree Mason; life mem, Nat Asn Advan Colored People; chmn, Oak Pk Soc Serv Orgn. **Honors/Awds:** Hon doctorate, Edward Waters Col. **Home Addr:** 3507 Southern Hills Dr, PO Box 300633, Kansas City, MO 64137. **Business Addr:** Pastor, First African Methodist Episcopal Church, 1111 N Eighth St, Kansas City, KS 66101, **Business Phone:** (913)371-2805.

**DANDRIDGE, BOB.** See DANDRIDGE, ROBERT L, JR.

## DANDRIDGE, ED

President (organization), chief executive officer. **Educ:** Tufts Univ, BA, hist, 1986; Univ Pa, Law Sch, JD, 1989. **Career:** Loeb & Loeb LLP, atty, 1989-91; Sawyer/Miller Group, prin, 1991-97; ABC Tv Network, vpres, 1997-2000; BrandSphere Partners, managing partner, 2000-08; Nielsen, chief commun officer, 2008-12; Nat Asn Investment Co, pres & chief exec officer, 2012-13; Collective, chief mkt officer, 2013-14; Marsh & McLennan Co Inc, chief commun officer, 2014-. **Orgs:** Co-chair, Mus African Art; bd dir, Coun Urban Professionals; bd dir, Coun Urban Professionals; bd dir, Clubmen Westchester; Exec Leadership Coun.

## DANDRIDGE, PROF. RITA BERNICE

Educator, writer. **Personal:** Born Richmond, VA. **Educ:** Va Union Univ, BA, 1961; Howard Univ, MA, 1963, PhD, 1970. **Career:** Morgan State Univ, asst prof Eng, 1964-71; Univ Toledo, asst prof Eng, 1971-74; Norfolk State Univ, Dept Eng & Foreign Lang, prof, 1974-. **Orgs:** Subscriber Mod Lang Asn; Col Lang Asn; Multi-ethnic Lit US African Am Rev; Nat Women's Studies Asn; Mod Lang Asn; Col Lang Asn. **Honors/Awds:** Roy A. Woods Outstanding Teacher Award, Norfolk State Univ, 1998; Regional Delegate to MLA, 2003-05; TIAA-CREF Va Outstanding Fac Awards; Recipient of various stipends and study grants, National Endowment for the Humanities. **Special Achievements:** Selected articles, "But Some of Us Are Brave", 1982; "Louise Meriwether", "Dictionary of Literary Biography", Afro-Am Fiction Writers after 1955, 1984, Vol 33; "Josephine Joyce Turpin, Richmond Writer", 1986; book, "Ann Allen Shockley, An Annotated Primary and Secondary Bibliography", 1987; book, Black Women's Blues, A Literary Anthology (1934-1988), 1992; "Debunking the Beauty Myth" in Terry McMillan's "Waiting to Exhale, Language, Rhythm and Sound", 1997; "Debunking the Motherhood Myth in Terry McMillan's Mama", 1998; "The Race, Gender", Romance Connection: "A Black Feminist Reading of African-American Women's Historical Romances", 2004; Selected one of 11 recipients of the TIAA-CREF Virginia Outstanding Faculty Awards. **Home Addr:** 1941 Lancing Crest Lane, Chesapeake, VA 23323-6649. **Business Addr:** Professor, Norfolk State University, 106 James Bowser Bldg 700 Pk Ave, Norfolk, VA 23504, **Business Phone:** (757)823-8891.

## DANDRIDGE, ROBERT L., JR. (BOB DANDRIDGE)

Basketball coach, basketball player. **Personal:** Born Nov 15, 1947, Richmond, VA; married Barbara. **Educ:** Norfolk State Univ, attended 1969; Hampton Univ, MA, coun. **Career:** Basketball player (retired), basketball coach; Milwaukee Bucks, 1969-77, 1981-82; Wash Bullets, 1977-81; Hampton Univ, asst coach, 1987-92; NBA Players Asn, dir, 1996-98; Am Basketball Asn, LongIsland, head coach, 2005-. **Business Addr:** Head Coach, The American Basketball Association, 9421 Holliday Dr, Indianapolis, IN 46260, **Business Phone:** (317)844-7502.

## DANDY, CLARENCE L.

Founder (originator), clergy, executive. **Personal:** Born Jan 7, 1939, St. Petersburg, FL; married Luagussie; children: Cynthia, Louis, Anthony, Jackie & Karlette. **Educ:** Full Gospel Minister Int Dallas, DD; Fla A&M Univ, attended 1959. **Career:** United Full Gospel Temple, founder, pres; Prayer Tower, Raleigh, NC, dir. **Orgs:** Chmn, bd dir Rev C Dandy Evangelistic Asn Raleigh. **Honors/Awds:** Recipient 1st Prize Trophy, Evangelist of the Year, United Full Gospel Temple, 1974. **Home Addr:** 4410 Bracada Dr, Durham County, Durham, NC 27705-7608. **Business Addr:** Founder, United Full Gospel Temple, 220 W Geer St, Durham, NC 27705, **Business Phone:** (919)688-0167.

## DANDY, DR. ROSCOE GREER

Government official, educator. **Personal:** Born Dec 20, 1946, Los Angeles, CA; son of Doris L Edwards and Roscoe Conkling; married Lesley A Dandy. **Educ:** Calif State Univ, BA, 1970; Univ Southern Calif, MSW, 1973; Univ Pittsburgh, MPH, 1974, MPA, 1975, DrPH, 1981; Harvard Univ, cert, 1981; Univ Ill, Urbana, IL, 1968; LaSalle Exten Univ, Chicago, IL, 1968. **Career:** Calif State Youth Authority, youth counr, 1971; Colo State Dept Health, pub health intern, 1974; Green Engineering Corp, health planning intern, 1975; Univ Pittsburgh, instr, 1977-80; Kane Hosp, admin health intern, 1979; USPHS, lt comdr, assoc dir, out-patient clin, 1980-81, pub health analyst & proj officer, 1993-; Cent Mich Univ, instr, 1981-; Vet Admin Hosp, asst chief trainee, 1981-83; Vet Admin, asst chief med admin, 1983-85, clin social worker, 1985-93; Columbia Inst Psychotherap, psychotherapist, 1989-91; Columbia Pac Univ, instr, 1990; Nova Southeastern Univ, instr, 1991; D.A. Wynne & Assocs Inc, 1991-94; San Rafael, Calif, 1990, Nova Univ, Ft Lauderdale, Fla, 1991; Nova Univ, Ft Lauderdale, Nova Southeastern Univ pub health, adj prof, 2010; Health Care Mgt Prog, prog dir & assoc prof. **Orgs:** Fel, Dr Martin Luther King Jr, Woodrow Wilson Found, 1971-73; Consult Jackson State Univ, Jackson, MS, 1977; Southern Christian Leadership Conf, 1973-; Nat Asn Advan Colored People, 1987-; Am Pub Health Asn, 1987-; Joint Ctr Polit Studies, 1986-; Brookings Inst, 1985; Fed Am Scientists, 1988-; Police community liaison Howard County Police Dept, 1989-93; Am Pub Health Asn; Nat Asn Social Workers. **Home Addr:** 23 Reybury Lane, Palm Coast, FL 32164, **Home Phone:** (386)313-6560. **Business Addr:** Senior Public Health Analyst, HRSA/Office of Minority Health, 18172 Parklawn Bdg 5600 Fisher Lane, Rockville, MD 20857, **Business Phone:** (301)443-6582.

## DANIEL, BERTHA

College administrator. **Educ:** Valdosta State Col, BS, 1991; Troy State Univ, MS. **Career:** Abraham Baldwin Agr Col, assoc prof Criminal Justice, Interim dir col serv & human resources, currently. **Orgs:** Proud Loving Individuals Giving Hand Teens, Chamber Com, Rotary, Tift County Comn C & Youth, City Govt Rep Libr Bd, & Friends United Educ III. **Home Addr:** 2019 Tyson Ave, Tifton, GA 31794, **Home Phone:** (229)382-4218. **Business Addr:** Director of College Services, Abraham Baldwin Agricultural College, ABAC 39 2802 Moore Hwy, Tifton, GA 31794, **Business Phone:** (229)386-7232.

## DANIEL, CELIA C.

Librarian. **Educ:** Concordia Univ, BA, black hist & Eng; McGill Univ, grad dipl, educ, MLS, libr & info sci. **Career:** Centennial Reg High Sch, Montreal, Can, teacher librn; Howard Univ, Founder Libr, assoc librn, head ref & instructions, currently. **Honors/Awds:** Teacher of the Year Award, 1994. **Business Addr:** Associate Librarian, Head of Reference and Instructions, Howard University, 500 Howard Pl NW Rm 102, Washington, DC 20059, **Business Phone:** (202)806-7446.

## DANIEL, COLENE YVONNE

Health services administrator. **Personal:** Born Apr 23, 1954, Cincinnati, OH. **Educ:** Univ Cincinnati, BS, speech path & audiol, 1977; Tex Woman's Univ, MS, healthcare admin, 1980; Johns Hopkins Sch Hyg & Pub Health, MPH, health policy, 1996. **Career:** Health Care Admin, residency, 1979; Veterans ADM Med Ctr, health systs specialist, 1980-82; AMR Med Intl Inc, asst hosp dir, 1982-86, mgt assoc, 1986-87; Univ Chicago Hosps, assoc dir, 1987-91; John Hopkins Health Syst, vip cre & cot servs, 1991-2002, pres's Coun urban Health, co-chair, 1998; DC Healthcare Alliance, 2002-03; Md gen hosp, pres & chief exec officer, 2004-; KSP Healthcare Group, pres, currently; Doctors Community Healthcare, regional chief exec officer, currently. **Orgs:** Healthcare Forum; Healthcare Forum Jour; Am Col Healthcare Execs; Johns Hopkins Med Servs Corp, bd trustee, 1995-97; John Hopkins Health Syst, Dome Circle ASO, 1995-97; Johns Hospkins Med & Parking, 1996-98; COL Notre Dame, bd trustee, 1993-99; Health EDUC Resource ORG, bd trustee, 1996-98; Hist E Baltimore COT Action Coaltion, bd trustee, 1994-98; Links, Harbor City Chap, 1997-2000; AFA Com Walters Art Gallery, 1994-97; PULSE COT Prog, bd adv opers, 1992-96. **Home Addr:** 9 E Lake Ave, Baltimore, MD 21212. **Business Addr:** President, Chief Executive Officer, Maryland General Hospital, 827 Linden Ave, Baltimore, MD 21201, **Business Phone:** (410)225-8000.

## DANIEL, DR. ELNORA D.

Educator, college administrator, college president. **Personal:** Born Nov 19, 1941, Oxford, NC; married Herman; children: 1. **Educ:** NC A&T Univ, BS, 1964; Teachers Col, Columbia Univ, MEd, 1968, EdD, 1975; Col William & Mary, 1972. **Career:** NY Med Ctr, nurse; Columbia Univ, teaching asst, 1976; Hampton Univ, prof & dean, sch nursing, 1980-91, adminr, interdisciplinary nursing ctr, 1985, exec vpres & provost, 1995-98; Chicago State Univ, pres, 1998-2008. **Orgs:** Econ Club Chicago; bd dir, Nat Asn Equal Opportunity Higher Educ; bd dir, Little Co Mary; bd mem, La Rabida C's Hosp; bd mem, Womens Bd Field Mus & Holds numerous memships; consult, W.K. Kellogg Found; consult, Oper Smile Int; fel, Am Acad Nursing. **Business Addr:** President, Chicago State University, 9501 S King Dr, Chicago, IL 60628-1598, **Business Phone:** (773)995-2000.

## DANIEL, EUGENE, JR.

Football player. **Personal:** Born May 4, 1961, Baton Rouge, LA. **Educ:** La State Univ, grad. **Career:** Football player (retired); Indianapolis Colts, right ctr back, 1984-96; Baltimore Ravens, right ctr back, 1997. **Honors/Awds:** Football News All American Football

Conference selection, 1985; American Football Conference Defensive Player of the Week. **Special Achievements:** TV Special: 1984 NFL Draft, 1984. Longest Interception Return in Colts history, Scoring on a 97-yard Interception against the New York Jets.

## DANIEL, GRISELDA
School administrator. **Personal:** Born Feb 7, 1938, Battle Creek, MI; daughter of Edward and Teritha; children: Cornell A, Gary L, Cheri A & Patrick H. **Educ:** Western Mich Univ, BS, 1973, MS, 1980. **Career:** School administrator (retired); Borgess Hosp, surg nurse, 1958-66; Kalamazoo St Hosp, attend nurse, 1966-70; Mich Dept Educ; Western Mich Univ, Col Gen Studies, counr & trainer, 1970-73, Martin Luther King Jr Prog, dir, 1975-80, asst, vpres acad affrs off & dir spl prog, 1980-88, asst dean, Grad Col, dir grad diversity prog, 1988-2005. **Orgs:** Pres, Int Mentoring Asn, 1988-89. **Home Addr:** 27847 County Rd 653, Gobles, MI 49055-9237, **Home Phone:** (269)628-5555. **Business Addr:** MI.

## DANIEL, JACK L.
Educator, administrator. **Personal:** Born Jun 9, 1942, Johnstown, PA; married Jerlean Colley; children: Omari & Marijata. **Educ:** Univ Pittsburgh, BS, psychol, 1963, MA, commun, 1965, PhD, commun, 1968; Stanford Univ, post doctoral grad, 1974; Harvard Univ, Inst Educ Mgt, post doctoral grad, 1986. **Career:** Cent Mich Univ, asst prof, 1967-68; Univ Pittsburgh, chmn, assoc prof, 1969-73, Col Arts & Sci, assoc dean, 1974-78, Undergrad Studies & Dean Students, assoc provost, 1987-92, interim dean Col Gen Studies, vice provost, acad affairs, 1992-, prof commun, 1999-, vice provost acad affairs & vice provost & interim dean stud affairs, 2001-02, vice provost undergrad studies & dean stud, 2002-05, vice provost, undergrad studies, 2005, Pitts Sch Arts Sci, distinguished serv prof, commun. **Orgs:** Numerous mem & positions held oraganizations incl Speech Commun Asn; Int Commun Asn; Soc Intercultural Educ Training & Res; bd mem, Red Cross Educ Ctrs; adv comt mem, Investing Now, 1988-; Louise Child Care Ctr, 1991 & 1992; Fla Educ Fund's Coun Elders, 1995-; bd dir, Hill House Asn, 1997-; secy, vpres & pres, Nat Commun Asn; NCA Finance Comt; secy, vpres & pres, NCA Black Caucus. **Home Addr:** 201 Woodcrest Dr, Sewickley, PA 15143. **Business Addr:** Professor, Vice Provost Academic Affairs, University of Pittsburgh, 4200 5th Ave, Pittsburgh, PA 15260, **Business Phone:** (412)624-4141.

## DANIEL, JAMES L., SR.
Consultant, executive. **Personal:** Born Nov 16, 1945, Brunswick, GA; married Brenda J; children: James Jr & Tonya. **Educ:** Tuskegee Inst, attended 1964; Brunswick Col, BA, 1976; Soc Cert Sr Advisors, cert sr advisor, 2008. **Career:** Sears Roebuck & Co, div mgr, 1968-76; Brunswick City, city comnr, 1972-76; Bellsouth, sales mgr, 1976-2000, sr acct exec, 1991-98; Southern Bell Tel, acct exec, 1978-80, serv consult, 1980-91; Stripe-A-Lot/Precision Pavement Marking & Maintenance Co, owner, 1986-; KMC Telecom, sales mgr, 2000-01, city dir, 2001; Best Designer Wear, owner, 2002-; Caretech Inc, chief exec officer, 2008-11; Home Helpers Woodstock, adminr, 2011-. **Orgs:** Pres & founder, Leaders Am Dem Soc, 1959; ex-officer, Brunswick Chamber Com, 1972-76. **Honors/Awds:** Frat Order Police, 1973; Brunswick City Community Award, 1976; Outstanding Service Award, Christ Mem Baptist Church, 1982. **Home Addr:** 504 Picabo St, Woodstock, GA 30189-7054, **Home Phone:** (770)592-7017.

## DANIEL, DR. JESSICA HENDERSON
Psychologist, college teacher, president (organization). **Personal:** Born Aug 2, 1944, San Antonio, TX; daughter of James E and Geraldine Thomas; children: Margaret. **Educ:** Fayetteville State Col, BA, hist, 1964; Univ Ill Urbana, MS, 1967, PhD, 1969; Harvard Univ, EdD. **Career:** Univ Ill, asst prof educ psychiat, 1969-70; Univ Ore, asst prof dept spec educ, 1970-72; Boston Col, ast prof educ psychiat, 1972-76; Harvard Med Sch, postdoctoral clin fel, 1974-76, instr psychiat, 1976-91, teaching fel, 1989, asst prof psychol, Dept Psychiat, 1991-; Boston C's Hosp, res assoc/psychiat, 1972-, dept psychiat, assoc dir leadership educ adolescent health, dir training psychol, currently; Judge Baker C's Ctr, psychologist, 1976-02, sr res assoc, currently; Harvard Univ, adj assoc prof psichiat, asst prof, currently; Boston Univ, Clin Psychol Prog, adj assoc prof psychol, currently. **Orgs:** Vice chmn, Bd Regist Psychologist, State Mass, 1984-89, chmn bd regist, 1989-93; mem bd, Brookline Arts Ctr, 1985-88; Tech Adv Comt Robert Wood Johnson Found, 1986-90; psychol consult Pub Schs Brookline, Cambridge, MA; Charles St AME Church; fel Am Psychol Asn; Mass Psychol Asn; Am Orthopsychiat Asn; cert, Am Bd Clin Psychol, 1999; Univ Ill, Am Psychol Asn, pres, Womens Div, Am Psychol Asn, 2001-02; leadeship coun, Girls Coalition Greater Boston, 2009; Leadership Inst Women Psychol; Task Force Adolescent Girls, Comt Advan Prof Pract; chair, Women's Caucus; Pub Interest Caucus; Early Career Psychologist Task Force; Kellogg Found; chair, Dr Martin Luther King Jr Observance; chair, Black Hist Month Observance Comt; Diversity Leadership Develop Workshop, 2011. **Special Achievements:** First African-American elected to the position of member-at-large on the APA Board of Directors. **Home Addr:** PO Box 605, Brookline, MA 02446, **Home Phone:** (617)738-5420. **Business Addr:** Director of Training in Psychology, Boston Children's Hospital, 300 Longwood Ave, Boston, MA 02115, **Business Phone:** (617)355-6734.

## DANIEL, REV. MARTHA
President (organization). **Educ:** Calif State Polytech Univ, BS, comput info systs, 1981; Univ La Verne, MBA, finance, 1983. **Career:** Atlanta Richfield Petrol Prod, systs analyst/proj lead, 1981-83; IBM Global Bus Serv, sr systs engr, 1983-85; Bekins Transp, mgr, 1985-87; Cable Valued Network, dir & IT admin, 1987-89; FDIC, first vpres & chief info officer, 1989-93; Aerojet Gen, chief info officer; ARCO; Info Mgt Resources Inc, founder, pres & chief exec officer, 1993-. **Orgs:** Bd dir & founding mem, Women Philanthropy Orange County United Way; chairwoman, Sch Bus Adv Coun, BAC, Calif Polytech Univ; trusteehip, an affil Int Women Forum; Orange County Nat Asn Women Bus Owners; Orange County Nat Asn Advan Colored People; Elite Serv Disabled Veteran Owned Bus Network, exec vpres. **Special Achievements:** Co author: On the Otherside of Midnight, 2000. **Business Addr:** Chief Executive Officer & President, Founder, Information Management Resources Inc, 85 Argonaut Suite 200, Aliso Viejo, CA 92656, **Business Phone:** (949)215-8889.

## DANIEL, MARY REED
Artist, painter (artist). **Personal:** Born Jan 1, 1946, East St. Louis, IL; married William J Daniel Sr; children: William J Jr. **Career:** Black Dimensions Contemp Am Art, publ & artist; Shows: Earl Graves Publ Co Black Enterprise Mag, Art Inst Sales & Rental Gallery, Milliken Rug Design Competition; Galerie Triangle; Lansburgh Ctr; Evans-Tibbs Collection; AMontgomery Ward Gallery; Tweed Mus; Paramaribo Suriname S Am; Hist City Hall, Harriet & Harmon Kelley Collection African Am Art. **Orgs:** Artist Guild Chicago; Artist League Midwest; S Side Community Art Ctr; Old Town Triangle Art Ctr Surface Design Asn; Chicago Artists Coalition. **Honors/Awds:** Honored, Afro-American Artists & Boston Public Library. **Home Addr:** 1391 N Milwaukee Ave, Chicago, IL 60622, **Home Phone:** (773)235-5477.

## DANIEL, SAMUEL J.
Hospital administrator. **Personal:** Born Sep 13, 1950, Leeward Islands. **Educ:** Columbia Univ, MD, 1978; Am Bd Internal Med & Gastroenterol, dipl, 1989. **Career:** N Gen Hosp, Internal Med Residency Prog, prog dir & chief Gastroenterol, 1994-99, med dir & dir med, 1998-2001, pres & chief exec officer, 2001-10; Gastroenterol, St Lukes-Roosevelt Hosp Ctr, postdoctoral fel; Mt Sinai Sch Med, assoc clin prof; RCHN Community Health Found, bd mem, currently; St. Lukes's & Roosevelt Hosp, Gastroenterol, fel. **Orgs:** Fel Am Col Gastroenterol, 1989; fel Am Col Physicians, 1994; Assocs Adv Coun, Am Col Physicians; bd dir, Boy Scouts Am; bd dir, Primary Care Develop Corp; New York Gastroenterol Asn; bd dir, League Vol Hosps & Homes; bd gov, Greater NY Hosp Asn; Prof Adv Comt New Horizons Scholars Prog; Selection Comt Lewis & Jack Rudin NY Mem Prize Med Sc; fel, NY Acad Med, 2004; bd trustee, Healthcare Asn NY; Heritage Affil Am Heart Asn Bd Trustees-New York Chap; chmn, bd dirs Community Health Alliance N Gen; Greater NY Regional Bd Dirs Nat Conf Community & Justice; adv bd, Upper Manhattan Physicians Against Cancer; fel Am Gastroenterol Asn, 2010. **Honors/Awds:** The Best Doctors in New York, NY Mag, 2000; Nation's Best Physicians, Network Journal and Black Enterprise Mag, 2001; Leon Bogues Award, Black & Latino Legislative Caucus, 2004; Good Scout Award, Boys Scout Am, 2002; Outstanding Leadership Award, 2006; Caribbean Luminary Award, Univ W Indies, 2007. **Business Addr:** Member of Board, RCHN Community Health Found, 1633 Broadway 18th Fl, New York, NY 10019, **Business Phone:** (212)246-1122.

## DANIEL, SIMMIE CHILDREY
Educator. **Personal:** Born Feb 9, 1934, Shorter, AL; daughter of Luther J (deceased) and Ora M. **Educ:** Ala State Univ, BS, 1957; Ind Univ, MS, 1967; St Louis Univ, spec study; Univ Nev, spec study. **Career:** Albany State Col, Albany Ga, exec sec, 1957-60; St Louis Pub Schs, St Louis Mo, bus teacher, 1963; El Reno Pub Schs, El Reno Okla, Eng teacher, 1963; Clark Co Sch Dist, Las Vegas Nev; Eldorado High Sch, teacher. **Orgs:** Nat Bus Educ Asn; Clark Co Classroom Teachers Asn; Nev State Educ Asn; Nat Vocational Educ Asn; Prof Col Women Asn; Nat Sorority Phi Delta Kappa Inc, 1973; Gamma Phi Delta Sorority, 1975. **Home Addr:** 3865 Tumbleweed Lane, Las Vegas, NV 89121, **Home Phone:** (702)456-8076.

## DANIEL, WENDY PALMER (WENDY PALMER)
Basketball player. **Personal:** Born Aug 12, 1974, Timberlake, NC; daughter of Melvin and Mary. **Educ:** Univ Va, BA, hist, 1996. **Career:** Basketball player (retired), basketball coach; Va Commonwealth Univ, asst women's basketball coach, 1993-96; Oveido, Spain, 1996-97; Club DKSK, Hungary, 1997-98; Utah Starzz, forward, 1997-99; Galatasaray, Turkey, 1998-99; Detroit Shock, rep, 1999-2002; Taranto, Italy, 2001-02; Orlando Miracle, forward, 2002; Conn Sun, 2003-04; San Antonio Silver Stars, forward, 2005; Seattle Storm, forward, 2006-07; Univ Ky, staff, 2007-09; Univ Va, asst coach, 2009; UNCG women's basketball team, head coach, 2011-. **Orgs:** Zeta Phi Beta. **Business Addr:** Head Coach, University of North Carolina at Greensboro, 1400 Spring Garden St, Greensboro, NC 27412, **Business Phone:** (336)334-5000.

## DANIEL, HON. WILEY YOUNG
Lawyer, judge, association executive. **Personal:** Born Sep 10, 1946, Louisville, KY; son of Lavinia and Wiley; married Ida Seymour; children: Jennifer, Stephanie & Nicole. **Educ:** Howard Univ, BA, 1968; Howard Univ Sch Law, JD, 1971. **Career:** Detroit law firm, Dickinson, atty; Wright Mc Kean & Cudlip, atty, 1971-77; Detroit Col Law, adj prof, 1974-77; Wayne County Neighborhood Legal Serv, dir, 1974-76; Gorsuch Kirgis Campbell Walker & Grover, atty, 1977-88; Univ Colo, Sch Law, adj fac, 1977-80, 2000-; Colo Personnel Serv Bd, dir, 1979-83; Iliff Sch Theol, dir & vice-chair, 1983; Popham, Haik, Schnobrich & Kaufman, partner & share holder, 1988-95; US Dist Ct, Dist Colo, chief judge, 1995-; Us Senate, chief judge, 2008-12, sr judge, 2013-. **Orgs:** Law J, 1970-71; Colo State Bd Agr, 1989-95; trustee, Denver Bar Asn, 1990-93; Nat Bar Asn; pres, 1992-93, Colo Bar Asn; Managing Ed Howard LLJ; Delta Theta Phi Law Frat, Alpha Phi Alpha Socl Frat; Sigma Pi Phi Fraternity; adj facul, Univ Denver Col Law; bd chair, Iliff Sch Theol; Am Inst Ct Found; Colo Trial Lawyers Asn; fel Am Bar Found; fel Colo Bar Found. **Honors/Awds:** Distinguished Service Award 1986, Sam Cary Bar Asn; Cs Legal Clinic Service Youth Award, 1995; USA Speaker Aboard, Nigeria, 1995; Speaker Abroad, Russia, 1997; Distinguished Service Award, Kappa Alpha Psi Fraternity, Denver Alumni Chap, 1999. **Special Achievements:** First African American, US Dist Ct, Dist Colorado. **Home Addr:** 2140 Monaco Pkwy, Denver, CO 80207. **Business Addr:** Chief Judge, US District Court, Rm A1038 Alfred A Arraj US Courthouse 901 19th St, Denver, CO 80294-3589, **Business Phone:** (303)844-2170.

## DANIEL, DR. YVONNE
Anthropologist. **Personal:** Born Oct 20, 1940, New York, NY; daughter of Orville and Kibbie Payne; children: H Douglas III, Kent, Terrence & Todd. **Educ:** Howard Univ; Calif State Univ, Hayward, BA, music, 1972; Mills Col, MA, dance, 1975; Univ Calif, Berkeley, MA, PhD, social & cult anthrop, 1989. **Career:** Calif State Univ, Hayward, lectr, 1973; Mills Col, lectr, 1976-86; Col Alameda, lectr, 1975-77, actg chair, 1977-89; Five Col & Smith Col, asst prof, 1989-91; Five Colege, prof dance, 1991-2001; Mills Col & Women's Leadership Inst, vis prof, 1999-2000; Smith Col, prof Dance & Afro-Am Studies, 2001-04; prof emer Dance & Afro-Am Studies, 2004-. **Orgs:** Cong Res Dance, 1975-92; Am Anthropologists Asn, 1984-97; fel Ford Found, 1991-92; World African Diaspora Asn, 1999; vis scholar, Mills Col, Womens Leadership Inst, 1999-2000; fel, Rockefeller Foundation. **Honors/Awds:** Univ Mass, Amhurst, 2001; Smith Col Black Students Award, 2004. **Special Achievements:** Author, Rumba: Dance & Social Change in Contemporary Cuba, Univ Ind Press, 1995; Dancing Wisdom: Embodied Knowledge in Haitian Vodou, Cuban Yoruba, and Bahian Candomble, Caribbean and Atlantic Diaspora Dance; Igniting Citizenship, 2011; Univ Ill Press; Articles published in CORD Dance Research Jour, Black Scholar, & Annals of Tourism; Performed with Nat Folklore Ensemble Cuba. **Business Addr:** Professor Emerita of Dance & Afro American Studies, Smith College, 17 New S St, Northampton, MA 01063, **Business Phone:** (413)585-3870.

## DANIELS, A. RAIFORD
Executive, educator. **Personal:** Born Dec 13, 1944, Columbia, SC; son of Willie L and Alma Gordon. **Educ:** Lincoln Univ, BA, 1966; Columbia Univ, NY, MBA, 1973, EdD, 1997. **Career:** Prudential Ins City Newark, mgt trainee group ins, 1966-67; Citibank, acct officer, Nat Bank Group, 1968-72; Corning Corp, NY, sr financial analyst, 1973-74; Bank Am, San Francisco, vpres, N Am Div, 1974-78; Prudential Ins Co, vpres corp finance dept, Capital Markets Group, 1978-88; Wilalm Group Ltd, managing prin & chief exec officer, currently; Bergen Community Col, prof, currently. **Orgs:** Columbia Club; Lincoln Univ Alumni; Minority Interchange NY; Am Soc CLU & ChFC; Naval Res Asn; pres, Nat Asn Advan Colored People, currently; Young Men's Christian Asn; Nat Naval Officers Asn; Newark Chamber Com; Nat Asn Rev Appraisers; Calder fel Calder Found, NY, 1972. **Honors/Awds:** Licensed Cert Gen Real Estate Appraiser, real estate & ins broker; registered invest adv & gen securities rep; Cert Rev Appraiser, register mortgage underwriter & broker. **Business Addr:** Managing Principal, Wilalm Group Ltd, 6 Bleeker St, Newark, NJ 07101, **Business Phone:** (201)622-8282.

## DANIELS, ALFRED CLAUDE WYNDER
Educator. **Personal:** Born Mar 22, 1934, Philadelphia, PA; married Ginger; children: Carmen & David & Jerry. **Educ:** Ariz State Univ, BS, 1965; Harvard Law Sch, JD, 1975. **Career:** Harvard Law Sch, asst dean, 1975-; NE HH Aerospace Design Co Inc, vpres; pvt pract atty. **Orgs:** Nat Asn Black Mfr; pres, Black Corp Pres New Eng; Urban League; Nat Asn Advan Colored People. **Home Addr:** PO Box 1695, Oak Bluffs, MA 02557-1695, **Home Phone:** (508)693-9713.

## DANIELS, ANTONIO ROBERT
Actor, basketball player. **Personal:** Born Mar 19, 1975, Columbus, OH; married Sonia; children: Jada. **Educ:** Bowling Green State, attended 1997. **Career:** Basketball player (retired), free agent; Vancouver Grizzlies, guard, 1997-98; San Antonio Spurs, 1998-2002; Portland Trail Blazers, 2002-03; Seattle Super Sonics, free agt, 2003-05; Wash Wizards, pt guard, 2005-09; New Orleans Hornets, guard, 2008-09; Minnesota Timberwolves, 2009-14; Philadelphia 76ers, 2010-11; Tex Legends D-League, 2010-12; Fox Sports, tv analyst, currently; Okla City Thunder, broadcast, currently. Actor: Shades of Grey, 2005; For Thy Love, 2006. **Orgs:** Nat Basketball Asn. **Business Addr:** Free Agent.

## DANIELS, REV. DR. C. MACKEY
Executive, baptist clergy. **Career:** Pastor (retired); Progressive Nat Baptist Conv Inc, pres, 1999-2002; W Chestnut St Baptist Church, pastor. **Business Addr:** Pastor, West Chestnut St Baptist Church, 1725 W Chestnut St, Louisville, KY 40203, **Business Phone:** (502)584-3664.

## DANIELS, CECIL TYRONE
Consultant, educator. **Personal:** Born Nov 23, 1941, Miami, FL; married Patricia Ann Robinson; children: Lee Ernest, Letitia Nicole & La Keitha Jonise. **Educ:** Fla A&M Univ, BA, 1964; Univ Northern Colo, MA, 1974. **Career:** Dade County Pub Sch Syst, prin, teacher, 1965-73, human rels coordr, 1970, asst prin, 1974-76; Univ Northern Colo, consult, 1975-76; Myrtle Grove Elem Sch, prin, currently. **Orgs:** Nat Alliance Black Sch Educr; Dade Co Schs Admin Asn; Dade Co Guid Asn; Fla A&M Alumni Asn; Univ Northern Colo Alumni Asn; vpres, Lions Club Int, 1977; Phi Delta Kappa; Big Bros Inc; Jack & Jill Am Inc. **Honors/Awds:** Service Award, WJ Bryan Elem PTA, 1976; Nominated Admin of the Year, 1976-77; Fulford Comm Award, 1976-77; Service Award, Fulford Elem, PTA, 1977; Service Award, Cub Scouts, 1977; Certificate for runner-up, Admin of the Year, 1977; Administrator of the Year, 1978; Ad Hoc Com Dade Co Sch Sys, 1980. **Home Addr:** 17240 NE 17th Ave, Miami, FL 33056-4911, **Home Phone:** (305)621-5532. **Business Addr:** Principal, Myrtle Grove Elementary School, 3125 NW 176th St, Miami, FL 33056, **Business Phone:** (305)624-8431.

## DANIELS, CURTIS A.
Salesperson. **Personal:** Born Apr 1, 1941, Italy, TX; married Cynthia A Epps. **Educ:** Bishop Col, BA, 1973. **Career:** Ingham Co Hosp, asst phys therapist, 1961-62; Titche-Goettinger, buyer, 1961-62; Fox & Jacobs, sales rep; Bishop Col, lectr. **Orgs:** Fox & Jacobs' "Million Dollar Circle", 1975; Omega Psi Phi, Mu Gamma Chap. **Home Addr:** 4913 Alta Oaks Lane, Lewisville, TX 75067.

## DANIELS, DARRELL B.
Administrator, association executive, chief executive officer. **Career:** Tampa-Hillsborough Urban League, cheif prog dir & actg chief exec officer, actg pres, currently. **Orgs:** Greater Tampa Chamber Com Found; Ethiopian N Am Health Professionals Asn. **Business Addr:** Acting President, Acring Chief Executive Officer, Tampa Hillsborough Urban League, 1405 Tampa Pk Plz, Tampa, FL 33605, **Business Phone:** (813)229-8117.

## DANIELS, DR. DAVID HERBERT, JR.
Physician. **Personal:** Born Sep 1, 1941, Little Rock, AR; married Doris; children: David, Dorothy, Doreen, Danny & Dora. **Educ:** Philander Smith Col, BS, 1968; Univ Ariz Med Sch, MD, 1967; Los Angeles Col Med Ctr, attended 1968. **Career:** Walter Reed Army Med Ctr,

Cardiovasc Disease, fel; David Grant Med Ctr, resident, internal med; Univ Southern Calif, internship; Cardiac Ctr Dir Cardiac Pulmonary Serv, physician cardiologist; Montclair & Chino Gen Hosp, physician; Pomona Valley Hosp Med Ctr, physician; San Antonio Community Hosp, physician. **Orgs:** Alpha Kappa Mu Nat Hon Soc, 1962; Beta Kappa Phi Nat Sch Hon Soc, 1962; dir, cardiac chmn, Cardiac Surg Comn Dr's Hosp; Am Col Cardiol; Am Col Physician; Am Col Cert Physicians; cert fel Am Col. **Home Addr:** 6837 Ramona, Alta Loma, CA 91701. **Business Addr:** Physician, 3535 Inland Empire Blvd Suite 27, Ontario, CA 91764, **Business Phone:** (909)941-2572.

### DANIELS, DICK. See DANIELS, RICHARD BERNARD.

### DANIELS, EARL HODGES
Journalist, writer. **Personal:** Born May 19, 1963, Tallahassee, FL; son of Earl and Betty. **Educ:** Fla A&M Univ, BS, sociol, 1987; Univ SC, Multicultural Newspaper Workshop, post grad study, 1989. **Career:** Ft Lauderdale Sun-Sentinel, news reporter, 1989-95; Fla Times-Union, Jacksonville, staff writer & bus writer, 1995-2005; writing consult, currently; Commun Solutions, Writer, proofreader & editing consult, 2005-; UPS, training supvr, 2006-; Internal Revenue Serv, seasonal clerk, 2006-11. **Orgs:** Nat Asn Black Journalists, 1990-; Kappa Alpha Psi Fraternity, 1982-; Stud Govt Asn; Fla A&M Univ Marching Band.

### DANIELS, DR. ELIZABETH
Dentist. **Personal:** Born Sep 23, 1938, Sebastian, FL; daughter of Levi and Addie Blackshear; married Jesse J Robinson Jr; children: Jennifer. **Educ:** Tenn State Univ, BS, bio chem, 1958; Howard Univ, MS, 1963; Univ Calif, PhD, 1968; Univ Conn, Sch Dent Med, DMD, dent, 1977. **Career:** Lockheed Propulsion Co, proposal writer, 1963-64; Pfizer Inc, med chemist, 1968-73; pvt pract, 1978-; Meharry Med Col, Sch Dent, asst prof, 1977-85, asst dean acad affairs, 1985-88, dept Periodont, assoc prof, 1988-89; pvt pract dentist, 1990-. **Orgs:** Nat Dent Asn, 1978-; Am Asn Dent Schs, 1978-89; Golden Heritage mem, Nat Asn Advan Colored People; vpres, Tenn State Univ Nat Alumni Asn, 1986-88; Howard Univ Alumni Asn; Church & Community Action; Portsmouth City Sch Bd, 1996-2004; pres, Nat Asn Advan Colored People, Portsmouth Br, 1997-2002; adv bd, Norfolk State Univ, Teacher Recruitment Proj, 1998-; VSBA, Legis, Policies & Resolutions comn, 1999-00; bd dir, Va Sch Boards Asn, 2002-07; pres, Va Sch Boards Asn, 2006; Adv Comn Educ Gifted, Commonwealth Va, 2001-04; Nat Soc Dent Practitioners; bd dir, Starbase Victory Mission & Vision; Nat Asn Advancment Colored People; Steering Comt Coun Urban Boards Educ. **Honors/Awds:** NASA Fel, Univ Calif, 1964-68; American Men and Women of Science, 1969; Outstanding Young Women of America, 1970. **Special Achievements:** First African American woman to graduate from Univ Connecticut Sch Dental Medicine; One of the first elected members of the Portsmouth City School Board in 1996; published an article, "The Effects of Environmental Pollutants on Enamel Hypoplasia and Dental Attrition", Hazard Waste Disposal Journal. **Home Addr:** 1502 Belafonte Dr, Portsmouth, VA 23701. **Business Addr:** Dentist, Private Practice, 4259 Greenwood Dr, Portsmouth, VA 23701, **Business Phone:** (757)488-4776.

### DANIELS, FREDERICK L., JR.
Banker, president (organization). **Personal:** Born Oct 9, 1965, Cleveland, OH; son of Gail M; married Yvette Kinsey; children: Kinsey & Kasey. **Educ:** Univ Va, BA, econ & eng, 1987. **Career:** First Nat Bank Atlanta, credit analyst, 1987-89; Wachovia Bank Ga, bus develop mgr, 1989-90, br mgr & banking officer, 1990-93; First Southern Bank, AVP & comm loan officer, 1993-; Citizens Trust Bank, vpres com lending, 1996-97, mgr, loan admin, 1997-2001, exec vpres, chief credit officer, 2010-; Metrop Atlanta Rapid Transit Authority DeKalb Co, com lending div mgr, 2002-03, first vpres, sr loan officer, 2003-10, chmn, 2010-. **Orgs:** Kappa Alpha Psi, Greenforest Baptist Church, 1980-; S DeKalb Bus Asn, bd dir, 1996-97, vpres, 1998, pres, 1999-2000; Partnership COT Action, bd dir, 1998-2002; bd chmn, 2002-; DeKalb Med Ctr, Hillandale, bd dir, 2001-. **Home Addr:** 6121 Magnolia Ridge, Stone Mountain, GA 30087, **Home Phone:** (770)469-8806. **Business Addr:** Senior Vice President, Senior Loan Officer, Citizens Trust Bank, PO Box 4485, Atlanta, GA 30302, **Business Phone:** (678)406-4000.

### DANIELS, GREG
Vice president (organization), executive, engineer. **Educ:** Albany State Univ, BS, maths. **Career:** Nissan N Am Inc, dir prod qual assurance & mfg, vpres mfg Smyrna Plant, sr vpres US mfg, 1982-2008; Ford Motor Co, Wayne Assembly Plant, indust engr. **Orgs:** Rutherford County Chamber Com, 1992; Exec comt, 100 Black Men Mid Tenn; alumnus, Leadership Rutherford County; exec bd mem, Albany State Univ Found; Rutherford County Boys & Girls Club. **Honors/Awds:** Outstanding Young Tennessean, Tenn Jaycees, 1992. **Special Achievements:** First African American to hold the position of senior vice president at Nissan North America Inc.

### DANIELS, JEROME ALVONNE
Football coach, executive, football player. **Personal:** Born Sep 13, 1974, Hartford, CT. **Educ:** Northeastern Univ, BS, Eng lang & lit gen, 1996; Concordia Univ-Irvine, MS, athletic admin & coaching, 2014; Grand Canyon Univ, PhD, psychol, 2016-. **Career:** Football player (retired), executive, coach; Ariz Cardinals, 1997, 1999, left guard, 1998; XFL New York/NJ Hitmen, 2000-01; Phoenix Col, offensive coordr & offensive line coach, 2010-12, head football coach, 2012-14; Ariz Sports Camps Fundraisers & Events, owner, 2011-; Grand Canyon Univ, higher educ counr, 2015-. **Orgs:** Nat Football League Alumni Asn, 1996; Nat Football League Players Asn, 1996. **Business Addr:** Higher Education Counselor, Grand Canyon University, 3300 W Camelback Rd, Phoenix, AZ 85017, **Business Phone:** (602)639-7500.

### DANIELS, JESSE
Engineer. **Personal:** Born Oct 14, 1935, Montgomery, AL; son of David M and Prince C Borom; married Ella McCreary; children: Jessica, Kenneth, Eric, Adrienne, Diane & Carl. **Educ:** AL State Univ, BS, 1961; Grad Credit, Auburn Univ, Emory Univ, Wake Forest Univ, Clemson Univ, GA Southern Col. **Career:** Engineer (retired); Ford Motor Co, design engr. **Orgs:** Eng Soc Detroit, 1963-78, 1978-83; Southeastern Mich Acapella Chorus, 1982-; Screen Actors Guild, 1984-; Nat Asn Advan Colored People, 1985-; Kappa Alpha Psi Fraternity; Prince Hall Masons. **Honors/Awds:** Two Nat TV Com Ford Motor Co, 1984; Distinguished Alumnus, AL State Univ, 1986; Narrator, Ford Col Recruiting Video. **Home Addr:** 11360 Auburn St, Detroit, MI 48228, **Home Phone:** (313)835-8945.

### DANIELS, JOHN W.
Lawyer, chairperson. **Personal:** Born Jun 11, 1948, Birmingham, AL; son of John and Kathryn; married Irma; children: John W III & Inez D. **Educ:** N Cent Col, BA, 1969; Univ Wis, MS, 1972; Harvard Law Sch, JD, 1974. **Career:** Quarles & Brady LLP, assoc, 1974-81, partner, 1981-, chmn emer, 2013; V&J Foods, chmn, dir, currently; Metro Milwaukee Chamber Com, dir, 1990-; N Milwaukee Bancshares, vchmn, 1992-98, chmn; Marshall & Ilsley Corp, dir, 2005-; Ralph Evinrude Found, dir; Greater Milwaukee Found, dir, chmn; Med Col Wis, dir emer; Milwaukee Symphony Orchestra, dir; Boys & Girls Clubs Milwaukee, dir. **Orgs:** Fel Nat Sci Found, 1969; fel Ford Found, 1970-71; bd Holy Redeemer Christian Acad, 1988-; nat vpres law students div, Am Bar Asn, 1973-74, Nat Coun, 1990-; Med Col Wis, 1991-, secy, 1995-; Am Col Real Estate Lawyers, 1994-96, nat treas, 1996-97, nat vpres, 1997-98, nat pres-elect, 1998-99, nat pres, 1999-2000; trustee, Evinrude Found, 1995-; N Cent Col, 2000-; founder, Golf Open, 2001-, chmn, fel; Anglo-Am Real Property Inst, 2002-; Am Col Mortgage Atty, 2002-; pres, Am Col Real Estate Lawyers; State Bar Wis; Milwaukee Bar Asn; pres, Milwaukee Young Lawyers Asn, 1981-82; bd chmn, Aurora Health Care. **Honors/Awds:** Mr Executive USA & Can, 1965-66; Outstanding Young Attorney, Milwaukee Jaycees, 1983; Outstanding Alumnus Award, N Cent Col, 1994; Human Relations Award, Nat Conf Christians & Jews, 2001; Award, Wis Asn Aro Lawyers, 2002; Humanitarian Award, St Francis C's Ctr, 2008; Friend of Hispanic Community Award, United Community Ctr, Pathfinder Award, African-Am Managing Partners Network, Legend of the Year, Milwaukee Community J, 2011; Spirit of Excellence Award, Am Bar Asn Comn, Friend of the University Award, Marquette Univ Alumni Asn, Excellence in Education Award, Milwaukee Pub Sch Bd Sch Dirs, Hall of Fame, Midwest Real Estate News mag, 2012; Midwest Urban Empowerment Leadership Award, National Managing Partner of the Year, Entrepreneur of the Year, 2013; Trustee of the Year Award, Wis Hosp Asn, 2014; Distinguished Executive Award, Wis Bus Hall Fame, 2015; Distinguished Alumni Award, Badger of the Year Award, Wis Alumni Asn, 2016. **Special Achievements:** Listed in The Best Lawyers in America; Listed in Chambers USA, 2003-; Named Wisconsin Super Lawyer, 2005-; Martindale-Hubbell AV Peer Review Rated. **Business Addr:** Chairman Emeritus, Quarles & Brady LLP, 411 E Wis Ave Suite 2040, Milwaukee, WI 53202-4497, **Business Phone:** (414)277-5103.

### DANIELS, DR. JOSEPH
Health services administrator. **Personal:** Born Mar 18, 1931, Linden, NJ; children: Joan & Jean. **Educ:** Lincoln Univ Pa, BA, 1953; Howard Univ Col Med, MD, 1957. **Career:** Med Ctr Jersey City, internship, 1957-58; Worcester City Hosp MA, 1958-59; Ancora Psychol Hosp, 1962-65; NJ Psychiat Hosp Ancora, attend psych, 1965-66; Salem Out-Patient Clin, Salem NJ, dir, 1966-67; Ment Health Ctr, Wyckoff WI, dir, 1967-70; E Orange Bd Educr, consult, 1970-75; In-patient Unit, Mt Carmel Guild, dir, 1970-71; NJ Col Med, clin asso prof psych, 1970-81; NJ Col Med, chief out-patient, 1971-77; Ctr Growth & Reconciliation Inc, med dir. **Orgs:** Beta Kappa Chi; Nat Sci Hon Soc, 1953; Youth Develop Inc, 1968-73; Northside Addict Rehab Ctr, 1969-71; Victory HSE Inc, 1970-77; bd trustee, Nyack Col, Nyack, NY, 1973-82; Newark Bd Educr, 1977-85; pres & bd chmn, Ministry Reconciliation Inc, 1981-85. **Honors/Awds:** American College Student Leaders, 1953; Outstanding Young Men of America, 1967; Psychodynamics & Psychopathlogy of Racism Publ, 1969. **Home Addr:** 20 Tuers Pl, Upper Montclair, NJ 07043. **Business Addr:** Medical Director, Center for Growth & Reconciliation Inc, 498 William St, East Orange, NJ 07019.

### DANIELS, KYSA
Journalist, public speaker. **Personal:** Born Sep 6, 1966, Houston, TX; daughter of Gregory and Judy Hunter; married Derwin; children: Ryan Gregory & Nicholas Adam. **Educ:** Tex A&M Univ, BA, jour, 1989; Eastern NMex Univ, MA, mass commun, 1990. **Career:** Houston Defender, reporter, 1990-92; KHOU-AM, news announcer, 1992; KBMT-TV, anchor & reporter, 1992-96; KSLA-TV anchor, 1996-99; CNN, overnight anchor, 2000-01; Clarion Commun, freelance speaker, writer, founder & pres, 2002-; Ga Perimeter Col, adj prof mass media, coordr mkg & pub rels; Atlanta J Const Faith & Values segment, feature writer, currently; col journalism instr & a newspaper guest columnist; Books: Substance and Sprit: A Collection of Poems, Quotes and Maxims to Strengthen Your Life. **Orgs:** Delta Sigma Theta Sorority, 1987-92; Big Bro/ Sister, 1990-92; SE Tex Asn Black Journalists, 1993-96; Nat Asn Black Journalists, 1999-2000; Parent/ Teacher Asn, 1999-; sponser, Women Women Int, 2000-; parish vpres, St Vincent de Paul Soc, 2002-; adv, Conyers-Rockdale Coun Arts, 2002-; Toastmasters Int, 2002-. **Honors/Awds:** Outstanding Graduate Award; Presidential Academic Scholar, Tex A & M Univ, 1985-89; Outstanding Mass Comm Grad, Eastern NMex Univ, 1990; Outstanding Young Professional, Spotlight Mag, 1995; Outstanding Journalist, Univ Memphis, 2001. **Special Achievements:** Author of Substance and Spirit (motivational book), 2002, guest columnist, Faith & Values section Atlanta Journal Const, 2002, moderator, Live Satellite Telecast at Centers for Disease Control, 2002, author, Then and Now Black Heritage Retrospect/ performing arts, 2002, has been featured in various national publications. **Home Addr:** 827 Cambridge Creek Dr SW, Conyers, GA 30094-5080, **Home Phone:** (770)761-5641. **Business Addr:** President, Founder, Clarion Communications, PO Box 1795, Conyers, GA 30012, **Business Phone:** (770)761-3955.

### DANIELS, LEE LOUIS
Movie producer. **Personal:** Born Dec 24, 1959, Philadelphia, PA; son of William and Clara Watson; married Billy Hopkins; children: Clara Infinity & Liam Samad. **Educ:** Lindenwood Col, St Charles, MO. **Career:** Nursing agency worker, 1978-79; Nursing Agency, mgr & owner, 1980, casting asst & talent mgr, 1981-; Lion's Gate Films, copres; film producer, 2000; Films: A Little Off Mark, 1986; Agnes & His Brothers, 2004; Shadowboxer, 2005; Producer: Monster's Ball, 2001; The Woodsman, 2004; Shadowboxer, producer & dir, 2005; Tennessee, 2008; Precious: Based on the Novel "Push" by Sapphire, producer & dir, 2009; Lee Daniels' The Butler, producer & dir, 2013; The Paperboy, dir & writer, 2012; TV Series: "Charlie Rose", 2006-13; "Media City", 2008; "Entertainment Tonight", 2008; "The Mo'Nique Show", 2009; "In the House with Peter Bart & Peter Guber", 2009; "The Daily Show with Jon Stewart", 2010; "Xpose", 2010; "The Oprah Winfrey Show", 2009-10; "Moving Pictures Live!", 2010; "The Wendy Williams Show", 2010; "Iconoclasts", 2010; "Cinema 3", 2010-13; "Oprah's Next Chapter", 2013; "Larry King Now", 2013; "Made in Hollywood", 2013; "The Hollywood Reporter Roundtables", 2013; Lee Daniels Entertainment, pres, dir, producer & chief exec officer, currently. **Honors/Awds:** Best Picture, Berlin Film Festival, 2002; Golden Globe nominee for Best Picture, 2002; Black Oscar, 2002; Best Picture, Nat Bd Review, 2002; Independent Spirit Award, 2005. **Special Achievements:** First film as a producer was the critically acclaimed film Monster's Ball, 2001; First African-American sole producer of an Academy Award-earning film. **Business Addr:** Director, Chief Executive Officer, Lee Daniels Entertainment, 39 W 131st St Suite 2, New York, NY 10037, **Business Phone:** (646)548-0930.

### DANIELS, LEMUEL LEE
Administrator, executive, vice president (organization). **Personal:** Born Dec 28, 1945, Montgomery, AL; son of Frank Hudson and Martha Daniels Johnson; children: Quintin. **Educ:** Southern Ill Univ, Carbondale, IL, BS, commun, 1968. **Career:** Merrill Lynch, Los Angeles, Calif, regist rep, 1976-78; A G Becker, Los Angeles, Calif, asst vpres, 1978-84; Drexel Burnham, Los Angeles, Calif, vpres, 1984-85; Bear, Stearns & Co, Los Angeles, Calif, assoc dir, 1985-94; Merrill Lynch, first vpres invest, 1994-99; Salomon Smith Barney, first vpres invest, 1999-, treas, currently; Deutsche Bank Securities Inc, financial advisor, vpres & client advisor; FINRA; Morgan Stanley, financial advisor; SEC, investment advisor. **Orgs:** Treas, bd dir, Los Angeles Arts Coun, 1989-; vice chair, Nat Asn Securities Prof, Task Force Rebuild Los Angeles; trustee, exec comt, Cross Roads Arts Acad, 1990-; bd mem, WEB Du Bois Sch, 1982-84; chancellor assoc, Univ Calif, La, 1978-80; sect, bd dir, Cottege Bound; bd dir, Greater Los Angeles African Am Chamber Com, 2005-; Investment Advisor Rep; Regist Investment Advisor. **Home Addr:** 6645 S Garth Ave, Los Angeles, CA 90056, **Home Phone:** (310)410-9898. **Business Addr:** Board Director, The Greater Los Angeles African American Chamber of Commerce, 5100 W Goldleaf Cir Suite 203, Los Angeles, CA 90056, **Business Phone:** (323)292-1297.

### DANIELS, LESHUN DARNELL, SR.
Football player. **Personal:** Born May 30, 1974, Warren, OH; married Alicia M; children: LeShun Jr. **Educ:** Ohio State Univ. **Career:** Minn Vikings, guard, 1997; Jacksonville Jaguars, guard, 2001. **Home Addr:** 865 Landsdowne Ave NW, Warren, OH 44485-2227, **Home Phone:** (234)600-5181.

### DANIELS, LINCOLN S., SR.
School administrator. **Personal:** Born Feb 17, 1932, Hickman, KY; son of James (deceased) and Viola (deceased); married Robbie L Davis; children: Karen Lee Trice, Lincoln Jr (deceased) & Terrence Leon. **Educ:** Philander Smith Col, BA, 1953; Wash Univ, MA, 1969. **Career:** School administrator (retired); St Louis Bd Educ, elem teacher, 1964-69, res statistician, 1973-75, Div Eval, div asst, 1975-80, admin asst, 1980-84, instrnl coordr, 1984-87, elem prin, 1987-97; St Louis Co Social Studies Implementation Proj, master teacher, 1966-69; St Louis Metro Soc Studies Ctr Wash Univ, res asst, 1966-69; Wash Univ, clin assoc, 1967-70, master teacher summer, 1970, res adv sum, 1970, supvr elem educ, 1970-73, coordr elem educ summer, 1971. **Orgs:** Phi Delta Kappa Ed Leadership Soc; Philander Smith Col Alumni Chap, 1966-68; Community Black Recruitment; Kappa Delta Pi Educ Hon Soc, 1969; pres, 1970-71, historian-reporter, 1971-72, Kappa Delta Pi St Louis; secy, St Louis Philander Smith Col Alumni Chap, 1970-74; Worshipful Master, Caution Lodge No 23, Prince Hall Masons, 1976; treas, 1976-78, pres-elect, 1978-79, pres, 1980, St Louis City Coun, Int Reading Asn; chmn, Block Unit No 375; Nat Urban League Confederation Block Units, 1976-; vpres, Midwest Region Philander Smith Col Nat Alumni Asn, 1977-79; pres, Metro-St Louis Philander Smith Col Alumni Chap; bd mem, Metrop Congregations United St. Louis, 1995-; vpres, Congregations Allied Community Improv, 1998-2000. **Home Addr:** 4640 Natural Bridge Ave, St. Louis, MO 63115-1923, **Home Phone:** (314)381-7939.

### DANIELS, LLOYD
Basketball coach, basketball player. **Personal:** Born Sep 4, 1967, Brooklyn, NY. **Educ:** Univ Nev, Las Vegas; Mt San Antonio Col, attended. **Career:** Basketball player (retired), coach; Mt. San Antonio, 1986-87; Topeka Sizzlers, 1987-88; Quad City, 1989-90; Miami Tropics, 1990-91; Greensboro City Gaters, 1991-92; Long Island Surf, 1991-92, 2000-02; San Antonio Spurs, shooting guard, 1992-94; Philadelphia 76ers, shooting guard, 1994-95; Los Angeles Lakers, shooting guard, 1994-95; Ft Wayne Fury, 1994-95, 1996-97; Limoges CSP, France, 1994-95; Scavolini Pesaro, 1995-96; Sacramento Kings, shooting guard, 1996-97; New Jersey Nets, shooting guard, 1996-97; Toronto Raptors, shooting guard, 1997-98; Polluelos de Aibonito, Pr, 1997-98, 1998-99; Galatasaray Istanbul, Turkey, 1997-98; Idaho Stampede, 1998-99; AEK Atene, Greece, 1998-99; Sioux Falls Skyforce, 1998-99; BayRunners, 1999-2000; Trenton Sh. Stars, 1999-2000; Tampa Bay T-Dawgs, 2000-01; Panteras de Miranda, Venezuela, 2000-01, 2002-03; Rida Scafati, Italy, 2001-02; Shanghai Sharks, China, 2001-02; Ovarense Aerosoles, Port, 2002-03; Strong Island Sound, 2005-06; Amateur Athletic Union Basketball, coach, currently. **Home Addr:** , NJ.

### DANIELS, MELVIN J. (MEL DANIELS)
Basketball player, basketball coach, basketball executive. **Personal:** Born Jul 20, 1944, Detroit, MI; son of Maceo and Bernice Clemmons; married Cecilia J Martinez. **Educ:** Burlington Jr Col, attended 1964; Univ NMex, attended 1967. **Career:** Basketball player (retired), basketball coach, basketball executive; Univ NMex Lobo, player, 1964-67; Minn Muskies, forward, 1967-68; Ind Pacers, ctr, 1968-74, dir player personnel; Memphis Sounds, ctr, 1974-75; NY Nets, ctr, 1976;

Ind State, asst basketball coach, 1978-80, asst coach, scout, 1983; Ind Pacers, dir player personnel, 1986-2009. **Orgs:** Am Quarter Horse Farm Circle M Ranch; Am Preview; Dash Cash bred stock Operating, 1972. **Home Addr:** 19789 Centennial Rd, Sheridan, IN 46069, **Home Phone:** (317)896-5380.

## DANIELS, PATRICIA ANN

Government official, founder (originator). **Personal:** Born Aug 6, 1940, Kaufman, TX; daughter of James Hiawatha Alexander and Mary Elizabeth Burnett Alexander; married Valjean; children: Barry M Alexander & Brette M. **Educ:** Los Angeles Jr Col Bus, Los Angeles, Calif, AA, 1964; Univ San Francisco, San Francisco Calif, BS, 1979. **Career:** City Berkeley, Berkeley, Calif, supvr, housing codes, 1968-80, supvr, parking collections, 1981-89, personnel-labor rels trainee, 1989-92, asst bldg & housing inspector; Sunday Sch, teacher & asst, community & potical; NCNW State Leadership Trainer, asst secy; Icanmindyourownbusiness.com, founder & chief exec officer. **Orgs:** Nat regional dir, first vpres, Far Western Region, Nat, 1989-; int pres, Gamma Phi Delta Sorority, Vol Serv, 1971-, currently; charter mem, Beta Sigma Chap, 1990-91, Sup First Anti-Basileus, 1992; pres, 1990-91, Calif Fedn Bus & Prof Women, Bay Valley Dist, 1983-; pres-elect, Diversity Task Force, Bay Valley Dist, 1983-; bd dir, Nat Forum Black Pub Admin, 1985-; charter mem, Nat Coun Negro Women, Alameda County Sect; bd dir, Local Black Women Organized Polit Action; Women's Missionary Union, prog dir, N Richmond Missionary Baptist Church; vpres, Housing Adv Comn Personnel Bd, City San Pablo; pres, Nat Mgt Action Team; Alameda County Sect NCNW. **Honors/Awds:** Rose Pin Award, Gamma Phi Delta Sorority, Nat, 1976; Woman of the Year, Far Western Region, Gamma Phi Delta Sorority, 1979; Dedicated Serv, Beta Sigma, 1986; Woman of the Year, Outstanding Community Serv, Nat Forum Black Public Admin, 1987; Local Woman of the Year, District Woman of the Year, Woman of Achievement, California Fedn of Business & Professional Women, 1988; Marks of Excellence, North Richmond Church, 1989. **Special Achievements:** First Vice President of the Women's Missionary Union; Author of two leadership manuals, Gamma Phi Delta Sorority. **Home Addr:** 1810 Hillcrest Rd, San Pablo, CA 94806-4134, **Home Phone:** (510)235-7827. **Business Addr:** Chief Executive Officer, Icanmindyourownbusiness.com, 1810 Hillcrest Rd, San Pablo, CA 94806, **Business Phone:** (510)235-7827.

## DANIELS, PHILLIP BERNARD

Executive, football player. **Personal:** Born Mar 4, 1973, Donaldsonville, GA; married Leslie; children: Davaris, Dakendrick, Damara & Dakiya. **Educ:** Univ Ga, social work. **Career:** Football player (retired), coach, executive; Seattle Seahawks, defensive end, 1996-99, right defensive end, 1997-98; Chicago Bears, defensive end, 2000-03; Wash Redskins, defensive end, 2004-10, dir player develop, 2012-; Philadelphia Eagles, defensive qual control & asst defensive line coach, 2016-. **Orgs:** Phi Beta Sigma Fraternity. **Home Addr:** Peanut Bland Rd, Donalsonville, IL 60607. **Business Addr:** Director of Player Development, Washington Redskins, 21300 Redskin Pk Dr, Ashburn, VA 20147, **Business Phone:** (703)478-8900.

## DANIELS, PRESTON A.

Consultant, broadcaster, mayor. **Personal:** Born Jan 1, 1945, Chicago, IL; married Patty; children: Preston A II. **Educ:** Drake Univ, BS, psychol, 1971, MS, health sci, 1972. **Career:** Des Moines, city coun, 1991, Iowa, mayor, 1997-2004; Iowa Dept Human Rights, dir, 2009-11; Employee & Family Resource's (EFR) Ct & Community, prog dir & consult; KFMG99.1, host. **Orgs:** Univ Iowa Adv Bd Addiction Technol; State Iowa Training Adv Bd Substance Abuse; League Cities; Iowa Dem Party; Metro Solid Waste Agency Bd; pres, Drake Neighborhood Asn; Nat Conf Black Mayors; Nat Conf Mayors; chair, Govs Task Force; bd mem, Iowa Empowerment Bd; League Iowa Human Rights Agencies; Nat Asn Human Rights Workers; co-organizer, Early Childhood Diversity Initiative. **Honors/Awds:** Professional Achievement Award, Grand view Col. **Special Achievements:** First African American mayor of Des Moines, IA. **Home Addr:** 2700 Scott Ave, Des Moines, IA 50317-1252, **Home Phone:** (515)261-0987.

## DANIELS, RANDY A.

Government official, educator, journalist. **Personal:** Born Jan 1, 1950?, Chicago, IL; married Justice Sallie Manzanet; children: 2. **Educ:** Southern Ill Univ, BS, govt & jour prog. **Career:** WVON radio, reporter, 1970-72, Africa Bur, chief, 1977-80; CBS News, nat corresp, 1972-82, foreign corresp, 1977-80; Jacaranda Nigeria Ltd, managing dir; City Col New York, adj prof jour; Canyon Johnson Urban Fund, sr vpres; Empire State Develop Corp, sr vpres & dep comnr econ revitalization; Columbia Univ's Grad Sch Jour, adj prof jour; New York Coun, Pres's Off, dir commun, 1986-88; Bahamas, secy to prime minister, 1988; NY govt, Empire State Develop Corp, Econ Revitalization, sr vpres, dep comnr, 1995; Canyon Johnson Urban Fund, sr vpres, 1999-2001; State Univ New York, vice chmn, 1997-; Pataki's Secy State, 2001; New York, secy, 2001-06; Gilford Securities Inc, Vice Chmn, 2007-. **Orgs:** Bd trustee, Exec & Fin Comt, State Univ New York, 1997; co-chair, Comn on Gen Educ & Charter Sch; Gov Patakiocos Weapons Mass Destruction Task Force; chair, S Shore Estuary Res Coun; Nat Asn Secretaries State; dep mayor, New York; chmn, Ny Real Estate Bd & Ny 911 Bd; Weapons Mass Destruction Task Force. **Business Addr:** Vice Chairman, Board of Trustee, State University of New York, 353 Broadway, Albany, NY 12246, **Business Phone:** (212)417-5800.

## DANIELS, RICHARD BERNARD (DICK DANIELS)

Football player, scout. **Personal:** Born Oct 19, 1944, Portland, OR; married Gloria; children: Sunde & Whitney. **Educ:** Pac Univ. **Career:** Football player (retired), scout; Dallas Cowboys, defensive back & return specialist, 1966-68; Chicago Bears, return specialist, 1969-70; Miami Dolphins, 1971, scout, 1972-75; Tampa Bay Buccaneers, head scout, 1975; San Francisco 49ers, scout, 1976-77; Wash Redskins, dir player personnel, 1978-84, 1985-89; USFL, Los Angeles Express, vpres player personnel, 1984; San Diego Chargers, asst gen mgr, 1990-96; Philadelphia Eagles, dir, football oper, 1996; St Louis Rams, col scout, 2000-09. **Home Addr:** , Del Mar, CA.

## DANIELS, RICHARD D.

Clergy. **Personal:** Born Jan 27, 1931, Micanopy, FL; married Doris B Bagley. **Educ:** Fla A & M Univ, BS, 1958. **Career:** Pastor (retired); St Luke AME, Gainesville, pastor, 1958-59; Silver Springs, 1959-64; St Stephens AME, Lees burg, Fla, 1964-71; Mt Zion African Methodist Episcopal Church, Ocala, pastor, 1971-72. **Orgs:** Deleg, Gen Conf, 1972; Nat Asn Advan Colored People; Masonic Lodge; Blood Bank Asn, Alachua Co; presiding elder, African Methodist Episcopal Church, 1973-. **Home Addr:** 2138 Pruitt St, Leesburg, FL 34748, **Home Phone:** (352)326-5437.

## DANIELS, DR. RON D.

Educator, association executive, executive director. **Personal:** children: Malik, Sundiata & Jeannette. **Educ:** Youngstown State, BA, hist, 1965; Rockefeller Sch Pub Affairs, MA, polit sci, 1967; Union Inst, Pol Sci, attended 1976, PhD, Africana studies; Univ Cincinnati, PhD, Africana studies. **Career:** Asn Neighborhd Ctr, Hag strom House, S Side Ctr, Camp Lexington, boys' prog dir, youth & young adult worker, camp counr, camp prog dir, 1961-64; Youngstown State Univ, educr, 1967-69; Freedom Inc, founder & chmn, 1968-74, exec dir, 1969-74; Perspectives Black, moderator & producer; WYTV, Youngstown OH, Ron Daniels Show, 1968-87; Kent State Univ, educr, asst prof African Am affairs & Pan-Am studies, 1971, 1981-86; Hiram Col, Ohio, educr, 1973; Pol Sci & Pan-African Studies, asst prof, 1974-77; Cornell Univ, educr, vis prof, 1979-80; Nat Rainbow Coalition, exec dir, 1987; Jesse Jackson Pres Campaign, southern regional mgr, 1988; Col Wooster, educr, vis assoc prof black studies, 1994; Inst Community Orgn & Develop, Youngstown, Ohio, exec dir; Ctr Const Rights, exec dir; syndicated columnist; Black Media Proj Progressive Mag, ed opinion writer; Black Collegion & Z Mag, contribr; Am Urban Radio Network, guest host, night talk; York Col, distinguished lectr; City Univ New York, distinguished lectr. **Orgs:** African Liberation Day Coord Com, 1972; convener, Ohio deleg Nat Black Polit Conv, Gary, IN, 1972; adj prof & mem bd dir, Ohio Inst Practical Pol, 1973; pres, Ohio Black Pol Assembly; pres, Nat Black Polit Assembly, 1974-80; cand, Mayor, 1977; Nat co-chmn, Nat Black Independent Polit Party, 1981-83; chmn, 1983-85; exec, Cong African People; founding training & proj eval consult, Episcopal Ch Gen Conv Spec Prog; coordr, Mid-W Regional Coalition; Coun Elders, Fed Pan-African Educ Inst; elder Marcus GarveySch; del No, Am Reg Steering Conf, 6th Pan-Africa Conf; Help Us Make A Natio Training Inst; Nat Econ Develop & Law Ctr; bd dir, Nat Jobs Peace Campaign; bd dirs, Greenpeace USA; bd dir, Nation Inst; co-chmn, Nat Malcolm X Commemoration Comn; bd dir, African Am Inst ResEmpowerment; nat chmn, campaign new tomorrow; independent cand Pres US, 1992; coordr, NH State Race Conf, 1994; steering comt, Nat African Am Ld shop summitt, 1994-96; exec coun, Nat Org comt, Millian March & Day Action, 1995; founder, Haiti Support Proj, 1995. **Honors/Awds:** Youngstown Black Polit Assembly-Freedom Inc Award, 1974; Minority Affairs Dir's Award, 1974; Model Cities Citizen Participation Orgn Award, 1974; Omega Psi Phi Community Service Award, 1979; McGuffey Center Community Service Award, 1982; African Cultural Weekend Award for Dedicated Leadership, 1985; Inter-Faith Community Action Committee Award, 1986; Inter-Denominational Clergy Women's Alliance Civic Award, 1986; First Williams Publishing Co Pioneer Award for Outstanding Contributions to Civil Rights in the Media, 1988. **Special Achievements:** First African American Executive Director of the Center for Constitutional Rights, 1993; first Distinguished Lecturer at York College of the City University of New York. **Home Addr:** 3135 95th St, East Elmhurst, NY 11369.

## DANIELS, TERRY L.

Business owner, manager. **Personal:** Born Jul 28, 1951, Shreveport, LA; son of Louis (deceased) and Annie (deceased); married Joyce E Hall; children: Shemetra Rachel & Nikki Renee. **Educ:** Southern Univ, A&M Col, BS, indust technol, 1973; Webster Col, MA, bus mgt, 1977; GE Advan Mfg Leadership Training, cert, 1984, 1994; Kodak Advan Mgt Training, cert, 1988; Int Mgt Develop Inst, 1998; Mich State Univ, cert, 1999. **Career:** Gen Elec Co, mgr, 1973-85, compressor mfg opers, mgr, 1985-88; Eastman Kodak, Frames & Struct, plant mgr, 1988-91, Site & Facil Group, div mgr, 1991-94; AT&T, gen mgr, dir, mfg, 1994-99; Lucent Technologies Inc, global purchasing, dir, 1999-2003; Gravograph New Hermes, global purchasing & qual systs, dir, 2003-05; IMC Holdings, global purchasing dir, 2005-08; DiversiTech Corp, sr planner-global procurement & scheduling, 2008-09; Robert Half Int, purchasing, sourcing, supply chain consult, 2009-10; TDOK Consult Group, owner & chief exec officer, 2010-. **Orgs:** Network Northstar Inc, 1991-; Int Facil Mgt Asn, 1992-; bd, chair, Nat Maintenance Excellence Award, 1992; Alliance Black Telecommunications Workers; Southern Univ Alumni Asn; chair, Boy Scouts Am W Sect Oteciana Coun. **Honors/Awds:** Youth Service Award, Black Achievers, 1984; Peak Award, Nat Maintenance Excellence Award, 1992. **Special Achievements:** Author: Maintenance Technology Magazine, p 24, 1992; Plant Eng Magazine, p 72, 1992. **Home Addr:** 644 Masters Dr, Stone Mountain, GA 30087, **Home Phone:** (404)879-2550. **Business Addr:** Owner, Chief Executive Officer, TDOK Consulting Group, 6220 Wurtenburg Ct, Stone Mountain, GA 30087, **Business Phone:** (404)372-4622.

## DANIELS, DR. WILLIAM JAMES

Dean (education), consultant, school administrator. **Personal:** Born Mar 7, 1940, Chicago, IL; son of William Hector McCoy and Ethel Cora Dent; married Fannie Pearl Hudson; children: Twanda Delois Christensen. **Educ:** Upper Iowa Univ, Fayette, IA, BA, 1962; Univ Iowa, MA, 1964, PhD, 1970. **Career:** Union Col, Schenectady, NY, asst prof, 1966-72, assoc prof, 1973-81, prof, 1982-88, assoc dean, 1983-88; Alfred E Smith, fel, 1970-71; Fulbright-Hayes, fel, Japan, 1973-74; US Supreme Ct, judicial fel, 1978-79; SUNY, adj prof, polit sci, Dept Afro-Am studies, 1970, Dept polit sci, adj prof, 1979; Rochester City Sch Dist, Mentor, 1980-2000; Rochester Inst Technol, Col Lib Arts, dean, 1988-98, prof polit sci, 1998-94, emer dean & prof. **Orgs:** Woodrow Wilson fel, 1962-63; Pres, Nat Conf Black Polit Scientists, 1972-73; vol mediator, 1981-88, chmn bd dir, Citizens law, order & justice, 1986-88; vpres, Am Polit Sci Asn, 1990-91; Asn Am Col; Am Asn Higher Educ; bd Chair, Rochester, Nat Urban League; Bd Chair, Hillside C's Ctr; arbitrator & mediator, Ctr Dispute Settlement; active mem, Rochester Inst Technol, 2012-; bd mem, Urban League Rochester NY Inc. **Home Addr:** 18 Audubon St, Rochester, NY 14610, **Home Phone:** (585)442-6017. **Business Addr:** Emeritus Professor, Emeritus Dean, Rochester Institute of Technology, 1 Lomb Mem Dr, Rochester, NY 14623-5603, **Business Phone:** (585)475-2938.

## DANIELS, WILLIE L.

Stockbroker, chief executive officer, founder (originator). **Career:** Bache Securities Inc, stockbroker; United Daniels Securities Inc, chief exec officer & founder, 1984-97. **Business Addr:** Chief Executive Officer, Founder, United Daniels Securities Inc, PO Box 617521, Orlando, FL 32861-7521.

## DANIELS-CARTER, VALERIE

President (organization). **Personal:** son of John and Katherine; married Jeffrey; children: Jeffrey. **Educ:** Lincoln Univ, BA, bus admin, 1978; Cardinal Stritch Col, Milwaukee, MBA, mgt, 1982. **Career:** Wis Nat Bank, retail & com lender, 1978; MGIC Invest Corp, auditor, 1981; Pizza Hut restaurants, 1997; V&J Holding Co Inc, pres & ceo, currently; Minority Franchise Assn Burger King Corp, pres, currently. **Orgs:** Star Bank; exec bd mem, Nat Franchisee Asn; Diversity Action Coun, Burger King corp; regional minister music, Church God Christ; U.S. Bank; AAA Mich & Wis Inc; Holy Redeemer Church God Christ; chief financial officer, Auxiliaries Ministries Church God Christ; Firstar Bank; Auto Club Group; AAA Wis; US Bank; Christian Stewardship Found; bd dir, Holy Redeemer Church God Christ. **Business Addr:** President, Chief Executive officer, V & J Holding Companies Inc, 6933 W Brown Deer Rd, Milwaukee, WI 53226, **Business Phone:** (414)365-9003.

## DANSBY, JESSE L., JR.

Educator. **Personal:** Born Aug 17, 1942, Bessemer, AL; son of Jesse L Sr and Ora L Martin; married Johnetta C Brazzell; children: Natasha Lynn & Mischa Anita. **Educ:** Tenn State Univ, BS, educ & biol, 1964; Univ Okla, Yale Univ, cert, human resource mgt, human rels, 1973; Univ Okla, MA, human rels, 1973; Indust Col Armed Forces, mgt cert, 1975; Air Command & Staff Col, mgt cert, 1977; Air Force Inst Tech Int Logistics, mgt cert, 1977. **Career:** Educator, Col Adminr (retired); Int Logistics Ctr, dir, Mid E & African prog, 1979-80; Defense Electronic Supply Ctr, dir installation serv, 1980-83; Kwang Ju Air Base S Korea, base comdr, 1983-84; HQ AirForce Logistics Command, dir inquiries & govt affairs off inspector gen, 1984-; Ind Univ, Richmond, IN, col adminr, dir diversity & multicultural affairs, 1989; Univ Ark, vis asst prof oper mgt, 2001. **Orgs:** Omega Phi Phi, 1962-; Greater Dayton Real Estate Investment Asn, 1980-; bd dir, Girl Scouts Am, 1982-; Indust Rel Asn, 1985-; Ancient EgyptianArabic Order Mystic Shrine. **Home Addr:** 1029 Collingtree Ct, McDonough, GA 30253-8808, **Home Phone:** (678)289-0721.

## DANTICAT, EDWIDGE

Writer, novelist. **Personal:** Born Jan 19, 1969, Port-au-Prince; daughter of Andre and Rose; married Fedo Boyer; children: Mira & Leila. **Educ:** Barnard Col, BA, fre lit, 1990; Brown Univ, MFA, creative writing, 1993. **Career:** Clinica Estetico, prod researcher; Soho Press, auth, currently; Courage & Pain, assoc producer; Books: Breath, Eyes, Memory, 1994; Krik? Krak!, 1996; The Farming of Bones, 1998, 1999; A Community of Equals, 1999; The Book of the Dead, 1999; Their Eyes Were Watching God, 2000; The Butterfly's Way, 2001; Walking on Fire, 2001; In the Flicker of an Eyelid, 2002; Behind the Mountains, 2002, 2004; After the Dance, 2002; The Dew Breaker, 2004; The Royal Diaries, 2005; Anacaona: Golden Flower Haiti 1490, 2005; Brother I'm Dying, 2007; Ghosts, 2008; Create Dangerously: The Immigrant Artist at Work, 2010; Haiti Noir, ed, 2011; Claire of the Sea Light, 2013; Film: Poto Mitan, writer, 2009; Girl Rising, writer, 2013. **Orgs:** Alpha Kappa Alpha Sorority Inc. **Honors/Awds:** Pushcart Short Story Prize, "Between the Pool & the Gardenias", 1995; Essence Fiction Award; Caribbean Writer Fiction Prize; Seventeen Mag Fiction Prize; Woman of Achievement Award, Barnard Col, 1995; Best Young American Novelists, "Breath, Eyes, Memory", 1996; American Book Award, The Farming of the Bones, 1999; The International Flaiano Prize; The Super Flaiano Prize, The Farming of the Bones; The Story Prize, "The Dew Breaker", 2005; The National Book Critics Circle Award, "Brother, I'm Dying", 2007; Dayton Literary Peace Prize, "Brother, I'm Dying", 2008; 15 Gutsiest Women of the Year, Jane Magazine; Langston Hughes Medal, City Col New York, 2011; OCM Bocas Prize, 2011; Honorary Degree, Smith Col, 2012; Honorary Degree, Yale Univ, 2013. **Business Addr:** Author, Soho Press, 853 Broadway, New York, NY 10003, **Business Phone:** (212)260-1900.

## DANTLEY, ADRIAN DELANO

Basketball player, athletic coach. **Personal:** Born Feb 28, 1956, Washington, DC; son of Geraldine Robinson and Avon; married Dinitri; children: Cameron, Kalani & Kayla. **Educ:** Univ Notre Dame, attended 1976. **Career:** Basketball player (retired), basketball coach; Buffalo Braves, 1976-77; Ind Pacers, 1977; Los Angeles Lakers, 1977-79; Utah Jazz, 1979-86; Detroit Pistons, 1986-89; Dallas Mavericks, 1989-90; Milwaukee Bucks, 1990-91; Breeze Milano, Italy, 1991-92; Towson Univ, asst coach, 1993-96; Denver Nuggets, asst coach, 2009-10; Eastern Mid Sch, guard, 2013-; Montgomery County Recreation League, referee. **Home Addr:** 9 Barn Ridge Ct, Silver Spring, MD 20906-1105, **Home Phone:** (301)924-4528. **Business Addr:** Guard, Eastern Middle School, 300 Univ Blvd E, Silver Spring, MD 20901, **Business Phone:** (301)650-6650.

## DANZY, PATRICIA LYNN

Consultant. **Personal:** Born Jul 26, 1958, Canton, OH; daughter of John Ball and Ruth; married Terry; children: DeWayne, Brian & Jamielle. **Educ:** Am Acad Procedural Coders, CPC, 1997. **Career:** MacDonald Psysicians Inc, client servs analyst, currently. **Orgs:** Coder, Am Acad Prof Coders, 1997. **Honors/Awds:** Good Hands Award, Allstate Ins Co, 1993, Performance Bonus, 1995, 1996. **Business Addr:** Professional Coding Consultant, Danzy Coding Consultants, 808 E Decker Dr, Seven Hills, OH 44131, **Business Phone:** (216)548-6454.

**DAPREMONT, DELMONT O., JR.**
Automotive executive. **Career:** Coastal Ford Inc, automobile dealer. **Business Addr:** Dealer, Coastal Ford Inc, 7311 Airport Blvd, Mobile, AL 36608, **Business Phone:** (205)344-4000.

**DAR, KIRBY DAVID DAR**
Football player, businessperson. **Personal:** Born Mar 27, 1972, Morgan City, LA; son of Kirby Sr. **Educ:** Syracuse Univ, attended 1995. **Career:** Football player (retired), coach, real estate agent; Miami Dolphins, wide receiver, 1995-98; New York/NJ Hitmen, XLF, 2001; Syracuse Soldiers, AIFL, head coach, 2006; HSBC, bus develop specialist, 2006-08; prog dir, 2011-; real estate agt, currently. **Home Addr:** PO Box 2872, Syracuse, NY 13220.

**DARA, OLU (CHARLES JONES, III)**
Musician. **Personal:** Born Jan 12, 1941, Natchez, MS; children: Nasir Jones (Nas). **Educ:** Tenn State Univ. **Career:** Trumpet player & coronetist; Okra Orchestra; Natchezsippi Dance Band; Actor: Kansas City, 1996; TV series: Mountain Stage, 2001; Jimmy Kimmel Live!, 106 & Park Top 10 Live, 2004; Solo albums: In the World: From Natchez to New York, 1998; Neighborhoods, 2001; Medicated Magic, 2002; Chinatown, 2003; Soundtrack: Civil Brand (writer: "Strange Things Happen Everyday" / performer: "Strange Things Happen Everyday"), 2002; A Prophet (performer: "Bridging the Gap"), 2009. **Honors/Awds:** New York Jazz Award for Stylistic Fusion; France's Django d'Or International Trophy in Blues category; three Audelco Awards; a Drama Desk nomination for "I Am a Man" by OyamO; induction into the Mississippi Musicians Hall of Fame, 2003. **Special Achievements:** Played with Art Blakely, Henry Threadgill, David Murray Octet, Don Pullen,Cassandra Wilson; staged "Blues Rooms" to strong acclaim in New York City and Fairfax, VA during the 1990s; First became known as a jazz musician. **Business Addr:** Musician, c/o Atlantic Records, 1290 Avenue of the Americas, New York, NY 10104, **Business Phone:** (212)707-2261.

**DARBY, DR. EMMA TURNER LUCAS**
School administrator, educator. **Personal:** Born Feb 5, 1949, Meridian, MS; children: Kamilah Aisha. **Educ:** Tougaloo Col, BA, 1970; Purdue Univ, MA, polit sci & govt, 1972; Univ Pittsburgh, MSW, social work, 1978, PhD, 1986. **Career:** Planned Parenthood, counr, 1973-75; St Francis Hosp, rehab specialist, 1975-76; Chatham Col, dir black studies, 1976-79, assoc vpres acad affairs, 1979-84; Presby Home C, consult, 1982-90; Carlow Univ, assoc prof, 1984-, prof, social work & Assoc Dean Sch Social Chg, 1994-2011; Community Col Allegheny Co, brd dir, 1998; Surface Stripe-ing & Painting LLC, co owner, 2003-; RIGHT Develop LLC, co owner, 2008-. **Orgs:** Bd dirs, YWCA Pittsburgh, 1982-86; pres, Pittsburgh Chap, Asn Study Afro-Am Life & Hist, 1983; bd dir, Training Wheels C Ctr, 1984-88; PA Blacks Higher Educ, 1987-; secy & pres, Nat Asn Social Workers; bd secy, Pittsburgh Coun Pub Educ; Girl Scouts SW Pa, 1988-90; Youth Build Pittsburgh, 1998-2000. **Honors/Awds:** Pittsburgh Professor Award, Talk Mag, 1982; TV prod, Career Trends for the 80's, 1983; Meritorious Service Award, Juvenile Ct Judges Comn & the Pa Coun; NIH Grant. **Home Addr:** 523 Arthur St, Pittsburgh, PA 15219. **Business Addr:** Co-Owner, Surface Stripe-ing and Painting LLC, 566 Soho St, Pittsburgh, PA 15219, **Business Phone:** (412)391-1886.

**DARBY, MATTHEW LAMONT**
Football player. **Personal:** Born Nov 19, 1968, Virginia Beach, VA; married Cheryl; children: Matthew & Marcus. **Educ:** Univ Calif, Los Angeles, BS, Afro-Am studies. **Career:** Football player (retired); Buffalo Bills, defensive back, 1992-93, 1995, free safety, 1994; Ariz Cardinals, strong safety, 1996-97. **Honors/Awds:** College Football All-American, 1991. **Home Addr:** 501 Sagecreek Ct, Winter Springs, FL 32708-2731, **Home Phone:** (407)327-7836.

**DARDEN, ANTHONY KOJO**
Manager. **Personal:** Born Jan 10, 1943, Birmingham, AL; son of Samuel (deceased) and Annie B Harris (deceased); children: 2. **Educ:** Wayne State Univ, AA, psychol, 1974, MA, social work, 1984; Detroit Inst Tech, BA, psychol, 1976. **Career:** Wayne State Univ, real estate, laws & sales, 1973; Wayne County Comt Col, Recognition Orgn first stud govt struct, managing ed, 1973, pres, 1974; Omaha Ins Co, ins, rules & law, 1975; Amway Corp, networking mkt, art & sci, 1989; City Detroit, prin cot serv, asst; Enterprising Bus Assoc Mkt, chmn; Mattah Movement, vpres, currently; Learning Unlimited Co LLC, dir & coordr, 2005-; PAOCC Africa Develop Group, dir, 2010-; D & D Enterprise Group LLC, owner. **Orgs:** Bd chair, 24 Hour Store Mkt Assoc; Shrine Black Madonna. **Special Achievements:** Co-organizer "The Open Door"; 25 Year of Service, Shrine of the Black Madonna. **Home Addr:** 2968 S Liddesdale St, Detroit, MI 48217-1113, **Home Phone:** (313)528-8201. **Business Addr:** Vice President, The Mattah Movement, 4911 Georgia Ave NW, Washington, DC 20011-4525, **Business Phone:** (202)723-3358.

**DARDEN, CALVIN RAMARRO**
Executive, vice president (organization), chairperson. **Personal:** Born Feb 5, 1950, Buffalo, NY; married Patricia Gail; children: Calvin Ramarro Jr, Tami & Lorielle. **Educ:** Canisius Col, BS, bus mgt, 1972; Emory Univ, Exec Develop Consortium, 1997. **Career:** United Parcel Serv ctr, customer serv supvr, 1974, sr exec, dist mgr N Nj, 1984-86, dist mgr Metro Jersey, 1986-91, dist mgr Metro Dist Columbia, 1991-93, vpres Pac region, 1993-95, vpres & corp strategic qual coordr, 1995-97, sr vpres, 1998-2005; Atlanta Beltline Inc, chmn, 2006-09; Darden Develop Group LLC, founder, chmn, 2009-15. **Orgs:** Pres, African Am Unity Ctrs; Atlanta Chap, 1996; Nat Urban League, 1997; Nat Urban League Black Exec Exchange Prog; 100 Black Men Metro, atlanta; chmn, deacons, Deliverance Temple Church God & Christ Atlanta, Ga; United Way Long Beach, Calif; bd dir, target Corp, Coca-Cola Enterprises; bd mem, Urban League Nat; bd mem, United Parcel Serv, 2001-05; Bd Target, 2003-; bd dir, Coca Cola Enterprises, 2004-; bd Cardinal Health, 2005-; bd mem, Atlanta Beltline Inc; chair bd trustee, vice chmn, Atlanta Police Found. **Home Addr:** 8155 Sentinae Chase Dr, Roswell, GA 30076, **Home Phone:** (770)993-3511. **Business Addr:** Boards of Trustee, Atlanta Police Foundation, 127 Peachtree St, Atlanta, GA 30303.

**DARDEN, DR. CHRISTINE MANN**
Aerospace engineer. **Personal:** Born Sep 10, 1942, Monroe, NC; daughter of Noah Horace Sr and Desma Chaney Mann; married Walter L Jr; children: Jeanne Riley & Janet Christine. **Educ:** Hampton Inst, BS, math, 1962, cert, teaching; Va State Col, MS, math, 1967; George Washington Univ, DSc, mech engineering, 1983. **Career:** Educator, administrator (retired); Russell High Sch, mathinstructor, 1962-63; Brunswick Co Sch, teacher, 1962-63; Norcom High Sch, teacher, 1964-65; Portsmouth City Sch, Va, teacher, 1964-65; Va State Col, math instr, 1966-67; NASA Langley Res Ctr, data analyst, 1967-73, aerospace eng, tech leader, sonic boom group, 1989-92, sr proj engr, advan vehicles div, dep prog mgr, HSR TU-144 prog, 1994-99, Aero Performing, dir, LARC asst dir planning, 2002-04, Off Strategic Communs & Educ, dir, 2004-07; Simmons Col, sr exec career develop fel, 1994. **Orgs:** Gamma Upsilon Omega Chap AKA, 1960-; Nat Langley Exchange Coun, 1979-; elder carver mem, Presby Ch, 1980-; chmn, Boundaries Comm Southern Va Presby Church, USA, 1983-88; pres, Hampton Roads Chap, Nat Tech Asn, 1984-88; moderator, Synod Mid-Atlantic Presby Churches, 1989-90; chmn, Presbytery Coun, Easter Va Presbytery, 1990-; secy, Aerocoustics Tech Comt, 1990-91, Am Inst Aeronaut & Astronauts; nat secy, Nat Tech Asn, 1990-92. **Honors/Awds:** The 20 Year Alumnus Award, Hampton Inst, 1982; Dr AT Weathers Tech Achievement Award, Nat Tech Asn, 1985; Dollars & Sense Mag, 100 Top Black Bus & Professional Women, 1986; Candace Award for Science & Technology, Nat Coalition 100 Black Women. 1987; Technol Transfer, NASA, 1990; Technical Achievements & Humanitarian Efforts, NC State Univ, 1990; NASA, EEO Medal, 1991; Dual Career Ladder Award, NASA Langley Research Center, 1991; Outstanding Women in Government Award, Women Sci & Eng, 1992; Langley Engineering Achievement Award, 1994. **Special Achievements:** Author or co-author of over 54 technical reports and articles. **Home Addr:** 1028 Barry Ct, Hampton, VA 23666, **Home Phone:** (757)838-7890.

**DARDEN, CHRISTOPHER ALLEN**
Writer, lawyer. **Personal:** Born Apr 7, 1956, Martinez, CA; son of Eddie and Jean; married Marcia Carter; children: Jenee, Chase, Christopher Jr & Tiffany. **Educ:** San Jose State Univ, BS, criminal justice admin, 1977; Univ Calif, Hastings Col Law, LLD, 1980. **Career:** Nat Labor Rels Bd, atty, 1980-81; Los Angeles Co Dist Attys Off, dep dist atty & prosecutor, 1981-95; Los Angeles Co, Spec Invests Div, asst head dep, 1988; Calif State Univ, fac; Southwestern Univ Sch Law, assoc prof, 1995-99; Darden & Assocs Inc, atty, 2000-; FOXX FIRM, coun, currently; writer: Contempt, co auth, 1996; Trials Nikki Hill, co auth, 1999; LA Justice, co auth, 2000; publ, Last Defense, 2002. **Orgs:** Fel Calif State Bar, 1980-; Los Angeles Co Asn Dep Dist Attys, 1986-87; pres & dir, Loved Ones Homicide Victims, 1987-; Nat Black Prosecutors Asn, 1989; Calif Bar, Criminal Law Sect, Exec Comt, 1994-97; John M Langston Bar Asn, 1995; life mem, Alpha Phi Alpha; Greek-lett fraternity; life mem, Nat Bar Asn; life mem, Am Trial Lawyers Asn. **Business Addr:** Attorney, Darden & Associates Inc, 5757 W Century Blvd Suite 700, Los Angeles, CA 90045, **Business Phone:** (310)568-1804.

**DARDEN, EDWIN CARLEY (EDWIN C DARDEN)**
School administrator. **Personal:** Born Sep 13, 1960, New York, NY; son of Eddie and Lee; married Lori; children: Leandra Ebonique & Jay Spenser. **Educ:** State Univ NY, Col Arts & Sci Geneseo, BA, Eng, 1981; Georgetown Univ Law Ctr, JD, 1997. **Career:** Capitol Publ, legal reporter, 1988-89; Georgetown Univ Law Ctr, assoc dir pub rels, 1989-97; Levi, Perry, Simmons & Loots, assoc atty, 1997-98; NY State Sch Brd Assn, sr staff atty, 1998-2002, Ctr Urban Schs Prog, dir, 2003-05; Nat Sch Boards Asn, sr staff atty, 1999-2003; NY sch bd Asn, Ctr Urban Schs Progs, dir, 2003-05; EdAdvocacy, founder; Ed Advocacy, managing partner, 2005-11; Appleseed, educ policy dir, 2006-14; Session Law Firm P.C, staff, currently; Bill & Melinda Gates Found, sr prog officer, 2015-. **Orgs:** Fed Bar Assn, 1996-; Am Bar Assn, 1997-; Nat Alliance Black Sch Educr, 1998-; pres, Educ Law Assn, 1998-; Parent Pub Schs Adv Bd; Mid-Atlantic Equity Assistance Ctr; Va Bar Assn, 1998-; chmn, Fairfax County Coun PTA Educ Comt, 1999-2000, vpres, 2000-; Nat Bar Asn. **Honors/Awds:** Educ Press Award First Place for Service, Educ Press As sn, 1988; Silver Inkwell Award, Intl Assn Bus Communicators, 1991; Coun Advan & Support Educ, Minority Prof Scholar, 1992; Americans United Separation Church & State, Madison-Jefferson Scholar, 1993. **Special Achievements:** Co-ed: Legal Issues & Educ Technol: A Sch Leaders Guide; US Supreme Ct brief: Eisenberg v Montgomery County Schs. **Home Addr:** 604 Stream Lane, Slingerlands, NY 12159-3008, **Home Phone:** (518)869-6964. **Business Addr:** Education Policy Director, Appleseed, 727 15th St NW 11th Fl, Washington, DC 20005, **Business Phone:** (202)347-7960.

**DARDEN, DR. JOSEPH SAMUEL, JR.**
Educator. **Personal:** Born Jul 25, 1925, Pleasantville, NJ; son of Joseph S Sr and Blanche Paige; married Barbara Cassandra Sellers; children: Michele Irene Darden Burgess. **Educ:** Lincoln Univ, AB, 1948; NY Univ, MA, 1952, EdD, 1963. **Career:** Clark Col, instr Biol Sci, 1952-55; Albany State Col, asst prof, Biol & Health Educ, 1955-64, chmn sci div, 1959-60; Kean Col NJ, prof & coordr, Health Educ, 1964-2002, chair, Health & Rec Dept, 1979-84; dir, Minority Enrollment, 1988-94, prof emer, 2003; Wagner Col, adj prof, 1966-88; Rutgers Univ, adj prof, Sex Educ, 1974-75; Mont Clair State Col, coun & educ leadership, 1975. **Orgs:** Vpres, Health Educ NJ Asn Am Alliance Health Phys Educ Recreation Dance, 1967; founder, NJ Health Educ Coun, 1967; ed bd, J Sch Health ASHA, 1969-72; vpres & chmn, Health Educ Div E DistAsn Am Alliance Health Phys Educ Recreation Dance, 1971-72; mem adv bd, Health Educ Am Alliance Health Phys Educ Recreation Dance, 1973-76; pres, E Dist Asn AAHPERD, 1974-75; gov coun Am Sch Health Asn, 1970-73; auth, lectr, workshop dir, radio & TV panelistsex educ; bd dir, Asn Advan Health Educ, 1975-78; E Dist Rep Alliance Bd, 1979-82; NJ Am Alliance Health Phys Educ Recreation Dance; Am Social Health Asn; SIECUS, Am Asn Sex Educrs, Counrs & Therapists; bd trustee, Planned Parenthood Metrop NJ; dipl, Am Bd Sexology, 1990-2000; founding fel Am Asn Health Educ, 1998. **Honors/Awds:** Distinguished Service Award, Am Sch Health Asn, 1971; Hon Fellow Award, NJ Asn Health, Physical Educ & Recreation, 1972; Hon Award, NJ Health Educ Coun, 1975; Distinguished Leadership Award, NJ Asn Health, Physical Educ & Recreation, 1975; Distinguished Service Award, Alpha Alpha Lambda Chap Alpha Phi Alpha, 1975; Dist Hon Award, E Dist Asn Am Alliance Health Physical Educ Recreation Dance, 1976; Outstanding Col & Univ Teacher of the Year, Eastern Dist Asn Am Alliance Health Physical Educ Recreation Dance, 1983; Alliance Hon Award, Am Alliance Health Physical Educ Recreation Dance, 1985; Charles D Henry Award, Am Alliance Health Physical Educ Recreation Dance, 1988; Prof Serv to Health Educ Award, Am Asn Health Educ & Am Alliance Health Physical Educ Recreation Dance, 1990; Edwin B Henderson Award, EMC, Am Alliance Health Physical Educ Recreation Dance, 1991; The Alumni Achievement Award, Lincoln Univ, 1993; Presidential Citation, Am Asn Health Educ & Am Alliance Health Physical Educ Recreation Dance, 1996. **Special Achievements:** Author: "Toward A Healthier Sexuality: A Book of Readings", 1996; ed, "Critical Health Issues Reader, Dubuque, Iowa", 2002, numerous articles and publications in state, regional & national. **Home Addr:** 1416 Thelma Dr, Union, NJ 07083, **Home Phone:** (908)688-5699.

**DARITY, JANKI EVANGELIA**
Manager, health services administrator. **Personal:** Born Beirut; daughter of William and Evangeline. **Educ:** Spelman Col, BA, polit sci, econs, 1980; Univ Tex, Austin Sch Law, JD, 1983; Harvard Univ, Sch Pub Health, MPH, policy & mgt, 1984. **Career:** Campbell, Davidson & Morgan, law clerk, 1981-82; Bechtel Group Inc, law clerk, 1982; Southern Union Gas Co, law clerk, 1983; Harper Hosp, admin fel, hosp admin, 1984-87; Mich Health & Hosp Asn, asst dir, legal & regulatory affairs, 1987-89; Henry Ford Hosp, dir urban health initiative, 1989-91; Henry Ford Health Systs, vpres, 1989-2000, corp dir community health develop, 1992-94, vp community develop, 1994-98, vpres community & bus develop, 1998; Consumers Union, atty, policy analyst, 2001-03; Kaiser Permanente, strategy develop & execution, mgt consult, 2003-07; Clorox Co, legal serv, legal proj mgr, 2007-. **Orgs:** Alpha Kappa Alpha Sorority Inc, 1979; Nat Bar Asn, 1981; Nat Health Lawyers Asn, 1983; Nat Asn Health Serv Execs, 1984; chair, Detroit Rotary Club Int, 1992; Womens Econ Club, 1992; 1st vpres bd dir, In-Site Horizon Field Trips Inc, 1992; Leadership Oakland, chair race & ethnic diversity steering community, 1993-97; bd dir, United Cerebral Palsy Metro Der, 1993-97; Leadership MI, 1993-94; Am Asn Univ Women, 1993; Leadership Am Alumni Asn, 1994; Asn Healthcare Philanthropy, 1994; Jr League Birmingham, 1996; Generation Promise bd dir, 1996-98; co-chair, Detroit United Negro Col Fund, Walk-A-Thon, 1997-98; chmn, Corp Develop, 1998; Harvard Club San Francisco. **Home Addr:** 5405 Carlton St Apt 204, Oakland, CA 94618, **Home Phone:** (510)654-5899. **Business Addr:** Legal Project Manager, The Clorox Co, 1221 Broadway, Oakland, CA 94612, **Business Phone:** (510)271-7147.

**DARITY, DR. WILLIAM ALEXANDER, SR.** **See Obituaries Section.**

**DARK, OKIANER CHRISTIAN**
Educator. **Personal:** Born Dec 8, 1954, Petersburg, VA; daughter of Marshall Christian Sr and Vivian Louise Rier Christian; married Lawrence; children: Harrison Edward. **Educ:** Upsala Col, E Orange, NJ, magna cum laude, BA, 1976; Rutgers Univ Sch Law, Newark, NJ, JD, 1979. **Career:** US Dept Justice, Antitrust Div, trial atty, 1979-84, Civil Div, trialatty, 1984; Dc, Spec Asst Us Atty; Portland, Ore, Asst Us Atty; Univ Richmond Law Sch, TC Williams Sch law, asst prof, 1984-87, from assoc prof to prof, Antitrust, 1987-90; Am Univ, Wash Col Law, vis prof & scholar, 1991-92; Willamette Univ Col Law, vis prof, 1994-95; US Atty's Off, asst USatty, 1995-2001; Howard Univ, Sch Law, assoc dean acad affairs, prof & interim dean, 2001-, Med Sch, Health Ethics course, lectr, legal issues health law. **Orgs:** Nat Bar Asn; adv bd, NBA Mag, 1988-; bd mem, Daily Planet, 1989-94; St Pauls Baptist Church, 1989-94; bd dir, Va Black Women Attorneys Asn, 1990-94; Penn State Bar Asn; NJ State Bar Asn; Va State Bar Asn; Ore State Bar Asn; Task Force Gender Fairness; bd trustee, YMCA, Portland, OR; bd dir, chair, NW Health Found; Link, Silver Spring chap; Mt Olivet Baptist Church; vice chair, chair, Montgomery County Comn Health, 2002-05; Peoples Community Baptist Church, Silver Spring, MD; bd mem, Soc Am Law Teachers; Montgomery County Adv Bd, Montgomery Cares Prog, currently; bd mem, Community Found Montgomery; pres, Links Inc, Silver Spring Chap; Peoples Community Baptist Church; bd trustee, law Sch Admis Coun; mem chair & standing comts, Asn Am Law Schs; Diversity Comt, ABA Sect Legal Educ & Bar; Nat Comn Fair Housing & Opportunity, 2008. **Special Achievements:** First African American tenured at the law school and the first African American woman tenured at the University. **Home Addr:** 2504 Locustwood Pl, Silver Spring, MD 20905. **Business Addr:** Professor of Law, Interim Dean, Howard University School of Law, 203 Houston Hall, Washington, DC 20008, **Business Phone:** (202)806-8003.

**DARKCHILD, RJ.** **See JERKINS, RODNEY.**

**DARKE, DR. CHARLES B.**
Dentist. **Personal:** Born Sep 22, 1937, Chicago, IL; son of Paul Olden and Annie Waulene Tennin; married Annetta; children: Charles B II; married Judith. **Educ:** Wilson Jr Col, AA, 1960; Meharry Med Col, DDS, 1964; Univ Calif, MPH, 1972. **Career:** Dentist (retired); Hosp Appointments: Mt Zion Hosp, St Mary Hosp, San Francisco Gen Hosp; Career Highlights: Dept Labor Job Corp Region 9, dent consult; Univ Calif, Sch Med, asst clin prof; Univ Calif, Sch Dent, lectr; San Francisco Gen Hosp, dir dent serv; San Francisco Gen Hosp, Satellite Health Ctrs, asst admin; San Francisco Health Dept, opers officer; part time pvt pract dentist; Calif State Univ, Fullerton, Fullerton, Calif, exec dir stud health & coun ctr; Hayes St Dent Group, gen dentist; Kaiser Found Hosps, sr consult. **Orgs:** State Bd Dent Examiners Calif; dir, Dent Ser San Francisco Gen Hosp, divout patient & community serv; Am Health Care, consult prepaid health plans; bd dirs, Calif C's Lobby; field consult, Joint Comn Accreditation Hosps; past pres, Northern Calif, Nat Dent Asn; bd dirs, Yorba Hill Med Ctr; sci task force, Chapman Univ. **Honors/Awds:** Outstanding Young Men of America, 1973. **Home Addr:** 7008 E Columbus Dr, Anaheim, CA 92807-4527, **Home Phone:** (714)281-8316. **Business Addr:** General Dentist, Hayes Street Dental Group, 2175 Hayes St, San Francisco, CA 94117, **Business Phone:** (415)668-8005.

**DARKINS, CHRISTOPHER OJI**
**Personal:** Born Apr 30, 1974, San Francisco, CA; married Paula; children: Andre. **Educ:** Univ Minn. **Career:** Football player (retired): Green Bay Packers, running back, 1996-97. **Honors/Awds:** Champion Packers, Super Bowl, XXXI; Champion Packers, Nat Football League, 1997.

**DARLING, HELEN MARIE**
Basketball player. **Personal:** Born Aug 29, 1978, Columbus, OH; daughter of Donald and Patricia Smith; children: Ja-Juan, Jalen & Nevaeh. **Educ:** Pa State, educ, 2000. **Career:** Cleveland Rockers, WNBA guard, 2000-03; Minn Lynx, 2004; Univ Memphis, asst coach, 2005-06; Charlotte Sting, guard, 2005-06; San Antonio Silver Stars, guard, 2007-; Amateur Athletic Union, head coach; Lady Tiger guards, acad coordr. D1 Shooters 2020 Elite Team, asst coach, currently. Books: "Hide 'n Seek Mondays", 2007; "Yummy Tummy Tuesdays", 2008. **Orgs:** Vol, Make-A-Wish Found, 2007-2008. **Business Addr:** Professional Basketball Player, San Antonio Silver Stars, 1 AT&T Ctr Pkwy, San Antonio, TX 78219, **Business Phone:** (210)444-5050.

**DARLING, JAMES JACKSON**
Football player. **Personal:** Born Dec 29, 1974, Denver, CO. **Educ:** Wash State Univ. **Career:** Philadelphia Eagles, 2000, left linebacker, 1997-98, linebacker, 1999; New York Jets, 2001-02; Ariz Cardinals, linebacker, 2003, 2006, linebacker, 2004, middle linebacker, 2005; free agt, currently. **Honors/Awds:** Two-time All-Pacific Ten Conf selection, 1995-96.

**DARNELL, EDWARD BUDDY**
Manager. **Personal:** Born Mar 4, 1930, Chicago, IL; son of Edward and Mary; married Gwendolyn Wilson; children: Glenn T & Gary L. **Educ:** Detroit Inst Technol, BA, psychol, 1968; Wayne State Univ, MSW, social work, 1971; Univ Mich, specialist geront, 1971. **Career:** Director (retired); Ford Motor Co, staff; Detroit Pub Sch Syst, dir; State Mich, social worker; Detroit City Airport, Off Civil Defense, dir, Detroit City Air Port, dep dir, 1991. **Orgs:** Imp first ceremonial master, Imp Coun Shriners, 1988; secy, United Supreme Coun, 1977; hon fel Phylaxis Soc, pres & founder, Great Lakes Chap, Mich; Advan Colored People; charter mem, Mich Aviation Hall Fame; Govs Air Serv Task Force; United Supreme Coun Benevolent Found, Philadelphia, Penn; bd dir, United Community Serv, Detroit, Mich; mem bd trustee, Hartford Memorial Baptist Church. **Honors/Awds:** Legion of honor, Prince Hall Shriners, 1973; Scottish Rite Hall of Fame, Prince Hall Scottish Rite, 1984; Humanitarian of the Year Award, Florence Ames Chap, 1990; Lee J Barrett Award, Detroit Metrop Visitors & Conv Bur, 1990, 1997; Honorary Citizen of Lovisville, 1991; Seagram's Vanguard Award, 1994; Honorary title of Captain, Capitol Heights Police Dept, Capitol Heights, Md, 1994; Honorary Past Grand Master; Grand Recording Secretary, United Supreme Coun, currently; pres, founder, Eagles Club - Commanders Rite. **Special Achievements:** Who's Who Among Black Americans, 1974. **Home Addr:** 584 Woodland St, Detroit, MI 48202, **Home Phone:** (313)867-3796.

**DARTSON, DR. MYRNA VANESSA**
Educator, physicist. **Educ:** Tex A&M Univ, PhD, 1998. **Career:** Pvt pract psychologist, currently; Paul Quinn Col, Dallas, adj psychol prof; Univ personal success, fac, currently. **Orgs:** Salesmanship Club. **Business Addr:** Psychologist, 4038 Lemmon Ave Suite 103, Dallas, TX 75219-3736, **Business Phone:** (214)219-1116.

**DASH, DAMON**
Music producer, executive director, actor. **Personal:** Born May 3, 1971, Harlem, NY; married Rachel Roy; children: Ava & Talullah Ruth. **Career:** Armadale vodka, owner; America Mag, owner; Pro-Keds sneakers, owner; Team Roc, owner; Tiret Watches, owner; Rachel Roy Clothing Line, owner; Dash Management, owner; Dash Di Bella Boxing, owner; Roc-A-Fella Rec, Co-founder, 1995, chief exec officer, 2003-05, consult, currently; Roc-A-Wear clothing line & Roc-A-Fella Films, founder, 1998; Dame Dash Music Group, founder, 2004-; BET, "Ultimate Hustler", producer; Films: Backstage, producer, 2000; Highlander: Endgame, actor, 2000; Paper Soldiers, dir, 2002; Paid In Full, producer & actor, 2002; Death of a Dynasty, producer, actor & dir, 2003; Jay-Z in Concert, chief exec officer, 2003; The Woodsman, producer, 2004; State Property 2, actor, 2005; Shadowboxer, producer, 2005; State Property 2, writer, dir & actor, 2005; Weapons, co-producer, 2007; Tennessee, exec producer, 2008; This Is Jim Jones, dir & exec producer, 2009; Red Apples Falling, actor & exec producer, 2009; Welcome to Blakroc, exec producer, 2009. **Orgs:** Juvenile Diabetes Res Found; Am Diabetes Asn. **Business Addr:** Owner, Dash Films, 825 8th Ave, New York, NY 10019-7472, **Business Phone:** (212)907-8031.

**DASH, DARIEN C.**
Executive. **Personal:** Born Jan 1, 1972?, New York, NY; son of Dennis and Linda; married Deborah; children: 3. **Educ:** Univ Southern Calif, BA, polit sci & leadership, 1993. **Career:** Digital Music Express, vpres sales, 1990; DME Interactive Holdings, pres, 1993-95, chmn, founder, chief exec officer, 1995-; Digital Mafia LLC, chief exec officer; VidShadow.com Inc, chief exec officer, 1999-. **Orgs:** Making Opportunities Upgrading Schs & Educ; pres, Alpha Phi Alpha Inc. **Business Addr:** Founder, Chief Executive Officer, DME Interactive Holdings Inc, 39 Broadway, New York, NY 10006, **Business Phone:** (212)422-6600.

**DASH, DR. HUGH M. H.**
Health services administrator. **Personal:** Born Feb 19, 1943, Brooklyn, NY; married Patricia Morris; children: Angela & Phillip. **Educ:** Morehouse Col, bus admin, 1969; Howard Univ, exec mgt, 1974; Ga State Univ, MA, pub health, 1984, PhD, 1992. **Career:** Citizens Trust Bank, com lending & credit officer, 1972-72; Interracial Coun Bus Opportunity, dep exec dir, 1972-75; Southern Conf Black Mayors, sr econ develop, 1975-76; Enterprises Now Inc, exec vpres, 1976-80; Prudential Health Care, regional dir & qual improv, 1980-; A Catalyst To Qual, owner; Hugh Dash & Co Inc, chief exec officer & chief financial officer; Metro Atlanta Off Supply Inc, chief exec officer. **Orgs:** Leadership Atlanta, 1978-; bd mem & pres, Atlanta Bus League, 1978-79, 1985; treas, White House Conf Small Bus, 1979-80. **Home Addr:** 1374 Dodson Dr SW, Atlanta, GA 30311, **Home Phone:** (404)758-0039. **Business Addr:** Regional Director, Quality Improvement, Prudential Health Care, 2859 Paces Ferry Rd Suite 330, Atlanta, GA 30339.

**DASH, JULIE**
Movie producer, movie director. **Personal:** Born Oct 22, 1952, Long Island, NY; married Arthur Jafa; children: Nzinga. **Educ:** City Col New York, BA, film prod, 1974; Am Film Inst, producing & writing fel, 1975, multimedia workshops, 1995; Univ Calif, Los Angeles, MFA, motion picture & tv prod, 1986. **Career:** Director, writer & producer; guest lectures, 1983-2000; Films: Working Models of Success, dir, 1973; Four Women, ed & dir, 1975; Diary of an African Nun, dir & ed, 1977; Illusions, ed, dir, writer & producer, 1982; Daughters of the Dust, dir, writer & producer, 1991; Praise House, 1991; Brothers of the Border, dir, 2004; Tupelo 77; Zora Neale Hurston: Jump at the Sun, producer, 2008; The Scarapist, 2009; Making Angels, 2010; TV series: Women: Stories of Passion, writer, dir & producer, 1997; Subway Stories: Tales from the Underground, writer, dir & producer, 1997; Funny Valentines, dir, 1999; Incognito, dir, 1999; Love Song, dir, 2000; The Rosa Parks Story, dir, 2002; Music Video: Thinking Of You, 1997; Love Is All Around, 1997; Geechee Girls Multimedia, founder, currently. **Orgs:** Hon mem, Alpha Kappa Alpha Sorority. **Honors/Awds:** Numerous honors & awards including Maya Deren Award, AFI; Black American Cinema Society Award for Illusions, 1985; Cinematography Award, Sundance Film Festival, 1991; Mirabella's 100 Fearless Women; Delta Sigma Theta Sorority's Lillian Award; Sojourner Truth Award; National Conference of Black Mayor's Literary Award; M.E.N.T.O.R Networks Award; Liberty Bell, The Coalition of 100 Black Women; The Black Oscar; Candace Award, Black Filmmaker's Hall of Fame; Women in Film Dorothy Arzner Award; Cinematography Award, Sun dance Film Festival; Third World Film Festival Award; Oscar Micheaux Award, Black Filmmaker's Hall of Fame; Black Cinema Society Award & Miami International Film Festival-Gold Medal; NAACP Image Award, 2002; Excellence in Cinematography Award, Cascade Festival African Films, 2005; USA Rockefeller Foundation Fellow, 2007; Family Television Award; New York Christopher Award; Guild Awards. **Special Achievements:** First African American woman to have a full-length general theatrical release in the United States; Book: Daughters Of The Dust: The Making Of An African American Woman's Film, 1992; Daughters of the Dust: A Novel, 1997; First African-American woman nominated in the category of Primetime Movies Made for Television. **Business Addr:** Director, Kino International Corp, 333 W 39th St Suite 503, New York, NY 10018, **Business Phone:** (212)629-6880.

**DASH, PROF. LEON DECOSTA**
Journalist, educator. **Personal:** Born Mar 16, 1944, New Bedford, MA; son of Leon Sr and Ruth; children: Darla & Destiny. **Educ:** Howard Univ, BA, hist, 1968. **Career:** Wash Post, reporter, 1966-71; W African Bur, chief, 1979-84, investigative reporter, 1984-98; Kenya Peace Corps, teacher, 1968-70; Univ Calif, San Diego, vis prof, 1978; Henry J Kaiser Family Found, fel, 1995-96; Univ Ill, Col Commun, Journalism & Afro-Am Studies, prof, 1998-2000, chair prof, 2000-01, Swanlund chair prof, 2002-03, Ctr Advan Studies, fac, 2003-09, Ctr Advan Studies, dir, 2009-14. **Orgs:** Co-founder, 1975-, fac advisor, 1998-, Nat Asn Black Journalist; Nat Ctr Disability & Journalism, 2010-. **Honors/Awds:** Robert F Kennedy Award, 1973; George Polk Award, Overseas Press Club, 1974; Balt-Wash Guild Award, 1974; Reporting Award, Capitol Press Club Intl, 1984; Africare Inter Nat Reporting Award, 1984; Distinguished Service Award, Md Social Serv Admin, 1986; General News Award, Nat Asn Black Journalists, 1986; Public Service Award, Wash-Baltimore Newspaper Guild, 1987; First Place Award, Investigative Reporters & Ed Orgn, 1987; President's Award, Wash Independent Writers, 1989; Special Citation, PEN Martha Al brand Nonfiction for "When Children Want Children"; Pulitzer Prize, Explanatory Jour, 1995; First Prize for Print, Robert F Kennedy Award, 1995; Media Fel, Henry J Kaisr Family Found, 1995-96; DHL, Lincoln Univ, 1996; Emmy Award, Nat Acad TV Arts & Sci, DC Chap, 1996; first prize, Harry Chapin Best Book Media Award, The World Hunger Year Orgn; Political Book Award, Wash Monthly Mag; Prevention for a Safer Society Literature Award, Nat Coun Crime & Delinquency, 1997; Teacher of the Year Award, Univ Ill, 2006. **Special Achievements:** Co-author: Shame of Prisons, 1972; author: When Children Want Children, 1989; Rosa Lee, 1996; Washington Post series, "Rosa Lee's Story". **Home Addr:** , IL. **Business Addr:** Swanlund Chair Professor of Journalism, Director, Center for Advanced Study, University of Illinois at Urbana-Champaign Center, 912 W Ill St, Urbana, IL 61801, **Business Phone:** (217)333-6729.

**DASH, STACEY LAURETTA**
Actor. **Personal:** Born Jan 20, 1966, Bronx, NY; daughter of Linda; married Brian Lovell, Jul 16, 1999, (divorced 2005); married James Maby, Feb 26, 2005, (divorced 2006); children: Lola & Austin; married Emmanuel Xuereb, Jan 1, 2007, (divorced 2010). **Career:** TV series: "Clueless", 1996-99; "The Strip", 1999; "A Pirate Looks at 15 to 20", 2001; "Eve", 2003; "Duck Dodgers", 2005; Secrets of a Hollywood Nurse, 2008; "American Dad!", 2008; "The Game", 2009; "Single Ladies", 2011; "The Exes", 2013. Films: Enemy Territory, 1987; Moving, 1988; Tenn Nights, 1989; Mo' Money, 1992; Renaissance Man, 1994; Illegal in Blue, 1995; Cold Around the Heart, 1997; Personals, 1999; Paper Soldiers, 2002; The Painting, 2002; View From the Top, 2003; Gangs of Roses, 2003; Ride or Die, 2003; Lethal Eviction, 2005; Getting Played, 2005; I Could Never Be Your Woman, 2007; Nora's Hair Salon II, 2008; Fashion Victim, 2008; Phantom Punch, 2009; Chrome Angels, 2009; Close Quarters, 2009; House Arrest, 2012; Dysfunctional Friends, 2012; Lap Dance, 2014; Patient Killer, 2014. **Honors/Awds:** Nominee, Young Artist Award, Best Young Supporting Actress - Feature Film for: Clueless (1995), 1996. **Business Addr:** Actress, PO Box 800487, Santa Clarita, CA 91380-0487.

**DATES, DR. JANNETTE LAKE**
Educator, college administrator. **Personal:** Born Jan 1, 1937?, Baltimore, MD; daughter of IMoses Lake and Lantha Alexander Lake; married Victor H; children: Karen, Victor Jr, Matthew & Craig. **Educ:** Coppin State Col, BS; Johns Hopkins Univ, MEd; Univ Md, College Park, PhD, educ admin, supv & curric, 1979. **Career:** Baltimore City Pub Sch Syst, classroom demonstration teacher, 1958-63, tv demonstration teacher, 1964-71; Morgan State Col & Goucher Col, instr, 1971-72; N Star TV ser, WBAL-TV, anchor & exec prod, 1972-73; Morgan State Univ, Commun Arts Prog, instr, 1972-77, coor dr tv proj, 1973-80, Dept Commun & Theater Arts, asst prof, 1977-80; WJZ-TV, panelist; Columbia Univ, Freedom Forum Media Studies Ctr, fel; Howard Univ, asst prof, 1981-85, Dept Radio, Tv & Film, Sch Commun, sequence coordr, 1981-85; State Col, Video Prod Serv, dir, 1985-87, Dept Lang, Lit & Jour, assoc prof, 1985-87, video prod serv dir, 1985-87; Howard Univ Sch Commun, assocdean, 1987-92, actg dean, 1993-96; Dept Radio, TV & Film, asst prof, 1981-85, assoc prof, 1990-98, prof, 1998-, John H Johnson Sch Commun, assoc dean, 1993-96, dean, 1996-2012; CPB Bd, 2013. **Orgs:** Comnr, Baltimore City Cable TV Comn, 1979-81; chairwoman, Educ Task Force, 1979-81; Baltimore Cable Access Corp, pres, 1982-86, vpres, 1986-88; Mayor's Cable Adv Comn, educ task force chairwoman, 1988-90; bd dir, Broadcast Educ Asn, Finance Comn, 1994, progchair, Nat Conf, 1996, bd dir, 1997-99, Secy treas bd, 1999-2000, vpres bd, 2000-01, pres bd dir, 2001-02; chmn, Black Col Commun Asn, 1997-2001; Vice-chmn, Accrediting Comt, Accrediting Coun Educ Jour & Mass Commun, 1998-99; vpres, Asn Educ Jour & Mass Commun, 2001-02, pres, 2003-04; Nat Black Media Coalition; Nat Commun Asn; Asn Commun Adminr; Speech Nat Commun Asn. **Home Addr:** 2107 Carterdale Rd, Baltimore, MD 21209, **Home Phone:** (410)664-8148.

**DATTY, JUNE.** **See DILLARD, DR. JUNE WHITE.**

**DAUGHTRY, REV. HERBERT DANIEL**
Clergy, public speaker. **Personal:** Born Jan 13, 1931, Savannah, GA; son of Alonzo Austin and Emmie Cheatham Williams; married Karen Ann Smith; children: Leah, Sharon, Dawnique & Herbert Jr. **Career:** African Peoples Christian Org, pres, 1982-; Nat Campaign Comm Rev Jesse Jackson, spec asst & confidant, 1983-84; The House Lord Churches, nat presiding minister, currently; Interdenominational Theol Sem, preacher; Mo Better Jaguars Football Team, mentor & pres; New York Jets football team, unofficial chaplain. **Orgs:** Bd dir, vice chmn, Bedford Stuyvesant Youth in Action, 1968; vchmn, Oper Breadbasket, 1969; co chmn, Ministers Against Narcotics, 1969; founder, Comn African Solidarity, 1977; founder, pres, Coalition of Concerned Leaders & Citizens to Save our C, 1977; bd dir, Randolph Evans Mem Scholar Fund, 1978-; chmn, Nat Black United Front, 1979-86, chmn emer, 1986-; bd dir, Black United Fund NY, 1980-; bd dir, Nat Rainbow Coalition, 1985-; bd dir, United African Churches NYS, 1988-; comnr, Black Leadership Comn on AIDS, 1989-; chmn, Asn Brooklyn Clergy Comt Devel, 1991-; founder & chmn, African Clergy & Elected Officials, 1991-; chmn, New York Citywide African Am Clergy Coun; Credentials Comt mem, Dem Nat Conv, 2004. **Honors/Awds:** Hon mem, Malik Sigma Psi Fraternity; Doctor Lett, Seton Hall Univ, 1980; Hon doctorate, State Univ of New York, 1992; The People's Pastor. **Special Achievements:** Author: Inside the Storm; No Monopoly on Suffering; Jesus Christ: African in Origin, Revolutionary & Redeeming in Action; My Beloved Community; Effectual Prayer and Dear 2pac; One of the principal lecturers at the 150th anniversary of the Virginia Theological Seminary; Host & principal speaker for the past 34 years on a weekly radio program aired Sunday mornings at 10:30 a.m. on New York City WWRL-AM. **Home Addr:** 366 Cumberland St, Brooklyn, NY 11238-1537, **Home Phone:** (718)857-2578. **Business Addr:** National Presiding Minister, Downtown Brooklyn Neighborhood Alliance, 415 Atlantic Ave, Brooklyn, NY 11217, **Business Phone:** (718)797-2184.

**DAUGHTY, MORRIS.** **See DAY, MORRIS EUGENE.**

**DAUPHIN, BOREL C.**
Insurance executive. **Career:** Williams Progressive Life & Accident Ins Co, chief exec.

**DAURHAM, ERNEST, JR.**
Chief executive officer, founder (originator). **Personal:** children: Barbara & Claudia. **Educ:** McCoy Barber Col, attended 1969; Dunbar Sch Cosmetol, attended 1969. **Career:** D-Orum Haircare Prod, founder & chief exec officer, 1979; Ernest Daurham Community Found, founder & head, 1991-; Daurham Inst Hair Technol, founder; Daurham Corp, founder, chmn & chief exec officer, currently. **Business Addr:** Founder, Chief Executive Officer, Daurham Corp, 8912 E Pinnacle Peak Rd, Scottsdale, AZ 85255, **Business Phone:** (623)-2427983.

**DAVE, ALFONZO, JR.**
Government official, real estate agent, business owner. **Personal:** Born Apr 2, 1945, St. Louis, MO; son of Alfonzo Sr and Pearl; children: Alfonzo III. **Educ:** Univ Colo, BA, 1967, Univ Calif, grad study. **Career:** Lic real estate; Al Dave & Assoc Realty, broker & owner; Alt Los Angeles Co Area Admin, state admin youth employ opportunity prog; previous assignments mgr, asst mgr, staff instr, case worker, job develop, employ interviewer; Employ Develop Dept, Calif's Workforce Agency, dep area admin, div chief; State's Employ Security Syst, sr off. **Orgs:** LA City Pvt Indust Coun, chp Youth & Young Adult Comn, Cent City Exec Comt, Summer Youth Employ Training Prog, Youth Opportunity Unlimited Task Force, Performance Eval Task Force, New Ad Hoc Progs Comn; Cent City Enterprise Zone Bus Adv Coun; Southern Calif Employ Round Table; LA Urban League Data Processing Training Ctr Adv Bd; Int Asn Personnel Employ Security; Personnel & Indust Rels Asn Inc; Nat Conf Christians & Jews; Community Rehab Industs; Alpha Kappa Delta; Alpha Phi Alpha; City LA Youth Serv Acad; Community Serv Ctr Prog; Rebuild LA Co-Chairperson Educ & Training Task Force; Los Angeles Demonstration Model Voc Educ, Workforce LA Steer Comt; Mus Afro-Am Arts; Los Angeles Transp Comn Job Develop & Training Task Force; Rebuild LA Educ & Training & Job, steering comt; Nickerson Gardens Empowerment Prog Adv Coun; New Prog Task Force, Los Angeles City PIC; Community Proj Restoration; vpres, bd dir, Mus African Am Art. **Honors/Awds:** Commendation, LA Co Probation Dept, 1975; North Hollywood Chamber of Commerce, 1977; Selected participant, 21st Annual Wilhelm Weinberg Seminar, Cornell Univ, 1979; Cash bonuses, State CA Managerial Performance Appraisal Program, 1986,

1988; Certificate, Mgt, Am Mgt Asn, 1974; Certificate, Mgt, State Personnel Bd, 1970; Selected US Conference Mayors make presentation "Remediation in the Inner City", 1988; Commendation, completion & instruction Masters Exec Excellence through EDD, 1988; The Eagle Award, Nat asn State Wrok Force Agencies, 2001. **Home Addr:** 326 Hillsdale St, Inglewood, CA 90302. **Business Addr:** Vice President, Museum African American Art, PO Box 8418, Los Angeles, CA 90008, **Business Phone:** (323)294-7071.

### DAVENPORT, ARTHUR. See FATTAH, HON. CHAKA.

### DAVENPORT, C. DENNIS
Lawyer. **Personal:** Born Dec 27, 1946, Lansing, MI; married Roselle Wilson; children: Ronald & Charlene. **Educ:** Mich State Univ, BA, 1969; Mich State Univ, MA, 1970; Univ Mich, JD, 1972. **Career:** Gen Motors Corp, atty, 1972-2001; Recruiting Comt, 1975-86; McDonald franchises, owner & operator, 1988-2001; Profeesional Develop Comt-Supvr lawyers, 1982-84; Legal Staff Qual Work Life Comt, chmn, 1983-86; Hawthorn Suites, owner, 2002-; Specialized Serv Inc, gen coun, 2006-. **Orgs:** Nat Bar Asn, 1973-; Mich State Bar, 1973-; Wolverine Bar Asn, 1973-; Southfield, Mich Econ Develop Comt, 2004-06; Nat Asn Advan Colored People; Kappa Alpha Psi Fraternity; State Bar Mich. **Honors/Awds:** Katrina Hotel Management Award, 2006. **Home Addr:** 2841 Briarcliff, Ann Arbor, MI 48105. **Business Addr:** General Counsel, Specialized Services Inc, 9920 Pulaski Hwy Suite 2, Middle River, MD 21220, **Business Phone:** (410)248-6093.

### DAVENPORT, CALVIN A.
Educator. **Personal:** Born Jan 15, 1928, Gloucester, VA; son of James Robert and Carrie Emalia Brook; married Beverly Jean Wills; children: Dean Darnell & Lynn Angela. **Educ:** Va State Univ, BS, 1949; Mich State Univ, MS, 1950; Nat Univ Mex, Mexico City, attended 1957; Mich State Univ, PhD, 1963; Univ Calif, Berkeley, CA, attended 1966; Harvard Med Sch, attended 1986. **Career:** Letterman Army Hosp San Francisco, med tech, 1953-55; Mich Dept Health, Div Labs, 1952-53, 1955-56; Mich State Univ, res asst, 1957-62; Va State Col, prof microbiol, 1963-69; Santa Ana Col, prof Biol; Calif State Univ, prof biol, 1969-92, prof emer microbiol, currently; Univ Calif, Irvine Col Bridge Prog Biomed Res, coordr, 1997-2002; African Sci Inst, consult & evaluator NSF. **Orgs:** Beta Kappa Chi Nat Sci Hon Soc, 1948-; Am Soc Microbiol, 1963-; Coordr, Coun Health Sci Educ, 1971-74; chmn, 1974; Accreditation Team Western Asn Schs & Cols, 1973-92; Orange Co Long Beach Health Consortium, 1973-83; CA State Employees Asn, 1973-; consult, Nat Inst Health Wash, 1973-; Am Pub Health Asn, 1968-92; Kappa Alpha Psi Fraternity; Iota Sigma Lambda Hon Soc; coordr, Health Manpower Educ Proj CA Univ Fullerton, 1974-75; Sr Comn Western Asn Sch & Col, 1976-79; eval panel bio phys & biochem, Nat Sci Found; consult & evaluator, Danforth Found, 1977-80; secy, Acad Assembly CA Univ & Col Med Tech Progs, 1978-79; Univ Minority Affairs Coun, 1981-85; Univ chmn, Acad Affirmative Actioomm, 1982-84; Univ dir incentive grants prog, Nat Action Coun Minorities Eng, 1983-84; dir, Univ " Investment People" prog, 1983-84; Univ AIDS educ, 1984-92; Minority Biomed Res, Support Adv Comm, Geront Res Inst, Univ Inst Health Educ & Training; Univ Health Professions Comm; Dept Long Range Planning Comm, Acad Assembly Calif State Univs & Cols; chair, CA Pub Health Lab dir Acad Assembly, 1990-92; chair, Dept Curric Comn, 1989-92; Univ Substance Abuse Educ Comn, 1991-92; bd trustee, Charles Drew, Univ Med & Sci, 1994-97. **Home Addr:** 124 S Carousel St, Anaheim, CA 92806, **Home Phone:** (714)630-2994. **Business Addr:** Professor Emeritus, California State University, 1 Univ Cir, Turlock, CA 95382.

### DAVENPORT, DR. CAROL A.
Educator. **Personal:** Born Aug 26, 1949. **Educ:** Norfolk State Univ, BA, eng, 1992; Old Dom Univ, MA, eng, 1994; Pa State Univ, PhD, educ, 2000. **Career:** Norfolk State Univ, asst prof eng, 1998-2008; Johnson C Smith Univ, assoc prof eng, 2008-. **Home Addr:** 2610 Rozzelles Landing Dr, Charlotte, NC 28214. **Business Addr:** Associate Professor of English, Department Chair, Rhetoric and Culture, Johnson C Smith University, SHB 205 100 Beatties Ford Rd, Charlotte, NC 28216, **Business Phone:** (704)378-1172.

### DAVENPORT, CHESTER C.
Executive. **Educ:** Univ Ga Sch Law, JD, 1966; Morehouse Col. **Career:** DC law firm Davenport & Seay, 1979-87; First City Properties, managing gen partner, 1973-76; Transp Policy & Int Affairs, asst secy, 1977-79; GTE Consumer Servs Corp, chmn; Georgetown Partners LLC, founder & managing dir, exec, 1988-; Trifork Inc, chief exec officer; Envirotest Systs Corp, dir, founder & chmn, 1990; Davenport Cellular Communs LLC, chmn; Basho Technologies Inc, exec chmn. **Orgs:** Trustee, Arch Found Univ Ga; bd mem, Trifork Inc; DC Bar; chmn, Envirotest Systs Corp; State Bar Ga; trustee, Morehouse Col. **Honors/Awds:** Co is ranked No 11 on the Black Enterprise list of Top 100 Industrial & Service company, 1994. **Business Addr:** Managing Director, Georgetown Partners LLC, 6903 Rockledge Dr Suite 214, Bethesda, MD 20817, **Business Phone:** (301)530-8110.

### DAVENPORT, DR. CHRISTIAN A.
Educator, editor, writer, editor, writer. **Personal:** Born Jun 4, 1965, New York, NY; son of Donn and Juliet Seignions. **Educ:** Clark Univ, BA, polit sci, 1987; Binghamton Univ, MA, polit sci, 1990, PhD, polit sci, 1992. **Career:** Univ Houston, asst prof, 1991-96; Univ Colo, Boulder, assoc prof polit sci, 1996-99, dir comparative polit ctr, 1997-99; Univ Md, Col Pk, sr fel, prof radical info & dir res, 1999-2003, Ctr Int Develop & Conflict Mgt, dir res, 1999-2003, assoc prof, 1999-2005, prof, 2006-08; Univ Mich, dir radical info proj, 2000-, dir stop our states, 2006-, dir illustrative info interface, 2010-; Univ Ulster, Transitional Justice Inst, vis fel, 2007; Stanford Univ, Ctr Advan Study Behav Sci (CASBS), residential fel, 2008-09; Univ Notre Dame, Kroc Inst Int Peace Studies, prof peace studies, polit sci & sociol, 2008-12; Conflict Consortium, co-founder, dir, 2012-; Univ Mich, Ann Arbor, prof polit sci, 2012-, fac assoc, ctr polit studies, 2012-; Peace Res Inst Oslo (PRIO), res prof, 2015-. Editor: Paths to State Repression: Human Rights Violations and Contentious Politics, 2000; Author: Repression and Mobilization, 2005; State Repression and the Domestic Democratic Peace, 2007; Media Bias, Perspective and State Repression: The Black Panther Party, 2010; How Social Movements Die: Repression and Demobilization of the Republic of New Africa, 2015. **Orgs:** Midwest Polit Sci Asn, 1991-; Am Polit Sci Asn, 1991-; Nat Black Polit Sci Asn, 1992-; Shape Cult Ctr, instr, 1993-95; Nat Popular Cult Asn, 1993-; Nat Coalition Blacks Reparations Am, 1993-; ed bd mem, Am Journ Polit Sci, 1994-; exec bd mem, African-Am Studies Prog, 1993-96, adv bd mem, Inst African-Am Policy Res, Univ Houston. 1994-96; W Dallas Detention Ctr, instr, 1995; Comparative Polit Ctr, Univ Colo; Ctr Int Develop & Conflict Mgt, 1999-2001; sr fel Ctr Int Develop & Conflict Mgt, Univ Md, Col Pk, 1999-2003; adv bd mem, codir, Minorities at Risk Data Proj, 2001-02; dir, Minorities at Risk Data Proj, Ctr Int Develop & Conflict Mgt, 2002-04; residential fel, Russell Sage Found, 2006-07; vis fel, Peace Res Inst Oslo, Ctr Study Civil War, 2007-2008; global fel, Peace Res Inst Oslo, Ctr Study Civil War, 2014-2017. **Business Addr:** Professor, Faculty Associate, University of Michigan, 426 Thompson St Rm 4246, Ann Arbor, MI 48104-2321, **Business Phone:** (734)764-6154.

### DAVENPORT, HON. HORACE ALEXANDER
Judge. **Personal:** Born Feb 22, 1919, Newberry, SC; son of William and Julia; married Alice I Latney; children: Alice D Ireland, Beverly A, Horace Jr & Nina D Arnold. **Educ:** Howard Univ, BA, 1946; Univ Pa, Wharton Sch Bus, MA, econs, 1947, LLB, 1950; Johnson C Smith Univ, LLD, 1979. **Career:** Gerber, Davenport & Wilenzik, atty, sole practr; Ct Common Pleas Montgomery County 38th Judicial Dist Pa, sr judge, 1976-. **Orgs:** Former dir, Cent Montgomery County, Bd Am Red Cross; former dir, GW Carver Community Ctr; former dir, Cent Montgomery County Coun Human Rel; former dir, Norristown Community Concerts; Vet Foreign Wars; Hist Soc Montgomery County; Norristown Br Nat Asn Advan Colored People; former mem, Norristown Repub Club; former dir, Norristown Sch Bd; dir, Citizens Coun Montgomery County; former dir, Norristown Art League; former dir, Montgomery County TB & Health Asn; former dir, Montgomery Hosp; former area capt, Salvation Army; former dir, Norristown Sch Bd Lay Rep, Area Voc-Tech Sch; solicitor, Montgomery County Election Bd, 1958-76; solicitor, Norristown Area Sch Dist, 1966-76; solicitor, Norristown Area Sch Authority, 1966-76; solicitor, Cent Montgomery County Area Voc-Tech Sch, 1968-76; dir, Nat Sch Bds Asn, 1969-76; dir, Pa Sch Bd Solicitors Asn, 1969, 1970, 1971, pres, 1972-73; trustee, Johnson C Smith Univ, Charlotte, NC; solicitor, Montgomery County Tax Claim Bur; Alpha Phi Alpha Fraternity; Sigma Pi Phi Fraternity; 33rd Degree Mason; Philadelphia Trial Lawyers Asn; Pa Bar Asn; Am Bar Asn; Nat Adv Vet Med Comt; Am Trial Lawyers Asn; Estates Planning Coun Montgomery County. **Honors/Awds:** Recipient of numerous community awards including the honor with a specialblack & gold stole recognizing his annuity donation to the Johnson C.Smith University by the Kresge Foundation. **Special Achievements:** First African American appointed to the bench in Montgomery County, PA. **Home Addr:** 118 S Schuylkill Ave, Eagleville, PA 19403-3144, **Home Phone:** (610)539-1081. **Business Addr:** Senior Judge, Court of Common Pleasure Montgomery County, PO Box 311, Norristown, PA 19404, **Business Phone:** (610)278-3181.

### DAVENPORT, DR. LAWRENCE FRANKLIN
Government official. **Personal:** Born Oct 13, 1944, Lansing, MI; married Cecelia Jackson; children: Laurence, Anita & Anthony. **Educ:** Mich State Univ, BA, 1968, MA; Fairleigh Dickinson Univ, PhD, 1975. **Career:** Lansing Community Col Mich, asst dir stud activ, 1968-69; Univ Mich, dir spec proj, 1969-72, asst dean, 1972; Nat Adv Coun Voc Educ, 1970, chmn, 1971; Nat Manpower Adv Coun, secy labor, 1972; Tuskegee Inst, vpres, 1972-74; San Diego Community Col Educ Cult Complex, pres, 1974-79; San Diego Comm Col Dist, provost, 1979-81; ACTION Agency, assoc dir domestic & anti-poverty opers, 1981-82; Dept Educ, Elem & Sec Educ, asst secy; Fla Atlantic Univ, exec vpres & chief operating officer, 2007; Fla AU Found Inc, exec dir; US, chief acad officer. **Orgs:** Comt, Martin Luther King Jr Fed Holiday Comt, 1985-86; Nat Adv Coun, 1973. **Honors/Awds:** Outstanding Young Citizen of San Diego, San Diego Jaycees, 1978. **Home Addr:** , Spring Valley, CA.

### DAVENPORT, REGINALD
Newspaper executive, auditor. **Personal:** Born Apr 5, 1948, Chicago, IL; son of Myrtle and Reginald C; married Stevelena. **Educ:** Southern Univ, BS, 1969; cert pub acct, IL, 1972. **Career:** Coopers & Lybrand, auditor, 1969-72; Beatrice Foods Co, internal audit supvr, 1972-74; NY Times Reg Newspaper Group, group controller, 1974-83, vpres & chief financial officer, 1983, sr vpres group, 1983-93, sr vpres opers, 1991, 1991, exec vpres opers, 1993. **Orgs:** Bd dir, Assoc Press, 1994-98. **Home Addr:** 10520 Roxburgh Lane, Roswell, GA 30076, **Home Phone:** (770)475-8032.

### DAVENPORT, RONALD R., SR.
Chief executive officer, executive. **Personal:** Born May 21, 1936, Philadelphia, PA; son of James and Beatrice McLemore; married Judith Loftin; children: Ronald R Jr, Judith Allison & Susan Ross. **Educ:** Pa State Univ, State Col, PA, BS, bus admin, 1958; Temple Univ Sch Law, Philadelphia, PA, LLB, 1962; Yale Law Sch, New Haven, CT, LLM, 1963. **Career:** Duquesne Univ Sch Law, Pittsburgh, PA, prof, 1963-70, dean, 1970-81; Buchanan Ingersoll, PC, Pittsburgh, PA, partner, 1982-84; Sheridan Broadcasting Corp, Pittsburgh, PA, founder, chief exec officer, 1972, chmn, 1972-; Am Urban Radio, co-chmn; Aramark Corp, bd dir, mem, 1980-; Harvard Univ, Vis Comt African Am Studies, chmn, currently; Pres's Comn White House, fel; Mellon Pvt Asset Mgt, dir; Momentum Equity Group LLC, adv bd; Baylock & Partners LP, dir. **Orgs:** Trustee, Comt Econ Develop, 1975-; bd mem, Allegheny Gen Hosp; bd mem, Nat Urban League; bd mem, Colgate Univ; bd mem, Boys & Girls Club; Friends Harry Reid; Urban League, nat dir; US Chamber Com, bd dir; Obama Victory Fund; bd mem, BNY Mellon Funds Trust, 2000-. **Home Addr:** 5837 Solway St, Pittsburgh, PA 15217-1228, **Home Phone:** (412)421-1547. **Business Addr:** Chairman of the Board, Sheridan Broadcasting Corp, 960 Penn Ave Suite 200, Pittsburgh, PA 15222, **Business Phone:** (412)456-4018.

### DAVID, GERALDINE R.
Government official. **Personal:** Born Sep 15, 1938, Helena, AR; married Odell Davis Jr; children: Cheryl, Vivian, Odel III, Eva, Darin, Vivian L Ross & Vivian L Ross. **Educ:** Univ Pine Bluff; Rust Col, Holly Springs, MS; Phillips County Community Col. **Career:** Elaine Jr HS, librn asst, 1967; Lake View Coop Assoc, bookkeeper, 1970; Lake View Elem Sch, librn asst, 1974; City Lake View, secy & treas, 1978-. **Orgs:** Bd dir, City Exec Comt, Lake View Med Clin, 1980-, E Ariz Area Aging, 1980-. **Home Addr:** Rte 2, PO Box 350 A, Lexa, AR 72355. **Business Addr:** Secretary, Treasurer, City of Lake View, Rte 1, Helena, AR 72342.

### DAVID, PATRICIA
Executive, financial manager. **Educ:** Fordham Univ, BS, finance, econs & acct, 1981; Fordham Gabelli Sch Bus, Doctorate Humane Lett, 2016. **Career:** Merrill Lynch, vpres & financial systs mgr, 1986-96; Salomon Bros, sr technol mgr; Citi, head diversity, instnl clients group, 1996-2010; JP Morgan Chase, managing dir & global head diversity, 2010-. **Honors/Awds:** Women Achievers, Young Women Christian Asn, 2000; Black Achievers in Industry, Young Women Christian Asn, 2002; Women Achievers Award, Young Women Christian Asn, 2005; Top Diversity Executive, Black Enterprise, 2014. **Special Achievements:** Publication: The Glass Hammer: Spotlight on People, 2007; 25 Influential Black Women, The Network Journal, 2012; Top 100 Most Influential Blacks in Corporate America, Savoy, 2012. **Business Addr:** Head of Diversity, Managing Director, JP Morgan Chase, 277 Pk Ave, New York, NY 10172, **Business Phone:** (212)270-6000.

### DAVIDDS-GARRIDO, NORBERTO, JR.
Football player. **Personal:** Born Oct 4, 1972, La Puente, CA; married Yasmin. **Educ:** Univ Southern Calif, grad. **Career:** Football player (retired); Carolina Panthers, right tackle, 1996-99; Ariz Cardinals, tackle, right guard, 2000. **Honors/Awds:** All-Rookie Team, Football Weekly, 1996. **Home Addr:** 5030 E Tenderrow Pl Unit B, Orange, CA 92867-1668.

### DAVIDSON, ADENIKE MARIE
Writer, educator. **Educ:** Col Holy Cross, Worcester, Mass, BA, Eng, 1989; Univ Calif, Los Angeles, MA, African Am studies, 1992; Univ Md, College Park, PhD, Eng, 2000. **Career:** Univ Cent Fla, asst prof, 1998-2005; Fisk Univ, assoc prof, 2005-12, prof, 2012-13; Del State Univ, dept chair eng & foreign lang, 2013-16, prof eng & gender studies, 2013-. **Honors/Awds:** UNCF/Mellon Foundation Fellowship, recipient, 2009. **Special Achievements:** Has written numerous journal articles as well as the book "The Black Nation Novel: Imagining Homeplaces in Early African-American Literature" (Third World Press, 2008). **Business Addr:** Department Chair, Professor of English, Delaware State University, Rm 204 1200 N DuPont Hwy, Dover, DE 19901, **Business Phone:** (302)857-6708.

### DAVIDSON, DR. ALPHONZO LOWELL, SR.
Educator, dentist. **Personal:** Born Dec 12, 1941, Fredericksburg, VA; married Carolyn; children: Alphonzo Jr & Stephanie. **Educ:** Howard Univ, BS, 1964, DDS, 1968, cert oral surg, 1973. **Career:** Howard Univ, Dept Oral Surg, asst prof; Howard Univ Hosp, attend oral surgeon; Prince George Co Hosp, assoc staff mem; pvt pract, currently. **Orgs:** Chi Delta Mu Fraternity, 1967; Oral Cancer Soc, 1968; Am Dent Soc, 1969; Robert T Freedman Dent Soc; Nat Dent Soc, 1969; Asn Mil Surgeons, 1970; Asn Interns & Residents Freedmen's Hosp, 1972; Am Soc Oral Surg, 1975; Am Bd Oral Surg, 1976; Dent Soc Anesthesiol, 1978; pres, DC Oral Surg Soc, 1979-80; Omicron Kappa Upsilon Pi Pi Chap, 1979-80; Sigma Phi Sigma; DC Dent Soc. **Home Addr:** 1668 Tamarack St NW, Washington, DC 20012, **Home Phone:** (202)723-2843. **Business Addr:** Dentist, 2811 Pa Ave SE Suite 2, Washington, DC 20020, **Business Phone:** (202)582-7275.

### DAVIDSON, ARTHUR B.
Administrator, government official. **Personal:** Born Dec 5, 1929, Detroit, MI; son of Arthur B and Idella; married Edith. **Educ:** Detroit Inst Technol, BA, 1964; Wayne State Univ, Pub Admin, 1970. **Career:** Human Resources Develop, area admin, 1964-68; Butzel Family Ctr Coord Serv, dir, 1968-70; City Detroit, planning admin, 1970-81, opers & mgt serv admin, 1981-82, dir admin serv & weatherization, 1982-88, asst dir, 1988; Dept Human Serv, dep dir, interim dep dir, 2002-. **Orgs:** Nat Asn Housing & Redevelop & Off, 1964; New Detroit Inc, 1970; treas, chmn finance, exec comt, OmniCare Health Plan Bd Trustees. **Honors/Awds:** Cert excellence, Urban League, 1965; Cert recognition, Greater Macedonia Baptist Church, 1965. **Home Addr:** 1449 E Larned, Detroit, MI 48207. **Business Addr:** Interim Deputy Director, City of Detroit Department of Human Services, 5031 Grandy Ave, Detroit, MI 48211, **Business Phone:** (313)852-5609.

### DAVIDSON, CAROL ANTHONY
Vice president (organization), executive, controller. **Educ:** St John Fisher Col, BS, 1976; Univ Rochester, MBA, 1988. **Career:** Arthur Andersen & Co, acct & auditing; Eastman Kodak Co, finance, auditing, acct, 1981-97; Dell Inc, chief compliance officer, vpres & corp controller & vpres internal audit, vpres audit, risk & compliance, 1997-2004; Tyco Int Ltd., sr vpres, controller & chief acct officer, 2004-12; DaVita HealthCare Partners Inc, dir; Pentair plc, dir, 2012-; Legg Mason Inc, dir, 2014-. **Orgs:** Bd mem, St. John Fisher Col; bd mem, Nat 4-H Coun; bd gov, Financial Indust Regulatory Authority. **Honors/Awds:** "Black Enterprise," The 100 Most Powerful Executives in Corporate America, 2010. **Business Addr:** Director, Legg Mason Inc, 100 Int Dr, Baltimore, MD 21202-1099, **Business Phone:** (877)534-4627.

### DAVIDSON, CLEATUS LAVON
Baseball player. **Personal:** Born Nov 1, 1976, Bartow, FL. **Career:** Baseball player (retired); GCL Twins, 1994-95; Elizabethton Twins, 1995-96; Ft Wayne Wizards, 1996-98; Minn Twins, 1999; New Britian Rock Cats; Mobile BayBears; Elmira Pioneers, infielder, 2003-04; N Shore Spirit, 2005; Long Beach Armada, 2008.

## DAVIDSON, EZRA C., JR.

Educator, dean (education). **Personal:** Born Oct 21, 1933, Water Valley, MS; son of Ezra C Sr and Theresa; children: Pamela, Gwendolyn, Marc & Ezra K. **Educ:** Morehouse Col, BS, 1954; Meharry Med Sch, MD, 1958. **Career:** LA Co Univ So CA Med Ctr, 1970-80; Martin Luther King Gen Hosp, chief serv, 1971-96; Univ So Calif Sch Med, prof, 1971-80; Univ Calif Los Angeles, chmn & chief-to-staff, 1971-96, prof, Obstet & Gynec, 1979-, Dartmouth Schs Med; Charles R Drew Univ Med & Sci, prof, 1971-, chmn dept ob & gynec 1971-96, assoc dean primary care, currently; Columbia Univ, fel. **Orgs:** Consult, Nat Found March Dimes, 1970-77; bd consult, Int Childbirth Educ Asn Inc, 1973-80; Nat Med Adv Com Nat Found March Dimes Inc, 1972-77; bd dir, Prof Staff Asn Found Martin Luther King Jr Gen Hosp, 1972-; examr, Am Bd Ob & Gynec, 1973-; Sec Adv Comt Pop Affairs, 1974-77; chmn, Serv Task Force, 1975-77; bd dir, Nat Alliance Sch Age Parents, 1975-80; bd trustee, 1989-, sec, 1975-77, chair, nat chmn; Alpha Omega Alpha Hon Soc; fel, Robert Woods Johnson Health Policy Inst Med Wash, DC, 1979-80; Ob & Gynec Nat Med Asn; pres, Assoc Profs Gynec & Ob, 1987-88; pres, Golden State Med Asn, 1989-90; sec, Am Col Ob & Gynec, 1983-89, pres-elect, 1989-90, pres, 1990-91; chmn, Obstet & Gynec Asn Southern CA, 1988-89; Food & DrugAdm, chair, adv com fertil & maternal health drugs, 1992-96; chair &sec's adv com infant mortality, Dept Health & Human Serv, 1992-95; Nat Acad Scis, Inst Med, 1991-; pres, Am Col Ob-Gynec; fel Am Col Surg; fel LA Ob-Gynec Soc; bd dir, Cs? Bur Southern Calif, pres, 1999-2002; bd dir, dir, Calif Wellness Found, chair, 1998-2000; pres, N Am Socs Pediat & Adolescent Gynec; chmn, Sect Obstet & Gynec Nat Med Asn; Fel Inst Med; fel Nat Acad Sci; Fel ad eundem Royal Col Obstetricians & Gynecologists; pres, Asn Acad Minority Physicians; chair, bd trustee, Blue Shield Calif Found; Acad Minority Physicians; bd gov, Jacobs Inst Womens Health; bd mem, Pac Ctr Law & Ethics, Sch Law, Univ Southern Calif; chair, Calif Technol Assessment Forum; adv comt, Reproductive Health Drugs Food & Drug Admin; Med Adv Bd Numera Inc. **Home Addr:** 800 W 1st St suite 2005, Los Angeles, CA 90012, **Home Phone:** (213)680-9532. **Business Addr:** Associate Dean, Professor, Charles R Drew University of Medicine & Science, 1731 E 120th St, Los Angeles, CA 90059, **Business Phone:** (323)563-4800.

## DAVIDSON, FLETCHER VERNON, JR.

Automotive executive. **Personal:** Born Feb 23, 1947, Portland, OR; son of Fletcher V Sr and Stella M; married Rosie Lee Tucker; children: Fletcher V III, Damion R & Crystal N. **Educ:** Los Angeles City Col, AA, tech engineering, 1966; Calif State Univ, Long Beach, BS, indust tech, 1972; Univ Southern Calif, MS, mgt sci, 1976. **Career:** McDonnell-Douglas Corp, draftsman, 1966-70, sr engr & syst analyst, 1970-73; Nat Asn Prof Organizers, vpres distrib & logistics opers, vpres & gen mgr; Toyota Motor Sales USA Inc, planning adminr, 1973-76, systs develop mgr, 1977-83, nat supply mgr, 1984-90, nat logistics planning mgr, 1991-92, vpres distrib & financial opers & gen mgr, 2001-, Customer Serv Div, group vpres & gen mgr, Prod Support Div, group vpres & gen mgr, currently; N Am parts Logistics Div, corp mgr, 1993-99. **Home Addr:** 1009 N Antonio Cir, Orange, CA 92869-1966, **Home Phone:** (714)771-7949. **Business Addr:** Group Vice President, General Manager, Toyota Motor Sales USA Inc, 19001 S Western Ave, Torrance, CA 90509, **Business Phone:** (310)468-4953.

## DAVIDSON, HEZEKIAH MILES

Executive. **Personal:** Born Jan 1, 1970. **Educ:** Univ Akron, bus admin & acct, 1991. **Career:** Household Finance Corp, loan originator, 1993-95; Crystal Brokerage Mortgage Co, loan originator & merchant coordr, 1995-97; Maj League Mortgage, mortgage consult, 1997-98; NationsBank / Bank Am, sr loan processor, 1998-99; Right Hand Mgt & Prod Inc, pres & chief exec officer, 1998-2011; Nat Relationship Tours, nat client mgr, 1999-2003; George Frasers PowerNetworking Conferences, proj mgr, 2002-03; Ohio Classic/Black Col All-Star Game, proj mgr, 2005; Citizens Healthcare Working Group Town Hall Meetings, nat proj mgr, 2005-06; Voices & Choices Northeast Ohio Town Hall Meetings I & II, nat proj mgr, 2005-06; Unified New Orleans Plan Community Cong II Meetings, nat proj mgr, 2006-07; Tom Joyner's Fantastic Voyage Cruise, team mem, 2009; Flicks Falls, proj mgr, 2008-10; Alpha Phi Alpha Homes Inc, mkt mgr, 2006-11. **Orgs:** mem, State Ohio Dept Developments, Entrepreneurship Roundtable; Northern Ohio Minority Bus Coun; Connected Int Meeting Professionals Asn; Akron Urban League Young Professionals Asn; Nat Youth Sports Prog; Miracle Tutoring & Learning Ctr; dir, Opportunity Parish Ecumenical Neighborhood Ministry Role Model Prog; group life supvr, Safe Landing Youth Shelter; Counr, Nat Youth Sports Prog; dir, Helen Arnold Community Learning Ctr, Adopt-A-Sch Prog; asst dir, Al Kaf & Isiserettes Youth Orgn; Mem, Al Kaf Shrine No 109; Mt Calvary Lodge No 76, Prince Hall F&AM; Proj mgr, Northern Ohio Minority Bus Coun, 2008. **Honors/Awds:** The 26 Best Bachelors of the Year, Ebony, 2003. **Home Addr:** 736 Ardella Ave, Akron, OH 44306.

## DAVIDSON, DR. KERRY

State government official. **Personal:** Born May 1, 1935, Water Valley, MS; married Betty Vanover; children: Mary Jaures & Elizabeth Jeanette. **Educ:** Morehouse Col, BS, polit sci & econs; Univ Iowa, MS, polit sci; Tulane Univ, PhD. **Career:** Southern Univ New Orleans, former chmn dept hist; Fisk Univ, chmn; La Bd Regents, comnr acad affairs, Sponsored Progs, dep comnr & proj dir, currently. **Honors/Awds:** Danforth Grant. **Special Achievements:** Author of 20th Century Civilization. **Home Addr:** 5511 Cong Blvd, Baton Rouge, LA 70808, **Home Phone:** (225)923-2130. **Business Addr:** Deputy Commissioner for Sponsored Programs, Louisiana Board of Regents, 1201 N 3rd St Suite 6-200, Baton Rouge, LA 70802, **Business Phone:** (225)342-4253.

## DAVIDSON, LURLEAN G.

Administrator, teacher. **Personal:** Born May 3, 1931, West Point, GA; married Ogletree; children: Marzette, Jerome, John, Darlene & Mary. **Educ:** Case Western Res Univ; Ohio Univ; Cleveland State Univ. **Career:** Sol Victory Mutual Life Ins, 1958-60; Parent Resource Ctrs Cleveland Bd Educ, dir; auditor; interviewer; election clerk; Cleveland Bd Ed, teacher; Davidson's Construct Co, secy, treas; Inner City Pride, pres. **Orgs:** Precinct Comt Woman, 1960-73; life mem, PTA, 1965; Glenville Area Coun Phyllis Wheatley Asn; Nat Asn Advan Colored People; Parent Adv Bd YMCA; Urban League; Jewish Coun. **Honors/Awds:** Outstanding Service Award, 1961; Outstanding Social Award, Certificate of Merit, Nat Asn Advan Colored People, 1962; Community Leadership Award, Coun City Cleveland, 1981. **Home Addr:** 1167 E Blvd, Cleveland, OH 44108-2973, **Home Phone:** (216)231-2226. **Business Addr:** Staff, Joseph F Landis School, 10118 Hampden Ave, Cleveland, OH 44108.

## DAVIDSON, RICK BERNARD

Banker. **Personal:** Born Oct 6, 1951, Nashville, TN; son of Robert and Beula Jones; married Izola Putnam; children: Sandra Putnam & Robert Derrick. **Educ:** Tenn Sch Banking, dipl, 1980; Univ Okla, ABA Com Sch Lending, dipl, 1983; Tenn Com Lending Sch, cert, 1988; Los Angeles State Univ, Grad Sch Banking S, cert, 1989. **Career:** Third Nat Bank, asst mgr, 1969-78; Com Union Bank, mgr, 1978-80; Com Union Bank, asst vpres & comn lending officer, 1981-84; Nashville City Bank, loan rev specialist, 1984; Citizens Savings Bank, asst vpres & com lending officer, first vpres, 1985-88, pres & chief exec officer, 1988-95. **Orgs:** Dir, Bethlehem Ctr, 1985-89, treas, 1986-88; pres, Mid Tenn Chap, Am Inst Banking, 1986-87; pres, Am Inst Banking, 1986-87; comnr, Tenn Serv Bd, 1987; treas, Uptown Nashville, 1989; dir, Proj Pencil, 1989; Legis Comn, 1989. **Home Addr:** 1009 S St, Nashville, TN 37203-4735, **Home Phone:** (615)254-0512.

## DAVIDSON, ROBERT C., JR.

Executive. **Personal:** Born Oct 3, 1945, Memphis, TN; son of Robert C Sr and Thelma; married Alice Faye; children: Robert C III, John Roderick & Julian L. **Educ:** Morehouse Col, BA, 1967, PhD; Univ Chicago, Grad Sch Bus, MBA, 1969. **Career:** Cresap, McCormack & Paget, sr assoc consult, 1969-72; Urban Nat Corp, co-founder & vpres, 1972-74; Avant Garde Enterprises, chief exec officer & exec vpres, 1974-75; R Davidson & Assoc, consult, 1975-78; Surface Protection Industs Inc, founder, pres, chief exec officer & chmn, 1978-2007; Broadway Financial Corp, dir; Jacobs Engineering Group Inc, dir, 2001-. **Orgs:** Bd dir, Los Angeles Chamber Orchestra; bd dir, C's Hosp Los Angeles; Young Pres's Orgn; Nat Asn Investment Cos; bd dir, Cedars-Sinai Med Ctr; trustee, Morehouse Col, 1997-; vpres, Urban Nat Corp; chmn & bd trustee, Art Ctr Col Design, 2010-; bd dir, Fulcrum Venture Capital Corp; bd mem, Broadway Fed Bank; bd dir, S Coast Air Qual Mgt Dist Brain Tumor & Air Pollution Found; adv coun, Univ Chicago Grad Sch Bus; bd dir, Mus Contemp Art; bd dir, Charles Drew Univ Sch Med; bd dir, Armory Ctr Arts; bd dir, African/Am Mus Art; bd dir, Big Bros Greater Los Angeles. **Home Addr:** 577 Woodland Rd, Pasadena, CA 91106, **Home Phone:** (818)793-7808. **Business Addr:** Director, Jacobs Engineering Group Inc, 155 N Lake Ave, Pasadena, CA 91101, **Business Phone:** (626)578-3500.

## DAVIDSON, RUDOLPH DOUGLAS (RUDY DAVIDSON)

Government official. **Personal:** Born Jul 19, 1941, Louisville, KY; son of Nathaniel and Catherine Ruffins; married Jean Slater. **Educ:** Univ Louisville, KY, sociol, 1979. **Career:** Westinghouse Learning Corp, Louisville, KY, mgr, 1966-70; Model Cities Prog, Louisville, KY, dir, oper mainstream, 1970-73; City Louisville, Louisville, KY, dir, Lou & Jeff County, directions opport, 1973-77, dir, Louisville, Jeff County, WEP, 1977-79, exec dir, Lou & Jeff County, CAA, 1979-83, dir solid waste mgt & serv, 1986-2003; Louisville Metro Govt, cabinet secy, pub works, 2003-06; independent civic & social orgn prof, cuurrently. **Orgs:** Lou & Jeff County Community Action Agency, 1983-; Jeff County Solid Waste Mgt Bd, 1985-; Nat Forum Black Pub Adminrs, 1989-; chmn, Mayor Jerry Abramson's Recycling Comt, 1989-; chmn, Mayor Jerry Abramson's Resource Recovery Proj Comn, 1990-; exec comt, Munic Waste Mgt Asn; pres, Ky Bluegrass Chap, Solid Waste Asn N Am; vpres, US Conf Mayors, Munic Waste Mgt Asn; vpres, W End Clubs Develo Ctr Bd; Cabinet Pub Works & Servs, Louisville-Jefferson County; pres, Shawnee Neighborhood Asn, 2008-; bd mem, Louisville Cent Community Ctr; Weed & Seed Steering Comt; pres, Fontaine Estates Homeowners Asn. **Home Addr:** 108 Fontaine Landing Ct, Louisville, KY 40212, **Home Phone:** (502)778-3050. **Business Addr:** Director, City of Louisville, 636 Meriwether Ave, Louisville, KY 40217, **Business Phone:** (502)574-3571.

## DAVIDSON, TOMMY

Comedian, actor. **Personal:** Born Nov 10, 1963, Washington, DC. **Career:** Standup comedian, currently; actor, currently; Films: Strictly Business, 1991; CB4, 1993; Ace Ventura: When Nature Calls, 1995; Booty Call, Plump Fiction, 1997; Woo, 1998; Pros & Cons, 1999; Bamboozled, 2000; Juwanna Mann, 2002; Funky Monkey, 2004; Black Dynamite, 2009; Dance Fu, 2011; Who Killed Soul Glow?, 2012. TV Series: "CBS Summer Playhouse", 1989; Kid 'n' Play, 1990; "In Living Color", actor, 1990-94, writer, 1993-94; "Tommy Davidson: Illin' in Philly", 1991; "The Best of Robert Townsend & His Partners in Crime", actor & writer, 1991; "Roc", "The 6th Annual Soul Train Music Awards", 1992; "The Commish", "Martin", "Yuletide in the 'hood", voice, "Mo' Funny: Black Comedy in America", "Soul Train Comedy Awards", "A Cool Like That Christmas", voice, 1993; "Duckman: Private Dick/Family Man", 1994; The Ren & Stimpy Show, 1996; "Boston Common", "Between Brothers", "Mad TV", "Space Ghost Coast to Coast", "Premium Blend", 1997, writer, 1999-2000; "Tonight at the House of Blues", "The Magic Hour", 1998; "Happily Ever After: Fairy Talesfor Every Child", "All That", 1999; "Malcolm & Eddie", 1999-2000; "All That", "Santa Who?", 2000; "The Proud Family", 2001-05; "Weakest Link", "Comedy Central Presents: The N.Y. Friars Club Roast of Hugh Hefner", 2001; "The Scream Team", "Platinum Comedy Series: Roasting Shaquille O'Neal", "The View", 2002; "Mad TV", "Hollywood Squares", "The Tonight Show with Jay Leno", 2003; "TV in Black: The First Fifty Years", voice, 2004; "The Sharon Osbourne Show", 2004; "Last Call with Carson Daly", 2004-05; "The Bernie Mac Show", 2004-05; "Inked", "Lilo & Stitch: The Series", "The Proud Family Movie", voice, "I Love the '90s: Part Deux", 2005; "In the Mix", "Comics Unleashed", 2006; "Everybody Hates Chris", 2007; "Live at Gotham", 2008; "NESN Comedy All-Stars", writer, 2009; "ComedyTV", 2010; "Black Dynamite: The Animated Series", 2011-14. **Honors/Awds:** Voted one of the Rising Stars of Comedy, 1990; TV Land Award, 2012. **Business Addr:** Actor, c/o William Morris Agency, 151 El Camino Dr, Beverly Hills, CA 90212-2775, **Business Phone:** (310)274-7451.

## DAVIDSON, U. S., JR.

Educator. **Personal:** Born Oct 28, 1954, Fulton, GA; son of U S Sr and Juanita; married Jacqueline J Martin; children: Brian Anthony. **Educ:** Parkland Community Col, AA, univ studies, 1975; NDak State Univ, BS, sec educ, 1978; Eastern Ill Univ, masters, guidance/coun, 1983, type 75, admin endorsement, 1986. **Career:** Champaign Community Unit Dist 4, instrnl aide, 1978-79, spec educ teacher, 1979-81, phys educ teacher, 1981-85, counr, 1985-88, dean studs, 1988-90, asst prin, 1990, prin, 1990; Osborne High Sch & NovaNET, prin. **Orgs:** Kappa Alpha Psi, 1974-; Phi Delta Kappa, 1983-; Asn Ill Mid Sch, 1990-; Champaign Human Rels Comn, 1990-; Champaign County Urban League, 1985-; Minority Teacher Recruitment Team, 1989-; Ill Mid Grades Planning Initiative Comt, 1991-; Comt Identify Minorities Bds & Comns, 1992-. **Home Addr:** 2602 Rachel Rd, Champaign, IL 61820. **Business Addr:** GA.

## DAVIDSON-HARGER, ESQ. JOAN CAROLE

Lawyer, teacher, executive. **Educ:** Univ Detroit, BA, 1975; Detroit Col Law, JD, 1983. **Career:** Detroit Bd Educ, urban adult teacher math, 1975-76; Ford Motor Co, NAAO, analyst, 1976-89; sole practr, atty, 1987-90; UAW Legal Serv, staff atty, 1990-91; Bloomfield Law Ctr PC, atty, 1991-. **Orgs:** Phi Alpha Theta, Hist Hon Soc, 1974; Nat Bar Asn, 1983-; vice pres, secy, United Methodist Women, 1985-90; leader/sponsor, Magnolia United Methodist Youth Group, 1985-89; Oakland Co Bar Asn, 1987-88; State Bar Mich, 1987-; Detroit Metrop Black United Methodist Scholar Fund, 1988-90; D Augustus Straker Bar Asn, 1991-. **Honors/Awds:** Service Award, United Methodist Women, 1988. **Business Addr:** Attorney, Bloomfield Law Center PC, 44060 Woodward Ave, Bloomfield Hills, MI 48302, **Business Phone:** (248)332-0222.

## DAVIE, DAMON JONATHON

Automotive executive. **Personal:** Born May 8, 1964, Detroit, MI; son of William and Alice; married Ruthanne; children: Damon & Daniel. **Educ:** Drake Univ, bus admin & mgt, 1985; Western Ill Univ, BA, communs & bus admin, 1988. **Career:** Pepsi Cola Co, mgt trainee, 1989-90; Rent-A-Ctr, acct mgr, 1990-91; Auto Club Group, minority vendor coordr, 1991-96; AAA Mich, minority vendor coordr, 1991-99; Perry Johnson Registrars Inc, CES-Carbon Emissions Serv, qual syst lead auditor, 1996-99; Ford-Detroit Chassis Plant, qual mgr, 1999-2004; TurboCare, qual syst consult, 2005-08; Wood Group, qual syst consult, 2005-08; Daimler Chrysler, lead qual specialist, 2005-08; Plymouth Industs, dir opers, 2008-11; D&P Global Solutions, qual & safety consult, 2008-12; Omnex Inc, consult & trainer, 2011-12; Hexagon Lincoln, qual engr, 2012-13; Faurecia Emissions Control Technologies, customer qual mgr, 2013-14; EASi, corp qual mgr, 2014-. **Orgs:** Vpres, Omega Psi Phi Fraternity Inc, Epsilon Beta Chap, 1987; comt mem, New Detroit Inc, 1996; United Way; Am Soc Qual; Nebr Safety Coun; Beatrice Chamber Com; Caribean Inst Qual Omnex Inc. **Honors/Awds:** ASQ Team Quality Award, 2006; Best of Plymouth Award, 2009. **Home Addr:** 22161 Marlow, Oak Park, MI 48237, **Home Phone:** (810)968-1641. **Business Addr:** Quality Engineer, Hexagon Lincoln, 5117 NW 40th St, Lincoln, NE 68524, **Business Phone:** (402)470-5000.

## DAVIE, TIMOTHY M. (TIM DAVIE)

Government official. **Personal:** Born Oct 14, 1955, Hopkinsville, KY; son of Barker W Sr; married Chloretha M. **Educ:** Ind Wesleyan Univ, BS (cum laude), bus mgt, 2003. **Career:** Government official (retired); Ft Wayne Fire Dept, fire fighter, 1981-84, lt, opers div, 1984-88, inspector, 1986-96, fire marshal, 1996-2000, fire chief, 2000-07; Lutheran Hosp Ind, security dir, dir environ care & lutheran health network vpres, 2007-; Int Asn Fire Chiefs, pres. **Orgs:** Nat Fire Protection Asn; Am Lung Asn, Regional Coun II, 1999-; Int Conf Biomed Ontology; Ind Fire Inspectors Asn; bd mem, Friends Lincoln Mus; Greater Progressive Baptist Church, Men Vision; comnr, Safety Village Survive Alive; bd dir, Am Heart Asn; bd mem, chief, Int Asn Fire Chiefs; Nat Fire Protection Asn; bd dir, Parkview YMCA; bd dir, Ind State Emergency Med Servs Comn, Lutheran Hosp bd dir, Pres Friends Lincoln Mus; chmn bd, Ind Fire Chiefs Asn; Paul Harris Fel; Allen County Community Libr; bd mem, Ft Wayne Ballet Inc; bd dir, Mad Anthony's C's Hope House & Ft Wayne C's Zoo; network vpres, Mad Anthony's C's Hope House; Allen County Local Emergency Planning Comt; Allen County Emergency Mgt Adv Coun; co-chairperson, Dist 3 Hosp Preparedness Planning Comt Inc, 2013. **Home Addr:** 322 NW Passage Trl, Ft. Wayne, IN 46825, **Home Phone:** (260)489-1449. **Business Addr:** Director, Lutheran Hospital of Indiana, 7950 W Jefferson, Ft. Wayne, IN 46804, **Business Phone:** (260)435-7014.

## DAVIES, REV. LAWRENCE A.

Mayor, clergy, association executive. **Personal:** Born Jul 7, 1930, Houston, TX; son of Lawrence A Sr (deceased) and Autrey Thomas Davies Miller; married Janice J Pryde; children: Lauren A (deceased), Karen M & Sharron L. **Educ:** Prairie View A&M Col, BS, 1949; Howard Univ Sch Relig, MDiv, 1957; Wesley Theol Sem, STM, 1961; Fredericksburg Bible Inst & Sem, DDiv, 1985. **Career:** Good Samaritan Baptist Church WA DC, pastor, 1956-60; Shiloh Baptist Church WA DC, asst pastor & relig ed dir, 1960-62; Shiloh Baptist Church Wash, assoc minister; Shiloh Baptist Church, pastor, 1962-; City Fredericksburg, city councilman, 1966-76, mayor, 1976. **Orgs:** Pres, Fredericksburg Area Ministerial Asn, 1965-66; Fredericksburg Baptist Ministers Conf, 1969-70; Rappahannock Citizen Corp, 1968-; VA Asn Ment Health, 1974-76; adv dir, Perpetual Am Bank, 1975-88; bd dir, Nat Conf Black Mayors, 1977-86, Nat Kidney Found VA, 1984-86; pres, VA Munic League, 1984-85, VA Conf Black Mayors, 1985-; founder, Fredericksburg Area Sickle Cell Asn; Fredericksburg Lions Club, Alpha Phi Alpha Frat, Prince Hall Masons, Gov's Comn Transp21st Century, 1986-88; bd visitor, Mary Wash Col, 1986-90; Commonwealth Transp Bd, 1990-. **Honors/Awds:** Young Man of the Year, Fredericksburg Jaycees, 1966; Citizen of the Year, Omega Psi Phi Frat, 1966; Citizenship Award, Fredericksburg Area Chamber Com, 1976; Man of the Year, VFW No 3103, 1977; Outstanding Service Award, Nat Asn Ment Health, 1979; Humanitarian of the Year Award, Mt Bethel Baptist Asn, 1984; Citizen of the Year, Alpha Kappa Alpha Sorority, Mid-Atlantic Region, 1990. **Special Achievements:** First African American mayor of City of Fredericksburg. **Home Addr:** 1301 Cardwell St, Fredericksburg, VA 22401, **Home Phone:** (540)373-

6226. **Business Addr:** Pastor, Shiloh Baptist Church, 801 Sophia St, Fredericksburg, VA 22401, **Business Phone:** (540)373-8701.

### DAVIS, DR. ABRAHAM, JR.

Educator, spokesperson, administrator. **Personal:** Born May 14, 1923, Beaufort, SC; son of Abraham and Everlena; married Jennie Howard; children: Silena, Wilkins Garrett Jr, James Wright & Joya Wright. **Educ:** Lancaster Sch Bible & Theol, diplo Bible & Theol, 1949; Houghton Col, BA, 1955; Temple Univ, MA, 1956; Univ Iowa; Pa State Univ; Western Res Univ, attended 1960; Ind Univ, Bloomington, PhD, 1971. **Career:** Educator, director (retired); Positive Ethnic Models & Ethnic Integration Col Curricula, lect, rhetorician; SC State Col Neg, speech therpst & instr, Orange, SC, 1956-58; Greenville Co Negro Pub Sch, co speech therpst, 1958-61; Houghton Col, instr Speech & Eng Compos, 1961-65; Ind Univ Bloomington, assoc teacher pub speaking, 1965-67; Houghton Col, assoc prof, prof speech, 1967-72; sabbatical lect, oral inter Afro-Am Lit & Rhet, 1972-73; Messiah Col, actg dean, 1973-74; Asbury Col, vis prof, 1973-74; Messiah Col, admin acad dean, 1975-80; Eastern Mennonite Col, Cross Cult Comn, coordr, prof, dir, 1980-85; Ctr Urban Theol Studies, prof speech & basic writing, 1986-87; Calvin Col, Grand Rapids, Dept Comn Arts & Sci, vis prof, 1987-88; Rockingham Pub Schs, dir human resources; Furious Flower Poetry Ctr, exec dir; James Madison Univ, prof Eng. **Orgs:** Volunt various organs. **Honors/Awds:** Pub Doctoral Dissertation & Abstract, An Accelerated Speech Curriculum for Selected Educational Dis adv td Negros, Dissertation Abstract, 1971; Speaker Regional & Nat Professional Speech Comm Asn, 1972; Speaker Nat Coun Teachers Eng, 1973; vis lectr, The Fundamentals of Oral & Written Commun, 1976; Speaker & oral interpreter of Afro-Am lit & rhetoric various chs, comm groups, pub assemblies, faculty In Serv. **Special Achievements:** Published books: "Review of Your God is Too White Journal of Am Sci Affiliation", 1971; "The Oratory of Negro Leaders 1900-1960 for Ethnic and Minoirty Studies Newsletter of WI State", 1972; "Black Jargon in White Am Journal of American Science Affiliation"; Article: "Evangelicals Listen, Please Listen Bridge", 1976; First director of multi-cultural services at EMU, 1980. **Home Addr:** 1285 Shank Dr, Harrisonburg, VA 22802-5534, **Home Phone:** (540)432-7295.

### DAVIS, ADRIAN

President (organization), administrator. **Educ:** Spelman Col, BA, polit sci & econs, 1973; Wayne State Univ, MEd, 1994, doctoral degree, educ leadership & admin/eval & measurement, 2012. **Career:** Mich Coun Social Studies, pres; House Delegates, deleg, 1993-; Nat Bd for Prof Teaching Stand, exec assoc, 1994-2003; Nat Coun Social Studies, pres, 2001-02, Nominations & Elections Comt, mem, currently; Detroit Pub Schs, asst prin, 2003-10, prin, 2010-11. **Orgs:** Nat Alliance Civic Educ; exec assoc assessment develop, Nat Bd Prof Teaching Stand; regional partner, AdvancED, 2011-. **Home Addr:** 17121 Village Dr, Redford, MI 48240. **Business Addr:** Commitee Member, The National Council for the Social Studies, 8555 16th St Suite 500, Silver Spring, MD 20910, **Business Phone:** (301)588-1800.

### DAVIS, ADRIANNE

Health services administrator, government official. **Personal:** Born Sep 6, 1945, Newark, NJ. **Educ:** Montclair St Col, BA, bus educ, MA, 1967. **Career:** W Side HS, instr, 1967-73; N Ward Ctr, 1973, exec dir, 2008-10, founder; Essex Co NJ, free holder large, 1982-87; County Col Morris, adj prof, 1983. **Orgs:** Consult, John Hay Whitney Found, 1973-74; chair, Essex County Col Personnel Communs, 1979; bd trustee, Essex Vty Col, 1979-80; Essex County Bd Freeholders, 1982, Budget Rev Comn, Essex County Bd Freeholders, 1983; Essex County Econ Develop Corp, 1983; vpres, Essex County Bd Educ, 2007; clerk, Essex County; secy, Caucus Educ Corp; bd mem, Christ King Prep Sch; vpres, Robert Treat Acad Charter Sch Bd Trustees, currently. **Honors/Awds:** Distingushed Service Award, Theatre Universal Images, 1980; Appreciation Award, Essex County Col, 1980; Citizens Appreciation Award, Community Womens Concerns Essex County, 1980; Dr Martin Luther King Recogonition Award, N Ward Ctr, 1983. **Home Addr:** 36 Hawthorne Pl, Montclair, NJ 07042. **Business Addr:** Secretary, Caucus Educational Corp, PO Box 155, Montclair, NJ 07042, **Business Phone:** (973)233-9890.

### DAVIS, AGNES MARIA

Manager, registered nurse, executive. **Personal:** Born Jun 3, 1927, Republic of Panama; daughter of Frederick (deceased) and Ellen (deceased); married Samuel Huntley; children: Alexander Dunker Jr & Ann Maria Dunker. **Educ:** St Francis Col, BS, 1984; Long Island Univ, MS, 1987; Sch Nursing, Jewish Hosp & Med Ctr Brooklyn. **Career:** Jewish Hosp & Med Ctr Brooklyn, supvr, 1961-65; Interfaith Med Ctr, full-time asst dir nursing, 1985-88; Clove Lakes Nursing Home, part-time supvr, 1992-; Senga Travel Inc, pres, currently. **Orgs:** Nursing Alumnae Bd, 1973-; exec bd mem, Staten Island Chamber Com, 1992-; chairperson, NAACOG; Elite Group. **Special Achievements:** Author: Fetal Alcohol Syndrome (In The Neonates), 1978. **Home Addr:** 38 Parkview Loop, Staten Island, NY 10314-1662, **Home Phone:** (718)494-5475. **Business Addr:** President, Senga Travel Inc, 1918 Victory Blvd, Staten Island, NY 10314, **Business Phone:** (718)816-6108.

### DAVIS, DR. ALFRED C., SR.

Commissioner, clergy, administrator. **Personal:** Born Mar 11, 1938, Vaiden, MS; married Mary L Mack; children: Alfred C Jr, Darlene, Frederick Jerome & Angel Aleeta. **Educ:** NW Training Ctr, Ore State, attended 1969; Tacoma Voc Tech, attended 1970; Trinity Hall Col & Sem York, DD, 1980. **Career:** New Jerusalem, asst pastor, 1958-61; Altheimer Meml Ch, asst pastor, 1961-64; Eastside Comm Church, pastor & founder, 1964-, minister, currently; Multi Serv Ctr, E side, ODI, asst dir, 1965; E side Comm Day Care Ctr, founder & admin, 1972-; Tacoma Housing Auth, minister. **Orgs:** Pres & exec officer, FORCE, 1973-; founder, majestic Aires Rehab Farm Yelm, 1975-; chmn, bd commr Tacoma Housing Authority, 1977-; pres, Tacoma Ministerial Alliance, 1978-80; bd mem, Nat Commn ERS Com Nahro's, 1979-; charter mem, Tacoma Club; Nat Asn Advan Colored People; Tacoma Urban League; chmn, Ministrial Alliance; evangelism & mem, adv bd toTMA Pres. **Honors/Awds:** Service to Mankind Award, Puget Sound Sertoma Club, 1980; Dist Serv to Mankind Award, BC-WA Dist NW Region Sertoma, 1980; Key to City of Tacoma, WA from Mayor Mike Parker, 1980. **Home Addr:** 6066 S Wapate Lake Dr, Tacoma, WA 98408, **Home Phone:** (253)475-2902. **Business Addr:** Pastor, Eastside Community Church, 4420 E Portland Ave, Tacoma, WA 98404, **Business Phone:** (253)472-3552.

### DAVIS, ALGENITA SCOTT

Lawyer, vice president (organization). **Personal:** Born Oct 1, 1950, Houston, TX; daughter of Althea Lewis and CB Scott; married John Whittaker III; children: Marthea & John IV; married Ardie Segars Jr; children: Summer Nicole, Daniel, Jacquelyn & Christina. **Educ:** Howard Univ, Sch Bus, BA, acct, 1971, Sch Law, JD, tax law & taxation, 1974. **Career:** US Govt Printing Off, clerk-typist, 1969-71; Howard Univ Dept Residence Life, grad fel, 1971-74; US Gen Acct Off, legal intern, 1972; Shell Oil Co, tax serv mgr, tax compliance dept, 1974-77, off legis & indust affairs, mgr, 1977-79, Tax Compliance Dept, tax atty, 1979; Burney Edwards Hall Hartsfield & Scott, partner, 1975-78; Port Houston Authority, gen coun, 1979-89; Tex Com Bank Shares, vpres & sr vpres, community affairs officers; JP Morgan Chase & Co, mgr, sr vpres & community affairs officer, 1989-2006; Tex Southern Univ Sch Bus, vis prof, 2003-06; Lewis Affiliated Inc, partner, 2004-; Thurgood Marshall Sch Law, vis prof, 2005-06; Houston Downtown Mgt Dist, founding chair & founding pres; Houston Habitat Humanity, exec dir. **Orgs:** State Bar Tex, US Tax Ct, US Southern Dist Ct & Fifth Circuit Ct Appeals, US Supreme Ct, Interstate Comm Commn, Fed Maritime Comn; charter mem, Nat Bar Inst; polit action comm, Houston Lawyers Asn, 1975-76; bd dir, Houston Lawyers Asn, 1976-77, 1985-88, pres, Houston Lawyers Asn, 1988-89; Black Women Lawyers Asn; Judicial Campaign Worker Domestic Rels Ct Cand, 1976; Speakers Bur Houston Bar Asn, 1978-79; rep single mem, Dist Coalition Houston Lawyers Asn, 1979; NBA Invest Corp, 1984-; fundraising chair; Comt-to-re-Elect Judson Robinson Counman-at-Large Position 5, 1985; NBA Women's Div vpres, 1987-89; chair & bd dir, Third Ward Redevelop Coun; past bd chair, Houston Area Urban League, 2008; Houston Chamber Com; Zeta Phi Beta; Nat Coun Negro Women; Links Inc; Jack 'n Jill Am; exec dir, Houston Habitat Humanity Inc, 2006-13; founding dir, William A Lawson Inst Peace & Prosperity; chair, Greater Houston Women's Found; chair, Cent Houston Housing & Parking Corp; TIRZ Zone No Nine; pres, Nat Bar Asn, 1990-91; City Planning Comn; adv bd, Kinder Inst Urban Res. **Honors/Awds:** Distinguished Christian Service, Sloan Methodist Ch, 1977; Distinguished Community Service, Trinity Methodist Ch, 1978; Distinguished Service Award, Nat Bar Asn, 1982; One of Houston's Most Influential Black Women, Black Experience Mag, 1984; Houston Lawyers Association Service Award, 1985, 1987, 1988; Young Achievers Award, Human Enrichment Life Prog, 1986, 1990; Woman of Distinction, Ebony Man Mag; Named one of 5 Outstanding Young Houstonian & Texan Designers, 1989; Ebony Mag, 100 Most Influential African Americans, 1991; Woman of Distinction, 1992; Woman on the Move, 1994; Super Achiever, Human Enrichment of Life Prog, 1997; Community Service Award, Houston Bus & Prof Men's Club, 1997; Community Service Award, 1997. **Home Addr:** 5011 Jackson St, Houston, TX 77004, **Home Phone:** (713)533-1694. **Business Addr:** Partner, Lewis Affiliated Inc, 5445 Almeda Rd Suite 400, Houston, TX 77004.

### DAVIS, ALISHA

Television news anchorperson. **Personal:** married Michael Roberts. **Educ:** Harvard Univ, BA, afro-am studies, 1996. **Career:** Newsweek, reporter, 1997-2001; CNN Int, guest commentator; MSNBC, guest commentator; Fox News Channel, gen assignment corresp; Oxygen, guest commentator; Headline News, anchor, 2001-04; CNN Headlines News, anchor, 2001-05; E! News Live, co anchor, 2004-05; MTV News, news reporter, currently; Actress: Total Request Live, 1998; The Miss Teen USA Pageant, 2004; Hope & Faith, 1980-2005; Girlfriends, 2005; The Sopranos, 2007; Hollywood Heat, 2008; ABC News, journalist, 2006-. **Business Addr:** News Reporter, MTV Networks, 1515 Broadway, New York, NY 10036, **Business Phone:** (212)258-8000.

### DAVIS, ALLISON JEANNE

Executive director, founder (originator). **Personal:** Born Apr 7, 1953, New York, NY; daughter of Walter and Doris Nelson; married Robert G Wright; children: Tyler & Cooper. **Educ:** Boston Univ, BS, jour, 1975. **Career:** WBZ-TV, Boston, MA, writer & producer, 1975-78; KDKA-TV, Pittsburgh, PA, on-air reporter, 1978-81; NBC, writer-producer, 1980-98; NBC News, producer, 1981-95; Today, NBC, producer, 1984-95; "Scholastic"-NBC News Video, developer, writer & producer, 1993-97; MSNBC.com, exec producer, 1998-2000; CBS Tv, sr vpres-creative, 1998-2002; "Reading Club", creator & exec producer; Howard Univ, adj prof, 2001-03; Nat Visionary Leadership Proj, founding bd mem & vpres, 2002-07; Jackie Robinson Found, vpres, chief operating officer & spec asst to chief exec officer, 2004-09, 2012-14; City Col New York, adj prof, 2005-06; Coopty Productions, founder, 2007-; Riverside Church, New York, dir commun & media, 2009-12; CUNY's Grad Sch Journalism, adj prof, 2010-11; Arts Horizons, actg exec dir, 2014-. **Orgs:** Founding mem, parliamentarian & vpres, Nat Asn Black Journalists; foundering bd mem, Nat Visionary Leadership Proj; bd mem, Poets & Writers. **Special Achievements:** Helped launch MSNBC; first executive producer of MSNBC on the Internet, 1994-97; contributor "Global News Perspectives on the Information Age" (2001); National News Emmy judge, 2009-. **Business Addr:** Arts Horizons, 1 Grand Ave Suite 7, Englewood, NJ 07631, **Business Phone:** (201)567-1766.

### DAVIS, ALONZO J.

Artist. **Personal:** Born Feb 2, 1942, Tuskegee, AL. **Educ:** Pepperdine Col, BA, 1964; Univ Calif, Los Angeles, post grad, 1966; BFA, 1971; Otis Art Inst, MFA, 1973. **Career:** La Unified Sch Ddist, instr, 1962-70; Brockman Gallery, owner & co-dir, 1967-73; Contemp Crafts Inc, consult, 1968-70; Mt San Antonio Col, instr, 1971-73; Padasena City Col, instr, 1971; Univ Calif, Los Angeles, lectr, 1973; Watts Towers & Art Ctr, consult, 1976-; Los Angeles Col Mus Art, consult, 1976; Calif State Univ, instr, 1976-; artist, currently; San Antonio Art Inst, 1991-92; Memphis Col Art, dean, 1993-2002; Ga Southern Univ; Perry Nicole Fine Art; Memphis Col Art; La Tech Univ. **Orgs:** Exec dir, Brockman Gallery Prod, 1973-; bd mem, Calif Confederation Arts, 1976-; bd mem, Comm Arts Develop Group, 1976-77; founder, Support Arts, 1976-; bd mem, Cult News Serv, 1977-; bd mem, Artists Econ Action; ed, Neworld Mag, 1977; Plaza Club, Memphis & Shelby County Pub Libr; Marbury Wing, Prince Georges County Courthouse. **Honors/Awds:** Grants, NEA, 1973-77; Inner City Mural Grant, 1974; Excellence in Celebrating Bamboo, Arts & Crafts Competition, Am Bamboo Soc, 2006. **Special Achievements:** Published "Black Artists of the New Generation", 1977. **Business Addr:** Artist, 4410 Oglethorpe St Suite 609, Hyattsville, MD 20781, **Business Phone:** (301)454-0433.

### DAVIS, ANGELA YVONNE

Activist, writer, educator. **Personal:** Born Jan 26, 1944, Birmingham, AL; daughter of B Frank and Sallye E; married Hilton Braithwaite. **Educ:** Univ Paris, attended 1964; Brandeis Univ, BA, 1965; Univ Frankfurt, attended 1967; Univ Calif, San Diego, MA, 1968; Humboldt Univ, PhD. **Career:** Educator, author, philosopher, actor & political activist; Univ Calif, Los Angeles, asst prof, philos, 1969-70, Santa Cruz, prof hist consciousness, prof emer hist consciousness & feminist studies, currently; San Francisco State Univ & San Francisco Art Inst, prof. Books: If They Come in the Morning: Voices of Resistance, 1971; Angela Davis: An Autobiography, 1974; Women, Race & Class, 1981; Women, Culture & Politics, 1989; The Angela Y Davis Reader, 1999; Are Prisons Obsolete?, 2003. Films: Fidel, 2001; The US vs John Lennon, 2006; Blues Legacies and Black Feminism: Gertrude; Narrative of the Life of Frederick Douglass; The Meaning of Freedom. **Orgs:** Founder & co-chairperson, Nat Alliance Against Racist & Polit Repression; nat bd dir, Nat Polit Cong Black Women; nat bd mem, Nat Black Womens Health Proj; Che-Lumumba Club; Phi Beta Kappa; Black Panthers Party; Cent Comn, Communist Party; adv bd, Prison Activist Resource Ctr; Stud Nonviolent Coord Comt; founding mem, Critical Resistance; Sisters Inside Inc. **Home Addr:** 269 Moultrie St, San Francisco, CA 94110. **Business Addr:** Professor Emerita of History of Consciousness & Feminist Studies, University of California Santa Cruz, 1156 High St Rm 430, Santa Cruz, CA 95064, **Business Phone:** (831)459-5332.

### DAVIS, ANITA LOUISE

County government official, association executive. **Personal:** Born Oct 3, 1936, Williamsport, PA; daughter of Malcolm Porter and Jessie Porter; married Morris S; children: Lynn M Lyles Jeyious (deceased), Wayne D Lyles & Mark E Lyles. **Educ:** Buffalo State Col, attended 1955 & 1979; Univ NDak, Grand Forks, AFB, 1969; Univ NH, attended 1971; Univ Buffalo, attended 1972; Tallahasee Community Col; Fla A&M Univ, BS, criminal justice, 1990. **Career:** Health & Rehab Servs Leon Start Ctr, adminr asst III, 1979-83; Fla Dept Labor, employ spec, 1983-87, civil rights specialist II, 1987-89; Leon County Bd Commissioners, chmn, 1993-94; Re-elected Leon City Bd Commissioners Dist, 1994; Nat Asn County Orgn, Elder Serv Inc, vol; Pride Ct Colanthes, Community/Civic Comt, vice chair; Leon County, Proj Community Task Force Drugs & Crime, comnr, dir community enrichment; BSA Suwanne Dist Risk Kids Coun, chmn; Citizens Ethics Reform, co-chair, currently. **Orgs:** Pres, Tallahassee Br, Nat Asn Advan Colored People, 1981-90; pres, Regional/Local Int Philo Coord, Philos Sigma Gamma Rho Sorority, Beta Delta Chap, 1982-88 & 1990-; vpres, Fla State Conf Nat Asn Advan Colored People Br, 1986-99; reporter, Beta Delta Sigma Chap, 1992; Nat Hookup Black Women; FSU Leadership Conf; Capital Women's Polit Caucus; pres, Capital City Dem Women's Club; coun mem, Suwanee Area Boy Scouts Am treas& bd dir, Black Develop Found; first vpres & comt chmn, CAO Head Start Overall Policy Coun; Criminal Justice Comn, BUILD Buffalo Inc; criminal justice chairperson, Nat Asn Advan Colored People; social dir, AD Price &Perry Sr Citizens; coordr, Masten Dist Block Club Asn. **Honors/Awds:** Lifetime Achievement Award, Acad Fla Trial Lawyers, 1987; Nat Leadership Award, Nat Asn Advan Colored People, 1989 & 1990; Martin Luter King Jr Community Leadership Award, Fla A&M Univ, 1991; Community Service Award, Fla Comn Human Rels Community, 1994. **Special Achievements:** First African-American woman elected to the Leon County Commission. **Home Addr:** 708 Bragg Dr, Tallahassee, FL 32305-6706, **Home Phone:** (904)574-3075.

### DAVIS, ANTHONY D.

Football player, football coach. **Personal:** Born Mar 7, 1969, Kennewick, WA; children: Anthony Jr, Anessa & Alexus. **Educ:** Univ Utah. **Career:** Football player (retired), coach; Univ Utah, 1988-92; Seattle Seahawks, linebacker, 1993; Kans City Chiefs, 1994-98; Green Bay Packers, 1999; Baltimore Ravens, 2000; Mid Am Naz Univ, linebackers, coaching staff, 2008-. **Honors/Awds:** Super Bowl Champion, 2000. **Business Addr:** Coaching staff, MidAmerica Nazarene University, 2030 E College Way, Olathe, KS 66062-1899, **Business Phone:** (913)971-3749.

### DAVIS, ANTHONY EBONEY (COUNCILMAN ANTHONY DAVIS)

School administrator. **Personal:** Born Paterson, NJ; son of Thomas and Dorothy; married Deanna Morris. **Educ:** Cheyney Univ, BS, 1999; Rutgers Univ, Sch Social Work. **Career:** Devernex Found, recreation counr, 1987-89; Chester County Prison, correction officer, 1989-90; Comar Inc, ment health counr, 1990-91; Resource Human Develop, supvr, 1990-96; N Philadelphia Health Syst, drug, alcohol counr, 1991-93; N Philadelphia Health Syst, clin counr, 1992-96; St Joseph's Hosp, Psychiat Dept, family clinician, caseworker, 1996-2001; Passaic County Community Col, SMT Col Bound Prog, asst dir urban educ col bound/gear up prog, currently; City Paterson, councilman, 2004. **Orgs:** Chair, Omega Psi Phi, Omega Teens, 1987-; founder, Concerned Role Model Scholar, 1989-; Cheyney Univ, Nat Alumni Asn, 1990-, Mentoring Prog, 1990-; treas, Caribbean Empowerment NJ, 1996-; County Comt, 1998-; E side HS Mentoring Prog, 1998; comnr, Paterson Bd Educ, 2000-; comnr, Paterson Rent Leveling Bd, 2000-; Nat Asn Advan Colored People; Rotary Club; Toastmasters Int; vpres, Paterson City Coun, 2010-; First Ward Councilman, currently. **Honors/Awds:** Congressional Record, House Rep, 2000; Resolution of the City, City Coun, 2000; Civilian Citation, Paterson Fire Dept, 2000; New Jersey Meritorious Service Award, UNCF, 2000; Caring Indeed Award, St Josephs Hosp Psychiatry Dept, 2000. **Special Achievements:** Volunteer to Feed Patersons homeless citizens. **Home Addr:** 125 Presidential Blvd 12H, Paterson, NJ 07522, **Home Phone:** (973)956-1529. **Business Addr:** Assistant Director, Club Advisor,

Passaic County College, 1 Col Blvd 155 Mkt St 3rd Fl, Paterson, NJ 07505, **Business Phone:** (973)684-5223.

### DAVIS, ANTHONY R.
Software developer. **Personal:** Born Aug 24, 1957, New Orleans, LA; son of Donald and Anna; married Theresa; children: Brittany Nicole & Bliss Monique. **Educ:** Southern Univ, BS, comput sci, 1980; Univ Colo, MS, telecommunications, 1997. **Career:** Am Bank, night transit operator, 1976-79, asst supv, transit opers, 1979-80; Western Elec, software developer, 1980-82; Honeywell, TID, programmer, 1982-85; AT&T Bell Labs, software engr, 1985-96; Lucent Technologies, software engr, 1996-. **Orgs:** Col Asn Black Prof Engrs & Scientists; Inst Elec & Electronics Engrs Comput Soc. **Special Achievements:** Virtual Local Area Networks: The New LAN Paradigm, thesis, 1997. **Home Addr:** 3707 S Truckee Way, Aurora, CO 80013-3457, **Home Phone:** (303)690-9277. **Business Addr:** Technical Staff, Lucent Technologies, 11900 N Pecos St Rm 31A 71, Westminster, CO 80234, **Business Phone:** (303)538-2405.

### DAVIS, ANTONE EUGENE
Football player, business owner. **Personal:** Born Feb 28, 1967, Sweetwater, TN; son of Milton Trice; married Carrie; children: Cailyn Marie, Dakota, Carley & Braden. **Educ:** Univ Tenn, urban studies, 1990. **Career:** Football player (retired), football coach, owner; Philadelphia Eagles, right tackle, 1991-93, 1995, left guard, 1994; Atlanta Falcons, right tackle, 1996, tackle, 1997; Green Bay Packers, 1999; Chilis restaurant, mgr, 2011; Univ Tenn, Vol Life, coordr, 2012-; Northwestern Mutual Financial Network, financial rep; Gridiron Grill Restaurant, owner; Rocky Top Holdings LLC, owner, currently. **Orgs:** Am Cancer Soc; Spec Olympics; Campus Crusade Christ; Jr Achievement & Community Found; Christian Athletes & S Lake Kids Hope USA. **Honors/Awds:** Jacobs Trophy, Univ Tenn, 1990; best blocker, southeastern Conference; Unanimous All-America honors. **Special Achievements:** TV Series: "ESPN's Sunday Night Football", 1993; "NFL Monday Night Football", 1993-94; "The Biggest Loser", 2011-12. **Home Addr:** , Knoxville, TN. **Business Addr:** Owner, Rocky Top Holdings LLC, 11435 Lake Louisa Rd, Clermont, FL 34711.

### DAVIS, ANTONIO CAMERON. See ANDREWS, REAL.

### DAVIS, ANTONIO LEE
Executive, basketball player, basketball coach. **Personal:** Born Oct 31, 1968, Oakland, CA; married Kendra; children: Antonio Jr & Kaela. **Educ:** Univ Tex, El Paso, attended 1990. **Career:** Basketball player (retired), coach, executive; Panathinaikos, Greece, 1990-92; Philips Milano Ital league, 1992-93; Ind Pacers, pt forward, 1993-99, agt; Toronto Raptors, ctr, 1999-2001, 2002-06, pt forward, 2001-02; Team USA, 2002; Chicago Bulls, ctr, 2003-04, power forward, 2004-05; New York Knicks, pt forward, 2005-06; MPA's basketball team, asst coach; ESPN, Nat Basketball Asn Broadcasts, studio analyst, 2012-. **Orgs:** Pres, NBA Players Asn, 2005. **Honors/Awds:** Silver Medal, Tournament Americas, 1989; Sears Community Service Award, 2000; NBA All-Star Award, 2001; African-American Ethnic Sports Hall of Fame, 2010.

### DAVIS, REV. ARNOR S. See Obituaries Section.

### DAVIS, HON. ARRIE W.
State government official, educator. **Personal:** Born Jul 21, 1940, Baltimore, MD; children: Joanne & Aria. **Educ:** Morgan State Col, BA, 1963; NY Univ, MA, 1966; Univ Baltimore, JD, 1969. **Career:** Judge (retired), educator; Baltimore City Pub Sch, Eng instr, 1964-69; Edmondson Senior High School, swimming coach; American Red Cross, water safety instructor; Supreme Bench Baltimore, bailiff, 1968-69; Judge Joseph Carter & Master Harry Sachs, law clerk, 1968-69; Baltimore City, asst atty gen, Criminal Appeals Div, 1971-79; Morgan State Univ, bus law instr, 1971-81; Villa Julie Col, law instr, 1972-80; Baltimore City, Dept Pub Safety & Correctional Serv, Div Correction, coun, 1979-81; Baltimore City, Dist Ct Md, Dist 1, assoc judge, 1981-83; Baltimore City, legis comt mem, 1989-91, exec comt, 1995-97, Civil Law & Procedure Comt, 1998-2001; Baltimore City Circuit Ct, 8th Judicial Circuit, assoc judge, 1983-90; City Baltimore, Ct Spec Appeals Md, judge, 1990-2010; Judicial Inst Md, bd dir, 2000-07; New Judges' Orientation, instr, 2000-. **Orgs:** Baltimore City Bar Asn; Md Bar, 1969; Md State Bar Asn; Am Bar Asn; Nat Bar Asn; Comt Study Sentencing & Correctional Alternatives Women Convicted Crime, 1987-88; Monumental Bar Asn; Baltimore City Bar Found; Wranglers Law Club, 1998-; chair, Harry A. Cole Judicial Coun; Md Bar Found, 1999-; State Comn Criminal Sentencing Policy, 2000-14; bd dir, Md Judicial Conf, 2000-07; bd dir, Acad St. James Episcopal Church. **Honors/Awds:** Legal Excellence Award, Waring Mitchell Law Society of Howard County, 1994; Legacy for Excellence in Litigation Award, Snyder Center, Univ Baltimore Sch of Law, 2003; Legal Excellence Award, J. Franklyn Bourne Bar Asn, 2004; Alumnus of the Year, Univ of Baltimore Sch of Law, 2004; Recognized as Distinguished Alumnus of Frederick Douglass Senior High School, Baltimore City Council, 2005; Hall of Fame, Nat Bar Asn, 2011. **Home Addr:** 5716 Charlestowne Dr, Baltimore, MD 21212-2415, **Home Phone:** (410)358-7187.

### DAVIS, ARTHUR, III
City planner, educator, consultant. **Personal:** Born Nov 12, 1942, Sampson County, NC; son of Arthur; children: Arthur Paris. **Educ:** Morehouse Col, BA, 1965; Carnegie-Mellon Univ, MA, 1966; Univ Pittsburgh, MPA, 1967. **Career:** City planner (retired), educator, consultant; NC Agr & Tech State Univ , asst prof, 1967-68, 1990-95; City Greensboro, sr planner, 1969-2005; Guilford Col, lectr, 1975-81; consult, 1975-; NC Agr & Tech State Univ, asst prof, plng & design, consult assoc; Carolina Eval Res Ctr, city, corp, church planner. **Orgs:** Bd NC Fels Bd, 1971-84; Nat Greene Sertoma pres & bd, 1971; bd & pres, Greensboro Interclub Coun, 1971-98; pres bd, Greensboro Credit Union, 1978; bd chmn, Greensboro Emp Co mem, 1978-82; Gen Greene Coun BSA, 1980-; secy, NC APA, 1980-86; bd secy, Am Plng Orgn, 1981-85; Grimsley PTA bd, 1982-86; United Arts Coun Bd, 1983-85; USOA Bd, 1985-90; Greensboro Visions I & II, 1986-92; bd mem, NC ASPA, 1987-; staff adv, Ole Asheboro Neighborhood Asn, 1989-; COM 100, 1989-; bd, Human Serv IST, 1989-95; adv bd GTCC, 1989-; County Resource Housing Bd, 1990-94; Minority Women Bus deveop Coun, 1990-; pres, Am Soc Pub Admin, 1991-92; BSA Eagle Rev Bd, 1991-; Ctr City Coun, 1995-; Morehouse Col Alumni Club; area rep, Exec Comt, Greensboro Neighborhood Cong; United Way Adv Coun; Old N State Boy Scouts Eagle Coun; Hayes Taylor YMCA Bd; Strategic Plng Comt; GTCC; Housing Greensboro Bd; Nat Greene Sertoma Bd; Metro YMCA Endowment Develop Comt; Bd Equalization & Rev, Guilford County Comnr; coun mem, City Greensboro. **Honors/Awds:** Community Service Award, A&T, 1974 & 1975; Univ S Jaycees, Am Plng Asn, A&T Univ, 1975; Men of Achievement, 1976; Award Greensboro, YMCA, 1978; Comm Serv Sertoma Int, 1981; numerous citations US Dept of Comm, President Leadership Award, 1983; Greensboro 100 Award, 1991; NBFPA Service Award Outstanding Citizen, 1992; Outstanding 100 Citizens, 1992; ASPA Outstanding Service Award, 1992; Sertoma Award, 1993; YPL Award, 1993; Carolina Peacemaker Award, 1993; Ole Asheboro Award, 1994; NC Credit Union Volunteer, 1994; City Service Award, 1995; Leadership 2000, 1996-98; Technology/Strategic Planning, 1997; Comm of 100 Service Award, 1997; NAACP Award, 1998; Sertoman of the Year Sertoma InterNat, 1998; Employee of the Yr, 1998; NAHRN Award, 1998, Hayes Taylor YMCA, 1999; City Service Award, 1999; Sertoma Award, 1999; Hayes Taylor YMCA, 2000; President's Award, NFBPA, 2001; Nat Green Sertoma, 2001; NC Neighbors Award, 2003; Carolina Peacemaker, 2002. **Home Addr:** 910 Ross Ave, Greensboro, NC 27406-2414, **Home Phone:** (336)273-3849. **Business Addr:** Council Member, City of Greensboro, 910 Ross Ave, Greensboro, NC 27406-2414, **Business Phone:** (336)273-3849.

### DAVIS, ARTUR
Politician, government official. **Personal:** Born Oct 9, 1967, Montgomery, AL; married Tara Johnson. **Educ:** Harvard Univ, BA, 1990; Harvard Law Sch, JD, 1993. **Career:** Mid Dist Ala, lawyer, pvt pract, 1993-94; Mid Dist Ala, asst to US atty, 1994-98; Southern Poverty Law Ctr, intern; pvt pract civil rights law; FOX Network, Birmingham, legal & polit commentator; US House Rep, Ala 7th Cong Dist, dem mem, 2003-11, Republican Party, 2012-. **Orgs:** Cong Black Caucus; Dem Cong Campaign Comt; co chmn, New Dem Network; co char, New Dem Coalition; fel Harvards prestigious Inst Polit. **Home Addr:** 550 14th Rd S Apt 424, Arlington, VA 22202, **Home Phone:** (571)319-0252. **Business Addr:** Republican Party.

### DAVIS, BARBARA D.
Executive. **Educ:** St Joseph Calumet Col; Ind Univ; Univ Wis. **Career:** Insland Steel Proj, off mgr, 1976-77, recruiter-counr, 1977-78, asst proj dir, 1978-79, dir, 1980; Gilbane Bldg Co, equal employ opportunity officer, 1982, corp affirmative action specialist, 1984-. **Orgs:** Ill Affirmative Action Officers Asn; chairperson, IAAOA Conf, 1985; liaison Black Contractors United/Chicago Urban League; consult, World's Fair Plan Affirmative Action; pres, Women Construct; consult, Int Women Econ Develop Corp; Ind Civil Rights Comn; vpres, Fair Share Orgn; consult, Women's League State Affil; Nat Asn Advan Colored People. **Honors/Awds:** Union Counselor Award, AFL-CIO Lake Co Cent Labor Union & United Steel Workers Am Local 1010; Affirmative Action Officer of the Year Award, Black Contractors United; Dedicated Service Award, Nat Coun Black Child Develop NY; Spec Award, Black Contractors United, 1985. **Home Addr:** 1054 Ralston St, Gary, IN 46406. **Business Addr:** Corporate Affirm Action Officer, 200 W Madison St Suite 700, Chicago, IL 60606.

### DAVIS, BELVA
Television show host. **Personal:** Born Oct 13, 1933, Monroe, LA; daughter of John Melton and Florence Howard Mays; married William Vince Moore; children: Steven Eugene & Darolyn Denise. **Educ:** Oakland City Col; San Francisco State Univ. **Career:** Anchor (retired); Oakland Naval Supply Depot, typist; Jet, freelancer, 1957; Sun Reporter, ed, 1961-68; Bay Area Independent, reporter; KSAN; KDIA, disc jockey; KNEW, 1964-66; KPIX-TV, anchor, 1966; KQED-TV, A Closer Look & Eve Ed, host, 1977-2012; Cont Commodity Serv Inc, interest rate specialist, 1978-82; KRON-TV, news anchor & urban affairs specialist, 1981; Chicago Bd Trade; Harris Trust & Savings Bank, govt securities rep, 1982-83; Dean Witter Reynolds, hedging & trading strategist, 1983-85, sr financial futures analyst, 1985-, vpres, 1985-92; CNBC, specialist, anchor, 1992-97; FOX News Channel, sr bus corresp; Wall St Week, co-anchor, currently. **Orgs:** Awards Comt, San Francisco Found, 1982-88; nat vpres, Am Fedn TV & Radio Artists, 1984-; bd mem, Howard Thurman Found; bd mem, Black Filmmakers Hall Fame; Links; bd mem, Commonwealth Club Calif, 1991-; bd mem, Blue Shield Calif, 1992-; bd mem, Metro YMCA; long-time mem & off, Am Fedn Tv & Radio Artists; Bay area community, serv Adv Coun Int Mus Women. 2008-; bd mem; Mus African Diaspora; bd mem, Inst Aging; bd mem, Fine Arts Mus San Francisco. **Honors/Awds:** Best newscast, Corporation for Public Broadcasting, 1978; Seven Emmy's No Cal TV Acad; National Journal Award, Nat Urban Coalition, 1985; Nat Journal Award, Ohio State Univ, 1985; Silver Circle Inductee, National Academy of Television Arts & Sciences, Northern Calif. Chapter, 1989, Governor's Award, 1995; Outstanding Journalism, Sigma Delta Chi, 1990; Honorary PhD, for television and community service work, 1996; Governor's Award, NC Chap, Nat Acad TV Arts & Sci, 1996; Lifetime Achievement Award, Nat Acad TV Arts & Sci; Lifetime Achievement Award, American Women in Radio & Television, Golden Gate Chapter, 1999; Belva Davis Diversity Scholarship, 1999; International Women's Media Foundation Courage Award, Lifetime Achievement Award Recipient, 2004; Former Vice President, American Federation of Television and Radio Artists; Chair Emeritus, National Equal Employment Opportunities; Lifetime Achievement Award, National Association of Black Journalists; Leadership Award, Coro Northern California, 2004; Lifetime Achievement Award, 100 Black Men of the Bay Area, 2005; Honorary member, Alpha Kappa Alpha Sorority Inc; Award for Excellent Broadcasting, Radio Television News Directors Association; Lincoln Award, Leon & Sylvia Panetta Institute, 2007; Inducted to the Bay Area Radio Hall of Fame, 2007. **Special Achievements:** First black female at KSAN; First Female African American television reporter on the West Coast; Author, Never in My Wildest Dreams: A Black Woman's Life in Journalism, 2010. **Home Addr:** 588 Sutter St Suite 297, San Francisco, CA 94102, **Home Phone:** (415)322-0405. **Business Addr:** Special Projects Reporter, KRON Channel 4, 1001 Van Ness Ave, San Francisco, CA 94109, **Business Phone:** (415)441-4444.

### DAVIS, BEN JEROME
Basketball player. **Personal:** Born Dec 26, 1972, Vero Beach, FL. **Educ:** Kans Univ, attended 1992; Univ Fla; Hutchinson Community Col, attended 1994; Univ Ariz, attended 1996. **Career:** Basketball player (retired); Phoenix Suns, power forward, 1996-97, 1999-2000; Continental Basketball Asn, Grand Rapids Hoops, 1997-98; NY Knics, power forward, 1997-99; Capitanes de Arecibo, Pr, 1998; Tau Ceramica, Spain, 1998; Continental Basketball Asn, Idaho Stampede, 1999; Brujos de Guayama, Pr, 2000; Am Basketball Asn, Kans City Knights, 2000; Makedonikos, Greece, 2000-01; Trotamundos de Carabobo, Venezuela, 2001; Cantabria Lobos, Spain, 2001-02; Roseto Sharks, Italy, 2002-03; Houston Rockets, 2003-04; Us Basketball League, Westchester Wildfire, 2004; Benfica, Port, 2005-06; Paysandu BB, Uruguay, 2006-07; Lechugueros de Leon, Mex, 2008-09; Liceo de Costa Rica, 2008-09. **Honors/Awds:** Virginia Player of the Year, Oak Hill Acad. **Business Addr:** Player, Liceo de Costa Rica00107, **Business Phone:** (506)2221-376.

### DAVIS, DR. BENNIE L.
Physician. **Personal:** Born Dec 7, 1927, Muskogee, OK; children: Benjamin & Duane. **Educ:** Samuel Huston Col, BS, 1947; Howard Univ, MD, 1952. **Career:** Homer G Philips Hosp, St Louis, internship, 1952-53, resident, 1957; Terre Haute IN, gen pract, 1953-54; Homer G Phillips Hosp, surg resident, 1953-55; urol resident, 1954-58; Pvt Pract Indianapolis, urologist, 1960. **Orgs:** AMA; Nat Med Asn; Alpha Phi Alpha Frat; Chi Delta Mu Sci Frat; Sigma P Phi Frat; Am Urol Asn; Ind Univ Med Ctr; Rotarty Club; Our Savior Luthern Church; Div Urol Meth Hosp Grad Med Ctr; Urol Sec Nat Med Asn; fel Am Col Surgeons, 1963. **Honors/Awds:** Diplomate, Am Bd Urol, 1961. **Home Addr:** 6007 Crows Nest Dr, Indianapolis, IN 46208. **Business Addr:** Physician, 2615 N Capitol Ave, Indianapolis, IN 46208.

### DAVIS, DR. BERTHA LANE
Educator. **Personal:** Born Sep 3, 1950, Mobile, AL; daughter of James Lane and Marie Woods Lane; married George W; children: Geoffrey J. **Educ:** Tuskegee Univ, BS, 1972; Coppin State Col, MEd, 1975; Univ Md, MS, 1977; Wash State Univ, PhD, 1983; Univ Pa, Naval War Col, further study, 2001. **Career:** Hampton Univ, dean Sch Nursing, 1991-96, asst dean res, 1998-2006, prof, 2012-; Admin HU Nursing Ctr/ Heath Mobile chair, Dept Grad Nursing Educ, 1985-91; Community Ment Health Psychiat Nursing Track, dir. **Orgs:** Chi Eta Phi Nursing Sorority, 1976-; Sigma Theta Tau Int, 1981-; Am Nurses Assn, 1981-; Fel Am Acad Nursing, 1991; Alpha Kappa Alpha Sorority, 2005; Acad Nursing Educ, Fel, 2007. **Special Achievements:** USAR AN LTC (retired) Corps, 2005; Operation Smile International, Medical Missions Support Team, Monrovia Liberia, 1987-88. **Home Addr:** 2 Haywagon Trail, Hampton, VA 23669, **Home Phone:** (757)850-3303. **Business Addr:** Hampton, VA.

### DAVIS, BETTYE J.
State government official, social worker, executive director. **Personal:** Born May 17, 1938, Homer, LA; daughter of Dan Ivory and Rosylind Daniel Ivory; married Troy J; children: Anthony B & Sonja Wade. **Educ:** St Anthony Sch Practical Nursing, GN, 1961; Grambling State Univ, BSW, 1972; Univ Alaska; UA Anchorage, post grad, 1977. **Career:** Social worker (retired), state rep; YWCA San Bernardino, asst dir, 1971-72; DFYS Anchorage, child care specialist, 1975-80; Alaska Black Leadership Educ Prog, dir, 1979-82; Anchorage Youth Serv Div Family, social worker, 1980; Anchorage Div Soc Serv, foster dr; Anchorage Bd Ed, vpres; State Alaska Div Family & Youth Servs, foster care coordr, 1982-89; Alaska House Representatives, 14th Dist, mem, 1991-93, 21st Dist, 1993-97, K Dist, mem, 2001-13; NCSL Health Comt, Nat Conf State Legislatures, presiding officer, 2007-08; Anchorage Sch Dist Sch Bd, seat a rep, 2016-. **Orgs:** N Future BPW Club Inc, 1978-79; Church Women United; Common Ground; pres, Anchorage Chap Delta Sigma Theta, 1979-80; bd dir, March Dimes, 1983-85; bd dir, Nat Caucus Black Sch Bd Mem, 1987-89; pres, Nat Sch Bd Asn, 1989-91; bd mem, YWCA Anchorage, 1989-90; bd dir, Alaska 2000 Educ Proj, 1991-; bd dir, Winning with Stronger Educ, 1991-; bd dir, Anchorage Ctr Families, 1992-; Anchorage Sch Bd: 1998-99; pres, Alaska Fed Bus & Prof Women, 1999-2000; Alaska Black Leadership Conf; treas, Alaska Women's Lobby; Blacks Govt; chairperson, Alaska Black Caucus; Anchorage Br Nat Asn Advan Colored People; League Women Voters; Alaska Women's Polit Caucus; Nat Asn Advan Colored People; Anchorage Zonta Club; life mem Delta Sigma Theta Sorority; life mem, Bus & Prof Women; Campfire; bd mem, Spec Olympics; Athena Socs, 1994-; Anchorage Zonta Club, 1994-; chair, Alaska Black Caucus. **Honors/Awds:** Woman of the Year, Alaska Colored Womens Club, 1981; Social Worker of the Year, Nat Foster Parents Asn, 1983; Child Care Worker of the Year, Alaska Foster Parent Asn, 1983; Political Awareness Award of the Year, Alaska Black Caucus, 1984; Outstanding Achievement Award in Education, Alaska Colored Womens Club, 1985; Outstanding Women in Education, Zeta Phi Beta, 1985; Outstanding Service Award, Alaska Black Caucus, 1986; Outstanding Political Awareness Award, Alaska Black Caucus, 1986; Community Service Award, Alaska Black Leadership, 1986; Caucus Member of the Year, Alaska Black Caucus, 1987; Boards manship Award, Asn Alaska Sch Boards, 1989; Outstanding Board Member Award, Asn Alaska Sch Boards, 1990; Woman of the Year, Alaska Bus & Prof Womens Club, 1990; Woman of Achievement Award, YWCA, 1991; Henry Toll Fellowship, Toll Fel, 1992; Outstanding Leadership Award, California Assembly, 1992; Grambling State University Hall of Fame, 2008. **Home Addr:** 2240 Foxhall Dr, Anchorage, AK 99504, **Home Phone:** (907)337-2034. **Business Addr:** Seat A Representative, Anchorage School District School Board, 5530 E Northern Lights Blvd, Anchorage, AK 99504, **Business Phone:** (907)742-4000.

### DAVIS, BEVERLY WATTS
Executive, administrator. **Educ:** Trinity Univ, San Antonio, BA, econs, polit sci, social sci; Webster Univ, Jeffersonville, MA. **Career:** Texan's War Drugs, statewide coord, Dir Prog; Community Mobilization, nat trainer; San Antonio Fighting Back, exec dir; San Antonio United Way, sr vpres; US Dept Health & Human Serv Nat Ctr Advan Prev,

consul; Ctr Substance Abuse Prev, Substance Abuse & Ment Health Serv Admin, US Dept Health & Human Serv, dir, 2003-. **Orgs:** Bd Trustee, chair, vice-chair, secy, Austin Reg Community Col; US Dept Housing & Urban Develop Nat Adv Comt; Nat Inhalant Abuse Prev Coalition; chair, Multi-Cult Affairs Comt Tex Com Alcohol & Drug Abuse; bd dir, NOWS Crime Prev Coalitions Americas chair; Tex Task Force local drugcontrol; founder & chair, Women's Chamber Com; sr vpres, United Way San Antonio & Bexar County; exec dir, San Antonio Fighting Back Anti-Drug Community Coalition. **Business Addr:** Director, Center for Substance Abuse Prevention, 1 Choke Cherry Rd Rm 4-1057, Rockville, MD 20857, **Business Phone:** (240)276-2000.

### DAVIS, BILLY, JR.
Entertainer, singer. **Personal:** Born Jun 26, 1938, St. Louis, MO; married Marilyn McCoo; children: Steven; children: 1. **Career:** Singer, recording artist, entertainer; solo artist, 1975-; performed as duet act, Marilyn McCoo & BillyDavis Jr, 1976-80; variety show: "The Marilyn McCoo & Billy Davis JrShow", CBS-TV, 1977; TV series; "It Takes a Thief", 1970; "The Love Boat", 1978; Let Me Have A Dream, 1982; "Grizzly Adams & the Legend of Dark Mountain", 1999; "The Jamie Foxx Show", 1999-2001; Thank You, Good Night, 2001; "Lifestyle Magazine", 2001; "VH-1 Where Are They Now?", 2002; "Hollywood Squares", 2002; "Pyramid", 2003; "Tavis Smiley", 2004; An Evening of Stars, 2004; Mississippi Rising, 2005; The Billy Davis Rhythm Machine, head, 2008; 2008 Camie Awards, 2008; My Music: My Generation-The 60s, 2008; Marvin Hamlisch Presents, 2010. **Orgs:** Fifth Dimension, mem, 1965-75; Bill Glass Ministries; Billy Graham & Luis Palau Ministries. **Honors/Awds:** Grammy Award with Marilyn McCoo, "You Don't Have To Be A Star",1977; Hollywood's Walk of Fame, 1997; Tokyo Music Festival, Grand Prize with Marilyn McCoo; Five Grammy Awards; Star on the Hollywood Walk of Fame; 14 Gold Records; Grammy Award for Best R&B Performance by a Duo or Group. **Special Achievements:** Guest appearance, The Trinity Broadcasting Network; Author: Up, Up, and Away: How We Found Love, Faith, and Lasting Marriage in the Entertainment World, 2004; The first African American married couple to host a network television series. **Business Addr:** Entertainer, William Morris Agency, 1325 Avenue of the Americas, New York, NY 10019, **Business Phone:** (212)586-5100.

### DAVIS, BILLY. See DAVIS, WILLIAM AUGUSTA, III.

### DAVIS, BING. See DAVIS, WILLIS H.

### DAVIS, DR. BRENDA LIGHTSEY-HENDRICKS
School administrator, president (organization). **Personal:** Born Dec 21, 1943, Fairfield, AL; daughter of Guy and Flora; married William R David; children: Tonia D Kelly, William R Jr, Scott, Frank B & Joye Lynn. **Educ:** Harlem Hosp Sch Nursing, dipl, nursing, 1964; Teachers Col Columbia Univ, BS, nursing, 1969, MEd, psychiat, 1972, EdD, curric & teaching, 1976. **Career:** President (retired); Riverside Community Col, dir & chairperson nursing, 1975, dean nursing educ, dean occup educ, dean grants & contract educ, Norco Campus, provost, pres, 1993-2006; Norco Col, pres, 2006-11, pres emerita, 2011-13. **Orgs:** Nat League Nurses, 1975-; Calif Community Col Adminrs, 1984-; Am Vocational Educ Asn, 1984-; Diamond Bar Black Women's Asn, 1985-; Nat Black Nurses' Asn, 1985-; pres, Inland Empire Black Nurses' Asn, 1986-; adv comt mem, Calif State Univ, San Bernardino, 1986; Black Hist ProgComt, DBBWA, 1986-. **Honors/Awds:** Training Grant NY State, 1968-69; Minority Scholarship Teachers Col Columbia, 1970; Training Grant Nat Inst Ment Health, 1971-75. **Home Addr:** 2149 S Indian Creek Rd, Diamond Bar, CA 91765. **Business Addr:** President, Riverside Community College, 2001 3rd St, Norco, CA 92860-2600, **Business Phone:** (951)372-7000.

### DAVIS, BRIAN KEITH
Basketball player, businessperson, basketball coach. **Personal:** Born Jun 21, 1970, Atlantic City, NJ; married Marsha; children: Brian Jr. **Educ:** Duke Univ, attended 1992. **Career:** Basketball player (retired), coach, businessperson; Fr League, Pau Orthez, 1992-93; NBA, Minn Timberwolves, small forward, 1994-95; Aliaga Petkim, 2000; Pan-Am Games team, 1994; Joy Game LLC, coach & dir basketball opers, 1994-; Blue Devil Ventures, managing partner, currently. **Orgs:** Nat Historic Trust. **Honors/Awds:** First Team All-ACC Tournament, 1992. **Special Achievements:** Only African American in NCAA history to play in four consecutive Final Four tournaments. **Business Addr:** Director Of Basketball Operations, Joy of the Game LLC, 158 S Waukegan Rd, Deerfield, IL 60015, **Business Phone:** (847)498-6646.

### DAVIS, BROWNIE W.
Insurance executive, president (organization). **Personal:** Born Mar 13, 1933, Philadelphia, PA; son of Brownie and Eloise; married Elba; children: Brenda & Bruce. **Educ:** City Col New York, NY, BA, 1957; Life Underwriter Trng Coun, grad advan underwriting & health ins. **Career:** Va Hosp Brooklyn, radioisotope tech; Farmingdale LI Unit, repub aviation supvr; Williamsburgh Steel Prod Co, draftsman off mgr; Macy's Rego Park, mgr in-charge, housewares; NY Life Ins Co, field underwriter; Guardian Life Ins Co Am, dist agency mgr; Manhattan Community Col, adj prof, 1986-; LaGuardia Community Col, adj prof, 1989; Brownie W Davis Agency Corp, pres, currently. **Orgs:** Pres, Queens Br First Nat Asn Life Underwriters; NY Life Agt Adv Coun, 1973-74; adv bd mem, Minority Bus Coun; Queens Chamber Com; bonding chmn, Asn Minority Bus Enterprises, vpres; pres, Cedar Manor Co-op, 1967-70; bd mem, NY Housing Auth, Symphony Orchestra; exec vpres, Nat Minority Bus Coun; Aetna Great Performance Club, 1986-88; bd mem, United Blackmen Queens; Black Achiever in Indust Harlem YMCA, 1974, chmn Bd Mgrs, 1979-82. **Honors/Awds:** Centurion, 1967-; Health Insurance Leader, 1967-75; National Quality Award for Life-Health, 1972-75; Group Insurance Leader, 1973; Company Honor Roll over 100 Consecutive Months; Black Achiever in Indiana, 1974; Leader Aetna Life & Casualty Region; Leadership Award, York Col, 1989. **Business Addr:** President, Brownie W Davis Agency, 22 Elm St, Woodmere, NY 11598, **Business Phone:** (516)569-7979.

### DAVIS, DR. BRUCE R.
Executive. **Personal:** Born Dec 27, 1963, Cordele, GA; son of Andrew Carter West and Eddie Mae; married Shawn Watson; children: Bruce Randall II & Br. **Educ:** Clark Col, BA, bus admin & acct, 1986; Atlanta Univ, MBA, finance, 1988. **Career:** Marathon Oil Co, staff acct, 1984-85; Univ Southern Calif, adj prof; Bank One, corp credit analyst, 1987; Bank Am, lender & asst vpres, 1988-93; Chevron Corp, staff res scientist; Davis, Marks & Assocs, sr engineering consult & founder; Appraisal Assocs, partner; Davis Productions, pres, consult; JPMorgan Chase Bank, vpres; PNC Bank Corp, vpres, pres; Davis Aircraft Prod Co, pres, vhief exec officer; Nat City Bank, community pres, 1993-; Community State Bank, vpres & invest officer, financial advisor; Community Futures Develop Corp, cult develop coordr, currently; Midbrook Indust Washers Inc, chief exec officer, owner; Davis Capital Inc, founder, pres & chief exec officer. **Orgs:** SPE Found, 1973-; golf comm chmn, Greater Jackson Chamber Community, 2002-; dir, fin comm, Jackson Non-Profit Support Ctr, 2002-; dir, mkt workgroup, Foote Hosp HIO Community, 2002-; dir, funding comm, Jr Achievement, 2003-; Fel Midtown asn; bd mem, Highfields Inc; cult develop advisor, SD&G Co. **Home Addr:** 3720 Colchester Rd, Lansing, MI 48906, **Home Phone:** (517)321-4520. **Business Addr:** Community President, National City Bank of Jackson, 101 E Mich Ave, Jackson, MI 49201-1434, **Business Phone:** (517)780-0507.

### DAVIS, BUNNY COLEMAN
Librarian. **Personal:** Born Mar 21, 1946, New Orleans, LA; daughter of Joseph and Elberta Plummer; children: Sean & Mark. **Educ:** Memphis State Univ, BS, educ, 1972; George Peabody Col Vanderbilt Univ, MLS, 1975. **Career:** Memphis City Schs, librn, 1972-85, 1988-; State Dept Educ, evaluator, 1985-88. **Orgs:** Nat Educ Asn; Alpha Kappa Alpha Sor Inc; Holy Rosary Outreach Prog. **Home Addr:** 5020 Pheasant Run Lane, Memphis, TN 38141-0206, **Home Phone:** (901)366-4635.

### DAVIS, DR. CARRIE LOUISE FILER. See Obituaries Section.

### DAVIS, CHARLES
Government official. **Personal:** Born Sep 4, 1944, Seattle, WA; married Lonear W Heard; children: Charles II & Jenise A. **Educ:** Calif State Univ, BS, bus, 1972. **Career:** Government official (retired), consultant; Hughes Aircraft Co, contract adm acct, 1966-73; City Compton, clerk, 1973-2003; consultant, currently. **Orgs:** Int Inst Munic Clerks, 1973-; Am Rec Mgt Asn, 1973-; Am Mgt Asn Adv Bd Compton & Br Salvation Army; exec bd, YMCA; S E Area Planning Coun; Calif City Clerks Asn; Compton Community Col Dist, trustee. **Honors/Awds:** Air force Craftmanship Award, Hughes Aircraft Co, 1971; Community Service Award, Compton Model Cities, 1974; Merit Award, Inner City Challenge Inc, 1974; Council Resolution of Appreciation, 1975. **Special Achievements:** First African American to receive "Certified Municipal Clerk" designation in the US, 1976. **Home Addr:** 334 W Palm St, Compton, CA 90220, **Home Phone:** (310)635-6316. **Business Addr:** Trustee, Compton Community College District, 1111 E Artesia Blvd, Compton, CA 90221.

### DAVIS, CHARLES
Basketball player, athletic director, athlete. **Personal:** Born Sep 7, 1949, New York, NY; married Linda; children: Sharrika DeVae & Sydney Rae. **Educ:** Wake Forest Univ, BA, Eng, 1971, MA, lib sci, 1997. **Career:** Basketball player, athletic player (retired); athletic dir; Cleveland Cavaliers, pt guard, 1971-72; Portland Trail Blazers, pt guard, 1972-73; Wake Forest Univ, sports marketer & acct exec, 1989, dir community progs, 1991-94, asst athletic dir, 1995-99; Bowie State Univ, athletics dir, 2000-02; NC Agr & Tech State Univ, athletics dir, 2002-04. **Orgs:** Millennium Fund. **Honors/Awds:** Wake Forest Sports Hall of Fame, 1984; Award of Excellence, Athletic Management Mag, 1996; ACC Men's Basketball Player of the Year, 1971. **Special Achievements:** First African American to be named the ACC Player of the Year; named to the ACC 50th Anniversary Men's Basketball Team, Second African American player in Wake Forest's history.

### DAVIS, CHARLES A.
Executive director, president (organization), executive. **Personal:** Born Sep 29, 1922, Mobile, AL; son of Robert and Clara; married Rosalie Dorsey; children: Charles Jr & Daphne Kaye. **Educ:** WVa State Col, attended 1944; Roosevelt Univ Chicago, polit sci, 1953; Chicago's Cent YMCA Col. **Career:** Journalist, pub rels consult, bus entrepreneur & civic vol; Jayson Bldg Corp, Phoenix Real Estate Group, Adco Asn, entrepreneur; dir advert, dir pub rel, city educ, sportswriter, reporter, dir, Highland Community Bank; Chicago Defender, 1946-59; Jayson Bldg Assoc, gen partner; Adco Assoc, founder & gen partner; ADCO II, partner; Charles A Davis & Assoc Inc, pres, currently. **Orgs:** Econ Club; life mem, Nat Asn Advan Colored People; Chicago Urban League; Alpha Phi Alpha Fraternity; Church Good Shepherd, 1934; exec dir, Nat Ins Asn, 1962; Pub Rels Socs Am, 1971; Coord Coun Community Orgn; Chicago Comn Human Rels; Chicago Econ Develop Corp;Cook County Comprehensive Health & Hosps; Allied Med Serv Gov Comn; Chicago Econ Develop Comn. **Home Addr:** 2121 W Howland Ave, Chicago, IL 60620. **Business Addr:** President, Charles A Davis & Associates LLC, 29340 Indust Way Suite D401, Evergreen, CO 80439-7853, **Business Phone:** (303)239-6276.

### DAVIS, CHARLES FRANKLIN
Sports manager, football player, executive. **Personal:** Born Nov 14, 1964, Elizabethton, TN; son of Franklin and Hildred; married Lisa Hales; children: Taylor & Parker. **Educ:** Univ Tenn, Knoxville, BA, polit sci, 1986, MA, hist, 1989. **Career:** Tenn Vols, defensive back, 1983-86; S Eastern Conf, fel, 1988; Univ Pac, asst football coach, 1989-90; USS Olympic Comt, asst to exec dir, 1990, dir, USS Olympic Training Ctr, 1990-94; Stanford Univ, asst athletic dir, 1994-96; 740 The Team, co-hosting, 2000-02 Turner Sports & NBC Sports, broadcaster; ESPN, sport analyst, 2004; Fox Sports S & Sunshine Network, analyst, 2006-; Tampa Bay Buccaneers, analyst, 2007-08; NFL Network, analyst, 2007-09; CBS, sideline reporter, 2001-02; TBS, leafd col football analyst; Golf Channel, commentator; Sun Sports; NBC; TNT; Atlanta Falcons preseason broadcasts, game analyst; NFL Network cohort Jim Mora, game analyst, 2007; Dick Stockton, game analyst. **Orgs:** Colorado Springs Opera Festival, bd, 1991-94; Colorado Springs Non Profit Ctr, bd, 1992-94. **Honors/Awds:** Accomplished Alumni Award, Univ Tenn Alumni Asn.

### DAVIS, DR. CHARLES RUDOLPH (CHUCK DAVIS)
Dancer, founder (originator), artistic director. **Personal:** Born Jan 1, 1937, Raleigh, NC; son of Tony and Ethel Davis. **Educ:** Howard Univ, BA, theatre & dance, 1968. **Career:** Babatunde Olatunji's Dance Co, dancer; Eleo Pomare's Dance Troupe, dancer; Bernice Johnson Dance Co, dancer; Chuck Davis Dance Co, founder, 1967; Am Dance Festival, Durham, artist-in-residence; African Am Dance Ensemble, founder & artistic dir, 1984-; Moments Black Inc; Am Dance Festival, Balasaraswati Joy Ann Dewey Endowed Chair, 2006; Cult Arts Safari, founder & facilitator. **Orgs:** Nat Asn Advan Colored People; bd mem, Int Asn Blacks Dance; NC Arts Coun, 1991; Brooklyn Acad Music, Brooklyn; Nat Endowment Arts. **Honors/Awds:** NC Artist Award, 1990; NC Award Fine Arts, 1992; NY Bessie Award; Brooklyn Acad Music Award; Dance for the Planet Award, 1998 & 2001; Honorary DFA, Medgar Evers Col, 1998; Nat Gov Award, 2000 & 2002; Kathryn H Wallace Award, 2000; Planet Award, The Advocacy Award, Durham Human Rels Comn, 2002; NC Dance Alliance Award, 2002; Commonwealth of Pennsylvania Legislative Black Caucus Award; Certicate of Excellence, AARP; NC Order of the Long Leaf Pine; Dance Magazine Award, 2004; Spirit of Hayti Trail Blazer Award, 2004. **Special Achievements:** Recognized by the Dance Heritage Coalition as one of the first 100 Irreplaceable Dance Treasurers in the US, 2000; Chuck Davis Day, declared in recognition on August 5, 2002 & January 1, 2007. His biographical profile was chronicled in The North Carolina Century: "Tar Heels Who Made a Difference 1900-2000". **Business Addr:** Founder, Artistic Director, African American Dance Ensemble, 120 Morris St, Durham, NC 27701, **Business Phone:** (919)560-2729.

### DAVIS, CHILI (CHARLES THEODORE DAVIS)
Baseball manager, baseball player. **Personal:** Born Jan 17, 1960, Kingston; son of William and Jenny; children: 3. **Career:** Baseball player (retired), baseball coach; San Francisco Giants, outfielder, 1981-87; Calif Angels, outfielder, 1988-90, 1993-96; Minn Twins, outfielder, 1991-92; Kans City Royals, 1997; NY Yankees, outfielder, 1998-99; Los Angeles Dodgers, hitting coach, 2010; Pawtucket Red Sox's, hitting coach, 2011; Oakland Athletics, hitting coach, 2011-; Ariz Diamondbacks, hitting instr & coach. **Home Addr:** 4227 Don Ortega Pl, Los Angeles, CA 90008. **Business Addr:** Hitting coach, Oakland Athletics, O co Coliseum 7000 Coliseum Way, Oakland, CA 94621, **Business Phone:** (510)638-4900.

### DAVIS, CHRISTINE R.
Executive, government official. **Personal:** Born Nashville, TN; married Steve G; children: Pamela E. **Educ:** Fisk Univ; Tenn State Univ; Boston Bus Col; Cath Univ Am. **Career:** Wash Bur Tuesday Pub Inc, dir; US Mem Cong, admn asst; Dem Nat Com, exec asst vice chrm; Comn Govt Opers House Representatives, staff dir. **Orgs:** Links Inc; Girl Friends Inc; Nat Press Club; Nat Coun Negro Women; Nat Coun Women; Delta Sigma Theta Sorority. **Honors/Awds:** Numerous awards from national, religious, educational, political, civic and congressional organizations. **Home Addr:** 5904 Ryland Dr, Bethesda, MD 20817, **Home Phone:** (301)897-4960.

### DAVIS, CLARENCE
State government official, educator. **Personal:** Born Sep 25, 1942, Wilkes County, GA; son of Clement Sr and Lola M McLendon; married Barbara J Holder; children: Wayne C, Clarence R, Cherylle M & Dawn T. **Educ:** Morgan State Univ, Baltimore, MD, BA, polit sci, 1968, MA, hist & social sci, 1978, currently pursuing doctorate educ. **Career:** House Delegates, 45th Dist, MD, 1983-07; state pres, Am Asn Retired Persons, Md, 2012. **Orgs:** Exec dir, Hamilton Ct Improv Assoc, 1968; suprv St Bernadine Comm Serv Ctr, 1971-72; res asst Friends Psychiat Res, 1972-75; Ways & Means Comt, 1983-07; bd mem Nat Assoc Sickle Cell Disease, 1984-87; steering comn, Nat Assoc Black Soc Wk, 1984-86; Joint Comt Protocol, 1987-2007; regional coordr, Nat Asn Black Vets; mem, Dorie Miller Veterans Foreign Wars Post, IBPOE W No 1043; Joint Expenditure Study Group Health, Housing, Econ Develop, & Environ, 1991; Md Affordable Housing Trust, 1992-97; Comn Study Ways Improve Financial Viability Racing Indust, 1997; vice chmn, Md Legis Black Caucus, 2001-07; Nat Conf State Legislatures; Nat Asn Concerned Veterans; Groove Phi Groove Social Fel Inc; Nat Asn Advan Colored People; Baltimore Red Line Community Adv Coun, 2006-07; Chair, Veterans Comn, Baltimore City, 2009-; hon mem, Morgan State Bears lacrosse. **Home Addr:** 1628 E 32nd St, Baltimore, MD 21218-3703, **Home Phone:** (410)366-0483.

### DAVIS, CLARENCE
Photojournalist. **Personal:** Born Dec 17, 1939, Atlanta, GA; son of Clarence and Trudie Goolsby; married Carol; children: Hazel C & Amanda Lael. **Educ:** Temple Univ, Philadelphia, Pa, attended 1959; Columbia Univ, New York, attended 1964; City Col, New York, NY, soc, 1975. **Career:** Columbia Univ, New York, NY, photogr asst, 1965-68; New York J News, Staff Photogr, 1968-72; Bergen Rec, Staff Photogr, 1972-73; New York Daily News, Staff Photogr, 1973-99, ed bd mem, 1990-91; Amsterdam News, Photo Consult, 1977-79; Rockland Community Col, prof photojournalism, 1984-95; New York Univ, Journalism Dept, prof photojournalism, 2000-04. **Orgs:** Arts Coun Rockland; bd directors, Arts in Public Places, 1987-90; New York Press Photogr Asn; US Senate News Galleries; founder, exec dir, mentor, The Africa Proj Inc, 1996-. **Honors/Awds:** New York Press Photographers Association, 1970, 1971, 1985, 1986, 1987, 1988, 1989, 1990, 1991, 1993 & 1994; Bergen Record Insight Award, 1972; New York Daily News Photo contest, 1977; New York City PBA Award, 1985; Daily News Photojournalism Award, 1987; Black Achievers in Industry Award, Harlem YMCA, 1988; Africa Project Focus Award, 1993 &1997; Pulitzer Nominations, "Boys in Danger" African-American Youth in Crises, 1990, "Fotorials" First photo editorial concept in US, 1991, "Terror at the Towers" World Trade Center bombing, 1993. **Special Achievements:** Three Pulitzer Prize nominations. **Home Addr:** 4 Dogwood Pl, Pomona, NY 10970. **Business Addr:** Founder,

Executive Director, The Africa Project Inc, PO Box 1451, Fayetteville, GA 30214, **Business Phone:** (678)428-2083.

### DAVIS, CLARENCE A.

Consultant, executive. **Personal:** Born Nov 29, 1941, New York, NY; children: Todd. **Educ:** Long Island Univ, BS, acct, 1967; CPA, 1975. **Career:** Spicer & Oppenheim, sr partner pub acct firm, 1967-90; NY Inst Clarence A Davis, fac, 1973-79; LIU Brooklyn Ctr, fac, 1974-80; Oppenheim, Appel, Dixon & Co, mgr, 1976, partnership, 1979, audit partner; Cub Scout Pack 999, cubmaster, 1977-81; Am Inst CPA Minority Recruitment Equal Opportunity Comn, chmn, 1977-83; Clarence A Davis Enterprises Inc, prin, 1990-98; Am Inst Cert Pub Accountants, chief financial officer, 1998-2000, chief exec officer, 2000-05, chief operating officer; Nestor Inc, chief financial officer, 1999-2000, dir, 2006-, interim chief exec officer, 2007, chief exec officer, 2007-09, pres, consult; Oneida Ltd, dir, 2005-06; Gabelli Global Multimedia Trust Inc, dir, 2006-; independent consult, 2006-07; Sonesta Int Hotels Corp, dir, 2009-; Pennichuck Corp, dir, 2009-; HPT SN Holding Inc, dir, mem audit comt & mem negotiating comt, 2009-; Tel & Data Sys Inc, independent dir, 2009-; Bizequity Corp, chmn& dir, 2011-; St Brigid's Elem Sch, chmn sch brd; St Brigid's CYO Track Team, track coach; Boy Scout Troop 999, asst scoutmaster; Gabelli SRI Fund, bd dir, trustee, currently; Gabelli Mutual Fund, dir, currently. **Orgs:** NY State Brd Pub Acct, 1984-; Am Inst CPA Future Issues Comn, 1984; Am Red Cross Liberty Fund, 2004; independent trustee, GDL Fund, 2006-; consult, Am Red Cross, 2005-06; NY St Soc CPA; Am Inst CPA; Nat Asn Black Acct; 100 Black Men; Kappa Alpha Psi Frat; Acct Pub Interest; Nestor Inc. **Honors/Awds:** Elected Archbishop Molloy High Sch Alumni Hall of Fame, 1984. **Special Achievements:** Article: "Accounting & Auditing Careers", The Black Collegian Mag, 1982. **Home Addr:** 444 Washington Blvd Apt 5320, Jersey City, NJ 07310-1905. **Business Addr:** Director, Gabelli SRI Fund, 1 Corporate Ctr, Rye, NY 10580-1422, **Business Phone:** (914)921-5100.

### DAVIS, CLARISSA. See DAVIS-WRIGHTSIL, CLARISSA.

### DAVIS, REV. CLIFTON DUNCAN

Singer, clergy, actor. **Personal:** Born Oct 4, 1945, Chicago, IL; son of Toussaint L'Ouverture and Thelma vanPutten; married Ann Taylor; children: Christian Noel & Holly Danielle; married Monica Durant. **Educ:** Oakwood Col, BA, theol, 1984; Andrews Univ, MDiv, 1988; Lincoln Univ, PhD. **Career:** Actor, singer, songwriter, minister, speaker; TV appearances: "A World Apart", 1971; "Love, American Style", 1971; "The Melba Moore-Clifton Davis Show", 1972; "Police Story", 1973 & 1977; "That's My Mama", 1974-75; "Amen", 1986-; "Amen", 1986-91; "The John Larroquette Show", 1993; Elizabeth City State Univ, Instnl Advan, interim vice chancellor, 1995-96; "The Jamie Foxx Show", 1996; "Living Single", 1997; "Sparks", 1997; "Malcolm & Eddie", 1997; "Party of Five", 1997; "Grace Under Fire", 1997; "The Sentinel", 1997; "The Gregory Hines Show", 1997; "Any Day Now", 1998; "In the House", 1999; Welcome Christ Ctr, Huntington Beach, co-pastor, 1999-2001; "City of Angels", 2000; "American Dreams", 2002; "Halloweentown High", 2004; "Half & Half", 2004; "Political Animals", 2012; "Mr. Box Office", 2012; "The First Family", 2013. Stage appearances: Scuba Duba, 1967; Horseman Pass By, 1969; Look to the Lilies, 1970; The Engagement Baby, 1970; Films: The Landlord, 1970; Two Gentlemen of Verona, 1971; Gus, Together for Days, 1972; Lost in the Stars, 1974; Scott Joplin, 1977; Clifton Davis Enterprises Inc, pres & chief exec officer, 1986-92; Any Given Sunday, 1999; The Painting, 2001; Kingdom Come, 2001; Max Keeble's Big Move, 2002; The Climb, 2002; The Engagement: My Phamily BBQ 2, 2006; Cover, 2007; What My Husband Doesn't Know, 2012; God's Amazing Grace... Is Just A Prayer Away, 2013. Christian Lifestyle Mag TV Prog, co-host; Trinity Broadcast Network, frequent guest host, 2000-08; The Most Soulful Sound, emcee & host. Clifton Davis Prods, founder; Welcome Am Inc, chief exec officer & pres; Clifton Davis Ministry, pastor, currently. **Orgs:** Actor's Equity; Am Fedn TV & Radio Artists; Screen Actors Guild; SCLC; NCF; Nat Am Advan Colored People; Freedom Fund SC, Nat Black Meeting Planners; 100 Black Men Am, Nat Black Educrs; hon mem chmn, Nat Parent Teacher's Asn, 1989-91. **Honors/Awds:** Theater World Award, 1971; Gold Record for Never Can Say Goodbye, 1971; Heart Torch Award, Am Heart Asn, 1975; Hon Doctor Ministry, Trinity Int Univ; DHL, Lincoln Col, Paine Col & Edward Waters Col; Distinguished Service Citation, UNCF, 1981; Oakwood College Distinguished Service Citation, UNCF, 1984; Legacy of the Dreamer Award, Southern Christian Leadership Conf, 1989; Distinguished Service Award, UNCF, 1990-92. **Special Achievements:** Grammy nomination for "Never Can Say Goodbye"; Tony Award nomination for Two Gentlemen of Verona; co-author of Lookin' Through The Windows; author, autobiographical essay, A Mason Dixon Memory; Listed in Who's Who In America. **Business Addr:** Pastor, Clifton Davis Ministry, 10624 S Eastern Ave Suite A-224, Henderson, NV 89052, **Business Phone:** (702)407-9060.

### DAVIS, CORA BOWIE

Executive. **Educ:** Howard Univ, BS, home econs, clothing & textiles, 1964. **Career:** Family Dollar Stores Inc, div vpres, 1988-96; Wal Mart Stores Inc, div merchandise mgr, 1996-98, vpres & div merchandise mgr, 1998-2006; independent retail exec. **Orgs:** Pres, Phi Alpha Omega Chap, Alpha Kappa Alpha Sorority Inc, 2008-10; adv bd, Northwest Ark Emerging Leaders, 2009-; pres, Tea Rose Found Northwest Ark, 2010-.

### DAVIS, FR. CYPRIAN. See Obituaries Section.

### DAVIS, DALE (ELLIOTT LYDELL DAVIS)

Basketball player. **Personal:** Born Mar 25, 1969, Toccoa, GA. **Educ:** Clemson Univ, bus mgt, 1991. **Career:** Basketball player (retired); Ind Pacers, forward & Power forward, 1991-97, 1999, ctr, 1998, 2000, 2005; Portland Trail Blazers, ctr, 2000-04; Golden State Warriors, ctr, 2004-05; Detroit Pistons, ctr, 2005-07. **Orgs:** Founder, Dale Davis Found. **Honors/Awds:** Clemson Ring of Honor, 2000; NBA Draft, 1991; Gold Medal, Summer Universiade, 1989. **Special Achievements:** Produced movie Playas Bal; Flim: Eddie, 1996; exec producer: Playas Ball, 2003; Derby in Black, 2007. **Business Addr:** Founder, Dale Davis Foundation, 514 NE 112th Ave, Vancouver, WA 98684, **Business Phone:** (360)260-9788.

### DAVIS, DANNY K.

Congressperson (U.S. federal government). **Personal:** Born Sep 6, 1941, Parkdale, AR; son of Mazzie and H D; married Vera Garner; children: Jonathan & Stacey. **Educ:** Ark AM&N Col, BA, 1961; Chicago State Univ, MS, 1968; Union Inst, PhD, 1977. **Career:** US Postal Serv, clerk, 1961-62; Chicago Bd Educ, teacher, counr, 1962-69; Greater Lawndale Conserv Comn, exec dir, 1969; Martin Luther King & Neighborhood Health Ctr, Chicago, dir trng, 1969-71; W Side Health Plng Orgn, manpower consult, 1971-72, exec dir, 1972-75; Miles Sq Community Health Ctr, spec asst pres, 1976; 29th Ward City Chicago, mem, alderman, chmn comn health, chmn comn zoning, alderman, 1979-90; Cook County, comnr, 1990-96; Chicago, mayor, 1991; US House Rep, congressman, 7th Cong Dist Ill, rep & congressman, 1996-. **Orgs:** Feelance consult, 1970-; lectr, Malcolm X Col, 1972-74; pres, W Side Asn Community Action, 1972-; Organizing Grp W Side State Bank Chicago, 1973-; pres, Nat Asn Community Health Ctr, 1977; mid-w rep, Speaker House Nat Asn Neighborhood Health Centers; Am Pub Health Asn; Lawndale People's Plng & Action Conf; comnr, Chicago Health Systs Agency; Cong Asian Pac Am Caucus; Cong Art Caucus; Cong Cancer Caucus; Cong C's Caucus; Cong Heart & Stroke Caucus; Cong Labor & Working Families Caucus; Cong Iraq Fallen Heroes Caucus; Cong Ment Health Caucus; Cong Pakistani Caucus; Rural Health Caucus; Cong Ukrainian Caucus; Cong Caucus Hellenic Issues; chair, Cong Postal Caucus; reg whip, Dem Caucus; Alpha Phi Alpha; Cong Black Caucus; Dem Socialists Am; pres, Cook County Bd; Deacon the New Galilee MB Church. **Honors/Awds:** Certificate of Merit, Pres Task force Youth Motivation, 1970; Achievement Award, Mont ford Pt Marine Asn, 1972; Community Service Award, United Concerned Parents, 1973; Best Alderman Award, IVI-IPO; Leon Des Press Award. **Home Addr:** 5956 W Race Ave, Chicago, IL 60644, **Home Phone:** (312)261-3164. **Business Addr:** Congressman, Representative, Illinois 7th District, 3333 W Arthington St Suite 130, Chicago, IL 60624, **Business Phone:** (773)533-7520.

### DAVIS, DARLENE ROSE (DARLENE DAVIS HEEP)

Lawyer, executive, secretary (office). **Personal:** Born Mar 9, 1959, New Orleans, LA; daughter of Benjamin Joseph and Estelle Cornish. **Educ:** Univ Grenoble, France, pub int law; Univ New Orleans, BA; Tulane Univ, JD; Univ Baltimore, LLM, grad tax prog. **Career:** Off Rep Jefferson, legis staff asst, 1993-; City Philadelphia, sr atty regulatory affairs, 2003-09; Pub Utility Comn, admin law judge, 2011-; US House Representatives, legis coun; Fed Judicial Ctr, researcher; Equal Employ Opportunity CMS; US Dist Ct New Orleans, Off Hon Louis Moore Jr, judicial clerk; Var Entities, ins defense coun; Dem Repub Congo, prog dir; US Dept Justice Wash DC, trial atty. **Orgs:** LOU State Bar Asn; NBA; League Women Voters; Alpha Theta Epsilon; agency coun, Wash DC; Alpha Theta Epsilon Hon Soc. **Honors/Awds:** Moot Ct Trial Team Mem; Int Law Jurisdiction, Highest Grade. **Special Achievements:** Contributor: Judicial Evaluations, FJC publ. **Home Addr:** PO Box 4350, Philadelphia, PA 19118-8350. **Business Addr:** Administrative Law Judge, Public Utility Commission Pennsylvania, 801 Market St, Philadelphia, PA 19107, **Business Phone:** (215)560-2105.

### DAVIS, DENICE FAYE

Executive. **Personal:** Born Mar 4, 1953, Flint, MI; daughter of Raymond Leverne Sr and Nita Jean Grier; married Kendall Blake Williams. **Educ:** Fisk Univ, Nashville, TN, attended 1972; Univ Detroit, Detroit, MI, BA, 1975; Univ Mich, Ann Arbor, MI, JD, 1978; Am Managed Care Rev Asn, Exec Leadership Prog, 1992. **Career:** Equitable Life Assurance Soc US, Equitable Real Estate Investment & Managing Co, contract specialist, 1979-84, real estate investment trainee, 1982-84; Denice Davis & Assoc, bus consult, lectr, 1984-87; Metmor Financial Inc, mgr, electronic fund transfer dept, 1988-89; United Am Healthcare Corp, Detroit, Mich, dir planning & develop, 1990-91, vpres, planning & develop, 1991-93, sr vpres, planning & develop. **Orgs:** Founder & mem, Alpha Kappa Alpha Sorority, 1974-; bd mem & head finance comt, Crenshaw Christian Ctr Alumni Asn, 1987-89; chaplain, parliamentarian, Pierians, 1990-; Bus Policy Rev Coun; Detroit Inst Arts; Roads Metrop Detroit; founder & mem, Theta Tau Chaper; Detroit Athletic Club. **Home Addr:** 2959 Mallery St, Flint, MI 48504, **Home Phone:** (313)232-2935.

### DAVIS, DENISE

Lawyer, executive, association executive. **Personal:** Born Lubbock, TX; married Ian Hancock; children: Colin & Chloe. **Educ:** Univ Tex, Austin, TX, BA, govt, 1989; Univ Tex Sch Law, JD, 1993. **Career:** Legis Coun; Senate Jurisp Comt, gen coun; Tex Judicial Coun, dir & coun, 1997-2000; Tex Senate, Off Lt Gov, gen coun, 2000-03; Tex House Reps, dep house parliamentarian & spec coun, 2003-04, house parliamentarian & spec coun, 2004-07, house parliamentarian & spec coun, 2009-10, chief staff, off speaker, 2010-12; ed bd, Am J Criminal Law; Baker Botts LLP, Corp Sect, spec coun, 2007-09; Davis Kaufman PLLC, partner, 2012-. **Orgs:** Town & Gown Club; Dyslexia Res Found; Links Inc; vol, Red Cross; chair, Task Force Ensure Judicial Readiness Times Emergency; KLRU Adv Bd; regional parliamentarian, Jack & Jill Am Inc; Dyslexia Res Found. **Honors/Awds:** Top 40 Under 40, Eclipse Mag; featured in Austin Woman Magazine; ranked #1 on the 2013 Rising Lobby Stars List published by Mike Hailey's Capitol Inside. **Business Addr:** Partner, Davis Kaufman PLLC, 508 W 14th St, Austin, TX 78701, **Business Phone:** (512)428-4558.

### DAVIS, DENYVETTA

Library administrator. **Personal:** Born Jul 26, 1949, Muskogee, OK; daughter of Denyfeaus and Hattie Bell Shipp; children: Melvin & Erma. **Educ:** Cent State Univ, Edmond, OK, BA, 1971, MEd, 1977; Atlanta Univ, Atlanta, GA, MLIS, 1974; Univ Okla, Norman, OK, attended 1990. **Career:** Langston Univ, Langston, cur, 1974-77; Okla Community Col, Okla City, librn, 1977-82; Ralph Ellison Libr, Metro Libr Syst, Okla City, librn, 1982-84; D'Ermel Enterprises, pres, 1984-; Metro Libr Syst, co-chair, dir libr opers, 1984-; Univ Okla, adj, 1990-. **Orgs:** Leadership Okla City, 1987-; pres, Literacy Coalition, 1989-90; vpres, NE Okla City Lioness Club, 1989-91; secy, Pub Libr Div, Okla Libr Asn, 1990-91; Am Libr Asn; vpres, Black Caucus Am Libr Asn Inc; chair, deleg elect comt, Govs Conf Libr, 1991; bd mem, Capitol Chamber Com. **Honors/Awds:** John Cotton Dana Public Relations Award, 1986, Young Visionary Leader, 1987, American Library Asn; Celebrate Literacy Award, International Reading Asn, 1988; Finer Womanhood Award, Zeta Phi Beta Sorority, 1988; Outstanding Community Service, Assault Illiteracy, 1988; Outstanding Community Service, HARAMBEE Inc, 1990; Governor's Community Service Award, 1999. **Business Addr:** Director of Library Operations, Metropolitan Library System, 300 Pk Ave, Oklahoma City, OK 73102, **Business Phone:** (405)606-3729.

### DAVIS, DIANA L.

Educator, editor. **Personal:** Born Aug 9, 1952, Akron, OH; daughter of Walter Sims and Margaret; married Henry Vance; children: Leon, Makeba, Kilemo, Ada & Henry. **Educ:** Cent State Univ, BA, 1974; Howard Univ, MA, 1983. **Career:** Prince George's County Pub Sch, social studies teacher, 1975-88, social studies coordr, 1988-91, prog coordr, 1991-95, community instr specialist, 1995-99, elem sch prin, 1999-2001; Houghton Mifflin, teacher consult, 1986; Ramapo Col, NJ, asst prof edu, prof; Monmouth Regional High Sch, supvr social studies, sch adminr, currently. **Orgs:** Nat Coun Social Studies, 1989; Nat Alliance Black Sch Educr; ed, Asn Afro-Am Life & Hist Black Studies Kit, 1997-98. **Home Addr:** 505 Ramapo Valley Rd, Mahwah, NJ 07430, **Home Phone:** (201)684-5425. **Business Addr:** Supervisor, Monmouth Regional High School, 1 Norman J Field Way, Tinton Falls, NJ 07724, **Business Phone:** (732)542-1170.

### DAVIS, DIANE LYNN

Executive. **Personal:** Born Apr 11, 1954, Detroit, MI. **Educ:** Wayne State Univ, Detroit, BS, 1981. **Career:** LI Farris Investment, Detroit, consult; Dow Chem Co, Midland, progmr, analyst; Candid Logic, Hazel Park, progmr; Gen Motors Corp, Warren, software engr; Electronic Data Systs, Detroit, syst engr mgr; Digital Equip Corp, Novi, info support systs, tele commun mgr; Fairfield Group, consult; Univ Detroit, Mercy, instr, 1987-; Ford Motor Co, 2007-. **Orgs:** Wayne State Univ Alumni Asn, 1981-; CYTCIP Adv Coun, 1988-, Detroit Urban League, 1989-; nat pres, Black Data Processing Assoc, 1992-. **Home Addr:** 19020 Fairfield St, Detroit, MI 48221, **Home Phone:** (313)341-9454.

### DAVIS, DONALD (DON DAVIS)

Executive. **Personal:** Born married Kiko; children: 3. **Career:** Music publ, actor, songwriter & rec producer; Groovesville music/BMI, 1963; Barclay Ltd Develop Co, partner, currently; United Sound Systs Rec Studio, owner, currently; First Independence National Bank, chief exec officer & chmn, currently. Produced albums: Detroit Soulman-Best Steve Mancha, 2000; Best Blue Break Beats, 2001; Ultraglide Black, 2001; Hometaping, 2002; Destiny Fulfilled, 2004; Cater 2 U, 2005; Girl, 2005; ID&T Dance Chart, 2005; Mesmerized, 2005. Recorded Live: Motortown Revue Collection, lead producer, 2005; Best Club Anthems, 2005; Complete Motown Singles, 2005; First Lady, 2005. Atlantic Unearthed: Soul Bros, 2006; Cult Club, 2006; Joy 94.9, 2006; Queer F**k, 2006; Blue Note Trip-Somethin Old, 2007; Blue Note Trip-Somethin Old Somethin Blue, 2007; Shakedown, 2007; Going Up, 2008; Stax Soul Power!, 2008; Ain't Gonna Bump No More / Disco Lady; All I Need Girl / Who's Making Love; Disco Lady / Love Better AM; I'm One Who Loves You / Harder You Love; Made Am; Ooh Ooh Dragon & Other Monsters; Our Love (Pocket) / Sweet Sherry; Reet Petite: 20 Greatest Hits; Shaft / Who's Making Love / Pvt No / Time Tight; Who's Makin' Love / Take Care Your Homework. **Orgs:** Bd mem, Detroit Renaissance; Detroit Economic Club; Local Initiatives Support Corporation; Booker T Washington bus Asn; co-chairperson, Fair Housing Ctr's, 2007. **Business Addr:** Chairman, First Independence Bank, 44 Mich Ave, Detroit, MI 48226, **Business Phone:** (313)256-8400.

### DAVIS, DONALD EARL, JR.

Football coach, football player. **Personal:** Born Dec 17, 1972, Olathe, KS; married Yannette; children: Dominique & Denay. **Educ:** Univ Kans, human develop, 1995. **Career:** Football player (retired), football coach, executive; New Orleans Saints, linebacker, 1996-98; Tampa Bay Buccaneers, 1998-2000; St Louis Rams, linebacker, 2001-02; New Eng Patriots, linebacker, 2003-06, asst strength & conditioning coach, 2007, team chaplain, 2008-; Living Waters Christian Church, Attleboro, Mass, teaching pastor; Pro Athletes Outreach, dir, 2008; Nat Football League Players Asn, regional dir, 2010. **Orgs:** Speaker, Iron Sharpens Iron. **Honors/Awds:** Super Bowl XXXVI, 2001; Super Bowls XXXVIII, 2003; Super Bowls XXXIX, 2004; Ernie Tavila Award, Athletes Action org, 2004; Most Valuable person.

### DAVIS, DR. DONALD FRED

Artist, educator. **Personal:** Born Jan 14, 1935, Baton Rouge, LA; son of Benjamin and Annabelle; married Anna Mae Eames; children: Anthony, Angela, Derek, Miriam & Michael. **Educ:** Southern La Univ, BA, 1959, MEd, 1966; Ariz State Univ, PhD, 1983. **Career:** Scotlandville High Sch, art instr, 1959-69; Community Advan Inc, art supvr, 1965; Istrouma High Sch, art instr, 1969-71; Baton Rouge Links Prog, 1972; La State Univ Lab Sch, art instr, 1972-87, col ed, 1987-89; Livingston Head Start, dir, 1990-95; Baton Rouge Recreation & Pks, art instr. **Orgs:** Nat Art Educ Asn; La Art Educ Asn; Phi Delta Kappa; Nat Asn Advan Colored People; United Methodist Church. **Honors/Awds:** Outstanding Contribution, Links Inc, 1972. **Special Achievements:** Authored "Contributions of four Blacks to art education in the South, 1920-70", 1983. **Home Addr:** 3116 Madison Ave, Baton Rouge, LA 70802-2159, **Home Phone:** (225)344-8504.

### DAVIS, DONALD GENE

Government official, educator, naval officer. **Personal:** Born Aug 29, 1971, Snow Hill, NC; son of Amos Artis and Mary Patricia; married Yuvonka; children: Ryan, Justin & Kyler. **Educ:** USAF Acad, BS, social sci, 1994; Cent Mich Univ, MS, admin, 1996; E Carolina Univ, MA, sociol, EdD, 2001. **Career:** USAF Acad, admis adv, 1994-95; Andrews Afb, serv officer, 1995-96, exec officer, 1996-97, 89th Airlift Wing, protocol duty officer, protocol flight line duty officer, 1997-98; Air Force Res Officer Training Corps Detachment 600, asst prof aerospace studies & commandant cadets, 1998-2001; Lenoir Community

Col, sociol instr, 1999-; St James Presby Church, lay minister, 2002-07; First Cong Dem Party, chair, 2003-08; Snow Hill, mayor, 2001-08; Pitt Community Col, sociol instr, 2007; E Carolina Univ, prof dept sociol, currently; Nc Senate, 2007-. **Orgs:** Nat Asn Advan Colored People, 1997-2000; USAF Acad Asn Grad, 1994-00; airforce cadet officer, Mentor Action Prog, 1995-97; Dem Nat Comn, 1997-2000; prog dir, Reach Tomorrow, 1992-2000; liaison officer, Metrop Admis Liaison, 1995-97; pres, African Heritage Asn, 1994-97; Greene County Interfaith Vols, 2001; St James Presby Church, Snow Hill, 2003; bd dir, NC League Munic; Z Smith Reynolds Found Adv Panel; bd visitor, E Carolina Univ, 2008-; NC Code Officials Qualification Bd, 2005; mem, Nc Senate, 2009-11. **Home Addr:** 413 W Greene St, PO Box 246, Snow Hill, NC 28580-0246, **Home Phone:** (252)747-2385. **Business Addr:** Candidate, Don Davis for NC Senate Campaign.

## DAVIS, DONALD W.

Lawyer. **Personal:** Born Feb 1, 1934, OK; married Marjorie D Williams; children: Lawrence, Wayne, Robert & Marjean. **Educ:** Univ Colo, BA; Univ WVa. **Career:** US Dept Interior; US Dept Lbr; Mntn Sts Tel Co, Denver; pvt pract atty. **Orgs:** Nat Bar Asn; Nat Bar Found; Am Bar Asn; Am Judictor Soc; lawyer Referral Comn; Com & Credit Comn, Okla Bar Asn; vice chmn, JJ Bruce Law Soc; Masons; Nat Asn Advan Colored People; bd dir, Urban League; coalition Civ Leadership; Baptist Church. **Home Addr:** PO Box 14750, Oklahoma City, OK 73113-1248, **Home Phone:** (405)428-0542. **Business Addr:** Attorney at Law, Private Practice, 1732 Northeast 36th St, Oklahoma City, OK 73111-5229, **Business Phone:** (405)427-8386.

## DAVIS, DR. DORIS ANN

President (organization), teacher. **Personal:** Born Jan 1, 1935; children: John, Rick, Kennedy & Shedrick. **Educ:** Univ Ill, BA; Northwestern Univ, MA; Univ Calif, Los Angeles, PhD. **Career:** Chicago & La, teacher; City Compton, elected city clerk, 1965-73, mayor, 1973-77; Daisy Child Develop Ctr, dir; Heritage Unlimited Inc, owner, chief exec officer, 1980-. **Orgs:** Bd dir, Southern Calif Clers Asn; Calif Teachers Asn; Southern Calif Clerk Asn, 1967-97; Int Muncpl Clerk Asn; Dem nat Policy Coun; St Calif Jnt Comn Rev Election Laws; educ res SWRL; pres, Davis Edgerton Asn; adv bd, Water Reclamation & Resource Recovery State Calif; chair bd dir, Welfare Info Serv; Calif Mus Sci & Indust; bd dir, Nat Advan Asn Colored People; Nat Urban League; Conf Negro Elected Officials; Phi Beta Kappa; Iota Lambda Phi; del, Calif, 1972; Dem Conv; Links Int League Women Voters; Welfare Info Serv; Med-Dent & Pharmaceut Aux; St Calif State Bar Ct; Int Studies Community; pres, La Chap, Nat Cong Black Polit Women; founder, Links, Harbor City; founder, Comn Status Women. **Honors/Awds:** Inductee Hall of Fame; Ron H Brown Award, African Am Trailblazers. **Special Achievements:** First African American woman to govern a metro city as the mayor of Compton, CA. **Home Addr:** 4206 E Rosecrans Ave, PO Box 5176, Compton, CA 90221. **Business Addr:** President, Heritage Unlimited Inc, 2221 E Rosecrans Ave, Compton, CA 90221-1715, **Business Phone:** (310)639-1596.

## DAVIS, EARL S.

Educator. **Personal:** Born New York, NY; son of Maurice and Evelyn Bryan. **Educ:** NC Cent Univ, Durham, NC, BA, 1951; NY Univ, NY, MSS, 1957; Long Island Consult Ctr, NY, cert, psycho anal psycho ther, 1968. **Career:** Dept Social Serv, NY, supvr, spec family coun, 1959-62; Travelers Aid Soc, NY, airport supvr, JFK, 1962-64; Lutheran Community Serv, NY, caseworker, dir group homes, 1964-68, dir social serv, 1968-71; St Christophers Sch, Dobbs Ferry, NY, dir treatment serv, 1971-72; NY Univ, asst dean, SSW, 1973-79, dir, IAAA, 1979-94; New York Univ, NYU Shirley M Ehrenkrenz, Sch Soc Work, consult spec prog, 1995, adj asst prof social work, currently. **Orgs:** One Hundred Black Men, NY City, 1973; UNESCO, 1982-84; bd dir, Rod Rogers Dance Co, 1986; bd dir, Carib Arts Festival Ensemble, 1989; bd dir, New Fed Theatre, 1990. **Home Addr:** 401 1st Ave, New York, NY 10010, **Home Phone:** (212)725-2019. **Business Addr:** Adjunct Assistant Professor of Social Work, New York University, NYU Shirley M Ehrenkrenz SSW, New York, NY 10003-6654, **Business Phone:** (212)998-5900.

## DAVIS, DR. EARLEAN R.

Educator. **Personal:** Born Dec 13, 1947, Sawyerville, AL; daughter of Roosevelt and Rosa Rutley; married Jimmy L; children: Patrice, Jesse & Jermaine. **Educ:** Stillman Col, BA, elem educ, 1969; Oakland Univ, teaching reading, 1976; Logos Grad Col, Christian coun, 1998, PhD, philos & human develop, 1998. **Career:** Pontiac Bd Educ, teacher, 1969-94; stud advocate, 1994-96, consult, 1996-99; Edison schs, asst prin, 1997-2000, prin, 2000-. **Orgs:** Nat Asn Advan Colored People; Int Reading Asn; Pontiac Educ Asn; Mich Educ Asn; Nat Educ Asn; Oakland County Reading Coun; Asn Supvr & Curric Develop; Pontiac Asn Sch Adminrs. **Home Addr:** 251 S Marshall St, Pontiac, MI 48342-3247, **Home Phone:** (248)335-0979. **Business Addr:** Principal, Edison Perdue Academy, 25 S Sanford Suite 104, Pontiac, MI 48342, **Business Phone:** (248)332-6500.

## DAVIS, EDITH G. WILLIAMS

Geophysicist. **Personal:** Born Apr 8, 1958, Passaic, NJ; daughter of James E and Ester Jean Rudolph; married Warren C Jr. **Educ:** Univ Miami, Coral Gables, FL, BS, geol & math, 1981; Stanford Univ, Stanford, CA, MS, geophys, 1983; Univ Tex, Austin, TX, Red McCombs Sch Bus, MBA, mkt, 1991; Baylor Univ, Waco, TX, EdD, curric & Instr emphasis, 2007. **Career:** Oxygen Isotopic Lab, coord, 1977, Dr Cesare Emiliani, 1977-78; US Geol Surv, geol field asst, 1980; Marathon Oil Co, geophys asst, 1981; US Geol Surv, explor geophysicist, 1981-82; Pa State Univ, dir sci; Mobil Oil Inc, explor geophysicist, 1983-86; Continental Airlines, Houston, Tex, gen sales reservation, 1987; Univ Tex, Grad Sch Bus, Dean off, Austin, minority stud affairs coordr, 1987-89; 3M Hq, St Paul, MN, mkt intern, 1988; Prime Network, Houston, Tex bus develop, 1990; House hold Faith, Tex Reservists Trust Fund, Houston, Tex, admin trust fund, 1991; Penn State Univ, dir, Summer Sci Prog, 1995; Harley-Davidson Motor Co, training mgr, 1997-2003; Ctr Astrophys, Space Physics, & Engineering Res, outreach educ coordr, 2004-07; Southwest Educ Develop Lab, sci achievement researcher, 2005; ABBA Mktg Exchange; co-founder; Tex Natural Resource Conserv Commn, prog admin; Univ Miami Sch Educ, Coral Gables, FL, Dept Teaching & Learning, vis asst prof, currently; Dept Defense, Ger, currently. **Orgs:** Miami Geol Soc, 1976-78; pres, United Black Students Organ, 1978-79; sci coord, Upward Bound Prog, 1979; Delta Sigma Theta Sor, 1979; AGU, 1981-82; AAPG, 1982-84; Am Asn Explor Geophys, 1982-84; vpres, MBA Women's Asn; Nat Blank Men Asn, rec Sec, 1987-; assistance prog adminr iii, Tex Natural Resource Conserv Comn, 1994-96; Asn Jr Leagues Waco; Phi Delta Kappa vpres mem, Baylor Univ, 2005-07; chairperson, Asn Teacher Educr Sci Educ SIG, 2007, 2008. **Honors/Awds:** John F Kennedy/Martin Luther King Scholarship Grant, 1977-80; President's List, 1978; United Black Students President's Award, 1978; Univ Miami Honors Scholarship, 1978; Shell Oil Scholarship Grant, 1978-80; Amer Geologic Union Award, 1981-82; fel US Geol Survey, 1981-82; fel Am Geol Inst, 1981-82; fel, Natl Black MBA, 1987; fel Consortium for Graduate Study in Management, 1988; Black History Difference Maker Award; Difference Maker Award, Va DuPuy, Waco Mayor & Don Wright, 2008. **Special Achievements:** First African American Female Geophysicist upon graduating from Stanford University. **Home Addr:** PO Box 141753, Austin, TX 78714, **Home Phone:** (512)239-1345. **Business Addr:** Visiting Assistant Professor, University of Miami School of Education, PO Box 248065, Coral Gables, FL 33124-2040, **Business Phone:** (305)284-3206.

## DAVIS, DR. EDWARD L.

Educator. **Personal:** Born Dec 6, 1943, Union Bridge, MD; married Carol Johnson; children: Tanya Lynn & Brian Patrick. **Educ:** Morgan State Univ, BS, math, 1965; Ohio Univ, MS, math, 1967; Johns Hopkins Univ, MS, mgt sci, 1973; NC State Univ, PhD, opers res, 1977. **Career:** Md Sen fel, 1961-65; Morgan State Univ, Math Dept, instr, 1970-73; Univ Cincinnati, Col Bus, asst prof, 1976-80; Atlanta Univ, Grad Sch Bus, assoc prof, 1980-88; NC A&T State Univ, asst prof; Atlanta Univ, assoc prof; Morgan State Univ, instr; NC Cent Univ, vis prof; AUS Air Defense Sch, Missile Sci Div, instr math; Univ Tex, El Paso, vis prof; Ohio State Univ, teaching asst; Bell Tel Lab, engr; Univ Tex, Austin, teaching & res scholar; Clark Atlanta Univ, Decision Sci Dept, prof decision sci, 1980-, dir econ develop ctr, 1983-2004, chmn, 1988-95, Bus Sch, actg dean, 1995-99, dean, 1999-2004, interim dean, 2007-; BECT 1 Group, chief exec officer. **Orgs:** Alpha Phi Alpha Fraternity, 1961-; Opers Res Soc Am, 1973-; Southern Fel Found, 1973-76; Am Inst Decision Sci, 1980-; Transp Res Bd, 1980-; taskforce mem, Atlanta C C, 1982-; Atlanta Bus League; Atlanta Neighborhood Fund; Kaufmann Entrepreneurial Educ Adv Bd; Black MBA Mag; AACSB Entrepreneur Affinity Group & several local adv comts. **Home Addr:** 1424 Niskey Lake Trail SW, Atlanta, GA 30331, **Home Phone:** (404)346-3837. **Business Addr:** Dean, Professor of Decision Sciences, Clark Atlanta University, Rm 100 223 James P Brawley Dr SW, Atlanta, GA 30314, **Business Phone:** (404)880-8000.

## DAVIS, DR. ELAINE CARSLEY (ELAINE ODEAL CARSLEY DAVIS)

Educator. **Personal:** Born Apr 15, 1921, Baltimore, MD; daughter of Stanley Carsley (deceased) and Corinne Baker Carsley (deceased); married R Clarke; children: R Clarke Jr & Lisa. **Educ:** Coppin State Col, BS, 1942; Morgan State Col, BS, 1943; Univ Md, LLB, 1950; Johns Hopkins Univ, MEd, 1955, PhD, attended 1958. **Career:** Douglass High Sch, math teacher; Baltimore City Pub Schs, 1942-74; Morgan State Col, instr, 1959-73; Baltimore Jr Col, instr, 1963-68; Loyola Col, instr, 1963-66; Johns Hopkins Univ, instr, 1964, assoc prof, dir educ, 1974-86. **Orgs:** Urban League, 1947; fel, Am Asn Univ Women, 1957; Phi Beta Kappa, 1958; bd trustee, Morgan State Col, 1965-67; chmn, bd trustee, Md State Col, 1967-73; United Negro Coll Fund, 1970; bd trustee, Goucher Col, 1972-75; Iota Phi Lambda, 1972; nat vpres, Pi Lambda Theta, 1973-78; Delta Sigma Theta; bd dir, Rouse Co, 1978-91. **Home Addr:** 711 Parks Height Ave, Baltimore, MD 21215, **Home Phone:** (410)358-4939.

**DAVIS, ELLIOTT LYDELL. See DAVIS, DALE.**

## DAVIS, EMANUAL

Basketball coach, basketball player. **Personal:** Born Aug 27, 1968, Philadelphia, PA; children: Jennifer & Tiffany. **Educ:** Del State Univ, attended 1991. **Career:** Basketball player (retired), coach; Philadelphia Spirit, Us Basketball League, 1991; Yakima Sun Kings, Continental Basketball Asn, 1992-93; Rockford Lightning, Continental Basketball Asn, 1993-94, 1995-96; Teamsystem Rimini, 1994-95; Houston Rockets, guard & pt guard,, 1996-98; Seattle Supersonics, pt guard, 1999-2001; Atlanta Hawks, guard & shooting guard, 2001-03; Awty Int Sch, coach, 2008-. **Honors/Awds:** Champion, Us Basketball League, 1991; Rookie of the Year, 1996; Defensive Player of the Year Award, Continental Basketball Asn. **Business Addr:** Coach, Awty International School, 7455 Awty Sch Lane, Houston, TX 77055, **Business Phone:** (713)686-4850.

## DAVIS, ERIC KEITH

Business owner, baseball player. **Personal:** Born May 29, 1962, Los Angeles, CA; married Sherrie; children: Erica & Sacha. **Career:** Baseball player (retired), business owner; Cincinnati Reds, outfielder, 1984-91; Los Angeles Dodgers, outfielder, 1992-93; Detroit Tigers, outfielder, 1993-94; Cincinnati Reds, outfielder, 1996; Baltimore Orioles, outfielder, 1997-98; St Louis Cardinals, outfielder, 1999-2000; San Francisco Giants, outfielder, 2001; Hitting From Heart Productions LLC, owner & founder, currently. **Orgs:** Eric Davis Youth Org; RBI Reviving Baseball Inner City; hon bd mem, Mult Myeloma Res Found. **Honors/Awds:** NL Gold Glove-CF, 1987, 1988, 1989; NL All-Star Team, 1987, 1989; Silver Slugger Award, 1987, 1989; Home Run Derby winner, 1989; World Series champion, 1990; NL Comeback Player of the Year, 1996; True Value Roberto Clemente Award, 1997; Jack Dunn Award, 1997; Fred Hutchinson Cancer Research Center, Hutch Award, 1997; Boston BBWAA, Tony Conigliaro Award, 1997; New York BBWAA, You Gotta Have Heart Award, 1997; Arete Award, 1997; Bob Chandler Courage Award, 1997; AL Comeback Player of the Year, 1998; Bob Bauman Physical Comeback Award, 1998; Espy Award as Comeback Athlete of 1998; inducted, Cincinnati Reds Hall of Fame, 2005. **Special Achievements:** Author: Born to Play: The Eric Davis Story, 1999; DVD: "Hitting from the Heart"; one of only two players ever to hit 25 or more home runs and steal 80 or more bases in a season, 2007. Producer: Harvard Park, 2012. 100 Years of the World Series, 2003. **Business Addr:** Owner, Founder, Hitting From The Heart Productions LLC, PO Box 90204, Long Beach, CA 90809.

## DAVIS, ERIC WAYNE

Radio host, football player. **Personal:** Born Jan 26, 1968, Anniston, AL; married Serena; children: Kevin, Nicolas, Daniel & Erica. **Educ:** Jacksonville State Univ. **Career:** Football player (retired), color analyst, host; San Francisco 49ers, defensive back, cornerback, 1990-91, left cornerback, 1991-95, color analyst, 2011, radio analyst, 2013; Carolina Panthers, left cornerback, 1996-2000, cornerback, 1999-2000; Denver Broncos, 2001; Detroit Lions, left cornerback, free safety, 2002; NFL Network, co host/analyst, 2012; KPIX-TV, color analyst; Comcast Sports Net Bay Area, analyst; 95.7 Game, co-host. **Honors/Awds:** Named to the NFC Defensive Player of the Month, 1993; All-Pro, 1995-97; Pro Bowl, 1995-96; Super Bowl champion, XXIX; Jacksonville State Athletic Hall of Fame, 1999; Alabama Sports Hall of Fame, 2013. **Special Achievements:** The highest drafted player in Jacksonville State history.

## DAVIS, DR. ERNESTINE B.

Educator. **Personal:** daughter of Henry B and Martha; children: Ella Michelle & Luther III. **Educ:** Tuskegee Univ, BSN, 1965; Med Col, GA, MSN, 1973; Univ Ala, EdD, 1979. **Career:** Orange County Med Ctr, supvr, 1969-71; Tuskegee Univ, pt instr, 1971-72; JA rew, obstet, maternal consult, 1973; Tuskegee Univ, instr, 1973-77; Univ Ala Weekend Col, asst prof, 1977-80; Univ Ala Capstone, asst prof, 1978-80; Univ N Ala, Col Nursing & Allied Health, prof, nursing, 1980-, RN & BSN, coord, currently, Presidential Mentors Prog, coordr, prog co-dir, advisor, currently. **Orgs:** Am Nurses Asn, 1965-; Med Col Geo Alumni Asn, 1973-; banquet com, Phi Kappa Phi Hon Soc, 1984-; Ala State Nurses Asn, chap human rights comn, 1985-89; treas, Univ N Ala, Nursing Hon Soc, 1986-; Soc Prof Nurses, 1988. **Home Addr:** 110 Colonial Dr, Florence, AL 35633, **Home Phone:** (256)767-5756. **Business Addr:** Professor, Coordinator, Traditional Option, Nursing, University of North Alabama College of Nursing & Allied Health, 2nd Fl Rm 203 Stevens Hall, Florence, AL 35632-0001, **Business Phone:** (256)765-4583.

## DAVIS, DR. ERNESTINE BADY

Nurse, educator. **Personal:** Born Apr 8, 1943, Atlanta, GA; daughter of Henry B and Martha; married Luther Jr; children: Ella Michelle & Luther III. **Educ:** Tuskegee Univ, BSN, 1965; Med Col, GA, MSN, 1973; Univ Ala, EdD, 1979. **Career:** Orange County Med Ctr, supvr, 1969-71; Tuskegee Univ, pt instr, 1971-72; JA rew, obstet, maternal consult, 1973; Tuskegee Univ, instr, 1973-77; Univ Ala Weekend Col, asst prof, 1977-80; Univ Ala Capstone, asst prof, 1978-80; Univ N Ala, Col Nursing, prof, 1980-, RN & BSN coord, currently, nursing, traditional, prof, Presidential Mentor's Acad, coord, proj dir, advisor. **Orgs:** Am Nurses Asoc, 1965-; Med Col Geo Alumni Asn, 1973-; Phi Kappa Phi Hon Soc, 1984-; chap human rights comn, Ala St Nurses Asn, 1985-; treas, Univ N Ala, Nursing Hon Soc, 1986-; Soc Prof Nurses, 1988; SREB Diversity Committee; bd dir, Phi Delta Kappa. **Special Achievements:** Ed, International Journal Of Nursing. **Home Addr:** 110 Colonial Dr, Florence, AL 35633, **Home Phone:** (256)767-5756. **Business Addr:** Professor, Former Assistant to the President for Minority Affairs, Director-PMA, University North Alabama College Nursing, 203 Stevens Hall, Florence, AL 35632-0001, **Business Phone:** (256)765-4583.

## DAVIS, ERROLL B., JR.

Chief executive officer, vice president (organization), executive. **Personal:** Born Jan 1, 1943?; married Elaine; children: 2. **Educ:** Carnegie-Mellon Univ, BSEE, 1965; Univ Chicago, MBA, finance, 1967. **Career:** Ford Motor Co, Detroit, corp finance staff, 1969-73; Xerox Corp Rochesterm, NY, 1973-78; Wis Power & Light Co, vpres finance, 1978-82, vpres, finance & pub affairs, 1982-84, dir, 1984-, exec vpres, 1984-87, pres, 1987-, chief exec off, 1988-90, chmn, 2000-06; Alliant Energy Corp Serv Inc, dir, 1982-2006, pres, 1990-2003, chief exec officer, 1990-2005, chmn, 2000-06; BP Corp N Am Inc, dir, 1984-2006, bd mem, 1991-; Alliant Energy Resources LLC, dir, 1988-, chmn, chief exec officer; WPL Holdings, pres & chief exec officer, 1990-98; PPG Industs Inc, dir, 1994-2007; BP PLC, dir, 1998-2010; Interstate Power & Light Co, chief exec officer, dir, 1998-, chmn, 2000-; Elec Power Res Inst Inc, dir; Indust Energy Applications Inc, dir; Edison Elec Inst, chmn, 2002-03, dir; Union Pac Rr Co Inc, dir, 2004-; Univ Syst Ga, chancellor, 2006-11; Gen Motors Co, dir, 2007-09, independent dir, 2009-15. **Orgs:** Selective Serv Appeal bd, 1982-01; adv bd, 1984-89, chair, 1987, campaign chmn, 1992, United Way; bd dir, Sentry Ins Co, 1988-97; bd mem, Competitive Wis, 1989-; life trustee, chmn, bd trustee, Carnegie Mellon Univ, 1989-; bd dir, Am Gas Asn, 1990-95; bd dir, Elec Power Res Inst, 1990-; bd dir, BP PLC, 1991-; bd mem, Amoco, 1991-98; bd dir, Asn Edison Illum Cos, 1993-; chair, 1994-95, bd Fel Wisc Asn Mfrs & Com, 1986-; Univ Wis, bd regents, 1987-94; bd mem, Brit Petrol, 1998-; chmn, Start Smart Dane Co, Dane Co; chmn, Am Soc Corp Execs, 1998-; bd mem, Union Pac, 2004-; adv bd, Fed Res Bank Chicago; bd mem, Indust Energy Applications; bd mem, Interstate Power & Light fel Southern Reg Educ Bd; bd trustee, Univ Chicago; fel US Olympic Comt Bd, 2004-08, founder, Davis Family Found; PBS Finance Comt, currently; Investment Subcomt, currently; Strategic Planning Adv Group, currently; Corp Support Adv Comt. **Home Addr:** 155 E Wilson St No 501, Madison, WI 53703. **Business Addr:** Board Member, Union Pacific Corp, 1400 Douglas St, Omaha, NE 68179, **Business Phone:** (402)544-5000.

## DAVIS, ESTHER GREGG

Consultant, school administrator. **Personal:** Born Oct 16, 1934, Chicago, IL; married Fred A Cooper. **Educ:** Hofstra Univ, BS, 1966; Northwestern Univ, PhD, 1974. **Career:** Va Tech, vis prof Educ, 1979-; Va Common wealth Univ, asst prof Educ, 1976-, consult, 1977-; Blue Cross Asn, dir assessment ctr, 1974-75; Chicago Bd Educ, teacher, 1970-71; NY Bd Educ, teacher, 1966-67; Richmond Pub Sch, ESEAT-TLE I Proj, consult, 1976-; Danforth Found, consult, 1976-77. **Orgs:** Phi Delta Kappa, 1973-; Am Mgt Asn, 1979; Mat Alliance Black Sch Educators, 1979. **Special Achievements:** Publ, "Intern Perception of Supervisory Support" ERIC, 1974; "Classroom Mgmt" Kappa Delta Pi Record, 1980-81; "Living Patterns of Urban Sch Administers"; "Lewin's Force Field Theory a model for decision making". **Home**

**Addr:** 3324 Shallowford Terr, Midlothian, VA 23112-4631. **Business Addr:** AUS Med Dept Personnel Sup Agency, VA Commonwealth University, 907 Floyd Ave, Richmond, VA 23284, **Business Phone:** (804)828-0100.

## DAVIS, ETHELDRA S.

Educator, school administrator, consultant. **Personal:** Born May 11, 1931, Marianna, AR; daughter of Luther Sampson and Fannie Sampson; children: Andrea & Robert. **Educ:** Los Angeles City Col, AA, 1951; Los Angeles St Col, BA, 1953; Univ Alaska, MA, 1964; Newport Univ, PhD, 1980. **Career:** Educator, school administrator, consultant (retired); Los Angeles Sch, teacher, 1953-58; Anchorage Sch, from teacher to asst prin, 1958-66, prin, 1967-80; Hew Region ten, field reader, 1967-70; Western Region, oeo consult, 1967-70; Juvenile Diversion Prog, exec dir, founder. **Orgs:** Alpha Kappa Alpha, NEA; ACPNA; NAESP; ISCPP; pres, Pan-Hellenic Coun Club Anchorage, 1960; dir, Child Develop Ctr Anchorage Community Action Agency; teacher, arts & crafts, YMCA; Home un-wed Mothers; Mayor's Adv Bd, 1968; Parks & Recreation Bd; bd dir, Camp fire; founder, United League Girls; Boy Scouts Am & Girls Scouts Am; Anchorage Neighborhood Watch, 1982-; founder, Nat Asn Advan Colored People, Youth Chapter. **Home Addr:** PO Box 210127, Anchorage, AK 99521, **Home Phone:** (907)338-5548.

## DAVIS, EUNICE J.

School principal. **Career:** N Dade Middle Sch, prin. **Honors/Awds:** Principal of the Year, Access Ctr, 2004; FCAT Academic Excellence award, 2006. **Home Addr:** 10125 NE 2nd Ave, Miami Shores, FL 33138-2349. **Business Addr:** Principal, North Dade Middle School, 1840 NW 157 St, Miami, FL 33054, **Business Phone:** (305)624-8415.

## DAVIS, FLASH. See DAVIS, WILLIE J.

## DAVIS, REV. FRANCE ALBERT

Clergy, educator, association executive. **Personal:** Born Dec 5, 1946, Gough, GA; son of John H and Julia Cooper; married Willene Witt; children: Carolyn Marie, Grace Elaine & France II. **Educ:** Univ Calif, BA, rhet, 1972; Westminster Col, BS, relig & philos, 1977; Univ Utah, MA, mass commun, 1978, fel; NW Nazarene Col, MMin, 1994. **Career:** St Paul Baptist Church, asst pastor, 1968; Univ Utah, instr, 1972, Dept Commun, adj assoc prof; Ctr St Baptist Church Oakland, Calif, cert ordination, 1971, assoc & youth minister, 1972-72; Calvary Baptist Church, pastor, 1973-, chief adminr; Intermountain Gen Baptist Conv, advisor, vpres. **Orgs:** Utah Opportunities Industrialization Ctr, 1974-; bd mem, Utah Bd Corr, 1975-, bd chmn, 1982-; bd mem, Nat Asn Advan Colored People, Salt Lake Br, 1975-77, 1985-; Albert Henry Educ Found, 1976-; chmn, Tribune Common Carrier Ed Bd, 1982; chmn, Martin Luther King Jr Holiday Comm Utah, 1985-86; chmn, Mignon Richmond Pk Comn, 1985-86; bd chmn, bd trustee, Salt Lake Community Col, 2007; exec bd, DIC/A; Nat Baptist Conv, SafricA Preaching. **Honors/Awds:** Pres Award, Salt Lake, Nat Asn Advan Colored People, 1975; Service Award, Beehive Elks, 1975; torch bearer, OIC/A, 1979; OIC Torchbearer Award, 1979; Black Scholars Outstanding Image Maker, 1986; DHL, Univ Utah, 1993; DHL, Salt Lake Community Col, 1997; DHL, Dixie State Col, 2002; McCarthey Silver Hope Award, Nat Multiple Sclerosis Soc, 2006. **Special Achievements:** Author: "Light in the Midst of Zion"; France Davis: "An American Story Told", 2007. **Home Addr:** 1912 Meadow Dr, Salt Lake City, UT 84121, **Home Phone:** (801)943-6145. **Business Addr:** Pastor, Calvary Baptist Church, 1090 S State St, Salt Lake City, UT 84111-4521, **Business Phone:** (801)355-1025.

## DAVIS, FRANK

Law enforcement officer. **Personal:** Born Mar 22, 1947, Claiborne County, MS; son of Green Lee and Mary Lee Barnes Triplett; children: Tracy & Gary. **Educ:** Alcorn State Univ, BS, 1972; Southern Univ, criminal justice, 1973. **Career:** Port Gibson, Miss, dep sheriff, 1968-78; Claiborne County, civil defense dir, 1978-79, Port Gibson Police Dept, asst chief police, 1978-79, sheriff, 1979-2012. **Orgs:** Treas, New Zion Lodge, 1976; hon mem, FBLA, 1980; Kiwanis Club, 1980; prof mem, Am Correctional Asn, 1983; Miss Sheriff's Asn; pres, NOBLE, MSchap, 1997; Police Pu suit Bd, 2003. **Honors/Awds:** Civil Defense Council, MS Civil Defense, 1978; Certificate of Merit, Aide-de-Camp, 1979; Mississippi Sheriff's Asn, 1988; MS Pkwy Commission Bd; MS Heritage Corridor Bd; Governor of the State of Missisippi, 1990; Citizenship Award, 1991. **Special Achievements:** The First sheriff elected in the Claiborne County; First president of the Mississippi Sheriff Association, 2000-01. **Home Addr:** Rte 1, PO Box 116, Hermanville, MS 39086.

## DAVIS, FRANK ALLEN

Chief executive officer, president (organization). **Personal:** Born Nov 17, 1960, Washington, GA; son of Joan A Johnson and Eugene N; married Elena Labarrere; children: Michael. **Educ:** Bucknell Univ, BS, elec engineering, 1982; Univ Ala, Birmingham, MBA, 1989; Tuck Sch Bus, Dartmouth, MBEP, 2004. **Career:** Westinghouse Control Div, div sales engr, 1982-85; Westinghouse Industs Mkt, asst sales engr, 1985-86, personnel consult, 1985-89, indust sls engr, 1987-89; Honeywell Inc, sr mkt spec, dir, 1989-92, nat distribr sls mgr, 1992-93; Siebe PLC Ltd, sr prod mkt mgr, 1993-94; Johnson Controls, nat end user sls, mktg mgr, 1994-95; Westinghouse Elec, dir; Delco Ventures, vpres, 1994-; Johnson Controls, group gen mgr, 1997-98, dir strategic planning, 1998-2000; Invensys, dir; Gerson Lehrman Group, New York, prin consult; Horizon Group Co, pres, chief exec officer, 2001-. **Orgs:** Alpha Phi Omega, 1984-; Nat Black MBA Asn, 1986-90; Am Mkt Asn, 1987-; Open Pit Mining Asn, 1987-89; Am Cancer Soc, 1990-91; Rockford Asn Minority Mgt, 1991-97; Northern Ill Minority Contractors Asn, 1995-97; Leaders Forum Milwaukee, 1997-98; Greater Atlanta Chamber Com, 1999-; S Reg Minority Bus Coun, 2002-; Ga Minority Supplier Develop Coun, 2005-; Inst Supply Mgt, 2005-06; Georgian Club, 2006-; Vindus, 2008-; bd dir, Bucknell Univ Alumni Asn, 2008-; Asn Strategic Planning, 2015-. **Home Addr:** 1927 Westover Lane NW, Kennesaw, GA 30152, **Home Phone:** (770)218-7354. **Business Addr:** President, Chief Executive Officer, Horizon Services Corp, 400 Galleria Pkwy Suite 1500, Atlanta, GA 30339, **Business Phone:** (205)249-8033.

## DAVIS, FREDERICK D.

Labor activist. **Personal:** Born Aug 6, 1935, Tulsa, OK; married Patricia; children: Grant Anthony, Frederick Douglass II & Mwindaace N Gai. **Educ:** Okla Univ. **Career:** McDonnell Douglas Aircraft Corp, 1956-. **Orgs:** Pres, Nat Asn Advan Colored People, Tulsa; pres, bd dir, Tulsa Area United Way; pub rel dir, Prince Hall Free & Accepted Masons; UAW, Const & Conv Deleg, 1975-; Paradise Baptist Church; Coal Creek 88 Masonic Lodge; pres, Tulsa Community Recreation Coun, 1972-74; chmn, Equal Oppurtunity Prog, 1974-75; Police Community Rels; Air Force Mem Found. **Special Achievements:** First Black & minority major Developer in the state of Oklahoma. **Home Addr:** 554 E 39th St N, Tulsa, OK 74106, **Home Phone:** (918)428-3591.

## DAVIS, GEORGE BERNARD

Educator, writer. **Personal:** Born Nov 29, 1939, Shepherdstown, WV; married Mary Cornelius; children: Pamela & George. **Educ:** Colgate Univ, BA, cult anthrop, 1961; Columbia Univ, MFA, creative writing, film, 1971. **Career:** Wash Post, DC, reporter, 1968-69; NY Times, NY, Sunday Dept, ed, 1969-70; Journalist/Auth, chief researcher/writer, 1972-2005; Bronx Community Col, City Univ NY, Bronx, asst prof, 1974-78; Rutgers Univ, NJ, Newark campus, asst prof, 1978, Dept Eng, assoc prof, prof emer, 1980-2015; Storytelling Age Interactive Technol, chief researcher/writer, 1985-95; Researcher: Interactive Narratives, chief researcher/writer, 1995-2005; Quest Digital Interactive, chief exec officer, 2012-; freelance writer var publ; Columbia Univ & Green haven Prison, teacher writing workshops; Black Swan Commun, co-founder & pres; Colgate Univ, adj; Columbia Univ, adj; Yale Sch Orgn & Mgt, adj. **Orgs:** Author's Guild; Grant NY Coun Arts; Nat Endowment Humanities; Authors League Am. **Special Achievements:** Author of numerous books. **Home Addr:** 101 Elmwood Ave, Mount Vernon, NY 10552. **Business Addr:** Chief Executive Officer, Quest Digital Interactive, 205 Yoakum Pkwy Unit 1010, Alexandria, VA 22304.

## DAVIS, DR. GLEN ANTHONY

Physician. **Personal:** Born Mar 18, 1972, Kalamazoo, MI; son of Charles and Clemetine (deceased). **Educ:** Univ Mich, BS, biomed sci, 1994; Univ Mich Med Sch, MD, 1998; Univ Notre Dame, Mendoza Col Bus, MBA, 2014. **Career:** Upjohn Co, lab asst, 1990; C's Hosp Mich, resident physician, 1998-2001; Bristol St Pediat, pediatrician, 2001-04; Pro Med Physician, pediatrician; S Bend Clin, pediatrician, currently; Borgess Health, pediatrician, 2004-05. **Orgs:** Golden Key Nat Hon Soc, 1991; Black Med Asn, 1994-98; Am Med Asn, 1994-; Am Acad Pediat, 1998-; Ind State Med Soc; bd trustee, S Bend Clin, 2014-. **Honors/Awds:** Ralph Gibson Award, Univ Mich Med Sch, 1998. **Special Achievements:** Host a TV segment called "Ask Dr. D?" on WSBT-TV. **Home Addr:** 200 Stratford Pl Apt G, Elkhart, IN 46516, **Home Phone:** (219)293-9458. **Business Addr:** Pediatrician, Board Of Trustee, South Bend Clinic, 211 N Eddy St, South Bend, IN 46617, **Business Phone:** (574)234-8161.

## DAVIS, GLENN

President (organization). **Career:** Acct mgr; proj mgr; sr consult; Bran Core Technologies, pres & chief exec officer, 1986-, consultant, 1991-2000. **Orgs:** Bd dir, GRTC; bd dir, Va Commonwealth Univ Alumni; asn dir, pres, & vpres, Asn Info Technol Profs; Comput Adv Comt Garfield Childs Mem Fund; VCU Adv Adopt-A-Sch Prog; ECPI Adv Comt. **Honors/Awds:** Entrepreneur of the year Award, Va Minority Supplier Develop Coun, 2004; Technology Award, Greater Richmond Technol Coun, 2003, 2004, 2005, & 2006; IBM Leadership Award; Information Systems Alumnus of the Year Award, Va Commonwealth Univ; Ernst & Youngs Emerging Company Award; Alumnus of the Year award, Virginia Commonwealth University. **Business Addr:** President, Chief Executive Officer, Bran Core Technologies, 501 E Franklin St Suite 301, Richmond, VA 23219-2323, **Business Phone:** (804)521-4041.

## DAVIS, GOLIATH J., III

Mayor, police chief. **Educ:** Rollins Col, BS, Behav Sci; Univ S Fla, MS, criminal justice; Fla State Univ, PhD, criminol; Harvard Univ John F Kennedy Sch Govt. **Career:** St Petersburg, Fla, Police Dept, asst chief admin serv bur, chief police, 1997-2001; Univ S Fla, adj prof criminol, currently; Midtown Econ Develop, dep mayor, 2003-. **Honors/Awds:** Community Leadership Award, Leadership St Pete Alumni Asn, 1998; Tampa Bay Ethics Award, Univ Tampa Ctr Ethics; Alumni Achievement Award in Law Enforcement, Rollins Col; Distinguished Alumni Award, Univ S Fla Pinellas County; Distinguished Citizen Award, Boy Scouts Am. **Special Achievements:** First African American police chief St Petersburg, Florida. **Business Addr:** Deputy Mayor, Midtown Economic Development, 175 5th St N, St. Petersburg, FL 33701, **Business Phone:** (727)893-7539.

## DAVIS, GRACE E.

Software developer. **Educ:** Grambling State Univ, BS, 1998; Univ Utah; Utah State Univ. **Career:** Salt Lake Conv & Visitors Bur, res asst, 1994-96; Tex Schs, Garland, teacher, 1999-2000; Baylor Univ Med Ctr, Dallas, Tex, police officer, 2001; Waterford Inst, educ software designer, currently. **Orgs:** Pub rels chmn, Blacks Collegiates & Assocs United, Utah State Univ, 1992-95; vol, Head Start, 1995; asst dir, Calvary Baptist Church, Saturday Sch Comput Reading Prog, 1998. **Honors/Awds:** Grambling State Univ, President's List, 1998. **Home Addr:** 1912 Meadow Dr, Salt Lake City, UT 84121, **Home Phone:** (801)943-6145. **Business Addr:** Teacher, Waterford Institute, 1590 E 9400 S, Sandy, UT 84093, **Business Phone:** (801)576-4900.

## DAVIS, GREGORY T.

Media executive. **Career:** Executive (retired); WRR Class 101.1 FM, gen mgr, 1993-2010. **Special Achievements:** First African-American to head up WRR-the only city-owned commercial station in the country. **Business Addr:** General Manager, WRR Classical 101.1 FM, 1516 1st Ave, Dallas, TX 75315-9001, **Business Phone:** (214)670-8888.

## DAVIS, GUY

Composer, guitarist, actor. **Personal:** Born May 12, 1952, New York, NY; son of Ossie (deceased) and Ruby Dee. **Career:** Films: Beat Street, 1984; TV series: "One Life to Live"; stage: Cotton Comes to Harlem; Mulebone, 1991; Trick the Devil, 1993; Ideas, 2004; Albums: Stomp Down Rider, 1995; Call Down the Thunder, 1996; You Don't Know My Mind, 1998; Butt Naked Free, 2000; Give In Kind, 2002, Chocolate to the Bone, 2003; Legacy, 2004; Skunkmello, 2006; Down At The Sea, 2007; Guy Davis On Air, 2007; Sweetheart Like You, 2009; The Adventures of Fishy Waters, 2012; Juba Dance, 2013. **Honors/Awds:** Best Acoustic Album of the Year; Best Acoustic Artist of the Year; Best Instrumentalist; BRIO Award, 1991; Keeping the Blues Alive Award, Blues Found, 1993; AUDELCO Award, 1993. **Business Addr:** Singer, Red House Records Inc, PO Box 4044, St. Paul, MN 55104, **Business Phone:** (651)644-4161.

## DAVIS, H. BERNARD

President (organization), automotive executive. **Personal:** Born Apr 30, 1945, Burnsville, AL; son of Leslie Holmes and Roxie Price; married Delphine Handley; children: Jason Henry & Jeanine Kianga. **Educ:** Mott Community Col, Flint, MI, AD, data processing, 1970; Univ Mich, Flint, MI, BBA, 1976; Mich State Univ, E Lansing, MI, MBA, bus admin, 1984; Pa State Univ, College Park, PA, exec mgt prog, 1989. **Career:** Gen Motors Corp, Corp Finance Staff, Detroit, Mich, dir prod cost anal, 1979-81; Gen Motors Corp, Oldsmobile Div, Lansing, Mich, from asst div comptroller to div comptroller, 1981-88; Powertrain Div B-O-C, Brighton, Mich, dir finance & bus planning, 1988-90; GM Engine Div, Brighton, Mich, div comptroller; Gen Motors Corp, Global Financial Shared Serv, exec dir, 1997-2001; DBD Consult & Mkt, pres & managing partner, 2004-; Fla Southern Col, exec residence, 2008-; Tower Solutions LLC, chmn bd & cso, 2012-13. **Orgs:** Treas, bd dir, Black Child & Family Inst, 1987-89; bd dir, Capital Area Found, 1987-89; vice chmn, Capital Area United Way, 1987; sr pastor, Alexander St Church God, 1988-89; Legacy Club M2M Asn; bd mem, His Nets. **Home Addr:** 7719 Flemingwood Ct, Sanford, FL 32771-8105, **Home Phone:** (407)330-2223. **Business Addr:** Executive in Residence, Florida Southern College, 111 Lake Hollingsworth Dr, Lakeland, FL 33801, **Business Phone:** (863)680-4111.

## DAVIS, HAROLD

Government official. **Personal:** Born Feb 29, 1932, New Orleans, LA; son of T D and Myrtle L Royal; married Barbara M; children: Harold Jr & Deborah Davis-Gillespie. **Educ:** Southern Univ, BA, polit sci & econs, 1952; Univ Calif, MPA, 1957; Univ Calif, Berkeley, MA, pub admin; Am Baptist Sem W, LLD. **Career:** Alameda Co, Calif, Redevelop Agency, relocation officer, 1961-63, asst exec dir, 1963-65, exec dir, 1965-68, chief asst welfare dir, 1968-72; City Oakland Housing Authority, chief exec officer, exec dir emer, currently. **Orgs:** Life mem, Alpha Phi Alpha; Nat Asn Housing & Redevelop Off, 1962; bd mem, Grad Theol Union, 1970 & 1994; trustee, 1997-, chmn, opers comt, nat bd dir & pres, Young Mens Christian Asn Retirement Fund, 1989-90; pres, Am Baptist Churches, 1988-89; chmn bd dir, C Hosp & res Ctr, Oakland, 1993-; life mem, Nat Advan Asn Colored People; Sigma Pi Phi Boule; Sire Archon, 1994-96; bd dir, Toastmasters Int; chmn bd trustee, Am Baptist Sem; pres & bd dir, Am Baptist Churches, USA; vpres, Ministers & Missionaries Retirement Bd Am Baptist Churches; bd, Young Mens Christian Asn, Berkeley CA; chmn, chmn bd, Y-USA. **Home Addr:** 691 Calmar Ave, Oakland, CA 94610. **Business Addr:** Trustee, YMCA Retirement Fund, 140 Broadway Fl 28, New York, NY 10005, **Business Phone:** (646)458-2400.

## DAVIS, HAROLD R.

Executive. **Personal:** Born Mar 25, 1926, High Point, NC; married Marva Lane; children: Stpehen, Craig, Brenda & Peggy J Slaughter. **Educ:** US Sch Admin, CLU, Am Col Life Underwriters, 1970; FLMI, Life Off mgt courses, 1976. **Career:** Executive (retired); NC Mutual Life Ins Co dist mgr, 1966-69; asst agency dir, 1969-72; self emp ins consult, Davis Financial Serv; regnl agency dir, 1973-77; vpres field opers, 1978-84; vpres mkt servs, 1984-88. **Orgs:** Am Soc CLU; vpres, Nat Ins Asn; bd dir, Durham, YMCA, 1979-83; bd dir, Life Ins Mkt & Res Asn, 1982-84. **Home Addr:** 5220 Peppercorn St, Durham, NC 27704, **Home Phone:** (919)477-7532.

## DAVIS, HERMAN E.

Executive, chief executive officer, educator. **Personal:** Born Mar 3, 1935, Carlton, AL; married Thelma; children: Millicent, Chiaka, Jennifer & Holly. **Educ:** Chicago State Univ, BE, bus educ, 1962; Roosevelt Univ, Chicago, MA, sch admin & supv, 1984. **Career:** Educator (retired), executive; New Direction Budgeting & Financial Serv Ctr Inc, pres; Du Sable High Sch, Chicago, teacher; Waddell & Reed Inc, rep; Chicago Pub Sch Syst, teacher; Gary Community Sch Syst, teacher; DuSable High Sch, teacher, 1962-94; Town Coopertown, Tenn, vice mayor, mayor, 2000-04, chmn econ develop bd, 2011-; Nashville Game Co, founder & chief exec officer, 2007-, owner, 2012-. **Orgs:** Pres, Asn Distrib Educ Coordinators, 1966; pres, Bryn Mawr & W Area Coun; S Shore Comn; chmn, Finance Comt S Shore Comn; Sigma Omega Chap Omega Psi Phi; Signal Corp. **Home Addr:** 7447 S Constance Ave, Chicago, IL 60649. **Business Addr:** Chief Executive officer, Owner, Nashville Game Co, 340 W Trinity Lane, Nashville, TN 37207-4917, **Business Phone:** (615)262-5139.

## DAVIS, HOWLIE R.

Executive. **Personal:** Born Sep 14, 1957, Charlotte, NC; son of Harry and Hattie B. **Educ:** Morehouse Col, BS, bus, 1979; Atlanta Univ, sch bus, 1980. **Career:** Clinton-Gore Presidential Transition Comm, 1992-93; White House, assoc dir personnel, 1993; US Dept Energy, White House liaison, 1993-96; Dem Nat Conv, dir security, 1996; Citzenship Educ Fund, proj dir, 1996; Presidential Inaugural Comm, dir spec serv until, 1997; Pub Pvt Partnership Inc, managing partner, 1997-98; CH2M HILL, sr vpres & dir local govt affairs, vpres & dir client develop, currently; Mayors, co-chairperson. **Orgs:** Alpha Phi Alpha Fraternity Inc; Bryce Harlow Found; bd mem, Int City & County Mgt Asn. **Home Addr:** 224 G St SW, Washington, DC 20024, **Home Phone:** (202)544-1002. **Business Addr:** Senior Vice President, CH2MHILL, 9191 S Jamaica St, Englewood, CO 80112, **Business Phone:** (720)286-2000.

**DAVIS, HUBERT IRA, JR.**
Basketball coach, basketball player, entertainer. **Personal:** Born May 17, 1970, Winston-Salem, NC; son of Hubert Sr; married Leslie; children: Elijah, Bobbie Grace & Micah. **Educ:** Univ NC, BA, criminal justice, 1992. **Career:** Basketball player (retired), coach, color analyst; NY Knicks, shooting guard, 1992-96; Toronto Raptors, shooting guard, 1996-97; Dallas Mavericks, shooting guard, 1997-98, pt guard, 1999-2001; Wash Wizards, shooting guard, 2001-02, pt guard, 2001; Detroit Pistons, shooting guard, 2002-04; NJ Nets, shooting guard, 2004; ESPN's Col Basketball Broadcasts, col basketball analyst, 2008-; NC Tar Heels, asst coach, 2012-; UNC Jr Varsity Team, head coach. **Orgs:** Carolina Basketball Coaching Staff, 2016-. **Honors/Awds:** Gold Medal, Summer Universiade, 1991. **Special Achievements:** TV appearance: College GameDay, 1986; New York Undercover, 1995; ESPN 25: Who's #1?, 2006; Pardon the Interruption, 2006; Mike & Mike, 2012; First round pick, No 20, NBA Draft, 1992. **Business Addr:** Basketball Analyst, ESPN, ESPN Plz 935 Middle St, Bristol, CT 06010, **Business Phone:** (860)766-2000.

**DAVIS, ISAAC (JOHN ISAAC EARL LAMONT DAVIS)**
Teacher, football player, football coach. **Personal:** Born Apr 8, 1972, Malvern, AR; son of John and Theresa; married Chandra; children: Gabrielle Nicole, Gisele Marie & Cameron. **Educ:** Univ Ark. **Career:** Football player (retired), coach, teacher; Ar Razorbacks, guard, 1990-93; San Diego Chargers, guard, 1994, right guard, 1995-97; New Orleans St, guard, 1997-98; Minn Vikings, guard, 1998; Las Vegas Outlaws, 2001; Chicago Enforcers, 2001; Memphis Maniax, 2001; Arkans Baptist Col Buffaloes, Offensive asst coach, 2007; John Horn High Sch, defensive line & track coach; Parkview Arts & Sci Magnet High Sch, asst coach & spec educ teacher, currently. **Orgs:** Athletes Educ Prog; founder, Block Against Hunger Found; Phi Beta Sigma fraternity. **Honors/Awds:** Honorary Captain, Razorbacks, 2010. **Business Addr:** Assistant Coach, Parkview Arts Science Magnet High School, 2501 Barrow Rd, Little Rock, AR 72204, **Business Phone:** (501)447-2300.

**DAVIS, J. MASON, JR.**
Lawyer. **Personal:** Born Jul 30, 1935, Birmingham, AL; son of Madeline Harris and J Mason; married June Carolyn Fox; children: Karen M & J Mason III; married June Fox. **Educ:** Talladega Col, BA, 1956; State Univ NY Law Sch, JD, 1959. **Career:** Sirote & Permutt PC, atty, 1960-, sr partner, currently; Univ Ala, Sch Law, adj prof ins & damages, 1972-97; Protective Indust Ins Co Ala Inc, chmn bd, dir, 1988-. **Orgs:** Gen Coun Nat Ins Asn, 1962-77; exec comn mem, Ala Dem Party, 1970-; exec Comn Birmingham Bar Asn, 1974-77; secy, Birmingham Bar Asn, 1978-79; pres, Nat Ins Asn, 1978-79; secy, Ala Dem Party, 1978-97; chmn, bd dir, Nat Ins Asn, 1979-81; Alpha Phi Alpha Fraternity, Nat Asn Advan Colored People, Sigma Pi Phi, Omicron Delta Kappa; chmn bd trustee, Talladega Col, 1981-88; pres, Birmingham Bar Asn, 1984-85; Ala State Bar, 1987-96; chmn, Birmingham Regional Chamber Com, 2001-02; chmn, United Way Cent Ala, 2002-03; Am & Nat Bar Associations; vice chmn, Birmingham Airport Authority; fel Am Bar Found. **Honors/Awds:** Dean Thomas W Christopher Award, Univ Ala Law Sch; Pres Citation Frontiers Am, 1962; Man of the Year, Alpha Phi Alpha Fraternity, 1973; Outstanding Serv Comm Serv Coun, 1973; Outdoor Recreation Achievement Award, US Dept Comm, 1975; Ala Recreation Parks Soc Lay Award, 1975; Outstanding Serv Univ Ala, Sch Law, 1977; Exemplary Dedication Higher Educ Ala Asn Col & Univ, 1982; Hon Doctor Law, Univ Buffalo Law sch, 2009; Honore, Journey Justice, Birmingham Bar Found, 2013; Honore, Ala Poverty Proj, 2013; Honoree "Lifetime Achievement Civil Rights", NAACP, 2013. **Special Achievements:** First African-American to practice as a senior partner of a major Alabama law firm. **Home Addr:** 9288 Briarmont Rd, Birmingham, AL 35205, **Home Phone:** (205)983-7074. **Business Addr:** Senior Partner, Attorney, Sirote & Permutt PC, 2311 Highland Ave S, Birmingham, AL 35255-5727, **Business Phone:** (205)930-5134.

**DAVIS, DR. JACKIE SOWELL**
Educator, high school principal. **Career:** PM High Sch, prin; Broadway High Sch, prin. **Business Addr:** Principal, Broadway High School, 1250 W Broadway Ave, Minneapolis, MN 55411-2533, **Business Phone:** (612)668-1850.

**DAVIS, JACKLEAN ANDREA**
Law enforcement officer. **Personal:** Born Feb 6, 1957, Cleveland, OH; daughter of Fredrick and LaFrench; children: Christina Katherine. **Educ:** Univ New Orleans. **Career:** Law enforcement officer (retired); New Orleans Police Dept, patrol officer, 1981-82, first dist, 1982, sixth dist, 1982-83, narcotic & drug abuse unit & vice unit, 1983-86, investr rape unit, 1984-86, investr homicide unit, 1986-91, sgt, 1991, lt. **Orgs:** Black Orgn Police; Nat Orgn Black Law Enforcement Exec; Int Asn Women Police; Int Asn Chiefs; Martha Grand Chap Order Eastern Stars. **Home Addr:** 4743 Knight Dr, New Orleans, LA 70127-3329, **Home Phone:** (504)246-0601.

**DAVIS, JAMES EDGAR**
Association executive, engineer, chief executive officer. **Personal:** Born Apr 30, 1948, Augusta, GA; son of Sarah N; married Kathleen Stitt; children: Esa & Veronica. **Educ:** NC St Univ, BS, civil engg, 1970, MS, civil engg, 1972; Univ NC, MS, master regional planning, 1972; Univ Md, PhD, course req, 1976; Fedn Exec Inst, 1982, Synectics, 1989, Univ Pa, 1991, Harvard Univ, attended 1992. **Career:** Southern Rwy Co, mgt trainee, 1970-72; Barton-Aschman Assocs, assoc, 1972-73; MITRE Corp, tech staff, 1973-74; US Dept Transp, chiefpre-award rev br, 1974-75, sr prog ayalyst, 1976-77, dir off grants asst, 1978-82, dep assoc adminr grants mgt, 1982-83, fed urban mass transp admin, 1974-83; Port Authority NY & NJ, asst dir rail transp, 1983-84; Sea-land Serv Inc, dir opers res, 1985-89; Am Soc Civil Engrs, asst exec dir, exec dir & chief exec officer, 1989-. **Orgs:** Fedn Sr Exec Serv; Can Sr Transp Mgt Prog, 1980; Am Mgt Asn; Am Soc Asn Exec; Greater Wash Soc Asn Exec; Coun Engg & Sci Soc Exec, Am Soc Civil Engrs. **Honors/Awds:** Silver Medal of Meritorious Achievement, The Secy Transp; The UMTA Adminr Bronze Medal Super Achievement; Represented USDOT in Riyadh, Saudi Arabia, 1978. **Special Achievements:** The first and only African American to serve as Executive Director of one of the oldest engineering societies, the American Society of Civil Engineers. **Home Addr:** 12625 Greenbriar Rd, Potomac, MD 20854, **Home Phone:** (301)765-2173. **Business Addr:** Executive Director, American Society of Civil Engineers - VA Office, 1801 Alexander Bell Dr, Reston, VA 20191, **Business Phone:** (703)295-6000.

**DAVIS, JAMES F.**
College administrator. **Personal:** Born Jan 29, 1943, Marion, SC; married Beverly A Hemmingway; children: Shean Askia & Donald Affonso. **Educ:** Johnson C Smith Univ, BA, 1964; Pepperdine Univ, MBA, 1977. **Career:** EF Hutton & Co Inc, 1968-71; SC Natl Bank, asst vpres, 1971-78; Rice Col, fac mem, 1978-79; Benedict Col, assoc vpres stud affair, 1979-, dean students, currently, co-chair. **Orgs:** Columbia Chamber Com, 1979; trustee mem, Benedict Col Fed Credit Union, 1979-; AUS Asn, 1979; Nat Assoc Col Deans Registrars & Admissions Officers, 1984; Am Asn Col Registrars & Admis Officers; Steering Comt Assessment Stud Acad Achievement; Nat Asn Stud Financial Aid Adminrs; Nat Asn Prof Women. **Home Addr:** 3909 Humphrey Dr, Columbia, SC 29223. **Business Addr:** Associate Vice President, Dean of Students, Benedict College, 1600 Harden St, Columbia, SC 29204, **Business Phone:** (803)253-5152.

**DAVIS, DR. JAMES R.**
School superintendent, auditor, executive. **Personal:** married Elaine; children: Tom, Matt & Jared. **Career:** Educator (retired); Hattiesburg Pub Sch Dist, supt, dir; James Daniel Assoc, managing partner; Farmington Twp auditor; Farmington Twp Dist 4, rep. **Orgs:** Pres, Nat Bd Educ Sci, US Dept Educ; bd dir, River Valley Country Club; bd dir, Allegheny Elec Coop; bd dir & Allegheny Dir, Tri-County Rural Elec Coop Inc. **Business Addr:** Allegheny Director, Tri-County Rural Electric Cooperative Inc, 22 N Main St, Mansfield, PA 16933-0526, **Business Phone:** (800)343-2559.

**DAVIS, JEAN E.**
Lawyer, administrator. **Personal:** Born New York, NY; daughter of Cynthia and Martin. **Educ:** Hunter Col, New York, NY, BS, 1961; Teachers Col, Columbia Univ, New York, MEd, 1966; Univ Wis Law Sch, Madison, Wis, JD, 1976; Boston Col. **Career:** Lincoln Hosp, Yeshiva Univ, Bronx, NY, cord, 1966-67; Maimonides Hosp, Brooklyn, NY, supvr, 1967-69; City Col, New York, NY, supv, counr, 1969-74; Off Solicitor, US Dept Labor, Civil Rights Div, Wash, DC, asst counsel, atty, adv, 1977-88, counsel, interpretations & advice, 1988-90; Drexel Univ, sr adv pres, 1990, chief staff & exec asst pres, Int Students & Scholars, dir. **Business Addr:** Chief Staff & Executive Assistant President, Drexel Univ, 3141 Chestnut St, Philadelphia, PA 19104, **Business Phone:** (215)895-2000.

**DAVIS, JEFF**
Chief financial officer, vice president (organization). **Educ:** Pa State Univ, BS, acct, 1984; Univ Pittsburgh, grad, MBA, 1992. **Career:** Peat Marwick, supv sr, 1984-87; Hillman Co, asst treas, 1987-96; Mckesson Gen Med, sr vpres & chief financial officer, 1996-98; WorldStrides, sr vpres & chief financial officer, 1998-2005; Wal-Mart Stores Inc, vpres finance-specialty div, 2006-07, vpres finance US store opers, 2007-08, sr vpres, finance & strategy, 2008-10, sr vpres & treas, 2010-13; Wal-Mart Stores Inc, exec vpres & Treas, 2013-14; Lakeland Tours LLC, chief financial officer; Walmart Stores US, exec vpres & chief financial officer, 2014-15; Darden, sr vpres & chief financial officer, 2015-. **Orgs:** Adv bd mem, Nat Asn Black Accountants; bd mem, First Tee Northwest Ark; bd mem, Wash Regional Hosp Found; bd visitor, Univ Pittsburgh, Joseph M. Katz Grad Sch. **Business Addr:** senior vice president, Chief Financial Officer, University of Virginia Darden School of Business, 100 Darden Blvd, Charlottesville, VA 22903, **Business Phone:** (434)924-7481.

**DAVIS, DR. JEWELNEL**
Executive, educator. **Personal:** Born Brooklyn, NY. **Educ:** Brown Univ, BA, relig studies, 1979; Yale Univ Divinity Sch, Mdiv; Univ Conn Sch Social Work, MSW. **Career:** Carleton Col, Northfield, MN, col chaplain; Colgate Univ, assoc univ chaplain; Columbia Univ, univ chaplain & assoc provost, 1996-, Earl Hall Ctr, dir, currently. **Orgs:** Pres, Coun Stud Affairs; Presidential Adv Comt, Sexual Assault; Harlem Congregations Community Improv Brd; advising officer, Stud Gov Bd groups, Columbia. **Business Addr:** University Chaplain & Associate Provost, Director, Columbia University, W710 Lerner Hall 2980 Broadway, New York, NY 10027, **Business Phone:** (212)854-1493.

**DAVIS, JOAN YVETTE**
Educator. **Personal:** Born Macon, GA. **Educ:** Bennett Col, BA, eng & hist; Ala Univ, JD. **Career:** Ala State Bd Educ, legal coun; Ala Dept Post sec Educ, gen coun & vice chancellor legal & human resources, 2002, Ala Technol Network, dir, chief exec officer, Ala Col Syst, interim chancellor, 2009, interim pres; Shelton State Community Col, interim pres, 2013; Delgado Community College, chancellor, currently. **Orgs:** Fel Montgomery Bar Asn; fel Ala Bar Asn; Montgomery Bar Asn; Ala Legis Educ Adv Comt. **Business Addr:** Chancellor, Delgado Community College, 615 City Pk Ave, New Orleans, LA 70119, **Business Phone:** (504)671-5000.

**DAVIS, DR. JOHN ALBERT**
Educator. **Personal:** Born Jan 6, 1935, LaGrange, GA; children: Greg, Deanna & Keith. **Educ:** Univ Calif, Los Angeles, BA, 1963, MA, 1965, PhD, 1971. **Career:** Educator (retired); Social Action Training Ctr, dir res, 1965; Univ Calif, asst prof, 1968; Univ Calif, Berkely, vis prof, 1971; Off Minority Affairs, Univ Southern Calif, 1972; Loyola Marymount Univ, assoc prof, sociol, Dept African Am Studies, chmn, prof. **Orgs:** Alpha Sigma Nu Soc Sci Hon Soc, 1970; bd mem, Los Angeles Childrens Bur, 1983-90, Milton F Williams Fund, 1980-86; pres, Crenshaw Neighbors, 1981-83. **Home Addr:** 4501 Circle View Blvd, Los Angeles, CA 90043.

**DAVIS, JOHN ALEXANDER**
Executive, civil rights activist. **Personal:** Born Jun 2, 1960, Bronx, NY. **Educ:** Columbia Univ NY, BA, 1982; Rutgers Law Sch Newark. **Career:** Century Pac Investment Corp, law clerk, 1985; Cohn & Lifland, law clerk, 1985-86; Integrity Life Ins, paralegal, 1986. **Orgs:** Trustee, bd gov, DeWitt Clinton Alumni Org, 1978-; nat bd mem, Nat Asn Advan Colored People, 1980-86, Youth Col Div, dir, 1986-; alumni officer, Columbia Univ, 1982-87. **Honors/Awds:** Roy Wilkins Scholarship, Nat Asn Advan Colored People, 1978; One of Fifty Future Black Leaders, Ebony Magazine, 1982; Best Legal Brief Frederick Douglass Moot Ct Competition BALSA, 1985. **Home Addr:** 1517 E Cold Spring Lane, Baltimore, MD 21218, **Home Phone:** (410)433-7936. **Business Addr:** Director, National Association for the Advancement of Colored People, 4805 Mt Hope Dr, Baltimore, MD 21215-3297, **Business Phone:** (410)580-5777.

**DAVIS, JOHN ISAAC EARL LAMONT. See DAVIS, ISAAC.**

**DAVIS, JOHN LEONARD**
Football player. **Personal:** Born May 14, 1973, Jasper, TX. **Educ:** Emporia State. **Career:** Football player (retired); Dallas Cowboys, 1995; Tampa Bay Buccaneers, tight end, 1997-99, Minn Vikings, tight end, 2000; Chicago Bears, tight end, 2001-03.

**DAVIS, JOHN W., III**
Financial manager, government official. **Personal:** Born Oct 29, 1958, Cincinnati, OH. **Educ:** Georgetown Univ, BS, 1980; ICMA City Mgt Sch; Harvard Univ; Ind Univ, attended 1986. **Career:** Georgetown Univ, assoc prof, 1979-80; Cincinnati City, contract acct, 1980-82; Dun & Bradstreet, financial analyst, 1981; Queen City Metro, comput programmer, 1982-85, analyst; SORTA, supt capital; Silverton City, chief fiscal & acct officer, 1982-87. **Orgs:** Nat Asn Accountants, 1982-87; Munic Fin Off Asn, 1982-87; Nat Asn Advan Colored People, 1983-87; Notary Pub State Ohio, 1984-87; bd trustee, OKI, 1984-85; Nat Budget Rev Bd; Nat Cash Mgt Comt; bd trustee, Cincinnati Br, Nat Asn Advan Colored People. **Home Addr:** 6616 Coleridge, Silverton, OH 45236.

**DAVIS, DR. JOHN W., JR.**
Church historian, executive director, clergy. **Personal:** son of John W and Virgie L; married Reba A; children: Misti D McNichols, John W III, Jarrett W & Ra-fel Jackson II. **Educ:** Univ Southern Miss, Hattiesburg, MS, Bachelor Degree, 1984; Int Bible Inst & Sem, Plymount, FL, Undergrad degree, 1985; Int Bible Inst & Sem, Plymount, FL, 1986; Trinity Col Bible & Theol Sem, Newburgh, IN, PhD, 2009. **Career:** Faith MB Church; New Educ Conv & Gen Miss Baptist State Conv Miss Inc, minister music; Gen Mississippi Baptist State Convention, pub rel dir, currently. **Orgs:** Bd mem & dir, Nat Baptist Conv. **Business Addr:** Public Relations Director, General Missionary Baptist State Convention, 3050 19th Ave, Gulfport, MS 39501, **Business Phone:** (228)392-3718.

**DAVIS, DR. JOHN WESLEY, SR.**
Clergy, president (organization). **Personal:** Born Aug 10, 1934, Laurel, WG; son of Willie (deceased) and Mary; married Virgie Louise Sumlin; children: John W Jr & Maurice Benard. **Educ:** Jackson State Univ, BMus, 1960; Am Bible Col, BPhB, 1967, MPhB & DD, 1968. **Career:** Jackson S Univ, scholar, 1956-60; Mt Olive D Cong, pres, 1968-80; Mt Moriah Missionary Baptist Church, pastor; Concord Missionary Baptist Church, pastor; St. Luke Missionary Baptist Church, pastor; New W Pt Missionary Baptist Church, pastor; Campbell Jr Col, instr; Pub Sch Syst, teacher; Greater Antioch Missionary Baptist Church, pastor, 1981-; Gen Missionary Baptist State Conv Miss Inc, exec asst. **Orgs:** Trustee, Mich Col Inst W Pt, 1975-85; life mem, Nat Asn Adv Colored People, 1981-; SCLC, 1981-; adv bd, Judge Baker, 1982; bd dir & adv bd, Nat Baptist Conv Inc; pres, New Educ State Conv; pres, Dist Cong; vpres, New Educ State Cong; parliametarian, Shiloh Dist Asn; adv bd, Gov MS Ceta Prog; vpres, Mt Olive Dist Cong Alumni Asn; Ministerial Biracial Alliance; adv bd, Miss Coop Exten Serv; Interdenominational Ministerial Alliance; Youth Ct Adv Bd; adv bd, Salvation Army Domestic Violence Shelter; Salvation Army; bd dir, Am Cancer Soc; counr, Youth Prison Ministry; chair, Pres Coun, NBC, USA Inc; pres, Jackson Co Interdemominational Ministerial Alliance; life mem, Nat Asn Advan Colored People; adv bd mem, Jackson County Youth Ct; trustee, MI Col & Inst. **Special Achievements:** Doctoral Dissertation "Christianity, A System Of Truth"; Author Of Daily Vacation Bible School Booklet. **Home Addr:** 3401 Westlane Dr, Gautier, MS 39553, **Home Phone:** (228)497-3137. **Business Addr:** Pastor, The Greater Antioch MB Church, 1028 Denny Ave, Pascagoula, MS 39567, **Business Phone:** (228)769-1044.

**DAVIS, JOHN WESLEY**
Lawyer, chief executive officer, executive. **Personal:** Born Nov 1, 1943, Detroit, MI; son of Dorris Miller; married Lorraine F; children: Aisha & Kiilu. **Educ:** Wabash Col, AB, 1964; Univ Denver, JD, 1971. **Career:** Int Asn Human Rights, EEO Prog, dir, 1975-76; Nat Bar Assn, EEO Prog, exec dir, 1976-78; John W Davis & Assocs, owner & chief exec officer, 1977-; Howard Univ, Reggie Prog, exec dir, 1980-84, law prof, 1978-85; Self Employed, atty, 1985-. **Orgs:** Life mem, Nat Bar Asn, NBA jour ed bd; Nat Asn Advan Colored People, life mem, 1979-, coop atty, 1977-; solicitor, GAO Personnel Appeals Bd, 1988-94; bd mem, DC Neighborhood Legal Serv, 1992-. **Honors/Awds:** Award Merit, Nat Asn Advan Colored People, 1975; Equal Justice Award, Nat Bar Asn, 1977; Certificateof Appreciation, 1980. **Special Achievements:** Law Review Article, NCCU Law Journal, The Supreme Court Rationale for Racism, 1976. Employment Discrimination Litigation Manual, 1977. **Home Addr:** 2219 William Mary Dr, Alexandria, VA 22308-1549, **Home Phone:** (703)780-5044. **Business Addr:** Attorney, 1003 K St NW, Washington, DC 20001, **Business Phone:** (202)783-3705.

**DAVIS, JOHNETTA GARNER**
Pathologist, school administrator, educator. **Personal:** Born Nov 1, 1939, Warrenton, VA. **Educ:** Teachers Col, BS, 1961; George Wash-

ington Univ, MA, 1969; Howard Univ, PhD, commun sci & dis, 1976. **Career:** Howard Univ, assoc dean, grad prof, 1978-96, assoc prof, prof commun dciences dis, 1972-78, emer prof, 1972-93; Am Speech & Hearing Asn, asst sec, prog develop, 1971-72; Fed City Col, asst prof, 1970-71; Teachers Col, instr, 1969-71; Wash DC Pub Schs, speech pathologist, 1961-68; Univ Md Col Pk, Grad Sch & Off Grad Recruitment Retention & Diversity, assoc dean & dir, 1993-2009, lectr grad studies, lectr family studies, currently. **Orgs:** Fed City Alumnae Chap Dist Sorority; Wash DC chap, The Soc Inc; Potomac Chap Links Inc; Am Speech-Lang & Hearing Asn, 1961-; DC Speech, Lang & Hearing, 1963-; task force on int grad educ Coun Grad Schs Task Force on MNY Educ; bd Stoddard Bapt Home, 1977-82; Sunday sch teacher, Mt Sinai Baptist Church, 1977-82; fac mem, Sch Pub Health. **Honors/Awds:** CCC-SP-L, Am Speech-Lang Hearing Asn, cert, 1962; US Office Educ, Fel, 1967; Outstanding Junior Faculty Award, DC Teachers Col, 1971; Outstanding faculty citation Students at DC Teachers Col, 1971; Frederick Douglass Honor Soc Howard Univ Chap, 1974; Outstanding Young Women in America, 1976; Outstanding Alumni Award, Howard Univ, Sch Communs, 1986; Howard Univ, establishment of the Johnetta G Davis Award for Best Mentor of Graduate Students, 1993; Administrator of the Year, Grad Stud Coun, 1992; Distinguished Service Awards, 1978-80, 1982, 1986, 1988, 1990; Prof Emerita, Howard Univ, 1996; Editors Award, J Contemporary Issues in Commun Scis & Disorders, 2000; Service Award, Univ Md, Grad Stud Govt, 2000; Merit Award, Univ Md, Black Fac & Staff Asn, 2000; Distinguished Alumnus, Howard University, 2006; President's Distinguished Service Award, University Maryland, 2006; ASHA Award, Am Speech-Lang-Hearing Asn, 2009. **Home Addr:** 519 Brummel Ct NW Apt 519, Washington, DC 20012-1846, **Home Phone:** (202)829-8808. **Business Addr:** Lecturer, Associate Dean & Director, University of Maryland, 2123 Lee Bldg, College Park, MD 20742-5121, **Business Phone:** (301)405-1000.

### DAVIS, JOHNNY REGINALD
Executive, basketball player, basketball coach. **Personal:** Born Oct 21, 1955, Detroit, MI; married Lezli; children: Reginald & Austin. **Educ:** Univ Dayton, attended 1976; Ga State Univ, BS, community develop, 1987; Union Inst & Univ Vt Col, MA, sports psychol, 1990. **Career:** Basketball player (retired), basketball coach, executive; Portland Trail Blazers, guard, 1976-78, asst coach, 1994-96; Ind Pacers, guard, 1978-82, asst coach, 2006-07; Atlanta Hawks, guard, 1982-84, 1986, dir community affairs, 1986-89, asst to pres, 1989-90, asst coach, 1990-93; Cleveland Cavaliers, guard, 1984-86; Los Angeles Clippers, asst coach, 1993-94; Philadelphia 76ers, head coach, 1996-97; NJ Nets, asst coach, 1997-99; Orlando Magic, from asst coach to head coach, 1999-2005; Minn Timber wolves, asst coach, 2005-06; Memphis Grizzlies, asst coach, 2007-09, interim head coach, 2009-11; Toronto Raptors, asst coach, 2011-13; Los Angeles Lakers, asst coach, 2013-14; Atlanta Hawks Found, asst, pres. **Home Addr:** 28 S Kaufman Stone Way, Biltmore Lake, NC 28715-7722, **Home Phone:** (828)633-0673. **Business Addr:** Assistant Coach, Los Angeles Lakers, Toyota Sports Ctr 555 Nash St, El Segundo, CA 90245, **Business Phone:** (310)426-6000.

### DAVIS, JONATHAN. See FAREED, KAMAAL IBN JOHN.

### DAVIS, JOSEPH SOLOMON
College administrator. **Personal:** Born Apr 8, 1938, Macon, GA; married Sarah Frances Striggles; children: Joan Yvette & Oscar Wendall. **Educ:** Tuskegee Inst, BS, MEd, 1968. **Career:** College administrator (retired); Boggs Acad, teacher ind arts, 1961-65; guid dir, 1965-67; Southern Asn Sec Sch, fel, 1967; Stillman Col, dir financial aid, 1967-76, 1981-95; dir, coun serv, 1976-81. **Orgs:** W Tuscaloosa Optimist Club, 1980-. **Home Addr:** 2608 32nd St, Northport, AL 35476-5218, **Home Phone:** (205)339-4313.

### DAVIS, DR. KATIE CAMPBELL
Educator. **Personal:** Born Sep 11, 1936, Lumber City, GA; married Ernest Jr; children: Theresa Lynn. **Educ:** Tenn State Univ, BA, 1957, MA, 1968; Univ Ill, PhD, 1974. **Career:** Teacher var pub sch; commun consult; Norfolk State Univ, prof speech & Eng, theatre arts, prof emer, currently. **Orgs:** Speech Comm Asn; Nat Advan Asn Colored People; Alpha Kappa Alpha Sorority; Am Asn Univ Women; pres, Norfolk State Univ Retirees Asn. **Home Addr:** 909 Amesbury Rd, Virginia Beach, VA 23464-3106, **Home Phone:** (757)467-1045. **Business Addr:** Professor Emeritus, Norfolk State University, 2401 Corprew Ave, Norfolk, VA 23504.

### DAVIS, KERY
Executive. **Educ:** Dartmouth Col, BA, polit sci; Cornell Law Sch, JD. **Career:** Basketball player; Reach Entertainment, gen mgr; Howard Univ, athletic dir; HBO, sr vpres sports prog. **Business Addr:** Senior Vice President, HBO Sports Programming, 1100 Avenue of the Americas, New York, NY 10036, **Business Phone:** (212)512-1168.

### DAVIS, HON. L. CLIFFORD
Lawyer, judge, educator. **Personal:** Born Oct 12, 1925, Wilton, AR; son of Augustus and Dora Duckett; married Ethel R Weaver; children: Karen Renae & Avis Janeth. **Educ:** Philander Smith Col, BA, bus admin, 1945; Atlanta Univ, Grad Studies Econs, 1946; Howard Univ, law sch, JD, 1949. **Career:** Davis Sturns & Johns, atty, 1949-; Gen Practioner Law, Ark, 1949-52; Paul Quinn Col, Waco, Tx, asst prof Bus, 1952-54; gen practr law, 1953-83, 2003-; Criminal Dist No. 2, judge, 1983-88; Johnson, Vaughn & Heiskell, off coun, gen coun, 1989-; Dist Judge, 1989-96; Tarrant County, sr dist judge, Tarrant County, 1994-2003; Clifford Davis Elem Sch, founder, currently. **Orgs:** Omega Psi Phi Frat; trustee, St Andrews United Methodist Church; pastmem bd, Tarrant Co Unit Fund; Tarrant County & Prec Worker's Coun; charter rev com City Ft Worth TX; adv coun, Tex Legal Serv Corp; Young Men Christian Asn; Nat Asn Advan Colored People; State Bar Tex; Supreme Ct US; US Ct Appeals Fifth & Eighth Circuits; life mem, Nat Bar Asn; Tex Bar Found Fel; Col State Bar Tex; Tarrant Co & Ft Worth/Tarrant Co Black Bar Asn; Ft Worth Black Bar Asn; L Clifford Davis Legal Asn.. **Honors/Awds:** Outstanding Achiever Award, Philander Smith Univ Alumni Asn, 1994; Living Legend in the Law, Jr Black Acad Arts & Letters, 1994; Marion Brooks' Living Legend Award, 1995; KRLD Radio Appreciation Community Service Award, 1996; Silver Gaval Award, Tarrant County Bar Asn, 1997; Arkansas Black Hall of Fame, 2007; Blackstone Award, Tarrant County Bar, 2015; Hall Fame, Nat Bar Asn; Lifetime Achievers Award, Tex Lawyers. **Special Achievements:** Opened First African American law office Tx; Living Legend in the Law presented by the Junior Black Academy of Arts & Letters, 1994; Legal Legend, Eclipse Magazine, 2007. **Home Addr:** 2101 Fleming Dr, Fort Worth, TX 76112, **Home Phone:** (817)451-5486. **Business Addr:** General Counselor, Johnson Vaughn & Heiskell, 5601Bridge St Suite 220, Fort Worth, TX 76112, **Business Phone:** (817)457-2999.

### DAVIS, LANCE ROOSEVELT
Executive. **Personal:** Born Dec 21, 1962, Orange, NJ; son of Roosevelt Jr and Joan Henson Roach. **Educ:** Johnson & Wales Univ, ASc, culinary arts, 1982, BA, food serv mgt, 1984. **Career:** APO Catering, owner & chief operator, 1983-84; Hyatt Regency, NB, corp mgr trainee, 1984-85, beverage mgr, exec steward, 1985-86, gourmet restaurant mgr, 1986-88, freelance food & beverage consult, 1987-89, Kans city, banquet mgr, 1988-89; Harrison CNF Ctr, from asst food & beverage dir to food & beverage dir, 1989-92; Lack mann Food Serv, Food Serv dir; South Pk Grille & Lounge, gen mgr, 2000-02; Wilmers Pk Renaissance, gen mgr, Food & Beverage, 2002-04; Lucky Strike Lanes, Lounge-W Nyack, New York, gen mgr, 2006-10; Castle Fun Ctr, gen mgr, 2011-12; Party Pl USA, vpres opers, 2012-. **Orgs:** Pres, Distrib Educ Club AME, Stan hope, NJ, 1979-80; founding father, Alpha Pi Omega Fraternity Inc, 1983; founding father, Omega Phi Delta Fraternity, 1984; bd mem, City CNL Glen Cove, NY, 1989-90; Bus Vols Arts, Middlesex County, 1984-85; Glen Cove Citizens Against Substance Abuse Inc, 1989-90; pres, Nat Asn Black Hospity Profs NY Chap, 1992-. **Home Addr:** 37 Forest Ave, Glen Cove, NY 11542, **Home Phone:** (516)676-3551.

### DAVIS, DR. LARRY EARL
Educational psychologist, dean (education). **Personal:** Born May 11, 1946, Saginaw, MI; son of Kires and Clara; married Shirley Salmon; children: Amani, Naeem & Keanu. **Educ:** Mich State Univ, BS, psychol, 1968; Univ Mich, MSW, group work, 1973, MA, psychol, 1975, PhD, soc work & psychol, 1977. **Career:** VISTA, New York, vol, 1969-72; Wash Univ, asst prof soc work & psychol, 1977-2001, E Desmond Lee chair ethnic & racial diversity; Univ Hawaii, sabbatical, 1988; Norfolk State Univ, adj fac, 1995-97; Univ Pittsburgh, Sch Soc Work, founder & ed, 2002-, chairholder Donald M. Henderson professorship, 2001-, dean, 2001-, Sandra Wexler dir, currently, Ctr Race & Social Prob, founder & dir, 2002-, Sch Arts & Sci, Dept Psychol, prof psychol, 2005-, Sch Health & Rehab Sci, prof rehab sci & technol, 2010-, Clin & Translational Sci Inst, prof, 2011-; Wash Univ, Bridges Mag, George Warren Brown Sch Social Work, E Desmond Lee prof racial & ethnic diversity, 1998, chairperson, 1998-2001; Ethnic & Racial Diversity, prof social work & psychol & E Desmond Lee chmn, E Desmond Lee prof, 1998. **Orgs:** Asn Black Psychologists, 1977-; Nat Asn Black Social Workers, 1977-; Nat Asn Social Workers, 1977-; Leadership St Louis, 1986; Coun Social Work Educ; Soc Social Work Res. **Honors/Awds:** Chancellor's 2007 Affirmative Action Award, 2007; Named Head of the University's new School of Race & Social Problems, Univ Pittsburgh, 2002. **Special Achievements:** Published & co-published numerous articles, including "Racial Composition of Groups," Social Work MA, 1979; "Racial Balance, A Psychological Issue," Social Work With Groups, 1980; "Minority Content in Social Work Educ, A Question of Objectives," Journal of Educ for Social Work, 1983; co-author, Race, Gender & Class: Guidelines for Practice with Individuals, Families, & Groups, Prentice-Hall, 1989; co-editor, Ethnic Issues in Adolescent Mental Health, Newbury Park, CA, Sage, 1990; Black & Single: Finding & Choosing a Partner Who is Right for You, Ballantine, 1998; Too Many Blacks, Too Many Whites: Is There A Racial Balance? Basic & Applied Social Psychology, 1995; Working with African-American Males: A Guide to Practice, Sage, 1999. **Home Addr:** 944 N Sheridan Ave, Pittsburgh, PA 15206, **Home Phone:** (412)441-6602. **Business Addr:** Dean, Professor, University of Pittsburgh, 2117 Cathedral Learning, Pittsburgh, PA 15260, **Business Phone:** (412)624-6304.

### DAVIS, LATINA
Basketball coach, basketball player, security consultant. **Personal:** Born Oct 8, 1974, TN. **Educ:** Univ Tenn, BS, 1996. **Career:** Tenn Maryville, teaching & running basketball camps; Atlanta, 1996-97; New Eng, 1996-97; Columbus Quest, guard, 1997-99; Unicoi Co High Sch, asst basketball coach; Lady Lakers, asst coach; E Tenn State Univ, asst coach; Watauga High Sch, basketball coach, 2003; security officer. **Home Addr:** , TN. **Business Addr:** Security Officer.

### DAVIS, LAWRENCE ARNETTE, JR.
Educator, college administrator. **Personal:** Born May 13, 1937, Pine Bluff, AR; married Ethel Louise Grant; children: Sonya, Lawrence III & Catherine. **Educ:** AM & N Col, BS, math, 1958; Univ Ark, Fayetteville, MS, math, 1960; Iowa State Univ, PhD, engineering math, 1973. **Career:** Chancellor (retired); AM & N Col, head col & pres, 1943, prof, 1961-68; MS Valley St Col, instr, 1960; NASA Advan Res & Technol summers, 1964 & 1965; NSF In-serv Inst, AM & N Col, dir, 1967-68; IA State Univ, grad teaching asst, 1969-71, Engr Res Inst, res asst, 1971-73; Univ AR, NASA Res Proj, dir, 1973-74; NASA Off Advan Res & Technol, admin specialist; Univ Ark, Pine Bluff, chmn & prof math & physics, 1976-, dean, arts & sci, dean, sci & technol, pres & interim chancellor, 1991-. **Orgs:** Soc Indust & Appl Mathematicians; Math Asn Am; Nat Asn Mathematicians; AR Acad Sci, 1966-68; AAAS; Am Asn Univ Prof; Am Asn Physics Teachers; BetaKappi Chi; Alpha Kappa Mu; bd mem, Jefferson County Indust Found; bd mem, Southern Regional Educ; bd mem, Fed Res Bd St Louis (Little RockBranch); bd dir, Jefferson Regional Med Ctr; bd dir, Ark Land & Farm Develop; pres bd advisors, Historically Black Cols & Univs. **Home Addr:** 208 W 34 St, Pine Bluff, AR 71601, **Home Phone:** (870)536-5007. **Business Addr:** Chancellor, University of Arkansas at Pine Bluff, 1200 N Univ Dr, Pine Bluff, AR 71611, **Business Phone:** (870)575-8000.

### DAVIS, LELIA KASENIA
Executive. **Personal:** Born Nov 7, 1941, Taft, OK; daughter of Willie Smith and Canzaty; married David Earl; children: Mark, Kasandra, Starla Smith Phillips, Canraty & Derrick. **Career:** Am Tech Inst, Muskogee, Okla, admin counr; City Taft, Taft Okla, mayor, 1973-; Okla C's Ctr Taft, currently. **Orgs:** Bd dir, Eastern Okla Develop Dist; pres, LeCon Org; chairwoman, Taft Parade Comn; adv bd dir, Dept Corrections; First Baptist Church Taft; vpres, Muskogee County Dem Women's Club. **Special Achievements:** First black woman to be elected mayor of a city. **Home Addr:** PO Box 248, Taft, OK 74463, **Home Phone:** (918)682-5003.

### DAVIS, LEODIS J.
Educator. **Personal:** Born Sep 25, 1933, Stamps, AK; son of Prentis and Mary Ann; married N June Wilson; children: Melonie & Leon. **Educ:** Univ Mo, Kansas City, BS, chem, 1956; Iowa State Univ, MS, biochem, 1958, PhD, biochem, 1960. **Career:** Tenn State Univ, asst prof chem, 1961-62; Howard Univ Med Col, asst prof biochem, 1962-67, assoc prof biochem, 1967-69; Iowa State Univ, res assoc, 1960-61, vis assoc prof, 1969, assoc prof biochem, 1969-76, prof chem, 1976-97, chmn chem dept, 1979-87, Col Lib Arts, asst dean, actg dean, Grad Col, sr assoc provost charg, 1988-89, Acad Affairs, assoc vpres, 1989-94, dir summer session, 1992-94, prof emer, 1997-. **Orgs:** Soc Sigma XI, 1960; Biochem Study Sect Ad Hoc Consult, 1970-; chem community minority affairs, Am Soc Biol, 1973; Aging Rev Comn, 1976-80; NIH Biochem Study Sect, 1976-81; Nat Res Coun Rev NSF Grad fel 1977-80; bd dir, Univ IA Credit Union, 1986-; Celluar & Molecular Basis Dis Rev Comm, 1986-90; Div Res Grants Adv Comm, 1993-97; HEW NIH Min Biomed Supp; bd dir & pres, Oakdale Res Pk; chair, Bd Control Athletics. **Honors/Awds:** Lederle Medical Faculty Award, US, 1967; UMKC Alumnus of the Year, 1986; Fogarty International Research Collaboration Award, Special Rev Community, 1992-93; Victor Wilson Scholar for academy achievement. **Home Addr:** 12012 Grand Ave, Kansas City, MO 64145-1493, **Home Phone:** (816)941-3091. **Business Addr:** Professor Emeritus, University of Iowa, E331 Chemistry Bldg, Iowa City, IA 52242-1294, **Business Phone:** (319)335-1350.

### DAVIS, LEONARD HARRY. See Obituaries Section.

### DAVIS, DR. LEROY, SR.
Administrator, executive. **Personal:** Born May 24, 1949, Orangeburg, SC; married Christine McGill; children: Tonya, Javette & Leroy Jr. **Educ:** SC State Univ, BS, biol, 1971; Purdue Univ, MS, microbiol, 1972, PhD, molecular biol, 1979. **Career:** President (retired); Sc State Univ, Talented & Gifted Workshops, prog dir, 1982-85, Acad Coun & Tutorial Prog, dir, 1983-86, Off Instnl Self-Studies, dir, 1987-90, vice provost acad admin, 1990-93, vpres stud serv, 1993-95, interim pres, 1995-96, pres, 1996-2002; Voorhees Col, Denmark, Sc, Ctr Excellence, exec dir, rural & minority health, distinguished prof, biol, currently. **Orgs:** Am Coun Educ; bd dir, Nat Col Athletic Asn; bd dir, Nat Asn Equal Opportunity Higher Educ; bd dir, Sc Aquarium; bd dir, Sc Sea Grant Consortium; bd dir, Southeastern Coun Foundations; chair, Sc Gov Sch Sci & Mathematics; Jessie Ball duPont Fund; chmn, comnr, Southern Asn Cols & Schs. **Business Addr:** Executive Director, Voorhees College, 430 Porter Rd, Denmark, SC 29042, **Business Phone:** (803)780-1234.

### DAVIS, LESTER E.
Architect, engineer. **Personal:** Born Aug 5, 1918, Tunica, MS; son of Emanuel and Carrie Ruth Jackson; married Annie B Debro; children: Dorothy J Wakefield. **Educ:** Kans State Univ, BS, archit engineering, 1950; Lincoln Univ, attended 1946. **Career:** Engineer (retired); USN Dept Naval Ship Yard, Vallejo, naval architect/struct, 1950-53; State Calif Dept Transp, bridge engr, 1953-75; Bay Area Rapid Transit Dist Ca, supr engr, struct/civil, 1975-86. **Orgs:** Life mem, Am Soc Civil Engrs; N Calif Coun Black Pr Engrs; regist pr engr, Civil Br St CA; life mem, Alpha Phi Alpha Fraternity; E Bay Struct Engrs Soc; Active Local Church & Civic Asn. **Home Addr:** 1000 E 14th St Apt 238, San Leandro, CA 94577-3791, **Home Phone:** (510)568-6647.

### DAVIS, LISA E.
Lawyer. **Personal:** Born Feb 6, 1960, Queens, NY; married Anthony Jamison; children: Marcus & Noelle. **Educ:** Harvard Univ, BA, Eng & Am lit, 1981; NY Univ Sch Law, JD, 1985. **Career:** Hon Constance Baker Motley, law clerk, 1985-86; Kramer Levin Naftalis & Frankel LLP, assoc, 1986-88; New York Univ Law Rev, staff mem; Frankfurt Kurnit Klein & Selz PC, assoc, 1988-93, partner, 1994-. **Orgs:** Intellectual Property Sect, Nat Bar Asn, 1993-; Black Entertainment & Sports Lawyers Asn; New York Bar; bd mem, Coun Urban Professionals, 2009-11; bd chair, Urbanworld Film Found, 2012; bd chair, Urban World Film Festival Found; bd mem, Coun Urban Prof; bd mem, S Orange Performing Arts Ctr. **Honors/Awds:** Top 50 Black Power Brokers in Entertainment, Black Lawyers, Black Enterprise Mag, 2002; Americas Top Black Lawyers, Black Enterprise Mag, 2003; Jacob K Javits Achievement Award, Bedford Stuyvesant Restoration Corp, 2003; 25 Influential Black Women in Business, Network J, 2007; Super Lawyer, Law and Politics magazine, 2009; Women Of Power Award, Nat Urban League; Attorneys at the Top, Network Js, 2011; Lawyer of the Year, Metrop Black Bar Asn; Super Lawyer, Law & Polit mag, 2011. **Special Achievements:** Well-known public speaker. **Business Addr:** Partner, Frankfurt Kurnit Klein & Selz PC, 488 Madison Ave 9th Fl, New York, NY 10022, **Business Phone:** (212)826-5530.

### DAVIS, LISA R.
Executive. **Personal:** Born Dec 2, 1961, Washington, DC; daughter of Doris and Lorenzo. **Educ:** Univ NC, Greensboro, BA, commun studies, 1983; Howard Univ, MBA, bus admin & pub admin, 1988. **Career:** Clinton/Gore Campaign, nat dep press secy, 1996; AARP, head of Pub rel & Commun, actg dep dir & dir commun; AstraZeneca Pharmaceut LP, vpres corp communs, 2006-10; MedImmune, vpres, 2010-. **Orgs:** Delta Sigma Theta, 1983-; Communs dir, Nat Bar Asn, 1986-89; staff dir, media & prof servs, Am Bar Asn, 1989-93; press secy, Dem Leadership Coun, 1993-96; Nat Press Club; Pub Rels Soc Am; fel Harvard Univs Inst Polit; trustee, Del Art Mus; bd mem, Nat Chamber Found; Am Bar Asn Standing Comt. **Business Addr:** Vice President, MedImmune, Gaithersburg, MD 20878.

**DAVIS, LUTHER CHARLES**
Consultant, sales manager. **Personal:** Born Sep 21, 1948, Key West, FL; son of Earl and Carol; married Sharon Ann Williams; children: Jason. **Educ:** Cornell Univ, BA, 1970. **Career:** Jewel Co Inc, buyer, 1977; Kraft Inc, Dairy Group, dist sales mgr, 1984; Mellin Ice Cream Co, vpres, 1985; Wis Milk Mkt Bd Inc, regional vpres. **Orgs:** Pres, Randallstown Optimist, 1990-91. **Home Addr:** 260 Iacuele Dr S, Kingston, RI 02879.

**DAVIS, MAJOR**
Administrator, association executive. **Personal:** Born Nov 6, 1931, Hartsville, SC; married Elsie M Luck; children: Shynethia Catrice & Trent Damone. **Educ:** Maricopa Tech Community Col, AA, 1973; Phoenix Col, AA, 1975; Ariz State Univ, BA, 1979. **Career:** USAF, jet test flight engr, 1951-72; ed, pub Phoenix Chronicle Newspaper, 1969; Youth Together Inc, founder & owner, 1970-; Miss Black Ariz Pageant, dir, 1971-; Miss Galaxy Int Pageant, nat dir, 1975-. **Orgs:** USAF Worlds Southern Hemisphere, 1968; Nat Asn Advan Colored People, 1970-; grand master, Alpha Grand Lodge, 1974-75; Phoenix Advert Club, 1976; Ariz Newspaper Asn, 1978; Phoenix Chamber Com, 1978. **Home Addr:** 4310 W Verde Lane, Phoenix, AZ 85031-3846, **Home Phone:** (602)272-5496. **Business Addr:** Owner, Youth Together Inc, 4310 W Verde Lane, Phoenix, AZ 85031, **Business Phone:** (602)272-5496.

**DAVIS, MARCIA**
Editor, writer. **Career:** Minneapolis Star Tribune, copy ed, 1989-92; Wasington Post, copy ed, Metro Desk, 1992-95, night police reporter, 1995-97, style assignment ed, 1999-2007, dist polit ed, 2007-09, dep nat ed, polit & govt desk, 2009-; Black Entertainment Tv, emerge mag sr ed, 1997-99. **Honors/Awds:** Marcia is one of the newspaper's most imaginative & passionate editors. **Business Addr:** Writer, Washington Post, 1150 15th St NW, Washington, DC 20071, **Business Phone:** (202)334-6000.

**DAVIS, DR. MARIANNA WHITE**
Editor, writer, educator. **Personal:** Born Jan 8, 1929, Philadelphia, PA; daughter of Albert McNeil White and Laura Bowman Frederick; children: Kenneth Renay. **Educ:** SC State Col, BA, eng, 1949; NY Univ, MA, eng, 1953; Boston Univ, DEd, eng, 1966. **Career:** Keenan High Sch, Columbia, teacher; SC Pub Sch, teacher, 1949-51, 1955-56, 1986-96; SC State Col, asst prof, 1956-64; Claflin Col, prof, 1966-69; Voorhees Col, vis prof, 1966-68; Boston Univ, vis prof, 1967; Univ Tenn, vis prof, 1969; Benedict Col, Eng prof & res, 1969-82, spl asst pres, 1987, Spec Proj & Self-Study, dir, chairperson, 1996-; ABC Devel Corp, co-founder & secy, 1972; Denmark Tech Col, actg pres, 1985-86; Davis & Assocs, pres, 1980-; N eastern Univ, Training Proj, coord, 1992-94; lectr, Ger, 1998, Italy, 2000. **Orgs:** Bd dir, Nat Coun Teachers Eng, 1958-80; exec comt, ADE Mod Lang Asn, 1976-79; exec producer, commr SC Educ TV, 1980-95; Pub Broadcasting Syst Adv Bd, 1981-83; Francis Burns United Methodist Ch; bd chmn, Columbia Urban League Bd, 1981-82; Nat Coun Negro Women; YWCA; life mem Nat Asn Advan Colored People; Moles; coord, Coalition Concerns Blacks Post Sec Educ SC; Alpha Kappa Alpha Sor; Order Eastern Star; chmn, SC Int Women's Yr Comn; founder, VICOS Women's League Comt Action; TISAWS; Civil Rights Comn Adv Bd, 1985-; Nat Publicity chair, Moles, 1988-92; bd educ, SC United Methodist Church, 1988-96; bd mem, bd visitors, Claflin Col; Sc Senate. **Home Addr:** 156 Aberdeen Ave, Columbia, SC 29203, **Home Phone:** (803)252-7509. **Business Addr:** Special Assistant to the President, Benedict College, 1600 Harden St, Columbia, SC 29204, **Business Phone:** (803)705-4379.

**DAVIS, MARIE H.**
President (organization), politician. **Career:** Foster City, elected mem, 1998-2000. **Orgs:** Pres, Nat Asn Advan Colored People, San Mateo County, 2002; Beautification Comt; Friends Libr. **Honors/Awds:** San Mateo County Women's Hall of Fame; Community Wall of Fame, inducted, 2002. **Home Addr:** 617 Cleveland St, Redwood City, CA 94061-1613, **Home Phone:** (650)341-4862. **Business Addr:** Elected Member, City of Foster City, City Hall, Foster City, CA 94404, **Business Phone:** (650)286-3200.

**DAVIS, DR. MARILYN ANN CHERRY**
Educator. **Personal:** Born Mar 26, 1951, Aiken, SC; daughter of Council Christopher and Sara Wilhelmena Walton (deceased); married Charles Douglas; children: Cheryl Maria. **Educ:** Hampton Inst, BA, 1973; Atlanta Univ, MA, 1977, PhD, polit sci, 1979. **Career:** Atlanta Jr Col, instr polit sci, 1977-79; Tuskegee Inst, asst prof polit sci, 1980; Bennett Col, asst prof polit sci, 1980-81; Spelman Col, fac, 1981-, chmn, 1984-85 & 1988-90, assoc prof polit sci, 1981-. **Orgs:** Am Polit Sci Asn, 1981-; Southern Polit Sci Asn, 1981-; Ga Polit Sci Asn, 1981-; Nat Conf Black Polit Scientists, 1981-; hon mem, Golden Key Nat Hon Soc; distinguished mem, Nat Soc Col Scholars, Spelman Col. **Home Addr:** 4140 Welcome All Terr, Atlanta, GA 30349-1926, **Home Phone:** (404)762-1036. **Business Addr:** Associate Professor, Spelman College, 350 Spelman Lane SW, Atlanta, GA 30345, **Business Phone:** (404)270-5649.

**DAVIS, MARILYNN A.**
Government official. **Personal:** Born Oct 30, 1952, Little Rock, AR; daughter of James Edward and Erma Lee Glasco. **Educ:** Smith Col, BA, econs, 1973; Univ Mich, MA, econs, 1976; Wash Univ, St Louis, MA, econs, 1980; Harvard Grad Sch Bus Admin, MBA, 1982. **Career:** State St Bank, Boston, sr credit analyst, 1981; Gen Motors Corp, Detroit, analyst, cent off financial staff, 1982-83; Gen Motors Corp, NY, sr financial analyst, overseas borrowing sect, 1982, sr financial analyst, financing, investment & financial planning sect, 1984, asst to GM group vpres, chief economist, 1984-86; Am Express Co, NY, vpres, risk financing, 1986-92; NY Housing Authority, dep gen mgr finance, chief financial officer, 1992-93; US Dept Housing & Urban Develop, asst secy admin, 1993-97; Fleet Boston Financial Corp, exec vpres & mgr consumer banking, 2000-02; Wilkins Mgt, sr mgr, 2002-06; Martha Schwartz Partners, chief exec officer, 2006-08; IMC Octave, managing dir, 2008-11; Self-Employed Exec Serv, exec advisor, 2011-; K2S Advisors, Partner, 2011-; Clark Atlanta Univ, Chief Staff & Spec Asst to Pres, 2015-. **Orgs:** Bd trustee, Studio Mus Harlem; chair, comt residence, Bd Counrs Smith Col; bd dir, Queens boro Soc Prev Cruelty to C; mgt assistance comt, Greater NY Fund/United Way. **Home Addr:** 4701 Connecticut Ave NW Apt 204, Washington, DC 20008, **Home Phone:** (202)364-6943. **Business Addr:** Chief of Staff, Special Assistant to the President, Clark Atlanta University, 223 James P Brawley Dr SW, Atlanta, GA 30314.

**DAVIS, MARION HARRIS**
Administrator, government official. **Personal:** Born Jul 27, 1938, Washington, DC; married Charles B; children: Alan Edward. **Educ:** Univ Pittsburgh, Grad Sch Public & Int Affairs, MPA, 1971; Am Univ, Wash, DC, attended 1970. **Career:** US Dept Housing & Urban Develop, Area Off Detroit, dep dir housing mgmt div; Off Secy Dept Housing & Urban Develop, Wash, DC, conf asst congr rltns officer, 1967-69; FHA Dept Housing & Urban Develop, Wash, DC, housing prog specialist mgt asst, 1969-70; Westinghouse Elec Corp, sr mgt consult, 1970-71; Dept Urban Renewal & Econ Develop, Rochester, NY, dir prog planning, 1971-72; Co Housing Off, Fairfax, Va, exec dir comt develop authority, 1972. **Orgs:** Nat Asn Housing & Redevelop Officials; Nat Inst Real Estate Mgt; Am Soc Planning Officials. **Honors/Awds:** Recip Carnegie Mid-Career Fellow Grad Sch Pub & Internatl Affairs, Univ Pittsburgh, 1970-71; Travel Study Award $3, 000, Grad Sch Ford Found, 1970-71. **Home Addr:** 18652 Santa Rosa, Detroit, MI 48221. **Business Addr:** Deputy Director, US Department Housing & Urban Development, 660 Woodward Ave, Detroit, MI 48226.

**DAVIS, MARK ANTHONY**
Basketball player. **Personal:** Born Apr 26, 1973, Thibodaux, LA. **Educ:** Howard Col, attended 1993; Tex Tech Univ, attended 1995. **Career:** Basketball player (retired); Minn Timberwolves, guard-forward & small forward, 1995-96; Philadelphia 76ers, guard-forward & small forward, 1996-98; Miami Heat, small forward, 1999; La Crosse Bobcats, 1999-2000; Golden State Warriors, guard-forward & small forward, 1999-2000; Viola Reggio Calabria, 2000; Dakota Wizards, 2001; Sioux Falls Skyforce, 2001-02; Phoenix Eclipse, 2002; Sta Lucia Realtors, 2002; Hapoel Galil Elyon, 2003-04; Maccabi Rishon LeZion, 2004; Wonju Dongbu Promy, guard-forward, 2005-06; Sci City Jena, 2007-08; Lappeenrannan NMKY, 2009-.

**DAVIS, MARTIN**
Clergy, teacher. **Educ:** Point Park Col, BA; Xavier Univ, Black Cath Studies, ThM. **Career:** Capuchin Franciscan Order, Soleman prof, 1964; St Augustine's Capuchin Franciscan Province, bro, 1968-; Moor Cath Parish, 1970; Lwrncvll Hawks Basketball Team, organizer; St Brigid/St Benedict Moor Church, bro; BlackInner-City Parochial Schs, teacher; Univ Md. **Orgs:** Nat Black Cath Clergy Caucus; Pittsburgh Dance Coun; bd trustee, Church Two Worlds. **Home Addr:** 220 37th St, Pittsburgh, PA 15201. **Business Addr:** Educator, University of Maryland, 620 W Lexington St, Baltimore, MD 21201, **Business Phone:** (410)706-3100.

**DAVIS, ESQ. MARVA ALEXIS**
Lawyer. **Personal:** Born May 19, 1952, Gretna, FL; daughter of Harold Kenon and Thelma Kenon Robinson; married Joseph E Roberts; children: Sheletha. **Educ:** Lincoln Univ, BS, 1974; Fla State Univ Col Law, JD, 1977. **Career:** Pub Defender's Off, Second Judicial Circuit, asst pub defender, 1977-85; Marva A Davis PA, atty, 1980; CEDO, gen coun, 1986-91; City Midway, city atty, 1986-87, 1992-2002; Fla A&M Univ, assoc gen coun, 1991; Chipola Rainbow Home Buildings Inc, coun; N Fla Educ Develop Corp, coun; Gadsden Senior Services Inc, coun; Gadsden Co, atty. **Orgs:** Pres, Barristers Asn; past bd mem, Tallahassee Women Lawyers Asn; past bd mem, Big Bend Hospice; bd mem, C Home Soc; Fla Bar Asn; Nat Bar Asn, 1977-; Acad Fla Trial Lawyers, 1983-. **Honors/Awds:** Outstanding Leadership, Capital Area Cot Action Agency, 1996; Hall of Fame. **Special Achievements:** First Associate General Counsels for the Florida Commission on Human Relations. **Home Addr:** 121 S Madison St, PO Box 551, Quincy, FL 32351, **Home Phone:** (850)875-9300. **Business Addr:** Attorney, Gadsden Co, 121 S Madison St, Quincy, FL 32353, **Business Phone:** (850)875-9300.

**DAVIS, DR. MATILDA LAVERNE**
Physician. **Personal:** Born Sep 23, 1926, Elizabeth, NJ; daughter of James T and Martha Hilton; married Robert M Cunningham; children: Robert, Dellena M & William Emory III. **Educ:** Howard Univ, BS, 1948, MD, 1951. **Career:** Harlem Hosp Ctr, resident; Karen Horney Horney Clin, post doctorate psychiat, 1967-71; Vet Admin Hosp, adjudication physician. **Orgs:** AMA; alumni mem, Howard Univ Med Sch; Nat Med Asn; life mem, Nat Asn Advan Colored People; charter mem, Howard Univ Med Alumni Asn; Nat Carrousels; Nat Contempo; fel Am Acad Family Physicians, dir, 1971-. **Honors/Awds:** Charter fellow, Am Acad Family Physicians, 1974; Physicians Recognition Award, Am Med Asn, 1980. **Special Achievements:** First women in the East in tennis 45 yrs & Older, Tennis Players 1979. **Home Addr:** 27 Dayton St, Elizabeth, NJ 07202.

**DAVIS, MELVIN LLOYD, SR.** **See Obituaries Section.**

**DAVIS, MICHAEL JAMES**
Judge. **Personal:** Born Jul 21, 1947, Cincinnati, OH; son of Chester L and Doris R Smith; married Sara Wahl; children: Michael & Alexander. **Educ:** Macalester Col, St Paul, BA, 1969; Univ Minn Law Sch, Minneapolis, JD, 1972; Macalester Col, Hon Doctor Laws degree, 2001. **Career:** Legal Rights Ctr, law clerk, 1971-73, atty, 1975-78; US Dept Health, Educ & Welfare, Off Gen Coun, Litigation Div, atty, 1973; Neighborhood Justice Ctr, Legal Rights Ctr, Minneapolis, criminal defense atty, 1974, mem bd; Legal Rights Ctr, criminal defense atty, 1975-78; William Mitchell Col Law, adj prof, 1977-81; Hennepin County Pub Defender's Off, asst pub defender, 1978-83; Univ Minn Law Sch, adj prof, 1982-; Hennepin County Munic Ct, judge, 1983-84; Hennepin Cty Dist Ct, judge, 1984-94; Minn Inst Legal Educ, 1990-; US Dist Ct, judge, 1994-. **Orgs:** Minn Civil Rights Comn, 1977-82; Am Inns Ct, 1992-; Minn Minority Lawyers Asn, 1980-; Nat Bar Asn, 1990-; Hennepin Cty Bar Asn, 1986; Minn State Bar Asn, 1986; Minn Lawyers Int Human Rights Comn, 1983-85; Minn Supreme Ct Racial Bias Task Force, 1990-93; Minn Supreme Ct, Closed Circuit TV Task Force, 1991; Atty Gen's Task Force Prev Sexual Violence Against Women, 1988-89; Hennepin Dist Cts, Fourth Judicial Dist, 1984-; Int Acad Trial Judges, 1996-; bd mem, Nat Asn Pub Interest Law Fels Equal Justice, 1997-; Eighth Circuit Jury Instr Comn, 1997-; US Asn Const Law, 1997-; Fed Bar Asn, 1994-; Fed Judges Asn, 1994-; Jack & Jill Am Inc, Rites Passage prog, youth mentor, 1998; pres, Minn Chap Fed Bar Asn, 2004-05; Omega Psi Phi Fraternity; adv bd mem, Jack Mason Law & Democracy Initiative. **Honors/Awds:** Outstanding Alumni Award, Macalester, 1989; Good Neighbor Award, WCCO Radio, 1989; Honorary Black Achievers Award; Law Student Scholarship in Judge Michael J Davis' Name, Minnesota Minority Lawyers Assn; Distinguished Service Award, William Mitchell Col Law, 2000; Judicial Professionalism Award, Hennepin County Bar Association, 2004; Citizen of the Year, Epsilon Rho Chapter, 2005. **Special Achievements:** Published "Civil Rights Advocate Doug Hall Retires from Legal Rights Center", 54 Hennepin Lawyer, 1985; "Strategies and Techniques: Court's Role in Promoting Settlement"; Civil Pretrial Practice Inst, MN Inst of Legal Education, 1993; "Jury Challenges Involving Issues of Race", MN Developments and US Supreme Ct Updates, MN State Bar Assn Continuint Legal Education, 1993; "Nominated for appointment: Judge Pamela Alexander", 62 Hennepin Lawyer 11, 1993; MN Supreme Court Closed-Circuit TV Task Force, writer of report adopted by the ct, 1991. **Home Addr:** Henn Co Govt Ctr, Minneapolis, MN 55401, **Home Phone:** (612)348-3677. **Business Addr:** Judge, US District Court, 15E US Courthouse, Minneapolis, MN 55415, **Business Phone:** (612)664-5070.

**DAVIS, MIKE (MICHAEL DAVIS)**
Basketball coach, basketball player. **Personal:** Born Sep 15, 1960, Fayette, AL; married Theresa; children: Mike Jr & Lateesha, Nicole (deceased); married Tamilya Floyd; children: Antoine. **Educ:** Ala Univ, attended 1983; Thomas Edison Col, BA, 1995. **Career:** Basketball player (retired), basketball coach; Milwaukee Bucks, player, 1983; Topeka Sizzlers, player, 1988-89; Pro basketball player, Switz & Italy, CBA, 1984-89; Miles Col, asst coach, 1989-90; Venezuela, 1990-91; Wichita Falls Texans, asst coach, 1990-94; Chicago Rockers, player & coach, 1994-95; AL Univ, asst coach, 1995-97; Ind Univ, asst coach, 1997-2000, Dept Intercollegiate Athletics, head coach, 2000-06; UAB Blazers, Univ Al, head coach, 2006-12; Tex Southern Univ, head coach, 2012-. **Business Addr:** Head Coach, Texas Southern University, 3100 Cleburne St, Houston, TX 77004, **Business Phone:** (713)313-7011.

**DAVIS, MILTON CARVER**
Lawyer, association executive. **Personal:** married Myrtle E; children: Milton & Warren. **Educ:** Tuskegee Univ, BS, 1971; Univ Iowa Sch Law, JD, 1974. **Career:** State Ala, asst atty gen, 1977; pvt pract atty, 1977-; Herman Lehman Found Scholar. **Orgs:** Pres, Alpha Phi Alpha Fraternity, 1993-96; World Policy Coun, 1996; Nat Bar Asn; Sigma Pi Phi Boule; fel Am Polit Sci Found; fel Ford Found. **Special Achievements:** First Ala resident elected as head of Alpha Phi Alpha; the oldest African-Am fraternity in the US. **Business Addr:** Attorney, Private Practice, 304 N Main St, Tuskegee, AL 36083, **Business Phone:** (334)727-6500.

**DAVIS, ESQ. MORRIS E.**
Lawyer, educator, manager. **Personal:** Born Aug 9, 1945, Wilmington, NC. **Educ:** NC Agr & Tech State Univ, BS, 1967; Univ Iowa, Col Law, JD, 1970; Univ Calif, Sch Pub Health, MPH, 1973. **Career:** US Dept Housing & Urban Devel, atty adv, 1970-72; J Black Health Perspectives, managing ed, 1973-74; Univ Calif, Inst Indust Rels, Labor Occup Health Prog, exec dir, 1974-80; US Merit Systs Protection Bd, admin judge, 1980-85; Law Off David P Corsi, atty law, 1986-88; arbitrator & mediator, atty, 1986-. **Orgs:** Calif Bar Asn; Iowa Bar Asn; Am Abritrator Asn; Am Pub Health Asn; Nat Acad Arbitrators; Nat Bar Asn; Nat Charles Houston Bar Asn; Alameda County Bar Asn; State Bar Calif; Am Arbit Asn; Fed Mediation & Conciliation Serv; Nat Mediation Bd; Calif Mediation & Conciliation Serv; Los Angeles City Employee Rels Bd. **Special Achievements:** Publication: "Health and Safety Provisions in Union Contracts", Minn Law Rev, 1981; "Problems Faced by Minority Workers", Boston: Little, Brown & Co, 3rd ed, 1994. **Home Addr:** 64 Ironwood, Oakland, CA 94605, **Home Phone:** (510)635-6705. **Business Addr:** Attorney, Arbitrator-Mediator, 315 Hanover Ave Suite 401, Oakland, CA 94605, **Business Phone:** (510)788-4698.

**DAVIS, DR. NATHAN TATE**
Jazz musician, educator, saxophonist. **Personal:** Born Feb 15, 1937, Kansas City, KS; son of Rosemary Green and Raymond E; married Ursula Broschke; children: Joyce Nathalie & Pierre Marc. **Educ:** Univ Kans, BME, 1960; Wesleyan Univ, CT, PhD, ethnomusicology, 1974. **Career:** Educr, Musician: Club St Germain, Paris, prof debut, Kenny Clark, 1963; Donald Byrd, Blue Note Club Paris, 1963; Chat Que Peche, Eric Dolphy, Paris, 1964; Europe; Belg Radio-TV, staff composer; Thelonius Monk Inst, dir; Univ Pittsburgh, Dept Music, prof music, emer prof music & dir, Jazz Studies, 1969-; Moorhead State Univ, prof jazz, 1969-; Penn Coun Arts fel, 1984; Recordings: Happy Girl, 1965; Nathan Davis Sextet Peace Treaty, 1965; The Hip Walk, 1966; Nathan Davis Quartet Rules of Freedom, 1968; Nathan Davis Quartet: Jazz Concert In A Benedictine Monestary, 1969; Makatuka, 1970; The 6th Sense in the 11th House, 1972; If, 1976; Suite for Dr. Martin Luther King, Jr, 1977; Faces of Love, 1982; London By Night, 1987; I'm A Fool To Want You, 1995; Two Originals, 1998; The Other Side of Morning, 2004. **Orgs:** Paris Reunion Band, 1985-89; Leading Roots; SACEM, Soc Composers, Paris, France; co-chmn ed com Inst Black Am Music Afro Am Bi Cen Hall Fame; founder, Int Acad Jazz Hall Fame & Sonny Rollins Int Jazz Arch, Univ Pittsburgh; dir, John F Kennedy Ctr's Jazz Ahead Prog; chair & founder, Univ Pittsburgh's Int Acad Jazz. **Honors/Awds:** Outstanding Educator, Kans City Alumni Asn, 1983; Faculty Award, Pennsylvania Coun Arts, 1984; Commonwealth Fund Award, 1985; Robert M Frankel Award of City Theatre, Pittsburgh, 1995; California University Award, 1995; DHL, Florida Mem Col; YWCA Racial Justice Award, 2003. **Special Achievements:** Created PhD deg prog Ethnomusicology, Univ Pittsburgh; created Jazz Prog, Univ Pittsburgh; created Jazz Prog, Paris-Am Acad Paris; author: Writings in jazz, 1992. **Home Addr:** 816 Lake Rd, PO

Box 21, Bradfordwoods, PA 15015-1330, **Home Phone:** (724)935-8206. **Business Addr:** Director of Jazz Studies, Professor Emeritus, University Pittsburgh, 110 Music Bldg, Pittsburgh, PA 15260, **Business Phone:** (412)624-4126.

## DAVIS, ESQ. NATHAN W., JR.

Lawyer. **Personal:** Born Dec 24, 1936, Ocean City, NJ; son of Nathan and Louisa; married Emma; children: Melode, Carla & Nathan III. **Educ:** Rutgers Univ, BA, polit sci, 1959; Howard Univ, Sch Law, JD, 1962. **Career:** Self-Employed, atty, 1974-84; State NJ, dep pub defender, 1984-; Egg Harbor Twp sch bd, pres. **Orgs:** Lay leader, Macedonia Methodist Church, 1974-; Atlantic Co Bar Asn, 1975-; pres, Egg Harbor Twp Bd Educ, 1984-; chmn, Munic Utilities Authority, 1991-; pres, Ocean City Ecumenical Coun. **Honors/Awds:** Service Award, Bd Educ, Egg Harbor Township, 1991 & 1992. **Special Achievements:** The first African American to practice law in Cape May County and be named to the Shore Memorial Hospital board of trustees; First African American to be elected as president of the Egg Harbor Township school board. **Home Addr:** 7022 Fernwood Ave, Egg Harbor Township, NJ 08234-5707, **Home Phone:** (609)927-3585. **Business Addr:** Deputy Public Defender, State of New Jersey, Finlaw Bldg 199 E Broadway 5th Fl, Salem, NJ 08079, **Business Phone:** (856)935-2212.

## DAVIS, NATHANIEL ALONZO (NATE ALONZO DAVIS)

Executive, president (organization), chief executive officer. **Personal:** Born Jan 25, 1954, Ft. McClelland, AL; son of Laura M and Jesse Jr; married Al Gene Redding; children: Taylor, Darren & Jasmine. **Educ:** Stevens Inst Technol, BE, 1976; Univ Pa, Moore Sch, elec engineering, MSEE, 1982; Univ Pa, Wharton Sch Bus, MBA, 1982. **Career:** AT&T Telecom Long Lines, engr, staff supvr, var other positions, 1976-81; MCI Telecommunications, dir, network engineering, 1983-86, vpres, financial oper, 1986-88, vpres, syst engineering, 1988-90, sr vpres, finance, 1990-92, sr vpres, chief financial officer, 1992-98, chief financial officer US opers, 1996-98; Nextel Commun, exec vpres, 1998-99; XM Satellite Radio Holdings Class A, bd dir, 1999-, chief operating officer, 2006-07, pres & chief exec officer, 2007-08; XO Commun Inc, pres & chief exec officer, 2000-03, Tele commun serv provider, 2002; RANND Adv Group, managing dir, 2003-05; Columbia Capital LLC, Exec Residence, 2003-06; Charter Commun, Independent dir & mem audit Comt, 2005-08, dir, 2005-; MCI Metro, pres, chief operating officer, Sr Vice Pres Network Opers, Sr Vice Pres Finance & Vice Pres Systs Develop, 2005-08; Unisys Corp, dir, 2011-; Earthlink Inc, Independent Dir, 2011; K12 Inc, online educ serv provider, Exec Chmn, 2013-, chief exec officer, 2014-. **Orgs:** Black MBA Asn, 1987; Black Data Proc Asn, 1988-90; Wharton Alumni Asn, 1989-; bd mem, Mutual Am Capital Mgt Corp; Bd Charter Commun, 2005-08; managing dir & owner, pres & chief operating officer, XM, 2006-; bd mem, Vibrant Solutions; Bd Telica Corp; Trustee, RLJ Lodging Trust, 2011. **Home Addr:** 2609 Geneva Hill Ct, Oakton, VA 22124-1534. **Business Addr:** Chairman, K12 Inc, 1375 Peachtree St, Atlanta, GA 30309, **Business Phone:** (404)815-0770.

## DAVIS, NIGEL S.

Banker. **Personal:** Born Oct 1, 1955, Bastrop, LA; son of Charles and Gladys T. **Educ:** Grambling State Univ, attended 1976. **Career:** Fed Res Bank Kans City, asst bank examr, 1977-82, bank examr, 1982-86, sr bank examr & managing examr, 1986-, asst vpres, currently. **Orgs:** Youth Task Group Vol Full Employ Coun, 1990; vol, Women's Employ Network. **Home Addr:** 8726 Ridgeway Ct, Raytown, MO 64138-3545, **Home Phone:** (816)356-1456. **Business Addr:** Assistant Vice President, The Federal Reserve Bank of Kansas City, 1 Memorial Dr, Kansas City, MO 64198-0001, **Business Phone:** (800)333-1010.

## DAVIS, NORMA JUNE

Educator. **Personal:** Born May 1, 1940, Jacksonville, FL; daughter of Myra and Maxie; married Leodis; children: Melonie Jones & L Elliott. **Educ:** Spelman Col, BA, 1961; Tenn state Univ. **Career:** Educator (retired); SNCC Atlanta, chmn, 1960; IA City Parks & Rec Comn, vchmn, 1972-76; Univ Iowa, Admin Serv Dept, coor dr info, 1975-76, coordr residence serv, 1976-84, asst dir residence serv, 1984-86, Affirmative Action, actg dir, 1985-86, asst to vpres fin, 1986-91, asst vpres fin & univ servs, 1991-97, Continuous Qual Improv, qual coordr. **Orgs:** Ad Hoc Commn Racism, Iowa City Sch Bd, 1971-72; secy & treas, Cedar Rapids Chap Links Inc, 1974-77; Kans City Friends Alvin Ailey, 2000-; Univ Ia African Am Coun; vice chair, Iowa City Parks & Recreation Comn; Iowa City Mgt Panel; Iowa City Bus & prof Women; bd dir, Iowa City Crisis Ctr; bd trustee, Iowa City Community Sch Dist. **Honors/Awds:** Distinguished Achievement Award, Univ Iowa, 1996. **Home Addr:** 12012 Grand Ave, Kansas City, MO 64145, **Home Phone:** (816)941-3091.

## DAVIS, NORMAN EMANUEL

Association executive. **Personal:** Born Apr 6, 1941, Waycross, GA; married Mineola James; children: Norman, Anthony & Corey V. **Educ:** Tuskegee Inst, BS, com industs, 1966. **Career:** Dial-A-Maid Inc, pres, 1978-80; Migrant & Seasonal Farm workers, exec dir, 1980-; Young Vol Action, dir; MECRR Activ Ctr, adjust instr; Davis Mkt & Assoc Inc; Tuskegee Model City, human resources develop; C Trust Fund, prog asst, dir community planning & econ develop; Waycross City, Dist I, comnr, 2006-; Recreation & Youth Serv, city dept head; Featherhood Initiative Prog, dir; Young Vol & Avtion Prog, dir; Migrant Worker Prog, dir. **Orgs:** Staff planner, Planning Comn; exec dir, City Tuskegee Migrant & Seasonally Employed Farm workers; city recreation proj City Tuskegee; F&A Mason32nd Degree, Shriner, Tuskegee Jaycees, Electrolex Club, Elks Lodge, Intl Guild Res Develop, Am Soc Planning Officials, Am Legion, Macon City Retardation & Rehab Exec Bd; adv bd, Macon Cty Medicare & Medicaid; Talent Search Adv Bd; Macon Cty Ment Health Bd; Tuskegee Planning Comn; Macon Cty Monumental & Hist Soc; Tuskegee-Macon Cty Youth Coun; Omega PsiPhi; served 2 yrs pres Wash Pub Sch PTA; pres, City Wide PTA; Macon Co Bd Educ; Model Cities soc planner City Tuskegee, 1969-78; dir & planner, Rec Dept; Young Vols & Action Prog; Migrant Worker Prog; Waycross-Ware County Chamber Com, 2011; Tuskegee Country Youth Coun; St. Paul Baptist Church. **Honors/Awds:** Legionnaire of the Year; Social Work Certificate for Suprvisions; State Mental Health Service Award; Youth Council Cert; Red Cross Campaign Fund Raising Certificate; Outstanding Achievement Award, City Tuskegee; Jaycees Scotman Award; Outstanding Achievement Award, Pro Plan Intl; Jaycees Outstanding Business Award, Outstanding Young Man of the Year; Macon City Council Retardation & Rehab Appreciation Certificate; Macon Cty 4 H Leadership Certificate; Joycees Scotsman & Outstanding Business Award. **Home Addr:** 801 N Marable Dr, Tuskegee, AL 36083, **Home Phone:** (334)724-9535. **Business Addr:** Commissioner of District 1, Waycross City, 1500 Clough St, Waycross, GA 31501, **Business Phone:** (912)338-8936.

## DAVIS, PERNELL

Football player. **Personal:** Born May 19, 1976, Birmingham, AL; son of George and Betty. **Educ:** Univ Ala, Birmingham, BA, Eng. **Career:** Football player (retired); Philadelphia Eagles, defensive tackle, 1999-2001; Frankfurt Galaxy, 2000; Cincinnati Bengals, 2002; Scottish Claymores, defensive back, 2002.

**DAVIS, PRESTON AUGUSTUS.** **See Obituaries Section.**

## DAVIS, REGINALD FRANCIS

Journalist, lecturer, writer. **Personal:** Born Aug 18, 1951, East Chicago, IN; son of James William and Frances Vivian Hyman Ford; married Toni Diane Holliday; children: Michael, Andrea & Paul. **Educ:** Purdue Univ, W Lafayette, IN, BA, commun; Northwestern Univ, Evanston, IL, MA, mgt, 1997. **Career:** The Times, Hammond, Ind, reporter, 1973-76; The Charlotte Observer, Charlotte, NC, copy ed, 1976-78; The Chicago Tribune, Chicago, Ill, 1978-, dep metro ed, 1987-92, assoc managing ed & mem ed bd; ABA Jour, Medill News Serv, asst managing ed, 2001-; Northwestern Univ, adj lectr, currently; Author: Contemporary Books, 1997; The Solo Dad Survival Guide, 1998; Raising Your Kids on Your Own. **Orgs:** Chicago Asn Black Journalists, 1988-; Nat Asn Black Journalists; Soc Newspaper Design. **Honors/Awds:** Academic Honorary, Phi Kappa Phi, 1973; Best Commentary Writing, Chicago Asn Black Journalists, 1994; Apex Awards, 2004, 2005 & 2006; Silver Award, Am Soc Bus Publs Eds, 2005. **Home Addr:** 539 S Harvey Ave, Oak Park, IL 60304, **Home Phone:** (708)848-3657. **Business Addr:** Assistant Managing Editor, ABA Journal, 210 S Clark St Suite 200, Chicago, IL 60604, **Business Phone:** (312)503-3800.

## DAVIS, REUBEN CORDELL

Football player. **Personal:** Born May 7, 1965, Greensboro, NC. **Educ:** Univ Nc. **Career:** Football player (retired); Tampa Bay Buccaneers, left defensive end & right defensive tackle, 1988-92; Phoenix Cardinals, left defensive tackle & right defensive end, 1992-93; San Diego Chargers, right defensive tackle, 1994-98.

## DAVIS, RICHARD C.

President (organization), educator, consultant. **Personal:** Born Sep 6, 1925, Los Angeles, CA; married Dolores Parks; children: Saundra, Marilyn & Jacqueline. **Educ:** Compton Col, AA, 1949; George Pepperdine Col, Los Angeles, CA, attended 1952. **Career:** Education(retired), adminr, coordr, supvr, counr; Los Angeles County Dept Parks & Recreation, recreation dir, 1948-52; Willow brook Jr High Sch, 1952-57; Compton Unified Sch Dist, teacher, 1952, 1967-70, supt, 1970-74; Ralph Bunche Jr High Sch, teacher, 1957-65; Tubman High Sch, continuing educ guid counr, 1965-66; Compton Sr High Sch, voc educ coun, 1966-67; C Welfare & Attend Servs, Sacramento County, Off Educ, consult. **Orgs:** Virtual life-long mem, Calif Asn Supervisors, C Welfare & Attendance, 1969, pres elect; Nat Educ Asn; Compton Sec Teachers Asn; Calif Continuing Educ Asn; Asn Compton Sch Adminr; Los Angeles County Dist Atty Adv Coun; cit adv com, Reg Planning Comn; agency exec Com, Welfare Planning Coun; chmn, Vandalism Prev Task Force; chmn, Feasibility Study YMCA; Del Am Home Owners Asn; PTA. **Home Addr:** 1862 Turmont St, Carson, CA 90746. **Business Addr:** 1623 E 118 St, Los Angeles, CA 90059.

## DAVIS, RICHARD H.

Lawyer, chairperson. **Personal:** Born Sep 12, 1943, Miami, FL; married Doreen D; children: LaRonda R & Richard QuinRo. **Educ:** Univ AZ, BS, pub admin, 1969, JD, 1972. **Career:** Woodrow Wilson Nat Fel Found, fel, 1969-72; Univ AZ, Col Law, lectr, 1973-; Chandle Tullar Udall & Redhair, assoc atty, 1972-80, partner, 1980; Mesch Clark & Rothschild PC, chmn, partner, currently; Black Stud Union, pres. **Orgs:** Am Bar Asn, 1972-; AZ Bar Asn, 1972-; bd dir, Soc AZ Legal Aid Soc, 1975-; Tucson Urban League, 1975-; Ododo Theatre, 1975-; comnr, AZ Athletic Comn, 1977-81; AZ Civil Rights Comn, 1977-78; pres, Tucson Urban League, 1977-78; bd dir, Pima City Bar Asn, 1978-80; Am Red Cross, 1980-83; YMCA, 1983-; fel Am Col Trial Lawyers; Sr Coun, Am Col Barristers; fel Am Col Trial Lawyers. **Honors/Awds:** Distinguished Citizen Award, NAACP Tucson, 1982. **Special Achievements:** First President of the Black Student Union. **Home Addr:** 5620 E S Wilshire Dr, Tucson, AZ 85711-4536, **Home Phone:** (520)790-3745. **Business Addr:** Partner, Chairman, Mesch Clark & Rothschild P C, 259 N Meyer Ave, Tucson, AZ 85701-1090, **Business Phone:** (520)624-8886.

## DAVIS, RICHARD O.

Automotive executive. **Personal:** son of Richard and Katherine. **Career:** Davis Buick-Jeep Eagle Inc, chief exec officer; Davis Automotive Inc, pres, currently. **Orgs:** GM Minority Dealer Asn, 1994-97. **Business Addr:** Owner, President, Davis Automotive Inc, 226 N Greenville Ave, Richardson, TX 75081, **Business Phone:** (972)235-1977.

## DAVIS, RICKY (TYREE RICARDO DAVIS)

Basketball player. **Personal:** Born Sep 23, 1979, Las Vegas, NV; son of Tyree III and Linda; married Vanessa Ramirez; children: Tyree Ricky V, Terez & Racquel Natale. **Educ:** Univ Iowa, attended 1998. **Career:** Basketball player; Charlotte Hornets, 1998-2000; Miami Heat, 2000-01, 2007-08; Cleveland Cavaliers, 2001-03; Boston Celtics, forward, 2003-06; Minn Timberwolves, guard, 2006-07; Los Angeles Clippers, 2008-10; Turk Telekom BK, 2010; Jiangsu Dragons, 2010; Chorale Roanne, 2011; Maine Red Claws (D-League), 2011-12; Piratas de Quebradillas, 2012; Erie BayHawks (D-League), 2013-14; free agt, currently. **Orgs:** Owner, Ricky Davis Found. **Business Addr:** Professional Basketball Player, Erie BayHawks Basketball, 110 E 8th St, Erie, PA 16501, **Business Phone:** (814)790-5600.

## DAVIS, ROB EMMETT

Executive, football player. **Personal:** Born Dec 10, 1968, Washington, DC. **Educ:** Shippensburg Univ, BA, criminal justice, 1992; Univ Wis, Green Bay, MA, appl leadership teaching & learning, 2013. **Career:** Football player (retired), exec; New York Jets, pract squad mem, 1993-94; Baltimore Stallions, defensive tackle, 1995; Kans City Chiefs, pract squad mem, 1996; Chicago Bears, defensive tackle, 1996; Green Bay Packers, defensive tackle, 1997-2007, capt, 2001-04, dir player develop, 2008-, dir player engagement, currently. **Honors/Awds:** Community Service Award, Green Bay Chamber Com, 1999; Athletic Hall of Fame, Shippensburg Univ, 2003. **Special Achievements:** USA Today All-Joe Team, 2006. **Business Addr:** Director of Player Engagement, Green Bay Packers, PO Box 10628, Green Bay, WI 54307, **Business Phone:** (920)496-5700.

## DAVIS, ROBERT ALAN

Government official. **Personal:** Born Detroit, MI; married Sheela. **Educ:** Univ Mich, BA, econs, 1981; Univ Detroit Mercy, MPA, pub admin, 1983; Drew Theol Sch, DMin. **Career:** City Detroit, Planner, 1984-86, dir human resources, 1986-97, exec asst mayor, sr exec, 1997-2001; Wayne County, Commun & Faith Based Initiatives dep dir, sr exec, 2001-03; Gov Off, Southeast Mich, sr adv & dir, 2003-07; State Mich, sr advisor, 2008-. **Orgs:** Child Care Coord Coun, pres, 1995-; pres, NW Activ Ctr, 1998-; pres, Univ Dist Community Asn. **Home Addr:** 18255 Oak Dr, Detroit, MI 48221, **Home Phone:** (313)342-0724. **Business Addr:** Senior Advisor, State of Michigan, State Capitol Lansing, Lansing, MI 48913.

## DAVIS, ROBERT E.

Government official. **Personal:** Born Nov 21, 1908, Kenansville, NC; married Bernice Shaw; children: Sandra Roberta. **Educ:** Fayetteville State Univ, BS, 1936. **Career:** Robesou Co Bd Educ, teacher, 1930-43; David Bros Wholesale Grocers, co-owner, 1940; City Maxton, city councilman, 1972-78; St NC, rep, 1978-80. **Orgs:** Master Masonic Lodge 86 Maxton, 1950-54; illustrous potentate Ouda Temple 147 Shriner, 1952-56. **Home Addr:** 134 3 St, PO Box 278, Maxton, NC 28364. **Business Addr:** Government Officer, Davis Bros Wholesale Grocers, Wilmington St, Maxton, NC 28364.

## DAVIS, ROBERT N.

Judge. **Personal:** Born Sep 20, 1953, Kewanee, IL; son of Robert Ezekiel and Rose; married Linda M Williams; children: Robert L. **Educ:** Univ Hartford, W Hartford, Conn, BA, 1975; Georgetown Univ Law Sch, Wash, DC, JD, 1978. **Career:** US Dept Educ, atty; US Atty, spec asst; CFTC, atty; Univ Miss, Sch Law, prof; Georgetown Univ, prof; J Nat Security Law, founder, currently; Univ S Fla; Georgetown Univ Law Ctr; Univ Memphis; Wash & Lee Univ; Stetson Univ Col Law, prof, 2001-04; US Ct Appeals Veterans Claims app by Pres George W Bush, judge, 2004-. **Orgs:** Am Arbit Asn; arbit panel mem, Us Olympic Comt; mediator, Us Postal Serv; Usn Res. **Honors/Awds:** Teacher of the Year, 1990; Scholar in Residence, Office of Gen Coun, US Olympic Comt, 1996. **Home Addr:** PO Box 815, University, MS 38677, **Home Phone:** (601)222-7361. **Business Addr:** Judge, United States Court of Appeals for Veterans Claims, 625 Ind Ave NW Suite 900, Washington, DC 20004-2950, **Business Phone:** (202)501-5970.

## DAVIS, RONALD

Executive, police officer. **Personal:** Born Sep 18, 1963, Columbus, OH; son of Arthur and Marva Berry; married Janeith Glenn; children: Veronica, Glenn & Destiny. **Educ:** Community Col Air Force, attended 1985; Univ Phoenix, attended 1990; Southern Ill Univ, BS, workforce educ & develop, 2001; Harvard Univ, John F Kennedy Sch Govt, Sr Execs State & Local Govt prog. **Career:** Oakland Police Dept, police officer, 1986-92, sergeant, 1992-97, lt, 1997-99, police acad dir, area comdr, capt, 1999-2005; US House of Representatives, mem; US Senate, mem; Diversity Expert Serv LLC, pres & chief exec officer, 2002-05; E Palo Alto Police Dept, police chief, 2005-. **Orgs:** Pres, 1999, region vpres, 1999-2002, San Francisco-Bay Area chap; chair, Nat Racial Profiling Task Force, 2000-02; Nat Org Black Law Enforcement Exec; Nat Comn Police Integrity, 2002-; Nat Conf State Legis; partner, Calif Dept Corrections & Rehab; police reform expert, US Dept Justice, Civil Rights Div; sr advisor, Police Assessment Resource Ctr; spec coun, Los Angeles Sheriff's Dept. **Home Addr:** 4110 Forest Hill Ct, Hayward, CA 94542, **Home Phone:** (510)209-3441. **Business Addr:** Chief of Police, East Palo Alto Police Department, 2415 Univ Ave, East Palo Alto, CA 94303, **Business Phone:** (650)853-3171.

## DAVIS, RONALD R. (RON DAVIS)

Association executive, manager, writer. **Personal:** Born Feb 5, 1942, Harlem, NY; son of Stanley A and Lauribel Diana; married Jean Williams; children: Yvette & Pamela. **Educ:** City Col. **Career:** US Track & Field; RCA, sect mgr; Afro-Am Vegetarian Soc, NY, pres, 1976, vegetarian activist; defensive driving instr, currently. **Orgs:** Afro-Am Vegetarian Soc; US Track & Field. **Special Achievements:** Author: Cdl Workbook: Everything You Need to Know to Pass Your Test. **Home Addr:** 55 Sheridan Ave, Mount Vernon, NY 10552-2530, **Home Phone:** (914)664-2066.

## DAVIS, RONALD U.

Executive, chief executive officer. **Career:** Tri-State Design Construct Co Inc, founder, chief exec officer & pres, 1975-. **Business Addr:** President & Founder, Chief Executive AOfficer, Tri-State Design Construct Co Inc, 7401 Old York Rd, Elkins Park, PA 19027, **Business Phone:** (215)782-8200.

## DAVIS, RONALD WESTON

Football executive, football player, vice president (organization). **Personal:** Born Sep 16, 1950, Camden, NJ; son of Arthur and Emma;

married Willabel; children: Ronald W II. **Educ:** Va State Univ, BS, educ, 1972, MED, 1975; Richard Bland Col, conv mkt & tourism mkt. **Career:** Football player (retired); San Fran 49ers, football palyer, 1972; St Louis Cardinals, football player, 1973-76; United Va Bank, retail & oper officer, 1976-84, br mgr; Metro Richmond Conv & Vis Bur, dep exec dir, sr vpres; Western Asn Conv & Visitors Bur, pres; Calif Conv & Visitors Bur, pres & chief exec officer; TSCentral Inc, nat prog exec, Conv Bur chief exec officer; San Mateo County Conv & Visitors Bur, sr vpres; Oakland Conv & Visitors Bur, pres & chief exec officer; Pa Conv Ctr Authority, sr vpres sales & customer rels, 2001-05; Parx Casino, chief diversity & inclusion officer, dir, 2005-. **Orgs:** Nat Football League Players Asn, 1976-85; bd dir, Metrop Bus League, 1977-84; pres & bd dir, Va State Univ Found, 1979-85; Guil field Church Finance Bd, 1985-89; Sr Community Develop Corp; Rotary Club; Guilfield Baptist Church; Kappa Alpha Psi Fraternity; active mem numerous Soc & Orgn. **Home Addr:** 2709 E Franklin St, Richmond, VA 23223-7904, **Home Phone:** (804)648-0898. **Business Addr:** Director, Parx Casino, 2999 St Rd, Bensalem, PA 19020, **Business Phone:** (267)223-3610.

## DAVIS, DR. RUSSELL ANDRE
School administrator, dean (education), president (organization). **Personal:** Born Sep 16, 1958, Wilmington, DE; son of Warren and Alberta. **Educ:** Hampton Univ, BA, 1980, MA, 1982; Univ Md, MEd, 1989, EdD, 1992. **Career:** Wash Sch Secretaries, dean studs, 1983-86; Prince George's Community Col, Frederick Community Col, Community Col Baltimore County; Howard Univ, instr Eng, 1986-88; Bowie State Univ, adj fac, Eng dept, 1988-, coordr psychol servs, 1989-90, dir coun & stud develop, 1990-92; Morgan State Univ, res assoc, 2002; Cecil Community Col, dir advising; Gloucester Co Col, vpres stud serv & interim pres, 2008-11. **Orgs:** Nat Educ Asn, 1980-; Nat Coun Teachers Eng, 1986-; chair, Am Col Testing Coun, 1986-; pres, Md Asn Multicultural Coun & Develop, 1988-92; Health Care Homeless, 1993-; bd dir, Nat Coun Black Am Affairs, Coun Am Asn Community Col, 2006-07; Gloucester County Prosecutor's Off. **Home Addr:** 6020 Harford Ave, Gwynn Oak, MD 21207, **Home Phone:** (410)744-1038. **Business Addr:** President, Gloucester County College, 1400 Tanyard Rd, Sewell, NJ 08080, **Business Phone:** (856)468-5000.

## DAVIS, RUTH A.
Government official. **Personal:** Born May 28, 1943, Phoenix, AZ; daughter of Anderson and Edith. **Educ:** Spelman Col, BS, sociol, 1966; Univ Calif, Berkeley, MSW, 1968; 34th Class Sr Sem, US Gov, grad, 1993; Aspen Inst, CO, grad. **Career:** Agency Int Develop, Pop Div, staff; Univ Calif, Berkeley, res asst; Foreign Serv, 1968-; consular off: Kinshasa, Zaire, 1969-71; Nairobi, Kenya, 1971-73; Tokyo, Japan, 1973-76; Naples, Italy, 1976-80; City Wash, DC, spec adv Int Affairs, 1980-82; State Dept's Oper Ctr, sr watch officer, 1982-84; Bur Pers, chief training & liaison, 1984-87; consultgen, Barcelona, Spain, 1987-91; ambassador to Repub Benin, 1992-95; Consular Affairs, prin dep asst secy, 1995-97; Foreign Serv Inst, dir, 1997-2001; US Foreign Serv, dir gen & dir human resources, 2001-03; Howard Univ, Diplomat-in-Residence Int Affairs, Distinguished Advisor, 2004; Africa Bur US Dept State, chief staff & Spec Adv, currently. **Orgs:** Pres, Thursday Luncheon Group; US Ambassador to Benin, 1992-95; career mem, Sr Foreign Serv; Career Ambassador, 2001. **Business Addr:** Chief of Staff, Senior Adviser, US Department of State, 2201 C St NW, Washington, DC 20520, **Business Phone:** (202)647-6575.

## DAVIS, SAMUEL C.
Journalist. **Personal:** Born Dec 10, 1959, Baltimore, MD; son of Sam Jr and Mammie Lee; married Gina Marie. **Educ:** Community Col, Baltimore, 1981; Coppin State Col, MA, eng, 1983. **Career:** Baltimore Sun, ed asst, 1980-84, sports reporter, 1984-92, local sports ed, 1992, asst sports ed, 1992-97, asst sports ed, 1995, dep sports ed, 1997-99, exec sports ed, 1999-2001, host, 1995-2005; tv host, 2000-05, asst managing ed sports, 2001-04, Recruitment & Staff Develop, asst managing ed, 2004-07, Budget & Admin, asst managing ed, 2007-; Morgan State Univ, adj prof, 2007-, page one ed/dir admin, 2011. **Orgs:** Trustee, Christian Mem Church; Nat Asn Black Journalists; refree, Int Asn Approved Basketball Officials, 1987-92. **Honors/Awds:** Carver High Sch, Hall of Fame. **Home Addr:** 5 Kimberly Ann Ct, Owings Mills, MD 21117, **Home Phone:** (410)581-3884. **Business Addr:** Assistant Managing Editor - Recruitment & Staff Development, The Baltimore Sun, 501 N Calvert St, Baltimore, MD 21278-0001, **Business Phone:** (410)332-6534.

## DAVIS, SHANI
Speed skater. **Personal:** Born Aug 13, 1982, Chicago, IL; son of Reginald Shuck and Cherie Davis. **Educ:** Northern Mich Univ, attended 2010. **Career:** Evanston Speedskating Club, speedskater, 1988-; Olympic speedskating ctr, Marquette, MI, currently. **Honors/Awds:** National Age Group Championship, 1995, 1997, 1999, 2000 & 2003; US Allround Champion, US Championships, 2003, 2004, 2005; Silver Medal, World Allround Long Track Championships, 2004; 1500 Meters World Champion, World Single Distance Championships, 2004; World Champion 1000m, 2004, 2007 & 2008, World Champion 1500m, 2007 & 2009; Bronze Medal, World Short Track Relay Team, World Short Track Championships, 2005; Silver Medal 1000 Meters, World Sprint Championships, 2005; 1000 Meters World Record Holder, 2005; Oscar Mathisen Award, 2005 & 2009; World Cup Winner, 58 times, 2005-2014; World Champion, World Allround Long Track Championships, 2005, 2006; 1000m Olympic Gold Medal, Olympic Winter Games, 2006; Olympic Gold & Silver Medalist, 2006 & 2010; Major Taylor Award, 2006; World Cup Overall Champion, 1000m, 2006, 2008-12 & 2014; Current World Record Holder, 1000m & 1500m, 2009; World Sprint Champion, 2009; Gold, Inzell, 1000 m, 2011; Bronze, Heerenveen, 1000m, 2012; Champion, Grand World Cup, 2014. **Special Achievements:** First African American to qualify for the Olympic Short Track Team; First black athlete to win a Winter Games Olympic Gold Medal in an individual event. **Business Addr:** Speedskater, Evanston Speedskating Club, 815 Dempster St, Evanston, IL 60201, **Business Phone:** (847)873-8980.

## DAVIS, DR. SHEILA PARHAM
Educator. **Personal:** Born Nov 30, 1954, Sumter, SC; daughter of James Franklin Sr and Mattie Mae Garvin; married Melvin; children: Deia Deneace & Danyetta Denise. **Educ:** Univ SC, ASN, 1975; Univ Ala, Huntsville, BSN, 1984; Univ Ala, Birmingham, MSN, cardiovasc nursing, 1985; Ga State Univ, Atlanta, PhD, nursing educ, 1993. **Career:** Huntsville Hosp, Huntsville, AL, critical care nurse, 1983-85; Univ Ala, Birmingham, AL, instr, 1985-89, asst prof, 1989-; Oakwood Col, Dept Nursing, chair, 1991-; Univ Miss Med Ctr, Jackson, Mich, assoc prof, prof nursing & asst dean doctoral studies specialties, currently; Online j ethics, founder & ed, currently. **Orgs:** Sigma Theta Tau, 1984; dir, Large, S Cent Asn Black SDA Nurses, 1988-; educ comt chair, Ala League Nurses, 1988-90; med temperance leader, S Pk SAC Church, 1988-; fel Am Nurses Asn, 1989-; publ commun comt mem, Asn Black Nurses Higher Ed, 1989-; inductee, Nat Hon Soc Nurses; assoc mem, Nat Acad Sci; bd mem, ANAC Publ; Fel Am Acad Nursing, 2008. **Home Addr:** 1533 Raymond Rd Apt 184, Jackson, MS 39204-4271. **Business Addr:** Associate Professor of Nursing, Assistant Dean for Doctoral Studies, University of Mississippi Medical Center, 2500 N State St, Jackson, MS 39216, **Business Phone:** (601)815-4010.

## DAVIS, SIDNEY LOUIS
Scientist. **Personal:** Born Jan 3, 1953, Kittery, ME; son of Sidney Louis and Wilhelmina Irene Ramsay; children: Jesse A & Joshua J. **Educ:** Bernadean Univ, ND, 1977; Anglo Am Inst Drugless Ther, ND, 1978; Univ State New York, BS, 1990. **Career:** Bible Sabbath Asn, naturopathic physician; USN, advan lab tech, 1983-03, res analyst, petty officer, atomic absorption analyst. **Orgs:** Ed, Proclaiming Sabbath More Fully, 1998-; knight, Imp House Sellassie, 1999-; Sodality Ark Int, 1999-; pres, Bible Sabbath Asn, 1999, bd dirs; Sabbath Africa Proj, 2000; Southern African Missiological Soc, 2001-. **Honors/Awds:** Knight de Bryan, 1999; Meritorious Ethiopian Order the Lion Judah, Imperial House Sellassie Solomonic Dynasty, 1999. **Special Achievements:** Proclaiming the Sabbath More Fully Sabbath Conferences, founder, 1998-; Seventh-day Adventist Feast day Internet Forum, founder, moderator, 2001; Sabbath in Africa Internet Forum, co-moderator, 2001. **Home Addr:** 72 John St, Reading, MA 01867, **Home Phone:** (847)452-1018. **Business Addr:** Director, Bible Sabbath Association, 2940 E Wis Apt J, Great Lakes, IL 60088, **Business Phone:** (847)785-0315.

## DAVIS, SONIA Y.
Vice president (organization), manager, executive. **Educ:** Univ Wis, Whitewater, BBA, 1987; Loyola Univ Chicago, MS, global human resources, 2000. **Career:** Northern Trust Corp, Corp & Instnl Serv Mgt Develop & Intern Prog, mgr, 1997-2002, vpres human resources sr consulant, 2000-09, human resources consult mgr, India, 2009-10, sr vpres human resources bus growth prog mgr, 2011-, Global Fund Serv, sr human resources bus partner, 2015-; Northern Oper Serv Pvt Ltd, human resources country mgr, India, 2010-11. **Orgs:** Co-chair, HRIR Alumni Asn; life mem, Alpha Kappa Alpha Sorority Inc; Soc Human Resource Mgt; life mem, Nat Black MBA Asn Inc. **Business Addr:** Senior Vice President, Senior Human Resources Business Partner, Northern Trust Corp, 50 S LaSalle St, Chicago, IL 60603, **Business Phone:** (312)630-6000.

## DAVIS, STACEY H. (STACEY DAVIS STEWART)
Executive. **Personal:** Born Mar 1, 1964, Atlanta, GA; daughter of Albert Miles and Myrtle Reid. **Educ:** Georgetown Univ, BA, econs, 1985; Univ Mich, MBA. **Career:** Merrill Lynch, sr assoc, 1987-90; Pryor, McClendon, Counts & Co, vpres investment banking, 1990-92; Fannie Mae Found, Housing & Community Develop Dept, pub affairs dir, 1992-95, southeast regional vpres, 1995-99, pres & chief exec officer, 1999-, sr vpres, 2007-; United Way Worldwide, exec vpres, Community Impact Leadership & Learning, pres, currently-. **Business Addr:** President, Chief Executive Officer, Fannie Mae Foundation, 4000 Wis Ave NW, Washington, DC 20016-2804, **Business Phone:** (202)274-8000.

## DAVIS, STEPHEN LAMONT
Football coach, football player. **Personal:** Born Mar 1, 1974, Spartanburg, SC. **Educ:** Auburn Col, grad. **Career:** Football player, football coach (retired); Wash Redskins, 1996, running back, 1997, 1999-2002, fullback, 1998; Carolina Panthers, running back, 2003-05; St. Louis Rams, running back, 2006; Carolina, 2008; Wash Redskins, 2009; Carolina Panthers, minority coaching intern, 2010-11. **Honors/Awds:** Three times Pro Bowl selection, 1999, 2000, 2003; Rushing Touchdowns Leader, 1999; One time All-Pro selection, 1999; Rushing Leader, Nat Football League, 1999, 2001; Champion, Nat Football League, 2003.

## DAVIS, STEVEN A.
Chairperson, chief executive officer, association executive. **Personal:** Born Jan 1, 1959; married Lynnda. **Educ:** Univ Wis, Milwaukee, BS & JD, bus admin; Univ Chicago, MBA, mkt & finance. **Career:** Kraft Gen Foods, Div Phillip Morris, mkt dir all Am gourmet, 1984-93; Tricon Global Restaurants, exec, 1993-2002; Pizza Hut Inc, Concept Develop, sr vpres, 2000-02; Yum! Brands Inc, Long John Silver's/A&W All-Am Food Restaurants, pres, 2002-06; Bob Evans Farms Inc, chairperson, dir & chief exec officer, 2006-14. **Orgs:** Bd mem, Walgreen Co, Dir; Embarq, 2009-15; dir, JobsOhio; Bd dir, Nat Restaurant Asn; bd mem, Arthur G. James Cancer Hosp; bd mem, Richard J Solove Res Inst Found; Columbus Partnership; bd mem, Turner 12, 2000-03; bd chair, Summerbridge Louisville educ assistance prog, 2003-06; bd dir, CenturyLink, 2006-09; Compete Columbus; chair, Oper Feed, 2007; bd dir, Marathon Petrol Corp, 2013-; bd dir, Albertsons Co, 2015-. **Honors/Awds:** "Black Enterprise," 75 Most Powerful Black Men in American Business, 2005; "Black Enterprise," The 100 Most Powerful Executives in Corporate America, 2010. **Business Addr:** Chairman, Chief Executive Officer, Bob Evans Farms Inc, 8111 Smiths Mill Rd, New Albany, OH 43054, **Business Phone:** (614)491-2225.

## DAVIS, TERRELL LAMAR
Football player, executive. **Personal:** Born Oct 28, 1972, San Diego, CA; son of Kateree; married Tamiko Nash. **Educ:** Univ Ga, BS, consumer econ. **Career:** Football player (retired), media exec; Denver Broncos, running back, 1995-2001, fullback, 2001; Super Bowl 50, capt, 2016-; Nat Football League Network, analyst, currently. **Honors/Awds:** Rookie of the Year, Football Digest, 1995; Super Bowl champion on XXXII, XXXIII; National Football League Offensive Player of the Year, Assoc Press, 1997-98; NFL Player of the Year, Sports Illustrated; National Football League Player of the Year, UPI; Most Valuable Player, Associated Press, 1998, Offensive Player of the Year, 1998; Espy Award for best National Football League Player, 1999; Colorado Sports Hall of Fame, 2004; Breitbard Hall of Fame, 2006; Pro Football Hall of Fame, 2007; Denver Broncos Ring of Fame, 2007; National Football League 1990s All-Decade Team; Denver Broncos 50th Anniversary Team. **Special Achievements:** Autobiography: TD: Dreams in Motion, 1998; Guest-starred on Disney Channel in an episode called "They Say It's Your Birthday" ; The Colbert Report, 2008. **Home Addr:** , Temecula, CA. **Business Addr:** Analyst, National Football League Network, 15th Fl 280 Pk Ave, New York, NY 10017, **Business Phone:** (212)450-2000.

## DAVIS, THEODIS C.
Marketing executive. **Personal:** Born Aug 19, 1946, Little Rock, AR; son of Tommy B and Matilda; married Faye E; children: Jessica, Ericka & Alyson. **Educ:** Ind Univ, masters, 1976. **Career:** Hankscrafts Motors, gen mgr; Gerber Prods, area mgr, Chicago dist, dir sls baby care, dir mktg baby care, vpres, baby care mktg, inventor. **Orgs:** Bd chmn, Urban League, Muskegon, Mich; Kappa Alpha Psi Fraternity; Frontiers Intl Serv Club; Kiwanis Intl; bd mem, W Shore Symphony. **Honors/Awds:** Numerous service & professional awards. **Home Addr:** 4084 Oak Hollow Ct, Muskegon, MI 49441, **Home Phone:** (231)780-3392.

## DAVIS, THURMAN M., SR.
Government official, administrator. **Personal:** Born Oct 11, 1936, Raleigh, NC; son of John C and Elizabeth Sr; married Loretta M White; children: Thurman Jr, Cynthia & Stephanie. **Educ:** Hampton Univ, BS, archit, 1960; AUS Engineering Sch; Fed Exec Inst. **Career:** Deputy Administrator (retired); US Gen Serv Admin, proj dir, exec asst comnr, PBS, 1979-83, real property operations, 1983-84, asst regional adminr, 1984-94, regional adminr, 1994-96, dep adminr, 1996; Dalton Dalton Little Newport, proj mgr, assoc, 1973-79; Archit & Transp Barriers Compliance Bd, chmn; Nat Capital Region, regional adminr; LiveWave Inc, dir; Hurt Norton & Assocs Inc, assoc; LoZart & Assoc LLC, managing dir, currently; Axxis Inc, venture advisor, currently. **Orgs:** Life mem, Alpha Phi Alpha Frat Inc, 1958-; Nat Am Soc Pub Admin, 1989-; Nat Forum Black Pub Adminr, 1993-; 100 Black Men Greater Wash, DC, 1995-; bd adv, Am Defense Int Inc; chmn, Found Advan Music & Educ; Nat Asn Advan Colored People; life mem, Sr Exec Asn. **Home Addr:** 14924 Emory Lane, Rockville, MD 20853, **Home Phone:** (301)460-1050. **Business Addr:** Venture Advisor, Axxis Inc, 1295 Bandana Blvd Suite 120, St. Paul, MN 55108-5116, **Business Phone:** (651)644-8280.

## DAVIS, TRAMAINE. See HAWKINS, TRAMAINE.

## DAVIS, TRAVIS HORACE
Football player. **Personal:** Born Jan 10, 1973, Harbor City, CA; children: David. **Educ:** Univ Notre Dame, psychol, 1997. **Career:** Football player (retired); Jacksonville Jaguars, defensive back & strong safety & free safety, 1995-98; Pittsburgh Steelers, safety & strong safety & free safety, 1999. **Honors/Awds:** Rookie of the Year, 1995.

## DAVIS, TROY
Football player. **Personal:** Born Sep 14, 1975, Miami, FL. **Educ:** Iowa State Univ. **Career:** Football player (retired); New Orleans Saints, running back, 1997-99; Hamilton Tiger Cats, Can Football League, running back, 2001-05; Can Football League, Edmonton Eskimos, running back, 2005-06; Toronto Argonauts, 2007. **Honors/Awds:** Consensus All-American, 1995 & 1996; Big 12 Offensive Player of the Year, 1996; E Div All-Star; All-Star; Grey Cup champion, 2005; College Football Hall of Fame, 2016. **Special Achievements:** First and only running back in NCAA football history to rush for 2,000 yards. **Home Addr:** 11861 SW 190th St, Miami, FL 33177.

## DAVIS, TYREE RICARDO. See DAVIS, RICKY.

## DAVIS, TYRONE
**Personal:** Born Jun 30, 1972, Halifax, VA. **Educ:** Va Univ. **Career:** Football player (retired); New York Jets, tight end, 1995-96; Green Bay Packers, tight end, 1997-2002.

## DAVIS, REV. TYRONE THEOPHILUS
Executive. **Personal:** Born Dec 10, 1948, Kansas City, KS; son of Morris T and Sara A Richardson; married Janice; children: Monette M, Natalie R & Tyrena E. **Educ:** Univ Cincinnati, BBA, acct, 1970; Lexington Theol Sem, MDiv, homiletics, 1976; Memphis Theol Sem, DMin. **Career:** Lexington-Fayette Co, exec dir, 1972-74; Phillips Mem CME Church, sr pastor, 1972-76; Parrish Temple CME Church, sr pastor, 1976-79; Urban League St Louis, acct, 1977-82; Jamison Mem CME Church, sr pastor, 1979-82; CME Church, admin coord, 1982-86, dir ann convocation, 2012; Wesley CME Church, sr pastor, 1986-88; Cong Nat Black Churches, comptroller, 1988, chief financial officer; Gen Bd Personnel Servs Inc, gen secy, 2010-; Opportunities Industrialization Ctr, exec dir; Inst Church Admin & mgt, fac facilitator; Sunday Sch Greenwood CME Church, men's Bible class teacher, sr assoc pastor; CME Community Develop Corp, pres; Zion Community Proj Inc, pres, currently. **Orgs:** Life mem, Alpha Phi Alpha Frat, 1968-; Lexington Fayette County, 1973-76; treas, KY Coun Churches, 1974-76; former treas, KY Conf Nat Asn Advan Colored People Chapts, 1975-76; Nat Asn Black Acct, 1981-91; treas, Beloit Br, Nat Asn Advan Colored People, 1986-; pres, Beloit Comm Ministers Fel, 1987-88; chair audit comt, Bd Trustees Lane Col, Jackson, TN; chair finance & audit comt, Bd Trustees Tex Col, Tyler, TX; secy, Bd Trustees Miles Col, Birmingham, AL; Bd Trustees Phillips Sch Theol, Atlanta, GA; chair bd dir, Zion Community Proj; Mobile Dist Southeast Ala Region; Greater Memphis CME Ministers Alliance & Urban

League. **Honors/Awds:** The 110% Award Merit Alpha Phi Alpha Frat, 1976; GW Carver Award, Sigma Gamma Rho Sor, 1984. **Home Addr:** 303 Derek St, Upper Marlboro, MD 20774, **Home Phone:** (301)249-7727. **Business Addr:** President, Zion Community Project Inc, PO Box 74, Memphis, TN 38101-0074, **Business Phone:** (901)261-3228.

### DAVIS, VIOLA

Actor. **Personal:** Born Aug 11, 1965, St. Matthews, SC; daughter of Dan and Mary Alice; married Julius Tennon; children: Genesis. **Educ:** RI Col, BA, theater, 1988; Julliard Sch Performing Arts, New York, cert actg, 1994. **Career:** Plays: Broadway: King Hedley Two, Seven Guitars; NY Shakespeare Fest: Everybody's Ruby, Pericles, As You Like It; OffBroadway: God's Heart; TV series: "City of Angels", 2000; "Judging Amy", 2000; "Traffic", 2000; "Providence", 2001; "The Guardian", 2001; "Third Watch", 2001; "Amy & Isabelle", 2001; "The Shrink Is In", 2001; "Kate & Leopold", 2001; "Law & Order: Criminal Intent", 2002; "The Division", 2002, "CSI: Crime Scene Investigation", 2002; "Far from Heaven", 2002; "Antwone Fisher", 2002; "Solaris", 2002; "Hack", 2003; "The Practice", 2003; "Century City", 2004; "Threshold", 2005; "Stone Cold", 2005; "Get Rich or Die Tryin'", 2005; "Jesse Stone: Night Passage", 2006; "Life Is Not a Fairytale: The Fantasia Barrino Story", 2006; "Jesse Stone: Sea Change", 2007; "Traveler", 2007; "Brothers & Sisters", 2008; "The Andromeda Strain", 2008; "Law & Order: Special Victims Unit", 2003-08; "United States of Tara", 2010; "Sofia the First", 2013; "How to Get Away with Murder", 2014-. Films: The Substance of Fire. 1996; Out of Sight, 1998; Traffic, 2000; The Shrink Is In, 2001; Kate & Leopold, 2001, Far from Heaven, 2002; Driving Fish, co-exec producer, 2002; Antwone Fisher, 2002; Solaris, 2002; Get Rich or Die Tryin, 2005; Syriana, 2005; World Trade Center. 2006; The Architect. 2006; Disturbia, 2007; Nights in Rodanthe, 2008, Doubt, 2008; Madea Goes to Jail, 2009; State of Play, 2009; Law Abiding Citizen, 2009; The Help, 2011; Extremely Loud & Incredibly Close, 2011; Won't Back Down, 2012; Beautiful Creatures, 2013; Prisoners, 2013; The Disappearance of Eleanor Rigby: Him, 2013; The Disappearance of Eleanor Rigby: Her, 2013; Ender's Game, 2013; The Disappearance of Eleanor Rigby: Them, 2014; Get on Up, 2014. **Orgs:** Drama Div's Group 22, 1989-93. **Honors/Awds:** Tony Award, 2001; DFA, RI Col, 2002; Los Angeles Drama Critics Circle Award, 2004; DFWFCA Award, Dallas-Ft Worth Film Critics Asn, 2008; HFCS Award, Houston Film Critics Soc, 2008; WAFCA Award, Wash DC Area Film Critics Asn, 2008; SLFCA Award, St. Louis Film Critics Asn, 2008; AAFCA Award, African-Am Film Critics Asn, 2008, 2011; NBR Award, Nat Bd Rev, 2008, 2011 & 2013; EDA Award, Alliance Women Film Journalists, 2008, 2011; Virtuoso Award, Santa Barbara Int Film Festival, 2009; Hollywood Film Award, Hollywood Film Festival, 2011; Satellite Award, 2011; NTFCA Award, N Tex Film Critics Asn, 2011; SEFCA Award, Southeastern Film Critics Asn, 2011; IFJA Award, Ind Film Journalists Asn, 2011; Black Reel Award, 2011, 2012; Screen Actors Guild Award, 2012; BET Award, 2012; Outstanding Performance Award, Santa Barbara Int Film Festival, 2012; IFC Award, Iowa Film Critics, 2012; Critics Choice Award, Broadcast Film Critics Asn, 2012; Crystal Award, Women Film Crystal, 2012; Career Achievement Award, Chicago Int Film Festival, 2012; Image Awards, Nat Asn Advan Colored People, 2012, 2013. **Business Addr:** Actor, Agency Performing Arts, 9200 Sunset Blvd Suite 900, Los Angeles, CA 90069, **Business Phone:** (310)273-0744.

### DAVIS, WALTER PAUL

Public relations executive, basketball player. **Personal:** Born Sep 9, 1954, Pineville, NC; married Susan Hatter; children: Hillary Elyse & Jordan Elizabeth. **Educ:** Univ NC, attended 1977. **Career:** Basketball player (retired), public relations executive; USA Men's Basketball Team; Phoenix Suns, guard, 1977-88; Denver Nuggets, self guard, 1988-91; Teams of Tomorrow, self guard, 1990-91 guard, 1989-91, 1992; community ambassador, 1992-, broadcaster; Portland Trail Blazers, 1991; ESPN Classic, broadcaster; Wash Wizards, adv scout; Univ NC, player; Wash Wizards, scout; Denver Nuggets, broadcaster; Denver Nuggets, small forward, 1991-92. **Orgs:** Nat Basketball Asn. **Honors/Awds:** Gold Medal, Olympic Games, Montreal, 1976; NBA Rookie of the Year, 1978; Pro Athlete of the Year, Phoenix Press Box Asn, 1979; 5-time mem, Western Conf All-Star Team; 37th National Basketball Association All Star Team; Phoenix Suns Ring Hon. **Business Addr:** Community Ambassador, Denver Nuggets, McNicholas Sports Arena, Denver, CO 80204-1799, **Business Phone:** (303)893-6700.

### DAVIS, WARREN B.

Educator. **Personal:** Born Sep 16, 1947, Gary, IN; son of Richard and Armenta; children: Kwame Inhatep & Ida Aisha. **Educ:** Defiance Col, BA, 1970; Bowling Green State Univ, BA, 1970, MA, 1971; Appalachian State Univ, develop educ specialists, 1984. **Career:** Mid-town Coffee Hse, Gary Youth Activ, prog dir, Trends Afro-Am Thought, teacher, 1969; USS Steel, laborer part time, 1967-69; Stud Develop Prog, coun, 1971-72; Bowling Green State Univ, assoc dir stud develop; Stud Develop Prog, coord coun serv, 1973; Defiance Col, instr, Afro-Am Hist II, 1973; Neighborhood Youth Corps, supvr; Coord Univ Toledo Tutorial Servs, Career Planning Ctr, supvr; Acad Support Serv, asst dir; Univ Toledo, assoc dean stud, dir stud develop, interim dir, sr dir stud develop, 1982-2008. **Orgs:** Am Pers & Guid Asn, 1971; Asn Counr Educ & Supvision, 1971; Minority Educ Serv Asn, Ohio; Nat Asn Develop Educ; bd dir, Coalition Qual Integrated Educ. **Honors/Awds:** Recipient Service Award, Minority Studs; Service Award, Bowling Green State Univ, 1977; Administrator of the Year, Boise State Univ, 1983. **Home Addr:** 914 Parkside Blvd, Toledo, OH 43607, **Home Phone:** (419)242-7970.

### DAVIS, WENDELL

Football player, football coach. **Personal:** Born Jun 27, 1973, Wichita, KS; married Tisha; children: Jackson. **Educ:** Univ Okla, sociol. **Career:** Dallas Cowboys, wide receiver, 1996-99; Washington Redskins, 1999; Can Football League, Calgary Stampeders, 2001; XFL, San Francisco Demons, 2001; Arena Football League, San Jose SaberCats, 2002, 2004; Grand Rapids Rampage, 2005; Ariz Rattlers, 2005; Maize High Sch, coach, 2007, 2008; Wichita Wild, asst coach, 2014 c, head coach, 2015. **Honors/Awds:** Arena Bowl title, 2002, 2004. **Special Achievements:** Film: 1996 NFL Draft, 1996. **Business Addr:** Head Coach, San Angelo Bandits, 1906 Sherwood Way, San Angelo, TX 76901, **Business Phone:** (325)942-3696.

### DAVIS, DR. WILLIAM

Educator. **Educ:** Talladega Col; Tuskegee Univ; Univ Idaho, PhD. **Career:** Professor, professor emeritus; Wash State Univ, Div Indust Res; Univ Tex Health Sci Ctr, pharmaceut dept; St Philip's Col, Natural Sci Dept, chmn & prof; Natural Sci Dept, prof, 1983-09, prof emer, 2010-. **Business Addr:** Professor Emeritus, St Philip College, SCI 216 K 1801 Martin Luther King Dr, San Antonio, TX 78203, **Business Phone:** (210)531-3545.

### DAVIS, WILLIAM AUGUSTA, III (BILLY DAVIS)

**Personal:** Born Jul 6, 1972, El Paso, TX. **Educ:** Univ Pittsburgh, grad. **Career:** Football player (retired); Dallas Cowboys, wide receiver, 1995-98; Baltimore Ravens, wide receiver, 1999-2000. **Honors/Awds:** Two-time SuperBowl champion.

### DAVIS, WILLIAM DELFORD

Chief executive officer, president (organization), radio broadcaster. **Personal:** Born Jul 24, 1934, Lisbon, LA; son of Nodie; married Ann; children: William, Duane & Lori; married Ann; children: 3. **Educ:** Grambling Col, BS, 1956; Univ Chicago, MBA, 1968. **Career:** City Cleveland, teacher; Cleveland Browns, 1958-59; Green Bay Packers, 1960-69; Joseph Schlitz Brewing co, sales & pub rels, 1964; Willie Davis Distributing Co, owner; All-Pro Broadcasting Inc, founder, dir, pres & chief exec officer, 1976-; MGM Resorts Int, dir emer, 1989-; MD Technologies Inc, pres & chief exec officer; W Beverage Co, founder; Fidelity Nat Financial Inc, independent dir, 2006-. **Orgs:** Bd dir, Schlitz Brewing; charter mem & dir, Exec Savings & Loan Asn; color analyst, KNBC Football Telecast; pub rel & prom work, Chrysler Corp; LA Co Spec Task Force; pres & dir, La Urban League; dir &bd mem, W Adams Comm Hosp; chmn, Cent Div LA Explorers, BSA; Career Coun Group; So Calif Businessmen's Asn; adv bd, Black Peace Officers Asn; Bicentennial Black Achievement Exhib; Spl LA Co Study Comn; toured VietnamSt Dept, 1966; bd dir, Sara Lee Corp, 1983-; bd dir, KMart Corp; bd dir, Dow Chem; trustee, Marquette Univ; trustee, Univ Chicago, emer trustee; bd mem, Alliance Bank; bd mem, Dow Chem, 1988-2006; bd mem, MGM Mirage, 1989-; bd mem, Johnson Controls, 1991-2006; bd mem, Metro-Goldwyn-Mayer, 1999-; bd mem, Manpower, 2001-; bd mem, Fidelity Nat Financial, 2003-; bd mem, K-Mart; bd mem, L.A. Gear; bd mem, Rally's Inc; bd mem, WICOR Inc; Pro Football Hall Fame Class; Kappa Alpha Psi Fraternity; bd dir, Grambling Col Found. **Home Addr:** 1710 E 111 St, Los Angeles, CA 90059. **Business Addr:** President, Chief Executive Officer, All Pro Broadcasting Inc, 161 N La Brea Ave, Inglewood, CA 90301, **Business Phone:** (310)330-3123.

### DAVIS, WILLIAM E., SR.

Architect, city planner. **Personal:** Born Dec 1, 1930, Camden, SC; son of Clarence Sr (deceased) and Margaret White (deceased); married Jacqueline Hawkins; children: William, Jr, Aia, Noma, Victor (deceased) & Brian. **Educ:** Howard Univ, BA, 1967; Columbia Univ, Pratt Inst NY, Mass Inst Tech, grad studies; City & Regional Planning Pratt Inst, MS, 1976. **Career:** US Treas Dept, 1958-66; RC Architects & Assocs, des & off mgr, 1967-68; F&M Shaefer Corp Brooklyn, arch designer, 1968-69; Brownsville Adv Planning Agency, planner, 1969-70; Urban Consults Inc, vpres, 1969-75; Volmer Assocs NY, arch & planner, 1971; City Boston Model City Admin, chief phys planning, 1972-75; Boston Model City, asst adminst, 1975; Onyx Consults Inc, pres, 1975-76; Mass Dept Pub Works, Bur Transp & Planning Develop, regional planner, 1976; US Dept Housing & Urban Develop, loan specialist, 1977-80; US Dept of Transp Fed Trans Admin, comm planner, 1980-87, prog mgr, 1987-; Manchester Cult Diversity Taskforce, pres. **Orgs:** Nat Tech Asn, 1968-75; Am Soc Planning Officials, 1969-77; founder, chair grad stud, Black Planners Network NY, 1970; Community Vol Asn Educ Adv C, 1971; prog mgr, SW Corridor Land Develop Coalition Proj Boston, 1971-75; conf ma planning dir, 1973-75; housing chmn, Roxbury Neighborhood Develop Coun, Boston, 1975; Dedham MA town mem Title I Educ Adv Coun, 1975-76; Greater Manchester Br Nat Asn Advan Colored People; vpres, Greater Manchester Black Scholar Found, 1987-; Martin Luther King Jr Speakers Bur, 1987-89; planning bd, Town of Auburn, NH, 1987-89; pres, Levi & Penelopia Kirkland Family Asn, 1990-94. **Honors/Awds:** Martin L King Fel, 1969-71; Commendation Urban Planning & Develop, Boston; Dirs Award for EEO, Volpe Nat Transport Ctr; Adminr Award, Am Turkish Friendship Asn, 1994; Gore Award, Superior Work Toward Reinventing Govt, 1994. **Home Addr:** 490 River Rd, Manchester, NH 03104, **Home Phone:** (603)624-0669.

### DAVIS, DR. WILLIAM L.

Educator, lawyer, association executive. **Personal:** Born Dec 30, 1933, Hopewell, VA; married Glenice Claiborne; children: Kevin & Todd. **Educ:** Morgan State Col, AB, 1955; Howard Univ, JD, 1961. **Career:** US Dept Navy, law clerk gen coun, 1960; US Dept Justice DC, trial atty, 1961-65; US Atty, asst, 1965-68; Neighborhood Legal Serv Prog Inc & Wash, desp dir, 1968-69, actg exec dir, 1969-70; United Planning Orgn, exec dir; UPO Wash DC, gen coun, 1970-73; Howard Univ, prof law, 1972. **Orgs:** Wash Bar Asn; Howard Law Sch Alumni Asn; mem bd dir, Independence Serv Corp; mem bd dir, Nat C's Island Inc; mem Bd dir, UPO Enterprises Inc; mem bd dir, Ed chief, UPO Comn Develop Corp; Howard Law J, 1960-61; Class Pres, 1960. **Honors/Awds:** Bureau of National Affairs Award; Bancroft-whitney Co & Lawyer's Cooperative Publishing Co Award. **Home Addr:** 1443 Locust Rd NW, Washington, DC 20012, **Home Phone:** (202)829-4354.

### DAVIS, WILLIAM R.

Educator. **Personal:** Born Apr 28, 1921, Cincinnati, OH; son of William and Florence; married Gladys Hamilton; children: William R Jr. **Educ:** Univ Cincinnati, BS, 1950; Ohio State Univ, MA, 1951; Northeastern Ill Univ, MA, 1969; Loyola Univ. **Career:** Educator (retired); Cincinnati Pub Recreation Comn, 1947-54; Oldtown Chicago Boys Club, athletic dir & prog dir, 1954-68; Loyola Univ Chicago, dir, instr, curric & instr, 1969, Proj Upward Bound, pres, 1981-82, actg dir, 1987-88; Chicago Pub Schs, from teacher to asst prin. **Orgs:** Nat Upward Bound Steering Comt, 1970-72; pres, Coun Col, 1970-74; chmn, Chicago Nat Col Fair, Nat Asn Col Admis Coun, 1973-75 & 1978-80; mem bd dir, Ill Asn Col Admis Coun, 1974-76; pres, Ill Asn Non-White Concerns Pers & Guid, 1977-78; pres, Ill Asn Col Admis Counr, 1981-82; Am Sch Health Asn; Am Asn Univ Profs; Nat Asn Higher Edn; Nat Asn Col Admis Counr; Phi EpsilonKappa; Phi Delta Kappa; Asn Supv & Curric Develop; Am Asn Coun & Develop (APGA); midwest reg rep Asn Non-White Concerns Coun & Develop; Ill State Bd Educ Adv Bd Pupil Personnel Serv. **Honors/Awds:** Presidential Award, Mid-Am Asn Educ Opportunity Prog Personnel, 1979; Presidential Award, Ill Asn Col Admis Counrs, 1982; Presidential Citation, Asn Multicultural Coun & Develop, 1984; Human Relations Award, Nat Asn Col Admis Counrs, 1984; Hon Degree Doctor of Humanities, Monrovia Col Monrovia Liberia W Africa, 1986. **Business Addr:** Director, Loyola University, 6525 N Sheridan Rd, Chicago, IL 60626, **Business Phone:** (773)274-3000.

### DAVIS, WILLIAM W.

Computer executive, chairperson. **Educ:** Southern Univ, BS, MBA; Dartmouth Col & Univ Miami, cert, exec mgt prog. **Career:** Pulsar Data Syst Inc, owner, founder & chief exec officer, 1983-99, pres, 1999-2000; Liberty Lending, co-founder, chief finance officer; Dupont, staff; Chevron, staff; Occidental Petrol Corp, staff; Spectrum Solutions Group Inc, prin & chmn, currently; Community Coun, pres, currently; Swiss Bank Corp, managing dir, currently. **Orgs:** Bd dir, Eefpg, currently. **Business Addr:** Chairman, Principal, Spectrum Solutions Group Inc, 1921 Gallows Rd Suite 360, Vienna, VA 22182, **Business Phone:** (703)752-3261.

### DAVIS, DR. WILLIE (BABAKUBWA KWEKU)

Museum director, educator, teacher. **Personal:** Born Oct 30, 1945, Memphis, TN; son of Willie and Mary; children: Willie Dell IV, Wendolyn Delores, Ayana Kai, Larry Smith, Lori Smith, Jackie Smith, Kathy Smith, Eric Smith & Debra Roper. **Educ:** Grand Valley State Univ, BS, 1971; Western Mich Univ, MA, 1974; Mich State Univ, PhD, 1982. **Career:** City Grand Rapids, maintenance worker, 1965-71; Grand Rapids Sch Dist, social studies teacher, 1971-76; Lansing Sch Dist Urban League, educ consult, 1976-80; Mich Dept Community Health, pub health consult, 1980-97; Lansing Community Col, adj prof, 1981-; Davenport Univ, adj prof, 1994-; Walker Fr Acad High Sch, teacher, 1998-2002; Davis Complex All Around African World Mus & Resource Ctr, dir, 2000-; Dianex Ltd, pres & chief exec officer, currently. **Orgs:** Pres, Black Asn State Employ, 1980-; Nat Asn Advan Colored People, Urban League, 1990-; pres, Nat Afr Am Hist Soc, 1992-; secy, EventLansing Regional Sister Cities Comm, 1995-; Asn Study Class African Civilizations, 1995-; chair health task force, Nat Asn Black Social Workers, 1995-; bd mem & secy, El Hajj Malik El Shabazz Acad, 1995-; pres, Nat Black United Front, Lansing chap, 1999-; Black Data Processing Asn; co-chair, Ghana Comt, Lansing Regional Sister City Comn; founder, Greater Lansing Minority Bus Asn; co-founded, Potter & Walsh Neighborhood Asn; past-pres, Neighborhood Youth & Parent Partnership Prog. **Honors/Awds:** Community Service Award, Negro Bus & Prof Women, 1992; Monty Award, Parent Support Network, 1993; Award of Appreciation, Mich St Univ, 1993; Certificate of Appreciation, Howard Univ, 2000. **Home Addr:** 1141 Lathrop, Lansing, MI 48912, **Home Phone:** (517)484-3858. **Business Addr:** Director, All Around African World Museum & Resource Center, 1136 Shepard St, Lansing, MI 48912, **Business Phone:** (517)214-1031.

### DAVIS, WILLIE CLARK

Football player, scout, lecturer. **Personal:** Born Oct 10, 1967, Little Rock, AR; married Veronica; children: Tiana, Jeremy & William. **Educ:** Cent Ark. **Career:** Football player (retired), scout, teacher; Kans City Chiefs, 1991, wide receiver, 1992-95, scout, 2006-; Orlando Thunder, 1992; Houston Oilers, wide receiver, 1996; Tenn Oilers, wide receiver, 1997-98; Univ Md, lectr, currently. **Honors/Awds:** Winning Touchdown, Mile High Stadium, Chiefs Victory Denver, 1994. **Business Addr:** Scout, Kansas City Chiefs, 1 Arrowhead Dr, Kansas City, KS 64129, **Business Phone:** (816)920-9300.

### DAVIS, REV. WILLIE FLOYD, JR.

Clergy. **Personal:** Born Sep 16, 1963, Bainbridge, GA; son of Willie Sr and Mary Beard; married Michelle R; children: Leslie Ann & Ashley LaShae. **Educ:** Monroe Community Col, attended 1983; State Univ NY, Brockport, BA, 1986; Rochester Real Estate Training Ctr, cert real estate sales, 1986; Children's Aid Soc, Nat Training Inst, cert human & teen sexuality training, 1991; NY State AIDS Inst, cert HIV/AIDS counsel, 1992; John Hopkins Univ, cert formative res, 1992; Monroe City Health, cert HIV/AIDS prev educ, 1993; Univ NC, cert continuing educ, 1993; Univ Rochester, cert crisis mgt resp, 1994. **Career:** Mt Olive Baptist Church, assoc minister, minister music, 1985-86; Pentecostal Memorial Baptist Church, assoc minister, minister music, 1986-91; Action Better COT, proj coordr, case mgr, housing coordr, 1989-92; Emmanuel Missionary Baptist Church, pastoral asst, assoc minister, minister music, dir christian educ, 1991-; Puerto Rican Youth Develop & Resource Ctr, dir prog opers, sr counr, 1992-94; Monroe Coun Teen Pregnancy, exec dir, 1992-2001; Cath Family Ctr, Cath youth orgn, prog dir, resource coordr, 1994-95; Baden St Settlement Rochester Inc, assoc exec dir, 1994-2001; Church Covenant United Church Christ, sr pastor, teacher, 1996-; FIGHT Village LLC, asst, 2004-; Neighborhood Network, dir, 2004-; Great Comn Worldwide Fel Churches & Ministries Int Inc, int presiding prelate & bishop, 2012-; All About Christ Network Inc, presiding prelate & bishop 2nd ecclesiastical jurisdiction, 2012; Cathedral Hope Community Church Inc, sr pastor & teacher, 2014-. **Orgs:** Exec dir, Monroe Coun Teen Pregnancy, 1989-; bd dir, Rochester Area Task Force AIDS, 1992-2001; sch health adv bd, John Marshall High Sch, 1994-; CHHA prof adv bd, Monroe City Health Dept, 1995-; bd dir, Zion Hill Found, 1995-; bd dir, CHANGE Collaborative, 1996-; bd dir, United Way Greater Rochester, 1996-; pres, chair, Black Leadership Comn AIDS, 1996-; Youth Services Qual Coun, 1996; adv bd, Catholic Family Ctr, 1997; New York State Gov Task Force, Out-of-Wedlock Births & Poverty, 1997-; Religious & Public Values Task Force, 1998-; bd dir, Action Better COT, 1998; Nat Campaign Prevent Teen Pregnancy; dir, Neighborhood Network Inc, 2004-. **Home Addr:** 35 Pebbleview Dr, Rochester, NY 14612, **Home Phone:** (716)621-8758. **Business Addr:** Executive Director, Monroe Council on Teen Pregnancy, 585 Joseph Ave, Rochester, NY 14621, **Business Phone:** (716)325-8123.

### DAVIS, WILLIE J. (FLASH DAVIS)
Lawyer, businessperson. **Personal:** Born Sep 29, 1935, Fort Valley, GA; married Carolyn Scoggins; children: Kristen & Roland. **Educ:** Morehouse Col, BA, 1956; New Eng Sch Law, JD, 1963. **Career:** Mass Comn Against Discrimination, field rep, 1963; Commonwealth Mass, asst atty gen, 1964-69; Dist Mass, asst US atty, 1969-71, US magistrate, 1971-76; pvt pract atty; Davis Robinson & White LLP, atty & founding mem, currently; Northeastern Univ Col Law Enforcement, lectr; Mass State Police Acad, staff. **Orgs:** Am Bar Asn; Am Judicature Soc; Alpha Phi Alpha; Sigma Phi Fraternity; Nat Asn Guardsmen; pres emer, Morehouse Col Nat Alumni Asn; vice chmn & chmn, Morehouse Col Bd Trustees; bd mem, Comt Pub Coun Servs, Commonwealth Mass; chmn, Comt Pub Coun Servs, Commonwealth Mass; bd mem, Mass Bay Transp Authority; chmn bd trustees, Morehouse Col. **Honors/Awds:** Ten Outstanding Young Men Award, Boston Jr C C, 1971; Hon Deg JD, New England Sch Law, 1972; Hon Deg DSc, Lowell Tech Inst, 1973; Southern Inter collegiate Athletic Conference Hall of Fame, 1998; Presidential Award of Distinction, Morehouse Col, 1999; Bennie Trailblazer Award, Morehouse Col, 2003. **Home Addr:** 61 Westbourne Rd, Newton Center, MA 02459-1617, **Home Phone:** (617)332-1571. **Business Addr:** Founding Member, Attorney, Davis Robinson & White LLP, 1 Faneuil Hall Market Pl Suite 304, Boston, MA 02109-1646, **Business Phone:** (617)723-7339.

### DAVIS, WILLIS H. (BING DAVIS)
School administrator. **Personal:** Born Jun 30, 1937, Greer, SC. **Educ:** DePauw Univ, Greencastle, Ind, BA, 1959; Dayton Art Inst, 1965; Miami Univ, Oxford, MEd, 1967; Ind State Univ, grad study, 1976. **Career:** Dayton Ohio Pub Schs, teacher, 1957-67; ESEA Title & III Living Arts Ctr, Dayton, OH, art dir, 1967-71; Black Hist & Cult Workshops, Ger Town, OH, vis artist & lectr ser, 1968; Bergamo Ctr, 1968-70; VISTA Prog; Auburn Univ, Ala, 1969; Wright State Univ, Dayton, OH, art instr, 1969-71; DePauw Univ, asst dean art & coordr black studies, 1970, asst prof art, 1971-76; Coord Black Studies, 1971; Miami Univ, assist dean grad sch, assoc prof art, 1976-78; Paul Robeson Cult & Perf Arts Ctr, dir, 1978-84; Cent State Univ, chmn art dept, 1978; Nat Conf Artists, pres & bd dir, currently. **Orgs:** Ohio Sec & Sr High Prins Asn Conf, Cleveland, 1970; Western Arts Asn, NAEA, Milwaukee, 1970; Black Studies Inst, Miami Univ, 1970; Va State Univ, Norfolk, 1970; Univ Cincinnati, Blue Ash Raymond Walters Br, 1972; HEW Inst Afro-Am Studies, Earlham Col, Richmond, 1972; Living Arts Prog, Dayton, 1972; Archdiocese Cincinnati Dayton Area Cath Schs, 1972; Purdue Univ, Lafayette, Ind, 1972; Univ Mass, 1972; Gov State Univ Nat & Endowment Arts Prog, 1972; Ind Pub Schs, Shortridge High Sch, Ind Arts Coun, 1972; Lafayette Community Ctr, Summer Arts Prog, Ind Arts Coun, 1972; Montgomery County Regional Arts & Cult Dist, Trustee, 1990-; Asn Am Cultures, SanAntonio, TX, 1994; Ctr Study & Develop Effective Pedag African-Am Learner, Tex Southern Univ, Houston, TX, 1994; African-Am Art Collectors Soc, Dayton Art Inst, 1995; Indianapolis Art Ctr, 2010; Am Craft Mus; Renwick Gallery; Md Inst Col Art & Design; Savannah Col Art & Design; Anacotia Mus; Nat Mus Art Senegal. **Honors/Awds:** Opus Award, 1996; Walk of Fame Award, Dayton, OH, 1996; Ohio Art Educator of the Year Award, Ohio Art Educ Asn, 1997; Honorable Doctorate of Fine Arts, Depauw Univ, 1997; Global Youth Peace, 1999; Ohioan Pegasus Award, 2001; Hall of Fame Award, Depauw Univ, 2001; Tolerance Award . **Special Achievements:** Publications: Communications LaRevue Moderne Mag article Paris, 1967; Mural Panorama on Black Hist Dayton Daily Newspaper, 1968; Cover Design for Educ Booklet on Black Hist Geo A Pflaum Pub, 1968; Calendar Illus for Nat Office for Black Cath, Washington, DC, 1972; represented in book "Black Artists on Art", 1972; Black Artist Documentary "Color It Black" Channel 13 WLWI-TV Indianapolis, 1972. Ceremony & Ritual: The Art pf Bing-Davis Retrospective Exhibit, Dayton, OH, 1996; Work shown in group juried competitive exhibitions one-man shows priv collections permanent museum collections. **Home Addr:** 201 Lexington Ave, Dayton, OH 45407. **Business Addr:** President, Board Director, National Conference Artists, PO Box 283, New York, NY 10030, **Business Phone:** (212)410-7892.

### DAVIS-CARTER, HOLLY
Entrepreneur. **Career:** Agency W Entertainment, Releve Entertainment, owner & prin agt, 2004-. **Business Addr:** Owner, Principal Agent, Agency West Entertainment, 6255 W Sunset Blvd Suite 923, Los Angeles, CA 90028, **Business Phone:** (323)468-9470.

### DAVIS-HALEY, DR. RACHEL T.
College teacher, educator. **Educ:** Loyola Univ, BS, educ, 1989; Xavier Univ, MS, curric & instr, 1993; Univ Md, College Park, PhD, curric & instr, 1998. **Career:** Univ Ga, Col Educ, asst prof; Univ New Orleans, Col Educ & human Develop, asst prof curric & instr, currently. **Business Addr:** Assistant Professor of Curriculum & Instruction, University of New Orleans, ED 342 Q 2000 Lakeshore Dr, New Orleans, LA 70148, **Business Phone:** (504)280-6000.

### DAVIS-HOWARD, VALERIE V.
Executive, consultant. **Educ:** Spelman Col, Atlanta, BA, econ; Univ Iowa, MBA. **Career:** Hartford; CIGNA; Amoco; Proctor & Gamble; Pepsi-Cola; Chase Manhattan Bank, asst vpres org develop; Univ Mich, training consult; Kaleel Jamison Consult Group Inc, 1998, mgr, sr consult, 2000-, vpres, 2002-; Human Resource Consortium LLC, consult, currently. **Orgs:** Am Soc Training & Develop; Nat Black MBA Asn; Org Develop Network. **Honors/Awds:** ASTD's New Guard, Am Soc Training & Develop, 2002. **Special Achievements:** She presents at national conferences & publishes articles on culture change & diversity; She volunteers her time to develop the empowerment of women & people of color. **Business Addr:** Senior Consultant, Vice President, The Kaleel Jamison Consulting Group Inc, 5 3rd St Suite 230, Troy, NY 12180, **Business Phone:** (518)271-7000.

### DAVIS-MCFARLAND, DR. E. ELISE
College administrator. **Personal:** Born Oct 18, 1946, Greensboro, NC; married Arthur C; children: Kira Jihan & William Joseph. **Educ:** Univ NC, BA, speech-lang path & audiol, 1968; Univ Va, MA & MEd, speech-lang path, 1971; Univ Wis, europ study prog, 1971; Harvard Univ, vis scholars prog, 1975; Univ Pittsburgh, PhD, speech-lang path, 1976. **Career:** Va State Univ, Dept Eng, instr, 1971-73; Univ Pittsburgh, Dept Psychol, res asst, 1973-76; Univ Houston, Dept Speech Pathol, asst prof, 1976-79; Col Charleston, Univ Affiliated Facil Prog, asst dir, 1978-79; Charleston Higher Educ Consortium, Educ Opportunity Ctr, dir, 1979-82; Charleston Trident Chamber Com, staff vpres, 1982-86; Citadel, dir in stres, 1985-93; Med Univ SC, teacher, assoc prof & prog dir, 1993-2002; Trident Tech Col, vpres stud serv, 2002-; Nat Coun Stud Develop, inst facilitator. **Orgs:** SC Health & Human Serv Fin Comn, 1984-; secy, SC Asn Elected &App Women Officials, 1984-; bd mem, Nat Rural Develop Fin Corp, 1985-; fel Am Speech-Lang Hearing Asn; Nat Asn Stud Personnel Admin; Am Col Personnel Asn; adv bd mem, bd mem & chair, Nat Black Asn Speech Lang & Hearing; secy, exec bd mem, Nat Coun Stud Develop; fel ASHA, Trident Tech Col. **Home Addr:** 204 Grove St, Charleston, SC 29403. **Business Addr:** Vice President for Student Services, Trident Technical College, 7000 Rivers Ave, Charleston, SC 29406, **Business Phone:** (843)574-6111.

### DAVIS-MILLIN, DR. MYRTLE A.
College teacher, pathologist. **Educ:** Tuskegee Univ, BS, chem & math, PhD, vet med, 1988; Univ Ill, PhD, toxicol, 1992. **Career:** Univ Maryland Sch Med, Dept Path, postdoctoral fel, 1992-94, asst prof, 2002-08; Lilly Res Labs, res advisor, 2002; Nat Cancer Inst, Div Cancer Treat & Diag, Toxicol & Pharamacol Br, chief, 2008-; ILAR J, co-ed; Toxicol Sci, assoc ed. **Orgs:** Inst Lab Animal Res Coun, Nat Acad Sci, 2012; Toxicol Path; Stoke-on-Trent City Coun; bd trustee, ILSI Health & Environ Sci Inst; NIH Study Sect, ALTX1. **Business Addr:** Chief, National Cancer Institute, 31 Ctr Dr Rm 3A44 MSC 2440, Bethesda, MD 20892, **Business Phone:** (301)496-4291.

### DAVIS-WRIGHTSIL, CLARISSA (CLARISSA DAVIS)
Basketball player, basketball coach, founder (originator). **Personal:** Born Jun 4, 1967, San Antonio, TX; married Jerald Wrightsil. **Educ:** Univ Tex, attended 1998. **Career:** Basketball player (retired), basketball coach; Goodwill Games, 1986, 1994; Pan Am Games, 1987; Ital Basketball League, 1989-90; Europ Cup Basketball Championship, 1990-91; Japanese Basketball League, 1991-93; Olympic Games, Barcelona, 1992; Turkish Basketball League, 1994-96; New Eng Blizzard, forward, 1996; Long Beach Stingrays, 1997-98; San Jose Lasers, 1998, Fenerbahce, Turkey, 1998-99; Phoenix Mercury team, WNBA, 1999; WNBA, San Antonio Spurs, dir devel, 1999-2002, WNBA, San Antonio Silver Stars, chief operating officer, 2002-06; Univ Tex Longhorns, asst coach, 2006-07; Rutgers Univ, asst coach, 2008-09. **Orgs:** Dir develop, Women's basketball, Spurs Found, bd dir, currently; athlete rep, USA Basketball Bd dir; pres & founder, head coach, TeamXpress Found, currently. **Home Addr:** 8900 Young Lane, Austin, TX 78737-3160. **Business Addr:** Founder, Head Coach, TeamXpress, 6705 Hwy 290W Suite 502, Austin, TX 78245, **Business Phone:** (512)619-0080.

### DAVISON, EDWARD LARRY
Lawyer. **Personal:** Born May 10, 1943, Akron, OH; son of Edward (deceased) and Marie Mapp Gordon; married Willa Rebecca Branham; children: Rebecca Marie & Christopher Larry. **Educ:** Univ Akron, assoc degree, 1967, BS, natural sci, 1973, JD, 1977. **Career:** Westinghouse R & D, lab technician, 1963-64; Gen Tire R & D, lab technician, 1964-67; Babcock & Wilcox, perf engr, 1967-76; Babcock & Wilcox CRD, cont mgr, 1976-89, sr cont mgr, 1989-. **Orgs:** Treas, pres, United Coun Corvette Clubs, 1983-91; pres, treas, planning & allocation Summit County United Way, 1984-89; Davison & Greene. **Honors/Awds:** Outstanding Achievement, Summit County Democratic Party, 1978; Award of Merit, Summit County United Way, 1980; Outstanding Achievement, United Coun Corvette Clubs, 1986. **Home Addr:** 1900 W Mkt St Suite G, Akron, OH 44313-6927, **Home Phone:** (330)867-0215. **Business Addr:** Attorney, 1562 Beeson St NE, Alliance, OH 44601, **Business Phone:** (330)823-6909.

### DAVISON, DR. JAMES, JR.
Psychologist. **Educ:** Shippensburg State Col, BA, psychol, 1976; Temple Univ, MEd, psychol, 1979; Univ Utah, PhD, psychol, 1986. **Career:** Calif State Prison syst, criminal justice syst; N Pk Col, asst prof psychol, 1983-84; Dept Youth Serv, dir connelly detention unit, 1985-86; Behav Mgt Corp, internship, 1986-87; Florence Gay Smith Found, internship, 1987-88, psychologist, 1987-89; Little Miracles Rehab Serv, clin dir, 1996-98; Olympia Fields Osteop Med Ctr, adj asst prof psychol, 1997-2000, clinician, 1997-2001; Ind State Prison, psychologist, 1999-2001, lead psychologist, 2001-02; Pvt Pract, psychologist, 2002-; Calif State Prison, psychologist, 2002-08; Mule Creek State Prison, psychologist, 2005-06, sr psychologist & supvr, 2008-; Calif Sch Forensic Studies, ct app expert panel mem juv delinq, 2009-10, adj asst prof psychol, 2009-. **Special Achievements:** Author, Prisoners of Our Past, 1993; Sweet Release: The Last Step to Black Freedom, 2008. **Business Addr:** Senior Psychologist, Supervisor, Mule Creek State Prison, 4001 Hwy 104, Ione, CA 95640, **Business Phone:** (209)274-4911.

### DAWES, DOMINIQUE MARGAUX
Gymnast, business owner. **Personal:** Born Nov 20, 1976, Silver Spring, MD; daughter of Don Arnold and Loretta Florence; married Jeff Thompson; children: 1. **Educ:** Stanford Univ; Univ Md. **Career:** Gymnast (retired), executive; gymnastics TV commentator; Hills Gymnastics, instr; Dominique Dawes LLC, pres, currently. **Orgs:** Elite, Hills Gymnastics, 1988-93; pres, Womens Sports Found, 2006- . **Honors/Awds:** Gold Medal, Uneven Bars & Vault; Fourth Place, Balance Beam 1993 World Championships; Gold Medal, All- around Vault Balance Beam, Uneven Bars, & fl Exercise 1994 & 1995 Nats; Most Outstanding, Hill's Gym, 1990-92; Bronze Medal Gymnastics, Olympic Games, 1992; Two Silver Medals, World Gymnastics Championships Competition, Birmingham, Eng, 1993; Silver Medalist, World Championship, 1994; Sportsperson of the Year, USA Gymnastics, 1994; Henry P Iba Citizen Award, 1995; Bronze Medalist, Atlanta Olympics, 1996; Essence Award, 1997; USA Gymnastics Hall of Fame, 1998; "Caring Hands, Caring Hearts" Award, Ronald McDonald House Charities & C Around World, 2003; Women of Distinction Award, AAUW, 2004; Gymnastics Hall of Fame Induction, 2005; Inducted into the USA Olympic Hall of Fame, 2008; Inducted into the International Gymnastics Hall of Fame, 2009. **Special Achievements:** Fourth-place Finish, All-around 1992 US Nat Championship; Fourth-place, All-around 1992 Olympic Trials; Finalist for the AAU Sullivan Award, 1994; First African American on US National gymnastics team, 1988 & US Olympic gymnastics team, 1992; First African American to Win individual Olympic Medal in Gymnastics, 1996; first African American to win a Best Actress Oscar, 2001; first African American to win an individual gold medal in the all-around competition in 2012. **Home Addr:** 129 Ritchie Ave, Silver Spring, MD 20910-5111, **Home Phone:** (301)589-8771. **Business Addr:** President, Womens Sports Foundation, Eisenhower Pk, East Meadow, NY 11554, **Business Phone:** (516)542-4700.

### DAWKINS, BRIAN PATRICK
Football player, executive. **Personal:** Born Oct 13, 1973, Jacksonville, FL; married Connie; children: Brian Jr, Brionni, Chonni & Cionni. **Educ:** Clemson Univ, grad. **Career:** Football player (retired), exec; Philadelphia Eagles, free safety & safety, 1996-2008; Denver Broncos, free safety, 2009, safety & corner back, 2010-11; Entertainment & Sports Programming Network, Nat Football League analyst, 2014- . **Honors/Awds:** National Football Conference Defensive Player of the Month Award, 2006; Seven Times Pro Bowler Selection, 1999 & 2001-02 & 2004-05 & 2006 & 2008-09 & 2011; NFL 2000s All-Decade Team, 2000; Whizzer White National Football League Man of the Year, 2008; Pro Football Hall of Fame, 2017. **Special Achievements:** The first player in National Football League history to record a sack, an interception, forced fumble and touchdown reception in a single game; The first player in National Football League history to record at least 30 interceptions and 30 forced fumbles. **Business Addr:** NFL Analyst, Entertainment & Sports Programming Network, 545 Mid St, Bristol, CT 06010, **Business Phone:** (860)585-2000.

### DAWKINS, JOHNNY EARL, JR.
Basketball player, basketball coach. **Personal:** Born Sep 28, 1963, Washington, DC; married Tracy; children: Aubrey, Gillian, Blair & Sean. **Educ:** Duke Univ, BA, polit sci, 1986. **Career:** Basketball player (retired), basketball coach; Duke Blue Devils, guard, 1983-86; San Antonio Spurs, guard, pt guard, 1986-89; Philadelphia 76ers, pt guard, 1989-94; Detroit Pistons, pt guard, 1994-95; Duke Univ, Athletic dept, admin intern, 1996, mens basketball, asst coach, 1998-99, assoc head-coach, 2000-08, player personnel dir, 2006-08; Duke games, Capitol Sports Network, radio color anal; Stanford Cardinal, men's basketball team, head coach, 2008-16; Univ Cent Fla, head coach, 2016. **Honors/Awds:** Duke Team MVP, 1983, 1984, 1985 & 1986; Freshman All-American, 1983; Consensus All-American, 1985 & 1986; CAA East Regional MVP, 1986; MVP ACC Tournament, 1986; National Player of the Year, Naismith Col, 1986; Duke Sports Hall of Fame, 1996. **Business Addr:** Head Coach, University of Central Florida, 4000 Central Florida Blvd, Orlando, FL 32816, **Business Phone:** (407)823-2000.

### DAWKINS, MICHAEL JAMES, JR.
Engineer. **Personal:** Born Nov 11, 1953, Chicago, IL; son of Willie and Willie Mae; married Cornelia A Long; children: Erika Michelle & Michael Jr. **Educ:** Univ Ill, Chicago, BS, 1978, MS, 1979. **Career:** Dow Chem Co, from res engr to sr res engr, 1979-86, proj leader, 1986-87, res leader, 1987-90, res assoc, 1990-. **Orgs:** AIChE, 1976-; adv bd, Soc Black Engrs LSU, 1982-; chmn, LSU SBE Adv Bd, 1982-84; minority liason, Ga Tech & LSU/Dow, 1983-; contact, Educ Enhancement/Dow, 1984-86; Nat Orgn Prof Advan Black Chemists & Chem Engrs. **Honors/Awds:** EIT Certification La, 1985. **Special Achievements:** Co-Author: "Coal slurry composition and treatment", 1989. **Home Addr:** 10038 Blakemore Ave, Baton Rouge, LA 70810-2545, **Home Phone:** (225)767-1691. **Business Addr:** Research Associate, Dow Chemical Co, 2030 Dow Ctr Abbott Rd, Midland, MI 48640.

### DAWKINS, SEAN RUSSELL
Police officer, football player, real estate agent. **Personal:** Born Feb 3, 1971, Red Bank, NJ. **Educ:** Univ Calif. **Career:** Football player (retired); Indianapolis Colts, wide receiver, 1993-97; New Orleans Saints, wide receiver, 1998; Seattle Sea hawks, wide receiver, 1999-2000; Jacksonville Jaguars, fullback & wide receiver, 2001; Minn Vikings, 2002; real estate, 2003; police officer. **Home Addr:** , CA.

### DAWKINS, STAN BARRINGTON BANCROFT
Dentist, educator. **Personal:** Born Jul 11, 1933, Jamaica, WI. **Educ:** City Col NY, BS, 1959; NY Univ Col Dent, DDS & MSD, 1963; FACD, 1990. **Career:** Dean (retired), self-employed dentist; Bird S Coler Metrop Hosp, chief prosthetics; New York Univ Col Dent, asst prof, assoc prof, group pract dir, dir advan educ prog, chair, asst dean. **Orgs:** Capt, City Col Track Team, 1957-59; capt, City Col Soccer Team, 1959; vpres, Omicron Kappa Upsilon, 1995; Am Dent Asn; NE Gnathological Soc; Am Radiol Soc; co-chair comm, Encourage Blacks Enter Med Prof; Greater New York Acad Prosthododtics; Am Prosthodontic Soc; New York Acad Dent. **Honors/Awds:** Outstanding Athlete Award, CCNY, 1959; CCNY Hall of Fame, 1974. **Home Addr:** 650 Malcolm X Blvd 13D, New York, NY 10037, **Home Phone:** (212)234-2896. **Business Addr:** Prosthodontist, 186 W 135th St, New York, NY 10030-2944, **Business Phone:** (212)926-4600.

### DAWKINS, DR. STEPHEN A.
Physician. **Personal:** Born Feb 27, 1960, Nashville, TN; son of Wilbert L Sr and Tinye L; married Arnika G; children: Brandon, Morgan-Brien & Paige-Nichette. **Educ:** Ga Inst Technol, BS, 1982; Morehouse Sch Med, MD, 1987; Columbia Univ, MPH, 1990. **Career:** Morristown Memorial Hosp, resident internal med; consult, 1987-90; Occup Health Serv, resident, 1988; NJ Dept Health, consult, 1988-90; NJ Bell, Med dir, 1989-90; Arkins Corp, owner, 1980-90; Occup Safety & Health Admin, occup med physician, 1990; Occup Health Int, Atlanta, physician, 1990-, Occup Med, dir, 2000; Caduceus Occup Med, Atlanta Med Ctr, med dir, 1999-. **Orgs:** Am Col Occup & Environ Med, Ga Chap; AMA; Med Asn Ga; Am Diabetes Asn; Arthritis Found; State Bd Worker's Compensation. **Business Addr:** Medical Director, Caduceus Occupational Medicine, 145 N Ave NE, Atlanta, GA 30308, **Business Phone:** (404)607-7677.

### DAWKINS, TAMMY C.

**Personal:** Born Aug 30, 1960, Washington, DC; daughter of Dan Lee Jenkins and Alfreda F Jenkins; married Fitzroy W; children: Danielle Charisse & Ayana Noelle. **Educ:** Howard Univ, BS, pharm, 1983; State Univ NY, Buffalo, DPharm, 1986. **Career:** Erie Co Med Ctr, staff develop pharmacist, 1987-88; Howard Univ, asst prof pharm pract, 1988-, Howard Univ Hosp, Pediat AIDS Clin Trials Group, pharmacist, currently; Dist Columbia AIDS Drug Awareness Prog, currently; NIH, resident; consult pharmacist, currently. **Orgs:** Am Soc Hosp Pharmacists, 1988-; Am Asn Col Pharm, 1989-90. **Honors/Awds:** Student Achievement Award, Asn Black Hosp Pharmacists, 1985; Rho Chi Nat Pharmacy Honor Soc, 1982; Academic Excellence Award. **Home Addr:** 1 Quail Ridge, Princeton Junction, MD 08550-2158, **Home Phone:** (609)799-2334. **Business Addr:** Assistant Professor, Howard University, Chauncey Cooper Hall, Washington, DC 20059, **Business Phone:** (202)806-7960.

### DAWKINS, WAYNE J.

Journalist, writer. **Personal:** Born Sep 19, 1955, New York, NY; son of Edward H and Iris C McFarquhar; married Allie Crump; children: Carmen Jamila; married Joyce Ingram. **Educ:** Long Island Univ, Brooklyn, NY, BA, jour, 1977; Columbia Univ, Grad Sch Jour, New York, NY, MS, journalism, 1980. **Career:** Trans-Urban News Serv, Brooklyn, NY, intern/reporter, 1978-79; Daily Argus, Mt Vernon, NY, reporter, 1980-84; Courier-Post, Cherry Hill, NJ, reporter, 1984-88, ed writer, 1988-91, columnist, 1991-56; Post-Tribune, Gary Ind, dep s lake ed, 1996-98; Daily Press, assoc edi, 1998-03, August Press, pres, 1992-; Auth, Black Journalists: NABJ Story, August Press, 1993 & 1997; Scripps Howard Sch Journalism, teacher; Hampton Univ, Hampton, Va, teacher; Rugged Waters: Black Journalists Swim Mainstream, August Press, 2003; Ed, Black Voices Commentary: Trotter Group, August Press, 2006. **Orgs:** Ed, co-founder, Black Alumni Network, 1990-; regional dir, 1984-89, scholar chmn, 1985-87, scholar comt, 1985-91, historian, 1991-, Nat Asn Black Journalists; co-founder, pres, treas, Garden State NJ, ABJ NABJ Affil, 1988-; Jour Alumni Asn, Columbia Univ, 1981-84; Trotter Group, 1992-; Publishers Mkt Asn, 1994; Columbia Univ Alumni Fedn Medal, 2004. **Honors/Awds:** Robert Harron Award, Columbia University GSJ, 1980; First-Place Award, NY State Asn Press, 1983; First-Place Award, NJ Press Asn, 1987; Journalism Alumni Award, Columbia University, 1990; Alumni Asn Award, Columbia Sch Jour, 1990; T Thomas Fortune Lifetime Achievement Awd, Golden State Asn of Black Journalists, 1994. **Special Achievements:** Author, Black Journalists: The NABJ Story, August Press, 1993. **Home Addr:** PO Box 6693, Newport News, VA 23606, **Home Phone:** (757)591-2361. **Business Addr:** President, August Press, 108 Terrell Rd, Newport News, VA 23606, **Business Phone:** (800)268-4338.

### DAWSEY, LAWRENCE LENEIR

Football player, football coach. **Personal:** Born Nov 16, 1967, Dothan, AL; married Chantal; children: Lawrence Jr & Dominque Arce. **Educ:** Fla State Univ, grad, 1991. **Career:** Football player (retired), football coach; Tampa Bay Buccaneers, wide receiver, 1991-95; New York Giants, wide receiver, 1996; Miami Dolphins, 1997; Tampa Cath High Sch, receivers coach, 1998; New Orleans Saints, 1999; St Louis Rams, training camp asst, 2001; Tampa Blake High Sch, receivers coach, 2002; La State Univ, grad asst, 2003; Univ State Fla, seminoles, receivers coach, 2004-06; Fla State Univ, wide receivers coach, 2007-09, PGC & wide receivers coach, 2010-13, co-offensive coordr & wide receivers, 2014. **Honors/Awds:** UPI NFL-NFC Rookie of the Year Award, 1991; NFL Rookie of the Year, Sports Illustrated & USA Today, 1991; Graduate Assistant at LSU on Nick Saban's staff, 2003. **Business Addr:** Co-Offensive Coordinator & Wide Receivers, Florida State University, 4202 E Fowler Ave, Tampa, FL 33620, **Business Phone:** (863)667-7000.

### DAWSON, DR. ALMA

Educator, librarian. **Educ:** Grambling State Univ, BS, sec educ, 1963; Univ Ore, MLS; Univ Mich, Ann Arbor, MI, AMLS, libr sci, 1974; Tex Women Univ, Denton, TX, PhD, libr sci & higher educ, 1996. **Career:** Natchitoches Parish La Sch syst, teacher & librn, 1964-69; Univ Mich, Mich, libr assoc, 1972-74; Prairie View A & M Univ, libr assoc, 1969-72, head serials dept, 1974-82, Dept Educ Technol, instr, 1980-82; La State Univ, head librn, 1982-94, instr, 1994-96, asst prof, 1996-2001, assoc prof, 2001-06, Sch Libr & Info Sci, Russell B Long prof, 2003-14, prof, 2006-14, prin investr & proj dir, 2009-12. **Orgs:** Beta Zeta Chap, Beta Phi Mu Nat Hon Soc; Phi Delta Kappa Hon Soc; Asn Col & Res Librns; Am Libr Asn; Asn Libr & Info Sci Educ; Lo Libr Asn; Asn Libr Collections & Tech Servs; Libr Res Round Table; fel Tex womens univ, Denton, 1990-91. **Home Addr:** , LA. **Business Addr:** Professor, Louisiana State University, 273 Coates Hall, Baton Rouge, LA 70803, **Business Phone:** (225)578-1463.

### DAWSON, ANDRE NOLAN

Baseball player, baseball executive. **Personal:** Born Jul 10, 1954, Miami, FL; son of Floyd and Mattie Brown (deceased); married Vanessa Turner; children: Darius & Amber. **Educ:** Fla Agr & Mech Univ. **Career:** Baseball player (retired), baseball executive; Montreal Expos, outfielder, 1976-86; Chicago Cubs, outfielder, 1987-92; Boston Red Sox, free agt, 1993-94; Fla Marlins, outfielder, 1995-96; Marlins orgn, spec asst pres, currently. **Orgs:** Fla A&M Univ Nat Alumni Asn. **Special Achievements:** Autobiography: If You Love This Game: An MVP's Life in Baseball, 2012. **Home Addr:** 10301 SW 144th St, Miami, FL 33176. **Business Addr:** Special Assistant to the President, Florida Marlins, 2267 NW 199th St, Miami, FL 33056, **Business Phone:** (305)626-7470.

### DAWSON, DR. REV. B. W.

College administrator, college president. **Career:** Selma Univ, actg pres, 1982-83, pres, 1986-94.

### DAWSON, BOBBY H.

Automotive executive, business owner, chief executive officer. **Career:** Freedom Ford Lincoln-Mercury Inc, pres & chief exec officer, currently. **Orgs:** Community Bus Partners. **Honors/Awds:** Company is 84 on Black Enterprise magazine's list of top 100 auto dealers, 1992. **Business Addr:** President, Chief Executive Officer, Freedom Ford Lincoln-Mercury Inc, 151 Woodland Dr SW, Wise, VA 24293-4623, **Business Phone:** (276)328-2686.

### DAWSON, DR. ERIC EMMANUEL

Government official. **Personal:** Born Dec 26, 1937, St. Thomas; son of Joseph E and Ann Olivia Forbes; married Betty Vanterpool; children: David, Diane & Eric Jr. **Educ:** NY Univ, BS, bus; Howard Univ, JD. **Career:** Senate VI, exec secy, 1965-67, 1968-71; Spec Asst to Gov, 1967-68; Sales Exec, 1971-72; Govt VI, sen, 1973-79, chief legal coun senate, 1983-84, sen, 1985-87, comnr econ develop & agr, 1987-94. **Orgs:** Caribbean Travel Orgn, 3rd vpres; VI Bar Asn, 1982-; chmn, VI Port Authority Gov Bd, 1987-94; Chmn, VI Indust Incentive Bd, 1987-94. **Home Addr:** 6966 Owen Dr, Melbourne, FL 32940-6629, **Home Phone:** (321)433-0944.

### DAWSON, HORACE G., III

Lawyer, food service manager. **Personal:** Born Oct 23, 1954, Durham, NC; son of Horace G Jr and Lula Cole; married Mildred L; children: H Greeley III & Mia Karisa. **Educ:** Harvard Univ, Harvard Col, BA, econs, 1976; Harvard Bus Sch, MBA, 1980, Harvard Law Sch, JD, 1980. **Career:** Baker & McKenzie, assoc, 1980-82; Summit Rovins & Feldesman, assoc, 1982-86; Reliance Group Holdings, staff coun, 1986-87; Telemundo Group Inc, vpres & asst gen coun, 1987-96; Hard Rock Cafe Int Inc, sr dir bus affairs, vpres bus affairs, gen coun & corp secy, 1996-2001, In-House Coun; Akerman Senterfitt & Eidson, coun, 2001-03; Darden Restaurants Inc, sr assoc gen coun, currently; Importante Gifts, vpres, Div Gen Coun; Red Lobster Seafood Co, exec vpres & gen coun, 2014-. **Orgs:** Am Bar Asn, 1980-; NY State Bar, 1980-; NY City Bar, 1980-; Coun Foreign Rels, 1989-96; Bd DIr, Cent Fla Chap, Urban League; Fla State Bar, 1994-; bd mem & secy, Darden Employees Fed Credit Union, 2009-14. **Home Addr:** 808 Brightwater Cir, Maitland, FL 32751-4215, **Home Phone:** (407)599-0870. **Business Addr:** Senior Associate General Counsel, Darden Restaurants Inc, 5900 Lake Ellenor Dr, Orlando, FL 32859-3330, **Business Phone:** (407)245-4000.

### DAWSON, HORACE GREELEY

Government official. **Personal:** Born Jan 30, 1926, Augusta, GA; son of Horace Greeley; married Lula M Cole; children: Horace G III & H Gregory. **Educ:** Lincoln Univ PA, AB, 1949; Columbia Univ, AM, eng & comparative lit, 1950; State Univ Iowa, PhD, 1961. **Career:** Southern Univ Baton Rouge, instr eng, 1950-53; NC Cent Univ, Durham, assoc prof Eng, dir pub rels, 1953-62; Uganda, cult affairs officer, 1962; Nigeria, cult affairs officer, 1964; Univ Lagos, Nigeria, vis prof, 1966-67; Us Info Agency, Liberia, pub affairs officer, 1967; US Dept State, sr sem foreign policy, 1970, cult affairs advisor, 1970-71; USIA/Africa, asst dir, dir, 1971-76, counr embassy pub affairs, dir, Philippines, 1979; Univ Md, vis prof, 1971-79; US Dept State, Botswana, ambassador extraordinary, plenipotentiary, 1979-83; Bd Examiners Foreign Serv, 1983-85; US Info agency, advisor dir, Off Equal Employ Opport & Civil Rights, dir, 1985-89; Howard Univ, PACE Prog, dir, pub affairs prog, 1989-91, Patricia Roberts Harris Pub Affairs Prog, dir, 1990-, Ctr Int Affairs, interim dir, 1993-94, asst pres Pub Affairs, 1994-95, Ralph J Bunche Int Affairs Ctr, actg dir, 1992, dir, 1997-. **Orgs:** Nat Asn Advan Colored People; Am Legion; vice chair, APA World Affairs Coun; sr bd stewards, Metrop Am Church; Asn Black Am Ambassadors; Coun Foreign Rels; World Affairs Coun, mem Alpha Phi Alpha; adv bd, Peace Corps; chmn, Franklin H Williams Memorial Internship Prog Coun Foreign Rels. **Honors/Awds:** Superior Honor Award, USIA, 1965 & 1989; hon doctorate, Lincoln Univ, 1990. **Special Achievements:** Author: "New Dimensions in Higher Education", 1961; "Handbook for High School Newspaper Advisors", 1961; "Race As A Factor in Cultural Exchange", "Exporting America", 1993; "First Black Diplomat," Foreign Serv J, Jan1993; First intercollegiate Greek-letter fraternity established for African Americans; numerous others. **Home Addr:** 1601 Kalmia Rd NW, Washington, DC 20012-1125, **Home Phone:** (202)722-5238. **Business Addr:** Director, Ralph J Bunche International Affairs Center, 2218 6th St NW, Washington, DC 20059, **Business Phone:** (202)806-4363.

### DAWSON, LAKE

Football player, executive. **Personal:** Born Jan 2, 1972, Boston, MA; married Lori; children: Bella, Myles & Leila. **Educ:** Univ Notre Dame, telecommunications. **Career:** Football player (retired), executive; Kans City Chiefs, wide receiver, 1994-97; Indianapolis Colts, 1999; Seattle Seahawks, pro personnel asst, asst dir pro personnel; Tenn Titans, dir pro personnel, 2007-11, vpres football opers, 2011-15, vpres player personnel, 2014-. **Business Addr:** Vice President of Player Personnel, Tennessee Titans, 460 Great Circle Rd, Nashville, TN 37228, **Business Phone:** (615)565-4000.

### DAWSON, DR. LAWRENCE E.

College administrator, school administrator, president (organization). **Career:** Am Coun Educ, dir mgt prog; Voorhees Col, pres, 1985. **Orgs:** Chair, Voorhees Col Bd trustee.

### DAWSON, DR. LEONARD ERVIN

Teacher, educational consultant, college president. **Personal:** Born Feb 5, 1934, Augusta, GA; married Laura R; children: Michael, Randall (deceased), Lavinia & Stephanie. **Educ:** Morris Brown Col, BA, Eng, 1954; Columbia Univ, MA, guid & coun, 1961, dipl, 1964; George Washington Univ, EdD, counr educ, 1974. **Career:** Educator (retired), consultant; Carver High Sch, teacher, 1956; Johnson Jr High Sch, head counr, 1964-67; Paine Col, prof, 1967-69, acad dean, 1969-70; US Dept Educ, educ prog specialist, 1970-71; RR Moton Memorial Inst, sr prog officer, 1971-77, exec vpres, 1977-80; United Negro Col Fund, dir spec proj, 1980-85; Voorhees Col, pres, 1985-2001; White House Initiative, sr consult, 2001-, dep counr & dir, 2004-. **Orgs:** Am Coun Educ; Am Mgt Asn; HBCU Capital Financing Adv Bd; United Negro Col Fund; Am Asn Higher Educ; bd trustees, Asn Episcopal Cols; Phi Delta Kappa; Alpha Phi Alpha; Nat Asn Advan Colored People; Nat Asn Equal Opportunity Higher Educ; Nat Educ Asn; Third St Bethel African Methodist Episcopal Church. **Honors/Awds:** Distinguished Alumni Award, Morris Brown Col, 1981, 1999; Awarded Order of the Palmetto by President of SC, 2001. **Special Achievements:** Author: "The Role of the Counselor, " The Columbia Owl, 1964; "Accountability & Federal Programs," United Board for Col Develop, 1976; "Goverance and the Small, Liberal Arts College," Moton Col Serv Bur, 1977; "Integrated Management Systems in United Negro College Fund Institutions", 1984; "The Next Ten Years: Who Should Benefit from Federal Support Available for Higher Education," a report prepared for the United Negro Col Fund, 1984. **Business Addr:** Senior Consultant, White House Initiative on Historically Black Colleges and Universities, 1900 K St NW Sixth Fl, Washington, DC 20206-5120, **Business Phone:** (202)502-7900.

### DAWSON, LUMELL HERBERT

Government official, executive director. **Personal:** Born Sep 5, 1934, Harrisburg, PA; married Jacquelyn Bourne; children: Anegla Lynn & Jeffrey Bourne. **Educ:** WVa State Col, BA, 1961. **Career:** NY City Dept Hr, supv caseworker, 1962-65; Voc Educ & Ext Bd, dir soc serv, 1965-70; Nassau County Comn Human Rights, assoc dir, 1970-; WVa State Col, recruiter, 1980-. **Orgs:** Omega Psi Phi Fraternity, 1958-; voc adv bd mem, State Univ NY, Farmingdale, 1979-85; voc adv bd mem, Hempstead High Sch, NY, 1980-; chair, Fund Raising Comn, Long Island Coalition Full Employ, 1980-; adv bd mem, Leadership Trng Inst, 1982-; EDGES Grp, 1985-; Christ First Presby Church, Hempstead, NY, 1987. **Honors/Awds:** Spec Recognition, Nassau County Comn Human Rights, 1983; Alumni Award, WVa State Col, 1986; Outstanding Contrib & Support, Oper Get Ahead, 1986; Achievement Award, Nat Asn Counties, 1986. **Home Addr:** 834 Barth Dr, Baldwin, NY 11510, **Home Phone:** (516)868-3402. **Business Addr:** Associate Director, Nassau County Commission Human Rights, 320 Old Country Rd, Garden City, NY 11530, **Business Phone:** (516)535-3557.

### DAWSON, DR. MARTHA E. See Obituaries Section.

### DAWSON, DR. MICHAEL C.

Editor, educator. **Personal:** Born Jan 1, 1951; married Alice Furumato. **Educ:** Univ Calif, Berkeley, BA, 1982; Harvard Univ, PhD, 1986. **Career:** Nat Black Election Study, co-prin investr, 1988; Nat Black Polit Study, prin investr, 1993-94; Univ Chicago, assoc prof, polit sci prof & chair, Ctr Study Race, Polit & Cult, founding dir & investr, William R Kenan Jr prof, 2001, Dept Polit Sci, John D MacArthur prof, John D MacArthur distinguished serv prof, currently; Harvard Univ, Dept Govt & African Studies, prof, 2002-05; Univ Mich; TheRoot.com, regular commentator; Du Bois Rev, founding co-ed. Books: Behind the Mule: Race & Class in African-American Politics, Princeton, 1994; Black Visions: The Roots of Contemporary African-American Political Ideologies, Chicago, 2001; Black Politics in the Early 21st Century; Fragmented Rainbow; Not in Our Lifetimes: The Future of Black Politics, 2011; Blacks In and Out of the Left: Past, Present & Future, 2013. **Orgs:** Bd dir, Social Sci Res Coun; Am Acad Arts & Sci; Black Civil Soc; Chair, Polit Sci Dept Univ Chicago; bd, Social Sci Res Coun & Am Acad Arts & Sci, 2006. **Home Addr:** 41 E 8th St Apt 1601, Chicago, IL 60605-2385, **Home Phone:** (312)431-8204. **Business Addr:** John D MacArthur Distinguished Service Professor, University of Chicago, Pick Hall 419 5828 S Univ Ave Suite 201, Chicago, IL 60637, **Business Phone:** (773)702-8932.

### DAWSON, DR. PETER EDWARD

Educator, physician. **Personal:** Born Nov 18, 1931, Plaquemine, LA; married Jean Lezama; children: Jonathan & Patricia. **Educ:** Xavier Univ, BS, 1954; Meharry Med Col, MD, 1962. **Career:** Utica Psychiat Ctr, resident psychiat; St Josephs Hosp Health Ctr, resident gen pract; St Joseph Hosp, internship res; La State Univ Sch Med, assoc prof; pvt pract, currently. **Orgs:** Charter mem, Am Acad Family Physicians; asst dir, So Infirmary; pres, Plaquemine Br; Nat Asn Advan Colored People, 1966-76; 32nd degree Mason; chmn, Test My Syremem BC; Alpha Phi Alpha Frat. **Honors/Awds:** Physician Recognition Award, 1969, 1972, 1975. **Home Addr:** 5825 Airline Hwy, Baton Rouge, LA 70805. **Business Addr:** Family Practice Physician, Private Practitioner, 58434 Meriam St, Plaquemine, LA 70764, **Business Phone:** (225)687-3344.

### DAWSON, RALPH CURTIS

Lawyer. **Educ:** Yale Univ, BA, 1973; Columbia Univ Law Sch, JD, 1976. **Career:** New York Supreme Ct, judge, 2013; Fulbright & Jaworski LLP, coun, co-chair, atty & partner, currently. **Orgs:** Am Bar Asn; NY State Bar Asn; Metrop Black Bar Asn New York; comt mem, Yale Univ Coun Comt Workplace Diversity, 2005-07; Departmental Disciplinary Comt First Judicial Dept; Wash DC Bar; Civil Rights Comt. **Business Addr:** Attorney, Partner, Fulbright & Jaworski LLP, 666 5th Ave, New York, NY 10103-3198, **Business Phone:** (212)318-3337.

### DAWSON, ROSARIO ISABEL

Actor. **Personal:** Born May 9, 1979, New York, NY; daughter of Greg and Isabel Celeste. **Career:** Films: Kids, 1995; Side Sts, 1997; Girls Night Out, 1997; He Got Game, 1998; Side Streets, 1998; Light It Up, 1999; Down to You, 2000; King of the Jungle, 2000; Sidewalks of New York, 2001; Josie & the Pussycats, 2001; Trigger Happy, 2001; Chelsea Walls, 2001; Love in the Time of Money, 2002; Ash Wednesday, 2002; Men in Black II, 2002; The Adventures of Pluto Nash, 2002; 25th Hour, 2002; Helldorado, 2002; This Girl's Life, 2003; Shattered Glass, 2003; The Rundown, 2003; Alexander, 2004; This Revolution, 2005; Sin City, 2005; Little Black Dress, 2005; Rent, 2005; A Guide to Recognizing Your Saints, 2005; Sin City 2, 2006; Killshot, 2006; Clerks II, 2006; A Guide to Recognizing Your Saints, 2006; Grindhouse: Death Proof, 2007; Descent, 2007, Killshot, 2008; Explicit Ills, 2008; Eagle Eye, 2008; Seven Pounds, 2008; Wonder Woman, voice, 2009; The Haunted World of El Superbeasto, voice, 2009; Percy Jackson & the Olympians: The Lightning Thief, post-production, 2010; Unstoppable, 2010; Girl Walks Into a Bar, 2011; Ten Year, 2011; The Zookeeper, post-production, 2011; Gimme Shelter, 2012; Fire with Fire, 2012; Trance, 2013; Gimme Shelter, 2013; Cesar Chavez, 2013; Parts Per Billion, 2013; Sin City: A Dame to Kill For, 2014; The Captive, 2014; Top Five, 2014; Justice League: Throne of Atlantis, 2015; Puerto Ricans in Paris, 2015; Henchmen, 2016; Unforgettable, 2017; The Lego Batman Movie, 2017. TV Series: "Punk'd", 2003; "Gemini Division", 2008; "Saturday Night Live", 2009; "SpongeBob SquarePants", 2009; "Five", 2011; "Daredevil", 2015; "Jessica Jones", 2015; "Luke Cage", 2015. **Hon-**

**ors/Awds:** Rising Star Award, Am Black Film Festival, 2004; Satellite Awards, 2005; Special Jury Prize, Sundance Film Festival, 2006; ShoWest Award, 2007; Image Awards, 2009; Streamy Awards, 2011; Community Service Award, 2013. **Business Addr:** Actress, Robbie Reed & Associates, 1635 N Cahuenga Fl 5, Los Angeles, CA 90028, **Business Phone:** (323)769-2455.

### DAWSON, SHED, JR.
Educator. **Personal:** Born Oct 6, 1973, Philadelphia, PA. **Educ:** Savannah State Univ, BS, sociol & psychol, 1995, MPA, leadership & human resources mgt, 2005; Ga Southern Univ, EdS, 2010. **Career:** Family Dollar Stores, store mgr, 1991-96; Ga State Bd Pardons & Paroles, parole officer, 1996-97; Bks-A-Million, receiving distrib mgr, 1996-98; Savannah State Univ, enrollment mgt specialist, 1998-2005, Acad Serv & Champ & Life Skills, dir, 2005-, asst athletic dir, 1998-2012, greek life coordr/l.e.a.d. instr, 2012-; Achievers Today & Tomorrow Inc, advisor, currently. **Orgs:** Beta Phi Lambda-Community Serv chmn, Alpha Phi Alpha Fraternity, 1995-; Prince Hall Mason, Sr Decon-Pythagoras Lodge no11, 1996-; Chap adv, Nat Asn Advan Colored People, Savannah Br Exec Comt, 1998-; March Dimes E Ga Div, Community Serv Comt, 1998-; staff coun exec comt-parliamentarian, Savannah State Univ, 2000-; Nat Col Testing Asn, 2000-; Mens Health adv bd, St Joseph Camdler Hosp, 2001-; chmn, Cult Competency & Diversity Comt; Ga Dist bd dir, 2003-. **Home Addr:** 12409 Largo Dr, PO Box 15172, Savannah, GA 31419, **Home Phone:** (912)220-5457. **Business Addr:** Assistant Athletic Director for Academic Services, Academic Coordinator, Savannah State University, 3219 Col St, Savannah, GA 31404-5255, **Business Phone:** (912)358-3433.

### DAWSON, WARREN HOPE
Lawyer. **Personal:** Born Oct 17, 1939, Mulberry, FL; married Joan Delores; children: Wendy Hope. **Educ:** Fla A&M Univ, BA, polit sci, 1961; Howard Univ Sch Law, JD, 1966. **Career:** Dawson & Assocs, coun to govt entities, atty & counr, founding partner, 1967-; Warren Hope Dawson & Assoc, atty. **Orgs:** Pres, Fla Chap Nat Bar Asn, 1979; Nat Bar Asn, 1979; Fla Bar Asn, 1980; standing comt legal asst, Am Bar Asn, 1980; adv bd dir, Tampa Bay Buccaneers, 1980; chmn, Hillbro County Civil Serv Bd; vpres, Tampa Chap Frontiers Int; Hillsborough County Bar Asn; Edgecomb Bar Asn; life mem, Fels Am Bar Found; past pres, Howard Univ; Nat Law Alumni Asn; past mem, Fla Supreme Ct Bench & Bar Comn. **Honors/Awds:** Whitney M Young Memorial Award, Tampa Urban League, 1979; The 100 Most Influential Blacks in America, Ebony Magazine, 1983; Unsung Hero Award, Tampa Orgn Black Affairs, 1991; Francisco A. Rodriguez Civil Rights Award, Edgecomb Bar Asn, 1991; Gertrude E. Rush Award, Nat Bar Asn, 1992; MLK Drum Major For Justice Award, Fed MLK Holiday Comn, 1993; Michael A. Fogarty Memorial In The Trenches Award, Hillsborough County Bar Asn, 2001; Hall of Fame, Nat Bar Asn, 2007; Distinguished Alumni Award, Florida A & M University, 1992; Awarded Honorary Doctorate of Humane Letters, FAMU, 2011; The Whitney M. Young Jr, Memorial Award, Tampa Urban League. **Special Achievements:** First African American hired in the National Labor Review Board's Tampa regional office; First African American assistant city attorney in Tampa, Florida. **Home Addr:** 3508 River Grove Dr, Tampa, FL 33610, **Home Phone:** (813)232-7891. **Business Addr:** Founding Partner, Dawson and Associates, 1467 Tampa Pk Plz, Tampa, FL 33605-4821, **Business Phone:** (813)221-1800.

### DAY, ERIC THERANDER, JR.
Law enforcement officer. **Personal:** Born Dec 15, 1952, Mobile, AL; son of Joseph and Ruby James; married Valerie Jones; children: Eric Therander Jr & Joaquin Kyron. **Educ:** Univ S Ala, BA, criminal justice, 1977, MEd, 1979. **Career:** Mobile Co Sheriff Dept, asst dir work release, 1977-79, dir work release, 1979-80, asst warden, 1980-81, asst planning officer, 1981-84, dir victim witness prog, 1984-85, dep sheriff, 1985-88; US Dept Justice, US Atty Off, Law Enforcement, Victim Witness, coordr, 1988-. **Orgs:** Southern States Correctional Asn; Lambda Alpha Epsilon; Alpha Phi Sigma; Ala Peace Officer Asn; Am Correctional Asn; vpres, Fel Christian Law Enforcement Officers; bd mem, 2nd vpres, Gulf Coast Fed Credit Union, 1985; chaplain, Southern Region Nat Black Police Asn, 1987; bd mem, Epilepsy Chap Mobile & Gulf Coast, 1988; Mobile United, 1989; Coalition Drug Free Mobile, 1990; Challenge 200, 1990; vice chmn, Summit Advan Values & Ethics, 1990; vpres, Blacks Govt, 1987; pres, Mobile Co Criminal Justice Soc, 1984-88; Mobile United; chmn, Human Resources Comt, 1992; Coalition Drug Free Mobile, 1992; chmn, bd mem, Youth Concerns Comn; chmn, Summit Advan Values & Ethics, 1992-93. **Home Addr:** 2409 Yerby Dr, Mobile, AL 36617-2326, **Home Phone:** (205)666-1519. **Business Addr:** Law Enforcement Victim Witness Coordinator, US Department of Justice, 63 S Royal St Suite 600, Mobile, AL 36602, **Business Phone:** (251)441-5845.

### DAY, JOHN
Entrepreneur, business owner. **Personal:** Born Jan 1, 1965; married Angela. **Career:** Hobo Shop, owner, 1996-. **Business Addr:** Owner, The HOBO Shop, 4407 S Ave, Capitol Heights, MD 20743, **Business Phone:** (301)735-7444.

### DAY, JOHN H.
Physicist. **Personal:** Born Jun 5, 1952, Savannah, GA; son of John H and Elsie M; married Agnes A Lasiter; children: Teresa; married Yardyne Jackson; children: Gregory Proctor. **Educ:** Bethune Cookman Col, BS, physics, 1973; Howard Univ, MS, physics, 1976, PhD, physics, 1982. **Career:** Martin Marietta Corp, Engr, laser optics div, 1973; Howard University, graduate teaching assistant/instructor, 1973-79; Dept Com, physicist, Nat bur stand, 1974-78; Dept Interior, US Geol surv, physicist, 1979-82; NASA, Goddard Space Ctr, engr, space technologist, energy conversion sect, 1982-88, sect head, energy conversion sect, 1988-90, asst br head, space power br, 1990-92, br head, space power br, 1992-98, chief technologist, appl engrg & technol dir, 1998-99, Elec Eng Div, chief, 1999-2012; Tex A&M Ctr Space power, adv bd, 1994-99; Capital Col Engrg, Dept Adv Bd, fac; Georgia Perimeter College, physics faculty, 2012-. **Orgs:** Interagency Advan Power Grp; Am Inst Aeronaut & Astronaut; Inst Elec & Electronic Engrs; AAAS; Am Phys Soc; Nat Soc Black Physicists; Sigma Pi Sigma Physics Hon Soc; Alpha Kappa Mu; Nat Hon Soc; Phi Beta Sigma Fraternity. **Honors/Awds:** Nat Science Foundation Fellowship Award, 1976-78; Graduate Fellowship Award, Howard Univ, 1979-81; Terminal Fellowship Award, Howard Univ 1980-82; NASA Outstanding Performance Awards, 1984-85, 1987, 1992-96; InterNat Cometary Explorer Group Award, 1985; InterNat Sun Earth Explorer Group Award, 1987; NASA Performance Management & Recognition System Awards, 1989-94; Gamma Ray Observatory Group Award, 1992; Goddard Exceptional Achievement Award, 1993; Upper Atmosphere Research Satellite Achievement Award, 1993; Geostationary Operational Environmental Satellite Group Award, 1994; Global Geospace Sci Satellite PSE Review Team Award, 1994; Hubble Space Telescope Servicing Mission Group Award, 1994; Landsat 7 Design Review Streamlining Team Award, 1995; X-Ray Timing Explorer Team Award, 1996; Tropical Rainfall Measuring Mission Team Award, 1998; NASA Medal of Exceptional Service, 1998; NASA Medal for Exceptional Service, 1998; Tropical Rainfall Measuring Mission Group Achievement Award, 1998; Outstanding Career Mentoring, 2001; Presdiential Meritorious Executive Award, 2004; NASA Corporate Recruitment Award, 2005; NASA Minority University Programs Distinguished Service Award, 2008; Goddard Diversity & Equal Opportunity Honor Award, 2010; Team Awards for Numerous Space Missions, 1982-2012. **Special Achievements:** NASA Space Photovoltaics Research & Technology Conference, 1983 & 1994; Presentations and publications include: Intersociety Energy Conversion Engineering Conference, 1987; Inst Elec & Electronic Engrs Photovoltaics Conf, 1987; Am Inst Aeronaut & Astronaut Small Satellite Symposium, 1993. **Home Addr:** 14507 Briercrest Rd, Bowie, MD 20720-4838, **Home Phone:** (301)464-4139. **Business Addr:** Chief, NASA Goddard Space Flight Center, Code 560 Bldg 23 Rm S-120, Greenbelt, MD 20771, **Business Phone:** (301)286-1852.

### DAY, MORRIS EUGENE (MORRIS DAUGHTY)
Composer, musician, actor. **Personal:** Born Dec 13, 1957, Minneapolis, MN; married Judith Jones; children: Evan, Derran & Tionna. **Career:** Films: Purple Rain, actor, 1984; Moving, actor, 1988; Heart and Soul, actor, 1988; The Adventures of Ford Fairlane, 1990; A Woman Like That, actor, 1997; Boys Klub, actor, 2001; Jay and Silent Bob Strike Back, 2001; West from North Goes South, actor, 2004; West from North Goes South, 2004; Moesha; The Adventures of Ford Fairlane; Jay & Silent Bob Strike Back; Graffiti Bridge. TV series: "227", 1989; "A New Attitude", 1990; "Da Boom Crew", 2004; "Eve", 2004; "I Love the '90s: Part Deux", 2005. Singles: "Color of Success", 1985; "The Oak Tree"; "Daydreaming", 1987; "Guaranteed", 1992; "The Character"; "Fishnet", 1988, #23; "Lovels a Game"; "Gimme Watcha Got"; "Circle of Love", 1992; "777-9311"; "Gigolos Get Lonely Too"; "Jungle Love"; "Jerk Out"; "The Bird"; "Get A Job", 2000; "It's About Time", 2004; "Chocolate"; "Shake!"; "Trendin". Albums: The Time, 1981; What Time Is It?, 1982; Ice Cream Castle, 1984; Pandemonium, 1990; Condensate, 2011. **Business Addr:** Actor, Singer, Reprise Records Inc, 3300 Warner Blvd, Burbank, CA 91505-4632.

### DAY, TERRY LEE
Football player, manager. **Personal:** Born Sep 18, 1974, Pickens, MS. **Educ:** Miss State Univ, BS; Holmes CC, grad. **Career:** Football player (retired), manager; NY Jets, defensive end, 1997-2000; Walmart, asst store mgr, currently. **Honors/Awds:** Hall of Fame Mem, Dedicated Football League, 2004. **Business Addr:** Assistant Store Manager, Walmart, 220 Veterans Memorial Dr, Kosciusko, MS 39090, **Business Phone:** (662)289-3422.

### DAY, TODD FITZGERALD
Basketball player, basketball coach. **Personal:** Born Jan 7, 1970, Decatur, IL; children: Natasha & Todd Jr. **Educ:** Univ Ark, attended 1992. **Career:** Basketball player (retired), basketball coach; Milwaukee Bucks, guard, forward, 1992-95; Boston Celtics, guard, forward, 1995-97; Miami Heat, guard, forward, 1997-98; La Crosse Bobcats, 1998-99; Phoenix Suns, 1999-2000; Minn Timberwolves, 2000-01; Ark RimRockers, 2004-05; APOEL, Cyprus, 2005-06; Argentino de Junin, Arg, 2006; Blue Stars, 2006-07; Ark Aeros, 2006-07; Premier Basketball League, Ark Impact, head coach, 2007; Memphis Acad Health Sci, coach, currently; Hamilton High Sch, alma mater, head coach; Team Penny, asst coach, currently. **Orgs:** Alpha Phi Alpha; Southwest Conf; Ark Sports Hall Fame. **Honors/Awds:** SWC Player of the Year, 1991. **Special Achievements:** NBA Draft, First round pick, No 8, 1992. **Business Addr:** Head Coach, Hamilton High School, 1165 Eaton Ave, Hamilton, OH 45013, **Business Phone:** (513)868-7700.

### DAYE, CHARLES EDWARD
Educator, lecturer. **Personal:** Born May 14, 1944, Durham, NC; son of Addie R and Eccleasiastes; married Norma S; children: Clarence L Hill III & Tammy H Roundtree. **Educ:** NC Cent Univ, BA, polit sci, 1966; Columbia Univ, JD, 1969. **Career:** US Ct Appeals Sixth Circuit, law clerk to chief judge, 1969-70; Covington & Burling, Wash, assoc, 1970-72; Univ NC, Sch Law, Chapel Hill, from asst prof to assoc prof, 1972-80, prof, 1981, 1985-91, Henry P Brandis Dist, prof law, 1991-, dep dir, 2006-; NC Cent Univ Sch Law, vis prof, 1980-81, dean & prof, 1981-85; Univ Nc, law sch prof & torts expert, henry brandis prof law, law prof; Univ Nc, Chapel Hill, dean, 2006. **Orgs:** Pres, 1976-78, exec secy, 1979-99, NC Asn Black Lawyers; bars mem, US Supreme Ct, NY, DC, NC; Triangle Housing Devel Corp, 1977-; chmn, Triangle Housing Devel Corp, 1979-91; bd dir, United Way Greater Durham, 1984-88; pres, Law Sch Admis Coun, 1991-93; Am Bar Asn; NC State Bar; NC Bar Asn; chmn, Asn Am Law Sch; chmn bd, NC Fair Housing Ctr; chmn, NC Poverty Proj; fel Am Bar Found. **Home Addr:** 3400 Cambridge Rd, Durham, NC 27707-4508, **Home Phone:** (919)489-9415. **Business Addr:** Professor of Law, University North Carolina School of Law, 5099 Van Hecke-Wettach Hall, Chapel Hill, NC 27599-3380, **Business Phone:** (919)962-7004.

### DAYS, BERTRAM MAURICE
Executive. **Personal:** Born Oct 1, 1952, Mobile, AL; son of Raymond N Sr and Hattie M; married Ava; children: Marcia Y Burke. **Educ:** Macalester Col, BA, 1974; Univ Rochester, MBA, 1976. **Career:** Univ Rochester, William E Simon Grad Sch Bus Admin, 1974-76, Cummins Engine Co, corp financial planning, 1976-80, mgr, financial admin, 1980-82, controller, serv prod, 1982-85, dir, bus develop, 1985-90, gen mgr, 1990-93; Hunter Industs, gen mgr, 1993-, vpres, currently. **Orgs:** Big Bro/Big Sister, 1982-85; William Laws Scholar Fndn, pres, 1985-88; Asn Qual & Participation, 1996-2001; Wake Co Schls/Bus Partnership, 2000-02; Am Mgt Asn, 2002-; bd dir, Raleigh Chamber Com, 2003-. **Home Addr:** 116 Bromfield Way, Cary, NC 27519, **Home Phone:** (919)362-6131. **Business Addr:** Vice President, General Manager, Hunter Industries Inc, 222 Gregson Dr, Cary, NC 27511, **Business Phone:** (919)380-6300.

### DAYS, DREW SAUNDERS, III
Government official, educator. **Personal:** Born Aug 29, 1941, Atlanta, GA; son of Drew S Jr (deceased) and Dorothea Jamerson (deceased); married Ann Ramsay Langdon; children: Alison Langdon & Elizabeth Jamerson. **Educ:** Hamilton Col, Clinton, NY, BA, Eng lit, 1963; Yale Law Sch, New Haven, CT, LLB, 1966. **Career:** Cotton Watt Jones King & Bowlus, Chicago, Ill, law assoc, 1966-67; Ill Civil Liberties Union, vol atty, 1966-67; Comayagua Honduras, peace cor psvol, 1967-69; NAACP Legal Defense & Educ & Educ Fund Inc, first asst coun, 1967-77; Agency Internal Develop Honduras, consult prog writer, 1968-69; Rockefeller Comn Latin Am, interpreter, 1969; Temple Univ & Philadelphia, asso prof law, 1973-75; SUS Dept Justice, asst atty gen, 1977-81 solicitor gen, 1993-; Yale Law Sch, fac, assoc prof, 1981-, Alfred M Rankin Prof Law, 1992-; Gen US, Solicitor, 1993-96; Morrison & Foerster Law Firm, Wash, counsel, 1997-. **Orgs:** Ill State Bar Asn, 1966; NY Bar Asn, 1970; Numerous memships incl Cong Black Caucus & Nat Conf Educ Blacks, 1972; trustee, Edna McConnell Clark Found, 1988-93; founding dir, Orville H. Schell, Ctr Int Human Rights, Yale Law Sch; bd dir, John D & Catherine T MacArthur Found; trustee, Hamilton Col; bd dir, Petra Found; Reginald Heber Smith Lawyer Fel Prog; Nat Asn Advan Colored People Legal Defense Fund; US Solicitor Gen, 1993-96; Smithsonian Inst Scholars Adv Panel, Smithsonian Black Hist Mus Coun; fel Am Acad Arts & Sci; life fel Am Bar Asn; Am Const Soc Law & Policy Bd Advisors; Am Law Inst; Amnesty Int; Const Proj Const Amendments Initiative; Coun Foreign Rels; Dem Cong Campaign Comt; Inter-Am Dialogue; Joe Lieberman Pres; John Kerry Pres; Kerry Victory, 2004. **Honors/Awds:** Judge Robert F Kennedy Memorial Human Rights Award, 1990; Fel, Am Acad Arts & Sci; Alfred M Rankin Professor of Law, Yale Law Sch, 1992-; Spirit of Excellence Award, Am Bar Asn, 1997; Hon Doctoral Degree, Univ NC Chapel Hill, 2003. **Special Achievements:** First African American justice of the Supreme Court, 1967; Published "Materials on Police Misconduct Litigation"; co-editor "Federal Civil Rights Litigation", Practicing Law Inst, 1977. **Home Addr:** 468 Whitney Ave Apt A21, New Haven, CT 06511, **Home Phone:** (203)787-7452. **Business Addr:** Alfred M Rankin Professor, Yale Law School, 127 Wall St, New Haven, CT 06511, **Business Phone:** (203)432-4992.

### DAYS, MICHAEL IRVIN
Journalist, editor. **Personal:** Born Aug 2, 1953, Philadelphia, PA; son of Helen Boles and Morris; married Angela P Dodson; children: Edward, Adrian, Andrew & Umi. **Educ:** Col Holy Cross, BA, 1975; Univ Mo, Sch Jour, MA, 1976. **Career:** Rochester Dem & Chronicle, reporter, 1978-80; Louisville Courier-Jour, reporter, 1980-84; Wall St Jour, reporter, 1984-86; Philadelphia Daily News, city hall, educ reporter, 1986-88, asst city ed, 1988-89, bus ed, 1989-91, asst managing ed, 1991-98, dep managing ed, 1998, managing ed, 2004-05, ed, 2005-11, ed, 2012-; Mc Cormick Tribune fel, 2002; Philadelphia Newspapers, vpres, 2005-09; Assoc Press Managing Ed, APME news ed, 2009-11; Philadelphia Inquirer, managing ed, 2011-12. **Orgs:** Pres, Louisville Asn Black Communicators, 1983; Nat Asn Black Journalists, 1985-87; pres, Philadelphia Asn Black Journalists, 1987-88; bd mem, PA SOC Newspaper Eds, 1991-93; Knight Ctr Specized Jour, 1998-. **Home Addr:** 324 Hamilton Ave, Trenton, NJ 08609, **Home Phone:** (609)394-7632. **Business Addr:** Editor, Philadelphia Daily News, 400 N Broad St, Philadelphia, PA 19101, **Business Phone:** (215)854-5984.

### DAYS, ROSETTA HILL. See Obituaries Section.

### DE GRAFF, JACQUES ANDRE
Executive. **Personal:** Born Nov 11, 1949, New York, NY; son of James Augustus and Beryl Hay; married Jacqueline Riley; children: Danielle Janet. **Educ:** Queensborough Community Col, Astoria, AA, 1971; Hunter Col, NY, BA, broadcast jour & mass commun, 1975; Develop Real Property, attended 1980; NY Univ, Real Estate Inst, attended 1981; Harvard Univ Community Develop Finance, attended 1981; NY Theol Sem, Mdiv, currently. **Career:** NY State Urban Develop Corp, New York, vpres finance, 1979-83; Packard Press Inc, NY, nat acct rep, 1985-86; Securities Press Inc, NY, vpres, 1986-88; De Graff Unlimited Inc, NY, managing partner, 1988-90; Bill Bradley, nat dep campaign mgr & dir deleg selection; Blueberry Treat Ctrs Inc, Brooklyn, exec dir, 1990; Canaan Baptist Church, pastoral staff, 1998-; Rev Al Sharpton Mayor, NY, campaign mgr, campaign coord, Nat Action Network, pres, currently. **Orgs:** Vice chmn, Adv Bd, Manhattan Urban League, 1987-; friend, Studio Mus, 1986-; 3rd vpres, Nat 100 Black Men NY Chap; Exec Adjunc, prestigious Hampton Univ Ministers Conf; chief protocol, Nat Action Network; African Am Adv Coun at Nielsen Media Res Inc, 2006. **Home Addr:** 60 Harbor Key Harmon Cove, Secaucus, NJ 07094, **Home Phone:** (201)866-5017. **Business Addr:** President, Rev Al Sharpton for Mayor, 16 Ct St 3rd Fl, Brooklyn, NY 11241, **Business Phone:** (718)834-4880.

### DE JONGH, PROF. JAMES LAURENCE
Educator. **Personal:** Born Sep 23, 1942, St. Thomas; son of Mavis Elizabeth Bentlage and Percy Leo. **Educ:** Williams Col, BA, 1964; Yale Univ, MA, 1967; NY Univ, PhD, 1983. **Career:** Rutgers Univ Newark, instr, 1969-70; City Univ New York, City Col New York, prof, 1970, Inst Res African Diapora Americas Caribbean, prof eng, dir, 1997-, prof emer, currently; Schomburg Ctr for Res in Black Cult, scholar, 2011-. **Orgs:** Dramatists Guild; Writers Guild Am E; Mod Lang Asn; Harlem Writers Guild; Zeta Psi Frat; Fel Ctr Black Studies Univ Calif Santa Barbara, 1981; Hon Fel Brookdale Ctr Aging Hunger Col, 1985. **Home Addr:** 6 Fordham Hill Oval Suite 9D, Bronx, NY 10468. **Business Addr:** Professor Emeritus, Director IRADAC, The City University of New York, 3110 Thomson Ave, Queens, NY 11101, **Business Phone:** (718)482-7200.

## DE LOATCH, RAVEN L.

Hospital administrator. **Educ:** E Carolina Univ Sch Med, MD, 1984. **Career:** Halifax Regional Hosp, chief staff, pvt pract, currently; Rural Health Group, Jackson, internist, currently. **Special Achievements:** First African Am chief of staff in Roanoke Rapids, NC. **Home Addr:** 937 Gregory Dr, Roanoke Rapids, NC 27870, **Home Phone:** (888)606-1286. **Business Addr:** Internist, Rural Health Group, 9425 NC Hwy 305, Jackson, NC 27845, **Business Phone:** (252)534-1661.

## DE PASSE, SUZANNE

Television producer, chairperson, chief executive officer. **Personal:** Born Jul 19, 1946, New York, NY; married Paul Le Mat; children: 3. **Educ:** Manhattan Community Col. **Career:** Motown Industs, asst exec, 1968, pres, 1980-; Lady Sings the Blues, co-author; Motown 25: Yesterday, Today, Forever, producer & writer, 1983; De Passe Entertainment Inc, co-chmn & chief exec officer, 1992-; Mini Series: "Lonesome Dove", "Small Sacrifices", 1989; "The Jacksons: An American Dream", 1992; "Return to Lonesome Dove", 1993; "Streets of Laredo", "Buffalo Girls", 1995; "Dead Man's Walk", 1996; "The Temptations", 1998; Series: "On Our Own", 1994-95; "Sister, Sister", 19959-99; "Smart Guy", 1996-99; exec producer, 1994-99; Motown 40: The Music Is Forever, producer & writer, 1998; Movies for Television: Happy Endings, 1983; Bridemaids, The Last Electric Knight, 1989; Someone Else's Child, The Loretta Claiborne Story, producer, 2000; Cheaters, producer, 2000; Zenon: The Zequel, producer, 2001; 32nd Nat Asn Advan Colored People Image Awards, producer, 2001; Essence Awards, producer, 2002; It's Show time at the Apollo, producer, 2002; Essence Awards, producer, 2003; 34th Nat Asn Advan Colored People Image Awards, producer, 2003; Soluna Proj, producer, 2004; Zenon: Z3, producer, 2004; The Black Movie Awards, producer & writer, 2005; The 2006 Black Movie Awards, exec producer, 2006; de Passe Jones Entertainment Group, co chairman. **Orgs:** Acad Motion Picture Arts & Sci; Am Fedn Tv & Radio Artists; trustee, Am Film Inst; Am Soc Composers & Publishers; Caucus Writers, Producers & dir; Debbie Allen Dance Acad; Humanities Prize; Los Angeles Chamber Com; Los Angeles Opera; Nat Asn Rec Arts & Sci; Nat Asn Tv Arts & Sci; New York Ballet; Producers Guild Am; Writers Guild Am. **Business Addr:** Chairman, Chief Executive Officer, De Passe Entertainment Inc, 5750 Wilshire Blvd Suite 640, Los Angeles, CA 90036, **Business Phone:** (323)965-2580.

## DE RUSSELL, MILICENT. See Obituaries Section.

## DE VEAUX, ALEXIS

Educator, writer. **Personal:** Born Sep 24, 1948, New York, NY; daughter of Richard Hill and Mae. **Educ:** Cornell Univ; Empire State Col, BA, 1976; State Univ NY, Buffalo, MA, 1989, PhD, women's studies, 1992. **Career:** New Haven Bd Educ, master artist, 1974-75; Sarah Lawrence Col, adj lectr, 1979-80; Norwich Univ, assoc fac, 1984-85; WabashCollege, Owen Dutson vis scholar, 1986-87; Essence Mag, ed-at-large, 1979-91; State Univ NY, Buffalo, NY, vis asst prof, 1991-92, asst prof, Dept Women's Studies, assoc prof & chair, currently. **Orgs:** Org Women Writers Africa Inc (OWWA). **Home Addr:** 186 Ashland Ave, Buffalo, NY 14222. **Business Addr:** Associate Professor, State University NY, 712 Clemens Hall, Buffalo, NY 14260-4630, **Business Phone:** (716)645-2327.

## DE VEAUX, STUART SAMUEL

Political consultant. **Personal:** Born May 19, 1970, Bronx, NY; son of Stuart and Jean. **Educ:** Howard Univ, attended 1990. **Career:** Republican Nat Comt, dep dir, spec asst co-chair; Black Americans Polit Action Comt; Calif Republican Party, spokesperson, commun dir, currently. **Orgs:** Nat Asn Advan Colored People. **Business Addr:** Spokesperson, Communication Director, California Republican Party, 1001 K St, Sacramento, CA 95814, **Business Phone:** (916)448-9496.

## DE'LEON, LUNDEN

Actor, fashion model, chief executive officer. **Career:** Actress, model, music entrepreneur, filmmaker & politician; Films: Surviving Paradise, 2000; Double D Avenger, 2001; Faux Pas, 2001; Cryptz, 2002; Deathbed, 2002; Ronny Camaro & Seven Angry Women, 2003; Mad Dawg, 2004; Pure, 2004; Irrebuttable Presumption, exec producer, 2004; Stifle, exec producer, 2009; Space Girls in Beverly Hills, 2009; Last of a Dying Breed, producer, 2009; Nurse Vicky, 2010; Kill Jill, 2010; 13 Miles to Hell, ed, 2010; Between Brothers, dir, 2011; Somebody's Child, therapist, 2012; Kindred Spirit, 2013; 12 Dog Days Till Christmas, 2014; Where Angels Dwell, Caravaggio and My Mother the Pope, Newton's Grace, forthcoming, 2015; Lake House, forthcoming, 2016. TV series: "Herzflimmern", 1998; "Livin'with Shuganah Shiksa"; "Vital Signs"; "The Ladies Room"; "Fury"; "Kickin Chicken"; "Just Shoot Me"; "Undercover", exec producer; "Veronica's Secret", exec producer; Dirrty Records, founder & chief exec officer, 2003-; Palmetto Film Studios, pres, 2008-14. **Orgs:** Pres, Dem Women's Coun, 2008. **Business Addr:** Chief Executive Officer, Founder, Dirrty Records, 468 N Camden Dr Suite 200, Beverly Hills, CA 90210, **Business Phone:** (310)860-5609.

## DEAN, ANGELA

Executive, fashion designer. **Educ:** Fashion Inst Design & Merchandising. **Career:** Deanzign Design Co, celebrity designer & bus owner, currently. **Orgs:** Bd dir, Fashion Inst Design & Merchandising Alumni. **Business Addr:** Celebrity Designer, Business Owner, Deanzign Design Co, 4725 W Wash Blvd, Los Angeles, CA 90016, **Business Phone:** (323)230-6761.

## DEAN, CLARA RUSSELL

School administrator. **Personal:** Born Sep 11, 1927, Greenville, SC; married Miles; children: Miles Jr, Angela, Jacquelynn, Barbara, Wanda & Patricia. **Educ:** Essex County Col, AAS, 1970; Rutgers, BA, psychol, 1970, MA, 1972; Felician Col, ASRN, 1972; Jersey City State, Nursing Sch, attended 1973. **Career:** Col Hosp Coun, bd mem & chmn affirm action, 1975-79; Col Med & Dent NJ, supv implimented dent clinic, 1977; Essex County, long range planning bd, 1983-; Bethune Acad, dir, 1984; Bethune Acad, pres. **Orgs:** Life mem, Nat Asn Advan Colored People; pres, Clara Dean Civic Asn, 1976-; Asn Bus & Prof Women, 1978-; ed comn, Greater Abyssian Church, 1980-; chairperson, Three City Wide Health Fairs, 1982-84; 100 Black Woman, 1982. **Honors/Awds:** Achievement Award, PATCH-Newark, 1981; Recognition Award, NAACP, Newark Br, 1983; Recognition Award, NJ State Commn for the Blind, 1985. **Home Addr:** 15 Birchwood Rd, Randolph, NJ 07869-2909, **Home Phone:** (973)895-3679. **Business Addr:** President, Bethune Academy, 26 Wash St, East Orange, NJ 07017-1315, **Business Phone:** (973)674-0660.

## DEAN, CURTIS

Hotel executive. **Career:** Marriott Int, area gen mgr, 1974-2009, Philadelphia mgr, 1995; Los Angeles mgr; Roberts Hotel Group, vpres, currently. **Business Addr:** Vice President, Roberts Hotel Group, St. Louis, MO.

## DEAN, DANIEL R.

Executive. **Personal:** Born Jan 23, 1941, Atlantic City, NJ; son of Edward and Cora L Harris; married Edna Geraldine Jeter; children: Tracey & Kevin. **Educ:** WVa State Col, BS, bus admin & mgt, 1963; Rutgers Univ, attended 1968; Pace Univ, attended 1977; Stonier Grad Sch Banking, cert, banking & financial support serv, 1983. **Career:** Citibank, NA New York, NY, oper officer, 1972-76, oper mgr, 1976-78, oper head, 1978-84; Citi corp USA Inc, Atlanta, relationship team mgr, vpres, 1969-89; D & E Floor Serv Inc, pres, 1988-. **Orgs:** Chmn bd dir, Frederick Douglas Liberation Libr, 1969-75; treas, Somerset County Comn Action Prog, 1973-76; trustee, Franklin Twp Libr Bd, 1975-78; pres, Super Golf Assoc, 1983-84; pres, Southern Snow Seekers Ski Club, 1985-88. **Home Addr:** 2501 Old Sewell Rd, Marietta, GA 30068, **Home Phone:** (770)565-1930. **Business Addr:** President, D & E Floor Serv Inc, 2501 Old Sewell Rd, Marietta, GA 30068-3458, **Business Phone:** (770)973-5029.

## DEAN, DIANE D.

Consultant, educator. **Personal:** Born Aug 26, 1949, Detroit, MI; daughter of Ada Spann and Edward Lesley. **Educ:** NC A & T State Univ, BS, 1971; Ind Univ, MS, 1973; Univ Calif, Los Angeles, CA, attended 1983; Case Western Res, cert, 1991; Harvard Grad Sch Educ, attended 1995; Cornell Univ, mgt develop cert, 2000. **Career:** Univ Miami, area coordr, 1973-75; Occidental Col, dir housing, 1975-78; Univ Southern Calif, asst dir admin, assistance & sch rels, 1978-80; Univ Calif, Los Angeles, from asst dir admin to assoc dir admin, 1980-85; Leadership Educ & Develop, dir opers, 1983-85; Nat Action Coun Minorities Engineering, dir incentive grants & educ & training scholar progs, 1985-90; Girl Scouts USA, mgt consult, 1990-95, develop consult educ & training; Columbia Bus Sch, Inst Non-profit Mgt, fac, 1998-. **Orgs:** Calif Asn Col; Univ Housing Officers, 1975-78; standing comt, Nat Asn Col Admin Counr, 1979-86; Black Womens Forum Los Angeles, 1980-; rep, Grad Mgt Admin Coun, 1981-85; Alpha Kappa Alpha; Calif Mus Afro-Am Art, 1984-; Studio Mus, Harlem, 1985-; co-chair, Region VI Nat Asn Stud Personnel Admin, 1985; Schomburg Soc, 1986-; Coun Concerned Black Execs, 1986; lifetime mem, Univ Calif Los Angeles Alumni Asn; NC A & T Alumni Asn; Urban League; lifetime mem, Cass Tech Alumni Asn; Nat Asn Advan Colored People; Corp Womens Network; Lit Soc, 1989-; Coalition 100 Black Women, 1991-; Nat Soc Fund Raising Execs; Am Soc Training & Develop; Nat Asn Female Execs; lifetime mem, Girl Scouts; Asn Girl Scouts Exec Staff, 1994-. **Home Addr:** 78 Orient Way Apt 2C, Rutherford, NJ 07070-4010. **Business Addr:** Faculty, Columbia Business School, 3022 Broadway, New York, NY 10027, **Business Phone:** (212)854-5553.

## DEAN, JAMES EDWARD

Educator, social worker, state government official. **Personal:** Born Mar 14, 1944, Atlanta, GA; son of Steve Sr and Dorothy Cox; married Vyvyan A Coleman; children: Sonya V & Monica A. **Educ:** Clark Col, BA, 1966; San Francisco City Col, attended 1966; Fisk Univ, attneded 1967; Atlanta Univ Sch Soc Work, MSW, 1968; Univ Ga, post grad studies, 1968; Emory Univ, post grad studies, 1976. **Career:** Government official (retired); Econ Opport Atlanta Inc, human res, 1965-66; Ga Gen Assembly, state rep, 1968-75; Clark Col, Atlanta, GA, dir alumni affairs, 1971-78; MBO, contract procurement specialist, 1978-80; Nat Urban League Inc, asst dir, 1980-82; BMC Realty Co, Atlanta, GA, mgt rep, 1982; State Ga Dept Transp, equal employ opportunity off, 1982-88, equal employ opportunity rev off, 1988-2006. **Orgs:** Atlanta Daily World Newspaper, 1960-70; Atlanta Inquirer Newspaper, 1962-68; vpres, Comm Serv Inc, Atlanta GA, 1982-89; Ctr Study Presidency, New York, 1988-89; sec & gov bd mem, Pine Acres Town & Country Club, 1989; pres, Hunter hills vols crime, 2004; Am Fedn Police; Nat Asn Social Workers; Nat Tech Asn; Southern Ctr Int Studies; Acad Cert Soc Workers; Leadership Ga Prog Found; Friendship Baptist Church; life mem, Alpha Phi Alpha Inc; HR Butler Lodge, Prince Hall Masonic Order; Atlanta Area Tech Sch Off-Campus Adv Comm; Atlanta Hist Socy; Frontiers Int Inc; Clark Atlanta Univ Alumni Asn, Atlanta Chap; Clark Atlanta Univ Nat Alumni Asn; Minority Worker Training Prog Clark Atlanta Univ; Joymen Club; bd dir, Atlanta Chap Univ N Asn; fel Nat Urban League. **Honors/Awds:** Alpha Kappa Delta Nat Soc Honour Soc, 1968; Gov Ga, Admiral Ga Navy, 1971; Gov Ga, Lt Colonel Aide de Camp, 1979, 1983 & 1991; Special Achievement Award, Dept Transp State GA, 1986, 1988 & 1996; Coun Religion & Int Affairs Fel; Outstanding Young Men Atlanta, Atlanta Jaycees; Southern Ctr Int Studies, Atlanta Black/Jewish Coalition; Presidential Citation, Clark Col; Social Action Leadership Award, N Ga Chap, Natl Asn Soc Workers Inc; Honorary State Trooper; Community Service Award, Women Morris Brown Col; Atlanta Univ Multi-Purpose Scholar Award. **Special Achievements:** A Study Comm Organization Techniques Utilized Three Self-Help Projects Securing Low-Income Involvement, 1968. **Home Addr:** 87 Burbank Dr NW, Atlanta, GA 30314-2450, **Home Phone:** (404)752-5427. **Business Addr:** District EEO Review Officer, State Georgia Department Transport, Atlanta, GA 30314, **Business Phone:** (404)755-8518.

## DEAN, DR. MARK E.

Vice president (organization), scientist, executive. **Personal:** Born Mar 2, 1957, Jefferson City, TN; son of James and Barbara; married Paula Bacon. **Educ:** Univ Tenn, BS, 1979; Fla Atlantic Univ, MSEE, 1982; Stanford Univ, PhD, elec engineering, 1992. **Career:** IBM Corp, dir archit, Power Personal Systs Div, 1993-94, vpres syst platforms, Interactive Broadband Systs, 1994-95, IBM fel & vpres, syst archit & performance, RS/6000 Div, 1995-97, IBM fel & dir, IBM Enterprise Server Group, Advan Tech Dev, 1997-2000, IBM TJ Watson Res Ctr, IBM fel & vpres systs, 2000-02, vpres, storage technol group, 2002-03, vpres, systs & technol group, 2003-04, almaden res ctr, 2004. **Orgs:** Bd trustee, Houston-Tillotson Col, 1977-; bd dir, Inroads Inc; bd advrs, Univ Tenn, Sch Engineering; bd advrs, Ga Tech; bd mem, Nat Soc Black Engrs; Phi Kappa Phi Hon Soc; Tau Beta Pi Engineering Hon Soc. **Special Achievements:** African-American to become an IBM Fellow. **Home Addr:** 17098 Holiday Dr, Morgan Hil, CA 95037, **Home Phone:** (408)782-0728. **Business Addr:** IBM Fellow, Vice President, IBM TJ Watson Research Center, PO Box 704, Yorktown Heights, NY 10598-0218, **Business Phone:** (914)945-1200.

## DEAN, TERRANCE

Writer. **Personal:** Born Detroit, MI. **Educ:** Fisk Univ, BA, commun, 1992. **Career:** New York Sun, Tennessean, writer; MTV; Men's Empowerment, founder & creator, currently; Young Men's Empowerment, founder & creator, currently; Young Women's Empowerment, founder & creator, currently; co-creator, The Gathering of Men, with Adeyemi Bandele; Terrance Dean Inc, pres, currently. Book: Reclaim Your Power, 2003; Straight from Your Gay Best Friend, 2010; Mogul, 2011. **Orgs:** Alpha Phi Alpha, Fraternity Inc; John Seigentheler Journalism Fel, Vanderbilt Univ, 2005. **Home Addr:** , Los Angeles, CA 90047. **Business Addr:** Writer, Mens Empowerment Inc, 2107 W Manchester Ave Suite 106, Los Angeles, CA 90047.

## DEAN, VYVYAN ARDENA COLEMAN

School administrator, educator. **Personal:** Born Jun 11, 1945, Ft. Benning, GA; daughter of Clarence and Dorothy Sims; married James Edward; children: Sonya V & Monica A. **Educ:** Palmer Memorial Inst, Sedalia, NC, dipl, 1962; Clark Col, BA, 1966; Atlanta Univ, MA, 1973; Ga State Univ, post grad advan studies, 1987; Atlanta Univ, post grad advan studies, 1987. **Career:** Atlanta Pub Sch Syst, Atlanta, Ga, teacher, 1966-, Atlanta Metrop Col, GED teacher, 1966-, John B Gordon Elem Sch & Charles R Drew Elem Sch, curric specialist, 1992-97; Marylin Elem Sch, curric specialist, 1997-98; SIA, City Atlanta Parks & Recreation, Atlanta, Ga, summer reading prog dir; Atlanta Pub Schs, SIA liaison, specialist, 1999-. **Orgs:** Vpres, Decatur/DeKalb Chap, Drifters, 1989-91, pres, currently; Nat Asn Educ Young C; Int Reading Asn; Ga Asn Educr; Nat Asn Educr; Atlanta Asn Educr; Curric & Supv Develop Asn; Pals, LINKS Interest Group; treas, Atlanta Chap, Circle Lets, 1982-91, pres, 1998-99; corresp secy, Inquirers Lit Club, 1983-91; Delta Sigma Theta Sorority, 1969-, sgt arms; AAE, AFT & Ga Adult Literacy Asn, 1970-; Friendship Baptist Church; Delta Sigma Theta; Nat Asn Advan Colored People; vol, United Negro Col Fund. **Home Addr:** 87 Burbank Dr NW, Atlanta, GA 30314-2850, **Home Phone:** (404)752-5427. **Business Addr:** Specialist, Atlanta Public Schools, 2250 Perry Blvd NW Suite 331, Atlanta, GA 30310, **Business Phone:** (404)792-5765.

## DEAN, WALTER R, JR. See Obituaries Section.

## DEAN, DR. WILLIE B.

Association executive. **Personal:** Born Mar 15, 1951, Potts Camp, MS; son of Mattie Delyta Brown and Eddie B; married Pamela Williamson; children: Cedric Lamont, Jarrod Wilberforce & Matthew Alexander. **Educ:** Univ Memphis, BS, educ, 1973; Univ Nebr, MBA, bus, 1993; Univ Minn, PhD, recreation & leisure serv, 2003. **Career:** Glenview YMCA, Memphis, Tenn, prog dir, 1974-75; YMCA Metrop Ft Worth, exec dir, 1975-81; Mc Donald YMCA, Ft Worth, Tex, exec dir, 1975-81; Mondanto YMCA, St Louis, Mo, vpres & exec dir, 1981-89; YMCA USA, natonal field exec, 1994-2001; YMCA Greater Cleveland, sr vpres opers & chief operating officer, pres, 2005-06; YMCA Arlington, pres & chief exec officer, 2007-12; KFAI Fresh Air Inc, exec dir, 2013-14; Univ Minn, teching asst; YouthCARE, exec dir, 2015-; Monsanto Co, vpres; Willie Dean & Assocs, owner, pres, currently; Omaha/Coun Bluffs YMCA, pres, chief exec officer; YMCA Mid-S, prog dir. **Orgs:** Jennings-N St Louis Kiwanis Club, 1981-89, pres, 1985; prog chmn, 100 Black Men Metro St Louis, 1983-89; Omega Psi Phi Frat Inc, 1983-89. **Honors/Awds:** Outstanding Young Man in America, 1976; Award of Administrative Excellence for Budget Management, National APD, 1985; Father of the Year, 100 Black Men off St Louis, 1985; Yes I Can Award, Metro Sentinel Newspaper, 1988; Best in North America Award, N Am YMCA Develop Officers, 1990; Executive Director of the Year Award, Iowa-Nebr APD Chap 43, 1993. **Special Achievements:** Publications: "Minorities, Women: Yes You Can Shatter the Glass Ceiling!", 1992; "Crisis Management Resource Package for YMCAs", 1995; "Barriers to Upward Mobility for African Americans in Leisure Services: A Case Study of the YMCA", 2004. **Home Addr:** 9244 Telford Bay, Minneapolis, MN 55443, **Home Phone:** (952)351-0986. **Business Addr:** Owner, President, Willie Dean & Associates, 10812 Yukon Ave S, Bloomington, MN 55438-3300, **Business Phone:** (952)941-1402.

## DEANDA, PETER

Actor. **Personal:** Born Mar 10, 1938, Pittsburgh, PA; married Fatima Salik, Apr 23, 1960, (divorced 1977); children: Allison & Peter; married Jacqueline Alexander, Nov 11, 1980, (divorced 1982); married Aeros Terra, Jun 21, 1987, (divorced 1992). **Educ:** Actors' Workshop. **Career:** TV Series: "One Life to Live", 1968-70; "Dan August", 1970; "Cutter", 1972; "Wide World Mystery", 1975; "Cannon", 1975; "Joe Forrester", 1976; "Police Woman", 1976; "Beulah Land", 1980; "What's Happening Now!", 1986; "Beverly Hills 90210", 1999; "Crusade", 1999; "Strong Medicine", 2003; Film: The Cool World, 1964; Lady Liberty, 1972; Come Back, 1972; Charleston Blue, 1972; The New Centurions, 1972; Advice to the Lovelorn, 1981; Banged Up, 2003. **Orgs:** Nat Asn Advan Colored People; Actors Equity Asn. **Honors/Awds:** Image Awards, Com Publ Black Drama Anthology, 1971. **Special Achievements:** Author of the Play "Ladies in Waiting". **Home Addr:** , Orlando, FL 32801. **Business Addr:** Actor, William Morris Agency, 1 William Morris Pl, Beverly Hills, CA 90212, **Business Phone:** (310)285-9000.

**DEAR, ALICE**
Executive director. **Personal:** Born Gary, IN. **Educ:** Howard Univ, BA, sociol, anthrop, 1969; Pace Univ, Lubin Sch Bus, MBA, financial mgt, 1977. **Career:** Pan Am World Airways, purser, flight serv specialist, flt attend, 1969-77; Irving Trust Co, vpres, int lending officer, 1977-89; African Develop Bank, US exec dir, 1994-2000; AM Dear & Assocs, pres, 2000-; Africa Millennium Fund LLC, vpres, 2001-03; Unique Afrique Inc, pres, 2006-2015; Preod Corp, assoc, 2008-09. **Orgs:** Bd mem, Africare; Alpha Kappa Alpha Sorority Inc; Rep to Un (DESA/ ECOSOC); Coun Foreign Rels; Global Summit Women, Int Planning Comt; Howard Univ Alumni Club New York; bd mem, Women's eNews; Int Univ Grand Bassam Found. **Business Addr:** President, Unique Afrique, 400 W 149th St Suite 2, New York, NY 10031-2819, **Business Phone:** (212)283-5231.

**DEARMAN, JOHN EDWARD (JOHN E DEARMAN)**
Judge. **Personal:** Born Mar 28, 1931, Troy, TX; son of Melvin and Jessie Mae Banks-Evans (deceased); married Ina Patricia Flemming; children: Tracy, Kelly, Jonathan & Jason. **Educ:** Wiley Col, BA, soc studies, 1950; Wayne State Law Sch, JD, 1954; Univ Calif, cert, labor arbitrator, 1973. **Career:** City Detroit, soc worker, 1957-58; Pvt Pract, atty, 1957-59, 1961-77; State Calif, judge; San Francisco Super Ct, judge; Hall Justice, Dept 18. **Orgs:** Nat Asn Advan Colored People; dir, Golden Gate Bridge Bd, 1966-70; comnr, metrop Transp Comn, 1970-75; dir, vpres, Family Serv Asn Am, 1968-72; pres bd, Family Serv Agency San Francisco, 1968-72; chmn, Black Caucus Family Serv Asn Am; pres, Family Serv Agency San Francisco. **Honors/Awds:** Judge of the Year, SF Trial Lawyers Asn, 1984; Humanitarian Judge of the Year, Calif Trial Lawyers Asn, 1984. **Special Achievements:** The longest-serving judge in San Francisco history. **Home Addr:** 217 Upper Ter, San Francisco, CA 94117. **Business Addr:** Judge, San Francisco Superior Court, Rm 204 400 McAllister St, San Francisco, CA 94102-4514, **Business Phone:** (415)551-3702.

**DEBARGE, CHICO (JONATHAN ARTHUR DEBARGE)**
Singer. **Personal:** Born Jun 23, 1966, Grand Rapids, MI; married Andrea Bordenave; children: Cheyann, Chicoco, Manny, Abrielle & Dontae. **Career:** Motown Rec, solo artist; Koch Rec, rec artist; Albums: Chico DeBarge, 1986; Talk to Me, 1986; Kiss Serious, 1988; Long Time No See, 1997; The Game, 1999; Free, 2003; Addiction, 2009; Songs: "Talk To Me", 1986; "The Girl Next Door", 1987; "Rainy Night", 1987; "Iggin' Me", 1997; "Love Still Good", 1997; "No Guarantee", 1998; "Virgin", 1998; "Soopa man Love"r, 1999; "Give You What You Want", 1999; "Listen to Your Man", 2000; "Playa Hater", 2000; "Home Alone", 2003; "Oh No", 2009. Films: Envy, 2005; Queen of Media, 2011. **Business Addr:** Recording Artist, Koch Records, 740 Broadway 7th Fl, New York, NY 10003, **Business Phone:** (212)353-8800.

**DEBARGE, EL (ELDRA PATRICK DEBARGE)**
Singer, actor. **Personal:** Born Jun 4, 1961, Grand Rapids, MI; son of Robert Louis Sr (deceased) and Etterlene; married Monique. **Career:** DeBarge Musical Group, vocalist, 1978-86; solo artist, 1986-; Solo Albums: El DeBarge, 1986; Gemini, 1989; In the Storm, 1992; Heart Mind & Soul, 1994; Paid in Full, 2002; Ultimate Collection, 2003; Kicking it old school, 2007; Who's Johnny?; All This Love; Love Me in a Special Way; Who's Holding Donna Now; Rhythm of the Night; Second Chance, 2010. Singles: "Who's Johnny", 1986; "Love Always", 1986; "Someone", 1986; "Starlight Express", 1987; "Somebody Loves You", 1989; "Real Love", 1989; "The Secret Garden", 1990; "All Through the Night", 1991; "After the Dance", 1991; "You Know What I Like", 1992; "My Heart Belongs to You", 1992; "Another Chance", 1992; "Where Is My Love", 1994; "Can't Get Enough", 1994; "Slide", 1994; "Where You Are", 1995; "Second Chance", 2010. TV Series: "Motown25: Yesterday, Today, Forever", 1983; "The 11th Annual American Music Awards", 1984; "Motown Returns to the Apollo", 1985; "Bandstand", 1985; "The Facts of Life", 1985; "Miami Vice", 1985; "The 13th Annual American Music Awards", 1986; "Soul Train", 1989; "The 4th Annual Soul Train Music Awards", 1990; "The 6th Annual Soul Train Music Awards", 1992; "Glee", 2009; "2010 Soul Train Awards", 2010; "Unsung", 2010; Actor: Miami Vice, 1985; Jumping the Broom, 2011. **Business Addr:** Vocalist, c/o Warner Bros, 3300 Warner Blvd, Burbank, CA 91505, **Business Phone:** (818)846-9090.

**DEBARGE, JONATHAN ARTHUR. See DEBARGE, CHICO.**

**DEBAS, DR. HAILE T.**
Surgeon, educator. **Personal:** Born Feb 25, 1937, Asmara; married Ignacia Kim. **Educ:** Univ Col Addis Ababa Ethiopia, BS, 1958; McGill Univ, Montreal, Can, MD, 1963; Ottawa Civic Hosp, internship, 1964; Vancouver Gen Hosp, surg residency, 1969. **Career:** Univ Glasgow, res fel; Univ Calif, Los Angeles, med res coun scholar gastrointestinal physiology; Univ BC, asst prof surg, 1971-75, assoc prof surg, 1976-80; Univ Calif, Los Angeles & Wadsworth Va Med Ctr, res fel, 1972-74, prof surg, 1980-85; Univ Wash, Seattle, prof surg, chief gastrointestinal surg, 1985-87; UCSF, AOA, vis prof, 1989; Univ Calif, prof & chmn surg, 1987-93; UnivTex Med Br, Galveston, vis prof, 1980; Univ Calif, San Francisco, dean, Sch Med, 1993-2003, chancellor, 1997-98, vice chancellor med affairs, 1998-, Dept Global Health Sci, exec dir, founding exec, 2003-10, dir, currently; Maurice Galante, distinguished prof surg emer, currently. **Orgs:** Fel Royal Col Physicians & Surgeons, Can, 1969-; Am Col Surgeons, 1984-; Am Gastro enterological asn, 1974-; Pac Coast Surg asn, 1982-; pres, Soc Black Acad Surgeons, 1998-99; Soc Surg, 1987-; dir, Am Bd Surg, 1990-97; Inst Med, 1990-; pres Int Hepato-Biliary-Pancreatic Assoc, 1991-92; fell AAAS, 1992; pres, Am Surg asn, 2001-02; Inst Med; chair, Coun Deans AAMC; Nat Acad Sci; fel Am Acad Arts & Sci; Un Comn HIV/AIDS; Governance Africa; bd regents, Uniformed Serv Univ Health Sci; mem adv comt, Dir Nat Insts Health; bd trustee, Aga Khan Univ; founding chair, Consortium Univs Global Health; dir, Univ Calif Global Health Inst. **Honors/Awds:** Essay Award, British Columbia Surgical Soc, 1965; Med Res Coun Canada Fel, 1972-74; William H Rorer Research Prize for Original Res So Calif Soc Gastroenterology, 1973; Golden Scalpel Award, Teaching Excellence Div General Surgery UCLA Sch Med, 1981; Kaiser Award Excellence in Teaching, UCSF Sch Med, 1991; fell, The Rockefeller Found, Bellagio Study & Conference Ctr; Named in honor of Haile T Debas; Abraham Flexner Award, Asn Am Med Col, 2004. **Home Addr:** 240 St Francis Blvd, San Francisco, CA 94127-1941, **Home Phone:** (415)753-0769. **Business Addr:** Director, University of California, 3333 Calif St, San Francisco, CA 94143-0443, **Business Phone:** (415)353-2161.

**DEBERRY, ANDRE**
Mayor. **Educ:** Jackson State Univ, BA, polit sci. **Career:** Motivational speaker; motivational teacher & trainer; baptist preacher; DeBerry & Bean Ins, owner; City Holly Springs Mayors Off, Northern Dist, mayor, currently; bd mem, Miss Econ Growth Alliance & Pt Presence, currently. **Orgs:** Holly Springs Chamber Com. **Business Addr:** Mayor, City of Holly Springs Mayor's Office, 160 S Memphis St, Holly Springs, MS 38635-2921, **Business Phone:** (662)252-4280.

**DEBERRY, DONNA**
Executive. **Educ:** Calif State Univ; Harvard Univ Sch, divinity prog. **Career:** Wyndham Int hospity Inc, sr vpres diversity & corp, exec vpres global diversity & corp affairs, asst chmn, 2000-04; Nike, vpres diversity, 2004-06; Global Diversity & Inclusion Executive Consultant, 2007-14; DRP Int, chief exec officer & founder; Walking Waking Journey, producer, 2009; Global Inclusion & Diversity Prog Mgr, Starbucks, 2014-. **Orgs:** Multicultural Food Serv & Hospitality Alliance; Nat Hisp Corp Coun; Us Hisp Chamber Com; Nat Coalition Black Meeting Planners; Nat Asn Black Hotel Owners, Operators & Develop; mem adv coun, eWomen Network Found; Nat Football League; US Olympic Comt. **Business Addr:** Global Inclusion, Diversity Program Manager, Starbucks, 2401 Utah Ave S, Seattle, WA 98134.

**DEBERRY, VIRGINIA**
Novelist, fashion model, vice president (organization). **Personal:** Born Wadesboro, NC; daughter of John and Juanita. **Educ:** State Univ NY, BA 1972; Fisk Univ. **Career:** Model (retired), novelist, executive; Eng teacher, Buffalo, NY; modelling; BB/LW, actg vpres; Hanes hosiery, spokeswoman; Great Dimensions newsletter, fashion ed; Maxima Mag, cofounder & ed chief; Maxima, chief ed; Co-author: St. Martin's Press, auth: Tryin' to Sleep Bed You Made, 1997; Far From Tree, 2000; Better Than I Know Myself, 2004; Warner Bks-Exposures (Marie Joyce); Gotta Keep Tryin', 2008; What Doesn't Kill You, 2009; Simon & Schuster. **Honors/Awds:** New Author of the Year Award, Go on Girl Book Club, 1997; Fiction Award, Black Caucus Am Library Asn, 1998; African American Literature Award, 2004; Open Book Award, African American Literary Awards Show, 2004. **Business Addr:** Novelist, DeBerry & Grant, PO Box 5224, Kendall Park, NJ 08824, **Business Phone:** (732)297-5867.

**DEBNAM, CHADWICK BASIL (CHAD DEBNAM)**
Consultant, association executive, president (organization). **Personal:** Born May 10, 1950, Clayton, NC; son of Clarence and Madie; married Mauria Fletcher; children: Andrea Dione. **Educ:** Pac Univ, Forest Grove, BS, polit sci, 1972; Portland State Univ, postgrad studies, 1973. **Career:** Mary Acheson House, prog dir, 1972-75; Urban Redevelop Corp, mkt dir, 1976-78; Three Sixty Degree Publ, pres, 1979-82; B Chadwick Ltd, pres, 1982; King Neighborhood Asn, chair, pres, currently. **Orgs:** Bd mem, Multnomah Co Charter Rev, 1982-84; chmn, Adv Steering Comt InnerNE YMCA, 1983-85; Albina Lions Club, 1983-; pres, Ore Bus League, 1984-87; Am Mkt Asn, 1986-87; chmn, Black Republican Coun Ore, 1986-88. **Home Addr:** 5215 NE Mallory Ave, Portland, OR 97211-2629, **Home Phone:** (503)281-6315. **Business Addr:** President, King Neighborhood Association, 5215 NE Mallory Ave, Portland, OR 97211, **Business Phone:** (503)281-6315.

**DEBRO, DR. JULIUS**
School administrator, educator. **Personal:** Born Sep 25, 1931, Jackson, MS; son of Joseph and Seleana; married Darlene Conley; children: Blair & Renee. **Educ:** Univ San Francisco, CA, BA, polit sci, 1953; Univ San Francisco Law Sch, attended 1957; San Jose State Univ, MA, sociol, 1967; Univ Calif, Berkeley, PhD, criminol, 1975. **Career:** JD Assocs, chief exec officer; NIH, fel, 1969-70; Narcotic & Drug Res Inc, res assoc, 1989-90; Univ Md, Inst Crim Justice & Criminol, asst prof, 1971-79; Comn Criminol & Criminal Justice Educ, Wash DC, prin investr, 1978-79; Dept Pub Admin, chmn, 1979-80; Clark Atlanta Univ, Dept Criminal Justice, dir, 1979-, profcriminol, chmn, 1985-86, chmn criminal justice admin, 1986-91; actg asst provost, 1992; Justice Quart dep ed; Atlanta Univ, fac; Univ Wash Grad Sch, Col Arts & Sci, Seattle, Wash, assoc dean, 1991-2002, adj prof am ethnic studies, Polit Sci dept, Law Soc & Justice Prog, prof, currently. **Orgs:** Dir, Spec Opportunity Prog, Univ Calif, Berkeley, 1968-70; chair, Metrop Atlanta Crime Comn, 1984-; Citizen's Rev Bd, Atlanta, Ga, 1985-; Cent Atlanta Progress Study Comn, 1986-87; Atlanta Anti-Crime Bd, 1987; chmn, Metrop Atlanta Crime Comn, 1987-88; investigative panel, Ga Bar Asn, 1988-90; fel Western Soc Criminol; Coun Higher Educ Criminal Justice; Alpha Phi Alpha; chmn, Drug Task Force, Fulton County, Ga; Am Soc Criminol. **Honors/Awds:** Herbert Bloch Award, Am Soc Criminol. **Home Addr:** 11531 36th Ave NE, Seattle, WA 98115. **Business Addr:** Professor, University of Washington, Gowen 107 202 Savery Hall, Seattle, WA 98195-3340, **Business Phone:** (206)616-3438.

**DECHALUS, LORENZO. See JAMAR, LORD.**

**DECLOUET, GLADYS HART (GLADYS HART DECLOUET-MIMS)**
Vice president (organization). **Personal:** Born Jacksonville, FL. **Educ:** Tuskegee Univ, BS, mech engineering; Univ Wis, Madison, MBA, finance & investment banking. **Career:** Conoco Inc, engr; Brit Petrol Inc (BP), div mgr mkt, 1995-98, distrib, finance, planning & bus develop; Jack in Box, vpres opers; BP Oil Co, div mgr mkt; Burger King Corp, N Am Co Opers, sr vpres, 2008-10. **Honors/Awds:** "The Diversity Journal," Women Worth Watching, 2010; "Black Enterprise", The 100 Most Powerful Executives in Corporate America, 2010. **Home Addr:** 2627 S Bayshore Dr Apt 2301, Miami, FL 33133-5451.

**DECOSTA-WILLIS, DR. MIRIAM**
Educator. **Personal:** Born Nov 1, 1934, Florence, AL; daughter of Frank A and Beautine Hubertt; married Archie W Willis Jr; children: Tarik Sugarmon, Elena S Williamson, Erika S Echols & Monique A Sugarmon; married Russell Sugarmon Jr; children: 4. **Educ:** Wellesley Col, BA, 1956; Johns Hopkins Univ, MA, 1960, PhD, romance lang, 1967. **Career:** Educator (retired); Owen Col, instr, 1960-66; Memphis State Univ, assoc prof span, 1966-70; Howard Univ, assoc prof span, 1970-74, prof, chmn dept, 1974-76; LeMoyne-Owen Col, prof, Romance Lang, prof span, dir du bois prog, 1979-88; George Mason Univ, prof span, 1989; Univ Md, dir grad studies, emer prof, 1999. **Orgs:** Coll Lang Asn; bd dir, MSU CtrRsch Women; Fedn State Humanities Couns; ed bd, Sage & Afro-Hisp Rev; life mem, Nat Asn Advan Colored People; chmn, exec bd mem, TN Humanities Coun, 1981-87; chmn, co founder, Memphis Black Writers Workshop; Memphis Arts Coun adv comt. **Honors/Awds:** Phi Beta Kappa, 1956; Johns Hopkins Fellowship, 1965; editor Blacks in Hispanic Literature Kennikat Pr, 1977; Outstanding Faculty Mem of the Year, Le Moyne-Owen Col, 1982. **Special Achievements:** First African American faculty member of Memphis State University, 1966; Author: Daughters of the Diaspora: Editor Blacks in Hispanic Literature Kennikat Pr, 1977; Afra-Hispanic Writers; Erotique Noire/Black Erotica; Homespun Images: An Anthology of Black Memphis Writers & Artists, 1988; Editor: The Memphis Diary of Ida B Wells, Beacon Press, 1994; Articles in CLAJ, Journal of Negro History, Black World Negro History Bulletin, Revista Inter americana, Caribbean Quart; Sage Afro-Hispanic Review; ed bd mem, Afro-Hisp Rev. **Home Addr:** 585 S Greer Suite 703, Memphis, TN 38111, **Home Phone:** (901)323-8870.

**DEE, MERRI (MARY DORHAM)**
Talk show host, radio broadcaster. **Personal:** Born Oct 30, 1936, Chicago, IL; daughter of John Blouin (deceased) and Agnes Blouin (deceased); children: Toya Dorham. **Educ:** St Xavier Univ, bus admin, 1950; Columbia Col, broadcasting & jour, 1960; Lewis Univ, PhD, 2000. **Career:** IBM; WBEE Radio, Harvey, Ill, radio host, 1966-68; WCIU TV, Channel 26, Chicago, Ill, tv show host, 1968; WSDM-FM, Chicago, Ill, Merri Dee Show, host, 1968-69; WSNS, Channel 44, Chicago, Ill, host, Merri Dee Show, 1969-71; WGN-TV, Chicago, Ill, air personality, anchor, 1972-84, reporter, dir community rels, mgr C's Charities, 1984-2008; Hillman's Foods, consumer adv, 1974-75; Kraft Foods, nutrit spokesperson, 1975-76 & 1979-80; WGN Broadcasting, newscaster & announcer. **Orgs:** Dir & co-founder, Athletes Better Educ; host, United Negro Col Fund; Telethon Chicago; Am Fedn TV & Radio Announcers; Ronald McDonald House Charities; Assoc Col Ill; Adoptions Unlimited; Jr Achievement; Gateway Charitable Found; Nat Tree Trust Found; Chinese Am Serv League; Ill Atty Gen's Violent Crime Victims Comn; States Atty's Adv Coun violence; Nat Col Summit; pres, leadership coun, Am Asn Retired Persons. **Honors/Awds:** Muscular Dystrophy Fundraising Trophy; National Association of Media Women Award; National Association of Black Accountants Recognition Award; Woman of the Year, Chicago Church Women's Fedn; Frederick D. Patterson Award, United Negro Col Fund, 1990; Little City Foundation Award, 1995; President's Award, Nat Asn Negro Bus & Prof Women's Club, 1995; Bethany Christian Service Award, 1995; Outstanding Media Person, AT&T; Outstanding Community Role Model, Kellogg's Corp; National Voice Award; Adoption Spokesperson Award, YMCA Metro Chicago; Outstanding Leadership Award; Woman of the Year, Today's Chicago Woman News; Mercedes Mentor Award, Chicago Mag; History Maker Award, Nat Hist Makers Asn; Silver Circle Award, Acad of TV Arts & Sci, 2001; Lifetime Achievement Award, Univ of Ill, Ctr on Women & Gender, 2003; Adoption Excellence Award, US Dept Health & Human Serv, 2004. **Special Achievements:** First African-American women to anchor the news in the Windy City. **Business Addr:** Director, Manager, WGN-TV Children's Charities, 2501 W Bradley Pl, Chicago, IL 60618-4718, **Business Phone:** (773)528-2311.

**DEE, RUBY. See Obituaries Section.**

**DEESE, DERRICK LYNN, SR.**
Radio host, football player. **Personal:** Born May 17, 1970, Culver City, CA; married Felicia; children: 4. **Educ:** El Camino Col, Torrance, CA; Univ Southern Calif. **Career:** Football player (retired), radio host; San Francisco 49ers, 1992-93, 1996, right guard, 1994, 1999, tackle, 1995, left tackle, 1997-98, 2000-03, right tackle, 1998-99; Tampa Bay Buccaneers, left tackle, 2004-05; Fox Sports Radio, nat radio host, 2004-. **Honors/Awds:** Champion, Super Bowl, XXIX. **Special Achievements:** Film: Super Bowl XXIX, 1995. **Business Addr:** National Radio Host, FOX Sports Radio, 10201 W Pico Blvd, Los Angeles, CA 90064, **Business Phone:** (310)369-6000.

**DEESE, GLENDA F.**
Government official. **Personal:** Born Selma, AL; children: 3. **Educ:** Concordia Col, AA, bus mgt, 2003. **Career:** Ala Dept Pub Safety, state trooper, 1980, trooper, 1981, asst dir, 2003; State Chief Driver License Examiner, capt, 1997, Admin Div, asst dir, 2003-06, major, 2006-; Safety Educ & Narcotics Unit; Ala Criminal Justice Training Ctr, corporal, 1988, asst basic training coordr, 1988, sgt, asst comdr, spec proj coordr, 2006-, opers & personnel; Hwy Patrol Div; George Wallace Community Col, consult; Deese & Assocs LLC, sole owner, currently. **Orgs:** Glenda Davis Deese Found; Mobile Youth Leadership Acad. **Home Addr:** , AL. **Business Addr:** Special Projects Coordinator, Major, Alabama Criminal Justice Training Center, Craig Field, Selma, AL 36701, **Business Phone:** (205)242-4263.

**DEESE, MANUEL**
Government official. **Personal:** Born Nov 8, 1941, Toomsboro, GA; married Jean Matthews; children: Eric & Byron. **Educ:** Morgan State Univ, BA, polit sci; Am Univ Sch Govt & Pub Admin, MPA. **Career:** Nat League Cities DC, policy analyst, 1969-71; City Alexandria, asst to city mgr, 1971-74; City Richmond, city mgr, asst city mgr opers, asst city mgr admin, 1974-77, asst city mgr opers, 1977-79, city mgr, 1979; Deese, Hastings & Miller, managing partner, 1983-. **Orgs:** Pres, Nat Forum Black Pub Admr, 1983-85; gov bd, Am Asn Pub Admin; bd dir, Richmond Regional Criminal Justice Training Ctr; bd, Intl City Mgt Asn; exec vpres, Blue Cross & Blue Shield Va; fel & bd mem, Nat Acad Pub Admin, 1983-; Kappa Alpha Psi. **Special Achievements:**

First black to be manager in City of Richmond. **Home Addr:** 6542 W Junaluska Rd, Richmond, VA 23225. **Business Addr:** Managing Partner, Deese, Hastings, & Miller, 700 E Main St Suite 1600, Richmond, VA 23219, **Business Phone:** (804)649-1121.

### DEESE, WILLIE A.

President (organization), executive, association executive. **Personal:** Born Jan 1, 1956; married Carol. **Educ:** NC Agr & Tech State Univ, BA, bus admin, 1977; Western New Eng Col, MBA, 1983. **Career:** Digital Equip Corp, 1976-92, site mgr; SmithKline Beecham Pharmaceut Philadelphia, vpres & dir, purchasing; Kaiser Permanente, vpres purchasing, 1996-97, sr vpres & dir purchasing, 1997; GlaxoSmith-Kline Pharmaceut PLC, sr vpres global procurement & logistics, 1992-2003; Merck, Mfg Div, exec vpres & pres, 2004-05, Global Procurement, sr vpres, 2005-08. **Orgs:** Dir, Dentsply Int Inc. **Honors/Awds:** "Black Enterprise," The 100 Most Powerful Executives in Corporate America, 2010; Beta Gamma Sigma National Business Achievement Award, 2011; Hon doctorate degree, Humanities, Nc A&T State Univ, 2011. **Business Addr:** Director, Dentsply Sirona International Inc, 221 W Philadelphia St, York, PA 17401, **Business Phone:** (800)877-0020.

### DEFRANTZ, DR. ANITA L.

Lawyer, association executive. **Personal:** Born Oct 4, 1952, Philadelphia, PA; daughter of Robert D (deceased) and Anita P. **Educ:** Conn Col, BA, polit philos, 1974; Univ Pa Sch Law, LLB, 1977. **Career:** US Women's Rowing Team, Olympics, Montreal, 1975-80, team capt, 1976; Juv Law Ct Philadelphia, atty, 1977-79; World Rowing Championships, 1978; Princeton Univ, adminr, 1979-81; Corp Enterprise Develop, coun, 1980-81; Los Angeles Olympic Organizing Comt, vpres, 1981-85; Staff Person, 1985-87; Amateur Athletic Found, pres, 1987-, dir, 1990-; OBN Holdings Inc, dir, 2003-; Western Asset Income Fund, dir, mem audit comt, 1998-; Western Asset Premier Bond Fund, trustee, mem audit comt, 2002-. **Orgs:** Exec bd, US Olympic Comt, 1977-, bd dir, 1996-; Int Olympic Comt, 1986-, exec bd, 1992-2001, vpres, 1997-2011; pres, LA84 Found Bd Dirs, 1987-2015; vpres, Women's World Cup, 1989; vpres World Rowing Fedn (FISA), 1993-2013; pres, Kids Sports, 1994-2012, bd mem; vpres, Int Rowing Fed, 1997-; dir, Women's FIFA World Cup, Los Angeles, 1999; chmn, Women & Sport Working Group; trustee, Conn Col; Int Comt Fair Play; Acad Sports; bd dir, Salt Lake City Olympic, Organizing Comt; C NOW, Fed Int Socs d'Aviron; bd mem, Vesper Rowing Club; bd mem, US Rowing Asn; trustee, Women's Sports Found; Southern Calif Olympian Soc; bd dir, Los Angeles Sports Coun; Alliance Women Coaches Adv Bd; hon chair, Am Rows; US Rowing Task Force Access, Affordability & Diversity. **Honors/Awds:** Olympic Torch Award, US Olympic Comt, 1988; honourable Doctor of Laws, Univ Rhode Island, 1989; Hall of Fame inductee, Conn Col, 1989; Major Taylor Award, 1989; Metrop Los Angeles YMCA, Martin Luther King Jr Brotherhood Award, 1990; Hon Award, Natl Asn of Women Collegiate Athletic Adminr, 1991; Jack Kelly Award, US Rowing's Bd Dirs, 1991; International Scholar-Athlete Hall of Fame, 1991; Doctor of Philanthropy Degree, Pepperdine Univ, 1992; Award of Excellence, Sports Lawyers Asn, 1992; Turner Broadcasting Trumpet Award, 1993; Billie Jean King, Contribution Award, 1996; Doctor of Laws, Mills Col, 1998; Doctor of Laws, Mount Holyoke Col, 1998; Abby J. Leibman Pursuit of Justice Award, Calif Women's Law Centre, 2008; Collegiate Rowing Coaches Association Hall of FameMedal of Hon, Int Softball Fed; Black Women of Achievement Award, Nat Asn Adv Colored People Legal Defense & Educ Fund; Award for Sports, Essence Mag; Silver Achievement Award for Pub Serv, Los Angeles YWCA; Numerous other awards. **Special Achievements:** Rowing Awards: Bronze Medal, Olympic Games, 1976; Silver Medal, World Championships, 1978; Six National Championships; Olympic Order Bronze Medal, 1980; One of Southern California's "Rising Stars", Los Angeles Times Mag, 1988; One of the 100 Most Powerful People in Sports, The Sporting News, 1991-97; First American woman and first African American to serve as vice president of the International Olympic Committee, 1997; 101 Most Influential Minorities in Sports, Sports Illustrated, 2003; First female president of the IOC in 2002; One of America's 100 Most Important Women, Ladies Home J. **Business Addr:** President, Director, Amateur Athletic Foundation, 2141 W Adams Blvd, Los Angeles, CA 90018, **Business Phone:** (323)730-4600.

### DEGENESTE, HENRY IRVING (HANK DEGENESTE)

Police officer, vice president (organization). **Personal:** Born Aug 16, 1940, Newark, NJ; son of William Henry and Olive Pansy Lopes; children: Michelle, Rene & Henry Jr. **Educ:** Fairleigh Dickinson Univ, attended 1962; Rutgers Univ, cert criminal justice planning & res, 1975; Fed Bur Invest, cert exec mgt, 1976; Columbia Univ, cert exec mgt criminal justice syst, 1976; Adelphi Univ, BA, bus admin, 1976; John Jay Col Criminal Justice, MPA. **Career:** Edmond Assocs, draftsman, 1962-65; Newark Pub Schs, sch teacher, 1962-65; US Postal Serv, staff, 1965-67; Port Authority NY & NJ, Law Enforcement, police officer, 1967-74, police sgt, 1974-76, police lt, 1976-78, police capt, 1978-81, police supt, 1981-88, dir pub safety & supt police, 1988-90; Prudential Securities, sr vpres & dir corp security & treas, 1990-2001; Prudential Financial, vpres dir global security, 1990-2005; Securtity Dirs Adv Group, managing partner, 2005-13; iJET Int, consult & mem security intelligence adv bd, 2005-; HDG Consult Inc, pres, 2013-. **Orgs:** Pres, Nat Orgn Black Law Enforcement Execs, 1982-83; bd mem, treas, YMCA Newark & Greater Essex County Nj, 1984-90; pres, Hudson County, NJ Chief Police, 1987-88; bd mem, treas, Urban League Hudson County Inc, 1987-2004; chmn, Tri-State Radio Planning Comt, 1988-90; comnr-treas bd, Comn Accreditation Law Enforcement Agencies, 1990-2000; bd mem, Offender Aid & Restoration Essex County Nj, 2001-; pres, Am Acad Prof Law Enforcement, 1989-91; NJ Coun Corrections, 1990; bd mem, NY & NJ Cargo Security Coun; bd mem, NJ Spec Olympics; bd mem, Mott Hall Sch Math, Sci & Tech Gifted & Talented Stud; bd mem, Police Exec Res Forum; Am Soc Pub Admin; Am Mgt Asn; Criminal Justice Educrs NY; Am Soc Indust Sec; Corp Justice & Opportunities Inc, 2011-; bd chair, Greater Ocala Community Develop Corp, 2013-; bd mem, Pub Policy Inst Marion County Fla, 2014-; bd mem, Police Fondation, 2014-; bd mem, Sonny Archer Law Enforcement Scholar Found, Inc, 2016-. **Honors/Awds:** New Jersey Pride Award, 1986; Three Police Commendation Medals; Meritorious Police Duty Medal; Port Authority Executive Director's UnitCitations; Whitney M Young Jr Award, Nat Urban League, 1986; Peace Medal UN, Black Achievers Industry Award, Harlem YMCA; United Nations Peace Medal. **Special Achievements:** Author, EMS and the Police Response to Terrorism, The Police Chief, May 1987; Urban Transit Center: Where Crime and the Homeless Meet, Law Enforcement News, 1987; Policing Transportation Facilities, Charles CThomas, Publisher, 1994. **Home Addr:** 40 Conger St, Bloomfield, NJ 07003, **Home Phone:** (201)748-2373. **Business Addr:** Consultant, Member, iJET International, 910F Bestgate Rd, Annapolis, MD 21401, **Business Phone:** (410)573-3860.

### DEGRAFFENREIDT, JAMES HENRY, JR.

Executive, lawyer, chairperson. **Personal:** Born May 8, 1953, Brooklyn, NY; married Mychelle Farmer; children: 4. **Educ:** Yale Col, BA, Am studies, 1974; Columbia Univ, Columbia Law Sch, JD, 1978; Columbia Bus Sch, MBA, 1978. **Career:** Northwood Baseball League, coach; McKenna, Wilkinson & Kittner, assoc; Hart, Carroll & Chavers, assoc; Wash Gas Light Holdings Inc, sr managing atty, 1986-91, sr vpres rates & regulatory affairs, 1991-94, pres, 2000-01, chief exec officer, 2001-09; Wash Gas Light Co, pres & chief operating officer, 1994-98, chmn & chief exec officer, 1998-2000, bd dir, 2000-09; Wash Gas Resources Corp, chief exec officer; Md, asst people's coun. **Orgs:** Dir, Wash Gas Light Co, 1994-2009; bd mem, Harbor Bankshares Corp, 1996-; bd mem, chmn, WGL Holdings Inc, dir, 2000-09; bd dir, Greater Wash Bd Trade; Bush-Cheney, 2004; bd dir, co-chair, Alliance to Save Energy, 2005-06; chmn & bd dir, Am Gas Asn, 2007-; dir, Vectren Corp, 2010-; bd mem, lead dir, Mass Mutual Financial Group; coach, St Matthews Athletic Asn; vpres & trustee, Walters Art Mus; trustee, Md Sci Ctr; Alliance Save Energy; mem bd, MedStar Health; Pete Coors Senate; Obama Am; bd trustee, Md Sci Ctr; Hillary Clinton Pres; John Kerry Pres; lead dir, mem exec comt, mem corp governance comt & mem human resources comt, Mass Mutual Life Ins Co;chmn, Md State Bd Educ. **Honors/Awds:** "Black Enterprise", The 100 Most Powerful Executives in Corporate America, 2010. **Business Addr:** Chairman, Chief Executive Officer, WGL Holdings Inc, 101 Constitution Ave NW, Washington, DC 20001, **Business Phone:** (703)750-2000.

### DEHART, HENRY R.

Engineer. **Personal:** Born Nov 11, 1931, Staten Island, NY; married Panzy Hawk; children: Henry & Linda. **Educ:** Polytech Inst NY, BCE, 1958. **Career:** Engineer (retired); NY City Dept Traffic, dir hwy design, 1992. **Orgs:** Past pres, Staten Island Br Nat Asn Advan Colored People, 1965; past comdr, Am Legion, 1966; Lic prof engr, NY; past warden, past dir, SS; lic lay reader, St Gabriels PE Church; acolyte master, St Gabriels Church. **Honors/Awds:** Friend of Howard Adward NY Club, Howard Univ Alumni, 1975; Past President Award, Staten Island Br, Nat Asn Advan Colored People, 1986; Bishop Cross Long Island Diocese, 1987; Meritorious Award for Community Service, 1987. **Home Addr:** 11006 214th St, Queens Village, NY 11429-1917, **Home Phone:** (212)749-0855.

### DEHART, DR. PANZY H.

Social worker. **Personal:** Born May 18, 1934, Cleveland County, NC; daughter of Henry Kilgore and Sallie Maude Hawk Owens; married Henry Ross; children: Henry Jr & Linda. **Educ:** Howard Univ, BA, 1956, MSW, 1958; George Mercer Sch Theol, Cert Christian Theol, 1997; NYU Grad Sch Social Work, PhD, 1999. **Career:** Social worker (retired); DC Dept Welfare, child welfare social worker, 1958-61; Vets Admin, clin social worker, 1961-65; Inwood House, supvr, 1966-68, 1970-72; NY City Dept Health, consult, 1968-70; NY Univ Med Ctr, rehab social worker, 1976-96. **Orgs:** Pres, Howard Univ Alumni Club, New York, 1970-74; bd dir, Parent Prep Inc, 1970-75; Queens Chap Jack & Jill Am Inc, 1973-87; dir, Jack & Jill Comput Assisted Lab, 1985-87; Concerned Citizens S Queens, 1987; Partnership Homeless, 1991-; Psychoanal Res Soc Sect VI, Am Psychol Asn, 1992-99; bd dir, Episcopal Charities Long Island Inc, 1996-02; St Gabriel's Episcopal Church, Hollis, Queens. **Honors/Awds:** Serv Award, Howard Univ Alumni Club, 1972; Nat Achievement Award, Lambda Kappa Mu Sorority, 1974; Serv Award, Jack & Jill Am Inc, Queens Chap, 1986. **Home Addr:** 11006 214th St, Queens Village, NY 11429-1917, **Home Phone:** (718)479-8315.

### DEHERE, LENNOX DOMINIQUE. See DEHERE, TERRY.

### DEHERE, TERRY (LENNOX DOMINIQUE DEHERE)

Government official, executive, basketball player. **Personal:** Born Sep 12, 1971, New York, NY. **Educ:** Seton Hall Univ, attended 1993. **Career:** Basketball player (retired); politician, restauranteur; Los Angeles Clippers, pt guard, 1993-97; Sacramento Kings, pt guard, 1997-99; Vancouver Grizzlies, shooting guard, 1999; N Charleston Lowgators, 2001-02; Jersey City Munic, at-large coun, 2001; Sanai's at Newkirk-Summit House, owner, currently. **Orgs:** Chmn, Jersey City Community Housing Corp; Jersey City Bd Ed, 2007-, vpres, 2009-10. **Honors/Awds:** Big East Men's Basketball Player of the Year, 1993; Conf Tournament MVP. **Business Addr:** Owner, Sanai's Restaurant, 510 Summit Ave, Jersey City, NJ 07306, **Business Phone:** (201)795-9393.

### DEION, NEON. See SANDERS, DEION LUWYNN.

### DEJESUS, EDWARD

Founder (originator). **Educ:** Fordham Univ, BA, polit sci, 1986; New Sch Social Res, MS, urban policy; Rutgers Univ, Ctr Strategic Urban Community Leadership Prog, MS, urban policy, 1993. **Career:** Ft Wash Mens, instnl aide, 1984-85; Harlems Mens, case mgr, 1985-91; Career Advan Prog, dir, 1987-91; CETE, dir, 1991-94; Higher Educ Fund, advan prog, 1987-91; Alianza Dominicana, Ctr Employ Training & Educ, dir, 1991-94; Phipps Community Develop Corp, dir youth fair chance, 1994-95; Nat Youth Employ Coalition, dir, 1995-99; US Dept Labor, consult, 1997-99; Youth Develop & Res Fund, dir, 1999-2010, founder & pres, 1999-2011; WK Kellogg Found, nat fel; Edward DeJesus Seminars & Consult, consult, 2010-13; STRIVE-DC, exec dir, 2013-14; Youth Advocate Progs Inc, Workforce Develop Progs & Policy, nat dir, 2014-. **Orgs:** Vice chair, Nat Youth Employ Coalition, 1995-99; Sar Levitan Ctr Youth Policies, John Hopkins Univ; Youth Build Transformation Acad; Nat Urban League; Rainbow Push Coalition; Calif Workforce Asn; New York Asn Training & Employ Professionals; Kappa Alpha Psi. **Honors/Awds:** Eli and May Rudin Community Service Award, 1993; One of the top 40 under 40 in the Wash Metrop Area, 2000; October 12th Ed DeJesus Day, named in honor, 2003. **Business Addr:** National Director, Youth Advocate Programs Inc, 2007 N 3rd St, Harrisburg, PA 17102, **Business Phone:** (717)232-7580.

### DEJOIE, CAROLYN BARNES MILANES

Educator, counselor, psychotherapist. **Personal:** Born New Orleans, LA; daughter of Edward Franklin Barnes and Alice Milanes Barnes; children: Deirdre Jeanelle, Prudhomme III & Duan Kendall. **Educ:** Xavier Univ La, BA; Nat Univ Mex, MA, 1962; Univ Wis, MSW, 1970; Union Grad Sch, PhD, 1976. **Career:** Wis cert marriage & family therapist, clin social worker; Southern Univ, instr, 1962-63; Va State Col, asst prof, 1963-66; Univ Wis Ext, admin specialist, 1967-68, asst pres, 1970-73, prof continuing educ & prof develop, 1973-92, prof emer currently; Human Rels Coun Serv, owner, dir, 1980-; psychotherapist Pvt Pract, 1980-; Sun & Shadows Publ Co, owner, 1987-; Lectura, 1994-; Itinerant Journalistic reporter, 1996-; Univ Havana, Socio-Econ Aspects Cuban Life, investr, 1996-97; Secular Humanists, Madison, Wis, founder, dir; Wis Bd Bar Examiners, rep, currently. **Orgs:** Foreign lang consult, Travenol de Mex Am Brit Cowdray Hosp Mex, 1959-62; exec dir, Centro Hispano-Americano Madison, 1978-79; ed adv bd mem, Jour Negro Educ, 1985-; exec bd, Nat Asn Advan Colored People, Madison WI, 1987-; exec bd mem, Negro Educ Rev, 1988-; vpres, Nat Asn Media Women, 1989-90; Univ League, 1995-; crespar, Johns Hopkins Univ, 1996-. **Home Addr:** 5322 Fairway Dr, Madison, WI 53711, **Home Phone:** (608)274-2152. **Business Addr:** Professor Emerita, University of Wisconsin Extension, 212 River Dr Suite 3, Wausau, WI 54403, **Business Phone:** (715)261-1246.

### DEJOIE, MICHAEL C.

Manager, executive. **Personal:** Born Apr 25, 1947, New Orleans, LA; son of Constant C Jr and Julia B. **Educ:** Grinnell Col, AB, 1968; Columbia Univ, Grad Sch Bus, MBA, 1977. **Career:** WWL-TV, consumer affairs reporter, 1968-70; Loyola Inst Polit, fel, 1970; CBS News, assoc producer, ed, 1970-78; AT&T Long Lines, mgr, int & pub serv advert, 1978-79, AT&T Long Lines AT&T Communs, mgr, bus advert, 1979-84, AT&T Communs, Southern Region Media Ctr, mgr, 1984-85; MCD Communs Consults Inc, owner, consult, 1986-; Southern Christian Leadership CNF, dir communs, 1991-94; WIGO-TV, "What's Going On? With Joseph Lowery, producer, 1992-94; Am Asn Retired Persons, Communs rep, currently. **Orgs:** Am Fed TV & Radio Artists, 1968-70; Shop Steward, Writers Guild Am E, 1970-78; Atlanta Asn Black Journalists, 1987, 1992-; Int Asn Bus Communicators, 1987-; bd mem, Black Pub Rels SOC Atlanta, 1988-90; bd mem, Coord Coun Atlanta Pub Rels Orgs, 1989. **Honors/Awds:** Various advertising awards, 1978-84; Silver Quill for Best Video Prod, IABC, Operator, 1985; Best Ed, Asn Black Journalist, 1994; Outstanding Young American. **Home Addr:** 11 Wiley, Cape May Court House, NJ 08210, **Home Phone:** (504)944-8383. **Business Addr:** Communications Representative, American Association of Retired Persons, 999 Peachtree St NE Suite 1100, Atlanta, GA 30309, **Business Phone:** (404)870-3780.

### DEJONGH, MONIQUE EVADNE JELLERETTE

Writer, graphic artist. **Personal:** Born Feb 26, 1959, Los Angeles, CA; daughter of Carole and Alphonso; married Robert Charles Jr; children: Dylan & Jordan. **Educ:** Mary Louis Acad, HS Dipl, 1977; Boston Univ, Sch Arts, assoc degree fine arts, 1984. **Career:** McGovern & Pivoda, Graphic Design Paste-up Artist, 1985-86; Times Sq Studios, Chyron Operator, 1987-90; Essence Mag, asst ed; NY Times Sunday Mag, asst art dir, 1986-87; Genigraphics Inc, comput graphic artist, 1987; Thing of Beauty Prod, 1987-88; Times Sq Studios, art dir, 1987-91; Geraldo, chyron operator, 1988-90; MTV Raps, comput graphic designer, 1989-90; Brownstone Underground, founder & art dir, 1990-; MTV Graphics, paintbox electronic designer, 1993-94; Doubleday Random House Publishers, auth, 1995-96; Essence Mag, asst ed, 2000-01; Evadne Earthworx Inc, Freelance Writer, 2002-. Book: How To Marry A Black Man. **Orgs:** Jack & Jill Am, Queens Chap, NY. **Special Achievements:** Whitney Houston & Disney, Touchstone, are making movie version of book, "How To Marry A Black Man". **Home Addr:** 19908 100th Ave, Hollis, NY 11423, **Home Phone:** (718)464-0417. **Business Addr:** Freelance Writer, Evadne Earthworx Inc.

### DELANEY, DALLAS

Executive, manager. **Personal:** son of Dallas Sr and Rosie; married Marcia; children: Brandon & Dallas Jr. **Educ:** Univ Kans, EE, AT&T Technologies, 1985. **Career:** Hallmark Cards, proj leader; AT&T; Windy City, chem & agr prods controls engr; Abbott Pk Finishing Goods Mfg, Global Pharma Opers, opers mgr, currently; Abbott Int Inc, mgr, New Prod Launch/Sourcing Group. **Home Addr:** 222 E Lincoln Ave, Libertyville, IL 60048, **Home Phone:** (847)918-8191. **Business Addr:** Operations Manager, Abbott Laboratories Co, 100 Abbott Pk Rd, Abbott Park, IL 60064-3500, **Business Phone:** (847)937-6100.

### DELANEY, DUANE B.

Government official. **Personal:** Born Washington, DC. **Educ:** Howard Univ, BA, sociol, 1977; Am Univ, MA, judicial admin, 1979; Georgetown Univ Law Ctr, JD, 1989. **Career:** Super Ct DC, spec asst clerk ct, 1989-91, dep clerk ct, 1991, dir civil div, 1991-93; actg dir social serv div, 1993-94, clerk, 1994-. **Orgs:** DC Bar Asn; bd dir, Nat Asn Ct Mgt; bd dir, Justice Mgt Inst; Phi Beta Kappa; Bar Supreme Ct; bd dir, Nat Asn Credit Mgt, 1999-2002; Urban Ct Managers Network, currently. **Business Addr:** Clerk of Court, Superior Court of the District of Columbia, Moultrie Courthouse, Washington, DC 20001, **Business Phone:** (202)879-1400.

### DELANEY, JOHN PAUL

Journalist. **Personal:** Born Jan 13, 1933, Montgomery, AL; married Anita Jackson; children: John Paul III & David Allen. **Educ:** Ohio

State Univ, BA, jour, 1958. **Career:** Atlanta Daily World, 1959-61; Atlanta Munic Ct, probation officer, 1961-63; Dayton Daily News, OH, 1963-67; Wash Star, reporter, 1967-69; NY Times, corresp, Wash Bur, 1969-74, Chicago bur, 1974-77, corresp, asst nat ed, 1977-80, dep nat ed, 1980-86, chief Madrid bur, 1987-89, sr ed; Univ Ala, chmn, jour dept, currently. **Orgs:** Publ Comn, Atlanta Br, Nat Asn Advan Colored People, 1961-63; Robert F Kennedy Journ Awards Comt, 1973-75, chmn, 1975; founding mem, Nat Asn Black Journalists; bd chmn. **Honors/Awds:** Special Scholarship, Ohio State Univ, 1957; First Place, Baltimore-Washington Newspaper Guild, 1968; Lifetime Achievement Award, New York Asn Black Journalists, 1992. **Business Addr:** Chairman, University of Alabama, PO Box 870172, Tuscaloosa, AL 35487-0172, **Business Phone:** (205)348-7155.

## DELANEY, WILLIAM F.
Government official. **Personal:** Born Mar 23, 1947, Washington, DC; children: Damon. **Educ:** Cath Univ Am; Atlanta Univ. **Career:** Women's Bur, spec asst dir; White House Pres Speech writing Off; Carter Campaign Pres, nat dir vol; City Atlanta Off Consumer Affairs, counr; Voter Educ Proj Atlanta, res asst; US Dept Labor, staff. **Orgs:** Wash Women's Forum, 1977; Metro Dem Women's Club, 1977; Nat Hook-up Black Women Inc, 1977. **Home Addr:** 6109 4th St NW, Washington, DC 20011-1315, **Home Phone:** (202)291-3440. **Business Addr:** Staff, US Department of Labor, Washington, DC 20210.

## DELANEY, WILMA I.
Executive, vice president (organization). **Educ:** Prairie View A&M Univ, BS. **Career:** Dow's Midland, Mich, Global Environ Technol Ctr, mgr; Dow N Am, Environ Qual, dir; Dow's pub policy rel; US Geog Leadership Team; Pub Affairs Leadership team; Dow Chem Co, environ & regulatory affairs, vpres; Dow Chem Co, Fed & State Govt Affairs, vpres, 2002; Mickey Leland Natl Urban Air Toxic Res Ctr, bd dir, currently; One World Holdings Inc, bd dir, currently. **Orgs:** EPA's Nat Adv Coun Environ Policy & Technol. **Business Addr:** Board of Directors, The Mickey Leland National Urban Air Toxics Research Center, 7000 Fannin St Suite 700, Houston, TX 77030, **Business Phone:** (713)500-3450.

## DELANY, SAMUEL RAY, JR. (K LESLIE STEINER)
Educator, writer. **Personal:** Born Apr 1, 1942, New York, NY; son of Samuel Ray and Margaret Cary Boyd; married Marilyn Hacker; children: Iva Alyxander Hacker-Delany. **Educ:** City Col NY, 1961. **Career:** Educator, writer, ed, prof. Novels: The Jewels of Aptor, 1962; Out of the Dead City, 1963; The Towers of Toron, 1964; City of aThousand Suns, 1965; The Ballad of Beta-2, 1965; Babel-17, 1966; EmpireStar, 1966; The Einstein Intersection, 1967; Nova, 1968; The Fall of the Towers, 1970; Dhalgren, 1975; Triton, 1976; The Jewel-Hinged Jaw, 1977;The Am Shore, 1978; Stars in My Pocket like Grains of Sand, 1984; Starboard Wine, 1984; Straits of Messina, 1989; The Jewels of Aptor, Three Tales, 1993; They Fly at Ciron, 1993; The Mad Man, 1994; Stars in My Pocket Like Grains of Sand, 1994; Hogg, 1995; LongerViews, 1996; The Motion of Light in Water, 1998; Shorter Views, 1999; Phallos, 2004; About Writing, 2005; Dark Reflections, 2007; Through the Valley of the Nest of Spiders, 2012; Books: Times Square Red, Times Square Blue, 1999. series: "Wonder Woman comic series", 1972; Univ Mass, prof comparative lit, 1988-99; Temple Univ, Col Lib Arts, Pa, prof eng, 2001-; Univ Buffalo, eng prof. **Home Addr:** 184 West 82nd St, New York, NY 10024, **Home Phone:** (212)580-1943. **Business Addr:** Professor, Temple University, Anderson Hall 10th Fl, Philadelphia, PA 19122-6090, **Business Phone:** (215)204-7344.

## DELAUDER, DR. WILLIAM B.
College president, educator, army officer. **Personal:** married Vermell Faulk; children: William Jr & Ellen. **Educ:** Morgan State Univ, BS, chem, 1959; Wayne State Univ, PhD, phys chem, 1968. **Career:** NC Agr & Tech State Univ, Col Arts & Sci, prof chem & chair, dean, 1976-87; Del State Univ, Dover, pres, 1987-2003; Comn Abraham Lincoln Study Abroad Fel Prog, exec dir, 2004-07; William B DeLauder Consult, Consult, 2004-. **Orgs:** Exec dir, Comn Abraham Lincoln Study Abroad Fel Prog, Partnership Cut Hunger & Poverty Africa, 2004; bd mem, Int Food & Agr Develop; Adv Comt Educ & Human Resources Dirate NSF; sr coun, Del State Chamber Com; bd dir, United Way Del; chair, NASULGC Task ForceInt Educ; NC Bd Sci & Technol; MARC Rev Comt; Nat Adv Coun; Nat Inst Gen Med Sci NIH; bd mem, Agr Nat Res Coun; bd dir, Nat Asn State Univs &Land-Grant Cols; bd dir, Coun Higher Educ Accreditation; Am Farmland Trust; Grand Opera House. **Honors/Awds:** Thurgood Marshall Award, 1994; Educational Leadership Award of the Thurgood Marshall Scholarship Fund, 1999; Order of the First State Award, Ruth Ann Minner, 2002; Wesley Medal, Wesley Col, 2005; hon degree, Kent State Univ; hon degree, Univ Del. **Business Addr:** President Emeritus, Delaware State University, 1200 N DuPont Hwy, Dover, DE 19901, **Business Phone:** (302)857-6060.

## DELCO, DR. EXALTON ALFONSO, JR.
Educator. **Personal:** Born Sep 4, 1929, Houston, TX; son of Exalton and Pauline Broussard; married Wilhelmina R; children: Deborah, Exalton III, Loretta & Cheryl. **Educ:** Fisk Univ, BA, 1949; Univ Mich, MS, 1950; Univ Tex, PhD, zool, 1962. **Career:** Educator (retired); Tes Southern Univ, instr, 1950-55, asst prof, 1957-60, res asst, 1958-62; Houston-Tillotson Col, assoc prof, 1963-66; Prairie View A & M Col, guest prof, 1964; Houston-Tillotson Col, Dept biol, head & prof biol, 1966-68, vpres acad affairs, 1967-85; Austin County Col, vpres acad affairs, 1985-93; Univ Tex-Austin, spec asst, off pres, 1995-96. **Orgs:** Vpres, exec secy & mem coun, Beta Kappa Chi Sci Hon Soc, 1962-68; dist comnr, Eagle Dist Boy Scouts Am, 1967-68; Austin Housing Auth Comn, 1967-69; Travis Co Grand Jury Assoc, Community Coun Austin & Travis Co, 1968-70, pres, 1982-85; pres, St Vincent de Paul Soc Holy Cross Church, 1968; Family Prac Residency Adv Comn Tex, 1968-84; vpres & pres, Phi Delta Kappa, 1969-72; Am Fisheries Soc; Am Soc & Ichthyologists & Herpetologists; Am Soc Limnol & Oceanog; Soc Sigma Xi; NY Acad Sci; Tex Acad Sci; Fel AAAS; Am Inst Biol Sci. **Honors/Awds:** Stoye Prize, Am Soc Ichthyologists & Herpetologists, 1960; Danforth Assoc Huston-Tillotson Col Campus, 1966; Nominated Harbison Award, Danforth Found, 1966; Piper Prof, 1967; Nat Urban League Summer Fel, Allied Chem Co, 1969; Outstanding Educator of America. **Special Achievements:** Author of Numerous Books. **Home Addr:** 1805 Astor Pl, Austin, TX 78721-1308, **Home Phone:** (512)926-2424.

## DELCO, WILHELMINA R.
State government official, educator. **Personal:** Born Jul 16, 1929, Chicago, IL; daughter of William P Fitzgerald and Juanita Heath Watson; married Exalton A Jr; children: Deborah Diane Agbottah, Exalton A III, Loretta Elmirle Edelen & Cheryl Pauline. **Educ:** Fisk Univ, BA, sociol, 1950. **Career:** Government official (retired), educator; Prov Hosp, rec clerk; Ill Bell Tel, serv rep; Teachers St Asn, TX, clerk; St Tex House Reps, rep, speaker pro tempore, 1991-95; Univ Tex, adj prof, currently. **Orgs:** bd trustee, Austin Independent Sch Dist, 1968; secy, Austin Ind Sch Dist, 1972-74; deleg, Tex Cath Conf, 1972-; deleg, Tex Asn Sch Bds, 1973; mem bd trust, secy, Aus Community Col, 1973-74; chmn, Higher Educ Comt, Tex House Rep, 1979; founding mem, Austin Community Col Bd, 1979; secy, vice chmn, Citizens Adv Comt Juv Ct; City Austin Hum Rels Comt; vol soc worker, Travis Cty Welfare Dept; bd mem, Vol Bur, Key Trnr; Well-Child Conf, Austin League Women Voters; mem adv comt mem, Tex Employ Comt, Tex Comt Human & Publ Pol; chmn, leg adv coun, mem exec comt, Southern Reg Ed; mem steering comt, exec comt, Ed Comt, States; vice chmn, State-Fed Assembly Nat Conf State Legis; vice chmn, bd trustees, Ed Testing Serv; vice chmn, Nat Black Caucus State Legis; Comn Stand Southern Asn Cols & Schs; chmn & bd trustee, ETS; chmn assembly legis, Nat Conf State Legis; trustee, Southern Ed Found; Nat Hon Soc; chair, House Higher Educ Comt; leader, Parent Teacher Asn. **Honors/Awds:** Outstanding Woman Austin American Statesman, 1969; Liberty Bell Award, Austin Jr Bar Asn, 1969; Public School Service Award, Zeta Phi Beta, 1970; Public Service Merit Award, Omega Psi Phi, 1971; Appreciation Arthur DeWitty Award, 1971; Coronat Medal, St Edwards Univ, 1972; Service Award, Tex Congress Parents & Teachers, 1973; Appreciation Award Blanton School, 1973; Service Award, Sakarrah Temple, 1973; Service Citation, Optimist Club E Austin, 1973; Tex Women's Hall of Fame, 1986; building named for her, Prairie A&M Univ, 1996; Legends of Texas, 1999; Recieved various honorary degrees from St Edward Univ, Lee Col, Southwestern Univ, Houston-Tillotson Col & Wiley Col. **Special Achievements:** First woman and the second African American to hold the second highest position in the Texas House of Representatives until 1993; First African American elected to public office in Austin, Texas. **Home Addr:** 1805 Astor Pl, Austin, TX 78721-1308, **Home Phone:** (512)926-2424. **Business Addr:** Adjunct Professor, The University of Texas at Austin, Department Educational Administration, Austin, TX 78712, **Business Phone:** (512)471-7551.

## DELCY, LUDGET (DAPPER LOU)
Photographer, fashion consultant. **Personal:** Born Brooklyn, NY. **Career:** Jakob Schlaeper, intern; DapperLou.com, founder & blogger young men's fashion. **Honors/Awds:** Essence Magazine, Black Style Now: Forty Fab Fashion Bloggers, Listee. **Special Achievements:** Featured in "Vogue Italia" and "GQ". **Home Addr:** 416A Hancock St, Brooklyn, NY 11216, **Home Phone:** (718)288-2856.

## DELEON, JOSE CHESTARO
Baseball player. **Personal:** Born Dec 20, 1960, Rancho Viejo. **Career:** Baseball player (retired); Pittsburgh Pirates, pitcher, 1983-86; Chicago White Sox, pitcher, 1986-87, 1993-95; St Louis Cardinals, pitcher, 1988-92; Philadelphia Phillies, pitcher, 1992-93; Montreal Expos, pitcher, 1995. **Home Addr:** 216 Brighton Ave, Perth Amboy, NJ 08861.

## DELEON, PRISCILLA
Executive. **Personal:** Born Apr 5, 1958, Watsonville, CA; daughter of Federico and Jessie; married Douglas Carter; children: Aaron Carter. **Educ:** San Jose State Univ, BBM, 1980. **Career:** Security Pac Bk, opers mgr, 1981; Atari Inc, travel cood, 1982-83; Sheraton Sunnyvale, mgt coord, 1983-86; San Jose Conv & Visitors Bur, sales res, 1986, sales mgr, 1986-96, nat sales mgr, 1996; Expo Group, San Jose, assoc dir sales, 2003-05; Santa Clara Conv-Visitor Bur, nat sales mgr, currently. **Orgs:** Nat Coalition Black Meeting Planners; Hotel Sales & Mktg Asn Int; Expo Group LP; bd mem, Int Asn Exhib Mgt. **Business Addr:** National Sales Manager, Santa Clara Convention & Visitors Bureau, 1850 Warburton Ave, Santa Clara, CA 95050, **Business Phone:** (408)244-9660.

## DELIBERO, SHIRLEY A.
Executive. **Career:** Green Line, Mass Bay Transp Authority, proj mgr & supt, 1976; Wash Metrop Area Transit Authority, dir bus serv, gen mgr; Dallas Area Rapid Transit, dep exec dir; NJ Transit, exec dir, 1990-98; MV Transp Inc, strategic advisor; Metrop Transit Authority Harris Co, pres & chief exec officer, 1999-2004; DeLibero Transp Strategies LLC, pres, 2005-. **Orgs:** Adv bd, Newark Performing Arts; Urban League; YMCA Black Achievers; Woman State Govt; Women Transit; vice chair & bd dir, Am Pub Transp Asn; nat chair, Conf Minority Transp Off, 2006-08. **Special Achievements:** First African American woman to chair the American Public Transportation Association. **Business Addr:** President, DeLibero Transportation Strategies LLC, 121 N Post Oak Lane Suite 1703, Houston, TX 77024, **Business Phone:** (713)683-7954.

## DELILLY, DR. MAYO RALPH, III
Pediatrician. **Personal:** Born Apr 3, 1953, Los Angeles, CA; son of Mayo R Jr and Irene Wood; married Carol Covyeau; children: Irene Rose & Lauren Marie. **Educ:** Williams Col, BA, biol, 1974; Howard Univ Col Med, MD, 1978. **Career:** Los Angeles County King-Drew Med Ctr, resident, 1978-81; pvt pract pediatrician, currently. **Orgs:** LA Pediat Soc, 1981; Big Bros Greater Los Angeles, 1981-90; med adv, Sheenway Sch, Los Angeles, 1983; Am Acad Pediat; Alpha Omega Alpha Hon Med Soc; fel Am Acad Pediat, 1984; vchmn, Pediat Comn, Calif Med Ctr, 1988. **Honors/Awds:** Acad Achievement Award, Howard Univ Med Sch, 1976; Med Alumni Award, Howard Univ Med Sch, 1978. **Home Addr:** 1400 S Grand Ave, Los Angeles, CA 90015-3048, **Home Phone:** (213)765-7500. **Business Addr:** Pediatrician, Private Practice, 1818 S Western Ave Suite 207, Los Angeles, CA 90006-5808, **Business Phone:** (323)733-4148.

## DELK, JAMES F., JR.
Automotive executive. **Personal:** Born Sep 10, 1948, Smithfield, VA; son of James (deceased) and Edith Majors; married Thelma Garvin; children: Darlene, Kim, Timothy & James. **Educ:** Temple Univ, Philadelphia, PA, assocs, elec engineering, 1969. **Career:** IBM, Philadelphia, PA, customer eng, 1969-71; William H Porter, Newark, Del, salesman, 1971-74; Vans Chevrolet, New Castle, Del, sales mgr, 1974-82; GeneralMotors, salesman; Fairlane Ford Inc, chief exec officer & owner, currently; Fairlane Lincoln-Mercury in Hackettstown, NJ. **Orgs:** Alpha Phi Alpha, 1967-; pres, Schuylkill County Dealer Asn, 1991-92; regional mgr, Black Ford & Lincoln Mercury Dealers Asn, 1991-93. **Business Addr:** Chief Executive Officer, Owner, Fairlane Ford Inc, 14585 Mich Ave, Dearborn, MI 48126, **Business Phone:** (313)846-5000.

## DELK, OLIVER RAHN
Educator, executive director. **Personal:** Born Feb 4, 1948, Staten Island, NY; son of James and Mary Dixon. **Educ:** Ind Univ, BA, psychol, 1974; Ga State Univ, MS, criminal justice, 1976. **Career:** Sears, Roebuck & Co, asst mgr, 1974-76; Southeast Br YMCA, Atlanta, community prog dir, 1976-77; Off Mayor Atlanta, tech assist specialist, 1977-79; Morehouse Col, dir govt rels; Communities Joined Action, bd dir; Fulton County Dept Health, contracts mgr, currently; Instnl Advan, vpres; Morris Brown Col, Interim vpres, 1998-99; Fulbright Group Study Abroad Proj, proj dir; Livingstone Col, campaign mgr. **Orgs:** Nat Asn Equal Opportunities Higher Educ, 1979-; Nat Asn Advan Colored People, 1979-; Omega Psi Phi Frat, 1979-; SCLC, 1979-; pres, Asn Fund-Raising Officers 1985; chmn, Budget & Fin, Water, Waste Water Treat Operators, 1985; United Negro Col Fund; Nat Socs Fund Raising Execs; Atlanta Regional Comn Environ Comt. **Home Addr:** 657 Francis Pl NW, Atlanta, GA 30318-5013, **Home Phone:** (404)792-7729. **Business Addr:** Contracts Manager, Fulton County Department of Health, 99 Jesse Hill Jr Dr SE, Atlanta, GA 30303, **Business Phone:** (404)730-1216.

## DELK, TONY LORENZO
Basketball player. **Personal:** Born Jan 28, 1974, Covington, TN; married Margie; children: Taylor. **Educ:** Univ Ky, attended 1986. **Career:** Basketball player, coach (retired), executive; Charlotte Hornets, point guard, 1997-98; Golden State Warriors, guard, point guard, 1998-99; Sacramento Kings, point guard, 2000; Phoenix Suns, 2001-02; Boston Celtics, shooting guard, 2002, point guard, 2003; Dallas Mavericks, shooting guard, 2004; Atlanta Hawks, shooting guard, 2005-06; Detroit Pistons, shooting guard, 2006; Panathinaikos Athens, Greece, 2006-07; Carolina Giants, 2008; Ky Wildcats, asst coach, 2009-11; NMex State Aggies, asst coach, 2011-13. **Orgs:** Omega Psi Phi Fraternity; pres & chief exec officer, Taylor Delk Sickle Cell Found, 2003-. **Honors/Awds:** Most Outstanding Player, NCAA-Div I, 1996; Player of the Year, SEC, 1996. **Business Addr:** President, Chief Executive Officer, Taylor Delk Sickle Cell Foundation, 418 Chapel Cove, Brownsville, TN 38012, **Business Phone:** (731)694-8727.

## DELK, YVONNE V.
Clergy. **Personal:** Born Apr 15, 1939, Norfolk, VA; daughter of Marcus T. **Educ:** Norfolk State Col, Norfolk, Va, BA, sociol & Relig Educ, 1961; Andover Newton Theol Sem, Newton Ctr, MA, MRE, 1963; Cincinnati Univ, Cincinnati, OH, attended 1966; New York Theol Sem, New York, NY, ministry doctor, 1978. **Career:** United Church Christ, Bd Homeland Ministries, Boston, MA, Philadelphia, PA, secy urban & black church, 1969-76; Harvard Divinity Sch, Cambridge, MA, vis lectr, 1976-77; United Church Christ, New York, NY, assoc constituency develop off church soc, 1978-79, affirmative action officer, 1980-81, exec dir, off church soc, 1981-90; Community Renewal Soc, exec dir, 1990-99; Harvard Divinity Sch & Sch Theol, Va Union Univ, vis lectr, 1999-2001; Sem Consortium Pastoral Educ, Chica, Ill, vis lectr, 2001-05; Ctr African Am Theol Studies, founding dir, currently. **Orgs:** Bd dir, Proj Equality; mem prog combat racism, World Coun Churches; adv comn, World Coun Churches Conv Justice, Peace & Integrity Creation; Nat Planning Comt C Poverty; coord comt mem, Choose Peace; bd dir, Franklinton Ctr; Covenant Acad Urban Ministry. **Honors/Awds:** Antoinette Brown Award, United Church Christ, 1979; DDiv, Chicago Theol Sem, 1986; DDiv, Ursinus Col, 1986; Excellence in Field of Religion, Howard Univ, 1987; Leadership & Service Award, Proj Equality, 1988. **Special Achievements:** In 1974, she became the First African-American woman to be ordained in the United Church of Christ; Articles on the Black church experience, racism, and human rights have appeared in many publications. **Home Addr:** 5201 S Cornell Suite 11E, Chicago, IL 60615, **Home Phone:** (312)493-0103. **Business Addr:** Director, Center for African American Theological Studies, 200 N Mich Ave Suite 502, Chicago, IL 60601, **Business Phone:** (312)726-1200.

## DELL, WILLIE J.
Government official, executive director, social worker. **Personal:** Born May 8, 1930, Weldon, NC; daughter of Willie Aikens and Emma F Grant; married Nathan; children: Wayne & Arthur Jones. **Educ:** St Augustines Col, BA, 1952; Richmond Prof Inst Col William & Mary, MSW, 1960. **Career:** Government official (retired); Social Serv Bur, social worker, 1953-58; Med Col Va, med social worker, 1961-66; Richmond Pub Health Dept, chief med soc worker, 1966-68; Va Commonwealth Univ, asst prof, 1968-74, grad social work prog prof; Richmond City coun, 1973; Univ Richmond, adj prof, 1978-96; Va St Conf, Nat Asn Advan Colored People, voter empowerment coord, 1978-2000; JJ & W Assoc Consult, co-owner, exec dir. **Orgs:** Pres, Black Ed Assoc, 1973-75; city coun mem, City Richmond Va, 1975; Pres, Richmond Chap Nat Asn Social Workers, 1975; bd mem, Commonwealth Psychol; bd mem, Richmond Chap ARC & Fam C Serv, Nat League Cities; VCU Grad Sch; Richmond Community Hosp; Proj Jump St, 1975-80; exec dir, Richmond Comm Sr Ctr, 1976-95; Nat Asn Advan Colored People; N Side Civil Asn; St Augustines Chap; Nat Assoc Black Soc Workers; past chmn, Reg III NBC Leo; Va Coun Soc Welfare Coun Human Rel; Del Ver Women Clubs, Delta Sigma Theta; pres, Nat Black Presby Caucus; pres, Richmond Chap Nat Causes Black Aged, 1980-89; Bd Southern Regional Coun, 1980-99; pres, Richmond Urban Inst, 1984-88; Diocese Richmond, Haitian Comn, 1990-95; Nat Presby Hunger Adv Comt, 1994-99; bd mem, Heifer Proj Int, 1996-; bd, St Joseph's Home; exec dir, Richmond Community

Sr Ctr. **Honors/Awds:** Omega Citizen of the Year Award, 1974; Govt Award, Metro Bus League, 1975; Delta's Civic & Polit Involvement Award, 1975; Distinguished Service Award, St Augustine's Col, 1982; Outstanding Woman Award, Govt Youth Mens Christian Asn, 1982; Good Govt Award Eta Tau Chapter, 1982; Outstanding Vol, Powhatan Correctional Ctr, 1988; Jeffrey B Spence Award, Va Ctr Inclusive Communities. **Special Achievements:** First African-American elected to Richmond City Council. **Home Addr:** 2956 Hathaway Rd, Richmond, VA 23225, **Home Phone:** (804)560-1564.

## DELLUMS, DR. LEOLA HIGGS (ROSCOE DELLUMS)

Lawyer. **Personal:** Born Dec 12, 1941, Berkeley, CA; daughter of Leo C and Esther Lee; married Ronald Vernie; children: Ronald Brandon, Erik Todd & Piper Dellums Ross. **Educ:** San Francisco State Univ, BA, sociol, 1966; Calif State Teaching Credential, adult educ, 1967; Georgetown Univ Law Ctr, JD, 1982. **Career:** Reporter & broadcaster, 1972-80; Inst Servs Educ, consult, 1976; Am Civil Liberties Union, develop dir, publicist, 1976-78; Zuko Interior Designs, Pub Rels, advert mgr, 1978-79; Congressman Mickey Leland, spec asst, 1983; Super Ct Dist, judicial law clerk, 1984-85; Assembly Calif Legis, prin consult, Assembly Off Res, Wash, Dist, rep, 1985-92; Wash & Christian, atty law, 1993-96; US Dept Com, 1996-97; pvt practr atty, 1997-. **Orgs:** Nat Bar Asn; PEN Bar; Calif State Soc; Am Bar Asn; Potomac Chap Links Inc; AKA Sorority; Cong Club; Am Soc Composers, Authors & Publishers; Berkeley High Sch Alumni Asn; US Supreme Ct Bar; DC Ct Appeals Bar; US Dist Ct, DC Bar; Nat Bd Trustees, Ctr Prevent Handgun Violence, Sasha Bruce Youth Work; Regional Addiction Prev Inc, Adv Bd; Rise Sister Support Coun Minority Breast Cancer Resource Ctr; San Francisco State Univ Alumni Bd. **Honors/Awds:** The Ella Hill Hutch Award, Black Women Organized for Political Action, 1992; Inductee, Berkeley High School Hall of Fame, 1992; The Sojourner Truth Meritorious Service Award, Nat Asn Negro Bus & Prof Womens Club Inc, 1991; AT&T Volunteer Activist Award of Wash DC, 1985; Annual Solid Image Award, 1999; Outstanding Leadership Award, Black Women Organized for Political action, 1999; Nat Sojourner Truth Meritorious Service Award; Hall of Fame, Black Filmmakers. **Special Achievements:** First black Pom-pom girl & the first black on the Homecoming Queen Court; Songs published under RREPCO Publishing Company; poetry published in "The Sheet"; prescriptive diagnostic research paper, "Teaching English as a Second Language to Native Born"; hosted local Emmy award-winning television show "Cloth-A-Thon", WGLA; co-hosted local Emmy award-winning television show, "The Place",WRC; published "Something More", 1999. **Business Addr:** Attorney, 5423 28th St NW, Washington, DC 20015-1241, **Business Phone:** (202)686-5156.

## DELLUMS, RONALD VERNIE

Civil rights activist, association executive, mayor. **Personal:** Born Nov 24, 1935, Oakland, CA; son of Verney and Willa (deceased); married Cynthia Lewis; children: Brandy, Erik, Piper, Pam & Michael; married Leola Roscoe Higgs; married Athurine. **Educ:** Oakland City Col, AA, 1958; San Francisco State Col, BA, 1960; Univ Calif, Berkeley, MSW, 1962. **Career:** Congressperson, association executive, educator (retired); Calif Dept Ment Hyg, psychiat social worker, 1962-64; Bayview Community Ctr, prog dir, 1964-65; Hunters Pt Youth Opportunity Ctr, assoc dir, dir, 1965-66; Bay Area Social Planning Coun, planning consult, 1966-67; San Francisco Econ Opportunity Coun, Concentrated Employ Prog, dir, 1967-68; Social Dynamics Inc, sr consult, 1968-70; US House Rep, 7th Dist Calif, mem, 1971-75, 8th Dist Calif, mem, 1975-93, 9th Dist Calif, mem & dem, 1993-98; Health care Int Mgt Co, pres, City Oakland, mayor, 2007-11; San Francisco State Col, lectr. **Orgs:** Alpha Phi Alpha; House Comt Nat Security, 1973; Mil Procurement Subcomt; chair, Cong Black Caucus; chair, House Comt Dist Columbia, 1979-93; chair, House Armed Svcs Comt, 1993-95; Permanent Select Comt Intel; Berkeley City Coun, 1967-70; fraternity's World Policy Coun. **Honors/Awds:** Mayors' Climate Protection Award, 2008. **Special Achievements:** First African American elected to Congress from Northern California; Author, Defense Sense: The Search for a Rational Military Policy, 1983; Third African-American Mayor of Oakland. **Business Addr:** Mayor, City of Oakland, 1 Frank Ogawa Plz 3rd Fl, Oakland, CA 94612, **Business Phone:** (510)238-3141.

## DELLUMS, ROSCOE. See DELLUMS, DR. LEOLA HIGGS.

## DELOACH, WENDELIN W.

Attorney general (U.S. federal government). **Educ:** Roosevelt Univ, BS & BA; Univ Denver, JD, 1987. **Career:** DeLoach Law Firm, atty, currently. **Orgs:** Bd mem, Colo Sch Family Ther. **Home Addr:** 2600 S Parker Rd, Aurora, CO 80014, **Home Phone:** (720)449-9848. **Business Addr:** Attorney, DeLoach Law Firm, 79 W Monroe St Suite 1314, Chicago, IL 60603, **Business Phone:** (773)783-2400.

## DELOATCH, DR. EUGENE M.

College administrator. **Educ:** Tougaloo Col, BS, math, 1959; Lafayette Col, BS, elec engineering, 1959; Polytech Inst Univ, MS, elec engineering, 1966, PhD, bioengineering, 1972; Doctorate, bioengineering. **Career:** Howard Univ, prof & chmn, elec engineering, Washington, DC, 1975-84; Am Soc Engineering Educ, pres, 2001-02; Morgan State Univ, sch engineering, Baltimore, Md, dean, 1984-; Knowledge Integration Mgt Ctr Excellence, Prin Investr. **Orgs:** Secy, Bd dir Technol & Econ Develop Corp Md; Ed bd J Engineering Educ; chmn, Coun Dean's Engineering Historically Black Col & Univs; Tech adv bd, Whirlpool Corp; Nat Acad Engineering. **Business Addr:** Dean, Morgan State University, 1700 E Cold Spring Lane, Baltimore, MD 21251, **Business Phone:** (443)885-3231.

## DELOATCH, MYRNA SPENCER

Association executive, teacher. **Personal:** Born Tarboro, NC; married Johnnie W; children: Chris, Tamyra & Ivan. **Educ:** Ag & Tech Univ, BS, home econ; Purdue Univ, spec cert. **Career:** Ag Ed Inst Chillan S Am, teacher; La Guardia House NY, dir food serv; Farmers Home Admin, home supvr; Rich Sq Training Ctr, home econ teacher; Telamon Corp, employ training specialist; NC Rural Educ Working Group, dir; Edgecombe Community Col, Dept Social Serv, human servs coord, Family & Consumer Sci Comm, currently. **Orgs:** Pres, Ebonette Club; Tarboro Community Outreach, bd dir; Delta Sigma Theta Sorority, 1959; employ interviewer, Employ Sec Commn, 1976-81; Tarboro Housing & Comm Develop Adv Bd, 1979-84; Tarboro Arts Coun; Tarboro City Sch Bd Educ, 1979-85; NC Coop Exten Serv, adv bd. **Honors/Awds:** Outstanding Citizenship, E Tarboro Citizen League, 1978; Past President Award, Ebonette Club, 1980; Meritorious Service, East Tarboro Citizens League, 1981; special Service Award, Black Voices, 1982; Meritorious Service Award, E Tarboro Citizens League, 1985; Hall of Fame. **Home Addr:** 508 Panola St, PO Box 1601, Tarboro, NC 27886-1601. **Business Addr:** Member, Edgecomb County, Edgecombe County Administrative Bldg, Tarboro, NC 27886, **Business Phone:** (252)641-7821.

## DELOATCH, DR. SANDRA J.

College administrator, dean (education), vice president (organization). **Personal:** Born Suffolk, VA; daughter of David and Essie. **Educ:** Howard Univ, BS, math, 1971; Univ Mich, MA, 1972; Ind Univ, PhD, 1977; Col William & Mary, MS, 1995. **Career:** Norfolk State Univ, Math Dept, instr, asst prof, 1972-83, prof & comput sci prog coord, 1983-91, Comput Sci Dept, prof & chair, 1991-99, Sch Sci & Technol, interim dean, prof comput sci & dean, 2000-, univ's Comput Sci founder, provost & vpres acad affairs, currently; Nat Security Agency, prin investr. **Orgs:** AAAS; Phi Beta Kappa, 1971-; team chair, Comput Sci Accreditation Comn, 1987-98; bd dir & chair, technol task force, Girl Scout Coun Colonial Coast, 2001-; bd zoning appeals, City Suffolk, 2002-; Asn Comput Mach; Inst Elec& Electronics Engrs Comput Soc; Va Modeling Anal & Simulation Ctr; bd mem, Ctr Excellence Space Data & Info Sci Space Coun; Nat Nuclear Security Admin cyber security; NSF, Nat Oceanic & Atmospheric Admin, NASA Langley Res Ctr, Dept Educ, Dept Energy. **Home Addr:** 106 Seabreeze Lane, Suffolk, VA 23435-1735. **Business Addr:** Dean, Professor of Computer Science, Norfolk State University, C-236 Brown Memorial Hall, Norfolk, VA 23504, **Business Phone:** (757)823-8561.

## DELPHIN, DR. JACQUES MERCIER

Physician, administrator. **Personal:** Born Apr 26, 1929, Cap Haitien; son of Alexander and Sonia; married Marlene Lavitola Mastroti; children: Patrick, Barthold, Beverly, Miriam, Matthew & Janice. **Educ:** Grad Sec Studies, BS, 1950; Univ Haiti, W Indies, med sch, 1957; Sch Med State Univ, Md. **Career:** St Luke's Hosp, intern, 1960; Hudson River Psychiat Ctr, resident, 1961-64; Poughkeepsie, pvt pract, 1968; St Francis Hosp, physician, 1968-; Dutchess Co Dept Ment Hyg, psychiat dir, 1969-73; St Cabrini Home W Pk, med dir, 1974-80; Ad Interim, comment health, 1973-74; Hudson River State Hosp, psychiat dir partial hosp, 1966-69; Community Ment Health Ctr, dir, 1969-74; Spectrum Behav Health, med dir, 1998-; pvt pract, currently. **Orgs:** Pres, Mid-hudson Br Psychiat Asn, 1972; fel APA, 1972; med lic NY State, 1967; AAPA; ACA Forensic Psychiat; Am Asn Adolescent Psychiat; Am Psychiat Asn. **Home Addr:** 132 N Ave Apt Suite 104, Pleasant Valley, NY 12569, **Home Phone:** (845)635-3942. **Business Addr:** Physician, Spectrum Behavioral Health Inc, 510 Haight Ave Suite 102, Poughkeepsie, NY 12603, **Business Phone:** (845)485-9098.

## DELPIT, JOSEPH A.

State government official, restaurateur, president (organization). **Personal:** Born Jan 9, 1940, Baton Rouge, LA; son of Thomas H (deceased) and Edmae Butler; married Precious Robinson; children: Joseph Jr, Thomas, Deidre, Desiree & Derrick. **Educ:** Southern Univ, bus admin, food & nutrit. **Career:** State legislature (retired); Chicken Shack Restaurant, owner & operator, 1959-; Baton Rouge City, city councilman, 1968-75; master ceremonies, 1972, 1976, 1984; Dist Dist 67, state rep, 1975, 1980, 1983, 1987; La House Rep, state rep, speaker, 1984; Joe Delpit Enterprises Inc, owner, currently; Chicken Shack Systs Inc, pres, currently; D & W Health Servs Inc, pres, currently; W T B Inc, secy, treas & chief financial officer, currently; Booker T. Wash Nursing Ctr; Gr Baton Rouge Develop Corp; Gen United Life Ins Co; Sports Unlimited Inc, co-owner. **Orgs:** Shriner Hon mem, John B Frazier Hon Soc, 1974; chmn exec comt, Greater Baton Rouge Port Comn, 2004; Mem bd dir, People's Savings & Loan Co; bd mem, St Francis Xavier Cath Church; bd mgt, Baranco Clark YMCA; life mem & former pres, Baton Rouge Chap, Nat Asn Advan Colored People, life mem; City Parish Bi-racial Comt; Cath Lay Cong; bd dir, Op Upgrade; bd mgt, Ment Health Soc; Capital Region Planning Comn; Mason; founder, La Legis Black Caucus; life mem, McKinley High Sch Alumni Asn, charter; former bd dir & former pres, Capital City Kids Baseball Clin; proj mgt chmn, Old McKinley Bldg Proj; Ment Health Soc Bd Mgt; Capitol Region Planning Comn; pres, House Appropriations; Labor & Indust Rels Educ; House Arts Adv; Parochial Affairs Comt; St. Francis Xavier Cath Church Finance Bd; Ment Health Soc Bd Mgt; hon mem, James M. Frazier Hon Soc; bd dir, Baton Rouge Sickle Cell Anemia Found. **Honors/Awds:** Outstanding Service Award, Baranco Clark YMCA, 1960; Baton Rouge Businessman of the Year, News Leader, 1961; McKinley High Alumni Award, 1968; Outstanding Academic Support, Southern Univ Am Women Soc, 1970; National Freedom Award, Nat Asn Advan Colored People, 1970; Outstanding Leadership in Business and Civic Community Service, Omega Psi Phi Frat Inc, 1971; Outstanding Service, Southern Univ Alumni Fed, 1973; Business man of the Year, 1973; Shriver Award for dedicated service to the poor, Off Econ Opportunity, 1973; La Educ Asn Award; Alpha Kappa Alpha Sorority Award; James M. Frazier Hon Soc; Southern Univ's Alumni Fedn; Southern Univ's Ctr Bus and Econ Develop; Outstanding Young Men of America; Louisiana Education Association Award; Alpha Kappa Alpha Sorority Award. **Special Achievements:** Listed in Outstanding Young Men of America; Louisiana Education Association Award in recognition of outstanding achievements in the field of political and social action; First African American Councilman to serve the City of Baton Rouge. **Home Addr:** 2323 Iowa St, Baton Rouge, LA 70802-7738, **Home Phone:** (225)344-6046. **Business Addr:** Owner, Joe Delpit Enterprises Inc, 725 Lettsworth St, Baton Rouge, LA 70802, **Business Phone:** (225)343-1687.

## DELPIT, DR. LISA DENISE

Educator. **Personal:** Born May 23, 1952, Baton Rouge, LA; daughter of Thomas H and Edmae Butler; children: Maya. **Educ:** Antioch Col, BA, psychol, 1974; Harvard Grad Sch Educ, MA, 1980, EdD, 1984. **Career:** Durham Child Develop Ctr, teacher, admin asst, 1972-77; Philadelphia Parent-Teacher Centers, facilitator, 1975-77; Antioch Col, lectr, 1976-79; La State Dept of Educ, supvr, 1977-79; Cambridge Pub Sch Syst, consult, 1980-81; Roxbury Community Col, consult, 1980-81; Cleveland State Univ, fac, 1981; EARTHWATCH Inc, prog adminr & evaluator, 1981-82; N Solomons Prov Govt, consult, 1982-83; Atari Res Lab, consult, 1983-84; Univ Alaska, asst prof, reading, lang & lit, 1984-88, Teacher Educ Prog, coordr, 1987-88; Mich State Univ, Sch Educ, assoc prof, 1988-91; Morgan State Univ, Inst Urban Res, sr res assoc, 1988-94; Urban Sites Writing Network, Site Coordr, 1990-94; Ga State Univ, Benjamin E Mays Prof & chmn, 1994-2002, Ctr Urban Educ Excellence, dir, 1994-2002; Fla Int Univ, Miami, Fla, prof, 2002-, Ctr Urban Educ & Innovation, exec dir & eminent scholar, currently. **Orgs:** Co dir, Univ Mass, Boston, 1979-81; mem, ed bd, Harvard Educ Rev, 1980-82; Dissertation fel, Am Asn Univ Women Educ Found, 1984; Nat Acad Educ Spencer Fel, 1988; Ctr Collab Educ; Mac Arthur Fel, 1990; Res support, Nat Black Child Develop Inst, Baltimore Chap, 1990-91; literacy comt, vice chmn, Nat Bd Prof Teaching Stds; co chair, African-Am Curric Infusion Comt Baltimore PS; Int Reading Asn; Phi Delta Kappa; Nat Coun Teaching Eng; Am Educ Res Asn. **Home Addr:** 93 Berkeley Rd, Avondale Estates, GA 30002. **Business Addr:** Executive Director, Florida International University, 11200 SW 8th St, Miami, FL 33199, **Business Phone:** (305)348-2000.

## DELSARTE, LOUIS J.

Artist, college teacher. **Personal:** Born Sep 1, 1944, Brooklyn, NY. **Educ:** NY Univ, Pratt Inst, BFA, 1967; Univ Ariz, MFA, 1977; Brooklyn Col, NY, cert, fine arts educ. **Career:** Col New Rochelle, adj prof, 1988-92; Morris Brown Col, asst prof, 1992, prof, 2003; Spelman Col, adj prof, 1992-94; Morehouse Col, Altanta, Ga, prof fine arts & humanities, instr art, adj prof, currently; Stella Jones Gallery, New Orleans; Howard Univ, artist-in-resident; Studio Mus, Harlem, artist resident. **Orgs:** Commun, NY Metrop Transit Authority, 2000-01. **Home Addr:** , GA, **Home Phone:** (404)524-3245. **Business Addr:** Adjunct Professor of Fine Arts & Humanities, Morehouse College, 830 Westview Dr SW, Atlanta, GA 30314, **Business Phone:** (404)681-2800.

## DEMAS, DR. WILLIAM F.

Educator. **Educ:** State Univ NY, MD. **Career:** MD Anderson Hosp & Tumor Inst, fel; Univ Tex Houston Br, instr; Akron City Hosp, Summa Health Syst, Div Radiotherapy, chief, currently, Radiation Ther Oncol Grp, prin investr, currently; Northeastern Ohio Univs Col Med, prof radiol, currently; Cancer Care Ctr, pres & chief exec officer, currently. **Orgs:** Am Bd Radiol; chair, Personnel & Compensation Comt; trustee, Akron Community Found; bd trustee, Northeastern Ohio Univ Col Med; fel, Am Col Radiol. **Home Addr:** 885 North Sawburg Ave, suite 108, Alliance, OH 44601. **Business Addr:** Chief, Radiation Oncology, Akron City Hospital, 525 E Mkt St, Akron, OH 44304, **Business Phone:** (330)375-3557.

## DEMBER, JEAN WILKINS

Counselor. **Personal:** Born Jan 29, 1930, Brooklyn, NY; daughter of William H Sr and Martha Marie Benson; married Clarence Robert; children: Clarence Jr, Judith, Regina, Lila, Theresa & Zelie. **Educ:** Lincoln Schl Nurses, 1950; Manhattan Bus Inst, cert secy, 1952; Empire State Col, Old Westbury, NY, 1983; Lincoln Univ, PA, MHS, 1988. **Career:** NY State Deleg Black Polit Assem, 1972, pres, 1981-82; Webb-Dember African Am Heritage, cur & co-founder, 1975-; Black Hist Cult Prog, presentor designer, 1978-; Nat Black Polit Assembly, Comn Prisons & Genocide, org vol, 1982-83; Nassau Community Col, Black Women Studies, adj prof, 1983-2002; Nat Urban League Long Island, career counr, Structured Educ Support Prog, 1989-92. **Orgs:** Adv bd mem, Nat Black Lay Cath Caucus, 1970-85; Econ Opport Coun Suffolk, 1972-84; founding mem, Tri Community Health Coun, 1974-82; designer White Racism Ment Health Comm SC Div Ment Health, 1977-82; State Youth Advocacy, 1980-84; Evangelization Community Nat Off Black Catholics, 1982-84; Uganda Human Rights League, 1982-86; NY State Multicultural Adv Comt, 1984-91; chairperson, Long Island Day Care Serv, 1986-88; Lincoln Univ Alumni Asn; African Cult Ctr, Los Angeles; Nat Black Alcoholism Coun, 1987-89; pres, LI Cath Interracial Coun, 1988-91; Reform Ment Health, add Racist, White Supremist & Police Brutality & Murders Psychosocial Pathol; founder, Afrikans United Sanity Now, 1992-; Shape Ctr Harambee Coun Elders, 1992-; consult, Inst African Wisdom IFA ORISHA Educ Ctr; bd dir, Inst Interracial Harmony, currently. **Honors/Awds:** Am Beautiful grant community prog, 1981; Nat Off Black Cath Evangelization Award, 1982; Citizen of Year, Chi Rho Chprt Omega Psi Phi Frat Inc, 1982; Martin L King Award, Pilgrim State Human Rights Comn, 1983; vol advocate African Relief Cath Church & broader community; Suffolk County, Jack & Jill Award, 1990; Nat Asn Negro Bus & Prof Women's Clubs Inc, Nat Sojourner Truth Award, Meritorious Serv, 1991; Outstanding Service, Asn Community Rels, 1992; Nat Asn Advan Colored People Serv Award, Auburn Prison, 1992; Natl Black Service Award, Alcohol & Substance Abuse, Long Island Chap, Cosco Williams, pres; Cert Serv, Kazi Shule & SHAPE Ctr, 1995-96; Cert Appreciation, Million Man March LOC, 1996; Houston, Tex Cert Appreciation, Foster Elem Sch, 1996; var nominations, ABI, 1997-01. **Home Addr:** 2621 Rosewood St, Houston, TX 77004-5337, **Home Phone:** (631)643-2667. **Business Addr:** Board Director, The Institute For Interracial Harmony.

## DEMBY, JAMES E.

Electrical engineer. **Personal:** Born Dec 24, 1936, Chesapeake, VA; married Mavis A Smith; children: James Jr, Ken & Len. **Educ:** Tuskegee Inst, attended 1957; Howard Univ, BS, 1961. **Career:** Norfolk Naval Shipyard, advancing positions, 1961; Norfolk Naval Shipyard, supvry elec engr, 1973. **Orgs:** Vpres, United Civic League, 1963-64; asst dist comnr, Tidewater Coun BSA, 1966; Naval Civilian Admin Asn; Nat Asn Naval Tech & Supvr; Chesapeake Chap, Nat Tots & Teens. **Honors/Awds:** Scout Exec Award, 1970; Super Performance Award, 1971; Beneficial Suggestion Award, 1971; Cert of Merit, 1971; Arrowhead Honor, 1971; Scouter's Key, 1971; Order of the Arrow, 1972. **Home Addr:** 4008 Sun Valley Cres, Chesapeake, VA 23321, **Home Phone:** (757)488-0116.

**DEMERITTE, DR. EDWIN T.**
Insurance executive, government official, teacher. **Personal:** Born Jun 25, 1935, Miami, FL; son of Arnold and Daisy; children: Edwin Jr, Kathy Wynn, Deborah Renee, Dianne Marie & Michelle. **Educ:** Fla A&M Univ, BS, MEd; Barry Col Miami, grad work guid & coun; Fla Atlantic Univ, grad work admin & supr; Nova Univ, Doc Prog Nat Educ D Prog. **Career:** N Dade Sr High Sch, teacher, 1958-63, dept head, 1963-65; Miami NW Sr High Sch, guid counr, 1966-67; Miami NW Adult Educ Cent, instr, 1966-69; Miami Edison Sr High Sch, asst prin guid, 1969-70; Hialeah Jr High Sch, prin 1/2 quinmester prog, 1973; Metrop Life Ins Co, sales rep sr acct exec; Dade County Pub Sch Syst, Miami, FL, dir, 1976-81; Kovack Securities, regist rep, govt rels chmn, currently; Conf Metrop life, pres, 1988, 1994-97. **Orgs:** Nat Conf Chris & Jews Violence & Youth, 1969; Nat Inst Pol & Commun Rel, 1970; Nat Asn Sec Sch Prin Ann Meeting, 1971-73; Nat Asn Life Underwriters, 1981-; Miami Asn Life Underwiters, 1981-; Fla Asn Life Underwriters, 1981-; Million Dollar Round Table, 1984-2003; trustee, Presby Church USA Found, 1991-96; Miami Dade Asn Insu & Financial Adv, pres, 2009-10, sr coun, 2009-10, treas, advocacy & govt rels chair; consult, S Region Educ Bd. **Honors/Awds:** Policies placed over 200 policy contacts Award, Metro Ins Co, 1983; Three Metropolitan SE Territory Award, 1983; Qualifying Life Member of the Million Dollar Roundtable, 1984; Kiwanis Fellow, Guidance Counseling; Boy Scouting Award, Community Service Recognition; Dade County School Board Award, Commendable Contribution Educ; National Sales Award, NALU, 1988, 1994-97; Nat Quality Awards, NALU, 1988, 1993-97; Awarded The LUTCF Designation, 1998; National Sales Achievement Award, 1998; National Quality Award, 1998; Million Dollar Round Table Honor Roll, 1998. **Special Achievements:** Million Dollar Round table, 1999, 2003. **Home Addr:** 5301 NW 18 Ave, Miami, FL 33142, **Home Phone:** (305)696-2677. **Business Addr:** Government Relations Chairman, Kovack Securities, 5301 NW 18 Ave, Miami, FL 33142, **Business Phone:** (305)696-2677.

**DEMESME, RUBY B.**
Military leader. **Educ:** St Augustine Col, BA, 1969; Univ NC, Chapel Hill, MSW. **Career:** Cumberland County, exec adminr, 1969-80; Us Dept Army, 1989; Us Off Personnel Mgt, cong fel, 1990; Us Dept Air Force, asst dep asst secy, actg dep asst secy, 1993, dep asst secy, 1994, asst secy, 1998-2001; IBM, sr defense fel, dir human capital solutions & defense practices; BearingPoint, pub serv bus transformation team, 2005-; Deloitte, sr exec advisor/strategist, 2009-; auth, mentor, & inspirational speaker. **Orgs:** Women Defense; SES Women's Appointees; Subgroup Women & C; Sen Black Legis Staff (Caucus); Nat Mil Family Asn; Delta Sigma Theta Sorority; chmn, Andrews Fed Credit Union Bd. **Honors/Awds:** Outstanding Students Teachers Award, 1968; Outstanding Performance & Cash Awards, 1985-97; Commanders Award for Exceptional Service, 1984; Superior Civilian Service, 1991; Meritorious Civilian Service Award, 1994-98; Air Force Orgnal Excellence Award, 1997; Cert Achievement, Secy Army, 1997; 25th Anniversary All Volunteer Force Award, 1998; Distinguished Alumni Award, Univ NCA, 1998; Distinguished Leader Award, Air Force Asn, 1998; Distinguished Service Award, Tuskegee Airmen, 1999; Distinguished Alumni Award, St Augustine's Col, 2000; Meritorious Civilian Service, 2001. **Home Addr:** 2701 Lena Crt, Oakton, VA 22124. **Business Addr:** Assistant Secretary of the Air Force, SAF/MI, 1660 Air Force Pentagon Rm 4E1020, Washington, DC 20330-1660, **Business Phone:** (202)697-2302.

**DEMILLE, DR. VALERIE CECILIA**
Businessperson, medical researcher, consultant. **Personal:** Born Jun 2, 1949, New York, NY; daughter of Arnold C and Annie M Clark. **Educ:** NC Cent Univ, BS, 1972, MS, 1974; Meharry Med Col, MD, 1977; Baruch Col, New York, MPA, 1991. **Career:** USAF Sheppard AFB, staff psychiatrist, 1981-83; USAF Vandenberg AFB, chief ment health serv, 1983-84; Woodhull Hosp, staff psychiatrist, 1985; NY Med Col & Lincoln Hosp, New York, NY, unit chief, 1985-87, staff psychiatrist, 1987-88; New York Dept Ment Health, New York, NY, staff assoc anal, 1990-91; Upper Manhattan Ment Health Ctr, exec dir, 1992; Life Mgt, consult, 1993-99; Stress Mgt Asn, Harlem & deMille Consult Agency, founder; Pet Groomer, 2000; New York Bur, chief. **Orgs:** LomPoc bus Women Network; dir press rel, Nat Asn Advan Colored People Legal Defense Fund.

**DEMPSEY, REV. DR. JOSEPH PAGE**
Clergy, school administrator, educator. **Personal:** Born Mar 8, 1930, Nashville, NC; son of Sidney H (deceased) and Irene Alice Vick (deceased); married Evelyntyne Humphrey; children: Denise P, Joseph T, Eric H & Kathy D. **Educ:** Fayetteville State Univ, BS, 1958; Shaw Div Sch, BD, 1964; NC Cen Univ, MA, 1971; Shaw Div Sch, MDiv, 1972; Jacksonville Theol Sem, Fla, DTh, 1982; Faith Evangel Lutheran Sem, Tacoma, Wash, DMin, 1988. **Career:** C E Perry High Sch, grammer teacher, 1958-61; Pastor var locations since, 1961; Oberlin Baptist Church, pastor, 1964-80, minister; B F Person High Sch, Franklin, 1964-67; Apex (NC) Consol High Sch, 1967-71; NC Cent Univ, instr, 1971-, assoc dir, 1988-; circle faith baptist church, pastor, 1980-84; Pine Grove Baptist Church, Creedmoor NC, pastor, 1986-87; Elem & High Sch, instr; Worthdale United Baptist Church Raleigh, NC, pastor; NC Cent Univ, Grad Sch Educ, adj asst prof, 1991-, Coun Ctr, assoc dir, currently. **Orgs:** Dir, YMCA, 1961-67; Boys dir Young Men s Christian Asn Min Bd, 1967-71; Wake Baptist Asn, 1964; NC Personnel & Guide Asn; Am Personnel & Guid Asn; Exec Com, Wake Co Dem Party; bd dir, NC Gen Baptist Con; bd dir, YMCA, 1967-; bd dir, Comm Day Carde Ctr; Goals Raleigh Educ Outreach; Raleigh-Wake Martin Luther King Celebration Comt, 1989. **Honors/Awds:** Teacher of the Year, 1967; Raleigh, NC Christian Family of the Year, 1972; Outstanding Service Award, NC Cent Univ, 1973-74. **Home Addr:** 1409 E Martin St, Raleigh, NC 27610-2611, **Home Phone:** (919)828-6935. **Business Addr:** Adjunct Assistant Professor, NC Central University, PO Box 19688, Durham, NC 27707, **Business Phone:** (919)560-6466.

**DENMARK, LEON**
Vice president (organization), executive director. **Career:** Apollo Theater Harlem, exec dir; Negro ensemble Co, producing dir; Newark Symphony Hall, exec dir; NJ Performing Arts Ctr, vpres programming; Nat Black Arts Festival, exec producer, 1999. **Business Addr:** Vice President for Programming, New Jersey Performing Arts Center, 730 Peachtree St Suite 500, Atlanta, GA 30308.

**DENMARK, ROBERT RICHARD**
Manager, government official. **Personal:** Born Apr 1, 1930, Savannah, GA; son of Robert and Gladys Church; married Mamie E Sampson; children: Gladys Reed. **Educ:** MTI Bus Col, cert, comput sci, 1978; Am River Col, AA, 1980; Univ San Francisco, BS, 1982. **Career:** Manager (retired); Fed Aviation Admin, air traffic control, 1969-71; Prudential Ins Co Am, spec agt, 1971-74; Dept Interior US Bur Reclamation, comput analyst & programmer, 1974-84, adp contract adminr, 1984; US Dept Interior Div Info Resources, comput consult, 1980-84; comput security mgr, 1988-94. **Orgs:** Chief Rabban Ancient Arabic Order Nobles Mystic Shrine N & S Am, 1982-; pres, Sphinx Club Alpha Phi Alpha Frat Inc, 1985; clusterleader Sacramento Area Strategy Team Lutheran Church Am, 1985-87; secy, 1987, pres, 1988-92Zeta Beta Lambda Chap Alpha Phi Alpha; pres, First Eng Lutheran Church Coun, 1987-; Nat Asn Adv Colored People, Black Data Processing Asn; mem exec bd, Div Aging; 32 Degree Mason Ancient Free & Accepted Masonic Cong; exec bd mem, Sierra Pac Synod, Evangel Lutheran Church, 1991-; bd dir, Sacramento Lutheran High Sch, 1994-97. **Honors/Awds:** Res proj, Univ San Francisco, A Study of the Potential of Off Automation, 1982; Outstanding Leadership Award, Lutheran Church Am First Eng Lutheran Church, 1982-84; Special Achievement Award, US Dept Interior, 1985-86; Outstanding Service Award, Div Data Processing Bur Reclamation, 1987; Meritorious Service, Zeta Beta Lambda Chap, Alpha Phi Alpha Fraternity Inc, 1988; Outstanding Serv, Sacramento Area Lutheran Ministry, Evangelical Lutheran Church Am, 1988; Performance Award, US Bur Reclamation, Dept Interior, 1988; Alpha Phi Alpha Man of the Year, Zeta Beta Lambda Chap, 1990; Outstanding Service Award, Bur Reclamation, 1991-92. **Home Addr:** 2100 63rd Ave, Sacramento, CA 95822, **Home Phone:** (916)429-8814.

**DENNARD, DARRYL W.**
Television journalist. **Personal:** Born Sep 18, 1957, New York, NY; son of Eleanor Adamson and Glenn W; married Darlene Gray; children: Autumn Simone. **Educ:** Fordham Univ, Bronx, NY, attended 1985; State Univ Col Buffalo, NY, BA, broadcasting, 1981. **Career:** US Customs Serv, Buffalo, NY, import specialist trainee, 1977-79; WGR-TV, Buffalo, NY, prod asst, 1980-83; WGRZ-TV, Buffalo, NY, news reporter, 1983-87; Ebony jet showcase, co-host; Ebony Man Mag, assoc ed; Good Day Chicago, anchor; Johnson Publ Co, Chicago, Ill, TV co-host, 1987; Black Enterprise Report, co-host & producer; Minority Bus Report, WGN-TV, host; WVAZ-FM, anchor; WCGI-FM, anchor; WGCI-AM, anchor; first trace commun, vpres, currently; Double D Productions Inc, owner, pres, chief exec officer, currently. **Orgs:** Nat Black Media Coalition, 1983-87; bd mem, Buffalo Urban League, 1985-87; State Univ NY Col Buffalo Alumni Asn, 1985-86; community adv bd, Community Dept, SUNY Col Buffalo, 1987; Young Bros christ youth ministry. **Honors/Awds:** Best Public Affairs Program, New York State Broadcasters, 1985; Best Newscast of the Year Award, United Press Int, 1986; Black Leadership Award, 1490 Enterprises, 1986; Young Pioneer Award, Northern Region Black Political Caucus, 1986; Media Award, Buffalo Public Schs, 1987; Special Service Award, Seek/EOP SUNY Col Buffalo, 1988; Merit Award, United Negro Col Fund, 1989; NAMD Communication of the year. **Home Addr:** 5400 S Hyde Pk Blvd Suite 14B, Chicago, IL 60615, **Home Phone:** (312)947-0434. **Business Addr:** Host, WGN-TV, 2501 W Bradley Pl, Chicago, IL 60618-4718, **Business Phone:** (773)528-2311.

**DENNARD, GLORIA A.**
Executive, association executive. **Educ:** Stillman Col, attended 1965. **Career:** Educator, administrator (retired); Birmingham Civil Rights Inst, bd dir; Jefferson County Pub Schs, dir libr serv; Jefferson County Bd Educ, dir media serv, dir instructiional media, 1988-2011. **Orgs:** pres, Nat Alumni Asn Stillman Col; bd dir, Sickle Cell Dis Asn Am Cent Ala Chap; bd mem, Birmingham Civil Rights Inst. **Home Addr:** 212 Westmoreland Cir, Fairfield, AL 35064, **Home Phone:** (205)925-9373. **Business Addr:** Board of Trustee, Stillman College, 3601 Stillman Blvd, Tuscaloosa, AL 35403, **Business Phone:** (205)349-4240.

**DENNING, JOE WILLIAM**
Mayor, government official. **Personal:** Born Nov 30, 1945, Bowling Green, KY; son of Marion E and Evelyn Huskey; children: Kita Denning Clements & Larecia Denning Bell. **Educ:** Ky State Police Acad, 1970; Western KY Univ. **Career:** City Bowling, city comnr, 1992-2004, 2007-11, mayor, 2011-. **Orgs:** BG Warren County Chamber Comt; KY League Cities; Nat League Cities; Bowling Green Chamber Comt; Bowling Green Sch Bd, 1975-92. **Special Achievements:** First African American member of the Bowling Green School Board in 1975. **Home Addr:** 525 Eastwood Ave Apt D, Bowling Green, KY 42103-1690, **Home Phone:** (270)782-1048. **Business Addr:** Mayor, City of Bowling Green, 1001 College St, Bowling Green, KY 42101, **Business Phone:** (270)782-1048.

**DENNIS, ANDRE L.**
Lawyer. **Personal:** Born May 15, 1943, Burton-On-Trent; married Julie B Carpenter; children: Matthew. **Educ:** Cheyney Univ, BA, 1966; Howard Univ Sch Law, JD, 1969; Hon Doctor Laws, 1993. **Career:** Lawyer (retired); Stradley Ronon Stevens & Young LLP, assoc, 1969-76, partner, 1976. **Orgs:** Bd mem, Independence Found, 1997-; bd mem, Nat Sr Citizens Law Ctr, 1995; bd mem, Philadelphia Facil Mgt Corp, 1994-99; pres, Philadelphia Capital Case Resource Ctr, 1993; chancellor, Philadelphia Bar Asn, 1993; pres, 1990-91, bd gov, chair, 1986, Vol Indigent Prog; bd trustee, Community Legal Servs, 1973-84; Philadelphia Bar Asn House Delegs, 1988-; fel Am Col Trial Lawyers, 1994-; bd adv, Philadelphia Lawyer Chap; fel Am Bar Asn; fel Am Col Trial Lawyers. **Honors/Awds:** Pro Bono Serv Award, Pa Bar Asn, 1991-92; Appreciation Award, BWEA, Montgomery County Chap, 1992; Equal Justice Award, Community Legal Servs, 1992; Cheyney Univ, Honorary Doctor of Laws, 1993; ML King Jr Humanitarian Award, Salem Baptist Church, 1993; Pro Bono Pub Award, Am Bar Asn, 1994; Alumni Achievement Award, Howard Univ, 1996; Civil Liberties Award, Am Civil Liberties Union Found, 1997; Hon fel, Univ Pa, 1999; Region III Advocacy Award, Nat Bar Asn; named a Pennsylvania Super Lawyer, 2007-08; First Union Fidelity Award. **Home Addr:** 19 Theresa Dr, Malvern, PA 19355-9668, **Home Phone:** (610)933-4192. **Business Addr:** Partner, Stradley Ronon Stevens & Young LLP, 2600 One Commerce Sq, Philadelphia, PA 19103, **Business Phone:** (215)564-8000.

**DENNIS, CAROLYN K.**
Executive. **Personal:** Born Nov 12, 1948, Hickory, NC; daughter of George Killian and Naomi Killian; married Michael; children: Brandon Thompson & Christopher. **Educ:** NC A&T State Univ, BS, acct, 1971; Univ Wis-Milwaukee, Exec MBA, gen, 1998. **Career:** Executive (retired); Gen Motors, acct supvr, 1972-76; Ford Motor Co, acct supvr, 1976-80; Miller Brewing Co, acct supvr, 1981-87, acct mgr, 1987-94, brewery controller, 1994-97, group dir opers & finance, 1997-2005. **Orgs:** Adv bd, Univ Wis, Sch Educ, 1998; Young Women Christian Asn, financial comt, 2000; mem chair, E Cooper Newcomers Club, 2011-12; comput trainer, E Cooper Community Outreach, 2011-12; bus mgr, Providence Baptist Church, 2013-. **Home Addr:** 3321 W Burgundy Ct, Mequon, WI 53092, **Home Phone:** (262)242-9463.

**DENNIS, CECELIA GRIFFITH**
Educator. **Personal:** Born Sep 23, 1943, Raleigh, NC; daughter of Cecil and Sadie; married William Thomas; children: Jason Maurice. **Educ:** St Augustine Col, BA, 1966. **Career:** Educator (retired); Somerset Co Bd Educ, teacher, 1966-74; Worcester Co Bd Educ, teacher, 1974-00, coordr teacher recruitment, 2000. **Orgs:** Delta Sigma Theta, 1963-03; Nat Asn Advan Colored People, Wicomico Br, 1985-02; bd mem, Community Found Eastern Shore, 1972-03; Delta Kappa Gamma, 1989-2000; secy, Wicomico Co Liquor Control Bd, 1990-03; Dem Club Wicomico Co, 1990-03; secy, YMCA Mid Shore, Corp Bd, 1990-03; Worcester Co Retired Teachers Asn, 2000-02; comt mem, Chesapeake Forest Citizens Adv Comt, 2002; Independent Retired Persons; AARP; comt mem, Chesapeake Forestry Adv Bd; Rural Legacy Adv Bd; Deacon Bd, Wicomico Presby Church; St Augustines Col Alumni; Human Rels Comt. **Home Addr:** 1004 S Delano Ave, Salisbury, MD 21801-8043, **Home Phone:** (410)749-9316.

**DENNIS, EDWARD S. G., JR.**
Lawyer. **Personal:** Born Jan 24, 1945, Salisbury, MD; son of Virginia Monroe and Edward S; married Lois Juliette Young; children: Edward Brookfield. **Educ:** US Merchant Marine Acad, BS, 1967; Univ Pa Law Sch, JD, 1973. **Career:** Lawyer (retired); Eastern Dist Pa, US Dist Ct, law clerk, 1973-75; Eastern Dist Pa, asst US atty, 1975-80; Hon Peter F Vaira, asst US atty, 1975-80; US Dept Justice, Criminal Div Narcotic & Dangerous Drug Sect, dep chief, 1978-80, chief, 1980-83; Eastern Dist Pa, US atty, 1983-88, asst atty gen, 1988-90, actg dep atty gen, 1989-2002; Morgan, Lewis & Bockius, sr partner, 1990. **Orgs:** Bd dir, Pub Broadcasting Sta, WHYY Inc, 1990; Citizens Crime Comn, 1990-; fel Int Soc Barristers, 1991; Am Col Trial Lawyers. **Honors/Awds:** Citizen of the Year, Omega Psi Phi Fraternity, 1987; Edmund J Randolf Award, atty gen US, 1988; Hobart C Jackson Award, Philadelphia Inter-Alumni Coun United Negro Col Fund, 1988; Reverend Dr Martin Luther King Award, Educr Roundtable Inc, 1988; Religious Liberty Award, Am Jewish Cong, 1990. **Special Achievements:** First African-American to hold position Assistant Attorney General of the Criminal Division. **Home Addr:** 118 S 21st St Apt 1301, Philadelphia, PA 19103-4427.

**DENNIS, DR. EVIE GARRETT**
School administrator, government official. **Personal:** Born Sep 8, 1924, Farmhaven, MS; daughter of Eugene and Ola Brown; married Philip; children: Pia E. **Educ:** St Louis Univ, BS, biol, 1953; Univ Colo, MA, educ, 1971; Nova Univ, EdD, 1976. **Career:** School administrator (retired), government official; Childrens Asthma Res Inst & Hosp, from res asst to res assoc, 1958-66; Denver Pub Schs, Lake Jr High Sch, counr, teacher, 1966-71, community specialist, 1971, dep supt, 1988, supt, 1990-94; Denver Voc Guid Inst, cons, 1971-72; Metro State Col, teacher, 1974. **Orgs:** Alpha Kappa Alpha; vpres, US Olympic Comt; bd trustee, US Sports Acad; US Track& Field Inc; chmn, El Pomar Found Awards Excellence Comn, 1983; deleg, Int Amateur Athletic Fed; Int Olympic Comt, 1992; Denver Pvt Indust Coun; Mayor's Black Adv Comt; chair, USA Track & Field Diversity & Leadership Comt; pres, Athletics Cong; vpres, Rocky Mountain Asn; Gov Bodies Coun. **Special Achievements:** Dennis was one of the first two women to reach the US Olympic Executive Committee and the first to serve as Vice President of the US Olympic Committee; She was the first woman and the first African American to head the 60,000-student district; She was the Chef de Mission for the United States Olympic Committee for two Pan American Games as well as the 1988 Olympic Games, a first for a woman in Olympic's history. **Home Addr:** 1313 Steele St Suite 801, Denver, CO 80206.

**DENNIS, HUGO, JR.**
Educator. **Personal:** Born Aug 5, 1936, Tortola; married Carmen Lydia Marrero; children: Tony, Hugh, Jancie, Reynaldo & Alex. **Educ:** Hampton Inst, BS, 1959; Univ Conn, attended 1968. **Career:** VI Pub Schs, math teacher, 1960; St Thomas-St John Fedn Teacher, pres, 1967; Cent Labor Coun VI, pres, 1976; VI legis, pres, 1983-84; VI Govt, actg comnr housing, 1986-. **Orgs:** Deleg, Third Const Conv VI, 1978; rep, Study Tour SAfrica, 1980; pres, AARP VI. **Home Addr:** PO Box 476, St Thomas00801. **Business Addr:** President, AARP Virgin Islands, 93B Estate Diamond, Christiansted00820, **Business Phone:** (340)713-2002.

**DENNIS, JAMES CARLOS**
Marketing executive, vice president (organization). **Personal:** Born Jun 21, 1947, Washington, DC; son of Sadie; married Tonya Redding; children: James Stratford. **Educ:** Fairfield Univ, BS, bus admin & mgt, 1969; USN, Officer Cand Sch, Newport, RI, comn lt, 1969; Harvard Bus Sch, Soldiers Field, MA, MBA, mkt & finance, 1974. **Career:** Gen Foods Corp, White Plains, NY, brand mgr, 1974-78; Warner-Lambert Co, Morris Plains, NJ, sr prod mgr, 1978-81; Heublein Spirits Grp, Hartford, Conn, vpres mkt, 1981-83; Hewlett-Packard, Palo Alto, Calif, dir mkt communs, 1983-89; Travelers Co, Hartford, Conn, vpres mkt corp commun, 1989; Northeast Client Serv, sr vpres; Paymap, chief operating officer; Cendant Mem Group, chief mkt officer & unit gen mgr, 1999-2001; First Data Card Serv & Paymap, chief operating

officer paymap & sr vpres, prod mgt, 2001-04; ACNielsen, sr vpres client serv, 2004-06; Citigroup, sr corp mkt; AXA Equitable Life Ins Co, sr vpres customer mkt, 2006-09; AXA China, chief mkt officer, 2009-12; J Dennis Advisors LLC, prin, 2012-. **Orgs:** Omega Psi Phi Fraternity, 1969-; bd mem, Conn Spec Olympics, 1990-; bd mem, Hartford Stage Co, 1990-. **Business Addr:** Principal, J Dennis Advisors LLC, 714 Bethpage Dr, McDonough, GA 30253-4020, **Business Phone:** (770)506-2417.

## DENNIS, KAREN

Athletic coach. **Personal:** Born Detroit, MI; children: Ebony. **Educ:** Mich state Univ, BA, pub affairs, 1977; MA, phys educ, 1979. **Career:** Spartans womens track & field, asst coach, 1977; Mich State Univ, asst coach, 1977-81, head coach, 1981-92; US Sports Festival, coach, 1985; World Univ Championships, asst coach, Duisburg, Ger, 1989; Pan Am Games, coach; 1991; US Women's Team, coach, 1991, asst coach, 1995, head coach, 2000; Univ Nev-Los Vagas, track coach, head coach, 1992-2002; Ohio State's, women's head coach, 1993-2005; World Championships squad, asst coach, 1995; Buckeyes, head coach; Ohio State Women's Track & Field & Cross Country, asst track coach, 2003-06, head coach, 2006-13, dir, 2014-. **Orgs:** Black Coaches Asn USA Track & Field Int Competition Comm; pres, Athletic Cong Womens Track Coaches Asn NCAA Womens Track & Field Comm NCAA Track Coaches Asn; dir, U.S. Track & Field & Cross Country Coaches Asn. **Honors/Awds:** District VIII, Coach Yr, 1992; USATF Pres Award, 1993; Dennis Conference Coach Yr hons; Big Ten and Great Lakes coach of the year. **Special Achievements:** District IV Coach Yr, 1982; Olympic Games, womens head coach, Sydney, Australia, 2000. **Home Addr:** 2108 Henniker Way, Las Vegas, NV 89134-0336. **Business Addr:** Director, c/o CBS Interactive, 235 2nd St, San Francisco, CA 94105.

## DENNIS, MICHAEL A.

Executive, vice president (organization), administrator. **Personal:** children: 3. **Educ:** Dartmouth Col, BS; Univ Va, Darden Sch Bus, exec prog; Univ Calif, Haas Bus Sch, Berkeley, CA. **Career:** AT&T, Corp Data Ctr, syst admin, 1981; Lucent Technologies, vpres US serv bus commun syst group, 2000; General Sports Venue LLC, owner, pres; Avaya Inc, sr vpres, 2002-; JNET Communications LLC, chief operating officer, currently. **Orgs:** Bd dir, Chair, INROADS, Cent NJ, 2003-05; exec bd, Univ Vt Burlington. **Business Addr:** Chief Operating Officer, JNET Communications LLC, 25 Independence Blvd, Warren, NJ 07059, **Business Phone:** (908)660-4410.

## DENNIS, DR. PHILIP H.

Physician, neurologist. **Personal:** Born Dec 1, 1925, St. Louis, MO; son of Herman and Nellie Helena Watters Holton; married Patricia; children: Pia Evene, Lisette Marie, Philip Herman & Michael Marion. **Educ:** Lincoln Univ, attended 1947; St Louis Univ, attended 1953; Meharry Med Col, MD, 1957; Cook County Grad Sch Med, 1986, APA (CME), 1988. **Career:** Consult psychiatrist, Ill Retirement Syst; City Hosp St Louis, internship, 1957-58; Southern Ill Community Col, instr, 1971-74; Homer G. Phillips, Renard, & Cochran Hosp, psychiat resident, 1972, 1979, 1980, 1982, 1985-86; Ment Health Ctr, dir, 1980-; SIU Edwardsville, coun, 1982-; Windsor Med Arts Ctr, pvt pract, currently. **Orgs:** Southern IllI Univ, Edwardsville; Family Serv Agency; Chamber Com, Kiwanis; Am Soc Clin Hypn. **Honors/Awds:** NIMH fel, 1958-59; Lovejoy Award; Golden Rule Award; Host for KATZ radio "Open Mike" 1968-81; Developer Pleasingly Soft Prods, 1982; Exhibitor oneman art & sculpture show. **Home Addr:** 6225 Sworm Lane, Edwardsville, IL 62025-4917, **Home Phone:** (618)656-1341. **Business Addr:** Neuropsychiatrist, Windsor Medical Arts Center, 100 N 8th St Suite 200, East St. Louis, IL 62201, **Business Phone:** (618)874-5016.

## DENNIS, DR. RODNEY HOWARD

Psychiatrist. **Personal:** Born Oct 3, 1936, Tampa, FL; son of Huerta W and Gussie Harris. **Educ:** NY Univ, Col Arts & Sci, BA, 1958; Howard Univ, Col Med, MD, 1962. **Career:** Kings County Hosp, Rotating Internship, 1962-63; Letterman Gen Hosp, gen med officer, 1964-65; Univ Calif, LA, Brentwood Va Hosp, psychiat res, 1965-67; Metrop State Hosp, physician, 1968-69; New York Sch Psychiat, Brooklyn State Hosp, psychiat resident, 1970-73; Kingsboro Psychiat Ctr, Brooklyn State Hosp, psychiat, 1973-83; Woodhull Med & Ment Health Ctr, consult & liaison serv, attend physician dept psychiat, 1986-. **Orgs:** Am Psychiat Asn; Brooklyn Psychiat Soc; NY Acad Sci; NY Univ Alumni Asn; Asn NY State Ment Hyg Phys & Dentists; AAAS, Acad Psychosom Med, Pi Lambda Phi Frat. **Home Addr:** 307 Decatur St, Brooklyn, NY 11233, **Home Phone:** (718)778-3598. **Business Addr:** Attending Physician, Medical Associates Woodhull PC, 760 Broadway, Brooklyn, NY 11206, **Business Phone:** (718)963-5841.

## DENNIS, DR. RUTLEDGE M.

Educator, sociologist. **Personal:** Born Aug 16, 1939, Charleston, SC; son of David Sr and Ora Porcher; married Sarah Helen Bankhead; children: Shay T, Imaro, Kimya & Zuri. **Educ:** SC State Col, BA, social sci & sociol, 1966; Wash State Univ, MA, sociol, 1969, PhD, sociol, 1975. **Career:** Pre Doctoral Teaching Assoc, Fel, 1970-71; Va Commonwealth Univ, Dept Sociol & Anthrop, coord, Afro AM studies, 1971-78, assoc prof sociol dept, 1978-89, assoc chmn, sociol dept & assoc prof, 1981-83; George Mason Univ, Dept Sociol & Anthrop, vis commonwealth prof, 1989-91, prof, 1991-; Wash State Univ, Dept Sociol, teaching assoc; George Mason Univ, Fenwick Fel, 2005-06, prof sociol & anthrop, currently; Elsevier Publ Co, ed, currently. **Orgs:** Alpha Kappa Mu Hon Socs, 1965; co-coordr, Southeastern Reg African Sem, 1973-76; pres, Black Educ Asn, 1974-75; comnr, Richmond Redevelop & Housing Authority, 1979-81; Sigma Xi, 1980; pres & life mem, Asn Black Sociologists, 1981-83; Adv, Alpha Kappa Delta Chapt, George Mason Univ, 1991-; co-coordr, Grad Prog, sociol dept, George Mason Univ, 1991-; NY Acad Sci; Am Sociol Asn; Southern Sociol Asn; Ba'Alay Keriyah Soc; chair, African-Am Acad, 1999-; life mem, Nat Asn Advan Colored People; Am Asn Univ Prof; George Mason Univ; Eastern Sociol Socs; chair, Socs Study Social Probs; co adv, Tau Chap Alpha Kappa Delta Sociol Hon Soc; chair, Race & Ethnic Minority Comt. **Special Achievements:** First Director of African American Studies at Virginia Commonwealth University. **Home Addr:** 3015 Sunset Ave, Richmond, VA 23221-3925, **Home Phone:** (804)358-8198. **Business Addr:** Professor, George Mason University, Robinson Hall B 315, Fairfax, VA 22030, **Business Phone:** (703)993-1431.

## DENNIS, SHIRLEY M.

Government official, chairperson, vice president (organization). **Personal:** Born Feb 26, 1938, Omaha, NE; married William D C; children: Pamela, Robin & Sherrie. **Educ:** Cheyney State Col, attended 1956; Real Estate Inst, 1959; Am Inst Planner, 1970; Temple Univ, AS, 1985; Lincoln Univ, hon doctorate laws, 1986; Morris Brown Col, hon DHL, 1988; Cabrini Col, BA, orgn mgt, 1996; West Chester Univ Pa, MBA, bus admin, 1998. **Career:** Government official, Chairperson, Vice president (retired); Tucker & Tucker, Philadelphia, sales & Off mgr, 1961-67; Redevelop Authority, Philadelphia, equal opportunity specialist, 1967-68; Urban League Philadelphia, housing dir, 1969-71; Housing Asn Del Valley, managing dir, chief exec officer, 1971-79; Pa Dept Community Affairs, exec dep secy, 1979, actg secy, 1979-80, secy, 1980-86; Women's Bur, US Dept Labor, dir, 1986-88; PECO Energy Co, Prgms & Dev, dir corp sponsorships, 1991-99; Cheyney Univ Pa, Instnl Advan, vpres, 1999-2001. **Orgs:** Pres, Nat Asn Advan Colored People Willow Grove Br, 1972-79; exec bd mem, PA State Conf NCP, 1974-80; Philadelphia Tribune Charities, 1978; co-chairperson, Philadelphia Housing Task force, 1978; chairperson, PA Housing Finance Agency, 1979-86; exec bd mem, Coun State Community Affairs, 1980-86; exec comt, Nat State Housing Finance, 1982-86; Coalition 100 Black Women, 1982-; founding mem, trustee, Abington Memorial Hosp, MLK COM, 1982; bd mem, Philadelphia Martin Luther King, Jr Asn Inc, 1985; Willow Grove Sr Citizens Ctr, 1990-2000; bd mem, Health Partners, 1993-2001; Mayors Comn Aging, 1994-2000; United Negro Col Fund, Philadelphia Regional Telethon, 1996; chair, Regional Performing Arts Ctr Oversight Comt, 1996-2000; Distinguished Daughters PEN, 1998-; dir, bd mem, Willow Grove Found. **Home Addr:** 1656 Easton Rd, Willow Grove, PA 19090, **Home Phone:** (215)657-7113. **Business Addr:** Director, Willow Grove Foundation, 1837 Harte Rd, Jenkintown, PA 19046.

## DENNISTON, PROF. DOROTHY L.

Educator. **Personal:** Born Aug 10, 1944, Springfield, MA; daughter of James H Hamer and Irma L Washington Hamer. **Educ:** Northeastern Univ, BA, eng, 1967; Simmons Col, MA, eng, 1975; Brown Univ, PhD, eng, 1983. **Career:** Sec Schs, teacher Eng, 1967-71; Simmons Col, asst dir admis, 1972-73, instr freshman, 1973-; instr Eng, 1979-80, assoc dean, 1974-80, 79-80; Univ Tenn, asst prof Eng, 1983-86; Brown Univ, Dorothy Danforth Compton fel, 1981-82, howard post doc fel, 1986-87, vis asst prof Eng, 1987-88, asst prof, 1988-94, assoc prof Eng, 1994-, assoc dean col, 1995-96, 1999-2000, assoc prof Africana Studies, 2000-, Wriston fel; Wheaton Col, vis cole Jr prof, 1993. **Orgs:** Alpha Kappa Alpha Sorority, 1963-67; Nat Asn Foreign Stud Affairs, 1972; Assn Study Negro Life & Hist, 1972-; Mod Lang Assn, 1975-; adv com scholars-internship prog, Martin L King Jr Ctr Social Chg, 1976-; fel Nat Fel Fund, 1976-79; Nat Asn Inter discipliny Ethnic Studies, 1977-; Univ Tenn, Knoxville, asst prof, 1983-86; standing comt black studies. Col Lang Asn, 1983-86; SE Lang Asn, 1984-86; col bd, Eng Compos Test Comt, 1984-87; Col Lang Asn, 1984-; Langston Hughes Ctr Arts, 1988-; NE Lang Asn, 1991-; fel Ford Found, 1993. **Home Addr:** 223 Transit St, Providence, RI 02906-3041, **Home Phone:** (401)331-8178. **Business Addr:** Associate Professor, Brown University, 70 Brown St Rm 336, Providence, RI 02912, **Business Phone:** (401)863-3739.

## DENSON, DR. ANDRE B.

Educational psychologist. **Personal:** son of Anders and Barbara; children: Marcus. **Educ:** Univ Nev, Las Vegas, PhD, 1995. **Career:** Clark County Parks & Recreational Dept, recreational aide; Community Col Southern Nev, adj prof math; Univ Nev, Las Vegas, adj prof; Charles I. W Mid Sch, prin; Southern Nev Officials Asn, sports off; Mojave High Sch, prin & region supt; Clark County Sch Dist Northeast Region Ctr, asst supt, currently, instr, basketball coach, dean students, asst prin, athletic adminr; Sierra Nev Col, adj prof. **Orgs:** Omega Psi Phi Fraternity; Phi Kappa Phi Hon Soc; youth group dir & facilitator, Parish Coun, 1984-. **Honors/Awds:** Alliance of Black Professionals Academics Award, 1985-88; New Teacher Award, 1989, Teacher of the Year Award, 1992, Clark County Sch Dist; 12th District Omega Man of the Year, 1994; Distinguished Men of Southern Nevada, 1998. **Home Addr:** 7859 Howard Dade, Las Vegas, NV 89129, **Home Phone:** (702)799-3120. **Business Addr:** Assistant Superintendent, Clarke County School District, 5708 Mountain Vista St, Las Vegas, NV 89146, **Business Phone:** (702)799-0899.

## DENSON, AUTRY LAMONT, JR.

**Personal:** Born Dec 8, 1976, Lauderhill, FL; son of Janice Franklin; married Elaine; children: Autry III, Elijah, Ashley & Asia. **Educ:** Univ Notre Dame, BS, bus, 1999. **Career:** Football player (retired); Tampa Bay Buccaneers, 1999; Miami Dolphins, running back, 1999-2000; Chicago Bears, 2001; Detroit Lions, running back, 2002; Indianapolis Colts, 2002; Montreal Alouettes, Can Football League, 2004; Pope John Paul II High Sch, Boca Raton, Florida, head football coach, 2010; Bethune-Cookman Univ, asst coach, 2011-13; Miami Ohio University, Oxford, running backs coach, 2014-. **Orgs:** Founder, Autry L Denson Run Your Goal Found, 1999; Nat Football Alumni Asn. **Honors/Awds:** Rookie of the Year, 1999; Most Valuable Player, Gator Bowl, 1999. **Special Achievements:** Sixth player in Notre Dame history to reach the 1, 000-yard mark in a season; Reached 1,176 yards mark in 1998 & ranked seventh in Irish history. **Business Addr:** Founder, Run For Your Goal Foundation, 5379 Lyons Rd, Coconut Creek, FL 33073, **Business Phone:** (800)307-8130.

## DENSON, DAMON MICHAEL

Clergy, football player. **Personal:** Born Feb 8, 1975, Aliquippa, PA; married Camille; children: 2. **Educ:** Univ Mich, physic educ. **Career:** Football player (retired), clergy, owner; New Eng Patriots, guard, 1997-99; Baltimore Ravens, 2000; Life Int Church, assoc pastor, currently; Boston church, minister; DamonDenson.com, owner, currently. **Business Addr:** Owner, DamonDenson.com, 550 N Cent Expressway Suite 183, McKinney, TX 75070, **Business Phone:** (443)650-8431.

## DENSON, FRED L.

Lawyer, executive director. **Personal:** Born Jul 19, 1937, New Brighton, PA; married Catherine; children: Kevin Terrence, Kelly & Kendra. **Educ:** Rensselaer Polytech Inst, BE, chem engineering, 1959; Georgetown Univ, JD, 1966. **Career:** WOKR-TV ABC, host black dimensions, 1972-; Urban League, Rochester, exec dir, 1970-71; Eastman Kodak Co, atty, 1967-70; Law Off Fred L Denson, atty, currently. **Orgs:** Bd mem, NY Pub Employ Rels Bd; exec dir, Nat Patent Law Asn; dir, Armarco Mkg; pres, Genessee Region Home Care Asn; chmn, adv coun, NY Div Human Rights Am Bar Asn; Nat Bar Asn; Monroe Co Bar Asn; Nat Patent Law Asn; Am Arbit Asn. **Honors/Awds:** Rochester Community Service Award, 1974-76. **Special Achievements:** Author, Know Your Town Justice Court. **Home Phone:** (716)872-3378. **Business Addr:** Attorney, Law Office Fred L Denson, 14 E Main St, Webster, NY 14580-0801, **Business Phone:** (585)265-2710.

## DENT, DR. ANTHONY L.

Scientist, college teacher. **Personal:** Born Apr 19, 1943, Indian Head, MD; married Joyce P Chesley; children: Antonette, Robert & Christopher. **Educ:** Morgan State Univ, BS, chem, 1966; Johns Hopkins Univ, PhD, phys chem, Heterogeneous catalysis & Infrared spectros catalytic surfaces, 1970. **Career:** Chemist (retired), educator, executive; Carnegie Mellon Univ, asst prof, assoc prof chem eng, 1970-78; DuPont Co, res engr, 1972; PQ Corp, sr res fel, 1979-2000, Mat Sci Dept, sr chemist, 1979-80; res & develop supvr, 1981-83; res & develop mgr, 1983-85; Silica Catalyst Res & Develop Dept, res & develop assoc, 1985-87, prin scientist, Silica Catalyst Res & Develop Dept, sr res fel, 1987-95, Explor Dept, sr res fel, 1995-2000; Dent Enterprises, founder, 2000-08; Cheyney Univ Pa, adj prof, 2002-; Nat Orgn Black Chemists & Chem Engrs, news mag, ed, 2004-, pres; PQ Intranet websites, webmaster; Cheyney Univ Pa, fac. **Orgs:** Beta Kappa Chi Hon Soc, 1963; Phi Lambda Upslon, 1967; Sigma Xi, 1968; Phi Beta Kappa, 1969; CMU Facil Senate, 1971-75; secy, treas, pres, dir, Pitts Catalyst Soc, 1972-81; chmn, Sch Admis Comt Western Pa Chap, John Hopkins Univ, 1972-75; pres, Pitts Chap, Alumni Asn, 1976-77; vice chmn, 5th N Am Catalyst Soc, 1977; secy-treas, dir, Philadelphia Catalysis Club, 1981-83; pres & regional chmn, Del Valley Chap Nat Orgn Black Chemists & Chem Engrs, 1983-89, 1989-93; fel Am Inst Chemists, 1986; bd dir, Nat Orgn Black Chemists & Chem Engrs, 1997-; chmn, Nat Sci Bowl, 1999-; AAAS, 1999-2000; Nat Res Coun Comt; Identification Adv Serv; co-chmn, I &EC Ann Chem Engr Symp; Am Inst Chem Engrs. **Honors/Awds:** Meritorious Service Awards, Nat Orgn Black Chemists & Chem Engrs, 1988, 1994, 2008. **Home Addr:** 1207 Dundee Dr, Dresher, PA 19025-1617, **Home Phone:** (215)830-0495. **Business Addr:** News Magazine Editor, National Organization for the Professional Advancement of Black Chemists & Chemical Engineers, PO Box 77040, Washington, DC 20013, **Business Phone:** (866)599-0253.

## DENT, DAVID J.

Educator, journalist. **Educ:** Morehouse Col, BA, polit sci, 1981; Columbia Univ Grad Sch Jour, MS, 1982. **Career:** Africana Studies Prog; New York Univ, assoc prof jour & mass commun, social & cult anal, Fac Resource Network, adv, workshop leader, currently; Author: Whose Reality: Million Man March Black Renaissance Noire, 1996; In Search of Black America, Discovering the African American Dream, Simon & Schuster, 2000; American Extremes; The Huffington Post. **Orgs:** Bd mem, Calhoun Sch. **Business Addr:** Associate Professor, New York University, 20 Cooper Sq Rm 488 6th fl, New York, NY 10003, **Business Phone:** (212)998-7592.

## DENT, GARY KEVER

Executive, administrator. **Personal:** Born Nov 18, 1950, Norfolk, VA; son of Kever H and Geraldine Brown; married Carman Stroud; children: Katina Arne & Travis Damon. **Educ:** Norfolk State Univ, BS, spec educ, 1972; Cent Mich Univ, MA, mgt & supv, 1983. **Career:** Detroit Diesel Allison-GMC, serv training rep, 1974-76; gen motors, Gen Motors Educ & Training, regional mgr, 1977-85, Gen Motors Personnel Progs & Serv, mgr, 1985-89, Gen Motors Cent Off Personnel, 1989-93; City Detroit, Human Resource Dept, dir, assoc vpres, 1994-2002; Wayne State Univ, asst vpres human resource, 2002-06; Univ Cincinnati, assoc vpres, chief human resources officer & sr assoc vpres, 2006-09; Pa State Syst Higher Educ, vice chancellor human resources & labor rels, 2009; prin, Devine Group Inc, currently. **Orgs:** Co-chairperson, Nat Asn Advan Colored People, 1980-; Aircraft Owner & Pilots Asn, 1985-; pres, Nat Black MBA Asn, Detroit; chairperson, Boy Scouts Am, Cent Sec, 1988-; Head Start; United Way; Am Soc Employers; Detroit Inst Arts; Jr Achievement; Communities Sch-Detroit; Soc Human Resources Mgt; CUPA-HR; Nat Asn African-Americans Human Resources. **Home Addr:** 16190 Shaftsbury Ave, Detroit, MI 48219, **Home Phone:** (313)538-4313. **Business Addr:** The Devine Group, Principal, 7755 Montgomery Rd Suite 180, Cincinnati, OH 45236, **Business Phone:** (513)792-7500.

## DENT, DR. PRESTON L.

Educator, businessperson, psychologist. **Personal:** Born Apr 30, 1939, Philadelphia, PA; son of William and Alice Livingston; married Imelda Velasco; children: David & Robyn Lynn. **Educ:** Pa State Univ, BS, psychol, 1961; San Francisco State Univ, MA, psychol, 1963; Univ Calif, Santa Barbara, PhD, educ psychol, 1971. **Career:** San Francisco City Col, Dept Psychol, grad instr, 1966-67; STIR Facil, Bunker-Ramo Corp, simulator flight contrl prog eng, 1966-67; TRW Systs Inc, Indus Rels Div, trainer, counr, equal opport prog off, 1967-68; Pierce Col, psychol instr, 1967-72; Univ Calif, Santa Barbara, asst chancellor, 1969-72; Univ Southern Calif, prof higher educ, 1972-86; Dent-Glasser Corp, pres, chief exec officer, 1984-; Col Lett Arts Sci, assoc dean, dir develop & sponsored res. **Orgs:** UN Asn; fel Am Coun Educ, 1971-72; Golden State Found; comnr, City Los Angeles, 1981-82; dir, Los Angeles Child Guid Clin; consult, MacNeal-Schwendler Corp; bd advrs, Am Int Nat Bank; Int Coun Psychol; Am Psychol Soc; AAAS; Am Asn Univ Admin; trustee, Paine Col. **Honors/Awds:** Outstanding Young Men of America Award, US Chamber Com, 1970; Kappa Delta Pi Ed Hon, Phi Delta Kappa Ed Hon; Distinguished Service Award, City Los Angeles; Sigma Xi. **Special Achievements:** Author: "A Study of Faculty and Student Opinions on Teaching Effectiveness Ratings", 1980. **Home Addr:** 32551 Seacliff Dr, Rancho Palos Verdes,

CA 90275-6160, **Home Phone:** (424)206-2597. **Business Addr:** President, The Dent-Glasser Corp, 544 Finney Ct Unit B, Gardena, CA 90248, **Business Phone:** (310)291-5143.

### DENT, RICHARD LAMAR

Football player, chief executive officer, football coach. **Personal:** Born Dec 13, 1960, Atlanta, GA; son of Horace and Mary; married Leslie; children: Mary Francis Sarah & R J. **Educ:** Tenn State Univ, attended 1983. **Career:** Football player (retired), assistant coach, chief executive officer; Chicago Bears, defensive end, 1983-93, 1995, asst coach, 2003; San Francisco 49ers, defensive end, 1994; Indianapolis Colts, 1996; Philadelphia Eagles, defensive end, 1997; RLD Resources LLC, chief exec officer, 1999-; First Commun, partner. **Orgs:** Bd mem, Nat Col Found; Ill Col Hall Fame; Ill Literacy Prog; Chicago Pk Dist; Better Boys Found. **Home Addr:** 4328 Luxemburg Dr, Decatur, GA 30034. **Business Addr:** Chief Executive Officer, RLD Resources LLC, 333 N Mich Ave Suite 2800, Chicago, IL 60601, **Business Phone:** (312)795-0798.

### DENTON, SANDRA

Singer, actor. **Personal:** Born Nov 7, 1964, Kingston; married Anthony Criss; children: Tyran & Egypt Jahnari. **Educ:** Queensborough Community Col, nursing. **Career:** Singer & actress; Salt-N-Pepa, rap group, mem, 1985-2002; actor, currently; Albums: Hot, Cool, & Vicious, 1986; A Salt with a Deadly Pepa, 1988; Brand New, 1998. Films: Stay Tuned, 1992; Who's the Man?, 1993; Jason's Lyric, 1994; Joe's Apartment, 1996; 3 AM, 2001; Love & a Bullet, 2002; The Perfect Holiday, 2007; Queen of Media, 2011. TV Series: "Saturday Night Live", 1994; First Time Felon, 1997; Linc's, 2000; "Oz", 2000-03; "The Salt-N-Pepa Show", exec producer, 2007; "Let's Talk About Pep", actress, writer & exec producer, 2010; "Are We There Yet?", 2011; "Sharknado 2: The Second One", 2014. **Orgs:** Salt-N-Pepa. **Honors/Awds:** Push-It was #37 on VH1 Hundred Greatest Dance Songs. **Special Achievements:** First female rapper to have a gold album; Ranked #83 on VH1's Greatest Women of Rock N Roll. **Business Addr:** Actress, William Morris Agency LLC, 151 El Camino Dr, Beverly Hills, CA 90212, **Business Phone:** (310)859-4000.

### DENTON, TIMOTHY JEROME, SR.

Football player. **Personal:** Born Feb 2, 1973, Galveston, TX. **Educ:** Sam Houston State Univ, grad, 1999; Blinn JC, grad; Univ Okla, grad. **Career:** Football player (retired); Atlanta Falcons, defensive back, 1996; Wash Redskins, defensive back, 1998-99; San Diego Chargers, cornerback, 2000; Arena football league, Dallas Desperados, 2002-03.

### DENYE, BLAINE A.

Educator, teacher, vice president (organization). **Personal:** Born Jun 27, 1933, Chicago, IL; son of Julius and Gladys; married Doris L Thornton; children: Paul & Iva. **Educ:** Roosevelt Univ, BA, 1960; Chicago Teachers Col, MEd, 1964. **Career:** Teacher, 1960-63; coun, 1963-69; Educ Prog Planning, dir, 1969-70; Model Cities Prog, dir, 1969-73; Manley HS Chicago, prin, 1973-86; Dist Ten, supt, 1986-89. **Orgs:** Chmn, Diaconate Bd, 1966; chmn exec coun, Trinity United Church Christ, 1973-75; chmn, Bldg Comt, 1974-80; chmn, Bd Long Range Planning; Phi Delta Kappa; vpres bd dir, Trinity; pres, Trinity Community Housing Corp; pres, Trinity Acres Housing Corp. **Home Addr:** 1067 W 97 St, Chicago, IL 60643-1578, **Home Phone:** (773)445-8089.

### DEPRIEST, DARRYL LAWRENCE

Lawyer. **Personal:** Born Sep 23, 1954, Chicago, IL; son of W LaVerne and Bertha Williams; married Colleen K Connell; children: Brennan Connell & Carlyle Ann. **Educ:** Harvard Col, Cambridge, MA, BA, cum laude, govt, 1976; Harvard Law Sch, Cambridge, MA, JD, 1979; Nat Inst Trial Advocacy, Boulder, Co, 1983. **Career:** Kirkland & Ellis LLP, summer Assoc, 1977; McCutcheon, Doyle, Brown & Enerson, summer Assoc, 1978; Us Fed Courts, judicial law clerk, 1979-80; Hon Robert E Keeton, USDJ, Boston, Mass, law clerk, 1979-80; Jenner & Block, Chicago, Ill, partner, 1980-88; Am Bar Asn, Chicago, Ill, gen coun, 1988-2006; Hill+Knowlton Strategies, sr consult, 2008-15; US Small Bus Admin, chief Coun, 2015-. **Orgs:** Am Bar Asn; Nat Bar Asn; Ill State Bar Asn; Cook County Bar Asn; Chicago Bar Asn; Am Corp Coun Asn; Am Soc Asn Execs; Chicago Soc Asn Execs; bd dirs, Chicago Pub Schs Alumni Asn; bd dirs, 1981-85, Schs & Scholar Comt, 1980-, Harvard Club Chicago; Harvard Club Boston; Assoc Harvard Alumni; bd dirs, Leadership Greater Chicago, fel mem bd dirs, Pres, 1988-96; bd mem, 1991-2008, bd chair, 1997-2008, Chicago Bd Ethics; bd dirs, 1995-2008, vice pres, 1998-2008, Chicago Area Found Legal Serv. **Honors/Awds:** Leadership Greater Chicago, 1987-88; 40 Under 40, Crain's Chicago Bus, 1989; America's Best & Brightest Young Business & Professional Men, Dollars & Sense Mag, 1989; Monarch Award, Achievement Law, Xi Nu Omega Chapter, Alpha Kappa Alpha Sorority, 1989. **Home Addr:** 2925 W Leland Ave, Chicago, IL 60625-3715, **Home Phone:** (773)583-1289. **Business Addr:** Senior Consultant, Hill+Knowlton Strategies, 222 Merchandise Mart Plz Suite 275, Chicago, IL 60654, **Business Phone:** (312)255-3129.

### DERAMUS, BETTY

Columnist, writer. **Personal:** Born Tuscaloosa, AL. **Educ:** Wayne State Univ. **Career:** Columnist, Writer: Wayne State, Detroit, instr, eng & Africana studies; Detroit Free Press, ed writer, 1979-87; Assoc Press, ed writer; Eugene Pulliam, fel, Sigma Delta Chi Found, 1986; Detroit News, columnist, 1987-2006; BBC, commentator, 2004; Essence, Time-Life, N Star J, Black World, writer; Detroit News, Detroit Free Press & Mich Chronicle, commentator; Books: Constant Search; Forbidden Fruit: Love Stories from Underground Rr & Freedom by Any Means: True Stories Cunning & Courage Underground Rr. **Orgs:** Founding mem, Detroit Chap Nat Asn Black Journalists. **Home Addr:** , Detroit, MI.

### DERAMUS, BILL R.

Businessperson. **Personal:** Born Jul 10, 1938, Timpson, TX; son of Lafayette and T J; children: William. **Educ:** Prairie View A&M Univ, BS, bus admin, 1961; Webster Univ, MS, mgt & human rels, 1983. **Career:** Marriott Int, dir human rels, reg dir hr, reg mgr & s cent reg brand dir courtyard; Marriott, gen mgr, 1991-96, franchisee; Capstone Mgt Serv, pres, currently; MPH Mgt, co founder. **Orgs:** Life mem, Alpha Phi Alpha; life mem, Nat Asn Advan Colored People; Nat Black MBA; bd, Int Franchising Asn; bd, Nat Asn Black Hotel Owners, Operators & Developers. **Honors/Awds:** Regional Manager of the Year, 1995. **Special Achievements:** First African Am franchisee for Marriott Intl, 1996. **Home Addr:** 826 Meadowglen Circle, Coppell, TX 75019, **Home Phone:** (972)393-7751. **Business Addr:** Business Owner, Courtyard Marriott, 4949 Regent Blvd, Irving, TX 75063, **Business Phone:** (972)929-4004.

### DERBIGNY, RHODA L.

Marketing executive, manager. **Personal:** Born Jul 19, 1960, Hagerstown, MD; daughter of Maylon A Campher Sr and Gloria M Weathers; married Curtis E; children: Dominique M. **Educ:** Hagerstown Jr Col, Hagerstown, AA, bus admin, 1981; Towson State Univ, BS, bus admin, 1984. **Career:** Household Finance Corp, Hagerstown, asst mgr, 1984-86; Goodwill Indust Inc, Hagerstown, dir community based serv, 1986-87; Citicorp, Hagerstown, unit mgr, 1987-89; Corning Inc, mkt develop specialist, nat sales mgr, 1989-. **Orgs:** Nat Asn Advan Colored People, 1987-89; bd mem, Southern Tier Asn Blind, 1990-; Soc Black Prof, 1990-. **Home Addr:** 11034 Staley Dr, Hagerstown, MD 21742-9730, **Home Phone:** (301)739-4536. **Business Addr:** National Sales Manager, Corning Inc, MP 21 2 2, Corning, NY 14831, **Business Phone:** (607)974-7823.

### DERRICOTTE, DR. EUGENE ANDREW

Dentist, educator, football player. **Personal:** Born Jun 14, 1926, Fostoria, OH; son of Clarence C and Bessie M Anderson; married Jeanne E Hagans; children: Robert. **Educ:** Univ Mich, BS, pharm, 1950, DDS, 1958. **Career:** Football player, dentist (retired); Univ Mich Wolverines, football player, 1944-48; USAF, dent surgeon & chief dent surgeon var air force bases, 1971-79; USAF Acad, command dent surgeon, 1979-84; USAF Hosp Chanute AFB, dir dent serv, 1984-85; Univ Tex Health Sci Ctr, San Antonio, asst prof, 1985-2000. **Orgs:** Am Dent Asn; Alpha Phi Alpha; Air Force Memorial Found. **Honors/Awds:** Hall of Honor, Univ Mich, 1987; Congressional Gold Medal, Wash, DC, 2007. **Special Achievements:** First African-American in University's Athletes; The First African-american To Play In The Offensive Backfield For The Michigan Wolverines Football Program. **Home Addr:** 3718 Morning Mist St, San Antonio, TX 78230-2129, **Home Phone:** (210)561-0280.

### DERRICOTTE, TOI

Educator, poet. **Personal:** Born Apr 12, 1941, Hamtramck, MI; daughter of Antonia Baquet and Benjamin Sweeney Webster. **Educ:** Wayne State Univ, BA, spec educ, 1965; NY Univ, MA, eng lit & creative writing, 1984. **Career:** NJ State Coun Arts & Md State Arts Coun, master teacher, 1973-88; Columbia Univ, educ consult, 1979-82; Writers Voice Ser Manhattan, poetry teacher, 1985-86; Old Dom Univ, assoc prof Eng lit, 1988-90; George Mason Univ, commonwealth prof eng dept, 1990-91; Univ Pittsburgh, Eng Dept, prof eng, 1991-; New York Univ, Creative Writing Prog, vis prof, 1992; Cave Canem found, Hist Workshop & Retreat African-Am Poets, co-founder, 1996; Mills Col, distinguished vis poet, 1998; Xavier Univ, Delta Sigma Theta Sorority Inc, endowed chair poetry, 1999-2000; New York Univ, MFA Prog, prof, currently; Books: The Empress of the Death House, 1978; Natural Birth, 1983; Captivity, 1989, second edition, 1991, third edition, 1993. **Orgs:** Fel poetry Nat Endowment Arts, 1984; MacDowell fel 1984; Grad Admin Comt; ACIE, 2007-2008; Pedag & Difference Comt; chancellor, Acad Am Poets, 2012. **Home Addr:** 1600 Williamsburg Pl, Pittsburgh, PA 15235. **Business Addr:** Professor of English, University of Pittsburgh, CL 517-D Cathedral Learning, Pittsburgh, PA 15260, **Business Phone:** (412)624-6527.

### DERRYCK, VIVIAN LOWERY

Government official. **Personal:** Born Jan 30, 1945, Cleveland, OH; daughter of Collins and Mary; married Robert J Berg; children: David P, Amanda Derryck Castel & Belinda Z Berg. **Educ:** Chatham Col, BA, 1967; Columbia Univ, attended 1969, master int affairs, 1990. **Career:** Multicultural heritage teacher African and Hisp Hist & Cult Prog, New York, african curric specialist, 1969-70; African-Am Studies Prog New York Community Col, Brooklyn, asst dir, 1970-71; Educ Develop Ctr, Cambridge, Massachusetts, proj dir, 1972-73; Univ Liberia, staff, sr researcher, instr, 1974-77; US House Representatives, res assoc, 1978; Carnegie Corp, consult, 1979; V.P.'s Task Force Youth Employ, sr assoc, 1979; US Secretariat World Conf Un Decade Women, dir, 1979-80; US Dept State, dep asst secy, 1980-82; Nat Coun Negro Women, exec vp, dir, 1982-84; US Agency Int Develop, asst adminr & AFR, consult, 1984-85; Nat Dem Inst Int Affairs, vpres, 1984-88; Wash Int Ctr, exec dir, 1988-89; African Am Inst, pres, 1989-95; African Leadership Forum, sr advr, 1996-98; Acad Develop, sr vpres, 1997-98; election observer, 1997-2005; Secure Support Girls' Educ & Maternal & child health, sirleaf admin; Acad Edu Develop, sr vpres & dir, currently. **Orgs:** Bd dir, Int Develop Conf, 1983-; bd trustee, African Ctr Develop & Stategic Studies, 1991-; bd dir, Constituency Africa, 1993-; adv comn vol foreign aid, US Agency Int Develop, 1993-97; Ctr Prev Action, 1994-97; bd dir, Meridian Int Ctr, 1998-; Coun Foreign Rels; Bretton Woods Comt. **Home Addr:** 1501 Farragut St NW, Washington, DC 20011-3831, **Home Phone:** (202)545-0022. **Business Addr:** Senior Vice President, Director, Academy for Educational Development, 1825 Connecticut Ave NW, Washington, DC 20009-5721, **Business Phone:** (202)884-8000.

### DESANDIES, DR. KENNETH ANDRE

Physician. **Personal:** Born Feb 16, 1948, New York, NY; son of Conrad and Elsie; married Karen Yvonne Grant; children: Kisha & Kanika. **Educ:** Hampton Inst, BA, 1969; Meharry Med Col, MD, 1973. **Career:** Hurley Hosp, intern, 1973-74; State Univ NY Downstate, resident; Kings Co Hosp, resident obstet & gynec, 1974-78; Group Health Asn, obstet & gynec attend, 1978-81; pvt pract, 1981; Inova Alexandria Hosp, physician. **Orgs:** Fel Am Col Obstet & Gynec, 1981; Nat Med Asn; Alfred St Baptist Church; pres, N Va Med Socs; Am Col Obstetricians & Gynecologists. **Honors/Awds:** Board Certificate, Am Col Obstet & Gynec, 1980; Am Col Obstet & Gynec Award, 1980, 1998; Physician Recognition Award, Am Med Asn, 1983-98; Patients Choice Award, 2011. **Business Addr:** Physician, 4600 Duke St Suite 332, Alexandria, VA 22304-2516, **Business Phone:** (703)823-5656.

### DESASSURE, CHARLES

Computer scientist, educator, association executive. **Personal:** Born Apr 19, 1961, Eutawville, SC; son of Moses and Emma Dessesso; married Gloria Sumpter. **Educ:** Claflin Col, BS, 1984; Orangeburg-Calhoun Tech Col, AS, 1989; Webster Univ, MA, 2000. **Career:** Tarrant County Col, Compensatory, remedial educ teacher, 1984-87, coordr, comput instr, 1988-90, Micro Comput Specialist, programmer, 1990-93, LAN adminr, 1993-96, Comput Field Technol, analyst, 1996-98, Marcus Cabler, info syst mgr, 1998-2001; Comput Sci & Info Technol, instr, 2001-09, dept chair, 2006-09, asst prof, 2010-. **Orgs:** Bd dir, former mem, St Jones Baptist Church; Phi Beta Sigma Fraternity, 1981-; pres, SC Youth & Col Conf, Nat Asn Advan Colored People, 1981-83; bd mem, El Ctr Col Comput Technol Adv Comt, 1993-97; Asn Corp Comput Tech Prof, 1997-; former mem, Orangeburg Calhoun Tech Col Adv Bd; Arlington City Youth & Families Bd, 1998-; Arlington-Sundown Kiwanis Club, 2000-. **Honors/Awds:** Creative Writing Contest Award, Claflin Col, 1981; Leadership Award Nat, Phi Beta Sigma, 1982; Outstanding Undergraduate of the Year, Southeastern Region, Phi Beta Sigma Fraternity Inc, 1982-83; Editor-in-Chief Leadership Award, Clafin Col, 1983; Outstanding Teacher of the Year, Mansfield Bus Col, Columbia, SC, 1988-89; American Legion Bronze Medal, Dept SC, 1993; Presidential Award for Leadership, SC NAACP Conf, 1993. **Special Achievements:** Cert Novell Adminr, CNA, 1995. **Home Addr:** 740 Taft Dr, Arlington, TX 76011. **Business Addr:** Instructor of Business & Technology Division, Assistant Professor, Tarrant County College, 1500 Houston St, Fort Worth, TX 76102, **Business Phone:** (817)515-3747.

### DESERT, ALEX

Actor, singer, writer. **Personal:** Born Jul 18, 1968. **Career:** TV series: "TV 101", 1988; "Free Spirit", 1988-89; "A Different World", 1990; The Flash, 1990; "Beverly Hills, 90210", 1990; "The Flash", 1991; "The Heights", 1992; "Lush Life", 1993; "The Ticket", 1994; "Galaxy Beat", 1994; "Boy Meets World", 2000; "Becker", 2003; "Harry Green and Eugene", 2004; "Reno 911!", 2008; "Wolverine and the X-Men", 2008; "Rita Rocks", 2008; "House M.D.", 2009; "The Avengers: Earth's Mightiest Heroes", 2009-10; "The LeBrons", 2011; "Let's Do This!", 2011; "Isabel", 2012; "In Session with Jonathan Pessin", 2012; "Let It Shine", 2012; "Grey's Anatomy", 2014; "Mom", 2014; "Scandal", 2014. Films: PCU, 1994; Swingers, 1996; Playing God, 1997; High Fidelity, 2000; Masked and Anonymous, 2003; Chicken Party, 2003; Death of the Day, 2004; Pretty Persuasion, 2005; Tomb Raider: Legend, 2006; Scarface: The World Is Yours, 2006; "The Sarah Silverman Program", 2007; Tomb Raider: Underworld, 2008; "Wolverine and the X-Men", 2008; "Rita Rocks", 2008; Bob Funk, 2009; Lego: The Adventures of Clutch Powers, 2010; Alexander and the Terrible, Horrible, No Good, Very Bad Day, 2014. **Business Addr:** Actor, c/o CBS Television Network, 51 W 52nd St, New York, NY 10019, **Business Phone:** (212)975-3247.

### DESHIELDS, DELINO LAMONT

Baseball player, baseball executive. **Personal:** Born Jan 15, 1969, Seaford, DE; married Michelle Elliott; children: Delino Jr, D'Angelo, Diamond, Denim & Delaney. **Educ:** Villanova Univ. **Career:** Baseball player (retired), baseball executive; Montreal Expos, infielder, 1990-93; Los Angeles Dodgers, 1994-96; St Louis Cardinals, 1997-98; Baltimore Orioles, 1999-2001; Chicago Cubs, 2001-02; Urban Baseball League, co-founder & vpres, 2007-; Billings Mustangs, hitting coach & mgr, 2009; Louisville Bats, mgr, currently. **Honors/Awds:** State Baseball Player of the Year, 1986; Rookie of the Year Award, 1990; Inducted Delaware Sports Museum Hall of Fame, 2006; Eastern Shore Baseball Foundation Hall of Fame and Museum, 2010. **Special Achievements:** Led National League in triples, 1997; 9-time top 10 finisher among NL base stealers, 1990-98. **Business Addr:** Manager, Hitting Coach, Billings Mustangs, 2611 9 Ave N Billings MT 59101, Billings, MT 59101, **Business Phone:** (406)252-1241.

### DESOUSA, DR. D. JASON

Chancellor (education), school administrator, vice president (organization). **Personal:** Born Sep 12, 1964, New York, NY; son of William and Catherine. **Educ:** Morgan State Univ, BS, sports admin, 1987; Bowling Green State Univ, MA, col stud coun & personnel serv, 1989; Ind Univ, EdD, higher educ admin, 1994. **Career:** Tuskee Univ, dir career develop, 1994-95; Ala State Univ, asst vpres stud affairs, 1995-99; Savannah State Univ, vpres stud affairs; Morgan State Univ, asst vpres acad affairs, assoc Prof Higher Educ; 2002-; Huston-Tillotson Univ, provost, vpres acad & stud affairs, 2008-09; Fayetteville State Univ, div acad affairs asst vice chancellor stud retention, 2012-; ed bd, NASAP J, currently. Author: Student Success in College: Creating Conditions that Matter. **Orgs:** Stud regent, Morgan State Univ Bd Regents, 1986-87; nat bd dir, Kappa Alpha Psi Fraternity Inc, 1986-88; Am Col Stud Personnel Asn, 1989-; fel Ford Found, 1990-91; pres, Nat Asn Stud Affairs Prof; co-coordr, Int Ctr Stud Success & Instnl Accountability; polemarch, Bloomington Alumni Chap; advisor, Alpha Chap. **Home Addr:** 720 Hammocks View, Savannah, GA 31410, **Home Phone:** (912)898-0561. **Business Addr:** Assistant Vice Chancellor of Student Retention, Morgan State University, 1200 Murchison Rd, Fayetteville, MD 28301, **Business Phone:** (910)672-2687.

### DESSASO-GORDON, JANICE MARIE

Government official, consultant, chief executive officer. **Personal:** Born Apr 10, 1942, Washington, DC; daughter of John F Ford (deceased) and Marie E Sheppard; married Harold J; children: Anthony, Mark, Cathy, Eugene C & Michael A. **Educ:** Univ DC, Wash, DC, BA, 1977. **Career:** Var fed govt agencies, Wash, DC, secy, 1960-70; US Dept Com, Wash, DC, prog analyst, 1971-76, Minority Bus Develop Agency, prog mgr; JD Consult Group, consult, currently. **Orgs:** Exec vpres, Holy Comforter-St Cyprian Community Action Group, 1988-; Bus & Prof Women's Asn, 1988-; Nat Asn Female Execs; pres & chief exec officer, Community Action Group. **Honors/Awds:** Outstanding Performance Award, US Dept Com, 1973, 1979, 1984, 1986, 1988 & 1990-94; Certificate of Appreciation, Nat Minority Supplier Develop Coun, 1981; Outstanding Service Award, Nat Minority Supplier Develop Coun, 1985 & 1987; Appreciation Award, Nev Econ Develop Co, 1988; One of the 25 individuals honored for NMSDCs 25th

Anniversary, 1997. **Special Achievements:** Annual 30-hour dancer, Washington DC Special Olympics for Mentally Retarded-Dance Marathon, 1983-89. **Home Addr:** 347 11th St SE, Washington, DC 20003, **Home Phone:** (202)546-1607. **Business Addr:** Consultant, JD Consulting Group, 347 11th St SE, Washington, DC 20003-0000, **Business Phone:** (202)546-1607.

### DESSELLE, NATALIE (NATALIE DESSELLE REID)
Actor. **Personal:** Born Jul 12, 1967, Alexandria, LA; married Leonard Reid; children: Sereno, Summer & Sasha. **Educ:** Grambling State Univ. **Career:** Films: Set It Off, 1996; BAPS, How to Be a Player, 1997; Sweet Hideaway, 2003; Killing of Wendy, 2009; Queen Victoria's Wedding, 2010; Let Lorenzo, 2011; Zoe Gone, 2014. TV Series: Family Matters, 1996; "Built to Last", 1997; "Getting Personal", 1998; "For Your Love", 1998-2000; "Yes, Dear", 2002; "ER", 2003; "Eve", 2003-06; "Resident Aliens", 2005; TV films: "Cinderella", 1997; Freaknik: The Musical, 2010; A Mother's Rage, 2013. **Business Addr:** Actress, c/o Schiowitz, Clay, Ankrum & Ross Inc, 1680 N Vine St Suite 614, Los Angeles, CA 90028, **Business Phone:** (323)463-7300.

### DEVARD, JERRI
Executive. **Personal:** children: 2. **Educ:** Spelman Col, BA, econs; Clark Atlanta Univ Grad Sch Mgt, MBA, mkt. **Career:** Pillsbury Co, brand mgt, group mkt mgr, 1983-93; Nat Football League, dir sales & mkt, minn vikings, 1992-94; Harrah's Entertainment, vpres sales & mkt, 1994-96; Revlon, vpres mkt color cosmetics, 1996-98; Citigroup, chief mkt officer, 1998-2003; Verizon Commun, brand mgt & mkt communs, sr vpres, 2003-05, sr vpres mkt & brand mgt, 2005-07; DeVard Mkt Group, pres, 2009-10; Nokia Corp, exec vpres & chief mkt officer, 2011-12; ADT, chief mkt officer, 2014-16. **Orgs:** Bd, Pepsi African-Am Adv; bd dir, Asn Nat Advertisers; exec comt, Am Advert Fed Bd; bd mem, Exec Leadership Coun; adv bd, PepsiCo, 2002-12; bd dir, Tommy Hilfiger Corp, 2004-06; bd trustee, Spelman Col, 2005-14; bd dir, Gurwitch Prod, 2009-11; bd dir, Belk, 2010-16; bd dir, Ad Coun, 2015-; bd dir, ServiceMaster, 2016-. **Special Achievements:** Named as one of Black Enterprise magazine's "75 Most Powerful African-Americans in Corporate America" in February 2005. **Business Addr:** Board of Trustee, Spelman College, 350 Spelman Lane SW, Atlanta, GA 30314, **Business Phone:** (404)681-3643.

### DEVAUGHN-TIDLINE, DONNA MICHELLE
Health services administrator. **Personal:** Born Sep 20, 1954, Houston, TX; daughter of Louise Robinson DeVaughn and Canary DeVaughn; married Eric; children: Joseph W. **Educ:** Southern Methodist Univ, BBA, 1977. **Career:** Prudential Ins Co Inc, assoc mgr acct, 1980-83, dir health care mgt, 1987-; Prudential Health Care Plan Inc, admin mgr claims, 1983-84, dir admin HMO, 1984-86; Memphis State Univ, health admin grad internship prog, preceptor, 1985-86; TX C's Hosp, dir, Plan Dir Mem Serv, currently. **Orgs:** Nat Asn Female Execs; vol, Big Bros/Big Sisters; Delta Sigma Theta. **Home Addr:** 7605 Lark Creek, Memphis, TN 38125. **Business Addr:** Director, Director of Member Services, Texas Children's Hospital, 1919 S Braeswood 6th Fl, Houston, TX 77030, **Business Phone:** (832)824-2315.

### DEVERS, YOLANDA GAIL
Entrepreneur, athlete. **Personal:** Born Nov 19, 1966, Seattle, WA; daughter of Larry and Adele; married Ron Roberts; married Mike Phillips; children: Karsen Anise. **Educ:** Univ Calif Los Angeles, BA, sociol, 1988. **Career:** US Olympic Team, track & field, 1988, 1992, 1996, 2000; Gail Force Inc, owner, currently; Phil Prod LLC, co-owner, currently. **Orgs:** Founder, Gail Devers Found. **Business Addr:** Owner, Gail Force Inc, 950 Herrington Rd Suite C, Lawrenceville, GA 30044-7217, **Business Phone:** (770)822-5641.

### DEVINE, FRANK E.
School principal. **Career:** Mathematics Civics & Sci Charter Sch, Philadelphia, prin, currently. **Home Addr:** 111 David Rd, Balacynwyd, PA 19004, **Home Phone:** (610)668-9025. **Business Addr:** Principal, Charter School of Philadelphia, 447 N Broad St, Philadelphia, PA 19123, **Business Phone:** (215)923-4880.

### DEVINE, JAMIE
Manager, vice president (organization), politician. **Personal:** married Tameika Isaac; children: Tamia & Jade. **Educ:** Benedict Col, BA, eng lang & lit, 1997; SC Community Develop Cert Inst, community econ develop. **Career:** Columbia Housing Authority, mgr, 1994-2005; lic realtor; Richland County Sch Dist One, chmn bd, 2013; Community Assistance Provider, pres & chief exec officer, 2015-. **Orgs:** Greater Columbia Chamber Com; vice chairman, Admin Comt; bd mem, Richland One; Omega Psi Phi Fraternity Inc; Sc Sch Bd's Asn; Community Assistance Provider Inc, vpres, housing develop, 2005-14. **Business Addr:** Vice President of Housing Development, Community Assistance Provider Inc, 9400 2 Notch Rd, Columbia, SC 29229, **Business Phone:** (803)771-0050.

### DEVINE, LORETTA
Actor. **Personal:** Born Aug 21, 1949, Houston, TX; daughter of James and Eunice O'Neal; married Lamar Tyler; married Glen Marshall. **Educ:** Univ Houston, BA, speech & drama educ, 1971; Brandeis Univ, MFA, theatre arts, 1976. **Career:** Films: Will, 1981; Little Nikita, 1988; Sugar and Spice, 1990; Livin'Large, 1991; Caged Fear, 1992; Amos & Andrew, 1993; The Hard Truth, 1994; Waiting to Exhale, 1995; The Preacher's Wife, 1996; Hoodlum, 1997; Lover Girl, 1997; The Price of Kissing, 1997; Urban Legend, 1998; Book of Love, 1999; Oper Splitsville, 1999; Urban Legends: Final Cut, 2000; What Women Want, 2000; Kingdom Come, 2001; I Am Sam, 2001; Book of Love, 2002; The Script, 2002; Baby of the Family, 2002; Dreamgirls, 2006; This Christmas, 2007; First Sunday, 2008; Spring Breakdown, 2009; Death at a Funeral, 2010; Lottery Ticket, 2010; For Colored Girls, 2010; Madea's Big Happy Family, 2010; Jumping the Broom, 2011; Politics of Love, 2011; In the Hive, 2012; A Very Larry Christmas, 2013; Comeback Dad, 2014; Welcome to Me, 2014; The Sound and the Fury, 2014; You're Not You, 2014. TV series: "A Different World", 1987-88; "The PJs", 1999-2008; "Introducing Dorothy Dandridge", 1999; "Boston Pub", 2000; "Life Is Not a Fairy Tale", 2006; Cable series: "Clover", 1997; "Don King: Only in Am", 1997; "Down in the Delta", 1998; "Funny Valentines", 1999; "As We Know It (Part II)", 2006; "Grey's Anatomy", 2005-13; "Eli Stone", 2008-09; "My Son, My Son, What Have Ye Done Miss Roberts", 2009; "Cold Case", 2009; "Legally Mad", 2010; "Death at a Funeral Cynthia", 2010; "Party Down", 2010; "Lottery Ticket Grandma", 2010; "For Colored Girls Juanita Sims", 2010; "Politics of Love Shirlee Gupta", 2010; "Glee Sister Mary Constance", 2011; "Madea's Big Happy Family", 2011; "State of Georgia", 2011; "Norm of the North", 2012; "Shake It Up!", 2012; "The Game", 2012; "The Cleveland Show", 2012; "The Soul Man", 2012; "The Client List", 2012-13; "Doc McStuffins", 2012-14; "Teachers", exec producer, 2013; "Psych", 2014; "Sirens", 2014; "Sullivan & Son", 2014; "Turbo FAST", 2014. **Orgs:** Alpha Kappa Alpha Sorority Inc. **Honors/Awds:** Image Award, Nat Asn Advan Colored People, 1996, 1997, 2001, 2003, 2004 & 2013; Black Reel Award, 2006; LA Femme Filmmaker Award, LA Femme Int Film Festival, 2010; Primetime Emmy, 2011; Gracie Allen Award, 2012. **Special Achievements:** Has earned an Image Award nomination and an Independent Spirit Award nomination for her work in the 2004 film Woman Thou Art Loosed; also nominated for Black Movie Award and Satellite Awards.

### DEVINE, TAMEIKA ISAAC (TAMEIKA ISAAC DEVINE)
Business owner, city council member. **Personal:** married Jamie L; children: Tamia. **Educ:** Hampton Univ, BS, bus mgt, 1994; Spring Valley High Sch; Univ SC Sch Law, JD, law, 1997. **Career:** Carolina Regional Legal Serv, staff atty; Jabber & Isaac PA, founder, partner, currently; Columbia City Coun, councilwoman, 2002-; Univ Phoenix, adj prof. **Orgs:** Am Bar Asn Young Lawyers Div, 1997-2007; SC Bar Asn; Richland County Bar Asn; pres, Columbia Lawyers Asn; secy, SC Black Lawyers Asn; bd mem, Am Red Cross SC Blood Serv; exec coun, SC Young Lawyers Div. **Honors/Awds:** Woman of Distinction Award, Area Girl Scouts, 2004; Lincoln C Jenkins Award, Columbia Urban League, 2005; Certificate Achievement enrollees, National League of Cities. **Special Achievements:** First African-American to win an at-large seat on on Columbia City Council; the First African-American female to be elected to Columbia City Council; youngest ever to be elected to Columbia City Council in either gender or race; Named as one of the Top 20 under 40 by the State newspaper. **Business Addr:** Partner, Founder, Jabber & Isaac PA, 1419 Richland St, Columbia, SC 29201, **Business Phone:** (803)254-8868.

### DEVOE, RONALD BOYD, JR. (RONNIE DEVOE)
Singer, real estate executive. **Personal:** Born Nov 17, 1967, Boston, MA; son of Ronald Sr and Florence E; married Shamari Fears. **Career:** New Ed, singer, 1983; Bell Biv DeVoe, singer, 1990-; Albums: Poison, 1990; Bel Biv DeVoe--Greatest Hits, 2000; BBD, 2001; RE/MAX Real Estate agency, owner, 2002-. **Home Phone:** (818)340-2300. **Business Addr:** Singer, c/o R D's Private Line, 19528 Ventura Blvd, Tarzana, CA 91356, **Business Phone:** (818)340-2300.

### DEWBERRY-WILLIAMS, MADELINA DENISE
Manager, teacher. **Personal:** Born Oct 18, 1958, Los Angeles, CA; daughter of Johnnie Mae Lemons and Clarence; married Ja Daun. **Educ:** San Jose State Univ, attended 1981. **Career:** San Jose Unified Sch Dist, teacher, 1980-81; Santa Clara Junvenile Hall, counr, 1981; Nat Med Enterprises, personnel coordr, 1981-87; Am Express TRS, mgr human resources; Silicon Graphic Comput Syst, mgr, employ progs, 1993; Advo Inc, regional dir human resources, 1999-; Alstom SA, human resources mgr, 2007-. **Orgs:** Vpres, 1986-87, Nat affirmative action, 1986-87; Nat conf, 1987-88; Int Asn Personnel Women; co-chair, United Christian Network, 1986-; dir Spirit Connections, 1986-; bd mem, Cities Schs, 1990-91. **Honors/Awds:** Outstanding Woman in Health Care, YWCA, 1986. **Home Addr:** 26 Egypt Rd, Ellington, CT 06029-2432, **Home Phone:** (860)870-1190. **Business Addr:** Regional Director, Advo Inc, 6955 Mowry Ave, Newark, CA 94560, **Business Phone:** (510)505-6500.

### DEWEY, GEORGE J.
Executive director. **Educ:** Morehouse Col, BA, econs, 1986; Vassar Col, BA, econs, 1988; Harvard Bus Sch, MBA, gen mgt, 1994. **Career:** PaineWebber inc, asst vpres, 1989-96; Citicorp Securities, acquisition finance dept, 1996-98; Salomon Smith Barneys Financial Entrepreneurs Group, pres, vpres financial entrepreneurs group, 1998-2001; Citigroup Global Markets Inc, invest banking dir, dir, 1998-2005; Royal Bank Scotland, managing dir, 2005-. **Orgs:** Hentor, Harvard Bus Sch; community partners, BMAD; bd mem, 100 Black Men Bay Area; By-Laws Comt; chair, Mentoring Comt; bd supervisors, ACERA, currently. **Business Addr:** Managing Director, Royal Bank of Scotland, 150 Spear St, San Francisco, CA 94105, **Business Phone:** (415)644-9759.

### DIANA, DIANA
Cosmetics executive, consultant. **Personal:** Born Mar 6, 1948, Jamaica, NY; daughter of William Griffin and Corinne. **Educ:** Northern Essex Community Col, child care & spec educ, 1971; Midlands Tech. **Career:** Black Angels Dive Club, pres, 1975-; DiAna's Hair Ego salon, owner, 1977-; SC AIDS Educ Network Inc, exec dir, 1986-2000, founder, 1987. **Orgs:** Nat Minority AIDS Coun, 1986-; Women's Callaborative Work Group, 1999; SC African Am HIV Coun. **Honors/Awds:** Black Maria Film & Video Festival, Juror's Award; Am Film Festival Awards; 11 other awards; "Heroes & Heroines", Mother Jones Mag. **Special Achievements:** Author: Bacteriology & Sanitation for the Personal Care Worker, 1988; AIDS & the Law, 1988; AIDS in the Workplace, 1990; Curlers & Condoms, 2003. **Business Addr:** Cosmetologist, Owner, DiAna's Hair Ego Salon, 7222 Highview Dr, Columbia, SC 29223, **Business Phone:** (803)788-8580.

### DIANE, MAMADI
Shipping executive, president (organization), chief executive officer. **Personal:** Born May 16, 1947, Conakry; son of Ibrahima and Nankoria; married Cynthia Horthense; children: Mori. **Educ:** Richer Col, Houlton, Maine, BA, 1970; George Washington Univ, MBA, 1982. **Career:** St John Int, Wash, DC, vpres, 1972-82; AMEX Int Inc, Wash, DC, founder, chief exec officer & pres, 1983-; Metrop Wash Airports Authority, dir; DC, mayor. **Orgs:** Bd dirs, US World Cup Organising Comt, 1994-, US Indust Policy Adv Comt, 1995; adv bd mem, Salam Sudan Found. **Honors/Awds:** Congresional Award, Cong Mervyn Dymally, 1988; Hon Mem, Natl Conf Black Mayors, 1989; Chevalier Odre, Natl du Leopard, Govt Zaire, 1990. **Home Addr:** 1800 Shepherd St NW, Washington, DC 20011-5344, **Home Phone:** (202)606-1696. **Business Addr:** President, AMEX International Inc, 1615 L St NW Suite 340, Washington, DC 20036, **Business Phone:** (202)429-0222.

### DIAZ, FRUITTA LOUISE
Educator. **Personal:** Born Dec 25, 1939, Jersey City, NJ; daughter of Antonio and Pearl; married Joseph W Jenkins; children: Tia Sinclair, William Perkins & Grantlin Perkins. **Educ:** St Peter's Col, BA, 1974; Trenton State Col, MED, 1976. **Career:** Thomas A Edison Col, asst dir, 1975-80; NJ City Univ, dir, 1981-. **Orgs:** Pres, 1989-, 1998-2001, Asn Col Bound Progs; bd trustee, 1995-2001, pres, 2000-01, Kenmare HS; Hudson County Perinatal Consortium, 1995-97; bd mem, First Unitarian Universalist Church Essex County, 1998-2001; NJ City Univ, Tower Club. **Business Addr:** Director Upward Bound, New Jersey City University, Vodra Hall 2039 Kennedy Blvd Rm 123, Jersey City, NJ 07305, **Business Phone:** (201)200-2338.

### DICK, GEORGE ALBERT
Manager. **Personal:** Born Jan 31, 1940, St. Thomas; son of Cleveland and Ruby Drummond; married Margaret Wesley; children: Pete, Dave, Charmaine & Sharon. **Educ:** Bellevue Sch Nursing, RMN, 1962. **Career:** Bellevue Hosp, stud nurse, 1959-62, staff nurse nurse, 1962-67; Beverly Hills Hosp, Dallas, Tex, staff nurse, supvr, 1967-77; Southwest Airlines Co, Dallas, Tex, ramp agent, 1977-79, flight info agt, 1979-83, flight info supvr, 1983-86, mgr. **Orgs:** Opers Comn Southwest Airlines, 1986-; pres, Third World Sports & Social Asn, 1974-76. **Home Addr:** 732 Havenwood, Dallas, TX 75232, **Home Phone:** (214)224-9430. **Business Addr:** TX.

### DICKENS, SAMUEL, III
Executive, chief executive officer. **Career:** Uchs Inc, vpres & chief operating officer; Premier Circuit Assembly Inc, pres & chief exec officer, dir, 1983-. **Orgs:** Bd trustee mem, NC Asn Community Col trustee, currently. **Home Phone:** (919)496-2759. **Business Addr:** President, Chief Executive Officer, Premier Circuit Assembly Inc, 5653 Macedonia Rd, Spring Hope, NC 27882-9382, **Business Phone:** (252)478-4111.

### DICKERSON, AMINA J. (JILL L DICKERSON)
Executive director. **Personal:** Born Feb 2, 1954, Washington, DC; daughter of Ann Lee Stewart and Julius James; married Julian Roberts. **Educ:** Emerson Col, 1972; Harvard Prog, arts admin, 1974; Am Univ, MS, art mgt, 1988. **Career:** Executive (retired); Nat Mus African Art, Smithsonian Inst, dir educ, 1975-82; Philadelphias Afro-Am Hist & Cult Mus, asst dir, 1983; Du Sable Mus African Am Hist & Cult, pres, 1985-89; Chicago Hist Socs, vpres educ & pub progs, 1989-96; Kraft Foods, sr dir corp community involvement, 1997-2009, dir corp giving, 2003, sr dir, Global Community Involvement, 2003-09; Dickerson Global Advisors, 2009-. **Orgs:** Bd mem, Harris Ctr Music & Dance at Millennium Pk; co-chair, Peer Network Int Giving Donor's Forum; vice chmn, Int Comt Coun Foundations; bd mem, Chicago High Sch Arts; bd mem, Congo Sq Theatre; consult, Nat Endowment to Arts; fel Newberry Libr; vice chair, bd trustee, Woods Fund Chicago, 2011; chair, governance comt, Womens Funding Network, 2012; Lloyd A Fry Found, 2014.

### DICKERSON, DR. BETTE JEANNE
Teacher, president (organization), educator. **Personal:** Born May 21, 1951, Philadelphia, PA; daughter of Rosa Anthony. **Educ:** Morehead State Univ, BA, sociol, 1972; Univ Louisville, MEd, spec educ, 1975; Wash State Univ, PhD, sociol, 1986. **Career:** Louisville Jefferson Co Bd Educ, teacher, 1972-78; Wash State Univ, res asst, 1978-81; Nat Urban League, intern prog dir, 1981-82; WK Kellogg Found, prog assoc, 1982-86; Delta Sigma Theta Sor Inc, found dir, 1986-90; Am Univ, dept chair, 1999, assoc prof, currently; Women's & Gender Studies Prog dir, currently; Am Univ Ronald E. McNair Post baccalaureate Achievement Prog, co prin investr; AU Women's & Gender Studies Prog, dir. **Orgs:** Eastern Sociol Soc; Delta Sigma Theta Sor; Phi Kappa Phi Hon Soc; Sociologists Women Soc; DC Sociol Soc; chair, Am Univ Diversity Comt; fac adv, Am Univ Alternative Break; Pres, Asn Black Sociologists; Ford Found's Black; Conf Local Arrangements Comt, Asn Black Sociologists, 1995-96; Exec Comt, Asn Black Sociologists, 1995-96; Conf Local Arrangements Comt, Asn Black Sociologists, 1995-96; exec coun mem, Am Sociol Asn Sect Racial & Ethnic Minorities, 1996-98; actg exec dir, Asn Black Sociologists, 1996; pres-elect & chair prog comt, Asn Black Sociologists, 1998-99; Wash Bk Forums Planning Comt, 1998-2007; pres, Asn Black Sociologists, 1999-2000; Task Force Comt & Comt Nominations, Am Sociol Asn, 1999-2001; Task Force Am Sociol Asn Statement Race, 2000-02; Wash Regional Task Force Racism, 2002-07; Sister-to-Sister Task Force, Sociologists Women ocs, 2002-06; Hist & Arch Comt, Asn Black Sociologists, 2003-08; Cult Race & Ethnic Minorities Comt, Southern Sociol Socs, 2003-05;Awards Comt, Sociologists Women Socs, 2006-07. **Home Addr:** 3919 Livingston St, Hyattsville, MD 20781, **Home Phone:** (301)864-0339. **Business Addr:** Associate Professor, American University, 4400 Mass Ave NW, Washington, DC 20016, **Business Phone:** (202)885-2479.

### DICKERSON, PROF. DENNIS CLARK, SR.
Educator, clergy. **Personal:** Born Aug 12, 1949, McKeesport, PA; son of Carl O and Oswanna Wheeler; married Mary Anne Eubanks; children: Nicole, Valerie, Christina & Dennis Jr. **Educ:** Lincoln Univ, BA, 1971; Wash Univ, MA, 1974, PhD, 1978; Hartford Sem, Memphis Theol Sem; Morris Brown Col, LHD, 1990; Vanderbilt Univ, Mdiv, 2007. **Career:** Forest Pk Community Col, instr, 1974; Penn State Univ, Ogontz Campus, instr, 1975-76; Williams Col, from asst prof hist to assoc prof hist, 1976-85; Payne AME Church Chatham NY, pastor, 1980-85; St Mark AME Church, Munford, Tenn, pastor, 1985-87; Rhodes Col, assoc prof hist, 1985-87; Carter Woodson Inst, Univ Va, vis scholar, 1987-88; Williams Col, assoc prof hist, 1987-88;

African Methodist Episcopal Church, historiographer, 1988-, gen off coun, currently; Stanfield, prof hist, 1992-; Gen Officers Coun, secy; Payne Theolo Sem, vis prof, 1992, 1996, 1998; Yale Divinity Sch, vis prof am relig hist, 1995; Vanderbilt Univ, James M Lawson Jr prof hist, currently. **Orgs:** Fel Nat Endownment Humanities, 1982; Moody Grant Lyndon B Johnson Found, 1983; Grant-in-aid Am Coun Learned Soc, 1983-84; Improved Benevolent Protective Order Elks World; Alpha Phi Alpha Fraternity; Nat Asn Advan Colored People; GRE Hist Comm Educ Testing Serv, 1990-96; bd corporator, Williamstown Savings Bank, 1992-; bd trustee, N Adams State Col, 1992-95; Am Soc Church Hist; Orgn Am Historians; Am Hist Asn; Southern Hist Asn; World Methodist Hist Soc; Wesley Hist Soc; bd trustee, Am Bible Study Soc, 1995-; Louisville Inst, 2004-05; fel Siemens Am Acad, Berlin Spring, 2014. **Home Addr:** 212 Aspenwood Lane, Nashville, TN 37221. **Business Addr:** James M Lawson Jr Professor of History, Vanderbilt University, 2301 Vanderbilt Pl, Nashville, TN 37235, **Business Phone:** (615)343-4329.

### DICKERSON, ERIC DEMETRIC
Football player, television show host, business owner. **Personal:** Born Sep 2, 1960, Sealy, TX; son of Richard Seal and Helen; children: Erica. **Educ:** Southern Methodist Univ, attended. **Career:** Football player (retired), TV show host, executive; Los Angeles Rams, running back, 1983-87; Indianapolis Colts, 1987-91; Los Angeles Raiders, 1992-93; Atlanta Falcons, 1993; ABC, Monday Night Football, sideline reporter, 2000; Original Mini's Inc, founder & co-owner, 2005-; KCBS, Sports Cent Team, commentator & analyst; Sporting Goods Co, owner. TV Series: 1st & Ten: The Championship, 1989; One on One, 2004; CSI: N, 2013; The Kid & I. **Orgs:** Spokesperson, Just Say No; nat chmn, Nat Lung Asn. **Home Addr:** , Phoenix, AZ. **Business Addr:** Co-owner, Original Mini's Inc, 9161 Walker St, Cypress, CA 90630, **Business Phone:** (714)828-0018.

### DICKERSON, ERNEST ROSCOE
Movie director, cinematographer, writer. **Personal:** Born Jun 25, 1951, Newark, NJ; children: 5; married Traci; children: Janet & Ernest. **Educ:** Howard Univ, Wash, DC, BA, archit & photog; New York Univ, Tisch Sch Arts, New York, NY, MFA, film, 1982. **Career:** New Line Cinema, dir & cinematographer; TV series: "Great Performances", 1990; "Futuresport", 1998; "Strange Justice", 1999; "Night Visions", 2001; "Our America", 2002; "Monday Night Mayhem", 2002; "The Wire", 2003; "hird Watch", 2004; "Good Fences", 2004; "The Wire", 2004; "Invasion", 2005; "Criminal Minds", 2005; "Crossing Jordan", 2005; "ER", 2005; "the L Word", 2005; "Miracle's Boys", 2005; "The Cradle", 2005; "Masters Of Horror", 2006; "Heroes", 2006""The Evidence", 2006; "For One Night", 2006; "CSI: Miami", 2006; "Weeds", 2007; "Lincoln Heights", 2007, 2008 & 2010; "Dexter", 2008, 2010, 2011, 2012; "Burn Notice", 2009; "In Plain Sight", 2009; "Law & Order", 2009; "Medium", 2009; "The Vampire Diaries", 2010; "Treme", 2010; "The Walking Dead", 2012; "Treme", 2012; Cinematographer: Joe's Bed-Stuy Barbershop: We Cut Heads, 1983; The Brother from Another Planet, 1984; Tales from the Darkside, 1984; Desiree, 1984; One Night with Blue Note, 1985; Krush Groove, 1985; She's Gotta Have It, 1986; Almacita di desolato, 1986; Enemy Territory, 1987; Eddie Murphy Raw, 1987; Negatives, 1988; The Laser Man, 1988; School Daze, 1988; Fright House, 1989; Do the Right Thing, 1989; Def by Temptation, 1990; Mo' Better Blues, 1990; Law & Order, 1990; Ava & Gabriel - Un historia di amor, 1990; Jungle Fever, 1991; Sex, Drugs, Rock & Roll, 1991; Cousin Bobby, 1992; Malcolm X, 1992; Tales from the Crypt Presents Demon Knight, 1995; Bulletproof, 1996; The Wire, 2002; Our America, 2002; Miracle's Boys, 2005; Director: Juice, 1992, co-writer; Surviving the Game, 1994; Tales from the Crypt Presents Demon Knight, 1995; Bulletproof, 1996; Ambushed, 1998; Blind Faith, 1998; Bones, 2001; Never Die Alone, 2004. **Orgs:** Am Soc Cinematographers. **Honors/Awds:** New York Film Critics Circle Award for Best Cinematography, 1989; IFP Gotham Award for Cinematography, 1991; Austin Gay & Lesbian International Film Festival Award, 1999; Grand Jury Award, 1999; Daytime Emmy Award, 2003. **Special Achievements:** Nominated for Mystfest Award, 1993; Black Reel Awards, 2000, 2004, 2005 & 2006. **Business Addr:** Director, Cinematographer, New Line Cinema, 116 N Robertson, Los Angeles, CA 90048.

### DICKERSON, COL. HARVEY G., JR.
Army officer, business owner, presbyterian clergy. **Personal:** Born Oct 24, 1926, Prairie View, TX; son of Ada Taminia Kilpatrick and Harvey G; married Gerthyl Raye Sanders; children: Glenda Joy (deceased) & Harvey G III. **Educ:** Prairie View A&M Col, BS, 1947; Syracuse Univ, MBA, 1961; Army Command & Gen Staff Col; Armed Forces Staff Col; Army War Col. **Career:** Army officer (retired), business executive; 1st Battalion, 75th Artil; Logistics budget officer; Logistics, dep chief staff; US Army Maintenance and Mat Agency; US Army Mil Personnel Ctr; AUS, officer, comptroller, second lt, 1947, 1948-77, financial adv, 1977-80 & 1985-90; ROCKS Inc, col, pres, 1975-; Corp Pub Broadcasting, vpres, 1980-85; Prairie View A&M Univ, dir inst develop & asst pres, 1990-; Dickerson & Assocs Inc, pres, col, currently. **Orgs:** Asn Syracuse Comptrollers, 1962-; Asn Govt Comptrollers, 1963-; APA Frate Inc, 1975-; Am Soc C/U & CHFC, 1985-; Nat Bus League Southern Mar, 1985-90. **Home Addr:** 12204 Dillard Pl, Ft. Washington, MD 20744-6101, **Home Phone:** (301)292-5332. **Business Addr:** President, Dickerson & Associates Inc, 12204 Dillard Pl, Ft. Washington, MD 77446, **Business Phone:** (301)292-5332.

### DICKERSON, JANET SMITH
Dean (education), educator, school administrator. **Personal:** Born Feb 13, 1944, New York, NY; married J Paul Stephens; children: Jill, Karin & Dawn. **Educ:** Western Col Women, BA, eng, 1965; Xavier Univ, MEd, educ guid, 1968; Univ Pa, EdD; Harvard Univ Inst Educ Mgt, cert, 1982. **Career:** Exec (retired); Cincinnati Pub Schs, Ach Jr High Sch, eng teacher, 1965-68; Sawyer & BloomJr High Schs, guid counr, 1968-71; Univ Cincinnati, Educ Develop Prog, teacher, counr, 1971; Earlham Col, Richmond, assoc dean stud, dir supportive serv & asst prof educ, 1971-76; Swarthmore Col, assoc dean & dir acad support progs, 1976-81, dean col, 1981-91; Duke Univ, vpres stud affairs, 1991-2000; Princeton Univ, vpres campus life, 2000-10. **Orgs:** Bd mem, Valentine Found, 1990-95; bd mem, NC Equity, 1992-95; Durham Chamber Com, human rels comt; Links Inc, 1993-; bd trustee, Guilford Col, 1993-; Reader, HWE proposals, 1978-81; Wallingford-Swarthmore Sch Brd, 1988-91; bd mem, Client Security Fund Commonwealth PA, 1983-88; consult, Davidson, Oberlin; consult, Scripps; consult, Brown; consult, Barnard; consult, Wesleyan; consult, Haverford; consult, Bowdoin; elder, Witherspoon St Presby Church; pres, cent Nj chap Links Inc; Prism Adv Bd; trustee, Childrens Defense Fund; Yale Univ; Univ Va; co-chair, Healthier Princeton Adv Bd; co-chair, Diversity Working Group; co-chair, Task Force Health & Well-Being; Alcohol Coalition Comt; Princeton admin, 2000; Univ Health Serv; Off Relig Life & Pace Ctr; Frist Campus Ctr; dean, Col Nancy Malkiel; co-chair, Diversity Working Group; staff diversity, 2006; co-chair, Task Force Health & Well-Being; Healthier Princeton adv bd; vpres & secy, Robert Durkee; co-chair, Alcohol Coalition Comt. **Home Addr:** 228 Sayre Dr, Princeton, NJ 08540-5852, **Home Phone:** (609)919-1363. **Business Addr:** Vice President, Princeton University, Princeton, NJ 08544, **Business Phone:** (609)258-3000.

### DICKERSON, JILL L. See DICKERSON, AMINA J.

### DICKERSON, LOWELL DWIGHT
Musician, educator. **Personal:** Born Dec 26, 1944, Los Angeles, CA; son of Charles Edward and Ethel Hartie (deceased). **Educ:** Calif State Univ, Los Angeles, BA, music, 1973; Boston Univ, Berkley Col Music; Univ Southern Calif, masters, music, 1989, MM, jazz studies, 1990; Univ Calif, Los Angeles, C Ph1, PhD, ethnomusicology, 1995. **Career:** Albums: Sooner or Later, 1990; Dwights's Right's, 1992; Windows; Los Angeles Musicians Union, piano musician; Am Univ Sharjah, Col Arts & Sci, vis prof, Performing Arts Prog, assoc prof, currently. **Orgs:** Pi Kappa Lambda, 1989. **Home Addr:** 308 Westwood Pl 2 Suite 349, Los Angeles, CA 90024, **Home Phone:** (310)441-5456. **Business Addr:** Associate Professor, American University of Sharjah, PO Box 26666, Sharjah26666, **Business Phone:** (971)6515-555.

### DICKERSON, MICHAEL DEANGELO
Basketball player. **Personal:** Born Jun 25, 1975, Greenville, SC; children: 2. **Educ:** Univ Ariz, attended 1998. **Career:** Basketball player (retired); Houston Rockets, shooting guard, 1998-99; Vancouver Grizzlies, shooting guard, 1999-2001; Memphis Grizzlies, shooting guard, 2001-03; Faymasa Palencia, 2009-10. **Honors/Awds:** Washington Mr. Basketball, 1994.

### DICKERSON, RALPH, JR.
Association executive, president (organization). **Educ:** Southern Ill Univ, BS, bus admin, 1969; Univ Wis, MBA. **Career:** Executive (retired); United Way, St Louis, Mo, staff, 1970-76; United Way, Madison, staff, 1977-81; United Way, Cleveland, Ohio, staff, 1981-84; United Way, Pittsburgh, Pa, staff, 1984-88; United Way New York, pres & chief prof officer, 1988-04. **Orgs:** Dir, Civic & Corp Orgn; Alpha Kappa Psi Hon Bus Fraternity; bd dir, Faith Ctr Community Develop; Visitors Comt, Sch Mgt & Urban Affairs, New Sch Social Res; dir, United Way New York; dir, NYC2012 Inc. **Business Addr:** Director, NYC2012 Inc, 2 Pk Ave 32nd St, New York, NY 10016, **Business Phone:** (212)251-2500.

### DICKERSON, RON, JR.
Football coach. **Personal:** Born Jan 1, 1948; married Jeannie; children: Ron, Rashawn & Causey. **Educ:** Univ Ark, attended 1996. **Career:** Football player, coach, (retired); Kans State, defensive back, 1969-71, cornerback coach, 1973-75; Miami Dolphins, 1972; Louisville Cardinals, cornerback coach, 1976-78; Pittsburgh Panthers, cornerback coach, 1979-80; Colo Buffaloes, cornerback coach, 1982-84; Penn State Nittany Lions, cornerback coach, 1985-90; Clemson Univ Football Team, defensive coordr, 1991-92; Temple Univ Football Team, head football coach, 1993-97; Southwest Mo State Univ, asst Coach; US Sports Acad, chair sport coaching; Ala state Univ, interim dirof athletics, 1998-99; Lambuth Univ, head football coach, 2010; Gardner-Webb Runnin' Bulldogs, head coach, defensive line coach, 2011-13. **Orgs:** Black Coaches Asn Nat Bd Dirs Fel Christian Athletes. **Honors/Awds:** All American Football Foundation Hall of Fame, 2003. **Special Achievements:** The author of 101 Defensive Back Drills; First Afrian-American head coach in Big South football history.

### DICKERSON, THOMAS L., JR.
Radio broadcaster, television journalist. **Personal:** Born Mar 1, 1949, Houston, TX; son of Thomas Sr and Della Dervis Collins; married Peggy Lou Deale; children: Traci Lauren & Troy Lewis. **Educ:** Baker Univ, Baldwin City, BA, jour, 1971. **Career:** Radio News, KPRC-AM, reporter, KLOL-FM, news dir, KCOH, KWTV-TV, Okla City, news reporter & anchor, 1973-75; KTRK-TV, news reporter, 1975-77; WJLA-TV, Albritton Commun, news reporter, 1977-79; KTRK-TV, Cap Cities ABC, Houston, news reporter outdoors ed, 1979-. **Orgs:** Houston Asn Black Journalists; Nat Asn Black Journalists; Int Asn Fire fighters. **Honors/Awds:** Robert F Kennedy, Requiem Dying Neighborhood, 1978; Austin Headliner, Parole Ser, 1991. **Home Addr:** 15819 Willbriar Lane 3, Missouri City, TX 77489, **Home Phone:** (281)265-3585. **Business Addr:** Outdoors News Editor, KTRK-TV, PO Box 13, Houston, TX 77001, **Business Phone:** (713)663-4559.

### DICKERSON, TYRONE EDWARD
Certified public accountant. **Personal:** Born Dec 18, 1943, Abington, PA; married Denise P. **Educ:** Cent State Univ, BS, acct, 1965; Harvard Grad Sch Bus, MBA, 1970. **Career:** Lucas Tucker & Co, CPA's, 1971-74; Urban Nat Corp, vpres, 1974-77; Mitchell & Titus CPA, partner, 1977-80; Tyrone E Dickerson CPA, owner, 1984-. **Orgs:** Life mem, Kappa Alpha Psi Fraternity, 1962-; Richmond Rotary Club; Nat Asn Black Accts, 1971-; Am Inst Cert Pub Accts, 1974-; NY State Soc CPA's, 1975-; bd mem, Va Soc CPA's, 1980-; chmn, Va Bd Accountancy; founding mem, Dennis, Dickerson & Wilkins Mgt Consults. **Home Phone:** (804)272-5082. **Business Addr:** Owner, Tyrone E Dickerson CPA, 2911 Kenbury Rd, Richmond, VA 23235, **Business Phone:** (804)272-1250.

### DICKERSON, DR. WARNER LEE
Educator. **Personal:** Born Jun 18, 1937, Brownsville, TN; son of George and Mary; married Arcola Leavell; children: Jarvis Fernando & Arletrice Mechele. **Educ:** Tenn State Univ, BS, math, 1961; Memphis State Univ, MS, math, 1969; Univ Sarasota, EdD, voc ed, 1979. **Career:** Educator (retired); Memphis City Sch, teacher, 1961-70; State Tech Inc, teacher, 1970-74, vpres, 1970-81, dept head develop studies, 1974-76, ed admin, 1976-78, dir admin affairs, 1978-81; Tenn State Dept Educ, Nashville, comnr voc educ, 1981-84; Tenn State Dept Educ, Memphis, educ consult, 1984-86; Fayette Co Bd Educ, Somerville, Tenn, supt, 1986-91; Prudential Memphis, affil broker, 1992-94. **Orgs:** Vpres, Memphis Br, Nat Asn Advan Colored People, 1977-79, 2nd vpres, Tenn State Conf; pres, OIC Memphis Br, 1977-81; bd dir, Am Voc Asn, 1980-83; Nat Asn Advan Black Am Voc Educ, 1982-84; Tenn Voc Asn; bd dir, Fayette Co, 1988; Phi Beta Kappa; Am Voc Tech Asn; bd mem, pres memphis chap, exec comt, Nat Asn Advan Colored People. **Honors/Awds:** Distinguished Teacher Award, State Tech Ins, 1971. **Home Addr:** 7681 Hunters View Dr, Olive Branch, MS 38654-5739, **Home Phone:** (662)893-1768. **Business Addr:** President, National Association for the Advancement of Colored People, 27 Brentshire Sq Suite A, Jackson, TN 38305, **Business Phone:** (731)660-5580.

### DICKEY, BERNESTINE D.
Aerospace engineer, manager. **Personal:** Born Jun 25, 1947, Redwater, TX; married William; children: Carl Vashun & William Shane. **Educ:** Prairie View A&M Univ, BS, phyiscs & math, 1969; Tex A&M Univ, ME, indust eng. **Career:** Dept Defense, Red River Army Depot, maintainability engr, 1970-74; US Aviation Syst Command, indust engr, 1974-77; Ford Aerospace, quality engr, 1977-82; Gen Elec Co, instrnl design specialist, manned space flight, 1982-93; Johnson Space Ctr, spacelab payload crew training mgr, spacelab mission mgr, aerospace engr, 1993-97; Lyndon B Johnson Space Ctr, int space st launch package mgr, 1997-. **Orgs:** Delta Sigma Theta; LaMarque chap, Nat Asn Advan Colored People; Tex City Music Hall of Fame. **Honors/Awds:** Outstanding Performance Award Spacelab Life Sci Mission, 1991; Lyndon B Johnson Cert of Commendation, 1992; Outstanding Performance Rating Award, 1993, 1995-99; Cert Readiness Group Achievement Award, 1994; Exceptional Serv Medal, NASA, 1995, 1999; Lauch Package Group Achievement Award, Flight 5A.1, 2001; Multipurpose Logistics Module Group Achievement Award, Marshall Space Flight Ctr, 2001; STS Flight Crew Recognition Award, 2001. **Home Addr:** 9314 Skyline Dr, Texas City, TX 77591-2939. **Business Addr:** Launch Package Manager, Johnson Space Center, 2101 NASA Pky, Houston, TX 77058, **Business Phone:** (281)483-0123.

### DICKEY, ERIC JEROME
Novelist, screenwriter. **Personal:** Born Jul 7, 1961, Memphis, TN. **Educ:** Univ Memphis, BS, comput syst technol, 1983; UCLA, attended 1997. **Career:** Aerospace Indus, software developer; Rockwell Int, software develop, 1983-92; Rowland Unified Sch Dist, educr, 1994-97; writer, novelist, 1992-; Published novels: Sister, Sister, 1996; Friends & Lovers, "Thirteen, 1997; Cappuccino, screenplay, 1997; Days Gone By; Milk in My Coffee, 1998; Cheaters, 1999; Liar's Game, 2000; Got To Be Real, 2000; Between Lovers, 2001; Mothers and Sons, 2001; Thieves Paradise, 2002; Movie: Cappuccino, 2000; Contributor: Got To Be Real, 2000; Mothers & Sons, 2000; Between Lovers, 2001; Griots Beneath the Baobab: Tales from Los Angeles, 2002; Black Silk, 2002; Thieves' Paradise, 2002; Gumbo: A Celebration of African American Writing, 2002; The Other Woman, 2003; Naughty or Nice, 2003; Drive Me Crazy, 2004; Genevieve, 2005; Voices from the Other Side: Dark Dreams II, 2006; Chasing Destiny, 2006; Storm, 2006; Sleeping With Strangers, 2007; Waking With Enemies, 2007; Pleasure, 2008; Dying for Revenge, 2008; Resurrecting Midnight, 2009; Tempted by Trouble, 2010; An Accidental Affair, 2012; The Education of Nia Simone Bijou, 2013; Decadence, 2013. **Orgs:** Alpha Phi Alpha, 1980-; Int Black Writers & Artists, 1993-; mentor, Proj Reach, 1996-. **Honors/Awds:** Edna Crotchfield Founders Award, Commitment as Literary Artist, 1995; Blackboard Bestsellers, Sister, Sister, 1996, Friends & Lovers, 1997; City of Pomona, Calif, Proclamation, 1998; NAACP Image Award, nominee, for literature, Liar's Game, 2001; Glyph Comics Awards, 2007. **Home Addr:** 6709 Latijera Suite 618, Los Angeles, CA 90045, **Home Phone:** (213)303-7891.

### DICKEY, DR. LEONEL
Dentist. **Educ:** San Francisco State Col, clin psychol; Meharry Med Col, DDS; Tex Col, BA. **Career:** Life Sci, col teacher; High Sch prin; teacher sci math; coach sports; pvt pract dentist, currently. **Orgs:** Pres, organizer & founder, Golden State Dent Asn; mem bd dir, San Francisco Dent Care Found; pres, N Calif Chap Meharry Med Col Alumni Asn; chmn coord, Meharry Med Col Western Regional Mounting & Fund Raising Event; pres, Parents Adv Comt-pac Heights Elem Sch; chmn, BenjFranklin Jr High Sch Parents Adv Comt Implementing Fresno Plan N Calif Chap Nat Dent Asn; chmn state coord, Meharry Alumni $88 MillionCampaign Fund Dr; organizer, Bay Area Tex Col Alumni Asn. **Honors/Awds:** Outstanding Alumnus Award, Meharry Med & Moll Tex Col; Community Service Award, Bay Area Howard Univ Alumni. **Special Achievements:** Author of several outstanding scientific papers. **Business Addr:** Dentist, 1845 Fillmore St, San Francisco, CA 94115, **Business Phone:** (415)567-2600.

### DICKSON, DR. CHARLIE JONES
Educator. **Personal:** Born AL; daughter of Edward Jones and Tommie A Jones; married Joe N; children: Jonathan, Chari & Jori. **Educ:** Tuskegee Inst, BSN, 1966; Ohio State Univ, MSN, 1969; Univ Ala, EdD, 1984. **Career:** Lawson State Jr Col, Dept Nursing, chair, 1969-70; Tuskegee Inst, instr, 1970-73; Univ Ala, Sch Med, Birmingham, AL, prof, prof emer, currently. **Orgs:** Am Nurses Asn, 1975-; Ala State Nurses Asn, 1975-; bd dir, Shelby Med Ctr, 1987-93; bd mem, Shelby County Red Cross, 1990-91; bd, Nat Coun State Bd Nursing Inc, area III dir, 1990-91; Delta Sigma Theta Sorority Inc; pres, Ala Bd Nursing, 1990-91, chairperson, continued competence & continuing educ comt, 2001; Ala Respiratory Prog, 1991; fel Am Acad Nursing 1994; chair, Nat Coun Exam Comt; bd dir, Nat Coun State Boards Nursing, pres, Ala Bd Nursing. **Home Addr:** 1021 Riverchase Pkwy W, Hoover, AL 35244, **Home Phone:** (205)988-5679. **Business Addr:** Professor Emeritus, University of Alabama at Birmingham, 1530 3rd Ave S, Birmingham, AL 35294-1210, **Business Phone:** (205)934-5428.

### DICKSON, DARYL M.
Executive, consultant. **Personal:** Born Detroit, MI. **Educ:** Univ Mich, ABEd, elem educ, 1972, MA, 1973, educ reading, PhD, educ psychol, 1978. **Career:** Garrett Automotive Group Allied Signal Automotive Sector ASI, group dir human resources, 1987-90; Allied Signal Inc, group dir human resources, 1990-92, dir mgt, 1991-93; Quaker Oats Co, vpres human resources, 1993-96; Bausch & Lomb Inc, sr vpres human resources, 1996-2000; Dickson Consult, exec consult, 2001-, pres & chief exec officer, emer pres; Mgt Leadership Tomorrow, vpres talent develop, 2011-. **Orgs:** Mem bd dir, Wilson Commencement Pk, 2000-06; chair, C Awaiting Parents, 2007-; mem bd gov, Al Sigl Ctr Found, 2007-; staff mem, Rochester Literacy Movement Exec Comt. **Special Achievements:** First African American on Bausch & Lomb's Management Executive Commitee. **Home Addr:** 34 Paige St, Rochester, NY 14619. **Business Addr:** Vice President, Management Leadership for Tomorrow, 5335 Wis Ave NW Suite 805, Washington, DC 20015, **Business Phone:** (202)751-2330.

### DICKSON, FRED R.
Executive. **Educ:** Univ Minn-Morris, BA, math & comput Sci; Univ St Thomas, exec leadership prog. **Career:** Prudential Financial, programmer analyst, programmer, 1983-87; Pillsbury Co, sr mgr, mgr, systs analyst, 1987-99; Blue Cross & Blue Shield Minn, New Technologies Group, dir, 1999-2001, CRM Systs & Technol, vpres, 2001-04, chief info officer, vpres, 2004-08; Security Health Plan, chief info officer, 2009-10; Coventry Health Care, vpres, info technol, 2010-13; AmeriHealth Caritas Family Co, sr vpres & chief info officer, 2013-. **Orgs:** Bd mem, Sabathani Community Ctr; fel Eagan Technol Task Force; bd mem, Minn Inst Pub Health; bd mem, Minn eHealth Adv Comt. **Honors/Awds:** Business Journal Corporate Executive Award, Blue Cross Blue Shield, 2006. **Business Addr:** Senior Vice President, Chief Information Officer, AmeriHealth Caritas Family of Companies, 100 Stevens Dr, Philadelphia, PA 19113, **Business Phone:** (215)937-8000.

### DICKSON, REGINALD D.
Association executive. **Personal:** Born Apr 28, 1946, Oakland, TN; son of Louis Smith and Mildred Smith; married Illona White; children: Kia, Brandon & Rachel. **Educ:** Univ MO, Columbia, 1966; Harris-Stowe Teachers Col, BS, 1969; Wash Univ, BS, bus, 1978; St Louis Univ, attended 1978. **Career:** St Louis Pub Sch Syst, tchr, 1969-73; INROADS Inc, dir, 1973-76, regional dir, 1976-80, exec vpres, 1980-83, pres, chief exec officer, 1983-93; Buford, Dickson, Harper & Sparrow Inc, chmn & founder, 2001-. **Orgs:** Co-chmn Salvation Army Tree Lights St Louis, 1977-78; area coordr, Boy Scouts Am, 1978; Metro Develop Comt Red Cross, 1980; chmn, exec comn Child Guid Ctr, 1982-83; bd dir, Am First Nat Bank, 1979-99; bd dir, Conf Educ, 1982-; Statewide Task Force Educ, 1984-; Urban League, 1986-, CORO Found, 1986-, Confluence St Louis, 1986-;audit & bd dir, Dollar Gen Corp, 1993-2007; bd dir, Huntington Preferred Capital Inc, 2008-; founding mem, St Louis Rhythm & Blues Preserv Soc; adv bd trustee, Found Stud Communs; life memship comt mem, Nat Asn Advan Colored People; bd dir, Heartland Bank; chmn, St. Louis Region Am Red Cross; co-chair, Family Investment Trust; United Way; bd dir, St Louis Community Col Found; African Am Leadership Comt, Harris Stowe State Col; bd regents, Southeast Mo State Univ; Boy Scouts Am; founder & chair, Black Leadership Roundtable; chmn bd, AmSouth Community Develop Corp; past chair, United Negro Fund Adv Bd; Queens Col Ctr New Workforce; Urban League Metrop St. Louis; Stud Commun Inc; Grand Ctr Inc; Area Resources Community & Human Serv. **Honors/Awds:** Participant Danforth Leadership Program St Louis, 1978-79; Distinguished Service Award, INROADS Inc St Louis, 1984; Distinguished Alumni Award, Harris-Stowe State Col, 1985; judge, Washington Univ's first annual John M. Olin Cup competition, 1989; Charles R. Drew Award, Am Red Cross; Salvation Armys William Booth Award; INROADS Hall of Fame; Mel Lowenstein Community Affairs Award. **Home Addr:** 4301 Roland Blvd, St. Louis, MO 63121, **Home Phone:** (314)381-3757. **Business Addr:** Chairman, Founder, Buford, Dickson, Harper & Sparrow Inc, 1 Metropolitan Sq, St. Louis, MO 63102, **Business Phone:** (314)725-5445.

### DIDLICK, WELLS S.
Educator. **Personal:** Born Jun 16, 1925, Middletown, OH; son of Brack and Lena; married Beverly Chavis; children: Wells S Jr, James S, Julie A & Gail J. **Educ:** Miami Univ, BA, 1952. **Career:** Educator (retired); Campus Inter-Racial Club Miami Univ, pres, 1950-51, pres stud fac coun, 1951-52; Woodlawn Planning Comm, comnr; Woodlawn Ohio, councilman; Cincinnati Bd Ed, teacher. **Orgs:** Zoning Bd Appeals Village Woodlawn, 1979; Gov Task Force Sch Discipline Cincinnati Sch Syst, 1979; Indus Rel Comm Village Woodlawn, 1980; Nat Asn Advan Colored People. **Home Addr:** 406 Snelling Rd, Raleigh, NC 27609.

### DIESEL, VIN (MARK SINCLAIR VINCENT)
Actor, writer. **Personal:** Born Jul 18, 1967, New York, NY; son of Delora Sherleen; married Paloma Jimenez; children: Hania Riley, Vincent Sinclair & Pauline. **Educ:** Theater New City; Hunter Col, creative writing. **Career:** Writer, director, actor & producer; Films: Awakenings, 1990; Multi-Facial, 1994; Strays, 1997; Saving Pvt Ryan, 1998; The Iron Giant, 1999; Into Pitch Black, 2000; Boiler Room, 2000; Pitch Black, 2000; Knock around Guys, 2001; The Fast & the Furious, 2001; Knockaround Guys, 2001; The Chronicles of Riddick: Dark Fury, 2004; The Pacifier, 2005; Find Me Guilty, 2006; The Fast & the Furious: Tokyo Drift, 2006; Babylon A.D, 2008; Rockfish, 2008; Los Bandoleros, writer, dir, producer, 2009; The Last Witch Hunter, 2015-; The Fast & the Furious: Fifth Gear, currently; Hannibal the Conqueror, currently. Producer: xXx, exec producer, 2002; A Man Apart, 2003; Life is a Dream, 2004; The Chronicles of Riddick: Escape from Butcher Bay, 2004; Hitman, 2007; Fast & Furious, 2009; Fast Five, 2011; Fast & Furious 6, 2013; Riddick, 2013; Life is a Dream, exec producer, 2014; Furious 7, 2015-; Fast 8, 2017; xXx: The Return of Xander Cage, 2017; One Race Films, founder, currently; Tigon Studios, founder, currently; Racetrack Records, founder, currently; Int Bus Mgt, actor, currently. **Honors/Awds:** Online Film Critics Society Award, 1999; OFTA Film Award, Online Film & Tv Asn, 1999; MTV Movie Award, 2002 & 2014; Spike Video Game Award, 2004; Video Software Dealers Association Award, 2005; CinemaCon Award, 2011; Star on the Walk of Fame, 2013; Teen Choice Award, 2015; People's Choice Award, 2016. **Business Addr:** Actor, International Business Management, 9696 Culver Blvd Suite 203, Culver City, CA 90232.

### DIGGA, RAH (RASHIYA FISHER)
Rap musician. **Personal:** Born Dec 18, 1972, Newark, NJ; daughter of Al Fisher and Brenda; married Young Zee; children: 1. **Educ:** NJ Inst Technol, elec engineering. **Career:** The Outsidaz & The Flip mode Squad, group mem; Albums: Dirty Harriet, 1999; Everything Is a Story, 2004; Classic, 2010; TV series: "Da Hip Hop Witch", 2000; "Michael Jackson 30th Anniversary Celebration", 2001; "Carmen: A Hip Hopera", MTV, 2001; "The Making of Thir13en Ghosts", 2002; "Its Black Entertainment", 2002; "Hip-Hop VIPs", 2002; "Queens of Hip Hop", 2003; "Dennis Miller", 2004; Say My Name, 2009; Michael Jackson NRJ 12 Tribute, 2009; Films: Da Hip Hop Witch, 2000; 13 Ghosts, 2001; Songs: "Tight", 1999; "Imperial", 1999; "Break Fool", 2000; "Party and Bullshit", 2003; Breakin' All the Rules, 2004; "Make It Hot"/"See It In Your Eyes", 2005; "New Shit", 2008; "Warning Shots", 2010; "This Ain't no Lil' Kid Rap", 2010; "Classic", 2010. **Special Achievements:** Nominee, Best Female Hip-Hop Artist, 2002, 2004; Nominee, People's Champ Award, 2006.

### DIGGS, CHRISTIAN EMANUEL
Founder (originator), entrepreneur. **Personal:** son of Clarence and Liz. **Educ:** Tex Christian Univ, Ft Worth, Tex, polit sci. **Career:** SandoteWebsites.com, chief exec officer & founder, 1997-. **Honors/Awds:** Kidpreneurs Award, Black Enterprises Entrepreneurs Conf, 2001. **Business Addr:** Chief Executive Officer, Founder, SandoteWebsites.com, 9804 Sophora Circle, Dallas, TX 75249, **Business Phone:** (972)709-1494.

### DIGGS, DEBORAH DOLSEY
Executive. **Educ:** Wayne State Univ, BA, sociol, BA, psychol; Ind Univ, philanthropy prog. **Career:** United Negro Col Fund, regional dir, 2007-08; Deborah Dolsey Diggs & Co, consult, 2008-. **Orgs:** Bd vpres, Riverfront E Alliance, Detroit; founding mem, Women's Comt; Charles H. Wright Mus African Am Hist; comt mem, Downtown Detroit Partnership-E Jefferson Proj; bd mem, Harwood Inst; vol, Detroit Pub Schs Reading Corps Prog; Women's Econ Club; Nat Asn Fundraising Execs; Regional Detroit Chamber Com. **Business Addr:** Consultant, Deborah Dolsey Diggs & Co.

### DIGGS, JOETTA CLARK
Track and field athlete, president (organization). **Personal:** Born Aug 1, 1962, East Orange, NJ; daughter of Joe Clark and Jetta; married Ronald; children: Talitha LaNae. **Educ:** Univ Tenn, recreation admin, 1984. **Career:** Track & field athlete(retired); Fitkidz, host & producer; Joetta Sports & Beyond LLC, pres, currently; NJ Atty Genl's Off, Drug Diversion Sect, spec investr. Books: Principles for Success; Life Lessons Learned From Track & Field. **Orgs:** Comnr sports, NJ Sports & Expos Authority; bd mem, Raritan Valley Community Col, 2001; bd mem, Bus Partnership Somerset County; exec dir, Joetta Clark Diggs Sports Found. **Home Addr:** , NJ. **Business Addr:** President, Joetta Sports & Beyond LLC, PO Box 6262, Hillsborough, NJ 08844, **Business Phone:** (484)851-3148.

### DIGGS, LAWRENCE J.
President (organization). **Personal:** Born Nov 2, 1947, Houston, TX; son of Louis Maurine. **Educ:** Antioch Univ, BA, 1989. **Career:** SDSU, Speaker, 1995-14; South Dakota Humanities Council, Scholar, 1999-2014; El Diggs, Musician, 1960-15; KFRC, announcer, 1968-70; KSFO, announcer, producer & reporter, 1970-72; KSFX, announcer; Quiet Storm Trading Co; Vinegar Connoisseurs Int, pres & founder, 1984-; Int Vinegar Mus, founder & cur; Int Vinegar Res Inst, founder & head; Sdak humanities coun, 1999-2012. **Orgs:** Med vol, Peace Corps, 1979-81; pres, Zen Yukai, 1982-83; Lions Club, 1992-; Am Fedn Radio & TV Artists; Media Alliance; Micros Soc; Nat Coun Returned Peace Corps Vol; bd dir, Soto Zen Mission. **Home Addr:** 104 W Carlton Ave, PO Box 41, Roslyn, SD 57261, **Home Phone:** (605)486-4536. **Business Addr:** Founder, President, Vinegar Connoisseurs International, 30 Carlton Ave, Roslyn, SD 57261, **Business Phone:** (877)486-0075.

### DIGGS, DR. ROY DALTON, JR.
Physician, surgeon. **Personal:** Born Mar 29, 1929, Detroit, MI; married Johnella Smith. **Educ:** Wayne State Univ, attended 1949; Meharry Med Sch, MD, 1953. **Career:** Vet Affairs Med Ctr, gen surgeon; Truman Med Ctr-W, gen surgeon; Hurley Hosp, intern, 1953-54; KS City Gen Hosp, resident, 1954-56; VA Hosp Buffalo NY, resident, 1958-61; Lapeer St Home, surgeon, 1961-63; pvt pract gen surgeon; Hurley Med Ctr, gen surgeon, currently; T Williams Clin, pvt pract, currently. **Orgs:** Am Bd Surg; fel Am Col Surgeons; Flint Acad Surg; fel Am Col Emergency Physicians; Mich State Col Human Med; AMA; Nat Asn Advan Colored People; Nat Urban League; Foss Ave Christian Sch; Flint Urban League; Omega Psi Phi Frat. **Honors/Awds:** Humanitarian Award Flint, Human Rels Comt, 1977. **Home Addr:** 2910 Crestwood Dr, Flint, MI 48503, **Home Phone:** (870)232-9849. **Business Addr:** General Surgeon, T Williams Clinic, 4250 N Saginaw St, Flint, MI 48503, **Business Phone:** (810)787-5621.

### DIGGS, SCOTT LEO. See DIGGS, TAYE.

### DIGGS, TAYE (SCOTT LEO DIGGS)
Actor. **Personal:** Born Jan 2, 1972, Rochester, NY; son of Jeffries and Marcia Berry; married Idina Menzel; children: Walker Nathaniel. **Educ:** Syracuse Univ, BFA, musical theater. **Career:** Films: How Stella Got Her Groove Back, 1998; The Best Man, 1999; House on Haunted Hill, 1999; Go, 1999; The Wood, 1999; The Way of the Gun, 2000; Mary Jane's Last Dance, 2001; Equilibrium, 2002; Brown Sugar, 2002; New Best Friend, 2002; Just a Kiss, 2002; Chicago, 2002; Malibu's Most Wanted, 2003; Basic, 2003; Drum, 2004; Rent, 2005; Cake, 2005; Slow Burn, 2005; 30Days, 2006; Days of Wrath, 2008; Between Us, 2012; Scooby-Doo! Music of the Vampire, 2012; The Best Man Holiday, 2013; Baggage Claim, 2013; The Best Man Wedding. TV series: "Law & Order", 1996; "New York Undercover", 1996; "Ally McBeal", 1997; "101 Dalmatians: The Series", 1997; "The Guiding Light", 1997; "The West Wing", 1999; "The Martin Short Show", 1999; "Ed", 2000; "Ally McBeal", 2001; "Punk'd", 2003; "The West Wing", 2003; "Kevin Hill", 2004-05; "Will & Grace", 2006; "Day Break", producer & actor, 2006-07; "Grey's Anatomy", 2007; "Private Practice", 2007-13; "The Super Hero Squad Show", 2009; "Better Off Ted", 2009; "New Girl", 2013; "Murder in the First", 2014; "The Good Wife", 2014. **Honors/Awds:** Blockbuster Entertainment Award, 2000; Critics Choice Award, 2003; Excellence in Film making Award, Chicago Int Film Festival, 2003; Screen Actors Guild Award, 2003; Image Award, 2005, 2009. **Business Addr:** Actor, c/o Burton Goldstein Co, 156 W 56th Suite 1803, New York, NY 10019-3878, **Business Phone:** (212)582-9700.

### DIGGS, REV. DR. WILLIAM P., JR.
Clergy, educator, teacher. **Personal:** Born Oct 19, 1926, Columbia, SC; married Clotilda J Daniels; children: Mary Lynne & William Jr. **Educ:** Friendship Jr Col, Rock Hill, SC, attended 1943; Morehouse Col, AB, 1949; Atlanta Univ, MA, 1951; Colgate-Rochester Div Sch, BD, 1955; MDiv, 1972; Friendship Jr Col, DD, 1973; Morris Col, LHD, 1973; McCormick Theol Sem, D Min. **Career:** Friendship Jr Col, Rock Hill, SC, instr, 1950-52, instr sociol, 1955-61, asst prof; Second Baptist Church, Leroy, NY, stud pastor, 1954-55; Galilee Baptist Church, pastor, 1955-62; Benedict Col, Columbia, SC, asst prof sociol, 1964-74; Morris Col, Sumter, SC, minister, asst prof sociol; Trinity Baptist Church, Florence, SC. **Orgs:** Pres, Florence Br, Nat Asn Adv Colored People, 1970-74; Am Asn Univ Prof; Alpha Kappa Delta Hon Sociol Soc; Community Rels Comn, Florence, SC; chmn, Community Action Agency, Florence, Co; Area Manpower Bd; Florence County Bd Health; trustee bd, Friendship Jr Col; trustee bd, Morris Col; bd mem, Morehouse Col; bd mem, ITC; bd trustee, Interdenominational Theol Ctr; Nannie Helen Burroughs Sch; Greater Florence Habitat Humanity. **Honors/Awds:** Recognition Dedicated Serv, Church & Community, 1969; Florence Outstanding Leadership Civic Econ Community Involvement, 1971; Citizen of the Year, Chi Iota Chap, Omega Psi Phi Fraternity, 1976; Outstanding Achievement & Serv, Omega Psi Phi Fraternity, 1976; Valedictorian, High Sch Class; Honored, Trinity Baptist Church, Florence; Honored, Zeta Phi Beta Sorority; Pee Dee Area Council Boys Scouts of America Whitney Young Award; SC AARP Andrus Award, Community Service; Building Bridges Humanitarian Award, Greater Florence Chamber Com; He has received the states highest civilian honor, the Order of the Palmetto; SC Black Hall of Fame. **Home Addr:** 1607 N Irby St, Florence, SC 29501-1524, **Home Phone:** (843)662-7845.

### DIJI, DR. AUGUSTINE EBUN
Psychiatrist. **Personal:** Born Jun 27, 1932; son of James and Cecelia Oyeloye; married Gladys Jean; children: Augustine E Angela, B Renee, Latisa & Tameka. **Educ:** Queen's Univ Belfast, Northern Ireland, BS, physiology, 1958, MD, 1961. **Career:** Royal Victoria Hosp, Belfast, Ireland, intern, 1962-63; Queen's Univ Belfast, Ireland, resident, 1963-67; Ghana Med Sch, instr physiology, 1967-69; Erie County Med Ctr, spec fel, 1969-70; Buffalo Psychiat Ctr, staff psychiatrist, 1970-72, unit chief, 1972-78, actg dept clin dir, 1978-79, actg exec dir, 1979, med dir, 1980-; Buffalo Gen Hosp, staff, 1971-; part-time pvt pract psychiat, 1971-; Med Dent Staff, pres, 1975-77, 1985-88; State Univ NY, Buffalo, clin asst prof, 1975-; Geneva B Scruggs Com Health Care Ctr, Buffalo, consult psychiat, 1985-89; Univ NY, Buffalo, asst prof emer & psychiat, currently; pvt pract, physician, currently. **Orgs:** Brit Med Asn, 1963-76; Royal Col Physicians, 1966-; Royal Col Psychiats, 1966-; AMA, 1970-; Am Psychiat Asn, 1970-; Nat Med Asn, 1971- Workers Compensation Bd, 1972-2001; World Asn Soc Psychiat, 1976-; pres, Med & Dent Staff Buffalo Psychiat Ctr, 1976-77, 1985-88; Western New York Psychiat Soc; life time mem, Med Soc County Erie. **Honors/Awds:** Belfast scholar, Queen's Univ, 1955-61; Milroy Medal, 1957; Hutchinson's Scholar, 1957-58. **Special Achievements:** Publ "Local Vasodilation Action of Carbon Dioxide on Blood Vessels of Hand", Queen's Univ, 1959; "The Local Effects of Carbon Dioxide on Human Blood Vessels", Queen's Univ 1960; dissertation "A Survey of the Incidence of Mental Disorder in the Mentally Subnormal" 1965; First black psychiatrist to open a private practice in the city of Buffalo. **Home Addr:** 194 Exeter Rd, Buffalo, NY 14221-3345, **Home Phone:** (716)634-4380. **Business Addr:** Physician, Private Practice, 655 Hertel Ave, Buffalo, NY 14207, **Business Phone:** (716)874-4975.

### DILDAY, HON. JUDITH NELSON
Educator, judge, actor. **Personal:** Born Mar 28, 1943, Pittsburgh, PA; daughter of Alberta Nelson and Frank Nelson; married James S; children: Ayana, Sekou & Zakia. **Educ:** Univ Pittsburgh, BA, 1966; Millersville State Col, grad credits fr; Boston Univ Sch Law, JD, 1974. **Career:** Judge (retired) actor; Pittsburgh Bd Educ, Fr teacher, 1966-70; Boston Model City, educ counr, 1970-71; Suffolk County Dist Atty, asst dist atty, 1974-75; Specialized Training/Advocacy Proj, coun, 1977; Stern & Shapiro, atty, 1977-80; Off Solicitor US Dept Interior, atty adv, 1980-81; pvt pract counr law, 1981-82; Mass Bay Transp Authority, asst gen coun, 1982-89; Burnham, Hines & Dilday, partner, 1989-93; Probate & Family Ct Mass, assoc justice, circuit judge, 1993-98; Probate & Family Ct, Middlesex County Div, judge, 1998-2009. **Orgs:** Bd mem, Mass Black Lawyers Asn, 1980-84; Steering Comt, Lawyer's Comt Civil Rights, 1980-; vpres, Psi Omega Chap, Alpha Kappa Alpha, 1984-86; bd dir, Women's Bar Asn, 1984-; deleg, State Dem Conv, 1986; Mass Bar Asn; treas, Nat Bar Asn Region I; Mass Black Women Attorneys, League Afro-Am Women; State Dem Conv, 1987-89; pres elect, Women's Bar Asn; 1989, pres, 1990-91; deleg, secy bd dir, Daniel Marr Boy's Club; gen coun, 100 Black Women, 1992; Nat Asn Women Judges; Mass Black Judges Asn; Boston Black Women's Lit Club; eucharistic minister, St Cyprian's Episcopal Church. **Honors/Awds:** Woman of the Year, Cambridge, YWCA, 1989; Legal Services Achievement Award, League Afro-American Women, 1991; Silver Shingle Alumni Award, Boston Univ Sch Law, 1991; Sojourner Truth Legal Service Award, Nat Asn Negro Bus & Prof Women, 1991; Drum Major for Justice MLK Award, 2001. **Special Achievements:** First African American to serve on the Probate and Family Court; First black female to serve as Assistant District Attorney for Suffolk County; one of four African American female judges in the Massachusettes judiciary. **Home Addr:** 10 Park Plz 7th Fl, Boston, MA 02124-1307. **Business Addr:** Judge, Commonwealth of Massachusetts, 210 2 Center Plz, Boston, MA 02108, **Business Phone:** (617)788-6600.

**DILDAY, WILLIAM HORACE, JR.**
Advertising executive, business owner, journalist. **Personal:** Born Sep 14, 1937, Boston, MA; son of William Horace and Alease Virginia Scott; married Maxine Carol Wiggins; children: Scott, Erika & Kenya. **Educ:** Boston Univ, BS & BA, 1960. **Career:** Int Bus Mach, opers supvr, 1964-68; Edgerton Germehausen & Grier Roxbury, personnel adminr & pub rel dir, 1968-69; WHDH Inc, dir personnel, 1969-72; WLBT-TV, gen mgr, 1972-84; WJTV, exec vpres & gen mgr, 1985-89; News, Press & Gazette, Broad Div, corp vpres, 1989-93; Jackson Clarion Ledger, columnist; Kerimax Commun, chief exec officer pres & owner, 1994-. **Orgs:** Pres, Jackson Urban League, 1978-79; bd dir, NBC TV Affilitaed Bd, 1979-83; bd dir, Nat Asn Broadcasters, 1981-84; bd dir, Jackson-Hinds Comprehensive Health Ctr; bd dir, Miss Ment Health Asn, Jackson; bd dir, Pvt Indust Coun; bd dir, Cong Black Caucus' Comn Brain Trust; finance chairperson, Boy Scouts Am, Seminole Dist, 1988-89; bd mem, Jr Achievement, 1988-89; bd mem, United Way, 1988-89; first Am bank, 1990-93 & 1994-2001; vpres, 100 Black Men of Jackson, 1991; founding chmn & bd dir, Miss First Minority Controlled Com Bank; founding mem, Nat Asn Black Journalist. **Honors/Awds:** Peabody Award for Documentary Reporting; National Mental Health Association Media Award; Two Iris Awards, Nat Asn Tv Prog Execs. **Special Achievements:** First African American General Manager Commercial Television Station; First African American elected to a Television network affiliate board of directors; First African American elected to National Association of Broadcasters Board of Directors; Who's who in America, 1977-95; Who's who in black America, 1975-76 & 1993-95. **Home Addr:** 855 Rutherford Dr, Jackson, MS 39206-2134, **Home Phone:** (601)366-7251. **Business Addr:** Owner, Kerimax Communications, 510 George St Fl 4405, Jackson, MS 39202-3027, **Business Phone:** (601)955-7558.

**DILDY, CATHERINE GREENE**
Educator, executive. **Personal:** Born Nov 21, 1940, Dinwiddie, VA; daughter of Bruce Greene Sr and Cora H Greene; married Alvin V; children: Jewel D Trotman. **Educ:** Elizabeth City State Univ, BS, 1964; Univ Va, attended 1968, 1990; Norfolk State Univ, attended 1981, 1989; Old Dom Univ, attended 1971, 1977, 1980, 1990. **Career:** Norfolk Pub Schs, physical educ resource, elem, 1964-70, health & physical educ, jr, 1970-79, health & physical educ, 1979-, driver educ coordr, intramural dir, city-wide health fair chmn, 1979-92, dance group sponsor, 1979-92; Tri City Tours, vpres. **Orgs:** Dist Sorority, pres, fin secy, 1960-, chair budget, May Week Social; Nat Educ Asn, 1964-; Va Educ Asn, 1964-; Norfolk Educ Asn, 1964-; Norfolk Chap Drifters Inc, pres treas, 1969-; Va Beach Chap Pinochle Bugs, fintreas, 1980-; Norfolk Chap Nat Epicurean, fin secy, 1988-. **Home Addr:** 5524 Connie Lane, Virginia Beach, VA 23462-1614, **Home Phone:** (757)497-8609. **Business Addr:** Vice President, Tri City Tours, 5524 Connie Lane, Virginia Beach, VA 23462-1614, **Business Phone:** (757)499-4335.

**DILL, DR. BONNIE THORNTON**
Dean (education), founder (originator), educator. **Personal:** Born Oct 5, 1944, Chicago, IL; daughter of Irwin Stanley Thornton and Hilda Branch Thornton; married Jack C Shuler; children: Allen Richard Kamau, Anika Hillary & Nandi Elizabeth. **Educ:** Univ Rochester, BA, 1965; NY Univ, MA, 1970, PhD, 1979. **Career:** Off Equal Opportunity-Northeast Region, field rep, 1965-67; City New York Community Develop Agency, community organizer & prog officer, 1967-68; City New York Human Resources Admin, prog develop & field supvr, 1968-70; New York Univ Ctr Human Rel, trainer (part-time), 1969-71; Bernard M Baruch Col, Dept Compensatory Prog, lectr & coun, 1970-77; Bernard M Baruch Col, Black & Hisp Studies Prog, adj lectr, 1972-73; New York Univ Sociol Dept, teaching asst, 1974-75, adj instr, 1976-77; Memphis St Univ, asst prof sociol, 1978-83, Ctr Res Women, dir & founder, 1982-88, assoc prof sociol, 1983-90, prof sociol, 1990-91; Univ Md-Col Pk, prof women's studies & affil prof sociol, 1991-, dean col arts & humanities, 2011-; Univ MD, Consortium Race, Gender & Ethnicity, founding dir, Women's Studies, prof & chair, 2003-; Consortium Race, prog & dir; Princeton Univ, vis prof distinguished teaching, 2009-; Ms Mag, chair; Author: Disparities in Latina Health: An Intersectional Analyses, 2006; Instituting a Legacy of Change: Transforming the Campus Climate through Intellectual Leadership, 2009; Emerging Intersections: Race, Class and Gender in Theory, Policy & Practice, 2009; Intersectionality: A Transformative Paradigm in Feminist Theory & Social Justice, forthcoming. **Orgs:** Vpres, Am Sociol Asn, 2005-08; Soc Study Social Probs; Asn Black Sociol; Sociol Women Soc; pres, Nat Women's Studies Asn, 2010-12; Nat Coun Res Women. **Special Achievements:** First woman to serve as dean of the College of Arts and Humanities. **Home Addr:** 34 Silver Moon Dr, Silver Spring, MD 20904, **Home Phone:** (301)879-0004. **Business Addr:** Professor & Dean, Chair, University of Maryland, 2101 Woods Hall, College Park, MD 20742, **Business Phone:** (301)405-6877.

**DILL, GREGORY**
College administrator, school administrator. **Personal:** Born Dec 8, 1958, Flint, MI; son of Charles and Doris. **Educ:** Eastern Mich Univ, BBA, mgt, 1987, MBA, strategic leadership, 1996. **Career:** Catherine McAuley Health Sys, mgr, 1989-93; Eastern Mich Univ, genforeman, 1993-95, mgr, stud org adv; Oak Pk Sch Dist, chief staff, 2005-08; Washtenaw County, dir admin opers, 2009-11, dir infrastructure mgt, 2011-15, interim dep adminr, 2015-. **Orgs:** Alpha Phi Alpha, 1984-; Nat Hons Soc. **Home Addr:** 3077 Ailsa Craig Dr, Ann Arbor, MI 48108-2060, **Home Phone:** (734)487-1953. **Business Addr:** Interim Deputy Administrator, Director of Infrastructure Management, Washtenaw County, 7858 Valleyview Dr, Ypsilanti, MI 48197, **Business Phone:** (734)973-4980.

**DILLARD, HOWARD LEE**
Government official. **Personal:** Born Jan 21, 1946, Clinton, KY; son of Samuel William and Rosie Pearl Smith; married Frances Louise Piper; children: Wynita M, Christina M, Howard L Jr & Tamra Deann. **Educ:** Draughon's Col, attended 1982. **Career:** Dillard & Hunt, Clinton, KY, partner & mgr, 1980-82; Dillard Contractors, Clinton, KY, owner, 1982-88; Excel Industs, Fulton, KY, staff, 1988-. **Orgs:** Exec comt mem, Hickman Co Parks & Recreation Bd, 1984; treas, Hickman County Dem Exec Comt, 1988-; bd dir, Hickman County Sr Citizens, 1988-; Clinton Ky City Coun, 1988-; Worshipful Master, Prince Hall Masons, 1991-. **Home Addr:** 319 Blair St A, Clinton, KY 42031, **Home Phone:** (270)653-4683. **Business Addr:** Staff, Excel Industries, 600 Col St, Fulton, KY 42041, **Business Phone:** (502)472-0360.

**DILLARD, DR. JUNE WHITE (JUNE DATTY)**
Teacher, association executive, lawyer. **Personal:** Born Sep 26, 1937, Youngstown, OH; daughter of John Ira; married Martin Gregory; children: Belinda Louise, Brian Martin & Stephen Jeffrey; married Martin Gregory. **Educ:** Univ Chicago, AB, educ, 1958; Chicago Teachers Col, MA, guid coun & educ, 1961; Howard Univ Sch Law, JD, 1975. **Career:** Chicago Pub Schs, teacher, 1958-61; State Ohio, Off Econ Oppor, field rep, 1967-70; Securities & Exchange Comn, Div Enforcement, clerk, 1975-77; Taylor & Over by assoc, 1978-80; JW Dillard Esquire, atty, 1980-; Dillard & Assoc PC, atty, owner, 1988-. **Orgs:** Exec Dir, Nat Asn Advan Colored People, Prince Georges County br; pres, Prince Georges Arts Coun; bd dir, Harriets List; bd dir, Alpha Kappa Alpha Sorority Inc; JFB. **Honors/Awds:** Top Ladies Distinction; Cable TV Commissioner; Service Award, Coalition Black Affairs; Outstanding Contribution Legal Community, Nat Bar Asn; Disting mem Award, Nat Bus League Southern MD; Frederic Douglass Civic Achievement Award, MD Black Repub Coun; President Award, Nat Asn Advan Colored People; Outstanding Service Award, Prince Georges County Govt. **Home Addr:** 13509 Pendleton St, Ft. Washington, MD 20744-5414, **Home Phone:** (301)292-2867. **Business Addr:** Attorney, Owner, Dillard & Associates PC, PO Box 839, Accokeek, MD 20607-0839, **Business Phone:** (301)292-1868.

**DILLARD, DR. MARTIN GREGORY**
Physician, educator. **Personal:** Born Jul 7, 1935, Chicago, IL; son of Manny Martin and Evelyn Farmer; married Patricia Rachelle Cheek; children: Belinda, Brian & Stephen. **Educ:** Univ Chicago, BA, 1956, BS, 1957; Howard Univ Med Sch, MD, 1965. **Career:** Michael Reese Hosp & Med Ctr, resident, internal med, 1965-69, fel, nephrology, 1969-70; fel, Michael Reese Hosp & Med Ctr, 1970; US Pub Health Serv, fel, 1969-70; Howard Univ Col Med, asst prof med, 1970-74, Admin, Planning & Exec Comt, 1976-, asst dean & clin affairs, 1984-; Howard Univ Hosp, Hemodialysis Unit, chief, 1970-76; Howard Univ Hosp, Dept Med, asst chmn educ, 1973-76; Health Care Coalition Nat Capitol Area, bd dir, 1982-; Howard Univ, prof med, Nephrol Div, med dir & asst dean clin affairs; Howard Univ Hosp, assoc prof med, Div Nephrol, chief, physician, currently. **Orgs:** Alpha Omega Alpha Hon Med Soc, 1965; Nat Bd Med Examr, 1966; Am Bd Internal Med, 1972; Am Bd Internal Med Nephrol, 1978. **Home Addr:** 6 Greentree Ct, Bethesda, MD 20817, **Home Phone:** (301)365-4348. **Business Addr:** Physician, Howard University Hospital, 1160 Varnum St NE Suite 211, Washington, DC 20017, **Business Phone:** (202)269-4200.

**DILLARD, DR. MELVIN RUBIN**
Administrator. **Personal:** Born Feb 26, 1941, Kendleton, TX; son of Vellas and Ruby Lee Taylor; children: Melvin II, Melvia & Melvis. **Educ:** Huston-Tillotson Col, BA, 1964; Prairie View A&M Univ, MA, 1973; Life Underwriters Training Coun, 1984. **Career:** Nat Western Life, gen agt, 1975-81, div mgr, 1975-97; Life Underwriter Training Coun, moderator, 1979-86. **Orgs:** Tex Leaders Round Table, 1970-91; E Million Dollar Round Table, 1977-97; Lone Star Leader, 1983-87; San Jac into Asn Life Underwriters, 1991-; bd mem, Houston Asn Life Underwriters; nat pres, Huston-Tillotson Alumni; bd mem, Tex Comt Corp; United Methodist Church Mission Bd & Pension Bd; regional 4 dir & chmn, Tex Asn Life Underwriters Community Serv; dist lay leader, United Methodist Ch-South Dist; Asn Health Ins Agt; vice chmn & bd trustee, Huston Tillotson Col; bd mem & treas, Coppertree Asn; bd mem, Tex Community Corp. **Home Addr:** 12039 Willow Trl, Houston, TX 77035. **Business Addr:** Divisional Manager, National Western Life Insurance, 2656 S Loop W Suite 585, Houston, TX 77054, **Business Phone:** (713)669-9313.

**DILLARD, THELMA DELORIS**
Government official, educator. **Personal:** Born Jan 6, 1946, Macon, GA; daughter of Hester Lou Newberry Bivins; children: Cartese. **Educ:** Ft Valley St Col, BS, bus educ, 1966; Voc Educ Cert Workshops, 1970; Ga Col, MS, spec educ, 1975, MS, bus educ, 1978, MS, elem educ, 1986. **Career:** Tenn Valley Authority, off asst, 1966; Macon Tech Inst, Eng & bus edcuator, 1966-70; Ft Valley St Col, teacher, 1970-71; Dudley Hughes Voc Sch, except educ, 1972-74; Cent High Sch, teacher except educ & voc technol, 1972-2011; Doctorate Educ Leadership, 2009. **Orgs:** Secy, Macon Nat Asn Advan Colored People, 1965-, pres, 1995-97; Zeta Phi Beta, 1965-; secy, Nat Asn Advan Colored People, 1965-, vpres, 1991; asst secy, Ga St Nat Asn Advan Colored People, 1978, parliamentarian, 1982; Ga Coalition Black Women, 1980-; bd dir, Area Planning & Develop Comn, 1980-; chmn, Rules Comn Macon City Coun, 1980-; asst secy, Ga Asn Black Officials, 1980-, vice chmn, 1983, chmn, 1987-, Jack & Jill Am, 1948; chmn, Bibb Bd Educ, Macon, Ga, spec educ dept, 1986-; chmn, Cherry Blossom Think Pink Comn, 1990-91; assoc mem, Jack & Jill, 1990-; chmn, Pub Property Comn, City Macon, 1992-; app mem, Dem St Comn Ga, 1983-; Lizzie Baptist Church. **Honors/Awds:** Fifty Most Influential Women, Nat Asn Advan Colored People Macon & Informer Mag, 1981; Outstanding Woman of the Year, Nat Asn Advan Colored People, 1983; 50 Most Influential Women, GA Coalition Black Women, 1984; Several Commission Service Awards from many orgn; Macon City Council Community Service Award, 2000; Earl T Shinhoster Freedom Award, Nat Asn Advan Colored People, 2000; James Wimberly Institute Award, 2004; Medgar Evers Award, 2007; Southeastern Regional Nat Asn Advan Colored People Community Service Award, 2007; Warner Robins Air Force Base Blacks in Government Appreciation Award; Macon Housing Authority Appreciation Award; Black Elected Officials Appreciation Award, Ga Asn; Outstanding Woman Award, Zeta Phi Beta Sorority; Douglass Theatre James Wimberly-Mattie Dunn Award, 2010; Drum Major of Justice Award, Evangel Ministerial Alliance, 2012. **Home Addr:** 290 Rogers Ave, Macon, GA 31204-2504, **Home Phone:** (478)745-9889. **Business Addr:** Board Of Member, Central High School, 1365 Dr MLK Ave, Mobile, AL 36603.

**DILLARD, VICTORIA**
Actor. **Personal:** Born Sep 20, 1969, New York, NY. **Career:** Films: Star Trek: The Next Generation; Murder in Mississippi, Coming to America, 1988; Porgy & Bess; Internal Affairs, 1990; Ricochet, 1991; Deep Cover, 1992; The Glass Shield, 1994; Killing Obsession, 1994; Out-of-Sync, 1995; Statistically Speaking, 1995; The Best Man, 1999; Ali, 2001; TV Series: "Star Trek: The Next Generation", 1987; "Nasty Boys", 1990; "Seinfeld", 1993; "Tribeca", 1993; "L. A Law", 1994; "Roc", 1994; "Chicago Hope", 1994; "LA Law", 1994; "Martin", 1995; "Moesha", 1996; "Spin City", 1996-2000; "The Ditch digger's Daughters", 1997; "Laugh-In"; "Family Law", 1999; "Commitments", 2001; "Law & Order", 2004; "Law & Order: Criminal Intent", 2007; "The Unusuals", 2009. **Home Addr:** , New York, NY. **Business Addr:** Actress, ABC - TV, 6100 Wilshire Blvd Suite 310, Los Angeles, CA 90048, **Business Phone:** (323)937-8600.

**DILLARD, WANDA J.**
Administrator. **Personal:** Born Apr 19, 1953, Bluefield, VA; daughter of Robert and Louise; children: Micah C. **Educ:** Columbus Univ, AS, 1980; Otterbein Col, BS, 1983; Cent Mich Univ, MS, 1988. **Career:** Riverside Methodist Hosp, dir minority health, 1981-95; Ohio State Univ Med Ctr, community develop dir, currently. **Orgs:** Columbus Black Women's Health Proj, bd/steering comt; bd dir, Livington Ave Collaborate, 1996-; coun, United Way Franklin County, Health Vision, 1996-; bd dir, Hannah Neil, 1998-; bd trustee, bd mem, Columbus Compact Corp, bus & inst rep, bd dir, Gov Comt; bd mem, Coun Healthy Mothers & Babies; adv bd mem, United Way Cent Ohio. **Home Addr:** 1089 Wildwood Ave, Columbus, OH 43219-2160, **Home Phone:** (614)258-7873. **Business Addr:** Director Community Development, The Ohio State University Medical Center, 370 W 9th Ave, Columbus, OH 43210, **Business Phone:** (614)292-5062.

**DILLENBERGER, R. JEAN**
Government official, executive. **Personal:** Born May 6, 1931, Maywood, IL; married John; children: Tsan. **Educ:** San Francisco State Univ, BA, 1963, MA, 1978. **Career:** Government official (retired); San Francisco St Univ, serv to minority stud; Ford Found, proj dir; Off Civil Rights, chief oper; US Dept Educ, actg dir higher educ div & dir elem & sec educ div regional off civil rights; dep regional dir, 1987-94. **Orgs:** Dir, Advocates Women, 1973-77; dir & treas, Consumers Coop Berkeley, 1977-83; dir & pres, Consumers Group Legal Serv, 1973-76; adv bd, Women Orgn Employ; Asn Fed Women Execs Speaking Engagements, Higher Educ Br, Off Civil Rights, HEW. **Honors/Awds:** Published "70 Soul Secrets of Sapphire, "Toward Viable Directions in Post secondary Education". **Home Addr:** 727 Gelston Ave, El Cerrito, CA 94530.

**DILLIHAY, DR. TANYA CLARKSON**
Psychiatrist. **Personal:** Born Aug 8, 1958, Columbia, SC; daughter of Zack C and Rachel Scott; married Otha R Sr; children: Otha R II, Elliot Clarkson & Adam Scott. **Educ:** Spelman Col, BS, biol, 1979; Meharry Med Col, MD, 1983. **Career:** Univ Sc, Wm S Hall Psychiat Inst, resident training, 1983-87; SC State Hosp, psychiat serv chief, pvt pract, currently. **Orgs:** Treas, Afro-Amer Psychiatrists SC, 1986, 1987; chief resident, psycho-social rehab WSHPI, 1987; Ladson Pres Ch Columbia SC; Spelman Col Club; Congaree Med Asn; Delta Sigma Theta Sorority. **Special Achievements:** Article: "Suicide in Black Children" published in Psychiatric Forum, 1989. **Home Addr:** 7812 Tradd St, Columbia, SC 29209. **Business Addr:** Pschiatrist, Private Practice, 220 Faison Dr, Columbia, SC 29203, **Business Phone:** (803)935-7639.

**DILLON, AUBREY**
Educator. **Personal:** Born Jan 25, 1938, Prentiss, MS; son of Louella Barnes Quinn. **Educ:** Edinboro State Col, BS, social studies, 1961, MEd, 1964. **Career:** Educator (retired); Playground dir, 1961-63; Erie, PA Sch Dist, teacher, guid counr, 1961-69; Erie Tech High Sch, tennis coach, 1965-68; basic adult educ coord, 1966-68; Edinboro State Col, assoc dean men, 1969-93; Edinboro Univ Penn, prof, prof emer, 1993, educ consult, jazzie bd dir. **Orgs:** YMCA asst boy's work, dir, 1964-66; dir, Human Awareness Lab, Edinboro, 1965; supr stud teachers; chmn, Black Studies Comn Edinboro, 1969-72; pres, Phi Delta Kappa Beta Nu Chap, 1987-88; Pa Govs Justice Comn; bd Incorporators, WQLN Educ TV; Erie ACT Community Ctr Bd; Presque Isle Jaycees; Erie Human Rel Educ Com; Erie Urban Coalition; Kappa Delta Phi; Nat Educ Fraternity; Alpha Phi Alpha Soc Fraterniyt; bd dir, Meadville, Pa Unity Ctr; NATO Community Educ Comn; Booker T Wash Community Ctr Scoutmaster; bd dir, Citizen Scholar Found; Pa Black Conf Higher Educ; Inner-Frat Coun Adv; Phi Delta Kappa Edinboro Univ PA; Edinboro Univ Human Rels Comn; bd dir, Jazz Erie; bd dir, Bay front Ctr Maritime Studies; bd dir, Pennbriar Tennis & Health Club; bd dir, Presque Marina Asn; bd dir, Roadhouse Theatre; bd dir, Edinboro Univ Pa Alumini Asn; Pa State Educ Asn; former reader mem, Erie Times-News Ed bd. **Honors/Awds:** Jaycee of the Month, 1966; Runner-up Jaycee Man of the Year, 1967; Alpha Kappa Alpha Sor Sweetheart, 1971; Freshman Advocate Nominee, First Year Experience, Univ SC, 1990-91. **Home Addr:** 222 Beech Lakeside, PO Box 506, Edinboro, PA 16412-0506, **Home Phone:** (814)734-3417.

**DILLON, COREY JAMES**
Football player. **Personal:** Born Oct 24, 1974, Seattle, WA; married Desiree; children: Cameron, Carly & Deavan. **Educ:** Univ Wash, grad. **Career:** Football player (retired); Cincinnati Bengals, running back, 1997-2003; New Eng Patriots, running back, 2004-06. **Honors/Awds:** All-Metro Player of the Year; JC Offensive Back of the Year, 1995; AFC Rookie of the Year, Nat Football League Players Asn, 1997; Pro Bowl selection, 1999-2000, 2001, 2004; Super Bowl Champion XXXIX. **Special Achievements:** Record holder for top rushing game in National Football League history, 278 yards vs. Denver in 2000; producer: Boomie, 2015.

**DILLON, VERMON LEMAR**
Teacher, president (organization), government official. **Personal:** Born Jun 5, 1958, New Orleans, LA; son of Willie L (deceased) and Ruby Mary Cross (deceased); married Gloria Wade; children: Charles A Wade & Micah Lemar. **Educ:** La State Univ, BS, 1981; Southern Univ, MS, 1983. **Career:** Nicholls State Univ, equip mgr athletics, 1981-82; Southern Univ, grad asst athletics, 1982-83; Bogalusa City Schs, teacher, 1984; La State Univ, asst athletic dir, 1984-85; Univ

New Orleans, dept athletics equip mgr, 1985-86; Cent State Univ, dept athletics equip Mgr, 1986-90; Off Youth Develop, Baton Rouge Parish, probation officer II, 1990; La Univ, Juv probation officer, 1990-93; Ohio Dist, chair, currently. **Orgs:** Founder, JC Crump & JJ Piper Memorial, 1979-; Phi Beta Sigma Fraternity; Shiloh Baptist Church Brotherhood, 1990-; comt leader, Undershepherd Shiloh Baptist Church, 1991-; pres, Prince Hall Masons; Kiwanis, 1992; Child support specialist Dept Human Serv, Dayton, Ohio, 1993; Glory ministries church; pres, vpres, bd dir, Mem Prince Hall Masons, Kiwanis 1995; trustee, Omega Baptist Church, Dayton, Ohio, 1996. **Home Addr:** 724 Lexington Ave, Xenia, OH 45385, **Home Phone:** (513)769-5277.

## DILWORTH, DR. MARY ELIZABETH

Educator, vice president (organization). **Personal:** Born Feb 7, 1950, New York, NY; daughter of Tom and Martha Lina Williams; married Clyde C Aveilhe. **Educ:** Howard Univ, BA, 1972, MA, 1974; Catholic Univ Am, EdD, 1981. **Career:** Nat Adv Coun Educ Pr Develop, educ res analyst, 1974-76; Nat Inst Advan Studies, sr prog analyst, 1978-82; Inst Study Educ Policy, res assoc, 1983-85; Howard Univ Hosp, coord educ & training; ERIC Clearing house Teacher Educ, dir, 1987-; Am Asn Cols Teacher Educ, Wash, sr vpres, 1986-2005, dir; Howard Univ, Wash, DC, adj fac, sch educ, 1989-90; Nat Bd Prof Teaching Stand, Higher Educ Initiatives & Res, vpres, 2005-11, consult, 2011-13; Dc Educ Licensure Comn, comnr, 2014-. **Orgs:** Am Educ Res Asn; bd mem, Nat Ctr Res Teacher Educ; Phi Delta Kappa; prog chair, Nat Coun Negro Women; Nat Asn Advan Colored People Task Force Teacher Training & assessment; secy, Div K, Am Educ Res Asn, 1991-92; ETS Vis Panel Res, 2001-; bd dir, Holmes Partnership; prin investr, NSF; Var Non Profit orgn, consult, 2013-. **Home Addr:** 1651 38th St SE, Washington, DC 20020. **Business Addr:** Vice President, National Board For Professional Teaching Standards, 1525 Wilson Blvd Suite 500, Arlington, VA 22209, **Business Phone:** (703)465-2700.

## DIMRY, CHARLES LOUIS, III

Football player, football coach, business owner. **Personal:** Born Jan 31, 1966, San Diego, CA; married Francine; married Erin; children: 6. **Educ:** Univ Nev, BS, exercise sci, 1988. **Career:** Football player (retired), coach, business owner; Atlanta Falcons, defensive back, 1988, right Cornerback, 1989, left Cornerback, 1990; Denver Broncos, defensive back, 1991, right Cornerback, 1992-93; Tampa Bay Buccaneers, defensive back, right Cornerback, 1994-97; Philadelphia Eagles, defensive back, right Cornerback, 1997-98; San Diego Chargers, left Cornerback, 1998, linebacker, left Cornerback, 1999; San Diego col, defensive backs coach, 2004-05; San Diego's Premiere Prep Football Show, corresp; Velocity Sports Performance, owner, 2006-. **Honors/Awds:** Ed Block Courage Award, 1996. **Special Achievements:** TV Series: "ESPN's Sunday Night Football", 1994-95; "NFL Monday Night Football", 1997. **Home Addr:** , Carlsbad, CA. **Business Addr:** Owner, Velocity Sports Performance, 151 Kalmus Dr Bldg C Suite 200, Costa Mesa, CA 92626, **Business Phone:** (714)640-3360.

## DINES, STEVE

Entrepreneur, executive. **Educ:** Univ Leeds, BSc, elec engineering; Univ Manchester, Inst Sci & Technol, MSc, commun. **Career:** Advan Micro Devices; Cirrus Logic, officer corp, vpres & gen mgr; Excess Bandwidth Corp, pres & chief exec officer; Azanda Network Devices, pres & chief exec officer; mSilica Inc, dir, pres & chief exec officer, 2009; Sand Hill Angels Inc, dir; Andigilog Inc, chief exec officer & pres, currently. **Business Addr:** President, Chief Executive Officer, Andigilog Inc, 8380 S Kyrene Rd Suite 101, Tempe, AZ 85284, **Business Phone:** (480)940-6200.

## DINGLE, DEREK T.

Editor, vice president (organization), founder (originator). **Personal:** Born Nov 2, 1961, Brooklyn, NY. **Educ:** Norfolk State Univ, BA, journalism; NY Univ, Mag Mgt Prog, cert. **Career:** Milestone Media Inc, co-founder, 1991-97; Black Enterprise, managing ed, 1987-90; exec ed, 2000-08; sr vpres, ed-in-chief, 2008-. **Special Achievements:** Author: "First in the Field: Jackie Robinson, Baseball Hero" (Disney-Hyperion, 1998); author: "Black Enterprise Titans of the B.E. 100s: Black CEOs Who Redefined and Conquered American Business" (Wiley, 1999).

## DINIZULU, ESQ. YAO O.

Lawyer. **Personal:** Born Jan 1, 1973. **Educ:** Fla A&M Univ, BA, pub admin, 1994; Univ Ill Col Law, JD, law, 1997. **Career:** PricewaterhouseCoopers, tax consult, 1997-99; Harris, Mitchell & Dinizulu LLC, founder & atty, 2000-07; Dinizulu Law Group Ltd, founder, 2008-; Dinizulu, founder. **Orgs:** Supreme Ct Ill; Asn Trial Lawyers Am; bd dir, Bethel New Life Inc, 2003-06; Kappa Alpha Psi Fraternity Inc; exec bd, Nat Black Law Stud Asn; bd dir, United Fire Protection Partners LLC; hearing bd mem, Atty Regist & Disciplinary Comn Supreme Ct Ill; vice-chair judicial evaluations comt, Cook County Bar Asn; Tort Litigation Comt; YLS Comt; Chicago Bar Asn; Minorities Profession; Ill Trial Lawyer's Asn; pres & regional vpres, Fla A&M Univ Nat Alumni Asn Chicago Chap; midwest regional officer & vpres, Fla A&M Univ Nat Alumni Asn; community rep, Alexander Bouchet Local Sch Coun; mem rep, HBCU Col Consortium; honored mem, Strathmore's Who's Who, 2003-04 Ed; panelist, Exhale Talk Show; Vol, Obama Ill; bd mem, Citizens New Horizon; Am Bar Asn; Ill Trial Lawyers Asn; Ill State Bar Asn; Univ Ill Stud Bar Asn; Civil Pract & Rules Comt; Civil Rights & Criminal Law Comt; bd dir, Universal Fire Protection; Univ Ill Col Law Fac. **Honors/Awds:** James Benton Parsons Scholarship Award, Just Beginning Found; Public Service & Academic Achievement, Nat Bar Asn Judicial Coun; Best Bachelor of the Year, Ebony, 2003; 40 under 40, Law Bull Publ Co, 2007; Rising Star, Super Lawyers Mag, 2012. **Business Addr:** Founder, Attorney, Dinizulu Law Group Ltd, 221 N LaSalle Suite 1100, Chicago, IL 60601, **Business Phone:** (312)384-1920.

## DINKINS, DAVID NORMAN

Mayor, educator. **Personal:** Born Jul 10, 1927, Trenton, NJ; son of William; married Joyce Burrows; children: David Jr & Donna Hoggard. **Educ:** Howard Univ, BS, maths, 1950; Brooklyn Law Sch, JD, 1956. **Career:** Dyett, Alexander, Dinkins, Patterson, Michael, Dinkins, Jones, atty-partner, 1956-75; NY State Assembly, state assemblyman, 1966; NY State Dem Party, dist leader, 1967-; City New York, pres bd elections, 1972-73, city clerk, 1975-85, Manhattan bor, pres, 1986-90, mayor, 1990-93; Columbia Univ, Sch Int & Pub Affairs, prof pract pub affairs, 1993-, bd adv, professorship, 2003-. **Orgs:** Bd dir, NY State Am Dem Action; Urban League; bd dir, 100 Black Men; bd dir, March Dimes; bd dir, mem steering comt, Asn Better NY; Manhattan Women's Polit Caucus; Nat Asn Advan Colored People; Black-Jewish Coalition; Vera Inst Justice; Nova Anorca & NY State Urban Develop Corp; bd trustee, Malcolm King Harlem Col; pres adv coun, Marymount Manhattan Col; exec comt, Asn Bar City NY; bd dir, Upper Manhattan Empowerment Zone; Hon Life Trustee, Community Serv Socs New York; Hon trustee, Harlem Hosp; Alpha Phi Alpha Fraternity; Sigma Pi Phi; bd dir & hon founders bd, Jazz Found Am; Church Intercession, New York; Asn to Benefit C; ACORN; C's Health Fund; Fedn Protestant Welfare Agencies; Nelson Mandela C's Fund; Posse Found; Amadou Diallo Found; chmn emer bd dir, Nat Black Leadership Comn AIDS; chmn emer bd dir, CFA; steering comt, ABNY; mem bd dir, Coalition Homeless; bd dir, Independent News & Media; bd dir, New York Global Partners; Coun Foreign Rels; hon life trustee, Community Serv Socs New York; hon trustee, Friends Harlem Hosp; bd dir, Brooklyn Law Sch Alumni; Reveille Club; Friars Club; Montford Pt Marine Asn; bd dir, US Tennis Asn; bd dir, New York Sports Comn. **Special Achievements:** First Black Mayor of a Major U.S. City. **Home Addr:** 215 E 68th St Apt 31D, New York, NY 10065-5730. **Business Addr:** Professor, Columbia University, Int Affairs Bldg Rm 1430, New York, NY 10027, **Business Phone:** (212)854-4253.

## DINKINS, TRACI

Advertising executive, vice president (organization). **Educ:** City Univ NY, Baruch Col, Zicklin Sch Bus, BBA, advert & broadcast prod. **Career:** Bates, planner, 1993-96; UniWorld Group, planner, 1996-97, dir, 2001-03; Omnicom Group, assoc dir, 1997-2003; Starcom MediaVest Group, GM Planworks, media dir & vpres, 2003-08; J3-Universal McCann, sr vpres & group strategy dir, 2008-09; Freelance Media Strategist, consult, 2010; Spike DDB, assoc media dir & media dir; African Am Advert, pres; Zenith Optimedia, sr vpres & group commun dir, 2010-11; Mindshare, managing dir & sr partner, 2011-13; MEC, Team AT&T, sr partner, acct dir, 2013-. **Honors/Awds:** Outstanding Women in Marketing & Communication, Ebony Mag, 2003; BE Top Women Executives in Advertising & Marketing, 2013. **Business Addr:** Account Director, Senior Partner, MEC, 825 7th Ave, New York, NY 10019, **Business Phone:** (212)474-0000.

## DISHER, SPENCER C., III

Executive. **Personal:** Born Sep 30, 1957, Florence, SC; son of Spencer C Jr and Annette Moorer; married Katherine Dowdell. **Educ:** Univ Wis-Madison, BSCE, 1980; Northwestern Univ, JL Kellogg Grad Sch Mgt, MBA, 1986. **Career:** ExxonMobil, proj engr, 1980-84; Continental Bank, pub finance assoc, 1985-86; Chevron, fel, 1985; Citicorp Investment Bank, assoc, 1986-87; Deutsche Bank, senior assoc, 1987-88; BT Securities, NY, assoc, 1987-88; Credit Nat, vpres; NABM LLC, sr vpres; Natixis, sr vpres portfolio mgr, currently; Fixed-Income Asset Mgt, 2012-. **Orgs:** Toastmasters, 1984-86; Nat Black MBA Asn, 1985-; Nat Asn Advan Colored people; founder, Wis Black Engr Stud Soc. **Home Addr:** 22 Ridge Rd, Hartsdale, NY 10530, **Home Phone:** (914)428-3325. **Business Addr:** Senior Vice President, Natixis, 1251 Avenue of the Americas 34th Fl, New York, NY 10020, **Business Phone:** (212)302-9147.

## DISHMAN, CRIS EDWARD

Football player, football coach. **Personal:** Born Aug 13, 1965, Louisville, KY; married Carmen; children: Bianca, Coy & Ethan. **Educ:** Purdue Univ. **Career:** NFC Champion Football player (retired), football coach; Houston Oilers, defensive back, 1988-96; Wash Redskins, 1997-98; Kans City Chiefs, 1998-99; Minn Vikings, football player, 2000; Miami Dolphins, coach, 2006; Menlo Col, defensive back coach, 2006, defensive coordr, 2007-; Oakland Raiders, coach, 2007; San Diego Chargers, asst defensive backs coach, 2009-; Baylor Bears football team, coach art briles, 2015. **Orgs:** NFL's Minority Coaching Fel prog. **Business Addr:** Assistant Defensive Backs Coach, San Diego Chargers, 4020 Murphy Canyon Rd, San Diego, CA 92123, **Business Phone:** (858)874-4500.

## DISMUKE, MARY EUNICE

Executive director, association executive. **Personal:** Born Feb 5, 1942, West Point, GA; daughter of Hattie Snow Pelleccitti and Hubert Hazes Moss; married Olin; children: Sonja & Monica. **Educ:** Ga State Univ, Atlanta, GA, BS; Wayne State Univ, Detroit, MI, MSW. **Career:** Detroit Compact, Detroit, Mich, dir; Mich Dept Labor & Econ Growth, Detroit, Mich, dir, urban affairs; Detroit Assoc Black Org, Detroit, Mich, exec dir. **Orgs:** Exec bd mem, Detroit Asn lack Social Worker; secy, Coalition Black Trade Unionists. **Honors/Awds:** Outstanding Leadership, Detroit Asn Black Social Workers, 1970; Leadership Am, 1985; Harriet Tubman Award, A Philip Randolph Inst & Coalition Black Trade Unionists, 1989. **Home Addr:** 18485 Vaughan, Detroit, MI 48219, **Home Phone:** (313)694-3272.

## DIUGUID, LEWIS WALTER

Newspaper executive. **Personal:** Born Jul 17, 1955, St. Louis, MO; son of Lincoln I and Nancy Ruth Greenlee; married Valerie Gale Words; children: Adrianne Renee & Leslie Ellen. **Educ:** Univ Mo-Columbia, Sch Jour, BJ, 1977; Univ Ariz-Tucson, attended 1984; Maynard Inst Jour Educ, Editing Prog Minority Journalists. **Career:** Kans City Times, reporter, photogr, 1977-80, gen assignment reporter, surburban reporter, 1980-82, Jackson County courthouse reporter, 1982-84, copy ed, automotive ed, 1984-85; Kans City Star, asst bur chief, Johnson County, 1985-87, Southland Bur chief & columnist, 1987-92, asst city ed & columnist, 1993-94, assoc ed, Metro Columnist, 1994-, diversity co-chair, asst minority recruiter, 1995-, vpres community resources, Kans City Star, currently; Kans City Asn Black Journalists, Urban Stud Journalism Acad, co-coordinator. **Orgs:** founding mem, treas, newsletter ed & Media Awards Comt chmn, pres, Kans City Asn Black Journalists; Nat Asn Black Journalists, 1985-; Nat Soc Newspaper Columnists; Trotter Group Black Voices Commentary; bd dir, Missourian Publ Asn, Univ Mo-Columbia; bd trustee, William Allen White Found, William Allen White Sch Jour & Mass Commun, Univ Kans-Lawrence; Univ Mo Alumni Asn; Kans City Stars ed bd. **Honors/Awds:** Unity Award, Lincoln University, 1979; Ark of Friends Award, 1990-92; Urban League, Difference Maker Award, 1992; Mental Health Award, Missouri Dept of Mental Health, 1991; Research Mental Health Service, Media Award, 1992; First Place Opinion Column Award, Kansas City Press Club, 1993; Ark of Friends Media Professional Award, 1993; Asn Media Award, Mo Community Col, 1993; Journalism Award, Wayside Waifs Humane Society, 1993; Mental Health Awareness Award, Mental Health Asn Kansas City, 1993; Public Affairs/Social Issues Unity Award, Lincoln Univ, 1993; Ark of Friends of Greater Kansas City Media Professional Award, 1994; Harmony Encourages Awareness, Responsibility, Togetherness Award, 1995; SCLC Evelyn Wasserstorm Award, Commitment to Causes of Freedom, 1996; Project Equality Individual Achievement Award, 1997; Black Achievers in Industry Award, 1997; James K Batten Knight-Ridder Excellence Award, 1998; MO Honor Medal for distinguished Service, Univ MO Columbia School of Journalism, 2000; Millennium Award, NAACP Branch 4071, 2000; Missouri Asn Social Welfare Community Service Award, 2001; Charles E Bebb Peace Merit Award, 2002; Peace Alliance Award, Kansas City Institute, 2002; Media Award, Kansas Correctional Asn, 2002; Journalism Award, Current Peace Society, 2002; Gail & Irving Achtenburg Civil Libertarian of the Year Award, 2002; Mary Lona Diversity Award, Black Chamber of Commerce of Greater Kansas City, 2003; Soldier Award, NAACP Branch 4071 in Moberly, MO, 2004; Award for Unwavering Support & Good Work, Kansas City Federation of Teachers & School-Related Personnel, Local 691, 2005; First African American Achievement Award for Literary Contributions, United Govt Wyandotte County/Kans, KS, 2005; Courage Award, Kansas City Task Force for a Season for Nonviolence, 2005; Toast for the Children Award, 2006; Mayors Committee for People with Disabilities Media Leadership Award, 2006; Maxey DuPree Humanitarian Kindest Kansas Citian Award, 2007; Spotlight Award for Outstanding Media Coverage of Social Welfare Issues, Mo Asn Social Welfare, Kans Chapter, 2007; University of Missouri-Columbia Faculty-Alumni Award, 2007. **Special Achievements:** Most Influential African-Americans in Greater Kansas City, 1992-97; Author, A Teacher's Cry: Expose the Truth About Education Today, 2004; Discovering the Real America: Toward a More Perfect Union, 2007. **Home Addr:** 1601 Walnut St Apt 402, Kansas City, MO 64108, **Home Phone:** (816)421-1743. **Business Addr:** Vice President, Community Resources, Editorial Board Member & Columnist, The Kansas City Star, 1729 Grand Blvd, Kansas City, MO 64108, **Business Phone:** (816)234-4723.

## DIVINS, CHARLES

Actor, fashion model. **Personal:** Born Jan 29, 1976, Dallas, TX. **Career:** Tommy Hilfiger, model; Films: Passions; Till We Stop Having Fun, 2007; The Gauntlet, 2011; Running in Circles, 2012; Four of Hearts, 2013. TV series: "Family Feud", 1999, 2004; "Passions", 1999, 2002-07; "Half & Half", 2002, 2005-06; "Soapography", 2004; "Passion for the Game", 2005; "Starting Over", 2005; "Ben Masters"; Episode dated 24 March 2003, 2003; "Soap Talk", 2003-06; "50 Steamiest Southern Stars", 2005; "Shooting the Police: Cops on Film", 2006; "101 Incredible Celebrity Slimdowns", 2006; "The Turn On", 2006; "Your LA", 2006, 2007; Dinner Party, 2008; "My Boys", 2008; "Melrose Place", 2009; "CSI", 2010; "Femme Fatales", 2011; Milk & Honey, 2012. TV shows: "50 Steamiest Southern Stars", 2005; "The 19th Annual Soul Train Music Awards", 2005; "101 Incredible Celebrity Slim downs", 2006; 1st Look, 2011. **Honors/Awds:** Winner, Male Spokesmodel. **Special Achievements:** Featured in commercials including GQ, Glamour, Cosmopolitan, Gear; appeared in the 2003 Alaye calendar. **Business Addr:** Actor, Passions, 30 Rockefeller Plz, New York, NY 10112.

## DIX, HENRY

Postmaster general, manager. **Personal:** Born Trenton, NJ. **Career:** US Postal Serv, Philadelphia Metrop Performance Cluster, clerk & mail carrier, 1976, postmaster, post off opers, sr mgr, Mid-Carolinas Dist, dist mgr & lead exec. **Business Addr:** District Manager, Lead Executive, United States Postal Service, 2970 Market St, Philadelphia, PA 19104-9991, **Business Phone:** (215)895-8000.

## DIXON, ARDENA S.

Educator. **Personal:** Born Feb 24, 1927, Baltimore, MD; daughter of Albert E Simmons Sr and Sedonia Parker Simmons; married Daniel E Jr; children: Deidre I (deceased), Stephanie Dixon-Barham & Eris I. **Educ:** Coppin State Col, BS, 1963; Loyola Col, MS, 1971. **Career:** Educator (retired); Baltimore City Pub Schs, classroom teacher, 1963-69, reading specialist, 1969-73; Baltimore City Dept Social Serv, social work asst II, 1965-78, SWAII, supvr, 1969-71; Baltimore City Pub Schs, edual specialist, 1973-74, asst prin, 1974-79, prin, 1979-98; Md State Foster Care Review Bd, chairperson SWII bd, 1988-96. **Orgs:** PSASA, 1973-; MAESA/NEA, 1973-; eastern regional dir, Phi Delta Kappa Sorority, 1983-87, chairperson, eastern region Xinos, 1992-93, supreme basileus, 1997-2001; NCNVV, 1983-; ASCD, 1985-; Urban League Perpetual Guild, 1987-; life mem, Nat Asn Advan Colored People, 1987-; vpres, Pinochle Bugs Social/Civic Club, Baltimore Co, 1988-; NANBPWC, 1992-; pres, Perpetual Scholar Found, 1993-; Nat Sorority, Phi Delta Kappa; chairperson, Southwest Region Bd No 2, Citizen Rev Bd C, Baltimore, MD, 2004. **Home Addr:** 1410 N Ellwood Ave, Baltimore, MD 21213, **Home Phone:** (410)675-1573.

## DIXON, DR. ARMENDIA P.

School administrator. **Personal:** Born Laurel, MS; daughter of L E Pierce; married Harrison D Jr; children: Harrison D III. **Educ:** Edinboro Univ, PA, MEd, sch admin, 1978; Kent State Univ, PhD, curric, instrnl & supv, 1993; Jackson State Univ, BA, Eng. **Career:** Kent State Univ, adj prof, 1984-85; Crawford Cent Sch, exec dir, asst prin, 1985-90, prin, 1992-93; Erie Pub Sch, Sec Edu, dir, 1993-; Edinboro Univ, Pa, Dr Gerald P Jackson Dept Acad Support Serv, dept chmn, acad adminr, currently, Dept Eng & Theatre Arts, prof, currently. **Orgs:** Pres, Dr. Martin Luther King, Jr Scholar Found, 1980-; bd mem, United Way, Meadville, 1984-95; bd mem, Am Red Cross, 1989-95; chair, AKA Scholarships, 1989; Edinboro Univ Alumni Bd, 1990-. **Honors/Awds:** Urban Teachers Award, 1985; Citizenship Award, 1993; Distinguished Alumni Award, Edinboro Univ, 2001; Numerous Service Awards. **Special Achievements:** Author: Parents: Full Partners in the

Decision-Making Process, NASSP Bull, 1992. **Home Addr:** 716 Jefferson St, Meadville, PA 16335, **Home Phone:** (814)336-3767. **Business Addr:** Professor, Academic Administrator, Edinboro University of Pennsylvania, 219 Meadville St, Edinboro, PA 16444, **Business Phone:** (814)732-2781.

### DIXON, ARRINGTON LIGGINS

Executive. **Personal:** Born Dec 3, 1942, Washington, DC; son of James and Sallie; married Sharon Pratt; children: Aimee & Drew. **Educ:** Howard Univ, BA, econs, 1965; George Washington Univ, JD, 1972; AUs Command & Gen Staff Col, attended 1989. **Career:** Univ DC, assoc prof, 1967-74; Mgt Info Syst, pres, 1967-74; Coun DC, chmn, mem, 1975-82; Brookings Inst, guest scholar, 1983; Planning Res Corp, vpres, 1983-85; Arrington Dixon & Assoc Inc, pres & prin owner currently; Nat Capital Planning Comn, mayor, 2011-. **Orgs:** Bd mem, Wash Ctr, 1983-86; advan studies, adv comt, Brookings Inst, 1983-; bd mem, Greater SE Comt Hosp Found, 1983-84, Anacostia Mus, 1984-; Chmn, Anacostia Coordr Coun; life Mem, Comt 100 Fed City; Nat Asn Advan Colored People; DC dem party offices; chmn & mem, Metrop Wash Coun; chmn & mem, Coun DC. **Honors/Awds:** Congressional Appt US Air Force Acad, 1963-65; Software, Statutes & Stare Decisis Howard Univ Law Journal 420, 1967; Scholarship, George Wash Univ Law, 1969-72. **Special Achievements:** Mr. Dixon appointed, Commission by Mayor Adrian Fenty. **Home Addr:** 2401 Shannon Pl SE, Washington, DC 20020, **Home Phone:** (202)889-1070. **Business Addr:** Mayor, National Capital Planning Commission, 401 9th St NW, Washington, DC 20004, **Business Phone:** (202)482-7200.

### DIXON, DR. BENJAMIN

School administrator, educator. **Personal:** Born Apr 18, 1939, Hartford, CT; son of Rose Carter Brown and Cue Benjamin; married Carolyn Holmes; children: Kevin, Kyle & Kimberly; married Carolyn. **Educ:** Howard Univ, BS, gen music, 1962; Harvard Univ, MAT, 1963; Univ Mass, EdD, educ leadership & admin, 1977. **Career:** Hartford Conn Pub Schs, teacher, 1963-74; Westledge Sch, W Simsburg Conn, teacher & adv, 1969-71; Educ & Instr Inc, Hartford, Conn, co-dir, 1971-73; Bloomfield Pub Schs Conn, asst supt, 1974-86, actg supt schs, 1986-87; Capitol Region Educ Coun, Windsor, Conn, asst exec dir, 1987-88; The Travelers, Hartford, Conn, dir Human Resouces, 1989-92; Conn State Dept Educ, Hartford, Conn, dep comnr Educ, 1992-98; Va Tech Univ, Blacksburg, Va, vpres, off Multicultural Affairs, 1998-2006, vpres emer, 2006; Sankofa Futures Consult LLC, training & consult, founder & pres, 2007-. **Orgs:** Pres, CT Assoc Pupil Personnel Adminr, 1983-84; bd dir, Univ MA Sch Educ Alumni Assoc; sec bd trustee, Stowe Sch; CT State Adv Comn Mastery Testing, Spec Educ, Gifted & Talented; treas bd dir, Hartford Dist Cath Family Servs; gov's appointee CT C's Trust Fund Coun; bd dir Educ & Instr Inc; bd trustees Metro AME Zion Church; Am Mgt Asn, 1989; Am Soc Personnel Admins, 1989; pres, Study Comn, Coun Chief State Sch Officers, WA, DC; chair, Capitol Community-Tech Col Found, Hartford, CT; Black Men's Soc, Hartford, CT; CT Awards Excellence Bd; CT Comn African-Am Affairs; Pi Kappa Lambda Nat Hon Soc. **Honors/Awds:** Achievement & Service Award, Bloomfield Concerned Black Parents for Quality Educ, 1987. **Special Achievements:** Virginia Tech's first vice president for multicultural affairs; co-author "Stress and Burnout, A Primer Spec Educ & Special Servs Personnel", 1981. **Home Addr:** 1104 Deerfield Dr, Blacksburg, VA 24060-1703, **Home Phone:** (540)961-9115. **Business Addr:** Vice President Emeritus, Virginia Tech, 332 Burruss Hall, Blacksburg, VA 24061, **Business Phone:** (540)231-1820.

### DIXON, BRANDON VICTOR

Singer, theatrical producer, actor. **Personal:** Born Sep 23, 1981, Gaithersburg, MD. **Educ:** Columbia Univ, BA; Brit Acad Dramatic Actg, attended 1999. **Career:** Actor, 1999-. Raise the Roof and WalkRunyFly, producer, 2014-. Stage: The Lion King, 2003; The Color Purple, 2005-06; Ray Charles Live, 2007; The Scottsboro Boys, 2010; Cotton Club Parade, 2011; Rent, 2012; Far From Heaven, 2012; Motown the Musical, 2013-14; The Scottsboro Boys, West End, 2014; Shuffle Along, Or the Making of the Musical Sensation of 1921 and All That Followed, 2016; Hamilton, 2016-. Television: One Life to Live, ABC, 2006; Law & Order: Criminal Intent, NBC, 2009; The Good Wife, CBS, 2010. Film: The Warrior and the Savior, 2013. Stage producer: Indomitable: James Brown; Burnt Sugar: The Arkestra Chamber; Of Mice and Men, 2014; Hedwig and the Angry Inch, 2014-15. **Honors/Awds:** Antoinette Perry Award, 2014; Drama Desk Award, 2014; I.A.L. Diamond Award for Achievement in the Arts, Columbia Univ. **Business Addr:** Noble Talent Management, 8 Hamilton Ct, Lawrenceville, NJ 08648.

### DIXON, CAROLYN D. See FAULKNER, CAROLYN D.

### DIXON, ERNEST JAMES

Executive, football player. **Personal:** Born Oct 17, 1971, York, SC. **Educ:** Univ SC, BA, psychol, 2003. **Career:** Football player (retired), executive; New Orleans Saints, linebacker, 1994, middle linebacker, 1995, 1996-97; Oakland Raiders, 1998; Kans City Chiefs, 1998-2000; Volvo S Atlanata, gen sales mgr, 2000-08; Mercedes Benz S Atlanta, gen sales mgr, 2008-. **Business Addr:** General Sales Manager, Mercedes Benz of South Atlanta, 3775 Royal S Pkwy, Atlanta, GA 30349, **Business Phone:** (770)964-1600.

### DIXON, GERALD SCOTT, SR.

Football player, football coach. **Personal:** Born Jun 20, 1969, Charlotte, NC; children: Gerald Jr. **Educ:** Garden City Comm Col; Univ Sc. **Career:** Football player (retired), coach; Cleveland Browns, 1993-94, right linebacker, 1995; Cincinnati Bengals, linebacker, 1996, right outside linebacker, 1997; SanDiego Chargers, left linebacker, 1998, linebacker, 1999-2001; Oakland Raiders, 2001; Sylvia Circle Elem Sch, phys educ teacher & little league coach, currently; Rock Hill High Sch, linebackers coach, currently. **Special Achievements:** Film: 1992 NFL Draft, 1992. **Business Addr:** Linebackers Coach, Rock Hill High School, 320 W Springdale Rd, Rock Hill, SC 29730, **Business Phone:** (803)981-1300.

### DIXON, REV. JAMES WALLACE EDWIN, II

Clergy, executive. **Personal:** Born Nov 12, 1962, Houston, TX; son of James Sr and Carrol; married Linda. **Educ:** Oikodome Sch Bibl Studies, BA, 2003; Houston Baptist Univ; Tex Southern Univ; Houston Grad Sch Theol, MDiv. **Career:** Northwest Community Baptist Church, pastor, 1981, sr pastor; GOOD GANG USA Inc, founder & exec dir; Dom Acad, founder & pres, currently. **Orgs:** Bd mem, Fel Christian Athletes; bd mem, United Way Tex Gulf Coast; pres ministers conf, pres social justice comn, Nat Baptist Conv Am; Nat Asn Advan Colored People; bd dir, Metrop Transit Auth; founder, James Dixon Ministries Inc; bd mem, METRO Univ Corridor Details & Drawings; Third vpres, Nat Asn Advan Colored People, Houston Br Bd Mems; Samaritan's Feet. **Honors/Awds:** Humanitarian Award, Prairie View A & M Univ, 1986; Tex Gospel Music Awards, Outstanding Community Serv; Olympic Games Touchbearer, 1996. **Home Addr:** 5903 Green Falls Dr, Houston, TX 77088-4104, **Home Phone:** (281)448-4709. **Business Addr:** President, Founder, Dominion Academy, 835 Lee Ave SW, Leesburg, VA 20175, **Business Phone:** (703)737-0157.

### DIXON, JIMMY

Government official, chairperson. **Personal:** Born Dec 9, 1943, Devereux, GA; children: Glenda, Thaddeus & Taranda. **Educ:** Ga Mil, 1972, 1974, 1976; Univ Ga, attended 1978; Ga Col, attended 1981. **Career:** Cent St Hosp, supvr, 1964-74; Sparta Parks & Recreation, dir, 1975-79; Hancock County Bd Educ, chmn, 1978-; Rheem Air Condition Div, storekeeper, 1979-. **Orgs:** Supt Jones Chapel AME Sunday Sch, 1971-; Jones Chapel AME Steward Bd, 1974-, Ga Sch Bd Asn, 1975-; Stolkin Temple 22, 1976-; Lebar Consistory 28, 1976; GSBA Positions & Resolutions Comn, 1979-; comt mem, Dem Party Ga, 1982-85; CAES Adv Coun, Univ Ga. **Home Addr:** 111 Turkey Run NE, Milledgeville, GA 31061. **Business Addr:** Chairman, Hancock County Board Education, PO Box 488, Sparta, GA 31087, **Business Phone:** (706)444-5775.

### DIXON, JOHN FREDERICK

Marketing executive. **Personal:** Born Feb 19, 1949, Boston, MA. **Educ:** Howard Univ, BA, 1971; Columbia Univ, Grad Bus Sch, MBA, 1973, Teacher's Col, EdM, EdD. **Career:** US Dept Agr, agr mkt specialist, 1971; fel, Columbia Univ, 1971-73; Xerox Corp, sls rep, 1973-74; Stand Brands Inc, asst prod mgr, 1974-76; Red-T Productions, co-founder, 1975-; Black Sports Mag, mkt dir, 1976-78; Essence Commun Inc, mkt & res serv dir; New York Col Technol, assoc prof, currently. **Orgs:** World mem Int House, 1971-; African-Am Inst, 1973-; Alliance Francaise-French Inst, 1975-78; Consult, Africa Mag, 1976; consult, Horn of Africa Mag, 1977-78; Am Mkt Asn, 1978-; Advert Res Found, 1978-; Media Res Dirs Asn, 1979-; NAACP, 1979-. **Honors/Awds:** Co-inventor "Claim to Fame" Black History Game, 1977; pub "Pony Goes After Young Blacks with 'follow the Leader' Tack", 1977; creator "Battle of New Orleans" 64-page fight Prog, Muhammad Ali vs Leon Spinks, 1978; established In-House Essential Media Ad Agency Essence Mag; Distinguished serv Award, Harlem Teams for Self-Help, 1979. **Home Addr:** 684 Riverside Dr Apt 4F, New York, NY 10031-5028, **Home Phone:** (212)694-9377. **Business Addr:** Associate Professor, New York City College of Technology, Rm N-1024 300 Jay St, Brooklyn, NY 11201, **Business Phone:** (718)260-5768.

### DIXON, JOHN M.

Executive, chairperson. **Personal:** Born Jan 25, 1938, Chicago, IL; children: Kwane Dubois. **Educ:** Univ Mont, BS, 1959; New Eng Sch Law, JD, 1966; Boston Univ, MBA, 1976. **Career:** Sonesta NY, regional sales mgr, 1968-70; Sheraton Mtr Inns, dir promotion, 1970-73; Hyatt Regency O'Hare, exec asst mgr, 1973; Burlingame CA, gen mgr, 1973; Hyatt Regency, resident mgr, 1974-; Hyatt Regency Cambridge, gen mgr, 1975-; J.W. Marriott Hotel, owner, Wash; Univ Md, Sch Bus & Technol, Dept Hotel & Restaurant Mgt, asst prof & chmn, 2000-. **Business Addr:** Chairman, Department of Hotel and Restaurant Management, University of Maryland Eastern Shore, Eastern Shore, Princess Anne, MD 21853, **Business Phone:** (410)651-2200.

### DIXON, JULIUS B.

Executive. **Educ:** Howard Univ, BBA, 1975. **Career:** AstraZeneca Pharamaceuticals LP, Cardiovasular Therapeut Area, regional sales dir, area sales dir, rcl, sr dir, 1992-2011; Boehringer Ingelheim, regional dir & sales regional dir, 2011-. **Business Addr:** Regional Director, Sales Regional Director, Boehringer Ingelheim, 2600 S Shore Blvd Suite 300, League City, TX 77573-2944, **Business Phone:** (281)334-3936.

### DIXON, DR. LEON MARTIN

Educator, health services administrator, physician. **Personal:** Born Nov 12, 1927, Brooklyn, NY; son of Leon M and Helen Moody; married Alfonso Baxter; children: Deborah, Carolyn Knight, Cynthia, Suzanne & Leon II. **Educ:** Howard Univ, BS, 1949, MD, 1953. **Career:** Med & Cardiol Colo Univ Sch Med, instr, 1963-65; US Walson Army Hosp, hosp comdr, 1973-77; Reynolds Metals Co, Macmillan Med Ctr, dir, 1977-97; Fitzsimons Army Med Ctr, resident, cardiovasc dis & internal med; Jersey City Med Ctr, resident internal med; Kings County Hosp Ctr, resident; Commonwealth Occup Safety & Health Asns, staff physician, currently. **Orgs:** Consult Disaster Planning, Reynolds Metal, 1977-91; Cardiol Med First Army Area, 1965-69; Chesterfield County Drug Abuse Adv Comn, 1979-80; chmn, Pub Health Prev Med Richmond Acad Med, 1980-81; Med Soc Va. **Honors/Awds:** Physician for Astronantical Prog, Gemini Mercury, NASA, 1965-69; articles publ in Physiology of Heart Meningitis, Congenital Heart Disease, Chem other of Tumors. **Home Addr:** 10900 Ramshorn Rd, Midlothian, VA 23113-1116, **Home Phone:** (804)272-6814. **Business Addr:** Staff Physician, Commonwealth Occupational Safety & Health Associations LLC, 5935 Hopkins Rd 1sr Fl, Richmond, VA 23234-5750, **Business Phone:** (804)743-7613.

### DIXON, LEONARD BILL

Executive. **Personal:** Born Aug 1, 1956, Albany, GA; son of Clarence and Ruby; married Adrian; children: Joseph & Rosalind. **Educ:** State Fair Community Col, Asn Arts Degree, AA, 1977; Southwest Baptist Univ, BS, sociol & psychol, 1980; Nova Univ, Ft Lauderdale, FL, MS, prog admin, 1990. **Career:** Dept Health & Rehab Servs, group leader, 1980-82, supvr, 1982-85, supt, 1985-90; Dep Juv Justice Serv, prog opers adminr, 1990-95; Wayne County Community Col, adj prof, exec dir, 1995-; Dept Community Justice, exec dir, 1995-2004; Mich Dept Human Serv, Bur Juv Justice, dir, 2004-07. **Orgs:** Pres, Nat Juv Detention Asn; Am Correctional Asn; Coun Juv Correctional Admin; adj staff mem, Nova Univ; Nat Juv Jus Group-C's Defense Fund; EEOC-Dade County; bd dir, Wellington Group; ACA Comt Fla Dist XI; bd Dir, Community Tree House, Detroit Mich; Boy Scouts Am; Nat Comt Assessment Minority C; bd dir, Mich Juv Detention Asn. **Home Addr:** 24420 Crescent Dr, 1326 St Antoine, Woodhaven, MI 48183, **Home Phone:** (313)967-2014. **Business Addr:** Director, Department of Human Services, PO Box 30037, Lansing, MI 48909, **Business Phone:** (517)373-2035.

### DIXON, DR. LOUIS TENNYSON

Manager, association executive, engineer. **Personal:** Born Dec 13, 1941; son of Eitel V and Enid L; married Lora M; children: Michael. **Educ:** Howard Univ, BS, 1968; Johns Hopkins Univ, PhD, 1973. **Career:** Ford Motor Co, prin res scientist, sr resscientist, 1973-76, mgr chem dept, 1976-78, prin staff engr, 1978-86, engineering assoc, 1986-89, mgr. **Orgs:** Am Chem Soc; Soc Automotive Engrs; Soc Mfg Engrs; Stand Engineering Soc; vpres, Int Club, 1966-67; chmn, People-To-People, 1967-68; pres, Phi Lambda Upsilon, 1972-73; SAE Int, currently; Nat Coop Lab Accreditation, pres, 2004-. **Special Achievements:** Publications: "Infrared Studies of Isotope Effects for Hydrogen Absorption on Zinc Oxide" Journal of America Chemistry Society, 1972; "The Nature of Molecular Hydrogen Absorbed on Zinc Oxide" Journal of Physical Chem, 1973; "Infrared Active Species of Hydrogen Absorbed by Alumina-Supported Platinum" Journal of Catalysis, 1975; "Hydrogen Absorption by Alumina-Supported Supported Platinum" Journal of Catalysis, 1975; "Foaming & Air Entrainment in Automatic Transmission Fluids" Soc of Auto Engr, 1976; "Fuel Economy -Contributor of the Rear Axle Lubricant" Soc Auto Engr, 1977. **Home Addr:** 37781 Rhonswood Dr, Northville, MI 48167-9023, **Home Phone:** (248)426-8533. **Business Addr:** Chairman, Finance Committee, SAE International, 400 Commonwealth Dr, Warrendale, PA 15096-0001, **Business Phone:** (724)776-4841.

### DIXON, MARGARET A.

Association executive, teacher, president (organization). **Personal:** Born Jan 1, 1920, Columbia, SC; married Octavius; children: Kevin, Karen & Edith. **Educ:** Allen Univ, BA, educ; Hunter Col, MA; NY Univ, MA; Fordham Univ, prof dipl educ leadership; Nova Southeastern Univ, PhD, educ. **Career:** Educator (retired); New York Sch, teacher, 1954-80; Brooklyn Col Teacher Educ prog, supv prin; Brooklyn Col, supv prin; SC State Dept Educ, consult, 1981-86; Ford Found Fel; US Off Educ grad fel; Allen Univ, assoc prof & dir teacher educ, 1981-86. **Orgs:** Bd strategic planning comm; Nat Retired Teachers Asn Task Force; literacy tutor; vol, Meals-on-Wheels; Minority Affairs Initiative, spokesperson, 1988-92, Am Asn Retired Persons, 1992-94, vpres, pres, 1996-; bd mem, Am Asn Homes & Servs Aging, 1998-. **Special Achievements:** First Black National President of The American Association of the Retired Persons (AARP). **Home Addr:** 13514 New Acadia Lane, Upper Marlboro, MD 20774.

### DIXON, ORA WRIGHT

Administrator. **Career:** US Fish & Wildlife Serv, Conserv Training Ctr, Nat Girl Scout coordr & course leader div educ outreach & LFCC Chair, microbiologist, educr, currently. **Orgs:** US Environ Protection Agency. **Business Addr:** Coordinator, LFCC Chair, US Fish & Wildlife Service, 698 Conserv Way, Shepherdstown, WV 25443-9713, **Business Phone:** (304)876-7314.

### DIXON, RAYMOND P (RAY DIXON)

Chief executive officer. **Career:** Family Automobile Group, Owner, chief exec officer, 1995-. **Business Addr:** Chief Executive Officer, Owner, Family Automotive Group, 33033 Camino Capistrano, San Juan Capistrano, CA 92675, **Business Phone:** (949)493-4100.

### DIXON, RICHARD CLAY

Government official, mayor, politician. **Personal:** Born Jan 1, 1942. **Educ:** Central State Univ, attended. **Career:** City Dayton, OH, city comnr, mayor, 1987-93; Ohio Dem Party, politician. **Orgs:** Trustee, Greater Dayton Regional Transit Authority; adv coun, Great Pk Conservancy. **Special Achievements:** Second African-American person to serve as mayor of Dayton. **Business Addr:** Board of Trustee, Greater Dayton Regional Transit Authority, 4 S Main St, Dayton, OH 45402, **Business Phone:** (937)425-8400.

### DIXON, ROBERT L.

Vice president (organization), executive. **Educ:** Ga Inst Technol, BS, elec engineering. **Career:** Procter & Gamble, Global Bus Serv, vpres; PepsiCo., sr vpres & global chief info officer, 2007-; SAP Global Ctr Expertise, founder. **Orgs:** Bd mem, WellPoint Inc; CIO Strategy Exchange; IT Sr Mgt Forum; Cash CIO Forum; bd advisor, IBM; P&G's Global Bus Coun; pres's adv bd, Ga Inst Technol, Atlanta. **Honors/Awds:** Academy of Distinguished Engineering Alumni, Ga Inst Technol, 2002; "Black Enterprise," The 100 Most Powerful Executives in Corporate America, 2010; Top Ten Breakaway Leader Award, Global CIO Exec Summit, 2012; 7HMG Strategy 2012 Transformational CIO Leadership Award. **Business Addr:** Senior Vice President, Chief Information Officer, 700 Anderson Hill Rd, Purchase, NY 10577-1401, **Business Phone:** (914)253-2000.

### DIXON, RODRICK

Singer, composer. **Personal:** Born Jun 22, 1966; married Alfreda Burke. **Educ:** Mannes Col Music, New York, BM, 1989, MM, 1991. **Career:** Lyric Opera Chicago, performer; Portland Opera, performer; Virginia Opera, performer; Columbus Opera, performer; Album: In Concert; Follow the Star; Sacred Land; Three Mo Tenors, 2001; Cook, Dixon & Young Volume One, 2005; Liam Lawtons Sacred Land, 2006; TRIPTYCH, 2009. **Honors/Awds:** Richard F. Gold Career Grant, Shoshana Found; "Tenor of the Year" Award, Mary Dawson Art Guild, 1991. **Special Achievements:** Appeared on Great Performances, PBS, 2001; earned rave reviews for his Dame Myra Hess Memorial Concert broadcast honoring Roland Hayes on WFMT-FM Chicago. **Business Addr:** Singer, DiBurke Inc, PO Box 571, Oak Lawn, IL 60454, **Business Phone:** (301)423-6505.

### DIXON, RONNIE CHRISTOPHER
Football player. **Personal:** Born May 10, 1971, Clinton, NC. **Educ:** Univ Cincinnati, criminal justice. **Career:** Football player (retired); New Orleans Saints, defensive tackle, 1993; Philadelphia Eagles, right defensive tackle, 1995, defensive tackle, 1996; New York Jets, defensive tackle, 1997; Kans City Chiefs, 1998.

### DIXON, DR. RUTH F.
Educator. **Personal:** Born Sep 22, 1931, Camden, NJ; married George Jr; children: Cheryl Yvette & Brian Duane. **Educ:** Rowan Univ, NJ, BS, 1953, MA, 1965; Univ Pa, EdD, 1977. **Career:** Educator (retired); Rutgers Univ, asst prof, chairperson educ opportunity, assoc prof educ, Acad Found Dept, prof & chair, 1971-98, prof emer; Camden City Schs, elem & sec teacher, admin; NJ St Dept Educ, supvr. **Orgs:** Educ consult, St Col, 1965-71; State Asn Adult Educ, 1965-; exec bd, Educ Opport Fund Prog, 1971-; bd educ, Lay Comn, 1972-; exec bd, Black Peoples Unity Movement, 1973-; Mayors Adv Coun, 1974-; Kappa Delta Pi, 1976; NJ Asn Black Educrs, 1978-; dir, Distinguished Am Educ & Community Serv, 1980; coun, Camden City Pvt Indust, 1983; BPUM Child Develop Ctrs Adv Comt, 1983; bd trustee, Camden City Col, 1984; coun, Nat Asn Notaries, 1984; bd dir, Soc Educ & Scholars, 1984; Our Lady Lourdes Commuity Adv Comt, 1984; Cable adv bd, City Spokane, 2003-06. **Honors/Awds:** Community Award, BPUM-EDC, 1973; Soc Educ & Sch, Phi Delta Kappa Nat Honor Soc, 1975; Kappa Delta Pi; Pi Lambda Theta Nat Honor Soc, 1975; BPUM Special Award for Outstanding Education, 1976. **Home Addr:** 1554 Ormond Ave, Camden, NJ 08103-2941, **Home Phone:** (856)963-2487.

### DIXON, SHEILA ANN
Government official. **Personal:** Born Dec 27, 1953, Baltimore, MD; daughter of Phillip Sr and Winona; married Thomas Hampton; children: Joshua & Jasmine. **Educ:** Towson State Univ, BA, early childhood educ, 1976; Johns Hopkins Univ, MS, educ mgt, 1985. **Career:** Tillman Learning Ctr, adult learning specialist, 1983-84; Quazar Int, intsales mgr, 1983-84; Md Dept Bus & Econ Develop, int trade specialist, 1986-99; Dem State Cent Comt, mem, 40th legis dist, 1986; Baltimore City Coun, mem, 4th dist, 1987-99, pres, 1999-2007, mayor, 2007-10. **Orgs:** Fel Urban Health Initiative; Baltimore City Tobacco Community Health Coalition; lifetime mem, Nat Asn Advan Colored People; Afr-Am Women's Caucus; hon chair, HERO AIDS WALK; Nat Black Caucus Elected Officials; co-founder Bethel AME Food Coop; Retired Sr Vols Prog Adv Coun; Inst Human Virol; Transplant Resource Ctr; Baltimore Pub Markets Corp; Living Classrooms Found; Walters Art Gallery; active mem, Bethel AME Church; trustee, Stewardess Bd; trustee, Baltimore Mus Art, 1999-. **Special Achievements:** First African-American female to serve as president of the City council, Baltimore's first female mayor. **Business Addr:** Trustee, Baltimore Museum of Art, Baltimore, MD.

### DIXON, T. TROY
Executive director, executive. **Personal:** Born New York, NY. **Educ:** Col Holy Cross, Worcester, MS, BA, econs, 1993. **Career:** Salomon Bros, trader; Credit Suisse, head pass-thru, 1999-2002; UBS Investment Bank, exec dir, 2002-06; Deutsche Bank Securities Inc, managing dir, 2006-13, RMBS Trading Group, head; Hollis Pk Partners LP, founder & chief investment officer, 2013-. **Orgs:** chmn, Todd Isaac Scholar Fund; Corp Banking & Securities Americas Exec Comt; Rates & Credit Trading Exec Comt; Securities Indust & Financial Markets Asn; bd mem, Apollo Theater Found Inc; Pres's Coun. **Honors/Awds:** "The Network Journal," 40 Under Forty Class, 2006; "Black Enterprise," 75 Most Powerful Blacks on Wall Street, 2011. **Business Addr:** Founder, Chief Investment Officer, Hollis Park Partners LP, 1540 Broadway 39th Fl, New York, NY 10036, **Business Phone:** (646)701-6465.

### DIXON, TAMECKA MICHELLE
Basketball player. **Personal:** Born Dec 14, 1975, Linden, NJ; daughter of Boo Bowers. **Educ:** Univ Kans, BA, child psychol, 1997; Univ Phoenix, MBA, bus admin, 2011. **Career:** Basketball player (retired); Istanbul; Turkey; Los Angeles Sparks, guard, 1997-2005; Nike Inc, endorsement rep, 1997-2005; Houston comets, 2005-08; Ind Fever, 2009; Edward Jones, financial advisor, 2011-12; Am Income Life, gen agt, 2011-.

### DIXON, TYNNA G.
Executive. **Personal:** Born Jul 16, 1969, Temple, TX; daughter of M C and Sandra Thomas; children: Andre & Daylan. **Educ:** Temple Col, attended 1989; Univ Mary Hardin Baylor, attended 1995; Baylor Univ, masters, theol, 2012. **Career:** First Natl Bank, data entry & customer svc rep, 1989-93; Tex Dept Human Serv, eligibility specialist, 1993-95; Tex Workforce Comm, case mgr, 1995-97; Cent Tex Worforce Ctr, workforce develop specialist, 1997-14; Mary Kay Beauty Consult, Beauty Consult, 2006-12; Towne Adams realtors, realtor, 2005-; Wesley United Methodist Church, Waco TX, pastor, 2012-. **Orgs:** Temple High S Prep Advy Cou, 1997-; Temple Health & Human Serv, 1997-; Bell County Transp Alliance, 1997-; Child Care mgt Adv Coun, 1998-99; Ebony Cult Soc, 1998-; Nat Asn Advan Colored People, 1999-2000. **Home Addr:** PO Box 1433, Moody, TX 76557-1433, **Home Phone:** (254)986-2559. **Business Addr:** Pastor, Wesley United Methodist Church, Waco TX.

### DIXON, VALENA ALICE
Executive, administrator. **Personal:** Born Jan 11, 1953, Philadelphia, PA; daughter of James and Alice; children: James. **Educ:** St Joseph Univ; Univ S Ala, attended 1976; W Chester State Univ, BS, educ, 1974; Temple Univ, attended 1979. **Career:** Mobile County Pub Schs, ed, 1974-79; Reading Sch Dist, ed, 1974-79; Urban League, Philadelphia Chap, employ counr, 1979-81; Temple Univ, cotre source spt, 1981-82; Crisis Intervention Network Inc, prog mgr, 1982-87; Greater Media Cable Philadelphia, community rels mgr, 1987-92; Philadelphia Housing Authority, pub affairs dir, 1992-98; Richmond Redevelop & Housing Authority, vpres family serv & community rels, 1998-. Richmond Redevelop and Housing Authority, external rels dir, 2012-. **Orgs:** Bd mem, Ctr Literacy, 1990-94; Philadelphia Pub Rels Asn, 1990-; Philadelphia Asn Black Journalists, 1990-93; Nat Black Media Coalition, 1990-92; bd mem, Korean & Am Friendship Asn, 1991-; pres, Am Women Radio &TV, Philadelphia Chap, 1992-; Nat Forum Black Pub Adminr, 1992-; Linda Creed Breast Cancer Found, 1993-. **Home Addr:** 205 Beaufont Ct, Richmond, VA 23225-5811, **Home Phone:** (804)276-2429. **Business Addr:** Vice President, Richmond Redevelopment & Housing Authority, 901 Chamberlayne Pkwy, Richmond, VA 23261-6887, **Business Phone:** (804)780-4200.

### DIXON, HON. WILLIE L.
Government official. **Career:** Teledyne-Brown Corp, Jackson, supvr; Wash County Dist 5, comnr, 1992-. **Orgs:** Bd dir, Mobile Community Action; bd mem, ACCA Transp; bd dir, Wash County Dist 10, 2007-2008. **Home Addr:** PO Box 67, Chatom, AL 36518. **Business Addr:** Commissioner, Washington County District 5, Hwy 43, Wagarville, AL 36585, **Business Phone:** (334)847-2208.

### DIXON, YVONNE T.
Government official, executive. **Personal:** Born Washington, DC. **Educ:** Earlham Col, BS, polit sci, 1971; NY Univ Sch Law, JD, 1974. **Career:** Nat Labor Rels Bd, atty advisor, spec asst to gen coun, spec coun to gen coun, dep asst gen coun, asst gen coun, actg dep gen coun, 1992-93, gen att, Off Appeals, dir, currently. **Orgs:** Fel mem, Bar of the Dc. **Honors/Awds:** Presidential Meritorious Executive Rank Award, 1999. **Special Achievements:** First African-American woman to head NLRB'S Office of Appeals. **Business Addr:** Director, National Labor Relations Board, Rm 1057 1717 Pa Ave NW, Washington, DC 20570, **Business Phone:** (202)273-3760.

### DOAN, LURITA ALEXIS
Government official, executive, founder (originator). **Personal:** Born Jan 4, 1958, New Orleans, LA; daughter of Lucien Victor Alexis Jr; married Douglas; children: Natalia & Alexandra. **Educ:** Vassar Col, BA, Eng, 1979; Univ Tenn, Knoxville, MA, renaissance lit, 1983; Defense Lang Inst, hons, 1989. **Career:** Southeastern La Univ, instr, 1983-85; Cath Univ Am, instr, 1985-86; Col, La & Va, adj prof, 1984; Unisys, programmer & trainer, 1986-90; New Technol Mgt Inc, pres, founder & chief exec officer, 1990-2005; US Gen Serv Admin, adminr chief, 2006-08; Fed News Radio 1500 AM, conservative commentator, 2008-10. **Orgs:** Enterprising Women Soc; Am Const Soc; Security Indust Asn; Am Red Cross; Nat Women Bus Ctr, DC; Rape Crisis Ctr; Young Entrepreneurs Orgn; Young Presidents Orgn; United Negro Col Found; Am Women Bus Ctrs; Cystic Fibrosis Found; Whitman Walker Clin; bd trustee, Vassar Col, 2002-; bd trustee, Shakespeare Theatre Wash, DC; Comt 200; Coun Competitiveness; Nat Asn Women Bus Owners; Nat Asn Female Exec; Women Technol Int; Minority Bus Network; Northern Va Technol Coun; Belizean Grove; World Pres's Orgn, 2008-; Jane Austen Soc N Am, 2008-; Screen Actors Guild & Am Fedn Tv & Radio Artists, 2008-; Int Asn Contract & Com Mgt, 2012-. **Honors/Awds:** National Directors Award, dept com, 2003; Committee of 200 Luminary Award, 2003; Visionary Award, Nat Found, 2003; National Womens Business Council Award, 2004; ABRAZO Award, 2008; Tri National Award, 2008. **Special Achievements:** First woman to hold the position in US Gen Admin; first African Americans to integrate into the private school system in New Orleans in the early 1960s; nominated by President George W. Bush to lead the GSA. **Business Addr:** Member, World President's Organization, 600 E Las Colinas Blvd Suite 1000, Irving, TX 75039, **Business Phone:** (972)587-1500.

### DOANES-BERGIN, SHARYN F.
Executive. **Personal:** Born Atlanta, GA; daughter of Onzelo Doanes; married Michael Edward; children: Jennifer Lee & Jessica Faye. **Educ:** Paine Col, BA, 1969; Atlanta Law Sch, JD, 1978, ML, 1979; Cent Mich Univ, MPA, 1983. **Career:** Executive (retired); Honeywell Info Syst, employee rels mgr; NY Times Regional Newspaper Group, Atlanta, employee rels mgr; Atlanta Ballet Inc, vpres human resources; Intergalactic Ltd, chief financial officer. **Orgs:** Ga Exec Women, 1980-87; vpres, Paine Col Alumni, 1982-87; vpres, Ga Leukemia Soc, 1984-87; trustee, Paine Col, 1983-88; Odyssey, 1985-. **Honors/Awds:** Black Achiever Award, Harlem YMCA, 1992. **Home Addr:** 120 Ketterings Trace, Tyrone, GA 30290-1648, **Home Phone:** (770)964-9921.

### DOBARD, DR. RAYMOND G., JR.
Educator. **Educ:** Xavier Univ, LA, BA, fine arts, 1970; Johns Hopkins Univ, MA, 1973, PhD, hist art, 1975. **Career:** Howard Univ, Col Arts & Sci, fac, 1975-, prof art, currently; Quilt Study Ctr, Univ Nebr, adj fac mem, currently; Johns Hopkins Univ, John Hay Whitney Found & Leopold Schepp Found fel; Thomas Mann artist-in-residence fel, city Lubeck, Ger, 1986. **Orgs:** Founding mem, bd dir, Va Quilt Mus, Harrisonburg, 1992-96; adv bd, Textile Mus, Wash, DC, 1993-96; adv bd, Int Quilt Study Ctr, Univ Nebr, Lincoln, 1997-98; Nat Quilt Study Group; adv, New African Am Art Mus, Baltimore, MD, currently. **Business Addr:** Professor of Art, Howard University, 2455 6th St NW, Washington, DC 20059, **Business Phone:** (202)806-7047.

### DOBBINS, LUCILLE R.
Executive. **Personal:** married George; children: Diane. **Educ:** Roosevelt Univ, acct, 1968; Ill Cert Pub Acct Cert, 1970. **Career:** Hyde Pk Fed Savings & Loan, asst treas, 1963-69; Blackman Kallick & Co, auditor, 1969-73; Harris Trust & Savings Bank, vpres, 1974-84; City Chicago Dept Plng, dep comnr, 1984-86; City Chicago Mayor's Off, chief financial planning officer; Resolution Resources Inc, chief exec officer, pres, currently. **Orgs:** Nat Soc Cert Pub Acct, Ill Soc Cert Pub Acct; nat adv bd, Black Career Women Inc, Lambda Alpha Intl Hon Land Econ Soc; bd mem, Rainbow PUSH Coalition. **Honors/Awds:** Entrepreneur of the Year, 1994. **Special Achievements:** First head of the sub-cabinet, 1985-86; First deputy commissioner in the Department of Planning. **Home Addr:** 9049 S Bennett Ave, Chicago, IL 60617, **Home Phone:** (773)221-1738. **Business Addr:** President, Chief Executive Officer, Resolutions Resources Inc, 225 W Ohio St Suite 350, Chicago, IL 60654, **Business Phone:** (312)822-0605.

### DOBBS, DR. JOHN WESLEY
Educator, association executive, army officer. **Personal:** Born Oct 8, 1931, Grenada, MS; married Mildred; children: Kiley & Kelly. **Educ:** Western Mich Univ, BA, 1954; Wayne State Univ, ME, 1960; Mich State Univ, PhD, 1975. **Career:** Hemp seatd Pub Schs, supvr sch; Mich Dept Educ, asst supt sch & community affairs; Detroit Sch Syst, teacher, counr, asst prin, prin; State Dept Educ, dir sch & community educ. **Orgs:** St Adv Coun Equal Educ Opportunity; St Task Force Coun Guid; coordr, Task Force Out Sch Out Work Youth; rep, Mich Comn Criminal Justice; ad com, Mich Hum Serv Network; Am Asn Sch Adminr; Nat Asn Advan Colored People; Urban League; Nat Alliance Black Sch Educr; Eastern Mich Univ; bd dir, Metro Detroit Youth Found. **Honors/Awds:** President Award, Nat Alliance Black Sch Educr; Outstanding Admin Award, Detroit Soc Black Educr; Resolution of Appreciation, State Mich Concurrent House of Rep, 1983; Outstanding Eductor, Leader & Humanitarian Award, Hemp stead, NY Bd Educ, 1986; Distinguish Educator in Support of Black Children Award Leadership & Training Inst Hemp stead, 1986; Mayor's Proclamation Outstanding Community Leader Village of Hemp stead Long Island, 1986. **Home Addr:** 1448 Farwood Dr, East Lansing, MI 48823-1868, **Home Phone:** (517)351-7478. **Business Addr:** Principal, Detroit School System, 900 Victors Blvd Atrium Off Ctr Suite 210, Ann Arbor, MI 48108, **Business Phone:** (313)487-3249.

**DOBBS, MATTIWILDA. See Obituaries Section.**

### DOBSON, BYRON EUGENE
Journalist, editor. **Personal:** Born Jan 26, 1957, Easton, MD; son of William Edward and Elizabeth Young. **Educ:** Bowie State Univ, Bowie, MD, BA, communs, 1979; Univ Ariz, Ed Prog, Minority Journalists, grad fel, 1985. **Career:** WEMD-Radio, Easton, MD, news asst, 1979-80; Boca Raton News, Boca Raton, FL, reporter, asst city ed, city ed, 1980-90; Tallahassee Dem, Tallahassee, FL, night city ed, 1990-, relig ed, assoc community conversation ed, metro ed, currently. **Orgs:** Kappa Alpha Psi Fraternity, 1984-; pres, charter mem, Palm Beach Asn Black Journalists, 1988-90; Nat Asn Black Journalists, 1990-; Blacks Communs, 1990-. **Honors/Awds:** Corene J Elam Communications Award, Bowie State Univ, 1979; Featured in The Bulletin, Minorities in the Newsroom, May-June, 1987. **Home Addr:** 2731 Blairstone Rd, Tallahassee, FL 32301, **Home Phone:** (850)942-6916. **Business Addr:** Associate Community Conversation Editor, Metro Editor, The Tallahassee Democrat, 277 N Magnolia Dr, Tallahassee, FL 32301, **Business Phone:** (850)599-2100.

### DOBSON, DOROTHY ANN
Social worker. **Personal:** Born May 10, 1934, Chester, VA; daughter of Alfred and Julia Morton; married James; children: Jacquelyn, Kimberley & Gina. **Educ:** NC A&T State Univ, Greensboro, NC, BS, 1957. **Career:** Social worker (retired); Monroe County Dept Social Serv, Rochester, NY, adult protection caseworker, 1958-89. **Orgs:** Pres, Jack & Jill Am Inc, 1964-66; bd dirs & comt, Girl Scouts Genesee Alley, 1970-80; bd dir, United Way Rochester, eval comt, 1975-; bd dir, YWCA, 1975-81; pres, NC A&T Alumni Asn, 1980-82; coordr, pres & founder, Greater Rochester AARP, 1989-; deleg, NY State, AARP Biennial Conv, San Antonio, 1992; deleg, Black Cath Cong, New Orleans, 1992; social worker, Emmelyn Logan-Baldwin, currently. **Honors/Awds:** Urban League of Rochester Community Service Award, 1977; Monroe County Human Relations Community Services, 1982; Black Catholic Family Award, 1983; Volunteer Service Award United Way of Rochester, 1984; Dedicated Service Award, NC A&T State University, 1987. **Home Addr:** 524 Rockingham St, Rochester, NY 14620-2520, **Home Phone:** (585)473-1758. **Business Addr:** Social Worker, c/o Emmelyn Logan-Baldwin, 171 State St Suite 400, Rochester, NY 14614, **Business Phone:** (585)232-2292.

### DOBY, ALLEN E.
Government official, executive director. **Personal:** Born Oct 26, 1934, MS; son of A; married LaFaye Ealy. **Educ:** Calif State Univ, Northridge, CA, BS, recreation admin, 1973; MPA prog. **Career:** County Los Angeles, asst recreation dir, 1959-62, recreation dir, 1962-70, dist recreation dir, 1970-75; Calif Community Col Syst, lectr, 1973-75; Cerritos Community Col, instr, 1974-76; City Compton, dir parks & rec, 1975-80; City Santa Ana, exec dir, 1980-1996. **Orgs:** Calif Parks Rec Soc 1961-; bd dir, Nat Recreation Parks Assoc, 1971-; bd dir, NRPA Ethnic Minority Soc, 1971-. **Home Addr:** 709 Balboa Ave, Laguna Beach, CA 92651-4105. **Business Addr:** Executive Director, City Santa Ana, 405 W 5th St Suite 366, Santa Ana, CA 92701, **Business Phone:** (714)571-4202.

### DODD, GERALDA
Business owner. **Personal:** Born Jul 4, 1957, Toledo, OH; married Thomas Edward Sellers Jr. **Educ:** Univ Toledo. **Career:** Integrated Steel, owner & chief exec officer, 1990; HS Automotive, chief exec officer, 1991; Heidtman Steel Prod, receptionist, inventory control mgr, purchasing mgr, vpres purchasing & admin; Thomas Madison Inc, chief exec officer, currently. **Orgs:** Past bd dir, Cent Mich Univ. **Honors/Awds:** Most Influential Women, Crain Commun Inc, 2007. **Special Achievements:** First African-American woman to break through the gender barrier in the traditionally male-dominated business of steel and metal stamping. **Home Addr:** 1630 Wellesley Dr, Detroit, MI 48203-1480, **Home Phone:** (313)368-0140. **Business Addr:** Chief Executive Officer, President, Thomas Madison Inc, 2301 Hubbell St, Detroit, MI 48227, **Business Phone:** (313)273-4000.

### DODDY, REGINALD NATHANIEL
Engineer, executive. **Personal:** Born Jul 2, 1952, Cincinnati, OH; son of Nathan and Mildred Peek. **Educ:** Northwestern Univ, BS, elec engineering, 1975. **Career:** Eastman Kodak Co, mfg engr, 1975-77; Mead Corp, mfg engr, 1977-79; RCA Corp, assoc mem staff elec engr, 1979-84; Cincinnati Milacron, systs controls engr, 1984-94, software engineering supvr, 1994-. **Orgs:** Toastmasters Club, 1976-77; Inst Elect & Elect Engr, 1977-; tech dir, RCA Minority Engineering Prog, 1980-83.

**Honors/Awds:** Nomination Outstanding Young Men of America, 1982-83; Community Service Award, Indianapolis Ctr Leadership Develop, 1982. **Home Addr:** 3595 Wilson Ave, Cincinnati, OH 45229, **Home Phone:** (513)221-1433. **Business Addr:** Software Engineer Supervisor, Cincinnati Milacron, 4165 Halfacre Rd, Batavia, OH 45103-3247, **Business Phone:** (513)536-2000.

## DODGE, DEDRICK ALLEN

Football player. **Personal:** Born Jun 14, 1967, Neptune, NJ; married Patrice; children: Chante, Dedrick Jr & Nyla. **Educ:** Fla State Univ, criminol. **Career:** Football player (retired), coach; London Monarchs, 1991; Seattle Seahawks, defensive back & safety, 1991, corner back, 1992; San Francisco 49ers, 1994-96; Denver Broncos, safety, 1997; San Diego Chargers, safety, 1998; Evangel Christian Sch, coach; Mulberry Sr High Sch, head coach; Victory Christian Acad, head coach; Ft Valley State Univ, defensive coordr.

## DODSON, ANGELA PEARL

Editor. **Personal:** Born May 24, 1951, Beckley, WV; daughter of William Alfred Sr and Kira Evelyn; married Michael Irvin Days. **Educ:** Marshall Univ, Huntington, W VA, BA, 1973; Am Univ, Wash, DC, MA, jour & pub affairs, 1979. **Career:** Charleston Gazette, intern, Charleston, WV, 1972; Huntington Advertiser, Huntington, WV, reporter, 1972-74; Gannett News Serv, Wash, DC, corresp, 1974-77, asst news, feature ed, 1977-79; Rochester Times Union, Rochester, NY, asst city ed, 1979-80; Wash Star, Wash, DC, night slot features ed, 1980-81; Courier J Louisville, KY, copy ed, 1981-82; Diocese Trenton, Black Caths, radio host, 1999; Maynard Inst Journalism Educ, consult; New York Times, New York, NY, copy ed, dep ed living sect, ed living sect, ed style dept, 1983-95, sr ed, news admin, consult ed, 1995-03, freelance consult ed, exec ed; Black Issues Bk Rev Mag, freelance ed write, 1999-03, exec ed, 2003-; Editorsoncall LLC, founder,currently; Hampton Univ, consult; Mercer County Community Col, adj fac. **Orgs:** Chap founder, Alpha Kappa Alpha, Marshall Univ, 1971-75; former nat secy, Nat Asn Black Journalists, 1977; fac mem, adv bd mem, Editing Prog Minority Journalists, 1982-; bd mem, Univs prestigious Chuck Yeager Scholars Prog; Am Press Inst; Am Soc Newspaper Ed. **Honors/Awds:** Black Alumna of the Year, Sons Marshall, 1988; Distinguished Alumna, Sch Jour, Marshall Univ, 1989; Black Achiever in Industry, Harlem YMCA, 1990; New York Asn Black Journalists, Feature Writing Award, 2000; Outstanding black alumna. **Home Addr:** 324 Hamilton Ave, Trenton, NJ 08609, **Home Phone:** (609)394-7632. **Business Addr:** Executive Editor, Black Issues Book Review, 350 5th Ave Empire State Bldg Suite 1522, New York, NY 10118-0165, **Business Phone:** (212)947-8515.

## DODSON, HOWARD, JR.

Executive, educator. **Personal:** Born Jun 1, 1939, Chester, PA; son of Howard and Lou Birda (Jones); married Jualynne White; children: Alyce Christine & David Primus Luta. **Educ:** Westchester State Col, BS, 1961; Univ Calif, Los Angeles, attended 1964; Villanova Univ, MA, hist & polit sci, 1964; Univ Calif, Berkeley, ABD, 1974. **Career:** Nat Credit Union Educ Fedn Ecuador, educ progs dir, 1964-66; Peace Corps, recruiter, 1964-67, dir spec recruiting, 1967-68, trng officer, 1968; UC Berkeley, grad fel, 1969-73; CA State Col, assoc prof, 1970; Inst Black World, res fel, 1970-71; Inst Black World, prog dir, 1973-74, exec dir, 1974-79; Shaw Univ, adj prof, 1975; Emory Univ, lectr, 1976-79; Black Studies Curric Develop, dir, 1980-83; Nat Endowment Humanities, asst to chmn, 1980-82; Schomburg Ctr Res Black Cult, chief, 1984-2010, dir libr, proj cur; Moorland-Spingarn Res Ctr, dir. **Orgs:** Alpha Phi Alpha, 1959-64; SC Hist Soc, Peace Corps Vol, 1964-66; Oakland Black Caucus, 1969-73; consult, Nat Endowment Humanities, 1979-80; chmn, chief exec officer, Black Theol Proj, 1982-84; bd dir, Inst Black World, Atlanta Assoc Int Ed; Ed Brain Trust Cong Black Caucus; Atlanta Univ Sch Soc Work; Nat Comn Citizens Educ; GA Assoc Black Elected Officials; ESEA; Nat Credit Union Fed Educr; African Heritage Studies Assoc; AssocStudy Afro-Am Hist; So Hist Assoc; bd overseers Lang Col New Sch Social Res; bd dir, NCBS; AHSA; dir, Howard Univ Libr Syst; Caribbean Res Ctr; bd drs, Apollo Theater Found; UNESCO Slave Rte Proj. **Honors/Awds:** PICCO Scholar, 1959-61; Grad Fel UC Berkeley, 1969-73; Res Fel Inst Black World, 1970-71; ASALH Service Award, 1976; Governor's Award for African Am Distinction, 1982; Doctor Humane Letters, Widner Univ, 1987; Honorary Doctorate, Widener Univ, 1987, Adelphi Univ, 2004, W Chester State Univ, 2004, City Univ New York, 2004, Villanova Univ, 2007. **Special Achievements:** Publications: "Censorship and Black America", 1984; A Public Forum on the Draft Proposal to the U.S. Congress for Commemorating the African Burial Ground, 1993; "The Black New Yorkers", 2000; "Jubilee", 2002; "In Motion", 2004; "Lest We Forget", 2007; "Ideology, Identity and Assumptions", 2007; "Cultural Life", 2007; "Origins", 2008; "The Black Condition", 2009; "Becoming American", 2009; "Six-volume Encyclopedia of African American History and Culture". **Home Addr:** 159 00 Riverside Dr W Suite 2M 70, New York, NY 10032, **Home Phone:** (212)927-9487. **Business Addr:** Chief, Schomburg Center for Research in Black Culture, 515 Malcolm X Blvd, New York, NY 10037-1801, **Business Phone:** (212)491-2200.

## DODSON, DR. JUALYNNE E.

School administrator, educator, association executive. **Personal:** Born Jan 4, 1942, Pensacola, FL; daughter of Benjamin White and Flora White; married Howard; children: Alyce Christine & David Primus Luta. **Educ:** Univ Calif, Berkeley, BS, 1969, MA, 1972, PhD, sociol, 1984; Warren Deem Inst, Educ Mgt Columbia Univ Sch Bus, 1985; Northwestern Univ, Scholar Residence. **Career:** Inst Black World, consult res assoc, 1970-71; Atlanta Univ Sch Social Work, instr, 1973-74, res proj dir, 1973-81, dir res ctr, 1974-80, from asst prof to assoc prof, 1974-82, founding dir, 1979-82, chair Dept Child & Family Serv, 1980-82; Am Sociol Asn, res fel appl social, 1980; Garrett Theol Sem, vis scholar, 1981-82; Union Theol Sem, dean sem life & assoc prof, 1982-88; Black Theol Proj, exec dir, 1985-88; Schomburg Ctr Res Black Cult, Post-doctorate Fel; Princeton Univ, Ctr Study Am Relig, Post-doctorate Fel; Univ Ga, Post-doctorate Fel; Mich State Univohn A. Hannah Distinguished Vis Professorship; Hunter Col, City Univ NY, sociol dept, vis assoc prof, 1989-90; Yale Univ, sr res assoc, African & African-Am Studies, 1990-91; Princeton Univ, Ctr Studies Am Relig, sr res fel, 1991-92; Univ Colo, relig studies, African Am studies, sociol, assoc prof, 1992-2002, dir, 1996-; Mich State Univ, African Am & African Studies, fac, Relig Studies Dept, dir, 1996-, prof, 2003-05, Dept Sociol prof, 2005-. **Orgs:** Elected deleg Coun, Social Work Educ, 1979-82; Am Acad Relig, 1981, 1983, 1984 & 1987; Nat Coun Convenor Feminist Theol Inst, 1982-83; Soc Sci Study Relig, 1982, 1983, 1986; consult, Nat Child Welfare Trng Ctr, Ann Arbor, Mich, 1983-85; chair & bd dir, Black Theol Proj, 1983-84; Nat Coalition 100 Black Women, 1984; NY State Black & Puerto Rican Legis Caucus Women's Conf, 1985; NY State Affirmative Action Adv Coun, 1985-86; leader, Black Church Studies & Stud Caucus Retreat Colgate Rochester Divinity Sch, 1985; adv bd, Asn Black Women Higher Educ, 1985-88; Soc Am Archivists, 1986; bd dir, Asn Study World African Diaspora; Collegium African Am Res; Afro-Am Relig Hist Grp; Int Sociol Asn; Caribbean Studies Asn; Womanist Theol Grp; Afro-Latin Am Res Asn; vis prof, Brown Univ, 1999; vis prof, Bates Col, 2002. **Honors/Awds:** Gubernatorial Appointee White House Conf on Families, 1980; Lucy Craft Laney Award, Black Presbyterians United UPCUSA, 1982; Spivack Fel, Am Sociol Asn, 1983; Medal of Honor, Outstanding Community Service One Church One Child Prog, Indianapolis, 1986; Delegate Intl Conf, Ecumenical Sharing Nanjing, China, 1986; Outstanding Faculty Member Award, MSU Senior Class Council, 2005-06; Global Competency Award, 2009. **Special Achievements:** Author: A Source book in Child Welfare, National Child Welfare Training Center, 1982; "An Afro-Centric Educational Manual," University of Tennessee Press, Knoxville, 1983; African Religious Traditions of Cuba; publications: Engendered Church: Women, Power, and the AME Church; Religion in the Americas: Religion, Rims, & Boundaries. Sacred Spaces and Religious Traditions of Orient Cuba. **Business Addr:** Director, Professor, Michigan State University, 101 Morrill Hall, East Lansing, MI 48824, **Business Phone:** (517)432-8669.

## DODSON, VIVIAN M.

Government official, mayor. **Personal:** Born Jan 22, 1934, Washington, DC; daughter of Brevard and Maefield Wilson; married Barke M; children: Tangie B & Kaphree A(deceased). **Educ:** Wash Col Music, Wash, DC, AA, 1956. **Career:** Government official, mayor (retired); Prince Georges County Communs, Upper Marlboro, Md, communs oper, 1973-89; Town Capitol Heights, Capitol Heights, Md, councilwoman, 1982-86, mayor, 1986-2002. **Orgs:** Girl Scouts Am, 1971; dir, Recreation Capitol Heights, 1982-; bd mem, Prince Georges County Munic League, 1983-; Mothers Move, 1984-; Citizen Move, 1986; Mid-County Youth Serv; Coun Black Mayors; Nat Coun Black Women; Prince Georges Munic Mayors; Nat Polit Cong Black Women, 1991; pres, Prince Georges Munic Elective Women, 1992-; Gov Parris N. Glendenings Comn, State Block Grants. **Home Addr:** 5635 Southern Ave, Capitol Heights, MD 20743, **Home Phone:** (301)336-2198.

## DODSON, WILLIAM ALFRED, JR.

Administrator. **Personal:** Born Feb 9, 1950, Beckley, WV; son of William A Sr and Kira E Walthall; married Judythe Irene Taylor; children: Daymon. **Educ:** Marshall Univ, BA, sociol, 1973; Ohio State Univ, MA, pub admin, 1981; Ohio Real Estate Sales Lic, attended 1997. **Career:** Tri-state OIC, instr, 1972-73; ACF Ind, instrl rel repr, 1973-75; Off Human Serv, field rep, 1975-77; Off Appalachia ODOD, housing rep, 1977-82; WCVO-FM, vol announcer, 1980-96; Off Local Gov Serv, ODOD, field rep/devel specialist, 1982-86; Columbus Metro Housing Authority, asst dir housing prog, 1986-88, MIS mgr, 1988-89, mgt analyst, 1989-93; Rhema Christian Ctr, exec vp & dir community rels, 1992-; Day spring Christian CDC, exec dir, 1993-; lic realtor, 1997-2005; exec dir, Dayspring Christian Community Develop Corp. **Orgs:** Elder, Rhema Christian Ctr, 1982, exec vp, 1992-; bd mem, Asn Developmentally Disabled, 1986-99; chmn, Neighborhood Serv Adv Coun, Columbus, 1989-90, 1993-94, vpres, 1991-93, bd dir, 1986-93; pres, Directions Youth, 1992-93; Christian Mgt Asn, 1993-, chair, 1999-; Christian Comm Dev Asn, 1993-; vice chmn, Northeast Area Comm, 1993-96, chair, 1996-98; pres, Nat Asn Church Bus Admin, 1994-96; vice chmn, Columbus State Community Col, 1994-99, chmn, 1998-99; trustee, Columbus Compact Corp, 1995-97; Urban Concern, 1995-; I-670 Develop Corp, 1996-98; bd trustee, Columbus Metro Area Community Action Org, 1998-, chair, 2000, comnr; cert church mgr, Christian Mgt Asn, 1997; bd dir, Heartland Bank. **Honors/Awds:** Nat Achievement Scholar, Nat Merit ETS, 1968; Outstanding Participant, Nat Alliance Bus Jobs Campaign Huntington Metro, 1975; Certified Economic Development Specialist, Nat Dev Council, 1984; Certified Public Housing Mgr, 1987; Community Achievement Award, Marshall Univ Alumni Asn, 1996; Church Manager Certificate, Christian Mgt Asn, 1997; Soldier Faith Award, Unity Economic Summit, 1999; Harvard Divinity Sch, Summer Leadership Inst, 2000. **Home Addr:** 5362 Pk Lane Dr, Columbus, OH 43231, **Home Phone:** (614)901-0870. **Business Addr:** Executive Vice President, Director of Community Relations, Rhema Christian Center, Rhema Christian Ctr 2100 Agler Rd, Columbus, OH 43224, **Business Phone:** (614)471-0816.

## DOGG, SNOOP (CORDOZAR CALVIN BROADUS, JR.)

Rap musician. **Personal:** Born Oct 20, 1971, Long Beach, CA; son of Vernell Varndo and Beverly; married Chante Taylor; children: Corde & Cordell. **Career:** Rap musician, currently; 213, mem with Nate Dogg & Warren G; Dr Dre's album, Chronic, vocalist, 1993; solo music career; Albums: Doggy Style, debut album, 1993; Murder Was Case, 1994; Tha Dogfather, 1996; Da Game to Be Sold Not to Be Told, 1998; Top Dogg, 1999; Last Meal, 2000; Films: Ride, 1998; Urban Menace, 1999; The Wrecking Crew, 1999; Baby Boy, 2001; Training Day, 2001; Bones, 2001; Wash, 2001; Old Sch, 2003; You'll Never Weiz This Town Again, 2003; Starsky & Hutch, 2004; Falling Up, 2009; "WWF Raw War", 2009; Arthur and the Revenge of Maltazard, 2009; The Big Bang, 2011; We the Party, 2012; Mac & Devin Go to High School, 2012; Turbo, 2013; Reincarnated, 2013; Scary Movie 5, 2013; Dispensary, 2015; autobiography: Tha Dogg Father: Times, Trials & Hardcore Truths Snoop Dogg, 1999; "Distant Shores", 2005; Racing Stripes, 2005; Boss'n Up, 2005; Korn Makes a Video, 2005; The Tenants, 2005; Arthur and the Invisibles, 2007; Hood Horror, 2006; "Arthur et les Minimoys", 2006; Boondocks: Macktastic, 2007; TV Series: "Entourage", 2004-08; "CSI: NY", 2005; "Monk", 2007; "Medium", 2008; "CSI: Miami", 2008; "Chuck", 2009; "The Boondocks", 2010; "Sanjay and Craig", 2015; Snoopadelic Films, owner, 2005-. Video games: Call of Duty: Ghosts, 2014. **Orgs:** Deion Sanders Primetime Shootout, 1994. **Business Addr:** Rap Musician, Firstars Artist Management, 14724 Ventura Blvd, Sherman Oaks, CA 91403, **Business Phone:** (818)461-1701.

## DOGGETT, REV. JEFFREY ROLAND

Chairperson, consultant. **Career:** Cleveland Comt, chairperson; Consult, currently; Providence Baptist Church, Cleveland, OH, pastor, Evangelism Team, ministry leader, currently. **Orgs:** Ohio Christian Educ Asn. **Home Addr:** 3626 Raymont Blvd, University Heights, OH 44118-2617, **Home Phone:** (216)321-3761. **Business Addr:** Ministry Leader, Providence Baptist Church, 12712 Kinsman Ave, Cleveland, OH 44120, **Business Phone:** (216)991-5315.

## DOGGETT, JOHN NELSON

Educator. **Personal:** married Haiping Tang. **Educ:** Claremont Men's Col, BA, polit sci, 1969; Yale Univ, JD, litigation & poverty law, 1972; Harvard Univ, MBA, int bus & strategy, 1981. **Career:** Legal serv litigator, 1972-74; State Bar Calif, Legal Serv Dept, dir, 1975-79; McKinsey & Co, US & Scand, mgt consult, 1981-83; mgt5 consult, 1983-93; IMDC Inc, 1983-93; Laguna Entertainment & Mkt Inc, chief operating officer & co-founder, 1994-97; Univ Tex, Red McCombs Sch Bus, Dept Mgt, co dir, sr lectr, currently, Exec MBA Prog, dir, 2000-; Univ Tex IC2 Inst, sr res fel, currently; IMA DEC Univ, Sch Bus, vis prof; Aoyama Gakuin Univ, vis prof; Thammasat Univ, vis prof; Dell Inc, judge; Idea to Prod, co founder; ApplyGenie Inc, 2010-11. **Orgs:** Bd mem, Gnumber; chmn, Rainforest Partnership; bd dir, Affinegy Inc; adv bd, Treehouse Inc; adv bd, Lend-a-Hand-India Inc; rep, Cent Tex Regional CCIC Adv Comt, 2005-09. **Business Addr:** Senior Lecturer, The University of Texas, 1 Univ Sta B6300, Austin, TX 78712-1178, **Business Phone:** (512)232-7671.

## DOGINS, KEVIN RAY

Football player. **Personal:** Born Dec 7, 1972, Eagle Lake, TX; married Erica Grace; children: Kiara & Kevin Jr. **Educ:** Tex A&M Univ-Kingsville. **Career:** Football player (retired); Tampa Bay Buccaneers, 1996-97, 2000, guard, 1998, left guard, 1999; Chicago Bears, 2001, left guard, right guard & ctr, 2002; Atlanta Falcons, ctr, 2003, Philadelphia Eagles, 2003; real estate agt. **Home Addr:** 3606 Cline Rd, Wharton, TX 77488-4604, **Home Phone:** (979)531-8824.

## DOLBY, EDWARD C.

Banker. **Personal:** Born Jan 1, 1945; married Dee; children: Ed, Terius & Jarvone. **Educ:** Shaw Univ, BA ,sociol, 1966. **Career:** Banker (retired); NC Nat Bank, consumer bank exec; Bank Am Carolinas, pres, 1970-2001; NationsBank Carolinas, pres, 1998; US Securities & Exchange Comn, dir, 2003; Edward C Dolby Strategic Consult Grp LLC, pres, 2002-; Family Dollar Stores, Inc, independent dir, 2003-. **Orgs:** Incoming chmn, Audit Comt, US Securities & Exchange Comn; chmn, Charlotte Chamber; bd trustee, Shaw Univ; Audit & Compensation Comt; NC Econ Develop Bd Peace Corps; bd dir, Found Carolinas. **Honors/Awds:** Hon DHL, Shaw Univ, 1997. **Special Achievements:** Highest ranking African American line mgr for NationsBank. **Business Addr:** President, Edward C Dolby Strategic Consult Group LLC, 6921 Out Bounds Dr, Charlotte, NC 28210-7319.

## DOLEY, AMBASSADOR HAROLD E., JR.

Executive. **Personal:** Born Mar 8, 1947, New Orleans, LA; son of Harold Sr and Kathryn; married Helena Cobette; children: Harold III & Aaron. **Educ:** Xavier Univ, BS, acct & bus; Harvard Univ, Grad Sch Bus, PM. **Career:** Bache & Co Inc, stock trader, 1968; Southern Univ, instr, 1970-77; Doley Securities Inc, chmn, pres, founder, 1973-; Doley Properties, pres; Southern Univ New Orleans, instr; Bache Halsey Stuart Inc, acct exec; Howard Weil Labouisse & Friedrichs Inc, asst vpres, 1974-75; Doley Securities LLC, founder, 1975; Minerals Mgmt Servs, dir, 1982-83; Interiors Minerals Mgt Serv, dir, 1982; African Develop Bank, exec dir, ambassador, 1983-85; Initial Pub Offering Conrail, Beleaguered Freight, co-mgr, 1987; Ivory Coast; Cent Venture Capital Corp, co-owner. **Orgs:** NY Stock Exchange; Pub Brdcst Syst WYES-TV; Inter racial Coun Bus & Opp; Am Family Asn IST; bd mem, Orgn Islamic Conf Adv Bd; adv bd, Lloyds London; Zeta Boule; NY Options Exchange; trustee, Clark-Atlanta Univ; trustee, Shaw Univ; LA Weekly Bd; US Africa Can Opera Co; Pop Resource CTR; LA State Mineral Bd; Un Comn Disarmament Educ; Conflict Resolution & Peace; Int Asn Univ Presidents; Barnes Found; Smithsonian Nat Mus African Art; Corp Coun Africa; pres's bd advisor, Historically Black Cols & Univs; Coun Foreign Rels; Clark Atlanta Univ, bd trustee; Interracial Coun Bus Opportunity; Africa Am Inst; chmn, International Adv Group, currently; Africare; San Antonio Econ Develop Found; Maj stockholder United Bank; nat bd mem, Asn Pub Broadcasters; board treasurer, WYES. **Business Addr:** Founder, Doley Securities Inc, 616 Baronne St 3rd Fl, New Orleans, LA 70113, **Business Phone:** (504)561-1128.

## DOLPHIN, DERRICK

Business owner. **Personal:** Born Jan 1, 1971. **Educ:** Skidmore Col, BA, psychol, 1992. **Career:** Ctr Alternative Sentencing & Employ Serv, dir employ unit; Source Youth Found, dep dir; Leonard Resource Group, dir youth serv; Youth Develop & Res Fund, co-owner, 1997-, exec producer, vpres, 2001-03; Dolphinity LLC, pres, founder, 2006; Job Corps, US Dept Labor, proj mgr, 2006-. **Orgs:** Am Youth Policy Forum; NY Asn Training & Employment Prof Inc; founder, PepNet Awarded Career Explor Proj; founder, Dolphinity BV. **Business Addr:** President, Founder, Dolphinity LLC, 114 F St N e Suite 203, Washington, DC 20002-0000.

## DOMINGO, COLMAN (COLMAN JASON DOMINGO)

Playwright, actor. **Personal:** Born Nov 28, 1969, Philadelphia, PA; son of Clarence Bowles and Edith Bowles. **Educ:** Temple Univ, BA. **Career:** Actor, dir & playwright, 1999-; Nat Theater Inst at Eugene O'Neill Theater Ctr, fac mem; Univ N Carolina at Chapel Hill & Univ Tex at Austin, educr; Afrobluesoulpower Theater Co, founder & artistic dir. Film actor: Around Fire, 1999; Desi's Looking a New Girl, 2000; Kung Phooey!, 2003; Freedomland, 2006; Miracle at St. Anna, 2008; Passing Strange, 2009; Red Hook Summer, 2012; Lincoln, 2012; Newlyweds, 2013; All Bright, 2013; HairBrained, 2013; Lee Daniels'

Butler, 2013; Time Out Mind, 2014; Selma, 2014; Beautiful Something, 2015; Birth a Nation, 2016. Tv actor: Big Gay Sketch Show, 2008-10; Knick, 2015; Justice, 2015; Fear Walking Dead, 2015-. Stage actor: Scottsboro Boys, New York; Young Vic, London; Blood Knot, Signature Theater Ctr, New York; Passing Strange, Broadway; A Boy & His Soul, Vineyard Theater, Tricycle Theater & Brisbane Powerhouse Theaters; Wild With Happy, Pub Theater. Stage dir: Seven Guitars, Actors Theater Louisville, 2015; Barbecue, Geffen Playhouse, 2016; A Band Angels, Off-Broadway Alliance; Exit Cuckoo, Working Theater; Single Black Female, New Prof Theater; Mamalogues, W.E.B. Dubois Inst at Harvard Univ. **Orgs:** Bd dirs, Vineyard Theater. **Honors/Awds:** Obie Award; Lucille Lortel Award; Theater Bay Area Cash Award; Chashama Area Award; New York Theater Workshop Residency at Dartmouth. **Special Achievements:** Author of plays, "A Boy and His Soul"; "Wild With Happy"; "Dot"; "Up Jumped Springtime". **Business Addr:** The Gersh Agency, 9465 Wilshire Blvd Sixth Fl, Beverly Hills, CA 90212.

### DOMINIC, IRWING
Government official, manager. **Personal:** Born Aug 12, 1930, Spartanburg, SC; son of Irvin and Jessie M Hall Hunt; married Catherine Virginia Chapman; children: Duane, Dwight, Denice, Deirdre, Deland & Damian. **Educ:** Bellevue Univ, BA, sociol, 1978; Univ Nebr, attended 1979, Creighton Univ Omaha, attended 1980. **Career:** Manager (retired); US Postal Serv, Omaha, NE, mail handler, 1974-79, assoc training & develop specialist eas-14, 1979-80, training & develop spec, eas-16, 1980-83, cleveland mgr training, eas-21, 1983-86, Hicksville, NY, mgr employ & develop, eas-23, 1986-88, Akron, OH, mgr training & develop. **Orgs:** Fourth degree, Knights Columbus, 1980; founding mem, Blacks Govt Omaha NE Chap, 1981-82; Phoenix Rising Toastmasters, 1982; educ adv, Nat Asn Postal Supvr, 1983; Phoenix Postal Supvr, 1983; A Plus, 1988. **Honors/Awds:** Super Performance Award, US Postal Serv, 1979, Managers Recognition Award, 1982; Spot Awards, 1996; Far Exceeds Merit Award, 1997. **Home Addr:** 1532 E 86th St, Cleveland, OH 44106-3748, **Home Phone:** (216)721-3764.

### DOMINO, ANTOINE DOMINIQUE, JR. See DOMINO, FATS, JR.

### DOMINO, FATS, JR. (ANTOINE DOMINIQUE DOMINO, JR.)
Musician, entertainer. **Personal:** Born Feb 26, 1928, New Orleans, LA; married Rosemary; children: Antoinette, Antoine III, Andrea, Anatole, Anola, Adonica, Antonio & Andre. **Career:** Rock & roll singer; songwriter; pianist; musician & concert performer, 1950-; Composer: The Fat Man, 1949; Ain't That a Shame, 1955; Blue Monday, 1956; I'm In Love Again, 1956; Whole Lotta Loving, 1958; I Want to Walk You Home, 1959; Be My Guest, 1959; I'm Gonna Be a Wheel Someday, 1959; Walking to New Orleans, 1960; Let the Four Winds Blow, 1961; Big Mouth, 1967; One For The Highway, 1968; Lady Madonna, 1968; Lovely Rita, 1968; Everybody's Got Something to Hide Except Me and My Monkey, 1969; Make Me Belong to You, 1970; New Orleans Ain't the Same, 1970; Sleeping on the Job, 1978; Whiskey Heaven, 1980; Alive & Kickin', 2006; hit records include: Blueberry Hill, 1956; Margie, 1959; Lady Madonna, 1968; Dick Clark Productions, partner, 1995-; I'm Walking; Grabow & Assocs, entertainer, currently. **Honors/Awds:** Awarded more than 20 Gold Records; Rock & Roll Hall of Fame, 1986; Grammy Lifetime Achievement Award, 1987; American Nat Medal of the Arts, Nat Endowment Arts, 1998; Lifetime Achievement Award, OffBeat Mag, 2007; Inducted to Louisiana Music Hall Fame, 2007; Inducted to Hit Parade Hall Fame, 2007. **Special Achievements:** The 25th Greatest Rock 'n' Roll Artist of all time by Rolling Stone; Appeared in numerous movies & TV shows including: The Big Beat, 1958; Shake, Rattle & Rock!; The Girl Can't Help It; Jamboree; "Ricky Nelson & Fats Domino: Live at the Universal Amphitheatre", 1985; Biography, "Blue Monday, Fats Domino & the Lost Dawn Of Rock 'n' Roll", written by Rick Coleman, Da Capo Press, 2006; "Statue of Fats Domino", French Quarter of New Orleans. **Business Addr:** Entertainer, Grabow & Associates, 4219 Creekmeadow Dr, Dallas, TX 75287, **Business Phone:** (972)250-1162.

### DONALD, ARNOLD W.
Businessperson, executive. **Personal:** Born Jan 1, 1955?, New Orleans, LA; married Hazel Roberts; children: Radiah, Alicia & Zachary. **Educ:** Carleton Col, BA, 1976; Wash Univ, St. Louis, BS, 1977; Univ Chicago Booth Sch Bus, MBA, 1980. **Career:** Monsanto Co, St. Louis, employee, 1977-98, sr vpres, 1998-2000; Merisant Co Inc, chief exec officer, 2000-03; Tabletop Holdings, chief exec officer, 2000-03; Juv Diabetes Res Found Int Inc, pres & chief exec officer, 2006-08; TransCanada Corp, chief exec officer & pres, 2008-13; Exec Leadership Coun, pres & chief exec officer, 2010-12; Carnival Corp, chief exec officer, pres & dir, 2013-. **Orgs:** Oil-Dri Corp Am Bd, 1997-2013; Crown Holdings, Inc., bd 1999-; Belden Inc. bd 2000-; Scotts Miracle-Gro Co bd, 2000-09; Laclede Gas Co bd, 2003-; Bank Am bd, 2013-; Am Corp bd; Atlast Holdings LLC bd; Bank Montreal, bd; Barnes-Jewish Hosp Inc. bd; BJC Health Systs, Inc., bd; Brit-Am Proj bd; Carleton Col bd; Crown Cork & Seal Co, Inc. bd; Donald Danforth Plant Sci Ctr bd; Eurasia Found bd; Global Velocity Inc. bd; Russell Brands, LLC, boar, DHR Int, Inc.; Merisant US, Inc., bd (chmn, 2000-15); Mo Bot Garden bd; Nat Sci Teachers Asn Adv Bd (chmn); Opera Theatre St. Louis bd; St. Louis Art Mus bd; St. Louis Sci Ctr bd; US Russia Bus Coun bd; United Way Greater St. Louis bd; Wash Univ bd. Trustee, Dillard Univ. **Special Achievements:** Agri-Marketer of the Year, 1996; Executive of the Year Award, Black Enterprise Magazine, 1997; Washington University Distinguished Alumni Award, 1998; Eagle Award, National Eagle Leadership Institute, 1999; Black Engineers President's Award, 2000; Maritime Person of the Year Award, 2015. **Business Addr:** Carnival Corp, 3655 NW 87th Ave, Miami, FL 33178, **Business Phone:** (305)599-2600.

### DONALD, ARNOLD WAYNE
Executive. **Personal:** Born Dec 17, 1954, New Orleans, LA; son of Warren Joseph Sr and Hilda Aline (Melancon); married Hazel Alethea; children: Radiah Alethea, Alicia Aline & Stephen Zachary. **Educ:** Carleton Col, BA, econ, 1976; Wash Univ, BS, mech engineering, 1977; Univ Chicago, MBA, finance, 1980. **Career:** Monsanto Co, sr exec 1977, sr mkt analyst, 1980-81, mkt res supvr, 1981-82, prod supvr, 1982-83, round-up prod mgr, 1983, mkt mgr, 1983-86, prod dir, 1986, specialty crops dir, 1986-87, lawn & garden bus dir, 1987-91, sr vpres, 1998-2000; Residential Prod Div, vpres, 1991-92; Crop Protection Prod Div, vpres & gen mgr, 1992-93; NA Div, Crop Protection Unit, group vpres & gen mgr, pres, 1995, sr vpres, 1998-2000; TransCanada Corp, chief exec officer & pres; Oil-Dri Corp Am, dir, 1997-2013; Crown Holdings Inc, dir, 1999-; Merisant Co Inc, dir, 2000-, chief exec officer, 2000-03, chmn, 2000-05; Tabletop Holdings, chief exec officer, 2000-03; Belden Inc, dir, 2000-; Scotts Miracle-gro Co, dir, 2000-09; Mo Bot Garden, bd trustee, chmn, currently; Carnival Corp & Plc, dir, 2001 & 2003, chief exec officer & pres, 2013-; Laclede Group Inc, dir, 2003-14; Merisant Worldwide Inc, chmn, dir, 2000-; Laclede Gas Co, 2003-; Russell Brands LLC, dir, 2004-; BMO Financial Corp, dir, 2009-; Bank Am Corp, dir, 2013-; Atlas Holdings LLC, operating partner, dir, currently; BJC Health Syst Inc, dir; Crown Cork & Seal Co Inc, dir; DHR International Inc, dir, currently; Global Velocity Inc, dir; Wind Pt Partner, exec advisor; Monsanto's Nutrit & Consumer sectors, pres; Agr Prod Div, pres; Merisant US Inc, chmn; Bank Montreal & Harris Financial Corp Efficas Inc, dir; Univ Chicago Booth Sch Bus. **Orgs:** Vpres, Nat Socs Black Engrs, 1976; Can Agr Chem Asn, 1983-86; Nat Lawn & Garden Distribr Asn, 1988-91; Theater Proj Co, bd mem, 1989-91; team capt, 1988-89, bd mem, 1989-91, Monsanto YMCA; Ecumenical Housing Prod Corp, bd mem, 1990-98; bd vpres, 1990-93, pres bd, 1993; bd mem, 1991-93, exec comt, Lindenwood Col, currently; comt mem, United Way Greater St Louis, 1991-93; bd mem, John Burroughs Sch, 1992-93; pres, Leadership Ctr Greater St Louis; exec comt, bd, Brit Am Proj; Jr League Adv Bd; Nat Adv Coun Wash Univ Sch Engineering; Elliot Soc; chmn bd, Merisant Co Inc, 2000-05; Am Col Personnel Asn; bd, Future Farmers Am; bd, 4-H Club; pres & chief exec officer, Juv Diabetes Res Found Int Inc, 2006-08; Nat Sci Teachers Asn Adv Bd; mem bd, Managers at Bridgewell Resources LLC; trustee, Donald Danforth Plant Sci Ctr; bd, Carleton Col, Wash Univ; bd, St. Louis Art Mus, Mo Bot Garden; bd, St. Louis Sci Ctr; bd, Opera Theatre St. Louis; bd, Boy Scouts Am Greater St. Louis Area Coun; bd, St. Louis Regional Com & Growth Asn; bd, Barnes-Jewish Hosp; bd, Grocery Manufacturers Am & St. Louis Sports Comn; bd, US Russia Bus Coun; bd, Eurasia Found; trustee, Dillard Univ & Atlas Found; Pres's Export Coun; Pres's Export Coun. **Home Addr:** 7 Huntleigh Woods, St. Louis, MO 63131-4818, **Home Phone:** (314)822-5115. **Business Addr:** Chairman, Missouri Botanical Garden, 4344 Shaw Blvd, St. Louis, MO 63110, **Business Phone:** (314)577-5100.

### DONALD, DR. BERNICE BOUIE
Judge. **Personal:** Born Sep 17, 1951, DeSoto County, MS; daughter of Perry Bowie and Willie; married W L. **Educ:** Memphis State Univ, BA, 1974; Memphis State Univ Sch Law, JD, 1979; Nat Judicial Col, evidence cert, 1984. **Career:** S Cent Bell, clerk's mgr, 1971-79; Staff atty, Employ Law & Econ Develop Unit, Memphis Area Legal Serv, Tenn, 1980; Memphis Area Legal Serv, atty, 1979-80; Shelby Co Govt Pub Defenders Off, asst pub defender, 1980-82; Gen Sessions Ct, judge, 1982-88; Shelby State Community Col, adj prof, 1984-89; S Bankruptcy Ct, Western Dist Tenn, judge, 1988-95; US Dist, Western Dist Tenn, judge, 1995-2011, Sixth Circuit, judge, 2011-. **Orgs:** Memphis Bar Asn; Tenn Bar Asn; co-chair, Courts Comt Memphis & Shelby County Bar Asn; Ben F Jones Chap Nat Bar Asn; Asn Women Attys; Nat Asn Women Judges, 1983-; Am Judges Asn, 1983-; chair, Gen Sessions Judges Conf Educ, 1987; bd dir, Memphis State Univ Law Alumni; chair, Comt Excellence Legal Educ; Zeta Phi Beta Sor, Alpha Eta Zeta Chap, 1983; bd dir, Shelby State Community Col, Criminal Justice Panel, Nat Conf Negro Women, Bus & Prof Women Clubs; assoc mem, Nat Ctr State Courts; JAD Div Am Bar Asn; chair, Comn Opportunities Minorities, ABA, Am Trial Lawyers Asn; Conf Spec Ct Judges; pres, Asn Women Attys, 1990; Nat Conf Bankruptcy Jes, 1988; Found Womens Rights Adv Bd; secy, Am Bar Asn, 2008-. **Honors/Awds:** Young Careerist Award, State Tenn Raleigh Bur Prof Women; Woman of the Year, Pentecostal Church of God in Christ; Martin Luther King Community Service Award; Citizen of the Year, Excelsior Chap Eastern Star; Community Service Award, Youth-Nat Conf Christians & Jews, 1986. **Special Achievements:** First African-American woman to hold an officer position in the American Bar Association; First black female in US to serve on Bankruptcy Court; First African-American female United States District Court Judge in Tennessee; Featured in Essence, Ebony, Jet, Dollar & Sense, and Memphis Magazine; participated on numerous TV shows to discuss legal and judicial issues; participated on numerous panels and forums dealing with legal process and the judiciary. **Home Addr:** PO Box 11010, Memphis, TN 38111. **Business Addr:** Judge, US District Court, 100 E Fifth St, Cincinnati, OH 45202, **Business Phone:** (513)564-7000.

### DONALD, ELVAH T.
Broker, executive, business owner. **Personal:** Born Pine Bluff, AR; daughter of Leon F Sr and Evelyn S; married Robert E. **Educ:** Univ Toledo, Mich State Univ, BEd, bus admin, 1970; Ohio State Univ, attended 1972; Mich State Grad Sch Bus, 1977. **Career:** NAB Exec Loan Prog, Dept Labor, Col Ind rels, dir, 1976-78; Toledo Bd Edu, teacher, 1970-71; Owens-Corning Fiberglas Corp, Human Resources, mgr, Logistics & Planning, mgr, 1971-83; Reynolds Real Estate Co, sales assoc, 1984-86; Loss Realty Group, assoc broker, 1986-92; Donald Co, realtors, pres, owner & broker, 1992-. **Orgs:** Founder & organizer, Gathering Profs, 1996-; pres, Bus Ladies Session, 1972-79; bd mem, Mid Am Bank, 1984-94; exec bd, Nat Asn Advan Colored People, Toledo Br, 1975-77; bd mem, WGTE Pub Broadcasting, 1992-94; chair, Preferred Properties, Inc, 1989-95; Columbus Bd Realtors, chair, Communs, 1997-; Toledo Bd Realtors, Prof Stand, 1993-; Independent Brokers Asn Cent Ohio, pres, 2002-04; chmn & vice chmn, advisor bd trustee, New Albany Chamber Com, 2008-10; bd mem, United Way Cent Ohio; Nat Asn Realtors & HUD, instr, At Home With Diversity; Cent Ohio Christian Sch bd dirs; Delta Sigma Theta Sorority; Ohio Asn Realtors; Choreographer Univ Dance Troupe; Symphony Orchestra; New Albany Realty Asn. **Honors/Awds:** Who's Who Am, 1986-99; Who's Who Among African Am Professionals, 1995-2008; Who's Who Black Columbus, 1999-2008; Outstanding Business Award, Blue Chip Found, 1999; Columbus Board Realtors Volunteer Service Award, 2000-02; Broker Year Columbus Board Realtors, 2006; DuPont Registry Featured Realtor, 2008; Montclair's Who's Who Real Estate. **Home Addr:** 4281 Olmsted Rd, PO Box 595, New Albany, OH 43054-0595, **Home Phone:** (614)855-4585. **Business Addr:** President, Broker, Owner, The Donald Co, PO Box 595, New Albany, OH 43054, **Business Phone:** (614)899-0094.

### DONALD, MAJOR GEN. JAMES E.
Commissioner, chairperson. **Personal:** Born Jackson, MS; married August; children: Jeff & Cheryl. **Educ:** Univ Miss, BA, polit sci & hist, 1970; Univ Mo, MPA, 1983. **Career:** US Pac Command, Hawaii, dir opers, 1995-96; 25th Inf Div, Asst Div Comdr Opers; USARPAC, Dep Comndg Gen; G-1, AUS Forces Command, Ft McPherson, GA, Dep Chief Staff; AUS Army, Pac, 1998-2000, 25th Inf Div, asst div comdr, Command Hawai, dir opers/J3; Ga Dept corrections, Off Ombudsman & Family Advocacy, corrections comnr, 2004; State Bd Pardons & Paroles, bd mem, 2009, chmn, 2011-. **Honors/Awds:** Distinguished Service Medal; Defense Superior Service Medal; Legion of Merit; Mississippi Trailblazer Award, 2010; Inducted Univ Miss Alumni Hall Fame. **Business Addr:** Chairman, State Board of Pardons & Paroles, 2 Martin Luther King Jr Dr SE Suite 458, Atlanta, GA 30334-4909, **Business Phone:** (404)656-4661.

### DONALDSON, JAMES LEE, III
Basketball player, businessperson. **Personal:** Born Aug 16, 1957, Heachem. **Educ:** Wash State Univ, BS, sociol/psychol, 1979. **Career:** Basketball player (retired), business person; Nat Basketball Asn, 1980-96; Seattle Super Sonics, 1980-83; San Diego Clippers, 1983-84; Los Angeles Clippers, 1984-85; Dallas Mavericks, 1986-91; Donaldson Clin, owner & dir, 1990-; New York Knicks, 1991-92; Utah Jazz, 1992-95; Iraklis Thessaloniki, 1993-94; Caja San Fernando, 1996-97; Snai Montecatini, 1997; Breogan, 1998, 1999; AEL 1964, 1998-99; Standing Above The Crowd, pres, 2009-; China Serv Centre, consult, 2012-13; Great Wall Int Sports Media Co, consult & partner, 2013-; Tsinghua Int Sch, consult, 2013-; All Star Basketball Int Group, pres & chief exec officer, 2014-; All Star Flyers, pres & chief exec officer, 2014-. **Orgs:** Boy Scouts Am; chmn, Cent Area Sr Ctr Christian Brotherhood Acad; Columbia Tower Club; CommunitiesSchs; Greater Seattle Chamber Com; bd mem, Magnolia Community Adv Coun; bd mem, Mill Creek Bus Asn; bd mem, Mt Zion Baptist Church Scholar Comt; bd mem, Mukilteo Chamber Com; Nat Asn Advan Colored People Tacoma; bd mem, Northwest Minority Bus Coun; spokesperson, Sno King Youth Club; Sound Transit Diversity Oversight comt; S Snohomish County Chamber Com; bd mem, Tacoma Pierce County Black Collective; Urban League Tacoma; exec comt, Wash State Mentors; Wash State Univ Gray; Werlin Reading Prog; dir, Tacoma Col Success Found, 2010; Wash Cult Exchange, 2013-; bd dir, Nat Basketball Retired Players Asn. **Business Addr:** Owner, Director, The Donaldson Clinic, 16030 Bothell-Everett Hwy Suite 200, Mill Creek, WA 98012, **Business Phone:** (425)745-4910.

### DONALDSON, DR. LEON MATTHEW
Educator, engineer. **Personal:** Born Aug 16, 1933, Burton, SC; married Merita Worthy; children: Carter & TaJuania. **Educ:** Ala State Univ, BS, 1963; Southern Univ, MS, 1966; Rutgers Univ, EdD, 1973; Auburn Univ; George Washington Univ; NC Cent Univ. **Career:** NASA, res assoc; TV McCoo High Sch, teacher, 1963-70; Corning Glass Works, chem eng, 1970-71; Stauffer Chem Corp, chemist; Int Bus Mach Corp, engr; Morgan State Univ, assoc prof chem, fac athletics rep. **Orgs:** Nat Asn Advan Colored People; Nat Educ Asn; Nat Sci Teachers Asn; Nat Coun Teachers Math; Ala Educ Asn; SC Educ Asn; Civitan Int; Fla & AM; Kappa Alpha Psi Fraternity Inc; NSF fel Ala State Univ, NC Cent Univ; NSF fel Southern Univ; EPDA fel Rutgers Univ; Wetlands Restoration Steering Comt. **Home Addr:** 3 Geary Ct, Baltimore, MD 21208-2022, **Home Phone:** (410)521-7940. **Business Addr:** Faculty Athletic Representative, Associate Professor, Morgan State University, 1700 E Cold Spring Lane, Baltimore, MD 21251, **Business Phone:** (443)885-3333.

### DONALDSON, DR. SHAWN RIVA
Educator. **Personal:** Born May 6, 1957, Camden, NJ; daughter of Richard and Cammee; children: Ayanna Bernice Polk & Layla Callie Polk. **Educ:** Univ Pa, BA, sociol, 1979, MA, sociol, 1979; Rutgers Univ, PhD, sociol, 1990. **Career:** Stockton Col, instr, 1980-90, asst prof, 1990-96, assoc prof, 1996-2005. **Orgs:** Vpres, pres, found bd mem, RSC NJ, coun black fac & staff, 1987-88, 2002-03, 2004-; family selection comt, Habitat Humanity, Atlantic County. **Home Addr:** 864 Pk Rd, Mays Landing, NJ 08330-1916, **Home Phone:** (609)625-5462.

### DONAPHIN, ALEXA B.
Architect, administrator. **Educ:** Howard Univ, BArch; Harvard Univ; Dartmouth Col, MBA. **Career:** Archit Health Sci & Com, architect, exec vpres, co-owner, currently. **Orgs:** Am Inst Architects. **Business Addr:** Executive Vice President, Principal, Architecture For Health Science & Commerce, 777 Old Saw Mill River Rd Suite 290, Tarrytown, NY 10591-6721, **Business Phone:** (914)347-2472.

### DONAWA, DR. MARIA ELENA
Pathologist, consultant. **Personal:** Born May 13, 1948, Detroit, MI; daughter of Milton Solese and Helen Solese; married John R Lupien. **Educ:** Howard Univ Col Pharm, BS, pharm & med, 1971; Howard Univ Col Med, MD, 1976. **Career:** Marco Pharm, pharmacist, 1971-72; Peoples Drug Stores Inc, regist pharmacist, 1972-73; Howard Univ Hosp, resident, 1976-80, chief resident, 1979-80; Abel Labs Inc, staff pathologist, 1980; Food & Drug Admin Bur Med Devices, spec med consult, 1980-83, assoc dir stands, 1983-86; Food & Drug Admin Ctr Devices & Radiol Health, asst dir device safety & risk mgt, 1980-86; Donawa Lifescience Consult, Rome, Italy, pres & founder, 1986-; Metro Lab, path dir, 1982-83; Uk Inst Qual Assurance, lead auditor; Med Device Technol mag, columnist; Technion Commns, prog mgr, 2003-06; Orbis Global solns, 2006-08; Gerson Lehrman Group Inc, council member, currently. **Orgs:** Precinct chairperson Dem Party, 1978-79; DC Gen Hosp, bd trustees, 1979-86, chairperson qual control comm, 1983-86, sec & mem exec comm, 1985-86; Global Harmonization Task Force; bd dirs, Regulatory Affairs Prof Soc; ISO TC 210, currently; ISO TC 194 Working Group 4, currently; Minn Med Technol Network; Israel Life Sci Indust; Qual & Regulatory Network. **Honors/Awds:** US Pub Health Service Achievement Award, 1983, Unit Commendation, 1985. **Special Achievements:** Network TV interview

ABC News TSS, Tampons & FDA May 2, 1984 and June 21, 1982; Selected media interviews; "The Case of Toxic Shock Syndrome, " Knowledge Transfer Round table US Public Health Service, 1984; Report Panel Presentations; articles "Toxic Shock Syndrome, Chronology of State & Federal Epidemiologic Studies and Regulatory Decision Making" with G Schmid, M Osterholm Public Health Reports Vol 99 No 4, 1984. **Home Addr:** Via Fonte di Fauno 22, RomeI-00153, **Home Phone:** (390)6574-314. **Business Addr:** President, Founder, Donawa Lifescience Consulting, Piazza Albania 10, Rome00153, **Business Phone:** (390)6578-266.

## DONEGAN, CHARLES EDWARD

Lawyer, educator. **Personal:** Born Apr 10, 1933, Chicago, IL; son of Arthur C Jr and Odessa Arnold; married Patty L Harris; children: Carter Edward. **Educ:** Wilson Jr Col, BA, 1953; Roosevelt, BSC, bus admin, 1954; Loyola Univ, MSIR, 1959; Howard Univ, JD, 1967; Columbia Univ, LLM, 1970. **Career:** US Comn Civil Rights, legal intern, 1966; Poor Peoples Campaign, legal coun, 1968; F B McKissick Enterprises, staff coun, 1969; State Univ NY, Buffalo, first asst prof law, 1970-73; Sunyab, Howard, Southern, NC cent, Isu & Ohio State, prof law, 1971; Ford Fel Columbia Univ Law Sch, 1972-73; NEH Post Doctoral Fel Afro Am Studies Yale Univ, 1972-73; Howard Univ, assoc prof law, 1973-77; Ohio State Univ, vis assoc prof, 1977-78; First US EPA, asst reg coun, 1978-80; Ill State Bd Educ, hearing officer, 1981-; Fed Postal Serv Arbitrator, La, 1982-84; Fed Res Bd, Arbitrated cases involving Dept Health & Human Serv; Social Security Admin, Gen Serv Admin, Police, Veterans Admin, Bell Atlantic, Duke Power, Libr Cong, Housing & Urban Develop; Munic, hearing officer, City Chicago, 1987; City Evanston; Southern Univ, prof law1980-84, vis prof law, 1992; Charles E Donegan & Assoc, atty law, 1984-, 2001, atty & arbitrator, 1984-; LA State Univ, Law Sch, vis prof, 1981; NC Ctrl Univ Law Sch, vis prof, 1988-89; Cook County, Circuit Ct Judge Cand, 2000; atty law, 2003. **Orgs:** Labor arbitrator Steel Inds Postal AAA, 1971-; consult US Dept Ag, 1972; asst coun, Nat Asn Advan Colored People, Legal Defense Fund Inc, 1967-69; hiring officer Var Govt Agy, 1975-; labor arbitrator, AAA, 1978; labor arbitrator FMCS, 1985; chmn, legal educ comt, Wash Bar Asn, 1984-91; DC Atty-Client Arbit Bd, 1990-91; adv comt, DC Educ, Ward 4, 1991; moot ct judge, Georgetown, Howard, Balsa, 1987-; vp, Columbia Law Alumni Asn, Wash DC, 1994-; pres, vp, Soc Labor Rels Prof, 1987-; NBA Arbit Sect News lett, Ed, 1997-; Nat Asn Securities Dealers; Nat Futures Asn; NY Stock Exchange; Nat Conf Black Lawyers; Wash Bar Asn; Indust Rels Res Asn; Soc Prof Dispute Resolution; Am Nat DC Chicago Bar Asn; Nat Asn Advan Colored People Urban League; Alpha Phi Alpha; Phi Alpha Delta; Phi Alpha Kappa; consult DC Govt Dept Pub Works; DC Consumer Claims Arbit bd; DC Super Ct; chmn emer adr sect, Nat Bar Asn, Arbit Sect, chair. **Honors/Awds:** Most outstanding Prof, Southern Univ Law Sch, 1982. **Special Achievements:** First African American mem elected to the DC, Labor & Employ Law Sect, steering comt, 1995-98; Donated papers to Amistad Res Ctr, Tulane Univ, New Orleans, LA; pub numerous articles in prof journals; Speaker & Partic at Nat & Regional Conf, Named one of top 45, 42, 56, 61 Lawyers in Wash DC Area, Wash Afro-Am Newspaper, 1993-96. Publications: Kansas Law Review, 1972; Cornell International Law Journal, 1972; A Seminar In Legal Aspects Of Minority Economic Development, 1975; New York Law Review, 1983; Afro Americans And The Evolution Of A Living Constitution, Panelist,1988. **Home Addr:** 4315 Argyle Terr NW, Washington, DC 20011, **Home Phone:** (202)829-7161. **Business Addr:** Attorney, Arbitrator, Charles E Donegan & Assoc, 601 Pa Ave NW Suite 900 S Bldg, Washington, DC 20005, **Business Phone:** (202)434-8210.

## DOOMES, DR. EARL

Chancellor (education), educator. **Personal:** Born Feb 8, 1943, Washington, LA; son of Othus Sr; married Mazie Marie LeDeaux; children: Elizabeth Denise, Edward Earl & Elliot Doyle. **Educ:** Southern Univ Baton Rouge, BS, 1964; Univ Nebr Lincoln, PhD, 1969. **Career:** Educator (retired), professor emeritus; Univ NC, NSF trainee, 1967-68; Northwestern Univ, post doctoral res, 1968-69; Macalester Col, from asst prof to assoc prof, 1969-77; Petrol Res Fund Grant Proposal, reviewer, 1970-80; Fla State Univ, res assoc, 1975-76; La State Univ, Nat Sci Found Fac, Sci fel, 1975-76; Southern Univ, Baton Rouge, assoc prof, 1977-82, prof chem, 1982-87, chmn, 1987-92, Col Sci, dean, 1992-99, acad affairs, assoc vice chancellor, 1999, trng & mentoring, dir, 2003-06, prof emer, 2006-; Minority Biomed Re Sport Prog Nat Inst Health, consult, 1979-92. **Orgs:** NSF Grants Prog, 1985; Exec Comt, Baton Rouge Sect ACS, 1986-88, Org Chem Div ACS, 1966-; Nsf (NSF) Panel Rev Proposals, Sci Mat K-8, Wash, D.C; NIH-MBRS Prog Site Visit Team, State Univ New York, Col at Old Westbury, Long Island, NY, 1990; NIH-MBRS Prog Site Visit Team, San Jose State Univ, San Jose, CA, 1991; chmn, NIH-MBRS Prog Site Visit Team, Bethune-Cookman Col, Daytona Beach, Fla, 1991; NIH-Res Centers Minority Insts (RCMI) Prog Site Visit Team, Fla A&M Univ, Tallahassee, 1994; NSF Instrumentation Rev Panel, Wash, DC, 1995; NIH-Res Initiation Minority Insts (RIMI) Rev Comt, 1996. Sigma XI, Res Soc, 1996-2005. **Home Addr:** 13302 London Dr, Baker, LA 70714-4668, **Home Phone:** (225)774-8284. **Business Addr:** Professor Emeritus Chemistry, Southern University-Baton Rouge, 3rd Fl J S Clark Admin Bldg, Baton Rouge, LA 70813, **Business Phone:** (225)771-2360.

## DORHAM, MARY. See DEE, MERRI.

## DORMAN, HATTIE LAWRENCE

Management consultant, college teacher, president (organization). **Personal:** Born Jul 22, 1932, Cleveland, OH; daughter of James Lyman Lawrence (deceased) and Claire Correa Lenoir (deceased); married James W L; children: Lydia, Lynda & James Lawrence. **Educ:** Fenn Col, Cleveland State Univ, attended 1958; DC Teacher's Col, attended 1964; Grad Sch, attended 1969; Howard Univ, BA, 1987. **Career:** IRS, clerk, tax specialist, mgt analyst, supvr, staff advisor, 1954-79; US Dept Treas, from spec asst to dep asst secy, 1978-79; Inter Agency Comn Women's Bus Enterprise, US Small Bus Admin, dep dir, 1979-83; US Small Bus Admin Off Comn & Govt Support, dir, 1983-85; Dorman & Assocs, owner, mgt consult, trainer, pres, chief exec officer, 1985; Univ DC, assoc prof continuing educ; Howard Univ, guest lectr continuing educ; Presial Transition Team, chief staff dep dir, 1992-93. **Orgs:** Trainer Nation's Capital Girl Scout Coun, 1972-; Pres Task Force Women Bus Enterprise, 1978-79; Wash Hosp Ctr, 1986-2000; bd dir, Wider Opportunities Women, 1993-2000; bd dir, Delta Housing Corp, 1997; Nat Asn Female Execs; Am Asn Black Women Entrepreneurs; Black Career Women Inc; sr exec assoc, Fed Exec Inst Alumni Asn; Am Sociol Asn; Nat Coun Negro Women; golden life mem, Delta Sigma Theta Sorority Inc; Nat Urban League; bd dirs, Girl Scouts USA; Am Soc Training & Develop; Howard Univ Alumni Asn. **Honors/Awds:** Monetary Performance Award, IRS, 1970-78; Mary McLeod Bethune Centennial Award, Nat Coun Negro Women; Monetary Performance Award, US Small Bus Admin, 1980, 1984, 1985; Boss of the Year Award, Am Bus Women's Asn L'Enfant Chap, 1981; other award & citations: Delta Sigma Theta; PTA's; Am Asn Black Women Entrepreneurs; Nat Asn Minority Women; Articles: "Survey of Support Patterns", Black Orgn Black Polit Appointees Benjamin E Mays Monogr ser, 1988; "Field of Small Bus Develop". **Business Addr:** President, Owner, Dorman & Associates, 7801 13th St NW, Washington, DC 20012-1306, **Business Phone:** (202)726-4681.

## DORMAN, DR. LINNEAUS C.

Scientist, chemist. **Personal:** Born Jun 28, 1935, Orangeburg, SC; son of John A Sr (deceased) and Georgia (deceased); married Phae Hubble; children: Evelyn S & John A. **Educ:** Bradley Univ, BS, chem, 1956; Ind Univ, PhD, org chem, 1961. **Career:** Chemist, scientist (retired); Regional Res Lab, chemist, summers, 1956-59; Dow Chem Co, res chemist, 1960-68, res specialist, 1968-76, sr res assoc, 1976-83, assoc scientist, 1983-92, sr assoc scientist, 1993-94. **Orgs:** Secy, Am Chem Soc, 1971-92; dir, counr; chmn, Midland Black Coalition, 1973-77; bd mem, Saginaw Valley State Col, 1976-87; Nat Org Black Chemist & Chem Engrs, 1978; chmn, Midland Area Campaign, 1981-84; bd trustee, Midland Found, 1981-90; bd dir, Comerica Bank-Midland, 1982-95; pres, Midland Rotary Club, 1982-83; life mem, Nat Asn Advan Colored People; vpres, Midland Found, 1988-90; Elected to Bradley Univ, Centurion Soc, 1993; United Negro Col Fund; Bradley Univ Coun, 1994; bd financial adv, Ind Univ, Dept Chem, 1994; Saginaw Valley Torch Club, 1995; bd mem, Midland County Hist Soc, 2001-; bd mgr, Midland County Hist Soc, 2001; exec coun, Ind Univ Alumni Asn, 2002. **Honors/Awds:** Dow Research Fellow, Ind Univ, 1959-60; Bond Award, Am Oil Chemist Soc, 1960; Central Res Inventor of the Year, Dow Chem Co, 1983; Honorary Doctor Science, Saginaw Valley State Univ, 1988; Outstanding Service, Am chem Soc, 1990; Percy L Julian Award, Nat Org Black Chemist & Chem Engrs, 1999; Distinguished Service Medallion, Saginaw Valley State Univ, 2002. **Special Achievements:** Received twenty-six U.S. patents for his inventions; Publishing many research articles in premier research journals. **Home Addr:** 2452 N Deer Valley Dr, PO Box 1732, Midland, MI 48642, **Home Phone:** (989)631-0213.

## DORN, MICHAEL

Administrator, actor, media executive. **Personal:** Born Dec 9, 1952, Luling, TX; son of Allie Lee and Fentress. **Educ:** Starfleet Acad, Klingon grad. **Career:** Actor, director, voice actor & producer; TV Series: "CHIPS", 1979-82; "Days of Our Lives", 1986-87; "Star Trek: The Next Generation", 1987-94; "Aladdin", animated, 1993; "Gargoyles", animated, 1994; "Superman", animated, 1996; "Cow & Chicken", animated, 1997; "Johnny Bravo", animated, 1997; "I Am Weasel", animated, 1999; "Spider man: The Animated Series", 2002; "The Grim Adventures of Billy & Mandy", 2002-04; "Spider-Man", 2003; "Megas XLR", 2004; "Duck Dodgers", 2005; "Diamond Boogie & Corporate Pigfall", 2005; "Too Close for Combat & Fins of War", 2005; "Justice League", 2005; "Danny Phantom", 2005; "Descent", 2005; "The Ultimate Enemy", 2005; "Family Guy", 2005; "Fallen Angels", 2006; "A I Assault", 2006; "Without a Trace", 2007; "Ben 10", 2007; "Squirrel Boy", 2007; "The Deep Below", 2007; "Night Skies", 2007; Fist of the Warrior, 2007; Films: Rocky, 1976; Jagged Edge, 1985; Star Trek: Generations, 1994; Time master, 1995; Star Trek: First Contact, 1996; Menno's Mind, 1996; Trekkies, 1997; Star Trek: Insurrection, 1998; The Prophet's Game, 1999; Mach 2, 2000; Ali, 2001; The Gristle, 2001; Face Value, 2001; The Santa Clause 2, 2002; Star Trek: Nemesis, 2002; Shade, 2003; Through the Fire, writer, 2002; Episodes of Star Trek: Deep Space Nine, dir, 1993; Episode of Enterprise, dir, 2001; Walking on Water, assoc producer, 2004; The Santa Clause 3: The Escape Clause, 2006; All You've Got, 2006; TV Episode voice: Good Duck Hunting & Consumption Overruled, Diamond Boogie & Corporate Pig fall, The Kids Are All Wrong & Win, Lose or Duck, Villain struck & Just the Two of Us, Diva Delivery & Castle High, The Ultimate Enemy, Reign Storm, Fright Knight, 2005; Heart of the Beholder, 2005; Descent, 2005; The Santa Clause 3: The Escape Clause, 2006; All You have Got, 2006; Fallen Angels, 2006; The Deep Below, 2007; Night Skies, 2007; Saints Row 2, 2008; Bionicle: The Legend Reborn, 2009; Batman: The Brave and the Bold, 2009; Public Enemies, 2009; StarCraft II: Wings of Liberty, 2010; Mass Effect 2, 2010; Three (Drei) Star, 2010; Adventure Time, Gork, 2010; It's a Trap, Lt Worf (voice), 2010; Castle, Dr. Carver Burke, 2011; Regular Show, Thomas Demon, 2012; Shady Lady Narrator, 2012; Trek Nation Himself, 2012; Transformers Prime, TBA, 2013; Young Justice Invasion, Kalibak, 2013; Strange Frame: Love & Sax Star, 2013. **Orgs:** Air Force Aviation Heritage Found. **Business Addr:** Actor, Agency Performing Arts, 9000 Sunset Blvd Suite 1200, Los Angeles, CA 90069, **Business Phone:** (310)273-0744.

## DORN, DR. REV. ROOSEVELT F.

Judge, clergy, mayor. **Personal:** Born Oct 29, 1935, Checotah, OK; married Joyce Evelyn Glosson; children: Bryan Keith, Renee Felicia & Rochelle Francine. **Educ:** Univ Calif Sch Law, Berkeley; Whittier Law, JD, 1969; Calif Judicial Col; Earl Warren Legal Inst, 1979, 1982; Southern Calif Sch Ministry, DDiv, 1998. **Career:** Judge (retired), mayor; Los Angeles County, dep sheriff super ct bailiff, 1961-69; City Los Angeles, asst city atty, 1970-79; Dorn Real Estate, owner, 1977-; Inglewood Jud Dist CA, Munic Ct, judge, 1979-80; Los Angeles County Super Ct, judge, 1980-97; First African Methodist Episcopal Church Los Angeles, assoc minister, 1991-; City Inglewood Calif, mayor, 1997-2010; Independent Contractor, legal & polit consult, 2010-. **Orgs:** Founder, First pres Inglewood Dem Club, 1977-79; Nat Asn Advan Colored People; Urban League; LA Co Bar Asn; Langston Bar Asn; Calif Black Lawyers Asn; Am Bar Asn; Lions Club; assoc minister, Atherton Baptist Church, Inglewood, CA; Calif Judges Asn; Nat Bar Asn; Los Angeles Trial Lawyers Asn; pres, bd dir, 100 Black Men Los Angeles Inc; John M Langston Bar Asn Judges Div; pres, Pres Emer, Nat Conf Black Mayors; bd dir, Young Black Scholars; Ordained Minister, First AME Church, Los Angeles; Nat Asn Advan Colored People; New Frontier Dem Club & Whittier Alumni Asn. **Honors/Awds:** Commendation for Outstanding Community Service, Senate CA Legislature, 1978; Commendation for Outstanding Service, CA State Assembly, 1979; Commendation for Outstanding Achievement, New Frontier Dem Club Inglewood Dem Club, 1979; Outstanding Service Award, field Juvenile Justice Nat Sor Phi Delta Kappa Inc, Delta Kappa Chap, 1983; Outstanding Contributions Support & Leadership for Youth Award, RDM Scholarship Fund Inc, 1984, 1985; Meritorious Service Youth Award, The Inglewood Teachers Asn, 1986; Dedicated Service & Guidance Award, Inglewood High School Student Body; Nat Top Ladies Distinction Humanitarian Award, 1987; Outstanding Service Award, Prairie View A&M Univ Alumni Asn, 1989; Most Valuable Judge Certificate, Los Angeles County, Central District, 1991-93; Commendation for Outstanding Leadership, Los Angeles Chief of Police, Willie L Williams, 1992; FAME Award, First African Methodist Episcopal Church, 1992; Distinguished Service Award, Nat Bar Asn Judicial Coun; Certificate of Appreciation, Los Angeles Southwest Col; Nat Honoree, Los Angeles Sentinel's Highest Award; Man of the Year Award, Because I Love You; Distinguished Service and Leadership Award, National Sorority of Phi Delta Kappa, 1997; Appreciation Award, North Inglewood Little League, 1997; Outstanding Community Leader Award, Prison Fellowship Los Angeles, 1998; Positive Role Model Award, Miracle Theatre and Upper Room Church, 1999; Los Angeles Black History Award, 2000; Outstanding Leadership Award, Black Law Students Asn, University of West Los Angeles School of Law, 2001-02; Economic Development Award, 100 Black Men, 2002; American Cancer Society Award, 2003; Man of Valor Civic Award, Los Angeles NAACP, 2003; Huntington Browne Real Estate Award, 2004; John M. Langston Bar Association Hall of Fame Award, 2004; Community Youth Sports & Arts Foundation Award, 2004; Harry A. Meir Center Award, 2004; Spirit of Peace Award, Stop the Violence, Increase the Peace Foundation, 2005. **Business Addr:** Associate Minister, First African Methodist Episcopal Church Los Angeles, 2270 S Harvard Blvd, Los Angeles, CA 90018, **Business Phone:** (323)730-7750.

## DORRELL, KARL

Football coach, football player. **Personal:** Born Dec 18, 1963, Alameda, CA; married Kim; children: Chandler & Lauren. **Educ:** Univ Calif, BA, 1987. **Career:** Football player (retired), coach; Dallas Cowboys, 1987; Univ Calif, Los Angeles, grad asst, 1988, head coach, 2003-07; Univ Cent Fla, wide receivers coach, 1989; Univ N Ariz, offensive coordr & wide receivers coach, 1990-91; Univ Colo, wide receivers coach, 1992-93, offensive coordr, 1995-98; Univ Ariz State, wide receivers coach, 1994; Univ Wash, offensive coordr, 1999; Denver Broncos, wide receivers coach, 2000-02; Miami Dolphins, wide receivers coach, 2008-10, quarterbacks coach, 2011; Houston Texans, quarterbacks coach, 2012-13; Vanderbilt, offensive coordinator & quarterbacks coach, 2014. **Honors/Awds:** Freedom Bowl, 1986; PAC-10 championship, 2005. **Special Achievements:** First African American head coach in the history of the UCLA Bruins college football team. **Home Addr:** , Nashville, TN. **Business Addr:** Offensive Coordinator, Quarterbacks Coach, Miami Dolphins, 2601 Jess Neely Dr, Nashville, TN 37212, **Business Phone:** (615)322-4653.

## DORSE, EARNESTINE HUNT

Judge. **Personal:** Born Jun 29, 1952, Memphis, TN; daughter of William Ernest and Jennie Hunt; married Fred O; children: Sharon, Denee A Spencer, Dionne Hunt, William Keys, Larry Benson & Yolanda Hunt. **Educ:** Clark Col, BA, 1974; Memphis State Univ, JD, 1984. **Career:** Sonnenschein, Carlin, Nath & Rosenthal, litigation paralegal, 1981-82; Memphis Area Legal Servs Inc, Family Unit, law clerk, 1983-84; Evans, Willis, Stotts, Kyles, independent legal asst, 1984-86; Perkins, Hanna & Assocs, Gen civil pract, 1986-87; Shelby County Pub Defender, asst pub defender, 1986-90; Nat Acad Paralegal Studies, 1989-90; Div I, City Ct, Memphis, judge, 1990-. **Orgs:** S Am Bar Asn; dir, Nat Bar Asn, Judicial Coun, Region VI, 1991-93; Nat Asn Women Judges; TN Bar Asn; Ben F Jones Chap Nat Bar Asn; pres bd, Memphis St Law; bd dir, Nat Coun Community Behav Healthcare; atty, Asn Women Attys. **Honors/Awds:** Zeta Achiever Award, Zeta Phi Beta Sorority Inc, 1990-91; Tennessee Asn of Blacks in Criminal Justice, Maybelline Shades of You, Nat Council of Negro Women, 10 Best Dressed, 1991; Sr Outstanding Community Service, AA Latting, 1992. **Special Achievements:** Researched and wrote the History of the Memphis Urban League, 1945-75; First black female judge in the City of Memphis; Second black female judge in the Tennessee. **Business Addr:** Judge, Administrative, City Ct Memphis, 201 Poplar Ave Rm LL06, Memphis, TN 38103-1945, **Business Phone:** (901)636-3441.

## DORSETT, ANTHONY DREW. See DORSETT, TONY DREW.

## DORSETT, ANTHONY DREW, JR.

Football player. **Personal:** Born Sep 14, 1973, Aliquippa, PA; son of Tony. **Educ:** Univ Pittsburgh, grad. **Career:** Football player (retired); Houston Oilers, defensive back, 1996; Tenn Oilers, free safety & corner back, 1997-99; Tenn Titans; Oakland Raiders, defensive back & free safety & strong safety, 2000-03; Toronto Argonauts, 2007; Omaha Nighthawks, 2010. **Special Achievements:** Films: Super Bowl XXXIV, 2000; Super Bowl XXXVII, 2003. TV Series: "The Mo'Nique Show", 2010.

## DORSETT, DR. KATIE GRAYS

State government official. **Personal:** Born Jul 8, 1932, Shaw, MS; daughter of Willie Grays and Elizabeth Grays; married Warren G; children: Valerie. **Educ:** Alcorn State Univ, BS, 1953; Ind Univ Bloomington, MS, 1955; Univ NC Greensboro, EdD, 1975; State Univ NY Buffalo, attended 1981; Univ Md Col Pk, attended 1983. **Career:** Educator, senator (retired); NC A&T St Univ, Sch Bus & Econ, assoc prof, 1955-87; Greensboro City Coun, 1983-86; Transp Inst NC A&T, res assoc, 1983-87; Guilford County Comn, 1986-92; Dept Admin, State Nc, secy, 1993-2001; Nc State Sen, 28th Dist, sen, 2003-10. **Orgs:** Greensboro Citizens Asn; Nat Asn Advan Colored People; League Women Voters; bd mem, Greensboro Nat Bank; bd mem, MDC Corp; NC Gene Assembly; bd mem, Guilford Tech Comm Col, 1978-, exec bd, Gen Greene Coun Boy Scouts, 1980-; trustee, 1983-93; comt mem & bd mem, Nat Asn Counties, 1991-93; bd mem, Sickle

Cell Dis Asn Am, 1993-; bd mem, NC Asn County Comnrs, 1997-99; pres, Nat Asn State Chief Admin, 1999-2000; trustee, NC A & T State Univ, 2001-; nat chair, Sickle Cell Dis Asn Am, 2002-. **Honors/Awds:** Outstanding Civic Leader, Greensboro Inter club Coun, 1978; TV Citizen of the Week, WGHP TV, 1978; One Comm Award, Feb One Soc, 1982; Outstanding Citizen Award, Negro Business & Prof Women, 1983; Outstanding Comm Leader, Mt Zion Baptist Church, 1983; Leader of the Year, Omega Psi Phi, 1983; Woman of the Year, Mt Zion African Methodist Espicol Church, 1984; Sojourner Truth Award, Negro Bus & Prof Women, 1985; Leadership Award, Negro Bus & Prof Women, 1986; Distinguished Alumni, Nat Asn Equal Opportunity, 1987; Leadership Award, Sigma Gamma Rho, 1987; Silver Anniversary Service Award, NC Community Col, 1989; Woman of the Year, Nat Asn Advan Colored People, 1989; Distinguished Service Award, NC Asn Black Cty Comnrs, 1995; Strong Men and Women, Virginia Power, 1998. **Special Achievements:** First African American woman ever elected for Greensboro City Council; first African American woman to hold a North Carolina Cabinet post; 10publications including "A Study of Levels of Job Satisfaction and Job Aspirations Among Black Clerical Employees in Greensboro & Guilford Co, North Carolina" 1976; "Training & Career Opportunities for Minorities & Women" Proceedings, 1984. **Home Addr:** 1000 N Eng St, Greensboro, NC 27405-6804, **Home Phone:** (336)275-0628. **Business Addr:** State Senator, North Carolina Senate 28th District, Rm 2106 Legis Bldg 16 W Jones St, Raleigh, NC 27601-2808, **Business Phone:** (919)715-3042.

### DORSETT, MARY ALICE

Community activist, consultant. **Personal:** Born Feb 4, 1926, Dade City, FL; daughter of James and Nannie Mae Johnson; married W Ray Hill; children: Dwayne Oswald Hill & Countess Charisse Clarke. **Educ:** Paine Col, attended 1946; Nat Traning & Prof Sch Women & Girls, Wash, DC, 1950. **Career:** Self-employed, 1951-; Prof Bailbonds; Gen Employ Agency; income tax consult; Dorsett's Tax Serv, owner, 1951-; Dorsett's Bail Bonds, 1952-73; Dorsett's Gen Employ Agency, 1955-73. **Orgs:** Nat Asn Advan Colored People, 1950-; Urban League, Tampa br, 1950-; founder, Faith Mission, 1962-73; Nat Coun Negro Women, 1965-; Community Health Clin, 1977; Tampa Orgn Black Affairs, 1999-; founder, Health & Educ Asn; Coun Negro Women, Grand Union Pallbearer Soc. **Honors/Awds:** Tampa Urban League Award, 1987; Plaque, Tampa Org on Black Affairs, 1983; plaque, Links, 1986, 1994, 2001; plaque, Hills Jr Coll, 1991; Susie Padgett Award, 1996; plaque, Hillsborough County Sheriff Dept, 1996; Dr. King Drum Major Award, Dr. Marting Luther King Commemoration Committe; White Rose Honoree, 1997; Dr King Drum Major Award, 1998; plaque, SDA Church, 1999; plaque, NAACP, 2001. **Special Achievements:** First African American woman to run for state legislator from Hillsborough County, Florida; Building named in her honor, 2001; First Black to operate a Professional Bail Bond Business and General Employment Agency; Tax Collector honor Mrs. Dorsett with Dedication of New Branch Office; Named in the Millennium Edition of "2,000 Notable American Women". **Home Addr:** 1102 W Grace St, Tampa, FL 33607-5518, **Home Phone:** (813)251-0042.

### DORSETT, TONY DREW (ANTHONY DREW DORSETT)

Football player. **Personal:** Born Apr 7, 1954, Rochester, PA; son of West and Myrtle; married Janet Simon; children: Shukura & Anthony Jr. **Educ:** Univ Pittsburgh. **Career:** Football player (retired), executive, sports speaker; Dallas Cowboys, running back, 1977-87; Denver Broncos, running back, 1988; Southwestern Drilling Mud Co, Midland TX, partner; Brooks Int Speakers Bur, sports speaker, currently; Touchdown Prod, pres; Tony Dorsett Foods, owner. **Orgs:** Jump-Rope-A-Thon, 1980; Nat Easter Seals Sports Coun; chmn, Am Heart Asn; United Way; United Negro Col Fund; Tex Dept Hwys & Pub Trans Seat Belt Prog, Dallas Civic Opera. **Honors/Awds:** Chic Harley Award, 1976; Sporting News Player of the Year, 1976; UPI Player of the Year, 1976; Walter Camp Award, 1976; Maxwell Award, 1976; Rookie of the Year, Sporting News, 1977; Player of the Year, Nat Football Conf, 1981; holds numerous team (Dallas) records; played in Pro Bowl, 1978, 1981-83; established record for longest run from scrimmage (99yards), 1983; Dallas Cowboys Ring of Honor; Professional Football Hall of Fame, 1994. **Special Achievements:** First player in NCAA history with four 1000 yard seasons; appeared in films including: Necessary Roughness, 1991; Kill Zone, 1993; The Big Bounce, 2004. **Business Addr:** Sports Speaker, Brooks International Speakers Bureau, 763 Santa Fe Dr, Denver, CO 80204, **Business Phone:** (303)825-8700.

### DORSEY, CLINTON GEORGE

Educator, clergy. **Personal:** Born Oct 29, 1931, New York, NY. **Educ:** Wilberforce Univ, OH, BS, educ, 1966; United Theol Sem Dayton, OH, Mdiv, 1970; Wright State Univ, Dayton, OH, attended 1973. **Career:** Educator (retired); AME Church, United Church Christ, 1962-68; Wright Patterson Afb, Dayton, Ohio, W Ohio Conf, United Methodist Church, pastor, 1969-74; Troy High Sch, Troy, Ohio, counr, 1975-92. **Orgs:** Pres, Clinton G Dorsey Assoc Motivational Human Devel; dist rep, Ohio Sch Counors Asn, 1971-76; consult, Dem Nom US Rep Fourth Cong Dist Ohio, 1976; bd mem, Miami County Ment Assn, 1976; adv bd criminal justice comn, Edison State Community Col, 1979; APGA leg prog proj trainer Amer Personnel & Guid Assn, 1980; bd mem, Miami County Habitat Humanity, 1992; chmn, Miami County Dem Party; Troy Civil Serv Comn. **Business Addr:** Owner, President, Clinton G Dorsey Assocs, 1334 Custer Ct, Troy, OH 45373-1601, **Business Phone:** (937)339-5028.

### DORSEY, DENISE

Graphic artist. **Personal:** Born Apr 24, 1953, Washington, DC; daughter of Lillian Miles and Willie K. **Educ:** Univ MD, College Park, BS, 1975. **Career:** Young Women Christian Asn, Baltimore, MD, aerobic instr, 1981-91; Afro-Am Newspapers, Baltimore, MD, graphic artist, prod mgr, currently. **Orgs:** Secy & treas, United Paperworkers Int Union, Local 111, 1988-95; bd dir, Charles St Dancers, 1991. **Honors/Awds:** Employee Owner of the Year, 2006. **Home Addr:** 3406 Kenyon Ave, Baltimore, MD 21213, **Home Phone:** (410)325-3969. **Business Addr:** Production Manager, Afro-Am Newspapers, 2519 N Charles St, Baltimore, MD 21218, **Business Phone:** (410)554-8288.

### DORSEY, ELBERT

Lawyer, library administrator, teacher. **Personal:** Born Oct 4, 1941, St. Louis, MO; son of Velmer and Juanita Jarrett Green; married Diane Elaine; children: Elbert Todd, Donielle Elaine, Daniel Christopher & Joseff Alexander. **Educ:** Harris-Stowe State Col, BA, 1966; St Louis Univ Sch Law, JD, 1973. **Career:** St Louis Community Col Dist, asst librn, 1965-66; St Louis Bd Educ, teacher, 1966-70; St Louis Legal Aid Soc, law clerk, 1971-72; Small Bus Admin, loan officer & atty, 1973-74; Collier, Dorsey & Williams, atty; Smith & Dorsey, atty, currently. **Orgs:** Historian Mound City Bar Asn; Judicial Conf Adv Comt, Eighth Circuit Ct Appeals; chmn & bd dir, Yeatman/Union-Sarah Joint Comn Health; Pole march St Louis Alumni Chap Kappa Alpha Psi Frat; chmn, adv bd, St Louis Comprehensive Health Ctr Home Health Bd. **Honors/Awds:** Ford Fel World Conf Peace, 1973; Dedication Award, Mound City Bar Asn St Louis, 1983; Humanitarian Award, St Louis Alumni Chap Kappa Alpha Psi, 1985. **Home Addr:** 48 Willow Brook Dr, St Louis, MO 63146, **Home Phone:** (314)432-0115. **Business Addr:** Attorney, Smith & Dorsey LLC, 3910 Lindell Blvd, St. Louis, MO 63108, **Business Phone:** (314)534-3800.

### DORSEY, HERMAN SHERWOOD, JR.

Consultant. **Personal:** Born Apr 5, 1945, Brooklyn, NY; son of Herman Sr and Loretta Rosa Kenney; married Maria Teresa Miller; children: Donna Michelle & Bryan. **Educ:** NY City Community Col, Brooklyn, NY, AA, mech tech, 1966; Brooklyn Polytech Inst, Brooklyn, NY, BS, mech engineering, 1972; NY Univ, Bronx, NY, BS, mech engineering, 1972; Duke Univ, Durham, NC, cert, exec mgt, 1988. **Career:** Consol Edison Co, NY, technician, 1966-72, from engr to sr engr, 1972-83, subsection mgr, 1983-86, mgr, steam generation planning, 1986-91, tech supt, 1991-93, Steam & Elec Sta, 1994, plant mgr, 2000; pvt int consult, 1992-; motivational speaker, 1995. **Orgs:** Am Soc Mech Engrs, 1972; liaison, Nat Action Coun Minorities Eng, 1989-98; Nat Republican Cong Comm & Frederick Douglass Republican Coun, 1990-; IDEA, Nat Planning Comt, 1991-93; vpres, bd mem, Tamiment Resort POA, 1991-94; chair, Steam Integrated Resource Plan, Consol Edison, 1992; cand prin asst secy, DOE, 1993; US Trade & Develop Team, 1995; first vice chair & bd mem, Am Asn Blacks Energy, 1996-98. **Honors/Awds:** Pi Tau Sigma, Scholastic Achievement, Pi Tau Sigma-Hon Mech Engineering Soc, 1972; Black Achiever in Indust, YMCA-Harlem Br, 1975; Cert Vis Prof, Black Exec Exchange Prog, Nat Urban League & Asn Cols, 1976, 1977, 1980-89; Cert, Shaping the Minds of Young Adults, Consolidated Edison, 1988; Ms Am Pageant judge, 1995; Consult Gingdao, China Power Co, 1995; James E. Stewart Award, Am Asn Blacks Energy, 2000. **Special Achievements:** Three technical papers published internationally, Int Dist Heating & Cooling Asn, 1988, 1989, 1991. **Home Addr:** 7 Elmwood Dr, Goshen, NY 10924, **Home Phone:** (845)469-2080. **Business Addr:** NY.

### DORSEY, IVORY

Public speaker, writer, executive. **Personal:** Born Apr 29, 1947, DeQuincy, LA; daughter of Walter E Wood and Mary L Wood; children: Edward Douglas (deceased). **Educ:** Southern Univ, BS, bus ed, 1970; Xerox Int Ctr Training & Mgt Develop. **Career:** Oglethorpe Univ, Atlanta, vis instr; Xerox Corp, customer rep, Houston, 1974-75, high vol syst rep, 1975-76, region prog support, Dallas, 1976-77, field sales exec, 1977-79, field sales mgr, Atlanta, 1979-81, mgr xerox store, Atlanta, 1981-84; teacher, pub schs; Golden Eagle Bus Servs Inc, speaker, trainer, consult & facilitator, pres & owner, 1984-; pub speaker, trainer, facilitator & auth; Bk: Universal Appeal: Bottom Line Benefit Diversity, 1994; Soft Skills Hard Times: A Handbk High Achievers, 2004. **Orgs:** Pres, Am Soc Training & Develop, 1992; adv bd, Atlanta Chamber Com Partners Bus & Ed, 1992; Gov's Small & Minority Bus Adv Comt, vice-chairwoman, 1992, dir, ann speakers sch, Nat & Ga Speakers Asn, 1995; Greater Atlanta Chap Am Soc; Sterling Who's Who; Delta Sigma Theta Sorority. **Honors/Awds:** Atlanta Tribune, Annual Salute Bus Owners, 1990; Trailblazer Award, Top Ladies of Distinction, 1991; Distinguished Past Resident, DeQuincy Chamber Com, 1991; Netterville Alumni Award, 1994; G. Leon Netterville Alumni Award in Business, Southern Univ, 1994; Professional Development Award, Am Soc Training & Develop, 1994; Atlanta Area Alumnus Achievers in Business, Southern Univ, 1995; Distinguished Alumni Award, Southern Univ, 1998; Delta Sigma Theta Leadership Award, 2005. **Home Addr:** 6522 Mitchell Lane SW, Mableton, GA 30126-5166, **Home Phone:** (404)944-0293. **Business Addr:** President, Founder, Golden Eagle Business Service Inc, PO Box 43447, Atlanta, GA 30336-0447, **Business Phone:** (404)881-6777.

### DORSEY, JOHN L., JR.

Lawyer. **Personal:** Born Sep 24, 1935, New Orleans, LA; married Evelyn. **Educ:** Dillard Univ, BA, 1963; Loyola Univ, Law Sch, JD, 1969. **Career:** New Orleans Legal Assistance Corp, atty, 1968-70; Dorsey & Marks, New Orleans, atty, 1970-; pvt pract atty, currently. **Orgs:** Nat Bar Asn; New Orleans Criminal Ct Bar Asn; Am Bar Asn; Nat Asn Advan Colored People; New Orleans Urban League; Lower & Ninth Ward Neighborhood Coun; Comt Alcholism & Drug Abuse Greater New Orleans; All Conf Football, 1961. **Home Addr:** 4917 N Prieur St, New Orleans, LA 70117, **Home Phone:** (504)949-4210. **Business Addr:** Attorney, Private Practice, 4948 Chef Menteur Hwy Suite 519, New Orleans, LA 70126-5029, **Business Phone:** (504)246-9726.

### DORSEY, JOSEPH A., JR.

School administrator, physician, educator. **Personal:** Born Apr 19, 1932, Baltimore, MD; married Alma K Edmonds; children: Dwain Kevin & Kyle Joseph. **Educ:** Springfield Col, BS, 1958; NY Univ, cert advan grad studies, 1959; Northeastern Univ, MEd, 1966; Boston Univ, DEd, exercise physiology & kinesiology, 1976. **Career:** Wayne County Gen Hosp, phys therapist, 1959-60; Andover Sch Syst, teacher & coach, 1960-68; Lawrence Gen Hosp, phys therapist, 1960-66; pvt pract phys therapist, 1960-; Boston State Col, Dept Phys Educ, assoc prof, chmn, 1968-76; Univ Lowell Dept Health, prof, chmn, 1976-; Andover Bd Health & Sch Syst, consult, 1977-78. **Orgs:** Bd dir, Andover ABC, 1977-; fel Am Col Sports Med; comt mem, Merrimack Valley Health Coun, 1978-. **Honors/Awds:** Coach of the Year, MA Asn Gymnastic Coaches, 1967-68; Citations State Rep & State Sen, 1968 & 1977; Andover Hall of Fame, Andover Sch System, 1977. **Home Addr:** 4 Talbot Rd, Andover, MA 01810, **Home Phone:** (978)475-1803. **Business Addr:** 1 Rolfe St, Lowell, MA 01854.

### DORSEY, TREDELL

Athletic coach. **Personal:** married Makasha; children: Justin & Jaden. **Educ:** Univ RI, BS, exercise sci & phys educ, 1998; Springfield Col, MEd, appl exercise sci, 2002; Argosy Univ Atlanta, PhD, orgn leadership, 2012; Col Strength & Conditioning Coaches Asn, cert, CSCCa; Nat Acad Sports Med, cert, CES; USA Weightlifting, cert, USA-TF & USAW. **Career:** Gateway High Sch, asst defensive backs coach, 1999-2000; Discovery Intermediate Mid Sch, head phys educ coach, track coach & health teacher; Amherst Col, strength & conditioning coach; Holy Cross, strength & conditioning coach; Ala State Univ, head strength & conditioning coach; Ga Tech Univ, asst dir player develop, 2000-04, Ga Tech Athletic Asn, asst dir player performance, 2002-04; Velocity Sports Performance, dir sports performance, 2004-05; Ga State Univ, head strength & conditioning coach, 2005-08; Del State Univ, asst athletic dir strength & conditioning, 2008-09; Ala State Univ, head strength & conditioning coach, 2008-10; Cleveland State Univ, head strength & conditioning coach, 2010-12; Univ Cent Fla, asst dir strength & conditioning, 2013-; Ga Southern Univ, dir strength & conditioning, 2016-. **Honors/Awds:** Master Strength and Conditioning Coach, Col Strength & Conditioning Coaches Asn, 2016. **Business Addr:** Assistant Director of Strength and Conditioning, University of Central Florida, 4000 Cent Fla Blvd, Orlando, FL 32816, **Business Phone:** (407)823-2000.

### DORTCH, HEYWARD

Executive. **Personal:** Born Jun 25, 1939, Camden, AL; son of Clarence and Alice; married Amelia; children: Derrick Terrell. **Educ:** Tenn State Univ, BS, 1966; Univ Cambridge, Cambridge Cert Risk Mgt Churches & Schs; Wayne State Univ, MS. **Career:** Mich Consol-Gas Co Ann Jobs & Careers Sem, founder & chairperson, 1982-94; Diversa Group Inc, founder & chief exec officer, 1995-. **Orgs:** Bd trustee, financial secy, chief fiscal officer, chairperson/insurance & real estate comt bd, non-profit housing corp, Ebenezer AME Church; facilities mgt advisory bd, Eastern Mich Univ, Col Technol; bd chair, Phenix Inc; entrepreneurship adv coun & chair, Northern High Sch; vpres & chief operating officer, Ebenezer A M E Church Non-Profit Housing Corp; vpres, Robert L Phillips Housing Corp; vpres, Robert Thomas Ltd Dividend Housing Asn Ltd Partnership; trustee & chief financial officer, Ebenezer AME Church Tutorial Prog. **Home Addr:** 15537 Thatcher St, Detroit, MI 48235-3123, **Home Phone:** (313)273-0904. **Business Addr:** Founder, Chief Executive Officer, Diversa Group Inc, 17515 W 9 Mile Rd, Southfield, MI 48075, **Business Phone:** (313)533-3870.

### DORTCH, THOMAS W., JR.

Executive, entrepreneur, writer. **Personal:** Born Apr 12, 1950, Toccoa, GA; son of Thomas Wesley Sr and Lizzie Porter; married Carol Warren; children: 4. **Educ:** Ft Valley State Col, BA, sociol, 1972; Clark Atlanta Univ, MA, criminal justice admin, 1985. **Career:** Dem Party Ga, Atlanta, assoc dir, 1974-78; Off US Sen Sam Nunn, Atlanta, admin aide, 1978-86, state exec asst, 1986-90, state dir, 1990-94; 100 Black Men Am, chmn emrites, 1994-2005; Atlanta Transp Systs Inc, founder & chief exec officer, 1994-; TWD Inc, Atlanta, founder & chief exec officer, 1994-; SWIG, pres; Cornerstone Parking, chmn & chief exec officer; LLC, chmn; FAD Consult, managing partner; Ga Asn Minority Entrepreneurs, co-founder; Greater Atlantic Econ Alliance, co-founder; Nat Cares Mentoring Movement, chmn, 1994-. **Orgs:** Bd mem, Ga Asn Minority Entrepreneurs; adv bd mem, Ga Asn Black Elected officials; founder, Nat Black Col Alumni Hall Fame Found; Assault Illiteracy Prog; Assault Illiteracy Prog; Atlanta Jewish/Black Coalition; bd mem, Friendship Force Int; chmn & bd dir, 100 Black Men Atlanta. **Business Addr:** Chairman, Chief Executive Officer, TWD Inc, 230 Peachtree St Suite 530, Atlanta, GA 30303, **Business Phone:** (404)521-1115.

### DOSS, CONYA

Singer. **Personal:** Born Cleveland, OH; children: Landon Blu. **Career:** Cleveland pub sch syst, teacher; Albums: A Poem About Ms. Doss, 2002; Just Because, 2004; Love Rain Down, 2006; Still, 2008; Blu Transition, 2010; A Pocketful of Purpose, 2012. Solo: "Coffee", 2002; "Good Good", 2000; "Starship", 2002; "You Really Hurt Me", 2003; "Missin' You", 2004; "Damn That", 2004; "Sweet Love", 2004; "Ain't Giving Up", 2005; "Here We Go Again", 2005; "Tell Me Why", 2006; "Let You Know", 2006; "What I'd Do", 2008; "It's Over", 2008; "Can't Stop", 2009; "Message", 2009; "What We Gone Do", 2010; "All In You", 2010, Wi-Fi, 2011; "Don't Change", 2012; "Where Do Go From Here?", 2012; "You Got Me", 2014. **Honors/Awds:** Soultracks Award, 2008. **Business Addr:** Singer, c/o Heliocentric Public Relations, 7137 Alvern St Suite 212, Los Angeles, CA 90045, **Business Phone:** (310)645-4246.

### DOSS, DR. JUANITA KING

Clinical psychologist. **Personal:** Born Jan 5, 1942, Baltimore, MD; daughter of Charles and Helen; children: Charles & Lawry. **Educ:** Howard Univ, Wash, DC, BS, 1963; Wayne State Univ, Detroit, MI, MSW, 1972; Union Inst, Cincinnati, OH, PhD, 1988. **Career:** Allied Health Serv, Mich, assoc dir, 1972-78; Southwest Detroit Hosp, Mich, dir planning & develop, 1978-80; Psychol serv clin, co-founder & prin partner, currently; Burdette & Doss Assocs, Mich, co-owner & clin dir, 1980-. **Orgs:** Steering comt, Wayne State Univ Sch Med. **Business Addr:** Clinical Director, Burdette & Doss Psychological Services, 17352 W 12 Mile Rd Suite 100, Southfield, MI 48076-2119, **Business Phone:** (248)559-0730.

### DOSS, ROD

Publisher. **Personal:** Born Pittsburgh, PA. **Educ:** Pittsburgh Tech Inst, attended. **Career:** New Pittsbugh Courier, sales rep, 1967, vpres, ed & publ, 1997-. **Orgs:** Bd mem, NNPA Foundation. **Home Addr:** 15219. **Business Addr:** Editor, Publisher, New Pittsburgh Courier, 315 E Carson St, Pittsburgh, PA 15219, **Business Phone:** (412)481-8302.

### DOSS, HON. THERESA

Judge, association executive. **Personal:** Born Oct 8, 1939, Myrtlewood, AL; daughter of Eddie E and Ida Richards; married James T Wahls; children: James Christopher Doss Wahls. **Educ:** Ohio Univ, AB, 1961; OH State Univ Col Law, JD, 1964; Wayne State Univ, MA, 2000. **Career:** Judge (retired); Cleveland Pub Sch, teacher, 1961; State Mich, law librn, 1964-65; Archdiocese Detroit,, community prog developer, 1965-66; State Mich, asst atty gen, 1966-76; Detroit Lighting Comn, comnr, 1974-76; Common Pleas Ct, judge, 1976-81; State Mich Thirty sixth Dist, judge, 1981-2003; Mich Judicial Tenure Comn, comnr, 1995-2001; vice chair, 2001. **Orgs:** Secy, Wolverine Bar Asn, 1967-68; jour adv comn, State Bar Mich, 1971-77, rep assembly, 1975-81, Wayne County Character & Fitness comt, 1971-75; pres, Nat Bar Asn, Women Sect, 1975-76; pres, Women's Lawyers Asn Mich, 1973-74; Mich Metro Girl Scouts Coun; Neighborhood Serv Orgn, 1977-87; pres, Mich Dist Judges Asn, 1991; Wayne County Dist Judges Asn; trustee, Tabernacle Missionary Baptist Church; Nat Asn Advan Colored People; Nat Coun Negro Women. **Honors/Awds:** Certificate of Distinction, Ohio State University Col of Law Alumni Asn, 1983; Nat Council of Negro Women, Outstanding Achievement in Law, 1976; United Methodist Women of Second Grace Methodist Church, Meritorious Achievement of Community Service in Jurisprudence, 1976; Humantarian Service Award, Rosa L Gragg Educational & Civic Club, 1986; Honored as Founding Member, Women Division of Nat Bar Asn, 1992; Scroll of Distinguished Women Lawyers Award, Natl Bar Asn, 2001. **Special Achievements:** First African-American woman appointed to a judgeship. **Home Addr:** 1331 Balmoral Dr, Detroit, MI 48203, **Home Phone:** (313)893-2436.

### DOSSMAN, DR. CURLEY M., JR.

President (organization). **Personal:** married Jennifer; children: Jonathan. **Educ:** Morehouse Col, Atlanta, BA, 1973; Washington Univ Sch Law, JD, 1976. **Career:** Office Fed Affairs & Spec Projects, inter-agency liaison officer, 1976-78; La State Planning Office, asst dir, 1978-84; AT&T, regional atty, 1984-94; Georgia-Pacific Found, sr dir, Community Progs Dept, pres, 1994-. **Orgs:** Chair, AAMI task force subcomt; Brown V Bd Educ; Phi Beta Kappa; pres, Morehouse Stud Gov Asn; nal bd dir & exec comn; bd dir, 100 Black Men Am Inc; La Bar Asn; Nat Bar Asn; Am Bar Asn; bd dir, Prof Asn Ga Educrs; bd dir, High Mus Art; bd dir, Atlanta Downtown Improv Dist; bd dir, treas, Great Schs Atlanta; bd dir, Nat Black Arts Festival; bd dir, Atlanta Victim Assistance Prog; bd dir, Leadership Atlanta; Atlanta Rotary; Kiwanis Club; Atlanta Pub Sch Syst Charter Rev Comn; chair partnerships comt, Univ Ga Task Force Black Males Higher Educ; Ga Partnership Excellence Educ; bd dir, Trust Pub Land, Atlanta; bd dir, Leadership Ga; adv coun, United Way Am. **Business Addr:** President, Georgia-Pacific Foundation, 133 Peachtree St NE, Atlanta, GA 30303, **Business Phone:** (404)652-4182.

### DOST, JANICE H. BURROWS

Manager, executive, association executive. **Personal:** Born Oct 24, 1944, Boston, MA; daughter of Bernice E Cross Howard and Lloyd F Howard; married Quentin C Burrows; children: Matthew Howard & Christopher Lynch; married William A. **Educ:** Harvard Univ, Cambridge, MA, BA, 1966; Univ Calif, Berkeley, Calif, MBA, 1987. **Career:** US Civil Serv Comn, Boston, MA, Wash, DC, personnel spec, 1966-68; US Gen Serv Admin, New York, NY, regional training officer, 1971-72; City Berkeley, Berkeley, Calif, personnel spec, 1974-76; Alta Bates Hosp, Berkeley, Calif, personnel dir, 1976-85; self-employed consult, human resource mgt, Berkeley, Calif, 1985-; Univ Calif, Berkeley, Calif, dir libr hum resources, 1988-. **Orgs:** Chm, Berkeley Unified Sch Dist Personnel Comn, 1978-79, 1987-91; pres, SF Chap, Calif Hosp Personnel Mgrs Asn, 1980-81; Dir, Humanities W, 1991; Pres, Healthcare Human Resources Mgt Asn Calif, 1984-85; vpres, Calif Sch Personnel Comnr Asn, 1991-92; Am Libr Asn; Indust Rels Res Asn; admin & mgt asn, human resources sect, 1998-99; Nat Forum Black Pub Adminr. **Special Achievements:** Author: Minority Recruitment and Retention in ARL Libraries, Association of Research Libraries, Office of Management Services, 1990; "Minority Recruitment and Retention in ARL Libraries", Office of Management Services, Association of Research Libraries, 1990; "Onward or Upward? Getting Ahead in an Unfair World", Proceedings of the Second National Conference of the Black Caucus of the American Library Association, 1994; "Training Student Workers in Academic Libraries, How and Why?", "Journal of Library Administration", Volume 212, #3/4, 1994. **Home Addr:** 991 Creston Rd, Berkeley, CA 94702-1501, **Home Phone:** (510)527-7216. **Business Addr:** Director Library Human Resources, University California, 110 Doe Libr, Berkeley, CA 94720-6000, **Business Phone:** (510)642-3778.

### DOTSON, ALBERT E., JR.

Lawyer. **Personal:** Born Jun 9, 1960, Detroit, MI; son of Albert E Sr; married Gail Ash; children: Ashley & Albert III. **Educ:** Dartmouth Col, AB, econs & hist, 1982; Vanderbilt Univ, JD, 1987; Univ de Granada. **Career:** Fine Jacobson Schwartz Block & Eng, assoc, 1987-90; Jenner & Block, assoc, 1990-93; Eckert Seamans, partner, 1995-98; Bilzin Sumberg Baena Price & Axelrod LLP, atty & equity partner, 1998-; Fed Judicial Nominating Comn, comnr, 2009-; Pres's Adv Comn Educ Excellence African Americans, comnr, 2014-. **Orgs:** Chmn, Miami Dade Col Found bd trustee, 2001-07; bd gov's, Big Bros & Big Sisters Greater Miami; pres, FedEx Orange Bowl Game; chmn trustee, Sweet Home Missionary Baptist Church; chmn bd, 100 Black Men Am, 1989-; Orange Bowl Comt, 1993-, pres, 2006-07. **Business Addr:** Equity Partner, Attorney, Bilzin, Sumberg, Baena, Price & Axelrod, LLP, 1450 Brickell Ave 23rd Fl, Miami, FL 33131-2336, **Business Phone:** (305)374-7580.

### DOTSON, BETTY LOU. See Obituaries Section.

### DOTSON, EARL CHRISTOPHER

Football player. **Personal:** Born Dec 17, 1970, Beaumont, TX; married Janell; children: Jared. **Educ:** Tex A&M Univ, Kingsville. **Career:** Football player (retired); Green Bay Packers, offensive tackle & right tackle, 1993-2002. **Honors/Awds:** Champion, Super Bowl, XXXI.

### DOTSON, HOWARD, JR.

Association executive. **Personal:** Born Jun 6, 1939, Chester, PA. **Educ:** W Chester State Col, BS, social studies, 1961; Villanova Univ, MS, hist & polit sci, 1964. **Career:** Peace Corps, staff, 1964; Inst Black World Atlanta, 1970-79, exec dir, 1974-79; Nat Endowment Humanities, consult, 1984; Schomburg Ctr Res Black Cult, coordr, chief, dir, 1984-2010; Howard Univ Libr, interim dir, 2010-; Moorland-Spingarn Res Ctr, actg dir, 2010-; Educ Life Acad, advisor, currently; New York Pub Libr's Schomburg Ctr Res, dir. **Honors/Awds:** Honorary Doctorate, Widener Univ, 1987; Honorary Doctorate, Adelphi Univ, 2004; Honorary Doctorate, W Chester State Univ, 2005; Honorary Doctorate, City Univ New York, 2006; Honorary Doctorate, Villanova Univ, 2007. **Special Achievements:** Published numerous articles. **Business Addr:** Director, Howard University Libraries, 500 Howard Pl NW, Washington, DC 20059, **Business Phone:** (202)806-4239.

### DOTSON, HON. NORMA Y.

Judge. **Educ:** Wayne State Univ, Detroit, MI, BS, MEd, JD. **Career:** Detroit Pub Schs, teacher; Norma Y Dotson, PC, atty; Patterson, Phifer & Phillips, coun; State Mich, 36th Dist Ct, judge, currently. **Orgs:** State Bar Mich; Asn Black Judges Mich; Mich Dist Judges Asn; Nat Bar Asn; Wolverine Bar Asn; Nat Asn Advan Colored People; Detroit Fedn Teachers; Wayne State Univ Alumni Asn; Phi Alpha Delta; Delta Sigma Theta Inc; Phi Delta Kappa; bd mem & vice chair, Nat Conf Artists; bd dir, Nat Healthcare Scholars Found. **Business Addr:** Judge, State of Michigan, 421 Madison Ave, Detroit, MI 48226-2358, **Business Phone:** (313)965-2200.

### DOTSON, PHILLIP RANDOLPH

Educator. **Personal:** Born Oct 10, 1948, Carthage, MS; son of Jim O R and Velma Ernest; married Judith Kerr; children: Philip T R, Tiffany M & Brian R. **Educ:** Jackson State Univ, BS, art educ, 1970; Univ Miss, Oxford, MS, MFA painting, 1972. **Career:** Le Moyne-Owen Col, Dept Art, chmn, 1972-87, chmn, div fine arts & humanities, 1988-96, prof & area coordr, instr, currently; Memphis Jack & Jill Exhib, cur, 1983-84; Spirit African Art S, Memphis State Univ, cur, 1983. **Orgs:** Sponsor, Cotton Carnival Asn, 1972-83; Planning mem, Memphis May Int Festival, 1972-73; rev mem, Tenn Arts Comn, 1975-76; Relig Comm Arts & Am Revolution, 1976, Chamber Com; arts adv bd, Mallory Knights Charitable Orgn, 1976-80; Col Art Asn, 1978-80; bd mem, Artist Sch Prog Arts Coun; bd dir, Round Table Memphis Mus Dir, 1982-; bd mem, Memphis Arts Coun, 1986-; bd mem, Memphis Arts Festival, 1989-. **Home Addr:** 1678 Newsum, Germantown, TN 38138, **Home Phone:** (901)756-0543. **Business Addr:** Professor, Area Coordinator, LeMoyne-Owen College, 807 Walker Ave, Memphis, TN 38126, **Business Phone:** (901)435-1305.

### DOTSON-WILLIAMS, HENRIETTA

Government official. **Personal:** Born May 27, 1940, Valden, MS; daughter of Fred Perteete and Woodsy; married Michael J Williams; children: Johnice, Mike, Angela Woodson, Earl Dotson Jr , Dennis & Clifford. **Educ:** Ill Extn Univ, attended 1960. **Career:** Government official (retired); Ill Bell Tel Co, operator spec eng clerk, 1960-68; Winnebago County Treas's off, tax clerk/cashier, 1970-71; Winnebago County Bd Dist 12, suprv, 1972; Northern Ill Area Agency Aging, secy regional planner, 1974-75; N Ill Women's & Ctr, coun, 1975-77; Ill Secy State, exam clerk, 1977-81; Energy Assistance Prog, energy specialist, 1981-2002; Black Corner Monthly TV Prog, former moderator; Rockford Fire & Police comn, comm, 2008-. **Orgs:** Elected mem, Winnebago County Bd, 1970-90; pres, Winnebago County Bd Health, 1983-85; Ill Asn Bd Health, 1984-86; secy, Burpee Mus, bd dir; bd dir, Klehm Arboretum & Bot Gardens; chmn, Winnebago County Intergovernmental Affairs Comn; pres, Winnebago County Bd Health; bd mem, Fire & Police Com, Ill; pres, Ill Asn Bd Health; mem, Childrens Develop Ctr; mem, Nat Coun Negro Women; mem, Nat Asn Advan Colored People; treas & founding mem, Direction Fel Missionary Baptist Church. **Honors/Awds:** Finalist Excalibur nomination, 2008. **Special Achievements:** Woman of the Month, Essence Mag, 1978; Nominee for Woman of the Year, Young Women's Christian Asn, 1982 & 1986; Led an Effort to Retain Dr ML King's Birthday as a Legal Holiday for Winnebago County Employees. **Home Addr:** 1202 Kent St, Rockford, IL 61102-2749, **Home Phone:** (815)964-2143.

### DOTTIN, DR. ROBERT PHILIP

Educator, biologist, founder (originator). **Personal:** Born May 23, 1943, Trinidad; son of William and Lena; married Gail; children: Melissa & Garreth. **Educ:** Univ Toronto, BS, microbiol, 1968, MS, med biophys & med cell biol, 1970, PhD, med genetics, 1974; Univ Mass, post doc, 1976. **Career:** Biologist, research director; MIT, post doctoral, 1974-76; Univ Copenhagen, vis prof, 1975; Pasteur Inst, vis prof; Karlova Univ, vis prof; Oxford Univ, vis prof; MIT, Johns Hopkins Univ, asst prof, 1976-82, assoc prof, 1982-87; Just Garcia Hill, dir, founder; prin investr; co-prin investr; Hunter Col, CUNY, New York, NY, Dept Biol, prof, 1986-, prog coordr, ctr study gene struct & function, 1986-88, dir, ctr gene struct & function, 1998-. **Orgs:** Genetics Study Sect; grantee, Nat Inst Health, 1984-; Am Soc Cell Biol; Nat Sci Found; Am Heart Asn; Am Soc Human Genetics, 1986; Am Soc Biochem & Molecular Biol, 1985; ed, publ, Coalition Advan Blacks BioMed Scis, CABBS, A Resource Diry; Sigma Xi, exec comt; Lodish lab alumni; Nat Insts Health/Nat Ctr Res Resources. **Business Addr:** Director, Hunter College, Hunter Col N Bldg Rm 932N, New York, NY 10065, **Business Phone:** (212)772-5171.

### DOTTIN, ROGER ALLEN

Executive. **Personal:** Born Jul 13, 1945, Cambridge, MA; son of Reuben and Eunice; married Marilyn Ames. **Educ:** Cambridge Sch Bus, dipl, 1965; Grahm Jr Col. **Career:** Econ Opportunity Atlanta Inc, ctr dir, 1970-73; City Atlanta Community Rels Comn, asst dir, 1974-76; Metro Atlanta Rapid Transit Authority, sr comm rels spec, 1976-84, mgr community rels, 1984-86; Dallas Area Rapid Transit, mgr cust servs, 1986-90; Metrop Atlanta Rapid Transit Authority, mgr & community coordr, lifetime hon mem. **Orgs:** Vice chair, Sponsor-A-Family Proj Atlanta, 1983-87; Atlanta Pub Schs Safety & Emergency Mgt Adv-Coun, 1984-86; co-chair, Atlanta Br Nat Asn Advan Colored People; Afro-Acad Cult Tech Sci Olympics, 1984-86; Conf Minority Transp Offs, 1985-; chmn, 1999, pres, Int Cust Serv Asn; ampbellton/Cascade Ys Men; Local Coord Coun Fulton Co Pvt Indust Coun. **Honors/Awds:** Outstanding Servce Award, John Harland Boys Club Atlanta, 1982; Community Serv Award, NAACP Atlanta Br, 1984; Outstanding & Dedicated Serv, Nat Asn Advan Colored People Atlanta Br, 1986; YMCA Minority Achievers Prog, Dallas YMCA, 1988; Jondelle Harris Johnson Humanitarian Award, NAACP, Atlanta, 2001. **Home Addr:** 4321 Wallace Ave SW, Atlanta, GA 30331-6537, **Home Phone:** (404)349-8379.

### DOUG, DOUG E. (DOUGLAS BOURNE)

Actor. **Personal:** Born Jan 7, 1970, Brooklyn, NY. **Career:** Films: Mo' Better Blues, 1990; Hangin' With the Homeboys, 1991; Jungle Fever, 1991; Class Act, 1992; Cool Runnings, 1993; Operation Dumbo Drop, 1995; That Darn Cat, 1997; Rusty: A Dog's Tale, 1997; Everything's Jake, 2000; Citizen James, 2000; Eight-Legged Freaks, 2002; Shark Tale, Voice, 2004; Snowmen, 2010; A Novel Romance, 2011; Detachment, 2011; TV series: "The New Music Report", writer, 1990; "Where I Live", co-producer, 1993; "Cosby", 1996-2000; "Citizen James", dir, writer & producer, 2000; "Law & Order: Special Victims Unit", 2004-12; "Harvey Birdman, Attorney at Law", 2005; "Conviction", 2006; "Wyclef Jean in America", 2006; "Pilot", 2006; "My Gym Partner's a Monkey", 2007; "Justified", 2010; "Bar Karma", 2011; "Blue Bloods", 2014. **Honors/Awds:** Nominee, Image Award, 1998, 1999, 2000; Nominee, Independent Spirit Award, 1992; Nominee, Young Artist Award, 1994. **Business Addr:** Actor, William Morris Agency, 151 El Camino Dr, Beverly Hills, CA 90212, **Business Phone:** (310)859-4000.

### DOUGLAS, ASHANTI SHEQUOIYA

Singer, actor, writer. **Personal:** Born Oct 13, 1980, Glen Cove, NY; daughter of Ken-Kaide Thomas and Tina. **Career:** Albums: Ashanti, 2002; Chapter II, Ashanti's Christmas, 2003; Concrete Rose, 2004; Collectables by Ashanti, 2004; The Declaration, 2008; TBA, 2011; Braveheart, 2014. Films: Bride and Prejudice, 2004; Coach Carter, 2005; John Tucker Must Die, 2006; Resident Evil: Extinction, You're Nobody till Somebody Kills You, 2007; Mutant World, 2014. TV series: " American Dreams", "Sabrina, The Teenage Witch", 2002; "Buffy The Vampire Slayer", WrestleMania XIX, The Proud Family, 2003; "Punk'd", Oxygen: Custom Concert, 2004; "The Muppets' Wizard of Oz", Las Vegas, All That, 2005; "Diamond Life", 2005; "Oprah Winfrey's Legends Ball", 2006; "What Perez Sez", World Series, NFL Thanksgiving Classic, 2007; BET Awards, 2008; "Access Granted", "The Morning Show with Mike & Juliet", MANswers, 2009; The Biggest Loser, 2010; "Extreme Makeover: Home Edition", 2010; "The Tonight Show with Conan O'Brien"; "Army Wives", 2013; "Law & Order: Special Victims Unit", 2013; "Christmas in the City", 2013. **Honors/Awds:** Grammy Award, Best Contemporary R&B Album, 2003; American Music Award, 2003; Teen Choice Award; Soul Train Lady of Soul Award. **Special Achievements:** Ranked as No 81 in FHM's "100 Sexiest Women in the World 2005" special supplement, 2005; Named #13 on the Maxim magazine Hot 100 of 2005 list; Ranked #37 on the Maxim magazine Hot 100 of 2008 list. **Business Addr:** Artist, c/o Murder Inc Records, PO Box 538, Glen Oaks, NY 11004.

### DOUGLAS, BETTY. See DOUGLAS, ELIZABETH (BETTY) ASCHE.

### DOUGLAS, BUSTER. See DOUGLAS, JAMES.

### DOUGLAS, CARL E.

Lawyer. **Personal:** Born May 8, 1955, Los Angeles, CA. **Educ:** Northwestern Univ, BA, polit sci, 1977; Univ Calif, Boalt Hall Sch Law, JD, 1980. **Career:** Fed Commun Comn, atty, 1980-81; Fed Pub Defender's Off, dep fed pub defender, 1981-86; Law off Orenthal James Simpson, atty, 1994-95; Law Offs Johnnie Cochran, managing atty, 1986-98; Douglas Hicks Firm (Douglas Law Firm), atty, pres, 1998-. **Orgs:** State Bar Calif; John M Langston Bar Asn; Consumer Attorneys Asn LosAngeles. **Honors/Awds:** Trial Lawyer of the Year, John M. Langston Bar Asn, 1994, 1996; Trial Lawyer of the Year, Consumer Atty Asn Los Angeles, 1996; Soaring Eagle Award, Am Asn Justice, Johnnie L.Cochran, 2013; Hall of Fame, Calif Asn BlacK Lawyers, 2013; Susan Miller Dorsey High School Hall of Fame. **Business Addr:** Attorney, The Douglas Law Firm, 8484 Wilshire Blvd Suite 548, Beverly Hills, CA 90211-3234, **Business Phone:** (323)655-6505.

### DOUGLAS, ELIZABETH (BETTY) ASCHE (BETTY DOUGLAS)

Artist, educator. **Personal:** Born Dec 22, 1930, Rochester, PA; daughter of Charles Ferdell and Irma Mae (Edmonds) Asche; married William Roy; children: Andrea Lynne, Vicki Jo & Nanette Rae. **Educ:** Carnegie Inst Tech, BFA, 1951; Univ Pittsburgh, MA, 1956; Univ Pa, attended 1979. **Career:** Tex Col, Tyler, Tex, asst prof, 1955-58; Good Publ Co, Ft Worth, Tex, art dir, 1958-61; Beaver PA Schls & Rochester PA Schs, teacher art, 1962-66; Geneva Col, Beaver Falls, Pa, asst prof, assoc prof, prof, coord humanities, 1966-96, prof emerita fine arts & humanities, 1996-; Douglas Art Gallery, prin artist & owner, 1975-. **Orgs:** Col Art Asn, 1969-2000; chairperson, Rochester Area Human Rel Comm, 1973-74; Arts rev Christian Scholars Rev, 1973-; co-chairperson, taskforce Juv Delinq SW Reg Planning Comm Govs Justice Comm, 1976-78; prog chmn, Brodhead Cult Ctr, 1977-78; secy & treas, Found Art, Theory & Educ (FATE), 1979-80; art comm, Merrick Art Gallery Asn, 1980-; Nat Conf Artists, 1980-2000; bd mem, Christian Scholars Revolution, 1985-95; Asn Integrative Studies, 1985-99; Hofstra Univ Conf Avant-Garde Lit & Art, 1985; bd mem, Christians Visual Art, 1986-91, 1994-99; chmn, Merrick Art Gallery Asn Catalog Comm; auth & ed, Catalogue Merrick Art Gallery, 1988; bd mem, Northland Pub Libr Found, 1989-92; bd mem, Greater Beaver Valley Cult Alliance, 1990-92; bd mem, Asn Integrative Studies, 1991-94; bd mem, Merrick Art Gallery, 1994, pres, 1997-99, 2000-; Trinity Episcopal Sch Ministry, 1996-99; bd mem, Sweetwater Ctr Arts, 1997-2000, adv, 2000-; resource artist, Intergenerational Arts Proj; butler, Lawrence & Mercer Counties, PA; Beaver chap, Women's Bus Network; bd mem, Beaver Valley Int Arts Festival, 2001-04; chairperson, Beaver Valley Int Arts Festival, 2001-02; bd mem, Rochester Chamber Com; Beaver County Chamber Com; adv, Guild Coun Pittsburgh Ctr Arts, 2004-; Am Fed Musicians Beaver Chap; Lincoln Pk Performing Arts Charter Sch, 2005; Midland PA Arts Coun, 2007-; Beaver Valley

Musicians Union, 2007. **Honors/Awds:** Achievement Award, Beaver Valley Service Club, 1978; Scholar of the Year, Geneva Col Fac, 1985; Woman of Distinction in the Arts, Beaver-Castle Girl Scouts Coun, 1989; Woman of Eminence, Hawthorne Club, 1999; Athena Award Nominee, Beaver County, 2000, 2002; Hall of Fame inductee, Am Fedn Musicians, Beaver Valley Chap, 2003; Elizabeth Asche Douglas Fund, Geneva Col, named in honor, 2003; biography referenced in Who's Who in the World, Who's Who Among African Americans, Who's Who in the East, the National Registry of Who's Who, the International Directory of Women in the Arts, Outstanding Educators of American, The International Biographical Centre, Cambridge, U.K., Outstanding Achievers of the 21st Century; Service to Arts Award, Guild Coun, Pgh Ctr Arts, 2006; Civic Appreciation Award, Beaver County Bar Asn, 2013; Dreammakers Award, Baden Acad, 2013. **Special Achievements:** Articles published in CIVA (Christians in Visual Arts) numerous times, 1983-, papers delivered annual meetings FATE Toronto 1984, Assoc Integrative Studies 1984, article published Leonardo's Last Supper, Christian Scholar's Review 1988, career documented in Archives of National Museum for Women in the Arts. **Home Addr:** 491-3 McKinley St, Rochester, PA 15074-1663, **Home Phone:** (724)775-4618. **Business Addr:** Professor Emerita of Fine Arts & Humanities, Geneva College, 3200 College Ave, Beaver Falls, PA 15010, **Business Phone:** (724)846-5100.

## DOUGLAS, FLORENCE MAUD

Physician. **Personal:** Born Mar 26, 1933; married Franklin E Mcfarlane; children: Valerie, Angela & Alychandra. **Educ:** Hunter Col, NY, BA, 1955; Howard Univ Col Med, MD, 1959; CA State Med Lic, 1960-. **Career:** Los Angeles Co Gen Hosp, intern, 1959-60, resident gen psychiat, 1960-62, residency child psychiat, 1963-65; pvt pract, 1965-; Los Angeles Co Gen Hosp Sch Nursing, consult, 1960-62; Los Angeles Co Juv Hall, consult, 1960-62; Montefiore Hosp NY, residency gen psychiat, 1962; Episcopal Ch Home C Pasadena, Calif, consult, 1963-67; Huntington Meml Hosp Pasadena, consult, 1965-66; Los Angeles Co Ment Health Arcardia Sch Syst, consult, 1965-67; Univ Calif, Irvine, assoc clin prof, 1989. **Orgs:** Southern Calif Psychiat Soc; AMA; Los Angeles Co Med Asn; Am Psychiat Asn; Nat Med Asn; Am AsnAdolescent Psychiat; Am & Orthopsychiatric Asn; Calif Med Asn; Black Psychiat So CA; Black Psychiat Am; Ment Health Develop Comt, United Way; bd mem, Calif Dept Rehab Southern Calif Psychoanal Asn; Am Asn Group Psychotheraphy; Col Psychol & Soc Studies; bd mem, Model Cities Child Care Ctr; Johnny Tillmon Child Develop Ctr, New Careerists; Inner City Students; Urban Corp Students; dipl, Am Bd Psychol & Neurol; bd cert Child & Adolescent Psychiat; examr Am Bd Psychiat & Neurol; fel Am Acad Child & Psychiat; bd cert & fel Forensic Med & Forensic Examr, 1997. **Honors/Awds:** Anna Bartsche Dunne Scholarship, Howard Univ Col Med, 1956-58; Distinguished Public Service Award, 1998. **Home Addr:** 4305 Torrance Blvd, Torrance, CA 90503, **Home Phone:** (310)370-5055.

## DOUGLAS, GABRIELLE CHRISTINA VICTORIA (GABBY DOUGLAS)

Gymnast. **Personal:** Born Dec 31, 1995, Virginia Beach, VA; daughter of Timothy Douglas and Natalie Hawkins. **Career:** U.S. women's jr gymnast, 2008-10, sr gymnast, 2011-. **Honors/Awds:** Level 4 All-Around Gymnastics Title, Va State Championships, 2004 ; Silver Medal on Balance Beam, U.S. Jr Nat Championships, 2010; Uneven Bars Champion, Pan Am Championships Guadalajara, Mex, 2010; Gold Medal, World Championships, Tokyo, Japan, 2011; Gold Medal in Uneven Bars, Silver Medal in All-Around, Bronze Medal in Floor Exercise, Visa Championships, St. Louis, Mo, 2012; Gold Medal in Uneven Bars and Team, Pac Rim Championships, Seattle, Wash, 2012; Gold Medalist in All-Around, Gold Medalist in Team, Olympic Games, London, Eng, 2012; Female Athlete of the Year, Assoc Press, 2012. **Special Achievements:** First female gymnast to have both the All-Around and Team gold medals in the same Olympics; first African American Olympian to receive the All Around gold medal in gymnastics; autobiography, "Grace, Gold and Glory: My Leap of Faith," Zondervan, 2012.

## DOUGLAS, GARY A.

Insurance executive, president (organization). **Educ:** St Cloud State Univ, BS; Eastern Mich Univ, MBA. **Career:** Nationwide Ins New York, regional vpres; Allied Ins, Cent States Region, regional vpres; Nationwide Agribusiness Ins Co, pres & chief operating officer, 2007-; Farmland Mutual Ins Co, pres & chief operating officer, 2007-; Nat Mutual Ins Co, vpres; AMCO Ins Co, vpres; Allied Property & Casualty Ins Co, vpres; Depositors Ins Co, vpres. **Orgs:** Bd mem, Iowa Ins Inst; bd mem, Boys & Girls Clubs Cent Iowa; nat co-chair, Farm Safety 4 Just Kids' Endowment Steering Comt; dir, Nationwide Agribusiness Ins Co, 2007-; dir, Farmland Mutual Ins Co, 2007-.

## DOUGLAS, HARRY E., III

Educator. **Personal:** Born Nov 8, 1938; children: 2. **Educ:** Univ Denver, BA, 1959; Univ Calif, Los Angeles, MPA, personnel, 1972; Univ Southern Calif, MPA, health serv, 1981, DPA, health admin & policy, 1983; Southern Calif Univ Health Sci, DHL, 2004. **Career:** Dept Pub Social Servs, proj dir, sr prog asst, mgt trainee, social worker, 1960-68; Univ Southern Calif, Los Angeles, training officer, 1968-69; Martin Luther King & Charles R Drew Med Ctr, personnel officer, 1969-71, dir allied health training, 1971-73; Cedars-Sinai Med Ctr, dir manpower training & develop, 1973-74; Calif Reg Med Prog, prog dir HS & EP, 1974-75; Howard Univ, Col Allied Health Sci, assoc dean & assoc prof, 1975-83, actg dean, 1981-82; Charles R Drew Univ Med & Sci, Col Allied Health, dean, 1983-94, Charles R Drew Univ Med & Sci, vpres acad affairs, 1994-95, exec vpres, 1995-2003, interim pres, 2004-05. **Orgs:** Consult, DHEW Div Health Manpower; adv & coun, Am Soc Allied Health Prof Nat Data Gathering Proj; health brain trust mem, Cong Black Caucus; mgt progs, nursing personnel George Wash Univ; tech rev comn, Calif Community Reg Med Progs; Calif St Dept Ed; ad hoc adv comn, Career Educ Health Occupations; Am Assoc Comn & Jr Col; Sch Allied Health Study; Charles R Drew Postgrad Med Sch; San Francisco Personnel Dept; Nat Inst Ment Health; Orange City Personnel Dept; Univ Calif, Los Angeles; Proj Allied Health Prof; bd dir, DC Coalition Health Advocates; treas, bd mem, Nat Assoc Allied Health; Dietetic Manpower Demand Study; Child-Find & Advocacdy Comn; chmn, Am Soc Allied Prof; DC Adv Comn Magnet Sch HealthCareers; assoc coord, Reg Leadership Ctr Allied Health Educ; Am Soc Pub Admin; Am Pub Health Assoc; Nat Soc Allied Health; Am Asn Higher Educ; Am Coun Educ; Am Soc Allied Health Professions; Am Soc Pub Admin; Asn Am Med Cols; Phi Delta Kappa; Western Col Asn; Asn Minority Health Professions Schs; chair, Charles R Drew Univ Med & Sci, 2004-05. **Special Achievements:** Numerous presentations & publs. **Home Addr:** 6405 S Halm Ave, Los Angeles, CA 90056-2229, **Home Phone:** (310)216-7805.

## DOUGLAS, HERBERT PAUL, JR.

Consultant. **Personal:** Born Mar 9, 1922, Pittsburgh, PA; married Rozell; children: Barbara Joy Ralston & Herbert III. **Educ:** Xavier Univ, attended 1942; Univ Pittsburgh, BS, 1948, MEd, 1950. **Career:** Managed night bus, fathers auto bus, 1942-45; Pabst Brewing Co, sales rep to dist mgr, 1950-63, markets mgr, 1965-68; Schieffelin & Co NYC, sales rep, 1963-65, nat spec mkt mgr, 1965-68, Nat Spec Mkts, vpres, 1968-; Schieffelin & Somerset Co, Urban Mkt Develop, vpres, 1977-80, consult, 1987-2005; Nat Asn Mkt Develop, vpres. **Orgs:** Pres & founder, Int Amateur Athletic Asn Inc, 1980-; Track & Field Club; Optimist Club; Philadelphia Pioneer Club; Nat Asn Advan Colored People; Nat Urban League; Omega Psi Phi Frat; Chris Atlete Club; Ebenezer Bapt Church; Sales Exec Club; emer trustee, Univ Pittsburgh. **Honors/Awds:** Black Athletes Hall of Fame, 1974; Beverage Ind Award Urban League Guild, 1974; Jesse Owens International Trophy Award, 1980; Univ Pittsburgh, Lettermen of Distinction Award, 1980; Univ Bicentennial Award, 1987; Black Achievement Award, 1987; Western Pa Sports Hall of Fame, 1988; Pa Sports Hall of Fame, 1992; Legacy Award, Univ Pittsburgh, 2000; History Makers Award, 2006; Alumni Hall of Fame, Taylor Allderdice High Sch, 2009. **Special Achievements:** Olympic Games, long jump Bronze medal, 1948; currently last athlete from Pittsburgh to win a medal in Olympic Games; Selected by Ebony success libr one of top 1000 Successful Blacks in US. **Home Addr:** 407 Rices Mill Rd, Wyncote, PA 19095, **Home Phone:** (215)885-2644.

## DOUGLAS, HUGH LAMONT

Football player, television broadcaster. **Personal:** Born Aug 23, 1971, Mansfield, OH; married Ayanna; children: Kayla Rachelle & Brianna Syann. **Educ:** Cent State Univ, grad. **Career:** Football player (retired), analyst; NY Jets, defensive end, 1995, right defensive end, 1996-97; Philadelphia Eagles, right defensive end, 1998-99, defensive end, 1999-2002, 2004; Jacksonville Jaguars, defensive end, 2003; WTXF-TV, reporter; BBC Am, six nations championship co-host, 2011; Entertainment & Sports Programming Network, nat football league studio analyst, 2011-13; 92.9 Game Sports Talk radio Sta, host, currently. **Orgs:** Founder, Hugh Douglas Found, 1999. **Honors/Awds:** AP National Football League Defensive Rookie of the Year, 1995; Defensive Rookie of the Year, Prof Football Writers Am, 1995; Alumni Pass Rusher of the Year, Nat Football League, 2000; Jack Edelstein Memorial Award, 2000, 2001; National Football Conference Champion, 2004. **Home Addr:** , Fayetteville, GA. **Business Addr:** Host, 92.9 The Game Sports Talk Radio Station, 1201 Peachtree St Suite 800, Atlanta, GA 30361, **Business Phone:** (404)898-8900.

## DOUGLAS, JAMES (BUSTER DOUGLAS)

Basketball player, boxer. **Personal:** Born Apr 7, 1960, Columbus, OH; son of William and Lula Pearl McCauley (deceased); married Bertha Paige; children: LaMar, Cardae & Arthur. **Educ:** Mercy Hurst Col; Coffeyville Community Col; Dayton Sinclair Community Col. **Career:** Boxer (retired), basketball player; Coffeyville Community Col Red Ravens, 1977-78, Sinclair Community Col, 1979-80. **Orgs:** Pres, Lula Pearl Douglas Found. **Home Addr:** 1229 Manchester Ave, Columbus, OH 43211-1367.

## DOUGLAS, DR. JAMES MATTHEW

Educator, college administrator. **Personal:** Born Feb 11, 1944, Onalaska, TX; son of Desso D and Mary L; married Tanya Smith; children: DeLicia, Erika & James. **Educ:** Tex Southern Univ, BA, math, 1966, JD, law, 1970; Stanford Univ, JSM, law, 1971. **Career:** Singer Gen Precision, programmer analyst, 1966-72; Tex Southern Univ, Thurgood Marshall Sch Law, asst prof law, 1971-72, prof law, 1981-95, interim provost & vp acad affairs, 1995, pres, 1995-99, distinguished proflaw, 1999-, pres, 2002-; Cleveland State Univ, Cleveland-Marshall Col Law, asst prof law, 1972-75, asst dean stud affairs, 1974-75; Syracuse Univ Col Law, assoc prof law & assoc dean, 1975-80; Northeastern Univ Sch Law, prof law, 1980-81; Tex Southern Univ, dean & prof, 1981-95, interim provost & sr vpres acad affairs, 1995, interim pres, 1995, pres, 1995-99, distinguished prof, 1999-, exec vpres, 2008-, exec vpres/interim gen coun, 2009-12, Govt Affairs & Community Rels, vpres, 2012-; Fla A & M Univ, interim dean, 2005-07. **Orgs:** State Bar Tex, 1970; Houston Jr Bar Asn; chmn, Educ Comm Sci & Tech Sect; Am Bar Asn; bd dir, Hiscock Legal Soc; fac adv, Nat Bd Black Am Law Students; bd dir, Gulf Coast Legal Found; Nat Bar Asn Comm Legal Educ; ed bd, Tex Lawyer; life mem, Houston Chamber Comm; bd dir, Law Sch Admis Coun; chmn, Minority Affairs Comt, Law Sch Admis Coun; fel Am Bar Found; fel Tex Bar Found; fel Nat Bar Found; fel Houston Bar Found; Parlimentarian Stud Bar Asn; adv, Alpha Phi Alpha Soc Fraternity; pres, Sophomore Class; pres, Stud Body; pres, Alpha Phi Alpha Soc Fraternity; Sickle Cell Found; Gulf Coast Legal Found; founding mem, 100 Black Men Metrop Houston; bd dir, IMANI House, 2000-; life mem, Nat Asn Advan Colored Prople. **Home Addr:** 5318 Calhoun Rd, Houston, TX 77021, **Home Phone:** (713)747-4737. **Business Addr:** Executive Vice President, Distinguished Professor of Law, Texas Southern University, 220 Hannah Hall 3100 Cleburne Ave, Houston, TX 77004, **Business Phone:** (713)313-1122.

## DOUGLAS, DR. JANICE GREEN

Physician, educator. **Personal:** Born Mar 19, 1943; daughter of Louis and Electa Green; married Thee Baltimore; children: 2. **Educ:** Langston Col, eng & music; Meharry Med Sch, Nashville, Tenn, MD, 1968, DDS; Vanderbilt Univ, NIH fel endocrinol, 1973. **Career:** Nat Inst Health, sr staff fel, 1973; Case Western Res Univ Sch Med, 1981-, prof med & prof physiol & biophys, 1984-; Univ Hosp Cleveland, corres, dir hypertension, 2003-. **Orgs:** Inst Med; Am Soc Clin Invest; Asn Am Physicians; fel Am Heart Asn; bd dir, Am Bd Internal Med; Int Soc Hypertension Blacks; Am Soc Clin Invest & Asn Am Physicians; Nat Acad Med. **Honors/Awds:** Intern of the Year, 1969. **Special Achievements:** First woman promoted to or appointed to the rank of professor of Medicine at Case Western Reserve University Medical School; Co-Authored : Pathophysiology of Hypertension in Blacks, Hypertension in Ethnic Populations. **Business Addr:** Professor, Case Western Reserve University, Rm W165 10900 Euclid Ave, Cleveland, OH 44106-4982, **Business Phone:** (216)368-4340.

## DOUGLAS, JOE, JR.

Government official, firefighter. **Personal:** Born Jun 9, 1928, Topeka, KS; son of Joseph J and Imogene Taylor; married Nathalia Jean Washington; children: Shelley Jolana & Douglas Wilder. **Educ:** Washburn Univ, attended 1949. **Career:** Firefighter (retired); City Topeka, firefighter, 39 yrs, app fire chief, 1983-89; USD No 501, bd mem, 1977-85. **Orgs:** Topeka Coun Churches; First Conf Chair Kans E Conf Clomm Relig & Race United Methodist Ch; bd dir, Boys Club Am, 1971-73; chmn, comt Adv, Comn Educ, 1975-76; bd pres, USD No 501, 1980-81 & 1983-84; bd dir, Boy Scouts Am; Mayor's Disaster Adv Coun, Mayor's Task Force Illiteracy, Sunset Optimists; Topeka YWCA. **Honors/Awds:** Dean, United Methodist Youth Fel Inst, 1971-73; Presidential Citation for Extraordinary Serv Boys Club Am, 1972-73; Kans Friends Educ plaque winner; Annual Local Govt Official Category, 1986. **Home Addr:** 1811 SE Ind Ave, Topeka, KS 66607, **Home Phone:** (785)233-8502.

## DOUGLAS, JOHN DANIEL

Government official, educator, association executive. **Personal:** Born Aug 18, 1945, Richburg, SC; son of James E and Alberta Cousar; married Mildred Barber; children: Maurice, Jermel, GiGi & LaShawn. **Educ:** Morris Col, BS, 1967; Winthrop Col, MEduc, 1976. **Career:** Chester Co Schs, teacher, 1967-68; Carolina Community Actions Inc, head start dir, 1968-70; York Co Family Ct, chief probation officer, 1970-75; Charlotte-Mecklinburg Sch, teacher, 1975-80; Rock Hill Sch Dist No 3, teacher, 1980-; York Co, councilman; Union Co Sch, NC, 1988-. **Orgs:** Pres, Rock Hill Nat Asn Advan Colored People, 1976-81; pol action chmn, Menzel Shiner, 1980-; councilman, York Co Dist No 4, 1980-; chmn, Destinations Human Serv Trans, 1982-; chmn, Pub Works York Co, 1982-; financial secy, Sterling Elk Lodge, 1983-; bd dir, SC Asn Counties, 1986; exec admin asst, SC Asn Elks, 1986; chair, N Cent Med Clin, 1999-2001. **Honors/Awds:** Service to Mankind, Rock Hill Nat Asn Advan Colored People, 1979; Community Service Award, Elk-Sterling Lodge No 344 Rock Hill, 1980; Scroll of Honor, Omega Psi Phi Fraternity, 1983; Humanitarian Menzel Shiner, 1984; Elk of the Year, 1986; Man of the Year, Rock Grove AME Zion Church, 1986; Man of the Year, Elks, 1988; ID Quincy New man Award for Outstanding Service, 1991. **Home Addr:** 1205 Ogden Rd, PO Box 11578, Rock Hill, SC 29730-4935, **Home Phone:** (803)517-0519. **Business Addr:** Councilman, York County District 4, PO Box 11578, Rock Hill, SC 29731, **Business Phone:** (803)296-3120.

## DOUGLAS, JOSEPH FRANCIS, SR.

Educator. **Personal:** Born Oct 31, 1926, Indianapolis, IN; son of Louis Joseph (deceased) and Marion Elizabeth Brabham (deceased); married Edna; children: Marian E, Joseph Jr, Marie A & Barbara J. **Educ:** Purdue Univ, BSEE, 1948; Univ Mo, MSEE, 1962. **Career:** Educator (retired); Rural Electrification Admin, 1948-56; Southern Univ, 1956-64; Am Mach & Foundry Co, 1964-66; Pa State Univ, engr instr, 1966-70, assoc prof, 1970-87; engr consult, 1987-92; Ministry Educ, Sci & Technol, math teacher; Penn State's Commonwealth, assoc dean. **Orgs:** Chmn, Inst Elect & Electronics Engrs, 1949-, dir, 1985-86; Reg prof engr, 1954-96, Am Soc Engineering Educ, 1969-80; bd dir, York Hosp, PA, 1982-92; adv bd, Pa State York, 1986-96; Nat Asn Adv Colored People; Human Rel Adv Coun; York-Adams Area Coun; Boy Scouts Am; Community Action Prog. **Honors/Awds:** The Role of the Engineering Teacher, Conf Rec, Tucson, 1972; Lind back Award for Distinguished Teaching, 1972; Recipient of a Centennial Medal of the IEEE in 1984. **Special Achievements:** Contributor, "Understanding Batteries," technical paper, Volunteers in Technical Assistance Publication (VITA), 1985; special biography, included in various publications on outstanding African American scientists; The First African American Professor of Engineering at Penn State University. **Home Addr:** 2755 Trout Run Rd, PO Box 236, York, PA 17406-6957, **Home Phone:** (717)755-8308.

## DOUGLAS, MAE ALICE

Executive director, association executive. **Personal:** Born Dec 26, 1951, Rowland, NC. **Educ:** Univ NC, Greensboro, NC, BA, sociol, 1972. **Career:** Comn Status women, adminr, 1973-74; CIBA-GEIGY Corp, eeo coord, 1974-77, personnel mgr, mgr human resources, 1983-86, dir human resources; Ciba-Geigy Corp; Cox Commun Inc, exec vpres & chief people officer & sr vpres & chief people officer, 1995-. **Orgs:** Leadership Greensboro Chamber Com, 1979-80; planning div, United Way, 1980; prof rev comt State Dept Pub Instr, 1981-82; Am Soc Personnel Admin; Women's Prof Forum; bd mem, Women Cable Telecommun Found; Socs Human Resources Mgt, Nat Asn African Am Human Resources; Grady Health Syst Found; bd dir, Nat Asn Multi-Ethnicity Commun. **Honors/Awds:** Outstanding Young Women of America, 1975; Outstanding Young Woman Greensboro Jaycettes, 1978; Outstanding Woman in Business, YWCA, 1980; Best Operator Women, Working Mother Media, 2003, 2004, 2005; First Pioneer Award, NAMIC, 2005; CTHRA's Excellence in HR Award, 2008; NAMIC Mid-Atlantic First Diversity Champion Award. **Home Addr:** 3302 Wedgewood Pl, Greensboro, NC 27403. **Business Addr:** Senior Vice President, Chief People Officer, Cox Communications Inc, 1400 Lake Hearn Dr, Atlanta, GA 30319, **Business Phone:** (404)843-5000.

## DOUGLAS, NICHOLAS

Government official, manager. **Career:** Bur Land Mgt-Dept of Energy, Bakersfield, Calif, div minerals chief, field mgr, sr policy adv, Minerals, Realty & Resources Protection, dist mgr, oil shale policy advisor, currently, atty, Las Vegas, Nev. **Orgs:** Sr Exec Asn; Soc Petrol Engrs AIME. **Home Addr:** 2510 Maylen Cir, Anchorage, AK 99516. **Business Addr:** Oil Shale Policy Advisor, Bureau of Land Management, 222 W 7th Ave Sutie 13, Anchorage, AK 99513, **Business Phone:** (907)271-5960.

**DOUGLAS, OMAR**
Administrator, football player. **Personal:** Born Jun 3, 1972, New Orleans, LA. **Educ:** Univ Minn, attended 1994; Univ St Thomas Sch Bus, MBA. **Career:** New York Giants, 1994, 1996-98, wide receiver, 1995; The MONY Group, hr intern & hr consult, 1998; Thomson Reuters, sr hr generalist, 1999-2002; The Thomson Corp, Jostens, hr mgr, 2002-03; Deloitte Consult, mgr, hr transformation, 2004-07; Gen Mills, hr mgr, 2007-09, sr mgr, 2009-10, dir talent & orgn effectiveness, 2010-13, dir human resources int, 2013-14; Nike, sr HR dir, 2014-, sr dir, 2015-. **Honors/Awds:** Athlete of the Year, 1994. **Business Addr:** Director Human Resources International, General Mills Inc, 1 Gen Mills Blvd, Minneapolis, MN 55426, **Business Phone:** (763)764-7600.

**DOUGLAS, DR. SAMUEL HORACE**
Educator. **Personal:** Born May 10, 1928, Ardmore, OK; children: Carman Irving, Samuel & Emanuel. **Educ:** Bishop Col, BS, 1950; Okla State Univ, BS, 1959; MS, 1963; PhD, 1967. **Career:** Praire View A&M Univ Tex, asst prof Math, 1959-63; dept chmn, 1962-63; felSci Fac, 1963-67; Grambling Col La, math prof, 1967-; dept chmn, 1967-. **Orgs:** Mem Panel Spl & Probs Minority Groups; Am Math Soc; London Math Soc; Math Asn Am; consult Com Undergrad Prog Math dir summer & inservice Insts Math, NSF-Grambling Col, 1968-71; vis lectr, vice chmn, La-Ms sect, Math Asn Am; Pi Mu Epsilon; Alpha Phi Alpha. **Honors/Awds:** Distinguished Service Award, Pi Mu Epsilon, 1970. **Home Addr:** PO Box 564, Grambling, LA 71245, **Home Phone:** (318)247-6796.

**DOUGLAS, SHANNON**
Executive, founder (originator). **Career:** First Impressions Group, founder, 1999; Mint Chocolate Entertainment, owner, currently. **Business Addr:** Owner, Mint Chocolate Entertainment, 13591 St Marys St, Detroit, MI 48227-1732, **Business Phone:** (313)835-7353.

**DOUGLAS, SHERMAN**
Basketball player. **Personal:** Born Sep 15, 1966, Washington, DC; married Denise; children: Demi. **Educ:** Syracuse Univ, Syracuse, NY, attended 1989. **Career:** Basketball player (retired); Miami Heat, guard, 1989-92; Boston Celtics, 1992-95; Dolpher's Dolphins, 1994-95; MBA, Milwaukee Bucks, 1995-97; Cleveland Cavaliers, 1997; NJ Nets, 1997-98, 1999-2001; Los Angeles Clippers, 1998-99.

**DOUGLAS, SUZZANNE**
Actor. **Personal:** Born Apr 12, 1957, Chicago, IL; daughter of Donald Sr and Lois Mae; married Roy Jonathan Cobb; children: Jordan & Victoria. **Educ:** Ill State Univ, attended 1978. **Career:** The Last Weekend, producer, 1998; Stage roles: Three Penny Opera, Broadway, co-star with Sting; Drowning Crow, world premiere; A Night in Tunisia; Jar the Floor, Charlotte Repertory Theatre; Agnes of God, George Street Playhouse; TV series: "Purlie", 1981; "A Man Called Hawk", 1989; "The Cosby Show", 1990; "The Knife and Gun Club", 1990; "Great Performances", 1991; "Against the Law", 1990-91; "ABC Afterschool Specials", 1991; "I'll Fly Away", 1992; "Condition: Critical", 1992; "American Playhouse", 1993; "Search for Grace", 1994; "The Parent 'Hood", 1995-99; "NYPD Blue", 1996; "Promised Land", 1997-98; "Touched by an Angel", 1999; "Student Affairs", 1999; "The Parkers", 1999-2000; Law & Order Special Victims Unit, 2001; "Sounder", 2003; "Law & Order: Criminal Intent", 2004; "Mad Hops", 2004; "The Good Wife", 2010; "Are We There Yet?", 2011. Films: Tap; I'll Do Anything; Chain of Desire; How Stella Got Her Groove Back; Inkwell; Jason's Lyric; The School of Rock, 2003. co-starred with Forrest Whittaker; Inkwell, featured lead, co-starred with Joe Morton; Touched By An Angel; The Parkers, recurring; stage role, Drowning Crow, world premiere; Sounder, The School of Rock; stage, A Night in Tunisia; Sunday on the Rocks, 2004; Changing the Game, 2012. **Orgs:** Camp Giddiup; Athletes Against Abuse; Jackie Robinson Found; Marylawn Oranges Acad, 1995; Royce Clayton Found Sickle Cell; UNCF; trustee, George St Playhouse, 2001-02; USTA, community spec populations; honorary mem, Delta Sigma Theta Sorority Inc; lifetime mem, Girl Scouts Am; Nat Coun Negro Women; lifetime mem, Sigma Alpha Lambda; lifetime mem, Jack & Jill. **Honors/Awds:** Mary Martin Award, 1987; Nat Asn Advan Colored People Image Award, Tap, 1989; Athletes Against Drugs; two time Image Award winner; Black Osca; Reel Award; Black Reel Award, 2004. **Special Achievements:** First African Am to play the head role in Wit, NJ Premiere, George St Playhouse. **Home Addr:** 504 Summit Ave, Maplewood, NJ 07040. **Business Addr:** Actress, 13400 Chandller Blvd, Sherman Oaks, CA 91401, **Business Phone:** (818)990-4706.

**DOUGLAS, WALTER EDMOND, SR.**
Association executive, car dealer. **Personal:** Born Aug 22, 1933, Hamlet, NC; married Retha Hughes; children: Petra, Walter Jr & Mark. **Educ:** NC Cent Univ, BS, acct, 1954, MBA, bus & acct, 1955; Wayne State Univ, Hon LLD, 2013. **Career:** Int Revenue Serv Data Ctr, br chief, 1968-69, asst chief syst div, 1969-70, chief mgt staff, 1970-71, asst dir, 1971-72; New Detroit, from vpres to pres, 1972-85; DHT Tranp Inc, pres, 1979-2002; Avis Ford Inc, chmn, 1986-; ACG, dir, chmn, 1997; Fed Home Loan Bank, Indianapolis, dir; Jaguar/Land Rover Dealer, pres, 2005-07; Tuskegee Inst. **Orgs:** Vice chmn, Henry Ford Health Syst, bd mem, 1979-2010; bd mem, Detroit Symphony Orchestra Hall, 1980-; bd mem, AAA Mich, 1991-2006; dir, Automobile Club Mich, 1992, chmn, 2003; chmn, Auto Club Group, dir, 1997-; chair, Health Alliance Plan, United Way; bd dir & former chmn, Skillman Found; bd dir, Oakland Univ Found; bd dir, NCCU Found; bd dir, AAA; bd dir, Henry Health Ford Syst; Found Southeast Mich; bd, Tiger Woods Found; chmn, Auto Club Group; chmn external affairs comt, Charles H Wright Mus African Am Hist; bd mem, Wayne State Univ Found; Community Found Southeast Mich; N Carolina Cent Univ Found & First Tee Mich; hon trustee, Henry Ford Health Syst Inc; Tuskegee Inst Ala; bd trustee, Community Found Southeastern Mich; WSU Sch Med. **Honors/Awds:** Liberty Bell Award, Detroit Bar Asn, 1975; Award from President Reagan Exemplary Youth Development Program, 1984; Honorary Doctorate, NC Cent Univ, 1998; Honorary Doctorate, Wayne State Univ, 2013. **Home Addr:** 1189 Lone Pine Woods Dr, Bloomfield Hills, MI 48302. **Business Addr:** Chairman, Avis Ford Inc, 29200 Telegraph Rd, Southfield, MI 48034, **Business Phone:** (248)355-7500.

**DOUGLAS, WILLARD H., JR.**
Judge. **Personal:** Born Feb 4, 1932, Amherst, VA; married Jane O Eggleston; children: Willard III & Wendelin Janna. **Educ:** Va Union Univ, AB, 1957; Howard Univ Sch Law, JD, 1962. **Career:** Judge (retired); Teamsters Union, admin asst bd monitors, 1960-61; US Copyright Off, staff atty, 1961-62; US Comn Civil Rights, staff atty, 1962-65; Pvt Pract, 1965-69; asst Commonwealth atty, 1969-74; Juv & Domestic Rels Dist Ct Commonwealth Va, chief judge, 1974-89; Richmond Juv Domestic Rels Dist, judge. **Orgs:** Am Bar Asn; Va State Bar; Old Dom Bar Asn; Richmond Criminal Law Asn; Richmond Trial Lawyers Asn; Va Trial Lawyers Asn; Kappa Alpha Psi Frat Bd Richmond Area Psychiat Clin; Richmond Epilepsy Found; Big Bros Ferrum Col Va Wesleyan Col; Lay Leader Wesley Memorial United Methodist Church; Asn Lay Leader Va Conf Bd Laity & Richmond Dist Eastern Prov; bd mem, Nat Coun Juv & Family Ct Judges, 1986-89; United Methodist Church, Judicial Coun, 1984-92; exec comt, World Methodist Coun, 2001-06. **Honors/Awds:** Achievement Award, Richmond Alumni & Petersburg Alumni, 1974; Man of the Year, Richmond Alumnae Delta Sigma Theta, 1974. **Special Achievements:** First African-American judge in Virginia; States First full time black Judge. **Home Addr:** 606 Edgehill Rd, PO Box 26941, Richmond, VA 26941, **Home Phone:** (804)321-4222.

**DOUGLASS, JOHN W.**
State government official, executive director. **Educ:** Lincoln Univ, BA, 1964; Johns Hopkins Univ, MA, 1966. **Career:** Rohm & Hass, fel, 1964; Gilman, fel, 1964; Morgan State Col, instr, 1966-68; Mutual Funds, salesman, 1967-68; RL Johnson Realty Co; Baltimore City Coun, clerk, 1967-68; Balitmore City Planning Dept, consult, 1970-71; Md House Delegates, mem, 1971-94; Md Dept Assessments & Taxation, dep dir, 1995-2003; State Retirement & Pension Syst Md, employee systs rep, 2004-,07 bd trustee, 2004-; Ideal Fed Savings Bank, vpres, currently. **Orgs:** New Dem Club, 1968-; Adj Neighborhood Improv Asn, 1969-; bd trustees, Md State Retirement & Pension Syst; chmn, Joint Budget & Audit Comt, 1975-88. **Honors/Awds:** Am Legion Award, 1956; Am Chem Soc Award, 1964; Norman E Gaskin's Prize, 1964; Eastern LI Ward, 1964; Certificate of Achievement, Morgan State Col, 1968, 1969. **Home Addr:** 1535 E North Ave, Baltimore, MD 21213-1428, **Home Phone:** (410)752-6653. **Business Addr:** Board of Trustee, Maryland State Retirement & Pension System, 120 E Baltimore St, Baltimore, MD 21202-1600, **Business Phone:** (410)625-5555.

**DOUGLASS, HON. LEWIS LLOYD**
Judge. **Personal:** Born Dec 12, 1930, Brooklyn, NY; son of Lloyd and Cornelia; married Doris Wildy; children: David & Lori. **Educ:** Brooklyn Col, BS, 1953; St John's Law Sch, JD, 1956. **Career:** Judge (retired); Eastern Dist New York, asst us atty, 1960; Fed Prosecutor's Off, asst US atty, 1961-65; Bedford-Stuyvesant Corp, dep dir, 1965; Housing Redevelop Agency, exec dept dir, 1965-68; Housing Develop Orgn, gen coun, 1968-71; Black Enterprise Mag, exec vpres, 1972-75; NY State Prison Syst, exec dep comnr, 1975-78; New York Criminal Ct, judge, 1978-82; New York Ct Claims, 1987-99; Supreme Ct NY, actg judge, 1982-87, judge, 1999; Kings County Foreclosure Mediation Part, judicial hearing officer, 2006; Petroff Law Firm. **Orgs:** Chair, NY State Comn Minorities; Phi Beta Sigma. **Honors/Awds:** Lifetime Achievement Award, New York Ct Claims, 2006. **Special Achievements:** Publication: "Investing in Real Estate", Black Enterprise, 1972. **Home Addr:** 16625 Powells Cove Blvd Apt 12, Whitestone, NY 11357. **Business Addr:** Judge, Supreme Court, 360 Adams St, New York, NY 11201-3712, **Business Phone:** (718)643-5086.

**DOUGLASS, M. LORAYNE**
Educator. **Personal:** Born May 11, 1927, Ft. Gibson, OK; daughter of Wallace McNac and Ollie Nivens McNac; married Carlton R. **Educ:** Langston Univ, BA, 1948; Okla Univ, MEd, 1956. **Career:** Educator (retired); Ponca City Okla Schs, classroom teacher, 1950-54; Okla City Schs, classroom teacher, 1954-63; Los Angeles Unified Sch Dist, coordr, consult, parent educ coordr & conf planner, curric adv, resource teacher, classroom teacher, 1963-87. **Orgs:** United Teachers Los Angeles, 1963-87; Founders Church Relig Sci, 1965-; Nat Sorority Phi Delta Kappa, Far Western, regional dir, 1983-87; life mem, Nat Asn Advan Colored People, 1987. **Home Addr:** 3501 Floresta Ave, Los Angeles, CA 90043, **Home Phone:** (323)291-1830.

**DOUGLASS, MAURICE GERRARD**
Football player, football coach. **Personal:** Born Feb 12, 1964, Muncie, IN; married Camela; children: Shiloh, Moses & Maurice. **Educ:** Coffeyville Community Col, attended; Univ Ky, attended. **Career:** Football player (retired), football coach; Chicago Bears, defensive back, 1986-94; New York Giants, 1995-96; Trotwood-Madison High Sch, head coach, 2001-; Springfield High Sch, head coach, 2014. **Home Addr:** 1021 Sunset Dr, Englewood, OH 45322-2252. **Business Addr:** Head Coach, Trotwood-Madison High School, 4440 N Union Rd, Trotwood, OH 45426, **Business Phone:** (937)854-0878.

**DOUGLASS, DR. MELVIN ISADORE**
Educator, clergy. **Personal:** Born Jul 21, 1948, Manhattan, NY; son of Isadore and Esther Tripp. **Educ:** Vincennes Univ, AS, early childhood educ, 1970; Tuskegee Inst, BS, early childhood & elem educ, 1973; Morgan State Univ, MS, urban elem educ, 1975; NY Univ, MA, orgn admin supv, 1977; Columbia Univ, EdM, curric & teaching, 1978, EdD, PhD, 1981; Harvard Univ, cert, urban sch leadership, 2003. **Career:** Queensboro Soc Prev Cruelty C Inc, child care worker, 1973-75; Bronx Pub Sch, dean stud & teacher, New York, 1973-75; Amistad Child Day Care Ctr, sch age prog dir, Jamaica, 1976-77; City Univ, head track & field coach, 1981-83; Beck Mem Day Care Ctr, admin dir, 1983-84; Dept Juv Justice, primary sch dept chair, 1984-85, ombudsman, 1985-88; John Jay Col Criminal Justice, adj instr, 1988-89; Stimson Mid Sch, chmn, eng, reading & social studies, 1988-; Col New Rochelle, adj instr, sociol & african am studies, 1992-2005; Long Island Inst Prof Studies, instr educ, 1998-; Metrop Col NY, adj prof, social sci, 1999-2005; Minority Educr Network Inc, founder, pres & chief exec off, 1999-; Douglass Group, founder & chief exec officer; Brooklyn Col Grad Sch Educ, adj asst prof, New York, 2000; Harvard Grad Sch Educ, prin facilitator, 2007. **Orgs:** Pres, fed Jamaica Track Club, 1973-; Nat Educ Asn, 1973-; bd dir, Black Exp Theatre, 1982-; Nat Black Child Devel Inst, 1982-; bd dir, Queens Coun Arts, 1983-86; bd dir, Nu Omicron Chap OPP Day Care Ctr, 1984-; Prince Hall Masonry; 100 Hundred Black Men; pres, bd dir, NY Transit Br NCP, 1984-90; co-chp, Educ Comm NY State Conf NCP 1986-89; chp, Anti-Drug Comm Metro Coun Nat Asn Advan Colored People Br, 1986-89; Jamaica EW Adolescent Pregnancy Prev Consortium, 1986-89; bd dir, Long Island Tuskegee Alumni Asn, 1986-, vpres, 1987-89; bd dir, United Black Men Queens County Inc, 1986-89; basileus Nu Omicron Chap OPP Frat, 1987-88; assisting minister, asst pastor, co-chair, educ comt, City Black Leadership Coun, New York, 1987-88; Calvary Baptist Church, 1987-91; bd dir, Dance Explosion, 1987-97; area policy bd no 12, Subunit 2, 1987-99; S Huntington Chmns Asn, 1988-; Queens adv bd, NY Urban League, 1988-93; Am Fedn Sch Adminrs, 1988-; Coun Adminrs & Supvrs, 1988-; community adv bd, City NY Dept Correction, Queens House Detention Men, 1991-94; community adv bd, Pub Sch 40, Queens, NY, 1992-97; Ancient Arabic Order Nobles Mystic Shrine; Omega Psi Phi Fraternity, Phi Delta Kappa Fraternity; SPP Fraternity; bd mem, Ny Cult Educ Trust Bd. **Home Addr:** 395 Stuyvesant Ave, Brooklyn, NY 11233, **Home Phone:** (718)778-4661. **Business Addr:** Chairman, Stimson Jr High School, 401 Oakwood Rd, Huntington Station, NY 11746, **Business Phone:** (631)425-5432.

**DOURDAN, GARY ROBERT**
Actor, musician. **Personal:** Born Dec 11, 1966, Philadelphia, PA; son of Robert Durdin and Sandy; married Roshumba Williams; children: Nyla (Jennifer Sutton) & Lyric (Cynthia Hadden). **Career:** Actor, currently, musician, record producer; Films: Weekend at Bernie's II, 1993; The Paper, 1994; Sunset Park, 1996; Playing God, 1997; Alien: Resurrection, 1997; Get That Number, 1997; Thursday, 1998; Scar City, 1998; The Weekend, 1999; Trois, 2000; Dancing in September, 2000; Imposter, 2002; Slipping Into Darkness, 2003; Black August, 2007; Perfect Stranger, 2007; TV films: "The Good Fight", 1992; "Laurel Avenue", 1993; "Keys", 1994; "Rendezvous", 1999; "King of the World", 2000; "Fire!", 2008; "The Magnificent Cooly-T", 2009. TV series: "A Different World", 1991-92; "Swift Justice", 1996; "Lyric Cafe", 2002; "Loco Motives", 2006; "Leaving Las Vegas", 2007; TV guest appearances: "New York Undercover", 1994; "The Office", 1995; "Swift Justice", 1996; "Lois & Clark", 1996; "Seven Days", 1999; "Soul Food", 2000; "CSI", 2000-08; Soundtrack: Billabong Odyssey, 2003; Christine, 2012. musician; record producer. **Honors/Awds:** Seattle Int Film Fest Citation Excellence Ensemble Cast Performance, New American Cinema Award, 2000; Image Award; Outstanding Supporting Actor Drama, 2003. **Business Addr:** Actor, Paradigm, 10100 Santa Monica Blvd Suite 2500, Los Angeles, CA 90067.

**DOVE, DR. PEARLIE C.** **See Obituaries Section.**

**DOVE, RITA FRANCES**
Poet, educator, writer. **Personal:** Born Aug 28, 1952, Akron, OH; daughter of Ray A and Elvira E; married Fred Viebahn; children: Aviva Dove-Viebahn. **Educ:** Miami Univ, Oxford, OH, BA, 1973; Univ Tuebingen W Ger, attended 1975; Univ Iowa, MFA, 1977. **Career:** Tuskegee Inst, writer residence, 1982; AZ State Univ, asst prof, 1981-84, assoc prof, 1984-87, full prof, 1987-89; Univ Va, full prof Eng, 1989-93, Commonwealth prof Eng, 1993-; Univ Va, Shannon Ctr Advan Studies, fel, 1989-; poet laureate, US, 1993-95; spec cons Poetry, Lib Cong Bicentennial, 1999-2000; poet laureate, Va, 2004-06. Poems: Ten Poems, 1977; The Only Dark Spot In The Sky, 1980; The Yellow House on the Corner, 1980; Mandolin, 1982; Mus, 1983; Thomas & Beulah, 1986; The Other Side of the House, 1988; Grace Notes, 1989; Selected Poems, 1993; Lady Freedom Among Us, 1994; Mother Love, 1995; On the Bus with Rosa Parks, 1999; Am Smooth, 2004; Sonata Mulattica, 2009; Collected Poems 1974-2004, 2016. Short stories: Fifth Sunday, 1985. Novels: Through The Ivory Gate, 1992. Drama: The Darker Face of the Earth, 1994. Essays: The Poet's World, 1995; "The Poet's Choice", The Wash Post, weekly column, 2000-02. **Orgs:** Bd mem, Nat Forum Phi Kappa Phi Jour, 1984-89; lit adv panel, Nat Endowment Arts, 1984-86; chair, Poetry Grants Panel, Nat Endowment Arts, 1985; bd dir, Asn Writing Prog, 1985-88; pres, Asn Writing Prog, 1986-87; assoc ed, Callaloo Jour Afro-Am Arts & Lett, 1986-98, adv ed, Gettysburg Rev, 1987-, Tri Quart, 1988-, Ploughshares, 1992-, Ga Rev, 1994-, Bellingham Rev, 1996-, Int Quart, 1997-, Poetry Int, 1997-, Callaloo Jour Afro-Am Arts & Lett, 1998-, Mid-Am Rev, 1998-, Hunger Mountain, 2003-, Am Poetry Rev, 2005-; PEN Club Am Ctr; chancellor Acad Am Poets, 2006-2011; adv bd, NC Writers' Network, 1991-99; Poet's Corner, Cathedral St John Divine, elector, 1991-2002; adv bd, Thomas Jefferson Ctr Freedom Expression, 1994-; adv bd, VA Ctr Creative Arts, 1994-; adv bd, Live Arts, Charlottesville, 1994-; adv bd, Civilization, Mag Libr Cong, 1994-97; Coun Scholars, Libr Cong, 1994-; consult, Woman to Woman Lifetime, Lifetime TV, 1994; sen Phi Beta Kappa, 1994-2000; bd mem, Charlottesville-Albemarle Opera Soc, 1995; adv bd, US Civil War Ctr, 1995-99; bd gov, Univ CA, Humanities Res Inst, 1996-2000; chair, poetry jury, Pulitzer Bd Columbia Univ, 1997; bd dir, Poetry Daily, 2002-; Am Heritage Dict Usage Panel, 2002-; adv bd, Stud Achievement & Advocacy Serv, 2002-; adv bd, DuBois Ctr Am Hist & Cult, 2005-; adv bd, Givens Found Afr Am Lit, 2005-; Chubb fel Yale Univ, 2007; Am Philos Soc; Am Acad Arts & Sci; Am Acad Arts & Lett. **Honors/Awds:** Presidential Scholar, The Pres US Am, 1970; Fulbright Scholar, US Govt, 1974-75; Literature Grant, Nat Endowment Arts, 1978, 1989; Portia Pittman Fel, Nat Endowment Arts, 1982; Guggenheim Fel, Guggenheim Found, 1983-84; Callaloo Award, 1986; Lavan Younger Poet Award, The Acad Am Poets, 1986; Pulitzer Prize for Poetry, Pulitzer Bd Columbia Univ, 1987; General Electric Foundation Award for Younger Writers, 1987; Ohio Governor's Award, 1988; Bellagio Residency, Rockefeller Found, 1988; Ohioana Book Award for Grace Notes, 1990; Literary Lion, NY Pub Libr, 1991; Ohio Women's Hall of Fame, 1991; Phi Beta Kappa Poet, Harvard Univ, 1993; Poetry Reading at The White House, State Dinner in honor of Nat Medal of Arts recipients, 1993; Va Col Stores Asn Book Award for Through the Ivory Gate, 1993; Woman of the Year Award, Glamour Mag, 1993; NAACP Great American Artist Award, NAACP, 1993; Renaissance Forum Award, Leadership Lit Arts, Folger Shakespeare Libr, Wash DC, 1994; Ohioana Book Award for Selected Poems, 1994; Distinguished Achievement Medal, Miami Univ Alumni Asn, 1994; Golden Plate Award, Am Acad Achievement, 1994; Carl Sandburg Award, Intl Platform Asn, 1994; The Kennedy Ctr Fund for New American Plays Award, 1995; Heinz Award in Arts & Humanities, 1996; National Humanities Medal / Charles Frankel prize, US

Pres, 1996; Literary Lion, New York Pub Libr, 1996; Honorary Doctor of Letters, Univ Pa, 1996; Honorary Doctor of Letters, Spelman Col, 1996; Honorary Doctor of Letters, Univ NC, 1997; Honorary Doctor of Letters, Univ Notre Dame, 1997; Honorary Doctor of Letters, Northeastern Univ, 1997; Sara Lee Frontrunner Award, 1997; Writers for Writers Award, Barnes & Noble, 1997; Distinguished Woman Award, Nat Asn Women Educ, 1997; featured author on Ugandan postage stamp, 1997; Levinson Prize, Poetry Mag, 1998; Honorary Doctor of Letters, Columbia Univ, 1998; Honorary Doctor of Letters, SUNY Brock port, 1999; Honorary Doctor of Letters, Washington & Lee Univ, 1999; John Frederick Nims Translation Prize, with Fred Viebahn, 1999; Library Lion, NY Pub Libr, 2000; Duke Ellington Lifetime Achievement Award, 2001; Honorary Doctor of Letters, Howard Univ, 2001; Honorary Doctor of Letters, Pratt Ins, 2001; Emily Couric Women's Leadership Award, 2003; Honorary Doctor of Letters, Skidmore Col, 2004; Common Wealth Award of Distinguished Service, 2006; Lifetime Achievement Award, Library of Virginia, 2008; Fulbright Lifetime Achievement Medal, 2009; Premio Capri, Italy, 2009; Hurston/Wright Legacy Award, 2010; National Medal of Arts, US Pres, 2011; hon doctorates, Duke University, 2012; hon doctorates, Emerson College, 2013; hon doctorates, Emory University, 2013; hon doctorates, Yale University, 2014; Furious Flower Lifetime Achievement Award, 2014; Carole Weinstein Prize, 2014; Poetry and People International Prize, Guangdong, China, 2015; Stone Award for Lifetime Achievement, 2016. **Special Achievements:** Youngest & first African-American Poet Laureate, 1993-95; Second African-American to win Pulitzer Prize in Poetry. Only poet to be awarded both the National Humanities Medal and the National Medal of Arts. Editor: The Best American Poetry 2000; The Penguin Anthology of 20th Century American Poetry, 2011. **Business Addr:** Commonwealth Professor, University of Virginia, 219 Byran Hall, Charlottesville, VA 22904-4121, **Business Phone:** (434)924-6618.

### DOVE, DR. SHIRLEY L.
Executive. **Educ:** NC Wesleyan Col, BA, bus admin; E Carolina Univ, MA; NC State Univ, Community Col Leadership, PhD; Lenoir Community Col, attended 1975. **Career:** Sampson Community Col; Lenoir Community Col, vpres instrnl progs, vpres acad & stud serv, dean stud serv, exec vpres, 1975-. **Orgs:** Steering comt, NC Asn Community Col Instrnl Adminir. **Business Addr:** Executive Vice President, Vice President of Academic and Student Services, Lenoir Community College, 231 Hwy 58 S, Kinston, NC 28502-0188, **Business Phone:** (252)527-6223.

### DOWD, MARIA DENISE
Beautician, executive, writer. **Personal:** Born CA; married Curtis V; children: Lauren & Janelle. **Career:** African Am Women Tour, founder & exec producer, 1991-2004; Warm Spirit, dir, 2002-; Soul Journeys Inc, pres & founder, 2009-; PromoTrends Inc, pres. **Orgs:** Presenter, Divinity Christian Church Retreat; health & wellness columnist, Turning Pt Mag. **Honors/Awds:** The Spirit of Madam CJ Walker Award. **Special Achievements:** Author & Editor of numerous books. **Home Phone:** (619)229-7766. **Business Addr:** General Manager, Sol City Beauty Co, PO Box 152555, San Diego, CA 92195-2555, **Business Phone:** (619)750-8232.

### DOWDELL, DENNIS, JR.
Manager. **Personal:** Born Mar 8, 1945; son of Marjorie and Dennis; married Equinetta Cox; children: Malaika, Arianne & Cicely. **Educ:** Cent State Univ, BS, hist & polit sci, LHD; Cleveland State Univ Col Law, JD. **Career:** Cleveland Bd Educ, teacher, 1968-71; Legal Serv Org Indianapolis Inc, staff atty, 1971-72; US Dept Labor, Off Solicitor, trial atty, 1972-76, asst coun, OSHA, 1976-78, co-coun, Black Lung, 1978-80; Am Can Co, Compliance Plans & Litigation, dir, 1980-84, sr exec leadership positions human resources; Am Nat Can, Performance Plastics Div, vpres human resources, 1985-91; Henry Ford Health Syst, corp vpres human resources; Longaberger Co, vpres & human resource mgr; Lanyap Squared LLC, pres; Nat Asn Black Automotive Suppliers, pres; Exec Leadership Coun, Inst Leadership develop & res, exec dir, 2004, pres; Memorial Sloan Kettering Cancer Ctr, Chief Human Resources Off, vpres chief human resources, currently; US Dept Labor, sr atty. **Orgs:** Chmn, pres coun, Cent State Univ; bd dir, Nat Urban League, Black Exec Exchange Prog; Nat Urban League; Nat Asn Advan Colored People; Am Bar Asn; Nat Bar Asn; nat pres, Cent State Univ Nat Alumni Asn; exec leadership Coun, Omega Psi Phi Frat; Cent State Univ Found; Leadership Detroit; Detroit Urban League; nat bd dir, Alzheimer's Disand Related Dis Asn Inc; pres, 100 Black Men Greater Detroit; bd dir, Exec Leadership Found; vice chmn, Nat Alzheimer's Asn; Memorial Sloan Kettering; exec dir, Exec Leadership Couns Inst Leadership Develop & Res; vchair, Nat Alzheimers Asn; pres emer, 100 Black Men Greater Detroit; chair, BEEP Prog. **Honors/Awds:** Donald McGannon Award, Nat Urban League, 1998; David McGannon Award, Nat Urban League; Corporate Award, Exec Leadership Coun; Lifetime Achievement Award, Nat Urban League; Whitney M. Young Award, Nat Urban League. **Home Addr:** , Stamford, CT. **Business Addr:** Vice President of Human Resources, Memorial Sloan-Kettering Cancer Center, 1275 York Ave, New York, NY 10065, **Business Phone:** (212)639-2000.

### DOWDELL, KEVIN CRAWFORD
Executive director, consultant, chief executive officer. **Personal:** Born Oct 7, 1961, Schenectady, NY; son of Crawford and Doris; married Tia; children: London. **Educ:** Princeton Univ, BSE, mgt syst engineering, 1983; Wharton Bus Sch, MBA, finance & mkt, 1985. **Career:** Gen Elec Co, eng fel, 1979-80; Johnson & Johnson, leadership fel, Wharton, 1983-85; Strategic Planning Assocs, sr assoc & sr consult, 1985-89; Arthur A she's Safe Passage Found, Wash, DC, exec dir, 1989-93; Home Box Off, dept head & vpres new bus develop, 1994-2001; Vol Media LLC, founder & cheif exec officer, 2001-03; Boys & Girls Club, Wash, DC, interim pres & chief exec officer, chief opers officer, 2006-09. **Orgs:** Lifetime mem, Asn Black Princeton Alumni; pres, Princeton Soc Black Engrs, 1982-83; vice chmn, Whitney Young Conf, Wharton, 1984-85; co-founder, bd mem, Arthur A she's Safe Passage Found, 1989; vice chair, US Tennis Asn Nat Jr Tennis League, 2006-; bd mem, Harlem Jr Tennis & Educ Prog; founder, adv bd mem, 15 LOVE tennis prog. **Home Addr:** 211 Madison Ave, New York, NY 10016, **Home Phone:** (212)213-6287. **Business Addr:** Chief Operations Officer, Boys & Girls Club Of Greater Washington, 8380 Colesville Rd Suite 600, Silver Spring, MD 20910-6259, **Business Phone:** (301)562-2028.

### DOWDY, JAMES H.
Executive. **Personal:** Born Jun 3, 1932, New York, NY; son of Gertrude and Edward; married Elsia M; children: James Jr. **Educ:** D&B Bus Sch. **Career:** Limosine Serv; Real Estate firm; Vending Co; Contracting Co, 1962; Harlem Commonwealth Coun, exec dir; Commonwealth Holding Co, pres, chief exec officer, 1970-92; Eastcoast Devel Corp, pres, chief exec officer; Eastcoast Develop Community Tech Serv Inc, chmn, pres, currently. **Orgs:** Chmn, Vanguard Nat Bank; bd dir, Freedom Nat Bank, New York; bd mem, Harlem Interfaith Coun Serv; Presidential Task Force, 100 Black Men; bd mem, Cathedral Church St John Devine; chmn, Boys Choir Harlem. **Home Addr:** 253 W 138 St, New York, NY 10030, **Home Phone:** (212)690-6209. **Business Addr:** President, Chief Executive Officer, Eastcoast Development Community Technical Services Inc, 1250 Maryland Ave SW Suite C10, Washington, DC 20024-2166, **Business Phone:** (202)554-1970.

### DOWDY, DR. JOANNE KILGOUR
Educator. **Personal:** Born Nov 22, 1959, Port-of-Spain; daughter of Lennox Kilgour and Kathleen Kilgour. **Educ:** Juilliard Sch, Theater Ctr, BFA, theater, 1987; Teachers Col, MA; Columbia Univ, MAT, 1988; Univ NC, PhD, literacy studies, 1997. **Career:** Adam Clayton Powell Jr Jr High Sch, NY, teacher, 1989; New Hanover High Sch, Wilmington, NC, drama dir, 1990-92; Shaw Univ, Ctr Alternative Progs Educ, Wilmington, NC, eng instr, 1993; Off Learning Disabilities, Univ NC, Chapel Hill, acad consult, 1993, reading & writing instr, 1995; Literacy S, Durham, NC, literacy consult, 1995-96; Durham Tech Community Col, reading instr, 1996-97; Ga State Univ, asst prof, 1997-2001; Kent State Univ, Col Educ, assoc prof, prof, literacy studies, 2001-15. **Orgs:** Founding mem, Trinidad & Tobago Tv Workshop; pres, Black Church & Domestic Violence Inst, 2001-03; adv bd, GED Scholars Initiative KSU, 2002-03; adv bd, Ctr Int & Intercultural Educ, Kent State Univ, 2002-03; adv bd, Six Dist Compact ABLE, 2002-09; consult, Alchemy Inc, 2009-11. **Business Addr:** Professor, Kent State University, 404 White Hall, Kent, OH 44242-0001, **Business Phone:** (330)672-0639.

### DOWELL, CLYDE DONALD
Government official. **Personal:** Born Aug 19, 1938, Gordonsville, TN; son of Frances and LC; married Daisy; children: Sherry Green, Clyde D II, Marilyn Barnes & Tonja Hale. **Educ:** Wayne State Univ, BS, 1971; MBA, 1975. **Career:** City Detroit, jr typist, 1962-71, jr acct, 1971-73, semi sr acct, 1972-73, sr acct, 1973-74, prin acct, 1974-79, head acct, 1979-85, acct mgr, 1985-86, dep budget dir, 1986-93, dir pub works, 1994-2005. **Orgs:** Am Pub Works Asn; Detroit Zool Soc; Founder's Soc-Detroit Inst Arts; Nat Asn Assessing officers, 1979-85; lifetime mem, Nat Asn Advan Colored People, 1981; Precinct deleg Dem Party, 1989-93; exec bd, Urban Forum-American Public Works, 1995. **Home Addr:** 20429 Ardmore, Detroit, MI 48235-1510, **Home Phone:** (313)864-1849. **Business Addr:** Lifetime Member, National Association for the Advancement of Colored People, 4805 Mt Hope Dr, Baltimore, MD 21215, **Business Phone:** (410)366-3300.

### DOWELL-CERASOLI, PATRICIA R.
Government official. **Personal:** Born May 13, 1957, Bethpage, NY; daughter of Norman and Kathryn; married Paul; children: Justin David. **Educ:** Univ Rochester, Rochester, NY, BA, 1978; Univ Chicago, Chicago, IL, MA, 1980. **Career:** Dept Planning, City Chicago, Chicago, Ill, city planner, 1981-86; Mayor Off, City Chicago, Chicago, Ill, develop sub cabinet staff dir, 1987-89; Dept Planning City Chicago, Chicago, Ill, dep comnr, 1989. **Orgs:** Bd dir, Midwest Ctr Labor Res, 1989-; Lambda Alpha Land Econ Soc, 1990-; Nat Forum Black Pub Adminrs, 1990-; exec dir, Mid-South Planning & Develop Comn. **Business Addr:** IL.

### DOWERY, MARY A.
Educator. **Personal:** Born KY. **Educ:** Psychoanal Inst Training & Res, attended 1945; Knoxville Col, attended 1950; Atlanta Univ, MSW, 1952; Columbia Univ, attended 1964; NY Univ, attended 1965; Tulane Univ, attended 1975; Union Grad Sch. **Career:** Educator (retired); Einstein Med Col; Comm Ment Col; Comm Ment Health; Urban Renewal, Mobilization Youth Inc; Residential Treat Adolescent Girls; Calif Youth Authority; NY City Bd Educ; NY City, protestant cnc; social worker, 1953-65; Personnel By Dowery, founder & operator, 1965-71; Black Greeting Card "Uhuru", orgn publ, 1968-71; Ball St Univ, asst prof, arch, 1971-74. **Orgs:** Delta Sigma Theta; Asn Personnel Agys, NY City, 1965-69; Am Mgt Asn; Nat Asn Social Workers; Coun Social Work Educ; 100 Black Women, 1975-77; League Women Voters; NY Soc Sickle Cell Anemia; AU Alumni; Knoxville Col Alumni Asn; United Day Care Ctr; Bethel Home Boys; reviewer Nat Endowment Humanities. **Special Achievements:** Partic Mike Wallace Show, 1964; published Greeting Card Mag, 1970; Et Cetero Mag, 1964; Black Enter, 1970; Income Mag, 1970; Daily News, 1972; BusWeek Peps, 1969. **Home Addr:** 120 W 97th St Apt 13J, New York, NY 10025-9226, **Home Phone:** (212)864-5936.

### DOWKINGS, WENDY LANELL
Editor. **Personal:** Born Jun 24, 1964, Ft. Meade, MD; daughter of Bennie and Jessie Marbury. **Educ:** Univ Tex, El Paso, TX, 1984; Univ Tex, Austin, TX, BA, jour, 1986. **Career:** Fort Worth Star Telegram, Fort Worth, Tex, intern reporting, 1985; Austin Am Statesman, Tex, copy ed, 1985-86; Hartford Courant, Hartford, Conn, copy ed, 1986-89; Philadelphia Inquirer, Philadelphia, Pa, copy ed, 1989-. **Orgs:** Nat Asn Black Journalists, 1986-; vol fair coordr, Hartford Neighborhood Housing Asn, 1988-89; Conn Asn Black Communicators, 1988-89; Philadelphia Asn Black Journalists, 1991-. **Home Addr:** 1 Franklin Town Blvd Suite 1508, Philadelphia, PA 19102, **Home Phone:** (215)981-0722. **Business Addr:** Copy Editor, Philadelphia Inquirer, 400 N Broad St, Philadelphia, PA 19130, **Business Phone:** (215)854-2432.

### DOWNIE, DR. WINSOME ANGELA
Educator. **Personal:** Born Apr 14, 1948, Kingston; daughter of Frank G and Marie Angela Crarey; married Norbert W Rainford; children: Damien & Ayana. **Educ:** Barnard Col, New York, NY, BA, 1970, MA; Columbia Univ, New York, NY, 1974, MA, 1977, MPhil, 1977, PhD, 1985. **Career:** Columbia Univ, New York, NY, Pres's Fel, 1974; Kingsborough Community Col, instr, 1975-78; State Univ, New York, New Paltz, NY, instr, 1978; Manhattan Col, Dept Govt, asst prof gov, 1978-, chairperson, currently; Village Montebello, trustee, 2001-07, Dep Mayor, 2005-07. **Orgs:** Bd dir, Martin Luther King Ctr, 1988-92; chair, Church & Soc Work Area, United Methodist Church, 1990-; exec bd, Jamaican Cult & Civic Asn Rockland, 1991-; comt mem, Jack & Jill Rockland County; chair, Compact Team Viola Sch, Suffern, Rockland, NY; Nat Asn Advan Colored People, Spring Valley; Manhattan's Urban Affairs Prog. **Home Addr:** 39 Rose Hill Rd, Monticello, NY 12701, **Home Phone:** (914)369-0805. **Business Addr:** Assistant Professor of Government, Chairperson, Manhattan College, Manhattan Col Pkwy, Riverdale, NY 10471, **Business Phone:** (718)862-7292.

### DOWNING, DR. BEVERLY
Educational consultant, administrator. **Educ:** Livingstone Col, BS, health & phys educ, 1978; Hampton Univ, MA, sec educ, 1980; Mid Tenn Univ, DA, pedag, 1991. **Career:** Kaplan Higher Educ, dir educ, 2006-07; Ky State Univ, chair, 2008-12, interim provost, Undergrad Educ, assoc provost, 2012-, asst vpres acad affairs, 2013-, vpres acad affairs, 2014-, Sch Educ, chair; St Augustines Col, Div Educ, chmn, currently. **Orgs:** KACTE insts, exec bd; Collab Ctr Literacy Develop, exec bd; Asn Citizenship Teaching, exec bd. **Business Addr:** Chairman, Saint Augustines College, 1315 Oakwood Ave, Raleigh, NC 27610-2298, **Business Phone:** (919)516-4096.

### DOWNING, DR. JOHN WILLIAM, JR.
Educator, physician, association executive. **Personal:** Born Mar 13, 1936, Phoebus, VA; son of John W Sr and Alice B; married Bessie; children: Kevin & Kimberlynn. **Educ:** More house Col, BS, 1957; Meharry Med Col, MD, 1961. **Career:** Cincinnati C's Med Ctr, fel pediat cardiol, 1967-70; Univ Cincinnati, instr Pediat, 1969-70; Howard Univ, from asst prof to prof emer, 1970-2002, chmn, dept pediat & child health, 1986-94; Asn Med Sch Pediat, dept chmn. **Orgs:** Dir, Pediat Cardiac Clin Howard Univ Hosp; consult, DC Gen Hosp; chmn profed, comn Am Heart Asn Nations Capital Affil; DC Med Soc; Am Heart Asn, 1974-; ch coun, Third St Ch God, 1974-; bd dir, Am Heart Asn Nations Capital Affil; dipl, Am Bd Pediats; fel Am Col Cardiol. **Honors/Awds:** Alpha Omega Alpha Hon Med Socs. **Special Achievements:** published numerous publications in medical litreary. **Home Addr:** 129 Tanners Pt Dr, Stevensville, MD 21666, **Home Phone:** (410)643-0062. **Business Addr:** Professor Emeritus, Howard University, 2041 Ga Ave NW, Washington, DC 20060, **Business Phone:** (202)865-6100.

### DOWNING, STEPHEN
Athletic director. **Personal:** Born Sep 9, 1950, Indianapolis, IN; son of William and Evana; married Doris. **Educ:** Ind Univ, BS, health phys educ & recreation, 1973; Ind Univ-Purdue Univ, Indianapolis, MS, coun & guid, 1977. **Career:** Boston Celtics, ctr, 1973-75; Ind Univ-Purdue Univ Indianapolis, acad counr, 1978-79; Ind Univ, adminstrator asst to athletic dir, 1978-2001; Tex Tech Univ, sr assoc athletic dir & internal affairs, 2001-11; Marian Univ, dir athletics, 2011-. **Orgs:** Active childrens summer groups; Tex Tech Univ Strategic Planning Comt; mem & grad exec mgt Training Prog, Nat Asn Col Dirs Athletics; Tex Tech Athletics Internal Commun Comt. **Honors/Awds:** Most Valuable Player, Big Ten Conf, 1973; Chicago Tribune Silver Basketball Award, 1973; NBA Champion, 1974; Converse All-Amer Team; NCAA 3rd place team; HS All-Amer; Indiana Hall of Fame, 1995; Indiana University Athletic Hall of Fame, 2009. **Home Addr:** 6433 Lakeside Woods Cir, Indianapolis, IN 46278. **Business Addr:** Director of Athletics, Marian University, 3200 Cold Spring Rd, Indianapolis, IN 46222, **Business Phone:** (317)955-6000.

### DOWNING, WILL
Singer. **Personal:** Born Jan 1, 1961, Brooklyn, NY; married Audrey Wheeler. **Educ:** Va Union Univ. **Career:** Albums: Will Downing, 1988; Come Together as One, 1989; A Dream Fulfilled, 1991; Love's the Place to Be, 1993; Moods, 1995; Invitation Only, 1997; Pleasures of the Night, 1998; All the Man You Need, 2000; Greatest Love Songs, 2002; Sensual Journey, 2002; Emotions, 2003; Christmas Love & you, 2004; Soul Symphony, 2005; The Best Of Will Downing: The Millennium Collection, 2006; After Tonight, 2007; Classique, 2009; Love, Lust, & Lies: An Audio Novel, 2010; Yesterday, 2011; Today, 2012; Tomorrow, 2012. Songs: "Sorry I"; "If She Knew"; "The Rhythm of you & me"; "Nothing has ever felt like this"; "When you need me"; "Where is the Love", Love, Lust, & Lies: An Audio Novel, 2010. **Orgs:** Spokesperson, Am Stoke Asn. **Honors/Awds:** Best Album of the Year, Blues & Soul Mag; Vocalist of the Year; Best Live Performer, 1992; NAACP Image Awards; International Association of African American Music Diamond Award, 2002. **Special Achievements:** Sang background vocals for artists such as: Nona Hendryx, Jennifer Holliday; Najee; Stephanie Mills; David Peaston; Billy Ocean; Art Porter; sang duets with Rachelle Ferrell, Mica Paris; performed for Prince Charles and Princess Diana at the Prince's Trust Concert; nominated for Soul Train Music Awards; Recognized by the Grammys (All the Man you need) & the National Association for the Advancement of Colored People Image awards for his excellence on the stage & in studio; Published a book: UNVEILED, 2005; conducts a charity bowling event called Strike against Stroke to raise funds toward greater stroke awareness & educ in the African American Community. **Business Addr:** Singer, c/o Concord Music Gropup, 23307 Commerce Prk Rd, Cleveland, OH 44122, **Business Phone:** (800)551-5299.

### DOWNS, CRYSTAL
Consultant, writer. **Personal:** Born Dec 29, 1964, Chicago, IL; daughter of Charles Edmond and Queen Esta Taylor. **Educ:** Chicago State Univ, Chicago, IL, attended 1987; Columbia Col, Chicago, IL, BA, 1989. **Career:** Am Jour Reprod Immunol & Microbiol, Chicago, ed intern, 1987-88; Essence Mag, New York, summer intern, summer, 1988; Alpha Kappa Alpha Sorority, Chicago, asst dir, assoc ed, 1989-92; self-employed, writer, ed consult, 1992-95; Chicago State Univ,

Chicago, IL, from exec asst to pres, 1995. **Orgs:** Nat Asn Black Journalists, 1990-; Alpha Kappa Alpha Sorority, 1984-; CASE; bd, Pub Allies; Womens Adv Group. **Home Addr:** 5470 S Harper, Chicago, IL 60615, **Home Phone:** (773)684-7678. **Business Addr:** IL.

## DOXIE, MARVIN LEON, SR.

Marketing executive, executive director. **Personal:** Born May 15, 1943, Youngstown, OH; son of Melvin and E Beatrice Boyd; married Beverly Owens; children: Monica Yvette & Marvin Leon Jr. **Educ:** Youngstown State Univ; Ohio Univ; Howard Univ, Sch Bus & Pub Admin, attended 1975; Prince George's Col, attended 1995. **Career:** Greater Wash Bus Ctr, vpres, 1973-82; Raven Systs & Res, Bus Develop, dir, 1982-83; DC Govt, Minority Bus Opportunity Comn, mkt mgr, 1983-85; Automated Sci Group Inc, mkt support dir, 1985-94; M L Doxie & Assocs, pres, 1994-95; Delon Hampton & Assocs, chartered, client rels, dir; C C Johnson & Malhotra Engrs Ltd, Corp Bus Develop, dir, currently. **Orgs:** Montgomery C High Technol Coun, 1989-95; bd dir, Silver Spring Chamber Com, 1990-95; AFCEA, 1989-95; DC Chamber Com, 1975; Md & DC Minority Supplier Develop Coun, 1989; Am Mkt Asn; Architect & Eng Coun, dir, 1996. **Honors/Awds:** Appreciation Award, DC Govt, 1985; Cert Appreciation, White House Conf Small Bus, 1986; Cert Appreciation, Montgomery C, Md Govt, 1997. **Home Addr:** 7202 Wendover Dr, District Heights, MD 20747-1742, **Home Phone:** (301)336-6136. **Business Addr:** Director Corporate Business Development, C C Johnson & Malhotra Engineers Ltd, 3700 Koppers St Suite 109, Baltimore, MD 21227-1020, **Business Phone:** (410)644-0130.

## DOZIER, LAMONT

Songwriter. **Personal:** Born Jun 16, 1941, Detroit, MI; married Barbara; children: Beau Alexandre, Paris Ray & Desiree Starr. **Career:** Holland Group Productions, Songwriter, currently; Albums: Out Here On My Own, 1973; Love & Beauty, 1974; Black Bach, 1974; Right There, 1976; Peddlin' Music on the Side, 1977; Bittersweet, 1979; Working On You, 1981; Lamont, 1981; Bigger Than Life, 1983; Inside Seduction, 1991; Reflections of Lamont Dozier, 2004; Aint Got No Stop Button; Songs: "Baby I Need Your Loving"; "Baby Love"; "How Sweet It Is"; "I Hear a Symphony"; "Its the Same Old Song"; "Reach Out Ill Be There"; "This Old Heart of Mine"; "Where Did Our Love Go"; "You Cant Hurry Love"; "You Keep Me Hangin On". **Orgs:** Trustee, NARAS, urrently. **Honors/Awds:** Numerous honors & awards including Grammy Award, Best Song Written Specifically for a Motion Picture or Television, for "Two Hearts", 1988; Rock & Roll Hall of Fame, 1990; BMI Icon Award, 2003; Billboard Magazine Award; SongWriter's Hall of Fame; Brit Award; BMI ICON Awards; Pioneer Award, Rhythm & Blues Found; Thornton Legacy Award, Univ Southern Califs Thornton Sch Music. **Special Achievements:** Grammy nomination for Best Traditional R&B Vocal Album. **Business Addr:** Songwriter, Holland Group Productions, 1800 N Highland Ave, Hollywood, CA 90028, **Business Phone:** (323)463-2391.

**DOZIER, MORRIS, SR.** See Obituaries Section.

## DOZIER, MORRIS CICERO

Architect. **Personal:** Born Dec 24, 1953, Heidelberg; son of Morris and Mary; married Patricia A; children: Tiffany, Yannic & Sakai. **Educ:** Kans State Univ, BArch, archit, 1978; Fla Inst Technol, MBA, 1986. **Career:** Blue Dot Energy Co, proj mgr, 1996-2000; Bruce McMillan AIA Architects PA, architect, 2000-, pres, currently; Pepper Tree Serv Inc, owner. **Orgs:** Gideons, 1998-; Am Inst Architects, 2000-; Nat Coun Archit Regist Bds, 2002-. **Home Addr:** 226 W 14th St, Junction City, KS 66441, **Home Phone:** (785)238-6816. **Business Addr:** President, Architect, Bruce McMillan AIA Architect PA, 555 Poyntz Ave Suite 295, Manhattan, KS 66502, **Business Phone:** (785)776-1011.

## DOZIER, DR. RICHARD K.

Architect, school administrator, naval officer. **Personal:** Born Jan 18, 1939, Buffalo, NY. **Educ:** La Tech Col, AA, 1962; Yale Univ, BArch, 1969, MArch, 1970; Univ Mich, PhD, 1990. **Career:** Hist Preserv Archit Tuskegee Inst Ala, pvt prac; Archit Off New Haven, Conn, pvt prac; Tuskegee Inst, chmn dept archit, 1976-79, prof archit hist, 1979-87; Yale Univ, asst prof archit, 1970-76; Archit var firms; Hist Afro-Am Archit & Archit, teaching & prof specialization; Morgan State Univ, assoc prof archit, 1987-91; Fla A&M Univ, sch archit, prof, 1991-92, assoc dean, 1991-96, prof archit, 1996-2007; Tuskegee Univ, Dept Archit & Construct Sci, assoc dean & head, 2007-. **Orgs:** Am Inst Architects; Nat Orgn Minority Architects; African Am preserv orgn; Ala Black Heritage Coun; Nat Trust Hist Preserv; resident fel WEB. vis fel DuBois Inst, Harvard Univ, 1999-2000; Asn African Am Mus; Asn Study African Am Life & Hist; Am Inst Architects; Nat Asn Advan Colored People. **Honors/Awds:** Nat Book Award, 1953; Leadership Award, Yale Univ, 1969; Honor Award, 1970; Res Fellow, Graham Found, 1970; Nat Endowment Arts Award; Conn Found Arts; Dissertation Award, Nat Educ Health, 1986; Fulbright Award, 2002; Leadership Award, Alabama Black Heritage Council, 2004. **Home Addr:** 3446 Paces Ferry Rd, Tallahassee, FL 32309, **Home Phone:** (850)894-2691. **Business Addr:** Associate Dean, Head, Tuskegee University, Rm 115 Willcox C Bldg, Tuskegee, AL 36088, **Business Phone:** (334)727-8329.

**DRAHER, DODIE T.** See WALBEY, THEODOSIA EMMA DRAHER.

## DRAIN, GERSHWIN ALLEN

Judge. **Personal:** Born Jan 1, 1949?, Detroit, MI. **Educ:** Western Mich Univ, BA, 1970; Univ Mich Law Sch, JD, 1972; Univ Nev, Reno, Nat Judicial Col, MJS, 1991. **Career:** Coun, Detroit Dept Transp, 1973-74; Fed Defenders Off, trial atty; Thirty Sixth Dist Ct, Detroit, judge, 1986; Recorder's Ct, Detroit, judge, 1987; Wayne County Circuit Ct, judge, 1997-12; Us Dist Ct Eastern Dist Mich, judge, 2012-. **Orgs:** Mich Judges Asn; Wolverine Bar Asn; Asn Black Judges Mich; Mich Bar Asn; Nat Asn Advan Colored People. **Home Addr:** 16558 Westmoreland, Detroit, MI 48219. **Business Addr:** Judge, United States District Court for the Eastern District of Michigan, 231 W Lafayette Blvd Rm 1013, Detroit, MI 48226, **Business Phone:** (810)341-9760.

## DRAINE, MICHAEL

Vice president (organization), pharmacologist. **Educ:** Alcorn State Univ, BS, biol, 1982; Shenandoah Univ, MBA, bus admin, 1994; Byrd Sch Bus, MA, bus admin. **Career:** Parke-Dewatt Labs-Comprehensive Med Systs, field sales specialist, 1982-83; Novartis Pharmaceut, pharmaceut sales specialist, Chicago & Northwest, 1984-86, hosp sales specialist, Wis, 1987, regional sales mgr, Mid-W Region, 1988-90, dir fed govt affairs, 1996-98, head, 1997; Sandoz Pharmaceut, mgr state govt affairs, 1991-96; Merck & Co, sr mgr, 1998-2002; State Govt Affairs, southeast regional dir, 2002-03, exec dir, 2004-06; VA-DoD, nat sales dir, 2006-08; AstraZeneca LP, sr dir, 2008-09; Daiichi Sankyo Inc, sr dir, 2009-10; Strategic Policy Mgt Group LLC, managing dir, 2010-12; AmeriHealth Caritas, dir, 2012-14; PerformRx, vpres, 2014-. **Orgs:** Chmn pub health comt, bd dir, Cong Black Caucus Found Inc; bd mem, Tigerlily Found. **Business Addr:** Vice President, PerformRx, 200 Stevens Dr, Philadelphia, PA 19113, **Business Phone:** (866)533-5492.

## DRAKE, JERRY

Teacher, football player. **Personal:** Born Jul 9, 1969, Kingston, NY. **Educ:** Ulster County Community Col; Hastings Col. **Career:** Football player (retired), teacher; Ariz Cardinals, 1995-97, 2000, defensive tackle, 1998-99, right defensive tackle, 1999; Durham High Sch, health teacher. **Honors/Awds:** McLaughlin Award, Bronco Most Valuable Player; Hall of Fame, Hastings Col, 2003.

## DRAKE, LAWRENCE M., II (LARRY DRAKE)

Executive, president (organization). **Personal:** Born Jun 10, 1954, Pittsburgh, PA; son of Lawrence M II and Jean Williamson; married Sharon Martin; children: Kia Nichol & Kory Lawrence. **Educ:** Fisk Univ, music; Ga State Univ, BA, sociol, 1977; Rockhurst Col, MBA, 1990; Fielding Grad Univ, PhD, media psychol. **Career:** Exec;Coca-Cola USA, region mgr, KC Region, 1985-87, acct group mgr, CCE liaison, 1987-88, group dir, NY Acct Group, 1990-91, vpres n, vpres mide-cent, 1999-2004, Coca-Cola Nigeria & Equatorial Africa, managing dir, pres, ceo; KFC, Div Pepsico Inc, vpres, admin, asst to pres, 1990-91, vpres, gen mgr, N Ctr Div, 1991-93, New Bus Develop, vpres, KFC Express Concepts, 1993-95; Cablevision Systs Corp, sr vpres & gen mgr, 1995-96; Dolman Technologies Group, exec vpres, coo, 1996-; Hope 360 Inc, Co-Founder, chief exec officer, chmn; Kraft Foods; KFC Restaurant Div; Haven Media Group, co-managed; Personnel Decisions Int, consult; AJIA Capital Holdings, investment adv; Saurus Partners LLC, sr partner; LEAD Prog, pres & chief exec officer, currently. **Orgs:** Alpha Phi Alpha Fraternity Inc, 1974-; Ga State Univ Alumnae Asn, 1985-; Rockhurst Exec Fels Asn, 1990-; bd dir, MAI Inc, 1990-; Exec Leadership Coun, 1991-; Nat Black MBA Asn, 1991-; Nat Conf Christian & Jews; Leadership Cleveland; Vine & Oak Found N Am; Cleveland Bus Roundtable; Calif Sci Cente; Coca-Cola Africa Found; bd mem, Crystal Stairs Inc; bd mem, Nat Conf Community Justice; Calif Sci Ctr; trustee, Jarvis Christian Col; Nehemiah Proj Ministries Int. **Home Addr:** 26600 George Zergon Dr Suite 514, Beachwood, OH 44122. **Business Addr:** President Nigeria, Equatorial Africa, The Coca-Cola Co, PO Box 1734, Atlanta, GA 30301, **Business Phone:** (800)438-2653.

## DRAKE, MAGGIE W.

Judge. **Personal:** daughter of Arthur and Margaret K Williams. **Educ:** Highland Pk Col, AA, 1971; Mercy Col Detroit, BS, 1976; Univ Detroit, JD, 1981; Judicial Col, DP, 1993. **Career:** Detroit Police Dept, st officer, sergeant, 1974-92; Corp Coun, asst, 1982-92; Detroit Recorders Ct, 1992-97; Wayne County Circuit Ct, judge recorder, third judicial circuit, 1997-2007, circuit ct judge, currently. **Orgs:** Mich Judges Asn, 1993-; Black Judges Asn, 1993-; Asn Trial Judges, 1993-; Wolverine Bar Asn, 1993-. **Honors/Awds:** Community Treatment Ctr, Distinguished leader, 1996-97; Blacks in Blue Award, Detroit Police Asn, Distinguished Leader, 1997; BM&E State Convention, Women Auxiliary, Distinguished Leader Award, 1996. **Business Addr:** Judge, Wayne Co Circuit Ct, 1441 St Antoine, Detroit, MI 48226, **Business Phone:** (313)224-2481.

## DRAKE, MICHAEL V.

Chancellor (education), educator, president (organization). **Personal:** Born Jul 9, 1950, New York, NY; married Brenda; children: 2. **Educ:** Stanford Univ, BA; Univ Calif, San Francisco, MD. **Career:** Univ Calif, Sch Med, sr assoc dean, Steven P. Shearing Distinguished Prof Ophthal, distinguished prof educ, sr assoc dean, vpres health affairs, 2000-05, chancellor, 2005-14; Ohio State Univ, pres, 2014-. **Orgs:** Nat Academies' Inst Med; Am Acad Arts & Sci; immediate past nat pres, Alpha Omega Alpha Hon Med Soc; immediate past chair bd dirs, Asn Acad Health Centers; elected mem, Inst Med (Nat Academies); elected mem, Am Acad Arts & Sci; Nat Col Athletic Asn, Div I Exec Comt; secy, Coun Presidents Asn Pub & Land-grant Univs (APLU), 2014-; bd, Rock & Roll Hall Fame & Mus Inc, 2015. **Honors/Awds:** UC San Francisco School of Medicine's Clinical Teaching Award, recipient; UCSF Alumnus of the Year, 2000; American Association of Medical Colleges, Herbert W. Nickens Award, recipient, 2004; UC San Francisco's Gold Headed Cane Society, inductee, 2003; The California Wellness Foundation, Champions of Health Professions Diversity, 2007; Burbridge Award for Public Service, recipient; Asbury Award (clinical science) and the Michael J. Hogan Award (laboratory science), recipient; University of California Presidential Medal, recipient, 2014; Received Numerous Honors & Awards For Teaching. **Special Achievements:** First African American to hold position of president at Ohio State University. **Business Addr:** President, Ohio State University, 281 W Lane Ave, Columbus, OH 43210, **Business Phone:** (614)292-6446.

## DRAKE, PAULINE LILIE

Association executive, government official. **Personal:** Born Jul 20, 1926, Cliffwood, NJ; daughter of Gabriel David Robinson and Daisy Etta Brown; married Howard William; children: Sidney Howard. **Educ:** NY Univ, attended 1946; Brookdale Community Col, NJ, attended 1985. **Career:** Providence Baptist Church Cliff wood, church clerk, 1957-65, youth chair dir, 1960-72; Order Eastern Star AF & AM, Monmouth, county dep, 1960-71, worthy matron, 1994-97; Order Sunbeam Youth Dept OES AF & AM, dep, 1972-82. **Orgs:** Vol, USO, 1942-45; pres, Matawan, Hadassah, NJ, 1979-81; pres, Monmouth County Veterans Foreign Wars Aux NJ, 1980-81; cert chmn, Southern NJ Reg Hadassah, 1981-85; publicity chmn, State NJ Ladies Aux Veterans Foreign Wars, 1981-82, 1988-89, voice democracy & youth activ chmn, 1984-85, sr vpres, 1990-91; jr girls unit chmn, NJ Ladies Aux Veterans Foreign Wars, 1982-83, safety chmn, 1983-84, safety chmn, 1986-87, guard, 1986-87, conductress, 1987-88, jr vpres, 1988-90, community activ chairperson, state pres, 1991-92; transfer & trackdown chmn, Southern NJ Region Hadassah, 1987-90, chaplain, 1988, JNF chairperson, 1990-91; grand conductress, mil order cooties, 1994-95; second vpres, Madison Twp Hist Soc, 1994-96; Monmouth County Pk Afro Am Comt; Aberdeen Twp Community Develop Comt; Concerned Citizens Aberdeen; grand sr vpres, Ladies Auxiliary MOC, NJ, 1995-96; pres, Madison Twp Hist Soc, 1996-02; bd dir, Ctr Holocaust Studies Brookdale Community Col, Lincroft, 1996-03; grand pres, Ladies Auxilairy MOC, NJ, 1997-98; pres, Matawan Women's Club, 2000-02; chair, E States Conf, Veterans Foreign Wars Rehab, 2002-03. **Home Addr:** 85 Kennedy Ave, Cliffwood, NJ 07721-1160, **Home Phone:** (732)566-3289.

## DRAKEFORD, JACK

Government official. **Personal:** Born May 14, 1937, Englewood, NJ; son of Margaret Harris; married Virginia Finley; children: Gina & Nancy. **Educ:** New York Univ, New York, NY, bus admin; Syracuse Univ, Syracuse, NY, pub admin. **Career:** City Englewood, firefighter, 1959-73; James E Hanson, Hackensack, NJ, ins broker & real estate agt, 1973-77; City Englewood, city clerk, 1977-85, city mgr; Englewood City Coun, pres, 1976, 1999, 2002 & 2004; DPW, act dir & act pub safety dir; City Englewood, councman, currently; Labor Union Local 108 RWDSU, consult, currently. **Orgs:** Englewood Hosp Bd Trustee; bd mem, City Councilman, Englewood; comnr, Bergen Co Housing Authority; chmn, bd mem, Northern Valley Dist Bergen Co Boy Scouts; exec bd mem, Bergen Co Girl Scouts; bd pres, Bergen Co Tech Schs; bd Habitat humanity Bergen Co; Englewood Housing Authority; bd pres, Bergen Co Tech Sch; bd mem, Libr Trustee Asn. **Honors/Awds:** Received approximately 20 awards from various organizations including: Englewood Chamber Com; Bergen County Nat Asn Advan Colored People; Bergen County Boy Scouts Am; Bergen County Urban League; Bergan County Black Bus & Prof Women. **Special Achievements:** First African American City Clerk and the First African American City Manager. **Home Addr:** 173 Lafayette Pl, Englewood, NJ 07631, **Home Phone:** (201)569-6066. **Business Addr:** President of Board, Bergen County Technical Schools, 327 E Ridgewood Ave, Paramus, NJ 07652, **Business Phone:** (201)343-6000.

## DRAKEFORD, TYRONNE JAMES

Football player. **Personal:** Born Jun 21, 1971, Camden, SC; married Cindi; children: Julian, James & Justus T. **Educ:** Va Polytech Inst & State Univ, BS, finance. **Career:** Football player (retired); San Francisco 49ers, 1994, 2001, defensive back, 1995, 1997, left cornerback, 1996; New Orleans Saints, right cornerback, 1998-99; Wash Redskins, cornerback, 2000. **Orgs:** Regional athletic dir, Boys & Girls Clubs Greater Wash, Prince William County. **Honors/Awds:** Champion, Super Bowl, 1995. **Business Addr:** Regional Athletic Director, Boys & Girls Clubs of Greater Washington, 4103 Benning Rd NE, Washington, DC 20019, **Business Phone:** (202)540-2300.

**DRAKES, MURIEL B.** See Obituaries Section.

## DRAPER, DR. EDGAR DANIEL

Educator. **Personal:** Born Aug 29, 1921, Brooklyn, MD; son of Andrew J Sr and Anniebelle Saunders; married Emma J Williams; children: Marie E, Yvonne T & Edgar D Jr. **Educ:** Howard Univ, BA, 1943; NY Univ, MPA, 1948, PhD, 1967. **Career:** Educator (retired); Tex Southern Univ, dir, instr, 1948-49; Tubman Col, pres, 1949-51; Baltimore Housing Authority, asst mgr, 1951-52; Morgan State Col, bus mgr, from asst to the pres, 1952-60; Conf African Resources NY Univ, asst dir, 1960-61; African-Am Trade Develop Asn, exec secy, 1961-62; UN Inst Pub Admin, dep chief, 1962-63; Gov Nelson Rockefeller, prog asst, 1963-66; Bor Manhattan Comm Col, City Univ New York, assoc dean, dean col, prof pub admin, 1967-70, pres, 1970-84. **Orgs:** Met Chap Am Asn Pub Admin; NY Plan; Nat Conf Christs Jews, 1970-; Coun Higher Educ Inst, 1972-; Pr Training Com & Com; BSA; Nat African Studies; Nat Ed Asn; Comparative Ed Soc; Am Asn Comm & Jr Col; Asn Asst Negro Bus; Urban League; Gov Libr Com; Interstate Compact Ed; Joint Legis Com; Host Radio WNYC-AM Open Door, 1973-74; chmn, 4th Round Table Conf Perspectives Pub Admin Sudan; NY St Gov Com Manpower, 1966; Am Soc Pub Admin; Baltimore Urban League; NY Univ Alumni Asn; Nat Asn Advan Colored People; Metrop Educ Coalition; mem phi beta sigma bro org; Baltimore Counon Foreign Affairs; task force, Baltimore City Pub Sch; exec secy, Adv Comt Gov's Libr Conf. **Home Addr:** 2728 Longwood St, Baltimore, MD 21216, **Home Phone:** (410)669-0835.

## DRAPER, REV. FRANCES MURPHY

Newspaper executive, clergy. **Personal:** Born Dec 18, 1947, Baltimore, MD; daughter of James E Wood Sr and Frances L Murphy II; married Andre Reginald; children: Kevin E Peck, Andre D, Andrea J & Aaron R. **Educ:** Morgan State Univ, BA, span educ, 1969; Johns Hopkins Univ, MEd, bus admin & pastoral coun 1973; Univ Baltimore, Grad cert Mgmt, 1979; Univ Md, MBA, 1981; Loyola Col, Baltimore, MS, pastoral coun, 1996; St Mary's Sem, theol; United Theol Sem, DMin. **Career:** Baltimore City Pub Schs, teacher, 1969-73; NJ Afro-Am, mgr, 1973-76; Merrill Lynch Pierce Fenner & Smith, acct exec, 1976-78; Morgan State Univ, asst vpres develop, instr, 1978-84; Afro-Am Newspapers, NJ ed, mgr, pres, 1986-99, treas & bd mem; Nat cert counr; John Wesley AME Zion Church, Baltimore, Md, pastor, 2002-. **Orgs:** Delta Sigma Theta Sor Inc, 1968-; dir, Afro-Am Newspapers, 1976-; vice chair, City Baltimore's Literacy Found, 1988-94, chair, 1995-; Nat Coalition 100 Black Women, 1989-; bd mem, United Way Cent MD, 1994-97; bd mem, Baltimore City Chamber Com, 1994-97; bd regents, Morgan State Univ, trustee; bd trustee, Loyola Col; pastoral counr, Brantley Group; elder, AME Zion Church;

cofounder, Gods Love Ministry; Network, 2000. **Honors/Awds:** Woman of the Year in Business, Zeta Phi Beta Sorority Inc, 1990; AFRAM, one of 15 women honored, 1992; The New Daily Record, Maryland's Top 100 Women, 1996, 1998; 21st Century Award, The InterNat Alliance for Women, 1998; Carroll Award, Loyola Col, 1998; Distinguished Black Marylanders Award, Towson State Univ. **Special Achievements:** One of the "Area's Most Influential Women, ", Baltimore Magazine, 1983; USA Today, one of the "People to Watch," 1987. **Home Addr:** , Baltimore, MD. **Business Addr:** Pastor, John Wesley Ame Zion Church, 1923 Ashland Ave, Baltimore, MD 21205-1535, **Business Phone:** (410)732-7020.

## DRAPER, DR. FREDERICK WEBSTER

Educator. **Personal:** Born Jul 10, 1945, St. Louis, MO; married Carrie Todd; children: Fred W II & Angela. **Educ:** Ind State Univ, BS, 1968, MS, PE, 1969, MS, personnel admin, 1972, EdD, 1976. **Career:** Proj Upswing IN, asst dir, 1969; GED Prog Off Econ Opport, supvr, 1972-73; asst phys educ & head cross country coach, 1969-; dir, ed progs; Sch HPER, State Univ, dir educ opportunity progs, prof; Ind State Univ, prof; Global Net Solutions, pres, chief exec officer, currently. **Orgs:** Chmn, Black Freshmen Orientation Prog, Ind State Univ, 1971-74; internship vpres, Ind State Univ, Stud Affairs, 1972-73; bd vpres, Ind State Black Expo; bd dir, Hyte Community Ctr; bd dir & treas, Ind Airport; fac adv, Kappa Alpha Psi; City Human Rel Comn; Sch Human Rel Comn; Boy Scout Troup Leader; pres, Hulman Reg Airport; bd dir, Civil Rights Comn; vice chmn, Ind Civil Rights Comn; chmn bd, Ind Black Expo. **Honors/Awds:** Outstanding Black Faculty Award, Ind State Univ, 1972-73; Dean's List, 1968; Alumni Club; All-conf intrack every year as an undergraduate. **Special Achievements:** One of Nations Most Eligible Bachelors, Ebony Mag, 1969. **Home Addr:** 131 Phoenix Dr, Terre Haute, IN 47803-1411. **Business Addr:** President, Chief Executive Officer, Global Net Solutions, 2626 E 46th St Suite 200, Indianapolis, IN 46205.

## DRAPER, DR. SHARON MILLS

Educator. **Personal:** Born Apr 11, 1952, Cleveland, OH; daughter of Vick and Catherine; married Larry E; children: Wendy, Damon, Cory & Crystal. **Educ:** Pepperdine Univ, BA, 1971; Miami Univ, MA, 1974. **Career:** Cincinnati Bd Educ, teacher, 1970-97; Mayerson Acad, Nat Teacher Yr Prog, assoc, currently. Author: Tears of a Tiger, 1994; Forged by Fire, 1997; Romiette & Julio, 1999; Teaching from the Heart, 1999; Sharon M. Draper: Embracing Literacy; Buttered Bones; Let the Circle Be Unbroken; Darkness Before Dawn, 2001; Not Quite Burned Out, But Crispy around the Edges, 2001; Double Dutch, 2002; The Battle of Jericho, 2003; We Beat the Street, 2005; Copper Sun, 2006; Fire from the Rock, 2007; November Blues, 2007; Just Another Hero; Out of my Mind, 2010. **Orgs:** Bd dir, Nat Bd Prof Teaching Stands, 1995; Women's City Club; Nat Coun Teachers Eng; Ohio Coun Teachers Eng Lang Arts; Conf Eng Leadership; Am Fedn Teachers; Int Reading Asn; Delta Kappa Gamma. **Home Addr:** PO Box 36551, Cincinnati, OH 45236, **Home Phone:** (513)731-8295. **Business Addr:** Associate, Mayerson Academy, 2650 Highland Ave, Cincinnati, OH 45219, **Business Phone:** (513)475-4100.

## DRAYTON, TROY ANTHONY

Radio host, football player, real estate executive. **Personal:** Born Jun 29, 1970, Harrisburg, PA; son of Stella. **Educ:** Pa State Univ, attended 1992, BS, labor & employ rels, 2008; Univ Phoenix, MBA, bus admin, 2011. **Career:** Football player (retired), real estate agt, radio host; Los Angeles Rams, tight end, 1993-94; St Louis Rams, tight end, 1995; Miami Dolphins, 1997-99; Kans City Chiefs, 2000; Green Bay Packers, 2001; Ocean View Realty, realtor agt, 2005-07; WQAM 560 FM, radio host, 2007-08, co-host, 2010-; Macken Realty, realtor agt, 2007-09; Acad High Sch, hist teacher, 2008-09; Fabian Realty Inc, realtor assoc, 2009-; Finsiders Radio Show, 2011-; Miami Dolphins & Sun Life Stadium, Youth & Community Progs, mgr, 2012-. **Honors/Awds:** Rookie of the Year, 1993; Pro Bowl alternate, 1994. **Business Addr:** Realtor Associate, Fabian Realty Inc, 20650 Highland Lakes Blvd, North Miami Beach, FL 33179-2274, **Business Phone:** (305)936-2416.

## DRAYTON-MARTIN, MICHELLE

President (organization), publisher, chief executive officer. **Educ:** City Col NY, BS, nursing; Hunter Col, MS, pub health; Nelson Rockefeller Sch Pub Policy, cert; Columbia Univ Sch Bus, cert exec mgt & pub policy. **Career:** Today's Child Commun Inc, chief exec officer, pres & publ, sr mkt prin, 1998-. **Orgs:** Chairperson, Nat Black Family Prom Coalition; Auxiliary to Nat Med Asn; bd mem, Child Care Inst; bd mem, Brooklyn Perinatal Network; bd mem, African-Am Well Being Proj; bd mem, Nat Commun Adv Coun March Dimes; Coalition 100 Black Women; First Day Coalition headed by United Way NYC; Nat Adv Coun. **Business Addr:** Senior Marketing Principal, President, Today's Child Communications Inc, 152 Madison Ave Suite 202, New York, NY 10016, **Business Phone:** (212)462-4716.

## DRE, DR. (ANDRE RAMELLE YOUNG)

Rap musician, music producer. **Personal:** Born Feb 18, 1965, Compton, CA; married Nicole Young; children: 2; married Sedale; children: Truth & Truly; children: Curtis Young & Andre Young Jr (deceased). **Career:** Composer; Back-up vocalist Stevie Wonder, 1977-80; Rene & Angela duo, 1980-87; solo artist, 1987; songwriter & producer Isley Brothers, Lalah Hathaway, Klymaxx, Sheena Easton; Composer: Grant Theft & Auto: Vice City, 2002; Album: Rene & Angela, 1980; Wall To Wall, 1981; Rise, 1983; Street Called Desire, 1985; The Best of Rene & Angela: Come My Way, 1996; A Street Called Desire & More, 1997; Classic Masters, 2002; Solo Albums: Sharp, 1987; It's The Real Thing, 1989; Angela Winbush, 1994; Mission to Please, 1996; Ultimate Collection, 2001; Greatest Love Songs, 2004; Produced: The Firm, 1997; The Slim Shady LP, 1999; Dr. Dre, 1999, 2001; The Marshall Mathers LP, 2000; The Wash, 2001; Get Rich or Die Tryin' for 50 Cent, 2003; 50 Cent: The New Breed, 2003; The Game: Documentary, 2005; 50 Cent: The Massacre Special Edition, 2005. **Business Addr:** Founder, Aftermath Recordings, 15060 Ventura Blvd Suite 225, Sherman Oaks, CA 91403, **Business Phone:** (818)385-0024.

## DRENNEN, GORDON, JR.

Auditor. **Personal:** Born Jul 15, 1947, Atlanta, GA; son of Gordon D Sr and Eliza Harris; married Diane Hatcher; children: Kimberly. **Educ:** Ft Valley State Col, BS, 1970; TX Southern Univ, MBA, 1971. **Career:** Wolf & Co CPA's, staff acct, 1971-73, sr acct, 1973-78; Tarica & Co CPA's, supvr, 1978-80, mgr. **Orgs:** Nat Asn Black Accts, 1973-; dir, Am Civil Liberties Union GA, 1986-; finance chmn, Ft Valley State Col Alumni Asn, 1986-; GA State Soc CPA's; consult, Nat Asn Community Health Ctrs, GA Asn Primary Health Care Inc; Kappa Alpha Psi Frat; selection comt, chair, Ga Asn Minority Entrepreneurs, 1987-; vice chair, finance comt, Nat Black Col Alumni Hall Fame Found Inc, 1990-; bd dir, treas, Ga Advocacy Off Inc. **Honors/Awds:** Distinguished Alumni Citation of Year, Nat Asn Equal Opportunity Higher Educ; Grad Fellowship, Texas Southern Univ, 1970-71. **Home Addr:** 4105 Jeffrey Dr, Atlanta, GA 30349-2523, **Home Phone:** (404)762-6543.

## DREW, CHARLENE ROSELLA. See JARVIS, CHARLENE DREW.

## DREW, KENNETH R.

Publisher, commissioner. **Career:** Commissioner (retired); Human right Comnr; New Voice NY, publ & chmn, 2003.

## DREW, LARRY DONNELL

Basketball player, basketball coach. **Personal:** Born Apr 2, 1958, Kansas City, KS; married Sharon; children: Larry II, Landon & Lindsey. **Educ:** Univ Mo, attended 1980. **Career:** Basketball player (retired), basketball coach; Detroit Pistons, guard, 1980-81; Kans City Kings, 1982-85; Sacramento Kings, 1986; Los Angeles Clippers, 1986-88; Scavolini Pesaro, 1988-89; Los Angeles Lakers, 1989-91, asst coach, 1992-99; Detroit pistons, asst coach, 1999-2000; Wash Wizards, asst coach, 2000-03; NJ Nets, asst coach, 2003-04; Atlanta Hawks, asst coach, 2004-10, coach, 2010-13; Milwaukee Bucks, head coach, 2013-14; Cleveland Cavaliers, asst coach, 2014-. **Orgs:** Bd mem, KC K's Red Cross; teacher, basketball camps, Kansas, Missouri. **Home Addr:** 4942 Densmore Ave, Encino, CA 91436.

## DREW, STEPHEN RICHARD

Lawyer. **Personal:** Born May 25, 1949, Detroit, MI; son of Richard T and Gwendolyn Mae Johnson; married Clarice Smith; children: Richard, Stephen, Anthony, Thomas & Sahara. **Educ:** Univ Mich, BA, 1971; Univ Mich Law Sch, JD, 1974. **Career:** Williams Klukowski Drew & Fotieo, assoc, 1974-77, partner, 1977-87; Drew, Cooper & Anding, Grand Rapids, Mich, partner, Atty, 1991-; US Dist Ct, cert facilitator, 1998. **Orgs:** Chmn, City Grand Rapids Comn Rels Comn, 1984-85; consult, spec investr, Saginaw Police Dept, 1985-86; Sigma Pi Phi, 1985-; judicial merit selection panel mem, US Ct Appeals 6th Circuit, 1986-; legal redresscomn, Nat Asn Advan Colored People Grand Rapids Chap, 1987-; trustee, judicial rev comt, 1987; vpres, pres, Grand Rapids Bar Asn, 1990-93; Am Bar Asn; Nat Bar Asn; Mich Trial Lawyers Asn; Am Trial Lawyers Asn; fel State Bar Mich; pres, Floyd Skinner Bar Asn, 1989-92; civil justice reform adv comt, US Dist Ct, 1991-; fel Am Col Trial Lawyers, 2002; fel Col Labor & Employ Lawyers; Inst Continuing Educ. **Honors/Awds:** Outstanding Volunteer Award, Nat Asn Advan Colored People Grand Rapids Chap, 1982; Patriotic Service Award, Secy US Treas, 1986; Grand Rapids Giant Award Justice; Civil Libertarian Year, W Mich Am Civil Liberties Union, 1989; Giant Giants Award, 1999; Champion of Justice Award, State Bar of Michigan, 2003. **Home Addr:** 2244 Burning Tree Dr SE, Grand Rapids, MI 49546-5513, **Home Phone:** (616)956-0257. **Business Addr:** Partner, Drew, Cooper & Anding, 125 Ottawa Ave NW, Grand Rapids, MI 49503-2898, **Business Phone:** (616)454-8300.

## DREW, THELMA LUCILLE

Government official, secretary (government). **Personal:** Born Flushing, NY; married Archer S Drew Jr; children: Richard Michael, Kenneth Edward, Joanne Michelle, Sheryln Liane & KimberlyTerese. **Educ:** Queens Col, Eng, attended 1949; Am Inst Banking, mgt, 1972; Empire State Col, NY, pub admin, 1980; Hofstra Univ, cert mus studies, 1985. **Career:** Secretary (retired); NY Tele Co, bus off rep, 1949-58; Smithtown Twp, town rec leader (1st black), 1965-69; Nat Bank N Am, banker & mgt, 1969-73; Suffolk Co, Dept Soc Servs, social welfare examr, 1973-77; Suffolk Co, Human Rights Comm, sr investr, 1977-82, Dept Consumer Affairs, asst dir; Serv Human Rights Comn, Suffolk County, comnr, 1981. **Orgs:** Pres, Nat Asn Advan Colored People Smithtown Br, 1966-82; Womens Equal Oppty Coun, 1980-; Womens Equal Rights Cong, 1980-82; bd dir, Long Isl Affirmative Act Plan, 1980-; Victims Inf Bur, 1980-; Inst Labor/Mgmnt Studies, 1979-; founding mem, 100 Black Women LI, 1980-; Nat Asn Female Exec, 1982-; Nat Asn Consumer Prot, 1982-; pres & chairperson, Suffolk County Black Hist Asn, 1982-; pres, secy & founding mem, Long Island Minority Coalition, 1982-; NY Div Human Rights Coun, 1983-; secy, Suffolk County, 1991; Suffolk Coalition, 2005. **Honors/Awds:** Leadership Award, Nat Coun Christ & Jews/LI, 1982; Community Service Award, Nat Coun Oppty Coun LI, 1983; Community Service Award, Nat Asn Counties/LIAAO, 1983; Woman of the Year, Womens Equal Rights comn, 1984; Candidate for presrecognisation Award, vlnt Rsm/Suffolk, 1984. **Home Addr:** 64 Brooksite Dr, Smithtown, NY 11787-4467, **Home Phone:** (631)265-4301.

## DREW-PEEPLES, BRENDA

Lawyer. **Personal:** Born Feb 28, 1947, Fresno, CA; daughter of Jesse Drew and Gladys Drew; married Horace; children: Cranford Thomas & Vanessa Leigh. **Educ:** Des Moines Area Community Col, AA, 1973; Drake Univ, BS, bus admin & mgt gen, 1975; Univ Iowa Col Law, JD, 1978. **Career:** Iowa City Attys Off, legal intern, 1978; Aetna Life & Casualty Ins Des Moines, claim rep, 1979; Legal Serv Corp, Iowa, atty, 1979-81; Polk Co Atty Off, asst co atty, 1981-83; Drew-Peeples & Assocs, atty, 2009-; Davenport Civil Rights Comn, dir & atty, coun & exec dir. **Orgs:** Iowa St Bar Asn, 1980-; Moderator Davenport Comm Forum, 1985; Quad Cities Vision Future; League United Latin Am Citizens Club; Nat Asn Advan Colored People; St Louis County Libr; Poor Peoples Campaign Steering Comt; E Side Adv Bd; Nat Youth Sports Adv Bd; Quad Cities Merit Employ Coun; Womens Encour Bd; Davenport Civil Serv Comn; Iowa Asn Human Rights Agencies; Int Asn Off Human Rights Agencies; Nat Asn Human Rights Workers; Greater Quad Cities Telecomm Corp Bd; Maternal Health Ctr Bd; Scott County Bar Asn. **Home Addr:** 901 Gaines St, Davenport, IA 52803, **Home Phone:** (319)322-7085. **Business Addr:** Attorney, Drew-Peeples & Associates, 125 Kirkwood Blvd, Davenport, IA 52803-4510, **Business Phone:** (563)344-9765.

## DREWRY, CECELIA HODGES

Educator, actor. **Personal:** Born New York, NY; daughter of George and Olive; married Henry N. **Educ:** Hunter Col, BA, Eng, 1945; Columbia Univ, MA, hist, 1948; Shakespeare Univ, Birmingham, Eng, cert, 1949; Northwestern Univ, PhD, oral interpretation lit, 1967; Univ Ghana, cert, 1969. **Career:** Educator (retired); Talladega Col, instr, 1945-47; Pent house Dance & Drama Theatre, NY, dir speech, 1948-52; High Sch Performing Arts, NY, teacher, 1952-59; Princeton High Sch, teacher, 1959-61; Rutgers Univ, assoc prof, 1962-70; Teachers Col Columbia Univ, vis instr, 1968; African & Afro-Am Studies Prog, chair person, 1969-70; Haverford Col, vis prof eng, var theatre appearances, 1977-89; Bk Club, founder; Princeton Univ, asst dean, asst prof. **Orgs:** AAVP; Am Asn Univ Women; MLA; SCA; trustee, Cedar Crest Col, PA; Carnegie Found Advan Teaching; Nat Asn Advan Colored People; Nat Coun Negro Women; Princeton Asn Human Rights; life mem, Nat Asn Child Care Professionals. **Honors/Awds:** Award for excellence in oral interpretation of literature, N western Univ Sch of Speech; Alpha Psi Omega Hon Soc; Danforth Asn; Honoree, Phi Delta Kappa; Distinguished Women Award, Delaware-Raritan Girl Scouts. **Special Achievements:** Appeared in plays and starred in a one-woman performance. Co-Author: Afro-American History: Past to Present, Scribner, 1971. **Home Addr:** 2 Glenview Dr, Princeton, NJ 08540-6006, **Home Phone:** (609)452-2855.

## DREXLER, CLYDE AUSTIN

Basketball player, basketball coach, broadcaster. **Personal:** Born Jun 22, 1962, New Orleans, LA; son of James Sr and Eunice Drexler Scott; married Gaynell Floyd; children: Clyde Austin, Kathryn Elise & Adam Eugene; children: Erica. **Educ:** Univ Houston, attended 1983. **Career:** Basketball player (retired), basketball coach, broadcaster; Portland Trail Blazers, forward, 1983-95; Houston Rockets, forward, 1995-98, Rockets Home Games, color commentator, currently; Univ Houston, head coach, 1998-2000; Drexler Holdings LLC, mgr; Nat Basketball Asn, shooting guard; Nmex State; Tex Tech; Univ Houston; Actor: "Michael Jordan: His Airness", 1999; "Like Mike 2: Streetball", 2006; "On the Shoulders of Giants: The Story of the Greatest Team You Never Heard Of", 2010; "The Dream Team", 2012. **Orgs:** Chmn, Blazer, Avia Reading Prog, 1988-; hon chmn, UNCF, Portland Region, 1988-91; Houston's Phi Slama Jama Dunking Fraternity. **Special Achievements:** Book: "Clyde the Glide", 2004; "Shrews Can't Hoop". **Home Addr:** 4045 Piping Rock Lane, Houston, TX 77027-3916, **Home Phone:** (713)621-5718. **Business Addr:** Color Commentator, Houston Rockets, 1510 Polk St, Houston, TX 77002, **Business Phone:** (713)627-3865.

## DREYFUSS, JOEL P.

Writer, editor. **Personal:** Born Sep 17, 1945, Port-au-Prince; son of Roger and Anne-Marie; married Veronica Pollard; children: Justin. **Educ:** City Univ NY, BS; Univ Chicago, urban jour fel. **Career:** NY Post, reporter, 1969-73; Assoc Press, reporter, 1969-71; Wash Post, reporter 1971-76; AP, reporter, 1973-76; Black Enterprise, exec ed, 1980-83; Emerge, contrib ed; Fortune, assoc ed, 1983-90; Tokyo bur chief, 1986-88; Bus Tokyo, New York, NY, managing ed, 1990-91; PC Mag, New York, ed, 1991-94; Info Week, ed-in-chief, 1993-96; Our World News, ed-in-chief, 1996-97; CMP Publ Inc, ed-in-chief; Red Herrings Inc, ed-in-chief, currently. **Orgs:** Coun Foreign Rels, 1986-; Japan Soc, 1988-; founding mem, Nat Asn Black Journalists, 1975-. **Honors/Awds:** Urban journalism fel, Univ Chicago, 1973; Coauthor (with Charles Lawrence III), The Bakke Case: The Politics of Inequality; Founder, Nat Asn Black Journalists; Coun Foreign Rel. **Business Addr:** Editor-in-chief, Red Herring Inc, 19 Davis Dr, Belmont, CA 94002-3001, **Business Phone:** (650)428-2900.

## DRIESSEN, DANIEL (DAN DRIESSEN)

Baseball player, baseball manager. **Personal:** Born Jul 29, 1951, Hilton Head Island, SC; married Bonnie; children: 3. **Career:** Baseball player (retired), baseball coach; Cincinnati Reds, infielder, 1973-84; Montreal Expos, infielder, 1984-85; San Francisco Giants, infielder, 1985-86; Houston Astros, infielder, 1986; St Louis Cardinals, infielder, 1987. **Home Addr:** PO Box 1001, Hilton Head Island, SC 29928.

## DRIESSEN, HENRY, JR.

Government official, executive. **Personal:** Born Sep 28, 1927, Hilton Head Island, SC; married Phoebe; children: Leon, Ann J & Bernard. **Educ:** Savannah State Col, BA, 1957. **Career:** Government official (retired); Driessen Groc & Serv Stat & Bottle Shop, merchant, 1958; Town Hilton Head, Ward 1 councilman. **Orgs:** Teacher Screven County High Sch, 1957-58; area dir, Bank Beaufort; dir, Palmetto Elec Coop Inc; past vpres, Hilton Head Island med Clin; postmaster, Happy Home Lodge No 125; past pres, Hilton Head Elem Sch PTA; past pres, McCracken High Sch; past dir, Hilton Head Island Chamber Com. **Honors/Awds:** Islander of the Month, Hilton Head Island Chamber Com; Business Community Service Award, Island Bus & Community Affairs Asn, 2005. **Home Addr:** 10 Alex Patterson Rd, Hilton Head Island, SC 29926-2164, **Home Phone:** (843)785-3913.

## DRIGGRISS, DAPHNE BERNICE SUTHERLAND

School administrator, school principal. **Personal:** Born New York, NY; married Harvey Sr; children: Harvey William Jr. **Educ:** NY Univ, attended 1944; Queens Col, City Univ NY, attended 1950; Adelphi Col Univ, BS, 1963, MA, 1971; Pace Univ, cert & MS, 1973. **Career:** Pub Sch 136 Queens, NY, asst prin, 1970; Pub Sch 116 Queens, NY, asst prin, 1974-78; Pub Sch 35 Queens, NY, asst prin, 1976-77; Pub Sch 132 Queens, NY, prin, 1978-. **Orgs:** Nat Asn Advan Colored People-JAMAICA, NY, 1950; Beta Omicron Chap Nat Sor Phi Delta Kappa Inc, 1966-; basileus Nat Sor Phi Delta Kappa Inc Beta Omicron Chap, 1975-77; Dist 29 treas Coun Spvrs & Adminrs, 1976-; NY City Elem Sch Prins Asn, 1979-; exec advisr, 1977-79; nat coordr int proj Nat Sor Phi DK Inc, 1981-; const chairperson Eastern Reg, 1984-

. **Honors/Awds:** Assiatant Principal Achievement Award, PTA PS #116 Queens, NY, 1977. **Home Addr:** 20312 119th Ave, Jamaica, NY 11412. **Business Addr:** Principal, Public School 132 Queens, 132 15 218 St, Springfield Gardens, NY 11413.

## DRISKELL, DAVID CLYDE

Curator, artist, educator. **Personal:** Born Jun 7, 1931, Eatonton, GA; son of George W and Mary L Cloud; married Thelma G Deloatch. **Educ:** Skowhegan Sch Painting & Sculpture, Maine, cert, 1953; Howard Univ, BA, 1955; Cath Univ, MFA, 1962; Ricks bur unsthistoriches Den Haag, Holland, 1964; Neth Inst Hist Art, art hist. **Career:** Talladega Col, assoc prof, 1955-62; Howard Univ, assoc prof, 1962-66; Fisk Univ, prof & chmn dept art, 1966-76; Univ Ife, Nigeria, vis prof, 1970; Amistad Res Ctr, Cur Aaron Douglas Collection, 1977-; Univ Md, prof art, 1977-95, chmn dept art, 1978-83, distinguished univ prof art, 1995-98, distinguished univ prof emer, 1998-; Bowdoin Col, vis prof; Univ Mich, vis prof; Queens Col, vis prof; Obafemi Awolowo Univ Ile-Ife, Nigeria, vis prof. **Orgs:** Col Art Asn Am; SE Mus Conf; Am Asn Mus; Am Fedn Arts; bd dirs, Nat Mus African Art; bd dirs, Am Fedn Arts. **Honors/Awds:** John Hope Award, 1959; Graphic Art Award, Corcoran Gallery of Art, 1965; Harmon Found Fel, 1964; Purchase Awards, Birmingham Mus Art, 1972; Tougaloo Col Gallery, 1973; Honorary Doctor of Humane Letters, Daniel Payne Col, 1977, Rust Col, 1991; Honorary Doctor of Fine Arts, Tougaloo Col, 1977, Bowdoin Col, 1989, State Univ NY, Old Westburg, 1989; President's Distinguished Service Award, Univ Md, College Park, 1997; Distinguished Alumni Awards in Art, Howard Univ; National Humanities Medal, 2000; Rockefeller Found Fel; Danforth Found Fel; David C. Driskell Prize, High Museum of Art, named in honor, 2005. **Special Achievements:** David C. Driskell Prize was established at the High Museum in Atlanta, Georgia, "The first national award to honor and celebrate contributions to the field of African-American art and art history", 2005; First Lt in AUS. **Home Addr:** 4206 Decatur St, Hyattsville, MD 20607-3758. **Business Addr:** Distinguished Professor Emeritus of Art, University of Maryland, 1202 Art Sociol Bldg, College Park, MD 20742, **Business Phone:** (301)405-2763.

## DRIVER, DAVID E.

Publishing executive, chief executive officer. **Personal:** Born Oct 17, 1955, Chicago, IL; son of Edward and Esther. **Educ:** Bradley Univ, BS, acct, 1976; Univ Chicago, Booth Sch Bus, MBA, finance, econs, 1979. **Career:** Arthur Young, mgr, cert pub acct, 1976-78; Baxter Int Inc, Arnar Stone Labs' Int, finance mgr, 1978-80; Am Hosp Supply Corp, finance mgr, 1978-80; Merrill Lynch, vpres, 1980-89; Noble Press, pres & publ, 1989-98; Prudential Bache Financial, vpres, 1998-2005; Loop Capital Markets, sr vpres, 2005-07; Visionary Forex, chief investment officer, 2008-10; Jackson Harbor Financial, prin, chief exec officer, 2012-; TJM Instnl Serv, sr vpres & contractor, 2012; "Bond Bears", Trading Club, consult-interest rates hedging/trading & managed futures, 2014-. **Orgs:** Bd mem, Better Boys Found, 1987-89; Points Light Found, adv coun, 1989-91; recruitment chmn, United Way Vol Ctr, 1990-92; bd mem, Breakaway, 1991-92; founder, Black Lit Soc; founding mem, Nat Asn Black Bk Publ; Phi Beta Sigma Fraternity Inc; Automated Trading Strategies; Black Enterprise Networked; Black Professionals Chicago; Bus Capital Start Up & Abbr; Coun Urban Professionals; Nat Black MBA Asn; Nat Asn Black Accountants; Univ Chicago Alumni Asn; Asn Black Found Execs; secy, Soc Ill Bk Publishers. **Special Achievements:** The Good Heart Book: A Guide to Volunteering, Noble Press, 1989; Defending the Left, nonfiction book, Noble Press, 1991. **Home Addr:** 3000 N Sheridan, Chicago, IL 60610. **Business Addr:** Chief Executive Officer, Harbor Financial of Houston, 229 N Jackson St, Houston, MS 38851, **Business Phone:** (662)456-5791.

## DRIVER, DONALD JEROME

Radio host, football player. **Personal:** Born Feb 2, 1975, Houston, TX; son of Marvin Jr and Faye Gray; married Betina; children: Cristian, Christina & Charity. **Educ:** Alcorn State Univ, BS, acct, MCS. **Career:** Football player (retired), host; Green Bay Packers, wide receiver & defensive back, 1999-2012; Marco Rivera, instr, 2002; WLUK-TV, co-host, 2004-; AM 620 WTMJ, co-host. **Orgs:** Founder, Donald Driver Found, 2001; Alpha Phi Alpha Fraternity. **Honors/Awds:** Conf Athlete of the Year Award; Nice Guy Award, 2000; Community Service Award, Green Bay Chamber Com, 2001; Most Valuable Player, Green Bay Packers, 2002, 2006; Walter Payton Man of the Year, Green Bay Packers, 2002; Nat Football Conf, Pro Bowl Team, NFL, 2002, 2006, 2007, 2011; Professional Achievement Award, The Sixth Annual Lee Remmel Sports Awards, 2003; Ed Block Courage Award, 2005; Galloping Gobbler Award, FOX Sports, 2009; Red Smith Award, 2010; Super Bowl Champion (XLV), Green Bay Packers, 2010; Humanitarian of the Year, Amvets, 2013; Donald Driver Way, Downtown Green Bay named in honor, 2013. **Special Achievements:** TV Show: Host: Inside the Huddle with Donald Driver; Annual Offense vs. Defense softball game. Radio show with AM 620 WTMJ. Author: Quickie Makes the Team, 2008; Quickie Handles a Loss, 2009; Quickie Goes to the Big Game, 2011; Driven, 2013. **Business Addr:** Co-Host, WLUK-TV, 787 Lombardi Ave, Green Bay, WI 54304, **Business Phone:** (920)494-8711.

## DRIVER, JOHNIE M.

Engineer, air force officer. **Personal:** Born May 8, 1933, Centerville, AL; son of McKelway and Daisy B Richard; married Odessa Wright; children: Dwaine Stuart & Courtney LaShay. **Educ:** Univ Ill, BS, elec engineering, 1961, MS, elec engineering, 1963. **Career:** Sperry UT Co, Salt Lake City, UT, proj engr, 1963-66; Jet Propulsion Lab Systs Div, mem, tech staff, 1966-99; self-employed, Software Oper Engr, currently. **Orgs:** Pres, Salt Lake City Nat Advan Asn Colored People, 1965-66; UT State Civil Rights Comn, 1965; Pasadena, Calif Nat Advan Asn Colored People; deacon, chmn, teacher Bible, SS Admin, leadership, Metrop Baptist Ch. **Special Achievements:** First Black to address Joint Session UT State Legislature, 1965. **Home Addr:** 3002 Grandeur Ave, Altadena, CA 91001, **Home Phone:** (626)797-6393. **Business Addr:** Software Operations Engineer, 3002 Grandeur Ave, Altadena, CA 91001-4704, **Business Phone:** (626)797-6393.

## DRIVER, RICHARD SONNY, JR.

Editor, publisher. **Personal:** Born Aug 16, 1926, Philadelphia, PA; son of Richard E Sr and Helen Birchett. **Career:** Free-lance advert & pub rels; Scoop USA, N Philadelphia, Pa, Newspaper ed, publ & owner, 1964-. **Orgs:** Nat Asn Advan Colored People; consult, United Black Bus Asn; bd mem, Black United Fund; Original Richard Allen Comt Inc. **Honors/Awds:** Distinguished Award, Nat Asn Advan Colored People, 1962; Citation Jazz, Home Club Am, 1971; Advertising Award, Lancaster Ave Bus Asn, 1973; City of Philadelphia Citation, City Philadelphia, 1995; Four Chaplains Legion of Honor Award, Chapel Four Chaplains, 1989; Service Award, Senator Pa, Pa legis Black Caucus, 1992; Service Award, Philadelphia City Coun, Mayor Philadelphia, 1995; US House of Representatives Citation, 1995; Pa State House of Representation Citation, 1995. **Home Addr:** 1220 N Broad St, Philadelphia, PA 19121, **Home Phone:** (215)232-5974. **Business Addr:** Publisher, Owner, Scoop USA, 942 N Watts St, Philadelphia, PA 19123, **Business Phone:** (215)232-5974.

## DRIVER, WILSONIA BENITA. See SANCHEZ, DR. SONIA BENITA.

## DRUITT, BEVERLY F.

Lawyer. **Personal:** Born Jun 5, 1947, Buffalo, NY; daughter of James and Florence; married Warren Little. **Educ:** State Univ NY, Buffalo, NY, BA, sociol & black stud, 1971; Rutgers Univ Sch Law, Newark, NJ, JD, 1974. **Career:** Reginald Heber Smith fel, 1964-76; N Miss Rural Legal Servs, Oxford, Miss, managing atty, 1974-77; Nat Labor Rels Bd, field atty, 1977-80, Div of Enforcement Litigation Off Appeals, sr atty, 1980-. **Orgs:** Treas, Nat Bar Asn, labor law sect, 1988-97, officer, chairperson; vpres, dir, EEO chair, pres, Nat Labor Rels Bd Profs Asn, 1990-97; pres, Nat Labor Rels Bd Prof Asn, 1992; treas, arbit sect, Nat Bar Asn, 2002-04; Nat chairperson, Bar Asn, govt lawyers div, chair, 2004-08; vice-chair, 2006-08; Nat Coun Negro Women; Nat Asn Female Execs; Nat Asn Advan Colored People; ed bd, Nat Labor Rels Bd; Supreme Ct US Am; State Miss Bar; Phi Beta Kappa; vpres, Legis & Pub Affairs Dir & EEO Chair. **Honors/Awds:** Special Act Award, NLRB, 1996, 2000, 2005-07. **Special Achievements:** First Black Woman to serve as president in National Labor Relations Board Professional Association. **Home Addr:** 7935 Lake Pleasant Dr, Springfield, VA 22153-2750, **Home Phone:** (703)912-6548. **Business Addr:** Senior Attorney, National Labor Relations Board, 1099 14th St NW Suite 8710, Washington, DC 20570, **Business Phone:** (202)273-3758.

## DRUMMING, SAUNDRA T.

Educator. **Educ:** Fla A&M Univ, BS, acct, 1971; Univ Ill, MA, acct, 1972; Univ Wis, PhD, acct, 1982. **Career:** Fla A&M Univ, assoc prof acct, currently. **Business Addr:** Associate Professor, Florida A&M University, WW-411 500 Gamble St, Tallahassee, FL 32307-5200, **Business Phone:** (850)412-7729.

## DRUMMOND, DAVID C.

Executive. **Personal:** Born Mar 6, 1963. **Educ:** Santa Clara Univ, BA, hist; Stanford Law Sch, JD. **Career:** Wilson Sonsini Goodrich & Rosati, partner, 1998; SmartForce, exec vpres finance & chief financial officer, 1999-2002; SSI Investments II Ltd, chief financial officer & exec vpres finance, 1999, dir, 2000-; Google Inc, partner, Corp Coun Off, gen coun, sr vpres corp develop, 2002-06, chief legal officer, 2002-, Alphabet, sr vpres corp develop, 2006-; PacketTrap Networks Inc, advisor; Ozy Media Inc, advisor; Next Autoworks Co, dir; V-Vehicle Co, dir; Rocket Lawyer Inc, dir; Kohlberg Kravis Roberts & Co, managing partner. **Orgs:** Bd dir, Uber Technologies Inc, 2013-; bd dir, Kohlberg Kravis Roberts & Co LP, 2014-; bd dir, Rocket Lawyer Inc; chmn, Google Ventures; chmn, Google Capital. **Special Achievements:** Google's first outside counsel. **Business Addr:** Senior Vice President of Corporate Development for Alphabet, Chief Legal Officer, Google Inc, 1600 Amphitheatre Pkwy, Mountain View, CA 94043, **Business Phone:** (650)253-0000.

## DRUMMOND, WILLIAM JOE

Educator, journalist, radio broadcaster. **Personal:** Born Sep 29, 1944, Oakland, CA; son of Jack Martin Sr and Mary Louise Tompkins; married Faye M; children: Tammerlin & Sean. **Educ:** Univ Calif, BA, 1965; Columbia Univ, Grad Sch Jour, MS, 1966; Univ Calif, Los Angeles, attended 1971. **Career:** Courier-Jour, Louisville, KY, staff writer, 1966-67; Los Angeles Times, staff writer, 1967-70, asst metrop ed, 1970-71, bur chief, New Delhi, India, 1971-74, bur chief Jerusalem, Israel, 1974-76, Wash Bur, staff writer, 1977-79, reporter; Nat Pub Radio, cor resp, 1979-83; Univ Calif, Berkeley, jour prof, 1983-; Christian Sci Monitor, spec corresp, 1992-97. **Orgs:** Nat Asn Black Journalists; Soc Prof Journalists; fel assoc press secy to Pres Carter, 1976-77. **Honors/Awds:** Journalism Award, Vision Mag, 1966; Edward M Hood Award, Nat Press Club, Wash, DC, 1982; Chancellor's Dist Lectr, Univ Calif, Berkeley, 1983; Sidney Hillman Foundation Award for Journalism Excellence, 1986; Award for Outstanding Coverage of the Black Condition, Nat Asn Black Journalists, 1989; Roy W Howard Award, Scripps Howard Found, 1991; Jack R Howard Award for Broadcasting Excellence, Scripps Howard Found, 1992; Excellence in Journalism Award, Soc Prof Journalists Northern Calif Chap, 1994; National Press Club Foundation Award; James Madison Freedom of Information Award, Soc Prof Journalists Northern Calif, 2014. **Home Addr:** 6700 Sobrante Rd, Oakland, CA 94611-1127, **Home Phone:** (510)339-1962. **Business Addr:** Professor of Journalism, University of California, 121 N Gate Hall Suite 5860, Berkeley, CA 94720-5860, **Business Phone:** (510)642-3383.

## DU BOSE, REV. ROBERT EARL, JR.

Clergy. **Personal:** Born Oct 9, 1927, Birmingham, AL; married Angela Grace Edwards; children: Robert III, Audrice, Gerald, Lucy & Angela. **Educ:** St Augustine's Col, Raleigh, NC, BA, BS, 1950; Seabury & Western Theol Sem Evanston, Lth, 1953. **Career:** Clergy (retired); St Andrew's Tuskegee, episcopal chaplain, vicar, 1953-56; Church Good Shepherd Montgomery, AL, vicar, 1956-61; Hist St Thomas' Epis Ch Phila, Pa, curate, 1961-62; St Cyprian's Epis Ch Phila, vicar, 1962-64; St Barnabas Epis Ch Phila, assoc rector, 1964-66; House Prayer Epis Church Phila, rector, 1966-76; Gen Conv Epis Ch, spl rep, 1970; Hist St Thomas' Episcopal & Ch, rector. **Orgs:** Active Qparticipant Bus Protest & Sit Ins With Dr M L King Montgomery AL, 1956-61; active partic, Selective Patronage Prog with Dr Leon Sullivan, 1961-64; founder Opport Indsl & Ctrs Am & Int, 1964, 1967; Comn Fin Property Epis Diocese PA, 1974-; Bishop's Task Force on Housing Epis Diocese PA, 1979-; St Thomas Hist Soc. **Honors/Awds:** Key Award Opport Indsl Ctr Phila, PA, 1969; Nat Distinguished Service Award, Alpha Phi Alpha Frat, 1970; Outstanding Service Award, Greater WOak Ln Coord Coun, 1970-71; Service Award, The Sch Dist of Philadelphia Wagner Hr High Sch, 1974; Hon DCL, St Augustine's Col, 1979. **Home Addr:** 3701 Conshohocken Ave, Philadelphia, PA 19131, **Home Phone:** (215)477-1234.

## DUAL, J. FRED, JR.

Executive, entrepreneur, president (organization). **Personal:** Born Apr 10, 1942, Chicago, IL; son of Joseph Frederick and Dorothy Marie Bowie; married Joyce Faye Metoyer; children: Leah, Joseph F III & Karen; married Mindy Lou Good. **Educ:** Northern Va Community Col, Annandale, VA, AA, 1974; Am Univ, Wash, DC, BS, mgt & bus admin, 1981; George Washington Univ, Wash, DC, 1982; Owner Pres Mgt Prog, Harvard Bus Sch, Cambridge, MA, 1991. **Career:** Booz Allen & Hamilton, Arlington, Va, assoc, 1981-85; Dual Inc, Arlington, Va, founder, pres & chief exec officer, 1983-. **Orgs:** Navy League US, 1988-95; Prof Servs Coun, 1990-91; Nat Training Systs Asn, 1993-; Nat Space Club, 1994-; Am Defense Preparedness Asn, 1995-; bd mem, Elk Hill Farm, Goochland, Va. **Business Addr:** President, Chief Executive Officer, Dual Inc, 9304 Falls Bridge Lane, Potomac, MD 20854-3950, **Business Phone:** (240)462-0225.

## DUAL, DR. PETER ALFRED

Management consultant, educator. **Personal:** Born Jan 27, 1946, Alexandria, VA; son of Peter Lloyd and Averlee Lucritia; married Toni Irene Nixon; children: Nikki Averlee, Peter Aaron, Tony Ahmaad & Alfred Michael. **Educ:** Lake Mich Col, AA, 1966; Western Mich Univ, BS, 1969, MA, 1971; Mich State Univ, PsyD, 1973; Univ Tex-Houston, MPH, 1975. **Career:** Univ TX, asst prof, 1973-75; assoc dir African-American Studies, 1973-75, Nat Pub Health fel, 1974-75; Univ MI, Grad Sch Pub Health, asst prof health behaviour, 1975-78, dir, asst to dean, 1978-80; Martin Luther King & Rosa Parks distinguished vis prof, 1987-88; Eastern MI Univ, Col health human serv, dean, prof health admin & pub health, 1980-83; San Diego State Univ, dean Col HTH, prof health serv, 1983-93; Panama Proj Hope, sr consult, 1985; Chinese Med Asn ROC, distinguished guest lectr, 1986; CAP Hahnnemahn Med Ctr, Philadelphia, provost, 1993-95; San Diego State Univ, teacher intl health, 1995-96, Sch Pub Health, grad prof pub health; CA State Polytech Univ, Sch Educ & Intergrative Studies, prof, Col Lett Arts & Social Sci, prof kinesiology, vpres acad affairs, Pomona, Calif, 1996-2000; E Washington Univ, provost & vpres acad affairs, 2000-02; Bethel AME Church Emmanuel Ctr, sr res scholar, 2002, ceo & sr res scholar; Ctr Acad Enrichment & Outreach, consult; Univ Nev Las Vegas, currently. **Orgs:** Am Asn Higher Educ; Am Pub Health Asn, 1971-; Active Nat Health Coun, 1979; Greater Detroit Area Hosp Coun, 1982; Mich Pub Health Asn; Adult Educ Asn; Nat Educ Asn; Am Soc Allied Health Professions; ASSD; Am Asn Higher Educ; Am Coun Educ; Rotary club; USAID; Alpha Pi Boule Chap; Sigma Pi Phi Frat; Phi Beta Delta Honor Soc Intl Scholars; bd dir, Joint-Health Policy, Scripps Res Found Inst, SDSU, 1988-93; Nat Coun Community & Edu Partnership, chmn & bd dir, Richard Allen Enterprises; chair bd trustee, Nat Coun Community & Educ Partnerships, 2001; chair, San Diego Pub Sch. **Home Addr:** 14222 S Murphy Rd, Cheney, WA 99004-9041. **Business Addr:** American Public Health Association, 800 I St NW, Washington, DC 20001, **Business Phone:** (202)777-2742.

## DUBE, THOMAS M. T.

Educator. **Personal:** Born Dec 25, 1938, Essexvale; married Ruth; children: Cengubuqotho & Thina. **Educ:** Univ Lesotho, BA, 1958; Univ S Africa, UED, 1960; CW Post Col Long Island Univ, MS, 1963; Univ Chicago, MA, 1972; Mich State Univ, MA, 1974; Univ Rochester, EdD, 1969; Cooley Law Sch, JD. **Career:** Western Mich Univ, asst prof social sci; Geneva Col Pa, asst prof; Rochester, NY, pre-sch teacher; Ministry African Educ, Rhodesia Africa, high sch teacher & elem sch teacher. **Orgs:** Rhodesian African Teachers Asn; Asn African Studies Am; founder mem, JairosJiri Inst Physically-Handicapped; founder, asst prin, Mpopoma African Community High Sch. **Home Addr:** 720 Bosker Ave, Kalamazoo, MI 49007. **Business Addr:** 337 Moore Hall, Kalamazoo, MI 49001.

## DUBENION, ELBERT D.

Scout, football player. **Personal:** Born Feb 16, 1933, Griffin, GA; married Marilyn Earl; children: Debra Lynn, Carolyn Ann, Susan Marie & Lisa Renee. **Educ:** Bluffton Col, BS, 1959. **Career:** Football player (retired), scout; Columbus Recreation Dept, 1960-67; Buffalo Bills, prof player & guard, 1960-68, flanker, 1960-67; Ohio Malleable Co Columbus, attendance dir, 1963-64; Atlanta Falcons, col scout. **Orgs:** Charter mem, Am Football League Hall Fame; Bills Silver Anniversary All-Time team. **Honors/Awds:** Most Popular Man May Day, 1959; Voted MVP three times Buffalo; American Football League Champion, All-Star Game, 1964 & 1965; Bill's most-valuable-Player Rookie, 1960; Greater Buffalo Hall of Fame, 1993. **Special Achievements:** The first player franchise hist to gain 1, 000 receiving yards in a season; The eighth person selected for the Bill's Wall of Fame, 1993. **Home Addr:** 513 Cherrington Rd, Westerville, OH 43081-3060, **Home Phone:** (614)523-3551.

## DUBOIS, COL. JOSHUA

Government official, clergy, religious leader. **Personal:** Born Jan 1, 1982, Bar Harbor, ME; son of W. Antoni Sinkfield. **Educ:** Boston Univ, BA, polit sci, 2003; Princeton Univ, MS, pub affairs, 2005. **Career:** Aide US Rep Rush Holt & served fel off US Rep Charles Rangel; Assoc Pastor Calvary Praise & Worship Ctr Cambridge, MA; Off Faith Based & Neighborhood Partnerships, head, 2009; Newsweek, Daily Beast, relig columnist; Sen Obama's Legis Off, US Senate. **Orgs:** Big Bro; Alpha Phi Alpha Fraternity. **Honors/Awds:** William Belden Noble Lecture, Harvard Univ. **Special Achievements:** Helped engineer Obama's participation in Rick Warren's Presidential Forum during the campaign, decision to use Saddleback church pastor for Obama's Inaugural invocation. **Business Addr:** Head, The White House, 1600

Pennsylvania Ave NW, Washington, DC 20500, **Business Phone:** (202)456-1414.

### DUBOSE, CULLEN LANIER

Administrator. **Personal:** Born Jul 5, 1935, Moss Point, MS; married Helena Joyce; children: Cheri, Cullen & Freddie. **Educ:** Tougaloo Col, attended 1956; Tri State Univ, BS, civil engineering, 1958; Mich State Univ, housing & finance, attended grad. **Career:** State MI, bridge design engr, Civil Engr, Struct Draftsman & Hwy Draftsman, 1958-69; State MI Housing Develop Authority, civil Engr, 1970; dir rehab, 1971-72; dir constr, 1972-73; dir mgt & mkt, 1974; Painia Develop Corp, chief operating officer, 1977-2008, pres, 1979-; Tougaloo Col, bd trustee, 2003-. **Orgs:** Tri State Col Alumni Club; W Side Action Ctr; Lansing Civic Ctr Bd; Omega Psi Phi Frat Inc; Nat Asn Advan Colored People; dir housing comt; Big Bro Lansing; Model Cities Policy Bd; past pres, Gov Milliken's Task Force Oper Break Through, 1970-71; Mich Econ Growth Authority, 2005-; Nat City Corp Mich Multi Cities; secy, Mich Housing Coun; bd dir, Detroit Investment Fund; Mich Minority Bus Develop Coun; African Am Asn Businesses & Contractors; bd dir, Univ Cult Ctr Asn; bd mem, Nat City Corp Mich Multi-Cities. **Honors/Awds:** Omega Psi Phi Citizens Award, 1966; NAACP Citizen Award, 1967. **Home Addr:** 6035 Exec Dr Suite 201, Lansing, MI 48911-5338, **Home Phone:** (517)393-5800. **Business Addr:** Board of Trustee, Tougaloo College, 500 W County Line Rd, Tougaloo, MS 39174, **Business Phone:** (601)977-7700.

### DUBRIEL, LISA M.

Executive. **Educ:** Nat Automobile Dealers Asn, training prog. **Career:** Antioch Ford Auto Ctr, pres, owner, currently. **Honors/Awds:** Ford's Blue Oval Certification. **Business Addr:** President, Owner, Antioch Ford Auto Center, 1400 W 10th St, Antioch, CA 94509-1438, **Business Phone:** (925)757-1771.

### DUBROY, TASHNI-ANN

College president, business owner. **Personal:** daughter of Emerson Coote and Greta Coote; married Dale Dubroy; children: Marli-Jolie. **Educ:** Shaw Univ, BS, chem, 2002; NC State Univ, PhD, chem, 2007; Rutgers, State Univ NJ-New Brunswick, MBA, mkt, 2010. **Career:** NC State Univ, grad res asst, 2002-04, teaching asst, 2002-06; BASF Catalysts LLC, res & develop chemist, 2007, technol analyst, 2007-09, procurement mgr, 2009-10; Tea & Honey Blends, COO, 2006-; Shaw Univ, assoc prof, dept chair, 2011-13, spec asst to pres, 2014-15, pres-elect, 2015, pres, 2015-; Element Beauty Bar, co-owner, 2013-. **Orgs:** Co founder, Brilliant & Beautiful Found, 2012; Am Chem Soc. **Special Achievements:** Contributor to scientific journals including "Journal of Physical Organic Chemistry". **Business Addr:** Shaw University, 118 E South St, Raleigh, NC 27601, **Business Phone:** (919)546-8300.

### DUCARD, MALIK

Vice president (organization), media executive. **Educ:** Columbia Univ, New York, BA, film & African Am studies, 1995; Univ Calif, Los Angeles, Anderson Sch Mgt, MBA, 2000. **Career:** Young & Rubicam New York, acct exec new bus, 1995-98; Goldman Sachs, summer assoc equites div, 1999; Metro-Goldwyn-Mayer, dir strategic & financial planning, 2000-02, exec dir bus develop & acquisitions, 2002-04, vpres worldwide home entertainment bus develop & acquisitions, 2004-05; Lionsgate Entertainment, vpres home entertainment acquisitions & bus develop, 2005-07; Paramount Pictures, vpres N Am digital distrib, 2007-09, Sr vpres digital distrib Americas, 2009-11; Google & YouTube, content bus develop, 2011-, Family & Learning, YouTube, global head, 2011-. **Orgs:** Bd dir, Bresee Found. **Honors/Awds:** "Hollywood Reporter," Next Gen Edition; "Business Insider," 25 Most Influential Blacks in Technology, 2013. **Business Addr:** Content Business Development, Google Inc, 1600 Amphitheatre Pkwy, Mountain View, CA 94043.

### DUCKETT, ESQ. GREGORY

Executive, health services administrator. **Personal:** Born Jan 26, 1960, Memphis, TN; son of Lavance Harris and Ocie; married Brenda Parker; children: Stephen Gregory & Kelsey Breanna. **Educ:** Carnegie-Mellon Univ, Pittsburgh, attended 1981; Oberlin Col, Oberlin, BA, 1982; Memphis State Univ Sch Law, Memphis, TN, JD, 1985. **Career:** US Congressman Harold Ford, Memphis, Tenn, staff asst, 1983-84; Shelby County Criminal Ct, Memphis, Tenn, judicial law clerk, 1984-85; US Sen Albert Gore Jr, Memphis, Tenn, staff asst, 1985, staff atty, 1985-86, state coun, 1985-87; City Memphis, Memphis, Tenn, dir, div pub serv, 1988, dir, Div Housing & Community Develop, 1988-91, chief ade officer, 1991; Baptist Mem Health Care, sr vpres & chief legal officer, 1992-; Clinton/Gore Transition Team, appointee, 1992. **Orgs:** Pres, Memphis State Univ Sch Law Stud Bar Asn, 1985; bd mem, Youth Villages, 1988-; bd mem, Leadership Memphis, 1989-; Tenn Adv Comt Lower Miss Delta Develop Comn, 1989; bd mem, Memphis Col Art, 1990-; bd dir, WONDERS; St Jude Liberty Bowl; bd dir, Fed Res Bank St Louis, Memphis Br; Memphis Col Art; hearing officer, Tenn Supreme Courts Bd Prof Responsibility, 1993-2003; Nat Civil Rights Mus; pres, Liberty Bowl Festival Asn, 2001; bd mem, Am Health Lawyers Asn & Health Servs Develop Agency; bd mem, Memphis Zool Soc; chmn, Shelby County Election Comn; bd mem & chmn, Tenn Hosp Asn, 2007; Liberty Bowl Festival Asn; vice chair, Memphis Redbirds Found; bd regents, Tenn's ninth cong dist, 2012-. **Home Addr:** 665 Tenn St Unit 412, Memphis, TN 38103, **Home Phone:** (901)854-9439. **Business Addr:** Senior Vice President, Chief Legal Officer, Baptist Memorial Health Care, 350 N Humphreys Blvd EAGLB2 5th Fl, Memphis, TN 38120-2177, **Business Phone:** (901)227-5233.

### DUCKETT, KAREN IRENE

Executive, president (organization), chief executive officer. **Personal:** Born Jun 12, 1947, Rochester, NY; daughter of Albert and Ann Maass; married Wardell; children: Chioke, Shani & Makiri. **Educ:** Ohio Univ, BFA, 1969; Yale Univ, Occidental Col, MA, urban studies, 1974; Woodrow Wilson Col Law, JD, 1981. **Career:** Xerox Corp, facil mgr, interior designer, proj mgr, 1969-73; City Flint, dir planning, 1973-75; City Atlanta, phys develop adminr, 1975-78; Duckett Van Devere & Assocs Inc, pres, chief exec officer, 1985-89; Duckett Design Group, pres & chief exec officer, owner, 1985-. **Orgs:** Secy bd dir, Metro Atlanta Coalition 100 Black Women, 1987-91; exec comt, Leadership Atlanta, 1986-91, 1996; Nat Orgn Minority Architects, 1990-; treas, Jack & Jill Am, 1990-; bd mem, Atlanta Chamber Com, 1993-96; bd mem, Women's Econ Develop Agency, 1994-, chair, 1995-96; bd mem, Atlanta Bus League, 1995-98; Harvard Black Law Students Asn. **Home Addr:** 685 Wilson Mill Rd SW, Atlanta, GA 30331-4150, **Home Phone:** (404)696-6798. **Business Addr:** President, Owner, Duckett Design Group Inc, 1632 Ware Ave, East Point, GA 30344, **Business Phone:** (404)592-4539.

### DUCKSWORTH, MARILYN JACOBY

Publishing executive. **Personal:** Born Jan 1, 1957, Stamford, CT. **Educ:** Tufts Univ, BA, 1978, MA, Eng, 1979; Tufts Univ, London, Eng, 1977. **Career:** Doubleday & Co Inc, publicity asst, 1979-80, assoc publicist, 1980-82, sr publicist, 1982-83, mgr publicity, 1983-85; GP Putnam's Sons, mgr publicity, 1985, dir publicity, 1985-87; GP Putnam's Sons & Grosset Grp, exec dir publicity, vp, assoc publ, 1987, sr vpres corp commun, currently; Penguin Group Inc, dir corp commun, sr vpres, assoc publ & exec dir. **Orgs:** trustee, Tufts Univ, 1993-2003; Col Lang Asn; Pub Publicity Assoc; Women's Media Grp; Whos Who US Execs. **Honors/Awds:** Scholastic Achievement Award, Black Educators Stamford, 1974; Nat Honor, Soc Hon Soc Sec Sch, 1974; Dean's List Tufts Univ, 1974-78; Langston Hughes Literary Award, Tufts Univ, 1978; Black Mgr Publicity, Doubleday & Co Inc, 1983-85; Black exec dir publicity, GP Putnam's Sons. **Home Addr:** 81 W N St, Stamford, CT 06902. **Business Addr:** Senior Vice President, Corporate Communications, Penguin Group Inc, 1855 Chicago Rd, Sturgis, MI 49091, **Business Phone:** (269)651-9488.

### DUDLEY, EUNICE MOSLEY

Executive. **Personal:** Born Selma, AL; daughter of Andrew M Mosley Sr and Eva O Murdoch Mosley; married Joe Louis Dudley Sr; children: Joe Jr, Ursula & Genea. **Educ:** Talladega Col, attended. **Career:** Dudley Cosmetology Univ, Kernersville, NC, dir, 1989; Dudley Prod Inc, Kernersville, NC, co-founder & chief financial officer, currently. **Orgs:** Boy Scout Camp, Winston Salem; Girl Scout Camp, Keyauwee; United Negro Col Fund; Bennett Col Scholar; NC Agr & Tech Univ; E Forsyth Citizens Human Servs; Providence Baptist Church, Greensboro, NC; comt organizing sch mgt, Africa Univ; bd mem, Community Found Greater Greensboro; Financial Secy Greater Greensboro/Reidsville club, NANPBW; Direct Selling Educ Found Bd. **Business Addr:** Chief Financial Officer, Dudley Products Inc, 1080 Old Greensboro Rd, Kernersville, NC 27284-8488, **Business Phone:** (336)993-8800.

### DUDLEY, HERMAN T.

Government official, army officer. **Personal:** Born Apr 4, 1924, Richmond, KY; married Ruth. **Educ:** BS, 1956. **Career:** Govt Off (retired); Detroit Engr Off Bur Archit, dir. **Orgs:** Regist architect, State Mich. **Honors/Awds:** The Congressional Gold Medal, Cong. **Home Addr:** 3322 Buena Vista, Detroit, MI 48238. **Business Addr:** 9th Fl Cadillac Tower, Detroit, MI 48226.

### DUDLEY, JOE LOUIS, SR.

Entrepreneur, chief executive officer, salesperson. **Personal:** Born May 9, 1937, Aurora, NC; son of Gilmer L and Clara Yeates; married Eunice Mosley; children: Joe Jr, Ursula & Genea. **Educ:** NC A&T State Univ, BS, bus admin, 1967. **Career:** Fuller Prod, staff, 1962, distribr, 1967, pres, 1976-94; Dudley Prod Inc, pres & chief exec officer, 1975-; Dudley Cosmetol Univ, founder, 1989-; DCU Inn, 1990; Dudley Beauty Sch Syst, owner, currently; Dudley Beauty Corp LLC, ceo, pres, currently. **Orgs:** Direct Selling Asn; Joe Dudley Fel; Dudley Ladies; Com PASS; bd dir, Am Health & Beauty Aids Inst; bd dir, Br Banking & Trust Financial Corp. **Home Addr:** 1808 Morgans Mill Way, High Point, NC 27265-9704, **Home Phone:** (336)886-5218. **Business Addr:** President, Chief Executive Officer, Dudley Products Inc, 1835 Eastchester Dr, High Point, NC 27265.

### DUDLEY, JUANITA C.

Social worker, administrator. **Personal:** Born Apr 14, 1929, Talladega, AL; daughter of Walter Thomas Strickland and Fannie Tanner; married Calmeze Henike; children: Rhonda Carroll Le Grice. **Educ:** Talladega Col, AL, BA, 1950; Atlanta Univ, GA, MSW, 1954; Southwestern Univ Law Sch, Los Angeles, CA, 1967. **Career:** Dr CH Dudley, Los Angeles, Calif, psychiat soc worker, 1954-; Govt VI, St Thomas, supvr pub assistance, 1957-59; Los Angeles County, adoptionconsult, 1963-66; Nat Urban League Inc, Los Angeles, asst regional dir, 1966-73; Los Angeles County Grand Jury, Calif, 1982-83. **Orgs:** Nat vpres, Girlfriends Inc; Wilfandel Club Inc; Circlelets Inc; Los Angeles County, Grand Jury; Los Angeles County Hosp Asn, consult, 1975-76; exec bd dir, Los Angeles Chap-March Dimes; chairperson, Pub Affairs Comt Los Angeles chap. **Home Addr:** 1743 Virginia Rd, PO Box 191399, Los Angeles, CA 90019, **Home Phone:** (323)737-5770. **Business Addr:** Social Worker, 3731 Stocker St Suite 204, Los Angeles, CA 90019, **Business Phone:** (213)299-2050.

### DUDLEY, RICKEY DESHUN

Football player. **Personal:** Born Jul 15, 1972, Henderson, TX. **Educ:** Ohio State Univ. **Career:** Football player (retired); Oakland Raiders, tight end, 1996-2000; Cleveland Browns, tight end, 2001; Tampa Bay Buccaneers, tight end, full back, 2002-04.

### DUDLEY-WASHINGTON, LOISE

Educator, teacher. **Personal:** Born Nov 1, 1944, Ft. Lauderdale, FL; daughter of Thomas and Clara Kirkland Morley; children: Keith & Renee. **Educ:** City Col NY, BS, 1978, MS, 1980, PhD, 1990. **Career:** MLK Health Ctr, mgr & MIS analyst, 1969-89; G&S Res Analyst, statistian, 1981-82; Childrens Cir Daycare Ctr, spec ed coord, 1982-88, dir proj; Giant Step, 1989-90; St Mary's Sch, spec educ teacher, 1990-92; NYC Sch Bd, Dist 9, pres, 1992-; Health & Hosp Corp, early intervention off designee. **Orgs:** Vpres, NYC Sch Bd, Dist 9, 1983-92; consult, Hosp Billing Syst; dir, Bronx Youth Action, 1985-. **Honors/Awds:** Outstanding Community School Board Member Bronx Democratic Club, 1985; Excellence in Education, NYS Coun Black Republicans, 1986, 1987; Community Service Award, Montefiore Health Ctr, 1988. **Home Addr:** 540 E 169th St Apt 15c, Bronx, NY 10456-2653, **Home Phone:** (718)588-8441. **Business Addr:** Early Intervention Official Designee, Health & Hospital Corp, 1805 Williamsbridge Rd, Bronx, NY 10462.

### DUE, TANANARIVE

Writer. **Personal:** Born Jan 5, 1966, Tallahassee, FL; daughter of John Dorsey Jr and Patricia Stevens; married Steven Barnes; children: Jason Barnes. **Educ:** Northwestern Univ, BS, jour; Univ Leeds, MA, eng lit. **Career:** Journalist & novelist; Miami Herald, feature writer & columnist, 1988-98; Auth novels: Between, 1995; My Soul to Keep, 1997; Black Rose, 2000; Living Blood, 2001; Good House, 2003; Freedom Family, 2003; Joplin's Ghost, 2005; Casanegra: A Tennyson Hardwick Story, 2007; Blood Colony, 2008; My Soul To Take, 2011; contribr to Naked Came Manatee, 1996; Antioch Univ, Los Angeles, MFA prog, assoc fac, creative writing, currently; Co-Auth: Devils Wake, 2012; Domino Falls, 2013; Blair Underwood Presents From Cape Town With Love. **Orgs:** Hurston-Wright Found. **Business Addr:** Associate Faculty, Antioch University, 400 Corporate Pointe, Culver City, CA 90230, **Business Phone:** (310)578-1080.

### DUFF, JAMAL EDWIN

Football player, actor. **Personal:** Born Mar 11, 1972, Columbus, OH. **Educ:** San Diego State Univ, grad. **Career:** New York Giants, defensive end, 1995-96; Wash Redskins, left defensive end & defensive end, 1997-98. Films: S.W.A.T, 2003; The Rundown, 2003; The Eliminator, 2004; Dodgeball: A True Underdog story, 2004; The Marine, 2006; The Lords Of The Underworld, 2007; The Game Plan, 2007; Blood: The Last Vampire, 2009; The Black Mamba, 2011; Minkow, 2011; Django Unchained, 2012, Minkow, 2014. TV series: "CSI: Crime Scene Investigation, 2006; "All Of Us", 2006; "In Justice", 2006; "The Game", 2007; "Two and a Half Men", 2010; "Traffic Light", 2011; "Melissa & Joey", 2011; "Revenge", 2011-12; "Sons of Anarchy", 2013; "Brooklyn Nine-Nine", 2013; "Haunted Hathaways", 2014; "Workaholics", 2014. **Honors/Awds:** Aztecs Outstanding Def Player Of The Year Awd, San Diegfo Univ. **Home Addr:** , Long Beach, CA.

### DUFFOO, DR. FRANTZ MICHEL

Scientist, physician. **Personal:** Born Mar 5, 1954, Port-au-Prince; son of Franck and Leonie Narcisse; married Marcia Sylvester; children: Brian Anthony, Christian Jason & Ashley Gabrielle. **Educ:** City Col NY, BS, 1977; Meharry Med Col, Nashville, TN, MD, 1980. **Career:** Brookdale Hosp Med Ctr, intern, resident internal med, 1979-82; Montefiore Med Ctr, clin fel, 1982-83, res fel, 1983-84; Internal Med Am Bd Internal Med, dipl, 1984-; Woodhull Med & Ment Health Ctr, attend physician & consult nephrol, 1984-92, chief nephrology assoc dir med, 1990-92; Am Bd Internal Med, dipl, 1986; State Univ NY Health Sci Ctr, Brooklyn, instr med, 1985-88, asst prof med, 1988-; New York Univ, adj asst prof, 1990-; St Mary's Hosp, dir internal med residency prog, dir med, 1992-97, secy, 1992; Cath Med Ctrs, Internal Med Residency Prog, dir, 1997; St Vincent Cath Med Ctr, physician, pvt prac, currently; Caritas Health Care Inc, physician. **Orgs:** New York Acad Scis, 1981-88; Am Col Physicians, 1985-92; Am Soc Nephrology, 1985-; Int Soc Nephrol, 1985-; New York Soc Nephrol; charter mem, Am Soc Hypertension, 1986-; charter mem, Int Soc Hypertension Blacks; Nat Kidney Found, 1989-; fel Am Col Physicians, 1992. **Home Addr:** 11432. **Business Addr:** Private Practice, Nephrologist, 8825 153rd St, Jamaica, NY 11432, **Business Phone:** (718)558-7150.

### DUFFY, EUGENE JONES

Association executive, executive. **Personal:** Born Aug 25, 1954, Columbus, OH; son of Franklin V and Helen Jones; married Norrene Johnson; children: Josie Helen & Rosa Patrice. **Educ:** Morehouse Col, BA, 1976; Univ Ibadan Nigeria; Univ Western Cape. **Career:** Dept Parks Recreation & Cult Affairs, dep comr; Off Contract Compliance, dir; City Atlanta, Off Mayor, dep chief admin officer; H J Russel & Co, Atlanta, GA, sr vpres, 1990-94; Levmark Capital, sr policy consult; Albritton Capital Mgt, exec vpres; Paradigm Asset Mgt co, exec vpres mkt & sr exec vpres, currently. **Orgs:** Nat League Cities, Nat Conf Black Pub Admins; trustee, Morehouse Col; YMCA; pres, Atlanta Univ Ctr Stud Coun; founding mem, 100 Black Men atlanta; Urban Consortium. **Home Addr:** 4810 Harris Trl NW, Atlanta, GA 30327-4412. **Business Addr:** Senior Executive Vice President, Paradigm Asset Management Co, 445 Hamilton Ave, White Plains, NY 10601, **Business Phone:** (914)368-5410.

### DUFRESNE, DAPHNE J.

Financial manager, executive. **Personal:** daughter of Jacques and Yolande; married Joseph Leonard Amprey III, May 15, 2004. **Educ:** Univ Pa, BS, 1994; Harvard Bus Sch, MBA, 1999. **Career:** Bank Scotland's Structured Finance Group, assoc dir; Weston Presidio Capital, prin, 1999-2004; Parish Capital Advisors, venture partner, 2005; RLJ Equity Partners, founding partner & managing dir, 2005-; JBD Holdings LLC, managing partner. **Honors/Awds:** The Network Journal, 40 Under 40, 2010; "Black Enterprise", Rising Stars 40 & Under, 2014. **Business Addr:** Managing Partner, RLJ Equity Partners LLC, 7315 Wisconsin Ave Suite 900e, Bethesda, MD 20814, **Business Phone:** (240)744-7856.

### DUGAS, A. JEFFREY ALAN, SR.

Physician. **Personal:** Born Aug 6, 1953; son of Lester and Laurenetta; children: Andrea & Jeffrey Jr. **Educ:** Morehouse Col, BA, biol, 1976; Atlanta Univ, attended 1977; Roosevelt Univ, attended 1979; Morehouse Col Sch Med, attended 1982; Rush Med Col, MD, 1984. **Career:** Michael Reese Hosp & Med Ctr, community rels ment health rep, 1978-79; Morehouse Sch Med, res asst, 1981-82; Rush-Presby St Lukes Med Ctr, intern, 1984-85, residency, 1985-87, instr med, 1987-; Coastal Emergency Servs, independent contractor, 1986-87; Provident Med Ctr, 1987; City Chicago, Bd Health, physician, 1988-91; Rush Med Col, asst prof, 1991-; William L Dawson Nursing Ctr, med dir, 1991-; Your Health & Wellness, owner, currently. **Orgs:** Chicago Med Soc; Ill State Med Soc; Am Col Physicians; Am Med Asn; Nat Med Asn, Cook County Physicians Asn; Crescent Counties Found Med Care; Southside YMCA, bd, vchair. **Honors/Awds:** Leading Young Black Doctor, Dollars and Sense Magazine. **Business Addr:**

Physician, Rush University Medical Center, 401 W Ontario St Suite 220, Chicago, IL 60654, **Business Phone:** (312)255-1580.

### DUGGER, CLINTON GEORGE

Clergy. **Personal:** Born Sep 8, 1929, Beacon, NY; son of William and Mary Anderson; married Virginia McLean; children: Michael Kerwin. **Educ:** St Augustine's Col, BA, 1959; State Univ NY, Albany, MSW, 1967. **Career:** Clergy (retired); Trinity Church, cur, 1962-65; Diocese Albany, diocesan officer, 1965-67; Berkshire Farm Boys, chaplain, 1967-81; St Luke's vicar, 1973-85; Hoosac Sch, chaplain, 1981-85; Church Redeemer, rector. **Orgs:** Lebanon Valley Lions Club; Rensselaer Comm Ctr Bd; Troy Church Home Bd; bd dir, Gould Farm, MA; bd mem, Episcopal Church Coun Ctr, 1986-92; Am Legion Post No 1683. **Honors/Awds:** MDiv, Philadelphia Divinity Sch, 1962; Man of the Year, Rotary, 1975; Chaplain Emer, Hoosac Sch, 1987; Dean of the Metrop Deanery, Diocese, 1987; Chaplain of Fire Dept, Rensselaer, 1992. **Home Addr:** 14401 State Rte 22, PO Box 148, New Lebanon, NY 12125-0148, **Home Phone:** (518)794-9740.

### DUGGER, EDWARD, III

Executive. **Personal:** Born Apr 14, 1949, Dayton, OH; son of Edward Jr and Wertha; married Elizabeth Harris; children: Cyrus Edward, Langston Reid & Chloe D'jenne. **Educ:** Harvard Col, BA (cum laude), 1971; Princeton Univ, MPA UP, pub affairs, 1973. **Career:** Irwin Mgt Co Inc, mgr real estate div, 1973-74; UNC Ventures Inc, pres & chief exec officer, 1978-; Remote Light Inc, Dir, 1990; UNC Partners Inc, pres & chief exec officer, 1990-; NISE!, founder & cheif exec officer, 2010-; Reinventure Capital LP, pres, 2014-. **Orgs:** UNC Ventures Inc, corp bd, 1978-97; Greater Boston YMCA, 1981-92; United Way MA Bay, 1981-87;Nat Asn Advan Colored People Legal Defense Fund, New Eng, bd dir, 1985-; Harvard Univ, comt univ res, 1985-; bd dir, New Eng Aquarium, 1988-; bd dir, Partnership, 1988-95; C's Mus, 1988-95; San Francisco Med Ctr, mgt comn, 1989-; Columbia Plaza Assocs, dir, 1989; Granite Broadcasting Co, corp bd, 1989-2007; chair, Envirotest Syst Co, corp bd, 1990-98; US Radio, LP, adv comt, 1990-96; bd dir, Beth Israel Hosp, Boston Mass, 1991-96; UNC Media Inc, 1991-97; bd dir, Boys & Girls Club Boston, 1993-; dir, chmn, Social Venture Network, 1993-; Boston Club, 1994-; MA Bus Roundtable, 1994-; Students Responsible Bus, 1994-; exec, Fed Res Bank Boston, Dir & Mem Exec bd, audit & econ Reserach Comts, 1995-2000; Mass Bus Roundtable, dir, Exec Comt, 1995-; dir, Boston Community Capital Inc, 1998-; chmn, Venture Comt, 1998-; adv bd mem, Bridges Ventures U. S. Sustainable Growth Fund LP, 2013; Sustainable Bus Network Mass, dir, 2013-. **Home Addr:** 54 Burroughs St, Jamaica Plain, MA 02130-4059, **Home Phone:** (617)522-4936. **Business Addr:** President, Chief Executive Officer, UNC Partners Inc, 54 Burroughs St, Boston, MA 02130, **Business Phone:** (617)522-2160.

### DUHANEY, TREVOR

Automotive executive. **Educ:** London Sch Econs, MA. **Career:** Ns Jamaica Ltd, br mgr, 1971-74; Deel Ford, sales assoc, sales mgr & gen mgr, 1974-78; Newport Lincoln Mercury, partner & gen mgr, 1978-80; Anthony Abraham Chevrolet, sales assoc, 1980-83; Potamkin Chevrolet, sales mgr & sales assoc, 1983-85; Potamkin World Ctr, partner & gen mgr, 1985-89; Duhaney Auto Sales, pres & chief exec officer, 1989-93; Duhaney Pontiac Buick GMC, pres & chief exec officer, 1993-2004; Duhaney Motors, pres & chief exec officer, 2004-. **Orgs:** Bd gov, Greater Miami Chamber Com; Rainbow PUSH Coalition; Nat Minority Automobile Asn; S Fla Automobile Asn. **Business Addr:** Chief Executive Officer, President, Duhaney Motors, 8300 NW 7th Ave, Miami, FL 33150, **Business Phone:** (305)751-9621.

### DUHART, HAROLD BOBBY, SR.

Engineer, manager. **Personal:** Born Dec 15, 1938, Macon, GA; married Margaret Roberts; children: Bobby & Lori Brewington. **Educ:** NC Agr & Tech Univ, BS, 1963; Ga Inst Tech, advan study. **Career:** City Durham, NC, eng redevelop officer, 1964-65; AUS Corps Engrs, space facil design engr, 1964-68; Dept HUD, eng munic proj mgr, 1968-70; US Environ Protection Agency, NC, state proj mgr; Duhart Bros Builders Inc, prin, currently. **Orgs:** Pres, Duhart Bros Enterprises Macon, GA, 1974-; Fed Water Pollution Control Asn; Equal Opportunity Comn EPA; assoc mem, ASCE; PTA; Task force Minority Bus EPA prog; YMCA; SW Atlanta Comn Asn; SABFO. **Honors/Awds:** Membership campaign Award, YMCA; Special Achievement Award, EPA, 1973. **Business Addr:** Principal, Duhart Brothers Builders Inc, 1867 Austin Rd SW, Atlanta, GA 30331-4802, **Business Phone:** (404)344-8740.

### DUKE, BILL (WILLIAM HENRY DUKE, JR.)

Administrator, movie director, actor. **Personal:** Born Feb 26, 1943, Poughkeepsie, NY; son of William Henry Sr and Ethel Louise Douglas. **Educ:** Dutchess Community Col, AA; Boston Univ, Sch Fine Arts, Directing & Actg, BA, 1964; NY Univ, Sch Arts, Actg & Directing, MFA, 1968; Am Film Inst, Sch Fine Arts, Film & Directing, MFA, 1971. **Career:** Films: Car Wash, 1976; Am Gigilo, 1980; Commando, 1985; Predator, 1987; No Man's Land, 1987; Action Jackson, 1988; Street of No Return, 1989; Bird on a Wire, 1990; Rage In Harlem, dir, 1991; Deep Cover, dir, 1992; Menace II Soc, 1993; Cemetary Club, dir, 1993; Sister Act 2, 1993; Sweet Potato Ride, exec producer, 1996; Hoodlum, exec producer, 1997; Susan's Plan, 1998; Payback, 1999; Foolish, 1999; The Limey, 1999; Fever, 1999; Never Again, 2001; Exit Wounds, 2001; Love & a Bullet, 2002; Red Dragon, 2002; National Security, 2003; Twisted, 2004; Yellow, 2006; X-Men: The Last Stand, 2006; The Pact, exec producer, 2006; Yellow, 2006; The Go-Getter, 2007; Prince Among Slaves, recreations dir, 2008; Cover, dir & producer, 2008; Level 26: Dark Origins, 2009; The Big Bang, post-production, currrently, Freaky Deaky, 2012; Battledogs, 2013; Clipped Wings, They Do Fly, 2014; Bad Country, 2014; Preying for Mercy, writer, 2014; Restored Me, 2015. TV Series: "American Playhouse", dir, 1989; "Raisin In The Sun", dir, 1989; "Karen Sisco", 2003-04; "Lost", 2006; "Every Man for Himself", 2006; "Battlestar Galactica", 2006; "Black Market", 2006; Am Playhouse Killing, dir; The Meeting, dir; Miracle's Boys; Get Rich or Die Tryin, 2005; "Battlestar Galactica", 2006; "Lost", 2006; "The Boondocks", 2007; "Cold Case", 2008; "My Own Worst Enemy", 2008; "The Blexicans ", dir, writer, 2015; "Tru Dattt", exec producer, 2014; Howard Univ, Dept Radio, TV & Film, chmn, 2000; Howard Univ, Dept Radio, TV & Film, chmn, 2000; Howard Univ, Dept Radio TV & Film, chair; Yagya Productions, Duke Media, founder & chief exec officer, currently. Books: Black Light: The African American Hero, 1994; Bill Duke's 24-Hours L.A. **Orgs:** Sundance Film Festival, 1992; Artist Against Homelessness; dir Guild Am; Writers Guild Am; Screen Actors Guild; Nat Endowment Humanities; Calif State Film Comn Bd; bd trustee, Am Film Inst, currently. **Home Addr:** 317 Las Casas Ave, Pacific Palisades, CA 90272, **Home Phone:** (310)454-3643. **Business Addr:** Founder, Chief Executive Officer, Yagya Productions Inc, PO Box 609, Pacific Palisades, CA 90272-0609, **Business Phone:** (310)230-4040.

### DUKE, RUTH WHITE

Educator. **Personal:** Born Dec 12, 1927, Hampton, VA; daughter of George David (deceased) and Lucille Lowry (deceased); married Everette L; children: Everette L Jr & Cecil Q. **Educ:** Va State Univ, BS, 1948; NY Univ, MA, 1951; James Madison Univ, attended 1970; Old Dom Univ, attended 1972; Norfolk State Univ, attended 1973; Va Polytechnic Inst & State Univ, attended 1975. **Career:** Educator (retired); Lunenburg High Sch, bus teacher, 1949-52; Sumner & Vashon High Sch, bus teacher, 1952-54; Norfolk State Univ, bus teacher, 1955-56; BT Wash High Sch, bus teacher, 1956-57; US Govt, civil serv worker, 1957-59; Jacox Jr High Sch, bus teacher, 1961-65; Norview High Sch, bus teacher, dept chp, 1965-86; Old Dominion Univ, supvr social studies stud teachers, 1989-91. **Orgs:** Pres, vpres, corresp secy, Va Beach Pinchole Bugs, 1972-96; secy church meetings, Bank St Mem Church, 1974-94; bd, chair by-laws, Girls Inc Tide water, 1975-93; nat fin secy, Pinochle Bugs Social & Civic Club, 1980-84, nat treas, 1988-92; volunteer admin off, Norfolk Cot Hosp, 1990-96; Pinochle Bugs Social & Civic Club Inc, Nat exec sec; treas nat exec sec, L & J Gardens. **Home Addr:** 1036 Fairlawn Ave, Virginia Beach, VA 23455, **Home Phone:** (757)461-2908. **Business Addr:** VA, **Business Phone:** (804)461-2908.

**DUKE, WILLIAM HENRY, JR.** See DUKE, BILL.

### DUKES, CARL R.

President (organization), automotive executive, founder (originator). **Educ:** Mich State Univ. **Career:** Joliet Dodge Inc, pres, owner, 1990-. **Orgs:** Bd dir, Joliet Region Chamber Com. **Business Addr:** President, Owner, Joliet Dodge Inc, 2617 W Jefferson St, Joliet, IL 60435, **Business Phone:** (815)729-3343.

### DUKES, HAZEL NELL

Executive, government official. **Personal:** Born Mar 17, 1932, Montgomery, AL; daughter of Edward and Alice; children: Ronald. **Educ:** Ala State Tchr Col, AA, 1950; Adelphi Univ, advan master prog, 1978. **Career:** Macys Dept Store, staff, 1950; Nassau County Atty Off, community organizer; Dem Natl Conv, deleg, 1976, 1980; New York Off-Track Betting Corp, pres, 1990-94; Presidential Elector, New York, 1992; New York Nat Asn Advan Colored People, pres, 1999-. **Orgs:** Metro-LINKS; bd dir, Coalition 100 Black Women; bd dir, St New York Martin Luther King Jr. Comn; Nat Bd, 1977-, pres, 1990-, Nat Asn Advan Colored People, bd trustee, St Univ New York; Westbury Negro Bus & Prof Women's Club; secy, Coun Black Elected Dem NY Dem Nat Comt; pres, New York Nat Asn Advan Colored People, 1989-92; vice-chair, Nassau County Dem Comt. **Honors/Awds:** Social Action Award, Delta Sigma Theta Sor Inc, 1976; Sojurner Truth Award, Nat Asn Negro Bus & Prof Women's Clubs Inc, 1977; Community Service Award, New York OIC, 1976; Salute to African American Women, Dollar and Sense Magazine, 1989; Award for Outstanding Contribution to Social Justice, New York Human Rights Comn, 1985; Award for Promoting Justice & Interracial Harmony, B'nai B'rith, 1990; honorary doctorate, Queens Col, 1990. **Special Achievements:** First African American to work for the Nassau County attorney's office; first black vice-chair of the Nassau County Democratic Committee. **Home Addr:** 10 W 135 St, New York, NY 10037-2610, **Home Phone:** (212)281-1215. **Business Addr:** President, National Association for the Advancement of Colored People, 270 W 96th St, New York, NY 10025, **Business Phone:** (212)344-7474.

### DUKES, LILLIAN A.

Vice president (organization). **Educ:** Carnegie-Mellon Univ, BS, elec engineering & math; Villanova Univ, MS, elec engineering. **Career:** GE Aerospace, engr, 1983-88; Am Airlines, analyst; Independence Air, vpres maintenance, 2003-06; Am Eagle Airlines Inc, Tech Serv, vpres, 2006-10, vpres heavy maintenance, 2010-11, pres Eagle Aviation Serv Inc, 2010-11; Village Vision Haiti Found, vpres bd dirs, 2010; Beechcraft, vpres Global Supply Chain, 2011-14; VP Heavy Maintenance Midwest Airlines Inc, dir tech serv, dir aircraft tech support; Atlantic Coast Airlines, vpres; Spirit AeroSystems, vpres bus opers & global customer support & serv, 2014-. **Orgs:** Adv bd mem, Achieving Women's Excellence Supply Chain Opers, Mgt & Educ, 2013. **Business Addr:** Vice President, Global Customer Support and Services, Spirit AeroSystems, 3801 S Oliver St, Wichita, KS 67210.

### DUKES, RONALD

Consultant, executive. **Personal:** Born Dec 27, 1943, Neelyville, MO; married Albertine A Elliott; children: Barry Girard. **Educ:** Lincoln Univ, MO, BS, 1964. **Career:** Continental Can Co, training supvr labor rels, 1969-71; Emerson Elec Co, corp human resources staff, sr corp recruiter, 1971-74; Am Motors Corp, corp dir recruiting & mgmt develop, human resources exec, 1974-78; Booz Allen & Hamilton, assoc, 1978-80; Heidrick & Struggles Inc, partner & shareholder, 1980-99; Ronald Dukes Assoc LLC, pres & founder, 1999-. **Orgs:** Bd dir, Heidrick & Struggles Inc, 1980-99; Phi Beta Sigma Fraternity; bd mem, Chicago Youth Ctrs, 1987, chmn bd, 1995-97, exec comt mem, currently; bd dir & chair audit comt, First NonProfit Ins Co; Chicago United Way & Crusade Mercy Pension Subcomt, 1995-2005; bd visitors, Peter F Drucker Grad Mgt Ctr; Detroit Athletic Club; Econ Club Chicago; Execs Club Chicago; Retirement Plan Subcomt United Way Metrop Chicago. **Honors/Awds:** Commendation Medal & Combat Badge for Vietnam Service, AUS, 1967. **Special Achievements:** Listed in the 1990 Harper & Row Book, "The Career Makers: America's Top 100 Recruiters". **Home Addr:** 1105 Alden Lane, Buffalo Grove, IL 60089-1306, **Home Phone:** (847)541-8716. **Business Addr:** President, Founder, Ronald Dukes Associates LLC, PO Box 4839, Buffalo Grove, IL 60089-4839, **Business Phone:** (312)357-2895.

### DUKES, SONYA

Vice president (organization). **Educ:** Univ NC, Kenan-Flagler Exec Leadership Prog, attended 2007. **Career:** Wells Fargo & Co, sr vpres, corp supplier diversity. **Orgs:** Bd dir, Greater Los Angeles African-Am Chamber Com; bd dir, Nc Gov's Conf Women; Charlotte Chamber Com, Exec Comt; Howard Univ Commun Entrepreneurship Resource & Res Adv Coun, Exec Comt; mentor, W Charlotte High Sch's Emerging Leaders Prog; mentor, Johnson C. Smith Univ, Stud Leadership Prog; Exec Leadership Coun. **Business Addr:** Senior Vice President, Corporate Supplier Diversity, Wells Fargo.

### DULANEY, MICHAEL FAULKERSON

Administrator, football player. **Personal:** Born Sep 9, 1970, Kingsport, TN; married Alisia. **Educ:** Univ NC, BA, commun & gen, 1993. **Career:** Football player (retired), administrator: Arena Football League, 1994-95; Chicago Bears, running back, 1995-96, fullback, 1997, 1998; Carolina Panthers, fullback, 1998-99; Rubbermaid, acct mgr, 2000-03; Schering-Plough Res Inst, prof sales rep, 2003-04; Synthes, spine consult, 2004-07; Globus Med, sr spine specialist, 2007-10; M4 Surg LLC, distribr prin, 2010-12; Rubbermaid Healthcare, clin acct exec-southeast, 2012-; Capsa Solutions, regional sales mgr-southeast, 2012-; Practical Solutions, treas. **Business Addr:** Clinical Account Executive-Southeast, Capsa Solutions LLC, 4253 NE 189th Ave, Portland, OR 97230, **Business Phone:** (704)728-4854.

**DULIN, JOSEPH.** See Obituaries Section.

### DULIN, DR. ROBERT OTIS, JR.

Clergy. **Personal:** Born Mar 24, 1941, Lawrence, KS; married C Hawice Allen; children: Shannon E & Robert O III. **Educ:** Anderson Col, BA, 1963, DDiv, 2005; Cent Bapt Theol Sem, MDiv, 1967. **Career:** Pastor (retired); Third St Church God, assoc minister, 1964-66; First Church God, pastor, 1967-69; Nat Bd Christian Educ, assoc secy, Family Life & Adult Educ, dir, 1969-74; Metrop Church God, assoc pastor, 1974, sr minister, pastor, 1976-2008; Nat Conf Community & Justice, staff, 1988-2002; Gen Assembly Church God Mich, southeastern regional pastor. **Orgs:** Life mem, Nat Asn Advan Colored People, 1979; vice chmn & bd dir, Charles H Wright Mus African Am Hist; bd dir, Youth Sports & Recreation Comn; bd dir, Franklin Wright Settlements; chmn, Mid-Night Golf Inc; Metrop Organizing Strategy Enabling Strength (MOSES); bd dir, Michs C & United Way Community Serv. **Honors/Awds:** Alumni Achievement Award, Cent Baptist Theol Sem, 1974; Distinguished Alumni Award, Anderson Univ, 1997. **Home Addr:** 18707 Glenwood Blvd, Lathrup Village, MI 48076-2505, **Home Phone:** (248)327-7681. **Business Addr:** Reverend, Metropolitan Church God, 13400 Schaefer Hwy, Detroit, MI 48227-3539, **Business Phone:** (313)273-5580.

### DUMARS, JOE, III

Basketball executive, basketball player, executive. **Personal:** Born May 24, 1963, Shreveport, LA; son of Joe Jr (deceased) and Ophelia; married Debbie; children: Jordan Taylor & Aren. **Educ:** McNeese State Univ, BA, bus admin, 1985. **Career:** Basketball player (retired), exec; Detroit Pistons, guard, 1985-99, vpres player personnel, pres basketball opers, 1999-; Joe Dumars Field house, owner, 1994-; Detroit Technologies, owner, chief exec officer & pres, 1996-2006; First Mich Bank, bd dir, currently. **Business Addr:** President of Basketball Operations, Detroit Pistons, Palace Auburn Hills 3 Championship Dr, Auburn Hills, MI 48326, **Business Phone:** (248)377-0100.

### DUMAS, KAREN MARIE

Municipal government official, executive. **Personal:** Born Oct 22, 1962, Detroit, MI; married Timothy L Cook; children: Kirby & Jason. **Educ:** Mich State Univ, East Lansing, BS, 1986. **Career:** Marx & Co, Bloomfield Hills, Mich, acct asst & media rels, 1986-87; City Highland Pk, Highland Pk, Mich, dir pub info, 1987-88; Images & Ideas, Detroit, Mich, pres & owner, 1988-; Athletes Exclusive Sports Mkt, assoc partner, 1996-; Mich Front Page, columnist, 2000-; Off Mayor, City Detroit, exec dir community rels, 2002-03; Detroit Dept Cult, Arts & Tourism, dir; Mich Chronicle, columnist, 2001-09; Next Detroit, prog host; Artifacts & Jazz Ctr, TV prog co host, 2006-11; WGPR-FM, from co-host to on-air host, 2006-09; WRCJ-FM, host, 2007-08; City Detroit, chief commun & external affairs, 2009-11; 910AM Superstation, air personality, 2016-. **Orgs:** Nat Asn Advan Colored People, 1983-; Riverfront Community Orgn, 1986-; Adcraft Club Detroit, 1987-; bd dir, ALERT, 1987-; Civic Searchlight Comn, 1990-; bd dir, Sickle Cell Detection Comn, 1990-; Nat Asn Black Journalists, Detroit Chap, 1991-; Black Advert, Radio & Tv, 1991-; bd dir, Sphinix Orgn, 2001-; Mich Film Comn; Arts League Mich; Tourism Econ Deveolp Ctr; commun comt mem, Detroit Riverfront Conservancy; Ed Adv Bd BLAC Mag & Ideas inc. **Honors/Awds:** Profiles of Success Award, State Mich, Dept Com, MBE, 1991; 25 Most Influential Women in Detroit, Women's Informal Network, 2001. **Home Addr:** 1771 Burns, Detroit, MI 48214-2848, **Home Phone:** (313)824-4757. **Business Addr:** President, Images & Ideas Inc, 258 Eliot Suite 300, Detroit, MI 48201-2414, **Business Phone:** (866)330-4585.

### DUMAS, MICHAEL DION

Sales manager, football player, football coach. **Personal:** Born Mar 18, 1969, Grand Rapids, MI; married Clemencia; children: Michael, Meela & Gabriela. **Educ:** Ind Univ, BA, sports mkt, 1991. **Career:** Football player (retired), coach; Houston Oilers, defensive back, 1991-92; Nat Football League, 1991-2002; Buffalo Bills, 1994; Jacksonville Jaguars, free safety, 1995; San Diego Chargers, free safety & strong safety, 1997-2000; Liberty Mortgage LLC, pres, 2003-05; Miami Dolphins, defensive coach, asst coach, 2005-08; Planet Fitness, dist mgr opers, 2008-09; ABS Bus Solutions, sr area sales mgr & training mgr, 2010-12; SpaceMan Home & Off, design mgr, 2012-.

### DUMAS, TONY

Basketball player. **Personal:** Born Aug 25, 1972, Chicago, IL. **Educ:** Univ Miss, Kansas City, attended 1994. **Career:** Basketball player (retired); Dallas Mavericks, shooting guard, 1994-96; Phoenix Suns, shooting guard, 1996-97; Cleveland Cavaliers, shooting guard, 1997-98; La Crosse Bobcats, Continental Basketball Asn, 1998; Sporting Athens, Greece, 1999-2000; Vip Rimini, Italy, 2001. **Special Achievements:** First round pick, No 19, NBA Draft, 1994; Only player in University of Missouri-Kansas City history to be drafted into the NBA.

## DUMAS, TROY T.

Football player, football coach. **Personal:** Born Sep 30, 1972, Cheyenne, WY. **Educ:** Univ Nebr-Lincoln, BA, human resources & family sci, 1995. **Career:** Football player (retired), football player coach; Kans City Chiefs, linebacker, 1996-97; St Louis Rams, 1997; Denver Broncos; Orlando Pradators, linebacker, 2000; Edmonton Eskimos, linebacker, 2001; Cheyenne Cent High Sch, asst linebackers and defensive ends coach; Doane Col, defensive coordr & middle, outside linebackers coach; Huskers.net, line backers coach, currently; Southeast Mo State Univ, linebackers coach, 2008; Kans City chiefs, NFL Minority Coaching Fel, 2008; Redhawks, linebackers coach. **Honors/Awds:** All-Am hons; Semi-finalist for the Butkus Award; Nebraska State Troopers Defensive Player of the Game. **Home Addr:** , Riverside, CA. **Business Addr:** Linebackers Coach, Huskers, 1 Memorial Stadium, Lincoln, NE 68588-0120, **Business Phone:** (402)472-4224.

## DUMMETT, DR. JOCELYN ANGELA

Pediatrician. **Personal:** Born Sep 15, 1956, Leicester; daughter of Kenneth J and Sheila A Waterman; children: Richard Anthony Hunte & Ryan William Hunte. **Educ:** Howard Univ Col Med, MD, 1980. **Career:** St Vincents Hosp, Internship, 1980-81; State Univ NY Downstate Med Ctr, resident, 1981-83; Downstate Med Ctr, clini instr, 1983-85; LBJ Sch Health Prog, preceptor; Health Sci Ctr Brooklyn, asst clin prof; Javican Pediat Assocs, co-founder, 1985-87; Orange Regional Med Ctr, Dept Pediat, vice chmn; Middletown Community Health Ctr Pediat, physician, currently; Catskill Regional Med Ctr, physician; Crystal Run Healthcare, pediatrician, currently. **Orgs:** Fel Am Acad Pediat; Brooklyn Pediat Soc; Nat Med Assoc; rec secy, Provident Clin Soc, 1984-88; med secy, Hanson Pl Seventh-day Adventist Ch, 1986. **Honors/Awds:** Excellence in Pediatrics, Howard Univ, Col Med, 1980; Recoginition Award, Nat Health Serv Corps, 1985. **Home Addr:** 714 Troy Ave, Brooklyn, NY 11203, **Home Phone:** (718)756-8793. **Business Addr:** Pediatrician, Crystal Run Healthcare, 300 Crystal Run Rd, Middletown, NY 10941, **Business Phone:** (845)703-6999.

## DUNBAR, ANNE CYNTHIA

Administrator. **Personal:** Born Sep 24, 1938, New York, NY; daughter of Eric Henry Hines and Adella Costilda Joseph; children: Christopher. **Educ:** Bor Manhattan Community Col, AA, 1967; Brooklyn Col, BA, sociol & urban affairs, 1975, MS, educ, guid & coun, 1977; Columbia Univ Sch Pub & Int Affairs, cert, 1985. **Career:** Citi-Bank/Canal St Training Ctr, asst, master, 1968-69; 1st Venture Corp NY, asst, vpres, 1969-70; City Univ NY, Hunter Col, SEEK Financial Aid Prog, dir, 1970-76; Ford-Whitfield-Young Scholarship Fund, founder, 1975; NY State Dept Correctional Servs, dir comt rel, asst dir, 1976-89; Dept HEW NIH Sickle Blood Dis Prog, consult, 1977-79; Girl Scouts US, Mgt consult, 1989-90; Univ NY, instr. **Orgs:** Volunteer, Womens Div Gov Off, 1969-71; chairperson, Spec Progs Handicapped Community Sch Bd 12, 1977-; trustee, Bronx Mus, 1981-; chmn bd, NY Urban League, 1983-; Am Personnel & Guid Asn; founder pres, Break Thru Art; pres, NAACP Parkchester Br; adv mem, NY City Businessman Coun Employ Ex-offender; educ sponsor, Coalition 100 Black Women; mem bd dir, Bronx Boys Clubs; NY State Catholic Conf Criminal Justice Adv Comt; Comt Sch Bd 12; Brooklyn Col Alumni Asn; Borough Manhattan Community Col Alumni Asn; Bronx Coun Arts; Womens City Club NY. **Honors/Awds:** Citation Comt Coord & Devel Northside Ctr Child Develop, 1972; "Ambassador of Love" Val-to-me Productions, 1974; Citation Achievement Eastern NY Correctional Facil Jaycees, 1974; Citation Activ Penal Reform Gamblers Anonymous Green haven Prison Chap, 1974; Cert Appreciation, Eastern NY Correctional Facil, 1975; Claire Joseph King Mem Citation, 1975; Each One Teach One Comt Serv Award, Harlem Prof & John Hunter Mem Camp Fund, 1975; Outstanding Serv Award, Eastern Br NAACP, 1975; honoree, Int Women's Year Nat Coun Negro Women Inc, Flatbush Sect, 1975; Citation Distinguished Servs Handicapped C; Community Serv Award, Schaefer Brewry Co, 1978; Citizen Year Award, Bronx Boys Clubs, 1979; Humanitarian Award, Parkchester Cardiac Diag Med Ctr, 1979; Leadership Award, City Coun NY, 1983; Distinguish Community Serv Coun Churches NY; Commun Serv Award, Consolidated Edison NY; Congressional Citation Rep Mario Biaggi, 1978. **Home Addr:** 1940 E Tremont Ave 6B, Bronx, NY 10462, **Home Phone:** (718)887-1192.

## DUNBAR, DR. JOSEPH C.

Educator, scientist. **Personal:** Born Aug 27, 1944, Vicksburg, MS; son of J C Sr and Henrienne M Watkins; married Agnes Estorge; children: Andrea & Erica. **Educ:** Alcorn Col, Lorman, MS, BS, biol, 1963; Tex Southern, Houston, TX, MS, zool, 1966; Wayne State Univ, Detroit, MI, PhD, physiol & pharmacol, 1970. **Career:** Tex Southern, Houston, Tex, res asst, 1964-66, instr biol, 1966-67; Wayne State Univ, grad teaching asst, 1968-69; Sinai Hosp Detroit, Mich, post doctoral, diabetes trainee, 1970-72, res assoc, 1972-81; Wayne State Univ, Detroit, Mich, from asst prof, 1972-78, assoc prof physiol, 1978-85, prof physiol, 1985-, assoc chmn, 1995-97, chmn physiol, 1998-2007, chief sci advisor, dean sch med, assoc vpres res, 2007-. **Home Addr:** 19224 Parkside, Detroit, MI 48221, **Home Phone:** (313)368-9451. **Business Addr:** Associate Vice President for Research, Professor, Wayne State University, 5275 Scott Hall 540 E Canfield, Detroit, MI 48201, **Business Phone:** (313)577-5600.

## DUNBAR, ROCKMOND

Actor. **Personal:** Born Jan 11, 1973, Berkeley, CA; married Ivy Holmes. **Career:** Films: Misery Loves Company, 1993; Punks, 2000; All About You, 2001; Kiss Kiss Bang Bang, 2005; Dirty Laundry, producer, 2006; Jada, The Family That Preys, Alien Raiders, 2008; Pastor Brown, 2009; Love Chronicles: Secrets Revealed, 2010; Echo at 11 Oak Drive, 2012; Highland Park, 2013; More to Love, 2014; Busted, 2014. TV series: "Earth 2", 1994-95; "The Good News", 1997; "The Wayans Bros.", "Two Guys, a Girl & a Pizza Place", 1998; "Pacific Blue", "The Practice", "The Pretender", "Felicity", 1999; "G vs E", 2000; "Soul Food", 2000-04; "Girlfriends", 2003-04; Hollywood Division, "North Shore", 2004; "Head Cases", 2005; "Prison Break", 2005-09; Heartland, Shark, "Grey's Anatomy", "CSI: Miami", 2007; "The Game", 2009; Private Practice, The Defenders, Terriers, 2010; The Chicago Code, Taste of Romance, The Closer, Sons of Anarchy, 2011; Director: The Great Commission, producer, 2003; Behind the Scenes: The Great Commission, 2003; Pastor Brown, 2009; The Game, 2009-14; Private Practice, 2010; The Defenders, 2010; Terriers, 2010; The Chicago Code, 2011; The Closer, 2011; A Taste of Romance, 2012; Raising Izzie, 2012; Doubt, 2013; For Richer or Poorer, 2012-13; Sons of Anarchy, 2011-13; The Mentalist, 2013. **Honors/Awds:** Black Reel Award, 2002. **Special Achievements:** Named one of "Television's 50 Sexiest Stars of All Time" by TV Guide. **Business Addr:** Actor, Showtime Networks Inc, 1633 E Broadway, New York, NY 10019, **Business Phone:** (212)708-1600.

## DUNCAN, GENEVA

Administrator. **Personal:** Born Aug 21, 1935, Cleveland, OH; married Dave L Sr; children: Jolette, Dave Jr, Brenda, Darnell, Darlynn & Kevin. **Educ:** Feen Col; Cleveland State Univ. **Career:** Ministerial Day Care Asn, dir social serv. **Orgs:** Crest Found; bd, HADC; Cuyahoga County Welfare Dept; Fed Comn & Planning; Comn Christmas bur; dir pub rels; Mt Nebo Baptist Church; Hough Area Coun; Glenville Area Coun; Hough Area Devel Corp; Crest Found. **Home Addr:** 3118 Eastwick Dr, Cleveland, OH 44118, **Home Phone:** (216)321-0862. **Business Addr:** Administrator, 2521 E 61 St, Cleveland, OH 44104.

## DUNCAN, JAMIE ROBERT

Football player. **Personal:** Born Jul 20, 1975, Wilmington, DE. **Educ:** Vanderbilt Univ, BA, human & orgn develop. **Career:** Football player (retired); Tampa Bay Buccaneers, 1999, linebacker, middle linebacker, 1998, 2000-01; St Louis Rams, linebacker, middle linebacker, 2002-03; Atlanta Falcons, linebacker, 2004; bus, currently. **Orgs:** Bus Prof Am; Stud Promoting African-Am Cult. **Honors/Awds:** SEC Legend of the Game, 2009. **Special Achievements:** Featured on a poster promoting the importance of educ titled. **Home Addr:** , Tampa, FL.

## DUNCAN, JOAN A.

Government official, executive director. **Personal:** Born Sep 8, 1939, Butte, MT; daughter of Dr Walter E and Alyce M Driver. **Educ:** Carroll Col, attended 1957; Syracuse Univ, attended 1958. **Career:** Carroll Col, asst dean women, 1961-67; RDMC Comn Action Agency; dir, Foster Grandparent Prog, 1969-75; MT Dept Labor & Indust, Chief Women's Bur & founder, 1975-81; City Helena, city comnr, 1982-86; MT Legis, 1983-87; Helena Food Share Inc, exec dir, 1987-91; Hennesys Dept Store, promos dir & personnal shopper, 1992-. **Orgs:** Bd dir, Model Cities, 1972-74; dir, Helena Area Econ Develop Inc, 1985-87; Rocky Develop Coun Inc, 1982-86; United Way, 1973-89; writer producer host Leg, 1979-; TV Prog, 1979; Women's Window R Dio 52 Stas, 1976-81; Guardian Culch TV Prog, 1982-86; Last Chance Press Club, 1976-; MT Dem Party, 1980-; Lewis & Clark Health Bd, 1983-86; Lewis & Clark County Tax Appeals Bd; MT Communities Found; co-chmn, Proj Progress, Jobs Helena's Future, 1990-; exec dir, MT Food Bank Network, 1991-92. **Honors/Awds:** Outstanding Young Women of America, 1970; Montana Carrying the Torchin Troubled Times, 1974. **Home Addr:** 1026 Woodbridge Dr, Helena, MT 59601-5476, **Home Phone:** (406)443-6549. **Business Addr:** Manager, Dillard's Inc, Capital Hill Mall, Helena, MT 59601.

## DUNCAN, DR. LOUIS DAVIDSON, JR.

Physician. **Personal:** Born Oct 26, 1932, Lancaster, SC; son of Louis and Minnie. **Educ:** Howard Univ, BS, 1954; Howard Univ Sch Med, MD, 1958. **Career:** Pvt pract physician, currently. **Orgs:** Med Surg Soc DC Inc; Nat Med Asn Mt Airy Baptist Ch; Phi Beta Kappa. **Business Addr:** Physician, 1105 Buchanan St NW, Washington, DC 20011-4428, **Business Phone:** (202)882-3221.

## DUNCAN, LYNDA J.

Government official. **Educ:** Motlow State Community Col, AS, 1984. **Career:** Ray Belue & Assocs, model & actress, 1974-77; Ebony-Essence-GQ-Madamoiselle, model, 1974-79; Univ Tenn, contract coord, 1978-81; City Tullahoma, ct clerk, 1982-86; WKQD FM/AM, mkt consult & copywriter, 1986-. **Orgs:** Cir player, Atlanta, Ga, 1974-76; fund raiser, Comm Action Guild, 1977-79; coord youth active, Mt Zion Baptist Church, 1977-79; sponsor, Black Hist Club Tullahoma High Sch, 1978-79; treas, bd dir, Tullahoma Day Care Ctr, 1979-81; chair, C&D Stamps Scholar Fund, 1982-86; bd dir, TENCO Develop Inc, 1986-. **Home Addr:** 321 S Polk St, Tullahoma, TN 37388-3856, **Home Phone:** (931)455-2198. **Business Addr:** Marketing Consultant, Copywriter, WKQD FM/AM, Westside Dr, Tullahoma, TN 37388.

## DUNCAN, PEGGY

Entrepreneur, consultant, spokesperson. **Educ:** Ga State Univ, Atlanta, BS, mkt, 1982, cert, train trainer, 1996. **Career:** Duncan Resource Group Inc, chief exec officer, 1997; consult, pres, currently; Int Bus Mach Corp, proj mgr, 1982-94; Prof Sound Corp Press, comput trainer, 1997-, prof speaker, 1997-; Digital Breakthroughs Inst, founder, lead trainer, 2013-. Books: The Time Management Memory Jogger, 2008; Conquer Email Overload with Better Habits, Etiquette and Outlook 2007, 2010; Just Show Me Which Button to Click! in PowerPoint 2007, 2011. **Orgs:** Nat Asn for Female Executives; Soc Govt Meeting Planners; Fla Dent Asn Ann Conf; Am Soc Asn Execs; Am Bar Asn Ann TechShow; Fla Soc Asn Execs; US Tennis Asn. **Business Addr:** Founder, Lead Trainer, The Digital Breakthroughs Institute, Atlanta, GA, **Business Phone:** (404)492-8197.

## DUNCAN, SANDRA RHODES

Executive, president (organization). **Personal:** Born Nov 16, 1944, Chicago, IL; daughter of Duplain W Jr and Doris Millaud; married Joan D; children: Sabrina, Otis Jr, Orrin, Omar & Ashea. **Educ:** Commonwealth Col Mortuary Sci, attended 1969; La State Univ, exec mgt, 1991. **Career:** Duplin W Rhodes Funeral Home Inc, lic, funeral dir, 1962-, pres; Airport Rhodes Transp Inc, pres, 1986-91; Rhodes Enterprises, pres, 1991-. **Orgs:** Chairwoman, Jr Achievement, 1992-93; Bus Coun New Orleans & River Region; World Trade Ctr; La Coun Fiscal Reform, Amistad Resh Ctr; New Orleans Ctr Creative Arts; New Orleans Chap Links; Nat Com Bank; pres, Dryades Savings Bank, 2006-; bd dir, Newcorp Bus Assistance Ctr, currently. **Home Addr:** 3720 Gentilly Blvd, New Orleans, LA 70122, **Home Phone:** (504)948-3181. **Business Addr:** Board of Director, NewCorp Business Assistance Center, 2924 St Bernard Ave, New Orleans, LA 70119, **Business Phone:** (504)208-1700.

## DUNCAN, SYDNEY REE

Executive. **Personal:** Born Sep 29, 1937, Dallas, TX; daughter of Elijah L and Fannie Earl Carter; children: Shirley, Michelle & Walter. **Educ:** Tex Southern Univ, BA, 1959; Univ Wis, attended 1961; Wayne State Univ, MSW, 1996. **Career:** Executive (retired); Pontiac Pub Sch, social worker, 1966-69; Homes Black C, prog dir, 1969-71, pres & chief exec officer, 1972; Sydney Duncan Consult, pres. **Orgs:** Acad Cert Social Workers; founding mem, adv bd, Nat Ctr Permanency African Am C; bd dir, Found Community Encour; community adv bd, 15th Cong dist; partic, White House Task Force Black Family, 1994; founder, Nat Ctr Homes Black C; Govs Task Force Cs Justice. **Home Addr:** 2570 Iroquois, Detroit, MI 48201, **Home Phone:** (313)824-7728. **Business Addr:** President, Sydney Duncan Consulting, 342 W Crescent Lane, Detroit, MI 48207, **Business Phone:** (313)446-9770.

## DUNCAN, TIM (TIMOTHY THEODORE DUNCAN)

Basketball player. **Personal:** Born Apr 25, 1976, St. Croix, VI; son of William and Lone; married Amy; children: Sydney & Draven. **Educ:** Wake Forest Univ, BA, psychol, 1997. **Career:** San Antonio Spurs, ctr & forward, 1997-. **Orgs:** Founder, Tim Duncan Found; Tim Duncan's Character Prog, Spurs Found. **Business Addr:** Professional Basketball Player, San Antonio Spurs, SBC Ctr 1 SBC Ctr Pkwy, San Antonio, TX 78219, **Business Phone:** (210)444-5000.

## DUNCAN, VERDELL E.

Executive, government official, labor relations manager. **Personal:** Born May 9, 1946, Arkadelphia, AR; children: Constanc Regina, Cameron Chad & Jacobi Edwin. **Educ:** Henderson State Univ, BSE, 1968; Eastern Mich Univ, MA, 1974, MA, 1976. **Career:** Greater Flint OIC, dir training, 1972-73; City Flint, flint police officer, 1973-77; City Flint Retirement, trustee retirement bd, 1977-79; CON-CAM Publ Corp, owner; City Flint Hurley Med Ctr, 1st ward councilman, adminr Cult Diversity; Acad Flint Charter Sch, Supt, 1999-2010, dir, currently; Ctr Educ Performance & Info, prin, 2009-10. **Orgs:** Urban League; Nat Asn Advan Colored People; Coun liason, City Flint Human Rels Comn; Mich Asn Hosp Personnel dir; bd mem, Partner In Progress; secy, Mich Asn Affirmative Action Off; pres/owner, Twin & Assoc, 1983-; Omega Psi Phi Fraternity; coordr, Hurley Med Ctr Employee Assistance Prog; bd mem, Community Recovery Ctr; bd mem, pres, Community Coalition; bd mem, Genesee County Fedn Blind. **Home Addr:** 6814 Colonial Dr, Flint, MI 48505-1965, **Home Phone:** (810)785-9289. **Business Addr:** Director, Academy of Flint Charter School, 4100 W Coldwater Rd, Flint, MI 48504-1102, **Business Phone:** (810)789-9484.

## DUNGEE, MARGARET R.

Teacher. **Personal:** Born Richmond, VA; married Winfred A; children: Veronica Dungee Abrams. **Educ:** Va Union Univ, BA, 1962; Va Commonwealth Univ, MA, 1971; Howard Univ; Univ Va. **Career:** Teacher (retired); Fairmount Sch, teacher, 1962-69; John B Caly Sch, 1969-70; Southampton, resource teacher, 1971-72; Westhampton, diag prescriptive teacher, 1972-74; Richmond Pub Schs, human rels adv specialist, 1974-; Thirteen Acres Residential Sch, spec educ 1981-86; Richmond Pub Schs Clark Springs, teacher, 1986-94; Va Union Univ, reading instr, 1994-2001. **Orgs:** Pres & vpres, PTA Fairmont Elem Sch, 1959-61; pres, Richmond Educ Asn, 1973-74; pres, Delta Sigma Theta, 1979-81; vol, McGuire Community Hosp; advan gift chmn, Va Fund Renewal Conf Am Bapt Church & Progressive Nat Bapt; pres, sr chair, 5th Baptist Church; pres, Mission Soc 5th Baptist Church; tutor reading, vol; BGC; ABCOTS; ABCOT USA; Church WM United. **Home Addr:** 1704 Joycelyn Ct, Glen Allen, VA 23060-3907, **Home Phone:** (804)264-5021.

## DUNGEY, MERRIN

Actor. **Personal:** Born Aug 6, 1971, Sacramento, CA; married Matthew Drake; children: 2. **Educ:** Univ Calif, Los Angeles, BA, 1993. **Career:** Film: Deep Impact, 1999; EDtv, 1999; The Sky Is Falling, 2001; Scream at the Sound of the Beep, 2002; L!fe Happens, 2011. TV Series: "Martin", 1995; "Babylon 5", "Living Single", "Party Girl", 1996; "ER", "Murphy Brown", 1997; "Seinfeld", 1998; "The King of Queens", 1998-2007; "The West Wing", "G vs E", 1999; "Friends", 2000; "Grosse Pointe", "Curb Your Enthusiasm", 2001; "Alias", 2001-03; "Malcolm in the Middle", 2000-04; "Summerland", 2004-05; "Boston Legal", "Grey's Anatomy", 2007; "90210", 2008-13; "Surviving Suburbia", 2009; "Better Off Ted", 2009-10; "Castle", 2010; "Hung", 2010; "Outlaw", 2010; "Revenge, 2012"; "Hollywood Heights", 2012; "How to Live with Your Parents (For the Rest of Your Life)", 2013; "Betrayal", 2013; "Brooklyn Nine-Nine", 2014; "Trophy Wife", 2014; "Shameless", 2014; "Rizzoli & Isles", 2014; "Chasing Life", 2014; "CSI: Crime Scene Investigation", 2014. **Honors/Awds:** UCLA Acting Award, American Theater Award, UCLA School of Theater, 1990. **Business Addr:** Actress, c/o The Disney Studios, 500 S Buena Vista St, Burbank, CA 91521, **Business Phone:** (818)560-1000.

## DUNGIE, RUTH SPIGNER

Consultant, administrator. **Personal:** Born New York, NY; daughter of William M Spigner and Fannie W Spigner; married Elias; children: Christopher David. **Educ:** Col New Rochelle, BA, 1975; New Sch Social Res, MA, 1980; Univ New Haven, MBA, 2002. **Career:** ROLM Co, Norwalk, Conn, mgr, employee rels, 1989-92; IBM, personnel prog admin, 1981-83, corp litigation mgr, 1983-85, EEO prog adminr, 1985-86, personnel res surv adminr, 1987-89, Global Employee Res, sr HR consult, 1992-. **Orgs:** Alpha Kappa Alpha Sor; Nat Black MBA; Greater Hudson Valley Chap Links Inc; Soc Human Resource Mgt. **Home Addr:** 205 Langdon Ave, Mount Vernon, NY 10553-

1443, **Home Phone:** (914)667-2257. **Business Addr:** Senior Human Resource Consultant, IBM Corp, 1 New Orchard Rd, Armonk, NY 10504-1722, **Business Phone:** (914)499-1900.

**DUNGY, ANTHONY KEVIN.** See DUNGY, TONY.

**DUNGY, DR. CLAIBOURNE I.**
Physician, educator. **Personal:** Born Jan 1, 1938, Chicago, IL; married Madgetta T; children: Kathryn & Camille. **Educ:** Eastern Ill Univ, BS, 1962; Univ Ill, MD, 1967; Johns Hopkins Univ, MPH, 1971. **Career:** Univ Colo, Dept Pediats, 1971-75; Univ Calif, Irvine, Dept Pediats, 1975-88, Div Gen Pediats, chief, 1976-80, 1985-88; consult, KOCE TV, 1980-88; Univ Iowa, Nat Health Law & Policy Resource Ctr, sr assoc dir, currently, Dept Pediat, prof pediat & epidemiol, 1988, Div Gen Pediat & Adolescent Med, prof pediat emer, dir, currently; Nat Inst Child Health & Human Develop, panel chair, currently. **Orgs:** Am Pub Health Asn, 1971-; Ambulatory Pediat Asn, 1973-; reg dir, Region XIII AAP Head Start Prog, 1974-75; Calif State Child Health Bd, 1977-82; consult, Brookhaven Nat Labs Marshall Islands, 1982-; bd, Urban League Orange County Chap, 1982-88; co chair, APA Region IX, 1987-88, Region VI, 1993-95; Asn Acad Minority Physicians, 1991-2004; bd dir, Goodwill Southeast Iowa, 1993-2003, bd chair, 2000-02; Am Pediat Soc, 1994-; Am Acad Pediat, 1975-, comt pediat res, 1995-2001, coun gov affairs, 1996-99; ed bd, Arch Pediat & Adolescent Med, 1996-2002; bd dir, Ambulatory Pediat Asn, 1996-99, Am Bd Pediat, 1999-; pres elect, 2005-06, pres, 2006-07; Acad Breastfeeding Med; Am Pub Health Asn; Midwest Socs Pediat Res; Univ Iowa Alumni Asn, currently. **Business Addr:** Professor Pediatrics Emeritus, Director Division of General Pediatrics & Adoles, University of Iowa, 2627 John W Colloton Pavilion 200 Hawkins Dr, Iowa City, IA 52242-1083, **Business Phone:** (319)356-3644.

**DUNGY, DR. MADGETTA THORNTON**
Educator, school administrator. **Personal:** Born Jan 1, 1942, Lynchburg, VA; daughter of Edgar T and Madge Meadors; married Claibourne I; children: Kathryn & Camille. **Educ:** Cornell Col, IA, BA, polit sci, 1964; Univ Colo, Boulder, CO, MA, educ, 1974; Univ Iowa Col Educ, PhD, 1997. **Career:** Educator, school administrator (retired); Chicago Urban Renewal Comn, field rep, 1964; Chicago Sch Bd, high sch teacher-counr, 1964-67; Univ Utah, admis counr, 1967-68; Stanford Univ, financial aids officer, 1968-70; Girl Scout Coun, dir mem serv, 1979-86, counr summer bridge prog; Univ Calif-Irvine, stud affairs officer; Univ Iowa Roy J. & Lucille A. Carver Col Med, assoc, stud affairs, dir, minority progs, 1988, asst dean fac affairs & develop, 2000-05. **Orgs:** Nat Asn Stud Personnel Admin, 1973-; Calif Asn Coun & Develop, 1975-88; Orange City Vis Nurses Asn, 1976-81; adv bd coun, Gifted & Talented, 1978-; dir Vols Agencies, 1979-86; charter mem, Jack & Jill Am, 1980-88; Links Inc, 1982-88; citizens adv coun, KOCE TV, 1983; Nat Asn Med Minority Educr Inc, 1989-; golden life mem, Delta Sigma Theta Sorority Inc; vpres, Orange City Chap; bd mem, IA Women's Found; Am Asn Higher Educ. **Home Addr:** 35 Lakeview Knl NE, Iowa City, IA 52240-9161, **Home Phone:** (319)351-9173.

**DUNGY, TONY (ANTHONY KEVIN DUNGY)**
Football player, football coach, broadcaster. **Personal:** Born Oct 6, 1955, Jackson, MI; son of Wilbur and Cleomae; married Lauren; children: Tiara, Jade, Eric, Jordan, Jason, Justin & James (deceased). **Educ:** Univ Minn, BA, 1977. **Career:** Football player, football coach (retired); Pittsburgh Steelers, safety, 1977-78, defensive asst, 1981, defensive backs coach, 1982-83, defensive coordr, 1984-88; San Francisco 49ers, 1979; NY Giants, 1980; Univ Minn, defensive backs coach, 1980; Kans City Chiefs, defensive backs coach, 1989-91; Minn Vikings, defensive coordr, 1992-95; Tampa Bay Buccaneers, head coach, 1996-2001; Indianapolis Colts, head coach, 2002-08; NBC Sports, Football Night in America, color analyst, 2009-. **Orgs:** Nat spokesperson, Am Diabetes Asn, African Am Prog & Sch Walk Diabetes campaign, 2003; Pres's Coun Serv & Civic Participation, 2007; adv coun, Faith-Based & Neighborhood Partnerships, 2009; Boys & Girls Club. **Honors/Awds:** AFC Champion, 1978, 2006; Professional Coach of the Yearr, Maxwell Football Club, 1997; Fatherhood Award, Nat Fatherhood Initiative, 2002; Super Bowl Coach of Year, XIII, XLI, 2007; Amos Alonzo Stagg Coaching Award, Us Sports Acad, 2007; inducted Society of World Changers, Ind Wesleyan Univ, DHL, 2008; Indianapolis Colts Ring of Honor, 2010; Pro Football Hall of Fame, 2016. **Special Achievements:** First African American coach to win Super Bowl; Youngest assistant coach in NFL history; Author: Quiet Strength. **Business Addr:** Color Analyst, Football Night in America.

**DUNHAM, CLARENCE E., JR.**
Consultant. **Personal:** Born Aug 29, 1934, Syracuse, NY; son of Clarence and Leona Shepard; children: Audrey, Tracey, Joi & Roderick Stubbs. **Educ:** Syracuse Univ, attended 1953; AUS, Comm Tech Teletype Sch, attended 1959. **Career:** Consultant (retired); W Elec Co Inc, 1953-69; NY Tel Co, commun consult, 1969-83; AT & T, asst mgr, 1983-87; Syracuse City Legislator, 2007. **Orgs:** Coun mem, Syracuse Neighbourhood Health Ctr; bd dir, Dunbar Ctr Social Serv Facil; pres, Grand St Boys; adv, Jr Achievement Orgn, 1972-73; Co Legislator, 1973; bd dir, PEACE Inc, 1974; bd dir, WCNY TV, 1974; adv bd, Bishop Foery Found, 1974; bd dir, Onondaga Neighborhood Leg Serv, 1975; bd dir, Metro Syracuse Bus Ind Educ Coun, 1975; exec com, Northern Region Black Pol Caucus; pres, Southwest Community Ctr, 1989. **Honors/Awds:** Citation from Jr Achievement, 1972; First runner-up in YMCA Black Achievement Award, 1973; YMCA Black Achievement Award, 1975. **Home Addr:** 824 S St, Syracuse, NY 13207-1817, **Home Phone:** (315)478-1058.

**DUNLAP, ERICKA**
Entertainer. **Personal:** Born Dec 29, 1981; married Brian Kleinschmidt. **Educ:** Univ Cent Fla. **Career:** Miss Am Orgn, beauty contestant, Career Country Music, currently; Crown Jewel Consult, pub rels specialist, currently. **Orgs:** Delta Sigma Theta Sorority; founder, Crown Jewwl Found. **Honors/Awds:** Miss Orlando, 2001; Miss Heart Florida, 2002; Miss City Beautiful, 2003; Miss Florida, 2003; Miss America, 2003, 2004. **Special Achievements:** The first African American woman to be crowned Miss Florida, 2004; Miss America, 2004.

**DUNLAP, DR. KAREN F. BROWN**
Journalist, president (organization), educator. **Personal:** Born Jul 13, 1951, Nashville, TN; daughter of Charles Fitzgerald and Mary Shute; married Henry L; children: Asim, Christopher & Asha; married Henry L. **Educ:** Mich State Univ, E Lansing, MI, BA, 1971; Tenn State Univ, Nashville, TN, MS, 1976; Univ Tenn, Knoxville, TN, PhD, jour, mass commun, 1982. **Career:** Nashville Banner, Nashville, TN, staff writer, 1969-71; Warner Robins Enterprise, Warner Robins, Ga, ed, 1973; Macon News, Macon, Ga, reporter, 1973-74; Tenn State Univ, Nashville, TN, asst prof com, 1975-85; Bickel Found, Karl A & Madira Bickel, fel, 1979-80; Nashville Banner, assoc ed, 1983-85; Univ S Fla, Sch Mass Commun, Tampa, Fla, asst prof, 1985-03; St Petersburg Times, staff writer, 1986-92; Fla Endowment Fund, McKnight fel, 1986-87; Poynter Inst, St Petersburg, Fla, assoc dir, 1989, dean & reporting, writing & editing fac, 1991, pres & managing dir, currently; Dunlap Realty Inc, pres & treas. **Orgs:** Soc Prof Journalists, 1980-; Asn Educrs Jour & Mass Communs, 1981-; Delta Sigma Theta Sorority, 1982-; Nat Asn Black Journalists, 1985-; bd mem, Newspaper Asn Am Found; Eckerd Youth Alternatives; bd dir, Times Publ Co. **Home Addr:** 4714 W Estrella St, Tampa, FL 33629-5518, **Home Phone:** (813)282-0453. **Business Addr:** President, Managing Director, Poynter Institute of Media Studies, 801 3rd St S, St. Petersburg, FL 33701, **Business Phone:** (727)821-9494.

**DUNMORE, CHARLOTTE J.**
Educator, social worker. **Personal:** Born Nov 16, 1926, Philadelphia, PA. **Educ:** Univ Pa, BS, 1949; Columbia Univ, MSSW, 1954; Brandeis Univ, Florence Heller Sch, PhD, 1968. **Career:** Boston Childrens Serv Asn, supvr adoption dept, 1957-62; Episcopal Comn Serv, social worker, 1962-64; Simmons Col, Sch Soc Work, assoc prof, 1967-77; Ment Health Ctr, consult, 1974; NIH, consult, 1975; Univ Pittsburgh, Sch Social Work, prof, 1977. **Orgs:** Bd mem, Nat Conf Social Welfare Nat Inst Ment Health Fel, 1964-67; bd mem, New EngMed Ctr Accreditation Comn Coun Social Work Educ, 1976-79; rev panel, Coun Int Exchange Scholars, 1976. **Home Addr:** 144 N Dithridge St, Pittsburgh, PA 15213-2659, **Home Phone:** (412)621-2097.

**DUNMORE, GREGORY CHARLES**
Journalist, fashion designer. **Personal:** Born Mar 24, 1958, Detroit, MI; son of Albert J and Jo Thompson. **Educ:** Nat Univ Mex, BA, span, 1979; Cornell Univ, BS, indust & labor rels, 1980. **Career:** Jo Thompson Productions Inc, dir, fashion designer, 1985-; MIC Chronicle Newspaper Agency, columnist, 1987-; Black Entertainment Tv, Line Productions, entertainment reporter; Mich Chronicle, Columnist, currently. **Orgs:** Int Ist Metro Detroit, vip pub rels, bd, 1990-; Harmonie Pk Playhouse, adv bd, 1987-; NAB, 1987-; APA, 1989-. **Honors/Awds:** Bachelor of the Year, Essence Magazine, 1992; MIC Winner, Beefeater Gin's Fashion & Jazz Competition; Fellow, MIC Opera Theatre; Congressional Intern Fellow, Congressman Crockett. **Special Achievements:** Producer, writer, director: "Jo Thompson: This Is My Life-Melodies and Madness!!!" one-woman show, Carnegie Hall, 1991; "Jo Thompson Show," New York's legendary Michael's Pub, 1992; fashion designer: Carlos Nina Haute Couture label. **Home Addr:** 640 Del St Apt 201, Detroit, MI 48202-4401, **Home Phone:** (313)874-4734. **Business Addr:** Columnist, Michigan Chronicle, 479 Ledyard St, Detroit, MI 48201, **Business Phone:** (313)963-5522.

**DUNMORE, DR. LAWRENCE ALFRED, JR.**
Executive, physician. **Personal:** Born May 17, 1923, Georgetown, SC; married Gloria Parker; children: Gwendolyn, Jacquelyn & Lawrence III. **Educ:** Howard Univ, MD, 1955; Johns Hopkins Univ, MPH, 1970; SC State Col, BS. **Career:** DC Gen Hosp; DC Govt Sec Stand Investments & Stand Ltd Partnership, exec dir. **Orgs:** Health Adv Planning Comt; adv bd, Shaw Health Ctr; Health Priorities Sub comt; DC Govt Adv Bd, Phys Asst Sch Allied Health Howard Univ. **Honors/Awds:** Distinguished Public Service Award, Govt DC, 1973; Outstanding Performance Award, Dept Human Resources, DC, 1974. **Home Addr:** 1911 Sudbury Rd NW, Washington, DC 20012-2228, **Home Phone:** (202)607-7375.

**DUNN, DAVID LEON**
Football coach, football player. **Personal:** Born Jun 10, 1972, San Diego, CA; children: 6. **Educ:** Fresno State Univ, grad. **Career:** Football player (retired); Cincinnati Bengals, kick returner, 1995-96, wide receiver, 1997; Pittsburgh Steelers, kick returner, 1998; Cleveland Browns, 1999; Oakland Raiders, kick returner, 2000, punt returner, 2001; Lincoln High Sch, head Football coach, currently. **Business Addr:** Football Coach, 4777 Imperial Ave, San Diego, CA 92113, **Business Phone:** (619)266-6500.

**DUNN, DAX**
Executive, consultant. **Educ:** Daytona Beach Community Col; Sch Natural Wellness, personal develop, interpersonal relationships skills, 2009-. **Career:** Am Mortgage Inc; RAD Financial Serv Inc, founder, pres & dir, 1999-2009; RAD Wellness, dir, 2010-; RAD-WEB, consult dietitian, 2011-; Me Do Con Yoga, instr, 2013-. **Business Addr:** Founder, President & Director, RAD Financial Services Inc, 1060 Sunset Strip Ave Suite A, Sunrise, FL 33313-6106, **Business Phone:** (954)587-2662.

**DUNN, JAMES EARL**
Educator, real estate agent. **Personal:** Born Apr 7, 1955, Tunica, MS; son of Robert and Helen; married Dorothy Mae Collier. **Educ:** Northwestern Jr Col, attended 1975; Ft Gordon Ga Community Sch, dipl, 1978; Delta State Univ, BS, 1978, MA, 1983; Ft Sill Field Artil Sch, dipl, 1981. **Career:** Tunica Jr High Sch, sch teacher, 1978-; County Tunica, bd supervisors, currently; lic realtor & real estate agt, currently. **Orgs:** Nat Guard Asn, 1978; Nat Asn Advan Colored People, 1980; Tunica County PTA, 1983; bd dir, Delta Coun; treas, Tunica Educ Asn, 1983-; Miss Asn Supvrs, 1984; bd dir, N Delta Planning & Develop Dist, 1987; NW Miss Asn Realtors. **Home Addr:** 1175 Hollywood Rd, PO Box 1463, Tunica, MS 38676, **Home Phone:** (662)363-1304. **Business Addr:** SUPERVISOR, Tunica County, 1300 Sch St, Tunica, MS 38676-9363, **Business Phone:** (662)363-2842.

**DUNN, JASON ADAM**
Football player, football coach. **Personal:** Born Nov 15, 1973, Harrodsburg, KY. **Educ:** Eastern Ky Univ, grad. **Career:** Football player (retired), football coach; Philadelphia Eagles, tight end, 1996-99; Kans City Chiefs, tight end, 2000-07; Lafayette High Sch Ky, offensive line coach, 2010-13; Ky State Univ, spec teams coordr, 2013-. **Orgs:** Dunn 4 Kids Found. **Business Addr:** Special Teams Coordinator, 400 E Main St, Frankfort, KY 40601, **Business Phone:** (502)597-6813.

**DUNN, JERRY MICHAEL**
Basketball coach. **Personal:** Born May 6, 1953, Raleigh, NC; son of Maelene Leake; married Gwendolyn; children: Nichole, Taylor & Morgan. **Educ:** Wyo Jr Col, assoc degree; George Mason Univ, BS, health & phys educ, 1981. **Career:** George Mason Univ, asst coach, 1977-83; Penn State Univ, asst coach, 1983-95, head coach, 1995-2003; Wva Univ, asst coach, 2003-07; Univ Mich Wolverine prog, assoc head coach, 2007-10; New York Knicks, asst head coach, 2012-13; Tuskegee, head coach, 2014-. **Orgs:** Nat Asst Basketball Coaches; Black Coaches Asn; bd dir, Second Mile Charity Organizer. **Business Addr:** basketball coach, Tuskegee Univ, Tuskegee, AL 36088, **Business Phone:** (334)727-8150.

**DUNN, LINDA SPRADLEY**
Publisher. **Educ:** George Washington Univ; Harvard Univ, MBA prog. **Career:** Int Bus Mach Corp, staff, 1983-94, bus unit mgr, health indust mkt & sales support strategy, mgr & founder; Women's Leadership Exchange, pres & ceo; Idamar Enterprises Inc, founder, pres & chief exec officer; Odyssey Media, founder, chief exec officer & publ, 1999-. **Orgs:** Bd mem, NJ Performing Arts Women's Bd; bd mem, Essex County Col Found Bd; bd mem, United Way Essex. **Special Achievements:** First African American and the First Female chair of the board of directors of the Essex County and Hudson United Way. **Business Addr:** Chief Executive Officer, Publisher, Odyssey Media, 2655 N Ocean Dr Suite 405, Singer Island, FL 33404, **Business Phone:** (561)881-0351.

**DUNN, MARVIN**
Educator, psychologist. **Personal:** Born Jun 27, 1940, De Land, FL; married Linda Irene Lacy; children: Wanda, Fredrick, Kimberly, Jafari & Dierdre. **Educ:** Morehouse Col, BA, psychol, 1961; Roosevelt Univ, Chicago, IL, MA, educ, admin & supv, 1965; Univ Tenn, Knoxville, TN, PhD, psychol, 1972. **Career:** Educator(retired), executive; Miami, psychologist, 1970-71; Fla Int Univ, Dept Psychol, from asst prof to assoc prof, chair, Inst Sexism & Racism, guide, 1972-2006; Cult & Human Interaction Ctr, dir, founder, 1973-; Acad Community Educ, founder & dir, 1981-; keynote speaker, US Info Serv, 1994; Overtown Community Garden, dir, 1999-; Overtown Neighborhood Partnerships Proj, tech asst; Roots City Proj, 2009; Camillus House Inc, Inst Homeless Studies, teacher, resident scholar, currently. Books: The Miami Riots of 1980: Crossing the Bounds; Black Miami in the Twentieth Century, 1997; The Beast in Florida: A History of Anti-Black Violence, 2012; The Beast in Florida: A History of Anti-Black Violence, 2013. **Orgs:** Treas, Fla State Asn Dist Ment Health Bd, 1975-76; bd dir, Dade Co Found Emotionally Disturbed Youth, 1975; bd dir, Transition Inc, 1976-; pres bd, Driver Improv Prog, 1976-; comnr, Eleventh Judicial Circuit Nominating Comn, 1977; pres & bd mem, Human Inter-Action Potential Inc; consult, HEWOCD Ford Found Early Admin Col Scholar; Nat Asn Black Psychologists; Dade Co Psychol Asn; vpres, Dade Co Ment Health Asn; vpres, Dade-Monroe Dist Ment Health Dept; bd dir, Ctr Dialogue; Fla Coun Community Ment Health; Goldberg Comn Violence, SAfrica; proj adv bd mem, Ctr Folk & Community Art; founder, Acad Community Educ; founder, Roots City. **Home Addr:** 3530 Crystal View Ct, Miami, FL 33133-4025, **Home Phone:** (305)857-9701. **Business Addr:** Resident Scholar, Teacher, Camillus House Inc, 336 NW 5th St, Miami, FL 33128, **Business Phone:** (305)374-1065.

**DUNN, REGINALD ARTHUR**
Judge. **Educ:** Loyola Law Sch, attended 1970. **Career:** Judge (retired); Calif Youth Authority probation officer, 1970, dep pub defender; Los Angeles City Attys Off, criminal trial dep, 1977, spec asst City Atty Burt Pines, 1981, Dept Water Power, criminal unit chief, 1984; Los Angeles County Super Ct, judge, 2002.

**DUNN, TRACI M.**
Executive, president (organization). **Educ:** Univ N Tex, Sch Merchandising & Hospitality Mgt, BS, 1994; Dallas Baptist Univ, orgn mgt. **Career:** Four Seasons Hotels & Resorts, human resorce mgr, 1995-98; Accenture, diversity specialist, 1998-2002; Compass Group, dir diversity, 2002-04; Dunn & Assocs, founder, pres, 2004-07; Timken, Global Inclusion & Talent Acquisition, dir, 2007-10; Huntington Nat Bank Inclusion, Talent & Org Effectiveness, sr vpres, 2011-13; Accenture, N Am inclusion & diversity lead, 2013-. **Orgs:** Bd & conf chair, Diversity Coun Carolinas; charlotte chap pres, Nat Asn African Am Human Resources; leadership comt, Univ City Community Bldg Proj; co-chair, Charlotte Chamber Black Prof Network; Diversity Best Pract Comt, Charlotte Chamber; bd mem, Urban League; adv comt, Nat Black MBA Asn. **Business Addr:** North America Inclusion & Diversity Lead, Accenture, 111 Wash St, Albany, NY 12210, **Business Phone:** (518)462-1576.

**DUNN, WARRICK DE'MON**
Football player, administrator. **Personal:** Born Jan 5, 1975, Baton Rouge, LA; son of Betty Smothers. **Educ:** Fla State Univ, BS, info technol, 1997; Emory Univ, Goizueta Bus Sch, MBA, 2013. **Career:** Football player (retired), analyst, executive; Tampa Bay Buccaneers, running back, 1997-2001, 2008-09, fullback, 2001; Atlanta Falcons, running back, 2002-07; ESPN, NFL analyst, 2010-11; ESPN3.com, color commentator, 2010-; Nat Football League, NFL legends coordr, 2013-. **Orgs:** Founder, Warrick Dunn Found, 1997-; bd trustee, Atlanta Falcons, 2010-. **Honors/Awds:** First-team All-ACC, 1994-96; Honorable mention AP All-American, 1995; Second-team AP All-American, 1996; AP NFL Offensive Rookie of the Year, 1997; PFWA Offensive Rookie of the Year, 1997; Pro Bowl selection, 1997, 2000, 2005; Named NFL Rookie of the Year by Football News, Pro Football Weekly, and Sports Illus, 1997; Named Offensive Rookie of

the Year, Assoc Press, Football Dig, and Col and Pro Football Newsweekly, 1997; Pro Bowl, 1997; Ed Block Courage Award, 1998; Atlantas Peach of an Athlete Award, Boy Scouts Am, 2003; Man of the Year, Atlanta Falcons, 2003; The Henry P Iba Citizen Athlete Award, 2003; Athlete of the Year, Frank Ski Kids Found, 2003; Walter Payton Man of the Year Award, 2004; Giant Steps Award; Jessie Tuggle Humanitarian Award, 2004; No. 1 Good Guy Award, Sporting News. Walter Payton Man of the Year Award, 2004; Home Depot Neighborhood MVP Award, 2006; Whizzer White NFL Man of the Year, 2007; Giving Back Pro of the Year Award, Am Youth Football, 2007; JB Award, NFL Players Asn, 2008; Bart Starr Man of the Year Award, 2009; Bank of America Local Hero, 2009; 11-Alive Community Service Award, 2010; Heisman Humanitarian Award, 2010; Jefferson Awards Outstanding Athlete in Service & Philanthropy, 2011; 10, 000 Rushing Yards Club. **Special Achievements:** 101 Most Influential Minorities in Sports, Issue Sports Illus, 2003. **Business Addr:** Founder, Warrick Dunn Foundation, 3413 W Fletcher Ave, Tampa, FL 33618, **Business Phone:** (813)964-0100.

### DUNNER, DR. LESLIE BYRON

Composer, conductor (music). **Personal:** Born Jan 5, 1956, New York, NY; son of Lloyd Bertram and Audrey Hemmings. **Educ:** Univ Rochester, Eastman Sch Music, Rochester, NY, BA, appl music, clarinet performance, 1978; Queens Col, New York, NY, MA, music theory & musicol, 1979; Univ Cincinnati, Col Conserv Music, Cincinnati, PhD, orchestral conducting, 1982. **Career:** Carleton Col, asst prof, 1982-86; Dance Theatre Harlem, princ guest coductor, 1987-95; Detroit Symphony, resident conductor, assoc coductor, asst coductor, 1987-98; New York Philharmonic, cover conductor, 1993-98, asst conductor to Kurt Masur, 1994-2001; Kwa Zulu Natal Philharmonic Orchestra, guest conductor, 1994-2014; Symphony Ns, music dir, 1996-99; Annapolis Symphony Orchestra, music dir, 1997-2003; Joffrey Ballet, music dir & prin conductor, 2003-09; Louisville Ballet, prin conductor, 2009-11; Orquestra Filarmonica de Jalisco, interim music dir, 2011. **Orgs:** Bd dir, Am Music Ctr, 1991-, music dir, 1998-. **Honors/Awds:** Third Prize, Arturo Toscanini Inter Nat Conducting Competition, 1986; Spirit of Detroit Award, 1988; Named Man of the Year, Delta Phi Beta, Detroit, 1988; James Weldon Johnson Award, Nat Am Advan Colored People, 1991; American Symphony Orchestra League Award, 1994; Distinguished Young Alumnus Award, Univ Cincinnati, 1996; Man of the Year, Spirit of Detroit Award, Zeta Phi Beta Sorority. **Home Addr:** 1310 Blackwalnut Ct, Annapolis, MD 21403, **Home Phone:** (410)295-0927.

### DUNNIGAN, JERRY A.

Educator, artist. **Personal:** Born Jul 28, 1941, Cleveland, OH; married Roberta; children: James, Jerome & Jeffrey. **Educ:** Dayton Art Inst, Univ Dayton, BS, 1965; Ky State Univ, MA, 1970. **Career:** Linden Ctr, instr, 1964-65; Akron Art Inst, art instr, 1969-70; E Tech High Sch Black Acculturation Prog, instr Black Art, 1970-71; Nathan Hale Jr High Sch, dept chmn. **Orgs:** Nat Conf Artists; numerous exhibs comt chmn, OH; Div World Festival Black Art, 1975. **Home Addr:** 7268 Glenshire Rd, Cleveland, OH 44146-5930, **Home Phone:** (440)786-0369. **Business Addr:** 3588 E Blvd, Cleveland, OH 44105.

### DUNNINGS, STUART J., III

Lawyer. **Personal:** Born Oct 29, 1952, Lansing, MI; son of Stuart J and Janet Taylor; married Cynthia Marie; children: Courtney R & Coral S M. **Educ:** Amherst Col, BA, 1974; Univ Mich Sch Law, JD, 1979. **Career:** Thomas M Cooley Law Sch, adj Prof, 1989-98; Dunnings & Frawley PC, atty, 1980-96, partner; Ingham County, prosecuting atty, 1997-2016, prosecutor, currently; Lansing Sch Dist, educr, 2005-. **Orgs:** Standing comt character & fitness, State Bar Mich, 1987-96; vpres, Nat Asn Advan Colored People, Lansing Br, 1993; Prosecuting Attys Asn Mich; Trinity AME Church; Cath Educ Found; bd mem, Girl Scouts Mich Capitol Coun; bd mem, Mich State Univ Col Law; Youth Violence Prev Coalition; bd dir, Local United Way; bd dir, Girls Scouts; bd mem, Prosecuting Atty Asn Mich; adv bd, State Community Corrections. **Special Achievements:** First elected Ingham County Prosecutor in 1996; First African-American to be elected to such office in Michigan. **Home Addr:** 500 Everett Dr, PO Box 10043, Lansing, MI 48915-1108. **Business Addr:** Prosecuting Attorney, Prosecutor, Ingham County, 303 W Kalamazoo St 4R, Lansing, MI 48923, **Business Phone:** (517)483-6272.

### DUNSON, DR. CARRIE LEE

Educator, school administrator. **Personal:** Born Apr 19, 1946, Kansas City, MO; daughter of Walter and Roberta King; children: Anthony & Darren Harris. **Educ:** Lincoln Univ, Jefferson City, MO, BS, psychol, 1974; Cent Mo State Univ, Warrensburg, MS, corrections, 1975, EdS, 1976; Univ Mo, Ka, PhD, 1992. **Career:** Educator (retired), adminr; USMC, Kans City MO, mail clerk supvr, 1967; Wash DC Police Dept, supvr doc, 1971; MO Div of Ins, Jefferson City, sec, test examr 1973; KC Futures 150, proj evaluator; Cent Mo State Univ, Warrensburg, instr criminal justice, 1975, asst prof indus security, 1978, dir equal employ, 1978-88, assoc prof criminal justice, 1992-2005, prof emer, 2005-. **Orgs:** Sponsor Sigma Gamma Rho Sorority, 1975; Asn Black Collegiates, 1975; Am Soc Indus Sect, 1978; Order Eastern Star KS Chap, 1973; Comn Human Rights, MO Comn Human Rights, 1976; co-chmn, Comn MO Affirmative Action Asn, 1979; Asn Black Women in Higher Educ, 1980; co-advisor, Cent's Am Criminal Justice Asn Lamda Alpha Epsilon, 1996; adv, LAE Club, 1998-; off univ affirmative action officer, Affirmative Action Off; arbitrator, Greater Kans City Better Bus Bur; Wash D.C. Police Dept; juv justice syst; Kans City Task Force Adv Bd & Pres's Comn Status Women. **Home Addr:** 4939 College Ave, Kansas City, MO 64130, **Home Phone:** (816)923-9638. **Business Addr:** Professor Emeritus, University of Central Missouri, PO Box 800, Warrensburg, MO 64093, **Business Phone:** (660)543-4111.

### DUNSTON, SHAWON DONNELL

Baseball player, athletic coach. **Personal:** Born Mar 21, 1963, Brooklyn, NY; son of Jack and Brenda; married Tracie; children: Whitnie, Jasmine, I'sha & Shawon Jr. **Career:** Baseball player (retired), baseball coach; Chicago Cubs, infielder, 1985-95, 1997, guest coach; San Francisco Giants, shortstop, 1996, spring instr, 2001-02; Pittsburgh Pirates, shortstop, 1997; Cleveland Indians, shortstop, 1998; San Francisco Giants, shortstop, 1998; St Louis Cardinals, shortstop, 1999-2000; New York Mets, shortstop, 1999; San Francisco Giants, spring instr, 2001-02; Dusty Baker Acad, instr, currently. **Home Addr:** 6145 N Sheridan Suite 157, Chicago, IL 60660. **Business Addr:** Instructor, Dusty Baker International Baseball Academy, PO Box 1461, Pollock Pines, CA 95726, **Business Phone:** (480)644-6372.

### DUPER, MARK SUPER (SUPER DUPER)

Football player. **Personal:** Born Jan 25, 1959, Moreauville, LA; married Renee; children: Tracy, Stacey, Mark II, Alexandria & Kirby. **Educ:** Northwestern State Univ-La, grad. **Career:** Football player (retired); Miami Dolphins, wide receiver, 1982-92; Miami Hooters, 1994. **Orgs:** Omega Psi Phi Fraternity Inc. **Honors/Awds:** All-Pro selection, 1983-84; Pro Bowl selection, 1983-84 & 1986. **Special Achievements:** Rated as number one receiver in AFC & number two in NFL by Sportsgames computer rating system. **Home Addr:** , Marksville, LA.

**DUPER, SUPER. See DUPER, MARK SUPER.**

### DUPRE, DR. JOHN LIONEL

Psychiatrist. **Personal:** Born Dec 6, 1953, New Orleans, LA; son of Antoine Joseph Jr and Leverne Boutte; married Yadira Gisella McGrath; children: Joya Gabrielle. **Educ:** Tulane Univ, New Orleans, LA, BS, biol, 1975, Sch Med, MD, 1978. **Career:** Univ Calif, San Francisco, internship, Langley Porter Neuropsychiat Inst, Calif, residency prog, 1979-83; San Quentin State Prison, San Quentin, Calif, staff psychiatrist, 1983-2013; San Francisco, Calif, pvt pract psychiatrist, 1983-; JohnGeorge Pavilion, psychiat emergency serv psychiatrist, 2001-13. **Orgs:** Former pres, Black Psychiatrists NC, 1985-89; Am Psychol Asn; NAMA. **Business Addr:** Psychiatrist, Private Practice, 192 Grand View Ave, San Francisco, CA 94114-2732, **Business Phone:** (415)454-1461.

### DUPREE, DAVID H.

Lawyer, educator. **Personal:** Born Aug 18, 1959, Knoxville, TN; son of William F and Eloise Edwards; married Aleathea A; children: 2. **Educ:** Howard Univ Sch Bus & Pub Admin, BBA, 1981; Howard Univ Sch Law, JD, 1984. **Career:** Howard Univ Acad Comput Servs, stud res asst, 1978-84, systs analyst, 1985-87; Self-Employed, res methodologist, 1979-; Law Off David Dupree, atty, 1985-; Howard Univ Sch Bus, instr, 1990-94; pvt pract, atty, currently; E Knoxville Bus & Prof, prin; Knoxville City Coun, 6th Dist, atty; Gardiner & Assocs, atty, currently. **Orgs:** Comput Law Asn, 1985-; DC Comput Law Forum, 1985-; Pa Bar Asn, 1985; Pa Supreme Ct Bar 1985-; Am Judicature Soc 1986; DC Bar Asn, 1986, Tax Ct US, 1986-, Am Bar Asn, 1986, DC Ct Appeals, 1986-; bd mem, Achievement Scholar Prog, 1986-; trustee bd, Greater Mt Calvary Holy Ch, 1988-; US Dist Ct, DC, 1989-; Delta Sigma Pi Bus Fraternity, 1980-; Phi Alpha Delta Legal Fraternity, 1984-. **Home Addr:** 3837 Bonnie View Ave, Knoxville, TN 37914-3971, **Home Phone:** (865)524-4930. **Business Addr:** Attorney, Gardiner & Associates, 5401 Kingston Pke Suite 520, Knoxville, TN 37919, **Business Phone:** (865)450-9819.

### DUPREE, EDWARD A.

Association executive, administrator, executive. **Personal:** Born Mar 24, 1943, Farmville, NC; son of David and Nellie Fields Lunsford; married Helen Roberts; children: Davido M. **Educ:** NC Cent Univ, BA, 1965; Howard Univ Sch Social Work, MA, social work, 1968. **Career:** Baltimore City Dept Social Serv, casework supvr, 1968-70; Model Cities Agency, Community Info Div, chief, 1970-80; Urban Serv Agency, Energy & Housing Progs, chief, 1980-. **Orgs:** NC Cent Univ Alumni Asn, 1966-; Howard Univ Alumni Asn, 1968-; Am Asn Blacks Energy, 1980-; House Resolution, Md House Deleg, 1980; City Coun Baltimore Resolution, Baltimore City Coun, 1982, 1987; Md Energy Dirs Asn, 1984-; Nat Forum Black Pub Admins, 1989-. **Honors/Awds:** Outstanding Md Energy Assistance Prog Dir, Md Dept Human Resources, 1987; Citizen Citation, City Baltimore, 1990; Vpres Citation, Vpres City Coun Baltimore, 1990. **Home Addr:** 2629 Cross Country Blvd, Baltimore, MD 21215-3824, **Home Phone:** (410)466-5570. **Business Addr:** Chief, Urban Services Agency, 501 E Fayette St Lower Level, Baltimore, MD 21202, **Business Phone:** (410)396-8413.

### DUPREE, KIA

College teacher, writer. **Personal:** Born WA; children: 1. **Educ:** Hampton Univ, BA, mass media arts; Old Dom Univ, MA, eng. **Career:** St. Martins Press, asst ed; Hampton Univ, Eng Dept, prof, Dept Univ Rels, staff. Books: Damaged, 2010; Silenced, 2011; Shattered, 2012. **Home Addr:** , Washington, DC. **Business Addr:** Professor, Hampton University, Hampton, VA 23668, **Business Phone:** (757)727-5000.

### DUPREE, SANDRA KAY (SANDRA DUPREE CAMPBELL)

Librarian. **Personal:** Born Jul 17, 1956, Warren, AR; daughter of Asibear and Erie Ingram; married Bobby Charles Campbel; children: David Russell. **Educ:** Univ Ark, Pine Bluff, AR, BA, 1978; Atlanta Univ, Sch Libr Sci, Atlanta, GA, MSLS, 1979; Tex Womans Univ, Denton, TX, 1985. **Career:** Pub libr, Columbus & Franklin Co, Columbus, OH, intern, 1979-80; Bradley Co Libr, Warren, AR, dir, 1980-81; Univ Ark, Pine Bluff, AR, instr, 1982; SE Ark Reg Libr, Monticello, AR, specialist, 1982-83; Univ Ark, Monticello, AR, asst librn, 1984-97, assoc librn, & dir, currently. **Orgs:** Am Libr Asn, 1980-; Ark Libr Asn, 1980-; head nominating comt, Southeast Ark Concert Arts, 1987-98; bd mem, Friends Monticello Br Libr, 1988-; bd mem, Ark Endowment Humanities, 1986-89. **Honors/Awds:** Honorary Member, Phi Kappa Delta, 1987. **Home Addr:** PO Box 312, Monticello, AR 71657-0312, **Home Phone:** (870)367-2234. **Business Addr:** Director, University of Arkansas-Monticello, 346 Univ Dr, Monticello, AR 71656, **Business Phone:** (870)460-1026.

### DUPREE, PROF. SHERRY SHERROD

Religious scholar, bibliographer, educator. **Personal:** Born Nov 25, 1946, Raleigh, NC; daughter of Matthew Needham and Elouise Heartley; married Herbert Clarence; children: Amil, Andre & Andrew. **Educ:** NC Cent Univ, BS, voc home econs, 1968, MA, educ media, 1969; Univ Mich, AMLS, librarianship, ES, instrnl technol; Univ Fla. **Career:** Eastern Mich Univ, vis prof educ media, 1974; Ann Arbor Pub Schs, media specialist, 1970-76; Univ fla, assoc ref librn, 1977-83; Inst Black Cult, proj dir, 1982-92; Santa Fe Community col, ref librn, 1983-99, libr user serv coorde, 1999-2002, prof behav sci, 2002, prof, 2011, stud develop instr, currently; Gospel Music Hall Fame & Mus, Detroit, archivist, 1995-; Gospel Music Traveling Exhib, cur, 1994-; Fla Humanities Coun, exhib consult; Bks & articles: "Libr Media Ctr & Classroom Displays", w/Hertha Jenkins, Media Spectrum, 1976; "Display For Schools", 1976; "Mini-Course Libr Skills", Univ Fla, 1983; "What You Always Wanted to Know About Card Catalog But Was Afraid to Ask", 3rd ed rev Displays Schs Inc, 1987; African-Am Holiness Pentecostal Movement: An Annotated Bibliog, Garland Publ, NY, 1996; African-Am Good News (Gospel) Music, w/Herbert C DuPree, Mid Atlantic Regional Press, 1993; Exposed !!!: FDL Bur Invest (FBI) Unclassified Reports Churches & Church Leaders, w/Herbert C DuPree, Mid Atlantic Regional Press, 1993; Biog Dict African-Am Holiness Pentecostals: 1880-1990, 1989; African Am Holiness Pentecostal movement: Annotated bibliog Garland Libr Social Sci, 1996; Silent Spokesman Bishop Robert Clarence Lawson/Stewart & DuPree, 1998; A proj Vanderbilt Divinity Libr funded by Asn Theol Schs with coop from archivists Soc Pentecostal Studies, web site, 1999. Organizing Black Am: An Encycl African Am Associations/Mjagkij, 2001; New Int Dict Pentecostal & Charismatic Movements/Burgess, 2002; League Innovations Presentation 2004; Encycl Am Gospel Music/McNeil, 2006; Encycl Relig Revivals/McClymond 2007; Encycl Christian Civilization/Kurian, 2008; Adv Bd mem textbk Becoming A Master Stud/Ellis, 2009; Libr Credit Workshop, Roadmap to African Am Ref Resources; spec collection, African-Am Pentecostal & Holiness Collection; Fla African Am Hist Task Force, goal 3 chairperson, 2011-12; UNESCO Educ Tours, dir, 2011-12; DuPree Pentecostal Holiness Ctr, dir 2011-. **Orgs:** MZeta Phi Beta Sorority Inc, 1967-; Nat Asn Advan Colored People 1977-; Alachua Libr League 1977-; Williams Temple Church God Christ; Fla Libr Asn, 1980-; pres, Univ Fla Libr Asn, 1981-82; Fla Asn Community Cols, 1983-; Am Libr Asn; Asn Col & Res Libr Fla Chapt; Black FOCUS; Soc Am Archivists, 1986-; Mid Atlantic Regional Gospel Ministries 1987-; Soc Pentecostal Studies, 1987-; Black Family Develop, 1990-; Int Platform Asn; chair, Rosewood Massacre Forum, 1994-; Alachua Regional Marine Inst (ARMI), 1994-; Relig Caucus, Fla Libr Asn, chair, 1994-96; ed bd, 1994-, pres, 2000-01, Soc Pentecostal Studies; Fla Asn Christian Librarians, 1996-; bd mem, Alachua County Hist Trust/Matheson Mus, 1996-01; Gospel Music Hall Fame & Mus Inc, archivist, 1996-; Univ Fla Ctr Autism & Related Disabilities (CARD), 1996-; pub serv rep, Col Ctr Libr Automation (CCLA), 1998-2002; Black Caucus Am Libr Asn Newsletter; Fla Dept State, State Hist Marker Coun, 1999-2001; Friends Marjorie Kinnan Rawlings Farms Inc, 2000-; consult, Mission Agencies Who Preserve Church Arch; 2000-01; Fla State Geneal Soc, 2005-; Fla Storytelling Guild, 2006-; Int Gospel Music Hall Fame & Mus. **Home Addr:** 1825 NW 22nd Terr, Gainesville, FL 32605, **Home Phone:** (352)373-2030. **Business Addr:** Professor, Bibliographer, Santa Fe Community College, 3000 NW 83rd St, Gainesville, FL 32606, **Business Phone:** (352)395-5407.

### DUPRI, JERMAINE (JERMAINE DUPRI MAULDIN)

Executive. **Personal:** Born Sep 23, 1972, Asheville, NC; son of Michael Mauldin and Tina; children: Shaniah Mauldin. **Career:** Albums: 12 Soulful Nights of Christmas, 1996; Life in 1472, 1998; Instructions, 2001; Welcome to Atlanta, 2001; Green Light, 2004; Get Your No, 2005; Gotta Getcha, 2005; Young, Fly & Flashy, Vol. 1, 2005; We Belong Together, 2005; TLC's CrazySexyCool; Mariah Carey's Daydream; Tv movie: Carmen: A Hip Hopera, MTV, 2001; Arista Rec, sr vpres, 2003-; So So Def Recordings, chief exec officer, founder, currently; Virgin Rec, urban music, exec vpres; Universal Music Group's Island Rec, urban music pres; American Gangster, co-prouduced & co-wrote, 2007. **Honors/Awds:** Songwriter of the Year, Am Soc Composers, Authors & Publishers, 1999. **Special Achievements:** Label acts include: Kriss Kross, Xscape, Da Brat, Yvette Michele; written and produced for: TLC, Mariah Carey, The Notorious B.I.G., Sylk Times Leather: Listed top ten richest people in Hip-Hop; Top 25 greatest southern artists by Ozone Magazine. Autobiography: Young, Rich and Dangerous: The Making of a Music Mogul; Books: Young Rich and Dangerous: The Making of a Music Mogul. **Business Addr:** Founder, Chief Executive Officer, So-So Def Recordings, 685 Lambert Dr NE, Atlanta, GA 30324, **Business Phone:** (404)888-9900.

### DURAND, DR. HENRY J., JR.

Educator. **Personal:** Born Jun 14, 1948, Griffith, GA; son of Henry J Sr and Mildred C; married Bonita Ruth Cobb; children: Anitra R, Kendra N, Aprille L & Leroy Alan Larkin. **Educ:** Denison Univ, BA, sociol, 1971; Xavier Univ, MEd, 1976; Univ Cincinnati, EdD, 1988; Harvard Mgt Develop Inst; Am Mgt Asn Exec Progs. **Career:** Cincinnati Bd Educ, teacher, reading spt, 1974-76; Univ Cincinnati, inr, actg dir, reading & study skills prog, 1976-80, Col Med, dir, learning resources, 1980-82; Bushido Training Prog, training dir, 1982-86; Northern Ken Univ, asst prof, sociol, 1987-90; State Univ NY Buffalo, Ctr Appl Pub Affairs, sr res assoc, 1990, Ctr Acad Develop, dir, 1990; Educ Opportunity Prog, currently. **Orgs:** Am Educ Res Asn; Am Asn Higher Educ; Am Asn Univ Adrs; Am soc Training & Develop; United Univ Professions. **Home Addr:** 153 Winspear Ave, Buffalo, NY 14215-1033, **Home Phone:** (716)835-8244. **Business Addr:** Director, State University NY Buffalo, 208A Norton Hall, Buffalo, NY 14260, **Business Phone:** (716)645-3072.

### DURAND, WINSLEY O., JR.

Consultant, engineer. **Personal:** Born Jul 29, 1941, Bunkie, LA; son of Winsley Sr (deceased) and Enola (deceased); married Sonya Marie; children: Winsley III & Janay. **Educ:** USL, attended 1963; Southern Univ, BS, 1968; Bradley Univ, attended 1974; Univ Ill, MBA, 1987. **Career:** Caterpillar Tractor Co, jr sales develop engr, 1968-70, app engr, rels rep mgr, 1974-, equal employ cord, 1977-, mgr tech recruiting, 1987-; Western Engg, acct cord, 1970-71, sales develop engr, 1971-72, sales, spec assignment employee rels, 1973; pvt investor; Caterpillar Inc, Peoria, Ill, qual improv cord, 1988, off bus practices consult, currently. **Orgs:** Civil Rights Movement, 1960-65; pres, Peoria Black

Polit Assembly, 1974-75; chmn, Voter Reg Dr, 1976; bd mem, Tri Co Labor Educ & Indust Coun, 1977; pres, Greater Peoria Big Bro & Big Sister, 1982; bd adv, Greater Peoria Found, 1986; bd mem, Peoria Pub Libr, 1987; pres, Greater Peoria Libr Bd, 1992; pres, Greater Peoria Pvt Indust Coun, 1993-95. **Honors/Awds:** Outstanding New manite for Leadership, 1963; Outstanding Marine of Year Award, 1965; Dress Blue & Leather Neck Award, 1965; Outstanding Marine Award, Outstanding Leadership Civilian Work Marines, 1969. **Home Addr:** 2834 W Knollwood Ct, Peoria, IL 61604-1821, **Home Phone:** (309)688-9204. **Business Addr:** Business Practices Consultant, Caterpillar Inc, 100 NE Adams St, Peoria, IL 61629-0002, **Business Phone:** (309)675-1000.

### DURANT, CELESTE MILLICENT

Media executive, executive. **Personal:** Born Apr 23, 1947, New York, NY. **Educ:** Grinnell Col, BA, hist, 1968; Columbia Univ Grad Sch Jour, MSJ, 1970. **Career:** Life Mag, publicity asst, 1968-70; Dayton J Herald, staff writer, 1970-72; La Times, staff writer, 1972; freelance writer; KCOP, exec producer; Univ Calif, Riverside, campus commun officer, currently, sr pub info officer, currently; Loyola Marymount Univ, dir commun & media rels, currently. **Orgs:** Pub Rels Soc Am, currently. **Honors/Awds:** Ohio Newspaper, Women's Feature Writing Award, 1971; Recip, La Press Club Award, 1974; Alfred I. duPont-Columbia Award. **Home Addr:** 3887 Latrobe St, Los Angeles, CA 90031. **Business Addr:** Director of Communications & Media Relations, Loyola Marymount University, 1 Loyola Marymount Univ Dr, Los Angeles, CA 90045, **Business Phone:** (310)338-7708.

### DURANT, KAREN

Executive. **Personal:** Born New York, NY; daughter of Frank and Frankie Jackson; children: Darren Emil Simon. **Educ:** NY Univ. **Career:** Columbia Rec, prom mgr, 1984-88; CBS Rec, mgr, 1978-88; Jive Rec Zomba Music, mgr, 1988-90; EMI Rec, dir, 1992-94; Rondor Music, creative mgr, 1992, exec dir, gen mgr, 1994-, vpres; Sleepercell Productions, specialist, 2000-08; Artist Direct Rec, a&r consult, 2001-03; Consult / Freelance, expert witness, 2004-11; Soundkillers LLC, consult, 2006-; Film Independent, producer, 2008-11; Model City, Music Supvr, 2009-10; Model City, Specialist, 2009-10. **Orgs:** Nat Acad Rec Arts & Sci. **Home Addr:** 1734 Madison Ave, New York, NY 10029. **Business Addr:** Executive Director, General Manager, Rondor Music International, 2440 Sepulveda Blvd Suite 119, Los Angeles, CA 90064, **Business Phone:** (310)235-4800.

### DURANT, KEVIN

Basketball player. **Personal:** Born Sep 29, 1988, Washington, DC; son of Wanda. **Educ:** Univ Tex, Austin, attended 2007. **Career:** NBA Seattle Supersonics, drafted, 2007, player, 2007-08; NBA Oklahoma City Thunder, player, 2008-16; NBA Golden State Warriors, player, 2016-; USA Basketball, player, 2010-. **Orgs:** Kevin Durant Charity Foundation, founder. **Honors/Awds:** Oscar Robertson Award, 2007; Adolph F. Rupp Award, 2007; Naismith Award, 2007; Wooden Award, 2007; National Player of the Year, Associated Press; NBA Rookie of the Year, 2008; FIBA World Championship MVP, International Basketball Federation, 2010; Gold Medal, FIBA World Championship, 2010; NBA All-Star, 2010-14; Gold Medal, Olympics, 2012; NBA MVP, 2014. **Business Addr:** Golden State Warriors, 1011 Broadway, Oakland, CA 94607, **Business Phone:** (510)986-2200.

### DURANT, BISHOP NAOMI C.

Clergy, broadcaster. **Personal:** Born Jun 23, 1938, Baltimore, MD; daughter of Bishop Clem Williamson and Ruth Martin; married Albert; children: George, Victoria, Rodney & Hope. **Educ:** Baltimore Col, DD, 1970. **Career:** New Refuge Deliverance Holiness Church Inc, sr pastor, founder & Presiding Prelate, 1967-; Churches Baltimore & Wash Area, overseer bishop; Radio Stas WBGR, WEBB, WSID, WUST, gospel disc jockey, 1968-73. **Orgs:** Advocates Baltimore, 1971; Ada Chaplian 1 Order Eastern Star. **Honors/Awds:** Hon BTH degree, MD Bible Col, 1972. **Home Addr:** 1 Belle Forte Ct, Pikesville, MD 21208. **Business Addr:** Senior Pastor, Founder Archbishop, New Refuge Deliverance Holiness Church Incorporation, 1100 St Paul St Bishop DuRants Way, Baltimore, MD 21202, **Business Phone:** (410)752-6524.

### DURANT, DR. THOMAS JAMES

College teacher. **Personal:** Born Apr 9, 1941, Mansfield, LA; son of Thomas J Sr and Lena B Jones; married Mary C Peyton; children: Thomas III, Timothee & Tyrone. **Educ:** Grambling State Univ, BS, 1963; Tuskegee Inst, MS, 1966; Univ Wis, Madison, PhD, rural sociol, 1973. **Career:** Professor emeritus (retired), professor; US Peace Corps St Lucia Proj, agr exten, 1963-65; Tuskegee Inst, res assoc, 1966-68; Univ Wis, res asst, appl demog lab, 1968-72; madison area tech col, adult basic educ recruiter, 1969; Va State Univ, assoc prof, 1972-73; La State Univ, assoc prof sociol, 1973-94, ed, Sociol Spectrum Sociol Jour, 1984 & 1995, prof sociol, 1995, dir African & African Am Studies, 1997-2001; prof emer. **Orgs:** Phi Beta Sigma Frat Inc, Omicron Beta Sigma, 1961-; Gamma Sigma Delta HonSoc, La State Univ, 1979-86; Omicron Delta Kappa Leadership Soc, La State Univ Chap, 1986; Nat Asn Advan Colored People; Am Sociol Asn; Southern Sociol Soc; Rural Southwestern Mid-S & Southern Soc; Mid-S Sociol Asn; Rural Sociol Soc; Southern Rural Soc. **Home Addr:** 7826 Wimbledon Ave, Baton Rouge, LA 70810, **Home Phone:** (225)766-8233. **Business Addr:** Professor, PO Box 17209, Jackson, MS 39217, **Business Phone:** (601)979-2434.

### DURANT-PAIGE, BEVERLY

Public relations executive, music publisher. **Personal:** Born New York, NY; daughter of Wesley Durant and Eunice Fuller; children: Desiree Spirit & Danielle Carrington. **Educ:** Hunter Col, attended 1974. **Career:** CBS Rec, New York, mgr publicity, 1978; Howard Bloom Pub Rels, New York, sr acct exec, 1983; PAIGE ONE Pub Rels, New York, pres & chief exec officer, 1985; Polygram Inc, sr dir nat publicity; Interscope Rec, vpres publicity, black music, Island Black Music, vpres media rels, 1998; Island & Def Jam Music Grp, vpres, 2000; Blackgospel Promo Inc, pres, currently. **Orgs:** Pub Rels Soc New York; life mem, Nat Asn Advan Colored People. **Honors/Awds:** The Lillian Award, Delta Sigma Theta, 1988; Award of Appreciation, New York Police Dept, 1989; Industry's Top Publicists, Ebony Mag. **Home Addr:** 2 Jade Ct, Pomona, NY 10970-2722, **Home Phone:** (845)364-9644. **Business Addr:** President, Blackgospel Promo Inc, 2 Jade Ct, Pomona, NY 10970, **Business Phone:** (845)659-1271.

### DURDEN, EARNEL

Football coach, automotive executive. **Personal:** Born Jan 24, 1937, Los Angeles, CA; married June E; children: Mike, Kevin & Allan F. **Educ:** Ore State Univ, BS, 1959; Calif State Univ, Long Beach, MA, 1969; Calif State Bd Educ, life dipl. **Career:** Football coach, automotive executive (retired); LA Co Pks & Rec, dir, 1959-60; Jr High Sch, teacher coach entrepreneurs, 1960-63; Compton High Sch, backfield coach wrestling coach, 1963-66; Compton Col, defensive backfield coach, 1966-68; Versity Long Beach, Calif State Univ, head fresh coach, asst defensive backfield coach, 1968-69; Univ Calif, off backfield coach, 1969-71; LA Rams, off backfield, 1971-73; Houston Oilers, off backfield, 1973-74; Gen Motors, automobile dealer; San Diego Chargers, backfield rec, 1974-87, offensive backfield coach; Spec Sport Prog Young Men, spec asst dir & organizer. **Special Achievements:** Recipient first black Joe Col, Ore State Univ, 1956-57; first black football coach, Calif State Univ, Long Beach; first black coach, La Rams; first black coach, Houston Oilers; first team, Pac Coast Conf, 1956-57; Author: "Paying the Price: A Life in Football ... and Beyond", 2016. **Home Addr:** 7988 Cinthia St, La Mesa, CA 91941-6331.

### DURE, GERARD

Beautician. **Personal:** Born Brooklyn, NY. **Career:** Gerard Dure Salon, owner & celebrity hairstylist, currently; TV show: The Look' with Gerard Dure, 2006. **Orgs:** Guest beauty advisor, Life & Styles. **Special Achievements:** First Black makeup & hair artist on television doing programs; Books: All About Beauty. **Business Addr:** Owner, Celebrity Hairstylist, Gerard Dure Salon, 635 W 125th St Suite 2, New York, NY 10027, **Business Phone:** (212)865-0201.

### DURHAM, C. SHELBY

Health services administrator, chief executive officer, president (organization). **Personal:** Born Jul 25, 1960, Crawl Hill; daughter of Coolidge and Julia L; married Melvin T Jackson. **Educ:** Bermuda Col, gen cert educ, 1977; NC Agr & Tech State Univ, BA, 1981; Howard Univ, MS, 1983. **Career:** Dept Educ, Bermuda, c devel diagnostician, 1981; Ministry Health & Social Servs, Bermuda, speech ther intern, 1983; Howard Univ, teaching asst, 1983-84; Speech Inc, speech pathologist, 1984-86; Keystone Rehab Systs, speech pathologist, 1986-87, dist dir, 1987-92; ROI Health Care Continuum, pres & chief exec officer, 1992-99; At Home Health Inc, pres & chief exec officer, 1996-. **Orgs:** ASHA, 1983-96; Nat Asn Women Bus Owners, 1995-96; NAFE, 1995-96; Nat Coun Negro Women Inc, 1995-96. **Home Addr:** 1 Plumtree Dr, Sewell, NJ 08080, **Home Phone:** (856)881-4327. **Business Addr:** President, Chief Executive Officer, At Home Health Inc, 461 N 3rd St 5th Fl, Philadelphia, PA 19123, **Business Phone:** (215)940-2980.

### DURHAM, REV. EDDIE L., SR.

Government official, clergy. **Personal:** Born Mar 17, 1946, Newellton, LA; son of Rev Albert E and Annie B Emerson; married Fannie Henderson; children: Eddie Jr & Robert; married Sarah. **Educ:** Harvard Univ, Cambridge, MA, attended 1967; Southern Univ, Baton Rouge, La, BA, eng, 1968; Univ Utah, Salt Lake City, Utah, MS, admin, 1974. **Career:** Shell Chem Co, technician & trainer; Burlington County Community Col, adj prof; Stauffer Chem Co, Dayton, NJ, mgt trainee, 1969-70; Agway Chem Co, Yardville, NJ, asst plant mgr, 1970-71; NJ Dept Labor, Trenton, NJ, claims reviewer, 1971-72, personnel asst, 1972-74, chief admin, 1974-76, admin dir, 1976-; Red Hot Publ Co, pres, 1989-; Home Income Reporter, newsletter, ed & publ, 1990-; Success Inc, pres, 1992; Saints Memorial Community Church, pastor, currently. **Orgs:** Polit Action Comn Willingboro, 1975-82; pres, Am Soc Pub Admin, NJ, 1976-77; dir, First Peoples Bank NJ, 1977-82; Willingboro Twp Coun, 1977-82; dir, Saints' Memorial Community Church, 1979-; Blacks Govt, 1984-; Forum Black Pub Admin, 1986-; dir, Better Day Care Ctr, 1986-. **Honors/Awds:** Service Award, Saints' Memorial Community Church, 1983 & 1984; Service Award, Cathedral Love, 1989. **Special Achievements:** Editor/publisher, Home Income Reporter Newsletter, 1990-. **Home Addr:** 15 Brunswick Lane, Willingboro, NJ 08046, **Home Phone:** (609)871-1006. **Business Addr:** Pastor, Saints Memorial Community Church, 11 S John F Kennedy Way, Willingboro, NJ 08046, **Business Phone:** (609)871-4779.

### DURHAM, DR. JOSEPH THOMAS

Educator, college teacher. **Personal:** Born Nov 26, 1923, Raleigh, NC; son of Watt Sr and Serena Hooker; married Alice Spruill; children: LaDonna D Stamper & LaVerne. **Educ:** Morgan State Col, AB, 1948; Temple Univ, EdM, 1949; Columbia Univ, EdD, 1963. **Career:** New Lincoln Sch, teacher, 1956-58; Southern Univ, prof, 1958-60; Coppin State Col, chmn educ, 1960-63, dean col, 1965-68, dean educ, 1975-76, lectr, adj prof; Albany State Col, dean & prof, 1963-65; Univ NH, vis prof, 1966; Ill State Univ, assoc dean educ, 1968-72; Howard Univ, dean sch educ, 1972-75; Md State Bd Higher Educ, dir inst approval; Community Col Baltimore, interim pres, pres, 1985-90, pres emer; Morgan State Univ, prof educ; United Holy Church Am Inc, Holiness Union, ed, 1980-2000; Montgomery County Human Rels, comnr, 1983-86. **Orgs:** Phi Delta Kappa; Alpha Phi Alpha. **Honors/Awds:** Fel Gen Educ Bd, 1953-54; Fel Dan forth Found, 1975; Presidential Leadership Medallion, Univ Tex, 1989; Policy Owner Good Citizenship Award, Mutual Trust Co, 1974. **Special Achievements:** The Story of Civil Rights as Seen by the Black Church, DC Cook Publishing Co, 1971. **Home Addr:** 13102 Morningside Lane, Silver Spring, MD 20904-3158, **Home Phone:** (301)989-9093.

### DURHAM, LEON

Baseball player, baseball manager. **Personal:** Born Jul 31, 1957, Cincinnati, OH; married Angela; children: Ashley Loren, Ian & Lance. **Career:** Baseball player (retired), baseball coach, actor; St Louis Cardinals, outfielder & infielder, 1976, 1980, 1989; Chicago Cubs, outfielder & infielder, 1981-88; Cincinnati Reds, infielder, 1988; St Louis Cardinals, infielder, 1989; Lake Elsinore Storm, Calif League, coach, 1996; Vancouver Canadians, Pac Coast League, coach; Edmonton Trappers, coach; Anaheim Angels, coach; Detroit Tigers, Toledo Mud Hens, hitting coach, 2001-. TV Series: "MLB All-Star Game", 1983; "National League Championship Series", 1984; "Little Big League", 1994. **Orgs:** Chicago Pub High Sch Athletic Prog. **Home Addr:** 3932 Dickson Ave, Cincinnati, OH 45229. **Business Addr:** Hitting Coach, Toledo Mud Hens Baseball Club Inc, 406 Wash St, Toledo, OH 43604, **Business Phone:** (419)725-4367.

### DURHAM, RAY

Baseball player. **Personal:** Born Nov 30, 1971, Charlotte, NC; married Crystal Hedgecoe; children: Kendra Amber & Trent Austin; married Regina; children: 4. **Career:** Baseball player (retired); Chicago White Sox, infielder, 1995-2002; Oakland Athletics, 2002; San Francisco Giants, infielder, 2003-08; Milwaukee Brewers, 2008; free agt, currently.

### DURR, DR. MARLESE

Educator, sociologist. **Personal:** Born Albany, NY; daughter of Moses and Mary. **Educ:** State Univ NY, Albany, NY, BA, 1978, MA, African & Afro-Am studies, 1979, MA, sociol, 1985, PhD, sociol, 1993. **Career:** Wright State Univ, asst prof sociol, 1994-2000, assoc prof sociol, 2000, Womens Studies Prog, dir, 2001-04, Dept Sociol & Anthrop, prof, currently. **Orgs:** Nat Asn Black Bus & Prof Women, Orgn, Occup & Work Sect Grad Comn; Eastern Sociol Soc; Asn Black Sociologists, 1998-2001; Sociologist Women Soc, 1998-2002; chair, Am Sociol Asn, 1999-2000; Am Sociol Soc; 2004-07; adv bd, Jour Southern Sociol Soc, 2004-07; Soc Study Social Probs, 2006-09; co-chair, Sister Sister. **Special Achievements:** Has published articles on topics such as Racial Submarkets for Employment, Social Cost and Entrepreneurship, Politics of Race, and Needs of Urban Entrepreneurs; Published Race, Work, and Family in the Lives of African American Men and Women; Textbook/Reader, edited by Marlese Durr and Shirley A. Hill. New York: Rowman & Littlefield; and The New Politics of Race: From Du Bois to The 21st Century; edited by Marlese Durr; West Port, Connecticut: Praeger Press; "The New Politics of Race: Du Bois to the 21st Century and Race, Work; "African American Women: Gender Relations, Work, and The Political Economy in The Twenty-First Century." Gender & Society, Vol. 16. No. 4. with Shirley A. Hill; Family-Work Interface.? in Race, Work, and Family in the Lives of African American Men and Women with Shirley A. Hill; "Social Networks and Occupational Mobility? Pp. 55-71 in The New Politics of Race: From Du Bois to the 21st Century. edited by Marlese Durr. West Port, Connecticut: Praeger Press; "Sex, Drugs, and HIV: Sisters of the Laundromat?; Gender & Society, Vol. 19. No. 6; "Identifying the Unique Needs of the Urban Entrepreneurs: African American Skill Set Development." Race & Society, Vol. 2, No. 2, with Thomas S. Lyons and Gregg A. Lichtenstein; "Does Race Matter?: The Determinants and Consequences"; Race & Society, Vol. 1, No, 2 With Cedric Herring, Hayward D. Horton, and Melvin E. Thomas.; "Social Costs and Inner-city Entrepreneurship". National Journal of Sociology Vol. No. with Thomas S. Lyons and Katharine Cornwell; "Racial Submarkets in Government Employment: African American Professionals in New York State.? Sociological Forum Vol. 12, No. 3, with John R. Logan. **Business Addr:** Professor, Wright State University, Millett Hall 255, Dayton, OH 45435-0001, **Business Phone:** (937)775-2275.

### DUSTER, BENJAMIN C., IV

Executive. **Personal:** Born Chicago, IL. **Educ:** Yale Univ, BA, Econs Maj & Appl Math Minor, 1981; Harvard Univ, JD & MBA, 1985. **Career:** M&A group, Wachovia Securities, managing dir, Salomon Bros Inc, vpres, 1981-97; Masson & Co LLC, partner, 1997-2001; River Cities Capital Funds, Mem Adv Bd, 1998-2004; Watermark Advisors LLC, owner, sr advisor, 2001-05, exec managing dir, currently; B Duster & Co LLC, owner. **Orgs:** Adv bd mem, Neenah Foundry Co, 1997-2001, 2003-06; Ill Bar Asn; chmn bd, Algoma Steel Inc, 2002-07; bd mem, Accuride Corp; dir, Jazz Air Holding GP Inc, 2010-11; dir, Catalyst Paper Corp, 2007-12; dir, RCN Corp, dir, Ormet Corp, dir, Accuride Corp, 2011-13; bd mem, dir, Chorus Aviation Inc, 2010-14; MFLEX, 2012-15. **Business Addr:** Owner, Watermark Advisors LLC, 330 E Coffee St, Greenville, SC 29601, **Business Phone:** (864)527-5960.

### DUSTER, TROY S.

Educator, association executive, administrator. **Personal:** Born Jul 11, 1936, Chicago, IL; son of Benjamin Cecil (deceased) and Alfreda M Barnett; married Ellen Marie Johansson. **Educ:** Northwestern Univ, BS, jour, 1957, PhD, sociol, 1962; Univ Calif, MA, sociol, 1959. **Career:** Northwestern Univ, lectr, 1962; Univ Calif, Riverside, asst prof, 1963-65; Stockholm Univ, res sociologist, 1966-67, Berkeley, CA, asst res sociol, 1967-70, asst prof, 1970-78, prof, 1979-99, dir Inst Study Social Chg, 1979-97, chmn, Dept Sociol, 1985-88, Pres's Task Force Black Stud Eligibility, chair, 1986-90; Am Sociol Asn, asn ed, 1968-70, 1974; Univ BC, vis assoc prof, 1969; London Sch Econs, Guggenheim Fel, 1971-72; Comtemporary Sociol asn ed, 1974-76; Ford Found, sr res fel, 1980; Kaiser Found Res Inst, dir, 1985-88; NY Univ, Dept Sociol, prof, 1999-; Inst Hist Prod Knowledge, dir, currently. **Orgs:** Dir, Nat Inst Ment Health Training Grant, 1971; Assembly Behav & Social Sci Nat Rsch Coun Wash, 1973, Community Clin Eval Narcotic Antagonists, Nat Acad Sci, 1973; Comt Probs Drug Dependence, 1978-82; S African Career Develop & Outreach Prog Comt, 1987-92; bd dir, Prev Inst, 1988-91; Am Sociol Asn, 1988-91, pres, 2005; bd dir, Stiles Hall, 1992-96; Sci Adv Panel, 1993; Health & Environ Res Adv Comt, 1994; Nat Adv Coun, 1995-; bd dir, Asn Am Cols & Univs, 1997-; Nat Adv Comt, 1998-; Am Asn Advan Sci Comt Germ-Line Intervention, 1998-2001; Nat Adv Comm, 2000-01; bd gov, Univ Calif, 2002-; pres, Am Sociol Asn, 2005, AAAS Am Asn Advan Sci Ethical Soc Issues Panel Genetic Ther Germline Intervention. **Honors/Awds:** DHL, Williams Col, 1991; Chancellor's Professor Award, Univ California, Berkeley, 1998; DuBois-Johnson-Frazier Award, Am Sociol Asn, 2001; Hatfield Scholars Award, 2002; Benjamin Hooks Award, 2003; C. Wright Mills Award, 2004; DSc, Northwestern Univ, 2005. **Special Achievements:** Author: "The Legislation of Morality", 1972; Co-author: "Cultural Perspectives on Biological Knowledge", 1984; "Backdoor to Eugenics", 2003; "Whitewashing Race: The Myth of a Color-Blind Society", 2005. **Home Addr:** 29 Wash Sq W Apt 4CN, New York, NY 94705, **Home Phone:** (212)505-5938. **Business Addr:** Professor, New York University, Rm 4143 295 Lafayette St, New York, NY 10003, **Business Phone:** (212)998-7400.

### DUTTON, CHARLES STANLEY
Movie director, actor. **Personal:** Born Jan 30, 1951, Baltimore, MD; married Debbi Morgan. **Educ:** Towson State Univ, BA, theatre drama, 1978; Yale Univ Sch Drama, MA, drama, 1983. **Career:** Plays: "Ma Rainey's Black Bottom", 1984; "Pantomime", 1986; "Fried Chicken Invisibility", 1987; "Joe Turner's Come & Gone", 1987; "Splendid Mummer", 1988; "The Piano Lesson", 1990; "Ma Rainey's Black Bottom", 2003. TV series: "Equal Justice; The Trial of Mary Phagan", 1987; "Roc", 1991-95; "Laurel Avenue", exec producer, 1993; "True Women", 1997; "First-Time Felon", dir, 1997; "Aftershock: Earthquake in New York", 1999; "For Love or Country: The Arturo Sandoval Story", 2000; "10, 000 Black Men Named George", 2002; "Conviction", 2002; "DC Sniper: 23 Days of Fear", 2003; "Something the Lord Made", 2004; "Land Ahoy", 2005; "The Fly Guys", singing group mgr; "Threshold", 2006-06; "Sleeper Cell", 2006; "House M.D.", 2006-07; "My Name Is Earl", 2007; "Under", dir, 2008; "Racing for Time", actor & dir, 2008; "CSI: NY", 2009; "Law & Order: LA", 2011; "Criminal Minds", 2011; "American Horror Story", 2011; "40 Minutes of Hell", 2012; "Longmire", 2012-14; "The Good Wife", 2012; "Zero Hour", 2013; "LA Live the Show", 2014; "The Following", 2014. Films: Crocodile Dundee II, actor, 1988; Q&A; Mississippi Masala, actor, 1991; Alien 3, actor, 1992; Distinguished Gentlemen, actor, 1992; A Low Down Dirty Shame, actor, 1995; Time to Kill, actor, 1996; Mimic, actor, 1997; Blind Faith, actor, 1998; Black Dog, actor, 1998; Cookie's Fortune, actor, 1999; Random Hearts, actor, 1999; D-Tox, actor, 2002; Ma Rainey's Black Bottom, actor, 2003; Gothika, actor, 2003; Against the Ropes, actor & dir, 2004; Secret Window, actor, 2004; The L.A. Riot Spectacular, actor, 2005; Suspect, 2007; The Third Nail, actor, 2008; The Express, actor, 2009; Legion, actor, 2009; Bad Ass, 2011; Powers, 2011; Least Among Saints, 2012; The Obama Effect, dir & writer, 2012; Learning Uncle Vincent, 2013; The Monkey's Paw, 2013; A Very Larry Christmas, 2013; Peeples, exec producer, 2013; Android Cop, 2014; Comeback Dad, 2014. **Honors/Awds:** Yale School of Drama, class marshal, 1983; Outer Critics' Circle nomination, 1985; Drama Desk Award, 1985; Theatre World Award, 1985; Tony nomination, Ma Rainey's Black Bottom; Tony nomination, The Piano Lesson, 1990; Image Award, Nat Asn Advan Colored People, 1994, 2003 & 2004; Grand Jury Award, 1999; Primetime Emmy Award, 2000, 2002-03; Black Reel Award, 2001, 2003. **Business Addr:** Actor, Twentieth Century-Fox Television, 5746 Sunset Blvd, Los Angeles, CA 90028, **Business Phone:** (310)859-4000.

### DUVALL, HENRY F.
Public relations executive. **Personal:** Born Jan 3, 1949, Washington, DC; son of Henry F Sr and Ruth C; married Deborah Hawkins; children: Cherie. **Educ:** Univ Md Col Jour, BS, 1975. **Career:** Albuquerque Jour, copy ed, 1975-76; Univ Md, staff writer, 1976-77; Potomac Elec Power Co, writer, 1978; Howard Univ, ed, 1978-81, media coordr, 1981-89, info officer, 1989-91; Am Red Cross, media rels assoc, 1991-92; coord press rels & pub info, Coun Great City Schs, dir commun, 1992-. **Orgs:** Nat Press Club; Nat Asn Black Journalists; Educ Writers Asn; Nat Sch Pub Rels Asn. **Honors/Awds:** Scholarship, Am Newspaper Publ Asn, 1974; Urban Educator Award; Multiple awards for Council Great City Schools; 7 Telly Awards. **Special Achievements:** Established Communications Department, Council of the Great City Schools, 1992, launched a national news service, Howard University, 1981. **Home Addr:** 8 Whitehall Ct, Silver Spring, MD 20901, **Home Phone:** (301)681-3858. **Business Addr:** Director of Communications, Council of the Great City Schools, 1331 Pa Ave NW Suite 1100N, Washington, DC 20004, **Business Phone:** (202)393-2427.

### DUVERNAY, AVA
Movie director, founder (originator), publicist. **Personal:** Born Aug 24, 1972, Long Beach, CA. **Educ:** University of California, Los Angeles, Bachelor's. **Career:** DVA Media + Marketing (formerly The DuVernay Agency), Founder and CEO, 1999-; Documentary "This is the Life," Director, 2008; BET Networks Music Documentary "My Mic Sounds Nice," Director, 2010; Essence Music Festival, Director, 2010; Feature film drama "I Will Follow," Director, 2011; ESPN documentary "Nine for IX," Producer and Director, 2013; Short films "The Door" and "Say Yes," Director, 2013. **Orgs:** African-American Film Festival Releasing Movement (AFFRM), Founder; Academy of Motion Picture Arts and Sciences, Member; Academy of Television Arts & Sciences, Member; Film Independent, Board Member; Sundance Institute, Board Member. **Honors/Awds:** "The Root" Magazine, The Root 100 Honorees, 2013; Independent Spirit John Cassavetes Award, 2013; theGrio's 100, 2013.

### DYAS, PATRICIA ANN
Firefighter, government official. **Personal:** Born Dec 6, 1952, Shreveport, LA; daughter of Henry and Martile; children: Patrick, Matthew, Elizabeth & William. **Educ:** Southern Univ, Shreveport, BS, 1976; Va Hosp Tuskegee, AL, clin training, grad, 1976. **Career:** Shreveport Fire Dept, Shreveport, La, firefighter, emergency med technician & fire inspector, 1981-, asst dir, fire prev, 1999-, chief; lic realtor. **Orgs:** Red Cross Safety Bd; bd mem, YWCA; Greater Shreveport Optimists Club; Shreveport Black Chamber Com. **Honors/Awds:** Outstanding Young Firefighter, Shreveport, 1987; Outstanding community service award, 1987-88; Outstanding Woman of the Year, Zeta Phi Beta, 1987; Distinguished Black Female award, Traveleers Coalition, 1988; St Abraham Baptist Church Outstanding young Christian woman, 1988. **Special Achievements:** First female to be promoted to the rank of captain and assistant fire chief in Shreveport. **Home Addr:** 2526 E Galloway Blvd C, Shreveport, LA 71104-2732, **Home Phone:** (318)424-4335. **Business Addr:** Chief, Bureau of Fire Prevention, 505 Travis St Suite 510, Shreveport, LA 71101, **Business Phone:** (318)673-6740.

### DYE, DR. CLINTON ELWORTH, JR.
Executive director, chief executive officer, association executive. **Personal:** Born Apr 9, 1942, Atlanta, GA; son of Clinton E Sr and Charlotte; married Myrtice Willis; children: Clinton E III & Trevin Gerard. **Educ:** Morehouse Col, AB, 1965; Atlanta Univ Sch Soc Work, MSW, 1969, PhD, MBA, 1983. **Career:** Lockheed Corp; Econ Oppor Atlanta, dir drug recov prog, 1971-73; Atlanta Regional Comn, coord drug & alcohol planning, 1973-76; Atlanta Urban League Inc, dir comn srv, 1976-79, dep exec dir, 1979-, vpres, 1979-90, pres & chief exec officer, 2001-08; Ga Dept Human Resources, sr mgt, 1990. **Orgs:** Gov's Adv Coun Ment Health, 1975-76; bd visitors, Grady Memorial Hosp, 1983-; Leadership Atlanta, 1971-; vchmn bd, Metro Atlanta Pvt Indust Owner, 1983-; bd mem, N Cent GA Health Syst Agency, 1981-84; Regional Devel Coun, 1979-83; Regional Educ Policy Comt; US Comn Civil Rights, Ga Adv Comt; Ga State Univ Dept Social Work Community Adv Bd. **Home Addr:** 405 Ivy Glen Ct SW, Atlanta, GA 30331, **Home Phone:** (404)349-3507. **Business Addr:** President, Chief Executive Officer, Atlanta Urban League Inc, 100 Edgewood Ave NE Suite 600, Atlanta, GA 30303, **Business Phone:** (404)659-1150.

### DYE, ERNEST THADDEUS
Football player. **Personal:** Born Jul 15, 1971, Greenwood, SC; married Rhonda F; children: Ariel. **Educ:** Univ Southern Calif. **Career:** Football player (retired); Phoenix Cardinals, tackle, 1993; Ariz Cardinals, tackle & left tackle & left guard, 1994-96, 1998; St Louis Rams, 1997. **Home Addr:** 600 Stirling Glen Ct, Alpharetta, GA 30004-8840, **Home Phone:** (678)566-3430.

### DYE, JERMAINE TERRELL
Baseball player. **Personal:** Born Jan 28, 1974, Vacaville, CA; married Tricia; children: Devin, Jalen & Tiara. **Educ:** Cosumnes River Col. **Career:** Baseball player (retired); Atlanta Braves, outfielder, 1996; Kans City Royals, 1997-2001; Oakland Athletics, 2001-04; Chicago White Sox, outfielder, 2005-09. **Business Addr:** Professional Baseball Player, Chicago White Sox, US Cellular Field, Chicago, IL 60616, **Business Phone:** (312)674-1000.

### DYE, HON. LUTHER V.
Judge. **Personal:** Born Sep 26, 1933, Winston-Salem, NC; son of Luther William and Mattie Harpe; married Doris Lee Hairston; children: Barry, Bryan, Lisa & Blake. **Educ:** State Univ, BS, NC A&T, 1955; Brooklyn Law Sch, LLB, 1960. **Career:** Chicago Title Ins Co, title officer, 1958-69; Demov Morris Levin & Shein, assoc atty, 1969-73; NY Life Ins Co, assoc coun off gen coun, 1974-86; pvt law pract, 1986-88; Civil Ct City New York, judge, 1988-94; New York Supreme Ct, prin law clerk, 1994-95; Supreme Ct, justice, 2003. **Orgs:** Macon B Allen Black Bar Asn; NY State Bar Asn; exec mem, Real Property Law Sect; Queens Co Bar Asn; Real Property Com Civil Rights Com & Admis Comn; Grievance Comn; Local Draft Bd Selective Serv Syst; Brooklyn Law Sch Alumni Asn; trustee, Housing Develop Corp Coun Churches. **Home Addr:** 19614 McLaughlin Ave, Holliswood, NY 11483, **Home Phone:** (718)464-3580.

### DYER, BERNARD JOEL
Publisher. **Personal:** Born Mar 23, 1933, Bronx, NY; son of Joel and Miariam Samuels; children: Ethelda, Bertha, Minia & Joel. **Educ:** NY Community Col, technol, 1957. **Career:** CDM Neighborhood Develop Inst, exec dir; Miami Weekly, Journey Mag, publ; Third World Media Corp, pres & chief exec officer. **Orgs:** Phi Tau, vpres, 1955-57. **Honors/Awds:** Dade Co Award, 1969; Nat Coun Churches, Nations Best Community Org, 1967; Hon Dr, Community Org; leadership fel, Ford Found, 1979. **Home Addr:** PO Box 470007, Miami, FL 33147, **Home Phone:** (305)571-1521.

### DYER, DR. CHARLES AUSTEN
Executive. **Personal:** Born Jul 24, 1936, St. Ann; son of Jacob Alexander and Marjorie Emma Lewis; married Edwina Weston; children: M Hakim & Adam L. **Educ:** Pratt Inst, Bachelor Indust Design, 1957; Yeshiva Univ, MS, 1962; City Univ NY, PhD, 1980. **Career:** Digital Equip Corp, comput educ, artificial intelligence; Charles A Dyer Assocs, owner, currently. **Special Achievements:** Author of Preparing for Computer Assisted Instruction 1972; Teaching Aid patented 1973; Articles & papers on artificial intelligence & computer-assisted instruction 1980-. **Home Addr:** 9895 Palace Hall Dr Apt 313, Laurel, MD 20723, **Home Phone:** (301)604-4750. **Business Addr:** .

### DYER-GOODE, DR. PAMELA THERESA
Physician, gynecologist. **Personal:** Born Oct 7, 1950, Philadelphia, PA; daughter of Kirby and Mabel Clyatt; children: Lisa, Shonn, Erica & Brian. **Educ:** Cheyney State Col, BS, biol & chem, 1971; Temple Univ Med Sch, MD, 1977; Temple Univ, attended 1985; Cert, Anti-Aging & Regenerative Med. **Career:** Planned Parenthood, physician & ambulatory, 1978-80; Gruiffree Med Ctr, physician & ambulatory care, 1980-82; Hahnemann Univ Hosp, resident; Med Col Pa & Hosp, chief med resident gynec; Broad St Hosp, ambulatory care physician, 1982-84; Southeastern Pa Transp Authority, indust med & claims specialist, 1986; pvt family pract, 1986-; Renew Medspa, founder & med dir, currently. **Orgs:** NOW; Coalition 100 Black Women; Pa Med Soc; AMA; Nat Med Asn; Friends Pa Ballet Co; Am Acad Anti-Aging Med; Am Acad Cosmetic Gynecologists; Am Acad Cosmetic Physicians; fel Anti-Aging & Regenerative Med. **Honors/Awds:** Distinguished Alumna Award, Cheyney State Col, 1986; Outstanding Alumna, St Maria Goretti High Sch, 1986; Philadelphia New Observer Women on the Move, ed presentation; Top Obstetricians and Gynecologists Award, Consumers Res Coun Am, 2008, 2009, 2010, 2011. **Home Addr:** 305 Penbree Cir, Bala Cynwyd, PA 19004, **Home Phone:** (610)664-9905. **Business Addr:** Founder, Medical Director, Renew Medspa, 241 S 6th St Suite 120, Philadelphia, PA 19106, **Business Phone:** (215)792-6377.

### DYKES, DEWITT S., JR.
Educator. **Personal:** Born Jan 2, 1938, Chattanooga, TN; son of DeWitt S Sr and Violet T Anderson; married Marie Draper; children: Laura Marie Christine. **Educ:** Fisk Univ, BA, 1960; Univ Mich, MA, 1961, PhD, 1965. **Career:** Mich St Univ, instr, Am Thought & Lang, 1965-69; Oakland Univ, asst prof hist, 1969-73, assoc prof hist, 1973-, dean's asst affirmative action, 1975-78, coordr Afro-Amer studies 1975-83; Univ SC Sch Pub Health, consult, 1977. **Orgs:** African Heritage Studies Asn, 1970; Asn Study Afro-Am Life & Hist; charter mem, 1978, bk rev ed, 1981-85, Afro-Am Hist & Geneal Soc, 1978; Alpha Phi Alpha Fraternity; bd ed, Detroit Perspective, A Jour Regional Hist, 1978-84; vice chmn, 1980-82, chmn, 1982-84, Hist Designation Adv Bd City; pres, Fred Hart Williams Geneal Soc, 1980-86; bd trustee, Hist Soc Mich, 1983-89; Nat Endowment Humanities, 1985; pres, Mich Black Hist Network, 1986-88. **Home Addr:** 19419 Bretton Dr, Detroit, MI 48223. **Business Addr:** Associate Professor, Oakland University, 416 Varner Hall, Rochester, MI 48309-4401, **Business Phone:** (248)370-2100.

### DYMALLY, LYNN V.
Government official, educator. **Personal:** Born Sep 8, 1958, Los Angeles, CA. **Educ:** Univ Calif, San Diego, BA, commun & sociol, 1979; Univ Redlands, MA, bus mgt, 1987; Whittier Col Sch Law, JD, law, 1988. **Career:** Network Data Processing, vpres, 1979-80; Drew Postgrad Med Sch, Prog Int Health & Develop, admin analyst, 1980-81; KBRT Radio, bus mgr, 1981-85; Grace Home Foster Care C, legal adminr, 1993-95; GB Data Systs Inc, legal coordr, 1995-97; Polit Strategies, polit consult, 1995-; Calif State Univ Fullerton, lectr, 1998; Compton Unified Sch Dist, bd trustee; Calif State Univ, Long Beach, Calif, adj assoc prof legal studies bus, 1997-2013, adj lectr, 1998-99, Polit Sci Dept, judicial internship advisor, 1999, lectr, 2000, Assoc Students, ASI Elections Bd Gov, fac rep, 2005-12, Black Bus Stud Asn, fac advisor, 2005-12; Fashion Inst Design & Merchandising, asst trainer, 1997-2001; Long Beach Community Col Sch Bus Admin, instr, 1998-2002; New Age Charter Sch, consult, 2005-; Calif State Univ, Dominguez Hills, Calif African Am Polit & Econ Inst, prog coordr, 2006-; Lynn Dymally Group/Dennis Wayne Grou, real estate broker, 2007-; Calif Inst Health & Social Serv Inc, consult, 2007-; Water Replenishment Dist, Div 3, bd dir, 2013-14; Mervyn M Dymally Legacy Inst Inc, pres. **Orgs:** Spec asst, Calif State Mus Sci, Summer Break & Ind, 1973-78; analyst, consult, Aid to Needy C Mother's Anonymous Inc, Calif State Social Serv Prog, 1979-; Calif League Women Voter, 1983-; staff, Youth Christ, 1983-; statewide co-chmn, Calif Rainbow Youth Coalition Jackson Pres, 1984; consult, Legis Black Caucus Found, 2002-; Calif State Univ, Long Beach, fac fel Ctr Community Engagement, comnr, Comn Status Women; Long Beach Bar Asn Found; bd gov, Long Beach Bar Asn, 2009. **Honors/Awds:** Co-instr, The Presidential Classroom, 1985. **Home Addr:** 223 S Acacia Ave Suite 206, Compton, CA 90220. **Business Addr:** President, The Mervyn M Dymally Legacy Institute Inc, 2337 E Poppy St, Long Beach, CA 90805.

### DYSON, REV. DR. MICHAEL ERIC
Educator, baptist clergy. **Personal:** Born Oct 23, 1958, Detroit, MI; son of Everett and Addie Mae; married Marcia Louise; children: Michael II & Maisha; married Brenda Joyce. **Educ:** Knoxville Col; Carson-Newman Col, BA, 1982; Princeton Univ, MA, relig, 1991, PhD, relig, 1993. **Career:** Princeton Univ, Mathy Col, asst master; Hartford Sem, fac mem, 1988; Chicago Theol Sem, instr, asst prof, 1989; Brown Univ, asst prof, 1993; Univ NC, Prof Comm; Columbia Univ, vis prof African Am studies, 1997-99; DePaul Univ, Ida B Wells-Barnett prof relig studies, 1999-2002; Univ Pa, Avalon Found prof humanities, 2002;ordained Baptist minister; Nat Pub Radio, commentator; CNN, commentator; Real Time with Bill Maher, commentator; Radio One, host, 2006-07; Georgetown Univ, univ prof, currently; Common Ground Found, bd dir; MSNBC, polit analyst, 2011; auth, currently; radio host, currently.Tv Series: "Tupac Shakur: Before I Wake...", 2001; "When the Levees Broke: A Requiem in Four Acts", 2006; "America: Imagine the World Without Her", 2014; "The Leftovers", 2014. Tv Movie: "Tupac: The Hip Hop Genius", 2004. **Orgs:** Democratic Socialist Am. **Home Addr:** 5313 S Drexel Ave, Chicago, IL 60615-4907. **Business Addr:** University Professor, Georgetown University, 37th & O St NW, Washington, DC 20057, **Business Phone:** (202)687-0100.

### DYSON, WILLIAM RILEY
State government official, educator, association executive. **Personal:** Born Jul 12, 1940, Waycross, GA; son of Edward James and Lula Lorene Williams; children: Sonia, Wilfred, Erick & Michael. **Educ:** Morris Col, BA, soc studies, 1962; Southern Conn State Univ, MS, urban studies, 1975, Sixth-Yr Degree, admin & supv, 1982. **Career:** Veteran s Wine & Liquor, clerk, 1962-67; Coffee County Bd Educ, teacher, 1968-69; New Haven Pub Schs Syst, Conn, teacher, adminr, 1970-2006; Douglas GA, Blackshear GA, teacher; State Conn, 94th Assembly Dist, House Representatives, state rep, 1976-2008; Chaudhary Charan Singh Univ, polit sci dept, fac. **Orgs:** Hillary's Conn Steering Comt; chmn, powerful Appropriations Comt; chair, Conn Comn Nat & Community; chair, Legis Mgt's Day Care; Capitol Child Develop Ctr; bd dir, Drugs Dont Work. chair, Black & Puerto Rican Caucus; vice chair, Int Affairs Comt. **Home Addr:** PO Box 2064, New Haven, CT 06521, **Home Phone:** (203)777-3460. **Business Addr:** State Representative, State of Connecticut, Rm 4032 Legis Off Bldg, Hartford, CT 06106-1591, **Business Phone:** (860)240-8585.

### DZIKO, TRISH MILLINES
Manager, association executive, executive. **Personal:** Born Jan 1, 1957, NJ; daughter of Patricia Millines; children: 4. **Educ:** Monmouth Col, BS, comput sci, 1979. **Career:** Comput Sci Corp, programmer; Microsoft Corp, software tester & developer, mgr, consult, database designer & prog mgr, 1990-95, sr diversity adminr, 1995-96; Technol Access Found, co-founder & exec dir, 1996-. **Orgs:** trustee, Monmouth col; treas, Greater Seattle Chap Links Inc, 2008; Wash State Charter Schs Comn, 2012; bd mem, Wash Technol Indust Asn, 2015. **Honors/Awds:** Arthur Ashe Award for community service, 1998; Honorary Doctorate in Humane Letters, Seattle Univ, 2001; NCAA Silver Anniversary Award, 2004. **Business Addr:** Co-Founder, Executive Director, Technology Access Foundation, 605 SW 108th St, Seattle, WA 98146, **Business Phone:** (206)725-9095.

# E

### E-40, E. (EARL STEVENS)
Rap musician. **Personal:** Born Nov 15, 1967, Vallejo, CA. **Career:** Albums: Federal, 1994; The Mail Man, 1994; In a Major Way, 1995; The Hall of Game, 1996; The Element of Surprise, 1998; Charlie Hustle, 1999; Loyalty & Betrayal, 2000; Grit & Grind, 2002; Break in News, 2003; That Fire, 2004; The Best of E-40: Yesterday, Today & Tomorrow, 2004; The Bay Bridges Compilation, 2005; My Ghetto Report Card, 2006; The Ball Street Journal, 2008; Revenue Retrievin': Day Shift, 2010; Revenue Retrievin': Night Shift, 2010; Revenue Retrievin': Overtime Shift, 2011; Revenue Retrievin': Graveyard Shift, 2011; The Block Brochure: Welcome to the Soil 1, Soil2, Soil 3, 2012; The Block Brochure: Welcome to the Soil 4, Soil 5, Soil 6, 2013; Sharp On All 4 Corners: Corner 1, Corner 2, 2014; Sharp On All 4 Corners: Corner 3, Corner 4, 2015. Films: The Breaks, 1999; Charlie Hustle, 1999; Obstacles, 2000; three Strikes, 2000; Malibooty, voice, 2003; Survival of the Illest, 2004; Hair Show, 2004, Lil Jon Makes a Video: Snap Yo Fingers, 2006; Dead Heist, 2007. TV: Soul Train, 1995; Blowin Up, 2006; 106 & Park, 2006; Punk'd, 2006; Wild 'n Out, 2006; Yo Momma, 2006; Def Jam: Icon, 2007; BET Hip Hop Awards, 2007; Def Jam: Icon, 2007; The Chain Epidemic, 2008; From G's to Gents (Season 2), 2009; Played by Fame (Season 1), 2009; Play Your Position, 2009; The Model Boss, 2009; One World Hip Hop Championship, 2009; Played by Fame, 2009; Sick Wid It Recs, co-founder; Cloud 9, owner; Microsoft, investor. **Orgs:** Founding mem, Click; founder, Sick Wid It Records. **Business Addr:** Recording Artist, Jive Recs, 137-137 W 25th St Fl 11, New York, NY 10001, **Business Phone:** (212)727-0016.

### EADDY, JOKATA
Activist. **Educ:** University of South Carolina-Columbia, Bachelor's, 2001. **Career:** National Coalition to Abolish the Death Penalty, Domestic Program Director, 2002-06; USAction, Field Manager; National Association for the Advancement of Colored People (NAACP), Senior Advisor to the President and Senior Director of Voting Rights. **Honors/Awds:** Center for Effective Government, Outstanding Public Interest Rising Star, 2008; "The Root" Magazine, The Root 100 Honorees, 2013. **Special Achievements:** In 2004, she led the campaign against the U.S. juvenile death penalty, which played a role in the landmark U.S. Supreme Court decision that abolished it; in NAACP position, is a strong advocate for voting rights.

### EADY, CORNELIUS
Poet, educator, writer. **Personal:** Born Jan 1, 1954, Rochester, NY; married Sarah Micklem. **Educ:** Monroe Community Col; Empire St Col; Warren Wilson Col, MFA, 1986. **Career:** St Univ NY, Stony Brook, assoc prof eng, dir, Poetry Ctr; Sarah Lawrence Col; NY Univ; City Col NY; Col William & Mary; Sweet Briar Col, Univ Notre Dame, assoc prof eng, 2005-10, Creative Writing Prog, dir, currently, Univ Mo, prof eng, 2010-; Poems: Kartunes, 1980; Victims of the Latest Dance Craze, 1986; BOOM BOOM BOOM, 1988; The Gathering of My Name, 1991; You Don't Miss Your Water, 1995; autobiography of a jukebox, 1997; Blackbird; Brutal Imagination, Putnam, 2001; Hardheaded Weather, 2008; John Simon Guggenheim Memorial Found, fel; Nat Endowment Arts, fel. **Orgs:** Co-founder, Cave Canem, vpres, 1996-2013. **Honors/Awds:** George Oppenheimer Award, Newsday, 2002; Pulitzer Prize nominee; Lamont Poetry Selection, Acad Am Poets Victims Latest Dance Craze; Strousse Award, Prairie Schooner; fel, from the Guggenheim Found; fel, Nat Endowment Arts; fel, Rockefeller Found; fel, Lila Wallace-Reader Digest Found; Nat Book Award, 2001. **Home Addr:** , Columbia, MO. **Business Addr:** Professor of English, University of Missouri, 1100 Carrie Francke Dr, Columbia, MO 65211, **Business Phone:** (573)882-2121.

### EADY, KERMIT
President (organization), chief executive officer, entrepreneur. **Educ:** Morgan State Univ, BA, sociol/econs; NY Univ, MSW. **Career:** Human Resources Admin, New York mgr/caseworker, 1965-68; Medger Evers Col, adj asst prof, 1968-75; Norfolk State Univ, Grad Sch Social Work, dir admis & recruitment, 1976-78; Black United Fund NY, founder, 1979-2003, pres & chief exec officer; Eady Assocs, pres & founder, 2003-. **Business Addr:** President, Founder, Eady Associates, PO Box 445, Catskill, NY 12414, **Business Phone:** (877)811-6444.

### EADY, LYDIA DAVIS
Vice president (organization), president (organization), media executive. **Personal:** Born May 4, 1958, IN; daughter of Henderson S and Ruth Vinita (deceased); married Jacques Wayne; children: Andrew & Matthew John. **Educ:** Howard Univ, BA, broadcast mgt & bus, 1980. **Career:** WUSA-TV, intern, 1979; WRTV ABC Indianapolis, Ind, news reporter, 1980-81; Johnson Publ Co, asst dir pub rels, 1981-83, dir prom, 1983-85, vpres prom, 1985-2004; Ebony & Jet Celebrity Showcase, assoc producer; Am Black Achievment Awards, prog coord exec; Joy Communs, pres, 2005-07, 2009-; Daystar Sch, dir advan, 2007-09; E Lake Mgt & Develop Corp, dir mkt, 2011-. **Orgs:** Quinn Chapel AME Ch Chicago, Ill; Execs Club Chicago; League Black Women; Women's Advert Club Chicago; Chicago Asn Black Journalists; trustee, Alder Sch Prof Psychol; bd adv, Jad Communs. **Honors/Awds:** Folio Circulation Direct Mail Award of merit; CEBA Award for Merit; Listed in: Who's Who in the World; Who's Who of Am Women; Who's Who of Black Ams; Woman Of Substance Award, Men Committed Better Community. **Special Achievements:** EBONY Guide To Historically Black Coll & Univs, author; mag articles spec events & press releases; represented Co at the White House; ABC-TV network special, Celebrate The Dream: 50 Years Of EBONY; associate producer of EBONY/JET Celebrity Showcase. **Home Addr:** 1137 S Pk Terr, Chicago, IL 60605, **Home Phone:** (312)203-4985. **Business Addr:** President, Joy Communications.

### EADY, DR. MARVIN P., JR.
Dentist. **Educ:** Ind Univ Sch Dent, DDS, 1990. **Career:** Dr Eady Family Dent PC, dentist & pres, 1990-. **Business Addr:** President, Dentist, Dr Eady Family Dentistry PC, 4646 W Jefferson Blvd Suite 140, Ft. Wayne, IN 46804, **Business Phone:** (260)459-1415.

### EAGAN, CATHERINE B.
Banker. **Personal:** Born Jan 14, 1954, New York, NY; daughter of James Doyle Davis and Adele Helen Dixon Cartey; married Jay Victor. **Educ:** Simmons Col, Boston, MA, BA, educ, 1975, Grad Sch Mgt, cert, 1996; Harvard Univ, Grad Sch Educ, Cambridge, MA, EdM, admin, planning, social policy, 1978; Am Inst Banking, Wayne State Univ, attended 1980; Word Faith Bible Training Ctr, grad, 2000. **Career:** Metrop Coun Educ, Roxbury, MA, Support serv dir, 1975-78; United Community Serv Detroit, MI, prog consult, 1978-80; Nat Bank Detroit, Detroit, MI, com credit analyst, 1979-82; Detroit Econ Growth Corp, dir com develop, 1982-93; Pvt Banking Div, Mich Nat Bank, pvt banking officer, 1993-95, vpres, 1993-98; Nat Australia Bank, pvt banking officer, 1995-98; Workplace Wisdom Publ, founder, 1999-; William Tyndale Col, chmn dept continuing educ & assoc prof prof studies, 1999-; Catherine Eagan Ministries, founder; Wealthy Women Club, chief exec officer, 1998-; Catherine Eagan Enterprises LLC, vpres, currently. **Orgs:** Life mem, Nat Asn Advan Colored People, 1982-; Harvard Club Eastern Mich, 1982; Women's Econ Club, 1983-; Econ Club Detroit, 1984; role model, Detroit Pub Sch Stud Motivation Prog, 1986-; finance chairperson, United Negro Col Fund Walkathon, 1986-; finance chairperson, Detroit Area Agency Aging, 1990-; Nat Speakers Asn; Christian Booksellers Asn; Women's Exec Golf Club; trustee, Int Third World Leadership Asn, 2000-04. **Honors/Awds:** Certificate of Nat Recognition for Trapper's Alley Project; Award of Nat Excellence, Va Park Shopping Ctr, US Dept Housing & Urban Develop; Certificate of Participation, Business Role Model, Detroit Pub Schs Stud Motivational Prog, 1985, 1987, 1988, 1989, 1990; African-American Business & professional Women's Award, Dollars & Sense Magazine, 1991; Testimonial Resolution from the Detroit City Council, 1993; Proclamation from Mayor Coleman A Young for her work in the City of Detroit, 1993. **Special Achievements:** Numerous speaking engagements, co-author of dominating money & How to discover our purpose in ten days, first African-American Private Banker and Officer to one of Michigan's largest banks. **Home Addr:** 24300 Civic Ctr Dr Apt 214, Southfield, MI 48033-2565, **Home Phone:** (561)391-5135. **Business Addr:** Chief Executive Officer, President, Catherine Eagan Enterprises LLC, 3200 N Fed Hwy Suite 222, Boca Raton, FL 33431, **Business Phone:** (561)338-0009.

### EAGLIN, FULTON B.
Association executive, army officer, lawyer. **Personal:** Born Nov 23, 1941, Ann Arbor, MI; son of Simon P and Marguerite Davis; married Jan Collins; children: Fulton Christopher, Jennifer Naomi & Jessica Marguerite. **Educ:** Eastern Mich Univ, Ypsilanti, BS, 1963; Harvard Sch Bus, Cambridge, MA, 1969; Harvard Law Sch, Cambridge, MA, JD, 1969. **Career:** Harvard Univ, 1969-72; self employed atty, 1975-80; Eaglin, Drukis & Green, atty, 1980-. **Orgs:** Mich Bar Asn; Ypsilanti & Washtenaw County Bar Asn; treas, Child Family Serv Washtenaw County, 1975-77; trustee, Washtenaw Community Col, 1976; Kiwanis Int; bd dir, Am Red Cross, Washtenaw County Chap, 1985-87; chmn bd dir, United Way Mich, 1988; Alpha Phi Alpha Fraternity; Sire Archon, 1990-92; bd gov, United Way Am, 1992-99; Gamma Rho Chap; Sigma Pi Phi Fraternity. **Home Addr:** 2770 Tulsa Ave, Claremont, CA 91711, **Home Phone:** (734)665-5355. **Business Addr:** Attorney, Eaglin Drukis & Green, 2610 E Arbor Rd, Ann Arbor, MI 48103, **Business Phone:** (734)665-5355.

### EAGLIN, RUTH
Government official. **Career:** US Dept Transp, White House Liaison, 2000; White House Off, exec asst dir presidential Personnel, currently. **Business Addr:** Executive Assistant to Director, Office of Presidential Personnel, White House, Washington, DC 20500, **Business Phone:** (202)456-6238.

### EALY, MARY NEWCOMB
Educator, financial manager. **Personal:** Born Aug 26, 1948, Charleston, MO; daughter of Gussie E Newcomb and Susie M Williams; married Willie R; children: Lisa Denise. **Educ:** Lake Mich Col, AA, 1968; Western Mich Univ, BS, 1972. **Career:** Fox's Jewelry, ed mgr, 1969-70; Shifren & Willens Jewelry, off coord, 1969; Benton Harbor Area Sch, secy, 1970-71, dept head coord social studies, 1973, teacher, 2004; Mich State Dept Educ, reviewer, 1975-; Sch Curr & Educ Leadership, res; Jordan Col Berrien Campus, adj prof, 1987-; La'Nise Productions, vpres, currently. **Orgs:** Pres, Essence Blackness, 1974-; Mich & Nat Educ Asn Rep Assembly, 1974-; Nat Educ Asn, Off Black Caucus, 1974-; adv, Excelsior Chap, Nat Jr Hon Soc, 1975-; exec comm, MEA, 1976-77; Phi Delta Kappa, 1976; Andrews Unit Chap; Am Asn Col Pharm; Delta Sigma Theta Sorority Inc, BH-SJ Alumnae Chap, 1983-; coord, Close-up Found, 1985-; vpres, Benton Harbor-St Joseph Alumnae Chap, Delta Sigma Theta, 1987-89. **Home Addr:** 777 E Napier Ave Apt D4, PO Box 844, Benton Harbor, MI 49022-6129, **Home Phone:** (414)395-3065. **Business Addr:** Vice President, La'Nise Productions, PO Box 844, Benton Harbor, MI 49023.

### EALY, MICHAEL (MICHAEL BROWN)
Actor. **Personal:** Born Aug 3, 1973, Silver Spring, MD; married Khatira Rafiqzada; children: 1. **Educ:** Univ Md, Col Pk. **Career:** Stage productions: Joe Fearless & Whoa-Jack; Films: The Lush Life, 2000; Kissing Jessica Stein, 2001; Barbershop, 2002; Bad Company, 2002; Justice, 2003; 2 Fast 2 Furious, 2003; November, 2004; Never Die Alone, 2004; Barbershop 2: Back in Business, 2004; Jellysmoke, 2005; Suspect, 2007; Put it in a Book, 2007; Miracle at St Anna, 2008; Seven Pounds, 2008; The People Speak, 2009; Takers, 2010; For Colored Girls, 2010; Firebird, 2011; Underworld: Awakening, 2012; Think Like a Man, 2012; Unconditional, 2012; Last Vegas, 2013; The Signal, producer, 2013; About Last Night, 2014; Think Like a Man Too, 2014. TV series: "Metropolis", 2000; "Law & Order", 2000; "Madigan Men", 2000; "Soul Food", 2001; "ER", 2002-03; "Their Eyes Were Watching God", 2005; "Sleeper Cell", 2005-06; "Suspect", 2007; "FlashForward", 2009; "The People Speak", 2009; "The Good Wife", 2010; "Californication", 2011; "Common Law", 2012; "Almost Human", 2013-14. **Honors/Awds:** WAFCA Award, Wash DC Area Film Critics Asn, 2002; Best Actor in TV Series Eyes Were Watching God, 2005; Black Reel Award, 2006; Nominee, Golden Globe Award, 2007; Nominee, Black Reel Award, 2008; Won Best Supporting Actor for For Colored Girls, 2010; AAFCA Award, African-Am Film Critics Asn, 2010. **Business Addr:** Actor, c/o Vic Ramos Management, 49 W 9th St Suite 5B, New York, NY 10011, **Business Phone:** (212)473-2610.

### EARL, ACIE BOYD
Executive, basketball player, business owner. **Personal:** Born Jun 23, 1970, Peoria, IL; son of Acie and Carolyn; married Tiffini; children: Kendra, Kenya, Keonna, Kacie & Kareem. **Educ:** Univ Iowa, BS, leisure studies, 1993. **Career:** Basketball player (retired), coach, executive, business owner, power forward & center; Boston Celtics, 1993-95; NBA Draft, player, 1993; Ace Prom & Mkt, vpres, 1993; Toronto Raptors, 1995-97; Milwaukee Bucks, 1997; La Crosse Bobcats, 1997-98; Qainwei Wyan, 1999; Paris Basket Racing, France, 1998; Sydney Kings, Australia, 1998-99; Qianwei Aoshen, 1999; Tuborg Pilsener, Turkey, 1999-2000; Turk Telekom, Turkey, 2000-01; Avtodor Saratov, Russia, 2001; UNICS Kazan, Russia, 2001-02; Darussafaka, Turkey, 2002; Slask Wroclaw, Poland, 2003; Arkadia Traiskirchen Lions, Austria, 2003; Learmie Jr Col Cheyenne, Wyo, asst coach, 2003; Black Hawk Jr Col Moline, Ill, asst coach, 2003 & 2004; Buducnost Podgorica, Montenegro, 2004; KB Peja, Kosovo, 2004; Waterloo Revolution, 2004; S E Jr Col Burlington, Iowa, asst coach, 2004; Nat Basketball Leagues Sydney Kings, player, 1998-99; Tijuana Dragons, coach, 2004-05; San Jose Sky Rockets, head coach & Asst Gen Mgr; asst coach, Rockford Lightning, 2005; Ohio Aviators ABA, coach; Cleveland Majic, coach, 2006-07; Quad City Riverhawks, vpres, asst coach, 2006; Apex Sports Group, coach, 2006; Solon High Sch, freshman boys basketball coach, 2007-11; Venom Productions, owner, 1993-. **Orgs:** Vpres, Ace Award, 1993-; camp dir, WAM JAM basketball camp, 1994; VenoSports Mgt, 1999; Nation Islam. **Honors/Awds:** Pre-season All Am, Playboy Mag, 1992-93; Big Ten Defensive Player of the Year, 1992; Chinese D2 Champion, 1999; Chinese D2 Best Import Player, 1999; Turkish League MVP, 2001; All Korac Cup top 5 players, 2001; Turkish League Best Import Player, 2001; Turkish League Defensive Player of the Year, 2001; Kosovo MVP of playoffs and regular season, 2004; Kosovo play Off Champion, 2004. **Special Achievements:** NBA Draft, first round pick, 1993; Nominee, John Wooden Award, 1992-93. **Home Addr:** 2301 14th Ave, Moline, IL 61265, **Home Phone:** (319)338-1460. **Business Addr:** Owner, Venom Productions, PO Box 1685, Moline, IL 61265, **Business Phone:** (888)836-6649.

### EARL, DR. ARCHIE, SR.
Educator. **Personal:** Born Nov 28, 1946, Suffolk, VA; son of Edward Jr and Thelma Virginia Gertude Williams; married Doristine Gause; children: Karen, Archie Jr & Keisha. **Educ:** Old Dom Univ, Mod Geom, cert, 1970; Norfolk State Univ, BS, 1971, Visual BASIC, Bus Commun, cert, 1999; Hampton Univ, MA, 1976; Univ Va, BASIC Comput Programming Teachers, cert, 1983; Col William & Mary, CAS, 1983; Col William & Mary, EdD, 1986; Christopher Newport Univ, Principle Real Estate, cert, 1989; Tidewater Community Col, comput programming, cert, 1995. **Career:** Hampton Univ, fel 1972-74, statist instr, 1983; Col William & Mary, fel, 1980-86, grad asst, 1983-85; Family Inns Amer, night auditor, 1985-86; City Col Chicago, math lectr, 1986; Saudi Arabian Govt, Dammam Saudi Arabia, Math instr, 1987; Christopher Newport Col, Newport News VA, asst prof Math, 1987-90; Norfolk State Univ, fac senate pres, fac salary issues res comt chair, asst prof math, 1991, assoc prof, currently; IEIC Press, auth, publ, 1993-. **Orgs:** Deacon & treas, Mt Pleasant Baptist Church, Williams burgs, 1983-86; Asn Study Higher Educ, 1986-; Math Asn Am, 1988-; Am Math Soc 1988-; Am Statist Asn, 1991; Am Asn Univ Prof, 1997-; Nat Asn Mathematics; Am socs engineering educ. **Special Achievements:** Published math/statistic textbooks, articles in textbooks, articles in ERIC (world's largest education related database), article in Norfolk State University Research Magazine; Made scholarly presentations at local, national, and international conferences; Conducted research in metallurgical and materials engineering at University of Alabama; website design and analysis at the Naval Medical Research Center and the Pentagon (DOD); computational science at Elizabeth State University and Norfolk State University; consultant, University of Virginia and Virginia State Department of Education; Served on the doctoral dissertation committee for several PhD candidates, supervising the methodology/results phase of their work. **Home Addr:** 4728 Barn Swallow Dr, Chesapeake, VA 23321-1233, **Home Phone:** (757)488-0271. **Business Addr:** Associate Professor of Mathematics, Mathematics Department, 700 Pk Ave, Norfolk, VA 23504, **Business Phone:** (757)823-9564.

### EARLES, DR. JULIAN MANLY
Executive. **Personal:** Born Nov 22, 1942, Portsmouth, VA; son of James and Deberry; married Zenobia; children: Gregory & Julian Jr. **Educ:** Norfolk State Univ, BS, physics, 1964; Univ Rochester Sch Med & dent, MS, radiation biol, 1965; Univ Mich, PhD, radiation physics, 1973, environl health; Harvard Bus Schs, Mgt Develop, 1978; Vaughn Col Aeronaut & Technol Queens, New York, hon degrees; Nova Southeastern Univ Ft Lauderdale, Fla, hon degrees; NC Agr & Tech State Univ Greensboro, Nc, hon degrees. **Career:** NASA Glenn Res Ctr, chief, 1965-2006, Nat Aeronaut & Space Admins, dir, 2003-05; Cleveland State Univ, exec residence, 2006-. **Orgs:** Mem adv bd, Rock & Roll Hall Fame; NMCP; Kappa Alpha Psi Fraternity; Advan Colored People, Nat Tech Asn; Nat Soc Black Engrs; Nat Soc Black Physicists; Develop Fund Black Students Sci & Technol; Sigma Pi Phi Fraternity. **Honors/Awds:** Excep achievement & outstanding leadership medals, NASA; Presidential Rank Award of Meritorious Exec; Distinguished Scholar Lectr, Jennings Found; hon ScD, Col Aeronaut, NY; hon Doctor of Pedag, Nova Southeastern Univ; hon DHL, NC A&T State Univ; Distinguished Hons Vis Prof at numerous univs throughout the Nation; Community Service Award. **Special Achievements:** Guest speaker, Black Hist month closing ceremony; over 28 publ, tech & educ; run over 10, 000 miles in the past 5 yrs & successfully completed 25 marathons incl the Boston Marathon; NASA's first black section head, first black office chief, first black division chief and first black deputy director; Journal: NASA's first health physics guides. **Home Addr:** , Beachwood, OH. **Business Addr:** Executive in Residence, Cleveland State University, 2121 Euclid Ave, Cleveland, OH 44115-2214, **Business Phone:** (216)687-2000.

**EARLES, DR. RENE MARTIN**
Physician, executive, association executive. **Personal:** Born Oct 31, 1940, New Orleans, LA; married Eve Evans; children: Robert & Andrea. **Educ:** Howard Univ, BS, biol & chem, 1963; Howard Univ Col Med, MD, 1967. **Career:** DC Gen Hosp, dermatologist, resident surg, 1968-70; Univ Wash, preceptorship, 1970-72; Rush Med Ctr, residency, 1972-75; Kemo Health Ctr, Chicago, Ill, chief dermatologist; Dr Earles LLC, chmn, head prod develop, 2001-. **Orgs:** Nat Med Asn, 1967-; chmn, Div Dermatol, Mt Sinai Med Ctr, Chicago Ill, 1979-81; bd dir, Region Four, Ill; Am Cancer Soc; past pres, Howard Univ, Alumni asn, Chicago; frat life, Kappa Alpha Psi; Sigma Pi Phi; Chicagoans; Saracens; Am Acad Dermat; Chicago Dermat Soc; Soc Investigative Dermat; Cook County Physicians Asn; bd mem, Am Health & Beauty Aids Inst. **Special Achievements:** Featured as one of top 100 African - American Doctors in the United States in Black Enterprise Magazine; Magazines including the Journal of the National Medication Association, Ebony, American Academy of Facial Plastic Surgery, Essence and the Journal of Dermatologic Surgery and Oncology. **Home Addr:** 4800 S Lake Park Ave Apt 701, Chicago, IL 60615-2046. **Business Addr:** Chairman, Head of Product Development, Dr Earles LLC, 2930 S Mich Ave Suite 102, Chicago, IL 60616-3270, **Business Phone:** (312)225-7200.

**EARLEY, KEITH HENRY**
Executive, lawyer. **Personal:** Born Feb 3, 1952, New York, NY; son of Charles and Wilma; children: Khary. **Educ:** Cornell Univ, BA, govt, 1974; Rutgers Law Sch, JD, 1977; Am Univ, MS, orgn develop, 2000; Fielding Grad Univ, MA, human & orgn systs, 2012, PhD. **Career:** Delta Found, staff atty, 1977-80; Boasberg Klores Feldsman & Tucker, bus & finance assoc, 1980-82; Fed Home Loan Mortgage Corp, coun, asst gen coun, assoc gen coun, 1982-98, vpres employ strategies & practices, 1998-2003; Early Interventions LLC, prin, 2003-08, 2013-; Finnegan Henderson, dir, diversity & inclusion, 2008-13. **Orgs:** Chmn, Am Bar Asn Minority In-house Coun Group. **Home Addr:** 8200 Jones Branch Dr, McLean, VA 22102, **Home Phone:** (301)468-3223. **Business Addr:** Principal, Early Interventions LLC, 6208 Montrose Rd, Rockville, VA 20852, **Business Phone:** (301)468-9343.

**EARLS, DR. JULIAN MANLY**
Association executive. **Personal:** Born Nov 22, 1942, Portsmouth, VA; son of James and Ida Deberry; married Zenobia N Gregory; children: Julian Jr & Gregory. **Educ:** Norfolk State Col, BS, phys, 1964; Univ Rochester, MS, radiation biol, 1965; Univ Mich, MPH, 1972, PhD, radiation physics, 1973; Harvard Univ Grad Sch Bus, PMD, admin, 1978. **Career:** Cuyahoga Comm Col, adj math, 1966; NASA, physicist, 1965-67, US Nuclear Regulatory Agency, radiation specialist, 1967-68, asst dep dir, 1992-2006; Cleveland State Univ, adj prof, 1973, exec residence, 2006-; Health Safety & Security Div, chief, 1983-88, Capital Univ, adj prof, 1984; Off Health Serv, dir, 1988; NASA Lewis res centre, dep dir, 2002; Glenn Res Ctr, dep dir, dir, 2003-05; Nance Col Bus Admin, exec-in-residence, 2006-. **Orgs:** Kappa Alpha Psi Frat Inc, 1963-; fel US Atomic Energy, 1964; Am Health Phys Soc Pub Info Comm, 1966-73; Am Nuclear Soc, 1966-; health phys consult, 1970-; Environ Pollution Cont Bd NASA, 1970-; US Nuclear Reg Comm Radiation Emergency Team, 1971-; chmn, Norfolk State Col Alumni Asn, 1971-72; exec safety bd, NASA, 1972-; Nat Urban League Black Exec Exchange Prog, 1973-; bd trustees, Inner City Protestant Par, 1974-76; Cuyahoga Community Col, 1987-; Ohio Environ Manpower Symp Strgn Comm, 1974-; pres, orgn Cleveland Chap NTA Inc, 1974-76; vis comm, Case Western Res, 1975-; chmn, Cleveland Bd Educ Occup Work Exp Adv Bd, 1975-77; nat pres, Nat Tech Asn Inc, 1976-77; bd overseers, Case Western Res, 1977-; Mayors Coun CETA Funded Prog, Cleveland, 1980-; bd dir Opportunity Ind Ctr Inc Tau Boule Sigma Pi Phi fraternity; life mem, Nat Asn Advan Colored People; Nat Soc Black Engrs; Nat Soc Black Physicists. **Honors/Awds:** Certificate of Merit, Fed Exec Bd, 1973; Award for BEEP, Nat Urban League, 1973-74; Distinguished Alumnus Award, Norfolk State Col, 1974; OIC Service Award, 1974; EO Award & Med NASA, 1974; Beta Kappa Chi Sci Hon Soc; Alpha Kappa Mu Honor; resolution passed by Cleveland City Council for Service to Community, 1978; Tech Achievement Award, Soc Black Mfg Engrs & Tech, 1978; Distinguished Service Award, Cleveland Jaycees; Distinguished Service Award, Nat Tech Asn, 1981; Humanitarian Award, Wittenberg Univ, 1983; Distinguished Service Award, Nat Asn Black Accts, 1984; Nat Black Col Alumni Hall of Fame, 1986; Nat Black Col Alumni Hall Fame, 1986-; Black Col Graduate of Distinction, Nat Urban League, 1987; Technical Achievement Award, Nat Technical Asn, 1987; Acad Excellence Commendation, Univ Miss, 1989; Distinguished Book In Science, Africa-Sci Inst, 1990; Sons of Mandela Award, Cleveland, Nat Asn Advan Colored People, 1990; NASA Medal for Exceptional Achievement, 1995; Strong Men and Women Excellence in Leadership, 1996; Cleveland All Star Salute, 1997; Honorary Doctor of Aeronautics Degree, 1999; Honorary Doctor of Pedagogy Degree, 2000; Salt Lake Olympics Torch Bearer, 2002; Honorary Doctor of Humane Letters, 2003; Presidential Rank Award of Meritorious Executive; hon degree, Vaughn Col Aeronaut & Technol, Nova Southeastern Univ, Nc Agr & Tech State Univ. **Home Addr:** 2566 Richmond Rd, Beachwood, OH 44122-1776, **Home Phone:** (216)765-0828. **Business Addr:** Executive-in-Residence, Cleveland State University, 2121 Euclid Ave, Cleveland, OH 44115-2214, **Business Phone:** (216)687-2000.

**EARLY, DELLAREESE PATRICIA. See REESE, DELLA.**

**EARLY, EZZARD DALE**
Automotive executive. **Personal:** Born Aug 15, 1953, Memphis, TN; son of Johne and Nicula B; married Joan; children: Ashley. **Educ:** Univ Tenn, BS, 1975; Univ St Thomas, MBA, 1984. **Career:** Mo Pac Rr, asst tech mgr, 1976-77; Conoco Inc, rail fleet super, 1978-84; Vista Chem Co, rail fleet mgr, 1984-85; Deerbrook Forest Chrysler Jeep Inc, pres, 1987-. **Orgs:** Fel Nat Automotive Dealers Asn, 2004-; pres, Conrad O Johnson Fines Arts Found; Lake Houston Cult Arts Coun; Rotary Club. **Business Addr:** President, Chief Executive, Deerbrook Forest Chrysler Jeep Inc, 22655 Hwy 59 N, Kingwood, TX 77339-4406, **Business Phone:** (281)359-4000.

**EARLY, DR. GERALD**
Writer, educator. **Personal:** Born Apr 21, 1952, Philadelphia, PA; son of Henry (deceased) and Florence Fernandez Oglesby; married Ida Haynes; children: Linnet Kristen Haynes & Rosalind Lenora Haynes. **Educ:** Univ Pa, Philadelphia, PA, BA, Eng lit, 1974; Cornell Univ, Ithaca, NY, MA, eng lit, 1982, PhD, eng lit, 1982. **Career:** St. Louis's Wash Univ, asst prof, 1982; Univ Kans, Minority fel, 1985-87; Randolph Macon Col Women, Lynchburg, VA, writer residence, 1990; Wash Univ, St Louis, MO, asst prof, instr, Am Cult Studies Prog, dir & co-dir, 1991-96, African & Afro-Am Studies Prog, dir, 1992-99, Merle Kling, prof, mod lett, currently, Ctr Humanities, dir, currently, Ctr Joint Proj Humanities & Social Scis, dir, currently, prof eng, currently, prof Am Cult Studies, currently, prof African & African Am Studies, currently; Nat Pub Radio, commentator. **Orgs:** Fel Am Acad Arts & Sci; invited fel Nat Humanities Ctr, 2001-02; consult, Ken Burns doc films Baseball, Jazz, Unforgivable Blackness: Rise & Fall Jack Johnson, War. **Honors/Awds:** The Passing of Jazz's Old Guard, Best American Essays, 1986; Whiting Foundation Writer's Award, Whiting Found, 1988; CCLM/General Electric Foundation Award for Younger Writers, 1988; National Book Critics Circle Award, 1994; Washington University's Arthur Holly Compton Faculty Award, 1997; Phi Beta Kappa Award for Distinguished Service to the Humanities, Phi Beta Kappa Soc, 2006; 2 times nominated, Grammy Award; Honored, Washington Univ, 2007; Distinguished Service to Education Award, Harris-Stowe State Univ, 2007; Excellence in the Arts Award, Arts & Education Council, St Louis, Missouri, 2008. **Special Achievements:** Tuxedo Junction: Essays on American Culture, 1989; Life with Daughters: Watching the Miss America Pageant, 1990; Daughters: On Family and Fatherhood, Addison-Wesley, 1994; One Nation Under a Groove: Motown & American Culture, 1994; Author: "How the War in the Streets Is Won Poems on the Quest of Love and Faith"; "The Culture of Bruising: Essays on Prizefighting, Literature, and Modern American Culture"; "Yes I Can The Sammy Davis Jr Story", 2001; "Rhapsodies in Black: Music and Words From the Harlem Renaissance", 2002. **Home Addr:** 420 W Swon, St Louis, MO 63119, **Home Phone:** (314)569-1423. **Business Addr:** Professor African & Afro-American Studies, Merle Kling Professor of Modern Letters, Washington University, McMillan Hall S102 1 Brookings Dr, St Louis, MO 63130-4899, **Business Phone:** (314)935-5576.

**EARLY, IDA H.**
School administrator. **Personal:** Born Nov 3, 1952, Dallas, TX; daughter of Oscar E Haynes and Thalia M Ephraim Haynes; married Gerald L; children: Linnet Kristin Haynes Husi & Rosalind Lenora Haynes. **Educ:** Univ Pa, BA, sociol, 1974; Cornell Univ, attended 1979. **Career:** Univ Pa, asst to the vice provost, 1975-77; Cornell Univ, admin asst to dir, 1980-82; John M Olin Sch Bus, admin asst, stud rels coordr, 1983-84, spec proj, dir, 1984; Wash Univ, spec proj, info & found, dir, 1982-93, alumni & develop progs dir, 1993-96, dir progs, 1998-2001, sr assoc dir, alumni & develop, 2001-07, secy bd trustees, 2007-; Duke Univ, interim dir, 2001-02; George Warren Brown Sch, interim dir, 2005-06. **Orgs:** Alpha Kappa Alpha, 1974-; bd mem, Wash Univ, Campus YMCA/YWCA, 1987-95; vpres fundraising, 1991-93, pres, 1996-98, Jr League St Louis; bd mem, UN Assoc, 1992-94; United Way Greater St Louis Allocations Panel, 1992-94; bd mem, Epworth C & Family Serv, 1993-99, 2001-05; bd mem, Eden Sem, 1993-2005; bd mem, Dance St Louis, 1993-; bd mem, Asn Jr Leagues Int Inc, 1993-95; Zoo Friends, 2004-; bd mem, Girls Inc, 2005-; bd mem, Webster Community Arts Found, 2003-; sr assoc dir, Alumni & Develop Progs; bd mem, St Louis Woman's Club, 2007-. **Honors/Awds:** First Year Minority Grad Fel, Cornell Univ, 1977; Difference Maker's Award, Bar Asn Metrop St Louis, 2001. **Special Achievements:** Co-author, "The Consortium for Graduate Study in Management", Selections, The Magazine of the Graduate Management Admission Council, winter 1986, p14-17; First African American president of the Junior League of St. Louis, 1996-98. **Home Addr:** 53 Jefferson Rd, Webster Groves, MO 63119, **Home Phone:** (314)963-0267. **Business Addr:** Secretary to the Board of Trustees, Washington University, 1 Brookings Dr, St Louis, MO 63130-4899, **Business Phone:** (314)935-5105.

**EARLY, JAMES COUNTS**
Government official. **Personal:** Born Jan 12, 1947, Ocala, FL; son of James Tweetie and Altobelle Hampton Flanders; married Miriam Stewart; children: Jah-Mir & JaBen. **Educ:** More house Col, Atlanta, GA, BA, 1969; Canal Zone Col, Panama Canal Zone, attended 1967; Howard Univ, Wash, DC, PhD, 1971; Georgetown Univ Advan Port Inst, Wash, DC, port, 1973. **Career:** Antioch Col, Wash, DC, assoc prof, 1976-77; Howard Univ, Wash, DC, WHUR Radio, producer, writer & host, 1978-83; Inst Arts & Humanities, Nat Endowment Humanities, Wash, DC, humanist adminr, 1978-83; Smithsonian Inst, Wash, DC, exec asst, asst secy pub serv, 1984-88, dep asst secy pub serv, 1989-90, actg asst secy pub serv, 1990-91, asst secy educ & pub serv, 1991-95, asst provost Educ & Cult Prog, 1995-, Anacostia Mus & Ctr African Am Hist & Cult, actg dir, Cult Studies & Commun Ctr Folk life Prog& Cult Studies, dir, 1995-. **Orgs:** Arena stage outreach bd, Arena Stage, 1988-; adv bd mem, Textile Mus, 1989; bd vis, Ctr Pub Policy, Union Inst, 1988; bd mem, Wash Moscow Citizens Exchange, 1988; bd, Fondo Del Sol Gallery, 1988; 651 Kings Majestic Theater, bd, 1991; Environ Proj, Wash, bd, 1992; Africa Policy Info Ctr, 1992; Crossroads Mag, ed adv comt, 1990; bd dir, Inst Policy Studies; bd dir, Trans Africa Forum; humanist adminr, Nat Endowment Humanities; bd dir, Childrens Studio Sch, 1993. **Home Addr:** 5108 13th St NW, Washington, DC 20011, **Home Phone:** (202)882-8208. **Business Addr:** Director of Cultural Studies & Communication, Folklore consultant & Researcher, Smithsonian Institution, 955 Lenfant Plz SW, Washington, DC 20560, **Business Phone:** (202)287-2166.

**EARLY, QUINN REMAR**
Vice president (organization), football player, executive. **Personal:** Born Apr 13, 1965, West Hempstead, NY; married Casandra; children: Quinn Camer & Chance. **Educ:** Univ Iowa, BA, com art, 1988. **Career:** Football player (retired), executive; San Diego Chargers, wide receiver, 1988-90; New Orleans Saints, wide receiver, 1991-95; Buffalo Bills, wide receiver, 1996-98; New York Jets, wide receiver, 1999; White Dragon Schs, teacher, 1997; Qpro Prod, design dir & vpres, 2002-03; Quinn Earl, owner, motivational speaker, currently; Choy Li Fut; Stroovy, cofounder pres, 2014-. **Orgs:** New Orleans Saints. **Special Achievements:** Published numerous articles, including for Inside Kung-Fu Magazine, on how Martial Arts can be used for a healthy lifestyle; Actor: The Baytown Outlaws, 2012, In the Blood, 2014, Cat Run 2, 2014. **Home Addr:** , CA. **Business Addr:** Design Director, Vice President, Charles Drew University of Medicine and Science, 663 Balboa Ave, San Diego, CA 92118, **Business Phone:** (619)972-8155.

**EARLY, ROBERT S.**
Educator, college teacher. **Personal:** Born Nov 10, 1935, New York, NY; son of Robert S Jr and Rose C Jarrett; married Elizabeth Graham; children: David & Matthew. **Educ:** Univ Hartford, BS, bus admin, 1957; Morgan State Col, attended 1956. **Career:** Executive (retired); RCA Global Comn, personnel admin, 1958-68; ColtIndus, mgr personnel & pub affairs, 1968-72; Paper Tech Found Western Mich Univ, rep; AMA, instr, 1969-70; Speakman Co, dir personnel & indust rels, 1972-74; Champion Int Corp, dir personnel, 1974-78; Columbia Univ, vpres human resources, 1978-94; Nat Urban League's Black Exec Exchange Prog, visprof, 1978-81; Del Community Col, employee rels instr. **Orgs:** Co chair, Planned Parenthood NY City, 1987, chair, 1989-93; bd pres, Today's Stud Tomorrow's Teachers, 1999-; chmn bd, Intercommunity Camp, Westport, Conn; bd dir, Higher Educ Retirement Community Asn; bd mem, Manhattanville Community Ctr; Metlife Higher Educ Adv Bd; voting bd mem, Empire Blue Cross & Blue Shield. **Home Addr:** 6504 Grand Pt Ave, Bradenton, FL 34201, **Home Phone:** (941)351-3626.

**EARLY, SYBIL THERESA**
Executive. **Personal:** Born Aug 25, 1952, Staunton, VA. **Educ:** Bradley Univ, MBA, 1972; Fashion Inst, commun, 1974. **Career:** United Airlines, flight attend; Winston Network TDI Inc, mgr, acct exec; ET Media Inc, owner, pres, currently; independent mkt & advert prof. **Orgs:** Nat Asn Female Execs; DuSable Mus. **Honors/Awds:** Winston Network Outstanding Sales Performance, 1981-82 & 1986, Salesperson of the Year, 1983; Assoc Mem of the Year Award, Am Health & Beauty Aids Inst. **Special Achievements:** First female and african-owned independent outdoor advertising firm representing 93% of the out-of-home vendors in the United States. **Home Addr:** 3719 N Broadway St Apt 2f, Chicago, IL 60613-4165, **Home Phone:** (773)281-0462.

**EARVIN, DR. LARRY L.**
College administrator, chief executive officer. **Personal:** Born Feb 23, 1949, Chattanooga, TN; son of William and Clara Ware; married Valerie Johnson; children: William Jarrett & Allyson Valeria Richardson. **Educ:** Clark Col, BA, 1971; Ga State Univ, MS, 1973; Emory Univ, PhD, 1982. **Career:** Clark Col, Atlanta Housing Policy Study, asst dir, 1973-75, Southern Ctr Studies Pub Policy, asst dir, 1975-81, assoc dir, 1981-84, Dept Social Sci, chair & tenured prof polit sci, 1981-87, interim dean fac & instr, 1987-88, Clark Atlanta Univ, dean col, 1988-89, dean undergrad studies, 1989-90, assoc provost & dean stud affairs, 1990-92, assoc provost & actg dean, Sch Arts & Sci, 1992-93, dean, 1993-2000; Houston-Tillotson Col, pres, 2000-, chief exec cofficer; SACS Comn Cols, vpres, chief exec officer. **Orgs:** Adv bd mem, Austin Conv & Visitors Bur, 2000-; bd mem, Tex Campus Compact, 2001-; bd mem, Capital Area United Way, 2001-; bd mem, Austin Area Urban League, 2001-; bd mem, Nat Asn Equal Opportunity Higher Educ, 2002-; Univ Senate, United Methodist Church, sen, 2002-; bd mem, Independent Cols & Univ Tex, 2002-; bd mem, Coun Independent Col, 2003-; bd dir, Coun Higher Educ Accreditation; bd mem, Comt Planning & Implementation Nat Asn Schs & Cols; bd mem, Educ & Instnl Ins Adminr. **Home Addr:** 446 Wynns Way SW, Atlanta, GA 30331. **Business Addr:** Vice President, Chief Executive Officer, SACS Commission on Colleges, 1866 Southern Lane, Decatur, GA 30033-4097, **Business Phone:** (404)994-6577.

**EASLER, MICHAEL ANTHONY (MIKE EASLER)**
Baseball player, basketball coach. **Personal:** Born Nov 29, 1950, Cleveland, OH; son of James Edward and Willie Mae; married Brenda Jackson; children: Misty, Shandi & Khyla. **Educ:** Cleveland State Univ. **Career:** Baseball player (retired), baseball coach; Houston Astros, 1973-75; Calif Angels, 1976; Pittsburgh Pirates, 1977-83; Boston Red Sox, outfielder, 1984-85; New York Yankees, outfielder, 1986-87; Philadelphia Phillies, outfielder, 1987; Nippon Ham Fighters, prof baseball coach, 1988-89; Milwaukee Brewers, hitting coach, 1992; Boston Red Sox, hitting coach, 1993; St. Louis Cardinals, hitting coach, 1999-2001; Jacksonville Suns, hitting coach, 2006; Las Vegas 51s, hitting coach, 2007; Los Angeles Dodgers, hitting coach, 2008; Buffalo Bisons, hitting coach, 2011-; New York Mets, Buffalo Bisons, hitting instr, currently. **Home Addr:** 8428 Dutch Hill Ct, Las Vegas, NV 89128-7623. **Business Addr:** Hitting Coach, New York Mets organization, Citi Field, Flushing, NY 11368, **Business Phone:** (718)507-6387.

**EASLEY, BILLY HARLEY**
Photojournalist. **Personal:** Born Oct 10, 1925, St. Louis, MO; son of William Harley and Myrtle Easley Edmondson; married Gladys Brown; children: Cassandra V. **Educ:** Tenn State Univ, Nashville, cert, 1944; Nashville Sch Photog, cert, 1949; Nashville Tech Sch, cert, 1975. **Career:** Photojournalist (retired); Tennessean, Nashville, Tenn, photojournalist, 1966-00. **Orgs:** Nat Press Asn, 1967-; Nat Asn Black Journalist, 1985-. **Honors/Awds:** Carter Goodwin Woodson Award-Negro History, 1969; Metro Firefighters Association Award, 1977; National Press Association Award, 1979; Gannett Award, Gannett Publishing, 1984; Gannett Award, Special Olympics Photo Competition, 1987. **Home Addr:** 1906 15th Ave S, Nashville, TN 37212, **Home Phone:** (615)298-2878.

**EASLEY, BRENDA VIETTA (BRENDA EASLEY WEBB)**
Association executive, executive. **Personal:** Born Jun 28, 1951, Buffalo, NY; daughter of James T and Lacetta Dixon; children: Cynthia Duncan, Bryon Duncan & Robert Webb. **Career:** Buffalo & Erie County Pub Libr, prin libr clerk, 1968-88; Cath Diocese Buffalo, dir, cent buffalo ministries & off black ministry, 1988. **Orgs:** Mem & chairperson, Nat Asn Black Cath Admin, 1989; reg coord, Nat Black

Cath Cong, 1989-; chair, mem, commun comt, Buffalo Area Metrop Ministers Bd Trustees, 1989-. **Home Addr:** 328 Normal Ave, Buffalo, NY 14213-2521, **Home Phone:** (716)884-1537. **Business Addr:** Director, Roman Catholic Diocese of Buffalo, 795 Main St, Buffalo, NY 14203, **Business Phone:** (716)847-8391.

**EASLEY, CHARLES F., SR.**
School administrator, consultant, vice president (organization). **Personal:** Born May 3, 1935, Dalton, GA; son of Oscar Sr and Bertha Kenyon; married Helen Saxton; children: Charles Jr & Tania Patrice. **Educ:** Knoxville Col, AB, 1956; Teachers Col, Columbia Univ, teacher cert, 1960; Atlanta Univ, Clark Atlanta Univ, MA, 1965; Ga State Univ, attended 1978. **Career:** School administrator (retired); Stephens Sch, counr social studies, asst prin, 1958-65; Morris Brown Col, dean stud & asst prof, 1965-74; Nat Urban League, fel prog, consult, 1967-73; Atlanta Jr Metrop Col, vpres stud affairs, 1974-97; Easley & Assoc, consult, 1997. **Orgs:** Phi Delta Kappa Educ Fraternity, 1972-; Warren Memorial Boys Club, 1980-86; bd trustee, secy, personnel & comt chair, Trinity Sch, 1980-; Leadership Atlanta, 1982-; pres & secy, W Fulton Rotary Club, 1985-94; nat pres, Nat Coun Presby Men, 1992-94; consult, Southwest Atlanta Youth Acad & Athletic Asn, 1992; W End Rotary Club, 1994-; vice moderator & vice chair, 215th Gen Assembly Corp, Presby Church, USA, 2003; dean & dir develop, Johnson C. Smith Theol Sem; Synod Sun; pres, Sheltering Arms; vice chair, Gen Assembly Coun; Personnel Subcomt Exec Comt; adv comt, Social Witness Policy; advocacy comt, Racial Ethnic Concerns. **Home Addr:** 787 Duffield Dr NW, Atlanta, GA 30318-7228, **Home Phone:** (404)792-2024.

**EASLEY, DAMION (JACINTO DAMION EASLEY)**
Baseball executive, athletic coach, baseball player. **Personal:** Born Nov 11, 1969, New York, NY; married Dawn; children: Rocky, Jazmin, Nathaniel & Jayce Derrick. **Educ:** Long Beach City Col, attended 1988. **Career:** Baseball player (retired), coach, executive; Calif Angels, infielder, 1992-96; Detroit Tigers, 1996-2002; Tampa Bay Devil Rays, 2003; Fla Marlins, 2004-05; Ariz Diamondbacks, 2006; New York Mets, 2007-08; Peoria Padres, asst coach, currently; Warrior Baseball Acad, exec dir, currently. **Orgs:** CIF champions, 1987. **Honors/Awds:** AL All Star Team, 1998; Silver Slugger Award, 1998; AL Leader in Assists, 1998; Hit for a Cycle, 2001. **Special Achievements:** AL Leader in Putouts by a Second Basemen, 1998. **Business Addr:** Executive Director, Warrior Baseball Academy, 1763 Upland Dr, Houston, TX 77043, **Business Phone:** (832)867-6265.

**EASLEY, JACINTO DAMION.** See EASLEY, DAMION.

**EASLEY, JACQUELINE RUTH (JACQUELINE EASLEY MCGHEE)**
Executive. **Personal:** Born Oct 21, 1957, Ames, IA; daughter of Dr Eddie V and Ruth Burton; married Odell McGhee; children: Carey Lucia & Ty Ellington. **Educ:** Carleton Col, BA, 1980. **Career:** Am Repub Ins Co, personnel assoc, 1980, asst vpres personnel, 1984; Terr Hill comn, 2007-; City Des Moines Planning & Zoning Comn, comnr, 2008-; US Bank, dir. **Orgs:** Bd dir, YWCA Des Moines, 1983, pres, 1987; United Way Cent IA, 1984; Minority Ed Braintrust, 1985; exec comt, Nat Asn Advan Colored People, 1987; chairperson, Metrop Transit Authority, 1990; bd mem, Des Moines Pub Schs, 1990-2000; bd trustee, Drake Univ, 1996-2009; chmn, Regional Workforce Investment Bd, 2010-; bd dir, Employee Family Resources; bd trustee, Des Moines Metrop Transit Authority; Child Care Asn Greater Des Moines; Willkie House; Roosevelt High Sch Found; Young Women's Christian's Asn; dir, Mercy Med Ctr; bd trustee, Blank Hosp; Am Heart Asn; Cent Iowa Workforce Investment Bd. **Honors/Awds:** Woman Achievement, 1984; YWCA of Des Moines, 1984; Des Moines Regist, Up & Coming Bus Leader, 1986; Excellence in Leadership, 1990; Outstanding Young Citizen, Des Moines Jaycess, 1990; Am Best and Brightest Bus Prof, 1992; Woman of the Year Award, 2009; Iowa Women's Hall of Fame, 2011; Outstanding Young Iowan, Iowa Jaycees; Outstanding Service to Youth, Zeta Phi Beta Sorority; Judge Luther Glanton Award, Jr League of Greater Des Moine. **Special Achievements:** First African American female to serve on the Des Moines School Board. **Home Addr:** 3113 Southern Hills Dr, Des Moines, IA 50321, **Home Phone:** (515)243-3803.

**EASLEY, KENNY MASON, JR.**
Football player, executive. **Personal:** Born Jan 15, 1959, Chesapeake, VA; son of Juanita; married Gail; children: Kendrick, Gabrielle & Giordanna. **Educ:** Univ Calif, Los Angeles, BA, polit sci, 1980. **Career:** Football player (retired), business person; Seattle Seahawks, strong safety, 1981-87; Makena Sport, owner; Foster-Easley Sports Mgt Group, owner; Roller Wheels Inc, owner; Alderwood Olds-Cadillac, owner, currently; Sherm's BBQ Inc, owner; Norfolk Nighthawks, part-owner; bus entrepreneur, currently. **Orgs:** United Cerebral Palsy. **Honors/Awds:** Pro Bowl, 1982, 1983, 1984, 1985, 1987; Defensive Player of the Year, Asian Football Confederation, 1983; Defensive Player of the Year, Nat Football League, 1984; Defensive Back of the Year, Nat Football League Alumni Asn; Football Hall of Fame, 1994; Virginia Sports Hall of Fame, 1998; College Football Hall of Fame; Seagram Sports Award; Seahawks Most Valuable Player; Defensive Rookie of the Year, Asian Football Confederation; Defensive Player of the Year, Asian Football Confederation; Seahawks Ring of Honor, 2002; Hampton Roads Sports Hall of Fame, 2010. **Special Achievements:** A four time All-Pacific 10 Conference selection, 1977, 1978, 1979 & 1980; Finished ninth in the Heisman Trophy balloting, 1980. **Home Addr:** 5420 247th Pl SE, Issaquah, WA 98027. **Business Addr:** Owner, Alderwood Olds-Cadillac, 3909 196th St SW, Lynnwood, WA 98036-5732, **Business Phone:** (425)774-0513.

**EASLEY, REV. PAUL HOWARD**
Clergy. **Personal:** Born Sep 7, 1930, Charleston, WV; son of Alexander Pamplin Sr and Estella Allen; married Sarita; children: Paul Jr, Verita Green & David Allen. **Educ:** WVa State Col, BS, 1956; Gammon Theol Sem, BD, 1959; Iliff Sch Theol, MTS, 1972; Interdenominational Theol Sem, Mdiv, 1974. **Career:** John Wesley United Methodist Church, 1955-56; Seebert Charge, 1956; Fairmont Trinity Methodist Church, pastor, 1959-61; Roncevert-White Sulpher Charge, pastor, 1961; AUS, chaplain, 1961-80; Clark Col, chaplain, 1980-81; Clark Atlanta Univ, Atlanta, GA, univ chaplain, 1980-2001; Ben Hill United Methodist Church, assoc pastor, currently. **Orgs:** Mil Chaplains Asn, 1962-; Am Correctional Chaplains, 1964-; Correctional Chaplains Asn, 1964-; Clin oral Asn, 1977-; Nat Campus Ministers Asn, 1980-; charter pres, Optimist Int, 1984-; pres, PTA Therral HS, 1984-85; Omega Psi Phi Fraternity; Free & Accepted Masons; Nat Asn Advan Colored People; WV Conf, United Methodist Ch; Am Legion; Community Coun Metrop Atlanta Inc; coun mem, United Methodist Church; pres, Therrell High Sch Atlanta; CRT Ga Tech; Churches Home Foun Atlanta, Ga; Youth Hope Builders Acad; Fulton Leadership Acad; Exec Secy Br YMCA, Charleston, W Va; Counr Bethlehem Youth Ctr; Migrant Minister, Va Coun Churches; Boy Scouts Am; Prog Leader Br Gray Y progs, Atlanta, Ga. **Home Addr:** 265 Camelot Dr, Fayetteville, GA 30214-3640, **Home Phone:** (770)460-6695. **Business Addr:** Associate Pastor, Ben Hill United Methodist Church, Kresge Hall 2099 Fairburn SW Rd Suite 201, Atlanta, GA 30331, **Business Phone:** (404)344-0618.

**EASON, REV. GREGORY V., SR.**
Clergy. **Personal:** Born Dec 24, 1960, Metter, GA; son of Rev William and Geneva; married Linda Tyson; children: Carmen & Gregory Jr. **Educ:** E Ga Col, Swainsboro, Ga, AA, 1981; Morris Brown Col, Atlanta, Ga, BA, polit sci, 1983; Turner Theol Sem, Interdenominational Theol Ctr, Atlanta, Ga, MDiv, 1986; Columbia Theol Sem, Decatur, Ga, ThM, 1988; Columbia Theol Sem, DMin, 2011. **Career:** St Mark & Hickman Tabernacle African Methodist Episcopal Church, Wadley & Augusta, Ga, sr pastor, 1984-86; St James African Episcopal Church, Thomsom, Ga, sr pastor, 1986-88; St James African Methodist Episcopal Church, Monticello, Ga, sr pastor, 1988-90; St Phillip African Methodist Church, Savannah, Ga, sr pastor, 1990-04; Flipper Temple African Methodist Episcopal Church, Atlanta, Ga, sr pastor, 2004-05; Big Bethen African Methodist Episcopal Church, Atlanta, Ga, sr pastor, 2005-. **Orgs:** Bd trustee, Morris Brown Col, Atlanta, Ga; bd trustee, Turner Theol Sem, Atlanta, Ga; bd mem, Sicke Cell Asn, Savannah, Ga; Alpha Phi Alpha Fraternity Inc; bd mem, Family Independence Adv Bd, Chatham County Dept Family & C Servs; vchmn & chair person, Savannah Dist Comt Preachers Ann Conf & Preachers Orders, 1990-2004; Int Socs Theta Phi; chairperson, Ga Ann Conf Bd Examiners, 1991-2004; chair person, Finance comt, Atlanta N Ga Ann Conf, 1991-2004; chair person, Ministerial Efficiency Comt Ga Ann Conf, 1991-2004; vpres, Connectional Coun African Methodist Episcopal Church, 2005-. **Special Achievements:** Author: Looking at Aids Through the Eyes of God, 1991; Dreams and Nightmares, 1995; Article: "A Small Boy with a Big Fish"; This Far by Faith: African American Spiritual Journeys, commentator. **Business Addr:** Senior Pastor, Big Bethel African Methodist Episcopal Church, 220 Auburn Ave NE, Atlanta, GA 30303, **Business Phone:** (404)827-9707.

**EASON, OSCAR J., JR.**
Government official, civil rights activist. **Personal:** Born Jun 30, 1930, San Antonio, TX; son of Oscar and Doris Lucille; married Lois Anne; children: Angela Green & Oscar III. **Educ:** Prairie View A&M Col, BS, mech engineering, 1956; St Mary's Univ, MS, engineering, 1970. **Career:** Pac Architects & Engrs Inc, sup gen engr, 1970-72; Environ Protection Agency, gen engr, 1973-74; USN, Trident Missile Syst, proj mgr, 1974-81; AUS, Corps Engrs, sup mech engr, 1981-91, Chief Engineering Div, asst to chief, 1991-. **Orgs:** Nat Soc Prof Engrs, 1972-; vpres, Northwest Coalition Against Malicious Harrassment, 1983-87; vpres, Seattle King City Dispute Resolution Ctr, 1983-92; bd mem, pres, Nat Asn Advan Colored People, Seattle, 1983-; Nat pres, Blacks Govt Inc, 1994; Black Leadership Forum, 1995-; chair, Comn African-Am Affairs, 2006; pres, State Conf, Nat Asn Advan Colored People, Alaska, currently; mem Seattle-King County Dispute Resolution Ctr Bd; Univ Wash Minority Community adv comt; Highline YMCA Bd; nat pres, Blacks Govt; chair, WA State Comn, African Am Affairs. **Home Addr:** 5507 S Leo St, Seattle, WA 98178-2262, **Home Phone:** (206)725-5303. **Business Addr:** Assistant to Chief, US Army Corps of Engineers, Engineering Div 4735 E Marginal Way S, Washington, DC 98134-2385, **Business Phone:** (206)764-3742.

**EASON-STEELE, ELAINE**
Founder (originator), television producer. **Career:** Rosa & Raymond Parks Inst Self Develop, co-founder, 1987-; TV series: "Signs & Wonders", producer, 1995; "Intimate Portrait", 2001; "The Rosa Parks Story", producer, 2002. **Business Addr:** Co-Founder, Rosa & Raymond Parks Institute for Self Development, 535 Griswold St Suite 111-513, Detroit, MI 48226, **Business Phone:** (313)965-0606.

**EASTER, ERIC KEVIN**
Publisher, media executive, executive. **Personal:** Born Jan 19, 1961, Baltimore, MD; married Tina Tamara Hamilton. **Educ:** Howard Univ, BA, jour, 1983. **Career:** DC Coalition Homeless, exec dir, 1984; Easter & Assocs, pres, 1985-88; Jackson PRS, press ast, 1988; Nat Rainbow Coalition, press secy, 1988-90; New African Visions, pres, 1989-; Songs My People Doc Proj, producer & co ed, 1990-92; Wilder PRS, press secy, 1991-92; One Media Inc, chair, chief exec officer & founder, 1995-2002; ONE Mag, Black Film Rev Mag, publ & ed-in-chief, 1992-95; Akin & Randolph Agency, creative consult, lit agt; Wash Area Lawyers Arts, exec dir, 2002-04; Washingtonpost.Newsweek Interactive, dir, Commun, 2004-06; Johnson Publ Co, chief digital strategy & vpres digital & entertainment, 2007-10; Rock Content LLC, chief content officer & partner, 2010-12; Nat Black Programming Consortium, chair & bd dirs, 2010-; Black Heritage TV, chief exec officer, 2013-. **Orgs:** Nat Asn Black Journalists, 1984-; Howard Univ Commun Alumni Asn, 1985-86; secy, WritersCorps; AT&T Consumer Adv Panel, 2012-; mem bd, Pub Media Platform, 2013-. **Honors/Awds:** Mayors Special Recognition, City NY, 1992; Sojourner Truth Award, Links, 1993. **Special Achievements:** Co-creator, "Songs of My People" book and exhibit, 1992; co-producer, Taste of DC Annual Festival, 1991-. **Business Addr:** Chairman of the Board, National Black Programming Consortium, 68 E 131st St Suite 7, New York, NY 10037, **Business Phone:** (212)234-8200.

**EASTER, FRED.** See EASTER, WILFRED OTIS, JR.

**EASTER, DR. MARILYN K.**
Educator. **Personal:** Born Jan 6, 1957, Oklahoma City, OK; daughter of William L Pettigrew and Delois Ann Pettigrew; married Walter. **Educ:** Univ Colo, BA, 1979; Denver Univ, MA, admin & mgt, MSW, 1981; Univ San Francisco, EdD, 1992. **Career:** Gen Dent, mkt mgr, 1982; Chabot Col, instr, 1985-87; Nat Univ, Oakland, CA, adj prof, 1985-89; Amador Adult Sch, instr, 1985-89; Chabot Comm Col, instr, 1987-89; Calif St Univ, lectr, 1987-99; St Mary's Col, mkt chair assoc prof, 1994-96; Col Notre Dame, from assoc prof to prof, 1994-99; Col Notre Dame, Belmont, CA, 1995-99; Univ Calif, consult & actg dir, 2000; San Jose St Univ, Dept Mkt & Decisions Sci, lectr, 1999-, assoc prof, 2002-08, prof, 2008-. **Orgs:** Nat Asn Girl Scouts Am, 1991-95; Phi Delta Kappa Fraternity, 1992-2008; chair, Nat Asn Female Execs, Calif Chap, 1984-86; chair, Skywest Toastmasters, Hayward, CA, 1984-86; Oakland Chamber Com, Oakland, CA, 1985-87; Am Educ Res Asn, Wash, DC, 1990-2007; Am Soc Training & Develop, 1993-97; Calif St Teachers Asn, 1994-; chmn, Col Notre Dame, SAFE, 1997-; Nat Asn Advan Colored People, 1997-; co-chmn, steering comt, Col Notre Dame, 1997-; Nat Asn African Am Studies, 1997-2007; Nat Asn Equality Higher Educ, Wash, DC, 1998-2004; Nat Sch & Safety Ctr, 1999-2004; Pleasanton Partnerships Educ, Pleasanton, CA, 2000-04; Acad & Activ Booster Club, Pleasanton, CA, 2000-04; Int Asn Bus Commun, 2002-07; Asn Prof Commun Consults, 2002-07; hon mem, Hon Socs Phi Kappa Phi, 2003-; hon mem, Golden Key Int Honour Socs, 2004-; hon mem, Beta Gamma Sigma, 2005-; Int Acad Bus Commun; Asn Prof Commun Consult; Nat Asn African Am Studies; Asn Bus Commun; Int Asn Bus Commun. **Business Addr:** Associate Professor, Business Communication Coordinator, San Jose State University, Bus Tower Rm 763, San Jose, CA 95192, **Business Phone:** (408)924-3530.

**EASTER, RUFUS BENJAMIN, JR.**
School administrator, executive director, technician. **Personal:** Born Oct 5, 1928, Hampton, VA; married Evelyn Wills. **Educ:** NY Univ, Hampton Inst; Temple Univ; Piano Tech Schs. **Career:** Hampton Univ, admin, 1950, Music Dept, instr, Auxiliary Enterprises, dir, Sch Lib Arts Educ, Dept Music, piano technician, currently; Va State Sch Deaf & Blind, curric developer, consult to supt, 1954; Hampton Asn Arts & Humanities, founder & exec dir, 1967; WVEC, consult community affairs radio & TV stas, 1970; Whittaker Mem Hosp, vet; Newport News Gen Hosp, vet. **Orgs:** Bd dirs, Asn Col & Univ Concert Managers; Peninsula Symphony Orchestra; Peninsula Community Theatre; Asn Coun Arts; Asn State & Local Hist; Asn Preserv Va Antiq; Bachelor Benedict Club; Eastern State Hosps Human Rights Comt & Hosp Adv Bd; Hampton-Newport News Community Serv Adv Bd; pres, Nat Alliance Ment Ill; chmn, Insight Enterprises Peninsula Ctr Independent Living. **Honors/Awds:** Man of the Year Award, Peninsula Vol Serv Bur, 1969. **Home Addr:** 1036 Mary Peake Blvd, Hampton, VA 23666-4548, **Home Phone:** (757)827-2794. **Business Addr:** Piano Technician, Hampton University, Dept Music Sch Lib Arts Educ, Hampton, VA 23668, **Business Phone:** (757)728-6508.

**EASTER, WILFRED OTIS, JR. (FRED EASTER)**
School administrator. **Personal:** Born May 26, 1941, New York, NY; son of Wilfred Otis Sr and Mae Smith; married Mary Moore; children: Allison Garner & Mallory; married Donna Maxey. **Educ:** Harvard Col, Cambridge, BA, hist, 1964; Univ Minn, Minneapolis, attended 1979. **Career:** Sports Illus Mag, New York, NY, advert prom, 1964-66; Windsor Mountain Sch, Lenox, Mass, teacher & coach, 1966-68; Carleton Col, Northfield, MN, assoc dean studs, 1968-76; Control Data Corp, Minneapolis, MN, opers prog mgr, 1979-86; Univ Calif, Berkeley, Calif, exec dir, 1986-; Mathematics, Engineering, Sci, Achievement prog(MESA), dir. **Orgs:** Nat Asn PreCol dir, 1986-; Nat Asn Minority Eng Prog Adminrs, 1986-; Northern Calif Coun Black Prof Engrs, 1986-; E Bay GO Club, 1986-; World Wildlife Fund, 1987-. **Home Addr:** 266 Adams St, Oakland, CA 94610, **Home Phone:** (510)444-1623. **Business Addr:** Executive Director, University California Berkeley, Lawrence Hall Sci, Berkeley, CA 94720, **Business Phone:** (510)642-5064.

**EASTMOND, ARLINGTON LEON, JR.**
President (organization). **Personal:** son of Arlington Leon Sr. **Career:** A L Eastmond & Sons Inc, chief exec officer; Easco Boiler Corp, chief exec officer, 1970-, pres & owner, 1981. **Orgs:** Nat Asn Advan Colored People; Urban League; Am Boiler Manufacturers Asn; Oil Heat Asn; Minority Students Bus Club. **Honors/Awds:** Ernest & Young, Minority Regional Manufacturer of the Year, 1977; MBDA, Minority Manufacturer of the Year, 1996; NYS Governor's Award, 1995; Star Lite, Little League Award. **Special Achievements:** Company is ranked 77 on Black Enterprise magazine's list of top 100industrial service companies; Nation's only African-American manufacturer of boilers and steel storage tanks. **Business Addr:** Owner, EASCO Boiler Corp, 1175 Legett Ave, Bronx, NY 10474, **Business Phone:** (718)378-3000.

**EASTMOND, JOAN MARCELLA**
Educator, president (organization). **Personal:** Born May 10, 1940, Brooklyn, NY; daughter of Evans E and Lerta Taylor; children: Brian S Malone. **Educ:** W Va State Col, BS, home econ, 1963; Cornell Univ, summer instr Afro Am Studies, cert, 1969; Lincoln Univ, master, human serv, 1988; Union Experimental Cols/Univ, PhD, 1988. **Career:** NY City Bd Educ, teacher, 1963-70; State Educ Opportunity Ctr, instr; Afram Asn, asst to pres, 1971-78; Bed ford Study Restoration Corp, dir youth employment, 1978-85; Ft Green Sr Citizens Ctr, dir youth workers, srctr, 1985-; Lincoln Univ, adj prof, field study coord, 1988-. **Orgs:** Pres, Soc Unlimited, 1964-; chmn, Cotilion Found Comm; Nat Asn Bus Prof Women's Clubs, 1980-; Fund Raising Comt, NY Coun United Negro Col Fund, 1980-84; chmn, Teens Found Comm, Jack & Jill Am, 1983-88; bd mem, Afram Assoc, 1987-, Health Watch, 1988-. **Home Addr:** 342 Macon St, Brooklyn, NY 11233-1008, **Home Phone:** (718)455-1577. **Business Addr:** Director, Ft Greene Sr Citizens Ctr, 966 Fulton St, Brooklyn, NY 11238, **Business Phone:** (718)638-6910.

**EASTON, EARNEST LEE**
School administrator. **Personal:** Born May 1, 1943, South Bend, IN; son of Booker Talifero and Mahalie Marie Johnson. **Educ:** Chicago

City Col, AA, 1968; Univ Ill, Chicago, BA, polit sci, gen, 1970; Syracuse Univ, Maxwell Sch Citizenship & Affairs, MPA, 1971; Cornell Univ, MA, am polit, 1975, PhD, am polit, 1978. **Career:** Vietnam Era Veteran, 1963-66; Code of Conduct Hon Veteran, 1963; Cornell Univ, Dept Govt, teaching asst, 1973-76, judicial admin, CT, 1976, prof philos, 1996-97; Entertainment related employ, 1978-; Veteran Affairs, lobbyist, 1983-; independent scholar, 1983-; writer, 1983-; cand, Us pres, 1996, 2000, 2004; Univ Pres Positions, presidency caliber cand, 1999; Foreign policy & licensing, consult; Countries World, regist consult, 1999. **Orgs:** Creative Living Ctr; Writer's Guild, Los Angeles, 1983-; Bd UN Asn Am, Los Angeles, 1983, S Bend, Ind, 1993; Songwriters Guild, 1985; Artist Embassy; Am Polit Sci Asn, 2007-. **Home Addr:** 407 Lincoln Way W, PO Box 533, South Bend, IN 46601, **Home Phone:** (219)239-3185. **Business Addr:** Writer, 407 Lincoln Way W, South Bend, IN 46601, **Business Phone:** (219)239-3185.

## EATMAN, JOSEPH W.

Executive. **Career:** Corp Off Syst Inc, pres; Workplace Solutions, owner, dealer prin, chief exec officer, 2002-; Off Concepts Inc, prin & pres. **Special Achievements:** Named Detroits Most Influential African American Leaders by Corp Magazine. **Business Addr:** Dealer Principal, Owner, Workplace Solutions, 30800 Telegraph Rd Suite 2985, Bingham Farms, MI 48025, **Business Phone:** (248)430-2500.

## EATMAN, DR. TIMOTHY K.

Social scientist. **Personal:** Born Dec 28, 1968, New York, NY; son of Charles and Lorraine; married Janet Quinones; children: Jasmin Africali & Jamila Grace. **Educ:** Pace Univ, BS, early childhood develop, 1991; Howard Univ, MEd, col stud develop, 1993; Univ Ill, Urbana-Champaign, PhD, educ policy studies, 2001. **Career:** Univ Ill, Comt Inst Coop, prog coordr, 1997-2000, proj coordr & researcher, 2000-; Univ Mich, Ctr Study Higher & Postsecondary Educ, postdoctoral scholar, 2001-; Imagining Am: Artists & Scholars Pub Life, proj dir res & policy, currently; Syracuse Univ, assoc prof higher educ & fac co-dir Imagining Am, currently. **Orgs:** Alpha Phi Alpha, 1987-; bd dir, Mt Pleasant Christian Asn, 1992-; Am Ed Res Asn, 1993-; Phi Delta Kappa, 1994-; Bros Acad, Leadership Team, 2000-; budget dir, Bros Acad Res Inst. **Home Addr:** 8 Jamar Dr, Fayetteville, NY 13066, **Home Phone:** (315)299-3396. **Business Addr:** Professor, Faculty Co-Director, Syracuse University, 203 Tolley Bldg, Syracuse, NY 13244, **Business Phone:** (315)443-8590.

## EATMAN-WILLIAMS, JANICE A.

Manager, counselor, association executive. **Personal:** Born Mar 3, 1959, Cleveland, OH. **Educ:** Northwestern Univ, BS, commun, 1981; Cleveland State Univ, Post Grad Work, 1986; Case Western Res Univ, MNO, 2001. **Career:** Welfare Rights Org, community rel specialist, 1984; Ohio Works, recruiter, 1985; Voc Guid Servs, employ & training specialist, 1985-88; Case Western Res Univ, intervention asst, 1987-90, asst dir & dir, 2014-; HE Davis Intermediate Sch, coordr youth resource ctr, 1989-96, prog coordr Proj, STEP-UP, 1996-98, asst dir Edu Serv Learning Progs, 1998, Ctr Civic Engagement & Learning, asst dir & dir proj, currently; Focus Group Sch, dir, Currently. **Orgs:** Northwestern Alumni Assoc Cleveland Chap, 1981-; pub rels consult, Group Dynamics Inc, 1982-83; vol, UNCF, 1983-; Messengers Joy Gospel Ensemble, 1984-86; planning comm, Martin Luther King Jr Day Celebration, 1984-85; Urban League Greater Cleveland Fund Develop Comm, 1984-85; grad adv, Alpha Kappa Alpha Sor Inc, 1985-88; publicity co-chair, Ways & Mean Comm AKA Prog Yrs, 1985, 1986; Northwestern Black Alumni Assoc, 1986; presenter, Carver Connection Adopt-A-Sch Prog, 1987-88; presenter, Career Days Cleveland Pub Sch, 1987-88; League Pk Ctr Bd Mgrs, 1995-98, 2000-, treas, 2001; trainer, Tutoring & Mentoring Progs, 1996-; adv, Black Greek, Case W Res Univ, 2000-. **Honors/Awds:** Vol Serv Award, HARAMBEE Serv Black Families, 1983; Vol Award, Cleveland Pub Sch, Carver Connection Adopt-A-Sch, 1988; Workshop presenter, Pittsburgh Civic Garden Ctr, 1988. **Home Addr:** 17802 E Pk Dr, Cleveland, OH 44119-2012, **Home Phone:** (216)481-7806. **Business Addr:** Assistant Director, Director of Project, Case Western Reserve University, 11038 Bellflower Rd, Cleveland, OH 44106-7083, **Business Phone:** (216)368-6960.

## EATON, THELMA LUCILE

Educator, elementary school teacher, college teacher. **Personal:** Born Dec 17, 1928, New Orleans, LA; daughter of T R W Harris and Inez Porter; married William; children: Maurice & Allison. **Educ:** Fisk Univ, BA, 1949; Xavier Univ, attended 1951; NY Univ, attended 1952; Univ Southern Calif, MSW, 1965, DSW, 1973. **Career:** Univ Southern Calif, Mini-Col, Admin Off Soc Work Prog; Dept Social Serv, staff develop officer training & supv; Suicide Prevent Ctr, psychiat soc worker; Orleans Parish Sch Bd, teacher nursery sch & elem sch; Whittier Col, chair dept sociol, anthrop & social work, prof, 1970-94, prof emer, currently; Calif State Sen Teresa Hughes Off, chief staff. **Orgs:** Am Asn Univ Prof; State Leason Comn Human Serv; Nat Asn Soc Work; Geront Soc; Soc Stud Social Prob; Coun Social Work Educ; Nat Coun Negro Women; adv bd, Rio Hondo United Way; Univ Southern Calif, Geront Ctr Serv Black Aged; Nat Caucus Black Aged; Greater LA Community Action Agency; bd dir, Young Women Christian Asn; Foster Grandparent Prog; Retired Sr Vol Prog; Rio Hondo Vol Ctr; pres, Awar Women Calif; Calif Demo State Ctr Comn, LA County Cent Comn; Alpha Kappa Delta Sorority; Alzheimer's Dis Educ Adv Comt; bd dir, Southwest Community Col Found; Calif Stud Aid Comn; Calif State Comn; dir, Nat Coalition 100 Black Women. **Honors/Awds:** Outstanding Educator of America, 1974; Notable American Award, 1976-77; Key to Whittier College, 1976; Outstanding Women of the Year, Success Ltd Gov Calif; Community Service Award, Assembly Black Women's Lawyers. **Home Addr:** 1644 Wellington Rd, Los Angeles, CA 90019-5940, **Home Phone:** (323)735-2244. **Business Addr:** Professor Emeritus, Whittier College, 13406 Philadelphia St, Whittier, CA 90608-0634, **Business Phone:** (562)907-4200.

## EAVES, DR. JOHN H.

College administrator, county government official, consultant. **Personal:** Born Jacksonville, FL; married Lisa; children: Isaac, Kyle & Keturah; married Cheryl Regina. **Educ:** Morehouse Col, BS, math, 1984; Yale Univ, MS, relig, 1987; Univ SC, PhD, educ admin, 1999. **Career:** Southern Educ Found, prog officer; Kennesaw State Univ, GA, asst prof educ leadership; Nat Centre Comput Animation Vols Youth Prog, nat dir; Johnson C Smith Univ, Charlotte, NC, adj instr; Davidson Col, asst dean; Clayton State Univ, Morrow, GA, asst dean; US Peace Corps, reg mgr, 1999-2006; First Tabernacle, assoc minister; Ger Marshall Fund, Am Marshall Memorial fel, 2001; Fulton County Comn, GA, Dist 1, chmn, 2007-; Argosy Univ, Higher Educ Prog, dir & asst prof educ, currently; TalentQuest, exec consult, 2011-; Post Col Conn & Davidson Col, Nc, adminr. **Orgs:** Chmn, Atlanta Sister Cities Comn; Atlanta Coun Int Rels; vis prof, Nat Urban League Black Exec Exchange Prog; chmn, Fulton County Comn; Am Marshall Memorial Fel Recipient; Fulbright Sr Specialist Grant Recipient; City Atlantas Adv Comt; fel, Am Marshall Plan Memorial; nat dir, Nat Col Athletic Asn; southeast regional dir, Peace Corps; Fulton County Econ Develop Div; Fulton County Youth Comn; champion, Grady Hosp Syst; Fulton County's groundbreaking SMART Justice Adv Coun. **Home Addr:** 1371 Cascade Falls Dr SW, Atlanta, GA 30311, **Home Phone:** (404)696-0191. **Business Addr:** Chairman, Fulton County Government, 141 Pryor St, Atlanta, GA 30303, **Business Phone:** (404)730-8206.

## EBANKS, MICHELLE

Chief executive officer, president (organization), periodical publisher. **Personal:** Born Dayton, OH. **Educ:** Univ Fla, BA, finance. **Career:** Knapp Commun; Conde Nast, corp bus mgr; Time Inc, financial dir, gen mgr, vpres corp div; Inst Economet Res, pres & chief exec officer; People en Espanol, pres; Essence Commun Inc, group publ, pres, 2001-. **Orgs:** Bd dir, mem finance comt & mem technol comt, Nordstrom Inc, 2011-; bd dir, YMCA's Arts & Lett Comt; Exec Leadership Coun. **Business Addr:** President, ESSENCE Communications Inc, 135 W 50th St 4th Fl, New York, NY 10020, **Business Phone:** (212)522-1212.

## EBBE, DR. OBI N. I.

Educator. **Personal:** Born Jul 8, 1949, Umuobom; son of Virginia Uduola and Ebbe Muoneke Ilonuma; children: Nneka I & Njideka J. **Educ:** Univ London, London, UK, GCE, A & level, 1967; Western Mich Univ, Kalamazoo, MI, BA, 1976, MA, sociol, 1977; Southern Ill Univ, Carbondale, IL, PhD, sociol, 1981. **Career:** Western Ill Univ, Macomb, Ill, asst prof, 1981; Univ Tenn, Chattanooga, TN, asst prof, 1981-82, prof, currently; Ohio Northern Univ, Ada, Ohio, asst prof, 1982-84; Valparaiso Univ Sch Law, Valparaiso, Ind, fel, 1984-85; Delta State Univ, Cleveland, Miss, assoc prof, 1985-87; State Univ NY, Brockport, NY, prof, 1987-2000;, Anthrop & Geog, Univ Tenn, Chattanooga, head, Dept Sociol, anthrop & geog, 2000-04, prof, 2004-. **Orgs:** Alpha Kappa Delta, Nat Sociol Hon Soc, 1975; Acad Criminal Justice Sci, 1981-; Am Soc Criminol, 1981-; Int Asn Organized Crime, 1985-; Acad Security Educr & Trainers, 1990-; Am Soc Indust Security, 1990-. **Home Addr:** 9015 Potomac Dr, Chattanooga, TN 37421, **Home Phone:** (423)503-3943. **Business Addr:** Professor, University of Tennesse, 306A Brock Hall Dept 2102 615 McCallie Ave, Chattanooga, TN 37403, **Business Phone:** (423)425-4411.

## EBO, ANTONA (ELIZABETH LOUISE EBO)

Clergy. **Personal:** Born Apr 10, 1924, Bloomington, IL; daughter of Daniel and Louise Teal (deceased). **Educ:** St Louis Univ, St Louis MO, BS, med rec admin, 1962, MHA Hosp Exec Develop, 1970; Aquinas Inst Theol, Dubuque, MA, MTh Health Care Ministry, 1978. **Career:** Franciscan Sister Mary, 1946-; St Clare Hosp, Baraboo, Wis, exec dir, 1967-71; St Marys Hosp Med Ctr, Madison, Wis, asst exec dir, 1970-74, chaplain, 1978-81; Wis Cath Health Asn, Madison, Wis, exec dir, 1974-76; St Marys Hosp Med Ctr, chaplain, 1978-81; Univ Miss Med Ctr, Jackson, Miss, chaplain, 1981-87; Franciscan Sisters Mary, St Louis Mo, counor, 1987-91; St Nicholas Church, pastoral assoc, 1992-; St Clare Hosp & Health Serv, adminr. **Orgs:** First group sisters partic March Selma, St Louis Archdiocese, 1965; St Louis Archdiocesan Human Rights Comn, 1965-67, 1989-99; Nat Black Sisters' Conf, 1968-, pres, 1979-81, secy, 1997-2001; vice chmn, Madison Urban League Bd dir, 1972-76; comnr, Madison Housing Authority, 1974-76; vice chmn, Wis Health Facil Authority, 1976; Nat Asn Cath Chaplains, 1979-; Comn Cath Health Care Ministry, 1987-88; Leadership Conf Women Relig, 1987-91; bd dir, SSM Health Care Syst, 1987-91; Leadership Conf Women Relig Task Force Women's Concerns, 1989-90; planning comt, St Louis Archdiocesan Nat Black Cath Cong, 1988-; bd dir, 1991-2002, exec comn, secy, 1997-2002, Cardinal Ritter Inst; St Louis Archdiocesan Human Rights Comn, 1991-99; pres, Nat Black Sisters Conf; Miss Cath Conf Soc Concerns Dept, 1991-94; Archbishop's Pastoral Coun, St Louis Archdiocese, 2003-; Franciscan Sisters Mary. **Honors/Awds:** Certificate of Commendation, Madison Urban League, Madison WI, 1976; Certificate of Commendation, Governor Patrick Lucey, Wis Health Facilities Authority, 1976; Delegate, Nat Black Catholic Congress, Jackson Diocese, St Louis Archdiocese, St Louis Archdiocesan Human Rights Comm, 1994; 1987, 1992, 1997, 2002; Harriet Tubman Award, Nat Black Sisters' Conf, 1989; Martin Luther King Jr Award, St Louis Archdiocese Human Rights Comn, 1994; Honorary Doctorate of Humane Letters, Loyola Univ, 1995; Living Legend Award, Nat Voting Rights Mus, 2000; Martin Luther King Jr Award, 2002; Distinguished Humanitarian, State Celebration Comn MO, 2002; Distinguished Citizen, 2005, St Louis Argus; Spiritual Leadership Award, Xavier Univ Inst Black Catholic Studies, 2005; Rabbi Heschel & Rev Martin Luther King Jr Award, Jews United Justice, 2005. **Special Achievements:** First black woman religious to head a hospital, when she took the helm at St Clare Hospital in Baraboo, WI, 1968; Her experience from the March from Selma to Montgomery in 1965 is included in the Library of Congress Exhibition "Voices of Civil Rights" and she is featured in the PBS documentary "Sisters of Selma Bearing Witness for Change". **Home Addr:** 8053 Hafner Ct, St Louis, MO 63130-1533, **Home Phone:** (314)567-0628. **Business Addr:** Pastoral Associate, St Nicholas Roman Catholic Church, 701 N 18th St, St Louis, MO 63103, **Business Phone:** (314)231-2860.

## EBONG, REGINA U.

Accountant. **Personal:** Born Dec 9, 1953, Jos, PL; daughter of Janet Chinweze and Francis Chinweze; married Ben; children: Nne, Ben, Victor & Francis. **Educ:** Univ Nebr, Omaha, NE, BS, acct, 1981, CPA cert, 1981, MBA, 1983. **Career:** Enron Corp, sr EDP auditor, 1981-86; cert pub acct, 1986-; Hayes & Assoc LLC, assoc, 1986-88; Regina Ebong CPA, managing owner & dir, 1988-2004; intensive leadership training prog, Omaha Chamber Com, Class13, 1991; Inter Securities Inc, investment adv rep; Chapkis & Mitchell, cert pub acct, 2004-06; Solomon Ross Grey & co, mgr, 2006-07; Kellogg & Andelson, vpres, 2007-10; Regina Chinweze Accountancy Corp, founder & pres, 2010-. **Orgs:** Cert Info Systs Auditor, 1982; Am Inst Cert Pub Accountants, 1983-; Nebr Soc Cert Pub Accountants; Inst Int Auditors, 1985-; vice chmn, Girls Inc, finance comn, 1988-90; State & Local Govt Acct comn, 1989-; bd mem, Voices C, 1992-; Calif Soc Cert Pub Accountants. **Honors/Awds:** Leadership Omaha, Omaha Chamber Com, 1991. **Home Addr:** 804 S 131 Ave, Omaha, NE 68154, **Home Phone:** (402)333-2549. **Business Addr:** President, Founder, Regina Chinweze Accountancy Corp, 11601 Willshire Blvd Suite 504, Los Angeles, CA 90025, **Business Phone:** (310)575-4875.

## ECHOLS, ALVIN E., JR.

Lawyer, executive director. **Personal:** Born Dec 5, 1930, Philadelphia, PA; son of Alvin and Rhydine; married Gwendolyn G; children: Donna G Kearse & Alison D. **Educ:** Va Union Univ, BS, 1955; Howard Univ, LLB, 1957. **Career:** Pvt law pract, 1957-63; N City Cong, exec dir, 1963-, mgr. **Orgs:** Comn Leadership Sem Prog, 1962; comnr, Human Rel Community, 1969; dept chmn, State Republican Party, 1971-75; Pa chap, Nat Coun Crime & Delinquency, 1971-75; Friends Free Libr, 1972-75; Health & Welfare Coun, 1974. **Honors/Awds:** Achievement Award Industrialization Center, 1966; Distinguished Merit Citation, Nat Conf Christian & Jews, 1967; Certificate of Appreciation, Personnel Dept, Philadelphia Med Col, Pa, 1972-; Greater Philadelphia Partnership, 1974; Philadelphia Asn Community Develop Corp. **Home Addr:** 1429 Dondill Pl, Philadelphia, PA 19122, **Home Phone:** (215)763-2346. **Business Addr:** Executive Director, North City Congress, 1438 N Broad St, Philadelphia, PA 19121-4326, **Business Phone:** (215)978-1300.

## ECHOLS, DORIS BROWN

Educator, accountant, teacher. **Personal:** Born Oct 8, 1928, Oakwood, TX; daughter of William P Brown and Tinnie Viola Davis; married James Jerome; children: Jennifer Diane. **Educ:** Hughes Bus Col, bus cert, 1947; Tex Southern Univ, BA, psychol, 1954; Berkeley Police Dept Acad, attended 1998. **Career:** Educator (retired); Hughes Bus Col, teacher, 1948; Berkeley Unified Sch Dist, teacher, 1965-84; World Savings & Loans, acct specialist auditor, 1984, teacher, 1995-98. **Orgs:** Vol asst, Sr Citizen Ctr, 1985-; nominating comt mem, Nat Asn Advan Colored People, Berkeley, 1985-; tutor & planning comm, Adult Lit Prog, Oakland, 1986-; vol, How Berkeley Can You Be Parade, 1997, 1998; choir mem, treas, class leader, Downs United Methodist Church; bd dir, World Savings & Loans. **Home Addr:** 1514 Lincoln St, Berkeley, CA 94703-1222, **Home Phone:** (510)849-1358.

## ECHOLS, JAMES ALBERT

Marketing executive, public relations executive, military pilot. **Personal:** Born Sep 14, 1950, Memphis, TN; son of Joseph Jr and Vellar C McCraven; married Dorothy Mae Mithcell; children: Justin Fitzgerald. **Educ:** Cent State Univ, BA, 1981. **Career:** AUS, sr race rels instr, 1976-77; Res Life Ins Co, ins agt, 1977-78; Nigh Gov Campaign, admin asst minority affairs, 1978; Off Gov, state affirmative action off, staff, 1979-; E & C Trades LTD, pres & chmn bd, 1980; USAR, career counr, 1986-; Hon Enterprises Inc, chmn bd. **Orgs:** Urban League OK City, 1977; Nat Asn Advan Colored People, 1978; vpres, OK Human Rels Asn, 1978; Veterans Foreign Wars; Econ Develop Task Force, OK City Urban League. **Honors/Awds:** Member for excellent scholarship, Phi Eta Sigma, 1978. **Home Addr:** 420 Wildewood Terr, Oklahoma City, OK 73105, **Home Phone:** (913)371-2454. **Business Addr:** Chairman, Honor Enterprises Inc, 2405 NW 39th Expy Suite 200-C, Oklahoma City, OK 73112, **Business Phone:** (405)524-8580.

## ECHOLS, MARY ANN

School administrator. **Personal:** Born Jan 17, 1950, Youngstown, OH; daughter of Otis A Snipes (deceased) and Mable Ross Snipes; married Robert L; children: Robert Jr, Cheri, Michael K & Anthony A. **Educ:** Youngstown State Univ, Youngstown, OH, BA, sociol, 1972, MS, educ, 1977; Kent State Univ, Kent, OH, PhD, couns psychol, 2000. **Career:** Youngstown Metrop Housing Authority, Youngstown, Ohio, leasing aide, 1973; Youngstown Area Urban League, Youngstown, Ohio, dir educ & employ, 1973-76; Northeastern Ohio Employ & Training Consortium, Youngstown, Ohio, personnel, equal employ opportunity officer, 1977-80; Youngstown State Univ, Youngstown, Ohio, asst minority stud serv, 1980-84, dir spec stud serv, currently. **Orgs:** Exec comt mem, chair review comt, Youngstown Area United Way; vpres, Associated Neighborhood Ctrs, 1984-89; bd dir, Help Hot line, 1977-80; bias review panel mem, Ohio State Dept Educ; cultural pluralism task force mem, Lake River Girl Scout Coun, 1983-85; bd dir, Burdman Group. **Home Addr:** 1350 5th Ave, Youngstown, OH 44504, **Home Phone:** (330)744-1027. **Business Addr:** Director, Youngstown State University, 410 Wick Ave Kilcawley Ctr, Youngstown, OH 44555, **Business Phone:** (216)742-3538.

## ECKSTINE, ED

Actor, executive. **Personal:** son of Billy. **Educ:** Boston Univ, Boston, MA, music & jour, 1972; Univ Southern Calif, Los Angeles, Calif, attended 1973. **Career:** Actor; Quincy Jones Productions, exec vpres & gen mgr, 1973-84; Arista Rec, vpres, artist & repertoire, 1985-86; Mercury/Wing/PolyGram Rec, pres, 1986-98; FTMB Develop, pres, 2000-10; Eckstine Career Consult, pres, 2005-; Album: "Skin Deep", 1989; TV series: "E! True Hollywood Story", 2007. **Business Addr:** President, Eckstine Career Consultation, Los Angeles, CA 90001.

## ECTON, VIRGIL E.

Association executive, administrator. **Personal:** Born Jul 7, 1940, Paris, KY; married Harriette Morgan; children: Virgil, Brian Keith & Blair Christina. **Educ:** Ind Univ, BS, educ, 1962; Xavier Univ, MEd, 1966; Harvard Univ, advan mgt prog, 1989. **Career:** Ohio Civil Rights Comn, asst dir educ & community rels, 1968-70; United Negro Col Fund Inc, area develop dir, 1970-75, eatern reg supvr, 1975-76, dep nat campaign dir, 1976-77, nat campaign dir, 1977-79, dep exec dir fund-raising, 1979-82, exec vpres & chief oper officer, 1982-90, actg pres & chief exec officer, 1990-91, sr exec vpres & chief oper officer,

1991-; sr exec vpres Develop; Howard Univ, vpres, 2001-09; Tuskegee Univ, vpres fed affairs & dir capitl campaign, 2011-. **Orgs:** Bd mem, Nat Soc Fund-raising Exec Found; founding mem, Nat Philanthropy Day Steering Comt; exec bd & vpres, Boy Scouts Am, Bergen Coun; bd mem, Community Access; adv bd mem, Int Parenting Asn; adv bd mem, Bede Sch; trustee, Dwight Englewood Sch; chair, Howard Univ Alumni Bd; exec vpres, Nat Asn Advan Colored People, currently; vice chair, Asn Fundraising Professionals; Community Access Inc; Outward Bound; Japan Soc; Sigma Pi Phi; Langley Sch; Dwight Englewood Sch. **Home Addr:** 10316 Hickory Forest Lane, Oakton, VA 22124, **Home Phone:** (703)319-1134. **Business Addr:** Vice President, Tuskegee University, 1200 W Montgomery Rd, Tuskegee, AL 36088, **Business Phone:** (334)727-8011.

## EDDINGS, JOHN R.

Government official. **Personal:** Born Feb 23, 1943, Corinth, MS; son of Rufus L and Malgline J; married Patricia J; children: Carla J. **Educ:** Univ Hampton, BS, 1965; Wayne State Univ, attended 1976. **Career:** Daimler Chrysler Corp, personnel rep, 1972-74; Detroit Pub Sch, substitute teacher, 1974-75; City Detroit, transp personnel officer, 1975-80, recreatoin personnel officer, 1980-82, Civic Ctr, dep dir, 1982-93, dep dir, human resources, 1993-94, city ombudsman, 1995-2004; Macomb County, ombudsman, 2005-06; Detroit City Charter Comn, cand, 2009. **Orgs:** Int Ombudsman Inst; pres, US Asn, 1999-2001; bd dir, US Ombudsman Asn; Nat Forum Black Pub Adminr; Soc Human Res Mgt; Am Soc Pub Adminr; Nat Hampton alumni Asn Inc; Nat Asn Advan Colored People; adv bd, TOFM Head start. **Home Addr:** 20535 Rutherford St, Detroit, MI 48235-2163, **Home Phone:** (313)836-4944. **Business Addr:** MI.

## EDDY, DR. EDWARD A.

Executive, educator. **Personal:** Born Feb 27, 1938, Kansas City, KS; married Joyce B Carter; children: Darrell, Duane & Aaron. **Educ:** Pittsburg State Univ, BS, 1962; Univ Kans, MA, theatre lit, hist & criticism, 1966; Kans State Univ, PhD, educ leadership & admin gen, 1982. **Career:** Educator (retired), instructor; Pub Schs KCK, instr, 1962-69; Univ KS, instr, 1969-73; Univ Kans, instr african am studies, 1970-73; Rockhurst, dir specprog, 1973-77; Rockhurst Univ, dean stud serv, 1977-84; Chicago State Univ, dean; Chevy Chase Nursing Ctr, adminr; N Pk Univ, dean students, 1994-98; Aurora Univ, diversity affairs dir, assoc prof masters educ progs, 1997-2003, assoc prof, educ dept, 2001-03; online instr, 2003-13; Mid-Am Christian Univ, adj instr, 2013-. **Orgs:** OE regl steering comt, TRIO Prog, 1973-75; field reader, OE Title III, Proposals, 1982-83; consult educ, MLK Jr Hosp KCMO, 1975-77; chair steering comt, Nat Asn Stud Personnel Adminr, 1977-84; Aacd mem, Am Asn Coun Dir, 1985; Nat youth conv staff Church God, 1985; guestsoloist, Oper PUSH Chicago, 1985; Higher Educ Comn Col, 1986-88. **Honors/Awds:** Founder & dir, Black Ethos Performing Arts Troupe, 1971; Key to City Kans City, KS, 1984. **Home Addr:** 730 Violet Lane, Matteson, IL 60443. **Business Addr:** Adjunct Instructor, Mid-America Christian University, 3500 SW 119th St, Oklahoma City, OK 73170, **Business Phone:** (405)691-3800.

## EDELER, PHYLLIS

Executive. **Personal:** Born Gary, IN. **Educ:** N Cent Col, BA; Loyola Univ Chicago, MS, indust rels. **Career:** Disability Servs Southwest, state dir human resources, 1998-99; Tree Life/Gourmet Award Foods, region vpres human resources, 1999-2004; RH Edelen Assoc, owner, 2005-; Tandy Brands Accessories Inc, vpres human resources, 2007. **Orgs:** Soc Human Resources Mgmt; Dallas Human Resources Mgmt Asn; Nat Asn African Am Human Resources; adv bd, Dallas Chap, Nat Asn African Am Human Resources; trustee, bd mem, Wheatland Community Learning Ctr; Bd Adjust City Duncanville. **Home Addr:** 809 Whitney St, Cedar Hill, TX 75104, **Home Phone:** (972)291-0976. **Business Addr:** Owner, R. H. Edelen Associates, 1130 Dula Cir, Duncanville, TX 75116-2104, **Business Phone:** (972)709-6189.

## EDELMAN, MARIAN WRIGHT

Educator, lawyer, president (organization). **Personal:** Born Jun 6, 1939, Bennettsville, SC; daughter of Arthur J Wright (deceased) and Maggie Bowen Wright; married Peter; children: Joshua, Jonah & Ezra. **Educ:** Univ Geneva, Switz, 1959; Spelman Col, BA, 1960; Yale Law Sch, LLB, 1963. **Career:** Lawyer, educator, activist, reformer, c's advocate & adminr; NAACP Legal Defense & Educ Fund, staff atty, 1963-64, dir 1964-68; Wash Res Proj Southern Ctr Pub Policy, founder, partner, 1968-73; Ctr Law & Educ Harvard Univ, dir 1971-73; Books: Families Peril: An Agenda Social Chg, auth, 1987; Measure Our Success: A Lett to My C & Yours, auth, 1992; Guide My Feet: Prayers & Meditations Loving & Working C, auth, 1995; I'm Your Child, God: Prayers C & Teenagers, auth, 2002. **Orgs:** Lisle fel, Soviet Union; DC, MS, Commonwealth Asns; bd trustee King Ctr; adv coun M L King Memorial Libr; Coun Foreign Rels; Aetna Life & Casualty Found; Yale Univ Corp; chair, bd trustee Spelman Col; bd dir March Dimes; bd mem, Ctr Budget & Policy Priorities; bd mem, Citizens Const Concerns; bd mem, Joint Ctr Polit & Econ Studies; bd mem, Nat Asn Advan Colored People Legal Defense & Educ Fund Inc; bd mem, US Comt UNICEF; bd mem, Robin Hood Found; bd mem, Aaron Diamond Found; Howard Univ Comn; Nat Comn C; founder & pres, prin spokesperson, C's Defense Fund, 1973-; Rathbun Vis Fel Stanford Univ, 2011; Poor People's Campaign Martin Luther King Jr; Southern Christian Leadership Conf. **Special Achievements:** First African-American woman to pass the bar exam in Mississippi. **Business Addr:** Founder, President, Children's Defense Fund, 25 E St NW, Washington, DC 20001, **Business Phone:** (202)628-8787.

## EDGAR, JACQUELINE L. (JACKIE L EDGAR)

Automotive executive. **Personal:** Born Nov 27, 1948, Lafayette, LA; daughter of Antoine LeBlanc (deceased) and Effie Matthews; married Allen L Sr; children: Rachael Marie, Allen L Jr & Lawrence (deceased). **Educ:** Holy Rosary Inst, attended 1966. **Career:** Auto Mart Linc-Merc, salesperson, 1973-76; J P Thibodeaux Olds, salesperson, 1976-80; Broussard Pontiac, salesperson, 1980-83; Edgar Chevrolet Inc, pres, owner, 1983-87; Edgar Ford Inc, pres. **Orgs:** Performance Inc, 1989-92; treas, Breaux Bridge Chamber Com, 1992; Lafayette Cath Serv Ctr, 1992; Rehabilitaion Ctr Acadiana, 1992; St Jude C Res Hosp Dream Home Comt. **Home Addr:** 103 Blue Ridge, Carencro, LA 70520, **Home Phone:** (337)886-7991. **Business Addr:** President, Jackie Edgar Auto Supercenter, 331 Northwest Blvd, Franklin, LA 70538, **Business Phone:** (337)332-2145.

## EDGERTON, BRENDA EVANS

Executive, financial manager. **Personal:** Born Jun 15, 1949, Halifax, VA; daughter of Elmer Keith and Bernice; married Raymond; children: Lauren & Eric. **Educ:** Pa State Univ, State Col, 1969; Rutgers Univ, NJ, BA, 1970; Temple Univ, Philadelphia, MBA, 1976. **Career:** Scott Paper Co, Philadelphia, PA, mgr money & banking, 1976-84; Campbell Soup Co, Camden, NJ, dir finance, 1984-86, asst treas, 1986-88, dep treas, 1988-89, vpres, treas, 1989-94, vpres bus dev, 1996-98; Frontier Corp, dir, 1993-; US Soup, vpres finance, 1994-96; Finance US Soup, vpres, 1994-96; Global Crossing N Am Inc, bd dir, 1993-; C&S Wholesale Grocers Inc, sr vpres & chief financial officer. **Orgs:** Philadelphia Treas Club, 1985-; Financial Exec Inst, 1989-; Nat Asn Corpe Treas, 1989; YWCA, 1989-. **Home Addr:** 3432 Manor Rd, Huntingdon Valley, PA 19006. **Business Addr:** Vice President, Treasurer, Campbell Soup Co, 1 Campbell Pl Suite 2400, Camden, NJ 08103-1799, **Business Phone:** (856)342-4800.

## EDISON, JOANNE

Business owner. **Career:** Jo's UpClose & Personal Clothing, owner, currently. **Orgs:** Nat Asn Women Bus Owners, Greater Detroit Chap. **Business Addr:** Owner, Jo's UpClose & Personal Clothing, 511 Beaubian St, Detroit, MI 48226, **Business Phone:** (313)895-1516.

## EDLEY, CHRISTOPHER FAIRCHILD, JR.

Educator, government official. **Personal:** Born Jan 13, 1953, Boston, MA; son of Christopher Sr and Zaida Coles; married Tana Pesso; children: Christopher III; married Maria Echaveste; children: Zara & Elias. **Educ:** Swarthmore Col, Swartmore, PA, BA, 1973; Harvard Law Sch, Cambridge, MA, JD, 1978; Harvard Kennedy Sch, Cambridge, MA, MPP, 1978. **Career:** White House Domestic Policy Staff, asst dir, 1978-80; US Govt, Secy Housing, Educ & Welfare, spec asst, 1980; Harvard Law Sch, prof, 1981-04, Civil Rights Proj, co-founder, 1996; Wash Post, part-time ed page staff, 1982-84; Dukakis Pres, nat issues dir, 1987-88; US Off Mgt & Budget, assoc dir econ & govt, 1993-95; Pres US, spec coun, 1995; Harvard Law Rev, ed & officer; Univ Calif, Berkeley, Boalt Hall Sch Law, dean & prof, 2004-, William H. Orrick Jr distinguished chair, currently, Chief Justice Earl Warren Inst Law & Social Policy, dir, currently; Nat Comn Equity & Excellence Educ, co chair, 2011-. **Orgs:** Bd managers, Swarthmore Col, 1980-; bd dir, Am Coun Ger, 1981-84; founding trustee, Working Assets Money Fund, 1982-84; steering comt mem, Boston Lawyers Comt Civil Rights, 1984-87; Comt Policy Racial Justice, 1984-; consult, Joint Ctr Polit Studies, 1988-; bd dir, Ctr Social Welfare Policy & Law, 1989-; Am Bar Asn; Nat Bar Asn; Coun Foreign Rels; exec comt bd, People Am Way; adj scholar, Urban Inst; fel, Nat Acad Pub Admin; bd testing & assessment, Nat Res Coun; fel, Nat Acad Pub Admin; fel, Coun Foreign Rel; fel, Am Acad Arts & Sci; fel, Am Law Inst; adv bd, Obama-Biden Transition Proj; US Civil Rights Comm, 1999-2005; Russell Sage Found, trustee; Century Found, trustee. **Business Addr:** Dean, Professor, University of California-Berkeley, 215 Boalt Hall, Berkeley, CA 94720-7200, **Business Phone:** (510)642-6483.

## EDMOND, ALFRED ADAM, JR.

Editor, journalist, educator. **Personal:** Born Mar 8, 1960, Long Branch, NJ; son of Alfred Adam and Virginia E Monroe; married Topaza L Watkins; children: Monique Marie Brown, Christine Lorraine, David Adam Robeson & Allyson E Watkins. **Educ:** Rutgers Col, Rutgers Univ, Nb, NJ, BA, studio art & econs, 1983; Stanford Univ, cert completion, strategic planning course publ execs, 2005. **Career:** Big Red News, Brooklyn, NY, managing ed, 1984-86; New York Daily Challenge Inc, assoc ed, 1985-86; Mod Black Men Mag, New York, NY, sr ed, 1986-87; Black Enterprise, New York, assoc ed, 1987, sr ed, 1987-89, bus ed, 1989-90, sr ed & admin, 1990-92, managing ed, 1992-95, vpres, exec ed, 1995-2000, sr vpres, ed-in-chief, 2000-10, sr vpres, multimedia ed-in-chief, 2010-14, sr vpres, chief content officer, 2014-15, sr vpres, exec ed-at-large, 2015-; ABC Radio Network, Am Urban Radio Networks, personal finance contribr, 2000-; Nightly Bus Report, Commentator, 2009-12; Rutgers Univ, adj prof; WVON-AM, host urban bus roundtable, 2010-12; A2Z Personal Growth Enterprises, GrownZone.com, co-owner, 2012-, relationship educ proponent & coach, 2015-; Alfred Edmond Jr. Collection Windsor Neckwear, partner, 2012-14. **Orgs:** NY Asn Black Journalists, 1985-; Nat Asn Black Journalists, 1987-; Am Soc Mag Ed, 1988-; bd mem, Rutgers Alumni Fedn, 1990; founding life mem, Rutgers African-Am Alumni Alliance, 1990-; Rutgers Alumni Mag, ed bd mem, 1991-; Soc Am Bus Ed & Writers Inc, 1994-95; life mem, Rutgers Alumni Asn, 1996-; bd mem, Leadership Enterprise Diverse Am. **Honors/Awds:** Unity Award for Excellence in Media, Lincoln Univ, Mo, 1989-90; Recognition of Excellence, Paul Robeson Cult Ctr, Rutgers Univ, 1990; Unity Award for Excellence in Media, 1991, 1992; NYABJ Journalism Award, Bus Reporting Magazines, 1992, 1994; Long Branch High School Alumni, Acad Hall of Fame, 1996; The Nation's 100 Most Influential Business Journalist, TJFR Bus News Reporter, 1998; Chapter Service Award, NY Asn Black Journalists, 2000; RAAA African American Alumni Hall of Fame, Rutgers African-Am Alumni Alliance, 2005; Rutgers University Hall of Distinguished Alumni, Rutgers Univ, 2010; Hiscox Small Business Star, Hiscox Small Bus Ins, 2015; Griot Award, NYABJ. **Home Addr:** 919 Pk Pl Apt 6E, Brooklyn, NY 11213-1808, **Home Phone:** (718)467-7213. **Business Addr:** Senior Vice President, Editor-in-Chief, Earl G Graves Publishing Co Inc, Ed Dept, New York, NY 10011-4355, **Business Phone:** (212)242-8000.

## EDMOND, DR. JANICE L. SUMLER

Educator, lawyer. **Personal:** Born Aug 10, 1948, New York, NY; daughter of Lucille Jones (deceased) and Ernest (deceased). **Educ:** Univ Calif, Los Angeles, BA, 1970, MA, 1971; Georgetown Univ, WA, PhD, 1978; Univ Calif Sch Law, Los Angeles, JD, 1985. **Career:** Spelman Col, Atlanta, Ga, vis prof, 1980-81; Lubic Mem Law Scholar, 1983-84; Reginald Heber Smith Fel, legal aid, 1985-86; Clark Atlanta Univ, Atlanta, Ga, assoc prof, assoc dean, 1986; Mack Haygood, McLean Attorneys, Atlanta, Ga, atty, 1989-95; Pine Lake, Ga, pvt pract; Huston-Tillotson Univ, prof US hist, 2002-. **Orgs:** Nat vice dir, life mem, Asn Black Women Historians, 1986-88 & 1988-90; Ga Asn Black Women Attys, 1987-; recruiter, Georgetown Univ, 1988-; Southern Hist Asn; Asn Study African Am Life & Hist; dir, William Edward Burghardt Du Bois; judicial fel Supreme Ct US; Orgn Am Historians. **Home Addr:** 4192 Kings Troop Rd, Stone Mountain, GA 30083. **Business Addr:** Professor of History, Huston-Tillotson University, 900 Chicon St, Austin, TX 78702-2795, **Business Phone:** (512)505-3000.

## EDMOND, PAUL EDWARD

Manager. **Personal:** Born May 29, 1944, Shreveport, LA; son of Clarence Lee and Juanita Brown Allen; children: Neeve E Samuels, Doran & Oran. **Educ:** Southern Univ, Baton Rouge, La, BS, 1968; Ind Univ, Bloomington, Ind, MS, 1973; Univ Mich, Ann Arbor Mich, 1976. **Career:** State Ind, Ft Wayne, Ind, hosp admin, 1969-71; Lincoln Nat Ins, Ft Wayne, Ind, personnel mgr, 1971-76; Miller Brewing Co, Milwaukee, Wis, corp indust rels mgr, 1976-, affirmative action recruiter. **Orgs:** Am Soc Personnel Asn, 1973-; Indust Rels Mgr Asn, 1979-; Personnel & Labor Rels Asn, 1980-; bd mem, OIC Am, 1986-; chairperson, United Way Allocation Community, 1986-; comn mem, Milwaukee Urban League, Long Range Planning, 1987-; Grambling Univ Accreditation Comn, 1987-; bd mem, Milwaukee Desegregation Community, 1988-; State Wis Educ Coun, 1988-. **Honors/Awds:** Outstanding Young Men, Ft Wayne Jaycees, 1973; Professional Achiever, Nat Career Ctr, 1974; Black Achiever, New York YMCA, 1982; President's Award, Miller Brewing, 1984. **Home Addr:** 3612 N Sherman Blvd, Milwaukee, WI 53216, **Home Phone:** (414)442-2774. **Business Addr:** Manager, Miller Brewing Co, 3939 W Highland Blvd, Milwaukee, WI 53201, **Business Phone:** (414)931-2337.

## EDMONDS, BEVELYN

Writer, educator. **Personal:** Born Feb 17, 1951, Chicago, IL; daughter of Walter D and Ann Clotee Hecek (deceased). **Educ:** Tuskegee Univ, BSN, 1973; Med Col, MSN, 1975; St Xavier, MA, 1990. **Career:** Ill Cent County Hosp, staff, 1979-86; St Xavier Univ, asst prof, 1981-90, grant adolescent study, 1982; Jackson Pk Med Ctr, staff, 1986-95; Health Staff, in-house, 1990-; St Frances Hosp, instr, 1990-94; Doctor's Hosp, educr, 1994-95; Dimensions Int, staff writer, 1995-. Author: "Registered nurses' attitudes toward caring for clients with mentally ill patients with a history of criminal activity", 1989. **Orgs:** Delta Sigma Theta Sorority, 1969-; People United Save Humanity, 1979-; Sigma Theta Tau, 1986-; Asn Black Nursing Fac, 1987-; County Serv Block Club. **Home Addr:** 3316A S Cobb Dr PO Box 322, Smyrna, GA 30080, **Home Phone:** (770)507-9251.

## EDMONDS, BOBBIE GRAY

Lawyer, judge. **Personal:** Born LA. **Educ:** Southern Univ A&M, Baton Rouge, La, BA, interior design; Southern Univ Sch Law, Baton Rouge, LA, JD, 1980. **Career:** McNeese State Univ, Lake Charles, LA, adj prof; Tex Wesleyan Univ, Ft Worth, adj prof; US Supreme Ct, US Fifth Circuit Ct Appeals, atty pract; US Dist Ct Eastern Dist Mich, atty pract; US Dist Ct Northern Dist Tex, atty pract; US Dist Ct Eastern Dist La, atty pract; Southwest La Legal Servs, exec dir & gen coun; Reginald Heber Smith fel, Wash, DC, staff atty, 1980; N La Legal Serv Corp, staff atty; Southwest La Legal Serv Corp, exec dir & gen coun, 1983; Law Offices Bobbie Edmonds, pvt pract atty, 1987-; Tarrant County Civil Serv Comn, hearing officer, 2002-; City Forest Hill, alt munic judge, 2003-; Urban Am Network, talk show host, 2004-06. **Orgs:** Mem & pres, Tarrant County Bar Asn; Tarrant County Family Bar Asn; educ chair comt & lifetime mem, Nat Asn Advan Colored People; Nat Asn Black Journalists. **Honors/Awds:** Lawyer of the Year, Tarrant County Black Bar Asn, 1996; St. John's Baptist Church Pastor's Choice Award, 1996; Justice Award, Arlington Br, Nat Asn Advan Colored People, 1998; Thurgood Marshall Criminal Justice Award, Nat Asn Advan Colored People, 1998; KKDA African American Hero; Outstanding Director of the Year Award; Eclipse 31 Dynamic Lawyers; Fort Worth Magazine Top Lawyer; Eldon Mahon Inns of Courts, 1996; Lawyer of the Year, Tarrant County Black Bar Asn; Phenomenal Woman from the Federation of Women. **Special Achievements:** Appeared on NBC Dateline, ABC 20/20, ABC Sunday Morning, CNN, ABC-WFAA-Channel 8, NBC-KXAS-Channel 5; record as the youngest executive director in the State of Louisiana. **Business Addr:** Attorney, Law Offices of Bobbie Edmonds, 100 E 15th St Suite 410, Ft. Worth, TX 76102, **Business Phone:** (817)332-6501.

## EDMONDS, CAMPBELL RAY

Government official, mayor. **Personal:** Born Jun 9, 1930, Hopewell, VA; son of VB and Mattie; married Louise Smith. **Educ:** Va State Univ, Trade Sch, 1954, bus & mgt, 1956; Chase Inc Cost & Anal, 1961. **Career:** Transp Safety Bd, 1966; Traffic Bd Hopewell, co-chair, 1966-76; Blue Ribbon Crime Task Force, chmn, 1981; Hopewell City Coun, councilman, 1982-86; Hopewell Va, vice-mayor, 1984-86. **Orgs:** Adjuant gen, Albert Mills Post No 1387, VFW, 1975; bd dirs, C C, 1977-; Home Builder's Asn, 1980; comnr, Veterans Affairs Va, 1981; Appomattox Basin Indust Develop Corp, 1983; bd mem, Hopewell/Prince George Chamber Com; bd dirs, Prince George County Heritage Fair; Hopewell Voters League; trustee bd, Friendship Baptist Church, 1964-; aide, Va State Assoc Pres, IBPOE W; Hopewell Redevelop & Housing Authority, 2006. **Honors/Awds:** Outstanding Service, Sunlight Eld Lodge Hopewell, 1969; Achievement Award, Va State Asn, Health Dept, 1982; Community Service, Hopewell Action Coun, 1985; Certificate of Merit, City Hopewell, 1986; Outstanding Citizenship Award, United Fund, 1987. **Special Achievements:** First African American to be elected to the Hopewell City Council on May 4, 1982. **Home Addr:** 1105 Winston Churchill Dr, Hopewell, VA 23860, **Home Phone:** (804)458-4028. **Business Addr:** Director, Hopewell Redevelopment & Housing Authority, 350 E Poythress St, Hopewell, VA 23860, **Business Phone:** (804)458-5160.

## EDMONDS, CURTIS

Government official. **Personal:** Born Jun 1, 1938. **Career:** Government official (retired); Detroit Fire Dept, dep chief, 1994. **Home Addr:** 20510 Heyden St, Detroit, MI 48219, **Home Phone:** (313)531-5298.

## EDMONDS, ELAINE

Executive director. **Educ:** Elizabeth Seton Col, AA, comput sci; Marymount Col, BS, bus admin. **Career:** Harlem YMCA, exec dir & sr exec dir; YMCA Greater New York, sr exec dir, fund develop, mgr, Capital Fund Develop; Advan Engine Mgt Inc, prin. **Orgs:** Black Achiever Indust. **Business Addr:** Senior Executive Director of Fund Development, YMCA Of Greater New York, 5 W 63rd St 6th Fl, New York, NY 10023, **Business Phone:** (212)630-9600.

### EDMONDS, HENRIETTA
Accountant. **Career:** Accountant. **Home Addr:** 8904 16th St, Silver Spring, MD 20910-2231.

### EDMONDS, KENNETH
Singer, music producer, composer. **Personal:** Born Apr 10, 1958, Indianapolis, IN; son of Marvin (deceased) and Barbara; married Tracey McQuarn; children: Brandon & Dylan Michael; married Denise; married Nicole Pantenburg; children: Peyton Nicole. **Career:** Edmonds Entertainment, co-founder; La Face Records, owner, 1998; singer & producer, currently. Albums: Lovers, 1986; Tender Lover, 1989; A Closer Look, 1991; For the Cool in You, 1993; The Day, 1996; Christmas with Baby face, 1998; Face2Face, 2001; Grown & Sexy, 2005; Playlist, 2007; Josie & the Pussycats, exec producer & music producer, 2001; The Spirit of Christmas, 2002; Love, Marriage & Divorce, 2014; Partners, 2014. Films: Soul Food, co-producer, 1997; Hav Plenty, co-producer, 1998; Light It Up, exec producer, 1999; Punks, exec producer, 2000; Josie & the Pussycats, exec producer, 2001; God Part II, 2005. TV: Soul Food, exec producer, 1997-; The Tonight Show with Jay Leno, 2005. Compilation: A Collection of His Greatest Hits, 2000; Love Songs, 2001; The Essential Babyface, 2003; Remix: The Other Side of Cool, 2005. **Honors/Awds:** Songwriter of the Year, Broadcast Music Inc, 1989, 1990, 1991, 1995; Platinum Award, 1990; BMI Film & TV Award, 1990, 1993 & 1996-97Trumpet Award, Turner Broadcasting Syst, 1998; ASCAP Award, 2000; Image Award, Nat Advan Am Colored People, 1998; Grammy Award, 1993-98, 2014; Image Award, Outstanding Drama Series, Nat Advan Am Colored People, 2002; BMI Icon, BMI Urban Awards; has won 51 BMI Awards; Star on the Walk of Fame, 2013. **Special Achievements:** Had a Federal highway named in his honor. **Home Addr:** , Beverly Hills, CA. **Business Addr:** Owner, Edmonds Entertainment, 1635 N Cahuenga Blvd, Los Angeles, CA 90028, **Business Phone:** (323)860-1550.

### EDMONDS, LISA I.
Lawyer. **Career:** Abbott Labs Co, Domestic Legal Opers, atty, currently. **Business Addr:** Attorney of Domestic Legal Operations, Abbott Laboratories Co, 100 Abbott Pk Rd Dept 32RA, North Chicago, IL 60064-3500, **Business Phone:** (847)937-6100.

### EDMONDS, TERRY
Writer, government official, advertising executive. **Personal:** Born Sep 9, 1949, Baltimore, MD; son of Naomi Parker; married Antoinette; children: Maga. **Educ:** Morgan State Univ, Baltimore, BA, Eng, 1973. **Career:** Md Mass Transit Admin, Baltimore, Md, pub rels specialist, 1978-82; Trahan, Burden & Charles Advert, dir pub rels, 1982-87; Joint Ctr Polit Studies Inc, Wash, DC, dir commun, 1985-87; Off Kweisi Mfume, press secy, 1987-88; Macro Systs, Silver Spring, Md, consult, 1988-89; Blue Cross Blue Shield, Md, mgr media rels, 1989-90; Univ Res Corp, subcontract mgr pub rels work, 1990-91; ROW Sci, task mgr pub rels proj, 1991-93; Off Donna Shalala, US Sec Health & Human Serv, sr speechwriter & dir speechwriting, 1993-95; Pres Bill Clinton, dep asst, pres speechwriter, 1995-97, dep dir speechwriting, 1997-99, asst pres & dir speechwriting; AARP, dir ed mgt, 2002-05; Time Warner Inc, exec speechwriter & sr mem corp commun team, 2005-; Corp Nat & Community Serv, speechwriter; NASA Adminr Charles Bolden, sr advisor & speechwriter; Columbia Univ, assoc vpres & ed dir. **Special Achievements:** First African American speechwriter to work in the White House for a President. **Business Addr:** Executive Speechwriter, Time Warner Inc, 1 Time Warner Ctr, New York, NY 10019-8016, **Business Phone:** (212)484-8000.

### EDMONDS, TRACEY E. (TRACEY ELAINE MCQUARN)
Executive. **Personal:** Born Feb 18, 1967, Los Angeles, CA; daughter of George McQuarn and Jacqueline; married Kenneth; children: Brandon & Dylan; married Eddie Murphy. **Educ:** Stanford Univ, BA, 1987; Southern Univ, PhD, bus, 2004. **Career:** Yab Yum Entertainment, owner & pres, currently; Edmonds Entertainment Inc, pres & chief exec officer, 1993-; Our Stories Films, pres & chief operating officer, 2006-; ALRIGHT TV, chief exec officer & pres, 2012-. films: co-producer, Soul Food, 1997; HavPlenty, co-producer & actor 1997; producer, Light It Up, 1999; Josie & the Pussycats, producer, 2001; The Lamb, producer, 2001; Who's Your Caddy, 2007; Good Luck Chuck, 2007; New in Town, producer, 2009; Jumping the Broom, 2011. TV series: "Soul Food", exec producer, 2000; "College Hill", 2004-07; "Lil Kim: Countdown to Lockdown", 2006; "DMX: Soul of a Man", exec producer, 2006; "Stage Black", exec producer, 2007; "College Hill: Interns", exec producer, 2007; "College Hill Atlanta ", exec producer, 2007; "College Hill: South Beach", exec producer, 2009; "Take Action", exec producer, 2013; "Walk This Way", exec producer, 2013; "With This Ring", exec producer, 2015; "Deion's Family Playbook", exec producer, 2015; "Blackstage"; Schoolin, co-creator; "Nashville", actor, 2015. **Orgs:** RIAA; Do Something; MAP; Mr Hollands Opus; bd trustee, Am Film Inst; bd dir, C Uniting Nations; Exec Comt, Nat Asn Advan Colored People; Ambassador, CARE; Obama for America. **Business Addr:** President, Owner, Yab Yum Entertainment, 1635 N Cahuenga Blvd 6th Fl, Los Angeles, CA 90028, **Business Phone:** (323)860-1520.

### EDMONDSON, JEROME
Business owner, writer, consultant. **Personal:** married Alena; children: Cherita, Aaron & William. **Educ:** Ark State Univ, AA, criminal justice; Cleary Col, BA, bus finance, 1990. **Career:** KFC, staff, 1987, mkt mgr & dir opers, 1994; A&W Foods, owner, 1996; CBN Entrepreneur Training Inst, founder, chief exec officer, 1998; Urban Hope Community Develop Corp, co-founder; Edmondson Assocs, pres, 1998-; EDN Global, pres, chief exec officer; TopTel USA, pres & ceo, 2012-; Cand DeKalb County chief exec officer 2012, DeKalb ceo, 2012-. **Orgs:** Bd dir, Resource Inst Atlanta; exec bd mem, Intl Third World Leadership Asn; UN rep, UN Hq, Geneva; tech assistance provider, US Small Bus Admin; bd mem, Urban Hope Community Develop Corp. **Business Addr:** Owner, Senior Partner, Edmondson Associates, 1777 NE Expy Suite 275, Lithonia, GA 30329, **Business Phone:** (770)879-0902.

### EDMUNDS, ALLAN L.
Teacher, president (organization). **Personal:** Born Jan 1, 1949?, Philadelphia, PA. **Educ:** Temple Univ, BA, MA, arts mgmt, 1975. **Career:** Philadelphia sch syst, art teacher; Tyler Sch art; Swarthmore Col, dept fine art, vis prof, 2009-11; A. L. Edmunds Assocs Inc, assoc, 1994-; Brandywine Graphic Workshop, founder & pres, 1972-; Pa State Arts coun, fel. **Orgs:** Fel getty mus mgt inst, 1997; adv comt, Ave Arts S. **Business Addr:** President, Founder, Brandywine Graphic Workshop, 730 S Broad St, Philadelphia, PA 19146, **Business Phone:** (215)546-3675.

### EDMUNDS, DAVID L., JR.
Lawyer, executive director. **Personal:** Born Mar 30, 1953. **Educ:** Univ Rochester, Col Arts & Sci, BA, 1975; Case Western Res Univ, Franklin Thomas Backus Sch Law, JD, 1978. **Career:** US Ct Appeals, Second Circuit; US Dist Ct, Western Dist, NY; US Supreme Ct; Neighborhood Legal Serv Inc, Reginald Herber Smith Community Lawfel, staff atty, 1978-81; Charles Drew Sci Magnet Sch, tutor; NY Dept Law, Prison Litigation Bur, dep asst atty gen, 1981-83, Claims & Litigation Bur, 1983-95; Damon & Morey, partner, 1985-2003; Buffalo Regional Off, dep asst atty gen-in-charge, 1986-; NY Supreme Ct, Appellate Div, Fourth Judicial Dept, chief coun, 2003-06; Phillips Lytle LLP, atty & spec coun, 2006-10; NY Liquor Authority, dep comnr, 2010-. **Orgs:** Pres, Minority Bar Asn Wyo, 1987-91; dir, Erie County Bar Asn, 2002-03; co-chair, Spec Task Force Minorities Legal Prof; chair, Civil Rights Comn, NY State Bar Asn; bd dir, Leadership Buffalo, class, 1989; bd trustees, First Shiloh Baptist Church; vice pres, Geneva Scruggs Health Ctr; vice pres, Erie County Col, Citizens Adv Coun; life mem, Nat Asn Advan Colored People; bd gov, Case Western Res Univ Law Sch; trustee, Medaille Col; trustee, C Found; Buffalo Econ Renaissance Corp; Leadership Buffalo; pres, Shiloh Housing Develop Corp; Sigma Pi Phi Frat, 2010. **Honors/Awds:** Buffalo Business First & Buffalo Law Journal Who's Who in Law; Lawyer Service Award, Minority Bar Asn Western New York; Trailblazer Award, Minority Bar Asn Western New York; The National Conference for Community and Justice Legal Service Award. **Special Achievements:** First African American to be elected President of the Bar Association of Erie County in the 120 year history of the professional organization. **Home Addr:** 72 Edge Pk Ave, Buffalo, NY 14216, **Home Phone:** (716)874-9316. **Business Addr:** Deputy Commissioner, New York State Liquor Authority, 80 S Swan St 9th Fl, Albany, NY 12210-8002, **Business Phone:** (518)474-3114.

### EDMUNDS, FERRELL, JR.
Football player, football coach. **Personal:** Born Apr 16, 1965, South Boston, VA; children: Trey. **Educ:** Univ Md. **Career:** Football player (retired), coach; Miami Dolphins, tight end, 1988-92; Seattle Seahawks, tight end, 1993-94; Dan River High Sch, coach, currently. **Honors/Awds:** Pro Bowl, 1989, 1990; All-Pro, 1989. **Business Addr:** Coach, Dan River High School, 100 Dan River Wildcat Cir, Dan River, VA 24586, **Business Phone:** (434)822-7081.

### EDMUNDS, DR. WALTER RICHARD
Oral surgeon, educator, association executive. **Personal:** Born Mar 25, 1928, Philadelphia, PA; son of Waltha and McKinley. **Educ:** Pa State Univ, BS; Howard Univ, Col Dent, DDS; Univ Pa, Grad Sch Med. **Career:** Pa Hosp, oral surgeon; Univ Pa Sch Dent Med, assoc prof oral path; Jefferson Med Col, Thomas Jefferson Univ, clin asst prof otolaryngol; Univ Penn, clin asst prof pathol; pvt pract, oral & maxillofacial surgeon, currently. **Orgs:** Bd mem, Eagleville Hosp; fel Am Col Oral & Maxillofacial Surgeons Soc Hill Club; Am Bd Oral Surgeons; Alpha Phi Alpha; Sigma Pi Phi; Chi Delta Mu; bd mem, Philadelphia City Dent Soc; New Era Dental Society, 1st pres. **Business Addr:** Surgeon, 257 S 4th St, Philadelphia, PA 19106, **Business Phone:** (215)925-8586.

### EDNEY, DR. NORRIS ALLEN
Association executive, college teacher, executive director. **Personal:** Born Jul 17, 1936, Natchez, MS; son of Willie Albert and Elizabeth Grayer; married Lillian Clark; children: Norris Allen II, Albert DeFrance & Alvin Darcell. **Educ:** Natchez Jr Col, AA, 1955; Tougaloo Col, BS, 1957; Antioch Col, MST, 1962; Mich State Univ, PhD, 1969. **Career:** Alcorn State Univ, Lorman, Miss, instr & asst prof biol, 1963-66, prof biol, 1969, chmn biol, 1972-79, USDA proj dir, 1972, dir grad studies, 1975, dir arts & sci, 1973, dean & biol prof, sch arts & sci, chmn dept biol, interim dean sch arts & sci, pres, 1997-2001, interim pres, 2010-11; Southwestern Athletic Conf, pres; Natchez-Adams Sch Dist Bd, pres, currently. **Orgs:** Mycological Soc Am; AAAS; Am Asn Univ Profs;bd mem, Miss Acad Sci; Alpha Phi Alpha Fraternity; sch bd mem, Ft Braden Sch; bd trustee, State Insts Higher Learning; bd trustee, bd mem, pres bd trustee, Natchez-Adams Sch Dist. **Home Addr:** 302 Eastmoor Dr, Natchez, MS 39120, **Home Phone:** (601)442-4172. **Business Addr:** School Board President, Board Of Trustee, Natchez-Adams School District, 10 Homochitto St, Natchez, MS 39120.

### EDNEY, TYUS DWAYNE
Executive, basketball player. **Personal:** Born Feb 14, 1973, Gardena, CA; married Shewan; children: Kennedi. **Educ:** Univ Calif, Los Angeles, BA, commun studies, 1995. **Career:** Basketball player (retired), executive; Sacramento Kings, pt guard, 1995-97; Boston Celtics, pt guard, 1997-98; Zalgiris Kaunas, Lithuania, 1998-99; Benetton Basket Treviso, Italy, 1999-2000, 2001-04; Ind Pacers, pt guard, 2000-01; Lottomatica Roma, Italy, 2004-05; Olympiacos, Greece, guard, 2005-06; Climamio Bologna, Italy, 2006-07; Azovmash Mariupol, Ukraine, guard, 2007-08; Cajasol Sevilla, 2008-09; Caja San Fernando, Spain, 2008; Turow Zgorzelec, Poland, 2009-10; Univ Calif, Los Angeles, dir basketball opers, 2010-. **Honors/Awds:** Champion, Nat Col Athletic Asn, 1995; Champion, Euroleague, 1999; Most Valuable Player, Euroleague, 1999; Champion, Lithuanian League, 1999; Frances Pomeroy Naismith Award, 1995; Import Player of the Year, 2002; Most Valuable Player, Ital Supercup, 2002-03; Most Valuable Player, Ital Cup, 2003; Athletics Hall of Fame, Univ Calif, Los Angeles, 2009; Hall of Honor, Pac-12 Conf, 2014. **Special Achievements:** TV appearance: Hope & Gloria, 1995; Films: Eddie, 1996. **Business Addr:** Director of Basketball Operations, University of California, Los Angeles, 405 Hilgard Ave, Los Angeles, CA 90095, **Business Phone:** (310)825-4321.

### EDUOK, DR. ETIM EFFIONG
Educator. **Personal:** Born Jul 10, 1949, Uyo; son of Ekanem and Ima E; married Victoria; children: Oto-Obong, Uyuho, Ekemini & Etim Jr. **Educ:** Univ Nigeria, Nsukka, BS, chem, 1975; Univ Ala, MS, chem, 1980; Tex Christian Univ, PhD, chem, 1991. **Career:** Univ Ariz, asst prof, 1991; Tex Christian Univ, fel, 1992; Concordia Col, assoc prof, 1992-93; Xavier Univ, assoc prof chem, 1994-96. Book: Copper Complexes which Catalyze the Air Oxidation of Organic Substrates, Univ Ala, 1980. **Orgs:** Am Chem Soc, 1977; Am Inst Chemists, 1986, Pkal, 1994; Phi Lambda Upsilon, 2004. **Home Addr:** 122 Harbour Town Ct, New Orleans, LA 70131, **Home Phone:** (504)433-0044.

### EDWARDS, DR. ABIYAH, JR. (ED EDWARDS)
Clergy. **Personal:** Born Dec 23, 1927, Princeton, KY; son of Ivory Bumpass (deceased) and Marcles (deceased); children: Ed III, Delesa, Carla, Cornell, Yahis, Edwina, Charise, Iva, Philip, SchaKerra, Leonard, Mark, Renita, Dontina, Jai & Sonya Sanford. **Educ:** Inst Divine Metaphys Res Inc, DD, 1971. **Career:** Ford Motor Co, Dearborn, Mich, 1949-65; UAW Local 600-Ford, cio, 1965-92; Kaiser Jeep; Enjoy Restaurant/Palace, creative consult, mgr, 1988-89; Third Baptist Church, assoc pastor; Inst Divine Metaphys Res Inc, recruiter & lectr; Universal Sch Spiritual Awareness, dean, currently. **Orgs:** Inst Divine Metaphys Res Inc. **Honors/Awds:** Vol Serv Award, Project Head Start, 1992. **Special Achievements:** Foundation of Universal School of Spiritual Awareness; Author, The Beauty of it All, 1995. **Home Addr:** 5300 Newport Ave, Detroit, MI 48213, **Home Phone:** (313)822-8415. **Business Addr:** Dean, Universal School Spiritual Awareness, 5300 Newport Ave, Detroit, MI 48213, **Business Phone:** (313)822-8415.

### EDWARDS, HON. REV. AL E.
State government official, real estate executive. **Personal:** Born Mar 19, 1937, Houston, TX; son of E L Sr and Josephine; married Lana Kay Cloth; children: Albert Ely II, Jason Kiamba & Alana Catherine Raquel. **Educ:** Tex Southern Univ, Houston, TX, BS, 1966; Tuskegee Inst, AL, cert corrective ther; Col Bibl Studies, Houston, TX, assoc degree sem. **Career:** Gen Foods Corp, acct mgr, 1958-80; Al Edwards Pub Rels Advert, pres, 1968-; Nat Asn Adv Colored People, pub rels, 1976-78; Al Edwards Real Estate & Mortgage Co, 1979-; State Tex, state rep, dist 85, 1979-82, dist 146, 1979-2007, 2009-11; Progressive New Hope Baptist Church, Houston, TX, assoc pastor. **Orgs:** Houston Bus & Prof Men; Dean Pledges Alpha Phi Alpha; founder, pres bd, Houston Team Tennis Asn, 1976-78; founder, Tex Emancipation Juneteenth Cult & Hist Comn; chmn, Jesse Jackson Pres Campaign, Tex, 1984; chmn, Tex Sen Dist 13Conv, 1984; Dem Nat Comn, 1984, chmn, 1995; nat vice chmn, Mondale Pres Campaign, 1984; Alpha Phi Alpha Fraternity; founder, Juneteenth USA; Tex chmn, Legis Black Caucus; chmn, Rules & Resolutions Comt; chmn, Budget & Oversight Ways; chmn, Means Comt; chmn, Appropriation Comt. **Home Addr:** 3108 S MacGregor Way, Houston, TX 77021. **Business Addr:** State Representative, Texas House of Representatives, 4913 Griggs Rd, Houston, TX 77054-4608, **Business Phone:** (713)741-8800.

### EDWARDS, ANTHONY QUINN
Football player, executive. **Personal:** Born May 26, 1966, Casa Grande, AZ; son of Derek and Tara; married Mary Ann; children: Tony, Torrey & Tynette. **Educ:** NMex Highlands Univ, grad. **Career:** Football player (retired); football exec; Philadelphia Eagles, wide receiver, 1989-90; Phoenix Cardinals, 1991-93; Ariz Cardinals Football Club, wide receiver & punt returner, 1995-97, dir player develop, sr dir player develop, 1999-. **Special Achievements:** TV Series: "NFL Monday Night Football", 1989-95; "TNT Sunday Night Football", 1992-95; "NFL on FOX", 1995. **Business Addr:** Senior Director of Player Development, Arizona Cardinals, PO Box 888, Phoenix, AZ 85001, **Business Phone:** (602)379-0101.

### EDWARDS, ANTONIO
Football player, football coach. **Personal:** Born Mar 10, 1970, Moultrie, GA; married Regina; children: Ashanti & Amahn. **Educ:** Valdosta State Univ, criminal justice. **Career:** Football player (retired), coach; Seattle Sea hawks, defensive end, 1993-97; NY Giants, 1997; Atlanta Falcons, 1998; Carolina Panthers, defensive end, 1999-2001; Las Vegas Outlaws, 2001; Valdosta State Univ; Philadelphia eagles, defensive line coach; Col Sch, defensive line coach, currently. **Home Addr:** 716 2nd St NW, Moultrie, GA 31768. **Business Addr:** Defensive Line Coach, Collegiate School, 103 N Mooreland Rd, Richmond, VA 23229, **Business Phone:** (804)740-7077.

### EDWARDS, ANTUAN MINYE
Football player, administrator. **Personal:** Born May 26, 1977, Starkville, MS. **Educ:** Clemson Univ, Bus Admin & Mgt, 1998. **Career:** Football player (retired); Green Bay Packers, 2001, defensive back, 1999, defensive back, left cornerback, 2000, defensive back, strong safety, 2002, free safety, strong safety, 2003; Miami Dolphins, free safety, 2004; St Louis Rams, free safety, 2004; New Eng Patriots, 2004; Atlanta Falcons, defensive back, strong safety, 2005; Wash Redskins, 2006; E2Athletics, owner, 2014-; Shrevepor, Owner & Dir Football Opers, 2015-. **Orgs:** Make-A-Wish C's Hosp, WI; Bornemann's Nursing Home; Geraldine Zuber Edwards Found, 2003-. **Honors/Awds:** Jim Thorpe Award.

### EDWARDS, AUDREY MARIE
Publishing executive. **Personal:** Born Apr 21, 1947, Tacoma, WA; daughter of Cyrill and Bertie; married Benjamin Williams. **Educ:** Univ Wash, BA, hist, 1969; Columbia Univ, MA, curric & media technol, 1973. **Career:** Coretta Scott King fel, Am Asn Univ Women, 1969; Fairchild Publ, prom news ed, 1977-79; Black Enterprise Mag, exec ed, vpres, ed opers, 1978-79, exec ed, vpres ed oper, 1990-; Family

Circle Mag, sr ed, 1979-81; Essence Mag, contrib writer, 1981-, exec ed; NY Univ, adj prof, 1982-; Prospect Heights, independent broker; New York Times Sunday Real Estate, journalist; Brown Harris Stevens Brooklyn, LLC, lic assoc real estate broker, 2008-. **Orgs:** Regional dir, Nat Asn Black Journalists, 1981-83; prog chair, NY Asn Black Journalists, 1983-. **Honors/Awds:** Unity Award, Media Lincoln Univ, 1985. **Special Achievements:** Author: The Picture Life of Muhammad Ali, F Watts, 1976; The Picture Life of Bobby Orr, F Watts, 1976; The Picture Life of Stevie Wonder, F Watts, 1977; Children of the Dream: The Psychology of Black Success, 1992; Co-op Board Members Get a Baptism by Fire. **Home Addr:** 426 Eastern Pkwy, Brooklyn, NY 11225, **Home Phone:** (718)756-1024. **Business Addr:** Real Estate Broker, Brown Harris Stevens Brooklyn LLC, 100 7th Ave, Brooklyn, NY 11215, **Business Phone:** (718)399-4119.

### EDWARDS, BESSIE REGINA
Executive, manager, real estate agent. **Personal:** Born Mar 14, 1942, Gates County, NC. **Educ:** City Univ NY, Brooklyn Col, BA, spec baccularate prog, 1980; New Sch Univ, BA & MA, human resource mgt, 1982. **Career:** Opportunity Industrialization, counr & teacher, 1975-80; Manhattan Cable TV, affirmative action officer, 1980-86; Paragon Cable, mgr trng & develop; BR Edwards Assoc Real Estate, broker & owner, 1988-2010, partner, currently; Event Organizer, 2000-12; Pizzazz Meeting & Event Planning Group, owner, 2000-. **Orgs:** Bd mem, NY Chap Coalition 100 Black Women; sec, Minorities Cable; sec, Women Cable; bd mem, EDGES; Womens City Club; Brooklyn Chamber Com, 1989-90; Nat Forum Black Pub Admin; Cent Brooklyn Jazz Consortium; Jazzmobile. **Honors/Awds:** Black Achiever, Time Inc The Parent Co, 1987. **Home Phone:** (917)744-9391. **Business Addr:** Partner, Pizzazz Meeting & Event Planning Group, 195 Willoughby Ave Suite 1006, Brooklyn, NY 11205, **Business Phone:** (718)638-8199.

### EDWARDS, BRENT HAYES
Historian, college teacher, writer. **Educ:** Yale Univ, BA, 1990; Columbia Univ, MA, 1992, PhD, 1998. **Career:** Rutgers Univ, prof; Columbia Univ (New York), Louis Armstrong Vis Prof Jazz Studies, Dept Eng & Comparative Lit, prof. **Orgs:** Ed bd mem, Transition & Callaloo. **Honors/Awds:** For "The Practice of Diaspora," received John Hope Franklin Prize of the American Studies Association, the Gilbert Chinard prize of the Society for French Historical Studies, and runner-up for the James Russell Lowell Prize of the Modern Language Association. **Special Achievements:** Author of: "The Practice of Diaspora: Literature, Translation, and the Rise of Black Internationalism" (Harvard UP, 2003); co-editor of: "Uptown Conversation: The New Jazz Studies" (Columbia UP, 2004); has published numerous journal articles on African American literature, Francophone literature, and theories of African diaspora; co-editor of journal "Social Text".

### EDWARDS, CARL RAY, II
Lawyer. **Personal:** Born Jul 14, 1947, Detroit, MI; son of Carl R and Alice; married Alice Jennings; children: Patrick Phillips, Kwameena, Tonya Jennings, Ronald G Watters, Saraun & CarlRay. **Educ:** Mich Lutheran Col, BA, bus & acct, 1970; Univ Detroit Mercy, MA, urban econs, 1972; Wayne State Univ, JD, civil, const & criminal law, 1974. **Career:** Philo, Atkinson, Darling, Steinberg, Edwards & Jennings, partner, 1973-82; Edwards & Jennings PC, pres, 1982-; Detroit Gen Hosp, lead coun; Battle Creek, Mich, lead coun. **Orgs:** Mich Bar Asn, 1975-; Asn Trial Lawyers Am, 1976-; exec bd mem, Mich Trial Lawyers Asn, 1976-, treas, secy, vpres, pres, 1987-88; Nat Bar Asn, 1985-; co-founder, Nat Conf Black Lawyers, Mich Chap. **Honors/Awds:** Praisal Citation, Nat Asn Equal Opport Higher Educ, 1981; Founder's Award, Mich Trial Lawyers Asn, Peoples Law Sch, 1989. **Special Achievements:** State Bar of Michigan delegation member of judges and attorneys on legal and constitutional fact-finding mission to USSR and People's Republic of China, 1988; Co-founder of the Michigan Trial Lawyers' Peoples Law School, operating across Michigan and established by the Association of Trial Lawyers of America and operating in over 18 states nationwide. **Home Addr:** 495 Lodge Dr, Detroit, MI 48214-4160, **Home Phone:** (313)331-2141. **Business Addr:** President, Edwards & Jennings PC, Globe Bldg 407 E Fort St Suite 605, Detroit, MI 48226-2940, **Business Phone:** (313)961-5000.

### EDWARDS, DR. CLAUDIA L.
Administrator, consultant. **Personal:** Born Bronx, NY; daughter of Mable and Joshua; children: Damon & Andre. **Educ:** Bronx Community Col, AA, 1980; State Univ NY, Purchase, BA, 1984; NY Univ, MS, 1988, MUP, Robert F Wagner Sch Pub Serv, 1988; Fordham Univ, PhD, philos, 2008. **Career:** New York Dept Social Serv, Proj Dir, 1984-86; United Way, vpres, 1989-91; Pace Univ, Michalen Inst, educ consult, currently; Newark Pub Sch Found, educ consult, 2005-06; Edwards Consult Group, pres & chief exec officer, 2008-; Edwards Consult Group, pres & chief exec officer, 2008-; St John Fisher Col, EdD Prog Exec Leadership, asst prof, 2009-; Ralph C Wilson Sch Educ, vis asst prof, 2014. **Orgs:** Trustee, Westchester Med Ctr; Westchester fund Women & Girls; exec, Asn Black found; Women Commun; Women Philanthropy; trustee, Bus & Prof Women Found; Reader's Dig Fund, assoc dir, 1991-93, exec dir, 1993-2004. **Business Addr:** Assistant Professor, St John Fisher College, 3690 E Ave, Rochester, NY 14618, **Business Phone:** (585)385-8000.

### EDWARDS, DANIEL
Business owner, executive. **Personal:** married Monica. **Career:** Morehead Manor Bed & Breakfast, inn keeper & owner, currently. **Orgs:** Pres, African Am Asn Inkeepers Int. **Business Addr:** Owner, Inn Keeper, Morehead Manor Bed & Breakfast, 914 Vickers Ave, Durham, NC 27701, **Business Phone:** (919)687-4366.

### EDWARDS, DELORES A.
Journalist, television producer. **Personal:** Born Sep 22, 1965, New York, NY; daughter of Nathaniel and Lucy Miller. **Educ:** Northeastern Univ, Boston, MA, BS, 1988; Columbia Univ Grad Sch Journalism, MS, 2000. **Career:** Columbia Univ Grad Sch Arts & Scu, grad adv, 1988-89; ABC News, Nightline, 20/20, prod assoc, 1989-92, assoc producer ABC C's Spec "Prejudice, " 1992, "Kids Crossfire, " 1994, "Live at White House, pres Clinton: Answering C's Questions, " 1994; All Am TV, segment producer, 1992-93; TV Prog Enterprises, segment producer, 1992-93; Pac Rim LTD, res consult, 1993; Arts & Entertainment Network, assoc producer "Biog, " producer; WGBH/GR Productions, assoc producer "Surviving Odds: To Be a Young Black Male Am, " 1994; Kelly Films, assoc producer "Fighting Destroyer Escorts, " "Proudly We Served: Men USS Mason, " 1994; Barwall Productions, producer "Barbara Walters Interviews a Lifetime, " 1994; ABC News, Murder Beverly Hills: Menendez Trial, researcher, 1994; PBS, Imaging Am, assoc producer, 1996; FOX5, Good Day New York, producer; Freelance Tv Segment Producer, New York, NY; marblehill media, dir, currently. **Orgs:** Nat Asn Broadcasters, 1988-; NY Asn Black Journalist, 1988-; Nat Asn Broadcast Employees & Technicians, 1989-; Soc Professional Journalists, 1990-. **Home Addr:** 630 W 246 St 1229, Bronx, NY 10463. **Business Addr:** Director, Writer, Marblehill Media, **Business Phone:** (917)439-8446.

### EDWARDS, HON. DENNIS, JR.
Judge. **Personal:** Born Aug 19, 1922, New York, NY; son of Dennis Sr and Gladys Wilson; married Dorothy Fairclough; children: Lynne Mosley & Denise Young. **Educ:** NY Univ, BA, 1941; Harvard Law Sch, JD, 1944. **Career:** New York Supreme Ct, law clerk, 1948-65; New York Criminal Ct, judge, 1965-. **Orgs:** Harlem Lawyers Asn, 1952; Dir, New York Co Lawyers Asn, 1961-65; Am Judicature Soc, Am Bar Asn; dir, Speedwell Soc C; Omega Fraternity; Elks; Masons; Nat Asn Advan Colored People; Urban League; YMCA; NY Bar Asn, 1944-. **Home Addr:** 409 Edgecombe Ave, New York, NY 10032, **Home Phone:** (212)283-7737. **Business Addr:** Judge, New York Criminal Court, 100 Ctr St, New York, NY 10013, **Business Phone:** (646)386-4500.

### EDWARDS, DIXON VOLDEAN, III
Football player. **Personal:** Born Mar 25, 1968, Cincinnati, OH; son of Dixon Jr; married Secola; children: Dixon IV & Taylor. **Educ:** Mich State Univ. **Career:** Football player (retired); Dallas Cowboys, linebacker, 1991-92, left linebacker, 1993-95; Minn Vikings, right linebacker, 1996-97, left linebacker, 1998; Miami Dolphins, linebacker, 1999; Sports Arts & Media Inc, pres, currently. **Special Achievements:** Films: Super Bowl XXVII, 1993; Super Bowl XXVIII, 1994; Super Bowl XXX, 1996; 1998 NFC Championship Game, 1999; Hood Angels, video producer, 2003. **Business Addr:** President, Sports Arts & Media Inc, 7750 N Macarthur Blvd Suite 120-347, Irving, TX 75063-7514.

### EDWARDS, DONALD PHILIP
Lawyer. **Personal:** Born Aug 27, 1947, Buffalo, NY; son of Robert D and Lorraine V Jarrett; married Jo Roberson; children: Nia & Domia. **Educ:** Morehouse Col, Atlanta, GA, BA, 1969; Boston Univ Sch Law, JD, 1973. **Career:** Nat Asn Advan Colored People Legal Defense Fund, fel, 1973-76; Thomas Kennedy Sampson Edwards & Patterson, partner, 1974-92; Law Off of Donald P Edwards, sole practr, 1992-; Clef Prod Inc, co-owner & chmn bd dir, 1993-97. **Orgs:** State Bar GA, 1973-; bd dir, Hillside Int Truth Ctr, 1978-83, chmn bd, 1980-83, trustee, 1995-98; bd adv, Atlanta Legal Aid Soc, 1981-85; bd mem, Atlanta Vol Lawyers Inc, 1983-84; pres, Northern Dist Litigation Fund, 1984-87; bd mem, Nat Bar Asn, 1984, 1985; pres, Gate City Bar Asn, 1984; chmn, Fulton County Dept Family & C Serv, 1990; dir, Nat Bar Asn, Region XI, 1986-87; vpres, Christian Coun Metrop Atlanta, 1988-92, pres, 1998; bd mem, Am Cancer Socs, Atlanta Unit, 1988-89; bd dir, Atlanta Int Mus Art & Design, 1989-91; trustee, Southwest Hosp & Med Ctr, 1990-; pres, Southwest Hosp Found Inc, 1992-95; 100 Black Men Atlanta Inc, 1993-; pres, Asn Metro Atlanta DFCS Bds, 1992-94; chair, S Atlanta Dist, Boy Scouts Am; bd mem, exec comm, Atlanta Area Coun, Boy Scouts Am, 1998-; Fulton County, 2003-; Asn Trial Lawyers Am; legal adv team mem, Ga Asn Black Elected Officials. **Honors/Awds:** Outstanding Community Service Award, Col Pk Neighborhood Voters League, 1980; Presidential Award, Nat Black Am Law Stud Asn, 1983; Civil Rights Award, Gate City Bar Asn, 1983; Lawyer of the Yr, DeKalb Cty Nat Asn Advan Colored People, 1984; Top 100 Atlantans under 40 Atlanta Mag, 1984; Thurgood Marshall Award Award, Nat Asn Advan Colored People, Atlanta Br, 1985; Leadership Atlanta, 1985; Black Pages Prof Achievement Award, 1992; Chief Justice Robert Benham Community Service Award, State Bar GA, 2000; Silver Beaver Award, S Atlanta Dist, Boy Scouts of Ame, 2000; The Donald P. Edwards Humanitarian Award, South Atlanta Sankofa Dist, 2003; Blessed Are The Peacemakers Award, World Council of Churches, 2004; Allen Award, Atlanta Interfaith Broadcasters, 2004; Gate City Bar Asn; "Hall of Fame", 2004; Father of the Year; "100 Most Influential African Americans in Atlanta". **Home Phone:** (404)758-8414. **Business Addr:** Practioner, The Law Office of Donald P Edwards, 170 Mitchell St SW, Atlanta, GA 30303-3424, **Business Phone:** (404)526-8866.

### EDWARDS, HON. DONNA F.
**Personal:** Born Jun 28, 1958, Yanceyville, NC; daughter of John; married Derek; children: Jared. **Educ:** Wake Forest Univ, BA, eng, span; Wake Forest Univ, Franklin Pierce Law Ctr, JD. **Career:** UN Develop Prog, Develop Forum, Dept Econ & Social Info, asst dir, 1980-82; Lockheed Corp, Goddard Space Flight Ctr, writer, 1982-86; Dc Super Ct Judge, clerk, 1989-90; Arca Found, exec dir, 2000-08; Us House Representatives, Dist 4, cand, 2006; Us House Representatives, rep, 2008-. **Orgs:** Md Dem Party; exec dir, Ctr New Democracy, 1994-96; founder & exec dir, Nat Network to End Domestic Violence, 1996-99; exec dir, Nat Network to End Domestic Violence, 1996-99; dir, Nat Network to End Domestic Violence; vol, Pub Citizen; Tom Lantos Human Rights Comn; Diversity Leadership Coun, 2010-; deleg, Dem Party Nat Conv, 2012; bd dir, League Conserv Voters. **Business Addr:** Congresswoman, 111th Congress, 318 Cannon House Office Bldg, Washington, DC 20515, **Business Phone:** (202)225-8699.

### EDWARDS, DONNA MARIA. See O'BANNO, DR. DONNA M. EDWARDS.

### EDWARDS, DONNIE LEWIS, JR.
Football player. **Personal:** Born Apr 6, 1973, San Diego, CA; married Kathryn. **Educ:** Univ Calif, LA, BA, polit sci. **Career:** Football player (retired), yoga instructor; Kans City Chiefs, linebacker, 1996-2001, 2007-08; San Diego Chargers, linebacker, 2002-06; yoga instructor. **Orgs:** Alpha Rho chap Zeta Beta Tau; dir, Greatest Generations Found; Child Abuse Prev Found; After Sch All-Stars; Best Defense Found; Jump Life. **Honors/Awds:** Pro Bowl selection, 2003; All-Pro selection, 2002 & 2004; NFL Alumni Linebacker of the Year, 2004; 20/20 club. **Special Achievements:** TV Series: "Inside the NFL", 2007. TV Series: "ESPN's Sunday Night Football", producer & actor, 1987; "NFL Monday Night Football", producer & actor, 1970; "NBC Sunday Night Football", producer & actor, 2006. **Home Addr:** , Rancho Santa Fe, CA.

### EDWARDS, DOROTHY WRIGHT. See Obituaries Section.

### EDWARDS, ELLA RAINO
Actor, storyteller. **Personal:** Born Oct 7, 1938, Kilgore, TX; daughter of John Henry Raino (deceased) and Lola B Taylor Raino (deceased); children: Bernard Otis Wright. **Educ:** Los Angeles Metrop Col, AA; John Robert Powers Sch Modeling, grad. **Career:** Films: Big Time, asst dir, 1977; Young Doctors in Love, 1982; The New Odd Couple, assoc producer, 1982-83; Who Is Julia?, 1986; Bad Dreams, 1988; House Party, Vital Signs, 1990; Sneakers, 1992; On Hope, 1994; Fire Down Below, 1997; TV series: Dead Men Tell No Tales, 1971; "The White Shadow", 1979-80; Thursday's Child, 1983; "Doogie Howser, M.D.", 1991; "Wanda at Large", 2003; "ER", 2008; Los Angeles Int House Blues Found Educ Tours Prog, consult & performance artist; Metrop Water Dist Southern Calif Educ Div, res, develop, perform water stories, 1998-99; story teller, currently. **Orgs:** Griot Soc Southern Calif; Tellers & Talkers; Nat Storytelling Asn; Nat Asn Black Storytellers; Screen Actors Guild; Am Fed TV & Radio Artists; Founding & charter mem, Fin Sec Kwanza Found; former mem & secy, Black Women Theatre W, 1984-86. **Honors/Awds:** Ohio Close School Boys Award, 1972-74; Community Service Award, Alpha Gamma Omega Chap, Alpha Kappa Alpha Award; Certificate Commendation, City Los Angeles, 1988 & 1995; Certificate of Recognition, Jenesse Ctr; Performance Bicentennial US, Shreveport Regional Bicentennial Comn, 1976; Bicentennial Minute Man Award. **Special Achievements:** Official storyteller of Allensworth State Historic Park, California's first town founded by African Am; Co-author: "Another Kind of Treasure: A Story of Dreams Fulfilled". **Home Addr:** 8722 Skyline Dr, Los Angeles, CA 90046. **Business Addr:** Storyteller, PO Box 1420, Studio City, CA 90001, **Business Phone:** (323)654-1922.

### EDWARDS, GENYNE
Secretary (government), executive. **Educ:** Purdue Univ, BA, orgn leadership & supv, 1995; Marquette Univ Law Sch, law degree, 2000; Marquette Univ, cert, assocs com real estate, 2005; Cardinal Stritch Univ, cert, prof coaching, 2010. **Career:** Secretary (retired), director; YWCA, Greater Milwaukee, pub policy dir, 2000; Lanier Law Offs Ltd, atty; Chicago Lawyers for the Arts, staff; Milwaukee Art Mus, staff; Woo Connections, prin consult, 2003-; Strive Media Inst, staff; Wisc Dept Tourism, dep secy, 2001-03; WYMS-Radio Milwaukee, 88Nine Radio Milwaukee, community rels dir, 2006-08; Mosaic Milwaukee Partnerships Prog, prog dir, 2006-10; Edwards Ingenuity, LLC, prin, currently; Cardinal Stritch Univ, African Am Leadership Prog, prog coordr, 2008-; Community Advocates Pub Policy Inst, advocacy consult, 2008-; Cardinal Stritch Univ African Am Leadership Prog & Neighborhood Leadership Inst, prog consult, 2008-; P3 Develop Group LLC, partner, 2011-; Walnut Way Conserv Corp, commun & develop consult, 2012-13. **Orgs:** Community bd, Marquette Univ Law Alumni Asn; community bd, Milwaukee World Festivals Inc; community bd, Ko-Thi Dance Co; community bd, Cult Alliance Greater Milwaukee; community bd, Milwaukee chap, Black Pub Rels Soc; Med Col Wis, 2011-; bd mem, Pearls Teen Girls, Inc, 2016-. **Honors/Awds:** Volunteer of the Year, Volunteer Ctr of Greater Milwaukee, 2003; Most Influential African-Americans in the Tourism Industry, Nat Publ-Black Meetings & Tourism, 2004; Community Advocate Award, Marquette Univ Ethnic Alumni Asn, 2016. **Special Achievements:** Featured in Milwaukee Mag as a "Top 35 under 35", 2003. **Business Addr:** Advocacy Consultant, Community Advocates Public Policy Institute, 728 N James Lovell St, Milwaukee, WI 53203.

### EDWARDS, GEORGE REGINALD. See Obituaries Section.

### EDWARDS, GERALD DOUGLAS
Executive. **Personal:** Born Jul 13, 1950, Chicago, IL; son of William Kenneth and Lucille Elizabeth; married Jada Denise Brooks; children: Candice Rae & Gerald Douglas. **Educ:** Heidelberg Col, BA, bus admin, 1972. **Career:** Ford Motor Co, gen supvr, 1983-86; Detroit Plastic Molding, from asst plant mgr to plant mgr, 1986-87; Engineered Plastic Prod Inc, chief exec officer, 1987-, pres, 2004; NamDiamonds Inc, chief exec officer; Clear Stone LLC, Namibia, Africa, founder. **Orgs:** Minority input comt, Mich Minority Bus Develop Coun, 1989-; bd dir, 1989-, bldg fund campaign chmn, 1990-, Sumpter Community Church God; dir, Minority Technol Coun Mich, 1992-. **Home Addr:** 2465 Traver Blvd, Ann Arbor, MI 48105. **Business Addr:** Chief Executive Officer, President, Engineered Plastic Products Inc, 699 James L Hart Pkwy, Ypsilanti, MI 48197, **Business Phone:** (734)485-6501.

### EDWARDS, GROVER LEWIS, SR.
School administrator, president (organization). **Personal:** Born Feb 21, 1944, Henrico, NC; son of Grover C; married Lucy Priscilla Moody; children: Reggie Lamont, Telsha Nicole, Kelsey Daneen & Grover Lewis Jr. **Educ:** Elizabeth City State Univ, Assoc, attended 1965; Shaw Univ, BS, 1976. **Career:** RCA Training Prog, electronics instr, 1969-73, supvr instrs, 1973-79; Northampton County Sch Bd, found mem, bd mem, 1972-, chmn, 1984-; Edwards & Assocs Bldg Contractors, owner & pres, 1976-79; Norfax Real Estate Corp, pres, 1983-. **Orgs:** Past youth adv, Nat Asn Advan Colored People, 1969; pres, Gaston Relig Civic Orgn, 1971; pres, Northampton Housing Asst Prog, 1972; Prince Hall Masonic Lodge, 1975-; NC Home Builders Asn, 1980; bd dir, NC Sch Bd, 1984-. **Honors/Awds:** Service Award, Northampton HS W, 1980; Service Award, Athlete Asn, Tri-City Chums, 1981; Outstanding Business Award, Northampton Co Nat Asn Advan Colored People, 1985. **Business Addr:** Chairman, Foun-

dation Member, Northampton County School Board, 701 N Church St, Jackson, NC 27845, **Business Phone:** (252)534-1371.

**EDWARDS, DR. HARRY**
Educator, consultant. **Personal:** Born Nov 22, 1942, St. Louis, MO; son of Harry and Adelaide; married Sandra Y Boze; children: Tazamisha Heshima Imara, Fatima Malene Imara & Changa Demany Imara. **Educ:** Fresno State Col, attended 1960; San Jose State Univ, BA, sociol, 1964; Cornell Univ, MA, sociol, 1966, PhD, sociol, 1972. **Career:** San Jose State, instr sociol, 1967-69, vis prof, 1966-68; Univ Santa Clara, instr sociol, 1967-68; Univ Calif, Berkeley, from asst prof to prof sociol, 1970-2000, prof emer, 2000-. **Orgs:** Nat Sports Inst Oslo Norway; Nat Sports Inst Moscow USSR; consult, San Francisco 49ers; player personnel coun & progs, Golden State Warriors, 1987-95. **Honors/Awds:** Man of the Year Award, San Francisco Sun Reporter, 1968; Russwurm Award, Nat Newspaper Publishers Asn, 1968; fellowship, Cornell Univ, 1968; Dist Scholar, Ore State Univ, 1980; Hon Doctorate, Columbia Col, 1981; Miller Scholar, Univ Ill, 1982; Dist Scholar, Norwegian Col Physical Educ & Sports Oslow Norway, 1983; Dist Scholar, Univ Charleston, 1984; Dist Visiting Scholar, Ind State Univ, 1984. **Special Achievements:** Author: "Revolt of the Black Athlete", 1970; "Sociology of Sport", 1973; "The Struggle that Must Be: An Autobiography", 1980. Contributor of essays to magazines, including Sports Illustrated & Psychology, The Struggle That Must Be, Black Students and The Revolt of the Black Athlete. **Home Addr:** 40573 Dolores Pl, Fremont, CA 94539-3636. **Business Addr:** Professor Emeritus of Sociology, University of California, 101 Zellerbach Hall, Berkeley, CA 94720, **Business Phone:** (510)642-9988.

**EDWARDS, HON. HARRY THOMAS**
Lawyer, judge. **Personal:** Born Nov 3, 1940, New York, NY; son of George H and Arline Lyle; married Pamela Carrington; children: Brent & Michelle. **Educ:** Cornell Univ, BS, 1962; Univ Mich Law Sch, JD, 1965. **Career:** Pvt pract, atty, 1965-80; Seyfarth, Shaw Fairweather & Geraldson, atty, 1965-70; Univ Mich Law Sch, prof, 1970-75, 1977-80; Nat Labor Rels Bd, Labor arbitrator, 1971-80; Harvard Univ Law Sch, prof, 1975-77; Harvard Inst Educ Mgt, 1976-82; Nat Rr Passenger Corp, chmn, 1978-80; Amtrak, bd dir, 1978-80, chmn bd, 1979-80; US Ct Appeals, Wash, DC, judge, 1980-94, chief judge, 1994-2001, sr judge, 2005-; NY Univ Sch Law, vis prof, 1990-; Duke Univ, Fac, 2009. **Orgs:** Am Law Inst; Am Bar Asn; Am Acad Arts & Sci; Am Judicature Soc; bd dir, Unique Learning Ctr; Alpha Phi Alpha; Quill & Dagger soc; bd dir, New York Univ Sch Law, Inst Judicial Admin; fel Am Bar Found. **Honors/Awds:** LLD, Williams Col; LLD, Univ Detroit; LLD, Georgetown Univ; LLD, Brooklyn Col; LLD, State Univ NY; LLD, John Jay Col Criminal Justice; LLD, Lewis & Clark Col; LLD, St Lawrence Univ; Soc Am Law Teachers Award, 1982; Whitney North Seymour Medal, Am Arbitration Asn, 1988; Robert J. Kutak Award, Am Bar Asn, 2004; Inaugural Distinguished Alumni Award, Univ Mich Law Sch, 2011. **Special Achievements:** Co-author: Labor Relations Law in the Pub Sector, 1985; The Lawyer as a Negotiator, 1977; Collective Bargaining & Labor Arbitration, 1979; Higher Educ & the Law, 1980; author of more than 75 scholarly articles. **Business Addr:** Senior Judge, US Court of Appeals, The E Barrett Prettyman US Courthouse, Washington, DC 20001-2805, **Business Phone:** (202)216-7380.

**EDWARDS, HERMAN LEE**
Football coach, football player. **Personal:** Born Apr 27, 1954, Fort Eatontown, NJ; son of Herman Sr (deceased) and Martha; married Lia Camara; children: Marcus, Gabrielle & Vivian. **Educ:** Monterey Peninsula Col, 1970; San Diego State Univ, BA, criminal justice, 1977. **Career:** Football player (retired), football coach; San Diego State, defensive back, 1975-76; Philadelphia Eagles, defensive back, 1977-85; Atlanta Falcons, defensive back, 1986; Los Angeles Rams, defensive back, 1986; San Jose St Univ, defensive backs coach, 1987-89; Minority Coaching fel, fell & head coach, 1989; Kans City Chiefs, scout, 1990-91, defensive backs coach, 1992-95, pro personnel scout, 1995, franchise annals, head coach, 2006-08; Tampa Bay Buccaneers, asst head coach, 1996-2000; New York Jets, head coach, 2001-05; ESPN, studio Nat Football League analyst, 2009. **Orgs:** Founder, Herm Edwards Youth Found, 1985, Herm Edwards Youth Football Camp, 1985; Diabetes Res Inst; Leukemia & Lymphoma Soc; Breast Cancer Res Found; charter mem, Fritz Pollard Alliance, 2003; Positive Coaching Alliance, 2003; Juvenille Diabetes Res Found, Kans. **Honors/Awds:** Second-team All-NFC honors, 1980; Big Brother of the Year, Catholic Big Brothers For Boys and Girls, NY, 2002. **Special Achievements:** Actor: "NFL Monday Night Football", 1970; "The Complete History of the Philadelphia Eagles", 2004; "Mike & Mike", 2005.

**EDWARDS, HORACE BURTON**
Executive, consulting engineer, social worker. **Personal:** Born May 20, 1925, Tuscaloosa, AL; married Patsy; children: Adrienne, Paul, David & Michael. **Educ:** Marquette Univ, BS, naval sci, 1947, 1948; Iona Col, MBA, 1972. **Career:** Politician, consultant, (retired), executive; Atlantic Richfield Co, controller mkt, 1968-72, mgr finance, opeartion anal, 1973-76, mgr planning, control transp div, 1976-79; ARCO Transp Co, vpres planning, control, 1978-80; ARCO Pipeline Co, pres, chief exec officer, chmn; Edwards & Assocs Inc, consult engr, owner, currently. **Orgs:** Trustee Leadership Independence, 1984-85, Kans Chamber Com Leadership, Kans, 1985-86; dir, pres Independence Ind, 1985; Assoc Oil Pipe Lines Exec Comn, Am Petrol Inst & Cent Comn Pipe Line Transp; pres, bd dir, Jr Achievement Montgomery County Independence Kans; bd dir, Kans Chamber Com & Indust, Independence Community Col Endowment Bd; trustee, Inst Logopedics, Wichita, Kans; Kans Independent Col Fund; Kans Coun Econ Educ; trustee, Tex Southern Univ Bus Sch Found; Nat Bar Assoc Adv Comn Energy & Environ Law Sect; bd dir, Am Assoc Blacks Energy; partic Nat Urban League's Black Exec Exchange Prog; Nat Asn Advan Colored People; Fla A&M Sch Bus; Indust Ctr Entrepreneurial Develop Roundtable; secy transp, State Kans. **Honors/Awds:** Distinguished Engr Alumnus Award, Marquette Univ, 1984; hon LHD, Tex Southern Univ, 1982; hon LLD, Stillman Col, 1984. **Home Addr:** 311 Rajah Rd, Independence, KS 67301. **Business Addr:** Consulting Engineer, Owner, Edwards Engineering Consultants LLC, 7665 N Port Washington Rd Suite 103, Milwaukee, WI 53217-3175, **Business Phone:** (414)228-8998.

**EDWARDS, JOHN L., SR.**
Educator. **Personal:** Born Oct 18, 1930, Muncie, IN; married Mavis J Jones; children: John & Robert. **Educ:** Ball State Univ, BS, 1953; Ariz State Univ, MA, 1959, EdD, 1965. **Career:** Julian Elem Sch, Phoenix, teacher, 1955-62; Ariz State Univ, grad asst, 1962-63, fac assoc, 1963-64, instr, 1964-66, asst prof, 1966-69, assoc prof, 1969-75, exten & prof Col, asst dean, 1973-, prof emer, 1996-. **Orgs:** New Enterprise Assocs, 1956; Ariz Educ Asn; Kappa Delta Pi, 1962; fac Adv, Kappa Alpha Psi; Ariz State Univ, 1962-72 & 1975; Int Reading Asn, 1963; Am Asn Univ Profs, 1964; bd dir, Asn Higher Educ, 1964; Desert Area reading coun, 1966; Phi Delta Kappa, 1966; bd mem, Southwestern Coop End Lab; bd dir, Jane Wayland Child Guid Ctr, 1969-75; Ariz Right Read Comn, 1971; Phoenix Citizens Bond Comt, 1975; chmn, Ariz Educ Asn Instr & Prof Develop Comn; Black Caucus. **Home Addr:** 5721 E Calle Camelia, Phoenix, AZ 85018-4617, **Home Phone:** (480)949-7035. **Business Addr:** Professor Emeritus, Associate Dean, Arizona State University, Univ Ex Acad Serv Bldg 200 E Curry Rm 201, Temple, AZ 85287, **Business Phone:** (480)965-7668.

**EDWARDS, JOHN LOYD, III**
Foundation executive, association executive. **Personal:** Born Feb 18, 1948, Nashville, TN; son of John Loyd Jr (deceased); married Faith; children: Adrian Joel, Nikita Michelle & Derek Traimain. **Educ:** Tenn State Univ, BA, fine art, 1968; Univ Tenn, Chattanooga, BFA, 1980. **Career:** Chattanooga Northstar Newspaper, writer & dir advert, 1981-83; Mary Walker Hist & Educ Found, exec dir, bd chmn, 1983-; Visual Media Productions, pres, 1985-; Joseph Johnson Ment Health Ctr, bd dir, 1988-; Chattanooga News Chronicle Inc, owner. **Orgs:** Hon life mem, US Jaycees, 1987-; Asn Study Afro-Am Life & Hist, 1985-; vpres, Lakeside Parent Teachers Asn, 1986-; Phi Beta Sigma Fraternity. **Honors/Awds:** Outstanding Community Achievement, Vietnam Era Veteran City Chattanooga, 1979; Public Relations Director of the Year, Tenn Jaycees, 1983-84. **Home Addr:** 3110 N St, Chattanooga, TN 37411, **Home Phone:** (615)622-7072. **Business Addr:** Owner, Chattanooga News Chronicle, 611 E Ml King Blvd, Chattanooga, TN 37403, **Business Phone:** (423)267-2313.

**EDWARDS, DR. JOHN W, JR.** **See Obituaries Section.**

**EDWARDS, KENNETH J., SR.**
Executive. **Personal:** Born Apr 5, 1947, Beaumont, TX; married Gloria J Holmes; children: Melissa R, Kenitha J & Kenneth J. **Educ:** Lamar Univ, BS, 1970. **Career:** Executive (retired); US Govt, reliablty engr, 1970-71; John Deere Co, serv rep, 1971-72, sales prom supr, 1972-73, territory mgr, 1973-76, div serv mgr, 1976-77, serv mgr consumer prod, 1977-79, div sales mgr, 1979. **Special Achievements:** First African-American owner of a Deere agricultural dealership. **Home Addr:** 4301 Summer Brook Dr, Apex, NC 27539-5795, **Home Phone:** (919)327-3072.

**EDWARDS, KEVIN DURELL**
Basketball player, basketball executive. **Personal:** Born Oct 30, 1965, Cleveland Heights, OH; married Femi Emiola; children: 3. **Educ:** Lakeland Community Col, attended 1986; DePaul Univ, attended 1988. **Career:** Basketball player (retired), basketball executive; Miami Heat, guard, 1988-93; NJ Nets, 1993-98; Orlando Magic, 1998-2000; Vancouver Grizzlies, 2000-01; DePaul Univ, dir community, corp & prof rels, 2010-. **Business Addr:** Director, DePaul University, 1 E Jackson Blvd, Chicago, IL 60604, **Business Phone:** (312)362-8000.

**EDWARDS, LEO DEREK**
Composer, educator, association executive. **Personal:** Born Jan 31, 1937, Cincinnati, OH; children: 1. **Educ:** Mannes Col Music, BS, 1966; Brooklyn Col, MA, 1969. **Career:** Shumiatcher Sch Music, chmn theory dept, 1965-76; Brooklyn Col, teaching fel, 1966-68; Mannes Col Music, part-time assoc teaching prof, 1968-; City Univ New York, fac, 1969-75; Mannes Exten Div, dir, 1976-80; Eugene Lang Col, fac, currently. **Orgs:** Soc Black Composers; Phi Mu Alpha Sinfonia; Music Teachers Nat Asn. **Honors/Awds:** Phi Mu Alpha composition contest winner, 1960; Joseph Dillon Memorial Award, 1966; Citation Music Teachers National Association, 1975; National Endowment for the Arts grant, 1976. **Special Achievements:** Compositions in a wide variety of genres performed throughout the US, Central and South America; works published by Willis Music Co. **Home Addr:** PO Box 20037, Park W Finance Sta, New York, NY 10025, **Home Phone:** (212)864-4777. **Business Addr:** Part-time Associate Teaching Professor, Mannes College The New School for Music, 150 W 85th St, New York, NY 10024, **Business Phone:** (212)580-0210.

**EDWARDS, LEWIS**
Administrator, vice president (organization). **Personal:** Born May 16, 1953, Philadelphia, PA; son of Robert Norman and Margaret Norman; married Joan Southerland; children: Amber G & Ariel D. **Educ:** Pa State Univ, State Col, Pa, BS, acct, 1974. **Career:** Fidelity Bank, Philadelphia, Pa, sr auditor, 1974-78; Chrysler First Inc, Allentown, Pa, asst vpres acq analyst, vpres acq, 1978-94; Nations Credit Corp, vpres & dir, govt affairs, 1994. **Orgs:** Bd mem, Big Brothers Big Sisters, 1986-. **Home Addr:** 308 E Mosser St, Allentown, PA 18109, **Home Phone:** (610)770-0208.

**EDWARDS, DR. LONNIE C.**
Physician. **Personal:** Born Asheville, NC; son of Lonnie Sr and Corrie Thomas; married Carrie Glover; children: Lonnette & Lonnie III. **Educ:** Morehouse Col, attended 1945; Howard Univ Sch Med, MD, 1948; Roosevelt Univ, MPA, 1974; Nova Univ, MPA, 1977. **Career:** Pvt pract gen surg, 1955-70, family pract, 1960; Fantus Health Ctr, assoc med dir, 1970-71, dir, 1970-71; Cook County Hosp, dir div ambulatory serv, 1971-73, assoc med dir, 1974-83; Fantus Health Ctr, dir employee health serv hosp coordr home health care prog, 1974-83; Roosevelt Univ, pub admin prog; Abraham Lincoln Sch Med, clin asst prof family pract; Chicago Med Sch, clin asst prof dept family, 1974-83; City Chicago, comnr health, 1984-89; Cook County Hosp, dir Ambulatory Care Div, dep med dir, 1989. **Orgs:** Am Hosp Asn; Health Serv Develop Grants Study Sect, Dept Health Educ & Welfare; Nat Asn Neighborhood Health Ctrs; Prairie State Med Soc; Am Med Asn; Ill State Med Soc; Chicago Med Soc; Indust Med Asn; Cent States Soc Indust Med & Surg; AAAS; Asn Admin Ambulatory Serv; Am Acad Family Physicians; Nat Med Asn; Cook Co Physicians Asn; Am Pub Health Asn; Am Hosp Asn; Nat Asn Health Serv Exec; bd vpres, prin speaker, English Speaking Grand Lodge, dir, Rosicrucian Egyptian Mus. **Honors/Awds:** Distinguished Service, Hisp Health Alliance, 1985; Community Service Award, Nat Asn Health Serv Exec, 1986; Community Service Award, Truman Col, 1976; Pres Award, Ill Pub Health Asn, 1988; Human Service Award, Pilsen Neighbors Community Coun, 1988. **Special Achievements:** Selection of an Organizational Model for Maximizing the Effectiveness of Coordination of the Components of Outpatient Services, 1977; Numerous papers presented to various professional orgns and publication including, Ambulatory Care in a Large Urban Hospital Governors State Univ Seminar March 1978; Oral Cavity Evaluation-A Part of Prenatal Care IL Medical Journal Lonnie C Edwards MD Pedro A Poma MD et al Feb 1979 Vol 155No 2. **Home Addr:** Bldg 200 Rm B110F No 111G, Hines, IL 60615.

**EDWARDS, LUTHER HOWARD**
Government official. **Personal:** Born Jan 6, 1954, Butler, AL; son of Lee J Sr and Alma Jackson; married Geraldine Palmer; children: Ashley Letitia. **Educ:** Livingston Univ, BS, 1972, ME, 1976. **Career:** James River Corp, Comp Info Serv; Town Lisman, coun man, vice-mayor. **Orgs:** Pres, Afro-Am Soc; vpres, Owen Love Bus Asn; Stud Govt Assn; Col Civilian; Men's Housing Coun; Intramural Sports Asn; Yearbk Staff; Host& Hostess Comn; Phi Mu Alpha Sinfonia Frat; sec, Lisman Vol Fire Dept, 1980-; secy, Pleasant Hill Lodge 950, 1980-; secy, Edwards Pride Royal Arch Masons, 1982-. **Honors/Awds:** Outstanding Man of the Year. **Home Addr:** 26 N 2nd Ave, PO Box 141, Lisman, AL 36912, **Home Phone:** (205)398-3398.

**EDWARDS, DR. MARVIN E.**
Executive, school superintendent, educator. **Personal:** Born Oct 2, 1943, Memphis, TN; son of Simeon and Edna; married Carolyn; children: Belinda, Melissa, Craig, Eric & Derick. **Educ:** Eastern Ill Univ, BS, 1967; Chicago State Univ, MS, 1969; Northern Ill Univ, CAS, 1973, EdD, educ leadership, 1974. **Career:** Proviso High Sch, Maywood, Ill, teacher, dean stud, chair, 1967-72; Lockport High Sch, prin, 1972-75; Lockport Fairmont Elem Schs, supt, 1975-76; Joliet Twp High Schs, asst supt, 1976-78; Richmond Pub Schs, Richmond, Va, asst supt, 1978-80; Joliet Twp High Schs, Joliet, Ill, supt, 1980-85; Topeka Pub Schs, Topeka, Kans, supt, 1985-88; Dallas Independent Sch Dist, Dallas, Tex, gen supt, 1988-93; Elgin Area Sch Dist U-46, Ill, supt, 1993-2002; Aurora Univ, prof educ, 2002-. **Orgs:** Am Asn Sch Admin; Ill Asn Sch Adminr; Elgin Area Sch Adminr Asn; Asn Supv & Curric Develop; Nat Alliance Black Sch Educr; Phi Delta Kappa; Nat Sch Pub Rels Asn; Northwest Suburban African Am Investment Club; Rotary Club Bartlett; Broadview Baptist Church; Kappa Delta Pi; Fac Senate; Grad Affairs Comt; Diversity Experiences Subcomt Conceptual Framework Comt; Coun Cert Prof Personnel. **Special Achievements:** Selected as 1 of 100 best school executives in the Nation, Executive Educator magazine, 1987; The Executive Educator 100 List, Executive Education Magazine, 1986, 1992. **Home Addr:** 4N681 Mountain Ash Dr, Wayne, IL 60184. **Business Addr:** Professor of Education, Aurora University, Inst 219, Aurora, IL 60506-4892, **Business Phone:** (630)844-4625.

**EDWARDS, MATTIE SMITH**
Educator. **Personal:** Born Apr 16, 1931, Roxboro, NC; married E Zeno MD; children: Zenia Colette & Tanise Indra. **Educ:** Elizabeth City State Univ NC, BS, 1949; NC Ctr Univ, MA, 1953; Duke Univ, EdD, 1970. **Career:** Newbold Sch Fayetteville St Univ, supr, teacher, 1953-58; Cleveland Co Sch NC, gen supvr, 1965-69, reading coord, 1965-69; Springfield Col MA, assoc prof educ, prof educ, 1969-85, co-chair, fac emer, currently. **Orgs:** Bd trustee, Bay Path Col Mass, 1974-89; adv commn, Educ Personnel StMass, 1978-81; Nat Advan Asn Colored People; vpres, Auxiliary Greensboro Med Soc, 1990-92; Links Inc. **Honors/Awds:** Award Appreciation, Elizabeth City St Univ, 1980. **Home Addr:** 4 Allwood Ct, Greensboro, NC 27410-5935, **Home Phone:** (336)852-4741. **Business Addr:** Faculty Emeritus, Springfield College, 263 Alden St, Springfield, MA 01109-3797, **Business Phone:** (413)748-3000.

**EDWARDS, MICHELLE**
Basketball player, basketball coach. **Personal:** Born Mar 6, 1966, Boston, MA. **Educ:** Iowa Univ, BA, lib arts, 1989. **Career:** Basketball player (retired), basketball coach; Cleveland Rockers, guard, 1997-2000; Seattle Storm, guard, 2000-01; Rutgers Radio Network, color analyst, 2002-03; Cleveland Rockers, color analyst, 2003-04; Rutgers Univ, coor opers, 2003-04, asst coach, 2004-05, assoc dir opers, 2005-06, dir opers, 2007-. **Orgs:** Advisor, YMCA. **Business Addr:** Director of operations, Rutgers The State University NJ, Louis Brown Athletic Ctr, Piscataway, NJ 08854-8053, **Business Phone:** (732)445-4251.

**EDWARDS, DR. MILES STANLEY**
Educator, school administrator. **Personal:** Born Mar 21, 1951, Ft. Wayne, IN; son of William Howard Sr and Wanda L Woods. **Educ:** Ball State Univ, BS, 1973, admin cert, 1983; Ind Univ, MSEd, 1978; Univ Akron, PhD, 1994. **Career:** Administrator (retired), educator; Ft Wayne Community Schs, teacher spec educ, 1973-75, competency resource teacher, 1976-87, chap I resource teacher, 1988-90, coordr multicultural resource ctr, 1990-92, chap I specialist, 1993-94; DeKalb Ga County Sch Dist, math teacher, 1975-76; Ohio State Univ, GE fel, 1980; Oper Bread basket Learning Acad, teacher, 1985-86; Univ Akron, instr multicultural educ, 1992-93; Wash Elem Sch, asst prin, 1994-99. **Orgs:** Exec Bd, Old Ft YMCA, 1973-75; life mem, Nat Alliance Black Sch Educr; Ind Black Expo-Ft Wayne Chap, 1982-; Asn Black Communicators, 1982-85; bd mem, Ministerial Alliance Scholar Found, 1983-02; bd mem-at-large, Ft Wayne Alliance Black Sch Educr, 1983-92; Phi Delta Kappa, 1985-; bd minority affairs, Ind State Teachers Asn, 1985-86; Nat Educ Asn, 1985-94; dist rep, Int Reading Asn, 1986; MLK Living Memorial, 1986-90; bd dir, Martin Luther King Montessori Schs, 1986-98; Urban League; life mem, Nat Asn Advan Colored People; pres, Ind Black Expo-Ft Wayne Chap, 1988-90; Pi Lambda Theta Nat Hon & Prof Asn Educ, 1988-; Asn Supv &

Curric Develop, 1989-2000; Nat Coun Teachers Eng, 1990-96; bd dir, Ft Wayne Cinema Ctr, 1991-97; vpres, Ft Wayne Cinema Ctr, 1994-95; Allen County Ft Wayne Hist Soc, 1994-2000; pres, Martin Luther King Montessori Schs, 1994-98; Alpha Phi Alpha, 1995-02; founding mem, African & African Am Hist Soc & Mus, 1998, treas, 2002-14; bd dir, Heartland Chamber Chorale, 2001, pres; vpres, Pi Lambda Theta, 2005-06. **Special Achievements:** Listed in Who's Who Among African Americans, Who's Who Among Educators in America & Who's Who in the World. **Home Addr:** 4921 Ind Ave, Ft. Wayne, IN 46807-3001, **Home Phone:** (260)745-0044. **Business Addr:** IN.

### EDWARDS, MONICA
Executive, business owner. **Career:** Morehead Manor Bed & Breakfast, co-owner & treas, innkeeper, currently. **Orgs:** NC Bed & Breakfasts & Inns; treas, African Am Asn Inkeepers Int, currently. **Business Addr:** Co-owner, Treasurer, Morehead Manor Bed & Breakfast, 914 Vickers Ave, Durham, NC 27701, **Business Phone:** (919)687-4366.

### EDWARDS, MONIQUE MARIE
Lawyer, consultant. **Personal:** Born Aug 13, 1961, New Orleans, LA; daughter of Lloyd C and Mary Ann B. **Educ:** St Mary's Dominican Col, BS, merchandising & mkt, 1982; Southern Univ Law Ctr, JD, law, 1986. **Career:** Hon Bernette J Johnson, law clerk, 1986-87; Travelers Co, supvr, 1987-94; Maher, Gibson & Guiley PA, 1994-99; Edwards, Valdez & Ellis LLC, managing partner; pvt pract atty, currently; LA Dept Natural Resources, secy mineral, energy bd & exec coun, 2004-10; Family First Med Clin, off mgr & gen coun, 2010-; Edwards Law Group, managing atty, 2012-. **Orgs:** Moot ct bd, Southern Univ Law Ctr, 1985; La State Bar Asn, 1986-; Nat Bar Asn, 1990-; secy, 1990-91, Paul C Perkins Bar Asn, vpres, 1991-92; exec bd, Orange Co Br, Nat Asn Advan Colored People, 1991-, Acad FL Trial Lawyers; banquet chairwoman, Southern Christian Leadership Conf Greater Orlando, 1991-; Fla Bar Asn, 1992; pres, Fla Chap Nat Bar Asn, 1995-96; la house rep, Natural Resources Comt. **Honors/Awds:** 40 under 40 Award, Orlando Bus Journal, 1998; President's Award National Bar Association; Distinguished Leadership Award, Southern Univ Law Ctr; Graduate of Leadership Baton Rouge, 2013. **Home Addr:** PO Box 2249, Gonzalez, LA 70707-2249. **Business Addr:** Office Manager, General Counsel, Family First Medical Clinic, 25073 Hwy 1, Plaquemine, LA 70764, **Business Phone:** (225)687-1772.

### EDWARDS, DR. NICOLE R.
Educator, manager, vice president (organization). **Personal:** Born Jan 1, 1974. **Educ:** Jackson State Univ, BA, commun studies; Univ Southern Miss, MA, commun; Tougaloo Col, PhD, higher educ admin & res. **Career:** Tougaloo Col, Dept Speech & Eng, asst prof; Jackson State Univ, vpres; Lane Col, Inst Res, dir, New Stud Orientation, coordr, dir instnl res, dir inst effectiveness, assoc vpres learning support, admin mgr, currently. **Orgs:** Brownie troop leader, 2001-02; adv bd mem, Jim Hill High Sch Parent Teacher Asn; Leadership Jackson Class, 2002; vol, Habitat Humanity. **Business Addr:** Associate Vice President for Learning Support, Director of Institutional Effectiveness, Lane College, 545 Lane Ave, Jackson, TN 38301-4598, **Business Phone:** (731)426-7599.

### EDWARDS, OSCAR LEE
Consultant, president (organization). **Personal:** Born Dec 8, 1953, Long Beach, CA; son of Lewis Allen and Susie Belle; married Anita Grace Johnson; children: Ivan Lewis, Oscar Jr & Christine. **Educ:** Univ Calif Los Angeles, BA, econ, 1978, MBA, finance & mkt, 1981; UW & Kellog Training Ctr, cert master trainer. **Career:** Crenshaw YMCA, prog dir, 1977-79; CZ & Assocs Inc, vpres admin, 1981-84; Pacifica Servs Inc, sr consult, 1984-85; Cent News WAVE Publs, dir mkt, 1985-87; Edwards Assoc, pres, 1987; TMG/SER Inc, pres, 1987-90; Triaxial Mgt Serv, bd dirs, 1989-; Edwards Assocs & Media Mktg Network, pres, 1990-92; Visionary Mkt Inc, bd dirs, pres, currently; Econ Opportunity Ctr, adv bd, currently. **Orgs:** Bank credit analyst, Bank Am, 1980; res asst, Mayor Bradley's Africa Task Force, 1981-82; chmn bd mgrs, Crenshaw YMCA, 1983-84; pres, LA Chap Nat Black MBA Asn, 1985-86; bd dir, UCLA Black Alumni Asn, 1986-90; adv bd, Drew Health Educ Proj, 1986-90; prog comt, UCLA Mgt Alumni Asn, 1987-; Cert NFL Contract Adv, 1987-90; bd advs, S Calif chap, UNF, 1989-91; prog comt, Am Mkt Asn, 1993-; Inst Mgt Consults, 1984-; pres, Site Coun, Intensive Learning Ctr, 1999; PR comt chair, Conf Minority Transp Officials, 1999; co-chair, Am Pub Transp Asn; Southern Calif Pub Rels Socs; Compton Athletic Found Inc, Advantage Cert Develop Corp, currently. **Home Addr:** 5439 Pepperwood Ave, Lakewood, CA 90712, **Home Phone:** (562)633-1840. **Business Addr:** President, Visionary Marketing Inc, 1850 Redondo Ave Suite 201, Long Beach, CA 90804, **Business Phone:** (310)498-0788.

### EDWARDS, PRENTIS
Judge. **Personal:** children: 4. **Educ:** Wayne State Univ, BA, 1960, JD, 1965. **Career:** Wayne County Friend Ct, staff atty, 1966-68; Community Legal Coun, Supv Atty, 1968-69; Wayne County, Mich, asst county prosecutor, 1969-72; pvt pract lawyer, 1972-76; Wayne County Juv Ct, regist & chief referee, 1976-83; 36th Dist Ct, Criminal Div, presiding judge, 1983-85; Recorder's Ct, Circuit Ct, Criminal Div, judge, 1985; State Mich, circuit ct, 3rd circuit, judge, 1994-2012; Mich House Representatives, legis affairs, 2003-06; Detroit City Coun, pub policy analyst, 2006; Wayne County Prosecutor's Off, asst prosecuting atty, 2006-11; Mich State Senate, Dist 4, community liaison, 2011; 36th Dist Ct, Detroit, judge, 2011-. **Orgs:** State Bar Mich; Wayne County Bar Asn; Asn Black Judges; Mich Judges Asn; chmn, Grant Schs Scholar Fund; bd mem, Sickle Cell Info Ctr; mentor, Isuthu Inst; Fel Chapel Church; Nat Asn Advan Colored People. **Business Addr:** Judge, 36th District Court, 421 Madison Ave, Detroit, MI 48226, **Business Phone:** (313)965-2200.

### EDWARDS, PRESTON JOSEPH, SR.
Publisher, chief executive officer. **Personal:** Born Jul 3, 1943, New Orleans, LA; married Rosa Hughes; children: Preston Jr & Scott. **Educ:** Dillard Univ, BA, 1965; Atlanta Univ, MBA, 1966. **Career:** Nat City Bank, asst cashier, 1966-69; Southern Univ, Baton Rouge, La, asst prof, 1969-71; Great Atlantic & Pac Tea Co, reg mgr, 1975-76; Interracial Coun Bus Opportunity, vpres, 1976-77; IMinority Inc, chmn & chief exec officer; Black Collegian Mag, founder, publ, 1970-, chief exec officer, currently; iMinorities Diversity Inc, founder, publ/chief exec officer, 1970-; Pac Tea Co, Affirmative Action Great Atlantic, regional mgr; First Nat City Bank, asst cashier. **Orgs:** Bd mem, Jr Achievment; pres, J Inc; publ, J Nat Tech Asn; founder, Nat Asn Cols & Employers bus adv coun, Xavier Univ; bd coun, Career Develop Minorities, Jr Achievement Urban League Greater New Orleans Cent Bus Dist Hist Landmark Comn Employ Mgmt Asn Found Orleans Pvt Indust Coun; founder, Black Collegian. **Honors/Awds:** Male Image Award, Phi Beta Sigma African-Am, 1991; Role Model of the Young Leadership Council, 2006; Hall of Fame, Jr Achievement Bus, 2014; DHL, Livingstone Col; Presidents Award, Employ Mgt Asn Found; Pericles Award, Employ Mgt Asn; Pioneers of Excellence Award, CEBA. **Home Addr:** 18 Fairway Oaks Dr, New Orleans, LA 70131-3336, **Home Phone:** (504)393-4717. **Business Addr:** Publisher, Chief Executive Officer, The Black Collegian Magazine, 140 Carondelet St, New Orleans, LA 70130, **Business Phone:** (504)523-0154.

### EDWARDS, RAYMOND, JR.
Judge. **Educ:** Calif State Univ, BA, police sci & admin, 1971, JD, 1977. **Career:** Judge (retired); Southern Dist Calif, Asst US atty, 1979-83, chief, criminal div, 1983-85; Ct Appellate Div, Presiding Judge, 1999; Los Angeles County, dep dist atty & investr; State Calif, Super Ct, San Diego County, judge. **Orgs:** Calif Judges Asn; pres, Calif Judges Found, 1998-99; Calif State-Fed Judicial Coun.

### EDWARDS, RENIA K.
Administrator. **Educ:** Shaw Univ, BS, bus admin & mgt, 1995; Northern Ill Univ, MS, sport mgt, 1998. **Career:** Northern Ill Univ, GA stud athlete supprt serv & compliance, 1996-97; Univ Iowa, acad counr, 1998-2001; Shaw Univ Lady Bears Softball Team, Raleigh, NC; Austin Peay State Univ, Clarksville, TN, acad advising intern; Va Tech, asst dir stud athelete acad support servs, 2001-04; Univ SC, div dir, stud-athlete develop, dir internal opers, 2004-10, athletics acad adv, swimming & diving, Track & Field, cross country, currently; Sc State Univ, asst athletics dir, 2010-12, assoc athletics dir compliance/internal opers, 2012-14; Miss Valley State Univ, athletics consult, 2014, sr assoc athletics dir compliance & stud-athlete affairs, 2014-. **Orgs:** Career coordr & adv, Minority Focus Group Men; Blacksburg Alumnae Chap, Delta Sigma Theta Sorority; bd mem, N4A, 1998-11; vol, Cent Intercollegiate Athletic Asn, 2000-12. **Business Addr:** Assistant Athletics Director, South Carolina State University, 300 Col St NE, Orangeburg, SC 29117, **Business Phone:** (803)536-8578.

### EDWARDS, ROBERT
Educator, school administrator. **Personal:** Born Jan 30, 1939, Slocomb, AL; children: Randel Keith & Robert Corey. **Educ:** Bethune-Cookman Col, BS, 1965; City Col NY, MS, 1973. **Career:** Youth Training Acad, dir, 1969; Progress Asn Econ Develop, dir, 1972; Opportunity Indus Ctr, br mgr, 1974; Dade Co Pub Schs, prin, 1987-90. **Orgs:** Exec counr, Asn Study Afro-Amer Life & Hist, 1971; bd dir, Lexia Sch Young Adults, 1974; bd dir, OURS Inc, 1974; Urban League, Nat Asn Adv Colored People; Nat Alliance Black Sch Educrs; Kappa Alpha Psi; Bethune-Cookman Col Alumni Asn; Asn Study Afro-Amer Life & Hist. **Home Addr:** 20515 E Country Club Dr Suite 1948, Aventura, FL 33180, **Home Phone:** (305)792-7097.

### EDWARDS, ROBERT LEE, III
Manager, football player, football coach. **Personal:** Born Oct 2, 1974, Tennille, GA; son of Robert Jr and Jeannette; married Tracy. **Educ:** Univ Ga, BA, econs, family & consumer sci, 1997. **Career:** Football player (retired), manager, coach; New Eng Patriots, running back, 1998-2000; Miami dolphins, 2002; Montreal Alouettes, runner back, 2005-07; Toronto Argonauts, 2007-08; Arlington Christian Sch, head coach, 2009-12; All-Am Resources, relationship mgr, 2010-12; STAR Training Acad, founder & gen mgr, 2010-; One 24 Online, independent contractor, 2011-13; Greene County High Sch, head football coach, 2012-. **Honors/Awds:** Jim Thorpe Courage Award, 2003; Halas Award, Pro Football Writers Asn; East Division All-Star, Can Football League, 2005, 2006; Florida-Georgia Hall of Fame. **Business Addr:** Head Football Coach, Greene County High School, 1002 S Main St, Greensboro, GA 30642, **Business Phone:** (706)453-2271.

### EDWARDS, DR. RONDLE E.
Educator, school superintendent. **Personal:** Born Jul 19, 1934, Richmond, VA; son of Irene Taylor and Alfred M; married Gloria Twitty; children: Cassandra L, Lanee D Washington & Ronda D. **Educ:** Va Union Univ, AB; Va State Univ, MA; Ohio Univ, PhD. **Career:** Ohio State Univ, postdoctoral study; Columbia Univ, postdoctoral study; Richmond Pub Sch, asst supt gen admin & pupil personnel, 1972-75, asst supt support serv, 1975-76; E Cleveland City Sch, supt, 1976-84; Portsmouth Pub Sch, supt, 1984-87; Va Dept Educ, asst st supt, 1987-92; Harper Collins, vpres, Sch Rel Develop, 1992-; Portsmouth Pub Sch, supt; J Sargeant Reynolds Community Col, City Richmond, bd mem, 2008-; Va Commonwealth Univ, adj fac mem; Univ Richmond, adj fac mem; Old Dom Univ, adj fac mem. **Orgs:** Richmond Rotary Club; trustee, Cleveland Scholar Fund; United Negro Col Fund; Phi Delta Kappa Prof Frat; Am Asn Sch Personnel Adminr; Am Asn Sch Adminr, Ohio Sch Bd Asn; expert witness before US House Rep Comn Educ & Labor; Nat Coun Accreditation Teacher Educ. **Honors/Awds:** Award for Excellence in Public Education, Delta Sigma Theta Sor; Outstanding Achievement Award, Kappa Alpha Psi Frat; Outstanding Achievement Award, Phi Delta Kappa; Man of the Year, Cleveland Club Nat Asn Negro Bus; Man of the Year, Prof Women's Clubs; Exec Educator's Recognition One of North America's Top 100 Educators; Ohio Univ Alumni Medal of Merit for Notable Accomplishments in Education Administration, 1986; authored 4 books; numerous presentations. **Home Addr:** 3320 Carney Farm Lane, Portsmouth, VA 23703. **Business Addr:** Board Member, J Sargeant Reynolds Community College, PO Box 85622, Richmond, VA 23285-5622, **Business Phone:** (804)371-3000.

### EDWARDS, RUTH MCCALLA
Educator, lawyer. **Personal:** Born Apr 23, 1949, Cleveland, OH; married Michael M; children: Ashaunda, Alanna & Kamala. **Educ:** Hiram Col, BA, 1971; Univ Cincinnati Col Law, JD, law, 1974. **Career:** Legal Aid Soc Cincinnati, atty & off mgr, 1974-77; Pvt Law Pract, atty, 1977-79; Hamilton County Pub Defender Comn, atty, 1979; Univ Cincinnati, atty, prog coord, paralegal prog, 1979-, assoc prof, legal studies, emerita, currently. **Orgs:** Admitted Ohio State Bar, 1974; Admitted Fed Bar So Dist Ohio, 1974; bd trustee, Cincinnati Tech Col, 1977-; Am, Cincinnati Bar Asns; pres, Black Lawyers Asn Cincinnati; bd mem, Legal Aid Soc Cincinnati; bd mem, officer Winton Hills Med & Halth Ctr; bd mem & officer, Comprehensive Comn ChildCare; bd mem, Cincinnati Tech Col; Alpha Kappa Alpha Sor; arbitrator, Better Bus Bur Arbit Prog; Asn Comn Col Trustees; secy, Cent Reg Minority Affairs Assembly Asn Comn Col Trustees; Am Asn Paralegal Educ Inc; chairperson bd trustees, Cincinnati Tech Col, 1983-84; bd mem & officer, Winton Hills Med & Health Ctr; arbitrator, Am Arbit Asn; chair, Cent Region Minority Affairs Comn Asn Conity Col Trustees. **Honors/Awds:** Hon Deg Tech Lett, Cincinnati Tech Col, 1985; Black Achievers Award, YMCA, 1985. **Home Addr:** 6433 Leopard Lane, West Chester, OH 45069. **Business Addr:** Associate Professor, University Cincinnati, 302 Carl H Lindner Hall, Cincinnati, OH 45221, **Business Phone:** (513)556-1590.

### EDWARDS, SHIRLEY
Administrator. **Career:** Compton Community Col, exec vpres acad affairs, 2003, Child Develop Ctr, dir, currently. **Orgs:** Bd mem, Ctr Community & Family Serv; mem bd trustee, Compton Community Col. **Business Addr:** Director, Compton Community College, 1111 E Artesia Blvd CDC, Compton, CA 90221, **Business Phone:** (310)900-1600.

### EDWARDS, SHIRLEY JEAN
Government official. **Personal:** Born Oct 23, 1949, Doddsville, MS; married Thomas; children: Darron, Thomas Jr & Cheryl. **Educ:** Miss Valley State Univ, BS, 1983. **Career:** Fannie Humer Day Care, secy bk keeper, 1969-79; Sunflower/Humphrey Co Progress, career counr, 1979-83; Sunflower County Schs, sch attendance officer, 1983-; City Ruleville, alderwoman, mayor, 1993-. **Orgs:** Nat Conf Black Mayors. **Honors/Awds:** Community Service Award, Nat Asn Advan Colored People, Sunflower County, 1983. **Home Addr:** 408 Juniper Lane, Ruleville, MS 38771-3219, **Home Phone:** (662)756-0474. **Business Addr:** Mayor, Sunflower County, 200 E Floyce, Ruleville, MS 38771-0428, **Business Phone:** (662)756-2791.

### EDWARDS, DR. SOLOMON
Educator. **Personal:** Born Apr 2, 1932, Indianapolis, IN; married Claudia; children: Gregory D & Risa M. **Educ:** Ind Univ, Indianapolis, IN, BS, 1954, MS, 1969, EdD, 1984. **Career:** Arts Festival, coord, 1956; NY City Dramatic Readers, dir, 1957-58; Ind Pub Schs, teacher; Purdue Univ, assoc fac, 1971-79. **Orgs:** Omega Psi Phi; Nat Asn Advan Colored People; Phi Delta Kappa Ind Univ. **Home Addr:** 2228 W 59th St, Indianapolis, IN 46228-1721, **Home Phone:** (317)257-0228.

### EDWARDS, DR. SYLVIA
Lawyer. **Personal:** Born May 9, 1947, Lackawanna, NY. **Educ:** State Univ Col Buffalo, BS, 1969; Howard Univ Sch Law WA, JD, 1973. **Career:** Employ Sect Dept Justice, trial atty, 1973-76; Off Spec Litigation Dept Justice WA DC, sr trial atty; Coun DC, legis coun, 1977-79; DC Law Rev Comn, sr atty, 1979-; Metrop Area Contractors Inc, atty. **Orgs:** Ny Bar Asn, 1974-; Pa Bar, 1974; Adv Comn Codification Wash DC, 1977-79; Nat Asn Black Women Atty, 1978; legis consult Comt Pub Serv & Consumer Affairs Coun DC, 1979. **Honors/Awds:** Special Achievement Award, Howard Univ Sch Law, 1972; Intl Moot Court Award, Howard Univ Sch Law, 1973; Special Achievement Award, Dept Justice Wash DC, 1975; Resolution Special Achievement, Coun DC, 1979. **Home Addr:** 1122 7th St NE, Washington, DC 20002, **Home Phone:** (202)544-1287. **Business Addr:** Attorney, Metropolitan Area Contractors Inc, 1114 Georgia Ave Suite 404, Wheaton, MD 20902, **Business Phone:** (301)933-6904.

### EDWARDS, TAMRA
City council member, executive. **Personal:** Born May 4, 1959; daughter of Cleveland Harrington and Vera Ford; married Oliver; children: Jeremy, O'Juan, Oliver III & Heather. **Educ:** Mott Community Col. **Career:** Econ Empowerment Inc, chief operating officer & chief exec officer, currently; Mott Community Col, presidential ambassador; Mortgage Financing; pub advocator; City Durham, councilwoman, 2003. **Orgs:** Vpres, YMCA; Salem Housing Orgn. **Business Addr:** Chief Operating Officer, Chief Executive Officer, Economic Empowerment Inc, 3162 Flushing Rd, Flint, MI 48504, **Business Phone:** (810)232-0470.

### EDWARDS, TERESA
Basketball player, athletic coach. **Personal:** Born Jul 19, 1964, Cairo, GA. **Educ:** Univ Ga, leisure studies, 1990. **Career:** American Basketball League, 1996; Atlanta Glory, player & head coach; Philadelphia Rage; Minn Lynx, 2003-04, asst coach, 2006; 2008 Summer Olympics, analyst NBC sports coverage; Univ Ga, Minn Lynx, guard; Women's Nat Basketball Asn, Minn Lynx, asst coach, 2007; USA Basketball, bd dir, 2009-12; Tulsa Shock, asst coach, 2011; Women's Nat Basketball Asn, Tulsa Shock, head coach, 2011-; 2012 Olympic Games, chef de mission; Atlanta Dream, asst, 2014. **Business Addr:** Head Coach, Women's National Basketball Association, 1 W 3rd St Suite 1100, Tulsa, OK 74103, **Business Phone:** (918)949-9700.

### EDWARDS, THEODORE ALLEN
Executive, vice president (organization). **Personal:** Born Jan 16, 1954, Chicago, IL; son of Theodore and Mary; married Katheryn; children: Christopher, Cara, Rachael & Casey. **Educ:** Northwestern Univ, BS, 1975; Kellogg Grad Sch Mgt, MM, 1988. **Career:** Ameritech Info Indust Serv, staff, 1978-90, opers div mgr, 1990-91, dir acct mgt, 1991-92, mkt pub serv, gen mgr, 1992, Opers Carrier Serv, vpres, 1993-96, Local Exchange Carriers, vpres sales, 1996-; Pricewaterhouse Coopers, sr consult, 2000-02; Another Time Inc, vpres, co-owner, 2003-05; Jpmorgan Chase Bank, vpres, relationship mgr, 2005-08; Rocket Learning, sr acct mgr, 2008-09; Chicago Career Tech, consult, 2010-. **Orgs:** Bd trustee, Hull House Asn, 1990-97; bd dir, COT Investment Fund, 1996-97; bd dir, Pioneer Clubs Am, 1997.

Home Addr: 19 N Kensington, La Grange, IL 60525, **Home Phone:** (708)354-3453. **Business Addr:** Vice President of Sales, Ameritech Information Industry Services, 350 N Orleans Fl 3, Chicago, IL 60654, **Business Phone:** (312)335-6595.

## EDWARDS, THEODORE THOMAS

Executive, social worker. **Personal:** Born Sep 8, 1917, Bridgeport, CT; son of Theodore and Maude; married Vivian Blackmon. **Educ:** Quinnipac Col, AA, 1941; NY Univ, BS, 1946; Columbia Univ, MSW, 1947; US Pub Health Hosp, attended 1956; Univ Chicago, grad work, 1959. **Career:** Government official (retired); Goldwater Hosp, med social worker, 1947-48; NJ Parole Bd, parole officer, 1949-55; US Probation-US Parole Comn, probation officer, 1955-77. **Orgs:** Youth Worker, NY Youth Bd, 1947; Nat Coun Crime & Del, 1955-80; life mem, Fed Probation Off Asn, 1956-80; co-founder, Narcotic Treat Ctr, 1956; Mid Atlantic St Conf Correction, 1956-80; Rotary Int, 1975-77; Am Correction Asn, 1975-80. **Honors/Awds:** Certificate of Appreciation, Newark Boys Club, 1969; Crox De Geurre; 4 Battle Stars. **Special Achievements:** First African American Federal Probation Officer, Newark NJ, 1955; Co-founder of first Private Narcotic Treatment Center, Newark, NJ, 1957; First Black Federal Probation Director, Paterson, NJ, 1975-77. **Home Addr:** 801 Elizabeth Ave Apt 5G, Newark, NJ 07112, **Home Phone:** (201)926-9473.

## EDWARDS, THEODORE UNALDO

Government official. **Personal:** Born Sep 18, 1934, New York, NY; son of Joseph Unaldo (deceased) and Mary A; married Ione L D; children: Donna M O. **Educ:** St Peter's Col, BS, 1955; Rutgers Univ, MSW, 1962; BARO Clin, cert, 1967. **Career:** US Ct/Justice Dept, probation officer, 1962-69; Harlem Child Guid Clin, clin dir, 1969-78; Community Serv Soc New York, exec dir, 1973-76; City New Rochelle Dept Human Serv, dep comnr, 1977-; Col New Rochelle, New York, NY, adj prof, 1979-. **Orgs:** Bd mem, Catholic Big Brothers New York, 1975-; comnr, Off Black Ministry Archdiocese New York, 1977-; bd mem, Salvation Army New Rochelle, 1985-; exec bd, Nat Asn Advan Colored People, 1985-; Omega Omicron Iota Chap. **Honors/Awds:** Community Service Award, Col New Rochelle, New York, NY, 1983-85; Spike Harris Service Award, New York Counselors, 1985. **Special Achievements:** Numerous publications including "Why Bartering", Voice Mag, 1981; "Budget Time", Voice Mag, 1981; "The City of New Rochelle Senior Population", 1986; Columnist for Tomorrow Newspaper, Westchester, NY. **Home Addr:** 18 Muir Pl, New Rochelle, NY 10801, **Home Phone:** (914)632-1455. **Business Addr:** Deputy Commissioner, City of New Rochelle, City Hall, New Rochelle, NY 10801, **Business Phone:** (914)654-2084.

## EDWARDS, DR. THOMAS OLIVER

School administrator, psychologist. **Personal:** Born Jan 4, 1943, Vanceboro, NC; son of Calvin and Blanche Ethel; married Loretta McFadden; children: Tomia, Kuturi, Loretta, Tiffany & Calvin. **Educ:** City Col NY, BA, 1965; NY Univ, MA, 1968; City Univ NY, MPh, 1980, PhD, 1981. **Career:** Peace Corps Costa Rica, vol, 1965-67; Alexander Burger Jr High Sch, teacher, 1967-71; Medgar Evers Col instr & lect, 1971-81, asst prof, 1981-84, assoc prof, 1984-, assoc dean admin, 1986-88, actg chmn, SocialSci Div, 1988-89; Medgar Evers Col, affirmative action officer, assoc prof, Dept Social & Behav Sci, chairperson, currently. **Orgs:** Baseball coach Rochdale Village Little League, 1979-; consult, Urban Strategies Inc, 1980-; consult, Hale House Prom Human Potential, 1983; bd dir, mem Medgar Evers Col Child Care Ctr, 1983-; adj prof, Col New Rochelle, 1984-85; regional officer, New York Chap, Asn Black Psychol, 1990-92; exec coun mem, United Partners Asn, 1990-92; pres, New York Asn Black Psychol, 1983-; chair, Nat Asn Black Psychol, Black Family Task Force; bd dir, Genesis Transitional Housing Ministries Inc. **Home Addr:** 17807 137th Ave, Jamaica, NY 11434, **Home Phone:** (718)527-0934. **Business Addr:** Chairperson, Associate Professor, Medgar Evers College CUNY, 1150 Carroll St Suite 400, Brooklyn, NY 11225, **Business Phone:** (718)270-6989.

## EDWARDS, TONYA

Basketball player, basketball coach. **Personal:** Born Mar 13, 1968, Flint, MI. **Educ:** Univ Tenn, educ, 1990. **Career:** Basketball player (retired), basketball coach; Northwestern Community High Sch, girl's basketball coach, 1990-95; played Turkey, 1994; played Israel, 1995-96; Columbus Quest, guard, 1996-98, interim head coach; Minn Lynx, guard, 1999; Phoenix Mercury, guard, 2000-01, radio commentator, 2004; Charlotte Sting, guard, 2001-02; Nat Women's Basketball League, asst coach, 2004; Phoenix Mercury games, radio commentator, 2004; Detroit titans, asst coach, 2006-08; Alcorn State Lady Braves, head women's basketball coach, 2008-; Nat Womens Basketball League, asst coach. **Business Addr:** Head Women's Basketball Coach, Alcorn State Lady Braves, 1000 Asu Dr, Lorman, MS 39096-7500, **Business Phone:** (601)877-6467.

## EDWARDS, TREVOR A.

Marketing executive, vice president (organization). **Personal:** Born Nov 28, 1962, London; son of Ossie and Joyce; married Carolyn Jarrett, Jan 1, 1991?; children: Justin & Jaden. **Educ:** Baruch Col, BA, bus, 1984, MBA, int mkt & finance, 1989. **Career:** Goldman Sachs, UK, spec trades group analyst, 1984-86; Colgate Palmolive, global bus develop mgr, 1986-92; Nike Inc, regional mkt mgr, 1992, foot locker's mkt mgr strategic accounts, 1993-95, dir mkt Americas, 1995-97, dir mkt Europe, 1997-99, vpres mkt Europe, Mid E & Africa, 1999-2000, vpres US brand mkt, 2000-02, vpres global brand mgt, 2002-06, vpres global brand & category mgt, vpres, 2006-, brand pres, 2013-. **Orgs:** Dir, Mattel Inc, 2012-; Nike Found. **Business Addr:** Brand President, NIKE, Inc., 1 Bowerman Dr, Beaverton, OR 97005-6453.

## EDWARDS, VERBA L.

Executive. **Personal:** Born Jul 15, 1950, Boligee, AL; son of George and Bertha Barker; married Roberta Mackel; children: Keith, Christopher & Raquel. **Educ:** Alcorn State Univ, BS, bus admin, 1973; Cent Mich Univ, MA, personnel admin, 1977. **Career:** Gen Motors Corp Chevy Truck Assembly Plant, coordr equal employ opportunity, gen supvr mfg, supvr indust rels, supvr hourly personnel admin, 1973-81; Gen Motors Corp Chevrolet Cent Off, div salaried personnel admin, 1981-83; Gen Motors Corp Saginaw Div, asst dir personnel, 1984-87; Wing Tips & Pumps Inc, pres, chief exec officer, 1987-. **Orgs:** Omega Psi Phi Frat, Nat Alliance Bus Col/Indust Rels Div, Nat Asn Equal Opportunity Higher Educ; Nat Black MBA Asn. **Honors/Awds:** Outstanding Young Men Am, Jet Mag. **Special Achievements:** Author of "Wing Tips and Pumps". **Business Addr:** President, Chief Executive Officer, Wing Tips & Pumps Inc, 2357 Belmont Ct, Troy, MI 48098-2352, **Business Phone:** (248)641-0980.

## EDWARDS, HON. WILBUR PATTERSON, JR.

Lawyer. **Personal:** Born Aug 28, 1949, Yokohama; son of Wilbur P Sr and Mary C; married Evelynne Swagerty, Jun 8, 1989; children: Arielle Belson & Marissa Avery. **Educ:** Harvard Col, BA, 1971; Boston Col Law Sch, JD, 1984; Southern New Eng Sch Law, JD, 2009. **Career:** Purity Supreme, real estate rep, 1971-73; Grand Union Co, real estate rep, 1973-74; Southland Corp, real estate mgr, 1974-79; Toys R Us, real estate mgr, 1979-81; Roche, Carens & De Giacomo, atty, 1984-88; McKenzie & Edwards PC, atty, 1989-; Jane Swift, actg gov, 2002; Mass Southeastern Housing Ct, assoc justice, 2002-; ALI-ABA Land Use Inst, guest lectr. **Orgs:** Mass Bar Lawyers Asn, 1984-, secy, 1985; Property Sect Coun, chair, Mass Bar Asn, 1984-; Mass Conveyancers Asn, 1988-; pres, Boston Col Law Sch Bar Alumni Network, 1990-94; Supreme Judicial Cts Judiciary/Media Comt & Trial Cts Interpreters Comt; bd mem, former pres, Mass Black Judges Conf; Boston Bar Asn; Mass Continuing Legal Educ; Boston Lawyers Group; bd mem, Mass Judges Conf. **Home Addr:** 23 Pine Rd, Sharon, MA 02067-1913, **Home Phone:** (781)784-6784. **Business Addr:** Associate Justice, Massachusetts Southeastern Housing Court, 289 Rock St, Fall River, MA 02720-3246, **Business Phone:** (508)677-1505.

## EFFORT, DR. EDMUND D.

Dentist. **Personal:** Born Jun 20, 1949, Chicago, IL; son of Beverley and Exzene; married Elaine Leaphart; children: Edmundson David & April Elaine. **Educ:** Univ Ill, BS, maj psychol, minor chem & physics, 1972; Univ Mich, DDS, 1977; US Dent Inst, orthod prog, 1988-90; Air War Col, attended 1998-99; Straight Wire Orthod Studies, attended 2003. **Career:** Pvt pract, dentist, currently. **Orgs:** Alpha Phi Alpha, 1969-89, pres, 1994-96; Am Dent Assoc, 1977-89; Nat Asn Advan Colored People, 1981-89, bd dir & chmn, Health Affairs, 1995-98; Urban League, 1981-89, Pa Dent Assoc, 1981-89; bd dir, Lemington Home Aged, 1984; Lions, 1985, Elks, 1986; Urban Youth Action, 1986-87, bd dir, United Cerebral Palsy, 1987, Connely Trade Sch, 1987, Eva P Mitchell Residense, 1987; coach little league baseball, Boys Club, 1989; bd dir, Boys & Girls Club, 1990-; Felixvs Casey, expert witness, 1992-93; chmn, Med Assistance Advi Comt, PDA; Reizenstein Mid Sch, PTO, pres, 1994; chmn, Probable Cause Comt, State Bd Dent, 2010; Am Dent Asn; Pa Dent Asn; life mem, Asn Mil Surgeons; Odontological Soc Western Pa; founding mem, Pittsburgh Chap Tuskegee Airman Inc, 2010; bd mem, Shady Side Boys & Girls Club Pittsburgh. **Honors/Awds:** Black Achievers News in Print Magazine, 1984; Three articles written for Talk Magazine, 1985; PA Air Commendation Medal PA ANG, 1986; Community Service Award, Upward Bound Proj, 1987; Good Samaritan Award, Am Red Cross, 1988; Martin Luther King Award, Hand-In-Hand Inc, 1990. **Business Addr:** Dentist, Edmund D Effort, Gateway Towers 320 Ft Duquesne Blvd Suite 215, Pittsburgh, PA 15222, **Business Phone:** (412)765-0199.

## EFFORT, ELAINE

Journalist. **Personal:** married Edmund D; children: 2. **Educ:** Univ Mich, BA, polit sci, MA, jour. **Career:** WUOM; KQV Radios, host & reporter, 1973-79, 1983-. **Orgs:** Co-founder, The Girl Scout troop. **Honors/Awds:** Won Numerous awards including: 2 Golden Quills; PA AP; Women In Communs; Pittsburgh Black Media Fedn awards. **Home Addr:** 1139 Mellon St, Pittsburgh, PA 15206-1525, **Home Phone:** (412)441-8319. **Business Addr:** Host, Reporter, KQV Radios, 650 Smithfield St, Pittsburgh, PA 15222, **Business Phone:** (412)562-5900.

## EGGLESTON, NEVERETT A., JR.

Real estate agent, association executive, executive. **Personal:** Born Richmond, VA; daughter of Neverett A Sr; married Jean Deloris; children: Neverett A III & Jayne. **Educ:** NC Agr & Tech State Univ, BS, 1955. **Career:** Mainstream Inc, pres; Golden Skillet, prin; Silas Lee & Assocs, prin; Eggleston's Hotel, pres & chief exec officer, 1960-; Eggleston Auto Serv Ctr, pres & chief exec officer, 1979-; Eggleston Develop Corp, pres & chief exec officer, 1992-; Coldwell Banker Dew Realty Inc, real estate agt. **Orgs:** Bd mem, Nat Bus League, 1970-, secy, currently; chmn bd, Minority Supplier Develop, 1978-; E & R Janitorial Serv Inc, 1978-; bd mgt, Radiantherm Inc; bd dir, Jefferson Sheraton Hotel; adv bd, Womens bank; Richmond Chamber Com; vpres, Capital Area Innkeepers Asn; bd dir & pres, Metro Bus League; bd dir, Richmond Urban League; bd dir, Richmond Community Action Prog; bd dir, Am Red Cross; chmn, People League Voters; bd dir, Greater Richmond Transit Co; United Givers Fund. **Honors/Awds:** Spoke Award and Spark Plug Award, Jr Chamber Com; Businessman of the Year Award, Metro Bus League; Martin Luther King Community Learning Week Business Recognition, 1982. **Home Addr:** 11207 Nuckols Rd Suite E Glen, Allen, VA 23059-5511, **Home Phone:** (804)527-3948. **Business Addr:** President, Chief Executive Officer, The Eggleston Corp, 2712 Seminary Ave, Richmond, VA 23220, **Business Phone:** (804)321-7159.

## EGIEBOR, SHARON E.

Journalist. **Personal:** Born Jun 11, 1959, Kansas City, KS; daughter of William David Patterson Sr and Lester Alois Wilborn; children: Marcus Iyobosa. **Educ:** Dallas County Community Col Dist, Mountain View Campus, AA, lib arts, 1979; Univ Tex, Arlington, BA, jour, 1983; Tex Woman's Univ, attended 2009. **Career:** Tex mag, managing ed; Dallas Times Herald, Dallas, Tex, reporter, 1983-87, copy ed, 1987, asst reg ed, 1987-88, asst city ed, 1988-90, ed writer, 1990, exec ed; Egiebor Expressions, owner, chief exec officer, 1994-; The Dallas Examr, exec ed, 2002-05. **Orgs:** Dallas-Ft Worth Asn Black Communicators; Nat Asn Black Journalists; fel, Kaiser Family Found HIV-Mini Media Health, 2004; fel, Casey Journalism Ctr C & Families, 2005. **Honors/Awds:** Times Mirror Scholar, Times Mirror Corp, 1982; Jack Butler Award, UTA-Sch Jour, 1983; Sch Bell Award, Tex State Teachers Asn, 1985; Inst Jour Educ Fel, Minority Journalists, 1987; Community Serv Award, Black State Employees Asn, 1990. **Home Addr:** 209 Longbranch Lane, Dallas, TX 75217, **Home Phone:** (214)391-8771. **Business Addr:** Owner, Chief Executive Officer, Founder, Egiebor Expressions, PO Box 2842, Cedar Hill, TX 75106, **Business Phone:** (972)291-8452.

## EGINS, PAUL CARTER

Manager. **Personal:** Born Sep 22, 1963, Columbus, GA; son of Paul C Jr and Jacquelyn Joy. **Educ:** Univ Ga, BS, biol, 1986; Fla A&M Univ, attended 1987. **Career:** Atlanta Braves, Class A, athletic trainer, 1988-89, minor league admin, 1990, asst dir, scouting & player dev, 1990-91; Colo Rockies Baseball Club, asst dir scouting, 1992, player dev, 1993-94, asst dir player personnel, 1995-97, dir player develop, 1997-2000, dir minor league opers, dir maj league opers, currently. **Orgs:** Kappa Alpha Psi Fraternity, 1989-; RBI Prog, 1995-; bd dir, Bichette Baseball World, 1996-. **Honors/Awds:** Denver's Fifty Finest, Cystic Fibrosis Found, 1997. **Home Addr:** 295 Holly St, Denver, CO 80246, **Home Phone:** (303)394-9702. **Business Addr:** Director of Major League Operations, Colorado Rockies Baseball Club, Coors Field 2001 Blake St, Denver, CO 80205-2000, **Business Phone:** (303)292-0200.

## EICHELBERGER, BRENDA

Teacher, executive director. **Personal:** Born Oct 21, 1939, Washington, DC. **Educ:** Eng & Bus Educ, BS; DC Teachers Col, attended 1963; Chicago State Univ, MS, 1973. **Career:** Wash DC Pub Sch Syst, teacher, 1964-65; Muscatine Community Sch Dist, teacher, 1966-67; Chicago Pub Sch Syst, teacher, librn, counr, 1967-77; Nat Alliance Black Feminists, div exec dir, 1976; Nat Col Educ, m equiv sch admin & supvr. **Orgs:** Dist Ten Teacher Coun, 1974-75; Chicago Chap Nat Black Feminist Org, 1974-76; adv bd mem, Blue Gargoyle Grp 1975; bd mem, Citz Comt, 1975-76; bd mem, Pro & Con Screening 1976; bd mem, Chicagoland Women's Fed Credit Union, 1976-; found, Black Womens's Ctr 1976-; bd mem, treas, Chicago Consort Women Educ Prog, 1976. **Home Addr:** 4940 SE End Ave Apt 7C, Chicago, IL 60615. **Business Addr:** Executive Director, National Alliance of Black Feminists, 202 S State St, Chicago, IL 60604.

## EILAND, MIKE

Television director. **Career:** Clear Channel Commun, Inc, Clear Channel Radio, community engagement dir, recruiting mgr, pub serv dir & air personality, currently. **Business Addr:** Recruiting Manager, Public Service Director, Clear Channel Communications Inc, 1301 Dublin Rd, Columbus, OH 43215-7009, **Business Phone:** (614)487-2512.

## EISLEY, HOWARD JONATHAN

Basketball coach, basketball player. **Personal:** Born Dec 4, 1972, Detroit, MI; married Tiyesh M; children: Kennedy & Howard. **Educ:** Boston Col, BS, commun. **Career:** Basketball player (retired), coach; Minn Timberwolves, point guard, 1994-95; San Antonio Spurs, point guard, 1995; Utah Jazz, point guard, 1995-2000, 2004-05; Dallas Mavericks, shooting guard, 2000-01; New York Knicks, point guard, 2001-04; Phoenix Suns, point guard, 2003-04; Los Angeles Clippers, point guard, 2005-06, asst coach, 2010-14; Denver Nuggets, point guard, 2006; Chicago Bulls, 2006; Wash Wizards, asst coach, 2014-16. **Honors/Awds:** NBA draft, 1994; Jazz nominee, 1997-98; Sportsmanship Award, Nat Basketball Asn, 1998-99. **Home Addr:** 72 Pleasant Ridge Rd, Harrison, NY 10528-1212, **Home Phone:** (914)670-0009.

## EJOGO, CARMEN (CARMEN ELIZABETH EJOGO)

Actor. **Personal:** Born Jan 1, 1973?, London; daughter of Charles Ejogo and Elizabeth Douglas; married Tricky, Aug 8, 1998; married Jeffrey Wright, Aug 1, 2001?, (divorced 2014); children: TK & Elijah. **Career:** Actress. Films: Absolute Beginners, 1986; Metro, 1997; I Want You, 1998; The Avengers, 1998; Tube Tales, 1999; Love's Labour's Lost, 2000; Perfume, 2001; What's the Worst That Could Happen?, 2001; The Brave One, 2007; Pride and Glory, 2008; Away We Go, 2009; Sparkle, 2012; Alex Cross, 2012; The Purge; Anarchy, 2014; Selma, 2014; Born to Be Blue, 2015; Fantastic Beasts and Where to Find Them, 2016. Vocalist and songwriter, 1990s. Television: Saturday Disney, 1993-95; Cold Lazarus, 1996; Colour Blind, 1998; Sally Hemings: An American Scandal, 2000; Boycott, 2001; Lackawanna Blues, 2005; Kidnapped, 2006-07; M.O.N.Y, 2007; Chaos, 2011; Zero Hour, 2013. **Honors/Awds:** Black Reel Award, 2006; Black Film Critics Circle Award, 2014; Black Reel Award, 2015; Image Award, 2015. **Business Addr:** Authentic Talent and Literary Management, 20 Jay St Suite M17, Brooklyn, NY 11201.

## EKE, DR. KENOYE KELVIN

Educator, vice president (organization). **Personal:** Born Sep 1, 1956, Rivers State; son of Joseph and Nancy Owen; married Joy Grimes; children: Kenoye Kelvin Joseph & Kebbin Henry Joseph. **Educ:** Ala A&M Univ, BA, polit sci, 1980; Atlanta Univ, MA, polit sci, 1982, PhD, polit sci, 1985; Harvard Univ, MA, 1988, 1990; Univ Wis-Madison, 1989. **Career:** Bethune-Cookman Col, Daytona Beach, Fla, asst prof, 1985-89; Savannah State Col, assoc prof & coordr polit sci, 1989-93, dir int progs, 1991-93, Sch Humanities & Soc Sci, dean & prof, 1993-98; Univ Fla, Ctr African Studies, res fel, 1991; Cheyney Univ, Acad & Stud Affairs, provost & vpres, 2002-; Calif State Univ, Monterey Bay, interim asst vpres acad progs; Ky State Univ, assoc vpres acad affairs & chief acad admin, Col Prof Studies, assoc vpres acad affairs & actg dean, vpres acad affairs & summer session chief operating officer; Lib Arts & Sci, dean; Savannah State Univ, coordr polit sci, prof. **Orgs:** Exec bd, African Asn Polit Sci, N Am Chap, 1987-; pres, Pan-African Awareness Asn, Volusia County, FL, 1988-89; benefits adv bd, Chatham County, Dept Family & C Serv, 1989-; Pew fac fel int affairs, Harvard Univ, 1992-93; fel Am Coun Educ, 1994-95; dir, Spectrum Initiative; dir, Savannah State Univ's Ctr Trade & Technol Transfer. **Home Addr:** PO Box 20565, Savannah, GA 31404, **Home Phone:** (912)354-6883. **Business Addr:** Director, The Spectrum Initiative, PA.

**EKECHI, FELIX K.**
Educator. **Personal:** Born Oct 30, 1934, Owerri; son of Ekechi Egekeze; married Regina; children: Kemakolam, Chidi, Okechukwu & Chinyere. **Educ:** Holy Ghost Col, Umuahia, Nigeria, Gd 2 teachers cert, 1955; Univ Minn, BA, 1963; Kans State Univ, MA, 1964; Univ Wis-Madison, PhD, 1969. **Career:** St Dominicks Sch Afara-Mbieri, Nigeria, headmaster, 1955-58; Mt St Marys Col, Azaraegbelu, Owerri, tutor, 1959-60; Alcorn A&M Col Lorman, MS, instr, 1964-65; KS State Univ, grad asst, 1964-65; Univ Wis-Madison, grad teaching asst, 1965-69; Kent State Univ, from asst prof to assoc prof, 1969-77, prof, 1978, African Studies Prog, dir, prof emer his, currently; Univ Port Harcourt, Alvan Ikoku Col Educ, Univ Nigeria, vis prof, 1983; Alvan/Ikoku Col Educ, vis prof, 1994. **Orgs:** Pres, Black Fac & Staff Asn, Kent State Univ, 1974; Am Bicentennial Comn, Kent, OH, 1976-77; Am Missons & Educ Nigeria; Am Philos Soc, 1979-83; cord, African Studies Prog Kent State Univ, 1985-; African Studies Asn; Igbo Studies Asn; Third World Studies Asn; Am Hist Asn. **Home Addr:** 1077 Gardenview, Kent, OH 44240. **Business Addr:** Professor Emeritus, Kent State University, 305 Bowman Hall, Kent, OH 44242-0001, **Business Phone:** (330)672-2882.

**EL WILSON, BARBARA**
Entrepreneur. **Personal:** Born Feb 17, 1959, Charlotte, NC; daughter of Joseph Robinson Sr (deceased) and Doreather Robinson; married Alex O; children: Parker Destino Wilson. **Educ:** Howard Univ, Drama Dept, BFA, theater, 1981. **Career:** Duke Ellington Sch Performing Arts, instr, 1981-82; Every Man St Theatre Co, prod stage mgr, 1983-84; No Neck Monster Theatre Co's prod, Sanctuary, DC, performer; Sugarfoots, owner & creator, currently. **Orgs:** Women's Pres's Educ Org; Sistermoms. **Honors/Awds:** Helen Hayes Award, 1988. **Home Phone:** (202)726-8142. **Business Addr:** Owner, Creator, Sugarfoots, 5738 7th St NW, Washington, DC 20011-2006, **Business Phone:** (202)723-8890.

**EL-AMIN, SA'AD (JEROYD X GREENE)**
Teacher, lawyer. **Personal:** Born Feb 10, 1940, Manhattan, NY; married Carolyn Adams; children: Je Royd W III, Nicole & Anissa. **Educ:** Univ Southern Calif, BA, 1965; Yale Univ, JD, 1969, MA, 1969. **Career:** Sheffield & Greene, assoc law firm, 1969-71; Greene & Poindexter Inc, sr law practr, 1971-75; Howard Univ, asst prof law, 1973-74; World Commun Islam W, nat bus mgr, 1975-76; city councilman, 1998-2003; Tawheed Prep Sch, teacher. **Orgs:** Nat Asn Criminal Defense Lawyer Bar US Supreme Ct, 1973; Nat Consult & Lectr Coun Legal Educ, 1974-75; pres, Adv Comt Am Muslims Propagation; Financial Asst Fund; Iman Consult Bd, Hon Elijah Muhammad Mosque 2; Am Bar Asn; Nat Bar Asn; Nat Donfer Black Lawyers; Old Dom Bar Asn; Va State Bar; Va Trial Lawyers Asn; Richmond Criminal Bar Asn; fel Urban Ctr, Columbia Univ. **Honors/Awds:** Lawyer of the Year, Nat Conf Black Lawyers, 1974. **Home Addr:** 3205 Noble Ave, Richmond, VA 23222. **Business Addr:** Teacher, Tawheed Prep School Inc, 1202 Oak St, Richmond, VA 23220, **Business Phone:** (804)344-3350.

**EL-KATI, MAHMOUD (MILTON WILLIAMS)**
Writer, educator, lecturer. **Personal:** Born Oct 30, 1936, Savannah, GA; son of Rufus Williams and Razzie Garvan; children: Erick, Stokley & Kamali. **Educ:** Wilberforce Univ, BA, 1960; Univ Wis, attended 1965; Univ Ghana, attended 1969. **Career:** Macalester Col instr; lectr, writer & community activist; Metrop State Univ, community fac mem; Macalester Col, prof hist, lectr hist, vis instr hist, distinguished lectureship Am studies, currently, prof emer hist, currently; KFAI, consistent commentator; KMOJ, consistent commentator; Educ Prog, black prison inmates; Several Prison Inst, 1966-. Books: Politically Considered: 50th Commemoration of the Supreme Court Decision of 1954, 2004; An Ode to Africa: Kwanzaa Keepsake Cards, 2005; The Hiptionary: A Survey of African American Speech Patterns with A Digest of Key Words and Phrases, 2009; Haiti: The Hidden Truth, 2010. **Orgs:** Vol, Urban League; Nat Asn Advan Colored People; SNCC; Cong Racial Equality; creative ed; dir, Way Community Ctr, 1967-71; co founder & dir, Mankato State Univ. **Honors/Awds:** Page One Award, Twin Cities Newspaper Guild, 1968; Urban League Award, 1969; EROS U-of-the-Streets, Merritt Col, 1969; Recognition Award, Univ Minn; Stillwater Black Inmate Pop, 1974; United Ways Award, Macalester Col, 1991; Zora Neale Hurston Award, Nat Asn Black Storytellers; Sankofa Award, Stairstep Found. **Home Addr:** 157 N Lexington Pkwy, St Paul, MN 55104. **Business Addr:** Professor Emeritus, Distinguished Lectureship in American Studies, Macalester College, Rm 311 Old Main 1600 Grand Ave, St. Paul, MN 55105, **Business Phone:** (651)696-6000.

**ELAINE, LILLIAN.** **See FISHBURNE, LILLIAN E.**

**ELAM, DEBORAH A.**
Vice president (organization). **Personal:** married Archie; children: 2. **Educ:** La State Univ, BA, sociol, 1984; Southern Univ, Baton Rouge, LA, MPA, 1987. **Career:** Gen Elec, human resources leadership prog, 1987, managing dir human resources, 1997-2002, vpres, 2006, chief diversity officer & pres, 2013-. **Orgs:** Gen Elec African Am Forum; Gen Elec Womens Network; Exec Leadership Coun; pres, Links, Fairfield County Chap; Nat Black MBA Asn; Fairfield County Community Found; Working Mothers Mag-Women Color Initiative; Elfun Community Found; pres, Fairfield County Alumnae Chap; pres, Delta Sigma Theta Sorority Inc; Jack & Jill Am; Nat Coun Negro Women. **Business Addr:** Vice President, Chief Diversity Officer, General Electric Co, 3135 Easton Tpke, Fairfield, CT 06825, **Business Phone:** (203)373-2211.

**ELAM, DONNA**
Consultant, chief executive officer, educator. **Personal:** Born Nov 5, 1951, Brooklyn, NY; daughter of Alfred and Patricia; married Ernest Kennedy; children: Dana Martin Hazel, Jaimee & Helen Hazel. **Educ:** York Col, BS, 1976; NY Univ, MS, educ, 1980, PhD, educ, 1995. **Career:** New York Pub Schs, spec ed teacher, 1979-81; Hemstead, NY, teacher, learning disabilities, 1981-85; New York Univ, Equity Assistance Ctr, asst dir, 1987-91, dir, 1991-97; Southeastern Equity Ctr, assoc dir, 1997, equity specialist; Univ S Fla, assoc dir, prog develop & external affairs, vis fac mem; Proact Search Inc, consult, currently; Training, Eval, Assessment & Mgt Consult, founder & chief exec officer, currently; Magnet Schs Am, educ consult, currently; Author: Why They Marched: The Struggle for the Right to Vote; From the Schoolhouse to the Jailhouse: Can We Stop It?. **Orgs:** Co-founder, Northeast Consortium Multicultural Educ, 1993-97; ed bd, Nat Asn Multicultural Educ, 1994-95; founder, Eastside Multicultural Community Sch, 1997-; hon bd mem, Fla Inst Peace Edu & Res, 1998-; charter pres, Fla Asn Multultural Educ, 1998-99; comnr educ, Fla State Charter Sch Rev Panel, 1999-; State Comnr, 2000-04; City Tuskegee, Mayors Off, adv bd develop & tech, 2000-; US Atty Generals Working Comt Hate Crimes, 2001-; exec bd mem, Fla Martin Luther King Jr Inst; bd mem, NY Univ; bd mem, comnr human rels, USA Africa Inst; vice chair, Fla Comn Human Rels, 2007-; Fla Regional Policing Inst; Martin Luther King Jr Inst Non-violence; FBI Diversity Task Force. **Home Addr:** PO Box 382, Thonotosassa, FL 33592. **Business Addr:** Consultant, Proact Search Inc, 126 N Jefferson St Suite 360, Milwaukee, WI 53202, **Business Phone:** (414)347-0200.

**ELAM, HARRIET (HARRIET L ELAM-THOMAS)**
Government official, ambassador. **Personal:** Born Boston, MA; married Wilfred J. **Educ:** Simmons Col, BS, int bus; Tufts Univ, Fletcher Sch Law & Diplomacy, MA, pub diplomacy. **Career:** Ambassador (retired), professor; Am Press & Cult ctr, dir, 1994; Am Embassy, counr pub affairs, 1995; USIA Foreign Serv, minister counr, 1997, actg dep dir, 1999; US Ambassador, senegal, 1999-02; Chief Mission, Guinea-Bissau, 2001-; Univ Cent Fla, dipl residence, 2003-05, dir diplomacy prog, currently; US Europ Command, sr adv grp, 2003-06. **Orgs:** Fel, Am Acad Diplomacy; bd, Cult Acad Excellence; bd, Orlando Philharmonic Orchestra; bd, Inst Int Educ. **Honors/Awds:** Numerous award & honors including US Government's Superior Honor Award; Alumnae Achievement Award, Simmons Col, 1988; USIA's Lois Roth Award, 1991; Special Achievement Award, 1991, 1993, 1994; Hon Doctorate Law, Am Int Univ, 2001; Superior Honor Award, Piraeus Cultural Asn; Group Superior Award; Meritorious Honor Award; Director Generals Cup. **Special Achievements:** Highest ranking American woman in all three of the US diplomatic missions in Belgium. **Home Addr:** 839 Timber Isle Dr, Orlando, FL 32828-6912. **Business Addr:** Director of Diplomacy Program, University of Central Florida, 4000 Cent Fla Blvd, Orlando, FL 32816, **Business Phone:** (407)823-2000.

**ELAM, DR. HARRY PENOY, JR.**
Pediatrician, physician, educator. **Personal:** Born Jul 31, 1919, Little Rock, AR; married Sallyann; children: Regina, Bernadette, Joanne, Susanne, Bernard & Christopher. **Educ:** Loyola Univ, BS, 1949, MD, 1953. **Career:** Cook Co Hosp, intern, 1953-54, resident, 1954-56, Neurol Serv C Div, assoc dir, 1956-57; Stritch Sch Med Loyola Univ, instr, 1956-57; attend physician, 1956-61; res fel, pediat neurol, 1957-59; St Vincent's Orphanage, attend staff, 1957; Mercy Hosp, jr attend staff, 1957; Stritch Sch Med Loyola Univ, dir; Charles F. Read Zone Ctr, med dir, asst clin prof, 1957; Ment Health Clin, Dept Ment Health, med dir, 1962; Univ Ibadon Nigeria, sr lectr, 1962; Stritch Sch Med Loyola Univ, asst prof, 1965, assoc clin prof, 1967; Mile Sq Health Ctr, med dir, 1967; Rush-Presbytery-St Lukes Med Ctr, assoc clin prof, 1971; Rush Col Med, prof pediat, assoc prof med; pvt pract, physician, currently. **Orgs:** Adv bd, Good Samaritan Sch Ment Retarded C, 1963-65; adv bd, United Cerebral Palsy Greater Chicago, 1966-; Chicago Met Interagy Comn, Dept Ment Health, 1967; Am Acad Cerebral Palsy, 1970; Alpha Omega Alpha Hon Med Soc, 1971; Inst Med, Chicago, 1975; Am Soc Adlerian Psychologists; Chicago Pediat Soc; Handicapped C Coun; Am Acad Pediat. **Home Addr:** 924 Sheridan Rd, Evanston, IL 60202, **Home Phone:** (847)864-3137. **Business Addr:** Physician, 924 Sheridan Rd, Evanston, IL 60202, **Business Phone:** (847)864-3137.

**ELAM-THOMAS, HARRIET L.** **See ELAM, HARRIET.**

**ELBA, IDRIS (IDRISS AKUNA ELBA)**
Disc jockey, actor. **Personal:** Born Sep 6, 1972, London; son of Winston and Eva; married Henne (Kime) Norgaard; children: Isan; married Naiyana Garth; children: Winston. **Career:** Nightclub DJ (sometimes as DJ Big Driis), 1991-; actor, 1994-. Film: Behind the Mask, 1997; Belle maman, 1999; Sorted, 2000; Buffalo Soldiers, 2001; One Love, 2003; The Gospel, 2005; Daddy's Little Girls, 2007; The Reaping, 2007; 28 Weeks Later, 2007; American Gangster, 2007; This Christmas, 2007; Prom Night, 2008; RocknRolla, 2008; The Human Contract, 2008; The Unborn, 2009; Obsessed, 2009; Legacy: Black Ops, 2010; The Losers, 2010; Takers, 2010; Thor, 2011; Ghost Rider: Spirit of Vengeance, 2011; Prometheus, 2012; Pacific Rim, 2013; Mandela: Long Walk to Freedom, 2013; Thor: The Dark World, 2013; Second Coming, 2014; No Good Deed, 2014; The Gunman, 2015; Avengers: Age of Ultron, 2015; Beasts of No Nation, 2015; Zootopia, 2016; The Jungle Book, 2016; The Take, 2016; Finding Dory, 2016; 100 Streets, 2016; Star Trek Beyond, 2016. Television: 2point4 Children, 1994; Space Precinct, 1994; The Bill, 1994-95; Absolutely Fabulous, 1995; Bramwell, 1995; Crucial Tales, 1996; The Ruth Rendell Mysteries, 1996; The Governor, 1996; Crocodile Shoes II, 1996; Silent Witness, 1997; Insiders, 1997; Family Affairs, 1997; Ultraviolet, 1998; Verdict, 1998; Dangerfield, 1999; In Defence, 2000; London's Burning, 2001; Law & Order, 2001; The Inspector Lynley Mysteries, 2002; Hack, 2002; The Wire, HBO, 2002-04; Queens Supreme, 2003; Soul Food, 2003; CSI: Miami, 2003; Girlfriends, 2005; Jonny Zero, 2005; Sometimes in April, 2005; World of Trouble, 2005; All in the Game, 2006; The No. 1 Ladies' Detective Agency, 2008; The Office, 2009; Luther, 2010-15; The Big C, 2010; Aqua Teen Hunger Force, 2011; Real Strength, 2011Playhouse Presents, 2015. **Orgs:** Acad Motion Picture Arts & Sci; Nat Youth Music Theatre (former). **Honors/Awds:** BET Award, 2010, 2011; Image Award, 2011, 2014; Black Reel Award, 2012; Golden Globe Award, 2012; Humanitarian Award, BAFTA/LA Britannia Award, 2013; Royal Television Society Television Award, 2014; Screen Actors Guild Award, 2015; Officer of the Order of the British Empire, 2016; Evening Standard British Film Award, 2016; Independent Spirit Award, 2016; Screen Actors Guild Award, 2016. **Special Achievements:** The Anti-Crime Ambassador for The Prince's Trust, 2009. **Business Addr:** The Artists Partnership, 101 Finsbury Pavement, London, GL EC2A 1RS.

**ELDER, GERALDINE H.**
Administrator. **Personal:** Born Sep 13, 1937, Chicago, IL. **Educ:** Morris Brown Atlanta, attended 1957; Loyola Univ Chicago, attended 1959; Emory Univ Atlanta, attended 1969; Ga State Univ, urban govt, admin, Am govt & polit, 1984. **Career:** Pope Ballard Uriell Kennedy Shepard & Foul, legal sec, 1964-65; Emory Comn Legal Serv Ctr, off mgr, 1967-70; Jackson Patterson Pks & Franklin, legal sec, 1970-73; Off Mayor City Atlanta, mayor's exec sec, 1974-76, chief staff, 1977-79; City Atlanta, dir, comm affairs, 1976-77, sec, v mayor, comnr parks & rec, 1985; Peoplesway.Com Inc, presidential diamond, 1984-; RMC Inc, sr exec dir; DeKalb County Sch, field trip clerk, currently; Intele-Travel & PlanNet Mkt, independent travel agt, 2015-. **Orgs:** Alpha Kappa Alpha Sorority; donor rels mgr, Ga Tech Alumni Asn, 2000-. **Honors/Awds:** Nominated for Outstanding Young Women of Am. **Home Addr:** 2050 Venetian Dr SW, Atlanta, GA 30311-4030, **Home Phone:** (404)758-8440. **Business Addr:** Field Trip Clerk, DeKalb County Board of Education, 1701 Mountain Indust Blvd, Stone Mountain, GA 30083, **Business Phone:** (678)676-1200.

**ELDER, LARRY (LAURENCE ALLEN ELDER)**
Radio host, business owner, lawyer. **Personal:** Born Apr 27, 1952, Los Angeles, CA; son of Randolph and Viola. **Educ:** Brown Univ, BA, polit sci, 1974; Univ Mich Sch Law, JD, 1977. **Career:** Litigation law pract; Laurence A Elder & Assoc, founder & owner, 1980-; Warner Bros TV, Moral Ct, host; PBS, Nat Desk, reporter; 790 KABC, talk-show host, 1994-2014; ABC Radio Networks, talk show host, 2002-07; Michael & Me, dir, writer, producer, 2004; MSNBC, Imus Morning, host; CRN Digital Talk Radio Networks, 2015; KRLA, host, 2015-; Townhall.com, columnist. **Honors/Awds:** AEGIS Award of Excellence, 1998; Telly Award, 1998; Emerald City Gold Award of Excellence, 1999; Hollywood Walk of Fame. **Special Achievements:** Author: "The Ten Things You Can't Say in Am", 2000; "Showdown: Confronting Bias, Lies, and the Special Interests that Divide America", 2002; "Stupid Black Men: How to Play the Race Card--and Lose", 2008; "Stupid Black Men: How to Play the Race Card and Lose", 2009; "Dear Father, Dear Son: Two Lives...Eight Hours", 2012. **Home Addr:** , CA. **Business Addr:** Owner, Laurence A Elder & Associates, 10061 Riverside Dr, North Hollywood, CA 91602, **Business Phone:** (800)222-5222.

**ELDERS, DR. M. JOYCELYN (MINNIE JOYCELYN LEE)**
Physician, educator. **Personal:** Born Aug 13, 1933, Schaal, AR; daughter of Curtis L Jones and Haller Reed Jones; married Oliver B; children: Eric D & Kevin M. **Educ:** Philander Smith Col, BA, biol, 1952; Brooke Army Med Ctr, RPT, 1956; Univ Ark Med Sch, MD, 1960, MS, biochem, 1967. **Career:** Professor, health administrator (retired); Univ Minn Hosp, intern-pediat, 1960-61; Univ Ark Med Ctr, resident pediat, 1961-63, chief res & peds, 1963-64, res fel pediat, 1964-67, asst prof pediat, 1967-71, assoc prof peds, 1971-76, prof pediat, Col Pub Health, distinguished prof, 2002, fac researcher, prof emer pediat; Ark Dept Health, dir, 1987-93; US Dept Health & Human Servs, surgeon gen, 1993-94; Ark C's Hosp, prof; US Educ Dept, spec asst to intergovernmental affairs dir. **Orgs:** Fel USPHS, 1964; Am Asn Adv Sci; pres, Southern Soc Pediat Res; Acad f Pediat; Cent Ark Acad Pediat; Am Diabetes Asn; Lawson Wilkins Endocrine Soc; Am Fed Clin Res; Ark Diabetes Asn; Endocrine Soc; assoc mem, FEBS Am Phys Soc; Am Bd Pediat, 1965; bd mem, N Little Rock Workman's Comp Comn, 1975-79; Ark Sci & Tech Comn, 1975-76; Human Growth Found, 1974-78; chmn memship comn, Lawson Wilkins End Soc, 1976; Human Embryologoy & Develop Study Sect, 1976-80; Nat Adv Food & Drug Comn, 1977-80; pres, Sigma Xi, 1977-78; Nat Pituitary Agency, 1977-80; bd dir, Nat Bank Ark, 1979; Maternal & Child Health Res Comn, HHS, NIH, 1981-; Ed Bd J Ped, 1981-; secy, AR Sci & Tech Comn, 1983-; bd mem, Noside YMCA, 1973-84; chair acad adv bd, Int Sex Worker Found Art, Cult, & Educ. **Honors/Awds:** Alumni Academic Scholar, Philander Smith Col, 1949-52; USPHS Career Develop Award, 1967-72; Distinguished Women in America, Alpha Kappa Alpha, 1973; Woman of the Year, Ark Democrat, 1989; Career Develop Award, NIH; DSc, Bates Col, 2002. **Special Achievements:** First person in the state of Arkansas to become board certified in pediatric endocrinology, 1978; first African American and only the second woman to head the U.S. Public Health Service, 1993; Author: "Joycelyn Elders, M.D", 1996; "From Sharecropper's Daughter to Surgeon General of the United States of America," 1997; First female and African American to be director of the Department of Health in Arkansas; first African American to serve in the position. **Home Addr:** Marcia Cove Suite 14, Little Rock, AR 72206, **Home Phone:** (501)888-4787. **Business Addr:** Emeritus, University of Arkansas School of Medicine, 4301 W Markham St, Little Rock, AR 72205, **Business Phone:** (501)686-7000.

**ELEAZER, DR. GEORGE ROBERT, JR.**
Psychologist. **Personal:** Born Oct 16, 1956, East Patchogue, NY; son of George Robert Sr and Virginia Lee Conquest; children: George III. **Educ:** Choate Sch, attended 1974; Tufts Univ, BS, 1978; Hofstra Univ, MA, 1978, PhD, 1984. **Career:** Freeport Pub Schs, intern psychologist, 1980-81; United Cerebral Palsy Suffolk, intern psychologist, 1981-82; Westbury Pub Schs, psychologist, 1982-84; William Floyd Pub Schs, psychologist, 1984; Mid Island Sch, psychologist; Longwood Cent Sch Dist, Mid Island, NY, psychologist, 1984-. **Orgs:** Pres bd, Bellport Local Action Ctr, 1980-81; co-chmn, S Country Sch Dist, 1982-, pre kindergarten adv bd, budget adv comt, 1997; Phi Delta Kappa, 1985; Brookhaven Mem Hosp Adv Coun, 1984-; treas, Middle Island Rotary Sch, Middle Island WV; adv bd, Brookhaven Mem Hosp, 1984-; bd dir, Bellport Rotary club, 1985-86, pres, 1991-92; St Mary Church, pres lay coun, 1998. **Honors/Awds:** Am Legion Award, S Country Schs, 1970; David Bohn Mem Sch Award, S Country Schs, 1970; Daniel Hale Williams Award, Tufts Univ, 1978. **Home Addr:** PO Box 255, Bellport, NY 11713, **Home Phone:** (631)286-1033. **Business Addr:** Psychologist, Longwood Central School District, 100 Longwood Rd, Middle Island, NY 11953, **Business Phone:** (631)345-9200.

**ELEWONIBI, MOHAMMED THOMAS DAVID**
Football player, football coach. **Personal:** Born Dec 16, 1965, Lagos; married Sareh; children: Grace & Dylan. **Educ:** Snow Col, attended 1987; Brigham Young Univ, BA, bus mgt, 1989. **Career:** Football

player (retired), football coach; Saanich Vampires, 1981-83; Saanich Hornets, 1983-84; Victoria Payless, 1984-86; Okanagan Sun, 1986-87; Brigham Young Univ, 1987-89; Wash Redskins, guard & offensive tackle, 1991-93; Barcelona Dragons, 1995; Philadelphia Eagles, offensive tackle, 1995-96; Can Football League, BC Lions, offensive line, 1997-2000; Winnipeg Blue Bombers, 2000-05; Winnipeg Rifles Jr Football, offensive line coach, 2003-04, currently; BC Lions, 2005-06; Nat Football League, offensive lineman. **Honors/Awds:** Outland Trophy, 1989; CFL All-Star, 1998; CFL West All-Star, 1998; CFL East All-Star, 2000; Cal Murphy Award, 2002.

### ELEY, RANDALL ROBBI

Executive, chief executive officer, president (organization). **Personal:** Born Jan 29, 1952, Portsmouth, VA; son of Melvin and Florence Eley. **Educ:** Yale Univ, BA, polit sci, 1974; Univ Chicago Law Sch, JD, 1977. **Career:** Kutak Rock & Campbell, assoc atty & partner, 1977-86; Edgar Lomax Co, pres, chief invest officer & portfolio mgr, 1986-. TV Series: "CNN"; "CNBC"; "Wall Street Week" & "The Nightly Business Report". **Orgs:** DC Bar, 1986; bd dir, YMCA, 1992; adv coun mem, Norfolk State Univ, Bus Sch, 1996; trustee, William & Mary Coll Endowment Asn, 1997. **Home Addr:** 5505 Seminary Rd Apt 418, Falls Church, VA 22041-2934, **Home Phone:** (703)671-9798. **Business Addr:** President, Founder, Edgar Lomax Co, 6564 Loisdale Ct Suite 310, Springfield, VA 22150, **Business Phone:** (703)719-0026.

### ELIE, MARIO ANTOINE

Basketball coach, basketball player. **Personal:** Born Nov 26, 1963, New York, NY; married Gina Gaston; children: Gaston, Glenn & Lauren. **Educ:** Am Int Col, BA, human rels, 1985. **Career:** Basketball player (retired), basketball coach; Milwaukee Bucks, 1985; Dart Killester, Ireland, 1986-87; CBA: Miami Tropics, 1987; Union De Santa Fe, Arg, 1987; Ovarense, Port, 1987-89; Albany Patroons, 1989-91; Youngstown Pride, 1990; Los Angeles Lakers, 1990-91; Philadelphia 76ers, shooting guard, 1990-91; Golden State Warriors, small forward, 1990-91, shooting guard, 1991-92; Portland Trail Blazers, small forward, 1992-93; Houston Rockets, small forward, 1993-98; San Antonio Spurs, shooting guard, 1998-99, small forward, 1999-2000; Phoenix Suns, shooting guard, 2000-01; San Antonio Spurs, asst coach, 2003-04; Golden State Warriors, asst coach, 2004-06; FOX Sports, TV host, 2006-07; Dallas Mavericks, asst coach, 2007-09; Sacramento Kings, asst coach, 2009-11; Brooklyn Nets, asst coach, 2011-13; Orlando Magic Nat Basketball Asn, asst coach, 2015-. **Orgs:** Juv Diabetes Found. **Honors/Awds:** Champion, Nat Basketball Asn, 1994, 1995, 1999; New York Basketball Hall of Fame, 2007. **Business Addr:** Assistant Coach, Orlando Magic, 8701 Maitland Summit Blvd, Orlando, FL 32810, **Business Phone:** (407)916-2400.

### ELIZEY, CHRIS WILLIAM

Computer executive, association executive, naval officer. **Personal:** Born Aug 3, 1947, Brooklyn, NY; son of Hollis and Dorris; married Georgia V Robinson; children: Christopher. **Educ:** DePaul Univ, BS, 1976; Univ Okla, ME, 1989; Univ Va, PhD, 1990. **Career:** AT&T, syst engr, 1970-76; RCA Commun, vpres, 1976-80; Centurian Systs, vpres, 1980-. **Orgs:** Vpres, Nat bank Pages, 1985; pres, secy, Bank data Processors Asn, 1986-88, 1990; vpres, Cleveland bus league, 1988; pres, Outer City Golf, 1990. **Business Addr:** Vice President, Centurian Systems Technology, 3030 Euclid Ave, Cleveland, OH 44115, **Business Phone:** (212)881-3939.

### ELLARAINO, BAKI

Entertainer, storyteller, actor. **Personal:** Born Oct 7, 1938, Kilgore, TX; daughter of Bernice Jefferson Ward and Myles Butler; married Ross Anderson; children: Kawi Scott Anderson & Omar Hakam Anderson. **Educ:** Weist Barron Hill, Burbank, CA, attended 1988; Los Angeles Valley Col, N Hollywood, course voice & diction, 1989. **Career:** Los Angeles Int House Blues Found's Educ Tours Prog, consult & performance artist; Allensworth State Hist Pk, off storyteller; Compton Unified Sch Dist Consult, Theatre Arts & Drama, instr; Young People's Actg Workshop, Los Angeles, CA, voice & diction coach, 1988-89, producer & dir, 1989; storyteller, 1989-; TV Series: "Ironside", 1970; "David Cassidy-Man Undercover", 1978; "The White Shadow", 1979-81; "The New Odd Couple", assoc producer, 1982-83; "Murder, She Wrote", 1986; "The Twilight Zone", 1986; "Amen", 1986; "Doogie Howser, M.D.", 1991; "Beverly Hills, 90210", 1991; "The Sinbad Show", 1994; "The Good News", 1997; "The Wayans Bros", 1998; "Wanda at Large", 2003; "ER", 2008. **Special Achievements:** Co-author & publisher, Another Kind of Treasure; Official Storyteller of Allensworth State Historic Park, Californias first town founded by African Americans. **Home Addr:** 8722 Skyline Dr, Los Angeles, CA 90046-1422, **Home Phone:** (323)654-1922. **Business Addr:** Storyteller, Los Angeles, CA 90001, **Business Phone:** (323)654-1922.

### ELLER, CARL LEE

Football player, executive. **Personal:** Born Feb 25, 1942, Winston-Salem, NC; son of Clarence McGee (deceased) and Ernestine; married Mahogany Jaclynne Fasnacht; children: Cinder, Regis & Holiday. **Educ:** Univ MN, Educ, 1963, cert C D counr, 1982; Metropolitian St Col, Inst Chem Dependency; Metrop State Univ, human serv, 1994. **Career:** Football player (retired), executive; Minn Vikings, defensive end, 1964-78; Seattle Seahawks, defensive end, 1979-80; Nbc tv, color analyst, 1980; lic drug & alcohol counr; Viking Personnel, employee consult, 1982; Nat Football League, health consult; Nat Inst Sports & Hmnts, founder & dir, 1981-; US Athletes Assoc, founder & exec dir, 1983-; Triumph Serv, exec dir, currently. **Orgs:** SAG/AFTRA Actors Talent Asn, 1969-; Fel Christian Athletes; bd mem, MN Coun Chem Dependency, 1982-; MN Inst Black Chem Abuse, 1982-; pres, NFL Alumni MN Chap, 1982-85; Citizens Adv Coun, State MN, 1984-; bd mem, Univ MN, 1984-; chair, Grants comn, 1983-86; Chem Dependency Div; State Dept Health Human Serv; Mayors Task Force Chem Dependency, 1985-; Triumph Life Centers, 1986; vpres, Nat Football League Alumni, Minn Chap, 1986-; consult, Nat Football; pres, Univ Minn M Club, 1990; pres, Retired Players Asn; N Minneapolis community; Alpha Phi Alpha Fraternity. **Honors/Awds:** All American, Univ Minn, 1962-63; Hall of Fame, Univ Minn M Club, 1963; George Halas Award, Best Defensive Lineman, 1969; Defensive Player of the Year, Nat Football League Players Asn, 1971; Key Man Award, Miltipleclerosis Soc, 1977; Minnesota Labor Award, Hubert H Humphrey, 1982; Good Neighbor Award, WCCO Radio, 1984; Minn Sports Hall of Fame, 1989; North Carolina Sports Hall of Fame, 1991; Pro Football Hall of Fame, inductee, 2004; College Football Hall of Fame, 2006. **Special Achievements:** Films: Super Bowl IV, 1970, The Black Six, 1974; Busting, 1974, Super Bowl XI, 1977, Super Bowl IX, 1975, My 5th Super Bowl, producer, 1984; Beating the Odds, author, 1985. **Home Addr:** 1035 Washburn Ave N, Minneapolis, MN 55411-3557, **Home Phone:** (612)529-8177. **Business Addr:** Executive Director, Triumph Service, 3735 Lakeland Ave N Suite 200, Robbinsdale, MN 55422, **Business Phone:** (612)522-5844.

### ELLERBE, BRIAN HERSHOLT

Basketball coach. **Personal:** Born Sep 1, 1963, Capitol Heights, MD; married Ingrid; children: Brian Jr & Morgan Ashleigh. **Educ:** Rutgers Univ, BA, urban planning, 1985. **Career:** Rutgers Univ, grad asst coach, 1985-86; Bowling Green State Univ, asst coach, 1986-88; George Mason Univ, asst coach, 1988-90; Univ SC, asst coach, 1989-90; Univ VA, asst coach, 1990-91, 1993-94; Loyola Col, Md, head coach, 1994-97; Univ Mich, interim head coach, 1997, head coach, 1997-2001; Motor City Educ Sportsplex LLC, founder & dir res & develop, 2001-04, vpres corp develop, 2004-08; Ellerbe Res & Consult LLC, owner, 2008-09; George Wash Univ, asst coach, 2009-10; DePaul Univ, asst mens basketball coach, 2010-13; Ellerbe Consult LLC, proj & consult serv, 2013-. **Orgs:** Nat Asn Basketball Coaches; founding mem, Nat Asn Coaches Equity & Develop. **Business Addr:** Project & Consulting Services, Ellerbe Consulting LLC, **Business Phone:** (773)576-8094.

### ELLERBY, WILLIAM MITCHELL

State government official. **Personal:** Born Sep 19, 1946, Manning, SC; married Sarah Croker; children: Clifford, Andre & Mitchell Jr. **Educ:** Benedict Col, Columbia, SC, BA, 1971. **Career:** Sears Roebuck, div mgr, 1971-73; Jackson Cty Head start, admin asst, 1973-74; Chevron USA Refinery, refinery oper, 1974; State Miss, state rep, 1984; LaFont Inn Pascagoula, sales & mkt. **Orgs:** Methodist Church, Omega Psi Phi; bd dir, Jackson Cty Area Chamber Com; VFW; Am Legion; Elks, Eve Lions Club; vpres, Moss Pt Boxing Asn; pres, Eastside Voting Precinct; city dem exec comt, comnr, Jackson Cty Port Authority; Nat Asn Advan Colored People; chair, church Rels Sub comn. **Honors/Awds:** Host Awareness 1985 WHKS Moss Point. **Home Addr:** 3712 Baywood Dr, Moss Point, MS 39563, **Home Phone:** (228)475-0263.

### ELLINGTON, E. DAVID

Media executive. **Personal:** Born Jul 10, 1960, New York, NY; married Wendy Marx. **Educ:** Adelphi Univ, BA, hist, 1981; Howard Univ, MA, comparative polit & govt, 1984; Georgetown Univ Law Ctr, JD, 1989; Cornell Univ, cert completion, 1990. **Career:** House Subcomt on Africa, 1980; Law Offices E David Ellington, atty, 1990-95; Pub Interest Commun, telemarketing dept; McKenna & Cuneo, law clerk; practiced at law firms specializing entertainment law; NetNoir Inc, co-founder, chief exec officer, chmn & pres, 1995-2001; 2i Capital Asset Mgt Co Ltd, adv brd, currently; Emory Capital Group LLC, partner, 2002-07, managing partner, 2007-09; GridSpeak Corp, co-founder & pres, 2009-. **Orgs:** Co-founder & chmn, OpNet, 1997-2002; comnr, Telecommunications Comn City & County San Francisco, 1997- 2002; bd dir, San Francisco Jazz Orgn, 1999-2002; White House Fel regional rev panelist, 1999; US Fed Trade Comn Adv Comt Online Access & Security, 2000; Bus Execs Nat Security, 2000-02; bd gov, Commonwealth Club Calif, 2000-02; San Francisco Workforce Investment Bd, 2002-08; charter mem, TiE-Silicon Valley, 2004-; bd dir, Temptation Foods, currently; State Bar Calif; chmn, Beverly Hills Bar Asn; trustee & comnr, San Francisco Employees' Retirement Syst, 2002-08; bd, SFERS Bd; Disadvantaged youth technol training prog, 1997-2002; charter mem, TiE-Silicon Valley, 2004-; Bus Execs for Nat Security; Commonwealth Club Calif, 2000-02; San Francisco Jazz Orgn; hite House Fel regional rev panelist; adv bd, Rutgers Univ, Ctr Media Studies. **Honors/Awds:** Black Enterprise magazine's Entrepreneurs Award, Business Innovator of the Year, 1996. UPSIDE magazine's Technology 'Elite 100', 1999 & 2000. **Business Addr:** Co-Founder, President, GridSpeak Corp, 555 12th St Suite 2040, Oakland, CA 94607, **Business Phone:** (510)463-8800.

### ELLINGTON, MERCEDES

Choreographer, television producer, educator. **Personal:** Born Feb 9, 1949, New York, NY; daughter of Mercer and Ruth V Silas. **Educ:** Metropolitan Opera Sch Ballet; Juilliard Sch Music, BS, 1960. **Career:** Dancer, choreographer, educr; June Taylor Dancers Jackie Gleason Show, dancer, 1963-70; New York Opera debut, 1977; Sophisticated Ladies, featured dancer, asst choreographer, 1980-83; Balletap Am, USA, artistic co-dir, 1983-85; Blues Night, choreographer, 1984-85, Juba, choreographer, 1985-86; USA aka DanceEllington Inc, dir; DancEllington, artistic dir, 1985-93; Alvin Ailey Am Dance Cen, jazz tap teacher; Indianapolis Symphony Orchestras Yuletide Celebration, choreographer; Broadway Cares Equity Fights AIDS Tribute To Spirit Harlem, Apollo Theater, dir, 2001; Tyrone Shoes, choreographer; No No Nanette, asst choreographer; Hellzapoppin, asst choreographer; Oh Kay!, asst choreographer; Happy New Yr, asst choreographer; Grand Tour, asst choreographer; Sophisticated Ladies; Night That Made Am Famous; Black Broadway; Wild Women Dont Get Blues; Tribute to Miss Peggy Lee at Carnegie Hall; Ain't Misbehavin-Mt Vernon, Columbus, GA, St Louis; 14 MUNY; Duke Ellington Ctr Arts, founder; DUKE ELLINGTON BIG BAND, co-founder, 2009; Mercedes Ellington Enterprises, pres, currently; Productions: Peter Pan; Wizard Of Oz; Meet Me In St Louis; Kiss Me Kate; Broadway: Play On!; Anything Goes; Symphony Space, "Wall to Wall Duke Ellington"; "Juba", AMAS Production Vineyard Theatre; Indianapolis Yuletide Celebration; Twist-George St Playhouse; Flims: George M!, dancer, 1970; So Fine, dancer, 1981; Once the Music Played, choreographer, pre-production, 2015. **Orgs:** Local 802, Songwriters Guild Am; Actors Equity Coun, 1984-85; local bd & nat bd mem, Am Fedn TV & Radio Artists; bd mem, Career Transitions Dancers; Actors Equity Asn; Am Guild Musical Artists; Screen Actors Guild; Soc Stage Dir & Choreographers; Soc Singers; Friars Club; nominating comt, TONY; co-founded, Maurice Hines; Home Harlem Radio City Music Hall Rockettes; bd dir, Career Transition Dancers; bd pres, Duke Ellington Ctr Arts. **Home Addr:** 3900 Ford Rd, Philadelphia, PA 19131. **Business Addr:** President, Mercedes Ellington Enterprises, 215 W 92nd St 8H, New York, NY 10025-7477, **Business Phone:** (212)724-5565.

### ELLIOTT, ANTHONY DANIEL, III

Conductor (music), cellist, educator. **Personal:** Born Sep 3, 1948, Rome, NY; son of Charlie Mae White and Anthony Daniel; married Paula Sokol; children: Danielle, Michelle, Marie & Cecille. **Educ:** Ind Univ Sch Music, performers cert, 1969, BMus, 1970. **Career:** Aspen Chamber Symphony, prin cello, 1970; Toronto Symphony Orchestra, sect cello, 1970-73; Univ MN, instr, 1973-76; Minn Orchestra, assoc prin cello, 1973-78; MacAlester Col, instr, 1974-76; Vancouver Symphony Orchestra, prin cello, 1978-82; Vancouver Youth Orchestra, 1982-83; CBC Toronto Orchestra; Detroit Symphony; Marrowstone Music Festival, asst music dir, 1986-87; Western MI Univ, assoc prof cello, 1983-87, music dir: univ opera, univ symphony orchestra; Johannessen Int Sch Arts, fac, 1985-93; Univ Houston, Sch Music, Houston, TX, assoc prof, 1987-91, prof, 1991-94; Houston Youth Symphony, Houston, TX, music dir, 1990-94; Eastman Sch Music, vis prof, 1994-95; Univ MI, Sch Music, Theatre & Dance, prof cello, 1994-. **Orgs:** Adv bd, Music Assistance Fund, NY Philharmonic, 1970-; adv bd, African Am Musical Opportunities Asn, 1973-78; asst music dir, Marrowstone Music Festival, 1981-87; conductor, TX Music Festival, 1991-92; Adv bd, Texaco-Sphinx Competition, 1998-; Chamber Music Socs Lincoln Ctr; Emerson Juilliard Cleveland & Concord string quartets; Quartet Can. **Home Addr:** 2020 Columbia St, Ann Arbor, MI 48104-6411, **Home Phone:** (734)668-7522. **Business Addr:** Professor of Cello, University of Michigan, 1100 Baits Dr 3056 Moore, Ann Arbor, MI 48109-2085, **Business Phone:** (734)764-2523.

### ELLIOTT, CATHY

Insurance executive. **Personal:** Born Jan 21, 1956, Holly Springs, MS; daughter of Mamon Jr and Magnolia Newsom (deceased). **Educ:** Univ Miss, Oxford, MS, BPA, 1977. **Career:** Cigna Corp, Dallas, prod underwriter, 1985-87; Wausau Ins Co, Dallas, reg casualty underwriter, 1987-; Hartford Ins Co, Memphis, casualty underwriter; Nationwide Ins Co, Memphis, comml line underwriter. **Home Addr:** 7318 Parkridge Blvd Suite 79, Irving, TX 75063, **Home Phone:** (214)506-7925. **Business Addr:** Regional Casualty Underwriter, Wausau Ins Co, 105 Decker Ct Suite 600, Irving, TX 75062-2272, **Business Phone:** (972)650-1955.

### ELLIOTT, DARRELL STANLEY, SR.

Lawyer, executive. **Personal:** Born May 11, 1953, Denver, CO; son of Frank and Mattie V; married Diane; children: Darrell S Jr & Clarke M. **Educ:** Univ Denver, BA, 1975, JD, 1978. **Career:** Anaconda Atlantic Richfield, landman, 1978-80; Goldfields Mining Corp, asst coun, 1980-81; Unocal, reg coun, mgr, 1981-83; Darrell S Elliott PC, founder, 1984-. **Orgs:** Alfred A Arraj Am Inn Ct, vip, 1993-; Colo Bar Asn; Am Bar Asn; Colo Trial Laywers Asn; Am Trial Lawyers Asn; Denver Bar Asn; Rocky Mountain Mineral Law Found. **Home Addr:** 1727 E 4th Ave, Denver, CO 80218-4049, **Home Phone:** (303)393-7929. **Business Addr:** Founder, Darrell S Elliott PC, 1600 Pennsylvania St, Denver, CO 80203-1303, **Business Phone:** (303)863-1600.

### ELLIOTT, DR. DEREK WESLEY

Historian, educator. **Personal:** Born Oct 3, 1958, Nashville, TN; son of Irvin Wesley Jr and Joan Louise Curl. **Educ:** Harvard Univ, AB, 1980; Univ Calif, Berkeley, CA, MA, 1985; George Washington Univ, PhD, 1992. **Career:** Smithsonian Inst, Nat Air & Space Mus, cur, 1982-92; Tenn State Univ, asst prof hist, 1992-98, assoc prof, 1998-. **Orgs:** Am Hist Asn, 1987-; Orgn Am Historians, 1987-; Soc Hist Technol, 1987-; Phi Kappa Phi Hon Soc. **Honors/Awds:** Robinson Prize Comn, Soc Hist Technol, 1991-94. **Special Achievements:** Review: Technology and Culture, Vol 34, No 2, pp. 465-467, Apr 1993. **Home Addr:** 840 Belton Dr, Nashville, TN 37205, **Home Phone:** (615)353-1834. **Business Addr:** Associate Professor, Tennessee State University, 3500 John A Merritt Blvd, Nashville, TN 37209, **Business Phone:** (615)963-5000.

### ELLIOTT, J. RUSSELL

Mechanical engineer, consultant, manager. **Personal:** Born Chicago, IL; son of J Russell and Blanche Smith; married Sharon Lomax. **Educ:** Chicago Tech Col, BSME, 1968; Northwestern Univ, MBA, 1975. **Career:** Mechanical engineer, consultant, manager (retired); Johnson & Johnson Co, mech engr, supvr, 1966-75, Baby Prod Co, grp engrg mgr, 1975-80, Ortho Pharmaceut Div, dir indust engrg, 1980-85, natl mgr package engrg, 1986-94; Bus Consult, opers & engrg, 1995; Personal Prod Co, chief indust engineering. **Orgs:** Chicago Urban League, 1967-75; bd trustee, Sigma Phi Delta Engr Frat, 1967-69; adv hs youth grp, Good Shepherd Church, 1969-75; bd deacons, Good Shepherd Congregational Church, 1969-75; bd trustee, Chicago Opportunity Industrialization Ctr, 1973-75; Int Orgn Pkg Professionals, 1986-; exec comn, bd dir, Bucks County Pa, Nat Asn Advan Colored People, 1992-94; bd dir, Simon Found Pa, 1992-94; Alpha Phi Alpha; adv Soc Black Engrs, Princeton Univ. **Honors/Awds:** Certificate of Merit, Chicago Asn Com & Indust, 1973-75.

### ELLIOTT, JOHN

Association executive, educator. **Personal:** Born Jun 30, 1931, Raleigh, WV. **Educ:** Wayne State Univ, BA; Univ Mich, MA. **Career:** Educator, association executive (retired); Detroit Sch Syst, teacher; Detroit Fedn Teachers, admin asst, exec vpres & pres emeritus; Am Fedn Teachers, vpres, 1984. **Orgs:** Am Fedn Teachers. **Home Addr:** 20044 Appoline St, Detroit, MI 48235, **Home Phone:** (313)341-3218.

### ELLIOTT, JOY

Journalist. **Personal:** Born St. Ann. **Educ:** Univ Wis, Mona, Jamaica, BS; New Sch Univ, MA, media studies; Univ Poitiers' Institut de Touraine, Tours, France, dipl; Univ Paris, Sorbonne, France, dipl. **Career:** Assoc Press, cub reporter, 1970-72; Reuters News Serv, corresp, ed, 1972-92; Nat Endowment Humanities, fel, 1981; Univ Mich, fel Un Pop Fund; freelance journalist, writer, ed, vol tv producer, currently; UN spec conferences Panama City, Panama, Rio de Janeiro, Brazil, Istanbul, Turkey, Dakar, Senegal & Rome, Italy, cutting-edge reporting & editing; Manhattan pub access tv, producer & crew mem; media specialist; Carib News, journalist. **Orgs:** Nat Asn Black Journalists; Int Asn Mass Commun Res; Coalition 100 Black Women; Soc Prof J, NY Sponsoring Comn; Nat Advan Asn Colored People; Legal Defense Fund; interim bd dir, NY Chap Univ WI Guild Gradmakers; bd mem, Carib News newspaper NY; Fel Un Correspondents Asn. **Home Addr:** 135 W 136th St Suite 1, New York, NY 10030. **Business Addr:** Journalist, Carib News, 220 E 63rd St, New York, NY 10021, **Business Phone:** (212)838-1550.

**ELLIOTT, LARRY DOC. See WORTHY, LARRY ELLIOTT.**

**ELLIOTT, LORI KAREN**
Lawyer. **Personal:** Born May 26, 1959, Patuxent River, MD; daughter of Winfred Anthony and Rhoda Graves. **Educ:** Ohio Univ, attended 1979; Univ Pittsburgh, BA, 1981, Sch Law, JD, 1984. **Career:** Legal Aid Soc Cincinnati, staff atty, 1984-89, sr atty, 1989-. **Orgs:** Womens City Club; Pa Bar Asn, 1984; Ohio Bar Asn, 1985; US Dist Ct Northern Dist Ohio, 1987; US Ct Appeals 6th Circuit, 1988; bd dir, Self, currently. **Home Addr:** 10 Journal Sq 3rd Fl, Hamilton, OH 45011, **Home Phone:** (513)541-6145. **Business Addr:** Senior Attorney, Legal Aid Society of Cincinnati, 901 Elm St, Cincinnati, OH 45202-1084, **Business Phone:** (513)241-9400.

**ELLIOTT, MISSY (MELISSA ARNETTE ELLIOTT)**
Rap musician, music producer, singer. **Personal:** Born Jul 1, 1971, Portsmouth, VA; daughter of Ronnie and Patricia. **Career:** Albums: Diary of a Mad Band, 1993; The Show; The After Party; The Hotel, 1995; Supa Dupa Fly, 1997; Da Real World, 1999; Miss E So Addictive, 2001; Under Construction, 2002; This Is Not a Test!, 2003; The Cookbook, 2005; Respect M.E., 2006; The Countdown, 2007; Block Party, 2009; Films: Family Matters, 1997; TheWayans Bros, 1997; Pooty Tang, 2001; Honey, 2003; Shark Tale, 2004; Just for Kicks, 2005; TBA, 2007; Songs: "The Rain", 1997; "Beep Me 911", 1998; "All N My Grill", 1999; "Get Ur Freak On", 2001; "Take Away", 2001; "Pussycat", 2003; "I'm Really Hot", 2004; "Teary Eyed", 2005; "We Run This", 2006; "Ching-a-Ling", 2006; "CSI: Miami ", 2008; "Shake Your Pom Pom", 2009; "Best Best", 2009; "2010 Late Night with Jimmy Fallon", 2010; "2010 Soul Train Awards", 2010; "Unstoppable", 2010. **Honors/Awds:** Grammy Award for Rap Solo, 2001; ASCAP Award, 2002; MTV Video Music Awards, Best Hip-Hop Video; American Music Award, Favorite Rap & Hip-hop Female, 2003, 2005; Grammy Award, 2003, 2004 & 2006; appeared on a ABC's Extreme Makeover, 2007. **Special Achievements:** Nominated for Grammy Award, 1998, 2000, 2002, 2003, 2004, 2006; two of hersingles ranked in the top five of the 2000s decade on Acclaimed music.net. **Business Addr:** Artist, c/o E & W Records, 75 Rockefeller Plz, New York, NY 10019-6917, **Business Phone:** (212)275-4000.

**ELLIOTT, MONTE RAY**
Executive director, association executive. **Personal:** Born Dec 17, 1952, Ft. Worth, TX; married Vernal; children: Makala & Monica. **Educ:** Tarrant County Col, AA, 1978; Tex Wesleyan Univ, BA, 1983. **Career:** Southwestern Bell, installer, 1971-73, test desk tech, 1973-75, PBX installer, 1975-78, mgr installation, 1978-88, mgr external affairs, 1988-92, area mgr external affairs, 1992-98, dir external affairs, 1998-2000, exec dir external affairs. **Orgs:** Co-chair, Tarrant County, United Negro Col Fund, 1992-93; bd mem, Nat Asn Advan Colored People, Ft Worth, 1992-99; Aviation Adv Bd, 1993-95; chair, Ft Worth Human Rels Comm, 1997-99; bd mem, Sr Citizens Tarrant County, 1997-2000; chair, adv bd, Tex Asn African Am Chambers, 1999-; John Peter Smith Hosp Bd, 2000-; chmn, bd dir, Ft Worth Metrop Black Chamber Com. **Honors/Awds:** Father of the Yr, Fort Worth Star Telegram, 1993; Distinguished Alumni, IMTerrell Alumni Asn, 1996; Trailblazer Award, Business News, 2000. **Home Addr:** 6333 Meadows W Dr, Fort Worth, TX 76132-1161, **Home Phone:** (972)292-0797. **Business Addr:** Chairman, Executive Director External Affairs, Fort Worth Metropolitan Black Chamber Commerce, 1150 S Fwy Suite 211, Ft. Worth, TX 76104, **Business Phone:** (817)871-6538.

**ELLIOTT, SEAN MICHAEL**
Basketball player, basketball executive. **Personal:** Born Feb 2, 1968, Tucson, AZ. **Educ:** Univ Ariz, attended 1989. **Career:** Basketball player (retired), basketball analyst; San Antonio Spurs, forward, 1989-93, 1994-2001, commentator, 2004-05; Detroit Pistons, 1993-94; ABC Sports, basketball analyst, 2003-04; ESPN, basketball analyst, 2004-05; Univ Ariz; Spurs Broadcasting, basketball analyst, currently. **Business Addr:** Basketball Analyst, San Antonio Spurs, 7338 Baltimore Ave Suite 108A, College Park, MD 20740.

**ELLIOTT, SHARON E.**
Executive. **Educ:** Northwestern Univ, BA, MA, personnel admin, 1973. **Career:** Bristol-Myers Squibb Inc, human resources mgr; AlliedSignal Inc, human resources mgr; Starbucks Coffee Co, human resources mgr, sr vpres, human resources, 1994-2000; Eastman Kodak Co, Rochester, NY, vpres & dir, human resources, 2001; Ingersoll-Rand Co Ltd, sr vpres, human resources, 2003-; AREVA, vpres, human resources, 2010-. **Business Addr:** Vice President, AREVA Inc, 7207 IBM Dr, Charlotte, NC 28262, **Business Phone:** (704)805-2000.

**ELLIS, BENJAMIN F., JR.**
Manager, insurance executive. **Personal:** Born Sep 17, 1939, Philadelphia, PA; son of Benjamine H and Tinner F; married Sylvia Ann Simmons; children: Letitia A, Wendy S, Benjamin III & Melanie R. **Educ:** Temple Univ, Asn Electronics, 1967, BS, bus admin, 1974. **Career:** Naval Air Eng Ctr, Philadelphia, proj admin, 1966-73; Penn Mutual Life Ins Co, bldg supt, 1973-76, bldg mgr, 1976-79, asst vpres bldg mgt, 1979-81 & second vpres, 1981-88, dept head, regulatory compliance, govt & commun Rel, 1990-; City Philadelphia, comnr pub property, 1988-90. **Orgs:** Toastmasters Int, 1967-73; Corp Fin Comt, BOMA Int, 1974-; dir, BOMA Philadelphia, 1978-; allocations comt, United Way Southeastern Penn, 1978-; dir, Philadelphia Ctr Older People, 1981-. dir, Citizens Coalition Energy Efficiency, 1983-. **Honors/Awds:** Outstanding Apprentice of Year, Naval Air Engr Ctr, 1965. **Special Achievements:** First Black Vice President of Penn Mutual Life Insurance Co, 1979. **Home Addr:** 6702 Wayne Ave, Philadelphia, PA 19119-3522, **Home Phone:** (215)842-0367. **Business Addr:** Second Vice President, The Penn Mutual Life Insurance Co, Independence Sq Suite 2G, Philadelphia, PA 19172, **Business Phone:** (215)956-8000.

**ELLIS, BENJAMIN F., JR.**
Military leader. **Personal:** Born Dec 7, 1941, East Palatka, FL; son of Benjamin F and Edna Pinkston (deceased); married Aaron Robinson; children: Eric B & Traci A. **Educ:** Fla A&M Univ, Tallahassee, FL, BS, 1963; Ariz State Univ, Tempe, AZ, MA, 1972. **Career:** Military leader (retired); AUS, Ft Levenworth, Kans, intelligence officer, 1973-75, Hawaii, battalion opers officer, 1975-78, Jackson State Univ, Jackson, Miss, sr asst prof mil sci, 1978-81, Ft McPherson, Ga, asst inspector gen, 1981-85, Norfolk State Univ, Norfolk, Va, cmdr Army/ROTC, prof mil sci, 1985-89; Norfolk State Univ, Norfolk, Va, asst dir/auxiliary enterprises, 1990-91; Norfolk State Univ, dir, placement & career servs, 1992; Black Collegian, contribr. **Orgs:** Nat Asn Employers & Cols. **Home Addr:** 1033 Belvoir Lane, Virginia Beach, VA 23464, **Home Phone:** (757)424-2726.

**ELLIS, CALVIN H, III. See Obituaries Section.**

**ELLIS, CLARENCE JACK**
Mayor. **Personal:** Born Jan 6, 1946, Macon, GA; son of William and Willie Mae Glover; children: 5. **Educ:** St Leo Col, FL, BA. **Career:** US Census Bur, 1988-91, exec; Pub access TV, host, producer; cable tv exec; City Macon, mayor, 1999-2007; hon consul, Uganda; World Conf of Mayors, vpres. **Orgs:** C.Jack Ellis Youth Found; Named one top leaders State Ga; chmn, Int Affairs Comt Nat Conf Black Mayors; Veterans Foreign Wars; Disabled Am Veterans; Nat Asn Advan Colored People. **Business Addr:** GA.

**ELLIS, DALE**
Basketball player. **Personal:** Born Aug 6, 1960, Marietta, GA; married Monique; children: Ashley. **Educ:** Univ Tenn, attended 1983. **Career:** Basketball player (retired); Dallas Mavericks, guard-forward, 1983-86; Seattle Super Sonics, 1986-91, 1997-99; Milwaukee Bucks, 1991-92, 1999-2000; San Antonio Spurs, 1992-94; Denver Nuggets, 1994-97; Charlotte Hornets, 2000. **Orgs:** Nat Basketball Asn.

**ELLIS, DOUGLAS D., JR.**
Executive, consultant. **Personal:** Born Jul 9, 1947, Chicago, IL; son of Douglas Sr and Dorothy Mae Rummage; children: Aaron Christopher; children: Anthony Marcus, Chad Dominick & Jonathan Thomas. **Educ:** Univ Ill, Chicago, BS, 1976; Roosevelt Univ, Chicago, Ill, MS, 1979; Ill Lic, cert pub acct, 1995. **Career:** Sergeant (retired), consultant; Chicago Police Dept, Chicago, Ill, sgt, 1972-2005; Goodman Segar Hogan Inc, asst vpres, 1974; City-Wide Cols, Chicago, Ill, instr, 1984-86; City Chicago, Bur Parking, Chicago Ill, dir, 1986-91; Carr & Assocs, Pub Acct Firm, managing partner, 1992; Dept Justice (Int Criminal Investigative Training Assistance Prog), tech adv; Albanian Nat Police & Ministry Pub Order, sgt; Dellis Acct & Bus Serv, consult, currently; Ellis-Gibson Develop Group, pres. **Orgs:** Cert instr, Chicago Police Acad, 1976-78; Ill CPA Soc, 1985-; bd adv deleg, Inst Munic Parking Cong, 1986-; mem dir, Nat Asn Black Acct, 1987-88; Nat Asn Cert Fraud Examrs, 1995-; Va Beach Develop Authority, 2001-; regional dir, TowneBank, 2005-, bd dir, 2010-; Hampton Roads Asn Com Real Estate; bd mem, YMCA. **Honors/Awds:** Dept Commendation, Chicago Police Dept, 1981; First Degree Black Belt, TaeKwon Do, 1995. **Home Addr:** 2838 Alexander Cres, Flossmoor, IL 60422-1702, **Home Phone:** (708)799-4337. **Business Addr:** President, Ellis-Gibson Development Group, 1081 19th St Suite 203, Virginia Beach, VA 23451-5600, **Business Phone:** (757)497-7700.

**ELLIS, DR. EDWARD V.**
Educator. **Personal:** Born Feb 9, 1924, Louisburg, NC; married Elizabeth Gill; children: Ednetta K, Bruce E & Gary D. **Educ:** Shaw Univ, BS, 1949; NC Col, MSPH, 1950; Univ NC, PhD, 1964. **Career:** Educator (retired), executive; Raleigh Pub Schs, Wake Co Health Dept, health educ, 1950-51; NC Cent Univ, instr, 1951-52; Dist od Columbia Tuberc Asn, assoc health educ, 1952-55; Pa Dept Health, Div Chronic Dis, health educ consult, 1955-63, Div Pub Health Educ, Community Health Sect, chief, 1963-64, dir, 1964-67; Ind St Col, fac mem, sch comn & health educ workshop, 1963; Pa St Univ, fac mem, 1964-65, Col Human Develop, assoc prof pub health, 1969-82, assoc prof, assoc dean, 1969-82, spec asst pres, 1970-71, ctr head, 1971-72, actg div dir, 1972-74; Univ Minn, Sch Pub Health, Grad Prog Health Educ, asst prof, 1967-69; Univ Md Eastern Shore, vice chancellor, vpres acad affairs, 1983-94, prof emer, 1994-, dir exploris; Exploris Mid Sch, dir, currently. **Orgs:** Bd dir, Pa Lung Asn, 1972-77; fel, Am Pub Health Asn, 1973-79; Pa Adv Comt Comprehensive Health Planning, 1973-74; chmn, Coalition Nat Health Educ Orgn, 1978-80; chmn, Nat Univ Exten Asn, 1976-77; Nat Health Nat Adv Comt Community Health Promotions, 1978-79; advisory coun, Am Coun Life Ins, 1978-81; Am Adult Educ Asn; Am Asn Univ Profs; Prog Develop Bd; Soc Pub Health Educ; Soc Pub Health Educ; Pa Pub Health; Cent Pa Health Coun; Ctr Comn Health Coun; Comn Higher Educ; Adv Comn, Pa & Dept Pub Health; Pa Community Nat Health Security; Nat Black Alliance; Am Cancer Soc; Coun Serv Inc Ctr Co; Family Planning Coun Cent Pa; Family Serv Asn Am; Human Rel Comm. **Home Addr:** 4613 Thom Leaf Ct, Raleigh, NC 27604, **Home Phone:** (919)870-5486. **Business Addr:** Director, Exploris Middle School, 401 Hillsborough St, Raleigh, NC 27603, **Business Phone:** (919)715-3690.

**ELLIS, ERNEST W. (AKBAR KHAN)**
Banker, musician. **Personal:** Born Dec 4, 1940, New York, NY; son of Edmund and Mabel; married Judy; children: Anthony, Darius Kenyatta & Edmund Kip. **Educ:** Hartman Inst Criminol, BS, 1963; Am Inst Banking, advan degree, 1977; Inst Far Eastern Affairs, cert, 1981. **Career:** Banker (retired), musician; Un, reporter gen assembly, 1962-64; Harmelin Agency, admin asst ins, 1964-66; Prudential, consultins, 1966-69; St Dept CIA, 1967-70; intelligence off; Chase, 2nd vpres; Galactic Int Ltd, chief exec off & pres, 1982-, independent composer & gourmet chef, 1998-. **Orgs:** Contrib ed, Assets Protection Mag, 1976-; vis prof, Wagner Col, 1976; vice chmn, Area Policy Bd 7, New York, 1979-81; vis prof, Upsala Col, 1981; Asst treas, Western Hem Life Ins Co, 1982-. **Honors/Awds:** New Star Vibist, Sound of Music, 1970; Outstanding Citizen Award, Chase Bank, New York, 1972; Clifford Brown Memorial Music Award, New York, 1976; Certificate of Merit, The Assembly State NY, 1981. **Home Addr:** 14055 Burden Cres, Jamaica, NY 11435-2339, **Home Phone:** (718)297-2590.

**ELLIS, GREGORY LEMONT**
Football player. **Personal:** Born Aug 14, 1975, Wendell, NC; married Tangerk Love; children: Tyann, Geremiah & Taliah. **Educ:** Univ NC, grad. **Career:** Football player (retired); Dallas Cowboys, right defensive end, 1998-99, 2005, left defensive end & defensive end, 2000-04, left outside linebacker & linebacker, 2006, left linebacker & linebacker & defensive end, 2007-08; Oakland Raiders, right defensive end & defensive end, 2009. **Honors/Awds:** Consensus All-American, 1997; Pro Bowler, 2007; Co-All-Iron Award Winner, 2007; AP Comeback Player of the Year, Nat Football League, 2007, PFWA Comeback Player of the Year, Nat Football League, 2007. **Business Addr:** Professional Football Player, Oakland Raiders, 7000 Coliseum Way, Oakland, CA 94621, **Business Phone:** (972)556-9900.

**ELLIS, BISHOP J. DELANO, II**
Clergy. **Personal:** Born Dec 11, 1944, Philadelphia, PA; son of Jesse Sr and Lucy Mae-Harris; married Sabrina Joyce Clinkscale; children: Jesse III, David Demetrius, Lillian Marion, Jessica Delana & Jasmine Delana. **Educ:** Birmingham Univ, doctor humanities, 1968; Pillar Fire Sem, doctor canon law, 1970; Mason Col, doctor divinity, 1984, Howard Univ, Wash, BA, sociol & hist; Nazarene Sem Inst, WVa, MR Ed; Morehouse Col, Atlanta, Ga, doctor divinity; Stafford Univ, London, eng, doctor philos. **Career:** Clergyman, Church God Christ; St James COGIC, pastor, 1976-78; Pentecostal Church Christ, sr pastor, 1989-; Joint Col African Am Pentecostal Bishops, pres & founder. **Honors/Awds:** Birmingham Univ Award. **Special Achievements:** Author: The Mother Church, 1984; Judicial ADM, 1979; A Handbook on Creating Episcopacy in the African-American Pentecostal Church; Creator & author of The Dress Code for Clergy Church of God in Christ, 1972; Founder, the Adjutancy, COGIC, 1970. **Home Addr:** 11655 Regent Pk Dr, Chardon, OH 44024-8333, **Home Phone:** (440)286-8756. **Business Addr:** Senior Pastor, Pentecostal Church of Christ, 10515 Chester Ave, Cleveland, OH 44106, **Business Phone:** (216)721-5934.

**ELLIS, JOHNELL A.**
Engineer, accountant. **Personal:** Born Sep 28, 1945, New Orleans, LA; married Audrey Baker; children: Kimberly Ogren & Sonja Montero. **Educ:** Calif State Univ, BS, Eng, 1968; Univ S Calif, MBA, 1972. **Career:** Bunker-ramo & Westlake, engr, 1968; TRW Sys, Redondo Bch, admin asst, 1969-72; Dart Ind, acquisitions spec, 1972-74; Rockwell Int, financial analyst, 1974; Getty Oil Co, staff engr, 1985; Bambini Stores, Beverly Hills, acct; Calif State Univ, instr. **Orgs:** Soc Petro Engr; Inst Elec & Electronics Engrs; Kappa Alpha Psi; Tau Beta Pi; Eta Kappa Nu. **Honors/Awds:** Award of Appreciation, Improvement Act Comn. **Home Addr:** 19637 Campaign Dr, Carson, CA 90746.

**ELLIS, KENNETH K.**
Executive. **Career:** Morgan State Univ, Phys Plant Dept, assoc dir, dir, currently. **Business Addr:** Physical Plant Director, Morgan State University, Wash Serv Ctr Rm 311, Baltimore, MD 21251, **Business Phone:** (443)885-3333.

**ELLIS, LADD, JR.**
Government official. **Personal:** Born Dec 23, 1946, Winnsboro, LA; son of Ladd and Christine; married Maryetta; children: Kimberlyn, Angela, Stanley, Chris & Sierra. **Educ:** Northeastern La Univ, BBA, acct, 1972; N Tex State Univ, attended 1975; Syracuse Univ, MPA, 1983; CPA Colo, attended 1983; Harvard Univ, attended 1992. **Career:** Internal Revenue Serv, from revenue agt to asst dir, 1972-94, comnr, currently, dist dir, currently. **Orgs:** Exec comt, Asn Improv Minorities, Asn Improv Minorities Internal Revenue Serv, 1983-; exec comt, Fed Exec Bd, Kans City, 1993-; Internal Revenue Serv; Nat Educ Adv Bd, 1994-. **Home Addr:** 4015 Kentshire Lane, Dallas, TX 75287-5015, **Home Phone:** (972)818-3265. **Business Addr:** District Director, Commissioner, Internal Revenue Service, 1100 Com St Rm 121, Dallas, TX 75242, **Business Phone:** (214)413-6010.

**ELLIS, LAPHONSO DARNELL**
Basketball player, broadcaster. **Personal:** Born May 5, 1970, East St. Louis, IL; married Jennifer; children: Elexis, LaPhonso Jr & Walter. **Educ:** Univ Notre Dame, BA, acct, 1992. **Career:** Basketball player (retired), broadcaster; Denver Nuggets, power forward, 1992-94, small forward, 1995, 1997; Atlanta Hawks, power forward, 1999-2000; Minn Timberwolves, small forward, 2000, power forward, 2001; Miami Heat, forward, 2001-03; ESPN, col basketball analyst, 2009-; Notre Dame Men's Basketball team, radio sports announcer, currently; Notre Dame Fighting Irish men's basketball radio broadcasts, color commentator. **Orgs:** Spokesman, Denver Boys and Girls Club. **Honors/Awds:** Sportsmanship Award, Nat Basketball Asn, 1999, 2000, 2001, 2002. **Special Achievements:** Named to NBA All-Rookie First Team, 1993; Appeared in the filming of a TV 411 segment called "SportsSmarts". **Home Addr:** , Mishawaka, IN. **Business Addr:** Radio Sports Announcer, Notre Dame Men's Basketball Team, 113 Joyce Ctr, Notre Dame, IN 46556, **Business Phone:** (574)631-7356.

**ELLIS, MARILYN POPE**
Educator. **Personal:** Born Jun 24, 1938, Newark, NJ; daughter of James Albert and Gladys Hillman; children: Kristina Pope. **Educ:** Calif State Univ, Hayward, BA, 1969; Univ Calif, Berkeley, MA, 1972. **Career:** Educator (retired), professor emeritus; Peralta Community Col, prof hist, 1973-76; Skyline Col, prof, hist, 1973-98, prof emer, 1998-. **Home Addr:** 67 Werner Ave, Daly City, CA 94014, **Home Phone:** (415)994-4649. **Business Addr:** Emeritus, Skyline College, 3300 College Dr, San Bruno, CA 94066, **Business Phone:** (650)738-4100.

**ELLIS, MICHAEL G.**
Industrial designer, educator. **Personal:** Born Oct 31, 1962, Detroit, MI; son of Dave C and Cumire Roberston; married Marietta Kearney. **Educ:** Ctr Creative Studies, Detroit, MI, BFA, indust design, transp,

1984; Wayne State Univ, MBA. **Career:** Ford Motor Co, Dearborn, Mich, designer, 1984-89, sr designer, 1989-92, design mgr, 1992-97, design dir, 1999-2007, GHIA, Turin, Italy, designer; Ctr Creative Studies, Detroit, Mich, instr, 1989-91; Wayne State Univ, Detroit, Mich, instr, 1990; Ford Ger, Cologne, Ger, designer, chief designer, 1999-2007; THINK, design dir, 2000-02; Independant Consult, prin, 2007-. **Orgs:** Porsche Club Am, 1989-; Founder's Soc, Detroit Inst Arts, 1990-; Ellis Indust Design LLC; bd dir, kIDs Innovation Studios; Automotive Design Community. **Home Addr:** 11335 Prest, Detroit, MI 48227. **Business Addr:** Member, Ellis Industrial Design LLC, 590 Cypress Hills Dr, Encinitas, CA 92024, **Business Phone:** (760)803-6604.

## ELLIS, REV. P. J.

Clergy, executive. **Personal:** Born Sep 13, 1911, AL. **Career:** Morning Star Baptist Church, minister & pastor, 1985. **Orgs:** Bd dir, 28th St YMCA, 1957-; pres, Bapt Ministers Conf LA So CA, 1959-62; moderator, LA Dist Asn, 1959-68; life mem, Nat Asn Advan Colored People; parliamentarian, Calif St Baptist Conv; Nat Baptist Conv USA Inc. **Home Addr:** PO Box 1130, Sugarloaf, CA 92386-1130, **Home Phone:** (213)728-1107.

## ELLIS, REHEMA

Television journalist, journalist. **Personal:** Born Dec 19, 1954?, NC; children: 1. **Educ:** Simmons Col, undergrad degree, 1974; Columbia Univ, MJ, 1977. **Career:** KDKA Radio and TV, Pittsburgh, PA, reporter; WHDH-TV, reporter and weekend anchor; NBC News, general assignment correspondent, 1994-, education correspondent, 2010-; NBC online, contributor. **Special Achievements:** Organizer of NBC's first annual Education Nation summit; covered the terrorist attacks of September 11, 2001, Hurricane Katrina, 2005, and the plane crash on the Hudson River, 2009. **Business Addr:** NBC News, 30 Rockefeller Plz, New York, NY 10112.

## ELLIS, RODNEY GLENN

State government official, lawyer, banker. **Personal:** Born Apr 7, 1954, Houston, TX; son of Eligha and O Theresa; married Licia Green; children: 4. **Educ:** Tex Southern Univ, BA, 1975; Lyndon B Johnson Sch Pub Affairs, MPA, 1977; Univ Tex Sch Law, JD, 1979; Xavier Univ, New Orleans; London Sch Econs. **Career:** Lt Govr Tex, admin asst, 1976-80; US Cong, admin asst, 1981-83; Apex Securities Inc, pres & chmn, 1987-; Houston City Coun; US Congressman Mickey Leland, chief staff; State Tex, Dist 13, sen, 1990-, chmn, Sen Comt, currently; McGlinchey Stafford Lang Coun, 1995-2001; Rice Financial Prod Co, partner; Tagos Group, shareholder; Tex Legis Internship Prog, founder. **Orgs:** State Bar Tex; Nat Bar Asn; Am Leadership Forum; Tex Lyceum; bd dir, ARC; Houston Int Univ; Soc Performing Arts; Houston READ Comn; Mickey Leland Ctr World Hunger & Peace; Nat Asn Advan Colored People; Nat Coun Energy Policy; US Secy Energy Adv Bd; Univ Tex Found Bd; bd dir, Ctr Policy Alternatives; Nat Comn Energy Policy, Univ Tex Law Sch Found Bd; bd dir, Ctr Policy Alternatives, Innocence Proj Inc; Coun Foreign Rels, Utley Found; bd dir, Rainbow PUSH Coalition; bd dir, Barbara Jordan Freedom Found; co chair, Comn to Engage African Americans Climate Chg; Senate State Affairs; Transp & Natural Resources comt; found bd, Univ Tex Sch Law; Houston City Coun. **Home Addr:** 2102 Sunset Blvd, Houston, TX 77005. **Business Addr:** Senator, Texas State Senate, 440 La Suite 575, Houston, TX 77002, **Business Phone:** (713)236-0306.

## ELLIS, DR. TELLIS B., III

Physician, founder (originator), college teacher. **Personal:** Born Dec 15, 1943, Jackson, MS; son of Tellis B Jr and Lucinda Jenkins; children: Tellis B IV. **Educ:** Jackson State Univ, BS, 1965; Meharry Med Col, MD, 1970. **Career:** Tufts Delta Health Ctr, med externship, 1969; Meharry Med Col, med internship, 1970-71, internal med residency, 1971-74; Univ Miss Med Ctr, cardiol fel, 1975-77; Jackson Cardiol Assocs PA, founding partner & physician, 1978-; Univ Miss Med Ctr, asst clin prof med, 1982-; Jackson Mem Hosp, staff physician; Cent Miss Med Ctr, staff physician; Miss Baptist Med Ctr, staff physician; Madison County Med Ctr, staff physician; River Oaks Hosp, staff physician; St Dominic-Jackson Memorial Hosp, staff physician. **Orgs:** Jackson Med Soc; Nat Med Asn; Asn Black Cardiologists; Kappa Alpha Psi Fraternity; pres, Miss Med & Surg Asn; fel Am Col Cardiol; Cent TexMed Found; Am Bd Internal Med; Jackson State Univ Alumni Asn; Pearl St AME Church. **Home Addr:** 6068 Huntview Dr, Jackson, MS 39206-2130, **Home Phone:** (601)982-4110. **Business Addr:** Physician, Professor, Jackson Cardiol Associates, 971 Lakeland Dr Suite 850, Jackson, MS 39216-4609, **Business Phone:** (601)981-8543.

## ELLIS, TERRY LYNN

Singer. **Personal:** Born Sep 5, 1966, Houston, TX; daughter of Lennie James and Evelyn Marie Patton. **Educ:** Prairie View A&M Univ, mkt. **Career:** En vogue, r & b singer, 1988-; Albums with Envogue: Born to Sing, 1990; Remix to Sing, 1991; Funky Divas, 1992; Run away Love EP, 1993; EV3, 1997; Masterpiece Theater, 2000; The Gift of Christmas. 2002; Soul Flower, 2004; Solo Albums: Southern Gale, 1995; Films: Batman Forever, 1995; TV series: "Saturday Night Live", 1992-97; Roc, 1993; "Sparks", 1997; "Happily Ever After: Fairy Tales for Every Child", 2000; "En Vogue Christmas", 2014. Singles: "Hold On", 1990; "Lies", 1990; "You Don't Have to Worry", 1991; "Don't Go", 1991; "Strange", "My Lovin' (You're Never Gonna Get It), Giving Him Something He Can Feel", "Yesterday", "Free Your Mind", 1992; "Give It Up", "Turn It Loose", "Love Don't Love You", 1993; "Runaway Lov"e, 1993; "Whatta Man", 1994; "Where Ever You Are", 1995; "What Did I Do To You"/"Back Down Memory Lane", 1996; "Don't Let Go" (Love), 1996; "Whatever", 1997; "Too Gone Too Long", 1997; "No Fool No More", 2000; "Riddle", 2000; "Losin' My Mind, Ooh Boy"; "I'll Cry Later", 2011. **Orgs:** Group mem, Cindy Herron, 2004-05. **Special Achievements:** She contributed a track called "Call on me" for the HBO Film "Disappearing Acts" with Wesley Snipes. **Business Addr:** Vocalist, c/o Atlantic Records, 1290 Ave of the Americas, New York, NY 10104, **Business Phone:** (212)707-2000.

## ELLIS, ZACHARY L.

Executive. **Career:** Ellis Co LLC, Kenner, La, pres, founder & mgr, 1974-. **Orgs:** Better Bus Bur; La Mineral Bd; Nat Roofing Contractors Asn; Nat Legal Resource Ctr. **Business Addr:** Founder, President, The Ellis Co LLC, 2201 Richland St, Kenner, LA 70062, **Business Phone:** (504)469-3295.

## ELLIS-SIMON, AMY

Executive director. **Personal:** Born Evanston, IL. **Educ:** Univ Mich, BA, hist, 1994. **Career:** Bank of Am Merrill Lynch & Co., managing dir, 1993-, Mid Markets & Multi-Prod Sales, head. **Orgs:** Co-founder, Global Markets & Investment Banking Women's Leadership Coun; founder & chairperson, Three Sisters Scholar Found; vice chair, Sponsors Educ Opportunity. **Honors/Awds:** "Crain's New York Business", 40 Under Forty, 2004; "Black Enterprise", 75 Most Powerful Blacks on Wall Street, 2011. **Special Achievements:** First African-American woman appointed managing director at Merrill Lynch. **Business Addr:** Managing Director, Bank of America Merrill Lynch & Co, 100 N Tryon St 18th Floor, Charlotte, NC 28255-0001, **Business Phone:** (800)432-1000.

**ELLISON, CHESTER LAUGHTON.** **See Obituaries Section.**

## ELLISON, DAVID LEE

Government official. **Personal:** Born Oct 11, 1955, Houston, TX; son of L T Sr and Alma L Shelton; married Lethia Fanuiel; children: Dayna Leigh, Chakira, Lyndsay Dalethia, Drew Leslye, Kenoel & Landon David Oran. **Educ:** N Tex State Univ, BS, sec educ, 1980; Univ N Tex, MA, pub admin, 1988. **Career:** City Denton, TX, urban planner, 1980-83, sr planner, 1983-87, asst city mgr, 1987-89; City Mankato, MN, asst city mgr, 1989-91; City Lubbock, asst city mgr, 1991-94; City Carrollton, asst city mgr, 1994-97; City Scottsdale, AR, asst city mgr, 1997-2001, 2007-11; City Sugar Land, asst city mgr, 2002-07; City Houston, bur chief pub health preparedness, 2007; City San Antonio, interim dir planning & community develop, 2011-12, asst city mgr, 2012-14; City San Antonio Airport Syst, aviation planner, 2014-. **Orgs:** Nat Forum Black Pub Adminrs; Int City Mgt Asn; Nat Trust Hist Preserv; pres, N Tex Chap Conf Minority Pub Admin, 1988; exec dir, City Mankato & Blue Earth County Housing & Redevelop Authorities, 1989-; Minn City Mgt Asn; bd dictectors, Nat Community Develop Asn; bd dir, Greater Mankato Area United Way; bd dir, Mankato Area Young Men's Christian Asn; Innovations group; San Antonio Youth Literacy. **Business Addr:** Assistant City Manager, City of San Antonio, San Antonio, TX 77487-0110, **Business Phone:** (210)207-6000.

## ELLISON, JERRY ERNEST

Business owner, football player. **Personal:** Born Dec 20, 1971, Augusta, GA; married Loretta. **Educ:** Univ Tenn, Chattanooga. **Career:** JBE Enterprises, chief exec officer; Tampa Bay Buccaneers, running back & fullback, 1996-98; New Eng Patriots, running back, 1999.

## ELLISON, KEITH

Editor, farmer. **Personal:** Born Jan 1, 1968?. **Educ:** Carnegie Mellon Univ, BS, elec engineering & math, 1987; Univ Pa, Wharton Sch Bus, MBA, mkt & entrepreneurial mgt, 1995. **Career:** IBM, mkt rep, 1987-93; Next Step Mag, founder, ed & co publ, 1995-; Wharton Small Bus Develop Ctr, dir consult, 1998-2000; Wharton Sch Bus, Univ Pa, lectr commun; farmer & prof speaker; Ellison Group, owner, currently. **Orgs:** Nat Speakers Asn. **Honors/Awds:** Golden Circle Award, 100% Club. **Special Achievements:** Taught Bus Develop to Renewable-Energy Firms, Beijing, China, 2002. **Business Addr:** Owner, The Ellison Group, 155 E Godfrey Ave Suite B206, Philadelphia, PA 19120, **Business Phone:** (215)924-9281.

## ELLISON, KEITH MAURICE

Lawyer, legislator. **Personal:** Born Aug 4, 1963, Detroit, MI; son of Leonard and Clida; married Kim; children: Amirah, Jeremiah, Elijah & Isaiah. **Educ:** Wayne State Univ, BA, econ, 1987; Univ Minn Law Sch, JD, 1990. **Career:** Pract atty, 1990-2006; Minn State House, US House Representatives, Fifth Cong Dist Minn, rep, 2007-; Dem-Farmer-Labor Party; Minn state Dem Party; Cong Progressive Caucus, co-chair. **Orgs:** House Fin Serv Comt; House Judiciary Comt. **Home Addr:** 1629 Bryant Ave N, Minneapolis, MN 55411, **Home Phone:** (612)529-1412. **Business Addr:** Representative, US House of Representatives, 2100 Plymouth Ave, Minneapolis, MN 55411, **Business Phone:** (612)522-1212.

## ELLISON, MARVIN R.

Executive, businessperson. **Personal:** son of Ivory and Ella; married Sharyn; children: 2. **Educ:** Univ Memphis, BBA; Emory Univ, MBA. **Career:** Convenience store, employee; dept store, janitor; plumbing supply co, driver; Target, oper roles, corp dir asset protection, 1987-2002; Home Depot, sr vpres global logistics, pres Northern Div, 2002-08, exec vpres US stores, 2008-15; J. C. Penney Co Inc, pres & chief exec officer, 2015-. **Special Achievements:** First African American on The Home Depot's executive team; board member, FedEx; former director, H.R. Block, former director; Ellison Family Gospel group, musician and contributor to four albums. **Business Addr:** J.C. Penney, 6501 Legacy Dr, Plano, TX 75024.

## ELLISON, NOLEN M.

College administrator, educator. **Personal:** Born Jan 26, 1941, Kansas City, KS; married Carole; children: Marc & Steven. **Educ:** Kans Univ, BA, hist, BS, psychol, & polit sci, 1963; Hampton Inst, MA, 1966; Mich State Univ, PhD, urban planning & instnl mgt, 1971. **Career:** Mich State Univ, Urban Affairs, assoc dir ctr, 1968-70, asst pres, 1970-71, admin intern; 20 Good Men, interim pres & exec dir, Kellogg Found Proj; Metrop Jr Col Dist, asst chancellor, 1971-72; Seattle Community Col, pres & chief exec officer, 1972-74; Cuyahoga Community Col, pres & Secy, 1974-91, bd trustee; Univ Mo, Henry W Bloch Sch Bus & Pub Admin, dir & prof urban affairs; Mo Shutte Endowed prof, 1992-2001; Seed Ctr KC, vol, chmn, bd dir, 2001-; prof emer, Pub Admin, 2004-; Samuel Rodgers Community Health Clin, consult, currently; Univ Mo, Carolyn Schutte Mo Prof. **Orgs:** Phi Delta Kappa, 1968-; Carnegie Coun Policy Studies Higher Educ, NY City, 1973-; adv bd, Educ Resources Info Ctr Clearinghouse Jr Col, Univ Calif, Los Angeles, 1973-; bd dir, Am Asn Community & Jr Cols Asn; Gov Bds, Univ & Col, pres, adv com, 1974-; bd overseers, Morehouse Med Prog, 1975; exec bd, N Cent Asn Col & Schs, 1977; Kellogg Found; nat adv bd, Qual Educ Minorities Network; nat adv bd, Am Asn Univ Professors; chair bd standing comt, Workforce Develop/P & E. **Home Addr:** 1710 N 90th St, Kansas City, KS 66112-1505, **Home Phone:** (913)299-2738. **Business Addr:** Professor Emeritus, University of Missouri, 5100 Rockhill Rd, Kansas City, MO 64110-2499, **Business Phone:** (816)235-2215.

## ELLISON, DR. PAULINE ALLEN

Government official, executive. **Personal:** Born Iron Gate, VA; married Oscar Jr; children: Oscar III, Paula Michelle & Karla. **Educ:** Am Univ, MPA; Wilberforce Univ, Dr, humanities, 1976; Livingstone Col, DHL, 1979; Howard Univ; Georgetown Univ; Fed Exec Inst. **Career:** NOVA Chap Jack & Jill Am, founder & pres, 1963-69; Housing & Urban Develop, 1965; Dept Housing & Community Develop, dir personnel DC redevelop land agency; Links Inc, nat prog dir, 1970-74, pres, 1974-78; Arling Chap Links Inc, vpres, adminr, consult, nat pres, 1974-78; Arlington Civil Serv Commn, commr, 1983-87; Cent Fidelity Banks Inc, dir, 1989-; Real Estate Ctr, mgt consult & realtor, 1994; Consult, fed & munic mgt, 1994; Drs Johnson & Ellison Ltd, consult; Arlington Hosp, adv; Wash performing Arts Soc, secy. **Orgs:** Beta Kappa Chi Nat Hon Sci Soc; bd dir, Nat Conf; Pi Alpha Hon Soc; chmn & bd dir, Fed Exec Inst Alumni Asn, 1972-76; bd dir, Nat Conf Christians & Jews, 1976-87; vpres, Arlington Community TV, 1986-87; pres, Int Serv Club Coun, 1986-87; pres, Northern VA Chap Minority Polit Women, 1986-87; chmn, Ethics Community & Outreach Community; secy, bd dir, Burgundy Farm Country Day Sch; Drafting Comt Black Econ Summit Meeting; chmn, Personnel Policy Comn Burgundy Farm Country Day Sch; pres, Girls 4-H Club; pres, Debating & Lit Club; pres, Sr Class; youth leader, Baptist Young Peoples Union & Baptist Training Union; Am Soc Pub Admin; Nat Asn Housing & Redevelop Officials; Nat Asn Suggestion Sys; life mem, Nat Asn Advan Colored People; adv, Northern VA Jr League; Pub Policy Comt; vpres, Hubert Humphrey's Comt; dir bd, Arlington Hosp. chair, consult, Civil Serv Comn. **Home Addr:** 2927 N Lexington St, Arlington, VA 22207, **Home Phone:** (703)534-6735.

## ELLISON, PERVIS

Basketball player, basketball coach. **Personal:** Born Apr 3, 1967, Savannah, GA; son of Arthur Ashe; married Timi; children: Seattle, Aja & Malik. **Educ:** Univ Louisville, BA, criminal justice, 1989. **Career:** Basketball player (retired), basketball coach; Sacramento Kings, forward-ctr, 1989-90; Wash Bullets, 1990-94; Boston Celtics, 1994-2000; Seattle Supersonics, 2000-01; Lawnside Jaguars, football coach; Life Ctr Acad, coach, currently. **Business Addr:** Coach, Life Center Academy, 2035 Columbus Rd, Burlington, NJ 08016, **Business Phone:** (609)499-2100.

## ELLISON, ROSALIND

College administrator. **Career:** S Bend Community Sch Corp, dir stud serv, 2004. **Business Addr:** Director of Student Services, South Bend Community School Corp, 635 S Main St, South Bend, IN 46601, **Business Phone:** (219)283-8064.

## ELLISS, LUTHER JOHN

Football player. **Personal:** Born Mar 22, 1973, Mancos, CO; married Rebecca; children: Kaden, Olivia, Christian, Noah, Isaiah, Isabelle, Sophia, Jonah, Micah, Elijah, Mia & Colsen. **Educ:** Univ Utah. **Career:** Football player (retired); Detroit Lions, right defensive tackle & left defensive end & defensive tackle, 1995-2003; Denver Broncos, 2004. **Honors/Awds:** Defensive Player of the Year, Western Athletic Conf, 1994; Consensus All-American, 1994. **Special Achievements:** TV Series: "Real Sports with Bryant Gumbel", 2011.

## ELLSWORTH, PERCY DANIEL, III

Football player. **Personal:** Born Oct 19, 1974, Drewryville, VA. **Educ:** Univ Va, grad. **Career:** New York Giants, defensive back, 1996-97, strong safety, 1998, free safety & safety, 1999; Cleveland Browns, free safety, 2000-01. **Home Addr:** 11261 Fortsville Rd, Drewryville, VA 23844, **Home Phone:** (434)658-4750.

## ELLY, ANDREW JACKIE

Manager, executive. **Personal:** Born Jul 24, 1949, Pascagoula, MS; son of Andrew Thomas and Augustine Rita Martin; married Faye Olivia Meggs; children: Christopher, Naturio, Shawn, Orin & Jacketta. **Educ:** Jackson County Jr Col, 1967; Savannah State Col, 1970. **Career:** Refinery, mech, 1975-87; Chevron USA, maintenance supvr, 1987-; Jackson County Mentorship Prog, bd mem, 1990-; Jackson County Utility Authority, City Moss Pt, bd dir, mem, currently. **Orgs:** Comnr, Gulf Coast Regional Waste Water, 1977-; pres, Jackson County Sickle Cell, 1982-; natl sec, Knights Peter Claver, 1988-94, 13th supreme knight, 1994-2000. **Honors/Awds:** Silver Medal, Knights of Peter Claver, 1978; Male Role Model of the Year, City Moss Pt, 1998. **Home Addr:** 5912 Meadow Dr, Moss Point, MS 39563, **Home Phone:** (228)475-3132. **Business Addr:** Board of Director, Jackson County Utility Authority, 11100 Hwy 57, Vancleave, MS 39565, **Business Phone:** (228)762-0119.

## ELMORE, ESQ. ERNEST ERIC

Lawyer. **Personal:** Born Aug 21, 1964, Jamaica, NY; son of Sheila. **Educ:** Cornell Univ, BA, polit sci & govt, 1986; Cornell Law Sch, JD, govt law, 1989. **Career:** US Fed Trade Comn, gen atty, 1990-; US Atty Off DC, spec asst us atty, 1999-2000. **Orgs:** Alpha Phi Alpha Fraternity Inc, 1983-; Nat Bar Asn, 1989-; Ny Bar, 1991-. **Home Addr:** 5 Whitehall Ct, Silver Spring, MD 20901-1059, **Home Phone:** (301)754-3707. **Business Addr:** General Attorney, US Federal Trade Commission, 600 Pennsylvania Ave NW, Washington, DC 20580, **Business Phone:** (202)326-3109.

## ELMORE, DR. RONN

Counselor, actor, writer. **Personal:** Born Apr 27, 1957, Louisville, KY; married Aladrian; children: Corinn, Christina & Cory. **Educ:** Antioch Univ, BA, pub rels & jour, 1981; Fuller Theol Sem, MA, theol, marriage & family coun, 1989; Ryokan Col, Doctorate, clin psychol, 1992. **Career:** Actor, dancer, model, currently; Evangelist Rev. E.V. Hill, exec asst; Gospel Ministry, ordained, 1986; Faithful Cent Church, asst pastor & dir coun ministries, 1984-94; Relationship Clin, dir; Relationship Enrichment Progs, founder & dir, 1989-; Ronn Elmore Ministries Inc, therapist, minister & auth, prin, 2000-. **Orgs:** Exec bd, One Church, One Child; charter mem, Am Asn Christian Counrs. **Honors/Awds:** Chrysalis Award, Minority AIDS Proj, 1988. **Special Achievements:** Author: How to Love a Black Man, Time Warner, 1996; How to Love a Black Woman, Time Warner, 1998; An Outrageous Commitment: The 48 Vows Of An Indestructible Marriage, Harpercollins, 2003; Mercy Mercy Me. **Home Addr:** 333 W Florence Ave, Inglewood, CA 90301. **Business Addr:** Minister, Author, Ronn Elmore Ministries Inc, 5050 Laguna Blvd Suite 112-423, Elk Grove, CA 95758, **Business Phone:** (916)760-0401.

## ELMORE, STEPHEN A., SR.
Auditor. **Personal:** Born Feb 24, 1952, Montgomery, AL; son of Clinton R Sr and Margaret L; married Linda J Pryor; children: Stephen Jr, Dana Pryor & Jonathan Clinton. **Educ:** Morehouse Col, BA, 1973. **Career:** Arthur Andersen & Co, staff auditor, 1973-75, from sr auditor to audit mgr, 1975-80; Wachovia Corp, asst dir audit, 1980-83, gen auditor, 1983, dep gen auditor, 1987; Citizens Trust Bank, bd dirs, 2003-; Smiley-Smith & Bright CPA's, partner; Environ Facil Authority, finance dir; Citizens Bancshares Corp, dir, 2003-. **Orgs:** Am Inst Cert Pub Accounts, 1977; Ga Soc Cert Pub Accountants, 1978; Nat Asn Black Accounts Inc, 1978; founding mem, Atlanta-Fulton Co Zoo Inc, 1985-91; Inst Internal Auditors, 1985; 100 Black Men Atlanta, 1991; bd dir, Univ Community Develop Corp, 1991-; dir, Am Diabetes Asn, 1992-96; treas, Nat Black Arts Festival Mem Guild, 1997; Morehouse Col Bus Dept Exec Mentorship Prog; Ala Socs Cert Pub Accountants; bd dir, Boys & Girls Club Montgomery; Morehouse Col Alumni Asn; Leadership Atlanta Alumni. **Home Addr:** 115 Shady Brooke Walk, Fairburn, GA 30213, **Home Phone:** (770)719-1492. **Business Addr:** Board of Director, Citizen Trust Bank, 75 Piedmont Ave, Atlanta, GA 30303, **Business Phone:** (404)653-2815.

## ELZEY, THOMAS J.
College administrator, chief financial officer, vice president (organization). **Personal:** married Monedia; children: Briana & Tommi. **Educ:** Bradley Univ, BS, econ; Carnegie Mellon Univ, MS, pub mgt & policy, 1977. **Career:** Howard univ, sr vpres & chief financial officer; Drexel Univ, sr vpres, treas & chief financial officer, 2001-, Drexel Univ Col Med, sr vpres, treas & chief financial officer, 2002-; Citadel, exec vice pres finance, admin & opers; SC State Univ, pres; Thrift Depositor Protection Oversight Bd, dep exec dir; Resolution Trust Corp, dep exec dir; Perry Investments, vpres; Chicago Pk Dist, asst gen supt, chief operating officer; Fed Govt, sr policy analyst. **Orgs:** Treas, Drexel Res Found; EDUCAUSE; Ford Found Fel, Carnegie Mellon Univ; Resolution Trust Corp Wash DC; gen mgr, chief exec officer, San Francisco Pub Utilities Comn; dep budget dir, budget dir, Chicago Off Budget Mgt. **Business Addr:** Chief Financial Officer, Senior Vice President, Drexel University, 3141 Chestnut St Main Bldg 310, Philadelphia, PA 19104, **Business Phone:** (215)895-2803.

## EMANUEL, BERT TYRONE
Executive, football player. **Personal:** Born Oct 26, 1970, Kansas City, MO; son of Ervin and Marilyn; married Teri; children: Sydni Brook, Cortni, Whitni, Brittni & Bert Jr. **Educ:** Rice Univ, BA, 2004. **Career:** Football player (retired); Atlanta Falcons, wide receiver, 1994-97; Tampa Bay Buccaneers, wide receiver, 1998-99; Miami Dolphins, wide receiver, 2000; Detroit Lions, wide receiver, 2001; New Eng Patriots, wide receiver, 2001; KAOS Worldwide, founder, pres & chief exec officer, 2005-. **Special Achievements:** NFL to clarify the rule regarding what constitutes a valid pass reception, "The Bert Emanuel Rule". **Home Addr:** , Missouri City, TX. **Business Addr:** President, Chief Executive Officer, Kaos Worldwide, 15 Bees Creek Ct, Missouri City, TX 77459-6734, **Business Phone:** (281)313-5267.

## EMBRY, WAYNE RICHARD
Executive, administrator, basketball player. **Personal:** Born Mar 26, 1937, Springfield, OH; married Terri; children: Debbi, Jull & Wayne Jr. **Educ:** Miami Univ Oxford, BS, educ, 1958. **Career:** Basketball player (retired), executive; Cincinnati Royals, basket ballplayer, 1958-66; Royals, team capt, 1963; Boston Celtics, basketball player, 1966-68; Milwaukee Bucks, basketball player, 1968-69, gen mgr, 1972-79, vpres & consult, 1977-85; Ind Pacers, vpres & basketball consult, 1985-86; Cleveland Cavaliers, vpres basketball opers, 1985-92, gen mgr, 1986-99; Michael Alan Lewis Co, chief exec officer; Toronto Raptors, sr adv, 2004-, interim gen mgr, 2006. Author: The Inside Game: Race, Power and Politics in the NBA, 2004. **Orgs:** Alpha Phi Alpha; ABU-USA Olympic Basketball Player Selection CommUS Olympic Team. **Special Achievements:** First African American general manager in NBA league history and the first black general manager of a major U.S. team sport; First African American NBA team president with the Cavaliers in 1994. **Business Addr:** Senior Advisor, Toronto Raptors, 40 Bay St, Toronto, ON M5J 2X2, **Business Phone:** (216)420-2100.

## EMEAGWALI, DALE BROWN
Research scientist. **Personal:** Born Dec 24, 1954, Baltimore, MD; daughter of Johnnie Doris and Leon Robert; married Philip; children: Ijeoma. **Educ:** Coppin State Col, BA, biol, 1976; Georgetown Univ, PhD, microbiol, 1981. **Career:** Nat Insts Health, postdoctoral fel, 1981-84; Uniformed Servs Univ Health Sci, postdoctoral fel, 1985-86; Univ Wyo, res assoc, 1986-87; Univ Mich, sr res fel, 1987-88, asst res scientist, 1989-91; Univ Minn, res assoc, 1992-95, sr res fel; Morgan State Univ, prof, 1996-; Morgan Dept Biol, State Univ, lectr, currently; doctoral fel Fund, Delta Sigma Theta Sorority; fel, Damon Runyon Walter Winchell Cancer Fund; fel, Am Cancer Soc; fel, Nat Sci Found. **Orgs:** Sigma Xi, 1983-; AAAS, 1985-. **Honors/Awds:** Biomedical Fellowship Award, Meharry Med Col, 1974; 3rd Place Award, Best Presentation, Beta Kappa Chi & Nat Inst Sci, 1976; Biomedical Research Award, Coppin State Col, 1976; Postdoctoral Fellowship Award, Nat Sci Found, 1981; Postdoctoral Fellowship Award, Am Cancer Soc, 1981; Scientist of the Year Award, Nat Tech Asn, 1996. **Special Achievements:** Co-author: "Evidence of a Constitutive and Inducible Form of Kynurenine Formamidase," Archives of Biochem Biophysics, 1980; "Sequence Homology Between the Structural Proteins of Kilham Rat Virus," Journal of Virol, 1984; "Purification and Characterization of Kynurenine Formamidase Activity from S Paravulus," Canadian Journal of Microbiology, 1986; "Modulation of Ras Expression by Antisense Non-ionic Deoxyoligonucleotide Analogues," Journal of Gene Research, 1989; "Amplified Expression of Three Jun Family Members Inhibits Erytholeukemia Differentiation Blood," 1990; National Technical Society, Scientist of the Year, 1996. **Home Addr:** 3713 Sylvan Dr, Baltimore, MD 21207-6364. **Business Addr:** Lecturer, Morgan State University, Rm G 57, Baltimore, MD 21251, **Business Phone:** (443)885-3715.

## EMEAGWALI, DR. PHILIP CHUKWURAH
Computer scientist, educator, mathematician. **Personal:** Born Aug 23, 1954, Akure; son of James N and Agatha I; married Dale Brown; children: Ijeoma, Nnamdi & Onyeamechi. **Educ:** Univ London, gen cert educ, 1973; Ore State Univ, BS, math, 1977; George Washington Univ, MS, environ engineering, 1981; George Washington Univ, Engr degree, ocean, costal & marine, 1986; Univ Md, MA, appl math, 1986; Univ Mich, Ann Arbor, PhD, sci comput, 1993. **Career:** Md State Hwy Admini, var hwy Engineering duties, 1977-78; George Washington Univ, res, 1979-82; US Nat Weather Serv & Univ MD, researcher, 1984-86; US Bur Reclamation, civil engineering & res math duties, 1986-87; Univ Mich, Ann Arbor, researcher, 1987-91; Univ Minn, Army High Performance Comput Res Ctr, res fel, 1991-93; Independent Consult, 1993-; PBS Futures TV Serv, sci consult meteorol episode. **Orgs:** Inst Elec & Electronic Engrs' Comput Soc; Asn Comput Mach; Soc Indust & Appl Math; adv bd, Nat Tech Asn; Am Phys Soc; Inst Elect & Electronics Engrs; Geo Sci & Remote Sensing Soc; Am meteorol Soc; Nat Soc Black Engrs; Nat Soc Prof Engrs; Prof Commun Soc; Soc Res Tech Commun; Aircraft Owners & Pilots Asn; US Parachute Asn; Balloon Fedn Am; Nat Aeronaut Asn; Am Inst Aeronaut & Astronaut; Aerospace & Electronic Systs Soc; Nat Air & Space Mus; Underwater Explorers Soc; Am Socs Civil Engrs; Nat Space Socs. **Honors/Awds:** Gordon Bell Prize, Inst Elect & Electronics Engrs Soc, 1989; Distinguished Scientist Award, Nat Soc Black Engrs, 1991; Certificate of Recognition Award, Mobil Corp & US Black Engr Mag, 1991, 1992; Distinguished Visitor, IEEE Comput Soc, 1993-96; Computer Scientist of the Year Award, Nat Tech Asn, 1993; Eminent Engineer, Tau Beta Pi Nat Engineering Hon Soc, 1994; InterNat Man of the Year Award, Minority Technol Coun Mich, 1994; Certificate of Appreciation Award, Sci Mus Minn, 1994; Distinguished Scientist Award, World Bank, 1998; Best Scientist in Africa Award of the Pan African Broadcasting Heritage & Achievement Awards, 2001; History's Greatest Scientist of African Descent, New African mag, 2004; Received Numerous Awards. **Special Achievements:** Extolled by the then U.S. President Bill Clinton as "one of the great minds of the Information Age? and described by CNN as "a Father of the Internet"; Author of Several Books. **Home Addr:** 1101 30th St NW Suite 500, Washington, DC 20007, **Home Phone:** (202)203-8724. **Business Addr:** Independent Consultant, 1101 30th St NW Suite 500, Washington, DC 20007, **Business Phone:** (202)203-8724.

## EMEKA, MAURIS L. P.
Business owner, executive. **Personal:** Born Apr 4, 1941, Fargo, AR; married Sunday A Bacon; children: Amon, Gabriel, Justin & Apollo. **Educ:** Fisk Univ; Ore State Univ; Univ Kans, BA, 1961; Univ Wash, MBA, 1970. **Career:** Bike Master Inc, pres; Bicycle Store, owner; Black Econ Union Kans City, asst dir; Black Econ Res Ctr NY, asst dir. **Honors/Awds:** Author of book and articles on Black & Banks. **Home Addr:** 397 W Palisade Ave, Englewood, NJ 07631.

## EMERSON, MELINDA
Chief executive officer. **Educ:** Va Polytech Inst & State Univ, BA, commun studies, 1994; Dartmouth Col, Tuck Sch Bus, Dartmouth, minority exec educ prog, 2003. **Career:** Va Tech, intern, 1992-94; WPXI-TV, assoc producer, 1994-95; NBC 10, producer, 1995-97; Urban League Philadelphia, ULYP vol, 1996-2003; 6ABC WPVI-TV, producer, 1997-99; Quintessence Multimedia, founder, pres & exec officer, 1999-; Bldg Your Bus with Melinda Emerson, pres, 2007-; smallbizchat, host, 2009-; Smallbiztrends.com, start-up columnist, 2010-11; SecondAct.com, careers columnist, 2010-12; New York Times, 2012-; Become Your Own Boss 12 Months, auth, 2015-. **Orgs:** Nat Asn Women Bus Owners; Womens Bus Enterprise Nat Coun; Nat Minority Supplier Develop Coun; Nat Urban League; Gift Life Donor Prog; Minority Organ & Tissue Transplant Educ Prog; Nat Speakers Asn, 2007-. **Business Addr:** President, Execuitve Officer, Quintessence Entertainment Inc, 4548 Mkt St, Philadelphia, PA 19139, **Business Phone:** (215)243-4125.

## EMMANUEL, ANTHONY
President (organization), executive. **Educ:** Rutgers Univ, BS, elec eng & BA, math, 1996. **Career:** Lucent Technol Inc, Inferno Bus Unit, syst engr; AlphaOne Comput Solutions Inc, multimedia developer & comput instr; Rutgers Col Eng, Dean's Off, develop specialist, currently; Rutgers Univ, Digital Media Lab, mgr, 1993-96; Hookt.com, digital media dir, 2000-01; Emmanuel Media Grp Inc, chmn, chief exec officer, chief tech officer, content designer & video producer, 2001-07; Miami C s Hosp, Info Architect, 2007-09; Brightstar Corp, SharePoint Architect, Currently. **Business Addr:** SharePoint Architect, Information Architect, Brightstar Corp, 9725 NW 117th Ave, Miami, FL 33178, **Business Phone:** (305)421-6000.

## EMMANUEL, DR. TSEGAI
College teacher. **Personal:** Born Mar 27, 1940; son of G Hiwet and Ghebray Leteyesus; married Karen; children: Sarah & Ribka. **Educ:** Un Statist Ctr, dipl statist, 1962; Okla State Univ, BS, prod mgt, 1968, MA, 1970; Atlanta Univ, dipl econs, 1972; Univ Mo, PhD, mgt & policy admin, 1978; Univ Minn, Info Systs Fac Develop Inst, dipl, 1986. **Career:** Un Econ Comm Africa, African Statist Anal Dept, Addis Ababa, Ethiopia, head, 1960-63; Peace Corps Prog Univ Utah, inter-cult studies advisor, 1969; Lincoln Univ, Jefferson City, asst prof, 1970-76, dir, Int Stud Affairs, 1974-76; Eastern Wash State Univ, Cheyney, from asst prof to assoc prof, 1976-80; Wash State Univ, adj prof, 1979-90; Grambling State Univ, Col Bus, dean, 1980-90, prof, 1980-; Alcorn State Univ, Col Bus, Alcorn, Miss, curric eval, 1987; U S Deleg to First African & African-Am Conf, ivory coast, 1990; LeMoyene-Owens Col, budget consult, 1991; Ga State Univ, Prom & Tenure, 1998-2006; Ga State Univ, Distant Learning Task Force, 2006; Ind Univ, Prom & Tenure, outside evaluator, 2007; Prom & Tenure, Mgt & Mkt Dept, 2009. **Orgs:** Mem-at-large, 1983-84, treas, 1984-85, secy, 1985-86, vpres & prog chmn, 1986-87, pres, 1987-88 & 1989-90, Southwest Bus Admin Asn; nominating comt, 1984-85, chmn, equal opportunities minorities, 1985-87, mem, articles & bylaws comt, 1985-88, chmn, articles & bylaws comt, 1987-88, bd dir, 1987-89, int affairs comt, 1990-91, Am Assembly Col Sch Bus; chair, Grambling Econ Develop Coun, 1986-87; Grambling Med Bldg Comt, 1986-87; Fac Appointment, Prom & Tenure Comt, 1989-90; vis comt mem, Clark Atlanta Univ, 1994; chair finance comt, Grambling State Univ Athletic Found Bd, 1994-95; chair, Fulbright Teacher Exchange Prog, 1994-2000; Mayor's Comt Econ Develop, 1995-; Southwest Fedn Admin Disciplines; secy, State Comm Corp, La; La Coun Black Econ Develop; pres, Grambling Chamber Com, 2005; vis comt mem, Southern Asn Cols & Schs, 2000; chair, Ga State Univ, Fac Handbk, 2000; chair, Ga State Univ, Curric Comt, 2000-08; Ga State Univ, Grievance Comt, 2005; bd mem, Eddie Robinson Mus, 2009; dean, Search Comt, 2009; Acad Econs & Finance; Int Acad Bus & Econs; Int Bus & Econs Res; Southwest Acad Mgt; Asn Global Bus; Int Acad Bus Disciplines; Southern Mgt Asn; Western Acad Mgt; Southwest Fedn Asn Div; Southwest Bus Symp; Mid-S Asn Bus Disciplines; Acad Bus Admin. **Home Addr:** 708 Hundred Oaks Dr, Ruston, LA 71270-2420, **Home Phone:** (318)251-1766. **Business Addr:** Professor, Grambling State University, R W E Jones Dr, Grambling, LA 71245-2715, **Business Phone:** (318)274-2275.

## EMMONS, CARLOS ANTOINE
Executive, football player. **Personal:** Born Sep 3, 1973, Greenwood, MS. **Educ:** Ark State Univ, BS, bus mgmt, 1995. **Career:** Football player (retired), executive; Pittsburgh Steelers, 1996-97, right outside linebacker, 1998-99, linebacker, 1999; Philadelphia Eagles, right linebacker & linebacker, 2000-03; New York Giants, linebacker, 2004-06, left linebacker, 2004-05, right linebacker, 2006; 51 Ways, chief exec officer, 2008-; Emmons LLC, pres, chief exec officer, 2008-; Wet Willie's, Atlanta, GA, owner, chief exec officer, currently. **Honors/Awds:** Most Valuable Player, Philadelphia Eagles, 2003; Teams Ed Block Courage Award, 2007. **Business Addr:** Owner, Chief Executive Officer, Wet Willie's Restaurant, PO Box 60127, Savannah, GA 31412, **Business Phone:** (912)232-5650.

## EMMONS, REV. RAYFORD E.
Clergy. **Personal:** Born Jun 25, 1948, Philadelphia, PA. **Educ:** St Charles Sem, BA, 1970. **Career:** Field work experience parochial schs, hosps, comm & parish church activ; Atlanta Univ, asst Cath chaplain, 1972; St Patrics Church Norristown, asst pastor, 1974-; Most Blessed Sanament Church, asst pastor, 1978-80; St Elizabeth Church Philadelphia, asst pastor, 1980; Cath Social Serv, staff; St Agatha, priest; St James Church, priest; St Cyril Alexandria, assoc pastor & parochial vicar; Our Lady Hope Parish, parochial vicar; St. Martin Tours Parish, parochial vicar, currently. **Orgs:** Nat Black Seminarians Asn, 1970-73; Nat Black Cath Clergy Caucus, 1974-; affil, Nat Black Cath Lay Caucus. **Honors/Awds:** Several appearances on local & national TV progs; speaker at civic & religious group affairs; featured in local newspapers; formerly involved in prison, hosp & youth work. **Special Achievements:** First African American priest ordained for Archdiocese of Philadelphia, 1974. **Home Addr:** 6161 N 5th St, Philadelphia, PA 19120. **Business Addr:** Parochial Vicar, Our Lady of Hope Rectory, 5200 N Broad St, Philadelphia, PA 19141-1628, **Business Phone:** (215)329-8100.

## ENDERS, MURVIN S.
Executive. **Personal:** Born May 19, 1942; son of Murvin Sr and Ruth King; married Linda; children: Murvin III, Kevin & Erik. **Educ:** Fisk Univ, Nashville, TN, BA, 1962; Univ Indianapolis, IN, MBA, 1981. **Career:** Executive (retired); Chrysler Corp, Indianapolis, Ind, var positions, 1962-77, personnel mgr, 1977-81, prod facil engr mgr, 1981-83, shift supt, 1983-84, mgr mfg engr, 1984-86, prod mgr, 1986-89, plant mgr, 1989-95; IWC Resources, vpres admin affairs, 1995-98, vpres hr, 1998-2003; Black Men Indianapolis Inc, exec dir; Black Men S Fla Inc, exec dir. **Orgs:** Bd dir, Christal House Acad; Econ Develop Comn; bd dir, Methodist Hosp Found; bd dir, Christian Theol Sem; bd dir, Bowen Found; bd dir, Univ Indianapolis; lifetime mem, Nat Asn Advan Colored People; Circle City Frontiers Serv Club; Alpha Phi Alpha Fraternity; Sigma Pi Phi Fraternity; bd dir, Conner Prairie Mus; bd dir, 100 Black Men Indianapolis Inc; Diversity Comt Chair, United Way Cent Ind; bd mem, Christel House Acad; trustee, Christian Theol Sem; comt chair, chap develop, Black Men S Fla Inc. **Home Addr:** 509 Kessler Blvd W Dr, Indianapolis, IN 46228, **Home Phone:** (317)251-2591. **Business Addr:** Board of Director, Conner Prairie, 13400 Allisonville Rd, Fishers, IN 46308, **Business Phone:** (317)776-6006.

## ENGLAND, ERIC JEVON
Football player. **Personal:** Born Apr 25, 1971, Ft. Wayne, IN. **Educ:** Tex A&M Univ, sports mgt. **Career:** Ariz Cardinals, defensive end, 1994, 1996, 1995; BC Lions, can, 2000; San Francisco Demons, 2001; Detroit Fury, 2002; New York Dragons, 2003; Toronto Argonauts, 2003-06. **Honors/Awds:** All-Star, Can Football League, 2003; East All-Star, Can Football League, 2003; Champion, Grey Cup, 2004.

## ENGLAND, DR. RODNEY WAYNE
Educator, physician, association executive. **Personal:** Born Jun 24, 1932, Mounds, IL; son of Lois and Katie; married Patricia R Shipp; children: Rodney, Michael, Stephen, John & Sarah. **Educ:** Univ Ill, BS, 1954, MD, 1956. **Career:** Pvt pract physician, 1962-; Minneapolis VA Health Care Syst, resident, 1962; Ancker Hosp, resident, 1962; Univ Minn, clin assoc prof internal med, 1978; Health E Clin Internal Med, St Paul, 1993; Vet Affairs Med Ctr, resident. **Orgs:** Dipl Am Bd Internal Med, 1964; bd dirs, Health E Corp. **Home Addr:** 10367 Lancaster Cove, Woodbury, MN 55129, **Home Phone:** (651)731-7708. **Business Addr:** Physician, Private Practitioner, 17 Exchange St W Suite 835, Woodbury, MN 55102-1036, **Business Phone:** (651)232-4200.

**ENGLISH, ALBERT JAY**
Basketball coach, basketball player. **Personal:** Born Jul 11, 1967, Wilmington, DE; children: A J III & A'Jen. **Educ:** Va Union Univ, Richmond, VA, 1990. **Career:** Basketball player (retired), coach; Wash Bullets, 1990-92; Stefanel Trieste, Italy, 1992-93; Rapid City Thrillers, Continental Basketball Asn, 1993; Rochester Renegade, Continental Basketball Asn, 1993-94; Burghy Roma, Italy, 1994; Olitalia Forli, Italy, 1994; Levallois, France, 1994-95; Baloncesto Salamanca, Spain, 1995-96; Rolly Pistoia, Italy, 1996; Besiktas, Turkey, 1996-97; Levallois, France, 1997-98; Paris Basket Racing, France, 1998-99; Richmond Rhythm, 1999; Aris, Greece, 1999-2000; Salem Community Col, head coach, 2004; Peak Mgt, dir basketball opers. **Honors/Awds:** Player of the Year, Del High Sch, 1986; Nat Player of the Year. Inducted in to Delaware Sports Museum and Hall of Fame, 2004.

**ENGLISH, ALEX (ALEXANDER ENGLISH)**
Basketball player, basketball coach, actor. **Personal:** Born Jan 5, 1954, Columbia, SC. **Educ:** Univ SC, attended 1976. **Career:** Basketball player (retired); basketball coach; Milwaukee Bucks, 1976-78; Ind Pacers, 1978-80; Denver Nuggets, 1980-90; Dallas Mavericks, 1990-91; Ital League, 1991; Basket Napoli, 1991-92; NBA Players Asn, dir player progs & v pres; Nat Basketball Players Asn, dir player prog; NBA & NBPA, interim exec dir, 1995; Flick2 Ltd, co-founder; Hoop life.com, chmn bd, vpres; tv ser: Midnight Caller, actor, 1989; Eddie, actor, 1996; Film: Definite Maybe, actor, 1997; FOX Sports Network & FOX Rocky Mountain, color commentator Denver Nuggets, 1997-98; NBA.com TV, analyst, coach, Philadelphia 76ers, 2008; Raptors, asst coach, 2004-11; SEC Network, color analyst, 2014; Sacramento Kings, asst coach, currently. **Orgs:** Kappa Alpha Psi Fraternity Inc. **Business Addr:** Assistant Coach, Sacramento Kings, Sleep Train Arena 1 Sports Pkwy, Sacramento, CA 95834, **Business Phone:** (916)928-0000.

**ENGLISH, HENRY L.**
Association executive, president (organization), chief executive officer. **Personal:** Born May 27, 1942, West Point, MS; son of Julie Pearl Smith and Flozell; married Denise Tulloch; children: Nkrumah, Kenya, Jumanne & Kamilah. **Educ:** Malcolm X Col, 1969; Univ NH, Durban, BA, 1972; Cornell Univ, Grad Sch Mgt, Ithaca, NY, MPA, 1974. **Career:** Kittrell Col, Kittrell, NC, asst dir, develop dir admis, 1974-75; Jackson Pk Hosp, Chicago, Ill, asst admin, 1975-77; S Chicago Community Hosp, Chicago, Ill, dir planning & mkt, 1977-85; bd mem, Black United Fund Ill Inc, Chicago, Ill, pres & chief exec officer, 1985-. **Orgs:** Fel, Woodrow Wilson Nat Fel Found, 1972-74; Co-Chmn, United Black Voters, IL, 1977-79; pres, COMPRAND Inc, 1981-85; pres, Coalition Save S Shore Country Club, 1980-84; Calumet Dist Comr, Boy Scouts Am, 1982-84; vpres, S Shore Comn, 1989-; bd dir, Black United Fund Ill; Nat Health Care Execs. **Home Addr:** 6810 S Crandon Ave Apt 1, Chicago, IL 60649, **Home Phone:** (773)324-5262. **Business Addr:** President, Chief Executive Officer, Black United Fund Illinois Inc, 1809 E 71st St, Chicago, IL 60649, **Business Phone:** (773)324-0494.

**ENGLISH, JO JO.** See ENGLISH, STEPHEN.

**ENGLISH, KENNETH**
Government official. **Personal:** Born Jul 29, 1947, Waycross, GA; children: Crystal Denise, Constance MaryAlice & Kenneth II. **Educ:** Morehouse Col; Ga State Univ. **Career:** US Dept Labor, Off Intergovernmental Rel, regional rep region IV, 1978-; Ny Ctr Engineering Design & Indust Innovation, dep dir; Ga Dept Labor, prog dir. **Orgs:** Pres, United Rubber Workers Union Local, 1969-78; bd dir, Urban League Albany Chap, 1970-78; vpres, GA State AFL-CIO, 1972-78; del, Mini-Conv Nat Dem Party, 1974; secy, State Charter Comn, GA Dem Party, 1974-75; chmn, Second cong dist Affirmative Action Comt, GA Dem Party, 1975-77; GA State Employ & Training Coun, 1975-77; secy, Albany-Dougherty Comn, Nat AsnAdvan Colored People Br, 1976-78; Dougherty County Dem Comt, 1976-78; Philip Randolph Inst Albany Chap, 1976-; chmn, Auditing Comt, GA Dem Party, 1977-78; chmn, Albany Urban League, 1977-78; GA State Crime Comn, 1977-78; Asn Fed Exec, 1978-; Indust Rel Res Asn, 1979-; bd mem, Southern Labor Hist Asn, 1979-; Nat & Hon Soc; Alpha Lambda Delta, GSU, 1979; Select Comn Rev GA State, 1979; vpres, Labor Studies Stud Asn, GSU, 1979-. **Honors/Awds:** Nominated for Who's Who in America National Jaycees, 1976. **Business Addr:** Program Director, Office of Integovernmental Relations, 148 International Blvd NE Suite 265 Rm 624, Atlanta, GA 30303, **Business Phone:** (404)232-3500.

**ENGLISH, LEONTENE ROBERSON**
Educator, executive. **Personal:** Born Dec 20, 1930, Lexington, TX; daughter of Timothy and Willie L Smith Roberson; married George; children: Byron D. **Educ:** Paul Quinn Col, BS, 1952; Hoston Tillotson Col, elem cert, 1953; Tex Southern Univ, MEd, 1962; Univ Houston, doctoral work, 1966; Prairie View Univ, admin cert, 1982. **Career:** Educator (retired); Lee County CSD, teacher, 1953-62; Temple ISD, teacher, 1962-78, prin, 1978-92. **Orgs:** Trustee, Wayman Chapel AME, 1984-; ed chair, Nat Asn Advan Colored People, 1988-; chairperson, Bell Co Retired Teachers Scholar, 1992-; TISD Grow Your Own Teacher Prog, 1996-; Homeless Aliance, Core Group, 1999-; chair, TISD Blue Ribbon Task Force Subgroup, 1999-; Ebony Cult Club, 1999-; mentor, TISD Vol Prog, 2000-01; Temple-Bell Retired Teachers Asn; Bethune Sch Rocking Reader Prog. **Home Addr:** 2109 E Ave E I, Temple, TX 76501, **Home Phone:** (254)742-2593.

**ENGLISH, DR. PERRY T., JR.**
Publisher, executive. **Personal:** Born Aug 12, 1933, Blountstown, FL; son of Perry Sr; children: Sharilynn & Lori Laverne. **Educ:** Cent State Univ, BS, 1956; Faculte de Med Univ de Paris, MD, 1965. **Career:** Publisher (retired); Ste Antoine Hosp, house physician, 1965-71; Friendship Med Ctr Ltd, asst exec dir, 1971-75, admin, 1975-77; St Lukes Family Health Ctr Inc, pres, 1977; Englewood Med Ctr Inc, pres, 1978-83; Beverly Hills Convalescent Ctr Inc, pres; Cook Co, phys assoc; Lopere Pub Co Inc, pres; Blair & Cole, Attorneys Law, adminr. **Orgs:** Am Pub Health Asn; treas, Chicago Investment Corp; vpres, Lake Vista Ctr; pres, Lope Redevelop Corp; treas, Am Leasing Corp; secy, LET Develop Corp; pres, Lope Re Int; treas, Madison Mgt Corp; pres, Lorgen Investment & Develop Corp; Med Group Mgt Asn; exec dir, AESULAPIUS Soc; Chicago Asn Com & Indust; Chicago Coun Foreign Affairs; treas, Consortium; Ill Econ Develop Comn. **Honors/Awds:** Award from 3rd Ward Democratic Party, 1976. **Home Addr:** 8045 S Calumet Ave Apt 1 T, Chicago, IL 60619, **Home Phone:** (773)651-9749. **Business Addr:** President, Beverly Hills Convalescent Center Inc, 123 N Wacker Dr Suite 1100, Chicago, IL 60606.

**ENGLISH, REGINALD**
Chief executive officer. **Career:** Intellisys Technol Corp, chief exec officer, 1983-, chmn. **Honors/Awds:** Black Enterprise 100's List, 1996. **Business Addr:** Chief Executive Officer, Intellisys Technology Corp, 11781 Lee Jackson Memorial Hwy, Fairfax, VA 22033, **Business Phone:** (703)691-4717.

**ENGLISH, DR. RICHARD ALLYN**
Educator. **Personal:** Born Aug 29, 1936, Winter Park, FL; son of Wentworth and Mary; married Ireita Geraldine Williams. **Educ:** Talladega Col, AB, 1958; Univ Mich, MA, 1959, MSW, 1964, PhD, 1970. **Career:** Univ Oslo Norway, summer fel, 1956; Univ Mich, Woodrow Wilson fel, 1958-59, lectr, 1967-70, asst prof, 1970-72, Sch Soc Work, asst dean, 1971-74, assoc prof social work, assoc vpres acad affairs, 1974, prof, 1983-; Flint Urban League, voc youth serv dir, 1959-61, actg dir, 1961-62; Neighborhood Serv Org Detroit, soc group worker, 1963-66; Wayne State Univ, lectr, 1965-67; Hebrew Univ, Paul Baerwald Sch Social Work, vis scholar & lectr, 1975; Univ Tex, Austin, RL Sutherland chair ment health & social policy; Howard Univ, dean & prof sch soc work, 1985-2003, interim provost & chief acad officer, 2003-04, provost & chief acad officer, 2004-. **Orgs:** Coun Social Work Educ; Nat Asn Soc Workers; Exec Comt Huron Valley Chap, 1971-72; Nat Asn Black Social Workers; Ann Prog Meeting Coun Social Work Educ; Coun Soc Work Educ, Re accreditation Teams Grad Sch Social Work, 1973-; elec & mem, House Dels Coun Soc Work Educ, 1974-77; Ann Prog Planning Comn Coun Social Work Educ, 1975-78; chmn, Am Soc Asn, 1977; elec pres, Coun Soc Work Educ, 1981-84; Prog Comt Sem Social Work Educ & Human Settlements; Int Asn Sch Social Work, 1980-90; Search & Screen Comt Exec; Oper Crossroads Africa Ghana; bd, Am Civil Liberties Union; adv panel, Refugee Policy Group; Spaulding C Emer Found, 1987-; bd mem, Nat Assembly Nat Vol Health Orgn, 1988-; bd mem, Int Asiation Social Welfare, 1988-; int comt, Coun Social Work Educ, 1989-; NASW task Force Child Welfare, 1990; Mem World Assembly Organizing Comt; ed chief, Encycl Social Work, 1999-2003; NASW Publication Committee, 2000-03. **Honors/Awds:** Co-ed, Human Serv Org; Beyond Path Res & Theoretical Perspectives Black Families; Distinguished Service Award, Nat Asn Black Social Workers, 1983, Presidential Award for Excellence in Social Work Education, 1997; Certificate of Appreciation, Coun Social Work, 1984; Distinguished Alumni Award, 1985; Whitney Young Jr Scholar Award, Western Mich Univ, 1987; listed, Who's Who in America; listed, Who's Who Among Black Americans; listed, Who's Who in the Midwest; listed. **Home Addr:** 2724 Abilene Dr, Chevy Chase, MD 20815-3051, **Home Phone:** (301)587-1257. **Business Addr:** Provost, Chief Academic Officer, Howard University, 601 Howard Pl NW, Washington, DC 20059, **Business Phone:** (202)806-7300.

**ENGLISH, STEPHEN (JO JO ENGLISH)**
Basketball coach, basketball player. **Personal:** Born Feb 4, 1970, Frankfurt. **Educ:** Univ SC, attended 1992. **Career:** Basketball player (retired), coach; Nat Basketball Asn Chicago Bulls, shooting guard, 1992-95; Continental Basketball Asn, Tri-City Chinook, 1992-93; Continental Basketball Asn, LaCrosse Catbirds, 1993-94; Minn Timberwolves, 1993; Australian Nat Basketball League, Adelaide 36ers, 1995; Continental Basketball Asn, Yakima Sun Kings, 1995-96; Besiktas, Turkey, 1996-97; Antalyaspor Muratpasa, Turkey, 1997-98; Continental Basketball Asn, La Crosse Bobcats, 1998-99; Maccabi Kiryat Motzkin, Israel, 1999-2000; Strasbourg IG, France, 2000-01; Besancon BCD, France, 2001; Continental Basketball Asn, Rockford Lightning, 2001-02; Scott Br High Sch, head coach, 2011-12; Sumter High Sch, head coach. **Business Addr:** Head Coach, Sumter High School, 2580 McCray's Mill Rd, Sumter, SC 29154, **Business Phone:** (803)481-4480.

**ENGLISH, WILLIAM E.**
Executive. **Personal:** Born May 18, 1936, Marianna, AR; son of Dan and Lorraine; children: William Jr, Romona, Cheryl & Amber. **Educ:** Univ Mich, BS, 1955. **Career:** Executive (retired); Group Health Mutual, underwriter, 1959-63; 3M Co, sales mgr, 1963-68; Ceridian, Bus Ventures, vpres, 1968-95. **Orgs:** Chair, Minnesota African Am Polit Caucus, 1993-; Men Are Responsible Cultivating Hope, 1994-; chair, Minneapolis Model Cities Prog, 1969-71; chair & bd trustee, Minneapolis Urban League, 1975-78; trustee, Livingstone Col, 1986-90; chair, Howard Univ Cluster Prog, 1988-90; chair, Minnesota African Am Polit Caucus, 1993-; Men Responsible Cultivating Hope, 1994-; Nat Urban League. **Home Addr:** 500 Cambridge, Minneapolis, MN 55443, **Home Phone:** (612)933-2936.

**ENGRAM, BOBBY (SIMON J ENGRAM, III)**
Football coach, football player. **Personal:** Born Jan 7, 1973, Camden, SC; son of Simon (deceased) and Dorothy; married Deanna; children: Bobbi, Phoebe, Dean & Trey. **Educ:** Pa State, BS, exercise sci, 1995. **Career:** Football player (retired), coach; Chicago Bears, punt returner, 1996, wide receiver, 1997-2000; Seattle Seahawks, wide receiver, 2001-08, tight end, 2001, 2003, 2007-08, fullback, 2003; Kans City Chiefs, 2009; Cleveland Browns, 2010; San Francisco 49ers, offensive asst coach, 2011; Pittsburgh Panthers, wide receivers coach, 2012-14; Baltimore Ravens, wide receivers coach, 2014-. **Honors/Awds:** Three time AP All American, 1993-95; Citrus Bowl MVP, 1994; Biletnikoff Award, 1994; Ed Block Courage Award, 2005. **Special Achievements:** Films: 1996 Outback Bowl, 1996; 1996 NFL Draft, 1996; 2005 NFC Championship Game, 2006. TV Series: "NFL on FOX", 1996-2000; "NFL Monday Night Football", 1996-2007; "TNT Sunday Night Football", 1997; "ESPN's Sunday Night Football", 1998-2003; "The NFL on CBS", 1999; "NBC Sunday Night Football", 2006-08. **Home Addr:** , Baltimore, MD. **Business Addr:** Wide Receivers Coach, Baltimore Ravens, 1 Winning Dr, Owings Mills, WA 21117, **Business Phone:** (410)701-4000.

**ENGRAM, SIMON J, III.** See ENGRAM, BOBBY.

**ENIS, CURTIS D.**
Executive, football coach, football player. **Personal:** Born Jun 15, 1976, Union City, OH; married Tiffanie; children: Samson. **Educ:** Pa State Univ, BA, recreational mgt, 1997; Cent State Univ, BA, parks recreation & leisure studies, 2014; NFL/NCAA Coaches Acad, leadership, 2014. **Career:** Football player (retired), coach, executive; Chicago Bears, running back, 1998-2000; Cleveland Browns, running back, 2001; Clopay Bldg Prod, receiving dept supvr, 2004-08, relationship officer, currently; Varsity Football Team, head coach, 2010; Bradford High Sch, Bradford, Ohio, asst football coach, 2009-10, head football coach, 2010-14; Anheuser-Busch, opers supvr, 2014-; ABInBev, oper mgr. **Honors/Awds:** Mr. Football Award, 1993. **Business Addr:** Operations Supervisor, Anheuser-Busch Companies Inc, 1 Busch Pl, St. Louis, MO 63118.

**ENIS, SHALONDA MOCHEA**
Basketball player. **Personal:** Born Dec 3, 1974, Celeste, TX; children: Chanse & Chase. **Educ:** Univ Ala, attended 1997. **Career:** Seattle Reign, ctr, 1997-99; Wash Mystics, 1999; Charlotte Sting, ctr & forward, 2000-03; Kumho Life Falcons, 2004-05. **Home Addr:** , TX. **Business Addr:** Professional Basketball Player, Charlotte Sting, 333 E Trade St, Charlotte, NC 28202, **Business Phone:** (704)688-8600.

**ENNIX, DR. COYNESS LOYAL, JR.**
Physician, educator. **Personal:** Born Feb 12, 1942, Nashville, TN; son of Coyness L Sr (deceased) and Blanche Nivens; married Katharine; children: Nicole & Kristina. **Educ:** Fisk Univ, BS, 1963; Meharry Med Col, Sch Med, Nashville, TN, MD, 1967. **Career:** Baylor Col Med, asst prof, surg; Baylor Col Med, postdoctoral fel, 1976-77; Cleveland Clin Educ Found, fel, 1974-76; Cardiovasc DisBaylor Col Med, researcher; Methodist Hosp, staff surg; Inst Rehab & Res, St Joseph Hosp; Va Hosp; St Lukes Hosp; Univ Calif, San Francisco, asst clin prof surg; Alta Bates Med Ctr, Ctr Cardiac Surg, med dir & chief cardiac surg, 1993-2002; E Bay Cardiac Surg Ctr, cardiac surgeon, 2001-05; E Bay Cardiac Surg Ctr, bus mgr, 2003; Ctr Cardiac Surg, cardiac surgeon, 2005-; Wash Hosp, thoracic & cardiac surgeon, currently. **Orgs:** Am Col Surg; Michael E DeBakey Int Cardiovasc Soc; Houston Med Forum; Harris Co Med Soc; Tex Med Asn; Houston Acad Med; Ama; Am Trauma Soc; Houston Surg Soc; Nat Med Asn; bd mem, Oakland Youth Work; bd mem, Holy Names High Sch; San Francisco Surg Soc; Pan Pac Surg Asn; Denton A Cooley Cardiovasc Surg Soc; dipl, Am Bd Surg; dipl, Am Bd Thoracic Surg; Soc Thoracic Surgeons; pres, Am Heart Asn; Am Lung Asn; pres & founder, Bay Area soc Thoracic Surg; hon nat fel, Robert Wood Johnson Found, 1998; Western Thoracic Surg Asn; Spring Tool Suite; chmn, Continuous Qual Improv Comt; bd dir, Marcus Foster Educ Fund, 2015-. **Home Addr:** 101 Sea View Ave, Piedmont, CA 94610-1246, **Home Phone:** (510)547-8945. **Business Addr:** Thoracic & Cardiac Surgeon, Washington Hospital, 101 Sea View Ave, Piedmont, CA 94610, **Business Phone:** (510)459-3547.

**ENOCH, HOLLACE J.**
Federal government official. **Personal:** Born Jul 9, 1950, Mathews, VA; daughter of William Jackson and Gladys Jackson; married Hurley. **Educ:** Va Union Univ, Richmond, VA, BA, 1972. **Career:** Nat Labor Rels Bd, Baltimore MD, field examiner, 1972-78; US Patent & Trademark Off, Arlington, Va, labor & employee rels specialist, 1978-81; Nat Labor Rels Bd, Washington, DC, labor rels officer, 1981-89, assoc exec secy; Va Union Univ, dir human resources & title ix coordr, currently. **Orgs:** Various leadership positions, Delta Sigma Theta Sorority, 1969-; Soc Fed Labor Rels Profs, 1978-89. **Home Addr:** 6235 Shackelford Ter, Alexandria, VA 22312, **Home Phone:** (703)941-4440. **Business Addr:** Director of Human Resources, Title IX Coordinator, Virginia Union University, 1500 N Lombardy St, Richmond, VA 23220, **Business Phone:** (804)257-5841.

**ENOCH, JOHN D.**
Editor, executive, president (organization). **Career:** Minority & Women Bus, publ, chmn & ed; Indust Paper Prod Inc, pres, 2002-; Gen Maintenance Co, owner. **Orgs:** Adv bd mem, Randolph Bank; adv bd, Morris Plan Bank. **Business Addr:** President, Industrial Paper Products Inc, 530 Chapel Hill Rd, Burlington, NC 27216-0210, **Business Phone:** (336)226-2457.

**ENSLEY, ANNETTE**
Executive director, president (organization), consultant. **Career:** Inverness Travel, exec vpres; Russell Reynolds Assocs, exec search firm; Mark McCormicks, Int Mgt Grp, sports mkt & mgt firm; Nathan Cummings Found, dir admin & human res, dir human rels 1989-, off mgr asst pres, currently; consult, currently. **Orgs:** Travel consult, Am Assoc Retired Persons; bd dir, assoc dir, Nat Conf Black Lawyers; trustee, Nathan Cummings Found. **Home Addr:** , Newyork, NY, **Home Phone:** (212)799-7542. **Business Addr:** Director of Administration & Human Resources, Nathan Cummings Foundation, 475 10th Ave 14th Fl, New York, NY 10018-9715, **Business Phone:** (212)787-7300.

**ENSLEY, CAROLE DENISE.** See NASH, NIECY.

**ENTERTAINER, CEDRIC THE (CEDRIC ANTONIO KYLES)**
Comedian, actor, writer. **Personal:** Born Apr 24, 1964, Jefferson City, MO; son of Kittrell Kyles and Rosetta; married Lorna R Wells; children: Croix Alexander & Lucky Rose; married Lorna Wells; children: Tiara, Croix & Rose. **Educ:** Southeastern Miss State Univ, BS, mass commun. **Career:** Films: Ride, 1998; Big Momma's House, 2000; The Smoker, 2000; The Original Kings of Comedy, writer, 2000; Kingdom Come, 2001; Dr Doolittle 2, 2001; Ice Age, voice, 2001; Barbershop,

2002; Serving Sara, 2002; Intolerable Cruelty, 2003; Barbershop 2, 2004; The Honeymooners, producer, 2005; Charlotte's Web, 2006; Code Name: The Cleaner, producer, 2007; Talk To Me, 2007; Welcome Home, Roscoe Jenkins, 2008; Street Kings, 2008; Madagascar: Escape 2 Africa, voice, 2008; Cadillac Records, 2008; All's Faire in Love, 2009; Caught on Tape, post-production, 2009; The Law, post-production, 2009; Dance Fu, 2011; Larry Crowne, 2011; Madagascar 3: Europe's Most Wanted, 2012; Chicago Pulaski Jones, post-production, currently; A Haunted House, 2013; Wild Card, 2014; A Haunted House 2, 2014; Top Five, 2014; A Fall from Grace, forthcoming, 2015; TV Show: "It's Showtime at the Apollo", 1987; "Comic View", 1992; "The Steve Harvey Show", 1996-2002; "The Proud Family", 2001; "Cedric the Entertainer Presents", 2002; "The Boondocks", 2007; "WWE Raw", 2009; "It's Worth What?", 2011; "Hot in Cleveland", 2011-14; "The Soul Man", 2012-15; Cedric's Barber Battle, 2015; TV Commercials: Bud Light advertisements, 2001; The Black Movie Awards, 2005; State Farm insurance, claims adjuster; Champ Car World Series, CTE Racing-HVM, part owner, 2005-. **Orgs:** Kappa Alpha Psi Fraternity Inc. **Home Addr:** , CA. **Business Addr:** Actor, Universal Citywalk, 100 Universal City Plz, Universal City, CA 91608, **Business Phone:** (818)622-4455.

### EPHRIAM, ESQ. MABLEAN DELORIS

Television show host, judge. **Personal:** Born Apr 23, 1949, Hazlehurst, MS; daughter of Robert and Mable; married Cassuis Paxton; children: 1. **Educ:** Pitzer Col, BA; Whittier Col Law, JD, 1978; Harvard Univ, eng, 1981. **Career:** Judge (retired), attorney, TV host; Los Angeles City, dep city atty, 1978-82; law pract, 1982; Divorce Ct, judge, 1999-2006; pvt pract atty, currently; Monet Lane Productions, TV show host, currently. Actress: Diary of a Mad Black Woman, 2005; Madea's Family Reunion, 2006; Madea Goes to Jail; 2009; "Justice with Judge Mablean", 2014; H.U.F. Awards, host. **Orgs:** Co-founder, Harriet Buhia Ctr Family Law, 1982; pres, Los Angeles Black Women Lawyers group; Hearing Examr, Civil Serv Comn; bd dir, Union Rescue Mission; Exec Comt, Los Angeles Co Bar & State Bar Calif Family Law Sects; Am Bar Asn & Nat Bar Asn; bd dir, Southern Calif Women's Dept/Retirement Ctr Comt; pres, Black Women Lawyers Asn; founder, Mablean Ephriam Found. **Home Addr:** , OH. **Business Addr:** Host, Monet Lane Productions, PO Box 3510, Hollywood, CA 90078.

### EPPS, ANNA CHERRIE

School administrator. **Personal:** Born Jul 8, 1930, New Orleans, LA; daughter of Ernest Cherrie Sr and Anna J Cherrie; married Joseph M Sr. **Educ:** Howard Univ, BS, 1951; Loyola Univ, MS, microbiol, 1959; Howard Univ, PhD, 1966. **Career:** Xavier Univ, asst prof & actg chmn med tech, 1954-60; Howard Univ, asst prof microbiol, 1961-69; Tulane Univ Sch Med, res fel, 1969, asst prof med, 1971, assoc dean students serv & prof med, 1980-97, Tulane Med Ctr, dir med, 1975, vpes, dean, 1997-2002, interim vpres acad affairs, 1999; Meharry Med Col, pres, chief exec officer vpres & dean acad affairs, 1994-96, dean & vpres acad affairs, 1997-2002, dean emer, 2002-, sr adv pres, 2002-, Dept Internal Med, prof, currently, interim pres, 2006-07; Johns Hopkins Univ Sch Med, asst prof; US Pub Health Serv Fac Res, res fel. **Orgs:** Asn Am Med Cols; NAMME; Am Soc Clin Pathologists; Am Soc Med Technologists; Georgetown Univ Bd Regents; Am Asn Blood Banks; Am Asn Univ Profs; Sigma Xi; Am Asn Univ Women; AOA mem; Bd Regents, Georgetown Univ; Nat Bd Med Examiners. **Honors/Awds:** hon doctorate, Meharry Med Col, 1996; Herbert WNickens MD Award, Asn Am Med Cols, 2003; Harold Delaney Educ Achievement Award, Am Asn Blacks Higher Educ, 2008; Recognition Award, NAMME; Award for Meritorious Research, Interstate Post grad Med Asn Am. **Special Achievements:** Published numerous articles and books; first woman to lead one of the nations major independent medical colleges; only African-American woman with a Ph.D. to become dean of a U.S. medical school. **Home Addr:** 769 Sinlcair Cir, Brentwood, TN 37027, **Home Phone:** (615)371-2404. **Business Addr:** Senior Advisor, Dean Emerita, School of Medicine, Professor, Inter, Meharry Medical College, 1005 Dr DB Todd Jr Blvd, Nashville, TN 37208, **Business Phone:** (615)327-6768.

### EPPS, DR. C. ROY

Association executive. **Personal:** Born Jun 6, 1941, Bronx, NY; son of Clarence and Alice; children: Leah, Roy III, Leslye Renee & Camara Rose. **Educ:** Wilberforce Univ, BS, 1963; Rutgers Univ, MS, 1970. **Career:** Civic & Urban League Greater NB, community social worker, 1967-68, asst dir, 1968-70, exec dir & pres, 1970-, pres & chief exec officer, currently; MA Inst Tech, fel, 1982. **Orgs:** Founding mem, NB Tomorrow, 1975-; founder, chmn & former mem, NB Develop Corp, 1976-94; pres & bd mem, NB Bd Ed, 1976-85; Greater Raritan Workforce Investment Bd, 1983-99; co-chair, Black Leadership Conf, 1986-; chmn, Eric B. Chandler Health Ctr, 1998-; Middlesex County Workforce Investment Bd, 1999-; bd trustee, Citizens Campaign, vice chmn; founder, bd NB Tomorrow; Nat Urban League's Exec Dirs Coun; exec dir, Urban League Greater Nb; Nj State Supreme Ct's Mt Laurel; former pres & bd mem, Nb Bd Educ. **Honors/Awds:** President Award, Eastern Reg Coun Urban League Exec, 1977-81, President Award, Nat Coun Urban League Exec, 1978-80; comm fellows prog, MA Inst Tech, 1981-82; Hon Doctorate, Upsala Col, 1994; NBT's Lifetime Community Service. **Home Addr:** 3 Palmetto Ct, New Brunswick, NJ 08901-3167, **Home Phone:** (732)545-1926. **Business Addr:** Vice Chairman, The Citizens Campaign, 450 Main St, Metuchen, NJ 08840, **Business Phone:** (732)548-9798.

### EPPS, DR. CHARLES HARRY, JR.

Physician. **Personal:** Born Jul 24, 1930, Baltimore, MD; son of Charles Harry Sr (deceased) and Marjorie Sue Jackson (deceased); married Roselyn Payne; children: Charles Harry III, Kenneth Carter, Roselyn Elizabeth & Howard Robert. **Educ:** Howard Univ, BS, chemistry, 1947, MD, 1955. **Career:** Physician, educator (retired); ABOS, dipl, 1964, examr, 1974-92; Am Bd Orthotics & Prosthet, examr, 1970-76; Howard Univ, prof, Div Orthop Surg, chief, CLG Med, dean, 1988-94, Health Affairs, vp, 1994-96, spec asst pres health affairs, 1996-2001, Howard Hosp, actg chief exec officer; Johns Hopkins Hosp, assoc prof orthop surg; Howard Univ Orthop Residency Training Prog, prog dir. **Orgs:** Pres, Am Orthop Asn; Gov Health Legisl & Vet Affairs Comt; Am Acad Orthop Surg; Kappa Alpha Psi Frat Bd Trustees; Sidwell Friends Sch Wash DC; Nat Asn Advan Colored People; bd dir Boys Club Metro Police; gov Am Col Surgeon; Ethical & Judical Coun, Am Med Asn, 1982-87; ABOS. **Honors/Awds:** Humanitarian Award, American Academy of Orthopaedic Surgeons, 2003. **Special Achievements:** Has contributed more than seventy publications and thirty book chapters; First African American member of the American Orthopaedic Association; First African American oral examiner, 1970-80. **Home Addr:** 1775 N Portal Dr NW, Washington, DC 20012, **Home Phone:** (202)829-4453.

### EPPS, DR. CONSTANCE ARNETTRES

Dentist. **Personal:** Born Feb 8, 1950, Port Chester, NY; daughter of Robert Gooden and Geneva Colbert Gooden; married Charles Ray; children: Charles R II & Menika Elyse. **Educ:** Bennett Col, BS, biol, 1971; Howard Univ Col Dent, DDS, 1979; Univ NC, Chapel Hill, NC, MPH, 1990. **Career:** Blood Res Inst Harvard Univ, coagulation technician, 1971-72; US Govt Torrejon Air Base Madrid, teacher, 1973-74; St Elizabeth Hosp, dent officer, 1979-80; NC Dept Human Resources, pub health dentist, 1980-86; Univ NC, Chapel Hill, NC, adj assoc prof, 1986-; Guilford Co, Dept Health, Greensboro, NC, pub health dentist, 1986-, dent dir, 1990-, clin supvr, 2003; Perry L Jeffries Assocs, Greensboro, NC, dentist, currently. **Orgs:** Am Dent Asn; Nat Dent Asn; Acad Gen Dent, NC Dent Asn, 1979; Old N State & Guilford Co Dent Asn, 1984-; treas, NC Pub Health Asn, 1986-87, vice chmn, 1987-88; High Pt Orgn Polit Educ; Delta Sigma Theta; Guilford Co Headstart Adv Comn; chmn dent sect, NC Pub Health Asn, 1988-; chair dir, First United Baptist Church, trustee, 1988-, chmn, trustee bd, 1990-95; dent dir, Greensboro Urban Ministry Med & Dent Clin, 1989-95. **Honors/Awds:** Dr Raymond L Hayes Scholarship Award, Howard Univ Dent Sch, 1979; Outstanding Young Women of America, 1982; Young Dentist of the Year, NC Dental Society 3rd District Nominee, 1988; Nal Asn of County Health Officials Recognition of Achievement, Homebound Dental Prog, 1988; Outstanding Coll Students of Amer, Delta Omega, Nat Public Health Honor Soc, 1990; A Consortium of Doctors, 1991; Belle Ringer Image Award, Bennett Col, 1997. **Home Addr:** 2024 Arden Pl, High Point, NC 27265-3225, **Home Phone:** (336)887-2774. **Business Addr:** Dentist, Perry L Jeffries & Associates, 871 Huffman St, Greensboro, NC 27405, **Business Phone:** (336)230-0346.

### EPPS, DOLZIE C. B.

Educator. **Personal:** Born Jan 1, 1907, Shreveport, LA. **Educ:** Dillard Univ, attended 1929; Wiley Col, Marshall, TX, AB, 1945; Columbia Univ, NY, MA, 1950. **Career:** Caddo Parish Sch Syst, teacher health & phys educ, 1935-73; La St Univ, Sch Med, bd dir, 1976-. **Orgs:** Inst Rev Comn Human Exp, Shreveport, LA; bd dir, Caddo-Bossier Ct Observers, 1976-; bd dir, Shreveport Negro C C, 1976-; bd dir, Nat Asn Advan Colored People,1976-; bd dir, Phi Delta Kappa Sorority (Beta Alpha Chap) 1976-; BTW Alumni Found Shreveport La. **Honors/Awds:** Community Service Award, Nat Coun Negro Women, 1976; Ann Brewster Community Service, Nat Asn Advan Colored People, 1978; Vacation Bible School Award, Galilee Bapt Church, 1979; Branch Service Award, Nat Asn Advan Colored People, 1980. **Special Achievements:** First Vice President of Family Coun & C Serv, 1976-. **Home Addr:** 4678 N Lake Dr, Shreveport, LA 71107-2944. **Business Addr:** Board of Director, Louisiana State University School of Medicine, 1501 Kings Hwy, Shreveport, LA 71103, **Business Phone:** (318)675-7571.

### EPPS, DR. EDGAR G.

Educator. **Personal:** Born Aug 30, 1929, Little Rock, AR; son of Odelle and Clifford Epps; married Marilyn Miller; children: Carolyn & Raymond. **Educ:** Talladega Col, BA, 1951; Atlanta Univ, MA, 1955; Wash State Univ, PhD, sociol, 1959. **Career:** Tenn State Univ, asst, assoc prof, 1958-61; Fla A&M Univ, prof, 1961-64; Univ Mich, res assoc, assoc prof, psychology, 1965-70; Tuskegee Univ, assoc dir Carver Res Found, chmn div soc sci, prof sociol, 1967-70; Harvard Univ, vis prof, 1969; Univ Chicago, Marshall Field IV prof Urban Educ, Marshall Field IV prof Urban Educ emer, currently, Consortium Chicago Sch Res, sr res assoc, currently; Univ Wis-Milwaukee, Sch Educ, dept educ policy & community studies, sr prof, currently; Salzburg Sem Am Studies Salzburg Austria, fac mem, 1975; book: Cultural pluralism, author, editor, 1974. **Orgs:** Chicago Bd Educ, 1974-80; bd dir, Southern Educ Found, 1976-88; consult, Chicago Pub Schs; co-chair, Nat Adv Comt, currently. **Home Addr:** 5825 S Dorchester Ave, Chicago, IL 60637, **Home Phone:** (773)643-5715. **Business Addr:** Senior Professor, University of Wisconsin-Milwaukee, Enderis Hall Rm 549 2400 E Hartford Ave, Milwaukee, WI 53211, **Business Phone:** (414)229-4740.

### EPPS, EVERN COOPER

Executive, vice president (organization), president (organization). **Personal:** Born Clarendon, AR. **Educ:** Mich State Univ, BA, eng & jour, MA, 1974; Emory Univ; Harvard Sch Bus. **Career:** High Sch, teacher, 1970; United Parcel Serv Found, strategic planning, delivery info, training, bus develop, assoc dir, 1974-98, pres & vice chair, 1998-2007, Corp Rel, vpres, currently. **Orgs:** Nat Urban League, Black Exec Exchange Prog; adv coun, Coalition 100 Black Women; bd mem, Atlanta Partners Educ; vice chmn bd, NW Ga Girl Scouts Coun; corp adv, United Way Am; Nat Black Arts Festival; Close-Up Found; Points Light Found; Links-Dogwood Chap; bd dir, Ctr Corp Citizenship; chmn Bd, Atlanta Partners Educ. **Business Addr:** Vice President, United Parcel Serv, 55 Glenlake Pkwy NE Bldg, Atlanta, GA 30328, **Business Phone:** (404)828-4147.

### EPPS, GEORGE ALLEN, JR.

Executive. **Personal:** Born Jul 3, 1940, Fallis, OK; son of George Sr (deceased) and George Ellen Doak; married Linda Edwards; children: Gregory Allen & Michael Conrad. **Educ:** Kans City Jr Col, Kans City, KS, 1958; Rockhurst Col, Kans City, MO, 1971. **Career:** Executive (retired); Bendix Mfg Co, electronic technician, 1962-65; Southwestern Bell, Kans City, Mo, lineman, 1965-68, facil engr, 1968-71, installation supvr, 1971-76, St Louis, Mo, plant mechanization supvr, 1976-79, dist mgr-I&M, 1979-85, dist mgr, admin serv, 1985-; Gundacker Realty, sales, 1985. **Home Addr:** 2309 Stacia Dr, Plano, TX 75025-4748.

### EPPS, OMAR HASHIM

Actor, movie producer. **Personal:** Born Jul 20, 1973, Brooklyn, NY; son of Bonnie Maria; married Keisha Spivey; children: K'mari Mae & Amir. **Career:** Wolf pak, co-founder, 1991-; Films: Juice, 1992; Daybreak, 1993; The Program, 1993; Major League II, 1994; Higher Learning, 1995; Deadly Voyage, 1996; Don't Be a Menace to South Central While You're Drinking Your Juice in the Hood, 1996; Scream 2, 1997; Blossoms and Veils, 1997; Breakfast of Champions, 1999; The Mod Squad, 1999; The Wood, 1999; In Too Deep, 1999; Love and Basketball, 2000, Brother, 2000; Dracula 2000, 2000; Absolute Zero, 2000; Perfume, 2001; Big Trouble, 2002; Tupac: Resurrection, documentary, 2003; Against the Ropes, 2004; Alfie, 2004; A Day in the Life, 2009; You, Me & The Circus, producer, 2011; TV series: "Daybreak", 1993; "Conviction", 2002; "House M.D", sound track performer, 2004-11; "Resurrection", 2014; "Resurrection: A Second Chance", 2014; "Mile High", producer. **Honors/Awds:** Silver Nymph, Best Actor, 1997; Image Award, Nat Asn Advan Colored People, 2007, 2008 & 2013. **Special Achievements:** Has been nominated for Black Reel Awards, Image Awards, Teen Choice Award sand MTV Movie Awards. **Business Addr:** Actor, c/o Endeavor Agency, 9701 Wilshire Blvd 10th Fl, Beverly Hills, CA 90212, **Business Phone:** (310)248-2000.

### EPPS, PHILLIP EARL

Football player, advocate. **Personal:** Born Nov 11, 1959, Atlanta, TX; married Janice; children: Rachael Renee, Phillip Jordan, Alexis Jonae & LaShaunta Nicole. **Educ:** Tex Christian Univ, BS, justice. **Career:** Football player (retired), advocate; Green Bay Packers, wide receiver, punt returner, 1982-88; New York Jets, wide receiver, 1989-90; Scott D Moore Juv Justice Ctr, juv probation officer, currently. **Honors/Awds:** Rookie of the Year, 1982. **Home Addr:** 212 Boulder Creek, Dallas, TX 75115. **Business Addr:** Juvenile Probation Officer, Scott D Moore Juvenile Justice Center, 2701 Kimbo Rd, Ft. Worth, TX 76111-3099, **Business Phone:** (817)838-4600.

### EPTING, MARION AUSTIN

Artist, educator. **Personal:** Born Jan 1, 1940, Forrest, MS. **Educ:** Los Angeles City Col, AA, 1965; Otis Art Inst LA Co, BFA & MFA, 1969. **Career:** Otis Art Inst, rep permanent collections; Univ Calif, fac; San Jose State Col, fac; Denison Univ, fac; Seattle Art Mus, fac; Calif State Univ, Chicago, Otis Art Inst, prof, prof emer, currently; Pvt collections: Bernie Casey, Dorothy Chandler, Claude Booker, Ruth Stoehr & James Bates. **Honors/Awds:** Recipient Numerous Awards. **Special Achievements:** Marion Epting Print Prize. **Business Addr:** Professor Emeritus, California State University, Ayres Hall 202, Chico, CA 95926, **Business Phone:** (530)898-6875.

### ERICSSON, DR. APRILLE JOY

Educator, engineer. **Personal:** Born Apr 1, 1963, Brooklyn, NY; daughter of Henry and Corrinne; married Mark Jackson. **Educ:** City Col NY, 1984; Mass Inst Technol, BS, aeronaut & astronaut engineering, 1986; Howard Univ, ME, 1990, PhD, mech engineering aerospace option, 1995. **Career:** Howard Univ, grad researcher, 1990-95; Women NASA Group; NASA Goddard Space Flight Ctr, altitude control systs analyst, 1992-2001 & aerospace engr, 1992-, instrument Mgr, currently; Bowie St Univ, adj prof, math, 1997-99; Howard Univ, adj prof, mech eng, 1999; NASA HQ, prog mgr & prog exec, 2001-. **Orgs:** Am Inst Aeronaut Astronaut, 1985-; Nat Soc Black Engrs, alumni mem, 1986-; Am Astronaut Soc, 1995; Women Aerospace, 1996, 2002; pres, Goddard Chap, Nat Tech asn, 1998-; Blacks Govt, 2000; Howard Univ, GSAS, Responsive PhD Initiative Task Force, 2000-02; bd dir, Forestville Mil Acad; bd dir, SECME; bd dir, HU Sci Engineering Math Prog; bd dir, HU Mid Sch Mathand Sci; bd trustee, Howard Univ; NASA GSFC Speakers Bur; exec, Combined Federal Campaign. **Special Achievements:** First African American female to receive a PhD in Mechanical Engineering from Howard University; First African American female to receive a Ph.D. in Engineering at NASA GSFC. **Home Addr:** 1958 2nd St NW, Washington, DC 20001, **Home Phone:** (202)232-5444. **Business Addr:** Aerospace Engineer, National Aeronautics & Space Administration, 300 E St NW Rm 5P50, Washington, DC 20059, **Business Phone:** (202)358-0832.

### ERVIN, DEBORAH GREEN

School administrator. **Personal:** Born Apr 4, 1956, Greenville, SC; daughter of David Green Jr and Annie V Williams-Green; married Larry Don; children: Sean Deon & Elanda Deliece. **Educ:** Berea Col, BA, 1977; Clemson Univ, MEd, 1986. **Career:** Clemson Child Develop Ctr, head teacher, 1978-81; Clemson Univ, admis counr, 1981-86, asst dir admis, 1986; Winthrop Univ, asst dir admis, 1987-92, assoc dir admis, 1992-. **Orgs:** Secy, 1989-90, vpres, 1991-93, Carolina's Asn Col Registr & Admis Officers; Southern Asn Col Admis Officers; Home Econs Adv Comn D W Daniel High Sch; Clemson Univ, Day Care Comn, Col Educ Fac Selection Comt; Cent City Optimists, 1990-. **Home Addr:** 1061 Cypress St, Rock Hill, SC 29730. **Business Addr:** Associate Director, Winthrop University, 701 Oakland Ave, Rock Hill, SC 29730, **Business Phone:** (803)323-2211.

### ERVIN, KATHRYN

Executive, educator. **Educ:** Wayne State Univ, BFA, theatre-actg, 1978; Ill State Univ, MFA, theatre- directing, 1980. **Career:** Mich State Univ, asst prof, 1985-89; Cal State Univ, San Bernardino, Theatre Arts Dept, prof & chair, 1989-. **Orgs:** Numerous theatre orgn; consult, pres, Black Theatre Network, mem, currently; Int Asn Theatre C & Young People; fel Calif Arts Proj; Calif Educ Theatre Asn; Asn Theatre Higher Educ. **Business Addr:** Professor, Chair, California State University, Performing Arts Bldg 5500 Univ Pkwy Rm 111, San Bernardino, CA 92407, **Business Phone:** (909)537-5892.

### ERVING, JOHN, JR.

Publisher, business owner. **Personal:** Born Jan 28, 1949, Philadelphia, PA; son of John and Juanita; married Margaret; children: Rena, Saeed, Brandon & Deborah. **Educ:** Univ Pa, attended 1973; Temple Univ, Fox Sch Bus & Mgt, Bachelor Bus Admin, bus law & econs, 1979. **Career:** Wal-Mart Stores, part time staff; Am Greeting Corp, sales mgr, 1982-84; Kraft Food Serv, territory mgr, 1984-96; JonMar Creations Inc, pres & chief exec officer, 1995-. **Orgs:** Co-founder, Asn Black Bus Students, 1973-; lifetime mem, Nat Asn Advan Colored People, 1990-;

Greeting Card Asn. **Home Addr:** 5 Edwards Ct, Lawnside, NJ 08045-1161, **Home Phone:** (856)546-0724. **Business Addr:** President, JonMar Creations Inc, PO Box 702, Lawnside, NJ 08045, **Business Phone:** (800)824-9886.

## ERVING, JULIUS WINFIELD, II

Basketball player, basketball executive, businessperson. **Personal:** Born Feb 22, 1950, Roosevelt, NY; son of Julius and Callie Mae Lindsay; married Turquoise; children: Cheo, Julius III, Jazmin & Corey (deceased); married Madden; children: 3. **Educ:** Univ Mass, attended 1971. **Career:** Basketball player (retired), speaker, executive; Univ Mass, player, 1968-71; All-Am & All-Yankee Conf, player, 1970-71; Va Squires, 1971-73, New York Nets, 1973-76, Philadelphia 76ers, 1976-87; DJ Enterprises, dir; Orlando Magic, exec vpres; RDV Sports, vpres; Erving Group Inc, owner, currently; Gold Stars Speakers Bur, speaker, currently; Film: The Fish That Saved Pittsburgh, actor, 1979; Philadelphia, actor, 1993. **Orgs:** Trustee, Clark Atlanta Univ; bd dir, Meridian Bancorp; bd dir, Saks Inc; bd dir, Williams Commun; bd dir, Converse Inc; bd dir, Darden Restaurants Inc; bd dir, Sports Authority. **Home Addr:** PO Box 25040 SW Sta, Philadelphia, PA 19147. **Business Addr:** Speaker, Gold Stars Speakers Bureau, 7478 N La Cholla Blvd, Tucson, AZ 85741, **Business Phone:** (520)742-4384.

## ESCO, FRED, JR.

Government official, insurance executive, mayor. **Personal:** Born Sep 13, 1954, Canton, MS; son of Fred Lee (deceased) and Ida M Hudson; married Fleta Marie Jones; children: Tamaria, Amaya, Freda, Kristie & Ariel. **Educ:** Miss Valley State Univ, BA, 1978; MS Baptist Sem, christianity. **Career:** Esco's Ins co, owner, pres & chief exec officer; City Canton, alderman, 1979-97, mayor, 2002-. **Orgs:** Thirty Two Degree Mason Prince Hall Affil, 1979-85; Elk Club Canton, 1979-85; Nat Bus League, 1979-85; Mason; Elks; vpres, Nat Asn Advan Colored People Canton, 1983-84; secy & treas, Optimist Club Canton, 1984-85; Boys & Girls Club; Hisp Outreach Canton, Mt. Zion Missionary Baptist Church. **Special Achievements:** First African-American male to be elected as Mayor. **Home Addr:** 378 S Monroe St, Canton, MS 39046-4727, **Home Phone:** (601)859-1959. **Business Addr:** President, Esco' s Insurance Co, 274 W Peace St, Canton, MS 39046, **Business Phone:** (601)859-8236.

## ESEONU, DR. DOROTHY N.

Educator. **Personal:** Born Sep 23, 1955, Obowo Imo; daughter of Benson and Iheomagwu Ogbonna; married Maxwell; children: Ihuoma, Chijioke, Chikezie & Amarachi. **Educ:** E Stroudsburg State Col, BS, 1977; Howard Univ, MS, 1981; Va Commonwealth Univ, PhD, org chem, 1989. **Career:** Va State Univ, asst prof, 1990-93, adj prof, currently; J Sargent Reynolds Community Col, adj prof, 1990-93; Va Union Univ, chem prog coordr, assoc prof chem, 1993-; chairing secy, 2006. **Orgs:** Bd mem, Advocates Inter cult Richmond, 1994-96; pres, IBO Women's Cult Asn, 1996-99; chmn, Am Chem Soc-Va Sect; Minority Affairs, 1999-; secy, treas, co-chmn, Va Sect Exec Comt. **Home Addr:** 14002 Bridgetown Cir, Chester, VA 23831, **Home Phone:** (804)768-0784. **Business Addr:** Associate Professor, Virginia Union University, Rm 322 Ellison Hall, Richmond, VA 23220, **Business Phone:** (804)257-5615.

## ESKRIDGE, REV. JOHN CLARENCE

School administrator, educator. **Personal:** Born Jun 6, 1943, Pittsburgh, PA; son of John William and Constance Mary Rideout; children: Aziza & Mark. **Educ:** Duquesne Univ, Pittsburgh, BA, 1966, MA, 1971; Pac Southern Univ Calif, PhD, philos, 1978. **Career:** Community Col Allegheny County, philos fac, 1969; Pittsburgh Child Guid Clin, prog dir, creative recreational arts prog, 1969-70; Community Col Allegheny County Campus, dir black studies, 1969-71, Colspeakers bur, 1978-88; "Le Sacre Corps", Dance Co, artistic dir, 1969-79; First Baptist Church Pittsburgh, bd deacons, 1970-73; Carlow Col, dir, 1973-74; Community Col, prof philos, 1978-; Hot Lix Concert Jazz Band, leader, producer, 1978-89; Pittsburgh High Sch Creative & Performing Arts, adv bd, 1979-90; Community Col Allegheny County, Dept Lang & Philos, chmn, 1983-; Orpheo Concert Latin Band, leader, producer, 1989-. **Orgs:** Pittsburgh Musicians Soc, 1967-; Soc Phenomenol & Existential Philos, 1967-80; Am Philos Asn, 1969-80; founding chmn, Hermeneutic Circle, 1977-80; bd dir, Inst Collective Behav & Memory, 1980-87; vpres, African Am Fedn Am, 1983-89. **Honors/Awds:** NDEA study fel Duquesne Univ, 1967-70; Fac Spl Service Award, Community Col Allegheny Co Stud Union, 1978; Col Blue Ribbon Fac Award, Comn Col Allegheny County, 1981-82. **Home Addr:** 359 McKee Pl, Pittsburgh, PA 15213. **Business Addr:** Chairman, Professor, Community College of Allegheny County, 808 Ridge Ave, Pittsburgh, PA 15212-6003, **Business Phone:** (412)237-4414.

## ESOGBUE, DR. AUGUSTINE O.

Educator, engineer. **Personal:** Born Dec 25, 1940, Kaduna. **Educ:** Univ Calif, BS, elec engineering, 1964; Columbia Univ, MS, indust engineering & oper res, 1965; Univ S Calif, PhD, systs engineering & oper res, 1968. **Career:** Com Minority Career Advs; Indust & Systs Eng, Sch Health Systs, GA Inst Tech Atlanta, prof; Morehouse Col Atlanta, adj prof community med; Atlanta Univ GA, adjuct prof math sci; Univ Southern Calif, res assoc engr & med, 1965-68; Water Resources Res Ctr, Univ Calif, develop engr, 1966-67; Opers Res & Mem Syst Res Ctr; Case Western Res Univ Cleveland, asst prof, 1968-72; Univ Assoc Inc & Environ Dynamics, consult, 1968-72; Ga Inst Tech, chmn, 1975, Sch Indust & Systs Eng, assoc prof, 1972-77, prof, 1977-; Univ Calif Berkley, distinguished prof indust engineering & opers res & mgt sci. **Orgs:** Fel, AAAS, 1972; Environ Adv Grp; exec comt, Atlanta Reg Comt, 1974-89; comr & vicechmn, Atlanta Sister Cities Comn, 1975; chmn, Atlanta-Lagos Sister Cities Comn, 1975-; chmn, New Cities Develop comn; Atlanta Sister Cities comn, 1993-; Leadership Atlanta, Atlanta Leadership Develop Corp, (Class1979); bd mem, United Way's External Funding Admiss comn, 1987-89; chmn, Coalition 100 Black Youth, Atlanta Chap, 1990-96; 100 Black Men Atlanta, Atlanta Chap, 1990-; chmn, ORSA Health Applications Tech Sect, 1990-92; co-chmn, Retention & Acad Excellence, Proj Success; chmn, Col 100 Mentorship Prog; bd dir, NigerianAm, 1993-98; chmn & bd dir, Am Nigerian int Comn, 1998-; adv bd, Task Force GANGS, City Atlanta, 1993-; adv bd, USA-AFRICA int comn Mfg Tech, 1996-; steering comn, US Summiton Africa, 1998-99; S Eastern Deleg US Nat Summit Africa, Wash DC, 1998-2000; co ord, Worldwide Network Nigerian Prof & Intellectual, Brain Drain-Brain Gain Inc, 1999-; fel Inst Elec & Electronics Engrs, 1999; fel Nigerian Acad Sci, 2000; bd trustee, Nigerians Diaspora Orgs Ams, 2001-; bd trustee, GA Coun int Visitors, 2003-; chmn, ORSA/TIMS Vis Lectr Prog; Panel Mem, Nat Res Coun, Nat Acad Sci; dir, Intelligent Systs & Controls Lab. **Home Addr:** 1510 Loch Lomond Trl SW, Atlanta, GA 30331-7428, **Home Phone:** (404)344-3789. **Business Addr:** Professor, Georgia Institute of Technology, Groseclose 0205 Rm 442 765 Ferst Dr NW, Atlanta, GA 30332-0205, **Business Phone:** (404)894-2323.

## ESPOSITO, GIANCARLO GIUSEPPE ALESSANDRO

Actor. **Personal:** Born Apr 26, 1958, Copenhagen; married Joy McManigal; children: 4. **Career:** Tv experience including: Go Tell It on the Mountain, 1984; The Exchange Stud; Finnegan Begin Again, 1985; Miami Vice, 1985; Rock a bye, 1986; Spenser: For Hire, 1987; Relentless: Mind of a Killer, 1993; Bakers field PD, 1993; The Tomorrow Man, 1993; Homicide: Life on the St, 1998-99; The St, 2000; Girls Club, 2002; 5ive Days to Midnight, 2004; NYPD 2069, 2004; Law & Order: Trial by Jury, 2005; South Beach, 2006; Ghost Whisperer, 2006; Bones, 2006; Las Vegas, 2006; CSI: Miami, 20006-08; Kidnapped, 2007; New Amsterdam, 2008; Breaking Bad, 2009-11; Leverage, 2010; Lie to Me, 2010; Detroit 1-8-7, 2010; Criminal Minds: Suspect Behavior, 2011; Once Upon a Time, 2011-14; Community, 2012-13; NYC 22, 2012; Revolution, 2012-14; Timms Valley, 2013; Axe Cop, 2013. theater experience incl: Maggie Flynn; Miss Moffet, 1974; The Me Nobody Knows; See saw; Zooman and the Sign, 1980; The Gentleman Bandit, 1981; Keyboard, 1982; Do Lord Remember Me, 1984; Balm in Gilead, 1984; Don't Get God Started, 1987; One for Dexter, 1991; Distant Fires, 1992; films incl; Running, 1979; Taps, 1983; Trading Places, 1983; Cotton Club, 1984; Sweet Lorraine, 1987; Sch Daze, 1988; Do the Right Thing, 1989; Mo' Better Blues, 1990; Night on Earth, 1992; Bob Roberts, 1992; Amos and Andrew, 1993; Fresh, 1994; Benders, 1994; The Usual Suspects, 1995; Smoke, 1995; Reckless, 1995; The Keeper, 1995; Blue in the Face, 1995; Waiting to Exhale, 1995; Loose Women, 1996; Calif, 1996; Trouble on the Corner, 1997; The People, 1997; The Maze, 1997; Twilight, 1998; Phoenix, 1998; Lulu on the Bridge, 1998; Stardust, 1998; Where's Marlowe?, 1999; Big City Blues, 1999; Speak Truth to Power, 2000; Josephine, 2001; Monkey bone, 2001; Pinero, 2001; Ali, 2001; Blind Horizon, 2003; Ash Tuesday, 2003; Noise, 2004; Doing Hard Time, 2004; A Killer Within, 2004; Hate Crime, 2005; Chupacabra: Dark Seas, 2005; I Will Avenge You, Iago, 2005; Back in the Day, 2005; Carlito's Way: Rise to Power, 2005; Derailed, 2005; Last Holiday, 2006; Sherrybaby, 2006; Rain, 2006; Racing Daylight, 2007; The Box, 2007; Mano, 2007; Feel the Noise, 2007; Gospel Hill, 2008; Xenophobia, 2008; Rabbit Hole, 2010; S.W.A.T.: Firefight, 2011; Certainty, 2011; Alex Cross, 2012; Dreaming American, 2012; Over / Under, 2013; Requiem for the Big East, 2014; Son of Batman, 2014; Batman: Assault on Arkham, 2014; Stuck, 2015-; The Jungle Book, 2015-; The Maze Runner: Scorch Trials, 2015-. **Orgs:** Screen Actors Guild. **Honors/Awds:** OBIE Award, for Zooman and the Sign, 1981; Theatre World Award, for Zooman and the Sign, 1981; Obie Award for Distant Fires, 1993. **Home Addr:** c/o 40 Acres & A Mule Filmworks Inc, 124 Dekalb Ave, Brooklyn, NY 11217, **Home Phone:** (718)624-3703. **Business Addr:** Actor, ATTN: Tood Noonan, 1501 Broadway Suite 703, New York, NY 10036, **Business Phone:** (212)382-2000.

## ESPY, ALPHONSO MICHAEL

Lawyer, government official. **Personal:** Born Nov 30, 1953, Yazoo City, MS; son of Thomas J Huddleston Jr; married Portia Denise Ballar; children: Jamilla Morgan, Michael William & Ian Michael E; married Sheila Bell; children: 2. **Educ:** Howard Univ, BA, 1975; Univ Santa Clara Law Sch, JD, 1978. **Career:** Law Pract Yazoo City, atty; Cent MS Legal Servs, mgr, atty, 1978-80; State Secy Off, dir pub lands & elections div, 1980-84; State Atty Gen Off, dir, Miss Off Consumer Protection Div, chief assst atty gen & dir, 1984-85; Miss Off Pub Lands, asst secy & dir; US House Reps, Second Dist, Miss, staff mem, 1987-93; USDA, secy agr, 1993-94; Dept Energy, sr adv; Butler, Snow, O'Mara, Stevens & Cannada, PLLC, lawyer, currently; Mike Espy PLLC, owner & lawyer, atty, counr & agr advisor, currently; AE Agritrade Inc, owner; Morgan & Morgan PA, atty. **Orgs:** Bd mem, Farm Found Inc; vice chmn, Dem Leadership Coun; Dem Caucus Whips Orgn; Miss Bar Asn; Magnolia Bar Asn; Am Bar Asn; chmn bd dir, Toxin Alert Inc; Enterprise Corp Delta; Afro-Am Sons & Daughters Hosp Found; Hope Community Credit Union; Masons; 100 Black Men Jackson Inc; Feed C Int Ministries; New Hope Baptist Church Jackson, Miss; advisor, Regional Venture Capital Fund. **Home Addr:** 124 Cherry Laurel Cir, Pearl, MS 39208, **Home Phone:** (601)368-3193. **Business Addr:** Owner, Lawyer, Mike Espy PLLC, Lamar Life Bldg, Jackson, MS 39201, **Business Phone:** (601)355-9101.

## ESPY, BEN E.

Lawyer. **Personal:** married Kathy; children: Elizabeth, Amy, Laura & Lynnette. **Educ:** Ohio State Univ, BA, polit sci, 1965; Howard Univ Law Sch, JD, 1968. **Career:** Allegheny Airlines, corp atty, 1968; State Atty Gen Off, Civil Rights Div, dep chief, 1972-74, Div Criminal Activ, 1974; pvt pract atty, 1977-; Columbus City Coun, pres, 1982-92; Ohio State, sen, 1992-2002, from asst minority leader to minority leader, 1994-2000; Columbus Youth Corps, founder, 1991-; Ohio Senate, asst minority leader, 1994-96, minority leader, 1996-2000. **Orgs:** Columbus Bar Asn; Ohio Bar Asn; Am Bar Asn; Sigma Delta Tau Legal Fraternity; Cath Diocese Found Adv Bd; Kappa Alpha Psi Fraternity; co-founder, Urban Christian Leadership Asn; founder, Columbus Youth Corps; vpres bd dir, Ohio State Univ Alumni Asn, 2001-; Prince Hall Freemason. **Honors/Awds:** Ohio Dem Party Meryl Shoemaker Award; Legislator of the Year, Ohio Hunger Task Force; Legislator of the Year, Franklin County Trial Lawyers Association; Neighborhood House Volunteer Service Award; Outstanding Community Leader Award, McDonald's Restaurant; Distinguished Service Award, Ohio State University, 2001. **Special Achievements:** Espy created "The Job Show", a cable TV prog produced by the City Columbus, which helps people find jobs. He established the annual City of Columbus-Martin Luther King, Jr. Holiday Celebration. **Business Addr:** Attorney, State of Ohio, 1350 Brookwood Pl, Columbus, OH 43209, **Business Phone:** (614)236-5968.

## ESPY, HENRY

Mayor, president (organization). **Personal:** son of Henry Sr and Willie Jean Huddleston; children: Chuck III, Jaye, Charisse & Paula. **Career:** Clarksdale, Miss, mayor, 1990-2013, city comnr; Clarksdale Separate Munic Sch District, trustee. **Orgs:** Pres, Nat Conf Black Mayors; pres, Century Funeral Home & Burial Asn. **Business Addr:** Mayor, City of Clarksdale, 121 Sunflower Ave, Clarksdale, MS 38614, **Business Phone:** (662)621-8164.

## ESPY-WILSON, CAROL

College teacher, founder (originator), engineer. **Personal:** Born Atlanta, GA; daughter of Mattie Espy and Matthew Espy; married John Sylvanus Wilson; children: Ayana, Ashia & John (Jay) Sylvanus III. **Educ:** Stanford Univ, BS, elec engineering, 1979; Mass Inst Technol, MS, elec engineering, 1981, EE, 1984, PhD, elec engineering, 1987. **Career:** MIT, post-doctoral stud, Res Scientist, Vis Scientist, res assoc, 1987-89; Boston Univ, Fac, 1990-2001; Univ Md (UMD) at Col Pk, Elec & Comput Engineering Prof & Speech Commun Lab dir; OmniSpeech, Founder & chief exec officer, 2009-; Acoust; "Acoustics Today", assoc ed; "Journal of the Acoustical Society of America", assoc ed. **Orgs:** Acoust Soc Am (ASA) Fel; Inst Elec & Electronics Engrs (IEEE); Harvard, Radcliffe Fel, 2008-2009; Speech & Lang Tech Comt; Lang & Commun Study Sect, 2001-04; Acoust Soc Am; chair, Speech Tech Comt, 2007-10; Nat Adv Bd Med Rehab, Nat Insts Health. **Business Addr:** Founder, CEO, OmniSpeech, 387 Technol Dr, College Park, MD 20742, **Business Phone:** (301)405-8861.

## ESSIEN, DR. FRANCINE

Educator, administrator. **Personal:** Born Philadelphia, PA. **Educ:** Temple Univ, BA, biol; Yeshiva Univ, Albert Einstein Col Med, PhD, genetics; Univ Conn. **Career:** Professor (retired); Univ Port Harcourt, fulbright prof; Rutgers Univ, Off Minority Undergrad Sci Progs, dir, 1988, Dept Biol Sci, biol prof, Off Diversity & Acad Success Sci, dir emer, currently. **Orgs:** NIH Black Scientists Asn; lifetime mem, Rutgers African-Am Alumni Alliance. **Business Addr:** Director Emeritus, Rutgers University, Nelson Lab, Piscataway, NJ 08854-8000, **Business Phone:** (732)445-6878.

## ESSIET, DR. EVALEEN JOHNSON

Educator, nurse. **Personal:** Born Jun 21, 1933, Roxboro, NC; children: Ata & Bodie. **Educ:** Montefiore Hosp Sch Nursing, dipl, 1955; Univ Pittsburgh, BS, nursing, 1965, MSW, 1971, PhD, higher educ, 1983. **Career:** George Wash Univ Hosp, Wash, DC, staff nurse psychol, 1955-58; Allegheny County Health Dept, supvr pub health nurses, 1958-63; Mone fine Hosp Sch Nursing, nursing fac, 1963-66; Home Wd Bruston Ctr, St Francis Hosp CMHC, dir, 1968-69; Clin Hempsted Hosp CMHC, dir out-patient, 1971-73; Community Col Allegheny County, prof nursing, 1973-. **Orgs:** Pub chair, Chi Sta Phi Nursing Sorority, 1981-85; pres, coun, E Johnson Essiet Corp, 1983-84; elder, Presby Church USA, 1985-. **Home Addr:** 827 Bell Ave, Braddock, PA 15104. **Business Addr:** Professor of Nursing, Community College of Allegheny County, 808 Ridge Ave, Pittsburgh, PA 15212-6097, **Business Phone:** (412)237-2525.

## ESSOKA, GLORIA CORZEN

College teacher, nurse. **Personal:** Born May 25, 1938, Philadelphia, PA; daughter of William B and Thelma S; married Modi; children: Jonathan Dumbe & Ndome Lynette. **Educ:** Jefferson Hosp Sch Nursing, dipl, 1959; Univ Pa, BSN, 1962; Univ Pa, MSN, 1964; NY Univ, PhD, nursing, 1981; Hunter Col, post masters practr paediatric nurse cert prog, 1996. **Career:** Va State Col, instr, 1964-65; Hunter Col, instr, 1971-73, assoc prof, 1983-2006; Seton Hall Univ, assoc prof, 1973-82, distinguished vis prof, currently, Chair, family health nursing & behav sci, currently; Univ Malawi, vis prof, 1991-93; cert paediat nurse practr, 1997. **Orgs:** Univ Pa Alumnae Asn, 1962-; Sigma Theta Tau, 1967-; Am Nurses Asn, 1973-; NY Univ Alumnae Asn, 1981-; Nat League Nursing, 1982-; St Mary's Hosp, bd trustee, 1981-89; Asn Black Nursing Fac Higher Educ, 1988-; Thomas Jefferson Univ Alumnae Asn, 1993; NCP, 1997; NONPF, 1997; Nj Nursing Initiative; Am Asn Cols Nursing. **Home Addr:** 1 Arverne Rd, West Orange, NJ 07052-2601, **Home Phone:** (973)731-1014. **Business Addr:** Chairman, Family Health Nursing, Seton Hall University, 400 S Orange Ave, South Orange, NJ 07079, **Business Phone:** (973)761-9306.

## ESTES, ELAINE ROSE GRAHAM

Librarian. **Personal:** Born Nov 24, 1931, Springfield, MO; daughter of James McKinley and Zelma Mae Smith; married John M Jr. **Educ:** Drake Univ, BS, 1953, teaching cert, 1956; Univ Ill, MS, 1960. **Career:** Librarian (retired); Des Moines Pub Libr, dir libr syst, 1956-95. **Orgs:** Pres, Iowa Libr Asn; pres, Des Moines Metro Libr Asn; Am Libr Asn; bd mem, Iowa Soc Preserv Hist Landmarks; bd trustee, Des Moines Art Ctr; bd mem, Des Moines Community Playhouse; adv coun, Dept Adult Ed; bd adv, Nat Trust Hist Preserv; Mayors Sister City Comn; bd mem, Des Moines Civic Ctr; Polk City Hist Soc; state vpres, Questers; pres, Terr Hill Soc, Gov Comn Restoration Gov Mansion; pres, charter mem, DM Chap Links Inc; basilius Sorority Beta Phi Mu Hon Libr Scholastic Soc; chap, City Des Moines Hist Dist Comn; Rotary 1987-; Nat Comn Future Dr Unake Univ, Task Force Libr & Learning Resources, 1987-88; pres, Willson Alexander Scott, Chap Questers, 1988-98; bd, Wallace House Found, 1989-95; pres, IUPLA, 1991; chair, hist comn, Des Moines Sesquicentennial Comn, 1992-94; vpres, State Iowa Questers, 1999-; chair, Tour Comn Int Quester Conv, 1999; Terr Hill Comn, 2001-; Terr Hill Comn, 2001; Des Moines Found, 2001-07; Proteus, Iowa Antique Asn, 2000-02, pres, 2003-04; Drake Univ Nat Adv Comn Cowles Libr; Iowa Gov's Centennial Found; Salisbury House Acq Comn; Drake Univ, 50-yr Alumni Comn, 2003; Iowa Questers Comt Textiles & Clothing Collection, 2007-10; Henry Wallace House Found. **Home Addr:** 944 9th St, Des Moines, IA 50309-1204, **Home Phone:** (515)244-1462.

## ESTES, SIMON LAMONT

Opera singer. **Personal:** Born Feb 2, 1938, Centerville, IA; son of Simon and Ruth Jeter; married Yvonne Baer; children: Jennifer, Lynn & Tiffany; married Ovida Stong. **Educ:** Univ Iowa, BMus; Juilliard Sch Music. **Career:** L-Beck Opera Co, singer; Hamburg Opera Co, singer; opera singer & bass baritone; Juilliard Sch Music, prof; Wartburg Col, distinguished prof & artist-in-residence, 2002-; Boston Univ, artist fac; Iowa State Univ, F. Wendell Miller distinguished artist residence; Des Moines Univ, adj clin prof global health. **Orgs:** Old Gold Singers, Univ Iowa; Am Opera Soc; Simon Estes Int Fund Children; Simon Estes Educ Fund; Simon & Westella Estes Educ Fund. **Honors/Awds:** Numerous awards & honors including First prize, Int Tchaikovsky Vocal Competition, Moscow; grant, Martha Bard Rockefeller Found; Tchaikovsky Medal, 1985; honoree, Fine Arts Award, career achievements; acclaimed appearance, Porgy, Metropolitan Opera's first prod Porgy & Bess; Honorary doctorates from Siena Col, Drake Univ, Univ Tulsa, Luther Col, Iowa State Univ; Honorary Colonel, Iowa Nat Guard; Distinguished Alumni Award, Univ Iowa Alumni Asn; The Simon Estes Music High School and choir, near Cape Town, South Africa, stress musical pursuits and are named in his honor; Dr. Martin Luther King, Jr. Achievement Award, 2014. **Special Achievements:** First African American member of the Old Gold Singers, became the first male African-American to sing a major role on the stage at Bayreuth, San Francisco Opera, San Sebastian Festival, Spain, performed all four of the Hoffman roles in Offenbach's Tales of Hoffman, Macbeth's Banquo, The Magic Flute, The Marriage of Figaro. **Business Addr:** Distinguished Professor, Artist-in-Residence, Wartburg College, 100 Wartburg Blvd, Waverly, IA 50677, **Business Phone:** (800)772-2085.

### ESTES-SUMPTER, SIDMEL KAREN

Executive, association executive, educator. **Personal:** Born Nov 27, 1954, Marysville, CA; daughter of Emellen Mitchell and Sidney Harrison; married B Garnett; children: Joshua Khalid & Sidney Rashid. **Educ:** Northwestern Univ, BSJ, 1976, MSJ, 1977. **Career:** Emory Univ, adj journalism prof; Chicago Daily Defender, reporter, 1974; Chicago Daily News, desk asst, 1975; Guam Cable TV, reporter & anchor, 1977-79; WAGA-TV, FOX 5 News, news producer, planning mgr, asst ed, exec producer, 1979-2006; BreakThrough Inc, chief exec officer, 1998-; Drew Berry & Assocs, Talent Rep, 2007-11; Clark Atlanta Univ, Adj journalism prof, 2010-; Atlanta Metrop State Col, Adj Mass Commun Prof, 2013-14. **Orgs:** Pres youth coun, Atlanta Chap Nat Asn Advan Colored People, 1970-72; pres, Atlanta Asn Black Journalists, 1985-87; comn mem, Leadership Atlanta, 1988-; bd mem, Atlanta Exchange, 1987-89; Ben Hill United Methodist Ch, sect leader, 1989-91; bd mem, Soc Prof Journalists, 1991; bd vis, Northwestern Univ, 1998-; immediate past pres, 1991-93, pres, 1993-95, regional dir, 1987-91, Nat Asn Black Journalists; bd mem, Atlanta Press Club, 1998-2000; bd mem, Medill Bd Advisors, 2000-12; bd mem, Northwestern Univ Alumni Asn, 2005-12; bd mem, consult, Atlanta Ctr Creative Inquiry, 2005; bd mem, consult, Frederick Douglass Family Found, 2010. **Honors/Awds:** Excellence in Community Science in Television Award, AAB, 1983; Chair Award, Atlanta Asn Black Journalists, 1985; Producer of the Year, Am Women Radio & TV, 1986; Media Woman of the Year, Nat Asn Media Women, 1988; YWCA Award for Women of Achievement, 1988; Proclamation of Sidmel Estes-Sumpter Day, Atlanta, Nov. 18, 1988; Community Award, Nat Asn Prof & Bus Women, 1989; Bronze Woman of the Year, Iota Phi Lombdo, 1989; Pioneer Black Journalist Award, Atlanta Asn Black Journalists, 1990; most interesting personalities, Whos Who in Black Atlanta; Top Young People of Atlanta, Outstanding Atlanta, 1991; Lifetime Achievement Award, Crisis Mag, 1992; 100 Most Influential Black Americans and Organizations, Ebony Mag, 1993; Silver Circle Award, Nat Tv Acad SE Chap, 2003; Women's Hall of Fame, Atlanta Bus League, 2003; Alumni Service Award, Northwestern Univ, 2004; 7 Emmy Awards; lifetime membership, Atlanta Association of Black Journalists; "40 Voices of Distinction", historic Atlanta Voice newspaper; Millenium Pacesetter Award, Atlanta Bus League. **Special Achievements:** First woman president of the National Association of Black Journalists, 1991; featured in a fabulous book published by Meredith Publications entitled, 50 Celebrate 50. **Home Addr:** 443 Chartley Trail, Atlanta, GA 30303, **Home Phone:** (404)294-1021. **Business Addr:** Executive Producer, WAGA-TV, 1551 Briarcliff Rd NE, Atlanta, GA 30306, **Business Phone:** (404)875-5555.

### ESTILL, DR. ANN H. M.

Singer, violinist, educator. **Personal:** Born Washington, DC; daughter of Don V and T Christine Smith. **Educ:** Western Mich Univ, BMus; Columbia Univ, Teachers Col, MA; NY Univ, DA, voice performance, 1982. **Career:** Kalamazoo Jr Symphony, violinist; Jersey City State Col, researcher & developer African & Afro-Am Class music, prof music; actor, currently. **Orgs:** Am Inst Music Studies Graz Austria; pres, Sigma Alpha Iota Prof Hon Frat Women Music, NY Alumnae Chap, 1963; prov officer, Al-Past Phi C; educ hon, Phi Delta Kappa; Kappa Phi Methodist Women; Nat Asn Teachers Singing. **Business Addr:** Actor, 1 Holly St, Jersey City, NJ 07305-4837, **Business Phone:** (201)434-5759.

### ETHEREDGE, JAMES W., JR.

Government official. **Personal:** Born Jun 6, 1941, Leesville, SC; married Vanetta Bing; children: Lorna V & William Craig. **Educ:** SC State Col, BS, 1963; Ind State Univ, Soc, attended 1966; Winthrop Col, polit sci, attended 1973; Univ SC, MPA, 1973. **Career:** City Rock Hill, social prog spec, 1969-70; Winthrop Col, part time instr, 1973-79; City Rock Hill, dir admin serv, 1971-80; City Charleston, dir admin serv, 1980-. **Orgs:** SC City & Cty Mgt Asn; SC Munic Asn; Am Soc Pub Admin; Omega Psi Phi Frat; Charleston United Way Agency; Charleston Bus & Prof Asn; Avery Inst. **Home Addr:** 2210 Longview Ct, Charleston, SC 29414-6716, **Home Phone:** (843)766-0684. **Business Addr:** Director, City of Charleston, PO Box 304, Charleston, SC 29402, **Business Phone:** (803)724-3743.

### ETHRIDGE, JOHN E., JR.

Chief executive officer. **Career:** J E Ethridge Construction Inc, Fresno, Calif, chief exec officer & chmn, 1971-. **Business Addr:** Chief Executive officer, Chairman, J E Ethridge Construction Inc, 1146 E Portland Ave, Fresno, CA 93720, **Business Phone:** (559)435-2391.

### ETHRIDGE, RAYMOND ARTHUR, JR.

Football player, executive. **Personal:** Born Dec 12, 1968, San Diego, CA; son of Vernolia Walker; married Wanda Yvette; children: Rayven. **Educ:** Pasadena City Col, BA, gen bus, 1991; San Diego State Univ, BA, criminal justice & psychol, 1994. **Career:** Football player (retired), executive; San Diego Chargers, 1992-94; Cleveland Browns, 1995; Baltimore Ravens, wide receiver, 1996-98; Living Water Lending, vpres opers, 2002-06; Sports Image Mgt, vpres bus partnerships, 2006-13; Southwest Home Health Serv, Bus Develop, 2013-15; Total Home Health INC, Buisness Develop, 2015-16.

### ETHRIDGE, DR. ROBERT WYLIE

School administrator. **Personal:** Born Nov 12, 1940, Monroe, MI; son of Claude Sr and Hazel Johnson; married Elizabeth Sneed; children: Stephan, Tracy & Michael. **Educ:** Western Mich Univ, BA, eng, 1962, MA, span, 1970; Univ Mich, Ann Arbor, PhD, educ admin & supv, 1979. **Career:** Detroit Pub Sch, teacher, 1962-69; Western Mich Univ, area coordr housing, 1969-72, from admin asst to pres, 1972-79; Emory Univ, sr officer, coordr equal opportunity prog, 1981, from asst vpres to assoc vpres, 1982-2000, adj asst prof, 1982-, Off Equal Opportunities Prog, vpres, pres, 2000-; Emory Fed Credit Union, chairperson emer; Rollins Col, consult; Univ Wis-Green Bay, consult; Ore State Univ, consult; Rensselaer Polytech Inst, consult; US Comn Civil Rights, consult; Tobacco Inst, consult; Brown & Williamson Co, consult; State Univ New York, consult; N Star Bor Sch Dist Fairbanks, consult; Alaska, consult; Fulton County Sch Dist, consult; Colo Springs Sch Dist, consult; New York Dept Educ, consult; New York Civil Serv Comn, consult; Centers Dis Control, consult; Internal Revenue Serv, consult; Environ Protection Agency, consult. **Orgs:** Sec bd trustee, 1979-81, bd dir, 1989-91, vpres, 1993-94, pres, 1994-96, Western MichUniv Alumni Asn; CUPA, NACUBO 1981-, Nat Asn Advan Colored People, 1981-; vpres, 1981-84, pres, 1984-88 & 1990-92, Am Asn Affirmative Action; bd mem, Nat Conf Planner, 1982-84; bd, Nat Assault Illiteracy Prog, 1983-; financial subcomt mem, United Way, 1984-; United Way-Health Serv Coun, 1984-85; United Way-Admis Panel, 1984-85; Ga Pub Rels Asn, 1985; Nat Inst Employ Equity, 1986-; chmn bd, Am Contract Compliance Asn, 1987-89; pres, Onyx Soc Western Mich Univ, 1989 & 1997-99; bd dir, & adv bd mem; 1994-99, treas, 1996-98, vpres, 1998-2001, Community Friendship Inc; bd dir, Ga Nursing Found, 1994-95; pres, WMU Onyx Soc, 1994-97, 1997-94; bd dir, 100 Black Men Dekalb, 1997-98; bership comt mem, Leadership Atlanta, 1997-99; Race Rels Comn, 1997-2001; bd mem, Am Contract Compliance Asn; bd mem, Leadership Conf Civil Rights; Asn Off Human Rights Agencies; bd dir, Emory Fed Credit Union; Rachel B. Noel Distinguished Fac Mem, Metro State Col Denver, Colo, 2006; 100 Black Men Am; DeKalb County Chap; Community Friendship; Leadership Atlanta; 2006 Rachel B Noel Distinguished Fac Mem, Metro State Col. **Home Addr:** 340 Rainbow Row Ct, Alpharetta, GA 30022, **Home Phone:** (770)640-8380. **Business Addr:** Vice President, Emory University, Admin Bldg 201 Dowman Dr Suite 305, Atlanta, GA 30322, **Business Phone:** (404)727-9867.

### EUBANKS, DAYNA C.

Journalist. **Personal:** Born Jun 7, 1957, Wichita, KS. **Educ:** Univ Kans, BS, jour, 1979; Univ Detroit Mercy Sch Law, cert, commun law. **Career:** KAKE-TV Wichita, KS, psa actress, 1975; KJHK Radio News, Univ Kans, reporter, vpres, Mondale trip, 1977; KJHK Radio, Univ Kans, newscaster, news ed, 1977-78; Audio-Reader Univ Kans, newscaster, broadcaster, reader, 1977-78; WREN-AM Topeka, KS, legislative reporter, 1978; WIBW-TV-AM-FM Topeka Kans, newscaster, reporter, photographer, weekend news anchor, TV & radio, 1978-79; KOOL-TV Phoenix, AZ, weekend news anchor, gen assignment reporter, reporter, 1979-81; WXYZ-TV ABC Detroit, MI, weekendnews anchor, field anchor, Good Afternoon Detroit, gen assignment reporter 1981-88; WJBK-TV, Detroit, MI, anchor, host of weekday talk show Dayna, 1988-92; FCN Ford Commun Network, global corp network anchor, reporter, host, producer, 1993-94; WKRC-TV, Cincinnati, anchor & reporter, 1994-2007; Tropaion Media Inc, independent contractor, 2008-; LOCAL 12 First at Four, anchor. **Orgs:** Am Women in Radio & TV, Nat Asn TV Arts & Sci, Nat Asn Black Journalists, Sigma Delta Chi, Women in Commun, SAG, Am Fed TV & Radio Artists, Delta Sigma Theta; lifetime mem, Nat Asn Advan Colored People; co-chair & co-org, Detroit Black-Jewish Leaders Forum; volunteer teacher & counr, "Who Said I Can't" Program; nat convention chairperson, nat exec bd mem, IAWS, 1979; adv, Judicial Bd GSP-Corbin Hall, Acad Success KU Studs; ku rep IAWS Nat Conv; rep, Asn Univ Residence Halls. **Home Addr:** 24153 Evergreen St, Southfield, MI 48075. **Business Addr:** Anchor, WKRC-TV, 600 N Mcclurg Ct 3202a, Chicago, IL 60611-3044, **Business Phone:** (312)925-1946.

### EUBANKS, KEVIN TYRONE

Jazz musician, guitarist. **Personal:** Born Nov 15, 1957, Philadelphia, PA; son of William and Vera. **Educ:** Univ Berklee Col Music, 1979. **Career:** Composer: Psalms from the Underground, 1996. Rebound: The Legend of Earl' The Goat' Manigault, 1996; The Dinner, 1997; The Week That Girl Died, 1998. Films: Longshot, 2000. TV Series: "The Tonight Show with Jay Leno", musical dir, 1994-2012; "Muppets Tonight", 1997; "Hollywood Squares", 1999-2003; "V.I.P.", 2000; "Days of Our Lives", 2002; "Girlfriends", guitarist, 2003; "Studio 60 on the Sunset Strip", 2006; "Tavis Smiley", 2010; "Hollywood Uncensored with Sam Rubin", 2012. TV Movie: WCW Road Wild '98, 1998; Auth, Creative Guitarist, Hal Leonard; recs include: "Turning Point"; "Spirit Talk"; "Spirit Talk 2"; "Revelations"; NBC-TV, The Tonight Show, musical dir, currently. **Orgs:** Kappa Alpha Psi Fraternity Inc; BMI Found. **Business Addr:** Musical Director, NBC-TV, 3000 W Alameda Ave, Burbank, CA 91523, **Business Phone:** (818)840-4444.

### EUBANKS, LEMELVA

Executive. **Career:** KLM Financial, pres. **Business Addr:** President, KLM Financial, 6573 Pembridge, West Bloomfield, MI 48322, **Business Phone:** (248)661-6316.

### EUBANKS, W. RALPH

Editor, publisher. **Personal:** Born Jun 25, 1957, Collins, MS; son of Warren R and Lucille; married Colleen Delaney; children: Patrick Warren, Aidan Joseph & Delaney Marie. **Educ:** Univ Miss, BA, eng & psychol, 1978; Univ Mich, MA, eng lang & lit, 1979. **Career:** Am Geophys Union, copy ed, 1979-84; Univ Va Publ, advisor & adj prof; George Mason Univadvisor & adj prof; Am Psychol Asn, journals mgr, 1984-89; Taylor & Francis, managing ed, 1989-90; Am Psychol Asn, APA bks, dir, 1990-95; Libr Cong, dir publ, 1995-2013; Univ Va, Va Quart Rev, ed, 2013-; Books: Ever Is a Long Time: A Journey Into Mississippi's Dark Past; Mississippi Yearning; Still Learning From Dad; DNA is Only One Way to Spell Identity; Separate But Unequal; Before He Had His Dream, King Wrote a Letter; A Trip Back Home for a Lesson in Justice; Are We Putting Reading & Democracy at Risk?; I Know What He Means; The House at the End of the Road. **Orgs:** Wash Ed Press, 1979-; stud adv, Howard Univ Bk Publ Inst, 1992-93; pres, Wash Bk Publ, 1996-97; fel New Am Found, pres, Sigma Tau Delta Col Hon Soc. **Honors/Awds:** Guggenheim Fellowship, John Simon Guggenheim Found, 2007; Bernard L Schwartz Fellowship, New Am Found. **Home Addr:** 3135 Quesada St NW, Washington, DC 20015, **Home Phone:** (202)537-9536. **Business Addr:** Director Publishing, The Library of Congress, 101 Independence Ave SE, Washington, DC 20540-3000, **Business Phone:** (202)707-5000.

### EUGERE, EDWARD J.

Pharmacologist, educator, association executive. **Personal:** Born May 26, 1930, New Orleans, LA; married Yolanda Rousseve; children: Edward, Jan, Gail & Lisa. **Educ:** Xavier Univ, BS, 1951; Wayne State Univ, MS, 1953; Univ Conn, PhD, 1956. **Career:** Numerous Co, pharmacist, 1951-57; Wayne St Univ, grad teacher asst, 1951-53; Univ Conn, 1953-56; Highland Pk Jr Col, lectr; Detroit Inst Technol, asst prof, 1956-57; Baylor Col Med, Tex Southern Univ, prof, 1957-; Sch Pharm, dean, 1968-70, Postdoctoral Study Myocardial Biol, 1973. **Orgs:** Harris County Pharm Asn; pres, Houston Pharm Asn; Am Heart Asn; Lone Star St Pharm Asn; pres, Houston Area Chi Delta Mu Prof Frat; Am Asn Col Pharm; Am Tex Pharm Asn; Houston Pharmcologists; bd Educ, Diocess Galveston Houston, 1974-77; Sigma Xi Soc; pres, Rho Chi Pharm Hon Soc, 1977; pres, Grand Jury Asn Houston-harris Co; pres, Cath Interracial Coun, Houston; Gulf Coast Area Child Develop Ctr; Am Asn Cols Pharm Chi. **Honors/Awds:** Fesler Research Award, Univ Conn, 1954-56; Travel Award, Detroit Inst Technol, 1957; Guide & Leadership Award, Sr Class Tex Southern Univ, 1968; Leadership Award, Houston Pharm Asn, 1971; Faculty Development Award, Tex Southern Univ, 1973. **Home Addr:** 3306 Calumet St, Houston, TX 77004-7846, **Home Phone:** (713)528-4209. **Business Addr:** Professor Pharmacology, Texas Southern University, 3100 Cleburne St Suite 1234, Houston, TX 77004, **Business Phone:** (713)313-7542.

### EURE, DEXTER D, SR. See Obituaries Section.

### EURE, DR. HERMAN EDWARD

Scientist, educator. **Personal:** Born Jan 7, 1947, Corapeake, IL; son of Grover T and Sarah Goodman; children: Lauren Angela & Jared Anthony. **Educ:** Md State Col, BS, 1969; Wake Forest Univ, PhD, biol, 1974. **Career:** Wake Forest Univ, Dept Biol, chmn, 1998-2006, prof biol, 1974-, chmn biol, 1998-2006, from asst prof to prof, chair dept, 2006-08, asst dean, 2006-, emer pr biol, 2013-. **Orgs:** Inst Ecol Univ Ga; Sigma Xi; Nat Asn Advan Colored People; Alpha Phi Alpha Frat Inc; Am Soc Parasitol; SE Soc Parasitol; Beta Nat Biol Hon Soc; Beta Kappa Chi Nat Hon Soc; fel Ford Found; fel NSF; fel African Sci Inst. **Home Addr:** 113 Brentwood Dr, Advance, NC 27006-9437, **Home Phone:** (336)998-4602. **Business Addr:** Professor, Assistant Dean, Wake Forest University, 226 Winston Hall, Winston Salem, NC 27109, **Business Phone:** (336)758-5571.

### EVANS, AKWASI ROZELLE

Publisher, editor. **Personal:** Born Oct 17, 1948, Dayton, OH; son of Garfield and Geraline Dale; children: Sherilyn Ronetta Scott. **Educ:** Univ Ky, BA, sociol, 1978; Tex Southern Univ Grad Sch, attended 1982. **Career:** Austin Area Urban League, job developer & instr, 1983-84; Capitol City Argus Newspaper, reporter, 1983-85; Villager Newspaper, reporter, 1985-87; NOKOA Observer Newspaper, publ & ed, 1987-. **Orgs:** Nat Newspaper Publ Asn, 1986-; fel Tex Publ Asn, 1986-, vpres, 1991-; pres bd dir, Nat Bus League, 1986-91; pres, founder, African Am Improv Corp, 1986-; bd dir, Multicultured Action Proj, 1990-; vpres, Black Arts Alliance, 1984-87; bd dir, Save Austin's Neighborhoods & Environs, 1984-87; Capital City African Am Chamber Com, 1999-; Coun Community Reconciliation, 1998-. **Honors/Awds:** Dewitty Overton Human Rights Award, Nat Asn Advan Colored People, 1990; Media Award, Tex Ment Health Ment Retardation, 1991; Sankhore Holistic Health Inst, Hon Doctorate, 1982; Abbie Hoffman Memorial Award, 1990; Leadership in Human Rights, Delta Sigma Theta, 1990; Phoenix Award, Friends of the Phoenix, 1990; A Phillip Randolph Messenger Award, 1999, 2000. **Special Achievements:** Poetry Anthology: "Periplum Austin," 1990; "Seem Southern to Me," 1977; "Perfect Circle," 1974. **Home Addr:** 5200 King Charles Dr, Austin, TX 78724, **Home Phone:** (512)927-0661. **Business Addr:** Publisher, Editor, NOKOA The Observer Newspaper, 1154 B Angelina St, Austin, TX 78767-1131, **Business Phone:** (512)499-8713.

### EVANS, ALBERT

Ballet dancer. **Personal:** Born Atlanta, GA. **Educ:** Sch Am Ballet; Terpsichore Expressions. **Career:** NY City Ballet, corps mem, soloist, 1991-, prin, 1995-; Ballet performances include: Phlegmatic in Four Temperaments; Episodes; Ash; Behind the China Dogs; The Unanswered Question; One Body; Ten Years of New Choreography; Broken Promises; George Balanchine's: Agon, Brahms Schoenberg Quartet; Concerto Barocco; Cortege Hongrois; Danses Concertantes; The Nutcracker; A Midsummer Nights Dream; Monumentum pro Gesualdo; Movements Piano Orchestra; Stravinsky Violin Concerto; Symphony C; Symphony Three Movements; Peter Martins: Ecstatic Orange; Fearful Symmetries; Les Gentilhommes; Jeu de Cartes; Reliquary; Swan Lake; Jerome Robbins: Gershwin Concerto; The Goldberg Variations; Twyla Tharps: The Beethoven Seventh; Christopher Wheeldons: Polyphonia; Liturgy; The Four Temperaments; Jazz; Klavier; Kevin O'Day; Open Strings; Ulysses Dove; Red Angels; Miriam Mahdaviani; Appalachia Waltz; John Alleyne; The New Blondes; Christopher d'Amboise; Circle Of Fifths; Garth Fagan; Ellington Elation; Eliot Feld; William Forsythe; The Lady with The Little Dog; Union Jack; Western Symphony; Who Cares?; The Sleeping Beauty; Slonimsky's Earbox; Todo Buenos Aires; Swerve Poems; Twilight; Correlazione; Concerto In Five Movements; Steel & Rain; Touch; Russian Seasons; Makin Whoopee. **Honors/Awds:** Full scholarship, Sch of Am Ballet. **Business Addr:** Dancer, NY City Ballet, 20 Lincoln Ctr Plz, New York, NY 10023-6913, **Business Phone:** (212)870-5656.

**EVANS, ALICIA (ALICIA A EVANS)**
Public relations executive, writer, executive. **Personal:** Born May 28, 1960, Brooklyn, NY; daughter of Simon Levan and Magnolia Ballard. **Educ:** Hofstra Univ, Hempstead, NY, BA, comun, 1982; NY Univ, cert, bus mgmt, 1984. **Career:** Fortunoffs, Westbury NY, promotional sales asst, 1977-84; CBS News, NY, prog transcriber, 1981; City Col New York, adj prof; Lockhart & Pettus Advert Agency, NY, acct exec, 1982-87; Dark & Lovely; Always Nat Hair Care, NY, dir pub rels, 1987; Lippe Taylor agency, vpres diversity div; Total Image Commun, founder & pres, chief exec officer, 1993-. **Orgs:** Nat Asn Female Exec, 1988, Pub Rel Soc Am, 1988; pres, NY Black Pub Rel Soc, 1990-; charter mem, pres, Black Pub Rels Socs New York. **Honors/Awds:** African American Achievement, NY, Million Dollar Boys Club, 1988; 1000 Notable Business & Professional Women, Am Biographical Inst, 1990. **Special Achievements:** News & Feature Editor, "The Satellite", Hofstra Univ, 1981, 1982; Producer copywriter, Con Edison, New York Utility Co, 1984; Copywriter brochure, Minority & Women's Div, New York Chamber of Commerce, 1984; Senior editor, "Homecoming", Army ROTC Publication, 1984-87; Producer/copywriter, Dark & Lovely Hair Care Products, 1987; Author: The Mosaica Guide for Cultural Communicators. **Home Addr:** 41 Ave, Westbury, NY 11590-2505, **Home Phone:** (516)997-5921. **Business Addr:** President, Founder, Total Image Communications, PO Box 731, Westbury, NY 11590-0731, **Business Phone:** (516)377-6146.

**EVANS, DR. ARTHUR L. See Obituaries Section.**

**EVANS, DR. BILLY JOE**
Educator, research scientist. **Personal:** Born Aug 18, 1942, Macon, GA; married Adye Bel; children: William & Carole. **Educ:** Morehouse Col, BS, chem, 1963; Univ Chicago, PhD, chem, 1968. **Career:** Woodrow Wilson fel, 1963-; Univ Chicago, res assoc, 1968; Univ Man, Dept Physics, fel, 1968-69; Nat Res Coun Can fel, Univ Man, 1968-69; Howard Univ, asst prof chem, 1969-70; Univ Mich, Dept Chem, asst prof, 1970-73, Dept Geol & Mineral, assoc prof, 1973-75, from assoc prof chem to prof chem, 1975-03, prof emer chem, prof emer, 2007-; Nat Bur Stand Alloy Phys Sect, consult, 1971-78; Alfred P Sloan res fel, 1972-75; BASF Wyandotte, consult, 1976-78; Danforth assoc, 1977-83; Humboldt sr fel, 1977-78; US Geol Surv, consult, 1980-84; Naval Res Lab, consult, 1986-; Atlanta Univ, Dept Chem, prof & chair, 1986-87; Am Soc Eng Educ, distinguished fac fel, 1988; Morehouse Col, Rauner prof chem & dir mat sci, 1998-99; Gallery Inventors, Tubman Mus, inductee; assoc, Chem Mfrs Asn, Danforth Found; Alexander Von Humboldt fel. **Orgs:** Sigma Xi, 1968-; Am Phys Soc; Mineral Soc Am; Can Mineral Asn; Am Geophys Union; Minorities Am Geophys Union; adv comt, Los Alamos, Nat Lab; Phi Kappa Phi, 1991; Am Chem Soc, Comt Prof Training, 1999-; math & phys sci directorate, Nat Sci Found, Adv Comn, 1999-, chair, 2001-02; Am Soc Eng Educ; Phi Beta Kappa; Nat Res Coun Can. **Home Addr:** 810 Oxford Rd, Ann Arbor, MI 48104-2637, **Home Phone:** (734)662-5468. **Business Addr:** Professor Emeritus of Chemistry, University of Michigan, 930 N Univ Ave, Ann Arbor, MI 48109-1055, **Business Phone:** (734)763-4228.

**EVANS, HON. CAROLE YVONNE MIMS**
Judge. **Personal:** Born Oct 1, 1951, Hendersonville, NC; daughter of Evans King and Mary Louise Valentine; married Michael Duaine; children: Tracey Renee, Michael Thomas & Karen Michelle. **Educ:** Wellesley Col, BA, 1973; Duke Univ Sch Law, JD, 1976. **Career:** Chambers Stein Ferguson & Becton, atty, 1976-88; C's Law Ctr, 1989-92; NC Resident Super Ct Judge, Judicial Dist 26th, NC, judge, 1992-; Mecklenburg County Dist, judge, 1992-2003; Mecklenburg County Super, judge, 2003-. **Orgs:** Bd dir, Charlotte Asn, Young Women's Christian Asn, 1978-80; bd dir, Planned Parenthood Charlotte Affil, 1979-80; bd dir, Charlotte Mecklenburg Urban League Orgn, 1979-81; Charlotte Mecklenburg Planning Comn, 1980-83; Charlotte Speech & Hearing Ctr, 1983-89; NC Bar Asn Bd Gov, 1986-89; mem bd, Bio-Ethics Resources Group, 1988-; mem bd, Leadership Charlotte, 1988-; bd dir, Found Carolinas, 1992-. **Home Addr:** 7900 Sunnyvale Lane, Charlotte, NC 28210-6767. **Business Addr:** Superior Judges, North Carolina Resident Superior Court, Mecklenburg County Courthouse 832 E 4th St Suite 9600, Charlotte, NC 28202, **Business Phone:** (704)686-0101.

**EVANS, CHARLOTTE A.**
Executive. **Personal:** Born Providence, RI. **Educ:** NY Inst Credit. **Career:** First Nat City Bank, switchboard operator, platform customer rep, off asst, asst mgr, 1971. **Orgs:** Nat Asn Bank Women; Urban Banders Coalition; former bd mem, Hamilton Day Care Ctr; former mem, Manhattanville Com & Ctr; former mem, Scitarnard Players Providence RI; Black Achievers YMCA; original mem, Am Negro Theatre NY; hon mem, Iota Phi Lambda Sorority; vpres & secy, NY Rinkeydinks. **Honors/Awds:** Luncheon Award, Iota Phi Lambda Sorority, 1970. **Special Achievements:** First African American women officer of any bank in NY. **Home Addr:** 78 Mineral Spring Ave, Pawtucket, RI 02860-2808, **Home Phone:** (401)723-2174.

**EVANS, REV. CLAY**
Clergy. **Personal:** Born Jun 23, 1925, Brownsville, TN; son of A Henry and Estanuly; married Lutha Mae Hollingshed; children: Diane (deceased), Michael, Ralph, Claudette & Faith. **Educ:** Chicago Baptist Inst; Northern Baptist Theol Sem; Univ Chicago Sch Div; Ar Baptist Col, Brewster Theol Clin & Sch Relig, DD. **Career:** Pastor (retired); WCFL AM Radio & TV, ministry; Fel Baptist Church, pastor, founder, 1958-2000; Bapt Ministers Conf, pres, 1964-66. **Orgs:** African Am Relig Connection, founder & pres; found nat bd chair, Oper PUSH, 1958, chair, 1971-76, chmn emer, currently; founding pres, Broadcast Ministers Alliance Chicago, 1975; trustee bd chair, Chicago Baptist Inst; bd mem, Nat baptist Conention, USA Inc. **Honors/Awds:** Featured soloist, Voice Choir Fellowship Missionary Baptist Church; Stellar Gospel Music Award, 1996; numerous honorary doctor of divinity degrees. **Special Achievements:** From Plough Handle to Pulpit, autobiography, 1992, 1997. **Home Addr:** 9657 S Indiana Ave, Chicago, IL 60628, **Home Phone:** (773)568-6033. **Business Addr:** Founder, Fellowship Missionary Baptist Church, 4543 S Princeton Ave, Chicago, IL 60609, **Business Phone:** (773)924-3232.

**EVANS, DAVID LAWRENCE**
Educator. **Personal:** Born Dec 27, 1939, Phillips County, AR; married Mercedes L Sherrod; children: Daniel & Christine. **Educ:** Tenn State Univ, BS, elec engineering, 1962; Princeton Univ, MS, elec engineering, 1966. **Career:** Boeing Com, elec eng, 1962-64; Lockheed, elec eng, 1964; Princeton Univ, teaching asst, 1964-66; IBM Corp, elec eng, 1966-70; Harvard Univ, admin officer, asst dean, 1970, sr admis officer, currently; Harvard Found, adv, 1981. **Orgs:** Bd trustee, St Georges Sch; gov bd, Princeton Grad Alum Asn; Inst Elec & Electronic Engrs; Am Audlgy Soc; Nat Asn Col Admis Couns; Alpha Phi Alpha Fraternity; Harvard Club Boston; Asn Black Princeton Alumni; Princeton Alumni Asn New Eng; Nat Merit Corp; adv, Harvard Found. **Home Addr:** 208B Sherman St, Cambridge, MA 02140-3231. **Business Addr:** Senior Admissions Officer, Harvard College, 8 Garden St, Cambridge, MA 02138, **Business Phone:** (617)495-1527.

**EVANS, DONALD LEE**
Football player. **Personal:** Born Mar 14, 1964, Raleigh, NC; son of Novella Scott and Rhuben; married Debra Jeffers; children: Donald Lee II, Novella Leeann & Jessica Nicole. **Educ:** Winston-Salem State Univ, BS, health & phys edu, 1993. **Career:** Football player (retired); Los Angeles Rams, 1987; Philadelphia Edges, right defensive end, 1988; Pittsburgh Steelers, 1990-93; NY Jets, left defensive tackle, defensive end, 1994-95. **Orgs:** Project Bundle Up, 1987-; United Way, 1987-; Life Life Mission, 1987-; ShareWarmth, Hunger Project, Donald Evans Schlorship Fund, Black Arts Supporter. **Honors/Awds:** All CIAA Football Champions, Winston-Salem St Univ, 1986; Black and-Gold Barae Player of the Month, Pittsburgh Steeler Fan Club, 1992. **Special Achievements:** Winston-Salem State Univ, Dean's List, 1992; LA Rams, Number One DraftPick, 1987. Film: 1987 NFL Draft, 1987. **Home Addr:** 604 Meadowland Rd, Kernersville, NC 27284, **Home Phone:** (919)785-1504.

**EVANS, DOUGLAS EDWARDS**
Football player. **Personal:** Born May 13, 1970, Shreveport, LA; married Myria L; children: Aymara & Doug. **Educ:** La Tech Univ, finance. **Career:** Football player (retired); Green Bay Packers, 1993, right cornerback, 1994-97; Carolina Panthers, right cornerback, 1998-2001, cornerback, 1999; Seattle Seahawks, defensive back, 2002-03; Detroit Lions, defensive back, 2003. **Orgs:** Make Wish Found. **Honors/Awds:** Rookie of the Year, 1993; Super Bowl Champion (XXXI). **Special Achievements:** Film: Super Bowl XXXII, 1998. **Home Addr:** 126 Southwood Dr, Bossier City, LA 71111-6047.

**EVANS, REP. DWIGHT**
State government official. **Personal:** Born May 16, 1954, Philadelphia, PA; son of Henry and Jean Odoms. **Educ:** Philadelphia Community Col, attended 1973; La Salle Col, attended 1975; Temple Univ, attended 1976. **Career:** Teacher & rep: Philadelphia Pub Sch Syst, teacher; Urban League Philadelphia, employ counr/bob developer; State Pa, Dist 203, state rep, 1981-; Dem Appropriations Comt, chmn, 1991-2010. **Orgs:** Tutorial prog, Admis Procedure Comt, La Salle Col; chmn, Black Stud League; 10th Ward Dem Exec Comt; City-Wide Polit Alliance; NW Polit Coalition; Philadelphia Coun Neighborhoods; consult, N Cent Community Ment Health Ctr, House Umoja, Coun Labor & Indust; Stenton Food Co-op Prog; bd trustee, Pa Pub Sch Employees Retirement Syst; bd dir, nat & Philadelphia chap Black Alliance Educ Options; bd mem, Visitors Bur; bd mem, Presby Found, Philadelphia; Nat Gov Assessment Bd; founder, Pa Legis Comn Restructuring Urban Schs; bd dir, Fox Chase Cancer Ctr; Nat Conf State Legis's Deficit Reduction Task Force; co chair, Nat Conf State Legis's Hunger Caucus; Concerned Black Men; Nat Adv Comt, Leadership Healthy Communities; founder, Ogontz Ave Revitalization Corp; Partnership A Healthy Am. **Special Achievements:** First African American candidate to seek the office of Governor of Pennsylvania, 1994. **Home Addr:** 7174 Ogontz Ave, Philadelphia, PA 19138-2053, **Home Phone:** (215)549-0220. **Business Addr:** State Representative, Pennsylvania House of Representatives, 512 E3 Main Capitol, Harrisburg, PA 17120-2203, **Business Phone:** (717)783-1540.

**EVANS, ELINOR ELIZABETH**
Marketing executive. **Personal:** Born Mar 6, 1948, Detroit, MI; daughter of Harold and Evelyn; children: Tracey D, Candace D & Kevin D. **Educ:** Wayne County Conn Col, AA, 1989; Wayne State Univ, BS, 1997. **Career:** City Detroit, Transportation Dept, auto mechanic, 1974-77, sr clerk, 1977-83, prin clerk, 1983-84; City Detroit, COBO Conf/Exhib Ctr, event coordr, 1984-87, asst sales mgr, 1987-93, sales mgr, 1993-96, asst dir mkt, 1996-99, dir mkt, 1999-. **Orgs:** Nat Asn Advan Colored People, 1965-; Am Soc Asn Execs, 1987-; Nat Coalition Black Meeting Planners, 1993-; Religious Conference Mgt Asn, 1993-; Int Asn Exhibit Mgrs, 1995-; Optimist Club Central Detroit, 1995-; Asn Convention Mkt Execs, 1997; Prof Convention Mgmt Asn, 1999-. **Honors/Awds:** Certificate of Appreciation, Distributive Educ Clubs Am, 1994; Connecticut Service Award, High Sch Com & Bus Admin, 1996; Otto Finestein Writing Excellence Award, Wayne State Univ, 1997. **Home Addr:** 16511 Lesure St, Detroit, MI 48235, **Home Phone:** (313)340-1237. **Business Addr:** Director of Marketing, COBO Conference/Exhibition Center, 1 Wash Blvd, Detroit, MI 48226-4499, **Business Phone:** (313)877-8777.

**EVANS, ELIZABETH**
Executive. **Personal:** Born Jun 6, 1941, Augusta, GA; daughter of Robert D Sherard and Geraldine Payne; children: Tina, Emmet & Ida. **Educ:** Capital Univ. **Career:** WTVN-AM, WBUK-FM, from asst to pub affairs dir, 1970; WTVN-TV, community rels dir, 1973; Q FM 96, dir pub affairs; Clear Channel Columbus, dir pub affairs. **Orgs:** Chmn, Adv Bd, Black Family Connections Adoption, 1987; Women's Health Month Adv Comt, 1988; founder, Mors Against Crack Inc, 1989; Cols Aids Task Force Coalition, Media, 1989; founder, exec, African Am Cancer Support Group, 1992; vol, Am Cancer Soc Reach to Recovery, 1992; Direction Youth Serv Bd, 1992; Ohio Breast & Cervical Cancer Coalition; Columbus Breast & Cervical Cancer Proj; Ohio Chap, Nat Black Leadership Initiative Against Cancer; bd mem, Am Cancer Soc; bd mem, Race for Cure; ML King Arts Complex, Women's Serv Bd; founder, African Am Cancer Support Group Inc-; Ohio Dept Health Cancer Epidemiol Prev & Control Prog Bur; Grant Med Ctr Cancer Libr Adv Bd; Columbus Open Shelter; United Way Proj Diversity Bd; Columbus Women's Roundtable. **Home Addr:** 2441 Natchez Dr, Columbus, OH 43209, **Home Phone:** (614)236-2274. **Business Addr:** Founder, African American Cancer Support Group Inc, King Arts Complex 867 Mt Vernon Ave, Columbus, OH 43203, **Business Phone:** (614)236-2274.

**EVANS, ERNEST (CHUBBY CHECKER)**
Singer, actor, dancer. **Personal:** Born Oct 3, 1941, Spring Gulley, SC; married Rina Lodder; children: 3. **Career:** Cameo-Parkway Rec, rec artist; TV series: "Midnight Special"; "American Bandstand"; "Mike Douglas"; "Disco mania"; "Ally McBeal"; Recordings: The Class, 1959; Dancing Dinosaur, 1959; The Twist, 1960; Pony Time, Dance the Mess Around, The Fly, 1961; Slow Twist in, 1962; Popeye the Hitchhiker, 1962; Dancin Party, 1962; Limbo Rock, 1962; Let's Twist Again, 1962; Bird land, 1963; Twist It Up, 1963; Loddy Lo, 1963; 40 Twist, 1988; 20 Twistin' Hits, 1989; Knock Down the Walls, 2008; Changes, 2013. Jingle Bells; Peppermint Twist; Twist & Shout; Twist in the Night Away; Dances: The Jerk; The Hully Gully; The Boogaloo; The Shake; The Fly; The Pony; The Huckle buck; Films: Dont Knock The Twist; Twist Around The Clock. **Orgs:** Am Soc Composers, Authors & Publishers; BMI; Screen Actors Guld. **Honors/Awds:** Grammy Award, 1961. **Special Achievements:** Pony Time ranked No. 1, 1961; The Twist ranked No. 1, 1962; the only artist to have 5 albums in the Top 12 all at once; the only artist to havea song to be No. 1 twice; the only artist to have 9 Double-Sided Hits. **Business Addr:** Singer, Paradise Artists, 108 E Matilija St, Ojai, CA 93023, **Business Phone:** (805)646-8433.

**EVANS, ETU**
Executive, business owner, executive director. **Personal:** Born Feb 2, 1969, Orangeburg, CA; son of Rosa. **Educ:** SC State Univ, social work, 1992; Parsons Sch Design, shoe design, 1994; Columbia Univ, MS, appl behav sci, 1996; Fashion Inst Technol, footwear & accessories design, 2000. **Career:** Medgar Evers Col, adj prof; Inst Youth Entrepreneurship, asst dir; Berkeley Col, Fashion Dept, adj prof; Etu Evans LLC, chief shoemaker, pres & founder, 1993-. **Orgs:** Founder, Solesville Found, 1998-; Omega Psi Phi Fraternity. **Honors/Awds:** Crains Small Business of the Year, 2004; Proj Enterprise; New York Entrepreneur of the Year, 2005; Nat Urban League; Man of Influence; New face of the Martell Cognac Rise Above ad campaign saluting visionary men; Citizen of the Year Award, Omega Psi Phi Fraternity Inc; TONY Shopping Award, Time Out NY; 30 Leaders of the Future, Ebony mag. **Special Achievements:** Burger King Everyday Heroes National Campaign Honor, 2005; adorned the feet of many high profile celebrities, including Halle Berry, Beyonce, Erykah Badu, Lil Kim & supermodels Ana Hickman, Tyra Banks, Iman & Roshumba Futher; first African-American to successfully compete in the high-end shoe design market; featured in a number of publications including Jet, Essence & Black Enterprise. **Business Addr:** Founder & President, Chief Shoemaker, Etu Evans LLC, 45 Wall St Apt 1822, New York, NY 10005-1950, **Business Phone:** (212)706-1286.

**EVANS, DR. EVA L.**
School administrator. **Educ:** Wayne State Univ; Mich State Univ, MA, 1970, PhD, 1977. **Career:** Sch adminr, dep supt (retired); teacher; asst prin; elem educ dir; asst supt-personnel; instr dep supt; E Lansing Pub Schs, dep supt. **Orgs:** Bd dir, Alpha Kappa Alpha, nat comt chmn, chap officer, vpres, int pres, 1994-98; Lansing Community Col Found; Lansing/E Lansing Links Inc.

**EVANS, FAITH RENEE**
Singer, actor. **Personal:** Born Jun 10, 1973, Newark, NJ; daughter of Richard Swain and Helene Evans; married Kiyamma Griffin; children: Chyna; married The Notorious BIG; children: Christopher; married Todd Russaw; children: Joshua & Ryder. **Career:** Singer, songwriter, record producer & actress; Albums: Faith, 1995; Keep the Faith, 1998; Faithfully, 2001; Faithfully (Japan Bonus Track), 2002; The First Lady, 2005; A Faithful Christmas, 2005; Faith: Remixed, Unreleased & Featured, 2006; Something About Faith, 2010; R&B Divas, 2012; Incomparable, 2014; The King & I. Films: Turn It Up, 2000; The Fighting Temptations, 2003; Soul Kittens Cabaret, 2011. TV series: "Orange Bowl Parade", 1997; "All That", 1999; Half & Half, 2004. **Honors/Awds:** Lady of Soul Award, 1996; MTV Video Music Award, 1997 & 1999; Soul Train Award, 1998. Grammy Awards, Duo or Group, 1998; African American Literary Award, 2009. **Business Addr:** Singer, c/o Capitol Records Inc, 1750 N Vine St, Hollywood, CA 90028, **Business Phone:** (323)462-6252.

**EVANS, GREGORY JAMES**
Manager. **Personal:** Born Feb 15, 1954, Chicago, IL; son of Johnnie and Willie. **Educ:** Wilbur Wright Jr Col, AA, 1975; Southern IL Univ, BA, philos, 1977; Southern Ill Univ, MS, health educ, 1979; DePaul Univ, Chicago, Ill, PhD, philos, 1988; DeVry Univ, Keller Grad Sch Mgt, MBA, consumer econs, 2009. **Career:** Am Cancer Soc, dir pub educ, coord, 1980-82; Oak Pk YMCA, phys ed instr, 1982-84, Adult & Sr Leisure Serv, mgr, 1984-2005; Am Cancer Soc, publ ed dir, 1982; Health & Sports Prod, dir, 1982-84; Randolph Tower Fitness Ctr, mgr, 1983-84; Village Oak Pk, mgr adult educ, 1986-; Spec Event Entertainment Group, pres, 1989-; Pk Dist Oak Pk, mgr adult & lsr eisure serv, 1984-2005; SpecEvent Entertainment, pres, 1989-; USA Track & Field, Ill Asn, chairperson, long distance running, 1989-, educ dir, 2012-; Frank Lloyd Wright Races, race dir, currently; New York Life Ins Co, agt, 2006-12; Race Dir Univ, pres & chief exec officer, 2012-; Farmers Ins, agt, 2013-14; NeriumInternational, brand partner, 2014-; Prof Race Mgt, pres, 2014-. **Orgs:** Ahn's Tae Kwon Do Asn, 1978; ice hockey coach vol, Oak Pk Hockey Asn, 1980-81; gen mem, Ill Interagency Coun Smoking & Disease, 1980-83; Nat Pub Ed Ctr; Am Cancer Soc, 1980; vpres, Ill Soc Pub Health Ed, 1981-82; Oak Pk Area Jaycees, 1984-; Ill Pk & Recreation Asn, 1984-; Nat Youth Sport Coach Asn, 1987; Am Asn Phys, Health & Recreation, 1989; Chicago Conv Bur & Tourism, 1990; TAC Ill, Long Distance Running Comn, 1990; bd regent, Sch Sports Mgt, NC State Univ, 1992-95; regent, Sch Sports Mgt, 1991-; coordr, Rd Race Directions Conf; USA Track & Field Ill, 1992-. **Honors/Awds:** Semi-Pro Football Champs, Cook County Cowboys, 1981; Cultural Arts Award, Jack & Jill Asn Am W Suburban Chap, 1986. **Home Addr:** 18 Woodsorrel, Woodridge, IL 60517, **Home Phone:** (630)515-0888. **Business Addr:** President, Chief Executive

Officer, Race Director University, 1697 Charlotte Cir, Naperville, IL 60302, **Business Phone:** (630)327-1619.

**EVANS, DR. GROVER MILTON, SR.**
Government official, public speaker, consultant. **Personal:** Born Mar 6, 1952, Jonesboro, AR; son of William and Georgia Lee; married Helen; children: Grover Jr & Siobhan. **Educ:** Ark State Univ, BA, music & health educ, 1992, Regional Leaders Prog; LaSalle Univ, PhD, nutrit coun, 1995. **Career:** Motivational speaker, educr, bus consult; Jonesboro Sun, journalist, 1974-77; KXRQ, news dir, 1982-83; City Jonesboro, city councilman, 1984; vice mayor, City Jonesboro, 1984-96; Self employed, consult & motivational speaker, 1992-; State Ark, Disability Determination Social Security Admin, dir, 1996-2002; DDSSA, dir, 1996-2002; Ark Rehab Serv & Dept Human Serv, spec consult syst design, 2002-06, voc educr, 2002-10; Evans & Assocs Co Ark LLC, chief exec officer, pres & founder, 2005-; VoiceAmerica Talk Radio-WTR LLC, talk show host/speaker, 2012-; Articles: "Wellness, Goal Setting; Believing in Yourself"; "Being the Best and other topics". **Orgs:** Chmn, Ark State Spinal Cord Comn, 1989-99; comnr, Ark Martin Luther King Jr Comn, 1993; comnr, Early Childhood Comn, 1989-93; Ark Child Placement Adv Comt, 1987-; Consumer Adv Coun Rehab Serv, 1986-92; liaison, Nat Orgn Disabilities, 1986-; Jonesboro Chamber Com Educ Comt, 1995; US Water Fitness Asn Inc, vice chmn, 1993-; interim dir, Capital Zoning Comn; adv coun, Educ C with Disabilities; bd dir, Cent Ark Chap Am Red Cross Asn; chmn, Ark Early Childhood Comn; co-chair, Dr. Martin Luther King Jr. Comn; secy, Ark Lit Bd; Strategic Planning Bd, Pulaski Tech Col; City Little Rock Workforce Investment Bd; Olmstead Steering Comt; City Little Rock Workforce Investment Bd Youth Coun; Ark Injury Prev Coalition, Ark Dept Health; dir govt serv, Open Doors Orgn, 2010-; State's Pub Health Performance Stand Assessment Comt, currently; Ark Substance Abuse Comt; Ark Supported Housing Bd; Ark Alzheimer's Bd; Gospel Soc Today Comt & TEFRA Comt; exec comt, vice chair, City Little Rock Community Housing Adv Bd; Cent Ark United Way Bd; state chmn, Govt Agencies United Way; Adv Coun Educ C with Disabilities; Our Lady Good Coun Parish; 4th Degree Knights Columbus; Little Rock Christian Men's Club; Am Dietitian Asn, & Ark chap. **Home Addr:** 1616 Brookwood Dr, Little Rock, AR 72202, **Home Phone:** (501)296-1615. **Business Addr:** President, Founder, Evans & Associates of Arkansas LLC, 1613 Jennifer Dr, Little Rock, AR 72212-3827, **Business Phone:** (501)224-1114.

**EVANS, GWENDOLYN**
Executive, president (organization), chief executive officer. **Personal:** Born Jan 1, 1943?, NC; daughter of James L and Talmadge Whitley. **Educ:** Essex Col Bus, cert, 1965; Rutgers Univ, BS, 1973. **Career:** Prudential Ins Co, vpres, agency career develop, var admin, tech & clerical assignments, 1962-74; Col Rels, assoc mgr, 1974-75; Equal Opportunity Specialist, 1975-76, assoc mgr, corp personnel admin, 1976, mgr, field serv personnel, 1978-89; Calif & Idaho Locally Deployed Agents Proj, dir, 1989-90, vpres, career develop, 1990-93, vpres, sales support, 1993-95, vpres, urban mkt initiative, 1995-97; Strategy Plus Results Inc, chief exec officer & pres, bd gov, currently. **Orgs:** Hampton Inst Cluster Prog, Va, 1975-77, dir, serv personnel, 1978-; dir, field off planning, Prudential Ins Co, 1982-; exec comt, bd mem, Nat Community Prev Child Abuse NJ Chap, 1983-88; Am Soc Develop NJ Chap, 1984-85; charter mem, Educ Ctr Youth Newark; Women Unlimited; adv bd, Prevent Child Abuse; bd mem, Community Day Nursery. **Home Addr:** 27 Midland Blvd, Maplewood, NJ 07040. **Business Addr:** Chief Executive Officer, President, Strategy Plus Results Inc, 784 Morris Tpke Suite 339, Short Hills, NJ 07078, **Business Phone:** (973)762-2143.

**EVANS, HARRY, III**
Television broadcaster. **Personal:** Born Jan 1, 1956, Compton, CA. **Educ:** Univ Calif, Los Angeles, MA. **Career:** Baltimore-Wash mkt, radio host; That Show with Those Black Guys, host, exec producer & creator, 1994-2004. **Orgs:** Alpha Phi Alpha. **Honors/Awds:** George Foster Peabody Award, 1997; Cameo Award, 1998, 1999. **Business Addr:** Television Show Host, Executive Producer & Creator, That Show with Those Black Guys, PO Box 52, Simpsonville, MD 21150, **Business Phone:** (301)596-7575.

**EVANS, HUGH**
Manager, football player. **Personal:** Born Jan 1, 1943. **Educ:** NC Agr & Tech State Univ, grad, 1962. **Career:** San Francisco Giants, football player; Nat Basketball Asn, referee, 1972-2001, front off asst supvr, currently. **Honors/Awds:** Pro Football Hall of Frame, 2003. **Business Addr:** Assistant Supervisor, NBA Official, 645 5th Ave 15th Fl, New York, NY 10022-5986, **Business Phone:** (212)826-7000.

**EVANS, DR. JACK, SR.**
College president, educator. **Personal:** Born Jan 1, 1938, Houston, TX; married Patricia; children: Jack Jr, Herbert Raye & David Paul. **Educ:** Southwestern Christian Col, grad, 1959; Eastern NMex Univ, hist & relig, 1961; Univ Tex, MA, hist & Eng, 1963; Harding Univ, LLD; Pepperdine Univ, LLD; Abilene Christian Univ, LLD. **Career:** Col Church Christ, assoc minister, 1959; Southwestern Christian Col, dean & instr hist, 1963-67, pres, 1967-. **Orgs:** Bd bir, David Lipscomb Univ. **Honors/Awds:** LLD, Harding Univ; LLD, Pepperdine Univ; LLD, Abilene Christian Univ; Listed in Who's Who in American College and University Administration and Who's Who in Texas Today. **Special Achievements:** First African American President of the only predominantly black Christian College; author/editor of the Evans-Barr Debate, the Curing of Ham, the Cross or the Crescent, Sermons that Save, Sinai or Zion, The Two Covenants; and co-author with Dr James Maxell, of Divorce and Remarriage and with G P Holt, of Sermons of the Crusades. **Business Addr:** President, Southwestern Christian College, 200 Bowser Cir, Terrell, TX 75160, **Business Phone:** (972)524-3341.

**EVANS, JAMES L.**
Administrator. **Personal:** Born Nov 11, 1954, Columbus, OH; son of Darlene; children: Erika Briana & Alonzo James. **Educ:** Univ Ky, BS, 1976. **Career:** Ohio Secy State, press secy, 1983-87; Franklin County Dem Party, exec dir, 1987-90; WSMZ-FM, news dir & opers mgr, 1990-. **Orgs:** Sigma Delta Chi; Ohio Asn Broadcasters; Nab, Cent Ohio Chap. **Home Addr:** 1309 Woodnell Ave, Columbus, OH 43219, **Home Phone:** (614)253-5491. **Business Addr:** News Director, WSMZ-FM, 510 E Mound St, Columbus, OH 43215-5571, **Business Phone:** (614)469-1930.

**EVANS, JOSH (MIJOSHKI ANTWON EVANS)**
Football player. **Personal:** Born Sep 6, 1972, Langdale, AL; children: Morgan G & Joshua J. **Educ:** Univ Ala, Birmingham, grad. **Career:** Football player (retired); Houston Oilers, defensive tackle, 1995-96; Tenn Oilers, 1997, right defensive tackle, 1998; Tennessee Titans, left defensive tackle, 1999, defensive tackle & left defensive tackle, 2001; NY Jets, right defensive tackle, 2002, 2003, 2004.

**EVANS, KAMIEL DENISE**
School administrator. **Personal:** Born Jan 22, 1971, Wichita, KS; daughter of M D Fisher and Lois J Kempson; married Mario W; children: Kamerin Lydell & Marissa Lee. **Educ:** Butler County Community Col, attended 1990; Friends Univ, BA, sci, 1993; Wichita State Univ, MA, educ admin, 1999. **Career:** Wichita Pub Sch, teacher, 1993-97, admin intern, 1997-99, asst prin, 1999-2000, Jackson Elem Sch, prin, currently; Adams Elem Sch, prin. **Orgs:** Pres, 1993-95, vpres, 1998-99, Zeta Phi Beta Sorority; Sigma Zeta; St Mark UMC, Strengning Black Church for 21st Century, 1998; Wichita Asn Black Sch Educr, 1998-; Kans Women Educ Leadership, 1999; Am Cancer Soc Breast Cancer Awareness Comt, 1999; Grow Your Own Teacher Speaker's Bur, 1999; KS Asn Elem Schs Principals, 1999-2000. **Home Addr:** 13403 E Mustang Cir, Wichita, KS 67230-7587. **Business Addr:** Principal, Wichita Public School, 2717 N Woodlawn, Wichita, KS 67220, **Business Phone:** (316)973-1200.

**EVANS, LEE EDWARD**
Athlete, athletic coach. **Personal:** Born Feb 25, 1947, Madera, CA; married Princess. **Educ:** San Jose State Univ, attended 1970. **Career:** Nigeria & Saudi Arabia, coach, 1975-97; Nigerian Nat Team, phys fitness couns, coach, 1975-80; All-African Team, sprint coach, 1977; Wash Univ, sprint coach, 2002; Univ Ala, head coach, 2008. **Orgs:** Olympic Track Team, 1968 & 1972. **Home Addr:** 1625 Santa Clara St, Vallejo, CA 94590.

**EVANS, LEOMONT DOZIER**
Football player. **Personal:** Born Jul 12, 1974, Abbeville, SC; married Felicia; children: Kamyia, Cierra & Lemont Jr. **Educ:** Clemson Univ. **Career:** Football player (retired); Wash Redskins, 1996-97, strong safety, 1998, Free safety, Safety, 1999; Los Angeles Xtreme, 2001; Houston Texans, safety, 2002. **Home Addr:** 142 Runneymede Dr, Blythewood, SC 29016-9593.

**EVANS, LEON, JR.**
Insurance executive, consultant. **Personal:** Born Jan 8, 1953, Union Springs, AL; son of Leon Sr and Annie Ruth Beasley; married Nyle Denise Hallback; children: Andrea Lactrice & Carlos LaRoy. **Educ:** Tuskegee Univ, BS, 1977; Samford Univ, MBA, 1985. **Career:** Consultant, executive (retired); New Eng Bankcard Assoc, mgr trainee, 1973-75; John Hancock Ins Co, life underwriter, 1977-80; Renaissance Advan Off Controls, cert instr, 1986; Blue Cross & Blue Shield Ala, Internal Audit Div, consult & mgr. **Orgs:** Team leader, Big Bros Big Sisters Fund Dr, 1985; vpres, Groove Phi Groove Grad Chap, 1985; consult, Jr Achievement Birmingham, 1985-86; Nat Black MBA Asn, 1986-; fel Life Off Mgt Asn, 1987; Leadership Develop Asn, 1988-; Birmingham Urban League, 1988-; bd trustee, Gateway, bd dir, 2008-, legacy coun, 2013-14. **Honors/Awds:** Award for Outstanding Leadership Junior Achievement, 1986. **Home Addr:** 700 71st Pl S, Birmingham, AL 35206, **Home Phone:** (205)706-9805. **Business Addr:** Board of Director, Gateway, 1401 20th St S, Birmingham, AL 35205, **Business Phone:** (205)510-2600.

**EVANS, LEON EDWARD, JR.**
Banker. **Personal:** Born Dec 28, 1942, Chicago, IL; son of Leon E Sr; married Doris J Davis; children: Aaron Gerard & Sheila Rene. **Educ:** Wilson Jr Col, Park Col, assocs degree, gen studies, 1963; Park Univ, BA, bus admin, 1975. **Career:** Continental Ill Nat Bank Chicago, bookkeeping clerk, 1963-67; Independence Bank Chicago, asst cashier, 1967-69; Exchange Nat Bank Chicago, asst cashier, 1969-70; Gateway Nat Bank Chicago, vpres cashier, 1970-72; Douglas State Bank, vpres, cashier, 1972-75; Community Bank Nebr, pres & ceo, 1975-88; City Omaha, Off Mayor, econ develop aide, 1988-89; Bus Consult Specialists, consult, 1989-90; Am State Bank, exec vpres, 1990-92, pres, ceo, 1992-98; Bus Consult Specialist LLC, managing consult, owner, 1998-. **Orgs:** Am Bankers Asn, Community Bankers Coun; bd mem, Boys Town; bd mem, Okla Bankers Asn, 1995-96; bd mem, Metropolitan Tulsa Chamber Comm, 1996-98; bd mem, Am State Bank; bd mem, Conn Grad Sch Community Banking, Okla City Univ. **Home Addr:** 2201 N Rosedale Ave, Tulsa, OK 74127-2708, **Home Phone:** (918)587-3502.

**EVANS, DR. LEROY WINSTON**
Lawyer. **Personal:** Born Dec 15, 1946, Houston, TX; married Robbie Moore; children: Anana Salisha. **Educ:** Univ Houston, BBA, 1969; Univ Calif, Boalt Hall Sch Law, Berkeley, JD, 1972. **Career:** EE Worthing Scholar, 1965; Martin Luther King fel, 1969; Shear man & Steal, assoc, 1972-74; Emergency Land Fund, atty, gen couns, 1974-; Consortium Develop Rural, Southern E, exec dir, 1977-79; Small Farm Develop Corp, admin dir, 1979-. **Orgs:** Asst secy, treas, bd mem, Riverfront Enterprises Inc; Nat Conf Black Lawyers; LABA; bd mem, Southern E YMCA; Dekalb County Young Dem; Dekalb County Nat Asn Advan Colored People; Calif Bar Asn; NY Bar Asn; Practicing Law Inst; Sigma Iota Epsilon. **Honors/Awds:** Distinguished Mil Grad, 1969. **Home Addr:** 711 Flat Shoals Ave SE, Atlanta, GA 30316.

**EVANS, MARI**
Educator, writer, association executive. **Personal:** Born Jul 16, 1923, Toledo, OH; children: William Evan & Derek Reed. **Educ:** Univ Toledo; Marian Col, LHD, 1975. **Career:** Ind Univ-Purdue Univ Indianapolis, instr black lit & writer-in-residence, 1969-70; Ind Univ Bloomington, asst prof black lit & writer-in-residence, 1970-78; Northwestern Univ, vis asst prof, 1972-73; Nightstar, 1973-78 & 1981; Purdue Univ, W Lafayette, vis asst prof, 1978-80; Wash Univ, St Louis, vis asst prof, 1980; Cornell Univ, vis asst prof, 1981-83, asst prof, distinguished writer, 1983-85; State Univ NY-Albany, assoc prof, 1985-86; Miami Univ, Coral Gables, vis distinguished writer, 1989; Spelman Col, Atlanta, writer-in-residence, 1989-90; ed Black Women Writers, 1950-80: producer, dir & writer tv prog "The Black Experience", WTTV, Indianapolis, 1968-73; Books: forjuveniles, incl JD, Doubleday, 1973, I Look at Me, Third WorldPress, 1974, Singing Black, Reed Visuals, 1976, Jim Flying High, Doubleday, 1979; The Day They Made Beriani; playwright of "River of MySong", 1977, "Eyes" (musical), 1979, 1989, 1995; "Boochie", 1979, "Portrait of a Man" & "Glide & Sons" (musical); Auth of poetry: Nightstar, 1973-78; A Critical Eval, Doubleday-Anchor, 1984; Bks: Rap Stories, 1974, Dear Corinne, Tell Somebody!, 1999, Singing Black Alternative Nursery Rhymes C, 1998, Dark& Splendid Mass, 1992; How We Speak; Poems: The Gospel Singers, Where HaveYou Gone, "I Am a Black Woman", 1970; "Continuum, Black Classic Press", 2007. **Orgs:** Consult, Discovery Grant Prog, Nat Endowment Arts, 1969-70; consult ethnic studies, Bobbs-Merrill Co, 1970-73; chmn lit adv panel, Ind State Arts Comn, 1976-77; chmn, Statewide Comt Penal Reform; bd mgt, Fall Creek PkwyYMCA, 1975-81; bd dirs, 1st World Found; Ind Corrections Code Comn; African Heritage Studies Asn; Authors Guild; Authors League Am. **Honors/Awds:** Contrib poetry textbooks, anthologies & periodicals; John Hay Whitney fel, 1965-66; Woodrow Wilson Found grantee, 1968; Ind Univ Writers Conf Award, 1970; 1st Annual Poetry Award, Black Acad Arts & Letters, 1970; MacDowell Fel, 1975; Copeland Fel, Amherst Col, 1980; Nat Endowment Arts Grantee, 1981-82; Gwen Brooks Award, 1989, 1996; Du Sable Mus Award, 1989; Hazel J Bryant Award, Midwest African-Am Theatre Alliance; Zora Neale Hurston Soc Award, 1993; Alainhocke-Gwen Brooks Award, US Inc, 1995; Zora Nealst Hurston-Paul Robeson Award, Nat Coun Black Studies Inc, 1996. **Special Achievements:** Int Literary Hall Fame Writers African Descent. **Home Addr:** 3137 Broadway St, Indianapolis, IN 46205-3951, **Home Phone:** (317)926-5229.

**EVANS, MEREDITH**
Library administrator, college teacher, librarian. **Educ:** Clark Atlanta Univ, BA, 1994, MS, 2000; NC State Univ, MA, 2003; Univ NC, Chapel Hill, PhD, 2006. **Career:** Atlanta Tech Col, lead librn, 2003-05; Robert W. Woodruff Libr, Atlanta Univ Century, cur printed mat, 2005-08; San Jose State Univ, fac mem, 2006-08; Wayne State Univ, fac mem, 2008-11; Estelle & Melvin Gelman Libr, George Washington Univ, dir Spec Collections Res Ctr, 2008-12; Univ N Carolina Charlotte, assoc univ librn Spec Collections Dept & Digital Progs & Collections unit, 2012-14; Wash Univ St. Louis, assoc univ librn, 2014-15; Jimmy Carter Presidential Libr & Mus, dir, 2015-. **Orgs:** Asn Col & Res Libr; Nat Coun Pub Hist Study African Am Life & Hist; Zeta Phi Beta Soc; Am Libr Asn. **Honors/Awds:** Harvard Leadership Institute of Academic Librarians, 2009; Association of Research Libraries Leadership fellowship, 2013; United Negro College Fund/Carnegie-Mellon fellowship. **Special Achievements:** Contributor, "New Review of Academic Librarianship", 2015. **Business Addr:** Jimmy Carter Presidential Library & Museum, 441 Freedom Pkwy, Atlanta, GA 30307-1498, **Business Phone:** (404)865-7100.

**EVANS, MIJOSHKI ANTWON.** See EVANS, JOSH.

**EVANS, MIKE (MICHAEL LEEROYALL EVANS)**
Basketball coach, basketball player. **Personal:** Born Apr 19, 1955, Goldsboro, NC; married Kim; children: Michael, Rachelle & D'Ambra. **Educ:** Kans State Univ, attended 1978. **Career:** Basketball player (retired), basketball coach; San Antonio Spurs, prof basketball player, 1979-80; Milwaukee Bucks, 1980-82; Cleveland Cavaliers, 1982; Denver Nuggets, prof basketball player, 1983-88, asst coach, 1993-94, 1997, 2001-02, dir player personnel, TV anal, 1994-97, interim head coach, 2001; Toronto Raptors, scout, 2006-07, asst coach, 2007-09; Halifax Rainmen, coach, 2010-11; Moncton Miracles, coach, 2011-12. **Orgs:** Prog dir, Playing Peace. **Business Addr:** Basketball Coach, Moncton Miracles, 740 Rue Main St, Moncton, NB E1C 1E6, **Business Phone:** (506)204-7730.

**EVANS, MILTON L., SR.**
Chief executive officer. **Personal:** Born Oct 9, 1936, Snow Hill, NC; son of Herbert Jr and Lula Vines; married Alice Corella Brown; children: Milton Jr, Alan, Glenn, Warren & Kenneth. **Educ:** Shaw Univ, BS, chem, 1960; Tuskegee Inst, MS, chem, 1964. **Career:** Gen Elec, res & develop mktg mgt, 1964-73, sect mgr compacts, 1974-78, sect mgr strategic planning, gen mgr, specialty elastomers, 1980-82; Envisionetics Inc, pres, head; High Tech Systs Inc, pres & chief exec officer, 1983-; Tire Conversion Technologies Inc, vpres planning & technol, pres & chief exec officer, currently. **Orgs:** Dir, Siena Col Bus Coun; Outreach Inc; Schenectady Pvt Indust Coun; New York Head Injury Assn. **Home Addr:** 42 Shadow Wood Way, Ballston Lake, NY 12019, **Home Phone:** (518)877-8027. **Business Addr:** President, Chief Executive Officer, High Technology Systems Inc, PO Box 751, Clifton Park, NY 12065, **Business Phone:** (518)877-8027.

**EVANS, PATRICIA P.**
Educator. **Personal:** Born Topeka, KS; daughter of Lucille Mallory Phelps (deceased) and C Kermit Phelps; children: Langston Phelps, Kimberly Dawn & Kristina Ann. **Educ:** Avila Col, Kans City, MO, BSCh, 1961; Columbia Univ, attended 1972. **Career:** St Mary's Hos, Kansas City, Mo, med technologist, 1962-68; Univ Ill Med Ctr, Chicago, Ill, clin teaching asst & asst supvr hematol, 1968-71; Mt Sinai Hosp, New York, NY, asst supvr abnorm hematol, 1971-72; Veterans Admin Hosp, Madison WI, med technologist, 1974-75; St Mary's Hosp, Madison, WI, med technologist, 1977-81; Methodist Hosp, Madison, WI, med technologist, 1981-82; Univ Hosp & Clin, Madison, WI, proj specialist oncol res 1982-86; Carbone Cancer Ctr, proj specialist human oncol; Univ Wis, Dept Pathol & Lab Med, sr lectr, 1986, Dept Pathol & Lab Med, emer prof, currently. **Orgs:** Am Soc Clin Lab Sci, 1961-; Am Asn Blood Banks, 1962-; Am Soc Clin Pathologists, 1962-; AAAS, 1968-; Wis Asn Clin Lab Sci, 1972-; Madison Soc Clin Lab

Sci, 1977-; Shorewood League Bd, 1977-94; chairperson & bd mem, Jack & Jill Am, 1979-84; girl scout leader, Girl Scouts Am, 1982-88; parent mem, Boy Scouts Am, 1983-90; Ctr for Health Sci Minority Affairs Comt, 1988-94; co-chair, Mem Comt, Wis Soc Clin Lab Sci, 1988-90; bd mem, W High Sch PTSO, 1989-93; Parent Adv Comt, W High Sch, 1989-93; publicity chmn, Wis Soc Clin Lab Sci State Conv, 1990; Biol & Med Sci Area Rev Comt, 1990-93; vpres bd, Shorewood League Bd, 1990-91; pres, Shorewood League Bd, 1991-92; Ctr Health Scis Comn Women's Issues, 1992-98; Women Sci, Engineering & Math Comt, 1994-; nom-chair, Shorewood League Bd, 1994; Am Asn Univ Women, 1995-; Univ Wis-Madison Acad Advan Selection Comt, 1995-; Stud Appeals Comt Undergrad Prog Med Sch, 1997-; bd trustee, Am Soc Clin Lab Sci Educ & Res Fund, 1998; mentor, Univ Wis, Madison Acad Staff Prog, 1998-; Am Soc Clin Lab Sci Comt Prof Affairs, 1999-2003; Preliminary Rev Comt, 2005-11; Univ Wis Retirement Asn. **Home Addr:** 3223 Topping Rd, Madison, WI 53705, **Home Phone:** (608)238-7380. **Business Addr:** Professor Emeritus, University of Wisconsin-Madison Campus, 1300 Univ Ave, Madison, WI 53706, **Business Phone:** (608)262-2468.

## EVANS, PAUL F.

Police officer. **Educ:** Boston State Col, BS; Suffolk Univ Law Sch, LLB, 1978; Mass Inst Technol. **Career:** Police (retired), executive; Boston Police Dept, dir patrol, detectives & chief sr supt, 28-yr veteran, dir, comnr, 1993-2003; Police & Crime Stand Directorate, Brit, dir; GardaWorld, managing dir, currently; Vought Aircraft Industs Inc, Qual Engr Proj Lead; ImClone Systs Inc, supvr-mfg; Segway Inc, owner. **Orgs:** Bd dir, YMCA; Boston Police Athletic League; Police Exec Res Forum; Mass Bar Asn; Int Chiefs Police; Pine St Inn; Police Exec Res Forum. **Business Addr:** Managing Director, GardaWorld, 1390 Barre St, Montreal, QC H3C 1N4.

## EVANS, QUANELL RALPH. See X, QUANELL.

## EVANS, ROBERT ORAN (ROB EVANS)

Basketball coach, basketball player. **Personal:** Born Sep 7, 1946, Hobbs, NM; son of Oscar and Gladys; married Carolyn Ann Marshall; children: Damon LaMont & Amber Sharon (Clifford Massey). **Educ:** Lubbock Christian Col, AA, 1966; NMex State Univ, BS, eng, 1968. **Career:** Basketball player (retired), basketball coach; Houston Colt 45s, baseball player; Dallas Chaparrals; Oakland Raiders, wide receiver, 1968; NMex State Univ, asst basketball coach, 1969-76; Tex Tech Univ, asst basketball coach, 1976-90; Okla State Univ, asst basketball coach, 1990-92; Nat Asn asst Basketball Coaches, pres, 1991; Univ Miss, head basketball coach, 1992-98; Ole Miss, coach, 1997, 1998; Ariz State Univ, Men's Basketball, head coach, 1998-2006; Ark, asst coach, 2007-11; Tex Christian Univ, asst coach, 2011-12; Univ N Tex, asst head coach, 2012-. **Home Addr:** 3426 E Cherokee St, Phoenix, AZ 85044. **Business Addr:** Assistant Head coach, University of North Texas, 1155 Union Cir Suite 311277, Denton, TX 76203-5017, **Business Phone:** (940)565-2000.

## EVANS, ROXANNE J.

Journalist. **Personal:** Born Jun 6, 1952, Omaha, NE; daughter of James W Martin and Margaret L Steele; married Kelly Randolph; children: James, Imani, Askia & Joshua. **Educ:** Howard Univ, Wash, DC, 1976; Drake Univ, Des Moines, IA, BS, jour, 1982. **Career:** Nat Urban League, Wash, DC, res asst, 1975-76; Des Moines Regist, Des Moines, IA, reporter, 1978-83; Austin Am-Statesman, Austin, Tex, reporter, 1983-88, chief ed writer, 1988-93; Dep press secy, Gov Ann Richards, 1994-95; Tex Gen Land Off, dir publ/environ educ, 1995-99; Tex Am Fedn Teachers, pub rels dir, 1999-2002; Dc Pub Schs, chief commun officer, 2004-06; Our Tex Mag, Ed-at-Large; Austin Independent Sch Dist, Commun Specialist, currently; Evans Commun Ltd, commun prof, 2011-; co-ed-in-chief, Tex Black Hist Preserv Proj, currently. **Orgs:** Pres, Austin Asn Black Communicators, 1989-; Soc Prof Journalists; Nat Asn Black Journalists. **Honors/Awds:** Texas School Bell Award, Tex State Teachers Asn, 1985-88; Phoenix Award, Friends of Phoenix, 1984; Investigative Reporting award, Iowa Associated Press Managing Editor. **Business Addr:** Editorial Writer, Austin American-Statesman, 166 E Riverside Dr, Austin, TX 78767, **Business Phone:** (512)445-3655.

## EVANS, RUTHANA WILSON

Association executive, educator, consultant. **Personal:** Born Mar 26, 1932, Roxie, MS; daughter of James (deceased) and Lueberta (deceased); married Lit Parker Jr; children: Cedric Glenn & Valerie Denise. **Educ:** Tougaloo Col, BS, 1955; Univ Ill, BA, 1965; NC Col, attended 1967; Delta State Col, MS, 1971; Delta State Univ, MS, psychometrist, 1977, AAA Coun, 1981; Admin Coursework, AA. **Career:** Consult; Shaw Sch, elem teacher, 1955-57; Nailor Elem Sch, teacher, curric chmn, 1957-60, teacher, librn, 1960-62, librn, 1963-64; Pre-sch Story Hour, librn, 1964-66; Bolivar County Dist 4, libr supvr, 1965-67; TV Jackson, ed, curric resources teacher, 1968-70; Parks & Pearman Elem Schs, librn, 1968-70, Org elem sch libr prog, 1969; Greenville Elem Sch, consult, 1970; MS Head Start, educ dir, 1970-79; Bolivar County Dist 4 Schs Titles I, counr, 1979-94; Bolivar County Headstart, psychometrist, 1985-94; Bolivar Schs, psychometrist; Cleveland Schs testing cord, 1986, consult, 1995; St Paul Baptist Church, grant writing networker; Bolivar County Community Action Prog Inc, consult, currently. **Orgs:** PTA, 1955; secy, Negro's Citizens Community Cleveland, 1957-61; job trainer, Neighborhood Youth Corps Cleveland, 1969; Nat Asn Advan Colored People; Phi Delta Kappa; Tougaloo Alumni Delta State Alumni; org inventory, classification systs, Head Start, 1970; ms personnel & guid Assoc, ms libr asn; trainer manpower prog, STEP, 1970-; secy, Womens Club, 1970; from treas to pres, Athena Soc Club, 1971-73; consult, Ind Pre-sch Activ, 1971; active, BSA; negro voters league, Baptist Training Union Cleveland, 1972-; treas, E Side HS Band Booster, 1972; Nat Coun Black Child Develop, 1975-78; CETA, 1977; MS Counsrs Assoc; Nat Educ Assoc; secy, St Paul Baptist Church; lay bd mem, Jake Ayers Case; Am Couns Asn; Delta Sigma Theta Sorority Inc. **Honors/Awds:** First runner-up to Miss, Tougaloo Col, 1955. **Home Addr:** 816 Cross St, Cleveland, MS 38732, **Home Phone:** (662)843-4741. **Business Addr:** Consultant, Bolivar County Community Action Program Inc, 810 E Sunflower Rd Suite 120, Cleveland, MS 38732, **Business Phone:** (662)846-1491.

## EVANS, STACEY LYN. See MORGAN, STACEY EVANS.

## EVANS, DR. THERMAN E.

Chief executive officer, physician, health services administrator. **Personal:** Born Aug 20, 1944, Henderson, NC; son of Irvin Sr and Constine; married Bernetta Jones; children: Thomas E Jr & Clayton. **Educ:** Howard Univ, BS, 1966, MD, 1971; United Christian Col, BA, MA, PhD, theol, 1999. **Career:** Oper PUSH, nat health dir; E River Health Ctr Wash, physician; Howard Univ, clin fac, asst prof; Univ Calif, vis Regents scholar; wash bur chief; CT GenIns Co, 2nd vpres & corp med dir; CIGNA, asst med dir, 1979-83, corp med dir, 1983-87, vpres & corp med dir, 1987; Whole Life Assocs Inc, founder & chief exec officer, 2004-; Author: What Are the Leading Causes of Life? A Prescription for Living at Your Highest and Best; How to Keep People From Getting On Your Last Nerve: A Prescription for Managing Stress; What In Hell Do You Want? A Prescription for the Spiritual Strength to Live Heaven on Earth; From Purpose to Promise Driven Life: A Prescription for Making the Difference You Were Born to Make; Co-Author: Lighten Up; Staying Strong. **Orgs:** Nat bd dir, Oper PUSH, 1983, rev & adv comt, var agencies Fed Govt; pres, bd dir, Wash DC Bd Educ; pres, Oper PUSH, Philadelphia Chap, 1983-86; bd dir, Southeastern PA Wellness Coun, 1987-88, Philadelphia Health Mgt Corp, 1988-; pastor, Morning Star Community Christian Ctr, 1998-99, sr pastor, 1990-; bd dir, Wellness Coun Am; bd dir, Nat Asn Health Serv Execs. **Home Addr:** 906 Rock Lane, Elkins Park, PA 19027, **Home Phone:** (215)576-8319. **Business Addr:** Founder, Chief Executive Officer, Whole Life Associates Inc, 1009 Chandler Ave, Linden, NJ 07036, **Business Phone:** (908)925-7979.

## EVANS, TIMOTHY C.

Judge. **Personal:** Born Jun 1, 1943. **Educ:** Univ Ill, BA, 1965; John Marshall Law Sch, JD, 1969. **Career:** Chicago Dept Invests, former dep comnr; Secy State Off, Cook County, Ill, chief hearing officer, 1973; Chicago, Ill, city alderman, 4th ward, 1973-91; atty, pvt pract, 1991-; Cook City Circuit Ct, chief judge, 2001-. **Orgs:** Chmn, Chicago City Coun. **Honors/Awds:** The 4Unsuccessful bid for mayor, Chicago, Ill, gen election, Harold Washington Party, 1989. **Special Achievements:** First black Chief Judge of the Cook County Circuit Court in Chicago; Became the first judge from Illinois to receive the William H. Rehnquist Award for Judicial Excellence from the National Center for State Courts, 2009; 10 Attorneys Who Raised The Bar Over the Last Decade, Chicago Daily Law Bulletin, 2010. **Home Addr:** 5040 S Ellis Ave, Chicago, IL 60615-2712, **Home Phone:** (773)624-4079. **Business Addr:** Chief Judge, Circuit County of Cook County, 50 W Wash St Suite 2600, Chicago, IL 60602, **Business Phone:** (312)603-6000.

## EVANS, VERNON D.

Auditor, accountant. **Personal:** Born Mar 7, 1950, Ft. Worth, TX; son of Rev Dellie (deceased) and Thelma; married Viola Ruth Cross; children: Victor, Vinikka McCoy, Vernessa Bowie & Shadetra Johnson; married Debbara. **Educ:** N Tex State Univ, BBA, MBA, acct, 1972. **Career:** Ernst & Ernst Cert Pub Acct, staff acct, sr acct, 1972-76; Cert Pub Acct, 1973; Ernst & Whinney, audit mgr & supvr, 1972-82; Evans McAfee & Co, managing partner, 1976-78; Cert Mgt Acct, 1980; Ft Worth Independent Sch Dist, chief internal auditor, 1982-86; Cert Internal Auditor, 1985; Ft Worth Int Airport Bd, Dallas, Tex, dir audit serv, 1986-94, dep exec dir admin serv, exec vpres & chief financial officer; Cert Fraud Examr, 1989; San Diego County Regional Airport Authority, vpres, treas & chief financial officer, 2003-. **Orgs:** Nat Asn Accountants, 1974-80; chair, United Way Allocation Com III, 1979-80; vpres, Nat Asn Black Accountants, 1979-81, pres, 1981-83; chmn, McDonald YMCA, 1980; treas, Metro Econ Develop Corp, 1980; dir-at-large, chmn, Southern Regional Dir, 1987-90, N Am Regional Dirs Comt, 1991-94; state dir, Tex Soc Cert Pub Accountants, 1988-90; founder & pres, Asn Airport Internal Auditors, 1989-91; Tex State Bd Pub Accountancy, vice chmn, 1991-98; adv bd, TCU, 1992-; bd trustee, Prof Develop Inst, 1992-; Inst Internal Auditors; Asn Govt Accountants; Govt Fin Officers Asn; Nat Forum Black Pub Adminr; acct dept ad bd, N Tex State Univ; bd dir, Ft Worth Black Chamber Com; bd dir, Day Care Asn; Jackie Robinson, YMCA, San Diego, CA; vpres, Ft Worth Chap. **Honors/Awds:** Outstanding Achievement Award, Sickle Cell Anemia Asn Tex, 1979; Outstanding Achievement Award, Nat Asn Black Accountants, 1979, 1987; Greek Image Award, Pan-Hellenic Coun, 1983; Henry A Meadows Volunteer of the Year Award, YMCA-MFW, 1983; Outstanding Service Awards, McDonald YMCA, 1985; Outstanding Service Awards, United Negro Col Fund, 1986; Chi Rho Award, YMCA-MFW, 1988; F M Miller Award, McDonald YMCA, 1989; National Achievement Award, Nat Asn Black Accountants, 1989; Outstanding Regional Director Award, Inst Internal Auditors, 1990; CPA of the Year Award, Fort Worth Chap Tex Soc CPA, 1990; Outstanding Professional Achievement, Fort Worth Chap Nat Asn Black Accountants, 1992; Outstanding Leadership, United Negro Col Fund, 1994; Earnest Anderson Award, McDonald YMCA, 1994; CFO of the Year, San Diego Business Journal, 2008. **Home Addr:** 808 Firewheel Trl, Ft Worth, TX 76112, **Home Phone:** (817)446-7200. **Business Addr:** Vice President & Treasurer, Chief Financial Officer, San Diego County Regional Airport Authority, PO Box 82776, San Diego, CA 92138-2776, **Business Phone:** (619)400-2880.

## EVANS, W. FRANKLIN

Educator, college president. **Personal:** Born Augusta, GA. **Educ:** Univ Ga, BS, entom, 1984; Ga State Univ, PhD, higher educ admin, 1994. **Career:** Tenn State Univ, asst dean/dir pub serv, 1998-2001; Drake State, dean, 2001-06; Elizabeth City State Univ, assoc vice chancellor acad affairs, 2006-08; Va Union Univ, vpres acad affairs, 2008-12; SC State Univ, vpres acad affairs, 2012-13, actg pres, 2013, interim provost, 2013-; Voorhees Col, pres, currently. **Orgs:** Nat Asn Advan Colored People; Black Family Preserv Group Inc; Nat Asn Black Sch Educr; Partnership a Drug-free Community; Toastmasters Int; adv bd mem, Black Family Preserv Group Inc; adv bd mem, Nat Asn Black Sch Educr; adv bd mem, Partnership a Drug-free Community; adv bd mem, Phi Mu Alpha Sinfonia; adv bd mem, Toastmasters Int; adv bd mem, chap pres; secy; assoc ed; area dir, coordr, Alpha Phi Alpha Fraternity Inc; Sickle Cell Asn; Boys & Girls Club. **Business Addr:** Interim President, South Carolina State University, 300 Col St NE, Orangeburg, SC 29117, **Business Phone:** (803)536-7000.

## EVANS, WARREN CLEAGE

Educator, lawyer, sheriff. **Personal:** Born Dec 30, 1948, Detroit, MI; son of E Warren and Gladys H Cleage; children: Erikka N & Nikki Lynn. **Educ:** Madonna Univ, Livonia, MI, BA, social sci, 1975; Univ Detroit Mercy, MA, criminal justice, 1987; Detroit Col Law, Detroit, MI, JD, 1987. **Career:** Wayne County Sheriffs Dept, dep officer, 1970, undersheriff, 1987-91; Univ Detroit Mercy, asst prof, 1988; Wayne County Comn, dir admin, 1991-92; Wayne County Prosecutor's Off, chief spec opers, 2002-03; City Detroit, police chief; Wayne County, sheriff, 2003-; Wayne Countys Dept Community Justice, dir; Univ Mich, staff, currently; Huron-Clinton Metrop Authority Bd Commissioners, gov, currently; Wayne County exec. **Orgs:** Pres, Detroit Bd Water Comners, 1989-. **Home Addr:** 14620 Scripps, Detroit, MI 48215, **Home Phone:** (313)824-2013. **Business Addr:** Governor, Huron-Clinton Metropolitan Authority, 13000 High Ridge Dr, Brighton, MI 48114-9058, **Business Phone:** (800)477-2757.

## EVANS, DR. WEBB. See Obituaries Section.

## EVANS, DR. WILLIAM E.

Educational consultant, educator, executive. **Personal:** Born Nov 28, 1931, Mebane, NC; son of Mozelle; married Gloria Battle. **Educ:** Hampton Inst, BS, 1954; Southern Conn St Col, MS, 1961; Bridgeport Univ, attended 1964; Yale Univ, Drug Educ, 1971; Univ Conn, PhD, 1985. **Career:** Educational consultant (retired); Laurel Ledge Sch, Beacon Falls Conn, teacher, 1957-58; Barnard Sch, Waterbury Conn, teacher, 1958; elem physical educ instr, 1958-59; Wilby High Sch, Waterbury Conn, phys ed & biol instr, 1958-67; Project Upward Bound, Univ Hartford, reading instr, 1966-67, curriculum coordr & reading instr, 1967-68, asst project dir, 1968-72; Community Action Agency, Waterbury, 1967; Waterbury Sch System, supvr health & physical educ, 1967-72; Waterbury Pub Sch, drug coordr, 1971; Mattatuck Community Col, Psychol Dept, 1971-72; Waterbury Dept Educ, dir educ grants, 1972-90; Waterbury Tercentennial Inc, stud coordr; New Opportunities Waterbury, Conn, educ consult; Univ Conn, educ consult. **Orgs:** Nat Asn Advan Asn Colored People; bd incorporator, Boy's Club Am; First United Bapt Church, deacon. **Honors/Awds:** Hampton Alumni Fel, 1967; Outstanding Alumnus Award, Hampton Inst, 1974; Univ Conn Found Fel, 1984. **Home Addr:** PO Box 264, Bena, VA 23018-0264, **Home Phone:** (804)642-0306.

## EVANS-TRANUMN, DR. SHELIA

School administrator. **Personal:** Born Aug 19, 1951, Durham, NC; daughter of George Watts Sr and Eunice Allen; married Howard James Jr; children: DeAnna. **Educ:** NC Cent Univ, Durham, NC, BA, eng, 1973; Long Island Univ, Brooklyn, NY, MA, eng, 1977; NY Univ, PhD, eng. **Career:** New York Bd Educ, Auxiliary Servs High Schs, dir, 1973-; NY Educ Dept, Off Sch & Community Serv, assoc comnr, assoc comnr educ emer, 1993-2010; United Fedn Teachers, New York charter sch, educ consult, 2011-, exec dir, currently. **Orgs:** Pres, New York Alliance Black Sch Educr, 1986-; Chancellor's Adv Comt Promote Equal Opportunity, 1987-; founder & dir, Educr Christ, AME Church, 1988-; chairperson, Multicultural Adv Bd, New York Bd Educ, 1988-; minister educ, Bridge St AME Church, 1988-; Delta Sigma Theta Sorority Inc; trustee, 2003-, chair, 2011-13, Casey Family Progs; Chair, Bd dir Nat Coun Educating Black C; bd trustee, Phelps Stokes Fund. **Home Addr:** 316 E 57th St, Brooklyn, NY 11203, **Home Phone:** (718)629-9240. **Business Addr:** Executive Director, United Federation of Teachers Charter Schools New York, 52 Broadway 10th Fl, New York, NY 10004, **Business Phone:** (212)598-6800.

## EVANZZ, KARL ANDERSON (KARL EVAN ANDERSON)

Editor, writer, journalist. **Personal:** Born Jan 16, 1953, St. Louis, MO; son of Adolphus Anderson and Bernice; married Alexandra Jane Hamilton; children: Aqila, Aaron, Kanaan, Arianna & Adrian. **Educ:** Westminster Col, BA, 1975; Am Univ, Wash Col Law, 1977. **Career:** St Louis Argus, nat corresp, 1974-80; Law Offs Lowe, Mark & Moffitt, law clerk, 1975-76; Harry T Alexander, law clerk, 1977-80; The Wash Post, news aide, staff writer; researcher, 1980-2008, on-line ed, 1986-; Books: The Messenger: The Rise & Fall Elijah Muhammad, author; I Am The Greatest Quotes Muhammad Ali, author; The Judas Factor: The Plot to Kill Malcolm X, author; Poetry: "Crevice of Illusion, " 1975; "The Judas Factor: The Plot to Kill Malcolm X, " 1992; "Elijah Muhammad: A Biography, " Pantheon, 1997; New Wave Books, publisher, 2008-. **Orgs:** Nat Newspaper Guild, 1980-; Nat Asn Black Journalists, 1992-95. **Honors/Awds:** Grant, Fund for Investigative Journalism, 1991. **Special Achievements:** Poetry published in Southern Exposure Mag, 1971; First Place Prize, for poetry, Proud Mag, St Louis, MO, 1970, 1971; Appeared on The Oprah Winfrey Show & MSNBC. **Home Addr:** PO Box 296, Ashton, MD 20861-0296. **Business Addr:** On-Line Editor, Washington Post, 1150 15th St NW 4th Fl News, Washington, DC 20071, **Business Phone:** (202)334-6000.

## EVE, ARTHUR O.

Government official. **Personal:** Born Mar 23, 1933, New York, NY; married Constance Bowles; children: Arthur Jr, Leecia Roberta, Eric Vincent, Martin King & Malcolm X. **Educ:** Erie Comm Col, Assoc; WVa State Univ, BS. **Career:** Government official (retired); NY State Assembly, assemblyman, 1966-79, dep speaker, 1979-2003; Ny Black & Puerto Rican Legis Caucus, founder, chmn, 1975-76; Western New York Legis Del, dean; State wide Leadership Summit, architect, 1993. **Orgs:** Chmn, NY State Black & Puerto Rican Leg Caucus, 1975-76; dep speaker, Assembly, 1979; founder, Black Develop Found & Black Bus Develop Corp; formed, Minority Coalition; Roswell Pk Inst; life mem, Nat Advan Asn Colored People; founder, former chmn, Northern Region Black Polit Caucus; founder, chmn, Buffalo Youth Planning Coun; Comt Aging, Comt Rules& Ways; chmn, Ny Chap Nat Rainbow Coalition; Ny Black & Puerto Rican Legis Caucus. **Honors/Awds:** President's Distinguished Service Award, State Univ New York, Buffalo, 1982; Legislator of the Decade Award, Hunters Col, 1984; leadership Award, ET Marshall Scholarship Foundation, 1986; Distinguished Leadership in Arts-in-Education Awards, Kennedy Ctr,

1988; Malcolm X Leadership Award, African People's Christian Orgn, 1991; Achievement Award, NY State Minorities Corrections Inc, 1992; Leadership Legislative Award, New York Asn Sch Psychol, 1992; Adam Clayton Powell Award, 2000. **Special Achievements:** First African American to win the Buffalo Mayoral Democratic Primary. **Home Addr:** 184 Jewett Pkwy, Buffalo, NY 14214, **Home Phone:** (716)832-3469.

### EVE, CONSTANCE B. (CONSTANCE BOYLES EVE)

Chairperson. **Personal:** Born Jul 14, 1932, Havoco, WV; daughter of George Bowles and Roberta; married Arthur O; children: Leecia Roberta, Arthur O Jr, Eric Vincent, Martin King & Malcolm X. **Educ:** WVa State Col, BA, eng & drama; New York Univ, MA. **Career:** New York Univ, asst libr, res div; Bennett Col Women, asst prof, eng & drama, dir, little theater; Erie Community Col, prof eng, prof emer eng; Buffalo Pub Schs, instr eng; Women Human Rights & Dignity Inc, chmn & founder, 1980-. **Orgs:** Chair stewardship, mem vestry, St Philip's Episcopal Church; Episcopal Diocese Horns Plenty Concert; bd dir, Martin House Restoration Corporation; Buffalo Chapter Links; Alpha Kappa Alpha Sorority; Buffalo Coun Churches. **Honors/Awds:** Martin Luther King Award, Alpha Kappa Alpha & Gamma Psi Omega; Outstanding Citizen of New York State Award, Bd Trustees State Univ New York, Albany; Citizen of the Year, Buffalo Eve News, 1997; Western New York Leader Award, YMCA, 1997; Outstanding Women in Ministry Award, Westchester Black Women's Caucus, 1997; The Western New York Women's Hall of Fame Award; Mary B Talbert Civic Award, 1998; Western New York Womens Hall of Fame Award; Nat United Way Alexis de Tocqueville Society Award, 1998. **Special Achievements:** Mrs. Eve is featured in the 1998 Fall Issue of Jet Magazine; Issue of Essence Magazine; Nominated for the 1999 National Conference for Community and Justice Citation Award. **Business Addr:** Founder, Chairperson, Women for Human Rights and Dignity Inc, 2278 Main St, Buffalo, NY 14214, **Business Phone:** (716)831-9821.

### EVE, ERIC V.

Public relations executive. **Personal:** married Felicia Stenhouse; children: 3. **Educ:** Hobart Col, BA; City Univ NY, Baruch Col, MA, polit mgt. **Career:** White House, spec asst pres, polit affairs, 1995-97; William Jefferson Clinton, asst polit affairs; Verizon Commun, vpres, 1996-2004; Citigroup, head community rels, exec dir & sr vpres community rels, 2004-10; City New York, fiscal off, chief operating officer, dep comptroller, 2010-12; RLM Finsbury, partner, 2012-15, sr advisor, 2015-; Ichor Strategies, founder & chief exec officer, 2015-. **Orgs:** Bd mem, Fel Cong Black Caucus Found Inc; bd trustee, bd mem, Brooklyn Pub Libr; bd mem, Hobart & William Smith Cols; bd mem, Union Theol Sem; bd mem, Vestry Trinity Wall St. **Business Addr:** Chief Executive officer, Founder, Ichor Strategies, 437 Madison Ave, New York, NY 10022, **Business Phone:** (646)484-5801.

### EVERETT, CHARLES ROOSEVELT

Manager. **Personal:** Born Dec 2, 1962, Philadelphia, PA; son of Charles R Sr and Precola C Aldrich; married Jean S; children: Christian C & Adrian F. **Educ:** Univ Pa, BA, urban studies & transp planning, 1984. **Career:** Gannett Fleming Transp Engrs, trans planning engr, 1985-88; Woolpert Consults, proj mgr, trans planning, 1989-91; Syracuse Metro Transp Coun, dir, 1991-94; Syracuse Hancock Int Airport, NY, Dept Aviation, aviation comnr, 1994-2002, dir city opers, 2002-; City Syracuse, Dir City Opers, 2002-05; Everett & Assocs LLC, pres & managing prin, 2004-08; Fed Aviation Admin, Dept Transp, Planning & Environ Div, Off Assoc Admin Airports, mgr nat planning & environ div, 2006-08, cong liaison, 2009-11; Tran-Systems Corp, vpres, 2008-09; AFCO AvPORTS Mgt LLC, airport gen mgr, 2011-13; Lehigh-Northampton Airport Authority, exec dir, 2013-. **Orgs:** Transp Res Bd, 1987-; treas, NY Upstate Sect, Inst Transp Engrs, 1993-94, secy, 1995, vpres, 1996, pres, 1997; Am Asn Airport Execs, 1994-; NY Aviation Mgt Asn, 1996-, vpres, 1997, pres, 1998-99; pres, Aviation Aerospace Educ Found, 1997-; Nat Soc Black Engrs; US Air Force ROTC Detachment 750; Airports Coun Int-N Am; bd mem, Am Asn Airport Execs; Asn Strategic Planning; Am Inst Aeronaut & Astronaut; sr mem, Aviation Coun Pa; bd mem, Int Coun Airshows. **Honors/Awds:** Past Presidents Award, New York Aviation Mgt Asn, 1998-99; Bill Shea Award, New York Aviation Mgt Asn, 2004. **Special Achievements:** Planning, Development & Operation of a Deicing Fluid Collection & Treatment System, Deicing Int Conf, UK, 1997, "Winter Operations, Regulators and Water Quality," "Terminal Expansion and Renovation: Discover The Airport," FAA Airports Conference, 1997, Syracuse Intl Airshow, USAF Thunderbirds, 1997, Syracuse Intl Airshow, Canadian Forces Snowbirds, 1998. Publications: Reconsidering the Airport Business Model, J Airport Mgt, 2014. **Home Addr:** 225 Lincoln Pk Dr, Syracuse, NY 13203-3114, **Home Phone:** (315)425-9648. **Business Addr:** Executive Director, Lehigh-Northampton Airport Authority, 3311 Airport Rd, Allentown, PA 18109-3040, **Business Phone:** (610)266-6000.

### EVERETT, CYNTHIA A.

Lawyer, district attorney, government official. **Personal:** Born Jan 1, 1958, Manchester, CT. **Educ:** Fla State Univ, BA, govt, 1978; George Washington Univ, Nat Law Ctr, JD, 1982. **Career:** Dade Co State Atty's Off, supv atty; Miami Dist, asst US atty; Us Attys Off Southern Dist Fla; City Opa Locka City Atty, atty; owner, Atty, 1999-. Village Pinecrest Fla, village atty, currently. **Orgs:** Women Lawyers Div, 1989-91; Fla Bar Asn, 1992-95; treas, Fla Chap Nat Bar Asn, 1993-; bd govs, Fla Bar Asn, 1994-; bd trustee, United Way Dade Co, 1994-; Nat Asn Advan Colored People; Miami Partners Progress; pres, Black Lawyers Asn Dade Co; Fla Asn Women Lawyers; chair, Rules Community; pres, Nat Bar Asn; Dade Co Chap; Community Stud Educ & Admis Bar; Fla Bar Bd Gov; Fla Munic Attys Asn Steering Comt; Fla & Dc Bars; S Fla Legal Guide, S Flas Top Attorneys Labor & Employ & Munic Law, 2005-. **Business Addr:** Village Attorney, Government attorney, Village Of Pinecrest Florida, 12645 Pinecrest Pkwy, Pinecrest, FL 33054-3596, **Business Phone:** (305)234-2121.

### EVERETT, ESQ. J. RICHARD

Lawyer. **Personal:** Born Oct 2, 1936, Montezuma, IN; married Bernice Knowings; children: Jocelyn & Jeannenn. **Educ:** Morehouse Col, BS, 1960; St John's Univ, Law Sch, LLB, 1967; Patent Off Patent Acad, US, 1968. **Career:** Lawyer (retired); Food & Drug Admin, anal chemist, 1961-66; Food & Legal Officer, 1966-77; Eastman Kodak Co, admin asst, 1974-76; US Patent Off, patent exam, 1967-69, patent atty, 1969-79, sr patent atty, 1980-90; patent counr, 1990-99. **Orgs:** Am Intellectual Property Asn; Monroe Co Bar Asn; Rochester Patent Law Asn; Nat Bar Asn; vol, Nat Patent Law Asn; NY City Bar Asn; Monroe Co Bar Asn. **Honors/Awds:** Wiley A Branton Award, Nat Bar Asn. **Special Achievements:** Only African American patent attorney at Kodak from 1970-85. **Home Addr:** 1 Circle Wood Rd, Rochester, NY 14625. **Business Addr:** 934 Bay Ridge Ave, Annapolis, MD 21403.

### EVERETT, ESQ. RALPH B.

Lawyer. **Personal:** Born Jun 23, 1951, Orangeburg, SC; son of Alethia Hilton and Francis G S Jr; married Gwendolyn Harris; children: Jason G (Heidi Jackson). **Educ:** Morehouse Col, BA, 1973; Duke Univ Law Sch, JD, 1976. **Career:** US Supreme Ct, law pract; NC Dept Justice, assoc atty gen, 1976; NC Dept Labor, admin asst legal affairs, 1976-77; Sen Fritz Hollings, spec asst, 1977-78, legis asst, 1977-83; US Senate, Comm Com, Sci & Transp, atty, dem chief coun & staff dir, 1983-89; US Senate, Comm Com, sci & transp chief coun & staff dir, 1987-89; Paul Hastings, Janofsky & Walker LLP, partner, 1989-2006, Fed Legis Pract Group, co-chair; US Int Telecommunications Union Plenipotentiary Conf, ambassador, 1998; ITU's Second World Telecommunication Develop Conf, vchmn; Joint Ctr Polit & Econ Studies, pres & cheif exec officer, 2007-13; Georgetown Ctr Bus & Pub Policy, sr indust & innovation fel, 2015-. **Orgs:** NC & DC Bars; US Ct Appeals DC Ct; US Tax Ct; US Ct Claims; US Supreme Ct; bd dir, Cumulus Media Inc; bd dir, Shenandoah Life Ins Co; Am Bar Asn; Alpha Phi Alpha; Alumni Bd Visitors, Duke Unv Law Sch; trustee, Nat Urban League; Ctr Nat Policy; Phi Beta Kappa; Phi Alpha Theta Int Hon Soc Hist; secy, Bd Ctr Nat Policy; Press Bd Advisors Historically Black Cols & Univs; vchmn, Commonwealth Va Waste Mgt Bd; chair, bd trustee, Hist Alfred St Baptist Church; Econ Club Wash; bd trustee, Va Sci Mus; Alpha Phi Alpha Fraternity. **Honors/Awds:** Earl Warren Legal Scholar; 150 Most Influential African Americans, Ebony mag. **Special Achievements:** The first African American to receive a partnership at the Paul Hastings, Janofsky & Walker LLP law firm. In 1982, Mr. Everett became the First African American to head a U.S. Senate Committee Staff, when he was appointed by Senator Ernest F. Hollings (D-SC) to be the Democratic staff director & minority chief counsel of the Committee on Commerce, Science & Transportation. **Home Addr:** 9310 Ludgate Dr, Alexandria, VA 22309-2740, **Home Phone:** (703)780-9492. **Business Addr:** Senior Industry, Innovation Fellow, Center for Business and Public Policy, Rafik B Hariri Bldg 37th O St NW, Washington, DC 20057, **Business Phone:** (202)687-3686.

### EVERETT, THOMAS GREGORY

Football player, athletic coach. **Personal:** Born Nov 21, 1964, Daingerfield, TX. **Educ:** Baylor Univ, BS, health & phys educ; Cooper Inst, biomechanics strength training. **Career:** Football player (retired), athletic coach; Pittsburgh Steelers, 1987-91; Dallas Cowboys, 1992-93; Tampa Bay Buccaneers, 1994-95; Thomas Everett Athletics, sports performance dir, sports performance specialist & athletic develop coach, currently. **Business Addr:** Athletic Development Coach, Sports Performance Specialist, Thomas Everett Athletics, Dallas, TX 75277, **Business Phone:** (214)803-2727.

### EVERS, JAMES CHARLES

Executive, government official, mayor. **Personal:** Born Sep 11, 1922, Decatur, MS; son of Jesse Wright and James; married Nannie Laurie; children: Pat, Carolyn, Eunice, Sheila & Charlene. **Educ:** Alcorn State Univ, BS, 1951. **Career:** Fayette, MS, mayor, 1969-89; MS State Senate, cand, 1975; MS, cand, gov, 1971; MS Nat Asn Advan Colored People, field secy, 1963-69; US House Reps, cand, 1968; Medgar Evers Fund, pres, 1969-, founder; WMPR 90.1 FM, sta mgr, Currently. **Orgs:** Dem Nat Com; adv bd, Black Enterprise Mag; exec comt, MS Munic Asn; bd dirs, SW MS Planning & Devel Dist; Govs Manpower Conf, 1974-; Social Sci; Philos Jurisp; Regional Coun Negro Leadership. **Honors/Awds:** Man of the Year Award, Nat Asn Advan Colored People, 1969; MS Lectr Cols Univs, Sociology & Humanities, 1964-; Nat Asn Advan Colored People Recipient Nine Hon Degrees Humanities; EVERS Author, 1970. **Special Achievements:** Author, Have No Fear: The Charles Evers Story, Wiley & sons, 1997; First African American black mayor of Fayette. **Home Addr:** PO Box 605, Fayette, MS 39069. **Business Addr:** Station Manager, WMPR 90.1 FM, 1018 Pecan Pk Circle, Jackson, MS 39286, **Business Phone:** (601)948-5835.

### EVERS, WILLIAM PRESTON

Executive, executive director. **Personal:** Born Apr 12, 1952, Trenton, NJ; married Patricia; children: Kelsey A & Justin A. **Educ:** Montclair State Col, BA, phys educ, 1975; Fairleigh Dickinson Univ, MBA, mkt mgt, 1981. **Career:** Chicopee Mills, sales rep, 1976-78; Ford Motor Co, regional mgr, mkt rep, 1978-95; Harley-Davidson Motor Co, dir dealer develop, 1995-99, dir field opers, sr dir sales admin & strategy, 1999-2014. **Orgs:** Kappa Alpha Psi Fraternity Inc, 1990; pres, Newark Alumni; Sigma Gamma Rho; Milwaukee Urban League. **Home Addr:** 7322 W Lafayette Pl, Mequon, WI 53092-1564, **Home Phone:** (262)242-3032. **Business Addr:** Director of Field Operations, Harley-Davidson Motor Co, 3700 W Juneau Ave, Milwaukee, WI 53208, **Business Phone:** (414)342-4680.

### EVERS-WILLIAMS, DR. MYRLIE LOUISE (MYRLIE LOUISE BEASLEY)

Association executive, social worker, government official. **Personal:** Born Mar 17, 1933, Vicksburg, MS; daughter of James Van Dyke Beasley and Mildred Washington; married Medgar Evers; children: 3; married Walter Edward. **Educ:** Pomona Col, BA, sociol, 1968. **Career:** Claremont Col, asst dir educ opportunity, 1967, dir planning & develop; Seligman & Latz, vpres; Atlantic Richfield Co, nat dir community affairs; Los Angeles Bd Pub Works, comnr; MEW Assocs Inc, pres, 2000; Medgar Evers Inst, founder. **Orgs:** Chairwoman, Nat Asn Advan Colored People, 1995-98; first Field Secy, Nat Asn Advan Colored People, Miss; Delta Sigma Theta sorority. **Honors/Awds:** Auth, Us Living, 1967; Tribute To A Black Am Award, Conf Black Mayors, 2002; hon doctorate, Pomona Col; hon doctorate, Medgar Evers Col; hon doctorate, Spelman Col; hon doctorate, Columbia Col; hon doctorate, Bennett Col; hon doctorate, Tougaloo Col; hon doctorate, Willamette Univ; hon doctorate, Howard Univ. **Special Achievements:** First female to Chair the NAACP, 1995. Books: Watch Me Fly: What I Learned on the Way to Becoming the Woman I Was Meant to Be; In the bestseller I Dream A World: Black Women Who Changed America; first African-American woman commissioner for the Los Angeles, 1987; first woman and lay person to deliver an invocation for the president of the United States, 2013. **Home Addr:** PO Box 71242, ARP Sta, Los Angeles, CA 90071, **Home Phone:** (714)624-7193. **Business Addr:** President, MEW Associates Inc, 15 SW Colorado Ave Suite 310, Bend, OR 97702, **Business Phone:** (541)330-6342.

### EWELL, HON. RAYMOND WHITNEY

Legislator. **Personal:** Born Dec 29, 1928, Chicago, IL; son of Whitney and Severine; married Joyce Marie; children: David, Marc & Raymond. **Educ:** Univ Ill, BA, hist, 1949, MA, hist, 1951; Univ Chicago, JD, 1954. **Career:** Alderman; Ill Gen Assembly 29th Dist, state repp, 1967-83; sr advisor, US Sen Carol Moseley Braun; sr advisor, John H Stroger; Williams Miller & Ferguson, atty, currently; teacher pub sch; gas sta operator, lobbyist, City Chicago; real estate, currently. **Orgs:** Cook Co Bar Asn; bd Chicago Conf to Fulfill These Rights; Fed Pub & Defender Prog; Nat Asn Advan Colored People; Nat Socs State Legislators; YMCA; chmn, Higher Educ Comt, Ill Legis Black Caucus; pres, Perry Ave Block Club; Urban League; PUSH; dir, St Carthage Grooming Sch Boys; Fourth Ward Young Dem; supvr, Seventeenth Ward Regular Dem. **Special Achievements:** First Black Caucus was formed and served as a state legislator. **Home Addr:** 7902 S Perry Ave Apt 3w, Chicago, IL 60620-1149, **Home Phone:** (773)783-2123. **Business Addr:** Attorney, Williams Miller & Ferguson, 9415 S State St, Chicago, IL 60619-7230, **Business Phone:** (773)660-4300.

### EWERS, DR. JAMES BENJAMIN, JR.

Educator, school administrator. **Personal:** Born Sep 29, 1948, Winston-Salem, NC; son of Mildred Jane Holland and James B; married Deborah Leu Froy; children: Christopher, Aaron & Courtney. **Educ:** Johnson C Smith Univ, BA, polit sci, 1970; Cath Univ Am, MA, educ, 1971; Univ Mass, EdD, 1980; Harvard Univ, Mgt Develop Prog, cert, 1996. **Career:** Ballou High Sch, Wash DC Pub Schs, social studies teacher, 1971-75; Stockton State Col, asst dir admis, 1976-78; Univ Md Eastern Shore, dir admin & registr, 1978-84; Livingstone Col, vpres stud affairs, 1984-87; Dillard Univ, vpres stud affairs, 1987-90; Savannah State Col, vpres stud affairs, 1990-94; Liberty County Sch Dist, Hinesville, Ga, fac mem; Miami Univ, Middletown, Ohio, assoc dean stud affairs, 1995-2009, dir community partnerships; Edward Waters Col, vpres stud affairs & enrollment mgt, 2009-12. **Orgs:** Alpha Phi Alpha, 1967-; Nat Asn Foreign Stud Affairs, 1981-; Am Asn Coun Develop 1982-; Miami Univ Community Fed Credit Union; Phi Kappa Phi, 1983-; life mem, Nat Asn Advan Colored People 1983-; Salisbury/Rowan Human Rel Coun, 1985-87; Am Asn Higher Educ, 1987; Middletown Civil Serv Comn, 1996-; bd dir, Middletown YMCA, 1996-2003; United Way; bd dir Middletown Red Cross, 1996-2003; bd dir, Middletown Regional Hosp, 1998-; fel, Kellogg, 1998; bd dir, Middletown Rotary Club, 1998-2001. **Special Achievements:** First African American president of the Middletown area YMCA. **Home Addr:** 4504 Rosewood Ct, Middletown, OH 45042-3862, **Home Phone:** (513)420-9199. **Business Addr:** Lifetime Member, National Association for the Advancement of Colored People, 4805 Mt Hope Dr, Baltimore, MD 21215, **Business Phone:** (410)580-5777.

### EWING, MAMIE HANS

Government official, administrator. **Personal:** Born Aug 15, 1939, Houston, TX; married Robert; children: Steve & Perry. **Educ:** UNiv Tex, Austin, BA, 1960; Prairie View A&M Univ, MEd, 1974. **Career:** Tex Dept Human Resources, supvr child welfare div, 1969-71, dir & EEO, 1973-75, dir, Civil Rights, 1975-77, feild liason officer, 1977-78, regional admin, 1978-; Austin Neighborhood Youth Corps, div exec dir, 1972-73; Tex Dept Aging & Disability Serv, adminr, 2004. **Orgs:** Bd dir, Tarrant Co United Way, 1979-80; Nat Asn Soc Workers; Asn Black Soc Workers; Alpha Kappa Alpha Sorority; Jack & Jill; Nat Asn Advan Colored People; pres, Beta Psi Omega; Mo City Links, 1985-. **Honors/Awds:** Recipient Meritorious Service Award, Travis Co Child Welfare bd, 1971; Trailbazer of the Year Award, Bus & Professional Womens Asn Tarrant Co, 1979; Achievement Award, Asn Black Social Workers, 1979; Outstanding Women, Tex Govt, Governor's Comn Women Govt, 1987; Outstanding African Am Alumnus, Univ Tex Austin, Ex-Studs Asn, 1990; Houston Works Member of the Year, 1994; Mayor's Public Private Partnership Award, 1996. **Home Addr:** 10607 Dunlap St, Houston, TX 77096-4726, **Home Phone:** (713)721-0511. **Business Addr:** Regional Administrator, Texas Department of Aging & Disability Services, 5425 Polk Ave, Houston, TX 77222-6017, **Business Phone:** (713)767-2401.

### EWING, PATRICK ALOYSIUS, SR.

Basketball player, basketball coach. **Personal:** Born Aug 5, 1962, Kingston; son of Carl and Dorothy; married Rita; children: Randi, Corey & Patrick Jr. **Educ:** Georgetown Univ, BA, 1985. **Career:** Basketball player (retired), basketball coach; New York Knicks, ctr, 1985-2000; Seattle SuperSonics, 2000-01; Orlando Magic, asst coach, 2001-02, 2007-12; Wash Wizards, asst coach, 2002-03; Houston Rockets, asst coach, 2003-06; Charlotte Bobcats, assoc head coach, 2013-. **Orgs:** New York City Bd Educ, Drop Out Prevention Prog, 1985; pres, NBA Players Asn, 1997. **Business Addr:** Associate Head Coach, Charlotte Bobcats, 333 E Trade St, Charlotte, NC 28202, **Business Phone:** (704)688-8600.

### EWING, SAMUEL DANIEL

Executive, investment banker, consultant. **Personal:** Born Topeka, KS; son of Samuel Daniel Sr and Jane Elizabeth Smith; married Brenda Jean Arnold. **Educ:** Univ Cincinnati, BSEE, 1961; Univ Conn, MSEE, 1964; Harvard Univ, MBA, 1968. **Career:** Gruss & Co, investment mgr, 1968-69; Salomon Bros, New York, NY, sr assoc, 1969-75; Bankers Trust Co, New York, NY, founding prin, vpres & dir, 1975-78; Fed Savings & Loan Ins Corp, Wash, DC, dir, 1978-80; Ewing Capital

Inc, Wash, DC, pres & founder, CCO, 1981-. **Orgs:** Fel Fin Analyst Fed; DC Securities Adv Comn; trustee, Annuity Fund Ministers & Retirement Fund Lay Workers; trustee, Pension Bds, United Church Christ Inc; trustee, United Church Bd Pension Assets Mgt; trustee, Peoples Congregational United Church Christ; chair, Diversity Comt, United Bd Pension Assets Mgt; chair, Investment Comt, Immigration & Refugee Serv Am; dir, United Church Bd Ministerial Assistance Inc; Comt Corp Social Responsibility; Investment Comt Pension Bd, United Church Christ; Exec Finance Comn, Juv Diabetes Found Int; Finance & Develop Comn; Harvard Club Wash, DC; Harvard Bus Sch Club Wash, DC; Harvard Bus Sch African-Am Alumni Asn; Nat Asn Investments Prof; bd mem, Shaw Heritage Trust Fund; bd mem; Juv Diabetes Found Int; trustee, Huston-Tillotson Col, Investment Comn; pres & founding prin, Broadcast Capital Fund Inc, Wash, DC, 1980-81; adv bd, UConn Sch Eng, currently; bd dir, Univ Conn Found, currently; Eng Dean's Adv Bd. **Home Addr:** 2722 Unicorn Lane NW, Washington, DC 20015-2234, **Home Phone:** (202)364-4564. **Business Addr:** President, Founder, Ewing Capital Inc, 2722 Unicorn Lane NW, Washington, DC 20015-2234, **Business Phone:** (202)364-3996.

### EWING, STEVEN R.
Chief executive officer, executive. **Educ:** Del State Univ, BA, eng, 1982. **Career:** Champion Fordland Inc, pres, 1993-2002; Wade Ford Inc, chief exec & owner, 2000-; Motortrend Cert Advantage Dealer, chief exec officer, 2009-; Wade Financial Serv inc, pres, 2015-. **Orgs:** Kappa Alpha Psi Fraternity, 1989; Nat Automobile Dealer Asn; Ga Auto Dealer Asn; Nat Asn Minority Automobile Dealers; Ford Motor Minority Dealer. **Business Addr:** Chief Executive Officer, Owner, Wade Ford Inc, 3860 S Cobb Dr SE, Smyrna, GA 30080-5537, **Business Phone:** (770)436-1200.

### EWING, ESQ. WILLIAM JAMES
Lawyer. **Personal:** Born Sep 10, 1936, New York, NY. **Educ:** Seton Hall Univ, BA, 1958, JD, 1961. **Career:** NJ & US Dist Ct, Dist NJ, admitted to bar, 1972; William J Ewing Law firm, 1972-; US Ct Appeals, Third Circuit, 1980; US Supreme Ct, 1981; NY & US Dist Ct, Southern, Northern & Eastern Dist NY, 1983; Essex County Prosecutors Off, dir spec invests; CBS Aspen Systs Corp, legal comput corp exec; Montclair, NJ, munic Prosectuor & asst town atty; NJ Ct, arbitrator; Super Ct, Annexed Arbit Proj; The Law Firm of William J Ewing, PC, NJ, currently. **Orgs:** Nj Bar Asn, 1972; New York Trial Lawyers Asn, 1983; NJ State Am Nat Bar Asn; Concerned Legal Asn NJ; reg dir, Young Lawyers Sect Nat Bar Asn; Attys Montclair; Nat Asn Advan Colored People; exec bd, Montclair Urban Coalition; Garden State Bar Asn; regional dir, Am Trial Lawyers Asn; life mem, Nat Asn Advan Colored People; Montclair Br Coun; chmn, Legal Redress. **Honors/Awds:** Outstanding Man of the Year, 1973; Distinguished Service Award, Garden State Bar Asn. **Home Addr:** 162 Lincoln St, Montclair, NJ 07042. **Business Addr:** Attorney, The Law Firm of William J Ewing PC, 70 Pk St Suite 200, Montclair, NJ 07042, **Business Phone:** (973)746-9898.

### EXUM, THURMAN MCCOY
Executive, educator. **Personal:** Born Mar 29, 1947, Seven Springs, NC; married Wanda R Edwards; children: Thurman Jr & Jermaine. **Educ:** NC A&T State Univ, BS, auto tech, 1969, MS; Colo State Univ, attended 1984; NIASE, Auto Serv Excellence, 1985, MS, indust educ, 1987. **Career:** Buick Div GM, dist serv mgr, 1971-78; GM Trng Ctr, instr, 1978-79; Pat Mullery Buick, dir serv, 1979; No VA Community Col, instr & auto, 1980-81; Metro Auto Emission Serv Inc, pres, 1981-85; DC Dept Transp, consult, 1981-; State Va, consult, 1982-; NJ Comm Col, consult, 1981; Texaco Oil Co, consult, 1981; Colo State Univ, consult, 1983-84; Dana Corp, Spicer Axle Div, Greensboro; NC A&T State Univ, Sch Technol, instr, 1985, dean & dir motor sports technol, adj instr, currently; Exum Motor Sports. **Orgs:** Consult, Nat Home Study Coun, 1981-82; vpres, Coun Auto Apprent Coordr, 1982-83; coordr, Nat Auto Dev Assoc, 1983; MD Qual Assurance Moratorium, 1984; N Am Emissions Control Conf, 1982-; coordr St MD Vehicle Admin, 1984-; Soc Automotive Engrs, 1986-. **Home Addr:** 3797 Kelford Dr, Greensboro, NC 27406, **Home Phone:** (336)334-7585. **Business Addr:** Adjunct Instructor, North Carolina Agricultural & Technical State University, 1601 E Market St Price Hall Suite 102-L, Greensboro, NC 27411, **Business Phone:** (336)334-2253.

### EXUM, DR. WADE F.
Health services administrator. **Personal:** Born Jan 31, 1949, Clayton, NC; son of Alfred D and Lucille E; married Carolyn Jan; children: Daniel E, Adam B & Cord H. **Educ:** Ottawa Univ, BS, biol, 1971; Univ Colo Med Ctr, MD, 1977; Univ Colo Grad Sch Bus Admin, MBA, 1986. **Career:** Reynolds Elect & Eng Co, indust hygenist, 1971-73; US Pub Health Servs, gen med off, 1977-80; Colo State Univ, stud health physician, 1980-81; IMB Corp, sr managing physician, 1982-90; US Olympic Comt, usoc dir, DCA, 1991-2000; Off Hearing & Appeal, pres, currently; Us Olympic Comt, exec dir; Us Olympic Comt, dir drug control admin. **Orgs:** Am Med Asn, 1980-; Nat Med Asn, 1980-; Am Occup Med Asn, 1982-90; bd dir, Athletes Against Drugs, 1992-; NCAA Sports Scis Subcomt, 1992-94; USA Olympic Team Deleg, 1992, 1996; bd dir, Colo Springs Downtown YMCA, 1993-; bd dir, Colo Springs Chamber Com, 1996; bd dir, Shaka Found, 1997; Am Bd Forensic Examiners; admin, Drug Control; Us Olympic Comt dir, Drug control; dir adminstration, Drug control. **Home Addr:** 807 Fontmore Rd, Colorado Springs, CO 80904-1603, **Home Phone:** (719)634-2258. **Business Addr:** President, Office of Hearings & Appeals, 121 S Tejon St, Colorado Springs, CO 80904-1603, **Business Phone:** (719)634-2258.

### EYES, DR. GREEN. See SIMPSON, DONNIE.

### EZOZO, AGRIPPA O.
President (organization), association executive. **Personal:** married Wanda; children: Aaron Oke & Zola Uzezi. **Educ:** Wudil Teachers Col, Kano St, Nigeria, pub educ; Calif State Univ, Dominguez Hills, BS, comput info syst; Univ Calif, Los Angles, MA, African areas studies. **Career:** Kundila Primary Sch, Kano, Nigeria, teacher; African Diaspora Found, pres & founder, 2001-; Black Church Rev mag, publ; League of Patriotic Nigerians, Los Angeles, Calif, exec dir; Univ Calif, Los Angeles, benefits & disability analyst; Venice Family Clin Found, dir human resources. **Orgs:** Pres, Univ Calif Los Angeles Black Fac & Staff Asn, 1991; co-chair, Calif delegation to Nat Summit Africa, Wash, DC; co-chair & exec bd mem, African Diaspora Found. **Business Addr:** President, Founder, African Diaspora Foundation, 36914 Jenna Lane, Palmdale, CA 93550, **Business Phone:** (661)285-7513.

# F

### FADULU, DR. SUNDAY O.
Educator. **Personal:** Born Nov 11, 1940, Ibadan; married Jacqueline F; children: Sunday Jr & Tony. **Educ:** Okla Baptist Univ, BS, biol, 1964; Univ Okla, MS, PhD, 1969. **Career:** Univ Nigeria, lectr pharmaceut microbiol, 1969-70; Univ Ife Nigeria, resdrug unit, 1969-70; Univ Okla Sch Med, res assoc hemat, 1970-71; Tex Southern Univ, asst prof, 1972, prof micro biol, currently, chmn dept biol, 2000. **Orgs:** Sigma Xi, 1968; Beta Beta Beta Biol Hon Soc, 1973; Nat Geog Soc, 1973; MedMycological Soc Am, 1974; Int Soc Human & Animal Mycol, 1975; Friends Youth Houston TX, 1975; Nat Inst Sci Beta Kappa Chi; Smithsonian Inst Recip Fac Res Grant Urban Resources Ctr Sickle Cell Res; Minority Bio med Res Nat Inst Health; bd trustee, dir, Riverside Gen Hosp. **Home Addr:** 20115 Wickham Ct, Katy, TX 77450-2232. **Business Addr:** Professor, Texas Southern University, 3100 Cleburne Dr 203 New Science Bldg, Houston, TX 77004, **Business Phone:** (713)313-7219.

### FAGBAYI, MUTIU OLUTOYIN
President (organization), chief executive officer, executive. **Personal:** Born Jan 9, 1953, Lagos; married Patricia Ann Russell; children: Jumoke & Yinka. **Educ:** Univ Dayton, BS, chem engineering, 1972; Pa State Univ, MS, chem engineering, 1978. **Career:** Eastman Kodak Co, res scientist, 1978-85, sr bus res analyst, 1987-89; Nat Ctr Educ & Econ, chief operating officer, 1992-95; Performance Fact Inc, Oakland, Calif, founder, pres & chief exec officer, 1997-; Penn Dept of Educ, consult, 2002-08. **Orgs:** Secy, Webster Rotary Club, 1982-84; pres, exec bd & admin, Rochester Chap Nat Orgn Prof Advan Black Chemists & Chem Engrs, 1983-, 1986-, 1987-92; bd trustee, Webster Montessori Sch, 1984-86; Tau Beta Pi Eng Nat Hon Soc; bd advs, Micro Soc; Oxford Int Roundtable, Oxford Univ. **Home Addr:** , Rochester, NY 14625, **Home Phone:** (716)671-4255. **Business Addr:** President, Founder & Chief Executive Officer, Performance Fact Inc, 333 Hegenberger Rd Suite 204, Oakland, CA 94621, **Business Phone:** (510)568-7944.

### FAGIN, DARRYL HALL
Manager, executive director. **Personal:** Born May 18, 1942, Washington, DC; married Susan; children: Elizabeth Peggy & Adam Vincent. **Educ:** Olivet Col, BA, polit sci, 1968; George Washington Univ, Nat Law Ctr, JD, 1971; Am Univ Wash Col Law, LLM, law, 2005. **Career:** Black Studs Union Olive t Col, charter pres, 1968; Indust Bank Wash, loan officer & asst cashier, 1973-74; Judge Sorrell, Super Ct DC, law clerk, 1974-75; Am Security Bank, legal researcher assoc coun, 1975-77; Equal Employ Opportunity Comn, law clerk, 1977-78; US House Representatives, leg asst, 1978-79, 1984-90; US Treas, Dept Treas, asst; Americans Dem Action, legis dir, 1991-2010. **Orgs:** Lawyers Com DC Arts Comn, 1971; Pub Protection Com Met Bd Trade, 1976; adv bd mem, Nat Jobs All Coalition. **Honors/Awds:** Legal Fellowship Award; Regional Huber Smith community law fellowship Washington DC, 1971; Special Achievement Award, Dept US Treas, 1981; Special Appreciation Award, Martin Luther King Fed Holiday Comn, 1988. **Home Addr:** 4506 Avondale St Apt 7, Bethesda, MD 20814-3535, **Home Phone:** (301)718-6247. **Business Addr:** Advisory Board Member, National Jobs for All Coalition, PO Box 96, Lynbrook, NY 11563, **Business Phone:** (203)856-3877.

### FAIN, CONSTANCE FRISBY
Lawyer, educator. **Personal:** Born Feb 11, 1949, Philadelphia, PA; daughter of William and Dorothy; married Herbert; children: Kimberly K. **Educ:** Cheyney Univ, Cheyney State Col, BS, educ, 1970; Tex Southern Univ, JD, 1974; Univ Pa, LLM, 1981. **Career:** Prev Law Ctr, Housing Div, Stud asst, 1971-72; US Atty, Dept Justice, law clerk, 1972-74; Funchess, Charles, Long & Hannah Law Firm, atty, 1975-76; Tex Southern Univ, Thurgood Marshall Sch Law, prof law, 1976-88, CLEO Prog, instr, 1976-78, Legal Skills Prog, dir, 1978-90, asst prof, 1979, assoc prof, 1982, prof, 1988-2005, Earl Carl prof law, 2005-, houston law firm, atty; CLEO Prog, instr-legal writing, 1977-78; Prof Liability & Anal, prof, 1991-98; Butterworth Legal Publishers; Glanville Publishers Inc; Dobbs Ferry, New York, consult reviewer law bks, 1994-97; Critical Thinking & Law, prof, 1999-2002; Law Offices, res asst. **Orgs:** Stud asst-housing div, Preventative Law Ctr, Houston, 1971-72; law clerk, Us Atty's Off-Dept Justice, 1972-74; State Bar Tex, 1975-; State Bar Pa, 1981-; adv bd mem, NH, 1994; adv bd mem, Butterworth Legal Publishers, 1994; fel, Tex Bar Found, 1995-2000; fel Tex Bar Found, 1995-2000; US Dist Ct, Southern Dist Tex; US Ct Appeals, fifth Circuit; US Ct Appeals, eleventh circuit; Am Soc Writers Legal Subj; Phi Alpha Delta Law Fraternity; Black Women's Lawyers Asn; dep dir pub works & engineering, city Houston; adv bd mem, publ co. **Home Addr:** 4306 Rosebud St, Houston, TX 77053, **Home Phone:** (713)434-0669. **Business Addr:** Earl Carl Professor of Law, Texas Southern University, 3100 Cleburne Ave, Houston, TX 77004, **Business Phone:** (713)313-7393.

### FAIR, TALMADGE WILLARD
Association executive. **Personal:** Born Jan 15, 1939, Winston-Salem, NC. **Educ:** Johnson C Smith Univ, BA, sociol, 1961; Atlanta Univ Sch Social Work, MSW, 1963. **Career:** Urban League Greater Miami Inc, assoc dir, 1963, pres & chief exec officer, 1964-; Atlanta Univ Sch Social Work, adj prof; Nat Urban League's Whitney M Young Jr, Ctr Urban Leadership, adj prof; Fla Int Univ, adj prof; Bethune Cookman Col, adj prof. **Orgs:** Pres, Miami Varsity Club, 1978-; Miami Citizens Against Crime Exec Comt, 1980-; pres, Community Blacks Org Labor, 1981-; Fla Reg Coord Coun Voc Educ, 1984-88, Beacon Coun Orgn Task Force, 1985; bd trustees, Fla Int Univ; chmn bd dir, Bayside Found; chmn, bd dir, Vis Indust; bd gov & exec comt, Greater Miami Conv & Visitor's Bur; City Miami Civil Serv Bd; Dade/Monroe WAGES Coalition's Eval Comt; bd gov & exec comt, Miami Coalition a Safe & Drug-Free Community; co-founder, Liberty City Charter Sch; Gov Equity Educ Task Force; chair bd dir, Miami-Bayside Found & Miami-Dade Empowerment Trust; vis Am embassies Egypt, Oman & UK, United State's Adv Comt Cult Affairs; Pres's Comn White House Fels-Miami Regional Selection Panel, 2011; mem bd, The Fla Family Partnership Inc. **Honors/Awds:** Outstanding Dedicated Service, Troop 40 Boy Scouts Am, 1984; Appreciation Award, Martin Luther King Develop Corp, 1984; Gratitude Valuable Contrib Econ Opportunity Family Health Ctr, 1984; Appreciation Award, Progressive Firefighters Asn, 1985; Certificate of Appreciation Outstanding Service, City of Miami; Outstanding Citizen Service Award, State of Fla; Presidential Excalibur Award, Family Christian Agency Am; Community Service Award, Greater Miami Region Nat Conf Christians & Jews, 1995; Community Service Award, Phillip Morris Co Inc, 1992; Award, Nat Network Social Work Managers Inc, 1989; Leadership Award, Greater Miami Chamber Com; National Education Award, 2010. **Special Achievements:** Author of numerous published articles in the Miami Herald, Miami Magazine, Tropic Magazine; host of both radio and television programs; interviewed by 60 Minutes, Tom Brokaw, Ebony Magazine and National Geographic. **Business Addr:** President, Chief Executive Officer, Urban League of Greater Miami Inc, 8500 NW 25th Ave, Miami, FL 33147, **Business Phone:** (305)696-4450.

### FAIR, TERRANCE DELON
Radio host, football coach, football player. **Personal:** Born Jul 20, 1976, Phoenix, AZ; married Sherlone; children: Herandre, Delon & Ariyah. **Educ:** Tenn State Univ, BS, psychol, 2010. **Career:** Football player (retired), coach, host; Detroit Lions, right cornerback, 1998-2001, kick returner, punt returner, 1998, cornerback, 1999; Carolina Panthers, 2002; Pittsburgh Steelers, 2005; St Louis Rams, defensive back, 2005; Phoenix Col, coach; Univ Tenn, defensive qual control asst; WNOX, co-host; Dr WCYQ, co-host, currently; Tenn Athletics, coach defensive qual control asst, currently. **Honors/Awds:** SEC All-Freshman honors in 1994; All-Rookie hons, Pro Football Weekly, 1998; Spec Team Player of the Week, Nat Football League, 1998, 1999; Spec Team Player of the Month, Nat Football League, 1998; All-Sec, Assoc Press & Football News; All-Am hon mention. **Special Achievements:** Pro Bowl alternate, 1998; Returned punt 82 yards for touchdown to set state record, 1993. **Business Addr:** Coach Defensive Quality Control Assistant, Tennessee Athletics, 1600 Phillip Fulmer Way Suite 201, Knoxville, TN 37996, **Business Phone:** (865)656-1200.

### FAIRLEY, JULIETTE S.
Writer. **Personal:** Born Jun 21, 1969, Chateauroux; daughter of James and Sophie. **Educ:** Univ Houston, BA, commun, 1988; Columbia Univ Jour Sch, MS, 1991; Univ Wis grad sch banking. **Career:** Eng lang translr, Paris, France; Gence Intl D'Image TV, news anchor; Bergen Rec, reporter; Bloomberg Bus News, producer; Am W In-Flight Media, prog host, 2001; sem producer; auth, currently; Author: Money Talks: Black Financial Experts Talk to You About Money, 1998; Cliff's Notes on Investing in Mutual Funds, 1999; Money Rules: Personal Finance in Your 20s & 30's, 2002; Cash in the City: Affording Martinis, Manolos & Manicures on a Working Girl's Salary, 2002; TV show: The Making of a Mulatto; Cha Ching Money Makers, host, 2005; Tv series: Double Cross, SAG webisode series; Hey Diddle Diddle; short films: Mulatto's Dilemma; Diary of a Mulatto Bride and Mulatto Saga. **Orgs:** NY New Media Asn; Author's Guild; Am Soc Journalists & Authors; NY financial Writers Asn. **Honors/Awds:** People's Choice Best Fiction Film, 2012; Best Romantic Comedy, NY, 2012. **Home Addr:** PO Box 28-6958, New York, NY 10128, **Home Phone:** (212)714-7723. **Business Addr:** Author, John Wiley & Sons, 111 River St, Hoboken, NJ 07030-5774, **Business Phone:** (201)748-6000.

### FAIRMAN, J. W., JR.
Administrator, association executive, executive. **Personal:** Born May 20, 1948, Cleveland, OH; married Jeanne Arthur Hester; children: Bridgette, Darrin & Victor. **Educ:** Hardin-Simmons Univ, BS, speech & phys educ, 1970; State Ill, Dept Personnel, admin & org behav, 1974; Chicago State Univ, MS, criminal justice, 1975; Am Abritration Asn, labor mgt, 1977; Harper & Row Publ Co, Hostage Negotiations, 1980; Harvard Univ, Cambridge, John F Kennedy Sch Govt, sr mgt state & local govt officials, 1994. **Career:** Ill Dept Corrections, warden, 1971-91; Chicago DART Work Release, coun, 1971-72, ctr supvr, 1972-77; Ill Dept Corr Work Release, dep supt, 1977-79, comn corr ctr supvr, 1972-77, correctional coun, 1971-72; Stateville Correct Ctr, asst supt, 1979; Pontiac Correct Ctr, warden, 1979-82; Joliet Correct Ctr, warden, 1982-91; Ill Dept Corrections, Sheridan Correctional Ctr, warden, 1991; Cook County Dept Corrections, Chicago, Ill, exec dir, 1991-96, Juv Temp Detention Ctr, acct supt, Bur Pub Safety & Judicial Coordrn, chief, currently; Calif Dept Corrections, chief exec officer & spec consult, 1997-2000; Calif Dept Corrections & Rehab, warden, 1997-2000; Fairman Consult Servs, consult, 1996-97, 2000-02, 2007-, pres chief exec officer, 2014-; Cook County Bd Commissioners, Pres's Off, Bur Pub Safety & Judicial Coordn, chief, 2002-07; Cook County Juv Temp Detention Ctr, supt, 2006-07; Nakamoto Group Inc, compliance reviewer, 2007-10; L-3 MPRI, sr int correctional trainer, 2010-11, dir opers, 2011-12. **Orgs:** Ill Correct Asn, 1979-; Am Correct Asn, 1980-; Nat Asn Blacks Criminal Justice, 1976-; Circuit Ct Cook County Prin's Comt, 1991-; Ill Atty Gen Comn Af-Am Males, 1992-94; Chicago Salvation Army Corr Servs, adv bd, 1993-; Off Cook Cty State's Atty Gay & Lesbian Task Force, 1993-; Will Cty Police Chiefs Asn; City Joliet, Ill Task Force Gangs; Nat Asn Blacks Criminal Justice; Asn State Correctional Admins; Ill Correctional Asn; Am Correctional Asn; Am Jail Asn. **Home Phone:** (708)460-1280. **Business Addr:** Chief Public Safety Officer, Office of the Chief Public Safety Officer, 69 W Wash Suite 2630, Chicago, IL 60602, **Business Phone:** (312)603-1160.

### FAISON, DEREK E.
Executive. **Personal:** Born Jul 14, 1948, Newport News, VA; son of Edgar and Carmena Gantt; married Wilma A; children: Natalye

& Marcus. **Educ:** Univ Colo, Boulder, CO, BS, bus admin & mkt, 1970; Colo State Univ, Ft Colins, CO, attended 1972; Univ Wis, cert. **Career:** Penn Mutual Life Ins Co, Denver, Colo, sales rep, 1970-72; IBM, Boulder, Colo, copier planning mfg, acct mgr, mkt mgr, prod planning mgr, 1972-81; Kids Nite Out Across Am, managing partner; E Smart Serv, mgr, bus develop & venture funding; Faison Off Prod Co, pres, chief exec officer 1981-2000, founder, currently. **Orgs:** Bd mem, Big Bro, 1988-; bd mem, Colo Black Chamber Com, 1990-; bd mem, Greater Denver Chamber Com, 1990-; bd mem, Deans Adv Bd Columbia Bus Sch, 1990-; bd mem, Denver Broncos Active Rooster, 1990-; bd mem, Univ Colo Found; vice chair, Mile High United Way; Colo Bus Sch Deans Adv Bd; Nat Off Prod Asn; Aurora Chamber Com; Univ Colo Athletic Mentoring & Big Bros. **Home Addr:** 2681 S Kenton Ct, Aurora, CO 80014, **Home Phone:** (303)750-1896. **Business Addr:** Founder & Chief Executive officer, president, Faison Office Products Co, 151 Farmington Ave, Hartford, CT 06156, **Business Phone:** (860)273-0123.

### FAISON, DONALD ADEOSUN

Actor. **Personal:** Born Jun 22, 1974, New York, NY; married Lisa Askey; children: 3; married CaCee Cobb; children: Rocco. **Career:** TV series: "Sesame Street", 1992; "New York Undercover", 1996; "Sabrina, the Teenage Witch", 1996-98; "Clueless", 1996-99; "Sister, Sister", 1998; "Felicity", 2000-02; "Scrubs", 2001-10; "Clone High", 2002-03; "Higglytown Heroes", 2004-05; "The Bernie Mac Show", 2005; "Saturday Night Live", 2007; "Scrubs: Interns", 2009; "Titan Maximum", 2009; "American Dad!", 2009; "FCU: Fact Checkers Unit", 2010; "Cubed", 2010; "The Exes", 2011; "Robot Chicken", 2005-11; "Love Bites", 2011; TV movies: "Supreme Sanction", 1999; "Robot Chicken: Star Wars", 2007; "Kim Possible", 2007; "The Boondocks", 2008; "The Law", 2009; "The Odds", 2010; "FCU: Fact Checkers Unit", 2010; "Cubed", 2010; "Love Bites", 2011; "The Exes", 2011-14; "Adventure Time", 2012; "TRON: Uprising", 2012; "Wedding Band", 2013; "A Snow Globe Christmas", 2013. Films: Juice, 1992; Sugar Hill, 1993; New Jersey Drive, 1995; Clueless, 1995; Waiting to Exhale, 1995; Academy Boyz, 1997; Can't Hardly Wait, 1998; Butter, 1998; Trippin', 1999; Remember ther Titans, 2000; Double Whammy, 2001; Josie and the Pussycats, 2001; Big Fat Liar, 2002; Molly Gun, 2003; Good Boy, 2003; Uptown Girls, 2003; Ravedactyl: Project Evolution, 2003; King's Ransom, 2005; Something New, 2006; Bachelor Party Vegas, 2006; Homie Spumoni, 2006; 15 Minutes of Fame, exec producer, 2008; Next Day Air, co-producer, 2009; Venus & Vegas, 2009; Skyline, 2010; Pitch Perfect, 2012; Kick-Ass 2, 2013; Stag, 2013; Wish I Was Here, 2014. **Honors/Awds:** BET Comedy Award, 2004, 2005. **Business Addr:** Actor, c/o Gold Marshak Liedtke & Associates, 3500 W Olive Ave, Burbank, CA 91505.

### FAISON, EUGENE M., JR.

Chairperson, chief executive officer. **Educ:** Hampton Univ, BS, 1970; Dartmouth Univ, Minority Bus Exec Prog, grad. **Career:** Equals Three Communs Inc, chmn & chief exec officer, 1982-; FSquareGlobal, co founder & prin, 2014-; Nutrit Labs Int, co-founder, chmn & dir. **Orgs:** Chmn, Agency mgt comt, bd dir, Am Asn Advert Agencies; chmn, Am Asn Advert Agencies Oper Success Diversity Adv Bd; Govt Rels Comt, Am Asn Advert Agencies; chmn, Empowerment Network Found; vice chmn & dir, Women Community Serv; bd mem, Friends Zambia; Pub Rel Soc Am. **Business Addr:** Chairman, Chief Executive Officer, Equals Three Communications Inc, 7910 Woodmont Ave Suite 200, Bethesda, MD 20814-3015, **Business Phone:** (301)656-3100.

### FAISON, FRANKIE RUSSEL

Actor. **Personal:** Born Jun 10, 1949, Newport News, VA; son of Edgar and Carmena Gantt; married Jane Mandel; children: Blake, Amanda & Rachel. **Educ:** Ill Wesleyan Univ, Bloomington, IL, BFA, 1971; NY Univ, MFA, 1974. **Career:** Films: Ragtime, 1981; CHUD, 1984; Coming to America, 1988; Mississippi Burning, 1988; Do the Right Thing, 1989; The Silence of the Lambs, 1991; City of Hope, 1991; Freejack, 1992; Sommersby, 1993; The Rich Man's Wife, 1996; The Thomas Crown Affair, 1999; Where the Money Is, 2000; Thirteen Conversations About One Thing, 2001; Hannibal, 2001; The Sleepy Time Gal, 2001; Red Dragon, 2002; Show time, 2002; Gods & Generals, 2003; In Good Company, 2004; Crutch, 2004; The Cookout, 2004; Messengers, 2004; White Chicks, 2004; Premium, 2006; My Blueberry Nights, 2007; Nick and Norah's Infinite Playlist, 2008; Adam, 2009; # Cirque du Freak: The Vampire's Assistant; For Sale by Owner; Splinter heads, 2009. TV movies: The Spider and the Fly, 1994; The Langoliers, 1995; Call Me Claus, 2001; TV series: "True Colors", 1990; "Prey", 1997-98; "The Wire", 2002; "Law & Order: Special Victims Unit", 2007. **Orgs:** Actors Equity Asn, 1972-; Screen Actors Guide, 1974-; Am Fedn TV & Radio, 1974-; local spokesperson, Orgn Prev Child Abuse, 1991. **Honors/Awds:** Tony Nomination, 1988; Drama Desk Nomination, 1988; Audelco Award, 1989; Hon Doctorate Degree, Ill Wesleyan Univ, 2002; FFCC Award, 2003. **Home Addr:** 15 Cloverhill Pl, Montclair, NJ 07042-4818. **Business Addr:** Actor, c/o Innovative Artists, 235 Park Ave S, New York, NY 10003, **Business Phone:** (212)253-6900.

### FAISON, SHARON GAIL

Marketing executive. **Personal:** Born Nov 21, 1955, Newport News, VA; daughter of Edgar and Carmena Gantt; married Melvin E Bryant; children: Sharonda M & Jai R. **Educ:** Norfolk State Univ, BA, math, 1982. **Career:** Int Bus Mach Support Ctr, PSR, 1983-86; Faison Off Prod Co, Co, vpres, 1986-2000. **Orgs:** Nat Off Prod Asn, 1982; Zeta Phi Beta, 1984-; Minority Enterprise Inc, 1986-; Greater Denver Black Chamber Com, 1986-. **Honors/Awds:** Grad Fast Track Prog, Minority Enterprise Inc, 1990; Cert Appreciation, Total Quality Mgt, 1990; Colo Bus of the Year, Minority Enterprise Inc, 1990. **Home Addr:** 12143 W 84th Pl, Arvada, CO 80005.

### FAKHRID-DEEN, DR. NASHID ABDULLAH

College administrator. **Personal:** Born Feb 24, 1949, Monticello, AR; son of N T Thompson and Mary Thompson; married Pauline Rashidah Williamson; children: Jashed, Ayesha & Yasmeen. **Educ:** Grand Valley State Univ, BA, 1978; Univ Baltimore, Sch Law, JD, 1988. **Career:** Nat Islam, minister, 1975-79; Grand Valley State Univ, asst dir adminr, 1979-83, asst dir, talent search, 1980-83; Bowie State Univ, coordr recruitment, assoc dir adminr, 1988-90; Ky State Univ, Frankfort, Ky, exec asst pres, 1990-91; Ohio Univ, coordr minority stud affairs, 1992-94; State Ky, Ky Community & Tech Col Syst, coordr minority affairs, 1994, syst coordr, cult diversity progs, prin investr, currently; SE Ky Community & Tech Col, consult, currently. **Orgs:** Gen bus mgr, Nat Islam, 1972-76; bd dir, Climbing Tree Sch, 1977-78; bd dir, Family Serv Outreach, 1982-83; Mid-Am Asn Educ Opportunity Prog Personnel; exec coun, Black Law Students, Univ Baltimore; admin Retention Comt; Moot Ct Bd, 1986-88; developer & presentator, CARE, Baltimore, Wash Metro Area; pres, Black Law Students Asn, Univ Baltimore Sch Law, 1987-88; bd regent, Ky Community & Tech Col Syst. **Home Addr:** 224 Boiling Springs Dr, Lexington, KY 40511, **Home Phone:** (606)224-3297. **Business Addr:** Principal Investigator, Kentucky Community & Technical College System, 300 N Main St, Versailles, KY 40383, **Business Phone:** (859)256-3260.

### FALANA, LOLA (LOLETHA ELAYNE FALANA)

Actor, singer, religious reformer. **Personal:** Born Sep 11, 1942, Philadelphia, PA; daughter of Bennett and Cleo; married Feliciano Tavares. **Career:** Show biz (retired); Dancing jobs on the East Coast; Frank Sinatra's Reprise Label & Motown Records; Golden Boy, dancer, 1964; Films: A Man Called Adam, actress, 1966; I'll Try Tonight, 1967; Black Tigress, 1967; When I Say That I Love You, 1967; The Klansman, 1974; Lady Cocoa, 1975; Dr Jazz, actress & dancer, 1975; Las Vegas, singer, 1976-89; Mad About You, actress, 1989; Faberge, spokesperson; Album: My Baby, 1965; TV series: The New Bill Cosby Show, 1972-73; "Laugh In"; "The Flip Wilson Show"; "The Streets of San Francisco", 1974; "Ben Vereen... Comin", 1974; "Ben Vereen... Comin' at Ya", 1975; "Lola", 1975; "Lola Falana Show", 1976; "The Joey Bishop Show"; "The Hollywood Palace"; "The Love Boat", 1978; Marooned, 1978; "Liberace: A Valentine Special, 1979; "The Big Show", 1980; "Capitol", actress, 1982; "Lola, Lola y Lollo", 1982; "Hotel", 1986; Practice Relig & Faith, currently; Capital Entertainment, Agent, Currently. **Honors/Awds:** Nominated for a Tony Award, 1975; CLIO Award, Tigress com campaign, 1976; Theater World Award, Most Outstanding New Performer, 1976; Entertainer of the Year, Am Guild Variety Artists, 1977; Black Filmmakers Hall of Fame; Oscar Micheaux Award, 1989. **Special Achievements:** Smashed nearly every Las Vegas nightclub attendance & box office record; First Lady of Las Vegas. **Home Addr:** , Las Vegas, NV. **Business Addr:** Agent, Capital Entertainment, 1201 N St NW Suite A-5, Washington, DC 20035-6661.

### FALES, SUSAN MARYA

Television producer, writer. **Personal:** Born Rome; daughter of Timothy and Josephine Premice (deceased); married Aaron Christopher Hill; children: one. **Educ:** Harvard Univ, BA, hist & lit, 1985. **Career:** TV Shows:"The Cosby Show, " apprentice writer, 1985-86; "A Different World, " story editor, 1986-87, co-producer, writer, 1987-93; "Central Park West, " tv series, writer, 1995; "Linc's, " exec producer & head writer, 1998-2000; For Real, feature film, actress, 2001; "Suddenly Susan, " writer; "Vogue, " "Town & Country, " and "Travel & Leisure, " writer; "Kirk", exec producer; "Suddenly Susan", consult producer, writer. **Orgs:** Bd trustee, Am Ballet Theatre; Studio Museum in Harlem; East Side House Settlement. **Honors/Awds:** Produces Guild of Americas Nova award, Friends Black Emmys; Excellence & Heritage Award, Dillard University. **Special Achievements:** Author Always Wear Joy, Harper Collins, 2003; Nominated for the Humanitas Award; Finalist for Zora Neale Hurston Richard Wright Legacy Award. **Home Addr:** 863 Pk AveApt 7E, New York, NY 10075-0380. **Business Addr:** Writer, Wpxn-Tv, New York, NY 10112, **Business Phone:** (212)664-4444.

### FANCHER, DR. EVELYN PITTS

Librarian. **Personal:** Born Birmingham, AL; daughter of D C Pitts and Nell Pitts; married Charles B; children: Charles Jr, Mark & Adrienne. **Educ:** Ala State Univ, BS; Atlanta Univ, MSLS, 1961; Peabody Vanderbilt Univ, EdS, 1969, PhD, 1975. **Career:** Librarian (retired); Lincoln High Sch, librn, 1951-56; Ala Agri & Mech Univ, librn, 1956; Tenn State Univ, librn, 1962-75, prof libr Sci, 1975, dir libr, 1976-89; Vanderbilt Univ, Kelly M Smith Res Collection, res librn, 1991-96. **Orgs:** Bd dir, Girl Scout, Cumberland Valley, 1980-84; Libr consult, USAID, Swaziland, 1982; bd mem, Tenn Adv Coun Librarians, 1983-89; pres, Tenn Libr Asn, 1984-85; SE Libr Asn; Am Libr Asn; Tenn Libr Asn; Tenn Higher Educ Comn Libry Tech Coun; Tenn Long Range Plng Comn, five yr plan libr; reviewer, Southern Asn Cols & Schs; life mem, Nat Asn Advan Colored People; Alpha Kappa Alpha Sorority; Nat Coalition 100 Black Women; Adv Coun Sr Citizens; pres, African-Am Church Historians Asn, currently; pres, Les Gemmes Inc; Southeastern Libr Network; Links Inc; Alpha Kappa Alpha Sorority; Mem Adv Coun, Sr Citizens Inc; First Baptist Church. **Home Addr:** 3948 Drakes Br Rd, Nashville, TN 37218.

### FANN, ALBERT LOUIS

Educator, actor. **Personal:** Born Feb 21, 1925, Cleveland, OH; son of Albert Louis and Beulah; married Barbara; children: Tracy King, Shelley Peterson, Melanie, Albert, Kacie & Scott; married Mi Mi Green. **Educ:** Cleveland Inst Music, 1959; Living Ministries Int, DD, 1981. **Career:** Actor, 1950-; Al Fann Theatrical Ensemble, exec dir, 1965-; Come Back, Charleston Blue, assoc producer, 1972. Films: Cotton Comes to Harlem, 1970; The French Connection, 1971; Come Back, Charleston Blue, 1972; The Super Cops, 1974; E Lollipop, 1975; God Told Me To, 1976; The Incredible Hulk, 1977; Thank God Its Friday, 1978; Love in a Taxi, 1980; Casino, 1980; Scouts Honor, 1980; Thornwell, 1981; Parasite, 1982; Happy Endings, 1983; The Jerk, Too, 1984; Creator, 1985; Brown and Midnight Brewster, 1985; Handsome Harrys, 1986; Crossroads, 1986; Return to Horror High, 1987; Moving, 1988; Curse II: The Bite, 1988; Half N Half, 1988; To Die For, 1989; Oh Henry, 1989; Nick Knight, 1989; Turner & Hooch, 1990; The Naked Gun 2 1/2: The Smell of Fear, 1991; The Fisher King, 1991; Frankie and Johnny, 1991; Stop Or My Mom Will Shoot, 1992; Stormy Weathers, 1992; Sharons Secret, 1995; Hefner: Unauthorized, 1999. TV Series: "Search for Tomorrow", 1970; "How to Survive a Marriage", 1974; "The Plastic Man Comedy/Adventure Show", 1979; "Hes the Mayor", 1986; "Home Improvement The Long and Winding Road: Part 3", 1991-99; "Bodies of Evidence", 1992; Ballad of Derrick Gordon, producer; "Night Court Opportunity Knock Knocks Part 2", 1992; "Seinfeld The Ticket", 1992; "Hangin with Mr. Cooper The Presentation", 1992; "Daves World The Insecurity System", 1993; "Home Improvement Death Begins at Forty", 1994; "Home Improvement Als Video", 1994; "Home Improvement The Old College Try", 1994; "Martin Movin on In", 1994-95; "Scrambled Eggs", 1995; "Empty Nest Stand by Your Man", 1995; "Martin Headin for Trouble", 1995; "A Miracle Happens Here", 1995; "Almost Perfect Gimme Shelter", 1997; "Frasier Where Every Bloke Knows Your Name", 1998; "Any Day Now", 1999; "The West Wing Mr. Willis of Ohio", 1999; "The Michael Richards Show The Consultant", 2000; "Felicity My Best Friend's Wedding", 2001; "Curb Your Enthusiasm Crazy-Eyez Killah", 2002; "Greetings from Tucson Home Sweet Home", 2003; "The Lady killers", 2004. **Orgs:** Screen Actors Guild, 1965-; Am Fedn TV & Radio Artists, 1965-; life-time hon mem, Nat Asn Advan Colored People, 1979; founder, Inst Artistic Develop, Higher Mind Training, 1986; blue ribbon panel judge, Acad Artists & Sci, 1987. **Business Addr:** Actor, Associate Producer, Al Fann Theatrical Ensemble, 6051 Hollywood Blvd Suite 207, Los Angeles, CA 90028-5496, **Business Phone:** (323)464-0187.

### FANN, CHAD FITZGERALD

Football player. **Personal:** Born Jun 7, 1970, Jacksonville, FL. **Educ:** Fla A&M Univ, BA, criminal justice; Univ Miss, grad. **Career:** Football player (retired); Phoenix Cardinals, tight end, 1993; Ariz Cardinals, tight end, 1994-95; San Francisco 49ers, tight end, 1997-99; Minn Vikings, 2000.

### FAREED, KAMAAL IBN JOHN (JONATHAN DAVIS)

Rap musician, actor. **Personal:** Born Apr 10, 1970, Brooklyn, NY; married Michele Daves. **Career:** A Tribe Called Quest, co-founder, 1988-; Albums with A Tribe Called Quest including: People's Instinctive Travels & the Paths of Rhythm, 1990; The Low End Theory, 1991; Midnight Marauders, 1993; Beats, Rhymes, & Life, 1996; The Love Movement, 1998; Solo Albums: Description of a Fool, 1989; Poetic Justice, 1993; Rhyme & Reason, 1997; Love Goggles, 1999; Amplified, 1999; Open The Mix tape: Abstract Innovations, 2008; The Renaissance, 2008; "Kamaal/ The Abstract", 2009; Singles: "Vivrant Thing", "High Rollers (feat. Consequence)", "Breathe & Stop", 1999; "For The Nasty (feat. Busta Rhymes & Pharrell)", 2005; "Work It Out", 2007; Films: Poetic Justice, 1993; Disappearing Acts, 2000: Prison Song, producer & writer, 2001; Brown Sugar, 2002; Death of a Dynasty, 2003; She Hate Me, 2004; Cadillac Record, 2008; Holy Rollers, 2010. TV series: "Happily Ever After: Fairy Tales for Every Child", 2000; "Disappearing Acts", 2000; "The Hip Hop Project", assoc producer, 2006. **Honors/Awds:** Best Dance Recording: "Galvanize", Grammy Awards, 2006; Nominee: Best R&B Song: "Honey", Grammy Awards, 1999; Best Hip-Hop Video: "Vivrant Thing", MTV Awards, 2000; Best Rap Solo Performance: "Vivrant Thing", Grammy Awards, 2000; Best Rap Album: (The Renaissance), Grammy Awards, 2010. **Business Addr:** Singer, Rapper & Actor, Hip Hop producer, c/o BMG Entertainment Inc, 1540 Broadway Fl 44, New York, NY 10036, **Business Phone:** (212)930-4000.

### FARLEY, DR. JONATHAN DAVID

College teacher, educator. **Personal:** Born Jan 1, 1970?, Rochester, NY. **Educ:** Harvard Univ, AB, math, 1991; Oxford Univ, PhD, math, 1995. **Career:** Math Sci Res Inst, fel, 1995-97; Vanderbilt Univ, asst prof to assoc prof, 2002; Mass Inst Technol, prof, vis assoc prof appl math, MIT affil, 2003-04; Harvard Univ, vis scholar, 2005-, math prof, currently; Stanford Univ Ctr Int Security, sci fel, 2005; Univ W Indies, prof, math & comp sci, currently. **Orgs:** Post-doctoral fel Math Sci Res Inst, 1995-97; Fel Ctr Int Security & Coop, 2005-06; scince fel Stanford Univ; Warren Group. **Business Addr:** Mathematics Professor, Harvard University, 1 Oxford St, Cambridge, MA 02138, **Business Phone:** (617)495-8477.

### FARLEY, WILLIAM HORACE, JR. See Obituaries Section.

### FARMER, CLARENCE, SR. See Obituaries Section.

### FARMER, FOREST JACKSON, SR.

Executive. **Personal:** Born Jan 15, 1941, Zanesville, OH; son of William J and Leatha D Randolph; married Rosalyn Farmer McPherson; children: Forest Jr & Christopher M. **Educ:** Purdue Univ, Lafayette, IN, BS, biol & phys educ, 1965. **Career:** Chrysler Motors Corp, 1968-88, Jefferson Assembly Plant, plant mgr, 1981, Newark, DE, assembly plant mgr, 1983, Sterling Heights, MI, plant mgr, 1984, dir advan mfg planning, 1986-87, Highland Pk, MI, gen plant mgr, 1987-88, Acustar, Troy, MI, pres, 1988-95; Trillium Teamologies, chmn, chief exec officer & pres, 1995-; Bing Mfg Inc, pres & chief exec officer, 1995-98; Farmer Group, chmn, pres & chief exec officer, 1998-; Regal Plastics Co, chief exec officer; Enerflex Solutions LLC, chmn, chief exec officer & pres. **Orgs:** Bd dir, Lubrizol Corp, 1997-2012; bd dir, Am Axle & Mfg Inc, 1999-; bd dir, Saturn Electronics & Engineering Inc, 2000-12; mem bd, Macomb Hosp Corp. **Honors/Awds:** Outstanding Businessman, 1989; 100 Black Men of America, 1989. **Business Addr:** Chairman & President, Chief Executive Officer, The Farmer Group, 35 W Huron St, Pontiac, MI 48342, **Business Phone:** (248)322-7079.

### FARMER, HARVEY RAY. See FARMER, RAY, JR.

### FARMER, HILDA WOOTEN

Banker. **Personal:** Born Apr 25, 1950, La Grange, NC; daughter of Elbert Wooten and Janie Wooten (deceased); married William E; children: William Jr & Courtney. **Educ:** NC Cent Univ, Durham, NC, BS, 1972. **Career:** Wachovia Bank, Goldsboro, NC, dealer credit mgr, asst vpres, 1987-. **Orgs:** Treas, Am Cancer Soc, 1986-91. **Home Addr:** 494 Hare Rd Rte 4, PO Box 90, Goldsboro, NC 27534-7966, **Home Phone:** (919)736-7193. **Business Addr:** Assistant Vice President, Sales Finance Department, Wachovia Bank & Trust Co, 301 E Ash St, Goldsboro, NC 27530, **Business Phone:** (919)735-0211.

**FARMER, NANCY A.**
Judge. **Educ:** Eastern Mich Univ; Detroit Col Law, law. **Career:** Thirty sixth Dist Ct, Detroit, chief judge & ct adminr, currently. **Orgs:** Workers Compensation Bd & Chairperson Mich Employ Bd Rev; trustee, Detroit Metrop Bar Asn; bd dir, St Francis Family Serv; Links Inc; Renaissance Chap. **Business Addr:** Chief Judge, Court Administrator, 36th District Court, 421 Madison Ave, Detroit, MI 48226, **Business Phone:** (313)965-8720.

**FARMER, RAY, JR. (HARVEY RAY FARMER)**
Football executive, football player. **Personal:** Born Jul 1, 1974, White Plains, NY; married Vernet B; children: Boyd & Kennedy. **Educ:** Duke Univ, BA, sociol, 1996. **Career:** Football player (retired), football executive; Philadelphia Eagles, left linebacker, 1996-97, 1998; Duke Univ, acad coordr, 2001; Atlanta Falcons, pro-scout, 2002-05; Kans City Chiefs, dir pro personnel, 2006-12; Cleveland Browns, asst gen mgr, 2013-14, gen mgr, 2014-15; Carolina Panthers; Comcast Sports Network, tv sports analyst. **Honors/Awds:** Inductee, Chiefs Hall of Fame, 1992; Pro Football Hall of Fame, 2008; Holds a Chief Record with 58 Career INT's. **Special Achievements:** Was a two-time All-Atlantic Coast Conference selection for the BlueDevils; was named to the conference All-Academic Team in 1994. **Home Addr:** 14452 Canterbury St, Overland Park, KS 66224-3934. **Business Addr:** General Manager, Cleveland Browns, 76 Lou Groza Blvd, Berea, OH 44017, **Business Phone:** (440)824-3434.

**FARMER, DR. ROBERT CLARENCE, SR.**
Physician. **Personal:** Born Jan 1, 1941, Rochester, PA; son of Francis Alexander and Ora Juanita McClain; married Linda Kay Hill; children: Saundra, Robert II, James & Wendy. **Educ:** Howard Univ, BS, 1963, MD, 1967. **Career:** Univ Pittsburgh, resident radiol, instr pediat radiol, 1973-74; St Francis Med Ctr, resident radiol, intern; Pittsburgh C Hosp, fel; Howard Univ, asst prof radiol, 1974-75, asst prof pediat, 1974-77; St Anthony Hosp, dir radiol, 1977-81; Fayette Co Hosp, dir radiol, 1978-83; Ft Stewart Hosp, dir radiol, 1980-81; Connellsville State Gen Hosp, dir radiol, 1982-85; Highlands Hosp & Health Ctr, dir radiol, 1985-2000; Farmer Diag Imaging Serv Inc, pres, health radiol, 1992-; HUA, pres, 1992-; African Am Chamber Com. **Orgs:** Life mem, Nat Asn Advan Colored People, 1953-; life mem, Alpha Phi Alpha Frat; Radiol Soc N Am, 1973-; Am Col Radiol, 1973-; Nat Med Asn, 1977-; Am Cancer Soc, 1983-; bd dirs, Am Lung Asn, 1985-; bd dirs, Comm Housing Resource, Bd Fayette City, PA; FROGS Club, Pittsburgh; pres, Fayette County, Nat Asn Advan Colored People, 1989-92; vpres, Pa State Conf Nat Asn Advan Colored People Br, 1989-91; pres, Rotary Club Connellsville; vpres, Pittsburgh Lay Conf Am Methodist Episcopal Church; pres, Gateway Med Soc Nat Med Asn, 1994-96; pres, Chi Delta Mu Fraternity Pi Chap, 1995-97; bd mem, Blue Cross Western Pa, 1996; bd mem, High Mark Corp, 1996-. **Honors/Awds:** Black Achiever of SW Pennsylvania 11th dist Debora Grand Chapter OES, 1988; Physician of the Year, Gateway Med Soc, 1999. **Special Achievements:** Publications "Carcinoma of the Breast; A Clinical Study", NMA Journal1969; "Immunological Responses in Infantile Cortical Hyperostosis, "Pediatric Rsch Vol 10 1976; "Immunological Studies in Caffey's Cortical Hyperostosis", Pediatrics 1977. **Home Addr:** 53 Colgate Dr, Rancho Mirage, CA 92270-3703, **Home Phone:** (760)324-9895. **Business Addr:** President, Farmer Diagnostic Imaging Service, 210 N Pittsburgh St, Connellsville, PA 15425-3233, **Business Phone:** (724)626-0610.

**FARMER, SHARON**
Photographer, government official. **Personal:** Born Jun 10, 1951, Washington, DC. **Educ:** Ohio State Univ, BA, photog & music, 1974. **Career:** White House, chief, White House Photog, 1993-99, dir, 1999-2001; Assoc Press, photo ed, photo supvr, 2001-04, Kerry Edwards 2004 Inc, campaign photogr, 2004-05; Am Univ, fac; Mt Vernon Col, fac; Ind Univ, fac. **Orgs:** Photog Ed, Assoc Press, 2001-04; mem, Delta Sigma Theta Sorority Inc, Ohio State Univ. **Special Achievements:** First Black Women to serve as White House Photographer. **Business Addr:** Photo Supervisor, Associated Press, 1150 18th St NW, Washington, DC 20036, **Business Phone:** (202)466-3973.

**FARR, D'MARCO MARCELLUS**
Football player, radio host. **Personal:** Born Jun 9, 1971, San Pablo, CA; married Cynthia; children: Grant Marcellus. **Educ:** Univ Wash, BA, soc & justice. **Career:** Football player (retired), host; Los Angeles Rams, defensive tackle, 1994; St Louis Rams, right defensive tackle, 1994-2000, defensive end, 1999; San Francisco 49ers, 2003-04; KSPN radio, D'Marco Farr Show, host, 2005-07; KTVI FOX 2, TV color commentary, 2008; 103.3 KLOU, 2008-16; 101.1 WXOS, 2008-16; 101 ESPN, color commentator & host, 2009-16; FSN, Best Damn Sports Show Period, co-host, 2009. **Honors/Awds:** Super Bowl champion XXXIV; Morris Trophy, 1993; Pro Bowl, 1999. **Business Addr:** Color Commentator, Host, 101 ESPN, 11647 Olive Blvd, St. Louis, MO 63141, **Business Phone:** (314)983-6000.

**FARR, MELVIN, SR. See Obituaries Section.**

**FARRAKHAN, LOUIS (LOUIS EUGENE WALCOTT)**
Social worker, clergy. **Personal:** Born May 11, 1933, Bronx, NY; son of Percival Clarke (deceased) and Sarah Mae Manning; married Khadijah; children: Mustapha, Joshua Nasir, Abnar, Louis Jr, Donna, Hanan, Maria, Fatimah & Khallada. **Educ:** Winston-Salem Teachers Col. **Career:** Minister; Us govt, social leader & critic; Final Call, founder, 1979; Nation Islam, minister & actg head, currently. **Honors/Awds:** Named to the list of the Greatest Chicagoans of the Century; Rev Dr Jeremiah A Wright Jr Lifetime Achievement Trumpeteer Award, 2007. **Special Achievements:** Independent Black Leadership in America, 1991; organized Million Man March, 1995; organized Million Family March, 2000; achieved fame in Bostonas a vocalist, calypso singer, dancer & violinist; book: A Torchlight for America, 1993; First African Americans to appear on the Ted Mack Amateur Hour. **Business Addr:** Minister, The Nation of Islam, 7351 S Stony Island Ave, Chicago, IL 60649, **Business Phone:** (773)324-6000.

**FARRAR, MOSES**
Business owner, writer. **Personal:** Born Dec 28, 1929, Richmond, VA; son of Percy B and Lavinia; married Naomi Boekhoudt; children: Muriel Locke, Regina Dyson, Valerie Dews, Miriam, Benjamin, Monique Marshall & Lisa Eaves. **Career:** Business owner (retired); Norfolk J & Guide, 1951-60; Philadelphia Inquirer, typesetter, 1961-63; Wescott Thomson, Philadelphia, Pa, typesetter, 1963-69; self-employed, 1969-92; Fifth Tabernacle, local pastor, currently. Books: What Black Christians Should Know (But Don't) About Christianity!; The Deceiving of the Black Race; A Non-Christian's Response to Christianity; The Hebrew Scriptures and the Greek Scriptures: The Vast Differences; Lavinia, My Mother; Clara Naomi, My Wife; The Hebrew Heritage of Black Africa; What Will It Take to Wake Us Up?; 40 Most FAQs to Hebrew Israelites with Answers; Rabbi Yeshua Ben Yosef (JOSHUA Son of Joseph): JESUS, Who Thought He Was Messiah!. **Orgs:** Temple Beth El's Fifth Tabernacle, 1973-76; Ninth Tabernacle, 1976-93; minister, Fifteenth Tabernacle, 1993-98; assoc minister, Seventh Tabernacle, 1998-2000; First Tabernacle, 2002. **Home Addr:** 437 E 22nd St Suite 1A, PO Box 100065, Brooklyn, NY 11210-0065, **Home Phone:** (718)287-7743.

**FARRELL, CHERYL LAYNE**
Banker, singer, advocate. **Personal:** Born Sep 10, 1955, Los Angeles, CA; married Wendell Charles; children: Nia Grace & Alexander Layne. **Educ:** Univ Calif, Los Angeles, Calif, BA, econs, 1987; Univ SC, Los Angeles, CA, Annenberg Sch, MA, commun mgt, 2000. **Career:** Writer, spokesperson, singer & advocate; Bullocks Dept Store, Los Angeles, Calif, dept mgr, asst buyer, 1977-79; Union Bank, Los Angeles, Calif, credit mgr, 1979-81, col recruiter, ops trainee, 1981-82; Bank Am, Los Angeles, Calif, asst vpres, 1982-84, vpres, cash mgt & govt serv, mgr, 1984-95, commun vpres, 1995-96; M&I Electronic Banking, Glendale, Calif, nat acct mgr, 1997; Juv Diabetes Res Found, parent advocate, 2003-; Providence Health & Serv, mkt commun consult, 2010-11; Syndicated Tv, tv spokesperson, 2001-08; TV Personality & Spokesperson: Jeopardy!, 2001-08; Cheryl Farrell Commun, corp commun consult, 2010-; Southern Calif Edison, corp commun contractor, 2012-13; Spokesperson: The Greater Contribution, 2008-10. **Orgs:** Dir pub rel, Los Angeles Urban Bankers, 1986-89; moderator, Morningside United Church Christ; Bank Am Speaking Club; vol, Big Sisters, Los Angeles; mem bd dir, LA Chap, Int Asn Bus Communicators, 2008-; healthcare advocate, speakers bur, music producer, Am Diabetes Asn; dir, Int Asn Bus Communictors, 2008-12; parent advocate-vol co-producer, music dir, Juv Diabetes Res Found, 2003-12. **Honors/Awds:** CINDY Award, Faces Diversity Video, 1996; Suggestion Award, Union Bank. **Special Achievements:** Hundred Most Promising Black Women in Corporate America, Ebony Mag. **Home Addr:** 638 Lindero Canyon Rd, PO Box 110, Oak Park, CA 91377, **Home Phone:** (818)516-3804. **Business Addr:** Corporate Communications Consultant, Cheryl Farrell Communications, 638 Lindero Canyon Rd, Oak Park, CA 91377.

**FARRELL, HERMAN DENNY, JR.**
State government official. **Personal:** Born Feb 4, 1932, White Plains, NY; son of Herman Sr and Gladys; married Theresa; children: Monique, Herman III & Sopia Llene. **Educ:** NY Univ, attended 1955. **Career:** Sup Ct Judge Confidential Aid, 1966-72; Mayor John Lindsay, asst dir local neighbor Govt, 1972-74; NY St Assembly, Ways & Means Comm, assembly man, 1974-, chmn, Assembly Banks Comt, 1979-94, mem, Temp Comt Interstate Banking, mem, 1983; New York County Dem Comt, county leader, 1981-; Financial Insts Nat Conf State Legislators, sub comt chmn, 1981-82; NY Dem Party, committeeman, 1970, 1983-93, vice chmn, 1982-92, chmn, 2001-; Electoral Col, elector, 2000. **Orgs:** Dem Nat Comt, 1988; hon mem, Tioga Carver Comm Found, 1989-95. **Honors/Awds:** Distinguished Legislator Award, St Parole Officers; NY Affirmative Action Coun's Award; Appreciation Award, Boricua Col; Childs Mem Church Award; NY St Ct Clerks Asn Award; Am Legion Cert Appreciation; Tioga Carver Comm Found. **Business Addr:** Assemblyman, New York State Assembly, 2541-55 Adam Clayton Powell Jr Blvd, New York, NY 10039, **Business Phone:** (212)234-1430.

**FARRELL, ROBERT C.**
Government official. **Personal:** Born Oct 1, 1936, Natchez, MS; married Essiebea; children: Mia Ann. **Educ:** Univ Calif, Los Angeles, BA, 1961, Grad Sch Jour. **Career:** Calif Eagle Newspaper, reporter; Los Angeles Sentinel Newspaper, reporter; Jet Mag, corresp; Star Rev News Watts, publ; State Assembly man Mervyn Dymally, consult, currently. **Orgs:** Dep city counman, Billy C Mills, 1963-71; admin co ordr, S Los Angeles Mayor Bradley's & Staff, 1969-73; Los Angeles City Coun man, 8th Dist, 1974-91; Radio & TV News Asn So, CA; Pub Rels Soc Am; Nat Asn Advan Colored People; Sigma Delta Chi; Legal Defense & Educ Fund; UCLA Alumni Asn; Urban League; pres, Baptist Ministers Conf Los Angeles & vicinity; pres, San Pedro Sect Nat Conf Negro Women. **Home Addr:** 1351 W 37 St, Los Angeles, CA 90007. **Business Addr:** Consultant, Capitol Office, PO Box 942849, Sacramento, CA 94249-0052, **Business Phone:** (916)319-2052.

**FARRINGTON, THOMAS ALEX**
Executive, executive director. **Personal:** Born Nov 12, 1943, Chapel Hill, NC; son of Osmond T and Mary; married Juarez Harrell; children: Christopher, Trevor & Tomeeka. **Educ:** NC Agr & Tech State Univ, BS, elec engineering, 1966; Northeastern Univ, Grad Sch Eng. **Career:** RCA Corp, 1966-69; Int Offshore Co Serv Inc, pres, 1969-; Input Output Comput Servs, pres, chief exec officer, 1969-94; Farrington Assocs Inc, pres & chief exec officer, 1994-; Prostate Health Educ Network, founder & pres. **Orgs:** Coun Foreign Rels, 1989-; dir, Boston Pvt Indust Coun; dir, Minority Bus Enterprise Legal Defense Fund; founder, Intelligent Transp Syst Consortium Inc; bd dir, Bankblackwell. **Honors/Awds:** Minority Contractor Yr, Dept Transp, 1984; Nat Minority Serv Indust Firm Yr, US Dept Com, 1986. **Special Achievements:** Top 100 Businesses, Black Enterprise; Special Achievement, Black Corporate Presidents of New England, 1988. **Home Addr:** 3100 Old Pineview Rd, Chapel Hill, NC 27516-5967. **Business Addr:** President, Chief Executive Officer, Farrington Associates Inc, 1 Adams Pl, Quincy, MA 02169, **Business Phone:** (781)487-7054.

**FARRIOR, JAMES ALFRED**
Football player. **Personal:** Born Jan 6, 1975, Ettrick, VA; son of James and Rebecca; married Iman. **Educ:** Va Univ, BS, psychol. **Career:** Football player (retired); New York Jets, right outside linebacker, 1997, linebacker, 1998-99, right outside linebacker & linebacker, 2000-01; Pittsburgh Steelers, right linebacker & left inner linebacker & linebacker & mid linebacker, 2002-11. **Orgs:** Founder, James Farrior Found. **Honors/Awds:** ACC Newcomer of the Week honors; Group AA co-offensive Player of the Year; All-Metro & All-State hons; ACC0 second team hons; Most Valuable Player, Pittsburgh Steelers, 2004; Pro Bowl, 2004 & 2008; Co-Player of the Year, The Richmond Times-Dispatch's; Bravo Award; Three Times American Football Conference Champion, 2005, 2008, 2010; Virginia Sports Hall of Fame, 2016. **Home Addr:** 5835 Indian Trl, Houston, TX 77057-1306. **Business Addr:** Professional Football Player, Pittsburgh Steelers, 3400 S Water St, Pittsburgh, PA 15203-2349, **Business Phone:** (412)432-7800.

**FARRIS, DR. ALICIA RENEE**
Executive director. **Educ:** Cent Mich Univ, attended 1998. **Career:** New Begginnings Consult Group, owner, currenlty; Univ Detroit Mercy, Lib Arts & Educ, Mich Inst Nonviolence Educ, adj prof, exec dir, currently; Restaurant Opportunities Ctr Mich, state dir. **Orgs:** Bd mem, adv bd mem, Mich Coalition Human Rights; bd mem, Detroit Community Justice Partnership; New Detroit Inc, Mich Inst Nonviolence Educ; Mich Neighborhood Partnership & Doing Develop Differently Metrop Detroit. **Home Addr:** , MI. **Business Addr:** Executive Director, University of Detroit Mercy, 8200 W Outer Dr, Detroit, MI 48219-3580, **Business Phone:** (313)494-6650.

**FARRIS, ESQ. DEBORAH ELLISON**
Lawyer. **Personal:** Born Dec 29, 1950, Williamsburg, VA; daughter of John M Jr (deceased) and Ethel Crawford (deceased); married J Randolph, Sep 15, 1978; children: James R II. **Educ:** Del State Col, BA, 1972; Antioch Grad Sch, MA, 1973; Howard Univ Sch Law, JD, 1976. **Career:** Off Gov Rick Perry, one-call bd, 2003; pvt pract atty, currently. **Orgs:** Nat pres, Nat Carrousels Inc, 1990-92; Black Women Atty Asn; local financial secy, Jack & Jill Am Inc; Nat Coalition 100 Black Women; Gov Task Force Tuberc; Dallas Youth Orchestra Bd; NBA; Girl Friends Inc; J L Turner Legal Soc; Dallas Youth Orchestra Bd; State Bar Tex; Nat Bar Asn; Tex Criminal Defense Lawyers Asn. **Business Addr:** Attorney, Private Practice, 4136 High Summit Dr, Dallas, TX 75244-6626, **Business Phone:** (972)484-2895.

**FARRIS, HON. JEROME**
Judge. **Personal:** Born Mar 4, 1930, Birmingham, AL; son of Willie Joe and Elizabeth; children: Juli Elizabeth & Janelle Marie. **Educ:** Morehouse Col, BS, 1951, LLD, 1951; Atlanta Univ, MSW, 1955; Univ Wash, JD, 1958. **Career:** Weyer Roderick Schroeter & Sterne, assoc, 1958-59; Weyer Schroeter Sterne & Farris, partner, 1959-61; Schroeter & Farris, partner, 1961-63; Schroeter Farris Bangs & Horowitz, partner, 1963-65; Farris Bangs & Horowitz, partner, 1965-69; Wash State Off, Ct appeals, judge, 1969-79, US Appeals Ct Judge, 9th Circuit, 1979-95. **Orgs:** Pres, Wash State Jr Community Col, 1965-66; trustee, Pacific NW Ballet, 1978-83; chmn, ABA Appellate Judges' Conf, 1982-83; chmn, State Fed Judicial Coun of Wash, 1983-87; adv bd, Nat Ctr for State Courts Appellate Justice Proj, 1978-81; founder, Univ Wash Law Sch, 1978-84; adv bd, Tyee Bd of Adv, 1984-; regent, Univ Wash, 1985-97; bd, Am Bar Found, 1987-, exec comt, 1989-; vis comt, Harvard Law Sch, 1996-; US Supreme Ct, judicial fel comm, 1997-; Int Judicial Rels, judicial conf comm, 1997-. **Honors/Awds:** Clayton Frost Award Jaycees, 1966; Order of Coif Univ Wash Law Sch. **Business Addr:** Circuit Judge, United States Court of Appeals for the Ninth Circuit, 1200 6th Ave Suite 1805, Seattle, WA 98104, **Business Phone:** (206)553-2672.

**FARROW, BILL. See FARROW, WILLIAM MCKNIGHT, III.**

**FARROW, DR. HAROLD FRANK**
Dentist. **Personal:** Born May 10, 1936, Pensacola, FL; married Virginia B; children: Heather & Vance. **Educ:** Tenn State Univ, BS, 1959; Howard Univ, DDS, 1970. **Career:** C's Hosp, Detroit, staff, 1970-71; Wayne Co Health Dept, proj prescad, 1971-72; pvt pract, dentist, 1972-. **Orgs:** Secy, Wolverine Dent Soc, 1974; pres, Wolverine Dent Soc, 1976; Wolverine Dent Soc, 1977; Am Dent Asn; Mich Dent Asn; DDDA; Nat Dent Asn; Chi Delta Mu Fraternity; Noble Marracci Temple no 13, Mystic Shrine, 1974; Nat Asn Advan Colored People, 1976; New Prospect Baptist Church; Howard Univ; N15 Metab Edsel Ford Inst. **Honors/Awds:** Achievement Honorary Award, Wolverine Dent Soc, 1974. **Home Addr:** 8241 Parkstone Pl, Naples, FL 34120-0614, **Home Phone:** (239)353-9275. **Business Addr:** Dentist, Private Practice, 334 Livernois St, Ferndale, MI 48220, **Business Phone:** (248)547-2040.

**FARROW, SALLIE A.**
Lawyer. **Personal:** Born Dec 31, 1942, Plainfield, NJ; daughter of James R Rivera and Sallie Mitchell Rivera; children: Richard H Staton Jr. **Educ:** Denver Univ, Denver, Colo, BA, 1974; Univ Nebr, Lincoln, Nebr, JD, 1976. **Career:** Mutual Omaha, Omaha, Nebr, asst gen coun, 1977-87; NY Life Ins Co, assoc counr, 1987-. **Orgs:** Kappa Delta Pi, 1973-; consult, ACE Counr SBA, Omaha, 1980-85; panelist, US Off Educ, Wash, DC, 1981; chairperson, Boys Scouts Am, Omaha, 1982; organizer, adv, Metro Sci & Eng Fair Inc, 1982-87; moot ct judge; Creighton Univ, 1983-87; consult, Omaha Pub Schs, Career Awareness, 1983-87; dir, Girls Club Omaha, 1985-87; ed, bar-jour, Nat Bar Asn, 1986-; comt mem, Omaha Bar Asn, 1986-87; Nat Bar Asn Memoirs & Legal Jour, 1986 & 1988; mentor, Legal Outreach, 1992-; vol, gen coun, Nat Coun Negro Women Greater NY, 1993. **Honors/Awds:** Outstanding Achievement, Girls Club Omaha, 1987. **Home Addr:** 1 Rockwell Pl Apt 1D, Brooklyn, NY 11217, **Home Phone:** (718)852-6131. **Business Addr:** Associate Counselor, New York Life Insurance Co, 51 Madison Ave Suite 10SB, New York, NY 10010, **Business Phone:** (212)576-7000.

**FARROW, WILLIAM MCKNIGHT, III (BILL FARROW)**
Executive. **Personal:** Born Feb 23, 1955, Chicago, IL; son of William McKnight Jr and Ruth Katherine Haven; married Sandra High; children: Ashley Marie, William McKnight IV & Justin Matthew. **Educ:** Augustana Col, Rock Island, BA, 1977; Northwestern Univ, Evanston, MBA, 1979. **Career:** Northwestern Mem Hosp, mgt fel, 1978; Arthur Andersen & Co, Chicago, sr consult, 1979-83; GD Searle & Co, Skokie, mgr acquisitions, 1983-85; Dart & Kraft Inc, Northbrook, dir strategy, 1985-86; First Nat Bank Chicago, vpres, head mkt, 1986-88; First Chicago Capital Markets, Chicago, managing dir, 1988-92; NOW, sr vpres, 1992; First Chicago CRE & Inst Bank, head mkt, 1992-96; First Chicago NBD Corp, sr vpres, prog exec, 1996-99; Bank One Corp, sr vpres, Head Treas Mgt, 1999-2000, sr vpres, Head E-Bus, 2000-01; Chicago Bd Trade, exec vpres & chief info officer, 2001; Winston & Wolfe LLC, owner; FC Partners Group, chief exec officer; Urban Partnership Bank, pres & chief exec officer, currently. **Orgs:** Reg facilitator, LEAD, 1979-91; bd dir, Ancilla Hosp Syst Inc, 1985-89; bd dir, Community Ment Health Coun, 1986-88; Chicago Bond Club, 1989-; bd dir, Inroads Inc, 1992-; chmn, United Way/Crusade Mercy, W Region, 1993-; Leadership Greater Chicago, 1994; bd dir, Cabrini Green Tutoring, 1995-; Life Directions Inc, 1995-; Ct Theatre, 1996-; bd dir, Fed Res Bank Chicago; trustee, Ill Inst Technol; dir, North-Shore Health Systs; bd dir, CoBank Inc, currently. **Home Addr:** 1734 Asbury Ave, Evanston, IL 60201-3502, **Home Phone:** (847)570-0331. **Business Addr:** Chief Executive Officer, President, Urban Partnership Bank, 7555 N Calif Ave, Chicago, IL 60645, **Business Phone:** (773)420-5050.

**FARROW, MAJ. WILLIE LEWIS.** **See Obituaries Section.**

**FATTAH, HON. CHAKA (ARTHUR DAVENPORT)**
**Personal:** Born Nov 21, 1956, Philadelphia, PA; son of Russell Davenport and Frances Brown; married Michelle; children: Chaka Jr; married Renee Chenault; children: Francis, Cameron, Chandler & Chip. **Educ:** Philadelphia Community Col; Univ Pa, Wharton Sch, Fels Inst Govt, MGA, 1986; Harvard Univ, JFK Sch Govt. **Career:** State Pa, state rep, dist 192, 1982-88, state sen, dist 7, 1988-94; Pa House Representatives, Dem Rep, 1983-88; US House Reps, Second Cong Dist Penn, congressman, 1994-; sr mem, US House Appropriations Comt; chmn, Cong urban Caucus. **Orgs:** Dem Cong Campaign Comt; Cong Black Caucus; Alpha Phi Alpha fraternity. **Business Addr:** Congressman, US House of Representatives, 2401 N 54th St, Philadelphia, PA 19131, **Business Phone:** (215)387-6404.

**FATTAH, FALAKA (QUEEN MOTHER FALAKA FATTAH)**
Association executive, founder (originator), writer. **Personal:** Born Dec 28, 1931, Philadelphia, PA; daughter of Percy Brown and Louise C Somers West; married David; children: Stefan, Robin, Kenneth, Chaka, Nasser & David. **Educ:** Whitern New Sch, Mse, 1949; Fleischers Art Sch, 1949; Temple Univ, attended 1953; Junto Evening Sch, course, 1956. **Career:** Self Employed Free Lance Writer, 1950-91; Philadelphia Bull Tribune Afro-Am Newspaper Pittsburgh Courier, journalist, 1952-68; Umoja Mag, ed, 1968-; Self Employed Urban Consult, 1970-91; Arthur A Little Assoc Off Jrvl Justice, consult, 1982-83; Eisenhower Found, Control Data, consult, 1982-83; House Umoja, chief exec officer, pres & founder, currently. **Orgs:** Exctr Comm Urban Affair Partnership, 1980-91; vice chmn, W Philadelphia Youth Coun Ctr, 1981-91; comm, Mayor's Drug Alcohol Comn, 1982-83; sec, Nat Ctr Neighborhood Enterprise, 1982-; bd dir, Exec Com Eisenhower Found, 1983-; bd dir, Mayonb Comn Women; Hist Soc Pa, 1983-; consult, Wilmington House UMOJA, 1987-91; consult Portland House UMOJA, 1989-91; exec comt, Greater Philadelphia Partnership; comnr, Mayors Comn Women & Mayors Drug & Alcohol Comn; life mem, Hist Soc Penn; bd mem, W Philadelphia Coun Ctr; adv bd, Bridge; vpres, Philadelphia Coun Neighborhood Orgn; cofound, Philadelphia Black United Front. **Honors/Awds:** Reduction of Gang Deaths in Philadelphia via vol; coordinator of "IV Gang War in 1974 Campaign"; Grace B Flandnau Award, Nat Coun Crime & Delinquency, 1981; Secretary's Award, US Dept Health & Human Serv, 1989; Presidential Recognition, Temple Award for Creative Altruism, Inst Noetic Scis, 1990. **Special Achievements:** Book: "World Without Violence". **Business Addr:** Founder, Chief Executive Officer, House of Umoja Inc, 5625 W Master St, Philadelphia, PA 19131, **Business Phone:** (215)473-5893.

**FATTAH, QUEEN MOTHER FALAKA.** **See FATTAH, FALAKA.**

**FAUCETT, BARBARA J.** **See Obituaries Section.**

**FAULCON, DR. CLARENCE AUGUSTUS, II**
Educator. **Personal:** Born Aug 8, 1928, Philadelphia, PA; son of Leroy C and Addie Robinson; married Jacqueline Beach; children: David Clarence. **Educ:** Lincoln Univ, attended 1948; Univ Pa, BMus, 1950, MA, music educ, 1952; Philadelphia Conserv Music, PhD, musicol, 1962. **Career:** Educator (retried); Sulzberger Jr High Sch, Philadelphia, chmn music prog, music teacher & chmn, 1951-63; Philadelphia Concert Orchestra, asst conductor & clarinetist, 1955-57; Cazenovia Col, Cazenovia, NY, asst prof & chmn, 1963-68; Morgan St Univ, Baltimore, prof music & chmn, 1968-93; Educ Testing Serv, art consult, 1974. **Orgs:** Del, Int Biog Ctr Arts & Commun Cong; Afro Am Music Health Prom DisPrev & Ther, Montreal, Can; Conf Nat Med Asn, 1984; Music Fund Soc Philadelphia; chair, Wholistic Ministry Churches, 1994; Pa Hist Soc; Sigma Pi Phi. **Honors/Awds:** Faculty Award, Morgan St Univ Promethan Soc, 1983; Int Biographical Cong Medal, Budapest, Hungary, 1985; Bronze Bar Award, 1987; IBC Silver Medal, Queen Eng, 1990. **Home Addr:** 617 Ridgeview Rd Runnymede, PO Box 670, Hockessin, DE 19707, **Home Phone:** (302)239-3665.

**FAULCON, DR. GADDIS J.**
Educator. **Personal:** Born Nov 29, 1950, Oxford, NC; son of Jack and Lucille; married Jeanette; children: Tina & Rukel. **Educ:** St Augustine's Col, BS, 1974; NC State Univ, MRR/MPA, 1981, EdD, 1994. **Career:** Garner Rd YMCA, phys dir, 1975-83; Elizabeth City St Univ, NNCT, asst dir, 1984-85; St Augustine's Col, from asst vpres stud affairs to vpres stud affairs, 1985-95; Christian Faith Ct, acad dean; Shaw Univ, asst prof, Dept Allied Health Professions, assoc prof & chair, currently, fac athletic rep, currently, dean, 2009-. **Orgs:** Adv bd, vpres, Wilton Elem Sch; adv bd, Nat Youth Sport, 1987-92; bd dir, NC St Univ, 1990-92; Boy Scouts Am, Occoneechee Coun, 1992-94; adv bd, St Augustine's Col, Still Going On; Family First Granville County, 1990-95. **Home Addr:** 4019 Eaton Rd, Kittrell, NC 27544, **Home Phone:** (919)693-1566. **Business Addr:** Associate Professor of Allied Health Professions, Chairman of Allied Health, Shaw University, 118 E S St, Raleigh, NC 27601, **Business Phone:** (919)546-8205.

**FAULDING, JULIETTE J.**
Financial manager, executive director, consultant. **Personal:** Born Aug 2, 1952, Jackson, MS; daughter of Vannette Johnson and Luella B Tapo. **Educ:** Univ Calif, Berkeley, attended; Tougaloo Col, BS, math & econs, 1974; Columbia Univ, MBA, finance, 1976. **Career:** Mobil Oil Corp, banking analyst, 1976-77, financial analyst, 1977-79, short term investr, 1979-81, sr financial analyst, 1981-88, financial advisor, sales & supply treasr, 1989-96; Air Line Pilots Asn, Sr Financial Analyst, 1999-2002; MaxPont LLC, financial consult, 2002-04; SERVE Inc, dep exec dir, 2005-08; Alpha Acad, financial consult, 2008-; St.Johns Episcopal Church, Bookkeeper, 2010-. **Orgs:** Comt mem, Boy Scout Troop 75, 1982-87; assoc adv, Explorer Post 75 Queens, NY, 1982-87; Black MBA Asn; Chantilly Pyramid Minority Stud Achievement Comt, minority achievement representatives. **Honors/Awds:** Distinguished Graduate Award, Nat Asn For Equal Oppurtunity, 1984. **Special Achievements:** Participant Black Exec Exchange Prog; 100 of the most promising Black women in corporate America. **Home Addr:** 15169 Stratton Major Ct, Centreville, VA 20120, **Home Phone:** (703)803-9422. **Business Addr:** Financial Advisor, Supply Treasurer, Mobil Oil Corp, 3225 Gallows Rd, Fairfax, VA 22037, **Business Phone:** (703)846-3704.

**FAULK, MARSHALL WILLIAM**
Football player, foundation executive. **Personal:** Born Feb 26, 1973, New Orleans, LA; son of Roosevelt and Cecile; married Linday Stoudt; children: Marshall Jr, Jaden, Brooklyn, Presley, Farrah, Mahlik, Kwuan & Hakim. **Educ:** San Diego State Univ, attended 1993. **Career:** Football player (retired), foundation executive; Indianapolis Colts, running back, 1994-98; St Louis Rams, running back, 1999-2005, fullback, 199; NFL Network, analyst, currently. **Orgs:** Founder, Marshall Faulk Found, 1994-. **Honors/Awds:** First-team All-American, 1991-93; Offensive Rookie of the Year, Nat Fotball League, 1994; UPI AFL-AFC Rookie of the Year, 1994; Pro Bowl, 1994-95, 1999-2000; Miller Lite Player of the Week, 1995; Daniel F Reeves Memorial Award, 1999-2001; Offensive Player of the Year, Nat Fotball League, 2000-01; Player of the Year, Nat Football League, 2001; Bert Bell Award, 2001; Breitbard Hall of Fame, San Diego Hall of Champions, 2009; Tenth-leading rusher of All-Time; Pro Football Hall of Fame, 2011; Super Bowl champion. **Special Achievements:** Films: The J-K Conspiracy, 2004; Field of Dreams 2: Lockout, 2011; Love Cures Cancer: Take a Chance on Love, 2009. TV Series: "Arli$$", 2000-01; "Point After", 2006; "Life in Pieces", 2016. **Business Addr:** Founder, Marshall Faulk Foundation, 448 W Mkt St Suite 201, San Diego, CA 92101.

**FAULKNER, CAROLYN D. (CAROLYN D DIXON)**
Manager, consultant. **Personal:** Born Aug 30, 1938, Mullins, SC; daughter of Rembert Gerald and Ollie Mae Smith; married Melvin; children: Lenora, Leonard & Tasheba. **Career:** Shirlon Indust, bookkeeper, 1958-63; J H Taylor Mgt, bookkeeper, 1964-75; Wedding Plan Plus Inc, pres & consult, 1966-; Oak Hill Indust, bookkeeper, 1976-80; Harry Zelenko, bookkeeper, 1981-91. **Orgs:** H & R Block, 1984-86; Block Asn, pres, 1987-; Asn Bridal Consults, 1989-; Brooklyn Chamber Com, 1990-93. **Honors/Awds:** Brooklyn Bor Pres, Proclamation, 1984; Edward Griffith Award, State Assemblyman, 1985; Certificateof Achievement, Asn Bridal Consults, 1990-91; mem, split Ron Brown Polit Club. **Special Achievements:** Cert travel agt, Sobelsohn Sch Travel, 1985; accredited cruise counsr, Cruise Line Intl Asn, 1990; profiency, Congressman Ed Towns, 1990; Performance, Brides Mag, 1993. **Home Addr:** 935 Schenck Ave, Brooklyn, NY 11207-9101, **Home Phone:** (718)927-2579. **Business Addr:** Member, Association of Bridal Consultant, 200 Chestnutland Rd, New Milford, CT 06776, **Business Phone:** (203)355-0464.

**FAUNTROY, REV. WALTER EDWARD**
Association executive, clergy, executive director. **Personal:** Born Feb 6, 1933, Washington, DC; son of William T and Ethel Vine; married Dorothy Simms; children: Marvin Keith. **Educ:** Va Union Univ, BA, cum laude, 1955; Yale Univ Divinity Sch, BD, 1958. **Career:** Pastor (retired); New Bethel Bapt Church, pastor, 1959-, pastor emer, 2009; Wash Bur Southern Christian Leadership Conf, dir, 1960-71, coordr hist, 1963-65; White House Conf Fulfill These Rights, vice chmn, 1966; DC City Coun, vice chmn, 1967-69; Poor People's Campaign, natl coordr, 1969; House Reps, DC deleg, 1971-90; Dem Nat Conv, deleg, 1972; Bus Enterprise Develop LLC, chmn, currently. **Orgs:** Pres, Nat Black Leadership Round table; chmn & bd dir, Southern Christian Leadership Conf; chmn, bd dir, vice pres, Govt Affairs, Martin Luther King Jr Ctr Soc Chg; Leadership Conf Civil Rights, 1961-71; founder & pres, Walter E Fauntroy & Assoc; chmn, DC Coalition Conscience, 1965; pres & founder, Model Inner City Community Org Inc, Wash, 1966-72; co-chmn, Free S Africa Movement; chair, Bipartisan & Bicameral Task Force Haiti; chmn, Cong Black Caucus, 1981-83; nat dir, 20th Aniv March Wash Jobs Peace & Freedom, 1983; co-chair, Sudan Campaign. **Honors/Awds:** Hubert H Humphrey Humanitarian Award, Nat Urban Coalition, 1984; LLD, Georgetown Univ Law Sch, Yale Univ & VA Union Univ. **Special Achievements:** First African-American to win a presidential primary. **Home Addr:** 4105 17th St NW, Washington, DC 20011. **Business Addr:** Emeritus Pastor, New Bethel Baptist Church, 8430 Linwood St C L Franklin Blvd, Detroit, MI 48206, **Business Phone:** (313)894-5788.

**FAUST, DR. NAOMI FLOWE**
Educator, writer, poet. **Personal:** Born Salisbury, NC; daughter of Christopher Leroy and Ada Luella Graham; married Roy Malcolm. **Educ:** Bennett Col, Greensboro, NC, BA, 1934; Univ Mich, Ann Arbor, MA; NY Univ, PhD. **Career:** Pub Sch Syst, Gaffney SC, elem teacher; Atkins High Sch, Winston-Salem NC, eng teacher; Bennett Col & Southern Univ, Scotlandville LA, instr eng; Morgan State Univ Baltimore, Md, prof eng; Greensboro Pub Sch, teacher; New York City Pub Sch, teacher; Queens Col, City Univ New York, prof eng & educ. **Orgs:** Am Asn Univ Profs; Nat Coun Teachers Eng; Nat Women's Book Asn; World Poetry Soc Intercontinental; NY poetry forum, Nat Asn Advan Colored People; Acad Am Poets; Am Asn Univ Women; Poetry Soc Am; City Univ New York. **Home Addr:** 112 01 175th St, Jamaica, NY 11433, **Home Phone:** (718)291-5338.

**FAVORS, DR. STEVE ALEXANDER, JR.**
School administrator, president (organization), vice president (organization). **Personal:** Born Dec 30, 1948, Texarkana, TX; son of Clarence and Irma; married Charlotte Edwards; children: Steve Jr & Jonathan. **Educ:** Tex A & M Univ, BS, pre-law, 1971, MS, stud personnel & guid, 1973, EdD, 1978. **Career:** Wiley Col, vpres stud affairs, 1977-81; Prairie View A & M Univ, asst prof educ, 1979-81; Dillard Univ, vpres stud affairs, 1981-85; Univ New Orleans, Dillard Univ New Orleans, Wiley Col, vpres stud affairs, 1985-90; Howard Univ, vpres stud affairs, 1990-98, actg athletic dir, 1994-96; Grambling State Univ, pres, 1998-2001; Tex A & M Univ, educr. **Orgs:** Nat Col Athletic Asn; United Way; Boy Scouts; Nat Asn Advan Colored People; Omega Psi Phi Fraternity Inc, 1970; charter mem, Tex Asn Blacks Higher Educ, 1974-78; prof counr, Tex Bd Examiners Prof Counselors, 1984; task force mem, Nat Asn Col Univ Personnel Adminr, 1989; Nat Asn Stud Personnel Adminr, Task Force, 1989-90; exec comm mem, Mid-Eastern Athletic Conf, 1990-98; bd trustee mem, Nat Order Omega, 1991-94; bd mem, Mid-S Delta Consortium, 1998-; SWAC Pres's Coun, 1998-; Am Col Personnel Asn; Nat Asn Personnel Workers; Tex Personnel & Guid Asn; Phi Delta Kappa; bd trustee, Univ La Syst; head, Black inst higher educ; Grambling State Univ community; Dist Columbia Chief Stud Personnel Asn; Am Asn Univ Adminr; Nat Asn Stud Personnel Adminr; Am Col Personnel Asn; Tex Asn Black Personnel Workers Higher Educ; Alpha Phi Omega Fraternity Inc; Barons, New Orleans Urban League Greater Metrop Urban League Wash, DC; Mt. Zion United Methodist Men's Asn, Boy Scouts Am, LeDroit Park Community Asn; Mayor New Orleans War Drugs Task Force. **Home Addr:** 103 Wayside Dr, Grambling, LA 71245, **Home Phone:** (318)247-1886. **Business Addr:** President, Grambling State University, 403 Main St, Grambling, LA 71245.

**FAW, BARBARA ANN**
School administrator. **Personal:** Born Jul 27, 1936, Cullen, VA; daughter of Bernard and Edna Wilkes; married Joseph A. **Educ:** Morgan State Univ, Baltimore, MD, BA, 1965; Howard Univ, Wash, DC, MA, 1966. **Career:** School administrator (retired); coord & sponsor small bus inst, 1967-70, chair woman Conf "Know your Rights", 1973; Baltimore Community Col, First Chancellor, 1986-; Community Col Baltimore, vpres admin, 1988-90, dean col, 1977-00, dean stud activ, 1973-77, admin asst to pres 1971-73, chmn dept bus admin, 1970-71, prof bus admin, 1965-71; Baltimore City Community Col, dir rels, 1990-2000; Sci Everyone, proj dir, 1992-2000. **Orgs:** Nat Coun Black Am Affairs Am Asn Community & Jr Cols, 1985-; presidential search comn, Community Col Baltimore, 1985-86; panelist, Conf Women's Career Paths Univ Baltimore, 1986; bd rev, Comn Mid States, 1987-; Nat Econ Asn; Sales & Mkt Asn; Am Asn Univ Prof; W Arlington Community Orgn; Mayor's Vol Cadre Educ; Task Force Role Scope & Commitment. **Home Addr:** 4413 Groveland Ave, Baltimore, MD 21215, **Home Phone:** (410)542-5260.

**FAY, TONI GEORGETTE**
Media executive, consultant. **Personal:** Born Apr 25, 1947, New York, NY; daughter of Allie Smith and George E. **Educ:** Duquesne Univ, BA, 1968; Univ Pittsburgh, MSW, 1972, MEd, 1973. **Career:** New York Dept Social Serv, caseworker, 1968-70; Pittsburgh Drug Abuse Ctr Inc, dir, 1972-74; Gov Coun Drug & Alcohol Abuse, Regional comnr, 1973-76; Nat Coun Negro Women, dir planning & develop, 1977-81; D Parke Gibson Assoc, exec vpres, 1981-82; AOL / Time Warner Inc, dir, 1981-92, community rels mgr, 1982, corp community rels & affirmative action, dir, sr advisor, vpres, 1982-2003 & corp officer, 1992-2000; Howard Univ, Ctr Excellence Advert, dir; TGF Assocs Inc, owner, pres, currently. **Orgs:** Corp Nat & Community Serv, 2000-01; US Comn, UNICEF; Cong Black Caucus Found; Franklin & Eleanor Roosevelt Inst; New York Coalition 100 Black Women; Exec Leadership Coun Found; vpres, Nat Coun Negro Women, 1977; Links Inc; Alpha Kappa Alpha Sorority; bd mem, secy, Appollo Theatre Found; bd mem, Nat Asn Advan Colored People Legal Defense Fund; bd mem, United Way Bergen Co; bd mem, vpres, Apollo Theater Found; Girls Scouts New York; bd mem, Franklin & Eleanor Roosevelt Inst; bd mem, Nat Hospice Found; bd mem, Nat Inst Literacy; bd mem, Nat Hospice Found, 2009; bd dir, Nat Asn Advan Colored People Legal Defense Fund; bd dir, Nat & Community Serv; Coro Found; Fedn Protestant Welfare Agencies; U.S Capitol Hist Soc; Quincy Jones Listen Up Found; Bethune Cookman Col. **Honors/Awds:** Dollars & Sense-100 Black Women Bus, 1986; American Twin Award, YWCA, 1987; Nat Asn Advan Colored People Corp Award, 1989; New York Women's Foundation Award, 1991; New York Women's Award, 1996; President Award, Cong Black Caucus Found, 1996; Listed in Whos Who of American Women, Whos Who in America & Whos Who in the World. **Special Achievements:** First African American officer elected by Time Warner Inc. **Business Addr:** President, TGF Associates Inc, 233 W Hudson Ave, Englewood, NJ 07631-1611, **Business Phone:** (201)816-9050.

**FEARN, JAMES E., JR.**
Lawyer. **Personal:** Born Feb 2, 1945, Chattanooga, TN; son of James E and Kayte Marsh; married Karen Edmunds; children: Jeremy Kahlil & Jonathan Kyle. **Educ:** Antioch Col, BA, 1968; Univ Chicago Law Sch, JD, 1971. **Career:** Seattle Legal Serv, staff atty, 1971-76; Dept Housing & Urban Develop, aso regional coun, 1976-78; Seattle City Atty Off, asst city atty, 1978-85, Land Use Div, dir, 1985-89; Tousley Brain, Land Use Sect, head, 1989-93; Seattle Commons, spec coun,

1993-94; Inst Local Govt & Pub Serv, dep dir, exec dir, 1994-97; Ogdon Murphy Wallace, coun; Housing & Urban Develop, atty; Seattle Housing Authority, Exec, gen coun, 2001-; pvt atty, currently. **Orgs:** Seattle Pks Bd; bd dir, Port Jobs; trust bd trustees, Mountains Sound Greenway; Sand Pt Blue Ribbon Comt; King County Conserv Futures Citizens Comt; Seattle Citizens Open Space Oversight Comt; Seattle Comprehensive Plan Adv Comt; Gov's Growth Mgt Task Force; Bldg Indust Legal Trust Fund Adv Comt; Hist Seattle Pub Develop Authority Coun; chair, Hist Seattle's Gov Coun. **Special Achievements:** Book: "Preserving Seattle's Rental Housing; Greater Northwest Law Use Review", 1985; "Transfer of Development Rights, Wash Asn Municipal Atty's Legal Notes", 1979; "Tenants Rights: A Guide for Wash State", 1976, 3rd edition, 1991. **Home Addr:** 1603 22nd Ave, Seattle, WA 98122, **Home Phone:** (206)328-2105. **Business Addr:** General Counsel, Seattle Housing Authority, 120 6th Ave N, Seattle, WA 98109-1028, **Business Phone:** (206)615-3570.

## FEARN-BANKS, KATHLEEN

Publicist, writer, educator. **Personal:** Born Nov 21, 1941, Chattanooga, TN; daughter of James E and Kayte M. **Educ:** Wayne State Univ, BA, jour, 1964; Univ Calif, Los Angeles, MS, jour, 1965; Univ Southern Calif, Los Angeles, CA, ABD PhD, 1981. **Career:** Univ Calif, Will Rogers Fel, 1964-65; NBC TV Network, Publicity Dept, mgr, media rels, 1969-90; KNXT-TV News LA, news writer, producer, 1968-69; KCBS TV news, news writer, producer & reporter, 1968-69; Los Angeles Ctn Col, instr, journ, eng, creative writing, 1965-; Los Angeles Times, feature writer, 1968; Univ Wash, Sch Commun, tenured assoc prof, 1995-; freelance motion picture publicist, currently; People to People, An Introd to Mass Commun, co-ed; Hist Dict, African Am TV, 2005; Co-author: Story Western Man; Author: Crisis Communications; A Case Book Approach, 1996, 2nd ed, 2001. **Orgs:** Pub Rel Soc Am, 1989-; Writers Guild Am; Publicists Guild; Acad TV & Sci; bd dir, vpres, Neighbors Watts; Delta Sigma Theta Sorority, chap vp; Asn Edu Journ & Mass Comm, 1990-; chair, Prof Freedom & Responsibility Ctr, 1998. **Honors/Awds:** CA Sun Magazine writers Award, Univ Calif, Los Angeles, 1965; Woman of the Year, Los Angeles Sentinel, 1986; Teacher of the Year, Sch Commun, Univ Wash, 1993, 1995; PR Professional of the Year, Pub Rels Socs of Am, 1999. **Special Achievements:** First African-American entertainer to host a successful television variety series when he headed NBC's "The Flip Wilson Show". **Home Phone:** (206)522-9236. **Business Addr:** Tenured Associate Professor, University of Washington, Rm CMU 133, Seattle, WA 98195, **Business Phone:** (206)543-7646.

## FEARS, EMERY LEWIS, JR.

Educator. **Personal:** Born Jul 23, 1925, Tuskegee, AL; son of Emery and Evadne Angers; married Jeanette Johnson; children: Cheryl; married Jeanette Johnson; children: Jason & Ashlyn. **Educ:** Howard Univ, BMusEd, 1951; Univ Mich Ann Arbor, MMus, 1962; Old Dom Univ, attended 1974. **Career:** Educator (retired); J S Clarke High Sch, New Orleans, LA, band dir, 1951-52; I C Nor com High Sch, Portsmouth, Va, band dir, 1952-72; Manor High Sch, Portsmouth, Va, band dir & curriculum specialist, 1972-74; Norfolk State Univ, Music DEPT, assoc prof music, dir bands, 1974-91, prof emeritus music, 1992. **Orgs:** Charter mem, 1960-, bd dir, 1978-82, 1984-86, Nat Band Asn; pres, southern div, 1980-82, Col Band dir Nat Asn; Am Bandmasters Asn, 1981-; Phi Beta Mus Nat Sch Bandmaster Frat, 1985-. **Home Addr:** 2605 Cecilia Terr, Chesapeake, VA 23323-3805, **Home Phone:** (757)487-6279.

## FEARS, HARDING H., JR.

Automotive executive. **Personal:** Born Apr 19, 1964, Detroit, MI; son of Harding Sr and Katherine; married Diane; children: Harding III. **Educ:** Tex Southern Univ, BA, telecommunications, 1987; Oakland Univ, attended 1992; Mich State Univ, MBA, mgt, 1997. **Career:** Bozell, Jacobs, Kenyon & Eckart, intern, 1987; ITT Teves N Am, mkt analyst, 1988-90; ITT Automotive, sr mkt analyst, 1990-94, mgr, bus mgr develop, 1995-97; Intermet Corp, dir mkt, 1997-2002, sr acct mgr, 2002-06; FormTech Industs LLC, mgr, mkt & sales, 2006-09; Magna Powertrain, acct mgr, 2011-. **Orgs:** Am Mkt Asn; Soc Auto Analysts; Auto Mkt Res Coun; Soc Competitive Intelligence Professionals; Nat Black MBA Asn; Soc Auto Engrs; Nat Black Media Coalition; Alpha Pi Alpha Fraternity Inc. **Home Addr:** 14942 Stahelin Ave, Detroit, MI 48223-3605, **Home Phone:** (313)493-0955.

## FEASTER, ALLISON SHARLENE

Basketball player, executive. **Personal:** Born Feb 11, 1976, Chester, SC; married Danny Strong; children: Sara. **Educ:** Harvard Univ, BA, econs, 1998. **Career:** ShadeTree Home Girls, Edgefield, SC, mentor, exec dir; Merrill Lynch, equities analyst; Anadia Sanitana, Port, 1998-99; Los Angeles Sparks, guard, 1998-2000; ASPTT Aix-en-Provence, France, 1999-2001; US Valenciennes Olympic, France, 2001-05; Charlotte Sting, guard & forward, 2001-06; Clean$mart Dry Cleaners, co-owner, 2005-11; Ros Casares Valencia, Spain, 2006-07; C.B. San Jose Leon, 2007-08; Ind Fever, 2008; Famila Wuber Schio, 2008-09; Club Deportivo Basket Zaragoza, 2009-11; Perfumerias Avenida Baloncesto, 2011-12; Uni Girona CB, 2012-13; C.B. Alcobendas, 2013-. **Home Addr:** 507 Dawley Dr, Fuquay Varina, NC 27526-4825. **Business Addr:** Professional Basketball Player, C.B. Alcobendas, City Hall Antela Stop, Alcobendas28100.

## FEASTER, BRUCE SULLIVAN

Executive director, lawyer. **Personal:** Born Jul 13, 1961, Flint, MI; son of John Alfred and Lillian Battle; married Deborah Mallory; children: Montez & Dante. **Educ:** Mich State Univ, BA, 1983; Univ Tex, Law Sch, JD, 1986. **Career:** WCNLS C's Ctr for Justice & Peace, founder, exec dir, currently; Detroit City Coun, atty, currently; SEIU Mich State Coun, polit & internal organizer, currently. **Orgs:** Alpha Phi Alpha; Metro Detroit Optimists; Nat Asn Advan Colored People; Detroit Urban League; Umoja-Nia; E Village Asn; Great New Mt Moraih Baptist Church; Conant United Methodist Church; True Rock Missionary Bapatist Church; Charles H Wright Maah; United Negro Col Fund; Mich Comt Juv Justice, 2000; bd mem, J Urban Youth Cult. **Honors/Awds:** Nat Mens Scholar; Turman Scholar; Optimist Club Scholar; Alpha Phi Alpha Scholar. **Home Addr:** 3487 Harvard Rd, Detroit, MI 48224, **Home Phone:** (313)885-4152. **Business Addr:** Attorney, Detroit City Council, 2 Woodward Ave Suite 314, Detroit, MI 48226, **Business Phone:** (616)224-9475.

## FEATHERSTONE, KARL RAMON

Law enforcement officer, football coach. **Personal:** Born Oct 13, 1964, Indianola, MS; son of Charles Edward and Jessie Mae; married Lorie; children: Kadin. **Educ:** Tex Southern Univ, BS, comput sci, 1985; Kaplan Univ, BS, criminal justice, 2009. **Career:** USMC, spec forces; St Clair Shores Police Dept, police officer; Lake view High Sch, varsity football asst coach, 1997-98; Royal Oak Kimball High Sch, varsity football asst coach, 1998-2001; Royal Oak Dondero HS, varsity football asst coach, 2001; Port Huron Pirates, football head coach, currently; Saginaw Sting, head coach, 2009. Oakland Univ, asst head football coach, 2015-. **Orgs:** Alpha Phi Alpha Fraternity. **Honors/Awds:** Championship, 2006; CIFL Coach of the year, 2007.

## FEEMSTER, JOHN ARTHUR

Physician. **Personal:** Born Sep 9, 1939, Winston-Salem, NC. **Educ:** Univ Minn, Knox Col, BS, 1959; Meharry Med Col, MD, 1963. **Career:** Vet Affairs Med Ctr, resident; Gen Surg Bronx Munic Hosp Ctr, resident gen surg; Univ Minn, gen surg resident, 1970, bd cert, gen surg, 1971; Wayne State Univ Sch Med, resident, 1974-75; Thorocic Cardiovasc Surg, bd cert, 1975; Am Col Surgeons, physician self fel, 1977; Am Col Angiol; Kirwood Gen Hosp, cheif dept surg; pvt pract thoracic & cardiovasc surg; C's Hosp Mich; 207th Evac Hosp, chief surg & spec serv; Meadowbrook Urgent Care. **Orgs:** Nat Med Soc; Am Col Emergency Physicians; vpres, Detroit Med Soc; Detroit Surg Soc; Detroit Surg Asn; Omega Psi Phi Frat; Alpha Omega Alpha Hon Med Soc; Nat Asn Advan Colored People; Founders Soc Detroit Inst Arts; Asn Mil Surgeons; Ama. **Honors/Awds:** Founders Soc Detroit Symphony Orch Young Investigator's Award, Am Col Cardiology, 1969; Fel, Oak Ridge Inst Nuclear Studies; Michigan Distinguished Citizen, Mich House Representatives, 1984; Doctor Recognition Award, Mercy Hosp, 1993. **Special Achievements:** Written more than 30 articles for medical journals. **Business Addr:** Doctor, Meadowbrook Urgent Care, 33722 Woodward Ave, Birmingham, MI 48009, **Business Phone:** (248)919-4900.

## FELDER, CAIN HOPE

Educator, clergy. **Personal:** Born Jun 9, 1943, Aiken, SC; son of James (deceased) and Lula Mae Landy (deceased); married Annette Hutchins; children: Akidah H; married Jewell Richardson Smith. **Educ:** Boston Latin Sch, dipl, 1962; Howard Univ, Wash, DC, BA, 1966; Oxford Univ, Mansfield Col, Oxford, Eng, dipl, theol, 1968; Union Theol Sem, New York, NY, Mdiv, 1969; Columbia Univ, New York, NY, MPhil, 1978, PhD, bibl lang & lit, 1982. **Career:** Black Methodists Church Renewal, Atlanta, Ga, nat exec dir, 1969-72; Morgan State Univ, Baltimore, Md, dir fed rels & assoc prof philos, 1972-74; City Col Baltimore, adj with Upward Bound, 1972-73; Coppin State Col, adj instr Philos, 1973-74; Grace United Methodist Church, New York, NY, pastor, 1975-78; Hunter Col City Univ New York, adj instr, 1976-77; Princeton Theol Sem, Princeton, NJ, instr, 1978-81; United Methodist Black Caucus; nat dir; Howard Univ Sch Divinity, asst prof, 1981-82, assoc prof, 1982-87, prof, New Testament Lang & Lit, 1987-, chair, 1999-, chair Doctor Ministry Prog, 2000-06; Books: The Journal of Religious Thought, ed, 1982-89. **Orgs:** Soc Bibl Lit; Soc Study Black Religion; Am Acad Religion; Middle E Studies Asn; bd dir, exec comt, chmn, Nat Convocation Planning Comt, Black ol Project; Union ol Sem Black Econ, chmn, 1969-70; Black Econ Develop Corp, Detroit, 1969-70; bd mem, Inter relig Found Community Orgn, 1970-72; bd mem, Inter religious Found Comn Orgn, 1970-72; mem, Cuba Resource Ctr, 1971; founder, Enterprises Now; founder, Narco House, drug rehab ctr, Atlanta, Ga; chair, New Testament Fac Group, Wash ol Consortium, 1984-86; Coun Univ Senate, Howard Univ, 1985-98; mem, Howard Univ Grad Sch Fac, 1985; mem, Fac Welfare Comt Univ Senate, Howard Univ, 1986; chmn, ol Search Comt, Howard Univ Sch Divinity, 1987; fac senate coun, mem, Howard Univ, 1987-1992; founder & chmn, Bibl Inst Social Chg, 1990-; founder, chmn, chief exec officer, Bibl Inst Social Chg, Washington, DC; Howard Univ, Chair Doctor Ministry Prog, 2000-06; mem, Fac Senate Coun, 2000-06. **Home Addr:** 4142 22nd St NE, Washington, DC 20018, **Home Phone:** (202)269-4311. **Business Addr:** Professor, Howard University School of Divinity, Rm 252 & 249 1400 Shepherd St NE, Washington, DC 20017, **Business Phone:** (202)806-0760.

## FELDER, HARVEY

Conductor (music), educator. **Personal:** Born Nov 2, 1955, Milwaukee, WI; son of Emma Bell and Harvey Jr. **Educ:** Univ Wis-Madison, BM, music, 1977; Univ Mich, MM, music, 1982. **Career:** Eastern Mich Univ, vis lectr, 1983-84; Haverford Col, col lectr, 1984-88, chair; Johns Hopkins Univ, univ symphony conductor, 1987-90; Wva Univ; Milwaukee Symphony Orchestra, asst conductor, 1988-95; St. Louis Symphony Orchestra, resident conductor, 1995-96; Tacoma Symphony Orchestra, music dir, 1995-, conductor laureate, 2014-; Swarthmore Col, artist residence; Univ Wis, artist residence; Wis Chamber Orchestra, artistic advisor; Fox Valley Symphony, music dir; Ann Arbor Summer Symphony, music dir; Haverford/ Bryn Mawr Symphony, music dir & conductor. APPEAR IN: saka Telemann Chamber Orchestra; Orquesta Sinfonica del Estados de Mex; Orquesta Sinfonica Nacional de Costa Rica; Mikkeli City Orchestra Finland; New Japan Philharmonic; Univ Conn, assoc prof & dir orchestral studies, 2012-. **Honors/Awds:** Citation of Excellence, Wis State Assembly; Distinguished Citizen Award, Wis Civic Music Asn; Distinguished Alumni Award, Univ Wis-Madison; Outstanding Achievement in the Arts Award, Tacoma's Arts Fund. **Home Addr:** 5509 N Milwaukee River Pky, Milwaukee, WI 53209, **Home Phone:** (414)228-6651. **Business Addr:** Music Director, Tacoma Symphony Orchestra, 738 Broadway Suite 301, Tacoma, WA 98402, **Business Phone:** (253)272-7264.

## FELDER, DR. JACK

Scientist, educator, army officer. **Personal:** Born Jan 1, 1939, Columbia, SC. **Educ:** NY State Univ, MS, biochem, PhD, biochem. **Career:** Educator (retired); Natich Labs, Boston, Mass, germ warfare specialist, 1964-66; Siemens Firm, Berlin, Ger, res scientist, translr, 1966-70; Harlem Prep, New York, fac, 1974; New York Pub Sch, 2001; Books: From the Statue of Liberty to the Statue of Bigotry, 1986; AIDS-US Germ Warfare at its Best with Documents and Proof, 1986; Who Really Assassinated Dr. Martin Luther King, 1987; Who Really Was Behind the Assassination of Malcolm X, 1988.

## FELDER, DR. LORETTA KAY (FELDER MCKELVEY)

Dentist. **Personal:** Born Apr 19, 1956, Sumter, SC; daughter of Daniel DeLeon Sr and Lorraine Perry; married Walter. **Educ:** Old Dom Univ, BS, biol, 1978; Howard Univ, DDS, dent, 1982. **Career:** U.S. Pub Health Serv Comn Corps, dent officer, 1982-85; Ruskin Migrant Health Care Inc, Hillsborough Co, Fla, dentist, 1982-84; Midlands Primary Health Care Inc, dent dir, 1985-88; Univ Dent PA, founder, dentist, chief exec officer, 1988-; Carolina Tribune Newspaper, Minority Health, assoc publ, 1992-. **Orgs:** Consult, SC Richland Co Gov Primary Health Task Force, 1984; Nat Dent Asn, 1985-87; bd dir, YWCA Sumter Area, 1986-88; Nat Coun Negro Women; Nat Asn Advan Colored People; bd dir, Big Bros & Big Sisters Inc, Greater Columbia; SC Dent Asn; Am Dent Asn; bd dir, SC Women's Consortium, 1996; vol, C Dent Clin; Conagree Med, Dent & Pharmaceut Asn; Cent Dist Dent Soc; Palmetto Dent Study Club; Columbia Dent Implant Asn; fel Acad Gen Dent; fel Pierre Fauchard Acad; vol, Richland County C's Dent Clin; Francis Burns United Methodist Church. **Honors/Awds:** Living the Legacy Award, Columbia NCNW, 1993; Prestigious Fellow Award, Acad Gen Dent. **Home Addr:** PO Box 50664, Columbia, SC 29250-0664. **Business Addr:** Dentist, Founder, University Dental PA, 3126 Devine St, Columbia, SC 29205-2431, **Business Phone:** (803)252-8101.

## FELDER-HOEHNE, FELICIA HARRIS

Educator, librarian. **Personal:** Born Knoxville, TN; daughter of Boyd S Ivey and Geraldine Celestine Harris; married Paul Arthur. **Educ:** Knoxville Col, BS; Atlanta Univ, MSLS, 1966; Univ Tenn, 1978. **Career:** SCLC, secy to Septima Poinsette Clark; McMinn County Schs, Eng teacher; Knoxville Col, admin asst, off pres & admin offices, 1960-63, asst to dir pub rel, 1963-65; Atlanta Univ, Trevor Arnett Libr, grad libr asst, 1965-66; United Presby Church, Bd Nat Missions, teacher/librn, summer study skills prog, 1968; Knoxville Col, Alumni Libr, head circulation servs, 1966-69; Univ Tenn, Knoxville, Tenn, prof & ref librn, 1969-. **Orgs:** Am Libr Asn; Alpha Kappa Alpha Sorority; Tenn Libr Asn; E Tenn Libr Asn; Int Womens Yr Decade, 1974-75; Nat Asn Advan Colored People; YWCA; Knoxville Col Alumni Asn; Knoxville Nativity Pageant Choir, 1975-95; Knoxville Black Officials Coalition, 1976-79; Beck Cult Exchange Ctr, charter mem, 1976-; Inter denomi Nat Concert Choir; Payne Ave Baptist Church; bd dir, Knoxville Community Chorus; pres, Spring Pl Neighborhood Asn, 1980-; relig task force, 1982 World's Fair; bd dir, UT Fed Credit Union, 1984-89; charter mem, Nat Mus Women Arts, 1985-; dir pub rels, Concerned Asn Residents E, 1988-90; Tenn Valley Energy Coalition, 1988-90; bd dir, Mentoring Acad Boys, 1996-; Knoxville Opera Guild, 1996-; bd dir & secy, Ctr Neighborhood Develop, 1998-2001; Common Ground, 1998-; asst lib dir, Payne Ave Bapt Church Media Libr, 1998-2001; bd dir, Knoxville Opera Co, 1999-; Knoxville's Promise: Alliance Youth, 1999-; Wall Tolerance, 2003-; chair, Neighborhood Asn Officers. **Home Addr:** 5413 Spring Pl Cir NE, Knoxville, TN 37924-2174, **Home Phone:** (865)525-5654. **Business Addr:** Professor, Research Librarian, The University of Tennessee, 145 John C Hodges Library 1015 Volunteer Blvd, Knoxville, TN 37996-1000, **Business Phone:** (865)974-0018.

## FELICIANA, DR. JERRYE BROWN

School administrator. **Personal:** Born Aug 20, 1951, Bethesda, MD; daughter of James Dudley Brown and Katie Glean McNair Brown; married Albert; children: Wayne, Jaison & Kyanna. **Educ:** George Washington Univ, BA, psychol, 1974; Trinity Col, MAT, 1976; Maple Springs Baptist Sem, MA, 1994, DMin, 1994, Howard Univ, PhD, 2005. **Career:** Georgetown Univ, asst dir upward bound 1977-78; US Dept Agr, consult, 1981; Trinity Col, asst dir for minority affairs 1983-84, dir, upward bound, 1978-89; Howard Univ, asst dir, stud support serv, 1989-2005; Maple Springs Baptist Bible Col & Sem, vpres finance & admin, Prof Coun & Psychol, 1992. **Orgs:** Chairwoman, DC Consol Educ serv, 1983-89; bd mem, 1983-, pres, 2003-04, exec bd, 2004-05, Mid-Eastern Asn Educ Opportunity Prog Personnel; mem bd dir, Ethel J Williams Scholar Comt, 1989-; Am Asn Christian Counors; Am Coun Asn. **Home Addr:** 5200 Vienna Dr, Clinton, MD 20735-2459, **Home Phone:** (301)868-1353.

## FELIX, ALLYSON

Track and field athlete, athlete. **Personal:** Born Nov 18, 1985, Los Angeles, CA; daughter of Paul and Marlean. **Educ:** Univ Southern Calif, BA. **Career:** Track and field athlete, 2001-. **Orgs:** USA Track & Field. **Honors/Awds:** Jesse Owens/Jackie Joyner-Kersee Award, 2005, 2007, 2010, 2012, 2015; IAAF World Athlete of the Year, 2012. Pan American Games, bronze medal, 2003; Summer Olympics, silver 200m, 2004 and 2008 and 400m Silver Medal, 2016; World Outdoor Championships, gold medal, 200m, 2005, 2007, 2009; World Outdoor Championships, gold medal, 4x400m, 2007, 2009, 2011; World Outdoor Championships, gold medal 4x100m, 2007, 2011; Olympic Games, gold medal 4x400m, 2008, 4x400m, 2012, 4x100m, 2012, and 4x400 and 4x100, 2016; Diamond League Championships, gold medal, 200m and 400m, 2010; World Outdoor Championships, silver medal, 400m, and bronze medal, 200m, 2011; Summer Olympics, gold medal 200m, 2012Diamond League Championships, gold medal, 200m, 2014, 2015; World Outdoor Championships, silver medal, 4x100m and 4x400m, 2015; World Outdoor Championships, gold medal, 400m, 2015. **Special Achievements:** Named to the President's Council on Fitness, Sports and Nutrition, 2012. Won more world championship gold medals than any other U.S. athlete. Won three Olympic gold medals in a single games, 2012. Active in Right to Play, Win with Integrity, and Let's Move Active Schools. **Business Addr:** USA Track & Field, 132 East Washington St Suite 800, Indianapolis, IN 46204, **Business Phone:** (317)261-0500.

## FELIX, DR. DUDLEY E.

Educator. **Educ:** Royal Col Physicians & Surgeons, Glasgow, LDS, 1967; Howard Univ, Wash, DC, DDS, 1978; Univ Pa, Med & Dent Cols; Philadelphia Gen Hosp. **Career:** Univ Pa Gen Hosp, Otorhinolaryngology & Temporo-Mandibular Joint Clin, resident & attending physician; Philadelphia Gen Hosp, Dept Oral/Internal Med, resident; Howard Univ, clinical instr oral & maxillofacial surg, 1969-73; Howard Univ, Div Dist Columbia Gen Hosp, dir sr studs, 1974; Meharry Med Col, fac mem sch dent, dir didactic prog oral diagnosis & oral med, head sect oral med; assoc prof, dept Endodontics & Oral Diagnostic Scis, currently. **Orgs:** Acad Fel, Am Acad Oral Med; Attend consult, Hubbard Hosp; lectr & attend consult, Dept Pediat Med, Meharry Med Col; guest lectr & attend consult, Tenn State Univ; fel Royal Soc Health, UK; Am Acad Gen Dent Surg, 1979; dipl, Am Specialty Bd Oral Med, 1981; Int Acad Prev Med, 1982; fel Int Acad Med Preventics, 1983; Am Cancer Soc; Am Soc Regional Anesthesia; Int Asn Pain Study; Am Asn Pain Study; Int Soc Adv Educ; co-chmn, fac eval comn, 1987, grievance comn, 1987, fac rep fac senate, 1988, fac coun, 1988, curric comn, 1988, Meharry Med Col; Am Asn Study Headache. **Home Addr:** 1500 Charlotte Ave, Nashville, TN 37203, **Home Phone:** (615)329-9797. **Business Addr:** Associate Professor, Meharry Medical College, 1005 Dr D B Todd Jr Blvd, Nashville, TN 37208, **Business Phone:** (615)327-6000.

## FELKER, REV. DR. JOSEPH B., JR.

Clergy, president (organization). **Personal:** Born Nov 25, 1926, Chicago, IL; son of Joseph; married Ruthie Crockrom; children: Cordelia & Jacquelyn. **Educ:** Univ Chicago, CBI, 1953; Ill Barber Col, MA, 1952; Bapt Theol Sem, BTH, 1956; McKenney Theol Sem. **Career:** Vet Barber Shop, pres, 1957-; reverend, 2004; Mt Carmel Baptist Church, pastor, 1957-2009, pastor emer, 2009-. **Orgs:** Moderator, Greater New Era Dist Asn Chicago, 1968-; treas, JH Jackson Libr; Nat Asn Advan Colored People; Urban League; treas, Mich Towers S; chmn, moderators, Bapt Gen State Conv, 1973-; chmn trustee, Chicago Baptist Inst, 1996-; dir, Mt Carmel Found Inc. **Honors/Awds:** CBI Cert of Achievement, 1971; Outstanding Leadership as Moderator, Chs, Greater New Era Dist Asn, 1973; Most Outstanding & Program Moderator of the Year, Midwestern Bapt Layman Fel Inc, 1974; Civic & Rel Work Hon, Fgn Mission Bd MB Conv, 1976; cert of recognition, Gen State Conv IL 25 Yrs of Denominational Christian Serv, 1977. **Home Addr:** 8229 S Clyde, Chicago, IL 60617. **Business Addr:** Pastor Emeritus, Mt Carmel Baptist Church, 2976 S Wabash Ave, Chicago, IL 60616-3227, **Business Phone:** (312)225-0510.

## FELTON, DENNIS

Basketball coach, executive. **Personal:** Born Jun 21, 1963, Tokyo; son of Sgt Edward and Nancy Klatt; married Melanie Smith; children: Jazz & Nile. **Educ:** Prince George Community Col, AA, 1983; Howard Univ, BA, radio, tv & film prod, 1985. **Career:** Oxon Hill High Sch, asst coach, 1984-85; Charles Co Community Col, asst coach, 1985-86; Univ Del, asst coach, 1986-90; Tulane Univ, asst coach, 1990-91; St Josephs Univ, asst coach, 1991-92; Providence Col, asst coach, 1992-94; Clemson Univ, from asst coach to assoc coach, 1994-98; Western Ky Univ, head coach, 1998-2003; Univ Ga, head coach, 2003-09; USA Basketball, asst coach, 2003; USA Basketball, asst coach, 2005; NJ Nets, asst coach, 2010; San Antonio Spurs, dir pro player personnel, 2010-11; Tulsa, asst coach, 2014-. **Business Addr:** Director of Pro Player Personnel, San Antonio Spurs, SBC Ctr 1 SBC Ctr Pkwy, San Antonio, TX 78219, **Business Phone:** (210)444-5000.

## FELTON, HERMAN J., JR.

College president, college administrator. **Personal:** son of Herman J Sr. **Educ:** Edward Waters Col, BA; Levin Col Law, Univ Fla, JD; Jackson State Univ. **Career:** Murray State Univ, dir develop, 2004-07; Livingston Col, vpres instnl advan, 2007-12, sr vpres, chief operating officer & vpres advan, 2012-16; Wilberforce Univ, pres, 2016-. **Orgs:** Kappa Alpha Psi, 1999-. Higher Education Leadership Foundation, co-founder and president, 2015-. **Business Addr:** Wilberforce University, 1055 N Bickett Rd, Wilberforce, OH 45384, **Business Phone:** (937)708-5704.

## FELTON, JAMES A.

Educator, administrator, art museum director. **Personal:** Born Jun 20, 1945, New York, NY. **Educ:** Bradley Univ, BA, 1967; Tufts Univ, MA, 1969. **Career:** Univ Mass, asst dir financial aid & dir financial aid; Metro Mus Art NY, intern treas dept. **Orgs:** Foreign Affairs & Scholar, Phi Mu Alpha Sinfonia; Mass Asn Col Minority Adminr. **Business Addr:** Assistant Director, University of Massachusetts, Boston Harbor Campus, Boston, MA 02125.

## FELTON, ZORA MARTIN

Educator, museum director. **Personal:** Born Jun 22, 1930, Allentown, PA; daughter of James William and Josephine Elizabeth Cobbs; married Edward P Jr; children: Erica, Eric & Edward. **Educ:** Moravian Col, Bethlehem, PA, BA, 1952; Howard Univ, Wash, DC, MEd, 1980. **Career:** Educator (retired); Sleighton Farm Sch Girls, Media, Pa, field counr, 1952; Dayton YWCA, Dayton, Ohio, dir teenage dept, 1952-58; SE Neighborhood House, Wash, DC, dir educ & group work, 1958-67; Anacostia Mus, Smithsonian Inst, WAsh, DC, chief educ & outreach servs dept, emerita, 1967-94. **Orgs:** African-Am Mus Asn; bd mem, Anacostia Coord Coun; Delta Sigma Theta Sorority; secy, Ethel James Williams Scholar Fund; ed bd, Ft Stevens Sr Ctr Newsletter. **Home Addr:** 1438 Whittier St NW, Washington, DC 20012, **Home Phone:** (202)882-8675.

## FELTUS, BISHOP JAMES, JR.

Clergy, bishop. **Personal:** Born Apr 16, 1921, Gloster, MS; son of James Sr and Lillie Packnette; married Hazel Luter; children: James III, Elliott, Percy, Erasmus, Riley (deceased), Joan F, Wilson, Gerald, Eunice Little & Michael. **Educ:** Xavier Univ, PhB, 1946; Campbell Col, BD, 1954, DD, 1955; Southern Univ, EdM, 1963; New Orleans Baptist Theol Sem, MRE, 1973, UBS, PhD, 1998. **Career:** Brit Honduras, dist supt dist 8, 1953-65, overseer, 1955; Orleans Parish Sch Bd, substitute teacher, 1954-74; First Church God Christ, pastor; Church God Christ United US, London, Jamaica, SafricA, founder, sr presiding bishop, 1974; Jurisdiction 2 Church God Christ, bishop. **Orgs:** Pres, Interdenominational Ministerial Alliance, 1987-; Dist Atty's Comt Against Drugs, 1988-89; Am Asn Christian Couns. **Honors/Awds:** Hon Civil Sheriff Orleans Parish, Paul Valteau, 1983; Awarded by Mayor Mo real, 1983; Long career performing good works daily benefit City New Orleans, adopted City Coun New Orleans, 1986; Civil Sheriff Dep, Paul Valteau; Col Staff to Gov Edwin Edwards State La, 1987; Cert Appreciation, Contribuiton City New Orleans, Mayor S Bartholomew, 1987; Commended & Cited City Coun contrib community & leadership exhibited, 1987; proclaimed Bishop James Feltus Jr's Day New Orleans; adopted Mayor S Bartholomew & City Coun New Orleans, 1987; Accomplishments Relig, The Nat Sorority Phi Delta Kappa, Alpha Theta Chap, 1990. **Home Addr:** 2742 Prentiss Ave, New Orleans, LA 70122, **Home Phone:** (504)288-9121. **Business Addr:** Bishop, Churches God Christ United, 2453 Josephine St, New Orleans, LA 70113, **Business Phone:** (504)523-6232.

## FENTRESS, SHIRLEY B.

Administrator, secretary (organization). **Personal:** Born Nov 16, 1937, Bolivar, TN; daughter of John Lester and Mammie Bernice Pankey; married Ernest; children: Sherral Mitchell & Willie F Mitchell. **Educ:** Tenn State Univ, attended 1957; Cortez Bus Col, attended 1968. **Career:** Administrator, director (retired); Frank Thrifty Grocery, owner, 1980-81; Frank Thrifty Liquor Corp, owner, 1981-84; City Col Chicago, dir payroll, 1989-95. **Orgs:** Sec New Philadelphia Baptist Courtesy Comn, 1972; co-chmn, capt, 1st Union Baptist Church Pastor Anniversary, 1985, chairperson, Pastors Anniversary, 1986-87; coordr, Crusade Mercy City Col Chicago, 1986-87; financial secy, Victory Christian Church Baptist, 1986. **Home Addr:** 308 S Hickory St, Glenwood, IL 60425-1816, **Home Phone:** (708)758-3862.

## FENTRESS-WILLIAMS, JUDY

Minister (clergy), religious educator. **Personal:** married Kevin; children: Samantha & Jacob. **Educ:** Princeton Univ, BA, 1984; Yale Univ, MDiv, 1990, PhD, 1999. **Career:** Hartford Sem, asst prof, 1993-98, prof, 1998-2002, dir Black Ministries prog, 1993-2002, fac Women's Leadership Inst, 1996-; Va Theol Sem, asst prof, 2002-05, assoc prof, 2005-. **Orgs:** Soc Bibl Lit; Asn Theol Schs fac grant selection panel, 2001-05; Conversations Relig & Theol ed bd, 2002-06; Adv Bd Off Relig Life at Princeton, 2003-. **Honors/Awds:** John A. Wade Prize, 1989. **Special Achievements:** Contributor, September 11: Religious Perspectives on the Causes and Consequences, 2002; Bakhtin and Genre, 2007; The Africana Bible, 2009; Teaching Our Story, Alban Institute, 2010. Author, Ruth, Abingdon Old Testament Commentaries, 2012. **Business Addr:** Virginia Theological Seminary, 3737 Sem Rd, Alexandria, VA 22304, **Business Phone:** (703)370-6600.

## FENTY, ROBYN RIHANNA. See RIHANNA.

## FERDINAND, DR. KEITH C.

Cardiologist. **Personal:** Born Dec 5, 1950, New Orleans, LA; son of Vallery Jr and Inola Copelin; married Daphne Pajeaud; children: Kamau, Rashida, Aminisha & Jua. **Educ:** Cornel Univ, telluride scholar, 1969; Univ New Orleans, BA, biol, 1972; Howard Univ, Col Med, MD, 1976. **Career:** US Pub Health Hosp, New Orleans, La, intern, 1976-77; La State Univ Med Ctr, New Orleans, La, internal med resident, 1977-79, cardiol fel, 1979-80; Howard Univ Hosp, Wash, DC, cardiol fel, 1981; Flint Goodridge Hosp, New Orleans, La, chief cardiol, 1981-85; Med Assocs, New Orleans, La, pvt pract, 1981-83; Xavier Univ, New Orleans, La, vis prof, 1981-82, assoc prof, 1982, prof; Health Corp, New Orleans, La, consult, 1982-85; Heartbeats Life Ctr, New Orleans, La, pvt pract, 1983-, med dir, currently; United Med Ctr, New Orleans, La, chief cardiol, 1985-, chief med staff, 1987-88; La State Univ, Med Ctr, New Orleans, La, clin instr, 1986-; Emory Univ, Dept Med, clin prof; Morehouse Sch Med, Dept Med, adj clin prof; Tulane Univ, Heart & Vascular Inst, prof clin med, currently. **Orgs:** Bd mem, Urban League Greater New Orleans, 1984; bd mem, Greater New Orleans Ment Health Asn, 1985-87; chair, Nat Forum Heart Disand Stroke Prev; bd mem, ABC Hurricane Relief Fund, 1987-; bd mem, Am Lung Asn, LA, 1987-; ed newsletter, ABC Hurricane Relief Fund, 1988-90; dir, ABC Hurricane Relief Fund, currently; Asn Black Cardiologists; fel Am Col Cardiol; vpres, La Med Asn, 1988-; pres, Am Heart Asn; Trilateral Comt, End Violence Black Community; Alpha Omega Alpha; pres, Orleans Div Am Heart Asn, 1989-; chm bd, ABC Hurricane Relief Fund, 1990-; pres, La State Bd Med Examiners, 1990-; New Orleans Charity Hosp Bd, 1990-; pres, Physicians Asn La Inc, 1992-; Nat High Blood Pressure Edu Prog Coord Comt; chair, Sect Four Sixth Report Joint Nat Comt; ALLHAT Data Safety & Monitoring Bd; chair, Bd Asn Black Cardiologists Inc; Ad Hoc Comt Minority Populations Nat High Blood Pressure Educ Prog Coord Comt, currently; dir, NHLBI Physician's Heath Network; Am Soc Hypertension. **Honors/Awds:** First Place, Unity Awards in Media, Lincoln Univ, Mo, 1982; Outstanding Service Award, LP Nurses, La, 1983; Black Man of the Year, New Orleans Asn Black Social Workers, 1985; Distinguished Service Award, Greater Liberty BC, 1987; Frederick Douglass Award, Nat Asn Negro Bus & Prof Womens Club New Orleans, 1988; One of the Top 100 Best Black Physicians in the United States, Black Enterprise Mag; Louis B Russell Jr Memorial Award, Am Heart Asn, 2004; Walter M Booker Community Service Award, ABC; Walter M Booker Community Service Award, Asn Black Cardiologists, 2004. **Business Addr:** Professor of Clinical Medicine, Tulane University School of Medicine, 1415 Tulane Ave 4th Fl, New Orleans, LA 70112, **Business Phone:** (504)988-6113.

## FERERE, DR. GERARD ALPHONSE

Educator, college teacher. **Personal:** Born Jul 21, 1930, Cap Haitien; son of Alphonse M and Marie Leroy; married Nancy Turnier; children: Magali & Rachel. **Educ:** Naval Acad, Venezuela, Ens, 1953; Villanova Univ, MA, 1967; Univ Pa, PhD, 1974. **Career:** Haitian Navy, naval officer, 1953-58; Haiti, lang teacher, 1958-63; SELF, transl/interpreter, 1964; St Joseph's Univ, prof, 1964-98; prof emer lang & lingustics, 1998-. **Orgs:** Founder, Coalition Haitian Concerns, 1982-; comnr, Haitian Am Pa Heritage Affairs Comn, 1991-95. **Home Addr:** 20136 Ocean Key Dr, Boca Raton, FL 33498, **Home Phone:** (561)883-0226. **Business Addr:** Professor Emeritus, St Joseph's University, 5600 City Ave, Philadelphia, PA 19131, **Business Phone:** (610)660-1000.

## FERGERSON, MIRIAM N.

Salesperson. **Personal:** Born Sep 15, 1941, Homestead, PA; daughter of James A and Miriam King; married Cecil; children: Melanie, John & Kinte. **Educ:** Va State Univ, BA, fr ed, 1964; Azusa Pac Univ, MA, marriage, family & child coun, 1975. **Career:** Art Educ Consult Serv, founder, admin consult, 1974-; Calif Super Ct Conciliation Ct, family counr, 1977-78; Youth Training Sch, youth counr, 1978-83; SanMar Group Homes, substance abuse social worker, 1983-. **Orgs:** Youth counr, Missionary Dept Messiah Bapt Church, 1982-86; mem bd, Christian Educ Messiah Bapt Church, 1983-; bd chmn, Friends Wm Grant Still Arts Ctr, 1983-; vpres, Arts & Cult 10th Councilmanic Dist Women's Steering Comn, 1984-85; consult, Dr Chas R Drew Hist Exhib Drew Med Sch, 1984-85; researcher, City Watts, Watts Towers Art Ctr, 1984-85; Calif Drug Free Youth, 1984; Rev Jesse Jackson Pres, 1984; vpres, Parent Adv Coun Fairfax High, 1984-85; ed consult, Watts Towers Jazz Festival Publ, 1986; liason 10th Dist Arts Adv Coun, 1986-87; founder, Friends Los Angeles SW Col Art Gallery, 1991; Friends Kerman Maddox City Coun, 1991; Friends Geneva Cox City Coun; pres, Trinity Mission Circle Messiah Church. **Honors/Awds:** Community Coun Serv Award, Westminster Presby Church, 1984-85; West Angeles Christian Acad Outstanding Volunteer Serv Award, 1986; Nat Conf Artists Outstanding Serv Award, 1987. **Special Achievements:** Article Golden State Life Ins Travel & Art mag, 1978; publ, "Artaculture: Masud Kordofan", Los Angeles SW Col, 1990; publ, "Tribute of Carter G Woodson", Cal State Dominguez Hills, 1991; publ, "Listen Rap Movement", Los Angeles SW Col, 1991; Hon co-chair, Watts Summer Festival Inc, 2004; TV Doc Watts Festival Recounted Univ Jenkins Prod, 1980. **Home Phone:** (213)936-7779. **Business Addr:** Administrative Consultant, Art Education Consultant Services, 1417 So Ogden Dr, Los Angeles, CA 90019.

## FERGUS, JOSEPH E.

Chief executive officer, president (organization), founder (originator). **Educ:** Norfolk State Univ, BS, elec engineering, 1982; Univ Ill, MS, elec engineering, 1984. **Career:** AT&T Labs, sr scientist; Commun Technologies Inc, founder, pres & chief exec officer, 1990-. **Business Addr:** Founder, President, Chief Executive Officer, Communication Technologies Inc, 3684 Ctrview Dr Suite 100, Chantilly, VA 20151, **Business Phone:** (703)961-9080.

## FERGUSON, CECIL L.

Graphic artist, designer. **Personal:** Born Mar 13, 1931, Chicago, IL; married Irene; children: Mark. **Educ:** Art Inst Chicago; Inst Design, Ill Inst Technol; Am Acad Art. **Career:** Artist (retired); Natural hist mus expos pk, janitor; Ebony Mag, asst art dir; Ebony Success Libr, designer; Johnson Publ, promotional illustrations & layouts; Los Angeles Co Art Mus, cur; Los Angels Southwest col, cur, 1985. **Home Addr:** 11638 S Artesian Ave, Chicago, IL 60655-1529, **Home Phone:** (773)445-5382.

## FERGUSON, DEREK TALMAR (DEREK FERGUSON)

Publishing executive, vice president (organization). **Personal:** Born Apr 20, 1965, Yonkers, NY; son of James and Roberta Lewis Pieck; married Regina Bullock; children: Reginald James, Maya & Peri. **Educ:** Univ Pa, Wharton Sch, Philadelphia, BS, econ, 1985; Harvard Bus Sch, Cambridge, MBA, 1990. **Career:** Coopers & Lybrand, New York, auditor, mergers & acquisitions analyst, sr acct, 1985-88; Urban Profile Commun, Baltimore, chief operating officer, co-founder, assoc publ, beginning 1988-91; Bain & Co, Cambridge, summer assoc & mgr, 1989; BMG Spec Prod, vpres fin opers; Bad Boy Worldwide Entertainment Group, chief financial officer, 1998; Cross Trainers Apparel; Covenant Bldg Serv; Life Music. **Orgs:** Black Wharton, 1984; vpres, AASO-Harvard Bus Sch, 1989-90; Youth Education Through Sports; fel New York Covenant Church. **Honors/Awds:** Maggie L Walker Award, Emma L Higgombothum Award, Black Fac & Admin, Univ Penn, 1985; Onyx Sr Hon Soc, Univ Penn, 1985; Cert Pub Acct, AICPA, 1988; Int Mar Corp Entrepreneurs Comp-Hon Mention, Univ Tex, Austin, 1990. **Special Achievements:** First African Americans to be promoted to manager at Bain & Co. **Home Addr:** 1900 Patterson Ave, Bronx, NY 10473, **Home Phone:** (718)589-3170. **Business Addr:** Chief Financial Officer, Bad Boy Worldwide Entertainment Group, 1440 Broadway 16th Fl, New York, NY 10018, **Business Phone:** (212)381-1540.

## FERGUSON, ELLIOTT LAROY, II

Sales manager, vice president (organization). **Personal:** Born Nov 26, 1965, Spokane, WA; son of Gwendolyn Cooper Williams and Elliott L Sr. **Educ:** Savannah State Col, BA, mkt & bus admin, 1988. **Career:** Savannah, Econ Develop, Authority, dir res, 1988-91; Savannah Conv & Visitors Bur, dir sales, 1991-92; Atlanta Conv & Visitors Bur, sales mgr, 1992-, vpres; Destination DC, vpres conv sales & serv, pres, chief exec officer, 2001-; Conv & Tourism Corp, Conv Sales & Serv, Wash, DC, Mem Dept, interim head, sr vpres, currently; Wash CTC, vpres sales. **Orgs:** Alpha Phi Alpha, 1988-; bd mem, Rape Crisis Ctr, 1991-92; S Atlantic 2000 Club, 1991-92; Destination Mkt Asn Int, 1995-, dir, 2012-; bd mem, March Dimes; mentor, Capital Chap; bd mem, DC Conv & Tourism Corp; chmn, Hospitality Alliance Wash; chmn, Wash Conv & Sports Authority; chmn, Hotel Asn Wash; chmn, Restaurant Asn Metrop Wash; Am Soc Asn Execs; Nat Coalition Black Meeting Planners; Relig Conf Mgt Asn; Prof Conf Mgt Asn; Int Asn Exhib Execs; Capitol Hill; Downtown Bus Improv Dist; Mil Bowl; bd dir, Franciscan Monastery USA Inc; active mentor, Capital Partners Educ; Capital Partners Inc; bd dir, US Travel Asn; bd dir, Dc's Taxicab Comn; bd dir, DC Jazz Festival; bd dir, Ryan Kerrigan "Blitz Better" Found; Brand USA Mkt Adv Group. **Home Addr:** 3920 Dogwood Farm Rd, Decatur, GA 30034-6435, **Home Phone:** (404)808-1656. **Business Addr:** President, Chief Executive Officer, Destination Marketing Association International, 2025 M St NW Suite 500, Washington, DC 20036, **Business Phone:** (202)296-7888.

## FERGUSON, FAY

Executive. **Personal:** children: Eric. **Educ:** Concordia Col, BA, eng, speech & drama, 1973; Ind Univ, MBA, 1978. **Career:** Mich City, teacher; Bozell & Jacobs, advert & sr acct exec; Burrell Commun Grp, mng partner, 1971-, co-chief exec officer, 2004-, mng partner acct mgt & opers, currently; Burrell Advert, acct supvr, 1984, vpres, 1986, vpres/acct dir, 1988, mgt supvr, 1992, dir, 1993. **Orgs:** Chicago Advert Fedn; Perspectives Charter Sch; bd gov, Chicago Coun; Am Asn Advert Agencies Inc; chair, Procter & Gamble Co; adv bd mem, TurnerPatterson; Am Diabetes Asn; Chicago Network, N Shore Chap

Links Inc. **Business Addr:** Co-Chief Executive Officer, Managing Partner, Burrell Communications Group, 233 N Mich Ave Suite 2900, Chicago, IL 60601, **Business Phone:** (312)297-9600.

### FERGUSON, JASON O.
Football player. **Personal:** Born Nov 28, 1974, Nettleton, MA. **Educ:** Univ Ga, grad. **Career:** Football player (retired); New York Jets, defensive tackle, 1997, left defensive tackle, 1998-99, nose tackle, 1999-2004, defensive tackle, 2000, right defensive tackle, 2002-04; Dallas Cowboys, nose tackle, 2005-07, defensive tackle & defensive end, 2005; Miami Dolphins, left defensive tackle, 2008, nose tackle, 2008-09. **Honors/Awds:** American Football Conference Defensive Player of the Week, 2003.

### FERGUSON, JOEL I.
Executive, real estate executive. **Personal:** married Erma. **Educ:** Mich State Univ, BA, elem educ, 1965. **Career:** Maxco Inc, dir, 1985-; Mich State Univ, bd trustees, mem, 1986-, chmn, 1992, 1996-; WLAJ-TV, pres, owner & founder, 1990-; Channel 53, cofounder & pres; Lansing, cofounder & pres; WFSL-TV, owner; Fox 47, owner; WSYM, founder; Mich Broadband Develop Authority, bd dirs, dir, 2002-; F&S Develop Co, founder & partner, chmn, currently; Blue Cross Blue Shield Mich Inc, vpres, dir; Capitol Bancorp, dir; Greektown Casino LLC, dir. **Orgs:** Dir, Greater Lansing Urban League OJT prog; bd dir, Fed Home Loan Mortgage Corp. **Special Achievements:** A U.S. Marine Corps veteran. **Home Addr:** 3412 Sandhurst Dr, Lansing, MI 48911, **Home Phone:** (517)882-2343. **Business Addr:** Founder, Partner, Ferguson Development LLC, 1223 Turner St Suite 300, Lansing, MI 48906, **Business Phone:** (517)371-2515.

### FERGUSON, JOHNNIE NATHANIEL
Banker, manager. **Personal:** Born Jan 17, 1943, Washington, DC; son of James H and Viola Cooper (deceased); married Delphine David; children: Michelle D. **Educ:** Univ Dist Columbia, AAS, comput sci, 1973; Harcourt Learning Direct, PC repair, 2000; Prof Develop Inst, real estate cert, 2003. **Career:** FBI, fingerprint tech, 1964-67; Riggs Nat Corp, Wash, DC, programmer, 1967-79, data processing supvr, 1979-90, banking officer & asst mgr, 1990-93, banking officer & mgr, 1993-98, asst vpres, sales mgr, 1998-2001, vpres, bus develop officer, 2001-. **Orgs:** Pres, Orr Elem Sch PTA, 1976-84; Wash, DC Asn Urban Bankers, 1977-83; pres, Riggs Nat Bank Club, 1979; treas, DC Cong Parents & Teachers, 1982-84; treas, Adv Neighborhood Comm 6C, 1982-; DC Fed Farmers & Consumers Markets, 1983-; DC Cong PTA, 1986; Nat Cong Parents & Teachers, 1987; treas, Kiwanis Club Eastern Br, 1988-92; chmn, Local Bd 1 Selective Serv Syst, 1988-01; vpres, DC Cong PTA, 1989-92; vpres, Kiwanis Club Eastern Br, 1990-91; secy, DC Comn Human Rights, 1990-91; bd mem, Anacostia/Cong Heights Partnership, controller, 1993-; Anacostia Bus & Prof Asn, 1994-2001; Area D Community Ment Health Asn, 1995-99; Hadley Mem Hosp Community Bd, 1996-99; deacon bd, church treas, financial secy & off adminr, St Matthews Baptist Church, 1999-2001; bd dir, Far SE Family Strengthing Collab Inc, Finance Comt, 2000-. **Honors/Awds:** Certification Appreciation, Am Cancer Soc, 1980; Certification Appreciation, DC Adv Coun Voc Educ, 1980; Certification Award, Benjamin G Orr Elem Sch, 1980-84; Meritorious Public Service Award, 1997. **Home Addr:** 1919 Ridge Pl SE, Washington, DC 20020-4626, **Home Phone:** (202)678-5212. **Business Addr:** Board Member, Far Southeast Family Strengthening Collaborative Inc, 2041 Martin Luther King Jr Ave SE Suite 304, Washington, DC 20020, **Business Phone:** (202)889-1425.

### FERGUSON, RALPH
Vice president (organization), automotive executive. **Personal:** Born Feb 23, 1955, Warner Robins, GA; son of Jordan Georgia and Jesse. **Educ:** Citadel Col, Charleston, SC, BS, educ, 1977; Ga Col, Milledgeville, GA, attended 1985. **Career:** Houston Bd Educ, Warner Robins, Ga, teacher, 1977-83; 20th Century Realty, Warner Robins, Ga, sales, 1981-84; J-Mac Olds, Warner Robins, Ga, sales, 1984-85; Eddie Wiggins F-L-M, Warner Robins, Ga, sales, 1985-86; Sumter Ford-L-M, Americus, Ga, co-owner & vpres 1986-; Pkwy E Ford, auto dealer, 1994-2003; Day Automotive, GSM, 2008-09; Wade Ford, sales prof, 2009-. **Orgs:** Citadel Alumni Asn, 1977-91; Alumni Football Asn, 1977-91; Black Ford Lincoln Mercury, 1986-91; pres, Ferguson Family Found, 1990-. **Home Addr:** PO Box 397, Warner Robins, GA 31099, **Home Phone:** (912)328-2515. **Business Addr:** Sales Professional, Wade Ford, 3860 S Cobb Dr SE, Smyrna, GA 30080, **Business Phone:** (770)436-1200.

### FERGUSON, RENEE
Journalist. **Personal:** Born Aug 22, 1949, Oklahoma City, OK; daughter of Eugene and Mary; married Ken Smikle; children: Jason. **Educ:** Ind Univ, BS, jour, 1971, MA, 1972. **Career:** Jackson State Univ, post stud intern, 1970; Kent State Univ, post stud intern, 1970; Indianapolis Star newspaper, writer, 1971-72; WLWI-TV Indianapolis, news reporter, 1972-76; WBBM-TV Chicago, news reporter, investigative reporter, 1977-82; CBS News, news reporter, NY & Atlanta, network news corresp, 1980; Nat Broadcasting Co, Chicago, Unit 5 investigative team, WMAQ-TV, investigative reporter, 1987-2008; Univ Chicago, benton fel, 1993-94; Harvard Univ, Nieman fel, 2006-07; US House Representatives, communications dir, 2011-13; Renee Ferguson Writing & Editing, bk doctor, 2013. **Orgs:** Bd dir, Asn C, 1975-78; bd mem, Big Sisters Am, Indianapolis, 1975-78; Alpha Kappa Alpha Sorority; Nat Orgn Women; Am Civil Liberties Union; Chicago Black Women's Lawyers Asn; bd dir, Investigative Reporters & Ed Inc; co founder, chicago chap, Nat Asn Black Journalists, 1978; Nat Acad Motion Picture Arts & Sci. **Special Achievements:** First African American woman to work as an investigative reporter in Chicago. **Home Addr:** , Chicago, IL 60615.

### FERGUSON, DR. ROBERT LEE, SR.
Consultant. **Personal:** Born Feb 18, 1932, Rascon San Luis Potoci; son of Booker T (deceased) and Corillea Jackson (deceased); married Ruby Evelyn Brewer; children: Robert Jr & Duane; married Raymonde Bateau Polk; children: Raymonde Polk-Wilson, Samuel Polk, Pierre Polk, Regina1 Polk & Carmel Polk. **Educ:** Bakersfield Col, attended 1951; Naval Aviation Preflight, Pensacola, FL, 1964; S western Col, AA, 1969; Naval Postgrad Sch, BA, 1973; Univ N Colo, MA, 1975; Pac Western Univ Los Angeles CA, PhD, 1986. **Career:** USN Hawaii, capt's steward, 1951-52; Heavy Attack Squadron, aircraft maintenance chief; USN, Bombardier Navigator, adv human minority rels psychol coun, 1967-77; INFO, naval flight officer, flighter squadron213, asst maintenance officer; NAS Miramar CA, asst dept head aircraft maintenance, 1973-75; USS Enterprise, asst dept head aircraft maintenance, 1975-78; NAS, Lemoore CA, officer charge aircraft maintenance, 1978-80; Left Brain Press, consult, auth; Fighter Squadron 124, dept head aircraft maintenance, 1980; Rail Co, sr logistics analyst; syst acquisition mgt consult; self-employed, 1988-. **Orgs:** Fleet Res Asn, 1963-65; mgr, Pk view Little League, Chula Vista, CA, 1969-77; Naval Aviation Tail hook Asn, 1972-; alumni, Naval Post grad Sch, 1973-; Veterans Foreign Wars, 1974-; alumni, Univ N Colo, 1975-; Nat Naval Officer Asn, 1977-; San Diego Mus Art; corresp chmn, African Arts Comm; Naval Aviation Mus, Pensacola, FL. **Honors/Awds:** Author: The Four-O (4.0) Sailor, self-publish, 1990. **Business Addr:** Consultant, Author, Left Brain Press, 604 Mariposa Cir, Chula Vista, CA 91911-2511, **Business Phone:** (619)421-8847.

### FERGUSON, ROGER W., JR.
Economist, president (organization), chief executive officer. **Personal:** Born Oct 28, 1951, Washington, DC; married Annette Nazareth; children: 2. **Educ:** Harvard Col, BA, econs, 1973; Harvard Law Sch, JD, 1979; Harvard Univ, PhD, econs, 1981. **Career:** Cambridge Univ, Frank Knox Memorial fel; Davis Polk & Wardwell, atty, 1981-84; McKinsey & Co, assoc partner & dir res, 1984-97; Fed Res Syst, bd gov, 1997-2006, vice chmn, 1999-2006; Swiss Re Am Holding Corp, head financial serv & mem swiss re's exec comt, 2006-08; Teachers Ins & Annuity Asn-Col Retirement Equities Fund (TIAA-CREF), pres & chief exec officer, 2008-. **Orgs:** Bd mem, Brevan Howard Asset Mgt LLP, 2010-; fel Am Acad Arts & Sci, 2010-; bd dir mem, Int Flavors & Fragrances, 2014-; Panel Econ Adv, Cong Budget Off, 2014-; bd mem, Gen Mills, 2015-; chmn, Conf Bd, 2015-; Am Philos Soc, 2016-; bd mem, Alphabet, Inc., 2016-; bd trustee, Comt Econ Develop; bd trustee, Inst Advan Study; bd trustee, Memorial Sloan Kettering Cancer Ctr; vice chmn, bd trustee, New York Econ Club; Coun Foreign Rels; Group Thirty. **Honors/Awds:** Bond Market Association, The Distinguished Service Award, 2002; Society of Government Economists and the American Economic Association, Economics in Government Distinguished Lecturer, 2004; NACHA, The George Mitchell Payments Systems Excellence Award, 2005; Abyssinian Development Corporation, The Renaissance Award, 2006; Global Interdependence Center, The Frederick Heldering Global Leadership Award, 2006, 2013; New York Association for Business Economics, The William F. Butler Memorial Award, 2006; Global Alternative Investment Management Forum (GAIM) and the Cambridge Endowment for Research in Finance (CERF), Global Financial Policy Award, 2007; Council for Economic Education, Visionary Award, 2009; "Black Enterprise," The 100 Most Powerful Executives in Corporate America, 2010; African American Chamber of Commerce of New Jersey, Business Achievement Award, 2011; Global Econ Achievement Award, 100 Black Men's, 2012; Achievement Award, Exec Leadership Coun, 2013; Adam Smith Award, Nat Asn Bus Econs, 2013; Chairman's Award, A Better Chance, 2013; Soaring Eagle Award, Eagle Acad Found, 2014; Trustee Leadership Award, Comt Econ Develop, 2014; honorary degrees, Lincoln Col, Webster Univ, Wash & Jefferson Col, Mich State Univ, Worcester Polytech Inst, St. Lawrence Univ, Univ Md, Baltimore County, Georgetown Univ & Metrop Col New York. **Business Addr:** President, Chief Executive Officer, TIAA-CREF, 730 3rd Ave, New York, NY 10017.

**FERGUSON, ROSETTA A.** **See Obituaries Section.**

### FERGUSON, SHERLON LEE
Executive. **Personal:** Born Mar 2, 1949, Richmond, VA; son of William Sr and Grace Brown; married Brenda Russell; children: Mia & Meaghan. **Educ:** Morgan State Univ, Baltimore, BS, math, 1971. **Career:** Blue Cross & Blue Shield, Baltimore, actuarial asst, 1971-73; Honeywell Inc, Baltimore, sr sales engr, 1973-83; FSCO Inc, Baltimore, pres & chief exec officer, 1983-. **Orgs:** Bldg Cong & Exchange Baltimore, 1973-; Am Soc Heating, Refrig & Air Conditioning Engs, 1973-; US Chamber Com, 1988-89; Better Bus Bur, 1988-; Minority Bus Develop Coun, 1988-; Asn Builders & Contractors, 1988-; Minority Supplier Develop Coun, 1988-. **Home Addr:** 919 E Belvedere Ave, Baltimore, MD 21212, **Home Phone:** (410)435-6320. **Business Addr:** President, Chief Executive Officer, FSCO Inc, 6927 Hardford Rd, Baltimore, MD 21234-7711, **Business Phone:** (410)668-3611.

### FERGUSON, ST. JULIAN
Musician, educator, salesperson. **Personal:** Born Apr 13, 1935, SC; son of Irene and Alonzo; married Albertha Simmons; children: Darian, Gerald & Bernard. **Educ:** SC State Univ, BS, 1957; Loyola Univ, MEd, 1971. **Career:** Tilden Tech High Sch, instr music teacher, 1965-69; Madison Elem, teacher, 1969-71; Chicago Bd Educ, teacher early remediation, 1971; Bryn Mawr Elem Sch, teacher, 1971; Coldwell Banker, sales assoc, 1993; Lower N Youth Ctr, music dir. **Orgs:** Nat Educ Asn; Ill Teachers Asn; Chicago Fed Musicians. **Home Addr:** 9956 S Union Ave, Chicago, IL 60628-1038, **Home Phone:** (773)230-8595. **Business Addr:** Sales Associate, Coldwell Banker, 11113 S Wern Ave, Chicago, IL 60643, **Business Phone:** (312)779-5400.

### FERGUSON, VALERIE C.
Hotel executive, vice president (organization). **Educ:** Univ San Francisco, BA, govt, polit sci, 1977. **Career:** Hyatt Hotel, Atlanta, clerk, gen mgr, 1977-95; Ritz-Carlton, Atlanta, gen mgr, 1994-98; Loews Philadelphia Hotel, reg vpres, 1998-2012, vpres brand mgt, 2012-13, managing dir, sr vpres opers; Loews Corp, regional vpres, 1998-2013; Denihan Hospitality Group, vpres opers, 2014-15; Walt Disney Parks & Resorts, Experience, Planning & Integration, dir lodging, 2016-. **Orgs:** Pa Travel Coun; Philadelphia Conv & Visitors Bur; Hist Philadelphia Inc; Urban League Philadelphia; Philadelphia Workforce Investment Corp; Sch Dist Philadelphia's Communities Schools & Widener Univ; chmn, Am Hotel & Lodging Asn; adv bd mem, Univ Del. **Honors/Awds:** Pioneer Award, Atlanta Bus League, 1991; Women of the Year, Network Exec Women Hospitality, 1993; Trumpet Award, Turner Broadcasting, 1994; Lodging Leader of the Year, Ga Hospitality & Trade Asn, 1998; Drum Major for Justice Award, Southern Christian Leadership Conference; Honorary Doctorate, Food Manufacturing Asn; Hospitality Leader of the Year, Diversity Institute, 2000; Hospitality Hotelier of the Year, Multicultural Black Culinary Alliance Food Serv & Hospitality. **Special Achievements:** First African American to hold the position of vice chairwoman American Hotel and Motel Association; Named to the Atlanta Business League's list of Top 100 Black Women of Influence; Named one of the 100 Most Influential Women in Travel for 1998 and 1999 by Travel Agent magazine; Selected as one of the Top 100 Women in Corporate America by Ebony Magazine. **Home Addr:** 9112 Quail Run Dr, Chattanooga, TN 37421-1347. **Business Addr:** Director of Lodging, Walt Disney Parks and Resorts, 1025 Grand Cent, Glendale, CA 91201.

### FERNANDES, JULIE A.
Government official. **Educ:** Univ Chicago, AB, 1987, Law Sch, JD, 1994. **Career:** Justice Dept, voting expert; White House Domestic Policy Coun, from spec asst to pres; Leadership Conf Civil Rights, sr policy analyst, 2002-08, spec coun; US Dept Justice, trl atty, Civil Rights Div & assoc coun asst atty gen civil rights; Raben Groups, prin health & educ & const & justice prac groups, currently. Alliance to End Slavery & Trafficking, dir, 2011-; Humanity United, dir; Open Soc Inst, sr policy analyst. **Orgs:** Karpatkin fell Nat Legal Dep, Am Civil Liberties Union; Am Const Soc. **Business Addr:** Principal, The Raben Group, 1640 Rhode Island Ave NW Suite 600, Washington, DC 20036, **Business Phone:** (202)466-8585.

### FERNANDES, MARY A.
Government official. **Personal:** married Paul; children: 3. **Educ:** Northeastern Univ, BA, human resource mgt. **Career:** Mass Bay Transp Authority, Exec Off Transp & Construct, dep secy Civil Rights & Prog Develop, currently; Silver Line Communs & Community Develop, asst gen mgr, currently. **Orgs:** Pres, bd mem, Boston Chap Conf Minority Transp Officials. **Business Addr:** Assistant General Manager, Massachusetts Bay Transportation Authority, 240 Southampton St, Boston, MA 02118, **Business Phone:** (617)222-1000.

### FERNANDEZ, DENISE BURSE
Actor. **Personal:** Born Jan 1, 1952, Atlanta, GA. **Career:** Film: Basquiat, 1996; On the One, 2005; The Juror, 1996; Funny Valentines, 1999; Preaching to the Choir, 2005; Peace, Love, & Misunderstanding, 2011. TV Series: "The American Experience", 1993; "New York Undercover", 1995; "Law & Order", 1999; "The Sopranos", 2000; "Cosby", 2000; "Third Watch", 2001; "100 Centre Street", 2001; "Law & Order: Special Victims Unit", 2001; "Law & Order: Criminal Intent", 2005; "One Life to Live", 2010; "House of Payne", 2006-11. **Business Addr:** Actress, Screen Actors Guild, 180 St Nicholas Ave Suite 21, New York, NY 10026, **Business Phone:** (212)663-5440.

### FERNANDEZ, JOHN PETER
Executive, manager. **Personal:** Born Oct 22, 1941, Boston, MA; children: Michele, Eleni & Sevgi. **Educ:** Harvard Univ, AB, govt, 1969; Univ CA, Berkeley, MA, sociol, 1971; Univ CA, Berkeley, PhD, indust sociol, 1974. **Career:** YMCA Dorchester MA, prog dir, 1965-69; AT&T NYC, Res & Mgt Devlopment, personnel supvr res, 1973-74, dist mgr, 1975-77, div level opers mgr, 1977-81, div mgr labor rels, 1981-84, human resoucres corp, 1987-88; Yale Univ, asst prof, 1974-75; AT&T Basking Rioge NJ, mgr mgt educ & develop, 1975-78; Bell PA, div mgr customer serv, 1978; Advan Res Mgt Consults Global LLC, pres & founder, 1981-; IMPACT Leadership 21, panelist, 2013. **Orgs:** Am Sociol Asn, 1973; Coun Concerned Black Exec, 1975-. **Honors/Awds:** Outstanding sophomore Govt Maj, Northeastern Univ, 1967; special careers fellow, Univ CA, Berkeley, 1969-73. **Special Achievements:** Author of 9 books; First Black division level operations manager. **Business Addr:** President, Founder, Advanced Research Management Consultants Global LLC, 701 W Allens Lane, Philadelphia, PA 19119, **Business Phone:** (215)247-4547.

### FERNANDEZ, PETER JAY
Actor. **Personal:** Born Aug 15, 1953, Brockton, MA; son of Barbara Julio; married Densie Burse. **Educ:** Boston Univ Sch Arts, BA, 1975. **Career:** TV Series: "The Prosecutors", 1996; "Hack", 2001; "Deep Vote", 2001; "Law & Order: Criminal Intent", 2001-11; "On the One", 2005; "Great Performances", 2008; "Fringe", 2009; "Damages", 2009; "Blue Bloods", 2010; "The Good Wife", 2010; "Body of Proof", 2011; "House of Cards", 2013; "Deception", 2013. Performed on stage with: Black & Hispanic Shakespeare Company, 1997; Classic Stage Co, New York, 1998; New York Stage & Film, 1998; Joseph Papp Public Theatre, 1997; Cincinnati Playhouse/Arena Stage, 1999; Via com Pictures, Adventures of Superboy, series regular, 1991-92; Jelly's Last Jam, Broadway, 1994; BET Movies & Starz USA Films, 1999; Fal Short, 2002; Films: In Till You Die, 1992; Funny Valentines, 1999; The Egoists, 2003; Preaching to the Choir, 2005; Deception, 2008; The Adjustment Bureau, 2011. **Orgs:** Actor's Equity Asn, 1975-; Screen Actors Guild, 1978-; Am Fedn TV & Radio Artists, 1978-; Non Traditional Casting Proj, 1990-; 52nd St Proj, 1989-. **Honors/Awds:** Helen Hayes Award, Best Actor in a Musical, nominee, 1999; Cincinnati Theatre Awards, Best Actor in a Musical, nominee, 1999. **Home Addr:** 180 St Nicholas Ave, New York, NY 10026, **Home Phone:** (212)663-5440.

### FERNANDEZ, TONY (OCTAVIO ANTONIO FERNANDEZ CASTRO)
Association executive, baseball player, minister (clergy). **Personal:** Born Jun 30, 1962, San Pedro de Macoris; married Clara; children: Joel, Jonathan, Abraham, Andy & Jazmin. **Career:** Baseball player (retired); Toronto Blue Jays, infielder, 1983-90, 1993, 1998-99 & 2001; San Diego Padres, infielder, 1991-92; New York Mets, infielder, 1993; Cincinnati Reds, 1994; New York Yankees, 1995-96; Cleveland Indians, 1997; Seibu Lions, 2000; Milwaukee Brewers, infielder, 2001; ordained minister, currently. **Orgs:** Founder, Tony Fernandez Found, 2002-. **Honors/Awds:** R Howard Webster Award as Syracuses Most Valuable Player, 1982-83; Rookie of the Year, Baseball Writers Asn Am, 1984; Labatts Blue Player of the Month, 1986; All-Star selection, 1986-89, 1992, 1999; Gold Glove Awards, 1986-89; World Series champion, 1993; Toronto Blue Jays Level of Excellence. **Home Addr:** Calle N Suite 3 B Restauracion, San Pedro De Marcoris21000. **Busi-**

**ness Addr:** Founder, Tony Fernandez Foundation, 1675 Market St Suite 211, Weston, FL 33326, **Business Phone:** (854)249-0524.

### FERNANDEZ-SMITH, WILHELMENIA
Singer. **Personal:** Born Jan 1, 1949?, Philadelphia, PA. **Career:** TV series: " La Boheme", 1980; Film: Diva, 1981; Singles: "Someone to Watch Over Me", 1987; "Motown 30: What's Goin' On!", 1990; Opera & Concert singer, currently. **Business Addr:** Opera & Concert Singer, 3280 Brighton Place Dr, Lexington, KY 40509, **Business Phone:** (859)225-0374.

### FERREBEE, THOMAS G.
Police officer, vice president (organization). **Personal:** Born Jan 24, 1937, Detroit, MI; married Irma; children: Gregory G, Debra L & Angela M. **Educ:** Iowa State Univ, BS, 1960; Eastern Mich Univ, MA, guid & coun, 1963. **Career:** Detroit Police Dept, comdr recruiting div & dir police recruitment & placement div, 1969; Ford Motor Co; Hamtramck HS, teacher; Chrysler Corp; Wayne County, dir human rels; Wayne County Community Col, mgr labor rels, dir cert; TGF Enterprises LLC, founder, 2001; CFS, vpres mktg, 2004. **Orgs:** Bd trustee personnel com, Childrens Hosp MI; Ctr Criminal Justice & Minority Employ Law Enforcement; consult, Minority Police Recruiting; Optimist Club Detroit; area activ chmn, BSA; Mich Pub Personnel Asn; Concerned Police Off Equal Justice. **Home Addr:** 15784 Ilene St, Detroit, MI 48238-1002. **Business Addr:** Vice President of Marketing, 8045 2nd Ave, Detroit, MI 48202.

### FERRELL, DUANE EDWARD
Basketball player, basketball executive, manager. **Personal:** Born Feb 28, 1965, Baltimore, MD; married Tina I; children: 4. **Educ:** Ga Inst Technol, BS, indust mgt, 1988. **Career:** Basketball player (retired), basketball exec; Yellow Jacket, 1985-88; Atlanta Hawks, forward & small forward, 1988-94; CBA, Topeka Sizzlers, small forward, 1989-90; Ind Pacers, small forward, 1994-97; Golden State Warriors, small forward, 1997-99; Vidya Media Ventures Inc, mgr; Wash Wizards, dir player prog & asst coach, 2001-04; Atlanta Hawks, player rels & progs mgr, 2008-. **Honors/Awds:** McDonald's All American, 1983-84; ACC Rookie of the Year, 1985; CBA Newcomer of the Year, 1990. **Special Achievements:** He was part of the 1982 National Championship team & led the number one ranked team in the country in 1988. **Home Addr:** 2345 Hamiltowne Cir, Rosedale, MD 21237-1451. **Business Addr:** Player Relations & Programs Manager, Atlanta Hawks, Verizon Ctr 601 F St NW, Atlanta, GA 30303, **Business Phone:** (404)878-3800.

### FERRELL, TYRA
Actor. **Personal:** Born Jan 28, 1962, Houston, TX; daughter of Rachel Johnson; married Don Carlos Johnson. **Educ:** Univ Tex, Austin, actg. **Career:** Broadway: The Lady and Her Music; Dreamgirls; Films: So Fine, 1981; Gimme an 'F', 1984; Lady Beware, 1987; School Daze, 1988; Tapeheads, 1988; The Mighty Quinn, 1989; The Exorcist III, 1990; Jungle Fever, 1991; Boyz n the Hood, 1991; Ulterior Motives, 1992; White Men Can't Jump, 1992; Equinox, 1992; Poetic Justice, 1993; The Perfect Score, 2004; Coochie, 2004; Boxed in, 2014. TV Series: "Reaching for the Stars", 1985; "Hill Street Blues", 1985; "Moonlight", 1985; "The Twilight Zone", 1985; "ABC After School Specials", 1986; "Hunter", 1986; "Mathnet", 1987; "The Bronx Zoo", 1987-88; "Side by Side", 1988; "Mr Belvedere", 1988; "The Neon Empire", 1989; "Quantum Leap", 1989; "Thirty Something", 1989-90; "City", 1990; "Full House", 1990; "The Trials of Rosie O'Neill", 1990; "You Must Remember This", 1992; "Better Off Dead", 1993; "The Cape", 1993; "ER", 1994; "The Cape", 1996-97; "Early Edition", 1997; "The Corner", 2000; "Soul Food", 2000; "The Shield", 2002; "Futility", 2003; "Law & Order: Special Victims Unit", 2003; "NTSB: The Crash of Flight 323", 2004. **Special Achievements:** She was listed as one of twelve "Promising New Actors of 1991" in John Willis' Screen World, 2005; nominee, Image Award as an Outstanding Actress in a Television Movie, 2005. **Business Addr:** Actor, Gersh Agency, 232 N Canon Dr, Beverly Hills, CA 90210, **Business Phone:** (310)274-6611.

### FERRER, JOSE
Executive. **Career:** Kwanzaa Fest Found, founder & chmn, 1981-. **Business Addr:** Chairman, Founder, Kwanzaa Fest, 800 Grand Concourse Suite 3CS, Bronx, NY 10461, **Business Phone:** (718)402-1419.

### FEWELL, RICHARD
Playwright. **Personal:** Born Feb 2, 1937, Rock Hill, SC; son of Thomas and Laura Steele; married Geraldine Whitted; children: Renee Lorraine & Ritchard Gerald. **Educ:** Univ Bridgeport, BA, 1976, MA, 1980. **Career:** Educr, playwright; US Postal Serv, mail classification & reqs & postal servs, 1992; Univ Bridgeport, part-time Eng instr, 1994; Sacred Heart Univ, Fairfield, Conn, adj instr; Housatonic Community Col, lectr eng, instr african-am lit & lit & compos, 1996-2007, part-time fac; Plays: Spunk; Amen Corner; Playboy Wi; To Kill A Mockingbird; 2020 BC, Good Morning; Best Church Frank St; Prometheus Fire, audience develop & new play advisor. **Orgs:** Pres, Alpha Sigma Lambda, 1975-76; bd mem, Nat Asn Advan Colored People, 1976-; Frank Silvera Writer's Workshop, 1978-90; bur chief Fairfield County; freelance writer, Fairfield County Advocate, contrib ed, Conn Update, 1982-83; bd dir, Bridgeport Arts Coun, 1982-85; community mem, Action Bridgeport community Develop, 1984-86; found mem, New Bridge Ensemble, 1986-; ed, Nat Alliance Postal & Fed Employees Newsletter & Local 808; African Am Family Forum, 1990-91; Inner City Newspaper, 1990-2001; Adv Comt, New Eng Found Arts, 1992; adv comt, Artists Trust, Cambridge, Mass, 1992-96. **Honors/Awds:** Bert & Katya Gilden Memorial Short Story Award, 1975; First Prize Article, Writer's Digest Creative Writing Contest, 1977; Literature Award, Conn Comt Arts, 1984; Publ Black Scholar, The Greenfield Review, Callaloo, Obsidian, Anthology Magazine Verse & Yearbook of American Poetry, The South Carolina Review, Okike (Nigeria), African Voices, African American Review; Others; author "Everything Happens Today; " Heritage Award, Arts & Humanities, Alpha Kappa Alpha Sorority, 1987; actor, Dot Playhouse, played role of "Rev Sykes" in To Kill a Mockingbird, 1988; poetry readings Stan Nishimura Performance Arts/New Haven, Conn, 1988-89; excerpts from unpublished novel published Mwendo (Iowa), Obsidian (NC) & Beanfeast (Conn); Grant, Conn Comn Arts, 1990; Nguzo Saba Award, Kwanzaa Seven Prod, 1996; Fairfield Review & On-Line Literary Mag, 1998; Poetry Readings: WPKN.FM, 1998; New Haven Free Pub Libr, 1998; Playwright Award, Conn Comn Cult & Tourism, 1999; Played role of "Luke" in Baldwin's "Amen Corner" HCC Performing Arts Ctr, 2000; Keeper of the Flame Award, Calvary Seventh-day Adventist Church, 2000; Distinguished Advocate for the Arts Award, 2001; Distinguished Alumni, Univ Bridgeport, 2002. **Special Achievements:** Played Lead Role in Independent Film, Good Morning, premiered at Yale University, 1991; play Coon Dog, was a finalist in Theodore Ward prize for playwriting, 1991; play Hats was in five finalist in Theodore Ward prize, 1997-98; play, Skyy Piece, premiere reading, 2000; play, Juggie Bones, Rich Forum, 2003; Dramatic concert reading, Stamford Ctr for the Creative Arts, 2004; "Skyy Piece" featured in the Lower Eas Side Festival/New York; Featured writer in African Voices Magazine's Cultural Circle Conference, 2011. **Home Addr:** 89 Yaremich Dr Suite A, Bridgeport, CT 06606-2554, **Home Phone:** (203)372-1774. **Business Addr:** New Play Advisor, Prometheus Fire, PO Box 17246, Stamford, CT 06907-7246.

### FIELDER, CECIL GRANT
Baseball manager, baseball player. **Personal:** Born Sep 21, 1963, Los Angeles, CA; son of Tina; married Stacey Lynn Granger; children: Prince & Ceclynn; married Angie; children: Grant. **Educ:** Univ Nev, Las Vegas. **Career:** Baseball player (retired), baseball manager; Toronto Blue Jays, infielder, 1985-88; Hanshin Tigers, infielder, 1989; Detroit Tigers, infielder, 1990-96; New York Yankees, 1996-97; Anaheim Angels, 1998; Cleveland Indians, 1998; Charlotte County Redfish, mgr, 2007; Atlantic City Surf, field mgr, 2008-; Torrington Titans, adv bd mem, 2011-. **Business Addr:** Field Manager, Atlantic City Surf, Bernie Robbins Stadium, Atlantic City, NJ 08401-1335, **Business Phone:** (609)344-8873.

### FIELDER, DR. FRED CHARLES
School administrator, dentist, association executive. **Personal:** Born Jun 16, 1933, Hattiesburg, MS; son of Ben and Quinnie White; married Vivian L Johnson; children: Fred Charles Jr. **Educ:** Tougaloo Col, BS, 1956; Meharry Med Col, DDS, 1960. **Career:** Hubbard Hosp, intern, 1960-61; Univ Mich, Miss, oper dent, 1964, Mich Inst Tech, fel, 1966; Meharry Med Col, Dept Oper Dent, instr, 1961-63, from asst prof to assoc prof, 1964-74; Meharry Med Col Dent Clin, supt, 1971; Meharry Med Col Sch Dent, asst dean, exec assoc dean, interim dean, 1992-93, dean, 1993-97, deam emer, 1997-; Meharry Med Col, Dept Oper Dent, prof & chmn. **Orgs:** Pres, Kappa Sigma Pi Honor Soc, 1961-62; Acad Oper Dent; fel United Health Found, 1963; Am Bd Oper Dent; fel Col Dentists; Am Asn Dent Schs; past zone vpres, Pan TN Dent Asn, 1968-75, st vpres, 1979; comm mem Manpower & Aux Am Asn Dent Schsn, 1969-70; coun Int Asn Dent Res, 1969-73; consul NC St, Bd Dent Exam, 1970; vpres, Omicron-Omicron Chap Omicron Kappa Upsilon Honor Dent Soc, 1970-72, pres, 1972-74; vpres, Capital City Dent Soc, 1972-74, pres, 1974-76; clin consult comn, AmDent Asn, 1979-; consult, Quarterly J Nat Dent Asn; Nat Dent Asn; Nashville Dent Soc; Tenn State Dent Soc; Asn Dent Res; Conf Oper Dentistry Educators; Clark Mem United Methodist Church; Schs Comn Cols Vis Comt; Am Dent Asn. **Honors/Awds:** Most Outstanding Soph Dental Student, Meharry Med Col, 1958; Chi Delta Mu Awards, 1958; Meth Scholarship Award; Mosby School Book Award; Caulk Prize, 1959; United Meth Scholar Award, High Sch Aver, 1959; Academy Dental Medical Award, 1960; Acad Gold Foil Award, 1960; Donley H Turpin Member Award, 1960; Mizzy Award Crown & Bridge, 1960; Pan TN Dental Association Award, 1960; Jos Frank Dental Award, 1960; Mosby Book Award, 1960; Caulk Prize, 1960; Nashville Dental Supply Prize, 1960; Snyder Dent Prize, 1960; Alpha Omega Award, 1960; Valedictorian Royal St HS, 1952; Recog & plaque one of l00 most valuable employees, Meharry Med Col, 1975; Dedication Recip Meharrian yearbook, 1964; Recog plaque Growth & Develop Meharry Col, 1971; Outstanding Faculty of the Year, Nat Alumni Asn, 1988; Student Appreciation Award, class of 1993; Fred C. Fielder, DDS Distinguished Dentist Award, Clark Mem United Methodist Church, named in honor, 2007; Pre-Alumni Council Award; Senior Dental Class Award. **Home Addr:** 4219 Drakes Hill Dr, Nashville, TN 37218, **Home Phone:** (615)876-1938. **Business Addr:** Dean Emeritus, Meharry Medical College, 1005 Dr DB Todd Jr Blvd, Nashville, TN 37208, **Business Phone:** (615)327-6000.

### FIELDER, PRINCE SEMIEN
Baseball player. **Personal:** Born May 9, 1984, Ontario, CA; son of Cecil and Stacey August; married Chanel; children: Jaden & Haven. **Career:** Minor League Baseball, Huntsville Stars, 2004; Minor League Baseball, Nashville Sounds, 2005; Maj League Baseball, Nat League, Milwaukee Brewers, 2005-11; Maj League Baseball, Am League, Detroit Tigers, 2012-13; Tex Rangers, 2014-. **Honors/Awds:** Minor League Player of the Year, USA Today, 2004; National League Hank Aaron Award, 2007; All-Star Game, 2007; National League Home Run Champion, 2007; Silver Slugger Award, 2007, 2011, 2012; All-Star Game, 2009; Most Valuable Player, Milwaukee Brewers, 2009; National League Runs Batted In Leader, 2009; All-Star Game, 2011; All-Star Game Most Valuable Player, 2011; All-Star Game, 2012; All-Star Home Run Derby Champion, 2009, 2012; AL Comeback Player of the Year, 2015. **Business Addr:** Professional Baseball Player, Texas Rangers, 1000 Ballpark Way, Arlington, TX 76011, **Business Phone:** (817)273-5222.

**FIELDING, HERBERT ULYSSES.** **See Obituaries Section.**

**FIELDS, ALVA DOTSON.** **See Obituaries Section.**

### FIELDS, BRENDA JOYCE
School administrator. **Personal:** Born Tacoma, WA; daughter of Betty Mewborn. **Educ:** Ohio State Univ, BA, psychol, 1981; Columbus Chamber Com, Leadership Columbus, leadership cert, 1989; United Way, Proj Diversity, bd develop cert, 1989; Col Bus, Ohio State Univ, Sch Pub Policy & Mgt, MA, 1994. **Career:** Columbus Recreation & Parks Dept, dance instr, choreographer, 1980-90; Ohio State Univ, pub inquiries asst, 1983-93, asst dir stud progs, 1993; Sphinx Sr Honoraries, Ohio Union, asst dir, 1994; Sullivant Gardens Capital Kids, site dir. **Orgs:** Leadership Columbus, Chamber Com; Ohio State Univ, Women Color Consortium, 1984-; Delta Sigma Theta Sorority Inc; bd trustee, Nat Assault Prevent Ctr; Truth-Douglass Soc, 1992; United Negro Col Fund, Ohio State Univ, 1992-. **Home Addr:** 1303 Doten Ave, Columbus, OH 43212. **Business Addr:** Site Director, Sullivant Gardens Capital Kids, 755 Renick St, Columbus, OH 43223, **Business Phone:** (614)645-5587.

### FIELDS, C. VIRGINIA
Government official. **Personal:** Born Aug 6, 1945, Birmingham, AL; married Henry. **Educ:** Knoxville Col, TN, BA, sociol, 1967; Ind Univ, MSW, 1969. **Career:** NY, social worker, 1971-88; City NY, coun mem, 1989-97; Manhattan Bor, pres, 1998-2006; social serv adminr, New York Work Release Prog; New York Univs Silver Sch Social Work, adj lectr. **Orgs:** Dir, C's Aid Soc; consult, Nat Bd YWCA; bd mem, Va Nat League Cities; bd mem, Jazz at Lincoln Ctr; bd mem, Am Mus Natural Hist; bd mem, Mus City New York; bd mem, el Museo del barrio; bd mem, Mus Art & Design; Alpha Kappa Alpha sorority; LINKS; Eastern Star; Abyssinian Baptist Church; pres & chief exec officer, Nat Black Leadership Comn AIDS Inc, 2008-; Ny AIDS Adv Coun, 2008-; US Dept Health & Human Serv Region II Health Equity Coun, 2011-; pres, Knoxville Col, Nat Alumni Asn, currently. **Business Addr:** President, Chief Executive Officer, National Black Leadership Commission on AIDS, Inc, 215 W 125th St 2nd Fl, New Yorkq, NY 10027, **Business Phone:** (212)614-0023.

### FIELDS, CLEO
Lawyer, politician. **Personal:** Born Nov 22, 1962, Baton Rouge, LA; son of Isidore and Alice; married Debra Horton; children: Brandon & Christopher. **Educ:** Southern Univ, BA, 1984; Southern Univ Sch Law, JD, 1987. **Career:** State La, sen, 1987-92; US House Representatives, Las 4th Cong Dist, congressman, 1993-97; Clinton-Gore presidential campaign, vol sr advisor, 1996; 14th Sen Dist LA, state sen, 1998-2008; Fields Law Firm LLC, founder, owner & Partner, 1998-; Cleo Fields & Assocs, pres & chief exec officer. **Orgs:** Founder, La Leadership Inst; chair, LA Legis Black Caucus, 2000-01; co-chair, Rainbow/Push Bd Trustee, gen coun, currently; Mt Pilgrim Baptist Church. **Business Addr:** Owner, Lawyer, The Fields Law Firm LLC, 2147 Govt St, Baton Rouge, LA 70806, **Business Phone:** (225)343-5377.

### FIELDS, DR. DEXTER L.
Psychiatrist, educator, consultant. **Personal:** Born Oct 12, 1944, Detroit, MI; married Margaret L Betts. **Educ:** Wayne State Univ Sch Med, BA, 1967, Col Med, MD, 1972. **Career:** Kirwood Gen Hosp & Hutzel Hosp, staff physician; Boston City Hosp, psychiat resident, 1972-73; Harvard Col, clin fel psychiat, 1972-74; Detroit Psychiat Inst, psychiat resident, 1973-75; NE Guid Substance Abuse Ctr, consult psychiatrist, 1974-76; Kirwood Ment Health Ctr, consult psychiatrist, 1976-80; Oper Hope, Community Ment Health Ctr, internal med resident & consult psychiatrist, 1976-77 & 1980; Detroit Bd Educ, consult; Recorder's Ct Psychiat Clin, consult & chief psychiat, 2002. **Orgs:** Black Psychiat Forum Boston, 1972-73; Black Psychiat Am, 1973; fel Solomon Fuller, 1974; chmn, Bal African, 2004; Friends Mod Art; adv bd, Found Jr Coun DIA; chmn, Friends African & African-Am Art; chmn, Nat Conf Artists Mich Chap; bd dir, Detroit Inst Arts, currently. **Home Addr:** 16000 W 9 Mile Rd Suite 207, Southfield, MI 48075, **Home Phone:** (248)569-9155. **Business Addr:** Board Director, The Detroit Institute of Arts, 5200 Woodward Ave, Detroit, MI 48202, **Business Phone:** (313)833-7900.

### FIELDS, EARL GRAYSON
Consultant, housing developer. **Personal:** Born Jun 18, 1935, Brooklyn, NY; son of Ralph Allen and Queena Rachel Grayson; married Pauline Hay; children: Cheryl, Mark & Leslie. **Educ:** CCNY, BA, 1968. **Career:** US Bur Customs, customs inspector, 1963-68; US Dept Housing & Urban Devel, multi family & col housing rep, 1968-72, model city rep, 1972-74, prog mgr, 1974-78; Century Housing Corp, housing & community develop consult; US Dept Housing & Urban Devel, Santa Ana, CA, mgr, field off mgr, comnr, 1978-94; EGP & Assocs Inc, pres; Housing & Community Devel, consult, 1978-94. **Orgs:** Vchmn Orange County Urban League, 1981-82; treas, co chmn, Bowers Mus Black Cult Coun, 1982-; Orange County Master Chorale, 1983-; chmnpolicy bd, Los Angeles Fed Exec Bd, 1988-92; Nat Asn Black County Officals; bd mem, Century Community Develop Inc; housing & community develop consult, Century Housing Corp. **Honors/Awds:** Cert Assoc, Minority Real Estate Devel, 1980; Integrity Knowledge Serv Inland Empire Mortgage Bankers Asn, 1981; Vol Award United Way Orange City, 1982; Patriotic Serv US Dept Treas, 1984; US Dept Housing & Urban Devel, Region IX, Mgr of the Year, 1989-90. **Home Addr:** 31081 Spoon Cir, Temecula, CA 92591-3975, **Home Phone:** (951)676-1049. **Business Addr:** President, EGP & Associates, PO Box 16233, Irvine, CA 92623.

### FIELDS, REAR ADM. EVELYN JUANITA
Government official. **Personal:** Born Jan 29, 1949, Norfolk, VA; daughter of Richard T Sr and Jerlean W. **Educ:** Norfolk State Univ, BS, math, 1971. **Career:** Government official (retired); Nat Oceanic & Atmospheric Admin, Atlantic Marine Ctr, Norfolk, Va, civilian cartogr, 1972; Nat Oceanic & Atmospheric Admin/Ship McArthur, comndg officer, 1989-90; Nat Oceanic & Atmospheric Admin/Comn Personnel Ctr, Sci & Technol fel, 1990-91; Nat Oceanic & Atmospheric Admin/Nat Ocean Serv/NGS, admin officer, 1991-94; Nat Oceanic & Atmospheric Admin/Nat Ocean Serv/C&GS, br chief, 1994-95; Nat Oceanic & Atmospheric Admin/Comn, Personnel Ctr, dir, 1995-97; Nat Oceanic & Atmospheric Admin/Nat Ocean Serv, dep asst admin, 1997-99; Nat Oceanic & Atmospheric Admin Off Marine & Aviation Opers, dir, 1999-2003, dir comn personnel, 1999-2002. **Orgs:** Nat Oceanic & Atmospheric Admin Asn Comned Officers, 1975-; life mem, Retired Officers Asn, 1980-; life mem, Res Officers Asn, 1997-; Nat Mil Family Asn, 1999-; hon mem, Zeta Phi Beta Sorority, 2000-; bd dir, Mariners' Mus. **Special Achievements:** First African American woman to hold National Oceanic and Atmospheric Administration Commissioned Officer Corps. **Home Addr:** 12 Rockingham Ct, Germantown, MD 20874-2223, **Home Phone:** (301)916-5526. **Business Addr:** Director, National Oceanic & Atmospheric Administration, 8403 Colesville Rd Suite 500, Silver Spring, MD 20910-3282, **Business Phone:** (301)713-3444.

**FIELDS, DR. EWAUGH FINNEY**
College administrator. **Personal:** children: Jamie Benjamin (deceased). **Educ:** Ky State Col, Frankfort, KY, BS, math; WVa Univ, Morgantown, WV, MA, sec educ; Temple Univ, Philadelphia, PA, EdD, math educ. **Career:** US Armed Forces Inst, Yokohama, Japan, algebra instr, 1956-57; Radio Corp Am, Camden, NJ, class C engr, 1959-63; Franklin Inst Lab, Philadelphia, Pa, res mathematician, 1963; Cinnaminson Jr & Sr High Sch, teacher & mathdept head, 1963-69; Rutgers Univ, Camden, NJ, adj instr, 1967; Temple Univ, Philadelphia, Pa, staff asst, 1967, matheduc, curric & instr, minority engineering educ, dean emer, prof emer; Gloucester County Col, Sewell, NJ, adj lectr, 1968-69; Drexel Univ, Philadelphia, Pa, asst prof math, 1969-72, assoc prof math, 1972-76, asst vpres acad affairs, 1973-76, prof math, dean, eve & Univ Col, 1986-92, Outreach & Access, vprovost, 1992-96, prof emer & dean emer, currently, Dept Mathand Comput Sci, staff, 1997-98; Univ Wash, Seattle, Wash, vpresminority affairs, 1976-77, assoc prof math educ, 1976-77; Univ Dist Columbia, Wash, DC, dean, the Univ Col, 1978-86, prof math, 1981-86, interim coordr acad affairs, 1983-84, actg provost & vpres acad affairs, 1984-85; Univ Nairobi, Nairobi, Kenya, exchange prof, 1985. **Orgs:** Nat Coun Teachers Math; Nat Inst Sci; Am Soc Engineering Educ; AAAS; Am Coun Educ; Am Asn Higher Educ; Nat Asn Remedial & Develop Educ; bd dir, Philadelphia Bus Corp. **Business Addr:** Professor Emeritus, Dean Emeritus, Drexel University, 3141 Chestnut St, Philadelphia, PA 19104-3020, **Business Phone:** (215)895-2000.

**FIELDS, FAYE F.**
Executive. **Personal:** married William. **Educ:** Univ Cincinnati, BS, nursing, 1972, MS, adult psychiat nursing, 1974, Col Bus, PhD, bus admin. **Career:** Integrated Resource Technologies Inc, founder, owner, pres & chief exec officer, 1986-; Univ med ctr, serv provider & adminr; Digital Equip Corp, mgt consult, sr mgt develop & internal orgn consult; Wash Nat Baseball Club, founding partner, currently. **Orgs:** Nat hon sorority; Sigma Theta Tau; fel Group Hosp & Med Serv; bd dir, Girl Scout Coun Nation's Capital; CareFirst BlueCross & BlueShield; bd dir, S Eastern Univ; Univ Cincinnati Alumni Asn; Small & Emerging Contractor Adv Forum. **Honors/Awds:** Emerging Business of the Year Award, Black Enterprise Mag, 2004; Small Business of the Year Award, DC Chamber of Commerce, 2004. **Business Addr:** President, Chief Executive Officer, Integrated Resource Technologies Inc, 1800 Diagonal Rd Suite 600, Alexandria, VA 22314, **Business Phone:** (703)931-3330.

**FIELDS, FELICIA J.**
Executive, vice president (organization), executive director. **Personal:** Born Jan 1, 1965?. **Educ:** Univ Mich, BA, psychol; Cent Mich Univ, MS, admin; Leadership Develop, cert; Personal Effectiveness, cert; Diversity, cert. **Career:** Ford Motor Co, 1986-, exec dir human resources, automotive opers & corp staffs, vpres human resources, 2005-08, group vpres human resources & corp servs, 2008-. **Orgs:** Ford Exec Coun Diversity; bd mem, Prof Women's Network; founding mem, Ford Multi Cult Alliance; bd dir, Nat Action Coun Minorities Engineering (NACME); Womens Health Adv Coun; vice chair, Governance Comt; Oakwood Hosp, Women's Health Adv Coun. **Business Addr:** Vice President of Human Resources & Corporate Service, Ford Motor Co, 1 American Rd, Dearborn, MI 48121, **Business Phone:** (313)429-0009.

**FIELDS, INEZ C.**
Lawyer. **Personal:** Born Hampton, VA; daughter of George Washington (deceased) and Sallie; married Frederick C Scott; children: Fred G (deceased). **Educ:** Boston Univ Law Sch, LLD, 1922. **Career:** Atty. **Orgs:** Life mem, Nat Asn Advan Colored People; hon mem, Hampton Woman's Serv League; Am Asn Univ Women; Catherine Fields Lit Club; Women's Forum; Old Dom Bar Asn; Va State Bar; Mt Olive Tent Lodge; Third Bapt Chap; Harry T Burleigh Comn Chorus; Delta Sigma Theta Sor. **Honors/Awds:** Appreciation Outstanding Commission Service Award, Plaque King St Comn Ctr; Plaque significant comn serv. **Special Achievements:** First women admitted to practice law in Massachusetts; Became the states first African American female lawyer. **Home Addr:** 5 George Ct, Hampton, VA 23663.

**FIELDS, KENNETH HENRY (KENNY FIELDS)**
Basketball player. **Personal:** Born Feb 9, 1962, Iowa City, IA. **Educ:** Univ Calif, Los Angeles, CA, BA, 1984. **Career:** Basketball player (retired); Univ Calif, Los Angeles, CA, Bruins, 1980-84; Milwaukee Bucks, 1984-86; Los Angeles Clippers, 1986-88; Jersey Shore Bucs, 1988; CBA, Grand Rapids, Tulsa.

**FIELDS, KIM VICTORIA**
Actor. **Personal:** Born May 12, 1969, New York, NY; daughter of Chip; married Johnathon Franklin Freeman; children: Sebastian Alexander Morgan; married Christopher Morgan; children: Quincy Morgan. **Educ:** Pepperdine Univ, BA, 1990. **Career:** TV Series: "Baby, I'm Back", 1978; "Diff'rent Strokes ", 1979; "The Comeback Kid", 1980; "Children of Divorce", 1980; "Diff'rent Strokes", 1979-81; "The Facts of Life"1979-88; "The Kid with the Broken Halo", 1982; "Pryor's Place", 1984; "The Golden Palace", 1992; "Martin", 1992; "Living Single", 1993-97; "Cupid", 1998; "Kenan & Kel", actress & dir, 1997-99; "Glow", 2000; ": Hidden Blessings", 2000; "Strong Medicine", 2000; "Strong Medicine", 2000; "The Drew Carey Show", 2001; "The Facts of Life Reunion", 2001; "The Steve Harvey Show", 2001; "Teen Talk", assoc producer, 2002; "The Division", 2004; "One on One", 2004; "Bow", 2005; "The Comeback", 2005; "Eve", 2006; "Anguilla Tranquility Fest", producer, 2007; "The Cleaner", 2008; "Meet the Browns", dir, 2009-10; "Holiday Love", 2010; "Lens on Talent", producer, 2010; "A Cross to Bear", 2012; "For Better or for Worse", 2014; "The Real Housewives of Atlanta", 2015-16; "Dancing with the Stars", 2016. Films: Uninvited Guest, 1999; Glow, 2000; Me & Mrs. Jones, 2001; Tall, Dark & Handsome, exec producer, 2004; Monster Mutt, 2011; What to Expect When You're Expecting, 2012; Victory Entertainment, pres & chief exec officer, currently. **Orgs:** W Angeles Church GodChrist; Am Fedn TV & Radio Artists; Screen Actors Guild; Delta Sigma Theta Sorority. **Honors/Awds:** Young Artist Award for Best Young Comedienne, 1981; Young Artist Award for Best Young Comedienne-Motion Picture or Television, 1982; Youth In Film Award, Best Actress; NAACP Image Award, Best Actress, 1985; Justice Dept Role Model of the Year Award, 1987. **Home Addr:** 9034 Sunset Blvd Suite 250, Los Angeles, CA 90069. **Business Addr:** Actress, Endeavor Talent Agency, 9701 Wilshire Blvd Fl 10, Beverly Hills, CA 90212.

**FIELDS, LYNN M.**
President (organization), executive. **Personal:** Born Jul 11, 1950, Philadelphia, PA; daughter of Barton A and Violet W. **Educ:** St Josephs Univ, Philadelphia, BS, 1975; Harvard Univ, John F Kennedy Sch Govt, Cambridge, MA, MPA, 1981. **Career:** Commonwealth Consults Inc, pres, dir, 1988-91; Philadelphia Gas Works, vpres, govt & community affairs, 1991-95, dir, communicationist pub rels, 1995-97; United Way SE Pa, loaned exec, 1997-98; Philadelphia Int Airport, dep dir aviation mkt & pub affairs, 1998-. **Orgs:** Bd trustee, parlimentarian, chair external affairs, 1978-96, Lincoln Univ; bd mem, Delta Sigma Theta Sorority Inc; chair pun rels comt, Dist Scholar Endowment Found; League Women Voters; Women Commun; Pub Rels Soc Am. **Home Addr:** 1602 E Yerkes St, Philadelphia, PA 19150, **Home Phone:** (215)548-0203. **Business Addr:** Deputy Director of Aviation Marketing & Public Affairs, Philadelphia International Airport, 8800 Essington Ave, Philadelphia, PA 19153, **Business Phone:** (215)937-6937.

**FIELDS, MARK LEE**
Executive, football player. **Personal:** Born Nov 9, 1972, Los Angeles, CA; children: 2. **Educ:** Los Angeles Southwest Col; Compton Col; Wash Univ. **Career:** New Orleans Saints, linebacker, right outside linebacker, 1995-2000, right linebacker, 1996-98; St Louis Rams, linebacker, 2001; Carolina Panthers, linebacker, left outside linebacker, 2002-04; Rose & Fields, partner & owner, currently; Juice N Right LLC, owner. **Orgs:** A Child Wish. **Honors/Awds:** Pro Bowl, 2000, 2004; Pac 10 Defensive Player of the Year; Winner of the ESPY come back Award. **Home Addr:** 5231 Citrus Cir, River Ridge, LA 70123. **Business Addr:** Owner, Partner, Rose & Fields Real Estate, 12725 W Indian Sch Rd Suite F-100, Avondale, AZ 85392, **Business Phone:** (623)907-1199.

**FIELDS, NATE**
Chief executive officer, president (organization). **Personal:** married Jackie. **Educ:** Johns Hopkins Univ, Paul H Nitze Sch Advan Int Studies, MA, int develop finance, 1975. **Career:** African Develop Found, vpres, 1995-2000, pres & chief exec officer, 2000-06, Africa opers, chief exec officer; Silatech, Doha, Qatar, managing dir prog opers, 2008-. **Orgs:** Africa Bur Us Aid; Int Youth Found; World Vision Int; Control Data Corp; Bluffton Univ; bd Mem, R.H. Donnelley Publ & Advert Inc. **Home Addr:** 236 N 2nd St, Hamilton, OH 45011-1659. **Business Addr:** Managing director, Silatech.

**FIELDS, DR. RICHARD A., SR.**
Consultant, executive. **Personal:** Born Apr 18, 1950, Washington, DC; married Sylvia Crisp; children: Kirstyn & Richard Jr. **Educ:** Hampton Inst, BA, 1971; Duke Univ, Sch Med, MD, med, 1975; Duke Univ, resident psychiat, 1978. **Career:** Dept Psychiat & Neurol AUS, chief, 1979-80; Neuse Ment Health Ctr, clin dir, 1980-82; E Carolina Univ, asst prof, 1980-82; Ga Regional Hosp Atlanta, supt, 1982-96; Emory Univ, asst prof, 1984-96; Morehouse Med Sch, adj clin assoc prof psychiat, 1984-96; Ctr Medicare & Medicaid Ser, US Dept Health, Baltimore, MD, psychiat consult, 1989-2003; Fields & Assoc Inc, founder, chief exec officer, pres, sr consult, 1996-; Joint Comn Accreditation Healthcare Orgs, survr, 1997-2003, hosp consult, 1999-2003; State & Psychiat Hosp Compliance Collab, exec dir, 2007-; GEO Columbia Regional Care Ctr, actg med dir, 2010-11. **Orgs:** Am Psychiat Asn, 1975-2007; Black Psychiatrists Am, 1977-, pres, 1984-88; pres, Ga Chap Am Assoc Admin Psychiat, 1987-88; fel Am Psychiat Asns, 1991; pres, Ga Psychiat Assoc, 1992-93; vice chair, APA Coun Psychiat Serv, 1994-96; Omega Psi Phi Fraternity; Nat Asn Advan Colored People; Nat coun community behav Heal Care; St Philip Ame Church, 1985-. **Honors/Awds:** Achievement Award for Excellence in Community Health Services, Upjohn, 1974; Outstanding Young Men of America, 1981; Festival of Hope Award for Efforts to Counter Stigma, 1989; Programmatic Achievement Award, Ment Health Asn Ga, 1994; Psychiatrist of the Year, Ga Psychiatric Physician Asn, 1994-95. **Home Phone:** (770)389-4248. **Business Addr:** Senior Consultant, Fields & Associates Inc, 150 St Marks Dr Suite 202, Stockbridge, GA 30281-1091, **Business Phone:** (770)389-3800.

**FIELDS, SAVOYNNE MORGAN**
Counselor, school administrator. **Personal:** Born May 26, 1950, Rocky Mount, NC; daughter of Charlie and Hazel C Brown. **Educ:** NC Agr & Tech State Univ, BS, psych, 1972, MS, guid, 1979. **Career:** Pub Libr High Pt NC, libr asst III, 1975-79; La State Univ, Eunice, counsr, coordr stud develop serv, 1979-82, minority recruiter, 1982-88, career placement coord, 1988-. **Orgs:** ASAP, 1979-; LAHSRP, 1982-; coord, LSUE's Black Hist Activ, 1982-; founding mem, LADE, 1982-; NAUW, 1983-; ACPA, 1984-; AACD, 1984; NAUW Historian, 1986-; rec & corresp sec, Chat-A-While Inc. **Honors/Awds:** First Black Recruiter, Louisiana State Univ, Eunice, 1982-; Matron of the Year, Little Zion Baptist Church, 1984; Little Zion BC Matrons President's Award, 1985; LADE Developmental Educ, LSUE, 1986; Outstanding Educator, Chat-A-While Club, 1987; Outstanding Developmental Educator, LSUE, LADE, 1988; Woman of the Year, NAUW, 1988. **Home Addr:** 113 Ave Acadians Suite 8, Opelousas, LA 70570, **Home Phone:** (337)942-7252. **Business Addr:** Coordinator, Louisiana State University, PO Box 1129, Eunice, LA 70535, **Business Phone:** (318)457-7311.

**FIELDS, VALERIE K.**
Chief executive officer. **Personal:** Born Raleigh, NC. **Educ:** Univ NC, Chapel Hill, BA, jour & mass commun; Covenant Bible Inst, Raleigh, NC, BTh, DTh, MTh, 2007. **Career:** Walt Disney World Resort, adminr; McDonald's Corp, adminr; Bridge Builders TV Prog, freelancer; Kushell Assocs Inc, freelancer; Onyx Greeting Cards, owner; VK Fields & Co, founder, chief exec officer, 1997-; Sch Jour & Mass Commn, Univ NC-Chapel Hill, adj prof, currently; Journalism & Mass Commun, adj prof; Univ NC, mass commun; Women's Forum N Carolina, vpres, 2013; bd, Women's Forum N Carolina. **Orgs:** Bd mem, Literacy Coun Wake County; vpres mkt, Nat Black MBA Asn; bd mem, chairwoman, Greater Raleigh Chamber Com; founder, Miracle Ministries Inc; bd dir, Christian Career & Bus Women Am; adminr, Ronald McDonald C's Charities N Carolina. **Business Addr:** Chief Executive Officer, V.k. Fields & Co Pr Pros, PO Box 18651, Raleigh, NC 27619, **Business Phone:** (919)829-5951.

**FIELDS, WILLIAM I., JR.**
Executive, association executive, vice president (organization). **Personal:** Born May 4, 1944, Frankfort, KY; son of William I Sr and Kathryn; married Faye Ford. **Educ:** Ky State Col, Frankfort, KY, BS, 1966; Univ Louisville, Louisville, KY, MS, 1971; Harvard Univ Grad Sch, bus exec prog. **Career:** Community Action Comn, Cincinnati, OH, coord field serv, 1971-72; Community Coun, Cincinnati, OH, planning assoc, 1972-74; Community Chest, Cincinnati, OH, assoc dir planning, 1974-77; United Community Planning Corp, Boston, MA, assoc exec vpres, 1978-81; ATE Mgt, Ridayh, Saudi Arabia, dir admin & personnel, 1981-83; Integrated Resource Technologies Inc, chief operating officer, currently. **Orgs:** Vpres, Health Planning Coun Greater Boston, 1979-81; vpres, dir, 1983-90, regional vpres, 1990, United Way Am, Wash, DC; Nat Forum Black Pub Admin, 1984-86; Big Bros Greater Wash, 1985-86; Orgn New Equality, 1985-; Literacy Vol Ill, 1990-; vpres, Am Soc Training & Develop, currently. **Home Addr:** 360 E Randolph St Apt 2208, Chicago, IL 60601. **Business Addr:** Chief Operating Officer, Integrated Resource Technologies Inc, 4601 N Fairfax Dr Suite 1200, Arlington, VA 22203, **Business Phone:** (703)931-3330.

**FIERCE, HUGHLYN F.**
Banker, president (organization). **Personal:** Born Brooklyn, NY; son of Millus and Helen; married Jewel Crews; children: Holly, Heather & Brooke. **Educ:** Morgan State Univ, BA, econ; NY Univ, MBA, advan prof cert, finance. **Career:** J P Morgan Chase, sr vpres, 1963-94; Chase Manhattan Bank, asst br mgr trainee, com loan officer, vpres, sr vpres, 1963-94; Freedom Nat Bank, NY, pres & chief exec officer, 1974-77; New York Univ, adj prof finance; Pace Univ Lubin Sch Bus; Jazz Lincoln Ctr, pres & chief exec officer, 2002-04. **Orgs:** Bd, Scudder Charitable Found; bd, Marymount Manhattan Col; NY State Comptroller's Invest Adv Comn, NY State Common Retirement Fund; bd dir, Baltic Am Enterprise Fund; bd dir, Parsons Brinkerhoff Inc; bd dir, Baltic Am Freedom Found; chmn & bd dir, Jazz Lincoln Ctr; bd mem, Czech & Slovak-Am Enterprise Fund, 1996-97; lifetime hon trustee, Am Mus Natural Hist, NY, currently. **Business Addr:** Honorary Trustee, American Museum of Natural History, Cent Pk W 79th St, New York, NY 10024-5192, **Business Phone:** (212)769-5100.

**FIERCE, MILFRED C.**
Educator. **Personal:** Born Jul 6, 1937, Brooklyn, NY. **Educ:** Wagner Col, BA, bus econ, 1960, MS, sec educ, 1967; Columbia Univ, MA, MPhil, PhD. **Career:** Educator (retired): Curtis High Sch; Vassar Col, dir Black Studies, 1969-71; Hunter Col, prof, 1973-81; Brooklyn Col, City Univ NY, Dept African Studies, prof & chair(retired), 1982-88. **Orgs:** Exec dir, Asn Black Found Exec Inc, 1976; NY St Col Proficiency Exam Comt African & Afro-Am Hist, fall, 1976; res dir, Study Comn US Policy toward SAfrica, 1979; African-Am Teachers Asn; African Heritage Studies Asn; Asn Study Afro-Am Life & Hist; Am Hist Asn; Orgn Am Historians; consult, Ford Found supported study group Southern Africa; Coun Foreign Rels, 1995. **Home Addr:** 835 Herkimer St, Brooklyn, NY 11233, **Home Phone:** (718)735-5932.

**FIFTY CENT (CURTIS JAMES JACKSON, III)**
Singer, actor. **Personal:** Born Jul 6, 1975, Queens, NY; son of Sabrina Jackson; married Shaniqua Tompkins; children: Marquise. **Career:** Albums: Get Rich or Die Tryin', 2003, 2005; The New Breed; In da Club, 2003; 21 Questions, 2003; P.I.M.P, 2003; The Massacre, 2005; Window Shopper, 2005; Hustler's Ambition, 2006; Date Movie, 2006; Little Man, 2006; Curtis, 2006; Before I Self Destruct, 2009. Films: 50 Cent: Bulletproof, 2005; Get Rich or Die Tryin', 2005; Home of the Brave, 2006; The Ski Mask Way, 2006; Righteous Kill, 2006; Before I Self Destruct, 2008; G-Unit, founder; Caught in the Crossfire, exec producer, 2009; Gun, 2010; Morning Glory, 2010; Vengeance, 2011; Odd Thomas, 2012; Fire with Fire, producer, 2012; Southpaw, 2015. TV Series: "The Wire", 2004; "The Simpsons", 2005; "50 Cent: The Money & the Power", 2008; "Entourage", 2009. **Business Addr:** Rap Musician, c/o Shady & Interscope Records, 2220 Colorado Ave, Santa Monica, CA 90404, **Business Phone:** (310)865-1000.

**FIGUEROA, BERNABE WILLIAMS, JR.** **See WILLIAMS, BERNIE.**

**FIGURES, DEON JUNIEL**
Football player. **Personal:** Born Jan 10, 1970, Bellflower, CA. **Educ:** Univ Colo, BA, sociology & criminol, 1993. **Career:** Football player (retired); Pittsburgh Steelers, defensive back, 1993, 1995-96, right cornerback, 1994; Jacksonville Jaguars, right cornerback, 1997-98. **Honors/Awds:** Big-8 Defensive Player of the Year, First Team All-American, Jim Thorpe Trophy Award, 1992; Jack Tatum Trophy, 1992.

**FIGURES, THOMAS H.** **See Obituaries Section.**

**FIGURES, VIVIAN DAVIS**
State government official, president (organization), chief executive officer. **Personal:** Born Jan 24, 1957, Mobile, AL; married Michael A; children: Akil Michael, Shomari Coleman & Jelani Anthony. **Educ:** Univ New Haven, W Haven, CT, BS; Jones Sch Law, Montgomery. **Career:** Mem-at-large, Dem Nat Comt; Dem Nat Conv, del, 1984, 1988, 1992, 1996, 2000, 2004; Ala State Dem Exec Comt, elected mem, 1986-; Perfect Print Inc, pres & owner; Mobile, AL, city councilwoman, 1993-97; Ala State Senate, sen, 1997-, minority leader, 2013-; Figures Legacy Educ Found, pres & chief exec officer, currently. **Orgs:** Ala New S Coalition; State Ala Hwy Safety Comn; adv bd, Ala Alcoholic Beverage Control Bd; several Senate Comts; Ala Womens Comn; Metrop Mobile Young Men Christian Asn; bd mem, Big Bros & Big Sisters Prog; bd mem, Homeless Coalition Mobile Inc; bd mem, Drug Ed Coun; Green Grove Missionary Baptist Church; vice chmn, Senates Local del &Vet Mil Affairs comt; bd mem, Mobile Area Chamber

Com; bd dir, Mobile Area Educ Found; bd mem, Habitat Humanity; bd mem, Salvation Army; adv bd, Ala Alcoholic Beverage Control Bd; Ala New S Coalition; bd mem, Prichard Boys & Girls Club; Gulf Coast Christian Ctr; Alpha Kappa Alpha Sorority Inc, 2002; Coalition 100 Black Women; Dem Nat Comt; Mobile City Coun. **Home Addr:** 2054 Clemente Ct, Mobile, AL 36617, **Home Phone:** (251)457-9008. **Business Addr:** Senator, Alabama State House, 11 S Union St Suite 736, Montgomery, AL 36130, **Business Phone:** (334)242-7871.

### FILER, HON. KELVIN DEAN

Superior court judge. **Personal:** Born Nov 25, 1955, Compton, CA; son of Maxcy and Blondell; children: Brynne Ashley & Kree Donalyn. **Educ:** Univ Calif, Santa Cruz, BA, polit, 1977; Univ Calif, Berkeley, JD, 1980. **Career:** Dep state pub defender, 1980-82; pvt pract, atty, 1982-; Super Ct, comnr, 2000-02; Munic Ct Compton, Calif, comnr; Super Ct, Compton, judge, currently. **Orgs:** Bd trustee, Compton Unified Sch Dist, 1981-93; bd dir, Compton Chamber Com, 1984-; pres, Compton Chamber Com, 1988-89; vpres, Compton Chamber Com; S Cent Bar Asn; Compton Br, Nat Asn Advan Colored People; Calif State Bar; Am Bar Asn; Nat Bar Asn; Calif Asn Black Lawyers. **Honors/Awds:** Outstanding Comm Support, Compton Police Dept, 1985; Black Family of the Yr, Coca-Cola Bottling Co, Los Angeles, 1988; Award of Honor, Los Angeles City Bd Supv, 1989; Martin Luther King Drum Major Award, Compton Youth Action Ctr, 1990; Spec Serv Mem, S Cent Bar Asn, 1993. **Special Achievements:** Successfully argued case before CA Supreme Court resulting in a unanimous opinion (People vs Taylor 1982 31 Cal 3d 483). **Business Addr:** Judge, Superior Court, 200 W Compton Blvd, Compton, CA 90220, **Business Phone:** (310)603-7714.

### FILES, LOLITA

Writer, manager. **Personal:** Born Jan 1, 1964, Ft. Lauderdale, FL. **Educ:** Univ Fla, BS, broadcast jour, 1985. **Career:** Acuderm Inc, mkt mgr, 1986-87; Great Atlantic Mgt, regional property coordr, 1988-91; Henry H. Filer Mid Sch, Eng teacher, 1990-91; KinderCare, nat commun mgr, 1992-96; 3BadShibas Entertainment, auth, screenwriter & producer, 1996-; DLI Enterprises LLC, chief exec officer, owner, 2008-; Books: Scenes from a Sistah, 1997; Getting to the Good Part, 1999; Blind Ambitions, 2000; Child of God, 2001; Tastes Like Chicken, 2004; Sex lies murder fame, 2006; Three For The Road, 2007; Short Stories: Roses, Red, Room 416, 2002; Bobby Q's Sauce, 2007; Standing Room Only, 2003. **Orgs:** Alpha Kappa Alpha Sorority Inc, 1983-; prof mem, PEN Am, 2014-. **Business Addr:** Writer, c/o Simon & Schuster, 1230 Avenue of the Americas, New York, NY 10020, **Business Phone:** (212)698-7000.

### FILLYAW, LEONARD DAVID

Educator, law enforcement officer. **Personal:** Born Jun 25, 1939, Brooklyn, NY; son of John David and Rose Rosalind; married Willie M Tate; children: Sharon, Denise & Tyrone David. **Educ:** John Jay Col Criminal Justice, AA, 1972, BA, 1973; Dowling Col, MEd, 1980; Liquid Oxygen Missile Sch. **Career:** Educator (retired); Brooklyn Union Gas Co, co rep, 1962-64; NY City Transit Police, police officer, 1966-97; NY City Police Acad, police instr, Social Sci Dept; Cent Islip Sch Dist, teacher, 1979. **Orgs:** Guardians Police Asn, 1964-; NCP, 1984-; UNCF, 1986-; Southern Poverty Law Ctr, 1984-; bd trustee, Cent Islip Libr; bd trustee, Cent Suffolk Libr; trustee, Suffolk County Coop Libr Syst; libr trustee, Cent Islip Sch Dist. **Home Addr:** 203 Leaf Ave, Central Islip, NY 11722, **Home Phone:** (516)234-0872.

### FINCH, GREGORY MARTIN

Lawyer. **Personal:** Born Sep 14, 1951, Madera, CA; son of Isaac and Deloma Dillard; married Shirley; children: Damon, Megan & Christopher. **Educ:** Univ CA, BA, soc & art, 1975; McGeorge Sch Law, JD, 1979. **Career:** Signature Law Group LLP, partner, atty, currently. **Orgs:** Calif State Bar, 1979; Deleg, St Bar Conv, 1983; pres, Active 20 & 30 Club 1, 1989; bd mem, Child & Family Inst, 1989-99; pres, Active 20 & 30, US & Can, 1990; AME Regional chmn, World Coun Serv Clubs, 1993; pres, Wiley Manuel Law Asn, 1994; bd mem, YMCA Greater Sacramento, 1996-; bd pres, YMCA, 1999-; bd dir, Sierra Adoption Servs, 1999-; bd dir, Rotary Club Sacramento, 2000-; Suiter Hosp Community Benifil comts; Suiter Hosp Med Affairs comt; secy, Natomas Planning Adv Coun; found bd, Sutter Hosp; chmn, Small Bus Advocacy Comn, Sacramento Chamber Com; bd mem, YMCA Super Calif; Region Med Policy Comt; Christ Unity Church. **Honors/Awds:** Rookie of the Year, Active 20 & 30 Chap 1, 1985. **Home Addr:** 1431 22nd St Suite D, Sacramento, CA 95816. **Business Addr:** Attorney, Partner, Signature Law Group LLP, 3400 Bradshaw Rd Suite A-4A, Sacramento, CA 95827-2614, **Business Phone:** (916)856-5800.

### FINCH, DR. JANET M.

Educator, chairperson. **Personal:** Born Jun 4, 1950, Nashville, TN; daughter of James W and Helen Ardis; married Harold William; children: Harold & Toria. **Educ:** Tenn State Univ, BS, math, 1972, MA, educ adult educ, 1978; Vanderbilt Univ, PhD, higher educ admin, 1985. **Career:** Nashville State Tech, educ specialist 1977-80, proj dir, 1980-81, dept head develop studies, 1981-85, asst dean gen studies, 1981-86; Mid Tenn State Univ, actg vpres for admin, 1985-87; Univ Ky, asst vice chancellor, 1986; Am Coun Educ fel, 1986-87; Motlow State Community Col, Tullahoma, TN, dean acad affairs 1988-91; exec asst pres, 1991; Belmont Univ, dir, opportunities admis, 1992-94; State Community Col, pres, 1994-96; Metrop Community Col, pres, 1996-98; Metro Schs, maths teacher, 1998-2000; Tenn State Univ, Dept Educ Admin, prof & dept head, 2000-. **Orgs:** Secy, Temple Child Care Develop Ctr, 1984-85; youth choir dir & pianist 15th Ave Baptist Church, 1985-; Youth Comt YWCA; hon mem, Phi Delta Kappa; Nat Educ Asn; Nat Asn Sec Sch Prin; Am Coun Educ; Am Coun Fel; Tenn Educ Asn. **Home Addr:** 221 Rising Sun Terr, Old Hickory, TN 37138, **Home Phone:** (615)847-8452. **Business Addr:** Professor, Head, Tennessee State University, L401 Avon Williams Campus, Nashville, TN 37209, **Business Phone:** (615)963-7038.

### FINGAZ, STICKY (KIRK JONES)

Rap musician, actor. **Personal:** Born Nov 3, 1973, Brooklyn, NY. **Career:** Actor, singer, producer, director; Rap group ONYX, mem; Albums: Bacdafu cup, 1993; All We Got Iz Us, 1995; Shut 'Em Down, 1998; Black trash: The Auto biography of Kirk Jones, 2000; Bacdafu cup Part II, 2002; Triggernometry, 2003; Cold Case Files, 2003; Decade, 2003; Sticky Fingaz: The Album, 2014. Films: Clockers, Dead Presidents, 1995; Ride, New Yorker, Le, 1998; Game Day, In Too Deep, Love Goggles, Black & White, 1999; Next Friday, 2000; Boricua's Bond, The Price of Air, Lock down, The Playaz Court, 2000; Lift, MacArthur Park, Flossin, 2001; LAX, Reality Check, 2002; Hot Parts (voice), Leprechaun: Back 2 Tha Hood (voice), Ride Or Die, Malibooty, 2003; Flight of the Phoenix, TrueVinyl, Gas, 2004; Over There, 2005; A Day in the Life, actor & producer, 2007; Nite Tales: The Movie, 2008; Karma, Confessions & Holi, Dough Boys, Order of Redemption, 2009; Steppin: The Movie, 2009; Breaking Point, 2009; A Day in the Life, actor, writer, producer & dir, 2009; Once Fallen, 2010; Hard Breakers, 2010; Caught on Tape, actor, writer, producer & dir, 2010; Immortal Cycle, 2010; The Dead Sea, 2011; Fanaddict, 2011; Changing the Game, 2012; Motel, 2013; Brooklyn Knight, actor, writer & dir, 2013; The Bag Man, 2014; The Dead Sea, 2014. TV series: "New York Undercover", 1995-97; "413 Hope St", 1997; "Nash Bridges", "The Parkers", 1999; "18 Wheels of Justice", 2000; "The Twilight Zone", Just Cause, "Carnivores", 2002; "The Shield", 2002-06; Platinum, "Inferno", 2003; "Blood & Water", 2004; "Over There", House of the Dead 2, CSI: Miami, 2005-11; "Orphans", 2005; "Conclave", 2006; "Monsters", 2006; "Blade: The Series", 2006; "Law & Order: Criminal Intent", "Tell Me You Love Me", 2007; "The Beast", 2009; "Burn Notice", 2009; "Raising the Bar", 2009; "NCIS: Los Angeles, 2010; "Rizzoli & Isles", 2010; "NYC 22", 2012. **Business Addr:** Actor, c/o William Morris Agency, 151 El Camino Dr, Beverly Hills, CA 90212, **Business Phone:** (310)859-4000.

### FINLAYSON, DR. ARNOLD ROBERT

Lawyer, administrator. **Personal:** Born Jun 30, 1963, Washington, DC; son of Joseph Arnold Jr and Patricia Glenn. **Educ:** Bowie State Col, BS, 1985; Howard Univ Sch Law, JD, 1989. **Career:** US Dept State, procurement analyst, 1987-90; Hon George W Mitchell, assoc judge, DC Super Ct, judicial law clerk, 1990-92; Shaw, Pittman, Potts & Trowbridge, govt contracts assoc, 1992; DC, secy; Freedom Info Act, Off Doc & Admin Issuances, adminr, dir, currently. **Orgs:** DC Bar Asn; Bar Commonwealth PA; US Ct Appeals Fed Circuit; Am Bar Asn; Kappa Alpha Psi Fraternity Inc. **Home Addr:** 441 4th St NW Rm 520, Washington, DC 20004, **Home Phone:** (202)737-1787. **Business Addr:** Director, Freedom Information Act Office, 1 Judiciary Sq 441 4th St NW Suite 520 S, Washington, DC 20001, **Business Phone:** (202)737-1787.

### FINLAYSON, DR. WILLIAM E.

Educator, physician, association executive. **Personal:** Born Sep 1, 1924, Manatee, FL; married Edith; children: Reginald & James. **Educ:** Morehouse Col, BS, 1948; Meharry Med Col, MD, 1953. **Career:** Physician (retired); Univ Minn, resident, 1958; Milwaukee Med Complex, teacher; pvt pract, 1958-97; Am Col Obstet & Gynec, fel, 1963; Am Col Surgeons, fel, 1964; Med Col Wis, fac; Univ Wis Med Sch, fac; Aurora Med Group, obstet & gynec. **Orgs:** Milwaukee Med Soc; House Del Wis Med Soc; pres, Milwaukee Gynec Soc; St Joseph's Hosp; Mt Sinai Med Ctr; Deaconess Hosp; Cream City Med Soc; Med Col Wis; bd dirs, Southeastern Wis Health Syst Agency; pres, Alpha Phi Alpha; Frontiers Int; life mem, Nat Asn Advan Colored Poeple; Urban League; We-Milwaukeeans; pres, YMCA local br; Greater Galilee Baptist Church; life mem, Nat Asn Advan Colored People; charter bd mem, pres, N Milwaukee State Bank. **Special Achievements:** United States Army's first Lieutenant; Founder of first black-owned bank in Milwaukee, 1971. **Home Addr:** 7320 N Pheasant Lane, River Hills, WI 53217. **Business Addr:** Charter Board Member, President, North Milwaukee State Bank, 5630 West Fond du Lac Ave, Milwaukee, WI 53216, **Business Phone:** (414)466-2344.

### FINLEY, DR. D. LINELL, SR.

Educator. **Personal:** Born Mar 27, 1948, Gunnison, MS; son of George Sr (deceased) and Celestine Hayes; married Janet D Duff; children: Sharriette & D. **Educ:** Jackson State Univ, Jackson, MS, BA, 1972; Atlanta Univ, Atlanta, GA, MA, 1974, PhD, 1981. **Career:** Atlanta Univ, Ford Found fel, 1972-75, asst prof, coordr polit sci prog, 1975-88, coordr, 1985-88; Rock Ages Baptist Church, pastor; Auburn Univ Montgomery, Montgomery, Ala, adj assoc prof, polit sci, 1988, polit sci prof; Univ Ala, Grade Prog, Maxwell AFB, adj fac, 1991, asst prof, adj prof, 2003-, polit sci; S lawn Baptist Church, pastor & adj prof, 2003-. **Orgs:** Nat Conf Black Polit Scientists, 1977-; Pi Gamma Mu Int Hon Soc Social Sci, 1978; Ala Polit Sci Asn, 1980-; Kappa Delta Pi Edu Hon Soc, 1982; Phi Delta Kappa Prof Educ Hon Fraternity, 1986; pres, post sec div, Ala Educ Asn, 1990-91; bd dir, Ala Educ Asn, 1990-91; bd dir, Cent Ala Laubach Literacy Coun, 1990-93; pres, Capitol City Civitan, Montgomery, Ala, 1990-91; Thirty Second Deg Mason, Phi Beta Sigma Fraternity; bd trustee, Univ Ala. **Home Addr:** 3458 S Water Mill Rd, Montgomery, AL 36116-1935, **Home Phone:** (334)279-5518. **Business Addr:** Assistant Professor, Auburn University Montgomery, 210L Goodwyn Hall, Montgomery, AL 36124-4023, **Business Phone:** (334)244-3741.

### FINLEY, MICHAEL HOWARD

Basketball player. **Personal:** Born Mar 6, 1973, Melrose Park, IL; married Rebekah; children: 3. **Educ:** Wis State Univ, bus mgt, 1995. **Career:** Basketball player (retired); Phoenix Suns, small forward, 1995-96; Dallas Mavericks, small forward, 1996-2004, shooting guard, 2004-06; San Antonio Spurs, shooting guard, 2005-06, 2007-08, small forward, 2006-07, 2008-10; Boston Celtics, small forward, 2010; Michael Finley Found, founder, 2003; Follow Through Productions LLC, financier & exec producer, 2009-; Finley & Friends, founder; NBA Media Ventures, Dallas Mavericks, asst vpres, currently. **Orgs:** Make-A-Wish Found. **Honors/Awds:** USA Basketball Male Athlete of the Year, 1993; NBA All-Rookie First Team, 1995-96; 2-Time NBA All-Star; NBA championship, 2007. **Special Achievements:** Film: Sanctum, co-producer, 2011; The Day, exec producer, 2011; LUV, 2012; Lee Daniels' The Butler, exec producer, 2013; Sneakerheadz, exec producer, 2015; The Benefactor, exec producer, 2015; Meet the Blacks, exec producer, 2016; The Birth of a Nation, exec producer, 2016; The First To Do It, exec producer, 2017; American Made, exec producer, 2017. **Home Addr:** , Dallas, TX. **Business Addr:** Assistant Vice President, Dallas Mavericks, 2909 Taylor St, Dallas, TX 75226, **Business Phone:** (214)658-7174.

### FINLEY, SANDRA JEAN KILLINGSWORTH

Consultant. **Personal:** Born Aug 14, 1950, Chicago, IL; daughter of Lee Hunter Killingsworth and Cleve Killingsworth; married Eddie Franklin; children: Bakari Khalid Ali. **Educ:** Loyola Univ, Chicago, IL, BA, 1972. **Career:** Chicago Bar Asn, Chicago, Ill, dir pub rel, 1977-79; Chicago Econ Develop Corp, Chicago, Ill, dir pub rel, 1978-79; 5100 Communs, Chicago, Ill, pres, 1980-; Sandra Finley Co, pres & entrepreneur, 1989-. **Orgs:** Fed Womens Prog, USAF, 1983; pres, bd chair, chief exec officer, League Black Women, 1987-89; bd mem, Brass Found, 1989-; bd mem, Chicago Chap, Nat Asn Advan Colored People, 1989-; bd mem, Chicago Youth Ctr, 1990-; Pub Prog Bd Comt, Field Mus Natural Hist, 1992; Chicago Bar Asn; Nat Black MBA Asn; Chicago Area Broadcast Pub Affairs Asn; bd mem, Ill Health Maintenance Org Guaranty Asn; chair, Union League Chicago's Comt; bd mem, Ill Health Maintenance Orgn Guaranty Asn. **Honors/Awds:** Kizzy Award, Kizzy Scholar Fund, 1979; National Council Negro Women Award, 1986; Chicago's Up & Coming, Dollars & Sense Mag, 1985; Entrepreneur of the Year, PUSH, 1988; Meritorious Commission Citation, City Chicago, 1985; AT&T Synergy Award, 1999; Outstanding Leader Award, YWCA, Chicago, 2009; Metropolitan Chicago Award, Racial Justice, YWCA, 2013. **Business Addr:** President, Entrepreneur, The Sandra Finley Co, 254 Cove Dr, Flossmoor, IL 60422-1977, **Business Phone:** (708)754-0825.

### FINLEY, SKIP

Executive. **Personal:** Born Jul 23, 1948, Ann Arbor, MI; son of Mildred V Johnson and Ewell W; married Karen M Woolard; children: Kharma Isis & R Kristin. **Educ:** Northeastern Univ, Boston, MA, 1971. **Career:** Skifin Gallery, Boston MA, owner, 1970-71; WHDH-TV, Boston MA, floor dir, 1971; WSBK-TV, Boston MA, floor mgr, asst dir, producer, 1971-72; WRKO-Radio, Boston MA, acct exec, 1972-73; Humphrey, Browning, MacDougall Advert, Boston MA, acct mgr, 1973-74; Sheridan Broadcasting Corp, sales mgr, WAMO AM/FM, 1974-75, gen mgr WAMO AM/FM, 1975-76, vpres/gen mgr SBC Radio Div, 1976-77, vpres, corp off, 1976-82, eastern sales mgr, 1977-79, exec vpres/gen mgr, 1979-81, pres, 1981-82; Albimar Omaha Ltd Partnership/Albimar Mgt Inc, Boston MA, pres & gen partner, 1982-95; KEZO AM-FM, Omaha, Nebr, gen partner, 1983-88; KDAB-FM, Ogden/Salt Lake City, UT, gen partner, 1985-90; WKYS-FM, Wash, DC, pres/gen mgr, 1988-95; AMR Urban Radio Networks, chief exec officer /chief operating officer, 1995-98; Answers & Solutions, pres, 1999-2003; Inner City Broadcasting Corp, dir, 2001-, vice chmn, 2003-. **Orgs:** Nat Thespian Soc; bd overseers, Vineyard Open Land Found; Martha's Vineyard Rod & Gun Club; Wash Area Broadcasters Asn; Nat Asn Broadcasters, 1990-94, vice chair, 1993-94; bd, Radio Advert Bur; dir, Nat Asn Black Owned Broadcasters; 1977-95; bd, Advert CNL, 1998-99; bd, Broadcasters Found Am. **Home Addr:** 35 Tower Ridge Rd, PO Box 2943, Oak Bluffs, MA 02557, **Home Phone:** (508)696-3742. **Business Addr:** Vice Chairman, Director, Inner City Broadcasting Corp, 3 Pk Ave 41st Fl, New York, NY 10016-5901, **Business Phone:** (212)447-1000.

### FINN, JOHN WILLIAM

School administrator, business owner. **Personal:** Born Apr 30, 1942, Lexington, KY; married Joan Washington; children: Jarell Wendell & Janelle Wynice. **Educ:** Ky State Univ, BS, 1966; Ind Northern Univ, MA, bus admin; MBA, 1971. **Career:** Gary Ind Schs, teacher, coach, recreation leader, 1967-69; Anderson Boys Club, activity dir, 1968-69; Univ Mich, asst dir housing, 1969-71, assoc dir housing, 1977-86; Diversified Educ Products, Gary, Ind, owner, pres, 1986-, admin asst supt, 1991-. **Orgs:** Mich Housing & Food Serv Officers; Mich Col Personnel Asn; Nat Asn Stud Personnel Admins; Asn Col & Univ Housing Officials; Am Asn Higher Educ; Am Asn Jr Col; United Fund; Boys Club Am; Nat Asn Advan Colored People; Kappa Alpha Psi Frat Inc; pres, Ann Arbor Sportsmen; Black Faculty & Staff Asn. **Honors/Awds:** All City-All State Football, 1968-69; Outstanding Young Men of Amer. **Special Achievements:** First African American in Administrative position in Housing Office Univ of Michigan. **Home Addr:** 431 Ryan Rd, Ann Arbor, MI 48103, **Home Phone:** (734)913-2064. **Business Addr:** School Administrator, 620 E 10 Pl, Gary, IN 46402, **Business Phone:** (219)881-5401.

### FINN, MICHELLE BONAE (MICHELLE FINN-BURRELL)

Athlete. **Personal:** Born May 8, 1965, Orlando, FL; married Leroy Russel; children: Cameron, Joshua & Jaden. **Educ:** Oak Ridge High Sch; Fla State Univ. **Career:** Athlete (retired); Track & field athlete. **Honors/Awds:** TAC/USA's National Indoor Champion, 1990; Hall of Fame, Fla State Univ, 1990; Gold medal, Barcelona Olympics, 400 Meter Relay, 1992; World Indoor Championships, Int Asn Athletics Federations. **Business Addr:** Field Athlete, US Olympic Track & Field Team, 200 S Capitol Ave Suite 140, Indianapolis, IN 46225, **Business Phone:** (317)261-0500.

**FINN-BURRELL, MICHELLE.** See FINN, MICHELLE BONAE.

### FINNEY, ERNEST A., JR.

Judge. **Personal:** Born Mar 23, 1931, Smithfield, VA; son of Ernet A Sr and Collen Godwin (deceased); married Frances Davenport; children: Ernest III, Lynn & Jerry. **Educ:** Claflin Col, BA, 1952; SC State Col Sch Law, JD, 1954; Nat Col State Judiciary, Reno, NV, grad, 1977; New York Univ Sch Law, sr appellate judges sem, 1985. **Career:** Judge (retired); SC Sumter County Courthouse 3rd Judicial Circuit SC, resident judge, 1976-85; SC Supreme Ct, assoc justice, 1985-94, chief justice, 1994-00; SC State Univ, interim pres, 2002-03; Finney Law Firm Inc, Atty, coun, currently. **Orgs:** Chmn bd, Buena Vista Devel Corp; Am Bar Asn; SC Bar Asn; Nat Bar Asn; Sumter County Bar Ass; Am Judicature Soc; Nat Asn Advan Colored People; Alpha Phi Alpha; United Meth Church Gen Coun Fin & Admin Legal Responsibilities Comn; chmn, bd trustee, Claflin Col; adv comt, Univ SC Sch Law; founder, Legis Black Caucus. **Honors/Awds:** Distinguished Service, City Sumter, 1970; SC Coun Human Rights, 1972; Alumnus Award, SC State Col, 1973; Civil Libertarian of the Year, ACLU, 1973; Citizen of the Year, Omega Psi Phi, 1973; Bedford-Stuyvesant New York Jaycee Award, 1974; Politic & Alumni Award, Claflin Col, 1974;

James M Dabbs Award, SC Council Human Rights, 1974; Selected to rep SC at Am Bar Asn Criminal Code Revision Conf, San Diego, 1975; Wateree Comn Action Inc Serv, 1975; SC Nat Asn Advan Colored People Native Son, 1976; Delta Sigma Leadership Serv, 1976; Service of Mankind Award, Emmanuel Meth Church, 1977; HHD, Claflin Col, 1977; LLD, Citadel; LLD, Johnson C Smith Univ; LLD, Morris College; DHL, Col Charleston; DHL, SC State Univ; Nat Asn Equal Oppt Higher Educ, 1986; Distinguished Alumni of the Year Award, Claflin Col, SC State Col; Award of Achievement, Alpha Phi Alpha, 1986; Honoree, SC Trial Lawyers Association, 1993; SC Order of the Palmetto, 1994; National Black College Hall of Fame, 1998; Honorary Degree: Claflin Univ, Johnson C Smith Univ, Morris Col, Col Charleston, Wofford Col, Francis Marion Univ, Univ SC. **Special Achievements:** First African-American Supreme Court Justice appointed to the South Carolina Supreme Court; First African-American to serve on the House Judiciary Committee. **Home Addr:** 24 Runnymede Blvd, Sumter, SC 29153. **Business Addr:** Attorney, Of Counsel, Finney Law Firm, 2117 Pk St, Columbia, SC 29201, **Business Phone:** (803)254-7408.

### FINNEY, DR. ESSEX EUGENE, JR.

Government official, executive. **Personal:** Born May 16, 1937, Michaux, VA; son of Essex Eugene Sr and Etta Francis Burton; married Rosa Ellen Bradley; children: Essex E III & Karen Finney Shelton. **Educ:** Va Polytech Inst, BS, 1959; Pa State Univ, MS, 1960; Mich State Univ, PhD, 1963. **Career:** Government official (retired); Rocky Mt Arsenal Denver County, br chief, 1963-65; Agr Res Serv USDA, res scientist, 1965-77, actg adminr, assoc adminr; Agr Mkt Res Inst, inst chmn, 1972-75; Beltsville Agr Res Ctr, asst dir, 1977-83, assoc dir, 1983-87; N Atlantic Area Asn, dir, 1987-89; Beltsville Agr Res Ctr, USDA, dir, 1989-92; Agr Res Serv, USDA, assoc admin, 1992-95, actg ARS adminr. **Orgs:** Princeton fel Woodrow Wilson Sch, Princeton Univ, 1973-74; Counman Town Glenarden MD, 1975; sr policy analyst, Off Sci Adv to Pres, 1980-81; bd dir, Prince George's Chamber Com, 1983-87; pres, Beltsville Org Prof Employees US Dept Agr, 1984-85; Bd Agr, Nat Res Coun, 1997-99; founder, Nat Adv Comt Off Professionals, 2003. **Honors/Awds:** CRC Press Handbook Transportation & Mkt Agr, 1981; Fellow, Am Soc AgrEngrs, 1983; Award Administration, Gamma Sigma Delta Univ MD, 1985; Outstanding Engineering Alumni Award, Penn St Univ, 1985; Elected, Nat Acad Engr, 1994. **Home Addr:** 11206 Chantilly Lane, Mitcheville, MD 20721-2438, **Home Phone:** (301)464-1206.

### FINNEY, KAREN

Government official. **Career:** Press Off First Lady, dep press secy; Dem Nat Commun Press Off, dir; The Hill, columnist, currently; MSNBC, polit analyst, currently. **Orgs:** Womens Leadership Forum Network; Teach Am; Womens Vote Ctr; Fr Am Founds prestigious Young Leaders prog; spokesperson & Dir Commun, Dem Nat Comt; sr fel & consult, Media Matters;, press Secy, strategic commun adv, Hillary Rodham Clinton. **Business Addr:** Columnist, The Hill, 1625 K St NW Suite 900, Washington, DC 20006, **Business Phone:** (202)628-8500.

### FINNEY, REV. DR. LEON D., JR.

Association executive. **Personal:** Born Jul 7, 1938, Louise, MS; married Sharon; married Georgette Greenlee; children: Kristin & Leon III (deceased). **Educ:** McCormick Theol Sem, doctor theol, MA, theol studies; Goddard Col, MA econs & urban community develop, 1974; Nova Univ, PhD, 1978. **Career:** Vis Sch Theol, vis prof, 1968-70; Luth Sch Theol, chair, 1969; Univ Chicago, fac lectr, fld instr, 1970-, prof; Fisk Univ, vis lectr, 1970-71; LA State Univ, cons; McCormick Theol Sem, prof, African Am Leadership Studies, 1993-; African Am Leadership Partnership, exec dir, 1993; Woodlawn Orgn, pres, 2002-, chmn & chief exec officer, currently; Univ IL, chair, Biochem & Infectious DisComm, 2002-, prof; Christ Apostolic Church, founder & pastor; Lutheran Sch Theol, prof; Northwestern Univ, prof; Presby Col Korea, prof; Lincoln S Cent Real Estate Group, chmn & prin; Chicago Pub Housing Authority, vice chmn; Chicago Pub Schs, Monitoring Comn Sch Desegregation, chmn. **Orgs:** Chicago United; vice chmn, bd dirs, Guaranty Bank & Trust Co Chicago Asn Com & Ind Black Ill Legis Lobby, 1976-; Chicago Urban League, 1970-; Nat Urban Coalition; deleg, White House Conf Balanced Growth & Small Bus; consult, Urban Develop, Chicago Econ Develop Comm; pres, Chicago Planning Comm; chair, comm adv community, Chicago Transit Auth; Woodlawn Community Develop Corp; Broadcast Ministers Alliance; Coun a Parliament World's Religions; vice chair, pastor Metrop Apostolic Community Church. **Honors/Awds:** Ford Found Grant, 1970; 10 Most Outstanding Young Men, Chicago Jr Chamber Com, 1970; Cert Merit, Cent State Univ Alumni Asn, 1971; Outstanding Alumni Award, Hyde Park HS, 1972; Distinguished Educator Award, 1972; Affirmative Action Merit Award, Breadbasket Commercial Asn, 1973; PACE Award, Pervis Staples, 1973. **Special Achievements:** One of four African American invited to Israel to study Israeli-Arab Rel, Israeli govt, 1973; Author, "Neighborhood Econ Develop-Myth or Fact," 1979; co-auth, "Comm Develop Policy Paper Struct Disinvestment: A Prob in Search of a Policy". **Business Addr:** Chairman, Chief Executive Officer, The Woodlawn Orgn, 6040 S Harper Ave, Chicago, IL 60637, **Business Phone:** (773)288-5840.

### FINNEY, MICHAEL ANTHONY

Executive, president (organization), chief executive officer. **Personal:** Born Oct 2, 1956, Flint, MI; married Gina Michelle Mickels. **Educ:** Saginaw Valley State Col, BBA, 1979; Cent Mich Univ, MA, human resources. **Career:** Deloitte Haskins & Sells CPA, admin asst, 1978-79; Stud Govt Saginaw Valley State Col, pres, 1978-79; J C Penney Co, merchandise mgr, 1979-81; Saginaw Valley State Col, admin rep, 1981-84; Thomson Saginaw Ballscrew Co, sr vpres & gen mgr, 1987-2000; Mich Econ Develop Corp Emerging Bus Sectors, vpres, 2000-02, pres & chief exec officer; City Saginaw, asst city mgr; Greater Rochester Enterprise, chief exec officer, pres, 2002-05; Ann Arbor SPARK, pres & chief exec officer, 2005-11; Mich Econ Develop Corp, pres & chief exec officer, 2011-15; State Mich, sr advisor econ growth, 2015; Community Ventures Resources Inc, pres & chief exec officer, 2015-. **Orgs:** State dir, Mich Phi Beta Sigma Fraternity, 1979-80; bd dir, Saginaw Valley State Col Alumni Asn, 1981-; bd dir, Big Bros, Big Sisters Saginaw Inc, 1982-83; Saginaw Jaycees, 1984-; Int City Mgrs Asn, Mich City Mgrs Asn; Detroit RiverFront Conservancy; bd dir, State Sci & Technol Inst; trustee, Washtenaw Community Col Found; trustee, Ann Arbor Area Community Found; Univ Mich Life Sci Inst; Off Technol Transfer & Col Engineering Ctr Entrepreneurship; Nat Adv Councils; bd dir, State Sci & Technol Inst, currently; bd dir, Mich Strategic Fund, currently; bd dir, Mich Econ Growth Authority, currently; bd dir, Gov Snyder's Talent Investment Bd, currently; bd dir, Washtenaw Community Col Found, currently. **Honors/Awds:** Outstanding Young Men, Am US Jaycees, 1979; Outstanding Achievement in Black Affairs, SVSC Black Stud Asn, 1983; Minett Distinguished Professor, Rochester Inst Technol, 2005; One of the 2007 Newsmakers of the Year, Crain's Detroit Bus; Outstanding Alumnus, Saginaw Valley State Univ, 2008. **Home Addr:** 415 Ardussi, Saginaw, MI 48602. **Business Addr:** President, Chief Executive Officer, Michigan Economic Development Corp, 300 N Wash Sq, Lansing, MI 48913, **Business Phone:** (517)241-1400.

### FINNEY, SARA VERNETTA

Television producer. **Personal:** Born Jan 25, 1957; married Robert L Johnson Jr. **Educ:** Univ Southern Calif, BA, broadcast jour. **Career:** Embassy Television; United Paramount Network, Parkers, exec producer, 2004; TV series: "What's Happening Now", 1985; "227", 1985; "Married with Children", 1987; "The Parent 'Hood", 1995-96; "Moesha", exec producer, 1996-99; "The Parkers", exec producer, 1999-2004; "Mo's House", 2006; "The Game", 2006-07; Writer: "The Jeffersons", 1982-85; "What's Happening Now!", 1985; "Mama's Family", 1986; "The Facts of Life", 1987; "Married with Children", 1989; New Attitude", 1990; "Family Matters", co-producer, 1993-95, producer, 1994-95; "The Parent 'Hood", supv producer, 1995-96. **Orgs:** Delta Sigma Theta Sorority. **Business Addr:** Executive Producer, United Paramount Network, 11800 Wilshire Blvd, Los Angeles, CA 90025, **Business Phone:** (310)575-7000.

### FINNIE, ROGER LEWIS, SR.

Football player. **Personal:** Born Nov 6, 1945, Miami, FL; married Debbie; children: Shannon Monique & Rogers Lewis Jr. **Educ:** Fla A&M Univ, attended 1969. **Career:** New York Jets, right tackle, offensive tackle, guard, defensive end, tight end, 1969-72; St Louis Cardinals, left tackle, 1973-78; New Orleans Saints, 1979. **Orgs:** Youth org; NFL Players Asn. **Honors/Awds:** Defensive Lineman of the Year; Ebony All-Am, Defensive Lineman; Trophy, Best Offensive Line NFL Fewer Quarterback Sacks. **Special Achievements:** Named Pittsburg All-Am, 1968; received game balls, NY Jets, 1969 & 1971. **Home Addr:** 3708 Australian Ave, West Palm Beach, FL 33407.

### FISCHER, LISA (MELONIE FISCHER)

Singer. **Personal:** Born Dec 1, 1958, Brooklyn, NY. **Career:** Luther Vandross, back-up singer; Albums: So Intense, Elektra Recs, 1991; Singles: "Glad To Be Alive", 1990; "How Can I Ease the Pain", 1991; "Save Me", 1991; "So Intense", 1992; "Colors of Love", 1993; solo artist, currently; "Human Beings", 2009. **Home Addr:** 3264 S Kihei Rd, Kihei, HI 96753-9605. **Business Addr:** Vocalist, c/o Atlantic Records, 1290 Ave of the Americas, New York, NY 10104, **Business Phone:** (212)707-2000.

### FISCHER, MELONIE. See FISCHER, LISA.

### FISCHER, WILLIAM S.

Musician, educator, publisher. **Personal:** Born Mar 5, 1935, Shelby, MS; son of R A Fisher and Willye; married Dolores Labrie; children: Darius, Marc, Bryan & Paul. **Educ:** Xavier Univ, New Orleans, BS, 1956; Colo Col, MA, 1962; Univ Vienna, Akademie Fur Musik & Darstellende; N Western Univ, Cyprus, PhD, meta physics, 1999. **Career:** Xavier Univ, assoc prof, 1962-66; Atlantic Rec, arranger & conductor, 1965-, music dir, 1968-70, rec producer, 1973-75; Newport Col & Cardiff Col, lectr, 1966-67; New York Pub Sch, 1967-75; New York, publ, 1967-; Arcana Rec, owner, 1971-; Albums: Circles, 1970; Akelarre Sorta, 1972; Omen, 1972. **Orgs:** Am Fedn Musicians, 1953; Am Soc Composers Authors & Publishers, 1964; Nat Asn Music Educ, 1964; exec dir, Soc Black Composers, 1971-. **Honors/Awds:** Grants: Edger Stern Family Fund Comn, 1963-65; Akademischer Austausdienst W Ger, 1964; Orgn Am States; Pan Am Grant, 1964; New Orleans Phil harmonic Comt, 1964-65; Fulbright Grant, 1965-66; Austrian Govt Grant, 1965; NY Coun Arts, 1971; Nat Endowment Arts, 1971. **Special Achievements:** Commissioned Film Score Elliott, A Feature Film, Back roads of Jackson, WO, 1987; commissioned to write Mass for a Saint, SBS of Bensalem, Pennsylvania, 1988; meditation on Mt St Helens for Orch, Ready Productions, 1990-91; Commission to write MASS, Parish Le Beau Louisiana, First Established, by People of Color, Founded, 1897; New Music for Violin/Saxophone Concertos using computer assimilated orchestra, "The Cross Bronx Concerto" and other CD's, 1995-96; Gazelle for Alvin Ailey Co12 yrs performance feature films for United Artists Inc and Born to Win; Emi: Studios London "Boardwalk". **Home Addr:** 1365 St Nicholas Ave Apt 13J, New York, NY 10033-6205, **Home Phone:** (212)923-4950. **Business Phone:** (212)923-4950.

### FISHBURNE, LAURENCE JOHN, III

Actor. **Personal:** Born Jul 30, 1961, Augusta, GA; son of Laurence John Jr and Hattie Bell Crawford; married Hajna O Moss; children: Langston Issa & Montana Isis; married Gina Torres; children: Delilah. **Educ:** Lincoln Sq Acad. **Career:** Films include: Apocalyse Now, 1979; Fast Break, 1979; Death Wish II, 1982; Rumble Fish, 1983; The Cotton Club, 1984; The Color Purple, 1985; Quicksilver, 1986; Nightmare on Elm Street III, 1987; Sch Daze, 1988; Red Heat, 1988; King of New York, 1990; Boyz in the Hood, 1991; Cadence, 1991; Deep Cover, 1992; Searching for Bobby Fischer, 1993; What's Love Got To Do With It, 1993; Higher Learning, 1995; Bad Company, 1995; Just Cause, 1995; Othello, 1995; Fled, 1996; Event Horizon, 1997; Hoodlum, 1997, The Matrix, 1999; Osmosis Jones, 2001; Biker Boyz, 2003; The Matrix Reloaded, 2003; Mystic River, 2003; The Matrix Revolutions, 2003; Five Fingers, 2005; Bobby, 2006; The Death & Life of Bobby Z, 2006; 21, 2008; Tortured, 2008; Days of Wrath, 2008; Black Water Transit, 2009; Armored, 2009; Predators, 2010; Contagion, 2011; The Colony, 2013; Man of Steel, 2013; Khumba, 2013; Ride Along, 2014; The Signal, 2014; Rudderless, 2014. TV movies: "Decoration Day", 1990; "Choices", 1992; "The Tuskegee Airmen", 1995; "Before Your Eyes", 1996; "Miss Evers' Boys", 1997; "Always Outnumbered", 1998; "Sex & the Matrix", 2000; "Decoded: The Making of 'The Matrix Reloaded", 2003; "Thurgood", 2011; "Have a Little Faith", 2011; TV series: "Pee-Wee's Playhouse", 1986-90; "Tribeca", 1993; "CSI: Crime Scene Investigation", 2008-11; "CSI: Miami", 2009; "CSI: NY", 2009; "Hannibal", 2013-14; "Black-ish", 2014. plays include: August Wilson's Two Train Running; The Lion in Winter, 1999; Assault on Precinct 13, 2005; Akeelah & the Bee, 2006; Fences, 2006; Without Walls, 2006; Thurgood, 2008; Producer: TriBeCa, 1993; Hoodlum, 1997; Once in the Life, 2000; Akeelah & the Bee, Mission: Impossible III, 2006; The Death and Life of Bobby Z, TMNT, Fantastic Four: Rise of the Silver Surfer, 2007; Tortured, Days of Wrath, 2008. **Honors/Awds:** Drama Desk Award for Outstanding Featured Actor in a Play, 1975-2000; Primetime Emmy Award for Outstanding Guest Actor - Drama Series, 1975-2000; Tony Award for Best Performance by a Featured Actor in a Play, 1976-2000; Best Actor in a Featured Role, 1992; Image Award, Nat Asn Advan Colored People, 1996, 1998 & 2012; CableACE Award, 1997; PGA Golden Laurel Awards; Television Producer of the YearAward in Longform, 1998; Blockbuster Entertainment Award for FavoriteSupporting Actor - Action Science-Fiction, 2000; MTV Movie Award for Best Fight, 2000; Drama Desk Award for Outstanding One-Person Show, 2001-25; Boston Society of Film Critics Awards for Best Ensemble Cast, 2003; Lifetime Achievement Award, 2005; Outstanding Performance by an Actor in a Supporting Role, 2006; Black Movie Award, 2006; Hollywood Film Award, 2006; Copper Wing Tribute Award, 2006; Special Award, ShoWest Convention, 2006, 2008; Career Achievement Award, Zurich Film Festival, 2011. **Special Achievements:** First Black to portray Shakespeare's Othello on silver screen. **Business Addr:** Actor, Michelle Marx Inc, 8756 Holloway Dr, Los Angeles, CA 90069.

### FISHBURNE, LILLIAN E. (LILLIAN ELAINE)

Naval officer. **Personal:** Born Mar 25, 1949, Patuxent River, MD; married Albert J Sullivan; children: Cherese. **Educ:** Lincoln Univ, BA, 1971; USN Women's Officers Sch; Webster Col, MA, mgt, 1980; US Naval Postgrad Sch, MS, telecommunications syst mgt, 1982; Indust Col Armed Forces, grad, 1993. **Career:** US Navy, 1973-2001; Naval Air Test Facil, Lakehurst, NJ, personnel & legal officer, 1973-74; Recruiting Dist, Miami, FL, Navy officer progs recruiter, 1974-77; Naval Telecommunications Ctr, Great Lakes, IL, officer in-chg, 1977; Command, Control & Commun Directorate Off Chief Naval Opers, asst head Joint Allied Command & Control Matters Br, 1982-84; Naval Commun Sta, Yokosuka, Japan, exec officer, 1984; Chief Naval Opers Command, Control & Commun Directorate, spec proj officer; Naval Comput & Telecommunications Sta, Key W, FL, 1992-93; Command, Control, Commun & Comput Systs Directorate Joint Staff, Pentagon, chief Command & Control Systs Support Div, 1993-95; Naval Comput & Telecommunications Area Eastern Pac Sta, Wahiawa, Hawaii, 1995; Space, Info Warfare, Command & Control Directorate-Chief Naval Opers, dir Info Transfer Div. **Orgs:** Zeta Phi Beta. **Special Achievements:** First African-American woman to hold the rank of Rear Admiral, U.S. Navy, 1998.

### FISHER, ALMA M.

Librarian. **Personal:** Born Dec 22, 1945, Learned, MI; married Eugene. **Educ:** Tougaloo Col, BA, eng, 1967; Dominican Univ, MALS, 1970. **Career:** Chicago Pub Sch Syst, teacher, 1967-69; Chicago Pub Libr Sys librn, staff, 1970-72; Tougaloo Col, archivist; Nat Endowment Humanities, comprehensive arch training prog; Tougaloo Col, sr archivist, 2004-. **Orgs:** Am Libr Asn; Mich Libr Asn; Mich Teachers Asn; Black Caucus ALA; Urban League; Nat Asn Advan Colored People; Utica Jr Col Alumni Asn; Soc Am Archivists; Archivists & Arch Color Roundtable. **Honors/Awds:** HBCU Arch Internship, 2001. **Home Addr:** 120 Rutherford Pl, Jackson, MS 39206. **Business Addr:** Senior Archivist, Tougaloo College, 400 W Co Line Rd, Tougaloo, MS 39174, **Business Phone:** (601)977-6140.

### FISHER, ANTWONE QUENTON

Movie director, movie producer, writer. **Personal:** Born Aug 3, 1959, OH; son of Edward Eklins and Eva Mae; married LaNette M; children: Indigo & Azure. **Career:** Director, author, poet, lecturer, college professor, movie producer & screenwriter; Terminal Island Fed Prison, guard; Sony Pictures Entertainment, security guard; author; Author: Finding Fish: A Memoir, 2001; Author: The Antwone Fisher Story (screenplay), 2002; Who Will Cry for the Little Boy?: Poems, 2003; A Boy Should Know ow To Tie A Tie: And Other Lessons For Succeeding In Life, 2010; Films: The Antwone Fisher Story, co-producer & screen writer, 2002; ATL, writer, 2006; My Summer Friend, writer, dir, 2009; Queen Victoria's Wedding, actor, 2010; This Life Of Mine The Leon T. Garr Story, writer, dir, producer, ed, cinematographer, 2011. **Home Addr:** 4832 Shenandoah Ave, Los Angeles, CA 90056-1057. **Business Addr:** Author, Screenwriter, c/o Author Mail William Morrow, 10 E 53rd St 7th Fl, New York, NY 10022.

### FISHER, FR. DAVID ANDREW

Educator, clergy. **Personal:** Born Sep 12, 1958, Columbus, OH; son of Morgan Cecil and Jean Otis Peck. **Educ:** Ohio Dominican Col, Columbus, OH, BA, philos, 1980; Pontif Gregorian Univ, Rome, Italy, STB, theol, 1983, STL, theol, 1985, STD, 2004. **Career:** St Paul Church, Westerville, OH, assoc pastor, 1985-87; SS Augustine & Gabriel, Columbus, OH, pastor, 1987-90; Xavier Univ; Univ Dayton; Rosemont Col; Ohio Dominican Col, Columbus, OH, prof philos, 1989-; St Joseph Cathedral, Columbus, OH, assoc pastor, 1990-; Cent State Univ, adj prof philos; Columbus State Community Col, Dept Humanities, prof, currently; St Johnny Padua Maronite Church, pastor, adminr. **Orgs:** Bd trustee, Alzhiemer Asn, 1986-89; bd trustee, St Stephen Comt House, 1988-90. **Home Addr:** 1945 Ardenrun Way, Columbus, OH 43219, **Home Phone:** (614)253-1039. **Business Addr:** Professor, Columbus State Community College, 550 E Spring St, Columbus, OH 43216-1609, **Business Phone:** (614)287-5056.

### FISHER, DEREK LAMAR

Basketball player, basketball coach. **Personal:** Born Aug 9, 1974, Little Rock, AR; son of John and Annette; married Candace; children: Tatum, Drew, Marshall & Chloe. **Educ:** Univ Ark-Little Rock, commun, attended 1996. **Career:** Basketball player (retired), coach; Los Angeles Lakers, pt guard, 1996-2003, 2007-12, shooting guard,

2003-04; Golden State Warriors, pt guard, 2004-06; Utah Jazz, shooting guard, 2006-07; Dallas Mavericks, pt guard, 2012; Okla City Thunder, shooting guard, 2012-14; New York Knicks, head coach, 2014-16. **Orgs:** Ame Cancer Soc; Big Bros Big Sisters; pres, Nat Basketball Players Asn; Amateur Athletic Union. **Honors/Awds:** Sunbelt Conference Player of the Year, 1996; Champion, Nat Basketball Asn, 2000-02, 2009-10; Shooting Stars champion, Nat Basketball Asn, 2004; Sportsmanship Award, Nat Basketball Asn, 2006-07. **Business Addr:** Head Coach, New York Knicks, Madison Sq Garden 2 Pa Plz, New York, NY 10121-0091, **Business Phone:** (212)465-6471.

**FISHER, E. CARLETON**
College teacher. **Personal:** Born Nov 3, 1934, St. Louis, MO; children: Victor, Bruce & Vernon. **Educ:** Howard Univ, BS, MS, 1957; Am Univ; Morgan State Univ, EdD, 1986. **Career:** Univ Chicago, numerical analyst, 1957-66; Int Bus Mach, personnel mgr, 1966-72; Univ Md, exec asst chancellor affirmative action, 1973-77; Notre Dame, exec dir minorities engr, 1977-78; Prudential Ins, dir, col rels, 1978-80; Affirmative Action, prof math, asst pres. **Orgs:** Kappa Alpha Psi; Am Guild Organists; pres & founder, Md Asn Affirmative Action Officers, 1975-77, 1983-85; Gold Seker Fel; Morgan State Univ, 1983-85. **Business Addr:** MD.

**FISHER, EDITH MAUREEN**
Entrepreneur, librarian, athletic coach. **Personal:** Born Jul 29, 1944, Houston, TX; daughter of Freeman and Ruby Jase. **Educ:** Los Angeles Trade Technol Col, AA, 1965; Univ Ill, Urbana-Champaign, MLS, 1972; City Univ NY, Queens Col, cert ethnicity & librarianship, 1975; Univ Pittsburgh, PhD, 1991. **Career:** Univ Calif, San Diego, La Jolla, cent univ libr, 1972-90; Contemp Black Arts Prog, adj lectr, 1981-90; Univ Calif, Los Angeles, Sch Libr & Info Sci, lectr, 1989; Eval & Training Inst, Los Angeles, Calif, consult & tech adv, 1991; Tenge Enterprises, Encinitas, Calif, pres & founder, 1991-2001; Am Lib Asn, consult, trainer, 1993-; UC San Diego, librn. **Orgs:** Pres, Black Caucus Am Libr Asn, 1988-90; San Diego County Black Chamber Com-GLA; Am Soc Training & Develop. **Honors/Awds:** President Award, Black Caucus Am Libr Asn, 1990; Counr Calif Libr Asn, 1987-90; Am Soc Training & Develop. **Special Achievements:** Author of "What Do I Read Next? Multicultural Literature", 1997. **Home Addr:** 656 Crest Dr, Encinitas, CA 92024.

**FISHER, DR. EDWARD G.**
Surgeon. **Personal:** Born Apr 22, 1932; son of Guy O D and Elisa Howell Dawes; married Judy Ann; children: Yvonne & Ronald. **Educ:** Brooklyn Col, BS, 1956; Howard Univ, Md, 1961. **Career:** Howard Univ, med officer, 1966-68; Operating Rm, Com Hadley Hosp, chmn; Howard Univ Hosp; Freedmens Hosp, instr, 1966-68; Greater SE Comn, active staff privileges; Inst Urban Living Wash, DC, med dir; Hadley Memorial Hosp, active attend physician; Full Gospel Church Lord's Missions Int Inc, pastor, currently; pvt prac, currently. **Orgs:** Med Care Eval Comn; DC Med Soc; DC Medico-chirugical Soc; Nat Med Asn; AMA & Interns & Residents Asn Freedmens Hosp; Nat Asn Interns & Residents; Polit Action Com; Urban League; Hon Med Soc, 1961; Dipl AmBd Surg; Joint Conf Hadley Hosp; Med Staff Hadley Mem Hosp; bd trustee, Hadley Mem Hosp; Alpha Omega Alpha; co-pastor, Full Gospel Church Lord's Missions Int Inc; chaplain, bd govrs, Med-Chi Socs Wash, DC, currently. **Honors/Awds:** Author of numerous publications; Co-author: Human Sexuality Christian Perspective, 1984; Moses & the Burning Bush, 2006. **Home Addr:** 11705 Bishops Content Rd, Mitchellville, MD 20721, **Home Phone:** (301)390-0024. **Business Addr:** Pastor, Full Gospel Church Lord's Missions International Inc, 3536 Minn Ave SE Suite 1, Washington, DC 20019, **Business Phone:** (202)575-5433.

**FISHER, DR. JUDITH DANELLE**
Consultant, physician. **Personal:** Born Feb 17, 1951, Sanford, NC. **Educ:** Howard Univ, Col Lib Arts, BS, 1974, Sch Med, MD 1975. **Career:** Howard Univ Hosp, psychiat, 1975-77; Hahnemann Med Col, psyciatricresident, 1976-78, fel, 1978-79; CMHC Hahnemann, med dir, 1979-80; Hahnemann Hosp Philadelphia, asst dir in-patient unit, psychol unit, 1980-81; pvt pract, 1980-; Cam Care Health Corp, psychol actg med dir, 1981-83; Eagleville Hosp, Women's In-Patient Unit, dir, 1983-84; Wake Co MHC, staff psychiat, 1984-85; NC Cent Bronx Hosp, Disability Determination Svcs, psychiat consult, 1985-; Jacobi Med Ctr, Community Psychiat, currently. **Orgs:** Am Psychiat Asn, 1981-; bd dir, Women Transition Philadelphia, 1982-84; Smithsonian Asn, 1984-; Nat Asn Disability Examrs, 1985-; Am Film Inst, 1986-; State NC Employees Asn, 1986-; Livingston Col Alumni Asn. **Honors/Awds:** NIMH Minority Fellowship, Am Psychiat Asn, 1976-78; Certificate of Recognition, Alpha Kappa Alpha Sorority Raleigh, 1985. **Home Addr:** 332 Bleecker St Suite F16, New York, NY 10014, **Home Phone:** (917)853-6209. **Business Addr:** Community Psychiatric, Jacobi Medical Center, 1400 Pelham Pkwy S, Bronx, NY 10461, **Business Phone:** (718)918-5000.

**FISHER, LLOYD B.**
Lawyer. **Personal:** Born Jan 13, 1942, Marthaville, LA; married Shirley T Little; children: Jawara M J. **Educ:** Purdue Univ, BS; Valparaiso Univ Sch Law, JD, 1973. **Career:** B002 Allen & Hamiltol, consult, 1969-70; City Gary, asst city atty, 1973-76; Gary & Opportunities Industrialization Ctr, vpres, bd dir, 1975; Lake Co Govt, pub defender, 1977-79; Lloyd B Fisher Atty Law, owner, pvt pract atty, 1979-. **Orgs:** Basileus Omega, Psi Phi Fraternity, Alpha Chi Chap, 1974-76; Am Bar Asn, 1974-; Nat Bar Asn, 1974-; pres, Lake County Opportunities Develop Found Inc, 1975-; Nat Asn Advan Colored People, 1976-; bd mem, Purdue Club, Club Lake County, 1976-; TMLA, 1979-80; asst to chmn, Criminal Law Sect, Nat Bar Asn, 1980; Bar Asn 7th Fed Cir; Ill State BarAsn; pub rels chmn, Comn Pack 23 23 Cub Scouts Am Gary; bd mem, Thurgood Marshall Law Asn. **Honors/Awds:** Certificate of Appreciation, Tolleston Community Coun, 1977; Certificate of Appreciation, Nat Asn Advan Colored People, 1977; Dedicated Service Award, Gary Opportunities Industrialtization Ctr, 1980. **Business Addr:** Lawyer, Lloyd B Fisher Attorney Law, 734 N Newton St, Gary, IN 46403, **Business Phone:** (219)938-8461.

**FISHER, RASHIYA. See DIGGA, RAH.**

**FISHER, RONALD L., SR.**
Banker, vice president (organization). **Personal:** Born May 19, 1951, Hamlet, NC; son of William and Elizabeth; married Del Johnson; children: Ron Jr & Lacy. **Educ:** NC Cent Univ, Dunham, NC, BS, finance, 1973; Univ Wis-Madison, Sch Bus, MBA, 1977. **Career:** Cameron Brown Mortgage Co, actg vpres, commerical real estate, 1977-80; First Union Nat Bank, vpres, cot lending, sr vpres, 1973-99, vpres, employee rels, 1980-89; Wachovia Bank, sr vpres, 1973-99; HBC Consult LLC, owner & pres, 1999-; Support Ctr, bus develop specialist, 2013-. **Orgs:** Bus adv bd, JC Smith Univ, 1986-; Charlotte Urban League, 1991-; 100 Black Men Charlotte, 1991-; bd mem, Charlotte Housing Authority Scholar Fund, 2000-08; fel Consortium Grad Study Mgt; treas, Athletes United Youth, 2000-10; bus develop officer, First Legacy Community Credit Union, 2012. **Home Addr:** 235 Elmhurst Rd, Charlotte, NC 28209-1150. **Business Addr:** Owner, President, HBC Consulting LLC, 1716 Wilmore Dr, Charlotte, NC 28216, **Business Phone:** (704)972-8063.

**FISHER, RUBIN IVAN**
College administrator, manager, vice president (organization). **Personal:** Born Sep 25, 1948, Baltimore, MD. **Educ:** Univ Conn, BS, 1971; Univ New Haven, MS, 1993. **Career:** Travelers Ins Co, asst dir personnel, adminr personnel, 1977-78; employ coun, 1974-77; Aetna Life & Casualty Ins Co, supr field controllers dept, 1972-74; Travelers, Hartford, Conn, ast dir, 1974-88; Black Col Serv, New Orleans, La, asst vpres, 1988-90; Saab Cars USA Inc, Orange, Conn, mgr, employ & training, 1990-93; Univ Pa, dir human resources-Univ Libr, 1993-98; Capital Community Col, dir human resources, 1998-, hr exec, affirmative action officer. **Orgs:** Soc Human Resources Mgt; Res Officer Asn Am; Urban League; Nat Asn Advan Colored People; Strategic Planning Community; accredited personnel specialist designation, Am Soc Personnel Admin-accreditation Inst, 1978; accredited prof, Human Resources designation Personnel Accreditiation Inst, 1987. **Home Addr:** 79 Strawberry Lane, Manchester, CT 06040, **Home Phone:** (203)647-1546. **Business Addr:** Director of Human Resources, Affirmative Action Officer, Capital Community College, 950 Main St Rm 214, Hartford, CT 06103-1234, **Business Phone:** (860)906-5000.

**FISHER, SHELLEY MARIE**
Educator. **Personal:** Born Jul 2, 1942, Gary, IN; daughter of Wendell Brumfield; married Alfred J; children: Tiffiny & Eric. **Educ:** Ind Univ, BS, 1964, MS, 1969. **Career:** Gary Community Sch Corp, adminr, 1969-10, Ernie Pyle Elem Sch, prin, currently; Northwest Acad Aerospace & Aviation Inc, founder & chief exec officer, currently. **Orgs:** Bd dir, Self-Marketing Inc, 1981-84; franchiser, Nat Employment Transmittal Inc, 1981-84; nat secy, Nat Tots & Teens Inc, 1981-85; 3rd vpres, Drifting Dunes Girl Scout Coun, 1986-; Alpha Kappa Alpha Inc; facilitator, Learning Indiana Dept educ. **Home Addr:** 1700 Taft St, Gary, IN 46404-2256, **Home Phone:** (219)949-8036. **Business Addr:** Principal, Ernie Pyle Elementary School, 2545 W 19th Pl, Gary, IN 46404-2698, **Business Phone:** (219)977-2142.

**FITCH, HARRISON ARNOLD**
Lawyer, association executive. **Personal:** Born Jul 4, 1943, Elizabeth, NJ; married Ruth Mckinney; children: Harrison A Jr & Robin L. **Educ:** Columbia Col, AB, 1965; Columbia Univ, LLB, 1968. **Career:** Boston Legal Assistance Proj, atty, 1968-69; Boston Univ, Sch Law, lectr, 1969; Good win Procter & Hoar Trustee Boston Five Cents Savs Bank, atty; Fitch, Wiley, Richlin & Tourse, partner. **Orgs:** Babson & Col; dir, Boston Legal Aid Soc Steering Com Lawyers Com Civil Rights Under Law; dir, MA Law Reform Inst; Boston Legal Assistance Proj; Gov's Ad Hoc Adv Com Judicial Appointments, 1972. **Home Addr:** 27 Sch St 4th Fl, Boston, MA 02180, **Home Phone:** (617)523-6663. **Business Addr:** Partner, Attorney, Fitch & Tourse, 189 State St Fl 5, Boston, MA 02109-2652, **Business Phone:** (617)557-3700.

**FITCH, MILTON FREDERICK TOBY, JR.**
State government official. **Personal:** Born Wilson, NC; son of Milton F (deceased) and Cora Whitted; children: Melanie & Milton III. **Educ:** NC Cent Univ, BS, 1969, Sch Law, JD, 1972. **Career:** NC House Representatives, rep, 1985; Dist 7B, super ct judge, 2001; Most Worshipful Prince Hall Grand Lodge, Free & Accepted Masons NC & Jurisdictions Inc, most worshipful grand master, 2003-; NC Cent Univ, football coach; Del State Col, mootball coach; Grand Lodge Jurisdiction N Carolina, most worshipful grand master; State N Carolina, house rep. **Orgs:** NC Bar; DC Bar; Mt Hebron Masonic Lodge #42; life mem, Nat Asn Advan Colored People; Joint Legis Comn Govt Opers; Adv Budget Comn; Workplace Safety Study Comn; Eastern N Carolina Sch Deaf Found; co chmn, State Personnel Study Comt; Joint Selection State Health Ins Comt; Clark Col, upward bound prog. **Honors/Awds:** North Carolina AFL-CIO; Youth for Social Change Award, Southerners; Community Service Award, NC Asn Black Lawyers; Albert L. Turner Award, NC Central Univ; Legislator of the Year Award, Nc Asn Educ Off Personnel. **Special Achievements:** First African American in the State of North Carolina to preside over the House; First Majority Whip & the First African American to be elected House Majority Leader. **Business Addr:** Most Worshipful Grand Master, Most Worshipful Prince Hall Grand Lodge of North Carolina Inc, 101 E Main St, Durham, NC 27701, **Business Phone:** (919)683-9636.

**FITCHUE, M. ANTHONY**
Educator, writer, dean (education). **Personal:** Born Dec 13, 1943, Kansas City, MO; son of Robert Anthony and Carrie Wilma Witherspoon F; married Leah Doretha White; children: Ebony Joy. **Educ:** Hampton Univ, BS, social sci educ, 1967; Columbia Univ, MS, jour prog, 1971, MA, adult educ, 1992; Harvard Univ, EdM, 1974; Columbia Univ, Teachers Col, EdD, adult educ & educ hist, 1995. **Career:** Dept Labor, Off Fed Contract Compliance, Wash, DC, spec asst to dir, 1979-81; US Info Agency, US Embassy, Bamako, Mali, attache cult, 1981-82; US Info Agency, US Consulate, Madras, Tamil Nadu, India, vice consult, 1982-85; PrattInst, Brooklyn, NY, asst dean, 1987-88; Col New Rochelle City, Univ NY, Iona Col, NY, adj prof, 1987-90; Chancellor, NY, consult, 1988; Le MoyneCol, Multicultural Affairs, dir, 1992-97; Suny Cortland, lectr, 1995-97; Southhampton Col, Multicultural Prog, dir, 1997-98; NYC, Bd Ed, Div FundedProg, res assoc, 1999; Morgan State Univ, Educ & Urban Studies, transfercoordr, asst dean, currently. **Orgs:** Int Fel, Grad Sch Journ, Columbia Univ, 1970-71; Policy fel, Leadership Insts Educ, George Wash Univ, 1974-75; Harvard-Radcliffe Alumni Against Apartheid; nat coordr, Nat Urban League; Proj coordr, Nat Urban League, 1987-90; comnr Ny MLKjr Comn, Syracuse, 1991-94; bd dir Metrop Sch Arts, Syracuse, 1991-95; vol Paul Robeson Performing Arts Ensemble, Syracuse, 1992; Corp mem United Way Cent New York, Syracuse, 1993-. **Business Addr:** Assistant Dean, Transfer Coordinator, Morgan State University, Banneker Hall- Rm 301D 1700 E Cold Spring Lane, Baltimore, MD 21251, **Business Phone:** (443)885-3333.

**FITTS, DR. REV. LEROY**
Clergy, educator. **Personal:** Born Jul 6, 1944, Norlina, NC; son of Johnnie and Louise; married Alice Louise Alston; children: Timothy, Leroy, Dietrich E, Angelique L & Leticia A. **Educ:** Shaw Univ, BA, 1967; Southeastern Baptist Theol Sem, MDiv, 1970; Va Sem, DDiv, 1975, DHL, 1990; Princeton Univ, attended 1984; Baltimore Hebrew Univ, MA, 1985. **Career:** First Baptist Church, Jacksonville, NC, pastor, 1968-72; First Baptist Church, Baltimore, Md, pastor, 1972-; Community Col, Baltimore, adj prof, 1978-80; Va Sem & Col, pres, 1981; Black Church Hist, St Mary's Sem & Univ, Baltimore, Md, prof. **Orgs:** Ed, Loft Carey Baptist Conv, 1975-90; Nat Asn Advan Colored People; Asn Study Negro Hist, 1978-; bd mgr, Va Sem & Col, 1980; bd mgr, St Marys Sem & Univ. **Special Achievements:** Author: Lott Carey First Black Missionary to Africa, 1978; A History of Black Baptists, 1985; article "The Church in the South & Social Issues", Faith & Mission vol II, No I, Fall 1984. **Home Addr:** 3912 The Alameda, Baltimore, MD 21218-2106, **Home Phone:** (410)366-3362.

**FITTZ, SENGA NENGUDI. See NENGUDI, SENGA.**

**FITZGERALD, HERBERT H.**
Detective, president (organization). **Personal:** Born Jul 17, 1928, Trenton, NJ; children: Darrel A & Denise A. **Educ:** Howard Univ Rider Col, bus admin & police admin, 1974. **Career:** Mercer Co, prosecutor, detective; Police Dept, Trenton, NJ, officer & detective. **Orgs:** Co Detectives Asn, NJ; pres, Bro Officers Law Enforcement Soc; NJ Narcotic & Enforcement Officers Asn; Int Narcotic Enforcement Officers Asn; Alpha Phi Alpha Zeta Iota Lambda Chap; Nat Asn Advan Colored People; comnr, Trenton Housing Authority, 1971; bd mem, Model Cities Policy Comn, 1972; Mercer County Alcoholism Prog, 1972; master mason, King David Lodge, Trenton, NJ; 32nd Degree Mason Ophir Consisteory 48, Trenton, NJ; adv bd mem, Union Indust Home Boys, Trenton, NJ; Frontiers Int Bd Gov Police Athletic League. **Honors/Awds:** Many certificates of commendation for meritorious service Trenton Police Dept; Drew Pearson Cultural Achievement Award. **Home Addr:** PO Box 397, Trenton, NJ 08603. **Business Addr:** Office of the County Prosecutor, Detective, Mercer County Court House, Trenton, NJ 08607.

**FITZGERALD, LARRY DARNELL, JR.**
**Personal:** Born Aug 31, 1983, Minneapolis, MN; son of Larry Sr and Carol (deceased); children: Devin. **Educ:** Univ Pittsburgh, attended 2002; Valley Forge Mil Acad, Wayne, Pa, attended 2002. **Career:** Ariz Cardinals, wide receiver, 2004-. **Orgs:** Founder, Larry Fitzgerald First Down Fund, currently; founder, Carol Fitzgerald Memorial Fund, currently. **Honors/Awds:** Fred Biletnikoff Award, 2003; Walter Camp Award, 2003; Paul Warfield Trophy, 2003; Big East Offensive Player of the Year, 2003; Unanimous All-American, 2003; Pro Bowl, 2005, 2007, 2008, 2008, 2010, 2011, 2012, 2013; Receiving Yards Leader, Nat Football Conf, 2008.Champion, Nat Football Conf, 2008; Most Valuable Player, Pro Bowl, 2009; Man of the Year, Walter Payton Nat Football League, 2012; Georgetown Lombardi Award, Nat Football League Players Association, 2013; Henry P. Iba Citizen Athlete, Rotary Club Tulsa, 2014. **Special Achievements:** Youngest NFL receiver to reach 11,000 career receiving yards. **Home Addr:** 6920 E Hummingbird Lane, Paradise Valley, AZ 85253-3643, **Home Phone:** (480)699-2513. **Business Addr:** Wide Receiver, Arizona Cardinals, 8701 S Hardy Dr, Tempe, AZ 85284, **Business Phone:** (602)379-0101.

**FITZGERALD-BROWN, BENITA. See MOSLEY, BENITA FITZGERALD.**

**FITZHUGH, BENJAMIN DEWEY**
Lawyer. **Educ:** Univ Ark-Fayetteville, BS, 1973, JD, 1976. **Career:** Law Offices Bennie O'Neil & B Dewey Fitzhugh, atty, 2003-. **Business Addr:** Attorney, Law Offices Of Bennie O'Neil & B Dewey Fitzhugh, 1423 Main St, Little Rock, AR 72114-4128, **Business Phone:** (501)374-3030.

**FITZHUGH, KATHRYN CORROTHERS**
Librarian. **Personal:** Born Feb 4, 1950, Warren, AR; daughter of Charles Edward and Billie Jean Burns; married Benjamin Dewey; children: Erica Janine. **Educ:** Univ Ark, Fayetteville, AR, BA, Fr, 1971; Univ Ill, Urbana-Champaign, Champaign, IL, MSLS, libr sci, 1976; Univ Ark, Little Rock, AR, JD, 1983. **Career:** US Dist Ct, Eastern Dist Ark, librn; Philander Smith Col, cataloger; Univ Ark, Grad Inst Technol, Little Rock, technol librn, 1977-79; US Ct Appeals, Little Rock, AR, br librn, 1980-83, 1989-92; Hon. George Howard, Jr, law clerk, 1983-84; Fitzhugh & Fitzhugh, Little Rock, AR, partner, 1985-87; Univ Ark-Little Rock, Pulaski Co Law Libr, ref, circulation libr, 1987-89, ref & spec collections libr, currently, prof, 2003, William H Bowen Sch Law, prof, currently. **Orgs:** Am Asn Law Librs, 1982-; Ark Bar Asn, 1983-; Ouachita Girl Scout Coun, 1986-88; Delta Sigma Theta Sorority, 1991-; Am Bar Asn, 1992-; Am Libr Asn, 1993-; Soc Southwest Archivists, 1994-; Soc Am Archivists; Mid-Am Asn Law Librs; pres, prog chmn, Southwestern Asn Law Librs; speaker, Ark Hist Asn; pres, S Western Asn Law Librs, 2002-03; Delta Sigma Theta; parliamentarian, W Harold Flowers Law Socs; speaker, Black Hist Comn Ark. **Honors/Awds:** Faculty Excellence Award, 2003. **Special Achievements:** Author: "Arkansas Practice Materials II: a Selective Annotated Bibliography," UALR Law Review 21, 1999, pp 363-412; "Federal Income Taxation" in, Specialized Legal Research, Aspen Publishers, Boston, 1999, 2003. **Home Addr:** 4715 Darragh Dr, Lit-

tle Rock, AR 72204-8425, **Home Phone:** (501)565-1994. **Business Addr:** Professor, University of Arkansas at Little Rock, 1201 McMath Ave, Little Rock, AR 72202, **Business Phone:** (501)324-9974.

### FITZPATRICK, ALBERT E.

Publishing executive, management consultant, dean (education). **Personal:** Born Dec 30, 1928, Elyria, OH; son of Ben and Mary; married Derien Lucas; children: Sharon, Karyle & Albert II. **Educ:** Kent State Univ, BA, jour & sociol, 1956. **Career:** Sports reporter, Elyria Chronicle Telegram; Akron Beacon J, reporter, 1956-58; Pulitzer Prize-Winning Coverage, Kent State Disturbance, dir, 1970; Akron Beakon J, farm ed, asst state ed, copy ed news desk, asst news ed, news ed, asst managing ed, managing ed, 1973-77; Pulitzer Jury, 1975-76, 1983; Akron Beacon J, exec ed, 1977-84; ed, Yr-Freedom J, Cuyahoga Community Col, Cleveland, 1978; NW Univ, Medill Sch Jour, assoc prof, 1979-80; Knight Ridder, dir minority affairs, 1985; Knight Ridder, asst vpres minority affairs, 1985-94, exec & ed; Albert E Fitzpatrick Leadership Develop Inst, dean, currently; Fitzpatrick Consults, chmn & chief exec officer, currently; Sch Journ & Mass Commun, adj prof, currently; Kent State univ, journalism adj prof; Northwestern Univ, Medill, assoc prof, sr fel; Howard Univ, Journalism Dept, interim chair. **Orgs:** Chmn bd, Wesley Temple, AME Church, 1965-84; pres, Buckeye Chap, Sigma Delta Chi, 1971; pres, Akron Press Club, 1981-83; pres, Nat Asn Black Journalists, 1985-87; chmn & minorities bd mem, Am Cancer Soc, Boy Scouts, Ctr Econ Educ; chmn, UNCF adv bd, 1989; chmn, Nat Asn Minority Media Exercise, 1990-; Am Soc Newspaper Ed; prof adv bd, Kent State Univ Sch Commun; chmn, Southern Newspapers Asn; founding chair, Nat Asn Minority Media Execs. **Honors/Awds:** Outstanding Alumnus Award, Kent State Univ, 1973; John S Knight Award, Sigma Del Ta Chi, Akron, OH, 1980; Frederick Douglass Award Lifetime Achievement, Nat Asn Black Journalists, 1984; Ida B Wells Award, Nat Asn Black Journalists, Nat Conf Ed Writers, Nat Broadcast Ed Asn, 1989; Community Service Award, Kent State Univ, 1991; Chairmans Citation, Nat Press Found, 2005; Robert G McGruder Award, 2005; Pulitzer Prize, Akron Beacon J; American Journalism Historical Association and National Press Foundation Awards; Kent State's Robert B. McGruder Distinguished Lecture Award; Inducted NABJ's Hall of Fame. **Special Achievements:** First African American to win the distinguished Ida B Wells Award. **Home Addr:** 435 Armante Ct, Akron, OH 44313, **Home Phone:** (330)945-7606. **Business Addr:** Dean, Leadership Development Institute, PO Box 19900, Detroit, MI 48219-0900, **Business Phone:** (313)993-1776.

### FITZPATRICK, B. EDWARD

Executive. **Career:** Puget Sound Chrysler-Plymouth Inc, Renton, Wash, pres, chief exec officer, 1986-; Puget Sound Dodge Renton, Wash, owner; Lexus Modesto, owner. **Business Addr:** Chief Executive Officer, Puget Sound Chrysler-Plymouth, 4622 W View Dr, Everett, WA 98203-2417, **Business Phone:** (206)226-0066.

### FLACK, DR. JOHN M.

Physician, educator. **Personal:** Born Jan 23, 1957, Hill AFT, UT; son of John and Bernezetta Littles; married Jennifer Schoats; children: Courtney, Christen, Cathryn, Catelyn & Carey. **Educ:** Langston Univ, BS, chem, 1978; Univ Okla, Sch Med, MD, 1982, Health Sci, chief med resident, 1986; Univ Minn, Sch Pub Health, MPH, epidemiol, 1990. **Career:** Univ Okla, chief med resident, 1982-86, instr med, 1986-88; Univ Minn, asst prof, 1990-92, chief, gen & prev med, 1992-94; Bowman Gray Sch Med, assoc prof surg, 1994-97; Vencor Hosp, former, vpres; Wake Forest Univ, Bowman Gray Sch Med, assoc prof; Hypertension Ctr, instr med, assoc dir; Wayne St Univ, assoc chmn & prof, 1997-88, Depts Internal Med & Community Med, prof, 1997-98, Dept Internal Med, assoc chmn, 1999-2000, assoc chmn acad affairs & chief qual officer, 2000-05, interim chmn, 2005-, Dept Community Med, faculty, 1999-, Cardiovasc Epidemiol & Clin Appln Prog, dir, acad affairs, chmn, currently, Dept Med, Div Clin Epidemiol & Translational Res, dir, 2006-; ECEA dir & assoc chmn, clin res & urban healthoutcomes, 2002-; Translational Res & Clin Epidemiol, chief; Nat Inst Environ Health Sci, prin investr; Nat Insts Health, prin investr; John D. Dingell Veterans Affairs Med Ctr, consult, 2004-; Detroit Med Ctr, chief, 2005-. **Orgs:** Res Ctr Minority, 1992-96; bd trustees, Int Soc Hypertension Blacks, 1995-; Nebr Dept Health, 1999; 100 Black Men, 2000-; Am Black Cardiologist; chair, Nat Kidney Found, KEEP comt, 2000-; Alpha Omega Alpha Med Hon Socs; fel Health Care Qual Effectiveness Res; bd, Coun Advan Diabetes Res Educ; Cardio renal Adv Panel Food & Drug Admin. **Honors/Awds:** Distinguished Alumni, 1993; Positive Image Award, Pee Dee Newspaper Group, 1995; Dr Daniel D Savage Scientific Award, 1998; One Best Doctors in Am, 1998, 2002, 2003; Distinguished Service Award, Nat Kidney Found, 2003; Distinguished Research Award, Int Soc Hypertension in Blacks; Pillar of Excellence Award, Mich Peer Rev Orgn, 2005; Crains Detroit Business Health Care Hero Award, 2005; Award for Excellence, Forest Dewey Dodrill, Am Heart Asn, 2007. **Special Achievements:** Authored more than 103 peer-reviewed manuscripts and book chapters; Manuscript reviewer for several prominent medical journals; special consultant to the metabolic and endocrinologic drug products FDA Advisor. **Home Addr:** 4489 Cranbrook Trail, Orchard Lake, MI 48323-1507, **Home Phone:** (248)681-5910. **Business Addr:** CECA Director, Associate Chairman, Wayne State University School Medicine, 4201 St Antoine Suite 2E, Detroit, MI 48201, **Business Phone:** (313)745-8244.

### FLACK, ROBERTA

Singer, songwriter. **Personal:** Born Feb 10, 1937, Asheville, NC; daughter of Laron LeRoy and Irene; married Stephen Novosel; children: Bernard Wright. **Educ:** Howard Univ, BA, music educ, 1958; Univ Mass, PhD. **Career:** Music & eng teacher 1959-60; Browne Jr High & Rabaut Jr High, teacher, 1960-67; piano teacher; Tivoli Club, pianist & singer; 1520 Club, pianist; singer & songwriter, 1968-; ABC TV spec, First Time Ever, star, 1973; OCL Songs From Neighborhood", 2005; Magic Lady Inc, singer & song writer, currently; Roberta Flack Sch Music, founder, currently; TV theme song, Valerie, writer; Albums: First Take, 1969; Chap Two, 1970; Quiet Fire, 1971; Will You Love Me Tomorrow, 1972; Where Love, 1972; Roberta Flack & Donny Hathaway, 1972; Killing Me Softly, 1973; Feel Like Making Love, 1975; Blue Lights Basement, 1978; Roberta Flack, 1978; Closer I Get To You, 1978; You Are My Heaven, Back Together Again & Don't Make Me Wait Too Long, 1979; Why Are You So Bad, 1980; Live & More, 1980; Roberta Flack Featuring Donny Hathaway, 1980; Bustin Loose, writer, 1981; I'm One, 1982; Tonight I Celebrate My Love, 1983; B To Love, 1983; Hits & Hist, 1984; If I'm Still Around Tomorrow, 1984; Roberta Flack, 1985; Oasis, 1988; Set Night To Music, 1991; Stop World, 1992; Roberta, 1995; Christmas Album, 1997; Friends, 1999; Holiday, 2003; Very Best Roberta Flack, 2006. **Orgs:** Sigma Delta Chi; trustee, Atlanta Univ; Delta Sigma Theta; Artist Empowerment Coalition. **Business Addr:** Singer, Songwriter, Magic Lady Inc, 236 5th Ave, New York, NY 10001-7606, **Business Phone:** (212)644-7218.

### FLAGG, DR. ELOISE ALMA WILLIAM

Consultant, educator. **Personal:** Born Sep 16, 1918, City Point, VA; daughter of Caroline Ethel Moody (deceased) and Hannibal Greenee (deceased); married J Thomas; children: Thomas L & Luisa Flagg Foley. **Educ:** Newark State Col, BA, 1940; Montclair State Col, MA, 1943; Columbia Univ, EdD, 1955; Newark State Col, LittD, 1968. **Career:** Teacher, assistant superintendent (retired), consult; Wash, grade teacher, 1941-43; Elem Sch, grade teacher, 1943-57, remedial reading teacher, 1957-63, from vice prin to prin, 1963-67; Newark State Col, adj instr eng, 1964; Sch Bd Educ Newark, vprin, prin & asst supt, 1967-83; Montclair State Col, Rutgers Univ, adj instr, 1982; Educ & Ed, consult, 1983-; Newark Pub Libr, John Cotton Dana lectr, 2004; E. Alma Flagg Scholar Fund Inc, consult; Hawkins St Sch, prin. **Orgs:** Kappa Delta Pi Hon Soc Educ, 1954; dir, YMWCA, 1964-73; educ chair, Proj Pride, 1980-; pres, League Women Voters Newark, 1982-84; Gov's Comm C Serv Planning, 1983-87; vpres, Newark Youth Art Exhib, 1988; vol, NJ Performing Arts Ctr, 1994; charter mem, Newark Preserv & Landmarks Comm; vpres, Share, NJ, 1996; Nat Hon Socs; Nat Coun Teachers Mathematics; Nat Coun Teacher Educ; Nat Surv Stud Engagement; Am Asn Univ Women; Alpha Kappa Alpha; Soroptimist Int Newark; Urban League Essex Co; Newark Sr Citizens Comn; life mem, Nat Asn Advan Colored People. **Honors/Awds:** Distinguished Service to Education, NSC Alumni, 1966; Citizenship Award, Weequahic Comm Coun, 1967; Roster Super Merit, E Side HS Alumni, 1969; Distinguished Service Award, Cosmopolitan, 1970; Adam Clayton Powell Education Award, NJ Alliance Black Sch Educr, 1981; E Alma Flagg Sch Newark, 1985; Sojourner Truth Award, Negro Bus & Prof Women, 1985; ESHS Distinguished Alumni Award, 75th Anniversary, 1986; Education Law Center Award, 1986; Distinguished Alumna Award, Teachers Col Columbia Univ, 1986; Dr E Alma Flagg School, Newark, NJ, named in honor. **Special Achievements:** First African-Am female prin in Newark, 1964; Published books like: Lines and Colors (poetry), 1979; Feelings, Lines, Colors (poetry), 1980; Twenty More with Thought & Feeling, 1981. **Business Addr:** Educational Consultant, Owner, E Alma Flagg Scholarship Fund Inc, 67 Vaughan Dr, Newark, NJ 07103.

### FLAGG, THOMAS J.

College teacher. **Educ:** Howard Univ, BA, mus; Columbia Univ, Teachers Col, MA. **Career:** College teacher (retired); Howard Univ, prof music, 1999-2003; Talladega Col, Ala, asst prof. **Orgs:** Emer mem, Attrus C Fleming Music Scholar Fund. **Business Addr:** Emeritus Member, Attrus C Fleming Music Scholarship Fund, PO Box 90213, Washington, DC 20090-0213.

### FLAKE, REV. DR. FLOYD H.

Educator, clergy, government official. **Personal:** Born Jan 30, 1945, Los Angeles, CA; son of Robert Booker Sr and Rosie Lee Johnson; married Margaret Elaine McCollins; children: Aliya, Nailah, Rasheed & Hasan. **Educ:** Wilberforce Univ, BA, 1967; Payne Theol Sem; Northeastern Univ Sch Bus; United Theol Sem, Dayton, OH, DMin. **Career:** Miami Valley Child Develop Centers, social worker, 1967-68; Bethel AME Church, pastor, 1968-70; Xerox Corp, mkt analyst, 1969-70; Lincoln Univ, dir stud affairs, assoc dean students, 1970-73; Sec Presby Church, pastor, 1971-73; Martin Luther King Jr Afro Am Ctr, Boston Univ, univ chaplain marsh chapel & dean students, 1973-76; Mt Zion AME Ch, pastor, 1974-75; Greater Allen Allen African Methodist Cathedral New York, sr pastor, 1976-; Allen Sr Citizen Complex, developer; Allen Christian Sch, founder; Allen AME Church, Jamaica, NY, pastor, 1976; US House Representatives, congressman, 1986-97; Edison Charter Schs, pres, 2000; Wilberforce Univ, pres, 2002-08; New York Post, columnist. **Orgs:** Life mem, Nat Asn Advan Colored People; ordained minister, African Methodist Episcopal Church; life mem, SCLC; bd mem, Fannie Mae Found; adv bd, FDIC; bd mem, NYC Olympics, 2012; Press Comn Excellence Spec Educ; Princeton Rev; NewYork City Investment Fund Civic Capital Corp; Fed Deposit Ins Corp Adv Comt Banking Policy; Bank Am Nat Adv Bd; sr fel Manhattan Inst Social &Econ Policy; adj fel, Adv Bd, Brookings Inst Ctr Urban & Metrop Policy; New York 2012 Olympic Comt. **Home Addr:** 1 Langley Lane, Old Wesbury, NY 11568, **Home Phone:** (212)225-3461. **Business Addr:** Senior Pastor, The Greater Allen Allen African Methodist Cathedral of New York, 110-31 Merrick Blvd, Jamaica, NY 11433, **Business Phone:** (718)206-4600.

### FLAKES, REV. GARLAND KAZELL

Clergy, business owner, law enforcement officer. **Personal:** Born Jun 12, 1963, Temple, TX; son of Myrtle L Captain; married Delena K Johnson; children: Brittany Alyse, Chaundra Dellouise, M'Kenzie Kay & Garland KaZell. **Educ:** Huston-Tillotson Col, Austin, TX, BA, govt & hist, 1985; Sam Houston State Univ, Huntsville, TX; Tex Lutheran Col, Seguin. **Career:** Tex Dept Criminal Justice/ID, Community Educ Prog, asst admin, 1980-90, Terrell Unit, chief classification, 1993-94, asst warden, 1994-97, sr warden, 1997-99; Flakes Family Serv, owner & dir, 1997-; Pleasure Island, Tex, comnr. **Orgs:** Comt Adv Panel, Indust Pk, 1998; assoc minister, Greater Good Hope, 1998-; bd dir, Nelson Credit Corp, 1998; counsr, Nat Inst Corrections, Therapeut Comt, Exec Training New Wardens, 1998; vol, Tex Youth Comn, 1999; vol, Prison Ministry, 1999; vol, Ct App Spec Advocate, 2000. **Home Addr:** 5140 Linda Lane, PO Box 13058, Beaumont, TX 77726, **Home Phone:** (409)892-0085. **Business Addr:** Founder, Director, Flakes Family Service, 5140 Linda Lane, Beaumont, TX 77708-2518, **Business Phone:** (409)892-0085.

### FLAMER, JOHN HENRY

School administrator, association executive. **Personal:** Born Oct 13, 1938, Philadelphia, PA; married Mary Elizabeth Holder; children: Crystal Flamer-Garrison, Dawn Flamer- Parks, Melanie Armstead-Williams, Tamiko Flamer-Rettle, Theodore, Todd, Timothy, John III & Christopher. **Educ:** Southern Ill Univ, BS, 1964, MS, 1975. **Career:** Southern Ill Univ, Job Corps, teacher, coach, 1965, bus affairs, asst vpres, 1968, Affirmative Action Minority Affairs, asst pres; Ill Youth, prin, 1967; EEO US Civil Serv, consult; Nat Affirmative Action Officers, pres, 1973. **Orgs:** State Ill; bd mem, Madison St Clair Co Urban League; pres, Metro Sickle Cell Anemia; Employ Adv Com Inland Steel; Alpha Phi Alpha; vpres, Ill Track & Field Coaches Asn; treas, Nat Black Alliance Grad & Prof Educ; Asn Health Recreation & Phys Educ; Ethnic Adv Comn; Nat Black Staff Network; pres, Ill Inter-col Cross Country Coaches Asn. **Home Addr:** 11 Saddlewood Lane, Edwardsville, IL 62025-2753.

### FLANAGAN, BETTY. See FLANAGAN, ELIZABETH.

### FLANAGAN, ELIZABETH (BETTY FLANAGAN)

Activist, association executive, president (organization). **Career:** Nat Retiree Coun Am Fedn State County & Munic Employees, Dist 47 Retiree Chap, pres, vice chair, 2004-. **Orgs:** Pres, Philadelphia Chap 47. **Special Achievements:** First Black female Retiree Council officer. **Business Addr:** Vice Chair, National Retiree Council of the American Federation of State County & Municipal Employees, 1625 L St NW, Washington, DC 20036-5687, **Business Phone:** (202)429-1000.

### FLANAGAN, DR. T. EARL, JR.

Dentist, president (government). **Personal:** Born Jan 20, 1937, Baltimore, MD; son of Thomas Earl Sr (deceased) and Marjorie B (deceased); married LaVerne M; children: Thomas III, Shelley & Brian. **Educ:** Howard Univ, BS, 1959, DDS, 1966. **Career:** Dentist (retired); pvt pract dentist, 1966; St Elizabeths Hosp, instr intern prog, chief dent officer, 1969; Dept Health & Ment Hyg, pres. **Orgs:** Nat Dent Asn; Am Dent Asn; Acad Gen Dentists; Am Dent Soc Anesthesiol; Am Asn Hosp Dentists State; RT Freeman Dent Soc; Md Dent Soc Anesthesiol; Nat Asn Advan Colored People; Urban League; Kappa Alpha Psi; Chi Delta Mu; fel Am Dent Soc Anesthesiol. **Honors/Awds:** Am Cancer Soc, Harold Krogh Award. **Home Addr:** 6 Homecrest Ct, Silver Spring, MD 20906-1861. **Business Addr:** Dentist, 905 Sheridan St, Hyattsville, MD 20783, **Business Phone:** (301)559-1300.

### FLATEAU, DR. JOHN

Executive director, dean (education). **Personal:** Born Feb 24, 1950, Brooklyn, NY; married Lorraine Witherspoon. **Educ:** Wash Sq Col NY Univ, BA, 1972; Baruch Col, master, 1977; City Univ NY, Grad Ctr, PhD, Am polit & pub policy. **Career:** NYS Comn Health Educ & Illness Prev, prin res analyst; Adult Educ Dist Coun 37 AFSCME & Hunter Col, City Univ NY, teacher, 1968-74; Prog Admin, BED-STUY Summer Prog, supvr, 1968-72; Harlem Youth Develop Ctr, comnwckr, 1976; NY State Assembly Albet Vann NY State Legis, admin asst; Black & Puerto Rican Caucus Inc NY State Legis, exec dir, 1977-78; chief staff to Mayor; NYC Districting Comn, comnr; Nat Black Lay Cath Caucus, youth chmns natl off black caths, bd dir; Bedford Stuyvesant Pastoral Planning Prog, vpres; Bed-stuyvesant Laymen's Convocation, pres; DuBois Bunche Ctr Pub Policy, sr fel, co found & exec dir; Medgar Evers Col, prof pub admin & dean external rels, dean sch bus & dean instnl advan, currently. **Orgs:** Urban Voter Educ Asn; Comm Educ Task Force; founding mem, Vanguard &Independent Dem Asn Inc 56th AD; Kings Co Dem Comn, 1972-; del, NY Judicial Conv 2nd Dist, 1972-; Nat Asn Advan Colored People; Alumni Asns NY Univ/Baruch Col; MLK Jr Alumn Asn; pres, JARM Res Assocs Ltd, 1979-; polit action chmn, Conv Planner Black Agenda Conv Brooklyn, NY, 1980; Black United Front NY Met Chap; Macon-macdonough-lewis-stuyvesant Block Asn; 592 Prospect Pl Tenants Asn; chair, Econ Empowerment Comt, Nat Asn Advan Colored People Brooklyn Br; sr vpres, NYS Urban Develop Corp; exec dir NYS Black & Puerto Rican Legis Caucus; Comnr, NYC Districting Comn; Advisor, NYS Legis Adv Task Force; chairperson, US Census Adv Comt. **Home Addr:** 368 MacDonough St, Brooklyn, NY 11233, **Home Phone:** (718)467-9085. **Business Addr:** Professor, Dean External Relations, Medgar Evers College, 1650 Bedford Ave Rm 2032C, Brooklyn, NY 11201, **Business Phone:** (718)270-5122.

### FLATTS, BARBARA ANN

Lawyer. **Personal:** Born Sep 27, 1951, New York, NY; daughter of Albert Sr and Amy Morris; children: Albert Paul & Amy Christina. **Educ:** Hampton Univ, BA, 1972; Am Univ Wash Col Law, JD, 1974. **Career:** Laborer's Dist & Coun, law clerk, 1973-74; US Dept Labor Benefits Rev Bd, atty adv, 1975-76; Off Corp Coun DC Govt, asst corp coun, 1976-80; US Dept Justice Environ Enforcement Sect, Land & Natural Resources Div, trial atty, 1980; New York Housing Auth Contracts Real Estate & Fin div, atty, 1984; Employ Security Bur, asst atty gen, 1986-87; NY Dept Law, Harlem Regional Off, asst atty gen charge, 1986-2001; NY Supreme Ct Queens County, atty, prin law secy, 2006-; York col, adj prof; City Univ New York, adj prof. **Orgs:** Exec comt bd dir, Coun Legal Educ Opportunity, 1973-75; pres, Am Univ Chap Black Am Law Stud Asn, 1974; Am Bar Asn, 1975-; past secy, Kappa Beta Phi Legal Asn, 1976; bd dir, Wash Urban League, 1977-80; bd dir, Girl Scout Coun Nation's Capital, 1977-81; Juv Justice Adv Comt DC, 1979-80; bd mem, Harlem Legal Servs, 1990-; Alpha Kappa Alpha Sor inc; Wa bar Asn; Alpha Kappa Alpha, Epsilon Pi Omega; connection community coordr Alpha Kappa Alpha; United Negro Col Fund; St Albans Congregational Church; Queens County Bar Asn. **Home Addr:** 15120 Jamaica Ave, Jamaica, NY 11432-3726, **Home Phone:** (718)454-5987. **Business Addr:** Principal Law Secretary, State of New York Law Department, 163 W 125th St 25th Fl, New York, NY 10271-0332, **Business Phone:** (212)961-4408.

### FLEETWOOD, THEREZ

Costume designer, business owner. **Educ:** Fashion Inst Technol, NY, fashion design. **Career:** Prod mgr, New York; designer, 1990-; Therez Fleetwood, owner & designer, currently. **Honors/Awds:** African-American Women of Triumph Award, Allstate Insurance Co; New Day Designer of the Year; One of the New York Museum's Top Designers for their "New York Gets Married" exhibit. **Special Achievements:** Designed the only Afrocentric costumes to be worn by Mickey and Minnie Mouse at Walt Disney World in Orlando;

Books: The Afro Centric Bride, A Style Guide, Amber Books; featured in an array of publications, including Elle, Italian Glamour, Women's Wear Daily, & The New York Times. **Home Addr:** , NJ. **Business Addr:** Owner, Costume Designer, Therez Fleetwood, Dallas, TX, **Business Phone:** (214)815-9325.

### FLEMING, ALICIA DELAMOTHE
Chief executive officer, executive, labor relations manager. **Personal:** Born New York, NY; married John A. **Educ:** NY Univ, BS, 1972, MS, 1980. **Career:** New York Univ Med Ctr, off mgr admin, 1966-79; Booz Allen & Hamilton, mgr non exempt personnel, 1979-81; Time Inc, employ counr, 1981-85; Non-Exempt Recruiting & Develop, mgr, 1985-; A D Fleming Group Inc, pres, 1989-, chief exec officer. **Orgs:** Women Human Resources Mgt, 1983; EDGES, 1985. **Home Addr:** 392 Cent Pk W Suite 19K, New York, NY 10025, **Home Phone:** (212)222-3513. **Business Addr:** President, A D Fleming Group Inc, Rm 720 139 Fulton St, New York, NY 10038, **Business Phone:** (212)227-0909.

### FLEMING, DR. ARTHUR WALLACE
Surgeon. **Personal:** Born Oct 1, 1935, Johnson City, TN; son of Smith George Sr (deceased) and Vivian Cecile Richardson; married Dolores Caffey; children: Arthur Jr, Robyn, Jon, Mark, Robert, Bernadette & Erik S. **Educ:** Ill State Norm Univ, attended 1954; Wayne State Univ, BA, chem, 1965; Univ Mich Med Sch, MD, 1967. **Career:** Detroit Inst Cancer Res, res asst, 1958-61; Walter Reed Army Med Ctr, thoracic & cardiovasc surgeon serv staff, 1972-83; Walter Reed Army Inst Res, dept surg staff, 1974-76, div exp surg chief, 1976-77, dir dept surg, 1977-83; Uniformed Serv Univ Health Sci, assoc prof surg, 1978-83; King-Drew Med Ctr, dir trauma ctr, 1983-, prog dir gen surg & chief surg, 1983-; Charles R Drew Univ Med & Sci, prof & chmn, Dept Surg, 1983; MLK Gen Hosp, chief surg, 1983; La County Martin L King Jr Drew Med Ctr, chief surg, 1983-. **Orgs:** Chmn, Dept Surg Charles R Drew Univ Med & Sci, 1983-; Trauma dirs comt, Los Angeles Co, 1984-; bd dir, Am Col Surgeons Soc Calif Chap, 1986-; pres, Soc Black Acad Surgeons, 1986-91. **Honors/Awds:** Hoff Medal for Research, 1974; Gold Medal paper, Forum on Progress in Surgery Southeastern Surgical Congress, 1977; The Surgeon General's "A" prefix Highest Military Medical Professional Attainment, 1981; The Legion Merit Investigative projects combat casualty care pioneering of autologous blood transfusions US Army, 1983; Meritorious Serv Award USAF, 1984; William Sinkler Award, Surgical Sect Nat Medical Asn, 1990; Friend of the Nurses Award, King-Dew Med Ctr Nursing Dept, 1990; Commendation, Dir Trauma Ctr, 1989; Lifetime Achievement Award, Charles Drew Univ. **Special Achievements:** He was one of three African American students accepted into a class of 200 medical students. **Home Addr:** 6671 Crest Rd, Rancho Palos Verdes, CA 90275-5425, **Home Phone:** (310)541-6770. **Business Addr:** Chairman, Charles R Drew University of Medicine & Science, 12021 S Wilmington Ave, Los Angeles, CA 90059, **Business Phone:** (310)668-4321.

### FLEMING, DAVID AARON
Architect, engineer, government official. **Personal:** Born Aug 21, 1963, Washington, DC; son of Alton Leonard and Charlotte Ann Long. **Educ:** Stanford Univ, BSEE, 1986, MSME, 1988; Ill Inst Technol, MAr, 1992; Northwestern Univ, PhD, 1991-. **Career:** Cong Black Caucus, cong intern, 1982; IBM, engr, 1983; Johns Hopkins Applied Physics Lab, engr, 1985-87; Veteran's ADM Hosp, product designer, 1988; General Electric, product designer, 1989; Amoco Oil, engr, 1989-92; Walt Disney Imagineering, designer imagineer, 1992-; Tek Designs Int, engr, 1996-; US Patent & Trademark Office, patent examiner, 1998-99. **Orgs:** Nat Soc Black Engrs, nat chap, 1989-91, nat publs chair, 1987-89; Nat Stud Support Coun Africa, nat co-chap, 1991-95; Alpha Phi Alpha Fraternity Inc. **Honors/Awds:** Gen Electric, Latimer Scholar; Consortium for Degrees for Minorities Eng, Fel, 1985; Nat Org Minority Architects, Scholar, 1989; Am Inst Architects, Roche Traveling Scholar, 1990; Walt Disney Imagineering, Imaginations Design Contest, firsst Place, 1992. **Special Achievements:** Co-designed robotic sign language machine "Dexter, The Fingerspelling Robotic Hand," 1988; 4 patents in US. **Business Addr:** Engineer, Tek Designs International, 506 12th St NE, Washington, DC 20002-6310, **Business Phone:** (202)543-7297.

### FLEMING, ELLIS T.
Executive. **Personal:** Born Mar 26, 1933, Baltimore, MD; son of Lewis and Lavanna; married Subenia Mae Pettie. **Educ:** Brooklyn Col, Indust Rels, 1957; CCNY, attended 1959; La SalleLaw Corresp United Laundry & Dry Cleaners Baltimore Course, 1963. **Career:** BlackNY Proc Dist, adminr dir mil personnel prog, 1957-62; Haryou-Act, asst exec dir prog, 1963-66; New Breed Ent, part-owner, 1966-70; Jackie Robinson Mgt Corp, 1972; org & prog consult, Bed Stuy Lawyers Asn, Gov Nelson Rockefeller, White House, 1972-73; United Laundry & DryCleaners Baltimore Inc, pres, 1998; Exchange Traded Funds Assoc BusCons, pres; Exchange Traded Funds Financial Serv, pres; Nat Bankers Asn; City Univ NY, Hostos Col, Bd Educ Health & Phys Educ Dept, consult exec dir; Span Am Merchants Asn; Congressman Edolphus Towns eleventh CD New York, spec asst. **Orgs:** Dir, E Flatbush Urban Planning Study, 1978-79; field coordr, Brooklyn Boro Pres, 1985; co-found & exec dir, Marcus Garvey Health Facil; chair, EF Comn Corp; found & pres, Comn EF Pres; Oper Breadbasket; Congr Black Caucus Round table; co-found, EF Church AVMerch Asn; Fed Block Asn; contrib writer, Consequences Powerlessness, Youth Ghetto; consult, Clothing Mfg & Retailers; lect bus comt; Planning Bd Regional Planning Asn NY, NJ, CT; White House Consult prog Black Am; gen adv, Nat Youth Movement; adv, Opportunity Ind Ctrs NY. **Honors/Awds:** Brooklyn Jaycees, 1964; Man of the Year Award. **Special Achievements:** Writer & contributor "Consequences of Powerlessness" authored Dr KennethClark; author "The Great Deluge". **Home Addr:** 2100 N Smallwood St, Baltimore, MD 21216-3220, **Home Phone:** (410)462-5590.

### FLEMING, GEORGE
School administrator, football player, government official. **Personal:** Born Feb 22, 1937, Dallas, TX; son of Lilla N and A R; married Tina Bradley; children: Sonja & Yemi. **Educ:** Univ Wash, Seattle, WA, BA, bus admin. **Career:** Football player, government official (retired); Wash Huskies, kicker, 1960-61; Oakland Raiders, 1961-62, Winnipeg Blue Bombers, 1963-65; Wash Sec of State, Olympia, WA, examiner foreign corps, 1965-66; Wash-Idaho area Pacific Northwest Bell US West Commun, Seattle, WA, employment asst, 1966-70, commun cons, Seattle area, 1970-73, personnels up, Wash-Idaho area, 1973-75, mgr econ develop, Wash-Idaho area, 1975; community develop mgr; State Wash, state rep, 1968-70, state sen, dist 37, 1971-91; US W Communs, Seattle, employee; Seattle Pub Schs, exec dir external rels, 1991-94, dir govt rels, 1995; Kings county, dept transp, dir gov rels. **Orgs:** Am Indust Develop Coun; pres, Pac Northwest Indust Develop Coun; Econ Develop Coun Puget Sound; bd dir, Randolph Carter; vice chair, Dem Caucus, 1973-80, chmn, 1980-88; adv bd, Urban, Racial, Rural & Disadvantaged Educ; pres, Econ Develop Coun Wash; Nat Asn Advan Colored People; Rainer Valley Enterprise Ctr; fiscal adv comt, Nat Conf State Legislators; bus adv comm, Puget Sound Chamber Com; dir, Econ Devel Execs Wash; Mason; bd dir, Seattle Sports Comn. **Special Achievements:** First African American to be elected to the Washington State Senate, 1970.

### FLEMING, GWENDOLYN R. KEYES
Lawyer. **Personal:** Born Nov 2, 1968, Livingston, NJ; daughter of Andrew and Ursula; married Randal; children: 2. **Educ:** Douglass Col, Rutgers Univ, BS, finance, 1990; Emory Univ Sch Law, JD, 1993. **Career:** DeKalb County, sr asst solicitor gen, 1993-94, solicitor gen, 1999-2004, dist atty, 2005-10; Fulton County, sr asst dist atty, 1994-97; New Birth Church, visitor, 1999-2010; Stone Mountain Judicial Circuit, dist atty, 2005-10; US Environ Protection Agency, regional adminr, 2010-13; US Environ Protection Agency, chief staff, 2013-15; Immigration & Customs Enforcement, Dept Homeland Security, prin legal advisor, 2015-. **Orgs:** State Bar Ga, 1993-; Ga Asn Black Women Attys, 1993-2010; DeKalb Lawyers Asn, 1996-2010; Leadership DeKalb, 1999-2010; pres, Ga Asn Solicitors-Gen, 2003-04; client, St. Phillip AME Church, 2008; bd mem, Ga Ctr Child Advocacy, 2007-10; Nat Asn Advan Colored People, DeKalb Chap; Nat Coun Negro Women, DeKalb Chap; chair, Admis Comt Emory Black Law Students Alumni Adv Bd; DeKalb County Domestic Violence Task Force, Subcomt DV Fatality Rev, chair, pres, Emory Alumni Assoc., Dist Atty's Asn GA; DeKalb Rape Crisis Ctr; pres, Emory Univ Sch Law Alumni Asn Exec Comt; Am Bar Asn. **Honors/Awds:** Award for High Academic Achievement, Dignity, Integrity, Service and Commitment to the Law in Georgia, Ga Asn Black Women Lawyers, 1993; Black Law Students Asn Distinguished Alumni Award, Emory Univ Sch Law, 1996; Communities of America Trail Blazer Award, 1998; Millennium Diva Award, 1999; Douglass Col Alumni Hall of Fame, inductee, 2001; Chief Justice Robert Benham Community Service Award, Ga Supreme Ct, 2001; Outstanding Atlanta, honoree, 2002-03; Award for distinguished service and leadership, DeKalb Rotary Coun, 2003; Emory Univ School of Law Distinguished Alumni Award, 2007; List of Georgia's 100 Most Powerful & Influential Women, Women Looking Ahead News Magazines. **Special Achievements:** First African-American woman elected to the offices of Solicitor-General and District Attorney in DeKalb County. **Business Addr:** Principal Legal Advisor, Immigration and Customs Enforcement, 500 12th St SW Stop 5600, Washington, DC 20536-5600, **Business Phone:** (703)603-3400.

### FLEMING, DR. JOHN EMORY
Museum director. **Personal:** Born Aug 3, 1944, Morganton, NC; son of James E and Mary E; married Barbara Durr; children: Tuliza & Diara. **Educ:** Berea Col, BA, 1966; Univ Ky, attended 1967; Univ Malawi; Howard Univ, MA, PhD, am hist, 1974; Univ Calif, Berkeley, Calif, Mus Mgt Inst. **Career:** Ky Civil Rights Comn, community serv & educ specialist, 1966-67; Peace Corps, Malawi, Africa, visual aids specialist & adminr, 1967-69; Youth Pride Inc, Dept Training & Educ, Wash, DC, supvr, 1970-71; US Civil Rights Comn, Fed Eval Div prog analyst, 1971-72; Howard Univ, Dept Hist, asst prof hist, 1974-78; Ohio Hist Soc, Columbus, OH, afro-am mus proj dir, 1980-88; Nat Afro-Am Mus & Cult Ctr, dir, 1988-98; Nat Underground Rr Freedom Ctr, dir & chief operating officer, 1998-2000; Cincinnati Mus Ctr, Union Terminal, Cincinnati, OH, vpres mus, 2001-07, dir emer, currently; Univ Cincinnati, Dept Hist, Cincinnati, OH, adj prof, 2005-07; Int African Am Mus, interim dir, 2009-; Miss Civil Rights Mus, sr consult, 2012. **Orgs:** Alpha Phi Alpha; Nat Asn Advan Colored People, 1974-87; sr fel Inst Study Educ Policy, Howard Univ, 1974-80; bd, J Negro Hist, 1982-96; vpres bd, Art Community Expression, 1984-87; bd, Columbus Area Leadership Prog, 1985-89; panel, Columbus Found, 1986-87; vpres, Ohio Mus Asn, 1989-90; bd mem, adv coun, Mus Trustee Asn, 1989-95; prog comt, Am Asn State & Local Hist, 1988; nomination comt, 1989; exec coun, vpres, Assoc Study Afro-Am Life & Hist, 1990-92; exec comt, Am Asn Mus, 1990-91; chair prog comt, MAP Survr & Accreditation Team Visitor, 1992; nominating comt, 1993; Hons Comt, 1994-97; bd mem, Am Asn Mus, 1990-95; pres & bd mem, African-Am Mus Asn, 1991-96; White House Conf Travel & Tourism, 1995; chair, Ohio Arts Coun; Ohio Becentennial Comn, 1996-03; Yellow Springs Hist Soc; nat pres, Asn Study African Am Life & Hist, 2007-09; Southern Hist Asn; Sigma Pi Phi; Ohio Travel Indust Adv Coun; Ohio Asn Hist Soc & Mus; Nc Hist & Lit Socs; adv panel, Nat Trust Hist Preserv; Nat Endowment Humanities; Nat Afro-Am Mus Found; Montgomery County Hist Socs Bd; Knight Found; Hist Rec Adv Bd; Getty Leadership Adv Comt; Greene County Hist Socs; Gail Res Publishers Adv Bd 6th Ed Afro-Am Almanac; Eastern Ill Mus Studies Adv Bd; Dr Martin Luther King Memorial Comt; Bicentennial Comn Northwest Ordinance & Const; Asn Mid-W Mus; bd trustee, Berea Col, 2007-. **Honors/Awds:** Distinguished Alumni Award, Berea Col; The Franklin H Williams Award for Outstanding Community Service, Nat Peace Corps; Lifetime Achievement Award, African Am Mus Asn; Carter G Woodson Award, Berea Col; Outstanding Professional Achievement Award, Ohio Mus Asn; Martin Luther King Award; Ohioana Outstanding Humanities Award for Distinguished Service to Ohio in African American History, Ohiano Libr. **Special Achievements:** Author: The Lengthening Shadow of Slavery: Historical Justification for Affirmative Action for Blacks in Higher Education, Howard Univ Press, 1976; Affirmative Action for Blacks in Higher Education, A Report, Howard Univ Press, 1978; The Case for Affirmative Action for Blacks in Higher Education, Howard Univ Press, 1978; A Summer Remembered: A Memoir, Silver Maple Publ, 2005. **Home Addr:** 1308 Corry St, Yellow Springs, OH 45387, **Home Phone:** (513)767-1259. **Business Addr:** Director Emeritus, Cincinnati Museum Center, 1301 Western Ave, Cincinnati, OH 45203, **Business Phone:** (513)287-7000.

### FLEMING, DR. JUANITA W.
Educator. **Personal:** Born Lincolnton, NC; daughter of Joseph and Bertha; married William; children: Billy & Bobby. **Educ:** Hampton Univ, BSN, 1957; Univ Chicago, MA, nursing educ, 1959; Univ Md, jour & human develop; Cath Univ Am, PhD, educ psychol, 1969. **Career:** DC Genl Hosp, head nurse, 1957-58; DC Bur PH, PH nurse, 1959-60; Freedman's Hosp Sch Nursing, instr, 1962-65; Howard Univ Dept Ped, PH nursing consult, 1965-66; Univ Ky, Col Nursing, prof nursing, asst dean grad educ, 1975-81, assoc dean & dir grad studies, 1982-85, assoc vice chancellor acad affairs, 1984-91, spec asst pres, acad affairs & prof nursing & educ, 1991-2001, prof emer, 2003-; Ky State Univ, fac mem, interim vpres acad affairs, 2003-06; prof emer, 2006-. **Orgs:** Nat Acad Sci Inst Med; Am Acad Nursing. **Home Addr:** 316 Exum Ct, Frankfort, KY 40601-3020. **Business Addr:** Professor Emeritus, University of Kentucky, 138 Leader Ave, Lexington, KY 40506-9983.

### FLEMING, JUNE H.
Government official, manager, association executive. **Personal:** Born Jun 24, 1938, Little Rock, AR; daughter of Ethel Thompson Dwellingham and Herman Dwellingham; married Roscoe L; children: Ethel & Roscoe Lee III. **Educ:** Talladega Col, BA, 1953; Drexel Univ, MLS, 1954; Stanford Univ, cert, 1974. **Career:** Government officer (retired); Brooklyn Pub Libr, br librn, 1954-55; Little Rock Sch Syst, librn, 1955-56; Phil Smith Col, assoc prof, 1960-66; Palo Alto Calif, dir librn, 1967-81; Palo Alto Calif, city mgr, 1992-2000; City Franklin, interim city mgr, 2012. **Orgs:** Soroptimsit Club, 1980-82; adv bd, YWCA, 1983-; Peninsula Links, 1986-; Delta Sigma Theta Rotary, 1988-; High St United Methodist Church; PDCCC Local Col Bd, 2013-. **Honors/Awds:** Woman of Vision Award, 1997. **Home Addr:** 200 Sheridan Ave Suite 303, Palo Alto, CA 94306, **Home Phone:** (650)321-6288. **Business Addr:** Interim City Manager, City of Franklin Virginia, 207 W 2nd Ave, Franklin, VA 23851, **Business Phone:** (757)562-8503.

### FLEMING, PATRICIA STUBBS
Social worker, federal government official. **Personal:** Born Mar 17, 1937, Philadelphia, PA; daughter of Fredrick D Stubbs and Marion Turner Stubbs; married Harold S; children: Douglass, Craig & Gordon. **Educ:** Vassar Col, BA, 1957; Univ Pa; Cranbrook Acad Fine Arts; NY Univ; Pa Acad Fine Arts. **Career:** Legis asst Rep Augustus Hawkins, 1971-73, Rep Shirley Chisholm, 1973-75, Rep Andrew Young, Comm Rules, US House Rep, 1975-77; Educ & Welfare, spec asst secy health, 1977-78; Legis US Dept Educ, asst sec, 1979-80, dep asst sec, 1980-81; James H. Lowry & Assocs, sr pub policy assoc, 1981-83; Rep Ted Weiss, admin asst, 1983-86; Sub comt Human Resources & Inter-Govt Rels, US House Rep, prof staff mem, 1986-93; Dept Health & Human Servs, spec asst secy, 1993-94; Interim Nat Aids Policy, coordr, 1994; White House, Off Nat AIDS Policy, dir, 1994-97; Patricia S Fleming Assocs, HIV & AIDS consult, artist, currently. **Orgs:** Pres, Prev Works Needle Exchange Nation's Capitol; Foundry Gallery. **Honors/Awds:** Education Policy Fel Prog, 1971-72. **Special Achievements:** Articles on same topics in a variety of Publishing. **Business Addr:** AIDS Consultant, Patricia S Fleming Associates, 6009 Mass Ave, Bethesda, MD 20816, **Business Phone:** (301)320-5420.

### FLEMING, PROF. RAYMOND RICHARD
Educator. **Personal:** Born Feb 27, 1945, Cleveland, OH; son of Theodore Robert and Ethel Dorsey; married Nancy Runge; children: John K, Peter C & Stephen R. **Educ:** Univ Notre Dame, IN, BA, 1967; Univ Florence, Italy, attended 1968; Harvard Univ, Cambridge, MA, 1969, PhD, comparative lit, 1976. **Career:** St. Mary's Col, Upward Bound prog, asst dir; Harvard Univ, Woodrow Wilson, Fel, 1968; Univ Notre Dame, Notre Dame Ind, ital instr, 1969-72; Univ Calif, San Diego Calif, asst prof, 1973-80; Alexander Von Humboldt Ger, fel 1978; Miami Univ, Oxford Ohio, assoc prof Ital, 1980-87, asst dean grad sch, assoc dean grad sch, 1985-87; Penn State Univ, Univ Pk, Pa, prof com lit & Ital, 1987-95; Fla State Univ, distinguished prof ital, Dept Inter disciplinary Humanities, prof, John Francis Dugan prof Mod Lang & Humanities, 1995-; Djerassi artist residence, Woodside, stint, Calif, 2003; Poetry: "Ice and Honey", Dorrance, 1979; "Diplomatic Relations", Lotus, 1982; "Keats, Leopardi and Holderlin: The Poet as Priest of the Absolute", Garland, 1987; Periodicals: "Richmond Times-Dispatch", 1987; "Journal of Blacks in Higher Education", 1993. **Orgs:** Dante Soc Am; Am Coun Learned Soc; Pac & Ancient Mod Lang Asn; pres, Am Conf Romanticism, 1998-2000; exec bd mem, Int Asn Study Ital Lang & Lit, 1998-2002. **Home Addr:** 4015 Kilmartin Dr, Tallahassee, FL 32308-2861, **Home Phone:** (850)668-1795. **Business Addr:** John Francis Dugan Professor of Modern Languages & Humanities, Florida State University, 432 Diffenbaugh Bldg Suite 1549, Tallahassee, FL 32306, **Business Phone:** (850)644-1758.

### FLEMING, VERN
Basketball player, basketball coach. **Personal:** Born Feb 4, 1962, New York, NY; married Michelle Clarke; children: Vern Jr. **Educ:** Ga Univ, attended 1984. **Career:** Basketball player (retired), basketball coach; Ind Pacers, guard, 1984-95, asst coach, 1999; NJ Nets, guard, 1995-96; Limoges, 1996-97.

### FLEMING, VERNON CORNELIUS
Manager. **Personal:** Born Dec 19, 1952, Louisa County, VA; son of William E and Josephine Robinson; married Gloria A Murray; children: Gino & Sean. **Educ:** Hampton Univ, BA, sociol, 1974; Col William & Mary, MBA, bus admin, 1980; AUS Command & Gen Staff Col, dipl, 1987. **Career:** Col William & Mary, asst prof mil sci, 1980-83; Procter & Gamble, pur mgr, 1983-84, sr pur mgr, 1984-95, pur grp mgr, 1983-2008, second vice chair, 2008; JM Smucker Co, mgr indirect pur, 2008-11; VCF Consult LLC, chief exec officer & pres, 2011; MeadWestvaco, sr mgr-indirect sourcing, 2011-13; Performance Food Group, dir strategic sourcing, 2013-. **Orgs:** Chmn bd dir, Williamsburg Head Start, 1982-83; Res Officers Asn, 1983-; Prime Mover, Purchases Support Grp, 1989-94; Louisa County Hist Soc, 2002; Inst Supply Mgt, 2012; pres, bd dir, Shady Grove Rosenwald Sch Inc, 2013; advisor, Customer Adv Bd -EnerNOC, 2016; bd dir, Goochland County Hist Soc, 2016; Kappa Alpha Psi Frat; cochmn, prog comt, Nat Black MBA Asn; Nat Hampton Alumni Asn; pres coun, Boy Scouts Am; bd dir & life mem, Kappa Alpha Psi Frat; chmn, Cert Comt, vice chmn, bd dir & vice chmn, Md, DC, Minority

Supplier Develop Coun; life mem, Kappa Alpha Psi Fraternity. **Honors/Awds:** Service Award, Peninsula League Youth, 1982; Officer of the Year, Cincinnati Chap Kappa Alpha Psi, 1985; Polemarch's Award, Cincinnati Chap Kappa Alpha Psi, 1987; Alumni of the Year, Hampton Univ Alumni Asn, 1995; Silver Beaver Award, Boy Scouts Am, 1996; Md/DC MSDC Chairman Award, 2001; Supplier Diversity Advocate of The Year, 2001; Purchases Crystal Award, Procter & Gamble. **Home Addr:** 8225 Elko Dr, Ellicott City, MD 21043, **Home Phone:** (410)418-5541. **Business Addr:** Second Vice Chairperson, Procter & Gamble, 11103 Pepper Rd, Hunt Valley, MD 21030, **Business Phone:** (410)785-5549.

### FLEMING-RIFE, ANITA

Consultant, president (organization), college teacher. **Personal:** Born Jan 10, 1946, Des Moines, IA; daughter of Charles R (deceased) and Mary C (deceased); married Donald Rife; children: Donnyta, Donald & Charles. **Educ:** Univ Northern Colo, Greeley, BA, commun, 1979, MA, jour, 1990; Southern ill Univ, Carbondale, PhD, jour, 1997. **Career:** KARK-TV, Little Rock, producer & resr, 1982-86; Univ Northern Colo, Greeley, teaching asst, 1986-88, asst prof, 1995-98, spec asst pres, currently; Southern Ill Univ, Carbondale, teaching & res asst, 1988-89; UN Secretariat, NYC, proj mgr & pub info officer, 1992-93; Pa State Univ, State Col, asst prof, 1998-2003; consult, Fleming-Rife Cons, State Col, 2003-04; Lock Haven Univ Pa, assoc prof, 2004-05; Clark Atlanta Univ, assoc prof, dir & chair mass media arts, 2005-; Un Oper Somalia, pub info officer; Penn State Univ, univ pres. **Orgs:** Nat Womens Studies Asn, 1987-89; Colo Womens Studies Asn, 1987-89. Asn Educrs Journ Mass Commun, 1989-; Black Grad Stud Asn, 1989-90; Alpha Kappa Alpha Sorority, Gamma Kappa Omega Chap, 1991; fel, AEJMC's Freedom Forum Teaching Workshop, Ind Univ, 1997; Ford Found, 1998; Asn Educ Jour & Mass Commun; pres, Asn Educ Journalism; Galesburg Regional Econ Develop Asn; chair, Europ Diversity Awards Comt, 2009-10; Col Communs Diversity Comt; Col Humanities; Social Sci Diversity Comt; bd dir, E Africa Community Ctr; chair, Nat Summit Africa Wash, 2000; UNC Pres Kay Norton's exec team; Human Resources Off; Equity & Diversity Coun & campus governance groups; chair, Equity & Diversity Award Comt; boards dir, Adventures Health, Educ & Agr Develop; Africa Agenda; E Africa Community Colo. **Home Addr:** 6805 Old Waterloo Rd Apt 832, Baltimore, MD 21227-6747, **Home Phone:** (410)457-5805. **Business Addr:** Special Assistant to the President for Equity & Diversity, University of Northern Colorado, 1862 10th Ave, Greeley, CO 80639, **Business Phone:** (970)351-1834.

### FLEMMING, CAROLYN

Librarian, editor. **Personal:** Born Jan 11, 1946, Orange, NY; daughter of James Ralph and Helen McCrary; married Ronald Howard I; children: Ronald H II, Solomon N J, Jasmin A K, Nimrod M, Jade C, Jewell C, Joy C, Janicka J, Jafrica & Jamaica B. **Educ:** Drake Col Bus, attended 1965; Va Union Univ, attended 1966. **Career:** Fine Print News, ed; Testing Dept, Va Union, 1966; Astara Inc, Mystery Sch, 1976; The Rosicrucian Order AMORC; Glendale Pub Libr, City Glendale, ed & libr adminr, currently. **Orgs:** Dir, Fashion Show Blacks Arts Festival, 1970; dir, Art & Show Black Arts Festival, 1970; NRA; Nu-Buff Sportsman Club; Regent Sportsman Club. **Home Addr:** 806 Fillmore Ave, Buffalo, NY 14212-1356, **Home Phone:** (716)855-3810. **Business Addr:** Editor, Library Administrator, Glendale Public Library, 222 E Harvard St, Glendale, CA 91205, **Business Phone:** (818)548-3999.

### FLEMMING, DR. CHARLES STEPHEN

Educator, ambassador, diplomat. **Personal:** Born Oct 30, 1948, St. Lucia; son of James and Mary Magdalene Whitney; children: Albert, Charles, Alika, Nadine & Sean. **Educ:** City Col NY, New York, NY, BA, 1977; NY Univ, New York, NY, MA, 1979, MPhil, 1984, PhD, 1985. **Career:** Malcolm King Col, New York, NY, instr, 1979-81; New York Univ, adj instr, 1981-84; Bronx Community Col, New York, NY, adj instr, 1981-89; Mission St Lucia UN, New York, NY, ambassador, 1984-89; Bronx Community Col, City Univ New York, adj asst prof polit sci, 1996-; Bronx Bor Pres's Off, dir res & real estate, 1998-; Prime Holdings, bd advisor; Ashlin Realty, prin broker, 2003; Briza Technologies Sr Exec Team, chief financial officer, currently; Ashlin Capital, pres & chief exec officer, currently. **Orgs:** Am Polit Sci Asn, 1980-; Caribbean Studies Asn, 1987-; Int Polit Sci Asn, 1988-; Int Studies Asn, 1988-; Int Asn Permanent Rep, 1989-. **Honors/Awds:** Commendation, City Govt New York, 1979; Pi Sigma Alpha Nat Polit Sci Hon Soc, 1980; Taraknath Das Prize, New York Univ, 1983. **Special Achievements:** Author: The Zone of Peace Declamation, 1985. **Home Addr:** Grand Central St, PO Box 4254, New York, NY 10163-6030, **Home Phone:** (212)208-4685. **Business Addr:** President, Chief Executive Officer, Ashlin Capital LLC, 44 Wall St 12th Fl, New York, NY 10005, **Business Phone:** (212)208-4685.

### FLEMMING, CLENTE

Banker. **Educ:** Univ SC, BS, bus, 1999. **Career:** Bank Am, sr vpres, personal exec, 1970-2000; Flemming Group Inc, founder, pres, 2000-; SC Community Bank, pres & chief exec officer, 2002-12. **Orgs:** Chmn & bd mem, City Yr, Inc; vpres, SC Diversity Coun; bd chmn, SC Am Red Cross; First Steps Ad bd; trustee, Zion Baptist Church Bd; exec dir, Columbia Chap 100 Black Men Am; chmn & bd mem, Columbia Soc Human Resource Mgt; Agency Head Salary Comn; bd mem, United Way midlands; comnr, SC State Housing Finance Authority; bd dir, SC Chamber Com. **Honors/Awds:** Distinguished Black Alumnus, Univ SC Black Alumni Coun; Professional of the Year Award, Columbia Soc Human Resource Mgt, 1995; Order of Palmetto, Gov SC, 1999; Lifetime Service & Achievement Award, Rudolph Canzater Scholarship Fund, Inc. **Special Achievements:** One of South Carolina's top 25 African-American influences by South Carolina Business, Vision magazine; Mayor and City of Columbia proclaimed December 8, 1999, as "Clente Flemming Day, ? and presented him with a Key to the City. **Home Addr:** 200 Hastings Pt Dr, Columbia, SC 29203-9101. **Business Addr:** President, Founder, The Flemming Group Inc, 3800 N Main St Suite D, Columbia, SC 29203-6446, **Business Phone:** (803)540-1929.

### FLEMMING, LILLIAN BROCK

Government official, educator. **Personal:** Born Jul 27, 1949, Greenville, SC; daughter of James Dennis and Lila Mae Martin; married Reverend J M; children: Rodrecus, Johnny, Tonjalyn, Sherretta, Davit, Ranando, Ebony, J M II & Emanuel. **Educ:** Furman Univ, BA, 1971; MEd, math educ, 1975; Furman Univ, honory doctor philos, 2014. **Career:** Southside High Sch, math teacher, 1971; Greenville County Schs, high sch math teacher, 1971-94, prof employ recruiter, 1995-; Greenville City Coun, pres, 1981-, vice mayor pro-tem, 1983-89; Donaldson Ctr, comnr, 1987-; City Greenville, Mayor Pro Tem, coun mem, 1989-2009, vice mayor pro tem, coun mem, 2011-; Bergamo, Italy, rep; Mountain View Baptist Church-Greenville. **Orgs:** Vpres, 1978-79, pres, 1979-80, Greenville County Educ Asn, 1978-79; bd dir, Sunbelt Human Advan Resource Ent, 1981-88; Dem Nat Conv, 1984, 1988; Nat Coun Negro Women; Nat Asn Advan Colored People; dir, Ronald McDonald House; Greenville Dem Women; Phyllis Wheatley Post Fells; Nat Edu Asn; Greenville Cent Area Partnership; Southernside Community Ctr; chmn bd, Southernside Block Partnership, 1994-; trustee, Furman Univ, 1995-2001; bd dir, Brockwood Sr Housing, chmn bd, 1996-; founder, Conf Black Munic Elected Officials SC, pres, 2000-02; pres, Munic Asn SC, 2003-04; bd dir, AdvanceSC, 2007-; pres, Blue Star Mothers Am, SC Chap 3, 2011-15; S.H.A.R.E. Action Agency Bd, 2007-15; Boy Scouts Blue Ridge Coun Bd, 2013-; Girl Scouts Mountains-Midlands Bd, 2014-. **Honors/Awds:** Teacher of the Year, Southside High Sch, 1974, 1976, 1993, 1994; Outstanding Secondary Educator America, 1976; Outstanding Woman of America, 1977; Community Service Client Council of Western Carolina, 1981; Citizen of the Year, Client Coun Western Carolina, 1982; Outstanding Black American, 1982; Human Rel Greenville County Educ Asn, 1984; Cooper White Humanitarian Award, Greenville County Educ Human Rel Comn, 1984; Outstanding Community Service, Epsilon Iota Zeta Chap Sor, 1984; Distinguished Service Award, Mt View Baptist Church, 1988; Political Service Award, SC Baptist Educ & Missionary Conv, 1988; Outstanding Phyllis Wheatley Post Fellow Award, 1989; William F Gibson Service Award, Greenville, Nat Asn Advan Colored People, 1990; Martin Luther King Leadership Award, Phyllis Wheatley Leadership Orgn, 1991; Community Service Award, Azah Temple, 1991; Sch Dist Greenville County, Third Runner-Up for Teacher of the Year, 1993-94; Woman of Distinction Award, Girl Scouts Blue Ridge Coun, 1994; Lillian Brock Flemming Leadership Award, Furman Univ; Women's Triumph Award for State & Local Govt, SC Gov Comn; 2000; Richard Furman Baptist Heritage Award, 2002; Bellsouth SC African American History Maker, 2004; Most Influential African American in Greenville, Nat Asn Advan Colored People, 2006; Amy Kay Stubbs Women of Achievement Award, YMCA, 2008; One of the 21 Jewels of Black History of Greenville County by Beyond Differences, 2008; Alumni Service Award, Furman Univ, 2012. **Special Achievements:** First Black to be elected vice mayor pro tempore in City of Greenville; First black to be elected mayor pro tempore in City of Greenville; First black female to be elected to Greenville City Council; First city council member to be elected to five consecutive terms since the 1960's; One of the first three African American women to attend Furman University in Greenville, South Carolina, 1967. **Home Addr:** 398 Oscar St, Greenville, SC 29601, **Home Phone:** (864)241-8677. **Business Addr:** Professional Employment Recruiter, District 2 Representative, Greenville County Schools, 301 E Camperdown Way, Greenville, SC 29601, **Business Phone:** (864)355-3976.

### FLETCHER, ALPHONSE, JR. (ALPHONSE BUDDY FLETCHER, JR.)

Chairperson, founder (originator), chief executive officer. **Personal:** Born Dec 19, 1965, New London, CT; son of Alphonse and Bettye; married Ellen K Pao; children: Matilda Pao. **Educ:** Harvard Col, AB, appl mathematics, 1987; Yale Sch Forestry & Environ Studies, MS, environ mgt, 2004. **Career:** Bear, Stearns & Co., vpres; Gen Elec Co's Kidder, Peabody & Co., sr vpres; Fletcher Asset Mgt Inc, founder, chmn & chief exec officer, 1991-. **Orgs:** Harvard Republican Club; pres, exclusive Phoenix SK club; Alphonse Fletcher Univ Professorship; trustee, Inauguration Pres-Elect Barack Obama; Nat Asn Advan Colored People. **Honors/Awds:** Bank St Col Educ, hon degree; Clarkson Univ, hon degree; Conn Col, hon degree; State Univ New York, Albany, hon degree; Ernst & Young New York City, Entrepreneur of the Year, 1999; Sponsors for Educational Opportunity, Leadership Award, 2002; United Negro College Fund, Extraordinary Black Man Award, 2004; Harvard Gay & Lesbian Caucus, Civil Rights Award, 2005; Morehouse College, Candle in the Dark, 2006; "Black Enterprise", 75 Most Powerful Blacks on Wall Street, 2011. **Home Addr:** , San Francisco, CA. **Business Addr:** Founder, Chairman, Fletcher Asset Management Inc, 48 Wall St, New York, NY 10005, **Business Phone:** (212)480-2141.

### FLETCHER, DR. ANTHONY M.

Cardiologist. **Personal:** son of Lawrence and Dr Patricia. **Educ:** Xavier Univ; Univ Cincinnati Col Med, MD, 1980. **Career:** George Wash Med Ctr, residency; Georgetown Univ Hosp, residency, fel cardiol; St Vincent Infirmary Med Ctr, cardiologist; pvt pract; Cardiol & Med Clin, cardiologist, internist, currently. **Orgs:** Exec coun, Heart Ball, 2002; Heart Walk; treas, Heartland Affil Bd; dir, Cath labs; bd gov, Am Col Cardiol; Am Bd Internal Med; pres, Little Rock Am Heart Asn Bd, currently. **Honors/Awds:** Worthen-Cornett Award, Am Heart Asn Cent Ark Heart Ball, 2003. **Business Addr:** Cardiologist, Internist, Cardiology & Medicine Clinic, 5315 W 12th St, Little Rock, AR 72204, **Business Phone:** (501)664-0941.

### FLETCHER, DR. BETTYE WARD

Management consultant, educator, administrator. **Educ:** Tougaloo Col, BA, sociol, 1970; Atlanta Univ, MS, social work, 1972; Univ Ala, DSW, 1986. **Career:** Ctr Substance Abuse Prev, comm chmn; Jackson State Univ, grad dean, vpres res & develop, 1999, interim pres, 1999-2000, prof social, Jake Ayers Inst Res, fac, currently; Prof Assoc Inc, founder, pres & chief exec officer, currently; Miss Dept Human Serv, exec dir, 2000; US Dept Health & Human Serv, Substance Abuse & Ment Health Serv Admin, Adv Coun, mem, currently; Miss Econ Coun, chief advan officer, principle investr & proj dir, dir human serv; Miss Urban Res Ctr, founder. **Orgs:** Bd dir, Community Matters Inc; bishop, United Methodist Church; pres, Miss Comn Status Women; bd trustee, Miss Low-Income Child Care Initiative. **Honors/Awds:** Honor doctorate, alma mater, 1999. **Special Achievements:** First woman & first sitting campus administrator to be named president at Jackson State University. **Business Addr:** President, Chief Executive Officer, Professional Associates Inc, 217B Katherine Dr, Flowood, MS 39232, **Business Phone:** (601)979-2434.

### FLETCHER, BILL. See FLETCHER, WILLIAM G, JR.

### FLETCHER, CLIFF

Executive. **Career:** WWWZ-FM, pres; WJNI-FM, gen mgr, currently. **Orgs:** SC Broadcasters Asn. **Business Addr:** General Manager, WJNI-FM, 5081 Rivers Ave, North Charleston, SC 29418, **Business Phone:** (843)554-1063.

### FLETCHER, GLEN EDWARD

Automotive executive. **Personal:** Born Aug 6, 1951, Auburn, NY; son of Merritt W and Naomi P; married Donna M Mattes; children: Kasha B & Garrison A. **Career:** New York State Elec & Gas, labourer, 1970-77; Motorla Commun, 1977-78; Fox Ford Co Inc, sales & sales mgr, 1978-, partner, gen mgr, currently. **Orgs:** Minority Ford Lincoln Mercury Dealers Asn. **Home Addr:** 6 Cherry St Rd, Auburn, NY 13021, **Home Phone:** (315)253-0532. **Business Addr:** President, General Manager, Fox Ford Co Inc, 1068 Arsenal St, Watertown, NY 13601, **Business Phone:** (315)782-7200.

### FLETCHER, JAMES ANDREW

Chancellor (education), executive, astrologer. **Personal:** Born May 8, 1945, Tulsa, OK; son of Howard Bruce and Edna Katherine; married Karen Kite; children: Howard Bruce, Jamie Katherine & Lancelot Lansing; married Maria Merissa; children: Jemila Pujadas & Aisha Pujadas. **Educ:** Mass Inst Technol, BS, aeronaut & astronaut, 1967; Harvard Grad Sch Bus Admin, MBA, 1972; Fairleigh Dickinson Univ, MS, mech engineering, 1973; LaSalle Univ, Chicago, LLB, 1977. **Career:** Gen Elec Corp, Syst Simulation Eng, engr, 1967-70; Gen Res Corp, systs analyst, 1969; Int Bus Mach Corp, mkt rep, 1972-73, fin prog adminr, 1974-76, lab controller, 1976-78, fin prog mgr, 1979-81, planning consol mgr, 1981-83, pricing mgr IPD, 1983, dir plans & controls, 1983-85, Syst Printing Bus Unit, chief financial officer; White House fel, Off Mgt & Budget, 1973-74, exec asst to dep dir; Burroughs Corp; Unisys Corp, staff vpres, pricing & bus anal, 1985-89, Communs Line Bus Mkt Div, vpres finance, 1989-90, Corp Fin Planning & Anal, vpres, 1990-91, vpres bus opers, 1991; Howard Univ, vpres bus & fiscal affairs, chief financial officer & treas, 1991-95; Univ Colo, Boulder, vice chancellor admin & finance, 1995-96; Morehouse Col, vpres bus & finance, 1997-2000; Entertainment Develop Corp, vpres & chief financial officer, 2000-01; Tex A&M Univ Syst, vice chancellor admin, 2001-; Idaho State Univ, vpres finance & admin, 2007-. **Orgs:** Bd mem, Am Friends Serv Comn, 1980-88, 1995-, mem exec comt, mem fin comn, 2001-; Gen Comt, Friends Community Nat Legis; White House Fels Asn, Nat Asn Advan Colored People; 100 Black Men Atlanta. **Honors/Awds:** George F Baker Scholar, Harvard Grad Sch Bus Admin, 1972; AFSC South Africa Trip Deleg, 1979, FWCC South Africa Trip Deleg, 1989; elected mem, Harvard Bus Sch Century Club. **Special Achievements:** Author: "A Quaker Speaks from the Black Experience, The Life and Collected Works of Barrington Dunbar, " 1980; co-author Friends Face the World, 1987. **Home Addr:** 490 Hickory Glen Lane, Atlanta, GA 30311. **Business Addr:** Vice President for Finance & Administration, Idaho State University, 921 S 8th Ave, Pocatello, ID 83209-8219, **Business Phone:** (208)282-2404.

### FLETCHER, LONDON LEVI

Football player. **Personal:** Born May 19, 1975, Cleveland, OH; married Charne; children: Paige, Brooke & Cortland Steele. **Educ:** St Francis Univ, attended; John Carroll Univ, grad. **Career:** Football player (retired); St Louis Rams, linebacker, 1998, mid linebacker, 1999-2001; Buffalo Bills, mid linebacker, 2002-06, linebacker, 2002; Wash Redskins, mid linebacker, 2007-09, 2012-13, linebacker, 2007, 2010. **Honors/Awds:** St. Louis Rams Rookie of the Year, 1998; Carroll Rosenbloom Memorial Award, 1998; Rams Roy Award, 1998; Champion, Nat Football League, 1999, 2001; BJ Blanchard Award, 2007; Walter Payton Man of the Year Award, 2009; Pro Bowl, 2009, 2010, 2011, 2012; Super Bowl champion (XXXIV); Combined Tackles Leader, Nat Football League, 2011; Defensive Player of the Year, Wash Redskins, 2011; Bart Starr Man of the Year Award, 2012. **Special Achievements:** NFL All-Time Record of Consecutive Starts at Linebacker; NFL All-Time Record of Consecutive Games Played at Linebacker. **Business Addr:** Professional Football Player, Washington Redskins, 21300 Redskin Park Dr, Ashburn, VA 20147, **Business Phone:** (703)478-8900.

### FLETCHER, LOUISA ADALINE

State government official. **Personal:** Born Jan 3, 1919, Independence, KS; daughter of Charles L Wesley and Anna T Wilson Wesley; married Allen T; children: Jerold W. **Educ:** Am Tech Soc, Chicago IL, cert, bus admin, 1938. **Career:** State governement official (retired); Usn Dept, Bremerton, WA, clerk typist, 1944-45; Campbell Grocery Store, Bonner Spring, KS, clerk, 1945-52; US Treas, Kansas City MO, graphotype operator, 1952-53; Dept Health, Educ & Welfare, Social Security Admin, Kansas City, Mo, clerk typist, 1954-65, reviewer, 1965-67, comput claims clerk supvr, 1965-75; Fletcher's Rentals, mgr; Kans Pub Employ, Rel Bd, 1977-85. **Orgs:** Pres, Nat Asn Advan Colored People KS State Conf, 1974, 1976 & 1978, regional chair person, 1977; Nat Asn Retired Fed Employ; bd dir, Nat Asn Advan Colored People Nat; Nat Comn preserve Social Security & Medicare; pres, Phys Ther Asst Bonner Springs, KS Sch, 1940-42. **Home Addr:** 101 N Neconi Ave, Bonner Springs, KS 66012, **Home Phone:** (913)422-2052.

### FLETCHER, MILTON ERIC

Executive. **Personal:** Born Feb 20, 1949, New Orleans, LA; son of Mertis Whittaker and Ervin Jr. **Educ:** Southeastern La, BA, mkt, 1971; Univ Phoenix, MBA, bus orgn mgt, 1997; Int Coach Fedn, prof cert coach; Coach Training Alliance, cert exec coach; NLP Coach Training Inst Calif, cert neuro-ling programming coach. **Career:** Detroit Diesel Allison, EEO rep, 1976-79; Gen Motors Bldg Div, staff asst, 1979-81; Gen Motors Tech Staffs, supvr, human resources mgt, 1981-85, supvr, recruiting, 1985-87, mgr, personnel placement, 1987-92; Gen

Motors, global mgr, human resources, 1990-2006; Saturn Corp, Powertrain plant, personnel dir, mgr, human resources, 1992-96; Great Minds Inc, chief success officer, currently; Gen Motors Corp, Warren, Mich, chmn human resources, mktg chmn, vpres human resources, Global Human Resources, mgr, 2001-2005; Spring Arbor Univ, adj prof, 2002-; Great Minds Coaching, pres, 2006-; NLP Coach Training Inst, career & leadership coach, 2006-10; Effective Leaders Prog, leadership coach, 2008-09; Detroit Revitalization FelsProg, exec leadership coach, 2012-. **Orgs:** Cot Case Mgt Serv Inc, pres bd dir, 1976-92; Southern Univ Bus & IDS Cluster, co-chmn, 1985-; Alpha Phi Alpha, 1988-2010; Gamma Lambda Chap, Educ Fund, 1988-; Hartford Memorial Baptist Church, deacon, 1987-92; Spruce St Bapt Church, deacon, 1992-; election & bd dir, 2008-2009, pres, 2010, Prof Coaches Asn Mich; immediate pres, Prof Coaches Asn Mich, 2010; pres, ICF Midwest Regional Adv Coun, 2012-13. **Home Addr:** 330 Village Vanderbilt, Nashville, TN 37212, **Home Phone:** (615)321-5237. **Business Addr:** President, Great Minds Coaching, 16500 N Pk Dr Suite 1811, Southfield, MI 48075, **Business Phone:** (248)569-9383.

## FLETCHER, PATRICIA LOUISE

Educator. **Personal:** Born Jun 20, 1938, Steubenville, OH; daughter of Clifford Mayo; married Lawrence; children: Anthony. **Educ:** Steubenville Sch Cosmetology, 1964; Franciscan Univ, attended 1969; WVa Univ, MA, 1972; Dayton Univ, attended 1979. **Career:** Steubenville City Sch, 1967-72, high sch supt, 1972-80; Garfield Elem Sch, prin, 1981-97; Grandparents Acad, founder. **Orgs:** Pres, Fair Housing, 1980-92; pres, Alpha Kappa Alpha Sorority, 1990; UN Asn USA, 1994; pres, bd adv, Franciscan Univ, 1995; pres, Asn Colored Women's Clubs & Youth Affil, 1996-98; pres, United Way Jefferson City, 1996; vpres, Jefferson Community Col, 1997; pres, Asn Childhood Develop; Nat Asn Advan Colored People; Nat Coun Women; trustee, Frederick Douglass Memorial & Hist Asn; bd trustee, Eastern Gateway Community Col. **Special Achievements:** Received Maureen C. Grady Award for Special Achievement. **Home Addr:** 420 Lauretta Dr, Steubenville, OH 43952. **Business Addr:** Board of Trustee, Eastern Gateway Community College, Jefferson County Campus, Steubenville, OH 43952, **Business Phone:** (740)264-5591.

## FLETCHER, ROBERT E.

Movie director, writer, lawyer. **Personal:** Born Dec 12, 1938, Detroit, MI; son of Robert and Rose Lillian; children: Kabenga. **Educ:** Fisk Univ, attended 1959; Wayne State Univ, BA, 1961; Nat Educ TV Film Training Sch, attended 1970; Com Film Workshop Coun, TV News Cinematography Prog, attended 1971; Nat Acad TV Arts & Sci/Third World Cinema Prod Inc, attended 1977; NY Univ Sch Law, JD, 1990. **Career:** No Student Movement Harlem, field organizer, 1963-64; Nat Stud Asn, Tutorial Prog, photographer & adminr, 1963; Harlem Educ Proj; SNCC, Miss, photojournalist, 1964-68; Miss Freedom Sch; freelance photographer, journalist & film maker, 1968-; Rod Rodgers Dance Co, chmn & bd dir, 1973-; Brooklyn Col, Dept Film Studies, adj prof, 1975-76; Cravath, Swaine & Moore, atty, 1991, retired; Finley, Fletcher & Pilch LLP, co-founder. Films: "A Luta Continua"; cinematographer & co-dir, 1971; O Povo Organizado, cinematographer, 1975; Vote for Your Life, producer & dir, 1977; Weatherization, What's It all About?; Voices of the Civil Rights Movement, panelist, 1980; TV series: "A Nation in View", co-producer; Photographic: "The Wiz", "Freddi Prinz Story"; Jet, Ebony, Ms, Redbook & Life; Cinematographer: PBS television Black Journal & Enterface. **Orgs:** Int Photographers Motion Picture Indust. **Special Achievements:** Author: "We're Gonna Rule!" The Movement, 1967; Co-author: Quiet War in Mozambique, 1973. **Business Addr:** Attorney, Finley, Fletcher & Pilch LLP, 19 Vestry St, New York, NY 10013-1975, **Business Phone:** (212)633-2373.

## FLETCHER, SYLVESTER JAMES

Executive. **Personal:** Born Apr 24, 1934, Ebony, VA; son of Saint Luke Sr and Christeal Bishop; married Catherine Moore; children: Karen Darlene & Keith Errol. **Educ:** Va State Univ, BA, agron & soil sci, 1956. **Career:** US dept of Agr, Soil Conserv Serv, suvy soil scientist, 1956-76; Natural Resource Dynamics, pres & mgr, cert prof soil scientist, 1976-; Mother Flercher's Inc, pres, 1983-; Energenesis Develop Corp, pres, 1986-90. **Orgs:** US & NJ Jaycees, nat dir, 1967-68; Newton Rotary, head var coms, 1976-; Soil Conserv SOC AME, 1956-83; NJ Soil Conserv SOC AME, pres, 1971-72; NJ ASN Prof Soil Scientists, charter pres, 1974-76; Soil Sci SOC AME, Agron SOC AME, 1956-; AMR Registry Cert Professionals Agron, Crops, Soils, 1980-; Nature Conservancy, NJ chp, bd trustee, 1994-2003. **Home Addr:** 9b Barrett Ave, Newton, NJ 07860-1902, **Home Phone:** (973)383-5668. **Business Addr:** President, Natural Resource Dynamics, 9B Barrett Ave, Newton, NJ 07860, **Business Phone:** (973)383-5668.

## FLETCHER, TERRELL ANTOINE

Football player, clergy. **Personal:** Born Sep 14, 1973, St. Louis, MO; married Sheree Zampino; children: Trey & Jodie. **Educ:** Univ Wis-Madison, BA, Eng lit, 1995; Southern Calif Sem, MA, relig studies, 2002. **Career:** Football player (retired), pastor; San Diego Chargers, running back, 1995-2002; City Hope Int Church, sr pastor, 2012-. **Orgs:** Chmn & spokesperson, Jr Achievement; sr pastor, City Hope Int Church, 2006-; chief exec officer, Wake Up Ur Dream, 2010-. **Special Achievements:** Author: " The Book of You", 2016. **Business Addr:** Senior Pastor, City of Hope International Church, 4999 Holly Dr, San Diego, CA 92120, **Business Phone:** (619)266-2626.

## FLETCHER, WILLIAM G., JR. (BILL FLETCHER)

Activist, president (organization). **Personal:** Born Jun 21, 1954, New York, NY; son of William G Sr and Joan Carter; married Candace S Carson; children: Yasmin Jwahir. **Educ:** Harvard Univ, AB, 1976. **Career:** Gen Mech shipyard, welder, 1977-80; Boston Jobs Coalition, organizer, 1980-81; Greater Boston Legal Servs, paralegal, 1982-86; Univ Mass Boston, adj fac, 1982-90; UAW, Dist 65, organizer, 1986-90; Nat Postal Mail Handlers Union, org secy, admin dir, 1990-91; E & S, SEIU, asst educ dir, educ dir, field servs dir, pub sector div dir, asst to pres, 1991-96; AFL-CIO, educ dir, 1996-99, asst to pres, 1999-2001; George Meany Ctr Labor Studies, vpres, Intl trade union devel progs, 2001-02; Ctr Labor Renewal, co-founder; Brooklyn Col, vis prof, currently; Trans Africa Forum, pres, 2002-, chief exec officer, currently. **Orgs:** Maine & Shipbuiling Workers Union, 1977-80; Boston Black United Front, 1980-81; Black Radical Cong, nat coord comt, 1998-, nat co-chair, 2001-; Popular Econs, adv bd, 2000-; Monthly Rev Found, dir, 2001-; United Peace & Justice, co-chair, 2002-, nat steering comt, 2003-; bd mem, BlackCommentator; leading mem, Dem Socialists Am. **Business Addr:** President, Chief Executive Officer, TransAfrica Forum, 1629 K St NW Suite 1100, Washington, DC 20006, **Business Phone:** (202)223-1960.

## FLETCHER, WINONA LEE

Educator. **Personal:** Born Nov 25, 1926, Hamlet, NC; daughter of Henry F Lee and Sarah Lownes Lee; married Joseph G; children: Betty Ann. **Educ:** Johnson C Smith Univ, Charlotte, NC, BA, 1947; Univ Iowa, Iowa City, MA, 1951; Ind Univ, Bloomington, PhD, 1968; Univ W Africa, Toga, Dahomey, Ghana, Nigeria, 1974. **Career:** Delwatts Radio, Electronics Inst, Winston-Salem NC, sec teacher, 1947-51; Ky State Univ, Frankfort, prof area coordr, 1951-78; Lincoln Univ, Jefferson City, Mo, dir costumer instr, summers, 1952-60; John F Kennedy Ctr, consult, 1978-; Ind Univ, Bloomington, prof theatre & afro-am studies, 1978-94, asoc dean col arts & sci, 1981-84, prof emer, currently; sr ed, Community Memories: A Glimpse African Am Life Frankfort, KY, 2003; Black Theatre Network, consult. **Orgs:** Dir cult affairs, Upward Bound, Ky State Univ, 1966-67; coordr, Am Col Theatre Festival, 1973-; chair, ATA's Black Theatre Prog, 1974-77; Ky Arts Comn, 1976-79; nat pres, Univ Col Theatre Asn, 1979-80; Nat Comn Theatre Educ, 1980-85; bd dir, Am Theatre Asn; US Nat Comn, Un Educ Sci & Cult Orgn, 1981-85; coordr, Kennedy Ctr Black Col Proj, 1981-84; adv bd mem, First Int Women Playwrights Conf, 1987-88; exec secy, Nat Asn Dramatic & Speech Arts; chair, Int Exchange Scholars; adv bd, Ind Arts Comn. **Home Addr:** 317 Cold Harbor Dr, Frankfort, KY 40601, **Home Phone:** (502)227-4482. **Business Addr:** Professor Emerita, Indiana University, 275 N Jordan, Bloomington, IN 47405-1101.

## FLEURANT, GERDES

Founder (originator), president (organization), educator. **Personal:** Born Jul 7, 1939, Port-au-Prince; son of Jacques Fabien Pradel and Fanie Jn-Charles; married Florienne Saintil; children: Herve & Maimouna. **Educ:** New Eng Conserv Music, BA, social sci, 1964; New Eng Conserv Music, BMus, organ, 1968; Northeastern Univ, MA, social, 1971; Tufts Univ, MMus, compos, 1980, Caribbean Cult & Music, PhD, 1987. **Career:** Educator (retired); Ecole Ste Trinite Haiti, dir gen music, 1959-64; Col St Pierre Haiti, social studies teacher, 1962-64; Brockton Schs, gen music teacher, 1968-70; Salem State Col, assoc prof sociol, 1971-89, prof sociol, 1989-; Brandeis Univ, lectr black music, 1973-74; Assumption Col, vis prof, sociol, 1976-77; Wellesley Col, vis prof, blackmusic, 1985, assoc prof, emer music, 2005-; dir, African Am studies; Brown Univ, vis prof, 1992; Leocardie & Alexandre Kenscoff Cult Ctr & Gawou Ginou Sch Mirebalais, HAITI, Gawou Ginou Found Inc, co-founder. **Orgs:** Consult City Boston Bilingual & Bicultural Phase II, 1976, RI BlackHeritage Soc Desegregation Prog, 1980-81; bd mem, Advocacy Comn Changes, 1980-83; ed bd New Eng Jour Black Studies, 1982-; bd mem, Cambridge Haitian Am Assoc, 1984-85; Cambridge Peace Comt, 1984-85; pres, Nat Coun Black Studies NE Reg, 1984-86; consult, Humanities Inst Belmont, Mass, 1987; Patriotic Coumbite Haitian Diaspora, 1987-91; bd chmn, CPDH, 1991-. **Home Addr:** 3485 Environ Blvd Suite 203, Lauderhill, FL 33319, **Home Phone:** (954)486-3485. **Business Addr:** Educator, Professor Emeritus, Wellesley College (Emeritus), Wellesley, MA 02481.

## FLINT, DR. CHARLEY

Educator. **Personal:** married Jeff; children: Matthew & Nathaniel. **Educ:** NC A&T Univ, BS; Rutgers Univ, MA, PhD, sociol. **Career:** NC A&T Univ, fac, 1972-74; Rutgers Univ, asst prof sociol, 1974-84; William Patterson Univ, Criminal Justice, coordr, currrently, Sociol Dept, prof & chair, 1984-, vpres, Grad Prog Sociol, dir; ALANA, founding coord. **Orgs:** Bd trustee pres, NJ Asn Corrections; secy bd dir, pres bd dir, YWCA Eastern Union County; bd dir, NJ Chap, Am Correctional Asn; vpres, NJ Asn Criminal Justice Educrs; Eastern Sociol Soc; Am Sociol Asn; Int Community Corrections Asn; Asn Black Women Higher Educ; panel mem, William Paterson Univ, bd mem, W E B DuBois Scholars Inst; co founder, Ctr Study White Am Cult. **Business Addr:** Professor, William Patterson University, Sci 328 300 Pompton Rd, Wayne, NJ 07470, **Business Phone:** (973)720-2368.

**FLINT, MARY FRANCES.** See Obituaries Section.

## FLIPPINS, GREGORY L.

Mayor. **Personal:** Born Jul 2, 1950, Shaw, MS. **Educ:** Delta State Univ, Grad, 1972; Valley State Univ. **Career:** Shaw MS, mayor; Internal Revenue, 2 1/2 yrs; Bolivar Co Neighborhood Youth Corp, counr; Chenault Chevrolet Co, car salesman; Housing Authority City Greenwood, exec dir, currently. **Orgs:** Fel, Inst Polit. **Home Addr:** 209 E Taft St, Greenwood, MS 38930-6253, **Home Phone:** (662)453-8817. **Business Addr:** Executive Director, Housing Authority City Greenwood, 111 E Wash St, Greenwood, MS 38935-1487, **Business Phone:** (662)453-4822.

## FLONO, FANNIE

Journalist. **Personal:** Born May 4, 1952, Augusta, GA; daughter of Prudence King and Adam. **Educ:** Clark Col, Atlanta, GA, BA, jour, 1974. **Career:** Greenville (SC) News, asst city ed, 1983-84; Charlotte (NC) Observer Newspaper, asst, state ed, 1984-86, asst Polit ed, 1986-88, Polit ed, 1988-90, night metro ed, 1990-91, city ed, 1991-93, edial writer & columnist, 1993-96, assoc ed, 1996-. **Orgs:** Charlotte Bus League, 1987-90; pres, Charlotte Area Asn Black Journalists, 1988, rec secy, 1990; prog comt, Nat Asn Black Journalists, 1990; dep regional dir, Region IV Nat Asn Black Journalists, 1990; Nat Asn Black Journalists, Nat Scholar co-chairperson, 1992-93 Fel Harvard Univ, 1998-99. **Honors/Awds:** Georgia School Bell Award, Ga Asn Educr, 1978; Investigative Reporting, reporter, First Place, United Press InterNat Ga, 1980; Investigative Reporting Editor 1st Place, NC Press Asn, 1988, 2nd Place, Column Writing, 1994; Fellow, Atlantic Bridge Found; Fel, Inst Educ Inquiry, 2003-04; Region III Hall of Fame, Nat Asn Black Journalists, 2007. **Special Achievements:** One of 24 American and foreign journalists chosen as a Nieman Fellow; One of nine American journalists selected for a study tour of China by the East-West Center, 2005; Book: Thriving in the Shadows: The Black Experience in Charlotte & Mecklenburg County, 2006. **Home Addr:** 9609 Manus Ct, Matthews, NC 28105, **Home Phone:** (704)563-6261. **Business Addr:** Associate Editor, Charlotte Observer, 600 S Tryon St, Charlotte, NC 28202, **Business Phone:** (704)358-5079.

## FLOOD, EUGENE, JR.

Executive, trader. **Educ:** Harvard Col, BA, econs, 1978; Mass Inst Technol, PhD, econs, 1983. **Career:** Stanford Univ, Graduate Sch Bus, instr, finance, 1982-87; Morgan Stanley Asset Mgt, portfolio mgr, 1987-99; Mas Inst Technol, dean; Nomura Sch Advanced Mgt; Int Mgt Inst, Tokyo; Geneva, lectr; Res Corp, res & develop group, mgr; Derivative Trading Group, mgr, 1990-91; mortgage-backed securities area, trader, 1991-95; Smith Breeden Assocs, dir, pres & chief exec officer, 1994-96; Teachers Ins & Annuity Asn Am, exec vpres; TIAA-CREF, exec vpres Diversified Financial Serv, 2011-12; Morgan Stanley Asset Mgt, portfolio mgr. **Orgs:** Nat Sci Found, Minority Fels in Econs; Soc Quantitative Analysts; trustee, Col Retirement Equities Fund; bd mem, Mass Inst Technol. **Home Addr:** 280 S Mangum St, Durham, NC 27701, **Home Phone:** (919)967-7221. **Business Addr:** Executive Vice President, Teachers Insurance and Annuity Association-CREF, 8500 Andrew Carnegie Blvd, Charlotte, NC 28262.

**FLORES, JOSEPH R.** See Obituaries Section.

## FLORES, LEO

Banker. **Career:** Enterprise Mortgage; Falcon Nat Bank, pres; Webb Country, auditor, currently. **Business Addr:** Auditor, Webb Country, 1000 Houston St, Laredo, TX 78040, **Business Phone:** (956)523-4000.

## FLOURNOY, VALERIE ROSE

Writer, consultant. **Personal:** Born Apr 17, 1952, Camden, NJ; daughter of Payton I Sr (deceased) and Ivie Mae Buchanan (deceased). **Educ:** Hobart & William Smith Col, Geneva, NY, BA, social studies, teaching cert, 1974. **Career:** Dial Bks Young Readers, asst ed, 1977-79; Silhouette Bks/Pocket Bks, sr ed, 1979-82; Berkley Publ Group/Second Chance at Love, ed consult, 1982-83; Vis A Vis Publ Co, 1985-; Books: The Best Time of Day, 1978; The Twins Strike Back, 1980; Patchwork Quilt, 1985; Until Summer's End, 1986; Tanya's Reunion, 1995; Celie & Harvest Fiddler, 1995; The Christmas Talisman. **Orgs:** Bd pres, Palmyra Bd Educ; Burlington County Prof Develop Bd; bd dir, Perkins Ctr Arts S Jersey; Black Women publ. **Home Addr:** 505 Arch St, Palmyra, NJ 08065, **Home Phone:** (856)829-9149.

## FLOWERS, JOYCE E.

Administrator. **Career:** Women Color Found & Health Ministries, bd dir. **Business Addr:** Member, Board of Directors, Women of Color Foundation & Health Ministries Inc, PO Box 3835, Southfield, MI 48037.

## FLOWERS, LETHON, III (LEE FLOWERS)

Football player. **Personal:** Born Jan 14, 1973, Columbia, SC. **Educ:** Ga Inst Technol. **Career:** Football player (retired); Pittsburgh Steelers, defensive back & free safety & strong safety, 1995-2002; Denver Broncos, safety, 2003. **Special Achievements:** Films: Like Mike, 2002.

## FLOWERS, DR. LOMA KAYE

Psychiatrist, educator, writer. **Personal:** Born Feb 27, 1944, OH; daughter of George W and Elsie; married Edgar Flowers Jr; children: George & Brandon. **Educ:** Western Res Univ, AB, biol, 1964; Case Western Res Univ, MD, 1968. **Career:** Psychiatrist (retired), consultant; San Francisco Gen Hosp, internship, 1968-69; Stanford Univ Med Ctr, residency psychiat, 1969-72, teacher, 1972-; Sch Health Bus Orgs, consult, 1970-; E Palo Alto Comm Health Ctr, dir ment health, 1971-73; Va Hosp San Francisco, chief ment hyg clin, 1973-77; Delaney & Flowers Dream Ctr, founder, 1981-, co-dir, 1983-; Host, BET Cable TV, "Dr Flowers Call", 1985-86; Univ Calif, clin prof psychiat, 1997; personal & prof develop consult, currently. **Orgs:** Vpres, 1983-85, chmn bd dirs, Asn Study Dreams, 1984-85; chair, San Francisco Sch Bd sch supt search, 1994-95; pres, Northern Calif Psychiat Asn, 1998-99; Negro Bus & Prof Women's Asn; Nat Asn Advan Colored People, Black Psychiat Am; SFUSD, PTSA; AMA; Am Psychiat Asn; Asn Study Dreams; Calif Med Soc; John Hale Med Soc; Nat Med Asn. **Honors/Awds:** Francis Hobart Herrick Prize, 1964; Phi Beta Kappa, 1964; Med Sch Faculty Award Research, 1968; Distinguished Fellow, Am Psychiat Asn, 1987; Univ Calif San Francisco Henry J Kaiser Teaching Award, 1996 & 2004; Special Recognition Award, Univ Calif San Francisco Clinical Faculty Asn, 1994; Distinguished Service Award, Emotional Educ consult, 2002; Presidents Distinguished Service Award, NCPS, 2002. **Special Achievements:** Author, "The Morning After: A Pragmatists Approach to Dreams," Psychiatric Journal, Univ Ottawa, 1988; author, "Psychotherapy Black & White," Journal Nat Med Assn, 1972; "The Dream Interview Method in a Private Outpatient Psychotherapy Practice," New Directions in Dream Interpretation, Suny Press, 1993; "The Use of Presleep Instructions and Dreams in Psyhcosomatic Disorders." Psychotherapy & Psychosomatics 1995; "The Dream Interview Method in Addiction Recovery, A Treatment Guide." Journal of Substance Abuse, Treatment, 1996; "The Changing Role of 'Using' Dreams in Addiction Recovery." Journal of Substance Abuse, Treatment, 1998. **Business Addr:** Personal and Professional Development Consultant, 1670 Plymouth Ave, San Francisco, CA 94127, **Business Phone:** (415)333-8631.

## FLOWERS, MICHAEL E.

Entrepreneur, lawyer. **Educ:** Bucknell Univ, BS, 1976; Ohio State Univ Col Law, JD, 1979. **Career:** Porter, Wright, Morris & Arthur, assoc, 1979-86, partner, 1987-95; Bricker & Eckler LLP, partner, 1995-2007; The Bus Lawyer, ed, 1997-98; Community Capital Develop Corp, dir, 1998-2002; Columbus Urban Growth Corp, dir, 2000-04; Krieger Automobile Dealerships, asst secy & dir; Keith B Key Enterprises LLC, vpres & chief legal coun, 2008-16; Steptoe & Johnson PLLC, Coun, 2016-. **Orgs:** Ohio Small Bus & Entrepreneurship Coun, 1991-92; gov coun, ABA Sect Bus Law, 1994-2001; deleg, The White House Conf Small Bus; secy, Columbus Bd trustee, 1998-2002; chair, Bus Law Sect Am Bar Asn, 1999-2000; Entrepreneurship Steering Comt,

Greater Columbus Chamber Com, 1999-2002; trustee, 2002-10, bd secy, 2009-10, Mt Carmel Health Syst; bd mem, Columbus Bar Serv Inc, 1999-2003; ABA J Bd Ed, 2005-; trustee, Columbus State Community Col; fel Am Bar Found; appointee, Gov Taft's Minority Bus Coun; Nat Bar Asn; Negotiated Acquisitions Comt, ABA Sect Bus Law; founding mem, ed bd, Bus Law Today; Am Bar Asn Comt Continuing Prof Educ; founding mem, ABA Africa Law Initiatives Coun; chair & bd secy, Mt Carmel Health Found Bd Trustees; chair, Capital Park Health Ctr Bd Trustees; deacon, Genessee Ave Church Christ; bd secy, Optimer Photonics Inc; exec, Capital Club; Am Law Inst; Phi Eta Sigma & Omicron Delta Kappa; minority bus exec prog, Tuck sch Bus; bd trustees, Nat Church Residences; Bd Trustee, Ohio State Bar Found; bd gov, Am Bar Asn, 2012-15. **Honors/Awds:** Columbus Jaycees Outstanding Young Citizen Award, 1988; Minority Small Bus Advocate of the Year, US Small Bus Admin, 1993; Bus First Forty Under 40 Award, 1993; Business Law Chair's Award, Am Bar Asn Sect, 1995; Distinguished Alumnus, Col Law, Ohio State Univ, 2001; Ritter Award for Professionalism, Ohio State Bar Found, 2005; Prof Achievement Award, The Ohio State Univ Alumni Asn, 2006; John Mercer Langston Bar Association Distinguished Leader Award, 2006. **Special Achievements:** Author: Basic Legal Issues Associated with Internet Start-Ups, Ohio Assembly of Councils Business Trade Journal, June, 2000; Updated ABA Diversity Plan Forges Ahead, The National Law Journal, July, 2000; Leading US Corporation Files Amicus Brief Favoring Diversity, The Metropolitan Corporate Counsel, March, 2001; US Lawyers Can Promote Democracy In Distant Places, Business Law Today, November/December, 2002; List of Nation's Top Lawyers, Black Enterprise Mag, 2003; Listed in Best Lawyers in Am, 2005-06. Published Numerous Books & Articles. **Business Addr:** Vice President, Chief Legal Counsel, Keith B Key Enterprises LLC, 3433 Agler Rd Suite 2000, Columbus, OH 43219, **Business Phone:** (614)476-3548.

### FLOWERS, MICHAEL E.

Lawyer. **Educ:** Bucknell Univ, BS, 1976; Ohio State Univ, JD, 1979; Tuck Sch Bus Dartmouth Minority, bus exec prog, 2001. **Career:** Porter WrightMorris & Arthur LLP, 1979-95; Bricker & Eckler LLP, partner, 1995-2007; KBK Enterprises LLC, vpres & chief legal coun/city exec, 2008-16; Steptoe & Johnson PLLC, atty, 2016-. **Orgs:** Gov coun, Am Bar Asn Sect Bus Law, 1994-2001; Secy, COSI Columbus Bd Trustees, 1998-02; Entrepreneurship Steering Comt, Greater Columbus Chamber Com, 1999-02; dir, Columbus Urban Growth Corp, 2000-04; Am Law Inst; Am Bar Asn Jl Bd Edit, 2005-; Nat Bar Asn; chair, founding mem, Ed Bd, Bus Law Today; ed bd, Bus law, Am Bar Asn; trustee & bd secy, Mt Carmel Health Syst; dir, Community Capital Develop Corp; bd mem, Columbus Bar Servs; Exec mem, Capital Club; Bus Law group; Fels Am Bar Found; bd trustees, Ohio State Bar Foundation, 2010-12; bd governor, Am Bar Asn, 2012-15. **Honors/Awds:** Distinguished Alumnus, Col Law Ohio State Univ, 2000; Honored, Am Law Inst, 2002; List Nations Top Lawyers, Black Enterprise Mag, 2003; Ohio Super Lawyers Listing, 2004-06; Ritter Award for Professionalism, Ohio State Bar Found, 2005; Professional Achievement Award, Ohio State Univ Alumni Asn, 2006; Listed Best Lawyers Am, 2005-06. **Special Achievements:** First African American elected chair of Bus Law section of the Amer Bar Asn Author of U.S. Lawyers Can Promote Democracy In Distant Places,"Business Law Today, November & December 2002; "Leading U.S. Corporation Files Amicus Brief Favoring Diversity", The Metropolitan Corporate Counsel, March 2001; "Updated ABA Diversity Plan Forges Ahead",The National Law Journal, July 2000. **Home Addr:** 1351 Camelot Dr, Columbus, OH 43220. **Business Addr:** Vice President, Chief Legal Counsel, KBK Enterprises, 4249 Easton Way Suite 220, Columbus, OH 43219, **Business Phone:** (614)476-3548.

### FLOWERS, RALPH LORENZO. See Obituaries Section.

### FLOWERS, DR. RUNETTE (RUNETTE FLOWERS WILLIAMS)

Pediatrician. **Personal:** Born Apr 2, 1945, Donaldsonville, GA; married W Alphonso. **Educ:** Dillard Univ, BA, biol, 1967; Tuskegee Inst, MS, 1969; Meharry Med Col, MD, 1973. **Career:** Emory Univ, residency, 1973-76; Grady Mem Hosp, resident, 1976; Dekalb Grady Clin, staff pediatrician, 1976-; Emory Univ & Sch Med, Dept Prev Med, asst prof, 1976-; Edwood-parent-child Ctr, consult, 1977-; Sch Nursing Ga Baptist Hosp, lectr, 1978-79; Nurse Practitioner Prog Emory, preceptor, 1978-79; S Dekalb Pediat, obstet & gynec, 1980-; WAGA Channel 5, resident tv pediatrician, 1994-. **Orgs:** Greater Atlanta Pediat Asn, 1978-; Health Syst Agency, Ga, 1980; Delta Sigma Theta Sorority Beta Kappa Chi Sci Hon Soc; Composite State Bd Med Examiners, 1983-; Fedn State Med Bd US, 1992-; Nat Bd Med Examiners. **Honors/Awds:** Most Outstanding Student & Grace M James Award, Pediat Meharry Med Col, 1973. **Home Addr:** 1465 Tulip Pl, Decatur, GA 30032-3143. **Business Addr:** Obstetrics & Gynecology Physician, South Dekalb Pediatrics Incorporation, 2855 Candler Rd suite 9, Decatur, GA 30034-1415, **Business Phone:** (404)243-9630.

### FLOWERS, DR. SALLY A.

Dentist. **Personal:** Born Jun 18, 1954, Detroit, MI; daughter of Willie Oscar and Mary Jane Perry James; children: Krystle Maria & Dawn Amber. **Educ:** Eastern Mich Univ, attended 1974; Howard Univ Sch Dent, DDS, 1978; Johns Hopkins Univ, MPH, 1980. **Career:** Pimlico Dent Clin, Baltimore, Md, assoc dentist, 1979-; Dr Roy Baptiste, Silver Springs, Md, assoc dentist, 1980-82; Dr Barbara Johnson, Wash, DC, assoc dentist, 1981-82; Capital Hill Dent Ctr, Wash, DC, assoc dentist, 1981-82; pvt pract gen dentist, 1982-. **Orgs:** Am Dent Asn, 1982-; Acad Gen Dent, 1982-; DC Dent Soc, 1982-; pres, Pin Pro High Golf Club, 1987-88; Rec secy, Kennedy St Asn Merchants Prof, 1989-91; Johns Hopkins Alumni; Howard Univ Alumni. **Home Addr:** 234 Main Sail Ct, Detroit, MI 48207-5008, **Home Phone:** (313)567-4866. **Business Addr:** Dentist, Private Practice, 250 Kennedy St NW, Washington, DC 20011, **Business Phone:** (202)726-5250.

### FLOWERS, SONNY. See FLOWERS, WILLIAM HAROLD, JR.

### FLOWERS, VONETTA (VONETTA JEFFERY)

Athlete. **Personal:** Born Oct 29, 1973, Birmingham, AL; married Johnny Mack; children: 3. **Educ:** Univ Ala, Birmingham, phys educ, 1997. **Career:** Bobsledder, athlete (retired); US Olympic Comt, bobsledder, 2006. **Honors/Awds:** Gold medal, women's bobsled, Winter Olympics, 2002; Victor Award, 2002; Live The Dream Award, 2002; 50 of the Most Inspiring African-Americans, Essence Magazine, 2002; 57 of the Most Intriguing Blacks, Ebony Magazine, 2002; 50 Most Beautiful People, People Magazine, 2002; Alabama Athlete of the Year, US Sports Academy, 2002; The Wilma Rudolph Athlete of the Year Award, Rainbow/PUSH Coalition, 2002; Honorary Member, Alpha Kappa Alpha Sorority; Recipient of the USOC Team of the Year, 2002; Dodge Nat Athletic Olympian Award, 2003; Bronze medal, FIBT World Championships, 2004; Winter Olympics, sixth, 2006; US Olympic Spirit Award; 50 Most Beautiful People; 5th at World Championships with partner Jean Prahm (Racine), 2005; Annie Glenn Award, 2006; Hearing Hear-O Award, 2006; Alabama Sports Hall of Fame, 2010. **Special Achievements:** First black athlete to win gold at the Olympic Winter Games; Author: Running on Ice: The Overcoming Faith of Vonetta Flowers. **Home Addr:** 1609 Jody Ct, Jacksonville, FL 32259.

### FLOWERS, WILLIAM HAROLD, JR. (SONNY FLOWERS)

Association executive, lawyer. **Personal:** Born Mar 22, 1946, Chicago, IL; son of Ruth C and W Harold; married Pamela Mays. **Educ:** Univ Colo, BA, 1967, Law Sch, JD, 1971. **Career:** Pvt pract atty, 1978-; Adams County, dep dist atty, 1977-78; pvt pract, 1979-; Holland & Hart, Cenver, Colo, partner, 1989-97; Hurth, Sisk & Blakemore LLP, partner, 1997-. **Orgs:** Bd dir, KGNU Radio Sta, 1981-84; bd dir, Colo Criminal Defense Bar, 1982-83; reg dir, Nat Bar Asn, 1984-85; vice pres, Nat Bar Asn, 1990-91; bd govs, Nat Bar Asn, 1985-95; exec bd, Boy Scouts Am, 1983-99; pres, Sam Cary Bar Asn; Comt Corrections Bd, 1984-90; Judicial Nominating Comt, 1988-94; bd dir, Colo ACLU, 1990; pres, Colo Trial Lawyers Asn, 1999-2000; Asn Trial Lawyers Am, exec comt, 2001-03; bd gov, Asn Trial Lawyers Am, 2002-03; bd dir, Coloradons Against Death Penalty, 2001-; Colo Am Civil Liberties Union; pres, Univ Colo Alumni Asn, 1994-95; bd dir, Univ Colo Found, 1996-02; vice pres, Colo Bar Asn, 2002-03; bd dir, Boulder County Bar Asn, 2003-04; Am Bd Trial Advocates; Am Asn Justice; vice pres, Colo Bar Asn; pres, Univ Colo, Boulder Alumni Asn; Univ Colo Found's Bd Dir. **Honors/Awds:** Community Service Award, Univ Co Alumni Asn, 1998; Outstanding Alumnus, Univ Colo Black Students Alliance, 1990; Award in Bus Community Action, Boulder County, CO, 1990; Presidential Award, Nat Bar Asn, 1987; Colorado Super Lawyers, 2006, 2007. **Home Addr:** 345 Mohawk Dr, Boulder, CO 80303. **Business Addr:** Partner, Hurth, Sisk & Blakemore LLP, 4860 Riverbend Rd, Boulder, CO 80308, **Business Phone:** (303)443-7900.

### FLOYD, CHRISTOPHER MICHAEL

Football player. **Personal:** Born Jun 23, 1975, Detroit, MI. **Educ:** Univ Mich, grad. **Career:** Football player (retired); New Eng Patriots, running back, 1998-2000; Cleveland Browns, running back, 2000.

### FLOYD, CLIFF, JR. (CORNELIUS CLIFFORD FLOYD)

Baseball player, radio host. **Personal:** Born Dec 5, 1972, Chicago, IL; son of Cornelius Clifford Sr and Olivia; married Maryanne Manning; children: 2. **Career:** Baseball player (retired); co-host; Montreal Expos, infielder, 1993-96, 2002; Florida Marlins, 1997-2002; Boston Red Sox, 2002; New York Mets, infielder, 2003-06; Chicago Cubs, outfielders, 2007; Tampa Bay Rays, 2008; San Diego Padres, 2009; FOX Sports Fla, broadcasting, 2010; Sirius XM Radio, co-host, currently. **Business Addr:** Co-Host, Sirius XM Radio, PO Box 33174, Detroit, MI 48232, **Business Phone:** (866)528-7474.

### FLOYD, DR. DEAN ALLEN

Physician. **Personal:** Born Mar 10, 1951, Loris, SC; son of Stephen J Sr and Ernestine; married Gail Payton; children: Anissa Deanne, Dean Allen II & Allycia Summer. **Educ:** Clemson Univ, BS, 1972; Med Univ SC, MD, 1976. **Career:** Palmetto Richland Memorial Hosp, resident family pract; Richmond Memorial Hosp, resident, 1977-80; Family Health Centers Inc, med dir, 1980-85; pvt pract, 1985-; SC State Health & Human Serv, health consult, 1985; Richland Community Health Care Asn Inc, Columbia, SC, physician, med dir, currently; Eau Claire Coop Health Centers, physician, currently. **Home Addr:** 2601 Millwood Ave, Columbia, SC 29205, **Home Phone:** (803)254-5940. **Business Addr:** Medical Director, Richland Community Health Care Association Inc, 1520 Laurel St, Columbia, SC 29201, **Business Phone:** (803)799-8407.

### FLOYD, ERIC AUGUSTUS (SLEEPY FLOYD)

Basketball player, basketball coach. **Personal:** Born Mar 6, 1960, Gastonia, NC. **Educ:** Georgetown Univ, polit sci & pub admin, 1982. **Career:** Basketball player (retired), basketball coach; NJ Nets, 1982-83, 1994-95; Golden State Warriors, 1983-87; Houston Rockets, 1988-93; San Antonio Spurs, 1993-94; Restaurant; Financial Mgt Co; Jr Varsity Boys Basketball, coach, 2004-05; Bedding Co, employer, 2013-15; JobsyWobsy, pres, 2015.

### FLOYD, JAMES T., SR.

Executive, association executive, football coach. **Personal:** Born Jan 1, 1935?, Laurens, SC; son of Willie J; married Barbara; children: James T Jr, Norman V, Kimberly U, Javonda A & Brittaine Nakkole. **Educ:** Allen Univ, BS, biol, 1957; Tuskegee Univ, MS, 1965. **Career:** Sanders High Sch, teacher, 1957-58, asst coach, head football coach, 1960-64; BeckHigh Sch, chmn sci dept, 1965-69; Union Carbide Corp, process engr, 1969-72; WR Grace & Co, process engr, 1972-75, equal assurance mgr, 1976-82, group leader eng, 1983; F & M Develop Enterprises Inc, owner, pres, chief exec officer, 1985-; James T. Floyd Construct, owner, pres, chief exec officer; Unlimited Gen Construct, owner, pres, chief exec officer. **Orgs:** Bd dir, Phillis Wheatly Asn; adv bd, USCG Col; adv bd, Dept Ment Health; founder, PBS Fed Credit Union. **Honors/Awds:** Elected the Twenty Fifth Nat Pres Conclave New Orleans, 1984; Selected to Ebony's 100 Most Influential Blacks in Am, 1985-87; Entrepreneur of the Year, 1990; Inducted Distinguished Service Chapter, 1987. **Home Addr:** 106 Brandon Way, Simpsonville, SC 29681, **Home Phone:** (864)297-3513. **Business Addr:** Chief Executive Officer, President, F & M Development Inc, 133 Bennett St, Greenville, SC 29601, **Business Phone:** (864)233-7732.

### FLOYD, DR. JEREMIAH

Executive, association executive, consultant. **Personal:** Born Jan 8, 1932, Laurens, SC; son of Willie James and Clairender; married Clara Brown; children: Camille & Edgar. **Educ:** Allen Univ, BS, 1956; NY Univ, MA, 1960, PhD, 1973. **Career:** Nat Sch Bds Asn, assoc dir; Evanston Pub Sch, prin, 1970-73; Nat Sch Bd Asn, dir urban & minority rel, 1973-76, form asst exec dir to assoc exec dir, 1976-78; Hands Sci Outreach, bd pres; Floyd Consult, sr partner & chief exec officer, prin, currently. **Orgs:** Bd dir, United Way Evanston, 1971-76; pres, NU Chap, Phi Delta Kappa, 1972-74; vpres, Northwestern Univ Alumni Educ, 1973-76; vice chmn, Montgomery Community Servs Partnership, 1986-95; State Adv Comt Adult Educ & Community Serv, 1986-88; Montgomery Col Gen Educ Adv Comt, 1988-. **Honors/Awds:** NSF fel, Nat Sci Found, Northwestern Univ, 1959-62; IDEA fel, Rockford Col, 1969; pres, Wilmette Sch Dist 39 Bd Educ, 1976; Montgomery County Bd Educ, MD, 1984; vpres, Montgomery County Bd Educ MD, 1985-86. **Business Addr:** Senior Partner, Chief Executive Officer, Floyd's Consulting, 5909 Aberdeen Rd, Bethesda, MD 20817, **Business Phone:** (301)229-4780.

### FLOYD, MALCOLM GREGORY ALI

Football coach, football player. **Personal:** Born Dec 19, 1972, San Francisco, CA. **Educ:** Calif State Univ, Fresno. **Career:** Football player (retired), coach; Houston Oilers, wide receiver, 1994-96; Tenn Oilers, wide receiver, 1997; St Louis Rams, wide receiver, 1997; San Diego Chargers, 2006-08; CK McClatchy High Sch Sacramento, Football coach, 2011-. **Business Addr:** Football Coach, C K McClatchy High School, 3066 Freeport Blvd, Sacramento, CA 95818, **Business Phone:** (916)264-4400.

### FLOYD, MARK STEPHEN

Lawyer, association executive. **Personal:** Born Nov 30, 1958, El Paso, TX; son of Columbus and Vardrene Bailey; married Lauren Generette. **Educ:** Stanford Univ, AB, music & polit sci, 1980; Columbia Law Sch, JD, 1983. **Career:** Sq Sanders & Dempsey, Cleveland, Ohio, partner, 1983-; Thompson Hine LLP, Labor & Employ Pract Group, vice chair, patner, Diversity Comt, chair, 2000-; Columbia J Art & Law, ed; DDR Corp, exec vpres, 2012-. **Orgs:** Exec comt mem, Cleveland Ballet, 1989-93; exec comt, legal coun, Cleveland Baroque Orchestra, 1992-96; steering comt mem, Cleveland Orchestra; tenor soloist, asst conductor, Mt Zion Congregational Church; bd trustees, Crains Cleveland Bus Top 40 Young Bus Leaders Under 40; bd trustees, Cleveland Bar Asn; bd trustees, Cleveland Inst; Am Bar Asn; Bd Gov, Ohio State Bar Asn. 2008-; Am Immigration Lawyers Asn; bd trustees, Urban League Greater Cleveland; chair, Cleveland Inst Music; parliamentarian, Coun Deleg, Ohio State Bar Asn; chmn, Club at Key Ctr; fel Litigation Coun Am. **Honors/Awds:** Ohio Super Lawyers Award, 2006-07, 2008, 2010; 40 Under 40 Outstanding Young Business Leaders, Crain's Cleveland Business. **Special Achievements:** Publications: Discrimination Damages: Controlling The Tax Consequences For The Plaintiff, 1999; Employment at Will: Job-Related Lawsuits Rapidly Overwhelming the Courts, 2000; Road to Becoming Law Long for OSHA, 2000; NLRB Ruling to Dramatically Impact Employers, 2000; Written Policy Can Help Control Technology Abuse, 2000; Supreme Court Ruling Moved Toward Favoring Arbitration, 2001; Employers' Responsibilities to Today's Citizen Soldiers, 2005; Preemptive Strike: Protecting Your Company's Employment Assets, 2005. **Home Addr:** 15101 Shore Acres Dr, Cleveland, OH 44110-1241, **Home Phone:** (216)531-9435. **Business Addr:** Partner, Attorney, Thompson Hine LLP, 3900 Key Ctr 127 Public Sq, Cleveland, OH 44114-1291, **Business Phone:** (216)566-5836.

### FLOYD, HON. MARQUETTE L.

Judge. **Personal:** Born Oct 14, 1928, Winnsboro, SC; son of Mary Brown; married Mildred L; children: 6. **Educ:** New York Univ, BS, 1958; Brooklyn Law Sch, LLB, 1960. **Career:** Judge (retired); Suffolk County, dist ct judge; Pvt Prac NY, atty; Ronek Pk Civic Asn, pres; Dist Ct Suffolk County, county ct, 1986; Ny State, Riverhead, NY, supreme ct, presiding justice, 1990-03. **Orgs:** Pres, N Amityville Rep Club; dir, chmn ACE Ctr; dir, Legal Aid Soc; dir, Sunrise Psychia Clin; dir & Key, Amityville Youth Orgn; secy, Eta Theta Lambda Chap; Alpha Phi Alpha Frat Inc; Suffolk Co Bar Asn; NY State Bar Asn; Dist Ct bd Judges Suffold County; Dist Ct bd Judges Nassau & Suffolk Co; Supreme Ct Justices; Suffolk County Charter Rev Comt; NY State Jury Syst Mgt Adv Comt. **Honors/Awds:** Community Serv Award, 100 Black Men Nassau & Suffolk, 1982; Schroll Hon Award, Nat Asn Bus & Prof Women, 1983; Achievement Award, Babylon Coun Black Republicans, 1985; County Ct Judge Yr, Suffolk County Ct Officers Asn, 1986; Judge Yr, Suffolk County Bar Asn, 1987; Man Yr, Suffolk County Police Conf, 1990. **Special Achievements:** First African American to be elected to dist ct Judge Suffolk County; First African American justice Ny Supreme Ct. **Home Addr:** 665 Comdr Ave, West Babylon, NY 11704. **Business Addr:** Supreme Court Judge, Suffolk County Supreme Court, 400 Carleton Ave, Central Islip, NY 11722, **Business Phone:** (631)853-6317.

### FLOYD, DR. SAMUEL A., JR.

Educator, college administrator, consultant. **Personal:** Born Feb 1, 1937, Tallahassee, FL; son of Samuel A and Theora Combs; married Barbara; children: Wanda LaVerne Green, Cecilia Ann Carruthers & Samuel A III. **Educ:** Fla A&M Univ, BS, 1957; Southern Ill Univ, Carbondale, MME, 1965, PhD, 1969. **Career:** Smith-Brown High Sch, Arcadia, Fla, band dir, 1957-62; Fla A&M Univ, Dept Music, music instr, asst dir bands, 1962-64; Southern Ill Univ, Carbondale, assoc prof, 1964-78; Fisk Univ, Inst Res Black Am Music, dir, 1978-83; Columbia Col, Chicago, Ctr Black Music Res, dir, 1983-90, 1993-2002, acad dean, 1990-93, interim vpres acad affairs & provost, 1999-2001, dir emer & consult, 2002-. **Orgs:** Am Musiological Soc; nat Coun mem, Col Music Soc, 1978-80; Pi Kappa Lambda; bd trustee, Soc Am Music, Sonneck Soc, 1990-93; vis comt, Vanderbilt Univ, Blair

Sch Music, 1990-; Southern Ill Univ; Fisk Univ; Columbia Col; vis comt, Univ Chicago, deptmusic, 1992-. **Home Addr:** 901 S Plymouth Ct Apt 206, Chicago, IL 60605-2040, **Home Phone:** (312)786-0362. **Business Addr:** Director Emeritus, Columbia College Chicago, 600 S Mich Ave, Chicago, IL 60605-1996, **Business Phone:** (312)344-7559.

**FLOYD, SLEEPY. See FLOYD, ERIC AUGUSTUS.**

**FLOYD, VERNON CLINTON**
Executive, engineer, educator. **Personal:** Born Nov 20, 1927, Chickasaw Terrace, AL; son of Nathan D and Ora A Ellis; children: Marjorie A & Victor C. **Educ:** Dunbar Trade Sch, Chicago, IL, 1946; Indust Training Inst, Chicago, IL, 1946; Tuskegee Inst, electronic, bus mgt, archit, mech drawing, AL, 1952. **Career:** Sta WMOZ, Mobile, AL, chief engr, 1953-65; Carver Tech Trade Sch, Mobile, AL, electronics instr, 1966-68; Community Educ Prog, Hattiesburg, Miss, 1988; Circuit Broadcasting Network, Hattiesburg, Miss, founder, owner & pres, 1969-; Elec Contractor, Hattiesburg, Miss, 1972-; Radio Broadcasting Sta, pres. **Orgs:** Adv chmn, Boy Scouts Am, 1971-73; BOAZ Lodge No 4, 1980; elec bd mem, City Hattiesburg, 1981-83. **Special Achievements:** First black-owned and operated radio station, Mississippi-WORV-AM in Hattiesburg. **Home Addr:** Rte 11 Box 2711 AA, Hattiesburg, MS 39401. **Business Addr:** President, Circuit Broadcasting Network, 1204 Graveline St, Hattiesburg, MS 39401, **Business Phone:** (601)544-1941.

**FLOYD, VIRCHER B.**
Teacher, educator, association executive. **Personal:** Born Apr 3, 1928. **Educ:** Earlham Col, BA, 1952, MA, 1954; Univ Pittsburgh, MSW, 1962. **Career:** Educator (retired); Pittsburgh Regional Off Penn Dept Pub Welfare, state social worker, 1961-63; Rural Community Develop Unit Tlaxcala Mex AFSC, dir, 1963-65; Peace Corps Bogota, Colombia, urban prog rep & staff, dir, 1968-70; Career Serv Off Earlham Col, asst prof & dir, 1970-75; Bogota Field Off, Columbia, field dir corresp, 1975-77; Child Reach Plan Int, Columbia, Nicaragua, Brazil, Liberia, Ecuador & Honduras, field dir, 1975-92; Foryth Tech Community Col Span, teacher, tutor. **Orgs:** Exec dir, Sewickley Community Ctr, 1956-60; Townsend Community Ctr, Richmond, Ind, 1965-68; vpres, Allegheny Co Fed Settlements; nat bd mem, Am Friends Serv Community, 1972-75; Acad Cert Social Workers. **Special Achievements:** Author of numerous publications. **Home Addr:** 810 Nightingale, Xenia, OH 45385, **Home Phone:** (937)376-5408.

**FLOYD, WILLIAM ALI**
Executive, football player. **Personal:** Born Feb 17, 1972, Jacksonville, FL; married Bonita; children: William, Thai & Jaden. **Educ:** Fla State Univ. **Career:** Football player (retired), executive; San Francisco 49ers, fullback, 1994-97; Carolina Panthers, fullback, 1998-2000; Fla State Univ, color analyst, 2008-; ISP Sports Network, color analyst, 2008-; Sunshine Network, color analyst; Able Body Labor, pub rels liaison, currently. **Orgs:** Community-benefit found; William Floyd's Bar None Found. **Honors/Awds:** All-Sun Coast & All-Pinellas County honor; Champion, Super Bowl, XXIX. **Special Achievements:** First Rookie in NFL history to score 3 touchdowns in a playoff game. **Home Addr:** , Orlando, FL. **Business Addr:** Public Relations Liaison, Able Body Labor, 20920 S Dixie Hwy, Miami, FL 33189, **Business Phone:** (305)971-7500.

**FLOYD, DR. WINSTON CORDELL**
Physician. **Personal:** Born Nov 13, 1948, Edgefield, SC; married Francena Pinckney. **Educ:** Tuskegee Inst, BS, 1969; Meharry Med Col, MD, 1973. **Career:** Cook County Hosp, internship, 1973-74; Meharry Med Col, resident, 1974-77, instr internal med, 1976-77; pvt pract internal med, currently; Anderson Memorial Hosp, attend staff; Palmetto Health Baptist Easley Hosp; Hart County Hosp; Oconee Memorial Hosp; Cannon Memorial Hosp; AnMed Health Eastside Internal Med, physician, currently. **Orgs:** Dipl, Nat Bd Med Examr, 1974; Am Bd Internal Med; AMA; Alpha Phi Alpha Frat; Cent Tex Med Found; owner, pres, Floyd Winston C Md Pa Inc. **Honors/Awds:** Cert, Am Bd Internal Med. **Business Addr:** Physician, AnMed Health Eastside Internal Medicine, 400 N Fant St Suite G, Anderson, SC 29621, **Business Phone:** (864)224-2197.

**FLUELLEN, VELDA SPAULDING**
Chief executive officer, executive, business owner. **Personal:** Born Feb 5, 1942, Durham, NC; daughter of John Lee White and Sarah Badie Spaulding White McEachin; married Arthur L; children: Randall, Tanya & Bryan. **Educ:** Hampton IST, BS, 1963, MS, 1969; NC Cent Univ, bus admin cert, 1974. **Career:** Phoenix High Sch, sci dept chmn, 1963-70; Hampton Inst, grad asst, 1969-70; NC Cent Univ, prof biol, 1970-75; Fluellen's Seafood House, owner, 1975-78; Tucson Jobs Corps, educ curric, 1979-80; IBM Corp, staff position purchasing, 1981-89; A&B Trading Co Inc, pres & chief exec officer, 1988-96; Art's BBQ & Vel's Catering Serv, co-chef & co-owner, currently. **Orgs:** Alpha Kappa Alpha Sorority, 1967-; Nat Coun Negro Women, 1970-92; Nat Asn Advan Colored People, 1981-88; Links Inc, 1981-; Resources Women, 1988-; golden life mem, Nat Asn Advan Colored People, 1988-; Chamber Com, 1988-; Tucson Metrop Conv Ctr & Viss Bur, 1988-; bd mem, Ariz Restaurant Asn, Tucson Chap, 1991-; bd mem, Pima Early Rising Execs, 1992-. **Home Addr:** 2802 W Magee Rd, Tucson, AZ 85742-1500. **Business Addr:** Owner, Vel's Catering Serv, 450 N Main Ave, Tucson, AZ 85701, **Business Phone:** (520)388-9295.

**FLUKER, ELAYNE M.**
Editor, executive. **Personal:** Born Queens, NY. **Educ:** Hampton Univ, BA, Eng, 1995. **Career:** Essence Mag, ed asst, 1997-99, senior editor, 1996-2004, asst ed, 1999-2000, arts & entertainment ed, 2000-02; Essence Commun, ed-in-chief, 2002; Suede Magazine, founding managing ed, celebrity proj dir, 2004-05; freelance celebrity talent booker, producer, writer, ed, 2005-06; Vibe & Vibe Vixen Mag, managing ed, 2006-07; IVillage.com, Beauty & Style & Entertainment channels, ed dir, 2007-08; Elite PA Serv, chief exec officer, currently; Brides.com, managing ed, 2008-; Conde Nast Digital, managing ed, 2008-10; Latina.com, dir digital, 2010; Black Enterprise, exec ed digital media, 2010-12; Martha Stewart Living, digital managing dir, 2012-14; ChicRebellion.tv, founder, chief exec officer, 2012-. **Special Achievements:** Tv Appearances: "The Today Show", "Nightline", "Extra", "Inside Edition", "CNN", "VH1", "FOX", "BET". **Business Addr:** Chief Executive Officer, Elite PA Services.

**FLUKER, DR. WALTER EARL**
Educator, clergy, administrator. **Personal:** Born Aug 26, 1951, Vaiden, MS; son of Clinton and Zettie; married Sharon; children: Wendy D, Tiffany M, Clinton & Hampton. **Educ:** Trinity Col, BA, philos & bibl studies, 1977; Garrett Evangelical Theol Sem, Mdiv, 1980; Boston Univ, PhD, social ethics, 1988. **Career:** Boston Univ, Whitney M Young fel, 1981-82; Harvard Univ, Andrew W Mellonfac fel, 1990-91; Vanderbilt Univ Res Coun, univ fel, 1990-91; Christian Friendship MB Church, assoc pastor, 1992-97; Morehouse Col, Colgate Rochester Divinity Sch, Howard Thurman Papers Proj, ed & dir, 1992-97, Dept Philos & Relig & Leadership Stud, exec dir, prof, Leadership Stud, chair, 1998, Leadership Ctr, exec dir, currently, Coca-Cola prof leadership studies, exec dir, currently; Vision Quest Inc, pres, founder & chief exec officer, 1997; Walter Earl Fluker & Assocs, founder; Harvard Divinity Sch, AA Relig Studies, Leadership Ctr, vis prof, 2001-02; US Embassy Speaker & Specialist Prog, speaker & lectr; The Sound of the Genuine: The Papers of Howard Washington Thurman, sr ed; Black Leaders and Ideologies in the South: Resistance and Non-Violence, co-ed; Tumber of A Strange Freedom: The Best of Howard Thurman on Religious Experience and Public Life, co-ed; Martin Luther King Jr, prof & dir; Eastman Kodak, consult & workshop leader; Goldman Sachs, consult & workshop leader; Sierra Leone, youth develop initiatives, consult; Salzburg Seminar, fac; Int Human Rights Exchange Programme, distinguished visitor; Univ Cape Town, Grad Sch Bus, vis prof, Educating Ethical Leaders for the Twenty-First Century, Cascade Books, ed; Books: The Stones that the Builders Rejected: Essays on Ethical Leadership from the Black Church Tradition; My People Need Me and volume II; Christian, Who Calls Me Christian?; Ethical Leadership: The Quest for Character, Civility and Community, 2009; Articles: "Looking For Martin: Black Leadership in an Era of Contested Post-Racism and Post-Blackness", 2013; "Leaders Who Have Shaped US Religious Dialogue: Howard Thurman", 2013; Columbia Theol Sem, vis prof; Princeton Theol Sem, vis prof. **Orgs:** Bd mem, Trinity Press Int; bd mem, Howard Thurman Educ Trust; bd mem, Toni Morrison Soc; Soc Christian Ethics; Soc Study Black Relig; Am Acad Relig; Nat Asn Advan Colored People; fac adv, Omicron Delta Kappa Soc; adv bd, Am Asn Cols, currently; bd, US News & World Report, Nat Selection Comt; Urban League Rochester; Lib Educ, bd; consult, Ford Found; pastor, St John's Congregational Church; dean, Lawless Memorial Chapel; DHL, Honoris Causa. **Home Addr:** 415 Montague Ave, Atlanta, GA 30331, **Home Phone:** (404)629-6819. **Business Addr:** Executive Director, Coca-Cola Professor of Leadership Studies, Morehouse College, 830 Westview Dr SW, Atlanta, GA 30314, **Business Phone:** (404)681-2800.

**FLYNN, H. WELTON**
Accountant. **Personal:** Born Dec 22, 1921, Blackville, SC; son of Inez M and Welton; children: Welton C & Gerald A. **Educ:** Golden Gate Univ, BA, 1951. **Career:** Government official (retired); H. Welton Flynn & Assocs, pub acct, 1949-2004; Pub Transp Comn, 1996; San Francisco Munic Transp Agency, chmn, 2000-04. **Orgs:** Alpha Phi Alpha Fraternity Inc, 1960; Nat Asn Advan Colored People, 1984; San Francisco Pub Utilities Comn, 1970-91; San Francisco Conv & Visitors Bur, chmn bd, 1992-; San Francisco Soc Acct, 1977. **Honors/Awds:** City's First African-American on any commission, 1970; Alpha Phi Alpha, Man of the Year, 1985, 1995, Humanitarian Medal, 1988; Nat Asn Advan Colored People Legal Defense Fund, Man of the Year, 1989; San Francisco Bus & Prof Women, Man of the Year, 1983; State Calif, State Bd Accountancy, 1949; inaugural Miriam Gholikely Award, MTC, 2004; American Public Transportation Asn Hall of Fame, 2006. **Special Achievements:** First chair of the FMTA Board of Director; Muni's Flynn Division named in honor. **Home Addr:** 1255 Post St Suite 807, San Francisco, CA 94109, **Home Phone:** (415)775-1255.

**FOARD, FREDERICK CARTER**
Publisher, executive. **Personal:** Born Mar 10, 1945, Philadelphia, PA; son of Howard A Sr and Adele; married Georgeanne Garrett; children: Nicole & Justin. **Educ:** Lincoln Univ PA, BA, psychol, 1967; Capital Univ Columbus, MBA, finance & mkt, 1976. **Career:** HRB Singer Div Singer Co, scientist, 1967-69; Schering Labs Schering Plough, mkt res analyst, 1969-71; Bristol Labs/Bristol-Myers Co, sr mkt res, 1971-73; Warren-Teed Pharm/Rohm & Haas Co, mgr mkt res, 1973-74, prod mgr, 1974-77; Smith Kline Beckman Corp, sr prod mgr, 1977-83, dir commun, 1983-87, dir mkt, 1986-88, vpres, cardiovasc mkt, 1987-91; Advan Commun Strategies Inc, Cherry Hill, NJ, pres & chief exec officer, 1991-99; Commun Media Inc, exec vpres, media opers mgt, 1999-2009, exec vpres, strategic insights, 2009-10, 2012; pres & chief exec officer, F Carter Foard & Assocs LLC, 2012-; UCI, dir, bus develop, 2014-; Shepherd's Village at Pk Ave, adminr, 2015-. **Orgs:** Omega Psi Phi Fraternity, 1963-; Am Mgt Asn, 1977-89; Nat Black MBA Asn, 1983-; Pharmaceut Adv Coun, 1986-93; corp mkt rep, Pharmaceut Manufacturers Asn, 1986-91; bd vice chmn, Nat Minority Health Asn, 1989-94; bd mem, Am Health Asn, Philadelphia Affil, 1990-94; bd mem, Health Policy Int, 1991-; Sigma Pi Phi Fraternity. **Honors/Awds:** Legion of Honor Chapel of Four Chaplains, 1981; MBA of the Year, 1990; Omega Man of the Year, 1992. **Home Addr:** 807 Monmouth Dr, Cherry Hill, NJ 08002, **Home Phone:** (609)779-8122. **Business Addr:** President, Chief Executive Officer, F Carter Foard & Associates LLC, 407 Monmouth Dr, Cherry Hill, NJ 08002.

**FOBBS, KEVIN**
Executive, public relations executive, consultant. **Personal:** Born Jan 11, 1954, River Rouge, MI; son of Booker Terry and Geraldine Jenna; married Patricia Marie Strunck; children: Katherine Marie Strunck. **Educ:** Eastern Mich Univ, BS, polit sci & jour, 1978; Wayne State Univ Law Sch, attended 1980. **Career:** Wayne Co Neighborhood Legal Serv, community outreach coordr, 1986-90; Fobbs & Strunck Communs, pres, 1989; Mich Repub State Comt, vice chmn; Soul Source, dir govt & civic affairs; Nat Urban Policy Action Coun, pres, founder, currently; WDTK, Kevin Fobbs Show, host; Examr.com Entertainment, Journalist, auth. Author: Is There a Lion in My Kitchen, 2014. **Orgs:** Exec bd mem, Detroit Asn Black Orgn, 1984-; Nat Asn Advan Colored People, ACT-BE Comn Jobs, Detroit Br, 1991-; Mich Gov John Engler's Action Team, 1992-; Mich Enterprise Zone Authority, 1992-; bd mem, Wayne Co Dept Social Serv, 1992-; bd pres, Habitat Humanity, Metro Detroit Br; bd mem, Int Br, 1992-; co-chair & co-founder, Am-Can Cons Coalition. **Home Addr:** 20418 Lichfield, Detroit, MI 48221, **Home Phone:** (313)342-8568. **Business Addr:** President, Founder, National Urban Policy Action Council, 12948 Farmington Rd, Detroit, MI 48150, **Business Phone:** (313)749-1659.

**FOGAM, PROF. MARGARET HANORAH**
Administrator, educator. **Personal:** Born Bali; daughter of Simon and Freida. **Educ:** Georgetown Univ, Wash, DC, BA, 1979; Clark-Atlanta Univ, GA, MA, 1985, ABD, 1985. **Career:** Clark-Atlanta Univ, Ga, admin asst, 1989-; Morris Brown Col, prof, 1999. **Orgs:** Am Asn Sociologists, 1985-; Nat Conf Black Polit Scientists, 1987-; Nat Asn Social Scientists, 1988-; Am Asn Polit Scientists, 1987-; sr sponsorship asst, Plan Cameroon. **Home Addr:** 780 Lexington Ave SW, Atlanta, GA 30310, **Home Phone:** (404)254-3284. **Business Addr:** Administrative Assistant, Atlanta University, Oglethorpe Hall Rm 326, Atlanta, GA 30314, **Business Phone:** (404)880-6674.

**FOGGS, REV. DR. EDWARD L.**
Clergy, executive director, minister (clergy). **Personal:** Born Jul 11, 1934, Kansas City, KS; son of Eddie and Inez Lewis; married Joyce; children: Lynette, Iris, Edward Elliot, Joy & Alycia. **Educ:** Anderson Col & Ball State Univ, AB, 1958; Anderson Univ, DDiv, 1984; Anderson Sch Theol & Christian Theol Sem. **Career:** Sherman State Church God, Anderson, Ind, pastor, 1959-69; Anderson Col, Afro-Am Studies Dept, adj fac, 1968-; Anderson Univ, adj fac, 1968-82; Urban Ministers Bd Ch Ext & Home Missions Church God, dir, 1970-75; Exec Coun Church God, assoc exec secy, 1975-88, exec secy & chief exec officer, 1988-; Church God Ministries, Anderson, gen dir, Leadership Coun, exec secy & distinguished minister-at-large, currently. **Orgs:** Pres, Inspirational Youth Conv, Nat Asn Church God, 1964-72; Family Serv Madison County, 1964-66; chmn, Ill Gen Assembly Church God, 1967-68; Contrib Nat Church Pub Bldg Bridges Racial Understanding, 1967; pres, Urban League Madison County, 1969-71; bd mem, Nat Conf Black Churchmen, 1971-72; key speaker, 5th World Conf Church God, Oaxtepec, Mex, 1971; Oper, PUSH, 1974-75; alt bd mem, Urban Training Ctr Christian Mission, 1974-75; Am Mgt Asn, 1976-; Black Exec Denominations Related Orgn & Communions, 1977-78; Nat Relig Adv Coun, Nat Urban League, 1978-; Planning Conf, Sixth World Conf Church God, Nairobi, Kenya, E Africa, 1978; Martin Luther King Jr Memorial Comt, 1987-88; bd mem, Community Hosp County, 1988-; Inner City Found Excellence Educ, 1988-; Anderson Area Chamber Com, 1988-; United Way Madison County, 1989-; convener, World Conf Church God, Wiesbaden, W Ger, 1991; Conv Speaker/Conf & Leader/Consult Church Work; Nat Asn Evangelicals; Mission Am. **Special Achievements:** Co-authored Study Guide Andrew Billingsley's Book "Black Families & the Struggle for Survival" 1974. **Home Addr:** 2104 Mimosa Lane, Anderson, IN 46011, **Home Phone:** (765)644-0168. **Business Addr:** Minister at Large, Church of God Ministries, 1303 W 5th St, Anderson, IN 46018-2420, **Business Phone:** (765)642-0256.

**FOGGS, JOYCE D.**
Educator, teacher, school principal. **Personal:** Born Feb 13, 1930, Indianapolis, IN; daughter of Wilbur Stone (deceased) and Marry Elizabeth Stone (deceased); married Edward L; children: Lynette, Iris, Edward Elliot, Joy & Alycia. **Educ:** Anderson Col, BS, 1954; Ball State Univ, MA, 1967. **Career:** Educator, principal, school administrator (retired); Park Pl Sch, Anderson, Ind, teacher; Dunbal Elem Sch, Kansas City, teacher, 1954-55; Westvale Sch, Anderson, Ind, teacher, 1959-60; Hazelwood Sch, Anderson, Ind, teacher, 1963-70; Anderson Community Sch, asst prin; Robinson Elem Sch, prin, 1988-89; Shadeland Elem Sch, prin. **Orgs:** Am Asn Univ Women, 1959-65; vpres bd trustee, Anderson-Anderson Stoney Creek Lib bd, 1967-; Delta Kappa Gamma Hon Soc Women Educ, 1973-; Kappa Delta Pi, 1973-; comnr, Gruenwald Home Hist Preserv, 1977; Nat Spiritual Life; dir, Women Church God; exec bd, Women Church God, 1978-; Urban League Madison Co, 1982-; comnr, Anderson Housing Authority, 1984-; Community Hosp Found, 1988-; Anderson Area Youth Choir, Anderson Community Schs Found bd, United Way Madison County allocations comt & Anderson Pub Libr trustee. **Home Addr:** 2104 Mimosa Lane, Anderson, IN 46011, **Home Phone:** (317)644-0168.

**FOLEY, REV. BASIL A., SR.**
Clergy, founder (originator). **Personal:** Born Jan 22, 1931, Indianapolis, IN; son of Lee and Alberta; married Loesther; children: Basil A Jr, Katrina R, Yvonne A, Brian & Kenneth G. **Educ:** Chicago State Univ, BA, 1979; McCormick Theol Sem, Mdiv, 1982. **Career:** Pastor (retired); Newman AME Church & Youth Found, founder & pastor, 1953; Tenth Episcopal Dist, pastor; Fourth Episcopal Dist, pastor, presiding elder; AME Quadrennial Gen Conf, 1976-96. **Home Addr:** 121 Ct St, Pontiac, MI 48342, **Home Phone:** (248)335-3699.

**FOLEY, STEVE**
Football player. **Personal:** Born Sep 11, 1975, Little Rock, AR; son of Robert; children: 1. **Educ:** Northeast La Univ, BS, sociol. **Career:** Football player (retired); Cincinnati Bengals, linebacker & left outside linebacker, 1998-2002; Houston Texans, right outside linebacker, 2003; San Diego Chargers, linebacker, 2004-06. **Honors/Awds:** Chargers Alumni Player of Week, 2004.

**FOLK, DR. FRANK STEWART**
Physician. **Personal:** Born Oct 2, 1932, Varnville, SC; children: 3. **Educ:** Hampton Inst, attended 1954; Brooklyn Col, BS, 1957; Howard Univ, Col Med, MD, 1961. **Career:** Freedman Hosp, res gen surg, 1962-66, med officer, 1969-70; Howard Univ, res gen surg, 1962-66, instr surg, 1969, res fel, 1969-70; US Pub Health Serv, asst resident, 1964-65, chief resident, 1967-68; DC Gen Hosp, chief resident, 1965-66, med officer, 1969-70; State Univ NY Health Sci Ctr , Brooklyn, internship, resident; St Barnabas Hosp, asst resident, 1966-67, assoc attend, 1970-, assoc dir surg, 1980-82; IBM, Brooklyn, med dir, 1971-75; Downstate Med Col, asst instr, 1973-76, clin instr, 1976-86; Hosp Joint Dis Med Ctr, asst attend, 1973-79; Brooklyn Jewish Hosp, asst

attend surgeon, 1973-81; NY State Athletic Comn, asst med dir, 1980, actg med dir, 1986; NY Med Col, asst prof surg, 1987; Health & Hosp Corp, dir, 2004; Clin Surg Health Sci Ctr, asst prof, 2004; State Univ NY-Downstate Col Med, asst prof; pvt pract, currently; Univ Hosp Brooklyn, clin asst prof surg, currently. **Orgs:** Num OthOrgns NG, 1962-66; Cert Nat Bd Med Examiners, 1966; NY State Med Bd, 1967; asst former State Senotor Basil Paterson, 1970; Goldberg-paterson Election Financial Com, 1970; exec bd, Provident Clin Soc, 1971; chmn, Regl Nat Med Asn, 1971-74; Kings Co Hosp comm Bd Thomas R Fortune, 1971-74; vchmn, United Dem Mens Club, 1971-75; mem exec, Com Unity Dem Club, 1972-; bd dir, NY City Health Hosp Corp Legis Med & Prof Capital; bd dir, Charles A Drew Health Clin, 1974; Am Bd Surg, 1977; Am Col Cardiol; cand, Am Col Surgeons; Nat Med Asn; NY Cardiological Soc; Asn Acad Surg; Manhattan Control Med Soc; Provident Clin Soc Brooklyn; AMA; founding mem, Am Trauma Soc; Bronx Co Med Soc; Howard Univ Med Alumni Asn; Empire State Med Soc; NY State Med Soc; Unity Dem Club. **Home Addr:** 490 New York Ave, Brooklyn, NY 11225, **Home Phone:** (718)363-6600. **Business Addr:** Clinical Assistant Professor, University Hospital of Brooklyn, 450 Clarkson Ave, Brooklyn, NY 11203, **Business Phone:** (718)270-1000.

**FOLKS, BYRON ALLEN.** **See ALLEN, BYRON.**

## FOLLMER, PAUL L.

Banker. **Career:** El Pueblo State Bank, pres & chief exec officer, currently. **Home Addr:** 7515 Riverton Dr NW, Albuquerque, NM 87120, **Home Phone:** (505)994-9443.

## FOLSTON, JAMES EDWARD

Football player. **Personal:** Born Aug 14, 1971, Cocoa, FL. **Educ:** Northeast La Univ, grad. **Career:** Football player (retired); Los Angeles Raiders, 1994; Oakland Raiders, 1995, 1996, right linebacker, 1997, left linebacker, 1998; Ariz Cardinals, 1999, 2001, linebacker, 2000. **Honors/Awds:** ULM Iron Man Award; Athletics Hall of Fame, 2010. **Home Addr:** 1450 Victoria Blvd, Rockledge, FL 32955.

## FOMUFOD, DR. ANTOINE KOFI

Pediatrician, physician, educator. **Personal:** Born Oct 16, 1940, Ngen-Mbo; son of Ngwabi; married Angelina Hirku; children: Antoine, Ngwabi & Nina B. **Educ:** Univ Ibadan Nigeria, Col Med, MD, 1967; Johns Hopkins Univ Sch Med, fel pediat, 1973; Johns Hopkins Univ Sch Hyg, MPH, 1974; Am Bd Pediat, cert, pediat, neonatal-perinatal med. **Career:** Johns Hopkins Hosp, Bayview Med Ctr, resident & internship; Howard Univ, Dept Pediat, from asst prof to assoc prof, 1974-92, dir, neonatology, 1986-, prof pediat, 1992-; Pediatrix Med Group, pvt pract, currently. **Orgs:** Affil Fel Franklin Sq Hosp, 1971-73; Johns Hopkins Med-Surg Soc, 1974-; med staff, Hosp Sick C, 1975-77; DC Med Soc, 1975-; Am Acad Pediat, 1975-; secy bd, Assoc African Physicians N Am, 1980-; Sect Perinatal & Neonatal Pediat Am Acad Pediat; Southern Med Assoc, 1985-90; AAAS, 1985-90; Southern Perinatal Assoc, 1985-90; World Cong Martial Arts, 1986-; fel Am Acad Pediats; adv trustee, Mt Wash Pediat Hospl Inc. **Honors/Awds:** Merit Award, Howard Univ Med Stud Coun, 1981; Outstanding Physician Residents, Dept Pediat Howard Univ Hosp, 1982; Med Productivity Award, Howard Univ Hosp, 1994. **Special Achievements:** Over 50 papers published in peer reviewed medical journals as of Dec 1994. **Home Addr:** 5722 Avery Park Dr, Rockville, MD 20855-1738, **Home Phone:** (301)618-2630. **Business Addr:** Director, Professor, Howard University Hospital, 2041 Ga Ave NW, Washington, DC 20060, **Business Phone:** (202)865-6100.

## FONROSE, DR. HAROLD ANTHONY

Consultant, physician, association executive. **Personal:** Born Aug 31, 1925, Brooklyn, NY; married Mary Elizabeth; children: Wayne, Mark, Drew & Ward. **Educ:** Adelphi Univ, BA, 1952; Cornell Univ, MS, 1954; Howard Univ, MD, 1958. **Career:** Internist, 1962-; A Holly Patterson Home, consult, 1962-70, dir; Am Bd Internal Med, dipl, 1968; A Holly Patterson Home, med dir, 1970; Mt Sinai med Fac Elmhurst Campus, attend staff physician. **Orgs:** NY St & Nassau Co Med Soc; Sigma Pi Phi Frat; Alpha Sigma Boule; Alphi Phi Alpha Frat; Am Col Geriatrics, 1971; past bd dir, Vanguard Nat Bank, 1972-76; fel Am Col Physicians, 1977; Nassau County Med Soc; Ny Med Asn; Bd Vanguard Nat Bank; Pre-Medlcal Hon Soc; Adelphi activitles-Biotogy Club. **Special Achievements:** Published "Digital is Withdrawal in Aged" J Geriatrics; "Role of Med Dir in Skilled Nursing Facility". **Home Addr:** 1063 Inverness Ave, Melbourne, FL 32940. **Business Addr:** Physician, Howard University College of Medicine, 520 W St NW, Washington, DC 20059, **Business Phone:** (202)806-6270.

## FONTAINE, DR. JOHN M.

Physician, educator. **Personal:** Born Apr 6, 1954; son of Antoine and Gisele. **Educ:** Univ Med & Dent NJ, attended 1979. **Career:** Nassau Co Med Ctr, Internal Med, intern, 1980, residency, 1982; Veterans Admin Med Ctr, cardiol fel, 1985, Pacemaker Clin, dir, 1985-90, Cardiac Arrhythmia Clin, dir, 1985-90, Electrophysiol Lab, dir, 1985-90; State Univ NY, Health Sci, asst prof med, 1985-90; Med Col Pa, Electrophysiol Serv, dir cardiac, 1990-96, asst prof med, 1990-96; Allegheny Univ, Hosp-Med Division, dir cardiac arrhythmia serv, 1996-, assoc prof med, 1996-; pvt pract, currently; Drexel Univ Col Med, assoc prof, currently. **Orgs:** Cardiac Electrophysiol Soc, 1987; mentors prog, Asn Black Cardiologists, 1992; Manuscript reviewer, J Pacing & Clin Electrophysiol, 1994; manuscript reviewer, J Am Col Cardiol, 1996; mentors prog, Nat Med Asn, 1996; bd gov, Am Heart Asn Southeastern PA Affil, 1996-99; bd dir, Asn Black Cardiololgists, 1990; Nat Inst Health, currently. **Home Addr:** 219 N Broad St, Philadelphia, PA 19107, **Home Phone:** (215)762-5080. **Business Addr:** Physician, Private Pactitioner, 3300 Henry Ave, Philadelphia, PA 19129, **Business Phone:** (215)842-7455.

## FONTAYNE, K. NICOLE (K NICOLE FONTAYNE-MACK)

Financial manager, executive. **Personal:** Born Chicago, IL; daughter of James and Carole Youngblood; married James L Mack; children: Cameron J Underwood. **Educ:** Univ Chicago, AS, 1976; Roosevelt Univ, BA, polit sci, 1978; Nova Southeastern Univ, MPA, 2009. **Career:** Int Harvester Credit, Albany, credit analyst, 1979-80; Farmers Ins Group, Santa Ana, supvr, 1980-81; Amerisure/Mich Mutual, Detroit, jula mgr, 1987; Amerisure Co, resource productivity mgr, 1991-94; City Detroit, dir info technol serv, 1994-99; Detroit Waldorf Sch, bd trustee; Broward Co Off, Ft Lauderdale, Off Info Technol, interim chief; Broward County Off, Off Info Technol, chief info officer, 1999-2008; Magellan Assocs LLC, prin, chief info officers, 2008-12; Syzygy Assocs LLC, Managing Partner, 2009-; Trophy Club Econ Develop Corp, vol dir/bd mem, 2010-12, Vol Vice Chair Blue Ribbon Panel, 2013-14; Dispute Resolution Serv Tarrant County, vol vpres, 2011-13; Everest Group, 2014; Dallas Area Rapid Transit, vpres, chief info officer, 2014-. **Orgs:** Word of Faith, 1985-; co-chairperson, Amerisure, United Way Campaign, 1990. **Honors/Awds:** Minority Achievement Award, YMCA, 1990. **Home Addr:** 15103 Faust, Detroit, MI 48223, **Home Phone:** (313)272-7641. **Business Addr:** Vice President, Chief Information Officer, Dallas Area Rapid Transit, 1401 Pacific Ave, Dallas, TX 75202, **Business Phone:** (214)979-1111.

**FONTAYNE-MACK, K NICOLE.** **See FONTAYNE, K. NICOLE.**

## FONTENOT, REV. ALBERT E., JR.

President (organization), chief executive officer, clergy. **Personal:** Born Oct 23, 1946, Alexandria, LA; son of Albert E Sr and Fay Scott; married Beverly; children: Kimberly, Michelle & Albert III. **Educ:** DePaul Univ, BA, 1979, MBA, 1985; Bethany Theol Sem, DMin, 1993. **Career:** Wieboldt Inc, buyer, 1967-75; Playskool Toy Co, vpres res & develop, 1976-81; Wilson Jones Co, vpres mkt, 1981-85; Eldon Off Prods, vpres mkt, 1985-91; Antioch Bapt Ch, Long Beach, Calif, deacon, 1986-89, assoc pastor, 1989-92; Eldon-Rubbermaid Off Prod, vpres sales, 1991-93; Mt Calvary Bapt Ch, Knoxville, Tenn, assoc pastor, 1992-94; Atapco Off Prod, vpres mkt, 1993-94, sr vpres sales & mkt, 1994-95, pres & chief exec officer, 1995; 1st Bapt Ch, Baldwin, Mo, assoc pastor, 1994-2002; Eagle OPG Inc, pres & chief exec officer, 1995-2001; Fels Inc, vpres & gen mgr technol accessories Group, 2001-05; 2nd Baptist Ch, Elgin, Ill, assoc minister, 2002-06; Rhinotek Comput Prods Inc, chmn, pres & chief exec officer, 2006-; Mt Moriah Baptist Church, Los Angeles, assoc minister, 2006-. **Orgs:** Bd trustee, Bethel Bapt Ch, 1982-85, bd dir, United Way Greater St Louis, 1995-2001. **Home Addr:** 28 La Linda Dr, Long Beach, CA 90807-3306, **Home Phone:** (562)989-9517. **Business Addr:** Chairman President, Chief Executive Officer, Rhinotek Computer Products Inc, 2301 E Del Amo Blvd, Carson, CA 90220-6304, **Business Phone:** (310)638-2500.

## FONTENOT, ALBERT PAUL, III

Football player. **Personal:** Born Sep 17, 1970, Houston, TX; married Stephanie. **Educ:** Baylor Univ, commun. **Career:** Football player (retired); Chicago Bears, defensive end, 1993, left defensive tackle, 1994, right defensive end, 1995, left defensive end, 1996; Indianapolis Colts, left defensive end, 1997-98; San Diego Chargers, defensive end, 1999-2001.

## FONTENOT-JAMERSON, BERLINDA

Manager. **Personal:** Born Jul 5, 1947, San Fernando, CA; daughter of Leroy and Velma Kyle; married Michael. **Educ:** Los Angeles Trade Technol Col, AA, 1972; Calif State Univ, Los Angeles, BA, indust psychol, 1978; Pepperdine Univ, Malibu, CA, MBA, 1984. **Career:** Southern CA Gas Co LA CA, sr prof recruiter, consumer affairs mgr, 1984-87, community rels mgr, 1987-92, personnel rels & diversity mgr, 1992-95, Pac Enterprises, corp diversity mgr, 1995; Sempra Energy, dir corp diversity affairs; ABC, dir diversity & corp human resources, 2005-; Walt Disney Co, dir; Fontenot-Jamerson Group, pres; OnePeoples Inc, dir corp diversity affairs. **Orgs:** Adv bd, Amer Asn Blacks Energy, currently; bd mem, Women Color, 1987-; bd mem, Careers Older Ams, 1987-; pres, bd mem, Mus African Am Art, 1988-; vpres, admin, DATACOM, 1988-; comt chair, Nat Asn Advan Colored People-LDF Black Women Achievement, 1989; bd mem, Coalition Women's Econ Develop; UNCF Blue Ribbon COM; Diversity & EEO Mgrs Network. **Honors/Awds:** Leadership Award, YWCA, 1985; Gold Award, United Way, 1986; Black Women of Achievement Merit Award, NAACP-LDF, 1986; Merit Award, Am Asn Blacks Energy, 1986, 1988; Certificate of Support, LA Urban League, 1988-94; Women in NAALR Merit Award; Coalition Women Economic Development Award, 1992; Clarke A. Watson Chairmans Cup Award, 1993. **Home Addr:** 6526 Copperwood Ave Suite 104, Inglewood, CA 90302, **Home Phone:** (310)215-9028. **Business Addr:** Advisory Board Member, American Association of Blacks in Energy, 1625 K St NW Suite 405, Washington, DC 20006, **Business Phone:** (202)371-9530.

**FONVIELLE, BILL.** **See FONVIELLE, WILLIAM HAROLD.**

## FONVIELLE, WILLIAM HAROLD (BILL FONVIELLE)

Chief executive officer, founder (originator), vice president (organization). **Personal:** Born Dec 18, 1943, Chicago, IL; son of William B and Elizabeth Brown; married Carole Lynn Sharoff; children: Michelle R Williams, Deanne V & Jonathan W. **Educ:** Shimer Col, BA, humanities, 1963; Northwestern Univ, postgrad philos, 1965; Yale Univ, Sch Orgn & Mgt, MBA, 1981. **Career:** J Walter Thompson Co, media buyer, 1966-68; Vince Cullers Adv Inc, media dir, 1968-70; Communicon Inc, pres, 1970-75; State Ill, publ info officer, 1975-77 & dir motion, picture TV prodn, 1977; Denver Reg Coun Govt, dir pub affairs, 1977-79; Goodmeasure Inc, vpres & dir consult, 1981-86; Forum Corp, vpres, 1986-94, sr vpres performance measurement, 1995-97; Performance Measurement Assocs Inc, owner, founder & chief exec officer, 1997-; Harvard Bus Sch, prof; Mass Prod Develop Corp, chmn; Chg Masters Int Ltd, sr assoc, 2005-; Rosabeth Moss Kanter. Author: The Changing American Workplace: Work Alternatives in the '80s, 1985; From Manager to Innovator: Using Information to Become an Idea Entrepreneur, 1988. **Orgs:** Dir, Apt Store Inc, 1968-70; dir, Lovespace Inc, 1972-75; trustee, Village Carol Stream, Ill, 1973-77; dir, Northeastern Ill Plng Comn, 1973-77; dir, Homes Pvt Enterprise, 1973-77; trustee, Garrett-Evang Theol Sem, 1974-76; secy, Ill-Ind Bi-State Develop Agency Comn, 1975-77; Accrediation comt Colo Pub Rels Soc Am, 1978-80; founder, Coun City & Co Communicators, 1978-79; chmn, Mass Prod Develop Corp, 1986-; MENSA, 1987-; founding mem, Greater Boston Chap Int Customer Serv Asn, 1987-; United Way Mass Bay, 1987-92; Orgn Develop Network, 1988-; dir, Horizons Fund, 1990-94; Handel & Haydn Soc, overseer, 1992-; Nat Black MBA Asn, 1998-; dir, Atlantic Vacation Homes Inc, 1998-; chmn, Career Collab, 2001-05; chmn, City Glovester Plan Implementation Rev Comn, 2002-; Am Mgt Asn; Pub Rels Soc Am; Int Customer Serv Asn; fel, Pub rel Socs Am; N Shore Asn Realtors; Nat Asn Realtors. **Home Addr:** 27 Old Salem Rd, Gloucester, MA 01930-4026, **Home Phone:** (978)281-1650. **Business Addr:** Chief Executive Officer, Founder, Performance Measurement Associates Inc, 115 Prospect St, Gloucester, MA 01930-3708, **Business Phone:** (978)283-5408.

## FONVILLE, CHAD EVERETTE

Baseball player. **Personal:** Born Mar 5, 1971, Jacksonville, NC. **Educ:** Louisburg Col. **Career:** Baseball player (retired), baseball coach; Montreal Expos, infielder, 1995; Los Angeles Dodgers, 1995-97; Chicago White Sox, 1997; Cleveland Indians, infielder, 1998; Boston Red Sox, infielder, 1999; New York Yankees, infielder; Lejeune High Sch, head coach, currently. **Business Addr:** Head Coach, Le Juene High School, 835 Stone St, Camp Lejeune, NC 28547, **Business Phone:** (910)451-2451.

## FONVILLE, DANNY D.

Government official. **Career:** Calif Dept Corrections, corrections officer, 1981-; Becton Dickinson Pub Safety, NIT Narcotics Identification, master trainer; Folsom State Prison, conflict mgt trainer, trainer trainers; Equal Employ Opportunity Affirmation Action, counr & trainer; Folsom State Prison Youth Diversion Prog, Dept Corrections State Calif, recruiter. **Orgs:** Blacks Govt; Correctional Peace Officer Found. **Honors/Awds:** Correctional Officer of the Year, State Calif, 1995; Correctional Officer of the Year, City Folsom, 1995; Meritorious Service Award, Int Asn Correctional Officers, 1995; Officer of the Year, Correctional Peace Officer Found, 1996. **Home Addr:** PO Box 761, Walnut Grove, CA 95690. **Business Addr:** Corrections Officer, California Department of Corrections, PO Box W, Represa, CA 95671.

## FOOTE, YVONNE

School administrator. **Personal:** Born Dec 24, 1949, Philadelphia, PA; daughter of Lorenzo L Alleyne and Alma Jenkens Alleyne; married Nathaniel A; children: Omar Y. **Career:** Del Valley Reg Planning Comm, cost acct, 1975-81; Thomas & Muller Co Inc, bookkeeper, 1982-84; Laborers Dist Coun Legal Fund, secy & bookkeeper, 1984-; Rawle & Henderson, Philadelphia, Pa, accounts payable coordr, bookkeeper, 1987-; Lawnside Bd Educ, pres. **Home Addr:** 307 John F Kennedy Blvd, Lawnside, NJ 08045-1037, **Home Phone:** (856)546-0290. **Business Addr:** Accounts Payable Coordinator, Bookkeeper, Rawle & Henderson LLP, Widener Bldg 16th Fl 1 S Penn Sq, Philadelphia, PA 19107-3519, **Business Phone:** (215)575-4200.

## FOOTMAN, DAN ELLIS, JR.

Football player. **Personal:** Born Jan 13, 1969, Tampa, FL; children: Dantavian Hicks. **Educ:** Fla State Univ. **Career:** Football player (retired); Cleveland Browns, 1993, defensive end, 1994, right defensive tackle, 1995; Baltimore Ravens, nose tackle, 1996; Indianapolis Colts, right defensive end, 1997, defensive end, 1998. **Honors/Awds:** Brian Piccolo Award for ACC player; New York Daily News All-Star Award. **Home Addr:** 1311 Windsor Pl, Jacksonville, FL 32205, **Home Phone:** (904)388-3577.

## FORBES, CALVIN

College teacher, educator. **Personal:** Born May 6, 1945, Newark, NJ; son of Jacob and Mary Short. **Educ:** New Sch Social Res; Rutgers Univ; Brown Univ, MFA, 1978. **Career:** Emerson Col, Boston, Mass, asst prof eng, 1969-73; Tufts Univ, Medford, Mass, asst prof Eng, 1973-74, 1975-77; Denmark, France & Eng, fulbright lectr, 1974-75; Univ W Indies, guest lectr, 1982-83; Howard Univ, Wash, DC, writer residence; Wash Col, Chester Town, Md, asst prof creative writing, 1988-89; Sch Art Inst Chicago, chair writing, prof lib arts, assoc prof, 1991-. Books: Blue Monday, 1974; From the Book of Shine, 1979; The Shine Poems, 2001. **Orgs:** Mod Lang Asn; fel, Nat Endowment Arts Grant, 1982-83; fel, DC Comn Arts, 1984; Col Lang Asn; fel, NJ State Coun Arts. **Business Addr:** Professor of Liberal Arts, Associate Professor, School of Arts Institute of Chicago, 37 S Wabash Ave, Chicago, IL 60603, **Business Phone:** (312)899-5100.

## FORBES, GEORGE L.

Lawyer, politician. **Personal:** Born Apr 4, 1931, Memphis, TN; son of Cleveland and Elnora; married Mary Fleming; children: Helen, Mildred & Lauren. **Educ:** Baldwin-Wallace Col, BA, 1957; Cleveland Marshall Law Sch, JD, 1961. **Career:** Lawyer (retired); City Cleveland, teacher, 1958-62, housing insp, 1959-63; radio talk show host, 1972-75; Cuyahoga Co Dem Party, co-chmn, 1972-78; Cleveland City Coun, councilman, 1963-89, coun majority leader, 1972-73, pres, 1972-89; Baldwin-Wallace Col, guest lectr, 1990-; Forbes, Fields & Assoc Co, founding partner & prin officer, 1971; Ohio Supreme Ct; Us Dist Ct Northern Dist Ohio; avid Sunday Sch, teacher. **Orgs:** Chmn, Oper Regist; Nat Asn Def Lawyers; Cuyahoga Bar Asn; Ohio State Bar Asn; Cleveland Bar Asn; Gtr Cleveland Growth Corp & Asn; Coun Econ Opportunity; Legal Aid Soc; pres, Nat Asn Advan Colored People, Cleveland Chap, 1992, grand jury foreman, 1994; Urban League; John Harlan Law Club; Greater Cleveland Safety Coun; NAT League Cities; UNF; Oversight Bd Bur Worker's Compensation; Nat Asn Bond Lawyers; Nat Bar Asn; bd trustee, Baldwin-Wallace Col. **Honors/Awds:** Citation Merit, 1967; Humanitarian Of the Year, 1968; Man Of the Year, 1969; Outstanding Polit & Civic Efforts, 1971; Ohio Asn Commodores, 1973; Distinguished Merit Award, 1976; Ohio Gov Award, 1977; Police Athletic League Outstanding Service Award, 1978; Outstanding Community Leadership Award, Black Affairs Coun, 1983; Black Prof Of the Year, 1987; Honorary Doctorate Degree, Baldwin-Wallace Col, 1990; Honorary Doctorate Degree, Cent State Univ, 1989; Martin Luther King Jr Crusader Of the Year

Award, 1989; Cleveland State Univ, Distinguished Alumni Award, 1990; In Tribute to Pub Service Award, Cleveland State Univ Maxine Goodman Levin Col Urban Affairs, 1994; Louis Stokes Community Visionary Award; NAACP's Highest Award, 2009. **Special Achievements:** The city renamed a free overnight summer and winter camp for Cleveland's youth as Camp George L. Forbes, Highland Hills. **Home Addr:** 11430 Bellflower Rd, Cleveland, OH 44106, **Home Phone:** (216)229-4878.

### FORBES, MARLON DARRYL
Football player. **Personal:** Born Dec 25, 1971, Brooklyn, NY. **Educ:** Pa State Univ, BA, 1995. **Career:** Football player (retired); Chicago Bears, Nat Football League, 1996, corner back, safety, defensive back, 1997-98; Cleveland Browns, Nat Football League, free safety, 1999.

### FORD, AILEEN W. See Obituaries Section.

### FORD, DR. ALBERT S.
Educator, dentist. **Personal:** Born Dec 31, 1929, Elizabeth, NJ; son of William H and Bessie M Lewis; married Mary Victoria Burkett; children: Albert S Jr, Stephen D, Teresa D esq, Kevin M & Richard E. **Educ:** WVa State Col, Seton Hall Univ; Meharry Med Col, DDS, 1958; Rutgers Univ, attended 1982; New Sch Social Res, New York, attended 1981; Nat Bd Dent Examiners, dipl. **Career:** Newark Comn Health Serv Group Dent Serv, dir; pvt pract, Roselle, NJ, 1962-; Fairleigh Dickinson Col Dent Med, Hackensack, NJ, assoc prof, 1980-90; Univ Med & Dent, Newark, NJ, assoc prof. **Orgs:** Bd mgt, Meharry Med Col; Am Dent Asn; vpres, Common wealth Dent Soc; Int Asn Begg Study Groups; Am Endodontic Soc; Acad Gen Dent; bd mem, NJ State Bd Dent Examiners NE Regional Bd Dent Examiners, 1979; pres, Nat Advan Asn Colored People; mem exec bd, Urban League; vpres, Sr City Housing Corp; adv bd, First Nat Bank Cent Jersey; Sigma Pi Phi Mu Boule; Omega Psi Phi; NJ State Bd Dent Examiners; fel Am Col Dentists; fel Royal Soc Health; vpres & chmn, Treat Planning Fairleigh Dickinson Univ Sch Dent. **Home Addr:** 4 Linden Lane, Scotch Plains, NJ 07076, **Home Phone:** (908)241-3175. **Business Addr:** Dentist, 1001 Chestnut St, Roselle, NJ 07203-1934, **Business Phone:** (908)241-3175.

### FORD, ANTOINETTE (TONI FORD)
Executive. **Personal:** Born Dec 14, 1941, Philadelphia, PA; married Melvin W. **Educ:** Laval Univ Que, attended 1960; Chestnut Hill Col, BS, 1963; Am Univ, MS, 1966; Stanford Univ, attended 1967; Harvard Bus Sch, MBA. **Career:** Nat Oceanog Data Ctr, oceanog, 1966-69; Ogden Corp, oceanog, 1969-71; Stanford Univ, oceanog; White House fel, 1971-72; Inst Serv Educ, develop dir, 1972-73; Multimedia Commun Co, pres, chief exec officer; Telspan Serv Inc, pres, chief exec officer, 1998; Harvard Univ, John F. Kennedy fel; Stanford Univ, Nat Sci Found Fel; Projected Reality Corp, pres, 1998-2004; Double Dutch Digital Publ; Double Nickels Theatre Co, founder & pres, currently. Author: Bye Willie. **Orgs:** Fel NSF, 1967; DC City Co, 1973-75; exec vpres, B & C Asn Inc; Harvard Univ Fel Inst Polit, 1975; pres, Clemency Bd, 1975; vol, Town Hall Educ Arts & Recreation Campus; bd dir, DC Pub Libr Found. **Special Achievements:** First African American woman White House Fellow. **Business Addr:** Founder, President, Double Nickels Theatre Co, 1901 Miss Ave SE Suite 206, Washington, DC 20020, **Business Phone:** (843)636-3863.

### FORD, AUSBRA
Educator, sculptor. **Personal:** Born Feb 28, 1935, Chicago, IL; son of Thomas and Carrie; married Thelma Wakefield; children: Rangi & Maji. **Educ:** Sch Art Inst, Chicago, BA, 1964, MFA, 1966; Ray Vogue Art Sch, attended 1977. **Career:** Chicago Pub Sch, art instr, 1964-68; Gary Pub Sch, art instr, 1966-68; Southern Univ, Baton Rouge, La, assoc prof art, 1968-69; Chicago State Univ, prof art, 1969-, emer fac, currently. **Orgs:** Nat Conf Artists, 1975-; pres & co-founder, Visual Artists Round table, 1983-; Smithsonian Nat Mus African Art; Chicago Field Mus; pres & founder, African Am Visual Arts Round table; Kemetic Inst Northeastern Ill Univ; Asn Study Class African Civilizations; bd dir, DuSable Mus African Am Hist; S Side Community Arts Ctr. **Home Addr:** 8215 S Crandon Ave, Chicago, IL 60617-1933, **Home Phone:** (773)375-9598. **Business Addr:** Emeritus Faculty, Chicago State University, 9501 S King Dr, Chicago, IL 60628-1598, **Business Phone:** (773)995-2000.

### FORD, HON. BARRY W.
Lawyer. **Personal:** Born Dec 23, 1946, Pontotoc, MS; son of Oliver and Annie; married Willie Mae Duke; children: 3. **Educ:** Miss Valley St Col, BA, 1964; Thurgood Marshall Sch Law, JD, 1977; Nat Judicial Col, attended 1991. **Career:** Lawyers Comt Civil Rights, 1977-70; Munic Ct judge, 1979-90; Pontotoc County Sch syst, teacher & coach, 1974; Ford & Ford, Tupelo, Miss, atty, 1979-91; Prentiss & Tishomingo Counties, state Itawamba, Lee, Monroe, Pontotoc, Miss, ct trial judge, serv Alcorn, 1990-2001; Pontotoc city, Judge, 1991; First Circuit Ct Dist, circuit ct judge; Baker, Donelson, Bearman, Caldwell & Berkowitz, PC, atty, shareholder, currently. **Orgs:** Magnolia Bar Asn; Miss Bar Asn; Litigation Coun Am; Am Inns Ct; bd dir, Baker Donelson Diversity Comt; Adv Bd Mem, Best Lawyers Inc; McDonald United Methodist Church. **Honors/Awds:** Drum Major for Justice Award, Southern Christian Leadership Conf, 1998; Mississippi Majesty Award, 2008; Professionalism Award, Capital Area Bar Asn, 2012. **Special Achievements:** First black to ever be elected circuit judge in the State of Mississippi. **Home Addr:** 195 Martin Luther King Dr, Pontotoc, MS 38863, **Home Phone:** (601)489-5650. **Business Addr:** Board of Director, Baker, Donelson, Bearman, Caldwell & Berkowitz PC, 100 Vision Dr 1 Eastover Ctr Suite 400, Jackson, MS 39211-7000, **Business Phone:** (601)351-2400.

### FORD, CHERYL
Basketball player. **Personal:** Born Jun 6, 1981, Homer, LA; daughter of Karl Malone and Bonita. **Educ:** La Tech Univ, health & educ, 2003. **Career:** Detroit Shock, forward, 2003-09; New York Liberty, 2013. TV series producer: "Best of Britain", 2013; "Olives with Your Tea", 2011; Death Wears a Red Hat", 2008; "Hunting Bears", dir, 2012; "Death Wears a Red Hat", dir, 2008. **Business Addr:** Professional Basketball Player, Detroit Shock, Palace Auburn Hills 2 Championship Dr, Auburn Hills, MI 48326, **Business Phone:** (248)377-0100.

### FORD, DR. CLYDE W.
Writer, chiropractor. **Personal:** Born Jan 1, 1951, New York, NY; son of John and Vivian. **Educ:** Wesleyan Univ, CT, BA, 1971; Western States Chiropractic Col, Portland, OR, PhD, 1980. **Career:** IBM Corp, systs engr, 1977; Chiropractor, 1980s-; Inst Training, Synthesis Found & Psychosynthesis Inst; Somatosynthesis Training & Res, founder, 1987-; Leading Edge, ed; writer, lectr, 1989-; Inst African Mythology, dir & founder, currently. Auth: Where Healing Waters Meet: Touching Mind & Emotion Through Body, 1989; Compassionate Touch: Body's Role Healing & Recovery, N Atlantic Bks, 1993; We Can All Get Along: 50 Steps You Can Take to Help End Racism, 1994; Hero with an African Face: Mythic Wisdom Traditional Africa, 1999; The Adventures of Kima and The Frog, Winslow Press, 2000; Columbia Univ, fac; Wash Univ, fac; Whiskey Gulf, Vanguard Press, 2010; Precious Cargo: A Novel Suspense, 2010; Brain/Mind Bulletin, Marilyn Ferguson, ed. **Orgs:** Founder, Nat Asn Advan Colored People, Northern Puget Sound region; founder, Inst Black World; pres, Found Advan Chiropractic Res. **Home Addr:** , Bellingham, WA. **Business Addr:** Director, Founder, The Institute for Somatosynthesis Training & Research, PO Box 3056, Bellingham, WA 98227-3056, **Business Phone:** (206)398-9355.

### FORD, DARRELL L.
Vice president (organization). **Personal:** married Melenese. **Educ:** Rutgers Univ, BS, psychol, 1987, JD, 1992, MBA, 2002. **Career:** AT&T Wireless, exec dir sales opers; Honeywell Int, vpres corp human resources, 2002-08; Shell Oil, vpres human resources-retail, 2008-12; Advan Micro Devices (AMD) Inc, sr vpres & chief human resources officer, 2012-15; Xerox, sr vpres & chief human resources officer, 2015-. **Orgs:** Soc Human Resource Managers; Am Bar Asn-Labor & Employ Sect; Soc HR Planning. **Business Addr:** Senior Vice President, Chief Human Resources Officer, Xerox, 45 Glover Ave, Norwalk, CT 06856-4505, **Business Phone:** (800)275-9376.

### FORD, DARRYL
Writer, radio host. **Personal:** Born Dec 27, 1953, Detroit, MI; married Cozette; children: Darryl II, Rhonda, Brandon, Chris, Rodney & Brionne. **Educ:** N Tenn Bible Col, BA, bibl studies, 2001. **Career:** Consult, ResuMAYDAY, 2007-09; minister music, Glory To Glory Family Christian Ctr, 2001-10; pastor, Kingdom Church Brockton 2010-11; gen mgr, WMSX New Power 1410AM Boston's Inspiration Sta, 2010-11, founder, chief exec officer, Promise Commun, 1998-. **Orgs:** Bd mem, IBTNW, 2002-03.

### FORD, DR. DAVID LEON, JR.
Educator, president (organization). **Personal:** Born Sep 25, 1944, Ft. Worth, TX; son of David Leon and Vernita V Williams; married Joan Sessoms; children: David III. **Educ:** Iowa State Univ, BS, 1967; Univ Wis, Madison, MS, 1969, PhD, 1972. **Career:** Aerospace firm, indust engr; Purdue Univ, asst prof mgt, 1972-75; Yale Sch Orgn & Mgt, vis assoc prof, 1980-81; Univ Tex Dallas, Dept Orgn Stud Strategy & Int Mgt, prof, currently; DL Ford & Assocs, pres, currently. **Orgs:** Soc Int Bus Fel; Asn Social & Behav Scientists, 1978-79; Leadership Dallas Alumni Assoc; Leadership Dallas Adv Coun, 1978-80; bd dir, Greater Dallas Housing Opportunity Ctr, 1978-80; budget comn, United Way Metro Dallas, 1979; dir, Pro Line Corp, 1981-84; chmn, bd dir, NTL Inst Appl Behav Sci, 1985-86; dean, exec develop inst, Nat Black MBA Asn; chair, Comt People Color, Acad Mgt; pres & life mem, Asn Social & Behav Scientists; Orgn Develop Network; SYMLOG Consult Network; chair, bd regents, Inst Cert Prof Mgrs; fac mem, Cent Eurasian Leadership Alliance; Leadership Dallas Alumni Asn; Inst Opers Res & Mgt Sci. **Home Addr:** 7636 Mullrany Dr, Dallas, TX 75248-1602, **Home Phone:** (972)380-9512. **Business Addr:** Professor, Organisational Studies, Strategy & International Management, University Texas Dallas, PO Box 830688, Richardson, TX 75083-0688, **Business Phone:** (972)883-2015.

### FORD, DEBORAH LEE
Educator, counselor. **Personal:** Born Sep 22, 1945, Decatur, IL; married David Franklin; children: Alisa, Bryan & Laquitta. **Educ:** Millikin Univ, music; Richland Community Col, bus. **Career:** AE Staley Mfg Co, messenger & off pool sec, 1964; Day Care Licensed Family Serv, suprv, owned, operated, 1972-78; US Dept Com, res crew leader, 1980; Decatur Sch Dist 61, noon suprv, 1983. **Orgs:** Dist secy, Title I, 1980; dist chairperson, Title I, 1981, 1982; task force mem, Comn Strategic Planning Group, 1984; asst leader, Pre-Sch Prog, Dove Inc, 1984; dir, Wedding Coord, 1984; bd mem, Mental Health Asn Macon Co Inc, 1985; bd mem, Family Serv, 1985; chmn, Educ Comt, Nat Asn Adv Colored People. **Home Addr:** 846 S Webster St, Decatur, IL 62521, **Home Phone:** (217)423-5647. **Business Addr:** School Board Member, Decatur School, Dist 61, Decatur, IL 62521.

### FORD, DR. DEBRA HOLLY
Physician. **Personal:** married Dr Kevin Michael Sr; children: 2. **Educ:** Howard Univ, BS, zool; Howard Univ Sch Med, MD, 1986. **Career:** Howard Univ Hosp, intern, 1987, resident gen surg, 1991, assoc prof surg & colon & rectal surg, currently, vice chmn, currently, chief gensurg div, pres, head, sect colon & rectal surg, currently; vice dir surg residency prog; Univ Tx Med Sch, fel colon & rectal Surg, 1994. **Orgs:** Am Col Surgeons; Am Soc Colon & Rectal Surg; surg Sect, Nat Med Asn. **Honors/Awds:** Kaiser-Permanente Teaching Excellence Award. **Special Achievements:** First African American female to become board certified in the field of colon and rectal surgery; first African American female to become a diplomate of the Board of Colon and Rectal Surgery. **Home Addr:** 11903 Shadystone Ter, Bowie, MD 20721-2592, **Home Phone:** (301)249-0880. **Business Addr:** Associate Professor & Vice-Chairman, Director, Howard Univ Hospital, 2041 Georgia Ave NW Towers Bldg Suite 4000, Washington, DC 20060, **Business Phone:** (202)865-3785.

### FORD, DONALD A.
Executive. **Personal:** Born May 15, 1928, Philadelphia, PA; married Christina K; children: Donald A, Douglas E & Christel A. **Educ:** Shaw Univ, BA, 1950; Am Int Col, MEd, CAGS. **Career:** Urban Educ Adv Third World, Westfield State Col, asst dir, 1971-74; Westfield State Col, asst dir students union, staff emer. **Orgs:** Kappa Alpha Psi Fraternity, 1946-2011; church decon, St John's Congreational Church, 1964-2011; bd dir, Mass Heart Asn Western Chap, 1971-73; Asn Col Unions Int, 1971-2011; chmn, Affirmative Action Comt, Westfield State Col, 1975; St John's Congreational Church Choir; Admis Comt, Westfield State Col. **Home Addr:** 83 Mandalay Rd, Chicopee, MA 01020-3923, **Home Phone:** (413)536-1425. **Business Addr:** MA.

### FORD, EVERN D.
Consultant. **Personal:** Born Apr 28, 1952, Salem, NJ; son of Daniel Sr. **Educ:** Goldey Beacom Col, BS, bus admin, 1997. **Career:** EI DuPont Co, human resources mgr, diversity consult, sexual harassment facilitator, 1990-2005; Pershing LLC; human resources dir; Montclair State Univ, Montclair, NJ, proj team lead, human resources, 2007; EDF & Assocs, Woodstown, NJ, prin consult & Human Resources, 2006-; County Salem, Salem, NJ, county adminr, human resources dir, 2012-14; Salem Community Col, dir off-campus programming, 2014-15. **Orgs:** Bd dir, Nj Sch Bd Asn; vpres, Salem County Voc Tech Sch; bd dir, United Way Salem County; chmn, Fund Distrib Comt; Dale Carnegie Grad Asst; dir, Educ Info & Resource Ctr; dir, Nat Sch Bd Asn. **Honors/Awds:** Big Brother of the Year Award. **Home Addr:** 16 Rockwell Lane, Woodstown, NJ 08098-1364, **Home Phone:** (856)769-0702. **Business Addr:** Principal Consultant, Human Resources, Edf Associates Inc, 957 Lantern Light CT, Tallahassee, FL 32312-9008, **Business Phone:** (850)422-0064.

### FORD, PASTOR FLORIDA MOREHEAD
Clergy. **Personal:** Born Feb 22, 1948, Altheimer, AR; daughter of Henry (deceased) and Ossie Morris (deceased); married Fred; children: Erika & Sonya. **Educ:** Univ Ark, Pine Bluff, AR, BS, 1969; Univ Ark, Fayetteville, MS, chem, 1972; Howard Univ Divinity Sch, Wash, DC, Mdiv, 1991. **Career:** Dow Chem Co, Midland, MI, mgr minority recruiting, 1972-87; Nat Soc Black Engrs, Alexandria, VA, exec dir, 1987-93; Ebenezer African Methodist Episcopal Church, assoc minister; US Dept Energy, consult, 1993-96; Shalom Enterprises Inc, chief exec officer, 1996-98; Shalom Ministries Worship Ctr, organizer, pastor, 1998-; FT Morehead Ministries LLC, founder & chief exec officer. **Orgs:** Alpha Kappa Alpha Sor; dir, Christian Educ New Jerusalem Church; adv comn, Nat Assoc Minority Eng Prog Admis, 1982; Nat Orgn Black Chemists & Chem Eng; indust adv bd, Nat Soc Black Eng; bd mem, Woman Woman Ministries; chaplain, Nat Asn Black Seminarians; Wash Urban League; Nat Asn Black Meeting Planners; founder & chief exec officer, city peace enterprises Inc. **Home Addr:** 1303 Gunpowder Ct, Ft. Washington, MD 20744. **Business Addr:** Pastor, Shalom Ministries Worship Center, 515 Kerby Hill Rd, Ft. Washington, MD 20744, **Business Phone:** (301)567-5505.

### FORD, HAROLD EUGENE, SR.
Politician. **Personal:** Born May 20, 1945, Memphis, TN; son of Newton Jackson and Vera Davis; married Dorothy Jean Bowles; children: Harold Eugene Jr, Newton Jake & Sir Isaac; married Michelle Roberts; children: Andrew & Ava. **Educ:** Tenn State Univ, BS, 1967; John A Gupton Col, AA, mortuary sci, 1969; Howard Univ, MBA, 1982. **Career:** Politician, executive (retired); Ford & Sons Funeral Home, vpres & mgr, 1969; TN House Rep, 1971-74; US House Rep, congressman, TN, ninth dist & eighth dist, 1975-97; Harold Ford Group, consult, 2004. **Orgs:** Nat Adv Bd, St Jude C Res Hosp; bd mem, Metro Memphis YMCA, Alpha Phi Alpha; chmn, Black Tenn Polit Conv; trustee, Fisk Univ; Rust Univ; Alpha Phi Alpha. **Honors/Awds:** Outstanding Young Man of the Year, Memphis Jaycees, 1976; Outstanding Young Man of the Year, TN Jaycees, 1977; Child Advocate of the Year, Child Welfare League Am, 1987. **Special Achievements:** First African-American to represent Tennessee in Congress. **Home Addr:** 7966 Fisher Island Dr, Miami, FL 33109. **Business Addr:** c/o N J Ford and Sons Funeral Parlor Inc, 12 S Pkwy W, Memphis, TN 36109-1635.

### FORD, HAROLD EUGENE, JR.
**Personal:** Born May 11, 1970, Memphis, TN; son of Harold Sr and Dorothy Bowles; married Emily Threlkeld. **Educ:** Univ Pa, BA, 1992; Univ Mich, JD, 1996. **Career:** Senate Budget Comt, staff, 1992; US Dept Com, spec asst, 1993; US House Rep, congressman, 1997-2006; Dem Leadership Coun, chmn, currently; Vis Proff, Tex univ, 2007; NBC Cable News, news analyst, 2008; Tenn, Rep; One Hundred Fifth four succeeding Congresses, dem, 1997-2007; Us Senate, 2006. Article: "The New York Times". **Orgs:** Black Americans Cong; Dem Party mem, U. S. House Representatives; Mt. Moriah-E Baptist Church; youngest mem Cong; Dem Nat Conv; bd selectors, Jefferson Awards Pub Serv; New York Pub Advocate Bill de Blasio, 2010; House Budget Comt; House Comt Financial Serv; New Dem Coalition; Cong Black Caucus; Blue Dog Coalition. **Business Addr:** Chairman, Democratic Leadership Council, PO Box 15244, Washington, DC 20003, **Business Phone:** (202)546-0007.

### FORD, HENRY (HANK FORD)
Administrator, athletic director, basketball coach. **Educ:** Univ Md Eastern Shore, attended 1969. **Career:** Adminr; athletic dir (retired); Univ Md-Eastem Shore, instr, basketball & swimming coach, 1972-73; Tuskegee Univ, asst prof & head basketball coach, 1973-75; Hampton Univ, head basketball coach, 1975-87; Alfred Univ, athletic dir; Howard Univ, athletic dir, 1996-2000; Savannah State Univ, athletic dir, 2001-04. **Orgs:** Nat Asn Col dir Athletics; Nat Asn Col Mkg Adminr; Nat Asn Athletics Develop dir; Nat Asn Div I-AA Athletics dir; MEAC baseball championships, 1997-99; chair, MEAC Athletic dir Orgn, 1998-2000; MEAC men's & women's Outdoor Track Championships, 2000. **Business Addr:** Atnletic Director, Savannah State University, 3219 College St, Savannah, GA 31404, **Business Phone:** (912)358-4338.

### FORD, HENRY
Football player. **Personal:** Born Oct 30, 1971, Ft. Worth, TX. **Educ:** Univ Ark. **Career:** Football player (retired); Houston Oilers, defen-

sive tackle, 1994-96; Tenn Oilers, 1997-98; Tenn Titans, 1999-2002; New Orleans Saints, 2003.

### FORD, HILDA EILEEN

Executive. **Personal:** Born Apr 19, 1924, New York, NY. **Educ:** Brooklyn Col, 1945; Col St Rose, 1971. **Career:** City Baltimore, dir personnel; NY St Off Employ Rels, chief negotiator; NY St Employ Serv, Dept Civil Serv, asst dir; Youth Opportunities Ctr, dir; New York Off of Employee Rels, asst dir, 1974-77; Civil Serv Comn, personnel dir, 1977-87. **Orgs:** Urban Serv Comn, Baltimore City; Secy Personnel, 1987-94; Gov's Exec Coun, 1987-94. chair, State Employees' Health Ins Adv Coun, 1987-94; Md Coord Comt Martin Luther King Jr Holiday, 1991-94; bd trustee, State Retirement & Pension Syst, 1987-94; Asbestos Oversight Comt, 1987-94; Interdepartmental Comt Minority Affairs, 1987-94; Govs Spec Comt Port Baltimore, 1987; Govs Construct Indust Employers Adv Coun, 1988-94; Subcomt Mandated Health Ins Benefits Govs Comn Health Care Policy & Financing, 1988-94; Govs Drug & Alcohol Abuse Comn, 1989-94; Md State Employees Risk Mgt Adv Coun, 1989-94; Task Force to Study Incentive Awards Prog State Employees, 1990; Task Force to Study Md State Police Salaries, 1990-91; Govs Task Force Self-Esteem, 1990-91; bd trustee, Goucher Col, 1981-94. **Home Addr:** 2305 Bayleaf Ct, Baltimore, MD 21209, **Home Phone:** (410)466-3190.

### FORD, JOHN NEWTON

Government official, insurance agent, consultant. **Personal:** Born May 3, 1942, Memphis, TN; son of Newton Jackson and Vera Davis; married Tamara Mitchell; children: Michelle, Sean, Kemba, Autumn, Theo & Victoria. **Educ:** Tenn State Univ, BS, 1964; Memphis State Univ, MS, pub admin fin, 1978. **Career:** Memphis, TN, city councilman, 1971-79; Tenn Gen Assembly, Tenn state sen, 1974-2005; Tenn State Senate, Dist 29, state sen, speaker pro tempore, 1987-2005; JF Assocs, pres. **Orgs:** Chmn, Senate Gen Welfare, Health & Human Resources Comn; Fin Ways & Means Comn; pres, NJ Ford & Sons Funeral Parlors; pres, Ford & Assocs; life mem, Nat Asn Advan Colored People; Nat League Cities; Nat Black Caucus; bd mem, Regional Sickle Cell Anemia Coun; State & Local Govt Comn; Alpha Phi Alpha. **Honors/Awds:** Outstand Citizens Award, Mallory Knights Charitable, 1974; Outstanding Accomplishment Award, Civil Liberty League, 1975; Community Achievement Award, Lutheran Baptist Church, 1976; Distinguished Graduate Award, Memphis State Univ, 1978. **Home Addr:** 981 Villiage Pk Cove, Memphis, TN 38120.

### FORD, JOHNNY L., II

State government official. **Personal:** Born Aug 23, 1942, Tuskegee, AL; married Joyce London; children: Johnny Jr, Christopher & Tiffany. **Educ:** Knoxville Col, BA, hist & sociol, 1964; Nat Exec Inst, attended 1965; Auburn Univ, MPA, 1977. **Career:** Multi-Man Dist, exec Bronx, 1967-68; Sen Robt Kennedy, polit campaign strategist, 1968; Tuskegee Model Cities Prog, exec coord, 1969-70; Atty Fred Gray, campaign mgr, 1970; Multi Racial Corp, asst dir, 1970-72; US Justice Dept Montgomery, state supr comn rel serv, 1971-72; City Tuskegee, mayor, 1972-96, 2004-08, 2012-; Ala House Rep, state rep, 1997; Johnny Ford & Assoc Inc, pres; Macon County, 82nd Dist, State Rep, 1998-2004. **Orgs:** Founder & dir gen, World Conf Mayors Inc; Nat Asn Advan Colored People; Kappa Alpha Psi; pres, Ala League Munic; pres, Johnny Ford & Assoc Inc; pres-emer & founder, Nat Conf Black Mayors; Ala Foreign Trade Comn; chmn, Nat Utility Alliance; Ala Munic Elec Authority; pres, Ala League Munic; Kappa Alpha Psi; founding pres, Tuskegee Optimist Club; Mt Olive Missionary Baptist Church; Ala Conf Black Mayors; founding co-chair, Nat Policy Alliance. **Honors/Awds:** Top Campaigner Award BSA, 1967; Young Man of the Year, Women's Reserve, 1967; Youngest Multi-Dist Exec in Nation BSA, 1967; Awarded The Key to more than 100 American Foreign Cities. **Special Achievements:** First African American mayor in Alabama & received 4 honorary doctorate degrees; Tuskegee's first African American mayor in 1972; Tv Movie: The Rosa Parks Story, 2002. **Home Addr:** 1203 Lakeshore Dr, Tuskegee, AL 36083-1939. **Business Addr:** Mayor, City of Tuskegee, PO Box 830687, Tuskegee, AL 36083-0687, **Business Phone:** (334)720-0515.

### FORD, HON. JUDITH DONNA

Judge. **Personal:** Born Aug 30, 1935, Eureka, CA. **Educ:** Univ Calif, Berkeley, BS, 1957; Boalt Hall Sch Law, JD, 1974. **Career:** Petty Andrews Tufts & Jackson, assoc atty, 1974-79; Consumer Fraud Crime Div, SF Dist Atty's Off, dir, 1977-79; San Francisco County, asst dist atty, 1978-80; Fed Trade Comn, dir, 1980-82; Alameda County Munic Ct, judge, 1982-98; State Calif Munic Ct Oakland-Piedmont- Emeryville Dist, judge, 1983-. **Orgs:** Chas Houston Bar Asn, 1974-; San Francisco Bar Asn, Lawyer Referral Serv Comt, 1976; NSF Software Auditing Workshop, 1976; Comn Admin Justice, 1976-79; deleg, San Francisco Bar Asn Lawyer Referral Serv Comn, 1976; chair, E Oakland Planned Parenthood Adv Comn, 1977-80; speaker, Bank Admin Inst, 1977; speaker, EDP Audit Controls Workshop, 1977; speaker, CPA Soc, 1977; speaker, Joint meeting IIA & EDPA, 1978; dir, Planned Parenthood, 1978-80; Calif Asn Black Lawyers, 1978-; chair, Black Women Lawyers, NCA Finance Comn, 1979-80; San Francisco Lawyers Comn, Urban Affairs, 1979-80; chair, San Francisco Bar Asn Comn, Legal Educ Comt, 1979-80; bd mem, Consumer Union, 1979-82; ref, St Bar Ct, 1979-82; consr, Law Ctr Bd Consr, 1979-83; radio & TV speaker, FTrade Comn, 1980-82; San Francisco Bar Asn Judiciary Comn, 1981-82; bd mem, judicial coun, Peralta Serv Corp, 1983-, 1991-94; chair, CTC Privacy & Access Subcommittee, 1995-96; adv comt, Judicial Coun Ct Technol, 1995-98; bd mem, Calif Judges Asn, 1996-98; Calif Judges Asn; Alameda County Trauma Rev Comn; US Magistrate Merit Selection Comn; trustee, Alameda County Law Libr. **Special Achievements:** Calif Criminal Law Procedure & Practice, co-author, chapters 4 & 6; Various TV & Radio appearances. **Business Addr:** Judge, Oakland-Piedmont Emeryville Municipal Court, 661 Wash St, Oakland, CA 94607, **Business Phone:** (510)268-7601.

### FORD, KENNETH A.

Association executive. **Personal:** Born Aug 10, 1949, Washington, DC; married Shirley Payne; children: Travelle. **Educ:** Howard Univ, BSCE, 1972, MCE, 1977. **Career:** Limbach Co, proj engr, 1972-75; Potomac Elec Power Co, env engr, 1975-77; Parametric Inc, prog dir, 1977-82; Wash Suburban Sanit Comn, planning mgr, 1982-84; Nat Asn Home Builders, mgr civil eng, prog mgr, 1984-2010. **Orgs:** Nat Soc Prof Engrs, 1977; adv bd, Utility Location & Coordr Coun, 1984; Bldg Seismic Safety Coun, 1984; bd dir, Black Sci Inc, 1984-85; Am Soc Civil Engrs; vice chair, Nat Asn Home Builders Pacifica Found Bd. **Home Addr:** 11303 Sherrington Ct, Largo, MD 20774-2317, **Home Phone:** (301)350-5253. **Business Addr:** Vice Chair, National Association of Home Builders, 1201 15th St NW, Washington, DC 20005, **Business Phone:** (202)822-0228.

### FORD, KISHA ANGELINE

Basketball player. **Personal:** Born Apr 4, 1975, Baltimore, MD. **Educ:** Ga Tech, BA, 1997; Baker Col, MBA, 2001. **Career:** NY Liberty, guard & forward, 1997-98; Orlando Miracle, guard, 1999; Satila, Sweden, 1998-99; Miami Sol, guard & forward, 2000-01; Nat Women's Basketball League, Alanta Justice, guard & forward, 2001-02. **Home Addr:** 5936 Applegarth Pl, Capitol Heights, MD 20743-4236, **Home Phone:** (301)420-6748.

### FORD, LISA DENISE

Chemist, educator. **Personal:** Born Aug 3, 1965, Memphis, TN; daughter of Samuel L. **Educ:** Fisk Univ, BS, chem, 1987, MA, chem, 1990. **Career:** Barrow-Agee Anal Lab, anal chemist, 1987-88; Cargill Corn Milling Div, qual control chemist, 1988; Fisk Univ, grad lab teacher's asst, 1988-89; MMES, Oak Ridge Nat Lab, grad res intern, 1989-90; MMES, Nuclear & Environ Plant, qual control chemist, supv chemist, tech support chemist, staff chemist, 1990-96; MMES, Gaseous Diffusion & Waste Mgt Plant, chemist, 1993-94; Millington Cent High Sch, teacher, chemist, 1996-98; Austin-E Magnet High Sch, teacher, chemist, 1998-. **Orgs:** Am Chem Soc, 1987; Nat Teachers Asn; Tenn Teachers Asn. **Honors/Awds:** MMES Certificate of Appreciation; Tennessee Quality Achievement Award; Environmental, Restoration & Waste Mgt Mission Success Award; Second Runner-up to Miss Fisk, Fisk Univ Libr, 1986-87; International Hall of Fame, Inventors Club of America; Advanced Technology Award, 1993; Y-12 Pathfinder Award, 1994. **Home Addr:** 7205 John Norton Rd, Knoxville, TN 37920-6629, **Home Phone:** (865)579-3165. **Business Addr:** Teacher, Chemist, Knoxville Co Schools, Andrew Johnson Bldg, Knoxville, TN 37914, **Business Phone:** (865)594-1911.

### FORD, MONTE E.

Vice president (organization), executive. **Personal:** Born Oct 3, 1959, Washington, DC. **Educ:** Northeastern Univ, Boston, BS, bus admin, 1982. **Career:** Am Airlines, sr vpres & chief info officer; Bank Boston; Digital Equip Corp; Bank Boston, sr mgt; Assocs First Capital Corp, exec vpres, 1997-2000; Aptean Software, exec chmn, chief exec; AMR Corp, chief info officer & pres, 2001; Meta Group Inc, Dir, 2003-04; Moneygram Int inc, Dir, 2006-08; Akamai, dir, 2013-. **Orgs:** Bd dir, Oncor; res bd mem, CIO Strategy Exchange; network partner, Brightwood Capital Advisors LP; principal Quest Objects Group LLC. **Honors/Awds:** "Fortune," 50 Smartest People in Technology; "Black Engineer," 50 Most Important African Americans in Technology; "Black Enterprise," The 100 Most Powerful Executives in Corporate America, 2010; CIO Hall of Fame, CIO mag. **Business Addr:** Director, Akamai Technologies, 150 Broadway, Cambridge, MA 02142, **Business Phone:** (877)325-2624.

### FORD, NANCY HOWARD

School administrator. **Personal:** Born Jul 29, 1942, Wilmington, DE; children: Sergio Howard & Charis. **Educ:** Cent State Univ, BS, 1964; Univ Del, MEd, 1972. **Career:** CT State Welfare Dept, welfare home economist, 1968; Seattle Pub Sch, teacher-home arts, 1968-70; Wilmington Pub Sch, teacher corps int, 1970-72; Cheyney State Col, assoc dean res life, 1972-76; Dept Pub Instr DE, educ specialist, nutrit, educ & training summer food serv prog. **Orgs:** Vol, US Peace Corps-Brazil, 1964-66; vol, Teacher DE Adolescent Prog Inc, 1971. **Honors/Awds:** Received numerous awards including: National Honor Soc Wilmington High Sch, 1960; Highest Ranking Student, Central State Univ, 1964; Certificate of Recognition, US Peace Corps Serv, White House, 1966; Am Can Society; National Gold Award, Pub Educ, 1992. **Special Achievements:** TV Show appearance "Keeping Kid's Out of Harm's Way" Tom Brokaws nightly news, 1994; Participated in national news conf, C Defense Fund, Am Sch Food Serv Asn, 1994. **Home Addr:** PO Box 9567, Wilmington, DE 19809-0567.

### FORD, NATHANIEL P., SR.

Executive director. **Personal:** Born Jul 31, 1961, SC; son of Phillip and Thomasina; married Crystal; children: Phillip, Whitney, Brittany & Taylor. **Educ:** Mercer Univ, BA, appl studies orgn leadership. **Career:** New York Transit Authority, train conductor, 1983-86, train dispatcher, 1986-88, dep line supt, 1988-90, supt dist night opers, 1990-92; San Francisco Bay Area Rapid Transit Authority, asst chief transp officer, 1992-97; Metrop Atlanta Rapid Transit Authority, sr vp opers, 1997-99, exec vp opers & develop, 1999-2000, gen mgr & chief exec officer, 2000-05; San Francisco Munic Transp Agency, exec dir & chief exec officer, 2006-; Jacksonville Transp Authority, chief exec officer, currently. **Orgs:** Vice chair, bd dir, bus mgt & fin, Am Pub Transp Asn; 2nd vice chair, bd dir, Conf Minority Transp Officials; bd mem, Atlanta Neighborhood Develop Partnership; bd mem, Ga Chamber Com; bd mem, Metro Atlanta Chamber Com; Oversight & Proj Selection Com, Transp Coop Res Proj; APTREX Inst Int Transit Cert Rev Bd; United Way Metrop Atlanta Alexis de Tocqueville Soc; chair, Transbay Joint Powers Authority; bd, Peninsula Corridor Joint Powers Bd; chmn, TransLink Reg Smartcard Mgt Grp; treas, Nat Asn City Transp Officials. **Business Addr:** Executive Director, Chief Executive Officer, Jacksonville Transportation Authority, 121 W Forsyth St, St.Jacksonville, FL 94103, **Business Phone:** (415)701-4720.

### FORD, DR. ROBERT L.

Educator, executive. **Educ:** Southern Univ & A&M Col, BS, chem, math, 1967; Purdue Univ, PhD, phys chem, 1972. **Career:** Xerox Corp, assoc scientist, 1967-75; Southern Univ A & M Col, asst prof chem, 1975-81, assoc prof chem, 1985-87, prof chem, 1987-2003, Ctr Energy & Environ Studies, dir, 1989-96, Res & Strategic Initiatives, vice chancellor, 1996-98; Pub & Pvt Orgn, assorted positions, 1971-; LA Dept Urban & Comm Affairs, Off Comm Serv, asst secy, 1982-84; Dillard Univ, asst prof chem, 1984-85; Neo-Tech S Inc, pres & chief exec officer, 1985-; LA Bd Regents, asst assoc comnr sponsored prog, 1999-2001; Justice & Sustainability Assocs, consult, 2002-; Ft Valley State Univ, vpres Advan & Res, 2003-04; LA & SBA SBIR Phase Zero Initiative, SUBR, proj trainer, 2005; Tex Southern Univ, Col Sci & Technol, parliamentarian, assoc provost res, 2005-07, prof chem, 2007-, vpres, interim chair, 2008-09, dir, STEM Educ & Outreach, partnership coordr, founding dir, vice chancellor, Res, chmn, Minority Serv Inst Res Partnership; W Va High Tech Found Consortium, 2006; DRF Industs LLC, pres & chief exec officer, 2007-; Global Bus Roundtable, vpres; Kauffman Found UEP Houston Proj, prin investr, 2011-12; Earl Carl Inst Legal & Social Policy Inc, pres. **Orgs:** Am Chem Soc; Nat Teaching Asn; Sigma Xi Scientific Res Soc; Nat Coun Univ Res Adminrs; Am Soc Trainers & Developers; Phi Delta Kappa Int; Tech Transfer Soc; Nat Org Prof Advan Black Chemists & Chem Engrs; bd mem & pres, La Health Freedom Coalition; chair & senate mentoring comt, Tex Southern Univ, Col Sci & Technol; bd mem, Bridging Digital Divide Inc; bd mem, Houston-Luanda Sister City Asn; adv bd, Greater Houston Area Am Red Cross Southeast Br & founding; treas, Minority Serv Inst Res Partnership; Thompson Elem Sch Site Based Decision-Making Comt; bd mem, World Youth Found, 2013-15. **Home Addr:** 11505 Archery Dr, Baton Rouge, LA 70815, **Home Phone:** (225)273-9113. **Business Addr:** Professor, Texas Southern University, Science Ctr - 403 F SC, Houston, TX 77004, **Business Phone:** (713)313-7621.

### FORD, SAM

Journalist. **Personal:** Born May 29, 1953, Coffeyville, KS; son of Kathleen Owens and Sammie; married Gloria Murray; children: Murry & Gina. **Educ:** Univ Kans, BS, jour, 1974; Univ Minn, attended 1976. **Career:** KMSP-TV, reporter, 1974-75; WCCO-TV, reporter, 1975-77; CBS News, corresp, 1977-87; ABC7/WJLA-TV, gen assignment reporter, 1987-. **Orgs:** Nat Asn Black Journalists, founding mem, 1975-; Lincoln Park United Methodist Church, 1997-. **Home Addr:** 250 12th St SE, Washington, DC 20003-1403, **Home Phone:** (202)544-0633. **Business Addr:** News Reporter, ABC7/WJLA-TV, 1100 Wilson Blvd, Arlington, VA 22209, **Business Phone:** (703)236-9552.

### FORD, REV. SAMUEL LEE

Clergy. **Personal:** Born Jan 26, 1942, Leland, MS; son of Van and Lena B; children: Lisa F Davidson, Samuel Leon & Monica F Stokes. **Educ:** MA, 1989. **Career:** W Canaan Baptist Church, sr pastor, 1976-. **Orgs:** Dir, Millington Action & Involvement, 1987-98; trustee, Tenn Sch Religion, 1989-92; pres, Friendship Dist Asn, 1990-; dir, Home Mission, TN Regular Bapt Missionary Ed, 1998-; adv bd, Tenn State Rep Barbara Cooper. **Home Addr:** 3033 Spring Hill Cove, Memphis, TN 38127-7420, **Home Phone:** (901)357-2273. **Business Addr:** Senior Pastor, West Canaan Baptist Church, 8715 Wilkinsville Rd, Millington, TN 38053, **Business Phone:** (901)872-2426.

### FORD, STACEY

Basketball player. **Personal:** Born Jan 14, 1969. **Educ:** Univ Ga, BA, 1991. **Career:** Portland Power, 1996-98; Columbus Quest, forward, 1996-98; Colorado Xplosion, 1998; Libertas Terms, 2000-01; New York Liberty, 2001; Sacramento Monarchs, forward, 2001-02.

**FORD, TONI.** See FORD, ANTOINETTE.

### FORD, VERNON N.

Executive, vice president (organization). **Personal:** Born Feb 15, 1945, Eupora, MS; son of Robert N and Nancy E Jones; married Angela Graves; children: Tatia Lynn & Erin Kimberly. **Educ:** Cent State Univ, Wilberforce, OH, BS, mkt, 1970. **Career:** Alcoa, Los Angeles, Calif, sales rep, 1973-77; Alcoa, Indianapolis, Ind, br sales mgr, 1977-79; Alcoa, San Francisco, Calif, sales mgr, 1979-84; Alcoa, Houston, Tex, sales mgr, 1984-87; Separations Technol Inc, Warrendales, PA, mgr sales & distribr, 1987-90; Cent State Univ Found, vpres, bd Dir, mem, currently; Vancouver Exten Co, Vancouver Wash, pres, 1990; Ford Cleaning Serv, pres & owner; Cent State Univ, Col Bus, Bus & Indust Adv Coun, chmn, Gen Alumni Asn, pres; Alcoa, Halethorpe Extrusions Inc, pres; Philadelphia Gear Corp, vpres sales & mkt; Harlem Globetrotter, exec vice-pres & chief operating officer; Bldg Maintenance Serv Inc, pres, currently. **Orgs:** Exec Leadership Coun, 1986-; chmn, MESO Adv Bd, 1990-; Rotary, 1990-; life mem, Kappa Alpha Psi Fraternity Inc; life mem, Nat Asn Advan Colored People; chmn, Col Bus & Indust Adv Coun; pres & bd mem, CSU, 2004; pres & bd mem, GAA, 2004. **Home Addr:** 1227 Sherman Ave, Pittsburgh, PA 15212, **Home Phone:** (412)321-2713. **Business Addr:** President, Building Maintenance Services Inc, 1955 Vaughn Rd Suite 105, Kennesaw, GA 30144, **Business Phone:** (770)218-2993.

### FORD, WALLACE L., II

Educator, government official, legal secretary. **Personal:** Born Jan 13, 1950, New York, NY; son of Wallace and Carmen; married Rikki E Langston; children: Wallace III. **Educ:** Dartmouth Col, BA, 1970; Harvard Law Sch, JD, 1973. **Career:** Columbia Univ, Sch Int & Pub Affairs, adj prof, currently; Fordworks Assocs Inc, owner & founder, currently; Lenox Terr Tenants Asn, pres, currently; Wall St, investment banker; WDCR radio, disc jockey; State Supreme Ct, NY, law secy; State Assembly Comm Banking, NY, coun; Amistad DOT Venture Capital Inc, exec vpres & gen coun; State Dept Com Div Minority Bus Develop, NY, dep comnr; State New York Mortgage Agency, exec officer & chief exec officer, pres; Int Bus Sch Bus Metrop Col, New York; Kaye Scholer law firm, atty, coun; New York, comnr bus; Drexel Burnham Lambert Inc, vpres; City NY, dept ports & trade, comnr; New York Dept Ports & Trade, comnr; Medgar Evers Col, Pub Admin Dept, interim chair, chmn, teacher; Pace Univ; John Jay Col; Harlem Lawyers Asn, pres; Am Cancer Soc, pres; GoodWorks Int LLC, pres & chief operating officer; Ideal Develop Inc, vpres oper & bus develop, bd dir; TurningPointMagazine.com, contrib columnist, contribr. **Orgs:** Dartmouth Alumni Coun; Dartmouth Black Alumni Asn; bd trustee, MalcolmKing Col; Nat Asn Securities Prof; bd dir, Urban League, Harlem Br, NY; mem fac, Sch Int & Pub Affairs, Columbia Univ; mem bd adv, Ctr Jazz Studies, Columbia Univ, currently; mem bd adv, United Way Int, emer mem; mem bd dir, Haitel SA; bd advisor, Dartmouth Col, Rockefeller Ctr; bd mem, Gridline Commun Holdings Inc; sr fel Harvard Law Sch. **Honors/Awds:** Listed Ebony

Mag 100 Leaders the Future, 1978; listed Time Mag Fifty Faces of the Future, 1979; Annual Award, Nat Housing Conf, 1984. **Special Achievements:** Author: The Pride, Dafina Bks, 2005; What You Sow, Dafina Bks, 2006. **Home Addr:** 425 Pk Ave, New York, NY 10022, **Home Phone:** (212)836-7314. **Business Addr:** Adjunct Professor, Columbia University, Int Affairs Bldg 13th Fl, New York, NY 10027, **Business Phone:** (212)854-3213.

### FORD, WILLIAM L., JR.

Executive. **Personal:** Born Jul 31, 1941, Kayford, WV; married Eleanor Holmes; children: Karen & Valerie. **Educ:** Russell Sage Evening Col, attended 1966; State Univ Albany, NY, attended 1968. **Career:** Mayfair Inc Albany, off mgr, 1968-70; WROW-WTEN Albany, chief acct, 1970-71; WROW Radio Albany, bus mgr, 1971; WKBW-TV & Radio Buffalo, bus mgr, 1971-76; WFSB-TV Hartford, vpres bus & admin affairs, 1976-78; Post-Newsweek Sta Mich Inc WDIV, vpres, sta mgr, 1978-83; Cellular Telecommun, vpres. **Orgs:** Bd dir, Better Bus Bur Met Detroit, 1979; Jr Achievement Southeastern Mich, 1979; Broadcast Fin Mgt Assoc, 1979; Comnr, Detroit Black United Fund, 1979; bd gov, Detroit Chap Nat Acad TV Arts & Sci, 1980; bd dir, Mich Asn Broadcasters, 1980. **Home Addr:** 136 Whippoorwill Lane, Rochester Hills, MI 48309.

### FORDE, FRASER PHILIP, JR.

Executive. **Personal:** Born Nov 24, 1943, Tuskegee, AL; son of Fraser Philip Sr and Joyce Nourse; married LaVerne M; children: Tracey R, Fraser III & Erika. **Educ:** Hofstra Univ, BBA, 1965; Pace Univ, MBA, 1980. **Career:** Dun & Bradstreet Inc, credit analyst, 1967-69; Bank & Opers Dept, educ trainee, 1969-70; Money Transfer Dept, asst group head, 1970-71; asst officer personnel rep, 1971-73; Morgan Guaranty Trust Co, asst treas, 1973-87, asst vpres, 1987-89, vpres. **Orgs:** Treas, 1980-; delegate, Central Islip Sch Dist Budget Adv Comt, 1981. **Home Addr:** 64 Dietz St, Central Islip, NY 11722, **Home Phone:** (864)967-3322.

### FORDE, JAMES ALBERT (JIM FORDE)

Health services administrator. **Personal:** Born Jan 23, 1927, Brooklyn, NY; married Gaille Faulkner; children: Janice Ross & Jacqueline Sullivan. **Educ:** Brooklyn Col, BA, eng, 1949; City Col NY, MPA, 1955; NY State Univ, doctoral courses, 1960; Ithaca Col, nursing home admin, 1975. **Career:** Serv Dept Ment Hyg, dir bur mgt, 1963-67; Bur Budget Serv, dir, 1967-68; NY State Dept Ment Hyg, Local Serv Div, asst comnr, 1968-71; Off Prog Planning & Coord, NY State Dept Ment Hyg, assoc comnr, 1971-74; Willowbrook Devel Ctr, actg dir, 1974-75; Mid-Hudson Reg Dept Ment Hyg, reg dir, 1975-76; Health Care Agency Cty San Diego, dep admin, 1976-79; San Diego Black Health Assoc, co-founder, pres, admin dir, 1978-; San Diego City Dept Health Serv, dir, 1979-86; SD Urban League, exec dir; Calif Black Health Network, exec dir, 1987-. **Orgs:** Am Pub Health Assoc, Calif Black Health Network, State Calif, Hypertension Adv Coun; consult, Fed Off Health Affairs, 1973; Willowbrook Rev Panel, 1975-78; bd mem, CD Reg Ctr Devlop ment Disabled, 1979-86. **Home Addr:** 917 Golden Crest Dr, DURHAM, NC 27704, **Home Phone:** (919)294-4227.

### FORDHAM, CYNTHIA WILLIAMS

Lawyer, administrative court judge. **Personal:** Born Dec 6, 1954, Philadelphia, PA; daughter of Paul and Ola N; married Jerome. **Educ:** Pa State Univ, BA, 1975; Univ Pa Law Sch, JD, law, 1979. **Career:** Philadelphia Bd Educ, substitute teacher, 1976; Comn Legal Serv, law clerk, 1977-78; Pa Dept State, asst gen coun, 1980-84; Pa Human Rels Comn, asst coun, 1984-91; Pa Pub Utility Comn, spec agt, 1991-93, admin law judge, 1993-. **Orgs:** Am Bar Asn, 1976-; Pa Bar Asn, 1979-; Nat Bar Asn, 1983-; bd, Greater Philadelphia Health Action, 1979-, chairperson, 2007; pres, bd dir, TSB Church Community Outreach Corp, 1986-; Clifford Scott Green Chap Nat Bar Asn Judicial Coun; bd mem, Penn African Am Law Alumni Soc; bd pres, Diversified Community Serv; bd mem, Marian Anderson Hist Soc; bd mem, Lincoln Day Educ Ctr. **Home Addr:** 1929 S 18th St, Philadelphia, PA 19145, **Home Phone:** (215)336-2275. **Business Addr:** Administrative Law Judge, Pennsylvania Public Utility Commission, Philadelphia Dist Off, Philadelphia, PA 19107, **Business Phone:** (215)560-2105.

### FOREMAN, DOYLE

Sculptor, educator. **Personal:** Born Jun 17, 1933, Ardmore, OK; married Selma J; children: Doyle Jr & Maia. **Educ:** Ariz State Univ; Calif Col Arts & Crafts, BFA, 1960. **Career:** Sculptor & educator (retired); Oakland Recreation Dept, arts & crafts specialist, 1957-60, landscape, gardening & land mgt, 1961-65; Univ Calif, Col V Santa Cruz, prof art & sculptor, 1968-2001; Merrill Co, fel, Art Dept, founding mem; Calif Col Arts & Crafts, 1969; Yard bird Publ Co, art ed, art dir, bd dir, 1971; art ed, Yard bird Reader. **Orgs:** Santa Cruz County Art Comn, 1972-74; City Santa Cruz Bicentennial Comn, 1975; comt chmn, Kaiser Ctr Gallery Oakland, 1968; Int Sculpture Ctr, 1968; Comn Inter-Campus Art, Univ Calif, 1984, 1991-94; City Santa Cruz Pub Arts Comn, 1999-. **Honors/Awds:** The Josie King Humanatarian Award; Outstanding Community Service Award from Mayor; MEXUS grant for Pecked Rock drawing site, San Ignacio, Baja, Calif, Univ Calif, Santa Cruz; Best in Show, Kaiser Ctr Gallery, Oakland Museum, Oakland, CA; Mini-Grant for Ethnographic Artist Series Totem, Univ Calif, Santa Cruz; Instructional Improvement Grant to complete film on African sculpture. **Special Achievements:** Most Imaginative Sculpture, Bechtel Int Ctr Show, Palo Alto Times; art work has been published in Song of Andoumboulou by Nathaniel Mackey, African American Art and Artists by Samella Lewis, and Art in the San Francisco Bay Area by Thomas All bright. **Home Addr:** 432 Spring St, Santa Cruz, CA 95060-2026, **Home Phone:** (619)253-5936.

### FOREMAN, GEORGE EDWARD, SR.

Clergy, boxer. **Personal:** Born Jan 10, 1949, Marshall, TX; son of J D and Nancy; married Mary Joan Martelly, Jan 1, 1985; married Andrea Skeete, Jan 1, 19821985); married Sharon Goodson, Jan 1, 19811982). **Educ:** Rice Univ. **Career:** Professional Boxer (retired), Preacher, Pastor, Bus Owner; Job Corps, boxer, 1960; prof boxer, 1969-77, 1987-99; Church Lord Jesus Christ, pastor, preacher, proprietor & ordained minister, 1977-; Big George's ranch, owner, 1994-. **Orgs:** Founder, George Foreman Youth & Community Ctr; Knock-Out Pediat Cancer. **Business Addr:** Preacher, Ordained Minister, The Church of Lord Jesus Christ, 2501 Lone Oak Rd, Houston, TX 77093, **Business Phone:** (281)590-7480.

### FOREMAN, JOYCE BLACKNALL

Entrepreneur. **Personal:** Born Jul 6, 1948, Thelma, TX; daughter of Roy and Betty Lockhart. **Educ:** Univ Tex, Dallas, sociol; El Centro Col, AA; Paul Quinn Col, BS, mgt. **Career:** Foreman Off Prod, Dallas, TX, pres, currently. **Orgs:** Mem bd dir, Tex Com Bank; mem bd mgt, Urban League; chairperson, Dallas Independent Sch Dists Minority Bus Adv Comm; Nat Asn Female Execs; Nat Asn Advan Colored People; Womens Bus Connection; mem bd dir, Channel 13; Dallas Assembly; Dallas Citizens Coun; Comn Educ Excellence; vice chmn, bd dir, DART; Chmn's Task Force State Fair Tex; Dallas Together Forum; Dallas ISD Adv Group Dist 6. **Honors/Awds:** Vendor of the Year, Dallas, Ft Worth Minority Bus Develop Coun, 1984; Quest for Success Award, Miller Brewing Co, Dallas Morning News, Dallas Black Chamber Com, 1985; Dreammaker Award, Southeast Dallas Bus & Prof Women's Club, 1985; Business Recognition Award, Iota Phi Lambda, 1987; Spotlighting Your Success for Women Business Owner, 1986; Champion 100 Gran Award, 1984; Up & Comer to Watch, Dallas Times Herald, 1987; Community Service Award, Sigma Gamma Rho Sorority, 1987; Trailblazer Award, S Dallas Bus & Prof Women's Club, 1989; Minority Business Advocate of the Year for State of Texas, Small Bus Admin, 1989; Doers Award, 1989; Women who make a difference, Minority & Women Bus Mag, 1990; Certificate of Recognition, Congresswomen Eddie Bernice Johnson, 1993; Entrepreneur of the Year, Dallas Weekly, 1994; African American Hero Award, KKDA Radio & Coca-Cola, 1994; Fort Worth Black Chamber Excellence Award, 1997; Outstanding Business Award, Tex Black Women Conf, 1998; Community Service Award, KRLD & Guaranty Bank, 2001; Business of the month, Dallas Post Tribune, 2003. **Business Addr:** President, Foreman Office Products Inc, 1926 Main St, Dallas, TX 75201, **Business Phone:** (214)749-0266.

### FOREMAN, PEGGY E.

Lawyer, executive. **Personal:** Born Feb 18, 1958, Houston, TX; daughter of Dave and Ella. **Educ:** Univ Pa, attended 1978; Univ Houston, BBA, 1981; Tex Southern Univ, Thurgood Marshall Sch Law, JD, 1985. **Career:** Peggy Foreman, atty, 1985-89; Burney & Foreman Attorneys at Law, partner, 1990-. **Orgs:** Am Bar Asn; Nat Bar Asn; State Bar Tex; Tex Young Lawyers Asn; Harris Co Young Asn; Houston Lawyers Asn; Houston Bar Asn; Young Lawyers Asn; Nat Asn Bond Lawyers; Tex Trial Lawyers Asn; Gulf Coast Black Women Lawyers Asn; Phi Delta Phi Legal Fraternity Alumni Chap; Thurgood Marshall Sch Law Alumni Asn. **Honors/Awds:** Special Recognition, Houston Bus & Prof Men's Club; Woman of the Year, Iota Phi Lambda Sorority Inc, Beta Delta Chap. **Special Achievements:** Author, Wills and Trusts in Texas, Harris County Young Lawyers Asn & Texas Lawyers Asn, 1989, Client Satisfaction, How to Thrive, Not Just Survive in a Solo/Small Firm Practice, State Bar of Texas, December 1993; numerous others. **Home Addr:** 2605 Calumet St Suite 2, Houston, TX 77004, **Home Phone:** (713)520-5447. **Business Addr:** Partner, Burney & Foreman Attorneys at Law, 5445 Almeda Suite 400, Houston, TX 77004-7197, **Business Phone:** (713)526-6404.

### FORMEY, SYLVESTER C.

Executive. **Career:** Airport Comn, vice chair, currently; Vanguard Safety Co, founder; Vanguard Distribr Inc, chief exec officer, pres, founder, secy, currently; Vanguard Int LLC, pres, chief exec officer & founder; Lighthouse Community Develop Corp Inc, chief exec officer; Vanguard Holdings Ltd, chief exec officer. **Orgs:** Bd mem, Creative Coast; bd mem, World Trade Ctr Savannah; bd mem, Med-Bank Found Inc. **Business Addr:** President, Vanguard Distributors Inc, 107 NE Lathrop Ave, Savannah, GA 31402, **Business Phone:** (912)236-1766.

### FORNAY, ALFRED R., JR.

Editor, writer. **Personal:** Born Jun 8, 1941, Cincinnati, OH; son of Alfred Sr and Marguerite Weatherford. **Educ:** Wilfred Acad Beauty & Hair Design, 1966; City Col NY, AAS, 1968; State Univ NY, Fashion Inst Technol, AAS, 1971. **Career:** Fashion Fair Cosmetics, creative dir & beauty/training dir, 1973-78; Revlon Inc, polished ambers collection, creative dir, 1978-80; Elan Mag, elan beauty ed, 1980-82; Ebony Mag, beauty & fashion ed, 1982-85; EM Mag, ed, 1985-88; Ebony Man, ed chief, 1985; Tuesday, beauty ed; Essence Mag, assoc beauty ed, 1972-73; Clairol Cosmetics, asst ethnic mkt mgr, 1971-72, mkt mgr; Am Visions Mag, fashion & beauty contrib writer, 1989-; Johnson Publ Co Inc, Fashion Fair Div, beauty/training, 1988-; Bus Week Careers Mag, contrib fashion & beauty writer, 1987-88; Procter & Gamble, Cover Girl cosmetic div, consult, 1992; New Rochelle HS Continuing Edu, tcr, cosmetics & color theory, 2003; Bks: Fornay's Guide to Skin Care & Makeup Women Color, Simon & Schuster Publishers, 1989; Amalgamated Publishers Spec Beauty Ed, 1996; BE Mag Article, 1997; BET Weekend Mag Article, 1997; African Am Woman's Guide to Success Makeup & Skincare, 1999; B Beautiful: African Am Teenager's Complete Beauty Guide, 2002; Luxe Living, Beauty Life, older women; spec asst to David Paterson, 2006. **Orgs:** NAB, NY Chap, 1984, 1991-93; Nat Beauty Culturist League, 1983; friend/former bd mem, Boys Choir Harlem; NY Asn Black Journalist, 1991-92; Authors Guild Inc, 1991-93; personal grooming & develop consult, Girls Choir Harlem, 1994-95. **Honors/Awds:** Alumni of the Yr Award, Fashion Inst Tech, 1976; Mortimer C Ritter Award, 1976; Judge, Miss World Beauty Pageant London, Eng, 1982; contrib, McGraw Hill Book Co Encyclopedia of Black Am, 1981; BBW articles, 1984; Award in Excellence Black Women in Publishing NY, 1986; contrib, Black State of the Arts, Love Child Publishing, 1991; East NY Club of Brooklyn Nat Asn Negro Bus & Prof Women's Club Inc, 1981; Black Women in Publishing Connections III, 1986. **Home Addr:** PO Box 1321 Grand Central Sta, New York, NY 10163-1321, **Home Phone:** (914)576-5010.

### FORNEY, MARY JANE

Social worker. **Personal:** Born May 23, 1949, Galesburg, IL; children: James LaMour. **Educ:** Sangamon State Univ, BA, child family community serv, 1977. **Career:** Springfield & Sangamon County, Community Action, admin asst, 1968-74; Ill Dept C & Family Serv, child welfare worker & soc serv planner, 1974-78; Child Care Serv, Family Serv Ctr, Sangamon County, dir, 1982-; Ill Dept Human Serv, Child Care & Develop Outreach, coord. **Orgs:** Coun mem, Head Start Policy Coun, 1974-76; Nat Asn Educ Young C, vpres, 1981-83; chmn, Mother's March-March Dimes, 1984 & 1985; Nat Asn Black Social Worker, 1974-; secy, Streetside Boosters Neighborhood Adv Bd, 1976-; comt mem, Springfield Reg Adv Bd, Dept C & Family Serv, 1981-; spec projs chmn, Delta Sigma Theta, 1983-; adv bd Chair, Sangamon County, Dept Pub Aid, 1985-; DPA Adv Bd, 1982-; vpres, exec bd, March Dimes; Ill Interagency Nutrit Coun; adv bd, Ctr Early Childhood Leadership. **Honors/Awds:** Founders Day Award, St John AME Church, 1979; Social Worker of the Year, Nat Asn Black Soc Workers, 1979; Vol Award, Am Lung Asn, 1981; Hall of Fame Award, Springfield Sangamon County Action Comt, 1981; Outstanding Young Women of Am, 1982; Mother's March Chairperson March of Dimes Award, 1985; YWCA Woman of the Year Award; March of Dimes 5 Year Service Award, 1987. **Home Addr:** 2612 Parsley Lane, Springfield, IL 62711-7015, **Home Phone:** (217)698-5388. **Business Addr:** Co-ordinator, Illinois Department of Human Services, 400 W Lawrence 2 W, Springfield, IL 62762, **Business Phone:** (217)785-9336.

### FORREST-CARTER, DR. AUDREY FAYE

College teacher, educator. **Personal:** Born Apr 1, 1956, Greenwood, SC; daughter of Willie Sr and Ruth B; married Ewing Carter III; children: Channing Kamille & Ewing IV. **Educ:** Bennett Col, BA, 1978; NC A&T State Univ, MA, 1979; Miami Univ, PhD, 1990. **Career:** NC A&T State Univ, teaching asst, 1978-79; Winston-Salem State Univ, instr, 1979-84, asst prof, 1990-91; Miami Univ, doctoral assoc, 1984-88; NC A&T State Univ, asst prof Eng, 1992-96; Courtesy Kids, owner, currently; Winston-Salem State Univ, assoc prof, dept Eng & foreign lang, interim chair, 2009-. **Orgs:** Nat Coun Teachers Eng; Conf Col Compos & Commun. **Special Achievements:** Fiction Novel: The Wages of Sin; Judge Not!. **Home Addr:** 6007 Deer Pk Cir, Greensboro, NC 27455-9230. **Business Addr:** Interim Chair, Winston-Salem State University, 601 Martin Luther King Jr Dr 220 Hall-Patterson Rm 308, Winston Salem, NC 27101, **Business Phone:** (336)750-2315.

### FORSTER, CECIL R., JR.

Executive. **Personal:** Born Nov 11, 1943, NY. **Educ:** Middlebury Col, BA, 1964; St John's Univ, JD, 1967. **Career:** Irving Trust Co, lender officers training prog, 1967-68; WINS Radio, prof, in-chg advert sales, gen mgr; Pepsi Cola Metropolitan Bottling Co, vpres, secy & gen coun, 1971-74; Westinghouse Broadcasting Co Inc, vpres bus affairs, 1977-81; Unity Broadcasting Network Inc, vpres, 1981-85; legal bus advisor, 1985-89; Pace Univ Sch Law, prof law, 1985-89; Nutrit & Syst Inc, sr vpres & interim admin corp opers, 1989, sr vpres law & human resources, 1989-90, sr vpres law & govt affairs, 1990-91; Patton Boggs & Blow, coun, 1991-93; Infinity Broadcasting Corp, vpres & gen mgr, 1993; SportsRadio WIP 610, vpres & gen mgr. **Orgs:** Bd trustee, AFTRA Health & Retirement Funds, 1975-; bd dir, Howard Mem Fund, 1976-; exec adv comt, Black Exec Exchange Prog, Nat Urban League, 1977-; Fund Improv Postsecondary Educ, 1989; 100 Black Men; Am Bar Asn; NY Bar Asn; Phi Alpha Delta Law Fraternity; Sigma Pi Phi Fraternity; bd dir, Found Excellent Sch, currently. **Home Addr:** Residences Pier 5 Penns Landing, Philadelphia, PA 19106, **Home Phone:** (215)351-4139.

### FORSTER, JACQUELINE GAIL

Insurance executive, management consultant. **Personal:** Born Jan 29, 1970, Queens, NY; daughter of Charles and Gloria; married Brian Michael Cooper. **Educ:** Cornell Univ, BA, govt & eng, 1991; Univ PA Law Sch, JD, corp law, 1995. **Career:** EPLI, writer; EG Bowman Co Inc, vpres & sales mgr, Bowman Specialty Serv, sr vpres; Bear Stearns, analyst. **Orgs:** Bd dir, Nat Asn Ins Women, 1998-; plng comn, Harlem Bus Alliance; Cornell Univ Alumni Group Houston. **Honors/Awds:** Harriet Tubman Leadership Award, 1998; 40 Under 40 Award, Network Jour, 2000. **Home Addr:** 400 Crown Cant Suite 553, Edgewater, NJ 07020, **Home Phone:** (201)943-8112.

### FORSYTHE, HAZEL WALDRON

College teacher. **Personal:** Born Georgetown; daughter of Rupert and Isolene; married Vibert; children: Vibh & Vahl. **Educ:** Bristol Univ, UK, BEd, nutrit, 1977; Okla State Univ, MS, 1984, PhD, home econs, 1987. **Career:** Okla State Univ, Grad Asst, 1983-85, Grad Assoc, 1985-87; Inst Human Develop, fac assoc, 1992-95; Acad Nutrit & Dietetics, prof, 1992-2015; Univ Ky, assoc prof nutrit & food sci, 1989-, dir, coord prog dietetics, 1997-2000, dir, dietetics internship, 1997-, chair, dept nutrit & food sci, 1999-2006, Grad Ctr Nutrit Sci, assoc prof, currently; dir grad studies, 2006-11. **Orgs:** Am Dietetic Asn, 1989-; Int Fed Home Econs, Prog Affil Comt; Autism Soc Am, Bluegrass Chap Prog Coordr, 1999-; Asn Family & Consumer Scis, Awards Comt, 2000, accreditation rev; Ky Dietetic Asn, pres, 2001-02; Am Asn Ment Retardation; Am Asn Family & Consumer Sci; Caribbean Asn Home Econ; Int Fedn Home Econ; Ky Asn Family & Consumer Sci; Ky Early Childhood Asn; Res Asn Minority Prof; Soc Int Nutrt Educr; Soc Nutrt Educ; Southern Early Childhood Asn; Caribbean Asn Home Economists; Brit Coun Int Fel; Kappa Omicron Nu; Phi Upsilon Omicron; Phi Kappa Phi; Phi Delta Kappa. **Home Addr:** 1000 Turnbridge Rd, Lexington, KY 40506-0054, **Home Phone:** (859)271-0618. **Business Addr:** Associate Professor, Director, University of Kentucky, Rm 204 Funkhouser Bldg, Lexington, KY 40506-0050, **Business Phone:** (859)257-3800.

### FORT, DR. EDWARD BERNARD

Administrator, educator. **Personal:** Born Jun 12, 1951, Detroit, MI; son of Edward Clark and Inez Corrine; married Lessie Covington; children: Clarke & Lezlie. **Educ:** Wayne State Univ, BS, hist, 1954, MS, educ admin, 1958; Univ Calif, Berkeley, PhD, 1964. **Career:** Detroit Pub Schs, curric coordr, 1964-67; Univ Mich, Ann Arbor, vis prof educ admin, 1965-66; Univ Mich, Dearborn, adj prof urban educ, 1968-71; Mich State Univ, vis prof, 1974; Inkster Mich Pub Schs, supt, 1967-71; Sacramento Calif City Schs, supt, dep supt, 1971-74; Univ Wis Ctr Syst, chancellor, 1974-81; NC A&T State Univ, chancellor, 1981-99, Dept Hum Develop & Serv, chancellor emer & prof, 1999-. **Orgs:** Bd adv, Fund Improv Post Sec Educ, 1979-81; NASA Adv Coun, 1991-; bd dir, Nat Inst Environ Health Sci, 1988-92; pres comn, Nat Col Athletic Asn, 1984-86; bd dir, Nat Asn Equal Opportunity Higher Educ, 1984-; Greensboro NC Chamber Com Exec Bd; adv coun, Thurman Zumwalt Found; founder, Millennium Leadership Initiative, Am Asn State Cols & Univs. **Home Addr:** 900 Bluford St, Greensboro, NC 27401. **Business Addr:** Chancellor Emeritus, Professor, NC A&T State University, Dowdy Admin Bldg 1601 E Market St Rm 107, Greensboro, NC 27411-1095, **Business Phone:** (336)334-7595.

## FORT, DR. JANE GERALDINE

School administrator, educator. **Personal:** Born Aug 27, 1938, Nashville, TN; daughter of William Henry and Geraldine Bennett; married George Joseph Morrison; children: Sekou Morrison. **Educ:** Fisk Univ, BA, 1958; Univ Mass, MS, 1960, PhD, 1962. **Career:** City NY, Join, dir res, psychologist, 1964; City Col & William Alanson White Inst, NY, res assoc, 1965; Harvard Univ Grad Sch Educ, res assoc, 1965-69; Newton MA Schs, Reading Prog, consult & psychologist, 1974-75; Brookline Pub Schs, Brookline, MA, consult & sr res assoc, 1977-81; Roxbury Comm Col, Roxbury, MA, staff assoc, prog develop, 1979-81; Univ Calif-Davis, lectr, researcher, 1981-83; Clark Col, prog mgr eval & dir, 1984-87; Morehouse Sch Med, Dept Comm Health & Prev Med, 1987-92; Meharry Med Col, Cancer Control Res Unit, Cancer Prev Awareness Prog, assoc dir & co-prin investr, 1995-97, asst dean stud affairs, 1998, Dept Med Educ, asst prof clin skills & competency, 1998-. **Orgs:** Numerous bds dirs; lect sem & conf coordr & chmn; alumni clubs; Alpha Kappa Alpha Sorority; Asn Black Psychologists; Am Psychol Asn. **Honors/Awds:** Ford Found Fisk Univ, early entrant, 1953; Founder Award, Asn Black Psychologist, 1987. **Special Achievements:** Journal : REACH-Meharry Community-Campus Partnership: Developing Culturally Competent Health Care Providers, 2006. **Home Addr:** 2712 Meharry Blvd, Nashville, TN 37208-2839, **Home Phone:** (615)329-9723. **Business Addr:** Assistant Professor, Meharry Medical College, 1005 Dr DB Todd Jr Blvd, Nashville, TN 37208-3599, **Business Phone:** (615)327-5941.

## FORTE, LINDA DIANE

Banker. **Personal:** Born Dec 25, 1952, Cleveland, OH; daughter of Delvin L and Bertha l; married Tyrone M Davenport; children: Lynette Davenport & Simone Perry. **Educ:** Bowling Green State Univ, BS, 1974; Univ Mich, MBA, finance & acct, 1982. **Career:** Comerica Bank, compensation analyst, 1977-80, loan analyst, 1980-83, asst vpres & mgr credit admin, 1983-87, asst vpres & lender, 1987-88, vpres & sr lender, 1988-92, vpres & alt group mgr, 1992-95, vpres & mgr, 1995-04, sr vpres bus affairs & chief diversity officer, 2004-. **Orgs:** Pres, Urban bankers Forum, 1975-; Nat Black MBA Asn, 1982-; bd dir, Black Family Develop Inc, 1987-93; vice chair, Detroit Youth Found; Mich's Women Found; dir, Econ Develop Corp, Detroit; Comerica Charitable Found; dir, Neighborhood Develop Corp, Detroit; Coleman A Young Found; Mich Women's Found; Detroit Symphony Orchestra; Comericas Mgt Coun Comerica, 2004-; Henry Ford Health Syst Found, 2011-. **Honors/Awds:** Minority Achiever Award, YWCA, 1984; Banker of the Year, Urban bankers Forum, 1988; Banker of the Year Award, 1990; H Naylor Fitzhugh Award, Nat Black MBA, 1996; Crain's Detroit Business 100 Black Business Leaders, 1998; Michigan's Most Powerful African Americans, Corp Mag, 2003; John Copeland Community Leadership Legacy Award, YMCA, 2005; Best Corporate Executive Award, Black Women's Contracting Asn, 2005; Most Influential African-American Women in Michigan Award, Women's Informal Network's, 2005; Aubrey W Lee Award, Urban Financial Services Coalition, 2005. **Home Addr:** 153 Keelson Dr, Detroit, MI 48215, **Home Phone:** (313)823-6737. **Business Addr:** Senior Vice President of Business Affairs, Chief Diversity Officer, Comerica Bank, 500 Woodward Ave, Detroit, MI 48226, **Business Phone:** (313)222-5076.

## FORTE, DR. MINNIE T.

Educator, association executive. **Personal:** Born Jan 1, 1916?, Goldsboro, NC; children: William, Lonnie & Minnie Mae. **Educ:** Fayetteville State Univ, BS, 1939; NC Cent Univ, MA, 1951, PhD, 1960. **Career:** Durham City Sch Syst, teacher, 1944-60; Fayetteville St Univ, elem teacher, 1960-62, prof elem educ, 1974-83; Shaw Univ, 1962-65; Oper Break Ctr C, dir, 1965-66; St Augustines Col, assoc prof coordr; Early Childhood Educ, 1966-74. **Orgs:** Chmn, Christian Educ; White Rock Baptist Church; vpres, New Hope Baptist Asn; life mem, Nat Educ Asn; adv stud, NEA CAE; spec asst & coordr, Early Childhood Educ, 1970-74; Nat Coun Accreditation Teacher Educ Evaluate, 1975; Fayetteville St Univ, 1975. **Home Addr:** 1612 Merrick St, Durham, NC 27701, **Home Phone:** (919)682-7393.

## FORTIER, DR. THEODORE T., SR.

Dentist, association executive, educator. **Personal:** Born Aug 15, 1926, San Diego, CA. **Educ:** Univ Calif, Los Angeles; Univ Pa; Howard Univ Col Dent, DDS, 1957; Acad Gen Dent, DDS. **Career:** Dentist (retired); US Pub Health Serv, fel; Los Angeles, dentist pvt pract; Continuing Dent Educ Univ SC Sch Dent, instr, 1968; Dent Dept Hollywood Pres Med Ctr, chief, 1972-74; Dent Asst Sch, instr, 1986-93; VSC Sch Dent, teaching staff; S Calif, Health Newsletter, app ed; pvt pract dentist. **Orgs:** Los Angeles Coun; Univ SC Med Ctr, Compton; PTA Sch Dentist, 1959-61; pres, Angel City Dent Soc, 1968-69; vpres, Dent Found Calif, 1971; bd dir, Los Angeles Dent Soc; fel Exam Comt, 1986-91; Acad Gen Dent; House Delegates Calif Dent Asn; pres, Kiwanis Club Angeles Mesa, 1976; gen chmn, Fund raising Dr Crenshaw YMCA, 1975, 1993; Omicron Kappa Upsilon; pres, SC Acad Gen Dent, 1987; trustee, Calif Dent Asn, 1986-89; pres, Crenshaw Chamber Com, 1993-94; Community Police Adv Comt Bd; Parlimentarian, Tuskegee airmen Los Angeles Chap; angel, Aviation Angel Tuskegee Airmen, 2007-; bd mem, Vector Control Bd; bd dir, Dent Co Calif Dent Asn. **Honors/Awds:** Dental Alumni of the Year, Howard Univ Col Dent, 1987; Dentist of the Year, Southern Calif Acad Gen Dent, 1992; Speaker of the Year Award, Recycling Black Dollars Inc; Honoree, The Sch Dent, 2002; Humanitarian Award, Acad Gen Dent, 2005. **Business Addr:** Dentist, 3701 Stocker St Suite 408, Los Angeles, CA 90008-5123, **Business Phone:** (323)295-6883.

## FORTSON, DANNY (DANIEL ANTHONY FORTSON)

Basketball player. **Personal:** Born Mar 27, 1976, Philadelphia, PA. **Educ:** Univ Cincinnati, attended 1997. **Career:** Basketball player (retired); Denver Nuggets, forward, 1997-99; Boston Celtics, 1999-2000; Toronto Raptors, 2000; Golden State Warriors, 2000-03; Dallas Mavericks, forward, 2003-04; Seattle SuperSonics, forward, 2004-07.

## FORTSON, WALTER LEWIS

Lawyer. **Personal:** Born Jul 16, 1951, Hatchechubbee, AL; son of Oscar and Sallie; children: Walter Lewis II & Clara Alexis. **Educ:** Ala A&M Univ, BS, 1973; Atlanta Law Sch, JD, 1979. **Career:** Fortson & Secret, partner, 1991; Fortson & Assocs, atty, 2003-. **Orgs:** State Bar Ga; regional dir, Nat Bar Asn; Gate City Bar Asn; Fountain City Bar Asn, 1995. **Home Addr:** 1039 McGill Pk Pl, Atlanta, GA 30312, **Home Phone:** (404)523-4567. **Business Addr:** Attorney, Fortson & Assocs, 4319 Covington Hwy Suite 212, Decatur, GA 30035, **Business Phone:** (404)289-7611.

## FORTUNE, DR. GWENDOLINE Y.

Writer, educator. **Personal:** Born Houston, TX; daughter of W Hermon Young and Mittie McCain; children: Frederic, Phillip & Roger. **Educ:** JC Smith Univ, BS, educ & social sci, 1948; SC State Col, MS, 1951; Roosevelt Univ, MPh, 1972; Nova Univ, EdD, 1979. **Career:** Chicago Pub Schs, teacher, 1954-66; Dist 68 Skokie Ill, team coord, 1964-70; Oakton Community Col, prof ethnic studies cord, 1970-84; Consult "Discovery", dir 1984-; poems & articles: "Dancing as Fast as We Can"; "Inner Scan"; Novels: Growing Up Nigger Rich, 2002; Family Lines, 2003. **Orgs:** Exec brd, Ill Coun Black Studies, 1980-83; exec comt, Ill Consult Ethnicity Educ, 1980-84; manuscript chair, Off-Campus Writers Workshop, 1990-; bd dir, Nc Writers' Network. **Home Addr:** 8620 NW 13th St Suite 71, Gainesville, FL 32653, **Home Phone:** (352)372-0021.

## FORTUNE-MAGINLEY, LOIS J.

Television producer. **Personal:** Born Mar 16, 1946, New York, NY; daughter of Roland K and Hilda O; married George H. **Educ:** Monteith Col, Wayne State Univ, PhD, 1968; New York Univ, MAT, 1969. **Career:** C's TV Workshop, assoc producer int dept, 1978-79, Philippines, resident producer, 1983, exec producer int dept, 1985-87, exec producer, 1988-90; Nickelodeon, Pinwheel ser, exec producer, 1979-82; UNESCO, Un Develop Prog, ETV, producer & consult, New Delhi, India, 1987-88; Galaxy Classroom, exec producer, 1990-96. **Orgs:** Adv panel, Nat Endowment Arts, 1983; bd mem, Int Film & TV Festival, 1986; judge, Nat Acad Cable Programming, 1987-88; Acad TV Arts & Sci, 1990; Women Film, 1993-; roundtable producer, Nat Acad TV Arts & Sci; coun mem, Dirs Guild Am; Am Film Inst. **Honors/Awds:** Certificate, Nat Acad TV Arts & Sci, 1976-77; Certificate of Merit, Nat Cath Asn Broadcasters & Allied Commun, 1981; 2 Ace Awards, Nat Cable TV Asn, 1982; Philippine Catholic Mass Media Award, 1983; Silver Medal, Baghdad Int TV Festival, 1988. **Home Addr:** 515 N Gertruda Ave Unit 5, Redondo Beach, CA 90277-2140, **Home Phone:** (310)374-5356.

## FOSKEY, HON. CARNELL T.

District court judge. **Personal:** Born Dec 7, 1956, Darlington, SC; son of Thomas and Sadie; married Francina Little. **Educ:** State Univ NY, BA, polit sci & hist, 1977; Calif Western Sch Law, JD, 1980; Boston Univ Sch Law, LLM Taxation, 1982. **Career:** Nassau Co Dept Social Serv, staff atty, 1982-83; Nassau Co Off Co Atty, dep co atty, 1983-89; Off Presiding Supvr, exec asst, 1989-90; Dept Planning & Econ Develop, interim comnr, 1990-91; Nassau Co Dist Ct, dist ct judge, 1992-, 9th Judicial Dist, Supv Judge, 2005-. **Orgs:** Bar Asn Nassau County; 100 Black Men Nassau/Suffolk; Am Inns Ct; Nat Asn Advan Colored People Lakeview Br; Union Baptist Church; Union Sr Citizen Plaza; Nassau County Bar Asn; Peninsula Couning Ctr. **Honors/Awds:** Nassau Black Hist Comt, Man of the Year, 1992; Dollars & Sense Mag, 100 Top Black Prof, 1992; Man of the Year, Nassau Black Hist Comt, 1992-. **Special Achievements:** The First African American to be named Supv Judge; The youngest person to be elected to the Nassau Co Dist Ct in 1991; First employed as the Interim Commissioner of Planning and Economic Development. **Home Addr:** 226 Erie Rd, West Hempstead, NY 11552-3906, **Home Phone:** (516)766-1631. **Business Addr:** Supervising Judge, State NY District Court Nassau County, 435 Mid Neck, Great Neck, NY 11023-1412, **Business Phone:** (516)566-2200.

## FOSTER, AUTHERINE JUANITA LUCY

Educator. **Personal:** Born Oct 5, 1929, Shiloh, AL; daughter of Milton Cornelius and Minnie Hosea; married Hugh Lawrence; children: Hugh, Anglea, Crazia & Chrystal. **Educ:** Selma Univ, teaching cert; Miles Mem Col, BA, eng, 1952; Univ Ala, MA, elem educ, 1992. **Career:** Eng teacher & substitute teacher, 1952-; pub speaker. **Orgs:** Bd mem, Birmingham Civil Rights Inst; Nat Asn Advan Colored People; Zeta Phi Beta. **Business Addr:** Board Member, Birmingham Civil Rights Institute, 520 16th St N, Birmingham, AL 35203, **Business Phone:** (205)328-9696.

## FOSTER, DR. BELLANDRA B.

President (organization). **Personal:** daughter of George (deceased) and Ella Pearl Benefield (deceased); married Michael; children: 2. **Educ:** Mich State Univ, BS, civil & environ engineering, 1983, PhD, civil & environ engineering, 1999; Wayne State Univ, MS, civil engineering, 1989; Univ Mich, cert, intelligent transp systs, 1993; Northwestern Univ, traffic & transp engr, 1999. **Career:** Bechtel Power Corp, struct engr, 1983-84; Oakland County Road Comn, design engr & civil engr, 1984-85; Mich Dept Transp, civil & transp engr, 1985-92; City Atlanta, Dept Pub Work, dir hwy st, 1992-93; BBF Engineering Serv PC, pres & prin engr, 1994-2014; First Priority Entrepreneurship Consult Serv, auth, entrepreneurship consult & prof speaker, 2008-12; BBFoster Consult PC, pres, 2014. Books: For Love and Money: Seven Guidelines for Achieving Success in Your Home and Business, Surviving a Climate of Hate: Valuing Yourself in Spite of Bullying, Racism and Sexism. **Orgs:** Family Victory Fel Church; founder, Help House, 2007-; Civil Engineering Dept Adv bd mem, Mich State Univ, 2008-11; Am Consult Engrs Coun; Detroit Athletic Club; Dwight D. Eisenhower Fel, Fed Hwy Admin; adv bd mem, Mich State Univ Prof; adv bd mem, Mich State Univ Alumni; Great Lakes Ctr Truck & Transit Res Scholar, Univ Mich; Fel, ENO Transp Found; MSU Col Engineering Alumni Adv bd mem, Mich State Univ, 2010-; Fel, King-Chavez-Parks; bd mem, Mich State Univ Eli Broad Col Bus Exec Forum, 2011-; exec bd mem, Queen's Found, 2014-; Int Coach Fedn, 2015. **Home Addr:** 29305 Bradmoor Ct, Farmington Hills, MI 48334, **Home Phone:** (248)538-5345. **Business Addr:** President, BBF Engineering Services PC, 24445 NW Hwy Suite 110, Southfield, MI 48075-2436, **Business Phone:** (248)262-5777.

## FOSTER, CLYDE

Executive. **Personal:** Born Nov 21, 1931; married Dorothy M Harri; children: Anitra, Edith, Clydis, Byron & Carla. **Educ:** Ala A&M Univ, BS, 1954. **Career:** Army Ballistic Missile Agency, Redstone Arsenal, 1957; Marshall Space Flight Ctr, mathematician, instr Comput Lab, 1960, chief, EEO Civil Serv Employees, 1972, instr, training courses; Ala A&M Univ, dir, Comput Sci Dept, est Data Processing Lab & undegrad degree prog Comput Sci, first State Ala Educ Syst Higher Learning, 1968-70; Dallas Co Sch Syst, Selma, sci teacher; Prep Tech, pres; Triana Indus Inc, founder, pres. **Orgs:** Petitioned Probate Judge, gained rejuvenation Triana, 1964; org Data Processing Assoc Inc, 1970. **Home Addr:** 380 Zierdt Rd, Madison, AL 35756-8206, **Home Phone:** (256)772-3553.

## FOSTER, DEBORAH

Executive. **Educ:** Tex Southern Univ, attended, 1983. **Career:** DC, law-related educ, state dir; St Law Inc, prog dir, 1997-2004, sr prog dir, 1997-. **Orgs:** Fel Nat Coun Social Studies; Fel Nat Coun Juvenileand Family Ct Judges; Fel Asn Supv & Curric Develop. **Business Addr:** Senior Program Director, Street Law Inc, 1010 Wayne Ave Suite 870, Silver Spring, MD 20910, **Business Phone:** (301)589-1130.

## FOSTER, DELORES JACKSON

School administrator. **Personal:** Born Jan 24, 1938, Halltown, WV; daughter of Daniel David Jackson and Mary Frances Taylor; married James Hadlei; children: James Jr & Arthur; married Robert L Bailey; children: Mark D. **Educ:** Shepherd Col, BA, 1960; Jersey City State Col, MA, 1974. **Career:** School administrator (retired); Page-Jackson High Sch, teacher, 1960-61; Dickinson High Sch, teacher, 1961-71, teacher coordr, 1971-73, guide counr, 1973-84, actg vice prin, 1982-83, vice prin, 1985-91, actg prin, 1986, guid counr vice prin, 1987; PS No 34, prin, 1991-2000; educ consult commun sch, 2001. **Orgs:** Corresp sec, Black Educr United, 1975; adv bd, Upward Bound Proj, St Peter's Col, Jersey City, Nj, 1975-79; leadership training United Church Christ, 1979; First vpres, Col Women Inc, 1979-81; pres, Col Women Inc, 1981-83, 1995-; vice chmn, cong Pk Ave Christ Church Disciples Christ, 1982-84; workshop leader, Nj Alliance Black Educ conf, 1983; pres, Cent Atlantic Conf United Church Christ, 1984-87; elected lay del, 15th Gen Synod OCC Am IA, 1985; lay deleg 16th Gen Synod, Cleveland, Ohio, 1987; adv bd, prin ctr Garden State, 1994-2001; Emanuel AME Church, 1998; asst dir, bd Christian Ed; Nj, prin & Supvr Asn; Nat Alliance Black Sch Educr; Delta Sigma Theta Sorority; EmpowermentChg. **Honors/Awds:** Honored as a lay woman in the United Church of Christ at 15th Gen Synod in Am IA, 1985; Summer Inst Prin, Geraldine R Dodge Foundation Award, 1993. **Special Achievements:** Co-author, Integrating the Classroom with the World of Work, 1980; Featured in doc, "Quicksand and Banana Peels", Dodge Found, 1998. **Home Addr:** 89 Hawthorne Ave, East Orange, NJ 07018, **Home Phone:** (973)678-3431.

## FOSTER, DR. E. C.

Educator, government official, teacher. **Personal:** Born Jan 4, 1939, Canton, MS; son of Hugh D (deceased) and Minnie L Pugh; married Velvelyn Blackwell; children: Garnet A & Sunyetta M. **Educ:** Jackson State Univ, BS, 1964; Carnegie-Mellon Univ, MA, 1967, DA, 1970; African-Am Inst, post-doctoral study. **Career:** Educator, government official (retired); Natchez Pub Sch, histroy teacher, 1964-65; Brushton Inner City Proj, community organizer, 1965-66; Pittsburgh Pub Sch, teacher, 1967-68; Tougaloo Col, interim vpres acad affairs; Jackson State Univ, prof hist, 1969, Fac Senate, chmn, Black studies, dir, 1971-73, dean; Jackson MS City Coun, pres, 1985-94. **Orgs:** Pres, Fac Senate, Jackson State Univ, 1974-79; bd mem, Farish St YMCA, 1976-79; assoc ed, J Negro Hist, 1978-; pres, Asn Soc & Behav Scientists, 1982; legis comm chmn, Local PTA, 1984; city Counman Jackson MS; Chamber Com; Vicksburg/Jackson Trade Zone Comn, 1987; bd dirs, MS Munic Asn, 1994-; vice chair, Nat League Cities Leadership Training Coun, 1994. **Honors/Awds:** Jackson State Univ Alumni Service Award, 1985; Man of the Year Award, Omega Psi Phi, 1985; NAEFO Presidential Citation Award, 1986; Dr Martin Luther King Service Award, JSU/SGA, 1986. **Special Achievements:** Author of approx 30 publications, 1969-85. **Home Addr:** 3335 Santa Rosa St, Jackson, MS 39209, **Home Phone:** (601)354-2060.

## FOSTER, EDWARD, SR. (ED FOSTER)

Manager, president (organization). **Personal:** Born Sep 27, 1945, Maplesville, AL; son of Mamie; married Jacqulyn E Grant; children: Edward & Forrest Cedric. **Educ:** Selma Univ, attended 1967; AL A&M Univ, BS, 1971; Rochester Inst Technol, MS, mfg technol, 1980. **Career:** Xerox Corp, prod supv, 1972-82; GTE Corp, sr qual supv, 1983-86; NCR Corp, prod mgr, 1986; Dell Comput, prod mgr 1, 2005-06; Energizer Battert Co, sr mfg supvr, 2007-08; Ingersoll Rand, supv, 2007; GREGG & Assocs, sr mfg supv, 2007-12. **Orgs:** Pres, AL A&M ALumni Assoc, 1981-82; vpres Rochester Chap, AL A&M Alumni Assoc, 1982-83; Am Mgt Assoc, 1984; Am Soc Qual Control, 1985; 32 degree Lodge 107 Masonic Temple, 1985; Surface Mt Tech, 1986. **Honors/Awds:** Outstanding Work Higher Ed NAFEO, 1983. **Home Addr:** 2941 Knollcrest Hill Lane, High Point, NC 27265.

## FOSTER, EZOLA BROUSSARD

Politician, educator. **Personal:** Born Aug 9, 1938, Louisiana, LA; married Chuck; children: 3. **Educ:** Tex Southern Univ, BS, bus educ, 1960; Pepperdine Univ, MS, sch mgt & admin, 1973. **Career:** Educator (retired), politician; Watts, Los Angeles, high sch teacher, 1963-85; City Bell, high sch teacher, 1985-96; Black Am Family Values, founder, 1987, pres, 1987-00; US presidential, vpres, 2000-02; Reform Party, 2000-02; conservative polit activist, currently; Constitution Party, currently. **Orgs:** John Birch Soc; Const Party's Nat Comt, 2002-04; chmn, Am Independent Party Orange County Cent Comt, 2004-06. **Home Addr:** , Los Angeles, CA 90066, **Home Phone:** (310)313-2637.

**Business Addr:** Member, Constitution Party National Committee, PO Box 1782, Lancaster, PA 17608, **Business Phone:** (717)390-1993.

## FOSTER, FRANCES SMITH

Executive director, educator. **Personal:** Born Feb 8, 1944, Dayton, OH; daughter of Quinton and Mabel; married Warren R; children: Lisa Ramirez, Krishna & Quinton. **Educ:** Miami Univ, BS, educ, 1964; Univ S Calif, MA, Brit & Am lit, 1971; Univ Calif, San Diego, PhD, Brit & Am lit, 1976; State Univ NY, Geneseo, LHD, 2010. **Career:** Cin Pub Schs, teacher, 1964-66; Detroit Pub Schs, teacher, 1966-68; Univ Southern Calif, teaching asst, 1969-70; Calif State Univ, lectr eng, 1970-71, admin fel, 1983-84; San Fernando Valley State Col, instr, 1970-71; Univ Calif, San Diego, instr, third col writing prog, 1971-72, prof, am lit, 1988-94; San Diego State Univ, lectr, 1971-72, asst prof afro am studies, 1972-76, asst prof, 1976-79, asst dean & dir, 1976-79, assoc prof, 1979-82, prof, 1982-88; Afro Am Studies Dept, fac coordr, 1972-74, chair, 1975-76; Youngstown Eng Festival, distinguished vis prof, Youngstown State Univ, 1987; Harvard Divinity Sch, res assoc & vis lectr, 1991-2000; Univ Mich, vis lectr, dearborn, 1994; Emory Univ, Inst Womens Studies, prof, 1994-96, Charles Howard Candler prof eng & womens studies, 1996-, dir, 1999-2002, chmn, 2005-08. Books: Witnessing Slavery: The Development of the Antebellum Slave Narrative, 1979; Behind the Scenes: Thirty Years a Slave and Four Years in the White House by Elizabeth Keckley, 1998; Concise Oxford Companion to African American Literature, 2001; The Family in Africa and the African Diaspora: A Multidisciplinary Approach, 2004; Love and Marriage in Early African America, 2007; Til Death or Distance Do Us Part: Love and Marriage in African America, 2009; The Development of the Ante-Bellum Slave Narrative; Incidents in the Life of a Slave Girl; The Norton Anthology of African American Literature; Still Brave: The Evolution of Black Women's Studies, 2010. **Orgs:** Exec dir, Philol Asn Pac Coast, 1981-84; Humanities Adv Coun; KPBS; San Diego State Univ, Career Plan & Placement Ctr, Adv Comm; Nat Asn Advan Colored People, Col Lang Asn; Mod Lang Asn; W Coast Women's Hist Asn; Phi Beta Kappa; Phi Kappa Pi; Althenoi Phi Kappa Delta; Alpha Kappa Alpha; Childrens Lit Asn; MELUS; Am Lit Asn; Am Studies Asn; Soc Study Am Women Writers; Fel Nat Endowment Humanities Res, Atlanta Univ, 1980-81; Fel Calif State Univ Admin, 1983-84; exec coun, Mod Lang Asn, 1995-96; Sr Fel Univ Leiden, Neth, 1997; Hon Fel, Inst Res Humanities, Univ Wis, Madison, 1998-; Sr Fel, Ctr Study Relig & Law, Emory Univ Sch Law, 2001-; Sr Fel, W.E.B. DuBois Inst, Harvard Univ, 2002-04; Fel Feminist Sexual Ethics Proj Brandeis Univ, 2003-; Dept Eng, 2005-08; Emory Univ Freshman Convocation Speaker, 2007. **Business Addr:** Charles Howard Candler Professor, Emory University, N 302 Callaway Ctr 537 Kilgo Cir, Atlanta, GA 30322, **Business Phone:** (404)727-6920.

## FOSTER, GEORGE ARTHUR

Baseball player. **Personal:** Born Dec 1, 1948, Tuscaloosa, AL; married Sheila; children: Shawna & Starr. **Educ:** El Camino Col, Torrance, CA. **Career:** Baseball player (retired); San Francisco Giants, outfielder, 1969-71; Cincinnati Reds, outfielder, 1971-81; New York Mets, outfielder, 1982-86; Chicago White Sox, outfielder, 1986; The George Foster Diamond Report, Radio Show; St. Lucie Legends, 1989; Orix Buffaloes, cross-checker scout, 2010. **Orgs:** Founder, George Foster HomeDisadvantaged C, Upper Dayton, OH. **Home Addr:** PO Box 11098, Greenwich, CT 06830.

## FOSTER, GLADYS M.

Lawyer. **Personal:** Born Jul 12, 1927, Brooklyn, NY; married John H Skidmore. **Educ:** Barnard Col Columbia Univ, AB, 1949; Columbia Law Sch, JD, 1953. **Career:** Lawyer (retired); Brooklyn, NY, pvt prac; Workmen's Compensation & Unemployment Ins Appeal Bd, atty; NY State Div Human Rights, sr atty. **Orgs:** Brooklyn Bar Asn; Brooklyn Women's Bar Asn; Vocational Adv Law Barnard Col; vpres, Nat Asn Advan Colored People; Barnard Col Alumni By-Laws Com; Crown Heights Asn; vpres, Nat Asn Col Women. **Home Addr:** 1353 Union St, Brooklyn, NY 11213-4240, **Home Phone:** (718)773-1308.

## FOSTER, GREGORY

Track and field athlete. **Personal:** Born Apr 4, 1958, Chicago, IL; married Karen Marie Houlemard. **Educ:** Univ Calif, Los Angeles, Calif, attended 1981. **Career:** Track & field athlete (retired); hurdler, 1977-92. **Orgs:** Asn Athletics Mgrs. **Honors/Awds:** Gold Medal, IAAF World Cup, 1981; Gold Medal, World Championships, 1983; Silver Medal, Summer Olympics, 1984; Gold Medal, Goodwill Games, 1986; Gold Medal, World Championships, 1987; Gold Medal, World Championships in Athletics, 1991; Gold Medal, IAAF World Indoor Championships, 1991; US Track & Field Athlete Hall of Fame, 1998; Bronze Medal. **Special Achievements:** Nominee, Jesse Owens Award, 1987; Foster won 11 national titles & broke the indoor world record twice; Only person in the history of the IAAF World Championships in Athletics to win three consecutive 110 meter hurdling titles. **Home Addr:** 4207 Corrales Dr, Florissant, MO 63034, **Home Phone:** (314)583-2483.

## FOSTER, GREGORY CLINTON

Basketball player. **Personal:** Born Oct 3, 1968, Oakland, CA; married Victoria; children: Victoria & Collette. **Educ:** Univ Calif, Los Angeles, attended 1988; Univ Tex, El Paso, attended 1990, BA, interdisciplinary studies, 2011. **Career:** Basketball player (retired), coach; Breogan, Spain, 1990; Wash Bullets, ctr & power forward, 1990-92; Atlanta Hawks, 1992-93; Milwaukee Bucks, power forward, 1993-94, 2001-02, asst coach, currently; Papagos Athens, Greece, 1993-94; Chicago Bulls, 1994-95; Minn Timberwolves, 1994-95; Utah Jazz, 1995-98, power forward, 1999; Seattle Supersonics, power forward, 1999-2000; Los Angeles Lakers, ctr, 2000-01; Ind Pacers, ctr, 2001-02; Toronto Raptors, ctr, 2002-03; Philadelphia 76ers, asst coach, 2013-14. **Orgs:** Nat Basketball Asn. **Honors/Awds:** Champion, Nat Basketball Asn, 2001. **Special Achievements:** TV appearance: Forget Paris, 1995; The 1997 NBA Finals, 1997. **Business Addr:** Assistant Coach, Milwaukee Bucks, 1543 N 2nd St 6th Fl, Milwaukee, WI 53212, **Business Phone:** (414)227-0599.

## FOSTER, DR. HENRY WENDELL, JR.

Consultant, school administrator, physician. **Personal:** Born Sep 8, 1933, Pine Bluff, AR; son of Henry W and Ivie Hill Watson; married St Clair Anderson; children: Myrna & Wendell. **Educ:** Morehouse Col, BS, biol, 1954; Univ Ark Sch Med, MD, 1958. **Career:** Receiving Hosp, Detroit, Intern, 1958-59; Larson Afb, chief, obstet & gynec, 1959-61; Malden Hosp, residency, surg, 1961-62; George W Hubbard Hosp, Meharry Med Col, Nashville, TN, obstet & gynec resident, 1962-65; John A Andrew Memorial Hosp, Tuskegee Inst, obstet & gynec chief, 1965-70; John A Andrews Mem Hosp, chief obstet & gynec, 1970-73; Meharry Med Col, Dept Obstet & Gynec, prof, chmn, 1973-90, dean, vpres, health affairs, 1990-93, actg pres, 1993-94, prof emer obstet & gynec, currently; Vanderbilt Univ Med Ctr, clin prof obstet & gynec; Pres Clinton Sr adv, Teen Pregnancy Reduction & Youth Issues, 1996-2001; Dir Ctr DisControl & Prev, expert consult, 1996-; Secy Dept Health & Human Serv, expert consult, 1996-; Meharry Med Col, prof emer, obstet & gynec, dean, currently. **Orgs:** Macon Co Med Soc; AMA; Nat Med asn; health policy fel Asn Acad Health Ctr, 1994-95; Nat Acad Sci Inst Med; dipl, Am Bd Obstet & Gynec; Alpha Omega Alpha; Robert Wood Johnson Found; chair, U.S. Comt Un Pop Fund; bd dir, Pathfinder Int; chair, Us Nat Libr Med; Kappa Alpha Psi Fraternity. **Home Addr:** 4140 W Hamilton Rd, Nashville, TN 37218-1829, **Home Phone:** (615)299-0188. **Business Addr:** Professor Emeritus, Meharry Medical College, 1005 Dr DB Todd Blvd, Nashville, TN 37208, **Business Phone:** (615)327-5524.

## FOSTER, IVADALE MARIE FOULKS. See Obituaries Section.

## FOSTER, REV. JAMES HADLEI. See Obituaries Section.

## FOSTER, JANICE MARTIN

Lawyer. **Personal:** Born Jun 14, 1946, New Orleans, LA; married John P; children: Suzanne & Sean. **Educ:** Chestnut Hill Col, AB, 1967; Tulane Law Sch, JD, 1970. **Career:** Loisana State Univ, bd supvr; Mercy Hosp & Mercy Baptist Med Ctr, chairwoman; Jones Walker Waechter Poitevent Carrere & Denegre LLP, partner & atty, currently. **Orgs:** vpres, Bd Liquidation, City Debt, 1979-99; bd dir, Metrop Area Safety Coun, 1990; Govs Task Force Higher Educ, 1990; bd supervisors, La State Univ, 1991-96; bd trustee, Xavier Univ, 1996-2002, chmn, 2000-01; bd trustee, Greater New Orleans Found, 1993-2000; bd trustee & chmn, Baptist Community Ministries, 2006-08; La Bar Asn; Am Bar Asn; bd dir, New Orleans Legal Aid Corp Sch Leadership Ctr New Orleans; La Univ Bd Supvrs; bd trustee, Mercy Hosp; bd trustee, Baptist Med Ctr; Nat Bar Asn; bd dir, Jr Achievement Civil Serv Comnm New Orleans; third ann class 50 Leadership Law honorees; advisor, IssueLab Found Ctr; chair bd trustee, Sch Leadership Ctr; Louis A. Martinet Soc; La State Bar Asn; New Orleans Estate Planning Coun. **Honors/Awds:** Monte M Lemann Award, 1984; Michaelle Pitard Wynne Professionalism Award, 1996; New Orleans City Business Leadership in Law Award, 2007; Young Leadership Council Role Model, 2007; Top Lawyers in New Orleans Magazine, 2009. **Home Addr:** 2682 Law St, New Orleans, LA 70117. **Business Addr:** Attorney, Partner, Jones Walker Waechter Poitevent Carrere & Denegre LLP, 201 St Charles Ave, New Orleans, LA 70170-5100, **Business Phone:** (504)582-8168.

## FOSTER, JENNIFER K.

Executive. **Career:** Ill Community Col Bd, Adult Educ & Family Literacy, sr dir, GED adminr, currently, GED Testing Admin, interim dir & state dir, currently, New Learning Opportunities Div, assoc dir, assoc vpres adult educ & workforce develop, proj lead, currently. **Orgs:** exec comt, Nat Adult Educ Prof Develop Consortium; exec comt, Nat Coun State Dirs Adult Educ; Nat Reporting Stand. **Business Addr:** Associate Vice President, Project Lead, Illinois Community College Board, 401 E Capitol Ave, Springfield, IL 62701-1711, **Business Phone:** (217)782-5645.

## FOSTER, JYLLA MOORE

Association executive, manager. **Personal:** Born Jan 1, 1954, Salisbury, NC; married Stan; children: Anjylla. **Educ:** Livingstone Col, BS, math, 1976; Ind Univ, MBA, mkt, 1978; Corp Coach Univ; Benedictine Univ, PhD, orgn develop. **Career:** IBM, systs engr, 1978-83, syst eng mgr, 1983-96, vpres opers, 1996-97, vpres sales small & medium bus Midwest, 1997, vpres global channels, 1998, vpres & client exec, 1998-2000, nat pres; Crystal Stairs Inc, Hins dale, Ill, founder, pres & chief exec officer, 2000-; CenterForInsight.com, chief exec officer; Global Inst Innovative & Collab Thinking, managing dir; Robinson Group Consult Inc, innovative leader & bus exec. **Orgs:** Pres, Zeta Phi Beta Sorority, 1973-; Int Asn Coaches; Am Soc Training & Develop; Nat Black MBA Asn; Info Technol Sr Mgt Forum; Nat Coun Negro Women; adv bd, Sigma Educ Found; Asn Training & Develop; Nat Speakers Asn; Int Coach Fedn; consortium fel Ind Univ. **Honors/Awds:** Hon DHL, Livingstone Col, 1999; Distinguished Alumna Award, Nat Asn Equal Opportunity Higher Educ, 2000; Most Influential African-Americans, Ebony mag; National Business and Professional Womens Corporate Hall of Fame; Distinguished Alumni Award, Nat Asn Equal Opportunity Higher Educ. **Special Achievements:** Author: DUE NORTH! Strengthen Your Leadership Assets, Crystal Stairs Inc, 2002. **Business Addr:** Chief Executive Officer, Crystal Stairs Inc, 5105 Goldleaf Cir Suite 150, Los Angeles, CA 90056, **Business Phone:** (323)299-8998.

## FOSTER, LLOYD L.

Scientist. **Personal:** Born Jul 3, 1930, Austin, TX; married Leatrice Norman; children: Lloyd Jr, Lionel Laird & Lyle Lerone. **Educ:** Huston-Tillotson Col, BS, 1951; Incarnate World Col, MS, 1966; Baylor Sch Med, cert physiol & mod instrumentation, 1967. **Career:** Scientist (retired); Brooks, AFB, med tech, 1963-64, biologist, 1964-70, res chemist, 1970-74, educ tech, 1974-76, res chemist, 1976-91, chief, eqal employ counr, collateral duty, 1981-91; St Philips Col, biol instr, 1966-01. **Orgs:** Nat Asn Equal Opportunity Higher Educ; Am Chem Soc; Nat Asn Advan Colored People; Phyllis Wheatley Area Optismist Club; Houston Tillotson Col Alumni Asn. **Honors/Awds:** Academic Achievement Award, Huston-Tillotson Col, 1974; Alumni Chapter Award, Nat Asn Black Cols, 1976. **Special Achievements:** First African-American Male to receive a masters degree from Incarnate Word College, San Antonio, Tex, 1966. **Home Addr:** 147 Morningview Dr, San Antonio, TX 78220-3118, **Home Phone:** (210)333-7463.

## FOSTER, PARRAN L., III

Association executive, executive. **Personal:** married Glenna. **Educ:** Johnson C Smith Univ, BS, biol, 1972; Temple Univ, PhD, sci educ, 1974. **Career:** Camden NJ Sch Dist, sci teacher, 1973-74; Marion Labs Inc & Marion Merrill, 1975-93; Phoenix Pharmaceut Inc, pres, chief exec officer, founder & chmn, 1994-2006; Lakefront Investments Inc, pres, 2006-; Akcess Inc, pres, chief exec officer, 2006-. **Orgs:** Chmn, Alma Mater Trustees Bd; founder & dir, Phoenix Scholar Found; Nat Kidney Found Womens Healthcare Comt; mem adv bd, Howard Univ Cancer Ctrs Community; chmn trustee, NC univ; bd trustee, Johnson C Smith Univ, 2000-. **Special Achievements:** First black-owned pharmaceutical marketing company in the United States. **Home Addr:** , MD. **Business Addr:** President, Chief Executive Officer, Akcess Inc, 13530 Rockaway Blvd S, Ozone Park, NY 11420, **Business Phone:** (718)738-2425.

## FOSTER, DR. PORTIA L.

Nurse, educator. **Personal:** Born Gadsden, AL; daughter of Porter and Myrtle Davenport. **Educ:** Sanford Univ, Birmingham, AL, BSN, 1979; Univ Ala Birmingham, Birmingham, AL, MSN, 1980, DSN, 1989. **Career:** Baptist Hosp, Gasden, AL, nurse, 1974-77; Univ Ala Hosp, Birmingham, AL, nurse, 1977-80; Jacksonville State Univ, Jacksonville, AL, educator, 1980-99; Gadsden State Community Col, Practical Nursing Prog, coordr. **Orgs:** Am Nurses Asn, 1980-; Nat League Nursing, 1980-; Numerous positions held, Etowah County Nurses Soc, 1980-; pres, Dist 4, Ala State Nurses Asn; bd dir, Ala State Nurses Asn; bd dir, Ala, League Nursing, 1989-; Phi Kappa Phi, 1989; Asn Black Nursing Fac Inc. **Home Addr:** 705 County Rd 71, Gadsden, AL 35903, **Home Phone:** (256)927-7578.

## FOSTER, ROBERT LEON

Executive. **Personal:** Born Mar 11, 1939, Atlanta, GA; married Ethel Doris Bolden. **Educ:** Morris Brown Col, BA, 1961. **Career:** Equal Employ Opportunity, officer, 1972-75, asst dir, 1975-78; Ctr Dis Control HEW, asst exec officer; LMI analyst. **Orgs:** Phi Beta Sigma Frat; Nat Asn Advan Colored People. **Home Addr:** 2954 Pine Valley Cir, Atlanta, GA 30344, **Home Phone:** (404)344-1097.

## FOSTER, DR. ROSEBUD LIGHTBOURN. See Obituaries Section.

## FOSTER, T. ELOISE

Secretary (office), government official. **Personal:** Born Richmond, VA. **Educ:** Howard Univ, BA; Am Univ, MBA; Harvard Univ, prog sr exec state & local govt, 1994. **Career:** Md Dept Fiscal Serv, fiscal analyst, 1978-84; Md Higher Educ Suppl Loan Authority, exec dir, 1984-87; Gov's Legis Off, legis officer, 1987-91; Md Dept Budget & Fiscal Planning, asst secy, 1991-95; Md Dept Budget & Mgt, dep secy, 1996-2000, secy budget & mgt, 2000-03, actg secy budget & mgt, 2007, secy budget & mgt, 2007-; Univ Md Baltimore, Sch Med, asst dean prog develop & bus affairs, 2003-07; T. Eloise Foster & Assocs, LLC, founder, 2005-. **Orgs:** Chair, Md Higher Educ Suppl Loan Authority, 1987-90; Gov's Prescription Drug Comn, 1990-91; Gov's Task Force to Study Md State Police Salaries, 1990-91; Gov's Task Force to Study Gambling, 1993-94; chair, Md State Employees Risk Mgt Adv Coun, 1993-94; bd trustee, Md Teachers & State Employees Suppl Retirement Plans, 1995-2004; Task Force Funding Md Sch Deaf, 1996; Task Force Educ Funding Equity, Accountability, & Partnerships, 1997-98; Task Force to Study Col Readiness Disadvantaged & Capable Students, 2000-01; Community Access Steering Comt, 2000-01; Judith P Hoyer Blue Ribbon Comn Financing Early Child Care & Educ, 2000-01; Smart Growth & Neighborhood Conserv Subcabinet, 2000-01; Gov's Exec Coun, 2000-03; Gov's Subcabinet C, Youth, & Families, 2000-03; Smart Growth Subcabinet, 2001-03; Gov's Coun Adolescent Pregnancy, 2000-03; Asbestos Oversight Comt, 2000-03; bd dir, Assistive Technol Guaranteed Loan Prog, 2000-03; Capital Debt Affordability Comt, 2000-03; Comn Correctional Stand, 2000-03; State Info Technol Bd, 2000-03; Gov's Task Force to Study Injured Workers Ins Fund, 2000; State Labor Rels Bd, 2000-03; Interdepartmental Comt Minority Affairs, 2000-03; Procurement Adv Coun, 2000-03; bd trustees, State Retirement & Pension Syst, 2000-03; Bd Revenue Estimates, 2000-03; chair, State Employees' Health Ins Adv Coun, 2000-03; Comn Educ Finance, Equity, & Excellence, 2000-02; Transit Policy Panel, 2000-03; Md Green Buildings Coun, 2001-03; Joseph Fund Bd, 2001-03; Comn Responsible Fatherhood, 2001-03; Task Force to Study Pub Sch Facil, 2002-03; Task Force to Study Md Agr Land Preserv Found, 2002-03; Gov's Comn Struct & Efficiency State Govt, 2003; Gov's Exec Coun, 2007-; C's Cabinet, 2007-; Smart Growth Subcabinet, 2007-; chair, bd trustee, Md Teachers & State Employees Suppl Retirement Plans, 2007-; Asbestos Oversight Comt, 2007-; Bay Restoration Fund Adv Comt, 2007-; Capital Debt Affordability Comt, 2007-; Climate Chg Comn, 2007-; Comn Correctional Stand, 2007-; Comn State Debt, 2007-; Interagency Disabilities Bd, 2007-; Md State Drug & Alcohol Abuse Coun, 2007-; Md Green Bldg Coun, 2007-; bd dir, Md Health Ins Plan, 2007-; Coord Coun Juv Serv Educ Progs, 2007-; Interdepartmental Comt Minority Affairs, 2007-; procurement Adv Coun, 2007-; bd trustee, State Retirement & Pension Syst, 2007-, admin comt, 2007-, investment comt, 2007-, corp governance comt, 2013-; Bd Revenue Estimates, 2007-; Md Sch-Based Health Ctr Policy Adv Coun, 2007-; opers & mgt adv comt, Md War 1812 Bicentennial Comn, 2007-; chair, State Employees' Health Ins Adv Coun, 2007-08; Task Force to Study Develop Disabilities Admin Rate-Payment Syst, 2007-08; Task Force to Study Group-Home Educ & Placement Practices, 2007-08; Task Force Health Care Access & Reimbursement, 2007-08; Comn to Develop Md Model Funding Higher Educ, 2007-08; Comn to Study Southern Md Transp Needs, 2007-08; Blue Ribbon Comn to Study Retiree Health-Care Funding Options, 2007-09; bd dir, Assistive Technol Guaranteed Loan Prog, 2007-09; Base Realignment & Closure Subcabinet, 2007-11; Md Bus Tax Reform Comn, 2008-10; Task Force to Study Procurement Health & Social Serv by State Agencies, 2008-10; Joint Legis & Exec Comn Oversight Pub-Pvt Partnerships, 2010-12; Task Force to Study Procurement Health, Educ, & Social Serv by State Agencies, 2010-12; Blue Ribbon Comn Md Transp Funding, 2010-12;

Work Group to Consider Gaming Abbr, 2012; Joint Comt Health Benefit Exchange Financing, 2012; Statewide Interoperability Exec Comt, 2008-; Md Integrated Map Exec Comt, 2009-; Md Green Purchasing Comt, 2010-; vice chair, Gov's Warrior to Worker Coun, 2010-; Md Health Care Reform Coord Coun, 2010, 2011-; Coun Procurement Health, Educ & Social Serv, 2012-; Md Subcabinet Pub-Pvt Partnerships, 2013-; Md Smart Growth Investment Fund Work Group, 2013-. **Special Achievements:** First African American woman to serve as chief budget officer of a state; named one of Maryland's Top 100 Women in 2002 and 2007. **Business Addr:** Secretary of Budget & Management, Office of Secretary, 45 Calvert St 1st Fl, Annapolis, MD 21401-1907, **Business Phone:** (410)260-7041.

## FOSTER, TONI

Basketball player. **Personal:** Born Oct 16, 1971. **Educ:** Univ Iowa, BA, 1993. **Career:** Phoenix Mercury, forward & ctr, 1997-99.

## FOSTER, WILLIAM K, SR. See Obituaries Section.

## FOSTER-GREAR, PAMELA

Executive. **Personal:** Born Feb 20, 1957, Cleveland, OH; daughter of Curtis and Margaret; married Lance Grear; children: Yejide Hadassah-Noni Grear. **Educ:** Cuyahoga Community Col, attended 1979; Columbus State Community Col, attended 1983; Fashion Inst Technol, cert, 1987; Dartmouth Col, Amos Tuck Sch, Minority Bus Exec Prog, cert, 1990. **Career:** Univ Property Devel, mgr, 1973-83; Ohio Dept Youth Servs, comput literacy instr, 1983-86; Foster Corp, pres & chief exec officer, 1986-. **Orgs:** Supporter, African Ctr, 1987-; bd mem, Light Ctr, 1989-; bd mem, Martin Luther King Jr Ctr Performing Arts, 1989-90; supporter, "I Know I Can" Prog, 1990-91; supporter, Southern Christian Leadership Conf, 1991-92; adv bd chairperson, Columbus Area Chamber Com, 1992-; mentorship prog, Jr Achievement, Ohio State Univ, Stud Devel Prog, 1992-; supporter & guest speaker, NE Career Ctr, 1992. **Home Addr:** 3346 Pine Valley Rd, Columbus, OH 43219, **Home Phone:** (614)475-5949. **Business Addr:** President, Chief Executive Officer, Foster Corp, PO Box 09191, Columbus, OH 43209, **Business Phone:** (614)774-4536.

## FOUCHE, LORI DICKERSON

President (organization). **Personal:** daughter of Judith Dickerson and Charles Dickerson; married Patrick. **Educ:** Princeton Univ, BA, hist, 1991; Harvard Bus Sch, MBA, gen mgt, 2000; Kellogg Sch Mgt Northwestern Univ, cert, integrated mkt, 2003. **Career:** Exec Protection Pract, underwriter, 1991-94, mgr, 1994-95, asst vpres, prod & training mgr, 1996-98; Parthenon Group, 2000-02; Com Ins, pres; Chubb & Son, vpres, 2002-03, exec, sr vpres strategic mkt mgr, 2003-06; Firemans Fund Ins Co, sr vpres mkt exec, 2006-07, sr vpres & chief operating officer, 2007-08, pres com ins, 2008-12, chief exec officer, pres, 2011-13; Prudential Financial, pres & chief operating officer, 2013-14, sr vpres & chief exec officer, 2014-. **Orgs:** Supreme Ct Nj Disciplinary Oversight Comt; Princeton Univs Minority Bus Asn Prog, mentor; bd mem, Girls Inc; Jack & Jill Am. **Business Addr:** Senior Vice President, Chief Executive Officer, Prudential Financial, 74 Highland Ave, Montclair, NJ 07042-1910.

## FOUCHE, LORI DICKERSON

Chief executive officer, president (organization). **Personal:** daughter of Judith Dickerson and Charles Dickerson; married Patrick. **Educ:** Princeton Univ, BA, hist, 1991; Harvard Bus Sch, MBA, 2000; Northwestern Univ Kellogg Sch Mgt, cert integrated mkt, 2003. **Career:** Chubb & Son, 1987-98, vpres & sr vpres, 2002-06; Parthenon Group, mgt consult, 2000-02; Fireman's Fund Ins Co., Com Ins, pres, head mkt spec lines, 2006-, chief operating officer, chief exec officer, 2011-13; Prudential Financial, pres, 2013-15; Allianz SE, US property casualty unit, chief exec officer, currently. **Honors/Awds:** "The Network Journal," 40 Under Forty, 2007; "Black Enterprise," The 100 Most Powerful Executives in Corporate America, 2010.

## FOULKS, DR. CARL ALVIN, JR.

Physician. **Personal:** Born Jun 10, 1947, Greensboro, NC; married Deborah Casandra Smith; children: Carl Jr, Dion & Cory. **Educ:** NC A&T State Univ, Greensboro, NC, chem; Howard Univ Col Pharm, Washi, DC, RPh; Howard Univ Med Sch, internal med, MD. **Career:** E Carolina Univ Sch Med, Greenville, NC, resident; Providence Hosp, chief resident; Univ Tex-Houston Health Sci Ctr, fel; MD Anderson Cancer Ctr, fel; Tex Med Ctr, fel; Cumberland County Med Clin, dir; pvt pract physician; Piedmont Health Ctr, Statesville, NC, physician, currently. **Orgs:** Nat Med Asn; Am Gastroenterol Asn; Am Soc Gastrointestinal Endoscopy; Am Col Physicians; Piedmont Healthcare. **Honors/Awds:** Hon, NC A&T State Univ. **Home Addr:** 2227 Kingswood Rd, Fayetteville, NC 28303, **Home Phone:** (919)483-1979. **Business Addr:** Physician, Piedmont Healthcare PA, 650 Signal Hill Dr Exten, Statesville, NC 28687-1845, **Business Phone:** (704)873-4277.

## FOUNTAIN, CHERYL GIBSON. See GIBSON, DR. CHERYL DIANNE.

## FOUNTAIN, TAMARA R.

Ophthalmologist, chairperson. **Personal:** Born Dec 3, 1962, Edwards AFB, CA. **Educ:** Stanford Univ, BA, human biol, 1984; Harvard Med Sch, MD, 1988. **Career:** Rush Univ, Dept Ophthal, asst prof, 1998-2003, dir med stud/primary care resident educ, 1999-2006, assoc prof, 2003-10, Oculoplastics Div, sect dir, 2005-, prof, 2010-; Northwestern Univ, Dept Ophthal, Div Surg, 2000-08; Univ Chicago, Div Surg, 2009-. **Orgs:** Bd trustees, Am Acad Ophthal, 2004; bd dirs, Ophthalmic Mutual Ins Co, 2007-, chmn bd, 2014. **Honors/Awds:** U.S. Presidential Scholar, Recipient, 1980; Scholastic Achievement Award, AKA Sorority, Recipient, 1982; National Achievement Scholar, Recipient, 1982; Stanford Overseas Program (Florence, Italy), Recipient, 1984; Aesculapian Club, Harvard Medical School, Selection, 1988; Harvard Medical School, Commencement Marshall 1988; National Eye Institute Grant, Recipient, 1992; University of Southern California, Fellow of the Year, 1996; Leadership Development Program, Inaugural Class American Academy of Ophthalmology, 1998; American Academy of Ophthalmology, Achievement Award, 2001; American Eye Study Club, Inductee, 2003; American Academy of Ophthalmology, Practice Management Division, Secretariat Award, October 2005; "Best Doctors," Recipient, 2005-; American Academy of Ophthalmology, Senior Achievement Award, 2008; American Academy of Ophthalmology, Membership Services Division, Secretariat Award, 2009; American Academy of Ophthalmology, Communications Division, Secretariat Award, 2009; "America's Top Ophthalmologists," 2010; American Society of Ophthalmic Plastic and Reconstructive Surgeons, Orkan Stasior Leadership Award, 2012. **Special Achievements:** Numerous presentations at scientific meetings. **Business Addr:** Ophthalmology Partners Ltd., 740 Waukegan Rd Suite 360, Deerfield, IL 60015, **Business Phone:** (847)945-6770.

## FOUNTAIN, W. FRANK, JR.

President (organization), vice president (organization). **Personal:** Born Jul 17, 1944, Brewton, AL; son of Willie Frank and Janie; married Sharma. **Educ:** Va Hampton Univ, BA, hist & polit sci, 1966; Univ Pa Wharton Sch, MBA, 1973. **Career:** Peace Corps, W Bengal, India, vol, 1966-68; Old Carco LLC, vpres govt affairs; Daimler Chrysler Corp Fund, pres; Daimler Chrysler Group, investment analyst, 1973, Corp Controller's Off, Treas's Off, Chrysler's Govt Affairs Off, vpres govt affairs, 1995-98, sr vpres govt affairs, 1998-2004, sr vpres external affairs & pub policy, 2004-; Wharton Sch, Univ Pa, overseer; Escambia Enterprises LLC, chmn; Dte Energy Co, dir, 2007-. **Orgs:** Bd dir, chmn, Detroit Pub Schs, 1999-2003; vice chair, Detroit Regional Chamber Com; Mus African Am Hist; trustee, Hudson-Webber Found; Mich Mfrs Asn; trustee, Community Found Southeast Mich; WTVS-Channel 56, Pub TV; Music Hall; Wharton Sch Bd Overseers; chair, Hampton Univ Bd trustee; chair, Metro Detroit Conv &Visitors Bur; chair, Citizens Res Coun Mich; Int Visitors Coun Metro Detroit; dir, Detroit Investment Fund; vice chair, New Detroit; Dennis W Archer Found; Econ Club Detroit; vice chair, Corp Coun Africa; Detroit Metro Sports Comn; Focus Hope Adv Bd; chair, Metrop Affairs Coalition; Mackinac Ctr Pub Policy Adv Bd; vice chair, Joint Ctr Polit & Econ Studies; Bus Coun Ala; dir, Downtown Detroit Partnership; bd chm, Africare, currently. **Business Addr:** Senior Vice President of Government Affairs, Daimler Chrysler Corp, 1000 Chrysler Dr, Auburn Hills, MI 48326-2766, **Business Phone:** (248)576-5741.

## FOUNTLEORY, MILLICENT

Editor. **Educ:** Wake Tech Community Col; Univ Ill, Urbana-Champaign, Am hist; Northwestern Univ, MSJ, BSJ, newspaper jour; Duke Univ, MA, lib arts & sci/lib studies. **Career:** Philadelphia Inquirer, copy ed news & features, 1980-82; Gannett Newspapers, asst news ed, 1985-86; News & Observer Publ Co, asst news ed & slot ed, 1986-11; eduPad, copy ed, 2011; NC State Univ, lectr, 2011-12; Newspaper Prof, ed, mgr, pub rels, advert, promotions, app ed, vol.

## FOURNIER, COLLETTE V.

Educator, photojournalist. **Personal:** Born Jul 21, 1952, New York, NY; daughter of Alexander and Cynthia Hubbard Mann. **Educ:** Rochester Inst Technol, Rochester, NY, AAS, photog illus, 1973, BS, biomed commun, 1979; Union Inst & Univ Vt Col, Montpelier, VT, MFA, visual arts prog, 2003. **Career:** RAETA TV21 WXXI, Rochester, NY, prod asst, engr trainee, 1979-81; Malrite Communs, TV 31, WUHF, Rochester, NY, sr film ed, 1981-82, TV 21, WXXI, prod asst, 1981-82; Community Darkroom, Rochester, NY, photog instr, 1982-88; About Time Mag, Rochester, NY, photojournalist, 1982-88; J, News Gannett, W Nyack, NY, photojournalist, 1988-89; Rockland J News, photogr & staff photogr, 1988-89, 1996-2000; Bergen Rec, Hackensack, NJ, staff photogr, 1989-91, freelance photogr, 2002; State Univ NY, Rockland Community Col, Art Dept, Suffern, NY, adj photog prof, 1992-, spec events coordr, Educ Asst Off Pres, 1992-94, Campus Communs & Photogr, 1994-; New York Post, freelance photogr, 1994-95. **Orgs:** Nat Asn Black Journalists, 1984-; Nat Press Photogr Asn, 1988-; Women's Caucus Arts, 1984-; NJ Press Photogr Asn, 1989-; mem, Kamoinge, African Am photogr collective; Univ Photogr Asn Am; panelist, Arts Coun Rockland; bd dir, Arts Alliance Haverstraw, currently. **Home Addr:** PO Box 462, Nyack, NY 10960-0462, **Home Phone:** (845)352-2648. **Business Addr:** Adjunct Faculty, Rockland Community College, 145 Col Rd, Suffern, NY 10901, **Business Phone:** (845)574-4549.

## FOUSHEE, PREVOST VEST

Marketing executive. **Personal:** Born Apr 26, 1952, Pittsburg, NC; son of Prevex and Cora Cotton; married Trudi McCollum; children: Prevost Jr & Ashlei. **Educ:** Fayetteville State Univ, BS, bus admin, 1977. **Career:** Pillsbury Corp, sls rep, 1978; Anheuser-Busch Inc, sls rep, 1978-79, area sls mgr, 1979-81, dist sls mgr, 1981-83, mgr, 1982, proj mgr, mgt develop, 1983-84, spec markets mgr, 1984-91, geog mkt mgr, 1991-92, prod mgr, Budweiser, 1992-94; Nat Light Ice King Cobra, brand mgr, 1994-97; Michelob Family & Specialty, dir, 1997, sr brand mgr. **Orgs:** Mkt comt, UNF, 1992; Bd dir, vpres, Employ Connection St Louis, retired. **Honors/Awds:** Black Achievers Award, Harlem YMCA, 1980; Yes I Can Award, Am Sentinel Newspaper, St Louis, 1990.

## FOWLER, BENNIE

Vice president (organization). **Educ:** Cent State Univ, BS, bus mgt; Ind Univ, MBA, opers mgt. **Career:** Jaguar Land Rover N Am LLC, chief operating officer & vpres advan & mfg engineering; Ford Motor Co, Global Qual & New Model Launch, global vpres, 1990-. **Orgs:** Founder, Powerstroke Athletic Club; Bd dir, Beaumont Hosps. **Honors/Awds:** "Black Enterprise," The 100 Most Powerful Executives in Corporate America, 2010.

## FOWLER, BENNIE W., II

Executive, vice president (organization). **Personal:** Born Jan 1, 1956, Augusta, GA. **Educ:** Cent State Univ, Wilberforce, OH, BS, bus mgt; Ind Univ, MBA, opers mgt. **Career:** Gen Motors Corp, 1978-86; Chrysler Corp, var mfg mgt positions; Ford Motor Co, St Thomas Assembly Plant, supt, 1990, N Am Prod Develop, exec dir, 2002-03; N Am Mfg Oper, Dir; Jaguar & Land Rover, vpres & chief operating officer, 2003-05, Advan & Mfg Eng, vpres, 2005, vpres global qual, 2006-10, group vpres global qual & New Model Launch, 2010-; Powerstroke Athletic Club, founder, chief exec officer. **Orgs:** Bd dir, Beaumont Hosps. **Business Addr:** Vice President of Advanced & Manufacturing Engineering & Quality, Ford Motor Co, 1 American Rd, Dearborn, MI 48126-0685, **Business Phone:** (313)322-3000.

## FOWLER, JAMES DANIEL, JR.

Executive. **Personal:** Born Apr 24, 1944, Washington, DC; son of James D and Romay Lucas; married Linda Marie Raiford; children: Scott & Kimberly. **Educ:** Howard Univ, Wash, DC, 1963; US Mil Acad, West Point, NY, BS, 1967; Rochester Inst Tech, Rochester, NY, MBA, 1975. **Career:** Xerox Corp, Rochester, NY, coord grad rels, 1971-74, mgr personnel admin, 1974-75; DP Parker & Assoc Inc, Wellesley Ma, sr consult, 1975-76; ITT World Hq, new York MY, mgr Staffing, 1976-78; ITT Aetna, Denver Co, vip dir admin, 1978; ITT Consumer Financial Corp, Minneapolis MN, sr vpres, dir admin, 1978-84, sr vpres, dir admin & mktg, 1984-87, exec vpres, dir admin & mkt, 1987-90, exec vpres, dir prod mgt, mkt & adm, 1990-92, exec vpres, dir adm, 1992; ITT Eductaional Serv Inc, dir, 1994-; Fowler & Assocs, pres, 1996-2000; Exec Leadership Coun & Found, pres, 2000; ITT Corp, sr vpres & dir human resources, 2000-02. **Orgs:** US Mil Acad W Pt, trustee, 1978-86, 1987-90; Asn MBA Exec; EXE Leadership coun, 1997-; charter mbr, bod; MR Financial Serv Asn; Am Soc Personnel Adm. **Honors/Awds:** Black Achiever Award, ITT, 1979. **Home Addr:** 10452 Bluff Rd, Eden Prairie, MN 55347, **Home Phone:** (612)944-2342. **Business Addr:** Director, ITT Educational Services Inc, 8911 Columbine Rd, Eden Prairie, MN 55347, **Business Phone:** (612)540-0840.

## FOWLER, JOHN D.

Educator, association executive. **Personal:** Born Mar 22, 1931, Clinton, NC; son of John D and Sallie L Howard; married Wilma J Butler; children: Ronald M, Valerie D Wall & Christopher E. **Educ:** Winston-Salem Cent Univ, attended 1954; State Univ New Paltz, MA, 1974; Northeastern Univ, educ studies; NC Cent Univ; Univ Vt. **Career:** Mt Pleasant Elem Sch, prin, 1955-58; CE Perry High Sch, teacher, 1958-63; W Pender Sch, 1963-64; Dunbar Elem Sch, 1964-65; Hudson City Sch Dist, asst prin, coordr; City Sch Dist, Rochester NY, vprin, 1985-. **Orgs:** NY State Reg Plan Asn; bd dir, Columbia County Exten Serv; Omega Psi Phi; life mem, Nat Educ Asn; Nat Advan Asn Colored People; vpres, Kiwanis Greater Hudson; chmn, Const By-Laws Com Van Rennselear Div Kiwanis Int; city Counman, 1980-85; Lt Gov, Kiwanis Int, 1981-82; County supvr, 1985; bd dir, Anthony L Jordan Health Ctr; Maplewood YMCA; Kiwanis Club Eastridge Irondequoit. **Honors/Awds:** Alumni scholarship Winston-Salem Central Univ, 1950; First black chosen from Columbia County to represent Northeast Synod; chairperson of many committees while on city council in Hudson NY, 1980-85; Administrator. of the Year, PTO of #6 School, 1988-89; Administrator of the Year Dag Hammarskjold-School No 6 1989-90; C E Perry High School, valedictorian, graduated withhonors. **Home Addr:** 247 Maplewood Ave, Rochester, NY 14613, **Home Phone:** (585)647-3726. **Business Addr:** Board of Member, Kiwanis Club of Eastridge Irondequoit, 745 Titus Ave Annex Bldg, Rochester, NY 14613, **Business Phone:** (585)544-5650.

## FOWLER, DR. QUEEN DUNLAP

School administrator. **Personal:** Born St. Louis, MO; children: Darnell Keith. **Educ:** Harris Teachers Col, BA, 1960; St Louis Univ, MEd, 1965, PhD, 1974, psychol, 1979. **Career:** WA Univ, St Louis, Mo, asst dir adm coord of rec & pub rels, 1969-79, lectr & instr, 1975-79, coord field studies, 1977-78; Sch Dist Wellston, Mo, supt, 1979-84; St. Louis Pub Schs, exec dir & chief adminr, Pupil Personnel Serv, 1984; educ consult; Wash Univ, prof & counr; Fowler & Assocs Consult Servs, pres, currently. **Orgs:** Urban League Metrop, St Louis, 1965-; bd dir exec bd, Girl Scouts Greater St Louis, 1978-; bd dir, United Way Greater St Louis, 1979-; nat nominating comt & nat prog plan comt, Am Asn Sch Admin, 1980-94; nat adv bd, Am Psych Asn, 1982-86; bd curators, Lincoln Univ, Jefferson City, MO, 1983-87; vpres, bd dir, Metro YWCA, 1984-; bd dir, Nat Asn Christians & Jews, 1984-88; exec bd, Alpha Pi Chi Bus & Prof Sor, 1984-; regional counr, Delta Sigma Theta Sorority, 1986-; YWCA, nat task force retirement, 1990-94; Bd Regents, 2004-09; gov coun rep, Am Coun Asn; rep, Asn Multicultural Coun Develop, 2006-; vpres, Gateway Chap Links; pres, St. Louis Top Ladies Distinction; Harris-Stowe Bd Regents; pres emer, St. Louis Coalition 100 Black Women. **Home Addr:** 14 Nob Hill Lane, St. Louis, MO 63130-2038, **Home Phone:** (314)994-1514. **Business Addr:** President, Fowler & Associates Consultant Services, 3565 Piedmont Rd NE, Atlanta, GA 30305, **Business Phone:** (404)231-1144.

## FOWLER, REGGIE (REGINALD DENNIS FOWLER)

Executive, business owner. **Personal:** Born Feb 1, 1959; son of Al and Eloise; children: 2. **Educ:** Univ Wyo, BA, soc work, 1981; Ariz State Univ, MBA. **Career:** Spiral Inc, founder & owner, 1989-; Kyrene OEM LLC, owner; Mobil Oil's, sales chem div; Minn Vikings, owner. **Honors/Awds:** Inducted, Sahuaro High School Alumni Cougar Foundation Hall of Fame, 1998; Rookie of the Year. **Special Achievements:** First African American principal owner of an NFL team. **Home Addr:** 6909 W Ray Rd Suite 9, Chandler, AZ 85226-1526, **Home Phone:** (480)625-3350. **Business Addr:** Owner, Minnesota Vikings, 9520 Viking Dr, Eden Prairie, MN 55344, **Business Phone:** (952)828-6500.

## FOWLER, DR. RONALD J.

Clergy. **Personal:** son of Robert L and Susie Bell; married Ella Le Joyce Sojourner; children: Cynthia DeAnne Fowler-Starks, Christine Denise Fowler-Mack & Ronald Joseph II. **Educ:** Kent State Univ, BS, educ, 1959, MS; Anderson Col Sch Theol, Mdiv, 1966; Pittsburgh Theol Sem, ThD; Jungian Inst, Zurich, Switz, Mdiv, 1966. **Career:** Detroit Pub Schs, teacher; Robert St Church God, assoc pastor; Arlington Church God, Akron, OH, sr pastor, currently. **Orgs:** Bd mem, Akron Pub Schs, 1988-2000; chmn, Anderson Univ Trustee Bd; bd mem, Anderson Univ Exec Comt; bd mem, Knight Found; mem bd dir, Nat City Bank. **Business Addr:** Senior Pastor, Arlington Church of God, 539 S Arlington St, Akron, OH 44306-1797, **Business Phone:** (330)773-3321.

**FOWLER, JUDGE WILLIAM E., JR.**
Judge. **Personal:** Born Nov 4, 1921, Akron, OH; son of William E Sr and Maude; married Norma June; children: Claude, John & Diane. **Educ:** Fordham Univ Sch Law, LLB, 1952. **Career:** Social Security Comn, admin law judge; US Dept Labor, admin law judge; Akron OH, city prosecutor, 1956-59; State OH, asst atty gen, 1959-61; US Dept Justice, spl asst atty gen, 1961-64; US Dept Labor, admin law judge, trial exam, 1964-66; US Nat Transp Safety Bd, chief adminstrv law judge; Bd Appeals & Rev, US cvl serv comm, 1966-69; Ohio Atty Gen Off, chief hwy div; Nat Transp Safety Bd, chief admin law judge, 1969-2012, chief judge, 1977-2012. **Orgs:** Housing Opportunities Coun, 1970-74; Fed Bar Asn; Toastmasters Club, 1970-75; dir, Fed Bar Asn, 1972-74; former pres, DC Ment Health asn, 1972-74; former pres, Fed Adminstrn Law Judges Conf, 1974-75; Am Bar Asn; Nat Bar Asn; Wash Bar Asn. **Honors/Awds:** Distinguished Service Award, DC Public Sch, 1985; Mary C Lawton Outstanding Government Service Award, Am Bar Asn, 2009. **Special Achievements:** First black pres Judges Conference. **Home Addr:** 1620 Underwood St NW, Washington, DC 20012-2832, **Home Phone:** (202)726-8223. **Business Addr:** Chief Administrative Law Judge, National Transportation Safety Board, 490 L Enfant Plz E SW Rm 4704, Washington, DC 20594, **Business Phone:** (202)314-6150.

**FOWLKES, DORETHA P.**
Real estate agent, real estate executive, manager. **Personal:** Born Apr 2, 1944, Meherrin, VA; children: Tracey. **Educ:** Va Commonwealth Univ, J Sargeant Reynolds, attended 1982. **Career:** RL Williams, sales assoc & off mgr, 1975-79; Robinson Harris, sales assoc, 1979-81; Fowlkes & Co Realtors, agt & pres, 1981-. **Orgs:** Pres, Ebony Ladies, 1975-77; pres, Richmond Bd Realtists, 1981-84; bd mem, N Richmond YMCA, 1983; bd mem, Zoning Appeals Bd, 1984; bd mem, Metro Bus League, 1985; pres, Va Assoc Realtist, 1985-; bd dir, Consol Bank & Trust. **Honors/Awds:** Business of Year, Metro Business League, 1982; Business Association of Year, Am Bus Women, 1984; Business person Youth, Nat Asn Advan Colored People, 1984. **Home Addr:** 2800 Hawthorne Ave, Richmond, VA 23222-3523, **Home Phone:** (804)329-1627. **Business Addr:** President, Agent, Fowlkes & Co Realtors, 2519 Chamberlayne Ave, Richmond, VA 23222-4214, **Business Phone:** (804)321-8000.

**FOWLKES, NELSON N., SR.**
Executive. **Personal:** Born Dec 26, 1934, Chattanooga, TN; son of Edward B Sr and Dorothy F Johnson (deceased); married Peggy Jackson; children: Errol A, Janet Fowlkes-Allen & Nelson Joseph. **Educ:** Cent State Univ, BS, chem, 1957; Univ Tenn, MS, biochem, 1970; Pac Lutheran Univ, attended 1974; Consortium Calif Univ & Col, MPA, 1982. **Career:** Letterman Army Med Ctr, chief clinl chem., 1974-75; Mich Biomed Lab, admin asst, 1976-78; St Agnes Med Ctr, lab mgr, 1978-80, planning asst, 1980-82, asst dir planning, 1982-84, dir res & planning, 1984-86, dir corp rel, 1986-; St Francis Hosp, dir, ambulatory clinics, 1992-2002; Johnson Chapel AME Church, co-proj coordr, 2003-09; PJ'S Travel Connection LLC, travel consult, 2007-. **Orgs:** Bus Adv Coun Sch Bus, 1980-89; treas, Alumni Trust Coun FSU, 1984-89; pres, Twentieth Century Golf Club, 1985-88; bd dir, Community Health Coun Inc, 2002; TEAM Referral Network, 2009-11; exec dir, Harrison Bryant Kearney Blvd Plaza Inc; vice chmn, Valley Small Bus Develop Corp. **Special Achievements:** Corporate Health Risk Mgmt: An Employer's Journal of Health Care Newest Tool to Reduce Health Care Costs Mkt, 1989. **Home Addr:** 2935 Juniper Dr, Corona, CA 92882-3656, **Home Phone:** (951)737-7851. **Business Addr:** Travel Consultant, PJ'S Travel Connection LLC, Dublin, CA.

**FOX, CHARLES WASHINGTON**
Writer, television producer, administrator. **Personal:** Born Jun 14, 1945, Clarksburg, WV; son of Charles W Jr and Lucille Eleanor Penister; married Judy Delores; children: Charles W IV, Renee Ann & Lori Michelle. **Educ:** Johns Hopkins Univ, MA, 1973. **Career:** Educator, writer, producer, consult; MPTV, Owings Mills, PBS, writer, 1972-75; WCVB-TV, producer, 1975-79; Quick Brown Fox Prod, owner & producer, 1979-90; WNEV-TV, CBS, producer, 1981-85; WRC-TV, NBC, producer, 1985-86; Am Univ, assoc prof, 1987-89; Morgan State Univ, fac; Baltimore Community Col, fac; Md Film Comn, dir, 1990-93; Worldnet TV & Film Serv, Global Satellite Tv Syst, dir, 1993-97; Ohio Univ Sch Flim, dir, 2002-; Am Univ, Morgan State Univ & Baltimore Community Col, film & commun. **Orgs:** Mgr, Commun & Outreach, Pres Off Diversity, Ohio Univ; dir, Md Film Comn, 1990-93. **Home Addr:** 943 S St NW, Washington, DC 20001, **Home Phone:** (202)332-3042. **Business Addr:** Director, Ohio University School of Film, Lindley Hall 378, Athens, OH 45701, **Business Phone:** (740)593-1000.

**FOX, PAULETTE**
Executive director. **Career:** Opportunities Industrialization Ctr New Brit Inc, owner, exec dir, 1985-. **Orgs:** Chairperson, African-Am Adv Comt, New Brit Mus Am Art Inc. **Home Addr:** 14 Andrews St, New Britain, CT 06051-3324, **Home Phone:** (860)826-1650. **Business Addr:** Executive Director, Owner, Opportunities Industrialization Center of New Britain Inc, 1 Grove St Suite 315, New Britain, CT 06053, **Business Phone:** (860)224-7151.

**FOX, AMBASSADOR RICHARD K., JR.**
Ambassador. **Personal:** Born Oct 22, 1925, Cincinnati, OH; son of Richard K Sr and Kathryn Lynch; married Jeanne Jones; children: Jeanne Alston, Jane Johnson & Helen Fields; married Catherine Mastny. **Educ:** Ind Univ, BA, 1949; Ind Univ Grad Sch, attended 1950. **Career:** Ambassador (retired); Urban Leagues St Louis, St Paul, 1950-56; Minn Comm Against Discrimination St Paul, asst dir, 1956-61; Dept State, spec asst to dep asst secy personnel, 1961-63, spec asst to dep under secy admin, 1963-65; US Embassy Madrid, counr admin affairs, 1965-70; Bur Ed Cult Affairs, dep asst secy, 1973-74, dep dir personnel, 1974-76, foreign serv officer & dep inspector gen, 1979-83; Sr Semnr Foreign Policy, 1976-77; US Ambassador Trinidad & Tobago, 1977-79. **Orgs:** Bd mem, Luth Human Rels Assoc Am, 1971-76, pres; vice chmn, DC Bd Higher Educ, 1972-76; bd trustee, Univ DC, 1976-77; chmn, bd dir, Wheat Ridge Found Chicago, 1979-88; pres, Am Foreign Serv Protective Asn, Wash, 1979-92; sr vpres visitor prog serv, Meridian Int Ctr, 1983-97; bd mem, Vesper Soc, CA; bd mem, Luther Inst, 1999-; Wash Inst Foreign Affairs; Am Acad Diplomacy; bd govs, Diplomatic & Consular Officers Retired, Bacon House; Nat Coun Int Vistors, 1998-; Minn Fair Employ Practices Comn; pres, Lutheran Human Rels Asn. **Honors/Awds:** Alpha Kappa Delta Hon Soc Indiana Univ, 1950; Superior Honor Awd Dept of State, 1964, 1983; Meritorious Honor Awd Embassy Madrid, 1970; Doctor of Laws, Valparaiso Univ, 1983; Wilbur Carr Award, Dept of State. **Home Addr:** 5124 Waukesha Rd, Bethesda, MD 20816, **Home Phone:** (301)229-6386. **Business Addr:** Member, National Council for International Vistors, 1420 K St NW Suite 800, Washington, DC 20005, **Business Phone:** (202)842-1414.

**FOX, RICK (ULRICH ALEXANDER FOX)**
Basketball player, actor. **Personal:** Born Jul 24, 1969, Toronto, ON; son of Diane Gerace; married Vanessa Willams; children: Kyle & Sasha Gabriella. **Educ:** Univ NC, attended 1991, BA, radio, tv & motion pictures; Kingsway Acad, attended. **Career:** Basketball player (retired), actor; Boston Celtics, shooting forward, 1991-97; Los Angeles Lakers, shooting forward, 1997-2004; E-Sports, franchise owner. Film: Blue Chips, 1994; Eddie, 1996; He Got Game, 1998; Collectors, 1999; Resurrection, 1999; Four Faces God, 1999; Holes, 2003; Mini's First Time, 2006; Meet Browns, 2008; Tyler Perry's Meet Browns, 2008; Hysteria, 2009; Paradi$e, currently; Back to School Mom, 2015; "Dope", 2015. TV: "Oz", 1997-2003; "1-800-Missing", 1998; "Arti$$", 2001; "St Time", 2003; "Fairly Odd Parents", 2003; "Kevin Hill", 2005; "Love Inc", 2005-06; "One Tree Hill", 2006; "Entertainment Tonight", 2006-09; "Dirt", 2007; "Ugly Betty", 2007; "Game", 2007-09; "Are You Smarter Than a 5th Grader?", 2008; "Up Close with Carrie Keagan", 2008; "Head case", 2008; "Party Down", 2009; "Melrose Pl", 2009-10; "Fox vs Fox", 2010; "Dollhouse", 2010; "The Guild", 2011; "Single Ladies", 2011-12; "The Big Bang Theory", 2011; "Dan Savage's New Threat to Rick Santorum", 2011; "Body of Proof", 2011; "Jake & Amir", 2011-13; "Mr. Box Office", 2012-13; "Franklin & Bash", 2012; "Hit the Floor", 2013; "The Glades", 2013; "Off Season: Lex Morrison Story", 2013; "Meet Me at a Funeral", 2014. **Honors/Awds:** NBA Finals Championship ring, 2000. **Business Addr:** Actor, William Morris Agency Inc, 1 William Morris Pl, Beverly Hills, CA 90212, **Business Phone:** (310)859-4000.

**FOX, THOMAS E., JR.**
Lawyer. **Personal:** Born Jul 22, 1963, Brooklyn, NY; son of Thomas and Juanita Aquart. **Educ:** Jackson State Univ, Jackson MS, BA, 1985; Harvard Law Sch, Cambridge MA, JD, 1988. **Career:** Nat City Bd Correction, NY, asst coun, 1985; Harvard Prison Legal Assistance Proj, Cambridge MA, stud atty, 1986; Brown & Wood Law Firm, New York NY, summer assoc, 1987; Hon Clifford Scott Green, Philadelphia PA, law clerk, 1988-89; White & Case Law Firm, NY, assoc, 1989; NYC Dept Educ, lawyer. **Orgs:** Nat Conf Black Lawyers; pres/chmn, Nat Black Law Stud Asn, 1987-88; NY State Bar. **Honors/Awds:** Allan Locke Scholar, Educ Found Phi Beta Sigma, 1984; Rhodes Scholar Finalist, State Miss, 1984; Agnes fel Nat Asn Advan Colored People, 1985-86; Earl Warren fel Legal Defense Fund, Nat Asn Advan Colored People, 1985-88. **Home Addr:** 17825 Leslie Rd, Jamaica, NY 11434-2732, **Home Phone:** (718)723-8967. **Business Addr:** Lawyer, New York Department of Education, Rm 21 9027 Sutphin Blvd, Jamaica, NY 11435-3647, **Business Phone:** (347)446-7808.

**FOX, ULRICH ALEXANDER. See FOX, RICK.**

**FOX, VIVICA ANJANETTA**
Television producer, actor. **Personal:** Born Jul 30, 1964, South Bend, IN; daughter of William and Everlyena; married Christopher Harvest. **Educ:** Golden West Col, AA, social sci. **Career:** Foxy Brown Productions, owners, currently; TV appearances: "Generations", 1989; "Beverly Hills 90210", 1991; "In the House", 1991; "The Fresh Prince of Bel Air", 1991; "Out All Night", 1992; "The Young & the Restless", 1994; "The Tuskegee Airmen", 1995; "Living Single", 1996; "Arsenio", 1997; "City of Angels", 2000; "Kim Possible: A Sitch in Time", voice, 2003; "Alias", 2004; "Loonatics Unleashed", 2005; "1-800-Missing", 2004-06; "Curb Your Enthusiasm", 2007-09; "All of Us", 2006; "Icons", 2006; "Little Britain USA", 2008; "Law & Order", 2008; "Da Kink in My Hair", 2009; "Degrassi Goes Hollywood", 2009; "True Jackson, VP", 2009-10; "Scooby-Doo! Mystery Incorporated", 2010-13; "Melissa and Joey", 2010-13; "Drop Dead Diva", 2010-13; "A Holiday Heist", 2011; "Raising Hope", 2012; "Sharknado 2: The Second One", 2014; "The Celebrity Apprentice 7", 2014; "Mob Wives", 2015; "Mann & Wife", 2015; "Sofia the First", 2015. Films: Born on the Fourth of July, 1989; Independence Day, 1996; Set It Off, 1996; Booty Call, 1997; Batman & Robin, 1997; Soul Food, 1997; Solomon; Why Do Fools Fall in Love, 1998; Teaching Mrs Tingle, 1999; Idle Hands, 1999; Double Take, 2001; Kingdom Come, 2001; Two Can Play That Game, 2001; Little Secrets, 2001; Juwanna Mann, 2002; Boat Trip, 2002; Ride or Die, 2003; Motives, 2004; Ella Enchanted, 2004; Blast, 2004; Getting Played, 2005; The Salon, 2005; The Hard Corps, 2006; Citizen Duane, 2006; Kicking It Old Skool, 2007; Father of Lies, 2007; Motives 2, 2007; Motives 2: Behind the Scenes, 2007; Natural Born Komics, 2007; Three Can Play That Game, 2008; Unstable Fables: Tortoise vs. Hare, 2008; Private Valentine: Blonde & Dangerous, 2008; Major Movie Star, 2008; Cover, 2008; San Saba, 2008; The Slammin' Salmon, 2009; Hollywood & Wine, 2009; Shark City, 2009; Caught On Tape, 2009; Junkyard Dog, 2010; Black November, 2012; It's Not You, It's Me, 2013; Home Run, 2013; Scooby-Doo! Stage Fright, 2013; Mercenaries, 2014; 30 Days in Atlanta, 2014; Cool Cat Saves the Kids, 2014. **Business Addr:** Actress, Foxy Brown Productions Inc, PO Box 3538, Granada Hills, CA 91394, **Business Phone:** (310)288-8000.

**FOXALL, DR. MARTHA JEAN**
Educator, nurse. **Personal:** Born Mar 17, 1931, Omaha, NE; daughter of Robert L Hammonds and Katrina Hammonds; married Pitmon Sr(deceased); children: Pitmon Jr & Mark. **Educ:** Bryan Mem Hosp Sch Nursing, RN, 1952; Univ Nebr, Omaha, BSN, 1954; MA, 1961; Univ Nebr Med Ctr, MSN, 1976; Univ NE Lincoln, PhD, 1979. **Career:** Immanuel Hosp Sch Nursing, staff nurse, 1952, teaching fac maternity nursing, 1953-68, assoc dir nursing educ, 1968-75; Div Nurs Midland & Luth Col Fremont NE, assoc dir, 1975-80; Univ Nebr Med Ctr, Col Nursing, assoc prof, 1980, Parent & Child Admin Educ & Sci Dept, mentor, prof, 2000-06, chmn, emer prof nursing, 2006-. **Orgs:** Am Nurses Asn; Immunization prog, Midland Luth Col, 1977; diabetic screening Omaha Area Chap, 1978; Lect "Aging & Sexuality" Midland Lutheran Col, 1979-80; chmn, CEU com NE League Nursing, 1979-80; res proj dir, Univ Nebr Med Ctr, 1979; chairperson, Com Ment Health Delta Sigma Theta Sorority, 1980; fel Am Acad Nursing (FANN); Am Nurses Asn Coun Nurse Researchers; Midwest Nursing Res Soc; Coun Grad Educ; Coun Admin Nursing; Phi Delta Gamma; Sigma Theta Tau. **Honors/Awds:** Sigma Theta Tau; Nat Hon Soc Nursing, 1979; Annual Alumni Award, Bryan Sch Nursing, 1997; Hon Doctorate, Midland Lutheran Col, 2000; Distinguished Alumnus Award, Col Nursing, Univ NE, 2002; Univ Nebr Med Ctr, Col Nursing, Borsheim's Peggy Carr Glass Plate, 2006. **Home Addr:** 5705 Willit St, Omaha, NE 68105-1851, **Home Phone:** (402)571-0243. **Business Addr:** Emeritus Professor, Chair, University Nebraska Medical Center, Rm 5041 985330 Nebr Med Center, Omaha, NE 68198-5330, **Business Phone:** (402)559-6608.

**FOXWORTH, DERRICK**
Police chief, government official, commander. **Personal:** married Linda; children: Teela & Derrick Jr. **Educ:** Univ Portland, BS, 1980. **Career:** Portland Police Bur, officer & uniform patrol, 1981-90, sgt, 1990-94, lt, 1994-96, capt, 1996-97, comdr, 1997-2002, asst chief, opers br, 2002-03, chief police, 2003-. **Business Addr:** Chief of Police, Portland Police Bureau, 1111 SW 2nd Ave Suite 1526, Portland, OR 97204, **Business Phone:** (503)823-0000.

**FOXX, ANTHONY (ANTHONY RENARD FOXX)**
Mayor, lawyer, government official. **Personal:** Born Apr 30, 1971, Charlotte, NC; son of Laura; married Samara Ryder; children: Zachary & Hillary. **Educ:** Davidson Col, BA, hist, 1993; NY Univ, Sch Law, JD, 1996; Mecklenberg County Bar Leadership Inst, grad. **Career:** Smith, Helms, Mullis & Moore Law Firm (Charlotte, NC), atty; US Sixth Circuit Ct Appeals, law clerk; US Dept. Justice, Civil Rights Div, trial atty; US House Representatives Comt Judiciary, staff coun; Hunton & Williams Law Firm, com litigator, 2001-09; Rep Mel Watt (D-NC), campaign mgr, 2004; City Charlotte, city coun, 2005, at-large rep; Budget, Housing & Neighborhood Develop, chair, 2005-07; NC, mayor, 2009-13; US secy transp, 2013. **Orgs:** Charlotte-Mecklenburg Development Corp, rep; coun rep, Meckenburg-Union Metropolitan Planning Organization. **Honors/Awds:** "The Root" Magazine, The Root 100 Honorees, 2013. **Special Achievements:** First African American student body president at Davidson College; nominated for US Secretary of Transportation by President Barack Obama. **Business Addr:** Secretary, US Department of Transportation, 1200 New Jersey Ave SE, Washington, DC 20590, **Business Phone:** (202)366-4000.

**FOXX, JAMIE (ERIC MARLON BISHOP)**
Actor. **Personal:** Born Dec 13, 1967, Terrell, TX; son of Louise. **Educ:** US Int Univ, San Diego, class music. **Career:** TV series: "In Living Color", 1991-94; "Roc", 1992-93; "Straight From the Foxx hole", 1994; "The Jamie Foxx Show", actor & writer, 1996-2001, producer, 1996-98, exec producer, 1998-2001; "Hangin' with Mr. Cooper", 1996; "Moesha", 1996; "Small Talk", exec producer, 2002; "Jamie Foxx Presents Laffapalooza", exec producer, 2003-06; "Redemption: The Stan Tookie Williams Story", 2004; "Chappelle's Show", 2004; "Jamie Foxx's Laffapalooza", producer, 2006; "Life Support", exec producer, 2007; "G's to Gents Top Ten Gentlemen's Club", exec producer & creator, 2008; "From G's to Gents", exec producer & writer, 2008-09; "In the Flow with Affion Crockett", exec producer & writer, 2011; "Night Tales", dir, 2011; "Apollo Live", exec producer, 2012. Films: Toys, 1992; The Truth About Cats and Dogs, 1996; The Great White Hype, 1996; Booty Call, 1997; The Player's Club, 1998; Any Given Sunday, 1999; Held Up, 1999; Bait, 2000; Ali, 2001; Date from Heaven, 2001; Shade, 2003; Breakin' All the Rules, 2004; Collateral Ray, 2004; Stealth, Jarhead, 2005; Unpredictable, 2005; The Kingdom, 2007; Intuition, 2008; Best Night of My Life, 2010; Album: Peep This, 1994; Miami Vice, Dreamgirls, 2006; The Soloist, Law Abiding Citizen, 2009; Valentine's Day, 2010; Due Date, 2010; Horrible Bosses, 2011; Rio, 2011; Kane & Lynch, 2012; Django Unchained, 2012; White House Down, 2013; The Amazing Spider-Man 2, 2014; A Million Ways to Die in the West, 2014; Horrible Bosses 2, 2014; Annie, 2014. Tours: The Unpredictable Tour, 2006; The Blame It Tour, 2009. **Honors/Awds:** Image Award, Nat Asn Advan Colored People, 1998, 2002 & 2005; Won Theatrical-Best Supporting Actor, 2002; Black Reel Award, 2002, 2005; FFCC Award, Fla Film Critics Circle, 2004; NBR Award, 2004; Academy Award, 2004; PFCS Award, Phoenix Film Critics Soc, 2004; AAFCA Award, African-Am Film Critics Asn, 2004; Hollywood Breakthrough Award, 2004; WAFCA Award, Wash DC Area Film Critics Asn, 2004; KCFCC Award, 2004; NYFCO Award, New York Film Critics, 2004; Seattle Film Critics Award, 2004; SEFCA Award, Southeastern Film Critics Asn, 2004; SLFCA Award, St. Louis Film Critics Asn, 2004; BSFC Award, 2004; BAFTA Award, Boston Soc Film Critics, 2005; Prism Award, 2005; Academy Award, Best Actor, 2005; OFTA Film Award, Online Film & Tv Asn, 2005; Oscar Award, 2005; NSFC Award, Nat Soc Film Critics, 2005; VFCC Award, Vancouver Film Critics Circle, 2005; Screen Actors Guild Award, 2005; BET Award, 2005, 2013; Critics Choice Award, 2005; Golden Globe, 2005; Golden Satellite Award, 2005; Sierra Award, 2005; Grace Award, 2005; ALFS Award, London Critics Circle Film, 2005; Favorite R&B/Soul Male Artist, American Music Awards, 2006; Jupiter Award, 2006; Best Music Video, Soul Train Awards, 2006; Best R&B/Soul Album, Soul Train Awards, 2007; Star on the Walk of Fame, 2007; Best Collaboration, BET Award, 2009; Record of the Year, Soul Train Awards, 2009; Best R&B Performance by a Duo or Group, Grammy Awards, 2010; MTV Generation Award, 2013. **Special Achievements:** TV sitcom No. 1 among African American viewers on WB network; fourth person in history who scored a No 1 album & won an Academy Award; first man of the millennium to host "Saturday Night Live" 1975; Is the first person to have been nominated for three acting awards at the Golden Globes in the same year; became one of the elite ten thespians to have been nominated for both a Supporting and Lead Acting Academy Award in the same year for their achievements in two different movies; Is only the second male in history to receive two acting Oscar nominations in the same year for two different movies; first African American to be nominated for two Oscars in the same year; second actor to win an Academy Award for "Best Actor" and to have had a No 1 billboard single; named one of People Magazine's "Hottest Bachelors" in 2006; amie Foxx hosted the 2009 BET Awards ceremony, 2009. **Business Addr:** Actor, c/o King

Management, 4477 Sherman Oaks Circle, Sherman Oaks, CA 91403-3818, **Business Phone:** (818)501-2800.

### FOXX, LAURA R.

College administrator. **Personal:** children: 1. **Educ:** Univ NC, Charlotte, BA, eng, Chapel Hill, MA, educ. **Career:** Davidson Col, Maj gifts officer, 1989-96; Nations Bank Found, pres, 1997; Bank Am Corp, exec dir & sr vpres; Foxx Co Inc, prin; Univ NC, Univ Advan, assoc vpres, chief advan officer, syst, bd gov; NC Cent Univ, instnl advan, interim vchancellor, 2007-09; Corp DevelopMint, sr coun, Higher educ div, currently. **Orgs:** Coun Advan Support Educ, Comn Philanthropy; trustee, Pub Libr Charlotte Mecklenburg County; pres, NationsBank Found; Charlotte Arts & Sci Coun; Leadership Charlotte; Dowd YMCA; vice chair, Financial Futures Found Inc; Catawba Riverkeeper Found; Andreas H. Bechtler Art Found & Mus; US Airways Educ Found Coun; Innovation Inst, McColl Ctr Visual Arts; corp bd diversity prog, UNC Sch Law; adv bd, Univ NC, Corp Opers, Carolinas Healthcare Syst. **Business Addr:** Senior Counsel, Higher Education Division, Corporate DevelopMint, exec Pk at Faber Pl 4000 Faber Pl Dr Suite 130, Charleston, SC 29405-8585, **Business Phone:** (843)853-9999.

### FOXX, NINA

Writer. **Personal:** Born Jamaica, NY. **Educ:** Hunter Col, BS, psychol; Baruch Col, MS, indust-orgn psychol; City Univ NY, PhD, indust-orgn psychol; Univ Wash, grad lit fiction cert; Farleigh Dickinson Univ, MFA, creative writing. **Career:** Books: Nina Foxx; Cynnamon Foster; Dippin' My Soul, 2000; Do The Write Thing, 2002; Get Some Love, 2003; Going Buck Wild, 2004; Marrying Up, 2005; Mama:Gone, 2005; Just Short of Crazy, 2006; NO Girl Needs A Husband Seven Days a Week 2007, Get some love, Marrying UP: The Stage Play 2008, BlackWords Online, "In Search of Color", columnist; Dippin' My Spoon; Do Right Woman, 2011; Black Issues Book Review, reviewer; Dell Comput Corp, designer; Brown Sugar IV, anthology, 2005; FoxxTale Productions LLC Producer, 2007. **Orgs:** Bd mem, Austin Cs Mus; Austin Writers League & Girls Scouts; Jack & Jill Am; Alpha Kappa Alpha Sorority; Capital Area Food Bank; El Buen Samaritano Episcopal Mission; Links Inc. **Business Addr:** Author, Writer, Foxx/Tale Productions, San Antonio, TX 78746, **Business Phone:** (415)246-5134.

### FOYLE, ADONAL DAVID

Entrepreneur, basketball player. **Personal:** Born Mar 9, 1975, Canouan; son of Jay Mandle and Joan. **Educ:** Colgate Univ, BA, hist, 1999; Orinda Univ, MS, sports psychol. **Career:** Basketball player (retired); Golden State Warriors, ctr, 1997-2008; Memphis Grizzlies, 2008-09; Orlando Magic, ctr, 2007-08, 2009-10; Adonal Foyle Enterprises, pres, currently. **Orgs:** Founder, Democracy Matters; founder, Kerosene Lamp Found Inc; Nat Basketball Players Asn. **Honors/Awds:** Most Outstanding Player, Five-Star Camp, 1992; McDonald s All American, 1993-94; Rookie of the Year, Patriot League, 1995; AP All-America, NCAA, 1996-97; Player of the Year, Patriot League, 1996, 1997; NBA Community Assist Award, Nat Basketball Asn, 2006; NBA Good Guys, Sporting News, 2006; World Sports Humanitarian Hall of Fame, 2009. **Business Addr:** President, Adonal Foyle Enterprises, 625 E Cent Blvd, Orlando, FL 32801.

### FRAME, GEORGE J.

Executive. **Career:** Ford Motor Co, Minority Dealer Opers, exec dir dealer develop; Jaguar Cars N Am, vpres, vpres admin, chief financial officer. **Orgs:** Bd dir, SCORE Asn. **Business Addr:** Executive Director of Dealer Development, Ford Motor Co, 1 Am Rd, Dearborn, MI 48126-2798, **Business Phone:** (313)322-3000.

**FRANCE, FREDERICK DOUG, JR.** See Obituaries Section.

**FRANCE, JO MARIE PAYTON-NOBLE.** See PAYTON-NOBLE, JOMARIE.

### FRANCIS, CHARLES K.

Executive, educator, physician. **Personal:** Born Newark, NJ. **Educ:** Dartmouth Col; Jefferson Med Col, Philadelphia. **Career:** Martin Luther King Jr Gen Hosp, chief cardiol; Col Physicians & Surgeons Columbia Univ, prof clin med; Harlem Hosp Ctr, chmn, dept med; Yale Univ, assoc prof; Yale-New Haven Hosp, Cardiac Catherization Lab, dir; Am Col Cardiol, fel; Am Col Physicians, fel; Univ Calif Los Angeles, David Geffen Sch Med, prof med; Univ Conn Sch Med, asst prof med; Mt Sinai Hosp, Hartford, Conn, chief cardiol; Univ Southern Calif Med Sch; Am Col Physicians, pres, 2004-05, bd regents, currently; NY Acad Med, Off Health Disparities, adj investr, currently. **Orgs:** Inst Med Nat Acad Sci; adv comm dir, NIH; pres, Am Heart Asn Western States Affil, Los Angeles County; chair, Coun Clin Cardiol Am Heart Asn; bd dir, Am Bd Internal Med; bd dir, NY Acad Med; chair, Bd Asn Black Cardiologists; co-chair, Working Group Coronary Artery Dis Blacks; pres, Am Col Physicians; Charles R Drew Univ Med & Sci, asst prof med, pres; NY Med Col, Ctr Health Disparities, dir; chair, Hypertensive Dis Comt, Am Col Cardiol; pres, Am Heart Asn, Conn Affil; nat bd dir, Am Heart Asn; chair bd, Asn Black Cardiologists; bd gov, Clin Ctr, NIH; Nat Adv Coun Nat Heart Lung & Blood Inst; prin investr, Urban Health Inst, Harlem Hosp Ctr; Agency Health Care Policy & Res. **Home Addr:** 125 Paterson St, New Brunswick, NJ 08903, **Home Phone:** (732)235-7855. **Business Addr:** Adjunct Investigator, New York Academy of Medicine, 1216 5th Ave, New York, NY 10029, **Business Phone:** (212)822-7288.

### FRANCIS, CHARLES S. L.

Government official. **Personal:** Born Sep 13, 1943, Kingston; son of Barbara and Claude; married Wilma Smith; children: Charles II, Michael, Erica & Aaron. **Educ:** Calif State Univ, BS, 1970; MCRP, 1977. **Career:** Fresno Model Cities Prog, proj develop specialist; Calif State Univ Fresno, adj prof; City Fresno, budget analyst, Fresno Pvt Indus Coun, exec dir & chief exec officer, currently; Fresno City Col, dir grant funded educ prog; County Brd Educ, pres, Training inst, dir, currently. **Orgs:** Regional chmn, Nat & Asn Planners, 1972-75; chmn, Sr Vol Prog, 1972-; full mem, Am Soc Planning Officials, 1972-; bd dir, Cent Valley YMCA, 1973-; chmn, Lincoln Elem Sch PTA; Affirmative Action Comm Fresno Co Bd Educ; pres, Alpha Phi Alpha Frat Iota Nu Lambda Chap, 1973-75; coordr, State Fed Liason Black Polit Coun, 1975-; exec officer, secy, Fresno Br, Nat Asn Advan Colored People; bd mem, Nat Asn County Training & Employ Prof, 1988-90; Leadership Fresno Alumni Asn; bus adv coun, CSUF-Sch Bus & Admin Sci; bd dir, Nat Asn Workforce Develop Prof; adv coun, Women to Women. **Honors/Awds:** Assn Students service & leadership award, 1970. **Home Addr:** 190 S Valentine Ave, Fresno, CA 93706, **Home Phone:** (559)268-1781. **Business Addr:** Director of Training Institute, Fresno City College, 1101 E Univ Ave, Fresno, CA 93741, **Business Phone:** (559)256-8272.

### FRANCIS, DR. CHERYL MARGARET

Association executive, vice president (organization). **Personal:** Born Sep 7, 1949, New Orleans, LA; daughter of Albert Jr; married F Daniel Cantrell. **Educ:** Loyola Univ, BS, educ, biol, 1971; Univ Chicago, PhD, educ admin, 1975. **Career:** Upward Bound Proj, prog dir, 1968-70; Headstart, recruiter, 1970; Scope Prog, teacher, 1970; MW Admin Ctr, res asst, 1971-74, dir, studs serv, 1972-73; Supt Schs, Skokie Ill, admin asst, 1974; Niles Twp Demoraphic Study, consult, 1974; Contracting Corp Am Educ Admin & Counr, dir, 1979-; City Chicago, Dept Human Servs, proj mgr, 1981-88, Title XX Prog, mgr, 1985-88; Bethel New Life, sr vpres progs, 1995-2001; Chicago Area Proj, assoc exec dir, 2006-15; Francis & Assocs, managing partner; Chicago Area Proj, assoc exec dir; Coll Urban Sci, Univ Ill, prof; Nat Com Cits Educ, midwest staff; Midwest Admin Ctr, Univ Chicago, res asst. **Orgs:** Am Educ Res Asn, Ford Fel Urban Adminr, 1971; Nat Fels Fund Fel 1974; United Way Chicago, mgr non profit consult unit, 1988-; Safer Found, vpres core progs, 2001-03; dir human develop, Steans Family Found, 2004; Nonprofit Financial Ctr, interim exec dir, 2004-06; bd secy, Chicago Opps Industrialization Ctr Inc, bd dir; Nat Alliance Black Sch Educ; Chicago Focus; Am Asn Sch Adminr; League Black Women; Shore Comn; AsnSupv & Curric; adv panel, Nat InstEduc Women's Aux Mary Bartelme HomeGirls; Chicago Jobs Coun; bd mem, Gads Hill Ctr. **Honors/Awds:** Louis J Twomney Award, Humanitarian Concern, 1971; Cardinal Key Hon Soc. **Home Addr:** 1508 W Jackson Blvd, Chicago, IL 60607, **Home Phone:** (312)226-3777. **Business Addr:** Executive Director, Nonprofit Financial Center, 29 E Madison St Suite 1005, Chicago, IL 60602-4415, **Business Phone:** (312)252-0420.

### FRANCIS, DELMA J.

Editor, executive, journalist. **Personal:** Born Dec 16, 1953, Lancaster, KY; daughter of George Jr and Marie Terry. **Educ:** Eastern Ky Univ, Richmond, KY, BA, jour, 1975; Univ Louisville, Louisville, KY, MS, community develop & pub admin, 1978. **Career:** Lexington Herald, Lexington, Ky, ed & reporter, 1975-76; Courier-J, reporter & ed; Louisville Times, Louisville, Ky, reporter, 1976-86; Hartford Courant, Hartford, Conn, asst bur chief, 1986-89; Richmond Times-Dispatch, Richmond, Va, asst city ed, 1989-94; Star Tribune, Minneapolis, Minn, asst features ed, reporter, 1994-2007; Osseo Area Schs, substitute teacher, 2008-11; Wordsmith, owner, 2007-; Minn Post, ed & reporter, 2007-. **Orgs:** Louisville Asn Black Communicators, 1977-86; alt dir, Nat Asn Black Journalists, 1979-; Choral Club Louisville, 1981-86; vpres, Conn Asn Black Communicators, 1987-89; Big Bros & Big Sisters, 1990-91; dir, Ebenezer Baptist Church Orchestra, 1990-94; Ebenezer Baptist Church Sanctuary choir, 1990-94; Richmond Festival Chorus, 1992-; Leigh Morris Chorale, 1994-; vpres, Twin Cities Black Journalists, 1995-; Minn Women's Press, freelancer, 2007-. **Home Addr:** 7401 79th Ave N, Brooklyn Park, MN 55445-2608, **Home Phone:** (612)898-3274. **Business Addr:** Editor & Reporter, Minn Post, 900 6th Ave SE, Minneapolis, MN 55414.

### FRANCIS, DR. E. ARACELIS

Educator, social worker. **Personal:** Born Dec 2, 1939, St. Thomas; daughter of Amadeo I and Ethanie Maria Smith. **Educ:** Inter-Am Univ, BA, 1960; Univ Chicago, Sch SS Admin, MA, 1964; Columbia Univ, Sch Social Work, DSW, 1979. **Career:** Director (retired), educator; Adelphi Univ, Sch Soc Work, asst prof, 1971-75; Child Welfare Div Vi, Dept Social Welfare, virgin island, exec dir off planning & develop, 1975-80; US Dept Health & Human Servs, fel, 1980-81; Univ Md, Sch Social Work & CP, asst prof, 1982-85; Coun Social Work Educ, Minority Fel Prog, dir, 1985-2007; Howard Univ, Sch Social Work, adj assoc prof, 1995-96, assoc asst prof, 1997-; Univ Vi, assoc prof social work, 2010-. **Orgs:** Am Pub Welfare Assoc, 1962-; Acad Cert Soc Workers, 1965-; vice chmn, State Manpower Serv Coun, 1976-80; bd dir, League Women Voters VI, 1977-80; pres, Nat Assoc Social Workers VI Chap, 1978-80; Caribbean Studies Assoc, 1981-85; chmn, Comm Minority Groups, Coun Soc Work Ed, 1982-85; chmn, Comm Inquiry Nat Assoc Social Workers Metro DC Chap, 1984-86; chairperson, Planning Comn, Nat Assoc Social Workers, 1987; rec secy, Union Black Episcopalians, DC chap, 1990-92; Minority Issues Conf; nominations comn, Vi Asn, 1991-92; World Assembly Planning Sub comt, 1991-92; bd dir, Metrop Wash Chap Nat Assoc Social Workers, 1992-94; pres, Metrop Chap Nat Assoc Social Workers, 1994-96; bd, Columbia Univ Sch Social Work Alumni, 1998-; chief, Bur Day Care Serv. **Home Addr:** 7836 Shepherd Hills Ct, Lorton, VA 22079-4325, **Home Phone:** (703)550-2750.

### FRANCIS, DR. EDITH V.

School administrator. **Personal:** Born Harlem, NY; daughter of James Audain and Iris; married Gilbert H; children: Deborah Ann Scott-Martin, Denise Tolbert & Dwayne H. **Educ:** Hunter Col, BA, MA, childhood educ, MS, guid; NY Univ, EdD, admin. **Career:** Ed Dept Media Ctr-Audio Visual Proj Ph I Stud Teacher Imp, adj pr, 1959-61; Stud Teaching, instr suprv, 1962-63, critic teacher, 1963-66; Elem Sch, teacher, 1963-66; Jr/Sr HS, suprv, 1967-68; Campus Schs, asst dir, 1968-69; Hunter Col Elem Sch, princ, 1968-69; NY City Bd Ed, consult, 1969-70; Except Gifted C Proj PS, coord, 1970-71; Princeton Reg Schs, prin, 1970-76, act spt schs, 1976-77; Hunter Col Dept Curr & Teaching; adj prof, 1971-72; US Dept HEW, consult, 1973-; Ed Testing Serv, tech asst consult 1975-; Ewing Twp Pub Schs, supt schs, 1977-87; Columbia Univ, Teachers Col, prof, practr, scholar, 1987-91; Irvington Pub Schs, supt schs, 1991-92; E Orange Pub Sch, dir, community & adult educ, 1992-2002, prin adult high sch, 2002. **Orgs:** Pres, Princeton Reg Admin Asn, 1974-75; chairperson ed comm Princeton Bicentennial Comm, 1974-77; bd dir, Pub Lib, 1976-77; Witherspoon Devel Corp, 1976-82; legis comm NJ; Am Asn Sch Admin, 1977-; bd dir, YWCA Trenton NJ, 1977-89; int pres Grand Basileus Zeta Phi Beta, 1980-86; bd examr, NJ Ed Dept, 1980-86; bd trustee Nat Assault Illiteracy, 1982-86; bd dir, Helene Fuld Hosp, 1982-86; gov task force Trenton NJ 1982-86; bd dir, Nat Merit Scholar Corp 1982-87; Nat Asn Suprv & Curric Devel; Nat Coun Admin Women Ed; CUNY Black Profs & Admin Women Ed; Am Asn Univ Profs; Sch masters NJ; NJ Ed Asn; NJ Coun Ed; Phi Beta Kappa; Links Inc, 1986-; pres, Cent NJ chap, 1997-; 18th Int Grand Pres, Delta Mu Zeta Chap. **Home Addr:** 4116 Melrose Ct, Melbourne, FL 32940-1472, **Home Phone:** (321)254-1939.

### FRANCIS, DR. GILBERT H.

Executive, educator. **Personal:** Born May 27, 1930, Brooklyn, NY; married Edith V; children: Deborah Scott Martin, Denise Tolbert & Dwayne H. **Educ:** St John's Univ, BBA, LLD; City Col; Hunter Col; City Univ. **Career:** Educator, executive (retired); US Dept Health Educ & Welfare Off Civil Rights, asst chief elem & sec educ br, 1967-73; NJ Div Civil Rights Dept Law & Pub Safety, dir civil rights, 1973-74; Super markets Gen Corp, dir equal employ opportunity, 1974-76; Comprehensive Compliance Servs, consult & pres, 1976; US Dept Educ, asst chief tech assistance, 1976-86; NJ State Dept Educ, educ prog specialist, 1986-97; NJ State Dept Treas, sr mgt specialist, 1997-2002; Niagara Univ, lectr; Hunter Col, lectr; Trenton State Col, lectr; Lehman Col, lectr; Sweet Briar Col, lectr; Nat Pan Hellenic Coun Inc, pres. **Orgs:** EDGES Group; nat comn co-chair, Assault Illiteracy Prog; bd dir, chair higher educ prog NJ Conf Br Nat Asn Advan Colored People; Nat Alliance Black Sch Educrs; life mem, Nat Asn Advan Colored People; Lions Intl; Frontiers Intl; legal comn Intl Asn Off Human Rights Agencies; Nat Asn Human Rights Workers, Comn One Hundred; comn affairs adv, Hunter Col Campus Schs, NYC; Phi Beta Sigma Frat Inc; pres, Nat Pan-Hellenic Coun Inc. **Home Addr:** 4116 Melrose Ct, Melbourne, FL 32940-1472, **Home Phone:** (321)254-1939.

**FRANCIS, HENRY MINTON.** See Obituaries Section.

### FRANCIS, JAMES L.

Government official. **Personal:** Born Dec 30, 1943, Cincinnati, OH; son of James L and Marjorie L Murphy; married Melanie Hall; children: Renee L & Darryl. **Educ:** Ohio Univ, Athens, OH, BA, polit sci, 1965; Howard Univ, Wa DC, gradstudies, 1967; Wright State Univ, Dayton, OH, 1976; Cent Mich Univ, Mt Pleasant, MPA, 1978. **Career:** Govt Employs Ins Co, Wa DC, claims examr; City Dayton, Ohio, field rep, human rels coun, 1970-71, asst to exec dir, human rels coun, 1971-72, supt, div property mgt, 1972-78, dir pub works, 1978-85, asst city mgr, admin servs, 1985-90, exec asst, clerk city comn, 1990. **Orgs:** Alpha Pi Phi Fraternity, 1963-; Westmont Optimist Club, 1984-; Intl City Mgrs Asn, 1985-; Sigma Pi Phi Fraternity, 1986-; bd mem, Nat Forum Black Pub Admin, 1987-96; bd trustee, OH Munic League, 1990-97; OH Adv Coun, US Civil Rights Comn. **Honors/Awds:** Readers Digest Found, Sister City Tech Asst Prog Monrovia, Liberia, 1986; Certificate of Merit, Louisville, Ky, Bd Aldermen, 1988; Marks Excellence Award, Nat Forum Black Pub Adminr, 1998. **Home Addr:** 5870 Access Rd, Dayton, OH 45431, **Home Phone:** (937)256-2789.

### FRANCIS, REV. DR. JAMES N.

Clergy. **Personal:** Born Mar 25, 1951, Kingston; son of David and Esther; married Edna Mc Intosh; children: Sharice, Crystal, James Jr & Justin. **Educ:** RCA Inst; New York Univ & Pace Univ; Lehman Col, BA, 1976; Merrill Lynch Sch Econ, MBA, 1983; Trinity Evangel, MA, bibl studies, 1991; Jacksonville Theol Sem, Dmin, 1996. **Career:** Wall St, vpres finance; Merrill Lynch, stockbroker; Wall-St, vpres finance; Merrill Lynch & Co; Monument Faith Ministries Church, pastor, sr paster & founder, currently, chmn, 1997-. **Orgs:** Chmn, Operation Reach Out Across Miami. **Honors/Awds:** Pastor of the Year, Church of God, 1996; Metro Miami Dade County, Key to the City, 1998; MIP Supervising Pastor Award, 2002. **Home Addr:** 19700 NE 22nd Ave, North Miami, FL 33180, **Home Phone:** (305)931-0751. **Business Addr:** Chairman, Monument of Faith Ministries Church, 1956 NW 183rd St, North Miami Beach, FL 33179-5044, **Business Phone:** (305)621-1354.

### FRANCIS, LIVINGSTON S.

Management consultant, educator. **Personal:** Born Dec 2, 1929, Brooklyn, NY; son of James R and Ethel Price; married Helen Owensby; children: Brian S, Ronald & Gary. **Educ:** Adelphi Univ, Garden City, NY, BS, MSW. **Career:** NYC Parks, Recreation & Cult Affairs, New York, asst comnr, 1960-69; Community Cou Greater New York, assoc exec dir, 1970-77; New York State Univ, Farmingdale, assoc adj prof, 1974-76; Adelphi Univ, Garden City New York, adj prof, 1976-80; YMCA Greater NY-Harlem Br, New York, exec dir, 1977-80; Greater New York Fund & United Way, dep exec dir, 1980-86; Fordham Univ, New York, adj prof, 1980-2000; Francis Livington & Assocs, owner, pres & chief exec officer, currently. **Orgs:** Reveille Club; Omega Psi Phi; chair emer & bd dir, N Gen Hosp; dir, United Hosp Fund; trustee, Helene Fuld Col Nursing; pres, Livingston S Francis Asn, Roosevelt New York, 1986-; exec dir, Asn Black Charities, New York, 1988-. **Home Addr:** 65 Bauer Ave, Roosevelt, NY 11575, **Home Phone:** (516)868-8598. **Business Addr:** President, Chief Executive Officer, Francis Livington & Associates, 65 Bauer Ave, Roosevelt, NY 11575, **Business Phone:** (516)546-8455.

### FRANCIS, DR. NORMAN C.

College administrator. **Personal:** Born Mar 20, 1931, Lafayette, LA. **Educ:** Xavier Univ, BS, 1952; Loyola Univ Law Sch, JD, 1955. **Career:** President (retired); Xavier Univ, dean men, 1957, dir stud personnel serv, 1963, asst to pres, 1964, exec vpres, 1967, pres, 1968-2015. **Orgs:** Fel Am Acad Arts & Sci; bd dir, WLAE-TV; Carnegie Found Advan Teaching; Am Assessment Higher Educ; chmn bd, Col Entrance Exam Bd, 1976-; chmn, La Recovery Authority; chmn, Educ Testing Serv; chmn, bd dir, Southern Educ Found; pres, Am Asn Higher Educ; pres, United Negro Col Fund; Nat Comn Excellence Educ; Nat Adv Res Coun, US Dept Health & Human Resources; Vatican's Pontif Coun Justice & Peace; adv bd, Soc St. Joseph; exec comt, Nat

Cath Educ Asn; bd trustee, Cath Univ Am; bd regents, Loyola Univ; bd dir, Nat Cath Coun Interracial Justice. **Special Achievements:** First African-American to enroll at Loyola University New Orleans. He was one of two African-American students selected to integrate Loyola University Law School in New Orleans, Louisiana. In 1955 became the school's first Black graduate. First African American and first layman to serve as president of Xavier in 1968. Nation's longest serving university president, with 56 years of service at Xavier and 47 of those years as president. He is the Longest-tenured current leader of an American University. **Home Addr:** 1630 King Dr, New Orleans, LA 70122, **Home Phone:** (504)282-7631.

### FRANCIS, PATRICK JOHN

Chancellor (education), association executive, manager. **Personal:** Born Sep 4, 1964, New Orleans, LA; son of Norman C and Blanche Macdonald; married Kristi; children: 3. **Educ:** Univ Notre Dame, South Bend, BA, Am studies, 1986; Univ Tex, Austin, TX, LBJ Sch Pub Affairs, MPA, pub affairs, 1988. **Career:** Sloan Fel Grad Study Pub Affairs, 1986-87; US Senate Com Labor & Human Resources, Wash, DC, intern, 1987; Tex Dept Agr, proj consult, 1988; House Res Orgn Tex House Representatives, researcher & writer, 1989; Tex State Auditors Off, asst state auditor, 1989-90; Tex Asn Sch Bd, asst dir govt rels, 1990-95; Off Gov Tex, Lt Gov Bob Bullock, spec asst to lieutenent gov, 1995-98; Legis Budget Bd, team mgr, 1999-2003; Univ Tex Syst, asst vice chancellor health affairs, 2003-. **Orgs:** Ed staff quart publ, Profiling Minority Alumni LBJ Sch Pub Affairs, 1990. **Home Addr:** 748 River Oaks Dr, Austin, TX 78748-3846, **Home Phone:** (512)280-8772. **Business Addr:** Assistant Vice Chancellor, University of Texas System, O Henry Hall 2nd Fl, Austin, TX 78701-2982, **Business Phone:** (512)499-4224.

### FRANCISCO, ANTHONY M.

Government official. **Personal:** Born Jun 30, 1960, Nashville, TN; son of Maurine E Moore and Anceo M; married Kimberly Statum; children: Alexandria Morgan. **Educ:** Univ Okla, Norman, BA, 1981; Univ Tex, Austin, SPPS, 1981; Syracuse Univ, Syracuse, NY, MPA, 1983. **Career:** Syracuse Housing Authority, NY, admin aide, 1983; City Kans, MO, mgt intern, 1983-84; City Okla, OK, mgt, budget analyst, 1984-86, financial enterprise budget officer, 1986-88, dir st maintenance, 1988-90, investment officer, 1990-; City Norman, OK, treas, 2002, finance dir, 1996-. **Orgs:** Christian Church, 1962-; local pres, Kappa Alpha Psi Fraternity, 1979-; Int City Mgt Asn, 1983-88; Ambassadors' Concert Choir, 1985-; local pres, Nat Forum Black Pub Admin, 1987-; bd mem, Okla City Metrop area Pub Schs Trust. **Home Addr:** 1313 NE 50th St, Oklahoma City, OK 73111-6619, **Home Phone:** (405)427-7010. **Business Addr:** Treasurer, Finance Director, City of Norman, 201 W Gray Bldg C, Norman, OK 73069, **Business Phone:** (405)366-5413.

### FRANCISCO, JOSEPH SALVADORE

Educator, physical chemist. **Personal:** Born Mar 26, 1955, New Orleans, LA; son of Joseph Salvadore Sr and Lucinda Baker; married Priya. **Educ:** Univ Tex, Austin, TX, BS, chem, 1977; Mass Inst Technol, Cambridge, MA, PhD, 1983. **Career:** Univ Tex, Robert Welch Undergrad Res fel, 1973-76; Univ Tex, jr fel, 1977; MIT, HEW fel, 1978-81; Univ Sydney, Sydney, Australia, vis lectr, 1981; St Edmund's Col, Cambridge Univ, res fel, 1983-85; Cambridge Univ, Cambridge, Eng, res fel, 1983-85; Mass Inst Tech, Cambridge, MA, provost post doctoral fel, 1985-86; Wayne St Univ, Detroit, Mich, asst prof chem, 1986-90, assoc prof, 1990-94; Alfred P Sloan Found, res fel, 1990-92; Calif Inst Technol, Planetary Sci Div, vis assoc, 1991-93; John Simon Guggenheim fel, Jet Propulsion Lab, 1993-94; Calif Inst Technol, Jet Propulsion Lab, vis scientist, 1993-94; Purdue Univ, prof phys chem & earth & atmosphere sci, 1995; Sterling Brownvis prof, Williams Col, 1998; Purdue Univ, William E Moore distinguished prof earth & atmospheric sci & chem, currently; Univ Bologna, Inst Advan Studies, sr vis fel; Univ Paris, vis prof; Uppsala Univ, vis prof; Nat Taipei Univ, Taiwan, chair & prof. **Orgs:** Fac adv, WSU, Nobcche Stud Chap, 1986-; vol, Inst Res Appreticeship Minority High Sch Students, 1987-; MIT Corp Visit Comn, 1987-; NASA HBCU Res Panel, 1987-; consult, Inst Defense Anal, 1988-; Sigma Xi, 1990-; Naval Res Adv Comt, Dept Navy, 1994-96; Army Sci Bd, 1996-; Am Phys Soc fel, 1998; AAAS fel, 2001; Nat Org Black Chemists & Chem Engrs; fel Am Chem Socs, pres, currently; Res fel, Cambridge Univ; Press Comt, Nat Medal Sci, 2011-12; Am Acad Arts & Sci; Aaas. **Home Addr:** 4663 Woods Edge Dr, Zionsville, IN 46077. **Business Addr:** William E Moore Distinguished Professor, Purdue University, 1393 H C Brown Bldg, West Lafayette, IN 47907-1393, **Business Phone:** (765)494-7851.

### FRANCO, JULIO CESAR ROBLES

Manager, baseball player. **Personal:** Born Aug 23, 1958, Hato Mayor. **Career:** Baseball player (retired), manager; Philadelphia Phillies, infielder, 1982; Cleveland Indians, infielder, 1983-88, 1996-97; Tex Rangers, infielder, 1989-93; Chicago White Sox, 1994; Chiba Lotte Marines, 1995, 1998; Cleveland Indians, 1996-97; Milwaukee Brewers, 1997; Tampa Bay Devil Rays, 1999; Samsung Lions, 2000; Atlanta Braves, 2001-05, 2007; New York Mets, infielder, 2006-07; free agt, currently; Mets rookie level, mgr. **Home Addr:** CF 16 B Libre Ing Cons, San Pedro de Macoris4023. **Business Addr:** Infielder, New York Mets, Shea Stadium, Flushing, NY 11368.

### FRANCOIS, DR. EMMANUEL SATURNIN

Surgeon, physician. **Personal:** Born Dec 23, 1938, Port-au-Prince; son of Saturnin F Ceau and Fausta Lauren Ceau; married Edda Gibbs; children: Randolph Emmanuel, Herve Daniel & Chantal Claire. **Educ:** Col St Louis De Gonzague, attended 1958; Univ Haiti, attended 1964. **Career:** Surgeon (retired); Harlem Hosp Ctr Columbia Univ, resident, 1966-72; Provident Hosp, 1972-73; pvt pract surgeon, 1973. **Orgs:** Baltimore City Med Soc; Med Chi Soc Md; AMA; Nat Med Asn; chmn, Asn Haitian Physician Abroad; Am Asn Automotive Med; Trauma Soc; Smithsonian Inst. **Business Addr:** Board Member, Founder, Association of Haitian Physicians Abroad, 1166 Eastern Pkwy, Brooklyn, NY 11213, **Business Phone:** (718)745-1015.

### FRANK, TELLIS JOSEPH, JR.

Executive, basketball coach, basketball player. **Personal:** Born Apr 26, 1965, Gary, IN. **Educ:** Western Ky Univ, attended 1987. **Career:** Basketball player (retired), coach, executive; Golden State Warriors, power forward, 1987-89; Miami Heat, power forward, 1989-90; Phonola Caserta, Italy, 1990-91; Minn Timberwolves, power forward, 1991-92, 1993-94; Pitch Cholet, France, 1994-95; TDK Manresa, Spain, 1995-96; Caja San Fernando, 1996-97; Leon Caja Espana, Spain, 1997-98; Scandone Avellino, Italy, 1998-99; Basket Livorno, Italy, 1999-2000; Longobardi Scafati, Italy, 2000-01; Hampton Univ, asst mens basketball coach, 2002, coaching staff, 2005-07; Harvard-Westlake Sch, Freshman Team, head coach, Varsity Team, asst coach, 2007-09; Atlanta Dream Women's Nat Basketball Asn, asst coach, 2015; Los Angeles City, asst mens basketball coach; Shooter Group LLC, dir sports progs, currently. **Honors/Awds:** Sun Belt Conference Player of the Year, 1987.

### FRANKLIN, ALLEN D.

Executive, educator. **Personal:** Born May 25, 1945, Berkeley, CA. **Educ:** Merritt Col, AA, 1966; San Francisco State Univ, BA, 1969; Univ Calif, Berkeley, MBA, 1971, PhD, 1974. **Career:** Lawrence Berkeley Lab, Math & Comput Dept, math programmer, 1969-71; Far W Lab, consult, 1972-73; Planning Dept City Hayward, consult, 1973-; Univ Calif, Berkeley, instr, 1973-74; Grad Sch Bus Admin; Calif St Univ, Hayward Sch Bus & Econ, pres, assoc dean & asst. **Orgs:** Caucus Black Economists/Nat Econ Asn; bd dir, Minority Bus Assistance Stud Develop Found; Asn comput Mach. **Honors/Awds:** Certificate of Honor, Bus Majors Asn, Calif St Univ, Hayward, 1974; Outstanding Young Man Am, 1975; Certificate of Appreciation, The Exchange Club Oakland, 1975. **Home Addr:** 2939 Galindo St, Oakland, CA 94601. **Business Addr:** Associate Dean, California State University, Hayward, CA 95380.

### FRANKLIN, ARETHA LOUISE

Songwriter, singer, actor. **Personal:** Born Mar 25, 1942, Memphis, TN; daughter of Clarence L and Barbara Siggers; married Glynn Turman; children: Clarence, Edward, Teddy & Kecalf; married Ted White. **Educ:** Julliard Sch, piano. **Career:** Gospel singer, 1952-61; Rhythm & Blues & Soul vocalist, 1960-84; Pop Music vocalist, 1985-; Albums include: Aretha, 1961; Electrifying, 1962; Tender Moving & Swinging, 1962; Laughing on the Outside, 1962; Unforgettable, 1964; Songs of Faith, 1964; Running Out of Fools, 1964; Yeah, 1965; Soul Sister, 1966; Queen of Soul, 1967; I Never Loved a Man, 1967; Once in a Lifetime, 1967; Aretha Arrives, 1967; Lady Soul, 1968; Live at Paris, Olympia, 1968; Aretha Now, 1968; Soul 69, 1969; Today I Sing the Blues, 1969; Aretha Gold, 1969; I Say a Little Prayer, 1969; This Girl's in Love with You, 1970; Spirit in the Dark, 1970; Don't Play That Song, 1970; Live at the Filmore West, 1971; Young, Gifted & Black, 1971; Amazing Grace, 1972; Hey Hey Now, 1973; Let Me Into Your Life, 1974; With Everything I Feel in Me, 1975; You, 1975; Sparkle, 1976; Sweet Passion, 1977; Almighty Fire, 1978; Diva, 1979; Aretha, 1980; Who's Zoom in Who, 1985; Aretha After Hours, 1987; Love All the Hurt Away, 1987; One Lord, One Faith, 1988; Through the Storm, 1989; A Rose Is Still A Rose, 1998; One Lord, One Faith, One Baptism, 2003; So Damn Happy, 2003; Jewels In The Crown: All-Star Duets With The Queen, 2007; Soundtrack including: In Good Company, 2004; "Entourage", 2005; Larry the Cable Guy: Health Inspector, 2006; Bobby, 2006; Gracie, 2007; Eye See Me, 2007; Films: The Blue Brothers, 1980; Blue Brothers 2000, 1998. R&B singles: "I Never Loved a Man", 1967; "Respect", 1967; "Baby I Love You", 1967; "Chain of Fools", 1967; "(Sweet Sweet Baby) Since You've Been Gone", 1968; "Think", 1968; "Share Your Love with Me", 1969; "Call Me", 1970; "Don't Play That Song (You Lied)", 1970; "Bridge Over Troubled Water", 1971; "Spanish Harlem", 1971; "Day Dreaming", 1972; "Angel", 1973; "Until You Come Back to Me (That's What I'm Gonna Do)", 1973; "I'm in Love", 1974; "Something He Can Feel", 1976; "Break It to Me Gently", 1977; "Jump to It", 1982; "Get It Right", 1983; "Freeway of Love", 1985. Filmography: Black Rodeo, 1972; The Blues Brothers, 1980; Listen Up: The Lives of Quincy Jones, 1990; Blues Brothers 2000, 1998; Tom Dowd & the Language of Music, 2003; The Zen of Bennett, 2012; Muscle Shoals, 2013. **Orgs:** Delta Sigma Theta Sorority Inc. **Honors/Awds:** Grammy Award, Best Female R & B Performance, 1967-74 (every year), 1982, 1986, 1988, 1989, 2004, 2006 & 2008; Hollywood Walk of Fame, 1979; American Music Award, 1984; Grammy Living Legend Award, 1991; Lifetime Achievement Award, R & B Found, 1992; Grammy Lifetime Achievement Award, 1994; Nat Medal for the Arts, 1999; honored by and appeared on "Divas Live, " VH1, 2001; Damon J Keith Soul & Spirit Humanitarian Award, 2003; Presidential Medal of Freedom, 2005; UK Music Hall of Fame, 2005; MusiCares Person of the Year, 2008; Vanguard Award, NAACP, 2008; GMA Gospel Music Hall of Fame, 2012. **Special Achievements:** Author: Aretha: From These Roots; first woman to be admitted to the Rock and Roll Hall Of Fame; performed at President Bill Clinton's presidential inauguration in 1992; song "R-E-S-P-E-C-T" ranked no 4 on Natl Endowment for the Arts & Recording Indust Asn of Am list of The 365 Songs of the Century, 2001; Nineth Greatest Rock 'n' Roll Artist of all time, Rolling Stone. **Business Addr:** Singer, William Morris Agency, 1 William Morris Pl, Beverly Hills, CA 90212, **Business Phone:** (310)859-4000.

### FRANKLIN, AUDREY DEMPS

School administrator. **Personal:** Born Mar 20, 1950, Ft. Meade, FL; daughter of John and Garnell Demps; married James; children: Wesley James. **Educ:** Benette Col, BS, 1972; NC Agr & Tech State Univ, MA, 1978. **Career:** Bennett Col, mgt info, 1973-90, employee benefits specialist, pres, 1990-, Alumnae Affairs, dir. **Orgs:** Financial secy, Bennett Col, NAA, 1991-98; pres, Alpha Kappa Alpha Sorority, 1998-; assoc mem, Jack & Jill Am, 1998; pres, Nat Alumnae Asn; Black Child Develop Inst Greensboro; NC Independent Cols & Univs. **Honors/Awds:** Alpha Kappa Alpha, Silver Award, 1997; Bennett Col, Susie W Jones, 1998. **Home Addr:** 3071 Renaissance Pkwy, Jamestown, NC 27282-8753, **Home Phone:** (336)858-5048. **Business Addr:** Benefits Specialist, Director-Alumnae Affairs, Bennett College, John Race Admin Bldg 2nd Fl 900 E Wash St, Greensboro, NC 27401, **Business Phone:** (336)517-2247.

### FRANKLIN, BERNARD W.

School administrator. **Personal:** married Shirley Lee; children: Jacori, Gabrielle & Allyson. **Educ:** Simpson Col, BA, relig, 1974; Western Md Col, MS; Columbia Univ Teachers Col, PhD. **Career:** Miami Univ, asst prof, 1983; Livingstone Col, chief exec officer, pres, 1989-95; St Augustines Col, chief exec officer, pres, 1995-99; Hood Theol Sem, chief exec officer, pres; Johnson C Smith Univ, asst vpres stud affairs; Delhaize Am Inc, dir, 1993-; RBC Ban corp, dir, 1998-; Va Union Univ, pres, 1999-2003; Nat Col Athletic Asn, sr vpres & vpres governance, 2003, exec vpres mem servs & stud-athlete affairs, currently. **Orgs:** Exec Comt, Nat Col Athletic Asn; vice chair, Div II Presidents Coun, Nat Col Athletic Asn; trustee, Simpson col; United Negro Col Fund; bd trustee, Simpson Col. **Business Addr:** Senior Vice President for Governance, The National Collegiate Athletic Association, 700 W Wash St, Indianapolis, IN 46206-6222, **Business Phone:** (317)917-6222.

### FRANKLIN, CLARENCE FREDERICK, JR.

Educator. **Personal:** Born Jan 30, 1945, Knoxville, TN; son of Clarence David Shell and Geraldine Franklin Waller; children: Carissa Racquel. **Educ:** Tuskegee Inst, attended 1963; Univ Tenn, attended 1964; Cooper Inst, BS, bus mgt, 1978. **Career:** Union Carbide Corp, machinist, 1968-79; Martin Marietta Inc, foreman, training admin. **Orgs:** VFW, 1962; alumni assoc, Tuskegee Inst; Optimist Club Mechanicsville; pres & mem, Optimist Club Mechanicsville, Lonsdale; CC Russell Masonic Lodge 262; Payne Ave Baptist Church; secy, 100 Black Men Inc, Knoxville, TN. **Home Addr:** 4258 St Lucia Lane, Knoxville, TN 37921, **Home Phone:** (865)909-0110. **Business Addr:** Training Administrator, Martin-Marietta Inc, Oak Ridge, TN 37831, **Business Phone:** (615)576-4366.

### FRANKLIN, COSTELLA M.

Nurse. **Personal:** Born Mar 14, 1932, Durham, NC; children: Saadia Ardisa, Kevin Leonard & Michale Bernard. **Educ:** Hampton Sch Nursing, attended 1953; Univ Calif. **Career:** Nurse (retired); Childrens Hosp, Wash, nurse, 1955-56; Childrens Hosp Los Angeles, asst head nurse, 1956-60; Daniel Freeman Hosp, asst head nurse, 1960-65; Coronary Care Memorial Hosp Long Beach, nurse, 1968-71. **Orgs:** Life mem, Blue Angels Social & Charity Club, 1968-; chair, Banneker Alumni Parent Asn Developmentally Disabled Adults, 1977; Calif Prof Nurses Asn; Calif Coun Retarded; Nat Asn Retarded C; SW Asn Retarded C; Except Children's Found Women's Aux; Except Adult Parent Guild. **Honors/Awds:** Los Angeles Press Club Award, 1962; Lane Bryant Vol Citizens Community Award, 1967; Calif state Senate Award, Senator James Wedworth, 1968; Merit Award, Long Beach Memorial Hosp Qual control, 1969; Citation award for outstanding achievement in community, 1971; Angel of the year Award, 1972; Distinguished Award, 1977; Sweetheart of the Year, New Decade, 1980. **Home Addr:** 1351 E Bankers Dr, Carson, CA 90746.

### FRANKLIN, DR. CURTIS U., JR.

Psychiatrist. **Personal:** Born Oct 30, 1929, Commerce, TX; married Rose Marie Henry; children: Curtis, III, Vicki, Lisa, William, Valerie & Rose Marie Jr. **Educ:** Prairie View A&M Col; Fisk Univ, BA, 1949; Howard Univ, Col Med, MD, 1953. **Career:** Homer G Phillips Hosp, internship residency, 1953; Doctor's Clin KC, prac internal med, 1960-64; Psychiat Receiving Ctr KC, residency psychiat, 1964-67; pvt pract psychiatrist, 1967-. **Orgs:** Psychiat consult, Swope Pkwy Health Ctr; Cath Family & Community Serv; Voc Rehab; Social Security Admin; asst clin prof, Univ Miss-KC Med Sch; diplomat, Am Bd Psychiat & Neurol; fel Am Psychiat Asn; AMA; Nat Med Asn; Miss Med Asn; Jackson Co Med Soc; KC Med Soc; Alpha Phi Alpha. **Home Addr:** 8135 Holmes Rd Suite 102, Kansas City, MO 64131, **Home Phone:** (816)363-1638. **Business Addr:** Psychiatrist, Private Practice, 4301 Main Suite 14, Kansas City, MO 64111.

### FRANKLIN, DON

Actor. **Personal:** Born Dec 14, 1960, Chicago, IL; son of Donald and Dorothy Jean; married Sheila Burke; married Kristine; children: 2. **Educ:** Studied actg under Soren Kirk, Zephyr Theatre; Dan LaMarte, Training Ctr Working Actor; studied voice under Robert Berthold, Joel Ewing. **Career:** NK & Co, head out-trade clerk; Films: Northville Cemetery Massacre, 1976; Growing Up Young, 1980; Somewhere in Time, 1980; Fast Forward, 1985; The Big Picture, 1989; Moving, 1988; Knightwatch, 1989; The Big Picture, 1989; Killor Be Killed, 1990; Between the Sheets, 2003; Hair Show, 2004; BlackDawn, 2005; An American Girl: Chrissa Stands Strong, 2009; The Shift, 2009; The Space Between, 2010; How to Make Love to a Woman, 2010; Any Day Now, 2012; TV series: "The Cosby Show", 1987; "Nightwatch", 1988; "Young Riders", 1990-92; "SeaQuestDSV", 1993-95; "SeaQuest 2032", 1993-96; "Chicago Hope", 1997; "Seven Days", 1998-2001; "The Bernie Mac Show", 2004; "CSI: Miami", 2005; "Frame Up", 2005; "NCIS", 2005-06; "Castle", 2010; "The Mentalist", 2012; "Bones", 2013; "Glee", 2013. TV movies: "Nasty Boys", 1989-90; "Fight for Justice: The Nancy Conn Story", 1995; "Asteroid", 1997; "Seven Days", 1998; "Anna's Dream", 2002. TV guest appearances: The Outer Limits, 1997; Living Single, 1997; Moesha, 1998; Girlfriends, 2001-02; The District, 2001-03; She Spies, 2003; Wild Card, 2003. Theatre: Playboy of the West Indies, The Tempest, Dealing, West Memphis Mojo, The Middle of Nowhere in the Middle of the Night, A Chorus Line, One Shining Moment, Kismet, Life of Bessie Smith, Pippin, Amen Corner. TV episode: Smoked, 2006; Shalom, 2006; Pilot, 2006; What If They Run?, 2006; Day Break, 2007; What If She's Lying?, 2007; Double Down, 2007; Blowback, 2007; "Journeyman", 2007; Half Load, 2009; "The Closer", 2009. **Orgs:** Screen Actors Guild; Am Fed Television & Radio Artists; Actors Equity Asn. **Honors/Awds:** Joseph Jefferson Nomination, Best Actor, The Middle of Nowhere in the Middle of the Night. **Home Addr:** 3815 S McLaughlin, Los Angeles, CA 90066, **Home Phone:** (310)397-1713. **Business Addr:** Actor, c/o Abrams Artists Agency, 275 Seventh Ave 26th Fl, New York, NY 10001, **Business Phone:** (646)486-4600.

### FRANKLIN, EUGENE T., JR.

Association executive, educator. **Personal:** Born Jun 8, 1945, Detroit, MI; married Beverly King. **Educ:** Ky State Col, BA, 1972; Univ Louisville, MEd, 1972. **Career:** KY State Univ, dir Title III proj, educ instr, 1972-74; Detroit Urban League, dir educ serv; Detroit Pub Sch, facilitator; Detroit Pub Sch, asst prin, currently. **Orgs:** Nat Educ Asn;

KY Ctr Bio-Psychosynthesis; Asn Teacher Educ; Am Inst Econ Res; Detroits Coalition Peaceful Integration; Com Desegregation; Frankfort-Franklin Co Comn Human Rights. **Honors/Awds:** Butzel scholarship Detroit Urban League, 1970; KY Sickle Cell Anemia Found, 1971; Recepient grad fel, Univ Louisville; Deans list KY State Univ. **Special Achievements:** First African American houseparents researchers KYC Child Welfare Research Found. **Home Addr:** 30734 Charleston Ct, Farmington Hills, MI 48331-1510, **Home Phone:** (248)788-3953. **Business Addr:** Facilitator, The Detroit Public School, 3031 W Grand Blvd Sch Center Bldg, Detroit, MI 48202, **Business Phone:** (313)494-7567.

### FRANKLIN, GAYLE JESSUP. See JESSUP, GAYLE LOUISE.

### FRANKLIN, DR. GRANT L.
Physician. **Personal:** Born Jun 21, 1918, Pauls Valley, OK; married Rita Bruckschlogi; children: Monique, Julie, Grant Jr & Carol Susan. **Educ:** Langston Univ, BS, 1941; Atlanta Univ, MS, 1947; Meharry Med Col, MD, 1951. **Career:** Hubbard Hosp, intern, 1951-52; Cleveland Veterans Admin & Case Western Res Univ Hosps, gen surg residency, 1952-56; Polyclinic Hosp, chief surg; Woman's Hosp, chief surg; Case Western Res Med Sch, sr clin instr surg; Cleveland Wade Veterans Admin Hosp, surg consult; pvt pract surgeon; Huron Road Hosp, assoc chief surg; United Hosp Ctr, urol specialist, currently. **Orgs:** Cert Am Bd Surg, 1957; Am Col Surgeons; 1959-; Cleveland Acad Med; Cleveland Surg Soc; Pan Am Surg Soc; Soc Abdominal Surgeons; AMA; Ohio Med Asn; Cleveland & Nat Med Asns; Nat Alumni Asn, Meharry Med Col; surgicalb staffs Lutheran Med Ctr; St Vincent's Med Ctr; St Luke's Hosp; adv bd, Cleveland Found; bd trustees, Summer Music Exp; life mem, Nat Asn Advan Colored People; PUSH; Am Urol Asn; Wva State Med Asn. **Honors/Awds:** Physician of the Year, Polyclinic Hosp Reunion. **Home Addr:** 2599 N Pk Blvd, Cleveland, OH 44106, **Home Phone:** (216)321-7297. **Business Addr:** Urology Specialist, United Hospital Center, 327 Med Pk Dr, Bridgeport, WV 26330, **Business Phone:** (681)342-1000.

### FRANKLIN, DR. HAROLD A.
Educator, executive. **Personal:** married Lilla M Sherman. **Educ:** Ala State Univ, govt & psychol, 1962; Univ Denver, Grad Sch Int Studies, MA, 1974; Auburn Univ, BA, hist; Univ Denver, MA, hist; Tufts Univ; Bradeis Univ. **Career:** Educator (retired); mgr; Ala State Univ, teacher, 1965; Tuskegee Inst, 1965-68; NC Agr & Tech State Univ, instr, 1969, vis prof, 1970; Ala Serv Ctr Black Elected Off, dir, 1969-70; Talladega Col, asst prof, 1968-92; Tuskegee Inst; Terry's Metrop Mortuary, mgr, currently. **Orgs:** Pres, Nat Asn Advan Colored People; E AL Planning Comn; Talladega County Overall Econ Comn; Black Coalition Talladega; Ala Dem Conf Boy Scouts Am; Ci tizen's Conf Pub Affairs; Ala Hist Comn Bd Adv; Ala League Adv Educ; treas, Star Zion AMEZion Ch; bd adv, Community Life Inst; Ala Crt Higher Edn; Ala Coun Human Rels; HAFS. **Honors/Awds:** Hon Doctorate Sigma Rho Sigma Honor Soc; Community Leadership & service Award; Phi Alpha Theta Int Honor Soc Hist; DAH, Auburn Univ. **Special Achievements:** First African-American to enroll at Auburn University, 1964. **Home Addr:** 1429 Autumn Lane C, Sylacauga, AL 35150-1625, **Home Phone:** (256)249-3378. **Business Addr:** Manager, Terry's Metrop Mortuary, 1702 Battle St W, Talladega, AL 35160, **Business Phone:** (256)362-2421.

### FRANKLIN, DR. HERMAN
School administrator. **Personal:** Born May 1, 1935, Mays Lick, KY; son of Arthur (deceased) and Margaret Taber (deceased); married LaRaeu Ingram; children: Stephen LaMonte. **Educ:** Ky State Univ, BS, 1960; Tuskegee Univ, MS, 1964; Ohio State Univ, PhD, 1973. **Career:** School administrator (retired); Ala Coop Exten Serv, asst agt, 1963-64; Tuskegee Inst, dir adult educ res proj, 1964-66; Ala State Off Econ Opportunity, Ala tech asst corp dir, 1966-70; City Tuskegee, AL, ex dir model cities, 1970-71; Ohio State Univ, Off Minority Affairs, admin assoc, 1971-73; Tenn State Univ, asst prof ext cont educ, 1973-74; Tuskegee Inst, dean studs, 1974-77; Southern Assoc Cols & Schs, consult, 1976-81; Gene Carter & Assoc, consult, evaluator, 1981-83; Mid States Asn Cols & Schs, consult, 1981-99; US Dept Educ, consult, 1982-83; Univ Md, vpres stud affairs, 1977-99, sr vpres, 1999-2001. **Orgs:** Charter mem & bd dir, chair, Pub Comn, Optimist Int; Lions Int, 1968-70; vice chair bd, JJ Ashburn Jr Youth Ctr, 1970-73; chair comn, Chamber Com, Tuskegee, 1970, 1974-77; bd dir exec, bd vpres, Chamber Com, 1975-77, 1976; presenter, Stud Servs Inst, 1979-80; presenter, Nat Asn Equal Opport Higher Educ, 1979-80; exec bd, Boy Scouts Am, 1984-. **Honors/Awds:** Graduate Fellowship, Tuskegee Inst, 1962-63; grad assistantship, Ohio State Univ, 1971-73; Patriotic Civilian Award, Tuskegee Inst ROTC, 1976; century mem, Boy Scouts Am, 1976, 1977; Outstanding Service Award, Lower Shore Asn Coun & Develop, 1983-84; Honorary Trustee Del-Mar-Va Council, Boy Scouts Am, 1985 & 1995; Boss of the Year, Bay Shore Chap, 1991; Distinguished Black Marylanders Award, 1999; Northeast Alumni Achiever, Tuskee Univ, 2001. **Home Addr:** 4743 Stratford Ct, Salisbury, MD 21804-2701, **Home Phone:** (410)341-6636.

### FRANKLIN, J. E.
Writer. **Personal:** Born Aug 10, 1937, Houston, TX; daughter of Robert and Mathie Randle; children: Olff & Malika. **Educ:** Univ Tex, Austin, BA, 1960; Union Theol Sem, 1973. **Career:** Playwright, 1964-; Freedom Sch, Carthage, Miss, primary sch teacher, summer, 1964; Neighborhood House, Buffalo, NY, youth dir, 1964-65; US Off Econ Opportunity New York, analyst, 1967-68; Univ New York, Herbert H Lehman Col, New York, lectr, 1969-75; Zora Neale Hurston Writer's Workshop of the New Fed Theatre, New York, NY, dir, 1970; Skidmore Col, Saratoga Springs, dir, 1979-80; Brown Univ, Providence, resident playwright, 1983-89; Harlem Sch of the Arts, fac mem, 1990-; Blackgirl Ensemble Theatre, founder & artistic dir, 1990-; Author: A First Step to Freedom, 1964; The In-Crowd, 1965; Mau Mau Room; Black Girl, play & film, 1971; The Prodigal Sister, 1976; Where Dewdrops of Mercy Shine Bright, 1983; Borderline Fool, 1988; Christchild, 1992. **Orgs:** Dramatists Guild, 1971-; fel Nat Endowment Arts, 1979; fel Rockefeller found, 1980. **Honors/Awds:** Media Women Award, 1971; Drama Desk Award, The Drama Desk, 1971; Dramatic Arts Award, Howard Univ, 1974; The Better Boys Foundation Playwriting Award, 1978; The Ajabei Children's Theater Annual Award, 1978; NEA Award, Nat Endowment, for the Arts, 1979; Rockefeller Award, Rockefeller Found, 1980; Writers Guild Award, Writers Guild Am, E, 1981. **Business Addr:** Writer, Victoria Lucas Associates, 888 7th Ave Suite 401, New York, NY 10019, **Business Phone:** (212)489-8008.

### FRANKLIN, JAMES E.
Football coach. **Personal:** Born Feb 2, 1972, Langhorne, PA; married Fumi Franklin; children: Ava & Addison Franklin. **Educ:** E Stroudsburg (Pa) Univ, BS, psychol, 1995; Wash State Univ, MA, educ leadership, 1999. **Career:** Kutztown (PA) Univ, Wide Receiver Coach, 1995-96; E Stroudsburg (PA) Univ, NCAA Div 2 Football Team, cornerback & safety coach, 1996; James Madison Univ, NCAA Div 1 Football Team, wide receiver coach, 1997; Wash State Univ, NCAA Football Team, tight end coach, 1998; Idaho State Univ, NCAA Football Team, wide receiver coach, 1999; Univ Md, NCAA Football Team, wide receiver coach, 2000-04, offensive coordr, asst. head coach, 2008-10; Green Bay Packers, NFL Team, wide receiver coach, 2005; Kans State Univ, NCAA Football Team, offensive coordr, 2006-07; Vanderbilt Univ, NCAA Football Team, head football coach, 2011-13; Penn State, 2014-. **Special Achievements:** First African American to be head coach of a major sport at Vanderbilt. **Business Addr:** Head football coach, Penn State Nittany Lions football, 204 Multi-Sport Facility, University Park, PA 16802, **Business Phone:** (814)865-0561.

### FRANKLIN, KIRK DWAYNE
Singer, actor. **Personal:** Born Jan 26, 1970, Ft. Worth, TX; married Tammy Renee Collins; children: Kerrion, Carrington, Kennedy & Caziah. **Career:** Mt Rose Baptist Church, minister music, 1981; Greater, Stronger Rest MBC, minister music, 1988; Grace Temple SDA Church, musician, 1988; wrotematerial & performed on I Will Let Nothing Separate Me, DFW Mass Choir, 1991, Live in Indianapolis, GMWA Nat Mass Choir, 1993; Albums: Gospo-Centric, 1993; He Say, She Say But What Does God Say?, 1995; R Kelly album, 1995; Kirk Franklin & The Family Christmas; Whatcha Lookin' 4, 1996; Produced album by gospel group, God's Property, God's Property from Kirk Franklin's Nu Nation, 1997; Any Given Sunday, 1999; Get on the Bus, 1999; Tour of Life; The Rebirth of Kirk Franklin, 2002; Hero, 2005; Kirk Franklin Presents: Songs for the Storm, Vol 1, 2006; Norbit, 2007; The Fight of My Life, 2007; Singles: "Looking For You", 2005; "Imagine Me", 2006; Declaration (This is It), 2007; Films: Kirk Franklin: The NuNation Tour, 1999; Sweating in the Spirit, 2005; TV: "Sister, Sister", 1998; "Something to Sing About", 2000; "Boycott", 2001; "The ProudFamily", 2003; "Access Hollywood", 2007; "Sunday Best", 2007, "Hello Fear", 2011; "Marvin Sapp"; "Mali Music"; "Marvin Winans"; "John P Kee"; "Rance Allen"; 22nd AnnualStellar Gospel Music Awards. **Business Addr:** Gospel Vocalist, c/o Gospo-Centric Records, 421 E Beach St, Inglewood, CA 90302, **Business Phone:** (310)677-5603.

### FRANKLIN, DR. LANCE STONESTREET
School administrator, executive director. **Personal:** Born Jul 3, 1962, Chicago, IL; son of Lawrence and Carrene Stonestreet; married Anita Valentina Martin; children: Lance Jabraan & Ian Jamaal. **Educ:** Wayne State Univ, BA, chem, 1986, MS, occup & environ health sci, 1988, PhD, civil & environ engineering, 1990; Harvard Univ Sch Pub Health, radiation safety, 2006. **Career:** Detroit Edison, asst indust hyg technician, 1986-87; Wayne Co Med Examr, chemist, 1987-88; Chrysler Corp, res assoc, 1988; Wayne State Univ, dir & radiation safety officer, 1988-2008; Franklin Environ Group, chief exec officer, 2005-08; KCP Found, fel, 1989; Va Tech, Environ Health, Safety & Res Support, dir, 2008-, asst vpres, 2016-. **Orgs:** ACGIH, 1989; Freemason, F&AM, PHA, 1990; Nat Asn Advan Colored People, 1992; AIHA Toxicol Community, 1992; bd mem, Samaritan Non-Profit Housing Asn, 1993; bd mem, Univ Dist Asn, 1995; Wayne Co Interview Bd, 1995; Omega Psi Phi, Fraternity; C Ctr, Black Family Develop; C's Inst Mich; Nat Safety Coun; Am Chem Socs; Socs Res Adminr; Wayne States Environ Health Acad Adv Comt; Nat Safety Couns Campus Safety Asn; chair, Wayne States Environ Sustainability Comt; treas, Campus Safety Health & Environ Mgt Asn, 1988-2014. **Honors/Awds:** Complete Program Award, Nat Safety Couns Campus Safety Div; Omega Phi Psi Scholar, 1985; Quality of Service Award, Wayne State Univ, 1993; Certificate of Congratulations, Off Govt, MI, 1993; Spirit of Detroit Award, City Detroit, 1993; King Chavez Park Scholar, State Mich. **Special Achievements:** Author: "Maudsley Reactive & Nonreactive Rats: Performance in an Operant Conflict Paradigm", Physiology & Behavior, Vol 72, 1992. **Home Addr:** 18084 Oak Dr, Detroit, MI 48221, **Home Phone:** (313)862-3865. **Business Addr:** Director, Virginia Tech, 675 Res Ctr Dr, Blacksburg, VA 24061, **Business Phone:** (540)231-9044.

### FRANKLIN, LINDA CHERYL KENNEDY
Journalist, business owner, radio broadcaster. **Personal:** Born Oct 7, 1950, Brooklyn, NY; daughter of Adam C Falcon and Marjorie J Edwards; married Lonnie; children: Kennedy M. **Educ:** Univ Nebr, attended 1969; Macalester Col, BA, psychol, sec educ, 1972. **Career:** KOLN/KGIN-TV Lincoln, intern, 1968; KMTV Omaha, news intern, 1968; KOWH-AM Radio Omaha, pub affairs mgr, 1972-73; WOW-AM Radio Omaha, news reporter, 1973-74; KGW AM Portland, news reporter, anchor, 1974-76; KING-TV Seattle, news reporter, anchor, 1976-92; LK Media, owner, 2000-; Seattle King County Pub Health, commun mgr, 1992-2001; Urban League Metrop Seattle, Educ Dept, prog mgr, 2006-10; James Wash Found & Cult Ctr, Mkt & Outreach, prog dir, 2012. **Orgs:** Seattle pres, AFTRA, 1976-; Nat Asn Advan Colored People, 1980-91; Am Fed TV & Radio Artists, local bd mem, 1988, nat bd mem, 1991; Nat Asn Black Journalists, 1989-; Tabor 100, Seattle, WA, grant adminr, 2013-14. **Honors/Awds:** Spot News Reporting Award, Sigma Delta Chi NW, 1979, 1983, 1988, 1990; Wash Educ Asn, Best Special Doc, 1990; Emmy Nomination, Outstanding Biog Doc, Natl Acad TV Arts & Sci, 1990. **Home Addr:** 403 8 45th Ave SW, Seattle, WA 98116. **Business Addr:** Reporter, Anchor, KING-TV, PO Box 24545, Seattle, WA 98124, **Business Phone:** (206)448-3875.

### FRANKLIN, MARTHA LOIS
Computer scientist. **Personal:** Born Nov 14, 1956, Nacogdoches, TX; daughter of William Sanders Jr and Ida Smith Sanders. **Educ:** Prairie View A&M Univ, Prairie View, Tex, BS, 1980; Am Inst Banking, Houston, Tex, 1987. **Career:** Texaco USA, Houston, Tex, programmer analyst, 1980-83; Gulf Oil Corp, Houston, Tex, sr bus analyst, 1983-85; City Houston, Houston, Tex, sr programmer analyst, 1985-86; Pennzoil Co, Houston, Tex, sr syst analyst, 1988-; Tex Com Bank, Houston, Tex, sr programmer analyst, Software Design, vpres, 1989-. **Orgs:** Ski Jammers, 1985-89; pres, Black Data Processing Assoc, Houston, TX, 1985-89; Houston Educ Asn Reading & Training, 1987-89, 1987-89, fin secy, 1990, Alpha Kappa Alpha, Omicron Tau Omega; Prairie View A&M Alumni, 1988-89; Toastmasters, 1989; vpres, Software Design, 1989; bd dir, United Negro Col Fund, Houston, TX, 1989-90. **Honors/Awds:** Nat Outstanding Sr, 1975; Member of the Year, Black Data Processing, Black Data Processing Assocs, 1990. **Home Addr:** 12101 Steeple Way Blvd Suite 602, Houston, TX 77065, **Home Phone:** (713)894-8320. **Business Addr:** Senior System Analyst, Pennzoil Co, 700 Milam Pennzoil Pl 9th Fl, Houston, TX 77002, **Business Phone:** (713)546-4178.

### FRANKLIN, OLIVER ST. CLAIR, JR.
Executive, financial manager. **Personal:** Born Oct 30, 1945, Washington, DC; son of Rev Oliver St Clair Sr and Hyla Turner; married Patricia E Mikols; children: Julien K. **Educ:** Lincoln Univ, BA, econs & lib arts, 1966; Edinburgh Univ, dipl, 1967; Oxford Univ, Balliol Col, Woodrow Wilson fel, 1970. **Career:** Univ Penn, Annenberg Ctr, Philadelphia, dir, 1972-77; independent film producer & critic, 1977-84; City Philadelphia, dep city rep, 1984-89; independent publ, 1989-; Hon Brit Consulate, hon consul, 1998-; RISA Investment Adv, founding partner, 1999-2003; Right Mgt Consult Inc, dir, 2001-; Int House Philadelphia, pres & chief exec officer, 2003-08; Franklin Investment Group, partner, 2008-; Electronic Ink Inc, vice chmn, 2009-; Pilgrim, Baxter, Greig & Assocs, Wayne, PA, vpres; Civil War Mus Philadelphia, co founder. **Orgs:** Pres, Philadelphia Chap, Oxford & Cambridge Soc, 1985-; bd mem, Opera Co Philadelphia, 1985-; bd mem, Afro-Am Hist & Cult Mus, 1985-; bd mem, Inst Contemp Art, 1986-; vpres, Int Protocol Asn, 1987-; bd adv, First Com Bank Philadelphia, 1989-; Franklin Inn, 1989; chair emer, City Fels, 1990; planning comt mem, Nat Asn Security Prof, 1990-; bd mem, Dynamis Therapeut, 2003; chair & bd gov, Civil War Mus Philadelphia, 2004; chmn, Acad Funds Trust Innovator McKinley Income Fund, 2007; chmn, Acad Asset Mgt, 2010; trustee, Philadelphia Found; trustee, Rosenbach Mus & Libr; trustee, Global Interdependence Ctr; trustee, S African Environ Trust; trustee, Sir Hans Koopler Trust, NY; dep dir pub affairs, Gov's Comn, Md; trustee, Phil Foundn; pres, Philadelphia Chap Oxford; pres, Cambridge Soc; chief trade & investment advisor, Brit Hon Coun; bd mem, Acad Asset Mgt; chmn, Acad Funds Trust Innovator Matrix Income Fund; Nat Asn Securities Professionals; Philadelphia Securities Asn; bd advisors, Genisys Group; pres, Philadelphia Chap Oxford & Cambridge Soc. **Honors/Awds:** Volunteer of the Year, Vol Action Coun, 1988; Distinguished Alumni, Nat Asn Equal Opportunity Higher Educ, 1989. **Home Addr:** 4023 Apalogen Rd, Philadelphia, PA 19129-5501, **Home Phone:** (215)844-4344. **Business Addr:** Vice Chairman, Electronic Ink Inc, 1 S Broad St 19th Fl, Philadelphia, PA 19107, **Business Phone:** (215)922-3800.

### FRANKLIN, PRESTONIA D. (ANU PRESTONIA)
Business owner. **Personal:** Born Mar 26, 1957, Portsmouth, VA; daughter of Preston and Barbara; married Joseph II. **Educ:** Howard Univ, attended 1978; Pac Sch Orient Med, Acupuncture, 2000; Integral Yoga Inst, Yoga Instr, 2002. **Career:** Khamit Kinks Inc, pres & founder, 1979-2008, consult, 1981-; Mexic Arte, Client, 2010. **Orgs:** Curriculum comt mem, Int Braiders Network. **Honors/Awds:** Recognition Award, Nat Braiders Guild, 1989; Best Conrows Award, Uhuru Sasa, 1979; Best Creation Award, Robert Fiance Beauty Sch, 1986; Bronner Bros, trend setters, 1990-91; Nat Braiders Guild Recognition Award, Wash, DC, 1995; Bronner Brothers Braiders Competition 1st & 2nd place, Atlanta, Ga, 1996; Bronner Brothers Braiders Competition 1st place, Fla, 1998; Natural Hair Stylist Hall of Fame Award, 2002; Women in the Black WIB nBus 2002 Award, 2002. **Special Achievements:** Cover of Essence Magazine, Angela Bassett's hair, Dec, 1992; Conver sesneaker commercial, En Vogue's hair, 1993; Clairol styling for black market, 1992; Hype Hair, September cover, 1994; And Daring Dos: A History of Extraordinary Hair, 1994; Celebrity makeup artist's Sam Fine's Fine Beauty: Beauty Basics and Beyond for African-American Women, 1999; Miki Taylor's Self-Seduction: Your Ultimate Path to Inner and Outer Beauty, 2003; The International Hairstyle Index, 2003. **Business Addr:** Founder, President, Khamit Kinks Inc, 400 Atlantic Ave, Brooklyn, NY 11201, **Business Phone:** (718)422-2600.

### FRANKLIN, DR. RENTY BENJAMIN
Educator, association executive, physiologist. **Personal:** Born Sep 2, 1945, Birmingham, AL; son of George and Pinkie; married Theresa C Langston; children: LaTania & Omari. **Educ:** Morehouse Col, BS, 1966; Atlanta Univ, MS, 1967; Howard Univ, PhD, 1972. **Career:** NSF, Med Educ Prog, grant reviewer; Morehouse Col, consult admis com; Atlanta Univ Ctr, pre-baccalaureate; Robert Wood Johnson Found, cons; NIH Cons St Augustine's Col, instr, 1967-69; Howard Univ Col Med, asst prof, 1972-77, Res fel, 1974; Univ MD Dent Sch, Dept Biomed Sci, assoc prof, 1980-86, Dept Physiology, prof, 1986-, Molecular & Cell Biol Track, dir, currently. **Orgs:** Sigma Xi Soc; Am Physiol Soc; AAAS; NY Acad Scis; Endocrinal Soc; Reproductive Endocrinol Study Sect, 1992-96, 2002-04, NIH Sci Rev Group, chmn, 1994-96, Integrative & Clin Endocrinol & Reproduction Study Sect, 2004-05. **Honors/Awds:** Outstanding Faculty Research Award, Howard Univ Col Med, 1976; Howard Hughes-Morehouse Distinguished Scientist Award, 1994; Distinguished African American Scientists of the 20th Century, 1996. **Special Achievements:** Author of over 100 science articles & abstracts. **Business Addr:** Professor, Director, University Maryland, Rm 4 E 36A 666 W Baltimore St, Baltimore, MD 21201, **Business Phone:** (410)706-7259.

### FRANKLIN, DR. REV. ROBERT MICHAEL, JR.
College president. **Personal:** Born Feb 22, 1954, Chicago, IL; son of Robert Michael and Lee Ethel; married Cheryl Diane Goffney; children: Imani Renee, Robert Michael III & Julian Michael DeShazier. **Educ:** Morehouse Col, BA, polit sci, 1975; Univ Durham, Eng, post grad studies; Harvard Univ Divinity Sch, MDiv, 1978; Univ Chicago, PhD, ethics, soc, relig & social sci, 1985. **Career:** FTE BE Mays fel, 1975-78; St Paul Church God Christ, asst pastor, 1978-84; St Bernards Hosp, prot chaplain, 1979-81; Prairie St Col, instr psychol, 1981; Univ

Chicago, instr rels & psychol, field ed dir, 1981-83; Harvard Univ, Divinity Sch, assoc dir ministerial studies, 1984-85, vis lectr ministry & Afro-Am relig, 1986-88; Colgate Rochester Divinity Sch, dean & prof black church studies, 1985-89; Emory Univ, Candler Sch Theol, asst prof, 1989-91, dir black church studies, 1989-, assoc prof ethics & soc, 1991, presidential distinguished prof social ethics, 2004-07, sr advisor community & diversity; Ford Found, Rights & Social Justice, prog dir, 1995-; Interdenominational Theol Ctr, pres, 1997-2002; Morehouse Col, pres, 2007-12, pres emer, currently; Stanford Univ's Martin Luther King, Jr. Res & Educ Inst, vis scholar. **Orgs:** Phi Beta Kappa, Morehouse Col, 1975; Am Acad Relig; Soc Sci Study Rels; Asn Sociol Rels; Soc Study Black Rels; asst pastor, life long mem, St Paul Church God. **Honors/Awds:** Honorary Degree, Bethune Cookman Univ, Bates Col & Swarthmore Col. **Special Achievements:** Publications: Criterion 1984; The Iliff Review 1985, Union Seminary Qtrly Review, 1986, Liberating Visions: Human Fulfillment and Social Justice in African-American Thought, Augsburg Fortress Press, 1990; "Crisis in the Village: Restoring Hope in African American Communities", 2007. **Business Addr:** President Emeritus, Morehouse College, 830 W View Dr S W, Atlanta, GA 30314, **Business Phone:** (404)681-2800.

### FRANKLIN, SHIRLEY CLARKE (SHIRLEY CLARKE)

Educator, chief executive officer, mayor. **Personal:** Born May 10, 1945, Philadelphia, PA; daughter of Eugene Haywood Clarke and Ruth Lyons White; married David McCoy; children: Kai Ayanna, Cabral Holsey & Kali Jamilla. **Educ:** Howard Univ, Wash, DC, BA, sociol, 1968; Univ Pa, Philadelphia, PA, MA, sociol, 1969. **Career:** US Dept Labor, Wash DC, contract officer, 1966-68; Talladega Col, Talladega AL, instr, 1969-71; City Atlanta, Atlanta, dir, comnr cult affairs, 1978-81, city mgr, chief admin officer, 1982-90, exec officer opers, 1990-91, Atlanta Comt Olympic Games, sr vpres external rels, 1991-97; A Brown Olmstead & Assoc, partner, 1996-; Shirley Clarke Franklin & Assoc, founder & chief exec officer, 1997-98; Urban Environ Solutions LLC, partner, 1998; GA Reg Trans Auth, vice-chair, 1999-2000; City Atlanta, mayor, 2002-10; Blogging While Blue, founder; Spelman Col, chair, 2011; Univ Tex, LBJ Sch Pub Affairs, vis prof ethics & polit values, currently. **Orgs:** Trustee, Atlanta Symphony Orchestra, 1977-81; GA Coun Arts, Atlanta, 1979-82; fel Atlanta Found, 1980; chmn, Abbr Arts Panel, Nat Endowment Arts, Wash, DC, 1980-82; bd dir, Nat Urban Coalition, Wash, DC, 1980-83; adv bd, GA Womens Polit Caucus, Atlanta, 1982-84; bd trustee, Nat Black Arts Festival, Spelman Col; bd dir, Atlanta Life Ins Co; bd dir, United Way Atlanta; bd dir, Atlanta Chamber Com; bd dir, Carter Ctr; bd, E Lake Comm Found; Charles Drew Charter Sch; King Baudouin; US Found; Paideia Sch; Comm Found; Nat Forum Black Pub Adminrs; Delta Sigma Theta Sorority Inc; Atlanta Conv & Visitors Bur; co-chair, United Way Metrop Atlantas Regional Comn; chair, Nat Ctr Civil & Human Rights; Robert Wood Johnson Found; bd dir, Mueller Water Prod; bd dir, Delta Air Lines; bd dir, Volcker Alliance; Nat Ctr Transp Systs; Comn a Healthier Am; pres, Ga Munic Asn; pres, Nat Conf Dem Mayors; Nat Coun Black Mayors; Pan Atlantic Ga Regional Alliance; US Conf Mayors; Am Civil Liberties Union; Atlanta Develop Authority; Atlanta Jazz Festival; secy, Atlanta Regional Commision; Black United Fund; Ga Coalition Black Women; Girl Scouts; Jack & Jill; Neighborhood Arts Ctr; Radcliffe Presby Church; secy, Regional Comn; African Episcopal St Thomas; Links Inc; Un Inst Training & Res; bd chmn, chief exec officer, Purpose Built Communities, currently. **Special Achievements:** First African American female mayor in 2001, as well as the first woman to be a mayor of a major southern city. **Home Addr:** 1258 Tuckawanna Dr SW, Atlanta, GA 30311-3122, **Home Phone:** (404)699-0544. **Business Addr:** Chairman of the Board, Chief Executive Officer, Purpose Built Communities.

### FRANKLIN, TAMARA SIMPKINS

Media executive, vice president (organization). **Educ:** Yale Univ, BS, eng; Harvard Univ, MBA; Nat Asn Multi-Ethnicity Commun (NAMIC), Exec Leadership Develop Prog, attended 2008; WICT Betsy Magness Leadership Inst. **Career:** Motorola, dir new bus develop & strategic mkt; Turner Broadcasting Systs, vpres bus develop; Scripps Network Interactive, sr vpres affil opers & new media distrib, 2009-14, exec vpres, 2014-. **Orgs:** Bd Women, Cable Telecommunications & Digital Hollywood's Women's Entertainment & Technol. **Business Addr:** Executive Vice President, Scripps Network Interactive, Knoxville, TN.

**FRANKLIN, WILLIAM B.** **See Obituaries Section.**

### FRANKS, CREE SUMMER (CREE SUMMER)

Actor. **Personal:** Born Jul 7, 1969, Los Angeles, CA; daughter of Don Francks and Lili Red Eagle; married Angelo Pullens; children: 2. **Career:** Albums: Womb Amnesia, w/Subject to Change, 1993; Street Faerie, 1999; TV series actor: Inspector Gadget, 1983-84; Bay Cove, 1987; A Different World, 1988-93; Sweet Justice, 1994; Camp Lazlo, 2004; TV series, voice: Ewoks, 1985; Tiny Toon Adventures, 1990-92; Rugrats, 1991; Gargoyles, 1994; Problem Child, 1993; Freakazoid!, 1995; The Twisted Adventures of Felix the Cat, 1995; Mortal Kombat: The Animated Series, 1995; Jungle Cubs, 1996; Project GeeKeR, 1996; The Incredible Hulk, 1996; 101 Dalmatians: The Series, 1997; Pepper Ann, 1997; Mummies Alive!, 1997; Pinky, Elmyra & the Brain, 1998; Histeria!, 1998; Batman Beyond, 1999; Sabrina the Animated Series, 1999; The Weekenders, 2000; Teachers Pet, 2000; Clifford the Big Red Dog, 2000; As Told by Ginger, 2000; Codename: Kids Next Door, 2002; My Life as a Teenage Robot, 2003; All Grown Up, 2003; Star Wars: Clone Wars, 2003; WordGirl, 2007-14; Curious George, 2007-11; The Marvelous Misadventures of Flapjack, 2008; The Goode Family, 2009; Curious George 2: Follow That Monkey!, 2009; DJ & The Fro, 2009; Infamous, 2009; The Super Hero Squad Show, 2009-11; Mad, 2010; Batman: The Brave and the Bold, 2010; The Drawn Together Movie: The Movie!, 2010; "Thundercats", 2011-12; Scooby-Doo! Mystery Incorporated, 2011; The Looney Tunes Show, 2011; "Young Justice", 2011-12; Naruto: Shippuden, 2011; "The Cleveland Show", 2011; "Pound Puppies", 2011-13; "Dan Vs", 2011-12; "Good Vibes", 2011; "Superman of Tokyo", 2012; "Robot and Monster", 2012; "The High Fructose Adventures of Annoying Orange", 2013; "Thunder and Lightning", 2013; "Beware the Batman", 2013; "Henry Hugglemonster", 2013; "Xiaolin Chronicles", 2013-14; "Rick and Morty", 2014; "Kung Fu Panda: Legends of Awesomeness", 2014; "Ben 10: Omniverse", 2014; "Sheriff Callie's Wild West", 2014; "Marvel's Avengers Assemble", 2014; "The Tom and Jerry Show", 2014; "The Boondocks", 2014; "Breadwinners", 2014; TV movies, voice: The Rugrats: All Growed Up, 2001; A Rugrats Kwanzaa Special, 2001; Elise: Mere Mortal, 2002; Film actor: Wild Thing, 1987; Tuesday Morning Ride, 1995; Film voice: The Care Bears Movie, 1985; Care Bears II, 1986; Rugrats in Paris, 2000; Atlantis, 2001; Final Fantasy X, 2001; The Wild Thornberrys Movie, 2002; Rugrats Meet the Wild Thornberrys, 2003; Rugrats Go Wild, 2003; Final Fantasy X-2, 2003; Clifford's Really Big Movie, 2004; Strange Frame: Love & Sax, 2011; Star Wars: Detours, 2012. **Special Achievements:** Nominated for Emmy award. **Home Addr:** 9348 Civic Center Dr Suite 407, Beverly Hills, CA 90210. **Business Addr:** Actress, c/o William Morris Agency, 1 William Morris Pl, Beverly Hills, CA 90212, **Business Phone:** (310)859-4000.

### FRANKS, GARY ALVIN

Real estate developer, politician, government official. **Personal:** Born Feb 9, 1953, Waterbury, CT; son of Richard and Janery Petteway; married Donna Williams; children: Jessica & Gary Jr; children: Azia. **Educ:** Yale Univ, BA, 1975. **Career:** GAF Realty, Waterbury, CT, pres; Conn Bd Alderman, mem, 1986-90; US House Representatives CT, Fifth Dist, rep, 1991-97; Gary Alvin Assocs, partner, 1999-. **Orgs:** Dir, Waterbury Chamber Comm; dir, Waterbury YMCA; dir, Waterbury Am Red Cross; dir, Waterbury Found; dir, Waterbury Opportunities & Indust Ctr; Congressional Black Caucus. **Honors/Awds:** Outstanding Young Man, Boy's Club; Man of the Year, Prof Women's Asn, Waterbury. **Special Achievements:** First African-American Representative to be elected from Connecticut; featured in New York Times, Wall Str Jour, Wash Post Style Section, LA Times, Boston Globe, Newsweek, Time Mag & USA Weekend Mag; appeared Meet the Press, Face the Nation, 20/20, Larry King Live, Night line, Today Show, BET, Crossfire & Eye to Eye with Connie Chung. First black Republican in Congress in nearly 50 years. **Home Addr:** 110 Midwood Ave, PO Box 2743, Waterbury, CT 06708, **Home Phone:** (203)574-3618. **Business Addr:** Gary Alvin Associates LLC, 1717 K St NW, Washington, DC 20036, **Business Phone:** (202)508-1066.

### FRASER, GEORGE C.

Entrepreneur, chief executive officer, writer. **Personal:** Born May 1, 1945, Brooklyn, NY; son of Walter and Ida Mae Baldwin; married Nora Jean Spencer; children: Kyle & Scott. **Educ:** Dartmouth Col, Amos Tuck Sch Bus, cert, MBEP, 1996. **Career:** Procter & Gamble, mkt mgr, 1972-84; United Way, Cleveland, OH, dir mkt communs, 1984-87; Ford Motor Co, Detroit, Mich, minority dealer develop prog, 1987-89; Success Source Inc, Cleveland, OH, pres, 1988-; FraserNet Inc, Cleveland, OH, pres, chmn & chief exec officer, 1988-; Auth: Success Runs Our Race; Complete Guide to Effective Networking African Am Community; Race Success: Ten Best Bus Opportunities Blacks Am. **Orgs:** Bd trustee, Ohio Bldg Authority; 100 Black Men Am; Nat Black MBA Asn; founder, Nat Ann PowerNetworking Conf; chmn, Phoenix Village Acad. **Honors/Awds:** Nat Volunteer of the Year, UNCF, 1982, 1983; Commendation for Outstanding Community Service, Ohio Senate & House Rep, 1985; First Place Award of Achievement for Community Events, Success Net, 1989; Communicator of the Year Award, Black Media Workers Cleveland, 1990; Communicator of the Year Award, Cleveland Chapter, Nat Asn Black Journalists, 1990; Communication Excellence to Black Audiences Award, 1991; City of Cleveland, Minority Business Advocate of the Year, 1991; Black Achiever of the Year, Voices of Cleveland, 1992; Black Professional of the Year, Black Professionals Asn Cleveland, 1992; DHL, Jarvis Christian Col, 1999; Architects of the Village Award, Allstate Insurance, 2000; Manager of the Year, Procter & Gamble; Honorary Doctorate Degree of Philosophy, CICA Int Univ & Sem; Honorary Doctorate Degree of Philosophy, OVID Univ & Sem. **Special Achievements:** City Cleveland, George C Fraser Day, Feb 29, 1992; First National speaker to have 4 speeches selected (over 10 yrs) by Vital Speeches to be published worldwide; One of the Top 50 Power Brokers in Black America, Upscale Mag. **Home Addr:** 4192 Cedar Ave Suite 107, Cleveland, OH 44103, **Home Phone:** (216)464-3699. **Business Addr:** Chairman, Chief Executive Officer, FraserNet Inc, 2940 Noble Rd Suite 203, Cleveland Heights, OH 44121-2242, **Business Phone:** (216)691-6686.

### FRASER, DR. LEON ALLISON

Physician. **Personal:** Born Nov 15, 1921, Winchester, TN; son of Phil E Sr and Dora L Seward; married Elizabeth Louise Smith; children: Leon Jr & Keith. **Educ:** Fisk Univ, BA, 1948; Howard Univ Sch Med, MD, 1952. **Career:** Physician (retired); Homer G Phillips Hosp St Louis, intern, 1952-53, resident, 1953-56; NJ State Dept Health, pub health physician, 1958-72, dir chronic dis, 1972-75; Trenton NJ Pub Sch, Med dir, 1982-94; pvt pract internal med, 1956-93. **Orgs:** Mercer Med Ctr Hosp Staff, 1956-; Mercer Co & NJ Med Socs, 1958-; Nat Med Asn, 1965-; Am Pub Health Asn, 1970-; Harvard-Radcliffe Parent's Asn, 1971-; life mem, Nat Asn Advan Colored People; life mem, Kappa Alpha Psi; trustee, Father's Asn Lawrenceville Prep Sch, 1972-75; Grand Boule Sigma Pi Phi Frat, 1986-; life mem, AMA. **Honors/Awds:** Alumni Achievement Award, Kappa Alpha Psi, 1968; published article: "Huntington's Chorea, Case Study", 1966; singles tennis champion, Mercer County Med Soc, 1982; golden merit award, Med Soc NJ, 2002. **Home Addr:** 421 Masterson Ct, Trenton, NJ 08618-1440, **Home Phone:** (609)882-5607.

### FRASER, THOMAS EDWARDS

Lawyer, executive. **Personal:** Born Sep 16, 1944, New York, NY; son of Thomas Augustus (deceased) and Vera Edwina; married Regina Stewart; children: Helena, Steven & David. **Educ:** Univ Wis, BS, 1969, MS, 1973; Univ Wis Law Sch, JD, 1979. **Career:** Pub Serv Comn Wis, legal clerk, 1977-79; United Airlines Inc, sr coun, 1979-; Stewart Collection Mkt, exec vpres, secy & gen coun, 1996-; Staridea Inc, coun, 1999-. **Orgs:** State Bar Wis, 1979-; State Bar Ill, 1979-; Ill Coun Col Attendance, 1984. **Honors/Awds:** America Best & Brightest, Dollar and Sense Mag, 1992. **Home Addr:** 6101 N Sheridan Rd Suite 16A, Chicago, IL 60660-2870, **Home Phone:** (773)743-3675. **Business Addr:** Senior Counsel, United Airlines Inc, 1200 E Algonquin Rd, Chicago, IL 60007, **Business Phone:** (847)700-4000.

### FRASIER, RALPH KENNEDY

Banker, lawyer, association executive. **Personal:** Born Sep 16, 1938, Winston-Salem, NC; son of Leroy B and Kathryn Kennedy; married Jeannine Marie Quick; children: Karen Denise F Alston, Gail S F Cox, Ralph K Jr, Keith L, Marie K & Rochelle D. **Educ:** Univ NC, 1958; NC Cent Univ, BS, com, 1962; NC Cent Univ, Sch Law, JD, 1965. **Career:** Wachovia Bank & Trust Co, Winston-Salem, NC, legal asst, 1965-66, asst secy, 1966-68, asst vpres, 1968-69, vpres, coun, 1969-70; Wachovia, vpres, coun, 1970-75; Huntington Nat Bank, Columbus, OH, exec vpres, gen coun, 1975-76, sr vpres, gen coun, 1976-83, secy, 1981-98, exec vpres, gen coun, secy, cashier, 1983-98, dir, 1998-2004; Huntington Bancshares Inc, gen coun, 1975-98, secy, 1981-98; Porter Wright Morris & Arthur LLP, atty, 1998-; Adatom.com Inc, dir, 1999-2001; Fraiser & Fraiser, Pa, Durham, NC, atty, 2001-; Columbus Bar Found, fel; Sigma Pi Phi Fraternity Inc, Brawley Fel. **Orgs:** NCA State Bar, 1965-; Nat Bar Asn, 1965-; trustee, Am Bar Asn, 1965-; vice chmn, Winston-Salem Transit Authority, 1968-74; chmn, 1974-75; OH Bar asn, 1976-; Columbus Bar Asn, 1976-; Columbus Urban League Inc, 1987-94; Greater Columbus Arts Coun, trustee, 1986-94; Riverside Methodist Hosps Found Inc, trustee, 1989-90; trustee, Grant Med Ctr; trustee, Grant/Riverside Methodist Hosp, 1996-97; vice chmn, 1995; chmn, 1996; treas, 1998-; Ohio Bd Regents; trustee, NC Cent Univ, 1994-2001; trustee, Nat Judicial col, Reno, Nev, 1996-; dir, Ohio HTH Corp, 1997; treas, 1998-2004; trustee OCLC Online Comput Libr Ctr Inc, Dublin OH, 1999; Nat Coun Col Law, Ohio State Univ; dir, Blackout Media Corp; dir, Columbus Found; bd mem, Directions Youth; bd mem, Inroads Columbus Inc; bd mem, Appalachian State Univ; bd mem, Nc Cent Univ; bd mem, Nc Family Serv Inc; bd mem, Community Mutual Ins Co; life mem, NAACP; life mem, Alpha Phi Alpha Fraternity Inc. **Honors/Awds:** Ritter Award, Ohio State Bar Found, 2002. **Home Addr:** 392 Walnut Cliffs Dr, Columbus, OH 43213-3531, **Home Phone:** (614)866-4652. **Business Addr:** Attorney, Porter Wright Morris & Arthur LLP, 3100 Huntington Ctr 41 S High St, Columbus, OH 43215-6194, **Business Phone:** (614)227-2125.

### FRAZER, DR. EVA LOUISE

Physician. **Personal:** Born Jun 30, 1957, St. Louis, MO; daughter of Charles Rivers Jr and Louise J Richardson Forrest; married Steven Craig Roberts; children: Steven Craig Roberts II, Christian Roberts & Darci Roberts. **Educ:** Univ Mo, BA, MD, 1981; PhD. **Career:** Mayo Grad Sch Med, intern, residency, 1984; St Mary's Health Ctr, physician, 1984-89; Barnes Care, physician, 1990, dir; pvt pract intern; Univ Mo, cur, 1984-90. **Orgs:** Nat Med Asn, 1984-; St Mary's Found Fund Bd; trustee, St Louis Univ; bd trustee, St Louis Art Mus, currently. **Honors/Awds:** Kaiser Merit Award; Univ Mo Alumni Award, 1985; UMKC School of Medicine Alumni Acheivement Award, 1985; Alumni Service Award, Univ Mo, 1994. **Home Addr:** 401 Pine St, Saint Louis, MO 63102. **Business Addr:** Board of Trustee, Saint Louis Art Museum, Forest Pk, 1 Fine Arts Dr, Saint Louis, MO 63110-1380, **Business Phone:** (314)721-0072.

### FRAZER, VICTOR O.

Lawyer. **Personal:** Born May 24, 1943, St. Thomas; son of Albert and Amanda Blyden; children: Kaaren Frazer-Crawford & Aileene. **Educ:** Fisk Univ, Nashville, TN, BA, 1964; Howard Univ Law Sch, JD, 1971. **Career:** Off Atty Gen DC, lawyer, 1974-78; Interstate Com Comn, lawyer; US Patent Off, lawyer; VI Water & Power Authority, gen coun, 1987-89; Congressman Mervyn Dymally, admin asst, 1989-91; Pvt Law Pract, 1991-; Mfr's Hanover Trust Co, banker; Comt Dist Columbia US House Rep, coun; One Hundred Fourth Cong, congressman, 1995-97; Manufacturers Hanover Trust Co, banking; Securtiy Trust Co; . **Orgs:** Nat Bar Asn; Am Bar Asn; Virgin Islands Bar, 1971; State Md Bar; State NY Bar; Dist Columbia Bar, 1971; Omega Psi Phi; coun, Comt DC. **Home Addr:** PO Box 5928, St. Thomas00803.

### FRAZIER, ADOLPHUS CORNELIOUS (AL FRAZIER)

Dean (education), football player. **Personal:** Born Mar 28, 1935, Jacksonville, FL; married Mary Charlene; children: Pamela & Eric. **Educ:** Fla A&M Univ, BS, 1968; Columbia Univ, MA, 1975. **Career:** Football player, assistant dean (retired); Toronto Argonauts, Can Football League, 1957; Ottawa Rough Riders, Can Football League, 1960; Denver Broncos Football Team, flanker back, kick returner, punt returner, 1961, kick returner, 1962, 1963; Lookout Mtn Sch Boys, prin supvr, 1964-67; York Col, City Univ NY, prof, dir financial aid, asst dean stud develop, asst dean, div inst advan, 2006; Reach Into Cult Heights Inc, chmn. **Orgs:** Nat Asn Advan Colored People, 1979; bd dir, Community Bd 12, 1979-; Rochdale Village, 1981; Jamaica Arts Ctr, 1982. **Honors/Awds:** Grey Cup champion, 1960; Delegate Queens City Judicial Conv, 1976-84; Sports Hall of Fame, Fla A&M Univ, 1979; Campaign Aide Pres Carter, 1980; Community Service Award, SO zone Park Women Asn, 1981; Elected Dist Leader 32nd Assembly Dist Queens Co NYC. **Home Addr:** 17240 133rd Ave, Jamaica, NY 11434, **Home Phone:** (718)723-2087.

### FRAZIER, CHARLES DOUGLAS (CHARLIE FRAZIER)

Educator, athletic coach. **Personal:** Born Aug 12, 1939, Houston, TX; son of Rebecca Brown; married Betty Alridge. **Educ:** Tex Southern Univ, BS, 1964, MS, 1975. **Career:** Football player (retired), coach; Houston Oilers & New Eng Patriots, prof football player, 1962-70; Rice Univ, receivers coach, 1975; Tex Christian Univ, receivers coach, 1976; Univ Tulsa, receivers coach, 1976; Houston Independent Sch Dist, asst football coach, reciever, currently. **Orgs:** Football Coaching Asn; Hiram Clark Civic Club; Houston Coaches Asn; Nat Asn Intercollegiate Athletics. **Home Addr:** 4018 Brookston St, Houston, TX 77045, **Home Phone:** (713)729-6171. **Business Addr:** Assistant Football Coach, Houston Independent School District, 4400 W 18th St, Houston, TX 77092-8501, **Business Phone:** (713)556-6005.

### FRAZIER, CLIFF

Writer, television producer, executive director. **Personal:** Born Aug 27, 1934, Detroit, MI; son of Larney and Willie Mae; children: Marcus & Aliya Noel. **Educ:** Wayne State Univ, BA, theatre, 1957. **Career:** Community Film Workshop Coun, exec dir, 1968-74; Third World Cinema, admin, 1972-78; Inst New Cinema Artists, exec dir/pres,

1976-86; Commun Indust Skills Ctr, dir, 1987-91; Owens Commun's, vpres, 1991-94; NY Metrop Martin Luther King Jr Ctr Nonviolence, exec dir, 1994-; Co-author: Arts Educ & the Urban Subculture, US Dept of HEW, 1967; Author: Talking Cinematically, 20th Century Fox, 1974; Discovery in Drama, Paulist Press, 1969; New York Metrop Martin Luther King, exec dir; Harriet Tubman Charter Sch, chair; Jr. Ctr Nonviolence, exec dir; Int Commun Asn Inc, founder & pres. **Orgs:** Comnr, Black Leadership comn on AIDS, 1996-; secy, African-Am Legal Defense & Educ Fund, 1997-; bd, Cable TV's Manhattan Neighborhood Network, 1998-; founder & pres, Int Communs Asn, 1990-; bd mem, chair, New Fed Theatre, 2001-; bd, Habitat for Humanity, 2002-; co-founder, chair, Harriet Tubman Charter Sch, 2002; chmn, bd mem, Dwyer Cult Ctr; founder, Immigration & U.S. Citizenship Prog. **Honors/Awds:** Man Borough Pres, Cliff Frazier Day Proclamation, 1976; Distinguished Serv Award, Am Film Inst, 1978; Emmy Award, NY Acad TV Arts & Sci, 1984; Outstanding Service, Int Radio & Television Soc, 1986; Special Commemoration New York City Comptroller, 1995; Special Citation, New York State Assembly, 1998; InterNat Peace Award, Kobe, Japan, 2007. **Home Addr:** 337 W 138th St Suite 6D, New York, NY 10030, **Home Phone:** (212)281-2592. **Business Addr:** Executive Director, New York Metrop Martin Luther King Jr, 576 E 165th St, Bronx, NY 10456, **Business Phone:** (718)589-7858.

### FRAZIER, CLYDE. See FRAZIER, WALT, JR.

### FRAZIER, REV. DAN E., SR. (DANIEL E FRAZIER, SR.)
Government official, clergy. **Personal:** Born Dec 23, 1949, Ypsilanti, MI; son of Horace and Mattie; married Evangelist Ilean; children: Dennis, Sharron, Evelyn & Daniel Jr. **Educ:** Linfield Col; LaVerne Univ; Portland State Univ. **Career:** NY Life Ins Co, field underwriter, 1976-78; Dorite Gen Contractors, owner-operator, 1978-80; Carter Mem Church, assoc pastor, 1981-84; Abundant Life Ministries, pastor & founder, 1984-; City San Bernardino, city councilman, 1984-88. **Orgs:** Bd mem, San Bernardino Redevel Agency, 1983-; Nat Asn Advan Colored People San Bernardino; corp bd mem, San Bernardino Community Hosp; polit affairs chair, Inland Empire Interdenominational Ministrial Alliance. **Honors/Awds:** Million Dollar Round Table Club, NY Life Insurance Co; Brought first communtiy-based police station to the city of San Bernardino, 1983; Comn achiever, A Phillip Randolph Inst, San Bernardino Chapt; Chosen Most Influential Black Metropolitan Precinct Reporter in the Inland Empire, 1984. **Home Addr:** 1084 Western Ave, San Bernardino, CA 92411, **Home Phone:** (909)884-8375. **Business Addr:** City Councilman, City of San Bernardino, 300 N D St, San Bernardino, CA 92418, **Business Phone:** (951)543-3839.

### FRAZIER, EUFAULA SMITH
Executive director, teacher, chief executive officer. **Personal:** Born Oct 16, 1924, Dodge County, GA; married Arthur Lee; children: Maurice, Noland, Edwin & Michelle. **Educ:** Fla Int Univ, BS, 1977. **Career:** Atlanta Life Ins Co, underwriter, 1951-53; Little Nook Beauty Parlor, owner, 1956-67; Michelles Grocery, owner, 1962-; Tenant Educ Asn, Miami, exec dir; community organizer, 1967-77; Dade County Pub Schs, teacher, 1982-95; Community Polit Screening Panel Inc, Black Coalition Concerned Citizens Inc, pres, dir; Hialeah Heights Civic, Club Inc, pres; African Descent Task Force Inc, dir. **Orgs:** Dir, Fla Tenant's Org; consult, S Fla Hlth Task Force, 1973-; Model Cities Task Force, 1971; consult, Nat Welafare Rights Org, 1969-; exec com mem, Metro-Dade Co Dem Comt, 1974; co-host, Dem Nat Conv, 1972; People's Coalition, 1972-; plng adv, Coun Countinuing Educ Women, 1971-74; Brownsville CAA, 1964-74; facilitator, Radical Relat Inst, 1973-74; dir, Tenant Educ Info Ctr, 1974; comm organizer, Family Health Ctr, 1969-72; Nat Asn Advan Colored People, 1972-77; Legal Serv Miami, 1974-77; Ment Health, 1975-77; alt Nat Dem Party Conv, 1976; chief exec officer, Beulah A G Smith Scholar Found, 2003. **Home Addr:** 4900 NW 32nd Ave, Miami, FL 33142-4138, **Home Phone:** (305)634-4479. **Business Addr:** Owner, Director, Michelles Grocery, 4929 NW 17th Ave, Miami, FL 33142, **Business Phone:** (305)634-3300.

### FRAZIER, FRANCES CURTIS
State government official. **Personal:** Born May 19, 1948, Philadelphia, PA; daughter of William Henry and Letiticia Patsy Thompson. **Educ:** Norfolk State Univ, BS, spec educ, 1972; Ohio State Univ, MA, learning disabilities & behav dis, 1973. **Career:** Ohio State Univ, grad sch, 1974-75; The Ohio Asn Retarded Citizens Inc, project coordr, 1976-79; Columbus Community Col, behav sci, 1981-85; County Arts Project Inc, exec dir, 1982-84; Ohio Dept Ment Retardation & Develop Disabilities, develop disabilities consult, 1983-87; Nat Assault Prev Ctr, spec needs consult, 1985-87; Ohio Dept Human Servs, prog admin cultural initiatives, 1990-94, exec staff, 1994-98; City Colombus, Community Rels Comn, comnr, currently; WomensWorkfcf Inc, consult; 1998-; Frances Curtis Frazier, consult, 1998-. **Orgs:** A Quality Sharing Inc, founder, spokesperson, 1979-84; Greater Columbus YWCA, co-chair, racial justice co policy, 1987-95; Women Color Sexual Assault Community Ohio, core group, 1989-94; Gov's Interagency Coun Women's Issues, steering comt, 1989-91; self-help developer, Nat Black Women's Health Project, 1989-, bd dir, 1993-; Riverside Hosp, black women's health prog steering comt, 1990-95; Women's Work as a Ministry, spokesperson, 1990-; Grailville/Nat Women's Task Force, 1992-96; US Civil Rights Comn, Ohio Adv Civil Rights Comn, 1992-97; sr assoc, Paul J Aicher Found, 1992-; prin, Rise Sister Rise; sr assoc, Everyday Democracy, 1995-. **Home Addr:** 3466 Bolton Ave, Columbus, OH 43227. **Business Addr:** Commissioner, City of Columbus, 1111 E Broad St Suite 302, Columbus, OH 43215, **Business Phone:** (614)645-1993.

### FRAZIER, HERMAN RONALD
Athlete, athletic director. **Personal:** Born Oct 29, 1954, Philadelphia, PA; son of Frances and Nathaniel; married Katie Nance. **Educ:** Ariz State Univ, Tempe, AZ, BS, polit sci, 1977. **Career:** Ariz State Univ, Tempe, Ariz, asst dir events & facilities, dir athletics facilities, asst dir opers, assoc athletics dir, sr assoc athletics dirbus & opers, 1977-2000; Univ Ala Birmingham, athletics dir, 2000-02; Univ Hawaii, athletics dir, 2002-08; Temple Univ, assoc athletic dir sports admin, 2008-. **Orgs:** Bd dir, advisory council, US Olympic Comt, 1984-; bd dir, Athletics Cong, 1984-; adv bd, Dept Econ Security, 1985-; bd dir, Fiesta Bowl, 1988, vice-pres, 1996, chmn, 1998, 1999; NCAA/USOC Task Force; Div I NCAA Football Issues Comt. **Home Addr:** 9841 S 46th St, Phoenix, AZ 85044. **Business Addr:** Associate Athletic Sports Administrator, Temple University, 1801 N Broad St, Philadelphia, PA 19122, **Business Phone:** (215)204-7000.

### FRAZIER, JACQUELINE. See FRAZIER-LYDE, HON. JACQUI.

### FRAZIER, DR. JIMMY LEON
Physician. **Personal:** Born Aug 29, 1939, Beaumont, TX; son of E Leon and Thelma Cooper; married Shirley A Jolley; children: Andrea Nichole, Daveed & Keith D. **Educ:** Tex Southern Univ, BS, 1960; Meharry Med Col, MD, 1967. **Career:** Beaumont Sch Dist Tex, teacher, 1960-63; NASA, aerospace engr, 1964; Good Samaritan Hosp & H C, intern, 1967-69, resident internal Med, 1971-72, staff, 1972; Pk DuValle Health Ctr, pract, 1968-69, 1972; Family practician, physician, 1971-; Wright State Univ Sch Med, admis com, 1978-80. **Orgs:** Alpha Phi Alpha, Am Acad Family Prac, Nat Med Asn, AMA, Ohio State Med Asn, Shriners-Prince Hall Mason; Dayton Ohio Montgomery Co Med Asn; Gem City Med Soc; dipl Am Bd Family Pract; fel Am Acad Family Physicians; Dayton Racquet Club; Nat Asn Advan Colored People. **Honors/Awds:** Achievement Award, Gem City Med Soc, 1999. **Home Addr:** 543 Valewood Lane, Dayton, OH 45405, **Home Phone:** (937)278-5075. **Business Addr:** Physician, 1401 Salem Ave, Dayton, OH 45406, **Business Phone:** (937)275-7409.

### FRAZIER, JORDAN
Business owner, automotive executive, association executive. **Personal:** Born Screven, GA; married Cora; children: Edward & Shayla. **Career:** Afro-Am Life Ins Co; Seaboard Coastline Rr; Roebuck Chrylser Plymouth, sales, 1975, used car mgr, 1979; Jim Bailey City Car Sales, finance mgr; Jim Burke Buick, finance mgr, 1980; Midfield Dodge, pres, owner & gen mgr, chief exec officer, 1990-. **Orgs:** Vulcan Kiwanis Club; bd mem, Boys Scouts Am; trustee, Miles Col; bd dir, Birmingham Regional Chamber Com. **Honors/Awds:** Small Business Person of the Year, Birmingham Chamber Com, 1996. **Special Achievements:** Listed 63 of 100 top auto dealers, Black Enterprise, 1992. **Business Addr:** Owner, President, Chief Executive Officer, Midfield Dodge Inc, 549 Bessemer Super Hwy, Midfield, AL 35228, **Business Phone:** (205)365-3511.

### FRAZIER, JULIE A.
Engineer. **Personal:** Born Dec 9, 1962, Cleveland, OH; daughter of Gerald N. **Educ:** Tuskegee Univ, BS, 1986. **Career:** Sherwin Williams Tech Lab, lab technician, 1984-85; AT&T Bell Labs, Atlanta, Ga, chem engineering asst, 1987-89. **Orgs:** Am Inst Chem Engrs, 1985-86; Vol Greater Cleveland Literacy Coalition, 1986-87; Assault Illiteracy Prog, 1986-87. **Home Addr:** 114 Brook Ridge, Doraville, GA 30340, **Home Phone:** (404)449-7352.

### FRAZIER, KENNETH C.
Chief executive officer. **Personal:** Born Dec 17, 1954, Philadelphia, PA; son of Otis. **Educ:** Pa State Univ, BA, polit sci, 1975; Harvard Law Sch, JD, 1978. **Career:** Drinker, Biddle & Reath, litigation dept, partner, 1978-92; Astra Merck, vpres, gen coun & secy, 1992-94; Merck & Co Inc, vpres pub affairs, 1994-96, vpres pub affairs & asst gen coun, 1997-99, vpres & dep gen coun, 1999, gen coun, 1999-2007, sr vpres, 1999-2006, exec vpres, 2006-07, pres Global Human Health, 2007-10, pres, 2010-, chief exec officer, 2011-, chmn, 2011; MedcoHealth Solutions Inc, mgr & dir, 2002. **Orgs:** Dir, Ethics Resource Ctr; adv bd mem, Univ Pa Law & Econs Ctr, 1978; dir, Exxon Mobil Corp, 2009-; bd mem, Cornerstone Christian Acad; bd mem, Ithaka; bd mem, Legal Serv New Jersey; adv bd mem, CorporateProBono.org; adv bd mem, Metrop Corp Coun; adv bd mem, Nat Legal Aid & Defender Asn; adv bd mem, Rand Inst Civil Justice; adv bd mem, Seton Hall Univ Health Law & Policy Ctr; Coun Am Law Inst; Am Bar Asn; Am Corp Coun Asn; Asn Gen Coun; Coun Foreign Rels; Pa Bar Asn. **Business Addr:** Chairman, Chief Executive Officer, President, Merck & Co Inc, 1 Merck Dr, Whitehouse Station, NJ 08889-0100, **Business Phone:** (908)423-1000.

### FRAZIER, DR. LEON
**Personal:** Born May 16, 1932, Orangeburg, SC; married Irlene Janet Sharperson; children: Angela, Chris & Celeste. **Educ:** SC State Univ, BS, 1955; Univ Okla, attended 1967; Ala A&M Univ, MS, guid & coun, 1968; Okla State Univ, EdD, educ psychol, 1971; Univ Okla, pub admin. **Career:** Aiken County Pub Schs, SC, teacher, 1954-56; USAF Electronics Training Ctr, Keesler AFB, MS, training instr, 1956-58; AUS Missile Sch RedstoneArsenal, instr, 1958-61, training admin, 1961-68, educ specialist, 1968-69; Ala A&M Univ, vpres acad affairs, dir, 1971-73, assoc prof, asst dean grad studies, 1971-73, prof psychol, vpres stud affairs, 1974-82, exec vpres, vpres admin serv, 1989-2006; State Ala, lic psychologist; Transworld Accrediting Comn Int, comnr, currently; comnr human serv, State Ala; founder & exec dir, Christian Workers Inst; US Dept Educ, proposal evaluating consult. **Orgs:** AAAS; Am Psychol Asn; Nat Educ Asn; Nat Rehab Asn; chmn, Nat Asn CollDeans Registrars & Admis Comn; Coun Acad Deans Southern States; Phi Delta Kappa Int Educ Fraternity; Ala Educ Asn; Ala Psychol Asn; adv comt mem, Madison County Ment Health Bd Prof; dir, Huntsville-Madison County Community Action Comn; vpres, Madison County Ment Health Asn; Madison County Community Coun Orgn; trustee, Huntsville Art League & Mus Asn; Madison County Dem Exec Comt; Nat Asn Advan Colored People; state dir pubrels, Church God Christ; trustee, deacon & dir finance, Gov Div Church God Christ; chair & bd dir, Okla State Univ, currently; vis team mem, Southern Asn Cols & Schs. **Honors/Awds:** Numerous community service awards. **Special Achievements:** Publication: Journals such as The Journal of Research and Development in Education, and the Journal of the Medical Association of the State of Alabama. **Home Addr:** 2811 Penland Ave NW, Huntsville, AL 35810, **Home Phone:** (256)852-4343. **Business Addr:** Commissioner, Transworld Accrediting Commission International, 231 E Alessandro Blvd Suite A-210, Riverside, AL 92508-6039, **Business Phone:** (951)901-5586.

### FRAZIER, LINK REGINA JOLLIVETTE. See FRAZIER, REGINA JOLLIVETTE.

### FRAZIER, RAMONA YANCEY
Manager, executive. **Personal:** Born Jun 27, 1941, Boston, MA; daughter of Raymond E Yancey Sr and Gladys E Springer Yancey; children: Pamela Rae. **Educ:** Howard Univ, BA Psychol, 1960; Simmons Col, BA Psychol, 1962; Pace Univ, BA, bus admin, 1984. **Career:** Brown Bros Harriman Co, employ mgr, 1969-73; Anchor Savings Bank, dir personnel, 1973-74; Boston Univ, personnel officer, 1974-77; Raytheon Co, mgr eeo, 1977; Anchor Savings Bank, asst vpres personnel officer, 1977-79; GAF Corp, dir eeo, 1979-84; Venator Group, dir personnel, 1984-87, corp mgr, 1987-98, dir, 1998-; InoMedic, chief human resources officer, 2006-09; TempusJets LLC, human resources mgr, 2010-; Orion Air Group LLC, human resource mgr, 2010-. **Orgs:** Former pres, EDGES Group Inc; Friend Mayor's Comn status Women NYC; Human Resources Planning Soc; Delta Sigma Theta; bd, Brookwood Childcare; JHRM; bd dirs, Brooklyn Young Women Christian Asn. **Honors/Awds:** Mary McLeod Bethune Recognition Award, Nat Coun Negro Women, 1989; Corporate Recognition, Nat Asn for the Advan of Colored People; Achievement, NYS Sen Velmanette Montgomery, 1998. **Home Addr:** 195 Willoughby Ave, Brooklyn, NY 11205, **Home Phone:** (718)636-8949. **Business Addr:** Human Resources Manager, Orion Air Group LLC, 1001 Providence Blvd, Newport News, VA 23602, **Business Phone:** (757)875-7779.

### FRAZIER, RAY JERRELL
Government official, broadcaster. **Personal:** Born Jun 27, 1943, Lake Providence, LA. **Educ:** Grambling Univ. **Career:** KLPL Radio, announcer; Town Lake Providence, councilman, 1974, state comnr, currently. **Orgs:** MW Prince Hall Grand Lodge F & AM LA Sunrise Lodge No 109; Nat Asn Advan Colored People. **Home Addr:** 400 Hudson, Lake Providence, LA 71254. **Business Addr:** State Commissioner, Town of Lake Providence, 201 Sparrow St, Lake Providence, LA 71254, **Business Phone:** (318)559-2288.

### FRAZIER, REGINA JOLLIVETTE (LINK REGINA JOLLIVETTE FRAZIER)
Manager, teacher. **Personal:** Born Sep 30, 1943, Miami, FL; daughter of Cyrus Martin Sr and Frances Reeves; married Ronald Eugene; children: Ronald II, Robert Christopher & Rozalynn Suzanne. **Educ:** Howard Univ, BS, pharm, 1966; Univ Miami, MBA, 1983. **Career:** Director, teacher (retired); Comn Drug Store Inc Miami, pharm intern, 1966; Peoples Drug Stores Inc, Wash, pharm intern, 1967-68, staff pharmacist, 1968-69; Nat Assoc Retired Teachers & Am Assoc Retired Persons Drug Serv Wash, chief pharmacist, staff pharmacist, 1969-70; Univ Miami Hosps & Clinics, sr pharmacist, 1970, dir, 1973-2007; Univ Fla, Col Pharm, preceptor; Fla A & M Univ Col Pharm, clin field instr. **Orgs:** Nat parliamentarian Assoc Black Hosp Pharmacists; Am Soc Hosp Pharmacists; Nat Pharmaceut Assoc; Pharm Adv Comt; Shared Purchasing Prog Hosp Consortium Inc; Fla Pharmaceut Assoc; adv comt, Fla & GA Cancer Info Servs; fel Women's Chamber Com So Fla Inc; Miami Forum; Metro Dade County Zoning Appeals Bd, 1977-88; pres, Links Found Inc, 1986-90; pres, League Women Voters, Am Assoc Univ Women; bd dir, United Negro Col Fund; bd dir, Nat Coalition Black Voter Participation; Alpha Kappa Alpha Sorority Inc; Gamma Zeta Omega Chapt; Carats Inc; Zonta Intl; Greater Miami I Club; Jack & Jill Am; Nat Asn Advan Colored People Legal Defense & Educ Fund; Hosp Consortium Inc; bd trustee, Greater Miami United Way; bd dir, Girl Scout Coun Trop Fla; exec bd, New World Sch Arts; life mem, YWCA Greater Miami-Dade; Jack & Jill Am Inc. **Honors/Awds:** Devoted Service Award, Links Inc, 1980; Community Headliner Award, Women Commun, 1984; Trail Blazer Award, Women's Community 100, 1984; Salute to Leadership Award, Agri Invest Fund Inc, 1986; Sarah A. Blocker Meritorious Community Service Award, Fla Memorial Col; Distinguished Community Service Award, Alpha Phi Alpha & Beta Lambda Chaps; Leadership Award, Antidefamation League; Bronze Medallion, Nat Conf Christians Jews. **Special Achievements:** One of the One Hundred Most Influential Black Americans, Ebony Magazines, 1987-90; One of the Americas Top 100 Black Business & Professional Women, Dollars & Sense Magazines selection, 1988. **Home Addr:** 1320 NW 88th St, Miami, FL 33147.

### FRAZIER, SHIRLEY GEORGE
President (organization). **Personal:** Born Brooklyn, NY; daughter of Albert Jr and Joan Branch; married John Beasley Jr; children: Genesis A. **Educ:** Essex County Col, AS, 1990; NY Univ, BA, jour, 1999. **Career:** Sweet Survival LLC, pres, 1989-. **Orgs:** Bd mem, Gift Asn Am, 1992-99; assoc mem, Gift Basket Profs Network, 1996-2001. **Home Addr:** 650 E 28 St, Paterson, NJ 07504-1831, **Home Phone:** (973)870-0450. **Business Addr:** President, Sweet Survival LLC, PO Box 91, Paramus, NJ 07653-0091, **Business Phone:** (973)279-2799.

### FRAZIER, WALT, JR. (CLYDE FRAZIER)
Basketball player, broadcaster. **Personal:** Born Mar 29, 1945, Atlanta, GA; son of Walter and Eula; married Marsha Clark; children: Walt III & Angel. **Educ:** Southern Ill Univ, attended 1967. **Career:** Basketball player (retired), commentator; New York Knicks, 1967-77; Cleveland Cavaliers, 1977-80; US Basketball League franchise, investor; US Vi Boat firm, boat capt, 1989; NY Knicks, TV anal & broadcaster; All Am Speakers, motivational speaker, currently; Walt Frazier Enterprises, pres; Just Men, New York, co-owner; Basketball Camp, Pawling, operator; Madison Sq Garden Network, color commentator, currently; Clyde Frazier's Wine & Dine, owner, 2012-; Films: Aaron Loves Angela, actor, 1975; Eddie, actor, 1996; Death of a Dynasty, 3 AM, actor, 2001; actor, 2003. **Home Addr:** 675 Flamingo Dr SW, Atlanta, GA 30311, **Home Phone:** (404)753-3325. **Business Addr:** Commentator, Madison Square Garden Network, 2 Pa Plz 15th Fl, New York, NY 10121-0091, **Business Phone:** (212)465-6741.

**FRAZIER, DR. WILLIAM JAMES**
Physician. **Personal:** Born Aug 20, 1942, Gary, IN; married Veronica; children: Kevin, Monica & Nicole. **Educ:** Fisk Univ, attended 1964; Ind Univ Sch Med, MD, 1968. **Career:** Baylor Univ Med Ctr, resident gen surg, 1970; Barnes Jewish Hosp S Campus, resident, 1975; Edinburg Regional Med Ctr; pvt pract urol, currently. **Orgs:** AMA; Dallas Co Med Soc; Am Col Surgeon; dipl, Am Bd Urol; Am Col Emergency Physicians; CV Roman Med Soc; Nat Med Asn. **Honors/Awds:** Publication: "Use of Phenylephrine in the Detection of the Opening Snap of Mitral Stenosis", Am Heart J, 1969; "Early Manipulation & Torsion of the Testicle", Jour Urol, 1975; bronze star for Meritorious Service. **Home Addr:** 6418 Royalton Dr, Dallas, TX 75230-3513, **Home Phone:** (214)368-3446. **Business Addr:** Private Pratice, 5215 Lobello Dr, Dallas, TX 75229, **Business Phone:** (214)552-6660.

**FRAZIER, DR. WYNETTA ARTRICIA**
Executive director, association executive. **Personal:** Born Jul 21, 1942, Mounds, IL; daughter of Willie J Williams and Annie L Fite Williams; married Sterling R; children: Renee, Tommie & Clifford. **Educ:** Gov St Univ, BS & MA, 1975; Univ Ill, CDA; Columbia-Pacific, San Rafael, Calif, PhD, 1989; DePaul Univ. **Career:** Univ Ill, Dept Educ, Early Childhood Res & Intervention Progs, asst dir, 1985; Gov Health Affairs, asst; Health Serv Adminr, sr health planner; Comp Health Planning Sub Area, exec dir; Lloyd Ferguson Health Ctr, asst adminr; Health Occup, dir; Chicago Comn Women, pres; Chicago Comn Human Rels, Comnr; Chicago Urban League, pres; Nat Asn Health Serv Exec, vpres. **Orgs:** Past pres, Nat pres, Nat Hook Up Black Women Inc, 2007, bd dir; Am Pub Health Asn; Nat Asn Neighborhood Health Ctrs; Auxiliary Cook Co Hosp; Kozminski Sch PTA; Sch Com Hyde Pk Kenwood Community Conf; Independent voters Ill; Health Comt; League Black Women; Afro Am Family & Community Serv; Chicago Forum; Nat Orgn Women. **Honors/Awds:** Clin Awards Chicago Med Soc, 1972-74; Who's Who Black Americans, 1987-88, 1991 & 1997; Award of Excellence, Chicago Consortium of Early Intervention Providers, 1997; Women of Achievement, International Churches of God in Christ, 1997; VIP Award, Illinois Parents Too Soon; Ten Outstanding Young People Award Chicago Jaycees; Citizen of the Week WJPC & WAIT radio stations; Ebony Award, U. S. Civil Rights Comn; Grant Chas Gavin Scholar. **Home Addr:** 5117 S Univ Ave, Chicago, IL 60615-3961, **Home Phone:** (312)643-5866. **Business Addr:** Board of Director, National Hook-Up of Black Women Inc, 1809 E 71st St Suite 205, Chicago, IL 60649-2000, **Business Phone:** (773)667-7061.

**FRAZIER-ELLISON, VICKI L.**
State government official. **Personal:** Born Oct 24, 1963, New York, NY; daughter of Thomas Gerald and Lurine; married Alvin. **Educ:** Cornell Univ, BS, 1985. **Career:** Bank NY, acct adminr, 1985-86; Mellon Bank, sales, serv supvr, 1986-88; AT&T Communs, acct exec, 1988-89; GTE Mobile Communs, opers, serv mgr, 1989-91; Md Lottery Agency, dep dir, 1991-. **Orgs:** Nat Asn Female Execs, 1991; First Baptist Church Guilford, chap, men & women's day, 1992, deaconess, 1996; Md Pub Fin Officers Asn; Govt Fin Officers Asn. **Honors/Awds:** Premier Achievement Award, Mellon Bank, 1987; Sales Achievement Award, AT&T Communs, 1988; Premier Serv Quality Award, GTE Mobile Communs, 1990. **Home Addr:** 454 Hawkridge Ln, Sykesville, MD 21784-7652, **Home Phone:** (410)552-3503. **Business Addr:** Deputy Director, Maryland Lottery Agency, 6776 Reistertown Rd Suite 204, Baltimore, MD 21215, **Business Phone:** (410)764-5761.

**FRAZIER-LYDE, HON. JACQUI (JACQUELINE FRAZIER)**
Business owner, boxer, lawyer. **Personal:** Born Dec 2, 1961, Beaufort, SC; daughter of Joe and Florence; married Peter; children: Peter Jr, Sable & John-Joseph. **Educ:** Am Univ, BA, justice; Villanova Univ, law degree, 1988. **Career:** Boxer (retired), business owner, lawyer; pub defender; prof boxer, 2000; Plymouth-Whitemarsh High, pres; Frazier-Lyde & Assocs LLC, owner, currently; Philadelphia Munic Ct, judge, 2008-. **Honors/Awds:** WIBA Light Heavyweight Title, 2001. **Business Addr:** Judge, Philadelphia Municipal Court, 1301 Criminal Justice Ctr 1301 Filbert St, Philadelphia, PA 19107, **Business Phone:** (215)683-7226.

**FREDERICK, WAYNE A. I.**
College president, college administrator, college teacher. **Personal:** children: 2. **Educ:** Howard Univ, BS, zool, MD, MBA. **Career:** Univ Conn Health Ctr, dir surg oncol & asst prof; Carole & Ray Neag Comprehensive Cancer Ctr, assoc dir, Dept Surg, fac; Howard Univ, 2006-, Col Med, assoc dean, Dept Surg, div chief, chief acad officer, provost, pres, 2013-. **Honors/Awds:** Recognized in 2014 by the U.S. Congress for his work in highlighting the health disparities that exist among African Americans and other underrepresented groups. **Special Achievements:** Author of numerous articles, book chapters, abstracts, and editorials.

**FREDERICKS, HENRY SAINT CLAIRE, JR.** **See MAHAL, TAJ.**

**FREDRICK, DR. EARL E., JR.**
Physician. **Personal:** Born Aug 13, 1929, Chicago, IL; son of Earl Eugene Sr and Lucille Ray; married Barbara Cartman; children: Earl E III & Erica E. **Educ:** Univ Ill, BS, 1951; Howard Univ, MD, 1958; IL State Med Lic, 1959-. **Career:** Univ Chicago, Food Res Inst, 1953; Ill Dept Pub Health, bacteriologist, 1953-55; Freedmans Hosp, med lab technician, 1956-58; Vet Affairs Lakeside M C, resident Internal Med; Cook County Hosp, rotating intern, 1958-59, resident Internal Med, 1959-61; VA Med Ctr, resident, internal med; Va Res Hosp, hemat fel, 1961-62; Physician Cook County Hosp, attended, 1963-73; Fredrick Ashley Clin, physican, internal med & hemat; St Francis Hosp, Dept Med, chmn, 1974-76, pres med staff, 1978-79; Anchor Org Health Maintenance, physician internal med, 1974-97, Anchor-Pk Forest Off, clin dir, 1982-85; pvt pract physician, currently; Roseland Community Hosp, consult staff; Provident Hosp; Louise Burg Hosp; Christian Community Health Ctr, physician, currently. **Orgs:** Alt deleg, AMA, 1987-95, deleg, 1997-2002; bd trustees, Ill State Med Soc, 1997-2000; Nat Med Asn; Cook County Physicians Asn; Clin Asn Internal Med Chicago Med Sch, 1963-73; Am Col Physicians, 1975-; bd mem, Chicago Found Med Care, 1977-83; bd trustees, Chicago Med Soc, 1977-85, vice chmn, bd trustees, 1983-85, Credentials & Elections Comn, Ethical Rels Comn, 2005-06, vice chair, Resolutions Ref Comn, 2005-06; chmn bd, Wash Park YMCA, 1977-80; S Suburban Soc Internal Med; Crescent County Found Med Care; Am Col Physicians; Am Soc Internal Med. **Honors/Awds:** Glucose 6-Phosphate Dehydrogenase Deficiency, A Review J, Nat Med Asn, 1962; honoree, Rotary Chicago SE; honoree, Sickle Cell Dis Asn, 2000; Pride in Profession Award, AMA, 2001; Primary Health Care Clinician Devotion Award, The Ill Primary Health Care Asn, 2009. **Home Addr:** 5300 S Shore Dr Apt 21, Chicago, IL 60615, **Home Phone:** (773)288-2026. **Business Addr:** Physician, Christian Community Health Center, 9718 S Halsted St, Chicago, IL 60628, **Business Phone:** (773)233-4100.

**FREE, KENNETH A., SR. (KEN FREE)**
Commissioner, administrator, consultant. **Personal:** Born Jun 8, 1936, Greensboro, NC; son of Lee W and Margaret McMurray (deceased); married Carolyn Carter; children: Delana, Kenneth Jr & Benjamin. **Educ:** NC A&T State Univ, BS, 1970. **Career:** Negro League, 1959-60; NY Mets Prof Baseball, minor leagues, 1960-64; Cent Motor Lines, Greensboro, NC, 1964-67; Greensboro Parks & Recreation, community ctr dir, 1967-70; NC Dept Natural & Econ Resources, pk & rec consult, 1970-78; Mid-Eastern Athletic Conf, Greensboro, NC, comnr, 1978-96; Eastern Intercollegiate Athletic Conf, comnr, 1996-2006. **Orgs:** Pres, NC Recreation Parks Soc, 1978; life mem, pres, Fayetteville Alumni Kappa Alpha Psi Fraternity, 1972-77; NCAA Div I Basketball E Regional Adv Comt, 1982-84; Nat Col Athletic Asn Comt Comts, 1984-86; Col Commissioners Asn; Univ Commissioners Asn; secy & treas, vpres, Univ Commissioners Asn; NCAA Div I Basketball Comt; Comt Basketball Issues; Mason/Morning Star Lodge 691; exec comt, Nat Asn Col dir Athletics. **Special Achievements:** First African-American appointed to the powerful NCAA Division I Men's Basketball Selection Committee, 1987. **Home Addr:** 2912 W Vandalia Rd, Greensboro, NC 27407, **Home Phone:** (336)299-6340.

**FREE, LLOYD BERNARD.** **See FREE, WORLD B.**

**FREE, VICKY L.**
Executive. **Educ:** Univ SC, BS, broadcast jour, eng & mass commun, 1992; Northwestern Univ, Kellog Sch Mgt, MBA, mgt, 2004. **Career:** McDonald's Corp, head, 2000-03, mkt dir, vpres, dir women's initiatives, 2002-05; Turner Broadcasting Syst Inc, vpres entertainment mkt, 2005-07, vpres emerging markets & promotions, 2007-09, 360 Consumer Mkt Adult Swim & Cartoon Network, vpres, 2008-11; Bet Networks, exec vpres mkt & chief mkt officer, 2011-; Sunrise Enterprise, Columbia, SC. **Orgs:** Bd mem, WEB DuBois Found, 2006-12; dir pub affairs, Richland County Govt Columbia, SC; mkt rep, Pitney Bowes Corp; Women Cable Telecommunications; YWCA Nat Bd Mem. **Honors/Awds:** Ebony Outstanding Women in Marketing & Communications Award, Ebony Mag, 2005; 25 Influential Black Women, Network J, 2012. **Business Addr:** Executive Vice President of Marketing, Chief Marketing Officer, BET Networks, 1235 W St NE, Washington, DC 20018-1211, **Business Phone:** (202)608-2000.

**FREE, WORLD B. (LLOYD BERNARD FREE)**
Basketball coach, basketball player, executive. **Personal:** Born Dec 9, 1953, Atlanta, GA. **Educ:** Guilford Col, attended 1975. **Career:** Basketball player (retired), basketball coach; Philadelphia 76er's, 1975-78, 1987-88, strengthing & conditioning coach, 1994, ambassador basketball, dir player develop, currently; San Diego Clippers, 1978-80; Golden State Warriors, 1980-82; Cleveland Cavaliers, 1982-86; Miami Tropics, 1987; Houston Rockets, 1987-88; Oklahoma City Calvary, 1991; Atlanta Eagles, 1991. **Business Addr:** Director of Player Development, Philadelphia 76ers, 3601 S Broad St, Philadelphia, PA 19148, **Business Phone:** (215)339-7600.

**FREELAND, ROBERT LENWARD, JR.**
Executive, singer. **Personal:** Born May 5, 1939, Gary, IN; married Carolyn J Woolridge; children: Robin & Brandon. **Educ:** Ind Inst Real Estate, cert, 1962; Ind Univ, Calumet Col, Whiting, IN, 1980, 1981. **Career:** Devaney Realtors, salesman, 1961-63; Mobil Oil Corp, sales engr, 1963-66; Len Pollak Buick, salesman, 1966-68; Four Roses Distillers Co, mkt rep, 1968-71; Black Horsemen Liquor Stores, owner, 1969-81; Ind state rep, 1973-74; Lake Co Govt Ctr, Lake Co Recorder, 1973-74; Gary Common Coun, city councilman, 1975-79, vpres, 1976, pres, 1977-79; Gary, police comnr, 1979-83; Calumet Twp Trustees, Gary, Ind, chief dep trustee, 1988. **Orgs:** Nat Asn Advan Colored People; Urban League; Frontiers Int; bd mem, Northwest Ind Regional Plan Comn, 1975-78. **Home Addr:** 3877 Madison St, Gary, IN 46408-2728, **Home Phone:** (219)884-4765.

**FREELAND, SHAWN ERICKA**
Manager. **Personal:** Born Sep 10, 1968, Jacksonville, FL; daughter of Leonard Harris Sr and Sharon Conley. **Educ:** Fla Community Col, AA. **Career:** WCGL, host; Gospel TV Video, exec producer, pub rels; Streetball Partners Int, event dir; UNC Media Jacksonville, prom dir; KJMS/KWAM, Clear Channel Commun, prom dir; NTR Enterprises, opers mgr, currently; Promotions Unlimited 2000 Inc, dir, currently. **Orgs:** Jacksonville Together; NCP. **Honors/Awds:** Community Service Award, Jacksonville Sheriff's Office. **Special Achievements:** Come Together Day, Metropolitan Park, 1992; Martin Luther King Jr Birthday Celebration, Jax Landing, 1992; Support First Coast First, 1992; Come Together Day, Jam 4 Peace, 1994; City of Jacksonville, Mayor's Office, Proclamation. **Home Addr:** 130 S Front St Suite 518, Memphis, TN 38103. **Business Addr:** Director, Promotions Unlimited 2000 Inc, 19111 W 10 Mile Rd Suite 205, Southfield, MI 48075, **Business Phone:** (248)372-7072.

**FREELON, NNENNA (CHINYERE NNENNA PIERCE)**
Jazz singer. **Personal:** Born Jul 28, 1954, Cambridge, MS; married Philip G; children: Deen, Maya & Pierce. **Educ:** Simmons Col, Boston, BA, health care admin. **Career:** Jazz singer, currently; Albums: Nnenna Freelon, 1992; Heritage, 1993; Listen, 1994; Shaking Free, 1996; Maiden Voyage, 1998; Soul call, 2000; Tales of Wonder: Celebrating Stevie Wonder, 2002; Live, 2003; Blueprint of a Lady, 2005; Better Than Anything, 2008; Homefree, 2010; Films: "What Women Want", 2000. **Orgs:** Spokeswoman, Nat Asn Partners Educ; Women Jazz Asn Inc. **Business Addr:** Recording Artist, c/o Ed Keane Assocs, 1140 Saratoga St, Boston, MA 02128, **Business Phone:** (617)846-0067.

**FREEMAN, DR. ALGEANIA WARREN**
College administrator, president (organization), chief executive officer. **Personal:** Born Jan 24, 1949, Dunn, NC; married Ernest; children: Ernest III. **Educ:** Fayetteville State Univ, BS, eng, 1970; Southern ill Univ, Carbondale, MS, speech path & audiol, 1972; Ohio State Univ, PhD, speech commun, 1977. **Career:** Americana Nursing Ctr, Decatur, Ill, speech pathologist, 1972-73; Norfolk State Col, Norfolk VA, eng instr, 1973-75; Ohio State Univ, Columbus, teaching assoc, 1975-76; NC A & T State Univ, Greensboro, asst prof, 1977; Norfolk State Univ, asst prof, prof, vpres advan, exec dir, dept chair, 1978-01; E Tenn State Univ, prof, 1987-90; Morgan State Univ, prof, 1990-92; Livingstone Col, pres, 2001-04; Univ Md Eastern Shore, sr fel, 2006-; Southern Calif Col, vpres advan & prog develop; Found Independent Higher Educ, vpres develop; Martin Univ, pres; Freeman Group, pres & chief exec officer; Wilberforce Univ, pres, 2014; Kellogg Col Women Color Leadership Develop Inst, prog dir, 2005-06; Norfolk State Univ, vpres; Morgan State Univ, E Tenn State Univ & Orange Coast Col, fac mem; Dept Speech Commun & Theatre Arts Nc A&T State Univ, asst prof & chair. **Orgs:** State dir, Theta Phi Beta, VA, 1980-82; exec dir, Nat Black Asn Speech Lang Hearing, 1982-84; pres, Nat Allied Health, 1985-86; Allied Health Study Comt, 1987-88; pres, Coalition 100 Black Women, San Diego chap, 1994; bd dir, CIAA, 2001-; bd mem, Found Carolinas, 2002-; int consult, WK Kellogg Found, S Africa; Nat Acad Scis; Statewide Task Force, VA; Calif Asn Instrnl Adminr; Kids Voting Va; Montebello Rehab Hosp, Univ Md Hosp Syst; Md Easter Seals; Friends Norfolk Juv Ct; Girl Scouts Eastern Tenn; sr fel Univ Md Eastern Shore; founder, Freeman Group; bd mem, Independent Cols Ind Inc; chmn, Wilberforce Bd trustee; HBCU community; U.S. Pentagon & Am Socs Allied Health; Wilberforce community. **Home Addr:** 1317 Baecher Lane, Norfolk, VA 23509. **Business Addr:** President, Wilberforce University, 1055 N Bickett Rd, Wilberforce, OH 45384-1001, **Business Phone:** (937)376-2911.

**FREEMAN, DR. ANTOINETTE Y.**
College teacher. **Educ:** PhD, 2002. **Career:** Huston Tillotson Col, asst prof; Boston Univ Sch Med; Mass Col of Pharm & Health Sci Univ, adj asst prof, currently. **Business Addr:** Adjunct Assistant Professor, MCPHS University, 179 Longwood Ave, Boston, MA 02115-5896, **Business Phone:** (617)732-2800.

**FREEMAN, ANTONIO MICHAEL**
Executive, football player. **Personal:** Born May 27, 1972, Baltimore, MD. **Educ:** Va Polytech Inst & State Univ. **Career:** Football player (retired), commentator; Green Bay Packers, wide receiver & kick returner & punt returner, 1995-2001, 2003; Philadelphia Eagles, wide receiver, 2002; Miami Dolphins, wide receiver, 2004; Comcast SportsNet Wash, commentator, currently. **Honors/Awds:** Champion, Super Bowl XXXI, 1996; Pro Bowl, 1998; All-Pro, 1998; Receiving Yards Leader, Nat Football League, 1998; Green Bay Packers Hall of Fame; Virginia Sports Hall of Fame, 2012. **Special Achievements:** Greatest play in the history of Monday Night Football, ESPN. **Business Addr:** Commentator, Comcast SportsNet, 7700 Wis Ave, Bethesda, MD 20814, **Business Phone:** (301)718-3200.

**FREEMAN, BRENDA**
Vice president (organization). **Educ:** Univ Md, BS, chem engineering, MBA, mkt & finance. **Career:** Mobil Oil Corp, mkt; Pepsico Inc, mkt; VH1, vpres, consumer mkt; ABC Radio Networks, exec dir mkt; MTV Networks, Nickelodeon, sr vpres, integrated mkt & promotions, 2002-; Turner Broadcasting Syst Inc, chief mkt officer; DreamWorks Animation, tv mkt, 2014-. **Orgs:** Women Cable & Tv (WICT); adv bd, Univ Md Col Engineering. **Business Addr:** Senior Vice President, MTV Networks, 1515 Broadway, New York, NY 10036, **Business Phone:** (212)258-6000.

**FREEMAN, BRIAN M.**
Executive. **Personal:** Born Apr 25, 1957, Hartford, CT; son of Walter and Shirley; married Constance L; children: Brian Mark Jr & Corey Cose. **Educ:** Calif Inst Technol, BS, mat sci, 1979. **Career:** Menasco Aerosystems, sr metallurgist, 1981-97, dir engineering, 1981-97; Curtiss-Wright Flight Systs, Tech Serv, vpres, 1997-2001; Curtiss-Wright Controls Inc, vpres, technol & mkt develop, 2001-12; Strategically Growing Businesses through Mergers & Acquisition, m&a exec, 2012-. **Orgs:** Am Soc Metals, 1981-; Soc Automotive Engrs, 1990-. **Home Addr:** 11065 Alderbrook Lane, Charlotte, NC 28270-1563, **Home Phone:** (908)876-8539. **Business Addr:** Vice President of Technology, Market Development, Curtiss-Wright Controls Inc, 15800 John J Delaney Dr Suite 200, Charlotte, NC 28277, **Business Phone:** (704)869-4600.

**FREEMAN, CLAIRE E.**
Government official, executive director, chief executive officer. **Personal:** Born Sep 24, 1943, Cleveland, OH; children: Whitney Blair Morgan - Woods & Shani T'Nai. **Educ:** Univ Calif, Riverside, BA, sociol & hist, 1969; Univ Southern Calif, MS, urban & regional planning, 1973. **Career:** City Inglewood, Housing Community & Develop Div, human affairs supvr, 1973-77; Calif Asn Realtors, housing & community develop mgr, 1978-80; Dept Housing & Urban Devlop, Community Planning & Develop, dep asst secy, 1981-84; Dept Housing & Urban Develop, asst secy admin, 1989; Cuyahoga Metrop Housing Authority, chief exec officer, 1990; Cuyahoga Metrop Housing Authority, chief exec officer, 1999, dir, 1995; Off Secy Defense & Civilian Personnel Policy, dep asst secy. **Orgs:** Chairwoman, bd trustee, Urban League Greater Cleveland, 1996; Housing Authority Ins Co, Coun Large Pub Housing Authorities, Dept Defense Qual Life Task Force. **Honors/Awds:** Outstanding Alumni, African American Support Group, Univ Southern Calif, 1983; Distinguished Serv Medal, Housing & Urban Develop, 1984; Meritorious Service Award, Nat

Asn Advan Colored People, 1987; Medal Outstanding Public Service Award, Secy Defense, 1987, 1989; State & Local Small Bus Advocate Award, US Small Bus Admin, 1992; Social Justice Crusader the Year Award, Southern Christian Leadership Conf, 4th Annual Martin Luther King Jr, 1992; Black Professional of the Year, Greater Cleveland, 1996. **Home Addr:** 12900 Lake Ave 609, Lakewood, OH 44107, **Home Phone:** (216)226-7775.

### FREEMAN, DARNELL. See KEMP, LEROY PERCY, JR.

### FREEMAN, DENISE
School administrator. **Personal:** married Barry; children: 4. **Educ:** Piedmont Col, Demorest, GA, BA; Inter-denominational Theol Ctr, Atlanta, GA. **Career:** Lincoln County sch bd, baptist minister, 1993-96; Lincoln County Bd Educ, chmn bd educ, 2006-. **Orgs:** Dist 1 rep, Lincoln County Bd Educ, 1992-96. **Home Addr:** PO Box 268, Tignall, GA 30668, **Home Phone:** (706)359-2232. **Business Addr:** Chairman, Lincoln County Board of Education, 423 Metasville Rd, Lincolnton, GA 30817, **Business Phone:** (706)359-3742.

### FREEMAN, DIANE S.
School administrator, educator. **Personal:** Born Springfield, MA; children: Urraca Jorge, Joaquin Arturo & Javier Akin. **Educ:** Cent Conn State Univ, BA, anthrop, 1970; Univ Conn, MSW, casework, 1977; Holyoke Community Col, AA; Wellesley Col, cert mgt, 1983. **Career:** Univ Hartford, social work consult, 1977, dir, sociol & multi cult studies prog, 1977-78, asst dir admin, 1978-80; Nh Col, Conn, instr, 1979-82; Eastern Conn State Univ, instr, 1981; Trinity Col, asst dir, career coun, 1981-84; Greater Hartford Community Col, dir, spec serv & ASTRA, 1984-87; Manchester Community & Tech Col, Social Div, asst prof, social serv prog, cord, 1987, Dept Social Serv & Hospitality, dept chmn & assoc prof, prog co ordinator, currently; Hartford Bd Educ, therapist, spec educ, 1989-91 . **Orgs:** New Eng Minority Women Admin Higher Educ, 1984-86. **Business Addr:** Associate Professor, Manchester Community & Technical College, Great Path MS Suite 4, Manchester, CT 06045-1046, **Business Phone:** (860)512-2781.

### FREEMAN, FRANKIE MUSE (MARIE FRANKIE MUSE)
Lawyer. **Personal:** Born Nov 24, 1916, Danville, VA; daughter of William Brown and Maude Beatrice Smith; married Shelby; children: Shelbe. **Educ:** Hampton Inst, attended 1936; Howard Univ, LLB, 1947. **Career:** Attorney (retired); US, polit appointee; US Treas Dept, clerk, 1942-44; Off Price Admin, statistician, 1944-45; Col Finger lakes, instr bus law, 1947-49; atty law, 1949-56; St. Louis Land Clearance & Housing Authorities, from assoc gen coun to gen coun, 1956-70; US Comn Civil Rights, comnr, 1964-79; Community Serv Admin, inspector gen; Freeman Whitfield Montgomery Staples & White, partner & atty; Montgomery Hollie & Assocs LLC, atty, currently; Nat Asn Advan Colored People, atty. **Orgs:** Am Bar Asn; Nat Bar Asn; Mound City Bar Asn; Lawyers Asn St Louis; Nat Asn Housing & Redevelop Officials; Nat Housing Conf; League Women Voters; pres, Delta Sigma Theta Sorority; bd dir, Nat Coun Negro Women; bd mem, St Louis Br; legal coun, Nat Asn Advan Colored People; bd trustee, Howard Univ, Laclede Sch Law, trustee emer; first vpres, Nat Coun Aging, bd chmn; bd mem, St Louis Region Nat Conf Christians & Jews; Am Red Cross; St Louis Bi-State Chapt; bd chmn, St Louis Urban League; Gateway Chap Links Inc; trustee bd, Wash Tabernacle Baptist Church; Citizens Comn Civil Rights; bd mem, United Way; bd mem, Metrop Zool Pk; bd mem, St. Louis Ctr Int Rels; World Affairs Councils Am; Girl Scouts US Am; YWCA Metro St Louis; treas, Wash Tabernacle Baptist Church; Bar Asn Metrop St. Louis; Mem Comn, Presidential Scholars, 2015. **Honors/Awds:** Recipient of numerous honors including Outstanding Citizen Award, Mound City Press Club, 1953; Hall of Fame, Nat Bar Asn, 1990; International Civil Rights Walk of Fame, 2007; received several honorary doctorate degrees from institutions that include Hampton Univ, Univ Mo-St. Louis, St Louis Univ, Wash Univ St. Louis & Howard Univ; St. Louis, Missouri Citizen of the Year, 2011; Spingarn Medal, NAACP, 2011; Spirit of Excellence Award, Am Bar Asn Comn, 2014. **Special Achievements:** First woman to be appointed to the United States Commission on Civil Rights; Honored by Dollars and Sense Magazine as one of America's Top 100 Women 1985; Author, A Song of Faith and Hope: The Life of Frankie Muse Freeman, 2003. **Home Addr:** 91 Waterman Pl, St Louis, MO 63112, **Home Phone:** (314)361-4385. **Business Addr:** Trustee Emeritus, Howard University Office of the Secretary, 2400 6th St NW Suite 440, Washington, DC 20059, **Business Phone:** (202)806-2250.

### FREEMAN, DR. HAROLD P.
Surgeon. **Personal:** Born Mar 2, 1933, Washington, DC; son of Clyde and Lucille; married Artholian C; children: Harold Paul & Neale Palmer. **Educ:** Cath Univ Am, BA, 1954; Howard Med Sch, MD, 1958; Am Bd Surg, diplomat. **Career:** Howard Univ Hosp, internship, 1958-59, resident, gen surg, 1959-64; Sloane Kettering Cancer Ctr, 1964-67; Columbia Presby Hosp, assoc attend surgeon, 1974-89; Breast Exam Ctr Harlem, med dir, 1979-; Harlem Hosp Ctr, attend surgeon, dir surg, dir surg, 1974-99; Columbia Univ, prof clin surg, 1989-; N Gen Hosp, pres & chief exec officer, 1999-, dir surg, 1999-; Nat Cancer Inst, Bethesda, sr advisor, currently; Am Cancer Soc, chief architect, currently; N Gen Hosp, chief surg & pres; Howard Univ, dir. **Orgs:** Soc Surg Oncol, 1975-; bd dir, Am Cancer Soc, 1978-; chmn, Nat Adv Comt Cancer Socio-Econ Disadvantaged Am Cancer Soc, 1986-88; Exec Coun Soc Surg Oncol, 1987-89; Gov Am Col Surgeons, 1988; nat pres, Am Cancer Soc, 1988-89; Alpha Omega Alpha, 1989; Exec Comt Am Col Surgeons, 1990; chair, PRS Cancer Panel, 1991-94; past chmn, US Pres's Cancer Panel; sr dir, NCI; founder & pres, Ralph Lauren Ctr Cancer Care & prev; fel, Am Col Surgeons; diplomat, Am Bd Surg. **Honors/Awds:** Harris Award, Outstanding Gentlemen Cath Univ, 1954; Prize in Psychaitry, 1958, trustee, 1993-, Howard Univ,; Daniel Hal Williams Award, Outstanding Achievement Chief Resident Howard Univ Hosp, 1964; National Boys Singles Tennis Champion, Am Tennis Asn, 1948; Honorary Doctor Sci: Albany Sch Med, 1989, Niagara Univ, 1989, Adelphi Univ, 1989; Catholic UNIV, Honorary Doctor Sci, 1989; Mary Lasker Award; Health Lifetime Achievement Award; American Cancer Society Medal Honor; Jill Rose Award; American Society Clinical Oncology Special Recognition Award; Other selected awards includes: The Mary Lasker Award for Public Service, Time Inc; CDC Foundation's Champion of Prevention Award; Jill Rose Award, Breast Cancer Research Foundation; Washington Cancer Institute's Spirit of Life Award; George Washington University Cancer Institute's Distinguished Public Service Award; Daniel Hale Williams Award, 2006; Harold P Freeman Award, American Cancer Society, 1990. **Home Addr:** 57 Sprain Valley Rd, Scarsdale, NY 10583. **Business Addr:** Founder, President, Harold P Freeman Patient Navigation Institute, 132 W 112th St, New York, NY 10026, **Business Phone:** (877)369-0902.

### FREEMAN, KERLIN R., JR.
Educator, association executive, army officer. **Personal:** Born Sep 24, 1930, Chelsea, MA; son of Lucille and Kerlin; married E Juanita Maybin; children: Leslie R, Beverly F & Alan K. **Educ:** Metro State Col, Denver Co, BA, elem educ, 1975; Lesley Col, Cambridge, Mass, MA, comput educ, 1985. **Career:** Educator (retired); Nat Asn Advan Colored People, human rels com, 1976-82, pres, 1977-82; Basilus, Xi Pi Chap Omega Psi Phi, recorder, 1977-81; XI Chap Omega Psi Phi, vice baselius, 1986-90; Colo Springs Dist no 11, elem sch teacher, NEA dir, 1990-92. **Orgs:** Int Asn Approved Basketball Officials, 1973-92; del, Dem Nat Conv, 1976; chmn, Mny Caucus CO Ed Assoc, 1982-; chmn human rel comm, City CO Springs, 1983-85; bd dir, CO Springs Edu Asn, 1985-91; United Teaching Prof CO Football Officials Asn, Black Ed Dist 11; bd dir, NEA, 1990-91; bd dir, CEA, 1990-91; regional dir, CSEA, 1991-92; at-large dir, CEA, Ethnic Mny Adv Coun, 1991-92; basileus, Xi Pi Chap, 1991-94; committeman, Pikes Peak Lodge No. 5, F&A Masons, Precinct 125. **Honors/Awds:** Non-Commd Officer of the Year USAF-ADC, 1970; Meritorious Service Medal, USAF, 1971; Voted One of Ten Most Influential Blacks in CO Springs. **Home Addr:** 3003 Greenwood Cir, Colorado Springs, CO 80910, **Home Phone:** (719)633-7193. **Business Addr:** CO.

### FREEMAN, KIMBERLEY EDELIN
School administrator, educator, psychologist. **Personal:** Born Jun 11, 1970, Laken Heath; daughter of Kenneth and Ramona Edelin; married Clyde III; children: Clyde IV & Czleb. **Educ:** Spelman Col, BA, 1992; Univ Mich, MA, 1995, PhD, educ psychol, 1998. **Career:** Rackham Grad Sch, Merit fel, 1992-97; Spencer Found, Dissertation fel, 1996-97; Frederick D Patterson Res Inst & UNCF, res scientist, 1997-99, exec dir, 1999; George Wash Univ, Columbian Col Arts & Sci, vis asst prof orgn sci & indust psychol; Brown Univ, fel; Howard Univ, Dept Human Develop & Psycho educ studies, asst prof, currently. **Orgs:** AERA Spec Interest Group, Res Focus Black Educ, 1993-2001; Am Educ Res Asn, 1994-2002; Am Psychol Asn, 1996-2001; Nat Alliance Black Sch Educ, 1998-2004; comer, AERA Comm Res Black Educ, 1999; assoc ed, Rev African Am Educ, 1999; NPEC, 2000; adv coun, Nat Ctr Educ Stats, 2001; Nat Black Grad Stud Asn, adv bd, 2001-04; Soc Res Child Develop, 2001; ed/adv bd, J Negro Educ. **Home Addr:** 6615 7th St NW, Washington, DC 20012, **Home Phone:** (202)882-0833. **Business Addr:** Assistant Professor, Howard University, HDPES ASA 305, Washington, DC 20059, **Business Phone:** (202)865-6510.

### FREEMAN, LAURETTA (LAURETTA FREEMAN HORN)
Basketball player, basketball coach. **Personal:** Born Mar 17, 1971, Mobile, AL; married Thomas Horn; children: Jamie. **Educ:** Auburn Univ, BBA, bus admin & mgt, 1993; Univ S Ala, MA, educ, 2008-. **Career:** Basketball player (retired), basketball coach; Atlanta Glory, forward, 1996-99; Auburn Univ, admin asst, 1999, asst coach, 1999-2004; Leflore High Sch, head track coach, 2004-06; St. Paul's Episcopal Sch, head varsity girls basketball coach, 2006-. **Business Addr:** Coach, St Paul's Episcopal School, 161 Dogwood Lane, Mobile, AL 36608, **Business Phone:** (251)342-6700.

### FREEMAN, LOUIS LAWRENCE (LOU FREEMAN)
Pilot, airline executive. **Personal:** Born Jun 12, 1952, Austin, TX; married Stephanie; children: Nikki & Stephen. **Educ:** E Tex State Univ, BS, sociol & psychol, 1974; Reese Afb, Tex, USAF pilot training, 1975. **Career:** Flight Training Squadron, Mather Afb, Calif, Co-Pilot, pilot, instr pilot, 1975-80; Southwest Airlines, Ariz, Ill, first officer, capt, Phoenix Pilot Base, asst chief pilot, 1989-92, chief pilot, 1992-. **Honors/Awds:** Squadron Pilot of the Year, 454th Flight Training Squadron, USAF; Winning Spirit Award; President's Award, Southwest Airlines; Corporate Trailblazer Award, Dollars & Sense Mag, 1993; Keynote speaker, Black Hist Month Celebration, Miami Int Airport, 1996. **Special Achievements:** The first black pilot to be hired by Southwest Airlines. His professional skills enabled him to become Southwest's First African American captain as well, and later, chief pilot for the Chicago pilot base of the airline, 1987; The First African American cadet corps commander in the school's ROTC (Reserve Officers Training Corps); First black second lieu- tenant to become a squadron scheduler and one of the first lieutenants to become an instructor pilot and supervisor of flying; One of only two black chief of pilots for a major air carrier In the United States. **Home Addr:** 2612 Wendy Dr, Naperville, IL 60565, **Home Phone:** (713)946-7798. **Business Addr:** Chief Pilot, Southwest Airlines, 5333 S Laramie Ave, Chicago, IL 60638, **Business Phone:** (773)284-5900.

### FREEMAN, MARIANNA
Basketball coach. **Personal:** Born Jul 30, 1957, Wilmington, DE; daughter of Marion L. **Educ:** Cheyney Univ, BS, 1979; Slippery Rock Univ, MS. **Career:** Del state Col, head coach, 1981-83; Univ Iowa, asst coach, 1983-93; Syracuse Univ, pres, asst coach, head coach, 1993-96; USA Jr World Championship Team, asst coach, 1998; USA World Championship Team, asst coach, 2002; Black Coaches Asn, pres & third head coach prog. **Orgs:** Bd dir, Black Coaches Asn, 1987-, chair; pres, Women's Basketball Coaches Asn, 1998-; Nat Coun Negro Women; chair, Nat Col Athletic Asn Rules Comm. **Home Addr:** 6031 Jerusalem Dr, Cicero, NY 13039.

### FREEMAN, MELINDA LYONS
Educator. **Personal:** Born Apr 22, 1956, Chapel Hill, NC; daughter of Eugene and Mary; children: Tyler Mason. **Educ:** NC Cent Univ, BSHE, 1982; Univ NC, Greensboro, NC, MEd, 1985. **Career:** Univ NC Hosp, cardiol tech; Alamance County Health Dept, nutritionist, outreach coordr health educr & technician, currently. **Orgs:** Local chap pres, Delta Sigma Theta Sorority, 1992; Int Childbirth Educr Assoc, 1993-97; Alamance Juv Crime Prev Coun, 1995; Nat Asn Advan Colored People, 1997-; trainer, NC Family Resource Coalition, 1997-; trainer & vol, NC Vol Families C, 1997-; comt chair, Alamance Child Abuse Prev Task Force, 1997-; Burlington Alumnae chap pres, Delta Sigma Theta Sorority, 1998-2002. **Home Addr:** 414 Tarpley St, Burlington, NC 27215-3877, **Home Phone:** (336)570-0373. **Business Addr:** Health Educator, Alamance County Health Department, 316 N Graham Hopedale Rd Suite B, Burlington, NC 27215, **Business Phone:** (336)513-5500.

### FREEMAN, MORGAN PORTERFIELD, JR.
Actor. **Personal:** Born Jun 1, 1937, Memphis, TN; son of Morgan Porterfield (deceased) and Mayme Edna Revere (deceased); married Jeanette Adair Bradshow; children: Alphonse & Saifoulaye; married Myrna Colley-Lee; children: Deena & Morgana. **Educ:** Los Angeles City Col, theater arts, 1960. **Career:** Stage appearances include: The Nigger-Lovers, 1967; Hello Dolly, 1967; Jungle of the Cities, 1969; The Recruiting Officer, 1969; Scuba Duba, 1969; Purlie, 1970; Black Visions, 1972; Sisyphus & the Blue-Eyed Cyclops, 1975; Cockfight, 1977; The Last Street Play, 1977; The Mighty Gents, 1978; White Pelicans, 1978; Coriolanus, 1979; Julius Caesar, 1979; Mother Courage & Her Children, 1980; Othello, 1982; All's Well That Ends Well, 1982; Buck, 1982; The World of Ben Caldwell, 1982; The Gospel at Colonus, 1983; Medea & the Doll, 1984; Driving Miss Daisy, 1987; The Taming of the Shrew, 1990. Films: Who Says I Can't Ride a Rainbow?, 1971; Brubaker, 1980; Eyewitness, 1980; Harry & Son, 1983; Teachers, 1984; Marie, 1985; That Was Then, This Is Now, 1985; Street art, 1987; Clean & Sober, 1988; Glory, 1989; Lean on Me, 1989; Driving Miss Daisy, 1989; Johnny Handsome, 1989; Robin Hood: Prince of Thieves, 1991; Unforgiven, 1992; Bopha, dir, 1993; The Shawshank Redemption, 1994; Outbreak, 1995; Seven, 1995; Kiss the Girls, 1997; Chain Reaction, 1997; Deep Impact, 1998; Hard Rain, 1998; Nurse Betty, 2000; Under Suspicion, 2000; Along Came a Spider, 2001; High Crimes, 2002; The Sum of All Fears, 2002; Dream catcher, 2003; Stage appearances include. Levity, 2003; Bruce Almighty, 2003; The Big Bounce, 2004; Danny the Dog, Edison, 2005; The Code, 2006; The Contract, 2006; 10 Items or Less, 2006; The Bucket List, 2007; Feast of Love, 2007; Gone Baby Gone, 2007; Evan lmighty, 2007; The Dark Knight, 2008; Thick as Thieves, 2008; Wanted, 2008; The Maiden Heist, 2009; Last Vegas, 2013; JFK: A President Betrayed, 2013; The LEGO Movie, 2014; Island of Lemurs: Madagascar, 2014; Transcendence, 2014; Lucy, 2014; Dolphin Tale 2, 2014; Momentum, 2015; Ted 2, 2015; London Has Fallen, 2016; Now You See Me 2, 2016. TV Series: "Electric Company", 1971-76; "Another World, 1982; "Hollow Image", 1979; "Attica", 1980; "The Marva Collins Story", 1981; "Ryan's Hope", 1981; "Another World", 1982-84; "The Atlanta Child Murders", 1985; "Resting Place", 1986; "Flight for Life", 1987; "Clinton & Nadine", 1988; "Mutiny", 1999; "Million Dollar Baby", 2004; "The Downward Spiral", 2005; "Slavery & the Making of America", 2005; "A Raisin in the Sun", 2008; "Stephen Fry in America", 2008; "Smithsonian Channel's Sound Revolution", 2008; "Through the Wormhole", 2010. **Orgs:** Actor's Equity Asn; Screen Actors Guild; Am Fedn Television & Radio Artists. **Honors/Awds:** Clarence Derwent Award; Drama Desk Award; Outstanding Featured Actor in a Play; Tony Award nomination; The Mighty Gents, 1978; Obie Award, Driving Miss Daisy, 1987; New York Film Critics Circle Award; Los Angeles Film Critics Award; Nat Soc Films Critics Award; Obie Awards, Mother Courage & Her C, Coriolanus, The Gospel at Colonus; Best Actor, Driving Miss Daisy, 1991; Image Award, Nat Asn Advan Colored People, Motion Picture Supporting Actor, 1998; Crystallris Award, 1998; Joseph Plateau Life Achievement Award, 2000; Hollywood Discovery Award for Outstanding Achievement in Acting, 2000; Philadelphia festival of World Cinema Lifetime Achievement Award, 2001; Special Prize for Outstanding Contribution to World Cinema, 2003; Nat Board Review Career Achievement Award, 2003; Academy Award, Best Supporting Actor, 2004; Crystal Globe Award, 2003; Lifetime Achievement Award, Miss Inst Arts & Letters, 2007; Kennedy Ctr Honors, 2008; Hon Degree, Brown Univ, 2010; Lifetime Achievement Award, Am Film Inst, 2011; Oscar, 2010; CinEuphoria, 2011; CinemaCon Award, 2013; Black Reel Award, received more than 50 awards. **Business Addr:** Actor, c/o William Morris Agency, 1325 Avenue of the Americas, New York, NY 10019, **Business Phone:** (212)586-5100.

### FREEMAN, DR. PAUL D.
Conductor (music). **Personal:** Born Jan 2, 1936, Richmond, VA; son of L H; married Cornelia Perry; children: Douglas Cornelia. **Educ:** Va State Univ; Eastman Sch Music, BM, 1956, MM, 1957, PhD Theory, 1963; Hochsch Fur Musik Berlin, addn studies. **Career:** Hochstein Music Sch, Rochester, NY, dir 1960-66; Opera Theatre Rochester, music dir, 1961-66; San Francisco Community Music Ctr, dir, 1966-68; San Francisco Little Sym, music dir, 1967-68; Dallas Sym Orchestra, assoc conductor, 1968-70; Detroit Sym, conductor-in-residence, 1970-79; Saginaw Sym, music dir; Helsinki Philharmonic Orchestra, prin guest conductor; Columbia Black Composers Ser, artistic dir; numerous recs; Chicago Sinfonietta, founder, music dir & conductor, 1987-; Victoria, BC, Can Symphony, conductor, 1979-89; Victoria Sym Orchestra, music dir emer, 1988-; Czech Nat Sym Orchestra, music dir & chief conductor, 1996-. **Honors/Awds:** Winner, Dimitri Mitropolous Int Conductors Competition, 1967; Special Spoleto Award, Festival Two Worlds, 1968; Distinguished Alumni Citation, Univ Rochester, 1975; Distinguished Citation Award, United Negro Col Fund; Koussevitzky International Recording Award, 1974; Nominee, Ebony Arts Award, 1989; LHD, Dominican Univ, 1994; LHD, Loyola Univ, 1998; Jubilate Award; Mahler Award, Europ Union Arts. **Special Achievements:** Numerous guest appearances in the US, Austria, England, Germany, Denmark, Norway, Sweden, Poland, Italy, Russia, Mexico, Israel, Finland/Yugoslavia, included in Time magazine's Top Five Classical Records Listing, 1974, has approximately 200 releases to his credit, was designated a History Maker, having been nominated by the DuSable Museum of African American History for his outstanding contributions to African American life, history & culture. On January 25, 2005 the Detroit Free Press published a story by music writer Mark Stryker entitled: A BLACK KEY: Conductor Paul Freeman, in town for the Sphinx Competition, adds color to the national classical music scene; First African-American orchestral director in the world. **Home Addr:** 405 N Wabash Ave Apt 4208, Chicago, IL

60611, **Home Phone:** (312)595-1303. **Business Addr:** Founder, Music Director, Chicago Sinfonietta, 70 E Lake St Suite 226, Chicago, IL 60601, **Business Phone:** (312)236-3681.

## FREEMAN, ROBERT, JR.
Government official, business owner. **Personal:** Born Milledgeville, GA. **Educ:** Ga Southern Univ, BS, MS, indust technol. **Career:** Freeman's Barber Shop, founder & owner, 1993-; Fed Govt, asst chief staff, currently. **Home Addr:** 245 Rock Creek Rd, gray, GA 31032-4821. **Business Addr:** Founder, Owner, Freeman's Barber Shop, 7923 Central Ave, Capitol Heights, MD 20743, **Business Phone:** (301)350-5399.

## FREEMAN, HON. RONALD J.
Judge. **Personal:** Born Aug 17, 1947, Winslow, NJ; married Carmen Martinez. **Educ:** Lincoln Univ, Pa, BA, 1969; Rutgers Law Sch, JD, 1972; State Univ NJ Sch Law. **Career:** Rutgers State Univ Col Ctr, staff asst, 1970; NJ Dept Law & Pub Safety, Div Civil Rights, Rutgers State Univ Sch Law Clin Prog, 1971; Camden Reg Legal Serv Inc, legal coun, 1972-73; NJ Dept Law & Pub Safety & Div Civil Rights, Rutgers Law Sch Clin Prog, sr field rep aide, 1972; Legal coun, comt legal serv phil, 1973; Glassboro State Col, adj fac, 1973; Freeman, Zeller & Bryant, gen partner, 1974-97; NJ Supreme Ct, state bd bar examr, 1989-97; Super Ct, 4th Vicinage, NJ, judge, currently. **Orgs:** Bar Supreme Ct, Pa, 1973; Bar US Dist Ct, E Dist, Pa, 1973; Bar US Ct, Appeals Third Ciruit, 1974; Bar Supreme Ct, NJ, 1974; Bar US Dist Ct, Dist NJ, 1974; chair, NJ Bd Bar Examr, 1989-97; chair, NJ Supreme Ct Comn Minority Concerns, 1999-2001; Pa Bar Asn; Am Bar Asn; Nat Bar Asn; Phil Bar Asn; Nat Conf, Black Lawyers; Phi Alpha Delta; NJ Bar Asn; Camden County Correctional Facil Adv Bd Comn; bd dir, Haddon Field Sch Creative & Performing Arts; Sigma Psi Phi, Delta Epsilon Boule; NCP; Nat Coun Juv & Family Ct Judges. **Home Addr:** 605 Covered Bridge Rd, PO Box 4205, Cherry Hill, NJ 08034-3138. **Business Addr:** Supreme Court Judge, Superior Court 4th Vicinage, Hall Justice, Camden, NJ 08103-4001, **Business Phone:** (856)379-2364.

## FREEMAN, SHIRLEY WALKER
Librarian. **Personal:** Born Jun 7, 1951, Jackson, MS; daughter of Leroy Walker Sr and Louise Luster; married N Trent; children: Jerry, Lamont, Courtney, Nate, Trevor, Kelli & Darwin. **Educ:** Livingston Col, attended 1970; Tougaloo Col, BS, 1973; Univ Ill, Urbana-Champaign, MLS, 1978. **Career:** Rowland Med Libr, ass librn, 1972-76; Univ Ill, grad teaching asst, 1976-78; Champaign Pub Libr, br mgr, librn, 1977-83; Columbus Metrop Libr, mgr, librn, 1983-, Freeman Construct Servs Inc, co-owner, currently. **Orgs:** Delta Sigma Theta Sorority, 1969-; Am Libr Asn; United Methodist Church; Black Caucus Am Libr Asn. **Home Addr:** 2881 Castlewood Rd, Columbus, OH 43209, **Home Phone:** (614)231-6386. **Business Addr:** Manager, Librarian, Columbus Metropolitan Library, 4371 E Broad St, Columbus, OH 43213, **Business Phone:** (614)645-2275.

## FREEMAN, DR. THOMAS F.
Clergy, educator, association executive. **Personal:** Born Jun 27, 1920, Richmond, VA; children: Thomas Jr, Carter & Carlotta. **Educ:** Univ Nigeria, Lagos; Univ Ghana, Ghana E Africa; Va Union Univ, BA, 1939; Andover Newton Theol Sch, BD, 1942; Univ Chicago, PhD, 1948; Howard Univ; Boston Univ; Univ Vienna, Austria; African Univ. **Career:** Rice Univ, vis prof; Concord Baptist Church, Boston MA, asst minister, 1939-40; Andover Newton, Turner fel, 1939-42; Pleasant St Baptist Church, Westerly RI, minister, 1940-44; Monumental Baptist Church Chicago, assoc minister, 1942-44; Univ C, fel, 1942-46; VA Union Univ, prof pract theol, 1944-49; Carmel Baptist Church, minister, 1944-50; Col Arts & Sci Tex Southern Univ, dept head philos, 1950-67, asst dean, 1968-70; Mt Horem Baptist Church, pastor, 1951; Model Cities Training Ctr Tex Southern Univ, dir, 1970-74; Tex Southern Univ, dir continuing educ; Weekend Col, dean. **Orgs:** Pres, Alpha Kappa Mu Nat Hon Soc, 1962-66; alumni dir, Alpha Kappa Mu Nat Hon Soc, 1966; bd dir, Andover Newton Alumni Asn; bd dir, Asn Churches; Nat Asn Advan Colored People; Boy Scouts; Urban League. **Honors/Awds:** Clarke Scholarship, VA Union Univ, 1939; Univ Faculty Member of the Year, Univ Divinity, 1950-51; Book Choices of The Pew, 1963; Tex Southern Univ-PI CC Award, Tex Southern Univ, 1974; DHL, Eastern Mass Univ; Faculty Member International Recognition Award, Tex Southern Univ, 1992; Margaret Ross Barnett Leadership Award, Houston Urban League, 1992; Thomas F. Freeman Honors College. **Special Achievements:** American Press co-author "From Separation to Special Designation", 1975. **Home Addr:** 3402 S McGregor Way, Houston, TX 77021-1230, **Home Phone:** (713)748-0436.

## FREEMAN, V. DIANE
Manager. **Personal:** Born Charleston, WV; children: Dione M & Kenisha J Manning. **Educ:** Univ Mich, BS, bus admin. **Career:** AT&T, operator; Gen Motors Corp, exec, sr mgr supplier diversity prog, 1990, vpres & asst secy; Ferguson Manning Assocs LLC, founder, chmn & chief exec officer, 2010-; Motor's Enterprise Inc, vpres & secy. **Orgs:** Native Am Bus Alliance; exec & finance comt mem, Mich Minority Bus Develop Coun; bd dir, Ctr Empowerment & Econ Develop, Ann Arbour, MI; bd mem, MMSDC; Nat Minority Supplier Develop Coun; Mich Minority Bus Develop Coun; Mich Hisp Chamber Com; Mich Womens Bus Coun; CEED; Edward Davis Found; Nat Asn Black Automotive Suppliers; Adv Bd Minority Bus News USA; Billion Dollar Roundtable Adv Bd; Tuck Sch Bus Adv Bd; Rainbow PUSH Coalition Adv Bd. **Honors/Awds:** President Award, Mich Minority Bus Develop Coun, 2003; Mentorship Award, 2003; Fifty Influential Minorities in Business, Minority Enterprise Advocate, 2004; Corporate Amiga Award, 2005; Corporate Champion of the Year Award, Mich Women Bus Coun, 2005; Diversity Champion Award, 2006; Advocate of the Year Award, Mich Minority Bus Develop Coun, 2007; Leadership and Service Award, MMBDC Bd Dirs, 2009. **Special Achievements:** First Black Women to hold her post at General Motors. **Business Addr:** Chairman, Chief Executive Officer, Ferguson Manning Associates LLC, 100 W Big Beaver Rd Suite 200, Troy, MI 48084, **Business Phone:** (248)524-0333.

## FREEMAN, WALTER EUGENE
Computer executive, manager. **Personal:** Born May 25, 1955, Hartford, CT; son of Walter and Shirley; married Marsha; children: Walter & Taylor. **Educ:** Boston Univ, BS, 1978; Cambridge Col, MS, mgt, 1991. **Career:** Pratt & Whitney Aircraft, buyer, 1979-84, sr buyer, 1984-87; Digital Equip Corp, purchasing specialist, 1987-90, purchasing consult, 1990-93; TM Industs, sales engr, 1993-94; Compaq Comput Corp, commodity mgr, 1994-97, procurement mgr, 1997-2000; Dell Inc, Worldwide Procurement, sr procurement mgr, 2000-04, fed bid, contracts & proposals mgr, 2004-06; Apple, applecare procurement mgr & sr procurement mgr, dir, corp procurement, 2006-. **Orgs:** Bd dir, Springfield Day Nursery, 1992-94; Nat Soc Black Engrs. **Home Addr:** 12811 Justin Trail, Houston, TX 77070-4664, **Home Phone:** (832)236-3412. **Business Addr:** Apple Care Procurement Manager, Apple Inc, 12545 Riata Vista Circle, Austin, TX 78727, **Business Phone:** (512)674-2000.

## FREEMAN, MAJOR GEN. WARREN L.
Military leader. **Personal:** Born Jackson, GA; son of Sara; married Barbara Ann; children: Kevin & Brandon. **Educ:** Pac Western Univ, BBA, mgt, 1982; AUs War Col, attended 1990; Nat Louis Univ, MS, mgt, 1993; Sr Res Component Officer Course, 1993; Harvard Univ, nat & int security mgt sem, 1996. **Career:** DC Army Nat Guard, dep brigade Comdr, 260th MP Brigade, DCARNG & chief staff, 1969-91; Aus, Comndg Gen DC Nat Guard, 1995-2002; Res Forces Policy Bd, army nat guard mem, 1997. **Orgs:** Kappa Alpha Psi; AUs War Col Alumni Asn; Nat Guard Asn US; Asn Aus; nat guard mem, Res Forces Policy Bd, 1997. **Honors/Awds:** Outstanding Young Men of America; hon doctorate of humane letters, Nat Louis Univ; Air Force Commendation Medal; Army Achievement Medal; Army Reserve Components Achievement Medal; National Defense Service Medal; Humanitarian Service Medal; Armed Forces Reserve Medal; Meritorious Service Medal; Legion of Merit; Army Commendation Medal; Distinguished Service Medal; US Meritorious Service Medal; Army Staff Identification Badge. **Home Addr:** , Mitchellville, MD 20721.

## FREEMAN, YAUSMENDA
Fashion model, actor, president (organization). **Personal:** Born Los Angeles, CA. **Educ:** Univ Calif, Berkeley, BA, archit; Van Mar Acad, camera tech, bus actg, Improv & Comedy; WLAC, voice coach. **Career:** Film: Still Bout It, 2004; Black Love; Forget Paris; TV Show: The George Lopez Show; The Martin Lawrence Show; Theatre Performance: A Woman's Worth; Diary of a Catholic Sch Dropout; The Wiz; The Grass Ainocot Greener; Indust: Women Talking; Mech of Life; African-Aerobics & Exotica; Knock Out Base Inc, pres & chief exec officer, 1996-2012; Prod Earth Inc, chief financial officer, 2012-. **Business Addr:** Chief Financial Officer, Products of the Earth Inc, 2405 Crane Ct, North Las Vegas, NV 89084-3143.

## FREEMAN-WILSON, KAREN MARIE
Judge, lawyer. **Personal:** Born Oct 24, 1960, Gary, IN; daughter of Travis Lee and Myrlin Delores Patterson; married Carmen Wilson Jr; children: 4. **Educ:** Harvard Col, Cambridge, MA, BA, 1982; Harvard Law Sch, Cambridge, MA, JD, 1985. **Career:** Lake Co Prosecutor's Off, Crown Pt, Ind, dep prosecutor, 1985-89; Lake Co Defender's Off, Crown Pt, Ind, pub defender, 1989; Ind Civil Rights Comn, Indianapolis, Ind, dir, 1989-92; Gary City Ct, presiding judge, 1995-2000; Hythiam Inc, bd dir, 2007; pvt pract, atty, civil & criminal litigation; atty gen, Ind, currently; Ind Civil Rights Comn, exec dir. **Orgs:** Vpres, Delta Sigma Theta Sorority, 1980-; Nat Coun Negro Women; chair, Israel CME Steward Bd, 1985-; Coalition 100 Black Women, 1990-; ceo, Nat Asn Drug Ct Profs, 2001; Am Bar Asn; Ind State Bar Asn; exec dir, Nat Drug Ct Inst, Wash, DC; Israel CME church, Gary; Delta Sigma Theta Sorority Inc; legal coun, Gary Urban Enterprise Asn, 1995-2006. **Honors/Awds:** Fifty Leaders of the Future, Ebony Mag, 1990; Bethune Award, Nat Coun Negro Women, 1990; National Award, Delta Sigma Theta Sorority. **Special Achievements:** In 2000, she was named one of the "Top 100 to Watch" by the National Democratic Leadership Council and was invited to address the 2000 National Democratic Convention in Los Angeles; First woman to lead the steel city of Gary, IN and the First African-American female mayor in the State of Indiana. **Home Addr:** 475 Garfield St, Gary, IN 46404, **Home Phone:** (219)882-4700. **Business Addr:** Attorney General, Indiana County, 302 W Wash St 5th Fl, Indianapolis, IN 46204, **Business Phone:** (317)232-6255.

## FREGIA, DARRELL LEON
Administrator, manager. **Personal:** Born Sep 8, 1949, San Francisco, CA; son of Gatson; married Deborah Brooks; children: Marque, Akil & Shani. **Educ:** City Col San Francisco, AA, gen educ, 1969; Stanford Univ, BA, sociol, 1972; Univ Wash, MHA, 1977. **Career:** San Mateo Co Probation Dept, Redwood City, Ca, adult probation officer, 1973-75; scholar grad sch, VPres Health Affairs Univ Wash, 1975-77; Va Hosp Seattle, adminr, intern, 1976; Group Health Coop E side Hosp & Med Ctr, adminr, 1977-78; Group Health Coop Fed Way Med Ctr, adminr, 1978-79; Group Health Coop Puget Sound Ctl Hosp & Med Ctr, asst hosp adminr, 1979-, asst comptroller, 1988-90; State Wash Employ Security Depat, risk mgr, 1990-97, fiscal mgr & policy coordr, 1997-; Sea Mar CHC Cannon House, adminr, currently. **Orgs:** Guiding Light Youth Mentorship Prog; Stanford Univ Buck Club, 1972-; Stanford Univ Alumni Asn, 1972-; life mem, Alpha Phi Alpha Frat Inc, 1977; Seattle Comn Col Curric Task Force, 1978; sec bd dir, Ctr Addiction Servs Seattle, 1978-; cons/analyst Pioneer Mgt Inc Seattle, 1978-; vpres bd dir, Paul Robeson Theatre Prod, 1980; Univ Wash Mentorship Prog, 1995-. **Honors/Awds:** Recipient Player of the Year Award, San Francisco HS AAA Basketball, 1967; Buck club athletic scholar, Stanford Univ Basketball, 1970-72; traineeship, US Dept Pub Health, 1975-77; Outstanding Young Man Am Award, US Jaycees, 1979. **Home Addr:** 9251 Renton Ave S, Seattle, WA 98118. **Business Addr:** Administrator, Sea Mar CHC - Cannon House, 1040 S Henderson St, Seattle, WA 98108, **Business Phone:** (206)788-3200.

## FREGIA, RAY, SR.
Executive. **Personal:** Born Nov 22, 1948, Beaumont, TX; son of Betty Thomas; married Jewell M Perkins; children: Ray Jr & Rik. **Educ:** Lamar Univ, BBA, 1971. **Career:** Ford Motor Corp, opers mgr; River View Ford Inc, vpres & operation mgr, currently. **Business Addr:** Vice President, Manager of Operations, Riverview Ford Inc, 2200 Rte 30, Oswego, IL 60543, **Business Phone:** (630)897-8900.

## FREISEN, GIL. See Obituaries Section.

## FRELOW, DR. ROBERT DEAN
Educator. **Personal:** Born Aug 1, 1932, Seminole, OK; married Maxine Camille Gibbs Badgett; children: Robert, Fred & Michael; married Rena Hersh. **Educ:** San Francisco State Col, BA, 1954; San Francisco State Univ, MA, 1964; Univ Calif-Berkeley, PhD, 1970. **Career:** Educator, Captain (retired): USAF, 1954-64; Oakland Unified Schs, teacher, 1960-66; Berkeley Unified Schs, asst, supt, 1966-70; Greenburgh Dist 7, asst supt, 1970-74, supt 1974; Pace Univ, 1974-90. **Orgs:** Am Asn Sch Admin, 1970; adj assoc prof, Pace Univ, 1973; bd dir, Westchester Arts Coun, 1982-87; Am Red Cross, 1985-86. **Home Addr:** 25A Hillside Terr, White Plains, NY 10601. **Business Addr:** Superintendent, Greenburgh Central Schools District 7, 475 W Hardale Ave, Hartsdale, NY 10530, **Business Phone:** (914)761-6000.

## FRENCH, HOWARD W.
Journalist, editor. **Personal:** Born Oct 14, 1957, Washington, DC; son of David Marshall and Carolyn Alverda; married Agnes Koffi; children: William Howard & Henry Nelson. **Educ:** Univ Mass, Amherst, BA, MA, 1979; Univ Hawaii, japanese. **Career:** Self-employed, Abidjan, Ivory Coast, conf translr, 1979-80; Univ Ivory Coast, Abidjan, Ivory Coast, asst prof eng, 1980-82; Wash Post, Abidjan, Ivory Coast, W Africa stringer, 1982-86; NY Times, New York, NY, metrop reporter, 1986-90, NY Times, Miami, FL, Caribbean corresp, 1990, bur chief, 1990-94; NY Times, w african bur chief, Abidjan Ivory Coast, 1994-98, Tokyo bur chief, 1999, sr writer & shanghai bur chief, 2003-2008; Int Herald Tribune, columnist; Columbia Univ Grad Sch Journalism, assoc prof, 2008-. **Orgs:** Nat Asn Broadcasters; Inst AMEs; African Studies Asn. **Honors/Awds:** Overseas Press Club of America's award, 1997. **Home Addr:** 1036 Obispo Ave, Coral Gables, FL 33134, **Home Phone:** (305)444-3130. **Business Addr:** Associate Professor, Columbia University Graduate School of Journalism, 809 Journalism MC 3801, New York, NY 10027, **Business Phone:** (212)854-0163.

## FRENCH, MARY ANN
Journalist. **Personal:** Born Aug 12, 1952, Washington, DC; daughter of David M (deceased) and Carolyn Howard (deseased); married Dennis M Marshall; children: French Scott; married Augustus Lindsey Palmer Jr. **Educ:** Boston Univ, attended 1970; Johns Hopkins Univ, attended 1979, Sch Advan Int Studies, MA, 1982. **Career:** Black Women's Comm Develop Found, dir prog admin, 1977-78; Wash Post, researcher, 1981-82, Wash, DC, reporter & staff writer, 1990, corresp, 1993-; Time Mag, reporter/researcher, 1982-84; Louisville Courier J, reporter, 1984-86; St Petersburg Fla Times, Wash corresp, 1986-88; Baltimore Sun, Wash corresp, 1988; Daily News, St Thomas, Vi, ed, 1989-90; Books: 40 Ways to Raise a Nonracist Child, 1996. **Orgs:** Fel Mod Media Inst, 1982; Louisville Assoc Black Communicators, 1984-86, Nat Assoc Black Journalists, 1984-, Wash Assoc Black Journalists, 1986-; Fel Duke Univ Ctr Pub Policy, 1993. **Home Addr:** 1643 Pk Rd NW, Washington, DC 20010, **Home Phone:** (202)265-1180. **Business Addr:** Correspondent, Staff Writer, The Washington Post, 1150 15th St NW, Washington, DC 20071, **Business Phone:** (202)334-7350.

## FRESH, EDITH MCCULLOUGH
Educator, counselor. **Personal:** Born Sep 23, 1942, Quincy, FL; daughter of Harry M McCullough (deceased) and Edith Anderson; married Frederick Anthony; children: Kevin W, Bradford, Carla & Eric. **Educ:** Ind Univ, AB, 1970; Univ Mich, MSW, 1972; Gestalt Inst Cleveland, dipl, 1977; Ga State Univ, MA, 1988, PhD, clin child & family psychol, 1993. **Career:** Proj Headline, Detroit MI, dir out patient treat, 1972-73; Pub Tech Inc, human resources spec, 1973-77; FL A&M Univ, asst prof, 1977-83; EM Fresh & Assoc, FL, sr assoc, 1977-83; Morehouse Sch Med, clin social worker, 1983-88; Spelman Col, clin social worker, 1988-90; Ga Ment Health Inst, Atlanta, GA, psychol int, 1990-91; New Found, marriage & family therapist, 1990-; DeKalb Col, N Campus, asst prof, 1991-94; Morehouse Sch Med Div dir, Biopsychosocial Med, 1994-, Dept Psychiat & Behav Sci, assoc prof, currently. **Orgs:** Acad Cert Social Workers, 1976-; Nat Asn Social Workers, 1976-; Nat Hook-Up Black Women, 1980-84; clin mem, Am Asn Marriage & Family Therapists, 1980-; site visitor, Comn Accreditation Marriage & Ther Educ, 1982-; vis staff, Gestalt Inst Cleveland, 1981-; bd mem, Ment Health Dist Bd II-B Leon City, FL, 1982-83; Am Asn Univ Women, 1983-85; chairperson, Ga Asn Marriage & Family Therapists Minority Affairs Task Force, 1991-94; ethics community, 1993-96, approved supvr, 2001, chair, 2003, Am Asn Marriage & Family Therapists; bd mem, Hillside Hosp. **Home Addr:** 2622 Peyton Woods Trl SW, Atlanta, GA 30311, **Home Phone:** (404)691-5462. **Business Addr:** Associate Professors, Morehouse School of Medicine, 720 Westview Dr SW, Atlanta, GA 30310-1495, **Business Phone:** (404)752-1500.

## FRETT, LA KESHIA (LA'KEISHA FRETT MEREDITH)
Basketball player. **Personal:** Born Jun 12, 1975, Carmel, CA; daughter of Raymond and Linda; married Dion. **Educ:** Univ Ga, consumer econs, 1997; Md Univ Col, MBA. **Career:** Basketball player (retired), basketball coach; Philadelphia Rage, forward, 1997; Los Angeles Sparks, 1999-2000; Sacramento Monarchs, 2001-03; Charlotte Sting, 2004; NY Liberty, forward, 2004-05; Univ Ga, asst coach, 2005-. **Business Addr:** Assistant Coach, University of Georgia Athletic Association, 1 Selig Cir, Athens, GA 30602, **Business Phone:** (706)542-9036.

## FRETWELL, CARL QUENTION, II
Law enforcement officer, government official. **Personal:** Born May 5, 1951, Ft. Worth, TX; son of Carl Q Sr and Georgetta Enge; married Constance D Barron. **Educ:** Tarrant County Jr Col, Ft Worth, AA, 1972; Tex Wesleyan Univ, Ft Worth, BBA, 1975; Univ N Tex, Denton, TX. **Career:** Tex Youth Coun, Crockett, caseworker I, 1975-76; Tex Youth Coun, Gainesville, caseworker II, sr dorm dir, 1976-82; Bd Pardons & Parole, Ft Worth, parole officer I, unit supvr, 1982-88; Tex Youth Comn, Ft Worth, parole officer II, parole officer III, off mgr,

1988-, ct liasons off, 1990, parole supvr, 1996-. **Orgs:** Prof mem, Tex Corrections Asn, 1976-97; Nat Asn Advan Colored People, 1978-; founder, Ft Worth Chap, Nat Asn Blacks Criminal Justice, 1986; Nat bd dir, 1988-; asst treas, 1989; Nat Asn Blacks Criminal Justice; bd dir, Boy Scouts, FortWorth, 1990; Nat treas, 1994. **Home Addr:** 1328 E Richmond St, Ft. Worth, TX 76104, **Home Phone:** (817)926-2114. **Business Addr:** Parole Supervisor, Texas Youth Commission, 4900 N Lamar Blvd, Ft. Worth, TX 78765, **Business Phone:** (512)424-6130.

## FRIDAY, JEFF

Entrepreneur, executive, movie producer. **Personal:** Born Jan 1, 1964, New York, NY; married Nicole; children: 3. **Educ:** Howard Univ, BA, finance; NY Univ, Leonard Stern Sch Bus, MBA, mkt, 1987. **Career:** Bristol Myers Int, mkt, 1987; Schiefflin & Sommerset, mkt, 1989; Mingo Group, vpres prom & event mkt, 1990; Acapulco Black Film Festival, founder, exec dir & producer, 1997-; UniWorld Films, pres, 1999; Am Black Film Festival, founder; One Week, co-exec producer, 2000; Film Life Inc, founder & chief exec officer, 2002-; Black Movie Awards, creator & exec producer, 2005; Playin' for Love, exec producer, 2013; Dog Eat Dog. **Honors/Awds:** Outstanding New Jerseyans Award, Kean Univ, 2003. **Special Achievements:** Featured in numerous publications included: Variety, Hollywood Reporter, Crains, Black Enterprise, Essence, The New York Times, The Los Angeles Times, NV magazine, VIBE & he has been profiled on WNBC-TV in New York; Recently named one of Black Enterprise magazine's "Top 50 Hollywood Power Brokers" and Ebony magazine's "150 Most Influential Blacks in America. **Home Addr:** , NJ. **Business Addr:** Founder, Chief Executive Officer, Film Life Inc, PO Box 688, New York, NY 10012, **Business Phone:** (212)966-2411.

## FRIERSON, DR. MICHAEL ANTHONY

Surgeon. **Personal:** Born Mar 2, 1961, Detroit, MI; son of Benjamin and Hattie Marie Chandler; married Jocrisshawn Gardner; children: Michael A II & Ashley Ryan. **Educ:** Univ MI, microbiol, 1983, Med Sch, Ann Arbor, MD, 1987. **Career:** Loyola Univ Med Ctr, internship, orthopaedic residency, 1992; Shriners Hosp, pediat fel, 1993; Ochsner Clin, partner, 1993-2000; Baton Rouge Gen Med Ctr, chief orthopaedic, 1999-2001; Bone & Joint Clin Baton Rouge Inc, 2000-, partner, 2001-; Our Lady Lake Found, pediat orthop specialist. **Orgs:** Alpha Phi Alpha, 1980-; E Baton Rouge Parish Med Asn; Am Bd Orthopaedic Surg. **Honors/Awds:** Walter P. Blount Pioneer Award, Pediatric Ortho Soc N Am, 1990; Army Achievement Medal. **Home Addr:** 9007 Highland Rd Unit 50, Baton Rouge, LA 70810, **Home Phone:** (225)767-3373. **Business Addr:** Partner, Bone & Joint Clinic, 7301 Hennessy Blvd Suite 200, Baton Rouge, LA 70808, **Business Phone:** (225)766-0050.

## FRIERSON, NINA

Accountant. **Business Addr:** Member, Board of Director, Women of Color Foundation & Health Ministries Inc, PO Box 3735, Southfield, MI 48037, **Business Phone:** (248)569-3532.

## FRIES, DR. SHARON LAVONNE (SHARON FRIES BRITT)

Educator. **Personal:** Born Jul 26, 1959, Chattahoochee County, GA. **Educ:** Univ Md, College Park, BA, family studies, 1981, PhD, educ, 1995; Ohio State Univ, MA, 1983. **Career:** Ohio State Univ, asst dir, 1981-82, stud develop grad asst, 1982-83; Towson State Univ, area coordr, 1983-85; Univ Md, Col Educ, prof, from asst to vpres stud affairs, chancellor, 1985-95, Dept Educ Policy & Leadership, asst prof, 1995-2003, assoc prof, 2004-, Higher Educ Stud Affairs & Int Educ Prog, dir, dept coun, higher educ & spec educ, 2013-15; Harvard Grad Sch Educ, vis prof, 1998-99; Johns Hopkins Univ, consult, race equity & diversity, 2001-; Us Secret Serv, consult, race equity & diversity, 2005-08; Princeton Univ, consult, race equity & diversity, 2006-; Mass Inst Technol, Provost Off, initiative fac race & diversity, 2008-10; Articles: "Retaining each other: Narratives of two African American women in the academy", 2005; "The black box: How high achieving Blacks resist stereotypes about Black Americans", 2007; "Advising through a Wave of Change", 2008; "Underrepresentatation in the academy: A study of race equity in three southern states", 2008; "Lessons from high-achieving students of color in physics", 2010; "Underrepresentation in the Academy and the Institutional Climate for Faculty Diversity", 2011; "mportant bridges to success for African-American students", 2012; "Important bridges to success for African-American students", 2012; "Learning race in a US context: An emergent framework on the perceptions of race among foreign-born students of color", 2014; "The acculturation experiences of foreign-born students of color in STEM", 2014; Book: Mentoring outside the line: The importance of authenticity, transparency and vulnerability in effective mentoring relationships; Black Within black: The perceptions of black immigrant collegians and their US college experiences, 2015. **Orgs:** Am Col Personnel Asn, 1981-; res bd, ACPA, 1985; directorate comn IX assessment stud develop mem, ACPA, 1986; Omicron Delta Kappa, 1989; chair, assoc staff rep, Black Fac, Staff Asn; Full Gospel AME Zion; Media & Ed Bd ACPA; Am Asn Affirmative Action Officers; Black Women's Coun Univ Md, Col Pk; consult, Univ MD Campus Prog & Off Campus Presentations; Am Asn Univ Prof; Asn Study Higher Educ; Am Asn Higher Educ; Am Asn Univ Professors. **Home Addr:** 10603 Foxlake Dr, Mitchellville, MD 20721. **Business Addr:** Professor, University of Maryland, 3112-F Benjamin Bldg, College Park, MD 20742-1165, **Business Phone:** (301)405-0186.

## FRINK, SAMUEL H.

Business owner, executive, association executive. **Personal:** Born Mar 20, 1944, La Grange, NC; son of E B and O W; married Juanita Vereen; children: Ivan & Chaun. **Educ:** NC Cent Univ, Durham, NC, BS, chem, 1966; Ford Motor Dealer Training, Va, 1986. **Career:** Business man (retired); Ford Motor Co, Fairfax, Va, sales rep, 1970-80; Maj Lincoln-Mercury, sales mgr, 1980-86; Bobby Gerald Ford-Lincoln-Mercury, partnership, 1991; Grand Strand Nissan, partnership, 1994; Lay-Fisher Chevrolet/Olds Inc, partnership, 1995; Conway Ford Inc, pres, 1986, partner; Grand Strand Nissan, partner; Gubernatorial designee, currently. **Orgs:** Exec bd mem, Boy Scouts Am bd visitors, Coastal Carolina Col, 1989-90; pres, Conway Area Chamber Com, 1990; adv coun mem, Horry County Youth, 2000, 1988-90; adv bd, Myrtle Beach Br Nat Bank SC, 1991; bd mem, Coastal Educ Found, 2003-; bd visitors, E Craig Wall Sr Col Bus Admin; secy/treas, exec comm, vice chair, acad stud affair comm, vchair, gov affair comm, Coastal Carolina Univ. **Honors/Awds:** Minority Small Businessman of the Year, 7 States of Southeast Region, 1990; Elks Americanism Award, Scouts Am, 1989; Businessman of the Year, Phi Beta Sigma Fraternity, 1988; Man of the Year, Cherry Hill Baptist Church, 1988. **Home Addr:** 1775 Dirty Br Rd, Conway, SC 29527-5115, **Home Phone:** (843)397-1283. **Business Addr:** Board of Trustee, Coastal Carolina University, PO Box 261954, Conway, SC 29528-6054, **Business Phone:** (843)347-3161.

## FRISBY, H. RUSSELL, JR.

Executive. **Personal:** Born Dec 28, 1950, Baltimore, MD; son of H Russell Sr and Kathryn T; married June J; children: H Russell III & James. **Educ:** Swarthmore Col, BA, 1972; Yale Law Sch, JD, 1975. **Career:** Cable, McDaniel, Bowie & Bond, assoc, 1975-77; Md Atty Gen's Off, asst atty gen, 1977-79; Fed Communs Comn, atty, 1979-83; Weil, Gotshal & Manges, assoc, 1983-86; Melnicove, Kaufman, Weiner & Smouse, partner, 1986-89; Venable, Baetjer & Howard, LLP, partner, 1989-95; Md Pub Serv Comn, chmn, 1995-98; Competitive Telecommun Asn, pres; CompTel/ASCENT, chief exec officer, pres, 1998-2005; Kirkpatrick & Lockhart, partner, 2005-06; Fleischman & Harding, partner, 2006-09; Stinson Morrison Hecker LLP, partner, energy & telecommunications atty, 2009-. **Orgs:** Bd dir, United Way Cent Md; bd dir, Baltimore Urban League; bd dir, Baltimore Mus Art; fel Am Bar Found, 1992; fel MD Bar Found, 1992; Founding chair, Baltimore City Chamber Com, 1993-94; Am Bar Asn; vice chair communs comm, Nat Asn Regulatory Comnrs, 1997-98; coun, Minority Bus Enterprise Legal Defense & Educ Fund Inc; Fed-State Joint Bd Universal Serv, 1997-98; bd dir, PAETEC Holding Corp, 2007-;independent dir, Pepco Holdings Inc, 2012-. **Home Addr:** 10729 Midsummer Lane, Columbia, MD 21044, **Home Phone:** (410)997-3786. **Business Addr:** Partner, Stinson Morrison Hecker LLP, 1201 Walnut St Suite 2900, Kansas City, MO 64106, **Business Phone:** (816)842-8600.

## FROHMAN, ROLAND H.

Dentist. **Personal:** Born Aug 18, 1928, Detroit, MI; married Alice F Hibbett; children: Roland Jr, Shelley & Jill. **Educ:** Wayne State Univ, BA, 1951; Howard Univ, DDS, 1955. **Career:** Dr Robert L Moseley, assoc, 1957-61; pvt prac dentist, 1961-; Harper Hosp Detroit, staff, 1968-; Roland H Frohman PC, dentist, 1980-. **Orgs:** Am Dent Asn; Wolverine Dent Asn; Mich State Dent Asn; Detroit Dist Dent Asn; Moors Club. **Honors/Awds:** Certificate Recognition by Mayor of Detroit for service in Mayors Youth Employment Program, 1968. **Home Addr:** 1500 Balmoral Dr, Detroit, MI 48203-1445, **Home Phone:** (313)368-4570. **Business Addr:** Dentist, Roland H Frohman PC, 13026 W McNichols, Detroit, MI 48235-4115, **Business Phone:** (313)864-9110.

## FROST, WILLIAM HENRY

Mayor. **Personal:** Born Apr 17, 1930, Maysville, NC; son of Philanders and Gracie Parlen Perry; married Ari Mae Jones; children: Warren, Leddia Frost Chapman, Aletha & Elroy. **Career:** US Civil Serv, Camp Lejeune, NC, warehouseman, 1955-65, chauffeur, 1965-68, radio dispatcher, 1968-77, bus driver, 1977-85; Town Maysville, NC, alderman, 1972-85, mayor, 1985-99. **Orgs:** Maysville Develop Corp, 1967-; bd, 1969-, Costal County Develop Bd, Sr Citizen Bd, pres, currently; chmn, Jone County, Dem Party; Meals Wheels. **Home Addr:** 86 Main St, PO Box 191, Maysville, NC 28555, **Home Phone:** (910)743-7231.

## FRY, DARRELL

Journalist, writer. **Personal:** Born Apr 16, 1963, Oklahoma City, OK; son of Jay D and Helen M Holmes Gray. **Educ:** Fla State Univ, Tallahassee, FL, BS, 1986. **Career:** St Petersburg Times, St Petersburg, Fla, sports writer, 1986-2002, Walt Disney Co, sports media dir, 2005-; Walt Disney World, sports media dir, currently. **Orgs:** Phi Beta Sigma Fraternity, 1984-; Nat Asn Black Journalists, 1986-. **Honors/Awds:** First Place, Fla Sports Writers Asn, 1987; Honorable Mention, AP Sports Ed, 1988, 1990. **Home Addr:** 8904 Hannigan Ct, Tampa, FL 33626, **Home Phone:** (813)920-3379. **Business Addr:** Sports Media Director, Walt Disney World, 1500 Epcot Resorts Blvd, Lake Buena Vista, FL 32830, **Business Phone:** (407)934-4000.

## FRYAR, REV. IRVING DALE, SR.

Clergy, football player, football coach. **Personal:** Born Sep 28, 1962, Mt. Holly, NJ; married Jacqueline M; children: Londen A, Irving Jr & Adrianne M. **Educ:** Univ Nebr; S Fla Bible Col & Theol Sem, bible study. **Career:** Football player (retired), pastor, speaker, coach; New Eng Patriots, wide receiver & Punt returner, 1984-92; Miami Dolphins, 1993-95; Philadelphia Eagles, 1996-98; Wash Redskins, wide receiver, 1999-2000; CNN & Sports Illus, football analyst; New Jerusalem House God, pentecostal minister, founder & pastor, 2003-; Robbinsville High Sch, head football coach, currently. **Orgs:** Bd dir, Christian Quart; partner, Kingdom Network; bd dir & spokesperson, Stop Child Abuse Now; founder, Irving Fryar Found, 1996-. **Honors/Awds:** Community Service Award, New Eng Patriots 1776 Quarterback Club, 1988; True Value & NFL Man of the Year, Philadelphia Eagles, 1996; Emmy Award; Bart Starr Man of the Year Award, 1998; Lloyd Ritter Community Service Award, Volunteer Center of Burlington County. **Special Achievements:** First player selected, NFL draft, 1984; Had featured in the Oliver Stone movie, On Any Given Sunday; Author of the book, Sunday Is My Day. **Home Addr:** 51 Applegate Rd, Jobstown, NJ 08041-2202. **Business Addr:** Founder, Pastor, New Jerusalem House of God, 400 Wash St, Jobstown, NJ 08060, **Business Phone:** (609)267-7600.

## FRYE, HON. HENRY E.

Educator, chief justice. **Personal:** Born Aug 1, 1932, Richmond County, NC; son of Walter A (deceased) and Pearl A (deceased); married Shirely Taylor; children: Henry E & Harlan E. **Educ:** NC Agr & Tech State Univ, BS, 1953; Univ NC Law Sch, JD, 1959; Syracuse Univ Law Sch, attended 1958; Am Arbit Asn, cert, com arbit & mediation. **Career:** US atty, NC, pract, 1959-63, asst, 1963-65; NCC Univ Law Sch, prof, 1965-67, instr; Frye & Johnson, atty; NC House Rep, mem, 1968-80; NC state, Senate, 1981-82; Supreme Ct NC, assoc justice, 1983-99, chief judge, 1999-2001; Brooks, Pierce, McLendon, Hunphrey & Leonard, LLP, counr, 2001-16; NC Agr & Tech State Univ, vis prof, currently. **Orgs:** Chmn, N Carolina Inst Polit Leadership, 2013; Greensboro Bar Asn; Am Bar Asn; NC Bar Asn; NC Asn Black Lawyers; Ame Bar Assoc; Am Judicature Soc; life mem, Nat Bar Asn; Kappa Alpha Psi Frat; former mem, secy bd mgt, Hayes Taylor YMCA; deacon, Providence Bapt Church; life mem, Nat Asn Advan Colored People; Elon Univ Sch Law. **Honors/Awds:** Hon doctorate, Shaw Univ, 1971; First NC A&T State University Alumni Excellence Award, 1971; Alumni Excellence Award, A&T State Univ, 1972; R R Wright Award, Nat Bankers Asn, 1983; Carolina Peacemaker Award, 1983; Charles D McIver Medal, UNC-Greensboro, 1986; Distinguished Alumnus Award, UNC-Chapel Hill, 1986; Charles McIver Award, University North Carolina at Greensboro, 1986; Lawyer of the Year, Asn Black Lawyers, 1988; Appellate Judges Award, NC Acad Trial Lawyers, 1989; Brotherhood Award, Nat Conf Christians & Jews, 1991; Greensboro Bus Leaders Hall of Fame, 1991; Outstanding Alumnus Award, University North Carolina Chapel Hill, 1995; Hon doctorate, NC A&T State University, 1983; Hon doctorate, Livingstone College, 1999; Hon doctorate, Fayetteville State University, 2000; Hon doctorate, East Carolina University, 2001; W E B DuBois Award, Association Social Behavioral Sciences, 2002; William Richardson Davie Award, University North Carolina Chapel Hill, 2002; Laurel Wreath Award, Kappa Alpha Psi, 2003; Liberty Bell Award, NC Bar Association, 2004; William H. Hastie Award for Excellence, Judicial Counsel of the NBA, 2004; Distinguished Service Award, Greensboro Bar Association, 2008; Hon doctorate, UNC Asheville, 2003; Hon doctorate, Florida Memorial College, 2004; Hon doctorate, UNC Greensboro, 2006; American Judicature Society Justice Award, 2006; Nc Award, 2007; John J Parker Award, North Carolina Bar Association, 2007; North Caroliniana Society Award, The North Caroliniana Society, 2008; Power of Justice Award, Business Leader Magazine & NC Bar, 2008; Power of Justice Award, Bus Leader Mag & NC Bar, 2008; Distinguished Service Award, Greensboro Bar Asn, 2008; North Carolina Award, 2009. **Special Achievements:** First African-American to be elected to the North Carolina House of Representatives in the Twentieth Century; First African-American to serveon the Supreme Court of NC; Elected one of Guilford Co 6 repin NC House, 1968. **Home Addr:** 1401 S Benbow Rd, Greensboro, NC 27406. **Business Addr:** Of Counsel, Brooks Pierce McLendon Humphrey & Leonard LLP, 2000 Renaissance Plz 230 N Elm St, Greensboro, NC 27401, **Business Phone:** (336)371-3188.

## FRYE, NADINE GRACE

Nurse. **Personal:** Born Greensburg, PA; daughter of Charles and Virgie Middles Grasty. **Educ:** Univ Pittsburgh, BSN, 1947, M Lit, 1951, PhD, 1987. **Career:** Nurse (retired); Western Psych Inst & Clin, Pgh PA, staff nurse & head nurse, 1948-50; Detroit Dept Health, Detroit MI, pub health nurse, 1951-53; Northville State Hosp, Nursing Educ Dept, instr/dir, 1953-56; Lafayette Clin, Detroit MI, dir nursing educ, 1956-57; Wayne State Univ, Detroit MI, instr, nursing, 1957-59; Mercywood Hosp, Ann Arbor MI, dir nursing educ 1959-61; Univ Mich Sch Nursing, asst prof, dir nursing, 1961-66; Western Psych Inst & Clin, Pittsburgh Pa, assoc dir cmh/mr nursing, 1969-73; Univ Pittsburgh Sch Nursing, prof Nursing, 1969-90. **Orgs:** Bd dir, 3 Rivers Youth Pittsburgh, 1971-77; consult St Agnes Cath Sch Pittsburgh, 1971-73; consult Univ S MS Sch Nursing, 1976; consult Univ Pittsburgh Sch Nursing, 1980-81; Am Nurses Asn, 1947; Alpha Kappa Alpha; Pittsburgh Club Nat Asn Negro Bus & Prof Women; Adv Community, Youth Ministry, Pittsburgh, PA, 1988-91; Int Sigma Theta Tau Hon Nursing Sorority; pres, Cong Bridge Clubs, 1996-99; secy & treas, Am Bridge Asn. **Honors/Awds:** Honor Award Kappa Alpha Psi, Pgh, Pa, 1943; Robert L Vann Mem Scholar, 1943; Alumni Award Univ Pittsburgh, 1980; Alumni Serv Award, Univ Pittsburgh, 1986. **Special Achievements:** One of first Black women admitted to Pittsburgh's nursing program, 1943. **Home Addr:** 6352 Aurelia St, Pittsburgh, PA 15206-4319, **Home Phone:** (412)441-6032.

## FRYE, REGINALD STANLEY

Executive. **Personal:** Born May 18, 1936, Yakima, WA; son of Elise Garrett and Virgil O; married Mikki Goree; children: Gregory, Martin & Trana. **Educ:** Los Angeles Community Col, Los Angeles, CA, 1956. **Career:** V O Frye Mfg, Seattle, Wash, salesman, 1959-64; Wash Natural Gas, Seattle, Wash, salesman, 1964-72; 3A Industs Inc, Seattle, Wash, pres & owner, 1972-2007. **Orgs:** Pres, Cent Contractors Asn, 1976-85; vice-chair, State Wash Off Minority & Women's Bus Enterprises Adv Bd, 1983-87. **Home Addr:** 2004 33rd Ave S, PO BOX 14029, Seattle, WA 98114-4915, **Home Phone:** (206)722-0472. **Business Addr:** President, Owner, 3A Industries Inc, 3101 Martin Luther King Jr Way, Seattle, WA 98114, **Business Phone:** (206)725-2200.

## FRYE, ROBERT EDWARD, SR.

Association executive, executive. **Personal:** Born Oct 11, 1936, Washington, DC; son of James E Jr and Alberta Edwards; married Deloris Ann Smith; children: Robert Jr & Amanda; married Rotha Isabel Holbert. **Educ:** Howard Univ, BSc, 1958; Am Univ, MPA, 1970; Fed Exec Inst, attended 1975. **Career:** AUS, Map Serv, cartogr, 1958-65; Wolf R & D Corp, proj mgr, 1965-69; Nat Bur Stand, comput syst analyst, 1969-73; US Consumer Prod Safety Comn, dir injury surveillance div, 1973-77, dir, hazard anal div, 1977-96, Off Planning & Eval, dir, 1997-99; Fairfax Co Sch Bd, mem-at-large, 1978-85, 1989-93, 1996-2003, vice chmn, 1998-99, chmn, 1999-2000; Nat Sch Bd Asn, consult, 1985-89. **Orgs:** Founding mem, Reston Black Focus, 1969-; Kappa Alpha Psi, Nat Fire Reporting Comt, Nat Fire Protection Asn, 1972-85; finance comt, 1982-85, VA Sch Bd Asn, 1989-93; Nat Caucus Black Sch Bd Mem, 1983-85, 1989; Fairfax County Comt 100, 1985-89; Fairfax Co Civil Serv Comt, 2005-; bd visitor, Long wood Univ, 2006-. **Honors/Awds:** Community Service Award, Urban League Nova Chap, 1981; Community Service Award, Nat Coun Negro Women, 1985; CPSC EEO Achievement Award, 1986; CPSC Chairman's Award, 1988, 1996; Community Service Award, Northern VA Alumni Chap, Omega Psi Phi, 1990, 2000; Fairfax County Community Service Award, 1992; CPSC Distinguished Service Award, 1993; Chairman's Commendation, 1995; Nova Alumni Award, Howard Univ, 1999; Community Hero Award, A & E Biography, 2002. **Home Addr:** 5514 Ivor St, Springfield, VA 22151-3211, **Home Phone:** (703)658-0526.

**Business Addr:** Board of Visitor, Longwood University, 201 High St, Farmville, VA 23909, **Business Phone:** (434)395-2000.

### FRYE, THOMAS JOHN (TOM FRYE)

Entrepreneur, chief executive officer. **Personal:** Born Jan 17, 1945, New York, NY; son of Thomas and Gloria; married Linda; children: Thomas Jr. **Educ:** Lincoln Univ, BA, 1969; John Marshall Law Sch, LLB, 1974. **Career:** Belranie Ins Co, claim adjuster & claim mgr, 1967-73; US Dept Labor, br chief, dep comnr, asst reg adminr, 1973-84; State Ill, dir, 1984-85; Zenith Ins Co, claim mgr, 1985-90; prof liability independent adjusting co, vpres; Frye Claims Consul & Admin Inc, founder & chief exec officer, 1990-; Ill Dept Labor, dep dir; Reliance & United Pac, claims rep, supvr & claims mgr; Statewide Legal Mal-pract Independent Adjusting Co, vpres. **Orgs:** Pres, San Francisco Indust Claim Asn, 1994-95; Minority Claim Assoc, exec dir, 1990-92. **Home Addr:** 836 Lakeshore Dr, Redwood City, CA 94065, **Home Phone:** (415)598-9159. **Business Addr:** Founder, Chief Executive Officer, Frye Claims Consultation & Administration Inc, 3500 Breakwater Ct Bldg A, Hayward, CA 94545, **Business Phone:** (800)322-3793.

### FRYSON, SIM E.

Chief executive officer, automotive executive. **Personal:** Born Jan 1, 1947?, Charleston, WV. **Educ:** WVa State Univ, BA, educ; Univ Detroit, Gen Motors Inst, assoc degree mkt & bus. **Career:** Int Bus Mach Corp; Kanawha County car dealership, sales exec, sales mgr; C & O Motors; Joe Holland Chevrolet, bus mgr; Sim Fryson Motor Co Inc, chief exec officer & pres, owner, 1995-; Auto Bus Keith Bateman. **Orgs:** Ashland Rotary Nissan Dealer Adv Bd; bd dir, Paramont Arts Theather; bd mem, Ashland Alliance; Shiloh Seventh-Day Adventist Church. **Home Addr:** 126 StoneyBrooke Dr, Ashland, KY 41101. **Business Addr:** President, Chief Executive Officer, Sim Fryson Motor Co Inc, 2565 Winchester Ave, Ashland, KY 41101, **Business Phone:** (606)329-2288.

### FUDGE, ANN MARIE

Executive, association executive. **Personal:** Born Apr 23, 1951, Washington, DC; married Richard Sr; children: Richard Jr & Kevin. **Educ:** Simmons Col, BA, retail mgt, 1973; Harvard Bus Sch, MBA, 1977. **Career:** Gen Elec, manpower spec, 1973-75; Gen Mills, mkt asst, 1977-78, asst prod mgr, 1978-80, prod mgr, 1980-83, mkt dir, 1983-86; Kraft Gen Foods, assoc dir strategic planning, 1986-89; Dinners & Enhancers div, from vpres mkt & develop to gen mgr, 1989-93; Kraft Foods, exec vpres, 1993-2000,; Pres Beverages Desserts & Post Div, 2000-01; Maxwell House Coffee Co, pres, 1994-2001; Young & Rubicam Brands, Young & Rubicam Advert, chmn, chief exec officer, 2003-07; Kraft Gen Foods, pres. **Orgs:** Nat Black MBA Asn, 1981-; Jr League, 1981-; Exec Leadership Coun, pres, 1994-96; Links; Comt 200; bd dirs, Allied Signal Inc; bd dir, Liz Claiborne; bd dir, Fed Res Bank New York; non-exec dir, Marriott Intl; bd dir, Honeywell International Inc, 2001-03; bd dir, Gen Elec; Coun Foreign Rels; bd dirs, Simmons Col; bd dirs, Harvard Bus Sch Alumni Asn; bd dirs, Catalyst Adv Bd; Boys & Girls Club Am; Partnership a Drug-Free Am; bd, Gen Elec; bd, Novartis; bd, Unilever; chair, US Progs Adv Bd Gates Found; trustee, Rockefeller Found; trustee, Brookings Inst; trustee, Coun Foreign Rels; Buzzient Inc; vice chair, Harvard Bd Overseers; trustee, Morehouse Col, 2006-. **Honors/Awds:** COGME Fellow, 1975-76; YWCA Leadership Award, 1979; Candace Award, 1992; Glamour Mag, Woman of the Year, 1995; Advert Woman of the Year, 1995; Alumni Achievement Award, Harvard Bus Sch, 1998; Achievement Award, Exec Leadership Coun, 2000; named by Fortune mag, one of 50 Most Powerful Women in American Business; Matrix Award, 2004. **Special Achievements:** First African-American woman to head a major advertising agency. **Business Addr:** Chairman, Chief Executive Officer, Young & Rubicam Brands, 285 Madison Ave, New York, NY 10017, **Business Phone:** (212)210-3000.

### FUDGE, MARCIA L.

Politician. **Personal:** Born Oct 29, 1952. **Educ:** Ohio State Univ, BS, bus admin, 1975; Cleveland Marshall Col Law, Cleveland State Univ, JD, 1983. **Career:** Pvt indust; Cuyahoga County; Cong USA; Cuyahoga County Prosecutor's Off, lawyer, pvt pract; dir, dir budget & finance & office admin; Us Rep Stephanie Tubbs Jones, 1999-2001; Warrensville Heights City, mayor, 2000-08; Ohio's 11th Cong Dist, US rep, 2008-; One Hundred Tenth Cong, dem. **Orgs:** Pres, Delta Sigma Theta Sorority, 1996-00, co-chair, Nat Social Action Comn; Zion Chapel Baptist Church; Dem Party; bd trustee, Cleveland Pub Libr; Shaker Heights Alumni Asn Hall Fame Class, 2003; Church God, Anderson, IN. **Special Achievements:** First Female and First African-American mayor. **Business Addr:** US Representative, Ohio's 11th Congressional District, 1019 Longworth House Off Bldg, Washington, DC 20515, **Business Phone:** (202)225-7032.

### FUERST, JEAN STERN

Educator. **Personal:** Born Sep 29, 1919, New York, NY; son of Charles F and Rose S; married Dorothy Braude. **Career:** Chicago Housing, dir res, 1943-52; Loyola Univ, prof social welfare policy, Sch Social Work, prof emer, currently. **Home Addr:** 5401 S Hyde Pk Blvd, Chicago, IL 60615, **Home Phone:** (773)324-3285. **Business Addr:** Professor Emeritus, Loyola University Chicago, 1032 W Sheridan Rd, Chicago, IL 60660, **Business Phone:** (773)274-3000.

### FUFUKA, TIKA N.Y.

Entrepreneur. **Personal:** Born Feb 21, 1952, Cleveland, OH; daughter of Mindoro Reed and Russell Reed. **Educ:** Cuyahoga Community Col, AA, AAB, 1973; Mich State Univ, BA, labor rels, 1975; Cleveland State Univ, int bus. **Career:** May Co, asst personnel dir, 1975-78; JC Penny, merchandiser, 1978-80; Joseph Horne, sports mgr, 1980-81; Higbee, fashion buyer, 1981-86; Mindoro & Assocs, exec vpres, 1982-; Fashion Bug, merchandise exec, 1986-92; Mindys Return Fashion, pres & chief exec officer, 1993-; Exec & Prof Protection Serv Inc, exec vpres, 1996; Legal Shield, independent assoc, 2012-. **Orgs:** Chair, Bus Women Comt, 21st Cong Dist Caucus, 1984; Urban League Greater Cleveland, 1984-90; Oper Push, 1987-90; Ohio Youth Adv, 1987-90; chmn bd, Black Focus, 1989-; Cleveland State Univ, BLK Aspiration Week Celebration Comn, 1990; Cleveland Opera, MAP Prog, 1990; Cleveland Female Bus Enterprise; Mayor's Census Task Force; 100 Bulk Women Coalition; Bulk Cong Caucus Braintrust; Asn MBA Exec; Black Prof Asn; Nat Asn Negro Bus & Prof Women; Nat Asn Female Execs; United Bulk Fund; Greater E Cleveland Dem Club; League Women Voters; Ohio Rainbow Coalition; Black Elected Dem Off Ohio; Cuyahoga Hills Boys Adv Coun; Nat Coun Negro Women; Nat Polit Cong Bulk Women; Career Beginning Prog, 1991-93; United Way Leadership Dev Prog Comt, 1992; vice chmn, Joint Comt Med Provider Impact State OH, 1992-; chmn, United Way Centralized Resource & Referral Serv, 1993; United Way Gen Assembly, 1993-96; Women Community Fed, 1993; Women App Off Proj, 1994; WCPN Radio, 1994; Planned Parenthood Greater Cleveland, 1995; Citizen League Cleveland, 1995; Friends Fed Libr, 1995; United Way Appeal Comt, 1996; Cleveland Mus Art, 1996; Pub Affairs Comt, Greater Cleveland Growth Asn, 1996; United Way Pub Policy Comt, 1997; Outstanding Young Am Nomination Comt, 1997; assoc, Nat Non-Profit Bd, 1997; Outstanding Young Woman Am, Nat Nomination Comt, 1997. **Honors/Awds:** Committee Award, Cleveland State Univ, 1991; United Way Leadership Award, 1991; Outstanding Young Man of America, Nat Nomination Comt, 1998; United Way Service Appreciation, 1998 & 2001; Community Relation Council Service Award, Cleveland Job Corps, 1998. **Home Addr:** 12001 Martin Luther King Jr Blvd, Cleveland, OH 44105, **Home Phone:** (216)491-8867.

### FUGET, DR. CHARLES ROBERT

School administrator. **Personal:** Born Dec 15, 1929, Rochester, PA; son of Clinton H and Mary Harris; married Enid Deane; children: Craig D; married Audra Blanding. **Educ:** Geneva Col, BS, 1951; Pa State Univ, MS, 1953, PhD, 1956. **Career:** Educator (retired); Esso Res & Eng, Linden, NJ, res chemist, 1955-56; Callery Chem Corp, Callery, Pa, res chemist, 1957-63; State Univ NY, Col, Buffalo, prof chem, 1963-64; Geneva Col, Beaver Falls, Pa, chmn, prof physics, 1964-71; AUS, Ballistic Res Labs, Aberdeen, Md, consult, 1968-69; Ind Univ PA, Sch Arts & Sci, assoc dean, 1971-76, Col Natural Sci & Math, dean, 1977-84, Stud Univ Affairs, actg vpres, 1984-85, Col Natural Sci & Math, dean, 1985-88; Pa Dept Educ, Harrisburg, Pa, dep secy, 1988-91; Ind Univ, Pa, interim pres, 1991-92; Pa Dept Educ, Harrisburg, Pa, dep secy, comnr, post-sec & higher educ, 1992-94; Bennett Col, interim pres, 2002, spec asst to pres Johnetta B Cole, 2002; Fisk Univ, interim pres, 2003-04. **Orgs:** Chmn, Pa Comn United Ministries Higher Educ, 1978-80; Ind Hosp Corp, 1978-83; bd govs, Gen Bd Higher Educ & Ministry, 1980-88, 1992-2000; bd dir, Ind Rotary Club, 1982-88; vpres, Univ Senate United Methodist Church, 1989-92; Nat Col Athletic Asn. **Honors/Awds:** Distinguished Service Award, Upper Beaver Valley Jaycees, 1969; Distinguished Service Award, Alumni Asn, Geneva Col, 1976; Presidents Medal of Distinction, Ind Univ, Pa, 1988; Hahnemann Univ, LHD, 1988; Geneva Col, DSc, hon, 1990; Ind Univ Pa, Hon Doctor Pub Serv, 1995. **Home Addr:** 859 W Boston Blvd, Detroit, MI 48202.

### FUGETT, JEAN SCHLOSS, JR.

Football player, executive, lawyer. **Personal:** Born Dec 16, 1951, Baltimore, MD; son of J R and Carolyn; married Carlotta; children: Joseph, Audie & Reggie. **Educ:** Amherst Col, BA, 1972; George Washington Univ Law Sch, JD. **Career:** Football player (retired), executive, lawyer, educator; Dallas Cowboys, tight end, 1972-75; Wash Redskins, tight end, 1976-79; Wash Post, intern; CBS Sports, football color commentator; Jean S Fugett Jr Firm, atty, 1981-2011; TLC Beatrice Int Holdings Co, chief exec officer & chmn, 1993-95; Baltimore lawfirm, founding partner; TLC Beatrice Int Food, mgr; Axum Capital Partners, managing dir, 2008-09; Fugett Baseball Group, founding partner, 2010-13; Towson Univ, adj prof, 2014-. **Orgs:** dir & vice-chair, McCall Pattern Co Mgt Comt; Leadership Coun Am Diabetes Asn Md Chap; Pres, Nat Football League Players Asn, 2005-; chancellor, Md Chap Sons Am Revolution. **Honors/Awds:** Pro Bowl, 1977. **Special Achievements:** Participated in Super Bowl X with Dallas Cowboys; first African Am to be inducted into the Md Soc of the Sons of the Am Revolution; He was the first African American to win Baltimore Catholic Athlete of the Year. **Business Addr:** President, National Football League Players Association, 2021 L St NW Suite 600, Washington, DC 20036-4909, **Business Phone:** (202)463-2200.

### FUHR, GRANT SCOTT

Hockey player, hockey coach. **Personal:** Born Sep 28, 1962, Spruce Grove, AB; son of Robert and Betty; married Corrine; children: 2; married Jill; children: Robert. **Career:** Hockey player, coach (retired); Edmunton Oilers, goalie, 1981-90; Nat Hockey League All-Star Game, 1984-86, 1988-89; Toronto Maple Leafs, goalie, 1991-92; Buffalo Sabres, goalie, 1992-95; Los Angeles Kings; St Louis Blues, 1995-99; St John Flames, 1999-2000; Calgary Flames, goalkeper, 1999-2000, goalkeeping consult, 2000-04; Phoenix Coyotes, goaltending coach, 2004-09. **Orgs:** Arthritis Soc Can; Lupus Can. **Honors/Awds:** NHL Second All-Star Team, 1982; Stanley Cup Champion, 1984, 1985, 1987, 1988, 1990; Gold Medal, Canada Cup Champion, 1984, 1987; Vezina Trophy, 1988; Silver Medal, World Championships, 1989; William M Jennings Trophy, 1994; Hockey Hall of Fame, 2003; Alberta Sports Hall of Fame, 2004. **Special Achievements:** First to be inducted into the Hockey Hall of Fame.

### FULGHAM, ROIETTA GOODWIN

Educator. **Personal:** Born Jan 28, 1948, Oakland, CA; daughter of Roy Alexander and Dovie Juanita Miles; children: Kendall Young Blood & Keia Syreeta. **Educ:** Utah State Univ, Logan, BS, 1966, MS, 1972. **Career:** Area Voc Ctr Ogden UT, off occups supvr, 1971-75; Yosemite Jr Col Dist Modesto, instr, 1975-76; Los Rios Comm Col Dist ARC, bus technol prof & chair, 1976-; Am River Col, bus prof, chairperson; Wang Labs Inc, support analyst, 1986; Westroots Bus Writing Syst, consult, 1986-2000. **Orgs:** Nat Western Calif Bus Educ Asn, 1976-; Nat Educ Asn, Calif Teachers Asn, 1976-; secy, Nat Asn Advan Colored People Cent Area Conf, 1976-87; St coun rep, Calif Teachers Asn, 1979-85; nat teller, Nat Asn Advan Colored People, 1980-81; secy, Utah St Univ Black Alumni Asn, 1980-; chairperson, Nat Asn Advan Colored People W Coast Region, 1982-83, Nat Asn Advan Colored People, ACT-SO Prog Sacramento Br, 1982-85; chairperson, Outstanding Bus Stud ProgCalif Bus Educ Asn, 1983; off mgr, IDS Fin Serv, 1985-86; vpres, Nat Asn Advan Colored People Calif St Conf, 1988-93; treas, NCP Sacramento Br, 1991-94; DeltaSigma Theta Inc, 1991-; pres, Growing Alternatives Foster Family Agency, 1995-2007; Nat Asn Advan Colored People Nat Youth Work Comn, 2000-02; pres-elect, Calif Bus Educ Asn, 2010-11; pres, Western Bus Educ Asn, 2011-; lifetime mem, Nat Asn Advan Colored People. **Home Addr:** 6600 Branchwater Way, Citrus Heights, CA 95621, **Home Phone:** (916)725-2779. **Business Addr:** Chairperson, American River College, 4700 Col Oak Dr, Sacramento, CA 95841, **Business Phone:** (916)484-8258.

### FULLER, ALMYRA OVETA

Scientist, college teacher. **Personal:** Born Aug 31, 1955, Mebane, NC; daughter of Herbert R and Deborah Evelyn Woods; married Jerry Caldwell; children: Brian Randolph Caldwell. **Educ:** Univ NC, Chapel Hill, BA, 1977, PhD, 1983; Univ Chicago, IL, postdoctoral study, 1987. **Career:** Univ NC, res asst, 1977-83; Univ Chicago, IL, instr & fel, 1983-87, res assoc, 1987-88; Univ Mich, Ann Arbor, asst prof, assoc prof, currently. **Orgs:** Alpha Kappa Alpha, Basileus Alumni Chap, 1977-78; co-founder Res Triangle, Nat Tech Asn, 1980-; asst dir, Summer Apprentice Res Prog, Univ NC, Chappel Hill, 1981-82; Sigma Xi, 1983-; AAAS, 1984-; Am Soc Microbiol, 1984-; Adv Comy Fel Prog, Line berger Cancer Res Ctr, 1989-; a bd regents, Ad Hoc Reviewer, 1989; Howard Hughes Doctoral Fel Panel, 1991. **Honors/Awds:** NTA Service Award, Res Triangle Chap NTA, 1983; Anna Fuller Fund Postdoctoral Award, 1983-84; Thornton Professional Achievement Award, Chicago chap, NTA, 1984; NIH Postdoctoral Research Award, Nat Inst Sci, 1984-86; Postdoctoral Research Award, Ford Found, 1986-87. **Special Achievements:** Author of many publications; Author of scientific publications, 1983-. **Home Addr:** 9398 Hidden Lake Circle, Dexter, MI 48130, **Home Phone:** (313)426-5722. **Business Addr:** Associate Professor, University of Michigan, 5641 Med Sci Bldg II, Ann Arbor, MI 48109-0620, **Business Phone:** (734)763-3531.

### FULLER, CHARLES

Playwright, writer. **Personal:** Born Mar 5, 1939, Philadelphia, PA; son of Charles Henry Sr and Lillian Anderson; married Miriam A Nesbitt; children: Charles III & David; married Claire Prieto. **Educ:** Villanova Univ, attended 1958; La Salle Univ, DFA, 1967. **Career:** Afro-American Arts Theatre, co-founder & co-dir, 1967-71; Playwriting Creative Artist Pub Serv, CAPS fel, 1975; Nat Endowment Arts, fel playwriting, 1976-77; Radio work: The Black Experience, dir, 1970-71; Stage writings: The Perfect Party, 1969; In My Many Names & Days, 1972; The Candidate, 1974; In the Deepest Part of Sleep, 1974; First Love, 1974; The Lay Out Letter, 1975; The Brownsville Raid, 1976; Sparrow in Flight, 1978; Zooman & the Sign, 1980; A Soldiers Play, 1981, 1982, 1983; Sally, 1988; Prince, Negro Ensemble Co Theatre Four, 1988; We, 1989; Films: A Soldier's Story, adaptation of play, 1984; Miles, 1994; TV series: "Roots, Resistance, and Renaissance", 1967; "The Sky Is Gray, American Short Story", 1980; "A Gathering of Old Men", 1987; "Urban Blight", 1987; "Sonnyboy", 1993; "Zooman", 1995; "The Badge", 1995; "Love Songs", 1997; "The Slave Dancer", 1998; Soldiers Story, author, currently; Chadama Ltd & Chadama II, pres & chief exec officer. **Orgs:** Writers Guild Am E. **Honors/Awds:** Rockefeller Grant Playwriting, 1976-77; Guggenheim fellowship for playwriting, 1977-78; Obie Award, Best Playwright, 1981; Audelco Awards, Best Playwright & Best Play, 1981, 1982; Theatre Club Award, Best Play; Pulitzer Prize for Drama, 1982; Best American Play Award, New York Critics, 1982; Outer Circle Critics Award, Best Play, 1982; Hazelett Award, Distinguished Artist, Pa Coun Arts; Edgar Award. **Special Achievements:** Nominee, Academy Award, screenwriting, Soldier's Story; Author of Snatch: The Adventures of David and Me, 2010. **Business Addr:** Author, William Morris Agency, 1350 Avenue of the Americas, New York, NY 10019.

### FULLER, COREY BUSHE

Football coach, football player. **Personal:** Born May 11, 1971, Tallahassee, FL; son of Vincent and Nina Dorsey. **Educ:** Fla State Univ, criminol & child develop. **Career:** Football player (retired), coach; Minn Vikings, left cornerback, 1995-98; Cleveland Browns, free safety & safety, 1999-2002, left cornerback, 1999-2002; Baltimore Ravens, right corner back & defensive back, 2003, left cornerback, 2004; E Gadsden High Sch, head football coach, 2010-12; Fla A&M Univ, defensive backs coach, interim head football coach, 2014-. **Business Addr:** Interim Head Football Coach, Florida A&M University, 1601 S Martin Luther King Jr Blvd, Tallahassee, FL 32307.

### FULLER, CURTIS D.

Composer, music arranger or orchestrator, musician. **Personal:** Born Dec 15, 1934, Detroit, MI; married Judith Patterson; children: Ronald, Darryl, Gerald, Dellaney & Wellington; married Catherine Rose Driscoll. **Educ:** Univ Detroit, Detroit Inst Arts; Wayne State Univ, BA; Bronx Comm Col, music theory; Henry St Settlement Inst, jazzmobile prog. **Career:** Yusef Lateef's Quintet; Dizzy Gillispie Orchestra; Quincy Jones Orchestra; Art Blakey "Jazz Messengers" Count Basie Orchestra; LITU, Long Island, NY, counr & Instr; Compositions: Smokin; Jacque's Groove; Sop City; People Places & Things; Crankin; Kwanza; Love & Understanding; A Caddy for daddy; Albums: New Trombone, Curtis Fuller with Red Garland, The Opener, Bone & Bari, 1957; Sliding Easy, Blues-ette, 1959; Meet The Jazztet, 1960; South American Cookin', The Magnificent Trombone of Curtis Fuller, Soul Trombone (Impulse! Records), 1961; Cabin in the Sky (Impulse! Records), 1962; Fire And Filigree (Bee Hive Records) with Sam Jones, Freddie Waits, Walter Bishop, Jr., Sal Nistico, Four on the Outside (Timeless Records), 1978; Curtis Fuller Meets Roma Jazz Trio (Timeless Records), 1982; Blues-ette, Part 2, 1993; Up Jumped Spring, 2004; Keep It Simple, 2005; I Will Tell Her, 2010; The Story of Cathy and Me, 2011; Down Home, 2012; Ny Summer Sch Arts, fac mem. **Orgs:** Local 802 Musicians Union; Broadcast Music writers. **Honors/Awds:** Downbeat Award; Pittsburg Courier Award. **Special Achievements:** Recorded World Award Shaefer Beer Award, recorded musical Cabin In Sky by Vernon Duke with the NY Phil Strings & Brass on ABC Paramount; performed at NY Radio City Jam Session 1973; performed at Tribute to Charlie Parker, 1975; performed at Newport Jazz Fest. **Home Addr:** 405 12 Atkins Ave, Neptune, NY 07753. **Business Addr:** Musician, 1864 7 Ave Suite 52, New York, NY 10026.

### FULLER, DORIS J.

Association executive, teacher, educator. **Personal:** Born May 26, 1945, Houston County, GA; daughter of Sim Clinton Jr and Bertha

Mae Clark. **Educ:** Morris Brown Col, BS, 1966; Univ San Francisco, attended 1969; Ga State Univ, MEd, 1975. **Career:** Atlanta Bd Educ, teacher, 1966-78, 1996; Southern Bell, asst mgr, 1978-94; Atlanta Metrop Col, adj instr & math, 1994; Benjamin Elijah Mays High Sch, teacher; Losoya Intermediate, teacher. **Orgs:** Vpres, Atlanta Alumnae Chap, DST Sorority, 1977-79; nominating comt chairperson, Southern Region DST Sorority Inc, 1978-80; pres, Magic Toastmasters TI, 1979, 1983, 1986; Southern Bell Speaker's Bur, 1980-94; State Youth Leadership Coord Dist 14 TI, 1981; rec sect mem, MBC Nat Alumni Asn, 1984-88; pres, Atlanta Chap MBC Alumni Asn, 1985-87; co-chairperson, Men's & Women's Unity Day Beulah Bapt Church, 1985; vpres, MBC Nat Alumni Asn, 1988-95. **Honors/Awds:** President's Award, Toastmasters Int, 1980; Outstanding Corp Alumni, NAFEO Wash DC, 1983; Presidential Citation, MBC Alumni Asn, Atlanta Chap, 1985; Outstanding Alumni MBC Student Govt Asn, 1985; Southern Bell Speakers Bureau Achievement Award, 1986; Southern Bell Best-of-the-Best Winner, 1988; Alumna of the Year, MBC Nat Alumni Asn, 1989; Woman of the Year, Beulah Baptist Church, 1997; Trustee of the Year, 1998. **Home Addr:** 2190 Star Mist Dr SW, Atlanta, GA 30311-5428, **Home Phone:** (404)344-2564. **Business Addr:** Teacher, Losoya Intermediate, Rm 101 1610 Martinez Losoya Rd, San Antonio, TX 78221, **Business Phone:** (210)882-1602.

### FULLER, GLORIA A.

Librarian. **Personal:** Born May 28, 1952, Brunswick, GA; daughter of Calvin Sinclair Atkinson Sr and Rosetta Frazier Atkinson; married Jimmy Lee; children: Gabrielle Amanda. **Educ:** SC State Univ, Orangeburg, SC, BS, 1974; Prince George's Community Col, Largo, Md, AA, 1980; Univ Md, College Park, Md, MLS, 1982. **Career:** Florence Sch Dist, Florence, SC, media specialist, 1974-75; Fedl Law Enforcement Trng Ctr, Brunswick, Ga, libr tech, 1975-76; Smithsonian Inst, Wash, DC, libr tech, 1976-83, libr, 1983-85; Defense Intelligence Agency, Wash, DC, info serv specialist, 1985-92; DIA Classified Libr, Database Servs Div, chief, 1992-. **Orgs:** Treas, fin secy, chair audit &chair reg his, Delta Sigma Theta Sorority, Inc, 1971-; Am Libr Asn, 1981-; Am Asn Law Libr, 1983-89; DC Online Users Grp, 1984-; Fed Libr Round Table, 1985-; ALA Black Caucus, 1988-89; FEDLINK Exec Adv coun, 1991-93; Armed Forces Libr Round Table, 1991; Fed Libr & Info ctr Comt, 1992-, Budget & Fin Working Grp, 1994-95; Community Open Source Prog Off (COSPO) Res Secretariat, 1993-96; Intelligence Community Librarians' Comt (ICLC); Emmanuel Baptist Church; Delta Sigma Theta Sorority Inc, MD jour, 1997-. **Honors/Awds:** Certification of Award for Exceptional Service, Smithsonian Inst, 1979-80, 1984-85; Letters of Appreciation, 1986, 1987, 1988, 1989 & 1994-95, Service Award, 1985, 1990 &1995-2000, Defense Intelligence Agency; Certificate of Recognition, Oper Desert Shield & Desert Storm, 1991; Community Open Source Prog Off, Certificate of Appreciation, 1995; Defense Intelligence Agency, Special Achievement Award, 1995-2002; Exceptional Performance Award, Central Intelligence Agency, 1995; Delta Sigma Theta Sorority Inc, 25 Years of Membership, 1996; Certificate of Appreciation in recognition of support to DIA & family mem employees who lost their lives as result of the Sept 11, 2001 terrorist attack on the Pentagon. **Home Addr:** 10715 Tyrone Dr, Upper Marlboro, MD 20772-4630. **Business Addr:** Chief, Defense Intelligence Agency, SVI-4 Rm E4-250, Washington, DC 20340-5100, **Business Phone:** (202)231-3231.

### FULLER, DR. HAROLD DAVID

Educator. **Personal:** Born Sep 1, 1937, Oklahoma City, OK; son of Andrew and Tisha Mae; married Annie Laurie Blood; children: April Beth & Jeremy David. **Educ:** Okla Univ, Norman, OK, BA, 1959; Ariz State Univ, Tempe, AZ, MA, 1968; EdD, 1992. **Career:** Educator (retired); USAF, Luke Air Force Base, airman, 1960-66; Roosevelt Sch Dist, Phoenix, AZ, teacher, 1964-68, community sch dir, 1968-71, asst prin, 1971-73; Mesa Pub Schs, Mesa, AZ, prin, 1973; Preside Sirrins Adult Day Health Care Bd. **Orgs:** Champaign chmn, Mesa United Way, 1990-91; pres bd, Mesa ARC, 1987-89; vice chair bd, Mesa United Way, 1987-89; pres bd, Mesa Family Young Men's Christian Asn, 1986-87; chmn bd, HEATS Found, 1990-; Preside Sirrino Adult Day Health Care. **Home Addr:** 1724 E Hope St, Mesa, AZ 85203-3925, **Home Phone:** (480)834-4959.

### FULLER, DR. HOWARD L.

Educator. **Personal:** Born Jan 14, 1941, Shreveport, LA; children: 3. **Educ:** Carroll Col, BS, 1962; Western Res Univ, MSA, social sci, 1964; Marquette Univ, PhD, sociol foundations educ, 1985. **Career:** Urban League, Chicago, Ill, staff, 1964; Oper Breakthrough, Durham, NC, staff, 1965-70; Malcolm X Liberation Univ, staff, 1970-74; labor organizer, 1974-76; Marquette Univ, Off Edu Opp, dir spec servs, 1976-83, Educ Opportunity Prog, assoc dir, 1979-83, Inst Transformation Learning, founder, dir & distinguished prof educ, 1995-, Inst Transformation Learning, dir; Wis Dept Employ Rels, secy, 1983-86; Milwaukee Area Tech Col, dean, 1986-88; Milwaukee Dept Health & Human Servs, dir, 1988-91; Milwaukee Pub Sch, supt, 1991-95. **Orgs:** Bd mem, Tran ctr Youth; Greater Milwaukee Edu Trust; Crusade Save Our C; bd dir, Johnson Found; Pew Forum Stand-based Reform; chair, Quest-Milwaukee; bd dir, Joyce Found; bd dir, Sch Choice Wis; bd dir, Advocates Sch Choice; sr fel Brown Univ, 1995-97; co founder & chair, Black Alliance for Educ Options, 2000-; chair bd, Alliance Choices Educ Milwaukee; chair bd, Leadership Acad; chair bd, Black Alliance Educ Options; chair, Charter Sch Rev Comt City Milwaukee; bd dir, Transcenter Youth. **Business Addr:** Director & Distinguished Professor of Education, Founder, Marquette University, Helfaer Bldg 750 N 18th St, Milwaukee, WI 53233, **Business Phone:** (414)288-5775.

### FULLER, JACK LEWIS

Fashion designer. **Personal:** Born Dec 30, 1945, Toombs County, GA; son of Mell and Elvera Gillis. **Educ:** Parsons Sch Design, BFA, 1965. **Career:** Edie Gladstone, asst designer; Kasper Joan Leslie, asst designer; Elliott Bass, Jardine Ltd, designer; Bleyle-By Jack Fuller, designer; Harlem Pub Schs, New York City Bd Educ, consult; Jack Fuller Ltd, partner, 1978. **Orgs:** New York City Bd Educ. **Honors/Awds:** Key to City Cincinnati, 1975-76; Rising Stars Fashion Show, Press Week, Plz Hotel, 1975; Urban League Designer of the Year, 1975; Pres Award, Univ Cincinnati, 1976. **Home Addr:** 107 W 25th St Apt 3D, New York, NY 10001-7210.

### FULLER, RANDY LAMAR

Football player, football coach, athletic director. **Personal:** Born Jun 2, 1970, Griffin, GA; married Gussie Carr; children: Ellington & Eden Haylee. **Educ:** Tenn State Univ, BS, criminal justice, 1994. **Career:** Football player (retired), football coach; Detroit Tigers, letterman, 1990-93; Denver Broncos, defensive back, 1994-95; Pittsburgh Steelers, 1995-97; Atlanta Falcons, 1998-99; Seattle Seahawks, 1999-2000; Tenn State Univ Tigers, defensive back coach; Sw De Kalb, defensive consult; Fulton, motivational speaker; DeKalb County sch, motivational speaker; Grace Heritage Christian Sch, Stone Mountain, head football coach, athletics dir, currently. **Orgs:** Co-found, Hometown Heroes Found; bd mem, Project Destiny DeKalb County; planning comt, Western Penn Sch Deaf. **Home Addr:** 2257 Patsy Lane, Columbus, GA 31903. **Business Addr:** Athletics Director, Head Football Coach, Grace Heritage Christian School, 1836 Rockbridge Rd, Stone Mountain, GA 30087, **Business Phone:** (615)963-5918.

### FULLER, VICKI L.

Vice president (organization). **Educ:** Roosevelt Univ, BS, BA; Univ Chicago, MBA, int finance & mkt. **Career:** Equitable Capital Mgt Corp, sr investment mgr to managing dir, 1985-93; AllianceBernstein LP, sr vpres & dir instnl mkt pub funds group 1994-; Alliance Capital Mgt Corp, sr vpres, 1994; NY Common Retirement Fund, chief investment officer, 2012-. **Orgs:** Dir, Apollo Theater Found Inc; Natl Coun Teacher Retirement, Corp Adv Comt; dir, Nominating Comt & Mem Planning & Environ Comt. **Business Addr:** Chief Investment Officer, New York State Common Retirement Fund, 253 W 125 St, Harlem, NY 10027, **Business Phone:** (212)531-5300.

### FULLER, DR. VIVIAN L.

Athletic director. **Personal:** Born Oct 17, 1954, Chapel Hill, NC. **Educ:** Fayetteville State Univ, BS, phys educ, 1977; Univ Idaho, MEd, 1978; Iowa State Univ, PhD, higher educ, 1985. **Career:** Univ Idaho, Bennett Col, 1978-84; NC A&T Univ, asst dir advisement progs to asst athletic dir, 1984-87; Ind Univ Pa, prof & assoc athletic dir, 1987-92; Northeastern Ill Univ, dir intercollegiate athletics, 1992-97; Tenn State Univ, intercollegiate athletics dir, 1997-99; Univ Md-Eastern Shore, dir athletics, 2000-03; Jackson State Univ, Jackson, Miss, athletics dir, 2003-13, assoc vpres Stud Affairs, currently. **Orgs:** Mgt Coun, Nat Col Athletic Asn; Peer Rev Comt; Initial Eligibility Stand Comt; Gender Equity Rask Force; Nat Youth Sports Prog; Black Women's Sports Found; Nat Asn Col dir Athletics; Delta Sigma Theta; Nat Asn Col Women Athletic Adminrs; Am Alliance Health, Phys Educ & Dance; Delta Sigma Theta Sorority Inc; Princess Anne & Salisbury Chamber Com. **Home Addr:** 5400 Kings Mill Dr, Salisbury, MD 21801, **Home Phone:** (410)548-4073. **Business Addr:** Athletic Director, Jackson State University, JSU Stud Ctr 2nd Fl, Jackson, MS 39217, **Business Phone:** (601)979-0833.

### FULLER, WILLIAM HENRY, JR.

Football player, radio broadcaster, executive. **Personal:** Born Mar 8, 1962, Norfolk, VA; married Precilla; children: Karen, Kalisa, Krystal & Kimberly. **Educ:** NC State Univ, BA, psychol, 1986. **Career:** Football player (retired), radio commentator, executive, football coach; Philadelphia Stars, Us Football League, 1984; Baltimore Stars, Us Football League, 1985; Houston Oilers, 1986, defensive end, 1987, right defensive end, 1988-89, left defensive end, 1990-93; Philadelphia Eagles, left defensive end, 1994-96; San Diego Chargers, left defensive end, 1997-98; Fulco Develop Inc, owner, chief exec officer & pres, currently; Frank W. Cox High Sch, asst coach; Va Destroyers Us Football League, radio commentator, 2011-. **Orgs:** University of North Carolina Educational Found; Juvenile Diabetes Found; Int & Norfolk Convention & Visitors Bureau. **Honors/Awds:** Pro-Bowl, 1991, 1994, 1995, 1996; University of North Carolina Sports Hall of Fame; mem, ACC's 50th Anniversary Football Team, 2002; Virginia Sports Hall of Fame, 2004; Most Valuable Player, Univ Nc. **Special Achievements:** Video Documentary: The Complete History of the Philadelphia Eagles. **Business Addr:** President, Chief Executive Officer, Fulco Development Inc, 500 E Main St, Norfolk, VA 23510.

### FULWOOD, SAM, III

Journalist. **Personal:** Born Aug 28, 1956, Monroe, NC; son of Samuel L Jr and Hallie Bernice Massey; married Cynthia Marie Bell; children: Katherine Amanda. **Educ:** Univ NC, Chapel Hill, BA, jour, 1978. **Career:** Charlotte Observer, NC, bus reporter, sports writer, police reporter, 1978-83; Baltimore Sun, bur corresp, Md, asst city ed, bus reporter, Africa corresp, ed writer, 1983-87; Atlanta Jour-Const, Atlanta, Ga, state polit ed, ed writer, asst bus ed, 1987-89; Los Angeles Times, Wash, DC, corresp, 1989-2000; Emerge Mag, columnist, 1990-92; Wash Bur Los Angeles, nat corresp, 1990; Nieman fel, Harvard Univ, 1993-94; Inst Polit fel, John F Kennedy Sch Govt, Harvard Univ, 2000; Case Western Res Univ, pres fel, 2003; The Plain Dealer, metro columnist; Case Western Res Univ; Ctr Am Progress, sr fel, currently. **Orgs:** Alpha Phi Alpha Fraternity, 1976-; mem bd advisors, Nieman Found; Parliamentational bd mem, 1989-90; Nat Asn Black Journalists; Assoc Press Socs Ohio; Black Media Asn, Charlotte, NC. **Honors/Awds:** Unity Awards in Media, 1st Political Reporting Lincoln Univ, 1988; founding contrib writer, Root; Break Through Award, Women, Men & Media, 1992; Pulitzer Prize-winning, 1992. **Special Achievements:** Author: "Walking From the Dream: My Life in the Black Middle Class," Anchor Books, 1996; "Full of It: Strong Words and Fresh Thinking for Cleveland", Gray & Company, 2004. **Home Addr:** 3004 Woodbury Rd, Shaker Heights, OH 44120, **Home Phone:** (216)272-9800. **Business Addr:** Senior Fellow, Center for American Progress, 1333 H St NW 10th Fl, Washington, DC 20005, **Business Phone:** (202)682-1611.

### FUNDERBURK, DR. WILLIAM WATSON

Physician. **Personal:** Born Aug 26, 1931, SC; son of William L and Florence; married Marilyn; children: William, Julie & Christina. **Educ:** Johnson C Smith Univ, BS, 1952; Howard Univ, MD, 1956. **Career:** Howard Med Sch & Hosp, staff, 1956-74, intern, 1956-57, resident Gen Surg, 1957-58, 1959-61, fel, 1962; Georgetown Univ Hosp, resident Gen Surg, 1958-59; Howard Univ, assoc dean stud affairs, 1970-72; Howard Univ, assoc prof surg, 1971-77; Ctr Ambulatory Surg med dir, 1977-84; Schmn, Dept Surg, Providence Hosp, DC, 2001-02; MedStar Wash Hosp Ctr, physician; self employed physician, currently. **Orgs:** Am Osteop Asn, 1956-; Nat Med Asn, 1956-99; Med Chi Soc, 1956-; DC Med Soc, 1989-; fel Am Col Surgeons. **Honors/Awds:** Certificate of Humanitarian Service, AMA, 1967; Distinguished Surgeon, Howard Dept Surg, 2000. **Home Phone:** (202)269-1143. **Business Addr:** Physician, 1160 Varnum St NE Suite 211, Washington, DC 20017, **Business Phone:** (202)877-3627.

### FUNDERBURKE, LAWRENCE DAMON

Basketball player, writer. **Personal:** Born Dec 15, 1970, Columbus, OH; son of Laura; married Monya Fairrow; children: Lawrence Elijah & Nyah. **Educ:** Ind Univ, 1990; Ohio State Univ, bus finance, 1994. **Career:** Basketball player (retired); Ambelopiki Afisorama, 1994-95; PAOK BC, 1995-96; Pau-Orthez, 1996-97; Sacramento Kings, forward, 1997-2004; Chicago Bulls, 2005. **Orgs:** Founder & Exec Dir, Lawrence Funderburke Youth Organ, 2000-. **Special Achievements:** Books:"Hook Me Up, Playa" & "The Triangle Formula of Success". **Business Addr:** President, Founder, Lawrence Funderburke Youth Organization, 1255 N Hamilton Rd Suite 135, Gahanna, OH 43230, **Business Phone:** (614)751-1541.

### FURLOUGH, JOYCE LYNN

Administrator, executive, vice president (organization). **Personal:** Born Mar 4, 1961, San Francisco, CA; daughter of Eddie Thompson and Geraldine; married Durrell; children: Durrell Jay Jr. **Educ:** Calif State Univ, Northridge, BS, health care admin, 1983. **Career:** Norrell, staff coordr; Pacificare Health Systs, sales rep, mkt mgr, proj mgr, mkt anal mgr, Serv & Develop, dir, Prod Develop, corp vpres mkt develop, 1985-00; Expedient Solutions, managing partner, 2000-04; Medicare Corp DEvelop, vpres, 1995-2000; Medicare Prod, Kaiser Permanente, nat dir, Secure Horizons Corp Mkt; Care More, gen mgr, vpres mkt & prod planning, currently. **Orgs:** Am Mkt Asn; Calif Asn Health Maintenance Orgn; Nat Female Exec Asn; Nat Coun Aging. **Business Addr:** Vice President of Market, Product Planning, Care More, 12900 Pk Plz Dr Suite 150, Cerritos, CA 90703, **Business Phone:** (877)211-6614.

### FUSE, BOBBY LEANDREW, JR.

Educator, high school teacher. **Personal:** Born Feb 17, 1952, Americus, GA; married Angela Michelle Lamar. **Educ:** Morehouse Col, BA, 1974; Mich State Univ, MA, 1975. **Career:** Col Urban Develop, grad asst to dean, 1974-75; Martin Luther King Jr Ctr, dir youth component, 1974-76; Atlanta Pub Sch, Atlanta Bd Educ, Frederick Douglass High Sch, teacher, 1976-; Fulton Co Dem Party, exec dir, 1977-78. **Orgs:** Jr Deacon Friendship Baptist Church-Americus, 1970-; Ga Baptist Conv, 1970-74; bd trustee, 1975; adv, Douglass HS Stud Govt 1977-85; Century Club Butler St, YMCA, 1981; fac mem, Martin Luther King Ctr Inst Non-violence, 1987; bd trustee, Martin Luther King Jr Ctr Nonviolent Social Chg Inc; youth coun adv, Nat Asn Advan Colored People; St John Lodge 17 F & AM; Holy Royal Arch Lodge 4 Americus; Nat Educ Asn; Nat Asn Sec Sch Principals; Asn Supv & Curric Develop; State Comn Life Hist Black Georgians; Mich State Univ Alumni Asn; Morehouse Col Alumni Asn. **Home Addr:** PO Box 6805, Americus, GA 31709-6805, **Home Phone:** (229)924-0708. **Business Addr:** Teacher, Atlanta Public School, Frederick Douglass High Sch, Atlanta, GA 30310, **Business Phone:** (404)799-1482.

### FUSE-HALL, ROSALIND

Dean (education), educator, college president. **Personal:** Born Atlanta, GA; married Jarvis Hall; children: Ifetoya Hall. **Educ:** Univ NC Chapel Hill, BS, admin criminal justice, 1980; Rutgers Sch Law, JD, 1983; Harvard Grad Sch Educ Inst, educ mgt, attended. **Career:** Presenter, public speaker; Hon William H Walls, Essex County Super Ct Newark, judicial law clerk; US Securities & Exchange Comn (New York), Enforcement Div, staff atty; St Lawrence Univ, asst dir minority affairs; Univ N Carolina syst, corp secy to bd gov, 1994-2002, assoc dean; N Carolina Cent Univ, exec asst to chancellor, 2003-07; Fla A&M Univ, chief staff to pres, 2007-12, interim exec dir title III progs, 2009-; Bennett Col, pres, 2013-. **Orgs:** Asn Black Women Higher Educ; Links Inc; bd dir, Community Found; co-chair, Asn Gov Bds; chair, Black Alumni Reunion; bd dir, BRIDGES; chair, United Negro Col Fund. **Business Addr:** President, Bennett College, 900 E Washington St, Greensboro, NC 27401, **Business Phone:** (336)517-2225.

### FUTRELL, DR. MARY ALICE FRANKLIN HATWOOD

Educator. **Personal:** Born May 24, 1940, Altavista, VA; daughter of Josephine Austin (deceased) and Josephine Hatwood; married Donald. **Educ:** Va State Univ, BA, 1962; George Washington Univ, MA, 1968, PhD, EdD, 1992. **Career:** Parker Gray High Sch, teacher, 1962-64; Ed Assoc Alexandria, pres, 1973-75; NEA Va Educ Assocs, pres, 1976-78, bd dir, 1978-80, secy-treas, 1980-83, pres, 1983-89; Alexandria's George Wash High Sch, headed bus educ dept, 1980; World Confederation Org Teaching Prof, bd dir, 1984-89, pres, 1989-93; Educ Int, pres, 1993-2004; George Wash Univ, Dept Educ Leadership, sr fel, 1989-92, Grad Sch Educ & Human Develop, dean, 1995-, prof educ, dir, currently. Articles: Education Record; Foreign Language Annals; Education Administration Quarterly. **Orgs:** Pres, Nat Educ Asn, 1983-89; adv bd, Esquire Regist, 1985; Task Force Teaching Carnegie Forum Educ & Econ, 1985; Nat Comn Role & Future State Cols & Univs; ed bd, Pro Educ Mag; Educ Adv Coun Metrop Life Ins Co; bd trustee, Joint Coun Econ Educ; NEA's Spec Comn Attacks Pub Educ; Select Comt Educ Black Youth; US Nat Comn United Nat Educ Sci & Cult Orgn; bd mem, Carnegie Found Improv Teaching; Kettering Found; Nat Comn Teaching & Am Future; chair, bd dir, Holmes Partnership; bd dir, Inst Educ Leadership; bd dir, Soc Study Educ; chap sponsor, Phi Delta Kappa, currently; bd dir, Nat Soc Study educ; Bethlehem Baptist Church; Nat Hon Soc; Delta Sigma Theta Sorority; pres, World Confederation Orgn; pres, Va Educ Asn; pres, Educ Int; pres, ERAmerica. **Business Addr:** Dean, Professor, George Washington University, 2121 I St NW, Washington, DC 20052, **Business Phone:** (202)994-1000.

# G

### G, WARREN (WARREN GRIFFIN, III)
Rap musician, television producer. **Personal:** Born Nov 10, 1970, Long Beach, CA; son of Ola Mae; married Tennille; children: 4. **Career:** Albums: Regulate. . . G Funk Era, 1994; Take a Look Over Your Shoulder, 1997; I Want it All, 2000; The Return of the Regulator, 2001; The Hard Way, 2004; In the Mid-Nite Hour, 2005; The G Files, 2009; Regulate...G Funk Era Pt. 2, 2014. Top 10 song: "Regulate"; Contributed songs to the movie soundtracks of "Poetic Justice" and "Above the Rim"; TV shows: "Parenthood"; "Clueless", 1997; "Little Richard", 2000; Barbershop 2: Back in Business, 2004; "All of Us", 2005; "Watsky's Making an Album", 2012; "Newsreaders", 2013. Films: Speedway Junky, 1999; Old School, 2003; Secret of Life, 2009; G-Funk Millennium 2000, rap artist, producer, currently. **Honors/Awds:** Grammy nomination; Nominated for MTV Movie Award for Best Song Regulate (Above the Rim), 1995. **Business Addr:** Rap Artist, G-Funk Millennium 2000, Los Angeles, CA 90024.

### GABBIN, DR. ALEXANDER LEE
Educator. **Personal:** Born Sep 6, 1945, Baltimore, MD; son of John and Dorothy Johns; married Joanne Veal; children: Jessea Nayo. **Educ:** Howard Univ, BA, 1967; Univ Chicago, MBA, 1970; Temple Univ, PhD, 1986. **Career:** Tech Construct Co, asst pres, 1968-70; Touche Ross & Co, staff auditor, 1970-72; Chicago Urban League, dep exec dir, 1972-74; Price Waterhouse & Co, auditor, 1974-75; Lincoln Univ, assoc prof, 1975-85; Nat Alliance African Am Athletes, exec officer; James Madison Univ, Sch Acct, assoc prof, 1985-95, dir, 1994-97, KPMG LLP prof acct, currently. **Orgs:** Ill Soc CPA's, 1978; Chicago Urban League; Kappa Alpha Psi; Am Acct Asn; Am Inst Cert Pub Accountants; Nat Asn Accountants, 1990-. **Home Addr:** 215 Campbell St, Harrisonburg, VA 22801. **Business Addr:** Professor, James Madison University, 423 Zane Showker Hall, Harrisonburg, VA 22807, **Business Phone:** (540)568-3093.

### GABBIN, DR. JOANNE VEAL
Educator. **Personal:** Born Feb 2, 1946, Baltimore, MD; daughter of Joseph and Jessie Smallwood; married Alexander L; children: Jessea Nayo. **Educ:** Morgan State Univ, BA, 1967; Univ Chicago, MA, 1970, PhD, 1980. **Career:** Catalyst Youth Inc, Chicago, IL, prog dir & instr, 1973-75; Lincoln Univ, Univ Pa, asst prof eng, 1977-82, assoc prof eng, 1982-85; James Madison Univ, Harrisonburg, VA, assoc prof Eng, 1985-86, Hons Prog, dir, 1986-, prof Eng, 1988-2005, Furious Flower Poetry Ctr, founder & exec dir, 1999-2009. Book: Sterling A. Brown: Building the Black Aesthetic Tradition, auth, 1994; A Revolution in African American Poetry, ed. **Orgs:** Chairperson, Toni Morrison & Supernatural, panel, Mid Atlantic Writers Asn, 1988; speaker, Creating a Masterpiece, Freshman Convocation James Madison Univ, 1988; Langston Hughes Soc, Zora Neale Hurston Soc; Mid Atlantic Writer Asn, MAWA Jour; Col Lang Asn; chairperson, Stud Emergency Fund, First Baptist Church, 1989-; chairperson, Va Found Humanities & Pub Policy; founder & organizer, Wintergreen Women Writers Collective. **Home Addr:** 215 Campbell St, Harrisonburg, VA 22801, **Home Phone:** (540)433-6015. **Business Addr:** Executive Director, Founder, James Madison University, 1151 Driver Dr MSC 3802, Harrisonburg, VA 22807, **Business Phone:** (540)568-6310.

### GABRIEL, BENJAMIN MOSES
Executive. **Personal:** Born Sep 17, 1931, Brooklyn, NY; married Rebecca; children: Shirley Ann, Janice, Brenda & Benjamin Jr. **Educ:** Cornell Univ; Empire State Univ, BS. **Career:** NY Transit Authority, reporter, 1957, supvr, 1968, mgr training ctr, 1971, contract compliance officer, 1973, supt, 1976. **Orgs:** Training coord, Asso Transit, 1971; campaign mgr, Local Sch Bd Elections, 1973, 1975; bd dir, Brooklyn Tuberc & Lung Asn, 1975; cand, dist leader 40th AD Dem Party, 1976; 100 Black Men; trustee, Lutheran Hosp, 1976; chmn, Labor & Indust, ENY Nat Asn Advan Colored People, 1976; vice chmn, bd dir, Asso Transit Guild. **Honors/Awds:** Community Service Award, Grace Bapt Church, 1974; Comm Serv & Transit Accomplishments, Elite Benevolent Soc, 1975; Doswell Mem Award, Asn Transit Guild, 1977. **Home Addr:** 1158 Sutter Ave Suite 1, Brooklyn, NY 11208, **Home Phone:** (718)827-1148. **Business Addr:** Superindent, NYCTA, 370 Jay St, Brooklyn, NY 11201.

### GADIKIAN, RANDOLPH L. (RANDY GADIKIAN)
Librarian, administrator. **Educ:** State Univ NY, Buffalo, BS, info systs mgt, 1979, MS, libr & info sci, 1981. **Career:** State Univ NY Col, Buffalo, E H Butler Libr, staff, 1982-99, coordr syst & technol, 1982-99, coordr comput assisted ref serv, coordr circulation serv, Emerging Technologies librn, Comput Serv liaison; State Univ NY, Fredonia Col, Daniel A Reed Libr, librn & dir libr serv, 1999-, Chautauqua-Cattaraugus Big Read, chmn. **Orgs:** Chair, State Univ NY Connect Adv Coun; bd mem, State Univ NY, Fredonia Col, Daniel A Reed Libr. **Home Addr:** , NY. **Business Addr:** Director of Library Services, Librarian, State University New York College at Fredonia, 280 Central Ave, Fredonia, NY 14063, **Business Phone:** (716)673-3181.

### GADSDEN, REV. DR. NATHANIEL J., SR.
Education reformer, manager. **Personal:** Born Oct 3, 1950, Harrisburg, PA; son of Nathaniel and Rosetta Robinson; married Carol L; children: David L & Nathaniel J III. **Educ:** W Chester Univ, BS, 1973; Columbia Pac Univ, MA, 1984; NJ Bible Inst; Hershey Med Ctr, clin pastoral educ; Harrisburg Hosp, clin pastoral educ; Columbia Pac Univ, PhD, 1986. **Career:** Pastor, Poet, Columnist, TV & Radio Show Host; Western Carolina Univ, resident hall dir, 1973-77; Child Abuse Hot line, case worker, 1977-80; Pa Dept Educ, equity coordr, 1980; planner alternative sentencing Pa, 1985; Help House Inc, Harrisburg, Pa, counr, 1989; Writer's Word shop Inc, dir, currently; United Way Capital Region, community bldg assoc, community impact mgr, currently; Imani African Christian Church, founder & pastor, currently; Harrisburg Univ Sci & Technol High Sch, counr, currently; Life Esteem, trained counr & family therapist. **Orgs:** Bd dir, Multi-Disciplinary Team Dauphin Co C & Youth; bd dir, Multi-Disciplinary Team Pa Dept C & Youth; bd mem, Comn Home Care Serv Inc; dir, Writers Word shop 1978-; host, WMSP-FM radio, 1979-; Nat Alliance Third World Journalists, 1980-; pres, Cent Pa Black Social Workers, 1982-84; host, WHP TV Channel 21, 1982-; bd dir, Metro Arts, 1982-; bd dir, Susquhanna Arts Coun, 1982; black adv bd, WITF-TV; bus assoc, Cent Pa Guid Assoc, 1984-; columnist, City News Harrisburg Pa, 1984-; Int Orgn Journalists; Harrisburg dir, Pa Black United Fund; bd dir, C Playroom Inc; minister, Community Chapel Church God Christ, Harrisburg, Pa; pres, Imani Ministerial Fel; dir, Nathaniel Gadsden's Writers Wordshop Found; bd dir, Perry County Housing Partnership; Rotary Int; Alpha Phi Alpha Fraternity. **Home Addr:** 1700 Mountain View Rd Apt 13, Harrisburg, PA 17102, **Home Phone:** (717)608-2312. **Business Addr:** Community Impact Manager, United Way of the Capital Region, 2235 Millennium Way, Enola, PA 17025, **Business Phone:** (717)724-4056.

### GADSDEN, ORONDE BENJAMIN
Football player, entrepreneur. **Personal:** Born Aug 20, 1971, Charleston, SC; married Bianke; children: Oronde II. **Educ:** Winston-Salem State Univ. **Career:** Football player (retired), executive; Indianapolis Colts; Drew Pearson Co, intern; Dallas Cowboys, wide receiver, 1995-96, 1997; Pittsburgh Steelers, wide receiver, 1996; Frankfurt Galaxy, wide receiver, 1997; Portland Forest Dragons, wide receiver, 1998; Arena Football League; Miami Dolphins, wide receiver, 1998-2003; Original Gear Inc, founder, 2000-06, DBA TotalLuxury Group, 2006-. **Orgs:** Vol, Habitat Humanity, 1999; vol, Big Bros & Big Sisters Broward County. **Business Addr:** Founder, Original Gear Inc, 500 Fashion Ave, New York, NY 10018-4502, **Business Phone:** (646)312-8982.

### GAFFNEY, DERRICK TYRONE
Football player. **Personal:** Born May 24, 1955, Jacksonville, FL; children: Jabar. **Educ:** Univ Fla, attended 1977. **Career:** Football player (retired); New York Jets, wide receiver, 1978-84 & 1987. **Orgs:** mem, Alpha phi alpha fraternity. **Honors/Awds:** Longest TD reception, Southeastern Conf, 1977. **Special Achievements:** First African-American to become the starter at the quarterback position for the Gators.

### GAFFNEY, LESLIE GALE
Executive. **Personal:** Born Feb 21, 1951, Cleveland, OH; daughter of George Douglas and Lucille Miller; married Kenneth Wilson Sr. **Educ:** Ky State Univ, BS, 1972. **Career:** R H Macy's, vendor inquiry mgr, 1979-84; Sony Corp Am, Corp Controllers, A/R proj mgr, 1984-85; Components Prod Co, oper mgr, 1985-86, accts payable mgr, 1986-87; Consumer Co Mid-Atlantic, oper mgr, 1987-88; Peripheral Prod Co, admin mgr, 1988-89, dir community affairs, 1989-2002; Broad Inst Mass Inst Technol & Harvard, dir commun, 2005-, graphics ed. **Orgs:** Exec comt, EDGES Group, 1988-; chair, adv bd, Nat Sci Found, Southern Calif Access Ctr, 1989-97; pre-col adv bd, NJ Inst Technol, 1992-; pres, Greater Montvale Bus Assn, 1992-; bd dir, Ky State Univ Alumni, 1993-96; bd dir, Com & Indust Asn NJ, 1996-. **Home Addr:** 1 Jesse Ct, Montville, NJ 07045, **Home Phone:** (973)331-1476. **Business Addr:** Director Of Communications, Broad Institute of MIT and Harvard, 320 Charles St, Cambridge, MA 02141-2023, **Business Phone:** (617)258-0900.

### GAFFNEY, MICHELE ELIZABETH
Zoologist, zoo keeper. **Personal:** Born Nov 13, 1960, Long Island, NY; daughter of Dr Floyd and Yvonne. **Educ:** Univ Calif-Davis, BS, 1982; Calif Polytech Univ, MS. **Career:** Zool Soc San Diego, Wild Animal Pk, sr mammal keeper, 1983-. **Orgs:** Comparative Nutrit Soc, 1998-. **Business Addr:** Senior Mammal Keeper, Zoological Society of San Diego, Wild Animal Pk, Escondido, CA 92027, **Business Phone:** (760)747-8702.

### GAFFNEY, THOMAS DANIEL
Executive, government official, association executive. **Personal:** Born Jun 19, 1933, Laredo, TX. **Career:** San Antonio Independent Sch Dist Sch Bd, vpres; US Govt, 23 yrs. **Orgs:** AFRES; San Antonio Mus Asn; Ruth Taylor Theater; Nat Asn Advan Colored People; 433 TAW & EEOC; 2851 ABGP & WELFARE Fund; LCL Adv Coun; Exec Comt UNCF; pres, Poverty Agency Bd; vpres, sch bd, 1973-77; San Antonio River Comn; Black Unity Coord Coun; life mem, BT Wash PTA; AFA; ACLU; Nat Caucus Black Sch Bds; NCOA. **Special Achievements:** First African American chairman of San Antonio Independent School District. **Home Addr:** 115 St John, San Antonio, TX 78202.

### GAINER, DR. FRANK EDWARD
Manager. **Personal:** Born Jun 18, 1938, Waynesboro, GA; son of Walter and Edith; married Alice M Ingram; children: Edward, Ervin & Todd. **Educ:** Morehouse Col, BS, 1960; Tuskegee Inst, MS, 1962; Iowa State Univ, MS, 1964, PhD, 1967. **Career:** Antibiotic Anal & Qual Control, mgr, 1978; Eli Lilly & Co, sec treas; JCG&M; M-MED, founder, 2000-; Fundamental Baptist Fel Asn, chief financial officer; Christian Heritage Ministries, founder, currently. **Orgs:** Asn chmn, Am Chem Soc, 1975; chancellor, Am Chem Soc, 1977; Sigma Xi; Beta Kappa Chi Hon Sci Soc; Nat Asn Advan Colored People; Urban League; secy, Mary Riggs Neighborhood Ctr, 1976; treas, 1977; bd dir, beginning, 1975. **Special Achievements:** Published science journals. **Home Addr:** 1810 W Kessler Blvd, PO Box 88842, Indianapolis, IN 46228-1817, **Home Phone:** (317)255-1284. **Business Addr:** Founder, M-MED, 3140 N Ill St, Indianapolis, IN 46208, **Business Phone:** (317)283-1454.

### GAINER, PROF. JOHN F.
Choral conductor, educator, composer. **Personal:** Born Aug 8, 1954, East Orange, NJ; son of Benjamin Franklin and Stella. **Educ:** Ariz State Univ, BA, 1980; Univ Ore, Sch Archit & Allied Arts, attended 1987. **Career:** Vocalist, musician, music dir, composer, music educr & consult; Dir & musician, 1968-; Ariz State Univ Gospel Ensemble, founder & dir, 1975-80; Lane Comm Col, music instr, 1984-85; Univ Ore, Sch Music, adj asst prof, 1983-99; Inspirational Sounds Community Choir, founder & dir, 1983-00; Ore Sym Orchestra & NW Community Gospel Chorus Gospel Christmas Concerts, 1999-; Northern Calif Mass Choir Gospel Music Workshop Am, staff music dir & soloist, 2001-; Federated Stores Inc, selling specialist, 2001-04; Almac Clin Technologies, admini asst & off coordr, 2004-06; Fair Housing Coun Ore, off mgr, 2007-. **Orgs:** Am Soc Composers Auth & Publ, 1972-; minister, Church God Christ Inc, 1979-; Ore Lane County Rainbow Coalition, 1983-88; precinct comm mem, Cent Dem Comm, 1984-88; Edwin Hawkins Music & Arts Sem, 1984-; chap rep & nat mass choir music comm, Gospel Music Workshop Am, 1986-. **Home Addr:** 13275 SW Brightwood St, Beaverton, OR 97005-1205, **Home Phone:** (503)626-6737. **Business Addr:** Office Manager, Fair Housing Council of Oregon, 506 SW 6th Ave Suite 1111, Portland, OR 97204, **Business Phone:** (503)223-8197.

### GAINES, HON. ADRIANE THERESA
Manager, executive, librarian. **Personal:** Born Aug 27, 1947, Mt. Vernon, NY; daughter of James McCoy and Dorothy McCoy. **Educ:** Fordham Univ, BA, commun & media studies, 1978. **Career:** Marine Midland Bank, secy & safekeeping dep, 1965-68; State Nat Bank El Paso, investment & sec dep, 1968-71; Rochester Inst Tech, asst info spec, 1971-72; Culinary Inst Am, asst librn, 1972-73; Unity Broadcasting Network, dircorp admin, 1973-82; NBN Broadcasting Inc, corp vpres, 1995; WWRL1600 AM, pres & gen mgr, 1995-. **Orgs:** Co-founder & bd mem, World Inst Black Comt CEBA Awards, 1978-; actg gen mgr KATZ AM WZEN FM Radio, 1982; comt bd dir, Coalition 100 Black Women, 1984-85; Women Cable, 1985; Adv Women Radio TV, 1982-; bd trustee, Apollo Theater Hall Fame, 1986-; adv comt mem, Schomburg Ctr Res Black Cult; bd mem, Aaron Davis Hall; bd mem, Joan Mitchell Found. **Honors/Awds:** Media Woman of the Year, Nat Asn Media Women, 1985; Leadership Award, Nat Asn for the Advan of Colored People, 1995. **Home Addr:** 218 W 138 St, New York, NY 10030. **Business Addr:** President, General Manager, WWRL 1600 AM, 333 7th Ave 14th Fl, New York, NY 10001, **Business Phone:** (212)631-0800.

### GAINES, AVA CANDA (AVA CANDA'CE GAINES)
Clergy. **Personal:** Born Feb 19, 1963, Madison, WI; daughter of George and Zelma Hamilton. **Educ:** Univ Dist Columbia, DC, 1983; Univ Tex, Dallas, Tex, BA, 1991; Southern Methodist Univ, Perkins Sch Theol, MA, theol studies, 2000. **Career:** St Paul CME Church, Chester, PA, sr pastor; Mt Pleasant Christian Methodist Episcopal Church, sr pastor, currently. **Orgs:** Recruiting comt, Nat Asn Advan Colored People, 1984; Black Polit Scientist Asn, 1986-. **Honors/Awds:** Ordained Elder, CME Church, 1989. **Special Achievements:** Author: Anybody Can Get the Holy Ghost, CME Church, 1986. **Home Addr:** 2601 W 9th St, Chester, PA 19013. **Business Addr:** Senior Pastor, Mt Pleasant Christian Methodist Episcopal Church, Hwy 360 W, Halifax, VA 24558, **Business Phone:** (804)476-6513.

### GAINES, BRENDA J.
Chief executive officer, president (organization), executive. **Personal:** Born Jan 1, 1949; daughter of DeLouise and Clarence. **Educ:** Univ Ill, Urbana-Champaign, BA, psychol & sociol, 1970; Roosevelt Univ, Chicago, IL, MA, pub admin, 1976. **Career:** U.S Dept Housing, dep regional admin, 1980-81, Asst Regional Adminr, 1981-83; Comnr Housing, Chicago, 1983-85; Harold Wash, dep chief staff, 1985-87; Head Govt & Community Rels, 1987-; Diners Club, N Am, vpres, 1992-94, Exec vpres Corp Card Sales, 1994-99, pres, 1999-2004, N Am Pres Diners Club Int, 1999-2004, chief exec officer, 2002-04; Off Depot Inc, dir, 2002-13; CAN Financial Corp, dir, 2004-; Tenet Healthcare Corp, bd dir, 2005-; NICOR Inc, dir, 2006-11; Fannie Mae, dir, 2006-; AGL Resources Inc, dir, 2011; Northern Ill Gas Co, dir; March Dimes & Econ Club Chicago, dir. **Orgs:** Bd mem, Diners Club Int Global; bd dir, Citibank Can; bd mem, Dr. Martin Luther King Jr. Boys &Girls Club; bd trustee, Nat Restaurant Asn Educ Found; bd trustee, Chicago Mus Sci & Indust; Comt 200, Exec Leadership Coun; Jr Achievement; Bd mem, Off Depot, 2002-; Bd mem, CNA Financial, 2004-; Bd mem, Tenet Healthcare, 2005-; Bd mem, Fannie Mae, 2006-; Bd mem, Nicor, 2006-11; AGL Resources, 2011-. **Business Addr:** Director, Fannie Mae, 3900 Wis Ave NW, Washington, DC 20016, **Business Phone:** (202)752-7000.

### GAINES, CASSANDRA JEAN
Executive, founder (originator). **Personal:** Born Feb 21, 1953, Oakland, CA; children: Annje Linaii Wilkerson. **Educ:** Connors State Col, attended 1979; Northeastern State Univ, attended 1989. **Career:** Roxy Theater, mgr; City Muskogee, multicult events coordr, 1996-; Roxy Theater, mgr; Black Town Tours, founder, 1997-; Nat Soul Food-Cook Off, founder & chief exec officer, 2008-; Womens health care, advocate. **Orgs:** Muskogee COC; Nat Asn Advan Colored People; Women Who Care; Nat Coalition Black Meeting Planners; Okla Human Rights, 2000; Travel Indust Asn, 2000; ed & mkt consult, Black Meeting & Tourism Mag; Muskogee Chamber Com. **Home Addr:** 2117 Okla St Suite 3, Muskogee, OK 74401, **Home Phone:** (918)682-8051. **Business Addr:** Founder, Chief Executive Officer, National Soul Food Cook-Off LLC, 2117 Okla St Suite 3, Muskogee, OK 74401, **Business Phone:** (918)684-6363.

### GAINES, COREY YASUTO
Basketball player, basketball coach, basketball executive. **Personal:** Born Jun 1, 1965, Los Angeles, CA. **Educ:** Univ Calif, Los Angeles, attended 1986; Loyola Marymount Univ, attended 1988. **Career:** Basketball player (retired), basketball coach, basketball executive; Quad City Thunder, 1988-89; NJ Nets, 1988-89; Omaha Racers, 1989-90; Philadelphia 76ers, 1989-90, 1994-95; Denver Nuggets, 1990-91; New York Knicks, 1993-94; Long Beach Jam, Am Basketball Asn, guard, asst coach, 2003-04, head coach, 2005-07; Calif Buzz, asst coach, 2004; Phoenix Mercury, asst coach, 2006-07; gen mgr & head coach, 2007-. **Business Addr:** Head Coach, General Manager, Phoenix Mercury, 201 E Jefferson St, Phoenix, AZ 85004, **Business Phone:** (602)252-9622.

### GAINES, CRYSTAL MONIQUE
Executive. **Personal:** Born Oct 14, 1972, Brooklyn, NY; daughter of J Kendall Flowers and LaVerne S; married Ludwig P. **Educ:** Hampton Univ, BS, mkt, 1994; George Washington Univ, MSPM, 2000. **Ca-**

**reer:** Soza & Co, prog mgr, bus develop, 1994-2000; G&B Solutions Inc, chief exec officer & chief human resources officer, 2001-08; mgt consult, 2008-13; Dell, acct exec, fed alliances, 2013-. **Orgs:** Proj Mgt Inst, 1998-; Tucker Plus Adv Bd, 2000-. **Business Addr:** Account Executive,Federal Alliances, Dell, 1 Dell Way, Round Rock, TX 78682, **Business Phone:** (512)338-4400.

### GAINES, ERNEST JAMES

Educator, writer. **Personal:** Born Jan 15, 1933, Pointe Coupee Parish, LA; married Dianne Saulney. **Educ:** Vallejo Jr Col; San Francisco St Col, attended 1957; Denison Univ, DLitt. **Career:** Books: Catherine Carmier, 1964; Catherine Carmier, 1966; Of Love & Dust, 1967; Bloodline, 1968; Of Love & Dust, 1968; The Autobiography of Miss Jane Pittman, 1971; A Long Day in November, 1971; In My Father's House, 1978; A Gathering of Old Men, 1983, 1987; A Lesson Before Dying, 1993; National Book Critics Circle Award for fiction, 1993; Oprah's Book Club, 1997; Mozart & Leadbelly: Stories & Essays, 2005. Univ Rennes, vis prof, 1969; Univ La, Lafayette, Dept Eng, prof & writer-in-residence, prof emer, currently. Short stories: The Turtles, 1956; Boy in the Double-Breasted Suit, 1957; Mary Louis, 1960; Just Like a Tree, 1963; The Sky Is Gray, 1963; A Long Day in November, 1964; My Grandpa and the Haint, 1966. Filmography: The Autobiography of Miss Jane Pittman, CBS Television, 1974; A Lesson Before Dying, 1999. **Orgs:** Am Acad Arts & Letters; fel MacArthur Foundation. **Honors/Awds:** Wallace Stegner fellow, 1957; National Endowment for the Arts grant, 1967; Solomon R. Guggenheim Foundation fellow, 1971; Gold Medal, Commonwealth Club CA, 1972, 1984; LA Libr Asn Award, 1972; Black Acad Arts & Letters Award, 1972; Award for Excellence of Achievement, San Francisco Arts Comt, 1983; Mac Arthur Fel, 1993; Louisiana Humanist of the Year, 1993; Nat Book Critics Circle Award, 1993; John D.and Catherine T. MacArthur Foundation fellow, 1993; Dos Passos Prize, 1993; Emmy Award for Best Television Movie, 1999; Chevalier in the Order of Art & Letters, France, 2000; National Governor's Arts Award, 2000; National Humanities Medal, 2000; Louisiana Writer of the Year Award, 2000; American Academy of Arts and Letters Department of Literature, 2000; Academy of Achievement Golden Plate Award, 2001; Ernest J. Gaines Award, Baton Rouge Found estab, 2007; Sidney Lanier Prize for Southern Literature, 2012; National Medal of Arts, 2013. **Special Achievements:** Published numerous articles. **Home Addr:** 128 Buena Vista Blvd, Lafayatte, LA 70503. **Business Addr:** Professor Emeritus of English, University of Louisiana, 400 E St Mary Blvd, Lafayette, LA 70504, **Business Phone:** (337)482-1848.

### GAINES, GRADY

Saxophonist. **Personal:** Born May 14, 1934, Waskom, TX. **Career:** Albums: Long Tall Sally; Send Me Some Lovin; Whole Lotta Shakin Goin On; Bring It On Home, Twisting The Night Away; Full Gain, 1988; Down & Dirty, Live At Tipitina's; Horn of Plenty, 1992; Jump Start, 2002; Songs: "Baby Work Out"; "The Night Time Is The Right Time"; "So In Love With You"; "I Can't Turn You Loose"; "Harlem Shuffle". **Honors/Awds:** Blues Heritage Award, Tex Blues Preserv Soc; Blues Artist of the Year, Juneteenth Festival, 1993; Best Blues, Best Horn Section, Best Funk/R&B, Houston Press, 2001; Local Musician of the Year, Houston Press, 2001; pvt parties, 2013-. **Special Achievements:** Honored by Texas Blues Preservation Society with its first annual Blues Heritage Award, citing him as being a Texas Blues Ambassador Around the World and a Pioneer in the Creation of Rock & Roll; in 1993, he played at one of President Clinton's inaugural parties. **Business Addr:** Saxophonist, Recording Bandleader, Gulf Coast Entertainment, 2017 W Gray St, Houston, TX 77019-3623, **Business Phone:** (713)523-7004.

### GAINES, HERSCHEL DAVIS

Educator. **Personal:** Born Oct 7, 1942, Parkin, AR; married Wilbert; children: Jacquelyn LaRue, Michelle LaRue & Genee La Rue. **Educ:** Univ Ark, Pine Bluff, BSE, 1962; Ark State Univ, MSE, 1979. **Career:** Phelix High Sch, eng teacher, 1962-69; Marion Sr High Sch, eng teacher, 1969-71; Mc Arthur Middle Sch, chmn eng dept, 1971-81; Jonesboro High Sch, asst prin, 1980-94; Ark State Univ, eng instr, supvr elem educ stud teachers, 1994; Williams Baptist Col, adj fac, adj instr eng. **Orgs:** Bd dir, Jonesboro Classroom Teachers Asn, 1972-; bd dir, Ariz Educ Asn, 1976-79; basileus anti-basileus & grammateus, Kappa Nu Omega Alpha Kappa Alpha Sor, 1976-80; affil rels comt, Nat Educ Asn, 1977-79; corr secy, Alpha Delta Kappa, 1979-; Adv Coun Upward Bound, Ariz State Univ, 1980-; app by Gov Bill Clinton to Employ Sec Div Adv Coun, 1981; nom comt, Crowley's Ridge Girl Scout Coun, 1981-83; educ comn, Crowley's Ridge Girl Scouts, 1981-83; bd dir, United Way Greater Jonesboro, 1985-86; pres, Ariz State Univ Fac Women's Club, 1985-87. **Honors/Awds:** Educ Award, Alpha Kappa Alpha Sor Jonesboro AR & AR Coun of AKA, 1976, 1978; Outstanding Young Educator Award, Jaycees Jonesboro, 1977; Silver Soror, Alpha Kappa Alpha, 1985; pres Nu Chap, Alpha Delta Kappa, 1994-96. **Home Addr:** 3605 Marzee Ann Dr, Jonesboro, AR 72401, **Home Phone:** (870)935-1528. **Business Addr:** Adjunct Instructor of English, Williams Baptist College, 60 W Fulbright Ave Maddox Ctr, Walnut Ridge, AR 72476, **Business Phone:** (870)886-6741.

### GAINES, JO EVA

Association executive. **Educ:** Salve Regina Univ, BA, educ; Providence Col, MA, guid & coun; Bridgewater State Col, career coun & sec admin. **Career:** City Newport, vice chmn; RI Asn Sch Comt, exec bd, 2001-, secy treas & vpres, 1958-2005, pres, 2013-; Salve Regina Univ, acad advisor. **Orgs:** Newport Sch Comt, 2000-; pres, St. Josephs Cath Church parish coun; Brown Univ Annenberg Inst Urban Educ Task Force; bd dir, Newport MLK Ctr; RI Comn Women; Big Sisters RI. **Honors/Awds:** National Association for the Advancement of Colored People Outstanding Educator Award; Howard Kay Award, Outstanding Sch Comt Serv. **Home Addr:** 227 Eustis Ave, Newport, RI 02840-3363, **Home Phone:** (401)846-7222. **Business Addr:** Member, Newport Public Schools, 15 Wickham Rd, Newport, RI 02840-4232, **Business Phone:** (401)847-2100.

### GAINES, JOHN A., SR.

Lawyer. **Personal:** Born May 23, 1941, Rock Hill, SC; son of John and Ernestine Moore; children: John A Jr & Janee Latrice. **Educ:** Benedict Col, BA, 1964; Howard Univ Law Sch, JD, 1968. **Career:** Rock Hill Model Cities Prog, adv & citizen, participation specialist, 1969-70; Nat Asn Advan Colored People Legal Defense Fund Inc, intern, 1970-71; pvt pract atty, 1971-; US Supreme Ct, lawyer civil rights & gen pract. **Orgs:** SCA State Bar; Nat Bar Asn; Nat Asn Advan Colored People Florence; APA Fraternity, 1963-; trustee, legal coun church & prayer coordr, New Life Assembly God; Small Bus Mgt Asn, 1976. **Honors/Awds:** American Jurisprudence Award, Bancroft-Whitney Co, 1968; Personalities of the South Award, Am Biographical Inst, 1970-71; Awarded Internship, Nat Asn Advan Colored People Legal Defense Fund Inc, 1970-71; Award recognizing membership Friendship 9, Friendship Jr College, 1979; Best Lawyers in America, Reveal Publ, 1979; Award Recognizing Membership in Friendship 9, Alpha Kappa Alpha Sorority, 1990; Pineville AME Zion Church Award, 1995; Pagel Award, York County Coun, Nat Asn Advan Colored People, 1999. **Home Addr:** 200 W Evans St Suite 211, Florence, SC 29501, **Home Phone:** (803)679-3035. **Business Addr:** Attorney, Private Practice, 200 W Evans St Suite 211, Florence, SC 29501, **Business Phone:** (843)679-3035.

### GAINES, MARY E.

Publicist, administrator. **Personal:** Born Boligee, AL; daughter of Mattie L Hamilton and Willie. **Educ:** Loop City Col, Chicago, IL, AA, 1970; Midwestern Broadcasting, Chicago, IL, dipl, 1972; Brewer State Jr Col, Fayette, AL, attended 1975; Univ Ala, Tuscaloosa, AL, BA, 1982. **Career:** WCBI-TV, Columbus, Miss, anchor producer & reporter, 1975-77; WNPT-Radio, Tuscaloosa, Ala, announcer, 1976-79; Fed Southern Co-ops, Epes, Ala, admin asst, 1977-79; WBRC-TV, Birmingham, Ala, reporter & ed, 1978-82; Arrington Mayor, Birmingham, Ala, off coordr, 1982-83; Ala Pub TV, Montgomery, Ala, TV producer, 1983-93; USDA Forest Serv Nat Forests Ala, pub affairs officer, currently. **Orgs:** SCLC & Nat Asn Advan Colored People, 1972-75; Youth Develop & BirminghamUrban League Bds, 1981-82; state coordr, Nat Asn Black Journalists, 1983-; founder, Central Ala Black Media Asn, 1988; Grand lady, Knights PeterClaver, Ladies Aux, 1990-; Faithful Navigator, KPC, Ladies Grace, 2002-; vpres, Knights PeterClaver Ladies Auxiliary, Gulf Coast Dist; Emancipation Proclamation Comt; secy, auditor, Archdiocesan Coun Catholic Women; treas, Knights PeterClaver Ladies Auxiliary; co-chair, Nat Black Catholic Cong. **Home Addr:** PO Box 1821, Montgomery, AL 36102-1821, **Home Phone:** (334)227-4517. **Business Addr:** Public Affairs Officer, USDA Forest Service, Supvr Off, Montgomery, AL 36107-3010, **Business Phone:** (334)832-4470.

### GAINES, DR. OSCAR CORNELL

Physician. **Personal:** Born May 21, 1954, Memphis, TN. **Educ:** Lambuth Col, BS, 1976; Meharry Med Col, MD, 1982. **Career:** AUS, capt & physician, 1983-87. **Orgs:** Prince Hall Mason Lodge, 1986; Alpha Phi Alpha. **Home Addr:** PO Box 995, Macon, GA 31202-0995. **Business Addr:** Physician, 225 Hidden Lakes Dr, Gray, GA 31032.

### GAINES, PATRICIA

Journalist, writer. **Career:** The Wash Post, reporter, 1978-2001; Laughing in the Dark: From Colored Girl to Woman of Color, author; A Journey from Prison to Power; the inspirational Moments of Grace: Meeting the Challenge to Change, author; speaker & prison reform activist; Nat Mag, freelancer & writer, currently; radio commentary writer, currently; Radio shows: "All Things Considered", commentator; "Blues and Notes", commentator. **Orgs:** Josephs House; Nat Asn Black Journalists; co founder, Brown Angel Ctr, currently. **Honors/Awds:** Excellence Award, Nat Asn Black Journalists. **Business Addr:** Reporter, Author, The Washington Post, 1150 15th St NW, Washington, DC 20071, **Business Phone:** (202)334-6000.

### GAINES, HON. PAUL LAURENCE

Executive, educator, mayor. **Personal:** Born Apr 20, 1932, Newport, RI; son of Albert P Sr and Pauline P Jackson; married Jo Eva Johnson; children: Jena, Patricia, Paulajo & Paul Jr. **Educ:** Xavier Univ LA, BEd, 1955; Bridgewater State Col, MEd, Coun, 1968. **Career:** Educator (retired); Newport RI Pub Sch, sch teacher, 1959-68; Newport RI Rogers HS, basketball coach, 1959-68; Newport RI Youth Corps, counr, 1960-66; Bridgewater State Col Mass, admin, 1968-96, asst to pres, 1983-96; Bridgewater State Grad Sch, Col prof, 1970-94, asst acad admin; Newport, RI, mayor. **Orgs:** Comnr, RI Ethics Comn, 1987-93; chair, Black Regt Enhancement Memorial Proj, 1997; Newport Br Nat Advan Asn Colored People; Newport Lions Club; Coun, 256 Knights Columbus; Urban League RI; RI Black Heritage Soc; bd trustees, St. Michael's Country Day Sch; bd, Newport Hist Soc; chair, Canvassing Authority, Newport, RI; chair, bd dir, Newport county ment health Ctr; Newport County Community Ment Health Ctr, chmn bd dir. **Honors/Awds:** Citizen of the Year, Omega Psi Phi Frat (Sigma Nu Chapt), 1981; George T Downing Award, RI, 1982; inductee, Newport Sports Hall Fame, 2002. **Special Achievements:** All-AM (Catholic) Basketball(District 3) Team, 1952-2000; First Black Sch Committee man Since, 1900; First Black City Council man, Newport City Council, 1977-81; First Black Mayor in New England, 1981; First Black Mayor State RI, 1981-83. **Home Addr:** 227 Eustis Ave, Newport, RI 02840-3363, **Home Phone:** (401)846-7222. **Business Addr:** Chairman & Board of Director, Newport County Community Mental Health Center, 127 Johnny Cake Hill Rd, Middletown, RI 02842, **Business Phone:** (401)846-1213.

### GAINES, RICHARD KENDALL

Insurance executive, consultant, chief executive officer. **Personal:** Born Apr 11, 1947, St. Louis, MO; son of Richard Harris and Jewell Gaines Harris; married Anne Marie Clarke; children: Kimberly & Yvette. **Educ:** Coe Col, BA, sociol, 1969; St Louis Univ, urban affairs. **Career:** City Des Moines, dep dir, 1969-70; St Louis Bd Educ, dir comn educ, 1970-73, pres, 1987-88; St Louis Univ, dir upward bound, 1973-76; Urban League Metrop St Louis, dir educ, 1976-77; state MO statewide Task force, 1984; St Louis Pub Sch, pres, 1987-88; Daniel & Henry Ins Brokers, vpres, dir; Richard K Gaines Inc, pres, chief exec officer, currently. **Orgs:** Jaycees St Louis, 1972-75; Am Personnel & Guid Asn, 1973-76; past pres, YMCA Men's Club City N, 1979-83; Nat Asn Life Underwriters; regist rep, Nat Asn Security Dealers; Independent Ins Agents MO; St Louis Bd Educ, 1983-89; bd dir, YMCA; past pres, St Louis Bd Educ, 1987-88; grand pharoah, pres, Royal Order Vagabonds Inc, 1992-96; bd dir, Tower Village Nursing Home, 1989; mem bd dir, Olympic festival comt, 1994; st Louis area boys scout, 1994; past chmn, black leadership roundtable, 1998-99, Nat Asn Advan Colored People SAB, St. Louis Pub Sch, 2009. **Honors/Awds:** Sales Award, Lincoln Nat Life Ins, 1977; Community Service Award, 1999. **Home Addr:** 1001 Highlands Plz Dr W Suite 429, St Louis, MO 63104. **Business Addr:** President, Chief Executing officer, Richard K Gaines Inc, 2324 N Florissant Ave, St. Louis, MO 63106-3149, **Business Phone:** (314)881-1969.

### GAINES, DR. SAMUEL STONE

Executive. **Personal:** Born Jan 25, 1938, Ft. Pierce, FL; married Theressa Ann Dillard; children: Andre, Arnold & Alwyn. **Educ:** Talladega Col, BA, 1960; McAllister Sch Embalming, attended 1961. **Career:** Fla Mortician Asn, pres, 1979-81; Epsilon Nu Delta Mortuary Fraternity, nat pres, 1982-84; Nat Funeral Dir & Morticians, nat pres, 1985-86; St Lucie Co Sch Bd, bd mem & chmn, currently. **Orgs:** Treas, Omicron Tau Chap Omega; treas, Fla Mortician Asn; St Lucie Co Sch Bd, 1972-; life mem, Omega Psi Phi Frat; golden hertigage mem, Nat Asn Adv Colored People; Grand Inspector Gen, 33rd degree Ancient & Accepted Scottish Rite Free Masonry Southern Jurisdiction; Asn Independent Funeral dir Fla. **Home Addr:** 1505 Ave Q, PO Box 831, Ft Pierce, FL 34950, **Home Phone:** (561)466-1025. **Business Addr:** Chairman, Board Member, School Board of St Lucie County, 2250 S Jenkins Rd, Ft Pierce, FL 34947, **Business Phone:** (772)462-8888.

### GAINES, SONJA

Commissioner, health services administrator, mental health counselor. **Educ:** Univ Md, BS, psychol; William Paterson Univ, BA, sociol & anthrop; Tex Women's Univ, MBA. **Career:** MHMR (Ment Health & Ment Retardation) Tarrant County (Tex), dir case mgt, 1988-1990, chief ment health serv, 1995-2014; Tex' Health & Human Serv Comn (HHSC), assoc comnr ment health, 2014-. **Orgs:** Leadership Ft Worth, 1997-; Tex Dept State Health Serv, Contracts Comt, 2009-; bus chair, Nat Alliance Ment Illness (NAMI), 2010-13; bd trustees mem, Ment Health Am, 2011-; Tex Dept State Health Serv, LANAC Comt, 2011-. **Business Phone:** (512)487-3417.

### GAINES, DR. THURSTON LENWOOD, JR.

Physician. **Personal:** Born Mar 20, 1922, Freeport, NY; son of Thurston Lenwood and Albertha Reubena Robinson; married Jacqueline Eleanor Kelly; children: Beverly Doreen, Terrell Lance & William Wesley. **Educ:** Howard Univ, attended 1943; NY Univ, BA, 1948; Meharry Med Col, MD, 1953. **Career:** Meadowbrook Hosp, E Meadow, internship; Veteran Hosp, med dir; SW Col Naturopathic med, adj prof; Hempstead, pvt pract surg, 1959-76; Assoc attend surgeon Nassau County Med Ctr, E Meadow, Long Island, NY, 1959-77; S Nassau Community Hosp, Oceanside, NY, dir prof educ & training, 1964-69; Mercy Hosp, Rockville Ctr, NY, dir surg educ, 1969-74; Western Mass Hosp, Westfield, Mass, chief prof serv, 1977-78; Soldiers Home Holyoke, med dir, 1979-88; pvt pract; elem sch teacher, currently. **Orgs:** Kiwanis Club Hempstead, NY, 1963-67; dep county med examr Nassau County, Long Island, NY, 1964-77; Hempstead Community Chest, Hempstead, NY, 1965; bd trustees Cath Hosp Asn, St Louis, MO, 1973-76; asst clin prof surg State Univ NY Stonybrook Med Sch, 1976-77; fel Am Col Surgeons; fel Int Col Surgeons; fel Am Col Utilization Rev Physicians, 1987. **Honors/Awds:** Diplomate, Am Bd Surg, 1963; Diplomate, Am Bd Qual Assurance Utilization Review Physicians, 1987; European-African-Middle East Campaign Medal; The Presidential Unit Citation. **Home Addr:** 35346 Summerholly Lane, Murrieta, AZ 92563-6709, **Home Phone:** (951)926-2352.

### GAINEY, LEONARD DENNIS, II

Association executive, consultant, president (organization). **Personal:** Born Aug 23, 1927, Jacksonville, FL; children: Leonard III, Derek & Kassandra. **Educ:** Morehouse Col, BA, 1949. **Career:** US Post Off Dept, Ft Lauderdale, Fla, carrier, 1953-66; Gaineys Bus Affairs, owner, 1953-66; Econ Opportunity Coord Group Inc, dep dir, controller, 1966-73; State Fla Ed Dept, fiscal officer, 1973-76; Urban League Broward City, pres, chief exec officer, 1976-81; Ken Thurston & Assoc Inc, bd mem, 1979-80; Omega Group Inc, mgr mgt consult br off; N Broward Hosp Dist, coordr, dir minority bus affairs, mgt consult, currently. **Orgs:** Nat Asn Health Servs Execs; Omega Psi Phi, 1957; Ed Community Ft Lauderdale Broward C C, 1980, Human Affairs Coun; Nat Coun Christians & Jews, 1980; chmn, Broward Co Human Rels Adv; Am Mgt Asn; Nat Soc Pub Acct; Nat Soc Tax Prof; Am Asn Prof Consult; Fla Asn Minority Bus Off; Nat ForumBlack Adminrs; Omega Psi Phi Fraternity Inc; zoning bd mem, City Lauderdale Lakes, Fla. **Honors/Awds:** Omega Man of the Year, Omega Psi Phi Fraternity; Citation Broward Co Human Rels Div, 1979. **Home Addr:** 6134 Grand Cypress Cir E, Coconut Creek, FL 33073-2343, **Home Phone:** (954)429-9022. **Business Addr:** Management Consultant, North Broward Hospital District, 303 SE 17th St, Ft. Lauderdale, FL 33316-2523, **Business Phone:** (954)759-7400.

### GAINOUS, FRED J.

College administrator, educator, president (organization). **Personal:** Born Jul 6, 1947, Tallahassee, FL; son of Eddie and Lucy; married Madie; children: Tamara, Nikki Meeks & Kelli. **Educ:** Fla A&M Univ, BS, agr educ, 1969; Univ Fla, MS, agr educ, 1972, educ specialist, 1974, PhD, 1975. **Career:** Fla A&M Univ, assoc prof educ, 1977-78, pres, 2002-04; Fla State Dept Educ, pro dir, 1978-79, coord, 1979-85; Kans State Dept Educ, asst comnr, 1985-87; St Peters burg Col, assoc vpres, 1987-88; Ala Col Systs, Dept Post sec Educ, chancellor, 1988-2002; Fla Agr & Mech Univ, pres. **Orgs:** Leadership Montgomery, 1993; Ala Comn Higher Educ Adv Coun; pres &chancellors, Ala Coun Col & Univ; Asn Community Col trustee; Jr Col & Trade Sch Authority; pres Acad, Am Asn Community Col, 1994; pres, Nat Coun State Dir Community Col, 1995; Leadership Ala, 1996; chancellor, Ala Col Syst; bd trustee, Faulkner Univ & Univ Fla; dir, Educ & Info Ctr, Fla; dir, Fla A&M Univ, 2002-05. **Business Addr:** President, Florida A&M University, 1601 S Martin Luther King Jr Blvd, Tallahassee, FL 32307, **Business Phone:** (850)599-3000.

### GAITAN, HON. FERNANDO J., JR.

Lawyer, judge. **Personal:** Born Aug 22, 1948, Kansas City, KS. **Educ:** Donnelly Col; Pittsburgh State Univ, BS, 1970; Univ Mo, Kansas City,

JD, 1974. **Career:** Chief judge (retried); Southwestern Bell Tel Co, atty, 1974-80; Sixteenth Judicial Circuit Ct, Mo, judge, 1980-86; Mo Ct Appeals, Western Dist, judge, 1986-91; Bur Prisons; US Justice Dept; pub defender; Legal Aid Soc; Sixteenth Judicial Circuit, Jackson City Ct House, judge; US Dist Ct, Western Dist Mo, chief judge, 2007-14; sr status, 2014-. **Orgs:** Mo Bar Asn; Kans City Bar Asn; Jackson County Bar Asn; Am Bar Asn; Nat Bar Asn; State & Nat Judicial Conf; St Lukes Hosp; De La Salle Educ Ctr; Ozanam Home Boys; Nat Asn Advan Colored People; Vol Corrections, Nat Conf Christians & Jews; Fed-State Jurisdiction Comt, 1997-2003; transferee judge, Multidistrict Litigation Panel; Just the Beginning Found, currently. **Honors/Awds:** One of the 500 leading judges in America, Lawdragon; Alumnus of the Year Award, Univ of Missouri-Kansas City; Outstanding Alumnus, Pittsburg State Univ; Difference Maker Award, Urban League of Greater Kansas City; Centurion Leadership Award, Greater Kansas City Chamber of Commerce; Missouri Walk of Fame; Reason to Believe Award, Kansas School District, Kansas City; Pittsburg State University Meritorious Achievement Award, 2009. **Special Achievements:** The first African-Am to serve as a Judge of the United States District Court for the Western District of Missouri; The youngest person ever app an Appellate Judge of the Missouri Court of Appeals-Western Dist. **Home Addr:** 131 W High St Rm 7552, Jefferson City, MO 65101-1557. **Business Addr:** Judge, US District Court Western District, Charles Evans Whittaker Ct House, Kansas City, MO 64108, **Business Phone:** (816)512-5630.

### GAITER, TONY, JR. (TONY BERNARD GAITER)
Football player. **Personal:** Born Jul 15, 1974, Miami, FL; son of Tony Sr and Mary. **Educ:** San Bernardino Valley Col, attended 1998; Univ Miami, BA, criminal justice. **Career:** Football player (retired); Nat Football League-Europe, Amsterdam Admirals; New Eng Patriots, wide receiver, 1997; Xtreme Football League, Orlando Rage, wide receiver; San Diego Chargers, 1998. **Honors/Awds:** Dade County Athlete of the Year; State Champion Thrice.

### GAITHER, BARRY (EDMUND BARRY GAITHER)
Arts administrator. **Personal:** Born Jan 1, 1944?, Great Falls, SC. **Educ:** Morehouse Col, BA; Ga State Univ; Brown Univ, MFA, 1968. **Career:** Spelman Col, lectr, 1968-69; Nat Ctr Afro-Am Artists, Mus, dir & cur, 1969-; Mus Fine Arts, Boston, cur, 1969-; Mass Col Art, lectr, 1970-71; Wellesley Col, lectr, 1971-74; Boston Univ, Afro-Am Studies, fac, 1971-83; Harvard Col, lectr, 1972-75; Univ Minn, Arts Leadership Inst, summer fac, 1989; Commission on Museums for a New Century; Commission on Equity and Excellence; Museums and Communities; American Alliance of Museums. **Orgs:** Am Asn Mus, 1984, 1986 & 2000; panel chmn, Pres George W Bushs Adv Bd; Historically Black Cols & Univs; dir & cheif cur, Mus Nat Ctr Afro-Am Artists, currently; panel chmn, Nat Endowment Arts, 1980-83; co-founder & pres, African Am Mus Asn. **Business Addr:** Director, Chief Curator, The National Center of Afro-American Artists, 465 Huntington Ave, Boston, MA 02115, **Business Phone:** (617)267-9300.

### GAITHER, DR. CORNELIUS E.
Dentist. **Personal:** Born Feb 28, 1928, Philadelphia, PA; son of Cornelius Hopson and Edith Albertha Robinson; married Anna Louise Whittaker; children: Cornelius, Carmen, Carol, John & Reginald. **Educ:** Lincoln Univ, AB, 1949; Meharry Med Col, DDS, 1953. **Career:** Salem Memorial Hosp, chief dent servs. **Orgs:** Rho Chap, Alpha Phi Alpha Fraternity; Chi Delta Mu, Med Dent Pharmaceut Fraternity; Salvation Army Serv Comt, 1958-; Aerospace Med Asn; S Jersey Med Dent Asn; Kiwanis Int: Christ Presb Church, 1970-; Sigma Pi Phi Fraternity. **Honors/Awds:** Other Award, Salvation Army; honoree, NJ State Colored Women's Federated Clubs; Parade marshal, Kiwanis Club, 1982. **Home Addr:** 968 Kings Hwy Apt R13, West Deptford, NJ 08086-9331, **Home Phone:** (856)467-0898. **Business Addr:** Dentist, 505 Auburn Ave, Swedesboro, NJ 08085, **Business Phone:** (856)467-0898.

### GAITHER, EDMUND BARRY. See GAITHER, BARRY.

### GAITHER, ISRAEL L.
Association executive, commander, chief executive officer. **Personal:** Born Oct 27, 1944, New Castle, PA; son of Israel L Sr and Lillian; married Eva D Shue; children: Michele Gaither Sparks & Mark. **Career:** USA Eastern Territory, Corps, 1964, DHQ, 1965, Corps, 1966, DHQ, 1975, div comdr, 1986, field secy, secy personnel, 1993, chief secy, 1997; S Africa Territory, territorial comdr, 1999; USA Eastern Territory, territorial comdr, 2002; Int HQ, chief staff, 2002-06, nat comdr comnr, 2006-. **Honors/Awds:** Honorary Doctor of Humane Letters, Asbury Col, 2005; Strong Men and Women Award, 2008. **Special Achievements:** First African American and youngest officer appointed as chief secretary for Salvation Army; first African to serve as territorial leader for the Salvation Army in South Africa; First African to receive the rank of CMSer; First African American to serve as Chief of the Staff, chief exec officer, comnr for the Salvation Army in 1865; First African-American to serve as a divisional commander. **Business Addr:** National Commander Commissioner, The Salvation Army in the United States of America, 615 Slaters Lane, Alexandria, VA 22313, **Business Phone:** (800)728-7825.

### GAITHER, JAMES W., JR.
Engineer. **Personal:** Born Dec 16, 1954, Battle Creek, MI; son of James W Sr and Marie Elizabeth Stubbs; married Susan Lynn Bryant; children: Anika Marie & James Bryant. **Educ:** Mich State Univ, East Lansing, Mich, BS, pkg engineering, 1981. **Career:** Revlon Prof Prod, Cincinnati, OH, tech pkg eng, 1982-84; Avon Prods Inc, New York, NY, indust engr, 1984-87, package develop adminr, 1987-89; Revlon Inc, NY, grp leader, package develop, 1989-92, mgr package develop, 1992-93; Colgate Palmolive, supvr package engineering, 1993-2000, global procurement mgr, 1993-2011, contract mfg mgr, 2000-07; Sujym LLC, pres, 2011; Conair Corp, package develop & purchasing, 2011-. **Orgs:** MSU Pkg Soc, Alumni, 1987-; Inst Pkg Profs, 1989-; Pkg coun, Am Mgt Asn, 1990-. **Special Achievements:** America's Best and Brightest Young Business & Professional Men, Dollars & Sense Mag, 1989. **Home Addr:** 22 Carolin Rd, Montclair, NJ 07043, **Home Phone:** (973)509-0522. **Business Addr:** Package Development & Purchasing, Conair Corp, 200 W Kensinger Dr, Cranberry Township, PA 16066, **Business Phone:** (724)584-5500.

### GAITHER, KATRYNA RENEE
Basketball player. **Personal:** Born Aug 13, 1975, Bronx, NY. **Educ:** Notre Dame Univ, attended 1997. **Career:** San Jose Lasers, ctr, 1997-99; CB Navarra, 1998-99; Becast Vicenza, 1999-2000; Brisaspor izmit, 2000-01; Ind Fever, 2000; Utah Starzz, 2000; Hanvit, 2001; DKSK Miskolc, 2002-03; Los Angeles Sparks, 2002; Wash Mystics, 2002; Tarbes GB, 2003-06; Dexia Namur, Belg League, 2006-07; EuroLeague Women All-Star Game, 2007; Dynamo Energie, 2007-08; ACP Livorno, 2008-09.

### GAITHER, MAGALENE DULIN
Educator. **Personal:** Born Jul 13, 1928, Mocksville, NC; daughter of Leroy Robertson and Edith Hazel Britton (deceased); married Troy Baxter Hudson; children: Eric Lynn Hudson Sr & Hazel Shanlon Hudson; married William Eugene. **Educ:** Bennett Col, Greensboro, NC, BA; NC Agr & Tech State Univ, Greensboro, NC, MS, adult educ. **Career:** Educator (retired); Buckingham County Training Sch, Dillwyn, Va, eng reading, 1950-51; Cent Davie High Sch, Mocksville, NC, eng hist, 1951-61; Unity High Sch, States ville, NC, eng teacher, 1961-70; N Iredell High Sch, Olin, NC, eng teacher, 1970-71; Davie High Sch, Mocksville, NC, eng teacher, community activist, 1971-83; Davidson County Community Col, Lexington, NC, instr, 1983-87. **Orgs:** Shiloh Baptist Church, 1938-; Nat Asn Advan Colored People, 1950-; Nat Educrs Asn, 1950-; chairperson, bd Nursing Home Advocacy, 1980-83; bd advs, Milling Manor Home Handicapped Women, 1985-; bd dir, Davie Co Arts Coun, 1979-81; co chairperson, Democratic Party, 1991-; Zeta Phi Beta Sorority Inc; pres, NC Asn Educrs, Davie Co Unit. **Home Addr:** 1938 US Hwy 64 E, Mocksville, NC 27028-7414, **Home Phone:** (336)998-8278.

### GAITHER, DR. THOMAS W.
Educator. **Personal:** Born Nov 12, 1938, Great Falls, SC. **Educ:** Claflin Col, BS, 1960; Atlanta Univ, MS, 1964; Univ Iowa, PhD, biol, 1968. **Career:** Cong Racial Equality CORE, field secy, 1960-62; Iowa City, forester, 1968; Slippery Rock State Univ, assoc prof, 1968-2007, prof biol, prof emer biol, dept chair, currently. **Orgs:** Bot Soc Am; Mycol Soc Am; AAAS; Soc Sigma Xi. **Honors/Awds:** Outstanding Young Member, Am Alpha Kappa Mu Nat Scholastic Hon Soc, 1972; Pacesetter Award, 2004. **Special Achievements:** USAF, 1960. **Home Addr:** 362 E Water St, Slippery Rock, PA 16057. **Business Addr:** Professor Emeritus, Slippery Rock University, 1 Morrow Way, Slippery Rock, PA 16057, **Business Phone:** (800)778-9111.

### GALBRAITH, ALAN SCOTT
Executive, football player, actor. **Personal:** Born Jan 7, 1967, Sacramento, CA. **Educ:** Univ Southern Calif, grad. **Career:** Football player (retired), actor, manager; Cleveland Browns, tight end, 1990-92; Dallas Cowboys, 1993, 1997, tight end, 1994; Wash Redskins, tight end, 1995-96; Green Bay Packers, 1998; Sacramento Kings, chaplain, currently; Cafe Barista Coffee House, gen mgr, currently. Film & TV Series: Macbeth: The Comedy, 2001; Duck, 2005; Dark Disciple, 2014; "The NFL on CBS", 1991; "ESPN's Sunday Night Football", 1991; "NFL Monday Night Football ", 1994-97; "NFL on FOX", 1995; "The NFL on NBC", 1997. **Honors/Awds:** Dallas Cowboys Super Bowl XXVIII Champions. **Business Addr:** Chaplain, Sacramento Kings, 1 Sports Pkwy, Sacramento, CA 95834.

### GALL, DR. LENORE ROSALIE
School administrator. **Personal:** Born Aug 9, 1943, Brooklyn, NY; daughter of George Whitfield and Olive Rosalie Weekes. **Educ:** NY Univ, AAS, 1970, Tisch Sch Bus & Pub Admin, BS, 1973, training & develop cert, 1975, SEHNAP, MA, counr educ, 1977; Teachers Col, Columbia Univ, EdM, 1988, EdD, 1988. **Career:** School administrator (retired); Ford Found, 1967-76; New York Univ, Grad Sch Bus, dep dir, 1976-79; Pace Univ Lubin Sch Bus, dir career develop, 1979-82; La Guardia Community Col, City Univ New York, asst prof, 1981-95; Yale Univ Sch Orgn & Mgt, dir career develop, 1982-85; Brooklyn Col, City Univ New York, asst to assoc provost, 1985-88, asst to provost, 1988-91; Fashion Inst Technol, asst to vpres acad affairs, 1991-94; New York, City Tech Col, City Univ New York, asst provost, 1994-2000; City Col Technol, New York, dean studs & acad serv, 2000. **Orgs:** Chairperson bd dir, Langston Hughes Comm Libr, 1975-79 & 1982-91; vpres, awards comn chairperson, 1976-99 & 1999-, pres, Dollars Scholars; dir, Placement Secretarial Develop Workshops, Col Placement Serv, 1978-81; prog chairperson, New Haven Chamber Com, 1984; bd dir, 1985, pres, 1989-93, Asn Black Women Higher Educ Inc; northeast sectional dir, 1993-96, nat vpres, 1996-, nat pres, 2003-, Am Asn Univ Women; Educ Hon Orgn, Kappa Delta Pi, 1986; Columbia Univ Chap, Phi Delta Kappa, 1986; Am Asn Univ Adminr, 1986; Nat Asn Women Educ; Nat Urban League; vpres, 1987-89, pres, 1989-93, Nat Coun Negro Women N Queens Sec; pres, Corona-E Elmhurst & Queens Chap Dollars for Scholars; bd dir, Libr Action Comt Inc; Langston Hughes Community Libr; trustee, Queens Bor Pub Libr; co-chair, Audience Develop Task Force, Dance Theatre Harlem; vpres, pres, Nat Asn Univ Women, 2002-06. **Home Addr:** 31-33 91st St, Jackson Heights, NY 11369, **Home Phone:** (718)565-7457.

### GALLAGHER, DR. ABISOLA HELEN
Psychologist, educator. **Personal:** Born Oct 13, 1950, Chicago, IL; daughter of Lee Roy and Lulla Mae. **Educ:** St Xavier Univ, attended, psychol, 1970; Northeastern Ill Univ, BA, psychol, 1972; Univ Wis, Whitewater, MS, coun, 1974; Rutgers Univ, EdD, coun psychol, 1983. **Career:** Univ Wis Systm Cent Admin, educ admin intern, 1974-75; Univ Winconsin-Parkside, counr-prog coordr, 1975-78; Douglass Col Rutgers Univ, asst dean stud life, 1981-85; Unlimited Potential, mgt consult, 1985-87; Rutgers Col, Rutgers Univ, residence dir, 1978-81, asst dean off acad serv, 1987-90; Jersey State Col, coun psycholgist, 1990-, Clin Pract, lic psychologist, 1994-; Abisola Gallagher-Hobson, dir, coun & wellness serv, 2004-; NJ City Univ, Coun & Wellness Serv, dir, currently. **Orgs:** Vpres, Asn Black Psychologists Nj Chap, 1983-87, 1989-; exec bd mem, Coalition 100 Black Women Nj, 1985; Asn Black Psychologists, 1985-87; Am Psychol Asn, 1987; NJ Psychol Asn, 1987; NJ Chap, Asn Black Psychologists, 1989-91; exec bd mem, Women's Resource Ctr, 1991-92; dir, Coun & Psychol Serv Ctr; Asn Univ & Col Coun Ctr dir; Nj Col Health Asn. **Home Addr:** 175 Slocum Ave, Englewood, NJ 07631-2221, **Home Phone:** (201)816-1173. **Business Addr:** Director of Health & Wellness, New Jersey City University, 54 Col St, Jersey City, NJ 07305-1597, **Business Phone:** (201)200-3165.

### GALLAGHER, MIKE JOHN
Media executive. **Personal:** Born Jan 19, 1945, Toledo, OH; married Mary. **Educ:** John Carroll Univ, bus, 1967. **Career:** Reams Broadcasting Corp, sr vpres, 1977-80; WABQ Inc, pres, 1980-87. **Orgs:** Alpha Kappa Psi, 1968. **Home Addr:** 18149 Clifton Rd, Lakewood, OH 44107.

### GALLON, DR. DENNIS P.
Educator, administrator. **Personal:** Born Monticello, FL. **Educ:** Edward Waters Col, BS, bus, 1964; Ind Univ, Bloomington, MS, bus, 1969; Univ Fla, PhD, higher educ, 1975. **Career:** Fla Community Col, prof, 1972-79, bus mgr, 1979-81, dean & voc ed, 1981-84, dean instr, 1984-85, Col Lib Arts & Sci, dean, 1985-, assoc vpres acad progs, Kent Campus, pres; Univ Fla, Doctoral Prog Higher Educ Admin, adj prof; Palm Beach Community Col, pres, 1997-2010; Palm Beach State Col, pres, 2010-; Workforce Alliance Inc, dir, Currently. **Orgs:** Am Soc Training & Develop; Jax Chamber Com; Fla Asn Community Col; Jax Urban League; Am Asn Community Cols; Southern Asn Cols & Schs' Comn Cols; Fla Asn Cols & Univs; Leadership Fla; Univ Fla Alumni Bd; dir, Tenet St Marys Inc; dir, Fla Blood Centers Inc. **Honors/Awds:** Community Leader of the Year Award, Northern Palm Beach County Chamber Com, 2002; Martin Luther King Jr Distinguished Leader Award, Nat Asn Advan Colored People-S Palm Beach Br, 2004; Whitney M Young Jr National Service Award, Gulf Stream Coun Boy Scouts Am, 2005; Silver Medallion Award, Nat Conf Community & Justice, 2007; Life Time Achievement Award, Urban League Palm Beach County, 2007. **Home Addr:** 593 Masters Way, Palm Beach Gardens, FL 33418-8491, **Home Phone:** (561)625-0190. **Business Addr:** President, Palm Beach State College, AD 00208 4200 Congress Ave, Lake Worth, FL 33461, **Business Phone:** (561)868-3350.

### GALLOT, RICHARD JOSEPH, SR.
Executive, government official. **Personal:** Born Jan 31, 1936, Swords, LA; son of Freddie and Loretta; married Mildred Bernice Gauthier; children: Daphne, Loretta & Richard Jr. **Educ:** Tyler Barber Col, attended 1961; Grambling State Univ, BS, acct, 1975; Southern Univ Law Ctr. **Career:** Gallo's Barbershop, barber, 1961; Gallo's Grocer & Liquor & Serv, owner, 1969-; Town Grambling, mayor, 1981-84; Gov's Comn Community Develop, 1985; Grambling State Univ a, prof, Dept Hist, chair; La House Representatives, 2000-07, state senate, 2011. **Orgs:** Pres, Grambling Chamber Com, 1967; dir, Grambling Fed Credit Union, 1973; parish coun, St Benedict Church, 1975; Lion's Club, 1983; La Bd Ethics; pres, La AAUW Stud Adv Coun; bd supvr, Univ La Syst, 2005-11; Alpha Kappa Alpha Sorority Inc. **Honors/Awds:** Businessman of the Year, Bus Dept, Grambling State Univ, 1981; Outstanding Black in Louisiana, Teal Enterprise, 1982; Author: A History of Grambling State University. **Home Addr:** 1604 Martin Luther King A, PO Box 148, Grambling, LA 71245, **Home Phone:** (318)247-6446. **Business Addr:** 310 S Trenton St, Ruston, LA 71270, **Business Phone:** (318)251-8480.

### GALLOWAY, JOSEPH SCOTT (JOEY GALLOWAY)
Football player, executive. **Personal:** Born Nov 20, 1971, Bellaire, OH. **Educ:** Ohio State Univ, bus & mkt. **Career:** Seattle Seahawks, wide receiver, 1995-99; Dallas Cowboys, 2000-03; Tampa Bay Buccaneers, wide receiver, 2004-08; New England Patriots, wide receiver, 2009; Pittsburgh Steelers, wide receiver, 2009; Washington Redskins, wide receiver, 2010-; Arena Football League, Columbus Destroyers, owner, currently; Smoothie Jct, owner, 2007-; NBC Sports, studio analyst; ESPN, football analyst, 2012; WBNS, co-host. **Orgs:** Make-A-Wish Found; founder, Joey Galloway Family Found, 2003-. **Business Addr:** Co-Founder, Smoothie Junction, 1120 E Kennedy Blvd, Tampa, FL 33602, **Business Phone:** (813)849-0189.

### GALVIN, DR. EMMA CORINNE BROWN. See Obituaries Section.

### GAMBLE, G. ARLIVIA BABBAGE
Vice president (organization). **Personal:** married Raymond; children: Angelique. **Educ:** Ky State Univ, BA; Austin Peay State Univ, MA, 1979. **Career:** Limra Leadership Inst Fel, 2004; State Farm Ins Cos, vpres agency & sales resources, currently. **Orgs:** Nat Asn Ins Women's Leadership Prog; co-chair, Nat African-Am Womens Leadership Inst; Hopkinsville-Christian County Chamber Com; bd trustee, Murray State Univ; exec leadership cabinet, GAMA; chair, Grace Missionary Baptist Church Trustees. **Honors/Awds:** Innovative Award, Ky Chamber Com, 1991; Outstanding Young Alumna Award, APSUNAA, 1998; Athena Award, Hopkinsville-Christian County Chamber Com. **Business Addr:** Vice President of Agency Sales Resources, Leadership Board, State Farm Insurance Cos, 1 State Farm Plz, Bloomington, IL 61710, **Business Phone:** (309)766-2311.

### GAMBLE, KENNETH
Executive, musician. **Personal:** Born Aug 11, 1943, Philadelphia, PA; married Dione La Rue. **Career:** Kenny Gamble & Romeos, lead vocal; Columbia Recs, rec artist, 1963; Philadelphia Music Found, bd dir; Philadelphia Int Recs, co-owner; Raising Horizons Quest Charter Sch, instr, currently; Albums: Gonna Take a Miracle, 1971; Back Stabbers, 1972; 360 Degrees Billy Paul, 1972; Drowning Sea Love, 1972; Ship Ahoy, 1973; Sound Philadelphia, 1973; Black & Blue, 1973; Dance Your Troubles Away, 1975; Wake Up Everybody, 1975; To Be True, 1975; Love Message, 1975; Survival, 1975; Family Reunion, 1975; Philadelphia Freedom, 1975; We Got Rhythm, 1976; Message Music, 1976; All Things Time, 1976; Jacksons, 1977; Travelin' at Speed Thought, 1977; Teddy Pendergrass, 1977; Unmistakably Lou, 1977; Goin' Places, 1977; When You Hear Lou, You've Heard It All, 1977; So Full Love, 1978; Life a Song Worth Singing, 1978; dentify Yourself, 1978; Teddy, 1979; Let Me Be Good to You, 1979; Live! Coast to

Coast, 1979; Yr 2000, 1980; TP, 1980; Sit Down & Talk to Me, 1980; Get Much Love You Can, 1981; Spirit's It, 1981; I'm Love Again, 1983; Keep It Comin', 1984; Expressway To Your Heart; Cowboys To Girls; I Can't Stop Dancing; Only Strong Survive; I'm Gonna Make You Love Me; One Night Affair; We'll Be United; Silly, Silly Fool; Don't Let Green Grass Fool You; Slow Motion; Me & Mrs. Jones; Regina; Drowning Sea Love; If You Don't Know Me by Now; 992 Arguments; I Miss You; When World's At Peace; That's How Long I'll Be Loving You; Backstabbers; Love Train; Love I Lost; Now That We Found Love; Yesterday I Had Blues; I'll Always Love My Mama; Love Money; Bad Luck; Don't Call Me Bro; Zach's Fanfare; Love Message; Am I Black Enough You; Sunshine; When Will I See You Again; Livin' Weekend; Wake Up Everybody; Enjoy Yourself; I Could Dance All Nigh; I Love Music; Love Epidemic; Stairway To Heaven; Show You Way to Go; Do It Any Way You Wanna; My One & Only Love; Rich Get Richer; Hope That We Can Be Together Soon; Ooh Child. **Orgs:** Asn Music; Broadcast Music; Am Fed Musicians; Nat Asn Rec Merchandiser; Rec Indust Asn Am; T. J. Martell Leukemia Found; AMC Cancer Res Ctr & Hosp. **Business Addr:** Co-Founder, Philadelphia International Records, 309 S Broad St, Philadelphia, PA 19107, **Business Phone:** (215)985-0900.

## GAMBLE, KENNETH L.

Government official. **Personal:** Born Apr 24, 1941, Marshall, MO; son of Ira J Sr (deceased) and Elizabeth Lane (deceased); married Shiela M Greene; children: Jerry L Swain, Andrew J Swain & Kendra L E. **Educ:** Morgan State Col, Baltimore, MD, attended 1962; Youngstown State Univ, Youngstown, OH, BA, 1971; Univ Akron, Akron, OH, MA, urban studies, 1975. **Career:** Univ Akron, Ctr Urban Studies, Akron OH, res asst, 1972-73; Trans Century Corp, Wash, DC, consult, Pub Housing, 1973; Canton Urban League, Canton, OH, assoc dir, housing & community serv, 1973-77; Toledo NHS, Toledo, Ohio, exec dir, 1977-80; City Saginaw, Saginaw, Mich, dir, dept neighborhood serv; Saginaw Housing Cms, dir, 1991-92, ade asst asst city mgr, 1993, dep city mgr. **Home Addr:** 1415 Brown St, Saginaw, MI 48601, **Home Phone:** (989)752-2448. **Business Addr:** Administrative Assistant, Deputy General Service, City Saginaw, Saginaw, MI 48601, **Business Phone:** (517)759-1224.

## GAMBLE, OSCAR CHARLES

Baseball player. **Personal:** Born Dec 20, 1949, Ramer, AL; married Juanita Kenner; children: Sean & Sheena. **Career:** Baseball player (retired), contributor; Caldwell Cubs, 1968; San Antonio Missions, 1969; Chicago Cubs, outfielder, 1969; Philadelphia Phillies, 1970-72; Cleveland Indians, 1973-75; New York Yankees, 1976, 1979-84; Chicago White Sox, 1977, outfielder, 1985; San Diego Padres, 1978; Tex Rangers, 1979; Baseball Page, contribr, currently. **Home Addr:** 2129 Edinburgh Dr, Montgomery, AL 36116-1313.

## GAMBLE, ROBERT LEWIS

Government official. **Personal:** Born Apr 27, 1947, Carroll County, GA; married Lucy Ann Dixon; children: Venus Marie & Athenia Marie. **Career:** USMC, printing press oper, 1966; United Parcel Serv, feeder driver, 1970; Whitesburg City, mayor. **Orgs:** Chmn, Carroll Co Pre-health Clin, 1981; vice-chmn, Carroll Co Voc Sch, 1984. **Home Addr:** PO Box 572, Whitesburg, GA 30185. **Business Addr:** Mayor, City of Whitesburg, PO Box 151, Whitesburg, GA 30185.

## GAMBLE, DR. WILBERT

Educator. **Personal:** Born Jun 19, 1932, Greenville, AL; married Zeferene Tucker; children: Priscilla Ann. **Educ:** Wayne State Univ, BS, 1955, PhD, chem, 1960. **Career:** NIH predoctoral fel, 1959; NIH post doctoral fel, Cornell Univ, 1960-62; NIH post doctoral fel, 1960 & 1968; Ore State Univ, asst prof, 1962-67, assoc prof, prof, biochem, prof emer, currently; Johnson Res Found, Univ Pa, vis prof, 1967-76; Univ Sci & Tech Kumasi Ghana, Ful bright prof, 1971-72; NIH, vis res worker, 1976-77 & 1983-84; IPA, invest, 1990-91. **Orgs:** Lehn & Fink Medal Advan Pharm Sci, 1955; Phi Lambda Upsilon Hon Soc, 1957; Sigma Chi Hon Soc, 1960; Am Soc Bio chem & Molecular Biol; Danforth Asn Danforth Found, 1969-. **Home Addr:** 4115 NW Dale Dr, Corvallis, OR 97330-2903, **Home Phone:** (541)753-3223. **Business Addr:** Professor Emeritus, Oregon State University, 2011 Ag Life Sciences Bldg, Corvallis, OR 97331-7305, **Business Phone:** (541)737-4511.

## GAMBRELL, HON. DONNA J.

Executive, association executive. **Personal:** Born Nov 26, 1954, Washington, DC; daughter of Louis and Betty Snowden. **Educ:** Towson State Univ, BS, 1977; NY Univ, MS, 2001. **Career:** US Govt Accountability Off, 1979-87; Fed Savings & Loan Ins Corp, chief, policy mgr, 1987-91; Resolution Trust Corp, sr claims specialist, 1989-91; Fed Deposit Ins Corp, community affairs off, NY region, 1991-96, dep reg dir, NY region, 1996-97, assoc dir consumer community affairs, 1997-2000, dep dir consumer community affairs, 2000-02, dep dir, compliance & consumer protection, 2002-07; Gulf Coast Region, 2006-07; Community Develop Financial Insts, dir treas, 2007-13; Donna Gambrell Enterprises LLC, Independent Contractor, 2014-; Fed Res Bank Atlanta, Vis Scholar, 2014-. **Orgs:** Women Housing & Finance, 2003-; bd mem, Corporation for a Skilled Workforce, 2008-14; adv bd, Smithsonian Anacostia Community Mus, 2012-15; bd dir, Southern Bancorp Inc, 2015-; Asn Enterprise Opportunity, 2016. **Honors/Awds:** Excellence Award, FDIC, Financial Education, 2001; Excellence Award, 2002; National Public Service Award, 2004. **Home Addr:** 512 F St Terr SE, Washington, DC 20003-2719, **Home Phone:** (202)547-5155. **Business Addr:** Independent Contractor, Donna Gambrell Enterprises LLC, 532 F St Terr SE, Washington, DC 20003.

## GANDY, WAYNE LAMAR

Broadcaster, football player. **Personal:** Born Feb 10, 1971, Haines City, FL. **Educ:** Auburn Univ. **Career:** Football player (retired), owner; Los Angeles Rams, right tackle, 1994; St Louis Rams, left tackle, 1995-96, right tackle, 1997-98; Pittsburgh Steelers, left tackle, 1999-2002, tackle, 1999; New Orleans Saints, left tackle, 2003-05; Atlanta Falcons, left tackle, 2006-08; CBS-Atlanta Sports, host, 2011-12; ESPN, color analyst, 2013-; Gandy Group, owner. **Orgs:** Nat Honor Soc. **Business Addr:** Color Analyst, ESPN Inc, Bristol, CT.

## GANEY, DR. JAMES HOBSON

Dentist. **Personal:** Born Apr 29, 1944, Plainfield, NJ; married Peggy S; children: Jayme & Christopher. **Educ:** Howard Univ Col Pharm, BS, 1969; NJ Col Dent, DMD, 1974. **Career:** Farleigh Dickinson Univ Dent Sch, fac, 1979; Steven Hobson, DMD, PC, gen dent, 1995-97; Bronx-Lebanon Hosp Ctr, Div Restorative Dent, dir, Gen Pract Resident Prog, co-dir, currently, Dept Dent, asst clin prof; pvt pract dentist, currently. **Orgs:** Am pharmaceut Asn; NJ Pharmaceut Asn; Nat Pharmaceut Asn; Am Dent Asn; NJ Dent Asn; Nat Dent Asn; Acad Gen Dent; Union Co Dent Soc; Plainfield Dent Soc; Commonwealth Dent Soc; Health Prof Educ Adv Counc State NJ, 1979; mem bd dir, Planfield Camp Crusade; Nat Asn Advan Colored People; Psi Omega Dent Frat; Chi Delta Mu Frat. **Honors/Awds:** Certificate of Merit, Howard Univ Col Pharm. **Home Addr:** 206 Broad St Apt 16, Bloomfield, NJ 07003-2683. **Business Addr:** Dentist, Bronx-Lebanon Hospital Center, 1770 Grand Concourse, Bronx, NY 10457, **Business Phone:** (718)901-8410.

## GANNAWAY, NANCY C. See HARRISON, NANCY GANNAWAY.

## GANSON, WESLEY

Educator. **Career:** John Trix Elementary Sch, prin. **Business Addr:** Principal, John Trix Elementary School, 13700 Bringard Dr, Detroit, MI 48205-1156, **Business Phone:** (313)852-8644.

## GANT, CRYSTAL M.

Educator, business owner. **Personal:** Born Jan 13, 1972, Detroit, MI; daughter of Marshall and Jewell; married Anthony Mitchell. **Educ:** Univ Detroit, BA, 1993, teacher cert, 1995; Univ Mich, attended 1998. **Career:** Detroit Bd Educ, educ, 1993-2003; Crystal Clear Images, pres & chief exec officer, 1996-. **Home Addr:** 3768 Leslie St, Detroit, MI 48238, **Home Phone:** (313)933-3700. **Business Addr:** Chief Executive Officer, Crystal Clear Images, 15627 W McNichols, Detroit, MI 48238, **Business Phone:** (313)272-8433.

## GANT, PHILLIP M., III

Executive, vice president (organization). **Personal:** Born Aug 21, 1949, Chicago, IL; son of Phillip M II and Naurice; married LaJule Steele; children: Kimberli & Lyndsay. **Educ:** Linbloor Tech, Chicago, IL; Univ Ill, Chicago, IL. **Career:** Foote Cone & Belding, Chicago, Ill, copywriter to vpres & creative dir, 1971-79; Young & Rubican Adv, New York, NY, sr copy writer, 1979-81; J Walter Thompson Adv, Chicago, Ill, vpres & creative dir, 1982-84; BBDO Chicago, Chicago, Ill, exec vpres & exec creative dir, 1984-87, chief creative officer, 1987-04. **Orgs:** Bd mem, Evanston, Ill, Community Daycare Ctr; bd mem, Evanston, Ill, Sch Little C. **Home Addr:** 935 Sheridan Rd, Evanston, IL 60202. **Business Addr:** Creative Chief, BBDO Detroit, 880 W Long Lake Rd, Troy, MI 48098.

## GANT, RAYMOND LEROY

School administrator. **Personal:** Born Jul 7, 1961, Paw Paw, MI. **Educ:** Ferris State Univ, BS, bus admin, 1984; Cent Mich Univ, MA, coun educ, 1998. **Career:** Ferris State Univ, mgt intern off Planning & develop, 1984-86, dir minority stud affairs, 1986-, prog coordr, officio, spec asst to pres, currently; Leona Group, L.L.C., vpres, mkt, commun & pub rels, regional vpres. **Orgs:** Bd dir, FSU Alumni; alumni bd dir & founder, Minority Stud Scholar Selection Comt; Phi Beta Sigma; S Eastern Mich Black Alumni Asn; Nebr Humanities Coun; Nat Endowment for Humanities. **Home Addr:** Canterbry Green Apt GUI 2, Big Rapids, MI 49307. **Business Addr:** Special Assistant to the President, Director of Minority Student Affairs, Ferris State University, Ferris State Col, Big Rapids, MI 49307, **Business Phone:** (231)591-3815.

## GANT, RICHARD E.

Actor. **Personal:** Born Mar 10, 1944, San Francisco, CA. **Career:** TV appearances: "Attica", 1980; "Internal Affairs", 1988; "The Cosby Show", 1989; "Miami Vice", 1989; "MacGyver", 1991; "False Arrest", 1991; "Reasonable Doubts", 1991, 1992; "Beverly Hills, 90210", 1992; "Roc", 1992; "Murphy Brown", 1992; "Condition: Critical", 1992; "L.A. Law"; "MenDon't Tell"; "Empty Nest"; "Seinfeld"; "The Tower"; TV Series: "Trade Winds", 1993; "Wings", 1993; "Lois & Clark: The New Adventures of Superman"; "Martin"; "MacShayne: The Final Roll of the Dice"; "Living Single"; "Picket Fences", 1994; "Trial by Fire"; "The Bonnie Hunt Show", 1995; "The Client", 1996; "Touched by an Angel", 1996; "Yes, Dear", 2004; "Eve", 2005; "Deadwood", 2005; "In Justice", 2006; "How I Met Your Mother", 2006; "The Bill Engvall Show", 2007; "American Dad!", 2007-11; "Boston Legal", 2008; "General Hospital", 2007-08; "General Hospital: Night Shift", 2007-08; "Cold Case", 2009; "Men of a Certain Age", 2009-11; "The Deep End", 2010; "The Middle", 2012; "The Mindy Project", 2012-14; "Family Time", 2012; "Bunheads", 2012; "Back in the Game", 2013; "The Game", 2013-14; "Bleach", 2014; "The Fright Night Files", 2014. Films: Night of the Juggler, 1980; Death of a Prophet, 1981; Krush Groove, 1985; Suspect, 1987; Collision Course, 1989; The Freshman, 1990; Rocky V, 1990; Love or Money, 1990; Stone Cold, 1991; Last Breeze of Summer, 1991; CB4, 1993; Posse, 1993; Jason Goes to Hell: The Final Friday, 1993; City Hall, 1996; Ed, 1996; The Glimmer Man, 1996; Raven, 1997; Bean, 1997; Built to Last, 1997; The Big Lebowski, 1998; Sour Grapes, 1998; Godzilla, 1998; Divorcing Jack, 1998; Johnny B Good, 1998; Nutty prof II, 1998; Kingdom Come, 2001; The Job, 2001; Smallville, 2002; The Partners, 2003; Lesser of Three Evils, 2005; Hood of Horror, 2006; Ezra, 2007; Norbit, 2007; Cover, 2007; Waiting for Forever, 2010; Ashes, 2010; Screwball: The Ted Whitfield Story, 2010; Fed elections Nigeria, campaign mgr. **Business Addr:** Actor, c/o Pakula King, 9229 Sunset Blvd Suite 315, Los Angeles, CA 90069, **Business Phone:** (310)281-4868.

## GANT, RONALD EDWIN (RON GANT)

Baseball player, baseball executive. **Personal:** Born Mar 2, 1965, Victoria, TX; married Heather Campbell; children: Ryan Edwin & Alexus. **Career:** Baseball player (retired), baseball executive, broadcaster; Atlanta Braves, outfielder & infielder, 1987-93; Cincinnati Reds, 1995; St Louis Cardinals, 1996-98; Philadelphia Phillies, 1999-2000; Anaheim Angels, 2000; Colo Rockies, 2001; Oakland Athletics, 2001; San Diego Padres, 2002; Oakland Athletics, 2003; TBS, baseball analyst, 2005; FSN S & Sport S Braves, baseball Analyst, currently; Fox Broadcasting Co, WAGA-TV, anchor, currently. **Home Addr:** 512 Mon-Terey, Victoria, TX 77904. **Business Addr:** Baseball Analyst, FSN South, 1175 Peachtree St NE Suite 408, Atlanta, GA 30361, **Business Phone:** (404)230-7300.

## GANT, TRAVESA EVETTE

Basketball player. **Personal:** Born Oct 10, 1971, Orange, TX. **Educ:** Lamar Univ, BA, kinesiology. **Career:** Basketball player (retired); Nanya Formosa Plastic, Taiwan, ctr, 1994-95; Olympiakos Volos, Greece, 1996-97; SC Alcamo, 1997-98;Los Angeles Sparks, 1997; Troglos Priolo, 1998-99; Elitzur Delek, 2000-01; Bne Yehuda Ziontronics, 2001-03; WooriBank Hansae, 2003; Shinhan Bank S-Birds, 2003; Kumho Life Falcons, 2005-06.

## GANT, WANDA ADELE

Administrator. **Personal:** Born Oct 4, 1949, Washington, DC; daughter of Monore E (deceased) and Adela Mills; married Ronald Gary; children: Richard W V & Ronald II. **Educ:** Cent State Univ, Wilberforce, OH, BS, 1971; Southeastern Univ Wash, DC, MBPA, 1982. **Career:** Gen Servs Admin, equal opportunity specialist, 1971-78; US Dept Labor, equal opportunity specialist, 1978-84; US Info Agency, fed women's prog mgr, 1984-89; USIA, int visitors exchange specialist, 1989-93; US Dept Justice, equal employ opporunity specialist, 1993-. **Orgs:** Outstanding Young Women Am, 1981; Nat Coun Negro Women, 1983-; Alpha Kappa Alpha, 1983; Fed Women's Interagency Bd, 1984; DC-Dakar Sister Cities Friendship Coun, 1985-; Am Asn Univ Women, 1986; Bus & Prof Women, 1986. **Honors/Awds:** Super Performance Duty, 1971; Outstanding Young Women Am, 1983. **Home Addr:** 7811 Harder Ct, Clinton, MD 20735. **Business Addr:** Specialist, US Department Justice, Rm 1246 10th Pa Ave NW, Washington, DC 20530, **Business Phone:** (202)616-4800.

## GANTT, HARVEY BERNARD

Architect, politician. **Personal:** Born Jan 14, 1943, Charleston, SC; son of Christopher and Wilhelmenia; married Lucinda; children: Sonja, Erika, Angela & Adam. **Educ:** Iowa State Univ, attended 1962; Clemson Univ, BArch, 1965; Mass Inst Technol, MA, city planning, 1970. **Career:** Am architect & Dem politician; Odell Assocs, intern; architect, 1965-70; Soul City, exp city, planner, 1970-71; Univ NC, Chapel Hill, lectr, 1970-72; Gantt Huberman Architects, prin partner, 1971-; Clemson Univ, vis critic, 1972-73; City Charlotte, city coun mem, 1974-83, mayor pro tem, 1981-83, mayor, 1983-87; US Senate, dem cand, 1990 & 1996; Nat Capital Planning Comn, chair. **Orgs:** AIA; Am Planning Asn; Charlotte Chap, Nat Asn Advan Colored People; NC Design Found; US Coun Mayors, uncommitted deleg, 1984 Dem Conv. **Home Addr:** 517 N Poplar St, Charlotte, NC 28202-1729, **Home Phone:** (704)376-8764. **Business Addr:** Principal Partner, Gantt Huberman Architects PLLC, 500 N Tryon St, Charlotte, NC 28202, **Business Phone:** (704)334-6436.

## GARBEY, BARBARO

Baseball player, athletic coach. **Personal:** Born Dec 4, 1956, Santiago de Cuba; married Kimberly Grutza; children: Isabel, Barbaro Jr & Gabriela. **Career:** Baseball player (retired), athletic coach; Detroit Tigers, amateur free agt, 1980, outfielder & infielder, 1984-85; Tex Rangers, outfielder & infielder, 1988; W Mich Whitecaps, hitting coach, 2003; Tenn smokies, hitting coach, 2007-08; Peoria Cheifs, hitting coach, 2009-. **Home Addr:** 14094 Woodside St, Livonia, MI 48154-5206. **Business Addr:** Hitting Coach, Peoria Cheifs, 730 SW Jefferson, Peoria, IL 61605, **Business Phone:** (309)680-4000.

## GARCIA, KWAME N., SR.

School administrator. **Personal:** Born Apr 4, 1946, St. Croix; married Grete James; children: Kenny, Sharifa, Khalfani, Gustavo, Luanda & Kwame Jr. **Educ:** Col VI, AA, 1967; NY Univ, BS, 1969; Univ Mass, MBA, 1973. **Career:** VI Bd Ed, mem, 1978-; Univ VI, asst prof & state dir coop ext serv, pres, vice chmn, 1979-. **Orgs:** Nat Sch Bd Asn, 1978-; bd trustee, VI Pub TV Syst, 1982-84, Col Vi, 1982-84; bd dir, Caribbean Food Crops Soc; bd dir, Caribbean Coun Higher Educ Agr. **Home Addr:** PO Box 1307, Kingshill00851, **Home Phone:** (770)808-0280. **Business Addr:** State Director, Assistant Professor, University of the Virgin Islands, RR 02, Kingshill00850-9781, **Business Phone:** (340)692-4091.

## GARCIA, DR. WILLIAM BURRES

Musician. **Personal:** Born Jul 16, 1940, Dallas, TX; son of Eural Clinton and Willie Mae Jefferson. **Educ:** Prairie View A&M Univ, attended 1961; N Tex State Univ, BMus, 1962, MmusEd, 1965; Univ Iowa, PhD, 1973; Carnegie-Mellon Univ, col mgt prog, 1984. **Career:** Educator (retired); Philander Smith Col, instr music, 1963-64; Langston Univ, asst prof music, 1965-69; Howard Univ, NEH fel, 1974; Miles Col, assoc prof music, 1974-77; Talladega Col, prof music, 1977-, chmn music dept, 1977-, chmn humanities div, 1981-85, actg acad vpres, 1982-83; Selma Univ, acad dean, 1986-87; Lane Col, prof music, 1987-93, choir dir, 1987-93, Ctr Acad Skills Develop, dir, 1987-92, chair div humanities, 1989-93; Calif State Univ, Long Beach, Calif, Inst Learning, asst prof, 1988; Langston Univ, prof music & chair music dept, conductor choirs, 1993-99; Ft Valley State Univ, prof music & chair dept fine arts, 1999-2001; Lincoln Univ, prof voice & choral music, 2001-10, chair music dept, 2001-03, artistic dir & conductor concert choir, 2001-07, chair visual & performing arts dept, 2003-06. **Orgs:** Phi Mu Alpha Sinfonia, 1965; Am Choral dir Asn, 1967-; bd mem, Div Higher Educ Disciples Christ, 1978-81; bd mem, Talladega Arts Coun, 1981-85; Nat Asn Teachers Singing; Nat Asn Music Educ. **Home Addr:** 2207 Pebble Beach Dr, Elkton, MD 21921, **Home Phone:** (410)620-5623.

## GARDINER, GEORGE L.

Librarian, administrator, dean (education). **Personal:** Born May 3, 1933, Cambridge, MA; married Reida B Dykes; children: Jesse B, Veronica, Lynne & George DeWitt. **Educ:** Fisk Univ Nashville, BA, 1963; Univ Chicago, MA, 1967, CAS, 1969. **Career:** Am Libr Asn Chicago, asst exec sec, libr admin div, 1967; IL State Univ, Norm Ill, refrence libr, 1967-70; Cent State Univ, Wilber force OH, dir libr, 1970-72; Oakland Univ, Rochester, Mich, prof, dean libr sci, 1972; Univ Mich Sch Libr Sci, Ann Arbor MI, vis prof, 1975; Oakland Univ Libr, prof emer, currently. **Orgs:** Am Lib Asn, 1967-; Am Soc Info Sci, 1979-; Nat Lib Asn, 1978-; bd mem, Normal Pub Lib Normal, Ill, 1968-70; Afro-Am Hist Comm Ill C Supt Pub Instr, 1969-70; Bd Black Col Prog Pontiac, 1974-; chmn bd, Mich Lib Consortium, 1978-79; chmn, Mich Coun State Libr Dir, 1979-80. **Honors/Awds:** First prize, Nat Essay Contest Am Missionary Asn, 1961. **Special Achievements:** Mem Lect, Harvard Univ, 2005. **Home Addr:** 6777 Cedarbrook Dr, Bloomfield, MI 48301, **Home Phone:** (248)851-4467. **Business Addr:** Professor Emeritus, Oakland University Library, 2200 N Squirrel Rd, Rochester, MI 48309-4401, **Business Phone:** (248)370-2100.

### GARDNER, AVA MARIA
Manager, executive. **Personal:** Born Jun 1, 1962, Ft. Sill, OK; daughter of John M and Essie W. **Educ:** Cameron Univ, BS, criminal justice technol, 1985. **Career:** Okla City Conv & Visitors Bur, conv sales mgr, 1987-93; Denver Metro Conv & Visitors Bur, sr citywide sales mgr, 1993-2003; Kans City Conv & Entertainment Ctrs, dir sales & mkt mgr, 2003; City Kans City, Mo, dir citywide mkt, currently. **Orgs:** Nat Coalition Black Meeting Planners, 1988-; Prof Conv Mgt Asn; Int Asn Assembly Managers; Am Soc Asn Execs. **Special Achievements:** First runner-up at the Miss Black America. **Home Addr:** PO Box 1273, Denver, CO 80202. **Business Addr:** Director of Citywide Marketing, City of Kansas City, Missouri, 414 E 12th St, Kansas City, MO 64106, **Business Phone:** (816)513-1313.

### GARDNER, BARRY ALLAN
Football player, executive. **Personal:** Born Dec 13, 1976, Harvey, IL; son of Jerry and Brenda. **Educ:** Northwestern Univ, BS, commun, 1999. **Career:** Football player (retired); Philadelphia Eagles, linebacker, 1999-2002; Cleveland Browns, 2003-04; New York Jets, 2005; New Eng Patriots, 2006; Contrado Partners, partner; free agt, currently; Athletes Performance, linebacker's combine coach, 2006-; NU Vision Investment Group, pres, 2008-; Triple Threat Performance, linebacker's combine coach, 2009-12; Inst Athletes, dir player develop, 2009-; Performance Enhancement Professionals, linebacker's combine coach, 2010-; BE GREAT initiative LLC, pres, 2011-; Football Univ FBU, youth & high sch linebacker coach & mentor, 2012-.

### GARDNER, DR. BETTYE J.
Educator. **Personal:** Born Vicksburg, MS; daughter of Janie Foote and Glover C. **Educ:** Univ, BA, hist, 1962, MA, hist, 1964; George Washington Univ, PhD, 1974. **Career:** Howard Univ, instr, 1964-69; Social Sys Intervention Inc, sr res assoc, 1969; Wash DC Bd Educ, consult, 1969; Black Hist Calvert Ct, consult; Wash Tech Inst, asst prof, 1969-71; Coppin State Col, dean arts & sci, 1981-87, Dept Hist, prof, 1982-, chmn, 1988-90. **Orgs:** Nat Asn Advan Colored People; Org Am Historians; Assoc Black Women Historians; exec coun, Assoc Study Afro-Am Life & Hist; Nat Educ Asn; Nat Coun Negro Women, 1980; assoc, Danforth Found, 1980-86; ed bd, J Negro Hist; exec counc, Asn Study Afro-Am Life & Hist; vpres, Asn Afro Am Life & Hist, 1993-95, nat pres, 1995-97; chmn, Educ Licensure Comn; Bethune House Fed Com; nat bd, Spec Cong Task Force; comnr, McLeod Bethune Coun House Nat Hist Site; Cong Task Force Slave Labor; prog chair, Nat African Am Mus's Nat Conf; Strategic Plng Comt, Sch Arts & Sci; Sabbatical Lead Comt; Appeals Comt CFRC; Centennial Planning Comt; African Am Hist Month Comt; Foundations Excellence; Celebrating Excellence, Planning Comt; Arts & Sci Strategic Planning Comt; Intellectual Life Comt. **Home Addr:** 6101 16th St NW Apt 309, Washington, DC 20011-1751. **Business Addr:** Professor, Coppin State University, Rm GJ 408 2500 W N Ave, Baltimore, MD 21216, **Business Phone:** (410)951-3439.

### GARDNER, CEDRIC BOYER
Executive, lawyer. **Personal:** Born Jul 22, 1946, San Antonio, TX; son of Tommie L and Willie Mae; married Sylvia Irene Breckenridge; children: Zayani Aisha, Bilal Amin, Cedric Ahmed & Saida Ujima. **Educ:** Calif State Univ, Los Angeles, CA, BA, 1975; Univ Kans Sch Law, JD, 1983. **Career:** Urban League Wichita, assoc dir, 1977-80; Shawnee Co Dist Atty, asst dist atty, 1983-84; Univ Kans, training mgr, 1984-85; Kans Dept Health & Environ, atty, 1985-. **Orgs:** Douglas Co, Nat Asn Advan Colored People, 1978-81, Urban League Wichita, 1980-87; Douglas Co Amateur Radio Club, 1984-87; Douglas Co Asn Retarded Citizens. **Honors/Awds:** Outstanding Service, Wichita Nat Asn Advan Colored People, 1980. **Home Addr:** 1511 W 26th St, Lawrence, KS 66046, **Home Phone:** (913)842-7461. **Business Addr:** Special Assistant Attorney General, Kansas Department of Health & Environment, 400 SW 8th Ave Suite 203, Topeka, KS 66603-3930, **Business Phone:** (785)296-1500.

### GARDNER, EDWARD GEORGE
Executive, business owner. **Personal:** Born Feb 25, 1925, Chicago, IL; son of Frank and Eva; married Bettiann; children: Gary, Guy, Tracy & Terri. **Educ:** Chicago Teachers Col, BA; Univ Chicago, MA. **Career:** Beauty supply salesman, part time, late 1950; Chicago Sch Syst, elem sch & asst prin, 1945-64; Soft Sheen Prod Inc, founder & pres, 1964-85; Garden Investment Partners, pres; E G GardnerBeauty Prod Co, owner; House Kicks, owner, currently. **Orgs:** Founder, Regal Theater; bd mem, Chicago Urban league. **Business Addr:** Owner, House of Kicks, 9535 S Cottage Grove Ave, Chicago, IL 60628, **Business Phone:** (773)721-4351.

### GARDNER, DR. FRANK W.
Executive, educator. **Personal:** Born Jun 12, 1923, Chicago, IL; married Elaine St Avide; children: Craig M, Glenn P & Susan M. **Educ:** Chicago Teachers Col, BA, 1948; De Paul Univ, MEd, 1953; Univ Chicago, attended 1958; Northwestern Univ, PhD, 1975. **Career:** Educator (retired); Chicago Pub Sch, teacher, 1948-54, prin, asst sec, 1968, dist supt, 1974-83; Betsy Ross Elem Sch Chicago, asst prin, 1955-65; Ray Elem Sch Chicago, prin, 1965-68; Loyola Univ Chicago, lectr. **Orgs:** Chmn St Clotilde Elem Sch Bd, 1966-69; Sch Study Comn Archdiocese Chicago, 1970-71; bd dir, Faulkner Sch Chicago, 1971-72; bd ed pres, City Chicago, 1984-89; dir, writing Title III Proposal Estab Independent Learning Ctr Ray Elem Sch; Chicago Urban League; Phi Delta Kappa; Am Asn Sch Personnel Admin; dir emer, Golden Apple Found, bd mem; pres, Chicago Sch Bd. **Honors/Awds:** Leadership Award, Harold Wash; Boys & Girls Club of Chicago; Outstanding Alumnus, De Paul Univ. **Home Addr:** 8426 S Indiana Ave, Chicago, IL 60619, **Home Phone:** (773)846-1996. **Business Addr:** Director Emeritus, Board Member, Golden Apple Foundation, 8 S Michigan Ave Suite 700, Chicago, IL 60603, **Business Phone:** (312)407-0006.

### GARDNER, HAROLD W.
President (organization), chief executive officer, vice president (organization). **Educ:** Mich State Univ, BA, indust mgt; Harvard Bus Sch, MBA, finance, 1974. **Career:** Ford Motor Credit Co, sr fin anal; Detroit Sci Ctr, dir finance; MCN Energy Group, mgr corp develop, 1989; Gareste Ltda, prin, 2003; Mich Consol Gas Co, vpres mkt, sales & regulatory affairs; DTE Energy, sr vp corp serv; Mich Consol Gas Co, vpres gas opers; DTE Energy Co, sr vpres & asst chmn; Zoro Mining Corp, chmn, pres, chief exec officer & chief operating officer, 2007-; Pac Copper Corp, dir, vpres bus develop, 2007-. **Orgs:** Dir, Boulder Resources SA, 1999; dir, Gareste Ltda, 2003; dir, PGM Internacional, Aravena SA, 2004; Bd trustee, Leader Dogs Blind; bd trustee, Heat & Warmth Fund; Am Red Cross Seastern MI Chap, Matrix Human Servs; Adult Well-Being Servs; Mich Higher Edu Fac Authority; bd mem, Heat & Warmth Fund; bd mem, Loyola High Sch; mem audit comt, Pac Copper Corp, 2007-. **Home Addr:** 22604 S 215th St, Queen Creek, AZ 85142-9347, **Home Phone:** (480)987-0645. **Business Addr:** Vice President of Business Development, Director, Pacific Copper Corp, 3430 E Sunrise Dr, Tucson, AZ 85718, **Business Phone:** (520)989-0021.

### GARDNER, HEIDE
Vice president (organization). **Personal:** children: James & Robert. **Educ:** Mt Holyoke Col, S Hadley, MA, BS, econs & polit sci, 1979. **Career:** Am Advert Fedn, sr vpres; AAF Mosaic Ctr on Multiculturalism, founder & exec dir, 1996-2003, Interpublic Group Co, dir diversity, 2003, sr vpres, chief diversity & inclusion officer, currently. **Orgs:** Exec dir, Mosaic Ctr, Am Advert Fedn, 1996-2003; vol dir, New York Coun Girl Scouts, Int Radio & Tv Found, Ad Club New York & New Fed Theatre; bd mem, Am Asn Advert Agencies Found; NBMBA Asn; Asn Hisp Advert Agencies; New York Urban League, 2012. **Business Addr:** Chief Diversity & Inclusion Officer, Interpublic Group, 1114 Avenue of the Americas, New York, NY 10036, **Business Phone:** (212)704-1200.

### GARDNER, HENRY L.
Government official, secretary (organization). **Personal:** Born Oct 29, 1944, Jacksonville, FL; son of Annie B. **Educ:** Univ Ill, Urbana-Champaign, IL, AB, 1967; Southern Ill Univ, Carbondale, MA, 1969. **Career:** City Oakland, Oakland, Calif, asst personnel analyst, 1971-73, admin asst, 1973-76, asst to city mgr, 1976-78, asst city mgr, 1978-81, city mgr, 1981; Asn Bay Area Govts, exec dir & secy, treas, currently; Gardner, Underwood & Bacon Llc, prin. **Orgs:** Am Soc Pub Admin; Int City Mgt Asn; Alameda City & Co Mgt Asn; pres, Nat Forum Black Pub Admin, 1987-89; bd, Alliance Redesigning Govt; Nat Asn Local Arts Agencies; Am Soc Pub Admin; Int City Mgt Asn. **Home Addr:** 924 Hillcroft Cir, Oakland, CA 94610, **Home Phone:** (510)444-5017. **Business Addr:** Executive Director, Secretary, Association of Bay Area Governments, 101 Eigth St, Oakland, CA 94607, **Business Phone:** (510)464-7900.

### GARDNER, LOMAN RONALD
Educator, business owner. **Personal:** Born Feb 9, 1938, Detroit, MI; son of Loman Sr (deceased) and Lillian; married Kay; children: Hansel, Loman III, Toi & Troy. **Educ:** Eastern Mich Univ, BFAE, 1964; Mich State Univ, MA, 1970, MS, 1976, PhD, 1985. **Career:** Mich Sch Syst, instr & counr; Boys Republic Training Sch, instr; Detroit Pub Sch, instr, Learning Disabled, spec educr; Battle Creek Pub Sch, sch adv; Fed Bur Invest, spec agent; Detroit Police dept, dep & acting chief investr; Tots & Toys Pre Sch, owner, dir; Loman Investigations, owner & investr. **Orgs:** Kappa Alpha Psi, 1960-; Mason, Prince Hall, 1972-; Mich Asn Learning Disabilities Educr, 1990-; life mem, NCP, 1992. **Home Addr:** 2046 Cleo Lane, Deltona, FL 32738, **Home Phone:** (386)574-1820.

### GARDNER, RODERICK F.
Football player, accountant. **Personal:** Born Oct 26, 1977, Jacksonville, FL. **Educ:** Clemson Univ, BEd, human resources mgt & serv, 2000. **Career:** Football player (retired); Wash Redskins, wide receiver, 2001-04; Gardner Enterprise LLC, pres, 2003-09; Green Bay Packers, wide receiver, 2005; Carolina Panthers, wide receiver, 2005; Kans City Chiefs, wide receiver, 2006; Atlanta Luxury Imports, sales consult, 2007-12; Cumberland Group, bus develop & acct exec, 2015-. **Orgs:** Founder, Roderick Gardner Found; NFL Players Asn. **Honors/Awds:** Most Valuable Player, All-Southeast, All-Fla, All-Area, All-Conf, All-Region & All-State; All-ACC hons; First Team All-Am, Coll & Pro Football News; Biletnikoff Award; Offensive Player of the Week, Nat Football Conf, 2001. **Business Addr:** Business Development Executive, Account Executive, Cumberland Group LLC, 300 Galleria Pkwy Suite 1600, Atlanta, GA 30339, **Business Phone:** (770)575-9280.

### GARDNER, WALTER
Government official. **Career:** Civil rights activist; Newton Community Improv Corp, pres, 1989; Newton County Bd Supervisors, Miss, bd supvr, 1991-. **Business Addr:** Supervisor, Newton County Board of Supervisors, 92 W Broad St, Decatur, MS 39327-8960, **Business Phone:** (601)635-3444.

### GARIBALDI, DR. ANTOINE MICHAEL
College president, college teacher, educational psychologist. **Personal:** Born Sep 26, 1950, New Orleans, LA; son of Augustin and Marie Brule. **Educ:** Howard Univ, BA, sociol, 1973; Univ Minn, PhD, educ psychol, 1976. **Career:** Holy Comforter-St Cyprian, elem teacher, 1972-73; Univ Minn, Col Educ, res asst, 1973-75; St. Paul Urban League St Acad, prin, 1975-77; Inst Educ Leadership, educ policy fel, 1977-78; Nat Comn Excellence Educ, staff, 1981-82; Nat Inst Educ, res assoc, 1977-82; Xavier Univ LA, Dept Educ, chmn, prof educ, 1982-89, Col Arts & Sci, dean, 1989-91, vp acad affairs, 1991-96; Howard Univ, provost & chief acad officer, 1996-2000; Educ Testing Serv, sr fel, 2000-01; Gannon Univ, pres, 2001-10; Univ Detroit Mercy, pres, 2011-. **Orgs:** Asn Black Psychologists; fel Am Educ Res Asn; fel Am Psychol Asn; Alpha Phi Alpha; Phi Delta Kappa; Phi Kappa Phi; Sigma Pi Phi, Chair, SAC 2006-08; pres, Univ Minn Black Stud Psychol Asn, 1974-75; Sci Bd, AUs, 1979-83; assoc ed, Am Educ Res J, 1982-84; consult, US Dept Educ, 1983-85; New Orleans Libr Bd, 1984-93, chmn, 1991-93; bd dir, J Negro Educ; co-chmn, Mayor's Found Educ, 1987-90; co-chmn, educ comm, Urban League Greater New Orleans, 1984-90; Metrop Area Comt, 1992-96, educ fund bd, 1991-96; bd dir, Am Libr Asn; Alpha Kappa Mu, Psi Chi; bd dir, Ctr Educ African-Am Males, 1991-92; bd dir, AAHE, 1995-03, chair, 2001-03; comt mem, AACTE, 1988-98; sr fel, Vpres Collaborations & Corp Secy, Educ Testing Serv, 2000-01; bd dir, ACE, 2006-08, comt on LIE, 2004-07; bd dir, Sr Thea Bowman Black Cath Educ Found; bd dir, chair 2002-, Coun Independent Col, chair 2006-08, vice chair prog, 2003-05; chmn, Social Action Comt, Sigma Pi Phi, 2006-08, vice chmn, 2008-10; bd dir, Asn Independent Col & Univ PA, 2008-; NACUBO, bd dir, 2006-12; chair, NCAA Exec Comm subcomt Gender & Diversity, 2008-2009, pres, NCAA Div II, 2005-09; bd trustee, Univ St Thomas, MN, 2004-; bd regents, Seton Hall Univ, 2007-10; bd dir, Acad Search, 2008-; Nat Rev Bd, USCCB, 2009-; pres, Asn Gov Bds Coun, 2009-; Acad Search Inc; Am Coun Educ; Qual Educ Minorities; Math, Sci, Engineering Network; Fraternity's Educ Comn, 2010-12; Nat Asn Col & Univ Bus Officers; chair bd dir, Am Asn Higher Educ; Educ Comn, 2010-12; Comn Young African Am Males, 2012-14. **Home Addr:** 204 Bay Mist Dr, Erie, PA 16505, **Home Phone:** (814)835-7403. **Business Addr:** President, University of Detroit Mercy, 4001 W McNichols Rd, Detroit, MI 48221-3038, **Business Phone:** (313)993-1245.

### GARLAND, JOHN WILLIAM
School administrator. **Personal:** Born Oct 24, 1944, Harlem, NY; son of John W and Amy; married Carolyn Farrow; children: Amy & Jabari. **Educ:** Cent State Univ, BA, polit sci, 1971; Ohio State Univ Col Law, JD, 1974. **Career:** Coastal Plains, dir legal servs, 1979-83; Hayes & White, PC, sr atty, 1983-84; Law Off John W Garland, atty, 1984-88; Univ DC, gen coun, 1988-91; Univ Va, spec asst atty gen, assoc gen coun, 1991-93, exec asst pres, 1993-96, assoc vpres intellectual property, 1996-97; Cent State Univ, pres, 1997-. **Orgs:** Bd dir, Nat Asn Col & Univ Atty; Nat Conf Black Lawyers; Asn Univ Technol Mgr; bd dir, Wash Lawyers Comm Civil Rights Under Law; bd dir, Nat Veterans Legal Servs Proj; ed bd, J Col & Univ Law; US Supreme Ct; Supreme Ct NC: Supreme Ct Va; Ct Appeals, DC; pres, US Ct Mil Appeals; LeDroit Pk Civic Asn, 1974-76; life mem, Disabled Veterans Am; trustee, Miami Valley Res Pk Found; trustee, Greater Dayton Pub TV; trustee, Southwestern Ohio Coun Higher Educ; chair, Am Coun Educ Ctr Advan Racial & Ethnic Equity; bd mem, Edison Mat Technol Ctr, Dayton, OH; bd dir, FifthThird Bank; Nat Afro Am Mus & Cult Ctr; Nat Coun Col Law Alumni Asn, Ohio State Univ; founding dir, Tawawa Community Develop Corp; founding dir, Legal Servs Coastal Plains. **Home Addr:** 1685 US Rte 42 E, Xenia, OH 45385, **Home Phone:** (937)376-9141. **Business Addr:** President, Central State University, PO Box 1004, Wilberforce, OH 45384-1004, **Business Phone:** (937)376-6011.

### GARNER, DR. CHARLES
Musician, educator. **Personal:** Born Jul 27, 1931, Toledo, OH; married Judith Marie Bonner; children: Kevin & Darchelle. **Educ:** Cleveland Inst Mus, Bmus, 1953; Boston Univ, MA, 1957; Yale Univ, adv stud; Columbia Univ, New York, NY, PhD, 1991. **Career:** Univ Hartford, Hartt Sch Music, instr, 1961-65; E & Midwest, numerous piano & ensemble recitals; Southern Conn State Univ, composer, arranger, prof music, 1968-96, prof emer. **Orgs:** Am Asn Univ Prof; Phi Delta Kappa; Kappa Gamma Psi; Kappa Alpha Psi; Am Soc Composers Authors & Pub. **Honors/Awds:** Recipient Am Fed of Mus; Mu Phi Epsilon Scholar, 1948; Friends of Mus Award, 1949; First place OH Mus Teacher Auditions; Ranney Scholar of Cleveland, 1949-52; Charles H Ditson Award, Yale Univ, 1968; Frances Osbourn Kellogg prize in counterpoint, Yale Univ, 1969; Charles Garner Recital Hall, Southern Conn State Univ, named in honor. **Home Addr:** 190 Corbin Rd, Hamden, CT 06517. **Business Addr:** Professor Emeritus of Music, Southern Connecticut State University, 501 Crescent St, New Haven, CT 06515, **Business Phone:** (203)392-5841.

### GARNER, CHARLIE, III
Football player. **Personal:** Born Feb 13, 1972, Falls Church, VA. **Educ:** Univ Tenn, BA, bus mgt. **Career:** Football player (retired); Philadelphia Eagles, running back & fullback & kick returner, 1994-98; San Francisco 49ers, running back, 1999-2000; Oakland Raiders, running back, 2001-03; Tampa Bay Buccaneers, running back, 2004-05. **Honors/Awds:** Eagles Ed Block Courage Award, 1995; Virginia's Player of the Year; Pro Bowl, 2000.

### GARNER, CHRIS (CHRISTOPHER WINSLOW GARNER)
Basketball player. **Personal:** Born Feb 2, 1975, Memphis, TN. **Educ:** Memphis Univ, attended 1997. **Career:** Basketball player (retired); Skallagrimur UMFS, Iceland, 1997; Toronto Raptors, guard, 1997-98; Idaho Stampede, 1998-99, 2002-03; Fort Wayne Fury, 1999; Quad City Thunder, 1999, 2001; Zalgiris Kaunas, Lithuania, 1999-2000; Memphis Houn'Dawgs, 2000-01; Columbus Riverdragons, 2001-02; Golden State Warriors, 2001; STB Le Havre, France, 2001; Detroit Pistons, guard, 2003-04; Maccabi Rishon LeZion, Israel, 2004; Maccabi Giv'at Shmuel, Israel, 2004-05; Paris Basket Racing, France, 2005; AEL Larissa, Greece, 2005-06; GS Larissa, Greece, 2005-06; Cholet Basket, France, 2006-07; Apollon Patras, Greece, 2007; Achilleas, Cyprus, 2007-08, 2009-10; Polpak Swiecie, Poland, 2008; Basket Kwidzyn, Poland, 2008-09.

### GARNER, EDWARD, JR.
Commissioner, executive. **Personal:** Born Dec 4, 1942, Skippers, VA; married Betty J; children: Erica P, Edward P & Elizabeth P. **Educ:** NC Agr & Tech State Univ, BS, 1967; Squadron Off Sch, USAF, 1972; Univ NC Law Sch Chapel Hill, JD, 1976; Air Command & Staff Col,

attended 1981; Air War Col, 1994. **Career:** Akzo Am Inc, corp atty, 1976-85; NC Dept Crime Control & Pub Safety, asst secy, 1985-89; NC Indust Comn, dep comnr, 1989-2004; Garner Mediation, owner, currently. **Orgs:** NC State Bar; Am Bar Asn; Air Force Asn; NC Asn Black Laywers; Aircraft Owners & Pilots Asn; Negro Airmen Intl Inc; Asn Trial Lawyers Am; NC Acad Trial Lawyers; USaFr & NC Air Nat Guard; chmn, bd dir, Asheville Buncombe Community Rels Coun; mem bd, YMI Cult Ctr Inc; Asheville City Personnel Comn; comt, NC bar asn; Govs adv comn Mil Affairs, 1985-89; Gov Waste Mgt Bd, 1985-89; Gov Minority Exec Coun, 1985-89; Civil Air Patrol, 1986-89; Pub Officers & Employees Liability Ins Comn, 1987-89. **Business Addr:** Owner, Garner Mediation, PO Box 155, Fletcher, NC 28732, **Business Phone:** (704)621-6167.

## GARNER, JAMES A.

Politician, president (organization), mayor. **Personal:** Born Jun 21, 1945, Garysburg, NC. **Educ:** Adelphi Univ, BS. **Career:** Republican Mayor Hempstead, New York, 1988-05; White House Conf, panelist, 2002; US Conf Mayors, pres, 2003-04; US Small Bus Admin, Nat Adv Coun, adv comts; Us Conf of Mayors, 2013; Pest-Control Co, founder. **Orgs:** Nat Asn Advan Colored People; Town Hemp stead Minority Adv Coun; Local Am Legion; trustee, Village Hempstead; One Hundred Black Men Nassau-Suffolk Inc; Am Legion; Dep Nassau County Comptroller Claims, Payroll & Health Benefits Comptroller George Maragos. **Home Addr:** PO Box 32, Hempstead, NY 11550, **Home Phone:** (516)489-3400.

## GARNER, JOHN W. See Obituaries Section.

## GARNER, DR. LA FORREST DEAN

School administrator. **Personal:** Born Aug 20, 1933, Muskogee, OK; son of Fannie M Thompson and Sanford G; married Alfreida Thomas; children: Deana Y, Thomas L & Sanford E. **Educ:** Ind Univ Sch Dent, DDS, 1957, MSD, 1959, cert, orthod, 1961. **Career:** Ind Univ, Sch Dent, assoc prof, 1967-70, prof & chmn, 1970, assoc dean, minority stud serv, 1987, Grad & Post Grad Dent Educ IUSD, dir, 1994-, IUPUI, ombudsman, prof emer orthod, currently; Va Hosp Dent Div, consult, 1979-; James Whitcomb Riley Hosp, orthod coordr, 1979-. **Orgs:** Bd dir, Vis Nurses Asn, Indianapolis, 1973-77; local pres, Omicron Kappa Upsilon Local Chap, 1974-75; fel Am Col Dent, 1974; bd dir, Am Cleft Palate Educ Found, 1975-79; Boys Clubs, 1976-; Sigma Xi, 1976; chmn, Coun Res, Am Asn Orthodontists, 1976-77; Boule, 1978-; bd dir, Park Tudor Sch, Indianapolis, Ind, 1980-; life mem, Nat Asn Advan Colored People, 1980-; chmn, United Way Ancillary Serv, 1984-85; pres, Am Asn Dent Res, 1984-85; bd dir, Indianapolis Zoo, 1987-; bd dir, Fall Creek Pkwy YMCA, 1989. **Honors/Awds:** Nat Pres Omicron Kappa Upsilon Nat Dent Scholastic, 1974-75; Garner Minority Student Scholarship, named in honor, Ind Univ, 2006; DSc, Ind Univ, 2007. **Special Achievements:** Author: "A Study of the Posture of the Tongue in Individuals With Normal Occlusion". **Home Addr:** 2416 N Capitol Ave, Indianapolis, IN 46208, **Home Phone:** (317)926-7073. **Business Addr:** Professor Emeritus of Orthodontics, Indiana University, 107 S Ind Ave, Bloomington, IN 47405-7000, **Business Phone:** (812)855-4848.

## GARNER, DR. MARY E.

Psychologist, chief executive officer. **Personal:** Born Paterson, NJ; children: Floyd Jr & Steven. **Educ:** William Paterson Col, BA, psycol, 1973; Fairleigh Dickinson Univ, MA, clin psycol, 1976; City Univ NY, PhD, 1983. **Career:** Passaic City Community, prof psycol, 1983; Fairleigh Dickinson Univ, prof psycol summers, 1982-84; William Paterson Col, prof psycol, 1982-; Paterson Dept Human Resources, spec asst to dir, 1982-83, dir, 1983-; Paterson Community Health Ctr Inc, chief exec officer, currently. **Orgs:** Pres, Preakness Hosp Bd Mgrs, 1982-84; chairwoman, Riverview Towers Tenants Asn, 1973-; Coalition Pub Acct, 1982-; Zonta Int, 1983-; Black Bus & Prof Assoc, 1983-; NJ Amer Psychol Asn; NJ Primary Care Asn. **Honors/Awds:** Community serv Social & Economic Change for All Inc, 1983, Modern Beautician's Asn, 1983, Black History Month Comt, 1984-85; President Award, Preakness Hosp Bd Mgrs, 1984. **Home Addr:** 85 Presidential Blvd 15C, Paterson, NJ 07522. **Business Addr:** Chief Executive Officer, Paterson Community Health Center Inc, 32 Clinton St, Paterson, NJ 07522, **Business Phone:** (973)790-6594.

## GARNER, DR. MELVIN C.

Lawyer. **Personal:** Born Feb 9, 1941, Philadelphia, PA; son of George L and Freida White; married R Patricia Grant. **Educ:** Drexel Univ, BS, elec engineering, 1964; NY Univ, MSEE, 1967; Brooklyn Law Sch, JD, 1973. **Career:** Darby & Darby PC, partner, 1958-10, assoc, 1982-85; IBM Poughkeepsie NY, jr engr, 1964-66; CBS Labs, Stamford, Conn, engr, 1966-69; Sequential Inf Sys Dobbs Ferry, NY, proj engr, 1969-70; Bell TelLabs Holmdel, NY, patent staff, 1971-73; Brumbaugh Graves Donohue & Raymond, atty, 1973-81; New York Bar, atty; New York Intellectual Property Law Asn, pres, 2003-04; United Supreme Ct, atty; Ct Appeals Second & Fed Circuits, atty; Darby & Darby, prin, currently; Am Intellectual Property Law Asn, pres, 2005-06; Leason Ellis LLP, partner, currently. **Orgs:** NY Intellectual Property Law Asn; Nat Patent Law Asn; Eta Kappa Nu; Elect Engrs Soc; Brooklyn Law Rev; exec comt, Hon. William C. Conner Inn Ct, 2008-; Regional Vpres, Alpha Phi Alpha Fraternity. **Honors/Awds:** Drexel Univ, 2005. **Home Addr:** 111 Ridge Rd, Hartsdale, NY 10530. **Business Addr:** Partner, Leason Ellis LLP, 1 Barker Ave 5th Fl, White Plains, NY 10601-1526, **Business Phone:** (914)821-8005.

## GARNER, NATHAN WARREN

Executive. **Personal:** Born Dec 25, 1944, Detroit, MI; married Indira S Licht; children: Mark C, Erica D, Vincent C & Warren C. **Educ:** Wayne State Univ, BS, 1966; Wayne State Univ, Grad Sch Educ, MS, MEd, 1971; Columbia Univ, Grad Sch Bus, MBA, 1975; Stanford Grad Sch Bus, finance mgt prog, 1984. **Career:** Scholastic Inc, dir mkt, mgt & res, 1969-78, pres, 1995-; Time Distrib Serv Inc, dir mkt, 1978-80; US Dept Educ, spec asst secy educ, 1980-81; Time-Life Films Inc, vpres, 1981-82; Preview Subs TV Inc, pres, 1982-83; Manhattan Cable TV Inc, vpres; Paragon Cable TV Manhattan, pres; USA Networks, vpres, 1986-94; Harlem charter sch, actg asst prin; Jimmy Carter's Secy Educ, spec asst. **Orgs:** Adv bd, Fla A & M Univ Entrepreneurial Develop Ctr, 1983-85; Cable TV Admin & Mkt Soc, 1983-85; Asn Better New York, 1984-85; bd dir, E Mid Manhattan Chamber Com, 1984-85; chmn, Nat Asn Minorities Cable, 1987-88; steering community, 21st Century Fund; Friends Alvin Ailey Dance Theatre Alumni Asn; pres, Exec Exchange Prog; adv group, Columbia Univ Bus Sch Telecommunications Policy Res & Infor Studies Prog. **Honors/Awds:** Black Achievers Award, Harlem YMCA Greater New York, 1983; Andrew Heiskell Award, Time Inc, 1986; Excellence in Communications, E Manhattan Chamber Com, 1987. **Home Addr:** 442 Pac St, Brooklyn, NY 11217-2203, **Home Phone:** (401)423-9859. **Business Addr:** President, Scholastic Inc, 555 Broadway, New York, NY 10012, **Business Phone:** (212)343-6100.

## GARNER, VELVIA M.

State government official, chairperson. **Personal:** Born Nov 21, 1941, Halsted, TX; daughter of Edgar and Mary Elizabeth McKenzie; married Edward J; children: Angela, Tonia & Edward. **Educ:** Prairie View A&M Univ, BS, nursing, 1963; Univ Colo, Denver, Colo, MS, nursing admin, 1974; DPA. **Career:** Assoc dir, chairperson (retired); Ben Taub Gen Hosp, Houston, Tex, team leader, 1963-64; Madigan Gen Hosp, Tacoma, Wash, team leader, 1964-65; St Joseph Hosp, Denver, Colo, clin supvr, 1965-73; Univ Colo, Denver, Colo, asst prof, 1974-80; Ment Health Ctr Denver, State Colo, Div Youth Servs, dir med & psychol servs, 1980-87, assoc dir; Colo State Parole Bd, vchair, 1987-92; Lookout Mountain Youth Servs Ctr, asst dir, until 1992; Gilliam Detention Ctr, dir, 1993, assoc dir, 2001-05; City & County Denver, gang model initiative coordr; Accent Learning Systs, educ progs dir. **Orgs:** Chair, Ment Health Corp Denver, 1985; Colo Community Corrections Adv Coun, 1987; Rocky Mt Ctr for Health Prom & Educ, 1987; NURSES Colo Corp, 1984, pres, 1988-90; vpres educ bd dir, Rite Passage, Ridge View Acad, 2001-11. **Honors/Awds:** Teacher of the Year Award, Studs, Univ Colo, 1975-76; Adv Coun Adolescent Health, 1982-87; Community Service Award, CBWPA, 1983; Certificate for Recognition for Outstanding Community Service, Joint Effort Found, 1983; Colo Black Women Polit Action, 1986-; Community Corrections Adv Coun, 1989. **Home Addr:** 20595 E 49th Ave, Denver, CO 80249-7466, **Home Phone:** (303)373-1068.

## GARNES, SAM AARON

Football player, football coach. **Personal:** Born Jul 12, 1974, Bronx, NY. **Educ:** Univ Cincinnati, criminal justice, 1997. **Career:** Football player (retired), coach; New York Giants, strong safety, 1997-2002; New York Jets, strong safety, 2002-04; Emerson High Sch, defensive coordr, 2005; Cologne Centurions, defensive backs coach, 2006; Sam Garnes Football Camps & Clinics, owner, 2007-09; Las Vegas Locomotives, defensive backs coach, 2009-10; Carolina Panthers, spec teams asst, 2010-11; Denver Broncos, asst sec coach, 2011-14; Denver Broncos, safeties coach, 2011-15; Chicago Bears, asst sec coach, 2011-, safeties coach, 2015-. **Home Addr:** , West Milford, NJ. **Business Addr:** Safeties Coach, Chicago Bears, 1920 Football Dr, Lake Forest, IL 60045, **Business Phone:** (866)805-8555.

## GARNETT, KEVIN MAURICE

Basketball player. **Personal:** Born May 19, 1976, Mauldin, SC; son of O'Lewis McCullough and Shirley; married Brandi Padilla; children: 2. **Career:** Minn Timber wolves, forward, 1995-2007, 2015-; Boston Celtics, 2007-13; Brooklyn Nets, 2013-15.

## GARNETT, RONALD LEON

Lawyer. **Personal:** Born May 27, 1945, Louisville, KY. **Educ:** Cent State Univ, BS, 1967; Columbia Univ, JD, 1970. **Career:** US Dist Judge Robert McRae, law clerk, 1971-72; Winthrop Stimpson Putnam & Robts, atty, 1972-73; Am Express Co, atty, 1973-74; US Atty's Off, asst US atty, 1974-77; GTE Corp, sr coun, 1977-82; New York, criminal ct judge, 1984-86; pvt pract atty, currently. **Orgs:** Ny Bar Asn, 1973-; Nat Basketball Asn, 1981; Nat Asn Criminal Defense Lawyers, 1986; Am Bar Asn; New York Co Lawyers Asn; Kappa Alpha Psi. **Home Addr:** 613 W 145th St, New York, NY 10031, **Home Phone:** (212)862-2265. **Business Addr:** Attorney, 299 Broadway Suite 1802, New York, NY 10007-1901, **Business Phone:** (212)587-5159.

## GARNIER, THOMAS JOSEPH

Auditor. **Personal:** Born Apr 7, 1942, New Orleans, LA; son of Thomas and Louisa; married Grace L; children: Thomas J III & Joshua DeJalma. **Educ:** Dillard Univ, BA, 1966; Okla Univ, attended 1970. **Career:** Chevron Oil Co, acct anal, 1966-68; Shell Oil Co, acct anal, 1968-69; Off Econ Opportunity TCA, acct supvr, 1969-70; Model Cities, City New Orleans, chief fiscal off, 1970-71; La State Dept Educ, dir auditing, 1972-76; Garniers & Garniers Inc, pres, 1976-88; Bur Alcohol Tobacco & Firearms, US Treas Dept, sr auditor, currently. **Orgs:** Asn Govt Acct, 1989-; Asn Cert Fraud Examiners, 1990-; High Technol Crime Invest Asn, 2000-; Int Asn Law Enforcement Intelligence Analysts, 2001-; Nat Org Black Law Enforcement Execs, 2001-; Nat Asn Blacks Criminal Justice, 2001-; Acad Acct Historians, 2002-; Inst Internal Auditors, 2002-. **Honors/Awds:** Employee of the Year, Scientific Prof, Fed Exec Bd, 1997; Cert Appreciation, ATF FBI, 1998; Letter of Commendation, ATF, 1999; Special Act Award, ATF, 2000; Letter of Recognition, FBI, 2002. **Special Achievements:** Author: Audit Manual-Policies & Procedures, 1973; Ten Most Wanted Audit Discrepancies, 1974; Financial Expert Witness (State & Federal Courts), 1993-. **Home Addr:** 5140 Promenade Dr SW, PO Box 310872, Atlanta, GA 30331-8478, **Home Phone:** (404)629-0886. **Business Addr:** Senior Auditor, Bureau of Alcohol, Tobacco, Firearms, 2600 Century Pkwy Suite 330, Atlanta, GA 30345, **Business Phone:** (404)417-2653.

## GARRETT, ALINE MAE

**Personal:** Born Aug 28, 1944, Martinville, LA. **Educ:** Univ Southwestern La, BA, 1966; Oberlin Col, Ohio, AM, 1968; Univ Mass, PhD, 1971. **Career:** Educator (retired); Proj Head Start, Lafayette LA, teacher, 1966; Psychometrist Lafayette Parish Schs, 1967; Univ Southwestern La, Summer Sch Fac, teacher, 1969 & 1970; Univ Southwestern La, Lafayette, assoc prof psychol, 1971; Univ Mass, Amherst, grad res asst; Univ LA, Lafayette, Psychol, full prof, 2001. **Orgs:** Am Psychol Asn; Nat Asn Black Psychol; Soc Res Child Develop; Psi Chi; SE Psychol Asn; LA Psychol Asn; bd dir, Nat Coun Black Child Develop; Grad Fac, 1971-; comn Acad Affairs & Stand, 1972; Equal Employ Opportunity Comn, 1972; fac senate, 1973-; Cath Soc Serv, 1973; coun teacher educ col educ, Univ Southwestern La, 1974-; adv bd, SGA- Univ Southwestern La, Child Care Ctr; adv bd, Health Adv Bd, Tri-Parish Progress Inc, 1974; cand, St Martin Parish Sch Bd, 1974; agency parent coun, SMILE Inc, 1974; by appointment Mayor Willis Soc & Econ Com St Martinville, 1974; bd dir, Lafayette Chap Epilepsy Found; Alpha Lambda Delta. **Honors/Awds:** Research grant to do family res, HEW Office Child Develop, 1974-75; SEPA Visiting Women Program, 1974-; Faculty advisor, Nat Honor Soc; Outstanding black citizen, Southern Consumers Educ Found Field Educ, 1975. **Home Addr:** 615 N Theatre St, St Martinville, LA 70582-3454, **Home Phone:** (337)394-4106.

## GARRETT, CAIN, JR.

Military leader, commander. **Personal:** Born May 11, 1942, Kilgore, TX; son of Cain Jr (deceased) and Everett V Woods Henry. **Educ:** Univ CO Boulder, BSEE, 1968; Naval Post Grad Sch Monterey, MSEE, 1973; Naval Post Grad Sch Monterey, elec engr deg, 1974. **Career:** Commander (retired); USN, elec engr, 1974, communs officer, 1968-70, opers dept head, 1970-72, lt comdr flag secy, 1974-77, oper analyst & admin officer, Navy Oper Test Facil, 1977-80. **Orgs:** Inst Elec & Electronics Engrs; Big Brothers Steering Com Boulder, 1964-68; tournament dir, US Chess Federation, 1989-; Sacramento Chess Club. **Home Addr:** 618 Lake Front Dr Apt 57, Sacramento, CA 95831-5502, **Home Phone:** (916)391-5595.

## GARRETT, CHERYL ANN

Government official, teacher, executive. **Personal:** Born Aug 31, 1946, Bethel Springs, TN; daughter of Robert Eugene Smith and Jewel Perkins King Smith; married Larry Eugene; children: Larry Eugene II, David Conrad & Cheryl Lynn. **Educ:** Grambling Univ, BS, 1969. **Career:** Memphis Pk Comn, community ctr dir, 1970-72; Cent State Hosp, coordr adj ther, 1972-74; Memphis City Schs, sub teacher, 1974-; CJH Resources Inc, dir, pres, 1983-; Nat Black Republican Coun, southern reg, vpres; Fixit Home Repair, admin asst, 1985; City Memphis, Memphis, TN, Cunningham Community Ctr dir, currently. **Orgs:** Dir, Comn Shelby Cty Civil Serv Bd, 1979-; vice chmn, TN Comn Status Women, 1980; state pres, TN Republican Assembly, 1980-; treas, S Shelby Republican Club, 1982-. **Honors/Awds:** Merit Award, Shelby County Republican Party, 1979; Key to City, Chattanooga, TN, 1981; Family Award, Shelby County Republican Party, 1983; State Coordr, Black Vote Div Regan & Bush, 1984 Campaign, 1984; Key to the City Memphis, City Government, Mayor Hackett, 1990; Best Program Award, TN Rec & Parks Asn, Ethnic Minority Soc, 1991. **Home Addr:** 4829 Daphne Rd, Memphis, TN 38118-7226, **Home Phone:** (901)794-1632. **Business Addr:** Executive Director, City Memphis, 3373 Old Allen Rd, Memphis, TN 38128-2700, **Business Phone:** (901)377-3037.

## GARRETT, DARRELL W.

Chief executive officer, vice president (organization), manager. **Personal:** Born Nov 16, 1966, New York, NY; daughter of Daniel and Lucy. **Educ:** Univ Calif, Berkeley, BA, archit, 1989; SJ State Univ, MS, civil engineering & construct mgt, 1992. **Career:** O'Brien Kriteberg, proj mgr, 1990-94; Luster CM; Combass, pres, chief exec officer, 1994-98; Paragon Co, co-founder, chief architect, lead developer; ViaNovus, co-founder, chief developer, sr vpres, 1998-. **Business Addr:** Senior Vice President, Co-Founder, ViaNovus, 1001 Marina Village Pkwy Suite 401, Alameda, CA 94501, **Business Phone:** (510)337-1930.

## GARRETT, DEAN HEATH

Entrepreneur, basketball player. **Personal:** Born Nov 27, 1966, Los Angeles, CA; married Natasha Denise Taylor. **Educ:** San Francisco City Col, attended 1986; Ind Univ, attended 1988. **Career:** Basketball player (retired), business owner; Minn Timberwolves, free agt, 1996-97, 1998-2002; Denver Nuggets, free agt, 1997-98; Golden State Warriors, 2002; Escape nightclub & Bellanote Restaurant, co-owner, currently. **Home Addr:** , Las Vegas, CA 90210. **Business Addr:** Co-owner, Bellanotte, 600 Hennepin Ave S Suite 170, Minneapolis, MN 55403, **Business Phone:** (612)339-7200.

## GARRETT, DENISE EILEEN (DEE DEE BRIDGEWATER)

Singer. **Personal:** Born May 27, 1950, Memphis, TN; daughter of Matthew; married Gilbert Moses; children: China; married Jean-Marie Durand; children: Gabriel; married Cecil Bridgewater; children: Tulani. **Educ:** Mich State Univ; Univ Ill, Urbana-Champaign. **Career:** Thad Jones/Mel Lewis Orchestra, lead vocalist; Albums: Afro Blue, 1974; Dee Dee Bridgewater, 1976; Just Family, 1978; Bad for Me, 1979; Keeping Tradition, 1992; Love & Peace: A Tribute to Horace Silver, 1995; Dear Ella, 1997; Victim of Love, 1998; Live at Yoshi's, 2000; This is New, 2002; Jai Deux Amours, 2005; Red Earth, 2007; Eleanora Fagan (1915-1959): To Billie with Love from Dee Dee Bridgewater, 2010; Midnight Sun, 2011. **Honors/Awds:** Tony Award, Best Supporting Actress, 1975; Grammy Award for Best Musical Show Album, 1976; Grammy Award, 1998, 2010; Commandeur de L'Ordre des Artes et des Lettres, 2007. **Special Achievements:** Played Glinda the Good Witch in The Wiz, on Broadway, 1975; named Ambassador to the United Nations Food and Agriculture Organization; First American to be inducted to the Haut Conseil de la Francophonie. **Business Addr:** Vocalist, c/o Verve Music Group, 1755 Broadway 3rd Fl, New York, NY 10019-3743, **Business Phone:** (212)331-2000.

## GARRETT, DR. E. WYMAN

Obstetrician, gynecologist. **Personal:** Born May 25, 1933, Newark, NJ. **Educ:** Morgan State Col, Balto, BS, 1955; Howard Univ Col Med, MD, 1961. **Career:** Newark Mini-Surgi-Site, owner & med dir; Freemdmen's Hosp, internship, 1961-62; Harlem Hosp NY City, resident obstet/gynecol; Newark City Hosp, resident; NJ Col Med & Dent, assoc prof obstet & gynec; Vecam Inc, owner. **Orgs:** Newark Bd Educ, 1967-70; All-Am Basketball Morgan State; Beta Kappa Chi; Nat Sci Soc; Alpha Kappa Mu; dir, Drive Increase Black & Puerto Rican Enrollment, NJ Col Med & Dent; Orgn Black Prof & Bus Women; Nat Hon Soc Morgan State HBCU. **Honors/Awds:** Man of the Year Award, 1972. **Home Addr:** 114 S 12 St, Newark, NJ 07107, **Home Phone:** (973)351-4220.

### GARRETT, EUFAULA
Manager, executive. **Career:** Magic Johnson Theaters, mkt dir, 1997-. **Business Addr:** Marketing Director, Magic Johnson Theaters, 9100 Wilshire Blvd, Beverly Hills, CA 90212, **Business Phone:** (310)247-1994.

### GARRETT, DR. JACQUELYN BREWER
Physician, dermatologist. **Personal:** Born Apr 28, 1961, Washington, DC; daughter of Marlene H Brewer; children: Jacquelyn Marie & Duane Jr. **Educ:** Howard Univ, BS, 1983; Howard Univ Col Med, MD, 1985; Wash Univ, MBA. **Career:** Barnes Hosp, internal med intern, 1985-86, dermat resident, 1986-89; pvt pract dermat, currently. **Orgs:** Mound City Med Forum; St Louis Dermat Soc; Nat Med Asn, Dermat Sect; St Louis Asn Realtors; Mo Asn Realtors; Nat Asn Realtors; St Louis Regional Mult Listing Serv; fel Am Acad Dermat. **Honors/Awds:** African American Women of Distinction Award, 2006. **Business Addr:** Dermatologist, Private Practice, 11125 Dunn Rd Suite 411, St. Louis, MO 63136, **Business Phone:** (314)355-7111.

### GARRETT, JAMES EDWARD, JR.
State government official. **Personal:** Born Feb 26, 1959, Shelbyville, IN; son of James Edward Sr and Patricia Joan; married Tonita; children: James E III, Chakeyla & Tamara. **Educ:** Ind State Univ, BA, 1981; Ind Univ; Purdue Univ, attended 1990. **Career:** Ind State Univ, resident asst, 1979-80; Ind Gen Assembly, house staff intern, 1981; Dayton Hudson Corp, Target Store, sales & floor mgr, warehouse mgr, 1981-85; Ind Dept Com, Div Energy, prog asst, 1985-89; US Sen Dan Coats, ast state dir, 1989-98; city councilman at large, City Shelbyville, Ind, 1995-99; Shelby County Bank, Community reinvestment act dir, 1999-2002; Shelby City Lifelong Learning Corp, exec dir, 2002; Ind Family & Social Serv Admin, exec dir, 2005-; State Ind, exec dir, 2005-. **Orgs:** Chap pres & state dir, Phi Beta Sigma Fraternity, 1978-,; Ind State Univ, Qual Life Study Comn, 1979; Coun Black Execs, 1990-; bd trustee, pres, Shelbyville Cent Schs, 1985-93; trustee, Second Baptist Church, 1986-; Shelby County Cot Corrections Bd, 1985-; bd mem, Bears Blue River Festival, 1984-2002. **Home Addr:** 219 4th St, Shelbyville, IN 46176-2526, **Home Phone:** (317)392-1813. **Business Addr:** IN.

### GARRETT, JAMES F.
Executive, chief executive officer. **Personal:** Born Greensboro, NC; son of Sharecropper; married Joyce; children: Rodney & Melanie. **Educ:** NC A&T State Univ, BS, elec engineering; Southeastern Univ, MBA. **Career:** Naval Sea Systs Command, Systs Electromagnetic Div, dir; NATO US Rep, chief tech spokesman; Sentel Corp, founder, chief exec officer & pres, 1987-2006; Bd Nat Coalition Minority Bus, pres & chmn; Total Mgt Group LLC, prin, 2006-. **Orgs:** NASA Minority Bus Adv Coun; bd dir, Eastern Choral Soc. **Business Addr:** Principal, Chief Executive Officer, The Total Management Group LLC, 1940 Duke St Suite 200, Alexandria, VA 22314, **Business Phone:** (703)486-5655.

### GARRETT, KATHRYN
Radiologist. **Personal:** Born Mar 26, 1955, Cincinnati, OH; daughter of Leonard and Naomi; married Audley Murphy; children: Hamadi & Mehari. **Educ:** Brown Univ, BA, 1976; Univ Cincinnati, Sch Med, MD, 1981, cert, pediat radiol. **Career:** Univ Cincinnati Hosp, Cincinnati, OH, residency, 1984-88; Med Ctr Radiol Group, physician, partner, 1989-. **Orgs:** Fla Bd Med, 1991-, chair, 1996; United Cerebral Palsy Cent Fla Inc, 1997; chair laws com, Fedn State Med Bds, 1996-97; C's Hosp Med Ctr; Am Bd Radiol, 1988, 1995-. **Honors/Awds:** Dr James R Smith Award, African American Physician of the Year, Nat Asn Advan Colored People, Orlando Chap, 1993, 1997; Summit Award, Cent Fla Women's Resource Ctr, 2004. **Home Addr:** 1008 Anchorage Ct, Winter Park, FL 32789, **Home Phone:** (407)645-0558. **Business Addr:** Radiologist, Medical Center Radiology Group, 20 W Kaley St, Orlando, FL 32806, **Business Phone:** (407)423-2581.

### GARRETT, LOUIS HENRY
Manager. **Personal:** Born Jul 16, 1960, Monroe, LA; son of Mattie M. **Educ:** La Tech Univ, attended 1983; Moody Bible Inst; US Army, New Orleans, LA, legal course, second MLC, 1991. **Career:** Public sch teacher; Miss La Pageant Inc, dir advert; Grambling State Univ, McCall Dining Hall, mgr, facilities mgt, planning & opers; Ouachita Parish Ct, dep clerk, currently. **Orgs:** Phi Beta Sigma Frat Inc; La State Educ; dir, Phi Beta Sigma Frat Inc; Ouachita Parish Election Comn; Comnr-in-Charge Ward 10, Precinct 8; Nat Asn Miss Am State Pageants, 1986-87; Monroe City Planning & Zoning Comn, 1990-96; Ouachita Regional Bd Adjustments, 1996-; Fac adv, GSU chap Gamma Beta Phi Hon Soc, 1998-2000; Nat Baptist Sunday Sch; Voc Bible Sch. **Honors/Awds:** Sigma Tau Delta Honor, Soc English, 1981-83; Phi Alpha Theta Honor, Soc History, 1982-83; La State Brother of the Year, Phi Beta Sigma Fraternity. **Special Achievements:** First African American member of the LA Pageant Board of Dir, 1986-87; Monroe Jaycee of the Quarter, Springboard of the Yr. **Home Addr:** 1605 Booth St, Monroe, LA 71201-8210. **Business Addr:** Ouachita Parish Clerk Court, Parish Court House, 4th Judicial Dist, Monroe, LA 71210-1862.

### GARRETT, MELVIN ALBOY
Marketing executive. **Personal:** Born Jun 1, 1936, Montclair, NJ; married Maryann Harris. **Educ:** Upsala Col Eng, Orange, NJ, attended 1964. **Career:** Eisle King Libaire Stout & Co, NYSE, mgr, 1957-60; Halevy H Simons Archit, pub rel coordr, 1962-63; Nat St Bank Newark, banking clerk, 1963; Becker Construct Co, acct, 1964-65; United Airlines, ticket agt, sales rep, acct exec, mktg mgr, 1965-. **Orgs:** Dist Comt Man, Montclair, NJ; Nat Asn Advan Colored People; Urban League; United Airlines Black Employees Asn; Black Prof Orgn; Alpha Kappa Psi Frat. **Honors/Awds:** Interliner of the Year, 1977; Detroit Interline Club, 1977; hon mem, Detroit Interline Club, 1978; Black Achiever Award, NY Harlem YMCA, 1980; Black Acheivers Indust, 1980; Ambassador of Goodwill, Detroit-WindsorInterline Club Inc; Salesman of the Year Award, United Airlines; Community Service Award, United Airlines; Leadership Award, United Airlines. **Home Addr:** 710 White Pine Cir, Lawrenceville, NJ 08648, **Home Phone:** (609)882-6746.

### GARRETT, DR. NATHAN TAYLOR, SR.
Executive, accountant, lawyer. **Personal:** Born Aug 8, 1931, Tarboro, NC; son of York and Julia; married Wanda June Jones; children: Andrea Mausi, Devron & Nathan Jr. **Educ:** Yale Univ, BA, psychol, 1952; Wayne State Univ, post grad acct & bus, 1960; NC Cent Sch Law, JD, 1986. **Career:** Accountant, attorney (retired), executive; Richard H Austin & Co Detroit, acct, 1958-62; Nathan T Garrett, CPA Durham, proprietor, 1962-75; NC Fund Durham, dep dir, 1964-67; Found Community Develop Durham, founder & exec dir, 1967-72; Garrett, Sullivan, Davenport, Bowie & Grant, staff; Garrett & Davenport, Cherry Beraert & Holland Llp, partner, 1975-98; NCCU Sch Bus, acct & law classes teacher; NC Mutual Life Ins Co, dir, 1978, brd chmn, 1995, emer, bd dir, currently. **Orgs:** Bd exec comn, Mech & Farmers Bank Durham, 1965-78; chmn investment comm, chair, Coop Asst Fund NY, 1970-88; bd exec comm, Opportunity Funding Corp, DC, 1970-77; tenured fac mem, Sch Bus NC Cent Univ; bd chair & exec comn, NC Mutual Life Ins Co Durham, 1977-; bd vice chair, Acad Affairs Comm, trustee emer, Duke Univ, 1978-90; corp mem, Triangle Res Inst Found, 1980-91; chmn, People Panel NC 2000 ComnFuture, 1983; NC State Bd CPA Examr, 1986-92; pres, NC Asn Minority Bus; shareholder dir, Garrett Davenport CPAs PC; bd pres, Scarboro Nursery Sch, 1989-91; pres, Nat Asn State Bds Accountancy Inc, 1992-93; bd mem, Mech & Farmers Bank; pres, Nat Asn Minority CPA Firms; bd chair, trustee, Fayetteville State Univ; chmn, Minority Develop Adv Comt. **Home Addr:** 3923 Northampton Rd, Durham, NC 27707, **Home Phone:** (919)489-4889. **Business Addr:** Director, North Carolina Mutual Life Insurance Co, 411 W Chapel Hill St, Durham, NC 27701, **Business Phone:** (919)682-9201.

### GARRETT, DR. PAUL C.
Government official, lawyer, executive. **Personal:** Born Feb 8, 1946, Charlottesville, VA; son of Marshall T and Pauline H; married Louise Lawson; children: Matthew L. **Educ:** Brown Univ, AB, 1968; Univ Va Sch Law, JD, 1971. **Career:** USAF, asst staff judge advocate, 1972-76; City Charlottesville, Va, asst city atty, 1976-80; Charlottesville Circuit Ct, clerk, 1981-2011. **Orgs:** Charlottesville Albemarle Bar Asn. **Home Addr:** 1833 Yorktown Dr, Charlottesville, VA 22901. **Business Addr:** Clerk of the Court, Charlottesville Circuit Court, 315 E High St, Charlottesville, VA 22902, **Business Phone:** (434)970-3766.

### GARRETT, RUBY GRANT
Executive. **Personal:** Born May 13, 1941, Covington, GA; daughter of Robert L and Lola Price; married William H; children: Victoria & Laran. **Educ:** Carver Voc Sch Practical Nursing, LPN, 1960; Atlanta Col Art, BFA, 1971; Ga State Univ, attended 1973. **Career:** Ruby G Graphics Design, owner, 1969-72; Eric Hill Assoc Planning, art dir design consult, 1971-72; G Designs Inc Adv PR, pres & owner, 1972-79; Grant-Garrett Comun Inc, pres, chief exec officer, 1979-. **Orgs:** Pres, Nat Alliance Mkt Developers, Atlanta Chap, 1982-83; bd mem, Enterprise Atlanta, 1983-85; comt chmn, Nat Alliance Mkt Developers, Atlanta Chap, 1983-87; bd, comt chmn, Atlanta Bus League, 1983-87; consult, speaker, Univ Ga Exten Serv, 1984; consult, Atlanta Jr Coll, 1984. **Home Addr:** 2121 Beecher Rd SW, Atlanta, GA 30311-2507, **Home Phone:** (404)758-6660. **Business Addr:** President, Partner, Grant Garrett Communication Inc, 2121 Beecher Rd SW, Atlanta, GA 30311-2507, **Business Phone:** (404)755-2513.

### GARRISON, JANNA
Association executive, association executive. **Educ:** Mich State Univ, BA, educ; Wayne State Univ, MA, labor & indust rels; Labor Col. **Career:** Detroit Pub Sch Syst, elem & middle sch teacher, 1978-87; Detroit Fedn of Teachers, negotiator, exec vpres, pres, chief exec officer, 1987-2007; City of Southfield, city coun mem, 2009-11; MG Consulting, employee & labor rels consult, 2014-. **Orgs:** Vpres, Mich Fedn Teachers & Sch-Related Personnel, 1996-; Delta Sigma ta Sorority; Phi Delta Kappa; AFT PreK-12 Teachers prog & policy coun; AFT Mem benefits comm; bd mem, Co/Op Optical & Black Caucus Found; Labor Adv Bd for Health Alliance Plan; Nat Asn Advan Colored People; Arab Community Ctr for Econ & Social Serv. **Business Addr:** President, Detroit Federation of Teachers, 2875 W Grand Blvd, Detroit, MI 48202, **Business Phone:** (313)875-3500.

### GARRISON, JEWELL K.
Educator. **Personal:** Born Nov 6, 1946, Dayton, OH; children: Brandon. **Educ:** Cent State Univ, BA, social work, 1969; Atlanta Univ, Grad Sch Social Work, MSW, 1972; Authentic Leadership, MSW, 2005. **Career:** Montgomery Co Juv Ct, probation counr, 1969-70; Cath Social Serv, sch social worker, 1970-71; Atlanta Pub Sch Syst, sch social worker, 1971-72; Montgomery Co C Serv Bd, dir staff develop, 1972-77; Wright State Univ Dayton, asst prof, 1977-84, Dept Social Work & Med Soc, asn prof & practicum coord, 1984-89; Community Connections, exec dir, 1989-92; New Futures Dayton Area Youth, dep dir, 1992-93; Columbus Med Asn Found, sr prog officer, 1993, dir progs, 2000-09; Franklin County Families & C's First Coun, consult, 2010; Ohio Grantmakers Forum, consult, 2010-12; JK Garrison & Co, managing dir, 2012-. **Orgs:** Secy, 1976-78, pres, 1977-80 Dayton Chap Nat Asn Black Social Workers; bd dir, 1977-83, 1984-93, bd dir chmn person, 1989-92, Dayton Urban League; First vpres, OH State Chap, Nat Asn Black Social Workers, 1978-81; reg trustee, Nat Urban League, 1988-91; vpres, bd dir, Community Connections, 1988-89; exec comt bd dir, New Futures Dayton Area Youth, 1988-89; bd mem, Dayton Area Coun Youth, 1988-90; Human Serv Collab, 1993-; bd dir, Prevent Inst, 1994-96; United Way Franklin City-Vision Coun, 1996-; chmn & dir prog, Columbus Med Asn Found, currently. **Home Addr:** 936 Harborton Dr, Columbus, OH 43228-9262, **Home Phone:** (614)851-8567.

### GARRISON, DR. JORDAN MUHAMMAD, JR.
Physician, surgeon. **Personal:** Born Nov 1, 1956, Montclair, NJ; son of Jordan Muhammad Sr and Kathleen Wallace; married Fitrah Muhammad; children: Khadijah & Naimah. **Educ:** Lehigh Univ, BS, chem, 1978; Univ Med & Dent NJ, MD, 1983. **Career:** Univ Hosp, Univ Med & Dent NJ, Dept Surg, surg intern, 1982-83, chief surg resident, 1985-89, clin prof surg, 1989-90; Danbury Fed Corrections Inst, U.S. Dept Justice, Fed Bur Prisons, chief med officer, 1983-85; Northern Surg Asn, surgeon, 1990-; St Clare's Hosp, gen surgeon; pvt pract, currently; Garrison Ctr Healthy Living, founder, currently. **Orgs:** Am Soc Bariatric Surgery; Soc Am Gastrointestinal & Endoscopic Surgeons; Am Med Asn; Nat Med Asn; fel Am Col Surgeons; AMA. **Honors/Awds:** Surgical Residents Teaching Award, 1983, 1988. **Business Addr:** Founder, Garrison Center for Healthy Living, 400 W Blackwell St, Dover, NJ 07801, **Business Phone:** (973)570-2221.

### GARRISON-JACKSON, ZINA LYNNA
Tennis player. **Personal:** Born Nov 16, 1963, Houston, TX; married Willard. **Career:** Tennis player (retired), tennis coach, mgr; Prof tennis player, 1982-97; Zina Garrison All Ct Tennis Acad, founder & chmn, pres & player develop coach, 1993-; Adult Training Camps & Clins, 1997-; USA Nat Team, head coach, 1999; Minority Excellence Training Camps, 1999-; Fed Cup, asst coach, 1999-; Womens Tennis Coach US Olympic Team Fed Cup, head coach, 2004-06; Ace Player Develop Prog, co-founder; Womens Sports Legend, partner; Taylor Townsend, coach, currently. **Orgs:** Founder, Zina Garrison Found, 1988; US Pres Coun Phys Fitness Sports, 1994; US Tennis Asn Tennis & Educ Fed Founding Bd; US Tennis Asn; US Tennis Asn Olympic Comt; Womens Tennis Asn; Alpha Kappa Alpha Sorority Inc. **Honors/Awds:** ITF Junior of the Year Award, 1981; Australian Open, Runner-up, 1987, winner, 1987, runner-up, 1989, 1990, 1992 & 1993; Olympics, Doubles, gold medal, Singles, bronze medal, 1988; Wimbledon, winner, 1988 & 1990; Family Circle Community Service Award, 1992; Family Circle Community Service Award, 1992; Tennis Educational Merit Award, 1993; USTA Bowl Service Award For Community Service, 1998; Texas Tennis Hall Of Fame, 1998; African-American Ethnic Hall of Fame, 2004; Texas Professional Athletes of All Time, 2004. **Business Addr:** Founder & President, Chairman, The Zina Garrison All Court Tennis Academy, 12335 Kingsride Suite 106, Houston, TX 77024, **Business Phone:** (713)857-3167.

### GARRITY, MONIQUE PAUL
Educator. **Personal:** Born Mar 26, 1941, Petite Riviere, NS. **Educ:** Mary Grove Col, BA, econs, math, 1963; Boston Col, PhD, econs, 1970. **Career:** Educator (retired); Metro Area Planning Coun, Boston, MA, state analyst, 1965; Univ Mass, from asst prof to assoc prof; Wellesley Col, asst prof, 1970-71; Econ Res Unit, instr; OECD Paris, cons.World Bank, spec rep, 2001; Haitian C, partner; Little Sisters St.Therese, partner. **Orgs:** Regional chmn, Caucus Black Econ, 1971-72; dir, Black Econ Res Ctr; Am Scholar Coun; Fulbright Hayes Sr Lectureship Ave, Univ Dakar, 1974-75; consult, Guinea-Bissau, 1978, HAS, bd mem; bd mem, Pact. **Home Addr:** 9 Chauncy St, Cambridge, MA 02138.

### GARTIN, CLAUDIA L.
Judge. **Career:** Judge (retired); 36th Dist Ct, Detroit, judge, 1987-2000. **Home Addr:** 2086 Hyde Pk Rd, Detroit, MI 48207-4999, **Home Phone:** (313)567-0824.

### GARTRELL, BERNADETTE A.
Lawyer. **Personal:** Born Jun 21, 1945, Plainfield, IN; daughter of Barnett (deceased) and Doryse Laws. **Educ:** Howard Univ, BA, 1967, Sch Law, JD, 1970. **Career:** US Dept Housing & Urban Develop, gen coun, atty-adv, 1970-71; DC Corp Coun, asst corp coun, 1971-73; Mitchell, Shorter & Gartrell, managing partner, 1973-85; Leftwich Moore & Douglas, coun, 1985-87; Gartrell, Alexander & Gebhardt, managing partner, 1987-92; DC Super Ct, Arbitrator & Mediator, 1990-; Gartrell & Assoc, owner, 1992-. **Orgs:** Bd dir, Trial Lawyers Asn Metrop, WA, DC; Am Trial Lawyers Asn; Md Trial Lawyers Asn; Nat Asn Black Women Atty; Nat Bar Asn, Greater Wash Area Chap, Women Lawyers Div; Wash Bar Asn; J Franklyn Bourne Bar Asn; Alpha Kappa Alpha; Md Bar Asn. **Home Addr:** 8016 Ellingson Dr, Chevy Chase, MD 20815, **Home Phone:** (301)776-9078. **Business Addr:** Owner, Gartrell & Associates, 8401 Colesville Rd Metro Plz 1 Suite 620, Silver Spring, MD 20910-3349, **Business Phone:** (301)589-8855.

### GARVIN-LESLIE, DR. PENOLA M.
Physician. **Educ:** Wayne State Univ, MD, 1991. **Career:** Oak wood Hosp & Med Ctr, Wayne State Univ, resident; Barbara Ann Ctr Family Medi, med dir, currently; pvt pract, currently. **Business Addr:** Physician, Barbara Ann Center for Family Medicine, 15565 Northland Dr Suite 1080 E, Southfield, MI 48075, **Business Phone:** (248)905-5470.

### GARY, HOWARD V.
Executive. **Career:** Howard Gary & Co, pres, prin & chief exec officer, 1980-. **Business Addr:** President, Chief Executive Officer, Howard Gary & CO, 4141 N Miami Ave Suite 307, Miami, FL 33127, **Business Phone:** (305)571-1380.

### GARY, KATHYE J.
Opera singer. **Personal:** Born Anderson, SC; daughter of Colletha Lee Richardson; children: Russell Alexander, William Rodney & Charles Reginald. **Educ:** Forrest Bus Col, secretarial sci, 1971; Morris Brown Col, elec engineering, 1988. **Career:** Morris Brown Col, admin asst, 1990-2000, dir alumni affairs, 2000; New York Harlem Opera Theatre, Actor, "Madame C.J., "; cast mem/understudy, 1994-; Mt Carmel Baptist Church, soloist, 1998-. **Orgs:** Advisor, Delta Omicron Int Music Fraternity, 1993-96; spec performer, Alpha Kappa Alpha, 1998-2002. **Honors/Awds:** Outstanding Young Women of America, 1981. **Home Addr:** 5112 Hantcrest Dr SW, Mableton, GA 30126, **Home Phone:** (678)402-5926.

### GARY, DR. LAWRENCE EDWARD
Educator. **Personal:** Born May 26, 1939, Union Springs, AL; son of Ed and Henrietta Mays; married Robenia Baker; children: Lisa Che, Lawrence Charles Andre & Jason Edward. **Educ:** Tuskegee Inst, BS, 1963; Univ Mich, MPA, 1964, MSW, 1967, PhD, 1970. **Career:** Mich Econ Opportunity Prog, staff asst, 1964; Univ Mich, lectr, asst prof, 1968-71; Howard Univ, asst vpres acad affairs, 1971-72, dir prof, dir, Inst Urban Affairs & Res, 1972-90, prof social work, 1985-; Va Commonwealth Univ, Samuel S Wurtzel prof, 1990-92. **Orgs:** Action bd, Am Pub Health Asn, 1973-74; bd dir, DC Inst Ment Hyg, 1976-84; ed bd, Jour Social Work, 1977-81; Health Brain Trust Black Cong Caucus, 1977-87; publ bd Coun Social Work Educ, 1982-87; consulted

Jour Social Work, 1985-90; social welfare adv bd, Nat Urban League, 1985-89; bd mgt, Howard Univ Press, 1987-; youth adv bd, Lilly Endowment Inc, 1987-; bd mem, Child Welfare Inst, 1988-91; ed bd, Jour Teaching Social Work, 1987-; bd trustees, St Paul Am Church, 1984-; adv bd, DC Comm Pub Health, 1984-87; vis comm, Sch Social Work, Univ Mich, 1991-; Alpha Phi Alpha Fraternity Inc; Coun Social Work Educ, 1992-95; chair, Fac Develop Comt, Howard Univ. **Honors/Awds:** Distinguished Alumni Award, Nat Asn Equal Opportunity Higher Educ, 1979; Eminent Scholar, Va State Univ, 1982; Outstanding Publication, Nat Asn Black Social Workers, 1983; Labor of Love Award, Nat Head Start Asn, 1984; Eminent Scholar, Norfolk State Univ, 1986; Henry & Lucy Moses Distinguished Visiting Professor, Hunter Col NY, 1986-87; Coun Social Work Educ, 1988-89; Founder's Medallion, Nat Asn Social Workers, 1988; Distinguished Alumni Award, Nat Asn Equal Opportunity Higher Educ, 1988; Alumni Merit Award, Tuskegee Univ Alumni, 1991; Outstanding Leadership and Community Service Award, Nat Asn Black Social Workers Inc, 1993; Galt Visiting Scholar, VA Dept Ment Health, 1994; Distinguished Scholar Social Work, Albany State Col, GA, 1994; Distinguished Research Award, Howard Univ, 1995; Distinguished Recent Contributions to Social Work Award, Coun Social Work Educ, 1996; Distinguished Alumni Award, Univ Mich, Ann Arbor, 2001; Mankind Award, Alpha Phi Alpha Fraternity Inc, 2001; Distinguished Alumni Service Award, University Mich, 2002. **Special Achievements:** Author: "Mental HTH: A Challenge to Black Community", 1978; "Black Men", 1981. **Home Addr:** 1213 Kathryn Rd, Silver Spring, MD 20904-2176, **Home Phone:** (301)622-3063. **Business Addr:** Professor, Howard University, 601 Howard Pl NW, Washington, DC 20059, **Business Phone:** (202)806-7300.

### GARY, DR. MELVIN LEE
Psychologist. **Personal:** Born Apr 12, 1938, Brownsville, PA; son of Joseph and Marie Hood; married Juneau Gloria Mahan; children: Joseph Tyler; married Lanetta Jean Scott. **Educ:** Haverford Col, BA, 1961; OH State Univ, MA, 1964, PhD, 1967. **Career:** Veterans Admin Hosp, psychol trainee, 1964-65; Ohio State Univ, res assoc, Dept Psych & Ctr Voc & Tech Educ, 1965-66; Temple Univ, asst prof, 1968-69; Rutgers State Univ, assoc dean stud affairs, 1971-72, assoc prof, dept psychol, 1973, off budget & planning, assoc dir, assoc dean & dean acad affairs, Livingston Col, 1977-80, fac sen. **Orgs:** AAAS; Am Asn Univ Professors; Am Psychol Asn; Asn Black Psychologists; Soc Psychol Study Social Issues. **Honors/Awds:** Hon men Woodrow Fels, 1961; Soc of Sigma Xi, 1968; fel, Am Coun on Educ Fel UCLA, 1974; 30 years of service honoree, Rutgers State University, 2000. **Home Addr:** 32 Bowsprit Dr, Bayville, NJ 08721.

### GARY, SEKOU M.
Lawyer. **Personal:** Born Jul 27, 1973, Raleigh, NC; son of Willie and Gloria. **Educ:** NC Cent Univ, BA, polit sci, 1995; Quinnipiac Univ Sch Law, JD, 1999. **Career:** The Law Firm of Gary Williams Lewis & Watson PL, partner & atty, 2002-; pvt pract, currently. **Orgs:** Kappa Alpha Psi Fraternity Inc; Nat Bar Asn; Fla Bar; Am Trial Lawyers Asn. **Business Addr:** Attorney, Partner, The Law Firm of Gary, Williams, Lewis, & Watson PL, 221 E Osceola St, Stuart, FL 34994, **Business Phone:** (772)283-8260.

### GARY, TANISHA NUNN
Lawyer. **Personal:** daughter of Willie and Gloria; married Sekou Gary. **Educ:** Spelman Col, BA, polit sci, 1996; Quinnipiac Univ Sch Law, JD, 1999. **Career:** Gary, Williams, Parenti, Finney, Lewis, McManus, Watson & Sperando, PL, assoc atty, 1999-. **Orgs:** Am Bar Asn; Nat Bar Asn; St Lucie Co Bar Asn; Alpha Kappa Alpha Sorority Inc; S FL Chap; Nat Alumnae Asn Spellman Col; Fla Bar, 2000; Fla Bar Asn; exec dir, Gary Found; fel Earl Warren Legal Educ Opportunity, 1997-99. **Business Addr:** Associate Attorney, Gary, Williams, Parenti, Finney, Lewis, McManus, Watson, & Sperando, PL, 221 SE Osceola St, Stuart, FL 34990, **Business Phone:** (772)283-8260.

### GARY, TIM
Manager, executive. **Career:** M A C Cosmetics Inc, br mgr, reg vpres, currently. **Business Addr:** Branch Manager, M A C Cosmetics Inc, 8465 Pk Meadows Ctr Dr, Littleton, CO 80124-5128, **Business Phone:** (303)799-3400.

### GARY, WILLIE E.
Lawyer, chairperson, chief executive officer. **Personal:** Born Jul 12, 1947, Eastman, GA; son of Turner and Mary; married Gloria Royal; children: Kenneth, Sekou, Ali & Kobie. **Educ:** Shaw Univ, BA, bus admin, 1971; NC Cent Univ Law Sch, JD, 1974; Shaw Univ, LLD, 1992. **Career:** Gary, Williams, Parenti, Finney & Taylor, atty & sr partner, 1975-; Gary Enterprises, pres; Gary Found, founder, 1994-; Black Family Channel, Maj Broadcasting Cable Network, chmn & chief exec officer, currently; Law Firm Gary, Williams, Lewis, Watson & Sperando PL, atty, currently. **Orgs:** Bd trustee, chmn, Shaw Univ, 1987-. Am Bar Asn; Am Bd Trial Advocates; Am Trial Lawyers Asn; Nat Bar Asn; bd dir, Nat Bar Inst; Sigma Delta Tau Legal Fraternity; Martin & St Lucie County Bar Asns; Urban League, Civitan Int; NAACP; Nat Urban League; United Way Martin County; Martin Memorial Hosp Found Coun. **Honors/Awds:** Black College Alumni Hall of Fame, 1993; National Alumni Council Achievement Award, United Negro Col Fund, 1993; NAACP Image Awards Key of Life, 1994; C Francis Stradford Award, Nat Bar Asn, 1995; Trumpet Award, Turner Broadcasting Co, 1997; Horatio Alger Award, 1999; Hon Doctorates Law degrees from eleven universities. **Special Achievements:** Donated 10 million dollars to Shaw University, the largest cash donation given to an African American university, 1992. **Home Addr:** 36 Rio Vista Dr, Stuart, FL 34996, **Home Phone:** (407)283-4920. **Business Addr:** Founder, The Gary Foundation, c/o Kids Carnival Toy Dr, Stuart, FL 34997, **Business Phone:** (772)283-2609.

### GASH, SAMUEL LEE, JR.
Football player, football coach. **Personal:** Born Mar 7, 1969, Hendersonville, NC; married Kate; children: Samantha Leigh & Samuel Kolby. **Educ:** Pa State Univ, lib arts. **Career:** Football player (retired), football coach; New Eng Patriots, running back & fullback, 1992-97; Buffalo Bills, running back & fullback, 1998-99, 2003; Baltimore Ravens, running back & fullback, 2000-02; New York Jets, asst running back coach, 2006; Detroit Lions, asst spl coach, 2007, running backs coach, 2008-12; Green Bay Packers, running back coach, 2014-15. **Honors/Awds:** Pro Bowl selection. 1998, 1999; Ed Block Courage Award, 1996; Super Bowl, Baltimore Ravens, 2000; Super Bowl champion XXXV. **Special Achievements:** Film: Super Bowl XXXV, 2001. **Business Addr:** Running Backs Coach, Green Bay Packers, 1265 Lombardi Ave, Green Bay, MI 54304, **Business Phone:** (920)569-7500.

### GASKIN, DR. FRANCES CHRISTIAN
Business owner, nurse. **Personal:** Born Feb 7, 1936, New York, NY; daughter of Clement J Christian and Therese Farrelly Christian; married Conrad A; children: Conrad II, Tracy & Troy. **Educ:** Fordham Hosp Sch Nursing, Bronx, NY, dipl, 1957; City Univ NY, Hunter Col, NY, BS, 1962; Adelphi Univ, Garden City, New York, NY, MS, 1970; Fordham Univ, New York, NY, PhD, 1982. **Career:** New York Univ, New York, NY, adj lectr, 1978-79; Long Island Univ, Brooklyn, NY, asst prof, 1979-81; Regents Col Prog Albany, NY, prof, 1981-82; Hostos Community Col, Bronx, NY, prof, dir, 1983-85; Melanin Plus, hair care & skin prod, 1986-; New York Tech Col, Brooklyn, NY, adj prof, 1991-; Univ New York, New Patty, asst prof, 1992-95; Brook haven Nat Lab, res scientist, 1993-; Frances Christian Gaskin Inc, founder & pres, currently. **Orgs:** Hunter Alumni Asn, 1962-; Adelphi Alumni Asn, 1970-; Fordham Alumni Asn, 1982-; Phi Delta Kappa Frat, 1982-; Sigma Theta Tau, Int Hon Soc, 1984-; Soc Cosmetic Chemists, 1988-; Black Nurses Asn Capital Dist; Nat Black Nurses Asn, 1991-. **Honors/Awds:** Drum Major for Peace, Justice Our Lady Charity RC Church, 1979; Mabel K Staupers (Nursing), Omicron Chap, Chi Eta Phi Soc, 1984; US Patent, protectant composition & method, US Patent & Trademark Office, 1989; presented personal experience as an inventor, State of NY Legislative Resolution, Senator Farlee, 1991. **Home Addr:** 91 Boerum St Apt 19T, Brooklyn, NY 11206, **Home Phone:** (518)434-1610. **Business Addr:** President, Founder, Frances Christian Gaskin Inc, 298 State St Suite 2a, Albany, NY 12210-2033, **Business Phone:** (518)434-4142.

### GASKIN, JEANINE
Manager, educator. **Personal:** Born Dec 11, 1945, Detroit, MI; married Harry Thomas III; children: Harry Thomas IV. **Educ:** Univ Mich, BA, 1971. **Career:** Manager (retired); Detroit News, personal asst, 1966-69; Detroit Bd Educ, teacher, 1970-71; Detroit Med Hosp, personal asst, 1971-74; Harper-Grace Hosp, Human Resources Dept, human resource rep, 1976. **Orgs:** Univ Mich Alumni Asn; ed com, Coleman Young Cent Conf Com; secy, Blenheim Forest Comt Coun; Northwest Orgn Detroit; Am Personal Guide Asn; Nat Employ Coun Asn; Asn Non white Concerns Personal & Guide; Fed Soc Detroit Inst Arts; Nat Hist Soc, 1975. **Honors/Awds:** National Honorary Society Award, 1964; Citizenship Award, 1964; Scholarship Award, 1964; Archdiocesan Development Fund Writing Award, 1964. **Home Addr:** 19345 Manor St, Detroit, MI 48221.

### GASKINS, DR. HENRY JESSE
School administrator, founder (originator). **Personal:** Born Feb 27, 1935, Washington, DC; son of William; married Mary Ann Brown; children: Phyllis, Gregory, Henry J II, Derek J & Kendra L. **Educ:** Int Univ, BA; Nova Col, PhD, educ, 1978. **Career:** Libr Cong, supvr, 1957-97; Freedom Youth Acad, pres, chief exec officer, founder, 1980-. **Orgs:** Intl Acad & Prof Soc. **Honors/Awds:** President of the US, Honored for After School Program, 1987; Southeast Neighbors Community Award, Outstanding Community Service, 1989; President of the US, Volunteer Action Award, 1990; Mayor Marion Barry, Certificate of Commendation, 1990; Education Award, Washington Space Business Round table, 1994; Sister Clara Mohammed Education Award; Delta Sigma Theta Educational Development Award; Lambda Kappa Mu Community Service Award; Kimberly Clark's, "Kleenex Says Bless You" Award; Dossier Magazine's Philanthropy Award; Newsweek Magazine, 's "Good Neighbor" and "Unsung Hero"Awards; Nat Asn of Blacks in Criminal Justice Award; The Questers, Inc.Distinguished Service Award; The Washington Space Business Round table Education Award; United Planning Organization's Martin Luther King, Jr.Community Service Award; Volunteer Action Award. **Business Addr:** President, Founder, Freedom Youth Academy Inc, 1600 Morris Rd SE, Washington, DC 20020, **Business Phone:** (202)889-1682.

### GASKINS, LOUISE ELIZABETH
Educator, executive. **Personal:** Born Jun 2, 1930, Raleigh, NC; daughter of Joseph B F Cutchin (deceased) and Claytae V Hall Watson (deceased); married Leonard; children: Pamela, Donna Wetherbee & Eric. **Educ:** NC Cent Univ, BS, 1951; Fitchburg State, MEd, 1972. **Career:** Educator (retired), executive; Atkins High Sch, math teacher, 1951-54; AEC Germ, teacher, 1957-58; Ger, teacher, 1959; Wash State, teacher, 1960-61; Ligon High Sch, teacher, 1961-62; Army Educ Ctr Ger, teacher, 1964; Ayer High Sch, teacher math, 1965-72; Ayer Jr High Sch, guid counr, 1972-75, prin, 1975-91; Ayer Pub Schs, teacher, counr & prin, 1975-91; Mass Teachers Asn, retirement consult, 1987-; Mass Teachers Retirement Syst, receptionist, 1994-; Commonweath Mass, teachers retirement bd receptionist, 1994-12. **Orgs:** Ayers Tchr Asn, 1965-91; Nat Educ Asn, 1965-; Mass Teachers Asn, 1965-; fac rep, Prof Asn, 1966-70; advr, Afro Am Cult Club, 1967-74; N Cent Mass Guide Asn, 1968-75; Mass Sch Couns Asn, 1968-75; mem, Adm Selec Team, 1970-73; mem, Prof Negot Team, 1970-75; chmn, Supt Sel Comt, 1971-72; mem, bd dir, Adven House, 1973-75; Mass Jr H Mid Sch Prin Asn, 1975-91; state deleg, Nat Educ Asn Conv, 1975-; dir, Mass Nat Educ Asn, 1976-85; Nat Sec Sch Prin Asn; New Eng Asn Black Educr; Black Polit Task Force; Mass Dept Educ Study Com Jr High & Mid Sch; Mass Dept Educ Eval Strategy Grp Handicapped Students; vpres Montachusett Region Nat Asn Advan Colored People, 1977-78; bd mem, Ctr Well Being Inc, 1980-; MTAR, 1991-. **Home Addr:** 35 Boston Rd, Groton, MA 01450-1861, **Home Phone:** (978)448-5351. **Business Addr:** Member, Massachusetts Teachers Association, 48 Sword St, Auburn, MA 01501, **Business Phone:** (508)791-2121.

### GASKINS, MARY ANN
School administrator. **Personal:** Born May 18, 1940, Washington, DC; daughter of Paul F Brown; married Henry J; children: Henry J II, Derek J & Kendra L. **Educ:** Nova Col, BA, educ, 1989. **Career:** Administrator officer (retired), executive director, co-founder; NASA Headquarter Adv, admin officer, 1964-95; Freedom Youth Acad Inc, co-founder & exec dir, 1980-. **Orgs:** Bd mem, Press First Youth Leadership Forum, 1990. **Honors/Awds:** Honored for After School Progam, Pres US, 1987; Volunteer Action Award, Pres US, 1990; Hall of Fame, DC Comn Women, 1993; Women Who Make A Difference Award, WKYS-FM/WDCA-TV, 1994; Education Award, Questors, Inc, 1995; Martin Luther King Jr Community Service Award, United Planning Orgn, 1996. **Home Addr:** 1405 34th St, Washington, DC 20020-2303, **Home Phone:** (202)575-6017. **Business Addr:** Executive Director, Freedom Youth Academy Inc, 1600 Morris Rd SE, Washington, DC 20020-6312, **Business Phone:** (202)889-1682.

### GASKINS, PERCELL MCGAHEE
Educational consultant, football player. **Personal:** Born Apr 25, 1972, Daytona Beach, FL; married Dionna; children: PJ & Hannah. **Educ:** NW Okla State Univ, social sci, 1993; Kans State Univ, BA, social sci. **Career:** Football player (retired), education consultant; St Louis Rams, linebacker, 1996; Carolina Panthers, linebacker, 1997; Charlotte-Mecklenburg Schs, parent advocate, behav specialist, 1999-; UTR consult, Behav Modification Specialist, develop urban community empowerment processes, behav mgt specialist & chief exec officer, 1999-; Garinger High Sch, asst, ec job coach, head coach, 2014-15; Percell Gaskins Solutionist, pres, chief exec officer, 2015-; Community Outreach Christian Ministries, youth leader; RTI progressive educ solution models; World Worship Church, youth pastor. **Honors/Awds:** All America Honors, Kans State; 4th Bowl Win, Holiday Bowl; The Carolina Panthers Character All. **Business Addr:** Parent Advocate, Charlotte-Mecklenburg Schools, PO Box 30035, Charlotte, NC 28230-0035, **Business Phone:** (980)343-6041.

### GASPARD, DR. PATRICE THERESA
Pediatrician. **Personal:** Born Jun 30, 1954, New Orleans, LA; daughter of Octave and Shirley; married LeRoy Maxwell Graham; children: Arianne Marie & LeRoy M III. **Educ:** Tulane Univ, BS, 1976, Sch Med, MD, 1980. **Career:** Fitzsimmons Army Med Ctr, pediat resident, 1980-83, fel, 1986-88; Ft Knox Ky, chief inpatient servs; Fitzsimmons Army Med Ctr, fel adolescent med; Adolescence Med Clin, Fremont Area Med Ctr, chief; Morehouse Sch Med, adj clin asst prof, pediats, 1997-; Kaiser Permanente, pediats & adolescent med, physician, currently; C's Healthcare Atlanta; pvt pract, currently. **Orgs:** Cert Am Bd Pediats, 1984; Am Acad Pediats; Am Med Asn, Nat Med Asn, Soc Adolescent Med; adv coun chair, bd dir, Mary Hall Freedom House Inc. **Special Achievements:** First black elected to Alpha Omega Alpha Honor Medical Soc at Tulane Univ. **Home Addr:** 245 Vista Dr, Cedar Knolls, NJ 07927-2032. **Business Addr:** Physician Pediatrics, Adolescent Medicine, Kaiser Permanente Glenlake, 20 Glenlake Pkwy, Atlanta, GA 30328, **Business Phone:** (404)364-7243.

### GASTON, DR. ARNETT W.
Clinical psychologist, educator. **Personal:** Born Apr 1, 1938, New York, NY; married Sandra; children: Robyn & Brett. **Educ:** John Jay Col Criminal Justice, BA, social sci, 1971; City Univ NY, MA, psychol, 1976, MPhil, psycholog, 1979, PhD, clin psychol, 1981. **Career:** Nat Inst Justice, vis fel; Prince Georges County, Md, dir corrections; Mayor's Crisis Task Force, exec asst comnr; Minimum Stand, bd rev; NY State Stand & Goals Criminal Justice Planning Comn; Honolulu Symphony Orchestra, 1957; composer; auth; musician; conductor; City Univ NY, John Jay Col Criminal Justice, prof psychol & forensic studies; New York Dept Corrections, first dep comnr, chief mgt planning, chief ricers island, comndg officer training acad, clin psychologist; Am Univ, Wash, DC, fac; W Pt Mil Acad; Univ Md, Dept Criminol & Criminal Justice, adj assoc prof, currently, fac, currently; W Pt Mil Acad, John Jay Satellite Prog, fac; Int Criminal Justice, consult, currently. **Orgs:** Nat Asn Black Psychologists; 100 Black Men; Nat Asn Black Criminal Justice; Am Psychol Asn; Am Correctional Asn. **Home Addr:** 6717 Robinia Rd, Camp Springs, MD 20748-2719, **Home Phone:** (301)449-8286. **Business Addr:** Adjunct Associate Professor, University of Maryland College Park, New York City Dept Corrections, College Park, MD 20742-8235, **Business Phone:** (301)405-1000.

### GASTON, LINDA SAULSBY (LINDA E SAULSBY)
Business owner, consultant, association executive. **Personal:** Born Jun 15, 1947, San Francisco, CA; daughter of Arvis Dixon Harris and Harvey Harris; married James; children: Loren & Leslie. **Educ:** City Col San Francisco, San Francisco, Calif, AA; Univ St New York, Albany, NY, BS, lib arts; St Mary's Col Calif, MA, lib studies. **Career:** Morris Davis & Co, mgr admin, 1978-80; Linda Saulsby Mgt Consult, Oakland, Calif, staff, owner, 1981-83; Coopers & Lybrand, Wash, DC, Tucson Ariz, dir personnel & admin, 1983-86; Nat Asn Black Acct, Wash, DC, nat exec dir, 1986-89; Gen Elec Co, mgr, gen mgr, pres, sr vpres, 1989-96; Exploratorium, dir human resources & orgn develop, 1997-99; Les Consult Group, orgn develop, strategic planning & human resources consult, 1999-; Univ Calif, Haas Sch Bus, lectr, 2005-; Univ San Francisco, Sch Prof Studies, lectr, 2005-; St Mary's Col Calif, actg prog dir, 2006-07, thesis adv, 2007-08, Commun Dept & Col Sem Dept, adj assoc prof, currently, Corp & Community Rels, regional dir; Sch Extended Educ, reg dir corp & community rels, currently; Univ Ariz, Eller Col Mgt, adj lectr, 2007-. **Orgs:** Bd dir, YWCA, Oakland, Calif, 1981-83; Tucson, Ariz, 1985-86; Howard Univ, Sch Bus Adv Bd, 1987-; pres, Longmead Crossing Homeowners Asn, 1988-; Nat Community Asn Inst, 1988-; Price Waterhouse & Co Minority Recruiting Task Force, 1989-; bd mem & chair, Fin Comt, E Bay Agency C, Oakland, Calif. **Honors/Awds:** President's Membership Council Award, Greater Wash DC Bd Trade, 1985. **Special Achievements:** Article Published: Managing Editor, Spectrum (Jour Nat Asn Black Acct), 1986-89; Perspectives, 1998; Co-Editor, Perspectives, 2001; Contributor, The Chronicle of Higher Education, 2007. **Home Addr:** 60 Sheridan St NE, Washington, DC 20011, **Home Phone:** (202)598-0065. **Business Addr:** Adjunct Associate Professor, Regional Director, Saint Mary's College of California, 1928 St Mary's Rd, Moraga, CA 94556, **Business Phone:** (925)631-4000.

**GASTON, MACK CHARLES**
Military leader, association executive. **Personal:** Born Jul 17, 1940, Dalton, GA; son of John and Felicia Gilliard; married Lillian Junaita Bonds; children: Sonja Marie; married Nancy; children: Jeff & Craig. **Educ:** Tuskegee Inst, BS, electronics, 1964; US Naval War Col, grad level cert, 1977; US Indust Col Armed Forces, dipl, 1983; Mary Mt Col, MBA, 1984. **Career:** Military leader (retired), executive; USN, comdr, 1964, electronic officer & combat info officer USS Buck, 1965-67, eng officer USS O'Brien, 1967-69, mat officer & squad engr destroyer sqd five staff, 1969-71, personal aide & aide asst navy dir res & develop test & eval off cno, 1971-73, exec officer USS Conyngham, 1974-76, comndg officer USS Cochrane, 1977-79; Br head jr off assignment Navy mil pers command, 1979-81, comndg officer USS Cone, 1981-82, head surface warfare tra br off cno, 1983-84; USN, dir equal opportunity div; USS Josephus Daniels, CG 27, comndg officer battle cruiser, 1986-88; Atlantic Command, comdr chief, 1988; Chief Naval opers strategic studies group, CNO Fel, 1988-89; Surface Warfare Manpower & training dir, 1989-90; Defense Nuclear Agency, comdr, field command, 1990-92; Naval Training Ctr, comdr, 1992-95; Electronic Data Systs, vpres navy rels, 1998-2007; Mack Gaston Consult LLC, pres & chief exec officer, 2007-. **Orgs:** Mil Officers Asn AmJr Deacon & Sunday Sch Teacher Hopewell Baptist Church, 1953-64; counr & career planner, Nat Naval Off Asn, 1977-; Sunday Sch Teacher Greater Zion Baptist Church, 1981-85; US Naval Inst, 1987-; Flag & Gen Officer's Mess, 1991-; pres, Great Lakes Navy & Marine Corps Relief Soc, 1992-; chmn, Great Lakes Combined Fed Campaign, 1992-; chmn, Drug Educ Youth, DEFY, 1992-; exec bd, United Way Lake County, 1992-; Northern Ill Coun Alcoholism & Substance Abuse, 1992-; bd dir, USO Ill, 1992-; exec comt, Lake County Econ Develop Comn, 1992-; Rotary One, 1992-; exec comt, Fed Exec Bd, 1992-; Naval Order US, 1992-; Surface Navy Asn; Nat Mil Family Asn, 1992-; bd dir, Am Red Cross, 1992-; Retired Officer's Asn, 1992-; Am Legion, 1993-; Tin Can Sailors, 1993-; Navy Club US, 1993-; Nat Strategy Forum; Navy Memorial Found; N Chicago Citizens Against Drugs & Alcohol Abuse; N Chicago C Future; Tuskegee Alumni Asn; Lake County Learns; trustee, Benedictine Univ; chair, Mil Officers Asn Am; Armed Forces Coun; Am Heart Asn; Union League Club; bd mem, Convio Inc. **Honors/Awds:** Ga Educ Hall of Fame, Dalton, 1990; Dalton Baugh Award, Mass Bay Area Navy League, 1992; Ga State renamed portion of N Dalton Bypass Hwy, Admiral Mack Gaston Parkway, 1992; Nat Image Inc President's Award, 1992; Wilkins Meritorious Service Award, Nat Asn Advan Colored People, 1994; James Kemper Humanitarian Service Award, Northern Ill Coun Alcoholism & Substance Abuse, 1994. Received Numerous Awards & Medals. **Home Addr:** 6315 Drill Field Ct, Centreville, VA 20121, **Home Phone:** (703)266-4170. **Business Addr:** Chair, Military Officers Association of America, 201 N Wash St, Alexandria, VA 22314, **Business Phone:** (703)549-2311.

**GASTON, DR. MARILYN HUGHES**
Physician, educator, administrator. **Personal:** Born Jan 31, 1939, Cincinnati, OH; daughter of Myron Hughes and Dorothy Hughes; married Alonzo; children: Amy & Damon. **Educ:** Miami Univ, AB, zool, 1960; Univ Cincinnati, Sch Med, MD, pediat, 1964. **Career:** Physician, educator (retired), administrator; Philadelphia Gen Hosp, intern, 1965; C Hosp Med Ctr, resident, 1967; Community Pediats, assoc prof, 1968-70; C Hosp Med Ctr, asst dir, 1968, assoc prof pediats, 1972; Cincinnati Comprehensive Sickle Cell Ctr, dir, 1972; Lincoln Heights Health Ctr, med dir, 1973; Inst Med, inductee, 1997; Howard Univ, asst clin prof pediats; NIH Sickle Cell Dis Br Nat Heart Lung & Blood Inst, depbr chief; US Pub Health Serv, asst surgeon gen, 1989-2003, rear adm, Bur Primary Health Care, dir, 1990-2002; Gaston & Porter Health Improv Ctr, co-dir, 2003-; Bur Primary Health Care, asst surgeon gen & dir. **Orgs:** Am Acad Pediat; United Black Fac Asn; Am Pub Health Asn; med adv bd, State Crippled C Serv; bd trustee, C Health Asn; Pi Kappa Epsilon; med dir, Comn Corps US Pub Health Serv; Nat Med Asn; Inst Med; dir, Bur Primary Health Care, 1990; 9 Tampa Leadership Meeting Prime Time Sister Circles Inc, 2008. **Honors/Awds:** Outstanding Black Women America, 1973; Outstanding Black Women Cincinnati, 1974; City's Young Leader of Health, 1974; Harriet Tubman Woman of the Year, 1976; Gaston H et al-Proph Penicillin in Sickle Cell Anemia, New Eng J, 1986; Ohio Womens Hall of Fame, 1990; NMAs Lifetime Achievement Award; Gaston Scholars, Univ Cincinnati, 1999; Nathan Davis Award, Am Med Asn; Commendation Medal, Pub Health Serv, Dept Health & Human Serv; Outstanding Service Medal, Univ Cincinnati; Distinguished Alumnae Award; Maryland Womens Hall of Fame, 2006; Phyllis Wheatly Award; Appreciation Award, Jack & Jill; NIH Directors Award; hon doctorates, Univ Pa; hon doctorates, Dartmouth Univ; hon doctorates, Univ Med & Dent Nj. **Special Achievements:** Marilyn Hughes Gaston Day, City Cincinnati, OH; First African American Woman to Direct a Public Health Service Bureau; Co-author of the book Prime Time: The African America Woman's Guide to Midlife Health and Wellness; First African American Woman to Direct Major Public Health Service Bureau, 1990. **Home Addr:** 8612 Timber Hill Lane, Potomac, MD 20854, **Home Phone:** (863)427-9599. **Business Addr:** Co-Director, The Gaston & Porter Health Improvement Center, 8612 Timber Hill Lane, Potomac, MD 20854, **Business Phone:** (202)403-6266.

**GASTON, PATRICIA ELAINE**
Journalist. **Personal:** Born Mar 26, 1959, Kansas City, MO; daughter of Charles and Camille Weems; married Keith; children: Erin Michelle & Jonathan. **Educ:** Kans City Community Jr Col, AA, 1979; Univ Kans, BA, journ, 1981; George Washington Univ, Tourism Admin, 2004. **Career:** Boston Globe, copy ed, 1981; Rochester Ny Dem & Chronicle, copy ed, 1981-86; Dallas Morning News, asst int ed, 1986-97; Wash Post, ed, 2000-. **Orgs:** Journ & Women Symp, 1993-95; Coun Foreign Rels, 2004. **Honors/Awds:** Pulitzer Prize, Int Reporting, 1994. **Home Addr:** 106 W Apollo Rd, Garland, TX 75040, **Home Phone:** (214)414-4670. **Business Addr:** Editor, The Washington Post, 1150 15th St NW, Washington, DC 20071.

**GASTON, PATRICK REGINALD**
President (organization), executive director. **Personal:** Born Aug 5, 1957, Port-au-Prince; children: 2. **Educ:** Univ Mass, BA, mgt, 1984; Northeastern Univ, MBA, 1992; Ecole Superieurede Com, int cert bus. **Career:** Bell Atlantic Commun Inc, asst vpres; Verizon Found, Strategic Alliances, exec dir, 1984-2003, pres, 2003-; Clinton Bush Haiti Fund, sr advisor. **Orgs:** Trustee, Nat Asn Advan Colored People; Found Univ W Indies; Nat Coalition Cancer Survivorship; World Inst Disability; pres & chmn, Am Cancer Soc; William B Price Unit; vol, St Jude C Res Hosp; Nat Cs Latino Inst; Nat Found Women Legislators; Nat Gov Asn; bd dir, Americas Charities; fel Aspen Inst; adv bd, PTA; vice chair, Metrop Mus Art; Exec Leadership Coun; dir & mem audit Comt, Bed Bath & Beyond Inc, 2007-. **Home Addr:** , Maplewood, NJ 07036. **Business Addr:** President, Verizon Foundation, 1 Verizon Way, Basking Ridge, NJ 07920, **Business Phone:** (800)360-7955.

**GATERS, DOROTHY L.**
Athletic coach. **Personal:** Born Jan 4, 1946, Beulah, MS; daughter of Charlie and Ethel. **Educ:** Crane Community Col, AA, 1966; DePaul Univ, BA, 1969; Gov State Univ, MA, 1975. **Career:** McDonald's All-Am Games, coach, 2011; Ill High Sch Asn, coach; John Marshall High Sch, teacher, asst coach, head coach, athletic dir, currently. **Orgs:** Ill Basketball Coaches Asn; Women's Basketball Coaches Asn; Chicago Basketball Coaches Asn. **Honors/Awds:** Coach of the Year, Ill Basketball Coaches Asn, Dist 22; Coach of the Year, Chicago Pub League Basketball Coaches Asn; Women's Basketball Hall of Fame, 2000; Morgan Wootten Lifetime Achievement Award, 2009. **Special Achievements:** Coach National Team US Youth Develop; First player in NCAA women's basketball history to record 2,500 points and 1,250 rebounds. **Business Addr:** Head Coach, Athletic Director, John Marshall High School, 3250 W Adams St, Chicago, IL 60624, **Business Phone:** (773)534-6471.

**GATES, DR. HENRY LOUIS, JR.**
Educator, editor, writer. **Personal:** Born Sep 16, 1950, Keyser, WV; son of Henry-Louis Sr and Pauline Augusta Coleman; married Sharon Lynn Adams; children: Maude Augusta & Elizabeth Helen-Claire. **Educ:** Yale Univ, BA, hist, 1973; Univ Cambridge, Clare Col, Cambridge, Eng, MA, Eng, 1979, PhD, Eng, 1979. **Career:** Time, London Bur, London, Eng, staff corresp, 1973-75; AmCyanamid Co, Wayne, NJ, pub rels rep, 1975; Yale Univ, New Haven, CT, lectr, Eng & Afro-Am Studies, 1976-79, from asst prof to assoc prof, Eng & Afro-Am Studies, 1979-85; Cornell Univ, Ithaca, NY, prof Eng, ComparativeLit & Africana Studies, 1985-88, WEB Du Bois Prof Lit, 1988-90; Woodrow Wilson nat fel, 1988-90; Duke Univ, Durham, NC, John Spencer Bassett Prof Eng & Lit, 1990; Harvard Univ, WEB Du Bois prof humanities, chmn, African-Am Studies, dir, WEB Du Bois Inst African-Am Res, dir, 1991-, Dept African & African Am Studies, chair, WEB Du Bois Prof Humanities, currently; Author: Figures in Black: Words, Signs & the Racial Self, 1987; The Signifying Monkey: Towards a Theory Afro-Amer Literary Criticism, 1988; Loose Canons: Notes on the Culture Wars, 1991; Colored People: A Memoir, 1994; The Future of the Race, 1996; Thirteen Ways of Looking At A Black Man, 1997; The trials of Phillis Wheatley, 2003; America Behind the Color Line: Dialogues with African Americans, 2004; Finding Oprah's Roots, 2007; In Search of Our Roots, 2009; Faces of Am, 2010; Tradition and the Black Atlantic, 2010; Black in Latin Am, 2011; Editor: Our Nig, 1983; Black Literature & Literary Theory, 1984; "Race", Writing & Difference, 1986; The Classic Slave Narratives, 1987; The Norton Anthology of African-American Literature, 1996; The Encycl of the African and African Am Experience, 1999; The Bondwoman's Narrative, 2001; Searching for Hannah Crafts, 2004; The Annotated Uncle Tom's Cabin, 2006; The African Am nat biog, 2008; Lincoln on Race and Slavery. Princeton, NJ, 2009; Encycl of Africa, 2010; Series Editor: The Schomburg Library of Nineteenth-Century Black Women Writers, 1988; Co-Editor: Transition: An International Review; Co-Compiler, Wole Soyinka: A Bibliography of Primary & Secondary Sources, 1986; The Trials of Phillis Wheatley: America's First Poet & Her Encounters with the Founding Fathers, 2003; In Search of Hannah Crafts: Critical Essays on the Bondwoman's Narrative, 2004; Civil Rights: An A-to-Z Reference of the Movement that Changed America, 2005; Race & Reason: Black Letters in the Enlightenment, 2007; Films: From Great Zimbabwe to Kilimatinde, 1996; The Two Nations of Black America, 1998; Wonders of the African World, 1998 & 2004; Leaving Cleaver, 1999; America Beyond the Color Line, 2004; African American Lives, 2006; Oprah's Roots: An African American Lives Special, 2007; African American Lives 2, 2008; Looking for Lincoln, 2009; Faces of America, 2010. **Orgs:** Coun Foreign Rels; bd dir, Lincoln Ctr Theater & Whitney Mus; bd dir, Europ Inst Lit & Cult Studies, 1990-; bd dir, Am Coun Learned Socs, 1990-; Am Antiqn Socs; Union Writers African Peoples; Asn Doc Ed; African Roundtable; African Lit Asn; Afro-Am Acad; Am Studies Asn; Asn Study Afro-Am Life & Hist; Caribbean Studies Asn; ColLang Asn; Mod Lang Asn; Stone Trust; Zora Neale Hurston Soc; Pulitzer Prize Bd; Am Civil Liberties Union Nat Adv Coun; Trans Africa Forum Scholars Coun; Ger Am Studies Asn; New Eng Hist Geneal Soc; Am Philos Soc; co-founder, Root, 2008; chair, Fletcher Found; bd mem, New York Pub Libr, Jazz at Lincoln Ctr. **Honors/Awds:** Carnegie Found fel Africa, 1970-71; Phelps fel, Yale Univ, 1970-71; Mellon fel, Yale Univ, 1973-75, 1983-; A Whitney Griswold fel, Yale Univ, 1980; Nat Endowment for the Humanities grants, 1980-84, 1981-82; Rockefeller Found fel, 1980-81; MacArthur Prize fel, Mac Arthur Found, 1981-86; Whitney Humanities Center fel, 1982-84; Afro-Am Cultural Center Faculty Prize, 1983; Ford Found grant, 1984-85; Zora Neale Hurston Soc Award for Creative Scholar, 1986; Honorable Mention, John Hope Franklin Prize, Am Studies Asn, 1988; Am Book Award, 1989; Anisfield Book Award for Race Rels, 1989; Candle Award, Morehouse Col, 1989; George Polk Award, 1993; Lilliam Smith Award, Southern Lit, 1994; Chicago Tribune Heartland Award, 1994; 22Honorary Degrees; Distinguished Editorial Achievement, Critical Inquiry, 1996; Tikkun Nat Ethics Award, 1996; The Richard Ellman Lectures, Emory Univ, 1996; Alternative Press Award for Transition, An Int Review, 1995; 25 Most Influential Americans, Time, 1997; Natl Medal of Arts, presented by President Clinton, 1998; Bologna New Media Prize, 1999; Multiculturalism Award, Fairleigh Dickinson Univ, 1999; Healthy Lifestyle Award, 2001; Josiah Willard Gibbs Award, 2002; Carl Sandburg Literary Award, 2004; William C. Nell Living Legend Award, Afro-American Museum, 2004; Henry James Award, 2004; PBS Channel Thirteen Annual Award, 2006; Graduate of Distinction, 2006; Inductee, Sons of the American Revolution, 2006; Ralph Lowell Award, Corp Pub Broadcasting, 2008; Alfred I. duPont Columbia University Award, 2014; The Parents Choice Awards-Gold Award; recipient of nearly 50 honorary degrees. **Special Achievements:** First African-American to Receive a Ph.D From the Cambridge University; First African American to be Awarded an Andrew W. Mellon Foundation Fellowship; First African American to Have His Genome Fully Sequenced. **Home Addr:** 22 Francis Ave, Cambridge, MA 02138. **Business Addr:** Professor of the Humanities, Director, Harvard University, 104 Mt Auburn St 3rd Fl, Cambridge, MA 02138, **Business Phone:** (617)496-5468.

**GATES, JACQUELYN BURCH**
Executive. **Personal:** Born Jul 12, 1951, Brooklyn, NY; daughter of Herman Knight and Blanca Knight; married Oliver F Shipe; children: 5. **Educ:** Univ Ill; Brooklyn Col, BA, hist, 1973; New Sch Univ, Trinity Theol Sem. **Career:** Agency Child Develop, family coun, 1973-76; NY State Supreme Ct, secy to supreme ct justice, 1976-77; JC Penny Corp Hq, employ placement rep, 1977-79; Revlon Inc, personnel admin & recruiter, 1979-81; Paramount Pictures Corp, mgr indust rels, NY, 1981-82; Pepsi Cola Co, mgr prof placement, 1982-83; PepsiCo Inc Purchase, NY, mgr corp rels; Nynex Mobile Communicators Co, Orangeburg, vpres, Qual & Ethics, 1990-93; Corp Cult Initiatives, dir, 1994-95; Dukes Energy, vpres div & ethics, corp officer, 2000-02; Univ Ala Huntsville, assoc vpres advan, 2008-10; World Bank Group, ethics consult, 2002-, ethics officer, 2002-03; Int Finance Corp, ethics consult, 2002-; Oakwood Univ, vpres advan & develop, 2004-06; SOARing LLC, owner, pres & chief exec officer, 2003-; Int Serv Coun Ala, exec dir, 2010-; NYNEX Corp, vpres ethics; Bell Atlantic, vpres, Ethics Compliance & Diversity; BodyBasic, chief operating officer; Senn Delaney Leadership Consult Group, officer; Time Warner, officer. **Orgs:** Pres, Nat Asn Negro Bus & Prof Women Club, 1987-91, planned giving dir; bd dir, bd mem, Oper Reachback; emer bd mem, Ethics Officer Asn, currently; vis prof, Black Exec Exchange Prog, Nat Urban League; past pres, Spelman Corp Womens Roundtable; NYNEX Multicultural Asn; bd dirs, Martin Luther King Sr, Citizen Ctr; past pres, Edges Group, 1993-96; adv bd, Bentley Univ; mem adv bd, Nat Asn Black Telecommunications Prof Inc; Black Women Film Preserv Proj., Jr Achievement's Blue Ribbon Ethics Panel; emer bd mem, Ethics Officer Asn; bd dir, Global Ties US, currently. **Honors/Awds:** Student Achievement Award, Brooklyn Young Adults NANBPW, 1965; Achievement Award, Alpha Cosmetologists of Brooklyn, 1979; Nat Youth Achievement Award, Nat Asn Negro Buss & Prof Women Clubs, 1980; Black Achiever, Indust Harlem YMCA, 1984; Sojourner Truth Award, E NY Club Brooklyn NANBPW, 1984; Business Award, Kings Co Club Nat Asn Negro Buss & Prof Women Clubs, 1986; Young Achiever Award, Natl Coun of Women of USA, 1986; New york YWCA, Acad Women Achievers, 1996, Frasernet-Woman of Grace, 2003, Levine Museum of the New South-Women's Hall of Fame, 2004. **Special Achievements:** Hundred Young Women of Promise in 21st Century, Good Housekeeping Mag, 1985; Top 100 Black Business & Professional Women in America, Dollars & Sense Mag, 1986; 100 Most Influential Black American, Ebony Mag, 1988-91; amed as one of the "Top 50? companies for Asians, Blacks, Hispanics and Native Americans by Fortune Magazine and named to Latina Style magazine's "Top 50? for professional Hispanic women. Bell Atlantic was also named as one of "America's Top 15? companies for women-owned businesses by the Women's Enterprise Business National Council and was recognized as a "Promising Practice? company by the President's Initiative on Race for its work with employee resource groups, EBONY-Women at the Top of Corporate America, 2001. **Home Addr:** , Gurley, AL. **Business Addr:** President, Chief Executive Officer, SOARing LLC, PO Box 353, Harvest, AL 35749-0353, **Business Phone:** (704)562-3941.

**GATES, JIMMIE EARL**
Journalist. **Personal:** Born Jun 3, 1956, Jackson, MS; son of Allen and Birdie Lee; married Pattie Denise Kendrick; children: April Jimel. **Educ:** Jackson State Univ, BS, 1981, MS. **Career:** Jackson Daily News, staff writer, 1983-86; USA Today, Rosslyn, Va, travel & health update line ed, 1986-87; Clarion-Ledger, Jackson, Miss, staff writer, legis reporter, 1987-. **Orgs:** Jackson Br Nat Asn Advan Colored Peopl, 1985-; pres & treas, Jackson Asn Black Journalists, 1990-91; Soc Prof Journalists, 1990-. **Honors/Awds:** Merit Award, Southern Inst Jour, 1985; AP Community Award, Asniate Press, 1985; AP Community Award SE Region, Asniate Press, 1985; Best of Gannett, The Gannett Corp, 1987. **Home Addr:** 4412 Will O Run Dr, Jackson, MS 39212-3650, **Home Phone:** (601)373-9799. **Business Addr:** Staff Writer, The Clarion Ledger, 311 E Pearl St, Jackson, MS 39205, **Business Phone:** (601)961-7212.

**GATES, LEE**
Judge. **Personal:** married Yvonne Atkinsonchildren: 4. **Educ:** Univ Nev, Las Vegas, BA, 1974; Univ Colo Sch Law, JD, 1977. **Career:** Dep dist atty, 1978-81; pvt pract, 1982-86, 1987-91; dep pub defender, 1986-87; chief dist ct judge, 1998-00; Eighth Dist Ct, judge, 1991-. **Orgs:** Clark County Bar Asn; Am Judges Asn; Nat Conf Metrop Courts. **Business Addr:** Judge, Eighth Judicial District Court, 200 Lewis Ave Dept 8, Las Vegas, NV 89155, **Business Phone:** (702)671-4338.

**GATES, OTIS A., III**
Executive. **Personal:** Born Feb 26, 1935, Chattanooga, TN; married Barbara L; children: George, Theresa, Todd & Khari. **Educ:** Harvard Col, AB; Harvard Grad Sch Bus Admin, MBA, 1968. **Career:** Kaufman & Boad Homes Inc, asst to gen mgr, 1963-64; MI Blue Shield, mgr comput systs & opers, 1964-66; Zayre Corp, mgr comput systs develop, 1966-68; Arthur Andersen & Co, 1969-76, partner, 1976-85; Quincy Geneva Community Develop Corp, proj mgr; Long Bay Mgt Co, chief financial officer, currently. **Orgs:** Youth Serv comt, Mass Bay United Way Fund, 1974-80; bd trustee, Univ Hosp, 1983-90; chmn, Jobs Youth Boston; bd dir, Danforth Mus; Harvard Bus Sch African Am Alumni Asn. **Home Addr:** 69 Main St, Framingham, MA 01702, **Home Phone:** (508)879-0549. **Business Addr:** Chief Financial Officer, Long Bay Management Co, 351 Mass Ave, Boston, MA 02115.

**GATES, DR. PAUL EDWARD**
Oral surgeon, college administrator, health services administrator. **Personal:** Born Aug 16, 1945, Keyser, WV; son of Henry Louis Sr and Pauline Coleman; married Gemina; children: Eboni, Jennifer & Aaron Pierce. **Educ:** Potomac State Jr Col, AA, 1964; WVa Univ, BA, 1966 WVa Univ Sch Dent, DDS, 1970; NY Univ Sch Dent, 1971;

Fairleigh Dickinson, MBA, 1992. **Career:** Harlem Hosp Ctr, resd, 1970-73; Fairleigh Dickinson Dent Sch, oral surgeon, 1973, asst clin prof, 1973-76, dir minority affairs, 1979-86, prof, 1986, asst vpres acad admin, 1986-87; Col Dent Med, actg dean, 1988-89; from asst to pres, health planning & policy, 1988-89; Bronx-Lebanon Hosp, dir, oral & maxillofacial surg & dept dent, 1990, assoc prof, chmn dent, health resources & serv admin, currently; Albert Einstein Col Med, assoc prof med, 1994-; St Joseph's Hosp, attg oral surgeon. **Orgs:** ADA Stud, 1966-70, 1973-77; Xi Psi Phi Frat; WVa Univ Alumni Asn; stud Am Dent Asn; Passaic Co Dent Soc, 1973-77; NJ Dept Dent, 1973-77; bd dir, INCAA, 1973-74; NJ Dent Soc, 1973; NJ Dept Dent, 1973-77; bd dir, INCAA, 1973-74; Am Bd Oral Surg Dipl, 1975; Am Soc Oral Surg, 1977; Am Soc Dent Anesthesiol; Am Asn Hosp Dent, 1977; NJ Soc Dent Anesthesia; Harlem Hosp Soc Oral Surg; ed, Jour Passaic Co Dent Soc; chief, oral & maxillacial surg & assoc chmn, Dept Dent St Joseph's Hosp & Med Ctr; bd trustee, St Joseph's Hops & Med Ctr, 1984-87; N Dent Asn Commonwealth Dent Soc; dir, mny scholar prog, Nat Dent Asn Found, 1990-92; bd Gov, WVa Univ, 2000-; bd trustee, Bronx AIOs Soc, 2001; bd dir, NY AHEC, 2001-; MAN Etc, Inc. **Honors/Awds:** Outstanding Young Men in America, 1970, 1980; Outstanding Oral Surgery Faculty Award, 1977-81; OKU Nat Dent Honor Soc, 1980; Am Coun Educ Fellow, 1984-85; "Minority Recruitment and Retention at FDU" Journal Nat Dent Asn, 1988; Fellow Am Col, Dentist, 1989; Outstanding Achievement, Bronx-Lebanon Hosp, Employees African Descent, 1992-93; Distinguished Practitioner Dentisty, Nat Acad Practice, 1997; Sixth Annual Achievement Award, Nat Pro-Am Inc, 1997. **Special Achievements:** Published "Meningitis as a Result Post Extraction Infection Report a Case". Journal Oral Surgery 1972; "Visceral Kaposis's Sarcoma presenting with Gingival Lesions" Oral Surgery Oral Med & Oral Pathology 1980, "Oral Lesions in Crohn's Disease, Report a Case" NY State Dent Jrnl, "The Dent Cartridge-Its Contents & Clinical Implications" DMD 1980, "Calcium Nutrition & the Aging Process, A Review" Journal Gerodontology, 1985, "The Dent Cartridge It's Contents & Clinical Implications" DMD, 1985. **Home Addr:** 12 Vizcaya Ct, Wayne, NJ 07470, **Home Phone:** (973)835-0593. **Business Addr:** Chairman of Dentistry, Bronx-Lebanon Hospital Center, Rm 2F 1770 Grand Concourse, Bronx, NY 10457, **Business Phone:** (718)901-8115.

## GATES, REGINALD

President (organization). **Educ:** Bishop Col, BA, speech commun; Prairie View A & M Univ, MS. **Career:** Bishop Col, admin; United Negro Col Fund, fundraiser & mkt specialist; Dallas County Community Col, sr acct exec; Ft Worth Metrop Black Chamber Com, pres & chief exec officer; Dallas Black Chamber Com, pres & chief operating officer, 1996-2010; Tarrant County Col Dist, vice chancellor commun & external affairs, 2010-. **Business Addr:** Vice Chancellor for Communications & External Affairs, Tarrant County College District, 1500 Houston St, Ft. Worth, TX 76102, **Business Phone:** (817)515-8223.

## GATES, YVONNE ATKINSON

Government official. **Personal:** married Lee; children: 4. **Educ:** Univ Nev, BS, polit sci & jour, 1978, MS, 1982. **Career:** Commissioner (retired): Clark County, Las Vegas, comnr, 2004-07. **Orgs:** Nev Asn Counties; bd dir, Inner City Games; Debt Mgt Comn; Las Vegas Conv & Visitors Authority; Clark County Sch Bd Trustees. **Special Achievements:** First African American female commissioner, Clark County, Las Vegas.

## GATEWOOD, DR. ALGIE C.

School administrator. **Personal:** Born Dec 17, 1951, Wadesboro, NC; son of Bessie M and Haywood J; married Elaine Thornton; children: Wendolyn Charmaine, Andrea Marzina & Algie Carver Jr; married Rosalyn. **Educ:** Livingstone Col, BA, social sci & hist, 1974; Appalachian State Univ, MA, higher educ & col admin, 1977; Univ NC, Charlotte, cert guid & coun, 1982; NC State Univ, EdD; Winthrop Univ, sch admin lic, 1994. **Career:** Anson Community Col, dir human resources develop, 1974-81, dir inst res, 1980-81, from actg dean students to dean students, 1981-97; Univ NC, gen admin, asst dir, 1997; Univ NC-State Educ Assistance Authority, Health, Educ & Welfare div, dir; Portland Community Col, Cascade Campus, pres, 2004-; Alamance Community Col, pres. **Orgs:** Phi Beta Sigma Frat; trustee, Ebenezer Baptist Church; vpres, NC Found Advan Health Progs; bd mem emer, Anson Regional Med Serv, 1997; Anson County Bd Educ; comn mem, NC Contract Progs Dent, Med & Optom; NC Allied Health Coun; NC trustee Asn; chair & bd dir, Urban League Portland; bd mem, Ore Trail Chap; exec bd mem, N W Athletic Asn Community Cols; bd, Portland Community Reinvestment Initiative Inc; Ore Asn Minority Entrepreneurs; chair, Portland State Univ's Grad Sch Educ Adv Bd; bd, Open Meadow Sch; Am Asn Community Cols Diversity & Equity Comn. **Home Addr:** 2509 Brick Hearth Dr, Hillsborough, NC 27278, **Home Phone:** (919)732-1395. **Business Addr:** President, Portland Community College, 705 N Killingsworth St CA SSB 209, Portland, OR 97217, **Business Phone:** (971)722-6111.

## GATEWOOD, ESQ. DIANE RIDLEY

Lawyer. **Personal:** Born Jun 20, 1951, St. Louis, MO; daughter of Benjamin James and Vera Delores (Dickerson) R; married Lamerol Alexander. **Educ:** Wash Univ, AB, 1973; Northwestern Univ Sch Law, JD, 1976. **Career:** Smith & McCullin, legal asst wilson, 1977-78; Albert Gallatin Edwards, securities analyst, 1978-87; Am Stock Exchange, new listings mgr, 1987-89; Moodys Investors Serv, vpres & sr analyst, 1989-97; New York Univ, adj prof, 1992-94; NY State Off Atty Gen, Investment Protection Bur, asst atty gen & chief regist, 1999-; US Dept Agr. **Orgs:** Pres, Asn Black Women Attorneys, 1991-93; Am Bar Asn; bd dir, Nat Asn Securities Professionals; Dc Bar Asn; Ill Bar Asn; Ny Bar Asn; Metrop Black Bar Asn. **Honors/Awds:** Book: The High Cost of Juvenile Justice, Fordham Urban Law J, 1993. 25 Influential Black Women in Business, Network J: Black Professionals & Small Bus Mag, 2006. **Home Addr:** 58 Rutland Rd, Brooklyn, NY 11225-5313, **Home Phone:** (718)462-4738. **Business Addr:** Assistant Attorney, Office of the Attorney General, 120 Broadway 23rd Fl, New York, NY 10271-0002, **Business Phone:** (212)416-8564.

## GATEWOOD, DR. WALLACE LAVELL

Economist, educator. **Personal:** Born May 31, 1946, West Bend, KY; son of Cecil and Minnie Lucas; married Sharon JM Oliver; children: Eboni, Shannon & Ashley. **Educ:** Berea Col, BS, indust arts technol, 1968; Oberlin Col, post-baccalaureate cert, econs, math, & polit sci, 1969; Wash Univ, MBA, mgt, labor, & HRM, 1971; Univ Ill, Urbana-Champaign, PhD, labor & ind rels, 1975. **Career:** Fla A&M Univ, Tallahassee, asst prof econs, 1974; Fla State Univ Tallahassee, asst prof mgmt labor rels, 1974-77; Morgan State Univ, Baltimore, assoc prof bus & econs, 1977-79; WL Gatewood & Assoc Consult Firm, pres, 1979-; FMCS, labor arbitrator, 1980; independent cert fin planner, 1980-; Univ Baltimore, assoc prof mgmt & labor, 1980-82; Baruch Col NYC, asst prof, 1982-84; Coppin State Col, Baltimore, assoc prof mgmt sci, 1984-86; Morgan State Univ, prof bus admin & mgmt, 1986-, chair, 1988-; Long & Foster Real Estate Inc, real estate agt, 1987-89; Century 21 Assoc Inc, real estate agt, 1989-; Morgan State Univ, prof; Villa Julie, fac; Lavell Consul & Performance Syst, founder & sr consult, 2001-; Strayer Univ, prof mgt, 2004-09; Sellinger Sch Bus, Loyola Univ, adj prof mgt, currently; Herballife Int, Independent Distribr, currently. **Orgs:** Am Soc Productivity Improv; Am Soc Training & Develop; Ind Rels Res Asn; Nat Black MBA Asn; Nat Econs Asn; employ adv comt, Baltimore Urban League, 1968-; Nat Asn Advan Colored People, Baltimore, 1980; acad mgmt, Asn Human Resources Mgt & Org Behav; exec bd, pres Md Chap, Asn Human Resources Mgt & Organisational Behav; Baltimore Mkt Asn; coordr, Nat Asn Advan Colored People Lect Ser, 1981-82; Howard County Comn Women, 1981-84; coordr, Mgt Sci Serv Coppin State Col, 1984-86; secy, Patapsco Valley Regional Coun Episcopalian Diocese, 1987-88; dir, Ctr Fin Success, 1986-; adv bd, Women Virtue Inc. **Honors/Awds:** Scholar, Berea Col, 1964-68; Post-Baccalaureate Fel, Oberlin Col, 1968-69; Consortium Fellowship, Washington Univ, 1969-71; Fellowship, Univ Ill, 1971-73; Res Intern, Congressional Budget Off, 1978; Fac Fel, Social Security Admin, 1979; Man of the Year, Soc for Advancement Mgt, Morgan State Univ, 1980; Advisor of the Year, Univ Baltimore, 1981. **Home Addr:** 12 Devlon Ct, Owings Mills, MD 21117-6124, **Home Phone:** (410)581-7033. **Business Addr:** Adjunct Professor, Loyola University, 4501 N Charles St Sellinger Hall 418, Baltimore, MD 21210, **Business Phone:** (410)617-2000.

## GATLIN, JUSTIN

Track and field athlete. **Personal:** Born Feb 10, 1982, Brooklyn, NY; son of Willie and Jeanette; children: Jace Gatlin. **Educ:** Univ Tenn, BA, sociol. **Career:** Track & field athlete, 2001-. **Special Achievements:** Co-holder the American record for the 4x100 meter race. **Business Addr:** USA Track & Field, 132 E Wash St Suite 800, Indianapolis, KS 46204.

## GATLING, CHRIS RAYMOND

Basketball player, business owner. **Personal:** Born Sep 3, 1967, Elizabeth, NJ. **Educ:** Old Dom Univ, attended 1991. **Career:** Basketball player (retired), business owner; Golden State Warriors, power forward, 1991-96, ctr, 1993-94; Miami Heat, power forward, 1996, 2001-02; Dallas Mavericks, power forward, 1996-97; NJ Nets, power forward, 1997-98, ctr, 1998-99; Milwaukee Bucks, ctr, 1999; Orlando Magic, power forward, 1999-2000; Denver Nuggets, power forward, 2000; Cleveland Cavaliers, power forward, 2000-01; CSKA Moscow, Russia, 2002; Scavolini Pesaro, Italy, 2003; Chris Gatling Recreation Ctr, owner, currently; Cut Me Twice Barbershop, Oakland, owner, currently. **Honors/Awds:** Bronze medal, FIBA World Championship, 1990; Silver medal, Goodwill Games, 1990; Sun Belt Conference Men's Basketball Player of the Year, 1990-91; NBA Draft, 1991; Jack McMahon Award, Golden State Warriors, 1993; NBA All-Star, 1997. **Special Achievements:** TV Series: ESPN SportsCentury, 2002-03, The Sport Jerks, 1998. Film: 1997 NBA All-Star Game, 1997. **Business Addr:** Owner, Chris Gatling Recreation Center, 285 Union Ave, Irvington, NJ 07111, **Business Phone:** (973)399-6597.

## GATLING, JOSEPH THEODORE

Lawyer, association executive, marine corps officer. **Personal:** Born Mar 11, 1947, Washington, DC; son of Arphelius and Inez Sr. **Educ:** Fed City Col, pol sci, 1974; Prince Georges Community Col, paralegal studies, 1987; Univ Md, JD, 1988; Disabled Am Veterans Nat Serv Officer Training Prog, 1992; Col Southern Md, 2004-. **Career:** Off Personnel Mgt, info specialist, 1980-83; Coun DC, admin asst, 1984; Arts Comn DC, arts info coord, 1985; DC Off Human Rights, prog specialist, 1985-86; Shiloh Bapt Church, Primary Dept Church Sch, supt, 1985-96; Bd Veterans Appeals, legal technician, 1987, asst chief hearing sect, 1988-89, chief, 1990-; Dept DC, Disabled Am Vet, nat serv officer, 1990-95, dept comdr, 1997-99; pvt pract atty, currently. **Orgs:** Chmn, Peoples Govt Assoc Inc, 1974-78; Nat Asn Advan Colored People, 1980-; master, Redemption Lodge No 24, PHA, 1997; staff vol, Wash Very Spec Arts, 1995; legal ministry, First Baptist Church Glenarden, 1997-, card ministry, 2004-; selection bd adv, Help Disabled War Veterans, 1999-2001; acad scholar chmn, Redemption Lodge No 24, F& AM, PHA, DC Jurisdiction, 2000-; thrice illustrious grand master, Prince Hall Grand Coun, Royal & Select Masters, 2000-02; W Grand asst dir pub rels, Most Worshipful Prince Hall Grand Lodge DC, F& AM, PHA, 2000-02, Emer W Grand Asst Dir Community Affairs. **Honors/Awds:** Charles Coleman Award, Fed City Col, 1973; Outstanding Service, Exec Off Mayor, 1985; Community Service Award, United Black Fund, 1986; Outstanding Service, Combined Fed Campaign, 1988-90; Outstanding Membership Achievement, Disabled Am Veterans, 1991; Certificate of Appreciation, US Marines Corp Reserve, Toys Tots Found, 1993; Certificate of Appreciation, Shiloh Baptist Church, 1993, 1995, 1996; Certificates of Merit, United Supreme Coun, Ancient & Accepted Scottish Rite Freemasonry, Southern Jurisdiction, PHA, 1994 & 1997; Lodge of the Year, Redemption Lodge No.24, F& AM, PHA, 1997; Community Service Award, US Dept Veterans Affairs Med Ctr, 1998; Certificate of Appreciation, Metro Police Boys & Girls Clubs, 1997 & 1998; Director's Recognition Award, Dept Vet Affairs Med Ctr, 2000. **Business Addr:** Legal Consultant, 2707 18th St NE, Washington, DC 20018-1309, **Business Phone:** (202)635-1151.

## GATLING, PATRICIA LYNN

Lawyer, executive director. **Personal:** Born Jan 16, 1960, Annapolis, MD; daughter of Virginia D and Luther C. **Educ:** Johns Hopkins Univ, BA, int studies, 1979; Univ Md, Sch Law, JD, 1982. **Career:** Kings Co Dist Atty, asst dist atty, 1983-86, Maj Narcotics Bur, exec asst, dist atty, 1992-96, dep dist atty, 1996; Spec Narcotics Ct, Sterling Johnson Jr, spec narcotics asst, 1986-87; Spec State Prosecutor, New York Criminal Justice Syst, spec asst atty gen, 1987-89; US State Dept Int Law Enforcement Acad, John Jay Col Criminal Justice, sr trainer, 2001-05; New York Comn Human Rights, comnr & chair & Exec Producer NY Voices Civil Rights Movement, 2002-15; Off Gov Andrew Cuomo, Dep Secy Civil Rights, 2015. **Orgs:** trustee, Ny Lawyers' Fund, 2000-; bd mem, Univ Md Francis King Carey Sch Law, 2014-; trustee, United African Cong, 2014-; pres, Nat Black Prosecutors Asn; Asn Bar City New York. **Honors/Awds:** Dr. Betty Shabazz Award, 2004. **Special Achievements:** Featured In Numerous Publications Including Black Enterprise, Emerge, Black Elegance, Essence, Aramica and Major Newspapers such as The New York Times, The Daily News and The New York Post. TV Shows: The Prosecutors, Second Chance; 25 Most Influential Black Women in Business, Network J Mag. **Home Addr:** 1175 York Ave Apt 2T, New York, NY 10021, **Home Phone:** (212)355-6035. **Business Addr:** Commissioner, Chair, New York City Commission on Human Rights, 40 Rector St 10th Fl, New York, NY 10006, **Business Phone:** (212)306-5070.

## GATSON, WILINA IONE

Secretary (office), president (organization). **Personal:** Born Apr 17, 1925, Galveston, TX; daughter of Willie Lee and Ina Ivory Sibley; children: Natalie & Kenneth. **Educ:** Univ Tex Med Br, Sch Voc Nursing, 1954, BSN, 1960; Tex Southern Univ, attended 1957. **Career:** Lecturer (retired); Moody State Sch Cerebral Palsied C, Univ Tex Med Br, nursing supr, guest lectr; John Sealy Hosp, LVN psychiat; St Mary's Hosp, US Pub Health Hosp, asst night supvr; Galveston Col, guest lectr; Jack & Jill Am Inc. **Orgs:** Nat Asn Advan Colored People-TNA; Am Nurses Asn; Nat Coun Negro Women Inc; Delta Signa Theta Sorority Inc; Ladies Aux Am Leg; bd mem, Univ Tex Med Br Alumni Asn, 2006-08, mem emer, 2008-; Versatile Dames; Sickle Cell Anemia Found; Officer First Union Baptist; Officer Courts Calanthes Chap; Heroines Jericho; co-chairperson, AARP; pres, Sickle Cell Found Inc. **Honors/Awds:** Outstanding student of the Year Award, Univ Tex Med Br, 1958; Distinguished Alumnus Award, Univ Tex Sch Nursing, 1989, Distinguished Alumnus Award, 1989, Hall of Fame, 1992; Only Black in Hall of Fame, Only Black Distinguished Alumnus. **Special Achievements:** First African American to graduate from University Texas Medical Branch Degree Nursing School, 1960; first African American to serve as Off in University Texas Nursing Alumni Asn, 1961-62. **Home Addr:** 1317 Ave L, Galveston, TX 77550, **Home Phone:** (409)762-3411.

## GAULT, WILLIE JAMES

Football player, athlete, actor. **Personal:** Born Sep 5, 1960, Griffin, GA; son of James Jr and Willie Mae Roberts; married Dainnese Mathis; children: Shakari Denise & Gabriel James; married Suzan Brittan. **Educ:** Univ Tenn, Knoxville, TN, mkt, 1983. **Career:** Football player (retired), athlete (retired), actor; US Olympic Team, track & field, 1980; US Nat Team, track & field, 1980-83; Chicago Bears, wide receiver, 1983-87; Superbowl champion Chicago Bears, 1986; Los Angeles Raiders, wide receiver, 1988-93; Winter Olympics Bobsleigh, 1988; US Olympic Bobsled Team, pusher, 1990-91. Films: Street of Dreams, 1988; Sporting Chance, 1990; Run for the Dream, 1996; Night Vision, 1997; Holy Man, 1998; Malaika, 1998; Darwin Conspiracy, 1999; Millennium Man, 1999; The Darwin Conspiracy, 1999; Room 302, 2001; The Sum of All Fears, 2002; Cottonmouth, 2002; SWAT, 2003; Cellular, 2004; Deuce Bigalow: European Gigolo, 2005; Shut Up & Shoot!, 2006. TV Series: "Bodies of Evidence", 1992; "Tales from the Crypt", 1993; "In the Heat of the Night", 1993; "Renegade", 1995; "Vanishing Son", 1995; "Hangin' with Mr. Cooper", 1996; "Baywatch", 1996; "18 Wheels of Justice", 2000; "The Pretender", 1997-2000; "The Steve Harvey Show", 2001; "Girlfriends", 2001; "Grounded for Life", 2002; "The West Wing", 2000-04; "Ned's Declassified School Survival Guide", 2004-07; "Fat Actress", 2005; Aloha Airlines, investor, 2005. **Orgs:** Chmn, Ministry Lay Witnesses Christ, 1983-; pub speaker, Schs & Churches; Lou Garrett Com, 1983; Distonia Com, 1985; Fair Housing Com, City Chicago; nat spokesperson, AIDS & Diabetes Asn; spokesperson, Long Beach Ballet Dance Camp, 1990-91; Willie Gault's Youth Enrichment Prog. **Home Addr:** 7700 Sunset Blvd Suite 205, Los Angeles, CA 90046, **Home Phone:** (310)827-5007. **Business Addr:** Actor, William Morris Agency, 9601 Wilshire Blvd, Beverly Hills, CA 90210, **Business Phone:** (310)285-9000.

## GAVIN, DR. JAMES RAPHAEL, III

Executive director, physician, executive. **Personal:** Born Nov 23, 1945, Mobile, AL; son of James R II and Bessie S; married Annie Ruth Jackson; children: Raphael Hakkim & Lamar Kenyon. **Educ:** Livingstone Col, BS, chem, 1966; Emory Univ, PhD, biochem, 1970; Duke Univ Med Sch, MD, 1975. **Career:** Nat Inst Health, staff assoc, 1971-73; Duke Univ Hosp, pathologist, 1975-76; US Pub Health Serv, comdr, 2 1/2 yrs active, 11 1/2 yrs reserves; Wash Univ Sch Med, assoc prof med, 1979-86; Univ Okla Med Ctr, prof med, chief diabetes sect; Okla Univ Health Sci Ctr, William K Warren prof Diabetes Studies, 1989-91; Mansfelder Metals Ltd, dir; Ind Univ Sch Med, clin prof med; Howard Hughes Med Inst, sr sci officer, 1991-2002; MSLT Del, dir, 2001-02; Morehouse Sch Med, pres, 2002-05; Baxter, dir, 2003-; Emory Univ, clin prof med & sr adv health affairs, 2005-; Healing Our Village Inc, exec vpres, 2005-07, chief med officer, chief exec officer, 2007-; Microislet Inc, pres & chief exec officer, 2006-07; ALR Technologies Inc, Sr Med Consult, 2013. **Orgs:** Life mem, Alpha Phi Alpha; bd dir, Am Diabetes Asn, 1983-87; bd dir, Alpha Educ Found, 1986-; nat prog dir & sr prog consult, Robert Wood Johnson Found, 1987-; Nat Diabetes Adv Bd, 1988-92; trustee, Okla Sch Sci, Math Found, 1992-; pres, Am Diabetes Asn, 1993-94; Nat Inst Diabetes & Digestive & Kidney Adv Coun, 1995-; trustee, Robert Wood Johnson Found, 1996-; Alpha Omega Alpha; Am Asn Acad Minority Physicians; Am Asn Physicians; Am Soc Clin Invest; Endocrine Soc; Omicron Delta Kappa Hon Soc; Sigma Xi Sci Hon Soc; trustee, Emory univ; adv bd, Invoy Technologies; Inst Med Nat Acad Sci. **Honors/Awds:** Clinical Teacher of the Year, Barnes Hosp Dept Med, 1981-82; William Alexander Leadership Award, Epsilon Lambda Alpha Phi Alpha, 1982; Special Achiever, St Louis Sentinel, 1982; Distinguished Alumnus of HBI, Nat Asn For Equal Opportunity, 1987; ed bd, Acad Med, 1994-; Outstanding Clinician in Field of Diabetes, Am Diabetes Asn, 1990; Banting Medal for Distinguished Service, Am Diabetes Asn, 1994; Internist of Year, Nat Med Asn, 1997; Living Legend in Diabetes Award, Am Asn Diabetes Educr, 2009. **Home Addr:** 8225 Buckspark Lane W, Potomac, MD 20854, **Home Phone:** (301)365-7658. **Business Addr:**

Senior Medical Consultant, ALR Technologies Inc, 7400 Beaufont Springs Dr, Richmond, VA 23225, **Business Phone:** (804)554-3500.

**GAVIN, L. KATHERINE**
School administrator, college administrator, association executive. **Personal:** Born Chicago Heights, IL. **Educ:** Chicago State Univ, BA, 1952; Columbia Univ, MA, 1963; Nova Univ, EdD, 1976. **Career:** School administrator (retired); Lincoln Sch, Chicago Heights Sch Dist No170, prin, 1966; Prairie State Col, child develop prog, 1968, dir personalized learning prog, 1970; Chicago Heights Sch Dist No 170, dean stud, classroom instr. **Orgs:** S Suburban Chicago Chap Links Inc; chair bd dir, Dr Charles E Gavin Mem Found; Nat Asn Advan Colored People, PUSH. **Honors/Awds:** Outstanding Citizens Award, PUSH; Outstanding Civic & Service, S Suburb Chicago Chap of Links Inc; Scholar Image Award, Fred Hampton Found; lifetime hon, ALUMNI Asn Gov State Univ; Hall of Fame Bloom Township High Sch, 1980; Recognition Award Outstanding Service, Prairie State Col. **Home Addr:** 20643 Western Ave, Chicago Heights, IL 60411, **Home Phone:** (708)481-3484.

**GAVIN, MARY ANN**
Government official. **Personal:** Born Aug 8, 1945, Elmhurst, IL; daughter of Vernus (deceased) and Evelyn Thomas-Wilford (deceased); married Joeneather; children: Charles A & Darrell E. **Educ:** Col St Francis, Il BA, 1973. **Career:** Social Security Admin, serv rep, 1973-76, claims rep, 1976-79, supvr, 1979-85, mgt info specialist, 1985-86, labor rels mgt analyst, 1986-89, sect chief labor rels, 1989-99, dir, Ctr Human Resources, 1999-2000, Civil Rights & Equal Opp, dir, 2000-. **Orgs:** Black Adv Coun, 1994-96; Womans Adv Coun, 1995-; Social Security Black Caucus, 1996; chair, Fed Exec Bd, Chicago, 2007-. **Home Addr:** 1920 Tawny Ct, Joliet, IL 60435, **Home Phone:** (815)729-4717. **Business Addr:** Director, Civil Rights & Equal Opportunity, Off Regional Comnr, Chicago, IL 60601, **Business Phone:** (312)575-6394.

**GAY, ALVIN C.**
Businessperson, executive. **Educ:** Univ Santa Clara, BA, polit sci, 1970; Univ Wis-Madison, African & African Am polit, 1970. **Career:** Ogilvy & Mather, sr partner, 1982-95; UniWorld Group, sr vpres, 1995-99; Footsteps LLC, partner, founder & chief exec officer, 2000-13; BLVD Content, managing partner, 2014-. **Orgs:** Dir's Guild Am, 1989-; bd dir, Archit Salvage Warehouse, 2014-. **Business Addr:** Board of Director, Architectural Salvage Warehouse, 4885 15th St, Detroit, MI 48208, **Business Phone:** (313)896-8333.

**GAY, BIRDIE SPIVEY**
Library administrator. **Personal:** Born Mar 13, 1918, Atlanta, GA; married Howard Donald. **Educ:** Morris Brown Col, attended 1939; Atlanta Univ Sch Libr Serv, attended 1962. **Career:** Brooks County, teacher, 1939-41; Eatonton, Ga, 1941-42; Moutlrie, Ga, teacher & librn, 1942-45; ER Carter Elem Sch, Atlanta, librn & media specialist, 1946-59. **Orgs:** Nat Educ Asn; Ga Am Libr Asn; com adminr, YWCA; solicitor, Cancer Dr, Easter, Retarded C, Muscular Dystrophy; Nat Advan Asn Colored People; United Negro Col Fund; Morris Brown Alumni Asn. **Honors/Awds:** Teacher of the year, ER Carter Sch, 1960-61; Outstanding Service plaque, Sigma Gamma Rho Sorority, 1970. **Home Addr:** 1874 Penelope Rd NW, Atlanta, GA 30314.

**GAY, EDDIE C.**
Chemical engineer. **Personal:** Born May 13, 1940, Starkville, MS; married Sylvia J; children: 3. **Educ:** Wash Univ, BS, 1962; St. Louis Univ, DSc, 1967. **Career:** Chemical engineer (retired); Argonne Nat Lab Battery Prog, group leader, 1941-75; Lithium & Chalcogen Cell Develop Argonne Nat Lab, asst engr, 1968-69; Lithium-chalcogen Cell Develop Argonne Nat Lab, problem leader, 1969-71; Argonne Nat Lab Battery Prog, mgr, 1975. **Orgs:** Electrochem Soc; Am Inst Chem Engr; sigma xi; Nat Orgn Prof Advanc Black Chemists & Chem Engr; Faith United Protestant Church. **Honors/Awds:** Thesis Award, Argonne Nat Lab; Technical Achiever of the Year, 2002. **Home Addr:** 229 Grant St, Park Forest, IL 60466-1013, **Home Phone:** (708)747-9367.

**GAY, HELEN PARKER**
Counselor, mayor, association executive. **Personal:** Born Mar 14, 1920, Rocky Mount, NC; daughter of Frank Leslie Parker Sr (deceased) and Dillie Virginia Shaw Parker; children: Leslie Claudius (deceased). **Educ:** Barber-Scotia Col; NC State Col. **Career:** Employ Security Comn NC, interviewer II; Rocky Mt City Coun, coun mem, 1987-, coun woman, 1983-2003, mayor pro tem, 1986, 1993, 1997, 2002; caterer. **Orgs:** Hon mem, Sigma Gamma Rho Sor Inc, 1986 Rocky Mt Moles Inc, 1988; hon life mem, Presby Women Rocky Mt, 1989; chmn, Region IV, 1991; pres, NC Black Elected Munic Officials, 1990-91; bd mem, NC League Cities, 1990-91; elder, clerk session, Mt Pisgah Presby Church, Rocky Mt, 1990-91, 1993-; bd mem, Community Shelter Homeless. **Honors/Awds:** Merit Award, Employ Security Comn NC, 1950, 1960. **Special Achievements:** First African American female to be elected and serve on the Rocky Mount City Council. **Home Addr:** 1629 King Cir, Rocky Mount, NC 27801-3643, **Home Phone:** (252)442-9346.

**GAY, TYSON**
Track and field athlete. **Personal:** Born Aug 9, 1982, Lexington, KY; children: Trinity. **Educ:** Barton Community Col, 2003; Univ Ark, 2005. **Career:** Track & field athlete, 1999-. **Special Achievements:** University of Arkansas record holder in 100m; American record holder in 100m and 4x100m; world record holder for 200m on a straightaway; first athlete from the University of Arkansas to win an NCAA 100m title. **Business Addr:** USA Track & Field, 132 E Wash St Suite 800, Indianapolis, IN 46204.

**GAYLE, CRUISE**
Advertising executive, manager. **Educ:** Fla A&M Univ; Harvard Bus Sch. **Career:** McKinsey & Co, exec dir intergrated mkt commun; Microsoft Corp, sr pub rels mgr, mgr diversity mkt & commun, currently. **Business Addr:** Manager of Diversity Marketing, Communications, Microsoft Corp, 1 Microsoft Way, Redmond, WA 98052-7329, **Business Phone:** (425)882-8080.

**GAYLE, DR. HELENE DORIS**
Physician, executive. **Personal:** Born Aug 16, 1955, Buffalo, NY; daughter of Jacob A and Marietta D. **Educ:** Barnard Col, New York, BA, psychol, 1976; Univ Pa, MD, 1981; Johns Hopkins Univ, Baltimore, MPH, 1981. **Career:** C's Hosp Nat Med Ctr, Wash, DC, pediat resident, 1981-84; Centers Dis Control, Epidemic Intelligence Serv, 1984-86; Atlanta, Ga, med epidemiologist, 1986-87; Centers DisControl, Ped & Family Studies Sect, med epidemiologist, 1987-89, Div HIV/AIDS, asst chief sci, 1989-90, chief, int activ, 1990-92, agency AIDS coordr & chief, 1992-94; Wash Centers Dis Control & Prev, assoc dir, 1994-95; Bill & Melinda Gates Found, Centers Dis Control & Prev, HIV, TB & Reproductive Health, dir, 1995-2002; Care USA, pres & chief exec officer, 2006; US Aid, bd mem, 2007-; Ctr Strategic & Int Studies, bd trustee, 2007-; Colgate-Palmolive Co, bd mem, 2010-; McKinsey Social Initiative, chief exec officer, 2015-; Centers Dis Control, Atlanta, Ga, researcher & epidemiologist. **Orgs:** Bd mem, ONE Campaign, 2006-; bd trustee, Rockefeller Found, 2009-; bd mem, Coca-Cola, 2013-; Am Pub Health Asn; Am Acad Pediat; Nat Med Asn; Int AIDS Soc; bd mem, Inst Med & Coun Foreign Rels; Delta Omega Soc; Am Med Women's Asn; Soc Pub Health Educ; Rotary Club Atlanta. **Honors/Awds:** National Merit Scholar Fellowship Award, 1981; Henrietta & Jacob Lowenburg Prize, 1981; Joel Gordon Miller Award, 1981; Administrators & Black Faculty Merit Award, Univ of Pa, 1981; Outstanding Unit Citation, 1989, 1990; US Pub Health Service Achievement Medal, 1989; Celebration of Public Service Award, 1990; Colgate-Palmolive Co, Model of Excellence, 1992; US Public Health Service, Outstanding Service Medal, 1992, Unit Commendation Medal, 1992; Serwa Award, Nat Coalition 100 Black Women, 1995; Poindexter Award, US Pub Health Serv, 1996; Medal of Excellence, Columbia Univ, 1996; Service Award, Nat Coalition 100 Black Women Inc, 1999; Woman of the Year Award, 100 Black Men Am Inc, 1999; Women Looking Ahead (WLA) 100s List Award, Women Looking Ahead Inc, 1999; Scroll of Merit Award, Nat Med Asn, 2000; DHL, Jackson State Univ, 2004; DSc, Pa State Univ, 2004; DSc, Smith Col, 2007; DSc, Meharry Med Col, 2007; DSc, Duke Univ, 2008; DHL, Mt Sinai Sch Med New York Univ, 2008; DSc, Morehouse Sch Med, 2008; DHL, Brandeis Univ, 2008; DSc, Agnes Scott Col, 2009; LLD, Columbia Univ, 2009; DSc, Oberlin Col, 2011; DSc, Xavier Univ La, 2016; Top 100 Global Thinkers, Foreign Policy mag; received numerous awards. **Business Addr:** Chief Executive Officer, McKinsey Social Initiative, 1200 19th St NW Suite 910, Washington, DC 20036.

**GAYLE-THOMPSON, DR. DELORES JOYCE**
Physician. **Personal:** Born Feb 28, 1938, Portland; daughter of William Ellison and Lucilda Rebecca; married Amos F; children: Colin & Allison. **Educ:** Howard Univ, Col Lib Arts, BS, 1963, Col Med, MD, 1967; Columbia Univ Sch Pub Health, MPH, 1984. **Career:** Howard Univ Hosp, resident; Freedmen's Hosp Wash, intern, 1967-68; Harlem Hosp, resident pediat, 1968-70, physician pediat clin, 1970-83, assoc dir; Columbia Univ, Col Physicians & Surgeons, asst prof pediat, 1990-. **Orgs:** Nat Med Asn; Ambulatory Pediat Asn; Am Pub Health Asn; Susan Smith McKinney Steward Med Soc; bd mem, White Plains Cot Fair Inc; exec bd, Fund Greater Harlem. **Honors/Awds:** Citation, Howard Univ Century Club, 1986; Civic Award, Friends E Portland Jamaica W Indies, 1986. **Home Addr:** 6 Topland Rd, Hartsdale, NY 10530-3009, **Home Phone:** (914)428-5724. **Business Addr:** Assistant Professor, Columbia University, 2960 Broadway, New York, NY 10027-6902, **Business Phone:** (212)854-1754.

**GAYLES, DR. JONATHAN**
College teacher. **Educ:** Morehouse Col, BA, psychol, 1991; Winthrop Univ, MS, sch psycho, 1993; Univ S Fla, PhD, appl anthrop, 2002. **Career:** Tougaloo Col, adj prof dept pshycol, 1993-94; Fla Educ Fund, prog officer, 1994-99; Univ S Fla, grad teach asst, Dept Anthrop, 1999-2002, grad teach asst, dept africana studies, 2000-02, asst prof dept anthrop, 2003-04; Ind Univ, Pa, teach fel, Dept anthrop, 2002; Ga State Univ, asst prof dept african-am studies, 2004-08, assoc prof, 2009, assoc dean, undergrad learning, 2012-. **Orgs:** Am Anthrop Asn; Socs Latin Am & Caribbean Anthrop; Nat Coun Black Studies; Socs Appl Anthrop; McKnight Doctoral Fel Alumni Asn; Coun Anthrop & Educ; Asn Black Anthropologists; Prof Asns, 2006-; Pres, McKnight Alumni Asn, 2005-06; Secy, McKnight Alumni Asn. **Business Addr:** Associate Dean, Georgia State University, 1 Pk Pl Suite 962, Atlanta, GA 30303, **Business Phone:** (404)654-5852.

**GAYLES-FELTON, DR. ANNE RICHARDSON**
Educator, college teacher. **Personal:** Born Jun 4, 1923, Marshallville, GA; daughter of Franklin J and Marion R; married Ambrose M. **Educ:** Ft Valley State Col, BS, 1943; Columbia Univ, MA, 1949, prof dipl, 1953; Ill Univ, EdD, 1961. **Career:** Lamson Richardson High Sch, teacher; Ark Baptist Col, Dept Sociol, head, 1947-50; Ft Valley State Col, instr, social sci, 1950-54; Stillman Col, dir stud teaching, 1951-52; Albany State Col, assoc prof social sci & educ, 1954-57; Fla A&M Univ, dir stud teaching, 1957-62, Dept Sec Educ, head, 1962-82, supvr interns, prof sec educ, 1982-03, prof emer, 2003-; Rust Col, assoc prof social sci; Ga Pub Schs, teacher. **Orgs:** First vpres, Asn Social & Behavioral Serv, 1961-62; exec comt, Soc Prof Educ, 1969-70; comt mem, Am Asn Teacher Educ Col, 1970-80; comt master teacher, Asn Teacher Educrs, 1982-85; USS/China Joint Conf Educ, Beijing, China, 1992; USS Mil Acad Appointments Bd; Citizen Ambassador Prog, People to People Int, 1992; Gov Bush's Task Force, Equity Educ Opportunity; DST; Pi Lambda Theta; Phi Delta Kappa; Kappa Delta Pi; Alpha Kappa Mu; Pi Gamma Mu; Nat Republican Party, Presidential Task Force; State Fla Gov Commemorative Celebration Comn Dr Martin Luther King Jr; Gov Bd Independent Col & Univ, State Fla; Gov Comn Qual Educ; Urban League; Republican Party Fla; Delta Sigma Theta Sorority; Grace Dodge Soc; chmn, Party's Bus Adv Coun. **Home Addr:** 4425 Meandering Way Apt 226, Tallahassee, FL 32308-5746. **Business Addr:** Professor Emeritus, Florida A&M University, 1500 Wahnish Way, Tallahassee, FL 32307, **Business Phone:** (850)599-8163.

**GAYNOR, GLORIA**
Singer. **Personal:** Born Sep 7, 1949, Newark, NJ; daughter of Daniel Fowles and Queenie May Proctor; married Linwood Simon. **Career:** Albums: Never Can Say Goodbye, 1975; I've Got You, 1976; Glorious, 1977; Park Ave Sound, 1978; I Have A Right, 1979; Stories, 1980; I Kinda Like Me, 1981; I Am Gloria Gaynor, 1984; The Power of Gloria Gaynor, 1986; I Will Survive, 1990; I Am What I Am, 1996; I Wish You Love, 2002; I Will Survive (Go), 2003; The Answer, 2006; Christmas Presence, 2007; We Will Survive, 2013. Singles: "Honey Bee", 1974; "Never Can Say Goodbye", 1974; "Reach Out I'll Be There", 1974; "Real Good People", 1974; "Walk On By", 1974; "All I Need Is Your Sweet Lovin'", 1975; "Casanova Brown", 1975; "If You Want It Do It Yourself", 1975; "How High the Moon", 1975; "Let's Make a Deal", 1976; "I Will Survive", 1978; "Substitute", 1978; "Anybody Want to Party", 1979; "Let Me Know (I Have a Right)", 1979; "Tonight", 1980; "Let's Mend What's Been Broken", 1981; "I Am What I Am", 1983; "Strive", 1984; "My Love Is Music", 1985; "Don't You Dare Call It Love", 1986; "Be Soft with Me Tonight", 1987; "I Will Survive", 1993; "Mighty High", 1997; "Never Can Say Goodbye 1998", 1998; "Last Night", 2000; "Just Keep Thinking About You", 2001; "I Never Knew", 2002; "The Power of a Woman In Love", 2006; "Hacer Por Hacer", 2008; Film: Pinay, American Style, 1979. TV series: "The Keith Harris Show", 1983; "Entertainment Express", 1983; "Prom Night", 1999; "The 2002 World Music Awards", 2002; "Pyramid", 2003; "Good Morning Australia", 2004; "When Disco Ruled the World", 2005; "Gray Matters", 2006; "The Artists Music Guild Presents: The AMG Heritage Awards", 2013. **Honors/Awds:** Grammy Award for Best Disco Recording for "I Will Survive", 1979; Radio Regenbogen for Lifetime Disco, 1999; Inducted into the Dance Music Hall of Fame, 2005; Honorary Spokesperson, American Diabetes Association, 2008; 30th anniversary of "I Will Survive.", 2009. **Business Addr:** Singer, c/o PolyGram Holding Inc, 825 8th Ave, New York, NY 10019.

**GAYTON, ESQ. GARY D.**
Lawyer. **Personal:** Born Feb 25, 1933, Seattle, WA. **Educ:** Univ Wa, BA, polit sci, 1955; Gonzaga Univ Sch Law, JD, 1962. **Career:** Western Dist Wash, asst US atty, 1962-65; Stern, Gayton, Neubauer & Brucker, atty PS, 1965; US Secy Transp, spec asst, 1977-79; Urban Mass Transp Admin, actg admin, 1979; Smothers, Douple, Grayton & Long, partner, 1979-81; Diamond & Sylvester, coun, 1981-93; Grigsby Branford Co, sr vpres, 1985-96; Gaitan & Cusack, coun, 1994-95; Siebert Branford Shank & Co LLC, sr vpres, 1996-, regional mgr; Cusack Knowles Ferguson PLLC, counr, 1996-2001; pvt pract, 2001; law firms State Wash, lawyer & partner, currently; Clinton-Gore Transp Transition Team; Optimos Inc, dir. **Orgs:** Am Bar Asn; Am Trial Lawyers Asn; King Co Bar Asn; Wash State Bar Asn; chair, Bar-Pac comt, admin comn, Resolution comn, legis comn, civil rights comn; Nat Bar Asn; bd mem, Universal Security Life Ins Co; Seattle Pk Comn; Seattle Repertory Bd; Seattle Ethics & Fair Camp Comn; Seattle King Co Bicentennial Comn; bd mem, Salvation Army; bd mem, NW Civic Cult & Char Orgns; bd mem, Nat Asn Advan Colored People; bd mem, Inst Black Am Music Inc; pres, Loren Miller Bar Asn; lobbyist, Am Pub Transp Asn, 1993-2000; chair, sr adv bd, 9th Circuit Judicial Conf, 2000-01; DC Bar Asn; charter mem, Nat Conf Black Lawyers; chair bd, YMCA, E Madison; asst secy bd, Wash C's Home Soc; Nat Comn Support Pub Schs; vice chair, Boy Scouts Am; Metrop Dem Club; Seattle Urban League. **Honors/Awds:** Outstanding Community Service Award, Loren Miller Bar Asn; Ethic Award, Cult Ctr, Univ Wash, 1977; Humanitarian Award, Sigma Delta Tau; Distinguished Alumni, Univ Wash, 2005; Distinguished Alumni Merit Award, Gonzaga Univ Sch Law, 2009. **Special Achievements:** First African-American student-body president, Garfield High Sch; first African-American captain of a varsity sports team, Univ Wash; First black Presidential contender. **Home Addr:** 2125 1st Ave, Seattle, WA 98121, **Home Phone:** (206)441-8423. **Business Addr:** Senior Vice President, Siebert Brandford Shank & Co LLC, 2107 Elliot Ave Suite 307, Seattle, WA 98121, **Business Phone:** (206)621-8903.

**GAYTON, RENDELLA LUCAS.** **See LUCAS, DR. RENDELLA.**

**GEARY, REGGIE (REGINALD ELLIOT GEARY)**
Basketball player, basketball coach. **Personal:** Born Aug 31, 1973, Trenton, NJ; married Candace; children: Quincy & Wesley. **Educ:** Univ Ariz, BA, polit sci & govt, 1996. **Career:** Basketball player (retired), basketball coach; Cleveland Cavaliers, guard, 1996-97; San Antonio Spurs, 1997-98; Quad City Thunder, 1998-99; Idaho Stampede, 1999-2000; Bnei HaSharon, Israel, 2000-01; Porto, port, 2001-02; JL Bourg-en-Bresse, France, 2002-03; BC Kyiv, Ukraine, 2003-04; Univ Ariz, asst coach, 2005, 2008-09; Wildcats, basketball opers, 2005-06; Anaheim Arsenal, asst coach & dir opers, d-league coach, 2006-08, head coach; SMU Athletic Dept, asst coach, 2009-11; Crest Ins Group, ins broker, 2010-11; Yokohama B-Corsairs, head coach, 2011-13; Chiba Jets, head coach, 2013-15; Mitsubishi Diamond Dolphins Nagoya, head coach, 2015-; Flowing Wells High Sch, head coach. **Business Addr:** Assistant Coach, Southern Methodist University, 6024 Airline Rd, Dallas, TX 75275, **Business Phone:** (214)768-4012.

**GECAU, DR. KIMANI JAMES**
Educator. **Personal:** Born Jul 17, 1947. **Educ:** Univ E Africa, BA, 1969; McMaster Univ, MA, 1970; State Univ NY, PhD, 1975. **Career:** McMaster Univ, teaching asst, 1969-70; State Univ NY Buffalo, teaching asst, 1970-72; State Univ Col, Buffalo, instr, 1970-71; Geneseo, instr, 1972-75; Univ Nairobi, lectr, 1975; Univ Zimbabwe, Harare, Media & Commun Studies, lectr, currently. **Home Addr:** PO Box 46158, Nairobi00200. **Business Addr:** Lecturer, Department of English, University of Zimbabwe, Mount Pleasant, Harare, **Business Phone:** (263)430-7757.

**GEE, AL.** **See GERMANY, ALBERT.**

**GEE, CAMMIE.** **See GIST, CAROLE ANNE-MARIE.**

### GEE, WILLIAM ROWLAND, JR.

Engineer, vice president (organization). **Personal:** Born Oct 4, 1940, Washington, DC; son of William Rowland and Marietta L Brittain; married Sadie H Phillips; children: Moira G Travis, Morris B, Cathy P Kearney, Julia E & W Rowland III. **Educ:** Howard Univ, BSME, cum laude, 1962; Oak Ridge Sch Reactor Tech, nuclear engineering, 1963; Stanford Univ, MS, appl mech, 1971; Loyola Col Baltimore, MBA, 1981. **Career:** US Atomic Energy Comn, proj engr, 1962-66; GE Breeder Reactor Develop, engr, 1966-73; Potomac Elec Power Co, mgr nuclear engineering, 1975-77, mgr generating engineering, 1981-89, vpres generating, engineering & construct, 1989-, Bus Performance & Technol, vpres, 1991. **Orgs:** Omega Psi Phi; ASME; ANS; Edison Elec Inst. **Home Addr:** 1006 Coral Berry Ct, Great Falls, VA 22066, **Home Phone:** (703)406-8470. **Business Addr:** Vice President, System Engineering, Potomac Electric Power Co, 1900 Pa Ave NW, Washington, DC 20068, **Business Phone:** (202)872-2000.

### GELLINEAU, VICTOR MARCEL, JR.

Marketing executive, business owner, entrepreneur. **Personal:** Born Nov 3, 1942, New York, NY; son of Victor M and Marcella Gonzalez; married Carole Joy Johnston; children: Victor M III, Maria M & Carmen E. **Educ:** Howard Univ, BA, 1967; Baruch Col Bus & Pub Admin, MBA, 1974. **Career:** Burlington Industs, salesman, 1967-69; Lever Bros, asst prod mgr, 1969-71; Am Home Prod, prod mgr, 1971-73; Zebra Assoc, vpres & dir acct mgt, 1973-76; Heublein Inc, mkt mgr, 1976-83; Ponderosa Inc, dir mkt, 1983-85; Gen Foods Corp, sr prod mgr, 1985-89; Carole Joy Creations Inc, pres, chierf exec officer & owner, 1985-, vpres, secy. **Orgs:** Omega Psi Phi Fraternity Inc, 1967-; Am Mgt Asn, 1970-; vis prof, Nat Urban League Beep Prog, 1974-; bd mem & pres, Artists Collective, 1978-83; bd mem & pres, Jr Achievement, 1978-; Nat Black MBA Asn, 1983-; facilitator Inroads; bd mem, adv, Hord Found Inc, 1988-; bd mem, United Way, 1989-98; pres, Minority Bus Asn, bd mem, 1990-00; bd mem & treas, Hispanic Asn greater Danbury, 2000-06. **Home Addr:** 10 Kilian Dr, Danbury, CT 06811, **Home Phone:** (203)790-8585. **Business Addr:** President, Chief Executive Officer & Owner, Carole Joy Creations Inc, 1087 Fed Rd Suite 8, Brookfield, CT 06804-1156, **Business Phone:** (203)740-4490.

### GEMEDA, DR. GULUMA

Educator, college teacher. **Educ:** Addis Ababa Univ, Ethiopia, BA, 1980, MA, 1984; Mich State Univ, PhD, 1996. **Career:** Addis Ababa Univ, lectr & asst prof, 1984-87, lectr & researcher, 1990-92; Mich State Univ, teaching asst, 1987-90 & 1992-95; N Mich Univ, vis asst prof, 1996-97; Univ Mich-Flint, Dept Africana Studies, chair, adj asst prof, 1998-2001, asst prof, 2001-; Book: The Rise of Coffee and the Demise Imperial Autonomy: The Oromo Kingdom of Jimma and Political Centralization in Ethiopia, Contested Terrain; Land, Agriculture and Social Class Formation in the Gibe Region, From the mid-nineteenth century to 1936, in State, Land and Society in the History of Sudanic Africa. **Orgs:** African Studies Asn; Int Conf Ethiopian Studies; Int Studies Asn; Am Polit Sci Asn; pres, Oromo Studies Asn. **Business Addr:** Asst Professor, University of Michigan-Flint, 303 E Kearsley St, Flint, MI 48502-1950, **Business Phone:** (810)762-3353.

### GENET, MICHAEL

Actor, writer. **Personal:** Born Aug 25, 1958, Washington, DC; son of Dewey Hughes and Jeanette Butler Adams; married Karen Charles Hughes; children: Jasmin G & Michael C Hughes. **Educ:** Julliard Sch Drama, 1977; Calif Inst Arts, BFA, 1980. **Career:** Writer & Actor; Off-Broadway: Pvt Wilkie in Charles Fuller's A Soldier's Play; August Wilson's Joe Turner's Come & Gone; The Colored Museum; Ma Rainey's Black Bottom; Earth & Sky; Creon in The Oedipus Plays; Broadway: Marius in Elton John & Ann Rice's "Lestat"; A Few Good Men; Hamlet; Northeast Local; Television: "As the World Turns", 1956; "All My Children"; "Happy End"; "New York Undercover", 1997; "The Equalizer", 1988; "Janick"; "Hallelujah", 1993; "American Playhouse", 1993; "The Forget-Me-Not Murders", 1994; "Law & Order", 1992-08; "Law & Order CI", 2003-10; "Hindsight" 2007; "Guiding Light"; "One Life to Live", 2010; "Another World"; "Tyler Perry's House of Payne", 2009; "Ugly Betty", 2010; "Law & Order: Special Victims Unit", 2011; "The Americans", 2013; Film: Simple Justice, 1989; Presumed Innocent, 1990; Close to Eden; Stranger Among Us; It Only Happens With You; Let It Be Me, 1995; One Fine Day, 1996; Booty Call; Deadline, 2001; 25th Hour, 2002; She Hate Me, 2004; Dream Street, 2005; The Verdict, 2008; Writer: "Hallelujah", 1993; She Hate Me, 2004; Talk to Me, 2007; Wall Street: Money Never Sleeps, 2010. **Honors/Awds:** John F Kennedy Ctr Award, New American Plays, 2000; Nominee, Essence Award Nominee Outstanding Writing Motion Picture, 2004; NAACP Image Award for Outstanding Writing in a Motion Picture, 2008. **Home Addr:** 400 W 43rd St Suite 5D, New York, NY 10036, **Home Phone:** (212)465-1519.

### GENTRY, ALVIN HARRIS

Basketball coach. **Personal:** Born Nov 5, 1954, Shelby, NC; son of G H and Bulah Mae; married Pat Sue DeLuca; children: Alexis; married Suzanne Harris; children: Ryan & Jack. **Educ:** Appalachian State Univ, mgt, 1977. **Career:** Univ Colo, asst coach, 1977-78, grad asst, 1978, staff, 1981-85; Baylor Univ, asst coach, 1980-81; Kans Univ, asst coach, 1985-88; San Antonio Spurs, asst coach & scout, 1988-89, head asst, 1999-2000; Los Angeles Clippers, asst coach, 1990-91, 1999-2000, head coach, 2000-03, assoc head coach, 2013-14; Univ Kans, asst; Miami Heat, interim coach, head coach, 1991-95; Detroit Pistons, from asst coach to head coach, 1994-2000; Phoenix Suns, from asst coach to head coach, 2003-13; Golden State Warriors, assoc head coach, 2014-15; New Orleans Pelicans, head coach, 2015-. **Home Addr:** 6358 Quail Track Dr, Scottsdale, AZ 85262. **Business Addr:** Head Coach, New Orleans Pelicans, 5800 Airline Dr, Metairie, LA 70003, **Business Phone:** (504)733-0255.

### GENTRY, DR. ATRON A.

Educator. **Personal:** Born Jan 1, 1938, El Centro, CA; son of Hannah and Horace. **Educ:** Pasadena City Col, AA, 1958; Calif State Polytech Col, attended 1959; Calif State Univ, Los Angeles, BA, 1966; Univ Mass, EdD, 1970. **Career:** Ctr Urban Educ Prog, dir, 1968-71; Univ Mass, Sch Educ, assoc dean, 1971-75; Apple Creek State Inst Oh, asst supt, 1975-76; Cleveland State Hosp Oh, supt, 1976-78; dir, Univ Mass, Boston Sec Schs; Hull Col Higher Educ Hull Eng, vis prof, 1981; Beijing Teachers Col, vis prof, 1986; Univ Mass Amherst, sch educ, prof educ, prof emer, 1999-. **Orgs:** Phi Delta Kappa, 1971; staff mem, organizing comt, Olympic Games, 1984. **Honors/Awds:** Citizen of the Year, Omega Psi Frat, 1967; Urban Service Award, Off Econ Apport US Govt, 1966; Urban Educ The Hope Factor Philadelphia Sounder, 1972; Dedication & Service, Boston Secondary Sch Proj, 1987; Dr. Carter G.Woodson Memorial Uplift Award, Tau Iota Chapter, Omega Psi Fraternity, 1988; Crispus Attucks Award, Nat Comt Commemoration Am Revolutionary War Black Patriot, 1991. **Special Achievements:** Author for Learning to Survive: Black Youth Look for Education and Hope; Co-editor, Equity and Excellence in Education; Voice-over in an animation TV series "Fat Albert and the Cosby Kids", 1972. **Home Addr:** 9 Sutton Ct, PO Box 3241, Amherst, MA 01004, **Home Phone:** (413)256-3522. **Business Addr:** Professor Emeritus, University of Massachusetts, 300 Massachusetts Ave, Amherst, MA 01003, **Business Phone:** (413)545-0111.

### GENTRY, LAMAR DUANE

Government official, mayor. **Personal:** Born Dec 19, 1946, Chicago, IL; children: Mark J, LaMar P & Carlos D. **Educ:** Southern Ill Univ, BA, polit sci, 1970; Univ Ill, JD, 1979. **Career:** Gov Ill, model cities specialist, 1970-72, dir, model cities, 1972-74, dir, prog planning & develop, 1974-75; Capital Develop Bd Ill, regional sch dist anal, 1975-76; City E St Louis, Ill, dir admin, 1979-, comnr community develop, 1981, actg comptroller, 1983, dep mayor, city mgr, 2001; pub & govt rels consult, currently. **Orgs:** Bd dir, E St Louis Community Develop Credit Union; bd dir, Boy's Club Springfield, IN, 1973-75; bd dir, Springfield Urban League, 1973-75; pres, Kappa Alpha Psi Springfield Alumni, 1974-76; bd dir, N Cent Prov; bd dir & life mem, E St Louis Alumni Chap.

### GENTRY, NOLDEN I., JR.

Lawyer. **Personal:** Born Aug 30, 1937, Rockford, IL; son of Nolden L and Omega; married Barbara J; children: Adrienne, Natalie & Brian. **Educ:** Univ Iowa, BS, 1960; Iowa Col Law, JD, 1964. **Career:** FBI, spec agt, 1964-65; Iowa, asst atty gen, 1965-66; Brick Gentry, atty at law, Bowers, Swartz, Stoltze, Schuling & Levis, founding partner, shareholder & atty, 1967-; Des Moines Housing Corp, pres; Greater Des Moines Chamber Com, legal coun; Iowa Sch Bd Asn, legal coun; Des Moines Develop Corp, legal coun; Delta Dent Iowa & Neighborhood Develop Corp, legal coun. **Orgs:** Treas, Phi Delta Phi, 1962-63, pres, 1963-64; State Bd Pub Instr, 1968-70; bd dir, Des Moines Independent Sch Dist, 1970-83, pres, 1974-75; bd dir, Delta Dent Plan Iowa, 1971-; bd dir, Univ Iowa Found, 1973-76; First Bank Des Moines, 1978-; bd dir, Simpson Col, 1987-91; bd dir, Iowa Pub TV Found, 1987-93; bd dir, Bankers Trust Co, 1989-99; bd dir, MidAmerican Energy Holding Co, 1989-99; Des Moines Skywalk Comn, 1991-96; bd dir, Nat I-Club, 2001-02; bd dir, Racing Asn Cent Iowa, 2002-; Polk County Bar Asn; Iowa State Bar Asn; bd mem, Des Moinse Independent Comn Sch Bd; bd mem, Greater Des Moines Comn Found; bd mem, Delta Dent Plan; bd dir, Mid-Iowa Health Found; bd dir, Univ Iowa Black Alumni Asn; Univ Iowa Alumni Asn; bd dir, First Bank Iowa; bd dir, Mid Am Energy; bd dir, Prairie Meadows; legal coun, Neighborhood Develop Corp; bd dir, Mid-Iowa Health Found; bd dir, Civic Ctr Greater Des Moines; Polk County & Iowa State Bar; Drake Relays Comn. **Honors/Awds:** Distinguished Alumni Award, Univ Iowa, 2005; lifetime hon dir, Iowa Law Sch Found. Honored by Des Moines Chap Links, Des Moines Human Rights Comn; Des Moines Nat Conf Community and Justice, Greater Des Moines Leadership Inst, Martindale Hubbell Legal Dir. **Home Addr:** 1517 SW Pleasantview Dr, Des Moines, IA 50315-2127, **Home Phone:** (515)282-0831. **Business Addr:** Attorney, Brick Gentry Bowers Swartz Stoltze Schuling Levis PC, 6701 Westown Pkwy Suite 100, West Des Moines, IA 50266-7703, **Business Phone:** (515)274-1450.

### GEORGE, ALLEN

Lawyer. **Personal:** Born Oct 13, 1935, New York, NY; married Valerie Daring; children: Gerald, Kenneth & Johnathan. **Educ:** NYH Univ, BS, 1964; NY Univ Grad Sch Bus, attended 1968; Howard Univ, JD, 1973; Cleveland State Univ, LLM, 1980. **Career:** Bur Credit Unions, credit union examr, 1965-66; IRS, revenue agt, 1966-69; Lucas & Tucker & Co, tax acct, 1969-70; Stand Oil Co, atty, 1973-77; Pittman George & Copeland Co LPA, pvt pract, 1978; Allen George & Assoc, atty, currently. **Orgs:** Treas, Phi Alpha Delta Law Fraternity, 1972-73; CuyahogaCo Bar Asn Bd; Glenville YMCA, 1976; bd mem, Cath Interracial Coun; Caribbean Comt Cult Club; Knights Columbus; Nat Bar Asn; Am Bar Asn; Ohio Bar Asn; Bar Asn Greater Cleveland; Cleveland Lawyers Asn. **Honors/Awds:** Published: "The Tax Treatment of The-cost of Class C Stock Purchases", Farmers Coop, 1971; Cleveland State Univ Col Law, 1975-76. **Business Addr:** Attorney, Allen George & Associates, 12200 Fairhill Rd Suite B411-13, Cleveland, OH 44120-1058, **Business Phone:** (216)421-0687.

### GEORGE, DR. ALMA ROSE

Surgeon general. **Personal:** Born Mound Bayou, MS; daughter of Phillip M; married Frederick Finch; children: Franklin. **Educ:** Meharry Med Col Sch Med, MD, 1960. **Career:** Detroit Gen Hosp, internship, 1960-61; Va Med Ctr, resident gen surg, 1965-66; Mercy Hosp, Samaritan Health Ctr, resident, gen surg, 1961-65; Wayne County: operates three surg out patient centers & a patient care mgt syst, currently; Alma George & Assocs, med practr, currently; Sinai-Grace Hosp; Harper Univ Hosp. **Orgs:** Pres, Detroit Med Soc; secy, pres, Wolverine St Med Soc; bd delegates, bd trustees, treas, pres, Nat Med Asn. **Honors/Awds:** The 100 Most Influential Black Americans, Ebony Mag, May, 1992. **Business Addr:** President, Medical Practitioner, Wolverine State Medical Society, 10730 W 7 Mile Rd, Detroit, MI 48221, **Business Phone:** (313)342-5189.

### GEORGE, CONSTANCE P.

Clergy. **Personal:** Born May 1, 1931, Farmville, VA; children: Otis Jr, Gary, Randall, Lisa Hamilton & Kirby. **Educ:** Col New Rochelle, BA, 1984; NYK Theol Sem, MDiv, 1988; United Theol Sem, DMin, 1994. **Career:** Westchester Med Ctr, chaplin consult; Grace Baptist Church, minister missions, exec minister & assoc pastor congregational care, assoc pastor emer sacred progs, currently. **Orgs:** Bd, YMCA, Mt Vernon; Westchester Childcare; United Black Clergy, Westchester; pres, Mt Vernon Coun Churches; Mt Vernon Human Rights Comn; spiritual life cmnr, Nat Baptist Conv USA; Alpha Kappa Alpha Sorority; Zeta Nu Omega Chap, Westchester County; NCP. **Honors/Awds:** Minister of the Year Award, Black Womens Health Proj, Westchester Chap, 1990; Wall of Honor Citation, Grace Baptist Church, 1991; Recognition Dedicated & Untiring Serv, United Black Clergy, Westchester, 1992; Cert Appreciation, Off County Exec, Westchester, County Women's Adv Bd, 1988; Serv Award, Westchester County Bd Legislators, Proclamation, 1992. **Special Achievements:** Sermon printed, Those Preaching Women, Ella P Mitchell, editor, 1985; First African Baptist ordained clergywoman raised in Mount Vernon, 1986. **Home Addr:** 153 S 5th Ave, Mount Vernon, NY 10550, **Home Phone:** (914)668-6857. **Business Addr:** Associate Pastor Emeritus, Grace Baptist Church, 1 Grace Plz 52 S 6th Ave, Mount Vernon, NY 10550, **Business Phone:** (914)664-2676.

### GEORGE, EDDIE, JR. (EDWARD NATHAN GEORGE)

Football player, television broadcaster. **Personal:** Born Sep 24, 1973, Philadelphia, PA; married Tamara Johnson; children: Eriq Michael & Jaire David. **Educ:** Ohio State Univ, landscape archit; Kellogg Sch Mgt, MBA, 2009. **Career:** Football player (retired), television broadcaster; Houston Oilers, running back, 1996; Tenn Oilers, 1997-98; Tenn Titans, 1999-2003; Dallas Cowboys, running back, 2004; G4 Network, G4 Sports, Training Camp host; Get Fit TN prog, spokeperson, 2006-. **Orgs:** R&B Groups. **Home Addr:** 4708 Stuart Glen Dr, PO Box 150283, Nashville, TN 37215-4820. **Business Addr:** Host, G4 Network, 12100 W Olympic Blvd, Los Angeles, CA 90064, **Business Phone:** (310)979-5000.

### GEORGE, EDWARD

Executive. **Personal:** married Cutie Bell; children: 5. **Career:** Amalgamated Transit Union, pres & bus agt, 1970-72; A New Beginning Church, owner, currently. **Orgs:** Bd mem, Legal Aid Soc San Joaguin Co, 1969-73; dir, Southeast Comm Asn, 1972-73; bd mem, A Phillip Randolph Ins, 1972-73; bd mem, KUOP FM Radio Sta Univ Pacific Stockton CA; pres, Nat Asn Advan Colored People Stockton; bd Mem, Cit Adv Com San Joaquin Co Planning Asn; adv bd, San Joaquin Co Manpower Prog; adv bd mem, Child Health Disability Prev Prog San Joaquin Co. **Home Addr:** 2420 Montclair St, Stockton, CA 95205, **Home Phone:** (209)463-4578. **Business Addr:** Owner, A New Beginning Church, 2393 E Sonora St, Stockton, CA 95205-6506, **Business Phone:** (209)943-3060.

### GEORGE, DR. GARY RAYMOND

State government official, attorney general (U.S. federal government). **Personal:** Born Mar 8, 1954, Milwaukee, WI; children: Grace Chevalier; married Patricia Schulz; children: 4. **Educ:** Univ Wis, Madison, BBA, acct, 1976; Univ Mich, Ann Arbor, MI, JD, 1979. **Career:** Arthur Young & Co, tax atty, 1979-80; WI State Senate, Dist Six, sen, 1980-2003; self-employed, atty, 1982-; WI Gubernatorial, cand, 1998; Senate President Pro Tempore 1999-2001; Gov Wis, cand, 2002; US House Representatives, Dist Four, cand, 2014. **Orgs:** Uniform State Laws Comt, 1981; Ed Block Grant Adv Comt, 1981; Ed Comt Bd, 1981; chmn, Pk W Redevel Task Force, 1981; Comn Uniform State Laws, 1981; co-chair, Joint Audit Comt, 1981-85; Educ Commun Bd, 1981-97; Milwaukee City Zoo Bd, 1981; Neighborhood Improve Develop Corp, 1982; bd trustee, Family Hosp Inc & Family Hosp Nursing Home Inc, 1983; chmn, Joint Fin Comt Ed Sub comt, 1983; co-chair, Joint Comt Fin, 1983-; Comt Develop Fin Authority, 1983; Alcohol & Drug Abuse Study Comt, 1983; State Supported Prog Adv Comt, 1983; Mayors Anti-Gang Initiative Task Force, 1984; Educ & State Insts; bd dir, Performing Arts Ctr, 1985; Wis State Bar; Dem Party Wis; Nat Caucus State Legislators; Coun State Govts; Milwaukee Forum; Nat Black Caucus State Legislators; Nat Asn Advan Colored People; Wis Spec Olympics; Sexual Assault & Child Abuse Study Comt; Am Indian Study Com, 1995; Milwaukee Child Welfare Partnership Coun, 1999-; Judicial Coun, 1999; Judiciary & Consumer Affairs; Biennial comt assignments, 2003; State Bar Wis. **Home Addr:** 1100 W Wells Suite 1711, Milwaukee, WI 53233, **Home Phone:** (414)271-9565. **Business Addr:** Senator, State Bar of Wisconsin, 1100 W Wells St, Milwaukee, WI 53233, **Business Phone:** (608)266-2500.

### GEORGE, DR. HERMON, JR.

Educator. **Personal:** Born Nov 22, 1945, Tampa, FL; son of Hermon Sr and Henrene Smith; children: Dahren Malcolm & Melissa Niani. **Educ:** Wilkes Col, Wilkes-Barre, PA, BA, polit sci, 1967; Middlebury Col, MA, span, 1968; Univ Calif, Irvine, CA, PhD, comparative cult, 1979. **Career:** Wartburg Col, Waverly, Iowa, instr Span, 1968-70; Fisk Univ, Nashville, Tenn, instr Span, 1970-71; Spelman Col, Atlanta, Ga, instr Span, 1978-81; Calif State Univ, Fresno, Calif, asst prof ethnic studies, 1978-81; State Univ NY, New Paltz, NY, asst prof black studies, 1981-85; Univ Northern Colo, Greeley, Colo, assoc prof & coordr, 1985-91; prof, 1991-. **Orgs:** Mem-at-large, exec bd, Nat Coun Black Studies, 1980-87; reviewer, Social Sci Jour, 1980-81, 1985-; reviewer, Sci & Soc, 1987-; regional ed, Western Jour Black Studies, 1991-96; Nat Conf Black Polit Scientists, 1988-89; Western Social Sci Asn. **Business Addr:** Professor, University of Northern Colorado, 501 20th St, Greeley, CO 80639, **Business Phone:** (970)351-1743.

### GEORGE, JASON WINSTON

Actor. **Personal:** Born Feb 9, 1972, Virginia Beach, VA; married Vandana Khanna; children: 1. **Educ:** Univ Va, BA, 1994; Temple Univ, MFA. **Career:** Films: Fallen, 1998; Barbershop, 2002; The Climb, 2002; Clock stoppers, 2002; Straighten Up America, 2003; Sledge: The Untold Story, 2005; Bewitched, 2005; Good Vibrations, 2005; You Did What?, 2006; Coffee, Tea, or Milk?, 2006; The Box, 2007; Three Can Play That Game, 2007; Race, 2008; Broken Windows, 2008; Playing for Keeps, 2012; TV series: "Sunset Beach", 1997-99; "Moesha", 1998-99; "Roswell", 2000; "Arliss", 2000; "Girlfriends", 2000; "Titans", 2000-01; "Friends", 2001; "OffCentre", 2001-02; "Jeremiah", 2002; "She Spies", 2003; "Abby", 2003; "Half & Half", 2002-03; "Boomtown", 2003; "Platinum", 2003; "Eve", 2003-06; "She Spies", 2003; "Without a Trace", 2005; "Stargate SG-1", 2005-06; "What About Brian", 2006-07; "House M.D.", 2007; "Shark", 2007; "ER", 2007-08; "Eli Stone", 2008-09; "Eastwick", 2009; "Inside the Box", 2009; "Grey's Anatomy", 2010-14; "Off the

Map", 2011; "Desperate Housewives", 2011; "Against the Wall", 2011; "The Closer", 2011; "Witches of East End", 2013; "Hit the Floor", 2013-14; "Mistresses", 2013-14. **Orgs:** Bd dir, Temple Univ's Sch Commun & Theater; bd dir, Am Fedn Tv & Radio Artists. **Business Addr:** Actor, c/o Writers & Artists Agency Inc, 8383 Wilshire Blvd, Beverly Hills, CA 90211, **Business Phone:** (323)866-0900.

### GEORGE, DR. LUVENIA A.
Musicologist, educator. **Personal:** Born Feb 26, 1934, Chicago, IL; daughter of Floyd D and Sweetie; married Henry H; children: Karen Marsha & Adrianne Rose. **Educ:** Howard Univ, Washington, DC, BEd, 1952; Univ Md, MEd, 1969, PhD, 1995. **Career:** DC Pub Schs, music teacher, 1954-92; Smithsonian Inst, res scholar, 1993-94, Duke Ellington Youth Proj, coordr, 1994-. Author: Teaching the Music of Six Different Cultures, 1986. **Orgs:** Organist, Sargent Presby Church, 1960-, elder, 1991-; pres, DC Music Educrs Asn, 1970-72; pres, DC Chap Am Choral dir Asn, 1978-80; Int Asn Jazz Educrs Resource Team. **Home Addr:** 7416 14th St NW, Washington, DC 20012-1502, **Home Phone:** (202)723-4408. **Business Addr:** Coordinator, Smithsonian Institute, 301 7th St SW, Washington, DC 20407, **Business Phone:** (202)633-8998.

### GEORGE, PAULINE L.
Executive. **Personal:** Born Apr 9, 1963, Cleveland, OH. **Educ:** Eastern Mich Univ, BA, 1985; Mich State Univ, MA, 1990. **Career:** WKYC TV-3 News, desk asst, weekend assoc producer, 1986; Continental Cablevision, telemarketing & sales, 1988-89; CNBC, affil rels acct exec, Midwest, 1989-90, affil rels regional mgr, Midwest, 1990-92, affil rels regional mgr, Nebr, 1992-93; CNBC/Am's Talking, reg dir Midwest & Can; GM R*Works, experiential mkt dir, 2005-11; Jack Morton Worldwide, vpres, acct dir-evaluations, 2011-; NBC Cable Networks, regional dir, Midwest & Can, currently. **Orgs:** Founding pres, Detroit chap, Nat Asn Minorities Cable; dir, nat bd dir, exec comt, 1997, Women Cable & Telecommunications, 1995-96; Cable TV Admin & Mkt (CTAM); Nat Asn Female Exec; Alpha Kappa Alpha Sorority. **Home Addr:** 2602 Beacon Hill Dr Suite 306, Auburn Hills, MI 48326. **Business Addr:** Regional Director, NBC Cable Networks, 2855 Coolidge Hwy Suite 201A, Troy, MI 48084, **Business Phone:** (810)643-9033.

### GEORGE, RONALD LAWRENCE
Football player. **Personal:** Born Mar 20, 1970, Heidelberg; married Julie. **Educ:** Stanford Univ, econ, 1992; UsaF Acad, grad. **Career:** Atlanta Falcons, linebacker, 1993, right linebacker, 1994-96, 1995; Minn Vikings, 1997; Kans City Chiefs, 1998-2000. **Honors/Awds:** All-American, 1992. **Special Achievements:** Film: 1993 NFL Draft, 1993.

### GEORGE, STUART
Executive, vice president (organization). **Educ:** Franklin Univ, BA, banking & finance. **Career:** State Teachers Retirement Syst Ohio, sr equity trader; Del Investments, sr vpres, head equity trading, 1997-. **Orgs:** Trader Forum; Wall St Friends; Buy-Side Equity Traders Roundtable; co-Chmn, Nasdaq Instnl Traders Adv Coun. **Honors/Awds:** "Black Enterprise," 75 Most Powerful Blacks on Wall Street, 2011. **Business Addr:** Senior Vice President, Head of Equity Trading, Delaware Investments, 2005 Market St 30, Philadelphia, PA 19103-7094, **Business Phone:** (215)255-2300.

### GEORGE, TATE CLAUDE
Basketball player, executive. **Personal:** Born May 29, 1968, Newark, NJ; children: Alexis & Jasmine. **Educ:** Univ Conn, attended 1990. **Career:** Basketball player (retired), exec; NJ Nets, 1990-93; Quad City Thunder, 1993-95; Milwaukee Bucks, 1995; Conn Pride, 1995-96; Rockford Lightning, 1996-97; Ft Wayne Fury, 1997; George Group, pres, chief exec officer, chmn bd dirs, currently. **Business Addr:** President, Chief Executive Officer, The George Group, 15 S Essex Ave, Orange, NJ 07050, **Business Phone:** (862)252-0664.

### GEORGE, DR. THEODORE ROOSEVELT, JR.
Physician. **Personal:** Born Dec 27, 1934, Cincinnati, OH; son of Theodore R and Christine Tatum; married Jeanne Sharpe; children: Theodore III & Blair. **Educ:** Howard Univ, BS, 1956, MD, 1960. **Career:** Freedman's Hosp, intern, 1961, resident, 1967; DC Gen Hosp, Howard Univ Hosp, WA Hosp Ctr, intern, resident Obstet & Gynec, physician; Howard Univ Col Med, asst prof; DC Gen Hosp, sr med officer; physician, currently. **Orgs:** Nat Med Asn, Med Soc DC, Chi Delta Mu Med Soc; Former Interns & Resd Freedmen's Hosp, Am Asn Gynec Laparoscopists, Alpha Phi Alpha Frat; WAGyn EC Soc; Medico-Chirurgical Soc; Pan AMA, Urban League; Jr Citizens Corps; Nat AsnAdvan Colored People; Police Boy's Club; MD Med Lic, 1960; DC Med Lic, 1965; trustee bd, St Paul Am Ch; Daniel Hale Williams Reading Club, 1972-; Southern Med Asn, 1980-; Howard Univ Med Alumni Asn. **Honors/Awds:** Natioanlional Competitive Scholarship, 1952-56; Dean's list, 1952-56; Representative Aviation Award, 1954; Dean's Cup, 1955; Presidents Cup, 1956; AFROTC Award, 1956; Outstanding Male Gradugate Student Counsel, 1956; Graduate Cum Laude, 1956; Natioanlional Medical Asn Scholarship, 1957; Psychiatric Award, 1960; Delivery in Elderly Primagravida Following Myomectomy, 1964; Vascular Systems Recovery of Red Blood Cells from the Peritonial Cavity, 1965; Concomittant Use of Stomaseptin & Metronidazole in the Treatment of Trichomonas Vaginalis Complicated by Moniliasis, 1966; Pelvic Exenteration, 1967; The Changing Role of Crean Section, 1969; Natioanl Medical Asn Award, 1967; American Physicians Recognition Award, 1972; American Academy of Family Physicians Award, 1974; Howard Univ Med Alumni Asn Award, 1974; American Cancer Soc Cert of Merit, 1975; Natioanl Fraternal Order of Police, 1976; Wyeth Teaching Award, 1993. **Home Addr:** 1840 Primrose Rd NW, Washington, DC 20012, **Home Phone:** (202)726-7534. **Business Addr:** Physician, General and Family Practice, 5505 5th St NW, Washington, DC 20011, **Business Phone:** (202)726-4847.

### GEORGE-BOWDEN, DR. REGINA
Educator. **Personal:** Born Mar 14, 1947, Durham, NC; daughter of Johnetta Holloway George and Reginald C George; married Marcel Bowden; children: Morris LaSalle. **Educ:** Tenn State Univ, BS, sociol, 1968; NC Cent Univ, MA, sociol, 1971; NC A & T Univ, MS, educ admin, MEd, 1977; NC State Univ, EdD, sociol, educ, 1989; Univ Ghana, Africa, fac study abroad educ, econs & sociol; Duke Univ, NC, Latin Am studies. **Career:** NC A&T State Univ, asst prof sociol, 1972-77; Shaw Univ, prof sociol & educ, 1990-2000; Durham Tech Community Col, laison teacher educ prog; NC Cent Univ, Teacher Liaison, dir campus ministries, currently; co chair, Durham Bus & Prof chain. **Orgs:** Sch bd mem, vice chmn, Durham Pub Schs; sr bd mem, NC Cent Univ; pres black caucus, chair profession, Southern Sociol Socs; pres fac senate, Shaw Univ; bd mem, Contemp Sociol J; Delta Sigma Theta; Durham Chap Girl Friends Inc; N Carolina Sociol Asn; Pi Gamma Mu; Nat Social Sci Hon Soc; Nat Educr Asn; Am Sociol Asn. **Home Addr:** 232 Monticello Ave, Durham, NC 27707, **Home Phone:** (919)490-1294. **Business Addr:** Director of Campus Ministries, North Carolina Central University, 1801 Fayetteville St, Durham, NC 27707, **Business Phone:** (919)530-6100.

### GERALD, PASTOR ARTHUR THOMAS, JR.
Clergy, school administrator. **Personal:** Born Oct 13, 1947, Boston, MA; son of Arthur (deceased) and Sarah; married Henrietta Williams; children: Arthur Michael & Alama Michelle. **Educ:** Lincoln Univ, attended 1967; Berkshire Christian Col, AB, Theol, 1970; Gordon Conwell Sem, MA, 1972; Salem State Univ, Humane Lett, Hon Degree. **Career:** Salem State Col, advisor afro-am soc, 1972-73, dir minority affairs, 1973-81, assoc dean acad affairs, 1981-; Minister gospel Jesus Christ, 1976; Massachusetts House Representatives; Twelfth Baptist Church, ministerial staff, assoc minister, interim pastor, pastor, 2010; Sch Bible, dean; youth dir, Norfolk House Centre. **Orgs:** Assoc minister 12th Baptist Ch; chair, Preschool Directorate Bd; chair, Human Resource Comt, Twelfth Baptist Church. **Honors/Awds:** Numerous Honors. **Special Achievements:** Thirteenth pastor of historic Twelfth Baptist Church. **Home Addr:** 31 Holyoke St, Lynn, MA 01905, **Home Phone:** (781)595-5522. **Business Addr:** Pastor, Twelfth Baptist Church, 150-160 Warren St, Roxbury, MA 02119, **Business Phone:** (617)442-7855.

### GERALD, DR. MELVIN DOUGLAS, SR.
Association executive, physician. **Personal:** Born Jul 17, 1942, Cerro Gordo, NC; son of Paul Sr and Mattie Vann; married Lenora Graham; children: Sonja Z & Melvin D Jr. **Educ:** Morehouse Col, Atlanta, BS, 1964; Howard Univ, MD, 1970; Johns Hopkins Univ, Sch Pub Health, MPH, 1974. **Career:** Freedmens Howard Univ Hosp, family med resident; Shaw Community Health Ctr, med dir, 1973-75; Howard Univ, asst prof, 1974-, dir, family pract, 1976-78; Gerald Family Care Assoc, physician, 1978-, pres & chief exec officer, currently; Providence Hosp, chmn, Dept Family Pract, 1989-93; Howard Univ Hosp Med, pres, 1996-98; G&G Family Care, pres & chief exec officer, currently; Columbus Regional Healthcare Syst, physician, currently. **Orgs:** Bd dir, Md State Cancer Soc, 1979-85; pres, DC Acad Family Physicians, 1992-94; chair, Dept FP, Prince Georges Hosp Ctr, 1994-98; pres, Howard Univ Med Alumni Asn, 1996-98; pres med staff, Howard Univ Hosp, 1996-98; bd dir, Am Acad Family Physicians, 1996-99; steering comt, Howard Univ. **Honors/Awds:** Received numerous outstanding awards. **Home Addr:** 11403 Dundee Dr, Mitchellville, MD 20721, **Home Phone:** (301)262-6674. **Business Addr:** Physician, Columbus Regional Healthcare System, 14508 James B White Hwy S, Tabor City, NC 28463, **Business Phone:** (910)653-7000.

### GERMAN, JAMMI DARNELL
Football player. **Personal:** Born Jul 4, 1974, Ft. Myers, FL. **Educ:** Miami Univ, grad. **Career:** Football player (retired); Atlanta Falcons, wide receiver, 1998-2000; Cleveland Browns, senior receiver & wide receiver, 2001. **Honors/Awds:** Mr Football Award, 1992; Walter Kichefski Football Award.

### GERMANY, ALBERT (AL GEE)
Disc jockey, administrator, executive director. **Personal:** Born Oct 23, 1942, Leeds, AL; married Jessica Khan; children: Mark & Shawn. **Educ:** Univ Pittsburgh, Geo Heide Sch Announcing, attended 1964. **Career:** WAMO, 1964-66; WZUM, Pittsburgh, 1966-68; WWRL, 1968-72; WOOK-AM, Washington Radio, 1968; WPIX, 1972; WLIB, NY, prog dir, 1973; Syndicated Radio Show Rap & Rhythm; Radio Station ZDK, co-owner; Nat Asn Radio & TV Announcers, exec dir, 1976-77; St Johns Antiqua Prof Black Announcers NY, West Indies pres. **Home Addr:** 180 E Pennywood Ave, Roosevelt, NY 11575.

### GERMANY, SYLVIA MARIE ARMSTRONG
College administrator. **Personal:** Born Jan 10, 1950, New Orleans, LA; married Plenty Morgan Jr; children: Jobyna Joidella & Adam Nathan. **Educ:** Southern Univ, New Orleans, BS, 1980, MA. **Career:** Orleans Parish Sch Bd, admin exec secy, 1977-80; Pre-Employ Prog, bus instr, 1980-81; Sidney N Collier Vo-Tech, bus instr, 1981-85; Oakwood Col, personnel assist, 1985, dir human resource mgt, dep title IX coordr, currently. **Orgs:** La Vo-Tech Asn, 1981-85; Am Soc Personnel Administrators, 1985-. **Home Addr:** PO Box 11452, Huntsville, AL 35814-1452, **Home Phone:** (256)726-7274. **Business Addr:** Director of Human Resources, Oakwood College, 7000 Adventist Blvd NW, Huntsville, AL 35896, **Business Phone:** (256)726-7274.

### GERREN, ASHLEIGH TAYLOR. See TAYLOR, GERREN.

### GERVIN, GEORGE
Basketball coach, basketball player, founder (originator). **Personal:** Born Apr 27, 1952, Detroit, MI; married Joyce; children: George Jr, Jared & Tia Monique. **Educ:** Eastern Mich Univ, attended 1972. **Career:** Basketball player (retired), coach, association executive; Va Squires, 1972-74; Phoenix Suns, 1974; San Antonio Spurs, 1974-85, community rels rep, 1992, asst coach, 1993, community rels dept, 1994; Chicago Bulls, 1985-86; Banco Roma, 1986-87; Quad City Thunder (CBA), 1989; TDK Manresa, 1989-90; George Gervin Youth Ctr Inc, founder, 1991-. **Orgs:** Continental Basketball Asn Quad City Thunder, 1989-90; NBA Hall Fame; George Gervin Youth Ctr Inc, founder, 1991-. **Home Addr:** 44 Gervin Pass, Spring Branch, TX 78070-6370. **Business Addr:** Founder, George Gervin Youth Center Inc, 6903 S Sunbelt Dr, San Antonio, TX 78218, **Business Phone:** (210)568-8800.

### GHENT, HENRI HERMANN
Writer, museum director, critic. **Personal:** Born Jun 23, 1926, Birmingham, AL; son of Reuben Gantt and Jennie Gantt. **Educ:** New Eng Conserv, Boston, MA, attended 1951; Mus Sch Fine Arts, Boston, MA, attended 1952; Longy Sch Music, Cambridge, MA, attended 1953; Univ Paris, France, attended 1960. **Career:** Martha Baird Rockefeller fel Music, 1957-58; Elegant Mag, New York, cult news ed, 1964-68; Inst Arts & Sci, Brooklyn, asst dir, 1968-69; Brooklyn Mus, Com Gallery, dir, 1968-72; Le Monde de la Musique, Paris, New York corres; Danser Mag, Paris; Ford Found Travel & Study fel, 1974-75. **Orgs:** Chief juror, Grad Stud Art & Design, Pratt Inst, Brooklyn, NY, 1972; chief juror, Dayton Art Inst, All-Ohio Painting Sculpture Biennial, 1972; consult, Nat Endowment Arts, Wash, DC, 1973-74; Nat Asn Advan Colored People. **Honors/Awds:** Marian Anderson Scholarship Award, 1951, 1952; Art Critics Award, Nat Endowment Arts, Wash, DC, 1973-74; Samuel H Kress Found Award in Arts Research; Achievement in the Arts Award, Nat Asn Advan Colored People, 1973. **Special Achievements:** Hon degree humanities, Allen Univ, Columbia, SC, 1966; Contributed significant articles on visual & performing arts to Le Monde de la Musique Paris, New York Times, Los Angeles Times, Cleveland Plain Dealer, Art Int, Lugano, Switz, Artforum, New York, Art in America, New York, Boston Globe, Village Voice, New York. **Home Addr:** 310 E 75th St Apt 1F, New York, NY 10021-3315, **Home Phone:** (212)472-1976. **Business Addr:** New York Correspondent, Le Monde de la Musique, 310 E 75th St, New York, NY 10021-3315, **Business Phone:** (212)472-1976.

### GHOLSON, DR. GENERAL JAMES
Musician, educator. **Personal:** Born Oct 15, 1944, Norfolk, VA; son of G James and Elsie; children: Christopher James. **Educ:** Mich State Univ, BM, 1966; Cath Univ, MM, 1970, DMA, 1975. **Career:** USN Band, Wash, DC, sect clarinetist & solist, 1966-70; Cath Univ, Wash, DC, grad asst, 1970-72; Opera Memphis, solo clarinet, 1972; Memphis State Univ, instr, asst prof, assoc prof clarinet, 1972-99, prof, 1999, retired; Memphis Woodwind Quintet, 1972-99, prof, 1999-; Memphis Sym, solo clarinet, 1975, prin clarinet. **Orgs:** Vol, SMART House; bd dir, Promise Acad, Memphis, 2004-08; Memphis Woodwind Quintet; bd mem, Eroica Ensemble. **Honors/Awds:** FLAME Award, Univ Memphis, 2007. **Special Achievements:** Author: The Seasonal Clarinetist; The Seasoned Clarinetist; videos: How to Make All West, Jamus, 1985; Kards in the Key of Kroepsch, Jamus, 1986; How to Make All Region a Breeze, Jamus, 1986; Project Solo, Jamus, 1987; First African-american Professor In The Rudi E. Scheidt School Of Music, 1972. **Home Addr:** 1311 Parkland, Memphis, TN 38111, **Home Phone:** (901)743-0109. **Business Addr:** Professor of Clarinet, University of Memphis, Suite 293 Music, Memphis, TN 38152, **Business Phone:** (901)678-3793.

### GHOLSON, ROBERT L.
Executive, president (organization). **Educ:** Tenn State Univ, BS, bus admin; Univ Memphis, MBA; Life Off Mgt Asn, cert, educ & mgt credits. **Career:** Universal Life Ins Co, memphis, pres, 1995-. **Orgs:** Bd mem, Memphis Boys Club; bd mem, Jr Achievement. **Home Addr:** 5111 Skippy St, Memphis, TN 38116-8340, **Home Phone:** (901)332-3564. **Business Addr:** President, Universal Life Insurance Co, 480 Linden Ave, Memphis, TN 38106, **Business Phone:** (901)775-0930.

### GHOLSTON, BETTY J. BLUE
School administrator, vice president (organization). **Personal:** Born Feb 1, 1942, Wagram, NC; married Willie Gunter; children: Lisa Regina, Betty Cornelia, Saranarda & Willie G Jr. **Educ:** NC Cent Univ, BS, com, 1963; NC Agr & Tech State Univ, MS, admin, 1979; Univ NC, further study, 1978. **Career:** Richmond County Schs, media specialist, 1968, job placement coordr, 1984; Cameron Morrison Sch, media specialist, 1968-77; Cameron Morrison Youth Ctr, proj dir & media specialist, 1977-83; NC Dept Correction, dir fed proj & educ spec; Scotland Spring Hill Twp, vice chmn, currently. **Orgs:** Bd Comnrs, Mayor Pro Tem Wagram, 1974-; founder, Wagram Br Libr, 1975; vpres, Cameron Morrison NCAE, 1982-83; rep, NC Coun Govt-Region N, 1982-; bd dir, Black Elected Munic Officials, 1983-84; vice chair, Scotland Co Bd Educ, 1986-98. **Honors/Awds:** Teacher of the Year, NC Dept of Youth Serv, 1977. **Home Addr:** 21681 Ctr St, Wagram, NC 28396, **Home Phone:** (910)369-2964. **Business Addr:** Vice Chair, Scotland County Government, 21681 Ctr St, Wagram, NC 28396, **Business Phone:** (910)369-2964.

### GIBBONS, DEVERON M.
Lobbyist, vice president (organization). **Personal:** children: 2. **Educ:** Univ Fla, BA, polit sci, 1995; Univ S Fla, MS, pub admin, 2006; Fla Agr & Mech Univ, JD, banking, corp, finance & securities law, 2017. **Career:** Mayor St Petersburg, spec asst; Holland & Knight, sr pub affairs adv, 2003-05; Amscot Financial Corp, vpres, pub affairs, 2004-. **Orgs:** Bd Gov, St Petersburg Area Chamber Com; chair, Chambers S Cent Coun; bd mem, local Nat Asn Advan Colored People; Water Leadership Adv Bd, Univ S Fla; bd mem, Worknet Pinellas; bd trustee, St Petersburg Col, 2006-. **Business Addr:** Vice President of Public Affairs, Amscot Financial Corp, 600 N Westshore Blvd, Tampa, FL 33609.

### GIBBONS, ELLA MAE TURNER. See TURNER-GIVENS, ELLA MAE.

### GIBBONS, GERARD
President (organization). **Personal:** married Nickye; children: Grant & Kenedi. **Educ:** Howard Univ, BA, mkt, 1989; Ariz State Univ, MBA, 1999. **Career:** Am Expressway, sales assoc, 1987-89; United Parcel Serv (UPS) Inc, package car driver, 1989-90, pres US sales, 1989-, acct exec, 1990-91, nat acct mgr, 1991-95, dir sales desert mountain region, 1995-99, vpres sales S Cent region, 1999-2001, vpres sales Southwest region. **Orgs:** Bd mem, Atlanta Women's Resource Ctr to End Domestic Violence; 100 Black Men Atlanta; Urban League's Black

Exec Exchange Prog. **Home Addr:** , Alpharetta, GA. **Business Addr:** President US Sales, United Parcel Service(UPS).

### GIBBS, JACK GILBERT, JR.

Lawyer. **Personal:** Born Aug 11, 1953, Columbus, OH; son of Jack Gilbert Sr and Ruth Ann; married Aloma C; children: Jack Gilbert III & Anna Louise. **Educ:** Mich St Univ, BA, 1975; Capital Univ Law Sch, JD, 1981. **Career:** Columbus Pub Schs, teacher, 1976-78; Ohio Atty Gen, legal intern, 1980-81; Ben Espy, law clerk, 1982; Self Employed, atty, 1982-; Supreme Ct Ohio, monitoring atty. **Orgs:** Sustaining mem & found fel Columbus Bar Asn, 1982-; Ohio St Bar Asn, 1982-; Am Bar Asn, 1982-; bd mem, pres, Hilltop Civic Coun Inc, 1987-93; chmn admin bd, Centenary United Methodist Church, 1987-95; Capital Law Sch Black Alumni, pres, 1990-; UNCF Star Panelist, star panelist, 1993-; Am Inns Ct, 1994-; bd counr, Capital Univ Law Sch, 2006-07. **Honors/Awds:** Community Service Award, Columbus Dispatch, 1988; Community Service Award, Ohio St Univ Bus Sch, 1989; Service Award, Capital Law Sch, 1990; Service Award, Hilltop Civic Coun Inc, 1994; David D White Award, African Am Law Alumni Asn, 2004. **Special Achievements:** Written serveral articles on Probate Law & Estate Planning. **Home Addr:** 3855 McDannald Dr, Columbus, OH 43230, **Home Phone:** (614)475-0569. **Business Addr:** Sustaining Member, Foundation Fellow, Columbus Bar Directory, 580 S High St Suite 300, Columbus, OH 43215-5644, **Business Phone:** (614)224-3191.

### GIBBS, DR. JEWELLE TAYLOR

Educator. **Personal:** Born Nov 4, 1933, Stratford, CT; daughter of Margaret P Morris and Julian A; married James Lowell Jr; children: Geoffrey Taylor & Lowell Dabney. **Educ:** Radcliffe Col, BA, social rels, behav sci, 1955, cert bus admin, 1959; Univ Calif, MSW, 1970, MA, psychol, 1977, PhD, psychol, 1980. **Career:** US Labor Dept, Wash, jr mgt asst, 1955-56; Pillsbury Co, Minneapolis, MN, mkt res analyst, 1959-61; Stanford Univ, psychiat, clin social worker, 1970-75, 1978-79; Univ Calif, Berkeley, prof, 1979-2000, Sch Social Welfare, prof emer, currently; Zellerbach Family Fund Chair Social Policy, Community Chg & Pract, Berkeley. Books: Young, Black & Male Am: An Endangered Species, ed, 1988; Preserving Privilege: California Politics, Propositions and People of Color; Children of Color: Psychological Interventions with Culturally Diverse Youth; Race and Justice: Rodney King and O.J. Simpson in a House Divided. **Orgs:** John Hay Whitney Opport Fel, Radcliffe Col, 1958-59; task force specp opulations, Pres Comn Ment Health, 1976-78; NIMH Pre-Doctoral Fel, Univ Calif, 1979-80; bd publs, Nat Asn Social Workers, 1980-82; bd regents, Univ Santa Clara, 1980-85; ed bd, Am J Orthopsychiatry, 1980-84; clinicalpsychol, pvt pract consult, 1983-90; consult, Carnegie Corp, 1983-87; fel, Bunting Inst, Radcliffe Col, 1985; bd dir, Am Orthopsychiatric Asn, 1985-88; Adv Bd, Nat Ctr C Poverty, 1987-95; fel, Am Psychol Asn, 1990; vpres, bd trustee, Radcliffe Col, 1991-95; ed bd, Int J SocialWelfare, 1998-2002. vpres, bd trustee, Van LobenSells Found, 1999-; bd dir, Theatre Works, 1999-2002. **Home Addr:** 857 Sonoma Terr, Stanford, CA 94305, **Home Phone:** (650)857-9005. **Business Addr:** Professor Emeritus, University of California, 120 Haviland Hall Suite 7400, Berkeley, CA 94720-7400, **Business Phone:** (510)642-1660.

### GIBBS, KAREN PATRICIA

Television news anchorperson. **Personal:** Born May 9, 1952, Boston, MA; daughter of James and Bertha. **Educ:** Roosevelt Univ, Chicago, BSBA, 1976; Univ Chicago Grad Sch Bus, MBA, finance & mkt, 1978. **Career:** CBOT, Mkt Reporter, 1970-76; Cont Commodity Serv Inc, interest rate specialist 1978-82; Chicago Bd Trade; Harris Trust & Savings Bank, govt securities rep 1982-83; Dean Witter Reynolds, hedging & trading strategist 1982-92, sr financial futures analyst 1985-, vpres, 1985-92; CNBC, specialist, anchor, 1992-97; FOX News Channel, anchor & sr bus reporter, 1992-2005; Md Pub Tv, co-anchor, 2005-05, personal finance & investing expert, 2012-; CME Group, 2005-06; Retirement Living TV, 2007-08; MoneyShow.com, video network host, 2009-11; Nightly Bus Report, contribr, 2011-12; Wall St Week, co-anchor, currently. **Orgs:** Bd dir, Henry Booth House 1981-85; bd dir, Chicago Lung Asn 1983-86; pres, Dorchester Condo Asn, 1984-89; Chicago Chap Nat Black MBA Asn, 1985-86; Nat Asn Security Prof; Chicago Pvt Indust Coun, 1990-92; Univ Ill Chicago, Col Med Corp Adv Bd; Off Invests & Audits; Pub Broadcasting Serv. **Home Addr:** 109 Homewood Ave, Allendale, NJ 07401-2217. **Business Addr:** Co-Anchor, Wall Street Week, Md Pub TV, Owings Mills, MD 21117.

### GIBBS, KEVIN CASEY

Executive, baseball player. **Personal:** Born Apr 3, 1974, Washington, DC. **Educ:** Old Dom Univ. **Career:** Yakima Bears, 1995; San Bernardino, 1995-97, 2000; Vero Beach Dodgers, 1995-96, 2000; Los Angeles Dodgers, 1996, 1999-2001; San Antonio Missions, 1997, 2000; Albuquerque Isotopes, 1998-99, 2000; Carolina, 2000; Colo Rockies, left field, 2001; Tampa Bay Devil Rays, 2002; Norwich Navigators, 2002; Camdan, 2003; Clearwater Threshers, 2004; Reading Phillies, 2004; Philadelphia Phillies, outfielder, 2004, 2011; Diamond Skills Baseball, founder & dir, currently; St John's High School, hitting and outfield coach. **Business Addr:** Director, Founder, Diamond Skills Baseball, 5509 Golf Lane, Rockville, MD 20852, **Business Phone:** (301)570-2833.

### GIBBS, MARLA (MARGARET THERESA BRADLEY)

Actor. **Personal:** Born Jun 14, 1931, Chicago, IL; daughter of Douglas Bradley and Ophelia Birdie Kemp; married Jordan Gibbs; children: Angela Elayne, Jordan Joseph Jr & Dorian Demetrius. **Educ:** Cortez Peters Bus Col, attended 1952. **Career:** Serv Bindery, receptionist, 1951-56; Kelly Girls, 1956; Gotham Hotel, switchboard operator, 1957; United Airlines, travel consult, 1963-74; Marla Gibbs Enterprises, pres, 1978; Hormar Inc, vpres, 1978; Marla's Memory Lanes, restaurant owner; actress, currently; Films: Sweet Jesus, Preacherman, 1973; Black Belt Jones, 1974; Passing Through, 1977; NobodysChild, 1986; Menu for Murder, 1990; Florence, 1990; Up Against the Wall, 1991; Last Breeze of Summer, 1991; The Meteor Man, 1993; Lily in Winter, 1994; Border to Border, 1998; Foolish, 1999; Lost & Found, 1999; TheVisit, 2000; Stanley's Gig, 2000; The Brothers, 2001; The Ties That Bind, 2006; The Heart Specialist, 2006; The What Goes Around Short Film 2009, 2009; "Just Like Family", assoc producer, 2009; Devil's Land, 2009; Sunnyview, 2010; Who Killed Soul Glow?, 2012; C'mon Man, 2012; Madea's Witness Protection, 2012; Forbidden Woman, 2013; Grantham & Rose, 2014. TV series: "The Jeffersons", 1975-85, writer, 1984; The Missing Are Deadly, 1975; "Barney Miller", 1975; "Arthur Hailey's the Moneychangers", 1976; YouCan't Take It with You, 1979; "Checking In", 1981; The Love Boat, 1981; "Pryor's Place", 1984; "227", producer, 1982, actress, 1985-90, writer, 1987-90; Menu for Murder, 1990; "A DifferentWorld", 1993; "In the Heat of the Night", 1993; "Empty Nest", 1993; Lilyin Winter, 1994; "Burke's Law", 1995; "Martin", 1995; "The Fresh Prince of Bel-Air", 1996; "101 Dalmatians: The Series", 1997-98; "The Hughleys", 1998-2002; "Martial Law", 1999; "Happily Ever After: Fairy Tales for EveryChild", 1999; "Dawson's Creek", 1999; "Touched by an Angel", 2000; "Judging Amy", 2001; "Mother's Day", 2001; "The King of Queens", 2002; "The Rerun Show", 2002; "Arli$$", 2002; "Profiles in Agenting", 2002; "Passions", 2004; "Listen Up", 2004; "ER", 2005; "Only Connect", 2005; "Cold Case", 2005; "It's Never Too Late", co-writer, 227's theme song 2006; "Lincoln Heights", 2008; "House of Payne", 2011; "Southland", 2012; "The First Family", 2012-13; "Mr. Box Office", 2013. **Orgs:** Treas, UGMAA Found; Crenshaw Pres: Sci Mind Church; Am Fedn TV & Radio Artists; hon mem, Alpha Kappa Alpha Sorority. **Honors/Awds:** Numerous honors & awards including Award, Nat Acad Arts & Sci, 1976; Award, Miss Black Culture Pageant, 1977; Award, United Negro Col Fund, 1977; Appreciation Award, La Sch Dist, 1978; Award, Women Involved, 1979; Tribute to the Black Woman Award, WISE, 1979; Community Service Award, Crenshaw High Sch, 1980; Award, Paul Robeson Players, 1980; Emmy Award, nominations, Outstanding Performance, supporting actress, 1981-85; Image Award, Nat Asn Advan Colored People, 1982; Golden Globe Nominee for Best Performance, 1985; Best Supporting Actress, 2000; EOTM Award, 2013. **Home Addr:** 8461 Vermont Ave, Los Angeles, CA 90068, **Home Phone:** (310)275-6028. **Business Addr:** Actress, Comedienne, c/o Buzz Halliday & Associates, 144 S Doheny Dr Suite 206, Los Angeles, CA 90048, **Business Phone:** (310)275-6028.

### GIBBS, NATHANIEL K.

Artist, painter (artist). **Personal:** Born Jun 15, 1948, Baltimore, MD; son of John W and Rosie M. **Educ:** MD Inst Col Art, BFA, fine arts, 1975; Am Univ, Wash, DC, MFA, fine arts, painting, 1981; Schuler Sch Fine Arts. **Career:** Baltimore City Mural Prog, 1981; Sch 33 Art Ctr, workshop instr, 1982-84; Studio 55 LLC, Solo Art Exhib; self-employed painter, currently. **Orgs:** Baltimore Charcoal Club Fine Arts, 1994; gov's adv comt, arts people with disabilities, 1998. **Business Addr:** Artist, Privately, 2432 W Coldspring Lane, Baltimore, MD 21215, **Business Phone:** (410)664-7249.

### GIBBS, ROBERT LEWIS

Circuit court judge, lawyer. **Personal:** Born Jul 26, 1954, Jackson, MS; son of William and Mary; married Debra; children: Ariana & Justis. **Educ:** Tougaloo Col, BA, 1976; Univ Miss, JD, 1979. **Career:** Southeast Miss Legal Serv, staff atty, 1979-80; Seventh Circuit Dist, asst dist atty, 1980; Miss Atty Gen, dep atty gen, 1980-90; Seventh Judicial Dist Miss, circuit judge; Hinds County Circuit Ct, judge, 1991-98; Hope Enterprise Corp, bd dir; First Com Bank, bd dir; Brunini, Grantham, Grower & Hewes LLC, partner, currently. **Orgs:** MS Bar, 1979-; Magnolia Bar Asn, 1979-; pres, Charles Clark Am Inns Ct, 1999-2001; Am Trial Nat Bar Asn, 1992-; Lawyers Asn, 1993-; Hinds County Bar Asn; Nat Bar Asn; Tougaloo Col Alumni Asn; pres, Miss Bar Found; pres, 100 Black Men Jackson; pres, Bar Asn Fifth Circuit; fel Miss Young Lawyers; Am Col Trial Lawyers; chmn, Miss Bar Asn; fel Am Bar Asn; Magnolia Bar Asn; Hinds County Bar Asn; Nat Bar Asn; bd mem, Jam Found Bd; Tougaloo Col Alumni Asn; bd mem, Metro Crime Comn; bd mem, Coha; Clarion-Ledger Ed bd; 100 Black Men Jackson Inc; pres, Charles Clark Chap Am Inns Ct; Fels Miss Young Lawyers; fel Am Col Trial Lawyers; bd chmn, United Way Capital Area; Mission Miss, Jackson Chamber Partnership; Jubilee! Jam, Festival Chair, 1998; William Winer Inst Racial Reconciliation; bd gov, Fifth Circuit Bar, 2000-02; chairperson, Ct Liaison & Judicial Admin Comt Miss Bar, 1999-2001; Miss Supreme Ct, Comn Bar Admis Rev; pres & bd dir, Jackson Conv & Visitors Bur; pres & bd dir, Hope Fed Credit Union; pres, New Life Women; pres, Arts Alliance; bd mem, Jubilee! Jam Found Bd; trustee, Leadership Jackson. **Honors/Awds:** Community Serv Award, Black Women Polit Action Forum, 1995; Outstanding Leadership, Serv & Dedication, Magnolia Bar Asn, 1998; Award Distinction, Univ Miss, 1988; Govt Serv Award, Magnolia Bar Assn, 1989; Award Appreciation, Tougaloo Col, 1991; Community Serv Award, Alpha Kappa Alpha, 1992; Thurgood Marshall Judge Award; Jack Young Sr Atty Award, Jackson Br NAACP; He ranked prestigious Best Lawyers Am dir; Vol Yr, Goodwill Industs, 2004; Distinguish Serv Award, Miss Bar Asn, 2004; Jackson Young, Sr Award, Jackson Br, NACCP, 2004; Lawyer Yr, 2007; Super Lawyers Top 50 Miss, Gen Litigation; Law-Related Pub Educ Award, Miss Bar Asn, 2007; Tourism Visionary Award, Jackson Conventions & Visitors Bur; Outstanding Leadership Award, Tougaloo Col; Community Servant Award, New Horizon; Professionalism Award, Capital Area Bar Asn; Image Award, Phi Beta Sigma Fraternity. **Home Addr:** 5962 Holbrook Dr, Jackson, MS 39206-2062, **Home Phone:** (601)940-0027. **Business Addr:** Partner, Brunini, Grantham, Grower & Hewes LLC, 1400 Trustmark Bldg 248 E Capitol St Suite 1400, Jackson, MS 39201, **Business Phone:** (601)960-6861.

### GIBBS, DR. SANDRA E.

Educator, association executive, administrator. **Personal:** Born Aug 16, 1942, Chicago, IL; daughter of Louis Shelby and Willa Marie Hurd. **Educ:** AM & N Col, AB, AM, Eng, 1964; Univ Ill, AM, Eng, 1971, PhD, Eng, 1974. **Career:** Cognitive/Engineering Psychologist; Little Rock Ark Pub Sch, high sch Eng teacher, 1964-70; Univ IL, teacher fresh rhtrc, 1970-71; Nat Coun Teacher Eng, prin investr, dir min affairs spec proj, 1973-77, dir spec progs & assoc exec dir, currently; IBM, exec consult; Enterprise Human Resources Integration Proj, proj dir. **Orgs:** Con AR Dept Educ Little Rock Ark, 1969; mem & adv bd, Prime Time Sch TV, 1975; consult, HEW Women's Proj Benedict Col, 1978-80; prop reviewer, Nat Endowment Humanities, 1979; Delta Sigma Theta Soc; Alpha Kappa Mu Hon Soc. **Honors/Awds:** Teachers Chairs of English Fellow, 1971; Crest Co Scholar, 1960-64; NDEA Fellow, 1966-67; Distinguished Alumni Citation, Nat Asn Equal Opportunity Higher Educ, 1986. **Special Achievements:** Publications: co-editor, A Celebration of Teachers, 1986, National Council of Teachers of English; "Black Novels Revisited," New Directions For Women, 1987; "Maria Stewart: Heroic Role Model," New Directions for Women, 1988; "A Symphony of Voices," Maryand English Journal, 1989; "Considering Diversity in Teaching Language and Literature," Michigan English Teacher, 1990; Zelma Watson George biographical sketch, Notable Black American Women. **Home Addr:** 1812 Braodmoor Dr, Champaign, IL 61821-5854. **Business Addr:** Associate Executive Director, Director of Special Programs, National Council of Teachers of English, 1111 W Kenyon Rd, Urbana, IL 61801-1096, **Business Phone:** (217)328-3870.

### GIBBS, WILLIAM LEE

Banker, chief executive officer, educator. **Personal:** Born Apr 11, 1945, Hinton, WV; son of William McKinley and Louise A; married Amporn Mankong; children: Vince Visuti. **Educ:** WVa State Col, BS, 1972. **Career:** Am Fletcher Nat Bank, vpres, 1972-82; BankSouth Corp, sr vpres, 1983-92; Stonier Grad Sch Banking, fac, 1984-; Citizens Trust Bank, pres & chief exec officer, 1992-97. **Orgs:** Assoc dir, Am Bankers Asn, 1982-83; bd mem, United Way Metrop Atlanta, 1992-; Atlanta Action Forum, 1993-; bd & exec mem, Cent Atlanta Prog Comt, 1993-; bd dir, Atlanta Life Ins Co; Atlanta Chamber Com; Am Bankers Asn Community Bank Coun; bd counors, Carter Ctr. **Honors/Awds:** The Pioneer Award, Atlanta Urban Bankers Asn; Honorary Commissioner of Agriculture, State Ind. **Home Addr:** 120 View Hill Ct, Atlanta, GA 30350, **Home Phone:** (770)992-2873. **Business Addr:** President, Chief Executive Officer, Citizens Trust Bank, 75 Piedmont Ave, Atlanta, GA 30303.

### GIBEL, RONALD L.

Executive, chief executive officer. **Career:** Urban Off Prod, pres, chief exec officer, currently. **Business Addr:** President, Chief Executive Officer, Urban Office Products, 251 W 39th St 18th Fl, New York, NY 10018-0766, **Business Phone:** (877)392-5477.

### GIBSON, DR. BENJAMIN F.

Judge, government official. **Personal:** Born Jul 13, 1931, Safford, AL; son of Eddie and Pearl; married Lucille Nelson; children: Charlotte, Linda, Gerald, Gail, Carol & Laura. **Educ:** Wayne State Univ, BS, 1955, LLM, 1980; Detroit Col Law, JD, 1960. **Career:** Judge (retired); City Detroit, acct, 1955-56; Detroit Edison Co, acct, 1956-61; State Mich, asst atty gen, 1961-63; Ingham County MI, asst prosecutor, 1963-64; Lansing MI, pvt pract law, 1964-79; Thomas Cooley Law Sch, prof, 1979-80; US Dist Ct Western Dist Grand Rapids, judge, 1979, chief judge, 1991-95, sr judge, 1996-99. **Orgs:** Grand Rapids Bar Asn; Mich Bar Asn; Black Judges Mich; Fedl Bar Asn; bd dir, Cooley Law Sch; United Way, Proj Blueprint; Floyd H Skinner Bar Asn; Fed Judges Asn; bd dir, Metrop YMCA; Peninsular Club; Beta Gamma fraternity, Sigma Pi Phi fraternity, Delta Theta Phi Law Fraternity; Grand Rapids Found. **Special Achievements:** First African-American appointed assistant prosecuting attorney in Ingham County, Michigan; First African-American professor of law at the Thomas M. Cooley Law School; First African-American Federal Judge & Chief Judge.

### GIBSON, BETTY M.

College administrator, government official. **Personal:** Born May 15, 1938, New Orleans, LA; daughter of Jerome G Greene Sr and Irene L Hannibal Greene; married Kenneth D; children: Tracy Jerome & Tamara Angelique. **Educ:** Ky State Univ, Frankfort, KY, BS, 1961; Eastern Ky Univ, Richmond, KY, MA, 1974. **Career:** College administrator (retired), government official; Fayette County Bd Educ; Lincoln Parish Bd Educ, Ruston, LA, music teacher, 1966-67; Franklin County Bd Educ, Frankfort, KY, music teacher, 1967-79; Va Beach Bd Educ, Va Beach, Va, music teacher, 1979-84; Ky State Univ, Frankfort, KY, asst vpres stud affairs, 1984-88; actg vpres stud affairs, 1988, vpres stud affairs, 1991-2000. **Orgs:** Frankfort Alumni Chap Alpha Kappa Alpha Sorority, 1967-; bd mem, Frankfort Arts Found, 1985-; Good Shepherd Church Parish Coun, 1986-; Top Ladies Distinction Inc; pres, Frankfort Lexington Links Inc, 1990-; dir, Lexington Diocese Comn Black Cath Concerns Comt, 1990-; pres, Beta Upsilon Omega Chap, 1977-78; bd dir, Salvation Army; personnel bd mem Ky State, 2006-10. **Home Addr:** 5400 Louisville Rd, Frankfort, KY 40601, **Home Phone:** (502)223-2746. **Business Addr:** Personnel Board Member, Kentucky State, 28 Fountain Pl, Frankfort, KY 40601, **Business Phone:** (502)564-7830.

**GIBSON, BOB.** See GIBSON, ROBERT.

### GIBSON, DR. CHERYL DIANNE (CHERYL GIBSON FOUNTAIN)

Physician. **Personal:** Born Oct 10, 1955, Detroit, MI; daughter of Dr George and Peggy; married Renzo Fountain; children: Anne Marie Frances Damron. **Educ:** Univ Mich, 1977; Wayne St Univ, MD, 1987. **Career:** Wayne State Univ Sch Med, residency, Mercy Hosp, attend physician, obstet & gynec, 1992-93; Detroit Riverview Hosp, attend physician, obstet & gynec, 1993-; Charles C Vincent Continuing Educ Ctr, med dir, obstet & gynec clin, 1994-; Macomb Hosp Ctr, attend physician obstet & gynec, 1996-; pvt pract obstet & gynec, currently; Oakland Univ, William Beaumont Sch Med, Dept Obstet & Gynec, asst prof, currently. **Orgs:** Nat Asn Advan Colored People, 1970-; Oak Grove Am Church, 1978-; Nat Med Asn, 1984-; Am Med Asn, 1984-; Am Col Obstet & Gynecol, 1984-; Mich St Med Soc, 1984-; Wayne County Med Soc, 1984-; Detroit Med Soc, 1984-; Int Corresp Soc Obstetricians & Gynecologists, 1988-; Southeastern mich Surg Soc, 1989. **Honors/Awds:** Community Service Award, Am Bus Women's Asn, 1995; Community Speaker for Women's Health Issues. **Special Achievements:** Mich Chronicle Newspaper, articles; Established Obstetrics & Gynecology Clinic in Detroit Public Schools for pregnant teens, 1994. **Home Addr:** 15201 W Mcnichols Rd, Detroit, MI 48235-3717, **Home Phone:** (313)837-0560. **Business Addr:** Assistant Professor, Oakland University, 2200 N Squirrel Rd, Rochester, MI 48309, **Business Phone:** (248)370-2100.

**GIBSON, DAMON O'KEITH**
Manager, executive, football player. **Personal:** Born Feb 25, 1975, Houston, TX; married Ruqayya; children: Damon Jr. **Educ:** Iowa Univ, BS, sociol, 1998. **Career:** Football player (retired), executive; Cincinnati Bengals, wide receiver, 1998; Cleveland Browns, 1999; Jacksonville Jaguars, 2001-02; Los Angeles Xtreme, 2001; Atlanta Falcons, wide receiver, 2002; Scottish ClayMores, wide receiver, 2002; Confidential, area mgr, 2009-; rottweilers breeder & trainer. **Honors/Awds:** Offensive Most Valuable Person. **Special Achievements:** TV appearance: H2O: Just Add Water, 2006. Films: The Marine, 2006; The Horseman, 2008. **Home Addr:** 2108 E Canyon Trace Dr, Houston, TX 77095-6551, **Home Phone:** (281)746-7279.

**GIBSON, DERRICK LAMONT**
Baseball player. **Personal:** Born Feb 5, 1975, Winter Haven, FL. **Career:** Baseball player (retired); Rockies, 1993; Bend Rockies, 1994; Asheville Tourists, 1995; New Haven Ravens, 1996-97; Colo Springs Sky Sox, 1997-99; Colo Rockies, outfielder, 1998-99; Calgary Cannons, 2000; Granted Free Agency, 2000; El Paso Diablos, 2001; Tucson Sidewinders, 2001; Duluth-Super Dukes, 2002; Long Island Ducks, 2003; Ark Travelers, 2004; Salt Lake Stingers, outfielder, 2004; Miss Braves, 2005; Richmond Braves, 2005; New Haven County Cutters, 2005-06.

**GIBSON, DR. EDWARD LEWIS**
Physician. **Personal:** Born Jun 6, 1932, Chicago, IL; married Nannette B; children: Joan, Edward Jr & Paula. **Educ:** Roosevelt UL, BS, 1953; Howard Univ Col Med, MD, 1957. **Career:** Physician (retired); Michael Reese Hosp, intern, 1957-58; Columbia-Presbyn Med & Ctr, resident, 1958-62; Columbia Univ, physician, asst prof anesthesiol; Bellevue Med Ctr, vis fel, 1962-64; Princeton Med Ctr, dir anesthesiol, 1967-74; Robert R Moton Memorial Inst, pract; physician, pvt pract. **Orgs:** AMA; Am Soc Anesthesiologists; Am Bd Anesthesiol. **Home Addr:** 47 Locust Lane, Princeton, NJ 08540-4001, **Home Phone:** (609)924-1043.

**GIBSON, ELVIS SONNY**
Consultant. **Personal:** Born Jul 15, 1937, Calvert, TX; married Sylvia M; children: Patricia Elaine. **Educ:** Pk Col, BA, social work, 1973. **Career:** US Dept Housing & Urban Develop, Fair Housing Enforcement, chief; Black United Appeal Inc; social eng consult, currently. **Orgs:** Pres, Black United Fund, Kans City, MO, 1976-; bd dir, Nat Black United Fund, 1978; chmn, Forum Social Expression Inc, 1980; chair, Charlie Parker Acad Arts, 1980; vpres, Black Hist & Geneal, 1980-; bd gov, Bruce Watkins Cult Ctr, 1989-. **Honors/Awds:** Jefferson Award, Taft Broadcasting Corp, 1986; Dr Martin Luther King Distinguished Community Service Award, Gov Mo, 1988; Carl R Johnson Humanitarian Award, Nat Asn Advan Colored People, 2008. **Special Achievements:** Published a book: "Mecca of the New Negro". **Home Addr:** 3550 Wabash Ave, Kansas City, MO 64109-2535, **Home Phone:** (816)861-9107. **Business Addr:** Social Engineering Consultant, Black United Appeal Inc, 3338 Benton Blvd, Kansas City, MO 64128-2021, **Business Phone:** (816)861-1222.

**GIBSON, DR. HARRIS, JR.**
Surgeon, administrator. **Personal:** Born Nov 19, 1936, Mobile, AL; son of Harris Sr and Maude Richardson; married Marva A Boone; children: Michael & Michelle. **Educ:** Ala State Univ, BS, 1956; Northwestern Univ, MS, 1957; Meharry Med Col, MD, 1961. **Career:** USPHS Hosp NY, internship, 1961-62; USPHS Hosp Boston, surg residency, 1962-66; USPHS, asst chief surg; Boston City Hosp Boston Univ, thoracicsurg residency, 1966-68; Cardio-Thoracic Assocs Inc, surgeon, 1969-; Winchester Hosp, chief thoracic surg; Boston Univ Med Sch, asst clinical prof surg; pvt pract cardiothoracic surg, currently. **Orgs:** Pres New Eng Med Soc Nat Med Asn, 1981-82; Middlesex E Dist Med Soc, Am Med Asn 1983-84; Am Med Asn, Soc Thoracic Surg. **Home Addr:** 6 Fox Hunt Lane, Winchester, MA 01890-3655, **Home Phone:** (781)729-2493. **Business Addr:** Surgeon, Thoracic Surgeon, Cardio-Thoracic Assocs Inc, 101 George P Hassett Dr Suite 2, Medford, MA 02155, **Business Phone:** (781)391-0050.

**GIBSON, JOANN**
Tutor, business owner. **Personal:** Born Jul 2, 1946, Detroit, MI; daughter of Frederick E and Loretta; married Ronnie L; children: Drew Allen & Dayna C Harris. **Educ:** Wayne County Community Col, attended 1977; Marygrove Col, Bus & Comput Sci, 1984. **Career:** Bendix Corp, staff, 1965-84; Dyna Path Systs, customer serv, 1984-91; Non-Stop Customer Serv, pres, 1992-09, freelance trainer & facilitator, 2010-12; Wayne State Univ, Detroit Employ Proj, bus consult, 1995-96; Girlbiz Prog, exec dir; Bloomfield, 2013-. **Orgs:** Nat Women's Hist Proj, 1990-; Northwest Area Bus Asn, 1991-; Women on Bd Comt, Detroit Women's Forum, 1995; interim exec dir, Nat Asn Women Bus Owners, 2004; Victory Village Ctr for Community Youth, bd mem, 1996-; adv bd, SBA-Women's Bus Develop Ctr, 1999-; dir, GeorgetownHouses Fox Hills Condo Asn, 2013-; tutor, Oakland Literacy Coun, 2013-. **Honors/Awds:** Business Person of the Month, Northwest Area Bus Asn, 1992, 1994; Jewels of Area D, Detroit Pub Schs, 1992; Mich Women's Historical Ctr & Hall of Fame, Michigan Women: Firsts & Founders; Nat Asn Women Bus Owners, Community Service Award, 1997; National Association of Women Business Owners Leadership Award, 1998; One of the 2006 Top 10 Michigan Business Women, NAWBO Greater Detroit Chapter; Spirit of Detroit Award, City Council of Detroit, Michigan; One of the Most Influential Black Women in Metropolitan Detroit, Women's Informal Network. **Special Achievements:** Listed as one of the Most Influential Black Women in Met Detroit, Women's Informal Network, 1999; Selected as Top 10 Michigan Women in Business by the Greater Detroit Chapter of The National Association of Women Business Owners, 2006; The ABC's of Customer Service, 26 words you can count on to inspire the best service possible. **Business Addr:** Freelance Trainer, Facilitator, Non-Stop Customer Service, 16634 Greenlawn St, Detroit, MI 48221-4912, **Business Phone:** (313)863-3901.

**GIBSON, DR. JOHN THOMAS**
Educator. **Personal:** Born Sep 19, 1948, Montgomery, AL; son of Herman F and L P; married Mayme Voncile Pierce; children: John Thomas Jr, Jerard Trenton, Justin Tarrance & Shayla Voncile. **Educ:** Tuskegee Univ, BS, educ, 1970, MEd, educ admin & finance, Distinguished Mil Grad, 1971; Univ Colo, Boulder, EdS, PhD, 1973; Harvard Univ, cert mgt, 1982. **Career:** President (retired), Professor; Tuskegee Inst, instr phys educ, 1971-72; Smiley Jr High Sch Denver, admin asst, 1971-73; Ala St Univ, dir lab exp, 1973-75, coordr fedrels, 1975-76, coordr, 1976-83, exec asst pres, 1983-86, vpres bus & finance, 1986, Admin & Finance Higher Educ, pres & prof, currently; Affirmative Action Comm Mont Elmore & Autauga Co, chmn, 1976-; Sci & Eng Alliance Inc, pres, 1999-2000; Ala A&M Univ, vpres, bus & finance, chief fiscal officer, 1992-96, pres, 1996-2005, prof, higher educ mgt & finance. **Orgs:** Bd mem, Bellingrath Exec Coun, 1976-; treas, bd trustee, First Congregational Chap, 1977-; secy, IBPOE Elks Southern Pride No 431, 1978; vice polemarch & polemarch, Montgomery Alumni Chap, Kappa Alpha Psi Inc, 1978-; Shaaban Temple No 103, 330 Mason, Optimist Int. **Home Addr:** 151 Heritage Lane, Madison, AL 35758-7975, **Home Phone:** (256)772-3172. **Business Addr:** Professor, Alabama A&M University, Presidential Suite Sch Bus, Normal, AL 35762-1357, **Business Phone:** (256)851-5000.

**GIBSON, JOHNNIE MAE**
Teacher, executive, government official. **Personal:** Born Mar 1, 1949, Caryville, FL; daughter of Alphonso Maldon and Rosa Lee Maldon; married Marvin; children: Tiffany Michele. **Educ:** Chipola Jr Col, FL, AA, nursing, 1968; Albany State Col, GA, BS, health phys educ, 1971; Ga State Univ, GA, MA, MEd, 1976. **Career:** Marianna HS, FL, high sch teacher, 1971-72; Albany, GA Police Dept, policewoman, Ct liaison officer, 1972-76; FBI, FL, spec agt, 1976-79; Fed Bur Invest, Wash, spec agt, 1979-82; Fed Bur Invest, White Collar Crime Div, supvry spec agt, 1981-82; Off Cong & Pub Affairs, supvry spec agt, 1982-87; Fed Bur Invest, unit supvr, 1987-88; Fed Bur Invest, fugitive & bank robbery supvr, 1988-89; Criminal Investigative Div FBI-Detroit, supvry spec agt, 1988-93; Unit Chief Bur, applicant invest unit, FBI head, 1993-99. **Orgs:** NOBLE, 1981-; Capital Press Club, 1982-; guest lectr, Hist Black Cols Univs, 1982-; vis lect, Urban League Black Exec Exchange Pgm, 1982-; Fed Bur Invest spokeswoman Fed Bur Invest Pub Affairs Off, 1982-; Int Asn Workforce Professionals, 1984; large Nat Assoc Media Women, 1985-. **Honors/Awds:** Several letters of commendation from Dir of FBI, 1978, 1980, 1981, 1989; Key to City of Louisville, KY, 1982; Honorary Kentucky Colonel, City of Louisville, 1982; Community Service Award, United Black Fund, Greater National Chapter, 1984; CBS movie, Johnnie Mae Gibson: FBI, 1986; Law Enforcement Pioneer Award, North State Law Enforcement Officers Association, 1988; Outstanding Support of Men & Women of the Air Force, The Air Force District of Washington, DC; Exceptional Performance Award, 1992-98. **Special Achievements:** The First Black Woman F.B.I. Agent.One of only two black female supervisors in the FBI. **Home Addr:** 8793 Brook Estates Ct, Lorton, VA 22079. **Business Addr:** Federal Bureau of Investigation, Headquarters, Washington, DC 20035.

**GIBSON, KALA J.**
Executive. **Educ:** Grand Valley State Univ, BBA, finance, 1994; Mich State Univ, Eli Broad Grad Sch Mgt, MBA, bus admin & mgt, gen, 2002. **Career:** Comerica Bank, vpres, mgr, sr vpres & bus banking group mgr, 1991-2011; Fifth Third Bank, affil head bus banking, Eastern Mich, affil head bus banking, 2011-13, sr vpres & head bus banking, 2013-. **Orgs:** Pres, dir, chairperson, Urban Fin Serv Coalition, Detroit Chap, 2006-, sr advisor; bd trustee, Charles H. Wright Mus African Am Hist; Phi Kappa Phi Hon Soc; Beta Gamma Sigma Hon Soc. **Honors/Awds:** Aubrey Lee Sr. Outstanding Banker Award; The Michigan Chronicle's Men of Excellence Award. **Business Addr:** Director, Senior Advisor, Urban Financial Services Coalition, PO Box 310722, Detroit, MI 48231.

**GIBSON, KENNETH ALLEN**
Mayor. **Personal:** Born May 15, 1932, Enterprise, AL; son of Willie Foy and Daisy (Lee); married Muriel Cook; children: Cheryl Fuller, JoAnn Danks & Joyce Williams. **Educ:** Newark Col, BS, civil eng, 1960. **Career:** NJ Hwy Dept, engr, 1950-60; Newark Housing Authority, chief engr, 1960-66; City Newark, chief struct engr, 1966-70; City Newark, 34th mayor, 1970-86; Rutgers Univ, instr, 1970; Gibson Assoc Inc, construct mgt firm, pres, currently. **Orgs:** Pres, US Conf Mayors, 1976-77; bd dir, Newark Urban Coalition; co-chmn, Bus & Indust Coord Coun; bd dirs, Newark Young Men's Christian Asn-Young Women's Christian Asn; Am Soc CE; Frontiers Int; Nat Asn Advan Colored People. **Honors/Awds:** Jaycee's Man of the Year Newark, 1964; Fiorello LaGuardia Award, New Sch; Jefferson Award, American Institute Public Service. **Special Achievements:** First African American president of the U.S. Conference of Mayors, 1976; First African American elected mayor of Northeastern U.S. city. **Home Addr:** 72 Tuxedo Pkwy, Newark, NJ 07106. **Business Addr:** President, Gibson Associates Inc, Renaissance Towers, Newark, NJ 07102, **Business Phone:** (201)624-2001.

**GIBSON, NELL BRAXTON**
Executive, administrator. **Personal:** Born Apr 9, 1942, Cordele, GA; daughter of John Thomas Braxton and Anne Thomas Braxton; married Bertram M II; children: Erika Anne. **Educ:** Tougaloo Col, attended 1961; Spelman Col, attended 1962; Calif State Univ Sacramento, attended 1964; Empire State Col, BA, 1982. **Career:** Gen Theol Sem, pastoral assoc, 1982-85; Episcopal Diocese New York, exec asst bishop, 1983-89; Episcopal Mission Soc, Parish Based Serv, dir, 1989-95; Nat Coun Churches, prog dir, 1995-96, assoc gen secy inclusiveness & justice, 1996-2000; mgt consult, 2000-. **Orgs:** Transafrica, 1984-; Black Diocesan Exec, 1986-; Metro-Manhattan Chap Links, 1990-; pres, New York Chap, Union Black Episcopalians, 1991-96 & 2000-03; St Mary's Episcopal AIDS Ctr; co-ordr, Episcopal Urban Caucus, 2005-; chair, Reparations Comt Episcopal Diocese New York; fel Trinity Wall St church, 2007. **Home Addr:** 100 W 94th St Apt 21-G, New York, NY 10025, **Home Phone:** (212)865-4596. **Business Addr:** Coordinator, Episcopal Urban Caucus, Pk W Sta, New York, NY 10025, **Business Phone:** (212)699-2998.

**GIBSON, OLIVER DONNOVAN**
Football player, football coach. **Personal:** Born Mar 15, 1972, Chicago, IL; son of Dave and Barbara. **Educ:** Univ Notre Dame, econ. **Career:** Football player (retired), coach; Pittsburgh Steelers, defensive tackle, 1995-98; Cincinnati Bengals, defensive tackle, 1999-2003, nose tackle & right defensive tackle, 1999, left defensive tackle, 2000-02; Tampa Bay Buccaneers, defensive tackle, 2004; Buffalo Bills, defensive tackle, 2004; Miami Northwestern High Sch, vol coach; Ariz Western Jr Col, asst; Proviso W High Sch, defensive line coach. **Honors/Awds:** USA Today High School Defensive Player of the Year, 1989; Unsung Hero Award, Nat Football League, 2001; Linemen of the Year Award, Nat Football Found; Nick Piet-rosante Award.

**GIBSON, REGINALD WALKER**
Lawyer, army officer, judge. **Personal:** Born Jul 31, 1927, Lynchburg, VA; son of McCoy and Julia Ann Butler; children: Reginald S Jr. **Educ:** Va Union Univ, BS, 1952; Univ Pa, Wharton Grad Sch Bus Admin, attended 1953; Howard Univ Sch Law, LLB, 1956. **Career:** Judge (retired); IRS Agt; Dept Treas, Internal Revenue Serv, agt, 1957-61; Dept Justice Tax Div, trial atty, 1961-71; Int Harvester Co, sr tax atty, 1971-76, gen tax atty, 1976-82; US Ct Fed Claims, judge, 1982-95. **Orgs:** DC Bar Asn; Fed Bar Asn; Ill Bar Asn; Nat Bar Asn; Claims Ct Bar Asn; emer mem J Edgar Murdock Am Inn Ct Taxation; Chicago Bar Asn; Ct Fed Claims Bar Asn; Am Judicature Soc; Just Beginning Found. **Honors/Awds:** Wall Street Journal Award, Ranking Student in Business Admin, 1952; American Jurisprudence Award, Excellence in Taxation & Trusts, 1956; Certificate of Award, US Atty Generals, 1969; Special Commendation for Outstanding Service in Tax Division, US Dept Justice, 1970; Listed in Whos Who in Black America, 1980, Whos Who in America, 1983; Distinguished Alumni of the Year, Howard Univ Sch Law, 1984. **Special Achievements:** First African American to serve as a Judge of the United States Claims Court in 1982. **Home Addr:** , Washington, DC.

**GIBSON, ROBERT (BOB GIBSON)**
Baseball player, sports promoter, baseball executive. **Personal:** Born Nov 9, 1935, Omaha, NE; son of Pack and Victoria; married Charline; children: Annette & Renee; married Wendy; children: Chris. **Educ:** Creighton Univ. **Career:** Baseball player (retired), baseball coach, speaker; St Louis Cardinals, pitcher, 1959-75, announcer, 1985-94, asst coach, 1995-97; New York Mets, coach, 1981-82; Atlanta Braves, asst coach, 1982-84; Am League, spec adv pres, 1998; Playing Field Promotions, speakers bur, sports speaker, currently. **Orgs:** Nat Baseball Hall Fame & Mus. **Home Addr:** 215 Belleview Blvd S, Bellevue, NE 68005. **Business Addr:** Sports Speaker, Playing Field Promotions, 960 Syracuse Ct, Denver, CO 80230, **Business Phone:** (303)341-7899.

**GIBSON, ROGER ALLAN**
Airline executive, vice president (organization). **Personal:** Born Jun 9, 1946, Oakland, CA; son of Betty J; married Patrice; children: Terrence, Kai & Jennifer. **Educ:** Merrit Col, attended 1973; Chabot Col, attened 1976; St Mary's Col, BA, mgt, 1986. **Career:** Airlines (retired); United Airlines, mgr inventory planning & control, 1979-86, MOC supply & syst dist, dir, 1986-87, dir inventory planning & control, 1987-89, dir, resource planning & control, 1989, dir, total qual, 1990-91, Mountain Region, head, Worldwide Cargo, leader, Worldwide Cargo, vpres, chief operating officer, Oakland Aircraft Mod Ctr, gen mgr, 1991-92, chmn cargo; NAME Mountain, vpres, 1992-; Sci & Technol Fund, independent dir, 1997-; Nuveen Investment Funds Inc, dir & chmn pricing comt, 1997-; Minn Munic Income Portfolio Inc, dir, 1998-; Cargo Portal Serv, co-founder; United Cargo, vpres & chmn, 2001-04. **Orgs:** Dir, Nat Jewish Health, Inc, 1976-; bd mem, Colo Uplife, 1993-; bd mem, Denver Area Coun Boy Scouts, 1993-; bd mem, Colo Nat Bank, 1995-; bd mem, Colo Ocean Journey, 1996-; bd mem, Denver Found, 1996-; bd mem, Denver Zool Found, 1996-; bd mem, Metrop State Col Denver, 1996-; bd mem, Nat Jewish Ctr, 1996-; bd dir, Nat Jewish Hosp; bd dir, Blue Skies; bd dir, First Am Funds, currently. **Home Addr:** 1020 15th St Suite 41A, Denver, CO 80202, **Home Phone:** (303)820-2979. **Business Addr:** Director, Minnesota Municipal Income Portfolio Inc, 800 Nicollet Mall, Minneapolis, MN 55402, **Business Phone:** (612)303-4772.

**GIBSON, TYRESE DARNELL**
Fashion model, actor, singer. **Personal:** Born Dec 30, 1978, Los Angeles, CA; son of Pricilla Murray; married Tarshimiah; children: Shayla Somer; married Norma Mitchell; children: 1. **Educ:** Fla A&M Univ, attended. **Career:** Albums: Tyrese, 1998; 2000 Watts, 2001; I Wanna Go There, 2002; Alter Ego, 2006; Open Invitation, 2011. Films: Guess, model, 1999; Baby Boy, 2001; Fast & Furious 2, 2003; Flight of the Phoenix, 2004; Four Brothers, 2005; Annapolis, 2006; Waist Deep, 2006; Alter Ego, 2006; Transformers, 2007; The Take, 2008; Death Race, 2008; Transformers: Revenge of the Fallen, 2009; Legion, 2010; Fast Five, 2011; Transformers: Dark of the Moon, 2011; Fast & Furious 6, 2013; Furious 7, 2015; Luke Cage, currently; The Big Test, film, currently; Boom, film, currently; HQ Pictures, owner. Tv Series: "First In", exec producer, 2009; "K-Town", exec producer, 2012-13; "Roll Models", exec producer, 2013. Books: How to Get Out of Your Own Way, 2012; Manology: Secrets of Your Man's Mind Revealed. **Business Addr:** Actor, Singer, BMG Records, 1540 Broadway, New York, NY 10036, **Business Phone:** (212)930-4000.

**GIBSON, WARREN ARNOLD**
Lawyer. **Personal:** Born Jul 16, 1941, Gary, IN. **Educ:** Ind Univ, BS, personnel mgt, 1965, Maurer Sch Law. **Career:** Montgomery Wards, supvr, 1966-67; Exxon Corp, employ rels rep, 1967-70; Dow Chem Co, atty. **Orgs:** Am Bar Asn; Nat Bar Asn; Mich Bar Asn; Midland Bar Asn; Alpha Phi Alpha; Urban League Black Exec Exchange Prog. **Honors/Awds:** Midland Jr Achievement, 1976-78. **Home Addr:** 2680 N Moreland Blvd Apt Suite 705, Cleveland, OH 44120-1496. **Business Addr:** PO Box 4378, Houston, TX 77210-4378.

**GIBSON, WAYNE CARLTON**
Executive. **Personal:** Born Oct 20, 1958, Fordyce, AR; son of Odis and Gertrude Thrower; married Ruthie N; children: Carla Roschelle. **Educ:** Henderson State Univ, BSBA, mgt & acct, 1980; Northwestern Univ, J L Kellogg Sch Bus, cert, petrol & energy econs & mgt, 1989. **Career:** Murphy Oil USA Inc, acct, 1980-84, sr div order analyst, 1984-86, supvr, Lease Rec & Div Orders, 1986-92, gen mgr corp purchasing, 1992, spec proj & permitting mgr, currently; Coldwell

Banker Robinson Real Estate, referral agt, currently. **Orgs:** Bd mem, El Dorado Sch Bd, 1990-; bd dir, Barton Libr, 1989-93; bd dir, S Ark Symphony, 1990-; bd dir, Salvation Army, 1985-; Nat Asn Purchasing Managers, 1992-; Am Mgt Asn, 1986-; Ark & El Dorado Bd Realtors, 1983-; bd dir, Union County Literacy Coun, 1991-94; Nat Asn Realtors; Ark Realtors; El Dorado Sch Bd. **Home Addr:** 710 White Oak Dr, El Dorado, AR 71730-8523, **Home Phone:** (870)862-0551. **Business Addr:** Referral Agent, Coldwell Banker Robinson Real Estate, 542 N Wash Ave, El Dorado, AR 71730, **Business Phone:** (870)862-9292.

## GIBSON, REV. WILLIAM M.

Educator, clergy. **Personal:** Born Sep 11, 1934, Hackensack, NJ; son of James and Evelyn Scott; married Jean J; children: Monica, Wayne, Wesley, Cayce & Jerrell Johnson. **Educ:** Rutgers Univ, BA, 1956; Boston Univ Sch Law, JD, 1959; Boston Col, MSW, 1966; Harvard Bus Sch, AMP cert, 1973; Va Union Univ Grad Sch Theol, MDiv, 1989. **Career:** US Dept Justice, asst US Atty, 1961-64; Boston Univ Law, dir law & poverty proj, 1966-70; Boston Univ Sch Afro Am Studies, assoc prof, 1968-71; Off Econ Opportunity, regional coun, 1970-72; FTC, regional dir, 1972-78; Fuller Ment Health Ctr, supt area dir; Boston, Metro Dist, dep distmgr; St Paul's Baptist Church, minister educ & singles; Med Col VA Hosp, Richmond, staff chaplain, 1990-91; VA Union Univ, Criminol & Criminal Justice Dept, instr, 1993-; Police Acad, recruit class chaplain, 1998; St Stephen's Baptist Church, pastor, currently. **Orgs:** Nat Asn Social Work, 1966; Acad Cert Social Worker, 1968; Mass Bar Asn, 1984; Sports Anglers Club, VA; Blue Waters Club Bermuda; Henrico County Community Criminal Justice Bd; Richmond Police Citizens Acad Bd. **Honors/Awds:** Outstanding Young 10 Men Award, Boston Jr CC, 1968; Young Lawyers Chair, Boston Univ Law Sch, 1969; Community Service Award, Roxbury YMCA, 1969; Outstanding Performance Award, FTC, 1972; Outstanding Govt Service Award, Nat Asn for the Advan of Colored People, Boston, 1975; Outstanding Service Award, Salvation Army, 1980; Samuel H James, Sr Theol Award, VA Union Sch Theol, 1989; Man of the Year, St Stephens Bapt Church, 1996. **Home Addr:** 3923 Dill Rd, PO Box 6102, Richmond, VA 23222, **Home Phone:** (804)321-3764. **Business Addr:** Pastor, St Stephen's Baptist Church, PO Box 689, Bowling Green, VA 22427, **Business Phone:** (804)633-9353.

## GIDDENS, RHIANNON

Musician. **Personal:** Born Feb 21, 1977; married Michael Laffan; children: Aoife & Caoimhin. **Educ:** Oberlin Conserv, undergrad degree, vocal performance, 2000. **Career:** Sankofa Strings (folk project), co-founder and frontwoman, 2005; Carolina Chocolate Drops, lead singer; solo artist, 2015-. Albums with the Carolina Chocolate Drops: "Dona Got a Ramblin Mind", Music Maker, 2006, "Genuine Negro Jig, 2010. Solo albums: "Tomorrow Is My Turn", 2015; "Factory Girl", 2015. **Special Achievements:** Appeared on TV special, "Another Day, Another Time: Celebrating the Music of Inside Llewyn Davis", 2014, a taping of a 2013 New York concert; appeared in a gospel concert in the In Performance at the White House series, 2014. **Business Addr:** Nonesuch Records, 1290 Avenue of the Americas, New York, NY 10104.

## GIDDINGS, REP. HELEN

State government official. **Personal:** Born Apr 21, 1945, Dallas, TX; daughter of Arthur and Catherine Warren Ferguson; married Donald; children: Lizette, Lisa & Stanley. **Educ:** Univ Tex, BA, bus, 1968. **Career:** Sears & Roebuck, training dir, 1975-77, personnel mgr, 1977-81, dir community affairs, 1979-81; Select Personnel, pres, 1981-86; Dallas Assembly, elected mem, 1981-; Tex House Representatives, dist 109, state rep, 1993-; Small bus owner, currently; Multiplex Inc, founder & pres, 1988-. **Orgs:** Dallas Symphony, 1980-; trustee, Dallas Alliance, 1981-, exec dir, 1987; pres, Dallas Black Chamber Com, 1981-92; secy, Dallas Hist Soc, 1983-; bd dir, Dallas Theatre Ctr, 1984-; exec dir, Leadership Dallas, 1985-86; Dist Six State Bar Grievance Comt; pres, Nat Order Women Legislatures, 2000-; chair bd, Dallas Black Chamber Com; vice chair, Dallas Transit Bd; African Am Mus; Dallas Summer Musicals; Dallas City Planning Comn; Nat Found Women Legislator; chair, African Am Mus Ann Ball; fel African Am Polit Cong; bd mem, Am Red Cross; bd mem, Casa De Los Amigos; bd mem, Consumer Credit Coun Serv; trustee, Dallas Alliance; chmn, Dallas Black Chamber Com; fel Dallas County Grand Jury; vice chair, Dallas Hist Socs; bd mem, Dallas Summer Musicals; bd, Dallas Symphony Orchestra; fel Goodwill Industs; bd mem, Greater Dallas Housing Opportunity Ctr; bd mem, Majestic Theatre Operating Co; pres, Trinity Chap Links; bd, Univ N Tex; vpres, Nat Order Women Legislators. **Business Addr:** State Representative, Texas House of Representatives, 1510 N Hampton Rd Suite 340, DeSoto, TX 75115, **Business Phone:** (972)224-6795.

## GIDDINGS, PAULA JANE

Educator, historian, writer. **Personal:** Born Nov 16, 1947, Yonkers, NY; daughter of Curtis Gulliver and Virginia Stokes. **Educ:** Howard Univ, WA, DC, BA, 1969; Bennett Col, DHL, 1990. **Career:** Random House, ed asst, 1969-70, copy ed, 1970-72; Howard Univ Press, assoc bk ed, 1972-75; Encore Am & Worldwide News, paris bur chief, France, 1975-77; NY, assoc ed, 1977-79; Essence, contrib & bk rev ed, 1985-90; Spelman Col, Atlanta, Ga, distinguished UNCF scholar, 1986-87; Rutgers Univ, chair womens studies, 1989-91; Barnard Ctr Res Women, fel, 1990-93; Princeton Univ, vis prof, 1992-93; Duke Univ, res prof, 1996-2000; Smith Col, African Am Studies, prof, 2001-, E. A. Woodson 1922 prof, currently; Books: "When & Where I Enter: The Impact of Black Women on Race & Sex in Am, 1984; In Search of Sisterhood, 1988; ed: Burning All Illusions. **Orgs:** Delta Sigma Theta Inc, 1967-; bd mem, Nat Coalition 100 Black Women, 1985-; Am Hist Asn, 1990; PEN, 1990-; Auth Guild Am, 1991; Century Club; New York Univ Inst Humanities, 1991-; Asn Black Women Historians; Nat Women's Studies Asn; fel Guggenheim Found, 1993; John Simon Guggenheim Found, 1993-94; fel Nat Humanitics Ctr, 1993-95; Womens WORLD. **Honors/Awds:** Ford Foundation Grant, 1982; United Negro Fund Distinguished Scholar, Spelman Col, 1986-87; Phi Beta Kappa Vis Scholar, 1996-97; Candace Award, Nat Coalition 100 Black Women, 1985; Alumni Award, Howard Univ, 1985; Westchester Black Womens Polit Caucus Award, 1986; Building Brick Award, New York Urban League, 1986; Anna Julia Cooper Award; hon degree, Wesleyan Univ CT, 1995; Anna Julia Cooper Award, Sage: A Scholarly Journal on Black Women. **Home Addr:** 34 Citation Dr, Durham, NC 27713-9158. **Business Addr:** Professor, Smith College, 17 New South St Wright Hall 203, Northampton, MA 01063, **Business Phone:** (413)585-3564.

## GIFFORD, DR. BERNARD R.

Educator. **Personal:** Born May 18, 1943, Brooklyn, NY; married Ursula M Jean; children: Antoinette & Bernard; married Guadalupe Valdes; children: Elizabeth. **Educ:** Long Island Univ, BS, 1965; Univ Rochester Med Sch, MS, 1968, PhD, radiation biol & biophys, 1972. **Career:** Russell Sage Found, resident scholar, 1977; New York Pub Sch Syst, dep chancellor & chief bus affairs off, 1973-77; New York Rand Inst, pres, 1972-73; Univ Rochester, vice pres & prof polit sci & pub policy; Univ Calif, Berkeley, chancellors prof & dean grad scheduc, 1983-89, Div Educ Math, Sci, Engineering & Technol, prof, currently, Int Educ, 2013-14, dir & chief instrnl officer, Consortium Leadership Educ Equity; Distrib Learning Workshop, pres, chief exec officer & instrnl officer, co-founder, 2001-; Apple Comput Inc, vpres educ; Books: Policy Perspectives on Educational Testing, Kluwer Academic Press, 1993; Testing Policy and Test Performance: Education, Language and Culture, Kluwer Academic Press, 1989, History in the Schools: What Shall We Teach? Macmillan, 1988. **Orgs:** US Atomic Energy Comn, Fel Nuclear Sci, 1965-71; app adj prof, pub admin, Columbia Univ, 1975-77; app adj lectr, Pub Policy, fel John F Kennedy Sch Govt, Harvard Univ, 1977-78; loeb fel Grad Sch Design; adv Comt, John F Kennedy Inst Polit, Harvard Univ; bd visitors, City Col New York; bd trustee, New York Univ; acad adv com, US Naval Acad; consult, Calif Supreme Ct, 1978-79; consult, Asst Secy Comn Planning & Develop, Dept Housing & Urban Develop, 1979; consult, Nat Acad Pub Admin, 1979-80; consult, Nat Inst Educ; bd dir, New York Urban Coalition; bd trustee, Ger Marshall Fund US; ed bd, Urban Affairs Quart; bd ed adv New York Affairs; ed bd, New York Educ Quart; ed bd, policy Anal; app adj & vis prof, Dept Urban Studies & Planning, Hunter Col, City Univ New York, Mass Inst Technol; founding fac chair, Calif State Univ Joint Doctoral Prog, currently. **Home Addr:** 111 St Felis St, Brooklyn, NY 11217. **Business Addr:** Professor, University of California, 4533 Tolman Hall Suite 1670, Berkeley, CA 94720, **Business Phone:** (510)643-4733.

## GIGGER, HELEN C.

Lawyer, counselor. **Personal:** Born Dec 24, 1944, Houston, TX; married Nathan J. **Educ:** Tex S Univ, BA, polit sci, 1965, JD, 1968. **Career:** Dean Law Sch, res asst; Houston Leg Found, legal intern; Okla City & Co Comm Act Prog Inc, prog analyst; State Okla, Crime Comn, legal coun, planner, asst munic counr, currenty. **Orgs:** Am Nat & Okla Bar Asns; secy, JJ & Bruce Law Soc; Am Judiccature Soc; EEOCoff Okla Crime Comn; OK Black Pol Cau; pres, Delta Sigma Theta Sor Inc; secy, Local & State Nat Asn Advan Colored People; Nat Scholar & Stand Com; Greater Cleves CME Church; chairperson, Church Prog; chairperson, RegVI Nat Asn Advan Colored People Conf, 1974; policy making com, Delta Sigma Theta Inc, 1975. **Honors/Awds:** Grad with Hons, 1961, 1965 & at top of Law Class, 1968; Parliament; Nat Delta Conv, 1973; Delta Cen Reg Parliament, 1974. **Home Addr:** 3309 E Forest Pk Dr, Oklahoma City, OK 73121-2225. **Business Addr:** Assistant Municipal Counselor, Oklahoma City Municipal Counselors office, 200 N Walker Ave, Oklahoma City, OK 73102-2232, **Business Phone:** (405)424-3644.

## GIGGER, NATHANIEL JAY

Lawyer, association executive. **Personal:** Born Jan 1, 1944, Elmore City, OK; son of Ernest and Katie Wyatt; married Helen Coleman; children: Nikolle Janelle. **Educ:** Langston Univ, BA, 1963; Tex Southern Univ, Houston, JD, 1967. **Career:** State Okla, asst state atty gen, 1970-79, dep atty dept human resources, 1979; Derryberry, Duncan & Nance Law Firm, mem, 1979-82; Nathaniel J Gigger Law Off, atty, 1982-. **Orgs:** Prince Hall Masons, 1967-; vice pres, State Conf Br Nat Asn Advan Colored People, 1972-77; state legal chmn, Int Benevolent Protective Order Elks, 1975-80; Mayor's Comn Bus Develop, 1976-79; exec bd mem, Community Action Agency, 1976-81; Asn Black Trial Lawyers, 1982-; bd mem, Okla Bus & Develop Coun, 1984-86; Northeast Okla City Chamber Com, 1987-; J J Bruce Law Soc. **Honors/Awds:** Roscoe Dunjee Humanitarian Award, Okla Nat Asn Advan Colored People, 1975; Outstanding Citizenship Award, Alpha Phi Alpha Fraternity, 1976; Outstanding Citizen Award, Okla City Set Club, 1981; Outstanding Lawyer Award, Nat Asn Advan Colored People Youth Coun, 1986. **Home Addr:** 3309 E Forest Pk Dr, Oklahoma City, OK 73121-2225, **Home Phone:** (405)528-7915. **Business Addr:** Owner, Attorney, Nathaniel J Gigger Law Office, 732 NE 36th St, Oklahoma City, OK 73105, **Business Phone:** (405)528-7915.

## GILBERT, ALBERT C.

Executive. **Personal:** Born Oct 19, 1924, Carlisle, PA; married Iris Boswell; children: Brenda, Richard, Walda Ann, Albert C III & Charles. **Educ:** Morgan State Univ, Baltimore, MD, BS, 1950; St John Col, Cleveland, OH, 1966; Cambridge Ctr, New York, NY, 1967. **Career:** Executive (retired); Continental Can Co, Cleveland, Ohio, hourly employee, finance secy, pres union, 1950, supvr, 1958, supt, 1964, mgr, 1969-74, special sales rep, 1974-83; Congressman Louis Stokes, Wash, DC, sr intern, 1985. **Orgs:** Vice chmn, Fibre Box Asn; bd mem, E Cleveland Sch, 1971-83; Nat Black Sch Bd; Nat Safety Coun; Citizens League Greater Cleveland; El Hasa Masonic Shrine 32 Degree Mason; Cleveland Chamber Com; Ohio Mfr Asn; bd dir, Rainey Inst Music; spec sales rep, Continental Group; pres, E Cleveland Kiwanis, 1987; Cuyahoga Co, Ohio, Western Res Agency Sr Citizens, 1987-93; bd mgrs, YMCA, 1988-94; club pres, club secy, lt gov, gov, Ohio Dist Kiwanis Int, 1991-93, 1994-95; pres, E Cleveland (FOPA) Fraternal Order Police Asn, 1996-99; E Cleveland Parks Inc. **Home Addr:** 2100 N Taylor Rd, Cleveland Heights, OH 44112-3002, **Home Phone:** (216)851-4109.

## GILBERT, DR. FRED D., JR.

College administrator. **Personal:** Born Dec 2, 1947, New Orleans, LA. **Educ:** Dillard Univ, BA, bus admin, 1970; Loyola Univ, MEd, educ admin, 1972; Iowa State Univ Higher Educ, PhD, pub admin, 1978. **Career:** Upward Bound Proj, admin dir, 1971-73; Upward Bound & Spec Serv Proj Univ, proj dir, 1973-75; IA State Univ, res asst, 1975-76, univ m housing area adv, 1976-77, TRIO dir, asst prof, 1978-; IA State Univ Col Ed, asst dean, 1987-; Des Moines Area Comm Col, dean urban campus, 1987-90, exec dir dist admin, 1990-92, exec dir res, found, grants & contracts, 1992-94, vpres res & develop, 1994-, exec dean; Mohave Community Col Neal Campus, campus dean, 2009-. **Orgs:** Bd dir, Ames Sch Dist Found; C & Families Iowa, Family Enrichment Ctr, IA Comprehensive Manpower Serv & Nat Coun Res & Develop. **Home Addr:** 1914 Stevenson Dr, Ames, IA 50010. **Business Addr:** Campus Dean, Mohave Community College-Neal Campus - Kingman, 1971 Jagerson Ave, Kingman, AZ 86409, **Business Phone:** (928)757-4331.

## GILBERT, JEAN P.

Educator. **Personal:** Born Aug 6, 1928, McDonald, PA. **Educ:** Bluefield St Col, BS, 1947; Univ Buffalo, EdM, 1955, EdD, 1962. **Career:** Clergy (retired); AL A&M Col, counr & lectr, 1956-57; Hampton Inst, dir testing, 1957-60; Univ IL, counr & educr, 1962-63; Brooklyn Col, asst prof, counr & educr, prof emer; SC St Col, counr & educr, 1964-65; Acad Develop Ctr Inc, founder. **Orgs:** Mem bd dir, DST Telecommunications Inc; Delta Sigma Theta; Pi Lambda Theta; Kappa Delta Pi; Am Psychol Asn; Am Personnel & Guid Asn; Nat Voc Guid Asn; Asn Non-White Concerns; Psychomet Dir Educ Prog Eval & Res JPG Consults Inc; JOB'S Prog; bd grdns bd dir, NY City Protestant; GS Coun Greater NY; mem bd, Gov NY St Personal & Guid Asn. **Honors/Awds:** James Foundation Grant, 1957; John Hay Whitney Foundation Grant, 1960; Women of Achievement Award, 1966; Outstanding Editors of America, 1974; Ford Found Grant. **Special Achievements:** Author of "Counseling Black Inner City Children in Groups". **Home Addr:** 4 Washinfton Sq Village, New York, NY 10001.

## GILBERT, SEAN

Football player. **Personal:** Born Apr 10, 1970, Aliquippa, PA; married Nicole; children: Deshaun, Sean Zacchaeus, Alea & Alexus. **Educ:** Pittsburgh Univ. **Career:** Football player (retired), executive, coach; Los Angeles Rams, right defensive tackle, 1992-94; St Louis Rams, right defensive end, 1995; Wash Redskins, right defensive tackle, 1996; Carolina Panthers, right defensive end, 1998, right defensive tackle & defensive tackle, 1999-2000, left defensive tackle & defensive end, 2001, 2002; Oakland Raiders, defensive line, 2003; I GOT Rec, chief exec officer, pres; Esquire Big & Tall Mens Clothing Store, partner; Sean Gilbert Assocs Inc, founder & pres, currently; Nerih Inc, chief exec officer; Obediah Rec LLC, owner, currently; S Mecklenburg High Sch, asst coach, currently. **Honors/Awds:** Carroll Rosen bloom Memorial Award, 1992; Rams Rookie of the Year Award, 1992; Pro Bowl, 1993; Pro Bowl alternate, 1995-96; Beaver County Sports Hall of Fame, 2009; Defensive High School Player of the Year, USA Today. **Home Addr:** , Charlotte, NC. **Business Addr:** President, Sean Gilbert & Associates Inc, 427 Franklin Ave, Aliquippa, PA 15001-3725, **Business Phone:** (724)378-0271.

## GILBERT, SHEDRICK EDWARD

Clergy. **Personal:** Born Jun 21, 1922, Miami, FL; married Wilma Wake; children: Janelle Gilbert Hall, Stephen & Jeffrey. **Educ:** Hampton Univ, BS, 1954. **Career:** US Post Off, lett carrier, 1956-78, supvr, 1978-84; St Agnes Episcopal Church, treas, 1967-94, asst deacon, 1984-. **Orgs:** OPP, 1952-; chmn, Diocese SE Fla, 1974-84, stewardship cms, 1983-85; pres, Booker T Wash Class 1938, 1988-; vpres, head prog, Algonquin Civic Club, 1989-; dir, St Agnes & Rainbow Village Corp, 1990-; chmn, Every Mem Canvas Campaign, 1990; Overtown Adv bd, 1991-; dir, eight week summer recreation prog, 1992; Jefferson Reaves Sr Health Ctr Comt; pres, dir, Algonquin Club. **Home Addr:** 3368 NW 51 Terr, Miami, FL 33142, **Home Phone:** (305)634-4321. **Business Addr:** FL.

## GILBERT, DR. SHIRL E., II

President (government), school administrator, chief executive officer. **Educ:** Harris Teachers Col, BS, elem educ & teaching, 1967; Southern Ill Univ, MS, educ admin & supv, 1974; Purdue Univ, PhD, superintendency & educ syst admin, 1984. **Career:** E Chicago Heights Pub Schs, supt, 1979-85; Indianapolis Pub Schs, supt, 1994; St. Louis Pub Schs, teacher, asst prin, prin; Chicago Heights Schs, dir guid & coun, dir curric, bus mgr, from adm asst to supt, asst supt, supt, 1979; Purdue Univ, asst dean, asst prof; Petersburg, supt; Indianapolis, supt, Matteson, supt; Philadelphia, supt; Recovery Sch Dist; La State Dept Educ, 2008-11; Baton Rouge Parish Schs, exec dir, 2010-13, exec adminr, 2009-; Tacoma Urban League, pres & chief exec officer; Sch Dist Pa, regional supt, currently. **Orgs:** Nat Adv Bd; Nat Ctr Res Eval, Stand Studs Testing; dir, Phi Beta Sigma Fraternity; Bd a Charter Syst; Am Asn Sch Adminr; Nat Alliance Black Sch Educr; Asn Supv & Curric Develop; life mem, Nat Asn Advan Colored People; life mem, Nat Urban League. **Special Achievements:** First African American superintendent of Indianapolis Public Schools. **Business Addr:** Regional Superintendent, School District of Philadelphia, 440 N Broad St, Philadelphia, PA 19130, **Business Phone:** (215)400-4000.

## GILCHRIEST, LORENZO

Educator, college teacher. **Personal:** Born Mar 21, 1938, Thomasville, GA; son of Willis Belle (deceased) and Mary Louise Belle (deceased); married Judith Graffman; children: Lorenzo David & Lorena. **Educ:** Newark State Col, BS, 1962; Pratt Inst, MS, 1967; Md Inst Col Art, MFA, 1975. **Career:** Senator Robert Kennedy Proj, Bedford Stuyvesant Youth Action, asst dir, 1965-67; Cornell Univ, guest prof, 1972-73; Baltimore Mus Art, art teacher adult prog, 1973-74; Morgan State Univ, guest artist print workshop summer, 1977; prof emer, 1997-; Towson State Univ, asst prof art dept. **Orgs:** Fel Int Artists Sem, 1962; Afro Am Slide Depository Samuel Kress Found, 1971; Gen Class Amateur Radio Lisc, 1976; Advan Class Amateur Radio Lisc, 1980; Am Radio Relay League. **Home Addr:** 1013 Woodbourne Ave, Baltimore, MD 21212.

## GILDON, JASON LARUE

Football player, football coach. **Personal:** Born Jul 31, 1972, Altus, OK; married Joy; children: Jason Jr. **Educ:** Okla State Univ, grad. **Career:** Football player (retired), football coach; Pittsburgh Steelers, linebacker, 1994, 1999, 2002, 1995, left outside linebacker, 1996-2003;

Jacksonville Jaguars, 2004; Peters Twp High Sch Dist, asst football coach, 2011-. **Honors/Awds:** Pro Bowl, 2000, 2001, 2002; All-Pro Selection, 2001; Pro Bowl American Football Conference Starters, 2002. **Business Addr:** Assistant Football Coach, Peters Township School District, 631 E McMurray Rd, McMurray, PA 15317, **Business Phone:** (724)941-6251.

## GILES, CHARLOTTE EMMA

Educator. **Personal:** Born Mar 29, 1937, Baltimore, MD; daughter of Samuel Hopkins and Phozie Dawson. **Educ:** Fisk Univ, BA, 1958; Ind Univ, MM, 1960, DM, 1970. **Career:** Tuskegee Inst, instr, 1958-59; Fla A&M Univ, asst prof music, 1960-65; Knoxville Col, assoc prof music, 1968-71; WVa State Col, Dept Music, fac, 1971-, interim chmn, 1971, prof & chair, currently, cult activ coord, dean, 1995-96. **Orgs:** Asn Performing Arts Presenters, 1978-; fel, Nat Endowment Humanities, 1979-80; bd mem, Asn Performing Arts Presenters, 1985-87; Gov's Comt Arts Educ, 1992; Consult, Cult Activ & Educ Assemblies comt; Wva State Univ Found Inc. **Home Addr:** 8 Downing St, Charleston, WV 25301, **Home Phone:** (304)346-4896. **Business Addr:** Professor, Chair, West Virginia State College, John W Davis Fine Arts Bldg Suite 203, Institute, WV 25112-1000, **Business Phone:** (800)987-2112.

## GILES, HENRIETTA

Television producer. **Personal:** Born Feb 23, 1962, Stanton, TN; daughter of Geraldine Maxwell and Jesse Cornelius. **Educ:** Univ Tenn Martin, Martin, Tenn, BS, 1984. **Career:** WTVF-TV, Nashville, Tenn, assoc producer, 1984-85, producer, 1988; WSOC-Radio, Charlotte, NC, copy writer, 1985-88; Odyssey Channel, Locked Out, host; TV serials: "Grammy Countdown", producer, 2000. **Orgs:** Nashville Asn Minority Communicators, 1989-; Nat Asn Black Journalists, 1990-. **Honors/Awds:** Award, Nat Asn Black Journalists, 2001. **Home Addr:** 317 Village Green Dr, Nashville, TN 37217, **Home Phone:** (615)367-4968.

## GILES, JAMES TYRONE

Judge. **Personal:** Born Jan 31, 1943, Charlottesville, VA. **Educ:** Amherst Col, BA, 1964; Yale Univ, LLB, 1967. **Career:** US Equal Employ Opportunity Comn, clerk, 1967; Nat Labor Rels Bd, field atty, 1967-68; Pepper Hamilton & Scheetz, assoc atty, 1968-74, partner, labor & employ, 1974-79; Fed Judiciary, Us Dist Ct Eastern Pa, dist judge, 1980-2008, US Dist Ct, Eastern Dist, Philadelphia, PA, judge, 1979-99, chief judge, 2001-07; ADR Options Inc, Mediator/Arbitrator, 2008-13; Pepper Hamilton LLP, coun, 2008-. **Orgs:** Fed Bar Asn; Philadelphia Bar Asn; Hist Dist Ct Rec Comt; fel Sigma Pi Phi; bd mem, Am Arbit Asn, 2009-; fel Independence Seaport Mus; fel Ctr Literacy & Lawyers Club Philadelphia; fel Am bar asn; fel Pa bar asn; fel Philadelphia bar asn; secy, Philadelphia Bar Asn Young Lawyers Sect; Civil War Mus. **Home Addr:** 346 Roumfort Rd, Philadelphia, PA 19119. **Business Addr:** Counsel, Pepper Hamilton LLP, 3000 2 Logan Sq, Philadelphia, PA 19103-2799, **Business Phone:** (215)981-4000.

## GILES, JOE L.

President (organization), chief executive officer, executive. **Personal:** Born Dec 6, 1943, Elrod, AL; son of Pinkie and Jessie; married Sarah Fisher; children: Alycia, Fredrick & Jolanda. **Educ:** Stillman Col, Tuscaloosa, AL, BA, 1966; Univ Detroit, Detroit, MI, MA, 1976. **Career:** Joe L Giles & Assocs, owner & pres, chief exec officer, founder, 1980-. **Orgs:** Bd dir, MYFO, 1981-83; dir placement, Kappa Alpha Psi, 1985-87; pres, Stillman Col Alumni Asn, 1988-90. **Home Addr:** 18105 Parkside, Detroit, MI 48221, **Home Phone:** (313)863-2046. **Business Addr:** Owner, President, Joe L Giles and Associates, 18105 Parkside St Suite 14, Detroit, MI 48221-2792, **Business Phone:** (313)864-0022.

## GILES, NANCY

Actor, comedian, writer. **Personal:** Born Jul 17, 1960, New York, NY; daughter of Thomas Jefferson and Dorothy Aileen Dove. **Educ:** Oberlin Col, Oberlin, OH, BA, 1981. **Career:** Theatre performance: Hey, Stay A While; The Best Of Second City; A Raisin the Sun; Mayor; Urban Blight; Police Boys; The Wacky Side Of Racism; Black Comedy; Notes Of A Negro Neurotic; Radio: The Jay Thomas Morning Show; Giles & Moriarty; The World According to Giles & Moriarty; TV series: "China Beach", 1988-91; "Delta", 1992; "Fox After Breakfast", 1996; "PB&J Otter", 1998; "Dream On; Fresh Prince"; "The Fresh Prince of Bel Air"; "LA Law; Spin City"; "Law & Order"; "The Jury"; "Hey, Joel"; "PB & J Otter"; Films: Off Beat, 1986; Ich und Er, 1987; Big, 1988; Working Girl, 1988; True Crime; Everythings Jake; Angie, 1994; Loverboy; Me & Him; New York Stories; Fear of a Black Hat, 1994; I'm Not Rappaport, 1996; True Crime, 1999; States of Control, 2001; Pop Life, 2002; Joshua; Superheroes; Before the Music Dies; Angie; CBS News Sunday Morning, contributor, currently. **Orgs:** Actors Equity Asn, 1983; Screen Actors Guild, 1984; Am Fedn TV & Radio Artists, 1984; hon mem, Alliance Women Veterans, 1989. **Honors/Awds:** Theatre World Award, Outstanding New Talent, Theatre World, 1985. **Special Achievements:** Writer and contributor to the Emmy award-winning "CBS News Sunday Morning", was the announcer and co-host of the alternative morning show "Fox After Breakfast"; Black Comedy: The Wacky Side of Racism (solo show), Mill Hill Playhouse, Trenton, NJ, 1999. **Home Phone:** (213)462-6565. **Business Addr:** Actress, c/o Bret Adams Ltd, 448 W 44th St, New York, NY 10036, **Business Phone:** (212)765-5630.

## GILES, TERRI LYNNETTE

Executive, manager. **Personal:** Born Miami, FL. **Educ:** Grambling State Univ, BS, mkt, 1988; Nova Southeastern Univ, MBA. **Career:** Bank Am, vpres, 1999-2010; Merrill Lynch Pierce Fenner & Smith Inc, 2010; Morgan Keegan & Co Inc, 2010-12; Regions Bank, 2010-; Cetera Investment Serv LLC, financial advisor, 2013-; Burger King World Hq, supvr, consumer response line, dept supvr, consumer response line, mgr, consumer rels; Herman Electronics, consumer serv mgr; Qual Solutions Personnel Servs, pres, founder, currently. **Orgs:** Soc Consumer Affairs Professionals, 1989-; Alpha Kappa Alpha Sorority Inc, 1990-; Nat Asn Female Execs, 1990-. **Honors/Awds:** Dollars & Sense Magazine, A Salute to America's Best & Brightest Business Professionals, 1992. **Home Addr:** 14800 SW 166th St, Miami, FL 33187. **Business Addr:** Financial Advisor, Cetera Investment Services LLC, 2800 Ponce De Leon Blvd, Miami, FL 33134.

## GILES, WILLIE ANTHONY, JR.

School administrator, educator. **Personal:** Born Mar 8, 1941, Conway, AR; married Carolyn Joan Williams; children: Dwayne, Keenon & Dana. **Educ:** Ark AM & N Col, BS, hist & govt, 1964; Univ Mich, MA, guid & coun, 1967; Univ Mo, EdS, educ admin, 1986; Univ Kans, EdD, educ policy & leadership. **Career:** Detroit Mich Sch Syst, teacher, 1964-67; Kans City MO Sch Syst, teacher, 1968-69; Humboldt High Sch, Kans City, Mo, Sch Syst, prin, 1969-70; Paseo High Sch, Kans City, Mo, Sch Syst, prin, 1971-75; NE High Sch, Kans City, Mo Sch Syst, prin, 1976-78; Kans City MO Sch Dist, dir admin servs, 1978-81 dir sec educ, 1981-85, dir, desegregation monitoring, 1985-86, assoc supt, 1986-; Indianapolis Pub Schs, dir instrnl serv, 1997, asst supt, 1999, dep supt, currently. **Orgs:** Bd mem, Whatsoever Cir Comm House; bd mem, Urban Serv Kans City, Mo; bd mem, Paseo Day care Serv; trustee secy, Paseo Baptist Church; Citizens Crusade Against Crime; Phi Delta Kappa; life mem, Nat Asn Advan Colored People; fel 100 Black Men; fel Indianapolis Urban League; fel Am Asn of Sch Adminr, fel Nat Asn Black Sch Educr; fel Ebenezer Baptist Church. **Honors/Awds:** Boss of the Year Award, Bus & Prof Women Starlight Chap, Kans City, Mo, 1978; Outstanding Educator Award, Alpha Phi Alpha Fraternity, 1980. **Home Addr:** 7145 E 69 St, Kansas City, MO 64133, **Home Phone:** (816)737-2788. **Business Addr:** Deputy Superintendent, Indianapolis Public Schools, 120 E Walnut St, Indianapolis, IN 46204, **Business Phone:** (317)226-4000.

## GILES-ALEXANDER, SHARON

Executive, entrepreneur. **Personal:** Born Sep 12, 1951, East Orange, NJ; daughter of William R and Althea B; married Willie L II; children: Willie L III & Jayson A. **Educ:** Morgan State Univ, BS, 1973; Rutgers Univ, MEd, 1975. **Career:** Newark Bd Educ, 1973-75; E Orange Bd Educ, teacher, 1975-77; EPC Int Inc, pres, 1977-2000; Advert Promotions, pres, 2001-05; Dionne Warwick Inst, teacher, econs & entrepreneurship, 2003-. **Orgs:** Am Mkt Asn; Advert Specialty, IST; Specialty Advert Asn; Fed Credit Union; New Hope Baptist Church; vpres econ develop, Coalition 100 Black Women; Nat Asn Female Exec; Nat Bus Coun; NCP; deleg, White House Conf Small Bus; Greater Newark Coc; E Orange cochran acad; Nat Asn Advan Colored People; Urban League. **Home Addr:** 189 Passaic Ave, Roseland, NJ 07068, **Home Phone:** (201)403-8780. **Business Addr:** President, EPC International Inc, 34 Woodland Rd, Roseland, NJ 07068, **Business Phone:** (201)403-2900.

## GILES-GEE, DR. HELEN FOSTER

Educator, college president. **Personal:** Born Oct 21, 1950, Fairfield, AL; daughter of Foster and Nannette Young; married Gilford Gee. **Educ:** Univ Pa, Philadelphia, BA, psychobiology, 1972, MS, sci educ, 1973, PhD, 1983; Rutgers Univ, NB, NJ, MS, zool, 1977. **Career:** Rutgers Univ, New Brunswick, NJ, teaching fellow, 1973-75; Stevens Inst Technol, Hoboken, NJ, sci teacher, Summer, 1974; Cheyney St Univ, Cheyney, Pa, assoc prof, 1975-86, chair biol, 1983-85; Univ, Towson, Md, exec asst pres & prof biol, 1986-92; Univ Syst Md, Aldelphi, Md, assoc vchancellor acad affairs, dir articulation, 1991-98; Towson St univ NY, Cortland, NY, Sch Prof Stud, Dean, 1998-2004; Keene St Col, pres, 2005-12, interim pres, 2012-; Univ Sci, Philadelphia, PA, pres, 2012-. **Orgs:** Pres, Cortland YWCA; vpres, pres Bd dir, Soc Col & Univ Planning, 1993-94; Leadership Md; Am Coun Educ & Planning Bd; pres, Am Asn Higher Educ, 1989-90; Am Assoc Inst Res; Nat Coun Measurement Educ; Omicro Delta Kappa, leadership hon soc; Phi Delta Kappa, hon fraternity; Pi Lambda Theta, hon soc, 1982-89; Sigma Xi, sci hon; steering comt, treas, Univ Am Syst Women's Forum, 1990-91; Fund Raising Comn, 1990-91; Am Asn Higher Educ; bd dir, Campus Compact; chair, Asn Am Cols & Univs; vice chair, Nh Charitable Found; chair, Nh Postsecondary Educ Comn; vice chair, Nh Col & Univ Coun; vice chair, Am Coun, Educ Comn Women Higher Educ; Nj ACE-Net Coord Bd. **Business Addr:** Interim President, Keene State College, Hale Bldg, Keene, NH 03435-1504, **Business Phone:** (603)358-2000.

## GILFORD, VERA ELAINE

Executive, consultant. **Personal:** Born Dec 20, 1953, Detroit, MI; daughter of James and Ruby. **Educ:** Mich State Univ, BA, bus admin & mgt, 1975; Tex Southern Univ, JD, 1978; Mediation Int Am, circuit civil mediator, 1995. **Career:** Off Chief Coun, atty, 1978-82; IRS, sr atty, 1978-87; Dept Justice, spec prosecutor, 1983; Off Dist Coun, sr atty, 1983-87; speaker, auth, bus leadership success coach, 1983-; Pete's Fountain & Bar, pres, 1987-; Gilford Broadcasting Co, chief exec officer, 1990-; Women Wisdom Inc, atty consult, currently; Vera Gilford Inc, auth, sink or swim & bus leadership & golf, 2012-. **Orgs:** Tax Sect, Fla Bar, 1982-; founder, Black Women Lawyers Asn; Nat Asn Broadcasters, 1991-95; Authors Guild, 1984-; Brickell Ave Lit Soc, 1993-; Exec Women's Golf League, 1994; bd mem, Fla Int Univ, 1995; bd pres, Miami Civic Chorale, 1995; Conflict Resolution Ctr Int, 1995; co-chmn, United Way Endowment, 2001. **Honors/Awds:** Outstanding Business Person, St John Cot Develop Corp, 1988; Most Significant Contribution to the Law Review Award, Tex Southern Univ, 1978. **Special Achievements:** Accumulated Earnings Tax, 1977; The Constitutionality of No-Fault Auto Ins, 1978; Proclamation Vera E Gilford Day, Miami, Fla, 1987; Author: Through Challenges Impacting Your Health Finances and Relationships. **Home Addr:** 100 Bayview Dr, Sunny Isles Beach, FL 33160. **Business Addr:** Business Executive, Leadership Coach, Vera Gilford Inc, PO Box 310265, Miami, FL 33231, **Business Phone:** (305)856-9340.

## GILKEY, BERNARD (OTIS BERNARD GILKEY)

Baseball player. **Personal:** Born Sep 24, 1966, St. Louis, MO; married Patrice; children: Jaelen & Caeven. **Educ:** St Louis Univ, attended 1984. **Career:** Baseball player (retired); St Louis Cardinals, outfielder, 1990-95, free agt, 2001; New York Mets, 1996-98; Ariz Diamondbacks, 1998-2000; Boston Red Sox, 2000; Atlanta Braves, 2001, free agt, 2001-. **Special Achievements:** Gilkey had a small role in the 1997 film Men in Black. **Home Addr:** 2200 Dunhill Way Ct, Chesterfield, MO 63005-4511. **Business Addr:** Free Agent, Atlanta Braves, Turner Field, Atlanta, GA 30315, **Business Phone:** (404)522-7630.

**GILKEY, OTIS BERNARD.** See GILKEY, BERNARD.

## GILL, GLENDA ELOISE

Educator. **Personal:** Born Jun 26, 1939, Clarksville, TN; daughter of Melvin Leo and Olivia Dunlop. **Educ:** Ala A&M Univ, BS, 1960; Univ Wis-Madison, MA, eng lit, 1964; Univ Iowa, PhD, eng & theatre, 1981. **Career:** Ala A&M Univ, asst prof eng, 1963-69; Univ Tex, El Paso, instr eng, 1970-75; Simpson Col, asst prof eng, 1981-82; Tuskegee Univ, assoc prof & dept head, 1982-83; Winston-Salem State Univ, assoc prof eng, 1984-90; Mich Technol Univ, assoc prof drama, 1990-2000, prof drama, 2000-06, prof emer drama, 2006-. **Orgs:** Delta Sigma Theta, 1958-; Nat Coun Teachers Eng, 1963-83; Conf Col Compos Comm, 1963-83; Am Soc Theatre Res, 1984-; Asn Theatre Higher Educ, 1987-; World Cong Theatre, 1989-; Eugene O'Neill Soc, 1998. **Home Addr:** 7584 Old Madison Pke NW Apt 13, Huntsville, AL 35806, **Home Phone:** (256)971-9399. **Business Addr:** Professor Emerita, Michigan Technological University, 1400 Townsend Dr, Houghton, MI 49931-1295, **Business Phone:** (906)487-1885.

## GILL, PROF. JACQUELINE A.

Librarian. **Personal:** Born Jun 4, 1950, New York, NY; daughter of Maude L Jones and Nathan S; children: Christopher B Aden; married Dana L Aden. **Educ:** Bor Manhattan Community Col, New York, AA, libr tech, 1976; Queens Col, Flushing, NY, BA, sociol, 1979; Pratt Inst, Brooklyn, NY, MLS, libr sci, 1982; City Col, New York, NY, MS, educ supv admin, 1989. **Career:** Little Red Sch House, libr asst, 1973-75; State Univ NY, Maritime Col, 1975-79; Maritime Col, Bronx, NY, serials asst, 1976-79; City Col, NY, res asst, 1979-83, librn instr, 1983-90, asst prof, 1990-98, assoc prof, 1979-, Acquisitions Div, chief, 1996-2000, ref librn & bibliog coordr, 2000-; Bor Manhattan Community Col, adj assoc prof, 1995-; eCrochet Passion, owner, hand crocheter & designer, 2007-. **Orgs:** Libr Asn City Univ NY, 1983-; Cognotes reporter, Am Libr Asn, 1989-91; rec secy, New York Black Librns Caucus, 1989-90; personnel admin secy, liaison JMRT, Am Libr Asn, 1989-91; Systs & serv secy, acquisition Syst comm mem, AmLibr Asn, 1990-91; CCNY Fac Senate Elections Comt, 1995-98; CCNY Fac Senate Affairs Comt, secy, 1995-98; N Am Serials Users Group, 1995-2000; NY Libr Asn, 1996-. **Honors/Awds:** PSC-City Univ New York Research Award Recipient, 1995-96; City Col City Women, 1999. **Home Addr:** 348 Van Name Ave, Staten Island, NY 10303. **Business Addr:** Owner, Hand Crocheter, Designer, eCrochet Passion, 348 Van Name Ave Staten Island, New York, NY 10303-2520, **Business Phone:** (347)934-3242.

## GILL, JOHNNY, JR.

Songwriter, composer, singer. **Personal:** Born May 22, 1966, Washington, DC; son of Johnny Sr and Annie. **Career:** New Ed, mem. Solo Albums: Johnny Gill, 1983; Chemistry, 1985; Johnny Gill, 1990; Provacative, 1993; Let's Get the Mood Right, 1996; Favorites, 1997; Ultimate Collection, 2002; Still Winning, 2011; The Game Changer, 2014. Singles: "Super Love", 1983; "When Something is Wrong with My Baby", 1983;"Tiger Beat", "Rub You the Right Way", 1990; "My, My, My", 1990; "Giving My All to You", 1991; "Slow & Sexy", 1992; "I Got You", 1993; "Long Way from Home", 1993; "Quiet Time to Play", 1994; "A Cute, Sweet Love Addiction", 1994; "Let's Get the Mood Right", 1995; "It's Your Body", 1995; "Love in an Elevator", 1995; "Give Love on Christmas Day", 1998; "In The Mood", 2011; "It Would Be You", 2011; "Just The Way You Are", 2012; "Behind Closed Doors", 2014; "Game Changer", 2015; "This One's for Me & You", 2015. Motion picture soundtrack. Contributor: Boomerang, Mo' Money, New Jack City; Filmography: Saturday Night Live; The Best of Keith Sweat, 2005; One on One, 2005; Behind the Music, 2005; R Uthe Gir, 2005. Tv series: "Cuts", 2005. Movie: The Ballad of Walter Holmes, 2006. **Orgs:** LSG & New Ed. **Honors/Awds:** Golden Note Award; 21st Annual Rhythm & Soul Music Awards, ASCAP. **Business Addr:** Vocalist, Motown/Universal Music Group, 2220 Colorado Ave, Santa Monica, CA 90404, **Business Phone:** (310)865-5000.

## GILL, KENDALL CEDRIC

Basketball player, basketball executive, boxer. **Personal:** Born May 25, 1968, Chicago, IL; married Wendy; children: Phoenix & Kota. **Educ:** Univ Ill, Urbana-Champaign, BA, speech commun, 1990. **Career:** Basketball player (retired), basketball analyst, boxer; Charlotte Hornets, guard, 1990-93, 1995-96; Seattle SuperSonics, 1993-95; NJ Nets, 1996-2001; Miami Heat, 2001-02; Minn Timberwolves, 2002-03; Chicago Bulls, 2003-04; Milwaukee Bucks, 2004-05; Comcast Sports Net, analyst, 2006-07; boxer, currently. TV Series: "Heaven Is a Playground", 1991; "My Brother and Me", 1994; "Of Boys and Men", 2008. **Orgs:** Founder, Kendall Gill House; NBA Pac Div Champion Seattle Supersonics team, 1993-94.

## GILL, REV. LAVERNE MCCAIN

Clergy, executive, writer. **Personal:** Born Oct 13, 1947, Washington, DC; daughter of Paul McCain and Mary McCain Williams; married Tepper; children: Jennette, Dylan & Tepper. **Educ:** Howard Univ, BA, 1969; Am Univ, grad studies, commun, 1973; Rutgers Univ, MBA, 1977; Princeton Theol Sem, MDiv, 1997, ThM, 1998. **Career:** US Senate, Sen Alan Cranston, legis aide, 1970-72; Lassiter & Co, vpres, 1973-77; Univ DC, assoc prof, 1979-82; Fed Res Bd Govs, budget analyst, 1983-86; Metro Chronicle Newspaper, ed, co-founder, 1986-94; McCain Media Inc, pres; Women's Radical Discipleship Ministries, founder, currently; Author: African American Women Congress: Forming & Transforming Hist, Rutgers Univ Press, 1997; Wash Post Article, Princeton Packet, July 8 1997; article, Lectionary Preaching Women Abingdon Press, 2000; Books: My Mother Prayed Me: Faith Journaling African Am Women Pilgrim, 2000; Daughter's Dignity: African Bibl Women, Virtues Women, Pilgrim Press, Cleveland, OH, 2000; Vashti's Victory, Pilgrim Press, 2003; Webster Church United Church Christ Soc Inc, Mich, guest speakers, sr pastor. **Orgs:** Congional Press Gallery, 1986-94; Nat Newspaper Publishers Asn; Capital Area Chap, Acad Arts & Sci; Am Film TV Radio Asn; Friends Rankin Chapel; African-Am Media Coalition; chaplain adminr, Chautauqua United Church Christ Soc Inc; founder & pres, Life Transformation Found Inc. **Honors/Awds:** Commendation, Fed Res Bd Governors, 1985; Montgomery Award, Nat Asn Advan Colored People, 1987; Mayors Community Service Award, 1991; Emmy Nomination, Nat Acad Arts & Sci, 1992; Borscht Found Fel, 1992; Jagow Preaching Award; Excellence in Homiletics Award, Princeton; Antoinette Brown Award for Excellence in Ministry; Social Responsibility Award. **Spe-**

cial Achievements: First African American to pastor the Webster United Church of Christ. Author Of Numerous Articles & Books. **Home Addr:** 5484 Webster Church Rd, Dexter, MI 48130, **Home Phone:** (734)426-5115.

## GILL, ESQ. NIA H.

Lawyer, politician. **Personal:** Born Mar 15, 1948, Glen Ridge, NJ; children: 1. **Educ:** Upsala Col, BA, hist & polit hist; Rutgers Univ Sch Law, JD; Foreign Policy Inst, Ctr Women Policy Studies, grad, 2006. **Career:** Gen Assembly, 1994-2001; Minority Whip, 1996-2001; NJ State Senate, state sen, 2002-; Gill & Cohen PC, atty, partner, currently; Am Dem Party, politician, currently; Senate Pres Pro Tempore, 2010-. **Orgs:** NJ State Bar Asn; Million Dollar Advocates Forum; chair, Com; vice chair, Judiciary Legislative Oversight; Legislative Servs Comn; NJ Legis Select Comt on Invest. **Business Addr:** State Senator, Senate President, New Jersey State Senate, 39 S Fullerton Ave 2nd Fl Suite 7, Montclair, NJ 07042, **Business Phone:** (973)509-0388.

## GILL, ROBERTA L.

Lawyer. **Personal:** Born Jun 25, 1947, Baltimore, MD; daughter of Robert and Rubye; children: Tara Maraj. **Educ:** Am Univ, Wash, DC, BA, int rels, 1969; Univ Chicago Law Sch, 1971; Univ Md Law Sch, JD, law, 1972; Johns Hopkins Sch Hyg & Pub Health, MPH, 1976. **Career:** Atty, pvt pract, 1972-88; E Baltimore Community Corp, coun, admin, 1979-83; Sickle Cell Dis Asn Md, admin, 1985-88; Off Atty Gen, asst atty gen, 1988-. **Orgs:** Delta Sigma Theta Sorority, 1967-; Baltimore Cable Access Corp, 1986-; Rafiki Na Dada, an all female acapella singing group, 1987-; Cooley's Anemia Found, secy, 1988-; pres, Nat Gill Family Reunion, 1996-. **Honors/Awds:** Outstanding Contributions, Sickle Cell Disease Asn Md, 1996. **Home Addr:** 3415 Callaway Ave, Baltimore, MD 21215-7122, **Home Phone:** (410)542-1674. **Business Addr:** Assistant Attorney General, State of Maryland Attorney General's Office, 200 St Paul Pl Suite 2700, Baltimore, MD 21202-2272, **Business Phone:** (410)468-2000.

## GILL, REP. ROSA UNDERWOOD

Educator, accountant, association executive. **Personal:** Born May 14, 1944, Wake County, NC; married Jimmie; children: Angie Rosharon & Natalie Denise. **Educ:** Shaw Univ, Raleigh NC, BS, math, 1968; NC Cent Univ, Durham, NC, attended 1978; NC State Univ, Raleigh, NC, attended 1979. **Career:** Educator (retired), State Employee; Nationwide Ins, Raleigh, NC, acct clerk, 1965-68; Johnson Co, Smithfield, NC, math instr, 1968-70; Wake Co Raleigh NC, math instr, 1971-80; State Govt Raleigh NC, acct I, 1980-; Wake Comt Pub Sch Syst, sch bd mem, vice chair, currently; NC Gen Assembly, rep, 2009-. **Orgs:** Secy, Dem Party Wake Co, 1974-78; girl scout leader, Girl Scouts Am, 1974-78; adv Stud Coun, 1975-80; girl scout leader, 1976-78; dem vice chmn, Dem Party Wake Co, 1978; bd mem, NC Sch Boards Asn; dir, Zeta Phi Beta Sorority Incorporation, NC State. **Home Addr:** 2408 Foxtrot Rd, Raleigh, NC 27610, **Home Phone:** (919)821-0425. **Business Addr:** Representative, North Carolina General Assembly, 16 W Jones St Rm 1303, Raleigh, NC 27601-1096, **Business Phone:** (919)733-5880.

## GILL, SAMUEL A.

Violinist. **Personal:** Born Nov 30, 1932, Brooklyn, NY; son of Everton and Clarendon. **Educ:** Juilliard Sch Music; Manhattan Sch Music, BA, music & MA, music educ, 1960; Univ Colo, DMus, 1989. **Career:** Basist (retired), assistant principal; Denver Symphony Orchestra, bass violin; Colorado Symphony Orchestra, bassist, asst prin. **Orgs:** Denver Symphony Soc. **Honors/Awds:** Shriner Syrian Temple Sym Social Award, Tilden High, 1950; Win of Down Beat International Crit Award, 1955. **Special Achievements:** Played with Max Roach; Coleman Hawkins; J J Johnson; Harry Belafonte Singers; Randy Weston Trio Master Mason Mt Evans Lodge; 32 Degree Mason Mountain & Plains Consist; among first of race to be engaged by major symphony, 1960; First African-American members of a major orchestra. **Home Addr:** 2620 Newport St, Denver, CO 80207, **Home Phone:** (303)388-5000.

## GILL, DR. WALTER A. (WALI HAKEEM)

Educator. **Personal:** Born Aug 16, 1937, Greenville, MS; son of Robert and Rubye C; married Frances Nichols; children: Valerie Palmer, Michelle Queen, Stacey Palmer, Danell & Daren. **Educ:** Morgan State Col, BS, 1960; Syracuse Univ, MEd, 1971, PhD, educ commun, 1977. **Career:** Sec sch art teacher, 1962-64, 1966-70, 1992-93, 1997-2002; Bowie State Col, asst prof, 1973-78; Morgan State Univ, asst prof, 1978-84; Univ Nebr, Omaha, asst prof, 1985-91; Millerville Univ, asst prof, 1994-96; Hickey Sch, art teacher, 1998-2001; Woodbourne Sch, art teacher, 2001-; Dual Image Consult, vpres, pres, currently. **Home Addr:** 4228 Evans Chapel Rd, Baltimore, MD 21211-1615, **Home Phone:** (410)366-7160. **Business Addr:** President, Dual Image Consultants, 4228 Evans Chapel Rd, Baltimore, MD 21211, **Business Phone:** (410)889-9100.

## GILL, DR. WANDA EILEEN

Federal government official. **Personal:** Born Feb 7, 1945. **Educ:** Va State Univ, BS, psychol, 1967; Univ Cincinnati, MA, psychol, 1968; Bowie State Univ, MEd, 1983; George Washington Univ, EdD, 1987. **Career:** Univ Cincinnati, Danforth Found fel, 1967-68; Georgetown Univ Sch Med, coordr, 1977-79; Bowie State Univ, dir, Coordr & Learning Skills Specialist, 1979-92; Mid States Asn Comn Higher Educ, assoc dir, 1993-94; Diverse Educ Solutions, Inc, pres, 1994-98; ED Expert Consult, 1998-2000; Inst Prof Develop, dir, 2000-01; OESE, sr adv & dir SIP, 2001-02; Off Innovation & Improv, prog mgt analyst, 2002-04; US Dept Educ, Technol Educ Progs Off, 2004-. **Orgs:** US Dept Educ Big Chap; African Am Fed Execs Asn; Asn Supv & Curric Develop; reg rep, gold mem, life mem, US Dept Educaiton Chap Blacks Govt; Am Educ Res Asn; conf chmn, Mid-Eastern Asn Educ Opportunity Prog Personnel, 1987-89; pres, MD Exec Coun Educ Opportunity, 1989-92. **Honors/Awds:** Oper Crossroads Africa, Spelman Col, 1964. **Special Achievements:** Authored 35 publications; Conducted the First National Evaluation of the National Guard Bureaus Challenge Program. **Home Addr:** 807 Manor House Dr, Upper Marlboro, MD 20774, **Home Phone:** (301)390-9113. **Business Addr:** Management Analyst, Technology in Education Program, US Department of Education, 400 Md Ave SW, Washington, DC 20003, **Business Phone:** (800)872-5327.

## GILLESPIE, BONITA

Business owner, educator. **Personal:** Born Jan 20, 1951, Knoxville, TN; daughter of James Edward and Hildritn Doris Johnson. **Educ:** Knoxville Col, Knoxville, TN, BS, acct, 1973; E Tenn State Univ, Johnson City, TN, MA, bus educ, 1976. **Career:** Martin-Maretta Energy Syst, Oak Ridge, TN, acct, 1978-86; Knoxville Col, Knoxville, TN, asst prof acct & mgt, 1986-; BG Acct, Knoxville, TN, owner & acct, 1987-; Gillespie Fin & Tax Serv, owner & pres, currently; Tenn Wesleyan Col, adj prof acct; Maryville Col adj prof acct; Nat Sch Bus & Technol, adj prof acct. **Orgs:** Charter mem, Nat Asn Black Acct, Knoxville Chap, 1980-; dir, S Cent Region, Zeta Phi Beta Sorority Inc, 1986-90; trainer & site coordr, Internal Rev Serv, Knoxville Off; Fel Nat Asn Pub Acct; Am Acct Asn; Nat Bus Educ Asn; Better Bus Bur Serv Greater E Tenn; Knoxville/Knox County Community Action Comt; Morningside Home Owners Asn; E Tenn Chap March Dimes. **Honors/Awds:** Distinguished Service Award, Knoxville Col Alumni Asn, 1983; Silver Service Award, IRS, 1990; Community Service Award, Knoxville Community Action Community, 1990 & 1994; Entrepreneur of the Year, Iota Phi Lambda Sorority, 2002-03. **Special Achievements:** One of the first businesses to participate in the City Knoxville Incubator Project at the old Moses school. **Home Addr:** 2518 Chillicothe St, Knoxville, TN 37921-7011, **Home Phone:** (615)673-0907. **Business Addr:** Owner, Accountant, Gillespie Financial & Tax Service, 3611 Western Ave, Knoxville, TN 37921-1637, **Business Phone:** (865)974-9674.

## GILLESPIE, MARCIA ANN

Editor, writer, consultant. **Personal:** Born Jul 10, 1944, Rockville Centre, NY; daughter of Charles M and Ethel Young. **Educ:** Lake Forest Col, BA, Am studies, 1966. **Career:** Time-Life Bks, Time Inc, researcher, 1966-70; Essence Mag, ed-in-chief, 1971-80; Ms Mag, New York, exec ed, ed-in-chief, commun consult, ed & writer, 1980-93; Ms Found Educ & Commun, Times Sq, consult, 1990-92, ed-in-chief, 1993-2001; Mothers Mag, ed-in-chief, ed emer, currently. exec ed, 1992-93; Liberty Media Women, pres, 1996; Univ WI, guest lectr & advisor to vice chancellor; Johnnetta B. Cole Inst, prof diversity residence, currently. **Orgs:** Nat Coun Negro Women; Am Soc Mag Ed; bd dir, Rod Rodgers Dance Co; Arthur Ashe Inst Urban Health; Black & Jewish Women, New York; guest lectr, Univ WI Sch Commun; adv tovice chancellor, Univ W Indies, Outreachto N Am; Studio Mus Harlem; Educ Equity Concepts, EEC; adv comt, Take Our Daughters to Work Day; adv brd, Feminist Press; bd dirs, Violence Policy Ctr, Wash, DC; adv bd, Girls, Re-Cast TV; adv bd, Feminists Animals Rights, FAR; adv brd, ISMN; adv bd, fel Aspen Inst; bd dir, New Fed Theater New York; Am Asn Mag Ed. **Honors/Awds:** Outstanding Alumni Award, Lake Forest Col, 1973; Matrix Award, NY Women Commun, 1978; Mary MacLeod Bethune Award, Nat Coun Negro Women; March of Dimes Award; Life Achievement Award, New York Asn Black Journalists; Matrix Awd from New York Women In Commn; Mary MacLeod Bethune Award from the National Council of Negro Women; National Magazine Award. **Special Achievements:** editor-in-chief of Ms. Magazine making her the first African American woman to achieve that position, 1992; Named one of the fifty faces for American Future Time Magazine, 1979; one of ten outstanding women in mag publ, 1982. Author: Maya Angelou: A Glorious Celebration, 2008. **Business Addr:** Board of Director, New Federal Theatre, 292 Henry St, New York, NY 10002-4804, **Business Phone:** (212)353-1176.

## GILLESPIE, DR. RENA HARRELL

Educational consultant, counselor. **Personal:** Born Oct 26, 1949, Starkville, MS. **Educ:** Miss State Univ, BS, 1972, PhD, 1981; Univ Cincinnati, ME, 1974. **Career:** Cincinnati Pub Schs, resident counr, 1972-74; Miss Univ Women, minority stud counr, 1974-78; Miss State Univ, residence hall dir, 1979-82; Miss Univ Women, Minority Doctoral Fel, 1978-81; Univ NC Chapel Hill, assoc dir health careers prog, 1983-86; Benjamin Eiijah Mays High Sch, support staff, counr, currently; self-employed, educ consult, currently. **Orgs:** United Methodist Local Bd Ministries, 1975-; Southern Col Personnel Asn, 1979-; Am Personnel & Guid Asn, 1980-; Asn Col Stud Personnel, 1980-; Nat Minority Health Affairs, 1984-; vol, Outreach Counr Econ Opportunities Atlanta Proj Delay, Teenage Pregnancy Prev Prog, 1987-; vol, Helpline Counr Ga Coun Child Abuse, 1987-. **Honors/Awds:** Outstanding Young Woman of America, 1984. **Home Addr:** 1735 Flintwood Dr SE, Atlanta, GA 30316-4129, **Home Phone:** (404)758-6724. **Business Addr:** Counselor, Mays High School, 3450 Benjamin E Mays Dr SW, Atlanta, GA 30331, **Business Phone:** (404)802-5100.

## GILLETTE, HON. FRANKIE JACOBS

Consultant. **Personal:** Born Apr 1, 1925, Norfolk, VA; daughter of Frank and Natalie Taylor; married Maxwell Claude. **Educ:** Hampton Inst, BS, 1946; Howard Univ, MSW, 1948. **Career:** Ada S McKinley Comm House Chicago, supvr, 1950-53; Sophie Wright Settlement, Detroit, prog dir, 1953-64; Concerted Serv Proj, dir, 1964-65; Univ Calif Soc Welfare Exten, prog coordr, 1965-68; US Comm Serv Admin, spec prog coordr, 1968-81; G & G Enterprises, pres, owner, 1978-. **Orgs:** San Francisco Bus & Prof Women, Inc, 1970-; dir, Time Savings & Loan Asn, 1980-90; vpres, San Francisco Handicapped Access Appeals Bd, 1982-87; chairperson, bd dir, NANBPWC Inc, 1983-87; pres, Nat Asn Negro Bus & Prof Women's Clubs Inc, 1983-87; life mem, Delta Sigma Theta Sorority; chairperson, San Francisco-Abidjan, Cote d'Ivoire Sister Cities Comm; vpres, Urban Econ Develop Corp, San Francisco, 1987-91; bd, San Francisco Conv & Visitors Bur, 1987-94, 1997-; comnr, San Francisco Human Rights Comn, 1988-92; trustee, Fine Arts Mus San Francisco, 1993-; Links Inc; bd dir, Mus African Diaspora, 2006, founder & trustee. **Honors/Awds:** Alumnus of the Year, Hampton Inst, 1966; Sojourner Truth NANBPWC Inc, 1980; publications The Organizer; The Governor NANBPWC Inc, 1978, 1981; Woman of the Year, Delta Delta Zeta Chapter, Zeta Phi Beta Sorority, 1991; "Lives of Accomplishment, " San Francisco Sr Ctr, 2003; MOAD, Certificate of Recognition, 2008; Certificate of Special Congressional Recognition, 2011; CA. Senate Certificate of Recognition 2011; City and County of San Francisco Certificate of Honor, 2010. **Special Achievements:** "Women Who Make It Happen" Frito-Lay and National Council of Negro Women, 1987. **Home Addr:** 85 Cleary Ct Suite 4, San Francisco, CA 94109, **Home Phone:** (415)563-8299. **Business Addr:** President, Owner, G & G Enterprises, 85 Cleary Ct Suite 4, San Francisco, CA 94109, **Business Phone:** (415)563-8299.

## GILLETTE, DR. LYRA STEPHANIE

Physician, obstetrician, gynecologist, obstetrician, gynecologist. **Personal:** Born Mar 1, 1930; children: 1. **Educ:** Barnard Col, AB, 1960; Howard Univ, MD, 1964; Columbia Univ, MPH, 1968. **Career:** Fr-Polycl Med S-Hl Ctr, resident, 1964-65; Harlem Hosp, resident, 1965-69; Obstet & Gynec, vis clinician & consult, 1969; Univ Vienna, guest physician, 1969; US PUSH, dept chief obstet & gynec, 1970; Martin Luther King Jr Hosp, dir ambulatory serv obstet & gynec, 1971; Watts Health Found, chief obstet & gynec; Univ S Calif, clin prof obstet & gynec, 1990; Los Angeles County, Dept Health Servs, med specialist; pvt pract, currently; Watts Healthcare Corp, physician, currently. **Orgs:** Chmn, Pub Health Comn, Am Med Women's Asn, 1977; consult, obstet & gynec, Device Panel FDA, 1976; dip, Nat Bd Med Examiners, 1965; Am Bd Obstet & Gynec, 1972; Am Col obstet & gynec, 1974; Los Angeles obstet & gynec Soc, 1973; Am Pub Health Asn, 1971; Asn Pub Health obstet & gynec, 1974. **Honors/Awds:** PHS grant, 1968; AMA Physician Rec Award, 1969. **Special Achievements:** Publication, "Management of Adenomatous Hyperplasia", OB World, 1977. **Home Addr:** 4483 Don Milagro Dr, Los Angeles, CA 90008. **Business Addr:** Physician, Watts Healthcare Corp, 10300 Compton Ave, Los Angeles, CA 90002, **Business Phone:** (323)357-6680.

## GILLIAM, ARLEEN FAIN

Labor activist. **Personal:** Born Jan 2, 1949, Huntington, WV; daughter of Cicero and Lorraine; married Reginald E Jr. **Educ:** Skidmore Col, BS, 1970; Mass Inst Tech, MBA, 1976. **Career:** Cong Budget Off, budget analyst, 1976-77; Labor US Dept Labor, exec asst, 1977-81; Am Fedn Labor & Cong Indust Orgn, asst dir dept soc sec, 1981-84, dir budget & planning, 1984-91, Planning & Personnel Policy, dir budget, 1991-96; Clinton-Gore transition team, 1992-; Am Fedn Labor & Cong Indust Orgn, asst pres, 1996, sr asst, currently. **Orgs:** Reston Chapter Links, 1977-87; Sloan Sch Bd Govs, 1989-95; Fairfax County Park Authority Bd, 1991-93. **Home Addr:** 10705 Regency Forest Dr, Vienna, VA 22181-2842, **Home Phone:** (703)620-2711. **Business Addr:** Senior Assistant, American Federation of Labor & Congress of Industrial Organizations, 815 16th St NW, Washington, DC 20006, **Business Phone:** (202)637-5235.

## GILLIAM, ART. See GILLIAM, HERMAN ARTHUR, JR.

## GILLIAM, DOROTHY BUTLER

Editor. **Personal:** Born Nov 24, 2013, Memphis, TN; married Sam; children: Stephanie, Melissa & Leah. **Educ:** Ursuline Col, Louisville; Sch Jour, attended 1961; Lincoln Univ, BA, 1957; Columbia Grad Sch Jour & grad, MA, 1961. **Career:** Ebony Mag; Johnson Publ; Jet, ed; The Post, gen assignment reporter, 1961-65, asst ed, 1972-79; Panorama WTTG TV, broadcaster, 1967-72; Am Univ & Howard Univ, lectr, 1967-68, writer, 1967-72; The Post, reporter, 1961-66, asst ed, 1979; Inst Journalism Educ, chmn; Va Commonwealth Univ Sch Mass Commun, distinguished Prof, 2000; Robert C Maynard Inst Journ Educ, bd dir, currently; Book: Paul Robeson All American, author, 1976. **Orgs:** Pres, Nat Asn Black Journalists, 1993-95; dir, Young Jour Develop Prog, 1997; Nat Asn Black Woman; Am Soc Newspaper Editors; bd mem, Fund Investigative Journalism; fel Freedom Forum. **Honors/Awds:** Grant, African-Am Inst, 1961; Anne O'Hare McCormick Award, NY Newspaper Womens Club; Jour of Year, Capital Press Clubs, 1967; Emmy award for Panorama; outstanding alumni, Lincoln Univ, 1973; Journalist of the Year award, Capital Press Club; Honor Medal, Univ Mo; Journalism Alumni of the Year Award, Columbia Grad Sch. **Special Achievements:** First black woman hired as a full-time reporter The Post. **Home Addr:** 1812 Upshur St NW, Washington, DC 20011. **Business Addr:** Board of Director, Robert C Maynard Institute for Journalism Education, 1211 Preserv Pkwy, Oakland, CA 94612, **Business Phone:** (510)891-9202.

## GILLIAM, FRANK DELANO, SR.

Football executive, football coach. **Personal:** Born Jan 7, 1934, Steubenville, OH; son of Ed and Viola; married Velma E; children: Frank Jr, Gayle & Michelle A. **Educ:** Iowa Univ, BA, 1957. **Career:** Football player (retired); Winnipeg & Vancouver Canadian Football League, pro football player, 1957-63; Iowa Univ, asst coach, 1966-70; Minn Vikings, scout, scouting dir, 1971-75, dir player personnel, 1975-94, vpres, sr consult & player personnel, 1994-2002. **Orgs:** Nat Asn Advan Colored People; Univ Iowa Alumni Asn; Univ Iowa Black Alumni Asn, Univ Iowa Lettermans Club. **Honors/Awds:** All-American, Nat Educ Asn, 1953, 1956; All Big Ten, 1956. **Home Addr:** 6730 Valhalla Way, Windermere, FL 34786-5625.

## GILLIAM, HERMAN ARTHUR, JR. (ART GILLIAM)

Executive. **Personal:** Born Mar 6, 1943, Nashville, TN; son of Herman Arthur Sr (deceased) and Leola Hortense Caruthers. **Educ:** Yale Univ, BA, 1963; Univ Mich, MBA, 1967. **Career:** Universal Life Ins Co, 1967-75, vpres, 1970; US House Representatives, 1975-76; Gilliam Commun Inc, chmn & pres, 1977-; 1340 WLOK, owner, currently. **Orgs:** Pres, Memphis Area Radio Stas; chmn bd, Black Bus Asn Memphis; chmn, Tenn Humanities Coun; bd mem, Nat Fedn State Humanities Coun; Soc Entrepreneurs; bd visitors, Memphis State Univ; bd trustee, LeMoyne-Owen Col, 1973; Treas Memphis Black Bus Asn; mem Tenn Asn; Nat Asn Broadcasters & Nat Asn Black Owned Broadcasters; treas & mem bd gov, Nat Acad Rec Arts & Sci. **Special Achievements:** First African American-owned Memphis radio station & city's first locally owned station. **Home Addr:** 840 Bluebird Rd, Memphis, TN 38116-4004, **Home Phone:** (901)332-3319. **Business Addr:** Chairman, President, Gilliam Communications Inc, 363 S 2nd St, Memphis, TN 38103, **Business Phone:** (901)527-9565.

**GILLIAM, JAMES H, SR. See Obituaries Section.**

**GILLIAM, SAM J., JR.**
Artist, arts administrator, painter (artist). **Personal:** Born Nov 30, 1933, Tupelo, MS; son of Sam and Estery; married Dorothy Butler; children: Stephanie, Melissa & Leah. **Educ:** Univ Louisville, BA, fine art, 1955, MA, 1961, painting, LHD, 1980; Northwestern Univ, LHD, 1990. **Career:** Wash Gallery Mod Art, 1964; Inst Contemp Art, 1965; 1st World Festival Negro Arts, 1966; Embassies, Wash Gallery Mod Art, artist, 1967; Corcoran Gallery, 1969; Martin Luther King Mem, exhib mus mod art, 1969; Harlem, exhibited studio mus, 1969; Venice Biennale, Italy, 1970; Whitney Mus Ann, painter, educr & artist, 1970; Art Inst Chicago, 1970; Pacy Gallery, NY, 1972; Maison de la Cult Rennes, France, 1973; Phoenix Gallery, San Francisco, 1974; Philadelphia Mus Art, 1975; Galerie Darthea Speyer Paris, 1976; Dart Gallery Chicago, 1977. **Honors/Awds:** Norman Walt Harris Prize, Art Inst Chicago; Doctor of Humane Letters, Univ Dist Columbia, 2006; Alumnus of the Year, Univ Louisville, 2006; National Endowment of the Arts Award. **Special Achievements:** First artist to introduce the idea of a painted canvas hanging without stretcher bars. **Business Addr:** Artist, 1900 Quincy St NW, Washington, DC 20011-5338.

**GILLIS, SHIRLEY J. BARFIELD**
Educator. **Personal:** Born Oct 2, 1943, Kinston, NC; daughter of George and Sarah Daughety; married Harvey; children: LaChale R. **Educ:** Elizabeth City State Univ, Elizabeth City, NC, BS, 1970; Eastern Conn State Univ, Willimantic, CT, MS, 1975; Southern Conn State Univ, New Haven, CT, attended 1990. **Career:** Teacher(retired). New London Bd Educ, New London, Conn, kindergarten teacher, 1970; Harbor Elem Sch, New London, Conn, Gen Elem, Kinder garden teacher, currently. **Orgs:** Chairperson, New London Educ Asn, 1975; pres, New London Educ Asn, 1980-81; Phi Delta Kappa, 1988-; corresondancy secy, Delta Kappa Gamma, 1989-; African Am Latino Coalition, 1989-; pres, New London Nat Asn Advan Colored People; Hist Black Col Alumni; pres, New London Alumni Chap, Delta Sigma Theta; founder & bd dir, Kente Cult Ctr; auxillary bd dir & vpres, Lawrence & Mem Hosp; corresp secy, New London Dem Party. **Special Achievements:** First African American President of the Auxiliary of Lawrence and Memorial Hospital. **Home Addr:** 340 Bayonet St, New London, CT 06320, **Home Phone:** (860)447-9536. **Business Addr:** Teacher, Harbor Elementary School, 432 Montauk Ave, New London, CT 06320, **Business Phone:** (860)447-6040.

**GILLIS, THERESA MCKINZY**
Manager, government official. **Personal:** Born Sep 16, 1945, Ft. Meade, FL; daughter of Arthur and Dezola Williams; married Eugene Talmadge; children: Reginald, Jarett & Jeraemy. **Educ:** Talladega Col, BA, 1967; Barry Univ, Miami, FL, MS, 1993. **Career:** Broward Employ & Training Admin, counr, mgr SYEP dir, 1976-82; Broward County Community Develop Div, citizen participation coordr, 1982-84, asst dir, dir, 1984-94; Proj & Community Coord, Pub Works Dept, Off Environ Serv, dir, 1994-; County Broward, br mgr; Newyork Intellectual Property Law Asn, pres. **Orgs:** SSO'S mem officer, Delta Sigma Theta Sorority, 1968-; Fla Community Develop Asn, 1984-; Nat Asn Counties, 1986-; Home Econs Adv Bd, BrowardSch Bd, 1987-89; comt mem, Mt Hermon AME Church Credit Union, 1988-; bd mem, Code Enforcement City Lauderdale Lakes, 1988-; Minority Recruitment Broward County Sch Bd, 1989; bd mem, City Lauderhill, Econ Develop Agency, 1996-; charter mem, Coalition 100 Black Women, Broward County Chap; adv bd mem, Lauderhill Pub Safety. **Home Addr:** 1350 SW 72nd Ave, Plantation, FL 33317-5073. **Business Addr:** Director, Public Works Department, 2555 W Copans Rd, Pompano Beach, FL 33069, **Business Phone:** (954)831-0706.

**GILLISPIE, WILLIAM HENRY**
Aerospace engineer, consultant. **Personal:** Born Jan 8, 1927, Hanna, WY; son of Nathan and Susie Anderson; married Laura; children: Vincent, Shiela & Richard. **Educ:** Lincoln Univ, BS, mech engineering, 1950; Wash Univ, Univ Mo Rolla & St Louis, grad study. **Career:** A/C Proj Off USA, ch test, 1953-61; USA Aviation Syst Comn, oper res anal, 1961-62, spec asst res & develop, 1962-63, dep chief observation helicopter field off, 1963-70, spec asst comndg gen prog mgt, 1970-73, mgr aircraft div, 1973; WHG Inc, prin, aerospace & mgt consult, 1989-; Army Aviation Systs Command, engr. **Orgs:** Mgt trans Aviation Res & Develop, 1960; command work act, AUS Mobility Comm, 1963; chmn, CFC camp USA Aviation Syst Comn, 1974; pres, Lincoln Univ Mo State chap, 1975-76; chmn, St Louis Sect, Am Inst Aeronaut & Astronaut, 1977; pres, Lincoln Univ Alumni Asn, 1979-85; Omega Psi Phi Fraternity. **Honors/Awds:** Army Civilian Merit Award, 1971; Section Leadership Award, Am Inst Aeronaut & Astronaut, 1977; Distinguished Alumni Award, Lincoln Univ, Mo, 1977; Army Commanders Award for Civil Service, 1980; Service Award, Am Inst Aeronaut & Astronaut, 1980; Presidential Award, Nat Asn Equal Opportunity Higher, 1985; Outstanding Service Award, Lincoln Univ, 1985; Commanders Award for Meritorious Achievment, 1988-89; Outstanding Service Award, Kinloch, Mo, 1998; Outstanding Service Award, Kirkwood, Mo Sch Bd, 1999. **Home Addr:** 1915 Claymills Dr, Chesterfield, MO 63017, **Home Phone:** (636)532-5171. **Business Addr:** Principal, Consultant, WHG Inc, 1915 Claymills Dr, Chesterfield, MO 63017, **Business Phone:** (636)532-5171.

**GILLOM, JENNIFER**
Basketball coach, basketball player. **Personal:** Born Jun 13, 1964, Abbeville, MS; daughter of Ella. **Educ:** Univ Miss, attended 1986. **Career:** Basketball player (retired), basketball coach; Ital League, Italy, 1987-91; Ancona, 1991-94; Messina, 1995-96; Phoenix Mercury, ctr, 1997-2002; Taronto, 2002; Los Angeles Sparks, forward, 2003, head coach, 2010-11; Xavier Col Prep, head coach, 2004-05, 2009-10; Minn Lynx, asst coach, 2008, head coach, 2009; USA Basketball Women's World Championship, asst coach, 2010-; Wash Mystics, asst coach, 2012; Conn Sun, asst coach, 2013-. **Orgs:** Mercury Community Rels Dept, 2001-02. **Home Addr:** PO Box 1921, Phoenix, AZ 85001, **Home Phone:** (602)332-7544. **Business Addr:** Assistant Coach, USA Basketball Women's World Championship, 5465 Mark Dabling Blvd, Colorado Springs, CO 80918-3842, **Business Phone:** (719)590-4800.

**GILLUM, ANDREW D.**
Commissioner. **Personal:** Born Jul 26, 1979, Miami, FL; son of Charles and Frances Gillum; married R Jai Howard; children: Jackson & Caroline Gillum. **Educ:** Fla A&M Univ, polit sci. **Career:** Fla Dem Party, dep polit dir; Tallahassee City Comn, comnr, 2003-, mayor pro tem, 2004-05; Capital Region Transp Planning Agency, chairperson, 2005; Fla A&M Univ, liaison & chief negotiator, currently; Fla Dem Party, state polit dir. **Orgs:** Bd dir, Mary Brogan Mus; bd dir, Keep Tallahassee-Leon County Beautiful; bd dir, Kids Inc; bd dir, Whole Child Leon Leadership Coun; bd dir, Riley House; Tiger Bay Club; Capital City Chamber; Leadership Tallahassee Class XXII; Capital City Child Care Consortium; nat dir, People Am Way Found Young Elected Officials Network; Black Youth Vote Coalition; Nat Asn Adv Colored People; Nat Coalition Black Civic Participation; chmn, Capital Region Transp Planning Agency, 2005; Econ Develop Coun; Fla League Cities; Cult Resources Comn Ways & Means Comt; exec comt mem, Big Bend 2006 Heart Walk; bd dir, Big Bend Community Based Care; bd dir, Mary Brogan Mus; bd dir, Keep Tallahassee-Leon County Beautiful; bd dir, Kids Inc; bd dir, Whole Child Leon Leadership Coun; ex officio mem, Riley House Bd Dirs; Capital City Child Care Consortium; nat dir, Young Elected Officials Network; People Am Way Found; chair, Blueprint 2000 Intergovernmental Agency, 2008-09; bd dir, Schott Found Pub Educ; bd mem, New World Found. **Honors/Awds:** Emerging Leaders Award, Cong Black Caucus Found Inc, 2003; The Fast Track 30 Leaders Who are 30 and Under, Ebony mag, 2004; Dr. Martin Luther King Jr. Leadership Award, Fla A&M Univ, 2010; 40/40 Young Alumni Award. **Special Achievements:** One of the citys Persons of the Year, Gainesville Sun, 1998; Listed in "The Fast Track 30 Leaders Who are 30 and Under " by Ebony, 2004. **Business Addr:** Commissioner, Tallahassee City Commission, Tallahassee City Hall 300 S Adams St, Tallahassee, FL 32301, **Business Phone:** (850)891-8181.

**GILLUM, RODERICK D.**
President (organization), public relations executive. **Personal:** Born Detroit, MI. **Educ:** Mich State Univ, BA, 1972; Northeastern Univ, Sch Law, JD, 1975; Mass Inst Technol, MS, mgt, 1985. **Career:** Gen Motors, atty, 1979, bd dir, secy & Asst gen coun, 1986-88, vpres corp responsibility & diversity, 1997-2009; Saturn Corp, mgr strategic planning, 1985-86, vpres, gen coun & secy, 1988-93; Motor Enterprises Inc, chmn bd & pres; State Mich Sen Arthur Cartwright, admin asst; Gen Motors Found, chmn; Detroit Econ Growth Corp, chmn; Detroit Econ Club, vpres; Saturn Corp, vpres & gen coun Jackson Lewis LLP, partner, shareholder, currently. **Orgs:** Cong Black Caucus Found; Chmn, Gen Motors Found; Chmn Bd, Charles H. Wright Mus African Am Hist; Co-Chair, Am Bar Asn Col Labor & Employ Law Opportunities Minorities Profession; bd trustee, W.K. Kellogg Found; dir, Invest Detroit; atty, Nat Labor Rels Bd Detroit; bd, Holcim Inc; Nat Urban League; Nat Coun LaRaza; Harvard Univ Kennedy Sch Govt Shorenstein Ctr; chair, Wash DC Martin Luther King; chair, Jr Nat Memorial Proj Found Inc; vice chair, Detroit Econ Growth Corp; chair, Joint Ctr Polit & Econ Studies; Firms Corp Diversity Coun; Corp Compliance; fel Am Bar Asns Col Labor & Employ Lawyer; WK Kellogg Found. **Home Addr:** 2737 Turtle Shores Dr, Bloomfield Hills, MI 48302-0768. **Business Addr:** Partner, Jackson Lewis LLP, 2000 Town Ctr Suite 1650, Southfield, MI 48075, **Business Phone:** (248)936-1900.

**GILLUM, DR. RONALD M., SR.**
School administrator, educator, association executive. **Personal:** Born May 21, 1939, Gates, PA; son of Roger O and Edna R; married Harriette A Coleman; children: Ronald Jr, Rhonda & Robin. **Educ:** Western Mich Univ, BS, 1963; Wayne State Univ, MEd, 1972, EdD, 1975. **Career:** Administrator (retired); Detroit Pub Sch, instr, 1963-69, teacher, 1963-70, admin, 1969-71; Wayne County Community Col, instr, 1969-71; Mich Dept St, dir prog develop, 1978-80; Boy's Club Am, recreation dir; Mich Dept Educ, Adult Educ, deputy dir, Lansing, Mich, 1980-83, dir, off Adult Exten Learning, currently; Detroit Col Bus, exec dir, 1996-; Wayne County Community Col, adj prof; Saginaw Valley Univ, adj prof; Western Mich Univ, adj prof; Black Child & Family Inst, exec dir; Nat Inst Literacy, bd dir; Rhonda Walker Found, state educ & univ adminr; Detroit Col Bus & Davenport Univ, adminr, currently. **Orgs:** Mich Alliance Black Sch Educr; Mich Asn Pub Adult Community Educ; Nat Alliance Black Sch Educr; co-founder, Black Teacher Workshops, Detroit; Urban League, Lansing; NAACP; PTA Lansing; bd dir, Am Asn Adult & Continuing Educ, 1987-; policy fel Educ Policy Fel Prog, Nat Inst Educ Leadership. **Honors/Awds:** Outstanding Leadership Award in Literacy, US Dept Educ, 1985; hon mem, Sheet Metal Workers Int Asn; Focus & Impact Award, Cotillion Club Inc, Detroit; Distinguished Service Award, Mich St Bd Educ, 1987; President Award, Mich Asn Adult & Continuing Educ, 1989. **Special Achievements:** Published articles, "Michigan is Learning How to Close Its Literacy Gap", Detroit Free Press, 1987; "Adult Literacy-Can We Handle the Problem", OPTIONS 1987. **Home Addr:** 7452 Gypsie Lane Apt 7, Lansing, MI 48917-1065. **Business Addr:** Director, Office of Adult Extended Learning, PO Box 30008, Lansing, MI 48909, **Business Phone:** (517)373-8358.

**GILMORE, DR. AL TONY**
Educator, manager, consultant. **Personal:** Born Jun 29, 1946, Spartanburg, SC; married Beryl Sansom; children: Jack S & Genevieve M. **Educ:** NC Cent Univ, BA, hist, 1968, MA, hist, 1969; Univ Toledo, PhD, Am hist, 1972. **Career:** Howard Univ, Dept Hist, assoc prof, prof, 1972-78; Inst Serv Educ, prog assoc; Univ MD, Col Pk Afro-Am Studies Prog, prof hist & dir, 1978-84; Nat Afro-Am Mus Proj, chief consult, 1982, dir; Asn Study African Am Life & Hist, researcher; Nat Educ Asn, sr prog officer, instr & prof develop specialist, 1985-89; Nat Educ Asn, mgr, sr prog officer, dir ctr human & civil rights, 1986-, historian & archivist emer; Human & Civil Rights div, sr prof assoc, 1989-2000; Leadership Training & Develop, mgr; Calif Comn Status African-Am Males, consult; Nat Endowment Humanities, consult; George Washington Univ, Estelle & Melvin Gelman Res Ctr, vis scholar. **Orgs:** Bd dir, Asn Study Afro Am Life & Hist, 1977-88; Org Am Historians; Am Hist Asn; Asn Study African-Am Life & Hist; pres, Forum Study Educ Excellence; bd dirs, Qual Educ Minorities Proj; Nat Coun Educ Black; bd mem, J African Am Hist; Qual Educ Minorities Proj; Am Hist Asn. **Special Achievements:** Author: Bad Nigger! The National Impact of Jack Johnson, 1975; Revisiting the Slave Community Revisited; The Natl Impact of Jack Johnson; The Life Times of Amos n Andy, in progress: A Social Hist; book reviews & articles have appeared in Wash Post; New Repub; Am Scholar; Lectured in Morehouse College, Harvard University, Brown University, Hampton University. **Home Addr:** 6108 Clearwood Rd, Bethesda, MD 20817-6002, **Home Phone:** (301)229-3753. **Business Addr:** Director, National Education Association, 1201 16th St NW, Washington, DC 20036-3290, **Business Phone:** (202)833-4000.

**GILMORE, JOHN T., JR.**
Real estate appraiser, educator. **Personal:** Born Aug 1, 1935, Prescott, AR; married Curley Usher. **Educ:** BS, 1957; MSIE, 1970; PhD, 1971. **Career:** Univ Ark, Dept Math Sci, prof, chair, 1982-96; Boeing Air Co, assoc engr, 1958-60, statist consult, comput prog consult; Gilmore Appraisal Serv, real estate appraiser, currently; Trinity Church, admin asst; Univ Ark Pine Bluff, dir eng; Diversified Unlimited Corp Inc, sec bd trustee. **Orgs:** Am Inst Indust Engr Inc; Pine Bluff Planning Comn; bd chmn, Trinity Church God Christ; Alpha Kappa Mu; Univ Nat Hon Soc; Beta Kappa Chi Sci Hon Soc; Alpha Pi Mu Indsust Eng Hon Soc. **Home Addr:** 902 Rosswood Colony Dr, Pine Bluff, AR 71603-0700, **Home Phone:** (870)536-2896. **Business Addr:** Real Estate Appraiser, Gilmore Appraisal Service, 1116 State St, Pine Bluff, AR 71603.

**GILMORE, MAHERSHALALHASHBAZ. See ALI, MAHERSHALA.**

**GILMORE, REV. MARSHALL B.**
Clergy. **Personal:** Born Jan 4, 1931, Hoffman, NC; married Yvonne Dukes; children: John M & Joan Michele. **Educ:** Paine Col, BA, 1957; Drew Theol Sem Madison, MDiv, theol, 1960; United Theol Sem, DMin, 1974; Tex Col, DDiv; Interdenominational Theol Ctr, DDiv. **Career:** Clergy, senior bishop (retired); Hudson Memorial CME Church, pastor, 1950; Bray Temple CME Chicago, Ill, pastor, 1960-62; W Mitchell St CME Church, 1962; Allen Temple CME Church, 1962-64; Phillips Temple CME Church, 1964-70; Payne Theol Sem Wilberforce, instr, 1972-73; CME Church, named Bishop, 1982; Christian Methodist Episcopal Church, Eight Episcopal Dist, sr bishop, 1994-2006. **Orgs:** Mem bd, Phillips Sch Theol, 1966-; vice-chair, Gen Connectional Bd, 1966-; bd trustee, Paine Col, 1969-; pres, Dayton Nat Asn Advan Colored People, 1971-72; rep, CME Church Consult Church Union; chair bd trustee, Tex Col; chair, Dept Evangelism, chair, Dept Personnel Serv. **Honors/Awds:** Doctor of Laws and Letters, Paine Col. **Home Addr:** 683 Beacontree Ct NW, Concord, NC 28027-7804, **Home Phone:** (704)786-3226. **Business Addr:** Member of the Board, Phillips School of Theology, 700 Martin Luther King Jr Dr, Atlanta, GA 30314, **Business Phone:** (404)527-7768.

**GILMORE, REV. DR. ROBERT MCKINLEY, SR.**
Educator, president (organization). **Personal:** Born May 14, 1952, Houston, TX; son of Marvin and Olan Yvonne; married Jacqueline Davis-Gilmore; children: Robert Jr & Reshun. **Educ:** Tex Southern Univ, BA, 1980, MA, 1981, MA, 1984; Univ Houston, PhD, educ, psychol, urban ministry, commun, 1985; Houston Grad Sch Theol, Mdiv, 1989. **Career:** KTSU & KPVU, radio producer & host, 1980-85; Tex Southern Univ, instr, 1981-83; City Houston, asst dir, 1982-84; Univ Houston, grad asst, 1982-85; Prairie View A&M Univ, asst prof, 1985-89; Houston Grad Sch Theol, urban ministry prog dir; Real Urban Ministry Inc, pres & chief exec officer, 2002-; Real Urban Counselors, Consults & Assocs, founder & pres, chief exec officer, 2009-; Real Productions, pres, 2011-; Real Publ Co, pres, chief exec officer. **Orgs:** Asst to pastor, Barbers Mem Bapt Church, 1979-89; pres, Real Prods, 1980-; consult, Baptist Ministers Asn, 1985-95; Phi Delta Kappa, Univ Houston, 1985-89; Prairie View A&M Univ, 1986-89; dir, Drug Training Prog Independent Missionary Baptist Asn; pres, One Church & One Child, 1988-90; pres, Real Educ Alternatives Leadership & Learning, 1989-91; drug educ consult, City Houston; Who DARE to LEAD, 2009. **Home Addr:** 11849 Spring Grove Dr, Houston, TX 77099, **Home Phone:** (281)983-0840. **Business Addr:** President, Chief Executive Officer, Real Urban Ministry Inc, St3232 Winbern St, Houston, TX 77004-4651, **Business Phone:** (713)741-6642.

**GILMORE, HON. VANESSA DIANE**
Judge. **Personal:** Born Oct 26, 1956, St. Albans, NY; daughter of Clifton and Laura H. **Educ:** Hampton Univ, BS, clothing & textile mkt, 1977; Univ Houston Col Law, JD, 1981. **Career:** Foleys Dept Store, fashion buyer, 1977-79; Univ Houston Col Law, adj prof, 1984; Sue Schecter & Assoc, atty, 1985-86; Vickery, Kilbride, Gilmore & Vickery, atty, 1981-94; Houston, Tex, pvt pract, 1981-94; US Courts, US dist Judge, 1994-. **Orgs:** Houston Bar Asn; chairperson church comn, Nat Asn Advan Colored People, 1989-93; pres & bd dir, YWCA, 1990-92; chairperson, LEAD, Links Inc, 1990-91; chairperson, Tex Dept Com, 1992-94; Univ Houston Alumni Bd, 1993-; chairperson, Texans N Am Free Trade Agreement. **Home Addr:** 3333 Allen Pkwy Unit 707, Houston, TX 77019-1838, **Home Phone:** (713)529-2249. **Business Addr:** Judge, US Courts, Rm 9513 515 Rusk St, Houston, TX 77002, **Business Phone:** (713)250-5931.

**GILOTH-DAVID, KING R.**
Clergy, editor. **Personal:** Born Dec 23, 1940, White Plains, NY; son of Henry and Frances Cook; married Mary Louise Hamill; children: Laura Lee (Larry), Daniel Louis (Sara), Matthew David (Kathy), Jonathan Henry & King David. **Educ:** Univ Notre Dame, BA, polit sci, 1963, MA, teaching, 1965. **Career:** Reformer Newspaper Inc, ed & publ, 1967-96; Northeast Africa Zion Media, ed, 1995-; Ethiopian Christian Spiritualist Church, founder, pastor, 1997-. **Orgs:** Dir, Christian Dem Ctr, S Bend, IN, 1964-87; chmn, Christian Dem Movement, 1968-; bd dir, St Joseph Col Comt Fed Credit Union, 1980-82; dir, Reg Fed Anti-Poverty Agency, 1980-82; dir, Ctr Christian Dem Socialism, 1987-; coord, Christian Dem Socialist Party, 1987-; secy, Tolton Soc, 1987-; mgr, secy, St Augustine Church Gospel Choir, 1988-; Volkswagen Remanufacturing Coop, 1988-; bd dir, Wash-Chapin African-Am Learning Prog, 1989-94; master mason, St Peter's Lodge 31, F&AM, Prince Hall, 1995-; bd dirs, S Bend Br Nat Asn Advan Colored People, 1996-97; S Bend Chap Ind Black Expo, 1997-98. **Honors/Awds:** US Deleg Christian Dem World Union, Rome. **Home Addr:** 1036 W

Jefferson Blvd, South Bend, IN 46601, **Home Phone:** (574)289-8127. **Business Addr:** Editor, Northeast Africa Zion Media, 1040 W Jefferson Blvd, South Bend, IN 46601.

### GILPIN, CLEMMIE EDWARD

Educator. **Personal:** Born Aug 12, 1942, Beaverdam, VA. **Educ:** Va State Col, BA, hist, 1966; Ohio Univ, MA, foreign affairs, 1970; Pa State Univ, PhD, community systs, 1998. **Career:** Nigeria Peace Corps, vol, 1966-68; Vista, recruit, 1969-71; Pa State Univ Harrisburg, instr, 1971-, asst prof community systs & Afro-Am studies, currrently, Sch Behav Sci & Educ, social sci prog coordr, currently; Penn State Harrisburg Model, founder & dir. **Orgs:** PA Sociol Soc; PA Prostate Cancer Coalition; UN Asn S cent PA; Voc Rehab Diversity Adv Comt; Harrisburg Area Community Col; fac adv, Black Stud Union; fac adv, Int Affairs Asn. **Business Addr:** Assistant Professor, Coordinator, Penn State University Harrisburg, 777 W Harrisburg Pke, Middletown, PA 17057-4898, **Business Phone:** (717)948-6208.

### GILTON, DR. DONNA L.

Educator, librarian. **Personal:** Born Jul 9, 1950, Lynn, MA; daughter of Charles W Sr and Hattie Franklin. **Educ:** Simmons Col, Boston, MA, BA, hist & elem educ, 1972, MS, 1975; Univ Pittsburgh, PA, PhD, libr sci, 1988. **Career:** Professor (retired), Emeritus Professor; Boston Pub Libr, Boston, MA, pre-prof asst, 1972-75, Codman Sq Br, librn I, 1975-78, Uphams Corner Br, librn II, 1978-79; Belize Teachers Col, Belize City, Belize, head librn, 1979-81; Univ Pittsburgh, Title IIB fel, 1981-82; Western Ky Univ, Bowling Green, KY, bus ref librn, 1984-88; Pa State Univ, Univ Pk, PA, bus ref librn & pattee libr, coordr, 1988-91; Univ RI, Grad Sch Libr & Infor Studies, from asst prof to assoc prof, 1992-2006, prof, 2006-14, prof emerita 2014-. **Orgs:** Belize Libr Asn, 1979-81; Spec Libr Asn, 1982-83, Pittsburgh Chap, 1982-83; Bus & Finance Div, 1982-83; Am Soc Info Sci, 1982-83; dir, Womens Missionary Socs, 1986-87, secy, 1988-91, ypd dir, 1990-91; Asn Res & Col Libr, 1987-; Am Libr Asn, 1987-; instr sect, Asn Res & Col Libr, 1987-, 1988-; Continuing Educ Comt, 1989-91; Asn Libr & Info Sci Educ, 1990-2014; Instr Diverse Pop Comt, 1991-95; coordr, Bd Christian Educ, First Church God, 1996-99, youth ministry coordr, 1996-98, jr church, 1996-98; RI Libr Asn, 1998-; Mass Black Librn Network, 1998-2014; Cornucopia Ri, 2006-14. **Special Achievements:** Author: Multicultural and Ethnic Children's Literature in the United States, 2006; Lifelong Learning in Public Libraries: Principles, Programs, and People, 2012. **Home Addr:** 16 Serenity Way, Peace Dale, RI 02879, **Home Phone:** (401)792-3888. **Business Addr:** Professor Emerita, University Rhode Island, Rm 9 Rodman Hall 94 W Alumni Ave, Kingston, RI 02881-0815, **Business Phone:** (401)874-4630.

### GILYARD-INGRAHAM, DR. GERALINE L.

Educator. **Personal:** Born Nov 24, 1938, Miami, FL; daughter of Robert and Rosabelle; married Arlington; children: Vanessa Henelle; children: Vanessa. **Educ:** Bethune-Cookman Col, BS, 1962; Fla Atlantic Univ, MS, 1967; Univ Miami, EdD, 1975. **Career:** Greenville Training Sch, 1962-63; Dade County Schs, 5th grade teacher, 1963-67, guid counr, 1967-70, human rels specialist, 1970-72, dir, admin servs, 1976-78, dir non-inst training, 1978-86, dir inst staffing, 1987-95; NOVA Southeastern Univ, adj prof, 1996-. **Orgs:** S Chap Negro Bus & Prof Women's Club; Top Ladies Distinction, Gamma Zeta Omega, Alpha Kappa Alpha, vpres, 1985-; United Methodist Women, coordr, Ed & Interp, 1997-2001; Col Gardens Homeowner's Asn, Historian, 1999-2003; chair personnel com, Wesley Found, Univ Miami, 1999-; Dania Beach Airport Adv Com, 2001-; chair person, Ebony Fashion Fair Comt. **Home Addr:** 744 SW 2 Pl, Dania Beach, FL 33004.

### GINUWINE (ELGIN BAYLOR LUMPKIN)

Actor, singer, dancer. **Personal:** Born Oct 15, 1975, Washington, DC; son of James II Lumpkin (deceased) and Sandra Lumpkin (deceased); married Tonya M Johnston; children: Dream Sarae Lumpkin & Story. **Educ:** Prince George Community Col, assoc degree. **Career:** Singer, Dancer, Actor; Films: Booty Call, 1997; The Best Man, 1999; Down to Earth, 2001; Barbershop, 2002; Juwanna Mann, 2002; Love Don't Cost a Thing, 2003; Deliver Us from Eva, 2003; Honey, 2003; Wild Hogs, 2007; Dark Rising: Bring Your Battle Axe, 2007; Grand Theft Auto IV, 2008; The Bachelor Party, 2011; The Ideal Husband, 2011; Magic Mike, 2012; Paid in Full, 2015; Chocolate City, 2015; Albums: Ginuwine..the Bachelor, 1996; 100% Ginuwine, 1999; The Life, 2001; The Senior, 2003; Back II Da Basics, 2005; I Apologize, 2007; A Man's Thoughts, 2009; TV guest appearances: "Moesha", 1996; "Martial Law", 1998; Single: "When We Make Love", 2005; Epic Records, rec artist, currently. **Business Addr:** Recording Artist, Epic Records, 550 Madison Ave 6th Fl, New York, NY 10022-3211, **Business Phone:** (212)833-8000.

### GIOVANNI, NIKKI, JR. (YOLANDE CORNELIA GIOVANNI)

Poet, educator. **Personal:** Born Jun 7, 1943, Knoxville, TN; daughter of Jones and Yolande Watson; children: Thomas Watson. **Educ:** Fisk Univ, BA, hist, 1967; Univ Pa, Sch Soc Work, attended 1967; Columbia Univ; Worcester Univ, LHD, 1972; Ripon Univ, DLitt, 1974; Smith Col, Dlitt, 1975. **Career:** Poet, writer, commentator, activist & educator, currently; Queens Col, asst prof black studies, 1968; Livingston Col, Rutgers Univ, assoc prof eng, 1968-72; Niktom, founder, 1970; Ohio State Univ, vis prof eng, 1984; Mt St Joseph, prof creative writing, 1985; Va Tech, vis prof eng, 1987-89, prof eng, 1989-, Gloria D Smith prof, 1997-99, distinguished prof Eng, 1999-; Warm Hearth Writer's Workshop, dir, 1988-; Books: Spin a Soft Black Song, 1971; Ego Tripping & Other Poems for Young People, 1973; Vacation Time: Poems for Children, 1980; Those Who Ride the Night Winds, 1983; Sacred Cows & Other Edibles, 1988; The Genie in the Jar, 1996; The Sun Is So Quiet, 1996; The Girls in the Circle (Just for You!), 2004; Poetry Speaks to Children: A Celebration of Poetry with a Beat, 2005; Lincoln and Douglass: An American Friendship, 2008; Hip Hop Speaks to Children: A Celebration of Poetry with a Beat, 2008; The Grasshopper's Song: An Aesop's Fable, 2008. Poetry: Black Feeling, Black Talk, 1968, 1970; Black Judgement, 1969; Re: Creation, 1970; My House, 1972; The Women and The Men, 1975; Cotton Candy on a Rainy Day, 1978; Woman, 1978; Those Who Ride The Night Winds, 1983; Knoxville, Tennessee, 1944; The Selected Poems of Nikki Giovanni, 1996; Love Poems, 1997; Blues: For All the Changes, 1999; Quilting the Black-Eyed Pea: Poems and Not Quite Poems, 2002; The Prosaic Soul of Nikki Giovanni, 2003; The Collected Poetry of Nikki Giovanni, 2003; Acolytes, 2007; Bicycles: Love Poems, 2009; 100 Best African American Poems, 2010; Chasing Utopia: A Hybrid, 2013. My House, 1972; The Women & the Men, 1975; Cotton C & Y on a Rainy Day, 1978; Those Who Ride the Night Winds, 1983; The Sun Is So Quiet, 1996; Love Poems, 1997; Blues: For All the Changes: New Poems, 1999; Quilting the Black-Eyed Pea: Poems & Not Quite Poems, 2002; The Prosaic Soul of Nikki Giovanni, 2003; Girls in the Circle, 2004; Lincoln and Douglass, 2008; Hip Hop Speaks to Children, 2008; The Grasshopper and the Ant, currently; Recordings: Truth Is On Its Way, 1971; Like a Ripple on a Pond, 1973; The Way I Feel, 1975; Legacies: The Poetry of Nikki Giovanni, 1976; The Reason I Like Chocolate, 1976; Cotton C&Y on a Rainy Day, 1978; Cotton Candy on a Rainy Day, 1978; Every Tone A Testimony, 2001; Nonfiction: Gemini: An Extended Biographical Statement on My First Twenty-five Years of Being a Black Poet, 1971; Sacred Cows & Other Edibles, 1991; Racism 101, 1993; Editor: Night Comes Softly: An Anthology of Black Female Voices, 1970; Gr & Mothers: A Multicultural Anthology of Poems, Reminiscences & Short Stories About the Keepers of Our Tradition, 1994; Fisk Univ, distinguished vis prof, 2007. **Orgs:** Nat Coun Negro Women; co-chair, Lit Arts Festival, State Tenn, 1986; bd dir, Va Found Humanities & Pub Policy, 1990-93; Soc Mag Writers; Nat Black Heroines PUSH; Winnie Mandela C's Fund Comt; Delta Sigma Theta Sorority; Omega Psi Phi. **Honors/Awds:** Woman of the Year, Ebony Mag, 1970; Woman of the Year, Mademoiselle Mag, 1971; Woman of the Year, Ladies Home Jour, 1972; Woman of the Year, Cincinnati Chapter YWCA, 1983; Inducted to Ohio Women's Hall of Fame, 1985; Distinguished Recognition Award, Detroit City Council, 1986; Silver Apple Award, Oakland Museum Film Festival, 1988; Community Volunteer of the Year Award, Warm Hearth Village, 1992; Black Women's Honor Society Award, Univ Southern Calif, 1994; Outstanding Woman of Tennessee; Tennessee Writers Award, Nashville Banner, 1994; Jeanine Rae Award, National Womens Music Festival, 1995; Tennessee Governor's Award, 1996; Langston Hughes Award, City Col NY, 1996; Parents' Choice Award, 1996; Appalachian Medallion Award, Univ Charleston, 1998; Image Award, NAACP, 2000; Distinguished Member Recognition Award, Delta Sigma Theta, Wilberforce, Ohio, 2000; City Council Resolution Honoring and Welcoming, Youngstown City, Ohio, 2000; Rosa Parks Women of Courage Award, 2002; Black Caucus Award, Am Libr Asn, 2003; Image Award for Outstanding Literary Work, NAACP, 2003; Honorary Citizen of Louisville Award, 2003; Honored in a Proclamation from the Mayor of Hartford which proclaimed that 10 April 2003 Nikki Giovanni Day, 2003; Atlanta Daily World 2nd Atlanta Choice Award, 2004; East Tennessee Writers Hall of Fame Award, 2004; Certificate of Appreciation, Delta Sigma Theta Sorority, 2005; Fourth Humanitarian Award, 2005; Lifetime Achievement Award, ALC, 2005; Certificate of Appreciation, Delta Sigma Theta Sorority, 2006; Women of Color Award, Va Univ Women Ctr, 2006; Honorary degrees: LHD, Wilberforce Univ, 1972; LittD, Ripon Univ, 1972; LittD, Univ Md, 1974; LittD, Smith Col, 1975; LHD, Col Mt St Joseph, 1983; LHD, Fish Univ, 1987; LHD, Mt St Mary Col, 1988; LHD, Ind Univ, 1991; LHD. Otterbein Col, 1992; Dr, Rockhurst Col, 1993; LHD, Widener Univ, 1993; LHD, Albright Col, 1995; LHD, Cabrini Col, 1995; LHD, Allegheny Col, 1997; LHD, Del State Univ, 1998; LHD, Martin Univ, 1999; LHD, Wilmington Univ, 1999; LHD, State Univ W Ga, 2000; LHD, Manhattanville Col, 2000; LHD, Cent State Univ, 2001; LHD, Pace Univ, 2002; LHD, Wva Uni, 2003; Coretta Scott King Award; Best Spoken Word Album, Nat Asn Radio and Tv Announcers; Rosa L. Parks Woman of Courage Award; Langston Hughes Medal for poetry; Women of Power Legacy Award. **Special Achievements:** Recorded six albums, including Truth Is On Its Way, 1972; Cotton Candy ona Rainy Day, 1978; tv appearances: Soul!, Natl Educ TV network, the Tonight Show; particip Soul at the Center, Lincoln Center Performing Arts New York City, 1972; contributor to numerous anthologies. **Business Addr:** Distinguished Professor of English, Virginia Tech University, 323 Shanks Hall, Blacksburg, VA 24061, **Business Phone:** (540)231-6501.

### GIOVANNI, YOLANDE CORNELIA. See GIOVANNI, NIKKI, JR.

### GIPSON, DR. BERNARD FRANKLIN, SR.

Surgeon. **Personal:** Born Sep 28, 1921, Bivins, TX; son of John Tom (deceased) and Alberta Rambo; married Ernestine Wallace; children: Bernard F Jr & Bruce Edward. **Educ:** Morehouse Col, BS, 1944; Howard Univ Col Med, Md, 1947; Am Bd Surg, dipl, 1954. **Career:** Surgeon, educator (retired); pvt pract surgeon, 1956-95; Atlanta Univ Syst Woodruff Libr, staff; Howard Univ, residency surg; Harlem Hosp, internship; Univ Colo, fac, clin assoc prof. **Orgs:** Kappa Alpha Psi fraternity, 1943; chmn, Dept Surg Mercy Med Ctr, 1968; life mem, Nat Asn Advan Colored People, 1980; chmn, Emancipation Proclamation Scholar Fund Newhope Baptist Church, 1974; New Hope Baptist Church, 1955-; Bd Deacons; Am Col Surgeons, Denver Acad Surg, Nat Med Asn; AMA; diplomat, Am Bd Surg; treas, Denver Med Soc; deleg, Colo State Med Soc; Am Cancer Soc; trustee, Denver Botanic Gardens, 1992. **Honors/Awds:** Community Service Award, Methodist Conf Western States, 1984; Frederick Douglass Award, Esquire Club, 1985. **Special Achievements:** Article Denver Post, 1984; Story my Life Denver Post Newspaper, 1984; The Bernard F. Gipson Sr, MD Papers (1947-2003). **Home Addr:** 2375 Monaco Pkwy, Denver, CO 80207-3453, **Home Phone:** (303)355-1765.

### GIPSON, CHARLES WELLS, JR.

Baseball player. **Personal:** Born Dec 16, 1972, Orange, CA. **Educ:** Cypress Jr Col, Calif. **Career:** Seattle Mariners, 1998-2002; Chicago Cubs, 2003; NY Yankees, outfielder, 2003; Tampa Bay Devil, 2004; Houston Astros, outfielder, 2005.

### GIPSON, HAYWARD R., JR.

Executive. **Educ:** Princeton Univ. **Career:** US intimate apparel unit, dir, mgr prod & vpres mkt; Playtex Inc, mktg exec & gen mgr; Corning, Vitro Intl, vpres & gen mgr, 1989; Playtex Apparel Inc, pres, 1994-. **Business Addr:** President, Playtex Apparel Inc, 700 Fairfield Ave, Stamford, CT 06904, **Business Phone:** (203)356-8000.

### GIPSON, DR. LOVELACE PRESTON, II

Dentist. **Personal:** Born Jan 9, 1942, Clarksdale, MS; married Amanda; children: Lovelace III, Tamitha, Teresa & Tinile. **Educ:** AM&N Col Dd, BS, 1963; St Louis Univ, attended 1965; Univ MO, attended 1966; Atlanta Univ, attended 1967; Univ Tenn Sch Dent, DDS, 1973. **Career:** St Louis & E St Louis Bd Educ, teacher, 1965-70; Hamilton Co Chattanooga Health Dept, staff dentist, 1974; pvt pract dentist; Firestone Dent Group PLLC, owner & dentist, currently. **Orgs:** Nat Bus League; PK Miller Youth Orgn, 1955; pres, Prof Corp, 1977; Nat Den Asn; Am Dent Asn; Memphis Shelby Co Dent Soc; Nat Asn Advan Colored People; UAPB Alumni Asn; Elks Lodge; Chickasaw Coun BSA; Urban League; hon del, Tenn Const Conv; Am Endodontic Soc; Founders Club Memphis Goodwill Boy's Club. **Honors/Awds:** Recipient, Ford Found Fel, St Louis Univ, 1965; NSF Grant, Univ MO & Atlanta Univ, 1966-67. **Home Addr:** 321 W Riveredge Dr, Cordova, TN 38018-7610, **Home Phone:** (901)759-3941. **Business Addr:** Dentist, Owner, Firestone Dental Group LLC, 1216 Thomas St, Memphis, TN 38107-1703, **Business Phone:** (901)525-3266.

### GIPSON, REVE

Writer, consultant, county commissioner. **Educ:** Los Angeles Valley Col, Van Nuys, Calif. **Career:** Freelance, writer & ed; KNBC News, Burbank, Calif, personal asst & news res, 1974-78; Capitol Recs, Los Angeles, Calif, publicist, 1978-87; Maze Featuring Frankie Beverly, Los Angeles, Calif, pub rels consult, 1987-; Los Angeles County, Dept Parks & Recreation Comn, comnr; County Pub Libr Comn, comnr, currently. **Orgs:** Nat Acad Recording Arts & Sci; Alpha Theta Chap, Beta Phi Gamma. **Honors/Awds:** Distinctive Women of Southern California, City Los Angeles; Dr Mary McLeod Bethune Award, County Los Angeles Bd Supvrs; Bill of Rights Speaker's Award, Bill Rights Commendation Comt; County Awards, Los Angeles City Coun; Organized M C Hammer Day in the City of Los Angeles; Founder, Annual "Youth on Parade" program. **Home Addr:** 4014 Don Diablo Dr, Los Angeles, CA 90008, **Home Phone:** (213)292-1493. **Business Addr:** Commissioner, County Public Library Commission, 7400 E Imp Hwy, Downey, CA 90242, **Business Phone:** (562)940-8418.

### GISCOMBE, DR. KATHERINE

Manager, vice president (organization). **Educ:** Univ Mich, BA, psychol, PhD, orgn psychol. **Career:** Unilever, group mgr consumer res, 1992-96; Catalyst, dir res, 1996-2000, sr dir res, 2000-06; vice pres res, 2006-13, vice pres global mem serv, 2013-. **Orgs:** Nat Asn Black Journalists; Acad Mgt; Closing Wealth Gap Initiative, 2012-15, Adv Bd, Womens Inter-Cult Exchange, currently. **Business Addr:** Vice President, Catalyst Inc, 120 Wall St 15th Fl, New York, NY 10005, **Business Phone:** (646)388-7731.

### GIST, CAROLE ANNE-MARIE (CAMMIE GEE)

Fashion model, singer. **Personal:** Born May 8, 1969, Detroit, MI; daughter of David Turner and Joan; children: 2. **Educ:** Northwood Univ, Midland, MI, BA, jr mkt & mgt. **Career:** Midland, Mich, club singer, currently; WORD Gospel Network, co-host gospel show, currently; Detroit Area Construct Co, exec asst; Wayne State Univ, fitness trainer, currently. **Honors/Awds:** Miss Michigan Pageant, winner, 1989; Miss USA Pageant, winner, 1990; Miss Universe Pageant, first runner-up, 1990. **Special Achievements:** First African American woman to be crowned Miss USA, 1990; First Miss Michigan to be crowned Miss USA, 1990. **Business Addr:** 5750 Wilshire Blvd Suite 225, Los Angeles, CA 90036, **Business Phone:** (213)965-0800.

### GIST, KAREN WINGFIELD

Educator. **Personal:** Born May 14, 1950, Harrisburg, PA; daughter of Raleigh Wingfield and Mary Gooden Wingfield; children: Maya Jemelle. **Educ:** Clarion State Univ, BS, 1972; Univ Pittsburgh, MEd, 1974; Calif State Univ, attended 1983. **Career:** NHS Fel, 1993; Pittsburgh Pub Sch, sec teacher, lit coach, Currently. **Orgs:** Instr, Community Col Allegheny County, 1974-84; fel Western Penn Writing-Proj, 1983-; Lambda Kappa Mu Sorority Inc Zeta Chap; Pittsburgh Fedn Teachers; Nat Coun Teachers Eng; Urban League; fel Carnegie Mellon Univ, Making Thinking Visible Proj, 1990-91; instr, Carlow Col, 1994-95. **Home Addr:** 128 Garlow Dr, Pittsburgh, PA 15235. **Business Addr:** Teacher, Pittsburgh Public Schools, 341 S Bellefield, Pittsburgh, PA 15213, **Business Phone:** (412)622-3500.

### GITE, LLOYD ANTHONY

Journalist. **Personal:** Born Oct 16, 1951, Houston, TX. **Educ:** N Tex State Univ, Denton, BS, polit sci, 1974; Southern Methodist Univ Dallas, attended 1977; Univ Mich, Ann Arbor, MS, radio, tv & film, 1980. **Career:** Journalist, writer (retired), executive; Nat Black Network, corresp, 1975-83; KNOK AM & FM, Dallas, news dir, 1977-78; Black Forum Dallas, host, producer, ABC prog, 1977-78; Sheridan Broadcasting Network, corresp, 1980-83; WTVS TV, Detroit, reporter, producer, 1981-83; Essence Mag, writer; Black Enterprise, writer; USA Today, writer; Gentlemen's Quart, writer; Working Woman, writer; Monthly Detroit, writer, 1981-2000; KRIV TV, reporter, producer, 1983-2001; Gite Gallery, owner & consult, 2001-. **Honors/Awds:** Essence Man, Essence Mag, 1976; Media Award, Press Club Dallas, 1977; One of the Most Outstanding Young Men in America, US Jaycees, 1978; One of the Fifty Leaders of the Future, Ebony Mag, 1978; Mentor of Year Award, Nat Asn Black Women Entrepreneurs, 1982; UNITY Award in Media, Lincoln Univ, 1982, 1983; Houston Press Club Aawrd for Media, 1984; National Association Black Journalists Award. **Business Addr:** Owner, Gite Gallery, 2024 Ala St, Houston, TX 77004, **Business Phone:** (713)523-3311.

### GITHIGA, REV. DR. JOHN GATUNGU

Chaplain. **Personal:** Born Jul 27, 1942, Muranga; son of Isaac Gitogo and Joyce Njeri; married Mary Nyambura; children: Rehema, Isaac Cyprian & June. **Educ:** Makerere Univ, theol dipl, 1974; Univ S, MDiv, 1979, Int Bible Inst & Sem, DREd, 1980; DMin, 1981; Church Army Col. **Career:** Diocese Nakuru, dir St Nicholars C Ctrs; St Paul's United Theol Col, dept head, pastoral theol, currently; African Asn Pastoral Study & Coun, founder & pres, 1985-88; St Cyprian Church, vice chair, 1986-91; Ecumencial Christian Fel, founder, pres, 1992-; Lakeview Ctr, tel crisis counr, Kairos spiritual dir, voluntary, 1992-;

Extended Arms Outreach Ctr, field counr juvenile offenders & their parents, 1992-96; Grambling State Univ, vice chair, chaplain; West Tex A&M Univ, chaplain & adj fac, currently; All Nations Christian Church Int Univ, chancellor & prof, pastoral theol, currently; Pensacola Jr Col, instr, currently. **Orgs:** Secy, Nat Christian Coun Kenya Youth Dept, Nakuru, 1966-68; Capt, First Nakuru Comp Boys Brigade, 1967-68; secy, Diocese Nakuru Youth Dept, 1968-71; pres, United Campus Ministry, Cursillo Secretarial, Diocese NW Tex; Univ W Fla Select Comt Minority Affairs, 1987-92; Martin Luther King Jr Celebration Comt, 1989; Ecumenical & Interfaith Comt, 1987-91; Greater Kiwanis Pensacola, 1988-92; Asn Theol Insts Eastern Africa, 1980-85; St Cyprian's Episcopal Church, 2002, vice chair, 2003-. **Honors/Awds:** Certificate of Appreciation for Presentation, Pensacola Jr Col, 1987; Certificate of Appreciation for Presentation, Kiwanis Club Greater Pensacola, 1988; Certificate of Appreciation for Planning, Martin Luther King Commemorative Comt, 1989; Kiwanis Certificate of Appreciation for Spiritual leadership and Service to Community, 1989. **Special Achievements:** Author, "The Use of Psychology in Pastoral Counseling in Africa," Theological Journal, 1982; The Spirit in the Black Soul, 1984; "Family in Transition," Beyond, July 1987; Initiation & Pastoral Psychology; Christ & Roots, 1988; co-author, Ewe Ki Jana (Oh Young Man), 1971. **Home Addr:** 2512 4th Ave, Canyon, TX 79015-4146. **Business Addr:** Adjunct Faculty, Chaplain, West Texas A & M University, 2521 4th Ave, Canyon, TX 79015, **Business Phone:** (806)655-3121.

### GITTENS, ANTHONY EDGAR (TONY GITTENS)

Executive director, educator. **Personal:** Born Dec 25, 1944, Brooklyn, NY; son of Henry Edgar and Rita; married Jennifer; children: Kai & Zachary. **Educ:** Howard Univ, BA, 1968; Union Grad Sch, PhD, 1976. **Career:** Univ DC, prof, 1971-96, prof emer, currently; Black Film Inst, dir, 1976-; DC Comn Arts & Humanities, exec dir, 1996-2008. **Orgs:** Wash DC Int Film Festival, 1986; DC Comn Arts & Humanities; secy, Mid Atlantic Arts Found. **Home Addr:** 1838 Ontario Pl NW, Washington, DC 20009-2109, **Home Phone:** (202)232-0619. **Business Addr:** Executive Director, District of Columbia Commission on the Arts & Humanities, 410 8th St NW 5th Fl, Washington, DC 20004, **Business Phone:** (202)724-5613.

### GITTENS, TONY. See GITTENS, ANTHONY EDGAR.

### GIVENS, SR. CLEMENTINA M.

Administrator. **Personal:** Born Nov 15, 1921, Baltimore, MD; daughter of James and Lavinia Nicholson. **Educ:** Sisters Loretto, St Louis, BS; Cath Univ, Wash, DC, MA, 1975. **Career:** Archdiocese Washington, DC, WA, DC, elem teacher, 1956-62; Archdiocese Miami, Miami, Fla, elem teacher, 1962-73; Archdiocese Wash, WA, DC, elem adminr, 1973-77; Archdiocese Baltimore, Baltimore, Md, 1977-79; Archdiocese Washington, DC, WA, DC, DC teacher, 1979-81; Archdiocese of Miami, Miami, Fla, sch adminr, 1981-88; St Patrick Cath Church, dir relig educ, currently; Off Black Cath Ministry, Rockford, Ill, dir. **Orgs:** Sch bd mem, Archdiocese Wash, DC, 1958-62; bd mem, sec, Archdiocese Wash; DC, 1973-77; black pastorial coun, Archdiocese Miami, 1981-88. **Home Addr:** 701 Gun Rd, Baltimore, MD 21227-3828. **Business Addr:** Director Religious Education, St Patrick Catholic Church, 3716 Garden Ave, Miami Beach, FL 33140, **Business Phone:** (305)531-1124.

### GIVENS, DR. DONOVAHN HESTON, JR.

Physician, educator, business owner. **Personal:** Born Dec 31, 1930, Chicago, IL; married Shirley; children: Linda, Rachel, Donna & Elizabeth. **Educ:** Univ Pa; Wayne State Univ; Univ Mich Med Sch, MD, 1961. **Career:** St Joseph Mercy Hosp, intern, 1961-62; St Joseph's, resident, 1962-65; Wayne State Univ, clin asst prof, 1965-; Oakland Internist Assoc, owner. **Orgs:** Nat Med Asn; Detroit Med Soc; Wayne Co Med Soc; Mich Med Soc; AMA; Am Soc Internal Med; Am Col Phys; Adv Plann Com Univ Out patient Clin, 1971-72. **Special Achievements:** Author: Urinary Salt Wasting in Chronic Renal Failure, Grace Hosp Billiton, 1970. **Home Addr:** 19480 Burlington, Detroit, MI 48223. **Business Addr:** Physician, 20905 Greenfield Suite 501, Southfield, MI 48075.

### GIVENS, DR. HENRY, JR.

College president. **Personal:** Born Jan 1, 1933; married Belma Evans; children: Stacey Woolfolk & Keith. **Educ:** Lincoln Univ, BA; Univ Ill, MA; St Louis Univ, PhD; Harvard Univ, postdoctoral studies, higher educ admin. **Career:** Webster Groves Sch Dist, teacher, prin; asst supt schs; Mo, asst comnr educ; Lincoln Univ, interim pres, 1987; Harris-Stowe State Univ, pres, 1979-2011. **Orgs:** Chair, Dr. Martin Luther King Jr. Statewide Celebration Comn, 1986-2011; bd dir, Am Asn State Cols & Univs; Asn Gov Bds, Mo Coord Bd Higher Educ; Nat Alliance Black Sch Educrs; Friends George Allen; Obama America; bd dir, Laclede Group; bd dir, Peabody Energy Corp, 2004-; consult, HBCU Capital Finance Prog Adv Bd; bd dir, St. Louis Regional Conv & Sports Complex Authority; Laclede Gas/Laclede Group; Peabody Energy Inc; Automobile Club Mo. **Honors/Awds:** Hon DHL, Lincoln Univ & St Louis Univ; has received more than 125 national, state and local awards and recognitions, including honorary doctorate degrees from Saint Louis University, Lincoln University and Washington University-St. Louis. **Special Achievements:** First African-American to serve Missouri as Assistant Commissioner of Education. **Business Addr:** President, Harris-Stowe State University, HGA 108 3026 Laclede Ave, St. Louis, MO 63103, **Business Phone:** (314)340-3366.

### GIVENS, JOSHUA EDMOND

Writer, marketing executive. **Personal:** Born Norfolk, VA. **Educ:** Northwestern Univ, BS, speech, 1975, MS, jour advert, 1977. **Career:** WGN-TV, promotional writer & news writer, 1974-75; Benton & Bowles Advert, acct exec, 1977-79; Nat Black Network Radio, acct exec, 1979-80; Ebony Mag, acct exec, 1980-81; Caldwell Reingold Advert, acct supvr, 1981; Revlon Inc, mkt mgr, 1981, ethnic retail mkt dir, 1981-86, ethnic retail mkt, vpres, 1987-93; Lou Roppolo & Assoc, ethnic mkt spec, mkt consult, mkt dir, 1993. **Orgs:** Nat Black MBA Asn NY Chap, 100 Black Men, NY Chap, Nat Asn Mkt Develop; Nat Asn Advan Colored People. **Honors/Awds:** Acad Scholar Northwestern Univ, 1971-77. **Home Addr:** 75 Union St Suite 2D, Hackensack, NJ 07601, **Home Phone:** (201)489-1853. **Business Addr:** Consultant, Lou Roppolo & Assocs Inc, Montvale, NJ 07645.

### GIVENS, LARRY (LAWRENCE GIVENS)

Vice president (organization). **Educ:** Wayne State Univ, BS, educ, 1962, MBA, 1968. **Career:** Chrysler Corp, vpres pub rel; Detroit Pub Sch, asst gen supt; AAA Mich, spokesperson, asst vpres human resources, dir corp rels, asst vpres corp rels & vpres corp rels; Detroit Empowerment Zone, exec dir, currently. **Orgs:** Bd dir, City Yr Detroit; bd dir, Covenant House Mich Corp; bd mem, Detroit Neighborhood Housing Serv Inc; bd mem, Starr Commonwealth C; vice chmn, Southfield Community Found; New Detroit Inc; Youth Connection; vice chmn, Horizon Health Syst; 100 Black Men Greater Detroit. **Business Addr:** Executive Director, Detroit Empowerment Zone, 65 Cadillac Sq Suite 2401, Detroit, MI 48226, **Business Phone:** (313)224-3968.

### GIVENS, LAWRENCE

Insurance executive, executive director, president (organization). **Personal:** Born Nov 30, 1938, Detroit, MI; son of Timothy and Senia Smith McClain; married Delores Clark; children: Kimberly, David, Lisa & Stefanie. **Educ:** Wayne State Univ, BA, educ, 1962, MBA, 1968. **Career:** Detroit Bd Educ, teacher, 1962-64; Chrysler Corp, vpres pub rels, 1964-82; Detroit Pub Schs, asst to gen supt, 1982-84; AAA Mich, dir corp rels, 1984-87, asst vpres corp rels, 1987-89, asst vpres hr, 1989-91, asst vpres corp rels, 1991-92, vpres corp rels, 1992-2000; Blackmond Givens Grp, pres, currently; Detroit Empowerment Zone Develop Corp, exec dir, 2001-05. **Orgs:** Pres, Bus Educ Alliance, 1989-91; secy, bd trustee, Horizon Health Systs, 1985-91; chmn, telethon, United Negro Col Fund, 1987-89; secy, bd dir, Efficacy Detroit, 1985-91; bd mem, Centrum Ins Co, 1983-91; bd dir, Henry Ford Village; Sloan Fel Chrysler Corp, 1968; pres, Covenant House Mich Life Skills Ctr-E; secy, Starr Commonwealth C; New Detroit Inc; bd mem, Henry Ford Bi-C Hosp; Gilda's Club; 100 Black Men Greater Detroit; Henry Ford Health Syst. **Honors/Awds:** Manager of the Year Award, Chrysler Corp, 1968; Outstanding Leadership Award, United Negro Col Fund, 1989; Pioneer Support Award, Mich Legis Black Caucus Found, 1996; Legacy Award, Mays Acad, 2000. **Special Achievements:** Minority Achiever of the Year, Detroit YMCA, 1985. **Home Addr:** 18711 Greenwald, Southfield, MI 48075, **Home Phone:** (810)569-8381. **Business Addr:** President, Blackmond Givens Group, 2990 W Grand Blvd, Detroit, MI 48202, **Business Phone:** (313)972-1554.

### GIVENS, LEONARD DAVID

Lawyer. **Personal:** Born Sep 10, 1943, Elmira, NY; married Patricia. **Educ:** Mansfield State Col, BS, 1961; Howard Law Sch, JD, 1971. **Career:** IBM, Owego, NY, admin asst, 1965-68; AFSCME, Wash, law clerk, 1968-69; NLRB, Wash, law clerk, 1970-71; Miller Canfield Paddock & Stone PLC, assoc, 1971-77, sr prin, 1978-, chief exec officer, 1991-94, Labor & Employ Law Pract Group, co-leader, dep leader, 2006-. **Orgs:** Am Bar Asn; Nat Bar Asn; labor sect coun mem, State Bar Mich; Detroit Bar Asn; fel, Mich State Bar Found; Oakland Co Bar Asn; labor coun, Mich State Bar Asn; bd mem, Nat Employ Labor Coun; Am Judicature Soc; bd dir, Homes Black C; bd mem, Detroit Regional Chamber; bd mem, Nature Conservancy Mich; Pres, Detroit Metrop Bar Asn, 2000-01; Chambers USA: Am's Leading Lawyers Bus, Employ & Labor, 2003-04; Wolverine Bar Asn; Greater Detroit Chamber Com; Am Labor & Employ Coun; bd mem, Mich Biotechnology Inst; Judicial Screening Comt; fel Col Labor & Employ Lawyers; Metrop Affairs Corp; vice chmn & bd mem, Metrop Affairs Coalition; Mich Biotechnological Inst; Fedn Girls Home; Law Jour Invitee Moot Ct Team; Col Labor & Employ Lawyers fel, 2003; Employ Law-Mgt & Labor Law-Mgt, 2012-. **Honors/Awds:** Crain's Detroit Bus, one Metro Detroit's Most Influential Black Bus Leaders, 1998; One of Southeastern Michigans 10 Best Lawyers, 1999; Listed in Labor and Employment Law Section, 2003-04; Published in America's Leading Lawyers for Business, 2003-05 editions; Published in The Best Lawyers in America, 2005-06; Mich Super Lawyers, Labor & Employ, 2006-; He was one of the Top 10 Nation's Most Powerful Employment Attorneys, 2009; Distinguished Service Award, State Bar of Mich, Labor & Employ Sect, 2010; Best Lawyers in America, Labor and Employment Law 2003-11; Dbusiness Mag, Tob Lawyers, Labor & Employ, 2011; Detroit Labor Law-Management Lawyer of the Year, 2012. **Home Phone:** (313)963-6420. **Business Addr:** Principal, Miller Canfield Paddock & Stone PLC, 150 W Jefferson Suite 2500, Detroit, MI 48226-4415, **Business Phone:** (313)496-7505.

### GIVENS, REGINALD ALONZO (REGGIE GIVENS)

Real estate executive, football player, administrator. **Personal:** Born Oct 3, 1971, Emporia, VA. **Educ:** Pa State Univ, grad. **Career:** Football player (retired), real estate broker; Baltimore Stallions, 1994-95; Toronto Argonauts, 1996-97; San Francisco 49ers, linebacker, 1998-99; Wash Redskins, 2000; Ocean View Realty, Fla, real estate broker, currently; Blitz, fitness & wellness coach & Owner, currently. **Honors/Awds:** Grey Cup, 1995-97; East All-Star, Can Football League, 1996. **Business Addr:** Real Estate Broker, Cape Cod Oceanview Realty, 414 S Orleans Rd, Orleans, MA 02653, **Business Phone:** (508)255-2202.

### GIVENS, ROBIN SIMONE

Actor. **Personal:** Born Nov 27, 1964, New York, NY; daughter of Reuben and Ruth Roper; married Mike Tyson; married Svetozar Marinkovic. **Educ:** Sarah Lawrence Col, 1984. **Career:** Actress, entrepreneur; Films: The Women of Brewster Place, 1989; A Rage in Harlem, 1991; Boomerang, 1992; Foreign Student, 1994; Blankman, 1994; Smoke, 1995; Blue in the Face, 1995; Secrets, 1997; Ride, 1998; Everything's Jake, 2000; Elite, 2000; Book of Love, 2000; Antibody, 2002; Head of State, 2003; A Cold Day in August, 2003; Flip the Script, 2005; Little Hercules in 3-D, 2006; Restraining Order, 2006; Queen of Media, 2008; The Family That Preys, 2008; Little Hercules in 3-D, 2008; A Mother's Prayer, 2009; Enemies Among Us, 2010; Unspoken Words, 2012; Double Sided, 2012; Airplane Vs Volcano, 2014; God's Not Dead 2, 2016. TV mini-series: The Women of Brewster Place, 1989. TV movies: Beverly Hills Madam, 1986; Dangerous Intentions, 1995; A Face to Die For, 1996; The Expendables, 2000; Spinning Out of Control, 2001; Hollywood Wives: The New Generation, 2003; Television series: "Head of the Class", 1987-91; "Angel Street", 1992; "Courthouse"; "Sparks", 1997-98. Forgive or Forget, host, 2000; Never Blue Productions, founder & dir, 1990; "Head of State", 2003; "Spy Games Reloaded", 2004; "Captive Hearts", 2005; "House of Payne", 2008; "Burn Notice", 2008; "The Game", 2008; "Everybody Hates Chris", 2008; "My Parents, My Sister & Me", 2010; "Chuck", 2011; "Reed Between the Lines", 2011; "Suburgatory", 2012; "Retired at 35", 2012 "90210", 2013; "Twisted", 2014; "Man Seeking Woman", 2016. **Honors/Awds:** ShoWest Award, 1991. **Business Addr:** Actress, Twentieth TV, 2121 Ave of the Stars 21st Fl, Los Angeles, CA 90067, **Business Phone:** (310)369-1000.

### GIVENS-LITTLE, AURELIO DUPRIEST

Clergy, manager. **Personal:** Born Nov 16, 1966, Charleston, SC; children: Kendall. **Educ:** Francis Marion Univ, BS, sociol, 1990; Interdenominational Theol Ctr, Gammon Theol Sem, MDiv, 1995, DMin, 2007. **Career:** Strayer Univ, adj prof humanities & philos; Abundant Life PPW Ctr Inc, pastor & exec dir, 1998-, bishop; Proj MEN Inc, chief exec officer, 2001-; Francis Marion Univ, coordr multicultural affairs, 2000-; grief counr. **Orgs:** Life mem, Alpha Pi Alpha Fraternity Inc; Suburban Lodge 213 F&A Masons, PHA; spec asst, life mem, coordr, Nat Asn Advan Colored People; Nat Conv Gospel Choirs & Choruses Inc; adv, treas, Greater Columbia Choral Union; Qual Unlimited Inc; dir, African Am Relig Affairs; Kershaw & Aiken Counties Ministerial Alliance; 100 Black Men Greater Columbia; African Am clergy; Abundant Life Augusta; Rosa Parks, prin organizer funeral serv; bd dir, Bros & Sisters United Chg Inc; SC Dist Bd Alphas. **Honors/Awds:** Outstanding Leadership Award, 2003. **Home Addr:** 50 Teaberry Lane, Elgin, SC 29045, **Home Phone:** (843)713-0608. **Business Addr:** Coordinator, Francis Marion University, PO Box 100547, Florence, SC 29501, **Business Phone:** (843)661-1188.

### GIVHAN, ROBIN DENEEN

Journalist, fashion editor. **Personal:** Born Sep 11, 1965, Detroit, MI; daughter of Robert and Stella Thompson. **Educ:** Princeton Univ, NJ, BA, 1986; Univ Mich, Ann Arbor, MI, MA, jour, 1988. **Career:** Detroit Free Press, staff writer, 1988-92, fashion ed, 1993-; San Francisco Chronicle, staff writer, 1992-93; Vogue mag; Wash Post, fashion ed, 2010. **Orgs:** Detroit Hist Soc, Costume Exhib Comt, 1990-91; Detroit Inst Arts, Founders Soc, 1989-91. **Honors/Awds:** Atrium Award, excellence in fashion writing, Univ Ga, 1990; Pulitzer Prize Winner, 2006. University of Michigan's Detroiter Hall of Fame, 2013. **Business Addr:** Fashion Editor, The Washington Post, 1150 15th St NW, Washington, DC 20071, **Business Phone:** (202)334-6000.

### GIVINS, ABE, JR.

Government official, educator. **Personal:** Born Apr 22, 1951, Columbus, MS; son of Abe Sr and Corine; married Linda Sue Robinson; children: Abe III, Ryan Eugene & Christel C. **Educ:** Cent State Univ, BS, educ, 1977. **Career:** Normandy Sch Dist, teacher, 1980-82; City Pine Lawn MO, alderman, 1982-, mayor, 1989; Ins Agency, ins broker, 1982-; St Louis Pub Schs, teacher biol, 1989-91, spec educ, 1989-91; Mo Dept Ment Health, residental therapist, 1991-. **Orgs:** Normandy Munic League, 1982-; MS Munic League, 1982-; Normandy Democ Club, 1982-. **Home Addr:** 4001 Treeshadow Dr, Saint Peters, MO 63376-3829, **Home Phone:** (636)379-2199. **Business Addr:** Alderman, City of Pine Lawn, 6250 Steve Marre Ave, Saint Louis, MO 63121.

### GLADDEN, DR. MAJOR P.

Orthopedic surgeon, educator. **Personal:** Born Dec 8, 1935, Chester, SC; son of Joseph and Isabelle Woodward; married Brenda Winckler; children: Miriam P & Paul B. **Educ:** Morgan State Univ, BS, 1957; Howard Univ, MD, 1961. **Career:** DC Gen Hosp, internship, 1961-62; Mt Alto Va Hosp, res training, gen surg, 1962-63; DC Gen Hosp, res ortho, 1963-64; Bronx Munic Hosp, residency ortho, 1964-66; Albert Einstein Col Med Bronx, instr, 1966-68; Howard Univ Col Med, asst prof, 1969-80; DC Gen Hosp, chief orthopaedic surg, 1968-80; Howard Univ Col Med, assoc prof ortho surg, 1980; Gladden & Manderson, pvt pract, currently. **Orgs:** Alpha Phi Alpha Frat; team physician, ortho consul, Howard Univ; vol, Orthopaedics Medico Prog Dominican Rep, 1978; examr, Am Bd Ortho Surg Chicago, 1979; vol, ortho surg Olympic Training Ctr Colo Springs, 1984; bd dir, Morgan State Univ Found, 1984; chief physician, DC Boxing & Wrestling Comn, 1984; fel Am Col Health Asn; found mem, Am Orthopaedic Soc Sports Med. **Home Addr:** 7315 Westminster Ct, University Park, FL 34201-2342, **Home Phone:** (941)360-9324. **Business Addr:** Surgeon, Gladden & Manderson, 1140 Varnum St NE Suite 108, Washington, DC 20017-2151, **Business Phone:** (202)526-5300.

### GLADMAN, CHARLES R., JR.

Government official. **Educ:** Univ Akron, assoc degree fire sci, 1977; Nat Fire Acad, exec fire officer prog, 1995. **Career:** City Akron Fire Dept, firefighter, 1973-79, lt & co officer, 1979-85, capt, 1986-89, dist fire chief, 1990-91, dep chief, 1992-96, fire chief, 1997-2007; United Black Firefighters Akron Inc Incorporator. **Special Achievements:** First African-American to be appointed fire chief, Akron.

### GLADNEY, DR. MARCELLIOUS

Dentist, consultant. **Personal:** Born May 14, 1949, West Point, MS; son of Robert and Annie; married Elizabeth F Jones; children: Scott, Tarik M & Tonia M. **Educ:** St Johns Univ, BS, pharm, 1972; Rutgers Univ, NJ, DMD, 1977; Univ Nebr, MS, 1993. **Career:** Eli Lilly & Co, pharm sales rep, 1972-74; US Pub Health Serv, asst dent surgeon, 1977-80; Mercer McDowel Dent Group, pres & founder, 1980-86; US Pub Health Serv, UNIT chief dent officer, 1991; PHS Indian Hosp, Indian Health Serv, pediat dent consult, currently. **Orgs:** Am Dent Asn, 1979-; Princeton WV Civitans, 1982-85; pres, Southern W Va Roadrunners Club, 1983-86; fel Am Acad Pediat Dent, 1995; Omega Psi Phi; Sigma Pi Phi; Nat Dent Asn; Am Acad Pediat Dent; vpres, NMex Asn Pediat Dent. **Special Achievements:** Book: Individual and Combined Anxiolytic Activity of Chloral Hydrate and Hydroxyzine in Mice. **Home Addr:** 1209 Bonita St, Grants, NM 87020, **Home Phone:** (505)876-4034. **Business Addr:** Pediatric Dentistry Consultant, PHS Indian Hospital, PO Box 649, Fort Defiance, AZ 86504, **Business Phone:** (928)729-8000.

### GLADWELL, MALCOLM
Writer, journalist. **Personal:** Born Sep 3, 1963, Hampshire; son of Graham and Joyce. **Educ:** Univ Toronto, BA, hist, 1984. **Career:** The Wash Post, sci & med writer, 1987-96, writer & reporter; Nat Jour Ctr, intern, 1992; New Yorker, staff writer, 1996-; Leigh Bur, auth & staff writer, currently; Author: David and Goliath: Underdogs, Misfits and the Art of Battling Giants; The Tipping Point: How Little Things Make a Big Difference, 2000; Blink: The Power of Thinking Without Thinking, 2005; Outliers: Book World; May be Geniuses Just Got Lucky; Secrets of their success; The Story of Success, 2008; The Sociology of Success; Why Some Succeed Wildly; What the Dog Saw, 2009. **Orgs:** Order Can. **Business Addr:** Author, Staff Writer, The Leigh Bureau, 92 E Main St Suite 200, Somerville, NJ 08876, **Business Phone:** (908)253-8600.

### GLANVILLE, DOUGLAS METUNWA (DOUG GLANVILLE)
Baseball player, manager. **Personal:** Born Aug 25, 1970, Hackensack, NJ. **Educ:** Univ Pa, BSE, sci & engineering, 1992. **Career:** Baseball player (retired), exec, analyst; Chicago Cubs, outfielder, 1996-97, 2003; Philadelphia Phillies, outfielder, 1998-2002, 2004; Tex Rangers, outfielder, 2002-03; New York Yankee, outfielder, 2005; GK Alliance LLC, pres, 2006-; Metrop Develop group, mgr & lead designer, currently; New York Times, opinionator contribr, 2008-; XM Radio, MLB Home Plate-Power Alley, baseball insider, 2009-10; HenryHolt/Times Bks, auth, 2010-; ESPN, baseball analyst, 2010-; TIME Ideas, columnist & contribr, 2011-. **Orgs:** Pres, co-founder, Glanville-Koshul Homes; exec sub com, Maj League Baseball Players Asn; Players Trust C, Boys & Girls Club Am; sponsor, Am Diabetes Asn, Philadelphia Phillies; founding mem, Philadelphia Futures Mentoring Prog; bd overseers, Pa Engineering. **Special Achievements:** The Game From Where I Stand, auth, 2010. **Business Addr:** President, GK Alliance LLC, 22W580 Poss St, Glen Ellyn, IL 60137, **Business Phone:** (630)433-6481.

### GLAPION, MICHAEL J.
Insurance executive, executive. **Personal:** Born May 15, 1947, New Orleans, LA; son of Armand P Jr and Alma Broussard; married Angeler Robert; children: Nicholas, Stacie Rose, Nina Simonne & Christopher. **Educ:** Xavier Univ La, BFA, 1969. **Career:** St Paul Fire & Marine Ins Co, com property underwriter, 1971-75; Medtronic Inc, mgr, risk mgt, 1975-78; Graco Inc, mgr risk mgt & ins, 1979-84; Harvest States Coop, dir risk mgt, 1982-88; Ins & Surety Specialist Inc, pres & chief exec officer, 1988-2002, staff, 2003-; Gillis, Ellis & Baker Inc, asst vpres, dir risk mgt serv, chmn, life mem, 2002-; Start Smart, LLC, currently. **Orgs:** Comnr, Richfield Human Rights Comn, 1971-74; bd mem & pres, Risk & Ins Mgt Soc MN, 1978-81; bd mem, N Community Br YMCA, 1979-84, chmn; bd mem, C's Home Soc MN, 1981-84; chmn, MN African Am Chamber Com, 1990-95; co-founder, MN Cult Diversity Ctr, 1991-97, vice chmn; bd mem & chmn, Turning Pt Inc, 1990-97; exec bd, Nat Asn Minority Contractors MN, 1993-95; pres, Prof Ins Agt Asn Minn, bd mem; New Orleans Blighted Housing Citizens Task Force; Ins Mgt Soc; bd dir, bd chair, Nat Safety Coun S La Chap; State Senate Dist 2 Adv Coun; E New Orleans Neighborhood Adv Comn; Marks Subdivision Neighborhood Asn; Independent Ins Agents & Brokers La; Independent Ins Agents Greater New Orleans; Mem Model Un; former pres & bd mem, MN Risk & Ins Mgt Soc; adv bd mem NAMC MN. **Honors/Awds:** President's Award, Nat Asn Minority Contractors MN, 1994; Man of the Year Award, Nat Asn Minority Contractors MN, 1994; Iron Man Award, North Community YMCA; N Community YMCA, 1995. **Home Addr:** 10935 N Hardy St, New Orleans, LA 70127-2837, **Home Phone:** (504)240-2165. **Business Addr:** Director Risk Management Services, Assistant Vice President, Gillis Ellis & Baker Inc, 1615 Poydras St Suite 600, New Orleans, LA 70112-1238, **Business Phone:** (504)619-5043.

### GLARE, DIANE
**Career:** Loyola Marymount Univ, asst prof African Am Studies. **Business Addr:** Assistant Professor of African American Studies, Loyola Marymount University, Los Angeles, CA 90045.

### GLASCO, DR. ANITA L.
Educator. **Personal:** Born Oct 24, 1942, Kansas City, KS. **Educ:** Univ Southern Calif, AB, polit sci, 1964; Harvard Univ, Law Sch, JD, 1967; Univ Chicago, MCL, 1970. **Career:** Univ Chicag, Ford Found, fel, 1968-70; Univ Dar Es Salaam Tanzania, consult; Univ Sofia, Bulgaria, consult; Zhongshan Univ, People's Repub China, consult; Moscow Conf Law & Econ Rels, consult; Smith & Glasco, pvt practr; Southwestern Univ Sch Law, adj fac, fac, 1972, prof law, 1975, prof emer, 2002-; SW, assoc prof law, 1972-75; Smith & Glascod partner, 1971-72; Lewis & Clark Col, vis prof law, 1975; Univ Wash, vis prof law, 1974; Univ Tenn knoxville, vis prof law, 1980; Irving D & Florence Rosenberg, prof law, 1997, prof emer, 1998; Ogletree Abbott Law Firm Llp, law sch prof. **Orgs:** Calif State Bar Asn, 1968-; Black Women Lawyers Asn; Calif Asn Black Lawyers; fel Inst Fr Lang & Civil Univ Geneva, 1968; fel Inst Fr Lang & Civil Univ Pau, 1969; fel Inst Fr Lang & Civil, Univ Paris, 1969; comparative law fel Univ Aix-Marseilles, 1969-74; chmn, Elect Minority Groups Sect Asn Am Law Sch, 1977; chmn, Minority Groups Sect Asn Law Sch, 1978; exec comt, Asn Am Law Schs Sect Int Legal Exchanges; Calif State Bar's Int Law Sect; bd dir, John M Langston Bar Asn. **Home Addr:** 14108 Tahiti Way Suite 622, Marina Del Rey, CA 90291. **Business Addr:** Professor Emeritus, SW University School Law, 675 S Westmoreland Ave, Los Angeles, CA 90005, **Business Phone:** (213)738-6717.

### GLASGOW, DOUGLAS G.
Educator, government official. **Educ:** Brooklyn Col, BA, 1959; Columbia Univ, MSW, 1961; Univ Southern Calif, DSW, 1968. **Career:** HEW Off Juv Delinq Youth Develop, LA, prin investr, 1968-69; Univ Calif Los Aageles, Ctr Study Afro-Am Hist Cult, interim dir, 1969-70, co-chaired; Coun Soc Work Educ, LA, Juv Delinq Comn, 1969-70; Univ Calif Los Angeles, Sch Soc Welfare, assoc prof, 1970-71, prof social policy & res; Howard Univ, Sch Soc Work, prof, dean emer, 1972-75; Nat Urban League Inc, wash oper, 1983; E Franklin Frazier Ctr Social Work Res Howard Univ, Wash, DC, scholar residence, currently; Univ Ghana Legon, vis prof; Makererre Univ Uganda, vis prof; Univ Md Baltimore, vis prof; Ministry Rehab, policy analyst & consult social develop. **Orgs:** Co-chmn, Black Fac Staff Univ Calif Los Angeles, 1969; Gls Comn Juv Delinq Adult Crime, 1969-70; bd dir, adv comt, Community Cols Guid, 1969, 1972-74; ed bd, NASW J Soc Worker, 1970-73; CSWE Struct Rev Comn, 1971-72; Rev Design Comn, 1972; vice chmn, Div Prog NCSW Cent Conf, 1973; US Prog Comt, ICSW, 1973; adv comt, Howard Univ, Inst Drug Abuse & Addiction, 1973; bd dir, United Black Fund Inc, Wash; Nat Asn Soc Workers; Int Coun Soc Welfare Inc; Acad Cert Soc Workers; Am Acad Polit & Social Sci; Nat Asn Black Soc Workers; Nat Asn Soc Workers; bd mem, Coun Soc Worker Educ; vpres, Nat Urban League; Black Men's Develop Ctr; Dc's Ment Health Reorganization Comn; Ment Health, & Teen Pregnancy Comn. **Honors/Awds:** Award, M J Palevsky Found, 1970; Fellow Award, Danforth Found, 1971; Sr Stipend Award, NIMH, 1975. **Home Addr:** 1746 Lamont St NW, Washington, DC 20010, **Home Phone:** (202)483-7455. **Business Addr:** Scholar in Residence, Howard University, School of Social Work, 2900 Van Ness St NW, Washington, DC 20008, **Business Phone:** (202)806-8213.

### GLASS, ERECKA TIFFANY
Law enforcement officer. **Personal:** Born Dec 8, 1965, Chicago, IL; daughter of Harry and Ruby. **Career:** Dept Corrections, dep sheriff, 1988-; Joel Hall Dance Ctr, jazz instr, 1997-98; Chicago Multi Cultural Dance Ctr, jazz instr, 1995-98. **Orgs:** Apostolic Church God, 1995-. **Home Addr:** 1056 N Monitor Ave, Chicago, IL 60651-2570, **Home Phone:** (773)626-3608. **Business Addr:** Sherrif, Cook County Dept Corrections, 2700 S California Ave, Chicago, IL 60608, **Business Phone:** (773)674-5201.

### GLASS, DR. ERNESTINE W MCCOY PICKENS
Educator. **Personal:** Born Dec 21, 1936, Braden, TN; daughter of Ernest W Williams and Rhobelia Alexander Williams; married William G Pickens; children: Marcus Christopher McCoy, Leslie, Reese & Todd. **Educ:** Tenn State Univ, BS, 1958; Atlanta Univ, MA, 1975; Emory Univ, PhD, 1986. **Career:** Educator (retired), professor emerita; Shelby County Bd Educ, Barret's Chapel High Sch, teacher, 1958-60; Casso polis High Sch, teacher, 1961-62; Weaver High Sch, teacher, 1964-71; John Overton High Sch, teacher, 1971-73; Atlanta Univ, commun skills instr, 1973-78; Clark Col, asst prof Eng, assoc prof, 1975-86; Clark Atlanta Univ, prof Eng, chair, dept Eng; Prof emer, currently. **Orgs:** Col Lang Asn Standing Comn, Eng Curric; Am Studies Asn; Nat Coun Teachers Eng; Toni Morrison Soc; Langston Hughes Soc; founding pres, Charles Waddell Chessnutt Asn; Am Lit Asn. **Home Addr:** 2808 Peyton Crossing Dr SW, Atlanta, GA 30311, **Home Phone:** (404)753-3109. **Business Addr:** Professor Emeritus, Emory University, 223 James P Brawley Dr, Atlanta, GA 30314, **Business Phone:** (404)880-8857.

### GLASS, GERALD DAMON
Basketball player, basketball coach. **Personal:** Born Nov 12, 1967, Greenwood, MS. **Educ:** Delta State Univ, Cleveland, MS, attended 1987; Univ Miss, attended 1990. **Career:** Basketball player (retired), basketball coach; Minn Timberwolves, 1990-92; Detroit Pistons, 1992-93; La Crosse Catbirds, 1993-94; Jcoplastic Napoli, Italy, 1994-95; NJ Nets, 1995; Charlotte Hornets, 1995-96; CSP Limoges, France, 1996-97; Ole Miss, coach staff; High Sch Alma Mater, heads coach; FIBA, Europe, 1997; Bnei HaSharon, Israel, 1998-99.

### GLASS, JAMES
Administrator. **Personal:** Born Jan 27, 1928, Birmingham, AL. **Educ:** Miles Col, Birmingham AL, attended 1951; Detroit Inst Technol, Detroit, MI, BA, sociol, 1976; Wayne State Univ, Labor Sch, Detroit, MI. **Career:** Chrysler Assembly Plant, 1952-54; Detroit Gen Hosp, 1952-55; Wayne County Juvenile Court, 1955-81; Todd Phillips C Home, 1965-78; AFSCME Coun 25, int vpres, elected 1981, pres, 1982-. **Orgs:** United Found; chmn, Coun 25 Exec Bd; exec bd mem, Mich AFL-CIO; vpres, int exec bd, AFSCME; Coalition Black Trade Unionists; governors appointee, Michi Job Training Coord Coun; bd dir, Nat Asn Advan Colored People; exec bd mem, Mich Trade Union Coun Histadrut. **Business Addr:** International Vice President, Michigan AFSCME Council #25, 1625 L St NW, Washington, MI 20036-5687, **Business Phone:** (202)429-1000.

### GLASS, RONALD EARLE
Actor. **Personal:** Born Jul 10, 1945, Evansville, IN; son of Crump and Lethia. **Educ:** Univ Evansville, BA, drama & lit, 1968. **Career:** Tyrone Guthrie Theater, co mem, 1968-72; TV Series: "Day of Absence", 1970; "Slow Dance on the Killing Ground", 1972; Beg, Borrow, or Steal, 1973; "Barney Miller", 1975-82; "Shirts & Skins", 1973; The Streets of San Francisco, 1974-76; Change at 125th Street, 1974; Let's Switch!, 1975; Foster & Laurie, 1975; "Crash", 1978; "The New Odd Couple", 1982-83; "Amen", 1989-91; "Rhythm & Blues", 1992; "Teen Angel", 1997; "Incognito", 1999; "Fire fly", 2002; "Sanford & Son", 1972; "Good Times"; All in the Family"; "The Streets of San Francisco", 1972; "The $10000 Pyramid", 1973; "When Things Were Rotten", 1975; "Hart to Hart", 1979; "The New Odd Couple", 1982-83; "Murder, She Wrote", 1984; Gus Brown & Midnight Brewster, 1985; "The Twilight Zone", 1985; "Amen", 1986; "Designing Women", 1986; Perry Mason: The Case of the Shooting Star, 1986; "227", 1987; "Family Matters", 1989; "Stat", dir, 1991; "Rugrats", 1992-2004; "Rhythm & Blues", 1992; "Mr. Rhodes", 1996; "The Practice", 1997; Teen Angel, 1997-98; Incognito, 1999; "Friends", 1999; "Twice In a Lifetime", 1999; "Yes, Dear", 2000; "Zoe, Duncan, Jack & Jane", 2000; Too Much Pressure, 2000; "Jack & Jill", 2000; "The Education of Max Bickford", 2001; "The Proud Family", 2001; "Fire fly", 2002-03; Secret History of Religion: Knights Templar, 2006; Secret History of Religion: Doomsday - Book of Revelation, 2006; "Shark", 2006-07; "Fable II", voice for Garth, 2008; "CSI: NY", 2011; "Major Crimes", 2013; "Agents of S.H.I.E.L.D.", 2013-14; "CSI: Crime Scene Investigation", 2014. Films: The Crazy World of Julius Vrooder, 1974; Deep Space, 1988; House guest, 1995; It's My Party, 1996; Back in Business, 1997; Unbowed, 1999; Deal of a Lifetime, 1999; Recess: School's Out, 2001; Serenity, 2005; Lakeview Terrace, 2008; Death at a Funeral, 2010; Strange Frame: Love & Sax, 2012; Just Another Man's Story, 2013. **Orgs:** Screen Actors Guild; Hollywood Acad TV Arts & Sci; Actors Equity Asn; Am Fedn TV & Radio Artists; Alpha Psi Omega Fraternity Inc; Al Wooten Jr. Heritage Ctr, chmn bd; bd trustee, Univ Evansville; Soka Gakkai Int. **Honors/Awds:** Blue Key Scholastic Honor Society; Alumni Certificate of Excellence, Univ Evansville, 1975; Dionysus Award, Hollywood Club Forum Int, 1977; Communtiy Award, La Sentinel Entertainment Writer Gertrude Gibson, 1975; Community Award, Phil Wilkes, Freddie Jett, 1976; William A Gumbertz Award, 1968; Medal of Honor, Univ Evansville; Pearl Le Compte Award; Distinguished Alumnus Award, Univ Evansville Alumni Asn, 2008. **Home Addr:** 8340 Delongpre B, Los Angeles, CA 90069. **Business Addr:** Actor, Mitchell K Stubbs & Associates, 8675 W Washington Blvd Suite 203, Culver City, CA 90232, **Business Phone:** (310)838-1200.

### GLASS, VIRGINIA M.
Consultant, executive director, association executive. **Personal:** Born Dec 14, 1927, Manila; daughter of Tomas N McKinney and Maria Moreto; children: Sidney & Luis. **Educ:** Fordham Univ; Columbia Univ, BA; Columbia Univ Sch Libr Sci; Hunter Col; Queens Col Sch, attended 1977. **Career:** Prom, Publicity, Community Devel & Educ, self-employed consult; Brooklyn Pub Libr, librn, 1949-52; NY City Sch Dist, high sch admin, 1952-70; San Diego City Sch, consult, 1970-72; Univ Calif, San Diego, consult, 1972-74; San Diego Human Rels Comn, educ coordr, 1974-78; City Col, dir community serv, 1978-80; LaJolla Country Day Sch, head librn, 1980-81; Mt. View Tennis Club, founder, pres; Black Tennis Mag, w coast ed; San Diego Urban League, dir, pub rels; Community Tennis Serv, pres, dir. **Orgs:** Exec comm, US Tennis Asn; co-founder, pres, San Diego Dist Tennis Asn; Contemp Black Arts, Univ Calif San Diego; Chrysler LeBaron Ser; cord, Jr Olympic Tennis; cord, Nat Jr Tennis League, San Diego; pres, Am Tennis Asn; Phoenix Challenge; Manila Liberation, Southern Calif Tennis Asn; Nat Conf Christians & Jews; Nat Asn Female Execs; Pac Womens Sports Found; Multicultural Participation Comt; co-founder, Mountain View Tennis Club; co-founder, San Diego Umpires Asn. **Honors/Awds:** Exec comm, US Tennis Asn; San Diego Dist Tennis Asn; Contemp Black Arts, Univ Calif San Diego; Chrysler LeBaron Ser; cord, Jr Olympic Tennis; Nat Jr Tennis League, Cord, San Diego; pres, Am Tennis Asn; Phoenix Challenge; Manila Liberation, Southern Calif Tennis Asn; Nat Conf Christians & Jews; Nat Asn Female Execs; Pac Womens Sports Found; Multicultural Participation Comt; co-founder, Mountain View Tennis Club; SCTA Lifetime Achievement Award, 2008. **Special Achievements:** Ranked first in the World, Womens 60s, 1989; Ranked 4 in the US Sr Women's Tennis & 2 in Southern California, 1989; Elected to Tennis Hall of Fame; First female president of the American Tennis Association; First Woman of Color to Serve on the USTA Executive Committee. **Business Addr:** President, Director, Community Tennis Service, 2690 Worden St Suite 84, San Diego, CA 92110-5861, **Business Phone:** (619)224-5746.

### GLAUDE, STEPHEN A.
Executive, executive director. **Personal:** Born Jul 25, 1954, Washington, DC; son of William Criss and Phyllis Taylor; married Rhonda Roland; children: Koya M, Shani & Khary. **Educ:** Morgan State Univ, BS, community develop, community ment health, 1977. **Career:** Capitol E Childrens Ctr, asst dir, 1977-79; DC Asn Retarded Citizens, voc evaluator, 1979-80; Nat Cong Community Econ Develop, pres & chief exec officer; Mens Ctr, Wash, DC, health educr, 1980-82; Men Can Stop Rape, exec dir & pres & chief exec officer, currently; Dir Constituent Serv, Coun DC, off chmn, 2009-10; DC, Mayor's Off Community Affairs, dir, 2011-14; US Dept Housing & Urban Develop, dep asst secy; Intergovernmental Rels, dep undersecretary; Coalition Nonprofit Housing & Econ Develop, exec dir, 2014-. **Orgs:** Founder & pres, Inst Life Studies, 1970-; chair & bd dir, Capitol E Cs Ctr, 1979; bd mem, Montgomery Ment Health Asn, 1980; exec dir, Nat Asn Neighborhoods, Wash, 1980-, pres; Pres Task Force Privaate Sector Initiatives, 1981; chair & fundraising mem develop comt, Black Child Develop Inst, 1984; Coun Black Econ Agenda, 1985; Nat Asn Advan Colored People; Neighborhood Coalition; Inst Life Studies; Natural Living Res Com Republican; off chmn, Dir Constituent Serv, 2009-10. **Honors/Awds:** Presidents Second Mild Award, 1977; Mental Health Community Service Award, 1977. **Special Achievements:** First African American to serve as President of the National Congress for Community Economic Development and to serve as Executive Director of the National Association of Neighborhoods. **Home Addr:** 3205c Ivy Wood Lane, Laurel, MD 20724-6076. **Business Addr:** Executive Director, Chief Executive Officer, Men Can Stop Rape, 1130 6th St NW Suite 100, Washington, DC 20001, **Business Phone:** (202)265-6530.

### GLEN, RODNEY. See WARD, RONNIE V.

### GLEN, ULYSSES, JR.
Government official. **Personal:** Born Aug 11, 1970, Cleveland, OH; son of Ulysses Sr and Janis W. **Educ:** Univ Cincinnati, BA, 1993. **Career:** Blue Cross/Blue Shield, sales coordr, mkt rep, 1994-96; Dc Govt, chief staff, 1996; Total HTH Care Plan, mktg mgr, 1996; Lottery & Charitable Games, Wash, DC, chief staff, 1996; off chief financial officer, Wash, DC, budget dir, currently. **Orgs:** Nat Asn Advan Colored People, 1993; Kappa Alpha Psi Fraternity Inc, vicepole march, 1996; Govt Finance Officers Asn; Asn Financial Professionals; Nat Forum Black Pub Adminr. **Home Addr:** 103 G St, Washington, DC 20024, **Home Phone:** (202)488-3153. **Business Addr:** Chief of Staff, Administrative Officer, DC Lottery & Charitable Games Control Bd, 2101 Martin Luther King Jr Ave SE, Washington, DC 20020-5731, **Business Phone:** (202)645-8000.

### GLENN, AARON DEVON
Football player, football coach. **Personal:** Born Jul 16, 1972, Humble, TX; married Devaney; children: Aaron II, Tristen & Rheagan. **Educ:** Tex A&M Univ, BA, bus, 1994. **Career:** Football player (retired), football coach; New York Jets, kick returner, left cornerback, 1994, 1997-98, left cornerback, 1995-96, 1999, 2001, corner back, 2000, pro personnel scout, col scouting, 2012-14; Houston Texans, left cornerback, 2002-04, 2010; Dallas Cowboys, right cornerback, corner back, 2005, free safety, 2006; Jacksonville Jaguars, right cornerback, defensive back, left cornerback, 2007; New Orleans Saints, left cornerback, 2008; Cleveland Browns, asst defensive back coach, 2014-; New Orleans Saints, sec coach, 2016-. **Orgs:** Nat Football League. **Honors/Awds:** Pro Bowl selection, 1997-98, 2002; Texans Player of the Year, 2002; Ed Block Courage Award, 2003; Houston Quarterback Club Awards; Foleys Texans Player of the Year; Pete Rozelle Awards; Most

Valuable Player XXXVI & XXXVIII; New York Jets All-Time Four Decade Team. **Business Addr:** Football Coach, New Orleans Saints, 5800 Airline Dr, Metairie, IN 70003, **Business Phone:** (504)733-0255.

## GLENN, CECIL E.

Educator, sociologist. **Personal:** Born Dec 18, 1938, Nashville, TN; children: Cecil LaVel & Gerald. **Educ:** Tenn A&I State Univ, BS; Northeastern Ill St Col, MA; Univ Colo, EdD, 1975. **Career:** Chicago Dept Educ, Pub Health Serv Civil Rights Envolvement; teacher; Higher Educ, area urban sociologist; Ment Health Inc, serv mental health, field chmn; Univ Colo, prof Soc Sci, head Ethnic Studies, assoc prof emer social; Colo MESA, bd mem, emer mem. **Orgs:** Chmn, Malcolm X Ment Inc; Nat Asn Advan Colored People. **Home Addr:** 2560 Krameria St, Denver, CO 80207-3437, **Home Phone:** (303)377-1922. **Business Addr:** Associate Professor Emeritus, University of Colorado, 1250 14th St, Denver, CO 80217.

## GLENN, DIANE

Banker, president (organization), chief executive officer. **Career:** Community Bank Lawndale, exec asst, exec dir, pres, chmn bd & chief exec officer, 1977-. **Orgs:** Bd dir & bd adv, Mid Am Leadership Found; bd mem & chair, ACCESS Community Health Ctr; Nat Bankers Asn; bd mem, Ill State Univ. **Business Addr:** President, Chief Executive Officer, Community Bank of Lawndale, 1111 S Homan Ave, Chicago, IL 60624-4346, **Business Phone:** (773)533-6900.

## GLENN, PATRICIA CAMPBELL

Manager. **Personal:** Born Dec 15, 1942, Brandon, MS; daughter of James Alvin and Ewnice Agnes Finch; children: Allison, Jennifer & Lee. **Educ:** Ohio State Univ, Columbus, BS, Eng educ, 1970; Montclair State Univ, MS, communs, 1999. **Career:** E High Sch, Columbus, teacher, 1971-74; Ohio Civil Rights Comn, Columbus, supvr, investr, 1974-78; US Dept Justice, regional dir, 1989-2000, sr mediator, 2001; US Dept Justice, regional dir, NY Region, 1989-2001; Fed Law Enforcement Training Ctr, hate crime training, 1992-; Nat Arson Task Force, coord, 1995; Univ Conflictology, Moscow & Komi, Russia, instr, 1996; US Dept Justice, regional dir, Chicago Region, 2001-; Conway County, spec U.S. marshal; Montclair State Univ, adj instr, currently. **Orgs:** Nat Coun Negro Women, 1980-; pres, Maj Charles L Hunt VFW Post, 1984-85; dist comnr, Boy Scouts, 1987-89; coordr, Church Aaron Task Force. **Honors/Awds:** Humanitarian Award, Columbus Metrop Community Action Org, 1980; Outstanding Performance Award, 1984; Human Relations Service Award, 1985; Kiwanis Award, Cert Appreciation, 1987; Silver Beaver, Chicago Area Coun, 1989; Outstanding Effort Hurricane Hugo, Fed Emergency Mgt Agency, 1990; 50 Outstanding Women in Justice, 1994; Outstanding Regional Dir, 1998; Award from NJ Assembly, 2000; Commendation, US Cong, 2001; Distinguished Service Award, US Dept Justice, 2003; Outstanding Regional Director Award; National Mother of the Year, Ashley Steward Retail Asn, 1998. **Special Achievements:** Yale Univ, lectured. **Home Addr:** 6231 Champlain Ane, Chicago, IL 60637-2523, **Home Phone:** (773)955-9724. **Business Addr:** Regional Director, US Department of Justice Community Relations Service, Rm 2130 230 S Dearborn, Chicago, IL 60604, **Business Phone:** (312)353-4356.

## GLENN, TARIK

Football player, president (organization). **Personal:** Born May 25, 1976, Cleveland, OH; married Maya. **Educ:** Univ Calif, Berkeley, BA, social welfare, 1999; Purdue Univ, Krannert Sch Mgt, MBA, exec educ prog. **Career:** Football player (retired), executive, advisor; Indianapolis Colts, left guard & right guard & offensive tackle & left tackle, 1997-2007; Dream Alive Inc, founder, 2001-, pres, 2011-; Univ Calif, Berkeley, stud athlete develop advisor, 2014-. **Honors/Awds:** Unsung Hero Award, Indianapolis Colts, 2000; Pro Bowl, 2004 & 2005 & 2006. **Business Addr:** Founder, President, Dream Alive Inc, 8836 Crystal River Dr, Indianapolis, IN 46240, **Business Phone:** (317)721-2618.

## GLENN, TERRY TYREE

Football player. **Personal:** Born Jul 23, 1974, Columbus, OH; children: 3. **Educ:** Ohio State Univ, hist. **Career:** Football player (retired); New Eng Patriots, wide receiver, 1996-2001; Green Bay Packers, wide receiver, 2002; Dallas Cowboys, wide receiver, 2003-07, tight end, 2005. **Orgs:** DARE prog. **Honors/Awds:** Fred Biletnikoff Award, 1995; Rookie of the Year, Sports Illustrated, 1996; Champion, Asian Football Conf, 1996, 2001; AFC Rookie of the Year, United Press Intl, 1996; Champion, Super Bowl, XXXVI. **Special Achievements:** First-team All-Big Ten, 1995; First-team AP All-American, 1995; Pro Bowl selection, 1999.

## GLOVER, AGNES W.

School administrator. **Personal:** Born Mar 6, 1925, Orangeburg, SC; daughter of Benjamin I Williams and Victoria; married Freddie V. **Educ:** SC State Col, BS, educ, 1956; Hunter Col, MS, 1973; Queens Col, MA, supr & admin, 1983. **Career:** School administrator (retired); Nat Sor Phi Delta Kappa Inc Beta Omicron Chap, third Anti Basileus, 1965-67, tamias, 1967-69, basileus, 1969-71, chmn bd dir Big Sister Educ Action & Serv Ctr, 1972; Hallet Cove Child Dev Ctr, dir. **Orgs:** Dir, Grosvenor DC, 1968-72; vpres, Flushing Br Nat Asn Advan Colored People, 1982, pres, 1974-78; Basileus Nat Sor Phi Delta Kappa Div Beta Omicron Chap, 1969-71, chmn bd dir, Big Sister, 1972-; life mem, Nat Asn Advan Colored People, 1987; SC St Col Chap Phi Delta Kappa, 1988. **Honors/Awds:** Serv & dedication Big Sister Educ Action Serv Ctr, 1978; Cert Appreciation La Guardia Community Col, 1981, Flushing Br Nat Asn Advan Colored People, 1984; Outstanding Serv, Flushing Br Nat Asn Advan Colored People, 1984; Outstanding Serv, Coun Supvrs & Admin of New York City, 1987; Dedicated Serv, The Nat Sorority of Phi Delta Kappa Inc, Beta Omicrom Chapter Big Sister Educ Action & Serv Ctr, 1987. **Home Addr:** 1453 Sifly Rd NE, Orangeburg, SC 29115, **Home Phone:** (803)534-9561.

## GLOVER, ANDREW LEE

Football player. **Personal:** Born Aug 12, 1967, New Orleans, LA; married Mary Harris; children: Andrew Keith & Christon Dion. **Educ:** Grambling State Univ. **Career:** Football player (retired); Los Angeles Raiders, tight end, 1991-94; Oakland Raiders, tight end, 1995-96; Minn Vikings, tight end & wide receiver, 1997-99; New Orleans Saints, tight end, 2000.

## GLOVER, DR. BERNARD ELLSWORTH

Dentist. **Personal:** Born Apr 9, 1933, Suffolk, VA; married Juanita Cross; children: Cheryl & Kevin. **Educ:** Morgan State Col, BS, 1959; Meharry Med Col, DDS, 1963. **Career:** St Elizabeth Hosp, internship, 1964; pvt pract, 1964-. **Orgs:** Bd mem, dir, Obici Hosp; bd mem & dir, Nansemon Credit Union; Suffolk City Forum; John L Mc Griff Dent Soc; Am Nat & Old Dom Dent Asn; Am Endodontic Soc; C C; Bi-racial Coun; Obia Hosp Staff. **Honors/Awds:** E end bapt ch Scholarship Award, Morgan State Col, 1955-59; Mosby Scholarship Award, 1962; Man of the Year, Kappa Alpha Si, 1974; Elks Award, 1975; John L. McGriff dental Society Leadership Award; Meharry Medical College President's Award; American Dental Association Award; Louise Obici Hospital Resolution for Dream Award, 2002; Appreciation Award; Certificate of Appreciation. **Home Addr:** 1213 White Marsh Rd, PO Box 1061, Suffolk, VA 23434-4046, **Home Phone:** (757)539-8118. **Business Addr:** Dentist, 811 E Washington St, Suffolk, VA 23434-3926, **Business Phone:** (757)539-7244.

## GLOVER, CHESTER ARTIS

Journalist. **Personal:** Born Sep 3, 1954, Detroit, MI; son of Artis O and Leona Johnson; married Mae Vaughn. **Educ:** Valencia Community Col, Orlando, FL, AA, 1977; Rollins Col, Winter Pk, FL, BS, 1982. **Career:** WCPX-TV Channel 6, Orlando, Fla, weekend assignment ed, 1980-83; Gov Press Off, Tallahassee, Fla, press aide, 1982; Stetson Univ, Deland, Fla, asst sports info, 1982-84; LAOOC-1984, Los Angeles, Calif, asst press chief, 1984; Orlando Sentinel, Orlando, Fla, staff writer, 1984-92; Allen & Assocs, Orlando, Fla, proofreader & copy ed, 1995-96; Saks Fifth Ave, Sales, 1996-98; Fla House Representatives, dist legis asst, 1998-2000; US House Representatives, dist cong caseworker, 2000-; Orange Co Dem Exec Comt, comt man, 2004-. **Orgs:** Assoc dir, Multicultural Resources, Orlando, Fla, 1989-; pres, Cent Fla Press Club, 1990-92; charter mem, Cent Fla Asn Black Journalists & Broadcasters, 1988-; educ chmn, Sentinel Commun Employees Fed Credit Union, 1990-91; Nat Asn Black Journalists, 1990-. **Home Addr:** 5807 Elon Dr, Orlando, FL 32808-1809, **Home Phone:** (407)290-0193. **Business Addr:** Committee Man, Orange County Democratic Executive Committee, 5807 Elon Dr, Orlando, FL 32808, **Business Phone:** (407)290-0193.

## GLOVER, REV. CLARENCE ERNEST, JR.

Educator, school administrator. **Personal:** Born Apr 19, 1956, Shreveport, LA; son of Clarence E Sr and Elizabeth Bradford. **Educ:** Grambling State Univ, BA, hist, 1978; Southern Methodist Univ, MTS, 1982; Harvard Univ, post grad, 1985. **Career:** St Duty CME Church, pastor, 1974-75; Wash Temple CME Church, pastor, 1978-80; Caddo Bossier Asn Retarded Citizens, instr & supvr, 1978-79; El Centro Col, campus minister, 1979-80; Clarence Glover Ministries Inc, pres, 1981-; Southern Methodist Univ, asst to chaplain, 1980-81, coordr intercultural educ African-Am stud serv, 1980-89; adj prof, African-Am Studies, 1987-93; Clarence Glover & Asn, prof lecturing & consul agency, 1987; Inter cult Educ & minority affairs, dir, 1990-94; Multicultural Educ Dallas Pub Schs, exec dir, currently. **Orgs:** African-Am cult consult Dallas Independent Sch Dist, 1980-; TX Asn CoI& Univ Stud Personnel Adminrs, 1980-; nat coordr Nat Black Christian Stud Leadership Consult, 1985-; third vpres TX Asn Black Personnel Higher Educ, 1985-; Nat Asn Advan Colored People; Christian Leadership Conf; Nat Asn Stud Personel Admin; Am Cancer African-Am Task Force; co-host Cable TV Show Relig Focus; lectr & consult African-Am Relig & Cult; Black Male-Female Rels; Life & Time Dr King Civil Rights Movement &Inter-Cult Rels & Racism; Nat Asn Multicultural Educ; Sankofa Educ Serv, chief exec officer. **Home Addr:** 7607 Caillet St, Dallas, TX 75209, **Home Phone:** (214)358-4316. **Business Addr:** Executive Director, Dallas Public Schools, 3700 Ross Ave, Dallas, TX 75204-5491, **Business Phone:** (972)925-3700.

## GLOVER, DANNY LEBERN (DANIEL LEBERN GLOVER)

Movie producer, actor. **Personal:** Born Jul 22, 1946, San Francisco, CA; son of James and Carrie Hunley; married Asake Bomani; children: Mandisa. **Educ:** San Francisco State Univ, BA, econs, 1968; Am Conserv Theatre; Black Box Theatre Co. **Career:** San Francisco Mayor's Off, researcher; actor; Stage: Master Harold & the Boys, 1982; The Island; Sizwe Bansi Is Dead; The Blood Knot; Suicide in B Flat; Macbeth; Nevis Mountain Dew; A Lesson From Alloes; Master Harold & the boys, 1982-83; Master Harold & the Boys, 2003; TV series: "Chiefs", 1978; "John Henry", 1987; "Lonesome Dove", 1988; "A Place at the Table", 1988; "A Raisin in the Sun", 1989; "How the Leopard Got His Spots", audio-visual, 1989; "Dead Man Out", HBO, 1989; "Hill Street Blues", guest appearance; "Lou Grant", guest appearance; "Many Mansions", Paris, guest appearance; "BJ & the Bear", guest appearance; American Heroes & Legends, 1992; "Civil War Journal", 1993; "Queen", 1993; "America's Dream", actor & exec producer, 1996; "Buffalo Soldiers", actor & exec producer, 1997; "Life by the Numbers", 1998; "Freedom Song", actor & exec producer, 2000; "The Henry Lee Project", 2003; "Henry Lee Good Fences", actor & producer, 2003; "Brothers & Sisters", 2007-08; "Back at the Barnyard", 2008; "My Name Is Earl", 2009; "Nite Tales: The Series", 2009; "Human Target", 2010; "Leverage", 2011; "Psych", 2011; "Touch", 2011; "American Dad!", 2013; "Muhammad Ali's Greatest Fight", 2013. Films: Escape from Alcatraz, 1979; Chu Chu& the Philly Fh, 1981; Iceman, 1984; Birdy, 1984; Places in the Heart, 1984; Witness, 1985; Silverado, 1985; The Color Purple, 1985; Lethal Weapon, 1987; Mandela, 1987; Bat 21, 1988; Lethal Weapon 2, 1989; To Sleep with Anger, 1990; Predator 2, 1991; Flight of the Intruder, 1991; A Ragein Harlem, 1991; Pure Luck, 1992; Lethal Weapon 3, 1992; Grand Canyon, 1992; Bopha, 1993; Angels in the Outfield, 1994; Gone Fishin, 1997; Buffalo Soldiers, TNT, 1997; Switchback, 1997; Lethal Weapon 4, 1998; Antz, 1998; Beloved, 1998; Prince of Egypt, 1998; Battu, 2000; Boesman & Lena, 2000; 3 AM, actor & exec producer, 2001; The Royal Tenenbaums, 2001; The Law and Mr. Lee, 2003; Saw, 2004; The Cookout, 2004; Missing in America, 2005; Manderlay, 2005; The Adventures of Brer Rabbit, 2006; The Shaggy Dog, 2006; Dream girls, 2006; Barnyard, 2006; Bamako, actor & exec producer, 2006; Honey dripper, 2007; Terra, 2007; Shooter, 2007; Poor Boy's Game, 2007; Africa Unite, exec producer, 2008; Trouble the Water, exec producer, 2008; Gospel Hill, 2008; Be Kind Rewind, 2008; Blindness, 2008; Saw V, 2008; Night Train, 2009; Down for Life, 2009; The Harimaya Bridge, 2009; 2012, 2009; Death at a Funeral, 2010; Dear Alice, 2010; Legendary, 2010; Alpha and Omega, 2010; Age of the Dragons, 2010; Mooz-lum, 2010; I Want to Be a Soldier, 2010; Five Minarets in New York, 2010; Donovan's Echo, 2011; Highland Park, 2012; Mentryville, 2012; Macbett, 2012; Prairie Bones, 2012; Chapo, 2012; Learning Uncle Vincent, 2013; Chasing Shakespeare, 2013; Alpha and Omega 2: A Howl-iday Adventure, 2013; Bad Asses, 2014; Rage, 2014; Beyond the Lights, 2014; Tula: The Revolt, 2013; Day Of The Mummy, 2014; Bad Asses on the Bayou, 2015; Checkmate, 2015; Scout, 2015; Gridlocked; 2015; Waffle Street, 2015; Andron: The Black Labyrinth, 2015; Dirty Grandpa, 2016; Complete Unknown, 2016; Mr. Pig, 2016; Andron-The Black Labyrinth, 2016; 93 Days, 2016; A Meyers Christmas, 2016; The Good Catholic, 2016; Monster Trucks, 2017-; Toussaint. **Orgs:** Mem bd dir, Ctr Econ & Policy Res. **Honors/Awds:** Black Filmmakers Hall of Fame; Theatre World Award, Master Harold & the Boys, 1982; Image Award, Nat Asn Advan Colored People, 1989; CableACE Award, 1989, 1996; hon degree, Paine Col, 1990; Nat Asn Advan Colored People, 1990, 1995, 1999; Independent Spirit Award, 1991; MTV Movie Award, 1993; Piper-Heidsieck Award, 1993; Lifetime Achievement Theatre Award, Nat Asn Advan Colored People, 2001; Lifetime Achievement Award, Jamerican International Film Festival, 2002; Lifetime Achievement Award, Los Angeles Pan African Film Festival, 2003; Humanitarian Of The Year, 2006; Festival President's Award, Karlovy Vary International Film Festival, 2008; DHL, Utah State Univ, 2010. **Special Achievements:** PBS, host, Celebrate Storytelling; United Nations Development Programme, Goodwill Ambassador, 1998-99. **Business Addr:** Actor, International Creative Management Inc, 10250 Constellation Blvd, Los Angeles, CA 90067, **Business Phone:** (310)550-4000.

## GLOVER, DIANA M.

Labor relations manager. **Personal:** Born Apr 19, 1948, Buffalo, NY. **Educ:** Cornell Univ, BA, sociol, 1971; Gen Motors Inst, lib arts cert, 1973. **Career:** Gen Motors Co Chev Div Tonawanda Motor, employ interviewer, 1973-74, ast supv employ, 1974-75, EEO rep, 1975-76, supr employee benefits, 1976, supr salaried pers admin, 1976-78, supr labor rel, 1978-, CPC Tonawanda Engineering Plant, asst Personnel dir; Jefferson Enterprises Inc, 1976. **Orgs:** Adv coord, Jr Achievement, 1975-78; Indust Rel Asn, 1976-80; Buffalo Urban League, 1976-; dir, Ctr Women Mgt, 1978-80; Nat Asn Advan Colored People, 1978-. **Honors/Awds:** Black Achievement Award, 1970. **Home Addr:** 38 St Paul St, Buffalo, NY 14209. **Business Addr:** Assistant Personnel Director, General Motors, PO Box 21, Buffalo, NY 14240.

## GLOVER, HON. DON EDWARD

Judge. **Personal:** Born Jan 1, 1944, Dermott, AR; son of Silas Sr and Lucinda; married Dorothy; children: Dorcedar & Doven. **Educ:** Univ Ark Pine Bluff, BS, bus admin, 1965; Howard Univ, Sch Law, JD, 1973. **Career:** Tulsa County Legal Aid, Baton Rouge Legal Aid, staff atty, 1973-78; N La Legal Aid, managing atty, 1978-80; Jamison & Glover Law Off, atty, 1981-83; Law Off Don Glover, atty, 1983-92; Elected Munic Judge, Dermott, 1986-88, 1989-92; 10th judicial dist, Circuit Judge, 1993-96, 1997-2000, 2001-04, 2004-. **Orgs:** Peace Corps, Vol Venezula, 1965-67; treas, St Paul Baptist Church; Dermott Area C C; bd chair, Morris Boaker Day Care Ctr; Ark Judicial Coun. **Honors/Awds:** Man of the Year, Dermott Area Chamber Com, 1989. **Home Addr:** 108 W Gaines St, Dermott, AR 71638, **Home Phone:** (501)538-5613. **Business Addr:** Circuit Judge, 10th Judicial Dist, Justice Bldg 625 Marshall St, Little Rock, AR 71654, **Business Phone:** (870)222-6885.

## GLOVER, DR. GLENDA B.

Dean (education), president (organization). **Personal:** Born Memphis, TN; married Charles; children: Candace & Dr Charles II. **Educ:** Tenn State Univ, BS, mathematics; Clark Atlanta Univ, MBA, 1976; George Washington Univ, PhD, econs & finance, 1990; Georgetown Univ Law Ctr, JD, 1994. **Career:** Potomac Elec Power Co, proj mgr tax admin & coordr investor rels, 1979-85; Big-Four CPA, acct,; Technol Appln Inc, vpres; Metters Indust, chief financial officer & sr vpres, 1985-90; Howard Univ, Dept Acct, chairperson & asst prof, 1990-94; Chapman Co, bd dir; Amervest Corp, bd dir; Harvard Bus Sch Mgt Alliance, bd dir; citigroup Stud Loan Corp, dir, 1998-; Jackson State Univ, Sch Bus, dean col bus, 1994-12; Tenn State Univ, pres, 2013-. **Orgs:** Founder, Nat Ctr Enterprise Zone Res, 1987; adv bd, Union Planters Bank Miss; bd examr, Am Inst Cert Pub Acct; bd dir, Lenox Group Inc, 2007-10; nat treas, bd dir, nat treas, Alpha Kappa Alpha Sorority; bd examr, Am Inst Cert Pub Accountants; Adv Bd, bd mem, Union Planters Bank Miss; bd mem, Nat Asn Advan Colored People; bd mem, MetroJackson Chamber Com; Nat Bar Asn; bd dir, Am Assembly Col Schs Bus; bd mem, Am Learning Corp; bd mem, First Guaranty Bancshares; chmn, Econ Anal Inc, 1998; chmn bd commissioners, Jackson (Miss) Airport Authority, 2002; dir, MobileBits Holdings Corp, 2012; dir, Pringo Inc, 2012. **Special Achievements:** One of two African American females to hold the economics Ph.D-CPA-JD combination in the nation. **Business Addr:** President, Tennessee State University, 3500 John A Merritt Blvd, Nashville, TN 37209, **Business Phone:** (615)963-5000.

## GLOVER, HAMILTON

Manager, executive, army officer. **Personal:** Born Feb 24, 1937, Atlanta, GA; son of Thomas R Sr and Lucile C. **Educ:** Morehouse Col, BA, 1957; Atlanta Univ, MBA, 1958. **Career:** Manager (retired); Mutual Fed Savings & Loans Asn, trainee, asst treas, 1958-60, asst treas, 1963, secy, treas, vpres-treas, sr vpres-treas, pres, 1994. **Home Addr:** 994 Willis Mill Rd SW, Atlanta, GA 30311-2433, **Home Phone:** (404)753-0827. **Business Addr:** President, Mutual Fed Savings & Loans Association, 205 Auburn Ave NE, Atlanta, GA 30303, **Business Phone:** (404)659-0701.

## GLOVER, JONATHAN A.

Executive. **Personal:** Born Asheville, NC. **Educ:** Catawba Col, bus admin. **Career:** Puma, sales rep, 1997-2000; Merrill Lynch & Co inc, financial adv, 2000-04; Morgan Stanley, financial adv, 2005-06; Mortgage Plng Grp, adv, currently; Toshiba Bus Solutions, software solutions specialist, 2013-. **Orgs:** Asheville Housing Authority; Asheville Bd Adjusts, Asheville City Coun; dir, chair, Fundraising Comm Kid's Voting Asheville, 2001-04; exec bd mem, Asheville-Buncombe Vision; chair, Diversity Adv Coun Carolina Day Sch; Univ NC, Asheville diversity efforts; vol, YWCA Women's Adv Bd & Caring C; NC Arboretum Soc. **Business Addr:** Software Solutions Specialist, Toshiba Business Solutions, 1 Town Sq Blvd Suite 215, Asheville, NC 28803, **Business Phone:** (828)681-5071.

### GLOVER, KEVIN BERNARD

Football player, executive. **Personal:** Born Jun 17, 1963, Washington, DC; married Cestaine; children: Maya Nikkole, Matthew Robert Romeo & Zaria. **Educ:** Univ Md, 1984. **Career:** Football player (retired), executive; Detroit Lions, ctr & guard, 1985-97; Seattle Seahawks, ctr & guard, 1998-99; Univ Md, Md Terrapins Football Team, dir character educ, coordr develop, alumni & community rels, currently. **Business Addr:** Director of Character Education, Maryland Terrapins Football Team, University of Maryland, 2601 Comcast Ctr Terrapin Trail, College Park, MD 20742, **Business Phone:** (301)314-9289.

### GLOVER, LA'ROI

Football player. **Personal:** Born Jul 4, 1974, San Diego, CA; married Spring; children: La'Roi Jr, Neomie & Sophia. **Educ:** San Diego State Univ, BA, pub admin, 1996; Fontbonne Univ, MBA, 2012. **Career:** Football player (retired), exec; Oakland Raiders, defensive tackle, 1996; New Orleans Saints, defensive tackle, 1997, 1999, right defensive tackle, 1998-2001; Dallas Cowboys, defensive tackle, 2002, 2005, right & left defensive tackle, 2003, defensive tackle, 2004; St. Louis Rams, defensive tackle, 2006-08, nose tackle, 2008, dir player progs, 2010-; Entertainment & Sports Programming Network, Analyst, 2009-. **Orgs:** Founder, LaRoi Glover Found, 1999. **Honors/Awds:** San Diego Co-Player of the Year; Lineman of the Year, Los Angeles Times; Player of the Year, Calif Interscholastic Fedn; Defensive Player of the Week, Nat Football league; Unsung Hero Awards, 1999; Man of the Year, St. Louise Saints, 1999; Inducted to Aztec Hall of Fame, 2010; Saints Hall of Fame, 2013; CIF Player of the Year; Lineman of the Year, Los Angeles Times. **Business Addr:** Director of Player Development, St. Louis Rams, 1 Rams Way St, St. Louis, MO 63045, **Business Phone:** (314)982-7267.

### GLOVER, LINDA F. See BAILEY, LINDA F.

### GLOVER, NATHANIEL, JR. (NAT GLOVER)

Law enforcement officer, executive. **Personal:** Born Mar 29, 1943; son of Nathaniel and Arsie B; married Doris J Bailey; children: Michael & John. **Educ:** Edward Waters Col, BS, social sci, 1966; Univ N Fla, MS, 1987; Fed Bur Invest Nat Acad, grad. **Career:** Law enforcement officer (retired); Jacksonville Sheriff's Off, 1966-2003, Detective Div, investr, 1969, sgt, 1974, head police hostage negotiation team, 1975-86, chief serv, 1986-88, dep dir police serv, dir police servs; polit democrat; police officer; Duval Co, Fla, sheriff; Jacksonville, Fla, sheriff, 1995-2003; bd trustee, interim pres, Edward Waters Col, 2008; Pres, Edward Waters Col, 2010-. **Orgs:** Edward Waters alumni; Omega Psi Phi Fraternity; Brotherhood Police Officers; Pres, St Stephen AME Church Bd; Bd dir, Habijax; Bd dir, United Negro Col Fund; Bd dir, Tiger Acad. **Business Addr:** President, Edward Waters College in Jacksonville, 1658 Kings Rd, Jacksonville, FL 32209-6199, **Business Phone:** (904)470-8000.

### GLOVER, ROBERT G.

Chemist, president (organization). **Personal:** Born Jul 4, 1931, Bradley, AR; married Mary; children: Mary, Andrew, Alvin, Shirley, Dedra & Robert. **Educ:** Univ Philadelphia, Printing Ink Inst LeHigh. **Career:** St Clair & Valentine Co; Printing Ink Inst LeHigh Univ, lab, staff; Qual Printing Ink Co, Houston, pres. **Orgs:** Litho Club; Craftsman Club, PTA Houston. **Special Achievements:** Only black owner of a firm which manufactures printing inks of all types for distribution throughout the world. **Business Addr:** President, Quality Color Printing Inks, 1803 Cleburne St, Houston, TX 77004-4129, **Business Phone:** (713)528-6976.

### GLOVER, SAVION

Dancer, actor. **Personal:** Born Nov 19, 1973, Newark, NJ; son of Yvette. **Educ:** Rye Country Day Sch, grad. **Career:** Broadway prods, "The Tap Dance Kid", 1985, "Black & Blue", 1989, "Jelly's Last Jam", 1992, "Bring in 'Da Noise, Bring in 'Da Funk", 1995; Films: Taps, 1988; Bamboozled, 2000; Happy Feet, choreographer, 2006; Happy Feet 2, choreographer, 2011. TV series: "Sesame Street", 1991-95; "Driving Me Crazy", 1988; "Dance in Am: Tap", 1989; "MMC", 1989; "Ebony & Jet Showcase", 1989; "Square One TV", 1990; "Black Filmmakers Hall of Fame"; "The Kennedy Center Honors"; "In a New Light '94", 1994; "Showbiz Today", 1996-97; "Late Show with David Letterman", 1997; "The Rosie O'Donnell Show", 1996-98; "Saturday Night Live", 1999; "Cedric the Entertainer Presents", 2003; "The Tonight Show with Jay Leno", 2005; "Russell Simmons Presents Def Poetry", 2005; "Dancing with the Stars", 2007; Not Your Ordinary Tappers, founder, 1997; Ti Dii, Dance Co, founder, currently; Music Box Theatre, 2016. **Honors/Awds:** Martin Luther King Jr Outstanding Youth Award, 1991; Dance Magazine Award, 1992; Nominated for Young Artist Award, 1994; Tony Award for Best Choreography, 1996; Nat Endowment for the Arts Grant, 1996; Best New Theater Star, Ent Weekly, 1996; Capezeo Award, 2004.

### GODBEE, THOMASINA D.

Research scientist. **Personal:** Born Apr 10, 1946, Waynesboro, GA; married Cornelius; children: William Jr & Cornelius Tremayne II. **Educ:** Paine Col, BS, 1966. **Career:** Butts Co Bd Educ, Jackson, Ga, chem instr, 1966-67; EI du Pont de Nemours & Co, lab tech, 1967-69; Grady Mem Hosp, lab tech, 1970-71; Univ Calif, Irvine, staff res assoc, nuclear physics, 1971-. **Orgs:** Nat Asn Advan Colored People; Paine Col Alumni Club; United Presby Women; Nat Asn Univ Women; Westminster United Presby Church, Soloist Paine Col Concert Choir, 1966; second vpres, scrapbook co-chm; first vpres, comm chmn, Nat Asn Univ Women. **Honors/Awds:** Eng & Soc Sci Awards, 1960, 1962; Natural Sci Award, 1961; Outstanding Serv to the Community Award, Nat Asn Univ Women, 1977; Spec Performance Award, Univ Calif, 1984. **Home Addr:** 3501 Stafford St, Hephzibah, GA 30815-6625, **Home Phone:** (706)790-6189. **Business Addr:** 3501 Stafford, Hephzibah, GA 30815.

### GODBOLD, DR. DONALD HORACE

School administrator. **Personal:** Born Oct 3, 1928, Detroit, MI; son of Eugene Quemado (deceased) and Alice Virginia Kinney (deceased); married Delores Roxanna Cofer; children: Michelle Roxanne, Donald Terrence Juan, Monique Toi & Darwyn Eugene. **Educ:** Wayne State Univ, BS, 1950, MEd, 1956; Univ Mich, Ann Arbor, PhD, 1967. **Career:** School administrator (retired); Wayne State Univ, teacher spec educ & supv teacher, 1953-67; Oakland Community Col, Orchard Ridge Campus, dean stud serv, 1967-68, provost & chief exec, 1968-70; Community Col Denver Auraria Campus, dean campus & founding chief exec, 1970-71, campus dir & chief exec, 1971-72, vpres & chief exec, 1972-73; Univ Northern Colo, guest prof sociol black hist & cult, counr, 1971-74; Merritt Col, pres, 1973-77; Peralta Community Col Dist, vice chancellor educ serv, supt, 1977-80, chancellor, 1980-88; independent consult, 1988-; Alameda Co Youth Develop Inc, George P Scotlan Youth & Family Ctr, exec dir. **Orgs:** Bd mem, Comn Urban Community Col, 1972-75; Am Asn Community & Jr Col; Adv Comt, Am Coun Educ, 1984-87; bd dir, Goodwill Indust Greater E Bay, 1975-86; bd dir, vpres & secy, New Oakland Comn, 1975-87; bd dir, Oakland Soc Prev Cruelty Animals, 1978-86; comt mem, Am Coun Educ Comn Col Athletics, 1977-80; City Oakland Pvt Indus Coun, 1978-88; chmn, Accreditation Team, Western Asn Sch & Col, 1979; bd dir, Cs Hosp Med Ctr, 1980-; Am Col Personnel Asn; Am Personnel & Guid Asn; Colo Asn Comunity Jr Col; Coun Except C; Nat Asn Stud Personnel Adminr; Mich Acad Sci Arts & Lett; Nat Voc Guid Asn; dir, Univ Mich Chap; Phi Delta Kappa; Wayne State Univ Col Educ Alumni Asn; Wayne State Univ Alumni Asn; Univ Mich Alumni Asn; Asn Calif Community Col Admin; bd mem, Urban League CO; bd dir, League Innovation Community Col, 1980-87; bd dir, Bay Area Black United Fund, 1981-87; Conv Adv Comn Calif Asn Community Col, 1983. **Home Addr:** 75 Mission Hills St, Oakland, CA 94605-4612, **Home Phone:** (510)553-1858. **Business Addr:** CA.

### GODBOLT, RICKY CHARLES

Military engineer, educator. **Personal:** Born Mar 7, 1959, Buckner, AR; son of Eddie B and Beatrice; children: LaKelya, LaChelya, Candice & Marcus. **Educ:** Cent Tex Col, AA, 1989; Pk Univ, BS, social psychol, 1993; Univ Phoenix, AA, MA, PhD, educ leadership, 2010. **Career:** AUS, track mech, 1978-80, electrician, 1981-86, mech, 1986-90, instr, 1990-93, chief eng, 1994-99; AUs Corps Engrs, prime power prod specialist, 1986-93, mech training sect instr leader, 2000-06; mech training instr, 2000-; Prince George's Community Col, part-time fac, prog dir, basic elec instr, 2001-, Construct & Develop Inst, dir, 2006-12, assoc prof, 2006-; Army Family Team Builder instr, 2002-; Assoc Builders & Contractors, craft training comt mem, 2007-10; Col Southern Md, dir, ctr trades & energy training, 2012-. **Orgs:** Prince Hall Masons, Samuel T Daniels Chap No 107, 1991-93, Mt Moriah Commandry No1, 1991-93; Shadrach Jackson Consistory No 156, 1992-94; Magnus Temple No3, 1992-94; Phylaxis Soc, 1992-, dir, mil affairs, 1996-; Eastern Stars, Majorie T Lancaster No 84, 1992-95; African Lodge, No 459, 1992-; Asn AUS, 1992-94; Retired Officers Asn, 1993-; Pk Col, Pinnacle mem, 1994; Fraternal Order Police, 1994-96; Prince Hall Masons, Zedekiah No167, 1994-; charter mem, Citizen's Flag Alliance, 1995-; AUS Warrant Officer's Asn, 1995-; Veterans Foreign Wars Post 6002, 1996-; first class operator, Nat Inst Uniform Licensing Power Engrs, 1996-; Nat Soc Black Engrs, 1996-; charter mem, Howard Bailey McAfee Heritage Soc Pk Col, 1997-; Lord Fairfax Silver chap, US Warrant Officer's Asn, 1997-; Am Legion Post No 0259, 1999-; Nat Black Social Workers; Asn Black Psychologists; Nat Asn Advan Colored People; Mt Vernon Lodge Odd fel; Disabled Am Veterans Chap No17, 2000-; Fraternal Order Police, Lodge No119, 2000-; Int Toast Masters, Ft Belvoir, Va chp, 2001-; Ft Belvoir Speakers Bur, 2001-; Mil Order World Wars, 2001-; Retiree Coun, 2001-; Ft George G Meade, MD chap, Retired Officers Asn, 2001-; Soc Am Mil Engrs, 2001-; Nat Asn Black Veterans, 2001-; Blacks Govt, 2001-; Oxon Hill Lions Club, 2002-; assoc mem, Fraternal Order Police Fed Lodge, 2002-; life mem, Disabled Am Veterans; Howard Bailey McAfee Heritage Soc. **Honors/Awds:** Honor Roll, Educ Ctr ANFB, 1991-92; Acad Scholarship, Asn AUS, 1992; Certificate Meritorious Service, Phylaxis Soc, 1993; Best Table Topic Award, Ft Belvoir, Va Toast Masters, 2001; 249th Engrs Commander's Coin Excellence, 2002. **Special Achievements:** NCO Quarter, 1983; First mechanic in history to win instructor year, 1992; First African-Am to win instructor year, 1992; First graduate sch for extended learning to become a member Howard Bailey McAfee Heritage Soc Park Col; First Afr Am mem Howard Bailey McAfee Heritage Soc, Park Col. **Home Addr:** 1210 Palmer Rd Apt 4, Fort Washington, MD 20744, **Home Phone:** (757)887-0734. **Business Addr:** Director Center for Trades and Energy Training, College of Southern Maryland, 8730 Mitchell Rd, La Plata, MD 20646, **Business Phone:** (301)934-2251.

### GODDARD, BERNIE. See ROHE, BERNIE.

### GODDARD, ROSALIND KENT

Librarian. **Personal:** Born Mar 7, 1944, Gadsden, AL; daughter of George and Nettye George Kent. **Educ:** San Francisco State Col, BA, 1965; Univ Calif, Los Angeles, MLS, 1982. **Career:** Los Angeles Pub Libr, Los Angeles, CA, sr librn, 1967-92, br mgr; Los Angeles Community Col, exec asst to chancellor, 1992-94, opers div, Human Resources, assoc dir, recruitment & training; Los Angeles Southwest Col, Los Angeles Comm Col, actg assoc dean, 1994; Los Angeles Trade Tech Col, actg assoc dean, 1996-97; Los Angeles City Col, Col Libr, ref librn, Learning Skills Ctr, instr, 1998-. **Orgs:** Calif Librarians Black Caucus, 1980-; Am Libr Asn, 1980-; Women Color, 1989-97; Nat Asn Advan Colored People, 1989-; comn mem, Calif Postsecondary Educ Comn, 1990-92; pres bd, Friends Watts Towers, 1997-; Asn Calif Community Col Adminr, 1997-98; ref libr fac, Los Angeles City Col. **Honors/Awds:** Staff Commendation, Los Angeles Pub Libr, 1969; Exceptional Leadership Award, Los Angeles Brotherhood Crusade, 1973; Outstanding Black Leader, La Communit Cols, 1993. **Home Addr:** 5268 Village Green, Los Angeles, CA 90016. **Business Addr:** Librarian, Los Angeles City College, 300A/103B 855 N Vt Ave, Los Angeles, CA 90029, **Business Phone:** (323)953-4000.

### GODETTE, FRANKLIN DELANO ROOSEVELT. See Obituaries Section.

### GODFREY, DR. FRANK EDEN

School administrator. **Personal:** Born Dec 23, 1944, Charleston, SC; married Andrea Ollivierra; children: Frank Jr, Marlin & Shannon. **Educ:** St Augustine, BS, bus, 1967; Tex Southern Univ, MBA, 1971; Harvard Univ, MPA, 1979, EdD, admin, planning, & social policy, 1983. **Career:** Tex Southern Univ, Ford fel, 1969-71; Hampton Inst, instr, 1971-75; Ctr Minority Bus Develop, assoc dir, 1972; NASA, contracting officer, negotiator & price analyst, 1974-80; St Leo Col, adj fac, 1975-78; NASA/Harvard Univ, EPM fel, 1978-79; Harvard Univ, res asst, 1980-82; Elliott Congregational Church, tutor, 1983; St Augustines Col, dir alumni affairs, 1984, Div Bus, head, Div Bus & Comput Sci, chairperson, 2008. **Orgs:** Nat Scholar, Alpha Kappa Mu, 1966; bd adv, Martin Luther King Open Sch, 1982-83. **Home Addr:** 2300 Havering Pl, Raleigh, NC 27604, **Home Phone:** (919)876-4791.

### GODFREY, RANDALL EURALENTRIS

Football player, business owner. **Personal:** Born Apr 6, 1973, Valdosta, GA. **Educ:** Univ Ga, BA, housing & consumer econ, 1996. **Career:** Football player (retired), executive; Dallas Cowboys, middle linebacker, 1996-2008; Tenn Titans, linebacker, 2000-02; Seattle Seahawks, linebacker, 2003; San Diego Chargers, linebacker, 2004-06; Wash Redskins, linebacker, 2007; Godfrey Funeral Home LLC, owner, 2005-. **Orgs:** Pres, Randall Godfrey Found, 1996, owner, 2005-; Nat Football League Players Asn, 1996; Ga Real Estate Investors Asn, 1996. **Honors/Awds:** Emil Karas Memorial Award for Most Inspirational Player. **Special Achievements:** TV appearance: NFL on FOX, 1994; 1996 NFL Draft, 1996; TNT Sunday Night Football, 1997; The NFL on NBC, 1997; NFL Monday Night Football, 1997-2001; ESPN's Sunday Night Football, 1998-2000; NBC Sunday Night Football, 2006. **Home Addr:** 3665 Moye Trl, Duluth, GA 30097. **Business Addr:** Owner, Godfrey Funeral Home LLC, 636 River St, Valdosta, GA 31601-5400, **Business Phone:** (229)242-9500.

### GODFREY, WILLIAM R.

Financial manager, insurance executive, auditor. **Personal:** Born May 18, 1948, Gay, GA; son of John W and Iula; married Joyce Lincoln; children: Runako, Kenan & Nyasha. **Educ:** Clark Atlanta Univ, BA, bus admin & finance, 1970; State Univ NY, Buffalo, MBA, mgt, 1973. **Career:** US Gen Acct Off, sr auditor, 1973-80; US Gen Serv Admin Off Inspector Gen, sr auditor, 1980, dis mgr, 1994-2011; Fulton Co, asst finance dir; GSA, sr advisor, 1994-97; William R Godfrey & Assocs Inc, currently. **Orgs:** Treas, Ment Health Asn Metro Atlanta, 1984-89. **Home Addr:** 215 Piedmont, Atlanta, GA 30308, **Home Phone:** (404)588-2254. **Business Addr:** Owner, William R Godfrey & Associates Inc, 215 Piedmont Ave Suite 2108, Atlanta, GA 30308, **Business Phone:** (404)588-2254.

### GOFF, DR. WILHELMINA DELORES

Association executive, counselor. **Personal:** Born Jun 18, 1940, Columbia, SC; daughter of William Earl and Katie Mae. **Educ:** Morgan State Col, BS, 1962; John Carroll Univ, MA, 1971; NY Univ; Cleveland State Univ, EdSD. **Career:** Hillcrest Ctr C Bedford Hills, counr, 1962-64; Cleveland Pub Sch, music teacher, 1964-78, guid counr, 1971-78; Cuyahoga Community Col, coordr, counr job corps, 1978-, assoc dir access & job corps act, 1979-80; Cleveland, asst dean stud personnel serv; Nat Coun Negro Women, dir prog & develop; Delta Sigma Theta Sorority, dep exec dir, 1977-82, regional dir. **Orgs:** Newsletter ed, Phi Delta Kappa Reg dir Delta Sigma Theta Sor, 1976-; pres, Ohio Asn Non-White Concerns Personnel & Guid, 1978-80; corresp secy & mem, large NE Ohio Personnel & Guid, 1978-80; bd mem & chmn, ed com Cleveland Nat Asn Advan Colored People, 1979-80; coordr speakers bur, Gr Cleveland Com IYC, 1979; pres, Delta Sigma Theta Tutoring & Nutrit Prog, 1986-; Carbondale Alumnae Chap. **Honors/Awds:** Award for Congressman Stokes Cleve, 1974; Pan-Hellenic Award, Cleveland, 1976; Outstanding Service, Delta New Orleans LA convention, 1979; Key to the City, Indianapolis Ind, 1980; Higher Educator Councilor of the Year NEOPGA, 1980; Outstanding Serv, Teen Father Prog, 1984; Proclamation, City Cincinnati, 1982; Outstanding Serv, OH Personnel & Guid Asn; Outstanding Serv, Dyke Col Stud Body, 1986; Outstanding Serv Youth & Educ, Cleveland Chap Negro Bus & Prof Women's Club, 1986. **Home Addr:** 29 Hawthorne Ct NE, Washington, DC 20017, **Home Phone:** (202)328-0474. **Business Addr:** Regional Director, Deputy Executive Director, Delta Sigma Theta Sorority Inc, 1707 New Hampshire Ave NW, Washington, DC 20009, **Business Phone:** (202)986-2509.

### GOGGINS, DR. HORACE

Dentist. **Personal:** Born May 14, 1929, Hodges, SC; son of Mattie Butler and Ulysses; married Juanita; children: Horace W Jr. **Educ:** SC State Col, BS, 1950; Howard Univ, DDS, 1955. **Career:** Dentist (retired); Rock Hill, SC, self-employed dent surgeon. **Orgs:** Nat Dent Asn; past pres, Palmetto Med & Dent Asn, 1973; SE Analgesia Soc; Tri County Dent Soc; Piedmont Dent Soc; Beta Kappa Chi Sci Soc; Rock Hill Planning Comn; Nat Asn Advan Colored People; Coun Human Rels; Mt Prospect Baptist Church deacon; Alpha Phi Alpha Fraternity; Sigma Pi Phi Fraternity; SC Dem Party; Am Legion Elks; secy, Nat Asn Advan Colored People. **Honors/Awds:** Doctor of the Year, Palmetto Dent Asn, 1983-84; Certificate of Appreciation, Delta Sigma Theta, 1992; Minority Business Person of the Year, 1994; Outstanding Service & Leadership Award, Rock Hill Br Nat Asn Advan Colored People, 1995; Humanitarian Award, Nat Asn Advan Colored People, SC, 2008. **Home Addr:** 1635 W Main St, Rock Hill, SC 29730. **Business Addr:** Dentist, 427 Dave Lyle Blvd, Rock Hill, SC 29730-4402, **Business Phone:** (803)328-0858.

### GOINES, DR. LEONARD

Musician, educator. **Personal:** Born Apr 22, 1934, Jacksonville, FL; son of Willie Mae LaMar and Buford; married Margaretta Bobo; children: Lisan Lynette. **Educ:** Manhattan Sch Music, BMus, 1955, MMus, 1956; Fontain bleu Sch Music France, cert, 1959; Columbus Univ, MA, 1960, dipl, 1961, EdD, 1963; New Sch Soc Res, BA, 1980; NY Univ, MA, 1980, Ctr Ment Health, 1983; Harvard Univ, CAS, 1984. **Career:** Educator (retired); New York Bd Educ, teacher music,

1959-65; Leonard Goines Quintet, trumpeter-leader, 1960-; Symphony New World, trumpeter, 1965-76; Bedford Stuyvesant Youth Action, dir music, 1965-66; Morgan State Col, assoc prof music, 1966-68; York Col City Univ NY, lectr, 1969; Manhattan Community Col, prof music, 1969-92; NY Univ, jazz hist lectr, 1970-88; City Univ New York, Queens Col, Afro-Am music lectr; Howard Univ, assoc prof music, 1970-72, WEB DuBois Inst, post-doctoral res fel, 1982-85; Shepard & Goines, partner org & educ arts consults, 1984-; Williams Col, vis prof music, 1984; Vassar Col, vis prof music, 1985; Lafayette Col Easton PA, distinguished vis prof music, 1986. **Orgs:** Folklore consult, Smithsonian Inst, 1974-76; jazz consult, Creative Artists Pub Serv Prog, 1980; bd trustees, Nat Asn Community Sch &Arts, 1982-85; chmn, spec arts sect panel Ny Coun Arts, 1982-85; jazz res consult, Nat EndowmentArts, 1983; music consult, US Info Agency, 1984; co-exec producer, BAM Majestic Theater, Brooklyn, NY, 1988-96; adv bd mem, Universal Jazz Coalition Inc; adv bd mem, Afro-Am Music Bicentennial Hall Fame & Mus Inc. **Honors/Awds:** Citizenship Winnipeg Canada, 1958; fac res grants, Howard Univ, State Univ NY, City Univ NY, 1971-73; first Annual NY Brass Conf for Scholar Award, 1973; develop series of music filmstrips for Educ Audio Visuals Inc, 1975; Public Service Award, US Dept of Labor, 1980; Col Teachers Fel, Nat Endowment for the Humanities, 1982-83; Scholar Incentive Award, City Univ NY, 1983-84; Hon writer & contrib articles to Groves Dict of Music & Musicians, Black Books Bulletin, first World, The Black Perspective in Music, Journ of African & Asian Studies, Black World, Downbeat, Music Educ Journ, Allegro. **Special Achievements:** Appointed To Preservation of Jazz Adv Comn by Secy of Smithsonian Inst, 1991-93. **Home Addr:** 221 W 131st St, New York, NY 10027, **Home Phone:** (212)862-1652.

## GOINS, MARY G.

Educator. **Personal:** Born Sep 8, 1929, Orange, TX; married Lee A Randle. **Educ:** BA, MA. **Career:** Instr & prin, 1961; Enterprise Jr High Sch, Compton, CA, prin. **Orgs:** Vpres, Compton Educ Asn, 1969-70; pres, Asn Compton Sch Course, 1970-71; secy, Asn Compton Unified Sch Adminrs, 1971-72; Asn Calif Sch Adminrs; Calif Pers & Guid Asn; PTA; officer Exec PTA. **Home Addr:** 19102 Northwood Ave, Carson, CA 90746.

## GOINS, ATTY. RICHARD ANTHONY

Educator, lawyer. **Personal:** Born Mar 1, 1950, New Orleans, LA; son of James Milton and Vivian Wiltz; married Nannette. **Educ:** Yale Univ, BA, hist, 1972; Stanford Univ & Law Sch, JD, 1975. **Career:** Stanford Univ, Sch Law, Reginald Heber Smith fel, 1975; New Orleans Legal Asst Corp, mgr & staff atty, 1975-77, dep dir, 1977-78, exec dir, 1978-81; Loyola Univ, Sch Law, asst prof, 1981-84; Hon Adrian G Duplantier, lawclerk, 1982; Adams & Reese, asst atty, 1984-87; Loyola Univ, Law Sch, adj prof, 1984-; atty, partner, 1987; Thomas More Inn Ct, barrister, 1988-2009; Comt Bar Admis, from asst examr to chmn, 1993-2010; Goins Aaron PC, atty, currently. **Orgs:** La State Bar Asn, 1975-; Calif State Bar, 1977-; Am Bar Asn Conf Minority Partners Majority/Corp Law Firm, 1990-; bd dir local chap, Fed Bar Asn, 1992-; Merit Selection Panel, Selection & Appointment US Magistrate, 1992-96. **Home Addr:** 4412 Mandeville St, New Orleans, LA 70112-4928, **Home Phone:** (504)286-3939. **Business Addr:** Attorney, Goins Aaron PC, 201 St Charles Ave Suite 3800, New Orleans, LA 70170, **Business Phone:** (504)569-1800.

## GOLDBERG, WHOOPI (CARYN ELAINE JOHNSON)

Activist, comedian, actor. **Personal:** Born Nov 13, 1955, New York, NY; daughter of Robert James Johnson Jr (deceased) and Emma Harris (deceased); married Alvin Martin, Jan 1, 1973, (divorced 1979); children: Alexandrea Martin; married David Edward Claessen, Sep 1, 1986, (divorced 1988); married Lyle Trachtenberg, Oct 1, 1994, (divorced 1995). **Career:** Stand-up comedian, Los Angeles, CA; Films: Citizen: I'm Not Losing My Mind, I'm Giving It Away, 1982; The Color Purple, 1985; Jumpin' Jack Flash, 1986; Burglar, 1987; Fatal Beauty, 1987; Clara's Heart, 1988; The Telephone, 1998; Homer & Eddie, 1989; Ghost, 1990; The Long Walk Home, 1990; Soap Dish, 1991; Sarafina, 1992; Sister Act, 1992; Made in America, 1993; Sister Act 2, 1993; Corrina, Corrina, 1994; Bogus, 1996; Eddie, 1996; The Associate, 1996; Ghosts of Mississippi, 1996; How Stella Got Her Groove Back, 1998; Girl Interrupted, 1999; Kingdom Come, 2001; Monkey bone, 2001; Rat Race, 2001; Blizzard, 2003; Pinocchio 3000, 2004; Super Babies: Baby Geniuses 2, 2004; Jiminy Glick in Lalawood, 2004; Racing Stripes, 2005; Whoopi: Backto Broadway-The 20th Anniversary, 2005; Doogal, 2006; Farce of the Penguins, 2006; Everyone's Hero, 2006; Homie Spumoni, 2006; It's Under My Skin, 2006; The Lasy Guy on Earth, 2006; Saturday Night Live: The Best of Saturday TV Fun house, 2006; If I Had Known I Was a Genius, 2007; Stream, 2008; Snow Buddies, 2008; Madea Goes to Jail, 2009; See You in September, 2010; Toy Story 3, 2010; For Colored Girls, 2010; A Little Bit of Heaven, 2011; The Contradictions of Fair Hope, 2012; Teenage Mutant Ninja Turtles, 2014; Top Five, 2014; Big Stone Gap, 2014; Black Dog, Red Dog, 2014. TV Series: "Star Trek: The Next Generation", 1987; "Baghdad Cafe", 1990; "Hollywood Squares", producer, 1998-2004; "Whose Line Is It Anyway?", 2000; "What Makes a Family", 2001; "Call Me Claus", 2001; "Madeline: My Fair Madeline", voice, 2002; "It's a Very Merry Muppet Christmas Movie", 2002; "Absolutely Fabulous", 2002; "Good Fences", producer, 2003; "Whoopi", producer, 2003; "Little burg", 2004; "Bear in the Big Blue House", 2005; "Just for Kicks", develop & exec producer, 2006; "Dawn French's Girls Who Do Comedy", 2006; "Everybody Hates Chris ", 2006; "Comic Relief seven times"; Academy Awards, host; Appearances on Moonlighting; "Scared Straight: 10 Years Later"; "Carol, Carl, Whoopi & Robin"; "An All-Star Celebration: The '88 Vote"; "Funny, You Don't Look 200"; "My Past Is My Own"; "Broadway: A Funny Thing Happened On the Way To The Forum"; "Cinderella"; Untitled IDT Entertainment Proj, 2006; "Sonotorious", 2006; "Law & Order: Criminal Intent", 2006; "If I Had Known I Was a Genius", 2006; "Everybody Hates Chris", 2006; "30 Rock", 2007-09; "Entourage", 2008; "Life on Mars", 2008; "A Muppets Christmas: Letters to Santa", 2008; "The Cleaner", 2009; "The Middle", 2012; "Suburgatory", 2012; "Robot Chicken", 2012; "666 Park Avenue", 2012; "Late Night with Jimmy Fallon", 2012-13; "Glee", 2012-14; "Sensitive Men", 2013; "Once Upon a Time in Wonderland", 2013-14; "A Day Late and a Dollar Short", 2014; "The 7D", 2014. HBO specials; Whoopi Goldberg Show; Roles: Star Trek: The Next Generation; Jumpin' Jack Flash; Toy Story 3; The View daytime talk show, moderator, 2007-; Guest Appearance in Shot Film: Liberian Girl. **Orgs:** Screen Actors Guild; Am Fedn TV & Radio Artists. **Honors/Awds:** NBR Award, 1985; Golden Globe Award, 1986, 1991; Academy Award Best Actress, 1985; Image Award, Nat Asn Advan Colored People, 1988, 1990, 1992-94, 1999 & 2004; Grammy Award, 1985; Kid's Choice Award, 1988, 1989, 1992-94; Humanitarian of the Year, Starlight Found, 1989; KCFCC Award, Kans City Film Critics Circle, 1990; Oscar Award, 1991; DFWFCA Award, Dallas-Ft Worth Film Critics Asn, 1991; Humanitarian Award, 1991; BAFTA Film Award, 1991, 2002; Saturn Award, 1991; Academy Award for Best Supporting Actress, 1991; American Comedy Award, 1991, 1993; TV Prize, 1992; Am Cinema Award, 1992; ShoWest Award, 1993; CableACE Award, 1993; Woman of the Year, 1993; People's Choice Award, 1994-96; Best Actress, Fantafestival, 1996; University of Vermont, hon degree, 1997; OFTA Television Award, Online Film & Tv Asn, 1997; Gay and Lesbian Alliance Against Defamation Vanguard Award, 1999; Ruby Award, Santa Barbara Int Film Festival, 2000; Star on Hollywood Walk of Fame, 2001; Star on the Walk of Fame, 2001; Crystal Award, 2001; Daytime Emmy Award, 2002, 2009; Tony Award, 2002; AFI Star Award, 2002; US Comedy Arts Festival, 2002; Gracie Allen Awards, 2003; Muse Award, New York Women Film & Tv, 2003; MVP of the Kinko's Celebrity Softball Game, 2003; British Academy Film Award; Hollywood Walk of Fame; Vision Award, 2008; Golden Apple Award, Casting Soc Am, 2011; Black Reel Award, 2014; Wilson Col, hon degree. **Special Achievements:** ABC's A Gala for the President, Ford's Theatre; Emmy Award nomination for hosting The 66th Annual Academy Awards; Broadway, A Funny Thing Happened on the Way to the Forum, 1997; Book: Alice, 1992; book 1997. The first African American to have received Academy Award nominations for both Best Actress and Best Supporting Actress; First African-American female to host the Academy Awards. **Business Addr:** Actor, Producer, Whoopi Inc, 4000 Warner Blvd Suite 405, Los Angeles, CA 90024.

## GOLDEN, ARTHUR IVANHOE. See Obituaries Section.

## GOLDEN, DR. CECILIA GRIFFIN

Educator, president (organization). **Personal:** married Ronald; children: Chaton, Jeryn & Adam. **Educ:** NY State Univ, Geneseo, BA, span educ; State Univ Albany, MS; State Univ Buffalo, PhD, social educ, 1998. **Career:** Rochester City Sch Dist, teacher, 1975-87, proj supvr reading, 1987-89; State Univ NY, Brockport, vis asst prof, urban ed specialist, 1989-91; Jefferson MS, HS, Edison Tech HS, vice prin, 1992-93; Andrew J Townson SchNo 39, prin, 1993-96; Rochester City Sch Dist, interim exec dir acad op, 1996-97, chief acad officer, 1997-; Southern Univ, asst provost, 2008-11; NY Coalition Childrens Ment Health Serv, pres. **Orgs:** Delta Kappa Gamma; Nat Alliance Black Sch Educr; Am Ed Res Asn; Asn Supv & Curric Develop; Phi Delta Kappa; Sch Admin Asn NY State; United Way Allegheny County; Rochester Women's Network; Urban League Rochester; YWCA Greater Pittsburgh, 2001-06; bd dir, WQED Multimedia Inc, 2003-; pres & chief exec officer, Vols Am Chesapeake, Lanham, 2006-; exec dir, Hillside Family Agencies, 2013-. **Home Addr:** 86 Langston Pt, Pittsford, NY 14534, **Home Phone:** (716)381-5839. **Business Addr:** President, Chief Executive Officer, Volunteers of America Chesapeake, 7901 Annapolis Rd, Lanham, MD 20706, **Business Phone:** (301)459-2020.

## GOLDEN, DONALD LEON

College teacher, lawyer. **Personal:** Born Jan 3, 1940, Walnut Cove, NC; children: Donna & Amber. **Educ:** Howard Univ, BA, 1972, Law Sch, JD, 1972. **Career:** US Atty's Off, law clerk, 1971; Judicial Panel Multi-Dist Litigation, temp researcher asst, 1971; Howard Law Sch Libr, 1971-72; US Dist Ct, law clerk, 1972-73; Covington & Burling, assoc, 1973-77; Howard Univ Law Sch, adj prof, 1974-81, prof, 1981-; Asst US Atty's Off, atty, 1977-81. **Home Addr:** 6012 28th St NW, Washington, DC 20015, **Home Phone:** (202)362-2484. **Business Addr:** Professor, Howard University Law School, 2935 Uptown St NW, Washington, DC 20008-1194.

## GOLDEN, JOYCE MARIE

Chief executive officer, chief financial officer, president (organization). **Personal:** Born Berkeley, CA; married William Paul; children: Shawn Patrick. **Educ:** Calif State Univ, Hayward, CA, BA, psychol, MBA, acct & finance. **Career:** Arthur Andersen & Co, sr acct, 1977-81; Bank Am, vpres & financial mgr, planning mgr, int banking controller, asst vp & acct mgr, 1981-86; Citi Corp Savings, dir acct, 1986-87; San Francisco Chronicle & Examr Newspapers, vpres & chief financial officer, 1987-93; SPG & Assocs, founder, pres & chief exec officer, currently. **Orgs:** Newspaper Asn Am; Am Womens Soc CPAs; vpres, Oakland Ensemble Theatre, 1986-89; Nat Asn Urban Bankers; vpres, Bus Vol Arts, 1990-93; treas, Bay Area Adoption Placement & Res Ctr, 1992-; vpres, Nat Geog Soc; nat bd mem, Women Inc; bd chair strategic planning, Financial Serv Coalition; Young Audiences Wash DC; bd mem, Dc Chamber Com, currently; Greater Wash Bd Trade, currently; Am Soc Asn Execs, currently. **Business Addr:** President, Chief Executive Officer, SPG & Associates, 7102 River Rd Suite 221, Bethesda, MD 20817, **Business Phone:** (301)320-3689.

## GOLDEN, LOUIE

Educator, association executive. **Personal:** Born May 2, 1940, Matthews, SC; married Batty Washington; children: Louis Shaun. **Educ:** Claflin Col, BS, math, 1963; Southern Ill Univ, MS, 1971. **Career:** Sterling High Sch Greenville, coach, teacher, 1963-65; Beck High Sch, coach, teacher, 1965-70; Carolina High Sch, coach, teacher, 1970-72; Riverside High Sch Greer, athletic dir, 1973; Greenville Co Sch Dist, Southside High Sch, athletic dir, head boys basketball coach, 2009. **Orgs:** Coack Clin SC Basketball; SC Educ Asn; Greenville Co Educ Asn; NEA Coun Math; SC HS League; master Mason; polemarch Kappa Alpha Psi Frat; Comn, Citizen week Co Coun; Pk & Tourist Comn Appalachian Coun Govt Pk & Recreation Comn Greenville C C; vice chmn, trustee bd, vice chmn fin com church treas, St Matthew United Meth Church; charter mem, Big Bros Big Sisters Upstate. **Honors/Awds:** South Carolina Athletic Coaches Association Hall of Fame, 1995; SCACA Athletic Director of the Year, 1998; Riverside High School gymnasium named in his honor; honored, Sc Gen Assembly, 2009; SCACA Coach of the Year and Region Coach of the Year. **Special Achievements:** First African American head coach prominent white school; First African American athletic dir Greenville Co Sch Dist; 750 winning percent basketball for ten years. **Home Addr:** 201 S Adams St, Taylors, SC 29687-2357, **Home Phone:** (864)244-8109.

## GOLDEN, MARITA

Novelist, college teacher. **Personal:** Born Apr 28, 1950, Washington, DC; daughter of Fancis Sherman and Beatrice Lee; married Femi Ajayi; children: Michael Kayode. **Educ:** Am Univ, BA, eng, 1972; Columbia Univ, MSC, Marita, 1973. **Career:** WNET Channel 13, NY, assoc producer, 1974-75; Univ Lagos, Nigeria, asst prof, 1975-79; Roxbury Community Col, Boston, MA, asst prof, 1979-81; Emerson Col, Boston, MA, asst prof, 1981-83; author, 1983-; George Mason Univ, Creative Writing Prog, sr writer, currently; Roxbury Community Col, fac; Va Commonwealth Univ, prof MFA creative writing prog, 1994-2001; Words Power LLC, novelist, pres, 2000-; Univ Dist Columbia, writer in residence, currently; Novels: Migrations of the Heart, 1983; A Womans Place, 1986; Long Distance Life, 1989; And Do Remember Me, 1992; Saving Our Sons, 1994; The Edge of Heaven, 1998; Skin Deep: Black & White Women on Race; A Miracle Everyday: Triumph & Transformation in the Lives of Single Mothers, 1999. **Orgs:** Exec dir, Inst Preserv & Study African-Am Writing, 1986-87; pres emer, African-Am Writers Guild; pres, Zora Neale Hurston/Richard Wright Found. **Home Addr:** 11506 Tommy Ct, Mitchellville, MD 20721. **Business Addr:** Novelist, Words of Power LLC, PO Box 4853, Largo, MD 20775, **Business Phone:** (301)683-2134.

## GOLDEN, MARVIN DARNELL

College teacher. **Personal:** Born Dec 9, 1955, Chicago, IL; son of Catherine L. **Educ:** DePaul Univ, Chicago, CA, polit sci, BA, 1978; Univ Ill, Chicago, CA, MPA, 1985. **Career:** Independent pub policy consult & orgr, 1955-97; Greenpeace, midwest regenergy campaigner, 1991-94; dir vol serv, 1998-2000; lawyers comt better housing, vol coordr, 1998-2000; Career Col Chicago, instr, 1999-2002; City Cols Chicago-Harry S Truman Col, instr, currently. **Orgs:** Am Psychol Asn, 1977-; Souvenir Prog Comt Chicago Sinfonietta Ann Benefit, 1991; Energy Justice Campaign, 1995-96; bd dir, Citizen Utility Bd, 1997-2001. **Home Addr:** 3550 N Lake Shore Dr, Chicago, IL 60657, **Home Phone:** (312)935-2164. **Business Addr:** Instructor, City Colleges of Chicago-Harry S Truman College, 1145 W Wilson Ave, Chicago, IL 60640-6063, **Business Phone:** (773)907-4000.

## GOLDEN, RONALD ALLEN

Insurance executive. **Personal:** Born Feb 6, 1944, St. Louis, MO; married Clementina Joyce Thompson; children: Stephanie, Lisa & Ronald. **Educ:** Southwest Mo State Univ, BS, 1970; Am Educ Inst, cert, casualty claim law assoc, 1979. **Career:** McDonnell & Douglas Corp, tool & parts control specialist, 1966-68; St Louis Bd Educ, teacher, 1968; Travelers Ins Co, supvr casualty prog claims, 1968-, sr claim law assoc, currently; Third World Band, bus mgr, 1973-; Simply US Bank, bus mgr, 1977-. **Orgs:** Am Fed Musicians Local, 1973-. **Honors/Awds:** Outstanding Freshman Award, Southwest Mo State Univ. **Special Achievements:** First black athlete to win track & field scholarship SMSU, 1962-66; first black in CP Claim St Louis Office Travellers Ins Co. **Home Addr:** 1554 Mendell Dr, St Louis, MO 63130, **Home Phone:** (314)727-5798. **Business Addr:** Senior Claim Law Associate, The Travelers Companies, 701 Mkt St, St Louis, MO 63101, **Business Phone:** (314)621-5540.

## GOLDEN, DR. WILLIE L.

Law enforcement officer. **Personal:** Born Aug 16, 1952, Miami, FL; son of Louise Smith and Willie S; married Myra E Jones; children: Bryan, Kyle, Christopher & William Justin. **Educ:** Southeast Fla Inst Criminal Justice, Miami, FL, cert completion, 1974; Miami-Dade Community Col, Miami, FL, AA, 1978; Biscayne Col, Miami, FL, BA, 1980; St Thomas Univ, Miami, FL, MS, 1981. **Career:** Police officer (retire); Metro-Dade Police Dept, Miami, Fla, police officer; Dade County Sch Syst, Miami, Fla, teacher, 1977-84; Dade County Citizen Safety Coun, Miami, Fla, instr, consult, 1984-; Fla Memorial Col, Miami, Fla, assoc prof, 1986-; Alexander & Alexander, Miami, Fla, pub rel consult, 1986-88; Metrop Police Inst, Miami, Fla, instr, 1987; Metro Dade PoliceDept, first lt. **Orgs:** Jr warden, Prince Hall Masons, 1974-; pres, Progressive Officers, 1975-; Dade County Police Ben Asn, 1975-; parliamentarian, Nat Black Police Asn, 1977-; chaplain, Phi Beta Sigma Fraternity, 1984-; Nat Asn Advan Colored People, 1984-; bd dir, S Fla Inst Traffic Safety Unlimited, 1985-; Prince Hall Shriner, temple, 149; Police Benevolent Asn; Univ Miami Med Adv Bd; Nat Orgn Black Law Enforcement Exec. **Home Addr:** 18910 NW 29th Pl, Miami Gardens, FL 33056, **Home Phone:** (305)621-0537.

## GOLDSBERRY, DR. RONALD EUGENE (RON GOLDSBERRY)

Automotive executive, chairperson, association executive. **Personal:** Born Sep 12, 1942, Wilmington, DE; married Betty; children: Ryan & Renee. **Educ:** Cent State Univ, BS, chem, 1964; Mich State Univ, PhD, inorg chem, 1969; Stanford Univ, MBA, fin & mkt, 1973. **Career:** Univ Calif, San Jose, asst prof chem, 1969-71; NASA Am Res Ctr, res chemist, 1969-72; Hewlett Packard Co, prod mgr, 1969-72; Boston Consult Group, mgt consult, 1973-75; Gulf Oil Corp, dir corp planning, 1975-78; Occidental Chem Corp, vpres bus develop, 1978-81, vpres & gen mgr surfacetreatment prods, 1981-83; Ford Motor Co, pres & chief operating officer, 1983-87; Parker Chem Co, pres, chief operating officer, 1983-87, gen mgr plastic & trim prod div, gen sales & mkt mgr, parts & serv, 1991-94, gen mgr customer serv, 1994-96, vpres & gen mgr, Global Customer Serv, 1997-99, vpres global bus strategy, 1999; Unumprovident Corp, dir, 1999-; Unum Group, dir, 1999-2015; OnStation Corp, chmn bd, 1999-2006, chief exec officer, 2002; Deloitte & Touche, consult, 2001-; UNC Ventures Inc, chmn. **Orgs:** Dir, Case Corp, 1998-; corp dir & mem audit comt, Can Tire Corp, 2014-; trustee, Cent State Univ; Nat Acad Engrs; bd mem, Cranbrook Educ Inst; bd mem, Mich State Univ Alumni Asn; bd mem, Black Exec Exchange Prog; Am Chem Soc; Nat Black MBA Asn; Nat Org Black Chemists & Chem Engrs; Asn Consumer Growth; Comn Devlop Asn; Am Mgt Asn; Econ Club; Greater Detroit Chamber Com; Omega Psi Phi Frat; bd trustee, WTVS Channel 56 Detroit; bd mem, Am Can Co; bd mem, Rockefeller Found; bd mem, Adrian Col; bd mem, William Beaumont Hosp; bd mem, Boy Scouts Am; bd mem, Mich State Univ Develop Fund; dir, adv coun, Stanford Grad Sch Bus; trustee, Rockefeller Found; chmn, Detroit Pub Tv; Vision 007 Youth Ctr Capital Campaign; United Way Southeastern Mich Virgil H. Carr Soc Cabinet Comt; Bd mem, Ex Primerica Corp; bd mem, Cent State Univ Found; bd mem, Mich State Univ Found; bd mem, Detroit Financial Adv Bd. **Honors/Awds:** Beta Kappa Chi Hon Soc, 1962; Alpha Kappa Mu Hon Soc, 1963; Omega Psi Phi Man of the Year, 1971; patent Ultraviolet & Thermally Stable Polymer Compositions, 1974; Outstanding Alumnus MI State Univ, 1983; Outstanding Alumnus NAFEO, 1983; Excellence in Management Award, Indust Week, 1985; Hon Dr, Cent State Univ, 1988; One of the top 25 black executives in the United States, Black Enterprise mag, 1988; Top 40 black executives, 1993; Top 50 Black Execs, Black Enterprise; Hon Dr, Adrian College. **Special Achievements:** Only the 2nd African-American vice president at Ford Motor Company, 1994. **Home Addr:** 3290 Chestnut Run, Bloomfield Hills, MI 48302. **Business Addr:** Director, Case Corp, 5729 Washington Ave, Racine, WI 53406, **Business Phone:** (262)636-6011.

### GOLDSON, ESQ. AMY ROBERTSON

Lawyer. **Personal:** Born Jan 16, 1953, Boston, MA; daughter of Irving E Robertson and E Emily Robertson; married Alfred L, Jun 24, 1974; children: Erin & Ava. **Educ:** Smith Col, BA, magna cum laude, 1974; Cath Univ Law Sch, JD, 1976. **Career:** Internal Revenue Serv, Off Chief Coun, Tax Ct Litigation Div, atty, 1976-77; Smothers, Douple, Gayton & Long, atty, 1978-83; Law Off Amy Goldson, atty, 1983-. **Orgs:** Gen coun, Cong Black Caucus Found, 1977-; bd dirs, Black Entertainment & Sports Lawyers Asn, 1986-; Nat Bar Asn, 1976-; Am Bar Asn, 1976-; chairperson, Mayor's Comt Entertainment, 1994; Wash Area Lawyers Arts, 1992-; bd dir, Wash Performing Arts Soc, 1987-, bd mem, SE Tennis & Learning Ctrand Recreation Wish List. **Honors/Awds:** First Group Scholar, Phi Beta Kappa, Smith Col, 1973. **Home Addr:** 4015 28th Pl NW, Washington, DC 20008-3801, **Home Phone:** (202)966-7531. **Business Addr:** Attorney, Law Off Amy Goldson, 4015 28th Pl NW, Washington, DC 20008-3801, **Business Phone:** (202)966-7531.

### GOLDSTON, BOBBY F.

Chief executive officer. **Career:** Family Ford Sales Inc, chief exec officer, currently. **Orgs:** T & G Assocs LLC. **Business Addr:** Chief Executive Officer, Family Ford Sales Inc, 1602 Florence Blvd, Florence, AL 35630, **Business Phone:** (256)764-3351.

### GOLDSTON, NATHANIEL R., III

Chief executive officer, executive. **Personal:** Born Oct 20, 1938, Omaha, NE; son of Nathaniel II and Mary Elizabeth; married A Darleen; children: Nathaniel IV, Steven & Kimberly. **Educ:** Univ Denver, BA, bus admin, 1962. **Career:** Catering Mgt Inc, food serv dir, dist mgr & regional vpres, 1963-74; Gourmet Serv Inc, pres & chmn bd, 1975, chmn & chief exec officer, currently. **Orgs:** Pres, 100 Black Men Am; pres emer & founding mem, 100 Black Men Atlanta; chmn bd, Tuskegee Inst Food Serv Task Force; bd dir, Atlanta Regional Comn; nat bd dir, Am Bus Coun; Atlanta Chamber Com, Am Mgt Asn, Pvt Indust Coun, Nat Restaurant Asn, Ga Hospitality & Travel Asn; chmn Bill Dickey Found & Ga Peace Officers Found; chmn, Nat Jr Golf Scholar Asn; bd mem, Sch Hospitality & Mgt Wiley Col; Univ Denver Alumni Asn; bd trustee, Univ Denver, 1990-. **Home Addr:** 4355 Candacraig, Atlanta, GA 30303, **Home Phone:** (770)752-8773. **Business Addr:** Chairman, Chief Executive Officer, Gourmet Serv Inc, 82 Piedmont Ave, Atlanta, GA 30303, **Business Phone:** (404)876-5700.

### GOLDWIRE, ANTHONY

Basketball player. **Personal:** Born Sep 6, 1971, West Palm Beach, FL; son of Willie and Betty. **Educ:** Univ Houston, sports mgt, 1994. **Career:** Basketball player (retired), basketball coach; Yakima Sun Kings, Continental Basketball Asn, 1994-96, 2002-04, 2005-06; Charlotte Hornets, guard, 1996-97; Denver Nuggets, 1997-98, 2001; Olympiacos, Greece, 1998-99; FC Barcelona, Spain, 1999-2000; Kans City Knights, Am Basketball Asn, 2000-01; Skipper Bologna, Italy, 2001-02; San Antonio Spurs, 2002-03; Wash Wizards, 2002-03; Gigantes de Carolina, Pr, 2003; Minn Timberwolves, 2003-04; Aris, Greece, 2004; NJ Nets, 2003-04; Criollos de Caguas, Pr, 2004; Detroit Pistons, 2005; Milwaukee Bucks, 2005, assn coach, 2010-13; Los Angeles Clippers, guard, 2005-06; Pamesa Valencia, Spain, 2006; Panellinios Gymnastikos Syllogos, Greece, 2006-07; Lokomotiv Rostov, Russia, 2006; Egaleo, Greece, 2006-08; Erie BayHawks, assn coach, 2014-. **Honors/Awds:** Championship, Continental Basketball Asn, 1995, 2003, 2006; Second All-Rookie Team, Continental Basketball Asn, 1995. **Business Addr:** Assistant Coach, Erie BayHawks, 110 E 8th St, Erie, PA 16501, **Business Phone:** (814)790-5600.

### GOLIDAY, WILLIE V.

Executive, chief executive officer, president (organization). **Personal:** Born Feb 22, 1956, Oxford, MS; married Mary Ann Cration. **Educ:** Jackson State Univ, BS, 1978, MBA, 1980. **Career:** Delta Capital Corp, investment analyst, 1980-82; Action Commun Co Inc, pres & chief exec officer; Moeller Mfg Inc, pres & chief exec officer. **Orgs:** Advisor Jr Achievement, 1981; Jacksonville State Univ Alumni Asn. **Home Addr:** 64 Milhem, Greenville, MS 38701, **Home Phone:** (601)334-3532. **Business Addr:** President, Chief Executive Officer, Action Communications Co Inc, PO Box 588, Greenville, MS 38701, **Business Phone:** (601)335-5291.

### GOLIGHTLY, LENA MILLS

Composer, radio producer, writer. **Personal:** Born Horse Cave, KY. **Educ:** Ky State Col, attended 1936. **Career:** Composer: "I Don't Worry", 1955; "Sugarpie Tears Easy Now", 1955; "Jack is Back", 1957; "Miss Bronzeville", 1961; "Eternal Flame", 1964; "Resurrection City USA", 1968; "Do Your Thing & I'll Do Mine", 1969; "King Dr", 1969; "I Had Too Much To Dream Last Night", 1970; Poems: Golden Chain of Friendship, 1967; Am You're Dying, 1969; WXFM-Radio, Chicago, IL, producer, 1966-; WBEE-Radio, Chicago, IL, producer, 1967; Ada S McKinley Comn Serv, active pub rels, 1967; Author: Premonition of Last Christmas, 1947, Top of the Mountain, 1967, The Seventh Child, 1967. **Orgs:** Nat Asn Media Women; Chicago Mus Asn; dir, Civic Liberty League IL; Nat Asn Advan Colored People; Urban League, AME Church; dir, Am Friendship Club; Chicago Mus Asn, 1965. **Honors/Awds:** Am Friendship Club Award, 1962-65; Award Merit, WVON, 1965, 1969; Awards Chicago, No Dist Asn Federated Clubs, 1966; WXFM, 1966; Carey Temple, 1966; WGRT Chicago, 1970; Nat Acad Best Dressed Churchwomen, 1972, 1973; Humanitarian Award, Baptist Foreign Mission Bur, 1973; Dr Martin Luther King Jr Humanitarian Award, Love Mem Missionary Baptist Church, 1974. **Home Addr:** 5333 S Michigan Ave, Chicago, IL 60615.

### GOLLADAY, MAMIE HOWARD. See HOWARD, DR. MAMIE R.

### GOLSON, BENNY

Musician, composer. **Personal:** Born Jan 25, 1929, Philadelphia, PA. **Educ:** Howard Univ, attended 1950. **Career:** Tenor saxaphonist, composer & arranger; Guggenheim Found, grant, 1995; Albums: New York Scene, 1957; Benny Golson's New York Scene, 1957; The Modern Touch, 1957; The Other Side of Benny Golson, 1958; Benny Golson and the Philadelphians, 1958; Gone With Golson, 1959; Groovin' with Golson, 1959; Gettin' With It, 1959; Meet the Jazz tet, 1960; Big City Sounds, 1960; The Jazztet at Birdhouse, 1961; The Jazztet and John Lewis, 1961; Take A Number From 1 to 10, 1961, 2007; Pop + Jazz = Swing, 1961; Here And Now, 1962; Another Git Together, 1962; Free, 1962; Turning point, 1962, 2005; Stockholm Sojourn, 1964; Tune In, Turn On to the Hippest Commercials, 1967; Killer Joe, 1977; Are You Real, 1977; I'm Always Dancin' to the Music, 1978; California Message, 1980; One More Mem'ry, 1981; Voices All, 1982; Playboy Jazz Festival, 1982; Moment to Moment, 1983; Nostalgia, 1983; Back to the City, 1986; Real Time, 1986; Benny Golson Quartet, 1990; Up Jumped Spring, 1990; I Remember Miles, 1992; Up Jumped Benny, 1997; Tenor Legacy, 1998; That's Funky, 2000; One Day Forever, 2001; Terminal 1, 2004; Free, 2004; The Masquerade is Over, 2005; The Many Moods Of Benny Golson, 2007; Three Little Words, 2007; New Time, New 'Tet, 2009; The Best of Benny Golson, 2009; Carribean drifting; Park Avenue Petite; Remembering Clifford Live; Domingo; The Brandenburg Concertos; The Philadelphians; Brown Immortal; The Athens Session; MASH; Mannix; Mission Impossible; Mod Squad; Room 222; Run for Your Life; The Partridge Family; The Academy Awards; The Karen Valentine Show; Des Femmes Disparaissent. **Honors/Awds:** American Jazz Masters Award, Nat Endowment Arts, 1995; BMI Music Award, 1998; Hon Doc, William Paterson College; Hon Doc, Berklee Sch Music, Boston, Mass; Mellon Living Legend Legacy Award, Mid Atlantic Arts Found, 2007; Outstanding Lifetime Achievement Award, Univ Pittsburgh Int Acad Jazz, 2007; International Academy of Jazz Hall of Fame, 2009. **Special Achievements:** Howard University Jazz Studies program created a prestigious award in his honor called the "Benny Golson Jazz Master Award" in 1996. **Business Addr:** Musician, Klose & Klose, 6399 Wilshire Blvd Suite 1002, Los Angeles, CA 90048, **Business Phone:** (323)653-7826.

### GOLSON, LEON

Executive director. **Career:** Midwest AIDS Prev Proj, prog dir, dep dir, candice moench; Red Cross HIV/AIDS African Am Instr prog, instr trainer. **Orgs:** Test counr, dir prev prog, HIV/AIDS Resource Ctr, 2007, Ypsilanti; test counr, Am Red Cross; Washtenaw Urban County Exec Comt; co chair, A4C. **Business Addr:** Director of Prevention Programs, HIV/AIDS Resource Center, 3075 Clark Rd Suite 203, Ypsilanti, MI 48197, **Business Phone:** (800)578-2300.

### GOMES, WAYNE MAURICE

Baseball player, executive. **Personal:** Born Jan 15, 1973, Hampton Roads, VA; married Melissa Marie Gilbert. **Educ:** Old Dom Univ, recreation & leisure studies. **Career:** Baseball player (retired), owner; Philadelphia Phillies, pitcher, 1997-2001; San Francisco Giants, 2001; Boston Red Sox, pitcher, 2002; Oakland Athletics, pitcher, 2004; Yucatan Leones & Saltilo Gigiantes, pitcher, 2005; Va Baseball Acad, owner, currently. **Orgs:** Phi Beta Sigma. **Business Addr:** Owner, Virginia Baseball Academy, 1322 LaSalle Ave Suite A, Hampton, VA 23669, **Business Phone:** (757)251-6367.

### GOMEZ, DENNIS CRAIG

Vice president (organization), labor relations manager. **Personal:** Born May 14, 1948, Suffern, NY; son of Carlos and Elizabeth; married Henrietta McAlister; children: Camille, Mark & Brian. **Educ:** Southern Ill Univ, BA, 1971. **Career:** Chase Manhattan Bank, credit corres, 1971-72; Centers Expertise, vpres; Allstate Corp, off oper super, 1972-73, claim super, 1973, div supvr, 1973-74, personnel asst, 1974-76, personnel div mgr, 1976-79, human resources mgr, 1979-80, personnel serv mgr, 1980-82, regional personnel mgr, 1982-86, human resource dir, customer rels dir, 1987-88, field human resources dir, 1989-97, financial asst vpres, 1997-2001, vpres human resources, 2002-08. **Orgs:** ASPA; Urban League Phila; Nat Asn Advan Colored People N Philadelphia br; chmn, OIC Fund Raising Montgomery Co, PA, 1985; CASA Lake County; Parent Coun Wake Forest Univ; bd mem, Boys & Girls Club Lake County; bd mem, Lake County Boys. **Home Addr:** 3 Robert Ct, Hawthorn Woods, IL 60047-9169, **Home Phone:** (847)438-2168. **Business Addr:** Vice President of Human Resources, The Allstate Corp, 2775 Sanders Rd, Northbrook, IL 60062, **Business Phone:** (847)402-6957.

### GOMEZ, JEWELLE L.

Writer. **Personal:** Born Sep 11, 1948, Boston, MA; daughter of John and Dolores LeClaire. **Educ:** Northeastern Univ, BA, 1971; Columbia Univ, MS, jour, 1973. **Career:** Columbia Univ, Ford Found fel, 1973; Hunter Col lectr, 1989-91; NY State Coun Arts, prog assoc, 1983-90, dir lit, 1990-93; New Col, lectr, 1993-94; Menlo Col, vis writer, 1993; Calif Arts Coun, artist in residence, 1994, 1995; Poetry Ctr & Am Poetry Arch San Francisco State Univ, exec dir, 1996-99; Cult Equity Grants Prog, San Francisco Arts Comn, dir, 2000-06; San Francisco Pub Libr, libr comnr, 2005-; Horizons Found, prog off, dir Grants & Community Initiatives, 2006-. Author: The Lipstick Papers, Grace Publs, 1980; Flamingoes & Bears, Grace Publs, 1986; The Gilda Stories, Firebrand Books, 1991; Forty Three Septembers, Firebrand Books, 1993; Oral Tradition: Poems Selected & New, Firebrand Books, 1995; Playwright "Bones & Ash: A Gilda Story", US tour, 1995-96; Don't Explain: Short Fiction, Firebrand Books, 1998. **Orgs:** Founding bd mem, Gay & Lesbian Alliance Against Defamation, 1988-90; bd mem, Open Meadows Found, 1989-; ed adv bd, Belle Lettres, 1990-96; ed adv bd, Multi-Cult Rev, 1991-95; adv bd, Cornell Univ Human Sexuality Arch, 1992-; bd mem, Coalition Against Censorship, 1993-; founding mem, Astraea Nat Lesbian Found; Open Meadows Found; fel Nat Endowment Arts, 1997; pres, San Francisco pub Libr; James C Hormel Endowment Comt; fel San Francisco Arts Comn. **Home Addr:** 206 Fairmont St, San Francisco, CA 94131. **Business Addr:** Program Officer, Horizons Foundation, 550 Montgomery St Suite 700, San Francisco, CA 94111, **Business Phone:** (415)398-2333.

### GOMEZ, DR. MICHAEL A.

Writer, college teacher. **Educ:** Univ Chicago, BA, hist, 1981, MA, African hist, 1982; PhD, African hist, 1985. **Career:** Wash Univ, St Louis, Mo, Dept Hist/African & Afro-Am Studies, asst prof, 1985-88; Spelman Col, Ga, Dept Hist, from asst prof to assoc prof, 1988-97; Spelman Col, dept Hist, chair, 1989-92, 1993-97, dir African Diaspora & World Core Curri Course, 1992-97; Univ Ga, Athens, DeptHist/African Am Studies, prof, 1997-99; NY Univ, Dept Hist & Dept Mid Eastern & Islamic Studies, prof, 1999-, chair, Dept Hist, 2004-07. Books: Pragmatism in the Age of Jihad: The Precolonial State of Bundu, 1992; Exchanging Our Country Marks: The Transformation of African Identities in the Colonial and Antebellum South, 1998; Reversing Sail: A History of the African Diaspora, 2005; Black Crescent: African Muslims in the Americas, 2005; Diasporic Africa: A Reader, 2006. **Orgs:** Adv bd, Consortium Inter-Instnl Collab in African & Latin Am Studies, 1989-97; dir, 2000-07, bd mem, 2000-09, Asn Study Worldwide African Diaspora (ASWAD); Ed Adv Bd, J African Hist, 2007-; Ed Adv Bd, 2007-10; Int Sci Comt Slave Rte Proj, 2009-; pres, UNESCO's Int Sci Comt, 2009-13. **Business Addr:** Professor, New York University, King Juan Carlos Ctr 53 Wash Sq S 7th Fl Rm 502, New York, NY 10012-1098, **Business Phone:** (212)998-8624.

### GOMEZ, TODD A.

Vice president (organization). **Educ:** Dartmouth Col, BA, econ, 1986; Northwestern Univ, Kellogg Sch Mgt, MBA, finance & real estate, 1991. **Career:** Nuveen Investments, vpres, 1996-2000; Chicago Housing Authority, chief financial officer, 2000-04; Banc Am Securities, managing dir, 2004-08; Bank Am Merrill Lynch, sr vpres, 2008-. **Orgs:** Adv bd mem, Enterprise Community Partners Inc; dir, Chicago Metrop Housing Develop Corp; bd mem, Supportive Housing Network; bd mem, Housing Partnership Develop Corp. **Honors/Awds:** "Black Enterprise," 75 Most Powerful Blacks on Wall Street, 2011. **Business Addr:** Senior Vice President, Bank of America Merrill Lynch, 1 Bryant Park 35th Fl, New York, NY 10036, **Business Phone:** (646)855-2639.

### GONA, DR. OPHELIA DELAINE

Research scientist, educator. **Personal:** Born Jul 4, 1936, SC; daughter of Joseph Armstrong and Mattie; married Amos; children: Shantha & Raj. **Educ:** Johnson C Smith Univ, BS, 1957; Yeshiva Univ, MS, 1965; City Col NY, MA, 1967; City Univ NY, PhD, biol, 1971. **Career:** Research scientist (retired); Cornell Univ Med Sch, lab tech, 1957-58; Eastern Dist High Sch Brooklyn, biol teacher, 1958-61; Peace Corps Vol Ghana, 1961-63; City Col NY, res asst, teacher asst, 1966-70; Montclair State Col, asst prof biol, 1970-77; NJ Col Med & Dent, asst prof anat; UMD-NJ Med Sch, assoc prof Anat, 1986, dir, 2001; NIH grant. **Orgs:** Educ consult, Hoffman LaRoche Pharms, 1972-73; AIBS, AAAS, Am Asn Anatomists, ARVO, NY Acad Sci. **Honors/Awds:** Distinguished Alumnus, Johnson Smith Univ, 2004; Golden Apple Award. **Special Achievements:** Author of scientific publications concerning comparative endocrinology of prolactin cataracts of the lens of the eye; Developer of computer-based instructional materials for Gross Anatomy, 1972-77. **Home Addr:** 831 Glendora Rd, Kissimmee, FL 34759-3251, **Home Phone:** (863)496-0661.

### GONSALVES, GREGG A.

Executive. **Educ:** Columbia Univ, New York, BS, mech engineering, 1989; Harvard Grad Sch Bus, MBA, 1993. **Career:** Mobil Oil Corp, Mkt & Refining Div, sales engr, 1989-91; Goldman Sachs & Co, Goldman Sachs' Mergers & Acquisitions Dept, assoc, 1993-97, Investment Banking Div, vpres, 1997-99, Goldman's Aerospace & Defense Sector, 1999-2007, managing dir, 2001-, partner, 2004-; Real Estate M&A Group, 2008; Integrated Capital LLC, investor, adv partner, currently. **Orgs:** Co-chmn, Jackie Robinson Found, 2006-; bd dir, A Better Chance; Columbia Univ's Fu Found Sch Engineering Appl Sci's Bd Visitors. **Honors/Awds:** "Black Enterprise," 75 Most Powerful Blacks on Wall Street, 2011; Ralph E Ward Achievement Award. **Business Addr:** Advisory Partner, Integrated Capital LLC, 11100 Santa Monica Blvd Suite 360, Los Angeles, CA 90025, **Business Phone:** (310)575-8801.

### GONZALEZ, ANITA LOUISE

Artist, educator. **Personal:** Born Feb 20, 1957, Newark, NJ; daughter of Cambell and Juanita Nash; children: Xochina Cora El Hilali. **Educ:** NY Univ, educ theatre, 1976; Fla State Univ, BA, theatre, 1979; Am Univ, MA, performing arts, 1979; Univ Wis, PhD, theatre, 1997. **Career:** Viacom, asst dir, 1983-86; NYPL Lincoln Ctr, film video activist, 1987-92; Urban Bush Women, performer, 1984-89; Bandana Women, artistic dir, 1985-95; New York Pub Libr Perfoming Arts Libr, film prod, 1985-89; Beloit Col, scholar residence, 1995-96; Conn Col, asst prof, 1997-99; Fla State Univ, asst prof, 1999-2004; State Univ NY, Dept Theatre Arts, assoc prof, 1999-2004; dir, writer & choreographer; Director: Dolores Prida, 1996; Tiye Giraud's Sugar Tit, 1998; State Univ New York, New Paltz, prof & provost fel, 2004-13; Art Boundaries Unlimited Inc, exec dir, 2006-; The Promise Keeper, 2008; Blood Wedding, 2009; Liverpool; Nobody; Junk Mail; Seens from the Unexpectedness of Love; Urinetown, The Musical; Heat; Migrant ImagiNations; Univ Mich at Ann Arbor, prof theatre, 2013-. **Orgs:** Bd dir, Mad Alex Arts Found, 1989-93; resident artist, Thompkins Sq Libr, 1986-90; artistic dir, Stack Motion Prod, 1987-92; resident artist, Tribeca Performing Arts Ctr, 1993-96; bd dir, Soc Dance Hist Scholars, 1998-2004; artist comt, Performance Studies Int, 1999-; Am Soc Theatre, 2000-; assoc mem, Socs Stage dir & Choreographers, 2006-; founder, Art Boundaries Unlimited; assoc mem, Dramatists Guild, 2009-. **Home Addr:** 187 Beechwood Dr, Crawfordville, FL 32327, **Home Phone:** (845)255-1205. **Business Addr:** Associate Professor,

State University of New York, CT 110 1 Hawk Dr, New Paltz, NY 12561, **Business Phone:** (845)257-3907.

**GONZALEZ, ANTHONY DAVID. See GONZALEZ, TONY.**

### GONZALEZ, CAMBELL
Engineer, financial manager. **Personal:** Born Aug 26, 1918, Tampa, FL; married Juanita Nash; children: Amelia, Anita & John. **Educ:** Howard Univ, BSEE, 1949; Stevens Inst, grad courses; Brooklyn Polytech, Newark Col Engineering. **Career:** Engineer, financial manager (retired); RCA, engr training, 1949, appl engr, 1950-55, design devel engr, 1955-70, proj engr, 1970-82; Col Financial Planning, Denver, Colo, CFP, 1983-86. **Orgs:** Inst Elec & Electronics Engrs; bd dir, YMCA, Orange, NJ; Alpha Phi Alpha Fraternity; planning bd, adv gr, Reading Twp; Sewer Adv Commn; teacher elder, Flemington Presby Church; pres, Inv Club Alumni; Rotary Club Flemington, NJ, 1990. **Honors/Awds:** Achievement Award, Howard Univ, 1957; Tech art pub, RCA Engr IRE Trans Electronics; Pat disclosure, RCA. **Home Addr:** 158 W Woodschurch Rd, Flemington, NJ 08822, **Home Phone:** (908)782-7841.

### GONZALEZ, TONY (ANTHONY DAVID GONZALEZ)
Football player, businessperson, executive. **Personal:** Born Feb 27, 1976, Torrance, CA; married Lauren Sanchez; children: Nikko; married October Tobie; children: Malia & River. **Educ:** Univ Calif, Berkeley, grad. **Career:** Football player (retired), executive; Kans City Chiefs, tight end, 1997-2008, running back, 1999; Atlanta Falcons, tight end, 2009-13; All-Pro Sci, co-founder, 2009; FitStar, trainer, 2013-; Nat Geog Channel, host, 2015; Sutra Restaurant, partner; Oliver Stone Prod, consult; Nat Football League Today, studio analyst, currently. **Orgs:** Tony Gonzalez Found. **Honors/Awds:** All-Pro, 1999-2004, 2006-08, 2012; Pro Bowl, 1999-2013; Alumni Tight End of the Year, Nat Football League, 2000, 2003; Presidential Volunteer Award, 2004; Pro Bowl All-Time Receptions Leader. **Special Achievements:** NFL Draft, First round pick, 1997; First tight end to ever catch 1,000 passes; First Tight End to reach 15,000 Receiving Yards; Second most consecutive games with a reception; Formed the "Tony Gonzalez Found"; The second-longest active string on the roster; Film & TV appearances: HBO, "Arliss", 2000; "The Jersey", 2000; "ABC, Married to the Kellys", 2004; "A.I. Assault", 2006; "Hard Knocks: Training Camp With The Kansas City Chiefs", 2007; "Celebrity Cooking Showdown", 2008; "Oprah Winfrey's The Big Give", 2008; "One Tree Hill", 2010; "NCIS", 2015; Spike TV, "Super gents"; "ABC, Extreme Makeover: Wedding Edition"; Introduced "Books and Buddies" prog; "Shock Wave"; Co-Author: "The All-Pro Diet", 2009. **Business Addr:** Professional Football Player, Atlanta Falcons, 4400 Falcon Pkwy, Flowery Branch, GA 30542, **Business Phone:** (770)965-3115.

### GONZAQUE, OZIE BELL
City commissioner. **Personal:** Born Jun 8, 1925, Thornton, AR; daughter of John Henry Woods and Wilie Lee Brown; married Roy Sylvester; children: Frieda Elaine, Barbara Jean, Bernadette, Roy Jr, Janet, Mary Nadene & Joseph Gregory. **Educ:** Southwest Col, cert; Univ Southern Calif, cert. **Career:** Fradelis Frozen Foods, Los Angeles, Calif, prod supvr, 1951-63; Dist Attys Evelle Younger, Joseph Busch & John Von DeCamp, adv coun mem, 1969-84; Atty Gen Evelle Younger, adv coun mem, 1971-83; Bur Consumer Affairs, advert & promotional policy vol, 1972-84; Juv Justice Ctr, vol, 1977-79; Los Angeles Housing Authority, comnr, 1986-95, 1998-2003, Housing Authority City Los Angeles, comnr, 1995-98, Community Develop Bank, City Los Angeles rep, 1995-2000; Housing Authority City Los Angeles, Los Angeles, chairperson, 1998. **Orgs:** Chmn bd, HACLA, 2003; Dir bd, S Cent Social Serv Corp; Community Develop Comn, County Los Angeles; pres, Southeast Businessmen's Booster Asn; bd dir, LA Community Develop Bank. **Honors/Awds:** Public Serv Award, ABLE, 1985; Woman of the Yr, State Calif Legis Body, 1989; People's Choice Award, People's Choice Inc, 1990; Achievement Award, NOBLE, 1990; Commissioner of the Yr, Nat Asn Housing & Redevelopment Officials, 1998; Woman of the Yr Award, Assemblywoman Maxine Waters; Meritorious Award, LAPD; Elizabeth B Wells Memorial Award. **Home Addr:** 10441 W Zamora Ave, Los Angeles, CA 90002, **Home Phone:** (213)567-5547. **Business Addr:** Commissioner, Los Angeles Housing Authority Department, 515 Columbia Ave, Los Angeles, CA 90017, **Business Phone:** (213)484-6772.

### GOOCH, JEFFREY LANCE
Executive, football player. **Personal:** Born Oct 31, 1974, Nashville, TN; married Tonya. **Educ:** Austin Peay State Univ. **Career:** Football player, exec; Tampa Bay Buccaneers, linebacker, 1996-2001, left linebacker, 1997-98, mid linebacker, 2004; Detroit Lions, linebacker, 2002-03; free agt, currently; Tampa Bay Storm, vpres football opers, currently. **Honors/Awds:** Most Valuable Player Award, Yale Lary Spec Teams. **Home Addr:** 12709 Seronera Valley Ct, Spring Hill, FL 34610-7658, **Home Phone:** (727)379-0310. **Business Addr:** Vice President of Football Operations, Tampa Bay Storm, 600 N Ashley Dr, Tampa, FL 33602.

### GOOD, MEGAN MONIQUE
Actor. **Personal:** Born Aug 8, 1981, Panorama City, CA; daughter of Leondis and Tyra Doyle; married DeVon Franklin. **Career:** Freedom Bridge Entertainment, co-founder; Films: House Party 3, 1994; Friday, 1995; Make a Wish, Molly, 1995; Eve's Bayou, 1997; The Secret Life of Girls, 1999; 3 Strikes, 2000; House Party 4: Down to the Last Minute, 2001; Awakenings 1, 2001; Awakenings 2, 2001; Ride Or Die, 2003; Deliver Us from Eva, 2003; Biker Boyz, 2003; DEBS, 2004; The Cookout, 2004; You Got Served, 2004; Roll Bounce, 2005; Venom, 2005; Waist Deep, 2006; Scarface: The World Is Yours, 2006; Miles from Home, 2006; Stomp the Yard, 2007; One Missed Call, 2008; The Love Guru, 2008; Saw V, 2008; The Unborn, 2009; Good Hair, 2010; Video Girl, 2011; 35 and Ticking, 2011; Jumping the Broom, 2011; Dysfunctional Friends, 2012; The Baytown Disco, 2012; Think Like a Man, 2012; The Obama Effect, 2012; Dick Little, 2012; Don Jon, 2013; Anchorman 2: The Legend Continues, 2013; Learning Uncle Vincent, 2013; Think Like a Man Too, 2014; Doctor Me, 2014. TV series: "Doogie Howser", "M.D"; "Amen"; "Just One of the Girls", 1997; "Blood for Blood", 1997; "The Famous Jett Jackson", 1998-2001; "Don't Stand Too Close to Me", 2000; "He Doth Protest Too Much", 2000; "Raising Dad", 2001; "My Wife & Kids", 2001; "The Parent Trap", 2001; "The Division", 2001-04; "The Jersey", 2002; "Graduation: Part 1", 2003; "Graduation: Part 2", 2003; "Here Comes Da Judge", 2003; "Jr.'s Risky Business: Part 1", 2003; "Jr's Risky Business: Part 2", 2003; "Kevin Hill", 2004-05; "Losing Isn't Everything", 2005; "Sacrificial Lambs", 2005; "Cardiac Episode", 2005; "Occupational Hazard", 2005; "Brick", 2005; Sundays in Fort Greene, producer, 2008; Miles from Home, producer, 2006; "House M.D.", 2007; "All of Us", 2007; "Cold Case", 2009; "The Game", 2011; "Californication", 2012; "Deception", 2013. Show: Cousin Skeeter, 1999-2003. **Honors/Awds:** Nominee, Image Award for Outstanding Youth Actor/Actress, 1998; nominee, Young Star Award, 1998; nominee, Black Movie Award, 2005; Independent Black Film Festival Award, 2006; nominee, Teen Choice Award, 2006. **Business Addr:** Actress, c/o Agency Performing Arts, 9200 W Sunset Blvd Suite 900, Los Angeles, CA 90069, **Business Phone:** (310)273-0744.

### GOODALL, HURLEY CHARLES
State government official, politician, army officer. **Personal:** Born May 23, 1927, Muncie, IN; son of Hurley Charles (deceased) and Dorene Mukes; married Fredine Wynn; children: Hurley E Jr & Fredrick. **Educ:** Ind Bus Col, attended 1949; Purdue Univ, time & motion courses, 1952. **Career:** Firefighter, government official (retired), politician; Muncie Malleable Foundry Co, 1944-50, time & motion steward, 1950-58; Muncie Fire Dept, fire fighter, 1958-78; Hur Co Inc, owner; Muncie Bd Educ, mem, 1970-78, pres, 1974-75; Del Co, IN, admin asst, 1978-80; Ind House Reps, St rep, 1978-92, asst fl leader, 1989-92; Muncie community, state legislator, 1978-92; Ball St Univ, vis fel & vis prof, Ctr Middletown Studies, vis scholar. **Orgs:** Pres, Whitely Community Coun, 1966-69; chair, Cent Reg, Nat Black Caucus Sch, 1972-78; bd trustee, Muncie Sch Bd Trustee, 1974-75, npres, 1974-75; bd mem, WIPB-TV Chan 49 Muncie PBS Sta, 1974-80; chmn, Ind Black Leg Caucus, 1980-92; Jobs Training Coord Coun; Gov Comn Minority Bus Develop; Muncie Human Rights Comn, 1961-67, chair, 1964-67; comt mem, Ind Sch Bd Asn; bd mem, Action Inc, 1966-75; coun mem, United Way Community Serv, 1971-72; Ind Sch Boards Asn, 1973-74, 1975; Roy C Buley Ctr, 1974-75; bd mem, Region Nat Caucus Black Sch, 1974-77; Muncie Opportunities Indust Ctr, 1978-82; Muncie Chamber Com Leadership Acad; Muncie C's Mus; Eastern Ind Pub Tv; Muncie chap Nat Asn Advan Colored People; Del County Emergency Med Serv; Ind Legis Black Caucus, 1980-92; Ind Caucus Black Dem Elected Officials, 1980-92. **Honors/Awds:** Muncie Black Hall of Fame, Multi-Serv Ctr Muncie, 1979; Government Service Award, OIC DE County, 1980; Horatio Alger Award, Muncie Boys Club, 1984; President's Medal, Ball St Univ, 1992; Nation Builder Award, NBCSL, 1992; Indiana Heritage Research Grant, Ind Hist Soc, 1999; Service Award, IN chap NAACP, 1999; Distinguished Hoosier Award, Ind Arts Comn, 2000; hon doctorate, Ball St Univ, 2007; Legislators of the Year; A Civil right Voice of Indiana, 2007. **Special Achievements:** He was one of the first two African-Americans selected to work for the fire department; He also was the first African-American selected to serve on the Muncie Community Schools Board of Education, 1970-78; co-author, History of Negroes in Muncie, 1974; Listed in Who is Who Among Black Americans, 1988; Inside the House, Ball St Press, 1995. **Home Addr:** 1905 E Carver Dr, Muncie, IN 47303-4011, **Home Phone:** (765)288-4757.

### GOODE, BRUCE T.
President (organization), chief executive officer. **Educ:** Univ Toledo, BS, finance. **Career:** Victory Capital Mgt, managing dir, 1976-; Goode Investment Mgt Inc, pres & chief exec officer, 1999-; Christian Hope Missionary Baptist Church, pastor; Faith Community Credit Union, pres; Pro Sports Advisors, portfolio mgr; EB Magic Fund, subadv, currently. **Orgs:** Bd trustee, Cleveland Restoration Soc; Cleveland Scholar Progs Inc; bd trustee, Univ Circle Inc. **Business Addr:** President, Chief Executive Officer, Goode Investment Management Inc, 1700 Terminal Twr 50 Pub Sq Suite 904, Cleveland, OH 44113-2207, **Business Phone:** (216)771-9000.

### GOODE, CALVIN COOLIDGE
Government official, business owner. **Personal:** Born Jan 27, 1927, Depew, OK; married Georgie M; children: Vernon, Jerald & Randolph. **Educ:** Phoenix Col, AA, 1947; Ariz State Col, BS, 1949; Ariz State Univ, MA, 1972. **Career:** Phoenix Union HS Dist, asst budget dir, 1949-69, sch community worker, 1969, sch bus mgr, asst property control dir; Calvin Goode & Asso Tax & Acct Srev, owner & oper, 1950-; Phoenix City Councilman, 1972-94; Phoenix City V Mayor, 1974, 1984. **Orgs:** Bd mem, Community Coun; dir, Investment Opportunities Inc; CTA, AEA, NEA; United Fund Budget Com; Phoenix Urban Leag; Nat Asn Advan Colored People; bd chmn, BT Wash Child Develop Ctr Inc; co-chmn, Child Care Proj Comm Coun; Omega Psi Phi Frat; Downtown Breakfast Optimist Club; Phoenix Elem Sch Bd; Neighborhood Improv Asn; bd mem, George Wash Carver Mus & Cult Ctr, 2008; Booker T Wash Child Develop Ctr. **Honors/Awds:** Hon Kachina Volunteer Award, 2004; Lifetime Achievement Award, named in honor, 2006. **Home Addr:** 1508 E Jefferson St, Phoenix, AZ 85034-2317, **Home Phone:** (602)253-5845.

### GOODE, FR. JAMES EDWARD
Clergy. **Personal:** Born Nov 18, 1943, Roanoke, VA. **Educ:** Univ State NY, Immaculate Conception Col, BA, philos, 1969; Col St Rose, MA, 1971; St Anthony Theol Sem, MDiv, 1972, MTh, 1974; Col St Rose, PhD; Univ Louvain Belg, post-doctoral studies, 1980; OFM, PhD. **Career:** Our Lady Charity, founding pastor & first black pastor, 1974-; City Univ NY, adj prof, 1975-, chaplain, 1975-; Ctr Positive Direction, dir, 1976-; Black Relig Expert Inst, co-dir; Directions J Black Church & Comm Studies, ed; Nat Black Cath Apostolate Life, founder & pres, currently; Survival & Faith Inst NY, cons; Juv Justice Task Force Ctrl Brooklyn, cons; lectr, psychol & theol; Solid Ground Franciscan Ministry, pastoral dir & founder; Serra High Sch, instr; Diocese Brooklyn, first pres; Immaculate Conception Sem, instr; Medgar Evers Col, assoc prof; Black Cath Affairs, coordr; San Francisco Comn Youth & C & Families, comnr; Chaplain Alpha Gamma Lambda Chap; Knight Peter Claver Ladies Auxiliary Ct, chaplain; Franciscan Handmaids Mary, spiritual consult; Mother God Franciscan Fraternity, spiritual asst & founder. **Orgs:** Elected mem, NY City Comn Sch Bd; Cent Brooklyn Youth & Family Servs; Juv Prev Progs Brooklyn; NY City Comn Planning Bd; Cult & Worship Adv Bd Nat Off Black Cath; Coalition Concerned Black Educrs NY; Black Ministers Coun; Nat Black Cath Clergy; Nat Asn Black Social Workers; EducTask ForcePositive Direction NY Urban Comn; hon mem, Cath Social Workers Asn; bd dirs, Off Black Ministry Diocese Brooklyn; bd dirs, Bldg Better Brooklyn; res fel Yale Divinity Sch; chair, City San Francisco Drug Abuse Conf; pres, San Francisco Housing Authority Comn; Off White House Deleg; life mem, Alpha Phi Alpha Fraternity; pres, Nat Black Cath Clergy Caucus; bd consults, Us Bishops Conf. **Honors/Awds:** DHL, VA Theol Sem; Martin Luther King Scholrship, NY Univ, 1975-76; Black Cath Leadership Award; named in honor, James E Goode Day, 1978; Nat Black Cath Clergy Tribute Award, 1979; lead, Nat Protest Prayer Serv Against Budget Cuts in Human Servs; Brother Joseph Davis Life Time Achievement Award, NBCCC, 1996 & 2002. **Special Achievements:** Numerous publs, "Catholicsm & Slavery in US" Labor Press, 1975; "Ministry in the 80's in the Black Comm" Liberation Press, 1980; The first Black Catholic Pastor in the Archdiocese of San Francisco; Preacher of First Black Cath Revival in US Chicago, 1974; proclamation, NY State Assembly; proclamation declaring Father James E Goode Day, Mayor of Brooklyn, 1978 & 1979. First black catholic priest, City of Roanoke; First Roman Catholic priest, Lincoln Center. **Business Addr:** Pastoral Director, Solid Ground Ministries, 440 W 36th St, New York, NY 10018-6326, **Business Phone:** (212)868-1847.

### GOODE, DR. REV. W. WILSON, SR.
Executive, army officer, mayor. **Personal:** Born Aug 19, 1938, Seaboard, NC; son of Albert and Rozelar; married Velma Helen Williams; children: Muriel, W Wilson Jr & Natasha. **Educ:** Morgan State Univ, BA, hist & polit sci, 1961; Univ Pa, Wharton Sch, MPA, 1968; Eastern Baptist Theol Sem, DMin, 2000. **Career:** Philadelphia Coun Community Advan, pres & chief exec officer, 1966-78; Pa Pub Utilities Comn, chmn, 1978-80; City Philadelphia, managing dir, 1980-82; City Philadelphia, mayor, 1984-92; Goode Group, pres & chief exec officer, 1992-; Goode Cause Inc, founder; US Dept Educ, secy regional rep, region III, probation officer, bldg maintenance supr, ins claims adjuster; Faith Based Initiatives Pub & Pvt Ventures, sr adv, sr dir, currently; Philadelphia Leadership Found, bd chmn, chief exec officer, currently. **Orgs:** Eastern Univ; chair, Free Libr Philadelphia; chair, Cornerstone Christian Acad; chair, Self Inc; vice-chair, Coun Leadership Found; co-founder, Black Polit Forum; Pa Pub Utility Comn, 1979, 1980, 1983; Philadelphia City Coun, 1999; chmn, Leadership Found Am; chmn, PLF; chmn, Self Inc; bd mem, Big Bros Big Sisters Southeastern Pa; Am's Promise Alliance; Eastern Univ, Palmer Theol Sem; Free Libr Philadelphia; Cornerstone Christian Acad; Southwest Leadership Acad Charter Sch; Communities Schs Philadelphia Inc; Partners Sacred Places; Sigma Pi Phi; Kappa Alpha Psi Fraternities. **Honors/Awds:** Numerous honorary degrees in US Universities; Purpose Prize. **Special Achievements:** First African American mayor of Philadelphia, PA; Author, In Goode Faith, autobiography, 1992. **Home Addr:** 2446 N 59th St, Philadelphia, PA 19131-1208, **Home Phone:** (215)878-2720. **Business Addr:** Chief Executive Officer, Board Chairman, Philadelphia Leadership Foundation, 2210 S 71st St, Philadelphia, PA 19142, **Business Phone:** (215)726-6047.

### GOODE, WILLIE K.
President (organization). **Personal:** married Adrianne. **Career:** Amco Disposal; Goode Trash Removal Inc, pres, 1991-; GTR Inc, pres, 1996-; Unity Disposal, pres, currently; Recycling LLC, pres, currently. **Business Addr:** President, Goode Trash Removal Inc, 4700 Lawrence St, Hyattsville, MD 20781-1029, **Business Phone:** (301)779-4208.

### GOODE, WILSON, JR. (W WILSON GOODE)
Government official. **Personal:** Born Aug 9, 1965, Philadelphia, PA; son of W Wilson and Velma W. **Educ:** Univ Pa, BA, alma mater, 1986. **Career:** Philadelphia Com Develop Corp, vpres, 1991-99; Philadelphia City Coun, city councilman at-Large, currently. **Orgs:** Alpha Phi Alpha Fraternity Inc, 1984-;chmn, Econ Develop Boards & Comts, 1992-99; Young Am Polit Comt, 1997-; dir, Amachi; Sigma Pi Phi fraternity; chair, Philadelphia City Coun. **Business Addr:** City Councilman At-Large, Philadelphia City Council, City Hall Rm 316, Philadelphia, PA 19107, **Business Phone:** (215)686-3414.

### GOODEN, C. MICHAEL
Chairperson, chief executive officer. **Personal:** married Diane Oksanen. **Educ:** Miami Univ, Oxford, OH, BS, appl sci, 1972; Moore Sch, Univ Pa, Philadelphia, PA, MS, engineering; Univ Pa, wharton exec mgt prog. **Career:** Integrated Systs Analysts Inc, co-founder, pres, chmn & chief exec officer, 1980-; Advent Lutheran Church, deacon, vpres & pres congregation. **Orgs:** Prof Serv Coun; Nsf's Bus & Opers Comt; Am Socs Naval Engrs; U.S. Chamber Com; ambassador, Dean Miam's Sch Engineering & Appl Sci; bd overseers, Sch Engineering & Appl Sci, Univ PA; bd overseers, bus & Opers, Nsf Adv Comt; bd dir, Smithsonian Inst Libr; vice-chair Libr Adv Bd; trustee, Miami Univ's bd trustee, 2012-. **Honors/Awds:** Hon Doctor Sci, Miami Univ, 1993. **Special Achievements:** Company ranked #34 on Black Enterprise's list of Top 100 Industrial/Service Companies, 1992. **Business Addr:** Chairman, Chief Executive Officer, Integrated Systems Analysts Inc, 2001 N Beauregard St Suite 600, Alexandria, VA 22311, **Business Phone:** (703)824-0700.

### GOODEN, CHERRY ROSS
Educator. **Personal:** Born Nov 7, 1942, Calvert, TX; daughter of John R and Ludia Beavers; children: Deron LeJohn & DeShaunda Lorraine. **Educ:** Tex Southern Univ, BS, elem educ, 1964, MEd, elem educ, 1972; Univ Houston, EdD, educ leadership & cult studies, 1991. **Career:** Houston Independent Sch Dist, teacher, 1964-76; Tex Southern Univ, Dept Curric & Instr, asst prof, assoc prof & interim chair, chap pres, assoc dean, dir, Gen Univ Acad Ctr, currently; Houston Univ, vis prof; Prairie View A&M Univ, vis prof. **Orgs:** Consult, Sch Dists State, 1981-; bd mem, Lockhart Tech Acad, 1984-86; Asn Teacher Educrs, 1986-; Asn Supv & Curric Develop, 1987-; Tex Southern Chap Phi Delta Kappa; treas, chaplain vpres & pres, Houston Chap Jack & Jill Amer; Humble-Intercontinental Chap Top Ladies Distinction; Hous-

ton Chap Nat Women Achievement; Alpha Kappa Alpha Sorority; Nat Alliance Black Sch Educrs, 1988-; founding mem, pres, Nat Asn Multicultural Educ, 2007-2009; life mem, Tex Asn Black Personnel Higher Educ; Int Reading Asn. **Home Addr:** 9200 W Bellfort St Suite 41, Houston, TX 77031-2316, **Home Phone:** (713)981-5026. **Business Addr:** Associate Professor, Interim Chairman, Texas Southern University Department of Curriculum & Instruction, ED 204 3100 Cleburne St, Houston, TX 77004, **Business Phone:** (713)313-1922.

### GOODEN, DWIGHT EUGENE
Actor, baseball player. **Personal:** Born Nov 16, 1964, Tampa, FL; son of Dan and Ella May; married Monica Harris; children: Devin, Darren, Ariel & Ashley; married Monique Moore; children: 2. **Career:** Baseball player (retired); NY Mets, pitcher, 1984-94; NY Yankees, 1996-97, 2000; Cleveland Indians, 1998-99; Houston Astros, 2000; Tampa Bay Devil Rays, 2000; Film: Batman Begins, 2005; TV Series: "1986 MLB All-Star Game", 1986; "2000 Official World Series", 2000; "Star-Crossed", 2002. **Home Addr:** 6700 30th St S, St Petersburg, FL 33712-5519.

### GOODEN, LINDA
Vice president (organization), executive. **Personal:** married Laird. **Educ:** Youngstown State Univ, BS, comput technol; Univ Md, BS, bus admin & MBA; Defense Systs Mgt Col, exec prog mgr, 1998. **Career:** Lockheed Martin, Info Systs & Global Serv, exec vpres, 2007-13; Nat Security Telecommunications Adv Comt, 2010-, exec vpres info systs, global solutions, pres info technol & vpres software support serv, 1997-2006. **Orgs:** Bd trustees, Eisenhower Fels; bd mem, exec bd eisenhower fels bd trustees, Armed Forces Commun & Electronics Asn (AFCEA) Int; bd mem, TechAmerica; bd mem, Univ Systs Md Bd Regents; bd dir, Automatic Data Processing (ADP) Inc. **Honors/Awds:** Women in Technology's Corporate Leadership Award, 2002; Federal 100 Eagle Award, Fed Comput Week, 2002; Black Engineer of the Year, US Black Engr, 2006; Greater Washington Government Contractor Awards, Executive of the Year, 2007; Top 50 Women in Technology, Corp bd mem, 2008; Maryland Business Hall of Fame, Inductee, 2008; The 100 Most Powerful Executives in Corporate America, Black Enterprise, 2010; 50 Most Powerful Women in Business, Fortune, 2009; Career Communications Hall of Fame, 2011; Hon doctor, pub serv degree, Univ Md; Hon doctor, pub serv degree, Univ Col. **Home Addr:** , Annapolis, MD. **Business Addr:** Executive Vice President, Lockheed Martin Corp, 6801 Rockledge Dr, Bethesda, MD 20817, **Business Phone:** (301)897-6000.

### GOODEN, LINDA R.
Association executive, executive director, executive. **Educ:** Youngstown State Univ, BS, comput technol, 1977; San Diego State Univ; Univ Md, BS, bus admin, MBA; Defense Systs Mgt Col, exec prog mgr course, 1998. **Career:** Lockheed Martin Australia Pty Ltd, dir; Lockheed Martin UK Ltd, dir; Lockheed Martin Corp, Software Support Serv, vpres, 1994-2006, It, pres info technol, 1997-2006, dep exec vpres info & technol serv, exec vpres info systs & global solutions, 2007-13; Gen Dynamics San Diego, engr; Prof Serv Coun, dir; Wash Gas Light Co, dir, 2013-. **Orgs:** Armed Forces Communs & Electronics Asn Int; Info Technol Asn Am; Univ Md, A. James Clark Sch Engr & Robert H. Smith Sch Bus Ctr Electronic Markets & Enterprises; Univ Md, Baltimore County; Prince George's Community Col Found; Md Bus Roundtable Educ; Exec Leadership Coun; bd trustee, Eisenhower Fels; Armed Forces Commun & Electronics Asn Int; TechAmerica; Univ Systs Md Bd Regents; dir & mem audit comt, Automatic Data Processing Inc, 2009-; Nat Security Telecommunications Adv Comt, 2010; Smithsonian Libr; mem adv bd, Millennium Corp, 2013-. **Honors/Awds:** Annual Peat Marwick High Tech Entrepreneur Award, 1994; Corporate Leadership Award, Women Technol, 2002; Eagle Award, Fed Comput Week, 2002; Hon Dr Pub Serv, Univ Md, 2005; Black Engineer of the Year, US Black Engr & IT Mag, 2006; Executive of the Year, Greater Washington Government Contractor Awards, 2007; Maryland Business Hall of Fame, 2008; Hon Dr Law, Morgan State Univ, 2010. **Special Achievements:** In 2010 Fortune magazine named her as one of the Top 50 Most Powerful Women in Business; Ms. Gooden was featured as one of Black Enterprise magazines 100 Most Powerful Executives in Corporate America for 2009; In 2008 Ms. Gooden was inducted into the Maryland Business Hall of Fame and named to Corporate Board Member magazines Top 50 Women in Technology. **Business Addr:** Director, Washington Gas Light Co, 101 Const Ave NW, Washington, DC 20080, **Business Phone:** (703)750-4440.

### GOODEN, DR. WINSTON EARL
Dean (education), clergy. **Personal:** married Kumea Shorter; children: Adia. **Educ:** Muskingum Col, BA, philos; Yale Univ Divinity Sch, Mdiv, 1973; Yale Univ, MS, PhD, clin & community psychol, 1980. **Career:** Pvt pract, clin psychol, 1984-; Univ Ill, Chicago, asst prof & assoc dean, 1995-2000; Fuller Theol Sem, asst prof, assoc prof psychol & dean, 2000-; Two Churches Conn, pastor; Unoja Juv Prog, co-founder & dir; Yale Univ, Black Church, pastor; United Community Church, New Haven, Conn, pastor; First AME Zion Church, assoc pastor. **Orgs:** Am Psychol Asn; Nat Coun Schs & Progs Prof Psychol; dir, Pasadena Hosp Asn. **Home Addr:** 180 N Oakland Ave, Pasadena, CA 91101, **Home Phone:** (626)584-5501. **Business Addr:** Associate Professor, Dean, Fuller Theological Seminary, 135 N Oakland Ave, Pasadena, CA 91182, **Business Phone:** (626)584-5200.

### GOODING, CUBA M., JR.
Actor, manager. **Personal:** Born Jan 2, 1968, Bronx, NY; son of Cuba Sr and Shirley; married Sara Kapfer; children: Spencer, Mason & Piper. **Career:** Films: Boyz N the Hood, 1991; Gladiator, 1992; A Few Good Men, 1992; Lightning Jack, 1994; Outbreak, 1995; Losing Isaiah, 1995; Jerry Maguire, 1996; As Good As It Gets, 1997; What Dreams May Come, 1998; A Murder of Crows, producer, 1999; Chill Factor, 1999; Instinct, 1999; Men of Honor, 2000; Pearl Harbor, 2001; Rat Race, 2001; Snow Dogs, 2002; Boat Trip, 2003; Psychic, 2003; The Fighting Tempations, 2003; Radio, 2003; Shadow boxer, 2005; Dirty, 2005; End Game, 2005; Norbit, 2006; What LKoveIs, 2006; Daddy Day Camp, 2006; American Gangster, 2007; Red Tails, 2012; The Butler, 2013; Machete Kills, 2013; Don Jon, 2013; Life of a King, 2013; Carry Me Home, 2014; Selma, 2014; Book of Negroes, 2015. TV series: "Murder Without Motive: The Edmund Perry Story", 1992; "Daybreak", HBO special, 1993; "The Tuskegee Airmen", HBO Movie, 1995; "Home on the Range", 2004; "Gifted Hands", 2009; "Firelight", 2012; "Guilty", 2013. Other: Hero Wanted, 2007; The Land Before Time XIII: The Wisdom of Friends, 2007; The way of War, 2008; The Devils Tomb, 2009; Lies & Illusions, 2009; Sacrifice, 2011; The Hit List, 2011; Red Tails, 2012; One in the Chamber, 2012. **Honors/Awds:** Broadcast Film Critics Association Award, Best Supporting Actor, 1996; Academy Award, Best Supporting Actor, 1997; American Comedy Award for Funniest Supporting Actor in a Motion Picture, 1997; Blockbuster Entertainment Award for Favorite Supporting Actor - Comedy/Romance, 1997; BFCA Award for Best Supporting Actor, 1997; CFCA Award for Best Supporting Actor, 1997; Nominee for Golden Globe Best Performance by an Actor in a Supporting Role in a Motion Picture, 1997; Golden Satellite Award for Best Performance by an Actor in a Supporting Role in a Motion Picture, Comedy or Musical, 1997; Screen Actors Guild Award for Outstanding Performance by a Male Actor in a Supporting Role, 1997; 50 most beautiful people in the world, People" magazine, 1997; Blockbuster Entertainment Award Favorite Supporting Actor, Drama/Romance, 1999; Hollywood Walk of Fame, 2002; Image Award, 2004; Carnie Award, 2005; Hollywood Walk of Fame, 2007; Received more than awards. **Home Addr:** , CA. **Business Addr:** Manager, Michael Rotenberg, 9460 Wilshire Blvd, Beverly Hills, CA 90212.

### GOODING, OMAR M.
Actor. **Personal:** Born Oct 19, 1976, Los Angeles, CA; son of Cuba Sr and Shirley. **Career:** TV series: "Just the Ten of Us", 1990; "Wild & Crazy Kids", 1990; "Hangin'with Mr. Cooper", 1992; "Blossom", 1992; "Thea", 1994; "Smart Guy", 1997; "Batman Beyond", 2000; "Static Shock", 2000; "Touched by an Angel", 2001; "The Division", 2002; "One on One", 2003; "Play makers", 2003-06; "Barbershop", 2005-06; "Mysterious Island", 2005; "Deadwood", 2006; "CSI: Miami", 2006; "Miami Trauma"; "Can Openers", 2009; "Grey's Anatomy", 2010; "Chase", 2011; "Family Time", 2012-14; "Single Ladies", 2012-14. Films: Ghost Dad, 1990; The Ernest Green Story, 1993; Freedom Song, 2000; Baby Boy, 2001; Verbal Communications, The Division, 2002; One on One, 2002-03; The Gospel, 2005; Lord Help Us, 2007; The Candy Shop, 2008; Knuckle Draggers, 2009; Alpha Males Experiment, 2009; Christmas in Compton, 2012; The Devil's Dozen, 2013; Holla II, 2013; Percentage, 2013; Lap Dance, 2014; Patterns of Attraction, 2014; Men, Money & Gold Diggers, 2014; Betrothed, 2014. **Honors/Awds:** Young Artist Award, 1992; Special Mention, Locarno International Film Festival, 2001; nomination, Image Award, 2006. **Business Addr:** Actor, c/o Talentworks, 3500 W Olive Ave Suite 1400, Burbank, CA 91505, **Business Phone:** (818)972-4300.

### GOODLOE, CELESTINE WILSON (CELESTE GOODLOE)
College administrator. **Personal:** Born May 7, 1954, Brooklyn, NY; married John W Jr; children: Jasmine R & Courtney M. **Educ:** Bennett Col, BS, 1976; Miami Univ, MS, 1982. **Career:** Bennett Col, admin counr, 1979-81; Miami Univ, grad asst, 1981-82; Col Wooster, asst dir, coord minority, 1982-84; Xavier Univ, assoc dir admin, 1984-, dir transfer recruitment & dir undergrad transfer admis, 2000-, stud financial assistance, currently. **Orgs:** Ohio Asn Col Admin Counrs, 1980-; panel partic, NACAC, 1982, 1985; Am Personnel & Guid Asn, 1981-82; local arrangement comt mem, OACAC Spring Conf, 1994; Nat Asn Foreign Stud Advs, 1994; local arrangements comt mem, Region VI, NAFSA Conf, 1996; Southern Ohio Transfer Coun, 1999; pres, Southern, Ohio Transfer Coun, 2000-; vpres, Greater Cincinnati Alliance Black Sch Educrs; Nat Alliance Black Sch Educrs. **Home Addr:** 1029 Elm Pk Dr, Cincinnati, OH 45216-2207. **Business Addr:** Director of Undergraduate Transfer Admission, Xavier University, 2nd Fl Schott Hall 3800 Victory Pkwy, Cincinnati, OH 45207-5311, **Business Phone:** (513)745-2016.

### GOODMAN, BOBBY. See GOODMAN, ROBERT O.

### GOODMAN, GEORGE D.
Association executive, executive director, mayor. **Personal:** Born Sep 13, 1940, Saginaw, MI; son of George V and Thelma Kaigler; married Judith A Mansfield; children: George & Mark. **Educ:** Eastern Mich Univ, BA, polit sci, 1963; MA, educ admin, 1970. **Career:** Eastern Mich Univ, instr, 1967-68; Univ Mich, asst dir admis, 1968-73, Opportunity Prog, dir, 1973-82; City Ypsilanti, chmn, 1969, mayor, 1972-82; Mich Munic League, exec dir, 1983, gov bd, 1990-93, pres, chief exec officer, 2005-08; Nat Acad Pub Admin, fel, 1998. **Orgs:** Life mem, Alpha Phi Alpha Frat; life mem, Nat Asn Advan Colored People; life mem, Ypsilanti Hist Soc; Emanon Club, 1967-; City Ypsilanti, 1967; bd mem, Huron Valley Girl Scout Coun, 1972-82; bd dir, Youth Understanding, 1973-78; bd dir, Ypsilanti Chamber Com, 1975-; Mid-Am Asn, 1978-; trustee, Starr Commonwealth, 1983-92, Trustee Emer, 2008-; chair, United Way Mich Bd Dir, 1987-; Ann Arbor Summer Festival Bd, 1988-96; Nat Gov Bd, Common Cause, 1990-94; pres, Mich Munic League Found, 1991; chmn, United Way Mich Bd, 1994-96; Nat League Cities, gov bd, Pub Technol Inc, 1996; Nat Asn Co; chair, Washtenaw County Community Col Found. **Honors/Awds:** Alumni Honors Award, Eastern Mich Univ Alumni Asn, 1972; Distinguished Service Award, Ypsilanti Area Jaycees, 1973; Public Service Achievement Award, Common Cause, 1987. **Home Addr:** PO Box 523, Mackinac Island, MI 49757-0523, **Home Phone:** (734)668-7901. **Business Addr:** Trustees Emeritus, Starr Commonwealth, 13725 Starr Commonwealth Rd, Albion, MI 49224, **Business Phone:** (800)837-5591.

### GOODMAN, HAROLD
Executive. **Personal:** Born Jun 3, 1954, Beaumont, TX; son of Harold C Sr and Gloria Lee; married Winford Jean McMillan; children: Preston & Winston Eugene. **Educ:** Prairie View A&M Univ, BA, mgt, 1976, MBA, 1978. **Career:** Fed Express Corp, mgr sta ops, 1982-84, sr ramp mgr, Houston Metro Dist, 1985-89, sr dist mgr, IAH Dist, 1989-91, managing dir, 1991-. **Orgs:** Bd dir, Oakland PIC, 1991-93; bd dir, Oakland Conv & Visitor's Bur, 1991-93; bd dir, Oakland Chamber Com, 1994-. **Home Addr:** 2815 Pk St, Berkeley, CA 94702-2315. **Business Addr:** Managing Director, Federal Express Corp, 1 Sally Ride Way, Oakland, CA 94621, **Business Phone:** (510)639-3808.

### GOODMAN, DR. JAMES ARTHUR
School administrator, consultant, chief executive officer. **Personal:** Born Apr 22, 1933, Portsmouth, VA; son of Accie and Viola James; married Gwendolyn Jones; children: James A Jr & Rhonda. **Educ:** Morehouse Col, AB, 1956; Atlanta Univ, MSW, 1958; Univ Minn, PhD, 1967. **Career:** Los Angeles City Health Dept, dir; Nat Acad Sci, Inst Med, Wash, DC, sr prof assoc, 1973-75; Univ Minn, Sch Social Work, Minneapolis, Minn, prof & dir, 1975-77; State Dept, Off Int Training, Wash, DC, dir, 1977-79; Univ Wash, vice provost; Inst Pub Mgt, Wash, DC, exec vpres, 1979-83; Morehouse Sch Med, assoc dean admin, 1980, vpres admin & policy, exec vpres, 1985-89, pres, 1989-91; Managed Health Care Syst, chief exec officer, chmn; prof consult; Rivera, Sierra & Co Inc, assoc consult, currently. **Orgs:** Ed adv bd mem, Ment Health Dig, 1971-73; bd dir, Atlanta Urban League, 1981-88; HealthSouth Inc, 1982-88; DeKalb County Hosp Authority, 1984-88; Nat Adv Coun Educ Health Prof, 1985-89; Rotary Int; Nat Accreditation Comt, Coun Social Work Educ; Nat Asn Social Workers; Acad Cert Social Workers; Coun Social Work Educ; Am Sociol Asn; bd mem, StarShine Academy District. **Home Addr:** 130 Morning Springs Walk, Fairburn, GA 30213. **Business Addr:** Board Member, StarShine Academy District, 3535 E McDowell Rd, Phoenix, AZ 85008, **Business Phone:** (602)957-9557.

### GOODMAN, KIM
Vice president (organization). **Educ:** Stanford Univ, BA, polit sci, & MS, indust engineering, 1987; Harvard Bus Sch, MBA. **Career:** Bain & Co, partner & vpres, 1987-2000; Dell Inc, vpres, head dell's software & peripherals bus, 2000-07; Am Express, Merchant Serv, N Am, exec vpres, global pres, 2007-13. **Orgs:** Dir, AutoNation Inc, 2007-10. **Honors/Awds:** "Black Enterprise," The 100 Most Powerful Executives in Corporate America, 2010.

### GOODMAN, KIM CRAWFORD
Vice president (organization), president (organization). **Personal:** Born May 1, 1965. **Educ:** Stanford Univ, BA, polit sci, MS, indust engineering; Harvard Bus Sch, MBA. **Career:** Bain & Co, partner & vpres, 1992-2000; Dell Inc, vpres & gen mgr, 2001-03, vpres, mkt & transactional sales, 2003-05, vpres, software & Peripherals, 2005-07; Merchant Serv Americas, exec vpres, 2007-10, pres, 2010-11; Am Express Co, pres, 2012-14. **Orgs:** Dir, AutoNation Inc, 2007-10. **Business Addr:** President, American Express Co, 200 Vesey St 50th fl, New York, NY 10285, **Business Phone:** (212)640-2000.

### GOODMAN, ROBERT O. (BOBBY GOODMAN)
Executive, military leader. **Personal:** Born Nov 30, 1956, San Juan; son of Robert Oliver Sr and Marylyn Joan Dykers; married Terry L Bryant; children: Tina & Morgan. **Educ:** US Naval Acad, Annapolis, MD, BS, opers anal, 1978; US Naval Post Grad Sch, Monterey, CA, MS, appl technol & space systs opers, 1987. **Career:** USN, A6E intruder bombadier/navigator (retired); Booz Allen Hamilton, sr assoc, 1992-2012; Sierra Nev Corp, prog mgr, 2012-13; S3 Inc, prog mgr, 2013-. **Orgs:** US Naval Acad Alumni Asn. **Business Addr:** Program Manager, S3 Inc, 1561 Vapor Trail, Colorado Springs, CO 80916, **Business Phone:** (719)591-5959.

### GOODMAN, RUBY LENE
Educator. **Personal:** Born Oct 15, 1957, Pinehurst, NC; daughter of James Leland and Magdaline Hough. **Educ:** Univ NC, Charlotte, BA, 1979; Fayetteville State Univ, cert, mid level educ, 1980; Univ NC, Pembroke, MA, 1992. **Career:** US Census, off asst; Sandhills Community Col, adult edur; Hoke Community Schs, educr, currently. **Orgs:** Nat Coalition Aviation Educ; Nat Acad Educ. **Home Addr:** 2850 N Shannon Rd, Shannon, NC 28386, **Home Phone:** (910)843-4753. **Business Addr:** Teacher, Hoke Community School, 310 Wooley St, Raeford, NC 28376, **Business Phone:** (910)875-4106.

### GOODNIGHT, PAUL D.
Artist, founder (originator). **Personal:** Born Dec 31, 1946, Chicago, IL; son of James Lockett and Esie Lockett; married Bernice Robinson; children: Aziza Robinson. **Educ:** Vesper George Col Art, attended 1971; Roxbury Community Col, attended 1972; Mass Col Art, BA, 1976, MFA, 1987. **Career:** Color Circle Art Pub Inc, founder & artistic dir, 1991-. **Honors/Awds:** Award Fellow, Artists Foundation, Boston, 1971; Nat Conf Artists Award, 1979; Unsung Heroes Award, Mus Afro-Am Hist, Boston, 1988; Artist of the Year Award, US Sports Acad, 1997; Honorary Masters Award, Mass Col Art, 1999; 21st Century Award, Urban League of Eastern Mass, 2000; Essence Award, Toyota & Essence Mag, 2000; African American Achievement Award, 2000. **Special Achievements:** Ten Artists at Their Best, Martin Luther King Libr, 1984; Work featured on tv shows, including: The Cosby Show, ER, Seinfeld; designed the World Cup poster, 1998. **Business Addr:** Founder, Artistic Director, Color Circle Art Publishing Inc, 791 Tremont St Suite N104, Boston, MA 02118, **Business Phone:** (800)254-1795.

### GOODRICH, HAROLD THOMAS
Educator, consultant. **Personal:** Born Aug 1, 1931, Memphis, TN; married Verastine; children: Ivan DeWayne & Michael Rene. **Educ:** Le Moyne-Owen Col, BS, 1957; Memphis State Univ, MA, 1969. **Career:** Educator (retired); Mitchell High Sch, Memphis, eng teacher, 1956-65, coordr, 1965-67; Adult Basic Ed, teacher, 1966; Adult Basic Educ, supvr, 1967-69; supvr instrs, 1967-74; Title I Consult, 1967-70; Consult AV, 1971; Nat Teacher Corps, team leader, 1972-74; Caplevlle Elem, teacher, 1974-76; Ross Elem, teacher, 1976-80; Crump Elem, teacher, 1980-85; Shelby County Schs. **Orgs:** Deleg, Nat Educ Asn, 1971, 1974; Chmn, Vis Com Southern Asn Col & Schs, 1974-76; Tex Educ Agency; Wis Technol Educ Asn; SCEA; TASCD; Asn Educ Commun & Technol, Asn Supv & Curric Develop, Dem, Omega Psi Phi; vpres, GAIA Invest Club; deacon, finance com, housing com Mt Vernon Bapt Chruch. **Honors/Awds:** Phi Delta Kappa Award, 1969; Outstanding Educator in America for 70's. **Home Addr:** Cadiz Lane, Hot Springs National Park, AZ 71909, **Home Phone:** (901)789-0326.

**GOODRICH, LINDA S.**
Educator, choreographer. **Personal:** Born Columbus, OH; married John O Roberts; children: 2. **Educ:** Ohio State Univ, MA, 1972, PhD, 1976; Mills Col, MFA, choreography & performance, 1982. **Career:** Dancing at Lugnasa, choreographer & dir; The Colored Museum, choreographer & dir; Jar the Floor, choreographer & dir; Cabin in the Sky, choreographer & dir; Raisin, choreographer & dir; For Colored Girls Who Have Considered Suicide When the Rainbo Was Enuf, choreographer & dir; Sisters, choreographer & dir; The Old Settler, choreographer & dir; A Thousand Cranes, choreographer; Viva Carnival show, producer, 2002; Venus, dir, 2002; Sideshow, producer, 2003; Pop Rocks, producer, 2006; Calif State Univ, chair & dance coordr, currently; Sacramento/Black Art Dance, founder, artistic dir & fac advisor, currently. **Orgs:** Bd mem, Celebration Arts Theatre. **Business Addr:** Chair, Dance Coordinator, California State University, 6000 J St, Sacramento, CA 95819-6069, **Business Phone:** (916)278-4784.

**GOODRICH, DR. THELMA E.**
Insurance executive. **Personal:** Born Apr 19, 1933, New York, NY; daughter of James and Evelyn; married Lawrence Hill. **Educ:** Baruch City Col, New York NY, attended 1952; Col Ins, New York, cert, 1960; Col New Rochelle, New York, attended 1985; Empire State Col, New York. **Career:** Fay Weintraub-Sterenbuck, New York, NY, secy, 1953; Thelma E Goodrich Inc, New York, owner & mgr, founder, 1959; Goodrich & Johnson Brokerage, New York, pres & chief exec officer, 1980-. **Orgs:** Iota Phi Lambda Sorority, 1975; New York Club Negro Bus & Prof Women, 1978; Bd chair, United Mutual Life Ins Co, 1983-86; bd mem, New York Property Fire Ins Orgn, 1983-; NY Auto Plan treas, E Harlem Renewal Agency, 1985-; dir, Aron Davis Hall, 1987-; dir, 100 Black Women, 1987-; pres, Harlem Bus Alliance, 1989; dir, Prof Ins Agents, 1989; pres, Coun Ins Brokers, 1989; chair, Greater Harlem Real Estate Bd, 1989; pres, Bus & Prof Women Club Inc, 1992. **Honors/Awds:** Community Service Award, New York City Bus & Prof Women, 1988; Community Service Award, New York State Black & Pub Rel Caucus, 1989; Community Service Award, Ins Women of New York State. **Special Achievements:** First vice president of New York Club, National Association of Negro. **Home Addr:** 6 E 130th St, New York, NY 10037, **Home Phone:** (212)368-5731. **Business Addr:** President, Chief Executive Officer, Goodrich & Johnson Brokerage, 360 W 125th St Suite 1, New York, NY 10027-4801, **Business Phone:** (212)865-5606.

**GOODSON, ADRIENNE M.**
Basketball coach, basketball player. **Personal:** Born Oct 19, 1966, Bayonne, NJ; daughter of Ralph Feuker and Margo. **Educ:** Old Dom Univ, BA, sec educ, mkt, 1989. **Career:** Basketball player (retired), educator; Banco de Credito, Brazil, forward, 1991-92; Unimed, Brazil, 1992-94; Ponte Preta, Brazil, 1994-95; Seara, Brazil, 1995-96; Atlanta Glory, 1996-98; Philadelphia Rage, 1998-99; Utah Starzz, guard, 1999-2002; San Antonio Silver Stars, guard, 2002-04; Houston Comets, unrestricted free agt, 2005; Charlotte Sting, 2005; ECPI Col Technol, freshmen admis presenter, currently. **Orgs:** Nat Championship squad. **Home Addr:** , Chesapeake, VA. **Business Addr:** Freshmen Admissions Presenter, ECPI College of Technology, 5555 Greenwich Rd Suite 300, Virginia Beach, VA 23462, **Business Phone:** (757)490-9090.

**GOODSON, ANNIE JEAN**
Government official, chairperson, president (organization). **Personal:** Born Camp Hill, AL; married Adolph. **Educ:** Ala State Univ, BS, 1954; Fisk Univ, grad study, 1956; Howard Univ Sch Soc Work, MSW, 1962; Univ Southern Calif, MPA, 1982. **Career:** Government official (retired); E Highland HS Sylocauga, Ala, pub sch teacher, 1954-56; DC Cs Ctr, teacher, 1957-58; DC Dept Pub Welfare, caseworker, 1958-60; Med Eval & Rehab Serv, chief, 1967-71; DC Dept Human Serv, chief spec serv div, 1971-76; Grp Ther St Elizabeths Hosp, Phelps-Stokes fel; DC Dept Hr, dep bur chief, 1976-80; Family Serv Admin, adminr, 1980-83; Comn Homelessness, Columbia, DC, exec dir, 1984-87, sr policy adv, 1987-95, actg comnr social serv, 1995-97; Links Inc, div social serv, actg comnr, hr, chairperson, currently. **Orgs:** Nat Asn Social Workers; psychiat soc worker, St Elizabeths Hosp, 1962-67; Acad Cert Social Workers; John Wesley Am Zion Ch; Delta Sigma Theta Inc Sor; chap pres, Montgomery Co Alumnae Chap, 1975-77; pres, Wash Carats, 1998-2000; pres, Capital City Links, 1999-. **Honors/Awds:** Nominee, Fed Woman's Award, 1975; Soror of Year Award, Delta Sigma Theta Sor, 1975; Lifetime Achievement, 1997; Nominee, Zeta Phi Beta Community Volunteer Service Award, 1998. **Home Addr:** 7914 13th St NW, Washington, DC 20012-1309, **Home Phone:** (202)882-8735. **Business Addr:** Chairperson, The Links Inc, 609 H St NE 5th Fl, Washington, DC 20002, **Business Phone:** (202)727-5930.

**GOODSON, DR. ERNEST JEROME**
Dentist. **Personal:** Born Dec 16, 1953, Concord, NC; married Patricia Timmons; children: Ernest Jerome Jr (Sonny) & Aaron Timmons. **Educ:** Univ NC, Chapel Hill, NC, BSD, 1976, Sch Dent, DDS, 1979; Univ Calif-San Francisco, MS, 1984; Harvard Univ, MPA, 2002. **Career:** Cent Piedmont Comm Col, fac, 1980; Univ London Royal Dent Hosp, fel dentsurg, 1980; Pasquotank-Perquimans- Cander-Chowan Dist Health Dept, dir dent serv; Univ NC Sch Dent, adj fac, 1981-82; Elizabeth City State Univ, lectr math, 1981-82; Nash-Edgecombe-Halifak Counties, dir dent serv, 1984-85; Fayetteville State Univ, lectr math, 1985-86; Acad Gen Dent, fel; pvt pract orthodontist, currently. **Orgs:** Tutor, First Baptist Math-Sci Tutorial Prog, 1986-; vpres, Minority Health Profs; bd mem, Cumberland Co ABC, 1990-94; found bd mem, Fayetteville State Univ; adv bd mem, United Nat Bank; dentist rep, Comm Health Serv, 1993-; adv bd, Leap Community; bd dir, Fayetteville Mus Art, 1994-; NC Teaching Fel Bd, 1994-; NC Dent Soc; Am Dent Asn; NC Asn Orthodontists; Southern Asn Orthodontists; Am Asn Orthodontists; World Fedn Orthodontists; Col Diplomates Am Bd Orthod; bd visitor, Univ NC, currently. **Honors/Awds:** Dentist of the Year, Old N State Dent Soc, 1997, Doctor of the Year, Cumberland County Minority Health & Legal Professionals; North Carolina State-Volunteer of the Year, College of Diplomates of the American Board of orthodontics, 2005; Professional of the Year, Fayetteville Business League, 2005; Citizenship Award, North Carolina dental Society, 2007; Harvey Beech Award, University of North Carolina, 2007; Harvey E Beech Outstanding Alumni Award, UNC Gen Alumni Asn, 2007; Small Business Excellence Award-Methodist University, 2009. **Special Achievements:** Research and publications include "Detection and Measurement of Sensory Illusions", Dept of Physiology, Univ of NC; "The London Experience", School of Medicine and School of Dentistry, 1981; "Dental Education in England" The Dental Asst 1981; "Orthodontics for the Public Health Dentist" NC Dental Public Health, 1986; "We Need More Than Money To Reform Public Education" THE CITIZEN, school news. **Home Addr:** 1801 Lakeshore Dr, Fayetteville, NC 28305, **Home Phone:** (910)484-6433. **Business Addr:** Orthodontist, 950 S McPherson Church Rd, Fayetteville, NC 28303, **Business Phone:** (910)483-2633.

**GOODSON, FRANCES ELIZABETH**
School administrator. **Personal:** Born Nashville, TN; married David; children: Shereen & David Hughes. **Educ:** Hofstra Univ, attended 1978; Negotiations Sem, attended 1979; Nat Asn Educ Negotiators, Negotiations Sem, attended 1980; Comput Educ, mgt sem, 1980; Nat Sch Bd Jour, Pub Rels Sem, attended 1983, Admin Eval Workshops, attended 1984. **Career:** Roosevelt Coun Parent Teachers Asn, pres, 1973-74; Legis Liaison Bd Educ, NYS, 1981-; Adv Coun Gov NYS, st human rights, 1984-, div women, 1995-; Roosevelt Pub Schs, bd educ, pres. **Orgs:** Bd mem, Adult Basic Educ, 1977-; Nat Caucus Black Sch Bd, 1978- bd dir, 1978-80, chair elect comn, 1982, exec vpres, 1986-87, 1987-88, Nat Caucus Black Sch Bd Mem; Elem Educ Accrediation Comm, 1983; bd dir, Nat Caucus Black Bd; NY St Liaison representing Roosevelt Bd Educ, 1982-; St Human Rights Adv Coun, 1983-84; vpres, Northeast Region Nat Caucus Black Sch Bd, 1983-84; vpres, 1983-84, pres, 1984-85, Roosevelt Bd Educ; Comn Child Care, 1984-; NY St Comn Child Care, 1985; Govt appointment NYS Comm Child Care, 1985; campaign coordr, co exec republican party, 1989 task force, NY St assembly, 1990; Nassau Cty Exec campaign reelection, 1990; res asst, Nassau City Off Women Servs, 1994; spec asst, Nassau City Off Minority Affairs, 1997-; local pres, Evangel Lutheran Church Am, 1998. **Honors/Awds:** Black Faces in High Places, 1979; Student Award, Frances E Goodson Award Est, 1980; Outstanding Member Award, NCBSBM, 1982; President Award Appreciation, 1983; National President Award, Nat Black Caucus, 1983-85; Dem Club of Roosevelt Award, 1984; Northeast Region VPres's Award, NCBSBM, 1984; National Woman of the Year Award, 100 Black Men Inc, 1985; New York State Senate Commendation Resolution, 1985; equalization rate-Roosevelt Pub Schs, NYS Legis law passed, 1988; Nassau City proclamation, Republican Party, 1988; NYS Assembly proclamation educ, 1988. **Special Achievements:** Poetry, Our World's Most Beloved Poems, 1985. **Home Addr:** 236 Beechwood Ave, Roosevelt, NY 11575-1634, **Home Phone:** (516)623-2794. **Business Addr:** President, Roosevelt Public Schools Board of Education, 2a Sch Lane, Roosevelt, NY 08555, **Business Phone:** (609)448-2798.

**GOODSON, JAMES ABNER, JR.**
Advertising executive. **Personal:** Born Jul 11, 1921, Cuero, TX; married Emma E; children: James III, Theresa Jasper, Johnny L & Jerome K. **Educ:** Metrop Col Los Angeles, attended 1943; Harold Styles Sch Radio Announcers, attended 1952. **Career:** Tire, salesman, 1940; BF Goodrich, 1944; Nat Rec Newspaper, publ & pres. **Orgs:** Pres, Cosmopolitan Rep Voters Club Inc; Nat Advan Asn Colored People; Urban League; Hollywood Community Police Coun, 1977, 81, Southside C C Los Angeles; Happiness Proj, Masonic Lodge, New Hope Baptist Ch; pres, JAGME Found. **Honors/Awds:** Exceptional Achievement Award, Nat asn Advan colored People, 1971; Personal & Professional Achievement Award, Hon Mike Roos 46th Assembly Dist, Hon Maxine Waters 48th Assembly Dist, Hon David Roberts 23rd Senatorial Dist, 1980; Cert Apprec County Los Angeles, 1980; Cert Commendation Republican Central Comn Los Angeles County, 1985; Plaque Appreciation Young Men's Christian Assoc, 1986. **Home Addr:** 545 W 111th St, Los Angeles, CA 90044, **Home Phone:** (323)755-8011. **Business Addr:** President, Jagme Foundation, 1605 N Cahuenga Blvd, Los Angeles, CA 90028, **Business Phone:** (323)962-2054.

**GOODSON, DR. LEROY BEVERLY**
Physician. **Personal:** Born Feb 11, 1933, Elyria, OH; son of Inez Louise Leach and Franklin Beverly; married Evelyn Wimmer; children: Earl, Kenneth & Parker. **Educ:** Univ Mich, BS, 1955; Univ Mich, MD, Med Sch, 1959; Kenyon Col, attended 1953. **Career:** St Rita's Hosp, intern, 1959-60; Community Hosp, Med Staff, 1960-; Carl S Jenkins, partner, 1960-61; Wilberforce Univ, med dir, 1960-62; pvt pract physician, 1963-72; Wright Patterson AF Base, 1966-68; Clark Co Drug Control Coun, med dir, 1971-; pvt pract physician, 1972-; Wright St Univ, consult, 1973-; HK Simpson Ctr Maternal Health, instr phys diag & anemia, 1973-; Wright St Univ, assoc clin prof; St Ritas Med Ctr, Flexible or Transitional Yr; family pract, 1975-; Alcohol Chem Detox Unit, med dir, 1975-83; Mercy Med Ctr Springfield; Oicc Primary Care Network, physician. **Orgs:** Ohio Acad Family Physicians, 1960-; secy, Clark Co Med Soc, 1968-70, pres, 1971; Oper Big Sister, 1968-70, pres bd, 1970; Am Red Cross, 1968-71, exec comt mem, 1969-71; Community Hosp Bd, 1968-71, exec comt mem, 1969-71; chmn bd, Ronez Apt Inc, 1972-74; Community Hosp, vpres, 1973; dipl, Am Bd Family Prac, 1973-; bd mem, St John's Nursing Home, 1980-; dipl, AMSADD, 1989. **Honors/Awds:** Outstanding Service to Community, Frontiers Int Inc, 1973; Service Award, Am Red Cross, 1971; Service Award, Community Hosp, 1971; 25 yrs Service Award, Alcohol, Drugs & Ment Health, 1993. **Home Addr:** . **Business Addr:** Physician, Oicc Primary Care Network, 2701 Moorefield Rd, Springfield, OH 45502, **Business Phone:** (937)399-6650.

**GOODSON, DR. MARTIN L., JR.**
Educator, association executive. **Personal:** Born Feb 14, 1943, Boligee, AL; children: Monique. **Educ:** Stillman Col, BS, 1964; Ind State Univ, MS, 1970; Ind Univ, EdD, 1975. **Career:** Rochelle High Sch, Lakeland, Fla, biol teacher, 1964-65; Woodrow Wilson, fel, 1964; Druid High Sch Tuscaloosa, physics teacher, 1965-66; Seagrams Distilling Inc, lab technician, 1967; Ind State Univ, instr, 1970-72; Ala State Univ, Huntsville, assoc prof, 1975-77; Delta Col, assoc prof, prof physics, 2004-. **Orgs:** Ala State pres, Nat Pres New Farmers Asn, 1959-60; keeper rec & seals, Omega Psi Phi Fraternity, 1963-64, secy, 1963-; adv, State Univ, 1968-75; pres, Nat Asn Advan Colored People Terre Haute, 1970-72; consult, Am Inst Physics, 1973-75; outside evaluator, Proj Impact State Ind, 1973-75; consult & evaluator, POT Modules, 1973-75; Phi Delta Kappa, 1974-; Outside Col Univ Ctr, Mich, 1977-; bd mem, Am Baptist Ol Sem, 1978-; Nat Asn Res Sci Teaching. **Honors/Awds:** Outstanding Service Award, Am Asn Univ Professors. **Special Achievements:** Journal Col Sci Teaching: "The Effect of Objective-Based Diagnostic Test on Physical Science Students", 1978. **Home Addr:** 3160 Ramond St, Saginaw, MI 48601-5931, **Home Phone:** (989)777-9533. **Business Addr:** Professor of Physics, Delta College, Rm D-156 1961 Delta Rd, University Center, MI 48710, **Business Phone:** (989)686-9255.

**GOODWIN, CURTIS LAMAR**
Baseball player. **Personal:** Born Sep 30, 1972, Oakland, CA. **Career:** Baseball player (retired); Baltimore Orioles, outfielder, 1995; Cincinnati Reds, 1996-97; Colo Rockies, 1998; Chicago Cubs, 1999; Toronto Blue Jays, outfielder, 1999. **Business Addr:** Professional Baseball Player, Toronto Blue Jays, 1 Blue Jays Way Suite 3200, Toronto, ON M5V 1J1, **Business Phone:** (416)341-1000.

**GOODWIN, DELLA MCGRAW**
Nurse, administrator, dean (education). **Personal:** Born Nov 21, 1931, Claremore, OK; daughter of James Edward McGraw (deceased) and Allie Mae Meadows (deceased); married Jesse F; children: Gordon Francis, Paula Therese & Jesse Stephen. **Educ:** Dunbar Jr Col, AA, 1952; Freedmen's Hosp Sch Nursing, Howard Univ, dipl nursing, 1955; Wayne State Univ, BSN, 1959, MSN, 1962. **Career:** Educator (retired); Detroit Receiving Hosp, hosp head nurse, 1958-60; Blvd Gen Hosp, Detroit, Mich, dir nursing, 1964-69; Paramedical Serv, Detroit, Mich, consult, 1969-72; Wayne County Community Col, Detroit, Mich, chair nursing, 1970-82, dean nursing & health, 1970-86; Health Systs Agency, 1979-81; Detroit Substance Abuse Coun, Della Goodwin & Co, pres & consult, 1986. **Orgs:** Health Coord Coun, 1979-84; Chair, Detroit Substance Abuse Coun, 1982-90; Detroit Health Comn, 1982-; Drunk Driving Task Force & Lansing, 1982; Cabinet Nursing Educ, Am Nurses Asn, 1984-88; Women's Conf Concerns, 1984; bd chairperson, pres, chief exec officer, Nat Ctr Advan Blacks Health Prof, 1988; Health Brain Trust, Mich Legis Black Caucus, 1988; bd dir, Southeast Mich Chap Am Red Cross, currently; pres, Comprehensive Health Planning Coun Southeastern Mich; Chi Eta Phi; Sigma Theta Tau Nursing Sororities; Detroit Dist Nurses Asn; Delta Sigma Theta Sorority; United Community Serv; Nat League Nursing; Mich Nurses Asn; Nat Ctr Advan Blacks Health Professions, currently. **Home Addr:** 19214 Appoline, Detroit, MI 48235-1213, **Home Phone:** (313)342-1522.

**GOODWIN, DONALD EDWARD**
Engineer, vice president (organization). **Personal:** Born May 5, 1949, Detroit, MI; son of James A and Thelma L; married Patricia Davis; children: Malik, Idris & Layla. **Educ:** Univ Mich, BS, mech engineering, 1971, Dearborn, Mich, MS, mgt, 1978; Duke Univ, dynamic mgt prog, 2005. **Career:** Engineer (retired); Cummins Engine Corp, prod engr, 1971-72; Chrysler Corp, prod engr, 1972-73, mgr, eng qual & reliability assurance, 1985-89, mgr, restraints eng, 1989-92, exec engr, LCP interior eng, 1992-94; Proving Grounds & Durability Testing, exec eng, 1994-98, Sci Labs Providing Grounds, vpres, 1999-2007; Ford Motor Co, prod engr, brakes & other, 1973-76, Pontiac DIV GM, proj engr, 1976-79, suv, powertrain reliability & other, 1979-85; Daimler Chrysler Corp, Develop Syst, dir, 1998, Sci Labs & Proving Grounds, vpres, 2007-08. **Orgs:** Am Soc Qual Control, 1985-91; NCP, 1989-; pres, Eng Soc Detroit, 1990; bd mem, Washtenaw United Way, 1996-98; bd trustee, New Calvary Baptist Church; dir, Chrysler Develop Syst; Vehicle Engineering Workforce Diversity Comt; DaimlerChrysler African Am Network; Nat Socs Prof Engrs' Indust Adv Group. **Honors/Awds:** MNY Achiever Award, Detroit YMCA, Chrysler Corp, 1989. **Special Achievements:** America's Best & Brightest Men, Dollars & Sense Magazine, 1996. **Home Addr:** 5765 Kirkridge Trail, Rochester Hills, MI 48306-2903, **Home Phone:** (313)377-2826. **Business Addr:** Vice President of Scientific Laboratories & Proving Grounds, DaimlerChrysler Corp, CIMS 483-05-02 Chrysler Dr E, Auburn Hills, MI 48326-2757, **Business Phone:** (248)576-2521.

**GOODWIN, JAMES OSBY**
Lawyer, president (organization). **Personal:** Born Nov 4, 1939, Tulsa, OK; married Vivian Palm; children: Jerry, Davey, Anna, Jeanne & Joey. **Educ:** Univ Notre Dame, BA, 1961; Univ Tulsa, JD, 1965. **Career:** Pvt pract atty; Okla Eagle Publ Co Inc, from publ to chief exec officer, pres, currently. **Orgs:** Bd chmn, Tulsa Comprehensive Health Ctr, 1973; ACLU Award Serv Chmn Tulsa City Co Bd Health, 1975; chmn, Tulsa Human Serv Agency, 1978-80; Tulsa City Co Bd Health; OK Bar Asn; Am Trial Lawyers; secy, vpres, Okla Trial Lawyers; Tulsa Co Bar Asn; Tulsa Co Legal Aid; Okla Press Asn. **Honors/Awds:** Award for Service as member board chairman, Tulsa Comprehensive Health Ctr, 1973; Great Spirit Award, March Dimes, 2000; Leadership Donar Award, Boy Scouts Am, 2001; Black Journalists Lifetime Achievement Award, Tulsa Asn, 2008. **Home Addr:** 8403 S Col Ave Apt 18-171, Tulsa, OK 74137-1450. **Business Addr:** President, Oklahoma Eagle Publishing Co, 624 E Archer St, Tulsa, OK 74120, **Business Phone:** (918)582-7124.

**GOODWIN, DR. JESSE FRANCIS**
Government official, chemist. **Personal:** Born Feb 7, 1929, Greenville, SC; son of Frances Byrd and Jesse; children: Gordon Francis, Paula Therese & Jesse Stephen. **Educ:** Xavier Univ, BS, Pharm, 1951; Wayne Univ, MS, 1953, PhD, 1957. **Career:** Wayne State Univ Col Med, res assoc, 1958-59; Wayne City Gen Hosp, clin bio chem, 1959-63; Gen Clin Res Ctr Childrens Hosp Wayne State Univ Sch Med, lab dir, 1963-73; Detroit Health Dept, dir labs; anal chemist. **Orgs:** Pres, Gamma Lambda Chap Alpha Phi Alpha Frat, 1972-76; bd trustees, Horizon Health Systs, 1982-; Detroit Osteop Hosp Corp, 1980-; Mary grove Col, 1977-93; 1st vpres, Det Br Nat Asn Advan Colored People, 1982-84, 2nd vpres, 1978-82, pres, Detroit chap; comnr, Mich Toxic Substance Control Comn, 1986-89; bd dirs, Mich Cath Conf, 1986-89; bd dirs, Am Asn Clin Chem, 1987-90; bd, Nat Acad Clin Bio chem, 1987; Detroit Archdiocesan Educ, adv comt, 1993-; bd trustees, Loyola High Sch, 1993-. **Honors/Awds:** Chairman MI Section, AACC, 1964; author, 36 Sci Publ, 1958-; Distinguished Service Award, Detroit Branch NAACP, 1983. **Home Addr:** 8447 Marygrove Dr, Detroit, MI 48221-2942, **Home Phone:** (313)342-7822.

### GOODWIN, MAC ARTHUR
Educator, consultant. **Personal:** Born Jan 31, 1942, Orangeburg, SC; son of Romie; married Junita; children: Bobbie Theresa, Michael Anthony & Gerard Arthur. **Educ:** Claflin Univ, BA, 1963; Univ SC, MAT, 1976. **Career:** Greenville County Sch Dist, teacher, 1964-65; Comt St Elem Jr High, art teacher, 1965-66; Carver High Sch, art teacher, 1965-70; Spartanburg High Sch, visual arts dept chmn, 1970-85; SC Dept Educ, fine arts consult & educ assoc, 1985-2000; Goodwin's Arts Consult, exec dir, currently. **Orgs:** Nat Visual & Performance Arts, Stands Comt, 1990-93; co-chmn, Nat Bd Pro Teaching Stand, 1990-; Col Bd, Arts Adv Comt, 1995-; pres-elect, 1999-2000, pres, 2000-03, pres, Nat Art Edu Asn; dir, Nat Supv & Admin Div; Art Edu Stands Develop Task Force; chair, Consortium Nat Prof Arts asns; vice chair, Nat Bd Prof Teaching Stds Early Adolescence through Young Adulthood/Art Stands; chair, SC African Am Monument Citizen Adv Comm; chair, SC Alliance Arts Edu; SC Gov's Sch Arts & Humanities; bd dir, State Dept Edu Rep; bd dir, Columbia Mus Art; bd dir, SC Arts Alliance; develop comt, Nat Assessment Educ Progress; Arts Assessment Framework Consensus; NAEP Visual & Performing Arts Assessment Task Develop Team; Arts Assessment Stand. **Home Addr:** 136 Jefferson Pl, Columbia, SC 29212, **Home Phone:** (803)772-6432. **Business Addr:** Executive Director, Goodwin's Arts Consulting, 1916 Asn Dr, Reston, VA 20191-1590, **Business Phone:** (803)772-6432.

### GOODWIN, MARIA ROSE
Historian, genealogist. **Personal:** Born Aug 27, 1950, Washington, DC; daughter of Thomas Cephas and Sarajane Cohron. **Educ:** George Washington Univ, MFA, 1974. **Career:** NAT Endowment Arts, prog specialist, 1974-89; US Dept Treas, Sales & Mkt Historians Off, US mint, historian, 1989-; Smithsonian's Anacostia Mus, African-Am geneal prof. **Orgs:** NAT Geneal SOC, counr, 1996-98; Treas Hist ASN, vip, 1996-98; Orgn AMR Historians, 1990-; Smithsonian Inst, vol staff, 1974-; Daughters Dorcas, 1990-; SOC Hist Fed GOV, 1991-; AFA Hist & Geneal SOC, guest speaker, 1996-. **Honors/Awds:** Smithsonian Inst, Vol Appreciation; Smithsonian & Anacostia, Ujim's Award. **Special Achievements:** Co-author, Guide to Black Washington, 1989-; FDR, Family Heritage Group, Anacostia Museum, 1988-95; Lecturer & Writer on conducting AFA Geneology RES; author of The Bones-Keeper's Journal, An African-American Geneology Sourcebook; Co-DRR "Hidden History Church Proj," Hist SOC WAS DC, 1990-92. **Home Addr:** 1219 46th St SE, Washington, DC 20019-5719, **Home Phone:** (202)584-7986. **Business Addr:** Mint Historian, US Department of the Treasury, 801 9th St NW, Washington, DC 20220, **Business Phone:** (202)354-7724.

### GOODWIN, MARTIN DAVID
Journalist. **Personal:** Born May 1, 1964, Tulsa, OK; son of James Osby and Vivian Edwina Palm; married Angela Denise Davis. **Educ:** Benedictine Col, Atchison, KS, BA, eng jour, 1986. **Career:** Okla Eagle, Tulsa, reporter, photogr, copy ed, 1983-86; Ithaca Jour, NY, reporter, copy ed, 1986-88; Courier-Jour, Louisville, Ky, reporter, copy ed; USA Today, rewrite ed & ed page asst, 1995-96; Courier Jour, asst metro ed, Ind state ed, reporter, bur chief, 1996; Star-Ledger, city ed; Middletown Jour, ed, 2003-; Cox Ohio Publ, managing ed presentation, 2006-. **Orgs:** Scholar comt mem, Nat Asn Black Journalists, 1986-; pres, Louisville Asn Black Communicators, 1988-98; Am Soc Newspaper Ed, 2003-; Diversity & Nomintating Comts. **Honors/Awds:** Soc Prof Journalists Award; Best of Gannett Award. **Home Addr:** 6487 Hughes Ridge Lane, Liberty Twp, OH 45011-1254, **Home Phone:** (513)779-4401. **Business Addr:** Editor, The Middletown Journal, 52 S Broad St, Middletown, OH 45042, **Business Phone:** (513)705-2834.

### GOODWIN, DR. NORMA J.
Executive, physician, educator. **Personal:** Born May 14, 1937, Norfolk, VA; daughter of Stephen and Helen. **Educ:** Va State Col, BS, 1956; Medical Col VA, MD, 1961. **Career:** Kings County Hosp Ctr Brooklyn, internship residency, 1961-65; Downstate Med Ctr, dir clin asst, asst prof clin, asst prof med, 1964-72; Nat Inst Health, fel nephrol, 1965-67; Kings County Hosp, Hemodialysis Unit, clin dir, 1967-69, 1969-71; Univ Hosp Downstate Ctr, attend physician, 1968-75; Health & Hosp Corp, vpres, sr vpres, 1971-75; Dept Family Pract, clin asst prof, 1972-; AMRON Mgt Consult Inc, pres, 1976-; New York Cith Health & Hosps, sr vpres ambulatory care, 1976-80; Howard Univ Sch Bus & Pub Admin, adj prof, 1977-; Health Power Minorities, founder, ed-chief, pres & chief exec officer, 2007-; US Centers Dis Control & Prev; Wm Wrigley Jr Co; CBS Corp; Medscape; Columbia Univ Teachers Col, adj prof; Columbia Univ, fac; Howard Univ, fac; Kings County Hosp, Den & State Univ NY, Downstate Med Ctr Brooklyn; State Univ New York, clin assoc prof, currently. **Orgs:** Staff, Kings County Hosp Ctr, 1965-; pres, Provident Clin Soc Brooklyn, 1969-72; charter mem, bd dir, NY City Comp Health Planning Agency, 1970-72; 2nd vpres, Nat Med Asn; first vpres, Empire State Med Soc State Chap Nat Med Asn, secy, speaker & house del, 1972-74, exec comn, 1974; founder & pres, Health Watch Info & Prom Serv Inc, 1984-2002; regional adv group, NY Metro Regional Med Prog; consult, Dept Health Educ & Welfare; Health Serv Res Study Sect Dept HEW; chmn, com comn med Kings Co Med Soc; 1st vice chmn, Bedford Stuyvesant Comp Health Plan Coun; NY Am & Int Soc Nephrology Am Pub Health Asn; bd trust, Atlanta Univ Ctr; NY Col Podiatric Med; bd dir, NY Asn Ambulatory Care; New York Heart Asn; Am Pub Health Asn; bd dir, Am Red Cross Greater NY; La Guardia Comt Col City Univ NY; Nat Asn Comt Health Ctrs Inc; Med Adv Bd Hypertension New York Health Dept; Leg Comn Med Soc Co Kings; subcom Hosp Emer Servs Med Soc Co Kings; Task Force Emer Med Care NY St Health Plan Comn; founder & pres, AMRON Mgt Consults Inc; Nat Asn Health Serv Execs; New York Health & Hosps Corp; advisor, Nat Insts Health; Nat Asn Advan Colored People; Am Heart Asn; Nat Task Force Prev & Treat Obesity; State Univ New York-Downstate Med Ctr. **Honors/Awds:** Nat Found Fellow, 1958; Jesse Smith Noyes & Smith Douglas Scholarships; Alpha Kappa Mu Nat Honor Soc; Beta Kappa Chi Nat Science Honor Soc; Soc Sigma Xi; author or co-author more than 30 publications; Health Watch News, brochures cancer & AIDS; Videos AIDS. **Special Achievements:** Recognition by Aetna a "Science and Technology Innovator", along with Health Power, in the Aetna book "Breaking Barriers", which features 44 individuals, groups and organizations out of more than 300 that had been featured over 27 years in the Aetna 2008 African American History Calendar; Has authored/co-authored more than 60 publications; Authoring an article, "Eliminating Health Disparities through a Nationally Unique Website" in the Inaugural Edition of Columbia University's online "Journal of Health Equity". **Business Addr:** President, Chief Executive Officer, Health Power for Minorities, 3020 Glenwood Rd, Brooklyn, NY 11210, **Business Phone:** (718)434-8103.

### GOODWIN, PASTOR ROBERT KERR
Association executive, executive director. **Personal:** Born Nov 15, 1948, Tulsa, OK; son of Edward L and Jeanne B Osby; married Ruth. **Educ:** Oral Roberts Univ, Tulsa, OK, BA, 1970; Univ Tulsa, MA, social psychol; San Francisco Theol Sem, Marin, CA, MA, philos, 1973; Tex A&M Univ. **Career:** Okla Eagle Publ Co, publ, 1973-81; Nat Univ Soc, Houston, Tex, regional sales mgr, 1985-87; lobbyist, dir pub affairs, 1985-89; Prairie View Tex A&M Univs, assoc vpres univ rels, 1985-89; Tex A&M Univ Syst, Col Sta, Tex, asst dep chancellor external affairs, 1987-89; US Dept Educ, White House Initiative HBCU's, exec dir, 1989-92; Historically Black Cols, staff, 1989-92; Nat Points Light Found, exec vpres & chief operating officer, 1992-95, pres & chief exec officer, 1995-2007; Okla churches, assoc pastor; Calif churches, assoc pastor. **Orgs:** Founding bd mem, Am's Promise Alliance Youth; bd mem, Generations United; bd mem, Nat Assembly; bd mem, PFLAG; bd dir, Salvation Army; exec dir, Historically Black Cols & Univs; asst dep chancellor, assoc vpres, Tex A&M Univ; Nat & Community Serv Coalition; Interdenominational Theol Ctr; Nat Urban FelsInc; Am Soc Asn Execs; Youth Understanding. **Honors/Awds:** Hon Doctorate Laws, Univ Md, Eastern Shore, 1990; Hon Doctorate Humane Lett, LeMoyne-Owens Col, 1990; Man of the Year, Nat Coun Christians & Jews; One of the 50 most influential people in the nonprofit sector, Non Profit Times; Award for Excellence in National Executive Leadership; Nat Assembly Health & Human Serv Orgn, 2001; Hon Dr, LeMoyne Owen Col; Hon Dr, Ripon Col. **Home Addr:** 3022 Barkley Gate Lane, Fairfax, VA 22031-1461, **Home Phone:** (703)208-0802.

### GOODWIN, STEFAN CORNELIUS
Anthropologist, educator. **Personal:** Born Feb 13, 1941, Norfolk, VA; son of S Cornelius and Dr Helen J; married Helen J. **Educ:** Tenn State Univ, BA, fr, 1960; NY Univ, MA, int rels, 1964; State Univ NY, attended 1971; Northwestern Univ, MA, anthrop, 1972, PhD, anthrop, 1974. **Career:** New York Col, social worker, 1961-62; Prudential Ins, actuarial corresp, 1963-65; Ministry Educ, Peace Corps vol, Nigeria, 1966-67; Inst Mod Lang, lectr, Saudi Arabia, 1968-69; Wayne State Univ, anthropologist, 1974-76; Morgan State Univ, anthropologist, 1976-2003, assoc prof Sociol & Anthrop, 2003-. **Orgs:** Bd mem, Baltimore Crisis Response Inc, 1996-99; pres & vpres, Baltimore Neighborhoods Inc, 1998-2001; chair, Task Force Study Hist & Legacy Slavery Md, Md Comn African Am Cult & Hist, 1997-2005; chair, Comn Coord Study, Commemoration & Impact Slavery's Hist & Legacy Md, 2001-05; life mem, Nat Asn Advan Colored People; Alpha Kappa Alpha; Alpha Kappa Mu; Pi Delta Phi; Sigma Rho Sigma; Alpha Kappa Delta. **Special Achievements:** Author: "Emergence of A Continent from Racial Dismemberment," Anthropologie Africaine, 1999; "Malta", Countries and Their Cultures, 2001; Malta, Mediterranean Bridge, 2002; African Legacies of Urbanization, 2004; Late Stone Age in the Nile Valley pub in Encyc of African History, 2004; Late Stone Age in the Nile Valley in Encyclopedia of African History, 2005; "Malta", Greenwood Encyclopedia of World Folklore and Folklife, 2006; African Legacies of Urbanization: Unfolding Saga of a Continent, 2006. **Home Addr:** 1213 Roundhill Rd, Baltimore, MD 21218-1448, **Home Phone:** (410)662-9771. **Business Addr:** Associate Professor, Morgan State University, 1700 E Cold Spring Lane, Baltimore, MD 21251, **Business Phone:** (443)885-3333.

### GOODWIN, THOMAS JONES
Baseball executive, baseball player. **Personal:** Born Jul 27, 1968, Fresno, CA. **Educ:** Calif State Univ, Fresno, CA. **Career:** Baseball player (retired), baseball coach, executive; Los Angeles Dodgers, outfielder & centerfielder, 1991-93, 2000-01; Kans City Royals, centerfielder, 1994-97; Tex Rangers, centerfielder, 1997-99; Col Rockies, centerfielder, 2000; San Francisco Giants, centerfielder, 2002; Chicago Cubs, centerfielder, 2003-04; Tampa Bay Devil Rays, 2005; Atlantic League, 2005; New York Mets, coach, 2012-; Lewisville Lizards, mgr; Lowell Spinners, coach, currently. **Orgs:** Baseball Am's Short Season All-Star Team, 1989; Pioneer League All-Star Team, 1989; Tex League All-Star Team, 1990; Boston Red Sox orgn, 2008-11. **Honors/Awds:** Gold Medal, Olympic Games, 1988; Silver Medal, Baseball World Cup, 1988. **Business Addr:** Coach, New York Mets, Citi Field 120-01 Roosevelt Ave, Flushing, MA 11368-1699, **Business Phone:** (718)507-8499.

**GOODWIN, VAUGHN ALLEN.** **See ABDULLAH, SHARIF.**

### GORDEN, GEN. FRED A.
Military leader. **Personal:** Born Feb 22, 1940, Anniston, AL; son of P J and Mary Ethel Johnson Harper; married Marcia Ann Stewart; children: Shawn Nicole & Michelle Elizabeth. **Educ:** US Mil Acad, BS, engineering, 1962; Middlebury Col, MA, span lang & lit, 1968; Armed Forces Staff Col; Nat War Col. **Career:** Military leader (retired); US Mil Acad, maj gen, 1962-96, brig gen, 1984, commandant cadets, 1987-89; Army Off Chief Legis Liaison, exec officer, 1980; Army Mil Dist Wash, comdr, 1993-95; Seventh Inf Div, asst div comdr; Off Asst Sec Defense Intl Security Affairs, dir; Div Artil Seventh Inf Div, comdr; Eighth AUS Korea, artil battalion exec officer; 25th Inf Div, field artil battalion comdr, inspector gen. **Orgs:** Adv Comt Minority Veterans; bd dir, USAA Ins Co; Alpha Phi Alpha Fraternity. **Honors/Awds:** Defense Distinguished Service Medal; Legion of Merit; Bronze Star Medal with V Device; Meritorious Serv Medal; Air Medal; Army Commendation Medal with one Oak Leaf Cluster; Alumnus of the Year, Am Asn Community & Jr Col, Middlebury Col, 1988; DHL, St Augustine Col, 1988; Candle in the Dark, Morehouse Col, 1989. **Special Achievements:** The First black commandant of cadets at the U.S. Military Academy, 1987. **Home Addr:** 500 N Fields Pass, Alpharetta, GA 30004-0945, **Home Phone:** (770)751-3119.

### GORDON, AARON Z., JR.
Educator. **Personal:** Born Oct 11, 1929, Port Gibson, MS; children: Aaron Jr, Aaryce & Alyta. **Educ:** Univ Mich, BS, 1952, PhD, 1974; Wayne State Univ, MA, 1956. **Career:** Ft Monmouth, assoc officers signal course, 1952; Commun Ctr Qualification Course, 1952; Teletype Operators Sch, asst officer in-chg; Message Ctr Clk Sch, officer in-chg; SW Signal Sch Training Ctr, Camp San Luis Obispo, CA; 3rd Inf Div AFFE Korea, commun ctr officer, asst cryptographic officer, 1953-54; Br Officers Advan Signal Officers Course, 1963; Command & Gen Staff Col Ft Leven worth; Air War Col Maxwell AFB; personnel officer, 1965; S1 5064 USAR Garr, 1967-69; 5032 USAR Sch, br officer advan course instr, 1969-71, dir, 1971-73; ICAF, 1974. **Orgs:** Asst dist leader, E Dist & Dist Leader, 1961-63; Health & Curric Workshop Detroit Pub Schs, 1963; Blue Star Mothers Detroit, 1963; comn chmn, Health& Phys Ed Teachers Inst Day E Dist, 1964; comt mem, Midwest Dist AAHPR Conv, Detroit, 1964; sch dist rep, Last Two Millage Campaigns Educ TV Teacher Channel 56 Detroit Pub Schs, 1964; bd dir, Troop 775 BSA, 1964; P gmd Educ Soc, Detroit, 1965; Detroit Orgn Sch Adminr & Suprs; Phi Delta Kappa; prog chmn, Detroit Sch Mem Club Metro; Detroit Sch Black Educ Admin; Nat All Black Ed; Mich Asn Elem Sch Admn Region 1; Carter Cath Methodist Episcopal Church, Detroit; coord, Ann Spelling Bee, 1967; partic, Maximizing Benefits from Testing Workp Test Admin, 1968; partic, Educ Admin Workshop, 1970-73; dir, Prof Skills Dev Workshop Metro Detroit Soc Black Educ Admin, Ann Arbor, 1973. **Honors/Awds:** Bronze Star Decoration; co-holder worlds record Outdoor Distance Medley Relay; co-holder world's record Indoor Distance Medley Relay; co-holder am record Indoor Two Mile & Relay, 1951. **Special Achievements:** Co-author: "Guide to Implementation of Unit of Smoking & Health", 1963. **Home Addr:** 3841 St Clair St, Detroit, MI 48214-4418, **Home Phone:** (313)821-0501.

### GORDON, PASTOR ALEXANDER H., II
Sports manager, athletic director, writer. **Personal:** Born Jun 13, 1944, Phoenix, AZ; son of Alexander Houston I and Elizabeth De-Louis Davis; married Loretta Perry; children: David Anthony & Ellen Alicia. **Educ:** Marquette Univ, BA, speech & radio TV, 1967; LaSalle Corresp Sch, dipl, bus admin, 1967. **Career:** WTMJ AM FM TV, prom intern & asst, sls prom & mdsg dir, 1965-69; Avco Broadcasting Corp, corp advert writer, 1969-70; WLWITV, prom & publicity dir, 1970-71; WPVI TV, audience prom dir, 1971-72; WPVI TV, mgr advert, 1972-74; WIIC TV, dir advert, prom & publicity, 1974-77; WPXI TV, dir co mmunity rels, 1977-79; Church God Prophecy, asst pastor, 1978-79, pastor, 1979-93; WPXI TV, acct exec, 1979-87; Pittsburgh Pirates Baseball Club, dir, community serv & sls, 1988; RobertoClemente Found, exec dir, 1993-. **Orgs:** Bd mem & treas, Braod casters Prom Asn, 1971-77; bd mem & vp, Pittsburgh Advert Club, 1975-77; pres, Mews Towne N Home Owners Asn, 1975-83; chaplain, Rotary Club Pittsburgh, 1977-80; United Way Allegheny County, allocations rev comt, 1977-81; bd mem & pres, Neighborhood CtrsAsn, 1977-83; chmn, Cub Scout Day Camp Comt, 1977-86; bd mem, Allegheny Trails Coun, Boy Scouts Am, 1977-93, 1997-; bd mem, Wilkinsburg comt Ministry, 1983-87; bd mem & vp, Three Rivers Youth Inc, 1988-92; treas & bd mem, Kingsley Asn, 1990-92; vice chmn-programming, Urban Scouting comt, 1990-93, chmn, Spring Roundup Recruitment Dr, 1990, 1991, 1992; bd mem, Mt Ararat Community Ctr, 1992-96; elder, Petra Ministries, 1995-98. **Honors/Awds:** Clio Awards Comm for Advertising, 1975; Golden Reel Award Pittsburgh Radio TV Club, 1976; California State Coll Alumni Assn, Special Service Award, 1980; Honorable Pastor Church of God of Prophecy Pa, 1980-81, 1983-84, 1987; Appreciation Award Allegheny Trails Council Boy Scouts of Am, 1985; Whitney Young Award for work with minority scouts, 1986; Silver Beaver Award, Boy Scouts of America, 1988; Salute to Negro League Baseball, The Homestead Grays and the Pittsburgh Crawfords, 1988; Boy Scouts of America, Special Appreciation Award, Greater Pittsburgh Coun, 1993. **Home Addr:** 133 Locust Ct, Pittsburgh, PA 15237. **Business Addr:** Executive Director, Roberto Clemente Found, 320 E N Ave, Pittsburgh, PA 15212, **Business Phone:** (412)231-2300.

### GORDON, BERTHA COMER
Educator, government official, nurse. **Personal:** Born Feb 27, 1916, Louisville, GA; married Carlton. **Educ:** NY Univ, BS, 1945; Hunter Col, MA, 1955. **Career:** NY City Dept Hosp, regist nurse, 1937-50; Manhattan Sch, teacher, 1950-52; coun, 1952-62; Eli Whitney Voc High Sch, dept head, 1962-69; Bronx, NY, from asst supt to supt, 1972-78; Morris High Sch, Bronx, prin. **Orgs:** NY City Admin Women Educ, 1970; pres & life mem, Nat Asn Advan Colored People; NY City Supt Asn; Am Asn Sch Admin; Am Voc Educ Asn; Am NY State City Dist 14 Nurses Asn; Dr Asn NY City Educ; exec bd mem, Asn Study African Am Life; Hist Hunter Col; NY Univ Alumni Asn. **Honors/Awds:** Hall of Fame, Kappa Delta Pi. **Home Addr:** 1002 Hall Ave, White Plains, NY 10604.

### GORDON, BRIDGETTE C.
Basketball player, basketball coach. **Personal:** Born Apr 27, 1967, DeLand, FL. **Educ:** Univ Tenn, polit sci, 1989. **Career:** Basketball player (retired), coach; Pool Comense, Ital League, 1990-96; Sacramento Monarchs, forward, 1997-98; Italy; Turkey; Fox SportsS, broadcaster; Stetson Univ, DeLand, Fla, asst coach, recruiting coordr, 2001-06; Women's Nat Basketball Asn, scout, 2006-07; Ga State Univ, recruiting coordr & asst coach, 2007; Wichita State Athletics, asst coach, recruiting coordr, 2015-. **Special Achievements:** She was the first freshman to ever lead Tennessee in scoring and brought home the program's first national title her sophomore year in 1987. **Business Addr:** Assistant Coach, Recruiting Coordinator, Wichita State University, 1845 Fairmount St, Wichita, KS 67260, **Business Phone:** (316)978-5541.

### GORDON, BRUCE S.
Executive, chief executive officer. **Personal:** Born Feb 15, 1946, Camden, NJ; son of Walter and Violet; married Genie Alston; children: Taurin S; married Tawana Tibbs. **Educ:** Gettysburg Col, Gettysburg, PA, BA, 1968; Univ Ill, Bell Advan Mgt, 1981; Univ Pa, Wharton Exec Mgt; Mass Inst Technol Sloan Sch Mgt, Boston, MS, 1988. **Career:** Bell Atlantic Corp, Arlington, Va, init mgt develop, 1968-70, bus off mgr, 1970-72, sales mgr, mkt, 1972-74, personnel supvr, 1974-76,

mkt mgt supvr, 1976-78, mkt mgr, 1978-80, div staff mgr, 1980-81, div opers mgr, 1981, div mgr, phone ctr, 1981-83, mkt mgr II, 1983-84, gen mgr, mktg & sales, 1985, vpres mkt, 1988-93; Bell Atlantic Network Serv, group pres retail, 1993-2000; 3PLex.com Inc, pres & chief exec officer; Verizon Commun, NY, pres, retail markets group, 2000-2003; NAACP, bd pres, chief exec officer 2005-07; Tyco Int Finance, dir, 2005-; CBS Corp, dir & mem compensation comm, 2006-; Northrop Grumman Corp, dir, Mem Compensation Comt & Mem Policy Comm, 2008-. **Orgs:** Founder, vpres, Alliance Black Mgrs; Toastmasters Int; bd trustee, Gettysburg Col; dir, Urban League, 1984-86; bd dir, Inroads Philadelphia, 1985-88; chair, United Negro Col Fund Telethon, 1985-86; vol, United Way, 1986-88; bd dir, Southern Co, 1994-2006; bd dir, Bar tech Personnel Servs, 1995; bd mem, Off Depot; bd, Bell Atlantic Nj; bd dir, EXE Leadership Coun; dir, Urban League; trustee, Alvin Ailey Dance Found; bd dir, Lincoln Ctr; Advert Coun Inc; non exec chmn, ADT Corp, 2012-; Friends Sen D'Amato 1998 Comt; chmn, Nat Eagle Leadership Inst; bd dir, Ad Coun. **Home Addr:** 1077 30th St NW Suite 209, Washington, DC 20005. **Business Addr:** Board of Director, Northrop Grumman, 2980 Fairview Pk Dr, Falls Church, VA 22042, **Business Phone:** (703)280-2900.

### GORDON, CHARLES D.
Housing developer, executive. **Personal:** Born Aug 10, 1934, Memphis, TN; married Hazel D Mannings; children: Debra, Charles Jr, Marshall, Kenneth, Derrick & Carlton. **Educ:** Univ Wyo; Tenn State Univ; Hampton Inst; Roosevelt Univ. **Career:** Chicago Hous Auth, clerk, mgt training prog, asst mgr, hous mgr I, housmgr II, 1961-; lectr var schs. **Orgs:** Nat Asn Housing & Redevelop Officials; Control Southside Community Workers; bd dir, Horizon House; Dist Ill Educ Coun; Area A Berea Coun Dep comnr hit, basketball league, hous invitational tour; bd dir, Afro-Am touch football league; bd dir, Housing Bowling League. **Honors/Awds:** Won commnr flag beautification grounds CIIA, 1971-74; Placed 3rd City Chicago beautiful grounds mgr Wentworth Gardens, 1974; Achievement plaque for outstanding achievement as hous mgr Community Wentworth. **Home Addr:** 8950 Cornell Ave, Chicago, IL 60617, **Home Phone:** (773)374-6064.

### GORDON, DR. CHARLES EUGENE
Educator, teacher. **Personal:** Born May 31, 1938, Gallatin, TN; married Barbara Gibbs. **Educ:** Hist Western Mich Univ, BS, 1962; Wayne State Univ, MEd, 1970; Univ Mich, PhD, higher educ admin, 1976. **Career:** Wayne State Univ, dir off spec stud serv progs, 1970-; Proj Upward Bound, dir, 1968-70; Detroit Youth Home, boys coun, supvr, 1965-67; Detroit Pub Schs, sec teacher social studies, spec educ, 1962-65. **Orgs:** Bd dir, ANWC; pres, Region V Trio Adv Coun; pres, Mich Coun Educ opp progs; exec bd mem, Nat Alliance officer grad & prof Educ; exec bd mem, Nat Asn Minority Fin Aid Admin; numerous prof & bus orgns; Am Asn Higher Educ; Am Pers & Guid Asn; Nat Coord Coun Educ Opp Progs; Nat Vocat Guid Asn; Mid-West Asn Educ Opp Prog Personnel; Mich Coun Educ Opp Progs; Nat Alliance Grad & Prof Educ; Am Educ Res Asn. **Home Addr:** 950 Whitmore 110, Detroit, MI 48203.

### GORDON, ESQ. CLAUDIA LORRAINE
Lawyer, secretary (organization). **Personal:** Born Jamaica. **Educ:** Howard Univ, BA, polit sci, 1995; Am Univ, Wash Col Law, JD, 2000. **Career:** Nat Asn Deaf Law Ctr, staff atty, advocacy leadership, 1989, Disability Community Off Pub Engagement at White House Off Pub Engagement, assoc dir, pub engagement advisor, 2013-; Civil Prac Clin, Wash Col Law; DC Serv-Ment Health Div, pub defender; Nat Black Deaf Advocates Asn, vpres; Nat Coun Disability, independent consult; US Dept Homeland Security Off Civil Rights & Civil Liberties, atty adv, sr policy adv; Off Fed Contracts & Compliance Progs US Dept Labor, spec asst to dir; Skadden fel; Gallaudet Univ, Gallaudet's Dept Social Work, lectr. **Orgs:** Bd trustee & secy, Lexington Sch Deaf & Ctr Deaf, 2004-; bd trustees, Gallaudet Univ, 2011; fel Golden Key Nat Hon Soc; fel Polit Sci Hon Soc; Black Law Stud Asn; vpres, Nat Black Deaf Advocates Asn; Black Deaf Advocates. **Honors/Awds:** Paul G Hearne & AAPD Leadership Award, 2002; Paul G Hearne Leadership Award, Am Asn People with Disabilities, 2003; Secretarys Gold Medal Award, 2006; Deaf Person of the Year, Deaf Life Mags, 2010. **Special Achievements:** First Black deaf female attorney in the US. **Business Addr:** Public Engagement Advisor, National Association of the Deaf, 8630 Fenton St Suite 820, Silver Spring, NY 20910-3819, **Business Phone:** (301)587-1788.

### GORDON, DARRIEN X. JAMAL
Football player. **Personal:** Born Nov 14, 1970, Shawnee, OK; son of James and Goldia; children: Jalil Tanyu Gamnje & Najim Tariq Gamnje. **Educ:** Stanford Univ, grad. **Career:** Football player (retired); San Diego Chargers, punt returner, 1993-96, right cornerback, 1993, left cornerback, 1994-96; Denver Broncos, punt returner & right cornerback, 1997-98; Oakland Raiders, strong safety, 1999, 2000, 2002; Atlanta Falcons, defensive back & strong safety, 2001; Green Bay Packers, 2002. **Honors/Awds:** Four Times All Pro Selection, 1994, 1996, 1997, 2001; Super Bowl Champion, XXXII, XXXIII. **Special Achievements:** Films: 1994 AFC Championship Game, 1995; Super Bowl XXIX, 1995; 1997 AFC Championship Game, 1998; Super Bowl XXXII, 1998; 1998 AFC Championship Game, 1999; Super Bowl XXXIII, 1999; Super Bowl XXXVII, 2003.

### GORDON, DWAYNE K.
Manager, football player, business owner. **Personal:** Born Nov 2, 1969, White Plains, NY; son of Bob; married Melissa. **Educ:** Univ NH, sociol, 1992; Nat Acad Sports Med, cert performance enhancement specialist, cert corrective exercise specialist, cert cert personal trainer. **Career:** Football player (retired), manager; Miami Dolphins, 1993; Atlanta Falcons, linebacker, 1993-95; San Diego Chargers, linebacker, 1995, 1996-97; New York Jets, left inside linebacker, 1997, 1999, linebacker, 1998, 2001; Three Amigos Pool Construct & Plastering, owner, 2003-05; New York Sports Club, fitness mgr, 2007-09, 2012-13, master trainer, 2013-14; 24 Hour Fitness, fitness mgr, 2009-12; LA Fitness, weekend gen mgr, 2012; Equinox, personal training mgr, 2014-. **Business Addr:** Personal Training Manager, Equinox, 895 Broadway, New York, NY 10003, **Business Phone:** (212)677-0180.

### GORDON, DR. EDMUND W.
Educator, college teacher, executive director. **Personal:** Born Jun 13, 1921, Goldsboro, NC; son of Tayloe and Mabel; married Susan Elizabeth Gitt; children: Edmund T, Christopher W, Jessica G & Johanna S. **Educ:** Howard Univ, BS, zool, 1942, Sch Divinity, BD, social ethics, 1945; Am Univ, MA, social psychol, 1950; Columbia Univ Teachers Col, EdD, child develop & guid, 1957. **Career:** Educator (retired), administrator; Yeshiva Univ, Ferkauf Grad Sch, Dept Spec Educ, chmn, 1959-60, Albert Einstein Col Med, res assoc prof pediat, 1961-68; Proj Head Start, dir div res & eval, 1965-67; Ferkauf Univ, Dept Educ, Psychol & Guid, chmn, 1965-68; Columbia Univ, Dept Guid, chmn, 1968-73; Teachers Col, dir div health serv sci & educ, 1970-73; Am J Orthopsychiatry, ed, 1978-83; Rev Res Educ, ed, 1981-84; Yale Univ, John M Musser prof psychol, John M Musser prof psychol emer, 1991-; City Univ NY Grad Sch, distinguished prof, educ psychol, 1992-96, Col Bd, sr adv to pres, 1992-98, exec dir acad affairs, 1998-2000; Teachers Col, Columbia Univ, vpres acad affairs & interim dean, 2000-01; Columbia Univ, Inst Urban & Minority Educ, Teachers Col, Richard March Hoe prof psychol & educ dir, 2001-, Richard March Hoe prof emer psychol & educ; Ctr Excellence Teaching & Learning, scholar-in residence, 2006-07; City Col New York, vis prof. **Orgs:** Fel life mem AAAS; fel Am Psychol Asn; fel Am Psychol Soc; fel Orthopsychiatric Asn; Asn Black Psychologists; AERA; trustee, Pub Educ Asn; trustee, Savings Bank Rockland County Monsey; AERA Plaque Life. **Honors/Awds:** Outstanding Achievements Award, Howard Alumni, 1973; elected, Nat Acad Educ, 1968; DHL, Yeshiva Univ, 1986; DHL, Brown Univ, 1988; DHL, Bank St Col, 1992; Teachers College Medal for Distinguished service to Education, Columbia Univ, 1993; Distinguished Career Contrib Award, Am Educ Res Asn, 1994; Hon Degree, Yale Univ; Hon DSc, Mt Holyoke Col; Hon DHL, Howard Univ, 1998. **Home Addr:** 3 Cooper Morris Dr, Pomona, NY 10970-3309, **Home Phone:** (914)354-5809. **Business Addr:** Richard March Hoe Professor Emeritus, Director, Columbia University, Inst Urban Minority Educ, New York, NY 10027, **Business Phone:** (212)678-3444.

### GORDON, EDWARD LANSING, III (ED GORDON)
Journalist. **Personal:** Born Aug 17, 1960, Detroit, MI; son of Edward Lansing Jr (deceased); married Karen Haney; children: Taylor. **Educ:** Western Mich Univ, BD, commun & polit sci, 1982. **Career:** Show: "Detroit Black Journal", host, 1986; "Black Men Speak Out: The Aftermath", host, 1992; "Conversations with Ed Gordon", host; "MSNBC", host; "BET Tonight", host, 2001-02; "Lead Story and Teen Summit", host; "Our World with Black Enterprise", host, 2006; "Weekly with Ed Gordon", hosy, 2010; WTVS-TV, prod asst, 1983-85, host, 1985-88; Black Entertainment TV, host, anchor, journalist, 1988-04, anchor & journalist, 2010-; NBC News, host, reporter, corresp; CBS-TV, corresp, 2004-05; Nat Pub Radio, host, 2005-10; Gordon Media Group, owner & chief exec officer, currently. **Honors/Awds:** Emmy Award, Acad Television Arts & Sci; Image Award, Na Asn Advan Colored People; Journalist of the Year Award, Nat Asn Black Journalists; Award for Merit Distinction & Excellence, Commun Excellence Black Audiences. **Special Achievements:** First journalist to interview former NFL star O J Simpson. **Business Addr:** Host, National Public Radio, 635 Mass Ave NW Suite 1, Washington, DC 20001, **Business Phone:** (202)513-3232.

### GORDON, GARTH
Executive, president (organization), founder (originator). **Career:** Phones Etc, founder & pres, 1994-. **Business Addr:** Founder, President, Phones Etc, 8263 Cswy Blvd Suite E, Tampa, FL 33619, **Business Phone:** (813)626-7931.

### GORDON, HELEN A.
Lawyer. **Personal:** Born Jul 20, 1923, NY; married Joseph A Bailey (deceased); children: Josette, Jonathan & Gordon C. **Educ:** Hunter Col, NY, AB, 1947; Brooklyn Law Sch, LLB, JD, 1950. **Career:** Pvt pract; AAA, arbitrator; City Col NY, lectr continuing educ; Gordon & Wilkins, atty, currently. **Orgs:** Bd trustee, Grahan Sch Child Hastings Hudson, NY; bd dir, E Tremone Child Care Ctr; Bronx & Women's Bar Asn; Gothamettes Inc; Ny Bar Asn, 1950-. **Home Addr:** 630 W 158 St, New York, NY 10032. **Business Addr:** Attorney, Gordon & Wilkins, 304 W 138th St, New York, NY 10030-2002, **Business Phone:** (212)690-2990.

### GORDON, JOI
Chief executive officer. **Personal:** daughter of Joyce Palmer; married Errol; children: Sydney & Nicholas. **Educ:** Univ Okla, BA, 1993, Radio & TB Broadcasting, Col Law, JD. **Career:** Bronx Criminal Ct, asst dist atty; Dress Success Worldwide, chief exec officer, 1999-. **Orgs:** Bd dir, Urban Brands; adv coun mem, Am Airlines; adv coun mem, Off Depot; adv coun mem, VOICE (imprint Hyperion Bks); adv coun mem, My Daughter's Keeper; Greater Queens Chap Links Inc, Am's Charities, 2007-. **Business Addr:** 32 E 31st St, New York, NY 10016, **Business Phone:** (212)532-1922.

### GORDON, LANCASTER
Basketball player. **Personal:** Born Jun 24, 1962, Jackson, MS. **Educ:** Univ Louisville, attended 1984. **Career:** Basketball player (retired); Los Angeles Clippers, 1984-88; Pensacola Tornados, 1988-89; La Crosse Catbirds, 1989-90; Sioux Falls Skyforce, 1990-91;Continental Basketball Association, 1988-91. **Home Addr:** , Jackson, MS 39201, **Home Phone:** (601)922-7496.

### GORDON, LEVAN
Judge. **Personal:** Born Apr 10, 1933, Philadelphia, PA; married Vivian J; children: Shari-Lyn L. **Educ:** Lincoln Univ Pa, AB; Howard Univ Law Sch, LLB; Pa State Univ. **Career:** Judge (retired); Gov Comn Chester, Pa, assoc coun, 1964; Philadelphia Housing Info Serv, exec dir, 1966-68; Pa Labor Rel Bd, hearing examr, 1971-74; Munic Ct Philadelphia, judge, Ct Common Please Philadelphia, judge, 1979; Temple Univ Sch Criminal Justice, instr; Georgetown Univ, Intensive Session Trial Advocacy Skills, instr; Ct Common Pleas, judge. **Orgs:** Alpha Phi Alpha; Zeta Omicron Lambda; Lincoln Univ Alumni Asn; W Philadelphia HS Alumni Asn; Philadelphia Bar Asn; Pa Bar Asn; Lawyers Club Phila; Am Judicature Soc; Am Bar Asn; Nat Bar Asn, Pa Conf Trial Judges; Philadelphia Tribune Charities; Philadelphia Tribune Bowling League; Chris J Perry Lodge Elks IBPOE W; Nat Bowling Asn; Am Bowling Cong; AFNA Preceptor Prog; Nat Asn Blacks Criminal Justice; World Asn Judges; bd dir, Nat Kidney Found; Men Malvern; bd trustee, supvr jr ushers, Tindley Temple United Methodist Church; Black Methodist Church Renewal; bd dir, Combined Health Appeal Am; bd dir, Nat Kidney Found, currently; bd trustee, alumni trustee, Lincoln Univ; Communities Sch Philadelphia Inc. **Honors/Awds:** Distinguished Service Award, Liberty Bell Dist Philadelphia Coun Boy Scouts Am; Community Service Award, Strawberry Mansion Civic Asn Puerto Rican; Achievement Award, Lincoln University Alumni; Man of the Year, Zeta Omicron Lambda Chap, Alpha Phi Alpha, 1975; Man of the Year Award, Asn Bus & Prof Women Philadelphia & Vicinity, 1984; Distinguished Service Award, McMichael Home & Sch Asn; Award of Excellence, Methodist Men Tindley Temple United Methodist Church, 1986; Hall of Fame, W Philadelphia High Sch. **Home Addr:** 906 E Slocum St, Philadelphia, PA 19150-3608, **Home Phone:** (215)276-8899.

### GORDON, PATRICK HENRY
Detective. **Personal:** Born Oct 22, 1959, Kalamazoo, MI; son of Henry and Griselda Daniel. **Educ:** Kalamazoo Valley Community Col, AA, 1983; Western Mich Univ, BS, 1985; Univ Md, MS, 2002. **Career:** Correctional officer, 1985-87; probation officer, 1987-99; chief case mgr, 1994-95; Off Corp Coun, investr, 1999-. **Orgs:** Criminal Justice Student asn. **Special Achievements:** Certified Notary for the District of Columbia. **Home Addr:** 7031 Palamar Turn, Lanham, MD 20783, **Home Phone:** (301)794-0014. **Business Addr:** Investigator, Office of the Corp Counsel, 441 4th St NW Suite 600 S, Washington, DC 20001, **Business Phone:** (202)727-3400.

### GORDON, RONALD EUGENE
Executive. **Personal:** Born Feb 22, 1946, Springfield, OH; married Felicity Ralph; children: Mark, Rebecca & Ryan. **Educ:** Cent State Univ, BS, 1973; Xavier Univ, MBA, 1976. **Career:** Continental Can Co, prod supvr, 1971-77; Formica Corp, prod supvr, 1977-79; Miller Brewing Co, prod supvr, 1979-. **Honors/Awds:** The Olubandek Dada Award, Dept Bus Admin, Central State Univ, 1973. **Home Addr:** 4917 Shady Pine Dr, Greensboro, NC 27455, **Home Phone:** (336)282-2364. **Business Addr:** Production Supervisor, Miller Brewing Co, PO Box 1170, Reidsville, NC 27320.

### GORDON, DR. SHERMAN A.
Clergy. **Personal:** Born May 27, 1972, Greenwood, MS; son of Turner Jr and Malissie C Price; married Marina Renee; children: Exodus Niaa & Eden Hill. **Educ:** Univ Calif, Santa Barbara, CA, BA, pre law & sociol, 1994; Claremont Sch Theol, Claremont, CA, MAR, relig, 1999; Univ Phoenix, MA, educ; United Theol Sem, DMin, 2001. **Career:** Marcus Garvey Elem sch, teacher, 1995; Brookins Comm AME Church, youth minister, 1995-97; New Philadelphia AME Church, sr pastor, 1997-; Univ Phoenix, educ instr; Family Faith Christian Ctr, founder & sr pastor, 2010-. **Orgs:** Counr, Upward Bound, 1992-94; pres, NuPower Community Outreach, 2001-02; pres, NuPhilly Invest club, 2001-03; pres, Nat Asn Advan Colored People, 2002-; dir, Men's Ministry Southern Calif A.M.E. 5th Dist; chmn bd, NuPower Community Outreach Serv Inc; comnr, City Carson's Fine Arts & Hist Comn; founder & chief exec officer, Sherman Gordon Ministries, 2004-; United Negro Col Fund Clergy Adv Bd; bd mem, First Church God Sch Ministry; bd mem, New Philadelphia AME Church. **Business Addr:** Senior Pastor, Family of Faith Christian Center, 345 E Carson St, Long Beach, CA 90807, **Business Phone:** (562)595-1222.

### GORDON, THOMAS FLYNN (TOM GORDON)
Baseball player. **Personal:** Born Nov 18, 1967, Sebring, FL. **Career:** Baseball player (retired); Kans City Royals, pitcher, 1988-95; Boston Red Sox, pitcher, 1996-99; Chicago Cubs, pitcher, 2001-02; Houston Astros, pitcher, 2002; Chicago White Sox, pitcher, 2003; New York Yankees, pitcher, 2004-05; Philadelphia Phillies, pitcher, 2006-08; Ariz Diamondbacks, pitcher, 2009-10. **Home Addr:** 1052 Highlands Ave, Avon Park, FL 33825. **Business Addr:** Professional Baseball Player, Philadelphia Phillies, Veterans Stadium, Philadelphia, PA 19148, **Business Phone:** (215)463-6000.

### GORDON, WALTER LEAR, III
Educator, lawyer. **Personal:** Born Mar 6, 1942, Los Angeles, CA; married Teresa Sanchez; children: Maya Luz. **Educ:** Ohio St Univ, BA, 1963; Univ Calif, Los Angeles, MPA, 1965, JD, 1973, PhD, polit sci, 1981. **Career:** Univ Calif Los Angeles Law Sch, eaching asst & res asst, polit sci dept, lectr, teaching asst & res asst, 1967-69, lectr polit sci dept, 1978-82; Calif State Univ at Los Angeles, Black Polit, Pan African Studies Dept, Teacher, 1969-71; pvt pract atty, 1974-; Gordon Law Firm, atty, currently. **Orgs:** Bd mem, SCLC W, 1980-85; Langston Bar Asn, 1986. **Special Achievements:** Publications: The Law & Pvt Police, Rand, 1971, Crime & Criminal Law also published several articles; The Nat Turner Insurrection Trials: A Mystic Chord Resonates Today, 2009; Author of numerous books. **Home Addr:** 1227 Westerly Terr, Los Angeles, CA 90026-2121, **Home Phone:** (323)662-9986. **Business Addr:** Attorney, The Gordon Law Firm, 2658 Griffith Pk Blvd Suite 176, Los Angeles, CA 90039-2520, **Business Phone:** (323)662-1243.

### GORDON-DILLARD, JOAN YVONNE
Educator. **Personal:** Born Oct 4, 1955, Eglin AFB, FL; daughter of Charles Robert and Lois Jackson; married Marvin Clinton. **Educ:** Fisk Univ, BA, 1977; La Sorbonne, Paris, France, cert, 1976; Ohio State Univ, MA, 1978, PhD, 1982. **Career:** Fel, Ohio State Univ, 1977; US Dept Labor, educ media specialist, 1979; Ohio State Univ, coordr res, develop & support, 1983-94; IBM, info developer, 1984-86, educ specialist, 1986-87, mkt rep, 1988-90, adv instr, developer, 1990-94; Lucent Technol, proj mgr distance learning, 1996. **Orgs:** Alpha Kappa Alpha Sorority Inc, 1978-; Asn Commun & Technol, 1982-85, 1993; Doug Williams Found, 1988-89; Minority Athletes Networking Inc, fund raising, 1990-; Crescent Moon Found, 1990-; Women Commun, 1991, 1993; team leader, IBM Aristotle Prog, 1992-. **Home Addr:** 1 Edgewater Rd, Cliffside Park, NJ 07010, **Home Phone:** (201)945-6310. **Business Addr:** Project Manager, Lucent Technol Inc, 140 Centennial Ave, Piscataway, NJ 08854, **Business Phone:** (908)457-7301.

## GORDON-REED, ANNETTE

College teacher. **Personal:** Born Nov 19, 1958, Livingston, TX; married Richard Reed; children: 2. **Educ:** Dartmouth Col, AB, 1981; Harvard Law Sch, JD, 1984. **Career:** New York Bd Correction, coun, 1987-92; New York Law Sch, Wallace Stevens Prof Law, 1992-2010; Rutgers Univ, Bd Gov Prof Hist, 2007-10; Harvard Univ, prof, 2010-; Harvard Law Sch, Charles Warren Prof Am Legal Hist, 2010-; Radcliffe Inst Advan Study, Carol K. Pforzheimer Prof, 2010-; Queen's Col, Oxford Univ, Harold Vyvyan Harmsworth Vis Prof Am Hist, 2014-15. **Orgs:** Am Acad Arts & Sci, fel, 2011-; Comn Humanities & Social Sci, Am Acad Arts & Sci, mem. **Special Achievements:** Author of "Thomas Jefferson and Sally Hemings: An American Controversy" (1997), "The Hemingses of Monticello: An American Family" (2008); coauthor of "Vernon Can Read! A Memoir" (2001), "The Most Blessed of Patriarchs: Thomas Jefferson and the Empire of Imagination" (2015); editor of "Race on Trial: Law and Justice in American History" (2002). **Business Addr:** Harvard Law School, Griswold 405, Cambridge, MA 02138-2801, **Business Phone:** (617)495-3894.

## GORDY, BERRY, JR.

Executive, television producer, composer. **Personal:** Born Nov 28, 1929, Detroit, MI; son of Berry Sr and Bertha Fuller; married Grace Eaton; children: Berry IV, Terry James, Hazel Joy, Kerry A, Kennedy W & Stefan K; married Thelma Coleman; children: Kerry Ashby; married Raynona Singleton. **Career:** Featherweight boxer; auto worker; composer; 3-D Rec Mart, owner; composer: You Made Me So Very Happy; Motown Rec Corp, founder & pres, 1959-88; Tamla Rec, founder; Motown Rec Co, founder & owner; Films: Lady Sings the Blues, 1972; Mahogany, dir, 1975; The Wiz, exec producer, 1978; The Last Dragon, producer, 1985; Soundtrack: Daddy Day Care, 2003; The Ital Job, 2003; Lord of War, 2005; Jarhead, 2005. **Orgs:** Dir Guild Am; chmn, Motown Ind entertainment complex. **Honors/Awds:** Bus Achievement Award, Interracial Coun Bus Opportunity, 1967; SecondAnnual American Music Award, 1975; Whitney M Young Jr Award, Los Angeles Urban League, 1980; exec producer film Berry Gordy's The Last Dragon, 1984; elected Gordon Grand Fel, Yale Univ, 1985; inducted into the Rock and Roll Hall of Fame, 1988; Junior Achievement U.S. Business Hall of Fame, 1998; hon degree, Mich State Univ, 2006; hondegree, Occidental Col, 2007; Michigan Rock and Roll Legends Hall of Fame, 2009; Songwriters Hall of Fame's Pioneer Award, 2013. **Special Achievements:** One of Five Leading Entrepreneurs of Nation, Babson Col, 1978; author, Berry Gordy: To Be Loved, 1994. **Home Addr:** Sarbonne Rd, Los Angeles, CA 90077.

## GORDY, DESIREE D'LAURA

Lawyer. **Personal:** Born Jul 14, 1956, Long Beach, CA; married Terry J Sr; children: Terry James Jr & Whitney Jade. **Educ:** San Diego St Univ, BA, 1978; Southwestern Univ Sch Law, JD, 1982. **Career:** Jobete Music Co Inc, in-house coun; Motown Productions Inc, in-house coun; Motown Rec Corp, in-house coun, 1983-88; State Bar Calif, 1983-; WORK Rec, Div MCA Rec, outside coun & bus affairs, 1987-90; Ice Cube & Pat Charbonnet, in-house coun, 1990-92; Law offices Desiree Gordy, lawyer, currently. **Orgs:** Vol, Bradley Gov Campaign, 1986; vol, All Africa Games Kenya, 1987; BlackWomen Lawyers Asn; John Langston Bar Asn; Calif Women's Lawyers Asn; Women Lawyers Asn Los Angeles; sponsor c underdeveloped nations. **Honors/Awds:** Top 100 Black Bus & Prof Women, 1986. **Home Addr:** 2259 Chelan Dr, Los Angeles, CA 90068. **Business Addr:** Lawyer, Law Offices of Desiree Gordy, 7095 Hollywood Blvd Suite 600, Los Angeles, CA 90028-6035, **Business Phone:** (323)874-3918.

## GORDY, SONJA M.

School administrator. **Career:** St Anthony Catholic Sch, admin asst.

## GORE, CEDRIC J.

Entrepreneur, software developer, musician. **Personal:** Born Jul 24, 1969, Brooklyn, NY; son of Roy and Lillian; married April Leite. **Educ:** Johnson & Wales Univ, AS, hospitality mgt; Fla Int Univ, BS, bus mgt. **Career:** Kapkin Communs, sr web developer, 1998-2000; Javakitty Media, pres, 1998-2002; CD Intelligence LLC, pres, chief technol officer, 2003-10; Crowd Fusion, support engr, 2011-12; Daily, QA engr, 2011-13, Fuzz Productions, QA engr, 2013-15; Refinery29 Inc, QA engr, 2015-. **Business Addr:** QA Engineer, Refinery29 Inc, 79 Leonard St, New York, NY 10013, **Business Phone:** (212)966-3112.

## GORE, DAVID L.

Lawyer. **Personal:** Born Dec 17, 1937, Horry County, SC; son of Samuel B and Sadie M Anderson; married Mary L Andrews; children: David Jr & Sheila. **Educ:** Allen Univ, BA, 1959; SC St Col, MEd, 1966; Howard Univ Sch Law, JD, 1969. **Career:** St. Helena High Sch, teacher, 1959-60; Palmetto High Sch, teacher, 1963-66; Nat Labor Rels Bd, legal asst to chmn, 1969-70; United Steelworkers Am, asst gen counr, 1970-81, dist counr, 1982-; Gore & Gore, 1999. **Orgs:** Ill Bar Asn; Pa Bar Asn; 3rd 6th 7th & 10th & DC Ct Appeals, US Supreme Ct; Phi Alpha Delta Legal Fraternity. **Home Addr:** 7209 Richard Rd, Darien, CT 60561-3564, **Home Phone:** (312)852-4886. **Business Addr:** Counsel District 7, United Steelworkers of America, 15 N MI Ave Suite 706, Chicago, IL 60601, **Business Phone:** (312)616-4224.

## GORE, JAMES ANTHONY

Executive. **Personal:** Born Jul 25, 1971, Brooklyn, NY; son of Roy and Lillian. **Educ:** Cleveland State Univ, BA, bus admin & finance, 1998. **Career:** WW Grainger, Internet Com Div, sales, customer serv, 1993-2000; Javakitty Media, co-founder, vpres, dir mkt & sales, 1998-2002; Ginyard Trucking, bus oper analyst; CD Intelligence, vpres, sales, 2002-. **Orgs:** Bd Adv, Gruuve Inc. **Business Addr:** Vice President, CD Intelligence, 1117 Peachtree Walk Suite 121, Atlanta, GA 30309-3950, **Business Phone:** (404)817-8050.

## GORE, JOHN MICHEL

Government official. **Personal:** Born Aug 6, 1955, Columbus, OH; son of John L and Rose M; married Judith Ann Jackson; children: Johnel Marie & Janee Michelle. **Educ:** Bowling Green State Univ, bus admin, 1976. **Career:** Government official (retired); Ohio State Auditor, welfare investr, 1976, asst auditor, 1978, asst auditor in-chg, 1984, field audit supv, 1987, asst audit mgr, 1990, asst dep auditor, 1992-; City Columbus, equal bus opportunity specialist, 1995-96, admin analyst II, 1996-97, regional exec dir, exec asst dir, 1997-08; Alpha Midwestern, regional exec dir, 2004. **Orgs:** Nat Asn Black Acct; Nat Asn Cert Fraud Examiners, 1992-; deacon bd & finance com, Free & Accepted Masons; Sec Baptist Church; UNF; Alpha Phi Alpha Fraternity. **Honors/Awds:** Exceptional Service Award, Alpha Phi Alpha, 1989, 1999; Man of the Year, Sec Baptist Church, 1990; Chapter Member of the Year, Nat Asn Black Accountants, Columbus, 1992-93. **Home Addr:** 424 Hanton Way, Columbus, OH 43213-4461, **Home Phone:** (614)475-9956.

## GORE, JOSEPH A.

School administrator, association executive. **Personal:** Born Supply, NC; married Gloria Gardner; children: Duane K. **Educ:** Livingstone Col, BS, 1952; Univ Mich, MS, 1960; Yale Univ, MPH, 1970; Univ Mass, EdD, 1977. **Career:** Mary Holmes Col, dean men & sci instr, 1956-58, dean students, 1959-62, acad dean, 1962-68, dir health servs, 1968-70, pres, 1972; Mary Holmes High Sch, prin, 1958-59; Tougaloo Col, acad dean, 1970-72; Brunswick Community Col, spec asst to pres, currently, Brunswick DESTINY Steering Comt, chairperson, currently. **Orgs:** FAFEO; Am Pub Asn; Nat Educ Asn; Clay City Chamber Com; bd dir, I M Hosp; bd trustee, Burnswick Community Hosp; Cape Fear Area United Way; Brunswick Co Parks & Recreation; Brunswick Community Col Found; gov appointee, Supply NC Coastal Resources Comn; pres, S Brunswick Islands Rotary Club; adv bd, Brunswick Co Div. **Home Addr:** PO Box 1257, West Point, MS 39773. **Business Addr:** Special Associate to President, Brunswick Community College, 50 Col Rd, Supply, NC 28462-0030, **Business Phone:** (910)755-7475.

## GORMAN, BERTHA GAFFNEY

Executive, association executive. **Personal:** Born Greenville, TX; daughter of Vivian Shoals and Bernice; married Prentice; children: Gregory G & Glen G. **Educ:** Sacramento Community Col & Am River Col, attended 1969; Calif State Univ, Sacramento, BA, commun, jour & related progs, 1973; Univ Uppsala, Sweden, int rels & affairs, 1973. **Career:** Sacramento Bee Newspaper, reporter, 1971-79; CA State Dept Ment Health, pub info officer, 1979-80; CA State Assembly, prin consult in-chg media, 1980-85; Lockheed Corp, Cala basas, dir issues mgt, 1985-2000, dir state local govt affairs, 1985-2000; State & Local Govt Affairs, Lockheed Martin, dir, 1995; CA State, Asn Secy External Affairs, Health & Human Serv Agency, assoc secy, 2000-04; Gaffney, Gorman & Assoc, dir, currently; Life Abbr & Educ Proj, pres & chief exec officer, 2012-. **Orgs:** Bd chair, Sacramento Regional Asst Dist, 1981-85; secy, Black Pub Rels Soc CA, LA, 1986-90; Black Women's Forum, LA, 1987; vice chair, Great Beginning Black Babies Task Force, LA, 1990-91; bd dir, Cares Clin, 2002; Legis Advocate CA, Nat Asn Advan Colored People, currently; bd dir, Am Cancer Soc, CA Div; Am Cancer Soc Mkt & Commun Comt, CA Div. **Honors/Awds:** Black Public Relations Society Honoree, 1991; PRSA Prism Award, 1994; IABC Merit Award. **Home Addr:** 18 Wensley Pl, Sacramento, CA 95835-2192, **Home Phone:** (916)419-7085. **Business Addr:** Associate Secretary, California Department of Health, PO Box 997413, Sacramento, CA 95899-7413, **Business Phone:** (916)654-3304.

## GOSLEE, DR. LEONARD THOMAS

Physician, pediatrician. **Personal:** Born Aug 5, 1932, Salisbury, MD. **Educ:** Howard Univ, BS; Boston Univ, MS; Meharry Med Col, MD. **Career:** Detroit Gen Hosp, internship, 1958-59; C's Hosp Mich, residency, 1959-62, chief residency, 1962-63; Laguardia Med Group Inc, physician, 1964-; pvt pract, currently. **Orgs:** Nat Med Asn; Am Acad Pediatrics; NY State Med Asn; Queens Col Med Asn; Am Asn Pediatrics; Sch Health Planning Prog; AMA. **Home Addr:** 639 W End Ave 11A, New York, NY 10025. **Business Addr:** Physician, 11218 Springfield Blvd, Jamaica, NY 11429, **Business Phone:** (718)479-6600.

## GOSS, CLAYTON

Playwright. **Personal:** Born Jan 1, 1946, Philadelphia, PA; children: 1. **Educ:** Howard Univ, Wash, DC. **Career:** Novelist & Playwright; Plays: "Homecookin"; "Of Being Hit"; "Space in Time"; "Bird of Paradise"; "Ornette"; "Oursides"; "Mars"; "Andrew"; Howard Univ, Washington, DC, playwright-in-residence & instr; Novels: Bill Pickett; Black Bulldogger. **Home Addr:** 6653 Sprague St, Philadelphia, PA 19119, **Home Phone:** (215)844-5017.

## GOSS, LINDA

Storyteller, folk artist, cultural historian. **Personal:** Born Alcoa, TN; daughter of Willie Louise McNair and Willie Murphy McNair; married Clay; children: Aisha, Uhuru & Jamal. **Educ:** Howard Univ, Wash, DC, BA, drama, 1969; Antioch Univ, Yellow Springs, OH, ME, educ, 1978. **Career:** Prof storyteller; Smithsonian Inst, several mus, performer; maj mus, festivals, univs, performer; Nat Asn Black Storytellers Inc, co-founder, officer & bd mem, 1982-; Rosenbach Mus, artist-in-residence, currently; PFPs Local Knowledge proj, featured artist, currently; E Tenn State Univ, Geier Found, vis prof, 2005. **Orgs:** Pres, Asn Black Storytelling, 1984-; pres, Hola Kumba Ya Cult Orgn, 1989-; founding mem, Keepers Cult; Zeta Phi Beta Sorority; lifetime mem, Griot Circle Md, 2007. **Honors/Awds:** Linda Goss Day, City Wash, DC, named in honor, 1983; Official Storyteller of Philadelphia, City Philadelphia, PA, 1984; Lind Goss Day, City Alcoa, TN, named in honor, 1986; Talk That Talk, anthology African-American storytelling, Simon & Schuster, 1989, Best Paperback of 1989, Publ Weekly, selected by Book of the Month Club for their Quality Paperback Club; Oracle Lifetime Achievement Award in Storytelling, Nat Storytelling Network, 2003; Leeway Transformation Award, 2006; Parson Fund Award, Benjamin A. Botkin Scholar Lecturer Award, Am Folk Life Ctr Libr Cong, 2006. **Special Achievements:** Co-author of The Baby Elopard book and cassette, Bantam/Doubleday/Dell, 1989. **Home Addr:** 6653 Sprague St, Philadelphia, PA 19119, **Home Phone:** (215)844-5017. **Business Addr:** Co-Founder, National Association Black Storytellers Inc, PO Box 67722, Baltimore, MD 21215, **Business Phone:** (410)947-1117.

## GOSS, TOM A.

Vice president (organization), athletic director, executive. **Personal:** Born Jul 6, 1946, Knoxville, TN; married Carol Goings; children: Anika, Fatima & Maloni. **Educ:** Univ Mich, Ann Arbor, BS, phys educ, 1968. **Career:** Procter & Gamble Corp, 1969; R J Reynolds Industs, regional mgr, 1970; Del Monte Corp, regional vpres, sales mgt staff; Faygo Beverage, Detroit, Mich, vpres sales & mkt; Nat Beverage Corp, exec vpres, 1987-93; PIA Merchandising, Irvine, Calif, pres & chief operating officer, 1993-97; Univ Mich, athletic dir, 1997-2000; The Goss Group Inc, managing partner & advisor, 1997, chmn, 2000-; Goss LLC, chmn, 2000-; Goss Group Marsh Inc, chmn, 2001; GMAC Ins Group, chmn, 2001; Goss LLC, chmn, 2001; Goss Steel & Processing LLC, chmn, 2003-; Bristol Logistics LLC, chmn, currently. **Orgs:** Bd mem, Nat African Am Ins Asn; vice chmn bd, dir, chmn, United Am Healthcare Corp, 2000-; bd mem, Nat African-Am Ins Asn; Barbara Ann Karmanos Inst; Boys & Girls Club Southeastern Mich; Detroit Tigers Baseball Adv Bd; United Am Healthcare Corp; Omni Care Health Plan Inc; bd chair, Detroit Workforce Develop Bd; trustee, African Am Experience Fund Nat Parks Serv & Found. **Business Addr:** Chairman, Goss LLC, 600 Renaissance Ctr Suite 1200, Detroit, MI 48243, **Business Phone:** (313)446-9636.

## GOSS, WILLIAM EPP

Executive. **Personal:** Born Feb 3, 1941, Baltimore, MD; married Charlotte H; children: Maisha, Zuri, Salah & Rasanah. **Educ:** Morgan State Univ, BA, 1968; Univ Chicago, Grad Sch Bus, MA, soc serv admin, 1970, MBA, 1975. **Career:** Talent Asst Prog Inc, asso dir, 1975-76, exec dir, 1976-; Minority Bus, mgt consult; Henry Booth House Settlement-Hull House Asn, ctr dir; Univ IL, Jan Addams Sch Work, field instr; Henry Booth House, pres & chief exec officer, currently. **Orgs:** Nat Asn Soc Workers; Asn Black MBA'S; Asn Black Soc Workers; bd dir, Hull House Asn. **Home Addr:** 6108 S Dorchester Ave, Chicago, IL 60637, **Home Phone:** (773)363-0611. **Business Addr:** President, Chief Executive Officer, Henry Booth House, 2929 S Wabash, Chicago, IL 60628, **Business Phone:** (312)225-0800.

## GOSS-SEEGER, DEBRA A.

Manager. **Personal:** Born Apr 21, 1958, San Francisco, CA; daughter of Waymond and Mildred Wilson; married Willie; children: Justin. **Educ:** Alameda Jr Col, AS, bus admin, 1986; Univ San Francisco, Calif, BS, bus admin, 1989; John F Kennedy Univ, MBA, orgn leadership, 2000; Univ Calif, Berkeley, Calif. **Career:** Xerox Corp, Sunnyvale, Calif, exec acct rep, 1975-80; Clorox Corp, Oakland, Calif, admin asst, 1980-85; Pac Gas & Elec Co, Berkeley, Calif, mkt mgr, sr community affairs mgr, 1989-99, maj acct rep; Hewlett-packard Co, mgr mkt commun, mgr prod mkt, mgr diversity & inclusion, 2000-05; Home Depot, mgr commun, sr mgr mkt, commun mgr, 2005-08; Lowe's Home Improv, mkt opers mgr, 2008-11; Microsoft, sr channel & partner mkt mgr, 2011-14; Intel Corp, prod mkt engr, 2014-. **Orgs:** Bd mem, NBMBAA Houston Chap, 2001-05; Brookhollow Baptist Church, 2004-07; Am Mkt Assoc; Nat Commun Assoc; exec comt mem, Nat Black MBA Asn. **Home Addr:** 1031 Chestnut St, Oakland, CA 94607. **Business Addr:** Product Marketing Engineer, Intel Corp, 2200 Mission Col Blvd, Santa Clara, CA 95052, **Business Phone:** (408)765-8080.

## GOSSETT, LOUIS CAMERON, JR.

Actor, social worker. **Personal:** Born May 27, 1936, Brooklyn, NY; son of Louis Sr and Hellen Rebecca Wray; married Hattie Glascoe; married Christina Mangosing; children: Sate; married Cyndi James; children: Sharron. **Educ:** NY Univ, BA, drama. **Career:** Actor, made Broadway debut in Take A Giant Step; The Desk Set, Broadway; Lost in the Stars, Broadway; Raisin in the Sun, Broadway; The Blacks; My Sweet Charlie; Carry Me Back to Morning side Heights; The Charlatan; Tell Pharoah; Roots; Murderous Angels, 1971-72; Chicago, 1996; TV series: "Inside", 1996; The "Inspectors", 1998; "Love Songs", 1999; "Strange Justice", 1999; "Dr Lucille", 2000; "For Love of Olivia", 2001; "Resurrection Boulevard", 2002; "What About Your Friends: Weekend Getaway", 2002; "Jasper, Texas", 2003; "Momentum", 2003; "Half & Half", 2004; "Solar Attack", 2005; "Lackawanna Blues", 2005; "Stargate SG-1", 2006; "Family Guy", 2006; "The Batman", 2007; "ER", 2009; "Psych", 2012; "Boardwalk Empire", 2013; "Miracle at Gate 213", 2013; "Extant", 2014; "Madam Secretary", 2014. Films: The Skin Game, 1971; The Laughing Policeman, 1974; It's Good to Be Alive, 1974; The White Dawn, 1975; Little Ladies of the Night, 1977; The Choirboys, 1977; The Deep, 1977; He Who Walks Alone, 1978; An Officer & a Gentleman, 1982; Jaws 3, 1983; The Guardian, 1984; Finders Keepers, 1984; Iron Eagle, 1985; Enemy Mine, 1985; Firewalker, 1986; The Principal, 1987; Iron Eagle II, 1988; Toy Soldiers, 1991; Diggstown, 1992; Monolith, 1993; Flashfire, 1993; Curse of the Starving Class, 1994; Iron Eagle IV, 1995; Managua, 1996; The Wall That Heals, 1997; Legend of the Mummy, 1997; The Highway man, 2000; Deceived, voice, 2002; Momentum, 2003; Solar Strike, Window, 2005; Club Soda, 2006; Daddy's Little Girls, 2007; Cover, 2007; Delgo, 2008; The BAMN Squad, 2008; The Perfect Game, 2008; The Least Among You, 2008; The Real Catch, 2008; Buttermilk Sky, 2008; Dog Jack, 2009; Shannon's Rainbow, 2009; The Least Among You, 2009; Smitty, 2010; Why Did I Get Married Too?, 2010; The Grace Card, 2010; A Fonder Heart, 2011; The Lamp, 2011; Smitty, 2012; Breaking at the Edge, 2013; A Fighting Man, 2014; Pride of Lions, 2014; Boiling Pot, 2014. **Orgs:** Motion Picture Arts & Sciences Acad; SAG; NAG; AEA; AFM; Alpha Phi Alpha; AGVA; Legal Defense Fund, Nat Asn Advan Colored People; pres, Eracism Foundation Inc, Currently. **Honors/Awds:** Donaldson Award, 1954; Primetime Emmy Award for role of Fiddler in Roots, 1977; Image Award, Nat Asn Advan Colored People, 1982, 1998; Oscar, Academy Awards, 1983; Golden Globe Award, 1983, 1992; Special Award, ShoWest Convention, 1983; Star on the Walk of Fame, 1992; Trumpet Award, 1997; Maverick Award, Taos Talking Picture Festival, 1997; Daytime Emmy Award for Outstanding Children's Special, 1998; Black Reel Award for Best Director, 2000; Lifetime Achievement Award, Temecula Valley Int Film Festival, 2004; Anniversary Award, TV Land Awards, 2007; Maverick Spirit Award, Ciniquest, 2009. **Home Addr:** PO Box 6187, Malibu, CA 90264. **Business Addr:** President, Eracism Foundation Inc, 30765 Malibu Coast Hwy, Malibu, CA 90265, **Business Phone:** (310)276-6700.

**GOTHARD, DR. BARBARA WHEATLEY**
Educator, school principal, government official. **Personal:** Born Nov 23, 1937, Springfield, IL; married Donald L; children: Donald Jr & Ann Marie. **Educ:** Mt Mary Col, Milwaukee, BA, 1959; Long Island Univ, Greenvale, NY, MS, 1972; Mich State Univ, PhD, 1977. **Career:** Milwaukee Pub Sch, art teacher, 1959-64; Union Free Sch Dist 4, Northport, NY, art teacher, 1966-71; Crimel Oakland Univ, Rochester, MI, free lance graphic artist, 1972-73; Cult Arts Events, Advisor Newspaper Utica, MI, ed, 1973-75; Utica Community Sch, art teacher, 1973-77; Utica High Sch, MI, assoc prin, 1977-; Mich State Univ, instr, 1980; Burger King Corp, Pub Affairs & Corp Social Responsibility Dept, 1983-89; Univ Calif, Sch Mgt, lectr & adj prof; Univ NC, Kenan-Flagler Bus Sch, lectr; Hill & Knowlton's Corp, Social Responsibility & Corp Sustainable Develop Groups, sr counr; Mid E & African Region, dir pub affairs; Dow Chem Co, global leader external affairs; Community Cols, bd gov, currently. **Orgs:** Bd dir, Meadow brook Art Gallery, Oakland Univ, 1973-76; bd dir, Xochipilli Gallery, 1974-76; Chairperson pub comn, Mich Asn Sec Sch Prin, 1977-; Nat Asn Sec Sch Prin, 1977-; Mich Coun Women Sch Admin, 1978-; vpres & gen mgr, Jackie Robinson Found; formerly mem adv bdAm Chamber Com-S africa; formerly mem adv bd, US Air Force Air Univ Bd; formerly mem bd gov, Calif Community Cols Syst; formerly chair, bd dirs, Space 4 Art; immediate past pres & co-chair artists coun exhib, Palm Springs Art Mus Artists Coun. **Honors/Awds:** Outstanding Young Women of Am, 1973. **Special Achievements:** Utica Cultural Arts Council Exhibits Paintings include Main Streams "74"Marietta College, OH, Detroit Artists Market "Woman Works" Univ of Michigan, Midwest Artists Milwaukee Performing Arts Center, Macomb CoBi-Centennial Exchange Program, Coventry, England; solo shows at Delta College, Univ City, MI, Art Gallery Central Michigan University, Mt MaryCollege, Milwaukee, WI, Xochipilli Gallery, MI; newspaper reviews prev collections, 1972-80; publ: "Art Tchr, Admin" Secondary Educ Today Jour ofthe MI Assn of Second Sch Prin 1978. **Home Addr:** 10787 Wilshire Blvd Apt 1504, Los Angeles, CA 90024, **Home Phone:** (310)441-1630. **Business Addr:** Board of Governors, Community Colleges, 1102 Q St Suite 4, Sacramento, CA 95814-6511, **Business Phone:** (916)445-8752.

**GOTHARD, DONALD L., SR.**
Automotive executive. **Personal:** Born Dec 2, 1934, Madison, WI; son of William H (deceased) and Lorraine M Williams (deceased); married Doris M Smith; children: Donald Jr & Ann Marie. **Educ:** Univ Notre Dame, BS, elec engineering, 1956; Res Officers Training Corp, attended 1956; GMI Tech, staff mgt prog cert, 1974. **Career:** Automotive executive (retired); United Technologies, consult; GM AC, Sparkplug Div, jr engr, prod engineering, 1956; Electron Div, design syst engr, Mace Missile Guid & Navig Equip, 1958-62; Buick Foundry, jr process engr, 1961; Apollo Ground Support Syst, engr, 1962-66; Apollo prog, systs engr & supvr, 1963-71; GM Delco, Electron Div, lab supvr; Apollo Guid Sys Lab, 1966-71; GM Auto, Electron Control Syst Develop, 1971; GM Instrumentation Sect, Test Dept, supvr engineering staff, 1972; GM Engineering Staff, asst mgr, 1973-76; GM Chevrolet, Motor Div, sr design engr, 1976-77, from asst staff engr to staff engr, 1977-82; GM Truck & Bus Engineering Opers, chief engr & elec components, 1982-85, exec engr & adv vehicle engineering, 1985-90; GM Res Lab, dir res admin serv, 1990-92; GM Design Ctr, exec prototype & process engineering, 1992-93; GM Mfg Ctr, Prototype Shops, dir qual & mfg eng, 1993-95. **Orgs:** Vol, YMCA Youth Basketball Prog, 1971-87; Meadow Brook Art Gallery Asn, 1972-80; Adv comt, Utica Community Sch Citizens, 1975-76; Soc Auto Engrs, 1976-2000; citizens comt educ & Financial needs & resources, Macomb Co Community Col, 1976; secy, Shelby Twp Cable TV Reg Comt, 1980-84; asst coach, Utica Eisenhower High Sch Girls Basketball, 1985-87; bd dir, Black Alumni Notre Dame, 1988-94; adv coun, Univ Notre Dame, 1989-; bd dir, Detroit Sci & Engineering Fair, 1992-99. **Home Addr:** 5510 Brookside Lane, Washington, MI 48094, **Home Phone:** (586)786-0035.

**GOTTI, IRV (IRVING DOMINGO LORENZO, JR.)**
Movie producer. **Personal:** Born Jun 26, 1970, Hollis, NY; married Debbie; children: Sonny & JJ. **Career:** Films: Rush Hour, 1998; Belly, 1998; Light It Up, 1999; Next Friday, 2000; Romeo Must Die, 2000; Bamboozled, 2000; Double Take, 2001; Down to Earth, 2001; Exit Wounds, 2001; The Fast & the Furious, 2001; The Wire, 2002; Friday After Next, 2002; Barbershop 2: Back in Business, 2004; Bride & Prejudice, 2004; Shall We Dance, 2004; Animal, 2005; Angel: One More Road to Cross, Composer, 2001; Mighty D-Block, composer, 2006. Singles: "Shit's Real", 1994; "Can I Live", 1996; "Can I Get A...", 1998; "Hot Spot", 1998; "What's My Name", 1999; "Holla Holla", 1999; "Come Back in One Piece", 2000; "Between Me and You", 2000; "What's Luv?", 2001; "I'm Real (Murder Remix)", 2001; "Ain't It Funny (Murder Remix)", 2001; "I Cry", 2001; "Always on Time", 2001; "Foolish", 2002; "Happy", 2002; "Down 4 U", 2002; "Mesmerize", 2002; "Gangsta Lovin", 2002; "Breakup 2 Makeup", 2004; "Infatuated", 2005. Albums: Heroes and Thieves, 2007; Gotti's Way, actor, 2007; Blunt/TVT Records, A&R rep, 1995; Def Jam Records, A&R rep, 1995-99; Top Dawg Prod, founder & chief exec officer; Murder Inc Records, founder & chief exec officer, 1999; The Inc Records, chief exec officer & founder. **Honors/Awds:** Two BMI Urban Awards; one BMI Pop Award, 2002.

**GOUDY, DR. ANDREW JAMES**
Teacher, vice president (organization), educator. **Personal:** Born Apr 15, 1943, Martins Ferry, OH; son of Bertha and Sidney. **Educ:** Ind Univ Pa, BS, chem, 1967, MS, chem, 1971; Univ Pittsburgh, PhD, phys chem, 1976. **Career:** Cameron City High Sch, teacher, 1968; Bald Eagle Nittany Hifh Sch, teacher, 1969; Canon Mcmillan High Sch, teacher, 1971; W Chester Univ, prof, 1977, chmn dept chem, 1983-87; Del State Univ, Dept Chem, prof & chairperson, currently; Hydrogen Storage Res Ctr, dir, currently. **Orgs:** Am Chem Soc, 1976-; Intl Asn Hydrogen Energy, 1982, Nat Asn Advan Colored People; Nat Orgn Black Chemists & Chem Engrs, 1990-95; Nat Hydrogen Asn; vpres, Capital City Rotary Club; fac mem, Del State Univ, 2001; pres, Dover Capital City Rotary, 2007. **Home Addr:** 1518 Manley Rd B36, West Chester, PA 19382. **Business Addr:** Professor, Chairman, Delaware State University, Luna I Mishoe Sci Ctr S 1200 N DuPont Hwy Rm 301, Dover, DE 19901, **Business Phone:** (302)857-6530.

**GOUGH, DR. WALTER C.** See Obituaries Section.

**GOULBOURNE, DONALD SAMUEL, JR.**
Social worker, administrator, executive director. **Personal:** Born May 5, 1950, New Rochelle, NY; son of Donald Samuel Sr and Girthel Grayson; children: Antoine Donald. **Educ:** Columbia Union Col, Takoma Pk, MD, BA, 1973; Columbia Univ Sch Social Work, NY, MS, 1977; Albert Einstein Col Med/Yeshiva Univ, post-grad cert, 1984. **Career:** New Rochelle Bd Educ, New Rochelle, NY, teachers asst, 1974-75; Wash Heights Community Ctr, NY, social work trainee, 1975-76; Family & C Serv, Stamford, Conn, clin social worker, 1977-79; Nat Health Serv Corps, Einstein Med Col, NY, social work coord, 1979-84; Dept Social Serv, Albert Einstein Col Med, NY, 1984-89; Lincoln Ave Clin, Guid Ctr, New Rochelle, NY, dir, 1989, exec dir. **Orgs:** USR Officers Asn, 1989; US Comn Officers Asn, 1989; Nat Asn Social Workers, 1989; Soc Clin Work Psychotherapists Inc, 1989; vol group leader, Minority Task Force AIDS, 1989; vpres, Westchester Townhouse Condominium Asn, 1989; prof coun, Community Adult Patients, 1989. **Honors/Awds:** Letter of Commendation, NY State Dept Health, 1981; Clin Asn Nomination, Dept Sociol, Herbert H Lehman Col City Univ NY, 1982; Service Citation, NY City Dept Pub Health, 1983; Certificate of Appreciation, Yeshiva Univ, 1986, 1987. **Home Addr:** 21 Clinton Ave, New Rochelle, NY 10801, **Home Phone:** (914)969-8306.

**GOULD, PROF. WILLIAM BENJAMIN, IV**
Lawyer, educator, association executive. **Personal:** Born Jul 16, 1936, Boston, MA; son of William Benjamin III and Leah Felts; married Hilda; children: William, V, Timothy & Bartholomew. **Educ:** Univ RI, AB, 1958; Cornell Law Sch, LLB, 1961; London Sch Econ, grad study, 1963; Univ Cambridge, MA, 1975. **Career:** United Auto Workers, asst gen counr, 1961-62; Nat Labor Rels Bd, atty, 1963-65; Battle, Fowler, Stokes & Kheel, mgt, 1965-68; Wayne State Law Sch, Detroit, prof law, 1968-71; Harvard Law Sch, vis prof law, 1971-72; Guggenheim, Fel, 1975; Rockefeller Found, Fel, 1975-76; Churchill Col, Cambridge, vis fel & lectr, 1975; Stanford Law Sch, Overseas Fel Churchill Col Cambridge, prof law, 1975, Charles A Beardsley, prof law, 1984-94, Charles A Beardsley, emer prof law, 2002-; Univ Tokyo, law fac, 1975, 1978; E-W Ctr, Honolulu, vis prof, 1982-83; Australian Nat Univ, vis prof, 1985; Europ Univ Inst, vis prof, 1988; Howard Law Sch, vis prof law, 1989; Univ Witwatersrand, vis prof, South Africa, 1991; Nat Labor Rels Bd, chair, 1994-98; Univ Hawaii Law Sch, vis prof law, 2005; Univ San Diego, Summer Law Study Abroad Prog, prof law, 2005. **Orgs:** Consult, U.S. Equal Employ Opportunity, 1966-67; First Fact-Finding Bd, 1967; Nat Acad Arbitrat, 1970-; Labor Law Sect; Am Bar Asn atty; racial discrim class act involving Detroit Edison Co Int Bro Teamsters; Am Fed Mus; del Dem Party mid-term conv, 1974; chmn, Nat Labor Rels Bd, 1994-98 Stanford Univ John S Knight Journalism; secy, Labor & Employ, Law Sect, 1980-81; Calif State Bar Ad Hoc Comt Wrongful Dismissal, 1983-84; chmn, Mayor San Francisco's Task Force Collective Bargaining, 1990-91; Future Worker/Mgt Rels Comn, U.S. Dept Labor & U.S. Dept Com, 1993-94; independent monitor, First Group Am Freedom Asn complaints, 2008-10; consult & spec advisor, U.S. Dept Housing & Urban Develop, 2011-12; chmn, Calif Agr Labor Rels Bd, 2014-. **Honors/Awds:** Cert Merit, Primer, Am Labor Law, 1983; Endowed Chair Holder, Charles ABeardsley Prof Law, 1984; LLD, Univ RI, 1986; LLD, Stetson Univ, 1996; LLD, DC Sch Law, 1996; 100 Most Influential Black Americans, 1996-98; LLD, Capital Univ, 1997; LLD, Rutgers Univ, 1998. **Special Achievements:** Author articles lab law & unions Stanford, Yale, Duke, Cornell, Penn & other law journals; Journals: Kissing Cousins?: The Federal Arbitration Act and Modern Labor Arbitration; Labor Issues in Professional Sports: Reflections on Baseball, Labor, and Antitrust Law; The Idea of the Job as Property in Contemporary America: The Legal and Collective Bargaining Framework; Japan's Reshaping of American Labor Law, Cambridge, 1984; On Labor Injunctions Pending Arbitration: Recasting Buffalo Forge: Black Workers in White Unions: Job Discrimination in the United States; Taft-Hartley Comes to Great Britain: Observations on the Industrial Relations; The Impact Upon Collective Bargaining Relationships. **Home Addr:** 711 Salvatierra St, Stanford, CA 94305-1020, **Home Phone:** (650)321-3128. **Business Addr:** Charles A Beardsley Professor Emeritus, Stanford Law School, 559 Nathan Abbott Way, Stanford, CA 94305-8610, **Business Phone:** (650)723-2465.

**GOVAN, REGINALD C.**
Lawyer. **Personal:** Born Dec 2, 1953, New York, NY; son of Oswald and Gwendolyn Minor. **Educ:** Carnegie-Mellon Univ, BA, econs & philos, 1975; Univ Pa Law Sch, JD, 1978. **Career:** Squire, Sanders & Dempsey, assoc, 1978-79; US Ct Appeals, 6th Circuit, Judge Nathaniel R Jones, sr law clerk, 1979-81; Manhattan Dist Atty, asst dist atty, 1981-83, sole practr, fed civil rights & genlitigation, 1983-85, 1987-89; US Sen, Com Judiciary, coun, 1985-87; US House Rep, Edu Labor Com, coun, 1989-95; Orgn Resource Couns Inc, sr consult, 1995-98; Freddie Mac, managing assoc gen coun, 1998-2012; Am Corp Coun Assn, vice chair, currently; Fed Aviation Admin, chief coun, 2014-. **Orgs:** Nat Bar Asn, 1984-; Wash Bar Asn, 1990-; chair, Dist Bar, 1991-94; Atty-Client Arbit Bd, 1991-94; Disciplinary Rev Com, 1991-93; Task Force Continuing Legal Educ, 1992-94; Metrop New York Black Bar Asn; Co-Chair, Ann Inst Employ Law; Mem, Adv Comt Labor & Employ Law; Vice-Chair, Am Corp Coun Asn. **Honors/Awds:** Co-chair, PLI Annual Institute on Employment Law. **Special Achievements:** One Nation, Indivisible: The Civil Rights Challenge for the 1990's, Wash, DC, Citizens' CMS on Civil Rights, 1989; "Framing Issues and Acquiring Codes: An Overview of the Legislative Sojourn of the Civil Rights Act of 1991", 41 The De Paul Law Review 1057, 1992; "Honorable Compromises and the Moral High Ground: The Conflict Between the Rhetoric and the Content of the Civil Rights Act of 1991", 46 The Rutgers Law Review 7, 1993; "The Politics of Principle: Why Employment-Law Reform is Floundering, "Organizations & People, 1996; "Alcohol At Company-Hosted-Events-Worth the Risk?" AACA Docket, 2003; "Employment Law is a Fishbowl: Coping with Less Privilege and Confidentiality", Employee Relations LJ, Vol 23, No 3(Winter 1997). **Home Addr:** 3311 Ross Pl NW, Washington, DC 20008-3332, **Home Phone:** (202)966-5567. **Business Addr:** Chief Counsel, Federal Aviation Administration, 800 Independence Ave SW, Washington, DC 20591, **Business Phone:** (866)835-5322.

**GOVAN, RONALD M.**
Physicist. **Personal:** Born Jan 20, 1931, Los Angeles, CA. **Educ:** Pac State Univ, Col Elec Engr, BSEE, 1962. **Career:** Univ SC, physics dept res assoc; Ryan Aircraft, elec main & calibration tech; Hughes Aircraft, elec fabric tech & elec main tech; USN ET2, main radar, sonar & commun equip; Univ S Calif, Los Angeles, physics dept asst res, 1962-64, chem dept instrument design, 1964-66; Rockwell Int Sci Ctr, staff assoc physics, 1966-; Univ Calif, Santa Barbara Dept Urban Aff, conf coordr, 1969. **Orgs:** Educ Coun Col & Univ Ventura Co; chmn local bd 81 selec serv, Ventura Co; bd dir, S Calif Comprehen Health Plan Bd; vpres, S Area Conf, Nat Asn Advan Colored People; vpres, Ventura County Nat Asn Advan Colored People; lab chmn, educ chmn; Camarillo Jaycees; chmn, John C Montgomery Forum Welfare; bd dir, Camarillo Boys Club; chmn, United Fund Ventura County Budget & Com Task Force; chmn, Ventura County Community Action Comn; Ventura County Criminal Justice Planning Deleg Conf Crim Just Sci & Technol Wash, DC, 1972; found pres, Camarillo Dem Club; Task Force On Excellence Educ Pomona, 1972; Calif State Dept Educ; lectr paid consult, Ventura Co Human Relat Comn; Task Force Housing Ventura Co Plann Dept; Equal Opport Comn; Calif State Personnel bd adv comt, Career Opport Develop; Gov's Conf Law Enforcement Stand Control Comt; Pub Spectros Group; Atmospheric Sci Group. **Honors/Awds:** Recipient Of Outstanding Contribution Award, Nat Asn Advan Colored People S Area Conf; Community Service Award; Outstanding Community Interest Award, 1967; Jaycee of Month award; Distinguished Service Award; Commendation for High Service. **Home Addr:** 8170 Redlands St Apt 301, Playa del Rey, CA 90293-8237. **Business Addr:** Staff Associate Physics, Rockwell International Science Center, 1049 Camino Dos Rios, Thousand Oaks, CA 91360.

**GOVAN, DR. SANDRA YVONNE**
Educator, college teacher, writer. **Personal:** Born Jul 28, 1948, Chicago, IL; daughter of Tanzel Romero and Sarah D Wilson. **Educ:** Valparaiso Univ, BA, 1970; Bowling Green Univ, MA, 1972; Emory Univ, PhD, 1980. **Career:** Luther Col, Decorah, IA, instr, 1972-75; Univ Ky, asst prof, 1980-83; Univ NC, assoc prof eng, 1983, Dept Eng, prof eng, emer, currently; Books: Connections, Links and Extended Networks: Patterns in Octavia Butler's Science Fiction. **Orgs:** Col Lang Asn, 1975-; Emory Univ Fel, 1975; Asn Study African-Am Life & Hist; Mod Lang Asn, 1980-; Langston Hughes Soc; coordr, Ronald E McNair Post baccalaureate Achievement Prog; founding mem, WinterGreen Women Writers Collective. **Home Addr:** 6508 Wickville Dr, Charlotte, NC 28215-4026, **Home Phone:** (704)535-4402. **Business Addr:** Emeritus, Professor, University of North Carolina, Dept of Eng, Charlotte, NC 28223-0001, **Business Phone:** (704)687-4218.

**GRACE, HON. BOBBIE H.**
Government official. **Personal:** Born Sep 29, 1945, Donaldsonville, GA; daughter of Willie Calvin Hutchins Sr and Helen Williams; married James Allen; children: Denise Renee George & Cheryl Lynette. **Career:** Government official (retired); City Dania Beach, mayor, comnr, vice mayor, 1989-97; Bell S, Info Technol, 1968-98. **Orgs:** Pres, Dania Beach Econ & Develop; vpres, Progress Dem Club; pres; Cent Broward Kiwanis; pres, N W Byrd Pointe Asn; Col Garden Homeowners Asn; Broward County Planning Coun; comnr, pres, Dania Beach Housing Authority; bd mem, Habitat Humanity; bd mem, Northwest Byrd Pointe Civic Asn; chairperson, Am Cancer Soc Relay Life Dania Beach, 2009-10; dir, Broward Black Elected Officials, 2011; mem, Broward County Charter Rev Bd; exec bd mem, Dania Econ Develop Corp. **Home Addr:** 110 NW 8th Ave, Dania Beach, FL 33004-2758, **Home Phone:** (954)396-0941.

**GRACE, GEORGE H.**
Executive, association executive, manager. **Personal:** Born May 20, 1948, Bartow, FL; son of DeeCee and Lillie Mae; married Regina Mobley; married Barbara Milton; children: Jerhonda J, Gregory & Keenyn. **Educ:** Tuskegee Univ, BS, 1971; Univ Miami, MS, 1978. **Career:** Gen Motors, Pontiac, MI, prod supvr, 1972-73; Bellsouth, Fla. regional mgr, 1974-. **Orgs:** Nat Asn Advan Colored People; Urban League; Hialeah Chamber Com; Omega Psi Phi Fraternity, 1973-98; Omega Psi Phi, 1973, grand keeper rec & seals, 1998, grand basileus, 2002-06, officer. **Honors/Awds:** The 100 Most Influential Black Americans, Ebony Mag, 2004. **Home Addr:** 16831 SW 111th Ct, Miami, FL 33157-4098. **Business Addr:** Member, Omega Psi Phi Fraternity Inc, 3951 Snapfinger Pkwy, Decatur, GA 30035, **Business Phone:** (404)284-5533.

**GRACE, HORACE R.**
President (organization). **Personal:** Born Jan 13, 1943, Timpson, TX; son of Robert and Lena Roberts Williams; married Margaret Richardson; children: April. **Educ:** Prairie View Univ, Prairie View, TX, BS, 1966; Va State Univ, Petersburg, VA, MS, 1976. **Career:** Fed Acquisition Consults, pres, 1982-; Pfizer Inc, sales mgr; Lawn Barber Landscaping, pres, 1982-, chief exec officer; Grace Investments, pres, 1985-; AMG Enterprises Inc, owner & pres; Grace Consulting bvba, Pres, 1998-. **Orgs:** Vice chmn, Tex Credit Union Comn, 1985-89; Christian Farm Bd, 1988-; Cent Tex Alliance Black Bus, 1988-; mem bd, Pvt Indust Coun, 1989-; United Way Bd, 1991; bd mem, pres, Clearwater Dist; bd mem, Cent Tx Workforce Develop Bd. **Home Addr:** 180 Mighty Oak Lane Rte 1, PO Box 25, Killeen, TX 76547-0065, **Home Phone:** (254)526-9200. **Business Addr:** President, Grace Consulting bvba.

**GRACE, DR. MARCELLUS**
Dean (education), educator, administrator. **Personal:** Born Oct 17, 1947, Selma, AL; son of Capp and Mary; married Laura Dunn; children: Syreeta Lynn & Marcellus Jr. **Educ:** Xavier Univ La, BS, pharm, 1971; Univ Minn, MS, hosp pharm, 1975, PhD, pharm admin, 1976. **Career:** Tulane Med Ctr Hosp & Clin, dir pharm serv, 1976-77; Xavier Univ, Col Pharm, asst prof, dir prof exp prof, 1976-78, dean prof, prof pharm admin, La Col Pharm, dean, 1983-99, Xavier Inst Bioenvironmental Toxicol, dir, 1983-98, prof pharm admin, 1999-2004; Howard Univ Col Pharm & Pharma col Sci, assoc dean serv ed, 1979-82, chmn dept pharm admin, 1982, Nursing & Allied Health Sci, prof pharm admin, Sch Pharm, assoc dean, 2004-06, PaCE Ctr, fac, currently; Xechem Int Inc, bd mem, 2005-; Meditab Pharmaceut LLC, founding mem & chief exec officer, 2007-; Treme Haircare LLC, co-founder. **Orgs:** New Orleans Hist Pharm Comn, 1983-98; pres, Asn Minority Health Prof Schs, 1987-89; pres, Minority Health

Prof Found; Nat Heart, Lung & Blood Inst Adv Coun, 1991-93; bd dir, Am Col Pharm, 1992-94; NY Acad Sci, 1991; bd dir, Ernest N Morial Asthma & Respiratory Dis Ctr, 1995-; bd dir, Alton Ochsner Med Found, 1996-; bd dir, Urban League Greater New Orleans, 1996-98. **Home Addr:** 5743 Louis Prima Dr W, New Orleans, LA 70128. **Business Addr:** Faculty, Howard University, 1100 Wayne Ave Suite 100, Silver Spring, MD 20910, **Business Phone:** (301)608-4100.

### GRACE, PRINCESTON
Automotive executive. **Career:** Montgomery Ford Lincoln Mercury Inc, exec, pres; Advantage Ford-Lincoln-Mercury Inc, pres & chief exec officer; Montgomery Ford Lincoln Mercury Inc, Montgomery, Ala, pres, currently. **Orgs:** Ford Motor Minority Dealers Asn. **Home Addr:** 4941 SW Bimini Cir N, Palm City, FL 34990-1231, **Home Phone:** (772)219-4839. **Business Addr:** President, Montgomery Ford Lincoln Mercury Inc, 4000 Eastern Blvd, Montgomery, AL 36116-2642, **Business Phone:** (334)613-5000.

### GRACE, SHERRY
Founder (originator), executive director, interior designer. **Personal:** Born Jan 1, 1954; married Willie Jr; children: Andre & Avery. **Career:** Interior designer; Mothers Incarcerated Sons Inc, founder, 2001-, exec dir, 2004; interior designer; Captivating Effects Interior Design, pres; Mothers Incarcerated Sons, pres, founder. **Orgs:** Mother's Day, 2001; Keynote speaker, Hardee Correctional Facil, 2006; keynote speaker, Chap 5135, Nat Asn Advan Colored People, 2005; treas, Mothers Incarcerated Sons. **Home Addr:** 2843 Oranole Way, Apopka, FL 32703-7858. **Business Addr:** Founder, Executive Director, Mothers of Incarcerated Sons Inc, 109 E Cumberland Cir, Longwood, FL 32779, **Business Phone:** (407)389-1416.

### GRADDICK-WEIR, DR. MIRIAN M.
Executive, vice president (organization). **Educ:** Hampton Univ, BA, psychol, 1976; Pa State Univ, MS, 1978, PhD, indust & orgn psychol, 1981. **Career:** AT&T Corp, staff corp human resources, 1981-88, spec asst to vice chmn, 1988-89, dir customer serv & consumer commun serv, 1991-93, vpres multimedia prod & exec human resources, 1994-95, vpres human resources, 1995-96, vpres human resources & bus effectiveness, 1996-98, chief human resources officer, 1998-99, exec vpres human resources, 1999-2004, exec vpres human resources & employee commun, 2004-06; Consumer Serv Co, chief human resources officer, 1998-99; Merck & Co Inc, sr vpres human resources, 2006-07, exec vpres human resources, 2008-; Yum Brands Inc, dir, 2012-; Harleysville Group Inc, dir, 2000-12. **Orgs:** Joint Ctr Polit & Econ Studies; Nat Med Fels Inc; Human Resources Policy Asn; Nat Acad Human Resources; Personnel Round Table & Cowdrick Group; fel Nat Acad Human Resources, 2001; adv bd mem, Ctr Advan Human Resource Studies, 2009-. **Business Addr:** Executive Vice President, Merck & Co Inc, 1 Merck Dr, Whitehouse Station, NJ 08889-0100, **Business Phone:** (908)423-1000.

### GRADDICK-WEIR, MIRIAN M.
Vice president (organization), executive, association executive. **Educ:** Hampton Univ, BA, psychol, 1976; Pa State Univ, MS, indust/orgn psychol, 1978, PhD, indust/orgn psychol, 1981. **Career:** AT&T, chief human resources officer, 1998-99, exec vpres human resources, 1999-2004, exec vpres human resources & employee commun, 2004-06; Merck & Co Inc, Global Human Resources, sr vpres, 2006-07, exec vpres, 2008-. **Orgs:** Dir, Harleysville Group Inc; bd mem, Joint Ctr Polit & Econ Studies; bd mem, Nat Med Fels Inc; bd mem, Harleysville Group Ins Co; bd mem, Human Resources Policy Asn; bd mem, Nat Acad Human Resources. **Honors/Awds:** HR Executive of the Year, 2001; The 100 Most Powerful Executives in Corporate America, Black Enterprise, 2010. **Business Addr:** Executive Vice President, Merck & Co Inc, 2000 Galloping Hill Rd, Kenilworth, NJ 07033, **Business Phone:** (908)740-4000.

### GRADY, GLENN G.
Executive, president (organization), chief executive officer. **Career:** Stroh Brewery Co, dir distribr, staff, 1963; Cimarron Express Inc, pres & chief exec officer, 1984-. **Business Addr:** President, Chief Executive Officer, Cimarron Express Inc, 21611 State Rte 51, Genoa, OH 43430, **Business Phone:** (419)855-7713.

### GRADY, WALTER E.
President (organization), chief executive officer, manager. **Educ:** Morehouse Col, Atlanta, Ga, bus admin, 1960; BS, bus admin, 1969; Roosevelt Univ, Chicago, Il, MBA, 1978; Am Inst Banking; Minority Bus Enterprise, cert; Chicago Minority Bus Develop Coun, cert; Nat Minority Suppliers Purchasing Coun, cert; US Dept Treas Minority Bank Deposit Prog, cert. **Career:** Us Postal Serv; Continental Ill Nat Bank & Trust Co, acct; Marcy-Newberry Asn, bus mgr, 1969-72; Seaway Nat Bank, Chicago, Ill, mgt trainee, 1972, bookkeeping mgr, pres & chief exec officer, 1980-2014. **Orgs:** Bd mem, Seaway Bank & Trust Co; bd mem, Seaway Bancshares Inc; bd mem, Ill Bankers Asn; bd mem, Boy Scouts Area Coun; bd mem, Comnr - Ill Comn Volunteerism; bd mem, Community Serv - 111th St YMCA; bd mem, Roosevelt Univ Bd Gov; bd mem, Roosevelt Univ Career Serv Adv Bd; bd mem, United Methodist Found; bd mem, Seaway Community Develop Corp; Nat Bankers Asn; Am Bankers Asn; Am Mgt Asn; Chicago Chamber Com; Chatham Lions; Econ Club Chicago; Crete United Methodist Church; Alpha Phi Alpha Fraternity; Alliance Bus Leaders & Entrepreneurs. **Business Addr:** President, Chief Executive Officer, Seaway National Bank, 645 E 87th St, Chicago, IL 60619, **Business Phone:** (773)602-4139.

### GRADY-SMITH, ESQ. MATTIE D.
Lawyer, government official. **Personal:** Born Apr 29, 1952, Blackstock, SC. **Educ:** Westchester Community Col, AAS, 1977; Mercy Col, BS, 1980; Pace Univ, MPA, 1982; Pace Univ Sch Law, JD, 1994. **Career:** Westchester County Dept of Social Serv, Admin Positions, 1973-91; Westchester Med Ctr, Risk & Ins Coordr, 1991-99; Westchester & Rockland Mediation Centers, cert mediator, cert lemon law arbitrator, 2004-11; Westchester County Off, EEO/AA, dir, 1999-2008; Westchester County, consult, hearing officer, 2008-10; Sole Proprietor, 2008-; Sc Fed Courts, Cert Mediator, 2013-; Midlands Mediation Ctr, vol mediator, 2013-. **Orgs:** Bus Coun Westchester, HR Coun; Westchester County Afr Am Adv Bd, Liaison; adv comt, City White Plains Youth Bur; mediator, Volunteer Coun Serv. **Home Addr:** PO Box 383, Tarrytown, NY 10591, **Home Phone:** (845)641-1105. **Business Addr:** Director, County of Westchester, 148 Martine Ave Suite 103, White Plains, NY 10601, **Business Phone:** (914)995-2141.

### GRAGG, LAUREN ANDREA
Manager, educator. **Personal:** Born Dec 20, 1967, Detroit, MI; daughter of J Robert and LaBarbara A. **Educ:** Cheonggang Acad, BA, MA, orgn commun & broadcast commun, 1997; Howard Univ, BA, 1989; Wayne State Univ, MA, commun pub rels. **Career:** Detroit Pistons, Palace Found, spec proj asst, 1990; EDS, serv rels analyst, 1990-93, pub rels rep, 1993-95, recruiter, 1995-98, prog mgr, 1998-99, mkt mgr, 1998-99, mgr, 2000, sr mkt rep, 1999-2000, eBusiness mkt mgr, 2001, mkt & bus develop mgr, 2001-02; pvt commun consult, 2001-02; Oakland Univ, Dept Rhet, Commun & Jour, spec lectr/instr, currently; Wayne State Univ, Grad Teaching Asst, 2003-06; Univ Toledo, vpres, 2006-08; A Living Lighthouse, bus consult, 2008-. **Orgs:** Howard Univ Alumni Asn; Delta Sigma Theta; Nat Urban League. **Home Addr:** 6301 Windhaven Pkwy Suite 110, Plano, TX 75093. **Business Addr:** Business Consultant, A Living Lighthouse.

### GRAHAM, ALBERTHA L.
Educator. **Personal:** Born Georgetown, SC; married Sam Ellison; children: Kezia Ellison. **Educ:** Morris Col, 1965; NY Univ, cert leadership develop training, 1968; Erikson Inst, MEd, 1971; Univ Pittsburgh, grad stud. **Career:** Educator (retired); Chopee High Sch, teacher, 1965-67, summer librn, 1966; Brook haven High Sch, head start teacher, 1967-68; Cent Brook haven Head Start Prog, dir, 1968-70; Suffolk County Summer Head Start Patchoque NY, dir, 1970; Kezia Enterprises, counr, owner; Calif Univ, Pa, state trng officer, assoc prof, prof, 2000-01, dir affirmative action & human rels, coun. **Orgs:** Nat Asn Educ Young Child; Nat Coun Black Child Develop; Pa Reg Adv Comn, Day Care Person Proj conduc EPI, 1973; Educ Com Pittsburgh Chap, Nat Asn Advan Colored People; nat pres, Black Women Asn Inc; vol & adv bd mem, Nat Coun Jewish Women Pittsburgh Sec Friends Indeed Proj, 1975-; African Am Inst; bd mem, Inst Women Ent; Nat Asn Women Bus Owners; Greater Pittsburgh Comn Women. **Home Addr:** 1207 Buena Vista St, Pittsburgh, PA 15212, **Home Phone:** (412)231-1801.

### GRAHAM, CHARLENE G.
Firefighter. **Personal:** married Derek; children: Jessica & Jennelle. **Educ:** Ferris State Univ. **Career:** Detroit Fire Dept, Res & Develop Div, div chief, dist chief, 1996-. **Orgs:** Alpha Kappa Alpha Sorority Inc. **Honors/Awds:** Certificate of Special Recognition; Golden Heritage Award; Detroit City Coun Testimonial Resolution; Proclamation, City Detroit Off Mayor; Recognition of Excellence Award, Nobel/Woman. **Special Achievements:** First woman to hold the rank of division chief in the Detroit Fire Department was an African American woman. **Home Addr:** 9216 Plainview Ave, Detroit, MI 48228-1766, **Home Phone:** (313)836-7394. **Business Addr:** Division Head, Detroit Fire Department, 250 W Larned St, Detroit, MI 48226, **Business Phone:** (313)596-2900.

### GRAHAM, DEMINGO
Football player, executive director. **Personal:** Born Sep 10, 1973, Newark, NJ. **Educ:** Hofstra Univ, BBA, mkt mgt & bus admin, 1998. **Career:** Football player (retired); San Diego Chargers, guard & right guard, 1998-2001; Houston Texans, guard & left guard, 2002-03; Dallas Cowboys, 2004; Chemistre Ent, Mkt & Creative Dir, 2009-. **Special Achievements:** Films: "By Any Means", 2016, "Kensho at the Bedfellow ", 2016. **Business Addr:** South Orange, NJ.

### GRAHAM, DONALD
Banker. **Personal:** Born Jan 28, 1947, Youngstown, OH; son of Morris and Katheryn; married Barbara; children: Anneke. **Educ:** Youngstown State Univ, BS, advert & pub rels, 1970; Xavier Univ, MBA, mkt, 1979; COL Mt St Joseph, acct cert, 1988. **Career:** Pitney Bowes Inc, sales, 1973; Ford Motor Co, zonal sales mgr, 1973-80; Fifth Third Bank Northeastern Ohio, mgr consumer lending div, bank dir, exec vpres, 1980-2008; Lakeland Community Col, adj prof bus, 2008-. **Orgs:** Omega Psi Phi Fraternity, 1968; pres, Nat Black MBA Asn, Cleveland, 1990-92; bd mem, Cleveland C's Mus, 1993-95; trustee, Urban League Cleveland, 1994-99; bd mem, Am Cancer Soc, 1995-; Urban Financial Asn, 1995-; trustee, Alumni Asn Youngstown State Univ, 1999; pres, Pepper Pike Civic League, 2000; vis comt, James J Nance Col Bus Admin, Cleveland State Univ, 2000-; trustee, Better Bus Bur, Cleveland OH, 2000-; Faith Fel Church; Northeastern Neighborhood Develop Corp; Williamson Col Bus Youngstown State Univ; dir, Veteran's Bus Coun Northern Ohio; dir, Minority Bus Assistance Prog. **Honors/Awds:** BLACK Achiever, YMCA, 1984; Outstanding Businessman, Dollar & Sense Magazine, 1993; Cleveland Growth ASN, Leadership Cleveland, 1997. **Home Addr:** 30700 Shaker Blvd, Cleveland, OH 44124, **Home Phone:** (216)831-5133. **Business Addr:** Adjunct Professor of Business, Lakeland Community College, 7700 Clocktower Dr, Kirtland, OH 44094, **Business Phone:** (440)525-7000.

### GRAHAM, GARTH N.
Government official, medical researcher, foundation executive. **Educ:** Fla Int Univ Miami, BS, biol; Yale Sch Pub Health, MPH; Yale Sch Med, MD, 2001; Mass Gen Hosp & Johns Hopkins. **Career:** Harvard Med Sch, fac; Univ Fla Sch Med, fac; Nat Health Info Technol Collab, chmn; US Dept Health & Human Serv, dep asst secy & head dept minority health; Univ Conn Sch Med, assoc prof, med; Univ Fla Sch Med (Gainesville), asst dean health policy & chief health serv res; Aetna Found, pres, 2013-. **Orgs:** Bd mem, N Am Thrombosis Forum; bd mem, Who Sci Group Equity Anal & Res; bd dir, Physicians Human Rights; Fed Coord Coun Comparative Effectiveness Res, Appointee. **Honors/Awds:** Kaiser Permanente, Future Thought Leaders in Healthcare; "The Root" Magazine, The Root 100 Honorees, 2013; Distinguished Millennium Visiting Scholar, Columbia Univ; Inaugural Credo Award, Am Col Cardiol; 20 People Who Make Healthcare Better, "Healthleaders" Magazine. **Special Achievements:** Authored Book: "The Role of Decentralization in Strengthening Equity in Healthcare," 2009; Widely published researcher, writer, and editor on disparities in healthcare-published in "Journal of American Medical Association," "Health Affairs," and "Circulation". **Business Addr:** President, Aetna Foundation, 151 Farmington Ave, Hartford, CT 06156, **Business Phone:** (860)273-6382.

### GRAHAM, GEORGE WASHINGTON
Government official. **Personal:** Born Feb 16, 1949, Kinston, NC; son of George W Sr and Mattie L; married Marilyn; children: Marilyn, George III, Alicia & Brandi. **Educ:** Fayetteville State Univ, BS, 1971; NC State Univ, MS, adult & community col educ, 1975, EdD, adult & community col educ, currently. **Career:** US Post Off, Fayetteville, NC, mail handler, 1967-71; Simone Jr High Sch, instr & athletic coach, 1971-72; Lenoir Community Col, Kinston, NC, adult basic educ dir, 1972-76, admin asst to pres & resource develop officer, 1977-79, chmn, currently; Dobbs Sch, Kinston, NC, exec dir, 1979-, chief exec dir; Lenoir County, bd comnr, mem, 1982-, chmn, currently; Eastern Nc Poverty Comt, exec dir; NC Dept Human Resources, Equal Opportunity officer; NC Dept Health & Human Serv, employee rels specialist. **Orgs:** Omega Psi Phi; Nat Asn Advan Colored People; St Augustus AME Zion Church; Jaycees, Masons, Kinston Rotary Club; NC Asn Black Elected Officials, Lenoir County Black Artist Guild; bd comnrs, Lenoir County; bd dir, Lenoir Mem Hosp; bd dir, United Way; Lenoir County Comn 100; bd dir, Lenoir County Health; NC Gen Assembly Spec Legis Comn Fairness Taxation; NC Asn County Comnrs Taxation & Finance Steering Comm; chmn, bldg comn, St Augustus AME Zion Church; bd dir, NC Asn County Comnrs; Greene Lamp Board. **Honors/Awds:** Teacher of the Year, 1971; Jaycee of the Month, 1973; Outstanding Educator of the Year, 1974; Outstanding Educator of America, 1974-75; Outstanding Black Educator, 1976; Jaycee Boss of the Year, 1979; Man of the Year, Omega Psi Phi, 1979; Distinguished Service Award Nominee, Kinston, Lenoir County Chamber Com, 1980; Governor's Award for Excellence Nominee, 1987. **Home Addr:** 419 Duggins Dr, PO Box 1082, Kinston, NC 28503, **Home Phone:** (252)527-6865. **Business Addr:** Chairman, Lenoir County, 130 S Queen St, Kinston, NC 28502, **Business Phone:** (252)559-6454.

### GRAHAM, GREGORY LAWRENCE
Basketball player, basketball coach. **Personal:** Born Nov 26, 1970, Indianapolis, IN. **Educ:** Ind Univ, attended 1993. **Career:** Basketball player (retired), basketball coach; Charlotte Hornets, guard & shooting guard, 1993; Philadelphia 76ers, shooting guard, 1993-95; NJ Nets, shooting guard, 1995-96; Seattle Supersonics, shooting guard, 1996-97; Cleveland Cavaliers, shooting guard, 1997-98; Idaho Stampede, 1997-98; Ft Wayne Fury, 1998-99; Boras Basket, Sweden, 1999-2000; Ind Alley Cats, head coach, 2005-06; Warren Cent High Sch, Teacher & Coach, 2008-15; Salve Regina Univ, asst coach, 2015-. **Orgs:** Am Basketball Asn. **Home Addr:** 9021 Butternut Ct, Indianapolis, IN 46260. **Business Addr:** Assistant Coach, Salve Regina University, 100 Ochre Pt Ave, Newport, RI 02840, **Business Phone:** (401)847-6650.

### GRAHAM, HELEN W.
Educator. **Personal:** Born New York, NY; daughter of Raymond and Pauline; married Fitzroy; children: Rosalyn & Shelle. **Educ:** Howard Univ, DC, BA, 1950; Hunter Col, New York, NY, MS, 1974. **Career:** Educator (retired); S Siegel Inc, New York, NY, off mgr, 1950-55; Brooklyn Bd Educ, Brooklyn, NY, teacher, 1962-89. **Orgs:** Treas, Nat Sorority Phi Delta Kappa Inc, Beta Omicron Chap, 1987-91; vpres, Key Women Am Inc, 1989-92; Protestant Teachers Asn; Nat Asn Univ Women. **Home Addr:** 134 29 166th Pl Suite 10A, Jamaica, NY 11434.

### GRAHAM, JAMES C., JR.
Executive director, chief executive officer, association executive. **Personal:** Born Aug 1, 1945, Ft. Wayne, IN; son of James C Sr and Marjorie Dickerson; married Cecelia; children: James C III (deceased), Joy, Angela, Margie & Audrey. **Educ:** Hillsdale Col, Hillsdale, Mich, BS, psychol, 1972; Nat Urban League Whitney M Young Exec Prog, New York, NY, dipl, 1984; Univ Wis; IBM Exec Develop Prog. **Career:** Metrop Human Rel Comn, Ft Wayne, Ind, dir, 1972-77; Madison Urban League, Madison, Wis, exec dir, 1977-83; Birmingham Urban League, Birmingham, Ala, dir, pres & chief exec officer, 1983. **Orgs:** Pres, Nat Urban League, Southern Coun CEOs, 1990-; Inclusiveness Comt, Govt Rel Comt, United Way; Alpha Phi Alpha Fraternity; Boy Scouts Am, Leadership Birmingham; Chamber Com Community Rel Comt; Southern Inst C & Families; chmn, PIC Nomination Comt, Pvt Indust Coun; Birmingham Youth Task Force. **Honors/Awds:** Martin Luther King Humanitarian Award, Madison, Wis. **Home Addr:** 5404 Cornell Dr, Irondale, AL 35210-2930, **Home Phone:** (205)956-5914. **Business Addr:** AL.

**GRAHAM, JAMES OTIS.** See GRAHAM, SCOTTIE.

### GRAHAM, JEFF TODD (JEFFERY TODD GRAHAM)
Football player, radio host. **Personal:** Born Feb 14, 1969, Dayton, OH. **Educ:** Ohio State Univ; Concordia Univ, polit sci; John Abbott Col, creative arts. **Career:** Football player (retired), radio host; Pittsburgh Steelers, wide receiver, 1991-93; Chicago Bears, 1994-95; New York Jets, 1996-97; Philadelphia Eagles, wide receiver, 1998; San Diego Chargers, wide receiver, 1999-2001; 1053 KISS-FM, Ottawa, eve dj, 2004-06, afternoon dr dj, 2006-09, music dir/announcer, 2009-. **Business Addr:** Announcer, Music Director, KISS FM, 2001 Thurston Dr, Ottawa, ON K1G 6C9, **Business Phone:** (613)736-2001.

### GRAHAM, DR. JO-ANN CLARA
Educator, college administrator. **Personal:** daughter of James Harold and Clara Polhemus. **Educ:** NY Univ, BS, 1962, MA, 1968, PhD, human commun, 1982. **Career:** City Univ NY, Bronx Community Col, prof commun arts & sci, 1970, dept chairperson & head humanities, chmn commun, div coordr humanities, prof emer. **Orgs:** Exec bd, NY State TESOL, 1970-73; comn panel, Am Arbit Asn, 1976; bd dir, Asn Black Charities, 1982; consult, Mayors Vol Action Ctr; NY

City Bd Educ; Maj NY City Law Firm; McGraw-Hill; Addison Wesley; Macmillan; N Hudson Lang Develop Ctr; Haryou-Act; vpres, G & S Assocs-Human Commun; bd mem, Hammond Mus; Cinque Art Gallery; Ernest Crichlow; Norman Lewis. **Home Addr:** 555 Kappock St, Bronx, NY 10463, **Home Phone:** (718)543-1479.

### GRAHAM, LADELL
Executive, president (organization). **Personal:** Born Oct 16, 1957, Shreveport, LA; son of Johnnie Lee and Corine Horton; married Gwendolyn Smith; children: Justin, Jonathan & Jasmine. **Educ:** Southern Univ, BBS, acct, 1981. **Career:** Assocs Corp, vpres, portfolio mgr, treas liaison & corp acct, 1981-87; Dean Witter, investment mgr, 1987-88; Am Capital Asset Mgt Inc, vice pres & portfolio mgr, 1987-90; Am Capital, investment vpres, 1988-90; Smith, Graham & Co, pres & chief investment officer, 1990-2000; Smith, Graham & Co Investment Advisors LP, founder, pres & chief investment officer, 1990-97; Champion Ctr, founder, 2000-. **Orgs:** Dist enrollment chmn, Boy Scouts Am, 1992; Nat Investment Mgrs Asn, 1995; Nat Asn Securities Professionals, 1995; Am Diabetes Asn, 1995; Tex Children's Hosp Develop Coun, 1995. **Home Addr:** 3902 Colony Woods Dr, Sugar Land, TX 77479-2842.

### GRAHAM, LARRY, JR.
Musician. **Personal:** Born Aug 14, 1946, Beaumont, TX; married Tina; children: Darric. **Career:** Dell Graham Jazz Trio, 1951-67; Sly & The Family Stone, bass play, 1967-73; Graham Cent Sta Mavimus Prod, founder & pres, 1973-77; Albums: Star Walk, 1979; One in a Million You, 1980; Just Be My Lady, 1981; Sooner or Later, 1982; Victory, 1983; Fired Up, 1985; Songs: "One in a Million You", 1980; "When We Get Married", 1980; "Guess Who", 1981; "Just Be My Lady", 1981; "Sooneror Later", 1982; "Don't Stop When You're Hot", 1982; "I Never Forget Your Eyes", 1983. **Orgs:** Jehovah's Witness. **Honors/Awds:** Top Star Award; Best Dress, 1973; Best Dress, 1973-74; Entertainer of the Year, 1975. **Business Addr:** Musician, Mister I Mouse Ltd, 920 Dickson St, Marina Del Rey, CA 90292.

### GRAHAM, MARIAH
Educator, executive, artist. **Personal:** Born Nov 3, 1946, SC. **Educ:** Sch Visual Arts, dipl, fashion illus, 1968. **Career:** Mariah Graham Illustrations, owner & bk & fashion Illusr, 1968-, pres, 1969-; New York Times, freelance artist, 1968-; Mary Mt Col, prof, 1977-; Fashion Inst Technol, instr, 1978-, fac; Greenwich Art Soc, fac, currently; Fordham Univ, adj prof art, 2000-07; Parsons Sch Design, adj prof, 2007-08; EF int Sch lang, adj fashion prof master's prog graphic design & fashion, 2010-. **Orgs:** Soc Illus; Graphic Art Guild; Drama & Guild Broadway. **Honors/Awds:** Certificate of Appreciation, Baruch Col, 1976; The One Show Merit Award, Art Direct Club, 1976; Certificate of Merit, Soc Illus, 1978; Certificate of Merit, New York Col, 1979. **Home Addr:** Rr 52, Jeffersonville, NY 12748, **Home Phone:** (845)482-4036. **Business Addr:** President, Owner, Mariah Graham Illustrations, PO Box 425, Jeffersonville, NY 12748, **Business Phone:** (845)482-4036.

### GRAHAM, ODELL
Scientist. **Personal:** Born Mar 31, 1931, Chicago, IL; son of James and Gertha Scott; married Loretta Harriet Lewis; children: Karyn, Cynthia & Jessica. **Educ:** Univ Calif, Los Angeles, BS, physics, 1961, MS, elec engineering, 1967, PhD, elec engineering, 1976. **Career:** Scientist (retired): Hughes Aircraft Co, Culver City, CA, res & asst, 1954-60, Canoga Pk, CA, div chief scientist, 1961-92; Alliant Techsystems, principle scientist, 1994-2007; Hycon Mfg Co, Monrovia, CA, elec engr, 1960-61; ATK Missile Systs Co, prin scientist, 1992; Graham Engineering Consult, engineering consult, 2010-. **Orgs:** Life sr mem, Inst Electronic & Elect Engr, 1972-; chmn, Los Angeles Chap Anten & Prop Soc Inst Elec & Electron Engr; Nat Asn Advan Colored People; exec comt mem, engineering dean's coun, Univ Calif, Los Angeles, 1987-; Tech Adv Comt, Hughes Univ; fel Inst Advan Engineering, 1981. **Honors/Awds:** Fel, Inst Advan Engineering, 1981; Engineering Merit Award, San Fernando Valley Engineering Coun, 1986; Black Engineer of the Year, Outstanding Tech Achievement, 1991. **Home Addr:** 3152 W Cumberland Ct, Westlake Village, CA 91362, **Home Phone:** (805)497-8419.

### GRAHAM, DR. PATRICIA G.
Educator. **Personal:** Born Mar 9, 1949, Saluda, SC; daughter of Eddie Roy and Lillian Leo Wertz. **Educ:** Rutgers Univ, BA, 1972; Antioch Col, MEd, 1974; Univ Mass, EdD, 1995. **Career:** Morrell Sch Girls, group leader, 1972-74; Widener Univ, coun, 1974-77; E Stroudsburg Univ, assoc prof, 1977, coun, 1977, Dept Acad Enrichment & Learning, prof, dept intercultural & interdisciplinary studies, dept chair & prof, prof emer, 1977-2013. **Orgs:** Pres, Pocono Chap, Phi Delta Kappa, 1994-95; Nat Asn Aadvan Colored People; Am Asn Coun & Develop; Am Asn Univ Prof; pres, Pa Asn Multicultural Coun; div Pa coun Asn; bd dirs, NE Pa Region, United Negro Col Fund; vpres, Asn Pa State Col & Univ Facul. **Honors/Awds:** Appreciation Award, Black Student Asn E Stroudsburg Univ, 1981; Chi Alpha Epsilon Honor Society Award, 1994; Martin Luther King Award, 2009; APSCUF Leadership Award, 2010. **Home Addr:** 426 Saw Creek Estates, Bushkill, PA 18324, **Home Phone:** (717)588-2892. **Business Addr:** Professor, Department Chair, E Stroudsburg University, Rm 1 Monroe Hall 200 Prospect St, East Stroudsburg, PA 18301-2999, **Business Phone:** (570)422-3211.

### GRAHAM, PAUL, JR.
Basketball player. **Personal:** Born Nov 28, 1967, Philadelphia, PA; married Rosa Marie Gonzales; children: Paul. **Educ:** Ohio Univ, attended 1989. **Career:** Basketball player (retired); Albany Patroons, shooting guard, 1990-91; Philadelphia Spirit, 1991; Altanta Hawks, shooting guard, 1991-94. **Home Addr:** N Marshall St, Philadelphia, PA 19120-3134.

**GRAHAM, PROF. PRECIOUS JEWEL.** See Obituaries Section.

### GRAHAM, RHEA L.
Geologist. **Personal:** children: 2. **Educ:** Bryn Mawr Col, BA, 1974; Ore State Univ, MA, 1977. **Career:** Sci Appln Int Corp, sr scientist; US Bur Mines, dir; State Nmex's Mining, Minerals Div Energy Minerals & Natural Resources Dept, adminr; Deuel & Assocs, sr engrg geologist; NMex Interstate Stream Comn, dir & mgr, currently. **Special Achievements:** First African American to be nominated as director for the US Bureau of Mines in its 84 year history, 1994. **Business Addr:** Director, Manager, New Mexico Interstate Stream Commission, 407 Galisteo St Bataan Memorial Bldg, Santa Fe, NM 87504-5102, **Business Phone:** (505)827-6160.

### GRAHAM, SAUNDRA M.
State government official, activist. **Personal:** Born Sep 5, 1941, Cambridge, MA; daughter of Charles B Postell and Roberta Betts Postell; children: Carl Jr, Rhonda, Tina, Darryl & David. **Educ:** Univ Mass, attended 1973; Harvard Univ. **Career:** Harvard Univ, Loeb fel; Riverside Cambridgeport Community Develop Corp, pres, 1971, co-founder; Cambridge City Coun, chairwoman Housing & Land Use Comt, 1972-88; State MA, vice mayor, 1976-77, counr, state rep, 1976-88; Multicultural Arts Ctr Comt, chairwomen, 1977-78; Graham & Parks Alternative Pub Sch, 1981; polit activist. **Orgs:** Bd dir, Cambridge Community Ctr, 1968; pres, Riverside Planning Team, 1970; Mass Legislators Asn; co-chair, Mass Coalition, 1983; Mass Black Legis Caucus; Mass Caucus Women Legislators. **Honors/Awds:** Distinguished Citizen Award, Mass Asn Afro-American Policeman, 1974; Award for Community Service, Boston Masons, 1974; Citations from Gov & Mass Secy State; National Sojourner Truth Award, Nat Asn Negro Bus & Prof Women's Clubs, 1976; Distinguished Citizen Award, Nat Asn Negro Bus & Professional Women's Clubs, 1976; Recognition Award, Cent Sq Cambridge Businessmen Asn, 1980; Woman of the Year, Boston Chap, Nat Orgn Women, 1982; The Graham and Parks Alternative Public School was named in her honor. **Special Achievements:** First African American woman representative from Cambridge to the State House. **Home Addr:** 189 Western Ave, Cambridge, MA 02139-3703, **Home Phone:** (617)491-4153.

### GRAHAM, SCOTTIE (JAMES OTIS GRAHAM)
Football player, executive director. **Personal:** Born Mar 28, 1969, Long Beach, NY; married Mary; children: Mylek & Marika. **Educ:** Ohio State Univ, BA, recreational educ, 1991; MA, black studies & black community, 1996. **Career:** Football player (retired), executive director; New York Jets, running back, 1992; Minn Vikings, running back, 1993-97; Cincinnati Bengals, running back, 1997; WBNS-TV, Sports Reporter, Sports Analyst, 1996-97; NFL Players Asn, regional dir, 1998-10, Dir Player Engagement, 2010-14; Sun Devil Athletics, sr assoc athletics dir, 2014-. **Orgs:** Reg dir, Nat Football League Players Asn, 1998-10. **Business Addr:** Director of Player Engagement, Director of Player Engagement, 1133 20th St NW Suite 600, Washington, DC 20036, **Business Phone:** (202)463-2200.

### GRAHAM, STEDMAN
Marketing executive, chairperson, chief executive officer. **Personal:** Born Mar 6, 1951, Whitesboro, NJ; son of Stedham Sr and Mary (deceased); married Glenda; children: Wendy. **Educ:** Hardin-Simmons Univ, BA, social work, 1974; Ball State Univ, MA, educ, 1979. **Career:** European Leagues, basketball player; B & C Assocs; Graham Gregory Bozell Inc, chief exec officer, 1996-; University of Illinois at Chicago, adj prof; adj prof; University of Chicago, Coker Col, distinguished vis prof, currently; Full Sail University, adj prof, currently; Temple Univ, adj prof, currently; S Graham & Assoc, chmn & chief exec officer, currently. Books: The Ultimate Guide to Sport Event Management and Marketing, 1995; You Can Make It Happen: A Nine Step Plan for Success, 1997; You Can Make It Happen Every Day, 1998; Teens Can Make It Happen: Nine Steps for Success, 2000; Teens Can Make It Happen Workbook, 2001; The Ultimate Guide to Sports Marketing, 2001; Build Your Own Life Brand!: A Powerful Strategy to Maximize Your Potential and Enhance Your Value for Ultimate Achievement, 2002; Move Without the Ball: Put Your Skills and Your Magic to Work for You, 2004; Who Are You?, 2005; Diversity: Leaders Not Labels: A New Plan for the 21st Century, 2006; Identity: Your Passport to Success, 2012. **Orgs:** Founder & exec dir, Athletes Against Drugs, 1985-; founder & dir, George Wash Univ, Forum Sport & Event Mgt & Mkt, 1994; co-founder, Youth Opportunity Movement; founder, Concerned Citizens Whitesboro; nat bd Jr Achievement; 7-Eleven Educ Is Freedom Found; Econ Club Chicago; founder, My Life About Found. **Business Addr:** Chairman, Chief Executive Officer, S Graham & Associates, 455 N Cityfront Plz Dr 15th Fl, Chicago, IL 60611, **Business Phone:** (312)755-0234.

### GRAIN, DAVID J.
Founder (originator), executive. **Educ:** Col Holy Cross, BA, Eng, 1984; Dartmouth Col, Amos Tuck Sch Bus, MBA, finance & strategy, 1989. **Career:** Morgan Stanley, High Yield Finance Dept, exec dir; AT&T Broadband's New Eng Region, sr vpres; Grain Commun Group Inc, founder & chief exec officer; Global Signal Inc, pres, 2002-06; Grain Mgt L.L.C., founder & managing partner, 2006-. **Orgs:** Nat Infrastructure Adv Coun, (app by Pres. Barack Obama), 2011; vice chair, Fla State Bd Admin, Investment Adv Coun; chmn, PRIM Investment Comt; bd dir, Southern Co; World Pres's Orgn; Bus Execs Nat Security; founding dir, Gateway Bank Southwest Fla; Nat Finance Comt Obama Am; bd trustees, Col Holy Cross; MBA adv bd mem, Amos Tuck Sch Bus Admin Dartmouth Col; US Tennis Asn. **Honors/Awds:** "Black Enterprise," 75 Most Powerful Blacks on Wall Street, 2011; Ten Outstanding Young Leaders Award, Boston Jaycees. **Business Addr:** Founder, Managing Partner, Grain Management LLC, 100 N Wash Blvd Suite 201, Sarasota, FL 34236, **Business Phone:** (941)373-0033.

### GRAMBY, SHIRLEY ANN
Manager, executive. **Personal:** Born , 1954, Hartford, CT; daughter of Sarge McCall Jr and Elizabeth McCall; married Charles E; children: Talib Eric & Shamar Terrell. **Educ:** BS, elem, spec educ, 1977; MA, admin & mkt, 1990. **Career:** OH BUR Workers Compensation, pub info asst, 1979-81; Indust CMS OH, mgt analyst, 1981-86; OH Dept Human Serv, prog planner, policy analyst, human serv specialist, 1986-; Sunrise Broadcasting, Power 106.3, WCKX Radio, prom dir, community events, dir, 1992-; WVKO, prom dir; Events Occasion, managing partner. **Orgs:** Co-chair, arts & lett, DST, 1988-90; exe vip, N E Linden Athletic ASN, 1989-90; bd mem, fundraising chair, Neighborhood House, 1989-; new prog com, United Way, 1989-; recruitment com, Leadership Columbus, 1990-; steering com, I Know I Can, 1990-; vip, Wilberforce UNIV Alumnae, Columbus cha, 1991-92; AMR Cancer SOC, Franklin Co Breast Cancer Task Force, 1990-91; Columbus Asn Black Journalists, 1st vpres, currently; Columbus Bridal Consults. **Honors/Awds:** James Penney Cash Award Outstanding Volunteers, 1987; Mayors Award, Outstanding COT Service, 1988; Jaycee of the Year, PRS's Award, Columbus Jaycees, 1989; Distinguished Service Award, DST, 1989-90; Walter & Marian English COT Service Award, 1990. **Special Achievements:** Showcasing Youth in the 90's, DST, Columbus Alumnae Proj, 1988-89; Afro Fair, 1990; Family Festival, Columbus Urban League, 1990-91; Greater Columbus Arts Festival, 1992; Celebrity Waiters, Comedy Night, 1991-92; Author: Boxing Championship. **Home Addr:** 7928 Oak Valley Rd, PO Box 1433, Reynoldsburg, OH 43068-6433, **Home Phone:** (614)475-5868. **Business Addr:** 1st Vice President, Columbus Association of Black Journalists, PO Box 1924, Columbus, OH 43216.

### GRANDBERRY, NIKKI V.
Public relations executive. **Educ:** Va Commonwealth Univ, BS, mass commun, 1975. **Career:** WJBK-TV, gen assignment reporter, 1978-86; WXYZ-TV, cohost "Company", 1994; Simons Michelson Zieve Inc, pub rels, pub rel partner, 1986-2009; Grandberry & Co, pr consult, 2008-; Adult Well-Being Serv, hiv/aids & sub abuse prev outreach worker, 2009-13; Nat Caucas & Ctr Black Aged, job counr, 2014-; Mediation Tribunal Asn, admin asst, 2014-; Detroit Pub Schs, substitute teacher. **Business Addr:** Administrative Assistant, Mediation Tribunal Association, 333 W Ft St Suite 1500, Detroit, MI 48226, **Business Phone:** (313)967-3348.

**GRANDERSON, ELZIE LEE.** See GRANDERSON, LZ.

### GRANDERSON, LZ (ELZIE LEE GRANDERSON)
Columnist, writer, journalist. **Personal:** Born Mar 11, 1972, Detroit, MI; son of Alma Miller; children: Isaiah; married Steve Huesing. **Educ:** Western Mich Univ, BA; Grand Valley State Univ. **Career:** Grand Rapids Press, writer; Atlanta J-Const, home design writer & sportswriter; S Bend Tribune; ESPN: Mag, freelance writer, 2003-04, NBA ed, 2004-, tennis ed, sr writer & columnist; ESPN, sr writer & contribr, 2004-; CNN, columnist & contribr, 2011-; ABC, contribr; ESPN.com, sr writer & columnist; Undefeated, sr writer; Northwestern Univ, lectr. **Honors/Awds:** Gay and Lesbian Alliance Against Defamation Award, 2009; Journalist of the Year, National Lesbian and Gay Journalists Association, 2011; The Institute of Politics, fellow; Hechinger Institute, fellow. **Special Achievements:** His TEDx talk, The Myth of the Gay Agenda, has been viewed more than one million times. **Business Addr:** ESPN, ESPN Plz, Bristol, CT 06010.

### GRANGER, EDWINA C.
Artist. **Personal:** Born Yonkers, NY; daughter of Paul Weldon and Christina White Weldon Small. **Educ:** NY Univ, courses & cert sculp ceramic, 1952; Caton Rose Inst Fine Arts, landscape anat, 1958; Art Stud League NY, portrait fig, 1962; N Mex Univ, compos abstract, 1965; Rutgers Univ, cert real estate, 1978. **Career:** Creative Arts McGuire AFB, teacher, 1963-64; exhibiting artist, 1964-69; Portugal & TTS Colonies People Exhibits, original pen & ink prints, 1973-80; Doll Shows Applehead, doll maker, 1976-80; Art work: The Spectators; African Market Place, 1990; Holiday Walk, 1990; Caribbean Dancer, 1990; Girl with Oranges; The Family; Lost in the Fog. **Orgs:** Nat Conf Artists Nat League Am Pen Women, 1965-81; Meadow Lands Race Track 3 Shows, 1979-84; Festival art consult, Garden State Art Ctr, 1980; Nat Asn Advan Colored People, 1985; Southern Christian Leadership Conf Women, 1988-92. **Honors/Awds:** Alexander Medal of Honor, Walton High Sch; Outstanding Achievement Art Award, NBPW, Willingboro, NJ. **Special Achievements:** Martin Luther King Show/Prints/Oils/Pen/Ink; Women Artists, p 33, 1990; Publication: Artist of GA Vol III, cover resume pictures, p 37-38, 1994; first prize in many art shows, Illinois, New Mexico, New York, New Jersey, and Azores. **Home Addr:** 7145 Chestnut Lane, Riverdale, GA 30274, **Home Phone:** (770)473-9955.

### GRANT, ANDRE M.
Lawyer, educator. **Educ:** Univ Iowa Col Law, JD. **Career:** Law Off Andre M Grant, prin & atty, currently; Chicago State Univ, asst prof criminal justice, currently. **Orgs:** N'Digo Found Scholar Comt; Cook County Bar Asn. **Business Addr:** Assistant Professor, Chicago State University, HWH 325 9501 S King Dr, Chicago, IL 60628, **Business Phone:** (773)995-2108.

### GRANT, ANTHONY T.
Banker, president (organization), chief executive officer. **Personal:** married Helen; children: Hamilton, Alexander, Kristina & Katherine. **Educ:** SC State Univ, BS, bus admin, 1982; Univ VA, Colgate-Darden Grad Sch Bus, com lending exec prog. **Career:** Bank Am, mgt trainee, 1982, bus banking div exec, pres multicultural banking group, chmn asset qual rev, regional com banking exec; Nations Bank, prof African Am banking group, chmn asset qual rev; Providence Search, consult; Grant Bus Strategies Inc, co-founder, chief exec officer, 2001-; Advan Am Cash Advan Centers Inc, dir. **Orgs:** Bd mem, BobbyPhills Fund; chmn, SC State Univ; bd trustee, chmn, United Negro Col Fund Campaign, Charlotte, NC; exec comt mem bd trustee, Nat Urban League; chmn & founding mem, 100 Black Men, Columbia, SC; bd mem, Fayetteville State Univ; bd mem, NC Citizens Bus & Indust; bd mem, United Way Cent Carolinas; bd mem, United Way Cent Carolinas Alexis de Tocqueville Socs; bd mem, United Way Am's Nat Leadership Coun; chmn, State's Comn Racial Rels. **Honors/Awds:** Order of the Palmetto, State of South Carolina, 1994; National Distinguished Alumnus Award, Alma Mater's; National Urban League's Volunteer Services Award; Randolph Canzater Lifetime Achievement Award; Donald H McGarmon Award, 1999; Hall of Fame, Omega Psi Phi fraternity, 1999; Tribute to Achievement Award, Maya Angelou/United Negro College Fund, 2001; Charlotte Post's People of Prominence Award, 2001; Eagle Award, Omega Psi Phi fraternity. **Home Addr:** 2114 Bermuda Hills Rd, Columbia, SC 29223-6733, **Home Phone:**

(803)518-5916. **Business Addr:** Chief Executive Officer, Chairman & Owner, Grant Business Strategies Inc, PO Box 23527, Columbia, SC 29244-3527, **Business Phone:** (803)419-8500.

## GRANT, ASHLEY
Business owner. **Career:** Artco Systs Inc, co-owner, currently. **Business Addr:** Co-owner, Artco Systems Inc, 1810 Forrest Pkwy Ave SE, Lake City, GA 30260, **Business Phone:** (404)635-9001.

## GRANT, DR. AUGUSTUS O.
Physician, educator. **Personal:** Born Jamaica; married Stephanie; children: Siobhan Earlyn. **Educ:** Univ Edinburgh, Scotland, MBChB, 1971; Univ Calif, San Francisco, CA, PhD, 1975; Univ Manitoba, Can, attended 1977; Duke Univ Med Ctr, Durham, NC, attended 1980. **Career:** Duke Univ Med Ctr, prof med, vice dean fac enrichment, currently; J Cardiovasc Electrophysiology, dep ed, currently; Am J Physiology Heart & Circulation, consult ed, currently. **Orgs:** Pres, Asn Black Cardiologists, 1992-94; pres, Am Heart Asn, 2003-04; Fel Am Heart Asn; fel Am Col Cardiol; Biophys Soc; Am Soc Clin Invest. **Home Addr:** 2562 Bittersweet Dr, Durham, NC 27705, **Home Phone:** (919)660-2200. **Business Addr:** Vice Dean, Professor of Medicine, Duke University Medical Center, 3116 N Duke St, Durham, NC 27704, **Business Phone:** (919)684-5948.

## GRANT, BRIAN WADE
Basketball player. **Personal:** Born Mar 5, 1972, Columbus, OH; married Gina; children: Amani, Elijah, Jaydon, Jonavan, Brian, Maliah & Anaya. **Educ:** Xavier Univ, orgn commun, 1994. **Career:** Basketball player (retired); Sacramento Kings, power forward, 1994-97; Portland Trailblazers, small forward, 1997-98, power forward, 1998-2000; Miami Heat, ctr, 2000-01, power forward, 2001-02, ctr, 2002-04; Los Angeles Lakers, ctr, 2004-05; Phoenix Suns, ctr, 2005-06; Boston Celtics, 2006. **Orgs:** Founder, Brian Grant Found. **Honors/Awds:** Horizon League Player of the Year, 1993, 1994; Rookie of the Year Award, 1994; NBA All-Rookie First Team, 1995; J Walter Kennedy Citizenship Award, 1999. **Special Achievements:** Film appearance: Eddie. **Business Addr:** Founder, Brian Grant Foundation, 650 NE Holladay St Suite 1600, Portland, OR 97232, **Business Phone:** (503)274-9382.

## GRANT, JUDGE CHERYL DAYNE
Lawyer, social worker, educator. **Personal:** Born Jan 3, 1944, Cincinnati, OH; married Daniel R; married Claude H Audley. **Educ:** Univ Cincinnati, BA, sociol & anthrop, 1966; Univ Cincinnati Law Sch, JD, 1973. **Career:** Memorial Community Ctr, social worker, 1966-68, pres; Cincinnati, police officer, 1968-70; Nat Asn Advan Colored People, scholar, 1970-73; Cincinnati Lawyers Housing, 1972; Legal Aid Soc, atty, 1973-74; Cong Thomas A Luken House Rep, admin aide, 1974-; Univ Cincinnati, Col Bus, asst prof, 1976-78; CD Grant & Assoc Co LPA, asst Ohio atty gen, 1979-80, Law owner; Off Munic Invest, chief invest; City Lincoln Heights, Ohio, dir legal serv; Hamilton County, asst pub defender; Southern Dist Ohio, asst US atty; ABC'S Law WCIN-RADIO, co-mod; Hamilton County Munic Ct, judge, 1997-. **Orgs:** Ohio Youth Adv Bd, 1974-77; Ohio Juv Justice Adv Comt, 1976-; Nat Asn Advan Colored People; bd dir, Womens City Club; bd mem, City Comn Justice & Corrections; pres bd, Community Ctr; Alpha Kappa Alpha Sorority; Elisha Chap - Ohio Eastern Stars & PHA; Zion Baptist Church; Black Career Women, Inc; Am Judges Asn; Cincinnati Bar Asn; Ohio Bar Asn; Am Bar Asn; Cincinnati Lawyers Club; Black Lawyers Asn Cincinnati; Regin Heber Smith fel Howard Univ; chairperson, Hamilton County Munic Ct Comt Technol; Ohio Judicial Conf; Ohio Asn Munic & County Judges; Univ Cincinnati Found Bd. **Honors/Awds:** Woman of Achievement Award, YWCA; Living Legend Award, Univ Cincinnati; African American Millennium Award, Harriet Beecher Stowe Hist Cult Asn; Edith Sampson Distinguished Political & Judicial Achievement Award, Mallory Hist Asn. **Home Addr:** 2181 Victory Pkwy Suite 106, Cincinnati, OH 45206, **Home Phone:** (513)751-5119. **Business Addr:** Judge, Municipal Court of Hamilton County, 1000 Main St, Cincinnati, OH 45202, **Business Phone:** (513)946-5165.

## GRANT, CHRISTINE S.
College teacher. **Educ:** Brown Univ, BS, chem engineering, 1984; Ga Inst Technol, MS, chem engineering, 1986, PhD, chem engineering, 1989. **Career:** NC State Univ, Fac Develop & Spec Initiatives, prof & assoc dean, currently; Am Inst Chem Engrs, fel, 2013. **Orgs:** Chair, Minority Affairs Comt Am Inst Chem Engrs. **Business Addr:** Professor, Associate Dean of Faculty Development and Special, North Carolina State University, Off Dean 115 Page Hall, Raleigh, NC 27695-7901, **Business Phone:** (919)515-7950.

## GRANT, CLAUDE DEWITT
School administrator, educator. **Personal:** Born Dec 20, 1944, New York, NY; son of Claude Allen and Rose Levonia Nelson; married Gloriana B Waters; children: Tahra Lore. **Educ:** US Armed Forces Inst, Ger; Bronx Comm Col, attended 1972; City Univ NY, Hunter Col, BA, psychol & jour, 1974; Iona Col, MS, jour & electronic publ, 1997; NY Institutle Photog, cert, Prof Photog, 2000. **Career:** NY Psychiat Inst, psych intern, 1973-74; Yonkers Youth Serv, adolescent counr, 1974-76; Jamaica Comm Adolescent Prog, assoc psychiatrist & sr social worker, 1976-79; Bronx Comm Col, coordr prog & cult affairs, 1979-86, Eng Dept, adj instr, 1991-, Bus & Prof Develop Inst, dir, coordrmkg & pub rels, founder, dir dir bus inst, 1986-99, pub rels, 1999-2007; Consult Plus comp, bus consult pract proprietor, 1991-, owner, 1992-. **Orgs:** Admin ed & fiscal officer, Blind Beggar Press, 1977-, bus mgr, co-founder, ed, designer; spec proj dir, Unity& Strength BCC, 1981-; Col Media Adv, 1982-, Assoc Ed Jour, 1983-; exec bd & pres, Bronx Coun Arts, 1968-2011; Col Jour Asn, 1984; freelance contrib, Essence Mag; freelance contrib, Amsterdam News; exec bd & vpres, Mind Builders Creative Arts Ctr, 1989-99; pres, Bronx Coun Arts Develop Corp, 1996-2000; Int Freelance Photogr Orgn, 2001-; Nat News Photogr Asn, 2002-; bd mem, Westchester/Fairfield PRSA Chap, 2008-11. **Honors/Awds:** Service Awards, Bronx, Conn, 1972, 1980, 1981, 1983, 1984; BCC Meritorious Service Awards, 1972-86; Certificate of Appreciation, US Comn Minority Bus Develop, 1992; Bronx Community Col Found, Faculty Research Award, 1993; Citation of Merit, Bronx Borough Pres Off, 1998; Cert of Graduation in Professional Photography, NY Inst Photography, 2000; Certificate of Recognition, City Univ NY, 2002, 2003, 2004. **Special Achievements:** Presented papers "Jazz, Lost Legacy of A People", University of California at Berkeley, "Creativity, Imagination Help Preserve Quality Programs on a Limited Budget", Bulletin of Associates of College Unions International, papers presented at BCC, 1986, Pace University, 1985, Howard University, 1987, books published are Keeping Time, 1981, Images in a Shaded Light, 1986, Just a Little Love, 2004; Journals: African Voices, Black Mask Magazine, Essence, Suburban Styles. **Home Addr:** 24 Bowbell Rd, White Plains, NY 10607-1106, **Home Phone:** (914)683-6792. **Business Addr:** Director of College Relations, Bronx Community College, Rm 16 Lang Hall W 181 St & Univ Ave, Bronx, NY 10453, **Business Phone:** (718)289-4124.

## GRANT, REV. DEBORA FELITA
Clergy. **Personal:** Born Jul 28, 1956, Georgetown, SC; daughter of Rev Joseph James and Lillie M Ward. **Educ:** Clark Col, Atlanta, Ga, BA, mass commun, 1981; Interdenominational Theol Ctr, Atlanta, Ga, Mdiv Pastoral Care & Coun, PhD, ministry, 1987. **Career:** SALT ministries, co founder; DHR & Div Youth Serv, Atlanta, Ga, ct serv worker, 1977-85; Interdenominational Theol Ctr, presidential scholar; Flipper Temple African Methodist Episcopal Church, Atlanta, Ga, youth pastor & asst minister; Morris Brown Col, Atlanta, Ga, chaplain; St John African Methodist Episcopal Church, pastor, currently. **Orgs:** Black Women Church & Soc, 1986-89; exec secy, Concerned Black Clergy Metro Atlanta, 1987-89; Nat Advan Asn Colored People, 1987-89; mentor & dir, African Methodist Episcopal Ministers Union, 1988-89; Nat Asn Col & Univ Chaplains, 1989; Nat Black Campus Ministers Asn, 1989; Southern Christian Leadership Conf Women, 1989; Turner Alumini Asn; Judicial Alternative, Ga; Black Women Church Soc; Women Ministry, Ga; Ga Charter Educ Found, Inc; N Ga Bd Examiners; dean, S W Ga Bd Examiners, currently. **Special Achievements:** First women to serve as chaplain at Morris Brown College; First woman to have been appointed to serve as dean in the 6th Episcopal District. **Home Addr:** 827 Lynn Cir SW, Atlanta, GA 30311-2354, **Home Phone:** (404)691-4338. **Business Addr:** Pastor, St John African Methodist Episcopal Church, 3980 Steam Mill Rd, Columbus, GA 31907, **Business Phone:** (706)682-6944.

## GRANT, ESQ. DENISE M.
Lawyer. **Educ:** George Washington Univ, BA, int rels & affairs, 1986; Georgetown Univ Law Ctr, JD, 1989. **Career:** Am Axle Mfg Inc; Abengoa Transmision Norte SA, borrower; Bank Am, NA, admin agt; Banco de Chile, borrower; IFH Pharma Corp; JBS USA LLC, borrower; Transelec SA, borrower; BBVA Securities Inc, sole lead arranger & bookrunner; Wells Fargo Bank, admin agt; Credit Agricole Corp & Investment Bank, admin agt; Citigroup Global Markets Inc, sole lead arranger & bookrunner; BBVA Bancomer SA, admin agt; Citibank NA, lead arranger, admin agt; Bank Tokyo-Mitsubishi UFJ Ltd, sole lead arranger; Citibank Del Peru SA, admin agt; Bank Ns, admin agt; Shearman & Sterling LLP, co-chairperson, currently, partner, currently. **Orgs:** Am Bar Asn; co chmn, Diversity Comt; trustee, Pingry Sch. **Honors/Awds:** Honored, Asn of Black Women Attorneys. **Special Achievements:** First African Am partner in the history of Shearman & Sterling. **Business Addr:** Partner, Shearman & Sterling LLP, Rm 1016 599 Lexington Ave, New York, NY 10022-6069, **Business Phone:** (212)848-7959.

## GRANT, DR. ELLSWORTH R.
Physician, oncologist. **Educ:** Univ Calif San Diego Sch Med, 1990. **Career:** Cedars-Sinai Med Ctr, resident, internal med, 1990-93; City Hope Natl Med Ctr, resident hemat & oncol, fel hemat & oncol, 1993-96; Pvt pract, hemat & oncol, currently; Elizabeth Ctr Cancer Detection, med dir, currently. **Orgs:** Dangriga Cancer Centre, founder. **Home Addr:** 1245 Wilshire Blvd, Los Angeles, CA 90017, **Home Phone:** (213)481-3948. **Business Addr:** Physician, Oncologist, 1338 S Hope St Lowr Level, Los Angeles, CA 90015, **Business Phone:** (213)742-5634.

## GRANT, ERNEST J.
Health services administrator, nurse, educator. **Personal:** Born Oct 6, 1958, Swannanoa, NC. **Educ:** AB Tech Col, dipl, practical nurse educ, 1977; NC Cent Univ, Durham, NC BS, nursing, 1985; Univ NC, Greensboro, NC, MS, nursing educ, 1993. **Career:** Univ NC Hosps, NC Jaycee Burn Ctr, Chapel Hill, licensed practical nurse, 1967, nursing educ clinician II, 1987-, clin educr, outreach nurse clinician; fel Am Acad Nursing, 2011. **Orgs:** Burn Ctr, QA Comt; bd dir, Am Nurses Asn, 2004-08; bd dir, Am Nurses Credentialing Ctr, 2004-07; pres, NC Nurses Asn, 2010; Am Asn Men Nursing; vice chair, bd chair, Nat Fire Protection Asn. **Special Achievements:** First African American male president of the North Carolina Nurse Association, 2010-11; First African American male to graduate from Licensed Practical Nursing program. **Business Addr:** Board Chair, National Fire Protection Association, 1 Batterymarch Pk, Quincy, MA 02169-7471, **Business Phone:** (617)770-3000.

## GRANT, GARY
Basketball coach, basketball player, president (organization). **Personal:** Born Apr 21, 1965, Canton, OH; married Tammie; children: Taryn Bree, Mahogany Simone & Piper. **Educ:** Univ Mich, BS, kinesiol, 1988. **Career:** Basketball player (retired), basketball coach, president; Los Angeles Clippers, guard, 1988-95; New York Knicks, 1995-96; Miami Heat, 1996-97; Yakima Sun Kings, 1997; Aris, Greece, 1998-99; Peristeri, Greece, 2001-02; Portland Trailblazers, guard, 1997-98, 2000-01, asst coach, 2002-03; ABA Valley Legends, pres; San Diego State Univ, asst coach, 2003-04; Mich Wolverines, 2010-11; So Cal Legends, pres & head coach, currently. **Home Addr:** 4253 Temma Ct, Calabasas, CA 91302-1879, **Home Phone:** (801)731-0857.

## GRANT, GARY RUDOLPH
Executive. **Personal:** Born Aug 19, 1943, Newport News, VA; son of Matthew and Florneza M. **Educ:** NC Cent Univ, BA, 1965; Shaw Univ, post grad; NC Wesleyan Col, post grad; Eastern NC Theol Sem, PhD, humanities, 1997. **Career:** Halifax Cty Sch, teacher, 1965-79; Tillery Casket Mfg Inc, gen mgr, 1979-; Flo-Matt United Inc, pres; Black Farmers & Agriculturalists Asn, pres, 1997-; Tillery community Halifax County Sch Syst, teacher; New York Dept Human Serv. **Orgs:** Bd mem, Concerned Citizens Tillery, 1979-85; NC Hunger Coalition, 1982-86; bd dir, Halifax City Bd Ed, 1982-86; chairperson, Comt Save Black Owned Land, 1983-; Environ Protection Agency's (EPA) Small Towns & Cities Adv Coun, 1996-98; bd mem & chairperson, African Am Environ Action Justice Network; co-dir, NC Environ Justice Network; planning comm mem, Who Owns Am Conf III, Land Tenure Ctr, Univ Wis-Madison; dir, Nat Land Loss Fund; Ctr Women Econ Alternatives; Environ Protection Agency, 1996-98; bd chairperson, Nat Black Family Land Trust, 2002. **Home Addr:** 815 Roanoke Dr, Halifax, NC 27839. **Business Addr:** President, Black Farmers Association, PO Box 61, Tillery, NC 27887, **Business Phone:** (252)826-2800.

## GRANT, DR. GEORGE C.
Library administrator. **Personal:** Born Oct 22, 1939, Memphis, TN; son of Willie L Sr and Clara Lawson; married Alice Morgan; children: Genine M & Melanie C. **Educ:** Owen Jr Col, Memphis Tenn, AA, 1959; Morehouse Col, Atlanta Ga, BS, 1961; Atlanta Univ, Atlanta Ga, MSLS, 1962; Univ Pittsburgh, SLIS, Pittsburgh, PA, PhD, 1981. **Career:** Owen Jr Col, Memphis Tenn, head librn, 1962-65; Southern Ill Univ, Edwardsville Ill, E St Louis Campus, chief librn, 1965-67, assoc dir libr, 1967-76; Morgan State Univ, Baltimore Md, libr dir, 1976-81; Stockton State Col, Pomona NJ, libr dir, 1981-86; Rollins Col, Winter Park Fla, dir librs, 1986; Four G Publ, pres & chief exec officer; Nc Cent Univ, dir libr, 2000-01; Jackson State Univ, dean, 2001-03; Ark State Univ, Libr & Info Servs, dean, 2003-; GrantHouse Publ, chief exec officer, currently. **Orgs:** Am Libr Asn, 1967-; 1971-, exec bd, 1980-, ed, newsletter, 1980-, ed, mem diry, 1984-, Black Caucus ALA; chair, 1982-86, adv comn, 1982-88, ALA Off Libr Outreach Serv; Fla Libr Asn, 1986-; bd dir, Cent Fla Soc ARO Heritage, 1987-89; steering comn, Preserve Eatonville Fla Community, 1988-90; steering comn, Cent Fla Libr Network, 1988-; adv comn, Fla State Libr, LSCA, 1988-; Urban Univ Libr Comt. **Honors/Awds:** Fel PhD Studies, Univ Pittsburgh, 1974-75; Coun Libr resources Acad, Libr Internship Yale Univ, 1975-76; Newsletter Black Caucus Ala, 1980-88; Mem Diry, Black Caucus ALA, 4th edition, 1984, 5th edition, 1986, 6th edition, 1988; BCALA Appreciation Award, 1989; Preserve Etonville Community Inc Serv Award, 1989; Eatonville Township Appreciation Award. **Special Achievements:** Compiler: Diry Ethnic Profs in Libr & Information SCI, FOUR-G Publishers Inc, 1991. **Home Addr:** 1650 Gladiolas Dr, Winter Park, FL 32792, **Home Phone:** (407)679-9331. **Business Addr:** Chief Executive Officer, GrantHouse Publishers, 2101 Green Leaf Dr, Jonesboro, AR 72401-9700, **Business Phone:** (870)934-0418.

## GRANT, DR. GWENDOLYN GOLDSBY
Counselor, writer. **Personal:** daughter of Ethel Lee and Esters; married Ralph T Jr; children: Ralph III, Sally-Ann & Rebecca. **Educ:** BS; MS, guid & coun; MS, behav sci; PhD, theol & educ. **Career:** Psychologist, sex educr, lectr; Essence, advice columnist; 21st Century Speakers Inc; TV appearances: Oprah; Montel Williams; Sally Jessy Raphael; MacNeil-Lehrer Newshour; Geraldo; Jenny Jones; Maury Povich Show; Jerry Springer Show. **Orgs:** Phi Delta Kappa; Phi Kappa Phi; Alpha Kappa Alpha Sorority; Nat Coun Negro Women; Nat Assc Black Journalists; diplomat, Am Bd Sexology; Nat Asn Black Journalists; Nat Coun Negro Women. **Honors/Awds:** Bobby E. Wright Community Service Award, Assc Black Psychologists. **Special Achievements:** Book: The Best Kind of Loving: A Black women's Guide to Finding Intimacy, HarperCollins publ, 1995. **Business Addr:** Psychologist, Writer, c/o 21st Century Speakers Inc, PO Box 1422, Gouldsboro, PA 18424, **Business Phone:** (570)842-3300.

## GRANT, HARVEY
Basketball coach, basketball player, baseball executive. **Personal:** Born Jul 4, 1965, Augusta, GA; married Beverly; children: Jerai, Jerian, Jerami & Jaelin. **Educ:** Clemson Univ, attended 1985; Independence Community Col, attended 1986; Univ Okla, attended 1988. **Career:** Basketball player (retired), basketball coach, executive; Washington Bullets, forward, 1988-93; Portland Trail Blazers, 1993-96; Washington Wizards, 1996-98, dir player develop; Philadelphia 76ers, 1999; Brevard Blue Ducks, head coach, 1999-2002; Am Nat Basketball Asn, player; Mid-Eastern Athletic Conf, asst coach. **Home Addr:** 11802 Woodbrook Ct, Bowie, MD 20721-4102.

## GRANT, HORACE JUNIOR
Basketball player. **Personal:** Born Jul 4, 1965, Augusta, GA; married Donna; children: Horace Jr; married Andrea; children: Naomi, Maia, Eva & Elijah. **Educ:** Clemson Univ, Clemson, SC, 1987. **Career:** Basketball player (retired); Chicago Bulls, forward, 1987-94; Orlando Magic, forward, 1994-99, 2001-02; Seattle SuperSonics, forward, 1999-2000; Los Angeles Lakers, forward, 2000-01, 2003-04.

## GRANT, IAN
Executive, president (organization). **Personal:** married Tanji. **Career:** Umoja Fine Arts Inc, founder & pres, currently. **Business Addr:** President, Founder, Umoja Fine Arts Gallery, 16250 Northland Dr Suite 104, Southfield, MI 48075-5226, **Business Phone:** (248)552-1070.

## GRANT, REV. DR. JACQUELYN
Educator. **Personal:** Born Dec 19, 1948, Georgetown, SC; daughter of Joseph James and Lillie Mae; married John W P Collier Jr. **Educ:** Bennett Col, Turner Theological Sem, BA, 1970; Union Theol Sem, MPhil, 1980, PhD, 1985. **Career:** Union Theol Sem, tutor & relief teacher 1975-77; Harvard Divinity Sch, assoc in res, 1977-79; Candler Sch Emory & Theol Univ, vis lectr, 1981; Princeton Theol Sem, vis lectr, 1985; Inter denominational Theol Ctr, Black Women Church & Soc Ctr, founder, 1981, prof, 1980, Fuller E Callaway prof Syst Theol, currently; Johnson C Smith Theol Sem, fac, currently. **Orgs:** Assoc minister, Allen AME Church, 1973-80; itinerant elder, African Methodist Episcopal Church, 1976, asst minister, 1980-82; Disserta tionfel, Fund for Theol Educ, 1979-80; DuBois fel, Harvard Univ, 1979-80; assoc minister, Flipper Temple AME Church, 1980-93; founder & dir, Black Women in Church & Soc Ctr, Interdenomi Nat Theol Ctr, 1981-; asst minister, Victory AME Church, 1993; bd dir, Black Theol Proj Am. **Home Addr:** 1235 Regency Ctr Dr SW, Atlanta, GA 30331, **Home**

**Phone:** (404)691-3052. **Business Addr:** Fuller E Callaway Professor of Systematic Theology, Director, Interdenominational Theological Center, BWCS Ctr 700 Martin Luther King Jr Dr, Atlanta, GA 30314-4143, **Business Phone:** (404)527-5712.

### GRANT, JAMES

School administrator, educator, association executive. **Personal:** Born Dec 28, 1932, Ruffin, SC; married Maggie Ruth Harrison; children: Christopher, Kevin & Karen. **Educ:** Adelphi Univ, BBA, 1959, MBA, 1973. **Career:** Adelphi Univ, asst controller, 1970-73, controller, 1973; City Univ New York, Medgar Evers Col, assoc dean admin, 1973-78, dean admin, 1978-79; State Univ NY Col, New Paltz, vpres admin. **Orgs:** Eastern Asn Univ & Col Bus Officers, 1970-; pres, Auxillary Compus Enterprises Inc, 1979-; pres, State Univ New York Bus Officers Asn, 1983-85; consult, Md State Higher Educ, 1984, 1985; consult, Mid States Asn, 1985. **Home Addr:** 826 Pepperidge Rd, Westbury, NY 11590, **Home Phone:** (516)997-5564. **Business Addr:** Vice President, State University of New York, 1 Hawk Dr, New Paltz, NY 12561, **Business Phone:** (845)257-7869.

### GRANT, NATHANIEL

Manager, executive. **Personal:** Born Sep 8, 1943, Washington, DC; married Patricia A; children: Monica D & Nathaniel D. **Educ:** Norfolk State Col, bus admin courses, 1966. **Career:** Communs Satellite, admin supvr, 1966-69; Am Assoc Univ Women, prod mgr, 1969-73; Nat Pub Radio, admin mgr, 1973-77; Neighborhood Reinvest Corp, dir, human resources, admin & training, div dir, 1995. **Orgs:** Nat Forum Black Pub Admin, 1984-87. **Honors/Awds:** Board Resolution for Outstanding Service, Neighborhood Housing Serv Am, 1982; Bd Resolution and Monetary Award, Neighborhood Reinvest Corp, 1986, 1988. **Home Addr:** 11908 Lanner Pl, Laurel, MD 20708-2810, **Home Phone:** (410)792-0606.

### GRANT, STEPHEN MITCHELL

Spokesperson, football player. **Personal:** Born Dec 23, 1969, Miami, FL; married Leslie R; children: Michael. **Educ:** WVa Univ. **Career:** Football player (retired); Indianapolis Colts, 1992-93, left linebacker, 1994-96, mid linebacker, 1997; TampaBay Buccaneers, 1997; SportsWorld, speaker; Tex Tech Univ football prog, chaplain, currently. **Orgs:** Face To Face Inc; preacher & motivational speaker, SportsWorld. **Honors/Awds:** Colts' Hard Nose Player of the Year, 1994. **Home Addr:** 20054 SW 123rd Dr, Miami, FL 33177-5217. **Business Addr:** Preacher, Speaker, SportsWorld, 1919 S Post Rd, Indianapolis, IN 46239, **Business Phone:** (800)832-6546.

### GRANT, TIMOTHY JEROME

Social worker. **Personal:** Born Aug 6, 1965, Greenville, SC; son of John M Sr and Mamie J Rosemond. **Educ:** Univ SC, Columbia SC, BS, 1983. **Career:** SC House Rep, Cola SC, legis aide, 1987-89; Richland County Dept Social Serv, Cola SC, social serv specialist I, 1987-89, social serv specialist II, 1989-90, social serv specialist III, 1990-93, work support specialist, 1993-96, assessment specialist, 1996-. **Orgs:** The alumni advisor chap, Phi Beta Sigma Frat; Notary Pub, SC Notary Pub; Outstanding Young Men Am, 1987, 1989; Outstanding Col Stud Am; Phi Beta Sigma Fraternity, life mem, 2000; Indian Waters Coun, Boy Scouts Am, Explorers counr. **Honors/Awds:** Undergraduate Brother of the Year, Phi Beta Sigma, 1986; Order of Omega Honor Soc, USC Greeks, 1987; Service Award, SC House Rep, 1987; Grad Brother of the Year for chapter, state & region, Phi Beta Sigma, 2000; Graduate Brother of the Year for S.C. & Southeastern Region, 2002. **Home Addr:** 7 Sterling Ridge Ct, Columbia, SC 29229-7731, **Home Phone:** (803)462-0346. **Business Addr:** Social Service Specialist, Richland Co, 3220 2 Notch Rd, Columbia, SC 29204.

### GRANT, DR. WILMER, JR.

Educator. **Personal:** Born Jul 29, 1940, Ahoskie, NC; married Ruth Dale Ford. **Educ:** Hampton Inst, BA, 1962; Ind Univ, MS, 1967, PhD, 1974. **Career:** Univ Toledo, asst prof, 1973-; Univ Mo, asst dean, 1972-73; Ind Mil Acad, instr, 1966; Ga Southern Col, instr, prof emer. **Orgs:** Am Phys Soc; Am Inst Physics; cent Ohio Black Studies Consortium; Nat Coun Black Studies; Alpha Phi Alpha, 1961-; bd trustees, Cordelia Martin Neighbourhood Health Ctr, 1974-76; Community Chest Budget Comn, 1975; Toledo Coun Bus, 1975-77; consult, DHEW, 1976; Asn Study Afro-Am Life & Hist, 1976-; Sigma Pi Phi, 1977-. **Honors/Awds:** Talent Contest, Omega Psi Phi, State Va, 1958; commendation, AUS, 1961; developer, "Famous Black Symphomic Composers & Their Works", 1976; certificate of merit, Kappa League, 1977. **Business Addr:** Professor Emeritus, Georgia Southern College, Landrum, Statesboro, GA 30460-8071, **Business Phone:** (912)478-8746.

### GRANT-BRUCE, ESQ. DARLENE CAMILLE

Lawyer. **Personal:** Born Apr 25, 1959, Jackson Heights, NY; daughter of Leonard and Lucille; married Raymond L. **Educ:** Brandeis Univ, BA, 1981; Georgetown Univ, JD, 1986. **Career:** Judge Mary Johnson Lowe Us Dist Ct New York, judicial clerk, 1984; Judge Paul Webber Super Ct, judicial clerk, 1985; Cullen & Dykman, assoc, 1986-87; Law Offic Lee H. Bostic, 1987-89; VI Dept Justice, asst atty gen, 1989-94; Nat Coun Crime & Delinq, gen coun, 1994-98; Coun DC, asst gen coun, 1994; US Dist Ct VI, spec master, 1996-99, spec master, currently; NY Assembly, assoc coun, 1998-99; Berkshire Farm Ctr & Serv Youth, gen coun, 1999-; Appellate Div, NY Supreme Ct. **Orgs:** Delta Sigma Theta Sorority; Am Bar Asn; Nat Bar Asn; NY Bar Asn; Macon B Allen Bar Asn; DC Bar Asn; Phi Delta Phi; bd trustees, Corona-E Elmhurst Civic Asn, 1987-89; vpres, Delta Sigma Theta Inc, 1990-92, legal adv, 1992-94; bd dir, Metro Black Bar Asn, 1997-2003; Legal Affairs Com, Am Correctional Asn, 1997; VI Bar Asn. **Honors/Awds:** Certificate of Appreciation, VI Dept Justice, 1993; Certificate of Service, Narcotics Strike Force, 1993; Earl Warren Legal Scholar, 1981; Coun Legal Educ Opportunities, 1981. **Special Achievements:** Should Prison Litigation Be Curtailed?, May, 1996, Focus-NCCD; Congressional Study on the DC Department of Corrections, Jan, 1996; Prison Litigation Reform Act, Corrections Today, August, 1998. **Home Addr:** 123 W 117th St Apt 3, New York, NY 10026-2283. **Business Addr:** General Counsel, Special Master, US District Court for VI, 210 W 137 St Suite 1, East Elmhurst, NY 10030, **Business Phone:** (212)371-9150.

### GRANTE, JULLIAN IRVING

Consultant, vice president (organization). **Personal:** Born Oct 18, 1950, Washington, DC; married Jo Draper; children: Jamil Patricia, Dusan Arthur & Blake Alexander. **Educ:** Univ Md, attended 1972; Southern Ill Univ, Carbondale, attended 1976. **Career:** Land'Or Int, vpres sales & mkt, 1980-88; J Irving & Draper, sr partner, 1988-; Grante Global Partners LLC, dir, chief legis strategist, 1990-; Am Wellness Alliance, sr partner & exec vpres, currently, sr bd mem & chief med advisor, 2004-. **Orgs:** Comm adv, Gov Commonwealth Va, 1986-; adv bd, dept Minority Bus Enterprise, 1995; Criminal Justice Serv Bd, 1994-2000; release rev comm, Dept Juv Justice, 1996-2000. **Honors/Awds:** Family Literacy Award, Barbara Bush Found, 1990; Recognition for Volunteerism in Education, White House Points Lights, 1992. **Home Phone:** (540)455-9929. **Business Addr:** Executive Vice President, Chief Medical Advisor, The American Wellness Alliance, 2103 E Parham Rd Suite 101, Richmond, VA 23228-2235, **Business Phone:** (804)262-6780.

### GRANTHAM, CHARLES

Educator, basketball player, chief executive officer. **Educ:** Cheyney State Univ, BS, social sci; Univ Pa Wharton Sch, MBA. **Career:** Univ Pa Sch Educ, doctoral course; Univ Penn, Wharton Sch, dir admis & fin aid, adj prof; Nat Basketball Asn, player, 1978-95; Nat Basketball Players Asn, exec dir, 1988-95; Univ Penn, adj prof, 2002-04; Seton Hall Univ, Stillman Sch Bus, adj prof, currently; Ceruzzi Sports & Entertainment Group Inc, pres & chief exec officer, currently. **Orgs:** Bd dir selection comt, USA Basketballs Dream Teams I & II; bd dir, Womens Sports Found & Sports Career Inc; Univ Penn, Wharton Sport Bus Initiative, Dept Legal Studies, sr fel, currently. **Business Addr:** President, Chief Executive Officer, Ceruzzi Sports and Entertainment Group Inc, 1 Penn Plz Suite 1932, New York, NY 10119, **Business Phone:** (212)268-5757.

### GRANTHAM, PROF. REGINA B.

Educator, chairperson. **Personal:** Born Nov 12, 1947, Philadelphia, PA. **Educ:** Pa State Univ, BS, MEd, commun sci & dis, gen. **Career:** State Univ New York, Cortland, Commun Dis & Sci Dept, assoc prof, 1993-, chair, currently. **Orgs:** Am Speech-Lang-Hearing Asn. **Business Addr:** Associate Professor, Chairperson, State University of New York College at Cortland, 38 Graham Ave, Cortland, NY 13045-0900, **Business Phone:** (607)753-5423.

### GRANTLEY, ROBERT CLARK

Executive, vice president (organization). **Personal:** Born Aug 30, 1948, Atlanta, GA; son of Robert Charles and Edith Clark; married Sandra Prophet; children: Michael & Robyn. **Educ:** Howard Univ, Wash, DC, BSEE, 1971; Cath Univ, Wash, DC, JD, 1983. **Career:** Challenger Res Inc, Rockville Md, electronics engr, 1971-73; Potomac Elec Power Co, Wash, DC, start-up engr, 1973-75, site mgr, 1975-78, construct coordr, 1978-84, mgr, Energy Use Mgt, 1974-87, vpres, Customer Serv, 1987-94; Pepco, group vpres customers & community rels, 1994-. **Orgs:** Wash DC Bar Asn, 1983-, Md Bar Asn, 1983-; bd dir, Levine Sch Music; bd dir, Greater Wash Urban League; bd dir, Leadership Wash; bd mem, DCWatch. **Home Addr:** 11005 Battlement LA, Fort Washington, MD 20744, **Home Phone:** (301)203-0747. **Business Addr:** Group Vice President, Pepco, 701 9th St NW Suite 6230, Washington, DC 20068, **Business Phone:** (202)872-3085.

### GRANVILLE, BILLY (WILLIAM GRANVILLE, III)

Football player, entrepreneur. **Personal:** Born Mar 11, 1974?, Trenton, NJ. **Educ:** Duke Univ, BA, sociol. **Career:** Football player (retired), Entrepreneur; Cincinnati Bengals, linebacker, 1997-2000; Houston Texans, linebacker, 2002; Northwestern Mutual Financial Network, financial rep, 2004-; Granville Financial Group, chief exec officer, owner, currently, managing mem, 2010-. **Orgs:** Bd visitor, Univ Houston, 2013-; bd dir, IBAT, 2013-; bd trustee, Rockwell Fund Inc, 2013-; bd trustee, Chinquapin Prep Sch, 2015-;bd, Greater Houston fel Christian Athletes; Soc Fin Serv Prof; Houston Estate & Fin Forum; NFL Alumni, Houston Chap; Nat Asn Ins & Financial Advisors. **Business Addr:** Chief Executive Officer, Owner, Granville Financial Group, 1980 Post Oak Blvd Suite 1500, Houston, TX 77056-2043, **Business Phone:** (866)850-4957.

### GRANVILLE, WILLIAM, JR.

Executive, school administrator, association executive. **Personal:** Born Dec 6, 1940, Warner Robins, GA; son of William Sr and Marian Hicks; married Jessica Katherine Hilton; children: Cheryl Lynn, Michelle Marie & William Lamont. **Educ:** Delaware State Col, BS, math, 1962; Princeton Theol Sem, MS, 2005. **Career:** Dept Army, mathematician, 1962-65; Mobil Res & Develop Corp, res math, 1965-69; Mobil Int Div, int planning anal, 1969-70, int rels exec, 1970-76; Mobil Oil Corp, mgr Middle East training oper, 1976-81, mgr tech transfer Middle E, 1981-; Mobil Int Consult Serv Inc, exec vpres, 1983; Granville Acad, founder & chmn, 1983-. **Orgs:** Woodrow Wilson Fel; bd trustee & bd dir, Rider Univ; bd dir, US Black Engr & US Hispanic Engr mag; Nat Asn Advan Colored People; Nj Educ Asn; founder, Metrop Trenton African Am Chamber Com; bd dir, Lawrenceville Sch; bd dir, Metro Trenton Nj Area Chamber Com; enrollment bd, Reasoning Mind. **Home Addr:** , VA. **Business Addr:** Founder, Chairman, Granville Academy, PO Box 7113, Ewing, NJ 08628, **Business Phone:** (609)403-0489.

### GRANVILLE, WILLIAM, III. See GRANVILLE, BILLY.

### GRATE, DR. ISAAC, JR.

Physician. **Personal:** Born Dec 20, 1952, Georgetown, SC; son of Isaac Sr and Beulah; married Frankie Lee Young; children: Chelsea. **Educ:** Howard Univ, attended 1974; Meharry Med Col, MD, 1978; Univ Calif, LA, Sch Pub Health, Grad Sch, attended 1980. **Career:** Martin Luther King Jr Gen Hosp, intern, 1978-79; Johns Hopkins Hosp, resident, 1980-82, fel, 1982; Tex Tech Univ, instr surg/em, 1982-84; St Lukes Episcopal Hosp, dir emergency svcs, 1985-87; Southeast Tex Emergency Physicians, partner, 1987-92; La Emergency & Trauma, specialist, 1992; Univ Tex, Health Sci Ctr, LBJ Gen Hosp, Houston, Tex, clin asst prof, currently; pvt pract, currently; Hermann Hosp, physician. **Orgs:** Affil fac, instr ACLS, Am Heart Asn, 1984-87; Houston Med Forum, 1987-92; Southwest Tex Emergency Physicians, 1987-92; Nat Med Asn; 1987-91; Univ Asn Emergency Physicians, 1992-97, Soc Teachers Emergency Med, 1992-97, fel Am Col Emergency Physicians, 1992-97; Nat Asn Advan Colored People, 1996. **Honors/Awds:** Dir Medical Educ Texas Tech Univ Sch of Medicine Div Emergency Medicine, 1982-85; Fellow Amer College Emergency Physicians, 1996-. **Home Addr:** 1212 Ripple Creek Dr, Houston, TX 77057-1763. **Business Addr:** Physician, Hermann Hospital, 6411 Fannin St, Houston, TX 77030, **Business Phone:** (713)704-4000.

### GRAUER, GLADYS BARKER

Artist, educator. **Personal:** Born Aug 15, 1923, Cincinnati, OH; daughter of Charles and Maude; married Solomon; children: Antoinette Baskerville, Edith, Edward & Leon. **Educ:** Art Inst Chicago, Rutgers Univ, attended 1945. **Career:** Educator (retired), artist; Essex Co Votech High Sch, teacher, 1974-88; Victoria & Albert Mus London; NJ State Coun Arts fel, 1985; Newark Mus, 1989-90; Essex Co Col, teacher, 1989-92; Newark Mus, artist resident, 1992; Art Coun Essel Co, artist resident; Rutgers Innovative Printmaking fel, 1993; artist, currently; paint & mixed media artist, currently; Jane Voorhees Zimmerli Art Mus;; Corp Art Galleries London; . **Orgs:** Alumni assoc, Art Inst Chicago, 1945-; Nat Educ Asn, 1974-; pres, Black Woman Visual Perspective, 1980-; bd mem, Newark Arts Coun, 1981-98; bd mem, City Without Walls Art Gallery, 1995-98; Nat Mus Am Art; Noyes Mus Art Oceanville; Morris Mus. **Home Addr:** 352 Seymour Ave, Newark, NJ 07112-2135, **Home Phone:** (973)923-7928. **Business Addr:** Artist, 352 Seymour Ave, Newark, NJ 07112-2135, **Business Phone:** (973)923-7928.

### GRAVENBERG, DR. ERIC VON

Educator, school administrator, vice president (organization). **Personal:** Born May 18, 1950, Oakland, CA; son of Allen and Myrtle LeBlanc; married Deborah Elaine; children: Roshan & Ashande. **Educ:** Calif State Univ, BA, black studies, 1972, MA, pub admin, 1974; Columbus Univ, PhD, educ admin. **Career:** Calif State Univ, Chico, dir educ opportunity prog, 1979-80; Calif State Univ Hayward, dir educ resource ctr, 1980-81; Off Chancellor Calif State Univ, asn dean educ progs, 1981-86; Univ Calif Riverside, dir undergrad admis, 1986, supt, dirunder grad admis, 1990-93; Renaissance Enterprises Pvt Consult Co, pres, 1989-; Inst Contemp Leadership, dean fac, 1989-91; Alliant Univ, assoc vp enrollment mgt, 1993-94, assoc vpres enrollment mgt & stud servs, vpres, ctr undergrad educ, 1996; Beacon Mgt Group, sr assoc, currently; Merritt Col, vpres stud affairs, currently. **Orgs:** Affirmative Action Comt Adv Bd, Univ Calif Irvine, 1985-86; bd mem, Western Asn Educ Opportunity Personnel, 1985-86; Nat Coun Access Serv Col Bd, 1985-; orgn develop consult, Calif State Univ-Chico, 1986; chmn minority affairs, Western Asn Col Admis Counr, 1988-; pres, Kevin Johnson's St Hope Acad. **Home Addr:** 12245 Langtry Cir, Moreno Valley, CA 92557, **Home Phone:** (909)488-0797. **Business Addr:** Senior Associate, Beacon Management Group, 155 S El Molino Ave Suite 103, Pasadena, CA 91101, **Business Phone:** (626)792-3492.

### GRAVES, ALLENE

Executive, president (organization). **Personal:** Born Jan 5, 1952, Washington, DC; daughter of Allen R and Eula D; children: Kym R Murray, Daquan Murray, Rico Plesant & Jamea Murray. **Educ:** Univ DC. **Career:** Shaw Proj Area Comt, admin asst, 1976-79; Am Coun Capital Formation, word processor, 1979-83; Acad Educ Develop, exec secy, 1983-84; Bergson, Borkland & Margolis, legal secy, 1984-85; Sherman & Lapidus, off mgr, 1984-86; Answer Staffing Serv Inc, pres & owner, 1987-, opers mgr, currently. **Orgs:** Secy, United Planning Orgn, 1972-76; Metrop Wash Temp Asn, 1989; Better Bus Bur; DC Chamber Com. **Home Addr:** 13001 St Gregory Ct, Bowie, MD 20721-2587, **Home Phone:** (301)218-3814. **Business Addr:** Operations Manager, President & Owner, The Answer Staffing Services Inc, 1325 G St NW Suite 500, Washington, DC 20005, **Business Phone:** (202)835-0190.

### GRAVES, AUTUMN ADKINS

College president, educator. **Personal:** Born Jan 1, 1973?, Monongahela, PA; daughter of Paul C Adkins and Maxine S Adkins; married R Vann Graves, Jan 1, 2010?. **Educ:** Univ Va, BA, rhet & hist, 1994; Teachers Col, Columbia Univ, MA, educ admin, 2000; NY Univ, cert fundraising; Univ Pa, EdD, 2012-. **Career:** Mercersburg Acad, dir spec progs; Breck Sch, upper sch counr & community serv coordr; Sidwell Friends Sch, upper sch dean, 2000-2003; Friends Sem, asst prin, 2003-09; Girard Col, pres, 2009-2012. **Orgs:** Philadelphia Film Off, Bd Mem; Public Health Mgt Corp, Bd Mem; Libr Co Philadelphia, Active Trustee; Shipley Sch Bryn Mawr, Active Trustee; World Class Greater Philadelphia, World Class Educ & Talent Develop Strategy Team, Team Mem; Jr League Philadelphia, Mem; Educ Admin Prog, Mentoring Scholar; Links Inc, Metro-Manhattan Chap.

### GRAVES, CAROLE A.

Politician, administrator, teacher. **Personal:** Born Apr 15, 1938, Newark, NJ; daughter of Jennie Valeria Stafford Anderson and Philip Burnett Anderson; married David Leon. **Educ:** Kean Col, Newark, BA, 1960; Rutgers Inst Labor & Mgt Rels, labor rels specialist cert, 1976. **Career:** Newark Sch Syst, Newark, NJ, spec educ teacher, 1960-69; Newark Teachers Union, Am Fedn Teachers, Newark, NJ, pres, 1968-95; Essex County Regist Deeds & Mortgages, am dem party politician, labor leader, 1995-2010. **Orgs:** Vpres, NJ State AFL-CIO; vpres, NJ State Indus Union Coun; vpres, Essex West/Hudson Central Labor Coun; vpres, NJ State Fedn Teachers; Rutgers Lacor Alumni Exec Bd; A Philip Randolph Inst; Coalition Labor Union Women. **Home Addr:** 40 Goldsmith Ave, Newark, NJ 07112, **Home Phone:** (973)923-8238.

### GRAVES, CLIFFORD WAYNE

Investment banker. **Personal:** Born Mar 30, 1939, San Francisco, CA; son of Wilbur Earl and Ruth Louise; married Anasa Briggs; children: Sharon & Diane. **Educ:** Univ Calif, Berkeley, CA, BA, 1961, M City

Planning, 1964. **Career:** City Santa Rosa, asst city planner, 1961-62; E Sussex Co, town planner & civic designer, 1964-66; San Francisco Bay Consult & Dev Comn, assoc planner, 1966-69; Univ Calif, Berkeley, lectr, 1968-69, spec proj officer, 1969-70; Comprehensive Planning Asst Div, dir, 1970-71; Howard Univ, lectr, 1970-73; Off Planning & Mgt Asst, dir & asst dir, 1971-72; Sec Comn Planning & Mgt, dep asst, 1972-74; Off Mgt & Budget, dep assoc dir, eval & prog implem; Co San Diego, chief admin officer, 1978-85; San Diego State Univ, assoc prof, 1979-85; Int Technol Corp, Torrance, Calif, dir planning, 1986-88; Grigsby & Graves Environ, San Diego, Calif, pres, 1988-, managing dir, 1988-02; Los Angeles Community Develop Dept, gen mgr, 2003-. **Orgs:** Am Inst Planners; Am Soc Planning Off; Am Soc Pub Admin; Nat Asn Planners; comnr, Port San Diego, 1990-. **Honors/Awds:** Distinguished Service Award, HUD, 1972; Wm A Jump Foundation Award, 1972; Student Award, Am Inst Planners, 1972. **Home Addr:** 7705 Hannum Ave, Culver City, CA 90230-6164, **Home Phone:** (310)313-4526. **Business Addr:** General Manager Economic Development, Los Angeles Community Development Department, 701 E Carson St, Carson, CA 90745, **Business Phone:** (310)233-4802.

## GRAVES, CURTIS M.
Manager. **Personal:** Born Aug 26, 1938, New Orleans, LA; son of Joseph F and Mabel Haydel; married Kay Bryant; children: Gretchen, Christopher & Gizelle; married Joanne. **Educ:** Xavier Univ; Tex Southern Univ, BA, 1963. **Career:** Stand Savs Asn Houston, mgr, 1962-66; Tex House Reps, elected, 1967-73; Leadership Inst Community Develop Wash, DC, training officer teaching state & local govt procedures; Nat Civil Serv League, managing assoc, dir continuing educ; NASA, dept dir civil affairs defense & inter govt rels div, dep dir acad serv pub affairs, chief educ & community serv, minority univ prog mgr, educ & comm affairs Br, chief, 1977-87; Howard Univ, govt affairs, spec asst; artistic photogr, currently. **Orgs:** Steering comt, Nat Congr Aerospace Educ; former pres, World Aerospace Educ Org; Wash Alumni Chap Kappa Alpha Psi Fraternity; pres, World Aerospace Educ Orgn, 1983-; bd mem, Ky Inst; Woodrow Wilson Fel Princeton Univ, 1985. **Honors/Awds:** Awards from the Coun Negro Women, Delta Sigma Theta Sorority, Nat Asn Col Women, City Los Angeles, Kappa Alpha Psi Fraternity, Tex Southern Univ, NY City Sch Syst, Nat Congr Aviation & Space Educ; Two hon doctorate degrees, Union Baptist Bible Sem; Frank G Brewer Trophy, 1989. **Special Achievements:** Published book: "Famous Black Americas, vol I & II". **Home Addr:** 5624 Mkt St, Houston, TX 77020.

## GRAVES, DENIQUE
Basketball player. **Personal:** Born Sep 16, 1975, Philadelphia, PA. **Educ:** Howard Univ, BS, social sci, teacher educ, 2008. **Career:** Basketball player (retired), basketball coach; Sacramento Monarchs, ctr, 1997; San Benardo, Brazil, Istanbul, Turkey, basketball player, 1999; Atlanta Justice; Orlando Miracle, 2001; Sofia Slavia, Bulgaria, 2001-02; Jiangsu, China, 2002; BC Power basket Wels, Austria, ctr, 2003; Binghamton Univ Bearcats, asst coach, 2008-09; Community Col Philadelphia, coach, 2010-11; Prodigal Pvt Security, site supvr, 2010-12; Keystone Col, asst women's basketball coach, 2012-13.

## GRAVES, DENYCE ANTOINETTE
Opera singer. **Personal:** Born Mar 7, 1964, Washington, DC; daughter of Charles and Dorothy Kenner; married David Perry; married Robert Montgomery; married Vincent Thomas; children: 1. **Educ:** Oberlin Col Conserv, 1984; New Eng Conserv Music, BMus, Aarst dipl, 1988. **Career:** Mezzo-soprano opera singer; Hansel & Gretel, 1989; Suzuki Madame Butterfly, Houston Grand Opera, 1990; Maddalena Rigoletto, DC, 1991; Carmen, Minn Opera, 1991; Concert Planet Earth, Sony Class, 1993; Hamlet, EMI, 1993; Recital Denyce Graves: Heroines de l'Opera romantique Francais, FNAC Music, 1993; Denyce Graves: A Cathedral Christmas, PBS Prod, 1998; Angels Watching Over Me, NPR Classics, 1998; Memorial, Carmen Productions, 2001; French Opera Arias, Virgin Classics, 2004; Kaleidoscope; Metro Opera, Dallas Opera, Opernhaus Zurich; Turk Rake's Progress, Chatelet, Paris; XM Satellite Radio, Voce di Donna, host, 2005; Amn Idol Underground, indust panelist, currently; Columbia Artists Mgt Inc, opera singer, currently. Albums: American Anthem, 2001; The Lost Days, 2003. **Orgs:** Panel mem, Am Guild Musical Artists; Wash Opera Open Forum, 1991; active supporter, African Nat Cong, Boston, 1985; panel mem, Black Entertainment tv. **Home Addr:** Suzanne Stephens Arts Serv, 1714 N Bryan St, Arlington, VA 22201. **Business Addr:** Opera Singer, Columbia Artists Management Inc, 165 W 57th St, New York, NY 10019, **Business Phone:** (212)397-6900.

## GRAVES, EARL GILBERT, SR.
Philanthropist, businessperson, publisher. **Personal:** Born Jan 9, 1935, Brooklyn, NY; son of Earl Godwin and Winifred (Sealy) G; married Barbara Kydd; children: Earl Gilbert Jr, John Clifford & Michael Alan. **Educ:** Morgan State Col, BA, econs, 1958. **Career:** Sen Robert F Kennedy, admin asst, 1965-68; Earl G Graves Ltd, founder, chmn & chief exec officer, currently; Earl G Graves Pub Co Inc, founder; Earl G Graves Assoc, founder; Black Enterprise Mag, founder & publ; Pepsi-Cola Wash, chmn & chief exec officer, 1990-98; Aetna Life & Casualty Co, dir; AMR Corp, dir; Chrysler Corp, dir; Federated Dept Stores Inc, dir, currently; Rohm & Haas Corp, dir, currently. **Orgs:** bd dir, Rohm & Haas Corp; Mag Pubs Asn; Nat Minority Purchasing Coun Inc; Nat Bd Exec Comt, Interracial Coun Bus Oppor; Nat Bus League; NY State Econ Develop Bd; exec comt, Greater NY Coun BSA; bd selector, Am Inst Pub Serv; trustee, Am Mus Natural Hist; Nat Asn Advan Colored People; SCLC Mag Publ Asn; Interracial Coun; Sigma Pi Phi; Statue Liberty Ellis Island Centennial Comt; visitingcomt, Harvard Univ, John F Kennedy Sch Govt; Pres's Coun Bus Admin, UnivVT; bd mem, New York Partnership; trustee, NY Econ Club; bd dirs, NYUrban Develop Corp; chmn, Black Bus Coun; exec comt, Coun Competitiveness; Stroh's Adv Coun; nat comnr, Nat Boy Scouts Am, 1990-95, vice pres exec bd; Nat Minority Bus Coun; tree coun, Bus Econ Develop; bd mem, New York Partnership; New Am Schls Develop Copr; Trans Africa Forum; Am Mus Natural Hist & lanetarium; Am Inst Pub Serv; Adv Coun, Character Educ Partnership; Steadman-Hawkins Sports Med Found; Nat Adv Bd, Nat Underground RR Freedom Ctr; trustee, Howard Univ; Aetna Inc; Aetna Found Inc; fel Yale Univ; fel Am Acad Arts & Sci, 2000; Omega Psi Phi; presidential comn, Nat Mus African Am Hist & Cult. **Honors/Awds:** Silver Beaver, 1969; 45 honorary degrees, including: LLD, Morgan St Univ, 1973, VA Union Univ, 1976, FL Memorial Col, 1978, J C Smith Univ, 1979, Wesleyan Univ, 1982, Talladaga Col, 1983, Baruch Col, 1984, AL St Univ, 1985, Mercy Col, 1986, Iona Col, 1987, Elizabeth City St Univ, 1987, Brown Univ, 1987, Lincoln Univ, 1988, Central St Univ, 1988, Howard Univ, 1989, Livingstone Col, 1989; Rust Col, 1974, Hampton Inst, 1979; Dowling Col, 1980; Bryant Col, 1983; St Josephs, NY, 1985; Morehouse Col, 1986; Silver Antelope, 1986; Suffolk Univ, 1987; Poynter Boy Scouts National Awards, Silver Buffalo, 1988; Meharry Med Col, 1989; Scroll of Honor, Nat Med Asn; Black Achiever, Talk Mag; Broadcaster of the Year, Nat Asn Black Owned Broadcasters; Earl G Graves School of Business & Management, named in honor; Spingarn Medal, Nat Asn Advan Colored People, 1999; Lifetime Achievement Award, Caribbean Tourism Org, 1999; Lifetime Achievement Award, Caribbean Tourism Org; Harvey C Russell Award, PepsiCo, 2005; Inducted into Junior Achievement US Business Hall of Fame, 2007; Silver Anniversary Award, Nat Collegiate Athletic Asn, 2009; Lifetime Achievement Award, Nat Asn Black Journalists. **Special Achievements:** Author, How to Succeed in Bussiness Without Being White, 1997; one of 100 Influential Blacks, Ebony Mag; one of 10 Most Outstanding Minority Businessmen in US, ex-Pres Nixon; one of 200 Future Leaders in US, Time Mag; one of Top 100 Business Lumanaries, TJFR, 1999; In 2002, Mr. Graveswas named by Fortune Magazine as one of the 50 most powerful and influential African Americans in corporate America. **Home Addr:** 8 Heathcote Rd, Scarsdale, NY 10583-4414. **Business Addr:** Chairman, Chief Executive Officer, Earl G Graves Ltd, 130 5th Ave Fl 10, New York, NY 10011-4399, **Business Phone:** (212)242-8000.

## GRAVES, EARL GILBERT, JR.
Publishing executive, basketball player. **Personal:** Born Jan 5, 1962, Brooklyn, NY; son of Earl G Sr and Barbara; married Roberta; children: Erika, Kristin, Earl G Jr & Theodore Daly. **Educ:** Yale Univ, BA, econ, 1984; Harvard Univ, Grad Sch Bus Admin, MBA, 1988. **Career:** Basketball player (retired), executive; Philadelphia 76ers, basketball player, 1984; Milwaukee Bucks; Cleveland Cavaliers, basketball player, 1984-85; Morgan Stanley, investment banker; Black Enterprise Mag, vpres advert & mkt, 1988-91, sr vpres advert & mkt, 1991-95, exec vpres, 1995-98, chief oper officer, 1995-2006, pres, 1998-, chief exec officer, 2006-; Earl G Graves Publ Co, pres, chmn & chief exec officer, currently; Auto Zone Inc, dir, 2002-. **Orgs:** Skull & Bones; Exec Comt, Nat Off Boy Scouts Am; bd dir, Aetna Found Inc; Educ Broadcasting Corp; Premier Automotive Group; Am Advert Fedn; bd dir, Mag Publishers Am; Skull & Bones Soc; bd dir, Thurgood Marshall Scholar Fund. **Honors/Awds:** Who's Who in America, 1974; Editorial Excellence Award for Business & Finance, 1996; AAF Jack Averett Volunteer Spirit Award; Hall of Achievement, Am Advert Fedn, 2002; National Award of Excellence, Minority Bus Enterprise; Named as One of Time Magazine's 200 future leaders of the Country; Received Honorary degrees from 53 Cols & Universities. **Business Addr:** President, Chief Executive Officer, Black Enterprise, 260 Madison Ave 11th Fl, New York, NY 10016, **Business Phone:** (212)242-8000.

## GRAVES, JOHN
Executive. **Career:** Detroit Lions, vpres. **Business Addr:** Vice President, Detroit Lions, 222 Republic Dr, Allen Park, MI 48101, **Business Phone:** (313)262-2222.

## GRAVES, JOHN CLIFFORD
Lawyer, chairperson. **Personal:** Born May 10, 1963, Brooklyn, NY; son of Earl Gilbert and Barbara Eliza Kydd; married Caroline Veronica Clarke. **Educ:** Colgate Univ, Hamilton, NY, 1982; Brown Univ, Providence, RI, BA, hist, 1986; Yale Law Sch, New Haven, CT, JD, 1989. **Career:** Cleary, Gottlieb, Steen & Hamilton, New York, NY, atty; Cath Big Bros Inc, pres; Graves Ventures, pres, chief operating officer & chief exec officer, currently; Mony Life Ins Co Am, dir; AXA Financial Inc, dir; AXA Equitable Life Ins Co, dir, currently; Earl G Graves Ltd, chief staff, currently. **Orgs:** Stud & Sponsor Partnership; Black Enterprise Entrepreneurs Conf, 1996; trustee, Meharry Med Col, Nashville; dir, Black Enterprise & Greenwich St Corp Growth Partners; Supvry Bd Daimler Chrysler AG; mem exec bd & exec comt, Nat Off Boy Scouts Am; bd dir, Aetna Found, AXA Financial. **Home Addr:** 112 Storer Ave, New Rochelle, NY 10801, **Home Phone:** (914)235-3360. **Business Addr:** Chief of Staff, Earl G Graves Ltd, 130 5th Ave 10th Fl, New York, NY 10011-4399, **Business Phone:** (212)242-8000.

## GRAVES, DR. LESLIE THERESA
Lawyer. **Personal:** Born Mar 27, 1956, Detroit, MI; daughter of Louis and Nora Mallett. **Educ:** Smith Col, Northampton, Mass, BA, 1977; Cath Univ, Wash, DC, JD, 1981. **Career:** State Mich, Detroit, workers compensation appeal bd mem, 1987-91; Wayne Co Community Col, gen coun; Wayne Co Circuit Ct, family div, dep juv regist, 1995, assoc ct adminr, currently. **Orgs:** State Bar Mich Comt Abbr Under-represented Groups Law, 1984-91; Women Lawyers Asn Mich, 1984-; exec bd, Wolverine Bar Asn, 1986, pres, 1990-91; bd dir, Brazel Dennard Chorale, 1988-; Int Visitors Coun, 1990-; Links Inc. **Honors/Awds:** Member of the Year, Wolverine Bar Asn, 1985; Private Attorney Involvement Award, WBA, 1990. **Home Addr:** 2016 Hyde Pk Dr, Detroit, MI 48207, **Home Phone:** (313)962-0250. **Business Addr:** Associate Court Administrator, Wayne County Circuit Court, 1025 E Forest Ave, Detroit, MI 48207-1024, **Business Phone:** (313)833-0197.

## GRAVES, RAY REYNOLDS
Judge, administrator. **Personal:** Born Jan 10, 1946, Tuscumbia, AL; son of Olga Wilder and Isaac; children: Claire Elise Glass & Reynolds Douglass. **Educ:** Trinity Col, BA, 1967; Wayne State Univ, JD, 1970. **Career:** Judge (retired); Pvt law pract, atty, 1970-81; Legal Aid & Defender Asn, dep defender, 1970-71; Liberson, Fink, Feiler, Crystal & Burdick, assoc, 1971-72; Patmon, Young & Kirk, assoc, 1972-73; Lewis, White, Clay & Graves PC, partner, 1973-81; Detroit Edison Co, staff atty, 1981, trial atty; Univ Detroit Law Sch, adj prof, 1981-85; US Bankruptcy Ct, judge, 1982-02, chief judge, 1991-95; BBK Ltd, managing dir & prin, partner, 2002-06; Eastern Dist Mich, judge Us bankruptcy ct, fed bankruptcy judge; Wayne County Corp Coun, prin tax atty; Wayne County Treas, prin tax atty. **Orgs:** Trustee, bd dir, Mich Cancer Found, 1979-83; bd gov, Nat Conf Bankruptcy Judges, 1984-88; fel, Am Col Bankruptcy, 1993; Christ Church Grosse Pointe, 1993-96; Sigma Pi Phi Fraternity, 1999-2001; fel Am Col Bankruptcy; Am Bankruptcy Inst; D. Augustus Straker Bar Asn, founder. **Home Addr:** 227 Iron St, Detroit, MI 48207, **Home Phone:** (313)656-2160.

## GRAVES, VALERIE JO
Executive, media executive, association executive. **Personal:** Born Feb 27, 1950, Pontiac, MI; daughter of Spurgeon and Edna Deloris Munson; married Alvin E Bessent; children: Brian. **Educ:** Wayne State Univ, attended 1973; NY Univ, Filmmaking Prog, 1985. **Career:** D Arcy MacManus & Masius Ad Agency, copywriter, 1974-75; BBDO Inc Ad Agency, copywriter, 1975-76; Kenyon & Eckhardt Boston Ad Agency, copywriter, 1977-80; Ross Roy Inc, vpres & assoc creative dir, 1980-85; J Walter Thompson USA Ad Agency, sr copywriter, 1981-82; Uniworld Group Inc, vpres, assoc creative dir, sr vpres, creative dir, sr vpres & chief creative officer, 1985-2005; Clinton/Gore Campaign, creative/media consult, 1992; Motown Rec LP, Corp Creative Serv, sr vpres, 1995-97; Vigilante agency, chief creative officer & creative dir, 2006; Nelson Commun Inc, creative dir, 1999-. **Orgs:** Mem bd, Harvard Univ Black Community & Stud Theater, 1979-80; Adcraft Club Detroit, 1982-; consult, Creative Network Inc, 1984-, dir, 1984-; Nat Asn Black Women Entrepreneurs, 1985; bd dir, Advert Club, New York, NY, 1996-; Creative Rev Comt, Partnership Drug-Free Am. **Honors/Awds:** Corporate Ad Award, 1981; Boston Ad Club Francis Hatch Award, 1981; Merit Award, Art Dirs Club New York, 1982; CEBA Award of Excellence, Black Owned Community Asn NY, 1983; Graphic Excellence Merchandising Graphics Award Competition, 1984; Notable Midwest Adwoman, Adweek Mag, Chicago, 1984; Creative Excellence to Black Audiences Award, CEBA, 1987-92; YWCA Academy Women Achievers, YWCA New York, 1989; Creativity Magazine Award; Chicago Radio Festival Award; Creative Excellence to Black Audiences Award. **Special Achievements:** One of the 100 Best and Brightest. **Business Addr:** Board Member, The Advertising Club, 989 Avenue of the Americas 7th Fl, New York, NY 10018, **Business Phone:** (212)533-8080.

## GRAY, ANDREW JACKSON
Executive. **Personal:** Born Jun 20, 1924, Charlotte, NC; married Lucille Jackson; children: Andrew Jr & Amizie. **Educ:** Morehouse Col, BA, 1946; NC State Univ, add studies. **Career:** Andrew J Gray Acct Firm, acct, 1962-; NC Con NAACP Br, auditor. **Orgs:** Nat Soc Pub Acct; NC Soc Acct; Nat Asn Enrolled Agt; Nat Asn Black Acct; Kappa Alpha Psi; Nat Asn Advan Colored People; St Paul Bapt Chi; YMCA. **Honors/Awds:** Hall of Fame Award, Charlotte Bus League, NAACP. **Home Addr:** 1342 Mulberry Ave, Charlotte, NC 28216, **Home Phone:** (704)372-3096. **Business Addr:** Accountant, Andrew J Gray Acct Firm, 2202 Beatties Ford Rd, Charlotte, NC 28216, **Business Phone:** (704)394-0179.

## GRAY, BEVERLY A.
Librarian. **Personal:** Born Aug 3, 1940, Boston, MA; daughter of Mark and Lula. **Educ:** Simmons Col, BS, social sci, 1962; Columbia Univ, MA, polit sci, 1964, MLS, 1965, cert african studies. **Career:** Harvard Univ, Africana bibliogr, 1965-67; Boston Univ, librn, African Studies Libr, 1967-72; Libr Cong, sr ref librn & African sect, area specialist, 1972-78 head, African sect, 1978-94, actg div chief, 1993, African & Mid Eastern Div, chief, 1994-. **Orgs:** African Studies Asn; exec bd, Africana Librns Coun; Mid E Librns Asn; Asn Jewish Libr; exec bd, Coop Africana Microfirm Proj; Am Libr Asn; Asn Study & Life African Am Hist. **Special Achievements:** Author, Uganda: Subject Guide to Publications, 1977; Africana Library Resources, In: Ethnic Collections in Libraries, 1983; Liberia During the Tolbert Eval A Guide, 1983; Africana Acquisitions at the Library of Congress, In: Africana Resources & Collections, 1989. **Business Addr:** Chief, Library Congress, 101 Independence Ave SE, Washington, DC 20540-1600, **Business Phone:** (202)707-2905.

## GRAY, BRIAN ANTON
Business owner, president (organization), chief executive officer. **Personal:** Born Apr 13, 1939, Philadelphia, PA; son of Cecil and Bertha; married Linda; children: Brian & Christian. **Educ:** Cheyney State Univ, BA, 1964; Howard Univ, MA, 1972. **Career:** Miller Brewing Co, mgr col rels, 1975-81; BG & Assocs Staffing Serv, pres & chief exec officer, 1981-; Howard Univ, dir personnel, 1982-91; Fed Home Loan Mortage Corp, staff; Metrop Wash Airports Authority, staff. **Orgs:** Omega Psi Phi Fraternity, 1962-; Employ Mgt Asn, 1982-; bd chmn, Bur Rehab, 1985-95; chmn & bd trustee, Nomination Comt, 1985-93; Soc Human Res Mgt, 1990-; Nation wide Interchange Serv, 1992-. **Honors/Awds:** Outstanding Volunteer, Montgomery County Gov, 1993; Outstanding Volunteer, Bur Rehab, 1993. **Home Addr:** 10112 Langhorne Ct Suite B, Bethesda, MD 20817-1250, **Home Phone:** (301)365-4138. **Business Addr:** President, Chief Executive Officer & Recruiter, BG & Associates Staffing Services, 10112 Langhorne Ct Suite B, Bethesda, MD 20827-0162, **Business Phone:** (301)365-4046.

## GRAY, DR. C. VERNON
Government official, college teacher, school administrator. **Personal:** Born Jul 30, 1939, Sunderland, MD; son of Major and Virgina; married Sandra Lea Trice; children: Michael V & Angela Parhem. **Educ:** Morgan State Univ, BA, 1961; Atlanta Univ, MA, 1962; Univ Mass, PhD, polit sci, 1971. **Career:** Professor (retired), advisor; Philander Smith Col, instr, 1961-66; Oakland Univ, instr, 1970-71; Joint Ctr Polit Studies, Wash, DC, staff, 1971-72; Morgan State Univ, chmn Polit sci, 1972-87, dir pub serv internship prog, 1972-87, assoc dean social sci, 1974-75, prof polit sci, chmn Polit sci & intl studies, 1984-87, internship cord, off campus advisor, currently; Goucher Col, vis prof, 1974; Univ Md, vis prof, 1978-81. **Orgs:** Exec coun, Nat Capitol Area Polit Sci Asn, 1976-; pres elect, Nat Conf Black Polit Sci, 1976-77; chmn, Polit Action Comm MD State Conf, Nat AsnAdvan Colored People, 1976-77; bd dir, Meals Wheels Cent Md, 1976; chmn, Ad Hoc Contribs Community Meals Wheels, 1976-77; pres, Nat Conf Black Polit Sci, 1977-78; nominating comm, Southern Polit Sci Asn, 1977-78; chmn, Ethnic & Cult Pluralism Award Comt, Am Polit Sci Asn, 1977-78; Polit analyst WJZ, WBAL, 1977-; host, producer Polit Power & People, 1977-80; speakers bur, United Way Cent Md, 1977-78; allocations panel, United Way Cent Md, 1977-78; adv comt, Ctr Urban Environ Studies, 1977-80; resources bd, Minority Energy Tech Asst Prog, Ctr Urban EnvironStudies, 1978; bd dir, Nat Policy Studies Goucher

Col, 1978; chmn progcomn, Alpha Phi Alpha, 1979-80; dir, Educ Activ Alpha Phi Alpha, 1979; Election Laws Rev Comm Md, 1979-80; Howard County Coun, coun man, 1982-, chmn co coun, 1985-, adminr, Off Human Rights, 2007-; bd dir, Natl Asn Counties, 1986-, health adv comt, 1992-93, pres, 1999-2000; chmn, United Negro Col Fund Howard Co Campaign, 1990-91; bd dir, pres, Md Asn Counties, 1992; bd dir, African Art Mus Md; bd dir, Howard Co Red Cross; bd dir, Howard Health Found; bd dir, NACO Financial Serv Ctr; NACO Taxation & Finance Steering Comt; Stanford Whos Who, Community; founder & chair, Healthy Family Howard Co; life mem, Nat Asn Advan Colored People. **Honors/Awds:** WEAA-FM Award Service, 1978; Community Service Award, United Way Cent Md, 1978; Appreciation Award, Calvert Co, Natl Asn Advan Colored People, 1978; Community Service Admin Cert Training, 1979; Certificate of Merit Black Womens Consciousness Raising Asn, 1979; Community Service Award, Howard Community Action, 1980; Award Distinguished Service, Natl Conf Black Polit Sci, 1980; Outstanding Faculty Award Community for Service, Morgan State Univ, 1980; Alpha Man of the Year, 1982; Ford Found Fellowship, Crusade Scholar, Southern Found Scholar; Citizen of the Year, Omega Psi Phi Fraternity,1987; Outstanding Service Award, Alpha Kappa Alpha Sorority, 1989; Honorary 4-H member; Outstanding Achievement Award, Md State Teachers Asn; Jewish Natl Fund Tree Life Award, Am Lung Asn; Lawmaker of the Year, 1993; Distinguished Black Marylanders Award, Towson State Univ. **Special Achievements:** First African-American black council member elected Howard County Council, 1982. **Home Addr:** 8502 Dark Hawk Cir, Columbia, MD 21045-5626, **Home Phone:** (410)992-6675. **Business Addr:** Advisor, Howard County, 6751 Gateway Dr Suite 239, Columbia, MD 21046, **Business Phone:** (410)313-6401.

## GRAY, CARLTON PATRICK

Football player. **Personal:** Born Jun 26, 1971, Cincinnati, OH; son of Patricia. **Educ:** Univ Calif, Los Angeles. **Career:** Football player (retired); Seattle Sea hawks, defensive back, 1993, left cornerback. 1994-96; Indianapolis Colts, left cornerback, 1997; New York Giants, defensive back, 1998; Kans City Chiefs, 1999, cornerback, 2000; Cincinnati Bengals, 2001.

## GRAY, DR. CAROL COLEMAN

Pediatrician. **Personal:** Born Jun 22, 1946, Wharton, TX; married James Howard; children: Nakia & James. **Educ:** Univ Tex Med Sch, BS, 1967, MD, 1972. **Career:** Walter Reed Army Med Ctr, pediat internship, 1972; Univ Md Med Ctr, pediat residency, 1977; Dallas Independent Sch Dist Proj Find, med coordr, 1979-83; Baylor Univ, Med Ctr, assoc attend, 1981-; Gray & Gray Mds, pvt prac, pediatrician, 1981-. **Orgs:** Am Med Asn; Nat Med Asn; CV Roman Med Soc; Nat Asn Advan Colored People. **Honors/Awds:** Civilian Achievement Award, Walter Reed Army Med Ctr, 1978; Black Women Against the Odds Award, Dallas Independent Sch Dist; Dream Maker's Award, Southeast Dallas Bus & Prof Women. **Special Achievements:** Second Annual Salute to America's Top 100 Black Business & Professional Women, Dollars & Sense Mag, 1986; Publications: "Wednesday's & Thursday's Children, Medical Assessment of the Child with a Handicap", Early Periodic Diagnosis & Treatment Programs. **Home Addr:** 10889 Carissa Dr, Dallas, TX 75218-1219, **Home Phone:** (214)348-8273. **Business Addr:** Pediatrician, Gray & Gray Mds, 3600 Gaston Ave Suite 760, Dallas, TX 75246, **Business Phone:** (214)826-6110.

## GRAY, CHRISTINE

Manager, executive. **Personal:** Born Hartford, CT; married Herman C; children: Dianne Greene & Donna F White. **Educ:** Admin Sch WAAC, attended 1943; Sch Comptometer, attended 1944; Exxon, math keypunch, 1971. **Career:** Kolodney & Meyers Hartford, payroll clerk, 1940-46; Hop Equip, customer serv rep, 1970-71; Credit Union, secy, 1965-67; Thompson & Weinman Co, asst off mgr, 1967-70; Union Co OIC, keypunch instr, 1971-73, 1975; Union Co Dept Youth Serv, secy; Union Co OIC, mgr spec; Employ Resource Specialist, 1981-83; Companion Aide, prog dir, 1985-94. **Orgs:** Charter mem, NCNW Vauzhall Sect; pres, Burnet Jr High PTA; Jr Dgt Ruler Emma V Kelly Elks, 1940-42; inter club pres, YWCA, 1942-45; jr clerk, Hopewell Bapt Church, 1941-46; secy, Concerned Citizens Vauxhall; secy, Citizens Coun Vauxhall; pres, Jefferson Sch PTA; pres, Nat Coun Negro Women Vauxhall Sect; chairlady, Consumer Educ NCNW; dist leader, Dist 8 Union Co Girl Scout Leader; bd mem, Union Co Anti-proverty bd; secy, Calvary Bapt Church, 1959-67, 1970-77; charter mem, Gary Family Asn; Cancer Soc; Comn Vacation Bible Sch; Calvary Bapt Sunday Sch; Census Bur, 1960-70; Calvary Bapt Ch, 1973; Historian Nat Coun Negro Women, Vauxhall Sect, 1980-; Mentor Vauxhall & Brookside African-Am Youth Lit Club; sr adv, Time Teens, 1988-90; sr adv, Togetherness Asn, 1991-. **Honors/Awds:** Gold pin Girl Scouts; Plaque, Nat Coun Negro Women Vauxhall Sect, 1972 & 1973; Cert, NCNW; Guest part, Esther Roll Theresa Merritt; Maude Johnson Cultural Award, 1976; Comn Serv Award, Nat Coun Negro Women, 1978; Comn Serv Award, Bethune Tradition, 1986; Comn Serv Award, Vauxhall Homecoming Asn, 1987; Study Comn Union Twp, Bd Educ, 1986. **Home Addr:** 29 Maple Ave, Vauxhall, NJ 07088-1209.

## GRAY, DERWIN LAMONT

Television show host, football player, association executive. **Personal:** Born Apr 9, 1971, San Antonio, TX; married Vicki; children: Presley & Jeremiah. **Educ:** Brigham Young Univ, BA, sports bus mgt; Southern Evangel Sem, Mdiv, apologetics. **Career:** Football player (retired), clergy; Indianapolis Colts, defensive back, 1993-97; Carolina Panthers, 1998; Fox TV Network, co-host, 2003; One Heart Time Ministries, co-founder, 1999-; Gathering, Pastoral leadership team; Evangel Church Alliance, minister, 2002-; Transformation Church, founder, exec elder, lead pastor, currently. Author: Hero: Unleashing God's Power in a Man's Heart, 2010; Limitless Life: You Are More Than Your When God Holds Your Future, 2013; Crazy Grace for Crazy Times Bible Study, 2015; The High-Definition Leader, 2015. **Orgs:** Founder, Derwin Gray Found, 1996-99; minister, Christian & Missionary Alliance. **Business Addr:** Lead Pastor, Executive Elder, Transformation Church, 8978 Charlotte Hwy, Indian Land, SC 29707, **Business Phone:** (803)835-0630.

## GRAY, DONNEE L.

Librarian, manager. **Personal:** Born Jul 4, 1951, Camp Springs, MD; son of Mattie; married Vedia Thompson; children: Marcus D. **Educ:** Charles County Community Col, attended; St Mary's Col Mar, BA, social sci, 1976. **Career:** US Nat Champions, head coach; NCAA basketball off, 1980; Int Tournament, Mozambique, Africa, head coach, 1985; Mid Atlantic Col Basketball Officials Asn, supvr officials, 1992; US Sen Libr, adminr, head legis ref asst, supvr legis info serv, Off Legis Clerk, senate validation clerk; Md Pub Sec Schs Athletic Asn, Supvr, Coordr, Div I col basketball referee; Big E, basketball off; Big Ten, basketball off; Big Twelve, basketball off; Conf USA, basketball off; Atlantic 10 conferences, basketball off; Cent Intercollegiate Athletic Asn, basketball off. **Orgs:** Chmn bd, US Senate FDL Employees Credit Union; bd mem, Cage Page Basketball Referee Publ; pres, Int Asn Approved Basketball Off Inc, 1991-; Nat Amateur Basketball Asn; Nat Col Athletic Asn; men's NCAA tournament, 1986; supvr, Mid-Atlantic Basketball Officials Asn; founder & dir, Mid-Atlantic Col Basketball Officials Asn. **Honors/Awds:** Basketball Official of the Year, CIAA, 1990, 1992; Hall of Fame, Col Southern Md, 2007. **Special Achievements:** Atlantic Coast CNF, Atlantic Ten CNF, Big East CNF, Colonial Athletic ASN, East Coast CNF, Mid-Eastern Athletic CNF, Southwest CNF, USA Basketball (FIBA); US Natl Champions, head coach, 1985; played for Charles County Community College for two seasons; one of the top basketball officials in the country. **Home Addr:** , Charles County, MD. **Business Addr:** Head, Legislative Reference Assistant, US Senate Library, B15 Russell Bldg, Washington, DC 20510-7112, **Business Phone:** (202)224-7106.

## GRAY, DR. EARL HADDON

Administrator, executive director. **Personal:** Born Apr 19, 1929, Richmond, VA; son of William Joseph (deceased) and Annie Baker Atkins (deceased); married Jane N Harris; children: Adrienne Anne. **Educ:** Va State Univ, Petersburg, Va, BS, acct, 1970, MEd, 1974. **Career:** Administrator (retired); Assoc Dir Stud Act, Petersburg, Va, assoc dir, 1966-70; VSC, Petersburg, Va, pers dir, 1970-71; Model Cities JTPA, Richmond, Va, dir, 1971-77; Plng & Eval, Bal State, asst dir, 1978-82; Res Div VEC, Richmond, Va, chief dir, 1982-85; Imp Coun, Detroit, Mich, imp potentate, 1986-88. **Orgs:** Chair, labor & indust comt, Nat Asn Advan Colored People, 1966-70; Comt Elderly, City Richmond, 1971-74; bd mem, Gold Bowl Classic, City Richmond, 1975-; Nat Assault literacy, New York, NY, 1984-; pres, Community Motivators Inc, New York, NY, 1988-; pres, Beta Gamma Lambda, 1998-; Ancient Egyptian Arabic Order Nobles Mystic Shrine, imp conv dir, 2000-02. **Honors/Awds:** Seagrams Vangard Award, Seagrams Co, 1985; DHL, Va Union Univ, 1988. **Home Addr:** 2930 Sem Ave, Richmond, VA 23220, **Home Phone:** (804)321-2722.

## GRAY, EARNEST L.

Executive, football player. **Personal:** Born Mar 2, 1957, Greenwood, MS. **Educ:** Memphis State Univ. **Career:** Football player (retired), executive; New York Giants, wide receiver, 1979-84; St Louis Cardinals, wide receiver, 1985; City Memphis, Fire Dept, occup safety & health admin coordr, currently. **Honors/Awds:** All National Football League Rookie Honors, UPI, Pro Football Weekly, Professional Football Writers Asn & Football Digest. **Home Addr:** 600 E Saguaro Dr, Benson, AZ 85602, **Home Phone:** (520)586-8771. **Business Addr:** Occupational Safety & Health Administration Coordinator, City of Memphis, 65 S Front St, Memphis, TN 38103, **Business Phone:** (901)636-1400.

## GRAY, EDWARD, JR. (ED GRAY)

Basketball player. **Personal:** Born Sep 27, 1975, Riverside, CA. **Educ:** Univ Tenn, attended 1994; Col Southern Idaho, attended 1995; Univ Calif, attended 1997. **Career:** Basketball player (retired); Atlanta Hawks, guard, 1997-99; Houston Rockets, 1999-2000; Gary Steelheads, 2000-01; Dakota Wizards, 2001-02.

## GRAY, FELIX GARY

Movie director, actor, movie producer. **Personal:** Born Jul 17, 1969, New York, NY. **Educ:** Los Angeles City Col; Golden State Col. **Career:** Video & film dir, 1990-; BET, Fox TV Networks, camera operator; W C & the Maad Circle, Coolio, TLC, Ice Cube, Dr Dre, music video; Films: Major League, actor, 1989; Murder Was the Case: The Movie, 1995; Friday, director, 1995; Set It Off, actor, exec producer, 1996; The Negotiator, 1998; Ryan Caulfield: Year One, 1999; Cypress Hill: Still Smokin, 2001; Babyface: A Collection of Hit Videos, 2001; The Italian Job, 2003; A Man Apart, producer & dir, 2003; OutKast: The Videos, 2003; Be Cool, producer, 2005; The Brazilian Job, 2006; Law Abiding Citizen, actor, 2009; Straight Outta Compton, dir, 2015; Furious 8, dir, forthcoming; Bragman Nyman Cafarelli, dir, currently; TV Series: "Ryan Caulfield: Year One", dir, exec producer, 1999; "Reel Comedy", 2002; "enemies", 2006; "MMA H.E.A.T.", 2009. **Special Achievements:** Nominee for Black Movie Award, 2005; Nominee for BET Comedy Award, 2005. **Business Addr:** Director, Bragman Nyman Cafarelli, 9171 Wilshire Blvd Penthouse Suite, Beverly Hills, CA 90210-5530.

## GRAY, ESQ. FRED DAVID, SR.

Lawyer, evangelist, preacher. **Personal:** Born Dec 14, 1930, Montgomery, AL; son of Abraham and Nancy; married Bernice Hill; children: Deborah, Vanessa, Fred David Jr & Stanley. **Educ:** Nashville Christian Inst; Ala State Univ, BS, 1951; Case Western Res Univ, JD, 1954. **Career:** Rosa Parks, atty; Dr Martin Luther King Jr, first civil rights atty; NAACP Legal Defense Fund Inc, coop atty; ala state rep, 1970-74; Tuskegee Univ, local gen coun; Gray, Langford, Sapp, McGowan Gray & Nathanson law firm, sr mem, sr partner, currently; pvt pract, currently. **Orgs:** Preacher, Newtown Church Christ, 1957; Rep, Ala State Legis, 1970-74; pres, Nat Bar Asn County Civil Attorneys, 1982-83; Bar comm 5th Judicial Circuit, 1983-86; pres elect, Nat Bar Asn, 1984-85; pres, Nat Bar Asn, 1985-86; pres, Ala State Bar Asn, 2002-03; Am Bar Asn; Omega Psi Phi Frat Inc; elder, Tuskegee Church Christ; chmn, bd trustees, Southwestern Christian Col; Ala Lawyers Asn; pres, Macon County Bar Asn; Nat Asn Col & Univ Attorneys; Nat Bar Inst; bd dir, Ala Exchange Bank; Int Soc Barristers; pres, Ala Bar Asn. **Honors/Awds:** The Man in the News NY Times, 1966; First Annual Equal Justice Award, Nat Bar Asn, 1977; Drum Major's Award, MLK Jr Mem Southern Christian Leadership Conf, 1980; Presidential Award, Nat Bar Asn, 1982; Legal Award, World Conf Mayors, 1985; Graduate of the Year; Case Western Res Univ, 1985; Man of the Year Award, Women Work Los Angeles Calif & Southwestern Christian Col, 1986; Charles Hamilton Houston Medallion of Merit, Wash Bar Assn, 1986; Spirit of Excellence Award, Am Bar Asn, 1996; America's Soaring Eagles Award, Minority Caucus Asn Trial Lawyers Am, 2003; Sarah T. Hughes Civil Rights Award, Fed Bar Asn, 2004; William Robert Ming Advocacy Award, 2006; C Frances Stradford Award, Nat Bar Asn; World Conference of Mayors Legal Award; Nat Bar Asn Equal Justice Award; Southern Christian Leadership Conference's Drum Major's Award. **Special Achievements:** First African-American to hold the position of President in Alabama State Bar Association. Elected to the House of Representatives in 1970, he was one of the first African Americans to serve in the Alabama Legislature since Reconstruction; Gray published his autobiography, Bus Ride to Justice: The Life and Works of Fred Gray. Film: Boycott, 2001; Selma, 2014. **Home Addr:** 1005 E Lakeshore Dr, Tuskegee, AL 36083, **Home Phone:** (334)727-2231. **Business Addr:** Senior Partner, Gray, Langford, Sapp, McGowan, Gray & Nathanson, 205 Bailey Bldg 400 S Union St, Montgomery, AL 36083-0239, **Business Phone:** (334)727-4830.

## GRAY, FRIZZELL GERARD. See MFUME, KWEISI.

## GRAY, HAROLD B.

Executive. **Personal:** married Linda. **Career:** Hercules Inc; Andersen Consult; Andersen Consult, info syst proj; Enterprism Solutions LLC, pres, chief exec officer; TechniData Am, pres & chief exec officer, bd dir, 1998-; Wilmington Econ Develop, dir, 2012-2014; United Way Del, vpres, resource develop. **Orgs:** Del Environ Appeals Bd. **Business Addr:** Chief Executive Officer, TechniData America LLC, 2 Little Falls Ctr, Wilmington, DE 19808-1668, **Business Phone:** (877)546-6523.

## GRAY, DR. JAMES E.

School administrator. **Career:** Natchez Jr Col, Natchez, Miss, acad dean & psychol instr & pres, currently. **Business Addr:** President, Academic Dean & Psychology Instructor, Natchez Junior College, 1010 N Union St, Natchez, MS 39120, **Business Phone:** (601)445-9702.

## GRAY, DR. JAMES HOWARD

Psychiatrist, physician, consultant. **Personal:** Born May 20, 1943, Kaufman, TX; son of Wilmer Oscar and Ocie Bell Blakemore; married Carol Coleman; children: Nakia & James. **Educ:** N Tex State Univ, BS, biol, 1966, MS, microbiol, 1967; Univ Tex Med Sch, MD, 1971; Johns Hopkins Hosp, Wilmer Ophthal Inst, attended 1978. **Career:** Bexar Co Hosp, internal med intern, 1971-72; Walter Reed Med Ctr Wash, 1972-75; Wilmer Ophthal Inst, Johns Hopkins Hosp, resident Ophthalmol, 1975-78; Khalili Hosp Ophthal, Dept Shiraz Iran, vis instr, 1978; Baylor Univ Med Ctr, assoc, 1978-; pvt pract ophthal, 1978-; Southwestern Med Sch, clin fac, 1979-88; Tex Instrument & Terrell State Hosp, eye consult, 1979-81; Univ Tex Health Sci Ctr San Antonio, resident, 1986-89; Univ Hosp-S Tx Med Ctr, resident Internal Medi. **Orgs:** Fee rev comt, Dallas County Med Soc, 1985-87; bd mem, Good St Baptist Church; Nat Asn Advan Colored People; YMCA; Am Heart Asn; Soc Prevent Blindness; Dallas Black Chamber Com; Am Med Asn; Johns Hopkins Hosp Resident's Asn; Wilmer Resident's Asn; Am Acad Ophthal; Tex Ophthal Asn; fel Am Col Surg; fel Am Acad Optom. **Honors/Awds:** Legis Merit Schol; Galaxy Starts Award, Dallas Independent Sch Dist; Social Serv Award; First Place & Best of Show Awards, Tex Med Asn; First Place Awards, SNMA Wyeth Nat Contest. **Home Addr:** 10889 Carissa Dr, Dallas, TX 75218, **Home Phone:** (214)348-8273. **Business Addr:** Ophthalmologist, Private Practice, 3600 Gaston Ave Suite 760, Dallas, TX 75246, **Business Phone:** (214)826-6110.

## GRAY, JERRY DON

Football player, football coach. **Personal:** Born Dec 16, 1962, Lubbock, TX; married Sherry; children: Jeremy, Jayden & Gray Jr. **Educ:** Univ Tex, BS, commun. **Career:** Football player (retired), football coach; Los Angeles Rams, defensive back, 1985, left corner back, 1986-91; Houston Oilers, right corner back, 1992; Tampa Bay Buccaneers, free safety, 1993; Southern Methodist Univ, defensive back coach, 1995; Tenn Oilers, defensive qual Control coach, 1997-99; Tenn Titans, defensive asst & qual control coach, 1999-2000 & 2011-13, defensive back coach, 1999-2000, defensive coordr, 2011-13; Buffalo Bills, defensive coordr, 2001-05; Wash Redskins, sec & corner backs coach, 2006-09; Seattle Seahawks, defensive back coach, 2010; Tex Longhorns, defensive back coach, 2011; Minn Vikings, defensive back coach, 2014-. **Orgs:** Jerry Gray Found, 2002. **Honors/Awds:** Pro Bowl selection, 1986-89; Most Valuable Player, Pro Bowl, 1989; Defensive Back of the Year, Nat Football Conf, 1989. **Business Addr:** Secondary Coach, Cornerbacks Coach, Washington Redskins, FedExField, Landover, MD 20785, **Business Phone:** (301)276-6050.

## GRAY, JOANNE S.

Educator, school administrator. **Personal:** Born Dec 19, 1943, Headland, AL; daughter of Charlie and Gussie Jones; married Kenneth Byron; children: Kina Carisse. **Educ:** Chicago City Col, AA, 1965; Chicago State Col, BS, 1970; Gov State Univ, MS, 1979. **Career:** Educator (retired); teacher, 1970-; Chicago Bd Educ, dist chair person sci fair, 1983-, sci dept chairperson, 1984, chairperson city wide acad Olympics, 1985-86, ECIA coord, 1986, teacher rep, local sch coun, 1991-93; Fermi Nat Lab & Chicago State Univ, Summer Inst Sci & Math Teachers, admin dir, 1990; Chicago State Univ, Anthony Sch, prin. **Orgs:** Bd dir, Pre-med & Allied Health Prog, Chicago State Univ, 1978-81; secy, vpres, Rebecca Circle United Methodist Women, 1980-86; Phi Delta Kappa, 1984-86; prog chmn, Nat Asn Biol Teachers, 1984; coord & facilitator, Nat Sci Educ Comn, 1984; sci curric bd gov, State Univ, 1986; bd mem, Womens Div Global Ministries, 1987; area teen adv, Top Ladies Distinction Inc, 1987-89; exec secy, bd dir, Chicago State Alumni Asn, 1989-; coord, Local Sch Improv Plan Sci, 1990-; bd dir, Chicago Orgn Autism, 1990-; chairperson, Vol Comt; Chicago Pub Sch Sci Fair, 1991-; co-chairperson, Judging Ill Jr Acad Sci State Exhib, 1991-; chairperson, Outstanding logy Teachers Awards Sub comt; pres, Nat Asn Biol Teachers Sect Role & Status Women & Minorities

Biol Educ, 1992-93. **Home Addr:** 11730 S Oakley Ave, Chicago, IL 60643-4726, **Home Phone:** (773)840-4603. **Business Addr:** IL.

## GRAY, JOHNNIE LEE

Football executive, football player. **Personal:** Born Dec 18, 1953, Lake Charles, LA; married Barbara. **Educ:** Allan Hancock Col, grad; Calif State Univ, Fullerton, grad. **Career:** Football player (retired), executive; Green Bay Packers, free safety, punt returner, 1975-80, strong safety, 1981-83; FOX affil, football analyst; Nat Football League, uniform inspector, currently. **Honors/Awds:** Hall of Fame, 1993. **Business Addr:** Uniform Inspector, Nat Football League, 345 Park Ave, New York, NY 10154, **Business Phone:** (212)450-2000.

## GRAY, JON R.

College teacher, lawyer, judge. **Personal:** son of C Jarrett Sr and Mai H. **Educ:** Grinnell Col, AB, 1973; Univ Mo, Kansas City Sch Law, JD, 1976. **Career:** Jackson County Circuit Ct (Sixteenth Judicial Circuit Mo), circuit judge, 1987-2007; Nat Inst Trial Advocacy, fac mem, 1987-; Shook, Hardy & Bacon, partner, 2007-; Am Arbit Asn, panel mem-com, 2008-; Emory Univ Sch Law, fac Kessler-Edison Prog; Mo Judicial Col, fac Kessler-Edison Prog. **Orgs:** Mo Bar, Kans City Metrop Bar Asn, Jackson County Bar Asn; Univ Mo-Kans City Alumni Asn; Mo W Bd Trustees; Nat Asn Advan Colored People; archon, Sigma Pi Phi, 1991-2015; chmn, Nat Bar Asn Judicial Coun, 2007-08; United Methodist Church Judicial Coun, 2004-12; bd mem, Urban League Greater Kans City; bd mem, Kans City Neighborhood Alliance & Friends Univ Mo-Kans City Conserv Music. **Honors/Awds:** Urban League of Greater Kansas City Difference Maker Award, the Urban League of Greater Kansas City, 2002; H. Michael Coburn Community Service Award, Legal Aid of Western Missouri, 2004; National Bar Association Presidential Award, 2008; Spurgeon Smithson Award, The Missouri Bar Foundation, 2014. **Special Achievements:** License to practice before the Missouri Supreme Court, the U.S. District Court, Western District of Missouri, and the U.S. Court of Appeals, Eighth Circuit. **Business Addr:** Shook, Hardy & Bacon LLP, 2555 Grand Blvd, Kansas City, MO 64108, **Business Phone:** (816)559-2272.

## GRAY, DR. JOSEPH WILLIAM, III

Physician, pediatrician, surgeon. **Personal:** Born May 31, 1938, Memphis, TN; married Jacquelyn Cooper; children: Joseph IV, Jaylynn, Jeffrey, Jerron & Jerome. **Educ:** St Augustine's Col, BA; Meharry Med Col, MD, 1963. **Career:** Santa Monica Hosp, intern, 1963-64; GW Hubbard Hosp, resident, 1966-69; pvt pract physician, 1985-. **Orgs:** Nat Med Asn; AMA; Toledo & Lucas Pediat Soc; Ohio Chap Am Acad Pediat; fel Am Acad Pediat; Am Bd Pediat; life mem, Nat Asn Advan Colored People; Sigma Pi Phi; Alpha Phi Alpha; Alpha Kappa Mu. **Home Addr:** 1 Aurora L Gonzalez Dr, Toledo, OH 43609, **Home Phone:** (419)241-4230. **Business Addr:** Physician, 2109 Hughes Dr, Toledo, OH 43606, **Business Phone:** (419)479-6060.

## GRAY, KAREN G. (KAREN GRAY HOUSTON)

Journalist. **Personal:** Born Montgomery, AL; daughter of Thomas W and Juanita Emanuel. **Educ:** Ohio Univ, Athens, OH, BA, psychol, 1972; Columbia Univ, New York, NY, MS, jour, 1973. **Career:** United Press Int, Boston, Mass, reporter, writer & ed, 1973-75; WHDH-AM, Boston, Mass, reporter, anchor, 1975-76; ABC News, New York, NY, radio anchor, 1976-81; NBC News, Wash, DC, radio & tv corresp, 1981-83; WCBS-TV, New York, NY, writer, assoc producer, 1984-87; WTOP Newsradio, Wash, DC, reporter, anchor, 1987; WTTG(FOX5), reporter, currently. **Orgs:** Nat Asn Black Journalists; Wash Asn Black Journalists; Capitol Press Club; reporters comt, Freedom Press. **Honors/Awds:** Persian Gulf War syndrome, Blinded American Veterans, named as honor; Best spot news coverage award, Sigma Delta Chi Society Of Professional Journalists, 1992, Chesapeake Associated Press Broadcasters Association and the Radio-Television News Directors Associations. **Business Addr:** Reporter, WTTG/FOX TV 5, 5151 Wis Ave NW, Washington, DC 20016, **Business Phone:** (202)244-5151.

## GRAY, KEITH A., JR.

Government official. **Personal:** Born Nov 3, 1947, Camden, NJ. **Educ:** Career Educ Inst, Cert, 1975; Pierce Jr Col, attended 1977; Rutgers Univ, attended 1983. **Career:** Conrail, customer rep, 1982; Juv In Need Suprv, counr, 1984; Cumberland City Welfare, intake maintenance, 1985; Bayside State Prison, furlough coordr, currently; Fairfield Twp Comm, mayor. **Orgs:** Adb bd Fairfield Twp Schs, 1983; leg comm adv Comm Women, 1984; bd dir, NJ Citizen Action, 1985; Nat Conf Black Mayors, 1985, NJ Asn Mayors, 1985, NJ Conf Mayors, 1985. **Honors/Awds:** Certificate NJ State Assembly, 1984; Certificate, SCOPE, 1984; Placque Concerned Citizens of Fairfield, 1984; Cert Concerned Citizens of Fairfield, 1984. **Special Achievements:** First African Woman to become mayor of Cumberland County. **Home Addr:** Rd 7 Rte 49, PO Box 373, Franklinville, NJ 08322.

## GRAY, KENNETH D.

College administrator, army officer, lawyer. **Personal:** Born Excelsior, WV; married Carolyn; children: 2. **Educ:** WVa State, BA, polit sci, 1966; WVa Univ, Morgantown, JD, 1969; Univ Va, law degree, 1975; AUS Command & Gen Staff Col. **Career:** Army officer (retired), educational administrator; AUS: Ft Ord, Calif, defense coun, judge advocate gen's corps, 1966-97, Vietnam, 1993, personnel mgt officer, asst judge advocate gen, 1993-97, Ct Mil Rev, chief judge, Legal Serv Agency, comdr, defense coun, legal assistance officer, Ft Ord, Calif, 1969, Vietnam, 1969, defense coun & command judge advocate, 1970, Ft Meade, Md, 1971; dep staff judge advocate, 1978, staff judge advocate, 1981-84, chief personnel, plans & training off, 1984, Pentagon, Minority JAG Prog, Personnel, Plans & Training Off, personnel mgt Offr, actg judge advocate gen, brig gen, spec asst to actg judge advocate gen, brig gen, 1991, maj gen; AUS Legal Serv Agency, comdr, 1991-93; AUS Ct Mil Rev, chief judge; Trial Judiciary, chief; Secy Army, Procurement Fraud Matters, rep; WVa Univ, vpres stud affairs, 1997-; Judge Advocate Gen's Sch, instr & sr instr. **Orgs:** Chair & fel, Am Bar Asn Found; fel, W Va Bar Found; Tex Bar Found; chair, Govt & Pub Sector Lawyers Div, Am Bar Asn; co-chair, Asn Pub Land Grant Univs Coun Stud Affairs; co-chair, Couns Exec Comt. **Special Achievements:** Only African-American general in Judge Advocates General Corps history. **Business Addr:** Vice President for Student Affairs, West Virginia University, 205 E Moore Hall, Morgantown, WV 26506, **Business Phone:** (304)293-5811.

## GRAY, REV. MACEO

Manager. **Personal:** Born Dec 22, 1940, Dallas, TX; married Annie P Hatcher; children: Karen & Kathleen. **Educ:** Prairie View Agr & Mech Univ, BS, elec engineering, 1963; Univ Mo; Dallas Theol Sem, ThM; Univ Miss, MSc, elec engineering; Rockhurst Col, MBA. **Career:** Bendix Corp, jr engr, 1963; Test Equip Design Dept, engineering supvr, 1969; Elec Prod, eng supr; AlliedSignal Aerospace Div, engineering prog mgr(retired), environ restoration prog, Mo; Marketplace Chaplains USA, part-time chaplain, region dir, 1998-, midwest region vpres, currently. **Orgs:** Jr Achievement Co, 1970; dir comn proj, Bendix Mgt Club, 1973-74; vpres, Spec Events Bendix Mgt Club, 1975-76; vpres, Camp Fire Bowling League. **Honors/Awds:** Chaplain of the Year, 1997; Dallas Theological Seminary Lewis Sperry Chafer Award; W E Hawkins Jr Award; received numerous outstanding service awards; The Fredrik Franson Award. **Special Achievements:** Author of "The Christian Comfort Companion" and "Passing on Your Christian Heritage to Your Children, Grandchildren and Generations to Come"; First president of Dallas Theological Seminary. **Home Addr:** 310 W Minor Dr, Kansas City, MO 64114-5545, **Home Phone:** (816)943-0275. **Business Addr:** Region Vice President, Marketplace Chaplains USA, 13795 N Mur Len Rd Suite 205, Olathe, KS 66062, **Business Phone:** (913)397-7757.

## GRAY, MACY (NATALIE RENEE MCINTYRE)

Actor, singer. **Personal:** Born Sep 6, 1967, Canton, OH; daughter of Otis Jones and Laura McIntyre; married Tracy Hinds; children: Aanisah, Tahmel & Cassius. **Educ:** Univ Southern Calif. **Career:** Macy Gray Music Acad, owner, 2005-; Albums: On How Life Is, 1999; The Id, 2001; The Trouble With Being Myself, 2003; The Very Best of Macy Gray, 2004; Live in Las vegas, 2005; Big, 2007; The Sellout, 2010; Covered, 2012; Talking Book, 2012; The Way, 2014; Films: Training Day, 2001; Spiderman, 2002; Gang of Roses, 2003; Scary Movie 3, 2003; Lightning in a Bottle, 2004; Around the World in 80 Days, 2004; Domino, 2005; Shadowboxer, 2005; The Crow: Wicked Prayer, 2005; Idlewild, 2006; The Paperboy, 2012; TV: "Ally McBeal", 2000; "MDs", 2002; "American Dreams", 2004; "Blue's Clue", 2004; That's So Raven, 2004; "American Dragon: Jake Long", 2005; "Duck Dodgers", 2005; "1-800-Missing", 2005; "Dancing With the Stars", 2009; Geffen Records Inc, singer, currently; Macy Gray Music Acad, 2005-. **Special Achievements:** Nominated Soul Train Awards, 1999; Nominated Grammy Award for Song of the Year & Record of the year, 2000; Nominated MTV Video Music Award for Best Hip-Hop Video, 2001; Nominated Billboard Awards, 2001; Nominated NAACP Image Award for Outstanding Actress in a Television Movie, Mini-Series or Dramatic Special, 2006. **Business Addr:** Singer, Geffen Records Inc, 9130 Sunset Blvd, Los Angeles, CA 90069, **Business Phone:** (310)278-9010.

## GRAY, MARCUS J.

Government official. **Personal:** Born Sep 22, 1936, Kansas City, MO; son of Marcus and Christina; married Abbey Dowdy; children: Marcus, III, Sean & Yolanda. **Educ:** Kellogg Community Col, BBA. **Career:** County clerk, 1964-72; Eaton Mfg, prod insp chief clerk qual con com trans clerk; Kellogg Co, mach operator; Cahoun County, county clerk regist, 1972-; Paradigm Cash Flow Solutions, partner, currently. **Orgs:** Exec comt, Calhoun County Dem Party; Haber & Comn Polit Reform Elections; sub comt chmn, Mich Non Partisan Election Comn; pres, Mich Asn County Clerks; pres, Nat Asn County Recorders & Clerks, 1979; United County Officer's Asn; pres, Battle Creek Area Urban League; pres, Battle Creek Area County Church; chmn, Calhoun-Barry Growth Alliance. **Honors/Awds:** Les Bon Amie Club Award, outstanding serv; certificate merit, Dem Party MI & Calhoun County Dem Women's Club; Clerk the Year, MI Asn County Clerks. **Home Addr:** 40 Maurer Dr, Battle Creek, MI 49037.

## GRAY, MARVIN W.

Lawyer. **Personal:** Born Aug 12, 1944, Chicago, IL; married Delia J; children: Derek, Jason & Meagan. **Educ:** Southern Ill Univ, BS, Eng, 1966; Chicago-Kent Col Law, Ill Inst Tech, JD, 1972. **Career:** Chicago Pub Sch, teacher, 1966, 1970-72; Aetna Life & Casualty Ins, claims rep, 1967-70; Montgomery & Holland, assoc & self-employed, 1967-79; Cook County, asst pub defender, 1972-74; Braud Warner & Neppl, assoc atty, 1974-75; Firm Ward & Gray, partner, 1975-76; Chicago Transit Authority, Law Dept, trial lawyer, 1987-91; Harth Vital Stroger Boarman & Williams, atty; Marvin W Gray Assocs, Chicago, Ill, pvt prac atty, currently. **Orgs:** Consult, Opera PUSH, 1973-74; coun, 10 Dist Omega Psi Phi Frat; Ill Trial Lawyers Asn; Phi Delta Phi Int Legal Frat; Nat Cook Co Ill; Am Bar Asn. **Honors/Awds:** Moran fund scholar, 1968; Ill Inst Tech scholar, 1970. **Home Addr:** 5125 S Drexel Ave, Chicago, IL 60615-3885, **Home Phone:** (773)643-4667. **Business Addr:** Attorney, Marvin W Gray Associates, 405 E Oakwood Blvd Suite 2L, Chicago, IL 60601-7511, **Business Phone:** (773)268-0900.

## GRAY, MEL (MELVIN JUNIUS GRAY)

Football player. **Personal:** Born Mar 16, 1961, Williamsburg, VA; children: Melanie & Devon. **Educ:** Coffeyville Community Col, grad; Purdue Univ, grad. **Career:** Football player (retired); Los Angeles Express, 1984; Okla, 1984; Ariz Outlaws, 1985; New Orleans Saints, running back, kickoff returner, 1986, kickoff returner, punt returner, 1987-88; Detroit Lions, kickoff returner, 1989, kickoff returner, punt returner, 1990-94; Houston Oilers, kickoff returner, punt returner, 1995-96; Tenn Oilers, 1997; Philadelphia Eagles, wide receiver, 1997. **Honors/Awds:** All-Decade Team, Nat Football League, 1990; Special Teams Player of the Year, Nat Football League Players Asn, 1991. **Special Achievements:** Film: 1991 NFC Championship Game, 1992. TV Series: "The NFL on NBC", 1979-97; "NFL Monday Night Football", 1988-90; "ESPN's Sunday Night Football", 1988-95.

## GRAY, MOSES W.

Automotive executive, football player. **Personal:** Born Apr 12, 1937, Rock Castle, VA; son of Moses Jr and Ida Young; married Ann Marie Powell; children: Tamara Ann & William Bernard. **Educ:** Ind Univ, BS, phys educ, 1961; Detroit Diesel Allison Apprentice Training Prog, 1967; Univ Mich, Gen Motors Inst. **Career:** Automotive Executive, Football player (retired); Indianapolis Warriors, New York Titans, 1961,62, prof football player; Gen Motors, Detroit Diesel Allison, Indianapolis, inspector, 1962-63, apprentice tool & die maker, 1963-67, journeyman tool & die maker, 1967-68, prod supvr, 1968-69, supvr-tool room, 1969-73, genl supv tool room, 1973-76, asst supt master mech, 1976-79, dir community rel, 1979-83, speedway plants, mgr mfg serv, 1983-90, speedway plants, gen supt mfg eng, 1990-92; Jr Achievement Advisor, Little League football coach, Thatcher Community Ctr; Little League basketball coach, Jewish Community Ctr. **Orgs:** Bd, Indianapolis Bus Develop Found; Black Adoption Comt; C's Bur Indianapolis; Child Welfare League Am; Indianapolis Urban League; Community Serv Coun, Ind Voc Tech Col; United Way Greater Indianapolis; Nat Asn Advan Colored People; Off Equal Opportunity, City Indianapolis; Channel 20 Pub Serv TV; Ind Black Expo; Black Child Develop Inst; United Way Agency Rel Adv Comt; Madame Walker Urban Life Ctr; Wilma Rudolph Found; pres, Indianapolis Chap Sigma Xi; pres, State Coun Adoptable C, 1972; pres, Black Adoption Comt, 1973; inaugural pres, Ind Asn Rights C, 1974; Ind Asn Rights C; Homes Black C, 1980; mem bd dir, Ind Univ Found; bd dir, pres, Asn Rights C Ind; asst dist comnr, Crossroads Am Coun; chmn, Ind Univs Neal Marshall Black Cult Ctr; Boy Scouts Am; co-chmn, United Negro Col Fund Telethon; "I" Men's Asn, Ind Univ; chmn, Neal-Marshall Black Cult Ctr, Ind Univ; Vol Bur; Mayor's Black Hist Month; Opportunities Industrialization Ctr; 100 Black Men Am Inc. **Home Addr:** 1313 Aggie Lane, Indianapolis, IN 46260-4096, **Home Phone:** (317)254-6569.

## GRAY, MYRON A.

Vice president (organization). **Personal:** children: 1. **Educ:** Univ Memphis, BA, bus; INSEAD, Fontainebleau, France, Advan Mgt Prog, grad; Yale Sch Bus, Advan Mgt Prog, grad. **Career:** United Parcel Serv Inc, package handler, 1978-84, package delivery driver, opers supvr, package div mgr delivery opers, 1989-95; Southeast Tex dist, vpres & chief operating officer, 1995-98; Rocky Mountain Dist, vpres & chief operating officer, 1995; Southwest Region, pres, 2002-04, N Cent Region, 2004-08, Americas region, pres, 2008-09, sr vpres US opers, 2009-10, pres US opers, 2010-. **Orgs:** Bd, Nat Urban League, Black Exec Exchange Prog; bd trustee, Dillard Univ; bd trustee, Miami-Dade United Way; dir, CLADEC; Nat Bd Gov; trustee, Boys & Girls Clubs Am (Southeast Region); bd trustee, Atlanta Police Found; United Parcel Serv Mgt Comt; bd, Fed Res Bank Atlanta; bd, Airlines Am. **Business Addr:** President, United Parcel Service, 55 Glenlake Pkwy NE, Atlanta, GA 30328.

## GRAY, ROBERT DEAN

Mayor, executive, chief executive officer. **Personal:** Born Jun 30, 1941, Clarksville, TN; son of R D and Willa M Bush; married Gloria Enochs. **Educ:** Miss Valley State Univ, BS, 1964; Tex Southern Univ, MS, 1968; Chevron Oil Co Bus Sch. **Career:** Bolivar County Sch Dist 3, teacher, coach, 1964-67; Tex Southern Univ, asst coach, grad asst, 1967-68; Bolivar County Head start Prog, dir, 1968-70; Shelby Chevron Serv St, owner, operator, 1968-78; City Shelby, mayor, 1976-97; Griffin Lamp Co, pres, chief exec officer, 1987-. **Orgs:** Bd dir, Munic Ass Miss, 1978-92; chmn, Munic Assn Serv Co Ins Pool; bd dir, Miss Inst ST Small Town, 1979-; bd dir, Miss Delta Coun, 1986-; vpres, Natl Conf Black Mayors, 1984-86; pres, Miss Conf Black Mayors, 1979-86; bd dir, Nat Assn Mfrs, 1989-91. **Honors/Awds:** Miss Valley State Univ, Sports Hall Fame Inductee, 1980. **Home Addr:** 1202 Lauderdale St, PO Box 145, Shelby, MS 38774-0145, **Home Phone:** (662)398-7326. **Business Addr:** President, Chief Executive Officer, Griffin Lamp Co, US Hwy Suite 61 S, Shelby, MS 38774, **Business Phone:** (601)398-7302.

## GRAY, DR. RONALD A.

Lawyer. **Personal:** Born Dec 15, 1952, Blackstone, VA; son of Archie and Mary Frances; married Doris; children: Avery & Lindsay. **Educ:** Ohio Univ, BA, econs, 1975; Case Western Res Univ, Col Law, JD, 1978. **Career:** Fed Trade Comn, staff atty, 1978-81; Am Express Co, staff atty, 1981-85, from assoc to managing coun, 1985-2004; Citigroup, dep gen coun, 2005, managing dir & gen coun, 2005-08, exec vpres & gen coun int cards, 2008-14; Opportunity Int, sr vpres, secy & global gen coun, 2015-. **Orgs:** Am Bar Asn, 1978-; bd mem, C Hope Found, 1991-94; bd mem, S African Legal Servs & Legal Assistance Proj, 1993-; vice chair, NY Bar Asn, Comt Minorities, 1994-97; bd mem, MFY Legal Servs, 1996-97; corp coun exec comt, NY State Bar Asn, 1997; Comn Multi-Discipline Pract, 1998-99; Kids Need Defense, 2011-14; City Bar Arbit Com. **Honors/Awds:** Gene Chapin Memorial Research Award, Ohio Univ, 1971; Harlem Achievers Award, Harlem YMCA, 1990; Harlem Black Achievers in Industry Award, 1998. **Special Achievements:** Publications: Companies Aim for Diversity, New York Law Journal, 1993; Employees at Risk, New York Law Journal, 1994; Chairman, Succeeding in the Business Card Market, Credit Card Inst, Executive Enterprises, 1997; Government and Marketplace Protections-Insolvent Carriers, ABA Forum on Air and Space Law, 1999. **Home Addr:** 630 Wellington Rd, Ridgewood, NJ 07450, **Home Phone:** (201)447-4205. **Business Addr:** Senior Vice President, General Counsel, Opportunity International, 550 W Van Buren Suite 200, Chicago, IL 60607, **Business Phone:** (312)487-5000.

## GRAY, RUBEN L.

Judge, lawyer. **Personal:** Born Nov 6, 1938, Georgetown, SC; married Jean E Dozier; children: Ruben Jr, Valencia & Valerie. **Educ:** SC State Univ, BS, 1961, JD, 1963; SC St Col, LLB, 1963. **Career:** SC Econ Opp Bd Inc, exec dir, 1968-70; Morris Col, vpres develop, 1970-73; Finney & Gray, atty; St SC Family Court 3rd Judicial Circuit Sumter County, judge, currently. **Orgs:** SC St Elections Comn; bd trustee, Sumter Sch Dist 17; Am Bankers Asn, NBA; SC Bar Asn; chmn, Sumter County Child Uplift Bd Inc; pres, Sumter Br Nat Asn Advan Colored People; UMCA; Goodfellows; Sumter County Black Polit Caucus; Sumter County Dem Exec Comt; trustee, Mt Pisgah Ame Church. **Honors/Awds:** Recipient, Community Leader of America Award, 1968. **Home Addr:** 110 S Wash St, Sumter, SC 29150, **Home Phone:** (803)934-0800. **Business Addr:** Judge, South Carolina Judicial Department, 108 N Magnolina St, Sumter, SC 29151-2636, **Business Phone:** (803)436-2373.

**GRAY, TORRIAN (TORRIAN DESHON GRAYBARTOW)**
Football player, football coach. **Personal:** Born Mar 18, 1974, Bartow, FL; married Elena Fullman; children: Tori. **Educ:** Va Tech, attended 1996. **Career:** Football player (retired), football coach; Va Tech Hokies football, 1992-96; Minn Vikings, defensive back, 1997-99; Univ Maine, defensive backs coach, 2000-01; Div I-AA Playoffs, coach, 2001; Univ Conn, defensive backs coach, 2002-03; Chicago Bears, defensive backs coach, 2004-05; Chick-fil-A, coach, 2006, 2009; Va Tech, defensive backs coach, 2006-, defensive sec coach, 2006-12, defensive sec & passing game coordr, 2013-; Orange, Kans, coach, 2007, 2008, 2010; Sugar, coach, 2011; Russell Athletic, coach, 2012; Sun, 2013; Mil, 2014. **Orgs:** Nat Col Athletic Asn. **Business Addr:** Defensive Secondary, Passing Game Coordinator, Virginia Tech, 901 Prices Fork Rd, Blacksburg, VA 24062-9001, **Business Phone:** (540)231-6285.

**GRAY, VALERIE HAMILTON**
Civil engineer, executive director. **Personal:** Born May 10, 1959, Houma, LA; daughter of Allen A and Lucia T Legaux; married Ian A; children: Adrienne Theresa & Ian Alexander. **Educ:** Univ Notre Dame, Notre Dame, Ind, BS, 1981; Corpus Christi State Univ, Corpus Christi, Tex, comput sci, 1987. **Career:** Texaco, USA, Harvey, La, proj engr, 1980-85; City Corpus Christi, Corpus Christi, Tex, neighborhood improv div supvr, 1985-88, engr II, 1988-89, water construct supt, 1989-95, storm water supt, 1995-, dir Storm Water & St Opers, Pub Works Dept, exec dir. **Orgs:** Am Soc Civil Engrs, 1981-; Am Water Works Asn, 1989-; Nat Soc Prof Engrs. **Honors/Awds:** Young Engineer of the Year, Nuects Chap Tex Soc Prof Engrs, 1994. **Home Addr:** 3329 New Bedford Dr, Corpus Christi, TX 78414, **Home Phone:** (512)992-6756. **Business Addr:** Director of Storm Water & Street Operations, Storm Water Department, 2726 Holly Rd, Corpus Christi, TX 78415, **Business Phone:** (361)826-1847.

**GRAY, WILFRED DOUGLAS**
Executive. **Personal:** Born Oct 1, 1937, Richmond, VA; son of Richard L and Lula B Duvall; married Shirley M Durant; children: Alden D & Kathleen Y. **Educ:** Dale Carnegie, Buffalo, NY, attended 1971; State Univ, NY, Buffalo, BA, 1974; Printing Indust Metrop Wash, Wash, DC, attended 1981. **Career:** Repub Steel, Buffalo, NY, scarfer, inspector, 1962-76; Buffalo Envelope, Buffalo, NY, sales rep, 1976-80; Envelopes Unlimited, Rockville, MD, sales rep, 1980-81; Gray Paper Prod Inc, Wash DC, founder, pres, Sales & Daily Opers, 1981-. **Orgs:** Chamber Com, DC, Nat Asn Advan Colored People; bd dir, Boys & Girls Clubs Greater Wash; Am Asn Retired Persons; Nat Asn Black Pub Officials; Upper Ga Ave Bus & Prof Asn; Nat Bus Forms Asn; Rotary Club Wash, DC. **Honors/Awds:** President's Award, Fed Envelope, 1979. **Home Addr:** 12201 Hazel Hill Cir, Ft. Washington, MD 20744. **Business Addr:** President, Gray Paper Products Inc, 214 L St NE, Washington, DC 20002-3536, **Business Phone:** (202)546-4919.

**GRAY-LITTLE, DR. BERNADETTE**
Educator, psychologist. **Personal:** Born Oct 31, 1945, Washington, NC; daughter of James Gray and Rosalie Lanier Gray; married Shade Keys Little; children: Maura M & Mark G. **Educ:** Marywood Univ, BA, 1966; St Louis Univ, MS, 1968, PhD, psychol, 1970. **Career:** Family Pract Ctr, Asst Dir & Supvr, 1971-76; Univ NC, from asst prof to assoc prof, 1971-82, dir, 1982-93, chair, 1993-98, sr assoc dean, 1999-2001, exec assoc provost, 2001-04, dean, col arts & sci, 2004-06, execu vice chancellor & provost, 2006-09; Kans Univ, Chancellor, 2009-. **Orgs:** Fac affil, Ctr Creative leadership, 1998-2004; Fel Am Psychol Asn; Sigma Xi; bd trustee, Online Comput Libr Ctr; bd mem, US Bank; Am Psychol Asn; Asn Pub & Land-grant Univs; exec comt, Asn Am Univs, 2013; Coun Foreign Rels. **Special Achievements:** First woman & First African American to lead the Kansas University. **Home Addr:** 229 Weaver Rd, Chapel Hill, NC 27514-5956. **Business Addr:** Chancellor, The University of Kansas, 230 Strong Hall, Lawrence, KS 66045-7518, **Business Phone:** (785)864-2700.

**GRAY-MORGAN, DR. LARUTH H.**
College administrator. **Personal:** Born Texarkana, TX; daughter of Hazel Johnson and Curtis Hackney; married Joseph; children: Diendra & Phillip; married Norris Gray; children: Phillip Anthony & Dierdra Alyce Gray. **Educ:** Howard Univ, BA, 1954; Columbia Univ, MA, 1957; Nova Univ, EdD, 1975. **Career:** New Rochelle New York Public Sch, chmn English Dept, Educ Support Ctr, prin, dir instructional serv, asst supt, 1980-83; Abbott Univ Free Sch District, supt sch, 1983-89; New York Univ, Metrop Ctr Urban Educ, dep dir, 1989, adj assoc prof, ed admin, 1990-, affil prof, 2003, dir external rels, 2003-. **Orgs:** Bd mem, comm White Plains, Young Women Christian Asn; Comt Aging City New Rochelle; chair, Urban Affairs Comm New York Asn Super & Curr Develop; vpres, New York State Eng Coun; pres, emer, bd dir Martin Luther King Child Care Ctr, 1980-; pres emer, Westchester Arts Coun, 1986-; bd dir, pres, bd trustee, New Rochelle Pub Libr Found, 1986-90 & 1993-95; bd dir & bd trustee, Katonah Art Mus; bd dir, New York State Alliance Art, 1989-91; bd dir, Westchester C's Asn & March Dimes, 1989-95; vpres, Westchester Coun Arts, 1987-94, exec vpres, 1996-99; Am Asn Sch Admin, Comt Minorities & Women, chair, 1990-; pres, Westchester Libr Syst, 1996-2000; pres, Methodist Art Coun, 2000-02; bd dir, Nat Alliance Black Sch Educs, currently; chair, Am Educ Res Asn, currently; US Serv Acad Rev Bd; chair, African Am Adv Comt; New York Comnr's Adv Panel C with Handicapping Conditions. **Home Addr:** 300 Pelham Rd 5K, New Rochelle, NY 10805-2208, **Home Phone:** (914)636-6154. **Business Addr:** Board of Director, National Alliance of Black School Educators, 310 Pa Ave SE, Washington, DC 20003, **Business Phone:** (202)608-6310.

**GRAY-WALKER, TRACEY**
Association executive, executive. **Personal:** married Derek; children: Tre. **Educ:** Fairleigh Dickinson Univ, BA, acct. **Career:** Touche Ross & Co, sr auditor; AXA Equitable Life Ins Co, vpres bus develop & opportunities, 1989-2008, chief diversity officer & sr vpres, 2008-. **Orgs:** Exec Leadership Coun; bd trustee, Nj Ctr Outreach & Serv Autistic Community; AXA Equitable's Diversity & Inclusion Coun; trustee, Autism Nj; Women's Bond Club. **Honors/Awds:** Autism Ambassador of the Year, Ctr Outreach & Serv Autistic Community, 2004; 25 Influential Black Women in Business, Network J, 2006; Women Worth Watching, 2008; Top Executive in America, Updtown Prof Publ, 2012; Women of Distinction, Girl Scouts Greater New York, 2012. **Business Addr:** Vice President, Chief Diversity Officer, AXA Equitable Life Insurance Co, 1290 Avenue of the Americas, New York, NY 10104, **Business Phone:** (212)554-1234.

**GRAYBARTOW, TORRIAN DESHON. See GRAY, TORRIAN.**

**GRAYDON, WASDON, JR.**
School administrator, executive director. **Personal:** Born Sep 22, 1950, Ft. Mammoth, NJ; son of Wasdon and Lenora; married Veronica Brooks; children: Tremayne & Jasmaine. **Educ:** Abraham Baldwin Agr Col, AS, sec educ, 1970; Ga Southern Col, BS, 1972; Valdosta State Col, 1974. **Career:** Spec Serv Prog, dir, 1973-76; Upward Bound Spec Serv Prog, dir, 1973-76, spec serv, min adv prog, 1983-87; Abraham Baldwin Agr Col, dir minority advising/TRIO Progs, 1983-2010, Ctr Multicultural Awareness, dir, stud support serv, 1997, Col Serv External Progs, interim dir, 2000-01; Tift Co, comnr dist 2, 1984-88; G&M Enterprises, partner, 1985-87; CAMP/HEP Progs, interim dir, 2002-03, Graydon Enterprises LLC, managing mem; First Community Bank Tifton, bd dir. **Orgs:** Phi Delta Kappa, 1975-83; bd mem, SW Ga Health Syst Agency Inc, 1976-81; Treas, Ga Asn Spec Prog Inc, 1980-84; consult, Ga Statewide Health Coord Coun, 1980-83; Tift Co Nat Asn Adv Colored People, 1980-87; trustee, Everette Temple CME Church, 1980-87; PROMISE Club, 1983-84; trustee, Tifton Tift Co Pub Libr, 1984-88; Tift Co Arts Coun, 1984-87; bd mem, Tifton-Tift Co United Way, 1986-88; Tifton-Tift Co C C, 1986-87; bd dir, Tifton-Tift Co Main State Prog, 1986-87; vice chair, Tift Co Dem Party; adv bd chairperson Intervention & Prev Serv, Inc; Tift County Hosp. **Honors/Awds:** GASPP Outstanding Service Award, 1983; SAEOPP Cert of Recognition, 1984; Manager of the Year, 1989-90; Leadership Ga Found Inc, 1991; Arts Citizen of the Year, Tifton-Tift County Arts Coun, 1994; Outstanding Serv Award, Univ Syst Ga, 1994; Pres Appreciation Award, ABAC, 2000-01; E Lanier Carson Leadership Award, ABAC, 2000-01, Humanitarian of Year, 4th dist Ga Funeral Serv Practitioners Asn, 2009. **Home Addr:** 4504 Raywood Dr, Tifton, GA 31793-8457, **Home Phone:** (229)386-2472. **Business Addr:** Director, Abraham Baldwin Agricultural College, 2802 Moore Hwy, Tifton, GA 31793, **Business Phone:** (229)386-3489.

**GRAYS, DR. MATTELIA BENNETT**
School administrator. **Personal:** Born Jul 26, 1931, Houston, TX; daughter of A B Bennett; married Horace; children: Karen. **Educ:** Dillard Univ, BA, 1952; Univ Mich, MA, spec educ; Pac Univ, Sacramento, EdD, educ admin, 1985. **Career:** Educator (retired); Rogers Educ Enrichment Ctr, prin, 1970-87; Houston Independent Sch Dist, Dist three supt, 1987; Continuous Progress Learning Corp, consult, educr admin operator; Univ Houston, supvr lab experiences teachers; Houston Pub Schs; Sorority's S Cent Region, pres & regional dir. **Orgs:** 18th int pres, Alpha Kappa Alpha Sorority Inc, 1970-74; Int Asn Childhood Educ; exec bd mem, Nat Pan Hellenic Coun Inc. **Honors/Awds:** AKA Sorority S Cent Region scholarship fund, named in honor. **Special Achievements:** Youngest person ever elected National President of the Alpha Kappa Omega Chapter Sorority in 1968. **Home Addr:** 7575 Cambridge St Apt 902, Houston, TX 77054-2034, **Home Phone:** (713)799-8038.

**GRAYSON, REV. DR. BYRON J., SR.**
Clergy, manager. **Personal:** Born Sep 3, 1949, York, PA; son of Charles F Sr and Hurline V Bridgette; married Jennifer Gibson; children: Cortella Jones, Paul Jones, Byron Jr & Nicolle. **Educ:** Howard Univ, BA, finance, 1971, MBA, bus, 1978, Sch Divinity, MDiv, 1995; United Theol Sem, DMin, cult issues an urban context, 2003. **Career:** Verizon, regulatory mgr, 1971-2001; Bell Atlantic, mgr, residence serv ctr, 1979-81, mgr, reg matters, 1981-97, sr specialist, Oper Serv, 1997; African Methodist Episcopal Church, ordained elder, 1997; St Jude AME Church, pastor, 1998-2012; Frederick City Police Dept, auxiliary police officer, currently; Frederick Community Col, bd trustee, currently. **Orgs:** Bd, Ed Partnership Technol Corp, 1991-96; elected comm, vice chmn, Adv Neighborhood Comm, 1988-95; Wash, DC Ward 3 Dem Comt, 1988-95; Alpha Phi Alpha Fraternity; Brown Memorial AME Church, asst pastor, 1995-98; Int Asn Police Chaplains. **Home Addr:** 1018 Eastbourne Ct, Frederick, MD 21702-5119, **Home Phone:** (301)353-9007. **Business Addr:** Board of Trustee, Frederick Community College, 7932 Opossumtown Pk, Frederick, MD 21702, **Business Phone:** (301)846-2400.

**GRAYSON, DEREK L., II**
Executive. **Personal:** Born Feb 11, 1971, Sandusky, OH; son of Derek Sr and Jill; married Carmen Felice; children: Miles & Noah. **Educ:** Morehouse Col, BA, bus admin, 1993. **Career:** Wachovia Bank, banking officer, 1993-97; Citizens Trust Bank, vpres, 1997-; Peachtree Nat Bank, vpres, 2004-06; Br Banking & Trust, vpres, 2006-08; Optimum Bus Consults Inc, pres & chief exec off, 2008-09; southeast bank, vpres Com Lender; Leadership DeKalb, 2008; US Small Bus Admin, Com Loan Specialist, 2009-10; Fifth Third Bank, vpres, 2010-. **Orgs:** Chmn bd dir, sec, S DeKalb Bus Incubator, 1998-; comnr, Stone Mountain Main St Comn; bd dir, chair, Habitate Humanity DeKalb, 1998-; Nat Asn Gov Guaranteed Lenders, 1999-; bd dir, Ctr Visually Impaired; treas bd dir, Anti-Prejudice Consortium; fel Atlanta Urban Bankers Asn. **Home Addr:** 4139 Idlewood Parc Ct, Tucker, GA 30084-7833, **Home Phone:** (770)414-5144. **Business Addr:** Vice President, Fifth Third Bank, 3344 Peachtree Rd Suite 800, Atlanta, GA 30326, **Business Phone:** (404)279-4532.

**GRAYSON, ELSIE MICHELLE**
Counselor. **Personal:** Born May 5, 1962, Fairfield, AL. **Educ:** Univ Ala, Tuscaloosa, BS; Univ Ala, Birmingham, MA, educ. **Career:** Child Ment Health Serv, teaching parent, 1983-84; Ala Dept Human Resources, social worker, 1984-. **Orgs:** Alpha Kappa Alpha Sor Inc; Omicron Omega Chapter; Eastern Star Corine Chap 257; choir dir, pres, asst teacher, New Mount Moriah Baptist Church. **Home Addr:** 322 Knight Ave, Hueytown, AL 35023, **Home Phone:** (205)744-4512. **Business Addr:** Social Worker, 1321 5th Ave S, Birmingham, AL 35202, **Business Phone:** (205)933-6045.

**GRAYSON, GEORGE WELTON**
State government official. **Personal:** Born Nov 1, 1938, Dixons Mills, AL; son of Aaron and Martha Harper; married Lucille Lampkin; children: Anthony, Reginald & Deirdre. **Educ:** Ala A&M Univ, BS, 1965, MS, 1968; Vanderbilt Univ, PhD, 1976. **Career:** Tenn Valley High Sch, Hillsboro, AL, teacher, 1966-67, guid counr & asst prin, 1967-68; Ala A&M Univ, biol instr, dept chmn, 1968-71; Ala House Reps, rep, 1983. **Orgs:** Ala New S Coalition; Synod Mid-South; Presbyterian Coun. **Home Addr:** 6398 Green Meadow Rd NW, Huntsville, AL 35810-4479, **Home Phone:** (256)852-9891. **Business Addr:** AL.

**GRAYSON, JENNIFER A.**
Executive. **Personal:** Born Apr 26, 1949, Union, SC; daughter of Martha Gist Gibson and Cortelyou Gibson; married Byron; children: Cortella, Paul, Byron Jr & Nicolle. **Educ:** SC State Univ, Orangeburg, SC, BS, 1972; George Washington Univ, Wash, DC, 1978. **Career:** Food & Drug Admin, Brooklyn, NY, consumer safety off, 1972-74; E Orange, NJ, consumer safety off, 1974-77; Rockville, Md, consumer safety off, 1977-90, actg br chief, 1990, br chief, 1990, actg assoc div dir, 1993-95; Bio-Reg Assoc, sr regulatory affairs specialist, Laurel, Md, 1995-96; Oncor Inc, sr regulatory affairs specialist, Gaithersburg, Md; Bio-Tech Imaging, vpres regulatory affairs, Frederick, Md, 1999-2003; US Food & Drug Admin, assoc div dir, 1972-95; Independent consult, currently. **Orgs:** Delta Sigma Theta Sorority, 1968-; first vpres, Alpha Wives Wash, DC, 1987-90; class leader, St Paul AME Ch, 1989-; historian, Missionary Soc/St Paul Ch, 1990-; first vpres, Missionary Soc/St Paul AME Church, 1991-95; Wash Conf, Ministers Wives, Spouses & Widows Alliance, 1994. **Home Addr:** 1018 Eastbourne Ct, Frederick, MD 21702, **Home Phone:** (301)846-0018. **Business Addr:** Independent Consultant, 1018 Eastbourne Ct, Frederick, MD 21702, **Business Phone:** (301)846-0018.

**GRAYSON, JOHN N.**
Executive. **Personal:** Born Sep 4, 1932, Brooklyn, NY; married Dorothy Lane; children: Lois, Theresa, Susan & April. **Educ:** BSEE, attended 1959. **Career:** Hughes Aircraft Co El Segundo CA, proj engr, 1955-62; Guid & Nav Lab TWR Sys Redondo Beach CA, bus mgr, 1962-71; Electronics Harward Opers, sub-proj mgr; prod line mgr mgr-manu engr test sec; Unified Ind Alexandria VA, dir energy probs proj minority bus enter, 1973; UNIVOX CA Co, pres. **Orgs:** Nat Assn Black Manu; Inst Elec & Electronics Engr Inc; chrtr pres, Consolidate Comn Action Asn; mem pres, Youth Motivation Task Force; Urban League; Nat Asn Advan Colored People; com sel-help group Mex Am Comm E LA; Orient-Am Caucus; ruling elder, Westminster Presb Ch LA; comnr, Gen Assembly United Presb Ch, 1969; moderator, Synod So Bca UPCUSA; chmn, com synod So CA; Gen Assembly Mission Coun UPCUSA; chmn, Sect Eval UPCUSA. **Home Addr:** 1932 Va Rd, Los Angeles, CA 90016-1730, **Home Phone:** (323)733-5706.

**GRAYSON, MEL**
Fashion designer, educator. **Personal:** Born Dec 3, 1950, Dallas, TX; son of Coot and Ruby Lee; children: Damon, Shannon Fields & Lillian Holmes. **Educ:** Trade-Tech Col, Los Angeles, CA, AA, 1971; Fashion Inst Design & Merchandising. **Career:** TV Serials: "Pride & Prejudice", costume desginer, 1990; "A Different World", costume desginer, 1990; House Party 3, costume desginer, 1994; "Bringing Up BayBay", production designer, 2005; Freelance fashion designer, 1972-74; ARPEJA, fashion designer, 1971-75; Bullock's Dept Store, visual merchandiser, 1975-77; Aaron Brothers Art Marts, mgr, 1977-86; fashion & costume designer, 1986-, Fashion Inst Design & Merchandising, prof, 2000-11; Pinky Rose Boutique, visual dir, currently; St Rage & Co, owner & designer, 1976-. **Orgs:** West Coast Fashion Alliance. **Home Addr:** 1140 N Gower St Suite 201, Hollywood, CA 90038, **Home Phone:** (323)856-8103. **Business Addr:** Owner, St Rage & Co, 1811 S Norton Ave, Los Angeles, CA 90019-6044, **Business Phone:** (323)419-4255.

**GRAYSON, STANLEY EDWARD (STAN EDWARD GRAYSON)**
Banker. **Personal:** Born Sep 11, 1950, Chicago, IL; son of George C Jr and L Elizabeth Smith; married Patricia Ann McKinnon; children: Lauren Ashley & Stephen Edward. **Educ:** Col Holy Cross, Worcester, BA, MA, 1972; Univ Mich Law Sch, Ann Arbor, MI, JD, 1975. **Career:** Metrop Life Ins Co, NY, atty, 1975-84; City New York, comnr financial servs, 1984-88, comnr finance & chief exec officer, 1988-89, dep mayor finance & econ develop, 1989-90; Financial Serv Corp, chmn, comnr, 1984-87; New York Indust Develop Agency, comnr, Chief Exec Officer, chmn; Goldman Sachs & Co, NY, Munic Bond Dept's Infrastructure & Gen Banking Group, vpres, 1990-96, managing dir, Munic Finance Dept, sr mem; Prudential Securities Inc, managing dir, mgr, pub finance, 1996; Prudential Equity Group LLC, vpres, 1990-96; Alliance Downtown New York Inc, dir; MR Beal & Co, pres, vice chmn, chief operating officer, 2002-. **Orgs:** NY State Bar Asn, 1977-; 100 Black Men, 1986-; bd dir, Boys Choir Harlem, 1987-91; bd dir, March Dimes NY, 1990-96; bd dir, Mus City NY, 1990-; bd dir, Region Plan Asn, 1990-95; firm's operating coun, 1990-96; bd trustee, Mgt Col, Tarrytown, 1991-96; bd dir, NY Downtown Hosp, 1991-95; bd trustee, Col Holy Cross, 1995-; bd dir, NY Outward Bound, 1995-; Comnr, Port Authority New York & NJ, 2008-; bd dir, TD Bank; bd dir, TD Bank US Holding Co; bd dir, Munic Securities Rulemaking Bd; bd dir, New York Cath Charities; bd dir, Brooklyn Info & Cult; bd dir, New York Sch Construct Authority; trustee, Churchill Sch & Ctr; Ny Bar. **Honors/Awds:** Crusader of the Year, 1972; Col Holy Cross, 1972; Man of the Year, Brooklyn Chamber Com, 1989; Hall of Fame, 1991. **Home Addr:** 601 E 20th St, New York, NY 10010. **Business Addr:** Vice Chairman, Chief Operating Officer, MR Beal & Co, 14 Wall St 17th Fl, New York, NY 10005-3801, **Business Phone:** (212)983-3930.

**GREAUX, CHERYL PREJEAN**
Entrepreneur, consultant, government official. **Personal:** Born Jul 30, 1949, Houston, TX; daughter of Evelyn F Jones; married Robert Bruce. **Educ:** Tex Southern Univ, BA, 1967; Univ Tex, MA, 1973.

Career: NASA Johnson Spacecraft Ctr, procurement specialist, 1968-71; Dept Labor, super compliance officer, 1973-80; Allied Corp, corp mgr, EEO Progs, 1980-85; Dean Witter Reynolds Inc, exec recruiter, 1986-88; USDA, civil rights dir, rural housing, 1995, Nat Alternative Dispute Resolution Prog, dir, civil rights dir; Greaux & Assoc, prin consult & partner, currently. **Orgs:** Delta Sigma Theta Sorority, 1965-; chmn, Fund Raising NJ Inst Tech, 1981-84; bd mem, Morris County Urban League, 1983-85; Coalition 100 Black Women, 1994; co-founder, Wash Edges Group Inc; Corp Womens Network. **Home Addr:** 2117 Vittoria Ct, Bowie, MD 20721-2818. **Business Addr:** Civil Rights Director, Greaux & Associates, 6323 Summerday Ct, Burke, VA 22015, **Business Phone:** (301)925-9167.

### GREAVES, MCLEAN

Chief executive officer. **Personal:** Born Sep 27, 1966, St. Thomas; son of Marion and Oswald (deceased). **Educ:** British Columbia Inst Technol, jour, 1986. **Career:** Int Bus Mach, Delrina Softkey Software, consult, 1993-96; Paper Mag, newmedia ed, 1995-96; PAPER Mag, Assoc New Media Ed, 1995-97; CBC TV, corresp, 1996-, exec producer, 2000-05; Columbia Sch Bus, lectr, 1997-98; Pratt Inst, lectr, 1998; Virtual Melanin Inc, chief exec officer & co-founder, 1995-99; HBO's urban internet div Vol.com, vpres content, 1999-2000; Nimble Co Inc, founder & chief exec officer, 2005-09; ZoomerMedia, Toronto, Can, vpres interactive, 2009-; Burning to Shine, producer. **Orgs:** Panelist, Comn Concerned Journalists, 1998. **Business Addr:** Vice President of Interactive, ZoomerMedia Ltd, 70 Jefferson Ave, Toronto, ON M6K 1Y4, **Business Phone:** (416)619-5517.

### GREAVES, WILLIAM

Writer, movie producer, administrator. **Personal:** Born Oct 8, 1926, New York, NY; son of Garfield and Emily Muir; married Louise Archambault; children: David, Taiyi & Maiya. **Educ:** City Col New York, attended 1945; Film Inst City Col, attended 1952. **Career:** Nat Film Bd Can, filmmaker, 1952-60; Can Drama Studio, artistic dir, 1952-63; UN TV, producer & dir, 1963-64; William Greaves Prods Inc, owner, 1964-, pres, currently; Black Jour, exec producer & co-host, 1968-70; Lee Strasberg Theatre Inst, instr, 1968-82; "Paul Robeson: A 90th Birthday Tribute", Shubert Theater, dir & co-producer, 1988; Films: Symbiopsychotaxiplasm: Take One, 1968; Ali, the Fighter, 1973; From These Roots, 1974; Ida B Wells: A Passion for Justice, PBS, 1989; Cinema Verite: Defining the Moment, 2000; Ralph Bunche: An American Odyssey, 2001; Symbiopsychotaxiplasm: Take 2 1/2, 2003. **Orgs:** NY Actors Studio; AFTRA; Am Guild Auth & Composers; DGA; co-founder, Nat Asn Black Media Producers, 1970; WGA; Equity Asn; SAG; Studio's Bd dir. **Honors/Awds:** Inductee, Black Filmmakers Hall of Fame, 1980; Special Recognition, Black Am Independent Film Festival, Paris, 1980; Indy Special Life Achievement Award, Asn Independent Video & Filmmakers; Dusa Award, Actors Studio, NY, 1980; Emmy Award, Nat Acad TV Arts & Sci; Four Emmy nominations; Conducted workshops for film directors & screen actors throughout the world; Ralph Bunche: An American Odyssey, selected for competition at Sundance Film Festival, 2001; Career Award, Full Frame Doc Film Festival, 2008. **Home Addr:** 475 W 57th St Apt 17A, New York, NY 10019-1778, **Home Phone:** (212)265-6150. **Business Addr:** President, William Greaves Productions Inc, Radio City Sta, New York, NY 10101-2044, **Business Phone:** (800)874-8314.

### GREELY, M. GASBY (GASBY GREELY BROWN)

Entrepreneur, financial manager. **Personal:** Born Oct 23, 1946, Detroit, MI; daughter of Wesley and Stella; children: Janine. **Educ:** Wayne County Community Col, AA, 1971; Wayne State Univ, BA, 1973; MIT, Advan Res, 1982; Harvard Univ, MPA, 1982. **Career:** WNET/Thirteen, mkt dir, 1983-87; Fox Tv, gen assignment reporter, 1987-89, financial corresp, 1989-93; Greenpeace, nat commun dir, 1993-95; Nat Urban League, vpres develop & commun, 1995-2000, sr vpres, 2001; Wash Opera Co, exec vpres & dir strategic res planning, 2000; Greenpeace, nat dir commun; Nat Urban League, sr vpres develop & commun; Gasby Group Inc, owner, chmn & chief exec officer, currently. **Orgs:** Pub Rel Soc Am, 1983-; Brooklyn Tabernacle, 1991-; Nat Press Club, 1993-; bd dir, Nat C Film Festival, 1996-; Nat Soc Fundraising Execs, 1997-; Nat Acad Tv Arts & Sci; Nat Asn Black Journalists. **Honors/Awds:** Alum of the Year, Nat Asn Community Col, 1989; Legacy Messenger, Black Career Women, 1997; Women of Industry Award, Nat Coun Negro Women. **Home Addr:** 40 Prospect Pk W, Brooklyn, NY 11215, **Home Phone:** (718)768-4486. **Business Addr:** Chairman, Chief Executive Officer, The Gasby Group Inc, 145 Fleet St, National Harbor, MD 20745, **Business Phone:** (301)292-2946.

### GREEN, A. C., JR.

Basketball player, president (organization). **Personal:** Born Oct 4, 1963, Portland, OR; son of A C Sr and Leola; married Veronique. **Educ:** Ore State Univ, BS, speech commun, 1985. **Career:** Basketball player (retired), pres; Los Angeles Lakers, forward, 1985-93, 1999-2000; Phoenix Suns, 1993-96; Dallas Mavericks, 1996-97; Miami Heat, 2000-01; AC Green Youth Found, founder & pres, currrently. **Orgs:** AC Green Youth Found; Athletes Abstinence Financial Destination Inc. **Business Addr:** President, AC Green Youth Foundation, 904 Silver Spur Rd Suite 416, Rolling Hills, CA 90274, **Business Phone:** (310)465-1470.

### GREEN, AHMAN RASHAD

Broadcaster, executive, football player. **Personal:** Born Feb 16, 1977, Omaha, NE; son of Glenda and Edward Scott; married Marie; children: 5. **Educ:** Univ Nebr, BA, geog, 2003. **Career:** Football player (retired), executive; Seattle Seahawks, running back, 1998-99; Green Bay Packers, 2000-06, 2009; Houston Texans, 2007-08; Omaha Nighthawks, 2010; Montreal Alouettes, 2011; Green Bay Blizzard, co-owner, 2012-; D1 Training Ctr, Green Bay Wis, co-owner; D1 Training Ctr Omaha Nebr, co-owner; WFRV-TV, sports commentator, currently. **Orgs:** Founder & pres, Ahman Green Found. **Honors/Awds:** Big Eight Offensive Freshman of the Year, 1995; Pro Bowl, 2001, 2002, 2003, 2004; All Pro, 2001, 2003; Rushing Champion, Nat Football Conf, 2003; Offensive Player of the Year, Nat Football Conf, 2003; FedEx Ground Player of the Year Award, 2003; All-Time Leading Rusher, Green Bay Packers; Hall of Fame Class, Univ Nebr, 2012; Hall of Fame Class, Green Bay Packers, 2014. **Home Addr:** 1750 Limestone Trl, De Pere, WI 54115-7973, **Home Phone:** (920)351-3306. **Business Addr:** Co-Owner, Green Bay Blizzard, 1901 S Oneida St, Green Bay, TX 54304, **Business Phone:** (920)405-1264.

### GREEN, REV. ALBERT LEORNES (AL GREEN)

Singer, executive, clergy. **Personal:** Born Apr 13, 1946, Forrest City, AR; son of Robert and Cora; married Shirley Kyles; children: Alva, Rubi & Kora. **Educ:** Lane Col, BA, music, 1976; Lemoyne Owen, BA, music, 1977. **Career:** Green Enterprises Inc, owner, pres, 1970; Bell then Hi-Rec, rec artist; Al Green Music Inc, owner, pres, rec artist, 1970-; Full Gospel Tabernacle Church, pastor, 1976-; Songs: "Rhymes"; "Lets Stay Together"; "Tired of Being Alone"; "How do You Mend a Broken Heart"; "Back up Train"; "Love & Happiness"; Broadway: Your Arms Too Short to Box with God, 1982. Albums: The Christmas Album, 1983; He is the Light, 1986; Love Is Reality, 1992; Gospel Soul, 1993; I Can't Stop, 2003; Everything's OK, 2005; Lay It Down, 2008; People Get Ready, 2009; Later with Jools Holland, 2010; Oh Happy Day: An All-Star Music Celebration. **Orgs:** NARAS, 1970-; AGVA, 1970-; spec dep, Memphis Sheriffs Dept, 1976-; honcapt, Bolling AFB, Wash DC, 1976-; pres, Lee County Pub Co, 1983-; Econ & Devel City Hall, 1984-; Rock & Roll Hall Fame. **Honors/Awds:** Tribute in the Music Ind Sullivan Award, 1982; Grammy Award for Precious Lord, NARAS, 1983; Grammy for I'll Rise Again, NARAS, 1984; Dove Award, Gospel Music Asn, 1984; Rock and Roll Hall of Fame, 1995; Grammy Lifetime Achievement Award, 2002; Gospel Music Hall of Fame, inducted, 2004; 100 Greatest Artists of All Time, Rolling Stone mag, 2004; Lifetime Achievement Award, BET Awards, 2009; Michigan Rock and Roll Legends Hall of Fame, 2009; Kennedy Center Honor, 2014. **Special Achievements:** Autobiography, Take Me To The River, 2009, A Road in Memphis named Reverand Al Green Road. **Home Addr:** PO Box 456, Memphis, TN 38101. **Business Addr:** Pastor, Full Gospel Tabernacle Church, 787 Hale Rd, Memphis, TN 38116, **Business Phone:** (901)396-9192.

### GREEN, ALEXANDER N. (AL GREEN)

Association executive, government official, politician. **Personal:** Born Sep 1, 1947, New Orleans, LA. **Educ:** Fla A&M Univ, attended 1971; Tex Southern Univ, Thurgood Marshall Sch Law, JD, 1974. **Career:** Harris Co, judge, justice peace, precinct 7, position 2, 1977-2004; Tex House Reps, Dist 9, rep, 2005-; Tex Southern Univ, Thurgood Marshall Sch Law, instr; Green, Wilson, Dewberry & Fitch Law Firm, co founder; US Congressman, Tex 9th, 2005-. **Orgs:** Pres, Nat Asn Advan Colored People, Houston, TX; Alpha Phi Alpha; State Bar Tex; bd mem, Urban League; bd mem, YMCA; Congressional Pakistan Caucus. **Honors/Awds:** Distinguished Service Award, Houston Citizens Chamber Com, 1978; Outstanding Leadership Award, Black Heritage Soc, 1981; Courageous Defender of Due Process for Educators, Am Fed Teachers, 1983; Ebony Magazines 100 Most Influential Black People, 2006; NAACP Fort Bend Branch Mickey Leland Humanitarian Award, 2006; Texas Black Democrats Profiles of Courage Award, 2007; AFL-CIO MLK Drum Major Award for Service, 2007; Texas Association of REALTORS Legacy Award, 2011. **Home Addr:** , Houston, TX. **Business Addr:** Representative, Texas House Representatives, 3003 S Loop W Suite 460, Houston, TX 77054, **Business Phone:** (713)383-9234.

### GREEN, ALLISON

Vice president (organization). **Educ:** Spelman Col, BA, psychol; Howard Univ, MA, coun psychol. **Career:** Vanguard, dir corp, human resources, 1999-2006; Wyeth Pharmaceut, dir corp diversity, 2006-09; Lincoln Financial Group, sr vpres & chief diversity officer, 2009-. **Orgs:** Bd dir, Main Line Chamber Com & Laurel House; sr Human Resources leadership team; bd dir, Urban League Philadelphia; bd dir, i4cp Diversity; Forum Exec Women; active mem, Alpha Kappa Alpha Sorority Inc.

### GREEN, ANITA LORRAINE

Banker, president (organization). **Personal:** Born Jul 18, 1948, Brooklyn, NY; daughter of Angus and Queen Esther; children: Corey James. **Educ:** Brooklyn Col, City Univ New York, NY, BA, econs, 1981. **Career:** Nat Urban League, prog develop specialist, 1972-82; Citicorp Diners Club, dir corp commun, 1981-89; Citibank FSB, vpres, community rels & CRA officer, 1990-98; Foster Green Morgan LLC, vpres mkt, 2002-; Anita Green Relocation Mgmt, pres, owner, currently. **Orgs:** Chairperson, Mus Sci & Ind, black creativity prog, 1992-; adv bd, DePaul Univ, Ctr Urban Educ, 1990-; bd mem, Ill Facil Fund, 1993-; bd mem, Life Directions; bd, Univ Chicago; Friends Against Aids; Life Directions; Mus Sci; Ind Adv Comn. **Honors/Awds:** Dollars & Sense Mag, Ams Best & Brightest Bus, Prof Men & Women, 1991; Mahogany Found, Community Relations Award, 1993-; YMCA Black & Hispanic Achievers of Industry Award, 1993; Success Guide, Top Ten To Watch, 1995; Today's Chicago Women, 100 Women Making a Difference. **Home Addr:** 1600 W 103 St, Chicago, IL 60643, **Home Phone:** (773)429-9890. **Business Addr:** Vice President Marketing, Foster Green Morgan LLC, 3148 S King Dr, Chicago, IL 60616-3940, **Business Phone:** (312)225-7224.

### GREEN, BERTRUM SCARBOROUGH. See GREEN, SCARBOROUGH.

### GREEN, BRENDA KAY

Educator. **Personal:** Born Dec 7, 1947, Baton Rouge, LA; daughter of Lillian White George and Jackson Willis. **Educ:** Southern Univ, Baton Rouge, LA, BS, 1969; Northwestern Univ, Evanston, IL, MA, attended 1973. **Career:** E Baton Rouge Parish Schs, Baton Rouge, La, dean stud, 1969-; E Baton Rouge Parish Dist Atty's Off, hon dist atty, 1983. **Orgs:** Pres, Beta Alpha Chap, Zeta Phi Beta, 1968, 3rd vpres, Mu Zeta Chap, 1976-80, first vpres, 1984-88; Nat Educ Asn, 1969-; La Educ Asn, 1969-72; Phi Delta Kappa, 1974-89; Nat Coun Negro Women, 1980-; La state dir, Zeta Phi Beta Sorority Inc, 1980-88, nat second vpres, 1988-92; chmn scholar, Nat Educ Found, ZOB, 1988-92. **Home Addr:** 1423 N 26th St, Baton Rouge, LA 70802, **Home Phone:** (504)383-2282. **Business Addr:** Dean of Students, Broadmoor High School, 10100 Goodwood Blvd, Baton Rouge, LA 70815, **Business Phone:** (225)926-7663.

### GREEN, D'TANYIAN JACQUEZ. See GREEN, JACQUEZ.

### GREEN, DARLENE

Government official. **Personal:** Born St. Louis, MO. **Educ:** Wash Univ, BS, bus admin. **Career:** City St Louis, budget dir, comptroller, 1995-, chief fiscal officer, currently; Incom Inc, sales coordr. **Orgs:** Zeta Phi Beta Sorority Inc; Nat Asn Black Accts; Nat Asn Advan Colored People; Govt Finance Officers Asn; Antioch Baptist Church; metrop St Louis bd dirs & finance comt, YWCA; bd dir, Employ Connection; St Louis Community Educ Task Force; Airport Comn; trustee, City Retirement Systs; Bd Estimate & Apportionment. **Honors/Awds:** Political Leadership Award, Young Dem St Louis City; Distinguished Service Award, Dr. Martin Luther King Jr State Celebration Comn, Miss; Nat Achievement Award, Nat Asn Black Accts Inc; Lifetime Achievement Award, Gateway Classic Sports Found; Shining Star Award, Nat Orgn Black ElectedLegis Women; Achievement Award, Sister to Sister Expo; Distinguished Community Service Award, Mound City Bar Asn; Community Service Award, St Louis Dist Christian Methodist Episcopal Church Ministerial Alliance, 2003; Political Leader of the Year Award, St Louis Metro Sentinel Journal, 2007. **Special Achievements:** First African American female comptroller of St. Louis; 52 Most Powerful People in St. Louis, 2008. **Home Addr:** . **Business Addr:** Comptroller, Chief Fiscal Officer, City of Saint Louis, City Hall 1200 Mkt St Rm 212, St Louis, MO 63103-2875, **Business Phone:** (314)622-4389.

### GREEN, DARRELL RAY

Football player, business owner. **Personal:** Born Feb 15, 1960, Houston, TX; married Jewell Fenner; children: Jarrel, Jared & Joi. **Educ:** Tex A&M Univ; St Pauls Col, BS, gen studies & social sci. **Career:** Football player (retired), business owner; Wash Redskins, cornerback, 1983-2002; Detroit Lions, 1987; Chicago Bears; Philadelphia Eagles, 1997; Ariz Cardinals, 1999; Darrell Green Enterprises, owner, 1997; Darrell Green Holdings LLC, owner, 2000; Intekras Inc, owner, currently; Trusted Solutions Group, owner, currently; Darrell Green Mortgage & Score Title & Escrow, owner, currently; WalkFitHealth Nation Fitness Ctr, owner, currently; Univ Mary Wash, spec asst, Stud-Athlete Develop & Pub Rels, 2013. **Orgs:** Big Bros Big Sisters Am, DC Chap; hon chmn, Am Red Cross, Northern Va Chap; founder, Darrell Green Youth Life Found, 1988; founder, Darrell Green Youth Life Learning Ctr, 1993-; bd mem, Baltimore-Wash 2012 Olympic Bid; Nat Football League Players Asn September 11th Relief Fund; bd mem, Loudoun Educ Found; Wolf Trap Found; Wash Bd Trade; Nat Spokesman, Marymount Univ; chair, Coun Serv & Civic Participation, 2003. **Business Addr:** Founder, Owner, Darrell Green Enterprises, 21515 Ridgetop Cir Suite 290, Ashburn, VA 20147, **Business Phone:** (703)547-7903.

### GREEN, DARRYL LYNN

Manager. **Personal:** Born Sep 29, 1958, Ypsilanti, MI; son of Clarence and Eleanor; children: Robert. **Educ:** Cent Mich Univ, attended 1978; Comput Learning Ctr, cert completion, 1988. **Career:** Alcoa Aluminum, inspector, 1979-91; Packard Bell, proj mgr, 1991-. **Home Addr:** 8265 Westbury Dr, Magna, UT 84044-2201, **Home Phone:** (801)579-3054. **Business Addr:** Manager, Packard Bell Electronics Inc, 8285 W 3500 S, Magna, UT 84044, **Business Phone:** (801)579-3054.

### GREEN, DR. DEBORAH KENNON

Lawyer. **Personal:** Born Aug 14, 1951, Knoxville, TN; daughter of George and Florence Jones; children: Joshua. **Educ:** Knoxville Col, BA, 1973; Georgetown Law Ctr, JD, 1976. **Career:** David N Niblack Wash, DC, law clerk, atty, 1976-77; DC Govt Rental Accommodations Off, hearing examr, 1977-78; Govt Oper Arrington Dixon, DC City Coun, comn clerk, 1978-79; Coun DC Off Arrington Dixon, leg asst to chmn, 1979-80; US Dept Labor, Safety & Health Div, Off Solicitor, sr atty, counr, Arlington, Va; pvt pract, currently. **Orgs:** County chmn, 7th Annual Conv Nat Asn Black Women Atty, 1978-; WV Bar Asn, 1979, Wash Bar Asn, 1980, Alfred St Baptist Church, 1989. **Honors/Awds:** Tuition Scholarship, Georgetown Law Ctr Wash DC, 1973-76; Earl Warren Legal Training Scholarship, 1973-74; Special Award of Merit, DC Bar, 1979; Meritorious Achievement Award, 1985, Federal Women's Program Award, 1990, Dept Labor; Exceptional Secretary Achievement Award, 1993. **Home Addr:** 3913 Terr Dr, Annandale, VA 22003, **Home Phone:** (703)256-9585. **Business Addr:** Counselor, Senior Attorney, US Department of Labor, 1100 Wilson Blvd, Arlington, VA 22209-2296, **Business Phone:** (202)693-9333.

### GREEN, DENNIS. See Obituaries Section.

### GREEN, DENNIS O.

Auditor, executive director. **Personal:** Born Nov 14, 1940, Detroit, MI; son of Arthur Salvador and Olive May Dean McCaughan; married Katherine F; children: Damon & Leslie. **Educ:** Wayne State Univ, BS, bus admin & finance, 1967; State Mich, CPA. **Career:** Arthur Andersen & Co, staff sr acct, 1967-69, audit mgr, 1971-73; Wells & Green Prof Corp, pres, 1969-71; City Detroit, finance dir, 1974-76; Off Mgmt & Budget Wash DC, assoc dir exec of the pres, 1977-78; Ford Motor Co, gen auditor, 1984-90; Citicorp, chief auditor, 1990-97; Citibank NA, chief auditor, 1990-97; Keiretsu Investments Inc, pres, currently; Celadon, founder & managing partner, currently; Coastal Banking Co, vice chmn, 1999-2011; Allete, dir, 2003-04; Adesa Inc, dir, 2004-; Gray Holdings, dir, currently; Venture Inc, dir & chm audit comt, currently; CBC Nat Bank, dir; Lowcountry Nat Bank, dir. **Orgs:** Inst Internal Auditors, 1984-; bd dir audit comt, Allete Inc, 2003-; Am Inst CPA's; Nat Asn Black Accountants; dir & pres, Olive Tree Found; dir & vpres, Boys & Girls Club Lowcountry; trustee, Beaufort Acad; Bd United Way Beaufort; pres, Boys & Girls Club Beaufort. **Home Addr:** 120 E 87th St No R102, New York, NY 10128. **Business Addr:** Director, Adesa Inc, 13085 Hamilton Crossing Blvd, Carmel, IL 46032, **Business Phone:** (317)815-1100.

### GREEN, DEREK

Fashion designer. **Personal:** Born Jan 1, 1968; son of Friendly and Gloria; married Sheri; children: Tori, Kyra & Riley. **Educ:** Art Inst,

Philadelphia, degree, fashion illus; Parsons Sch Design, BA, fashion design. **Career:** Am Eagle Outfitters, head designer; Tommy Hilfiger USA Inc, head designer & fashion designer, 1997-2000; Derek Green Designs, founder & head designer, 2006-. **Home Addr:** 100 W 119th St Apt 3A, New York, NY 10026. **Business Addr:** Head Designer, Founder, Derek Green Designs, 350 5th Ave Suite 6603, New York, NY 10118, **Business Phone:** (212)273-3300.

### GREEN, DRAYMOND (DRAYMOND JAMAL GREEN)

Basketball player. **Personal:** Born Mar 4, 1990, Saginaw, MI; son of Raymond and Mary Babers. **Educ:** Mich State Univ, attended 2012. **Career:** Ruben Daniels Mid Sch, Saginaw, MI, janitor; NBA Golden State Warriors, drafted, 2012, player, 2012-; Team USA, player Summer Olympics, 2016. **Honors/Awds:** Big Ten Player of the Year, 2012; NABC National Player of Year, 2012; First Team All American, 2012; Big Ten Jesse Owens Male Athlete of the Year Award, 2012; All-Defensive First Team, NBC, 2015; All-NBA 2nd Team, 2016; Big Ten Sixth Man of the Year; NBA championship (with Golden State), 2015; Olympic gold medal, 2016. **Special Achievements:** In 2014-15 NBA season, became the first Warriors player to average a block, steal, and a three-point shot per game. **Business Addr:** Golden State Warriors, 1011 Broadway, Oakland, CA 94607, **Business Phone:** (510)986-2200.

### GREEN, DR. EDDIE L.

School administrator, school superintendent. **Personal:** Born Mar 7, 1942, Houston, TX; son of Matthew and Mary Rose; married Jacqueline; children: Shelley & Bryce. **Educ:** Grambling State Univ, BS, bus educ, 1963; Wayne State Univ, MA, bus educ, MEd, 1970, EdD, 1993. **Career:** Govt off (retired); Detroit Pub Schs, teacher, bus educ dept head, 1979-81, dir, asst prin, prin, 1981-85, asst dir, 1985-89, area asst supt, 1989, area supt, 1989-97, interim dep supt, 1997, dep supt, 1997-, interim gen supt, 1998, chief exec officer, 1999; Murray-Wright, supt. **Orgs:** Pres, Mich Bus Educ Asn, 1967-; pres, Delta Pi Epsilon, 1975-; news lettered, Phi Delta Kappa, Detroit, 1980-; consult, NAPE, 1984; Automotive Aftermarket Suppliers Asn, 1989-; MASA, 1989-; Mich Asn Sec Sch Prin, 1989-; Detroit Pub Schs Ninth Grade Restructuring Prog, 1992; Asn Supv & Curric Develop, 1996-; bd dir, Horizons-Upward Bound Cranbrook Kingswood Schs, 2000. **Home Addr:** 3200 Cambridge Ave, Detroit, MI 48221, **Home Phone:** (313)861-9282.

### GREEN, ERNEST G.

Investment banker. **Personal:** Born Sep 22, 1941, Little Rock, AR; son of Ernest G Sr and Lothaire S; married Phyllis; children: Adam, Jessica & McKenzie Ann. **Educ:** Mich State Univ, BA, 1962, MA, 1964. **Career:** Adolph Inst, apprenticeship, 1965; A Philip Randolph Educ Fund, dir, 1968-76; US Labor Dept, asst secy labor, 1977-81; Green & Herman, partner, 1981-85; E Green & Assocs, owner, 1985-86; Lehman Bros, investment banker, 1987, managing dir pub finance, 1985-; Albert Shanker Inst, bd mem. **Orgs:** Bd mem, Winrock Int; Omega Psi Phi; chmn, AfriCare; chmn, African Devel Found; chair, Nat Asn Securities Profs; Sigma Pi Phi; Nat Asn Advan Colored People; Winthrop Rockefeller Found; Boy Scouts Am; African Develop Found. **Honors/Awds:** Eagle Scout Award, 1956; Rockefeller Public Service Award, Princeton Univ, 1976; Spingarn Award, Nat Asn Advan Colored People; Hon Doctorates, Tougaloo Col, 1979, Mich State Univ, 1994, Cent State Univ, 1996; Congressional Gold Medal; Distinguished Eagle Scout Award. **Special Achievements:** Member of the Little Rock Nine; First black students ever to attend classes at Little Rock Cent High School in Little Rock; First black to graduate from the school, 1958. **Business Addr:** Managing Director, Lehman Brothers, 800 Conn Ave NW Suite 1200, Washington, DC 20006, **Business Phone:** (202)452-4700.

### GREEN, GEORGIA MAE

Lawyer. **Personal:** Born Apr 15, 1950, Knoxville, TN; daughter of George Edward (deceased) and Florence Jones (deceased). **Educ:** Knoxville Col, BA, 1972; Howard Univ, Sch Law, Wash, DC, JD, 1976. **Career:** Dept Corrections, atty. **Orgs:** WVa Bar Asn, 1979-; conv cochmn, Nat Asn Black Women Atty, 1980-; first vpres, Am Fed Govt Employees Local 1550, DC Dept Corrections Union, 1984; DC Bar Asn. **Honors/Awds:** WVa Ambassador of Good Will Among All People, WVa Secy St, 1979. **Home Addr:** 3913 Terr Dr, Annandale, VA 22003-1868, **Home Phone:** (703)256-9585. **Business Addr:** Attorney, Department of Corrections, 1923 Vt Ave NW, Washington, DC 20001, **Business Phone:** (202)673-7316.

### GREEN, GERALDINE D. (GERALDINE DOROTHY GREEN)

Lawyer, executive director. **Personal:** Born Jul 14, 1938, New York, NY; daughter of Edward and Lula. **Educ:** City Col NY Baruch Sch Bus, BBA, 1964; St John's Univ Law Sch, JD, 1968. **Career:** Coopers & Lybrand CPA's, tax acct, 1966-68; IBM Corp, staff atty, 1968-72; Atlantic Richfield Co, sr atty asst corp secy, 1972-80; Calif State Bar Comn Corp, 1974-76; Calif Corp Comnr, 1980-83; Rosenfeld Meyer & Susman, partner, 1983-85; Burke, Robinson & Pearman, atty coun, 1985-86; Law Off Geraldine D Green, 1987-99; LA Traffic Comn, comnr; Bus Law & Fin, Dillard Univ, Fla Memorial Col, vis prof; Green Mgt Consults, pres, 1999-2001; Asn Advan Disabled Am, exec dir, 2001-03; Disabled Am Inc, exec dir, 2003-. **Orgs:** Pres, Beverly Hills/Hollywood Br Nat Asn Advan Colored People, 1979-82; spec coun, Los Angeles Urban League; Youth Motivation Task Force. **Honors/Awds:** Community Service Award, Los Angeles Urban League, 1973; Freedom Award Cit, Nat Asn Advan Colored People, 1973; Certificate of Achievement, YWCA, 1976; Certificate of Appreciation, City Los Angeles, 1981; Certificate of Appreciation, Calif State Senate, 1984; Geraldine D Green Day in City of Los Angeles, 1984; Certificate of Achievement, Calif State Legis, 1986. **Home Addr:** 500 Shatto Pl Suite 630, Los Angeles, CA 90020-1707, **Home Phone:** (213)362-6999.

### GREEN, GLORIA J.

Lawyer. **Personal:** Born Dec 8, 1954, Atlanta, GA; daughter of Alfred Sr and Mattie; children: Avery Dyan Kelley & Jennifer. **Educ:** Duke Univ, Durham, NC, BA, 1976; Georgetown Univ Law Ctr, Wash, DC, JD, 1979. **Career:** Securities & Exchange Comn, Wash, DC, from atty to sr atty, 1979-86; Fed Home Loan Bank Atlanta, Atlanta, Ga, vpres, dep gen coun & dir legal servs, 1986-96; Atlanta Housing Authority, dep gen coun & chief legal off, 1998-2014; GJGreen, experienced atty, consult & mediator, 2014-. **Orgs:** Bd dir, Wesley Community Ctrs, 1988-93; bd dir, S DeKalb Young Men Christian Asn, 1990-; bd dir, DC Express Track Club, 1990-; trustee, Kelley's Chapel United Methodist Church, 1990-; Nat Coalition 100 Black Women, 1989-93; pres, PTSA. **Honors/Awds:** Leadership Award, Partners With Youth, South Dakalb Young Men Christian Asn, 1992; Service Award, DC Express Track Club Inc, 1991-98. **Business Addr:** Attorney, Consultant & Mediator, GJGreen, 3105 Lions Club Lane, Lithonia, GA 30038-2297, **Business Phone:** (770)593-3102.

### GREEN, HAROLD, II

Football player, businessperson. **Personal:** Born Jan 29, 1968, Ladson, SC; son of Harold Sr. **Educ:** Univ SC, BS, retail mkt, 1989. **Career:** Football player (retired), business person; Cincinnati Bengals, Fullback, 1990-91, running back, 1992-95; St Louis Rams, running back, 1996; Atlanta Falcons, running back, 1997-98; Pro Bowl Motors, vpres, currently. **Orgs:** Founder, Green Team Found, 1993-; bd dir, Univ SC; Sisters Charity Found; Nat Retail Adv Bd. **Honors/Awds:** Heisman Trophy; Pro Bowl, 1992; Athletic Hall of Fame, Univ Sc, 2006. **Special Achievements:** Film: 1990 NFL Draft, 1990; 1998 NFC Championship Game, 1999. **Business Addr:** Vice President, Pro Bowl Motors, 1231 Broad River Rd, Columbia, SC 29210, **Business Phone:** (803)772-4768.

### GREEN, HUGH DONELL

Football player, business owner, football coach. **Personal:** Born Jul 27, 1959, Natchez, MS. **Educ:** Univ Pittsburgh, attended 1980. **Career:** Football player (retired), Football coach, Bus owner; Tampa Bay Buccaneers, linebacker, 1981-85; Miami Dolphins, linebacker, 1985-91; Barcelona Dragons, Nat Football League Europe, asst defensive coach, 2003; Luxury Car Rental Co, owner, currently.

### GREEN, HYDIA LUTRICE

Banker. **Personal:** Born Dec 24, 1963, New Orleans, LA; daughter of Jimmie Lee and Mertis Marie Flanders. **Educ:** La State Univ, Baton Rouge, LA, BS, mgt. **Career:** First Union Nat Bank, asst br mgr; County Savings Bank, Columbus, OH, dir mkt; Corp One Inc, staff, currently. **Orgs:** Chamber Com, 1988-; Civitan, 1989-, Sertoma, 1989-; third vpres, Zeta Phi Beta Sorority Inc, 1982-; jr achievement, Proj Bus Inst, 1989-. **Honors/Awds:** Zeta of the Year, Zeta Phi Beta Sorority Inc, 1986; Outstanding Young Women Am, 1987; Nat Collegiate Greek Merit Award, 1987. **Home Addr:** 6621 Pauline Dr, New Orleans, LA 70126-1040, **Home Phone:** (904)645-9053. **Business Addr:** Staff, Corporate One Inc, 12 Werville Sq Suite 352, Westerville, OH 43081-2919, **Business Phone:** (740)965-8225.

### GREEN, ISAAC H.

Chief executive officer. **Educ:** Duke Univ, AB, econs & hist, 1983; Columbia Univ, MBA, finance & bus econs, 1985. **Career:** NCNB Nat Bank, fundamental analyst, 1985-88; NCM Capital Mgt, sr vpres, dir investments & dir res, 1988-93; Loomis Sayles Value Equity Mgt Div, exec vpres & managing dir, 1993-2000; Piedmont Investment Advisors LLC, pres, chief exec officer, chief investment officer & portfolio mgr, 2000-. **Orgs:** Chairperson & bd mgr, Piedmont Investment Advisors LLC; bd mem, UNC Sch Arts Bd trustee; bd mem, Durham Acad Bd trustee; bd dir, Uplift Proj Inc. **Business Addr:** President, Chief Executive Officer, Piedmont Investment Advisors LLC, 300 W Morgan St Suite 1200, Durham, NC 27701, **Business Phone:** (919)688-8600.

### GREEN, JACQUEZ (D'TANYIAN JACQUEZ GREEN)

Football player, football coach. **Personal:** Born Jan 15, 1976, Ft. Valley, GA. **Educ:** Univ Fla, BS, parks, recreation & leisure studies, 1998. **Career:** Football player (retired), football coach; Tampa Bay Buccaneers, punt returner & kick returner, 1998-2001, 2003; Wash Redskins, punt returner, 2002; Detroit Lions, wide receiver, 2002; Gibbs High Sch, offensive coordr-asst hc, 2006-08; Lincoln High Sch, Tallahassee, Fla, offensive coordr-asst hc & head boys & girls track coach, 2009-12, offensive coordr & wide receivers, 2014-; Valdosta High Sch, asst football coach, wide receivers coach, 2013-14. **Honors/Awds:** SEC Championship, 1995, 1996; Bowl Alliance National Championship, 1996; Consensus All-American, 1997; Rookie of the Year, 1998; Knoxville News-Sentinel SEC All-Freshmen Team. **Special Achievements:** An avid video game player, who once won the annual Madden Bowl in back-to-back seasons. **Business Addr:** Offensive Coordinator, Gibbs Senior High School, 850 34th St S, St. Petersburg, FL 33711-2297, **Business Phone:** (727)893-5452.

### GREEN, JAMES

Basketball coach. **Personal:** Born Jul 8, 1960; children: Bryan. **Educ:** Univ Miss, BS, math educ, 1983. **Career:** Univ Idaho, asst coach, 1988-90; Tex A&M Univ, Col Sta, asst coach, 1990-92; Alab Univ, asst coach, 1992-94; Iowa State Univ, asst coach, 1994-96; Univ Southern Miss, head basketball coach, 1996-2004; Miss Valley State Univ, head men's basketball coach, 2005-08; Jacksonville State Univ, head coach, 2008-. **Business Addr:** Head Basketball Coach, Jacksonville State University, 700 Pelham Rd N, Jacksonville, AL 36265, **Business Phone:** (256)782-5535.

### GREEN, DR. JAMES L.

Ophthalmologist, educator. **Personal:** Born Feb 2, 1945, Hampton, VA; son of James; children: Timothy B & Jenifer L. **Educ:** Hampton Inst, BA, 1967; Meharry Med Col, MD, 1973. **Career:** Hubbard Hosp, intern, 1973-74, resident, 1975-77; Vet Admin Hosp, chief retina sect, 1978-79; Univ Ill, asst prof clin ophthal, 1980, resident, fel vitreous surg, 1979-81, asst prof ophthal, 1980-; Michael Reese Hosp & Med Ctr, attend surgeon, 1981-; Retinal Vitreal Consults, pract; Mercy Hosp & Med Ctr, chief retina serv, 1986-, chair ophthal, 2006-; Univ Chicago, clin assoc prof. **Orgs:** Fel Am Acad Opthal, 1979-; Am Bd Opthal, 1979-; Nat Med Asn; Chicago Opthal Soc; Ill Asn Ophthal; Vitreous Soc. **Honors/Awds:** Rowe Award in Ophthalmology, 1973; Merk Award, 1973. **Special Achievements:** Numerous publications. **Home Addr:** 721 Marion Ave, Highland Park, IL 60035, **Home Phone:** (847)266-1889. **Business Addr:** Chair, Mercy Hospital and Medical Center, 2525 S Mich Ave, Chicago, IL 60616-2477, **Business Phone:** (312)567-2000.

### GREEN, JARVIS R.

Executive, accountant. **Personal:** Born Feb 20, 1953, Tuskegee, AL; son of Jerry and Johnnie Lewis; married Desiree E; children: Kawanna. **Educ:** Ala Agr & Mech Univ, BS, 1976. **Career:** Brandon, Smith & Jones CPA Firm, sr acct; Atlanta Minority Bus Develop, construct acct; Atlanta Housing Authority, progs mgr; AGE Indust, exec vpres; AGE Enterprises Ltd, vpres, currently; Ryjohn, owner. **Orgs:** Fin secy, 100 Black Men Dekalb; finance & finance comn, Omega Psi Phi Fraternity; Dekalb Chamber Com; Geo Minority Supplier Div Coun; Better Bus Bur; US Chamber Com. **Honors/Awds:** Certificate of Appreciation, Christmas July Com; State Small Business of the Year Candidate, US Bus Acad. **Home Addr:** 1833 Fairpointe Trace, Stone Mountain, GA 30088-4025, **Home Phone:** (770)987-1107.

### GREEN, JOHN M.

Historian. **Personal:** Born May 11, 1932, Lawton, OK; son of Johnny M and Jannie McClanahan; married Melanie; children: John M & Tiffny E. **Educ:** Lincoln Univ, attended 1953; Wayne State Univ, BA, 1977. **Career:** Santa Fe Rr, chair car, 1954-55; State Mich, meter vehicle oper, 1956-64; Automobile Club Mich, supvr-legal, 1964-80; Hist Res Repository Inc, exec dir, founder, 1986-. **Orgs:** Dean pledges, Alpha Phi Alpha, 1953; Financial Forum, 1966; historian, Mus African Am Hist, 1984-86; bd mem, AAA Housing & Transp Trust, 1985-; historian, African Am Sports Hall Fame, 1992-94; Founding Comt & Retired Int Underground Rr Monument Collab, 1999-. **Honors/Awds:** Senate Res, Mich Legis, 1968; House Res, 1987; Resolution, Wayne County, MI, 1988; Senate, Mich Legis, 1990. **Special Achievements:** Negroes in Michigan History, 1968, 3rd reprint, 1985; Black Nobel Prize Winners, poster, 1985; International Black Nobel Prize Winners, poster, 1994; African Historical Tins; Cake Walk, Come Join Us Bro, Henry O Flipper, 1993-94. **Home Addr:** 387 Piper Blvd, Detroit, MI 48215-3037, **Home Phone:** (313)822-9027. **Business Addr:** Executive Director, Historical Research Repository Inc, PO Box 15364, Detroit, MI 48215-0364, **Business Phone:** (313)822-9027.

### GREEN, JONATHAN

Artist. **Personal:** Born Aug 9, 1955, Gardens Corner, SC; son of Melvin and Ruth J. **Educ:** Sch Art Inst Chicago, BFA, 1982. **Career:** Jonathan Green Art Collection LLC, pres & dir, 1985-; Works: Bathing, Norton Gallery, 1990; Silver Slipper Club, Morris Mus Art, 1990; Christening, Greenville Mus Art, 1991; Corene, Gibbes Mus Art, 1995; Vessels, Mc Kissick Mus, 1998; Personal Treasures Bernard & Shirley Kinsey, CA African Am Mus, Los Angeles, Calif, 2006; Jonathan Green Studios Inc, owner, currently. **Orgs:** Comn mem, Chicago Acad Arts, 1990-95; vpres, Colier County United Arts Coun, 1992-94; comm mem, Share Our Strength, 1993-95; Mus Am Folk Art, 2000-03; chmn, Nat Adv Coun, Afr Am Res Libr & Cult Ctr, 2002-; bd visitor, Col Arts & Sci, Howard Univ, 2003-; life mem, Gem Socs Naples, 2004-. **Honors/Awds:** Martin Luther King Jr Humanitarian Award, City Beaufort, 1993; Alberta G Peacock Award, 1996; honorary doctoral degree, Univ SC, 1996; Clememte C Pickney Award, SC House Reps, 1997; Certificate of Honor, City Portland, 1998; Order of the Palmeto Award, Columbia, SC, 2002; History Makers Award, Chicago, IL, 2002; Palmetto Civilian Award, 2002; Century of Achievement Award, Mus Am, 2003; Man of Distinction Award, Educ Found Collier County, 2003; Honorary Chair, Sch Art Inst Bare Walls, 2003; Century of Achievement in Art Award, 2003; Honorary Chair, Bare Walls Event, 2004; Honorary Chair, United Arts Coun of Collier County, 2004; The Eagle Award, SC Asn of Community Develop Corp, 2005; Named honorary International Ambassador of the Arts, State of Fla, 2005; Man of the Year, Gulfshore Life Mag, 2005; Annual National Arts Programs Award, Links Inc, PA, 2006; Artist of the Year, Penn Center Inc, 2007; Alummi Hall of Fame, Beaufort High Sch, 2007; Life Award; NAACP Image Awards, 2009; Elizabeth ONeill Verner Award for Life Time Achievement, 2010. **Home Addr:** , Naples, FL 34114. **Business Addr:** Director, President, Jonathan Green Studios Inc, 295 Seven Farms Dr Suite C-214, Daniel Island, SC 29492, **Business Phone:** (843)410-1383.

### GREEN, KIM M.

Vice president (organization), executive. **Personal:** married Jimmy Carter; children: Jessica. **Educ:** Hampton Univ, BA, mkt; London Sch Bus. **Career:** Chubb Group Ins Co, underwriter, 1983-85; Alexander & Alexander New York, 1985-90; MGIS, founder; Aon Risk Serv Inc, sr vpres, 1995-; Willis Ltd, exec vpres; AT&T Inc, asst mgr. **Orgs:** Exec Leadership Coun; bd dir, Hampton Univ; Independent Col Fund New York; Links. **Business Addr:** Senior Vice President, Aon Risk Services Inc, 199 Water St, New York, NY 10038, **Business Phone:** (212)441-1000.

### GREEN, LARRY A.

Administrator, vice president (organization), president (organization). **Personal:** Born Jul 22, 1952, Canton, GA; son of Jimmie Edwards and Cornelius; married Doris. **Educ:** Ga State Univ, attended 1974; Northwestern Univ. **Career:** A&M Rec, nat prom dir, 1974-80; MCA Rec, midwest regional mgr, 1980-85; Whlfield Assoc, consult, 1988-91; Chrysalis Rec, midwest regional mgr, 1985-88; St Chrysostoms Episcopal Church, assoc rector; First Baptist; Winston & Green, vpres, 1991-2010; Lumen Legal, sr acct exec, 2011-12; LAGLAW, founder, pres, 2012-. **Orgs:** Bd mem, Chicago Youth Ctrs, 1992-96; 100 Black Men Chicago, 1998-; bd mem, Chicago Area Coun Boy Scouts, 1995; bd mem, La Salle St Cycle, 1998-; bd mem, Goodman Theatre Discovery, 2000-; St Chrysostoms Church, eucharitic minister; Nat Bar Asn Network; 100 Black Men Chicago; Youth Guid Bd; Episcopal Deacon Saint Chrysostom's Episcopal Church Chicago. **Home Addr:** 333 E Ontario, Chicago, IL 60611. **Business Addr:** Vice President, Winston & Green, 111 W Washington St Suite 841, Chicago, IL 60602, **Business Phone:** (312)201-9777.

## GREEN, LEE
Planner. **Career:** Lee Green Fin Planning, fin planner, currently. **Business Addr:** Financial Planner, Principal, Lee Green Financial Planning, 3011 W Grand Blvd Suite 2410, Detroit, MI 48202-3096, **Business Phone:** (313)870-1000.

## GREEN, LESTER L.
Writer, electrical engineer, executive. **Personal:** Born Jun 27, 1941, Lynchburg, VA; married Lucille Withers. **Educ:** Howard Univ Sch Archit & Engr, Wash, DC, attended 1966; BSEE, 1966. **Career:** Am Tel & Tel Co, Silver Spring, MD, transmsn man, 1964-65; Elect Switching Syst Western Elect Co, proj engr, 1966-; Comm Commun Res Inc, pres, 1973-. **Orgs:** Chmn bd dir, Community Commun Syst, Baltimore, 1970-; chmn, Cablecommunication Task Force Develop Reg Learning Ctr, Morgan State Col, Baltimore, 1973-74; indust mem rep, WE Co Howard Univ Cluster; Soc Cable TV Engr; Inst Elect & Electronic Engrs; Alpha Phi Alpha Frat; Urban Reg Learning Ctr Policy Bd; exec bd, NW Baltimore Corp; charter mem, Pk Heights Comm Corp, Baltimore; charter mem & vpres, Beacon Hill Tenants Asn, Baltimore; charter mem, Oxford Manor Tenants Asn, Wash, DC. **Honors/Awds:** Citizenship & Leadership Award, Howard Univ, 1961; Cost Reduction Award, WE Co, 1974. **Special Achievements:** Author: The Design and Economics of an Urban Cable & Distrbution Systems, 1973. **Home Addr:** 737 Stoney Spring Dr, Baltimore, MD 21210.

## GREEN, LILLER
School administrator, association executive. **Personal:** Born Dec 1, 1928, Atlanta, GA; daughter of Walter and Henrietta; married William Clarence; children: Pamela A & Jan A. **Educ:** Morgan State Univ, BA, 1951; Bryn Mawr Col, MSW, 1953. **Career:** C Adolescents, Psychiat Clin, dir social work, 1957-59; Child Study Ctr, dir social work, 1959-60; Bryn Mawr Col, field instr, consult, 1963-65; Ivy Leaf Sch, dir, founder, 1965-2008. **Orgs:** Grace Baptist Ch; golden life mem, Delta Sigma Theta; life mem, Nat Advan Asn Colored People; bd dir, YWCA, 1983-85; Elem Educ Study Group, 1985-86. **Honors/Awds:** Eliza Jane Cummings Award, Morgan State Univ, 1951; Richard Allen Award, Community Serv Mother Bethel AME, 1982; Zeta Outstanding Woman of the Year, Beta Delta Zeta, 1983; Citizen of the Year, Omega Psi Phi, 1985; Community Service Award, Nat Advan Asn Colored People, 1990; Minority Enterprise Special Achievement Award, 1991; Outstanding Alumna Award, Morgan State Univ, 1991; Sadie T Alexander Community Service Award, Delta Sigma Theta, 1991; Bryn Mawr College Community Service Award, Black Alumnae Coordinating Comn Grad Sch Social Work & Social Res, 1992; Education of the Year Award, Philadelphia Chap Nat MBA Asn, 1992; National Kwanzaa Award, Philadelphia area, Kujichagulia, 1994; Excellence in Education Award, Phila Coun Clergy, Presented MLK Memorial Serv, 1995. **Home Addr:** 5902 Devon Pl, Philadelphia, PA 19138-1510, **Home Phone:** (215)844-4409. **Business Addr:** Founder, Ivy Leaf School, 1196 E Wash Lane, Philadelphia, PA 19138-1099, **Business Phone:** (215)848-3020.

## GREEN, LISA A.
Law enforcement officer. **Personal:** Born Charleston, SC; daughter of Edward Jr and Mary LM (deceased). **Educ:** Claflin Univ, BA, 1986. **Career:** Charleston City Sheriff's Off, training coordr sgt, 1997-99, Patrol Div, lt, 1999-. **Orgs:** Palmetto State Law Enforcement Officers Asn; SC Law Enforcement Officers Asn; Nat Orgn Black Law Enforcement Officers. **Honors/Awds:** Albert T Leppert Memorial Award, Civitan Int, 1997. **Special Achievements:** First African American Female Lieutenant in Charleston City Sheriff's Office, 1996. **Home Addr:** PO Box 42362, Charleston, SC 29423, **Home Phone:** (843)343-8619. **Business Addr:** Lieutenant, Charleston County Sheriff, 3505 Pinehaven Dr, Charleston, SC 29405, **Business Phone:** (803)554-4700.

## GREEN, LISA R.
Journalist, vice president (organization). **Personal:** Born Nov 2, 1964, Evanston, IL; daughter of Rev Albert W (deceased) and Elease W. **Educ:** Eastern Ill Univ, jour, 1986. **Career:** Rockford Regist Star, reporter, 1986-90, asst city ed, 1990-91, city ed, 1991-93, asst bus ed, 1993, bus editor, currently; Zion Gazette, ed, 1997; NBC Int Ltd, NBC News Channel Inc, NY, sr producer broadcast stand, NBC broadcast stand exec; vpres stand & practices; attorney, currently. **Orgs:** Nat Asn Black Journalists, 1988-; big sister, Big Brother/Big Sister Prog, 1992-97; YMCA-Booker, Wash Ctr, Black Achievers Steering Comt, 1993-98; New Zion Missionary Baptist Church; Salter Ensemble; Am Soc Newspaper Ed. **Honors/Awds:** Black Achievers, Black Achiever of the Year, 1994; Gannett Midwest Newspaper Group, 1994; ed mem, Unity 94 Journalist Conv, Atlanta. **Home Addr:** 4504 Trevor Cir, Rockford, IL 61109, **Home Phone:** (815)874-8127. **Business Addr:** Attorney, Lisa R Green Attorney, 5390 Manhattan Circle, Boulder, CO 80303, **Business Phone:** (303)928-2332.

## GREEN, LITTERIAL MAURICE
Basketball player, basketball coach, basketball executive. **Personal:** Born Mar 7, 1970, Pascagoula, MS. **Educ:** Univ Ga, attended 1992. **Career:** Basketball player (retired), basketball coach, basketball executive; Orlando Magic, 1992-94; Quad City Thunder, 1994-96, 1997-98; Detroit Pistons, 1996-97; Milwaukee Bucks, 1997-98; Cleveland Cavaliers, 1999; Marinos de Oriente, 1999-2000; Polluelos de Aibonito, 2000; Egepen Altay, 2001; Unia Tarnow, 2001; Zlatorog Lasko, 2001-02; Southern Crescent Lightning, World Basketball Asn, coach, 2003; St Louis Steamers, head coach; Chattanooga Steamers, head coach, 2005; Comcast Sports, color analyst; ESPN Col Basketball, analyst; Pract Pros Basketball Camps, founder; Am Basketball Asn Team, consult; St Basketball Asn, Jr SBA, Youth Basketball & Camps & Clins, dir, currently. **Honors/Awds:** Coach of the Year, World Basketball Asn, 2004. **Business Addr:** Director, Street Basketball Association LLC, 12138 Cent Ave Suite 390, Mitchellville, MD 20721, **Business Phone:** (301)218-1048.

## GREEN, DR. RICHARD CARTER
Counselor, business owner. **Personal:** Born Oct 28, 1947, Brooklyn, NY; married Florence Elayne Parson; children: Damani Saeed Tale, Taiesha Tene Tale & Khalid Abdu Tale. **Educ:** Central State Univ, BA, psychol, 1969; Wright State Univ, MA, personnel coun, 1980, MS, 1983. **Career:** Montgomery County Juv Ct, probation officer, counr, 1969-11; AUs 1st Lt Inf, instr offensive tactics, 1970-72; Montgomery Co Juv Ct, probation counr, 1972-73; Tale Retail & Wholesale Co, owner, 1985-2012; Nicholas Residential Treat Ctr, family resource counr, treat coordr, 1973-. **Orgs:** Omega Psi Phi Frat Inc, 1966-; Greater Dayton Jaycees, 1972; Nguzo Saba Family Educ & Unity Club, 1980-; master mason Prince Hall Free Masonry Ancient Sq Lodge 40, 1982-; lectr Child Discipline & Residential Treat, 1984-; fel Menninger Found, 1985. **Honors/Awds:** Certificate of Participation, seminary Adolescence Menninger Found, 1978; Outstanding Young Men of Am, US Jaycees, 1980; Comput Today & comput Literacy Sinclair Comt Col & Comput Tech, 1983; Gerontological Counseling Wright State Univ, 1985; Licensed Professional Counselor, OH Counr and Social Worker Bd, 1985. **Home Addr:** 811 Neal Ave, Dayton, OH 45406, **Home Phone:** (937)277-8438. **Business Addr:** Family Resource Counselor, Treatment Coordinator, Nicholas Residential Treatment Center, 5581 Dayton Liberty Rd, Dayton, OH 45418, **Business Phone:** (513)496-7109.

## GREEN, RICKEY
Basketball player. **Personal:** Born Aug 18, 1954, Chicago, IL; children: Kandyce. **Educ:** Vincennes Univ, attended 1973; Univ Mich, attended 1975. **Career:** Basketball player (retired); Golden State Warriors, guard, 1977-78; Detroit Pistons, guard, 1978; Hawaii Volcanos, guard, 1979-80; Billings Volcanos, guard, 1980-81; Utah Jazz, guard, 1980-88; Charlotte Hornets, guard, 1988-89; Milwaukee Bucks, guard, 1989; Ind Pacers, guard, 1989-90; Philadelphia 76ers, guard, 1990-91; Boston Celtics, guard, 1991-92. **Home Addr:** , Chicago, IL.

## GREEN, ROBERT DAVID
Football coach, football player. **Personal:** Born Sep 10, 1970, Washington, DC; children: 4. **Educ:** Col William & Mary. **Career:** Football player (retired), football coach; Wash Redskins, running back, 1992; Chicago Bears, running back, 1993-96; Minn Vikings, running back, 1997; Oxon Hill High Sch, head football coach & athletic dir, health teacher, currently. **Business Addr:** Head Football Coach, Athletic Director, Oxon Hill High School, 6701 Leyte Dr, Oxon Hill, MD 20745, **Business Phone:** (301)749-4300.

## GREEN, ROBERT LEE
Association executive, educator. **Personal:** Born Nov 23, 1933, Detroit, MI; son of Thomas and Alberta; married Lettie Cornelius; children: Robert, Melvin & Kurt. **Educ:** San Francisco State Col, BA, gen psychol, 1958, MA, educ psychol, 1960; Mich State Univ, PhD, educ psychol, 1963. **Career:** Southern Christian Leadership Conf, educ dir, 1965-67; USOE Grant Chicago Adult Educ Proj, dir, 1967; Mich State Univ, prof urban affairs, 1968-73, Col Urban Develop, dean, 1973-82, Urban Affairs Prog, prof & dean, prof emer & dean emer, currently; Ctr Urban Affairs, dir, 1968-73; NCJW Ctr Res Educ Disadvantages, Hebrew Univ, Jerusalem, vis lectr, 1971; Univ Nairobi, Kenya, 1971; Univ DC, pres, 1983-85; Nev Chmn "My Bro's Keeper", clark county, 2014; Cuyahoga Community Col, Ctr Urban Educ, dir, currently; Robert L Green & Assocs, founder, currently. **Orgs:** Am Psychol Asn; Am Asn Black Psychologists; Am Res Asn; bd dirs, Martin Luther King Jr Ctr Nonviolent Social Chg; Phi Kappa Phi Nat Hon Soc Ct app comt; consult & facilitator several ann summits, Nat African Am Sch Bd Mem. **Honors/Awds:** Inter Nat Ghandi-King-Ikeda Award, Morehouse Col, Atlanta, Ga, 2002; Distinguished Alumni Award, Mich State Univ, 2004; Distinguished Psychologist Award, Asn Black Psychologists, 2009; Living Legends Award, Nat Alliance Black Sch Educr. **Special Achievements:** Author of numerous books, including The Urban Challenge: Poverty & Race & Metropolitan Desegregation; Expectations: How Teacher Expectations Can Increase Student Achievement, 2000; Published many articles; First African American dean in Michigan State University. **Business Addr:** Professor Emeritus, Dean Emeritus, Michigan State University, Kellogg Ctr Garden Level, East Lansing, MI 48824-1022, **Business Phone:** (517)355-1855.

## GREEN, ROY CALVIN
Football player, radio host, actor. **Personal:** Born Jun 30, 1957, Magnolia, AR; children: Miyosha & Candace. **Educ:** Henderson State Univ, grad. **Career:** Football player (retired), co-host; St Louis Cardinals, kick returner, 1979, free safety, 1980, wide receiver, 1981-87; Phoenix Cardinals, wide reciever, 1988-90; Cleveland Browns, 1991; Philadelphia Eagles, wide receiver, 1991-92; KXAM, co-host, currently. **Honors/Awds:** Sporting News National Football Conference All-Star Team, 1979, 1983-84; Pro Bowl, 1983-84; Associated Press first-team, 1983-84; All-Pro selection, 1983-84; Hall of Honor, Henderson State Univ, 1997; Gold Ribbon Award for Best Community Service, Canadian Association of Broadcasters; Gold Ribbon Award for Best News, Public Affairs and Documentaries, Canadian Association of Broadcasters. **Special Achievements:** First National Football League Player to Start Both Ways Including Wide receiver & Defensive back in 21 years; TNT Sunday Night Football, 1990; Hollywood Wasteland, 2012; Film: Walking the Halls, 2012; While Expecting Cassius, 2014. **Business Addr:** Co-Host, KXAM, 4725 N Scottsdale Rd Suite 234, Scottsdale, AZ 85251, **Business Phone:** (480)423-1310.

**GREEN, RUTH A.** **See Obituaries Section.**

## GREEN, SAUL A.
Consultant, lawyer. **Personal:** Born Jan 1, 1947; children: 1. **Educ:** Univ Mich, BA, 1969, Law Sch, JD, 1972. **Career:** US Attys Off, asst, 1973-76; Wayne County, corp coun, 1989; Mich Supreme Ct, atty, 1998; Atty Off, Eastern Dist Mich, US atty, 1994-2001; Minority Bus Group, leader, 2001-04; Univ Mich Law Sch, adj prof, 2002-; Miller, Canfield, Paddock & Stone PLC, prin, 2001-, sr coun, currently; City Detroit, mayor, 2008-11. **Orgs:** Sixth Circuit Judicial Conf; life mem, Nat Asn Advan Colored People; Am Bar Asn, 1973-; bd dir, Wolverine Bar Asn, 1985-90, secy, 1986-87, pres, 1988-89; Open Justice Comn, 1998-; pres, Univ Mich Alumni Asn, 2001-03; Pub Interest/Pub Serv Fac Fel, 2009-10; Tabernacle Missionary Baptist Church; fel State Bar Found. **Honors/Awds:** Distinguished Service Award, 1989; Trailblaizer Award, Wolverine Bar Asn, 1991; Esteemed Alumni Award, 1994; Leonard F. Sain Alumni Award, Univ Mich Alumni Asn, 1994; Damon J. Keith Community Spirit Award, Wolverine Bar Asn, 1998; Champion of Justice Award, State Bar Mich, 1999; Wade Hampton McCree Jr Award, Fed Bar Asn, 2002; Frank J. Kelley Distinguished Public Servant Award, 2002; Name done of Michigan Most Powerful African-American Leaders, Corp Mag, 2003. Trailblazer Recipient, 2005. **Special Achievements:** First African American to hold post of US Attorney in Detroit; Top federal prosecutor in the Eastern district of Michigan; The Best Lawyers in America, Listed in the Criminal Defense Law Sect, 2005-06, 2006. **Home Addr:** 2769 Oakman Blvd, Detroit, MI 48238-2530, **Home Phone:** (313)935-6390. **Business Addr:** Senior Counsel, Principal, Miller Canfield Paddock & Stone PLC, 150 W Jefferson Suite 2500, Detroit, MI 48226-4415, **Business Phone:** (313)963-6420.

## GREEN, SCARBOROUGH (BERTRUM SCARBOROUGH GREEN)
Baseball player, baseball executive. **Personal:** Born Jun 9, 1974, Creve Coeur, MO. **Educ:** Meramec Jr Col. **Career:** Baseball player (retired), baseball coach; St Louis Cardinals, outfielder, 1997; Tex Rangers, 1999-2000; Kans City Royals, outfielder; Howard Payne Univ, Yellow Jackets, wide receivers coach, currently; Brownwood High Sch, running backs coach, currently; Greenville High Sch, football & baseball coach, currently. **Business Addr:** Football & Baseball Coach, Greenville High School, 1 Vardry St, Greenville, SC 29601, **Business Phone:** (864)355-5500.

## GREEN, SEAN CURTIS
Basketball player, athletic trainer, executive. **Personal:** Born Feb 2, 1970, Santa Monica, CA. **Educ:** NC State Univ, attended 1987; Iona Col, BA, commun, 1991. **Career:** Baseball player (retired), executive; Ind Pacers, guard, shooting guard, 1991-93; Philadelphia 76ers, shooting guard, 1993-94; Utah Jazz, shooting guard, 1994; Rapid City Thrillers, 1994-95; Jcoplastic Napoli, 1995, 1996; Puerto La Cruz, Venezuela, 1994, 1997; Jerusalem, israel, 1995; Teorematour Milano, Italy, 1995-96; Portland Mountain Cats, 1996; Napoli, Italy, 1997; Santeros de Aguada, 1997; Manila, Philippines, 1997, 2000; Darussafaka, Turkey, Istanbul, 1998-2000; JDA Dijon Basket, France, 2000-01; Guanare, Venezuela, 2002; trainer, 2000-; Chelsea Piers, personal trainer/ basketball coach, 2001-14; Green Storm Fitness LLC, founder, chief exec officer & trainer, 2004-; Convent Sacred Heart, head coach, 2010-14; Crossroads Sch Arts & Sci, head coach boys jv basketball, 2014-. **Special Achievements:** Appeared in numerous television commercials, primetime TV shows & 2 off Broadway productions. **Business Addr:** Chief Executive Officer, Trainer, Green Storm Fitness LLC, 123 Green St Suite 2, Brooklyn, NY 11222.

## GREEN, SIDNEY
Basketball player, basketball coach. **Personal:** Born Jan 4, 1961, Brooklyn, NY; married Deidra; children: LaShawn & Taurean. **Educ:** Univ Nev, Las Vegas, NV, BA, sociol, 1983. **Career:** Basketball player, basketball coach (retired); Chicago Bulls, forward, 1983-86; Detroit Pistons, 1986-87; New York Knicks, 1987-89; Orlando Magic, 1989-90; San Antonio Spurs, 1990-92; Charlotte Hornets, 1992-93; Long Island Univ, coach, 1995-97; Univ N Fla, coach, 1997-99; Fla Atlantic Univ, head coach, 1999-2005; Ind Univ, asst coach, 2005, 2009; Southampton Col, men's basketball team, head coach; free agt, currently. **Orgs:** Co-founder, Shoot Stars Found; founder, SIDS and Kids. **Honors/Awds:** Big West Conference Player of the Year, 1983; NCAA All-American Second Team, 1983; Nat Spirit of Love Award, Nat Basketball Asn Players Asn, 1989; UNLV Hall of Fame, 1994; Atlantic Sun Conference Coach of the Year, 2002. **Special Achievements:** First player drafted in franchise history by the Orlando Magic, 1989.

## GREEN, STERLING S.
Executive, real estate developer, government official. **Personal:** Born Oct 8, 1946, Washington, DC; married Sophie Ann Pinkney; children: Sterlicia Sophia & Tamika Tamara. **Educ:** Williams Col, MA, 1964; USASATC & S, Ft Devens, MA, 1967. **Career:** Government offficer (retired), real estate; United House Prayer, ordained elder, 1967, asst minister, 1971; DC Govt Adv Neighborhood Comm, vice chmn & comnr, 1978-85; United House Prayer, ordained apostle, 1984, Bishop W McCollough, dir spec proj, 1991-2001; Long & Foster Real Estate Inc, realtor, currently. **Orgs:** Elected adv neighborhood Comn, 1978; bd mem, SHAW Proj Area Comn, 1979; deleg DC Fed Civic Asn, 1979; Mayors Comn Coop Econ Develop, 1980; Nat comm mem McCollough Property Invest Comn, 1980; from asst exec dir to exec dir, McCollough Scholar Col Fund, 1984. **Home Addr:** 606 Emmanuel Ct NW Apt 302, Washington, DC 20001-3426, **Home Phone:** (202)842-4869. **Business Addr:** Realtor, Long & Foster Real Estate Inc, 7301 Ga Ave NW, Washington, DC 20012-1719, **Business Phone:** (202)882-2121.

## GREEN, THOMAS E.
State government official. **Personal:** Born Sep 9, 1940, Bronxville, NY; son of Grace and Louis T; married Patricia S; children: Thomas II & Jennifer. **Educ:** State Univ, Winston-Salem, NC, BS, 1963; AFL-CIO Labor Studies Ctr, Silver Spring, Md, attended 1972; Univ Utah, attended 1976. **Career:** Mfr Traders Trust Co, asst mgr, 1966-69; Recruitment Training Prog, field rep, 1969-71; Westchester Affirmative Action Agency, White Plains, NY, exec dir, 1970-90; NY Dept Labor, job training specialist, 1973-83, assoc employ consult, 1983-90, dep dir, 1990, Off Community Serv, County Opers Div, asst dir, currently. **Orgs:** Relocation dir, Urban Renewal Agency, 1962-64; resource consult, US Dept HEW, 1964-69; proj dir, pres, Community Juv Delinq & Youth Develop, 1964-70; prog dir, Urban Educ Ctr, 1965-68; consult, Southern Ill Univ, 1966-67; consult & proj dir, Cent State Univ, 1967-68; prog dir, Urban League Westchester, 1969-70; Int Asn Personnel Employ Security, 1983; exec bd mem, Nat Asn Pub Sector Equal Opportunity Officers, 1987-. **Honors/Awds:** The 32 degree United Supreme Coun 33 AASR Free Masonry USA; Community Service Award, Westchester & Rockland Boy Scouts Am. **Special Achievements:** Author 2 years study Juvenile Delinquent & Youth Development Program, 1965-66. **Home Addr:** 16 Winthrop Ave, New Rochelle, NY 10801-3407, **Home Phone:** (914)592-7924. **Business**

**Addr:** Assistant Director, Office of Community Service, Slot Suite S 1330, Little Rock, AR 72203-1437, **Business Phone:** (501)682-8715.

**GREEN, VERNA S.**
Executive, chief executive officer, president (organization). **Personal:** Born Oct 9, 1947, Columbus, GA; daughter of Evelyn Robinson Crouch and Oscar L Crouch; children: Grant Langston & Jason Wayne. **Educ:** Wayne State Univ, Detroit, MI, BS, bus admin, 1973; Mich State Univ, E Lansing, MI, MBA, 1976. **Career:** Gen Motors Corp, Detroit, Mich, orgn develop specialist, 1970-76; Vis Nurse Asn, Detroit, Mich, personnel dir, 1976-79; Detroit Med Ctr, Detroit Mich, asst dir mkt, assoc dir pub affairs, dir support serv, mgr training & develop, 1979-82; Booth Am Co, WJLB-FM, WMXD-FM, Detroit, vpres, gen mgr, pres, 1982-97; Evergreen Commun, vpres, gen Mgr, 1997-92; Crouch-Green Consult, partner, 1999-; Detroit Black Chamber Com, pres & chief exec officer, currently. **Orgs:** Nat Asn Advan Colored People, 1982-; Urban League, 1982-; alumni bd, Wayne State Univ Bus Sch; res comn, Nat Asn Broadcasters; Leadership Detroit, Grad Class No 7, 1986; bd mem, YWCA Metrop Detroit, 1986-87; Women's Advert Club, 1986-87; Mich Asn Broadcasters, 1987-; adv bd, Wayne State Univ Jour Inst Minorities, 1987-; bd mem, Detroit United Fund, 1987; Mich Women's Forum, 1987-; bd mem, C's Aid Soc, 1989; bd mem, YMCA Metrop Detroit, 1990; Detroit Sports Comn, 1992-; bd mem, Detroit Econ Growth Corp, 1994-; bd dir, MAB, currently; bd mem, Nat Asn Broadcasters, 1995-. **Business Addr:** President, Chief Executive Officer, Detroit Black Chamber of Commerce, 1274 Libr St Suite 1-B, Detroit, MI 48226, **Business Phone:** (313)309-3316.

**GREEN, VICTOR BERNARD**
Football player, consultant, radio broadcaster. **Personal:** Born Dec 8, 1969, Americus, GA; married Esther; children: 3. **Educ:** Int Tech Inst, Tampa, Fla, assocs mkt degree, 1988; Copiah-Lincoln Jr Col, Wesson, Miss, Assocs Arts Degree, 1990, attended 2001; Univ Akron, BA, polit sci & criminal justice, 1993; Nassau Community Col Garden City, New York, attended 2000; Charter Oak State Col New Brit, Conn, attended 2002. **Career:** Football player (retired), coach, consult, chief exec officer; New York Jets, strong safety, 1993-2002, left safety, 1999-2000, 2006; New Eng Patriots, safety, 2002, free safety, 2002-03; New Orleans Saints, free safety, 2003-04; Integral Munic Serv Corp, independent consult, 2005; TDC Corp, independent consult, 2005; Fox Sports Radio, NFL game analyst, 2005; Water Engineering Serv, independent consult, 2005; CSS Sports Nite, NFL game analyst, 2006-07; Safeguard Printing & Promotional Prod, sales & partner, 2006-; J Artur cellars, owner, 2006-; Mt. Pisgah High Sch, defensive backs coach, 2008; Tampa Bay Buccaneers, asst defensive backs coach intern, 2009, pro scout, 2009-10; Class Act Sports, pres & chief exec officer, 2010-; Pharmanex/NuSkin, distribr & rep, currently; real estate investor, currently. **Orgs:** Prof partner, Victor Green Found, 1995-; prof partner, Youth Develop, 1995-; bd mem, Frank ski Youth Found, 2005-06; Vital Health Care Group, 2009-. **Business Addr:** Professional Partner, Victor Green Foundation, 802 Jamont Circle, Alpharetta, GA 30022, **Business Phone:** (770)291-0558.

**GREEN, VINCENT E.**
Government official, educator, chief executive officer. **Personal:** Born Aug 10, 1957, Brooklyn, NY; son of Robert and Ozzie; married Fannie; children: Franklin Hartzog, Donna Hartzog, Doris Hartzog & Erika J. **Educ:** Cheyney Univ Pa, polit sci & govt, 1977; John Jay Col Criminal Justice, New York, NY, BS, criminal justice, 1979; Brooklyn Col, New York, NY, MS, polit sci, 1998; N Western Sem, PhD, theol & ministerial studies, 2014-. **Career:** New York Transit Authority, Spec Inspector, 1980-81; NY City, Dept Invest, dep comnr & supervising inspector, asst comnr, 1981, dep comnr, asst supvr, dep inspector gen, spec dep us marshall, supv inspector gen, 1981-2010; New York Cols, adj prof, 1990-; Dept Parks & Recreation, inspector gen, 1991; Col New Rochelle, Sch New Resources, adj prof, 1992; John Jay Col, Adj Prof, 2006-08; Wagner Col, Adj Prof, 2008-; G-Sq Consult Serv LLC, chief exec officer, 2009-; City Univ New York, dir vendor integrity & invests, 2010-; G-Sq Security Guard Training Acad, exec dir, 2015-. Author: Government Ethics and Law Enforcement: Toward Global Guidelines; Combating Unethical Practices in Government, Commerce and Society. **Orgs:** Dept Interior, Training Comn, co-chair, Recruitment & Retention Comn, chair, Advy Bd, Equal Employ Opport & Sexual Harassment, coun; Mayors Steering Comt Monitory, Woman Bus Enterprise Prog; pres, Toast Master Int; Nat Orgn Black Law Enforcement Execs; Nat Orgn Cert Fraud Examiners; Nat Inst Govt Purchasers; Fraternal Order Police; Soc Prof Investr; Nat Rifle Asn. **Business Addr:** Founder, Chief Executive Officer, G-Square Consulting Services LLC, 888c 8th Ave Suite 424, Washington, DC 10019.

**GREEN, WALTER**
Business owner. **Personal:** Born Sep 5, 1924, Coconut Grove, FL. **Educ:** Miami-Dade Col Sch Continuing Educ, attended 1972. **Career:** Walt's Laundromat, owner, 1972-80; real estate investor, 1947-80. **Orgs:** Pres, Black Grove Inc; New Frontiers Environ Understanding; Human Commun & Social Justice, 1970-80; pres, Grove Golfers Asn, 1960-70; Proj Area Com HUD, 1967-70; dir, Black Grove Com Design Ctr, 1970-76; exec comt, Int Optimist Club Coconut Grove, 1972-76; Coconut Grove Planning Task Force, 1974-76; Man Proj Comt, 1976. **Honors/Awds:** Conf partic in 1st Nat Seminar on Environmental Quality & Social Justice in Urban Am The Consrvtn Found, 1972; Voice of Am Intervw for W African Nats, 1976. **Special Achievements:** Co-author: History of Black Grove: A Planning model for America, 1973. **Home Addr:** 14901 Dunbar Ave, Miami, FL 33176. **Business Addr:** Laundry Self Service, Walt's Laundromat, 3571 Grand Ave, Miami, FL 33133-4924, **Business Phone:** (305)443-0652.

**GREEN, WILLIAM ERNEST**
Lawyer, executive. **Personal:** Born Nov 19, 1936, Philadelphia, PA; married Loretta Martin; children: Billy, Roderic & Nicole. **Educ:** Univ Pittsburgh, BS, chem, 1957; Duquesne Univ Sch Law, LLB, 1963. **Career:** NY & US Patent Off, admitted; Palo Alto Area Chap Am Red Cross, dir; Palo Alto CA, atty pvt pract, Calif; Us Steel Corp, Appl Res Labs, chemist, 1957-61, patent coordr, 1961-63; Sybron Corp, assoc patent coun & assoc gen coun, 1963-71; City Planning Comn Rochester, NY, chmn, 1966-71; Boise Cascade Corp, asst gen coun, 1971-74; William green Assocs, founding partner, atty, 1998-; Williams Co Inc, dir, 1998-; AIM Broadcasting, LLC, vpres, gen coun & secy, currently; Williams Co Inc, dir, 1998-, Ramsell Holding Corp, bd mem. **Orgs:** Palo Alto City Plann Comn; Charles Houston Bar Asn; Palo Alto Area Bar Asn; San Mateo Co Bar Asn; Bar Peninsula Patent Law Asn; SF Patent Law Asn; Am Bar Asn; chmn bd trustees, World Inquiry Sch; rep, County & Regional Plann Couns; Community Chest; Rochester Urban League; Rochester Health Serv Corp; Ind Training Sch; Rochester Monroe Co Chapnned Parenthood League Rochester & Monroe Co; PTA Bd Sch 1; managing ed, Law Rev Duquesne Univ Sch Law; dir, Philanthropic Ventures Fund, bd dir, Flowers Heritage Found; bd dir, Kids Common; State Bar Calif; United Way. **Honors/Awds:** Record Folette Greeno Public Award, 1966; NY State Jaycees Distinguished Service Award, 1967. **Home Addr:** 550 Hamilton Ave, Palo Alto, CA 94301-2010, **Home Phone:** (650)321-9992. **Business Addr:** Attorney, Founder, William Green & Associates, 425 Sherman Ave Suite 100, Palo Alto, CA 94306, **Business Phone:** (650)321-9992.

**GREEN, WILLIE AARON**
Football player, actor. **Personal:** Born Apr 22, 1966, Athens, GA. **Educ:** Univ Miss, attended. **Career:** Football player (retired), actor; Detroit Lions, wide receiver, 1991-93; Tampa Bay Buccaneers, 1994; Carolina Panthers, wide receiver, 1995-96; Denver Broncos, wide receiver, 1997-98; Miami Dolphins. Films: Sheffey, 1977; Diggstown, 1992; "Lizzie McGuire", 2002; Terra Firma, 2008. **Honors/Awds:** Superbowl Champion.

**GREEN-CAMPBELL, DEARDRA DELORES**
Financial manager, association executive, executive. **Personal:** Born Jan 21, 1959, Gary, IN; daughter of Herman W and Harriet L; married Thomas L; children: Evan T. **Educ:** Western Mich Univ, attended 1977; Purdue Univ, attended 1978. **Career:** Stuart James Corp, stock broker, 1983-84; Charles Schwab & Corp, vpres, 1984-91; D Campbell & Co, pres, 1991-; Financial Mgt Column, Atlanta Tribune, columnist, 1991-; Wind Enterprises Inc; Womens Econ Develop Agency Inc, exec dir, currently. **Orgs:** Hundred Black Women, 1991-; Atlanta Bus League, 1991-; Nat Asn Female Exec, 1991-. **Honors/Awds:** Chairmans Club, Charles Schwab & Corp, 1989, 1990; featured, Who's Who Among Black Americans. **Special Achievements:** Profiled, Women and Technology; profiled, Atlanta Business Chronicle. **Home Addr:** 103 Adrian Pl NW, Atlanta, GA 30327-4003. **Business Addr:** Executive Director, Women's Economic Development Agency Inc, 675 Metrop Pkwy Suite 2026, Atlanta, GA 30310, **Business Phone:** (678)904-2201.

**GREEN-GUYTON, LOUISE**
Banker, manager. **Personal:** Born Mar 4, 1948, Tyro, MS; daughter of Eldridge Green and Ruth; children: Curtis G & Patrice Y. **Educ:** Univ Memphis, bus admin, 1967; Univ Detroit-Mercy, BS, 1986. **Career:** Comerica Inc, staff, 1968-, sr internal bank auditor, consumer compliance officer, vpres pub affairs, 1999-, compliance mgr, currently. **Orgs:** Financial adv, Southern Christian Leader Conf, 1982-; Delta Sigma Theta, 1995-; life mem, Nat Asn Advan Colored People, 1995-; bd pres, New Hope Community Develop Corp, 1995-; vpres, Black Caucus Found, 1999-; bd dir, Heat & Warmth Fund; bd dir, Rosa Parks Scholar Found; adv bd, Abayomi Community Develop Corp, 1999-; adv bd, Mich Coalition Human Rights, 2001-; adv bd, Community Legal Resources; adv bd, First C's Finance Fund; bd mem, Detroit Community Health Connection Inc, 2003-; vol, Detroit Convoy Hope; trustee, Lewis Col Bus; bd visitor, Sch Social Work at Wayne State Univ, founder, Greater Works Found; Greater Burnette Baptist Church. **Honors/Awds:** Minority Achievers Award, YMCA, 1996; Spirit of Detroit Awards, City Detroit, 1997, 2000; Most Influential African American Women in Metropolitan Detroit, Women's Informal Network, 2000; Community Builders Award, 2001; Hon Doctor, bus admin, Lewis Col Bus; Women of Excellence Award, Mich Chronicle; Volunteer of the Year Award, CEED, 2011. **Special Achievements:** Notable Speaker at Women's Religious Conferences & Leadership Seminars. **Home Addr:** 20255 Greenview, Detroit, MI 48219, **Home Phone:** (313)532-4432. **Business Addr:** Vice President Public Affairs, Comerica Inc, PO Box 75000, Detroit, MI 48275-3352, **Business Phone:** (313)222-8620.

**GREENE, AURELIA**
State government official. **Personal:** Born Oct 26, 1934, New York, NY; daughter of Edward Henry and Sybil Russell Holley; married Rev Jerome A; children: Rhonda James & Russell Sobers. **Educ:** Rutgers Univ, Livingston Col, BA, community develop, 1975. **Career:** Public agency administrator, public official, assembly woman (retired), executive; Bronx Area Policy Bd No 6, exec dir, 1980-82; NY State Assembly, 1982-2009, 76th Assembly Dist, female dem dist leader, 77thAssembly Dist, assemblywoman, 2003-09, Dep Bronx Bor, pres, 2009-; Antioch Co, lectl; NY State, asst majority leader, dep majority leader, chair banking standing comn; dep dir, Morrisanis Community Corp. **Orgs:** Distinguished leader, 76th Assembly Dist, Bronx, 1979-82; Community Sch Bd No 9, 1985; exec officer, Bronx Unity Dem Club, 1986; educ adv, Morrisania Educ Coun, 1986; secy, Bronx County Dem Party, 1992-; secy, Bronx County Exec Comt, 1996-; chmn, Ny Assembly Bronx Deleg, 2002-; chmn, Ny Assembly Women's Caucus, 2003-; Nat Asn Advan Colored People; Urban League; chairwoman assembly's bronx deleg; Rules; Ways & Means; ranking mem educ comt; Bronx Urban League; Bronx Women's Polit Action; chair, State Assembly's Bronx Deleg; Assembly Bronx County; Bronx County Judicial Conv; Ny Asn Black & Puerto Rican Legislators. **Honors/Awds:** Numerous awards & honors including Woman of the Year, Nat Asn Advan Colored People; Brotherhood Award, New York State Employees; Organization Impact Award, Alpha Kappa Alpha; Distinguished Community Leadership Award, Morrisania Educ Coun; Gold Helmet, NY State Head Injury Asn, 1994. **Special Achievements:** Author, Motor Vehicle Leasing Act; First Chairwoman of the Assembly Standing Committee on Banks. **Home Addr:** 1248 Teller Ave, Bronx, NY 10456-3202, **Home Phone:** (718)588-4667. **Business Addr:** President, Office of the Bronx Borough President, 851 Grand Concourse Suite 301, Bronx, NY 10451, **Business Phone:** (718)590-4036.

**GREENE, DR. BEVERLY A.**
Clinical psychologist, educator. **Personal:** Born Aug 14, 1950, NJ; daughter of Samuel and Thelma. **Educ:** NY Univ, BA, psychol, 1973; Marquette Univ, educ psychol, 1974; Adelphi Univ, Derner Inst Advan Psychol Studies, MA, clin psychol, 1977, PhD, clin psychol, 1983; ABPP. **Career:** NY Bd Educ, sch psychologist, 1980-82; Kings County Hosp, Impatient Child & Adolescent Psychol Servs, dir, Prof Child Psych, sr psychologist, clin asst, 1982-89; Univ Med & Dent NJ, Newark, supv psychologist, clin ast prof psychiat, 1989-91; St John's Univ, assoc clin prof psychol, 1991-93, assoc prof, 1993-95, prof, 1995-. **Orgs:** Int Neuropsychol Soc, 1979-87; NY Asn Black Psychologists, 1980-; NY Coalition Hosp & Inst Psychologists, 1982-91; Nat Asn Black Psychologists; Asn Women Psychol; NY State Psychol Asn, 1984-85; Task Force Diversity Clin Psychol, 1991-92; co-chair, Continuing Educ, 1991-93; Am Psychol Asn, Task Force Ment Health Ethnic Minority Women, 1992-; Women Color Task Force, 1992-; fel Acad Clin Psychol, 1998; Am Bd Prof Psychol; fel Am Psychol Asn. **Home Addr:** 26 St Johns Pl Suite 3, Brooklyn, NY 11217, **Home Phone:** (718)638-6451. **Business Addr:** Professor, St John University, Marillac Hall Rm 409 Queens Campus 8000 Utopia Pkwy, Queens, NY 11439, **Business Phone:** (718)990-1538.

**GREENE, CECIL M., JR.**
Executive. **Personal:** Born Oct 10, 1932, Pass Christian, MS; married Joaquina Lizama; children: Joaquina Deborah & Cecil Gregory. **Educ:** Cent State Univ, BS, 1952; Knoxville Col, chem. **Career:** Executive (retired); Univ Chicago, Argonne Nat Lab, res technician, 1956-66, adminr, job evaluator, 1966-71; Enroci Fermi Inst, admin asst, 1966-71; Montgomery Ward & Co, Corp EEO Prog, mgr, 1971; City Col Chicago, registr; Timmons Realty Co, property mgr & salesperson; Knoxville Col, placement dir & dir admin serv. **Orgs:** Chicago Urban Affairs Coun, 1971-; Nat Urban Affairs Coun, 1971-; Nat Alliance Businessmen; Col Placement Asn; Chicago Ment Health Asn; Wabash YMCA; Nat Asn Advan Colored People; Kappa Alpha Psi Frat; personnel comn, S Shore Comn; bd mem, Crawford-sebastian Community Develop Coun Inc. **Home Addr:** 209 Lecta Ave Apt 3, Fort Smith, AR 72901-3580.

**GREENE, CHARLES ANDRE**
Executive. **Personal:** Born May 17, 1939, Blockton Junction, AL. **Educ:** Tex Southern Univ, Sch Bus; Wayne State Mortuary Sch, mortuary sci. **Career:** Dist gov, Dist 4 Nat Funeral Dirs & Mortcns Asn, 1973-74; Genesee Co Funeral Dir Asn, vpres; Greene Home Funerals, pres, 1998. **Orgs:** Bd dir, Greater Flint Opport Indust Controls Inc; Vehicle City Lodge No 1036 IBPOE W; Tall Pine Counc BSA; Epsilon Nu Delta Mortuary Frat; chmn, Educ Com Nat Funeral Dir & Mortcns Asn, 1972-73, fel Flint City Charter Comn, 1975; fel Bishop Airport Authority; elected fin chmn 5th Ward Charter Rev Comn, 1974; asst exec secy, Nat Funeral Dir & Mortcns Asn Inc, 1974; Foss Ave Baptist Church; found dir, Foss Ave Fed Credit Union; Wayne State Univ Alumni Asn; Tex Southern Univ Alumni Asn; Urban League Urban Coalition; Cent Optimist Club. **Home Addr:** 4430 St James Ct Apt 4, Flint, MI 48532-4260. **Business Addr:** President, Greene Home Funerals, 2210 M L King Ave, Flint, MI 48503-1030.

**GREENE, CHARLES EDWARD.** **See GREENE, JOE.**

**GREENE, CHARLES LAVANT**
Educator. **Personal:** Born Feb 22, 1938, Headland, AL; married Delores Johnson; children: Charles L. **Educ:** Univ Akron, OH, BS, biol, 1962; Univ Pittsburgh, PA, MSW, 1967; Akron Law Sch, OH, JD, 1977. **Career:** E Akron Comm House, coord comm level, 1967-68; CAC Prog, Syracuse NY, dep dir admin, 1968-70; Kent State Univ, asst prof, 1970-, asst prof & coord vol & comm serv, 1971-72, asst prof & asst dean stud life, 1972-, vpres, Human Resources, 1989. **Orgs:** Vpres, Urban Affair Tomorrow's People Consult Firm, 1972-; bd mem, Urban League Akron, OH, 1977-; bd mem, Fair Housing Contact Serv, Akron, OH, 1977-; bd mem, Ment Health Asn Summit Co, Akron, OH, 1977-80; bd mem, Alpha Homes Inc, Akron, 1979-; bd secy, Ebony Blackstar Broadcast Corp, 1980; Magnet Schs Task Forces; Col & Univ Personnel Asn; Akron Bar Asn; Am Bar Asn; chmn, bd trustee, Community Action Coun; bd trustee, United Way Portage County; Area Agency Aging. **Home Addr:** 1166 Winhurst Dr, Akron, OH 44313, **Home Phone:** (330)867-8132.

**GREENE, CLIFTON S.**
Executive, trader. **Personal:** Born Oct 21, 1920, Georgetown, SC; son of Wally and Janie; married Irene. **Educ:** SC State Col, attended 1940. **Career:** Executive (retired); Cliff Greene's Wines & Liquors Brooklyn, owner, 1948-74; Wally-Thel Inc, pres, 1959-69; Greenoung Enterprises, pres, 1966; Green-Harris Enterprises Inc, chmn, chief exec officer, 1966; Ebony Enterprises Inc, pres, 1972. **Orgs:** Pres, sole stock holder Nu-way Investors Corp; life mem, Nat Asn Advan Colored People; Urban League; Prince Hall Mason 32nd Degree; Shriner; Wid's Son Lodge suite 11; Long Island Consistory suite 61; Imp Coun; AEAONMS Inc; Am Legion; 100 Black Men Inc; Retired Army Officer's Asn; Ft Hamilton Officer's Club. **Honors/Awds:** First Black in US to file with FCC for UHF TV station; First Black or white to build multi-million dollar housing for elderly in Bedford Stuyvesant, Brooklyn; published "Unique & Mae" magazine; various articles, Stock Market Fundamentals, 1966. **Home Addr:** 1333 President St, Brooklyn, NY 11213, **Home Phone:** (718)493-7028.

**GREENE, EDITH L.**
Government official. **Personal:** Born Oct 29, 1919, Darlington, SC; daughter of Cohen Galloway Sr and Olivette Mazone Galloway; married Isaac Jr; children: Doris, Robert Allen, Elouise, Isaac, Frank, Jean, Cohen, Mae, Fred, Gennette & Don. **Career:** Town Bolton, Bolton, NC, mayor. **Orgs:** County coun pres, Exten Homemakers Club, 1950-78; leader, 4-H Club, 1970-79; League Women Voters, 1976-80; VFW Ladies Auxilary, 1977-; Eta Phi Beta, 1980-. **Home Addr:** PO Box 129, Bolton, NC 28423, **Home Phone:** (919)655-8482.

## GREENE, FRANKLIN D.

Automotive executive, president (organization). **Personal:** Born Jan 23, 1950, Hot Springs, AR; son of John H and Jessie L Muldrow. **Educ:** Col Ozarks Pt Lookout, MO, BS, 1972. **Career:** Cit Financial Serv, customer serv rep, 1972-73; Ford Motor Co, Kans City, MO, zone mgr, 1973-81; Indian Springs Ford, Kans City, MO, pres, 1981-83; Repub Ford Inc, pres, 1983-; Columbus Ford, Mercury, Columbus, KS, pres, 1987-; Zodiac Lounge, Springfield, MO, pres, 1988-90; Qual Ford Inc, W Des Moines, IA, pres & owner, 1989-; B & G Automotive Group, partner. **Orgs:** Bd dir, Big Bros & Sisters Springfield, MO, 1985-; pres, Sch Ozarks Springfield Alumni Asn, 1986-87; bd mem, Metro Credit Union, 1987-; bd mem, Am Red Cross, 1987-; bd mem, Minority Breakfast Club, 1990-; pres, Black Ford Lincoln Mercury Dealers Asn, 1991-; Kappa Alpha Psi Fraternity, 1994; adv bd, Bankers Trust Des Moines; athletic bd, Drake Univ; Partners Econ Progress; bd mem, W Des Moines Police Adv Bd. **Honors/Awds:** Athletic Hall of Fame, Col Ozarks, 1986; Meritorious Achievement Award, Col Ozarks, 1989. **Special Achievements:** Republic Ford listed as one of Black Enterprise's Top 100 Auto Dealers, 1984-91. **Home Addr:** 3408 Timberlane, West Des Moines, IA 50265. **Business Addr:** President, Quality Ford Inc, 1271 8th St, West Des Moines, IA 50265, **Business Phone:** (515)273-4256.

## GREENE, ESQ. GABRIELLE ELISE

Businessperson, chief executive officer, association executive. **Personal:** Born Jun 17, 1960, New York, NY; daughter of Gregory Frame Simms Ainspac and Patricia Ann Simms; married W Michael; children: Savannah Elise. **Educ:** Princeton Univ, BA, 1981; Harvard Bus, MBA, 1987; Harvard Law Sch, JD, 1987; Woodrow Wilson Sch, urban studies prog. **Career:** Bain & Co, consult, 1982-84; UNC partners, prin, 1987-91; Commonwealth Enterprise Fund, 1991-94; Black Enterprise/Greenwich St Venture Capital Fund, prin, 1998-2000; Crown Servs, chief financial officer, 2000-02; Villanueva Co, chief financial officer, 2002-; Whole foods mkt, dir, 2003-; Bright Horizons Family Solutions Inc, bd dir, 2006-08; Citigroup, prin; HPB Assocs, prin; Celestial Seasonings Inc, found; Crown Serv, chief financial officer; Gluecode Software, chief financial officer, 2002-05; Rustic Canyon/Fontis Partners, gen partner, 2005-; Johnson Prod Co, interim chief exec officer, 2011-13. **Orgs:** Nat Black MBA Asn, 1988; treas, Social Justice Women, 1989-91; Boston Partnership Steering Comt, 1992-; Boston C Mus, 1993; Milbank Memorial Fund; Mass State Bar; adv bd, Chela Financial Serv; bd dir, Stage Stores Inc, 2010-; dir, Indymac Bank; Boston Cs Mus; Boston Partnership; fel Aspen Inst; Safe Securities; Zoria Farms; Johnson Prod; Aspen Inst, Henry Crown fel. **Honors/Awds:** First Annual Scholarship Recipient, Nat Black MBA Asn, 1985; 100 Most Infulential People in Boston, Roxbury Chamber Com, 1994-95. **Home Addr:** 80 Clifton St, Belmont, MA 02478-3363. **Business Addr:** Director, Bright Horizons Family Solutions Inc, 200 Talcott Ave S, Watertown, MA 02472, **Business Phone:** (617)673-8000.

## GREENE, GRACE RANDOLPH

Government official. **Personal:** Born Oct 5, 1937, Washington, DC; children: Denise, Samuel T, Michael T, Annette, Wayne, Katerina, Grace E & Deloris. **Career:** Dept Housing & Community Develop, actg mgr-mgt aide, 1969-82; Adv Neighborhood Comn, comnr, 1982-84. **Orgs:** Co-chairperson, Libr Cent Baptist Church, Women's Dept Cent Baptist; vol, Friends & Anacostia Libr, 1984. **Home Addr:** 1924 Naylor Rd SE, Washington, DC 20020-6852.

## GREENE, GREGORY A.

Financial manager, executive director, auditor. **Personal:** Born Aug 29, 1949, Boston, MA; son of Harry and Edna; married Pearline Booth; children: Adria. **Educ:** Northeastern Univ, Boston, BS & MA, bus admin, 1972. **Career:** Director (retired); Arthur Andersen, Boston, MA, staff auditor, 1972-75; Arthur Andersen, Cincinnati, OH, sr auditor, 1976-77; Philip Morris Inc, New York, NY, coordr, mgr financial servs, 1977, dir corp acct, 1994. **Orgs:** Simon Found Pa. **Home Addr:** 1582 Revere Rd, Yardley, PA 19067, **Home Phone:** (215)493-0906. **Business Addr:** Director of Corporate Accounting, Philip Morris Inc, 120 Pk Ave 21st Fl, New York, NY 10017, **Business Phone:** (212)880-3239.

## GREENE, DR. HORACE F.

Physician, administrator, association executive. **Personal:** Born May 5, 1939, Tuscaloosa, AL; married Stephanie Rodgers; children: Amanda, David & Jason. **Educ:** Fisk Univ, BA, 1960; Meharry Med Sch, MD, 1964. **Career:** Johns Hopkins Hosp, internal med resident; Rollman Psychiat Inst, psychiat resident; Reynolds Memorial Hosp; Area Chamber Com Ment Health Ctr, dir adolescent serv, dir youth serv, clin dir, staff psychiatrist, supvr, 1970-74; Georgetown Univ SchMed, asst prof clin & psychiat, 1970; Va Hosp Wash, Drug Treat & Res Prog, consult, 1971; Howard Univ Sch Med, Residency Training Prog, consult, 1973; Alexandria Community Ment Health Ctr, dir, 1971-74; Bur Ment HealthServ, NHA, DC, dep admin chief, 1974; Vet Admin Hosp, consult dept psychiat, 1974; N Va Prison Aftercare Prog, consult, 1974-75; Behav Health Care, med dir; Urban Resources, consult; Kidd Int, consult; pvt pract physician, currently; Greater SE Wash Community Hosp, med dir. **Orgs:** Adv Coun Eastern Area Alcohol Educ & Training Prog Inc; Beta Kappa Chi HonSci; Kappa Alpha Psi Fraternity Inc; pres, ALL Progress Psychiat; Wash Psychiat Soc; Am Psychiat Asn; Wash Soc & Adolescent Psychiat; PsychiatAdv Coun, Ment Health Admin Wash; chmn, Prof Adv Comt, Ment Health AsnInc; Wash Coun Child Psychiat; APA Task Force Psychosurgery; nominatingComt, Wash Psychiat Soc, 1974; Peer Rev Comt, Wash Psychiat Soc; Nat MedFedn; Wash Hosp Ctr, vice chmn clin affairs, Dept psychiat, 1987-. **Honors/Awds:** A Ford Foundation Scholarship; Distinguished Alumni Hall of Fame. **Business Addr:** Physician, 4600 Connecticut Ave NW, Washington, DC 20008, **Business Phone:** (202)363-9116.

## GREENE, JEHMU

President (organization), executive director. **Personal:** Born Jun 22, 1972, Washington, DC. **Educ:** Univ Tex. **Career:** Ctr Policy Alternatives Youth Voices Proj & Nat Stud Voter Educ Day, prog dir, 1996-97; Urban Hang Suite, founder, managing dir, 1997-2001; Dem Nat Comt, dir womens outreach, 1998-2000, southern polit dir, 1998-99; Rock Vote, dir, 2000, pres, 2000-05, exec dir, 2005-; Proj Vote, nat dir, 2006-07; JSG Strategies, prin, 2007-14; Womens Media Ctr, pres, 2009-10; Fox News Channel, contribr, 2010; Univ Tex Neighborhood Prog, exec dir tex young dem & vol coordr. Television & Radio programs: "The O'Reilly Factor"; "MTV News"; "The Daily Show"; "Anderson Cooper 360"; "Dennis Miller Live"; "CBS Evening News"; "NBC Nightly News"; "Bloomberg Television"; "Tavis Smiley". **Orgs:** Exec Comt, Youth Vote Coalition; Bd Am Prospect; adv bd mem, Partnership Pub Serv; adv bd mem, Vote Am; adv bd mem, White House Proj Vote; adv bd mem, Run, Lead Proj & Freedom's Answer; co-founder & adv bd mem, Econ & Pub Policy Orgn Young Adults; pres, Womens Media Ctr; Citizens Debate Comn; bd dir, Am Prospect Mag; bd dir, Demos; bd dir, Youth Vote Coalition; adv bd mem, Campus Green Vote; credentials comt, 2004 Dem Nat Conv; Citizen's Debate Comn; founder, womens advocacy orgn, 2005; secy, US Nat Comn, Un Educ Sci & Cult Orgn, Secy, 2010; bd mem, 2030 Ctr. **Special Achievements:** First African-American president, Rock Vote Organization. **Business Addr:** Executive Director, President, Rock the Vote, 10635 Santa Monica Blvd Suite 150, Los Angeles, CA 90025, **Business Phone:** (310)234-0665.

## GREENE, JEROYD X. See EL-AMIN, SA'AD.

## GREENE, JERRY LOUIS

School administrator. **Personal:** Born Mar 30, 1957, Albany, NY; son of Ollie and Lucius; married Renee; children: Ashley Renee. **Educ:** Los Angeles Metrop Col, AA, 1981; Dekalb Community Col, attended 1981; Univ Md, AA, 1986. **Career:** Ft McPherson Ga Commun, comput operator, 1984-85; Camp Tango Korea, comput operator, 1984-85; US Training Mission, Soudi Arabia, comput operator, 1984-86; Defense Intelligence Agency, watch officer, 1986-89; White House Mil Off, oper officer, 1989-93; White House Commun Agency, opers officer, 1993-95; Defense Intelligence, head commun opers, supt, 1995-. **Honors/Awds:** Defense Meritorious Award, 1995. **Special Achievements:** Hand Selected by the White House Support the President; Recognized by VIPAI Gore for Superb Briefing; First NCO to be selected to work in the Presidents Operation Ctr; Top 5% of Army to be Nominated to work at the White House. **Home Addr:** 3424 Ascot Ct, Woodbridge, VA 22192, **Home Phone:** (703)680-7222. **Business Addr:** Superintendent, Defense Intelligence Agency, Rm 1D866 Pentagon, Washington, DC 20040, **Business Phone:** (202)697-3066.

## GREENE, JOANN LAVINA

Educator, psychiatrist, nurse. **Personal:** Born Columbus, OH; daughter of Lacy Davis and Lavina Allen Davis; children: David. **Educ:** San Jose State Univ, BS, 1969; Univ Calif, San Francisco, MS, 1970; Univ Southern Calif, PhD. **Career:** Psychiatrist (retired); VA Hosp Ment Hyg Clin, head nurse, 1970-72; San Jose State Univ, instr psychiat nursing, 1972-74; W Valley Col, instr psychiat tech prog, 1974-76; W Valley Mission Col, dir psychiat tech prog, 1976-99. **Orgs:** Alpha Kappa Alpha Sor, 1960-62; CNA, 1972-; ANA, 1972-; FACCC; Phi Kappa Phi; Sigma Theta Tau; pres, Calif Asn Psychiat Tech Educrs, 1980-83. **Honors/Awds:** Delta Sigma Theta Scholarship; NIMH Fellowship; Dean's List, President Scholar, Phi Kappa Phi; Florence Nightingale Award, 2 years; Sigma Theta Tau Nat Nursing Hon. **Home Addr:** 43512 Ocaso Corte, Fremont, CA 94539-5632, **Home Phone:** (510)657-2815.

## GREENE, JOE (CHARLES EDWARD GREENE)

Football coach, actor. **Personal:** Born Sep 24, 1946, Elgin, TX; son of Cleo Thomas; married Agnes; children: Major, Delon & JoQuel. **Educ:** N Tex State Univ, attended 1968. **Career:** Football player (retired), football coach (retired), motivational speaker, actor; Pittsburgh Steelers, defensive tackle, 1969-81, spec asst player personnel, 2004-; CBS-NFL Today, color commentator, 1983; Pittsburgh Steelers, asst coach, 1987; Miami Dolphins, defensive line coach, 1992-96; Ariz Cardinals, asst coach, 1999; Films: The Black Six, actor, 1974; Horror High, 1974; Lady Cocoa, 1975; Fighting Back: The Story of Rocky Bleier, 1980; Smokey & the Bandit II, 1980; All the Marbles & The Steeler & the Pittsburgh Kid, 1981. **Honors/Awds:** Col All Stars, Sporting News, 1968; NFL Eastern Conf All Stars, Sporting News, 1969; Defensive Rookie of the Year, Nat Football League, 1969; AFC All Stars, Sporting News, 1970-74, 1979; Pro Bowl, 1970-76, 1978, 1979, 1981; Defensive Player of the Year, Kans City Comt 101 Awards, 1972, 1974 Nat Football League, 1972, 1974; Defensive Most Valuable Player, Newspaper Enterprise Asn, 1972, 1974; Super Bowl; Nat Football Hall of Fame, 1987; Pittsburgh Pro Football Hall of Fame, 2011. **Special Achievements:** Acted & appeared in numerous TV commercials. **Home Addr:** 5109 Lippizaner Dr, Flower Mound, TX 75028-1626, **Home Phone:** (972)298-0128. **Business Addr:** Special Assistant for Player Personnel, Pittsburgh Steelers, 100 Art Rooney Ave, Pittsburgh, PA 15212, **Business Phone:** (412)432-7800.

## GREENE, DR. LIONEL OLIVER

**Personal:** Born Apr 28, 1948, Brooklyn, NY; son of Lionel Oliver Sr and Dollie Chapman. **Educ:** Calif State Univ Los Angeles, BA, 1970; Stanford Univ, PhD, neuropsychology, 1978; MIT, bioastronautics, 1980. **Career:** NASA, res scientist, 1973-77, 1979-81; Mass Inst Tech, res assoc, 1977-79; Lockheed Missiles & Space Co, res scientist, 1981-84; MacDonnell Douglas Astronaut, sr eng scientist, 1984-85; Univ Santa Clara, vis prof; AT&T Bell Labs, sr engr sci human factors, 1985-; lectr, Stanford Univ, 1979-84; adj prof, Fla A&M Univ; vis prof, San Jose State Univ; NIH, ROI Level Rev, 1995; Greene's Admin & Statist Servs, chief exec officer, 1995-; Nat Inst Clin Res, dir Biostatistics, 1998-; Boys & Girls Clubs, dir technol, 1999-; Mt States Biomed Res Inst, vpres, 2007-2008; NeuroFocus dir Neuroscience. **Orgs:** Soc Neuroscience, 1978-; Mission Spec Astronaut cand, 1978; Aerospace Med Asn, 1979-; Asn Black Psychologists; Am Defense Preparedness Asn, 1986-; FCC Radiotlphn Lic DJ, 6 Yrs; bd dir, Goodwill Indus Am Inc, 1992-; bd dir, Lafayette Prog, 2004-; bd dir, gotCOM, 2005-; vpres, Stanford Alumni Assoc. **Honors/Awds:** Nat Acad Sci Bethesda Md; Honor Soc, Mensa Soc, 1980-; NASA Sci Achievement Award, Top secret Clearance, Defense Investigative Servs. **Special Achievements:** 15 research publications 1975-; Ebony Magazine Bachelor, Ebony Magazine, 1980; 2; Recorded 2 jazz LP's; FAA Pilots License 1972; Reviewer of Papers, NIH, 1988-; Guest Panelist, Our Voices/BETV, 1991. **Home Addr:** 4287 Beltline Rd 149, Addison, CA 75001, **Home Phone:** (214)489-5683.

## GREENE, MARY ANN

Criminologist, president (organization). **Personal:** Born Aug 25, 1934, Los Angeles, CA; daughter of George Buford and Gladys Buford. **Educ:** Univ Calif, Los Angeles, BA, 1956; Pepperdime Univ, MA, 1979. **Career:** Probation director (retired), governor appointee; Los Angeles County, placement officer, 1961-73; community develop analyst, 1973-76; SW Community Col, prof, 1974-77; Los Angeles County, Probation Dept, supvr, 1976-81, sr dir II, 1981-92; Baldwin Hills Conservancy, chair, 2002-03, pres gov bd, gov bd appointee, currently. **Orgs:** Pres, Calif Probation, 1978-81; Parole Correctional Asn; pres, Blair Hills Asn, 1997-; pres, Los Angles chap; Culver City Employees Asn; Yvonne Brathwaite Burke; Sierra Club Calif; bd mem, Santa Monica Mountains Conservancy. **Honors/Awds:** Resolution Honoring Service, Blair Hills Asn, Calif Park Serv, 2002; Resolution Honoring Service, Baldwin Hills Conservancy, 2003; Woman of The Year. **Special Achievements:** Led development of urban park in Los Angeles. **Home Addr:** 5969 Wrightcrest Dr, Culver City, CA 90232, **Home Phone:** (310)838-6100. **Business Addr:** Governor Appointee of the Board, Baldwin Hills Conservancy, 3578 C Eastham Dr, Culver City, CA 90232, **Business Phone:** (310)558-5593.

## GREENE, MARY PENDER

Psychotherapist. **Educ:** NY Univ, BS, pre-social work, 1972; NY Univ, Silver Sch Social Work, MSW, 1974. **Career:** Brooklyn Psychiat Ctr Outpatient Clin, Supvr; Ment Health Clin at C's Aid Soc, Dir; Jewish Bd Family & C's Serv, Chief Social Work Serv, asst exec dir, 1984-2010; consult, clin supvr, pvt psychotherapist pract, relationship expert, prof speaker & career, exec coach, 1983-; MPG Consult, pres, currently. **Orgs:** Martha K. Selig Educ Inst, Exec Training Cabinet Mem; Ny Educ Social Work Bd; Founding Mem, Anti-Racist Alliance; Citizens Comt C New York; Asn Black Social Workers; Nat Asn Social Workers; Am Group Psychother Asn; Am Asn Sexuality Educr, Counselors & Therapists; Soc Sex Ther & Res; Black Agency Execs. **Honors/Awds:** The 25 Most Influential Black Women, Network J, 2007; Human Services Council Leadership Award, 2008; Distinguished Alumni Award, New York Univ, Silver Sch Social Work, 2009; Organizational Excellence Award, Nat Network Social Work Managers, 2010. **Special Achievements:** Known as a therapist to prominent New York residents; co-edited book, "Racism & Racial Identity: Reflections on Urban Practice in Mental Health & Social Services", Routledge, 2006. **Home Addr:** 1165 E 31st St, Brooklyn, NY 11210, **Home Phone:** (212)245-2510.

## GREENE, MAURICE LAMONT

Athlete, businessperson. **Personal:** Born Jul 23, 1974, Kansas City, KS. **Educ:** Univ Kans, attended. **Career:** Athlete (retired), Businessperson; Race youth found, founder, 2001-; Adidas, athlete, 2008; USA track & field inc, track & field athlete; Mo Greene Entertainment, owner, UCLA Bruins, vol asst coach, currently.TV Series: "Playing It Safe", 2002. **Orgs:** United Negro col fund. **Home Addr:** Granada Hills, Los Angeles, CA 91344. **Business Addr:** Founder, President, Mo Greene Entertainment, 348 Hauser Blvd, Los Angeles, CA 90036, **Business Phone:** (323)936-1530.

## GREENE, NATHANIEL D. (NATE GREENE)

Executive. **Personal:** married Roberta. **Educ:** St Mary's Univ, MA, econs, 1972. **Career:** Empire Ford Inc, Spokane, Wash, pres & owner, 1986-2003; Ministry Inst, Gonzaga Univ, exec dir. **Orgs:** Pres, Eastern Wash Univ, Bus Adv Coun; Northwest Ford Dealers Advert Asn; bd dir, Spokane Pub Facil, 2004-07; vice chair, bd dir, Wash Econ Develop Finance Authority, 2007-; bd trustee, Discovery Sch; vice chair, Spokane Pub Facil. **Home Addr:** 2716 Elliott Ave Apt 901, Seattle, WA 98121-3512, **Home Phone:** (206)441-1617. **Business Addr:** Board of Directors, Vice Chairman, Washington Economic Development Finance Authority, 1000 2nd Ave Suite 2700, Seattle, WA 98104-1046, **Business Phone:** (206)587-5634.

## GREENE, NELSON E, SR. See Obituaries Section.

## GREENE, PAMELA D.

Chief executive officer. **Career:** Greene Enterprises & Mkt LLC, owner & chief exec officer, currently. **Home Addr:** 7439 Woodrow Wilson, Detroit, MI 48206, **Home Phone:** (313)871-9260. **Business Addr:** Owner, Chief Executive Officer, Greene Enterprises & Marketing LLC, 21751 W 9 Mile Rd, Southfield, MI 48075, **Business Phone:** (248)358-3179.

## GREENE, RONALD ALEXANDER

Executive. **Personal:** Born Nov 1, 1945, Greenwood, SC; married Margaret St Mark; children: Ronald Jr & Jennifer. **Educ:** SC State Col, BS, 1968. **Career:** Blue Cross Blue Shield, programmer analyst, 1975-76, mgr data entry, 1976-78, coordr, 1978-79, mgr telecommunications, 1979. **Home Addr:** 579 Rosewood Dr, Orangeburg, SC 29115, **Home Phone:** (803)536-9959.

## GREENE, TALIB KWELI. See KWELI, TALIB.

## GREENE, REV. WILLIAM

Clergy, minister (clergy). **Personal:** Born Sep 13, 1933, Rowland, NC; son of Joe and Margaret Brunson; married Wilhelmenia O; children: Wanda. **Educ:** Anchorage Community Col, AA, 1982; Alaska Pac Univ, BA, 1983. **Career:** Shiloh Missionary Baptist Church, Anchorage, AK, chmn, 1974-79, admin, 1979-85; Alaska, chaplain, 1980-; Eagle River Missionary Baptist Church, minister, pastor, 1985-. **Orgs:** Pres, Interdenominational Ministerial Alliance, 1987-90; pres, Chugiak Food Pantry, 1988-; chair, Black Educ Task Force, 1988-92; chair, Minority Community Rels Police Task Force, 1988-; pres, Chugiak & Eagle River Ministerial Alliance Asn, 1999. **Honors/Awds:** Man of the Year Award, Alaska State Asn Colored Women, 1987; Outstanding Leadership Award, Alaska Black Caucus, 1988; Hon Doctor Divinity, Arkansas Baptist Col, 1997; Four Star Chaplain Award, US Chaplains Asn, 1999; Spec Appreciation Award, Minority Community Police Rels Task Force, Anchorage, AK, US Dept Justice Community Rels Serv, 1999. **Home Addr:** 7310 E 17th Ave, Anchorage, AK 99504-2707, **Home Phone:** (907)337-4168. **Business Addr:** Pastor, Eagle

River Missionary Baptist Church, 16050 Lesmer Ct, Eagle River, AK 99577-5188, **Business Phone:** (907)694-6142.

**GREENE, DR. WILLIAM HENRY L.**
Educator. **Personal:** Born Jul 28, 1943, Richburg, SC; son of Malachi and Mattie Macon; married Ruth Lipscomb; children: Omari & Jamila. **Educ:** Johnson C Smith Univ, BA, 1966; Mich State Univ, MA, 1970, PhD, 1972. **Career:** Univ Mass, asst prof, 1972-76, dir serv teacher educ, Ctr Urban Educ, 1974-76; Fayetteville State Univ, asst to chancellor, dir develop & univ rels, 1976-79; Johnson C Smith Univ, dir career coun & placement, 1979-83; Livingstone Col, pres, 1983-88; Gaston Col, assoc dean curric & fac develop, 1989-91, dean & instr, 1991-92, assoc vpres curric & instr, dean lib arts & sci, 1992-2000; Ohio State Univ, dir develop & asst to vice provost minority affairs, 2000, coordr, reunion, currently; Navy Race Rels Sch, founding dir. **Orgs:** NC Intern Coun, 1986; bd dir, Salisbury-Rowan Chamber Com, 1986; exec bd, Fayetteville Bus League, 1986; Phi Delta Kappa; Omega Psi Phi; Sigma Pi Phi; Salisbury Rowan Symphony Soc; Gaston County, Youth Men's Christian Asn; Salisbury Youth Men's Christian Asn; First Union Nat Bank; dir, Gaston County Mus Art & Hist; dir, Mint Mus; NC Chap, Am Heart Asn; dir, Gaston County Family Servs; Asn Supv & Curric Develop. **Honors/Awds:** Outstanding Black Educr, Black Caucus, 1976; Advisor of the Year, Fayetteville State, 1978-79; Achievement Recognition Award, Am Heart Asn, 1984; Community Service Award, Charlotte, NC, Zeta Phi Beta, Delta Zeta Chap, 1984. **Home Addr:** 1000 Clifton St, Charlotte, NC 28216, **Home Phone:** (704)333-5068. **Business Addr:** Director of Development, Reunion Coordinator, Ohio State University, Enarson Hall 154 W 12th Ave, Columbus, OH 43210, **Business Phone:** (614)292-6446.

**GREENE, WILLIE LOUIS**
Baseball player. **Personal:** Born Sep 23, 1971, Milledgeville, GA; son of Lathrop Bura (deceased) and Rhoda Lou Emma Putnam (deceased). **Career:** Baseball player (retired); Montreal Expos, 1990; Cincinnati Reds, infielder, 1992-98; Baltimore Orioles, 1998; Toronto Blue Jays, infielder, 1999; Chicago Cubs, infielder, 2000.

**GREENE-THAPEDI, DR. LLWELLYN L.**
Judge. **Personal:** Born Guthrie, OK; daughter of Latimer Hamilton and Fannye M Gaines; children: Severn Latimer Deck, Letha Llwellyn Deck, Sheryl Renee Deck, Andre Martin & Anthony Isaac. **Educ:** Langston Univ, BA; Univ Sask, MA; Loyola Univ, JD. **Career:** Judge (retired); Univ Sask, Can, instr, 1971-72; Amoco Oil Co, atty, 1976-81; Chicago State Univ, instr bus law, 1977-78; pvt pract, atty, 1981-92; State Ill, Circuit Ct Cook Co Judicial Circuit, judge. **Orgs:** Delivery Legal Serv Standing Comn, Ill State Bar Asn, 1976-85; pres, Cook County Bar Asn, 1988; bd dir, Pub Interest Law Internship, 1982-83; bd dir, Chicago Bar Asn, 1983-85; bd dir, Ill Inst Continuing Legal Educ, 1985-87; Citizen's Adv Comn Circuit Ct, 1987; Ill Trial Lawyers Asn, 1978-88; bd dir, Nat Bar Asn, 1987-88; pres, Cook County Bar Asn, 1987-88; mem hearings comn, Atty Regist & Disciplinary Comn, 1989-90; Urban League; Nat Asn Advan Colored People; Delta Sigma Theta; former pres, Black Lawyers Cook County Bar Asn. **Honors/Awds:** Meritorious Service Award, 1983; Award, Nat Asn Equal Opportunity Educ, 1984; Legal Assistance Found Award, 1984; Richard E Westbrook Award for legal excellence, 1986; Kizzie Award, 1987; Martin Luther King Teen Leadership Award, 1988. **Business Addr:** Judge, Illinois Courts, 50 W Washington St, Chicago, IL 60602, **Business Phone:** (312)603-6194.

**GREENFIELD, ELOISE**
Writer. **Personal:** Born May 17, 1929, Parmele, NC; daughter of Weston W Little and Lessie; married Robert J; children: Steven & Monica. **Educ:** Miner Teachers Col, attended 1949. **Career:** US Patent Off, clerk typist, 1949-56, supvr, 1956-60; DC Unemploy Compensation Bd, secy, 1963-64; Case Ctrl Tech Work & Trng Opportunity Ctr, 1967-68; DC Dept Occup & Prof, adminr, 1968; DC Writers Workshop, staff mem, 1971-74; DC Comn Arts, writer in residence, 1973; freelance writer, currently; Books: Bubbles, 1972; She Come Bringing Me that Little Baby Girl, 1974; Sister, 1974; Me & Nessie, 1975; First Pink Light, 1976; Africa Dream, 1976; I Can Do It by Myself, 1978; Talk About a Family, 1978; Darlene, 1980; Grandmama's Joy, 1980; Grandpa's Face, 1988; Night on Neighborhood St, 1991; Big Friend, Little Friend, 1991; I Make Music, 1991; Lisa's Daddy & Daughter Day, 1991; My Doll Keshia, 1991; My Daddy & I, 1991; Koya DeLaney & the Good Girl Blues, 1992; Aaron & Gayla's Alphabet Book, 1993; William & the Good Old Days, 1993; Sweet Baby Coming, 1994; Honey I Love, 1995; On My Horse, 1995; Easter Parade, 1998; The Friendly Four, 2006; Brothers & Sisters, 2008; Poems: Honey, I Love & Other Poems, 1978; Daydreamers, 1981; Nathaniel Talking, 1988; Under the Sunday Tree, 1988; Angels, 1988; I Can Draw a Weeposaur & Other Dinosaurs, 2001; In the Land of Words, 2004; Non-fiction: Rosa Parks, 1973; Paul Robeson, 175; Mary McLeod Bethune, 1977; Childtimes: A Three Generation Memoir, 1979; Alesia, 1981; For the Love of the Game: Michael Jordan & Me, 1997; How They Got Over: African Americans & the Call of the Sea, 2003. **Orgs:** African Am Writer's Guild; Authors Guild; Black Lit Umbrella; Inst Preserv & Study African Am Writing, 1984. **Honors/Awds:** Carter G Woodson Book Award, 1974; NY Times Outstanding Book; Irma Simonton Black Book Award, 1974; Jane Addams Children's Book Award, 1976; Coretta Scott King Award, 1978; Recognition of Merit Award, 1978; American Library Association Notable Book; Award, Nat Black Child Develop Inst, 1981; Award, Black Women in Sisterhood for Action, 1983; Washington DC Mayor's Art Award for Literature, 1983; Grants, DC Comn Arts & Humanities; lifetime achievement citation, Ninth Ann Celebration Black Writing, 1993. **Special Achievements:** Citation, Coun Interracial Books C; Citation, DC Asn Sch Librarians; Citation, Celebrations in Learning; short stories & articles for Negro Digest, Black World, Scholastic Scope, Ebony Jr, Negro Hist Bull, num children's Books; producer of children's recordings, 1982; works reviewed & dramatized on public TV (Reading Rainbow); was inducted into the National Literary Hall of Fame for Writers of African Descent. **Business Addr:** Author, PO Box 29077, Washington, DC 20017, **Business Phone:** (202)529-6116.

**GREENFIELD, MARK STEVEN**
Executive director, artist. **Personal:** Born May 24, 1951, Los Angeles, CA; son of Russell E and M Geraldine. **Educ:** Calif State Univ, Long Beach, BA, art educ, 1973; Calif State Univ, Los Angeles, MFA, painting & drawing, 1987. **Career:** Ca State Univ, biol dept illus, 1971-73; May Co Dept Stores, asst dir, 1973-77; Los Angeles County Dept Parks & Recreation, pk dir, 1973-79; Wing-foot prod, owner, 1975-; Rosey Grier's Giant Step, art instr, 1976-81; Brockman Gallery Prods, art coordr, 1977-78; Los Angeles Police Dept, artist, 1980-93; Watts Towers Arts Ctr, dir cult affairs, 1993-2002; Cult Affairs City Los Angles, art ctr dir, 1993-95, adminr; Los Angeles City Col, art instr, 1997-; Harbor Art Ctrs, LA, dir, 2002-04; LA Munic Art Gallery, exec dir, 2004-; Exhibs: "Crenshaw Consciousness", 1987; "Iconography-Banner Ser", 1999; "Iconography", 2000; "Blackatcha", 2000. **Orgs:** Pres, Calif African Am Geneal Soc, 1993-; bd mem, Los Angeles Art Asn, 1995-; bd mem, Watts Village Theater Co, 1997-; bd mem, Korean Am Mus, 1998-; founder, Black Creative Professionals Asn. **Home Addr:** 1250 Long Beach Ave Suite 206, Los Angeles, CA 90021, **Home Phone:** (213)623-3868. **Business Addr:** Director, Harbor Arts Center, 201 N Figueroa St Suite 1400, Los Angeles, CA 90012, **Business Phone:** (213)202-5500.

**GREENFIELD, DR. ROBERT THOMAS**
Physician. **Personal:** Born Washington, DC; son of Robert T Sr and Avis; married Wilma Sue Robertson; children: Kimberly, Karyn, Robert III, Richard, Brian & Ashley M. **Educ:** Howard Univ, BS, 1954, Col Med, MD, 1958. **Career:** Madigan Gen Hosp, intern, 1958-59; Freedmen's Hosp, res phys obstet & gynec, 1963-67; Howard Univ, Col Med, clin instr, 1976-; Howard Univ Hosp, resident obstet & gynec; Madigan Army Med Ctr, resident; Georgetown Univ, instr clin, 1978-; Drs Greenfield, Booker Chartered, physician, pres, 1969-; Chartered Health Plan, med dir, founder, 1987-90. **Orgs:** Bd dir, Columbia Hosp Women, 1981-85; Joint Perinatal Site Visit Task Force, Wash, DC, 1982-85; chief staff, Columbia Hosp Women, 1983-85; chmn, bd dir, Colmesh Inc, 1985-86; adv bd, DC Maternal & Infant Health; Joint Venture Med Staff & Columbia Hosp; vchmn, chmn, Wash, DC, Sect Dist IV, Am Col Obstet & Gynec, chmn, Perinatal Mortality Comn; Mayor's Comt Infant Mortality, 1990; founder, med dir, Chartered Health Plan, 1998-. **Honors/Awds:** Alpha Omega Alpha Med Scholastic Frat. **Home Addr:** 2010 Spruce Dr NW, Washington, DC 20012, **Home Phone:** (202)726-9364. **Business Addr:** Surgeon, Washington Hospital Center, 3300 Pa Ave SE, Washington, DC 20020, **Business Phone:** (202)877-3627.

**GREENIDGE, DR. KEVIN C.**
Educator, physician. **Personal:** Born Feb 5, 1952, New York, NY; married Dawn; children: Christopher & Ryan. **Educ:** Howard Univ, BS, 1973; Harvard Univ, MPH, health servs admin, 1977; State Univ NY, MD, 1977. **Career:** Martin Luther King Jr Gen Hosp, internship; Emory Univ Sch Med, resident; New York Eye & Ear Infirmary, dir resident training, 1983-87, adj surgeon, 1985-91, assoc attend surgeon, 1991-; Metrop Hosp Ctr, chief, dept opthalmol, 1987-91, dir, glaucoma serv, 1987-96; Beth Israel Med Ctr, asst attend, 1987-; Long Island Col Hosp, chmn ophthalmol, 1996-, fac; SUNY Brooklyn Health Sci Ctr; Wills Eye Hosp, fel; Kings Co Med Ctr, Dept Opthalmol, chmn, prof; Univ Hosp Brooklyn, Dept Opthalmol, dir; SUNY Brooklyn HSC Opthalmol Residency Prog, Dept Opthalmol, dir, 1996-; State Univ New York Downstate Med Ctr, prof & chmn, 1996, prof emer, currently; Coney Island Hosp, fac; Brooklyn Veterans Admin Med Ctr, fac; Kingsbrook Jewish Med Ctr, fac; Brookdale Univ Hosp Ctr, fac; Eye Inst W Fla, glaucoma specialist, 2005-. **Orgs:** Legis comm, New York Co Med Soc, 1985-89; adv bd dir, Am Soc Contemp Ophthal, 1987-; pres, Int Glaucoma Cong, 1991; assoc examr, Am Bd Ophthal, 1991-; deleg, Nat Med Asn, 1992-94; chair, Manhattan Cent Med Soc, Managed Care Comt, 1993-96; rep, mem bd trustee, Skills Transfer Adv Comm, Am Acad Ophthal, 1993, 1994-2000; alt deleg, Med Soc State NY, Am Med Asn; bd mem, Int Found Optic Nerve Disease; bd mem, Cong Glaucoma Caucus Found Inc; bd dir, African Diaspora Maritime, currently; bd mem, Glaucoma Res Found. **Home Addr:** 101 Greenway N, Forest Hills, NY 11375-6039. **Business Addr:** Glaucoma Specialist, Eye Institute of West Florida, 1225 W Bay Dr, Largo, FL 33770, **Business Phone:** (727)581-8706.

**GREENLEAF, LOUIS E.**
Government official. **Personal:** Born Apr 9, 1941, Newark, NJ; married Cynthia Robinson Conover; children: Bridget, Michael A, Brectt & Towanna. **Educ:** Essex Co Col, AS, 1973; John Jay Col Criminal Justice, BS, 1975; Rutgers Sch Law, JD, 1978. **Career:** Pvt Law Practr, atty, 1983-86, 1994-97; Newark City, police dept, 1968-86, police dir, 1986-88; Essex County Prosecutors Off, chief investigators, 1988-94; Weights & Measures, supt, 1997-. **Orgs:** NJ Bar Asn, 1985-; Nat Orgn Black Law Enforcement Execs; bd trustee, Garden State Bar Asn; bd dir, Newark Emr Servs Families. **Home Addr:** 49 Sagamore Lane, Bordentown, NJ 08505-4458, **Home Phone:** (609)298-6690. **Business Addr:** Superintendent, Office of Weights & Measures, 1261 Routes 1 & 9 S, Avenel, NJ 07001-1647, **Business Phone:** (732)815-4842.

**GREENWOOD, DR. CHARLES H.**
Administrator, president (organization). **Personal:** Born Jul 30, 1933, Anderson, IN; son of Lida M Lampkins and Huddie; married Theresa M Winfrey; children: Lisa Renee & Marc Charles. **Educ:** Ball State Teachers Col, BS, 1956; Colo Col, attended 1958; Ball State Univ, MA, 1961; Ind Univ, EdD, 1972. **Career:** Ball State Univ, grad asst, 1958-59, instr, 1961-63, assoc prof, 1973-, asst dean undergrad prog, 1974-84, Sch Continuing Educ, asst dean, 1984-; E Chicago Pub Schs, teacher, 1959-61; N Ill Univ, vis prof, 1973-74; Ind Univ Alumni Asn, Singing Hoosiers Alumni Coun, pres, 2005-10, bd mem, currently. **Orgs:** Bd mem & vpres, pres, Family Coun Serv, 1961-71; bd mem, Col Ave Methodist Church, 1961-71, 1975-78; bd mem, secy, Muncie Housing Authority, 1968-78; bd trustee, All Am Family Inst, 1971-73; Am Asn Higher Educ, 1974-; Asn Supv & Curric Develop, 1974-78; Asn Acad Affairs Admin, 1974-78; Phi Delta Kappa, 1976-; secy, YMCA Bd, 1978; Adult Educ Asn Ind, 1978; vpres, Jr Achievement, 1979-81; vpres & pres, Kiwanis Club Muncie Ind, 1980-81; lt gov Wapahanai Div, 1982-83; evaluator, Am Coun Educ, 1984; bd dir, E Cent Ind Community Singers, 1985-86, 1998-99; gov, SigmaIota Epsilon, 1986; gov, Ind Dist Kiwanis Int, 1990-91; educ coord Acad Comn Leadership; liaison officer, Liason Adv Bd, Midwest rep; dir, Aerospace Educ USAF CAP Aux Ind Wing; bd dir, Ball Mem Hosp, 1996-2005; Int Chmn Coun & Conv Munic, Kiwanas, int bd mem, United Way, 1997; Ind Blacks Higher Educ; Am Asn Blacks Higher Educ; Sigma Iota Epilson; NUCEA; Loaned Exec United Way, 2001-04; diversity comt, Kiwanis Int, 2001-04; Kiwanis Adv Bd Riley Hosp. **Honors/Awds:** Nat Bronze Award Jr Achievement, 1980; Outstanding Minority Fac, Ball State Univ; Distinguished Lt Gov Kiwanis Int, 1983; Sagamore of the Wabash, 1991; Outstanding Black Alumni Award, Ball State Univ, 1991; Distinguished Alumnus Award, Ind Univ Singing Hoosiers, 2001. **Home Addr:** 2504 W Lincolnshire Dr, Muncie, IN 47304, **Home Phone:** (765)288-2002. **Business Addr:** President of Singing Hoosiers Alumni Council, Associate Professor and Assistant Dean, Ball State University, 2000 Univ Ave Letterman 131, Muncie, IN 47306, **Business Phone:** (765)285-5776.

**GREENWOOD, DAVID KASIM (DAVE GREENWOOD)**
Basketball player. **Personal:** Born May 27, 1957, Lynwood, CA; married Joyce; children: Tiffany Crystal Marie. **Educ:** Univ Calif, Los Angeles, BA, hist, 1979. **Career:** Basketball player (retired); Chicago Bulls, 1979-85; San Antonio Spurs, 1986-89, 1990-91; Denver Nuggets, 1989; Detroit Pistons, 1990. **Orgs:** Taught basketball clinics Western US, 1980; Nat Basketball Retired Players Asn. **Home Addr:** 18857 Whitney Pl, Rowland Heights, CA 91748-4873.

**GREENWOOD, EDNA TURNER**
Editor. **Personal:** Born Shiner, TX; daughter of David Koontz and Mamie; married Wilbert; children: Ronald Vann Turner; married Norris. **Educ:** Tucker Bus Col, St Louis, MO, 1953. **Career:** Editor (retired); Good Publ Co (magazines, Jive, Bronze Thrills, Hip, Soul Confessions, Sepia & Soul Teen) Ft Worth, Tex, ed dir; circulation mgr, ed, 25 yrs. **Orgs:** Baker Chapel Am Ch; Nat Asn Advan Colored People; Ft Worth C C; bd mem, Neighborhood Action Comm, Tarrant Action Aging; bd mem, United Ctrs. **Honors/Awds:** Award Margaret Caskey Women in Commun, Ft Worth Prof Chap Women Commun, 1977. **Home Addr:** 5950 Alexandria Sky Lane, Fort Worth, TX 76119, **Home Phone:** (817)478-9813.

**GREENWOOD, MONIQUE**
Business owner, editor, writer. **Personal:** Born Jun 22, 1959, Washington, DC; married Glen Pogue; children: Glynn. **Educ:** Howard Univ, BA; Simmons Grad Sch Bus, MBA. **Career:** Fairchild Prods, staff, 1981-96; Akwaaba Bed & Breakfast, pres & chief exec officer, 1995-; Essence Mag, lifestyle dir & style dir, 1996-98, exec ed, 1998-2000, chief ed, 2000-01; Mirrors Coffee House, owner/operator, 1999-; Akwaaba by the Sea, owner/operator, 2001-; co founder & Author: Go On Girl! Book Club Guide to Reading Groups, 1999; Having What Matters: The Black Woman's Guide to Creating the Life You Really Want, 2001; Life Under New Management: How to Fire Your Job & Become Your Own Boss. **Honors/Awds:** Points of Light Award, Pres George W Bush, 2001. **Business Addr:** Owner, Akwaaba Mansion Bed & Breakfast, 347 McDonough St, Brooklyn, NY 11233-1012, **Business Phone:** (718)455-5958.

**GREER, BAUNITA M.**
Chief executive officer, executive. **Educ:** Am Univ, BSBA, acct, 1979. **Career:** Daniel & Bell Inc, treas & bd dir; New York Sch Continuing & Prof Studies, adj prof; Cromwell, Miller & Greer Inc, pres & founder, 1993-99, prin, 1994-2004, chief exec officer, currently; Wall St Conferences Inc, pres, exec, currently; NY Stock Exchange, examr; GRW Capital Corp, exec, chief exec officer, currently. **Orgs:** Nat Asn Securities Professionals NY Chap, 1995-2004; Nat Asn Investor Corp; dir, New York Soc Security Anal, 2000-06; Toastmaster Int, 2005-07. **Business Addr:** Executive, Chief Executive Officer, GRW Capital Corp, 1010 Vt Ave Suite 710 2nd Fl, Washington, DC 20005, **Business Phone:** (202)628-0880.

**GREER, DONOVAN ORLANDO**
Football player. **Personal:** Born Sep 11, 1974, Houston, TX. **Educ:** Tex A&M Univ, grad. **Career:** Football player (retired); New Orleans Saints, defensive back & corner back, 1997; Atlanta Falcons, corner back, 1997; Buffalo Bills, defensive back & corner back, 1998, 1999-2000; Wash Redskins, corner back, 2001; Detroit Lions, corner back, 2002.

**GREER, EDWARD M.**
Real estate agent. **Personal:** Born Mar 8, 1924, Gary, WV; married Jewell Means; children: Gail Lyle, Michael & Kenneth. **Educ:** WVa State Col, BS, 1948; George Washington Univ, MS, 1967. **Career:** Greer & Assoc Realtors, broker & owner, currently. **Orgs:** Asn AUS Mil Order World Wars; Nat Asn Uniformed Serv; Disabled Am Veterans; Nat War Col Alumni Asn; dir bd, Realtors; bd dir, Am Cancer Soc; Kappa Alpha Psi Fraternity Retired Officers Asn. **Honors/Awds:** Alumnus of the Year, WVa State Col, 1963. **Home Addr:** 3134 Mesa Verde Lane, El Paso, TX 79904, **Home Phone:** (915)755-2244. **Business Addr:** Owner, Broker, Greer & Associates Realtors, 3134 Mesa Verde Lane, El Paso, TX 79904, **Business Phone:** (915)751-4293.

**GREER, ERNEST LAMONT**
Lawyer, vice president (organization). **Educ:** Harvard Univ, AB, govt, 1988; Northwestern Univ, JD, 1991. **Career:** US Ct Appeals Sixth Circuit, judicial clerk, 1991-92; Greenberg Traurig, Atlanta managing shareholder, vpres, 2013-15, pres, 2015-. **Orgs:** co-pres, Trinity Sch Parents Asn, 2007; co-chair, Am Jewish Comt, 2010; co-chair, Families First, 14th Ann Dining a Difference Dinner, 2012; Ga Chamber Com First Atty Chmn, 2014; bd dirs, Achieve Atlanta, 2015-; bd trustee, C Healthcare Atlanta, 2015-; bd dirs, Atlanta Police Found, 2016-; vice chair, Atlanta Hist Ctr, 2016-; Bd trustees mem, Woodruff Arts Ctr; bd dirs mem, Ctr Civil & Human Rights; dir, Buckhead Coalition; Rotary Club Atlanta; Sigma Pi Phi Fraternity Inc (Kappa Boule); Nat Asn Guardsmen Inc, Atlanta Chap; Kappa Alpha Psi Fraternity Inc; co-chair, Grady White Coat Gala; secy, 100 Black Men Atlanta Inc; comt mem, Ga Competitiveness Initiative; gen coun, Nat Asn Minority Contractors, Atlanta. **Honors/Awds:**

Super Lawyers magazine, "Rising Star", 2005-06, "Top 100 Lawyers in Georgia", 2011, 2013, 2014, "Georgia Super Lawyers", listee, 2007-2014; Boss of the Year, Atlanta Chap NALS Inc, 2006; NFL Alumni 2007 Difference Maker Award, Cystic Fibrosis Found, 2007; "Georgia Trend" magazine, Legal Elite, 2008-13; "MCCA Rainmaker" Award, Winner, 2012; "Business to Business" magazine, IMPACT Leader Award, 2012; "Atlanta Business Chronicle", Who's Who in Law and Accounting, listee, 2012; "Atlanta Business Chronicle", 100 Most Influential Atlantans, 2012-14; "BTI Client Service All Stars", Federal Regulations, Listee, 2014; Atlanta Hawks African-American Trailblazer Awards, Honoree, February 4, 2014; "James" magazine, 100 Most Influential Georgians, 2014; "The Best Lawyers in America", Mass Tort Litigation/Class Actions--Defendants, 2013-15; National Bar Association "Sankofa" Award, Recipient, 2014; A. T. Walden Outstanding Lawyer, Gate City Bar, 2014; "The Atlanta Business Chronicle" Most Admired CEO--Professional Services, Winner, 2014; Whitney M. Young, Jr. Service Award, Atlanta Area Coun, Boy Scouts Am, 2015; 16th Annual Justice Robert Benham Award for Community Service, State Bar Ga, 2015. **Special Achievements:** Co-Author & Co-Editor, Toxic Mold Litigation, Lawyers & Judges Publishing, Second Edition, 2009. **Business Addr:** GreenbergTraurig, Terminus 200, Atlanta, GA 30305, **Business Phone:** (678)553-2100.

### GREER, HAROLD EVERETT (HAL GREER)

Basketball coach, basketball player. **Personal:** Born Jun 26, 1936, Huntington, WV; son of William; married Mayme; children: 3. **Educ:** Marshall Univ, Huntington, WV, attended 1958. **Career:** Basketball player (retired), basketball coach; Syracuse Nationals, guard, 1958-63; Philadelphia 76ers, guard, 1964-73; CBA, Philadelphia Kings, coach, 1980-81. **Home Addr:** 7900 E Princess Dr Apt 1021, Scottsdale, AZ 85255-5824, **Home Phone:** (480)473-9774.

### GREER, KARYN LYNETTE

Television journalist. **Personal:** Born Jun 20, 1962, Chicago, IL; daughter of Ronald Virgil and Jeanette Brenda Crossley; married Tony; children: Kyle & Tyler. **Educ:** Univ Ill, Champaign, IL, BA, broadcast jour & speech commun, 1984. **Career:** WCIA-TV, Champaign, Ill, asst dir newscasts, 1983-84; WICD-TV, Champaign, Ill, weekend anchor & reporter, 1984-86; WCSC-TV, Charleston, SC, weekend anchor & reporter, 1986-89; WGNX-TV, Atlanta, Ga, weeknight anchor & med reporter, 1989-99; Wxia Tv-11 Alive, anchor & reporter, 1999-. **Orgs:** Magnolia Chap, Links Inc; bd dir, Arthritis Found; bd dir, Volleyfest; bd dir, Atlanta 2 Day Walk Breast Cancer; bd govs, Nat Acad TV Arts & Sci, currently; Alpha Kappa Alpha Sorority Inc, 1982-; pres, Atlanta Press Club; bd mem, Arthritis Found; Greater N Atlanta Chap Jack & Jill Am Inc; Sport Giving. **Honors/Awds:** Revlon Kizzy Award; Black Woman Hall of Fame, 1990; First Place Feature, Atlanta Asn Black Journalists, 1990; Emmy Award, Specialty Reporting, 1991, Best Newscast, Collab Writing, Nat Acad TV Arts & Sci; Best of Gannett, Best Newscast. **Special Achievements:** one of Atlanta's 100 Women of Influence by the Atlanta Business League, 2008. **Business Addr:** Anchor, Reporter, Wxia Tv-11 Alive, 1611 W Peachtree St NE, Atlanta, GA 30309, **Business Phone:** (404)892-1611.

### GREER, DR. ROBERT O., JR.

Pathologist, dentist, writer. **Personal:** Born Mar 9, 1944, Columbus, OH; son of Robert O Sr and Mary A; married Phyllis Ann Harwell. **Educ:** Miami Univ, Oxford, OH, BA, 1965; Howard Univ, DDS, 1969; Boston Univ, ScD, 1974, MA, creative writing, 1988. **Career:** Boston Univ Hosp, residency, 1971-73, path fel, 1974; Univ Colo Health Sci Ctr, Dept Path, asst prof, 1974-77; Univ Colo Health Sci Ctr, Dept Path, assoc prof, 1977-80, prof, chmn, 1984-; Mile High Med Soc, secy, 1978-79, pres, 1983-85; Univ Colo Sch Dent, Div Oral Path & Oncol, prof & chmn, 1980-; Western States Regional Path Lab, pres & chief pathologist; Bks: Ltd Time, 2000; Isolation & Other Stories, 2002; Heat Shock, 2003; Devil's Hat band, 2004; Fourth Perspective, 2004; Devil's Red Nickel, 2005; Resurrecting Langston Blue, 2005; Devil's Backbone, 2006; Mongoose Deception, 2007; Blackbird, Farewell, 2008. **Orgs:** Bd dir, Miami Univ Alumni Asn, 1984-; Am Cancer Soc. **Home Addr:** 1375 Williams St, Denver, CO 80218, **Home Phone:** (303)377-1665. **Business Addr:** Professor, Chairman, University of Colorado School of Dental Medicine, Rm L26 130 13065 E 17th Ave, Aurora, CO 80045, **Business Phone:** (303)724-6982.

### GREGG, HON. HARRISON M., JR.

Lawyer. **Personal:** Born Sep 24, 1942, Longview, TX; son of Harrison and Ola Timberlake; married Arizona Johnson; children: Sherri Kimberly. **Educ:** Tex Southern Univ, BA, 1968, JD, 1971. **Career:** Gregg Okehie & Cashin, atty, 1972-; Tex Paralegal Sch, instr, 1976-; State Tex, second admin region, 4D master judge, 1987-; pvt pract, currently; Harris County Atty's Off, asst county atty, currently. **Orgs:** Houston Bar Asn; Tex State Bar; Houston Lawyer Asn; Tex Criminal Defense Lawyers; Harris Co Criminal Defense Lawyers; Nat Bar Asn; Am Bar Asn; vol, UNCF. **Honors/Awds:** Phi Alpha Delta. **Home Addr:** 3442 Eldorado Blvd, Missouri City, TX 77459. **Business Addr:** Assistant County Attorney, Harris County Attorney's Office, 1019 Cong St Fl 16, Houston, TX 77002, **Business Phone:** (713)274-5169.

### GREGG, LUCIUS PERRY, JR.

Executive. **Personal:** Born Jan 16, 1933, Henderson, NC; son of Lucius Sr and Rachel; married Doris Marie Jefferson. **Educ:** US Naval Acad, BS, elec engineering, 1955; Mass Inst Technol, MS, aeronaut, 1961; Cath Univ, doctoral cand, 1963; Grinnell Col, hon DSc, 1973; Aspen Inst Exec Prog, 1974; Harvard Univ Bus Sch, Advan Mgt Prog, 1975. **Career:** USAF, pilot, 1956-59; Andrews Afb, mission comdr, 1961; USAF Off Sci Res, proj dir space tech, 1961-65; Northwestern U, assoc dean Scis & dir res coordr, 1965-69; Alfred P Sloan Found, prog officer, 1969-71; 1st Nat Bank Chicago, vpres, 1972; 1st Chicago Univ Finance Corp, pres, 1972-74; Nat Pub Affairs, vpres & Dir, 1979; Citibank, vpres govt rels, 1979; New York Daily News, vpres, pub affairs, 1985; Hughes Aircraft Co, vpres. **Orgs:** Bd mem, Fermi NatAccel Lab, 1967-77; Econ Club Chicago, 1967-; acad bd US Naval Acad, 1971-; Tulane Univ Bd Visitors, 1972-; Univ Club Chicago, 1972-; Nat Acad Sci Found Com Human Resources, 1973-; Harvard Univ Trsts Vis Comm physics, 1973-; pres, Com White House Fellows Midwest Reg Selec Com, 1974-; Garrett Theol Sem, 1974-; bd dir, Corp Pub Broadcasting, 1975-; Chicago Coun Foreign Rel, 1975-; Harvard Club Chicago, 1975-; Roosevelt Univ, 1976-; Harvard Bus Sch Chicago, 1977; MIT Trsts Vis Con Aero & Astronaut; founder, Found Study Am Technol Leadership, 1999; bd dir, Amistad Res Ctr Inc, currently. **Special Achievements:** Listed in Who's Who in Science & Engineering, 2006; Listed in Who's Who in Business, 2006; Listed in Who's Who in the World, 2006. **Home Addr:** 8953 S Paulina, Chicago, IL 60620. **Business Addr:** Board of Director, Amistad Research Center Inc, 6823 St Charles Ave, New Orleans, LA 70118, **Business Phone:** (504)862-3222.

### GREGORY, DICK. See GREGORY, RICHARD CLAXTON.

### GREGORY, COL. FREDERICK DREW, SR.

Military leader, astronaut. **Personal:** Born Jan 7, 1941, Washington, DC; son of Francis A and Nora Drew; married Barbara Ann Archer(-deceased); children: Frederick D Jr & Heather Lynn Gregory Skeens. **Educ:** USAF Acad, BS, 1964; George Washington Univ, MS, info systs, 1977. **Career:** Military service (retired), airforce official; Vance Air Force Base, rescue pilot, 1965-66; Da Nang Air Base, rescue pilot, 1966; NASA Astronaut; USAF, helicopter & fighter pilot, 1965-70; USAF & NASA, res test pilot, 1971-78, astronaut, 1978-92, spacecraft comdr, 1989; Shuttle Avionics Integration Lab, 1979-83; Spacelab 3 mission, piloted challenger, 1985; NASA, assoc adminr, 1992-2001, assoc adminr, Off Space Flight, 2001-02, dep adminr, 2002-05, actg adminr, 2005. **Orgs:** Soc Exp Test Pilots; Order Daedalians; Tuskegee Airmen Inc; Air Force Assoc; Am Helicopter Soc; Nat Tech Asn; USAF Acad Asn Graduates; Omega Psi Phi; Sigma Pi Phi; Air Force Acad Asn Grad; Order Daedalians; Asn Space Explorers; Photonics Lab Fisk Univ; Engineering Col, Howard Univ; bd trustee, Md Space Ctr; Nat Tech Asn; Tuskegee Airmen Inc; bd dir, Young Astronaut Coun; Va Air & Space Ctr Hampton Roads Hist Ctr; Air Force Asn; Sigma Pi Phi Fraternity; Nat Tech Asn; challenger, Ctr Space Sci Educ Am Helicopter Socs. **Honors/Awds:** Distinguished Nat Scientist Award, Nat Soc Black Engrs, 1979; Two NASA Distinguished Service Medals; Three NASA Space Flight Medals; NASA Outstanding Leadership Award, NASA; Distinguished Alumni Award, George Wash Univ; Top 20 Minority Engineers, 1990; IRA Eaker Fel, Air Force Asn; President Medal, Charles R Drew, Univ Med & Sci; Meritorious Service Medal; Distinguished National Scientist Award, National Society Black Engineers, 1979; Presidential Rank Award, 2003; Ira Eaker Fel, Air Force Asn; Univ DC, Hon Doctorate Sci, 1986. **Special Achievements:** First Black Man to Command a Space Shuttle. **Home Addr:** 506 Tulip Rd, Annapolis, MD 21403-1326, **Home Phone:** (410)263-3837. **Business Addr:** NASA-JSC, 2101 NASA Rd 1, Houston, TX 77058, **Business Phone:** (202)358-0001.

### GREGORY, KARL DWIGHT

Executive, consultant, educator. **Personal:** Born Mar 26, 1931, Detroit, MI; son of Bertram and Sybil; married Tenicia Ann Banks; children: Kurt David, Sheila Therese & Karin Diane. **Educ:** Wayne State Univ, BA, econ, 1952, MA, finance, 1957; Univ Mich, PhD, econ, 1962. **Career:** Detroit Housing Comn, tech aid-acct, 1951-53; Fed Res Bank St Louis, economist, 1959; Wayne State Univ, prof, 1960-61, 1964-68; Fiscal economist Off Mgt & Budget, Wash DC, economist, 1961-64; Oakland Univ, Sch Bus Admin, prof in & strategic planning, 1968-96, distinguished prof emer econs; Fed Self Determination, exec dir, 1968-69; Accord Inc Housing Rehabil Detroit, pres, chief exec officer, bd chmn, 1970-71; S Univ NY Buffalo, vis prof, 1975; Cong Budget Off, exec staff, sr economist, vis scholar, 1974-75; 1st Independence Nat Bank, inter impres, 1980-81; Karl Dwight Gregory & Assoc, managing dir; KDG & assocs, mgt & econ consult, Managing Dir, currently. **Orgs:** Brown Univ, postdoctoral fel, micro econ; Dir, Nat Econ Asn, Black Econ Res Ctr, 1968-75, Inner City Bus Improv Forum, 1968-87; dir, chief org, chmn bd, 1st Independence Nat Bank, 1970-81; bd trustee Protestant Episcopal Diocese Mich, 1972-74, 1981-87, 1990-92; dir Inner City Capital Formation, 1973-86; Detroit Capital Access Ctr, 1973-86; adv comm US Census Black Pop, 1976-79; US Trade Negotiations Tokyo Round, 1978-81; dir, Detroit Br Fed Res Bank Chicago, 1981-86; Barden Cable vision Detroit, 1982-94; Detroit Metro Small Bus Investment Corp, 1982-85; Detroit Econ Growth Corp, 1982-94; bd trustee Oakland Cty Bus Attraction & Abbr Comn, 1983-84; mem Gov's Entrepreneurial Comn, Lansing, 1984-88; Gov Blanchard's Entrepreneurs & Small Bus Comn, 1984-89; vpres, Econ Club Detroit, 1984-89; first vice chair, Mich Minority Technol Coun, 1988-96; dir Detroit Urban League, 1989-92; Detroit Alliance Fair Banking, 1992-; chief exec officer, chmn bd, Greater BIDCO, 1990-96; Mich Gov Engler's Coun Econ Advisors, 1992-96; chair, Adult Well Being Serv, 1999-; Mem community impact cabinet United Way Southeast Mich, 2006-; Booker T. Wash Bus Asn, Nat Econ Asn. **Home Addr:** 18495 Adrian, Southfield, MI 48075, **Home Phone:** (248)569-7387. **Business Addr:** Managing Director, KDG & Associates.

### GREGORY, MICHAEL SAMUEL

Administrator. **Personal:** Born Dec 25, 1949, Barbourville, KY; son of Royal and Dorothy; married Linda Joy McCowan; children: Arron K, DaNiel K & Brittany M. **Educ:** Ken State Univ, BS, 1973, MPA, 1974; Univ Min, advan grad study, 1981; Ohio State Univ, advan grad study, 1982. **Career:** Ken State Univ, Coop Educ, asst dir, 1973-74, dir, 1974-77; St John's Univ, career planning dir, 1977-81; Ohio State Univ, law placement dir, 1981-87; Columbus Urban League, sr prog dir, 1987-; Nat Urban League, sr job placement leader, 1988, affil, 1992; Creative Med Personnel, chief exec officer. **Orgs:** Columbus Urban League; NCP; AM Soc Personnel ADRs; Columbus C's Hosp Develop Bd; NAT Urban League; Ohio Soc Prevent Blindness Bd. **Honors/Awds:** Ken State Univ, Alpha Mu Gamma Honor Soc, 1972; DPT Housing & Urban Develop Fellowship, 1973; Big Ten Univs, CIC Fellowship, 1980; Ohio State UNIV, Black Law Students ASN, 1987. **Home Addr:** 3060 Breed Dr, PO Box 452, Reynoldsburg, OH 43068, **Home Phone:** (614)863-1711. **Business Addr:** Chief Operations Officer, Creative Medical Personnel, PO Box 578, Brice, OH 43109-0452.

### GREGORY, RICHARD CLAXTON (DICK GREGORY)

Entrepreneur, lecturer, civil rights activist. **Personal:** Born Oct 12, 1932, St. Louis, MO; son of Presley and Lucille Franklin; married Lillian Smith; children: Richard Jr (deceased), Michele, Lynne, Paula, Pamela, Stephanie, Gregory Jr, Christian, Ayanna, Miss & Yohance. **Educ:** Southern Ill Univ, attended 1956. **Career:** MC Roberts Show Club, 1959-60; Us Postal Serv; Roberts Show Bar, 1961; Chicago Playboy Club, 1961; Esquire Club, Chicago, entertainer; night club Apex Robbins, owner; TV guest appearances Jack Parr Show, others; rec include: Dick Gregory in Living Black & White; Dick Gregory; The Light Side-Dark Side; lectr; Am Prog Bur, lectr, 1967-; Peace & Freedom Party Presidential Candidate, 1968; Dick Gregory Health Enterprises, Chicago, founder, 1984-; Films: Sweet Love, Bitter, 1967; Panther, 1995; Children of the Struggle, 1999; The Hot Chick, 2002; One Bright Shining Momen, 2006; Albums: In Living Black and White, 1961; East & West, 1961; Dick Gregory Talks Turkey, 1962; The Two Sides of Dick Gregory, 1963; Dick Gregory Running for President, 1964; So You See We All Have Problems; Dick Gregory On, 1969; The Light Side: The Dark Side, 1969; Dick Gregory's Frankenstein, 1970; Live at the Village Gate, 1970; At Kent State, 1971; Caught in the Act, 1974; The Best of Dick Gregory (1997); Books: From the Back of the Bus, 1962; Nigger, 1964; What's Happening, 1965; The Shadow That Scares Me, Write Me In, No More Lies, 1971; Dick Gregory's Political Primer, 1971; Dick Gregory's Natural Diet for Folks Who Eat Cookin, 1973; Dick Gregory's Bible & Tales with Commentary, 1974; Up From Nigger, 1976; The Murder of Martin Luther King Jr, 1977; Co-author: Callus On My Soul, 2000; Dick Gregory's Bible Tales; Dick Gregory's Natural Diet for Folks Who Eat; Murder in Memphis; co-author, African American Humor; daring Black leader. **Orgs:** Alpha Phi Alpha. **Honors/Awds:** Winner No Mile Championship, 1951, 1952; Outstanding Athlete, So Ill Univ, 1953; Ebony-Topaz Heritage & Freedom Award, 1978; Doctor of HumaneLetters, Southern Ill Univ, Carbondale, 1989; numerous other honorarydoctoral degrees; Smile of the Year Award, Angel City Dental Soc, 1999. **Home Addr:** Long Pond Rd, Plymouth, MA 02360. **Business Addr:** Founder, Dick Gregory Health Enterprises, 39 S LaSalle, Chicago, LA 60603.

### GREGORY, ROBERT ALPHONSO

Executive. **Personal:** Born Jun 21, 1935, Hertford, NC; married Barbara Ann White; children: Alan & Christopher. **Educ:** Elizabeth City State Univ NC, BS, 1956. **Career:** Rheingold Breweries Inc, acct sales rep, 1963-68; Faberge Inc, acct exec, 1968-72; 3M Duplicating Prod Div, area sales rep, 1972-74, nat mkt coordr, 1974-75; 3M Copying Prod Div, nat sales develop coordr, 1975-; Off Sys Div 3M, competitive anal supvr, 1980-82; Syst Bus Develop Unit, OSD 3M, mkt develop supvr, 1982-83; LES Ed Mkt OSD 3M, nat pub sector mkt coordr, 1983-2001; US Ct Appeals, 2001-. **Orgs:** Chap organizer, Alpha Phi Alpha Frat Inc, 1955-56; presenter, St Paul C C, 1974; family mem, St Paul Urban League, 1975-76; nat coordr, Copying Prod Div 3M, 1975-80; finance com spokesman, Guardian Angels Parish Coun, 1977-80. **Special Achievements:** Author, Marketing researh books, 1974-75, awareness bullet, 1975-80, competitive awareness bks, 1977-80, prod, VTR Ser Competition, 3M Copying Prod Div, 1979-80. **Home Addr:** 10200 City Walk Dr Suite 247, St. Paul, MN 55129-6906, **Home Phone:** (651)501-9671. **Business Addr:** Executive, 3M Co, 1101 15th St NW, Washington, DC 20005, **Business Phone:** (202)331-3967.

### GREGORY, JUDGE ROGER L.

Lawyer, judge. **Personal:** Born Jul 17, 1953, Philadelphia, PA; son of George L and Fannie Mae Washington; married Carla Eugenia Lewis; children: Adriene Leigh, Rachel Leigh & Christina Leigh. **Educ:** VA State Univ, BA, 1975; Univ Mich, JD, 1978. **Career:** Butzel, Long, Gust, Klein & Van Zile, assoc atty, 1978-80; Hunton & Williams, assoc atty, 1980-82; Wilder & Gregory, co-founder, managing partner, 1982-2001; US Ct Appeals Fourth Circuit, judge, 2000-16, chief judge, 2016-. **Orgs:** State Bar Mich, 1978; Va Bar Asn, 1980; dir, Indust Develop Authority, 1984-91; dir, Richmond Metro Chamber Com, 1989-91; pres, Old Dom Bar Asn, 1990-92; bd visitors, VA Common wealth Univ, past rector, 1985-93; VA State univ Found Bd, 1993-; Richmond Renaissance, chair exec comt, 1993-; bd visitors, VA State Univ, 1993-; bd dirs, Richmond Bar Asn, 1989-93; dir, Rich food Holding, 1994-; bd, Rich food Holding, 1994-; bd visitors, Left VA State Univ, 1996; bd, Christian C's Fund, 1997-; bd dir, Richmond Metrop Chamber Com; bd dir, VA Asn Defense Attys, 1996-; Fourth Circuit Judicial Conf; Omega Psi Phi fraternity; Sigma Pi Phi fraternity. **Honors/Awds:** Honor Society, Alpha Mu Gamma, 1973; Honor Society, Alpha Kappa Mu, 1974; Top 75 Black College Students America, Black Enterprise Mag, 1975; 100 Most Influential Richmonders, Richmond Surroundings Mag, 1990; Proclamation of Achievement, VA State Univ, 1991; Humanitarian Award, Nat Conf Christians & Jews, 1997; Virginia Law Foundation fellow. **Special Achievements:** First African American appointed to the U.S. Court of Appeals for the Fourth Circuit. **Business Addr:** Chief Judge, US Court of Appeals for the Fourth Circuit, 1100 E Main St Suite 501, Richmond, VA 23219, **Business Phone:** (804)916-2700.

### GREGORY, MOST REV. WILTON DANIEL

Clergy, archbishop. **Personal:** Born Dec 7, 1947, Chicago, IL; son of Wilton D Sr and Ethel D Duncan. **Educ:** Niles Col Loyola Univ, BA, 1969; St Mary Lake Sem, STB, 1971, Mdiv, 1973, STL, 1974; Pontif Liturgical Inst Sant'Anselmo Rome, Italy, SLD, 1980. **Career:** St Mary Lake Sem, teacher; Titular Bishop Oliva; Archdiocese Chicago, auxiliary bishop, 1983-93; Cath Diocese Belleville, bishop, 1994-2005; archbishop, Atlanta, 2005-. **Orgs:** Cath Theol Soc Am; N Am Acad Liturgy; Midwestern Asn Spiritual dir; Cath Theol Soc Am, 1980; N Am Acad Liturgy, 1981; Midwestern Asn Spiritual dir, 1981; chair, 1990-93, educ, 1993, doctrine, 1994, Bishops Comm Liturgy; bd trustee, Archdiocese Chicago Seminaries; pres, US Conf Cath Bishops, 2001-04. **Business Addr:** Catholic Archbishop of Atlanta, Catholic Diocese Belleville-Chancery Off, 222 S 3rd St, Belleville, IL 62220-1985, **Business Phone:** (618)277-8181.

### GRESHAM, DARRYL WAYNE

Vice president (organization). **Personal:** Born Feb 4, 1958, Pittsburgh, PA; son of James and Lillian; married Renee; children: Desra, Darian, Taylor, Catheryn & Averry. **Educ:** Carnegie-Mellon Univ, BS, mech engineering, 1982; Duke Univ, Grad Global Leader Prog, 2011.

**Career:** Abbott Diagnostics Global Mkt, clin chem mkt, dir, 2000-02, Abbott Labs, Sales & Serv, area dir, 2002-05, Abbott GmbH KG & Co, com training, EMEA, dir, 2005-07; Abbott Diagnostics, 1985-2010; Abbott Labs-SafricA, 2007-10; Biomerieux Inc, vpres US clinical sales, 2015-. **Orgs:** Nat Socs Black Engrs; Black MBA Asn; Nat Sales Network; Black Bus Netwok; exec comt mem, Black Bus Network; Bd Mem, Triangle Vol Ctr. **Honors/Awds:** Black Achievers Award, YMCA, 2000; NSN Lifetime Achiever Award, 2011. **Home Addr:** 12412 Beauvoir St, Raleigh, NC 27614. **Business Addr:** Vice President - US Clinical Sales, Biomerieux Inc, 100 Rodolphe St, Durham, NC 27712, **Business Phone:** (919)479-3642.

### GREY, MAURICE E.

Executive. **Career:** Edwards Sisters Realty Assocs, pres, partner, real estate broker, currently. **Orgs:** Bd mem, Harlem Bus Alliance Inc. **Home Addr:** 114 Pinecrest Dr, Hastings on Hudson, NY 10706-3702, **Home Phone:** (914)478-4808. **Business Addr:** Real Estate Broker, President, Edwards Sisters Realty Associates, 740 St Nichols Ave, New York, NY 10031-4002, **Business Phone:** (212)281-8830.

### GRIER, ARTHUR E., JR.

Executive. **Personal:** Born Mar 21, 1943, Charlotte, NC; married Linda Clay; children: Anthony & Eugene III. **Educ:** Fla A&M Univ; Cent Piedmont Community Col; Cincinnati Col Mortuary Sci, 1969. **Career:** Arthur E Grier & Arthur Grier Jr. Trust, pres; Grier Funeral Serv, owner, currently. **Orgs:** Funeral dir & Mort Asn NC; Western Dist Funeral dir & Mortuary Asn NC Inc; Nat Funeral Dir p Mort Asn NC Inc; bd mem, Nat FD; chmn, Funeral dir & Mort Asn NC Inc; Black Caucus; Big Bros Asn; Epsilon Nu Delta Mortuary Frat; Grier Heights Masonic Lodge No 752; Ambassadors Social Club; bd dir, Big Bros Asn; vpres, Western Dist Funeral dir; Eastside Coun. **Home Addr:** 2718 Monroe Rd, Charlotte, NC 28205, **Home Phone:** (704)343-0637. **Business Addr:** Owner, President, Grier Funeral Serv, 115 John McCarroll Ave, Charlotte, NC 28216, **Business Phone:** (704)332-7109.

### GRIER, BOBBY

Football coach, executive director. **Personal:** Born Nov 10, 1942, Detroit, MI; married Wendy; children: Chris & Michael James. **Educ:** Univ Iowa, BS, phys educ. **Career:** Football coach (retired), exec dir; Northwestrn Univ, offensive coord; Pittsburgh Panthers, defender; Kettering High Sch, Waterford, Mich, asst coach, 1966-69; Martin Luther King High Sch, Detroit, Mich, head coach, 1970-73; Eastern Mich, running backs coach, 1974-77; Boston Col, running backs coach, 1978-80; New Eng Patriots, offensive backfield coach, 1981, col scout, 1982-84, offensive backfield coach, 1985-92, dir pro scouting, 1993-94, dir player personnel, 1995-96, vpres player personnel, 1997-99; Houston Texans, assoc dir pro personnel, 2000-11, Sr Personnel Advisor, 2012-. **Business Addr:** Associate Director of Pro Scouting, Houston Texans, 2 Reliant Pk, Houston, TX 77054, **Business Phone:** (832)667-2000.

### GRIER, DAVID ALAN

Actor. **Personal:** Born Jun 30, 1956, Detroit, MI; son of William Henry and Aretas Ruth Dudley; married Christine Y Kim; children: Luisa Danbi; married Maritza Rivera. **Educ:** Univ Mich, BA, 1978; Yale Univ Sch Drama, MFA, 1981. **Career:** Films: A Soldiers Story, 1982; Streamers, 1982; Beer, 1984; From the Hip, 1986; I'm Gonna Git You Sucka, 1988; Boomerang, 1992; The Player, 1992; Blank man, 1992; In the Army Now, 1994; Jumanji, 1995; Tales from the Hood, 1995; McHale's Navy, 1997; Stuart Little, 1999; The Adventures of Rocky & Bullwinkle, 2000; Damned If You Do, 2000; Return to Me, 2000; East of A, 2000; 3 Strikes, 2000; 15 Minutes, 2001; I Shaved My Legs for This, 2001; How to Get the Man's Foot Outta Your Ass, 2003; Tiptoes, 2003; The Woodsman, 2004; Instant Karma; Bewitched, 2005; Little Man, 2006; Kissing Cousins, 2006; The Poker House, 2008; An American Carol, 2008; Dance Flick, 2009; Astro Boy, 2009; Something Like a Business, 2010; Hoodwinked Too! Hood vs. Evil, 2011; Peeples, 2013. Theatre: "Jackie Robinson; A Soldier's Play"; "Dream Girls; A Funny Thing Happened on the Way to the Forum", 1996-98; TV series: "In Living Color", 1990; "Preston Episodes", producer, 1995; "Premium Blend", writer, 1997; "Damon", 1998; "DAG", 2000; "Buzz Light year of Star Comm &", 2000; "Stress Test", 2000; "The X Files", 2000; "Hollywood A.D.", 2000; "Angels in the Infield", 2000; "The X Files", 2000; "King of Texas", 2002; "Chapter Forty-Two", 2002; "SesameStreet", 2002; "Crank Yankers", 2002; "Boston Public", 2002; "Tough Crowd with Colin Quinn", 2002; "King of Texas", 2002; "The Sweet Hair after", 2003; "Life with Bonnie", 2003; "The Sweet Hair after", 2003; "Boomerang", 2003; "Assaulted Nuts", 2003; "Rock Stars Do the Dumbest Things", 2003; "Cedric the Entertainer Presents", 2003; "The Truth True feld", 2004; "The Muppets Wizard of Oz", 2005; "The Muppets' Wizard of Oz", 2005; "My Wife & Kids", 2005; "The Bahamas: Part 2", 2005; "The Bahamas: Part 1", 2005; "The Davey Gee Show", producer, writer & actor, 2005; "Crank Yankers", 2002-05; "Thugaboo: Sneaker Madness", voice, 2006; "Thugaboo: A Miracle on D-Roc's Street", 2006; "Gym Teacher: The Movie", 2008; "Bones", 2010; "Law & Order: Special Victims Unit", 2010; "Happy Endings", 2013; "Randy Cunningham: 9th Grade Ninja", 2013; "The Watsons Go to Birmingham", 2013; "The Soul Man", 2014; "Comedy Bang! Bang!", 2014; "Bad Teacher", 2014; Movie: Road Hard, 2015. **Honors/Awds:** Theatre World Award for Musical, The First, 1981; Best Actor, Film Venice Film Festival, 1983; Emmy Award, 1990-94; Bronze Wrangler Award, Western Heritage Award, 2003; Groundbreaking Show, TV Land Awards, 2012. **Special Achievements:** Tony Award Nomination for The First, 1982. **Home Phone:** (212)744-5734. **Business Addr:** Actor, United Talent Agency, 9650 Wilshire Blvd Suite 500, Beverly Hills, CA 90212-2401, **Business Phone:** (310)273-6700.

### GRIER, JOHN K.

Executive, president (organization). **Personal:** Born May 15, 1950, Charlotte, NC. **Educ:** Andrews Univ, MA, 1976. **Career:** Lake Region Off Supply Inc, pres, currently. **Business Addr:** President, Lake Region Office Supply Inc, 65 Cadillac Sq Blvd Suite 2200, Detroit, MI 48226-2844, **Business Phone:** (313)963-2626.

### GRIER, JOHNNY

Manager, engineer. **Personal:** Born Apr 16, 1947, Charlotte, NC; son of Walter and Ruth Minor; married Victoria Miller; children: Lowell. **Educ:** Univ DC, Wash, DC, BA, 1987, MA, 1991. **Career:** Chesapeake & Potomac Tel Co, Wash, DC, engr; Verizon Tel Co, engr, through 2002; Nat Football League, New York, NY, referee, 1981-2004, dir, officiating off, 1981-2004, supvr officials, currently; Mid-Eastern Athletic Conf, supvr, football officials, 1998. **Orgs:** Awards comt, Pigskin Club Wash, DC, 1980. **Honors/Awds:** Butch Lambert Award for officialing, Nat Football Found, 2000. **Special Achievements:** First African-American referee in the history of the NFL with the start of the 1988 NFL season. **Home Addr:** 11905 Berrybrook Terr, Upper Marlboro, MD 20772-5323, **Home Phone:** (301)868-3069. **Business Addr:** Supervisor, National Football League Officiating Office, 280 Pk Ave, New York, NY 10017, **Business Phone:** (212)450-2000.

### GRIER, MARRIO DARNELL

Football player. **Personal:** Born Dec 5, 1971, Charlotte, NC. **Educ:** Clemson Col; Univ Tenn, Chattanooga. **Career:** Football player (retired); New Eng Patriots, running back, 1996-97, fullback, 1997; Colo Crush, running back, 2003.

### GRIER, MICHAEL JAMES

Scout, hockey player, hockey coach. **Personal:** Born Jan 5, 1975, Detroit, MI; son of Bobby and Chris; married Anne M; children: 3. **Educ:** Boston Univ. **Career:** Hockey player (retired), scout; Edmonton Oilers, right wing, 1996-2002; Wash Capitals, 2002-03; Buffalo Sabres, forward, 2003-05, 2009-11; San Jose Sharks, 2006-09; Chicago Blackhawks, pro scout, currently; St Sebastian's Sch, asst coach, Currently. **Honors/Awds:** All-Hockey East All-Star, 1994-95; Bronze Medal, Men's World Ice Hockey Championships, 2004; Lifetime, Hockey God. **Home Addr:** 638 Horse Point Rd, Belgrade, ME 04917-3032, **Home Phone:** (207)465-7483. **Business Addr:** Assistant Coach, St Sebastian's School, 1191 Greendale Ave, Needham, MA 02492, **Business Phone:** (781)449-5200.

### GRIER, PAMELA SUZETTE

Actor. **Personal:** Born May 26, 1949, Winston-Salem, NC; daughter of Clarence Ransom and Gwendolyn S Samuels. **Career:** Films: The Big Doll House, actress, 1971; The Bird Cage, actress, 1972; Black Mama, actress, White Mama, actress, 1973; Coffy, actress, 1973; Foxy Brown, actress, 1974; Friday Foster, actress, 1975; Sheba Baby, actress, 1975; Greased Lightning, actress, 1977; Fort Apache: The Bronx, actress, 1981; Something Wicked This Way Comes, actress, 1983; Stand Alone, actress, 1986; Posse, actress, 1993; Escape From LA, actress, 1996; Jackie Brown, actress, 1997; In Too Deep, actress, 1999; Holy Smoke, actress, 1999; Fortress 2, actress, 1999; Snow Day, actress, 2000; Wilder, 2000; 3 AM, actress, 2000; Ghosts of Mars, 2001; Bones, actress, 2001; Love the Hard Way, actress, 2001; Pluto Nash, actress, 2002; The Adventures of Pluto Nash, 2002; Baby of the Family, actress, 2003; Back in the Day, 2005; Bad Girls Behind Bars, 2005; The Invited, 2010; Just Wright, 2010; Larry Crowne, 2011; Woman Thou Art Loosed: On the 7th Day, 2012; The Man with the Iron Fists, 2012; Mafia, 2012. TV movies: Roots: The Next Generations, actress, 1979; Badge of the Assassin, actress, 1985; A Mother's Right: The Elizabeth Morgan Story, actress, 1992; Family Blessings, actress, 1996; Hayley Wagner, actress, Star, actress, 1999; Feast of All Saints, actress, 2001; First to Die, actress, 2003; Earthlings, actress, 2003. TV series: "Miami Vice", 1985; "Crime Story", 1986; "The Cosby Show", 1987; "Fresh Prince of Bel Air", 1994; "Martin", 1995; "The L Word", 2004-09; "Smallville", 2010. Plays: Fool for Love, 1986; Lincs, Show time, 1998; Ladies of the House, 2008. pre-production: Old School Gangstas; Rose, 2016; Grandmothers Murder Club, 2017. **Orgs:** Acad Motion Picture Arts & Scis; Screen Actors Guild; Am Fedn TV & Radio Artists; Actors Equity Asn. **Honors/Awds:** Image Award, Nat Asn Advan Colored People, 1986, 1998-06; Satellite Awards, 1998; Career Achievement Award, Acapulco Black Film Festival, 1999; Golden Slate Award Best Female Performance, 2000; Daytime Emmy Awards, 2000; Susan B. Anthony 'Failure is Impossible' Award, 2001; Black Reel Awards, 2002; Film Trumpet Award, 2003; Master of Cinema, RiverRun Int Film Festival, 2008. **Special Achievements:** Golden Globe Nominee, 1998. **Business Addr:** Actress, Innovative Artists Talent, 1505 10th St, Santa Monica, CA 90067-6022, **Business Phone:** (310)656-0400.

### GRIER, ROSEY (ROOSEVELT GRIER)

Football player, actor, community activist. **Personal:** Born Jul 14, 1932, Cuthbert, GA; son of Joseph and Ruth; married Beatrice Lewis; children: 1; married Margie Hanson; children: Denise, Roosevelt Kennedy & Cheryl Tubbs. **Educ:** Pa State Univ, BS, 1955. **Career:** Football player (retired), actor; New York Giants, right defensive end & right defensive tackle, 1955-62; Los Angeles Rams, right defensive tackle, 1963-68; Nat Gen Corp, pub rels dir; Films: The Thing with Two Heads, 1972; Skyjacked, 1972; Rabbit Test, 1978; The Glove, 1979; Roots, 1979; TheGong Show Movie, 1980; Reggie's Prayer, 1996; TV series: The Seekers, 1979; Concrete Cowboys, 1981; The List, 1983; The Simpsons, 1999. **Orgs:** Anti-Self-Destruction Prog; Soulville Found; Direction Sports; Teammates; Giant Step; Kennedy Found Ment Retarded; Are You Committed?, founder, 1984; Nat Col Athletic Asn; Alpha Phi Alpha fraternity; prog adminr community affairs, Milken Family Found; Co-founder, American Neighborhood Enterprises. **Honors/Awds:** Pro Bowl, 1956-60; Member of Los Angeles Rams Fearsome Foursome, 1963-67; Distinguished Alumni Award, Penn State, 1974; Alumni Fellow Award, 1991; New Jersey Sports Hall of Fame. **Special Achievements:** Author: The Rosey Grier Needlepoint Book for Men, Walker, 1973; The GentleGiant: An Autobiography, 1986; Rosey Grier's All-American Heroes:Multicultural Success Stories, 1993. **Business Addr:** Actor, William Morris Agency, 1 William Morris Pl, Beverly Hills, CA 90212, **Business Phone:** (310)859-4000.

### GRIFF, ROBERT OTIS. See GRIFFITH, ROBERT OTIS.

### GRIFFEY, GEORGE KENNETH. See GRIFFEY, KEN, SR.

### GRIFFEY, GEORGE KENNETH, JR. See GRIFFEY, KEN, JR.

### GRIFFEY, KEN, SR. (GEORGE KENNETH GRIFFEY)

Sports manager, consultant, baseball player. **Personal:** Born Apr 10, 1950, Donora, PA; married Alberta Littleton; children: George Jr & Craig; married Valarie. **Career:** Baseball player (retired), consultant, sports manager; Cincinnati Reds, outfielder, 1973-81; New York Yankees, outfielder & infielder, 1982-86; Atlanta Braves, outfielder & infielder, 1986-88; Cincinnati Reds, outfielder & infielder, 1988-90; Seattle Mariners, outfielder, 1990-92, spec asst player develop, hitting coach, 1992; Dayton Dragons, batting coach, 2010; Bakersfield Blaze, mgr, 2011; Cincinnati Reds, spec consult, currently. **Honors/Awds:** World Series champion, 1975, 1976; All-Star, 1976, 1977, 1980; Most Valuable Player MLB All-Star Game; 1980; Cincinnati Reds Hall of Fame, 2004. **Business Addr:** Special Consultant, Cincinnati Reds, Cinergy Field 100 Cinergy Field, Cincinnati, OH 45202, **Business Phone:** (513)421-4510.

### GRIFFEY, KEN, JR. (GEORGE KENNETH GRIFFEY, JR.)

Baseball player. **Personal:** Born Nov 21, 1969, Donora, PA; son of Ken Sr and Alberta Littleton; married Melissa; children: Trey Kenneth & Taryn Kennedy. **Career:** Baseball player (retired), consultant; Seattle Mariners, outfielder, 1989-99, 2009-10; Cincinnati Reds, 2000-08; Chicago White Sox, 2008; Mariners front off, spec consult, 2011-. **Orgs:** Hon co-chair, Aircraft Owners & Pilots Asn. **Home Addr:** 8216 Princeton Glendale Rd Suite 103, West Chester, OH 45069-1675. **Business Addr:** Professional Baseball Player, Cincinnati Reds, Cinergy Field, Cincinnati, OH 45202, **Business Phone:** (513)421-4510.

### GRIFFIN, ARCHIE

Football player, association executive, football coach. **Personal:** Born Aug 21, 1954, Columbus, OH; son of Margret and James; married Bonita; children: Anthony, Andre & Adam. **Educ:** Ohio State Univ, BS, indust mgt, 1976. **Career:** Football player (retired), football coach, association executive; Cincinnati Bengals, running back, 1976-82; US Football League, Jacksonville Bulls, 1983-85; Ohio State Univ, Columbus, OH, spec asst to athletic dir, 1985-87, asst dir athletics, 1987-94, assoc dir athletics, 1994; Ohio State Univ Alumni Asn, pres & chief exec officer, 2004-; Wendy's High Sch Heisman, spokesman, currently. Dayton Dragons, owner. **Orgs:** Founder, Archie Griffin Scholar Fund; co-founder, Archie & Bonita Griffin Found Fund; Columbus Found; Columbus Youth Found; Adv Bd ADA's Advocacy Leadership Coun, Am Diabetes Asn; James Cancer Hosp & Res Inst; hon chair, C's Hunger Alliance Endowment Fund, 2006. **Honors/Awds:** The Big 10 Most Valuable Player Award, 1973-74; Heisman Trophy Winner, 1974-75; Player of the Year, United Press Int, 1974-75; Harley Award, 1974-75; Walter Camp Award, 1974-75; Maxwell Award, 1975; Man of the Year, Sporting News, 1975; Varsity O Hall of Fame, 1981; Col Football Hall of Fame, 1986; Rose Bowl Hall of Fame, 1990; High School Hall of Fame, 1996. **Special Achievements:** Only player in NCAA history to start in four Rose Bowl games in a single career; Ranked No. 21 on ESPN's Top 25 Players In College Football History list, 2007; First player & one of two all-time to start in four Rose Bowls. **Business Addr:** President, Chief Executive Officer, The Ohio State University Alumni Association Inc, 2200 Olentangy River Rd, Columbus, OH 43210-1035, **Business Phone:** (614)292-2200.

### GRIFFIN, BERTHA L.

Business owner, president (organization). **Personal:** Born Feb 8, 1930, Blythewood, SC; daughter of Lula Woodard Cunningham and Dock Cunningham; married James; children: Wayne, Denise E Bryant & Geoffrey L. **Educ:** Greystone State Hosp, NJ state psychiat technician training course, 1956; Riverton Bio-Anal Lab Sch, Newark, NJ, 1959. **Career:** Greystone State Hosp, Newark, NJ, psychiat technician, 1953-56; Drs Burch& Williams, Newark, off mgr, 1957-63; Girl Friday Secretarial Sch, Newark, dir, 1963-71; Newark Manpower Training, Newark, dir, 1971-73; Porterhouse Cleaning, Edison, NJ, pres, 1973-. **Orgs:** Secy, Nat Asn Negro Bus & Prof Women, 1961-63; Nat Key Women Am, 1978-83; secy, Edison, NJ Bd Edn, 1978-84; delegate, White House Conf Small Bus, 1980; Small Bus Unity Coun & NJ Braint Trust Comn Small Bus; Minority Bus Enterprise Legal Defense Educ Fund Inc. **Honors/Awds:** Minority Business Woman of the Year, Newark Minority Bus Develop Ctr, 1984; Entrepreneur of the Year, YMCA, NJ, 1987; NJ Black Achievers, 1987; Venture Magazine, 1988; Recognition award, Nat Coun Negro Women, 1987. **Home Addr:** 1 Newburgh Dr, Edison, NJ 08817, **Home Phone:** (908)382-9160. **Business Addr:** President, Porterhouse Cleaning & Maintain, 6 Moyse Pl, Edison, NJ 08820-1513, **Business Phone:** (201)769-0997.

### GRIFFIN, DR. BETTY SUE

Educator, executive. **Personal:** Born Mar 5, 1943, Danville, KY; daughter of Allen James and Elise Taylor. **Educ:** Fisk Univ, BS, 1965; Ore State Univ, MS, 1976, PhD, 1985; Harvard Univ, exec leadership training; Wharton Sch, PA, exec leadership training; Univ Tex, Austin, exec leadership training; Stanford Univ, exec leadership training. **Career:** Over brook High Sch, Philadelphia, teacher, 1968-70; Model Cities, Portland, OR, placement dir, 1970-72; Ore State Univ, dir, field prog, 1972-, prof educ psych, dir teacher training prog; Ky Dept Educ, dir teacher internship prog, 1986-89, exec advisor; Griffin Group, founder, pres & chief exec officer, currently. **Orgs:** Delta Sigma Theta; Phi Kappa Phi; Eastern Star; pres, Nat Forum Black Pub Adminr, Bluegrass Chap; bd mem, Ore Gov Comn, 1978; bd mem, Gov's Com Voc Educ; bd mem, Gov's Comn Black Affairs, Ore; bd dir, Ky Long Term Policy Res Ctr; bd mem, Urban League, Lexington; Gov Scholars Prog; Girl Scouts Prog, Louisville; Nat Coun Negro Women; dir, Ky Beginning Teacher Internship Prog; bd mem, OASIS Inc; bd mem, ARCHS; consult, Mo Home Care Union. **Home Addr:** 462 Mcdowell Ave, Frankfort, KY 40601-3824, **Home Phone:** (502)695-0848. **Business Addr:** Founder & President, Chief Executive Officer, Griffin Group, 500 Merd Capital Plz Twr Suite 1728, Frankfort, KY 40601, **Business Phone:** (502)564-3678.

**GRIFFIN, BOBBY L.**
Executive, accountant. **Personal:** Born Jan 28, 1938, Prospect, TN; son of Frank and Kathleen Hogan; married Betty Wilson; children: Barbara, Lindonna & Bobbi. **Educ:** Tenn State Univ, BS, 1963; Cent Mich Univ, MA, 1985. **Career:** US Postal Serv, DC, sr acct, 1958, chmn bd dir, currently. **Orgs:** Master Mason, Charles Datcher Lodge 15, Prince Hall Affil, Wash, DC; Sigma Iota Epsilon Bus Mgt Fraternity; Tenn State Univ Alumni Asn; Cent Mich Univ Alumni Asn. **Home Addr:** 4803 Newland Rd, Suitland, MD 20746-1424, **Home Phone:** (301)420-3044. **Business Addr:** Chairman, US Postal Service, Rm 2P530 475 Lenfant Plz SW, Washington, DC 20260-0546, **Business Phone:** (202)268-3251.

**GRIFFIN, EDDIE**
Actor, movie director. **Personal:** Born Jul 15, 1968, Kansas City, MO; son of Eddie Sr and Doris Thomas; married Carla, Jan 1, 1983, (divorced 1984); children: Eddie Jr; married Rochelle, Jan 1, 2002; married Nia Rivers, Sep 8, 2011. **Educ:** Kans State Univ. **Career:** TV series: "Malcolm and Eddie", composer, producer & writer, 1996-2000, dir, 1999-2000; "The Year Without a Santa Claus", 2006; "Eddie Griffin: Freedom of Speech", exec producer, 2007; "Eddie Griffin: Going for Broke", writer, 2009; "Eddie Griffin: You Can Tell 'Em I Said It", exec producer & writer, 2011; Films: Metor Man, 1993; Foolish, 1999; Picking Up the Pieces, 2000; Double Take, 2001; John Q, 2002; Scary Movie 3, 2003; Prod, My Baby's Dadd, actor, writer & producer, 2004; Who Made the Potatoe Salad?, 2005; Date Movie, 2006; Irish Jam, 2006; Norbit, 2007; Redline, 2007; I'm Rick James, 2007; Urban Justice, 2007; Beethoven's Big Break, 2008; Young World, 2009; Hollywont, 2010; Bunyan and Babe, 2010; A Typical Love, 2012; Highway, actor & exec producer, 2012; How Sweet It Is, 2013; Last Supper, 2014. **Special Achievements:** Was number 64 on Comedy Central's list of the 100 Greatest Stand-ups of All Time; Nominee, Image Award, 2000. **Business Addr:** Actor, c/o United Paramount Network, 11800 Wilshire Blvd, Los Angeles, CA 90025, **Business Phone:** (310)575-7000.

**GRIFFIN, DR. ERVIN VEROME, SR.**
College president. **Personal:** Born May 15, 1949, Welch, WV; son of Roy and Martha; children: Ervin Jr. **Educ:** Bluefield St Col, BS, teacher educ, 1971; Western Ill Univ, MS, col stud coun & personnel serv, 1974; Va Polytech Inst & State Univ, cert advan grad study higher educ, 1979, EdD, community & jr col educ, 1980. **Career:** McDowell Co, Bd Educ, spec educ teacher, 1971-72; Western Ill Univ, asst head resident adv, 1972-74; SW Va Community Col, dir stud financial aid, 1974-78; Va Polytech Inst & St Univ, counr, 1978-79; SW Va Community Col, coordr co-curricular activ, 1979-84; Patrick Henry Community Col, dir stud develop, 1984-89; WVa St Community & Tech Col, vpres stud affairs, 1989-, pres, sr pres, 2004-06; Halifax Community Col, pres & chief exec officer, 2006-. **Orgs:** Am Col Personnel Asn; Am Asn Non-White Concerns; Am Personnel & Guid Asn; elected to Comm XI, Directorate Body Am Col Personnel Asn, 1984-87; bd dir, Tazewell Co Helpline, 1984-86; Martinsville-Henry Co, Nat Asn Advan Colored People, 1985-86; Martinsville-Henry Co Men's Roundtable, 1985-86; OIC Inc Charleston, 1991; pres, W Vir Asn, Stud Personnel Adminr, 1991-92; Nat Asn, Stud Personnel Adminr; Charleston OIC; WV SC Res & Develop Corp; bd adv, Southeastern Regional CMS Drug & Alcohol; exec bd, WVa, Asn Stud Personnel Adminr, 1992-93; Temple Faith Ministries, Cross Lanes, WVa; bd dir, Charleston Lions Club; Am Asn Community Cols; bd trustee, St Francis Hosp; Alpha Phi Alpha Fraternity Inc; Sigma Pi Phi Fraternity; Psi Chi Hon Soc; Phi Theta Kappa Hon Soc. **Honors/Awds:** Outstanding Young men of America, Jaycees SVCC, 1978; "The Pareto Optimality Problem", Minority Educ, 1981; "Adults Making the Commitment to Return to School" 1985; "Cocurricular Activities Programming, A Tool for Retention and Collaboration" 1985; Innovative Practs & Develop, Vocational Sex Equality, a monograph, 1988; The Alliance for Excellence: A Model Articulation Between the Community Coll and the Black Church, 1988; Award Excellence, Alliance for Excellence, 1989; Meritorious Service Award, Patrick Harvey Community Col, 1989; W Va St, Col, Adminr of the Year, 1991-92; Innovative Prog Award, W Va Asn Stud Personnel Adminr, 1991-93; Retention Excellence Award, Noel Levitz Ctr Stud Retention, 1991; Excelsior High Sch Nat Alumni Award, 1991; Outstanding Service Award, WVSC SGA, 1989-91; Outstanding Alumni Brother of the Year, Alpha Phi Alpha Fraternity Inc; Governors Living the Dream Award, Wva Martin Luther King Holiday Comn; Administrator of the Year, Wva State Col Stud Govt Asn; Community Impact Award, Wva Minority Bus Develop Ctr. **Special Achievements:** Publications/presentations: Innovative Pract & Develop Stud Mentoring, 1990; Bluefield St Col, A Time of Crisis and Reflection, 1991; keynote speaker: The Legacy of the Past & Challenges of the Future, Mingo County EOC, 1992; numerous others; First African Amrican administrator Soutwest Va Community College; First African American administrator Patrick Henry Community College; First African American President of Halifax Community College. **Home Addr:** 807 Elvira Rd, Dunbar, WV 25064, **Home Phone:** (304)768-5430. **Business Addr:** President, Chief Executive Officer, Halifax Community College, 100 Col Dr, Weldon, NC 27890, **Business Phone:** (252)536-4221.

**GRIFFIN, EURICH Z. (EURICH ZWINGLI GRIFFIN)**
Air force officer, lawyer. **Personal:** Born Nov 21, 1938, Washington, DC; son of Eurich and Lucille; children: Jennifer & Eurich III. **Educ:** Howard Univ, BA, 1967; Harvard Law Sch, JD, 1970. **Career:** US Fifth Cir Court Appeals Judge Paul H Roneyd, law clerk, 1971; Carlton, Fields, Ward, Emmanueal, Smith & Cutler, atty; Joyner & Jordan-Holmes, atty, sr atty, currently. **Orgs:** Am Bar Asn; Nat Bar Asn; Hillsborough Co; Fla Bar Asn; pres, Harvard Club W Coast Fla; St Petersburgh Kiwanis Club, 1971-74. **Home Addr:** 1260 Corinth Greens Dr, Sun City Center, FL 33573-8057, **Home Phone:** (813)223-9294. **Business Addr:** Senior Attorney, Joyner & Jordan-Holmes, 1112 E Kennedy Blvd, Tampa, FL 33602, **Business Phone:** (813)229-9300.

**GRIFFIN, FLOYD LEE, JR.**
State government official, executive, army officer. **Personal:** Born May 24, 1944, Milledgeville, GA; son of Floyd and Ruth Sr; married Nathalie Huffman; children: Brian E & Eric B. **Educ:** Grupton Jones Col, AS; Tuskegee Inst, BS, bldg construct, 1967; Fla Inst Tech, MS, contract procurement & mgt, 1974; Army Command & Gen Staff Col, attended 1979; Nat War Col, attended 1989. **Career:** Colonel (retired), state governement official, business owner; AUS, col, 1967-90; Slater's Funeral Home Inc, vpres, 1990, pres; Wake Forest Univ, Asst Prof, Mil Sci; Winston-Salem State Univ, asst prof, Mil Sci; Central State Hosp Found Inc, vice chair, 1991-; Ga State Senate, sen, 1994-98; Milledgeville, mayor, 2002-06. **Orgs:** Am Legion, 1967-; life mem, Omega Psi Phi Fraternity, 1979-; Prince Hall Free & Accepted Masons, 1985-; Sigma Pi Phi Fraternity, 1995-; bd dir, Nat Ctr Missing & Exploited C, 2006-; Trinity CME Church; Nations War Col Asn; 100 Black Men Am; bd trustee, Ga Mil Col; bd dir, Nat Conf Black Mayors. **Home Addr:** 103 Coventry CT, Milledgeville, GA 31061, **Home Phone:** (478)453-1030. **Business Addr:** Vice President, Slater's Funeral Home Inc, 244 N Wayne St, Milledgeville, GA 31061, **Business Phone:** (478)452-2412.

**GRIFFIN, GREGORY O., SR.**
Lawyer. **Personal:** married Debra; children: Greg Jr, Alexis Ivana & Christopher Michael. **Educ:** Morehouse Col, Atlanta, GA, BA, polit sci, 1980; Univ Pittsburgh Sch Law, Pittsburgh, PA, JD, 1983; Boston Univ Sch Law, Boston, MA, LLM, taxation, 1984. **Career:** Judicial Syst, Pittsburgh, Pa, chief prosecutor, 1981-83; AG Gaston Enterprises Inc, Birmingham, Ala, assoc gen couns, 1984-85; Birmingham, Ala, pvt pract atty, 1985-86; Legal Servs Corp Ala Inc, Selma, Ala, 1986-87; Off Atty Gen, Montgomery, Ala, Civil Litigation Div, Utilities Litigation Div, asst atty gen, 1987-; Ala State Univ, Montgomery, Ala, adj prof, income tax acct, 1989-; Ala Bd Pardons & Paroles, chief legal coun, 1995, chief coun, Legal Div, atty, 1995-2014; Montgomery County Ala, circuit judge, 2014-. **Orgs:** State Pa Bar Asn; Dist Columbia Bar Asn; State Ala Bar Asn; Tax Law Rev, Boston Univ Sch Law, 1983-84; 11th US Circuit Ct Appeals; US Dist Ct, Northern Dist Ala; Dist Columbia Bar; bd mem, Ala Bd Pardons & Paroles; bd mem, Ala Educ Tv Found Authority. **Honors/Awds:** Martin Luther King Jr Scholarship to Europe, Student Body Pres, Morehouse Col, Atlanta, GA; Law Sch Scholastic Scholar, winner, First Year Oral Argument, received honors in Oral Advocacy, judge, First Year Arguments, Univ Pittsburgh Sch Law, Pittsburgh, PA. **Home Addr:** 100 N Haardt Dr, Montgomery, AL 36105-1646, **Home Phone:** (334)318-5132. **Business Addr:** Chief Counsel, Attorney, Alabama Board of Pardons & Paroles, 301 S Ripley St, Montgomery, AL 36130-2405, **Business Phone:** (334)242-8710.

**GRIFFIN, JEAN THOMAS**
Educator, college teacher. **Personal:** Born Dec 26, 1937, Atlantic City, NJ; daughter of Clifton Washington and Alma Washington; married James A; children: Lillian Hasan, Tallie Thomas, Karen Brondidge, James A IV & Wayne. **Educ:** Temple Univ, BA, psychol, 1969, MEd, psychol, 1971, EdD Ed, psychol, 1973; Univ PA, Physicians Alcohol Educ Training Prog, 1976. **Career:** Yale Univ, asst prof dir, 1972-76; Nat Training Lab, training internship, 1973; Yale Univ, clin internship, 1975; Solomon Canter Fuller MHC, clin dir, 1976-77; Union Grad Sch, core prof, 1976-; Univ Mass Boston, assoc prof to prof, 1979-93, Union Inst & Univ, Grad Col, prof, currently. **Orgs:** Comm racism & sexism Nat Educ Asn, 1975; Women's Career devel Polaroid Corp, 1977; trainer, Nat Training Lab, 1977-83; pres bd, Women Inc. 1977-84; consult, ed, Univ Okla Col Nursing, 1978-81; fel Am Ortho psychiat Asn, 1978-85; assoc, Black Psychiat Eastern Rep, 1979; consult, training Bank Boston, 1980-84; Racism Workshop Boston State Col, 1981; adv to dir, Roxbury Community Sch, 1981-82; Fullbright Fel Barbados, 1994. **Honors/Awds:** Grant Prof Growth & Devel, 1974; Fellow Mellon Faculty Devel Award, 1982; article W African & Black Am Working Women published Journal Black Psychol, 1982; chapter in Contemporary Blk Marriage, 1984; numerous publications including Exploding the Popular Myths Review of Black Women in the Labor Force Equal Times, 1982; Kelloge Foundation Award, 1993. **Home Addr:** 1927 Kuehnle Ave, Atlantic City, NJ 08401-1703, **Home Phone:** (609)348-6383. **Business Addr:** Professor, Union Inst & University, 440 E McMillan St, Cincinnati, OH 45206, **Business Phone:** (513)861-6400.

**GRIFFIN, JUNE ESTHER.** **See BACON-BERCEY, JUNE ESTHER.**

**GRIFFIN, LEONARD JAMES, JR.**
Football player, football coach. **Personal:** Born Sep 22, 1962, Lake Providence, LA. **Educ:** Grambling State Univ. **Career:** Football player (retired), football coach; Kans City Chiefs, defensive end & left defensive end & right defensive end, 1986-93; Grambling State Univ, strength coach, currently; W Ouachita High Sch, teacher & defensive line coach. **Business Addr:** Strength Coach, Grambling State University, PO Box 4252, Grambling, LA 71245.

**GRIFFIN, LULA BERNICE**
Educator, association executive. **Personal:** Born Oct 16, 1949, Saginaw, MI. **Educ:** Tuskegee Inst, BSN, 1971; Univ Mich, attended 1974; Med Col Ga, MS, nursing, 1977. **Career:** Univ Ala, Hosp B'Ham, staff psychiat, 1971-73; Lawson State Community Col, Birmingham, AL, nursing instr, level II coordr, 1974-85; Cooper Green Hosp, Birmingham, AL, staff high risk nursing, 1982-83; Community Hosp, Birmingham, AL, staff. **Orgs:** Chi Eta Phi Sorority, 1969; Help One Another Club Inc, 1981; secy, Tuskegee Inst Nurses Alumni, 1982; vol diaster serv, Am Red Cross, 1984-85; Am Nurses Asn; Ala State Nurse Asn; Sixth Ave Baptist Church. **Honors/Awds:** Cert Psychiat & Ment Health Nurse, Am Nurses Asn, Cert Bd Psychiat & Ment Health Pract, 1985-89. **Home Addr:** 54 Lodengreen Dr, Birmingham, AL 35214, **Home Phone:** (205)791-0036. **Business Addr:** Nurse Instructor, Lawson State Community College, 526 Beacon Crest Cir, Birmingham, AL 35209.

**GRIFFIN, MICHAEL D.**
Automotive executive, engineer, president (organization). **Personal:** Born May 11, 1958, McKeesport, PA; son of Wilbur and Thelma Webb Taborn; married Brenda Olive. **Educ:** Rensselaer Polytech Inst, Troy, NY, BS, mech engineering, 1980; Univ Pa, Wharton Sch, Philadelphia, Pa, MBA, finance & mkt, 1988. **Career:** Gen Motors, sr design eng, 1980-88, sr mkt analyst, N Am passenger cars, 1988-90, asst prog mgr large & luxury vehicles, 1990-92, sr design engr, 1992-95, vehicle systs engr, 1995-2001, Vehicle Body Systs Troubleshooting, team leader, 2001-03, Vehicle Component Catalog Database, prog lead, 2003-04, Door Closing Efforts Qual-Reliability-Durability Focus, team leader, 2004-05; Essential Sound Prod Inc, founder, pres & chief financial officer, 2005-. **Orgs:** Soc Automotive Engrs, 1980-86; co-chairperson, bus corp comt, Nat Black MBA Asn, Detroit Chap, 1990-. **Honors/Awds:** US Patents (3 total), US Patent Office, 1984, 1985, 1986; Fel General Motors, 1986-88. **Home Addr:** 2616 Winter Pk Rd, Rochester Hills, MI 48309-1352, **Home Phone:** (248)210-3347. **Business Addr:** Founder, President, Essential Sound Products Inc, PO Box 81998, Rochester, MI 48308-1998, **Business Phone:** (248)375-2655.

**GRIFFIN, PERCY LEE**
Administrator, football player. **Personal:** Born Dec 10, 1945, Tougaloo, MN; son of Percy L and Mary F Perry Gray; married Andrealene Myles A; children: Gregory T. **Educ:** Jackson St Univ, BS; Ind Univ, MS, recreation admin. **Career:** Jackson State & Univ Alumni Asn Indianapolis, vpres; Detroit Lions, 1969; Indianapolis Capitols, football player, 1969-74; Indianapolis Caps Pro-Football Team, owner, pres, 1976-; City Indianapolis, Resource Recovery Coun, adminr. **Orgs:** Small Bus Asn. **Honors/Awds:** Small College All-Amer Pitts Courier. **Home Addr:** 6051 Gifford St N, Indianapolis, IN 46228, **Home Phone:** (317)257-1163. **Business Addr:** Administrator, Department of Public Works, 2700 S Belmont Ave, Indianapolis, IN 46226, **Business Phone:** (317)633-5401.

**GRIFFIN, PLES ANDREW**
Executive, government official. **Personal:** Born Apr 5, 1929, Pasadena, CA; married Lora Lee Jones. **Educ:** Univ Calif, BA, 1956; Univ SC, MS, 1964. **Career:** Pasandena Settlement Asn, exec dir, 1953-59; Pasadena Sch Dist, educr, coun, 1960-66; Pasadena City Col, coun, 1964-66; US Off Educ, consult, 1969-; Calif Dept Educ, adminr, Health Prom Off, chief off intergroup rels; Rand Corp, consult. **Orgs:** Nat All Balck Sch Educrs; Asn Calif Sch Adminr; Asn Calif Intergroup Rel Educrs; Nat Asn Advan Colored People, Sacramento Urban League; Alpha Phi Alpha; Episc Church. **Home Addr:** 1014 Foxhall Way, Sacramento, CA 95831-1709, **Home Phone:** (916)427-1489. **Business Addr:** Chief, California Department of Education, 721 Capitol Mal, Sacramento, CA 95814, **Business Phone:** (916)445-9482.

**GRIFFIN, ROBERT LEE, III**
Football player. **Personal:** Born Feb 12, 1990, Okinawa Prefecture; son of Robert Jr and Jacqueline Ross; married Rebecca Liddicoat, Jul 6, 2013; children: Reese Ann. **Educ:** Baylor Univ, BS, polit sci. **Career:** National Football League (NFL), Washington Redskins, Quarterback, 2012-.TV Series: "The League ", 2012.

**GRIFFIN, RONALD CHARLES**
Educator. **Personal:** Born Aug 17, 1943, Washington, DC; son of Gwendolyn Jones-Points and Roy John; married Vicky Lynn Tredway; children: David Ronald, Jason Roy & Meg Carrington. **Educ:** Hampton Inst, BS, 1965; Harvard Univ, Eng Dept & Pre-Law, 1965; Howard Univ, 1968; Univ VA, LLM, 1974. **Career:** Off Corp Coun Dist Columbia Govt, legal intern, 1968-69, legal clerk, 1969-70, asst corp coun, 1970; JAG Sch AUS, instr, 1970-74; Univ Ore, asst prof; Notre Dame Univ, vis prof, 1981-82; Washburn Univ, prof law, prof law emer, currently; Queens Univ, vis prof law; Fla A&M Univ, prof, currently. **Orgs:** Legal Educ Com Young Lawyers Sect Am Bar Asn; Young Lawyers Liaison Legal Educ & Admis Bar Sect Am Bar Asn; Bankruptcy Com Fed Bar Asn; Ore Consumer League, 1974-75; grievance examr Mid-W Region EEOC, 1984-85; pres, Cent States Law Sch Asn, 1987-88; vice chairperson, Kans Continuing Legal Educ Comm, 1989-90, chmn bd, 1996-99, bd mem, Brown Found, 1988-; chair bd, Mid-W People Color Legal Scholar Conference Inc, 2001-05. **Honors/Awds:** Rockefeller Found Grant; Outstanding Young Men Am Award, 1971; Outstanding Educators Am Award, 1973; Int Men Achievement, 1976; Outstanding Young Man Am Award, 1979; William O Douglas Award Outstanding Prof, 1985-86, 1994-95; Phi Kappa Phi Honor Soc; Phi Beta Delta Inter Nat Honor Soc. **Special Achievements:** Books: A Prairie Perspective on Global Warming and Climate Change: The Use of Law, Technology and Economics To Establish Private Sector Markets to Complement Kyoto", 2008; "NAFTA", Encyclopedia of the Great Plains, 2004; "Bureau of Alcohol, Tobacco, and Firearms", 2002; "The Importance of Reinventing Oscar: Versions of Wilde during the Last 100 Years", 2002; "The Trials of Oscar Wilde: The Intersection Between Law and Literature" in Processes of Institutionalisation: Case Studies in Law, Prison and Censorship, 2001. **Home Addr:** 155 South Court Ave Apt 2701, Orlando, FL 32801. **Business Addr:** Professor Emeritus, Washburn University Law School, Rm 310 1700 SW Coll Ave, Topeka, KS 66621, **Business Phone:** (785)670-1060.

**GRIFFIN, VIRGIL**
Politician. **Educ:** Boston Univ, BS, music pedag, 1981; Johns Hopkins Univ, Carey Bus Sch, MBA, bus admin, 2003. **Career:** Freddie Mac, dir cong rels, 1986-2008; Boeing Co, dir, govt opers, 2009-. **Orgs:** Bd dir, secy, Cong Black Caucus Found Inc, 2005-12; bd mem, Boeing's Employees Community Fund, 2011-; US Govt Rels & Pub Affairs. **Business Addr:** Board Member, Boeing's Employees Community Fund, 100 N Riverside, Chicago, IL 60606, **Business Phone:** (312)544-2000.

**GRIFFIN, WARREN, III.** **See G, WARREN.**

**GRIFFIN, WILLIAM MICHAEL, JR.** **See ALLAH, RAKIM.**

**GRIFFITH, DARRELL STEVEN**
Executive, basketball player. **Personal:** Born Jun 16, 1958, Louisville, KY. **Educ:** Univ Louisville, KY, commun, 1980. **Career:** Basketball player (retired), executive; Utah Jazz, 1980-93; Metro Enterprises Inc, founder & pres, currently; Univ Louisville, spec asst to pres, currently.

**Business Addr:** Founder, President, Metro Enterprises Inc, 8055 Nat Tpke, Louisville, KY 40214-4803.

### GRIFFITH, ELWIN JABEZ

Educator. **Personal:** Born Mar 2, 1938; married Norma Joyce Rollins; children: Traci. **Educ:** Long Island Univ, BA, mod lang, 1960; Brooklyn Law Sch, JD, law, 1963; NY Univ, LLM, int law, 1964. **Career:** Mod HS, teacher, 1955-56; Chase Manhattan Bank, asst couns, 1964-71; Cleveland Marshall Law Sch, asst prof, 1968; Teachers Inst & Annuity Asn, asst coun, 1971-72; Drake Univ, asst dean & asst prof, 1972-73; Univ Cincinnati, Col Law, assoc dean & prof, 1973-78; DePaul Law Sch, dean & prof, 1978-85; Fla State Univ, Col Law, prof, 1986-, Tallahassee Alumni prof, currently, Caribbean Law Inst, dir, 1988. **Orgs:** Barbados Independent Com, 1966; Bedford-Stuyvesant Jr C C, 1970-72; Black Exec Exchang Prof, 1971; Ny Bar Asn, 1963-; Am Bar Asn; Am Law Inst; ed bd, Caribbean Law & Bus; Cook County Bar Asn; arbitrator, Am Arbit Asn Cincinnati, Ohio & Chicago, Ill; advisor, Caribbean Students Asn; advisor, Black Law Students Asn; Summer Judicial Clerks Comt; chmn, Int Progs Comt; Fac Recruitment Comt; Adv Search Comt FSU Pres; chmn, Provost Search Comt; dir, Ill Inst Continuing Legal Educ, 1978-85; bd dir, Leadership Coun Metrop Open Communities Chicago, Ill, 1980-85; bd mgr, Chicago Bar Asn, 1981; speaker, Pre-Law Conf, Drake Univ, 1982; Mayor's Comt Ethics, City Chicago, 1984; exec dir, Caribbean Law Inst, 1988-; Fla Human Rights Advocacy Comt, 1989-; Am Law Inst; UWI Campus Coun, Barbados, 1996-; chmn, 1996-97, dir, Fla Asn Vol Agencies Caribbean Action; Am Immigration Lawyers Asn; adv bd mem, Chicago Vol Legal Serv Found. **Home Addr:** 2440 Monaco Dr, Tallahassee, FL 32308-5913, **Home Phone:** (850)656-6681. **Business Addr:** Tallahassee Alumni Professor, Florida State University, BK Roberts Hall Rm 336, Tallahassee, FL 32306-1601, **Business Phone:** (850)644-7731.

### GRIFFITH, DR. EZRA E. H.

Physician, educator. **Personal:** Born Feb 18, 1942; son of Vincent and Ermie; married Brigitte Jung. **Educ:** Harvard Univ, BA, 1963; Univ Strasbourg, MD, 1973; Albert Einstein Col Med, residency. **Career:** Fr Polyclinic Health Ctr, internship, 1973-74; Albert Einstein Col, chief res psychiat, 1974-77; Yale Univ, Sch Med, asst prof, 1977, assoc prof, 1982-91, Psychiat & African & African-Am Studies, prof, 1991, med dir, 2003, Clin Affairs, dep chmn, 1996; Conn Ment Health Ctr, assoc dir, 1986-89, dir, 1989-96, prof emer & sr res scientist in psychiat, dep chair for diversity & orgn ethics, currently; Yale Psychiat Quart, ed-in-chief, Dep Chair for Clin Affairs, currently; ed, J Am Acad Psychiat & Law, 1999-. **Orgs:** Bd dir, Black psychiat Am; Am Psychiat Asn; Am Acad Psychiat & Law; FALK fel; traveling fel Solomon Fuller Inst, 1976; fel WK Kellogg Found, 1980; pres, Am Acad Psychiat & Law, 1996-97; pres, Am Orthopsychiatric Asn, 1997-98; mem & ed bd, Hosp & Community Psychiat. **Honors/Awds:** Seymour Pollack Award, Am Acad Psychiat & Law, 2005; Isaac Ray Award, Am Psychiat Asn, 2010; Golden Apple Award, Am Acad Psychiat & Law, 2011. **Special Achievements:** Assoc ed, Diversity & Mental Health, 1995; ed, Journal of the American Academy of Psychiatry and Law; "Race and Excellence: My Dialogue with Chester Pierce", Univ IA Press. Ethics In Forensic Psychiatry, 1998; Race and Excellence: My Dialogue with Chester Pierce, 1998. **Home Addr:** 6 Marlborough Rd, North Haven, CT 06473-2927, **Home Phone:** (203)281-0403. **Business Addr:** Professor Emeritus, Senior Research Scientist, Deputy Chair for Diversity and Organizational Ethics, Yale University, 300 George St Suite 901, New Haven, CT 06511, **Business Phone:** (203)785-2018.

### GRIFFITH, HOWARD THOMAS

Football player, executive, broadcaster. **Personal:** Born Nov 17, 1967, Chicago, IL; married Kim; children: Howard II. **Educ:** Univ Ill, BA, speech commn, 1991. **Career:** Football player (retired), tv show host, football analyst; Los Angeles Rams, 1993, fullback, 1994; Carolina Panthers, fullback, 1995-96; Denver Broncos, fullback & wide receiver, 1997, fullback, 2000; Nat Football League, analyst; Nat Football League Europe football leagues, analyst; Big Ten Network, med rel mgr, other prim analyst & studio commentator, currently. **Orgs:** Bd dir, Nat Able Network Inc. **Honors/Awds:** Nat Football League championship rings in Super Bowl XXXII & Super Bowl XXXIII. **Special Achievements:** Third All time rusher in Illinois history. Book: "Laying it on the Line", 2001. Films: 1996 NFC Championship Game, 1997; 1997 AFC Championship Game, 1998; Super Bowl XXXII, 1998; 1998 AFC Championship Game, 1999; Super Bowl XXXIII, 1999. **Business Addr:** Studio Commentator, Big Ten Network, 600 W Chicago Ave Suite 875, Chicago, IL 60654, **Business Phone:** (312)665-0700.

### GRIFFITH, JOHN A.

Educator, government official, mayor. **Personal:** Born Dec 14, 1936, Greensburg, PA; married Patricia Cuff; children: Pamela, Gail & Jennifer. **Educ:** Ind Univ, BS, educ, hist & geog, 1960; Fairleigh Dickinson Univ, MBA, bus mgt, 1985; Seton Hall Univ, guid counr. **Career:** Regional public affairs manager, educator, counselor, (retired), executive; Asst Beaver Co, PA, social worker, 1960-62; Allen crest Juv Detention Ctr, Beaver, PA, counr, 1963-64; Nutley Pub Sch, NJ, teacher & football coach, 1964-68; Montclair Pub Sch, NJ, guid counr, 1968-69; Newark Day Care Ctr, pres; Kean Col, NJ, adj prof personnel mgt; Montclair Bd Educ, 1979-85; PSE & G, personal develop mgr, 1980-89, mgr employ develop progs, 1989-91, regional pub affairs mgr, 1991-2003; Montclair Twp Coun, dep mayor & councilman, 1988-992. **Orgs:** Edges Inc, 1970-; trustee, Urban League Essex Co, NJ, 1970-; pres, Bd Ed Montclair, NJ, 1979-85; adv bd, Nat Bank, 1979-; Am Soc Training & Develop, 1980-; founder, Montclair African Heritage Parade & Festival, 1990; Int Coun Bus Opportunities, 1985-; pres, Bloom field Better Human Rels Coun; YMCA; Montclair Fund Educ Excellence; bd dir, Katharine Gibbs Sch; Nj State Bd Educ; chairperson bd gov, Union County Col; NJ State Bd Educ; trustee, Newark Boys Chorus Sch. **Honors/Awds:** Seventy five Achievers, Black Media Inc. **Home Addr:** 23 Stephen St, Montclair, NJ 07042, **Home Phone:** (973)746-5136. **Business Addr:** Member of State Board of Education, NJ Department of Education, PO Box 500, Trenton, NJ 08625-0500, **Business Phone:** (609)292-4469.

### GRIFFITH, JOHN H.

Educator. **Personal:** Born Aug 28, 1931, Pittsburgh, PA; son of Cicero and Doris; married Euzelia Cooper; children: Nell & Ronald (deceased). **Educ:** Lincoln Univ, PA, BA, 1954; Atlanta Univ, Atlanta, MA, 1964; US Int Univ, San Diego, PhD, 1979. **Career:** Coahoma Jr Col, Clarksdale MS, instr, basketball coach, 1955-63; Atlanta Univ, instr summer sch, 1964; City Sch Dist, Rochester, NY, counr, Manpower Develop & Trng Prog, 1964-66, head counr, 1966-67, dir testing, 1967-68, plng & res dir, 1968-71; San Diego City Schs, asst dir plng & res dept, 1971-76, dir plng & res, 1976-84, dir res, 1984-. **Orgs:** Phi Delta Kappa Educ Fraternity, 1966-; San Diego Sch Admin Asn; Am Asn Sch Adminrs; Am Educ Res Asn; Asn Calif Sch Admin. **Home Addr:** 6970 Tuckaway St, San Diego, CA 92119, **Home Phone:** (619)469-8095. **Business Addr:** Director, San Diego Unified School District, 4100 Norm St Annex 7B, San Diego, CA 92103, **Business Phone:** (619)725-5672.

### GRIFFITH, REGINALD WILBERT

Architect, consultant, association executive. **Personal:** Born Aug 10, 1930, New York, NY; married Linden James; children: Courtney, Crystal & Cyrice. **Educ:** Mass Inst Technol, BA, architect, 1961, MA, city planning; Inst Int Educ, attended 1962. **Career:** Boston Redevelop Authority, architect, 1962-67; MICCO, dep exec dir, 1967-70; Howard Univ, prof, planning, 1970, chmn dept city reg planning, 1971-74; Nat Capital Planning Comn, comnr, vice chmn, 1975-79, exec dir, 1979-2000; USAID, sr policy advisor, 2000; Reg Griffith Asso, owner city planner architect; Am Inst Planners, vpres, 1977; Millennium Inst, bd founder, city planner & community develop consult, treas, currently. **Orgs:** Bd dir, Am Soc Planning Officials, 1974-76; bd dir, Am Planning Asn Found, 1971-; bd dir mem, Am Inst Architect; Georgetown Day Sch, 1972; chmn, Urban Trans Comn Consortium Univ, 1972-73; Mass Inst Technol Educ Coun, 1971; adv panel, City Baltimore, Md; bd dir, Wash DC Comn Arts Humanities; Corp DC Agenda; bd mem, DCWatch; traveling fel, Inst Int Educ. **Home Addr:** 3003 Van Ness St NW, Washington, DC 20008, **Home Phone:** (202)364-0067. **Business Addr:** Treasurer, Millennium Institute, 1634 Eye St NW Suite 300, Washington, DC 20006, **Business Phone:** (202)383-6200.

### GRIFFITH, ROBERT OTIS (ROBERT OTIS GRIFF)

Chief executive officer, football player, talk show host. **Personal:** Born Nov 30, 1970, Lonham, MD; married Amethyst. **Educ:** San Diego State Univ, BS, elec engineering power/laser optics, 1993. **Career:** Football player (retired); Minn Vikings, defensive back, 1994-2001, 2008; Cleveland Browns, defensive back, 2002-04; Ariz Cardinals, defensive back, 2005-06; CBS Channel 8, co-host, currently; Matador Enterprises Inc, chmn, pres & chief exec officer, 2002-; Nico's Steakhouse, owner, currently; United Football League, Sacramento Mountain Lions, dir pro personnel. **Orgs:** Player rep, Nat Football League Player's Asn, 1995-98; founder, Robert Griffith Found, 1998; exec mem, Nat Football League Player's Asn, 1998-2006. **Business Addr:** Chairman & President, Chief Executive Officer, Matador Enterprises Inc, 3525 Del Mar Heights Rd, San Diego, CA 92130-2122, **Business Phone:** (858)663-3405.

### GRIFFITH, YOLANDA YVETTE

Basketball player. **Personal:** Born Mar 1, 1970, Chicago, IL; children: Candace. **Educ:** Palm Beach Community Col, 1991; Fla Atlantic Univ, attended 1993. **Career:** Basketball player (retired), basketball coach; DJK Wildcats, Aschaffenburg, Ger, 1993-97; Long Beach Stingrays, forward, 1997-98; Chicago Condors, forward, 1998; Sacramento Monarchs, forward, 1999-2007; Lavezzini Basket Parma, Italy, 2000-02; UMMC Ekaterinburg, Russia, 2003-06; Seattle Storm, 2008-09; Ind Fever, adj asst coach, 2009; Ivy League univ, Dartmouth, asst coach, 2011-13; Lafayette Leopards, assitant coach, 2013-. **Orgs:** Founder, Girlz Inc. **Business Addr:** Assistant Coach, Lafayette Leopards, Kirby Sports Ctr 1st Fl, Easton, PA 18042, **Business Phone:** (610)330-5515.

### GRIFFITHS, ERROL D.

Advertising executive, salesperson, vice president (organization). **Personal:** Born Feb 5, 1956, Kingston; son of Canute U; married Joan M Nealon; children: Justin & Jason. **Educ:** Col City NY, BA, 1977; Fordham Univ, MBA, 1988. **Career:** Benton & Bowles Inc, media planner, 1977-80; Dancer Fitzgerald Sample, acct exec, 1980-82; HBO Inc, dir affil rels, 1982-85; Am Visions Mag, sales rep, 1985-86; Johnson Publ Co, vpres & advert dir, 1986-97; Disney Adventures, eastern ad sales mgr, 1997-2002, Disney Mag, advert sales exec, dir ad sales, 2002-. **Home Addr:** 220 E 87th St Apt 1G, New York, NY 10128-3142, **Home Phone:** (212)410-7020. **Business Addr:** Director of Advertising Sales, Disney Adventures & Disney Magazine, 114 5th Ave, New York, NY 10011, **Business Phone:** (212)807-5430.

### GRIGGS, ANTHONY G.

Football player, football coach, executive. **Personal:** Born Feb 12, 1960, Lawton, OK; married Bethann; children: Loren, Alexiss, Aaryn & Alexander. **Educ:** Villanova Univ, BA, commun, 1983; Ohio State Univ, commun, 1982. **Career:** Football player, football coach (retired), social worker; Philadelphia Eagles, right inside linebacker, 1982-85; Cleveland Browns, right inside linebacker, 1986-88; KansCity Chiefs, linebacker, 1989; Pittsburgh Steelers, asst strength conditioning coach, coordr player develop, dir player develop, 1992-2005; AG Squared Networks Inc, owner, pres, 1998-; Pres, Legends Found, 2009-; Crons Brand, Nat Trainer Crons Achievers Prog, 2009-; Payables 101, Vpres Bus Develop, 2010-; AthleteTrax LLC, Dir Team Alliance, 2013-; Quinnipiac Univ, teacher; Athlete Transition Inst, dir, consult; N side Christian Health Ctr, bd mem; AG Found, founder & exec dir, currently. **Honors/Awds:** Philadelphia Eagles Man of the Year, 1985. **Business Addr:** Founder, Executive Director, AG Foundation, PO Box 101261, Pittsburgh, PA 15237, **Business Phone:** (412)281-5146.

### GRIGGS, HARRY KINDELL, SR. See Obituaries Section.

### GRIGGS, JOHN W.

Executive. **Personal:** Born Dec 20, 1924, Birmingham, AL; married Leola; children: Sylvia & Linda. **Career:** E Linwood Lawnview Dev Corp, pres. **Orgs:** Bd trustee, Cleveland Model Cities, 1967-73; chmn, Model Cities Housing Comt, 1967-73; United Steel Workers Am & Jone Laughlin Steel Corp, 1970-72; mem past, Jr Sr Warden Upper Lawnview St Club, 1971-72. **Home Addr:** 3686 Mt Laurel Rd, Cleveland, OH 44121, **Home Phone:** (216)382-1960.

### GRIGGS, JUDITH RALPH

Educator. **Personal:** Born May 2, 1946, Pittsburgh, PA; married Phillip L. **Educ:** Cheyney Univ, PA, BS, 1968; Carnegie-Mellon Univ, MA, eng, 1969; Univ Pittsburgh, PhD, curric & supv. **Career:** Westinghouse HS St & Kieran Elem Sch Pittsburgh, teacher, 1968; Pittsburgh St Acad Prog, teacher, 1969-70, head teacher actg dir, 1971-72; Duquesne Univ, Coun & Learning Dept, asst dir, 1972-75, adv, assoc dir, affirmative action officer, adminr, dir, currently. **Orgs:** Founder, Together Inc, 1967-71; bd dir, Harambee Bookstore, 1969-71; An Psychol Guid Asn; educ consult, Pittsburgh Model Cities; adv bd, sec adv bd WDUQ Radio Sta & TV Sta Duquesne Univ; adv bd, Action Prog Pt Pk Col; fac, adv, Blck Stud Unoin Duquesne Univ Gospel Choir; Alpha Kappa Alpha Sor; Sixth Mt Zion Baptist Church; secy & bd mem, Alpha House, Pittsburgh; Phi Kappa Phi; bd trustee, Holy Family Inst. **Home Addr:** 772 Greenfield Ave, Pittsburgh, PA 15217. **Business Addr:** Director, Affirmative Action Officer, Duquesne University, 600 Forbes Ave, Pittsburgh, PA 15282, **Business Phone:** (412)396-6661.

### GRIGGS, DR. MILDRED BARNES

Educator. **Personal:** Born Mar 11, 1942, Marianna, AR; married Alvin Scott; children: Scott & Paul. **Educ:** Ark A M & N Col, BS, 1963; Univ Ill, MEd, 1966; Univ Ill, EdD, 1971; Clinton Jr Col, PhD. **Career:** Champaign Sch Dist, teacher, 1966-68; Univ Ill Col Educ, asst prof of voc & tech educ, 1971-76, Div Home Econs Educ, assoc prof, 1976, dean, 1995-2000, prof emer, currently. **Orgs:** Delta Sigma Theta Sorority, 1960-; Phi Delta Kappa, 1976-; consult, Nat Inst Educ, 1979-80; vpres, Am Home Econs Asn, 1979-81; Urban League; Nat Asn Advan Colored People. **Honors/Awds:** Recipient Outstanding Undergraduate Teaching Award, Univ Ill, 1975. **Special Achievements:** First African American Dean of the College of Education. **Home Addr:** 1508 Sussex Ct, Champaign, IL 61821-6987, **Home Phone:** (217)359-9020. **Business Addr:** Professor Emeritus, Dean Emeritus, University of Illinois, Education Bldg Suite 38, Champaign, IL 61820, **Business Phone:** (217)333-0960.

### GRIGSBY, ALICE BURNS

Librarian. **Personal:** Born Monroe, LA; daughter of Alex A and Ollie Hamilton Burns; married John; children: Myron. **Educ:** Southern Univ, Baton Rouge, BS, 1961; La State Univ, MLS, 1964; Univ Southern CA (USC), MPA, 1972; Univ CA, Los Angeles (UCLA), attended 1984. **Career:** Carroll High Sch, teacher, librn, 1961-65; Fresno County Libr, bookmobile librn, 1965-67; Univ Southern CA, bus sch librn, 1967-71; Santa Ana Col, ref librn, libr technol instr, 1971-84; El Camino Col, cataloging, systs develop libr, 1984-99; instrnl serv div, actg dean, 1999-03; dir learning resources, currently. **Orgs:** Chap pres, Alpha Kappa Alpha Sorority, 1959-; trustee, finance comt, Holman United Methodist Church, 1971-; nat vpres, past Nat Historian, past area VI dir, Top Ladies Distinction, Nat Stand Chmn, 1977-; Los Angeles City/CA demo cent comts, 1990-2000; bd mem, CA Asn Libr Trustees & Comnrs, 1992; vpres & pres, Inglewood Unified Schs Bd, 1997-2009; S State Systs Adv Bd, 1997-2003; pres, Southern Regional Occup Ctr Bd, 1999-2001; Calif Teachers Asn; Calif Sch Boards Deleg Assembly; pres, Inglewood Pub Libr Bd; nat officer, TLOD Serv Orgn; Southern Univ Alumni, Los Angeles Chap; adv bd, S State Coop Libr Syst. **Honors/Awds:** Outstanding Member, Southern Univ, La Chap, 1987; Assembly Dist (female) Democrat of the Year, 1988; Women's Wall of Fame, El Camino Col, 1999; Service Award, Nat Women's Polit Caucus/South Bay, 1999; Outstanding Educational Endeavors Award, 2004; Southern Ca Chaps Education Award, Nat Coun Negro Women, 2005; Service Award, Inglewood, Compton & Los Angeles City Couns; Inglewood Educators Award, Phi Delta Kappa, 2005. **Special Achievements:** Third IUSD bd mem to serve three, four-yr terms during her career and will retire from the bd at the end of the yr. **Home Addr:** 10901 Ardath Ave, Inglewood, CA 90303-2404, **Home Phone:** (323)779-5827. **Business Addr:** Director of Learning Resources, El Camino Community College, E Wing Rm 110 Schauerman Libr Main Fl, Torrance, CA 90506, **Business Phone:** (310)660-3525.

### GRIGSBY, CALVIN BURCHARD

Investment banker, lawyer, educator. **Personal:** Born Dec 24, 1946, Osceola, AR; son of Janever Burch and Uzziah P; married Cheryl; children: James, Janene & Calvin Jr. **Educ:** Univ Ariz, BA, econ & polit sci, 1968; Univ CA, Berkeley, CA, JD, 1972; Univ Pa, Wharton Sch, cert regulatory & complaince, 2003. **Career:** Pillsburg, Madison & Sutro, corp lawyer, 1972-75; Univ San Francisco, securities law prof, 1975-76; Itel Corp, nat mkt mgr, munic finance, 1975-79; Fiscal Funding, chief exec officer & gen coun, 1979; Grigsby & Assocs, chief exec officer & pres, 1981-. **Orgs:** Calif Bar Asn, 1972-; Fed Bar Asn; bd dir, Bond Mkt Asn; Charles Houstion Bar Asn, 1973-; vice chair, Nat Asn Securities Prof, 1985-; Nat Bar Asn, 1987-; bd trustee, San Francisco Symphony, 1987-; bd dir, Boalt Hall Alumni Asn, 1987-; bd trustee, UC Berkeley Found, 1990-; bd chmn, Fiscal Funding Co; bd chmn, Civic Improv Corp; Nat Asn Advan Colored People. **Special Achievements:** Author: "Fiduciary Duties of Bank Trustees," Calif Law Rev, 1972; "Buy, Borrow or Lease?" 1988; Speaker at Public Admin Conf, New Orleans, 1988. **Home Addr:** 2406 Saddleback Dr, Danville, CA 94111, **Home Phone:** (925)837-6066. **Business Addr:** President, Chief Executive Officer, Grigsby & Associates, 311 Calif St Suite 320, San Francisco, CA 94104, **Business Phone:** (415)676-2400.

### GRIGSBY, DAVID P.

Executive. **Personal:** Born Mar 6, 1949, Greenville, MS; children: Reginald, Kayla Ann & Jasohn. **Educ:** Miss Valley State Univ, BS, 1970; AMA Mgmt Acad Saranac Lake NY, mgmt, 1971; St Johns Univ Jamaica NY, MBA, 1973; Donald T Regan Sch Advan Fin Mgmt, 1984; Donald T. Regan, Sch Advan Financial Mgt, cert, financial mgt, financial mgt & mkt, 1987. **Career:** NBC TV NY City, coord, sales develop & prom, 1971-73; Metromedia TV Sales, NY City, dir, res & sales prom, 1973-75; Arbitron TV NY City, acct exec, easterntv sales, 1975-78; WENZ-AM Drum Commun Inc, pres, 1978-81; Merrill Lynch Pierce Fenner & Smith, investment broker, asst vpres, sr financial consult, 1981-89; Prudential Securities, first vpres investments, 1993;

RSL Group Int Inc, founder, pres & chief exec officer; Baron Capital Partners LLC, partner, prin, managing mem & exec vpres bus develop, 2008-11; Sr Life Ins Co, AGA Ins, team mgr, 2004-07; MRI Pharmaceut, founding partner; Grigsby Group LLC, managing mem & chief exec officer, 2007-; TGG Global Consult, LLC, managing mem & chief exec officer, 2012-; Cadiz Capital, LLC, Acquisitions & Investor Rels, pres, 2012-. **Orgs:** Second vpres, bd dir, Nat Asn Black Owned Broadcasters, 1979-81; adv bd mem, US Small Bus Admin Reg III, 1979-81; TV All C/Viewer Prom Ctr, 1979-80; chmn media comn., Fed Arts Coun, 1979-80; Manhattan Stockbrokers Club, 1984-; adv bd mem, US Small Bus Admin Reg II, 1984-87; selection comt, Small Bus Person Yr Reg II, 1985-87; issues specialist White House Conf Small Bus, 1986; publ speaker, broadcasting, Temple Univ, Hunter Univ, Union Univ, Howard Univ; Caribbean Hotel Asn; founding mem, Presidential Adv Comt; chief technol officer, Caribbean Tourism Orgn; St Lucia Hotel & Tourism Asn; Nat Ins Corp. **Honors/Awds:** Outstanding Sales US Arbitron TV Sales, 1977; Outstanding Service to Youth Salvation Army Boys Club, 1979; March of Dimes Service Award, Nat Found March Dimes, 1979; Award of Appreciation "To Be Ambitious Gifted & Black", Hunter Col, 1979; Certificate of Appreciation, Small Bus Admin, 1979 & 1981; Award of Appreciation, Asn Black Acct, 1984; Outstanding Officer, Governor Award NY Militia Award; President's Club Merrill Lynch. **Special Achievements:** Listed in Baron's Who's Who in Global Banking & Finance. **Home Addr:** 360 W 22nd St, New York, NY 10011. **Business Addr:** Executive Vice President of Business Development, Partner, Baron Capital Partners LLC, 17134 Downing St Suite 301, Gaithersburg, MD 20877, **Business Phone:** (240)277-8799.

## GRIGSBY, JEFFERSON EUGENE, III

Educator, city planner. **Personal:** Born May 30, 1944, Charlotte, NC; son of Jefferson Eugene Jr (deceased) and Rosalind; married Sharon; children: Jefferson Eugene IV & Jenna. **Educ:** Occidental Col, AB, sociol, 1966; Univ Calif, Los Angeles, MA, sociol, 1968, PhD, sociol, 1971. **Career:** Los Angeles 2000, staff consult, 1986-88; 2000 Partnership, staff consult, 1989-91; Univ Calif, Los Angeles, Grad Sch Archit & Urban Planning, prof, 1971-, Ctr Aro Studies, actg dir, 1991-92, dir, 1992-96; The Planning Group, pres, 1972-; Advan Policy Inst, dir, 1996; Nat Health Found, pres & chief exec officer, 2002-04. **Orgs:** Bd ed, J Black Studies, 1971-80; exec comt, HUD Scholars, task force, 1980-81; exec comt, Am Col Sch Planning, 1985-91, bd mem, 1988-91; bd mem, Am Gov Bd Cols & Univ; bd trustee, Occidental Col; bd educ, J Am Planning Asn, 1988-92; bd dir, 1010 Develop Corp, 1991-; co-chair, Rebuild LA Task Force Land Use & Transp, 1992; bd mem, Kaiser Found Hosps & Kaiser Found Health Plan Inc, 2004; bd mem, Calif Hosp Med Ctr & Occidental Col, currently. **Home Addr:** 4012 Farmouth Dr, Los Angeles, CA 90027-1314, **Home Phone:** (323)664-0810. **Business Addr:** President, Chief Executive Officer, National Health Foundation, 1 Kaiser Plz, Oakland, CA 94612, **Business Phone:** (213)538-0723.

## GRIGSBY, DR. MARSHALL C.

Clergy, school administrator, executive. **Personal:** Born Aug 18, 1946, Charlotte, NC; son of Eugene and Thomasina; married Harriet; children: Rosalyn Kimberly & Michelle Alexandria. **Educ:** Morehouse Col, BA, polit sci, 1968; Univ Chicago Div Sch, MTh, 1970, DMn, 1972. **Career:** Black Legis Clearing House, exec dir, 1970-72; First Unitarian Church Chicago, assoc minister, 1970-75; S Shore Community Planning Asn, proj dir, 1972; Asn Theol Sch, assoc dir, 1973-75; Howard Univ Sch Relig, asst dean & assoc prof, 1976-85; Benedict Col, pres, 1985-93; Hampton Univ, exec vpres, 1993-94, provost & chief exec officer, 1993; Grigsby & Assocs LLC, founder & owner, 2001, pres & chief exec officer, currently. **Orgs:** Fel Southern Fels Fund Inc, 1968-71; fel Fund Theol Educ Inc, 1969-71; Soc Study Black Relig, 1973-; consult, Asn Theol Schs, 1975-; nat selection panel, Fund Theol Educ Inc, 1976; consult, Relig Div Lilly Endowment, 1977-; Nat Coun Negro Women, 1979-; Columbia City Bd SC Nat; Jr Achievement Greater Columbia; bd trustee, ETV Endowment SC; bd trustee, USA Funds; chief higher educ specialist, Educ Comt U. S. Cong; sr legis assoc, US House Comt Educ & Workforce, 1993-2001; Am Soc Appraisers; managing consult, Coun OpportunityEduc; trustee, United Stud Aid Funds Inc; pres, Educ Res Systs; adv bd mem, Asn Pub & Land-grant Univs (APLU) Off Access & Success (OAS) Adv Bd. **Business Addr:** President, Chief Executive Officer, Grigsby & Associates LLC, 3703 Gawayne Ter, Silver Spring, MD 20906, **Business Phone:** (301)598-2090.

## GRIGSBY, TROY L.

Federal government official. **Personal:** Born Oct 25, 1934, Holly Grove, AR; son of Velma May Ammons and Roy Vell; children: Shari, Gloria, Alexis & Troy Jr. **Educ:** Wayne State Univ, BA, 1958, MUP, 1964. **Career:** Federal Government officer (retired); State Mich Dept Pub Welfare, social worker, 1959-62; Ypsilanti Mich Dept Urban Renewal, asst dir, 1962-64; Inkster Mich Dept Planning & Urban Renewal, asst dir & dir, 1964-68; Greater Cleveland Growth Asn, mgr community dev, 1968-71; State OH Dept Urban Affairs, dep dir, 1971-72; State OH Dept Econ & Community Develop, dep dir, 1972-75; Dept Community Develop Highland Pk, Mich, admin, 1976-79; US Dept HUD Omaha, NE, dep area mgr, 1979-82; US Dept HUD Milwaukee, WI, mgr, 1982-86; US Dept HUD Okla City OK, dep mgr, 1986-97. **Orgs:** Am Soc Planning Offs; Mayor's Comn Crisis Welfare, 1968; Mayor's Comn Urban Transp, 1968; Cleveland City Club, 1969-71; Cleveland Citizens League, 1969-71; bd dir, Plan Action Tomorrow Housing, 1970-71; Cleveland Contractor's Asst Corp, 1970-71; Mayor's Comn Trans & Redevelop, 1970-71; secy, OH State Bd Housing, 1971-75; OH Dept Transp Adv Comt Highways, Terminals & Parking, 1971-72; Gov Housing & Community Develop Adv Comn, 1971-74, staff dir; OH Water & Sewer Rotary Comn, 1971-75; state rep, Appalachian Reg Comn, 1971-75; OH Comprehensive Health Planning Adv Coun, 1972-74; Govs Conf Task Force Nat Regional Develop Policy, 1973; dir, Dayton State Farm Develop Bd, 1973-75; Coun State, Housing Fin Agencies Task Force Nat Housing Policy, 1973-74; Coun, State Community Affairs Agencies, 1974; Fed Reg Coun Task Force Inter Govt Rels, 1974; Okla Gov's Small Bus Conf Community, 1987-90; chair, Okla City Weed & Seed Prog, 1996-97; Church Redeemer vestry, 1999-2002, 2005; Okla Episcopal Church Diocean coun, 2000-04; chair, NE Home Ownership Consortium, 2000-02. **Honors/Awds:** Plaque Recognizing Outstanding Service, Mil Fed Officials Asn, Wisconsin, 1986; Governors Certificate of Recognition, Okla, 1988; Certificate of Appreciation, Okla Civil Rights Comn, 1990; numerous others. **Home Addr:** 11600 Richaven Rd, Oklahoma City, OK 73162-2987, **Home Phone:** (405)728-8229.

## GRILLO, LUIS

Manager, sports manager, basketball player. **Personal:** Born Oct 10, 1948, Washington, DC. **Career:** Basketball player, referee (retired); Sports mgr; Natl Basketball Referee Asn.

## GRIMES, CALVIN M., JR.

Executive. **Educ:** Boston Pub Sch Sst. **Career:** Grimes Oil Co Inc, Boston, MA, pres, chief exec officer & treas, 1999-. **Orgs:** Nat Minority Supplier Develop Coun Inc. **Business Addr:** President, Treasurer, Grimes Oil Co Inc, 40 Waldron's Bottom Rd Bldg 2, West Tisbury, MA 02575-0276, **Business Phone:** (617)825-1200.

## GRIMES, DARLENE M. C.

Executive. **Personal:** Born Jul 23, 1960, Boston, MA; daughter of Calvin M and Leah E Christie. **Educ:** Lesley Col, Cambridge, BS, 1983. **Career:** Grimes Oil Co, Boston, secy, currently. **Home Addr:** 29 Catawba St, Boston, MA 02119, **Home Phone:** (617)445-7917. **Business Addr:** Secretary, Grimes Oil Co, 40 Waldrons Bottom Rd Bldg 2, West Tisbury, MA 02575-0276, **Business Phone:** (617)825-1200.

## GRIMES, DOUGLAS M.

Lawyer, executive. **Personal:** Born Aug 11, 1942, Marshall, TX; married Bernadette. **Educ:** Calif St Col, BA, 1965; Howard Univ Sch Law, JD, 1968. **Career:** Ill Nat Bank & Co, Chicago, admin asst, 1968-70; Univ Ill, Col Law, asst prof law & dir, Community Involvement, 1970-71; Grimes, Barnes & Gill, atty, 1971-; City Gary, asst city atty; Gary City Ct, pub defender, judge; Douglas M Grimes PC, owner & atty, currently. **Orgs:** Deleg, Nat Black Assembly Conv, 1972-74; Police Civil Serv Comn; Gary Fire Comn; pres, Legal Aid Soc Gary; pres, Thurgood Marshall Law Asn; legal adv mem, Minority Businessmen's Steering Comt; legal adv, Lake County Corner; Gary Jaycees; adv bd mem, Urban League NW Ill Inc; Gary Frontiers Serv Club; secy, treas, bd mem, Gary Leased Housing Corp; Ill St Black Assembly; Gary chap, Ill St Black Assembly; bd dir, Gary Gus Resource Ctr; Chicago Jaycees, Southend Jaycees; legal & coun, Ill Jaycees; corp coun mem, City Gary; Gary Sch Bd Trustees. **Home Phone:** (219)938-5395. **Business Addr:** Attorney, Owner, Douglas M Grimes PC, 6941 Ironwood Ave, Gary, IN 46403-1216, **Business Phone:** (219)939-9511.

## GRIMES, NIKKI (NAOMI MCMILLAN)

Writer. **Personal:** Born Oct 20, 1950, Harlem, NY; daughter of James and Bernice McMillan. **Educ:** Rutgers Univ, Livingston Col, NB, NJ, BA, Eng, 1974. **Career:** Unique NY Mag, New York, NY, contrib ed, 1977-78; Cult Coun Found, New York, NY, lit consult, 1978-79; Swed Educt Radio, Stockholm, Sweden, writer, co-host, 1979-80; AB Exportspaok, Stockholm, Sweden, proof reader, translr, 1980-84; freelance writer, 1984-88; Walt Disney Co, Burbank, CA, ed, 1988-90; Elizabeth Harding, writer, currently; Author: Essence, Todays Christian Woman, Book Links; Books: When Daddy Prays; Malcolm X: A Force for Change; Parents' Choice Honors for Is It Far to Zanzibar? Aneesa Lee & the Weaver's Gift; Book for the Teen Age; Quick Pick for Reluctant Young Adult Readers; 100 Books for Reading & Sharing; Horn Book Fanfare; Bank Street Children's Book; Poems, 1970; Growin', 1977; Something on My Mind, 1978; Disney Babies Bedtime Stories; From a Childs Heart, 1993; Portrait of Mary, 1994; Meet Danitra Brown, 1994; C is For City, 1995; Come Sunday, 1996; It's Raining Laughter, 1997; Wild, Wild Hair, 1997; Jazmin's Notebook, 1998; A Dime A Dozen, 1998; My Man Blue, 1999; Hopscotch Love, 1999; At Break of Day, 1999; Is It Far to Zanzibar, 2000; Shoe Magic, 2001; A Pocketful of Poems, 2001; Bronx Masquerade, 2002; Talkin' About Bessie, 2002; When Daddy Prays, 2002; Under the Christmas Tree, 2002; Danitra Brown Leaves Town, 2002; Tai Chi Morning, 2004; A Day with Daddy 2004; What is Goodbye?, 2004; Danitra Brown, Class Clown, 2005; Dark Sons, 2005; Welcome, Precious, 2006; The Road to Paris, 2007; Oh, Brother!, 2007; Barack Obama: Son of Promise, Child of Hope, 2008; Make Way for Dyamonde Daniel, 2009; Rich: a Dyamonde Daniel Book, 2009; Voices of Christmas, 2009; A Girl Named Mister, 2010; Almost Zero: a Dyamonde Daniel Book, 2010; Notable Social Studies Trade Book; Planet Middle School, 2011. **Orgs:** Soc C's Bk Writers & Illusrs; Authors Guild. **Honors/Awds:** NAACP Image Award Finalist for Malcolm X: a Force for Change, 1993; Featured author, Nat Book Festival, 2003; 2003 Kerlan Award; Coretta Scott King Author Award for Bronx Masquerade; CSK Author Honor Awards, Talkin' About Bessie, Jazmin's Notebook; Children's Literature Council of California Award for Body of Work; ATB Best Children's Book Award; IMAGE Award Finalist; Best Book of the Year, New York Public Library; Coretta Scott King Author Award, 2003; Golden Dolphin Award, Southern Calif C's Book Asn, 2005; NCTE Award for Excellence in Poetry for Children, 2006; Bank Street College Children's Book of the Year Award; Horace Mann Upstanders Award for Almost Zero: a Dyamonde Daniel Book, 2011. **Home Addr:** 1222 Magnolia Ave, PO Box 172, Cororna, CA 92879, **Home Phone:** (505)268-6257. **Business Addr:** Writer, Curtis Brown Ltd, 10 Astor Pl, New York, NY 10003, **Business Phone:** (212)473-5400.

## GRIMES, VONI BUSTER

School administrator, president (organization). **Personal:** Born Dec 23, 1922, Bamberg, SC; son of Mittie and McKinley; married Lorrayne; children: Johnsie Silas, Edgar Gibson, Naomi Davis, Beverly Devan & Toni Gibson. **Educ:** Pa State Univ, attended 1951, cert, 1973; Univ Ky, cert, 1982, 1983 & 1985. **Career:** School administrator (retired); Philadelphia Ship Yard, sheet metal mechanic, 1942-44; York Hoover Corp, sheet metal worker, oper, 1947-49; Cole Steel Equip/Litton Ind, supvr, 1949-70; Pa State Univ/York Campus, dir bus serv, 1970-88; Golden Personal Care Inc, pres. **Orgs:** Himyar Temple No. 9, PHA, 1951-; master, Soc Friendship No. 42, PHA, 1956-; Nimrod Consistory No. 9, PHA, 1956-; bd dir, Indust Mgt Club, 1965-; budget chmn, York Co Red Cross, 1978-; secy, adv bd, White Rose Motor Club, AAA, 1980-; mgr, City York Bus Entrepreneur Resource Ctr, 1983-; adv, bd pres, York Co Voc-Tech Sch, 1985-88; pres, E York Lions Club, 1988-89; bd dir, 70001 (for drop-out students); lay leader Small Mem AMEZion Church. **Honors/Awds:** Voni B Grimes Day, named in honor, 1984; "Voni B Grimes Gym", named in honor, 1984. **Special Achievements:** Author, "Bridging Troubled Waters", 2008. **Home Addr:** 60 Hillery Ct, York, PA 17402, **Home Phone:** (717)751-2736. **Business Addr:** President, Golden Personal Care Inc, 58 E Cottage Pl, York, PA 17401-3141, **Business Phone:** (717)854-2123.

## GRIMSLEY, ETHELYNE

Administrator, consultant. **Personal:** Born Jun 13, 1941, Clayton, AL; married Calvin H; children: Kelvin & Karen. **Educ:** NY Community Col, AS, 1975. **Career:** Staten Island Develop Ctr, social work, 1962-80; NJ Sch Assoc, 1980-, Nominating Comt, 2004-06; Roselle Sch Bd, mem bd; Lankmark Travel, travel consult; chmn, Zoning bd, Bor Roselle. **Orgs:** Pres, Union City Sch Bd Asn, 1983-85; Nat Advan Asn Colored People; Union City Negro Bus & Prof Women's Club; pres, First Lady's Club. **Honors/Awds:** Women of Achievement Award, Leadership & Community Serv Phileman Baptist Church, 1983. **Home Addr:** 2281 Ludlow St, Rahway, NJ 07065, **Home Phone:** (732)381-1088. **Business Addr:** Chairman, Zoning Board, Borough of Roselle, 210 Chestnut St, Roselle, NJ 07203, **Business Phone:** (908)634-4540.

## GRINER, BRITTNEY (BRITTNEY YEVETTE GRINER)

Baseball player. **Personal:** Born Oct 18, 1990, Houston, TX; daughter of Ray and Sandra; married Glory Johnson, Jan 1, 2015?, (divorced 2016). **Educ:** Baylor Univ, BA, 2013. **Career:** Professional basketball player, WNBA Phoenix Mercury, 2013-, Zhejiang (China), 2013-14, Beijing (China), 2014-15; USA Basketball, player on European tour, 2011; USA Basketball Women's National Team, player, 2012-. **Honors/Awds:** Gatorade Texas Girls High School Player of the Year, 2009; Texas Miss Basketball, Texas Association of Basketball Coaches, 2009; WBCA National High School Player of the Year, 2009; Parade Magazine High School Player of the Year, 2009; USA Today High School Player of the Year, 2009; Brittney Griner Day, Houston, TX, May 7, 2009; Big 12 Freshman of the Year, 2010; Big 12 Defensive Player of the Year, 2010, 2011, 2012, 2013; Big 12 Player of the Year, 2011, 2012, 2013; ESPN.com, National Player of the Year, 2012; Honda Cup, 2012; Associated Press National Player of the Year, 2012, 2013; Naismith Trophy, 2012, 2013; Wade Trophy, 2012, 2013; Wooden Award, 2012, 2013; Ann Meyers Drysdale Player of the Year, 2012, 2013; WNBA Western Conference All-Star Team, 2013, 2014, 2015; WNBA Western Conference Player of the Week Award, 2014, 2015; WNBA Defensive Player of the Year, 2014, 2015; WNBA championship with the Phoenix Mercury, 2014; FIBA World Championships, gold medal with Team USA, 2014; HRC Visibility Award, 2015. **Special Achievements:** Number one overall pick in the 2013 WNBA draft; holds NCAA records for career blocked shots (748) and dunks by a female player (118). **Business Addr:** Phoenix Mercury, 201 East Jefferson St, Phoenix, AZ 85004, **Business Phone:** (602)462-2849.

## GRISHAM, ARNOLD T.

Banker, administrator. **Personal:** Born Dec 3, 1946, Chicago, IL; son of John and Gladys; married Jane; children: Kristine & Jonathan. **Educ:** De Paul Univ, BS, mgt, 1970, Grad Sch Bus, MBA, finance, 1973. **Career:** Continental Ill, second vpres, 1975-81; Wells Fargo, exec vpres, 1981-99; Wells Fargo Corp Serv, vpres & dep mgr, 1981-82, vpres & mgr, 1982-86; Wells Fargo Bank, Oakland, Calif, vpres & loan team mgr, 1986-88, regional vpres, 1988-89, sr vpres & regional mgr, 1989-94, exec vpres, 1994; Civic Bank Com, pres, coord & chief lending officer, 1999-2001; Civic Ban corp, bd mem; Korn & Ferry Int, partner, managing dir, 2000-01; Grisham Group LLC, managing partner, 2002-06, pres, chief exec officer; Alta Alliance Bank, pres & chief exec officer, 2006-10, dir, currently; Western Alliance Bancorporation, exec vpres, 2006-10; Tri-Valley Bank, chmn, pres & chief exec officer, 2011-. **Orgs:** Pres, Marcus Foster Educ Inst, 1989; chmn, Cult Diversity Comt, Wells Fargo Bank, 1990; bd mem, Wells Fargo Bank; bd regents, Holy Names Col, 1991-; United Negro Col Fund, E Bay Adv Comt, 1991-; chair, Fin Comt, Hanna Boys Ctr, 1992-; adv bd, E Oakland Youth Develop Ctr; Exec Leadership Coun; co-chair, Parents Coun, More house Col, Atlanta, GA; found bd, C Hosp Oakland; adv bd, Col Fund Northern Calif; adv coun, De Paul Univ Col Com, Exec Leadership Coun, Wash, DC; bd mem, Fed Res Bank San Francisco, 2008-10; trustee, DePaul Univ, 2011-; Founder & Comt Chmn, Last Mile Found, 2003-. **Home Addr:** 7831 Hansom Dr, Oakland, CA 94605, **Home Phone:** (510)635-7513. **Business Addr:** Chairman & Chief Executive Officer, President, Tri Valley Bank, 3160 Crow Canyon Rd, San Ramon, CA 94583.

## GRISSOM, MARQUIS DEAN

Baseball player. **Personal:** Born Apr 17, 1967, Atlanta, GA; married Tia. **Career:** Baseball player (retired), baseball executive; Montreal Expos, outfielder, 1989-94; Atlanta Braves, 1995-96; Cleveland Indians, 1997; Milwaukee Brewers, 1998-2000; Los Angeles Dodgers, 2001-02; San Francisco Giants, 2003-05; Chicago Cubs, 2006; Marquis Grissom Baseball Asn, founder, currently; Wash Nat, coach, 2009. **Home Addr:** Hwy 100, Hogansville, GA 30230, **Home Phone:** (706)637-6213. **Business Addr:** Founder, Marquis Grissom Baseball Association Inc, 1400 Veterans Memorial Hwy Suite 134-257, Mableton, GA 30126, **Business Phone:** (770)745-1244.

## GRIST, ARTHUR L.

Educator. **Personal:** Born Apr 29, 1930, Tampa, FL; son of Edwin and Eleanor; married Nancy Jackson; children: Michelle, Arthur & Michael. **Educ:** Ohio State Univ, BS; Univ Mich, MPH. **Career:** Cleveland Div Health, pub health sanitarian, 1955-61; Health Zoning & Housing, consult, 1961-65; Southern Ill Univ, Carbondale, fac, 1961, Edwards ville, asst vpres, 1965-70, asst pres, 1970-76, spec asst vpres bus affairs, 1976-79, asst prof, 1968-82, assoc prof emer, 1982-. **Orgs:** Black Caucus Health Workers, 1969-71; treas, St Louis Health Syst Agency, 1970-78; vpres, St Clair City Health & Welfare Coun, 1974-80; Edwardsville City Planning Comn, Zoning Bd Appeals, 1975-81; pres, Metro E Health Serv Coun Inc, 1978-80; City Edwards ville Pk & Recreation Bd, 1985-86; Alderman Ward 4 Edwardsville, Ill, 1986-93; life mem, Kappa Alpha Psi; Am Pub Health Asn; Nat Environ Health Asn; Madison Co Red Cross; YMCA; United Fund; United Way; treas,

Metro E Labor Coun; vpres, Alliance Reg Community Health MO, Ill; Reg Adv Group, Ill; Reg Med Prog. **Home Addr:** 1912 McKendree Dr, Edwardsville, IL 62025-2650, **Home Phone:** (618)656-8965. **Business Addr:** Associate Professor Emeritus, Southern Illinois University, PO Box 1122, Edwardsville, IL 62026-1653, **Business Phone:** (618)650-2000.

## GRIST, RONALD

Executive. **Personal:** Born New York, NY; son of Arthur and Ena; married Joyce Foust. **Educ:** City Col NY, BBA. **Career:** Aetna Bus Credit, New York, NY, vpres; Fidelity Bank, Philadelphia, PA, sr vpres; Fidelcorp Bus Credit Corp, New York, NY, exec vpres; CIT Group/Credit Finances Inc, exec vpres, chief fin officer. **Home Addr:** 1921 Lark Lane, Cherry Hill, NJ 08003, **Home Phone:** (856)429-5073.

## GROCE, CLIFTON ALLEN

Football player, football coach. **Personal:** Born Jul 30, 1972, College Station, TX. **Educ:** Tex A&M Univ, BA, econs, parks, recreation & leisure studies, 1994. **Career:** Football player (retired), coach; Indianapolis Colts, running back & fullback, 1995-98; New Eng Patriots, 1998; Cincinnati Bengals, fullback & running back, 1998-2000; Navasota Independent Sch Dist, running back coach, 2010-; Sheldon ISD, d-line, 2014-. **Business Addr:** Running Back Coach, Navasota Independent School District, 705 E Washington Ave, Avenue Navasota, TX 77868, **Business Phone:** (936)825-4200.

## GROFF, PETER CHARLES

Government official. **Personal:** Born Apr 21, 1963, Chicago, IL; son of Regis and Ada; married Regina C; children: Malachi Charles & Moriah Cherie. **Educ:** Univ Redlands, BA, 1985; Univ Denver Law Sch, JD, 1992; Univ Denver, PhD, 2008. **Career:** XM Satellite Radio, co host; Groff/Ellison Polit Report, ed chief; City Denver, asst councilwoman A Haynes, 1991-94; Ray Romer Gov Campaign, polit dir, 1994, City Denver, sr asst to mayor, 1994-96; Univ Denver, exec dir & sr lectr, 1996-; Vadent Evans LLC, coun, 2000-; State Colo, state rep, 2001-03, Colo Senate, 33rd dist, 2003-09; Campbell Chap AME Church, pastor, currently; MCG2 Consult LLC, prin; Nat Alliance Pub Charter Schs (NAPCS), pres & chief exec officer, 2011. **Orgs:** Founding fel, Future Focus, 1996-; exec bd, Urban League Denver, 1998-; Colo Unity, comt chair, 1998-; Shorter AME Church, sr steward, 2000-; founder & exec dir, Univ Denver, CO, ctr African Am Policy; vis fel, Johns Hopkins Univ Sch Educ, 2011; dir, Ctr Faith-Based & Neighborhood Partnerships. **Special Achievements:** First African-American to hold the position of President of the Senate in state history. **Home Addr:** 1400 Pontiac St, Denver, CO 80220, **Home Phone:** (303)355-0126. **Business Addr:** Founder, Executive Director, University of Denver, 2199 S University Blvd, Denver, CO 80208, **Business Phone:** (303)871-2000.

## GROFF, REV. REGINA COLEEN

Educator, clergy. **Personal:** Born Jul 17, 1971, Brooklyn, NY; daughter of John and Bonita Darby; married Peter; children: Malachi Charles & Moriah Cherie. **Educ:** Duke Univ, BA, philos, 1993; Duke Divinity Sch, Mdiv, 1996; Univ Denver, PhD, educ, 2004. **Career:** St Marys Acad, religion teacher, comn service dir, 1996-98; Barney Ford Elem Sch, reading asst, 1998-99; Jr Achievement, ed mgr, 1999-2000; Shorter Community African Methodist Episcopal Church, assoc minister christian educ, sr assoc minister & asst late Reverend Langston Boyd; Campbell African Methodist Episcopal Church, pastor, 2004-09; Grand Canyon Univ, online instr, 2010-; MCG2 Consult, chief acad officer, 2011-. **Orgs:** Colorado Coalition Against Domestic Violence; Nat Coalition Against Domestic Violence; Women Ministry & Rocky Mountain Dist; Future Black Women Leaders Colo; Colo Black Women Political Action. **Home Addr:** 1400 Pontiac St, Denver, CO 80220, **Home Phone:** (303)355-0126. **Business Addr:** Chief Academic Officer, MCG2 Consulting, 13024 Queen Chapel Rd, Woodbridge, VA 22193.

## GROOMES, DR. FREDDIE LANG

School administrator, educator. **Personal:** Born Jacksonville, FL; married Dennis A McLendon Sr; children: Linda Walton & Derek R. **Educ:** Fla A&M Univ, BS, coun & guid, 1962, MEd, coun & guid, 1963; Fla State Univ, coun & human systs, PhD, 1972. **Career:** Proj Upward Bound, coordr, counr, 1965-68, assoc dir, 1968-70; Fla A & M Univ, dir inst res, 1970-72; Fla State Univ, exec asst pres, dir human affairs, assoc prof, Human Serv & Studies, exec asst & dir equal opportunity & Pluralism vpres acad affairs, Off Univ Human Resources, exec asst to pres, 2003 retired. **Orgs:** Consult, Hewitt Assoc Inc; Am Coun Educ; Col & Univ Pers Asn; chmn, Fla Gov Comn Status Women; Fla Human Rels Comn; Fla Coun Indian Affairs; exec bd, Am Asn Affirm Action; trustee, Edward Waters Col; nat secy & nat parliamentarian, Alpha Kappa Alpha Sorority Inc; chmn, Fla Gov's Comn Status Women; Fla's Const Rev Comn; W. K. Kellogg Found, Nat Leadership Bd. **Honors/Awds:** Rockefeller Fel, 1976; Outstanding Educators Am; Kappa Delta Pi Nat Hon Soc. **Home Addr:** 3306 Wheatley Rd, Tallahassee, FL 32305, **Home Phone:** (850)576-4060. **Business Addr:** Assistant to the President, Florida State University, 301 Westcott Ave Admin Bldg, Tallahassee, FL 32306-1370, **Business Phone:** (850)644-5283.

## GROOMS, DR. HENRY RANDALL

Engineer, manager. **Personal:** Born Feb 10, 1944, Cleveland, OH; son of Leonard D and Lois Pickell; married Tonie Marie Joseph; children: Catherine, Zayne, Nina, Ivan, Ian, Athesis, Shaneya, Yaphet, Rahsan, Dax, Jevay & Xava. **Educ:** Howard Univ, BS, civil engineering, 1965; Carnegie-Mellon Univ, MS, civil engineering, 1967, PhD, civil engineering, 1969. **Career:** DC Hwy Dept Wash, DC, hwy engr, 1965; Peter F Loftus Corp Pittsgh, PA, struct Engr, 1966; Blaw-Knox Co Pittsgh, PA, struct engr, 1967-68; Rockwell Int Downey, Calif, struct engr, 1969-2006, engineering mgr; Boeing Integrated Defense Systs, engineering mgr, Strength S Struct Anal & Design, sr mgr, currently. **Orgs:** Kappa Alpha Psi, 1963-; Tau Beta Pi, 1964-; Am Soc Civil Engrs, 1965-; Sigma Xi, 1967-; scoutmaster, Boy Scouts Am, 1982-88; coach, Youth Basketball, 1984-; coach, Youth Soccer, 1985-; Watts Friendship Sports League, 1990-; co-founder, Proj Reach Scholar Found, 1994-; Watts Friendship Sports League. **Honors/Awds:** Col Recruiter of the Year, 1979-80; Engineer of the Year, Rockwell Int Space Div, 1980; Alumni Merit Award, Carnegie-Mellon Univ, 1985; Honoree, Western Res Hist Soc, Cleveland OH, Black Hist Arch Proj, 1989; Outstanding Engineering Volunteer Award, 1999; Elected fellow of the African Scientific Institute, 2002; Golden Torch Awards, Nat Soc Black Engr, 2004. **Special Achievements:** Author & co-author of 19 technical papers. **Home Addr:** 17608 Sidwell St, Granada Hills, CA 91344-1053, **Home Phone:** (818)360-6606. **Business Addr:** Senior Manager, Strength S Structural Analysis & Design, Boeing Integrated Defense Systems, 5301 Bolsa Ave, Huntington Beach, CA 92647, **Business Phone:** (714)896-5195.

## GROOMS, LEJUANA HARDMON. See HARDMON, LADY.

## GROOMS-CURINGTON, TALBERT LAWRENCE, SR.

Government official. **Personal:** Born Oct 21, 1956, Dayton, OH; son of James and Lucy M Grooms; children: Talbert L Jr. **Educ:** Sinclair Col, AS, lib arts, 1981; Wilberforce Univ, BS, mgt; Univ Dayton, MEd. **Career:** Wright Patterson AFB, acct, finance asst, 1975; Dayton Metrop Housing Authority, purchasing agt, 1977, purchasing assoc dir, 1987, asset mgt dir, currently; Miami Univ, Ohio, purchasing mgr, 1986; Wilberforce Univ, prof, currently; Grooms Curington Group LLC, pres, chief exec officer, 2005-. **Orgs:** Vice regional dir, Phi Beta Sigma; Beta Xi Sigma Chap; Citizens Fed Bank, CRA Bd; bd mem, United Way; Kiwanis Club; Nat Asn Housing & Redevelop Officials; Nat Purchasing Coun; Nat Asn Black Accountants; Nat Asn Blacks Govt; Cong Adv Coun; Nat Asn Advan Colored People; vice regional dir, Phi Beta Sigma Fraternity; Purchasing Mgr's Asn; Nat Pres, Wilberforce Univ Alumni Assoc. **Home Addr:** 5146 Weddington Dr, Dayton, OH 45426-1961, **Home Phone:** (937)248-0217. **Business Addr:** Director, Contracts, 400 Wayne Ave, Dayton, OH 45410, **Business Phone:** (937)910-7600.

## GROSVENOR, VERTAMAE

Writer, journalist. **Personal:** Born Apr 4, 1938, Hampton County, SC; children: Kali & Chandra. **Career:** Elan Mag, contrib ed; Essence Mag, contrib ed; Plain Brown Rapper, 1975; SC Arts Comn, Lit Task Force; Penn Ctr, writer-in-residence; Amsterdam News, Chicago Courier, writer food column, currently; Nat Pub Radio's Cult Desk, corresp, "Seasonings", host, currently; Bks: Vibration Cooking, 1970; Thursday & Every Other Sunday Off, 1972. **Orgs:** People United to Save Humanity. **Honors/Awds:** Robert F Kennedy Award; Ohio State Award; Columbia Award; DuPont-Columbia Award, 1990; Communications Excellence to Black America Award, 1991; National Association of Black Journalists Award, 1992. **Special Achievements:** Has written for The New York Times, The Village Voice, The Washington Post, Life, Redbook, Ebony, and Viva; Appeared on various TV programs including The Phil Donahue Show, The Today Show, ABC's Nightline, BET's Our Voices, and The Galloping Gourmet; Had a featured role in Julie Dash's American Playhouse movie, Daughters of the Dust, for which she was also a language consultant. **Business Addr:** Correspondent, National Public Radio, 635 Mass Ave NW, Washington, DC 20001, **Business Phone:** (202)513-2000.

## GROTH, CHAD

Executive. **Personal:** Born Apr 25, 1970, Minneapolis, MN; son of Karl; children: Chazz Marie. **Educ:** Minneapolis Tech Col, attended 1992. **Career:** Minn Timberwolves, player liaison, 1989-93; W Coast Hoops Report.com; Harlem Globetrotters, dir scouting & mgr basketball opers, 1993, vpres Stand & Player Personnel & chief scout, currently; Chad Groth Found, exec dir, currently; Area Codes Basketball Serv, founder, 2008-. **Orgs:** Pres, Area Codes Basketball Scouting Serv; dir, Areacodesbasketball.com. **Home Addr:** PO Box 44732, Ahwatukee, AZ 85064-4732, **Home Phone:** (602)753-5669. **Business Addr:** Vice President of Standards & Player Personnel, Scout, Harlem Globetrotters, 400 E Van Buren St Suite 300, Phoenix, AZ 85004-2257, **Business Phone:** (602)258-0000.

## GROVES, DR. DELORES ELLIS

School administrator. **Personal:** Born Jan 29, 1940, Shelby County, KY; daughter of David Irvin and Mary Powell; married Clyde; children: Angela D Payden & Robin L Ham. **Educ:** Spalding Col, BS, educ, 1966; John Carroll Univ, MA, educ, 1972; Cleveland State Univ, admin cert, 1979; Univ Akron, EdD, 1996. **Career:** Sch adminr (retired); Case Western Res Univ, professsional fel, 1998-99; Shaker Heights City Sch Dist, teacher/ adminr, elem prin, 1970-2000; Independent-Self Employed, educ consult, 2000-; Eagle Heights Acad, adminr, 2003-05; Asn Supv & Curric Develop, consult & trainer, 2006. **Orgs:** Pres & organizer, VIP's Social & Civic Club, 1973-75; dean pledges, Phi Delta Kappa Sorority, 1979-80; Phi Delta Kappa Fraternity, 1981-; consult, Cuy Sp Educ Serv Ctr, 1983-85; deleg & co rep, OAESA, 1984-87; health fair coordr, Shaker Heights Int Group, 1985; fund raiser & co-chairperson, Delta Sigma Theta, 1985-87; NAESP, 1978-; deleg rep assembly, 1985-87, nat nominating chair person, NABSE, 1986; Olivet Inst Bapt Church; pres, Shaker Heights Interest Group, 1991; bd mem, Cleveland C's Mus, 1992-94; pres, Links Inc, cleveland chap, 1993-, treas, 1994-97; bd mem & secy, Gt Clev Delta Fund Life Develop Ctr, 1997-; adminr, Eagle Heights Acad, 2003-05. **Home Addr:** 3616 Rolliston Rs, Shaker Heights, OH 44120.

## GROVES, HARRY EDWARD. See Obituaries Section.

## GRUNDY, CHESTER

Administrator. **Personal:** Born Aug 22, 1947, Louisville, KY; children: 2. **Educ:** Univ Ky, attended 1969. **Career:** Ky State Univ, Frankfort, interim vpres stud affairs; Univ Ky, UK African-Am Stud Affairs, dir, currently, Martin Luther King Jr Cult Ctr, dir Multicultural Stud Programming, stud affairs officer, currently. **Orgs:** Co-founder, Roots & Heritage Festival, Martin Luther King Jr celebration; Civil Rights Movement. **Business Addr:** Dir UK African-Am Stud Affairs, University of Kentucky, 557 Patterson Off Twr, Lexington, KY 40506-0027, **Business Phone:** (859)257-5641.

## GRUNDY, DALLAS A.

Executive director, administrator. **Personal:** Born Oct 24, 1972, Philadelphia, PA; son of Donald and Yolande. **Educ:** Rutgers Univ, BS, civil engineering, 1995, MBA, mgt info syst & mkt, 1999. **Career:** Mt Zion AME Ch, consult, 1987-; Taylor, Wiseman & Taylor, engineering-in-training, 1992-96; MBS Enterprises, co founder, vpres, 1995-99, exec vpres, 2000-; Hackensack Meadowlands Develop Comn, team leader, 1997-98; Lucent Tech, mkt strategy & staff oper mgr, 1997-98, staff oper mgr, 1998-2000; BCT Partners, founder & partner, 1999-; Somerset Christian Col, dir bus affairs, 2004-06; Rutgers Grad Sch Educ, assoc dean, finance & admin, 2006-; Univ Penn, Penn Law, assoc dean, bus affairs, 2015-. **Orgs:** Pres, Rutgers Chap Nat Soc Black Engrs, 1994; pres, Rutgers Nat Black MBA Asn, 1997-98; Renaissance Econ Develop Corp, 2000-; asst youth dir, First Baptist Ch Youth Ministry, 2000-; fel leadership prog, Partnership NJ, 2005-; chairperson, First Baptist Church Tech Adv Bd; founding trustee, Lawnside Educ Found; fel AABHE Leadership & Mentoring Inst, 2012-. **Home Addr:** 52 Almond Dr, Somerset, NJ 08873, **Home Phone:** (732)568-0698. **Business Addr:** Chief Operating Officer, BCT Partners Inc, 105 Lock St, Newark, NJ 07103, **Business Phone:** (973)622-0900.

## GUEST, WILLIAM, II

Singer. **Personal:** Born Jun 2, 1941, Atlanta, GA. **Career:** Gladys Knight and the Pips, mem; TV Series: "Operation: Entertainment", 1968; Della, 1969; "The Hollywood Palace", 1969; "The Andy Williams Show", 1970; "The Ed Sullivan Show", 1968-71; "Toast of the Town", 1968-71; "Bandstand", 1970-85; "Flip", 1972-73; "The Gladys Knight & the Pips Show", 1975; "Dinah!", "The Richard Pryor Special?", 1977; "The Midnight Special", 1973-80; "The Third Annual Black Achievement Awards", 1980; "Barbara Mandrell and the Mandrell Sisters", 1981; "The Suzanne Somers Special", 1982; "The 25th Annual Grammy Awards", 1983; "The 4th Annual Black Achievement Awards", 1983; "Benson", 1984; "The 11th Annual American Music Awards", 1984; "Too Pooped to Pip", 1984; "Solid Gold", 1985; "Ebony/Jet Showcase", 1986; "The 7th Annual Black Achievement Awards", 1986; "The 12th Annual People's Choice Awards", 1986; "The New Hollywood Squares", 1987; "Soul Train", 1971-88; "When A. Lansing Loves a Woman", 1996; "Murphy Brown", 1996. **Honors/Awds:** Inductee, Rock and Roll Hall of Fame, 1996; Lifetime Achievement Award, Rhythm & Blues Found, 1998. **Business Addr:** Vocalist, c/o MCA Records, 70 Universal City Plz 3rd Fl, Universal City, CA 91608, **Business Phone:** (818)777-4500.

## GUFFEY, EDITH A.

Statistician, executive, association executive. **Personal:** Born Sep 16, 1953, Kansas City, KS; married Jerry. **Educ:** Baker Univ, BA, sociol & psychol, 1975; Univ Kans, MSW, concentration admin & social work, 1987. **Career:** Div Family Serv, State Mo, child support investr, 1977-79; Kans City, Mo, child support enforcement officer, 1977-79; Rape Victim Support Serv, Douglas County, Kans, dir & co dir, 1982-84; Kans Dept Social & Rehab Serv, Home & Community-Based Serv, case mgr home & community based serv, 1983-84; Univ Kans, Off Stud Rec, asst to dir, 1984-87, asst dir, 1987-90, assoc dir admis, 1991; United Church Christ, secy, 1990-99, exec officer, assoc gen minister, 1999, chief operating officer, 1991-2011, Kans & Okla, conf minister, 2013-; Pa Conf United Church Christ, interim assoc conf minister, 2012. **Special Achievements:** First African American female & lay person to hold the post of secy of the 1.5 million-mem group of United Church of Christ. **Business Addr:** Conference Minister, Conference Director, United Church Christ, 1245 Fabrique, Wichita, KS 67218-3529, **Business Phone:** (316)686-4331.

## GUICE, REV. GREGORY CHARLES

Counselor, clergy. **Personal:** Born Nov 13, 1952, Detroit, MI; son of Rufus and Corrine Bowens; married Deena Dorsey; children: Merrin & Morgan; married Francine. **Educ:** Ky State Univ, Frankfort, KY, BA, hist & sociol, 1975; Marygrove Col, Detroit; Ctr Humanistic Studies, Detroit, MI, MA, clin psychol, 1986. **Career:** St Theresa Sch, Detroit, Mich, teacher, 1983-86; Black Family Devt Inc, social worker, 1986-88; Don Bosco Home for Boys, Detroit, Mich, social worker, 1988-89; Gesu Sch, Detroit, Mich, counr & teacher, 1989; specialist & family counr, 1990-93; Detroit Unity Temple, rev, spiritual counr, co-minister; Unity Christ Church, Ft Wayne, Ind, sr minister; Unity Church Lake Orion, unity minister, 2000-. **Orgs:** Co-founder, 'Be The Best That You Can Be', 1986-; jr deacon, Prince Hall Masonic Lodge, 1989-; bd mem, Unity Inst; bd mem, Unity Village. **Honors/Awds:** Mason of the Year, Prince Hall Lodge, 1990, 2007; Michiganian of the Year award, Detroit News, 2008. **Special Achievements:** Selected as one of the 10 Best Educators, Ebony Magazine, 1988; listed in "Who's Who in Black America", 2000, 2003. **Home Addr:** 16586 Trinity Ave, Detroit, MI 48219, **Home Phone:** (313)531-9137. **Business Addr:** Reverend, Unity Minister, Unity Church of Lake Orion, 3070 Baldwin Rd, Orion Township, MI 48359, **Business Phone:** (248)391-9211.

## GUICE, LEROY

Judge. **Personal:** Born Dec 12, 1944, Fayette, MS; married Rosemary Thompson; children: Cliff & Cedric. **Educ:** Co-Lin Jr Col, continuing educ, 1976; Miss Col, continuing educ, 1984; Univ Miss, 1984. **Career:** USAF, aircraft frame tech, 1964-68; Thomasville Furniture Co, plant production supvr, 1972-85; Jefferson County, justice ct judge, 1984-; bus owner. **Orgs:** Brother, United Methodist Church, 1972-; mason, brother Jefferson Lodge, 1984; judge, Justice Ct Judges Asn, 1984-. **Home Addr:** 1011 Hwy 33 Rt 2, PO Box 35, Fayette, MS 39069-5483, **Home Phone:** (407)654-2496. **Business Addr:** Judge Justice Court, Jefferson County District 1, PO Box 1047, Fayette, MS 39069.

## GUIDRY, DAVID

Executive. **Personal:** Born Aug 20, 1957, Palmetto, LA; son of Raphael and Agnes; married Ava Dejoie; children: Raphael, Amber & Bryce. **Educ:** La Tech Univ, attended 1977; TH Harris Voc Tech, assoc, 1978; Dartmouth Univ, Amos Tuck Sch Bus. **Career:** Bibbins & Rice Electronics, technician, 1979-82; Guico Mach Works, pres & chief exec officer, 1982-. **Orgs:** Bd mem, Gulf S Minority Purchasing Coun, 1989; Chamber Com, 1989; La Regional Vo-Tech Bd, 1990; app mem, Gov Task Force African Trade & Finance, 1992; Black Econ Develop Coun, 1990; bd mem, Harvey Canal Indust Asn, 1991; adv bd,

W Jefferson Tech Col; gov app, La Workforce Develop Comn, La Econ Develop Coun, La Hwy Safety Comn; vice chair, Jefferson Bus Coun; bd, Meadowcrest Hosp; bd dir, Fed Res Bank Atlanta, New Orleans br; Boy Scouts Am; La Minority Bus Coun; Bur Govt Res, chmn; Secy Univ New Orleans Found; Exec Cabinet, Chamber New Orleans & River Region; bd dir, People's Bank; bd dir, La C's Mus; Northshore Bus Coun; bd dir, vice chmn audit comt, First Bank & Trust, currently; trustee, Baptist Ministries Found, currently; chmn, bd commissioners Port New Orleans; Christian Health Ministries Found Bd trustee, currently; bd dir, Idea Village, currently. **Home Addr:** 1608 Longbridge Dr, Marrero, LA 70072, **Home Phone:** (504)348-2075. **Business Addr:** President, Chief Executive Officer, Guico Machine Works Inc, 1170 Destrehan Ave, Harvey, LA 70058, **Business Phone:** (504)340-7111.

## GUILFORD, DIANE PATTON

Librarian. **Personal:** Born Feb 15, 1949, Detroit, MI; daughter of Kathleen Droughn and Nesbitt B; married Samuel. **Educ:** Ky State Univ, Frankfort, KY, BA, 1970; Atlanta Univ, Atlanta, GA, MSLS, 1971. **Career:** Librarian (retired): Atlanta Pub Libr, Atlanta, GA, asst br head, 1971-73; Frostproof Pub Libr, Frostproof, Fla, consult, 1972; Romulus Community Schs, Romulus, Mich, media specialist, 1973-77; Fairfax County Pub Schs, Springfield, VA, head libr, 1978-04. **Orgs:** Vpres, Nat Coun Negro Women, Reston Chap, 1982-83; chairperson, Southeastern Libr Asn, Outstanding Southeastern Authors Comt, 1987-89; vpres, Alpha Kappa Alpha/Lambda Kappa Omega Chap, 1990-91; chairperson, Va Libr Asn, Sch Libr Sect, 1991-92; charter mem, Old Dom Chap, The Links. **Honors/Awds:** Human Relations Award, 1986, Commendation for Prof Excellence, 1987, Fairfax County Schools; Am Library Asn Award for Programs for Youth in Sch & Public Libraries, 1994. **Home Addr:** 11808 Foxclove Rd, Reston, VA 20191, **Home Phone:** (703)476-4917.

## GUILLAUME, DR. ALFRED JOSEPH, JR.

Educator, chancellor (education), executive. **Personal:** Born Apr 10, 1947, New Orleans, LA; married Bernice Forrest; children: Alfred III. **Educ:** Xavier Univ LA, 1968; Brown Univ, AM, 1972, PhD, 1976. **Career:** Fulbright-Hays Teaching Asst, Int Inst Educ, 1974-75; Xavier Univ, coord admis, 1977-78, dean freshman studies, 1978-80, dean arts & sci, 1980; Humbol dt St Univ, vpres acad affairs, staff emer, 1994-99; Ind Univ, S Bend, exec vpres acad affairs; United Way St. Joseph County, interim pres, chief exec officer, currently. **Orgs:** Bd, Coun Develop Fraternity LA, 1976-; Baudelaire & Nature, S Cent Mod Lang Asn Conv, 1977; asst treas, Col Lang Asn, 1978-81; sect chmn, S Cent Mod Lang Asn, 1978-79; pres, LA Col Hon Coun, 1980-81; gov appointee & mem acad adv coun, Develop Fr LA; La Athenee; assoc mem, Sociedad Nacional Hispanica; presentor & discussion leader, Competency Assessment Teacher Educ; panelist, Ed Testing Serv Workshop Testing, Dallas, Tex; consult, Methods Improving Oral Commun Target Lang. Am Conf Acad Deans, Nat Asn Col Deans Registrars & Admis Officers, La Coun Deans Arts & Sci; Asn Am Col; Am Asn Teachers Fr; Col Lang Asn; bd dir, United Way St. Joseph County; pres, Fischoff Nat Chamber Music Asn. **Special Achievements:** Conversation with Leopold Sedar Senghor on His Poetry & Baudelaire's, French Review 1978; The Baudelairian Imagination, Positive Approaches to Nature", Coll Lang Assoc Jrnl 1979; To Spring (Au Printemps), New Laurel Review, 1980; Women and Love in the Poetry of the Free People of Color, South Central Modern Lang Assoc Conv, 1980; The Emotive Impulse & the Senghorian Response to Nature, Coll Lang Assoc Conv, 1980; Literature in Nineteenth Century LA, Poetry & the Free People of Color, Jambalaya Public Library Lecture Series, 1980; Jeanne Duval as the Cornerstone of the Baudelairian Imagination, South Central Modern Lang Assn Convention, 1982; Love Death & ith in the New Orleans Poets or Color, Southern Quarterly, 1982; Joanni Questi, Monsieur Paul, LA Literature 1984; Le Divin Mystere, Religious Fervor in the Literature of the Free People of Color, Southern Conf on Christianity in Literature 1984. **Home Addr:** 7523 Wayfarer St, New Orleans, LA 70126, **Home Phone:** (504)286-0898. **Business Addr:** Interim President, Chief Executive Officer, United Way of St. Joseph County, 3517 E Jefferson Blvd, South Bend, IN 46615-2282, **Business Phone:** (574)232-8201.

## GUILLAUME, ROBERT (ROBERT PETER WILLIAMS)

Actor, television producer. **Personal:** Born Nov 30, 1927, St. Louis, MO; married Donna Brown; children: 1; married Marlene; children: 2. **Educ:** St Louis Univ; Wash Univ. **Career:** Theater appearances: Fly Blackbird, 1962; No Place to Be Somebody, 1969-70; Fire in the Mindhouse, 1970-71; Purlie, 1971-72; Benito Cereno, 1975-76; Guys & Dolls, 1976; Don Juan, 1977; The Phantom of the Opera, 1990. Films: Super Fly TNT, 1973; Seems Like Old Times, 1980; The Kid with the Broken Halo, 1982; The Kid with the 200 IQ, exec producer, 1983; Prince Jack, 1985; Wanted: Dead or Alive, 1987; Christmas, producer & dir, 1988; Lean On Me, 1989; Death Warrant, 1990; The Meteor Man, 1993; First Kid, 1996; The Land Before Time VIII: The Big Freeze, voice, 2001; 13th Child, 2002; The Adventures of Tom Thumb & Thumbelina, voice, 2002; Extreme Skate Adventure, voice, 2003; Big Fish, 2003; Unchained Memories, 2003; The Lion King 1 1/2, voice, 2004; Half-Life 2, voice, 2004; Kingdom Hearts II, voice, 2005; Jack Satin, 2005; Mugabe the Musical, 2007; Satin, 2008; The Secrets of Jonathan Sperry, 2009; Satin, 2011; Columbus Circle, 2012. TV series: "Soap", 1977-79; "Benson", 1979-86; "North & South", 1985; "John Grins Christmas Special", exec producer & dir, 1986; "Perry Mason: The Case of the Scandalous Scoundrel", 1987; "Fire & Rain", 1989; "The Robert Guillame Show", exec producer & actor, 1989; "Sports Night", 1998; "Sports Night", 1998-2000; "His Body guard", 1998; "The Happy Prince", 1999; "Moesha", 2000; "Quo Vadimus", 2000; "La Forza Del Destino", 2000; "Bells & a Siren", 2000; "April Is the Cruelest Month", 2000; "Draft Day: Part 2-The Fall of Ryan OBrian", 2000; "All This & Turkey Too", 2000; "8 Simple Rules for Dating My Teenage Daughter", 2003; "Every Picture Tells a Story", 2003; "Century City", 2004; "To Know Her", 2004; "Half-Life 2", voice, 2004, 2006-07; "CSI: Crime Scene Investigation", 2008; "Storyline Online", 2008. **Orgs:** Screen Actors Guild; Am Federation Television & Radio Artists. **Honors/Awds:** Emmy Award for Outstanding Supporting Actor in a Comedy, 1978-79; Emmy Award for Oustanding Lead Actor in a Comedy, 1984-85; Star on the St. Louis Walk of Fame, 1999; Image Awards, Nat Asn Advan Colored People; Golden Nymph, Outstanding Male Actor, 2001; Interactive Achievement Award, 2005; Star on the Hollywood Walk of Fame. **Special Achievements:** Only African American actor to win the Lead Comedy Actor award. **Home Addr:** 4925 Palo Dr, Tarzana, CA 91356. **Business Addr:** Actor, Peters Entertainment Production Inc, 1438 N Gower, Los Angeles, CA 90028.

## GUILLEBEAUX, TAMARA ELISE

Administrator, educator. **Personal:** Born Philadelphia, PA. **Educ:** Butler Univ, BA; NY Univ, MA; Pa Ballet Co Sch Dance; Judimar Sch Dance; Marion Cuyjet; Essie Marie Dorsey Sch Dance. **Career:** Metrop Opera, Lincoln Ctr, Develop Dept, admin, 1986-96; Macy's, Consult, 2007-. **Orgs:** Alpha Kappa Alpha Sor Inc; bd dir, Saraband Ltd; dir, Scholar Develop Saraband Ltd, 1985-; Nat Asn Female Exec; spec adv, bd dir, Robin Becker & Co; panelist, NY Found Arts, 1992-95; Nat Coalition 100 Black Women, 1994-96. **Honors/Awds:** Rosenblith Scholarship Award; soloist 51st Boule, Alpha Kappa Alpha Sor, 1984; partic, Int Olympics Black Dance Art Festival, 1984. **Business Addr:** Consultant, Macy's, PO Box 8113, Mason, OH 45040.

## GUILLORY, KEVEN

Television news anchorperson, journalist. **Personal:** Born Feb 20, 1953, Berkeley, CA; son of Emma Crenshaw and Jesse; married Arleigh Prelow; children: Alison & Kara; married Donna Barati; children: Maiya. **Educ:** Col Alameda, 1972; Univ Calif, Berkeley, CA, BA, eng, 1974; Stanford Univ, Stanford, CA, fel, 1991. **Career:** KALX, KRE, reporter, producer; KDIA, dir, producer; KSOL, San Mateo, Calif, news/pub affairs reporter, 1974-75; KBLX, Berkeley, Calif, news dir, 1976-79; K101, San Francisco, Calif, pub affairs dir, 1979-80; Youth News, Oakland, Calif, teacher, 1980-82; KITS, news & pub affairs dir; KALW, news dir; KQED Inc, San Francisco, Calif, producer/reporter, founding mem, 1985-2012; Northern Calif Pub Broadcasting, producer, 1985-2012; Journalist, 2003-12. **Orgs:** Mem, Nat Asn Black Journalists, 1981-; former pres, bd mem, Bay Area Black Journalists Asn, 1983-; RTNDA, Radio Tv News Dirs Asn; Bass Anglers Sportsmen Soc; bd mem, Crisis Support Serv Alameda County; chmn bd, Youth Radio Int. **Honors/Awds:** Associated Press News Award for Feature News, Associated Press, 1989, 1990; John Knight Journalism Fellowship, Stanford University, 1990-91. **Home Addr:** 2015 Woolsey St, Berkeley, CA 94703-2527, **Home Phone:** (415)553-2368.

## GUILLORY, LINDA SEMIEN

Business owner. **Personal:** Born Oct 4, 1950, Lake Charles, LA; daughter of Leo Semien and Adeline Semien; children: Tina G & Ashley F. **Educ:** Univ Colo, BA, 1985. **Career:** Mountain Bell, mgr, 1970-85; Transformative mgt, Inc, pres, owner; Handz Designs, owner, currently. **Orgs:** Bd mem, Coun Black Comt, 1988-91; vpres, Coun Black Prof, 1989-90; bd mem, Denver Victims Serv Ctr, 1989-; Mayor's Comt Employ, 1992-. **Honors/Awds:** Continued Leadership in Pluralism Award, 1987; Dedication to Women of Color Project Award, US West, Inc, 1989. **Special Achievements:** Published manual, Myth and Methods for Managing a Multi-cultural Workforce, 1989. **Home Addr:** 40 Watch Hill Dr, Colorado Springs, CO 80906, **Home Phone:** (719)226-8047. **Business Addr:** Owner, Handz On Designs, PO Box 7040, Denver, CO 80207-0262, **Business Phone:** (303)333-0187.

## GUILLORY, DR. WILLIAM A.

Executive director, educator. **Personal:** Born Dec 4, 1938, New Orleans, LA; children: William Jr & Daniel S. **Educ:** Dillard Univ, BS, 1960; Univ Calif, Berkeley, CA, PhD, 1964. **Career:** Howard Univ, asst prof, prof chem, 1965-69; Naval Ord Sta, consult, 1967-76; EPA, adv com, 1972-75; Prof Black Chemists & Chem Engrs, nat chmn, 1972; Nat Acad Sci, consult, 1973-74; Drexel Univ, assoc prof, prof chem, 1969-74; Univ Utah, assoc prof, chem, 1974-76, prof & chmn, dep chem, 1976; Innovations Int Inc, chief exec officer, owner & founder, 1983-; Ctr Creativity & Inquiry, exec dir, currently. **Orgs:** Post doctoral fel Nat Sci Found, Paris, 1964-65; fel Alfred P Sloan Found, 1971-73; adv panel, NSF, 1974-77; Beta Kappa Chi; Sigma Xi; Alpha Chi Sigma; Am Phys Soc; AAAS; NY Acad Sci; Phi Kappa Phi; Am Chem Soc. **Honors/Awds:** Outstanding Educators America, 1972; Merit Award, City New Orleans, 1974; Danfort Found Asn, 1975. **Special Achievements:** Presented over 4, 000 seminars, N & S Am, Gt Brit, Europe, Mex, Asia Pac &Can; facilitated seminars over 300 corps; author of numerous publications, including, "EMPOWERMENT" and "The Living Organization --- Spirituality in the Workplace". **Home Addr:** 1610 Park Pl, Park City, UT 84098-7512, **Home Phone:** (435)649-7818. **Business Addr:** Executive Director, The Center for Creativity and Inquiry, 5442 South 900 East Suite 551, Salt Lake City, UT 84117, **Business Phone:** (800)693-3594.

## GUILMENOT, RICHARD ARTHUR

President (organization), executive, accountant. **Personal:** Born Mar 15, 1948, Detroit, MI; married Melanie Williams. **Educ:** Fisk Univ, BA, 1970; Northwestern Univ, MBA, 1972. **Career:** Ted Bater Adv, acct exec, 1972-74; BBDO Adv, acct supvr & vpres, 1974-77; Mingo Jones Guilmendt, vpres & dir client serv, 1977-79; Warner Am Satellite Ent Co, vpres mkg, 1980-82; GCI, chief exec officer & pres, currently. **Orgs:** Adv, Amsterdam News, 1977-82; dir, Nat Urban League, 1978-81; barileur, Omega Psi Phi. **Home Addr:** 90 Grandview Ave, Great Neck, NY 11020-1510, **Home Phone:** (516)487-6308. **Business Addr:** President, Chief Executive Officer, GCI, 92 Grandview Ave, Great Neck, NY 11020, **Business Phone:** (516)482-0152.

**GUINIER, CAROL LANI.** See GUINIER, LANI.

## GUINIER, LANI (CAROL LANI GUINIER)

Educator, lawyer. **Personal:** Born Apr 19, 1950, New York, NY; daughter of Ewart and Eugenia Paprin; married Nolan A Bowie; children: Nikolas. **Educ:** Radcliffe Col, BA, 1971; Yale Law Sch, JD, 1974. **Career:** US Dist Judge, Damon Keith, clerk, 1974-76; Us Dept Justice, 1977-81; Wayne County Juv Ctr, referee, 1976-77; US Dept Justice, Civil Rights Div, 1977-81; NAACP Legal Defense Fund, 1981-88; New York Univ, adj law prof, 1985-89; Univ Pa, from assoc law prof to prof, 1988-92; Harvard Law Sch, law prof, 1998-2001; Bennett Boskey, law prof, 2001-. Books: The Tyranny of the Majority: Fundamental Fairness in Representative Democracy, 1994; Becoming Gentlemen: Women, Law Schools and Institutional Change, 1997; Turning a Civil Rights Setback into a New Vision of Social Justice, 1998; Who's Qualified?: A New Democracy Forum on Creating Equal Opportunity in School and Jobs, 2001; The Miner's Canary: Enlisting Race, Resisting Power, Transforming Democracy, 2002; Tyranny of the Meritocracy: How Wealth Became Merit, Class Became Race and Higher Education Became a Gift from the Poor to the Rich, 2015. **Orgs:** Asst Coun, Nat Asn Advan Colored People Legal Defense & Educ Fund Inc, 1981-88; Am Law Inst, 1996-; Penn Nat Comn Soc, Community & Cult, 1996-98; trustee, Open Soc Inst, 1996-; prin investr, RACETALKS; bd dir, Juv Law Ctr, Philadelphia, PA, 1992-98; bd dir, Juv Law Ctr, 1992-98; Asn Am Law Sch, 1992-93; adv Comt, Southern Regional Coun, 1992-95; bd dir, NOW Legal Defense Fund, 1990-96; Stanford Univ, Ctr Advan Study Behav Sci, fel, 2009. **Business Addr:** Bennett Boskey Professor of Law, Harvard Law School, 1563 Mass Ave, Cambridge, MA 02138-2996, **Business Phone:** (617)495-8304.

## GUITANO, ANTON W.

Executive, president (organization), auditor. **Personal:** Born Jul 5, 1950, Brooklyn, NY; son of Whitney J and Blanche Epps; married Leslie Marie Ferguson; children: Jessica Lynn, Jennifer Whitney & Jason. **Educ:** St Peters Col, Jersey City, BS, 1971; NY State Dept Educ, cert pub acct, 1979. **Career:** Price Waterhouse, NY, sr auditor, 1971-78; CBS Inc, NY, sr dir auditing, 1978-83, vpres finance & gen auditor, 1988, sr vpres, chief financial officer, 1996-2000, exec vpres, opers & chief financial officer, 2005-07; CBS Tv Network, controller; CBS Tv Stas, NY, controller, 1983-86, sr vpres, vpres finance, exec vpres opers & chief financial officer; CBS Tv Network, NY, controller, 1986-88, Viacom TV Stas Group, sr vpres & chief financial officer; CBS Radio, sr exec vpres opers & chief financial officer, 2007-09; CBS Local Media, chief operating officer, 2009-. **Orgs:** Am Inst Cert Pub Acct, 1979, NYSSCPA, 1979; pres, Walden & Country Woods Homeowners Asn, 1980-84; Broadcast Financial Mgt Asn, 1983, Nat Asn Broadcasters, 1983; bd gov, NY State Chap, Inst Internal Auditors, 1995-98; Financial Exec Inst, 1995; NY Internal Audit Indust Comn, 1995. **Home Addr:** Crane Rd, Carmel, NY 10512. **Business Addr:** Executive Vice President of Finance and Operations, Chief Operating Officer, CBS Radio Inc, 1271 Avenue of the Americas Fl 44, New York, NY 10020, **Business Phone:** (212)649-9600.

## GULLATTEE, ALYCE C.

Physicist, physician, educator. **Personal:** Born Jun 28, 1928, Detroit, MI; married Latinee G; children: Jeanne, Audrey & Nat. **Educ:** Univ Calif, BA, 1956; Howard Univ Col Med, MD, 1964. **Career:** St Elizabeth's Hosp, rotating internship, 1964-65, gen prac, 1965-66, residency psychiat, 1965-68, med officer psychiat, 1968-71; Howard Univ Col Med, asst prof, assoc prof, psychiat & behaviorial sci, clin asst prof, prof; Family Pract, 1970-, physician; Nat Inst Ment Health, Addictive Substances Abuse, career teacher, 1974-77; DC Gen Hosp, internship; George Washington Univ Hosp, resident. **Orgs:** Med bd, J Nat Med Asn, 1967-; rec secy, All Psychiat Progress, 1967-70; consult, Juv & Domestic Rels Ct, Arlington County, 1968-; Hosp Dels, Nat Med Asn, 1968-75; consult, EEO, 1969-70; chief consult, Drug Educ Prog, Juv Ct, Arlington, 1969, vchmn, 1969-70, chmn elect, 1970-71, chmn, 1971-72; observator consult, Coun Int Orgn, Am Psychiat Asn, 1969-73; chief consult, Arlington County Drug Abuse Treat Prog, Prelude, 1969-; chmn ad hoc comn, HEW, Poor C & Youth, 1969-; co-coordr, Drug Abuse Sem, Nat Coun Juv Ct Judges, 1970; rep Am Psychiat Asn, Chicago, 1970; Nat Psychiat Consult & Prog Develop; Nat Coun Negro Women, 1972-; Com Psychiat & Law, Am Psychiat Asn, 1973-; chmn Prog Comt, Am Psychiat Asn, 1974-75; chmn, Grad Com Int Progs, Howard Univ, 1974-; chmn, Comt Int Med, Nat Med Asn, Med-surg Soc, 1974-78; sr adv & co-founder, Stud Nat Med Asn, Wash; Nat Inst Drug Abuse Task Force, 1975-; Psychiat-Neurol Secy, Nat Med Asn. **Honors/Awds:** Academic Honors Zoology, Univ Calif, 1956; Citizens Award, Outstanding Contributions to Community, Santa Monica Nat Asn Advan Colored People, 1960; First Award Clinical Acumen, Howard Univ, Col Med, 1964; Magna Cum Laude Internship Award, St Elizabeth Hosp, 1965; Outstanding Teacher Award, Howard Univ, Col Med, 1973; Career Teacher Award, Nat Inst Ment Health, 1974-; Outstanding Black Woman of 1970, Nat Med Asn; nominee TV Emmy Award, Wash Chap Nat Acad TV Arts & Scis, NBC Spl The Disabled Mind; fel, Inst Soc, Ethics & Life Scis Hastings-on-Hudson, 1975-77. **Special Achievements:** Selected as member by the President of US for Nat Adv Com Juvenile Justice & Delinquency Prevention, US Dept Justice, 1975-76. **Home Addr:** 6408 16 St NW, Washington, DC 20012, **Home Phone:** (202)726-7692. **Business Addr:** Professor, Howard University College of Medicine, 2041 Georgia Ave NW, Washington, DC 20060, **Business Phone:** (202)865-6611.

## GULLIVER, ROBERT E.

Executive, vice president (organization). **Educ:** Cornell Univ, BS, indust & labor rels, 1992; Dartmouth Col, Amos Tuck Sch, MBA, 1997; Univ Pa, Wharton Sch, Securities Indust Inst, attended 2008. **Career:** GTE Serv Corp (now Verizon), human resources assoc, 1992-94; GE Capital, human resources specialist retailer financial serv, 1994-95; PwC Consult, 1997-99; Citigroup, dir human resources, 1999-2004; Wells Fargo, exec vpres & head human resources, 2004-10; Nat Football League (NFL), chief human resources officer, exec vpres, 2010-. **Orgs:** Bd mem, Am Red Cross; bd mem, Community Sch Arts, Charlotte, NC. **Business Addr:** Chief Human Resource Officer, Executive Vice President, National Football League, 280 Park Ave, New York, NY 10017.

## GUMBEL, BRYANT CHARLES

Television broadcaster. **Personal:** Born Sep 29, 1948, New Orleans, LA; son of Richard Dunbar and Rhea Alice LeCesne; married June Carlyn Baranco; children: Bradley Christopher & Jillian Beth; married Hilary Quinlan. **Educ:** Bates Col, BA, 1970. **Career:** Black Sports Mag, ed, 1971, ed-in-chief, 1972; KNBC-TV, weekend sportscaster, 1972-73, sportscaster, 1973-76, sports dir, 1976-81; NBC's Rose Bowl Parade & coverage, co-host, 1975; NBC, Grandstand Show, co-host, 1976; Super Bowl XI, co-host, 1977; 19-Inch Variety Show, 1977; KNBC, per& co-host, 1977; NBC, co-host, 1982-97; Olympics, Seoul, S Korea, host, NBC, 1988; CBS, host, 1997-98; CBS, co-host, 1999-2002; PBS Show, co-host, 2002; HBO, host, currently; WABC-TV, guest host, 2006; NFL Network, announcer, 2006-08. Films:

The Weather Man, 2005. TV series: "Major League Baseball All-Star Pregame Show", writer, 1981; "Cosby", 1999; "Real Sports with Bryant Gumbel", writer, 2005. **Orgs:** Am Fedn Tv & Radio Artists; SCS-BA; NATAS. **Honors/Awds:** Emmy Award, 1976, 1977, 2006, 2007; Golden Mike Award, Los Angeles Press Club, 1978, 1979; Edward R Murrow Award, Overseas Press Club, 1984; Frederick D Patterson Award, United Negro Col Fund; Martin Luther King Award, Cong Racial Equality; NAACP Image Awards; Inter Nat Journal Award; Africa's Future Award, US Comm United Nations C's Fund; Alfred I DuPont-Columbia University Award, 2005; Peabody Award; Leadership Award, African-Am Inst; Trumpet Award. **Special Achievements:** Guest appearances in various films including: The Weather Man. **Home Addr:** , Westchester, NY. **Business Addr:** Host, NBC, 30 Rockefeller Plz, New York, NY 10112, **Business Phone:** (212)664-4444.

### GUMBEL, GREG
Actor, television journalist. **Personal:** Born May 3, 1946, New Orleans, LA; son of Richard and Rhea Alice LeCesne; married Marcy Kaszynski; children: Michelle. **Educ:** Loras Col, BA, eng, 1967. **Career:** Am Hosp Supply Co, sales rep, 1968-73; WMAQ-TV, Chicago, sports anchor, 1973-81; ESPN, SportsCenter, co-anchor, 1981-89; CBS TV, NFL Today show, co-host, 1990-94, NBC Sports, host & play-by-play announcer, 1994-98, sportscaster, 2002; NFL Preview, host, currently; NFL Live, Olympic Winter Games, host, 1994; Tv show: "play by play", announcer, 1991-92. **Honors/Awds:** Recieved 3 Emmy Awards. **Special Achievements:** Selected to host 1994 Winter Olympic Games in Lillehammer, Norway; First black play by play announcer at a Super Bowl, 2001; Actor: Ebony Jet Showcase, 1982; 1999 AFC Championship Game, 2000; The Best Man Holiday, 2013. **Home Addr:** Intl Mgmt Group 22 E 71st St, New York, NY 10021-4911. **Business Addr:** Host, Play-by-Play Announcer, NBC-TV, c/o Scott Cooper, New York, NY 10112, **Business Phone:** (212)664-4444.

### GUMBY, DR. JOHN WESLEY
Educator. **Personal:** Born May 22, 1942, Harrisburg, PA; son of William H and Anna E; children: John W Jr & Angela D. **Educ:** Cheyney State Univ, BS, 1968; Western Md Col, MEd, 1975; Columbia Univ, PhD, 1998. **Career:** Harrisburg City Schs, varsity football coach, head track coach, 1968-70, span teacher, 1968-74, sec prin, 1975-97. **Orgs:** NAACP, 1960-; Chosen Friends Lodge No 43 (PHA), 1963-, chaplain, 2014-15; dir, Sible town Reunion Comt, 1972-; Phi Delta Kappa, 1975-; basileus, Omega Psi Phi Frat Inc, 1981-82. **Home Addr:** 2204 Chestnut St, Harrisburg, PA 17104-1335.

### GUNDY, ROY NATHANIEL, JR.
Computer scientist. **Personal:** Born Sep 26, 1967, Philadelphia, PA; son of Elizabeth. **Educ:** Drexel Univ, BS, com engineering opers mgt, 1991. **Career:** Channel 6, talk show panelist, 1983-85; Bonatsos, database analyst, 1987-; Thomas Jefferson Univ Hosp, micro comput technician, 1987-88, ic analyst, 1992-; Devon Systems Int Inc, network analyst, 1988-89; Johnson & Johnson, dir stands strategies & emerging technol, currently. **Orgs:** Philadelphia Regional Introd Minorities Engineering, 1982-; Region 2 programs chair, Nat Soc Black ENRs, 1986-; guide right chair, Kappa Alpha Psi, 1990-; Philadelphia Area Comput Soc, 1992-. **Honors/Awds:** Achievement in Commun Indust, Nat Black Media Coalition, 1983; Sales Achievement, Timberland Co, 1986; Scholar, Kodak, 1987-88; Scholar, Club Cornucopia, 1988-90. **Home Addr:** 1834 W 73rd Ave, Philadelphia, PA 19126, **Home Phone:** (215)387-3789. **Business Addr:** Director, Stands Strategies & Emerging Technology, Johnson & Johnson Co, 1 Johnson & Johnson Plz, New Brunswick, NJ 08933.

### GUNN, DR. ARTHUR CLINTON
Educator. **Personal:** Born Apr 29, 1942, New Castle, PA; son of John O Sr and Magnolia Hill Murray. **Educ:** Wilberforce Univ, Wilberforce, OH, BS, educ, 1964; Atlanta Univ, Atlanta, GA, MS, libr sci, 1969; Univ Pittsburgh, Sch Libr & Info Sci, Pittsburgh, PA, PhD, 1986. **Career:** Educator (retired); City Univ NY, fac; Del State Col, Dover, DE, librn, 1969-71; Howard Univ, Wash, DC, librn, 1971-76; Univ Md, Col Pk, Md, adj prof, 1972-76; Univ Pittsburgh, Pittsburgh, Pa, librn, 1983-86; Wayne State Univ, Detroit, Mich, prof, 1986-, Clark Atlanta Univ, Sch Libr & Info Studies, dean, 2004. **Orgs:** Am Libr Asn, 1969-; Am Libr & Info Sci Educ, 1986-; consult, Gen Motors Corp, 1988-; pres, Asn African-Am Librn, 1988-; chair, Govt Rels Comt, Asn Libr & Info Sci Educ; interim libr dir, Atlanta Univ Ctr. **Home Addr:** 630 Merrick St Suite 810, Detroit, MI 48202, **Home Phone:** (313)831-9707.

### GUNN, GLADYS
School administrator, teacher. **Personal:** Born Apr 28, 1937, Columbus, GA; daughter of John R and Jessie. **Educ:** Cent State Univ, BS, elem educ, 1959; Miami Univ, Med, 1964; Ohio State Univ, attended 1972. **Career:** School administrator (retired); Dayton Pub Schs, teacher, 1959-66, federally funded prog, interviewer, 1966-69, assoc personnel, 1969-71, coordr, 1982-86, spec asst admin & ident grants, 1986-92; Ohio Youth Comn, asst supt educ serv, 1972-73; CSU W & CSU Training Ins, dir, 1973-77; Cent State Univ, dir training inst & employ prog, 1977-78, coordr, SDIP, 1978-80, Dept Health & Human Serv, spec asst, 1980-81. **Orgs:** Am Asn Sch Admin, 1989-92; life mem, Nat Asn Advan Colored People, 1990-, educ comt chair, 1999-; officer, Alpha Kappa Alpha Sorority; Soroptimist Int; assoc supvr & currriculam develop, Phi Delta Kappa; Subcomt Educ Ad Hoc Comt Civil Rights; City Dayton Comm Ed; bd mem, Daymont Ment Health Prog; elected mem Inner W Priority Bd; bd mem, Comprehensive Manpower Training Ctr; League Women Voters. **Honors/Awds:** Presidential appointment, Nat Adv Coun Women's Educ Prog, 1978-80; pres appt Spec Asst, Spec Grps, 1980-81; Miley O. Williamson Award of Distinction, 1999; The Ohio Dr. Martin Luther King, Jr. Holiday Comn, 1990-98, chair, 1996-98. **Home Addr:** 4237 Catalpa Dr, Dayton, OH 45405-1717, **Home Phone:** (937)278-0447.

### GUNN, WILLIE COSDENA THOMAS
Educator, counselor. **Personal:** Born Dec 24, 1926, Seneca, SC; daughter of Fletcher Gideon and Mattie Riley Gideon; married Willie James; children: John Henderson Thomas III. **Educ:** Benedict Col, BS, 1946; Univ Mich, MA, educ, 1967, MA, guid, 1970; Urban Bible Col, Detroit, MI, Dr, 1987; Reed Bus Col, bus cert. **Career:** Emerson Jr HS, teacher common learnings & sci, 1956-64; Flint Sch Syst; Headstart Prog, supvr, 1965; Title I Oper Summer Prog, supvr, 1967-73; MI State Univ, teacher supvr, 1962-64; Emerson Jr HS, guid counr, 1964-76; Mott Col, instr social sci, 1969-78; Flint Open Sch, guid counr, 1976-82; Jordan Col, instr social sci dept, 1981; Southwestern HS, guid counr, 1982-88; Southwestern Acad, guid counr. **Orgs:** Flint City Adv Comt League Women Voters; Voter Educ Coalition Drug Abuse Task Force; bd dir, WFBE Pub Radio Station; bd dir, Nat Asn Media Women; life mem & pres, Zeta Phi Beta Sor; life mem & pres, Nat Sor Phi Delta Kappa; Am Asn Univ Women; life mem, Nat Asn Negro Bus & Prof Women; exec bd, prog chmn, Nat Asn Advan Colored People, Urban League, Africa Care, Nat Coun Negro Women; Genesee Area Asn Couning Develop; United Teachers Flint; Nat Educ Asn; Michigan Educ Asn; exec bd, Dimes Birth Defects Found, currently; Metropolitan Chamber Com, 1984-; 2nd vpres, Top Ladies Distinction, 1985-; Numerous Service & Achievement Awards; pub rels dir, Black Panhellenic Coun, 1987-. **Home Addr:** 1511 Church St, Flint, MI 48503, **Home Phone:** (313)234-0514.

### GUNTER, LAURIE. See Obituaries Section.

### GURLEY, ANNETTE DENISE
Administrator. **Personal:** Born Aug 24, 1955, Chicago, IL; daughter of C W Jackson and Rutha; married William Jr; children: Gregory Sheldon. **Educ:** Univ Ill, Chicago, BA, elem educ, 1977; Chicago State Univ, MS, reading, 1992; Concordia Univ, MA, admin & supv, 1995. **Career:** St Justin Martyr Sch, teacher, 1977-85; Chicago Pub Schs, teacher, 1985-90, teacher facilitator, 1990-94, elem area instr officer, currently; Michele Clark Mid, asst prin, 1994; DePaul Univ, instr, 1998-99; CPS Pub Schs, Michele Clark Prep Magnet High Sch, prin & area instrnl officer, 2001-07, chief officer, Teaching & Learning Chicago Pub Schs. **Orgs:** Treas, Progressive Community Church, 1983-; Jack & Jill Am, Chicago Chap, 1991-; presenter, Nat Mid Sch Asn, 1991-; chmn, Gregory Scholar Awards Comm, 1995-; Chicago Prin Asn, 1997-; teen sponsor, Jack & Jill Am, Chicago Chap, 1998-. **Home Addr:** 16719 Merrill Ave, South Holland, IL 60473-2628, **Home Phone:** (708)474-0693. **Business Addr:** Chief Officer, Chicago Public Schools Office of Teaching and Learning, Chicago Public Schools, 42 W Madison St 3rd Fl, Chicago, IL 60603, **Business Phone:** (773)553-2517.

### GUTHRIE, CARLTON LYONS
Automotive executive, executive, chief executive officer. **Personal:** Born Sep 15, 1952, Atlanta, GA; married Dawn-Marie; children: Carille & Adam. **Educ:** Harvard Col, BA (Hons), econs, 1974; Harvard Bus Sch, MBA, gen mgt, 1978. **Career:** Jewel Co Chicago, internal consult, 1978-80; McKinsey & Co, Chicago, sr assoc, 1980-82, sr consult; James H Lowry & Assoc Chicago, exec vpres, 1982-85, chief operating officer; Trumark Inc, co-owner, pres, chief exec officer & chmn, 1985-2001; Trumark Engineering, pres; Spectra LMP LLC, co-chmn; SPECTRA LLC, co-chmn; Philadelphia Nat Bank; Procter & Gamble, salesman; Detroit Chassis LLC, pres & co-chmn, currently; Guthrie Investment Group, vpres, currently. **Orgs:** Dir, Ctrs New Horizons Chicago, 1980-, Urban League Lansing MI, 1986-; dir, Gifted & Talented Educ Prog, Ingham County Church, 1986-; chmn bd, Single Parent Family Inst, Lansing, MI, 1987-; bd dir, Joyce Found, Chicago Ill, 1991-; bd dir, Shorebank Corp; dir, Initiative Competitive Inner City; pres, Nat Asn Black Automotive Suppliers; adv bd, Gov's State Univ Sch Bus; adv bd, Joint Ctr Polit & Econ Studies; bd dir, Trumark Inc; co-founder, Runners Club, Chicago. **Honors/Awds:** Extrepreneur of the Year, Chivas Regal/Seagrams, 1990; Mich Mfr of the Year, 1991; Trumark Inc: Supplier of the Year, Nat Minority Supplier Develop Coun, 1992. **Home Addr:** 1230 E 46th St, Chicago, IL 60653, **Home Phone:** (312)373-5006. **Business Addr:** President, Co-Chairman, Detroit Chassis LLC, 6501 Lynch Rd, Detroit, MI 48234, **Business Phone:** (313)571-2100.

### GUTHRIE, MICHAEL J.
Executive, president (organization). **Personal:** Born Sep 19, 1950, Lithonia, GA; son of Willie and Mary; married Valorie C Walker; children: Lauren & Kayla. **Educ:** Harvard Col, AB, 1972; Harvard Law Sch, JD, 1975. **Career:** Sonnenschein, Carlin, Nath & Rosenthal, atty, 1975-79; Johnson Products Co Inc, sr atty, 1979-83, vpres corp planning, 1983-85; Trumark Inc, co-owner, exec vpres, 1985-; Uptilt Inc, 1985; Guthrie Investment Corp, pres, currently; Detroit Chassis LLC, co-founder, co-chmn, pres & chief exec officer, currently; Spectra LLC, co-chmn, pres & chief exec officer, currently; Spectra LMP LLC, co-chmn, pres & chief exec officer, currently. **Orgs:** Bus adv bd, found bd, Lansing Comm Col; Eli Broad Grad Sch Mgt, Mich State Univ; pres, Nat Asn Black Automotive Suppliers; Jr Achievement Mid-Mich; Jr Achievement Southeast Mich; Physicians Health Plan Mid-Michigan; Govs Task Force Entrepreneurship & Small Bus; Mich Coun Voc Educ; Single Parent Family Inst; bd dir, Detroit Chassis LLC; Black Child & Family Inst Lansing; Children's Aid Soc Detroit; E Side Indust Coun Detroit; Comerica Bank Mich Cent Region. **Home Addr:** 3538 Sylvan Glen Dr, Okemos, MI 48864, **Home Phone:** (517)347-1111. **Business Addr:** President, Chief Executive Officer, Detroit Chassis LLC, 6501 Lynch Rd, Detroit, MI 48234-4140, **Business Phone:** (313)571-2100.

### GUY, ANGELA
Vice president (organization). **Educ:** Pa State Univ, BA, psychol; Harvard Kennedy Sch, exec women's leadership develop prog. **Career:** Levi Strauss & Co; Johnson & Johnson; SoftSheen-Carson L'Oreal USA, vpres sales, sr vpres sales, sr vpres & gen mgr, sr vpres diversity & inclusion, 2004-. **Orgs:** Nat Exec Women; indust partner, Am Health & Beauty Aids Inst; Harvest Hope Family Serv Network Inc; Am Conf Diversity; adv bd, Coalition 100 Black Women, NYC; Delta Sigma Theta Sorority Inc; Exec Leadership Coun; Asia Soc Bus Coun. **Business Addr:** Senior Vice President, General Manager, SoftSheen-Carson, 575 5th Ave 19th Fl, New York, NY 10017, **Business Phone:** (212)818-1500.

### GUY, ANGELA E.
Vice president (organization). **Educ:** Pa State Univ, BA, psychol; Harvard Univ, exec educ cert. **Career:** Levi Strauss & Co, Sales; Johnson & Johnson, vpres sales, 1999-2004; Softsheen-Carson, vpres Sales, 2004-07, Div L'Oreal USA, sr vpres sales, 2004-08, sr vpres & gen mgr, 2008-11; L'Oreal USA Inc, Diversity & Inclusion, sr vpres, 2012-. **Orgs:** Nat Exec Women; indust partner, Am Health & Beauty Aids Inst; bd mem, Harvest Hope Family Serv Network, currently; Am Conf Diversity; bd mem, Nat Coalition 100 Black Women; Delta Sigma Theta Sorority Inc; Asia Soc's Bus Coun. **Business Addr:** Senior Vice President, L'Oreal USA Inc, 575 5th Ave, New York, NY 10017, **Business Phone:** (212)818-1500.

### GUY, BUDDY (GEORGE GUY)
Guitarist, business owner, songwriter. **Personal:** Born Jul 30, 1936, Lettsworth, LA; son of Sam and Isabell. **Career:** Blues guitarist; Albums: Hoodoo Man Blues, 1965; A Man & the Blues, 1968; I Was Walking Through the Woods, 1974; Pleading the Blues, 1979; Stone Crazy!, 1981; Buddy Guy, 1983; Buddy Guy on Chess, Vol one, 1988; Damn Right, I'veGot the Blues, 1991; Sweet Tea, 2001; Blues Singer, 2003; Jammin' BluesElectric & Acoustic, 2003; Chicago Blues Festival 1964, 2003; DJ Play MyBlues, 2003; A Night of the Blues, 2005; Bring 'Em In, 2005; Everyday WeHave the Blues, 2006; Can't Quit the Blues, 2006; Live: The Real Deal, 2006; Goin Home: A Tribute to Fats Domino, 2007; Skin Deep, 2008; The Definitive Buddy Guy, 2009; Living Proof, 2010; Buddy Guys Legends, owner, currently.Film: In the Electric Mist, 2009; TV Series:"Jack's Big Music Show", 2006. **Home Addr:** , IL. **Business Addr:** Owner, Buddy Guys Legends, 700 S Wabash Ave, Chicago, IL 60605-2111, **Business Phone:** (312)427-1190.

### GUY, GEORGE. See GUY, BUDDY.

### GUY, JASMINE
Dance director, actor. **Personal:** Born Mar 10, 1962, Boston, MA; daughter of William and Jaye Rudolph; married Terrence Duckette; children: Imani. **Educ:** Alvin Ailey Dance Theatre. **Career:** Alvin Ailey Am Dance Theater, dancer; Atlanta Ballet Junior Co, dancer; TV Series: "A Different World", actor, 1987-93, writer, 1990-92, dir, 1992; "Queen", 1993; "A Century of Women", 1994; "NYPD Blue", 1995; "Living Single", 1996; "America's Dream", 1996; "Perfect Crime", 1997; "Linc's", 2000; "Feast of All Saints", 2001; "Call Me Claus", 2001; "Carrie", 2002; "Dead Like Me", 2003-04; "Haunted", 2004; "That's So Raven", 2006; "My Parents, My Sister & Me", 2009; "The Vampire Diaries", 2009-14; "Drop Dead Diva", 2010; "Let's Stay Together", 2012; "Kasha and the Zulu King", 2012; "My Other Mother", 2014; "If Loving You Is Wrong", 2014-. Films: School Daze, 1988; Harlem Nights, 1989; Boy Meets Girl, 1993; Klash, 1995; Cat's Don't Dance (voice), 1997; Madeline, 1998; Guinevere, 1999; Lillie, 1999; Diamond Men, 2000; Grease; Chicago, 2000; The Law of Enclosures, 2000; Dying on the Edge, 2001; The Violet Hour, 2003; Ways of the Flesh, 2006; video: I Was a Network Star, 2006; That's So Raven, 2006; Tru Loved, 2008; Dead Like Me, 2009; Stomp the Yard 2: Homecoming, 2010; October Baby, 2011; What About Us?, 2012, actor & exec producer, 2012; Scary Movie 5, 2013; Big Stone Gap, 2014; Sick People, 2016; The Substitute Spy, 2016. **Honors/Awds:** Image Award, Nat Asn Advan Colored People, 1990-95; Best Actress in a Comedy Series, for A Different World, 1990. **Special Achievements:** Albums: Jasmine Guy, 1990; "Try Me", 1990; "Another Like My Lover", "Just Want to Hold You" & "Don't Want Money", 1991. **Business Addr:** Actress, Stone Manners Agency, 6500 Wilshire Blvd Suite 550, Los Angeles, CA 90048, **Business Phone:** (323)655-1313.

### GUY, LYGIA BROWN
Executive, executive director. **Personal:** Born Apr 23, 1952, Charleston, SC; married Peter Steele; children: Aja. **Educ:** Spelman Col, attended 1972; Fashion Inst Am, AA, merchandising & design, 1973; Pepperdine Univ, BA, sociol, 1974. **Career:** Chelsa Rec, promotional coordr, 1975; Greedy Rec, promotional coordr, 1976; ABC Rec, promotional coordr, 1977; Connections, dir & owner, co-personnel agt, 1984; RCA Rec, merchandising mgr. **Orgs:** Nat Asn Advan Colored People, 1969; Acad Country Music, 1980; Am Fed TV Radio Artists, 1980; Nat Acad Rec Arts Sci, 1982; Black Music Asn. **Honors/Awds:** Promotional Manager of the Year Award, BRE Mag, 1984. **Home Addr:** 73 W Altadena Dr, Altadena, CA 91001.

### GUY-SHEFTALL, BEVERLY
Publisher, educator, writer. **Personal:** Born Jan 1, 1946, Memphis, TN; daughter of Ernestine Varnado and Walter. **Educ:** Spelman Col, BA, 1966; Atlanta Univ, MA, 1970; Emory Univ, PhD, 1977. **Career:** AL State Univ, fac, 1968-71; Spelman Col, prof Eng & women's studies, 1971-; Women's Res & Resource Ctr, Anna Julia Cooper prof Eng, 1981; SAGE: A Scholarly Jour Black women, founding co-ed; speaker; Emory Univ Inst Women's Studies, adj prof, currently; Women's Res & Resource Ctr & Anna Julia Cooper Prof Women's Studies, dir, currently. **Business Addr:** Founding Director, Spelman College, 350 Spelman Lane S W, Atlanta, GA 30314-4399, **Business Phone:** (404)681-3643.

### GUYNES, THOMAS V.
Football player. **Personal:** Born Sep 9, 1974, Marion, IN. **Educ:** Univ Mich. **Career:** Football player (retired), executive; Ariz Cardinals, tackle, 1997-98; Berlin Thunder, Europe, tackle, 2000-01; Detroit Seminoles, 2008; Washtenaw County Sheriff Dept, dep. **Orgs:** Omega Psi Phi; Prince Hall mason. **Honors/Awds:** Ernie Siegler Award, M Club Chicago, 1995. **Business Addr:** Football Player, Detroit Seminoles, PO Box 40235, Redford, MI 48239.

### GUYTON, REV. BOOKER T., SR.
Executive, school administrator. **Personal:** Born Dec 27, 1944, Clarksville, TX; son of Raymond Sr; married Mary Allen; children: Booker Jr, Roxann, Keisha & Katrina. **Educ:** Univ Pac, BS, educ, 1971, MA, relig, 1972. **Career:** Facil Mgt & Inst Personnel Develop, dir; Humanities & Intercultural Ed Div, chmn; Mgt Serv, from admin asst to vp; affirm action officer; Johnson & Johnson, supvr mfg; John F Kennedy Ctr, exec dir; Fed Teacher Corps prog, teacher intern; Parks

Chapel African Methodist Episcopal Church, pastor, prin, presiding elder, currently; San Joaquin Delta Community Col, instr. **Orgs:** N Stockton Rotary; Assoc Calif Community Col Admin; Calif Comm Serv Asn; Nat Ed Asn; CA Sch Bd Asn; Off Black Caucus Nat Ed Asn; Kappa Alpha Psi; bd dir, Dameron Hosp Found; pres, McKinley Improv Asn; State Coun Oppurtunity Indust Ctr State Calif. **Home Addr:** 148 W 8th St, Stockton, CA 95206, **Home Phone:** (209)463-0142. **Business Addr:** Presiding Elder, Principal, Parks Chapel African Methodist Episcopal Church, 476 34th St, Oakland, CA 94609, **Business Phone:** (510)654-8758.

### GUYTON, PATSY
Educator, nun. **Personal:** Born Jun 16, 1949, Mobile, AL; daughter of Wes and Marie Johnson. **Educ:** Bishop State Jr Col, Mobile, AL, assoc psychol, 1969; Ala State Univ, Montgomery, AL, BS, Hist, 1971; Springhill Col, TIPS, Mobile, AL, attended 1983; Univ New Orleans, MTh, theol, 1994. **Career:** Boca Raton Mid Sch, Boca Raton FL, teacher, 1971-75; Christian Benevolent Ins Co, Mobile AL, debit mgr, 1975-76; St Mary's C Home, Mobile AL, child care worker, 1976-79; Marion Corp, Theodore AL, personnel specialist, 1979-82; Parish Social Ministry, Mobile AL, coordr, 1982-88; Most Pure Heart Mary Church, dir relig educ, coordr ministries, 1988-92, Relig Educ, assoc dir, 1992-. **Orgs:** Alpha Kappa Alpha Sorority, 1970-; bd mem, Valentine Award, Cath Social Servs, 1982-; relig educ consult, Archdiocese Mobile AL, 1985-; bd mem, Nat Asn Lay Ministry, 1985-; inter parish coun, Black Cath Cong & Nat Asn Black Sisters; prog coordr, Cath Enrichment Ctr, 2003-; Sisters Christian Community relig order. **Home Addr:** PO Box 161191, Mobile, AL 36616-2191, **Home Phone:** (205)452-2537. **Business Addr:** Program Coordinator, Office of Multicultural Ministries, 3146 W Broadway, Louisville, KY 40211-1441, **Business Phone:** (502)776-0262.

### GUYTON, TYREE
Artist, painter (artist). **Personal:** Born Aug 24, 1955, Detroit, MI; son of George (deceased) and Betty Solomon; married Jenenne Whitfield; children: Tyree Jr, Towan, Omar, James & Tylisa. **Educ:** Marygrove Col; Wayne State Univ; Ctr Creative Studies, Detroit, MI. **Career:** Ford Motor Co, Dearborn, Mich, inspector; Northern High Sch, Master Residence Art Prog, Detroit, Mich, teacher; Heidelberg Proj, Detroit, Mich, pres, 1987-; painter, sculptor, currently. Solo Exhibs: Alexa Lee Gallery, Ann Arbor, Mich, 1994, 1995; Front Room Gallery, Detroit, Mich, 1988; Group Exhibs: Minn Mus Am Art, St Paul, 1996; Ctr Galleries, Detroit, Mich, 1995; Urban Inst Contemp Art, Grand Rapids, Mich, 1994; numerous others; featured var bks. **Honors/Awds:** Summer Youth Assistance Prog Award, Detroit, MI, 1989; Spirit of Detroit Award, Detroit City Coun, 1989; David A Harmond Award, City of Detroit, 1989; Comn Resolution Award, Wayne County, 1990; Testimonial Resolution Award, City of Detroit, 1990; Michiganian of the Yr, State Mich, 1991; Michigan Artist of the Year, Gov John Engler, State Mich, 1992; Humanity in the Arts Award, Ctr for Peace & Conflict Studies, Wayne State Univ, 1992; Volunteer Community Service Award, Youth Vol Corps, 1995; House of Representatives Resolution No 117, State Mich, 1995; Int Artist Award, Wayne County, 2003; hon doc, Fine Art, Detroit Inst Arts. **Home Addr:** PO Box 19377, Detroit, MI 48219, **Home Phone:** (313)532-6156. **Business Addr:** President, Heidelberg Project, 3600 Heidelberg St, Detroit, MI 48207, **Business Phone:** (313)974-6894.

### GUYTON, WANDA MARIE
Basketball coach, basketball player. **Personal:** Born Oct 14, 1968; daughter of Johnny Sr. **Educ:** Univ Southern Fla, attended 1989. **Career:** Basketball player (retired), basketball coach; NEC, Japan, forward, 1989-90; Tenerife, Spain, 1990-92; NEC, Italy, 1992-96; Womens Nat Basketball Asn, World Championship team, 1997-98; Houston Comets, 1997-98; Back-To-Back Womens Nat Basketball Asn Champions, 1997-99; Eastern Conf champions, 1997-99; Lead both teams to playoffs, 1997-2000; Detroit Shock, 1999; Univ S Fla, asst coach, 2000-01; Ger DBBL, Wasserburg, 2004-07; TSV Wasserburg Ger, asst coach & head coach, 2007-08, 2010-. **Orgs:** Womens basketball team, 1984-85, 1986-87 & 1988-89. **Home Addr:** Am Wuhrbach 27, Wasserburg83512. **Business Addr:** Assistant Coach, TSV Wasserburg Womens Basketball Team, Froschlanger 49, Wasserburg83512, **Business Phone:** (498)071-6223.

### GUZMAN, JUAN ANDRES CORREA
Baseball player, executive. **Personal:** Born Oct 28, 1966, Santo Domingo. **Career:** Baseball player (retired); Los Angeles Dodgers, 1985; Toronto Blue Jays, 1991-98; Baltimore Orioles, 1998-99; Cincinnati Reds, 1999; Tampa Bay Devil Rays, 2000; Kingdom Teaching, owner, 2009-.

### GWYNN, FLORINE EVAYONNE
Physician, counselor, administrator. **Personal:** Born Jan 16, 1944, Beckley, WV; daughter of Flauzell Calhoun and Jean Daisy Wright; married Herman L; children: Towanna M, Catherine S, Alvin, Calvin & Robert. **Educ:** Beckley Col, AS, 1970; Blue field State Col, BS, 1977; WVa Col Grad Studies, MS, 1982; WVa Union Col Law, Morgan Town, attended 1989. **Career:** Raleigh County, youth/sr citizens dir, 1969-72; Fed Prison Women, fed correctional officer, 1972-75; Nutrit Elderly, proj dir, 1979-80; Raleigh County Comn Aging, exec dir, 1980-81; Social Security Admin, hearing asst, 1982-; Blue field State Col, Criminal Justice Prog, asst prof, 1982-; N Cent Wva Community Action Asn, Kingwood, WVa, counr/coordr; Floettas Inc, pres; Another Way Inc, clin dir, lead therapist, currently. **Orgs:** Blue field State Col Alumni, 1977-; WV Col Grad Studies, 1979-; bd dir, Domestic Violence Ctr, 1984-; treas, Raleigh County Rainbow Coalition, 1984-; Phi Alpha Delta Law Fraternity, 1986-; coordr, Tygart Valley Baptist Asn Sunday Sch Cong, 1988-, Youth Action Inc, 1989-; bd mem, Sex Equity-Teen Pregnacy Proj, 1989-; vpres, Florence Crittenton Home & Serv, Wheeling, WV; pres, Tygart Valley Dist Baptist Asn Women's Conv. **Home Addr:** 1401 Anderson Ave, Morgantown, WV 26505-2321, **Home Phone:** (304)598-3246. **Business Addr:** Lead Therapist, Another Way Inc, 530 W Main St, Uniontown, PA 15409, **Business Phone:** (724)437-3024.

# H

### HABER, LOIS E.
Banker, executive. **Educ:** Arcadia Univ, BA, 1971. **Career:** Banker (retired); Del Valley Financial Servs Inc, pres & chief exec officer, 1978-2003; consult. **Orgs:** Chair bd mem, Ctr Women's Bus Res; chair, Nat Found Women Bus Owners; retired bd chair, Arcadia Univ, 2005-10; mem bd dir, AUI Fine Foods, 2014-; Chair Adv Coun, Arcadia Univ Sch Global Bus, 2015-. **Honors/Awds:** Woman Business Owner of the Year, Philadelphia Chap Nat Asn Women Business Owners; Penn Honor Roll of Women, 1996; Penn Top Women in Bus, 1997; Honorary Doctor of Humane Letters, 2016. **Special Achievements:** First alumna to be elected Chair of the University's Board.

### HABERSHAM-PARNELL, JEANNE
Educator. **Personal:** Born May 20, 1936, New York, NY; daughter of Paul and Ethel; children: Richard. **Educ:** Howard Univ, BA, 1958; Columbia Univ, MA, 1972. **Career:** Educator; Amsterdam News, Dawn Mag, Black Am, syndicated columnist; Inner City Broadcasting, WLIB & WBLS & WHCR, producer & host City Lights; WNYE Bd Educ Radio & TV, educ programmer & producer; Int Magnet Sch, admin asst, asst prin, dir, 1990-93; IMPACT II, Bd Educ citywide, dir. **Orgs:** NYC 100 Black Women; Metrop Jack & Jill Alumni; Harlem YWCA, bd mem; Opera Ebony, bd mem; Lincoln Ctr, adv educ comt; Am Fed TV & Radio Artists; Howard Univ Hall Restoration Comt; Nat Storytelling Asn. **Home Addr:** 2301 5th Ave Apt 2KK, New York, NY 10037, **Home Phone:** (212)234-3417.

### HACKETT, BARRY DEAN (DINO HACKETT)
Football player, executive. **Personal:** Born Jun 28, 1964, Greensboro, NC; married Cindy; children: Dustin Marie & Jax. **Educ:** Appalachian State Univ, BA, criminal justice, 1986. **Career:** Football player (retired), executive; Kans City Chiefs, linebacker & left inside linebacker, 1986, right inside linebacker, 1987-91; Seattle Seahawks, 1993; Hackett Properties Inc, pres, currently; Hackett Builders, founder. **Honors/Awds:** Ed Block Courage Award, 1986. **Business Addr:** President, Hackett Properties Inc, 813 Granite St, Greensboro, NC 27403-4352, **Business Phone:** (336)272-1251.

### HACKETT, DINO. See HACKETT, BARRY DEAN.

### HACKETT, OBRA V.
Educator, school administrator. **Personal:** Born Sep 9, 1937, Osyka, MS; son of James and Letha T Williams; married A Carolyn Evans; children: Obra V Jr. **Educ:** Jackson State Univ, BS, 1960; Atlanta Univ, MA, 1967; Miss State Univ, attended 1968. **Career:** Henry Weathers HS, math teacher, 1960-62, asst prin, 1962-64; Carver HS, counr, 1965-66; Utica Jr Col, voc counr, 1966-69, dean studs, 1969-73; Jackson State Univ, dir pub info, 1973-77, dir develop, 1977-84, asst dean career coun & placement, 1987-89, actg dir, career coun & placement, 1989-91, dir, 1991-92, pres, currently; JSU Dev Found, exec secy, 1984-87. **Orgs:** Charter mem, Col Pub Rels Asn MS, 1970; bd dir, Hinds Co Heart Asn, 1974-79; secy bd dir, Goodwill Indus MS, 1979-; comnr, scouting Seminole Dist Andrew Jackson Coun BSA, 1979-83; pres, Callaway HS PTA, 1986-87; Third vpres, Jackson Coun PTA, 1986-88; key communicator JPS, 1986-; first vpres, Jackson Coun PTA, 1988-90; treas, Jackson State Univ, Nat Alumni Asn, 1996-98; pres, Jackson Coun PTA, 1990-91; Jackson State Univ Nat Alumni Asn Inc, treas; bd mem, Miss PTA, 1990-, pres, 1997-99. **Home Addr:** 509 Woodson Dr, Jackson, MS 39206, **Home Phone:** (601)362-3016. **Business Addr:** Director, Jackson State University, 1400 J R Lynch St, Jackson, MS 39217, **Business Phone:** (601)979-2121.

### HACKETT, WILBUR L.
Manager. **Personal:** Born Oct 21, 1949, Winchester, KY; married Brenda. **Educ:** Univ Kent, BA, 1973. **Career:** Louisville Reg Criminal Justice Comn, comn coordr; Gen Election Louisville, supvr, 1973; Black Baron Construct Inc, staff, currently. **Orgs:** Adv Comt, Russel Area Youth; adv bd, Urban League Youth Prog; vpres, Concerned Young Men Louisville; adv bd, Proj WayOut; Sickle Cell Anemia Found Kent; Comn Restoration Black Hist; bd dir, Erwin House. **Honors/Awds:** Hon mention All-SEC Linebacker. **Special Achievements:** First black captain in SEC University of Kentucky. **Home Addr:** 6718 Fernhaven Rd, Louisville, KY 40228-1209, **Home Phone:** (502)239-9091. **Business Addr:** Owner, Black Baron Construction Inc, 3020 Bardstown Rd, Louisville, KY 40205, **Business Phone:** (502)418-7809.

### HACKEY, REV. GEORGE EDWARD, JR.
Law enforcement officer. **Personal:** Born May 19, 1948, Bethesda, MD; son of George Edward Sr and Doris Plummer; married Dory Ann Gray; children: Derick, Cari & George III. **Educ:** Montgomery Col, Rockville, MD, AA, gen educ, 1969; Towson State Univ, Towson, MD, BS, sociol, 1971. **Career:** Montgomery County Dept Recreation, Rockville, Md, playground dir, 1962-70; Montgomery County Bd Educ, Rockville, Md, bldg monitor, 1971-73; Montgomery County Dept Police, Rockville, Md, community rels officer; United Methodist Church, pastor, Sharp Street, MD, pastor, Indian Head, MD, currently. **Orgs:** Treas, Montgomery County African-Am Employees Asn, 1989-; Montgomery County Police Asn; chaplain, pres, Montgomery County Coalition Black Police Officers, 1974-; chaplain, pres, Great & Respectable Black Orgn, 1980-; mentor, Seneca Valley High Sch Models & Mentors Prog, 1990-; John Wesley United Methodist Church, exec officer. **Home Addr:** 19200 Bonmark Ct, Germantown, MD 20874, **Home Phone:** (301)540-9380. **Business Addr:** Pastor, United Methodist Church, 19 Mattingly Ave, Indian Head, MD 20640-1743, **Business Phone:** (301)743-2312.

### HACKLEY, DR. LLOYD VINCENT
School administrator, executive, administrator. **Personal:** Born Jun 14, 1940, Roanoke, VA; son of David W Sr (deceased) and Ernestine Parker (deceased); married Brenda L Stewart; children: Dianna Hackley-Applin & Michael R. **Educ:** Mich State Univ, BA, polit sci, 1965; Univ Colo, psychol, 1967; Univ NC, polit sci, PhD, 1976; Govt Exec Inst, Sch Bus Admin, Univ NC, Chapel Hill, 1980. **Career:** USAF Acad, coach track & cross country, 1974-78, assoc prof, course dir polit sci, 1974-78; Univ NC, Gen Admin, assoc vpres acad affairs, 1979-81; Univ NC, Chapel Hill, fac govt execs inst sch bus admin, 1980-81; Univ Ariz, Pine Bluff, chancellor chief exec officer, 1981-85; Univ NC, Gen Admin, vpres stud serv & spec prog, 1985-88; Fayetteville StateUniv, Fayetteville NC, chancellor, 1988, chancellor emer, 2003-; NC Community Col Syst, pres; Tyson Foods Inc, dir, 1992-11; Br Banking & Trust Corp, dir, 1992-10; Lloyd V Hackley & Assocs Inc, chief exec officer & pres, 1997-; Nat Character Counts! Coalition, chair, 1999, consult; Blue Cross & Blue Shield, NC, dir, 2003. **Orgs:** Exec comn Triangle World Affairs Ctr, 1978-79; bd dir, United Fund Carrboro, Chapel Hill, 1978-80; bd trustee, Village Co Found, 1980-81; exec comt, NC Comn, Int Educ, 1980-81; mem adv bd, Nat Ctr Toxicol Res, 1983; adv comt, Univ Ariz, Grad Inst Tech, 1983; chmn, sub comt curric & stud matters Ariz Qual Higher Educ Study Comn, 1984; chmn, sub comt mid & jr high schs Ariz Educ Stand Comn Elem & Sec Schs, 1983-84; vpres, United Way Jefferson Co, 1985; vpres bd dir, Ariz Endowment Humanities, 1984-85, 1985-86; chmn, Ariz Adv Comm to US Comn Civil Rights, 1985; Strategic Planning Team, Cumberland Co, Bd Educ, 1989; Fayetteville Area Econ Develop Corp; chmn, Pres Clinton's Adv Bd Historically Black Col & Univs; chair, NC Child Advocacy Inst. **Home Addr:** 1303 Yaupon Dr, Fayetteville, AR 28301, **Home Phone:** (919)486-1958. **Business Addr:** Chief Executive Officer, President, Lloyd V Hackley & Associates Inc.

### HACKMAN, LUTHER GEAN
Baseball player. **Personal:** Born Oct 10, 1974, Columbus, MS. **Career:** Baseball player (retired); Colo Rockies, 1994-99; St Louis Cardinals, 2000-02; San Diego Padres, pitcher, 2003; Cleveland Indians, 2003; Pittsburgh Pirates, 2004; Samsung Lions, 2005; Milwaukee Brewers, 2007; Uni-Pres 7-Eleven Lions, 2008, 2009-10; Olmecas de Tabasco, 2009.

### HACKNEY, L. CAMILLE
Executive, vice president (organization). **Educ:** Princeton Univ, BA, econs; Harvard Bus Sch, MBA, 1994. **Career:** Merrill Lynch & Co, financial analyst, 1990-92; HBO, mkt anal dept & independent consult, 1994; Warner Music Group, sr dir new media mkt develop, 1994-96; Elektra Entertainment Group, vpres strategic mkt new media, 1996-2004; Atlantic Rec, SVP Brand Partnerships & Com Licensing, 2008-12; Atlantic Rec/Warner Music Group, EVP Brand Partnerships & Licensing/Head GBPC, 2012-. **Orgs:** Tutor, mentor, Time To Read. **Business Addr:** Vice President of Strategic Marketing and New Media, Elektra Entertainment Group, 75 Rockefeller Plz 16th Fl, New York, NY 10019, **Business Phone:** (212)275-4000.

### HADDEN, EDDIE RAYNORD
Lawyer, pilot. **Personal:** Born May 25, 1943, Many, LA; son of Eddie and Emma Cross; married Kay Dupree; children: Eugene. **Educ:** Univ Tex, El Paso, BA, jour, 1965; George Washington Univ, incomplete MBA, 1971; Hofstra Univ Sch Law, JD, 1979. **Career:** Orgn Black Airline Pilots Inc, gen coun, 1972-; Eastern Airlines, pilot, 1972-89; JF Small Adv, vpres, 1973-74; pvt pract lawyer, 1980-; Aircraft Owners & Pilots Asn, regional counl, 1985-; Knowledge Systs Inc, 1990-; Fischer Porter Thomas & Reinfeld, atty, currently. **Orgs:** Vpres, Bergen Co NJ, Nat Asn Advan Colored People, 1980-83; pres, Bergen Co NJ Urban League Housing Auth, 1981-85; bd dir, Org Black Airline Pilots Inc, 1981-85; city councilman, City Englewood NJ, 1983-86; bd govs, Englewood, Chamber Com, 1990; bd mgr, Englewood Community Chest, 1990; chmn educ outreach, Alpha Phi Alpha fraternity, Kappa Theta Lambda Chap, 1990-; vice-chair, Community Resource Coun; NJ State Bar Asn; Bergen Co Bar Asn; Rotary Int; pres & chief exec officer, Nat Urban League; secy, Defense Ad Hoc Comt. **Honors/Awds:** Elected official, Englewood NJ City Coun, 1983; Youth Service Award, Tuskegee Airman Inc; Nat Conv, 1984; Rare Bird Award, Airline Pilots Asn, 1975; National Civic Achievement Award, Tuskegee Airmen Inc. **Home Addr:** 125 Jane St, Englewood, NJ 07631, **Home Phone:** (201)568-8145. **Business Addr:** Attorney At Law, Fischer Porter Thomas & Reinfeld, 180 Sylvan Ave 2nd Fl, Englewood Cliffs, NJ 07632, **Business Phone:** (201)569-5959.

### HADDOCK, MABLE J.
Consultant, educator. **Personal:** Born Jun 20, 1948, Clover, VA; daughter of Nephew R Staten; children: Kevin. **Educ:** Mercy Col, BA, 1974; NBC Fell Kent State Univ, MA, 1979; Wharton Bus Sch, cert, Pub Brdcst Mgt, 1982. **Career:** HEOP Mercy Col, asst dir, 1974-76; NBC, writer, res, 1977-78; Canton Cult Ctr, urban arts dir, 1978-80; producer: The Fannie Lou Hamer Story; Mandela; State Black Am, 1984; Ohio State Univ, Columbus, lectr, 1988-; Dialogue Mag, Columbus, contribr & writer; Nat Video Resources Rockefeller Found, consult, cur, 1990-91; Black Am Facing Millennium, 1997; Charles H Revson fel, 2005-06. **Orgs:** Women Commun, Ohio Arts Coun Minority Arts Task Force, 1980-82; consult, Ohio Arts Coun, 1980-82; bd dir, YWCA, 1982; bd, Columbus Cable Comm, 1982-83; Columbus Comm Cable Access, 1983-; bd mem emer, Nat Black Programming Consortium, founding dir, 1980-, pres & chief exec officer, founder, 1980-2012; Pa Coun Arts; Nat Endowment Arts; Jerome Found. **Honors/Awds:** Women of Achievement, YWCA, 1997; Participated conf on Media in Africa held in Senegal, 1981; Minority Arts Award, Ohio Arts Coun; Award of Excellence, Urban League, 1996; Kool Achiever Award, Unsung Heroes; Black Studies Heritage Award; NAMAC Media Award, 1998; Trailblazers Award, black film.com, 2002; Best Documentary, 2003; Special Jury Prize, 2003; Emmy Award, 2003; International Documentary Association Award, 2003. **Special Achievements:** Selected by the UN as rep on "Seminar on the Intensification of Int Media Action for the Immediate Independence of Namibia" held in Brazzaville, Congo, 1985.

### HADDON, JAMES FRANCIS
Investment banker. **Personal:** Born Aug 12, 1954, Columbia, SC; son of Wallace James and Ida Beatrice; married Sezelle Antoinette Gereau; children: Madeleine Louise & James Douglass. **Educ:** Wesleyan Univ, BA, 1976; Stanford Univ, MBA, 1980. **Career:** Mellon Nat Corp, real

estate analyst, 1976-78; Blyth Eastman Paine-Webber, assoc, 1982-83; Paine-Webber, vpres, 1984-89, managing dir, 1989; Smith Barney Shearson Inc, managing dir & mgr infrastructure group, currently. **Orgs:** Sponsors Econ Opportunity Mentor Prog, 1984-; Bd mem, Nat Asn Securities Prof, 1991-. **Home Addr:** 924 W End Ave, New York, NY 10025, **Home Phone:** (212)662-5344. **Business Addr:** Managing Director, Smith Barney Shearson Inc.

### HADLEY, DR. SYBIL CARTER
Lawyer. **Personal:** Born Dallas, TX; married Roy E Jr; children: Lauren Elizabeth & Dustin Carter. **Educ:** Univ Houston, BA, 1985; Univ Va, JD, 1988. **Career:** Fulton County Bd Elections & Regist, chair & chief registr, 1996-; Swift, Currie, McGhee & Hiers, sr assoc atty, partner, 1997; Insley & Race, litigation partner; Home Depot, dir legal, 2000-05, dir litigation dept; home based bus; PSA Healthcare, gen coun, 2009-11; Pediat Serv Am, litigation coordr, atty, currently. **Orgs:** Peachtree Presby Church; bd mem, JB Moore Soc Int Law; Legal Assistance Prog; Post-Conviction Assistance Prog; Trial Advocacy Prog; Nat Legal Aid & Defender Asn; Leadership Acad Women Color Attys; State Bar Ga. **Special Achievements:** First woman chair & chief registrar of Fulton County Board of Elections & Registration. **Home Addr:** 5980 Wellington Ave, Gainesville, GA 30506-3443, **Home Phone:** (770)533-9897. **Business Addr:** Litigation Coordinator, Pediatric Services of America, 6 Concourse Pkwy Suite 1100, Atlanta, GA 30328, **Business Phone:** (770)441-1580.

### HADNOTT, BENNIE L.
Consultant, executive, president (organization). **Personal:** Born Nov 23, 1944, Prattville, AL; son of James and Flora; children: Danielle & Johnathan. **Educ:** Bernard M Baruch Col, BBA, acct, 1971; Iona Col, MBA, acct & finance, 1976; NY Dept Educ, cert, 1976; Nj State Bd Accountancy, cert, 1979. **Career:** AICPA, mgr, 1976-81; Pace Grad Sch Bus, asst prof acct; Rutgers Univ, asst prof acct; Watson Rice LLP, managing partner & chief exec officer, 1981-2000; Watson Rice Consult Group Inc, pres; PIC Coun Bergen Co, treas; BCA Watson Rice LLP, owner, managing partner & sr consult, 1982-, Exec Comt, chmn, currently; Watson Rice Consult Group Inc, pres, currently; Tondah Consult Group, pres, consult. **Orgs:** Am Inst Cert Pub Acct; Asn Govt Accts; NY & NJ Intergovt Audit Forum; Munic Fin Officers Asn US & Can; Ny Soc Cert Pub Acct; dir-at-large, State & Local Govt & Health Care Community; Govt Acct & Auditing Educ Subcomt; Am Inst Cert Pub Acct; Fed Acquistion Comn, Wash, DC; Acct Future Issues Community; treas, Berger Co Br, Nat Asn Advan Colored People; NJ Bd Accountancy; Nat Asn Black Accts; pres, Hadnott Found. **Home Addr:** 810 Columbus Dr, Teaneck, NJ 07666-6609, **Home Phone:** (201)833-6234. **Business Addr:** Senior Consultant, Managing Partner, BCA Watson Rice LLP, 5 Penn Plz 15th Fl, New York, NY 10001, **Business Phone:** (212)447-7300.

### HAGAN, GWENAEL STEPHANE
Executive. **Personal:** Born Oct 9, 1960, Evreux; son of Willie D and Suzanne J Boule; children: Gael Y. **Educ:** Colo Univ-Boulder, BS, acct, 1982; Marquette Univ, MBA, 1988; Colo State Univ, MBA; CPA. **Career:** KMPG, auditor, 1982-83; Jones Intercable, sr auditor, 1983-85, bus mgr, 1985-86, cable TV syst mgr, 1986-88, dir new prod develop, 1988-90; Mind Exten Univ, vpres, bus develop, 1990; Microsoft, internet mkt mgr, 1994-96; Int Channel, vpres new bus develop, 1996-98; Online Syst Serv Inc, sr vpres strategic develop; Webb Interactive Serv, sr vpres strategic develop, vpres corp develop, 1998-2001; AccelX BV, gen mgr; Jabber Inc, chief financial officer, 2001-04, chief operating officer, 2002; Sales & Bus Develop, sr vpres, 2004-06; Mural Consult, prin, 2006; SolarGlass Window & Door, owner, 2006-; Hagan Ventures LLP, prin, currently. **Orgs:** Com chmn, vpres, bd mem, Nat Asn Minorities Cable, 1984-; bd mem, Namaste Solar, 2013-; bd mem, Hunger Free Colo, 2014-. **Business Addr:** Principal, Hagan Ventures LLC, 500 Hagan Ave, New Orleans, LA 70119, **Business Phone:** (504)262-0400.

### HAGAN, WILLIE JAMES
School administrator, educator. **Personal:** Born Dec 17, 1950, Montgomery, AL; son of Oliver and Dorothy Marie Wright; married Constance Marie Diaz; children: Lynea Marie Diaz. **Educ:** Conn Univ, Storrs, CT, BA, 1973, PhD, psychol; Univ Calif, Los Angeles, MA, fine arts, 1975. **Career:** Univ Conn, Storrs, CT, lobbyist, dir govt rels, 1986-90, actg vpres, 1990, assoc vpres, 1990; Dept Higher Educ, Hartford, CT, asst dir legis servs; Calif State Univ, Dominguez Hills, interim pres, 2012, pres, 2013; Calif State Univ, Fullerton, vpres admin, 1996-, finance & chief financial officer, currently. **Orgs:** Govt Rels & Commun Officers, 1982-87. **Home Addr:** 8850 E Foxhollow Dr, Anaheim, CA 92808-1671, **Home Phone:** (714)281-1860. **Business Addr:** Vice President Administration & Finance, Chief Financial Officer, California State University, Langsdorf Hall 805, Fullerton, CA 92834, **Business Phone:** (714)278-2115.

### HAGEMAN, HANS ERIC
Educator, lawyer, executive. **Personal:** Born Jan 1, 1957?, Chicago, IL; son of Lynn and Leola; married Bernadette Baptiste; children: Jamila & Viclar. **Educ:** Princeton Univ, BA, 1980; Columbia Univ Sch Law, JD, 1983; Mil Police Officer Basic Sch, attended 1983. **Career:** Thacher Proffitt & Wood, assoc, 1985-86; NY Co Dist Atty, asst dist atty, 1986-89; US Senate, minority chief coun & staff dir, 1989-90; Neighborhood Defender Serv Harlem, chief coun, 1991-92; E Harlem Sch Exodus House, co founder & exec dir, 1992-2001; Sulaxmi Sch Girls, founder, 2002-; Off Spec Narcotics Prosecution New York, asst dist atty; Emily N Carey Harbor Sch, exec dir, founder & head, 2002-09; Nat Police Corps, consult; Hans Hageman & Assocs, prin, 2010-, chief exec officer & founder, currently; Brownstone Fitness, co-founder, chief excitement officer; Jitegemee Inc, exec dir. **Orgs:** Treas, Bd, Harlem Congregation Community Improv Inc, 2000; trustee, Bill Traylor Found, 2001-; bd mem, Police Corps, 2001-; chair bd, founder & chief exec officer, Salus Found Inc; trustee, Harlem Episcopal Sch; adv mem, Bill Traylor Found; exec dir, Boys & Girls Harbor Inc, 2002-09; bd trustee mem, Harlem Acad. **Home Addr:** 1250 5th Ave, New York, NY 10029, **Home Phone:** (212)369-9542. **Business Addr:** Chief Executive Officer, Founder, The Salus Foundation Inc, PO Box 543, New York, NY 10026, **Business Phone:** (212)663-1105.

### HAGEMAN, IVAN
Educator. **Personal:** son of Rev and Leola. **Educ:** Harvard Univ, BA, social anthropol; Harvard's Grad Sch Educ, Med. **Career:** Klingenstein fel, Columbia Univ; fel, Rockefeller Found; Martin Luther King High Sch; East Harlem Sch, Exodus House, co-founder & head, currently. **Orgs:** Charter Sch Inst, State Univ, Albany. **Business Addr:** Co-Founder, Principal, East Harlem Sch, 309 E 103rd St, New York, NY 10029, **Business Phone:** (212)876-8775.

### HAGER, JOSEPH C., JR.
Educator. **Personal:** Born Jun 11, 1944, Washington, DC. **Educ:** Marist Col Poughkeepsie, NY, BA, 1967; Sherwood Sch Music Chicago, cert music, 1960; cand MA. **Career:** Am Univ, camp cour, 1960-61; Family & Child Servs; Marist House Formation St Joseph Novitiate, asst dir music; St Mary Parish, Poughkeepsie, instr, 1964-65; Marist Col, asst dir music, 1965-66; Marist Col, dir music, 1966-67; Mt St Michael Acad Bronx, sec educ teacher, 1967-70; Emmaculate Concoption, Bronx, teacher adult educ, 1968; New Rochelle High Sch relig, CCD training instr, 1968-69, sec teacher, 1968-70, CCD curric developer, 1969-70; Our Lady Perpetual Help, Pelham NY, teacher, 1968. **Orgs:** Staff consult, Nat Off Black Cath, 1970-73; exec dir, Nat Black Cath Clergy Caucus, 1970-73; dir relig educ, St Benedict Moor Wash DC, 1973-74; Alpha Kappa Psi Frat; DC bicentennial com; Nat Educ Asn; Nat Cath Educ Asn; Nat Black Cath Clergy Causus; bd mem camping progs, Family & Child Servs; Delta Psi Omega; Nat Off Black Caths; consult, DESIGN; Carter G Woodson Comn; Nat Black Churchmen Comt. **Home Addr:** 426 Jefferson St NW, Washington, DC 20011, **Home Phone:** (202)723-7404. **Business Addr:** Educator, Woodward Building Archdiocese, 733 15 St NW Suite 725, Washington, DC 20005.

### HAGGINS, JON
Fashion designer, writer, television show host. **Personal:** Born Sep 5, 1943, Tampa, FL; son of John and Willie Mae. **Educ:** Fashion Inst Tech, AAS, fashion, media, 1964. **Career:** Fashion designer, motivational speaker, host, producer, writer; Off Ave, designer, 1966; Jon Haggins Inc, pres & fashion designer; Procter & Gambles Ultra Detergents, spokesperson; Travel eTV & Travel eTV eMagazine, producer & host, 1999-2010; GlobeTrotter Jon Haggins TV, producer & host, 1999-; Kandu Productions, owner, 1999-; New York Lifestyles Mag, Contrib travel & restaurant writer, currently. Books: African Am Travel Guide To Hot, Exotic & Fun filled Places, 2007; Yes I Can Jon Haggins Memoir, 2008; Jon Haggins Inspirational Bk 2, 2008. **Orgs:** Beaujolas Socs Hon; adv bd mem, I Can Still. **Business Addr:** Producer, Host, GlobeTrotter Jon Haggins TV, PO Box 20902, New York, NY 10023, **Business Phone:** (646)463-1519.

### HAGINS, OGBONNA
Entrepreneur, educator. **Personal:** Born Feb 22, 1966, Philadelphia, PA; son of Paul (deceased) and Anne (deceased); married Sheena Lester; children: Atamusi Kamau & Atamanu Zaki. **Educ:** Temple Univ, attended 1984; Community Col Philadelphia, attended 1987. **Career:** Educator (retired), Executive; Davis Poole & Sloan, jr draftsman, 1984-87; The Salkin Group, working drawing specialist, 1987-89; Murray Archit, archit designer draftman, 1987-94; Dobbins High Sch, Sch Dist Philadelphia, archit design& drafting teacher, 1991-96; Reconstruction Inc, mentor; Philly Word Magazine, ed-in-chief, chief exec officer. **Orgs:** Philadelphia Fed Teachers, 1991-96. **Home Addr:** 4133 N Franklin St, Philadelphia, PA 19140-2207.

### HAGLER, REV. GRAYLAN S.
Clergy. **Personal:** Born Mar 1, 1954, Baltimore, MD. **Educ:** Oberlin Col, Ohio, BA, relig, 1976; Chicago Theol Sem, Mdiv. **Career:** United Church Christ, ordained, 1980; Ministers Racial, Social & Econ Justice, nat pres; Plymouth Congregational United Church Christ, pastor & sr minister, currently. **Orgs:** Develop dir, Neighborhood Assistance Corp Am; pres, Ministers Racial Social Econ Justice. **Business Addr:** Pastor, Senior Minister, Plymouth Congregational United Church Christ, 5301 N Capitol St NE, Washington, DC 20011, **Business Phone:** (202)723-5330.

### HAGLER, MARVIN (MARVELOUS MARVIN HAGLER)
Actor, boxer. **Personal:** Born May 23, 1954, Newark, NJ; son of Robert James Sims and Ida Mae (Lang); married Bertha Joann Dixon; children: Charelle, Celeste, James, Marvin Jr & Gentry; married Kay Guarrera. **Career:** Boxer (retired), actor; Boxer, 1980-87; Films: Indio, 1989; Indio 2-La rivolta, 1991; Cyber flic, 1997; Virtual Weapon, 1997; Notti di paura, 1997; Night of Fear; Ring of Fire: The Emile Griffith Story, 2005; TV: "WrestleMania XIV", 1998. **Orgs:** Prof middleweight boxer, world boxing champion, World Boxing Asn, 1980-88; Boxing Asn; World Boxing Coun.

### HAGOOD, HENRY BARKSDALE
Real estate developer, executive, government official. **Personal:** Born Aug 19, 1942, Wilson, NC; son of Emmett B Sr and Aurelia Muir; married Theresa Holder; children: Gabrielle Toles. **Educ:** Mich State Univ, BA, 1965. **Career:** Millender Ctr Asn, developer; Signet Develop Co, develop mgr; Walbridge Aldinger, dir bus develop; Detroit Housing Dept, mayor's exec liaison; Detroit Water & Sewerage Dept, admin asst, Contract & Grant Div; City Detroit, Community & Econ Develop Dept, dir; City Detroit, Mayor's Off, exec asst to Mayor Young; Farbman Group, vpres; Tecknowledge Group LCC, managing partner, currently; City Detroit, Dept Planning & Develop, dir develop activ, currently. **Orgs:** Detroit Econ Growth Corp Exec Comt; Econ Develop Corp; Downtown Develop Authority; Detroit Neighborhood Housing Serv; bd dir, Highland Pk YMCA; bd dir, Franklin Wright Settlement; New Detroit Inc; vice-chmn, Housing & Construct Comt. **Honors/Awds:** Distinguished Service Award, Southeastern Michigan Builder's Asn, 1992; Board of Recognition, Univ Citizens District Coun; Outstanding Service Award, Detroit Neighborhood Non-Profit Housing Corp; Outstanding Service Award Leadership, Area Coun Citizens Dist Coun. **Home Addr:** 2711 W 7 Mile Rd, Detroit, MI 48221-2221, **Home Phone:** (313)342-5257. **Business Addr:** Director of Development Activities, City of Detroit, 65 Cadillac Sq Suite 2300, Detroit, MI 48226, **Business Phone:** (313)224-6380.

### HAGOOD, JAY
Football player, football coach, football executive. **Personal:** Born Aug 9, 1973, Easley, SC. **Educ:** Va Polytech Inst & State Univ, attended 1997. **Career:** Football player (retired), football coach, exec; New York Jets, tackle, 1997-98; Miami Dolphins, 1998; San Diego Chargers; New Orleans Saints; NFL Europe, Frankfurt Galaxy, 1999-2000; Berlin Thunder, 2001; Centurions, NFL Europe, 2001; NFL Europe, Cologne Centurions, offensive asst coach, 2005; Jay Hagood Football Camp, founder & owner, 2008-.

### HAGWOOD, GERALDINE. See HOUSE, N. GERRY.

### HAILE, ANNETTE L.
Executive. **Personal:** Born Oct 3, 1952, Latrobe, PA; daughter of Edith Hill. **Educ:** John Carroll Univ, Cleveland, BS, biol, 1974; Baldwin Wallace Col, Berea, MBA, bus, 1978. **Career:** IBM Corp, Bethesda, dir, US Mkt & Serv, dir prod scheduling, vpres customer fulfillment, 1974-2007; John Carroll Univ, bd dir, mem, 2006-; Haile Consult LLC, owner, 2008-11. **Orgs:** Bd trustee, Studio Theatre; bd mem, United Arts Orgn; bd exec, Acad Affairs & Planning Comts; African Am Alliance. **Home Addr:** 3976 Georgetown Ct NW, Washington, DC 20007. **Business Addr:** Board of Director, John Carroll University, 1 John Carroll Blvd, University Heights, OH 44118, **Business Phone:** (216)397-1886.

### HAILEY, CEDRIC RENARD. See HAILEY, K-CI.

### HAILEY, JOJO (JOEL HAILEY)
Singer, writer. **Personal:** Born Jun 10, 1971, Charlotte, NC; children: 1. **Career:** Jodeci, mem; Ki-C & JoJo, mem, 1997-; Albums: Money Man, 2007; Wadsyaname, 2007; Films: Don't Be a Menace to South Central While Drinking Your Juice in the Hood, 1996; Soul Food, 1997; Shake, Rattle & Roll: An American Love Story, 1999, "After Hours: The Movie", 2011; TV series: "Martin", 1993; "Malcom & Eddie", 1997; "The Jamie Foxx Show", 1998; "Live with Regis & Kathie Lee", 2004; "Cribs", 2005; "Karaoke Revolution Presents: American Idol", 2007; "From Siberian Deeps", 2008; "K-Ci & JoJo: Come Clean", 2010. **Honors/Awds:** American Music Award, 1999; Blockbuster Award, 1999. **Business Addr:** Singer, MCA Records Incorporation, 70 Universal City Plz, Universal City, CA 91608.

### HAILEY, K-CI (CEDRIC RENARD HAILEY)
Singer. **Personal:** Born Sep 2, 1969, China Grove, NC; children: 1. **Career:** Jodeci, mem; K-Ci & JoJo, mem duo, 1997-. Albums: I'm Alright Now, 1983; Jesus Saves, 1984; God's Blessing, 1985; Love Always, 1997; All My Life, composer, 1998; It's Real, 1999; X, 2000; Save the Last Dance, 2001; Emotional, 2002; My Book, 2006; Ballad Collection for Lovers, 2007; Love, 2008; Playlist Your Way, 2008. Films: Soul Food, 1997; After Hours, 2013. Soundtrack: "Eddie", 1996; "Bullet proof", 1996; "Deliver Us from Eva", 2003; "Alpha Dog", 2006. **Business Addr:** Recording Artist, Universal Music Group, 2220 Colorado Ave, Santa Monica, CA 90404, **Business Phone:** (310)865-5000.

### HAILEY, PRISCILLA W.
Publisher. **Personal:** Born Oct 22, 1947, GA; married Howard L; children: Tasha M. **Educ:** Savannah State Col, BS, 1969. **Career:** Head Start, teacher, 1967-68; Dublin Ga Bd Educ, teacher, 1969-70; Kaiser Gypsum Co, credit secy, 1969; Medium Newspaper, Seattle, assoc publ, 1970-; Tiloben Publ, pres, currently. **Orgs:** Bd dir, treas, Tiloben Publ Co Inc; Nat Asn Advan Colored People; Black Educ & Econs Conf; team capt, Neighborhood Cancer Soc; Nat Educ Asn, 1969-70; Ga Educ Asn, 1969-70; vol acct inner city residents & vol trainer typesetter, Garfield HS Messenger, 1970-71; trainer & supr, Seattle Univ Minority Stud Newspaper, 1971-73. **Honors/Awds:** Model Cities Citizen Participation Award; Black Community Unsung Hero Award. **Home Addr:** 2710 31 Ave S, Seattle, WA 98144. **Business Addr:** President, Accountant, Tiloben Publishing Co Inc, 2600 S Jackson St, Seattle, WA 98144, **Business Phone:** (206)323-3070.

### HAILSTOCK, SHIRLEY
Writer, association executive. **Personal:** Born Newberry, SC; daughter of Eugene and Hattie. **Educ:** Howard Univ, Wash, DC, BS, chem; Fairleigh Dickinson Univ, MBA, chem mkt. **Career:** Rutgers State Univ, NJ, adj prof acct; Middlesex Co Col, prof, novel writing; Women Writers Color, officer. **Orgs:** Bd mem, pres, Romance Writers Am, 1988-2003. **Home Addr:** PO Box 513, Plainsboro, NJ 08536-0513.

### HAINES, CHARLES EDWARD
Arts administrator, college teacher, radio broadcaster. **Personal:** Born Apr 20, 1925, Louisville, KY; son of William and Willie M Warfield; children: Charles Jr. **Educ:** Ind Univ, AB, 1950, MFA, 1953 & MA, 1959. **Career:** Free lance, adv art; AUS, corp engr, 1944-46; WTTS radio; WTTV, Bloomington-Indianapolis, sta's artist, 1949; WLWI; WTHR TV, Indianapolis, Ind, art dir, 1959-; Purdue Univ, Indianapolis, lectr, 1969-; Ind Univ, grad asst, lectr; Sarkes Tarzian Inc, art dir; Avco Broad, art dir; Crosley Broad, art dir; Marian Col, lectr. **Orgs:** Col Art Asn Am; dean, Dean's Select Comn Search & Screen; Herron Sch Art Indianapolis. **Honors/Awds:** Black Expo Feat, Ebony Mag, 1957; Bronze Star, Rhineland Campaign; Art Work in Basketball Hall of Fame; painting in Atlanta Univ Collection. **Home Addr:** 3508 Sherburne Lane, Indianapolis, IN 46222, **Home Phone:** (317)926-9641. **Business Addr:** Art Director, WTHR TV, 1000 N Meridian St, Indianapolis, IN 46204, **Business Phone:** (317)655-5740.

### HAIR, PRINCELL
Vice president (organization). **Personal:** Born Feb 2, 1967, Ft. Lauderdale, FL; married Jodie; children: 5. **Educ:** Fla Int Univ, BS, broadcast jour; Emory Univ, MBA, 2006. **Career:** WPLG-TV Miami, producer, 1990-91; WSVN-TV Miami, producer, 1991-92; WDIV-TV Detroit, producer, 1992-93; WBBM-TV, exec producer news, 1993-95; WCPX-TV Orlando, Fla, asst news dir, 1995-97; WMAQ-TV, news dir, 1997-98; WBAL-TV Baltimore, news dir, 1998-2001; Viacom TV Stas Group, news dir; KCBS-TV, news dir; CNN/US, exec vpres & gen mgr, 2003-04, sr vpres, prog & talent develop, 2004-08;

Turner Broadcasting Inc, sr vpres; Comcast SportsNet, sr vpres, News Oper & studio prog, Comcast's 10 RSNs, 2008-; NBC Sports Group, sr vpres news and talent, 2012; Drexel Univ, adj assoc prof, currently. **Orgs:** Bd dir, Radio & Tv News dir Asn; bd visitor, Fla A&M Univ's Sch Journalism & Graphic Commun; Nat Asn Black Journalists; Nat Black MBA Asn; Nat Asn Broadcasters. **Home Addr:** 510 Grove Pk Pl, Roswell, GA 30075-6873. **Business Addr:** Adjunct Associate Professor, Drexel University, 3141 Chestnut St, Philadelphia, PA 19104, **Business Phone:** (215)895-2000.

### HAIRSTON, ABBEY GAIL

Lawyer. **Personal:** Born Oct 15, 1955, Chicago, IL; daughter of Horace W and Rosietta. **Educ:** Drake Univ, BA, 1976; Univ Iowa Col Law, JD, 1980. **Career:** Fla Rural Legal Serv, staff atty, 1980-82, supv atty, 1982-84; Palm Beach Co Fla Sch Bd, atty & gen coun, 1988-93; Nova Univ, adj prof, 1984-92; Barry Univ, adj prof, 1991-93; Alexander, Bearden, Hairston & Marks, partner, 1994; Seyfarth Shaw Law Firm, partner, 2000-05; DC Pub Sch, gen coun, 2006-07; Thatcher Law Firm LLC, atty, 2008-; Epstein, Becker & Green PC, partner. **Orgs:** Am Bar Asn; Asn Trial Lawyers Am; Fed Bar Asn; Nat Bar Asn; Outstanding Lawyers Am; Steering Comt Litigation Sect, DC Bar Asn; chmn, Bd Gov, Fed Bar Asn; Md Bar Asn. **Honors/Awds:** One of Washington's 50 Best Lawyers, Washingtonian Mag, 1997; Outstanding Lawyer in America, 2003. **Special Achievements:** Book: "The Leave and Disability Coordination Handbook", 1997. **Home Addr:** 2424 Portage Rd, Silver Spring, MD 20906, **Home Phone:** (301)460-3355. **Business Addr:** Attorney, Thatcher Law Firm LLC, 7849 Belle Point Dr, Greenbelt, MD 20770-3338, **Business Phone:** (301)441-1400.

### HAIRSTON, DR. EDDISON R., SR.

Dentist. **Personal:** Born Apr 4, 1933, York, PA; married Audrey Barnes; children: Eddison Jr & Robert Eugene. **Educ:** Lincoln Univ, AB, 1954; Howard Univ Dent Sch, DDS, 1962. **Career:** Pvt pract dentist, 1963-; Howard Univ Comm Dent Chronically Ill & Aged Prog, clin asst prof, 1967; Armstrong Dent Asst Prog, consult, 1973-74; Eddison R Hairston Sr DDS PC, dentist, 1984-. **Orgs:** Robt T Freeman Dent Soc; Am & Nat Dent Asns; DC Dent Soc; Am Soc Dent C; Omega Psi Phi; Wash Urban League; bd trustee, pres, Nat Asn Advan Colored People.Chap Gen Alumni Asn. **Business Addr:** Dentist, Eddison R Hairston Sr DDS PC, 3417 Minn Ave SE Suite 1, Washington, DC 20019-2358, **Business Phone:** (202)584-3331.

### HAIRSTON, HAROLD B.

Government official. **Personal:** Born Jan 1, 1940; married Anne; children: Harold Jr & Jennifer. **Career:** Philadelphia Fire Dept, 1964, fire comnr, 1992-2004; CBS 3, KYW-TV CBS 3, Pub Safety Consult, on-air consult, 2004-; Lab Charter Sch, chmn. **Orgs:** Int Asn Black Fire Fighters; Boca; Nat Fire Protectors Asn; CORA Serv inc; Variety Club Del Valley; Police Athletic League; Am Red Cross Southeastern Pa; Del Valley Burn Found; Dad Vail Regatta; Young Scholars Charter Sch. **Special Achievements:** First appointed Commissioner of the Philadelphia Fire Department, 1992. **Home Addr:** 823 W Mount Airy Ave, Philadelphia, PA 19119-3329, **Home Phone:** (215)248-0666. **Business Addr:** On Air Consultant, KYW-TV CBS 3, 1555 Hamilton St, Philadelphia, PA 19130, **Business Phone:** (215)977-5300.

### HAIRSTON, JERRY WAYNE, SR.

Baseball player. **Personal:** Born Feb 16, 1952, Birmingham, AL; son of Sammy; married Esperanza Anellano; children: Jerry Jr, Justin, Scott & Stacey Lynn. **Educ:** Lawson St Jr Col, Birmingham, AL. **Career:** Baseball player (retired), baseball coach; Chicago White Sox, outfielder, 1973-77, 1981-89; Pittsburgh Pirates, outfielder, 1977; Bristol White Sox, hitting coach, currently. **Home Addr:** 3770 1st St W, Birmingham, AL 35207. **Business Addr:** Hitting Coach, Bristol White Sox, 1501 Euclid Ave, Bristol, VA 24201, **Business Phone:** (276)645-7364.

### HAIRSTON, JERRY WAYNE, JR.

Baseball player. **Personal:** Born May 29, 1976, Naperville, IL; son of Jerry; married Tanaha; children: Jackson,Kara & Jessica. **Educ:** Southern Ill Univ. **Career:** Baltimore Orioles, outfielder, 1998-2004; Chicago Cubs, outfielder, 2005-06; Tex Rangers, outfielder, 2006-07; Cincinnati Reds, 2008-09; New York Yankees, 2009; San Diego Padres, 2010; Wash Nationals, 2011; Milwaukee Brewers, outfielder, 2011; Los Angeles Dodgers, 2012-13; free agt, currently. **Orgs:** Jehovah's Witnesses, 2000. **Special Achievements:** First African American to be a third-generation major-leaguer. **Business Addr:** Professional Baseball Player, Milwaukee Brewers, 1 Brewers Way, Milwaukee, WI 53214, **Business Phone:** (414)902-4400.

### HAIRSTON, JOSEPH HENRY

Lawyer. **Personal:** Born May 8, 1922, Axton, VA; son of James and Julia; married Anna L Allen; children: Nancy R, Naomi, JoAnn & Victoria M. **Educ:** Univ Md, BS, 1957; Am Univ, JD, 1960; Georgetown Univ, LLM, 1961. **Career:** Lawyer (retired); Off Solicitor Dept Labor Washington, atty, 1960-61; IRS, sr exec, Opers Div, dir, 1976-85. **Orgs:** Founder & pres, Nat Neighbors, 1969, 1975; exec com, DC Fed Citizens Asn, 1970-73; bd dir, Wash Bar Asn, 2005-08, 2009-; treas emer, Nat Bar Asn, 2007-; treas, Coordinating Coun, Cooperative Bapt Fel; DC Bar Asn; Am Bar Asn; treas, trustee, Baptist Sr Adult Ministries; vpres, Nat Lawyers Club, Neighbors Inc; vice chmn, moderator, Takoma Park Bapt Church; del, Shepherd Park Citizens Asn; Shepherd PTA; Takoma PTA; Officers Club, Walter Reed Army Med Ctr; Nat Asn Uniformed Serv; Comner, District Columbia Advisory Neighborhood Comn; trustee, DC Bapt Found; ex-bd, exec comm, DC Bapt Convention; co-chair, DC Postal Advisory Comm; chmn, Wash Gas Co, Citizens Advisory Comm; bd dir, Am Inst Parliamentarians. **Honors/Awds:** First African-American attorney apptd sr exec, Office of Chief Counsel, IRS. **Special Achievements:** First Black Army Helicopter Pilot in Military. **Home Addr:** 1316 Floral St NW, Washington, DC 20012-1718, **Home Phone:** (202)723-1025.

### HAIRSTON, RALEIGH DANIEL

Social worker, clergy. **Personal:** Born Nov 15, 1934, Amonate, VA; son of Samuel Hardin and Elsie Wilson; married Helen Carol Covington; children: John Lesley Daniel & Karen Nancy. **Educ:** Bluefield State Col, BS, 1959; Atlanta Univ, MSW, 1962; Bexley Hall Episcopal Sem, MA, 1969; Case Western Res Univ, MA, 1975; Colgate Rochester Divinity Sch, DMin, 1978. **Career:** Boston Univ Med Sch, Psychiat Dept, adj asst prof, 1970-71; Cleveland Metro Gen Hosp, proj adr, 1972-77; St Simon Cyrene Episcopal Church, rector, 1977-81; Emmanuel Episcopal Church, interim rector, 1982; Cleveland Munic Ct, probation officer, 1982-85; Veterans Admin Hosp, med social worker, 1985-88; Calvary Episcopal Church, asst priest, 1989-91; City Wash Child & Family Servs, social worker, 1989-94; St Augustine's Col, Raleigh, NC, chaplain, 1995-98; St Marks Episcopal Church, rector, Priest Charge, 2001-05. **Orgs:** National Association for the Advancement of Colored People, currently; Nat Asn Social Workers; Asn Black Social Workers; Union Black Episcopalians; former Am Fed State, Country & Munic Employees; Interdenominational Ministerial Asn; Diocese Ohio CMS Ministry, 1975-77; Diocese Southern Ohio CMS Ecumenical Rels, 1979-81; life mem, Kappa Alpha Psi Fraternity. **Honors/Awds:** Sigma Rho Sigma Honor Fraternity Social Sciences, Bluefield State Col, 1959; Firestone Scholarship, Bexley Hall Episcopal Sem, 1965; Human Services Volunteer Award, City Lincoln Heights, Ohio, 1980; Distinguished Service Award, St Augustine's Col, 1998. **Special Achievements:** A Study of Formal Training Provided, Employment, and the Availability of Jobs for Negro High School Graduates in Tampa, Florida, unpublished thesis, 1962, Atlanta Univ, GEO; Author, Blacks & the Episcopal Church in the Diocese of Ohio, unpublished dissertation, May 1978, Colgate Rochester Divinity School, NY. **Home Addr:** 222 Mohawk Trl, Wilmington, NC 28409-3415, **Home Phone:** (910)791-4057. **Business Addr:** Priest in Charge, Saint Mark's Episcopal Church, 601 Grace St, Wilmington, NC 28401, **Business Phone:** (910)763-3292.

### HAIRSTON, DR. SANDRA WATSON

Physician. **Educ:** Univ NC, Chapel Hill, MD. **Career:** York Hosp, York, Pa, resident physician; Am Bd Internal Med, internal med; Johns Hopkins Community Physicians, Wyman Pk Med Ctr, internal med physician, currently. **Business Addr:** Physician, Johns Hopkins Community Physicians, 3100 Wyman Pk Dr Suite 170, Baltimore, MD 21211, **Business Phone:** (410)338-3421.

### HAIRSTON, WILLIAM

Artistic director, writer, administrator. **Personal:** Born Apr 1, 1928, Goldsboro, NC; son of William Russell and Malissa Carter; married Enid Carey; children: Ann Marie. **Educ:** Univ Northern Colo, Greeley, Colo, BA, polit sci; Columbia Univ, New York; NY Univ. **Career:** Greenwich Mews Theatre, New York, prod coordr, 1963, co producer, 1963-64; New York Shakespeare Festival, theatre mgr & adminr, 1963-66; Ford Grant, Arena Stage, Washington, DC, asst to exec dir, 1965-66; Dem Nat Comt, radio news ed & corresp, 1968; DC, Exec Off Mayor, Off Personnel, exec mgr, 1970-90; DC Pipeline, Washington, DC, publ & ed, 1973-79; Books: The World of Carlos, 1968; Sex & Conflict, 1993; Ira Aldridge, 1998; Spaced Out: A Space Adventure, 1998; Showdown At Sundown, 1998; History of the National Capital Area Council, 1998; Passion & Politics, 2001; Playwright: Swan-Song of the 11th Dawn, 1962; Walk in Darkness, 1963; Curtain Call, Mr Aldridge, Sir!, 1964; Black Antigone, 1965; Ira Aldridge, 1988; Double Dare, 1995; Poems: Poetry & Prose of Passion & Compassion, 2002; Anthologies: Echoes of Yesterday; Best Poems of 1995; A Voyage to Remember; Forever & A Day; Fields of Gold; Essence of a Dream; Tracing Shadows; The Scenic Route; Journey Between Stars; Scriptwriting for US Info Agency: Apollo 11-Man on the Moon; Media Hora; Festival of Heritage; Jules Verne vs Real Flight to the Moon; Operation Money-Wise; TV series: "Harlem Detective", 1953; Films: Take the High Ground, 1953; Jerico-Jim Crow. **Orgs:** Exec bd, Dramatists Guild; Nat Capital Area Coun; Boy Scouts Am. **Honors/Awds:** Theatre Admininistration Grant, Ford Found, 1965-66; Literary Study Grant, Nat Endowment Arts, 1967; Playwrights Festival Award, Group Theatre, Seattle, WA, 1988; The Silver Beaver Award, Boy Scouts Am, Nat Capital Area, 1988; Multi Cultural Playwrights Festival Winner, 1988; Meritorious Public Service Award, DC, 1990; Creative Achievement Award, Univ Northern Colo, 2005. **Home Addr:** 5501 Sem Rd, Falls Church, VA 22041-3901, **Home Phone:** (703)845-1281.

### HAKEEM, WALI. See GILL, DR. WALTER A.

### HAKIM, AZ-ZAHIR (AZ-ZAHIR ALI HAKIM)

Business owner, football player. **Personal:** Born Jun 3, 1977, Los Angeles, CA. **Educ:** San Diego State Univ, grad. **Career:** Football player (retired); St Louis Rams, 1999, wide receiver, 1998, 2000-01; Detroit Lions, wide receiver, 2002-04, 2006; New Orleans Saints, wide receiver, 2005; San Diego Chargers, wide receiver, 2006; Miami Dolphins, 2007; Las Vegas Locomotives, 2009; Quickies, owner, 2009. **Honors/Awds:** Second-team All-WAC, 2005; Super Bowl champion (XXXIV); All-Pro, 2000. **Special Achievements:** Films: Super Bowl XXXIV, 2000; Super Bowl XXXVI, 2002. **Business Addr:** Owner, Quickie Burger, 1000 S State Rd 7, Hollywood, FL 33021, **Business Phone:** (954)981-9464.

### HALE, REV. CYNTHIA LYNNETTE

Clergy. **Personal:** Born Oct 27, 1952, Roanoke, VA; daughter of Harrison and Janice Hylton. **Educ:** Hollins Col, Hollins, Va, BA, Music, 1975; Duke Divinity Sch, Durham NC, MDiv, 1979; United Theol Sem, Dayton OH, Doctorate Ministry, 1991. **Career:** Fed Correctional facilities, Colorado & NC, Chaplain, 1979-85; Ray Hope Christian Church, Decatur, Ga, pastor, founder & sr pastor, currently. **Orgs:** Nat Coun Churches, New York, 1978-83; vpres, bd dir, Greenwood Cemetery Co, 1979-80; pres, Nat Convocation Christian Church, 1982-88; Gen Bd Christian Church, 1982-88; vpres, Concerned Black Clergy; bd dir, Christian Coun Metrop, Atlanta, 1989; Proj Impact, DeKalb; chief advisor, Nat Consortium Black Women Ministry; life mem, Disciples; bd trustee, Hollins Univ, 2006; co-chair, Women Ministry Obama; secy bd, Beulah Heights Univ; chair, City Hope Ministries Inc; co-chair, Samuel DeWitt Proctor Conf; chair, 21st Century Vision Team Christian Church. **Honors/Awds:** Outstanding Young Woman Am, 1982, 1986-88; Liberation Award, Nat Convocation CCDC, 1984; The Religious Award, Ninety-Nine Breakfast Club, 1990; The Religion Award, DeKalb Br, Nat Advan Asn Colored People, 1990; Inducted Martin Luther Kind Bd Preachers, Morehouse Col, 1993; Chosen Award, Atlanta Gospel Choice, 1998; Inducted into the African Am Biographies Hall of Fame; Profiles of Prominence Award, Martin Luther King, 2000; Outstanding Religious Leader Award, Alpha Kappa Alpha; Outstanding Ga Citizen, Ga Secy State; Ga Goodwill Ambassador; Church of the Week, 700 Club; Spiritual Enlightenment Award; Religious Leadership Award, Sisters African Descent; Pinnacle Leadership Award, Fortitude Educ, Cult Develop Found Inc, 2007; Christian Excellence Award, Yolanda Adams Morning Radio Show; Trombone Award, Rainbow Push Coalition; Excellence Award, Alpha Phi Alpha Fraternity; Hon DDiv, Bethany Col; Hon DDiv, Northwest Christian Col. **Special Achievements:** First female chaplain to serve in an all male institution; Author: I'm A Piece of Work: Sisters Shaped by God. **Home Addr:** 1909 Sheldon Lane, Conyers, GA 30094, **Home Phone:** (770)761-0728. **Business Addr:** Founder, Senior Pastor, Ray of Hope Christian Church, 2778 Snapfinger Rd, Decatur, GA 30034-2439, **Business Phone:** (770)696-5100.

### HALE, DERRICK F.

State government official. **Personal:** Born Jul 9, 1963, Detroit, MI; son of Thomas and Mildred Hall; married Cleo; children: Christina, Nicole & Derrick II. **Educ:** Wayne State Univ, BA, mass communs, 1995. **Career:** WDIV Channel 4, sports intern, 1987-88; Mich State Rep Michael J Bennane, legis aide, 1989-96; Fourteenth Dist, Mich, State Rep, 1997-02; Congressman Sander Levin, campaign coordr, 1998. **Orgs:** Wayne State Univ Alumni Asn; USA Boxing Asn; bd mem, Northwest Young Men's Christian Asn; Nat Black Caucus State Legislators; methodist mem, Nat Asn Advan Colored People, currently; founder, pres, Derrick F Hale Found; Coun State Govs; Coalition Labor Union Women; St Stephens AME Church; Am Coun Young Polit Leaders; Motor City Blight Busters; pres, Eighth Precinct Community Coun; pres, Eighth Precinct BUOY; vice chair, Mich Family Forum; Old Redford Asn; NAACP; Wayne State Alumni Asn; River Rouge Clean Up; 8th Precinct Community Rels; Brightmoor Concerned Citizens; House of Representatives, 1996. **Honors/Awds:** Volunteer of the Year, Eight Precinct Community Rels, 1998; Murray-Wright Hall of Fame, inductee, 1998; Legislator of the Year, Mich Minority Women's Network, 2000; Certificate of Recognition, Detroit Bd Police Comnrs, 2005; Spirit of Detroit Award, Detroit City Coun, 2005. **Special Achievements:** American council of young political leaders, selected as ambassador to South Korea, 1999. **Home Addr:** 18505 W 8 Mile Rd, Detroit, MI 48219, **Home Phone:** (313)592-8667. **Business Addr:** State Representative, Michigan House Representative, N 693 HOB, Lansing, MI 48909, **Business Phone:** (517)373-1705.

### HALE, GENE

Executive, founder (originator), president (organization). **Personal:** Born Apr 19, 1946, Birmingham, AL; son of Matt and Minnie; married Cecelia L Davis; children: Reginald, Kevin & Crystal. **Educ:** Calif State Univ, Dominguez Hills, Los Angeles, CA, BS, bus admin, 1980. **Career:** Co-founder, Fourth Ann Black Bus Day Luncheon; G&C Equip Corp, Gardena, Calif, founder & pres, 1981-; Gence, pres & chief exec officer, currently; G&C Serv & Supply Corp, pres & chief exec officer, currently. **Orgs:** Adv bd, Hist Black Col, 2004; chmn, Cong Task Force Minority Bus Set Asides Pvt Sector; chmn, Greater Los Angeles African Am Chamber Com; adv coun chmn, Calif Dept Transp; chmn, Century Freeway Employ Adv Comt; chmn, Fedn Minority Bus Asn; co-chmn, Calif Dept Transp Employ Comt; dir, Gardena Valley Chamber Com; adv comt mem, Entrepreneurial Prog Disadvantaged Youth; adv bd, Calif Pub Utilities; chair, Greater Los Angeles African Am; expert coun, Dept Com; adv bd, AT&T Technol Bd; comnr, City Los Angeles; dir, Los Angeles Conv & Visitors Bur; Calif Small Bus Bd; bd advisors, Historically Black Cols & Univs; chmn, Los Angeles African Am Chamber Com; chmn, Gardena Police Found; Pres Export Coun. **Home Addr:** 13235 Ruthelen St, Gardena, CA 90249, **Home Phone:** (213)770-5615. **Business Addr:** Founder, President, G&C Equipment Corp, 1875 W Redondo Beach Blvd Suite 102, Gardena, CA 90247, **Business Phone:** (213)515-6715.

### HALE, HILTON I.

Insurance agent. **Personal:** Born May 17, 1956, Columbus, OH; son of Phale D Sr and Cleo I. **Educ:** Northwestern Univ; Atlanta Univ; Morehouse Col; San Diego State, BA, bus, econ & commun, 1979; Am Col, chartered life underwriter, 2002. **Career:** United Parcel Serv, indust engr, 1979-81, revenue auditor, 1981-85; H & R Block, tax preparer, 1983-85; Hilton I Hale & Assoc LLC, chief exec officer, 1985-. **Orgs:** Columbus Life Underwriters Asn, 1986-; Ohio Asn Life Underwriters, 1986-; Nat Asn Underwriters, 1986-; King's Men, 1989-91; treas, Hilliard Dem Club, 1997-98; pres, Linden Kiwanis, 1998-99; Life Underwriters, Polit Action Community, 1998-99; Rainbow & PUSH Coalition, 1998-99; Nat Asn Ins & Financial Advisors, 2000-; Thursday Club, 2000-; ambassador, Am Heart Asn, 2007-08; ambassador, Am Stroke Asn, 2007-08; Northwestern Basketball Alumni. **Honors/Awds:** The Nat Quality Award, The Nat Asn Life Underwriters & Life Ins Mkt & Res Asn, 1993, 1997, 1998; Executive Council Award, NY Ins Co, 1987, 1988; Centurion Award, 1988; Quality Award, 1997, 1998; Award of Excellence, Columbus East High Sch Class of 1974, 2004; Sr NYLIC Designation, NY Life Ins Co, 2005; Community Serv Award, Black Pages Ohio, 2006. **Special Achievements:** Columbus Corporate Challenge Basketball Champions, 1987. **Home Addr:** PO Box 9863, Columbus, OH 43209-0863, **Home Phone:** (614)238-3021. **Business Addr:** Chief Executive Officer, Hilton I Hale & Assoc LLC, 897 E 11th Ave Suite A, Columbus, OH 43211-2757, **Business Phone:** (614)291-4253.

### HALE, DR. JANICE ELLEN

Educator, research scientist. **Personal:** Born Apr 30, 1948, Ft. Wayne, IN; daughter of Phale D Sr and Cleo Ingram; children: Keith A Benson Jr. **Educ:** Spelman Col, BA, sociol & elem educ, 1970; Interdenominational Theol Ctr, MRE, Christian educ, 1972; Ga State Univ, PhD, early childhood educ, 1974; Rockefeller Univ, post doctoral study, 1978; Univ Calif, post doctoral study, 1979; Yale Univ, post doctoral study, 1981. **Career:** Third Ave Child Develop Ctr, teacher, 1968; Model Cities Child Develop Prog, res & curric coord, 1972; Econ Opportunity Atlanta Head Start Child Develop Prog, educ coord, 1973; Ga State Univ, grad res asst, 1973-74, lectr dept early childhood educ, 1974; Clark Col, from asst prof to assoc prof, 1974-81; Univ Calif, lab comparative human cognition, res fel & vis lectr, lectr, commun prog, 1979; Yale Univ, Dept Psychol, res assoc, dept psychol, 1979-81, res affil, 1981-83, afro-am studies prog, lectr, 1980-81; Univ Conn Storrs, lectr, psychol dept, 1980; Cleveland State Univ, Dept Specialized Instrnl Progs, assoc prof, 1984-90; Jackson State Univ, assoc prof, early childhood educ, 1981-84; Coordr Early Childhood Educ Degree Prog, assoc prof, 1984-90; Wayne State Univ, prof, early childhood educ, 1991-; Inst Study African Am Child, (ISAAC) founding dir, 2006-. **Orgs:** Founder, Visions C, African-Am Early Childhood Educ Res Demonstration Prog, 1986-93; gov bd mem, Nat Asn Educ Young C, 1988-92; Mich Asn Educ Young C; Nat Asn Educ Young C; Nat Black Child Develop Inst Nat Alliance Black Sch Educr, 2006-. **Special Achievements:** Books Nominated for the Pulitzer Prize, 1995, 2001. **Home Addr:** 30336 Stratford Ct, Farmington Hills, MI 48331-1608, **Home Phone:** (248)661-4339. **Business Addr:** Professor, Wayne State University, 213 Educ Bldg, Detroit, MI 48202, **Business Phone:** (313)577-0954.

## HALE, KIMBERLY ANICE

Librarian, college administrator. **Personal:** Born Dec 6, 1962, Champaign, IL; daughter of Emery S White and Margaret I. **Educ:** Univ Ill, Urbana-Champaign, BS, sociol criminol, 1985, MS, lib & info sci, 1989. **Career:** Columbia Col Libr, Chicago, acquistions librn, coordr collection develop, 1989-2002; head collection mgt, 2002-08, actg dir, 2008, head libr mkt, 2008-13, head community engagement & spec initiatives. **Orgs:** Alpha Phi Omega Serv Fraternity, 1983-; Asn Col & Res Libr, 1988-; Asn Libr Colections & Tech Servs Div, 1988-; Am Libr Asn, 1988-; Women dir Chair, 1998-2001; Ref & User Servs Asn, 2003-04; Libr Admin & Mgt Asn, 2003-; Libr Fundraising Adv Comt; Ill Libr Asn Intellectual Freedom Comt; Electronic Res Comt; Columbia Col Chicago Curric Comt; Libr Fundraising Adv Comt; Ill Libr Asn Intellectual Freedom Comt. **Home Addr:** 5200 N Sheridan Rd Apt 730, Chicago, IL 60640, **Home Phone:** (773)561-8860. **Business Addr:** Head of Community Engagement and Special Initiatives, Columbia College Library, 624 S Mich Ave 3rd Fl E Rm 307B, Chicago, IL 60605, **Business Phone:** (312)369-7355.

## HALE, MARNA AMORETTI (MARNA HALE LEAKS)

Educator. **Personal:** Born Jan 13, 1951, Columbus, OH; daughter of Phale D Sr and Cleo Ingram; married Emanuel; children: Richard W Hale Pace, Deante George & Deandre George. **Educ:** Spelman Col, BA, eng lit & educ, 1973; John Carroll Univ, MA, eng Lit, 1992; Case Western Res Univ, attended 1993. **Career:** AT&T Technologies, sect chief training, 1977-87; Allen-Bradley Co Inc, srinstrnl developer, 1987-92; Data Corp Bus Systs Inc, training consult, 1994-96; Ernst & Young LLP, Prof & Orgn Develop, consult, 1998-2000; Intellinex, opers load & prog leader, sr mgr progs; City Cleveland, Div Water, proj dir, currently, Dept Pub Utilities, proj dir, 2003-14; Phale Hale Educ Consult Inc, pres, currently; Endeavor Group, consult, 2014-. **Orgs:** Int Soc Performance Improv, 1977-; Am Soc Training & Develop, 1992-98; Nat Writer's Asn, 1992-; Nat Spelman Alumni Asn, 1997-; Mgt Alliance; Am Water Works Asn; ECKANKAR. **Home Addr:** 4430 S Meadow Lane, Cleveland, OH 44109-3676, **Home Phone:** (216)661-6434. **Business Addr:** Project Director, City of Cleveland, 1201 Lakeside Ave, Cleveland, OH 44114, **Business Phone:** (216)664-3130.

## HALES, EDWARD EVERETTE (ED HALES)

Lawyer. **Personal:** Born Feb 13, 1932, Leechburg, PA; son of Charles and Bertha. **Educ:** Baldwin-Wallace Col, BA, govt & hist, 1955; Univ Wis, Law Col, JD, 1962. **Career:** Ford Motor Co-United Auto Workers, permanent umpire; Pac Bell, arbitrator; St Ak Pub Employees, arbitrator; State Minn, legal asst, atty gen, 1962-63; City Racine, asst city atty, 1965-67; Goodman Hales & Costello, atty, 1965-73; Hales Harvey & Neu, atty, 1973-79; Hales Hartig, atty, 1979-; Int Fel, consult; VISTA, consult; St Mich OEO, consult; IAUrban Res Ctr, consult; AIM Jobs, bd pvt consult; City San Diego, atty, currently. **Orgs:** Spec arbitrator, Bd Arbit US Steel Corp United Steel Workers Am; spec arbitrator, Fed Mediation Serv; spec arbitrator, Wiss Employ Rel Comn; spec arbitrator, Bd Arbit St Minn, Nat Asn Advan Colored People; Urban League; Nat Bar Asn; Am Bar Asn; WIS St Bar Asn; WIS Coun Criminal Justice; WIS Higher Educ Aids Bd; WIS Univ Merger Implementation Com; Alpha Phi Alpha; chmn, Fin Com Bd Regents Univ Wis Syst, 1975-77; pres, Bd Regents Univ Wis Syst, 1977-79; bd trustee, Asn Gov, Bds Univ & Col, 1977-; selection com US 7th Circuit & Judicial Ct, 1978-79; bd dir, Pub Broadcasting Serv, 1979-80; bd trustee, Asn Pub Broadcasting, 1979-; arbitrator, Am Arbit Asn, 1980-; bd trustee, Ripon Col, Ripon, Wi, 1980-; St Wis, Investment Bd, 1987-90; St Wis, Racing Comn, 1988-90; Ford Motor Co & United Automobile Workers, permanent umpire; US Postal Serv; Nat Asn Lett Carriers; Los Angeles Pub Employees Union; dir, Asn Gov Boards Univs & Cols; Bd Attorneys Prof Responsibility. **Honors/Awds:** Urban Service Award, 1967; Effort Award Kings Daughter Club, 1974. **Home Addr:** 4350 La Jolla Village Dr Suite 300, San Diego, CA 92121. **Business Addr:** Attorney, City San Diego, 4089 Porte De Palmas Suite 118, San Diego, CA 92122-5120, **Business Phone:** (619)546-4348.

## HALES, DR. MARY A.

Educator, bail bond agent. **Personal:** Born Jul 27, 1953, Fayetteville, NC; daughter of Jack E Melvin and Dorothy M Allen; children: Michelle, Mario & Dominique. **Educ:** Fayetteville State Univ, BS, psychol, 1981, elem educ & math, 1989, EdD, 2008; Cert Educ Admin & Supvr, 1994. **Career:** Foxe's Surety Bail Bonding Co, admin chief, 1978-81; Fayetteville Tech Inst, adult basic educ instr, 1981-88; WFBS Radio, radio commun operator, 1982-83; HSA Cumberland Psychiat Hosp, ment health counr, 1985-87; All Am Bail Bonding Co, owner & agt, 1987-; Long Hill Elem Sch, sixth grade teacher, 1989-90; Montclair Elem Sch, Fayetteville, NC, fourth grade teacher, 1990; Coun Real Estate, sales agt, 1994-; Margaret Willis Elem Sch, Fayetteville, NC, asst prin; Howard Hall Class Elem Sch, asst prin; Ferguson-Easley Elem Sch, Sch Math & Sci, prin, currently. **Orgs:** Vpres, Cumberland Co Chap Bail Bondsmen, 1978-81; notary pub State NC, 1980-; NC Asn Adult Educr; NC Bail Bondsmen Asn; NC Asn Educr; Nat Educ Asn; NC Coun Teachers Mathematics; Asn Teacher Educr; Fayetteville Jaycees; US Jaycees; athletic club, Fayetteville State Univ, 1993-; NC Asn Realtors; Fayetteville Area Bd Realtors; NC Asn Sch Adminr; Nat Dean's List; Alpha Kappa Mu Nat Hon Soc; Kappa Delta Pi Int Hon Soc Educ. **Home Addr:** 3490 Hastings Dr, Fayetteville, NC 28311-7626, **Home Phone:** (910)482-3390. **Business Addr:** Principal, Ferguson-Easley Elementary School, 1857 Seabrook Rd, Fayetteville, NC 28301, **Business Phone:** (910)483-4883.

## HALEY, CHARLES LEWIS

Football player, football coach. **Personal:** Born Jan 6, 1964, Gladys, VA; married Karen; children: Princess Kay, Charles Jr & Brianna. **Educ:** James Madison Univ. **Career:** Football player (retired), football coach; San Francisco 49ers, defensive end & left outside linebacker, 1986-91, 1998-99; Dallas Cowboys, 1992-96; Detroit Lions, right defensive end, 1992-96, asst coach, 2001-02. **Orgs:** Alpha Phi Alpha Fraternity; Xi Delta Chap. **Honors/Awds:** Division I-AA All-American, 1984-85; Pro Bowl, 1988, 1990-91, 1994-95; Football Digest, Defensive Player of the Year, 1990, 1994; Defensive Player of the Year, UPI NFC, 1990-94; Virginia Sports Hall of Fame, 2006; Super Bowl Champion; Dallas Cowboys Ring of Honor, 2011; Pro Football Hall of Fame, 2010-11; San Francisco 49ers Hall of Fame. **Special Achievements:** Tv appearance: Cooking with the Legends, 2009. **Business Addr:** 2121 George Halas Dr NW, Canton, OH 44708, **Business Phone:** (330)456-8207.

## HALEY, DAMON L.

Founder (originator), executive. **Educ:** Univ Calif, BA, econs, 1988; Univ Mich, Stephen M Ross Sch Bus, MBA, finance, 1992. **Career:** Occidental Col, admis officer, 1989-90; Reebok, marketer; Nike, mkt mgr, 1996-99; Chevron Corp, sr financial analyst, 1992-96; Nike, western region mkt mgr, 1996-99, consult, 2013, Global & USA Brand Basketball, consult, 2014-; Urban Mkt Corp Am, co-founder, 1999-, chief strategist, sr vpres & chief exec officer, currently; UMCA Sports & Entertainment, managing partner, 2000-12; Troika, sports acct dir, 2013-14; Something Big Tech, consult, 2015-; MeTyme Network, chief strategy officer, 2016-. **Orgs:** Adv bd mem, Econ Opportunity Ctr; eMarketing Asn Network; Cal Alumni Asn; Sports Indust Network; Pub rel & Commun Professionals; Sports Mkt & PR Pros. **Business Addr:** Chief Executive Officer, Chief Strategist, Urban Marketing Corp of America, 1450 S Fairfax Ave, Los Angeles, CA 90019, **Business Phone:** (323)934-8622.

## HALEY, DAVID

State government official, lawyer. **Personal:** Born Oct 29, 1958, Kansas City, KS; married Michelle; children: 4. **Educ:** Morehouse Col, BA, 1980; Howard Univ Law Sch, JD, 1984. **Career:** Kans Citys Ward 3, Precinct 4, precinct committeeman, 1988-; Kans State House Representatives, rep, 1995-2000; Kans Sen, 4th Dist, sen & pub affairs coun, 2001-; Five Star Speakers Bur, pub affairs counr, speaker. **Orgs:** Kans Vet Med Asn; bd mem, Habitat Humanity, 1994; bd mem, Northeast Action Group, Kans City Kans, 1994; bd mem, Planned Parenthood, Greater Kans City, 1994; bd mem, Turner House, Kans City Kans, 1994; Redistricting; Pub Health & Welfare; State Tribal Rels; Re-codification; Rehab & Restoration; Early Childhood Coord Coun; Corrections & Juv Justice comts; Senate Assessment & Taxation; Kans Sentencing Comn; bd dir, Kaw Valley Habitat Humanity; Area Voc Tech Sch Adv Bd; Kans Atty Gens FATAL Task Force; fel Ctr Policy Alternatives, 2000; Ranking Dem Senate Judiciary Comt, currently. **Home Addr:** PO Box 171110, Kansas City, KS 66117, **Home Phone:** (913)579-1490. **Business Addr:** State Senator, Kansas State Senate 4th Dist, 936 Cleveland Ave Rm 424 E, Kansas City, KS 66101, **Business Phone:** (913)321-3210.

**HALEY, GEORGE WILLIFORD BOYCE.** **See Obituaries Section.**

## HALEY, PROF. JOHNETTA RANDOLPH

College administrator, educator, musician. **Personal:** Born Mar 19, 1923, Alton, IL; daughter of John and Willye Smith; children: Karen Douglas & Michael. **Educ:** Lincoln Univ, BS, 1945; Southern Ill Univ, Edwardsville, MM, 1972; Univ Ill; Univ Mich, Georgetown; Univ Montpellier, France. **Career:** Educator, professor, college administrator (retired), professor emeritus; Lincoln HS, vocal & gen music teacher, 1945-48; Turner Jr HS, vocal music teacher & choral dir, 1950-55; Nipher Jr HS, vocal, gen music teacher & choral dir, 1955-71; Title I Prog Culturally Disadvantaged C, teacher black hist/music, 1966; Human Develop Corp, prog specialist, 1968; St Louis Coun Black People, interim exec dir, 1970; Sch Fine Arts, Southern Ill Univ, Edwardsville, grad res asst, 1971-72, asst prof music, 1972-77, prof music, 1982, prof emer, currently, dir, Emerita St Louis Br, chmn, 1982-92, chief exec officer, chmn emerita, currently; Tex Southern Univ, vis prof, 1977. **Orgs:** Am Asn Univ Prof; Col Music Soc; Music Educrs Nat Conf; Ill Music Educrs Asn; Nat Choral Dir Asn; Mu Phi Epsilon; Asn Teachers Educrs; Mid-WestKodaly Music Educrs; Orgn Am Kodaly Educrs; Artist Presentations Soc; Pi Kappa Lambda; supreme parliamentarian, Alpha Kappa Alpha, 1945-; pres, St Louis chap, Jack &Jill Inc; pres, Las Amigas Social Club; Friends St Louis Art Mus; Top Ladies Distinction Inc; United Negro Col Fund Inc; UrbanLeague; co-founder, St Louis Coun Black People; St Louis Mayors Comm Protection Innocent; Pilot Counr Aide Prog St Louis Pub Sch Delinq Stud; adv bd, Help Inc; chmn, Ill Comm Black Concerns Her Educ; bd trustee, Lincoln Univ, 1974-83; bd trustee, Stillman Col, 1984-; vol, Am Red Cross, 1986-2011; bd dir, Asn Gov bds Univs & Cols; bd dir, Links Inc; bd dir, Southern IllUniv Friends Music; bd dir, St. Louis area Red Cross; pres, Bd Curators, Lincoln Univ; St. Phillips Lutheran Church. **Special Achievements:** First female CEO of a of Southern Illinois University campus; First female president of the Board of Curators at Lincoln University; First woman elected president of the Congregation. **Home Addr:** 1926 Bennington Common Dr, St. Louis, MO 63146-2555, **Home Phone:** (314)275-8138. **Business Addr:** Chairperson Emerita, Southern Illinois University, Edwardsville, IL 62026, **Business Phone:** (618)650-2000.

## HALL, AARON

Singer. **Personal:** Born Aug 10, 1964, Bronx, NY. **Career:** Singles: "Don't Be Afraid", 1992; "Get a Little Freaky with Me", "Let's Make Love", 1993; "I Miss You", "When You Need Me", 1994; "Curiosity", "Scent of Attraction (duet w/Patra)", 1995; "Toss It Up (Makaveli w/ Aaron Hall, Danny Boy, K-Ci & JoJo)", 1996; "All The Places (I Will Kiss You)", 1998; "Why You Tryin' to Play Me", 2000; "Bye Baby", 2011. Albums: The Truth, 1993; Inside of You, 1998, Adults Only: The Final Album, 2005. **Orgs:** Part trio, Guy. **Honors/Awds:** The 3rd Annual Soul Train Music Awards, 1989-92; BET Awards 2009, 2009. **Special Achievements:** Appeared in movie, New Jack City, 1991. **Business Addr:** Vocalist, Singer.

## HALL, DR. ADDIE JUNE

School administrator, educator, clergy. **Personal:** Born Apr 11, 1930, Houston, TX; daughter of Milton Gray and Aniece Clair Ware; children: Sharmane C & LeRoy B Jr. **Educ:** Bethune Cookman, BA, 1955; Columbia Univ, Teachers Col, MA, 1962; Fla State Univ, PhD, 1975; Emory Univ, cert, theol, 1981, Candler Sch Theol, Mdiv, 1999. **Career:** Professor (retired), evangelist, author; Agat Guam, instr, 1955-58; Escambia City Sch Bd, instr, 1959-69, curric coordr, 1969-71, instr coordr, 1971-73; United Methodist Church, minister, 1971-; FL State Univ, grad instr, 1973-74, instr, 1974-75; Pensacola Jr Col, asst prof, 1975-78, prof, 1980, dir adult educ & prof, 1978-90, Minority Recruitment & Retention, dir, 1990-95, prof behav scis, 1991-95; evangelist & auth, 1995-. Books: The Wife / The Other Woman; Must I Tell It? I Gotta Tell It!. **Orgs:** Kappa Delta Pi, 1972-; Phi Delta Kappa, 1974-; parliamentarian, FL State Adv Coun, 1983-; adb bd, Dept Corrections Reg, 1983-; Nat Asn Advan Colored People; Tiger Bay Club; FL Admin, 1983; TV appearances Adult Educ, Black Hist, 1983 & 1984; Radio Western Bay Plenty Dist Coun, 1983 & 1984; journalist, Delta Sigma Theta, 1985-; marcher, March Dimes, Arthritis, Leukema Soc; lectr & counr, Churches Schs Inst; Nat Polit Cong Blackwomen, Am Asn Adult & Continuing Educ, US Senate Educ Adv Coun; pres & chair, Pensacola Chap Links Inc, 1988-92; Waterfront Mission Bd, 1990; Societas Docta Inc; Code Enforcement Bd, 1990-95; Adv Bd, Solid Waste Environ, 1990-93; vpres, Bayside Optimist Club, 1991; prin, Pensacola Polit Cong Black Women Inc. **Home Addr:** 2612 N 13th Ave, Pensacola, FL 32503, **Home Phone:** (850)438-0250.

## HALL, ALBERT

Baseball player. **Personal:** Born Mar 7, 1958, Birmingham, AL. **Career:** Baseball player (retired); Cleveland Indians, left fielder; Atlanta Braves, outfielder, 1981-88; Maj League Baseball, 1984, 1987; Pittsburgh Pirates, outfielder, 1989. **Home Addr:** 1628 Spaulding Ishkooda Rd, Birmingham, AL 35211-5520, **Home Phone:** (205)925-6321.

## HALL, ALFONZO LOUIS

President (organization). **Personal:** Born Jun 20, 1954, Statesboro, GA; son of Collis and Beaulah Coleman; married Lori Linell; children: Lyndon, Jordan & Marjani. **Educ:** Ind Wesleyan Univ, BS, sociol & psychol, 1976; Gen Motors Inst, advan ops plan, 1984, mfg cert, 1986, MS, 1988; Univ Pa Sch Bus, attended 1987; Univ Mich Sch Bus, attended 1989. **Career:** Gen Motors, gen supv press room & metal assembly, 1982-85, supt mfg, 1985-88, engr--charge model systs, 1989-92, prod mgr, Pontiac Luxury Car Div, 1992, actg plant mgr, 1992-93, loaned exec, 1993-94, plant mgr, 1994; Int Agile Mfg LLC, pres & chief exec officer, 2002-. **Orgs:** PNC Bank Urban Adv Bd; prog rev bd, Agility Forum, Le high UNV; Urban League Pittsburgh; Jr Achievement SW Pa Inc; exec adv bd, Penn State McKeesport Campus; ENG SOC Detroit; vip, Explorer Scouts AME, Clinton Valley & Oakland County Coun; founding mem, Mission Inc; 32nd Degree Mason, Prince Hall Masonic Order. **Business Addr:** Chief Executive Officer, President, International Agile Manufacturing ING LLC, 11021 Clito Rd W, Statesboro, GA 30459-2989, **Business Phone:** (912)587-2212.

## HALL, ANTHONY W., JR.

Government official, politician. **Personal:** Born Sep 16, 1944, Houston, TX; son of Anthony William Sr and Quintanna Alliniece; married Carolyn Joyce Middleton; children: Anthony William III & Ursula Antoinette. **Educ:** Howard Univ, BA, 1967; Thurgood Marshall Sch law, JD, 1982. **Career:** Harris County Comn Bray Houston, asst, 1971-72; Tex State House Representatives, 1973-79; Houston City Coun, 1979-89; Metrop Transit Authority, chmn, 1990-92; Williamson Gardner Hall & Wiensenthal, partner; Jackson Walker LLP, partner, 1998-; State Tex, state rep; City Houston, city coun mem & atty, 1998-2004, prin legal advisor, chief admin officer, 2004-10; El Paso Corp, dir, 2001-; Coastal Corp, bd dir, 1999-2001; Houston Endowment Inc, bd dir, currently, chmn, 2010-; pvt prac law, 2010-. **Orgs:** Rules Budget & Fin Coms, Tex Dem Party; state dem exec comt man Sen Dist 13; del, 1972, 1974, 1976, 1980; Dem Nat Conv; Kappa Alpha Psi; nat pres, Sigma Pi Phi Fraternity, bd trustee; Nat Munic League; brd mgr, YMCA Houston; Masons, Shriner, OES, Houston Bus & Prof Mens Club; bd dir, vpres, pres, Riverside Lions Club; exec bd mem, United Negro Col Fund, Gr Zion Baptist Church; Nat Bar Asn; Tex Bar Asn; Am Bar Asn; Houston Bar Asn; Houston Lawyers Asn; chmn, Boule Found; bd dir, Houston Symphony; bd dir, Boy Scouts Am-Sam Houston Area Coun, adv bd; bd dir, Ensemble Theatre; bd dir, Tex Cult Trust; bd dir, Jr Achievement Southeast Tex Inc; bd dir, Jr Achievement Worldwide; pres, Am Leadership Forum; bd dir, Houston/Gulf Coast; State Bar Tex. **Honors/Awds:** Fifth Wards Enrichment Prog Heart Houston; Black Achiever Award, YMCA, 1972; Citation for Outstanding Comn Serv, Natl Asn Advan Colored People, 1972; Cotton Hook of the Year Award, ILA Local872, 1973; Barbara Jordan Leadership Award; Hometown hero Award; Junior Achievement Gold Leadership Award; Distinguished Service Award, Am Pub Transit Asn; Marks of Excellence Award, Nat Forum Black Pub Adminr. **Special Achievements:** First African American & Minority Chairman of Metropolitan Transit Authority. **Home Addr:** 3709 Rio Vista St, Houston, TX 77021-1513, **Home Phone:** (713)748-6273. **Business Addr:** Attorney, 4 Houston Ctr, Houston, TX 77010, **Business Phone:** (713)739-0137.

## HALL, ARSENIO

Television talk show host, actor, comedian. **Personal:** Born Feb 12, 1956, Cleveland, OH; son of Fred and Annie; children: Arsenio Jr. **Educ:** Ohio Univ, Athens, OH; Kent State Univ, BA, gen speech,

1977. **Career:** Actor, writer currently; Stand-up comedian; Films: Amazon Women on the Moon, 1987; Coming to America, 1988, Harlem Nights, 1989; Black Dynamite, 2009; The Hero of Color City, 2013. TV series: "Movie Macabre", 1982; "The Half Hour Comedy Hour, host", 1983; "Thicke of the Night", 1984; "The New Love, American Style", 1985; "Motown Revue", 1985; "Alfred Hitchcock Presents", 1986; "The Real Ghost Busters", 1986-87; "Solid Gold', 1987; "The Late Show', host, 1987; "Uptown Comedy Express", writer, 1987; "Comedy Club", writer, 1987; "The Arsenio Hall Show, host & exec producer", 1989-94, 2013; "MTV Video Music Awards 1990", 1990; "A Party for Richard Pryor", writer, 1991; "Soul Train Comedy Awards", writer, 1993; "Arsenio", 1997; "Martial Law", 1998-2000; "Norm", 2000; "The Proud Family Movie", 2005; "Scooby-Doo! Pirates Ahoy!", 2006; "The Tonight Show with Johnny Carson. **Honors/Awds:** American Comedy Award, 1989; Image Award, Nat Asn Advan Colored People, 1990; People's Choice Award, 1990; Star on the Walk of Fame, 1990. **Home Addr:** 10250 Constellation Blvd, Los Angeles, CA 90067. **Business Addr:** Actor, M L Management Associates Inc, 1740 Broadway Fl 15, New York, NY 10019-4315, **Business Phone:** (212)333-5500.

### HALL, BENJAMIN LEWIS, III

Lawyer, educator. **Personal:** Born Mar 13, 1956, Laurens, SC; son of Benjamin Lewis II and Lilease Rogers; married Saundra Turner; children: Benjamin Lewis IV & Zachary Bass. **Educ:** Univ Southern Calif, BA, 1977; Duke Divinity Sch, Mdiv, 1979; Rheinische Friedrich Wilheims Univ, Bonn, Fed Fulbright Rep Ger Scholar Deutscher Akademischer Austausch Dienst, 1982; Duke Univ Grad Sch, PhD, 1985; Harvard Law Sch, JD, 1986. **Career:** Vinson & Elkins LLP, trial lawyer, spec coun, 1986-92; US Dist Ct, 1987; US Ct Appeals; US Supreme Ct; Univ Houston Law Ctr, adj prof law, 1987-; S Tex CLG Law, adj prof law, 1991; City Houston, city atty, 1992-95; O'Quinn & Laminack, atty, 1995-2000; Hall Law Firm LLP, founder, partner, 2000-; Bell St Chapel, minister, currently. **Orgs:** Fel Ger Res, Bonn Univ, 1980; fel, Duke Black Grad, 1979-80; fel James B Duke Grad, 1980-81; fel Black Doctoral Dissertation, 1982-83; State Bar Tex; shell fel, Lambarene; bd mem, Tex Bd Legal Specialization; exec bd mem, Nat Asn Advan Colored People; bd dir, Am Red Cross Houston Chap, 1988-91; bd dirs, Conrad Blucher Inst forSurveying & ScienceCorpus Christi, 1988-91; Houston Lawyer's Asn, 1986-; Nat Bar Asn, 1988-; Am Bar Asn, 1987-; Houston Jr Chamber Com, 1988-92; Tex Asn Defense Coun, 1990-92; Houston Bar Asn, 1987-; HBA Mem Comt, 1994-95; Col State Bar Tex, 1993-; Hon Comt, Sickle Cell Asn, 1994-; bd dir, Am Diabetes Asn, 1994-95. **Honors/Awds:** Rockefellar Scholar Award, 1977-78; Duke Merit Scholar Award, 1977-79; Benjamin E Mays Scholar Award, 1978-79; DADD Scholar to Germany, 1981-82; Shell Fellow to Lambarene, Gabon, Africa, 1982-83; Merrill Griswold Scholar, 1986; Outstanding Texan Award, 1993, 1995 & 1999; NAACP Alex Award. **Special Achievements:** Bar admissions: TEX, South District of TEX, Fifth Circuit Court of Appeals, DIS, USS Supreme Court. **Business Addr:** Partner, The Hall Law Firm LLP, 530 Lovett Blvd, Houston, TX 77006, **Business Phone:** (713)942-9600.

### HALL, BRIAN EDWARD

Executive. **Personal:** Born May 5, 1958, Cleveland, OH; son of William D and Virginia; married Susan Reed; children: Monika, Jordan & Tristen. **Educ:** Univ Cincinnati, BBA, 1980; Baldwin-Wallace Col, MBA, 1987. **Career:** Industrial Inventory Solutions LLC, chmn, chief exec officer & owner, currently, 2004-; Innogistics LLC, interim exec dir, chmn & cheif exec officer; Indust Transp Inc, chmn, pres & chief exec officer. **Orgs:** Founder, Tremont Elem Sch Adv Group; co-chmn & exec dir, Comn Econ Inclusion, 2012; secy & governance chmn, Rock & Roll Hall Fame; Press Coun Found; exec dir, Greater Cleveland Partnership; bd dir, Cleveland-Cuyahoga County Port Authority. **Home Addr:** 16260 S Pk Blvd, Shaker Heights, OH 44120, **Home Phone:** (216)751-1023. **Business Addr:** President, Chief Executive Officer, Industrial Transport Inc, 2330 E 79th St, Cleveland, OH 44104, **Business Phone:** (216)881-5643.

### HALL, CARLA

Television show host, chef, fashion model. **Personal:** Born May 12, 1964, Nashville, TN; married Matthew D Lyons; children: Stepson Noah. **Educ:** Howard Univ Bus Sch, acct, 1986; L'Academie de Cuisine, Gaithersburg, Md, cert. **Career:** Fashion model; Henley Pk Hotel, Externship, sous chef, 1996-; State Plaza, exec chef; Wash Club, exec chef; Alchemy Caterers (Silver Spring, MD), founder, 2001-; Reality TV show "Top Chef" season 5, contestant (runner-up), 2008; Documentary, "Paint Your Plate!", actor, 2010; Reality TV show "Top Chef: All-Stars", contestant, 2011; TV show "The Chew", co-host, 2011-. **Special Achievements:** Author of "Cooking with Love: Comfort Food that Hugs You," Atria Books (2013).

### HALL, CARLA

Restaurateur, television show host, chef. **Personal:** Born May 12, 1964, Nashville, TN; married Matthew Lyons, Jan 1, 2006?; children: Noah. **Educ:** Howard Univ, BA; L'Academie de Cuisine, MD. **Career:** Price Waterhouse, CPA; runway and print model; Henley Park Hotel, Washington, D.C., sous chef; The State Plaza Hotel, exec chef; The Washington Club, exec chef; Alchemy Caterers, owner, 2001-; taught classes at CulinAerie, Sur la Table and L'Academie de Cuisine; Top Chef, competitor; The Chew, ABC, co-host, 2011-; Carla Hall Petite Cookies, owner; Carla Hall's Southern Kitchen, New York, owner, 2016-. **Orgs:** Pajama Prog; GenYouth; Edible Acad New York Bot Garden; Food & Finance High Sch, New York. **Honors/Awds:** Daytime Emmy Award, 2015. **Special Achievements:** Author, Cooking with Love: Comfort Food That Hugs You, 2011; Cooking with Carla: New Comfort Foods from Around the World, 2014. Active with World Central Kitchen Chef Network, DC Central Kitchen, the USO, St. Jude's Children's Research Hospital, Feeding America, Women Chefs and Restaurateurs. **Business Addr:** Carla Hall's Southern Kitchen, Barclays Ctr, Brooklyn, TN 11217.

### HALL, CHARLES HAROLD

Administrator, association executive. **Personal:** Born Mar 10, 1934, Sapelo Island, GA; son of Charles and Beulah; married Margaret; children: Ronald Charles & Reginald Harold; children: Chuckie, Lori, Reginald & Ronald. **Educ:** Morehouse Col, BS, 1955; DT Watson Sch Psychiat, dipl, phys ther, 1956; Air Univ, USAF, cert, 1957. **Career:** VA Hosp, supvr phys therap, 1961-69; Therapeutic Serv Inc, pres & cheif exec officer, 1970-; Total Living Care Inc, adminr, 1976-; Dev Corp, Jefferson Twp, Ohio, treas, 1970-; Dayton Metropolitan Housing Authority, 1985-. **Orgs:** Nat Asn Advan Colored People, 1960-; secy, Chap Am Phys Therap Asn, 1967-; bd dir, BS Am, 1972-. **Honors/Awds:** Super Performance Award, Va Hosp; Outstanding Service Award, Am Phys Therap Asn; Delta Sigma Theta Business Man of the Year Award, 1992; National Business League Award, 1992; Robert G Dicus Award, pvt prac phys therap, 1992. **Special Achievements:** First African American Chief & chmn OH Chapter Am Phys Therap Asn, 1967-69; first black treas pvt pract; first black pres pvt prac sect; first black to win most prestigious award for private practice physical therapist, 1992; inductee, Order of Military Medical Merit. **Home Addr:** 45 Riverside Dr, Dayton, OH 45405, **Home Phone:** (513)835-5812. **Business Addr:** President, Professional Therapeutic Services, 45 Riverside Dr, Dayton, OH 45405, **Business Phone:** (513)228-9202.

### HALL, DR. CHRISTINE C. IIJIMA

President (organization), chief executive officer, college administrator. **Personal:** Born Mar 31, 1953, Colorado Springs, CO; daughter of Roger Leroy and Fumiko. **Educ:** Los Angeles Harbor Community Col, Wilmington, CA, AA, 1972; Calif State Univ, Long Beach, CA, BA, 1974; Univ Calif, Los Angeles, Los Angeles, CA, MA, 1975, PhD, social psychol, 1980. **Career:** Univ Calif, Irvine, Irvine, Calif, stud affairs officer, 1979-81, coun psychologist, 1981-86, dir, stud develop, 1983-86; Am Psychol Asn, Wash, CC, dir, off ethnic minority affairs, 1987-89; Ariz State Univ W, Phoenix, AZ, assoc vprovost, 1989-96; Asian Am Psychol Asn, pres, 1995-97; Glendale Community Col, assoc dean, 1998-2000; Maricopa Community Col, dir employee serv, 2000-13; Happijobs, pres & ceo, 2008-. **Orgs:** Mem chair, bd dir, Asian Am Psychol Asn, 1987-89; Asn Black Psychologist; Am Psychol Asn; Japanese Am Citizens League; bd dir, Am Cancer Soc, Glendale Chap, 1990-; bd, Planned Parenthood Northern & Cent Ari; bd, Ariz Humanities Coun; bd gov, State Bar Ariz; mem comt, bd dir, Asian Pacific Am Studies prog. **Business Addr:** President, Chief Executive Officer, HAAPIJOBS, 5025 N Central Ave Suite 210, Phoenix, AZ 85012.

### HALL, DANA ERIC

Football player, football coach, executive. **Personal:** Born Jul 8, 1969, Bellflower, CA; married Carrie; children: Johnathan & Dana Jr. **Educ:** Univ Wash, BS, polit sci, 1993. **Career:** Football player (retired), coach, executive; San Francisco 49ers, free safety, 1992-93, defensive back, 1994; Cleveland Browns, defensive back, 1995; Jacksonville Jaguars, strong safety, 1996-97; Total Community Develop, exec dir, 1997-; Wash Mutual Home Loans, vpres emerging markets, 2002-07; Mt San Antonio Col, asst football coach, 2003; ins & annuity consult, 2008-; San Bernardino Valley Col, defensive backs coach, co-defensive coordr, 2010-; Chaffey Col, coach, currently. **Honors/Awds:** Champion, Super Bowl XXIX, San Francisco 49ers. **Business Addr:** Coach, Chaffey College, 5885 Haven Ave, Rancho Cucamonga, CA 91737, **Business Phone:** (909)652-6000.

### HALL, DARNELL KENNETH

Police officer, athlete. **Personal:** Born Sep 26, 1971, Detroit, MI; son of Nelson; married Karen; children: 3. **Educ:** Blinn Col. **Career:** Athlete, 1991-; US Olympic Team, track & field, 1992; Detroit Police Dept, policeman, 1999-; Think Detroit Pal, comnr, asst athletic dir, currently; Detroit Police Athletic League, track comnr; Detroit PAL, youth develop officer. **Orgs:** Chmn, Mich Asn Amateur Athletic Union. **Honors/Awds:** Michigan state championship, 1990; Gold Medalist, 4X400 relay, Olympic Games, Barcelona, 1992; Gold Medal, World Indoor Championships, 1993, 1995. **Business Addr:** Police Officer, City of Detroit, 1301 3rd St, Detroit, MI 48226, **Business Phone:** (313)596-2200.

### HALL, DAVID

Vice president (organization), school administrator, educator. **Personal:** Born May 26, 1950, Savannah, GA; son of Ethel Glover and Levi Hall; married Marilyn Braithwaite; children: Rahsaan, Sakile & Kiamsha. **Educ:** Kans State Univ, BS, polit sci, 1972; Univ Okla, MA, human rels, 1975, JD, 1978; Harvard Law Sch, LLM, 1985, SJD, 1988. **Career:** Univ Okla, instr, 1975-79; Fed Trade Commun, staff atty, 1978-80; Univ Miss Law Sch, asst prof law, 1980-83; Univ Okla Law Sch, assoc prof law, 1983-85; Sabbatical res, S Africa, 1992; NE Univ Sch Law, assoc prof law, 1985-88, assoc dean acad affairs, 1988-92, assoc dean & prof, 1988-98, dean sch law, 1993-98, provost & sr vpres, 1998-2002, prof law, 2003-. **Orgs:** Nat Conf Black Lawyers, 1978-80; Okla Bar Asn, 1978-; atty, Fed Trade Commun, Chicago, IL, 1978-80; Am Bar Asn; bd dir, Legal Serv Corp, 2003; chmn, C Serv Roxbury; Mass Bar Asn; Nat Consumer Law Ctr; Gang Peace Inc; Inst Affirmative Action; Mass Civil Liberties Union; Civilian Rev Bd; Educ Develop Ctr; Asn Am Law Schs; Boston Bar Asn; Nat Black Wholistic Socs; Black Fac & Staff Orgn; Asn Am Law Schs; African Cult Socs; Trans-Africa Forum Scholars Adv Coun; Comn Equal Justice; Northeastern Univ Comt. **Home Addr:** 130 Rocky Knoll Dr, Stoughton, MA 02072-1082, **Home Phone:** (781)297-9316. **Business Addr:** Professor of Law, Northeastern University School of Law, 39 Cargill Hall, Boston, MA 02115, **Business Phone:** (617)373-3668.

### HALL, DR. DAVID ANTHONY, JR.

Dentist. **Personal:** Born Sep 19, 1945, San Francisco, CA; married Pamela C; children: David III & Darryl C. **Educ:** Southern Univ, BS, 1967; Meharry Med Sch, DDS, 1972. **Career:** Pvt pract dentist, 1973-; Health Power Asn, dentist, 1972-73. **Orgs:** ADA, NDA pres, Pelican State Dent Asn, 1980; life mem, Meharry Med Coll Alumni Asn; LDA 6th Dist Dent Asn; Capital & City Dent Asn, Scottlandville Jaycees; Baton Rouge Alumni, Kappa Alpha Psi; Mt Zion 1st Bapt; Southern Univ Alumni Asn; La State Bd Dent, 1994-. **Home Addr:** 934 Elysian Dr, Baton Rouge, LA 70810-2616, **Home Phone:** (225)766-3498. **Business Addr:** Dentist, 1137 Brookhollow Dr, Baton Rouge, LA 70810, **Business Phone:** (225)752-6925.

### HALL, DAVID MCKENZIE

Manager, executive, educator. **Personal:** Born Jun 21, 1928, Gary, IN; son of Alfred M and Grace Elizabeth Crimiel; married Jacqueline V Branch; children: Glen D (deceased) & Gary D. **Educ:** Howard Univ, BS, acct, 1951, MS, educ soc, 1966; NC Agr & State Univ, Greensboro, NC; Mass Inst Technol, Cambridge, MA, cert, 1976; Kennedy Western Univ, PhD, bus admin, 2002; USAF Squadron Officers Sch Air Command & Staff Col; Air War Col; Indust Col Armed Forces. **Career:** Educator (retired); Air Force Acct & Fin Ctr, Comput Opers Chief; Mil Airlift Command; Scott AFB IL USAF, dep base cmd, 1974-75, base cmd, 1975-76; Air Force Logistics Cmd, USAF, dep cmptrlr, 1976-77, cmptrlr, 1977-83; Delco-Remy Div Gen Motors, dir dp, 1983-84; Saginaw Div Gen Motors, gen mgr 1983; Electr Data Systs Corp, acct mgr, 1985-88; Electronic Data Systs, Saginaw, Mich, reg mgr, 1988-93; N wood Univ, prof, 1993-97; Saginaw Valley State Univ, Col Bus & Mgt, executivec-in-residence, 1997-2007; Hall & Assocs, owner, 1999-. **Orgs:** Mem, Boy Scouts Am, 1942-; Air Force asn, 1960-83; bd mem, Saginaw Community Found; Life mem, Nat Asn Advan Colored People; Kapa Alpha Psi; Community Affairs Comt, 1988-; exec bd mem, St. Mary's Hosp, 1989-93; St. Mary's Adv Bd, 1997-2003; Mil Officers Asn; co chair, Saginaw County's Promise; fel, Saginaw Valley State Univ; trustee bd, Bethel AME Church Trustee Bd. **Home Addr:** 49 W Hannum Blvd, Saginaw, MI 48602-1938, **Home Phone:** (989)791-1192. **Business Addr:** Executive in Residence, Saginaw Valley State University, 7400 Bay Rd, Saginaw, MI 48710-0001, **Business Phone:** (989)964-6076.

### HALL, DELILAH RIDLEY

School administrator, president (organization), vice president (organization). **Personal:** Born Aug 23, 1953, Baton Rouge, LA; daughter of Samuel Sr and Mamie Jones; married Holmes G Sr; children: Holmes, Byron, Marsha, Michael & Monica R. **Educ:** Jarvis Christian Col, BS, 1975; E Tex State Univ, MS, 1977. **Career:** E Tex State Univ, coordr, 1975-77; Long view Independent Sch Dist, ind instr, 1978; Jarvis Christian Col, Hawkins, TX, upward bound prog counr, 1978, asst dean acad affairs, 1980, asst pres, 1981-, interim vpres, 1991-, Title III coordr & assist pres, pres, Church Finance Coun, currently. **Orgs:** JCC/SCI Nat Alumni & Ex-Stud Asn, 1975; secy, Hawkins Elem PTA, 1985-87; Nat Asn Historically Black Cols & Univs; Zeta Phi Beta Sorority Inc. **Home Addr:** PO Box 37, Hawkins, TX 75765, **Home Phone:** (903)769-2769. **Business Addr:** Title III Coordinator, Assistant president, Jarvis Christian College, Hwy 80 E 7631 Private Rd, Hawkins, TX 75765-1470, **Business Phone:** (903)769-5700.

### HALL, DELORES

Actor. **Personal:** Born Kansas City, KS; married Michael Goodstone. **Educ:** Harbor Jr Col, LACC. **Career:** Actress & singer; Broadway Show: Your Arms Too Short To Box With God; Godspell; Hair; Bread, 1972; The Best Little Whorehouse in Texas, 1982; Age of Aquarius; night club performer. TV Series: "Diagnosis Murder", 1993-95. Films: Scrooged, 1988; Leap of Faith, 1992; Lethal Weapon 3, 1992. **Honors/Awds:** Antoinette Perry Award, 1977; Tony Award, Best Actress, 1977; Toro Award, Young Woman Am; nominated for Joseph Jefferson Award for Actress in a Revue for "Street Dreams", 1983. **Home Addr:** 3100 S Vermont Ave Suite 357, Los Angeles, CA 90007-3039. **Business Addr:** Actress, c/o William Morris Agency, 151 El Camino Dr, Beverly Hills, CA 90212, **Business Phone:** (310)859-4000.

### HALL, DR. DOLORES BROWN

School administrator, educator. **Personal:** Born Brooklyn, NY; married Kirkwood M; children: Alexander Chapman. **Educ:** Brooklyn Hosp Sch Nursing, RN, dipl, 1962; Long Island Univ, BS, 1966; Adelphi Univ, MS, 1969; NY Univ, PhD, 1977. **Career:** Medgar Evers Col NIMH Res Proj, proj dir, 1975-77; Del State Col, assoc prof, 1977-79; Health & Human Serv, NIMH St Elizabeth Hosp, dir nursing ed, 1979-84; Edison State Col, Nursing Prog, assoc dean & dir, 1984; Geront Soc Am, fel, 1985; Seton Hall Univ, asst prof, currently. **Orgs:** Workshop leader Del Home Aged, 1976; bd dir, Good Shepard Home Health Aide Prog, 1977-79; Ment Health Plan Task Force, 1978-79; US Pub Health Serv Cont EdReview Comn, 1980-83; consult, Charles Drew Neighborhood Health Ctr. **Home Addr:** 8 Belmont Cir, Trenton, NJ 08618-4454, **Home Phone:** (609)989-9604. **Business Addr:** Assistant Professor, Seton Hall University, 400 S Orange Ave, South Orange, NJ 07079, **Business Phone:** (973)761-2152.

### HALL, EDDIE LEON, JR.

Automotive executive. **Career:** Briarwood Ford Inc, owner & pres, currently. **Business Addr:** Owner, President, Briarwood Ford Inc, 7070 E Mich Ave, Saline, MI 48176-9514, **Business Phone:** (734)429-5478.

### HALL, ELLIOTT SAWYER

Lawyer, automotive executive. **Personal:** Born Jan 1, 1938, Detroit, MI; son of Odis and Ethel B; married Shirley Ann Robinson; children: Fred, Lannis & Tiffany. **Educ:** Wayne State Univ, Detroit, Mich, BA, polit sci, 1961, JD, 1963. **Career:** Govt Wayne Co, Mich, Detroit, Mich, chief asst prosecutor, 1983-85; Dykema Gossett Spencer Goodnow & Trigg, Detroit Mich, law partner, 1985-87; Ford Motor Co, Dearborn Mich, lawyer, lobbyist, vpres govt affairs, vpres dealer develop, 1987-2001; Georgetown Univ, bd mem; Clark Atlanta Univ, bd mem; Dykema Gossett PLLC, atty; Chrysler Corp, lawyer; Wayne County, chief asst prosecutor. **Orgs:** Pres, Nat Asn Advan Colored People, 1972; pres, United Black Coalition, 1974-75; chmn bd dir, Constituency Africa, 2006-; pres, Detroit Metrop Bar Asn; pres, Wolverine Bar Asn; bd mem, Georgetown Univ; Clark Atlanta Univ; chmn, Joint Ctr Polit & Econ Studies; bd mem, Cong Black Caucus Found; bd chmn, Music Hall Ctr Performing Arts. **Honors/Awds:** Distinguished Alumnus Award, Corporate Leadership Award, Wayne State Univ. **Special Achievements:** First African American Chief Assistant Prosecutor for Wayne County, Michigan; First African American Corporation Counsel for the City of Detroi; Auto Company's First African-american Vice President, Playing A Major Role In Expanding Its Minority-dealer Network Of Assets. **Home Addr:** 2770 Unicorn Lane NW, Washington, DC 20015-2234, **Home Phone:** (202)244-1975.

### HALL, EVERETT

Executive, fashion designer. **Personal:** son of Eugene. **Educ:** Howard Univ. **Career:** Everett Hall Designs, founder, owner, designer, 1982-; Black Label Boutique, Wash, DC, founder, 1994-; GQ, Wash, DC, founder, 1995-. **Special Achievements:** Nominated as a finalist for the Cutty Sark Award; Has been featured on CNN Style, E Television, FOX Philadelphia & Main Floor. **Business Addr:** Designer, Owner, Everett Hall Designs, Chevy Chase Pavillion, Washington, DC 20015, **Business Phone:** (202)362-0191.

**HALL, FRANCES WHITE**
Chief executive officer, president (organization). **Educ:** Univ Tenn, Knoxville, BFA, commun design, 1974; Amos Tuck Grad Sch Bus, Dartmouth Col, post grad, 1999. **Career:** Hall Commun Inc, pres & chief exec officer, 1980-; HCI Construct Supply LLC, pres, 2013-15; TYCO SimplexGrinnell, govt bus develop rep, 2014-. **Orgs:** Knoxville Area Chamber Partnership; City Knoxville Equal Bus Opportunity Bd; HUD Minority Bus Coun; Univ Tenn Chancellors Assocs; Knoxville Tourism & Sports Corp; Tennesseans Arts; Knoxville Mus Art; Sr Citizens Home Assistance Ctr; City Knoxville Equal Bus Opportunity Comt; Knoxville Urban Area Transp Plng Title VI & Environ Justice Comt; Knoxville Area Chamber Partnership Bd, 1999-2002; Exec Womens Asn; Press Adv Comt; Tenn Econ & Community Develop Telecom Adv Bd; Alpha Kappa Alpha Sorority. **Business Addr:** Government Business Development Representative, TYCO SimplexGrinnell, 50 Technology Dr, Westminster, MA 01441, **Business Phone:** (800)746-7539.

**HALL, FRED, III**
Financial manager, government official, president (organization). **Personal:** Born Feb 9, 1945, St. Louis, MO; married Pattie M Burdett; children: Fred IV & Rose M. **Educ:** Sinclair Col, AS, engineering technol, 1968; Univ Dayton, BS, engineering technol, 1976; Wright State Univ, MBA, 1992. **Career:** Gen Motors Corp, Delco Prod Div, lab tech, 1968-73, sales coordr, 1973-78, sales engr, 1978-85, mkt analyst, 1985-; Greene Co Bd Elections, pres, chmn, currently. **Orgs:** Bd mem, Camp Fire Girls, 1975-77; city comnr, City Xenia, 1977, 81-; sec, Xenia Wilber force Dem Club, 1979-82; pres, Wilberforce Xenia Optimist Club, 1981-82; chmn, bd zoning appeals, City Xenia, 1982-83, 1985; vpres, Chi Lambda Chap Alpha Phi Alpha, 1984-85; pres, Chi Lambda Chap, Alpha Phi Alpha, 1986-87; dep mayor, City Xenia, 1984-; plng comn, chmn, City Xenia, 1984, 1992-93; pres, city comn, City Xenia, 1989-90; bd mem, Boys & Girls Clubs, 1992-93. **Honors/Awds:** Award for Excellence in Community Activities, General Motors Corp, 1979; Citizen of the Year, Omega Psi Phi Fraternity, 1992. **Home Addr:** 582 Kathys Way, Xenia, OH 45385-4882, **Home Phone:** (937)372-3723. **Business Addr:** Chairman, President, Greene County Board Elections, 651 Dayton Xenia Rd, Xenia, OH 45385, **Business Phone:** (937)562-7470.

**HALL, HANSEL CRIMIEL**
Executive. **Personal:** Born Mar 12, 1929, Gary, IN; son of Alfred M (deceased) and Grace Eliz (deceased); children: Grace Jean. **Educ:** Ind Univ, BS, 1953; Indust Col Armed Forces, nat security mgt cert, 1971; Blackstone Sch Law, B Laws, 1982. **Career:** Internal Revenue Serv, officer, 1959-1964; Gasoline serv sta operator, realtor, 1964-1969; US Dept Housing & Urban Develop, prog specialist, 1969-73, dir, FH & EO div Minn, 1973-75, div Ind, 1975-79; US Dept Interior, dir off human resources, 1979-88; Korean War Veterans Educ Grant Corp, chief financing officer; Crimiel Commun Inc, pres, chief exec officer, 1982-2011. **Orgs:** Pres, Crimiel Ltd Consult, 1979-; pres, Minn-Dakota Conf; golden heritage mem, Nat Advan Asn Colored People, 1981-86; pres & bd dir, Riverview Towers Homeowners Asn, 1985-87; life mem, Ind Univ Alumni Asn; Omega Psi Phi; life mem, Veterans Foreign Wars; elected bd, Korean War Veterans Asn, 1992-95; pres, Minn State Asn Parliamentarians, 1997-99; Res Officers Asn. **Home Addr:** 1920 S 1st St, Minneapolis, MN 55414, **Home Phone:** (612)332-2685. **Business Addr:** President, Crimiel Communications Inc, PO Box 14648, Minneapolis, MN 55414-0648, **Business Phone:** (612)332-2685.

**HALL, HAROLD L.**
Executive, president (organization). **Career:** Delta Enterprises Inc, Greenville Miss, chief exec, pres, proj mgr, chief operating officer, currently. **Business Addr:** Chief Operating Officer, Delta Enterprises Inc, 819 Main St, Greenville, MS 38701, **Business Phone:** (601)335-5291.

**HALL, HORATHEL**
Consultant, educator, artist. **Personal:** Born Dec 3, 1926, Houston, TX; married Howard D; children: Kenneth A, Admerle J & Horace D. **Educ:** Prairie View A&M Univ, BA, 1948; NM Highlands, Las Vegas, MFA, 1962. **Career:** Educator (retired); Worthing High Sch, art teacher & dept chmn, 1951-80; Tes Southern Univ, art prof, 1964-79; W African States Art Res, fel, HISD, 1975; Houston Comm Col, art prof, 1975-77; Adept New Am Folk Gallery, crafts consult, 1977-79; Eliza Johnson Home Elderly, crafts consult, 1977-79; Houston Independent Sch Dist, art teacher & artist, 1980-. **Orgs:** Affil mem, Nat Art Educrs Asn, 1951-80; vpres, Con Temp Hand Weavers Houston, 1968-69; secy, E Sunny Side Civic Club Houston, 1970-80; secy, Orgn Black Artists, 1975-80; treas, Houston Art Educrs Asn, 1976-80; affil mem, Nat Conf Artists, 1976-80; spec publ, Black Artist Generation, 1977; Arts & Rural & Isolated Elderly Univ, KY, 1980. **Honors/Awds:** J. Eugene Grigsby Jr Award, Nat Art Educ Asn, 1984; Outstanding Service Award, Tex Southern Univ. **Special Achievements:** Published "Contemp Concepts of the Liberian Rice Bag Weave", vol 27 no 2, Con temp Hand weavers of Tex Inc, 1975; Arrow mont Scholar, Pi Beta Alumnae Club, Gatling burg, Tenn, 1980. **Home Addr:** 5035 Mayflower St, Houston, TX 77033, **Home Phone:** (713)734-0755. **Business Addr:** Artist, Houston Independent School District West, 9215 Scott St, Houston, TX 77051, **Business Phone:** (713)733-3433.

**HALL, IRA D.**
Executive director, president (organization), chief executive officer. **Personal:** Born Jan 1, 1945. **Educ:** Stanford Univ, BS, elec eng; Stanford Univ, Stanford Grad Sch Bus, MBA. **Career:** Louis F Rothschild, Unterberg, Towbin Inc, sr vpres; Int Bus Machs, chief exec officer & pres, 1985-98, Corp, dir intl oper, treas, 1990-98, Int Bus Mach World Trade Corp, controller, Int Bus Mach World Trade Ctr Ins Corp, chmn & chief exec officer; Texaco, Alliance Mgt, gen mgr, 1998-99, treas, 1999-2001, Head Finance Dept, 2001-; Southern New Eng Telecommunications Corp, dir, 1995-; Oce Imagistics Inc, dir, 2001-; Tampa Elec Co, dir, 2001-04; Reynolds & Reynolds Co, bd dir, 2002-; Utendahl Capital Mgt LP, pres & chief exec officer, 2002-04, sr adv, 2005-; Pepsi Bottling Group Inc, dir, 2003-; Ameriprise Financial Inc, dir, 2005-09; Publishers Clearing House, bd dir; Teco Energy Inc, bd dir, 2001-04; Southern New Eng Tel Co, dir; Am Express Funds, dir; Williams Co Inc, dir; Imagistics Int Inc, bd dir; Praxair Inc, dir, 2004-. **Orgs:** Chmn, Exec Leadership Coun, 2000; bd dir, Jackie Robinson Found; gov, US Postal Serv Audit Comt; mem dean adv coun, Stanford Sch Bus; trustee emer, Stanford Univ; dir, Jackie Robinson Found Inc. **Business Addr:** Director, Chairman, Praxair Inc, Worldwide Headquarters, Danbury, CT 06810, **Business Phone:** (716)879-4077.

**HALL, JACK L.**
Administrator, law enforcement officer. **Personal:** Born Feb 11, 1941, Cairo, IL; son of J K and Clemmie Lee; married Effie D; children: Marvin D & Marilyn R Goldwire. **Educ:** Lansing Community Col, assocs, criminal justice, 1961; Mich State Univ, BA, criminal justice, 1979; W Mich Univ, MPA, 1992. **Career:** Adminr (retired); Benton Twp Police Dept, patrolman, 1962-67; Mich Dept State Police, flint post, 1967-69, niles post, 1969-74, detroit MINT, personnel & training divisions, 1974-85, Ionia post, 1985-87; hq, 1987-92; Mich Dept Corrections, internal affairs mgr, 1992-2002. **Home Addr:** 11475 Upton Rd, Grand Ledge, MI 48837-9187, **Home Phone:** (517)627-5355.

**HALL, JAMES LAMONT. See HALL, LAMONT.**

**HALL, LT. GEN. JAMES REGINALD, JR.**
Military leader, administrator. **Personal:** Born Jul 15, 1936, Anniston, AL; son of James Reginald Sr and Evelyn Dodson; married Helen Kerr; children: Sheila A, James R III & Cheryl D. **Educ:** Morehouse Col, Atlanta, GA, BA, polit sci, 1957; Shippensburg State Univ, Shippensburg, PA, MS, pub admin, 1975; Kennedy Sch Govts, Sr Managers Prog, 1988; AUS War Col. **Career:** Military leader (retired), trustee; AUS, lt gen; mem, vice chair, Atlanta Committee for the Olympic Games, 1996; Morehouse Col, Campus Opers, vpres, asst secy; chair, Phys Plant Comt; OCS prog, 1958. **Orgs:** Alpha Phi Alpha Fraternity, 1954-; Prince Hall Mason, 1962-; pres, Nat Alumni Asn, 2002-06, trustee, exec, Morehouse Col; exec comt; audit comt; trusteehip & governance comt & Ad Hoc Comt Land Acquisition. **Home Addr:** 115 N Dr, Fairburn, GA 30213, **Home Phone:** (770)461-5154. **Business Addr:** Trustee, Morehouse College, 830 Westview Dr SW, Atlanta, GA 30314, **Business Phone:** (404)681-2800.

**HALL, DR. JARVIS A.**
Administrator. **Personal:** married Rosalind Fuse; children: Ifetoya. **Educ:** NC A & T State Univ, BA, 1979; Univ Mich, Ann Arbor, MI, MA, pub policy, 1982; Duke Univ, PhD, polit sci, 1993. **Career:** Teacher, St Lawrence Univ, Wash univ Lee Univ; NC Cent Univ, Dept Polit Sci, chmn, 1998-2005, dir, Inst Civic Engagement & Social Chg, assoc prof, currently. **Orgs:** Chair, Polit Action Comt NC Nat Asn Advan Colored People; bd mem, NC Ctr Voter Educ; bd mem, Carolina Justice Policy Ctr; dir, Acad Community Serv Learning Pro; Nat Civic League. **Business Addr:** Associate Professor, North Carolina Central University, 109 Edmonds Classroom Bldg 1801 Fayetteville St, Durham, NC 27707, **Business Phone:** (919)530-7256.

**HALL, DR. JEFFREY MAURICE**
Surgeon. **Personal:** Born Oct 31, 1958, Ypsilanti, MI; son of James and Maureen; married Janet R; children: Elliott Joshua. **Educ:** Univ Mich, BS, 1981; Univ Mich Med Sch, Ann Arbor, Mich, MD, 1985. **Career:** Henry Ford Hosp, resident; Wayne State Univ, fel, 1990-91; Hand Surg Assocs Mich, PC, surgeon, currently; Providence Hosp; St John Hosp & Med Ctr; St John Macomb Hosp, currently; Oakland Regional Hosp, physician, currently; Hand Surg Assoc Mich, physician, currently. **Orgs:** Am Med Asn, 1991; Am Asn Surg Hand, 1995; fel Am Col Surgeons, 1996; Am Bd Med Specialties Bd Surg. **Honors/Awds:** Cand for Chevron Scholar, Univ Mich, 1979; Citizen of the Week, WWJ Radio, 1995. **Home Addr:** 7304 Westchester, West Bloomfield, MI 48322, **Home Phone:** (810)661-8921. **Business Addr:** Medical Doctor, Surgeon, Hand Surgery Associates of Michigan PC, 19701 Vernier Rd Suite 210, Harper Woods, MI 48225, **Business Phone:** (313)640-7999.

**HALL, DR. JESSE J.**
Educator, association executive. **Personal:** Born Dec 16, 1938, Clover, SC; married Nancy Thorne; children: Nathaniel Craig & Yoland Yevette. **Educ:** State Teachers Col, Fayetteville, NC, BS, 1962; Univ NV, MEd, 1970; Univ San Francisco, attended 1984. **Career:** Educator (retired); Washoe Co Sch Dist, Orvis Ring & Sierra Vista Schs, prin, 1971-72, Glen Duncan Sch, prin, 1972-80, Lloyd Diedrichsen Sch, prin, 1981-84. **Orgs:** Int Reading Asn, 1962; Phi Delta Kappa, 1968; NV State Textbk Comn, 1969-79; Nat Asn Elem Sch Prin, 1971; NV Asn Sch Admn, 1972; Equal Opportunity Bd, UNR, 1980; bd dir, panel chmn, United Way NV, 1972-78; Nev Parents Teachers Asn. **Honors/Awds:** Man of the Year, Second Bapt Church, Reno, 1978; Distinguished Service Award, NAACP, 1978; Dist Service Award, Negro Bus & Prof Women's Asn, 1980; received numerous awards. **Special Achievements:** First African American teacher in the in the Washoe County School, 1962; First black administrator; First African American principal, 1970. **Home Addr:** 3125 Villa Marbella Cir, Reno, NV 89509-6603, **Home Phone:** (775)828-0401. **Business Addr:** Principal, Lloyd Diedrichsen School, 1735 Del Rosa Way, Sparks, NV 89431, **Business Phone:** (775)353-5730.

**HALL, JOEL**
Artistic director. **Personal:** Born Apr 20, 1949, Chicago, IL; son of Louis and Emma Lee. **Educ:** Northeastern Ill Univ, BA, sociol, 1972. **Career:** Dance: "Nightwalker", 1978; "Now You See It, Now You Don't", 1998; "El Gato Negro", 1992; "The Crossing", 1997; "Y-2 Day", 1999; Joel Hall Dancers & Ctr, artistic dir, prin choreographer, chief instr, exec dir & owner, 1974-; jazz dance, instr; Wayne State Univ; Ny Univ; Northern Ill Univ; Western Mich Univ; Chicago City Theatre Co, co founder. **Home Addr:** 3438 Elaine Pl Suite 2, Chicago, IL 60657, **Home Phone:** (773)528-0435. **Business Addr:** Artistic Director, Chief Instructor, Joel Hall Dancers & Center, 5965 N Clark St, Chicago, IL 60660, **Business Phone:** (773)293-0900.

**HALL, DR. JULIA GLOVER**
College teacher. **Personal:** Born Philadelphia, PA; daughter of Harold Heywood and Isabel Dickson; married William Francis Jr; children: William Francis III (deceased) & Michael David. **Educ:** Temple Univ, Philadelphia, PA, BA, 1968; Wharton Sch, Univ Pa, Philadelphia, PA, MA, 1969; Univ Pa, Philadelphia, PA, PhD, sociol, 1973; Harvard Univ, attended 1978. **Career:** Dept Justice, Govs Justice Comn, Harrisburg, PA, proj evaluator, 1974-79; Drexel Univ, Philadelphia, PA, assoc prof, psychol & sociol, 1982-91, prof criminal justice, 1991-; State Correctional Inst, Graterford, PA, coordr concerned srs & gray panthers, 1986-; Pa Bd Probation & Parole, trainer, 1988-; Pa Family Caregiver Support Prog, Geront Soc Am, prin investr & proj dir, 1988; Nat Inst Corrections, consult, 1989-; US Dept Health & Human Servs, prin investr & proj dir, 1989-91. **Orgs:** Nat Sci Found fel, Univ Pa, 1968-73; dir, Southern Home Servs; pres, Pa Asn Criminal Justice Educrs, 1990-93; convenor, Gray Panther chap, Graterford, Pa, 1989-; pres & bd mem, Pa Prison Soc, 1996-; chmn, Victim Offender Reconciliation Prog Graterford; Pa Legis Adv Comt; chair, Paul C Griffins Memorial Fund; advisor, Eta Iota, Drexel chap Alpha Phi Sigma & Nat Criminal Justice Hon Soc; chair, sub comt, Juv Life Without Parole; chair, Pa Coalition Fair Sentencing Youth. **Business Addr:** Professor, Drexel University, 3141 Chestnut St PSA 220, Philadelphia, PA 19104-2816, **Business Phone:** (215)895-2472.

**HALL, KATHRYN LOUISE (KATHRYN HALL-TRUJILLO)**
Chief executive officer, health services administrator, public speaker. **Personal:** Born Jul 19, 1948, Moscow, AR; daughter of Chester and Corrine Starks; children: Kennya Thornburg, Eddie Stokes & Tamu Green. **Educ:** Univ Calif, Los Angeles, BA, sociol, 1973, MPH, 1975; DDiv, metaphorumministry, 1999. **Career:** Calif State dept Health, health prog adv, 1975-82; Calif State Dept Serv, regional oper mgr, 1982-83; Independent Consult, 1982-; Family Health ProgInc, Long Beach, adv, 1983-84; Health Choice Inc, Portland OR, regional mgr, 1984-86; Calif State Dept Health Serv, health prog adv, 1986-90; Ctr Community Health & Well-Being, founder & dir, 1988-; City Univ LosAngeles, Grad Sch Life, Health & Environ Sci, adj prof; Earth Mama Healing, speaker, currently; Birthing Proj USA, founding dir, chief exec officer, currently. **Orgs:** Am Pub Health Asn; patic, Resources Person's Network, Off Minority Health; bd, Sacramento YWCA; chmn health comt, Black Advocates State Serv; Nat Coun Negro Women; Sacramento Black Infant Health Adv Comt; Bereaved Parents USA; Normandy United Methodist Church. **Home Addr:** 4041 Inyo Ave, Sacramento, CA 95820, **Home Phone:** (916)451-8567. **Business Addr:** Director, Founder, The Center for Community Health & Well-Being Inc, 1900 T St, Sacramento, CA 95811, **Business Phone:** (916)558-4800.

**HALL, PROF. KIM FELICIA**
Educator. **Personal:** Born Dec 25, 1961, Baltimore, MD; daughter of Lawrence Harold and Vera Webb. **Educ:** Hood Col, Frederick, BA, 1983; Univ Pa, PhD, renaissance studies, 1990. **Career:** Dem Nat Conv, commun coordr, 1984; Univ Pa, grad fel, 1985-86; Folger Inst, Wash, DC, fel, 1986; Comt re-elect Clarence Blount, campaign coordr, 1986; Friends Vera P Hall, publ rels dir, 1986-87; Woodrow Wilson Nat Fel Found, Mellon dissertation fel, 1988-89; Georgetown Univ, Wash, DC, lectr, 1989-90, asst prof, 1990-96, assoc prof eng, 1995-; Ford Found, fel, 1991-92; Folger Shakespeare Libr, Folger Inst fel, 1991; NEH Newberry Libr, postdoctoral fel, 1996-97; Fordham Univ, Thomas F X Mullarkey chair lit, 2001-; Swarthmore Col, vis instr; Barnard Col, prof, currently. **Orgs:** Vpres, Grad Eng Asn, Univ Pa, 1985-86; secy, Grad Eng Asn, 1984-85; Mod Lang Asn Shakespeare Div chair, 2000; Shakespeare Asn Am; Renaissance Soc Am; Mellon Fel Humanities, Woodrow Wilson Nat Fel Found; Soc Study Early Mod Women. **Home Addr:** 90 LaSalle St Apt 9A, New York, NY 10027, **Home Phone:** (212)665-0774. **Business Addr:** Professor, Barnard College, Barnard Hall 411 3009 Broadway, New York, NY 10027, **Business Phone:** (212)854-0729.

**HALL, KIRKWOOD MARSHAL**
Health services administrator. **Personal:** Born May 13, 1944, Montclair, NJ; son of Marshal Eugene and Alice Chapman; married Dolores Brown; children: Malaika Estelle, Dalili Talika & Alexander Chapman. **Educ:** Va Union Univ, BA, sociol, 1967; Pittsburgh Theol Sem, Mdiv, 1974; Univ Pittsburgh, Sch Pub Health, MPH, 1978. **Career:** Hill Ment Health Team, ment health clinician, 1970-74; Western Psychol Inst & Clin, dir, 1974-75; NJ Dept Pub Advocate, Div Ment Health, supvr, field rep, 1975-77; Proj Sail, dir, 1977-79; Univ Med & Dent Newark, NJ, ment health clinician, 1980-82; Henry J Austin Health Ctr, clin supvr, ment health. **Orgs:** Asst dir, Black Campus Ministries Inc, 1971-; chmn, Neighborhood Community Health Care, 1974; elder, Unification Assoc Christian Sabbath, 1976-80; assoc pastor, Union Bapt Church Trenton, NJ, 1981-; vpres, Samuel DeWitt Proctor Greater NJ Alumni Chap, Va Union Univ, 1983-84; assoc pastor, St Paul AME Zion, Trenton NJ, 1987-. **Home Addr:** 8 Belmont Cir, Trenton, NJ 08618, **Home Phone:** (609)989-9604. **Business Addr:** Clinic Supervisor, Henry J Austin Health Centre, 321 N Warren St, Trenton, NJ 08618.

**HALL, HON. L. PRISCILLA**
Judge, lawyer. **Personal:** daughter of Shelvin Jerome and Lucy Mae. **Educ:** Howard Univ, BA, 1968; Columbia Univ Sch Journ, MS, hons, 1969; Columbia Univ Sch Law, JD, 1973. **Career:** Gen Elec, corp atty, 1973-74; NY Supreme Ct, Appellate Div, First Dept, 1974; NY County, asst dist atty, 1974-79; Us Dist Ct, 1978-2005; NYC Dept Employ, inspector gen, 1979-82; NY State Dept Law, asst atty gen, 1982; NYC Human Resources Admin, inspector gen, 1982-86; Criminal Ct New York, judge, 1986-90; NY Supreme Ct, Kings County, actg justice, 1990; NY Ct Claims, judge, 1990-94; NY State Supreme Ct, justice, 1994-, Kings County, Criminal Div, admin judge, 2008-09, Appellate Div, Second Judicial Dept, assoc justice, 2009-; Fordham Univ Sch Law, adj prof, 2001-04; bd dir, Faith Ctr Community Develop Inc.

**Orgs:** NYS Asn Women Judges; Metrop Black Bar Asn; Asn Black Women Attys; Columbia Law Sch Asn; New York Bar Asn; Brooklyn Bar Asn; Brooklyn Womens Bar Asn; Asn Bar City New York; Ny Bar Found; Supreme Ct Justices Asn City New York; chmn & bd dir, Achievement First Charter Sch Crown Heights; Judicial Friends; Columbia Sch Law Asn. **Business Addr:** Administrative Judge, New York State Kings County, Supreme Ct Bldg, Brooklyn, NY 11201, **Business Phone:** (347)296-1061.

### HALL, LAMONT (JAMES LAMONT HALL)
Teacher, football player. **Personal:** Born Nov 16, 1974, Clover, SC; children: 2. **Educ:** Clemson Univ, BA, hist. **Career:** Football player (retired), teacher; Tampa Bay Buccaneers, 1998; Green Bay Packers, tight end, 1999; New Orleans Saints, tight end, 2000-02, 2004-05; Atlanta Falcons, 2003; Clemson Univ, teacher, 2007-. **Business Addr:** Teacher, Clemson University, Clemson, SC 29634, **Business Phone:** (864)656-3311.

### HALL, LEMANSKI
Football player, sports manager. **Personal:** Born Nov 24, 1970, Valley, AL. **Educ:** Univ Ala, criminal justice. **Career:** Football player (retired), sports manager; Ala Crimson Tide football team, 1990-93; Houston Oilers, linebacker, 1995-96; Tenn Oilers, 1997; Chicago Bears, 1998; Dallas Cowboys, 1999; Minn Vikings, 2000-02; Ensworth High Sch, fitness instr; D-1 Sports Training, dir opers, D1 Huntsville, recruiting coordr, currently. **Orgs:** Actg pres, Tenn NFL Alumni Asn; pres, Tenn Chap, Nat Football League Retired Players Asn. **Business Addr:** Recruiting Coordinator, D1 Sports Training, 7242 Bailey Cove Rd, Huntsville, AL 35802, **Business Phone:** (256)880-1717.

### HALL, LEWIS J.
Executive. **Career:** NY State Educ, coordr; Univ State NY, Scholar & Grants Admin, supvr, currently. **Business Addr:** Supervisor, University of the State of New York, 1400 Wash Ave, Albany, NY 12234, **Business Phone:** (518)442-3300.

### HALL, MELVIN CURTIS
Executive, lawyer. **Personal:** Born Jun 2, 1956, Tulsa, OK; son of Isiah and Eunice Jean Taylor; married Alicia Williams; children: Natasha Marie & Tenia Shanta. **Educ:** Langston Univ, BA, social sci educ, 1978; Univ Okla, Col Law, JD, 1981. **Career:** Cleveland County Dist Atty, asst dist atty, 1980-83; Okla Human Rights Comn, exec dir, 1983-87; US Ct Appeals, Tenth Circuit; Riggs Abney Neal Turpen Orbison & Lewis, partner, 1988-; Univ Okla, adj prof, currently. **Orgs:** Okla Bar Asn, 1982-; Okla City Asn Black Lawyers, 1986-; bd mem, Southwest Ctr Human Rels Studies, 1987-; bd mem, Progress Independence, 1988-; bd mem, Okla St Chamber Com & Indust, 1989-; chmn, regent, Regent, Univ Okla, 1992-99; exec comt, Southwest Ctr Human Rels Studies; bd dir, Arvest Bank. **Honors/Awds:** Blue Ribbon Award, Metropolitan Fair Housing Coun Okla City, 1985; Certificate Appreciation, US Dept Housing & Urban Develop, 1986; A CHamlin Tribute, Okla Legislative Black Caucus, 1987; Certificate Appreciation, Marion Anderson Middle Sch, 1987; Plaque Appreciation, APhilip Randolph Okla, 1990; Melvin C. Hall Leadership & Scholarship Award, Univ Okla, 1999; Trial Blazer Award, Univ Okla, Black Alumni Soc, 2000; The Melvin C. Hall Scholarship Award, Langston Univ, 2002; Certificate of Appreciation, Delta Sigma Theta Sorority Inc, 2010; Plaque of Appreciation, Univ Okla Col Law Bd Visitor, 2011; Ada Lois Sipuel Fisher Diversity Award, Okla Bar Asn, 2013. **Home Addr:** 4001 Buckingham Dr, Norman, OK 73072-1771, **Home Phone:** (405)364-3541. **Business Addr:** Partner, Riggs Abney Neal Turpen Orbison & Lewis, 5801 N Broadway Ext Suite 101, Oklahoma City, OK 73118, **Business Phone:** (405)843-9909.

### HALL, DR. MORRIS B., JR.
Lawyer. **Personal:** Born Oct 26, 1975, Port Huron, MI; son of Morris and Terry; children: Matea Kearns & Dontae Bassham. **Educ:** Univ Mich, BA, polit sci, 1997, BA, psychol, 1997; Wayne State Univ, JD, 2001. **Career:** N Am Lighting, QS 9000 stand engr, 1999-; H&L Develop Co LLC, pres & chief exec officer, 2000-. **Orgs:** Rules comt, Aggressive Diversified Investment Group, 1998-; Nat Asn Investors Corp, 1998-; Soc Automotive Engineering, 2000-; Am Trial Lawyers Asn, 2001-; Am Soc Mech Engrs. **Honors/Awds:** Young Man of the Year, Port Huron Men's Club, 1990, 1993; Outstanding Student Athlete, Jim Wilhelm Scholarship, 1993; Distinguished Mediator, Straus Inst Dispute Resolution, 2001. **Home Addr:** 25363 Bridle Path Lane, Farmington Hills, MI 48335. **Business Addr:** President, Chief Executive Officer, H&L Development Co LLC, PO Box 2211, Farmington Hills, MI 48333-2211, **Business Phone:** (810)523-5456.

### HALL, PAMELA VANESSA
Financial manager, consultant. **Personal:** Born Jul 2, 1954, Ann Arbor, MI; daughter of James D and Maureen. **Educ:** MI State Univ, BA, 1976. **Career:** AJC Bus Consul, financial consult, 1980-98; Am Express, fin adv, 1998-2003; Charter One Securities, financial consult, 2003; New York Life, financial serv prof, 2004-. **Orgs:** Metro Womens Civic Coun, 1997-; Nat Asn Advan Colored People, Ypsilanti/Willow Run Br, 1998-2001, 2nd vp, 2001-02; planning comnr, Wastenaw County Planning Comn, 2001-02. **Home Addr:** 2016 Main St Suite 2101, Houston, TX 77002. **Business Addr:** Financial Services Professional, Consultant, New York Life, 3200 Southwest Freeway Suite 1900, Houston, TX 77027-7611, **Business Phone:** (713)499-7605.

### HALL, DR. PERRY ALONZO
School administrator, executive director. **Personal:** Born Sep 15, 1947, Detroit, MI. **Educ:** Univ Mich, BA, psychol, 1969; Harvard Univ, PhD, educ & soc policy, 1977. **Career:** Ford Found, doctoral fel, 1971; Northeastern Univ, instr, 1974; Wayne State Univ, prog coordr, 1974-76, asst prof, 1977-80, centre black studies, actg dir, dir, 1980-; Univ NC Chapel Hill, African & afro am studies, assoc prof, currently. **Orgs:** Substance Abuse Comn, New Detroit Inc, 1974-; exec bd mem, Nat Coun Black Studies, 1978; consult, Chicago Ctr Afro-Am Studies & Res, 1982; consult, State Mich, Off Substance Abuse Serv, 1982; adv bd mem, Equal Opportunity Ctr, 1983-. **Honors/Awds:** Outstanding Young Men of Am, 1980. **Special Achievements:** Publications: Beyond Afrocentrism Alternate for Afro American studies; Western Journal of Black studies, 1991; Toward a Dramaturical Analysis of Historical Transformation in African American Musical culture; A Black Culture journal, 1991; Systematic & Thematic Principles, 1996; In the Vineyard: Working in African American Studies, Univ Tenn Press, 2004. **Home Addr:** 9209 Grandmont, Detroit, MI 48228. **Business Addr:** Associate Professor, University of North Carolina, 170 E Franklin St 3395 Battle Hall, Chapel Hill, NC 27599-3395, **Business Phone:** (919)537-3188.

### HALL, REGINA
Actor. **Personal:** Born Dec 12, 1970, Washington, DC; daughter of Odie and Ruby. **Educ:** NY Univ, MS, journalism, 1997. **Career:** Films: The Best Man, 1999; Love & Basketball, 2000; Scary Movie, 2000; Scary Movie 2, 2001; The Other Brother, 2002; Paid in Full, 2002; Malibu's Most Wanted, 2003; Scary Movie 3, 2003; Six Months Later, 2005; King's Ransom, 2005; The Honeymooners, 2005; Danika, 2006; Scary Movie 4, 2006; The Elder Son, 2006; First Sunday, 2008; Superhero Movie, 2008; Law Abiding Citizen, 2009; Mardi Gras, Death at a Funeral, 2010; Blondie: The Florence Ballard Story, 2011; Mardi Gras: Spring Break, 2011; Think Like a Man, 2012; The Best Man Holiday, 2013; About Last Night, 2014; Think Like a Man Too, 2014; . TV guest appearances: Loving, 1992; "New York Undercover", 1997; "NYPD Blue", 2000; "Disappearing Acts", 2000; "Ally McBeal", 2001-02; "Bygones", 2002, "What I'll Never Do for Love Again", 2002; 'Untitled Cedric the Entertainer Project", 2008; "Law & Order: Los Angeles", 2010-11; "Untitled Martin Lawrence Project", 2012; "Second Generation Wayans", 2013; "Married", 2014. **Honors/Awds:** Festival Award, San Diego Film Festival, 2006; Hollywood Award, Acapulco Black Film Festival, 2014. **Business Addr:** Actress, c/o Writers & Artists Agency, 8383 Wilshire Blvd Suite 550, Beverly Hills, CA 90211, **Business Phone:** (323)866-0900.

### HALL, DR. REGINALD LAWRENCE
Physician, educator, orthopedic surgeon. **Personal:** Born Jun 19, 1957, Whiteville, NC; son of Lawrence and Vera; married Ranota Thomas. **Educ:** Baltimore Polytech Inst, 1975; St Vincent Col, BS, chem, 1979; Duke Univ Sch Med, 1983. **Career:** Duke Univ Med Ctr, res, 1983, jr asst res, 1985, res orthop surg, 1989; Med Col Wis, Milwaukee, fel, 1990; St Vincent Col, chem lab asst; Mayor's Coordr Coun Criminal Justice Baltimore, work & study alumni develop off intern; Mass Transit Admin Baltimore, Res & Planning Dept, intern, mayor's coordr coun criminal justice; St Vincent Col, chem lab asst, work & study alumni develop off; summer fel Cornell Med Col; Durham Regional Hosp, Duke Univ Med Ctr, phlebotomist, res fel div ped cardiol, clin chem lab orthop surg resd, asst prof, cur, pvt pract, physician, currently. **Orgs:** Black Stud Union, Freshman Orientation Comn, Dean's Col Sub comm, Res Adv Coun, Alumni Telethon, Duke Univ Med Sch Admis Comn, Davison Coun Stud Govt, Stud Nat Med Asn, Am Med Stud Asn, Dean's Minority Affairs Subcomt; adv, Duke Univ Undergrad Premed Soc; Am Bd Orthopaedic Surg. **Honors/Awds:** CV Mosby Book Award; Analytic Chem Award. **Home Addr:** 120 William Penn Plz Suite 900, Durham, NC 27704, **Home Phone:** (919)220-5255. **Business Addr:** Physician, Durham Regional Hospital, PO Box 1500, Butner, NC 27509, **Business Phone:** (919)575-3900.

### HALL, ROBERT L.
Government official, mayor. **Personal:** Born Apr 1, 1937, Stuart, FL; married Rose Ann. **Career:** City Stuart, supt parks & cemetery; City Stuart, mayor, comnr. **Orgs:** Pres, Martin Co Dem Mens Club; potentate, Fla St Nursing Home Investr; chmn, Ombudsment Comn nursing home; Stuart Vol Fire Dept; 32 degree Mason; Shriner; So Asn Cemeteries; Pk Personnel Asn; Mason. **Honors/Awds:** Many awards from Civic & Church Organizations; Award for Serving as Commissioner & Mayor City Stuart; Award for Voters Registration Participation Super of Election. **Home Addr:** PO Box 1622, Stuart, FL 34995.

### HALL, ROBERT L.
Educator, curator. **Personal:** Born Miami, FL. **Educ:** Fisk Univ, Nashville, TN, BS, arts, 1972; George Washington Univ, Wash, DC, MAT, mus educ, 1975. **Career:** Fisk Univ Mus Art, Nashville, Tenn, cur, 1973-84; Anacostia Community Mus, Smithsonian Inst, Anacostia Mus & Ctr African Am Hist & Cult, assoc dir educ & visual arts specialist, 1984-, cur new visions, 1990-. **Orgs:** Am Asn Mus; African Am Mus Asn; Commonwealth Asn Mus; advisor, US Holocaust Mus; advisor, Presidents's Comt Arts & humanities. **Business Addr:** Associate Director for Education, Curator New Visions, Anacostia Community Museum, 1901 Ft Pl SE, Washington, DC 20020, **Business Phone:** (202)633-4868.

### HALL, RONALD E.
Executive, president (organization), chief executive officer. **Educ:** Western Mich Univ, BS, math; Wayne State Univ, MBA. **Career:** New Detroit Inc, exec; New Ctr Stamping, chmn & chief exec officer, 2003; Renaissance Capital Alliance, pres & chief exec officer; Bridgewater Interiors, pres & chief exec officer, currently; United Am Health care Corp, dir. **Orgs:** Pres, Mich Minority Bus Develop Coun, 1992-98; Casino Adv Comm; bd dir, St John Hosp & Med Ctr; chmn, Am Diabetes Asn Mich; 100 Black Men; Native Am Bus Alliance; Detroit Empowerment Zone; chmn, Southeastern Mich Jr Achievement; Walsh Col Pres's Advs Coun; bd dir, United Am Health careCorp; Booker T Wash Bus Asn; Bus Enterprise Develop Ctr; pres, Mich Amateur Athletic Asn; Metrop Growth & Develop Corp; Detroit Urban League; Va Pk Community Investment Asn; vice chmn, Family Serv Detroit & WayneCo; Rotary Club; Child Care Coord Coun Detroit/Wayne Co. **Business Addr:** President, Chief Executive Officer, Bridgewater Interiors LLC, 4617 W Fort St, Detroit, MI 48209-3208, **Business Phone:** (313)842-3300.

### HALL, SARAH N.
Lawyer. **Career:** Nat Conf Bar Examiners, pres & chair; WVa Bd Law Examiners, vpres & staff; atty law, currently. **Orgs:** Wva Bd Law Examiners. **Home Addr:** 28 Elkhorn St, PO Box 605, Welch, WV 24801-0605, **Home Phone:** (304)436-6200. **Business Addr:** Member, West Virginia Board of Law Examiners, Davidson Bldg 910 Quarrier St Suite 212, Charleston, WV 25301, **Business Phone:** (304)558-7815.

### HALL, SHARON
Manager, executive director, association executive. **Personal:** children: Christopher & Casey. **Educ:** Morris Brown Col, Atlanta, BS, 1978; Univ Southern Calif, MBA, 1982. **Career:** Procter & Gamble, brand mkt, staff, 1978-80; Allen & Hamilton, mkt mgr; Booz, Allen & Hamilton, strategy clients its mkt pract, 1982-84; Avon Prod, staff, gen mgr, 1984-94; Spencer Stuart, Atlanta, consult, 1997, Diversity Pract, co-founder, 1999, head off & partner, 2001-, off mgr, exec consult, bd dir, mgr, currently. **Orgs:** Bd mem, Urban League, Greater Kansas City; fel firm worldwide bd dir. **Honors/Awds:** Chairman Award, 1990 & 92; Hall the Q-Firm Award, 2000; Women Worth Watching, 2006; Women on Wall Street Conference, 2010; Black Enterprise Women Power Summit, 2014. **Special Achievements:** First African American woman to run a major search firm. **Home Addr:** , Atlanta, GA. **Business Addr:** Managing Director, Spencer Stuart, 2 Alliance Ctr, Atlanta, GA 30326, **Business Phone:** (404)504-4400.

### HALL, HON. SHELVIN LOUISE MARIE
State court judge, lawyer. **Personal:** Born Jun 15, 1948; daughter of Shelvin Jerome and Lucy M; married Ephraim M Martin. **Educ:** Hampton Univ, Hampton, Va; Boston Univ Sch Law, Boston, MA, JD. **Career:** Pvt practice atty; US Congressman Mickey Leland, legislative dir, 1980; Ill Dept Human Rights, sr atty, 1982, gen coun, 1984; Cook County, circuit ct judge, 1991-99; Ill Appellate Ct, appellate judge, 1999-, First Div & Fourth Div Appellate Ct, presiding justice. **Orgs:** Pres, Houston Lawyers Asn, 1977-78; pres, Baptist Gen State Conv Ill, 1995-2006, chair, Ill Judicial Coun Nat Bar Asn, 1998-99; educ & exec comt, Supreme Ct Ill Judicial Conf; Nat Asn Advan Colored People Legal Defense Fund & Educ Fund; nat vpres, Nat Bar Asn; chair, Young Lawyers Div; chair, Admin Law Sect; exec comt, Mem Bd Gov & Creator Interdenominational Prayer Breakfast, 1985; chair, Ill Judicial Coun; Cook County Bar Asn; Nat Bar Asn; Lutheran Family Mission; Legal Asst Found Chicago; Judges Asn; Nat Asn Women Judges; Ill State Bar Asn; vpre, Cook County Bar Asn; Women's Bar Asn Ill; Black Women Lawyer's Asn Greater Chicago; Chicago Bar Asn; Am Bar Asn; Delta Sigma Theta Sorority; Bars Supreme Ct Ill, Tex & US; Friendship Baptist Church; dir, Church Youth Dept; chair, Christian Care Dept; chair, Dept Christian Educ; Black Women Lawyers Asn Greater Chicago. **Business Addr:** Appellate Judge, Illinois Supreme Court, Appellate Ct Bldg 55 Symphony Way, Elgin, IL 60120, **Business Phone:** (847)695-3750.

### HALL, SOPHIA H.
Judge. **Personal:** Born Jul 10, 1943, Chicago, IL. **Educ:** Univ Wis, Madison, BA, hist, 1964; Northwestern Univ, Sch Law, JD, 1967. **Career:** McCoy, Ming & Black, assoc, 1967-76; Stanley Kusper Jr, admin asst; Mitchell, Hall, Jones & Black, PC, shareholder, 1976-80; munic, 1980-81; P.I., munic, 1981-82; State Ill, Circuit Ct Cook County Judicial Circuit, Criminal div, 1981-82, Chancery Div, 1983-86, Juv Justice & C Protection Dept, Admin Presiding Judge, 1994-01; Loyola Univ Chicago Law Sch, adj fac, 1996; Circuit Ct, judge, currently. **Orgs:** US Dist Ct Northern Dist Ill Bar Asn, 1967; bd dir, Nat Ctr State Cts, 1988-94; past pres, Nat Asn Women Judges, 1989-90; chair, Civil Damages Awards Comt, Ill Task Force; bd mem, State Justice Inst, 1998; chair, NAWJ Comt Task Force Family Violence; past pres, secy, treas & third vpres, Ill Judges Asn; Comt Circuit Ct Cook County; Judicial Admin Div, Am Bar Asn; Ill State Rep, chair person, Nat Conf State Trial Judges; Chicago Bar Asn; life mem, Nat Asn Advan Colored People; Zonta Club Southside Chicago; Chicago Network. **Honors/Awds:** Outstanding Jurist, John Marshall Law Sch, 1992; Distinguished Service Award, Nat Ctr State Cts, 1995; Todays Chicago Woman Hall of Fame; Civil Rights Award, Cook County Bar Association. **Special Achievements:** First Women Presiding Judge Within the Circuit Court of Cook County, 1993; Publ: Declaratory Judgments, Chicago Bar Record, November, 1991; Interlocutory Injunctions, Chicago Bar Record, Jul/Aug, 1992. **Business Addr:** Judge, Circuit Court.

### HALL, SYDNEY JAY, III
Lawyer. **Personal:** Born Feb 27, 1959, Sumpter, SC; son of Sidney and Loretta. **Educ:** Howard Univ, BBA, 1982, JD, 1987. **Career:** Firemans Fund/Am Express, para-legal, 1978-81; Am Express, spec asst vpres finance, 1982; Travelers Ins, claims adjuster, 1987; Freistat & Sandler, assoc, 1987; Hall Sydney J Law Off, atty, 1992-. **Orgs:** Nat Bar Asn; Am Bar Asn; Calif State Bar; Md State Bar; Penn State Bar; founder, Asa T Spaulding Ins Soc, 1990. **Honors/Awds:** Int Youth in Achievement Award, Cambridge, Eng; Leadership, San Mateo, 1992. **Home Addr:** 251 Topsail Ct, Foster City, CA 94404, **Home Phone:** (415)345-2497. **Business Addr:** Attorney, Sydney J Hall Law Office, 1308 Old Bayshore Hwy Suite 220, Burlingame, CA 94010, **Business Phone:** (650)342-1830.

### HALL, TAMRON
Talk show host, journalist. **Personal:** Born Sep 16, 1970, Luling, TX; daughter of Mary Newton. **Educ:** Temple University, B.A. in Broadcast Journalism. **Career:** KTVT (Dallas, TX), Reporter; WFLD-TV, Reporter, 1997-07; MSNBC, General Reporter and Fill-in Anchor, 2007-; News program "The Big Picture," co-host (with David Shuster), 2009-10; MSNBC's "NewsNation with Tamron Hall," Host, 2010-; NBC "Today," Correspondent; Investigation Discovery "Deadline: Crime with Tamron Hall," 2013-. **Orgs:** National Association of Black Journalists, Member. **Honors/Awds:** Temple University, Lew Klein Alumni in the Media Award, 2010; "The Root" Magazine, The Root 100 Honorees, 2013. **Special Achievements:** Hosted the Westminister Dog Show in 2009 and 2010; featured in media such as "Ebony" magazine, "Uptown" magazine, "Heart & Soul" Magazine, BET's "The Ed Gordon Show," Huffington Post, and AOL Black Voices.

### HALL, TANYA EVETTE
Association executive. **Personal:** Born Aug 12, 1966, Stratford, NJ. **Educ:** Drexel Univ, BS, hospitality admin/mgt, 1988. **Career:** Penn Tower Hotel, 1989-97; Philadelphia Conv & Visitors Bur, Multicultural Affairs Cong, exec dir, 1997-2012; Aetna, Northeast & Mid-Atlantic

Regions, community rels dir, regional dir, 2012-. **Orgs:** Nat Coalition Black Mkt Planners, 1989-; bd mem, Hospitality Sales & Mkt Asn Int, 1995-97; womens ministry dir, Impacting Your World Christian Ctr. **Honors/Awds:** Emerging Leader, Ebony Mag, 1996; African Am Leader, Philadelphia Tribune; 40 Under 40, Philadelphia Bus Jour; Mover & Shaker, Am Women's Heritage Soc; secy, Garth Solutions Inc; secy, PHLCVB; committee member, Meeting Professionals International. **Business Addr:** Community Relations Director, Aetna Inc, 151 Farmington Ave, Hartford, CT 06156, **Business Phone:** (860)273-0123.

**HALL, TERRY L.**
Administrator. **Personal:** Born Feb 23, 1957, Port Huron, MI; daughter of Richard and Audrey Pack; married Morris B Sr; children: Morris B & Antwan L. **Educ:** Northwood Univ, BBA; Baker Col, MBA, 1998. **Career:** DTE Energy, admin supvr, 1981-. **Orgs:** Nat Asn Advan Colored People, 1999-; United Way Citizen's Review Comt, 2000-; Port Huron Scholarship Asst Comt, 2001-; Mich Freedom Trail Comn, comnr, 2002-. **Home Addr:** 2690 Whitney Pl, Ft. Gratiot, MI 48059, **Home Phone:** (810)385-7619. **Business Addr:** Aministrative Supervisor, DTE Energy-Belle River Power Plant, 4505 King Rd, Detroit, MI 48226-1279, **Business Phone:** (810)326-3203.

**HALL, TRACEE K. (TRACEE HALL CROCKETT)**
Government official. **Personal:** Born Feb 13, 1973; children: 2. **Educ:** Ariz State Univ, BA, social, 1995, MPA, 2000. **Career:** City Phoenix Parks, youth counr, 1997; City Phoenix, asst, mgt intern, 2000-01, Aviation Dept, bus outreach proj mgr, 2001-04, sr asst to mayor, 2004-08, Aviation Dept, proj mgr, 2008-09, prog mgr, 2009-, dep chief staff, City Phoenix Parks & Recreation Dept, actg dep dir, 2012-; Everchanging Woman LLC, founder & chief exec officer. **Orgs:** Black Bd dir Proj; bd mem, Conf Minority Transp Off Ariz; bd mem, Ariz Coalition Adolescent Pregnancy & Prev; mentor, Young Families CAN; community mem, Community Alliance Black Stud Support, Ariz State Univ; adv group mem, Sistas Planned Parenthood Cent & Northern Ariz; adv coun mem, Ariz State Univ; bd mem, Suns Nite Hoops; Nat Forum Black Pub Adminr; Delta Sigma Theta Sorority Inc. **Business Addr:** Acting Deputy Director, City of Phoenix Parks & Recreation Department, 200 W Wash St 11th Fl, Phoenix, AZ 85003, **Business Phone:** (602)262-6011.

**HALL, DR. WILLIE GREEN, JR.**
Dentist. **Personal:** Born May 23, 1947, Prattville, AL; son of Willie G Sr and Kattie R; married Cheryl F Wesley; children: Darius & Dashia. **Educ:** Howard Univ, BS, 1971, DDS, 1978. **Career:** Peoples Drug Store, pharmacist & asst mgr, 1969-72; Stand Drugs, pharmacist, 1972-74; Syracuse Community Health Ctr, dentist, 1979-80; Southeast Dent Asn, partner & pres, 1984-91; E River Health Asn, dent dir, 1980-88; Lake Arbor Dent Asn, partner, 1991; CW Funding, owner; Dentist, pvt pract, currently. **Orgs:** Nat Dent Asn, 1986-; Am Dent Asn, 1986-; Nat Pharm Asn, 1986-87; Alpha Omega Psi Phi Fraternity, 1986-; Robert T Freeman Dent Soc, 1986-; Howard Univ, Pharm & Dent Alumni Asns; DC Dent Soc, 1988-; Int Asn Orthod, 1988-; Acad Gen Dent, 1989-; Campbell African Methodist Episcopal Church, Wash, DC; Nat Asn Entrepreneurs, Cert Mortgage Investors. **Honors/Awds:** Volunteer Award, DC Dept Recreation Spec Act, 1984; Capital Head Start Community Award, 1984; Award for Volunteer Service, Wash Srs Wellness Ctr, 1986. **Home Addr:** 4513 Holmehurst Way, Bowie, MD 20720-3455, **Home Phone:** (301)805-9788. **Business Addr:** Dentist, Aesthetic Dental Care Inc, 12164 Cent Ave Suite 221, Mitchellville, MD 20721, **Business Phone:** (301)249-8885.

**HALL-KEITH, JACQUELINE YVONNE**
Judge. **Personal:** Born Jan 8, 1953, Detroit, MI; daughter of William H and Evelyn V Callaway; married Luther A; children: Erin Yvonne. **Educ:** Gen Motors Inst, bus indus admin, 1976; Detroit Col Law, JD, 1980. **Career:** Gen Motors Corp, col co-op, 1971-76; Ford Motor Co, mgt trainee, 1976-78, personnel analyst, 1978-80, Gen Coun, staff atty, 1980-84; State Mich, Dept Labor, admin law judge/magistrate, 1984-94; Mich Dept Civil Rights, atty-at-law, dir, off legal affairs, 1994-. **Orgs:** State Bar Mich; Wolverine Bar Asn; GMI & DCL Alumni Asn; Asn Black Judges Mich; Nat Asn Advan Colored People; delsprite sponsor, Delta Sigma Theta Sorority, 1984-95; bd dir, 1988-91, pres, 1993-94, Top Ladies Distinction; mentor, Nolan Mid Sch, 1993-94; coun mem, State Bar Mich, Alternative Dispute Resolution Sect; bible study instr, Fel Chapel; Mich State Bar Asn. **Home Addr:** 19521 Burlington Dr, Detroit, MI 48203-1453, **Home Phone:** (313)368-8253. **Business Addr:** Attorney-at-Law, Director, Michigan Department of Civil Rights, 3054 W Grand Blvd Suite 3-600 Cadillac Pl, Detroit, MI 48202, **Business Phone:** (313)456-3700.

**HALL-TRUJILLO, KATHRYN.** **See HALL, KATHRYN LOUISE.**

**HALL-TURNER, DEBORAH**
Health services administrator. **Personal:** Born Jun 6, 1951, Detroit, MI; daughter of Herbert and Haroline; married Michael G Sr; children: Michael G Turner. **Educ:** Mercy Col Detroit, BSN, 1973; Case Mgt Soc Am, cert, 1994. **Career:** Wayne County Pt Care Mgmt, dir qual assurance, 1988-91; Mercy HealthServs, sr mgr qual mgmt, 1991-93, dir qual servs, 1993-94, dir accrediation, regulation, 1994-95; Mich Peer Rev Orgn, dir state gov progs, 1995-96, dir behav health prog & managed care eval, 1996-. **Orgs:** Pres, Asn Managed Care Nursing, bd mem, 1993-; treas, Thea Bowen Wellness Inst, 1995-; Black Nurses Asn; Mich Asn Health Plans. **Home Addr:** 20515 Vernier Suite 4, Harper Woods, MI 48225, **Home Phone:** (313)417-0929. **Business Addr:** Director Behavioral Health Program, Michigan Peer Review Organisation, 22670 Haggerty Rd Suite 100, Farmington Hills, MI 48335-2611, **Business Phone:** (517)796-6469.

**HALLIBURTON, CHRISTOPHER**
Executive. **Personal:** Born Apr 27, 1958, New York, NY; son of Norman and Camille Simonette; married Jocelyn Cooper. **Educ:** Tufts Univ, BA, hist & polit sci, 1980. **Career:** Aetna Life Ins, EBR, 1980-84; Tannenbaum-Harber, acct exec, 1982-84; Mayer & Meyer Assocs, acct exec, 1984-89; Crossroads Films, sales rep, 1989-91; 900 Frames, exec producer, 1991-93; Relativity Rec, dir video prod, currently; Adrock Inc, prin, 1997-2002; Corcoran Group, assoc broker, 2003-04, sr assoc broker, 2012-13; Warburg Realty Harlem, exec vpres managing dir, 2004-08, sr vpres, 2004-10; Maison Int, sales dir, 2010-11; City Connections Realty, assoc broker, 2011-12; DHS Develop Corp, prin, 2010-; Halstead Property LLC, assoc broker, 2013-. **Orgs:** Real Estate Bd New York; Tufts Univ Alumni Assoc; Us Tennis Asn. **Home Addr:** 105 Duane St, New York, NY 10007, **Home Phone:** (212)566-4094. **Business Addr:** Director of Urban Product Marketing, Relativity Records, 79 5th Ave 16th Fl, New York, NY 10003, **Business Phone:** (212)337-5317.

**HALLIBURTON, WARREN J.**
College teacher, writer, editor. **Personal:** Born Aug 2, 1924, New York, NY; son of Richard H and Blanche Watson; married Marion Jones; children: Cheryl, Stephanie, Warren Jr & Jena; married Francis Fletcher. **Educ:** NY Univ, BS, 1949; Columbia Univ, MEd, 1975, DEd, 1977. **Career:** Prairie View Agr & Mech Col, Prairie View, Tex, Eng instr, 1949; Bishop Col, Dallas, Tex, Eng instr, 1951; Inst int Educ, 1952; New York New York, Recorder, reporter & columnist, 1953; Brooklyn New York, teacher & dean high sch, 1958-60; New York Bd Educ, coordr, 1960-65; New York Dept Educ, assoc, 1960-65; McGraw Hill Inc, New York NY, ed, 1967; Hamilton-Kirkland Cols, Clinton New York, vis prof Eng, 1971-72; Columbia Univ, Teachers Col, New York New York, ed, res assoc & dir scholarly j, govt prog, 1972-77; Ethnic Studies Ctr, 1972-77; Reader's Dig, New York, New York, ed & writer, freelance ed & writer; Books: American Majorities and Minorities: A Syllabus of United States History for Secondary Schools, Arno, 1970; They Had a Dream, 1970; America's Color Caravan, 1970; The Picture Life of Jesse Jackson F Watts, 1972 & 1984; The History Black Americans, Harcourt, 1973; The History of Black Americans, 1973; Harlem: A History of Broken Dreams, Doubleday, 1974; Pathways to the World of English, Globe, 1974; The Fighting Redtails: America's First Black Airmen, illustrated by John Gampert, Contemporary Perspectives, 1978; Flight to the Stars: The Life of Daniel James, Jr, Contemporary Perspectives, 1979; The Tragedy of Little Bighorn, F. Watts, 1989; Nomads of the Sahara, Africa Today Series, Crestwood, 1992; Africa's Struggle for Independence, Africa Today Series, Crestwood, 1992; African Wildlife, Africa Today Series, Crestwood, 1992; Celebrations of African Heritage, Africa Today Series, Crestwood, 1992; African Industries, Africa Today Series, Crestwood, 1993; African Landscapes, Africa Today Series, Crestwood, 1993; Africa's Struggle to Survive, Africa Today Series, Crestwood, 1993; City & Village Life, Africa Today Series, Crestwood, 1993; Clarence Thomas:Supreme Ct Justice, Enslow, 1993; Historic Speeches African Americans, F. Watts, 1993; New Worlds Lit, co-ed; Novels: The Heist, 1969; Cry, Baby!, 1969; Some Things that Glitter, 1969. **Home Addr:** 22 Scribner Hill Rd, Wilton, CT 06897.

**HALLUMS, BENJAMIN F.**
Educator. **Personal:** Born Mar 6, 1940, Easley, SC; married Phyllis; children: Jacqueline, Bernard & Maisha. **Educ:** BA, 1970. **Career:** Quinnipiac Col, coun, 1971-75, asst prof fine arts, 1972-75, asst prof black studies, 1973-75; Sch Ment Retarded, coun, 1972-73; Allied Health Prog, coun, 1974. **Orgs:** Asn Black People Higher Educ, 1970-75; Conn Liason Prog, 1973; Minority Col Couns, 1973; Eastern Alliance Black Couns, 1974-75; Nat Black Col Choir Ann Fest; rep, United Ministry Higher Educ; Nat Quinnipiac Col Choirs; secy, Coalliation Black Prin, 1975; vpres, Couples Inc. **Home Addr:** 100 State St Suite 40, North Haven, CT 06473. **Business Addr:** College Counselor, Quinnipiac College, 275 Mt Carmel Ave, Hamden, CT 06518, **Business Phone:** (203)582-8200.

**HALYARD, DR. MICHELE YVETTE**
Physician, accordionist. **Personal:** Born Apr 13, 1961, Buffalo, NY; married Kevin Robinson. **Educ:** Howard Univ, BS, zool, 1982; Howard Univ Col Med, MD, 1984. **Career:** Howard Univ Hosp, resident radiation oncol, 1984-87; Mayo Clin Col Med, fel radiation oncol, 1987, assoc prof radiation oncol, physician, currently. **Orgs:** Nat & Am Med Assocs; Phi Beta Kappa Hon Soc; Alpha Omega Alpha Med Hon Soc; Alpha Kappa Alpha Sor Inc; Links Inc. **Honors/Awds:** Am Med Women's Asn Award Scholar Achievement; Grandy Award for Internal Medicine; Award for Clinical Excellence in Psychiatry; Frederick M Drew Award for Outstanding Performance in Radiation Therapy; article "The Use of Intraoperative Radiotherapy and External Beam Therapy in the Mgt of Desmoid Tumors", w/Jo Ann Collier-Manning MD, Ebrahim Ashayeri MD, Alfred Goldson MD, Frank Watkins MD, Ernest Myers MD in J Nat Med Asn, 1986. **Business Addr:** Physician, Associate Professor of Oncology, Mayo Clinic, 13400 E Shea Blvd, Scottsdale, AZ 85259, **Business Phone:** (480)301-8000.

**HAM, DARVIN**
Basketball player, basketball coach. **Personal:** Born Jul 23, 1973, Saginaw, MI; son of Wilmer Jones; married Deneitra; children: Darvin Jr, Donovan & Dominic Jr. **Educ:** Tex Tech Univ, attended 1996. **Career:** Basketball player (retired), basketball coach; Denver Nuggets, small forward, 1996-97; Ind Pacers, small forward, 1996-97; Wash Wizards, small forward, 1997-98; CB Granada, Spain, 1999; Milwaukee Bucks, small forward, 1999-2002; Atlanta Hawks, shooting guard, 2002-03, asst coach, 2013-; Detroit Pistons, small forward, 2003-05; Dallas Mavericks, FOX Sports Southwest, studio analyst; Talk N Text Phone Pals, Philippines, 2006; Dallas Mavericks, forward, 2007; Albuquerque Thunderbirds, forward, 2007-08, asst coach, 2008-10; Austin Toros, 2008; NMex Thunderbirds, head coach, 2010-11; Los Angeles Lakers, asst coach, 2011-13. **Honors/Awds:** Champion, Nat Basketball Asn, 2004. **Home Addr:** 1296 W Wesley Rd NW, Atlanta, GA 30327-1439. **Business Addr:** Assistant Coach, Atlanta Hawks, 101 Marietta St NW Suite 1900, Atlanta, NM 30303, **Business Phone:** (404)878-3800.

**HAM, DR. DEBRA NEWMAN**
Educator, historian. **Personal:** Born Aug 27, 1948, York, PA; daughter of Earl F and Eva Mitchell Owens; married Lester James Sr; children: Lester James Jr & Leslyn Jaye. **Educ:** Howard Univ, BA, hist, 1970, PhD, hist, 1984; Boston Univ, MA, hist, 1971. **Career:** Nat Arch, Wash, archivist, black hist specialist, 1972-86, NVA Comm Col, adj prof, 1986-88, Libr Cong, specialist, african-am manuscript historian, 1986-95, guest cur; Morgan State Univ, prof, hist, 1995-; Author: The Emergence of Liberian Women in the Nineteenth Century, 1984; Black History: A Guide to Civilian Records in the National Archives, 1984; The African-American Mosaic: A Guide to Black History Resources in the Library of Congress, editor, 1993; African American Odyssey: Quest for Full Citizenship, editor, 1998. **Orgs:** Founding mem, African-Am Hist & Geneal Soc, 1978-; publ dir, Asn Black Women Historians, 1987-90; exec coun, Asn Study Afro-Am Life & Hist, 1990-96; ed bd, Soc Am Archivists, 1990-92; Adv Comt African-Am Interpretation Monticello, 2003-. **Home Addr:** 8613 Magnolia St, Laurel, MD 20707, **Home Phone:** (301)953-1899. **Business Addr:** Professor, Speaker, Morgan State University, 313 Holmes Hall, Baltimore, MD 21251, **Business Phone:** (443)885-1788.

**HAM-YING, DR. JOHN MICHAEL**
Physician, educator. **Personal:** Born Mar 16, 1956, Gainesville, FL; son of John Russel and Dorothy McClellan; married Franeco Cheeks. **Educ:** Oakwood Col, BA, biol, 1977; Meharry Med Col, MD, 1981. **Career:** King Drew Med Ctr, asst med dir, 1984-85; Los Angeles Doctors Hosp, exec staff secy, 1984-85; S Eastern Col Osteopath Med, asst clin prof, 1985-96; Hendry Gen Hosp, attend physician, 1985-96; Clewiston Community Health Ctr, asst med dir, 1985-87; Fla Community Health Centers Inc, med dir, 1987-89, chief med officer, 1989-96; Alpha Health Plan, chief med officer, currently; Bur Primary Health Care, clin consult; Pine Hills Family Health Ctr, physician, currently; Community Health Centers Inc, vpres & chief med officer, currently. **Orgs:** Am Med Asn; Am Acad Family Physicians, FL Chap, 1983; charter mem, T Leroy Jefferson Med Soc, 1990-96; chmn med ethics subcomt, Fla Acad Family Physicians, Fla Asn Community Health Centers; bd dir, Am Bd Family Pract. **Home Addr:** 3933 Country Club Dr SuiteA, Orlando, FL 32808, **Home Phone:** (863)983-6117. **Business Addr:** Vice President, Chief Medical Officer, Community Health Centers Inc, 110 S Woodland St, Winter Garden, FL 34787-3546, **Business Phone:** (407)905-8827.

**HAMBERG, DR. MARCELLE R.**
Physician. **Personal:** Born Jul 4, 1931, Anderson, SC; son of Robert Clark and Pauline Hamlin; married Cheryl Jones; children: Marcelle Jr & Gabrielle. **Educ:** Hampton Inst, BS, 1953; Meharry Med Col, MD, 1957. **Career:** Internship, 1958; Hubbard Hosp Meharry Med Col, surg resident, 1959, resident urol, 1962; Univ Louisville, instr urol, 1967; Meharry Med Col, Div Urol, chief, 1976, assoc prof, 1974-82; Memorial Hosp Cancer All Dis; pvt pract physician, currently. **Orgs:** Sloan-Kettering Cancer Ctr, 1962-63; Newman Van High Spl; Fed Cancer Urol; Hosp Cancer & Allied Dis, 1962-63; Am Bd Urol, 1968; Am Urol Asn, SE, 1969. **Home Addr:** 1916 Patterson St Suite 603, Nashville, TN 37203, **Home Phone:** (615)327-2400. **Business Addr:** Physician, 4474 Clarksville Pike, Nashville, TN 37218, **Business Phone:** (615)876-3821.

**HAMBERLIN, DR. EMIEL**
Teacher. **Personal:** Born Nov 8, 1939, Fayette, MS; married Minnie; children: Emiel III & Mark. **Educ:** Alcorn State Univ, BA, biol, 1964; Univ Ill, MEd, voc educ, 1978, PhD, hort, 1982; Northwestern Univ, adv studies, 1993. **Career:** Chicago Pub Schs, Biol & Hort Environ Studies, prin, prof & teacher, 1964-; Jean Baptiste Pointe De Sable High Sch, teacher, currently. **Orgs:** Omega Psi Phi Fraternity, 1964-; Nat Geog Soc, 1970-; Oper PUSH, 1972; Nat Biol Asn, 1974-; Int Wild life Fedn, 1974-; Ill Teachers Asn, 1975-; Phi Delta Kappa, 1976-; Ill Sci Teachers Asn, 1978-; hon mem, Kappa Delta Pi, 1979-; bd mem, Ada McKinley Highland Spec C, 1980. **Honors/Awds:** Teacher of the Year, City Chicago, 1971; The Governors Award, World Flower Show, 1972; Outstanding Secondary Educator of America, 1974; Professional Personnel in Environmental Education, Ill Environ Educ Asn, 1975; Omega Man of the Year, 1977; Those Who Excell Award, State Ill, 1977; Illinois Teacher of the Year, 1977; Outstanding Educator Award, Lewis Univ, 1980; Phi Delta Kappa Educator, 1981; Ill Master Teacher, Governor Ill, 1981; State of Illinois Master Teacher Award, 1983; Ora Higgins Leadership Award, 1985; Distinguished Alumni of Black Universities, Nat Asn Equal Opport Higher Educ, 1986; Outstanding Achievements as an Educator in Horticulture, Mayor H Wash, 1986; One of the Heroes of Our Time Newsweek, Newsweek Mag, 1986; City of Chicago Teacher of the Year; Who's Who Among Black Americans - Educators, 1988; Kohl Family Foundation International Educator, 1992; Golden Apple Found Acad Fel, 1992; National Teachers Hall of Fame, 2001. **Home Addr:** 8500 S Winchester Ave, Chicago, IL 60620, **Home Phone:** (773)233-8509. **Business Addr:** Teacher of Biology and Horticulture, Jean Baptiste Pointe DeSable High School, 4934 S Wabash Ave, Chicago, IL 60615, **Business Phone:** (773)535-1100.

**HAMBLIN, ANGELA**
Basketball player, basketball coach. **Personal:** Born Sep 30, 1976, Gary, IN; children: 3. **Educ:** Univ Iowa, BA, eng, 1998. **Career:** Basketball player (retired), basketball coach; Lew Wallace Hornets, guard, 1994; Wash Mystics, guard, 1998; Detroit Shock, guard, 1998-99; Lew Wallace High Sch, basketball coach, currently. **Business Addr:** Basketball Head Coach, Lew Wallace High School, 415 W 45th Ave, Gary, IN 46408-3998, **Business Phone:** (219)980-6305.

**HAMBRICK, DARREN**
Football player. **Personal:** Born Aug 30, 1975, Lacoochee, FL. **Educ:** Univ SC, grad. **Career:** Football player (retired); Dallas Cowboys, 1998, linebacker, 1999-2001; Carolina Panthers, linebacker, 2001; Cleveland Browns, linebacker, 2002; Tampa Bay Storm, 2007. **Honors/Awds:** All-SEC, 1996; Pasco County Athlete of the Decade. **Special Achievements:** Best football player in Pasco County History.

**HAMBRICK, HAROLD E, JR.** **See Obituaries Section.**

**HAMBRICK-DIXON, DR. PRISCILLA J.**
Psychologist. **Educ:** Univ Mich, MA, develop psychol, PhD, educ & psychol; Albert Einstein Col Med, child clin psychol & child ment

health res. **Career:** Todays Child mag, ed bd; Hunter Col, Dept Educ Found & coun prog, asst prof, assoc prof, currently. **Orgs:** Nat Res Coun; Nat Acad Sci & Ford Found. **Special Achievements:** First psychometrician. **Business Addr:** Associate Professor of Educational Foundations, Hunter College, 695 Pk Ave, New York, NY 10065, **Business Phone:** (212)772-4627.

## HAMBY, EDWINA HARRIS

College administrator, businessperson. **Educ:** Fisk Univ, BA, eng lang & lit, 1968; Federal City Col/Univ DC, MA, reading & admin higher educ, 1973; Jackson State Univ, PhD, urban higher educ & hist higher educ, 2008. **Career:** Bowie State Col, dir freshman & sophomore basic studies div; Vanderbilt Univ, assoc dir sponsored res & training; Meharry Med Col, assoc prof & founding dir AHEC Prog Tenn, 1981-88; City Univ New York, vpres, dean & univ assoc dean acad affairs, 1988-2000; Fisk Univ, dean admis & exec dir alumni affairs & develop, 2001-03, vpres instnl advan, 2011-; Tougaloo Col, vpres instnl advan, 2004-08; WDH Resource Group Inc, partner, 2010-. **Special Achievements:** Served as the national director of research, International Association of Firefighters/AFL-CIO; served as the vice president of resource development, Boys & Girls Clubs of Middle Tennessee; experienced grants developer, writer, and administrator. **Business Addr:** Advancement House, 1000 17th Ave N, Nashville, TN 32708, **Business Phone:** (615)329-8768.

## HAMER, DR. JUDITH ANN

Executive, writer, manager. **Personal:** Born Jan 3, 1939, Brooklyn, NY; daughter of Frank Leslie Thompson and Martha Louise Taylor Thompson; married Martin J; children: Kim T, Fern S & Jill T; married Bill Buckley. **Educ:** Cornell Univ, BA, eng lit, 1960; Smith Col, MAT, 1961; Columbia Univ, PhD, educ, 1982. **Career:** CCNY, instr, 1971-76; Columbia Univ, adj instr, 1977-83; Learning Int, consult writer, 1984-86; UBS-Paine Webber Inc, dp trainer, 1986, training mgr, corp training dept, div vpres; Town Westport, Conn, mem, currently; Sienna Commun, pres, 2011-. **Orgs:** Coalition 100 Black Women Stamford, Conn; learning officer, Rockefeller Found, 2001-05; grant writer, Neighborhood Studios Fairfield County, 2007-11; C 21st Century. **Home Addr:** 19 Webb Rd, Westport, CT 06880, **Home Phone:** (203)226-9942. **Business Addr:** Member, Town of Westport, 110 Myrtle Ave, Westport, CT 06880, **Business Phone:** (203)341-1000.

## HAMER, STEVE (STEVIE RAY HAMER)

Basketball player, basketball coach. **Personal:** Born Nov 13, 1973, Memphis, TN; children: Malachi. **Educ:** Univ Tenn, attended 1996. **Career:** Basketball player (retired), basketball coach; Boston Celtics, ctr, 1996-97; Suntrust Bank, teller; Apostolic Christian Sch, asst coach, currently. **Orgs:** First Apostolic Church, 1999-. **Home Addr:** , Knoxville, TN. **Business Addr:** Assistant Coach, Apostolic Christian School, 5020 Pleasant Ridge Rd, Knoxville, TN 37912-0379, **Business Phone:** (865)523-5261.

## HAMILL, MARGARET HUDGENS

Educator. **Personal:** Born Mar 9, 1937, Laurens, SC; children: Beatrice Chauntea. **Educ:** Benedict Col, BA, 1958; St Peter's Col, Ed dipl, 1962. **Career:** No 5 Pub Sch, educr, 1966-68; Frank R Conwell, educr, 1968-74; Joseph H Brensinger, educr, 1974-. **Orgs:** Sch rep NJ Educ Asn, 1985-; adv, Tauette Club, 1985-; bd dirs, Bayonne Chap Nat Conf Christians & Jews, 1985-; pres, Young Women's League Friendship Bapt Church, 1986-; First vpres Bayonne Youth Ctr Inc, 1986-; sgt-of-arms Tau Gamma Delta Sor Psi Chapt. **Honors/Awds:** Community Service Award Bayonne, Nat Asn Advan Colored People, 1979; Brotherhood Award Nat Conf, Christians & Jews, 1985; Mary McLeod Bethune Award, 1985. **Home Addr:** 42 W 18th St, Bayonne, NJ 07002, **Home Phone:** (201)437-9229. **Business Addr:** Staff, Joseph H Brensinger, 128 Duncan Ave, Jersey City, NJ 07306, **Business Phone:** (201)547-5703.

## HAMILTON, ART

State government official, lawyer. **Personal:** Born Jan 1, 1947, Phoenix, AZ; children: 3. **Educ:** Phoenix Col. **Career:** Pub affairs rep; Ariz State Legisl, Phoenix AZ, state rep, Dist 22, House Minority Leader, 1993-99; Nat Coun State Legislatures, pres; Salt River Proj, sr pub affairs rep; Hamilton Gullett Davis & Roman LLC, patner & pub affairs consult, pres, currently; Art Hamilton Group LLC, founder, 2008-. **Orgs:** Found State Legis, Nat Conf State Legis; founding mem, mem emer, State Legis Leaders Found; Dem Nat Comt; chmn, Phoenix Sky Harbor Aviation Adv Bd, currently; Ariz State Bar Bd Gov; Labor's Community Serv Agency Maricopa County; bd dir, Phoenix C Hosp; Int Brotherhood Elec Workers; life mem, Nat Asn Advan Colored People, Maricopa County br; Advocacy Govt Rels; 1996 Dem Nat Conv; Ariz House Representatives; chmn, City Phoenix. **Special Achievements:** First African-American and only Arizonan to be elected President of the National Conference of State Legislatures. **Home Addr:** 140 E Lamar Rd, Phoenix, AZ 85012-1026. **Business Addr:** Founder, Art Hamilton Group LLC, 2575 E Camelback Rd Suite 860, Phoenix, AZ 85013, **Business Phone:** (602)381-6574.

## HAMILTON, ARTHUR LEE, JR.

President (organization), newspaper editor. **Personal:** Born Oct 19, 1957, Detroit, MI; son of Arthur and Lucy; married Marilyn; children: Kyala, Omar, Arlinda, Chineca & Mike. **Educ:** S Western Mich, attended 1979; Northern Mich Univ, attended 1984; Jackson Community Col, assoc, 1987. **Career:** Oracle Newspaper, staff writer, 1979-81; Huron Valley-Monitor Newspaper, ed, 1985-87; Snow Bird Newspaper, staff writer, 1988-89; Lakeland Pen Newspaper, ed, 1993-; Fathers Behind Bars Inc, pres & founder, currently. **Orgs:** Chmn & publicity, Nat Asn Advan Colored People, 1992-93; pres & founder, Fathers Behind Bars Inc, 1993-; Numens Masonic Lodge, 1993-. **Home Addr:** 525 Super St, Niles, MI 49120, **Home Phone:** (269)684-5715. **Business Addr:** President, Founder, Fathers Behind Bars Inc, 525 Super St, Niles, MI 49120, **Business Phone:** (616)684-5715.

## HAMILTON, DR. AWILDA

Educator, dean (education). **Educ:** Howard Univ, BA; Ohio Univ, MA, 1972; Univ Akron, PhD, 1980. **Career:** Univ Cent Fla, fel, 2004-05; Ohio Bd Regents, prin investr; Kent St Univ, Col & Grad Sch Educ, fac mem, prog cord, spl asst to dean, assoc prof, assoc dean, currently, Dept Educ Found & Spec Serv, chmn, currently. **Orgs:** Fel Am Coun Educ, 2004-05; bd dir, Kent State Univ Found. **Business Addr:** Associate Dean, Department Chairman & Board of Director, Kent State University, 409 White Hall, Kent, OH 44242-0001, **Business Phone:** (330)672-0576.

## HAMILTON, BOBBY JEROME

Football player. **Personal:** Born Jul 1, 1971, Columbia, MS; son of Billy (deceased) and Charlene. **Educ:** Southern Miss Univ. **Career:** Football player (retired); Seattle Sea hawks, 1994-95; Amsterdam Admirals, 1996; New York Jets, defensive end & left defensive end, 1996-99, 2006; New Eng patriots, defensive end & left defensive end, 2000-03; Oakland Raiders, defensive end & linebacker & defensive tackle, 2004-05; Cleveland Browns, defensive lineman & defensive end, 2007. **Honors/Awds:** Super Bowl champion, XXXVI, XXXVIII.

## HAMILTON, CHARLES VERNON

Educator. **Personal:** Born Oct 19, 1929, Muskogee, OK; son of Owen and Viola Haynes; married Dona Louise Cooper; children: Valli & Carol. **Educ:** Roosevelt Univ, Chicago, IL, BA, 1951; Loyola Univ, Sch Law, Chicago, IL, JD, 1954; Univ Chicago, Chicago, IL, MA, 1957, PhD, 1964. **Career:** Educator (retired); Tuskegee Univ, Ala, asst prof, 1958-60; Rutgers Univ, Newark, NJ, asst prof, 1963-64; Lincoln Univ, Oxford, Pa, prof, 1964-67; Roosevelt Univ, Chicago, Ill, prof, 1967-69; Columbia Univ, NY, prof polit sci, 1969-97; Metrop Appl Res Ctr, dir; Ford Found, consult. **Orgs:** Bd trustee, Twentieth Century Found; Bd Nat Asn Advan Colored People, 1975; bd ed, Polit Sc Quart, 1975; fel Am Acad Arts & Sci, 1993. **Home Addr:** 55 Barnard Rd, New Rochelle, NY 10801, **Home Phone:** (914)636-1437. **Business Addr:** Professor of Political Science, Columbia University, 420 W 118th St Rm 727, New York, NY 10027, **Business Phone:** (212)854-4518.

## HAMILTON, DEAN

Entrepreneur, founder (originator). **Educ:** St Stanislaus Col, Georgetown. **Career:** NetExpress; Ventel Inc; LPCom Inc; Subspace Commun, co found & chief exec officer; Ascend Communs, gen mgr; Co-Sine Commun, founder, pres & chief exec officer; Quicksilver, chief exec officer & founder; SubSpace Commun Inc, co-founder, chief exec officer & pres; Gale Technologies, chief technol officer, currently. **Honors/Awds:** One of the Top 8 Technology CEO's to Watch, www.Forbes.com, 1999. **Business Addr:** Chief Technology Officer, Senior Vice President - Engineering & Product Management, Gale Technologies Inc, 2350 Mission Col Blvd, Santa Clara, CA 95054, **Business Phone:** (408)980-4800.

## HAMILTON, EDWARD N. (ED HAMILTON)

Sculptor. **Personal:** Born Feb 14, 1947, Cincinnati, OH; married Bernadette S Chapman; children: Edward III & Kendra Jenelle. **Educ:** Louisville Sch Art, attended 1969; Univ Louisville, attended 1971; Spalding Col, attended 1973. **Career:** Iroquois High Sch, teacher, 1969-72; Louisville Art Workshop, 1972; Louisville Speed Mus, lectr, 1974; self-employed sculptor; Ed Hamilton Studio, owner, pres, dir, incorporator, currently. **Orgs:** Alpha Phi Alpha Fraternity; Mayors Adv Panel Pub Art; Nat Conf Artists, 1980; bd mem, Renaissance Develop Corp; St Georges Episcopal Church; Art Circle Asn; bd mem, St Frances High Sch, Louisville; exec bd, Thomas Clark Hist Ctr; Frankfort, KY; gov, Ky Mil Mus Frankfort, KY; bd mem, Ky Minority Businessmen; Episcopal Diocese, KY; Community Arts/Fund Arts; Speed Art Mus; bd mem, Ky Hist Ctr. **Honors/Awds:** Kentucky Black Achievers Award, 1980; Governor Artist Award, 1996; Bronze St Frances of Row, St Frances of Row Ch Louisville; Bronze of Whitney M Young Jr, comn by Ky State Alumni, 1998; Bronze portrait bust of Medgar W Evers, comn by Don Coleman Advert Co, Detroit, Mich; Governors Awards in the Arts, 1991; "Lift Award", Canaan Community Development Corporation; Best of Louisville Magazine 2005 Readers Choice Award for Visual Artist Annual Smith Award; Doctor of Humane Letters from Spalding University, 2000; Gallery of Great Black Kentuckians, 2001; DA Honorary Degree, Univ Louisville, 2004; DA Honorary Degree, Western Ky Univ, 2004; Arthur M Walters Champion of Diversity Award, Urban League Diversity Award, 2005; Xmas Tree Ornament for Mrs Laura Bushs Christmas Tree at the White House, 2008. **Special Achievements:** Numerous exhibitions, group shows, pub comn works in pvt collections including, Owensboro Mus Fine Art; Memphis State Univ Gallery; Washington Design Ctr; JB Speed Art Mus; Gibellina Mus in Palermo Italy; One of eight jurors for the International Andrew Young Memorial; Nat Comn Joe Louis, Cobo Hall in Detroit, MI; Booker T Wash, Hampton Univ; Amistad Memorial, New Haven, CT; The Spirit of Freedom Memorial, Wash, DC, 1998; "The Birth of an Artist, a journey of discovery", 2006; Abraham Lincoln Memorial, 2009; "Creating the Lincoln Memorial at Waterfront Park", 2009; "Ed Hamiltons Lincoln", 2009; Created the first Isaac Murphy Award given through the local NAACP. **Home Addr:** 122 S 43 St, Louisville, KY 40212. **Business Addr:** Owner, Ed Hamilton Studio Inc, 543 S Shelby St, Louisville, KY 40202-3602, **Business Phone:** (502)587-7709.

## HAMILTON, DR. FRANKLIN D.

Educator. **Personal:** Born Oct 30, 1942, Aucilla, FL; son of Verdell and Esther; children: Kayla, Ebony & Nikki. **Educ:** Fla A&M Univ, BS, chem & biol, 1964; Univ Pittsburgh, PhD, biochem, 1969; State Univ NY, Stony Brook, pos-doctoral, molecular biol, 1969. **Career:** ExpertNet, prin investr; Univ Pittsburgh, USPHS fel, 1964-69; State Univ NY, USPHS fel, 1969-71; Univ Tenn, from asst prof to assoc prof, 1971-79; Atlanta Univ, assoc prof, 1979-88; Univ Calif, Berkeley, vis prof, 1986-89; Fla A&M Univ, Div Sponsored Res, dir, 1989, Environ Scis Inst, prof chem, currently, vpres res, currently. **Orgs:** Vicechair, Sci Adv Comn Nat Asn Equal Opprtunity Higher Educ; consult, Nat Inst Health; consult, Robert Wood Johnson Fund; consult, Premed, Rev Comn, United Negro Col Fund; AAAS; Am Soc Cell Biol; comn mem, MARC Rev Comn, Nat Inst Gen Med Sci; comn mem, NSF Pre-doctoral Fel Rev Comn; coun mem, Am Soc Biochem & MSI Biol, 1988-91; exec bd mem, Phi Beta Sigma Fraternity Inc. **Home Addr:** PO Box 271, Lloyd, FL 32337-0271. **Business Addr:** Professor of Chemistry, Vice President for Research, Florida A&M University, 1515 Martin Luther King Blvd, Tallahassee, FL 32307, **Business Phone:** (850)561-2134.

## HAMILTON, HARRY EDWIN

Lawyer, football player. **Personal:** Born Nov 29, 1962, Jamaica, NY. **Educ:** Pa State Univ, BA, lib arts, 1984. **Career:** Football player (retired), lawyer; NY Jets, 1984-87; Tampa Bay Buccaneers, defensive back, 1988-91; atty, currently. **Business Addr:** Attorney, 307 Silo Ridge Ct Apt 301, Odenton, MD 21113-3271, **Business Phone:** (813)237-8545.

## HAMILTON, HOWARD W.

Executive. **Personal:** Born Jul 21, 1948, Chicago, IL; son of Howard and Etta Mae; children: Howard, Christina, James & Olivia. **Educ:** Parsons Col, BA, 1971; Columbia Univ, MBA, 1979. **Career:** E R Squibb Pharmaceut, field sales, 1972-77; Lederle Labs, prod prom mgr, 1979-80; Schering Labs, prod mgr, 1980-83; Abbott Labs, sr prod mgr, 1984-93; Essilor Am, group mkt mgr, 1994-95; gen mgr, 1996-; Johnson & Johnson Vision Care Inc, Spectacle Lens Group, dir mkt, 1998-. **Orgs:** Parlimentarian, Action Alliance Black Prof, 1988-90; pres, bd trustee, 1989-92, Actor's Summer Theatre; pres, 1991-92, African Am Action Alliance. **Home Addr:** 3806 Deckford Pl, PO Box 11321, Charlotte, NC 28211, **Home Phone:** (704)366-8330. **Business Addr:** Director of Marketing, Johnson & Johnson Vision Care Inc, 5568 Airport Rd NW, Roanoke, VA 24012-1311, **Business Phone:** (540)362-2020.

## HAMILTON, J LEONARD. See HAMILTON, LEONARD.

## HAMILTON, JOHN M.

Executive. **Educ:** Morehouse Col, BA, finance, 1979. **Career:** Advan Bank, vpres lending, pres & chief exec officer, chmn, 1991-2013; MECU Baltimore Inc, vpres lending & collections, 2013-, pres & chief exec officer, 2015-; Wash Shores Savings Bank, FSB, Orlando, Fla, chief exec officer; Presidents' Roundtable Inc, pres & chmn. **Orgs:** Dir bd, Univ Md, Baltimore, MD; bd mem, Am's Community Bankers; bd mem, Sinai Hosp; bd mem, UMB Bio Pk. **Business Addr:** President, Chief Executive Officer, MECU of Baltimore Inc, 7 E Redwood St, Baltimore, MD 21202, **Business Phone:** (410)752-8313.

## HAMILTON, JONNIE

Association executive, nurse. **Educ:** Oakland Univ, DNP, nursing, 2015. **Career:** Sch-based health ctr, St John Health Syst, Detroit, Mich, Pediat nurse practr, 1996-2010; St. John Providence Health Syst, nurse practr, 1996-2011; Chi Eta Phi Sorority Inc, regional dir, 2000-04; Middlewest Region, dir, 2002-04; Marcus Garvey Acad, Napoleon B Jordan Ctr Health, clin dir & Pediat nurse parctr, currently. **Orgs:** Nat Black Nurses Asn, 1974-2014; Chi Eta Phi Sorority Inc, 1987-2011, middlewest regional dir, 2000-04; Lambda Chi Chap; pres, Mich Nurses Asn; Am Nurses Asn; Sigma Theta Tau Nursing Hon Soc; Nat Asn Advan Colored People; Providence Hosp Nurses Alumnae Asn, 2000-12; vpres, Detroit Black Nurses Asn, 2001-11; RNAIM, 2005-11; chair, Delta Sigma Theta Sorority Inc, 2009-10; Coalition Mich Orgn Nursing. **Honors/Awds:** Advanced Practice Nurse Excellence Award: Mich Nurses Asn, Nat Black Nurses Asn, Chi Eta Phi Sorority Inc; Crain's Health Care Heroes, 2011. **Business Addr:** Clinic Director, Pediatric Nurse Practitioner, Napoleon B Jordan Center for Health Care, Rm 506 2301 Van Dyke St, Detroit, MI 48214, **Business Phone:** (313)866-9973.

## HAMILTON, LEONARD (J LEONARD HAMILTON)

Basketball coach. **Personal:** Born Aug 4, 1948, Gastonia, NC; son of John and Bennie Ruth (deceased); married Claudette; children: 2. **Educ:** Univ Tenn-Martin, BA, phys educ, 1971; Austin Peay State Univ, MA, phys & health educ, 1973. **Career:** Austin Peay State Univ, asst coach, 1971-74, full-time asst, 1973-74; Univ Ky, asst coach, 1974-86, asst coach, 1980, asst head coach; Okla State Univ, head coach, 1986-90; Univ Miami, Coral Gables FL, head coach, 1991-2000; Wash Wizards head coach, 2000-01; Fla State Univ, head coach, 2002-. **Orgs:** Kappa Alpha Psi Fraternity. **Business Addr:** Head Coach Basketball, Florida State University, 525 Stadium Dr W, Tallahassee, TN 32306, **Business Phone:** (850)644-2525.

## HAMILTON, LISA GAY

Actor. **Personal:** Born Mar 25, 1964, Los Angeles, CA; daughter of Ira Winslow Jr (deceased) and Tina; married Robin DG Kelley. **Educ:** NY Univ, BA, theatre; Juilliard Sch Drama, BFA, 1989. **Career:** Actress, producer, director; Films: Krush Groove, 1985; Reversal of Fortune, 1990; Naked in New York, 1993; Palookaville, 1995; Drunks, 1995; Twelve Monkeys, 1995; Nick & Jane, 1997; Drunks, 1997; Life Breath, 1997; Jackie Brown, 1997; Beloved, 1998; True Crime, 1999; Ten Tiny Love Stories, 2001; The Sum of All Fears, 2002; The Truth About Charlie, 2002; Beah: A Black Woman Speaks, dir & producer, 2003; Nine Lives, 2005; Conviction, 2005; Honeydripper, 2007; Deception, 2008; The Soloist, 2009; Beastly, Mother and Child, 2010; TV appearances: Way Cool, 1991; Law & Order, 1995; "Homicide: Life on the Street", 1993; "New York Undercover", 1994; All My Children, 1994; Clarissa, 1995; One Life to Live, 1996; The Practice, 1997-2003; "The Defenders: Choice of Evils", 1998; "Ally McBeal", 1998; Swing Vote, 1999; "A House Divided", 2000; "Hamlet", 2000; "Sex & the City", 2002; "The L Word", 2004; "ER", 2005; "Law & Order: Special Victims Unit", 2006-07; "Without a Trace", 2006; "Numb3rs", 2007; "Law & Order: Special Victims Unit", 2006-07; "Men of a Certain Age", 2009-11; "Beastly", 2011; "Take Shelter", 2011; "Southland", 2012; "Lovelace", 2013; "Grey's Anatomy", 2013; "Go for Sisters", 2013; "Life of a King", 2014. **Honors/Awds:** Documentary Award, AFI Fest, 2003; Bronze Leopard Award, Locarno Int Film Festival, 2005. **Business Addr:** Actress, c/o Paradigm Agency, 10100 Santa Monica Blvd Suite 2500, Los Angeles, CA 90067, **Business Phone:** (310)277-4400.

**HAMILTON, LYNN**
Actor. **Personal:** Born Apr 25, 1930, Yazoo City, MS; daughter of Louis and Nancy; married Frank S Jenkins; children: 1. **Educ:** Goodman Theatre, BA, 1954. **Career:** TV appearances: "The Practice"; "Sanford & Son", 1972-77; "Roots I", I; "The Waltons"; "227"; "Golden Girls"; "Amen"; "Generations"; "Gunsmoke"; "The Rockford Files"; "Hunter"; "Murphy Brown"; "Rituals"; "Generations"; "Dangerous Women"; "Oh, Mama!", 2002; "Sins of the Father", 2004; "Dangerous Women"; "Judging Amy", 2004; "Cold Case", 2009; Films: Shadows, 1959; Lady Sings the Blues; Buck & the Preacher; Bro John; Leadbelly; Legal Eagles; The Vanishing; Baby's Breath, 2003; stage appearances: Only In America, 1959; The Face of a Hero, 1960; The Miracle Worker; The Skin of Our Teeth. Flim: Shadows, 1959; Brother John & The Seven Minutes, 1971; Buck and the Preacher & Lady Sings the Blues, 1972; Hangup, 1974; Leadbelly, 1976; The Jesse Owens Story, 1984; Legal Eagles, 1986; The Vanishing, 1993; Beah: A Black Woman Speaks, 2003. **Honors/Awds:** NAACP Image Award; Trail Blazer Award, Nat Asn Advan Colored People; Living Legend Award, Nat Black Theatre, 2003. **Home Addr:** 1042 S Burnside Ave, Los Angeles, CA 90019, **Home Phone:** (213)933-4198. **Business Addr:** Actor, The Levin Agency, 8484 Wilshire Blvd, Beverly Hills, CA 90211, **Business Phone:** (213)653-7073.

**HAMILTON, MICHAEL ANTONIO**
Football player, salesperson, executive. **Personal:** Born Dec 3, 1973, Greenville, SC. **Educ:** NC Agr & Tech State Univ, BA, appl sci, biol, gen, 1996. **Career:** Football player (retired); San Diego Chargers, linebacker, 1997-99; Miami Dolphins, 2000; Cleveland Browns, 2000; Boston Sci, field clin rep, 2003-05, sales rep, 2005-06; St. Jude Med, sales rep, 2006-16, sales consult, 2016-; Bigkidd Int Sports, owner, 2011-. **Business Addr:** Sales Consultant, St. Jude Medical, 1 St Jude Medical Dr, St Paul, MN 55117-9983, **Business Phone:** (651)756-2000.

**HAMILTON, DR. PAUL L.**
Educator. **Personal:** Born Apr 1, 1941, Pueblo, CO; children: Askia Toure. **Educ:** Univ Denver, BA, 1964, MA, 1972; Univ N Colo, EdD, 1975. **Career:** Educator (retired); York St Cafe, mng partner; Denver Pub Schs, teacher, 1964-91, prin, 1991-95; State Colo, rep, 1969-73; Univ Denver, instr, 1971, lectr & res asst, 1971-72, adj prof hist, 1982-96; Univ Colo, instr, 1995-96; Hamilton Educ Consults, pres, currently; Power Learning Systs, dist dir, 1995; Critical Thinking Skills Inst, pres, currently; Rochester New York health facil, bus consults, currently; People Skills Inst, Exec Consult & Adv Bd mem, currently; Colo State Legis; Books: African People's Contributions to World Civilizations: Shattering the Myths Vol 1. **Orgs:** Asn Study Class African Civilizations; Nat Alliance Black Sch Educrs; Univ Denver Nat Hon Soc; pres, Renaissance Publs, 1993; dir, Rev. Jesse Jackson's Denver PUSH-EXCEL prog. **Home Addr:** 2811 Vine St, Denver, CO 80205-4633, **Home Phone:** (303)296-6997. **Business Addr:** President, Hamilton Education Consultants, 2811 Vine St, Denver, CO 80205, **Business Phone:** (303)296-6997.

**HAMILTON, PHANUEL J.**
Government official. **Personal:** Born Aug 3, 1929, Detroit, MI; children: Thieda E, Deborah & Gregory. **Educ:** Eastern Mich Univ, BA, 1951; Northwestern Univ, grad sch speech; DePaul Univ; Chicago State Univ; Ky Christian Univ, MA, 1973. **Career:** Teacher, 1956-64; Community Youth Welfare, dir, 1964-66; Cook County OEO, dir, 1965-66, OEO, manpower, 1966-69; Human Motivation Inst, consult, 1969; Chicago Mayor's Off Sr Citizens, dir field serv, 1970-, dir individual serv. **Orgs:** Am Asn Retarded Persons, 1973-75; Nat Coun Aging, 1974-75; Cerontological Soc, 1975; Nat Asn Soc Workers; Nat Asn Community Develop; Kappa Alpha Psi; Sigma Phi; Pi Kappa Delta; Urban League; Nat Asn Advan Colored People; Shiloh Baptist Church Mgt Develop. **Home Addr:** 6847 S Clyde Ave Apt 1, Chicago, IL 60649-1608.

**HAMILTON, RAINY, JR.**
Architect, business owner. **Personal:** Born Sep 22, 1956, Detroit, MI; son of Rainy Sr and Bernice Hodges. **Educ:** Univ Detroit, Mich, BS, archit, 1978, bachelors archit, 1979. **Career:** Schervish, Vogel & Merz, PC, Detroit, Mich, partner, 1979-90; Smith, Hinchman, & Grylls Assocs Inc, assoc & proj mgr, 1990-93; Hamilton Anderson Assoc, owner, 1994-, pres. **Orgs:** Am Inst Architects, 1979-; liaison, Minority Resources Comt, Am Inst Architects, 1989-; Detroit chap, pres, 2001-; founding mem, Mich Nat Orgn Minority Architects; State Mich Bd Architects & Bd surveyors; Univ Commons Orgn; Univ Dist Community Asn Bd. **Honors/Awds:** Young Architect of the Year, Detroit chap, Am Inst Architects, 1988; Outstanding Achievement Award for Building Design & Construction, Eng Soc, 1999; Merit Award, Mich Chap Am Soc Landscape Architects, 2000-01; Spec Community Initiative Award, Mich Soc Planning, 2002; Environ Achievement Award, Mich Environ Mgt Asn, 2003. **Special Achievements:** Hamilton Anderson Associates as one of the "Future 50" companies in metropolitan Detroit from over 6, 400 establishments; INC Magazine also named the firm as one of the nation's fastest growing companies for 1999; Hamilton Anderson Associates was featured in the list of the Twenty Largest Architectural Firms in Crain's Detroit 2000 at the 17th spot. **Home Addr:** 17505 Parkside, Detroit, MI 48221-2716, **Home Phone:** (313)862-7200. **Business Addr:** President, Owner, Hamilton Anderson Associates, 1435 Randolph St Suite 200, Detroit, MI 48226, **Business Phone:** (313)964-0270.

**HAMILTON, ROY L.**
Educator. **Personal:** Born Jul 11, 1958, Baton Rouge, LA; son of Shirley I Wilson; children: Johnny F. **Educ:** Morehouse Col, BA, hist, 1980; Univ Wis-Milwaukee, MA, Am hist, 1981; Ind Univ, PhD, Am hist, 2006. **Career:** CIC Minority fel; Ind Univ, Albert L Kohlmier fel; Univ Wis, Advan Opportunity Prog fel; Ind State Univ, asst dir upward bound prog, 1984-89; Purdue Univ Calumet, dir educ talent prog, 1988-89, McNair Prog, dir, 1989-, lectr ethnic stud prog, 1995, Educ Oppurtunity Progs, asst vice chancellor EOP, 2003-, assoc vice chancellor, 2013-14; Calumet Col St Joseph, adj fac degree completion prog, 1994-2001. **Orgs:** Mid-Am Asn Educ Opportunity Progs; Kappa Alpha Psi; Ind Coalition Blacks Higher Educ; Northwest Ind Symphony Orchestra Chorus; Christ United Methodist Church; Black Methodist Church Renewal (BMCR); Phi Delta Kappa; bd dir, Rose S Child Day Care Ctr; Monarch Awards Found; Xi Nu Omega Chap; Boys & Girls Clubs Northwest Ind, bd mem, 2010-. **Home Addr:** 3709 W 15th Ave, Gary, IN 46404, **Home Phone:** (219)944-1671. **Business Addr:** Assistant Vice Chancellor, Purdue University Calumet, 2200 169th St, Hammond, IN 46323-2094, **Business Phone:** (219)989-2779.

**HAMILTON, RUFFIN, III**
Executive, football player. **Personal:** Born Mar 2, 1971, Detroit, MI; married Dena; children: Whitney. **Educ:** Tulane Univ. **Career:** Football player (retired), exec; Green Bay Packers, linebacker, 1994; Papa Hamp's Antique Furniture Restoration, owner, 1996-; Atlanta Falcons, linebacker & mid linebacker, 1997-99. **Business Addr:** Owner, Papa Hamp's Antique Furniture Restoration, 4742 Longfellow Dr, Baton Rouge, LA 70805, **Business Phone:** (225)356-5886.

**HAMILTON, SAMUEL CARTENIUS**
Lawyer. **Personal:** Born Mar 29, 1936, Hope, AR; married Flora Elizabeth; children: Leslie Terrell, Sydne Carrigan & Patrice Alexan. **Educ:** Philander Smith Col, BS, 1958; Howard Univ, JD, 1970. **Career:** Roy M Ellis & Louise Eighnie Turner Gen Prac Law, Silver Spring, Md, assoc; Montgomery Co MD, asst states pros atty; U.S. Dept Housing & Urban Develop, atty; Lilver Spring MD, pvt pract law; Legal Aid Clin US Dist Attys Off DC; Off Chief Coun Fed Hwy Admin Litigation Div, legal intern; Ft Detrick MD, res asst; Hamilton & Assocs, atty, currently. **Orgs:** MD State Bar Asn; Am Bar Asn; Nat Bar Asn; pres, Frederick Co Br Nat Asn Advan Colored People; vpres, Md State Conf Nat Asn Advan Colored People Br; co-chmn; Comm Uphold State Pub Accomodation law; Prince Hall Masons; Kappa Alpha Psi Soc Frat; Phi Alpha Delta Legal Frat; bd dir, Comn Action Agency; founding mem, J. Franklyn Bourne Bar Asn. **Honors/Awds:** Frederick Co Award for Service & Leadership, Stud Bar Asn, Howard Univ Sch Law; Outstanding Citizen Award, Am Legion; Outstanding Service Award, Nat Asn Advan Colored People; Service Award, Prince Hall Masons. **Special Achievements:** First African American Assistant States Attorney for Montgomery County Maryland. **Home Addr:** 14 Hilltop Rd, Silver Spring, MD 20910, **Home Phone:** (301)565-0432. **Business Addr:** Attorney, The Law Office of Samuel C Hamilton, 8401 Colesville Rd Suite 620, Silver Spring, MD 20910-3396, **Business Phone:** (301)589-3000.

**HAMILTON, BISHOP WILBURN WYATT**
Executive, baptist clergy. **Personal:** Born Jan 28, 1931, San Antonio, TX; son of E E; married Joy Helena; children: Sharyn Maxine Smith, Tom Jack Bell (deceased), Marvyn Stanley Bell & Helena Joy. **Educ:** Simpson Bible Col, BS, social sci, DD; San Francisco City Col, AA; Golden Gate Univ, MBA; Simpson Col San Francisco, doctor divinity. **Career:** Am Pres Line, terminal chief, 1965-69; San Francisco Housing Authority, actg exec dir & pres; San Franciso Redevelop Agency, exec dir, 1969-71, asst exec dir admin, 1971-74, dep exec dir, 1974-77, exec dir, 1977-; Greater Victory Temple Church, sr pastor; Northern Calif Church God Christ, dir youth serv; San Franciso Redevelop Agency, exec dir; Hamilton Memorial COGIC, San Franciso, pastor; Church God Christ Inc, founding Pastor, gen secy bd, currently; Northwest Ecclesiastical Jurisdiction Calif, Seaside, Calif, prelate, currently; Calif Northwest Jurisdiction, founding bishop; San Francisco Redevelop Agency, exec dir. **Orgs:** Secy, San Francisco Interdenom Minstrial Alliance; judge field fac, CORO Found; pres, Northern Calif Region, Nat Asn Housing & Redevelop Officials; pres, Pac Southwest Region, Nat Asn Housing & Redevelop Officials;Nat Asn Advan Colored People; St Mary's Hosp Comt Bd. **Business Addr:** Prelate, California Northwest Ecclesiastical Jurisdiction, 874 36th Ave, Oakland, CA 94601, **Business Phone:** (510)547-8315.

**HAMILTON-ROSE, LESSIE**
Educator, administrator. **Career:** Rochester City School District, Flower City Sch No 54, prin, currently. **Business Addr:** Principal, Rochester City School District, 36 Otis St, Rochester, NY 14606, **Business Phone:** (585)254-2080.

**HAMITER, UHURU A.**
Security guard, football player. **Personal:** Born Mar 14, 1973, Kingstree, SC. **Educ:** Del State Univ, grad. **Career:** Football player (retired); Ferris Juv Detention Ctr, security off; England Monarchs, 1998; New Orleans Saints, defend, 1998-99; Philadelphia Eagles, 1998, defend, 2000-02; Chicago Bears, 2001; Houston Texans, defend, 2002. **Honors/Awds:** Rookie of the Year, 1998.

**HAMLAR, JOCELYN B.**
Banker, executive. **Personal:** Born Jan 8, 1954, Columbus, OH; daughter of David Duffield and Maxine Eloise Harbour (deceased); married Roy Clark; children: Morgan Allison & Sydney Erin; married Leighton J Toney. **Educ:** Boston Univ, BS, mkt, 1976, MS, pub rels, 1981. **Career:** Bank New Eng, asst mkt off, 1978-80; WNEV-TV, prod asst, 1979-81; United Community Planning Corp, commun dir, 1981-82; Am Hosp Assn, mkt commun specialist, 1982-83; WXRT-FM Radio Sta, dir mkt & adv & prom, 1983-86; LaSalle Nat Bank, vpres, dir pub rel, 1986-91; WBEZ-FM, dir mkt, 1991-93; ABN Amro N Am Inc, dir corp communs, vpres, 1993-97; LaSalle Bank Corp, sr vpres corp commun & dir comms, 1992-2007; Blue Cross & Blue Shield Asn, mkt & commun mgr, 2008-16; Peer Serv Inc, substance abuse counr, 2016-. **Orgs:** Bd dir, Next Theatre, 1989-91; bd dir, Child Care Ctr Asn, 1990-; bd dir, Remains Theatre, 1992-93; adv bd mem, Pub Allies, 1995-; bd dir, Chicago Coun Urban Affairs, 1999-; presidents adv coun, Harold Wash Col, Chicago, Ill, 1999-; bd dir, Hubbard St Dance Chicago, 2000-. **Honors/Awds:** Black Achievement Award, Greater Boston YMCA, 1979; Kizzy Award, Black Women Hall of Fame Found, 1987, 1990. **Home Addr:** 18 Williamsburg Rd, Evanston, IL 60203, **Home Phone:** (847)679-8142. **Business Addr:** Substance Abuse Counselor, Peer Services, 906 Davis St, Evanston, IL 60201, **Business Phone:** (847)492-1778.

**HAMLAR, PORTIA YVONNE TRENHOLM**
Lawyer, college teacher, executive director. **Personal:** Born Apr 30, 1932, Montgomery, AL; daughter of Harper Councill Sr (deceased) and Portia Lee (deceased); children: 1. **Educ:** Ala State Univ, BA, 1951; Mich State Univ, MA, 1953; Univ Detroit Sch Law, JD, 1972; Wayne State Univ. **Career:** Lawyer (retired); Detroit Pub Schs, vocal music instr, 1953-71; Univ Mich, acad counr, 1957-58; Pontiac High Sch, vocal music instr, 1963-65; Hyman Gurwin Nachman & Friedman, legal secy, 1966-68; Univ Detroit, law rev staff, 1970-72; Mich Appellate Defender, legal researcher, 1971-73; Am Bar Asn Lawyers Housing Prog, admin asst, 1973; Gr Watts Model Cities Housing Corp, legal coun, 1973; DE Law Sch Widener Univ, asst prof law, 1980-82; Mich State Bar Atty Grievence Comn, assoc coun, 1982-; Chrysler Corp, labor & environ coun, atty; Univ Wis, asst chancellor, dir equity & affirmative action; Univ Detroit Sch Law, adj prof law, prof law; Hazardous Mat Mgt J, ed bd. **Orgs:** Organist & choir dir, St Andrews Presby Church, 1955-72; lit & res, Am Bar Asn Comn Real Property Law, 1971-72; ABA Comn OSHA Law, 1978-; Am Asn Affirmative Action; Resources Counr Occup Safety & Health Lawyers Group; Mich State Bar; Detroit Bar Asn; Delta Sigma Theta; Kappa Beta Pi; Alpha Kappa Mu; Mu Phi Epsilon. **Special Achievements:** Publ: Landlord & Tenant, 1971; "HUD's Authority to Mandate Effective Management of Public Housing", 1972; Defending the Employer in OSHA Contests, 1977, "Minority Tokenism in American Law Schools", 1983. **Home Addr:** 29266 Wellington Rd W, Southfield, MI 48034-4571.

**HAMLIN, ARTHUR HENRY**
Educator. **Personal:** Born Jan 4, 1942, Bastrop, LA; son of Augustine and Elmore; married Deloris E; children: Eric & Erica J. **Educ:** Grambling State Univ, BS, 1965; Northeast La Univ, MA, 1970. **Career:** CTA, bus oper, 1966-67; Morehouse Parish Sch Bd, teacher-coach, 1966-; City Bastrop, gym super, 1973-76, councilman, 1977-; Morehouse Parish Drug Free Schs & Communities, coordr. **Orgs:** Oper Greenview Club, 1971-72; pres, Morehouse Community Improvment Org, 1973; pres, Morehouse Concerned Citizens, 1979; secy, Club21, 1981; Gents Civic & Social Club. **Home Addr:** 2302 Bonnie Ave, Bastrop, LA 71220-4101, **Home Phone:** (318)281-3118. **Business Addr:** Teacher Coach, Morehouse Parish School, PO Box 872, Bastrop, LA 71220, **Business Phone:** (318)281-5784.

**HAMLIN, DAVID W.**
Manager. **Personal:** Born Jan 1, 1989?, Pittsburgh, PA. **Educ:** Carnegie Mellon Univ, master pub mgt. **Career:** Hills Dept Store, hard lines merchandise mgr, 1976-80; Equitable Gas Co, buyer, 1980-90; Duquesne Light Co, dir minority bus develop, 1990-96; Carnegie Mellon Univ, dir purchasing serv & supplier managment, 1995-98; Rutgers Univ, exec dir univ procurement servs, 1998-2005; McCann-Erickson USA Inc, vpres, supplier diversity, 2006-13; Cartesian, Sr Procurement Consult, 2013-15; THG Hamlin Group, owner, 1985-, Consult, 2015-. **Orgs:** Nat Purchasing Mgt Asn, 1980-; chmn, Pittsburgh Regional Minority Purchasing Coun, 1980-; Nat HBCU Conf. **Honors/Awds:** Man of the Year, Black Opinion Magazine, 1989; Excellence Award in Business, Minority Business Opportunity Comm, 1993. **Business Addr:** Owner, THG The Hamlin Group, 1 Holly Manor Ct, Helmetta, NJ 08828-1165, **Business Phone:** (732)241-4508.

**HAMLIN, ERNEST LEE**
Clergy. **Personal:** Born Dec 9, 1943, Sussex, VA; son of Arish L and Elma Roseanna; married Pamela Diane Carter; children: Kevin, Rafael & Cherry. **Educ:** Va Union Univ, BA, 1970, Sch Theol, Mdiv, 1974; Presby Sch Christian Educ, MA, 1976; Va Commonwealth Univ, pastoral educ, 1977. **Career:** Mt Zion Baptist Church, asst pastor, 1971-79; Janie Porter Barrett Sch, counr, 1973; Med Col Va, counr & chaplain, 1976-77; Smithdeal-Massey Bus Col, consult & counr, 1978; Richmond Pub Schs, Substitute teacher, 1979-83; Aid & Restoration Hospitality House, house mgr, 1979-87; Jerusalem Baptist Church, interim pastor, 1980; Bethesda Baptist Church, pastor, 1981-83; Richmond Va Sem, theol & christian educ, prof, 1982-89; Ebenezer Baptist Church, supply pastor, 1984; Rutledge Col, admis rep & educ consult, 1984; Union Hill United Church Christ, pastor, 1986-89; Christian Educ Ministries, pres, chief exec officer, 1990-, exec dir, 1997; Emmanuel-St Mark's United Church Christ, pastor, 1990-92; Tubman-King Community Church, sr pastor, 1992; Open Door United Church Christ, interim pastor, 1994; Pembroke Manor United Church of Christ, interim pastor, currently; Warwick United Church Christ, assoc pastor, 2003-. **Orgs:** Bd mem, World Ministries, 1974-90; bd mem, United Church Christ, 1974-90; bd mem, Christian educ lectr local churches, 1974-90; bd dir, Richmond Chap, 1981-85; bd dir, Southern Christian Leadership Conf, Va State Unit, 1982-90; chairperson, United Negro Col Fund, 1983; exec secy, East Side Ecumenical Fel, 1990-91, exec vpres, 1991-92; bd dir, OIC Metro Saginaw, 1990-92, exec vpres, Northeast Ministerial Alliance, 1991-92; bd dir, One Church One Child MIC, 1991-92; bd dir, Habitat for Humanity, 1992-; Elon Homes C Campaign Comt; Covenant Asn; Mission Coun; Halifax Ministerial Asn; Halifax Habitat Humanity; United Black Christians; Nat Asn Black Achievers; Kappa Alpha Psi. **Home Addr:** 148 Springwood Dr, Daytona Beach, FL 32119-1425, **Home Phone:** (904)760-0567. **Business Addr:** Interim Pastor, Pembroke Manor United Church of Christ, 600 Independence Blvd, Virginia Beach, VA 23462, **Business Phone:** (757)490-8290.

**HAMM, PAULA**
Executive. **Career:** Symantec Corp, Security Prod Mgt, sr dir, 2003, Symantec Educ & Bus Critical Serv, vpres, currently. **Business Addr:** Vice President, Symantec Corp, 20330 Stevens Creek Blvd, Cupertino, CA 95014, **Business Phone:** (408)517-8000.

**HAMMER, M. C. (STANLEY KIRK BURRELL)**
Actor, dancer, singer. **Personal:** Born Mar 30, 1962, Oakland, CA; son of Louis Burrell Sr; married Stephanie Fuller; children: Akeiba Monique, Sarah Brooke, Stanley Kirk, Jeremiah & Samuel. **Career:** Albums: Feel My Power, 1987; Let's Get It Started, 1988; Please Hammer, Don't Hurt 'Em, 1990; Too Legit to Quit, 1991; The Funky Headhunter, 1994; Inside Out, 1995; Family Affair, 1998; Active Duty, 2001; Full Blast, 2003; Look Look Look, 2006; Borat: Cultural Learnings of America for Make Benefit Glorious Nation of Kazakhstan, 2006;

DanceJamTheMusic, 2009; Better Run Run, 2010; See Her Face, 2011; Gangnam Style"/"2 Legit 2 Quit, 2012. Tv series: "The Surreal Life", 2002; "Dance Fever", 2003; "I Married", 2004; "Praise the Lord", 2006; "LOOK", 2006; "So Long", producer, 2006; "Hammertime", 2009; "Uncle Grandpa", 2016; Internet Startup DanceJam.com, co-founder & chief strategy officer, 2008; Oakland Athletics, bat boy; Holy Ghost Boys, rap group, singer; Bust It Records, founder; solo performer, currently. **Honors/Awds:** Grammy Award, 1990; Image Award, Nat Asn Advan Colored People, People's Choice Award; Billboard Diamond Award; Soul Train Music Award, 1991; Living Legends of Hip Hop Award, Hip Hop Intl, 2008; People's Choice Award; Image Award, Nat Asn Advan Colored People; Billboard Diamond Award; Soul Train Music Award, 1991; Stellar Award, 1997; MTV Video Music Award, 2005; Hip Hop Award, 2008; Shorty Award, 2009; Second Annual Shorty Award, 2010; BET Hip Hop Award, 2010; Gravity Summit Social Media Marketer of the Year Award, 2010; American Music Award, 2012; George and Ira Gershwin Award, Univ Calif, Los Angeles, 2013. **Business Addr:** Recording Artist, c/o Capitol Records Inc, 1750 N Vine St, Los Angeles, CA 90028-5209, **Business Phone:** (323)462-6252.

## HAMMETT, WILLIE ANDERSON

Basketball coach, educator. **Personal:** Born Apr 19, 1945, Sumerton, SC; married Marian; children: Jamal. **Educ:** Hudson Valley Comm Col, AAS, 1966; WV St Col, BS, bus admin, 1968; State Univ NY, Albany, MS, coun & guid, 1971, EdS, 1977. **Career:** Educator (retired), coach; Troy Sch Syst, guid coun & basketball coach, 1969-71; Hudson Valley Community Col, coun & asst basketball coach, 1971-72, dir educ opportunity prog, 1972, vpres stud affairs, 1972-2003. **Orgs:** Bd dir, Camp Fire Girls, 1969-72; vpres, Troy Jaycees, 1969-72; bd trustee, Troy YWCA, 1972-; pres, NA-MAL Enterprises Inc, 1977-79; Coun Black Am Affairs, 1977-; bd dir, Samaritan Hosp, Troy, NY, 1978-; vice chairperson, exec bd, NY State Spec Prog Personnel Assoc, 1979-; Troy Boys & Girls Club; St Anne's Inst Albany; bd mem, Troy Savings Inc. **Honors/Awds:** Listed in Outstanding Young Men of America, 1972. **Home Addr:** 15 Tamarach Lane E, East Greenbush, NY 12061.

## HAMMOCK, ESQ. EDWARD R.

Government official, lawyer. **Personal:** Born Apr 20, 1938, Bronx, NY; married Jeanne Marshall; children: Erica, Rochelle & Regina. **Educ:** Brooklyn Col, BA, 1959; St John's Univ Law Sch, LLB, 1966. **Career:** Youth Coun Bur, caseworker, 1960-63; Supreme Ct Kings County, probation officer, 1963-66; NY Homicide Bur, asst dist atty, 1966-69; Daytop Village Inc, exec dir, 1969-72; Dept Law, NY State Criminal Invest, Attica Prison Riot, spec asst atty gen, 1971-73; NY City Dept Invest, dep comnr, 1973-76; Manhattan Dist Atty, assistance prosecutor; NY State Parole Bd, chief exec officer & chmn div parole, 1976; St John's Univ Sch Law, adj prof, prof; Nat Inst Drug Abuse, spec consult; Proj Return Inc, bd dir; pvt prac, atty, currently; Queens County Dist Atty, exec asst dist atty; John Jay Col Criminal Justice, fac; Col New Rochelle, fac; Hammock & Sullivan PC, atty, currently. **Orgs:** 100 Black Men; NY Lawyers Asn; NY State Bar Asn; pres, Stud Bar Asn, St.John's Univ, Sch Law. **Home Addr:** 11270 175 Pl, Jamaica, NY 11433-4139, **Home Phone:** (516)285-4141. **Business Addr:** Attorney, Hammock & Sullivan PC, 15408 Northern Blvd Suite 2G, Flushing, NY 11354, **Business Phone:** (718)358-6400.

## HAMMOCK, HON. JIMMY

Executive, association executive. **Career:** Phi Beta Sigma Fraternity Inc, Int Gen Bd, int treas, int pres, 2009-; Alcorn State Univ, pres, 2013-. **Orgs:** Beta Theta Boule; bd dir, Phi Beta Sigma Nat Found Inc. **Special Achievements:** Honorarii Alcornite Societatis Award. **Home Addr:** 1081 Hickory View Dr, Morristown, TN 37814-1581, **Home Phone:** (423)581-5364. **Business Addr:** President, Alcorn State University, 1000 ASU Dr, Lorman, MS 39096-7500, **Business Phone:** (601)877-6100.

## HAMMOND, DR. BENJAMIN FRANKLIN

School administrator, educator, microbiologist. **Personal:** Born Feb 28, 1934, Austin, TX; son of Virgil Thomas and Helen Marguerite Smith. **Educ:** Univ Kans, BA, 1954; Meharry Med Col, DDS, 1958; Univ PA, PhD, microbiol, 1962. **Career:** Oak Ridge Inst Nuclear Studies, postdoctoral fel, 1963; Univ Pa Sch Dent Med, Periodont Microbiol Lab, Dept Microbiol, prof, 1970-91, chmn, 1972-85, dir, 1980-91, assoc dean acad affairs, 1984-91, prof emer microbiol, 1991-; Nat Insts Health, nat adv dent res coun, 1975-78; R Metcalf Chair Marquette Univ, distinguished vis prof, 1986; Hahnemann Univ Col Med, Med Col Pa, prof med & dent med, 1991-97; Oral Microbiol Testing Serv, dir, 1991-94; Temple Univ Sch Dent, Oral Microbiol Testing Serv Lab, dir emer, 1996-, res prof, 1998-2009, clin prof periodont microbiol, currently. **Orgs:** Bd mem, Hist Soc PA; Mus Art Philadelphia; Nat Adv Dent Res Coun, NIH, 1975-78; vpres, Am Asn Dent Res, 1977, pres, 1978-79; Racquet Club Philadelphia; Union League Philadelphia; Metrop Opera Guild; bd mem, Philadelphia Mus Art; Am Soc Microbiol; bd dir & trustee, Atwater Kent Mus Philadelphia, 1999; Philadelphia Club; bd dir, Arthur Ross Gallery, 2001; bd dir, Am Poetry Ctr, 2001. **Honors/Awds:** EH Hatton Int Asn Dental Res, 1959; Lindback Award Distinguished Teaching, Univ PA, 1969; Medaille D'Argent City Paris France, 1976; Deans Lect, NW Univ Med Ctr, 1987; Hon Pres, Int Asn Dent Res, 1978; Hon Membership, Societe Francaise de Parodontologie. **Home Addr:** 560 N 23rd St, Philadelphia, PA 19130, **Home Phone:** (215)561-8539. **Business Addr:** Professor Emeritus, University of Pennsylvania, 240 S 40th St, Philadelphia, PA 19104, **Business Phone:** (215)707-5857.

## HAMMOND, BRANDON LA RON

Actor. **Personal:** Born Feb 6, 1984. **Career:** Films: Menace II Society, 1993; Strange Days, 1995; Waiting to Exhale, 1995; What's Love Got to Do With It; The Fan, 1996; Space Jam, 1996; Mars Attacks, 1996; No Easy Way, 1996; Soul Food, 1997; Blue Hill Avenue, 2001; Summer Blame, actor, writer & director, 2006; TV Series: "The Gregory Hines Show", 1997-98; TV Films: "Love, Lies & Lullabies", 1993; Coach, 1994; Dr. Quinn, Medicine Woman, 1996-98, "Road to Galveston", 1996; "Our America", 2002. **Honors/Awds:** Image Award, Nat Asn Advan Colored People, 1998. **Special Achievements:** Nominee, Young Artist Award, 1998, 2003; Nominee, Young Star Award, 1998. **Business Addr:** Actor, c/o William Morris Agency Inc, 151 S El Camino Dr, Beverly Hills, CA 90212, **Business Phone:** (310)274-7451.

## HAMMOND, DR. CAROL H. (CAROL HOWARD)

Educational psychologist. **Personal:** Born Oct 14, 1935, Knoxville, TN; daughter of D N Howard; married James M; children: Endea Thibodeaux, Atty Renata Craig, Rona Smith & James M Jr. **Educ:** Oakwood Col, BA, 1957; Univ Md, MEd, 1981; Howard Univ, PhD, 2000. **Career:** Abney Chapel SDA Sch, prin, teacher, 1959-60; Bekwai Overseas Cs Sch, teacher, 1962-68; Columbia Union Col, loan supvr, 1974-77, adj prof, psychol, 1998-; Slingo Adventist Sch, teacher, 1977-98; Bowie State Univ, adj prof & counr psychol & educ, 2001-. **Orgs:** Bd Ed, K-12, 1986-88. **Special Achievements:** Conducted Family Life Seminars in US, Bermuda & Africa, 1980-, author; Precious Memories of Missionaries of Color, co-author of "The School & Community Resources: A Cooperative Venture," published in Journal of Adventist Education, 1985, Marriage, Family, & Singleness, Advent Press, 1986, "Motivation: the Key to Success," pub in Educamus, 1993, conducted Parenting Seminar, John Nevins Seventh-day Adventist School, 1999. **Home Addr:** 3200 Fullerton St, Beltsville, MD 20705, **Home Phone:** (301)572-7536. **Business Addr:** Adjunct Professor, Counselor of Psychology & Education, Bowie State University, 14000 Jericho Pk Rd, Bowie, MD 20715-9465, **Business Phone:** (301)860-4000.

## HAMMOND, FRED

Gospel singer. **Personal:** Born Jan 1, 1961, Detroit, MI; married Kimberly; children: BreeAnn & Darius Sean. **Career:** Gospel vocalist; composer; producer; Face to Face Prod Co, owner, 1992-; FHammond Music, label founder; Albums: I'm Going On, 1985; Go Tell Somebody, 1986; On The Winning Side, 1987; Will You Be Ready?, 1988; Ordinary Just Won't Do, 1989; State of Mind, 1990; Number 7, 1991; I Am Persuaded, 1991; Deliverance, 1993; Matters of the Heart, 1994; The Inner Court, 1995; Gospel Greats, 1995; The Spirit of David, 1996; Pages of Life: Chapters 1&2, 1998; Purpose By Design, 2000; In Case You Missed It And Then Some, 2001; Christmas Just Remember, 2001; The Commissioned Reunion Live, 2002; Speak Those Things: POL Chapter 3, 2002; Hooked on the Hits, 2003; Somethin 'Bout Love, 2004; Praise & Worship, 2006; Free to Worship, 2006; Love Unstoppable, 2009; God, Love & Romance, 2012; United Tenors, 2013. Singles: "Let the Praise Begin", 1998; "Power", 1998; "King of Glory", 2001; "All Things Are Working", 2001; "We Have Not Forgotten", 2003; "Celebrate", 2004; "By Faith - with Sean Combs", 2005; "Better Than That' with The Singletons", 2007; Films: Zero Option, 2009. **Honors/Awds:** Numerous honors & awards including 6 Dove Awards, 4 Stellar Awards & a Grammy Award. **Special Achievements:** His release Free To Worship bombarded Billboards No 1 position on the Gospel Charts, and was hailed as one of the years best selling gospel albums for 2006. **Business Addr:** Gospel Vocalist, Face to Face Productions, 21421 Hilltop St Suite 20, Southfield, MI 48034, **Business Phone:** (248)354-5151.

## HAMMOND, JAMES A. (JAS A HAMMOND)

Executive. **Personal:** Born Nov 11, 1929, Tampa, FL; son of William and Lucile V; married Evelyne L Murrell; children: Kevin, Gary & Lisa. **Educ:** Hampton Univ, BS, indust voc educ, elec, 1951; US Command & Gen Staff Col, attended 1971; Indust Col Armed Forces, attended 1974. **Career:** Executive (retired); Hammond Elec Contracting Inc, pres, 1951-65; Community Rels City Tampa, admin dept head, 1965-70; Ala Nellum & Assocs Inc, vpres, 1969-73; Impact Asn Inc, pres, 1972-74; Walter Industs Inc, dir progs, 1974-89; Impac Commun Inc, pres & chief exec officer, 1983-86; Automation Res Systs Ltd, vpres, 1990-97. **Orgs:** Dir, Comn Fed Savings & Loan Asn, 1967-; Tampa Urban League, 1967; Am Asn Affirmative Action, 1977-81; chmn, City Civil Serv Bd, 1980-87; Comn Access Legal Syst, 1984; Kappa Alpha Psi Fraternity; Nat Asn Advan Colored People; comnr, Unemploy Appeals Comn, State Fla. **Home Addr:** 2505 E 19th Ave, Tampa, FL 33605-2823, **Home Phone:** (813)248-6225.

## HAMMOND, DR. JAMES MATTHEW

Military leader, educator. **Personal:** Born Jul 10, 1930, Kenansville, NC; married Carol Howard; children: Endea Renee, Renata Melleri, Rona Meiata & James Matthew Jr. **Educ:** Oakwood Col, BA, biol & chem, 1953; SC State Univ, MSc, 1960; Cath Univ Am, MA, 1975; Friendship Col, DDiv, 1963; S Ill Univ, PhD, 1973. **Career:** Atkins HS, guid counr, 1960-61; Sci Dept Bekwai Teachers Col, chair, 1961-68; Seventh Day Adventist Church Sierra Leone, pres, 1968-70; SDA Church N Ghana, exec dir, 1972-74; Pan African Dev Coop, brd mem, 1981; Columbia Union Col, teaching fac, 1974-06, chair, dept psychol, 1982-, emer prof, 2006-, adj prof, currently; Md Defense Force; Pa Mil Res, briggen, currently; adj prof, Univ Dc; Grad Sch Educ, adj prof; Howard Univ, adj prof; Sch Divinity, adj prof; Bowie State Univ, adj prof, currently; Sligo Adventist Sch, adj prof. **Orgs:** Psi Chi, 1989; bd mem, Pan African Develop Coop, 1981; Md Defence Force, 1991; Am Psychol Assoc, 1986; chaplain, Ltc, Civil Air Patrol, 1983; Nat Bd Cert Counselors Inc. **Home Addr:** 3200 Fullerton St, Beltsville, MD 20705-3215, **Home Phone:** (301)572-7536. **Business Addr:** Department Chairman, Columbia Union College, 7600 Flower Ave, Takoma Park, MD 20912, **Business Phone:** (301)891-4000.

## HAMMOND, JOHN B., III

Activist. **Personal:** married Yoko; children: Therese Morgan, John B & Yoji William. **Educ:** Mass Inst Technol, BS, mech engineering; Emory Univ, MBA, finance & gen mgt; Mass Inst Technol, Sloan Sch Mgt, PhD. **Career:** Booz Allen Hamilton, sr mgr, orgn chg & develop, independent consult; Emory Univ's Eve MBA prog, assoc dean & dir; MIT's Sloan Sch of Mgt; Harvard Univ's Kennedy Sch of Govt; Emory Univ's Goizueta Bus Sch, orgn develop & strategic commun. **Orgs:** Chief operating officer, Asn Black Cardiologists Inc; chmn & chief exec officer, S African am Bus asn US; Emory Univ's presidential comn Status Minorities; bd mem, Nat Black Herstory Task force; pres & chief exec officer, 100 Black Men Am Inc, 2007-; Pub Broadcast Atlanta. **Business Addr:** President, Chief Executive Officer, 100 Black Men of America Inc, 141 Auburn Ave NE, Atlanta, GA 30303-2503, **Business Phone:** (404)688-5100.

## HAMMOND, REV. KENNETH RAY

Clergy, educator. **Personal:** Born Jul 28, 1951, Winterville, NC; son of Hoyt and Mary Letha Tucker (deceased); married Evelyn Louise Patrick; children: Kennetta & Brandon. **Educ:** E Carolina Univ, BA, hist, 1973, MA, educ, 1983, CAS, coun educ, 1985; Shaw Univ, Mdiv, 1978; NC State Univ, ABD, 1986. **Career:** Mendenhall Stud Ctr E Carolina Univ, asst & prog dir, 1973-74, prog dir, 1974-85; Cedar Grove Baptist Church, pastor, 1974-79; Mt Shiloh Baptist Church, pastor, 1980-91; E Carolina Univ, asst dir, Univ Unions, 1985-88, assoc dir, Univ Unions & Stud Activ, 1988-91; Union Baptist Church, Durham, NC, sr pastor, 1992-; Shaw Divinity Sch, adj prof; United Christian Bible Inst, adj prof; youth minister, Mt Shiloh Baptist Church. **Orgs:** Alpha Phi Alpha Fraternity, 1971; Phi Alpha Theta, Hon Hist Soc, 1972; Asn Col Unions Int, 1973-91; Nat Asn Campus Activ, 1973-91; Nat Baptist Conv, 1975-91; chmn, Pitt Co Adolescent Sexuality Task Force, 1979-81; bd dir, Pitt Co Arts Coun, 1984-86; NC Asn Couns & Devel, 1985-91; NC Col Personnel Asn, 1986; Am Asn Coun & Devel, 1987; Am Col Personnel Asn, 1987; Interdenominational Ministerial Alliance Durham; secy, Area III, Am Baptist S; chair exec bd, E Cedar Grove Baptist Asn; pres, Shaw Univ, Divinity Sch bd trustee; pres, Nat Theol Alumni Asn; bd dir, 1st Citizens Bank, 1989-91; bd dir, Greenville Utilities Comm, 1989-91; gen bd, Gen Bapt State Conv, NC; bd dir, Habitat Humanity; bd dir, Downtown YMCA Durham; regional bd mem, Am Baptist Churches S; Pres Ministers Coun, vice moderator, Area III, 1999; vice chmn, Exec Comm, Gen Baptist State Conv, 1996; adv bd, Mech & Farmer Bank City, 1999; gen bd, Lott Carey Foreign Missions Conv; Duke Univ Health Systs; New Vision Community Develop; Joyland Found; Unicorn Bereavement Ctr; Mech & Farmers Bank; pres, Cong Christian Educ; pres, Shaw Divinity Sch Nat Theol Alumni Asn; bd mem, Global Scholars Acad; bd mem, Union Independent Sch. **Home Addr:** 211 November Dr, Durham, NC 27712-2438, **Home Phone:** (919)383-8061. **Business Addr:** Senior Pastor, Union Baptist Church, 904 N Roxboro St, Durham, NC 27701, **Business Phone:** (919)688-1304.

## HAMMOND, DR. MELVIN ALAN RAY, JR.

Dentist. **Personal:** Born Feb 6, 1949, Austin, TX; son of Melvin Sr and Helen Bernice Rucker; married Elloree Sanora Lawson; children: Melvin III. **Educ:** Huston-Tillotson Col, BS, 1971; Howard Univ Col Dent, DDS, dent, 1975. **Career:** Harris Co Hosp Dist, staff dentist, 1981-83; pvt pract dentist, 1981-; Melvin A R Hammond DDS & Assocs, gen dentist, currently. **Orgs:** Omega Psi Phi Fraternity, Rho Beta Beta, 1976-; vpres, Charles A George Dent Soc, 1984-85; pres, Gulf States Dent Asn, 1989-90; Am Tex & Nat Dent Asns; Houston Dist Dent Soc; Gulf States Dent Asn; Charles A George Dent Soc. **Honors/Awds:** Outstanding Young Men of America, 1982; Estelle Coffey Young Mem Award; Robert Hardy Jr Mem Award. **Home Addr:** 4414 Roseneath Dr, Houston, TX 77021-1617, **Home Phone:** (713)747-3345. **Business Addr:** General Dentist, Melvin AR Hammond & Associates, 1213 Hermann Dr Suite 840, Houston, TX 77004-7018, **Business Phone:** (713)523-1666.

## HAMMOND, DR. PAMELA V.

Educator. **Personal:** married Gary John; children: Jason W (Camille C) & Alexis S. **Educ:** Tuskegee Univ, BS, nursing, 1972; Univ Md, Baltimore, MD, MS, maternal child nursing, 1978; Old Dom Univ, PhD, educ leadership, 1992. **Career:** Coppin State Univ, fac mem & consult; Norfolk State Univ, fac mem & consult; Christopher Newport Univ, fac mem; Tuskegee Univ, consult; Fayetteville State Univ, consult; Bowie State Univ, consult; Winston-Salem State Univ, consult; NC A & T Univ, consult; Bethune-Cookman Univ, consult; Del State Univ, consult; NC Cent Univ, consult; Hampton Univ, Sch Nursing, chairperson, asst dean, res assoc, dean, 1998, 2007, Nursing Ctr, adminr, prof, provost, 2009-14; Va State Univ, interim pres, 2014-. **Orgs:** Bd mem & exec dir, Nat League Nursing; Veterans Admin; bd mem, Am Acad Nursing; bd mem, Acad Nursing Educ; Reaffirmation Accreditation Comt, SACS; adv coun, Ctr Sci Rev Comt; Nat Adv Coun Minority Health & Health Disparities; Nat Libr Med Environ Health Info Partnership; Va Bd Nursing; adv coun, Future Nursing Va; chair, Nat Inst Aerospace Bd dir, currently; Va Space Grant Consortium Bd dir, currently; New Am Cols & Univs Consortium, currently; Coun Independent Cols Va Inc, currently; bd trustee, Tinina Q Cade Found, currently; adv bd, WK Kellogg Found Proj Success, currently. **Special Achievements:** First Woman in Virginia State University nearly 133-year history to serve as president. **Business Addr:** Interim President, Virginia State University, 1 Hayden Dr, Petersburg, VA 23806, **Business Phone:** (804)524-5070.

## HAMMOND, ULYSSES BERNARD

Chief executive officer, vice president (organization), school administrator. **Personal:** Born Feb 18, 1951, Washington, DC; son of Eliza Jones and Cleveland; married Christine Pointer; children: Damon Moore & Shayna. **Educ:** Kenyon Col, Gambier, OH, BA, 1973; Wayne State Univ, Detroit, MI, MPA, 1975; Wayne State Univ Law Sch, Detroit, MI, JD, 1980. **Career:** Black Stud Union, resident advisor, sr class pres, founding mem, dep chairmen, chmn; Chelsea Groton Bank, corporator; Citizens Res Coun Mich, Detroit, Mich, res asst, 1974-75; Detroit City Coun, Detroit, Mich, spec proj asst, 1975-78; Wayne County Circuit Ct, Detroit, Mich, ct exec, 1978-83; Mich Supreme Ct, Lansing, Mich, assoc state ct adminr, 1983-90; DC Ct, Wash, DC, chief exec officer, 1990-2000; Conn Col, vpres admin, 2000-15. **Orgs:** Pres, Optimist Club N Detroit Found, 1980-83; bd mem, Boys & Girls Club Lansing, 1988-90; Lansing Chap, 1989-90; Conf State Ct Adminr, 1990-96, bd dir, 1996-, bd mem, 1995-; Nat Asn Ct Mgt 1990-, bd dir, 1996-, bd mem, 1995; Nat Bar Asn, 1991-; vice polemarch, Kappa Alpha Psi; Bar Asn DC, 1991-; bd mem, Anthony Bowen YMCA, Wash, DC, 1994-; second vice polemarch, WAS chap, 1996-; bd trustee, Kenyon Col; SE CT Sci Ctr Bd, 2000; New London Rotary, 2000-; bd mem, SE CT COC, 2001-; vpres, NCP, New London Chap, 2001-; bd mem, United Way New London, 2001-; pres, Martin Luther King Jr Scholar Trust Fund; chmn, Lawrence Memorial Hosp; chmn, United Way Southeastern Conn; chmn, Chamber Com Eastern Conn; Conn Hosp Asn; Conn Mirror; Thames Club. **Special Achievements:** First African American to administer an appellate and general jurisdiction court system in the country. **Business Addr:** Member, Rotary Club of New London, PO Box 654, New London, CT 06320.

**HAMMOND, VERLE B.**
Executive, military leader. **Personal:** Born Mar 20, 1934, St. Augustine, FL; son of Genevieve M and Elzer T; married Eleanor; children: Veronne Williams, Anthony & Pamela Holmes. **Educ:** Fla Agr & Mech Univ, BS, math & physics, 1956; Fla State Univ, MBA, opers res & systs anal, 1971. **Career:** AUS Col, mil officer, 1956-84; Innovative Technol Inc, army prog mgr, 1984-85, vpres & dir opers, 1985-88, sr vpres & gen mgr, opers group, 1988-89; Successful logistics, founder, 1989; Innovative Logistics Tech Inc, founder, 1989, pres & chief exec officer, 2010-12; uKarma Corp, dir, 2010; INNOLOG, founder & chief exec officer, dir, 2012. **Orgs:** Info Technol Unit, 1984-; Retired Mil Officers Asn; exec comt, Contract Servs Asn Am; adv bd, Enterprise Fed Savings Bank, 1995; bd dir, Fairfax Co Coc, 1998-; co-founder, Verle & Eleanor Hammond Found, 2002; bd trustee, treas, Univ DC, 2005-; Parren J Mitchell Founds Lifetime Achievement Award; Messiah United Methodist Church. **Business Addr:** Founding Chairman, Innovative Logistics Techniques Inc, 4000 Legato Dr Suite 830, Fairfax, VA 22102-7838, **Business Phone:** (703)766-1419.

**HAMMOND, DR. W. RODNEY**
Psychologist, administrator. **Personal:** Born Jan 12, 1946, Hampton, VA; son of William R Sr and Mildred; married Andrita J Topps; children: William Rodney III. **Educ:** Univ Ill, Champaign & Urbana, BS, 1968; Fla State Univ, MS, 1970, PhD, psychol, 1974; Harvard Univ, post-doctoral, 1990. **Career:** Fla State Univ, instr, 1973; Univ Tenn, asst prof psychol, 1974-76; Meharry Med Col CMHC, asst prof psychiat, 1976-83, dir c serv, 1976-83; Wright State Univ, assoc prof & asst dean, Sch Prof Psychol, 1983-96; Ctr Dis Control & Prev, Div Violence Prev, Atlanta, Ga, dir, 1996. **Orgs:** Fel Am Psychol Asn, 1975-, bd prof affairs, 1988-90, bd educ affairs, 1991-94; pres, bd trustee, Asn Advan Psychol, 1991; Ohio Develop Disabilities Planning Coun, 1986-88; bd dir, Am Asn Gifted C, 1986; chmn, Montgomery County Bd Ment Retardation, 1989-; bd dir, Prevent Child Abuse Am, 2001-. **Honors/Awds:** Outstanding 100 Seniors, Univ of IL Champaign & Urbana, 1968; President's Award for Outstanding Contribution in Teaching Research and Service, Wright State Univ, 1986; Fellow and Diplomate, American Board of Medical Psychotherapists, 1987; Fellow, Inter Nat Society for Research on Agression, 1992; Fellow, American Psychological Asn, 1994; Outstanding Article interesting research and policy issues on adolescence, to researchin adolescence, 1994; Outstanding Contributions to Health, OH Commission Minority Health; Top Ten African American Male, Dayton Parity, 2000; US Dept of Health and Human Services Secretary Award, 2001; Nicholas Hobbs Award & Meritorious Research Service Award, Am Psychol Asn, 2010. **Home Addr:** 267 Lakeshore Dr, Berkeley Lake, GA 30096-3060, **Home Phone:** (770)248-9820.

**HAMMONDS, ALFRED**
Executive. **Personal:** Born Feb 6, 1937, Gary, IN; married Pearlena J Donaldson; children: Alfred Jr & Danelle J. **Educ:** Bus Col, Hammond, IN, cert acct, 1963; Am Inst Banking, attended 1968. **Career:** Executive (retired); HC Lyttons & Co, salesman, 1961-63; Gary Nat Bank, baker asst vpres & br mgr; Gainer Bank, vpres & regional financial mgr. **Orgs:** Am Inst Banking; exec bd, Gary Frontiers Serv Club; vpres, Urban League; US Selective Serv Bd No 44. **Home Addr:** 1641 W 14th Ave, Gary, IN 46404.

**HAMMONDS, EVELYNN M.**
Educator, college administrator. **Personal:** Born Jan 1, 1953?, Atlanta, GA. **Educ:** Spelman Col, BS, physics, 1976; Ga Inst Technol, BS, elec engineering, 1976; Mass Inst Technol, MS, physics, 1980; Harvard Univ, PhD, hist sci, 1993. **Career:** Mass Inst Technol, prof; Harvard Col, Arts & Sci, fac mem, 2002-08, Sr vice provost fac develop & diversity, 2005-, dean, 2008-13; Harvard Univ, Barbara Gutmann Rosenkrantz, prof, hist sci & African Am studies, 2013-. **Orgs:** Sigma Xi, Distinguished Lectr, 2003-05; Broad Inst Harvard & MIT; bd mem, Social Sci Res Coun; bd mem, Bd Overseers Mus Sci Boston; bd mem, Asn Am Cols & Univs; Asn Women Sci, fel; Nsf s Comt Equal Opportunities Sci & Engineering. **Business Addr:** Professor, Harvard University, Cambridge, MA, **Business Phone:** (617)495-1560.

**HAMMONDS, GARFIELD, JR.**
Law enforcement officer, chairperson. **Career:** US Drug Enforcement Agency, spec agt, 1969-94; Ga Dept Juv Servs, comnr, 1994-95; Dep C & Youth, head, 1994-95; Ga State Bd Pardons & Paroles, chmn, 1996-97. **Orgs:** Kappa Alpha Psi Fraternity; 100 Black Men, Atlanta; Int Asn Chiefs Police; Nat Orgn Black Law Enforcement Execs; undercover agt, US Drug Enforcement Admin, 1969-94; Dept c & health, 1994; bd mem, Ga State Bd Pardons & Paroles, 1995-96, 2002-; Dept Juv serv. **Business Addr:** Board Member, chairman, Georgia State Board of Pardons & Paroles, 2 Martin Luther King Jr Dr SE Suite 458, Atlanta, GA 30334-4909, **Business Phone:** (404)656-5651.

**HAMMONDS, JEFFREY BRYAN**
Scout, baseball player. **Personal:** Born Mar 5, 1971, Scotch Plains, NJ; children: 3. **Educ:** Stanford Univ, Palo Alto, CA. **Career:** Baseball player (retired), scout; Baltimore Orioles, outfielder, 1993-98; Cincinnati Reds, outfielder, 1998-99; Colorado Rockies, outfielder, 2000; Milwaukee Brewers, outfielder, 2001-03; San Francisco Giants, outfielder, 2003-04; Washington Nationals, outfielder, 2005; San Diego Padres, scout, currently. **Home Addr:** , Weston, FL. **Business Addr:** Scout, San Diego Padres, Petco Pk 100 Pk Blvd, San Diego, CA 92101, **Business Phone:** (619)795-5000.

**HAMMONDS, TOM (TOM EDWARD HAMMONDS)**
Basketball player, race car driver. **Personal:** Born Mar 27, 1967, Ft. Walton Beach, FL; married Carolyn; children: Tommy Jr, Keelan & Kaison. **Educ:** Ga Tech Univ, attended 1989. **Career:** Basketball player (retired), race car driver; Wash Bullets, forward, 1989-92; Charlotte Hornets, 1992-93; New York Knicks; Denver Nuggets, 1993-97; Minn Timberwolves, 1997-2001; Tom Hammonds Chevrolet, Darlington SC, owner; Nat Hot Rod Asn, race car driver, 2003, 2007-; TK & K Enterprises, owner, 2011-. **Orgs:** Crestview Church God. **Business Addr:** Owner, TK & K Enterprises, 122 Windsor Dr, Crestview, FL 32539.

**HAMMONS, WILLIAM, II**
Entrepreneur. **Educ:** San Francisco State Univ. **Career:** LoveLife Found, media producer, co-founder, currently, Urban Advantage Consult LLC, gen mgr, 2009-12. **Business Addr:** Co-Founder, Media Producer, LoveLife Foundation, PO Box 70351, Oakland, CA 94612, **Business Phone:** (510)663-5683.

**HAMPTON, CHERYL IMELDA**
Journalist. **Personal:** Born Portsmouth, VA; daughter of George Livingston and Helen Bowen; children: Reed Thomas Smith & Adrienne Smith Brown. **Educ:** Syracuse Univ, BS, 1973; Northwestern Univ; Columbia Univ, Grad Sch jour, 2008. **Career:** Regional Learning Ctr, outreach coord, 1981-87; Syracuse Herald J/Herald Am, ed asst, 1987-88, staff writer, 1988-89, asst city ed, 1989-90, asst to managing ed, 1990-92, asst managing ed, 1991-92; Orange County Regist, asst managing ed, 1992-96, dep ed/nights, 1996-97; Nat Pub Radio, dir news staffing & admin, 1997-2008, Dir, Journalism Recruiting, 2009-11; CIH Inc, editing, recruiting, mgt consult, 2011-; Auth: Health & Wealth: Poverty & Disin Onondage County, 1989. **Orgs:** Bd dir, Jr League Syracuse, 1981-82; pres, League Women Voters Cent New York, 1983-87; NY Fair Women's Exec Coun, 1986-92; bd dir, Vol Ctr, Syracuse, NY, 1986-92; Nat Asn Black Journalists, 1989-; African Cult Arts Coun Bowers Mus Cult Art, 1993-97; Nat Asn Minority Media Exec, 1992; vice chair mem, Nat Press Club; pres, Jour & Women Symp, 2000. **Honors/Awds:** Woman of Achievement, Syracuse Post Standard, 1986; Special Achievement Award, Urban League of Onondage County, 1989; Best Story Written Against Deadline, 1989; Syracuse Press Club, Best Investigative Story, Best Series, 1990; Prism Award, Rape Crisis Ctr, 1991. **Business Addr:** Director, National Public Radio, 635 Mass Ave NW, Washington, DC 20001-3753, **Business Phone:** (202)513-2211.

**HAMPTON, DR. DELON**
Consulting engineer, president (organization), chief executive officer. **Personal:** Born Aug 23, 1933, Jefferson, TX; son of Uless (deceased) and Elizabeth Lewis (deceased). **Educ:** Univ Ill, Urbana-Champaign, BSCE, 1954; Purdue Univ, West Lafayette, MSCE, 1958, PhD, 1961; Purdue Univ, Hon Doctor Engineering, 1994; NJ Inst Technol, Hon Doctor Sci, 1996; Howard Univ, civil engineering professorship. **Career:** Consult activities, 1961-; Kans State Univ, asst prof, 1961-64; Eric H Wang Civil Engineering Res Fac, assoc res engr, 1962-63; IIT Res Inst, sr res engr, 1964-68; Howard Univ, Wash, DC, prof civil engineering, 1968-85; Gnaedinger, Banker, Hampton & Assoc, pres, 1972-74; Delon Hampton & Assoc, Chartered, Wash, DC, pres, chmn bd & chief exec officer, 1973-. **Orgs:** Vpres, Housing & Pub Facil, Montgomery County Chamber Com, 1983-85; pres, ASCE Nat Capital Sect, 1984-85, dist dir; bd, Wash DC Chamber Com, 1985-86; chmn, exec comn, Am Soc Civil Engrs, Engr Mgt Div, 1985-89; vpres, Am Consult Engrs Coun, 1987-89; pres Forum, Montgomery Col Found, 1987; bd, Dist 5 dir, Am Soc Civil Engrs, 1991-94, pres-elect, 1998-99, pres, 1999-2000; hon mem, Am Soc Civil Engrs, 1995; assoc mem bd gov, Am Pub Transit Asn; transp Coord, Community, Greater Wash Bd Trade; counr, Nat Acad Engineering; fel Am Acad Arts & Sci; Distinguished Engineering Alumnus & Old Master, Purdue Univ; chmn, Civil Engineering Res Found's Corp Adv Bd & Prof Activ Comts; bd dir, Nat Bldg Mus; bd dir, CEC Memorial Bd; chap hon mem, Chi Epsilon; eminent engr mem, Tau Beta Pi. **Honors/Awds:** Nat Acad Engr; Edmund Friedman Professional Recognition Award, Am Soc Civil Engrs, 1988; Business Man of the Year, Govt DC, Office Human Rights, 1988; Distinguished Alumnus, Civil Engineering Alumni Asn, Univ Ill, 1990; Outstanding Journal Paper Award, Jour Mgt Engineering, Am Soc Civil Engrs, 1990; President Award, DC Coun Engr & Archit Soc, 1991; James Laurie Prize, Am Soc Civil Engrs, 1997; Alumni Award, Col Engineering, Univ Ill, 2000; Theodore R Hagans Jr Memorial Achievement Award, Outstanding Award, Los Angeles Coun Black Consult Engrs. **Special Achievements:** First African American president of American Society of Civil Engineers; Featured in Philadelphia Electric Co's permanent exhibit of 24 outstanding black engrs from 1962-. **Home Addr:** 12804 Brushwood Terr, Potomac, MD 20854-1004, **Home Phone:** (301)926-2993. **Business Addr:** President, Chief Executive Officer, Delon Hampton & Associates, 900 7th St NW Suite 800, Washington, DC 20001, **Business Phone:** (202)898-1999.

**HAMPTON, FREDERICK M.**
College teacher. **Educ:** Winston-Salem State Univ, BS, elem educ, 1979; NC A&T State Univ, MS, educ admin, 1984; Appalachian State Univ, EdS, educ admin, 1988; Univ NC, Greensboro, EdD, educ admin, 1991. **Career:** Elem sch teacher & prin; Dir community educ; Rockingham County, teacher; Cleveland State Univ, Dept Coun, Admin, Supv & Adult Learning, assoc prof, 1991-; Article: Parent Involvement in Inner-City Schools-The Project Fast Extended Family Approach to Success, 1998. **Orgs:** Am Educ Res Asn; Am Asn Sch Adminr; Mid-Western Educ Res Asn; Cleveland State Univ, Black Fac & Staff Orgn, 2003-; Col Educ Technol Comt; Col Educ Petitions Comt; PEW Roundtable. **Business Addr:** Associate Professor, Cleveland State University, 2121 Euclid Ave JH 290, Cleveland, OH 44115-2214, **Business Phone:** (216)687-3828.

**HAMPTON, GRACE**
Educator. **Personal:** Born Oct 23, 1937, Courtland, AL. **Educ:** Art Inst Chicago, BAE, 1961; Ill State Univ, MS, 1968; Ariz State Univ, PhD, 1976. **Career:** Ill State Univ, Art Educ, prof; Northern Ill Univ, fac; Sch Art Inst Chicago, fac; Calif State Univ, Sacramento, fac; Nat Endowment Arts Wash, asst dir, 1983-85; Univ Ore, fac; Pa State Univ, Art Educ & Integrative Arts, sr fac mentor & prof, currently, head african am studies, currently. **Orgs:** Nat Art Educ Asn; Nat Conf Black Artist; artist-in-residence, Hayden House Phoenix; presented papes local & nat confs; del, Festac, 1977. **Home Addr:** 1220 N 44 St Apt 15, Phoenix, AZ 85008. **Business Addr:** Professor, Pennsylvania State University, 314 Old Main, University Park, PA 16802, **Business Phone:** (814)865-5906.

**HAMPTON, DR. JANET J.**
College teacher. **Educ:** Univ Kans, BA, 1958; Mexico City Col, MA, 1961; Cath Univ Am, PhD, 1985. **Career:** Educator (retired); George Washington Univ, assoc prof Spanish, adj ast prof med, 2006, assoc prof emer spanish, 2006-. **Business Addr:** Associate Professor Emeritus of Spanish, George Washington University, 2121 Eye St NW, Washington, DC 20052, **Business Phone:** (202)994-1000.

**HAMPTON, KYM**
Singer, basketball player, actor. **Personal:** Born Nov 3, 1962, Noraville, KY. **Educ:** Ariz State Univ, BA, theatre, 1985. **Career:** Basketball player (retired), actor, singer; Vigo, basketball player, 1985-87; Barcelona, 1987-89; Valencia, Spain, 1989-91; Bari, 1991-92; Chanson, Japan, 1992-93; Aix-en-Provence, France, 1993-94; Avellino, 1994-95; Sive Pavia, Italy, 1995-97; NY Liberty, basketball player, 1997-99; New York Liberty's Fan Development, leader, currently; Films: She Hate Me; TV Series: "Sharp Talk", 2005. **Orgs:** Women's Nat Basketball Asn. **Honors/Awds:** Sun Angel Athlete of the Year Award, 1984; Ariz State Univ Hall of Fame, 1989; Italian League, All-Star Team, 1992, 1995, 1996; Yolanda Jackson Giveback Award, 2002. **Business Addr:** PO Box 80351, Brooklyn, NY 11208, **Business Phone:** (347)735-7973.

**HAMPTON, LEROY**
Pharmacist, executive director. **Personal:** Born Apr 20, 1927, Ingalls, AR; married Anne; children: 5. **Educ:** Univ Colo, BS, pharm, 1950; Denver Univ, MS, chem, 1960. **Career:** Pharmacist (retired), executive director; Dow Chem Co, Colo, chemist, 1953-67, Midland, recruiting mgr, mgr minority employ rels, issues mgr health & environ sci res, 1967-86; Saginaw Valley State Univ, dir affirmative action; part time pharmacist, 1986-05. **Orgs:** Am Chem Soc; Midland Kiwanis Club; United Way; Dow's Community Action Panel. **Home Addr:** 2206 Burlington Dr, Midland, MI 48642-3895, **Home Phone:** (989)631-0127.

**HAMPTON, OPAL JEWELL**
Educator. **Personal:** Born Jul 4, 1942, Kansas City, KS; daughter of William A Blair and Mary Overton Blair; children: Kenton B. **Educ:** Emporia State Univ, BSE, 1966; Azusa Pac Univ, MA, 1974. **Career:** Educator (retired); Kans City United Sch Dist, teacher, 1964-66; Pasadena United Sch Dist, Pasadena, Calif, teacher, 1966-97, curric resource teacher & sci resource teacher, 1997; literacy coach, 2002. **Orgs:** Usher, First AME Church, 1966-; regional dir, 1987-91, Nat Sorority Phi Delta Kappa Inc; life mem, Nat Asn Advan Colored People. **Home Addr:** 1030 Chevron Ct, Pasadena, CA 91103-1009, **Home Phone:** (626)798-7053.

**HAMPTON, PHILLIP G., II**
Lawyer. **Personal:** son of Philip G; married Audrey. **Educ:** Mass Inst Technol, BS & MS, chem engineering, 1977; Univ Chicago Law Sch, JD, 1980. **Career:** US Patent & Trademark Off, asst comnr trademarks, 1994-98; Gardner Carton & Douglas LLP, atty & partner, 1998-2004; Dickstein Shapiro LLP, Intellectual Property Group, partner, 2004-; Howard Univ Sch Law, adj prof, currently; Haynes & Boone LLP, administrative partner, Off Admin Leader, Sr Coun, 2012-. **Orgs:** Chair, Nat Bar Asn, 1989-91; bd mem-at-large, Nat Bar Asn, 1991-94; mem exec comt, Nat Bar Asn, 1990-93; mem vis comt, Univ Chicago, 1995-98; pres, Am Intellectual Property Law Educ Found, 2002; chair mem comt, Am Intellectual Property Law Asn, 2004-07; co chair, Trademark Legis Comt; DePaul Univ Col Law; US Patent & Trademark Off; US Ct Appeals Fed Circuit; US Ct Fed Claims; Am Bar Asn; DePaul Univ Col Law; Intellectual Property Law Sect Am Bar Asn; gen coun, Wash Bar Asn. **Honors/Awds:** Top Minority IP Partner, Diversity & the Bar, 2003; America's Top Black Lawyers, Black Enterprise Mag, 2003. **Business Addr:** Attorney, Partner, Dickstein Shapiro LLP, 1825 Eye St NW, Washington, DC 20006-5403, **Business Phone:** (202)420-2200.

**HAMPTON, PHILLIP JEWEL**
Educator, executive director. **Personal:** Born Apr 23, 1922, Kansas City, MO; son of Cordell Daniels and Goldie Kelley; married Dorothy Smith; children: Harry J & Robert Keith. **Educ:** Kans State Col, Manhattan, attended 1946; Drake Univ, attended 1949; Kans City Art Inst, BFA, illus qualifications, 1951; Kansas City Univ, attended 1952. **Career:** Savannah State Col, dir art, assoc prof, 1952-69; Southern Ill Univ, Edwardsville, prof painting, 1969, prof emer, currently; Collectors Choices: African Art, 1998, African Am Art Works, 1999. **Orgs:** Instr, painting Jewish Ed Alliance, Savannah, 1967-68; bd mem, Savannah Art Asn Savannah, GA, 1968-69; Citizens Adv Coun, Edwardsville, IL, 1973-74; St Louis Art Mus, workshop, 2001; St Louis Artists' Guild; St Louis Art Mus; Contemp Art Mus, St Louis; Art St Louis. **Honors/Awds:** Certificate of Excellence, Savannah Chap Links, 1960; Danforth Association Danforth Found, 1980-86; Governors Purchase Award, IL State Fair, 1991; Retrospective Exhibition, King-Tisdell Cottage Found Inc, Savannah, GA, 1995; AKA Sorority Inc; Salute to Black Men Awdars, Omicron Eta Omege Chapter Award, 2001. **Home Addr:** 832 Holyoake Rd, Edwardsville, IL 62025-2315, **Home Phone:** (618)656-6018. **Business Addr:** Professor Emeritus, Southern Illinois University, 1 Hairpin Dr, Edwardsville, IL 62025, **Business Phone:** (888)328-5168.

**HAMPTON, RANDALL C.**
Banker, chief executive officer, president (organization). **Personal:** married Phyllis; children: 1. **Educ:** Ill State Univ, BS. **Career:** Executive (retired); Asset Mgt Group, exec vpres, 1997; LaSalle Bank Corp, Instnl Trust Serv, exec vpres, 1997-2007; Arial Capital Mgt, vice chmn, 1997; ABM AMRO Asset Mgt N Am, pres & chief exec officer, 2000. **Orgs:** Bd dir, chmn, Ctr New Horizons, 1982, capital campaign chmn, 2006-07; bd mem, Chicago State Univ; trustee, Olympia Fields Pension Fund; bd mem, United Way Metrop Chicago; bd mem, Art Inst Chicago Adv Bd; bd mem, Chicago Housing Authority; trustee, Ill Inst Technol; Chicago Community Trust; Leadership Qual Educ; African Am Legacy Initiative; bd mem, Nat Asn Securities Professionals; chmn, Centers New Horizons Civic Bd, currently. **Business Addr:** Chairman, Centers for New Horizons Civic Board, 4150 S King Dr, Chicago, IL 60653, **Business Phone:** (773)373-5700.

### HAMPTON, DR. ROBERT L.

Educator. **Personal:** Born Nov 18, 1947, Michigan City, IN; son of T L and Annie A Williams; married Cathy M Melson; children: Robyn & Conrad. **Educ:** Princeton Univ, BA, sociol, 1970; Univ Mich, MA, sociol, 1971, PhD, sociol, 1977. **Career:** Univ Mich, Dept Sociol, teaching asst, 1971-74, Univ Mich Exten Serv, teaching asst, 1972-74; Conn Col, instr, 1974-76, from asst prof sociol, 1976-83, 1983-89, dean, 1987-94, Family Studies, prof, prof sociol, 1989-94; Harvard Med Sch, lectr ped, 1980-94; Univ Md, dean undergrad studies, assoc provost acad affairs, prof sociol & family studies, 1994-2003; City Univ NY, York Col, Dept Social Sci prof & pres, 2003-06; Tenn State Univ, provost, chief operating officer & exec vpres, 2006-08, prof sociol, 2006-12, vis instr, 2013-. Am Intercontinental Univ, vpres acad affairs, 2011-12. **Orgs:** Woodrow Wilson fel 1970; pre-doc fel Ford Found, 1970-74; consult, Urban Inst, 1975; chmn, Oper Develop Corp, 1977-78; Danforth Asn, Danforth Found, 1979; consult, Women Crisis, 1979-82; NIMH Post Doc fel 1980; NRC fel Nat Res Coun, 1981; consult, C Hosp, Boston, 1982; Rockfeller Fel Rockefeller Found, 1983; mem exec comt, Peguot Community Found, 1983-86; pres, Child & Family Agency, 1987-90; New London County Child Sexual Abuse Task Force; United Way Southeastern CT, 1992-95; Prince Georges County Supt Schs, Adv Comt; Inst Women's Policy Res, Adv Comt; founder, Inst Domestic Violence African Am Community, 1993-; Asn Black Sociologists; Am Sociol Asn; Am Prof Soc Abuse C; Int Soc Prev Child Abuse & Neglect. **Honors/Awds:** Hartman Mentoring Scholar. **Special Achievements:** Publications: Issues in Children's and Families' Lives: Family Violence Prevention and treatment, 1999; Understanding the Origins and Incidence of Spousal Violence in North America, 1999; Working Towards a Culturally Competent Model of Research for Domestic Violence in the African American Community, 2001; The Encyclopedia of Primary Prevention and Health Promotion, 2003; Domestic Violence in the African American Community: An Analysis of Social and Structural Factors, 2003; Beyond Cultural Sensitivity: Rethinking, Racial, Ethnic, and Religious Understanding in America, 2004; The Mark of the Urchins, 2006; Evaluating Domestic Violence Intervensions For Black Women. **Home Addr:** 265 Pk Lane, Douglaston, NY 11363. **Business Addr:** Visiting Instructor, Tennessee State University, 3500 John A Merritt Blvd, Nashville, TN 37209, **Business Phone:** (615)963-5558.

### HAMPTON, RODNEY CRAIG

Football player. **Personal:** Born Apr 3, 1969, Houston, TX. **Educ:** Univ Ga. **Career:** Football player (retired); New York Giants, 1997, running back, 1990-96. **Honors/Awds:** Season Opener, Univ Ga, 1988; Natl Player of the Week, Sporting News; ESPN Player of the Game; SEC Player of the Week, 1989; Pro Bowl, 1992-93; Super Bowl XXV Champion; Hall of Fame, Florida-Georgia. **Home Addr:** 1415 North W Loop, Houston, TX 77055. **Business Addr:** 10024 Homestead Rd, Houston, TX 77016, **Business Phone:** (713)983-6043.

### HAMPTON, RONALD EVERETT

Law enforcement officer. **Personal:** Born Jan 5, 1945, Washington, DC; son of Memory J and Annie L Hunt; married Quintina M Hoban; children: Candace, Jasmine & Ronald Quinten. **Educ:** Am Univ, Wash, DC, BS, 1978. **Career:** Police officer (retired); US Air Force, Dover Air Force Base, staff sgt, 1968-72; Washington, DC Metrop Police Dept, Washington, DC, police officer, 1972-95; consult-educr, Carter Ctr Emory Univ. **Orgs:** Regional chmn, Eastern Region, Nat Black Police Asn, 1982-84, nat chmn, 1984-86, exec dir, 1987-; bd dir, Am Civil Liberties Union; Adv Comt, Capital Punishment Proj; bd mem, Amnesty Int; Fed Bd, Drug Policy Found Law Enforcement Comt. **Home Addr:** 303 Allison St NW, Washington, DC 20011-7307, **Home Phone:** (202)882-3023. **Business Addr:** Executive Director, National Black Police Association, 3100 Main St Suite 256, Dallas, TX 75226, **Business Phone:** (855)879-6272.

### HAMPTON, THOMAS EARLE, II

Government official. **Personal:** Born Sep 28, 1950, Greenville, SC; married Sheila Dixon. **Educ:** Morgan State Univ, BA, polit sci & govt, 1973; Univ Baltimore, MPA, 1984. **Career:** Baltimore Mayor's Off, admin aide, 1974-83; "Inside Criminal Justice Syst", pub affairs radio show, host & coord, 1979-83; Md Real Estate Comt, sales consult, 1981; Md Mass Transit Admin, Off Pub Affairs, community rels officer, 1983, sr govt rels off, 1983-2003, lobbyist, currently; Baltimore City Community Col, exec asst to pres, currently. **Orgs:** Kappa Alpha Psi Fraternity, 1971-; Nat Forum Black Pub Adminr, Md Chap; chmn, Mayor's Cable TV Adv Conf; bd dir, 10th Dist Dem Orgn; Conf Minority Trans Officials; Mayor's Cable Commun Adv Comt. **Home Addr:** 603 Winans Way, Baltimore, MD 21229-1431, **Home Phone:** (410)947-0110. **Business Addr:** Lobbyist, Maryland Mass Transit Administration, 6 St Paul St, Baltimore, MD 21202-1614, **Business Phone:** (410)539-5000.

### HAMPTON, WILLIE L.

Funeral director. **Personal:** Born May 9, 1933, Montgomery County, TN; son of G F and Geneva L. **Educ:** Ky Sch Mortuary Sci, MS, 1970. **Career:** Winston Funeral Home, lic fun dir & embalmer, owner & oper, 1969-. **Orgs:** So Ky Econ Opportunity Coun; Russellville City Coun; Men's Welfare League; 32 Deg Mason; Am Legion; Ra Coun Exec Bd; mem bd dir, Elec Plant Bd. **Honors/Awds:** First Black appointed bd dir Elec Plant Bd; City park named honor. **Home Addr:** PO Box 122, Russellville, KY 42276. **Business Addr:** Owner, Winston Funeral Home, 162 S Morgan St, Russellville, KY 42276-1941, **Business Phone:** (270)726-2055.

### HANCOCK, DARRIN

Basketball player. **Personal:** Born Nov 3, 1971, Birmingham, AL. **Educ:** Garden City Community Col, attended 1992; Univ Kans, attended 1993. **Career:** Basketball player (retired); Maurienne, France, 1993-94; Charlotte Hornets, small forward, 1994-96; Milwaukee Bucks, small forward, 1996; San Antonio Spurs, 1996-97; Omaha Racers, CBA, 1997; Milwaukee Bucks, 1997; Atlanta Hawks, 1997; Ft Wayne Fury, CBA, 1997-2000; NJ Shore Cats, USBL, 1998; Kans City Knights, ABA, 2000-01; Dodge City Legend, 2000 & 2002-03; Gary Steelheads, CBA, 2001-03 & 2004-05; Sioux Falls Skyforce, CBA, 2003-04; Pa Valley Dawgs, 2004; Kans Cagerz, USBL, 2005. **Honors/Awds:** NJCAA Player of the Year, 1992; USBL Post Season MVP, 2003.

### HANCOCK, HERBIE (HERBERT JEFFREY HANCOCK)

Musician. **Personal:** Born Apr 12, 1940, Chicago, IL; son of Wayman and Winnie Griffin; married Gudrun Meixner; children: Jessica. **Educ:** Grinnell Col, BA, music, 1960, BS, elec eng, 1960; Manhattan Sch Music, MA, music; Roosevelt Univ. **Career:** Albums: Takin' Off, 1962; Inventions & Dimensions, 1963; My Point of View, 1963; Maiden Voyage, 1965; Speak Like a Child, 1968; Herbie Hancock, 1968; The Prisoner, 1969; Mwandishi, 1970; Crossings, 1972; Sextant, 1973; Thrust, 1974; Death Wish, 1974; Dedications, 1974; Flood, 1975; Man-Child, 1975; Secrets, 1976; The Herbie Hancock Trio, 1977; V.S.O.P.: The Quintet, 1977; Sunlight, 1977; Direct Step, 1978; The Piano, 1978; Live Under the Sky, 1979; Monster, 1980; Herbie Hancock Trio, 1981; Quartet, 1981; Double Rainbow, 1981; Lite Me Up, 1982; Future Shock, 1983; Sound System, 1984; Village Life, 1985; Jazz Africa, 1986; Third Plane, 1986; Songs for My Father, 1988; Perfect Machine, 1988; Dis Is Da Drum, 1994; Jamming, 1994; The New Standard, 1995; 1+1, 1997; Gershwin's World, 1998; Future 2 Future, 2001; Directions In Music: Live at Massey Hall, 2002; V.S.O.P.: Live Under the Sky, 2004; Possibilities, 2005; The Essential Herbie Hancock, 2006; River: The Joni Letters, 2007; Then and Now: the Definitive Herbie Hancock, 2008; The Imagine Project, 2010; Thelonious Monk Inst Jazz, chmn, currently; Harvard Univ, Charles Eliot Norton Prof Poetry, 2014-. **Orgs:** Co found, Rhythm Life Orgn, 1996; co founder & bd dirs, Bayview Hunters Point Ctr Arts & Tech; chmn, Thelonious Monk Inst Jazz; Alzheimer's Found Am; Elizabeth Glaser Pediatric AIDS Found. **Honors/Awds:** MTV Award, 1983-84; Gold Note Jazz Awards, Nat Black MBA Asn, 1985; French Award, 1985; BMI Film Music Award, 1986; U.S. Radio Award, 1986; GBMI Film Music Award, Colors, 1989; Miles Davis Award, 1997; Soul Train Music Award, 1997; Grammy Award, Best Jazz Instr Perf, Gershwin's World, 1998; Grammy Award, Best Jazz Instrumental Album, Directions In Music, 2002; NEA Jazz Masters Award, 2004; Downbeat Magazine Readers Poll Hall of Fame, 2005; Album of the Year, 2007; Harvard Foundation Artist of the Year, 2008; Alumni Award, 2010; Kennedy Center Honors Award, 2013. **Special Achievements:** VH1's 100 Greatest Videos Rockit is 10th Greatest Video in 2001, was one of the first mainstream musicians to use an Apple computer in creating music in the early 1980s, author of The Buddha In Your Mirror. **Business Addr:** Chairman, Thelonious Monk Institute of Jazz, 5225 Wisconsin Ave NW Suite 605, Washington, DC 20015, **Business Phone:** (202)364-7272.

### HANCOCK, MICHAEL B.

City council member, president (organization). **Personal:** married Mary Louise Lee; children: 3. **Educ:** Hasting Col, BA, polit sci; Univ Colo, Grad Sch Pub Affairs, MA, pub admin. **Career:** Urban Leage Metrop Denver, pres & chief exec officer, 1999-06; Denver City Coun, Dist 11, city coun pres, currently; Jornae Enterprises, pres & chief exec officer. **Orgs:** Chmn, Coun Econ Develop Comt; vchmn Technol Comt; Pub Works; FasTracks Mass Transp; Denver City Coun; Blue Print Denver; Investment Comts; City's Pub Safety Comn; co-chair, City's Airport Rev Comn; chmn, Bond Implementation Comt. **Special Achievements:** Co author: Standing in the Gap: Leadership for the 21st Century, 2004. **Business Addr:** City Council President, Denver City Council, 4730 Oakland St Suite 200, Denver, CO 80239, **Business Phone:** (303)331-3872.

### HAND, JON THOMAS

Football player, president (organization). **Personal:** Born Nov 13, 1963, Sylacauga, AL; married Tanya. **Educ:** Univ Ala. **Career:** Football player (retired), association founder; Indianapolis Colts, defensive end & Right defensive end, 1986-93, defensive end, 1994; 4J Enterprises LLC, owner, currently. **Orgs:** Founder & bd dir, JT's Hand, 1997. **Home Addr:** PO Box 40296, Indianapolis, IN 46240-0296. **Business Addr:** Founder, JTs Hand, 911 East 86th St Siute 110, Indianapolis, IN 46240, **Business Phone:** (317)255-0570.

### HANDWERK, JANA D.

Insurance agent, financial manager. **Personal:** Born Nov 22, 1959, Kingston; daughter of Vera M; married A Bernard Williams; children: 2. **Educ:** Brown Univ, BS, appl mathematics & econs, 1981; Univ PA, Wharton Sch, MBA, finance & int bus, 1985. **Career:** OND Financial Solutions, CLU, ChFC; Cowan Financial Group, MassMutual, CLU, ChFC; Mass Mutual Life Ins Co, investment adv rep & agt; Cowan Financial, pres; Am Col, Chartered Financial Consult & Chartered Life Underwriter; Financial Educr Inc, Fifth Ave Financial, founding prin, currently, investment advisor rep, 1987-. **Orgs:** Socs Financial Serv Professionals; chartered financial analyst, cand CFA prog, Asn Investment Mgt & Res. **Home Addr:** 100 Pk Ave Fl 6, New York, NY 10017, **Home Phone:** (212)685-1499. **Business Addr:** Founding Principal, Financial Educators Inc, 530 5th Ave 14 Fl, New York, NY 10036-5101, **Business Phone:** (212)642-4808.

### HANDY, DELORES

Television news anchorperson. **Personal:** Born Apr 7, 1947, Little Rock, AR; daughter of George G and Myrtle Carr; married James Lawrence Brown. **Educ:** Univ Ark, attneded 1970. **Career:** FKAAY Radio, Little Rock, reporter & announcer, 1970-72; WHBQ-TV, Memphis, reporter & anchorperson, 1972-73; KABC-TV, LA, reporter, 1973-74; CBS-KNXT-TV, reporter & anchorperson, 1974-76; WJLA-TV Channel 7, Six O'clock News, co-anchor, 1976-78; WTTG-TV Channel 5, Wash, DC, Ten O'clock News & Black Reflections, anchorperson & host; Channel 7, Boston, brdcst journalist; Channel 2, Boston, producer, news anchor & host; Channel 68, Boston, producer, news anchor & host; Monitor Channel, news anchor; CNN Headline News, news anchor; WBUR, anchor, World of Ideas, fill-in host, currently; WNUR, brdcst journalist & news anchor, currently. **Orgs:** Hollywood-Beverly Hills Chap, Nat Asn Media Women; Am Women Radio & TV; Radio & TV News Asn Southern Calif; charter mem, Sigma Delta Chi AR Chap; bd dir, Jr Citizens Corps; exec comt, Nat Capital Area March Dimes; vol, Big Sisters Am Wash DC Chap; Wash Chap Am Women Radio & TV. **Honors/Awds:** Journalist of the Year Award, Capitol Press Club, 1977; Awards, Nat Coun Negro Women; Awards, United Black Fund Excellence Community Service; Award for Journalistic Achievement, Univ DC; Emmy Award, America's Black Forum Special Jesse Jackson, 1985; Emmy Award, Channel 7-Boston, 1987; Journalist of the Year, Washington Press Club; New York InterNat Film Festivals Award; New York International Film Festivals Awards. **Special Achievements:** Honored on 350th anniversary of Black Presence in Boston as one of 350 people who represented Black Presence in Boston 1988; Induction in the "Silver Circle" of the National Academy of Television Arts and Sciences for 25-years of excellence in television. **Home Addr:** Longfellow Pl Suite 2, Boston, MA 02114. **Business Addr:** Anchor, Fill-In Host of World of Ideas, WBUR, 3rd Fl 890 Commonwealth Ave, Boston, MA 02215, **Business Phone:** (617)353-0909.

### HANDY, JOHN RICHARD, III

Saxophonist, composer, college teacher. **Personal:** Born Feb 3, 1933, Dallas, TX; son of Pauline Conner and John R; children: John Richard IV. **Educ:** City Col NY, 1960; San Francisco State Col, BA, 1963. **Career:** Saxophonist, Composer, Educator: Mod Jazz Groups, Rhythm & Blues Bands, San Francisco-Oakland, Calif, 1948-58; Carnegie Recital Hall, concerts, 1962, 1967; Monterey Jazz Festival, 1964-66; Hollywood Bowl, Calif, 1966; Santa Clara Calif Symphony, 1967; Newport Jazz Festival, 1967; Antibes Jazz Festival, 1967; San Francisco prod Opera, head jazz band, 1967; Mus Dept San Francisco St Univ, part time fac mem, 1968-80, Artist-in-Residence, 1998-2002; La Red Hot Rec, 2000; San Francisco State Univ, fac; Stanford Univ, fac; Univ Calif, Berkeley, fac; San Francisco Conserv Music, fac; Albums: In the Vernacular, 1959; No Coast Jazz, 1960; Jazz, 1962; Live at the Monterey Jazz Festival, 1965; The 2nd John Handy Album, 1966; Quote Unquote, 1967; New View, 1967; Projections, 1968; Projections, 1968; Two Originals: Karuna Supreme/Rainbow, 1975; Hard Work, 1976; Carnival, 1977; Where Go the Boats, 1978; Handy Dandy Man, 1978; Excursion in Blue, 1988; Centerpiece, 1989; Very First Recordings, 1994; Live at the Monterey Jazz Festival, 1996; Live at Yoshi's Nightspot, 1996; John Handy's Musical Dreamland, 1996; Live at Yoshi's Nightspot, 2000; Side person: Charles Mingus Big Band: Alice's Wonderland, 1958; Mingus Ah Uhm, 1959; Blues & Roots, 1959; Mingus Ah Um; Mingus Dynasty; Jazz Portraits; Time is Running Out, 1976; Various Artists: From Spirituals to Swing, 1967; Brass Fever, 1977; Mingus Dynasty Group: Epitaph & Char in the Sky, 1979-89; Jazz Mine, 1980; Garland, 1981; OaklandJazzThere Festival, artistic director, 2000. Movie Sound tracks: All About the Benjamins, 2002; TV Sound tracks: The Bernie Mack Show, 2002; NPR, BBC, BET. **Orgs:** Music dir, Jazz Arts Soc, 1960-61; San Francisco Interim Arts Adv Comt, 1966-67. **Honors/Awds:** Downbeat Poll Award; 1st Place Award, Rec World All-star Band, 1968; Music Makers Award, San Francisco Music Ctr, College Alameda, 1986; Inducted into Bay Area Blues Society Hall of Fame, 1992; Lifetime Achievement Award, San Jose Jazz Soc, 1995; Jazz Note Award, Russian River Jazz Festival, 1996; Jazz Legends Award, 1996; Bill Graham Life time Achievement Award, Bay Area Music, 1997; Jazzie Award, Jazz on the Hill Festival, 1998; Contribution to the Arts Award, San Francisco Bd Supervisors, 1998; Honors Award, Allen Temple Baptist Church, 1998; Black History Month Award, College Siskiyous, Calif, 1998; Contribution to the World of Music Award, Mc Clymonds High Sch Alma Mater, Oakland, Calif; The Beacon Award, SFJAZZ, 2009. **Special Achievements:** Grammy nominations; inducted into the Alumni Hall of Fame San Francisco State University, 2006. **Home Addr:** 4100 10 Redwood Rd Suite 251, Oakland, CA 94619, **Home Phone:** (510)638-8234. **Business Addr:** 618 Baker St, San Francisco, CA 94117.

### HANDY, LILLIAN B.

Executive, chief executive officer, president (organization). **Educ:** Morgan State Univ; Univ Calif & Southeastern Univ. **Career:** Arthur Young & Co, mgt consult; Electronic Data Systs Inc, mgt consult; TRESP Assocs Inc, founder, pres, chief exec officer, 1981-. **Orgs:** Chair, Minority-Owned Bus Tech Transfer Consortium; bd trustee, Alexandria Hosp Found, Va; bd visitor, NC Agr & Tech State Unit, AT&T; Greensboro Delta Sigma Theta Sorority; Nat Aeronaut & Space Admin. **Business Addr:** Chief Executive Officer, President, TRESP Assocs Inc, 4900 Seminary Rd Suite 700, Alexandria, VA 22311.

### HANDY, REV. DR. NORMAN A., SR.

Clergy, minister (clergy). **Personal:** Born Washington, DC; married Carolyn K; children: Angela, John, Nancy Murray & Norman Jr. **Educ:** Univ DC, BA; Howard Univ Divinity Sch, MDiv, 1989; Wesley Theol Sem. **Career:** Priv pract marriage & family therapist, Wash, DC, Columbia, Md; City Coun, Baltimore, Md, 1995; Marriage & Family Therapist; Unity United Methodist Church, dir, sr minister, pastor, 2001-; City Coun Baltimore, rep 6th Councilmanic Dist. **Orgs:** Pres, Black United Methodist Preachers; co-chmn, City-Wide Liquor Coalition; co-chmn, Coalition Beautiful Neighborhoods; pres, Harlem Pk Neighborhood Coun; Md State Adv Coun Alcohol & Drug Abuse; Prince George's County Task Force Group Living Facil; Sykesville Town Home Asn; Strategic Planning Prog Baltimore-Wash Conf; Pan-Methodist Coalition; youth counr, Md Training Sch Boys; youth counr, Boy's Village, Cheltenham, Md; youth counr, Ionia Whipper Home Girls, Wash, DC; pres, Black United Methodist Preachers; Chaplain Interdenominational Ministerial Alliance, Baltimore. **Honors/Awds:** Best of Baltimore (Clergy-Activist Category), City Paper, 1991; Maryland's Most Beautiful Person, Baltimore City, 1992; Whitney Young Jr Award for Community Serv, Baltimore Urban League, 1995. **Business Addr:** Senior Minister, Pastor, Unity United Methodist Church, 1433 Edmondson Ave, Baltimore, MD 21223, **Business Phone:** (410)728-4826.

### HANDY, STEPHEN

Clergy, executive director. **Personal:** married Shelley; children: Janay, Stephen Jr & Noah. **Educ:** Dillard Univ, BA; Tenn State Univ, MBA; Vanderbilt Divinity Sch, MDiv. **Career:** United Methodist Publ House, exec dir, 2000-; McKendree United Methodist Church (Nashville, TN), lead pastor, 2009-. **Special Achievements:** Blog creater--www.pastorhandy.blogspot.com.

**HANES, WENDELL L.**
Television producer, entrepreneur. **Personal:** Born Jan 1, 1971; son of Odessa and Eugene; married Lesley Aisha Stephens. **Educ:** Brown Univ, cult media, 1993. **Career:** Bang Music, composer, musician & sound designer; Volition Sound Branding, pres & rep, currently.

**HANEY, DON LEE**
Television news anchorperson. **Personal:** Born Sep 30, 1934, Detroit, MI; married Shirley; children: Karen Lynn & Kimberly Joy. **Educ:** Wayne State Univ, MI, Radio-TV Arts maj, 1959, polit sci & law, 1974. **Career:** WSJM, staff announcer, 1956-57; CKCR, staff announcer, 1957-59; WQRS-FM; WLIN-FM; WGPR-FM, prog dir, 1959-60; WCHD-FM, 1960-63; WJR, staff announcer, 1963-68; CFPL-TV, host weekly pub affairs prog, 1967-68; WXYZ-TV, Haney's People, host, 1967-81; KUAR pub radio, Little Rock, Ark, weekday announcer, currently. **Orgs:** New Detroit Inc Commun Comt; bd dir, Am Fedn TV & Radio Arts Union; bd dir, Sudden Infant Death; bd mem, Equity Justice Coun; chmn, Mus Dyst Asn Am; Detroit City Airport Comn. **Home Addr:** 265 E Boston Blvd, Detroit, MI 48202, **Home Phone:** (313)883-3906. **Business Addr:** Weekday Announcer, KUAR Public Radio, 5820 Asher Ave Suite 400, Little Rock, AR 72204-1099, **Business Phone:** (501)569-8485.

**HANKIN, NOEL**
Management consultant. **Personal:** Born Apr 30, 1946, Kingston; son of Iris Penso and Ivanhoe; married Gwendolyn Diaz; children: Arana & Loren. **Educ:** Fordham Univ, New York, NY, attended 1969; Queens Col, Queens, NY, BA, sociol, 1968; NY Univ, attended 1970; Wharton Sch Bus, mkt cert, 1985. **Career:** Young & Rubicam, New York, NY, acct exec, 1970-72; Best Friends, New York, NY, prin, 1970-87; Benton & Bowles, New York, NY, acct exec, 1972-74; Hankin & Smith, New York, NY, prin, 1974-76; Ogilvy & Mather, New York, NY, vpres, acct supvr, 1978-86; Miller Brewing Co, Milwaukee, Wis, brand mgr, Miller Lite, 1986-88, dir mktg rel, 1988-94, dir ethnic mktg, 1994-96, dir, corp rel, 1996-97; Schieffelin & Somerset Co, vpres corp affairs, 1997-2001, vpres, multicultural mkt, 2001-03; Moet Hennessy USA, sr vpres, multicultural initiatives, 1997-2010. **Orgs:** Founder, secy & bd dir, Thurgood Marshall Scholar Fund, 1987-2011; Chair, New York Urban League 2000-05; 100 Black Men; bd advisors, Historically Black Cols & Univs. **Honors/Awds:** Black Achievers Award, YMCA-NYC, 1984; CEBA Award, Word Inst Black Comm, 1985, 1989, 1990; Black Book Award Outstanding Bus Person, 1989; Fundraising Award, UNCF, 1989; Nat Am Advan Colored People Community Service Award, 1992; Men Who Dare Award The Family Acad; Top 100 Alumni, Queens Col, 1998; Support Network Corporate Award, 2001; Concord Family Serv; Community Serv Award, 2002; Community Service Award, Nat Am Advan Colored People Community Service Award, 2005; NatUrban League Guild Legacy Award, 2005; Hon Doctor Humane Letters, Medgar Evers Col, City Univ NY. **Special Achievements:** Appointed by President Clinton to Commission of Historically Black Colleges & Universities, 1994-01. **Business Addr:** Principal, Hankin Consultants Inc, 27 Harding Terr, Sag Harbor, NY 11963, **Business Phone:** (917)536-2104.

**HANKINS, DR. ANDREW JAY, JR.**
Radiologist. **Personal:** Born Jul 15, 1942, Waukegan, IL; son of Andrew Sr and Julia Lampkins; married Margaret Roberts; children: Andrea Marie, Corbin Keith & Trent Allen. **Educ:** Univ Iowa, BA, 1964; Univ Mich, Med Sch, MD, 1968. **Career:** Michael Reese Hosp & Med Ctr, intern, 1968-69; Univ Chicago, resident, 1971-74; Dept Radiol, Univ Chicago, instr, 1974-75; Milton Community Hosp, staff radiol, 1975-84; SW Detroit Hosp, radiologist, 1975-80, vchmn, dept radiol, 1980-83, chmn, radiol, 1984-90; Wayne State Univ, clin asst prof, 1977-85; Southwest Detroit Hosp, vchief med staff, 1988-89; Goodwin Ervin Hankins & Assoc PC, pres, 1988-90; Mich Health Ctr, radiologist, 1991; Henry Ford Hosp, sr staff physician, 1991-. **Orgs:** Vpres, Goodwin Ervin & Assoc PC, 1980-87; consult, radio pharmaceut drug adv comn, FDA, 1982-84; pres, Equip Lsng Firm Hankins Ervin Goodwin & Assoc, 1984-89; Hartford Mem Baptist Church, 1984-; Nat Asn Advan Colored People; Detroit Med Soc, Nat Med Asn & Wayne County Med Soc; RSNA, SNM, & AIUM; Iowa Black Alumni Asn; YMCA; Big Ten Conf, Adv Comn, 1988-94; bd govrs, Downtown Detroit YMCA, 1991-96; alumni bd dir, Univ Iowa, 1994-; Detroit Athletic Club, 1997-. **Honors/Awds:** Omicron Delta Kappa Univ Iowa Cir, 1963; Nile Kinnick Scholar, Univ Iowa, 1963-64; Phi Beta Kappa Alpha Chap Iowa, 1964; Big Ten Medal of Honor, Univ Iowa, 1964; Sloan Found Scholar, Univ Mich Med Sch, 1964-68; Distinguished Young Alumni, Univ Iowa Alumni Asn, 1977. **Home Addr:** 1325 Joliet Pl, Detroit, MI 48207-2833, **Home Phone:** (313)393-9673. **Business Addr:** Senior Staff, Henry Ford Hospital Radiology, Sterling Hgts 14500 Hall Rd 2799 W Grand Blvd, Detroit, MI 48208, **Business Phone:** (800)436-7936.

**HANKINS, ANTHONY MARK**
Fashion designer. **Personal:** Born Nov 10, 1968, Elizabeth, NJ; son of Willie and Mary Jane. **Educ:** Pratt Inst, fashion design, 1988; Ecole de la chambre Syndicale de la Couture, 1989. **Career:** Yves St Laurent, design asst, 1989-90; Willi Smith; Adrienne Vittadini, design asst, 1990-91; JC Penney Co, Los Angeles, qual control inspector, 1991-92, Dallas, first in-house designer, JC Penney, 1992-94; Ramone Moya Ltd, fashion dir, vpres, partner, owner, 1994; Univ NTex, exec residence, 1995; Anthony Mark Hankins Inc, founder, sr vpres & design dir, 1998-; Antthony Design Originals, founder & owner currently. **Orgs:** SPCA Tex, 1995-; adv bd, Easter Seals, 1995-; bd dir, Attitudes & Attire, 1995-; Design Industs Found Fighting AIDS, 1996; S Dallas Bus & Prof Women's Youth Club, 1996; Good Morning Tex, Channel 8, 1996; MacDill Afb, Black Hist Comt, 1996; Black Retail Action Group, 1996. **Honors/Awds:** Hon Citizen, Jackson, Miss, 1996; Fabric Of Dreams Fashion Show, MacDill Air Force Base, 1996; Fashionetta, AKA Sorority, Inc, 1996; State of Oklahoma Citation, 1996; Turner Broadcasting Trumpet Award, 1996; Absolute Vodka Award, Dallas Design Intiative, 1996; Bus Achievement Award, Black Retail Action Group, 1996; Trailblazer Award, Nat Assn Negro Bus & Prof Women, 1995; Award of Excellence, New Jersey Education Asn, 1995; Trumpet Awards, Young Star Award, 1997; Bus Week Entrepreneur of the Year, 1998; Quest for Success Award, Black Chamber Com, 1998. **Special Achievements:** First In-House Designer, JC Penney Co, 1992-94; 3 the Wall Street Journal 1995; Newsweek's top 100 People to Watch in 21st century, 1997; Featured in Business Week Magazine 1997; The Fabric of Dreams, Motivational Biography, Dutton Books Publishing, 1998. **Home Addr:** 5450 Gaston Ave, Dallas, TX 75214, **Home Phone:** (972)594-7117. **Business Addr:** Design Director, Founder, Senior Vice President, Anthony Mark Hankins Inc, 5450 Gaston Ave, Dallas, TX 75214, **Business Phone:** (214)887-1777.

**HANKINS, BENJAMIN B., JR. (BEN HANKINS)**
Chief executive officer. **Personal:** Born Newport News, VA. **Educ:** Univ Va, BA, 1987; Univ Baltimore, MBA, 1993. **Career:** Axiom Resource Mgt Inc, pres & chief exec officer, 1996-; AITHERAS LLC, Partner, 2010-. **Orgs:** Bd trustee, St Paul Col; bd dir, Walter Ridley Scholarship Fund, Univ Va; co-founder, Commonwealth Real Estate Info Serv, 2010. **Business Addr:** President, Chief Executive Officer, Axiom Resource Mgt Inc, 5111 Leesburg Pke, Falls Church, VA 22041, **Business Phone:** (703)379-0412.

**HANKINS, HESTERLY G., III**
Educator, computer scientist. **Personal:** Born Sep 5, 1950, Sallisaw, OK; son of Hesterly G II and Ruth Faye Jackson. **Educ:** Univ Calif, Santa Barbara, BA, sociol, 1972; Univ Calif, Los Angeles, MBA, mgt info systs, 1974; Golden Gate Univ, postgrad study, 1986; La Verne Univ, postgrad study, 1987. **Career:** Xerox Corp, appln programmer, 1979-80; Eng Div, comput programmer, 1981-84; Ventura Col, instr, 1983-84; Golden Gate Univ, instr, 1984; Naval Air Sta, spec asst, 1984-85; PMTC, comput scientist, 1985-88; Chapman Col, instr, 1985; De Anza Col, instr, 1985; W Coast Univ, fac, 1987-88; W Coast Univ, Dept Bus Mgt, fac, 1987-91; Defense Contract Mgt Dist, Mgt Info Systs, sr analyst, 1988-94; Nat Univ, writing instr, 1994-, Dept Comput Soc, fac, currently. **Orgs:** Sec, Alpha Kappa Psi, 1977-, life mem; Fed Mgrs Asn; ICTIP; IEEE Compu Soc; Int Platform Asn; YM/WCA Benefit Jr Rodeo Asn; City Oxnard United Methodist Church; Combined Fed Campaign Keyperson; Asn Compu Mach; Fed Mgrs Asn; Nat Univ Alumni Asn; UCSB Alumni Asn; Grad Stud Mgmt Asn; bd dir, Int Whos Who & Whos Who Prof; Nat Asn Acct; Am Biog Inst; Calif Asn Acct. **Home Addr:** Los Angeles Intl Airport, Los Angeles, CA 90045. **Business Addr:** Faculty, National University, 9920 La Cienega Blvd Suite 300, Inglewood, CA 90301, **Business Phone:** (800)628-8648.

**HANKS, CAMILLE.** **See COSBY, CAMILLE OLIVIA HANKS.**

**HANLEY, J. FRANK, II**
Lawyer. **Personal:** Born Mar 11, 1943, Charlotte, NC; son of Robert D and Frank; children: Laura Elizabeth & Melinda Lee. **Educ:** Hampton Univ, BA, 1965; NC Cent Univ Sch Law, LLB, 1968. **Career:** State Ind, dep atty gen, 1969-71; Stand Oil Div Am Oil Co, real estate atty, 1971-72; Marion Co, dep prosecutor, 1972-73; Ind Employ Security Div, mem rev bd, 1974-78; pub defender, 1985-88; J. Frank Hanley II Inc, atty, currently. **Orgs:** Marion Co Bar Asn; Indianapolis Bar Asn; Nat Org Social Security Representatives. **Special Achievements:** Tennis Doubles Champion, Cent Inter-Atlantic Asn, 1965; Tennis Doubles Champion, Nat Collegiate Athletic Asn Atlantic Coast, 1965. **Business Addr:** Attorney, J Frank Hanley II Inc, 4279 Lafayette Rd, Indianapolis, IN 46254, **Business Phone:** (317)290-1800.

**HANNA, CASSANDRA H.**
Educator, musician. **Personal:** Born Jan 1, 1940, Miami, FL. **Educ:** St Augustine Col, BA, 1961; Univ Miami, MusM, 1971; Ind Univ. **Career:** Episcopal Church St Agnes, organist, choir dir; Miami Dade Comm Choir; Concerts radio & TV, co-dir; Comm Col Fla; pianist-lectr recitalist; Cassie's Cookies, pres; Miami Dade Community Col, assoc prof music, srprof music, currently. **Orgs:** MENC; NEA; FEA; FCME; NFHAS; FHEA; Alpha Kappa Alpha; Phi Kappa Alpha; AABWE; Nat Guild Organists; pres, Cardiney Corp/Diversified Investments; Music Teachers Nat Asn; Fla State Massage Ther Asn. **Home Addr:** 18320 NW 38th Ct, Opa Locka, FL 33055, **Home Phone:** (305)621-2057. **Business Addr:** Senior Professor, Miami Dade Community College, 11380 NW 27th Ave, Miami, FL 33167-3418, **Business Phone:** (305)347-1456.

**HANNAH, JOHNNIE, JR.**
Computer executive, college teacher. **Personal:** Born Nov 20, 1970, Akron, OH; son of Johnnie and Joanne. **Educ:** Howard Univ, BBA, info systs, 1993; Heidelberg Col, MBA, 2000. **Career:** GeuCorp, syst anal, 1993-96; United Way, Great Toledo, dir info syst, 1996-98; City Toledo, tech serv coordr, adminr, 1998-; Heidelberg Col, adj Instr, 2002-. **Orgs:** Upward Bd Prog, 1989; InRoads Alumni Asn, 1993; chair, Black Data Processing Assoc, Toledo Chap, 1996; bd mem, African Am Christian Fel Asn, 1996; vpres mem serv, Black Data Processing Asn, 1997; Nat Asn Advan Colored People, 1997; Greater Toledo Urban League, 1997; ONYX, 1997; Asn Info Technol Professionals, 1997; Pres Summit Americas Future, deleg, 1997; bd mem, KEVIN; founding mem, City Toledo Found Future. **Home Addr:** 2207 Rockspring Rd Apt D, Toledo, OH 43614-1644, **Home Phone:** (419)865-3565. **Business Addr:** Adjunct Instructor, Heidelberg College, 310 E Market St, Tiffin, OH 44883-2462, **Business Phone:** (419)448-2221.

**HANNAH, DR. MARC REGIS**
Electrical engineer, vice president (organization), scientist. **Personal:** Born Oct 13, 1956, Chicago, IL; son of Hubert and Edith. **Educ:** Ill Inst Technol, BS, elec engineering, 1977; Stanford Univ, MS, elec engineering, 1978, PhD, elec engineering, 1985. **Career:** Silicon Graphics, co-founder & mem tech staff, 1982-85, co-founder, vpres & chief scientist, 1997; SongPro, chief technol officer, 2002-; Nintendo Game Boy, chief technol officer; Pulsent Corp, vice pres prod archit; Rondeau Bay, partial owner; Omniverse Digital Solutions, vpre technol devel, currently. **Orgs:** Inst Elec & Electronics Engrs; Magic Edge; ACM, Northern Calif Coun Black Prof Engrs, Nat Tax Asn; trustee, Ill Inst Technol; adv bd, Venture Choice Inc; adv bd, Oasis Capital Partners Inc; adv bd, Betawave Corp. **Home Addr:** 474 O Connor St, Menlo Park, CA 94025. **Business Addr:** Advisory Board, Venture Choice Inc, 2225 E Bayshore Rd 260, Palo Alto, CA 94303, **Business Phone:** (650)320-7691.

**HANNAH, MOSIE R.**
Banker. **Personal:** Born Jul 11, 1949, Lake City, SC; married Doris Horry; children: Michelle & Brandon. **Educ:** Voorhees Col, BS, maths, 1970; Univ Mich, Grad Sch & Banking, attended 1981; Univ Okla, Retail Banking Sch, attended 1983. **Career:** Senior vice president (retired); Fleet Financial Group, br mgr, 1973-75, asst vpres, 1975-79, vpres, 1979-84, sr vpres, 1984-04; Bank Am, sr vpres, 1971-09; BOA, sr vpres, 2009. **Orgs:** Dir, United Neighbourhood Ctrs Am; Vstg Nurses Serv Monroe County; Rochester Bus Opportunites Corp; allocaties Com United Way Greater Rochester; Bank Am Assoc & Alumni Network. **Home Addr:** 31 Crystal Springs Lane, Fairport, NY 14450.

**HANNAH-JONES, BEVERLY K.**
Architect, chief executive officer. **Personal:** married Carlton. **Educ:** Mich State Univ, civil engineering, 1980; Lawrence Technol Univ, BS, archit, 1985; BArch, 1988, MArch, 2000. **Career:** Albert Kahn Family Co, archit designer, 1985-92; Hannah & Associates Inc, chief exec officer, 1993-; TAG Holdings LLC, vpres bus develop, 2009-12; Hannah-Neumann Smith LLC, managing partner, 2013-. **Orgs:** Delta Sigma Theta Sorority; Am Inst Architects; bd mem, Mich State Fire Safety Bd; Nat Asn Negro Bus & Prof Womens Club Inc. **Business Addr:** Chief Executive Officer, Hannah & Associates, Inc, 12801 Auburn St Suite 103, Detroit, MI 48223, **Business Phone:** (313)837-8457.

**HANNAHAM, FRED P.**
Engineer. **Educ:** PE. **Career:** Pvt pract, engr, currently. **Business Addr:** Professional Engineer, 4 Fordham Hill Oval Suite 14H, Bronx, NY 10468-4716, **Business Phone:** (718)367-3027.

**HANSBERRY-MOORE, VIRGINIA T.**
Educator. **Personal:** Born Jan 26, 1930, Ocala, FL; daughter of L T Thompson (deceased) and Beatrice (deceased); married Clarence; children: Katrina Veronica; married James. **Educ:** Fla Mem Col, St Augustine, FL, BS, elem educ, 1951; Masters Admin Supv, Melbourne, FL, cert, 1977. **Career:** Broward Co Sch Syst, Ft Lauderdale, Fla, teacher, 1951-84. **Orgs:** Gen chairwoman, Zeta Phi Beta Sorority, 1948-; Youth worker, First Baptist Church Piney Grove, 1951-; bd dir, Fla Endowment Fund Higher Educ, 1984-; dist dean, Christian Educ; supv dir, State Pageantry (CE); Nat First vpres, 1984-90; bd dir, Zeta Dove Found Inc. **Home Addr:** 3511 NW 23rd St, Ft. Lauderdale, FL 33311, **Home Phone:** (954)735-3511. **Business Addr:** Board Director, Zeta Dove Foundation Inc, PO Box 15811, Plantation, FL 33318.

**HANSBURY, VIVIEN H.**
Educator, president (organization). **Personal:** Born Feb 5, 1927, Richmond, VA; daughter of Arthur J and Mary Spain; married Horace Trent; children: Horace A Trent, Sandra Lewis & Vernard Trent; married Leonard Andrew Hansbury. **Educ:** Va State Univ, BS, 1966; Temple Univ, MEd, 1970, prin cert, 1972. **Career:** Educator (retired); fiscal acct, 1950-62; Del County Intermediate Unit, teacher, mentretarded & learning disability, 1966-68, supvr spec educ, 1968-69; Pa State Univ, counr, 1969-74; Sch Dist Philadelphia, educ teacher, 1974-76, Pre-Sch Handicapped, prog mgr, 1976-78, instr advr, 1978-84, resource teacher, consult, 1984-92; NIA Psychol Asn, educ consult, 1982-; coordr assault illiteracy, 1983-, northeastern sectional dir, 1988-; Tutor Mayor's Comn Literacy, 1984-90; PFT Retirement Chap Travel, Educ & Cult Comt, dir. **Orgs:** Den mother Boy Scouts Am, 1957; dir, Pinn Memorial Baptist Church, 1985-91; pres, Philadelphia chap Pan-Hellenic Coun, 1982; exec bd, Philadelphia Opportunities Industrialization Ctr, 1984-; pres, Wynnefield Residents Asn, 1992; Northeastern Fedn Women; pres, Philadelphia Coalition Federated Women, 1988-90; finance secy, Pa Fedn, 1986-90; Nat Asn Univ Women; Kappa Omega Zeta; Zeta Phi Beta; vpres, ed, Phil Delta Kappa, 1990-93; pres, Monday Eve, 1984-90; pres, Thirty Clusters, 1985-87; Nat rep, Civil Rights, Zeta Phi Beta Sorority, 1986-92, Black Family, dir, 1992-; pres, Sigma Pi Epsilon Delta, Philadelphia Chap, Grad Div, 1987-; pres, Top Ladies Distinction, Philadelphia Chap, 1988-93; pres, Phi Delta Kappa Fraternity, Univ Pa Chap, 1990-94; scholar comt mem, Phi Delta Kappa Nat Sorority, 1990-; nat mem-at-large, Nat Asn Colored Women's Clubs, 1992-; secy, Pinochle Bugs Social & Civic Club, Philadelphia Chap, 1992-; pres, Va State Univ Alumni Asn, Philadephia Chap, 1993-; treas, Top Ladies Distinction, Area II, 1993-; Nat Coun Negro Woman, Philadelphia Local; chmn, Travel Educ & Cult Comt; Philadelphia Fedn Teachers; Am Fedn Teachers. **Home Addr:** 2246 N 52nd St, Philadelphia, PA 19131-2313, **Home Phone:** (215)877-4232. **Business Addr:** Director, Philadelphia Federation of Teachers, 2246 N 52nd St, Philadelphia, PA 19131, **Business Phone:** (215)877-4232.

**HANSEN, JOYCE VIOLA**
Writer. **Personal:** Born Oct 18, 1942, Bronx, NY; daughter of Austin and Lillian Dancy; married Matthew Nelson. **Educ:** Pace Univ, NY, BA, eng, 1972; NY Univ, NY, MA, eng educ, 1978. **Career:** Educator (retired), writer; New York Bd Educ, teacher, 1973-95; Empire State Col, teacher, 1987-95; Auth: The Gift-Giver, 1980; Home Boy, 1982; Yellow Bird & Me, 1986; Which Way Freedom, 1986; Out From This Place, 1986; Between Two Fires: Black Soldiers in the Civil War, 1993; The Captive, Scholastic, 1994; I Thought My Soul Would Rise & Fly, 1997; Breaking Ground Breaking Silence, 1998; Women of Hope, 1998; The Heart Calls Home, 1999; Bury Me Not in a Land of Slaves, 2000; One True Friend, 2001; Freedom Roads, 2003; African Princess: The Amazing Lives of Africa's Royal Women, 2004; Home Is With Our Family, 2010. **Orgs:** Soc C's Bk Writers, 1980-; Auth's Guild. **Home Addr:** , SC.

**HANSEN, STANLEY S., JR.**
Educator, executive director. **Educ:** State Univ NY Col, Oneonta, NY, BS, sec educ, 1975, Brockport, NY, MS, educ & coun, 1979. **Career:** NY State Educ Dept, Off Higher Educ, exec coordr, K-16 Initiatives & Access Progs, exec dir, 1990-. **Business Addr:** Executive Director,

New York State Education Department, 89 Washington Ave, Albany, NY 12234, **Business Phone:** (518)474-3719.

### HANSFORD, LOUISE TODD

Publisher. **Personal:** Born Nov 6, 1944, Cincinnati, OH; daughter of James and Josephine; children: Eric. **Career:** The Andrew Jergens Co, secy, 1963-68; Procter & Gamble, org effectiveness consult, 1968-90; Fine Arts By Todd, owner, pres & chief exec officer, 1990-. **Orgs:** Valley Forge Federated, 1967-69; NAT Coun Negro Women, 1984-86; founder, Black Aware & Concerned, 1973-78; Atlanta BUS League, 1997; NAT Conf Artists, 1997; NAT Black Arts Festival, 1996; co-chair, Mayors Masked Ball, 1997; Atlanta COC. **Honors/Awds:** Atlanta BUS League, Outstanding Achievement BUS, 1997. **Special Achievements:** Woman of Enterprise Awards, Avon Products, nominated, 1998. **Business Addr:** President, Chief Executive Officer, Fine Arts by Todd, 1240 Old Chattahoochee Ave NW, Atlanta, GA 30318-3740, **Business Phone:** (404)351-5553.

### HANSON, JOHN L., JR.

President (organization), media executive, radio journalist. **Personal:** Born Aug 5, 1950, Detroit, MI; son of Lavinia Collins and Thomas Collins; married Latischa M; children: Kacey & Michael C Scott. **Educ:** Huston Tillotson Col, BS, econs/bus admin, 1972. **Career:** KHRB-AM Lockhart, disc jockey, 1970-71; John Hanson & Assocs, pres, chief exec officer, 1974-; KUT radio, announcer & sr host-producer, 1974-, Austin, disc jockey, 1974-80, producer/host, 1980-, producer Black Am radio ser, 1980-, exec producer, interim gen mgr, 1984-, admin serv officer, 2001-; Univ Tex, adj lectr, 1985-91; Thats My Song, pres, 2009-; Genesis Energy Group, dir, 2011-; KUTX Radio, on-air announcer, 2013-. **Orgs:** Pres, John Hanson & Assoc, 1974-; bd dir, Black Arts Alliance, 1985; bd dir, Camp Fire, 1985; pres, Austin Asn Black Communicators, 1986-87; bd dir, Nat Asn Black Journalists, 1987-89, adv, currently. **Home Addr:** 1301 Warrington Dr, Austin, TX 78753. **Business Addr:** Host, Producer, KUT Radio, PO Box A0704, Austin, TX 78712, **Business Phone:** (512)471-8260.

### HANSPARD, BYRON COURTENAY, SR.

Football player. **Personal:** Born Jan 23, 1976, Dallas, TX; married Yolanda Sargent. **Educ:** Tex Tech Univ, attended 1996. **Career:** Football player (retired); Atlanta Falcons, kick returner, 1997, running back, 1999; Tampa Bay Buccaneers, 2002-05. **Honors/Awds:** Big 12 Offensive Player of the Year, 1996; Doak Walker Award, 1996. **Special Achievements:** Films: 1995 Weiser Lock Copper Bowl, 1995; 1996 Builders Square Alamo Bowl, 1996. **Home Addr:** 713 Pine Hollow Dr, Desoto, TX 75115-6360, **Home Phone:** (972)223-7181.

### HAQQ, KHALIDA ISMAIL

School administrator. **Personal:** Born Jul 11, 1946, Cape Charles, VA; children: Hassana, Majeeda, Thaky, Hussain, Jaleel & Jameel. **Educ:** Rutgers Univ, NCAS, BA, psychol, black studies, 1980; Rutgers Univ, GSE, MEd, coun psychol, 1983; Nova Southeastern Univ, EdD. **Career:** Rutgers Univ, counr, 1976-80, res asst, 1981-82; Plainfield Brd Ed, sub teacher, 1980-81; Nb HS, career ed intern, 1982; Caldwell Col, coun, 1982-84, cord coun, tutor, 1984-; Rider Col, eop asst dir, counr, 1985-; Mercer Co Community Col, dir, pres, currently. **Orgs:** Irvington Parent Teachers Asn, NJ Asn Black Ed, 1980-, Asn Black Psychologists, 1982-, NJ Ed Opportunity Fund Prof Asn, 1982-, Am Asn coun & Develop, 1982-; Nat Asn Advan Colored People, 1985, Community Awareness Now, 1986-, Mercer County Black Dem Caucus, 1986; leadership adv bd Rutgers Minority Community. **Home Addr:** 31 Reading Ave, Trenton, NJ 08618. **Business Addr:** Director, President, Mercer County Community College, WWC Stud Ctr 238 JKC Rm 324, West Windsor, NJ 08550, **Business Phone:** (609)586-4800.

### HARALSON, LARRY L.

Government official, manager. **Personal:** married Irene Williams; children: Kimberly & Ashley. **Educ:** Memphis State Univ, Memphis, TN, BBA, bus admin, 1972. **Career:** Nat Bank Com, Memphis, TN, main off br mgr, 1978-79; First Tenn Bank, Memphis TN, sales & br mgr, 1979-87; Memphis City Govt, Memphis, TN, city treas & dir, 1988. **Orgs:** Chmn, Tenn Jaycees Personal Growth Sweepstakes, 1986; bd mem, Shelby County Bd Equalizations, 1990-; bd mem, White haven Community Develop Corp, currently; 100 Black Men Memphis Inc, currently. **Home Addr:** 2022 Oak Valley Rd, Memphis, TN 38116, **Home Phone:** (901)398-5323.

### HARBIN-FORTE, HON. BRENDA F.

Judge. **Personal:** Born Apr 19, 1954, Meridian, MS; daughter of Woodroc and Sophie; married Napolean; children: Ken M. **Educ:** Univ Calif, Berkeley, BA, 1976; Boalt Hall Sch Law, Univ Calif, Berkeley, CA, JD, 1979. **Career:** Legal Aid Soc Alameda Co, law clerk, 1977-78; Alameda Co Pub Defender, law clerk, 1978; Moore & Bell, law clerk, 1978-79; Harris, Alexander, Burris & Culver, assoc, 1982-84; Hastings Col Law, adj prof law, 1983-84; Thelen, Marrin, Johnson & Bridges, assoc, 1984-89, partner, 1990-92; Munic Ct State Calif, Co Alameda, Oakland-Piedmont-Emeryville Judicial Dist, judge, 1992-; CJER?s B E Witkin Judicial Col, dean, 2000-02; Juv Ct, Super Ct Calif, Co Alameda, presiding judge, currently. **Orgs:** Vpres, Calif Asn Black Lawyers, 1987-89, press's spec asst judicial, 1992-; exec bd mem & newsletter ed, Charles Houston Bar Asn, 1988, adv bd, 1993-; master, Edward J McFetridge Am Inn Ct, 1993-, chairperson, 1994-95; fel, Am Bar Found, 1993-; assoc trustee, Alta Bates Med Ctr Community Mem, 1994-; Am Bar Asn. **Home Addr:** 11040 Lochard St, Oakland, CA 94605, **Home Phone:** (415)635-2145. **Business Addr:** Presiding Judge, Superior Court of California, 400 Broadway, Oakland, CA 94605, **Business Phone:** (510)268-7373.

### HARDAWAY, ANFERNEE DEON (PENNY HARDAWAY)

Basketball executive, basketball player. **Personal:** Born Jul 18, 1971, Memphis, TN; son of Fae H; children: Ashton & Latanfernee. **Educ:** Univ Memphis, BA, prof studies, 2003. **Career:** Basketball player (retired), analyst; Orlando Magic, guard-forward, 1993-99, point guard, 1993-97, shooting guard, 1997-99; Phoenix Suns, shooting guard, 1999-2004; NY Knicks, shooting guard, 2004, small forward, 2004-06; Miami Heat, small forward, 2007-08; Nat Basketball Asn, analyst, currently; barbershop, owner; beauty salon, owner. **Orgs:** Penny Hardaway Found; nat spokesman, UNICEF. **Honors/Awds:** National High School Player of the Year, Parade Mag, 1990; Great Midwest Player of the Year, 1992, 1993; Schick Rookie Game, Most Valuable Player, 1994; NBA All-Rookie Team, 1994; NBA Rookie Challenge Most Valuable Player, 1994; NBA All-Star, 1995, 1996, 1997, 1998; All-NBA First Team, 1995, 1996; All-NBA Third Team, 1996; Gold Medal, Men's Basketball Olympics, Atlanta, 1996; Rich & Helen DeVos Community Enrichment Award, 1997. **Special Achievements:** First round, third pick, NBA Draft, 1993; Film appearance: Blue Chips, 1994; Gold medal, US Olympics Men's Basketball, 1996; featured on, "Cribs", MTV show, 2001. **Home Addr:** , Phoenix, AZ. **Business Addr:** Analyst, National Basketball Association, 645 5th Ave, New York, NY 10022, **Business Phone:** (212)407-8000.

### HARDAWAY, DR. ERNEST, II

Oral surgeon, educator, executive director. **Personal:** Born Mar 3, 1938, Col, GA; son of Ernest and Virginia L. **Educ:** Howard Univ, BS, 1957, DDS, 1966, oral surg, 1972; Johns Hopkins Univ, MPH, 1973. **Career:** Howard Univ, asst prof oral & maxillofacial surg, 1970; US Pub Health Serv, 1977-80; Bur Med Serv, dep dir, 1980; Pub Health Wash DC, from dep comnr to comnr, 1982-84; Mile Sq Health Ctr Inc, actg vpres, finance & admin affairs, 1984; Fed Employee Occup Health Prog HHS Region V, dir, 1985; Fed Employee Occup Health Prog, asst regional health adminr, 1985, dir, 1986-89, Chicago & Kans City, 1989-90; chief financial officer, coun comt entrepreneurial govt off Mgt & Budget, Wash, 1991-2001; Int Inst Bus Technol Inc, dir enterprise govt; Univ Ill, Col Bus, Comt Acad affairs, chmn, 2001-, bus adv coun. **Orgs:** Chief policy coord, Bur Med Serv, 1978; adv bd mem, Int Inst of Bus Technologies Inc, currently. **Honors/Awds:** Commendation Medal, US Pub Health Serv, 1973; Pub Health Serv Plaque, 1980; Meritorious Serv Medal; Outstanding Unit Citation Commendation Medal, US Pub Health Serv; Dentist of the Year, 1983; Distinguished Dentist of the Year, Nat Dent Asn, 1984; Fel, Am Col Dentists; Nat Dent Asn Found; Fel, Int Col Dentists; Fel, Am Asn Oral & Maxillofacial Surgeons; Fel, Acad Dentistry Int; Distinguished Service Awards. **Home Addr:** 2778 Unicorn Lane NW, Washington, DC 20015. **Business Addr:** Director of Enterprise Government, Advisory Board Member, International Institute of Business Technologies Inc, 1629 K St NW Suite 300, Washington, DC 20006, **Business Phone:** (202)463-9499.

### HARDAWAY, JERRY DAVID

Scout. **Personal:** Born Oct 23, 1951, Memphis, TN; son of Jerry D and Bennie Louise Carter; married Lisa A Mills; children: Jason D & Jheri D. **Educ:** Southern Ill Univ, BS, speech edu, 1974; Grambling State Univ, MA, sports admin, 1979. **Career:** Southern Ill Univ, co-capt, 1973; Memphis State Univ, asst football coach, 1975-77; Grambling State Univ, asst football coach, 1978-83; Univ Calif, Berkeley, asst football coach, 1984-86; Carolina Panthers, area scout, 1995; Ariz Cardinals, prof football team, area scout, 1996-. **Home Addr:** 107 Covington Sq Dr, Cary, NC 27513, **Home Phone:** (919)467-8199. **Business Addr:** Scout, Arizona Cardinals, 8701 S Hardy Dr, Phoenix, AZ 85284, **Business Phone:** (602)379-0101.

### HARDAWAY, PENNY. See HARDAWAY, ANFERNEE DEON.

### HARDAWAY, TIMOTHY DUANE, SR.

Basketball player, basketball coach, business owner. **Personal:** Born Sep 1, 1966, Chicago, IL; son of Donald; married Yolanda Adkins; children: Tim Jr & Nia. **Educ:** Univ Tex, attended 1989. **Career:** Basketball player (retired), basketball coach, owner; Golden State Warriors, guard, 1989-96; Miami Heat, guard, 1996-2001; Dallas Mavericks, guard, 2001-02; Denver Nuggets, guard, 2002; Ind Pacers, guard, 2003; Waterloo Kings, guard, 2005; Fla Pit Bulls, pres, gen mgr, co-owner & head coach, 2006; Trinity Sports & Entertrainment Group, co-founder & chief basketball opers adv, bus owner, currently; Trevor Proj, instr; YES Inst, instr; Detroit Pistons, asst coach, 2014-. **Orgs:** Co-founder, Support Group. **Business Addr:** Owner, Trinity Sports & Entertainment Group, 116 E 16th St, New York, NY 10003, **Business Phone:** (212)673-6465.

### HARDEMAN, DR. CAROLE HALL, SR.

Executive director. **Personal:** Born Muskogee, OK; daughter of Ira D Hall Sr and Rubye Hibler Hall; children: Paula Suzette. **Educ:** Fisk Univ, BA, music; Univ Okla, MA, 1975, PhD, sec educ admin, 1979; Harvard Univ, MLE Prog, 1988. **Career:** Okla State Regents Higher Ed, Regents doctoral fel, 1975-79; Univ Okla, Col Educ & Human Rels, vis prof, 1980-85; SW Ctr Human Rels Studies, exec dir, 1982-85; Adroit Publ Inc, pres; Twelve Inc staff; LeMoyne-Owen Col, vpres acad affairs, 1990-92, vpres res & develop, 1992-97; Nat Alliance Black Sch Educr, Res Round table Monographs, ed; Langston Univ, assoc dean educ, grad prof educ & behav sci, 1997-; Hall Hardeman Assocs, owner, 2006-; Ind Univ, vis prof, 2007; Univ Okla, vis prof, 2007-. **Orgs:** Founder, Okla Alliance Black Sch Educr, 1984; exec bd, Nat Alliance/Black Sch Ed, 1996-; Fel Links Inc; Jack & Jill Inc; Nat Alliance Black Sch Educr; Urban League; Nat Asn Advan Colored People; NAMPW; Am Asn Sch Adminr; Asn Supv & Curric Develop; AERA; Alpha Kappa Alpha; Young Women Christian Asn; Asn Women Math; Nat Task Force Multicultural Ed; Memphis Arts Coun Comt 100; bd dir, Planned Parenthood; bd dir, Southern Region Planned Parenthood, exec bd, 1994-; Memphis May, Memphis Literacy Coun; Okla Urban League; bd dir, Okla Philharmonic Soc; United Way Res & Convening Comt; Nat Coun Accreditation Teacher Educ; Bd Examiners Cent Okla; bd dir, Ambassadors Concert Choir; founding dir, Ctr Effective Pedag Diverse Learners; bd mem, Capitol Chamber Com; chmn, Langston Univs Ira DeVoyd Hall; Rubye Hibler Hall Endowed Lect Ser; comt mem, United Way Cent Okla, 2004-12; chair, found bd dir, Action Youth Outreach, 2010-11. **Home Addr:** 4425 Rankin Rd, Oklahoma City, OK 73120, **Home Phone:** (405)607-4229. **Business Addr:** Associate Dean of Education, Graduate Professor, Langston University, 4001 Lincoln Blvd Page Hall Suite 312B, Oklahoma City, OK 73050, **Business Phone:** (405)466-3394.

### HARDEMAN, JAMES ANTHONY

Social worker, administrator. **Personal:** Born Feb 2, 1943, Athens, GA; children: Maria & Brian. **Educ:** Howard Univ, BA, 1967; Univ Tex, Austin, BA, anthrop social welfare, 1970; Boston Col, MSW, 1973; Harvard Univ, MPA, 1974; Brandeis Univ, PhD, 1995. **Career:** Norfolk Prison Colony, dep supt classificaion & treat, 1972-77; Norfolk Prison Colony, psychiat social worker, 1972-74; Charles Drew Family Ctr, ment health admin dir, 1974-75; Dept Corrections, prison warden, 1975-78; Northeastern Correctional Ctr, supt, 1977-78; Dept Ment Health, sr social worker, 1978-79; Mayflower Coun Ctr, psychiat social worker, 1978-79; New Bedford Human Serv, clin consult, 1978-79; Commonwealth Mass, dep dir planning social serviced, 1979-83; Ex-Off Human Serv State House Boston, dep dir planning, 1981-06; Polaroid Corp, mgr corp employee asst prog, 1983-88, mgr, 1988-98; Workplace Violence Interventions & Strategies, exec dir & founder, 1998-; Family Continuity, sr clinician, 2007-; Boston, Mass, pvt pract, currently. **Orgs:** Bd dir, Boston Col, 1981-83; pres, Boston Col Grad Sch Social Work Alumni Asn, 1981-83; vpres, Nat Asn Social Work, Mass, 1982; bd mem, Mayflower Ment Health Asn, 1983-92; Cath Charities, 1983-85; Crime & Justice Found Boston, 1985; founder, S Shore Womens Ctr. **Home Addr:** 128 Bettencourt Rd, Plymouth, MA 02360-4202, **Home Phone:** (617)746-6021. **Business Addr:** Executive Director, Workplace Violence Interventions & Strategies, PO Box 4066, Plymouth, MA 02361, **Business Phone:** (508)746-0660.

### HARDEN, CEDRIC BERNARD

Football player. **Personal:** Born Oct 19, 1974, Atlanta, GA. **Educ:** Fla A&M Univ. **Career:** Football player (retired); San Diego Chargers, defensive end, 1998-99; Orange Rage, 2000-. **Honors/Awds:** Rookie of the Year, 1999. **Home Addr:** 8184 Wenonga Ct, tallahassee, FL 32311.

### HARDEN, MARVIN

Painter (artist), artist, educator. **Personal:** Born Austin, TX; son of Theodore Roosevelt and Ethel Sneed. **Educ:** Univ Calif, Los Angeles, BA, fine arts, 1959, MA, creative painting, 1963. **Career:** Univ Calif, Los Angeles, exten instr art, 1964-68; Los Angeles Harbor Col, eve div instr art, 1965-68; Ceeje Galleries, Los Angeles, 1964, 1966-67; Univ High Adult Sch, instr art, 1965-68; Minneapolis Inst Arts, 1968; Calif State Univ, Northridge, prof art, 1967-97, prof emer, 1997-; Santa Monica City Col, eve div instr art, 1968; Occidental Col, Los Angeles, 1969; Eugenia Butler Galleries, Los Angeles, 1971; Irving Blum Gallery, Los Angeles, 1972; David Stuart Galleries, Los Angeles, 1975; Calif State Col, Bakersfield, 1976-77; James Corcoran Gallery, 1978; Marvin Harden, Paintings & Drawings, 1979, 1982-83. John Simon Guggenheim Memorial Found Fel, 1983; One man shows: Whitney Mus Am Art; Irving Blum Gallery; Los Angeles Munic Art Gallery; Newport Harbor Art Mus; Eugenia Butler Galleries; James Corcoran Gallery; David Stuart Galleries; Ceeje Galleries; Rath Mus, Geneva, Switz; Armory Ctr Arts, Pasadena, CA; Brand Lib Art Ctr; Group shows: Brooklyn Mus; Chicago Mus Contemp Art; Equitable Gallery, NY; Nagoya City Mus, Japan; Tel Aviv Mus Art; Contemp Art Asn, Houston; Philadelphia Civic Ctr Mus; San Francisco Mus Art; High Mus Art; US State Dept Tour USSR; Franklin Furnace NY; San Diego F Art Gallery, 1995; Cheney Cowles Mus, Spokane, 1995; Davis & Cline Gallery, 2003. **Orgs:** Fel Nat Endowment Arts, 1972; co-founder, Los Angeles Inst Contemp Art, 1973; Grants Comt Los Angeles Inst Contemp Art, 1978; bd dir, Images & Issues Mag, 1980-83; fel John Simon Guggenheim Mem Found, 1983; Los Angeles Munic Art Gallery Asn Artist's Adv Bd, 1983-87; Nat Endowment Arts Visual Arts Fel Painting Panel, 1985; chmn, Los Angeles Cult Affairs Dept, Peer Rev Bd, Visual Arts Grants, 1990. **Honors/Awds:** Art Council Award, Univ Calif, Los Angeles, 1963; San Diego Jewish Community Center, 1966; National Endowment for the Arts, Artist's Fel, 1972; Los Angeles All City Art Festival, 1973; Awards in Visual Arts Fellowship, 1983; Distinguished Professor Award, 1984; Exceptional Meritorious Service Award, 1984, Calif State Univ, Northridge. **Special Achievements:** Elected to First Los Angeles Institute of Contemporary Art Exhibitions Committee, 1974. **Home Addr:** PO Box 1793, Cambria, CA 93428. **Business Addr:** Professor Emeritus, California State University at Northridge, 14637 Titus St, Panorama City, CA 91402, **Business Phone:** (818)677-2242.

### HARDEN, DR. ROBERT JAMES, SR.

Physician. **Personal:** Born Jul 16, 1952, Washington, GA; married Margaret Ellanor Hemp; children: Robert Jr & John Phillip. **Educ:** Univ Ill Chicago, BS, 1975; Meharry Med Col, MD, 1979. **Career:** Weiss Memorial Hosp, med intern, 1980-81; US Pub Health Serv, asst surgeon gen, 1981-83; Timberlawn Psychiat Hosp, psychiat resident, 1984-87, child & adolescent fel, 1987-89; pvt pract physicain psychiat, currently. **Orgs:** Resident mem exec coun, Tex Soc Psychiat Physicians, 1986-87. **Honors/Awds:** S01 W Ginsburg Fel Group for the Advancement of Psychiatry, 1987-89. **Home Addr:** 2312 Limestone Lane, Garland, TX 75040, **Home Phone:** (214)530-1117. **Business Addr:** Psychiatry Physician, Private Practitioner, 2222 W Spring Creek Pkwy Suite 202, Plano, TX 75023-4183, **Business Phone:** (972)985-9975.

### HARDIE, ROBERT L., JR.

Executive. **Personal:** Born Oct 22, 1941, Portsmouth, VA; son of Robert L Sr and Janie Norman; married Marianne Lowry; children: Levon, Robin & F Gary Lee. **Educ:** Hampton Univ, BS, 1963; Univ Md, Southern Ill, MBA. **Career:** AUS Security Agency Warrenton, chief elect engr, 1964-66; Bunker-Ramo Corp, Silver Spring, syst integration engr, 1966-69; Vitro Lab Automation Inc, Silver Spring, proj leader, 1969-72; Raytheon Serv Co, Hyattsville, sr systs engr, 1972-73; Systs Consult Inc, Wash, sr systs engr, 1973-75; Sci Mgt Asn Inc, prog mgr, 1975-85; Eval Res Corp Int, sr systs engr, 1985-86; Fairfax, sr electro magnetic engr; Sentel Corp, Va, chief exec officer & chmn, 1986-. **Orgs:** Inst Elec & Electronic Engrs, 1965-77; Am Soc Naval Engrs, 1974-; Navy League, 1974-87; Naval Inst; pres, Greenbelt Jaycees, 1973-74; chmn, Greenbelt Comn; Rels Adv Comt, 1974-76; Met Wash Coun Govts, 1975; vpres, Greenbelt Labor Day Festival Comt; bd dir, Camp Springs Boys & Girls Club, 1979-80; Greenbelt Rep Transp Citizen Adv Comt; Nat Asn Minority Bus, 1984. **Home Addr:** 6713 Robinia Rd, Camp Springs, MD 20748, **Home Phone:** (301)449-3630. **Business Addr:** Chairman, Chief Executive Officer,

Sentel Corp, 6713 Robinia Rd, Camp Springs, MD 20748-2719, **Business Phone:** (504)384-6120.

## HARDIN, DR. EUGENE

Educator, physician, executive director. **Personal:** Born Dec 6, 1941, Jacksonville, FL; children: Jeffrey & Gregory. **Educ:** Fla A&M Univ, BS, pharm, 1964; Univ S Fla, MD, 1977. **Career:** Walgreens, asst mgr, pharmacist, 1964-66; Va Hosp, staff pharmacist, 1966-74; King-Drew Med Ctr, Dept Emergency Med, physician specialist, 1980, asst prof, emergency med, 1980, vice chmn, 1990-93, Residence Training Prog, dir, 1990, chmn; Charles R Drew Univ Med & Sci, Dept Emergency Med, chair & assoc prof; Carson Med Group, primary care doctor. **Orgs:** Med dir, Carson Med Group, 1981; Nat Med Asn, 1984-92; Am Med Asn, 1984-; Drew Med Soc, 1985-92; Carson Chamber Com, 1985; SCLC, 1986; Martin Luther King Hosp, Joint Prac Comt, chmn, 1987; Am Col Emergency Physicians, 1990; dir, Calif Coun Emergency Med Residency, 1991; med dir, King-Drew Med Ctr, Physicians Assistance Prog. **Home Addr:** PO Box 901, Harbor City, CA 90710, **Home Phone:** (213)518-2737. **Business Addr:** Primary Care Doctor, Carson Medical Group, 357 E Carson St, Carson, CA 90745, **Business Phone:** (310)668-4519.

## HARDIN, DR. HENRY E.

Educator, businessperson, clergy. **Personal:** Born Jan 1, 1912, Ft. Motte, SC; son of Henry and Betsy Green; married Carrie; children: Isadora Wallace & Henrietta Butler. **Educ:** Benedict Col, BA, 1944, BD, 1945; NY Univ, MA, 1947, Ed D; Union Theol Sem City Col, NY, grad. **Career:** St Paul Bapt Church, pastor; Morris Col, Sumter, SC, prof, dean trustees head col, 1970, pres, 1971-73, dean & dir col financial aid prog, Centennial Celebration SC Bapt Conv, instr, chmn, currently. **Orgs:** Nat humanities fel Duke Univ, 1971; mem on staff, Colgate-Rochester Sem on Black Ch Curric, 1969; pres, Comn on Equal Opp. **Business Addr:** Chairman, Morris College, 100 W College St, Sumter, SC 29150, **Business Phone:** (803)778-1620.

## HARDIN, DR. JOHN

Educator. **Personal:** Born Sep 18, 1948, Louisville, KY; son of Albert A (deceased) and Elizabeth Hansbro (deceased); married Maxine Randle; children: Jonathan Rico. **Educ:** Bellarmine Univ, BA, hist, 1970; Fisk Univ, MA, hist, 1972; Univ Mich, PhD, hist, 1989. **Career:** Three Univ Fel, Fisk Univ, 1970-72; Univ Louisville, adj fac, 1972-84; Ky State Univ, instr, 1972-74 & 1976-78, asst prof, 1976-84, area coordr, 1978-80, vis asst prof, 1980-81, Wesleyan Col, vis fac; Eastern Wash Univ, asst prof, 1984-91, assoc prof, 1990-91; Spokane Community Col, instr, 1989; Potter Col Arts, Humanities & Social Scis, asst dean, 1997-2002; Western Ky Univ, instr, 1972-78, assoc prof, 1991-2009, asst dean, 1997-2002, asst to provost diversity enhancement, 2002-05, prof hist, 2009-, pres acad affairs; Univ Louisville, Spokane Community Col, vis fa; Books: Fifty Years of Segregation: Black Higher Education in Kentucky 1904-1954, 1997; Onward and Upward: A Centennial History of Kentucky State University 1886-1986, 1987; Six biographical entries were included in The Encyclopedia of Louisville, co-ed, 2001, Community Memories: A Glimpse of African Americans in Frankfort, Kentucky, co-ed, 2003. **Orgs:** Mem exec, community Ky Asn Teachers Hist, 1976-80 & 1991-; life mem, Phi Beta Sigma, 1980-; state dir, Phi Beta Sigma Fraternity Inc, 1981-83; club pres, Frankt Kiwanis Club, 1983-84; Ky Hist Preserv Rev Bd, 1983-84, Publ Adv Community Ky Hist Soc, 1983-84, Nat Coun Black Studies, 1984-; Ky Hist Soc, 1984-; Nat Asn Advan Colored People, 1984-; ed adv bd mem, Filson Club Hist Quart, 1989-92; Ky Oral Hist Comn, 1995-, comn chair, 2006-09; Phi Alpha Theta Hist Hon Soc; Ky African Am Heritage Comn, 2006-; bd dir, chair, African Am Mus. **Home Addr:** 2424 Tipperary, Bowling Green, KY 42104-4558, **Home Phone:** (270)781-6992. **Business Addr:** Professor of History, Western Kentucky University, 223A Cherry Hall 1906 Col Heights Blvd Suite 21086, Bowling Green, KY 42101-1086, **Business Phone:** (270)745-2233.

**HARDIN-DIGGS, MARIE D. See Obituaries Section.**

## HARDING, JOHN EDWARD

Executive, manager. **Personal:** Born May 28, 1938, Nashville, TN; son of James A and Helen E; married Delores Evon Kelly; children: Sheri Daley. **Educ:** Tenn A&I State Univ, BS, civil engineering, 1960. **Career:** AUS, dirate Civil Engr, Ohio, civil engr, 1960-67; Air Force Logistics Command, Ohio, civil engr, 1967-71; VI Dept Pub Works, St Thomas VI, comnr, 1971-75; VI Port Authority, St Thomas VI, dir engr, 1975-77, exec dir, 1975-91. **Orgs:** Am Soc Civil Engrs; Airport Operators Coun Int; Am Asn Port Authorities; Southeastern Airport Mgrs Asn; Southeastern & Caribbean Port Authorities; Am Asn Airport Execs. **Home Addr:** Estate Wintberg 1-143-57, St Thomas00801, **Home Phone:** (809)775-5395.

## HARDING, MICHAEL S.

Executive, association executive. **Personal:** Born Sep 5, 1951, St. Louis, MO; son of Derwood and Katie; children: Lindsey, Michael & Morgan. **Educ:** Cent Mo State Univ, BS, 1973; Univ N Fla, indust technol & mfg, 1982; Pepperdine Univ, MBA, 1987; Univ Mich, Bus Sch, mfg exec prog, 2000. **Career:** Executive (retired), lecturer; Anheuser-Busch Inc, prod mgt trainee, 1973-74, prod supvr, 1974-80, from asst supt to supt, 1980-85, pkg mgr, 1985-90, sr asst plant mgr, 1990-95, plant mgr, 1996-2006, vpres plant opers, 1998-2006, vpres US brewery Opers, 2001-06, packaging group, pres & chief exec officer, 2006; Precision Printing & Packaging Inc, chmn & chief exec officer; Jesse H. Jones Grad Sch Bus, Rice Univ, lectr mgt, currently. **Orgs:** Kappa Alpha Psi Fraternity, 1973-; Nat Black MBA Asn, 1991-; bd trustee, Columbia E Houston Med Ctr; bd mem, Sam Houston Area Coun Boy Scouts Am; Nat Beverage Pkg Asn; dir, Nat Safety Coun, 2001-03; dir, Anheuser-Busch Inc, 2001; dir, Anheuser-Busch Co Environ, Health & Safety Policy Comt, 2001; dir, Mathews-Dickey Boys & Girls Club, 2004. **Honors/Awds:** Black Achiever of Business & Education Award, NJ YMCA, 1988. **Special Achievements:** Completed Production Management Training Program, Anheuser-Busch Inc, 1973. **Business Addr:** Chairman, Chief Executive Officer, Precision Printing and Packaging Inc, 801 Alfred Thun Rd, Clarksville, TN 37040, **Business Phone:** (931)920-9000.

## HARDING, ROBERTA

Educator, lawyer. **Educ:** Univ San Francisco, BS, 1981; Harvard Law Sch, JD, 1986. **Career:** Univ Ky, Col Law, from asst prof to assoc prof, 1991-99, prof law, Willbert D Ham prof law, currently; Capital Case consult, 1997-; Wake Forest Univ Sch Law, vis assoc prof, 1997; Univ Ga Sch Law, vis assoc prof law, 1999. **Orgs:** Calif Bar, 1986-; Am Bar Asn, 1986-; ABA Sect Individual Rights & Responsibilities, 1991-; Am Asn Law Schls, 1991-; AALS Sect Human Rights, 2001-; bd mem, Ky Chap Am Civil Liberties Union, 2003-. **Business Addr:** Willburt D Ham Professor of Law, University of Kentucky, College of Law Bldg Rm 255 620 S Limestone, Lexington, KY 40506-0048, **Business Phone:** (859)257-1880.

## HARDISON, BETHANN

Activist, business owner, fashion consultant. **Personal:** Born Sep 30, 1942, Brooklyn, NY; married Donald McFadden; children: Kadeem Hardison. **Educ:** NY Univ Art Sch; Fashion Inst Technol. **Career:** New York garment dist, saleswoman, 1960; fashion model, 1967-81; Click, booking agt, 1980-81; activist, 1981-; Bethann Mgt Co Inc, New York, pres & creative dir, 1984-; tv exec producer, 1996; Vogue Italia, ed at large, 2010-. **Orgs:** Black Girls Coalition, co-founder, 1988-94, 2014-. **Special Achievements:** Fitting model for Willi Smith; barrier-breaking model in magazines like "Allure", "Harper's Bazaar", and "Vogue;" Versailles fashion face off, participant, 1973; promoted diversity in the fashion industry; co-executive producer of sitcoms, "Between Brothers", "Livin' Large". **Business Addr:** Bethann Management Co., Inc., 345 E 18th St, New York, NY 10003, **Business Phone:** (212)925-2153.

## HARDISON, KADEEM

Actor. **Personal:** Born Jul 24, 1965, Brooklyn, NY; son of Donald McFadden and Bethann; married Chante Moore; children: Sophia Milan. **Career:** Model, actor, currently; TV series: "A Different World", actor & dir, 1987-93; "Between Brothers", 1997; "Static Shock", 2000; "Just Shoot Me!", 2000; "Livin'Large", 2002; "Abby", 2003; "One on One", 2005; "My Name Is Earl", 2006; "Born a Gamblin Man", 2006; "Just for Kicks", 2006; "House M.D", 2006-07; "Everybody Hates Chris", 2007-09; "Living Single"; "Girlfriends", 2007; "Under One Roof", 2008; "Greek", 2009; "Cold Case", 2009; "Ghost Whisperer", 2010; "Family Guy", 2012; "Cult", 2013. TV movies: "Fire & Ice", 2001; "Red Skies", 2002; "Life Is Not a Fairytale: The Fantasia Barrino Story", 2006; "Ricochet", 2011. Films: Sch Daze, 1988; Def By Temptation, 1990; White Men Can't Jump, 1992; Panther, 1995; Vampire in Brooklyn, 1995; The Sixth Man, 1997; Drive, 1997; Blind Faith, 1998; Dancing in September, 2000; Thank Heaven, 2001; Thirty Years to Life, 2001; Instinctto Kill, 2001; Who's Your Daddy?, 2001; Thank Heaven, 2001; Dunsmore, 2001; Red Skies, 2002; Showtime, 2002; Biker Boyz, 2003; Face of Terror, 2003; Who's Your Daddy?, 2003; Love Hollywood Style, 2006; The Cassidy Kids, 2006; Bratz, 2007; The Sweep, 2008; Sister Switch, 2009; The Dark Party, dir, screenplay & co-exec producer, 2013; Some Other Time, 2013; Android Cop, 2014; Sister Switch, 2015; B C Butcher, 2016. Video recordings include: The Imagination Machines, 1992; CBS-TV Sch break Special; Word's Up; co exec producer & actor: Showtime Special; Blind Faith, 1998; Dunsmore, 2003; I Was a Network Star, 2006. **Honors/Awds:** Nat Asn Advan Colored People Image Award, 1989; Image Award for Outstanding Lead Actor, 1991; Image Award, Outstanding Lead Actor in a Comedy Series, 1992; Image Award, Outstanding Actor in a Television Movie, Mini-Series or Dramatic Special, 2007. **Special Achievements:** Has acted as director for A Different World. **Business Addr:** Actor, c/o Bethann Management Co Inc, 36 N Moore St, New York, NY 10013, **Business Phone:** (212)925-2153.

**HARDISON, RUTH INGE. See Obituaries Section.**

## HARDMAN, ARTINA TINSLEY

Government official. **Personal:** Born Jul 13, 1951. **Career:** Saunders Memorial African Methodist Episcopal Church, officer; Detroit City Councilwoman Alta Tinsley Talabi, staff; Detroit Job Corps Ctr, health care supvr; Detroit Mich House Rep, Dist 3, state rep, currently. **Orgs:** Chmn, Mich Legis Black Caucus; Coalition Against Bill Bd Advert Alcohol & Tobacco; Fedn Youth Servs; Nat Asn Advan Colored People; Empowerment Zone Community Prev Coalition. **Business Addr:** State Representative, Michigan House Representatives, Rm SO587 House Off Bldg, Lansing, MI 48909-7514, **Business Phone:** (517)373-1776.

## HARDMAN-CROMWELL, DR. REV. YOUTHA CORDELLA

Educator, association executive, administrator. **Personal:** Born Jan 10, 1941, Washington, DC; daughter of Esther Willis Jubilee; married Oliver W; children: Darnell Whitten, Dwayne Whitten, Debra Whitten & Michael. **Educ:** George Washington Univ, AA, 1960, BS, math, 1963; Troy State Univ, AL, MS, educ, 1971; Univ Va, EdS, math & educ, 1984; Howard Univ, Mdiv, 1986; Am Univ, PhD, 1992. **Career:** Mountain Home Primary Sch, ID, second grade teacher, 1964-67; Garrison Elem, DC, second grade teacher, 1967-68; Fledgling Sch AL, first grade teacher, 1968-70; Misawe Dependents Sch Japan, chmn Math dept & teacher, 1972-75; Elmore County High Sch, AL, math teacher, 1975; Stafford Sr High Sch, Va, math teacher, 1976-79; Germanna Comm Col, assoc prof math, 1979-86; Woodlawn United Methodist Church, Va, pastor, 1986-89; Howard Univ Sch Divinity, coor dr, Field Based Fel Prog, 1987-91, lectr practical theol, 1989-91; Am Univ Sch Educ, adj fac, 1989-95; Ford Fel Prog, dir, 1987-; Wesley Theol Sem, Dept Pract Ministry & Mission, dir, assoc prof, 2002-. **Orgs:** Chmn, Polit action Orange County, Nat Asn Advan Colored People, 1978-86; comm Planning, Nat Asn Advan Colored People, Dist Nine, VA, 1979-84; bd mem, Orange County Recreation Asn, 1979-80; Orange County Libr Bd, 1982-84; Benjamin Mays Fel Howard Univ Divinity Sch, 1984-86; Anderson Fel, 1985-86; Women Color Doctoral Fel, 1989-90; pres, Black Caucus, Va Conf UMC, 1986-88; consult, secy, Churches Transitional Communities, 1987-; Va Conf Comm Relig & Race, 1987-, chairperson, 1990-; vice chmn, SEJ Comm Relig & Race; bd dir, Edna Frazier Cromwell Scholar Fund Inc; bd dir, Hardman-Cromwell Ministries Inc; bd dir, U St Theatre Found; bd dir, Uplift; bd dir, Reconciling Congregations Prog; Nat Methodist Fel, 1990-91; bd dir, ethics & prof adv comt, Vis Nurses Asn; Asn Theol Field Educ; Acad Homiletics; bd mem, AMERC, 2002-; vice chmn, Asn Theol Field Educ, 2003-05; Trinity United Methodist Church, Alexandria, VA; bd dir, Appalachian Ministries Educ Resource Ctr. **Honors/Awds:** Outstanding Teacher, Dept Defense Dependent Sch, Japan, 1974; Service Award, Nat Asn Advan Colored People, Orange County, 1982, 1983; Henry C Maynard Award; Staff Award, Am Univ, 1989-90; Distinguished Alumni, Howard Univ Sch Divinity, 2001; Graduation Speaker, Am Univ, 1993; Distinguished Alumni, Howard Univ Sch Divinity, 2001. **Special Achievements:** Publ: Power and Sexual Abuse in Ministry, 1991; Living in the Intersection: Black Women Writers, 1994; Interrogation and Accusation, 1995; Change is Coming: How Shall We Respond?, 1995; Using Maps With Children, 1997; If Mary Came Again, 1999; Faith Link & Faith Now, 1999; Not In My Church, 1998; Make It Plain: Make It Portable: Effective Sermon Images, 2000; Freedom From " In Negro Preaching of the Nineteenth Century", 2000; Response, 2001; In Transforming the City, 2002; Imaging the Sermon, 2003. **Home Addr:** 2015 13th St NW, Washington, DC 20009. **Business Addr:** Director, Associate Professor, Wesley Theological Seminary, 4500 Mass Ave NW, Washington, DC 20016-5690, **Business Phone:** (202)885-8618.

## HARDMON, LADY (LEJUANA HARDMON GROOMS)

Basketball player. **Personal:** Born Sep 12, 1970; married Wendell C Grooms Jr. **Educ:** Univ Ga, attended 1992. **Career:** Basketball player (retired), coach; Deniz, Turkey, 1993-94; Bologna, Italy, 1994-95; Schio, Italy, 1996-97; DKSK, Hungary, 1995-96; Utah Starzz, guard, 1997; Sacramento Monarchs, guard, 1998-2004, scout, 2005; Arlington Christian Sch, coach.

## HARDNETT, CAROLYN JUDY

Librarian. **Personal:** Born Aug 12, 1947, Washington, DC; daughter of Freddie P and Ada West. **Educ:** Hampton Inst, Hampton, VA, 1969. **Career:** First & Merchants Nat Bank, Pentagon & Arlington, VA, 1968-70; Chicago Tribune, Wash, DC, libr asst, 1970-76, librn, 1976-85; Univ Dist Columbia, Sch Libr Sci, Lorton Col Prog: Profile a Spec Libr Newspaper, guest lectr, 1982; KY State Univ, Sch Libr Sci, News Media Libr Workshop, lectr, 1984; Baltimore Sun, Baltimore, MD, chief librn, 1985; St Petersburg Times, news researcher; BET Publ, res dir; Newseum, sr researcher, currently. **Orgs:** SLA, 1977; Secy, treas, Spec Librs Asn, News Div, 1982-83, conf planner, 1983-84, chair, 1984-85, dir, Baltimore Chap, 1986-88, bd dir, 1987-89; Nat Asn Black Journalists, 1985-; parliamentarian, Asn Black Media Workers, Baltimore Chap, 1985-86. **Honors/Awds:** Award of Merit, Spec Librs Asn, News Div, 1985; Certificate of Recognition, Black Enterprise Prof Exchange & Networking Forum, 1989; Joseph F Kwapil Memorial Award, 2007. **Special Achievements:** Reference and Information Gathering in a Special Library (Newspaper) 1983; Participated in several Regional Newspaper Workshops in 1983 and 1984. **Home Addr:** 1008 Dartmouthglen Way, Baltimore, MD 21212. **Business Addr:** Senior Researcher, Newseum, 1101 Wilson Blvd Suite 12, Arlington, VA 22209, **Business Phone:** (703)284-3544.

## HARDWICK, CLIFFORD E., III

Government official, educator. **Personal:** Born Sep 4, 1927, Savannah, GA; son of Clifford E Jr (deceased); married Beautine Williams; children: Clifford IV & Kenneth Allen (deceased). **Educ:** Savannah State Col, BS, biology, 1950; Univ Pittsburgh, MA, LittM, 1959; Howard Univ; NC Col; Atlanta Univ; Univ Ga; SC State Univ; Mott Leadership Inst; Morris Brown Col, LLD, 1975. **Career:** Beach High Sch, Biol Dept, chmn; Savannah-Chatham County Bd Educ, supvr sec educ; Effingham City Training Sch, teacher; instr, phys sci lectr, geninorganic chem, 1951-52; Springfield Terr Elem Sch, teacher, 1952-53; Alfred E Beach High Sch, Biol Dept, chmn, 1953-61; Sec Educ, supvr, 1961-68; Comm Educ Savannah, dir community educ, 1968-70; Univ Ga, Continuing Educ Prog, asst prof, dir, 1970-97, asst prof emer, 2003-, Neighborhood Continuing Educ Ctr, dir; Savannah State Univ, interim vpres stud affairs, 1999; Coastal Ga Ctr Continuing Ed ASC & SSC, asst dean; City Savannah, alderman emer. **Orgs:** Am Methodist Episcopal Church, itinerate elder, 1980; Nat Univ Ext Asn; Nat Comt Sch Educ Asn; Ga Adult Educ Coun; adv comt, Adult Basic Ed; Alpha Phi Alpha; pres, Greenbriar C Ctr, Savannah Tribune; dir, Carver State Bank; exec bd, Savannah Chap, Nat Asn Advan Colored People; Comn Christian, Ed St Philip AME Church; Savannah State Col Alumni Asn; Cardiovasc Nutrit Comn; chmn emer, vchmn, bd dir, Am Red Cross Savannah Chap; Hospice Savannah Bd; Am Heart Asn; exec comt, Coastal Area Coun Boy Scouts Am; United Way Allocations Panel; Nat Eagle Scout Asn-Boy Scouts Am; Exec Comt Savannah Olympic Support Coun; Asn Study Afro-Am Life & Hist; Community Cardiovasc Coun; bd, Carnegie Libr; Old Ga Conf African Methodist Episcopal Church; exec vpres, Martin Luther King, Jr. Observance Day. **Honors/Awds:** Man of the Year, Alpha Phi Alpha, 1962; Model Cities Recognition Award, 1971; Citizen of Day, WTOC, 1974; Cirus G Wiley Distinguished Alumnus Award, Savannah State Col, 1974; Community Service Award, Savannah Bus League, 1976; Honorary Doctor of Laws Degree, Morris Brown Col; Jefferson Award for Public Service Certificate of Excellence, 2009. **Special Achievements:** First African American elected to serve as foreman on grand jury, 1974. First African American to be appointed Supervisor of Secondary Education by the SavannahChatham County Board of Education. He was the highest ranking African American in the local public school system. The City & County honored him by proclaiming Sunday, October 24, 1982 as "Clifford Hardwick Day" in Savannah and Chatham County. First African American to be selected Chairman of a major Red Cross Chapter and Blood Center in the US. **Home Addr:** 1926 Archer St, Savannah, GA 31405-3708, **Home Phone:** (912)233-3735.

## HARDWICK, GARY C.

Movie producer, screenwriter, movie director. **Personal:** Born Detroit, MI. **Career:** US Dept Justice, Calif, atty; TV Serials: "Hangin' with Mr. Cooper", writer, 1992; "Where I Live", 1994; "Tall Hopes", 1993; "Thea", 1993; "South Central", 1994; "Me & the Boys", 1994; "Matt Waters", 1996; "In the House", 1997; "Trippin'", 1999; "Todd McFarlane's Spawn", Writer, 1999; "The Brothers", 2001; "Deliver Us from Eva", 2003; "Universal Remote", 2007; Movie producer: "Me &

the Boys", 1994; "Where I Live", 1994; "In the House", 1998; "Matt Waters", 1996; "Universal Remote", 2007; Director: "Where I Live", 1993; "Thea", 1993; "South Central", 1994; "The Brothers", 2001; "Deliver Us from Eva", 2003; "Universal Remote", 2007; Screenplay: Color of Justice; Lc Soul Unlimited; Road Dogs; Shooting Blanks; Sons of the Hammer; The Williams Family; Uncle Ray; Author: Cold Medina, 1996; Double Dead; Supreme Justice & Color Of Justice; The Executioner's Game; Citycide. **Special Achievements:** First African-American class president of Wayne State Law School. **Home Addr:** , Los Angeles, CA 00000.

## HARDWICK, DR. LINDA T.

School administrator, administrator. **Educ:** Cent State Univ; Case Western Res Univ; Univ Akron, MA, multicultural educ, PhD, educ. **Career:** Miles Standish Elem Schs, asst prin; Cleveland Munic Sch, prin; Forest Hill Parkway Acad, prin; Kent State Univ, adj prof; Richmond Heights Local Schs, supt, 2009-2012.

## HARDWICK, OMARI LATIF

Actor. **Personal:** Born Jan 9, 1974, Savannah, FL; son of Clifford IV and Joyce; married Jennifer Pfautch, Dec 20, 2012?; children: Nova. **Educ:** Univ Ga. **Career:** San Diego Chargers, National Football League, developmental squad member; security guard; substitute teacher; actor, 2000-; Bravelife (a production company), founder & pres, 2010-. Films: "Sucker Free City", 2004; "Beauty Shop", 2005; "Gridiron Gang", 2006; "The Guardian", 2006; "Next Day Air", 2007; "Miracle at St. Anna", 2008; "Next Day Air", 2009; "Kick-Ass", 2010; "The A-Team", 2010; "I Will Follow", 2010; "For Colored Girls", 2010; "Middle of Nowhere", 2012; "Sparkle", 2012; "Things Never Said", 2013; "The Last Letter", 2013; "A Christmas Blessing", 2013; "Reach Me", 2014; "Lap Dance", 2014; "Chapter & Verse". TV series: "Saved", 2006; "Dark Blue", TNT, 2009-10; "Being Mary Jane", 2013-14; "Power", 2014-. **Orgs:** Plan B. Inc. Theater Group, founding mem; Los Angeles Actor's Lounge. **Special Achievements:** Author of more than 400 poems; Omari Hardwick bluapple Poetry Corner, founder, 2011-. **Business Addr:** Bravelife Films, PO Box 393, Pasadena, CA 91102.

## HARDY, CHARLIE EDWARD

Insurance executive. **Personal:** Born Jan 19, 1941, Montgomery, AL; son of William H and Sarah W; married Lillie Pearl Curry; children: Randall Charles & Christa Valencia. **Educ:** Ala State Univ, BS, sec educ, 1962; Ind State Univ, attended 1967; Am Col, Life Underwriter Training Coun Fel, ins & financial serv, 1972; Univ Phoenix, MAOM, orgn mgt, 2005. **Career:** Brewton City Sch Syst, dir bands, 1962-66; Macon City Pub Sch, dir bands, 1966-69; MetLife, sr acct exec, 1969-2000, sr sls rep, assoc br mgr, 1988; Tuskegee Univ, consult, 2005-10; Ala State Univ, consult, 2005-10, prof, mgt & mkt, 2005-, chmn fac senate, 2010-; Great Black Speakers, motivational speaker, 2013-; John C Maxwell Leadership Team, leadership develop consult, 2015-; Fin Plng pract grp, owner. **Orgs:** Nat Assoc Life Underwriters, 1969; life mem, Million Dollar Round Table, 1971; legis liason Tuskegee Civic Asn, 1989; Fin Comt, City Tuskegee, 1997; chmn, MetLife Multicultural Career Initiative Southern Territory, 1997; pres, Tuskegee Univ, Tuskegee Area Chamber Com, 2004; chmn & bd dir, Comt, 2001; Nat Asn Advan Colored People; Tuskegee Civic Asn; 33 Degree Mason Shriner; life coach, COREMAP Syst; life mem, Alpha Phi Alpha Frat Inc; deacon Greenwood Missionary Baptist Church; life mem, Nat Asn Advan Colored People, Econ Consult Macon County Chap. **Honors/Awds:** Outstanding Alumnus Award, Ala State Univ, 1972; Alpha Man of the Year, Alpha Phi Alpha Frat Inc, 1975; Salesman of the Year, Metropolitan Life Montgomery Dist, 1979; Alpha Man of the Year, Alpha Phi Alpha Frat Tuskegee, 1984; Distinguished Alumnus Award, Ala State Univ, 1985; Inducted, Veteran for 20 Yrs Serv, Metropolitan Life & Affiliated Companies 1989. **Home Addr:** 1201 Howard Rd, PO Box 830330, Tuskegee, AL 36088-2976, **Home Phone:** (334)727-4198. **Business Addr:** Owner, Financial Planning Practice Group, PO Box 830330, Tuskegee, AL 36083, **Business Phone:** (334)727-4198.

## HARDY, DARRYL GERROD

Football player. **Personal:** Born Nov 22, 1968, Cincinnati, OH. **Educ:** Univ Tenn. **Career:** Football player (retired); Ariz Cardinals, 1992, linebacker, 1994-95; Ottawa Rough Riders, 1994; Dallas Cowboys, 1994-95, 1997; Seattle Seahawks, 1997. **Honors/Awds:** Champion, Super Bowl, XXX. **Business Addr:** Free Agent, Atlanta Falcons, 4400 Falcon Pkwy, Flowery Branch, GA 30542, **Business Phone:** (770)965-3115.

## HARDY, DR. DOROTHY C.

School administrator, founder (originator), teacher. **Personal:** Born Town Creek, AL; daughter of Odis Cal and Lorean Cal; children: Althea J Mootry (deceased). **Educ:** Ala State Univ, BS; Xavier Univ, MEd; Univ Cincinnati, EdD. **Career:** Sch administrator (retired), director counsel; Cent State Univ; Univ Cincinnati, Groups & Univ Progs, asst dean stud, 1973-77; Cincinnati Life Adj Inst, pres, 1980-83; Ohio Dept Ment Health, community div bus admin, 1983-84; Univ Ohio, prof; Southeast Mo State Univ, prof, 1984-89; Hardy Residential Rentals, 1986-96; Single Parent Prog, Cape Girardeau Area Voc Tech Sch, coordr, 1991-95; Univ N Ala, adj prof eng, 1997; Northwest-Schs Community Col, eng teacher, 1997-98; Intergenerational Writer's Guild, teacher, 1999-; Kans State Univ, asst prof & employ recuitment specialist; Univ Cincinnati, instr. **Orgs:** Human Involvement Prog, 1979; bus acct, Madisonville Job Training, 1982; consult, Archdiocese Greater Cincinnati, 1983; Prog Assoc Econ Develop; minority coordr, Issues 2 & 3 Citizens Gov Richard F Celeste, 1983-84; training dir, Mondale/Ferraro Camp, 1984; Shoals Life Adjust Inst, founder, 1999. **Honors/Awds:** Brodie Researcher Award, 1000 Plus, 1975; Outstanding Community Service, 1976; Outstanding Women, Nat Asn Adv Colored People, 1981; Cert of Merit, Pebble in the Pond, 1985; Golden Poet Award, 1986; Alumni of Distinction, Ala State Univ, 1997; Pub Exhib, Southeast Mo State Univ, 1999. **Special Achievements:** Background Player, "The Jesse Owens Story", Paramount Studio for ABC-TV, 1984; Fiction published in the Summerfield Journal Castalia Publishers & Ellipsis, Literary Journal; Poetry published in Essence Magazine, 1989, 1991-93; Southwest Missouri State Univ Museum Exhibit, Black Women: Against the Odds, 1996. **Home Addr:** 901 N Pine St, Florence, AL 35630-3342, **Home Phone:** (256)767-2487.

## HARDY, EURSLA DICKERSON

Teacher, educator. **Personal:** Born May 5, 1933, Thibodaux, LA; daughter of Albertha Lucas Dickerson and McNeil Dickerson; married McHenry Jr; children: Timothy Wayne. **Educ:** Grambling State Univ, BS, elem educ, 1955; Northwestern Univ & Grambling State Univ Libr Sci, attended 1967; Prairie View A&M Univ, MA, lib sci. **Career:** Educator (retired); Cohn Elem Sch, teacher & basketball coach, 1955; W Baton Rouge Parish, Port Allen, teacher, 1956-58; Herndon High Sch, teacher, 1958; Newton Smith Elem Sch, teacher & librn, Caddo Parish Sch Brd, Shreveport, teacher, librn, 1958-85. **Orgs:** Founder, orgnr, 1990, Sigma Rho Omega Chap, Alpha Kappa Alpha Sorority, 1990-92, anti basileus, 1990-92; bd mem, Allendale Bunch, YWCA, 1991-92; bd dir, Northwest, La YWCA, 1992-96; exec bd mem & corres secy, Shreveport Art Guild & Friends Meadows Mus Art, Centenary Col, 1994-95; bd dir, Caddo Parish Career Ctr, 1997-99; vice grandlady, Lady Auxillary St Peter Claver; steering comt mem, CWW; Vol Docent Meadows Mus Centenary Col; Mentorship Prog, Green Oaks Lab High Sch; Tutorial Prog Vol, George P Hendrix Elem Sch, Newton Smith Elem Sch; Esquirettes Social Club; pres, Green Oaks Teaching; Prof Magnet Scholar FND Inc; bd mem & vpres, CADDO Parish Sch, Dist 2; bd mem, Shreveport Art Guild, Friends Meadows Mus Ar; bd mem, Caddo Career & Technol Ctr; David Raines Community Health Ctr; charter mem, Friends Lib; pres, chmn, Theatre Performing Arts Shreveport; pres, Newton Smith First Fac. **Honors/Awds:** Bookworm Reading Club Librn Award, 1977-78; PTA Service Award, Newton Smith Elem, 1985; Recognition of Faithful Serv Educr Award, Caddo Assn Educr, 1985; Area Retreat AKA Cert Award, Hostess Chap, 1993; Outstanding Grad Basileus Award, S Cent Reg, Alpha Kappa Alpha Sorority Inc, 1994; Outstanding Grad Prog Serv Award, 1994; AKA Educ Advan Fund, 4 Stars Chap Award, 1994; Outstanding Community Serv Recog, Shreveport past Mayor Hazel Beard, 1994; Woman of the Year Award, Zeta Phi Beta, 1997; Best Dressed Award, Times Newspaper, 1998; Sigma RhoOmega Chap, Alpha Kappa Alpha Sorority Inc. **Special Achievements:** You Are in The News, Outstanding Comm Service Recognition. **Home Addr:** 106 Holcomb Dr, Shreveport, LA 71103-2026, **Home Phone:** (318)424-0540. **Business Addr:** School Board Member Dist 2, Vice President, Caddo Public School, 1961 Midway Ave, Shreveport, LA 71130-2000, **Business Phone:** (318)603-6300.

## HARDY, DR. FREEMAN

Educator, college teacher. **Personal:** Born May 22, 1942, Winona, MN; married Cozetta Hubbard; children: Tonya & Tasha. **Educ:** Ark AM & N Col, BS, 1964; Howard Univ, DDS, 1970; Georgetown Univ, MSc, 1974. **Career:** AR AM & N Col, lab instr, 1964; Howard Univ, instr, 1970-72; Howard Univ Col Dent, asst prof, 1974-77, assoc prof, 1977-83, prof, 1983-. **Orgs:** Diag & Treat Plng Rem Partial Dentures, 1976; Comparison Fluid Resin & Compression Molding Methods Processing Dimensional Changes, 1977; Consult, Howard Univ Hosp; Oral Cancer Soc, Chi Delta Mu; Omicron Kappa Upsilon; ADA; Robert T Freeman Dent Soc; NDA; Am Col Prosthodontics; AADR; IADR; Sigma Xi; DC Dent Soc; Alpha Phi Alpha. **Home Addr:** 2929 Marlow Rd, Silver Spring, MD 20904, **Home Phone:** (301)890-6663. **Business Addr:** Assistant Professor, Howard University College of Dentistry, 2041 Ga Ave, Washington, DC 20060.

## HARDY, DR. KENNETH V.

Educator. **Educ:** Pa State Univ, BS, 1973; Mich State Univ, MS, 1974; Fla State Univ, PhD, 1980; Family Ther Inst, Wash, DC, cert, 1986; Ment Res Inst, Family Ther Training Prog, 1989. **Career:** Fla State Univ, Ment Health Ctr, coun psychologist, 1977-80; Appalachee Community Ment Health Serv, ment health therapist, 1978-80; Univ Del, asst prof, 1980-83; VaPolytech & State Univ, adj prof, 1985-88; Syracuse Univ, Dept Marriage & Family Ther, prof, 1990-, Clin Training & Res, dir, 1990-95, Marriage & Family Ther Summer Inst, dir, 1993-, Dept Child & Family Studies, chmn, 1995-96; Family Ther Inst New Jerseym, vis fac, 1991-; Ackerman Inst Family, sr fac, 2000-04; Jour Marital & Family Ther, ed bd; Jour Family Psychother, ed bd; Jour Family Coun, ed bd; Jour Divorce, ed bd; Eikenberg Inst Relationships, dir; Drexel Univ, Couple & Family Ther Dept, prof, currently. **Orgs:** Prog dir, Comprehensive Youth Serv, 1974-76; dir, Southeast Delco Family Young Men Christian Asn, 1981-83; fel, dep dir, Comn Accreditation Marriage & Family Ther, Am Asn Marriage & Family Ther, 1983-84, exec dir, 1984-90, actg exec dir, 1985-88; Nat Coun Family Rels; Am Family Ther Acad; Am Asn Marriage & Family Ther Lic Bd; Ctr Res Women Wellesley Col; dir, Ctr C, Families, & Trauma. **Special Achievements:** Books: Revisioning Family Therapy: Race, Class, and Gender in Clinical Practice; Teens Who Hurt: Clinical Interventions for Breaking the Cycle of Violence. **Business Addr:** Professor, Drexel University, 245 N 15th St 1601 Cherry St Rm 710, Philadelphia, PA 19102, **Business Phone:** (267)359-5521.

## HARDY, KEVIN LAMONT

Football player, business owner, football coach. **Personal:** Born Jul 24, 1973, Evansville, IN; married Terrie; children: 2. **Educ:** Univ Ill, grad. **Career:** Football player (retired), coach; Jacksonville Jaguars, outside linebacker & right linebacker & left linebacker, 1996-2001; Dallas Cowboys, left linebacker, 2002; Cincinnati Bengals, middle linebacker, 2003-05; South Beach club venture, owner, currently; Southern Ill Univ, head coach, currently. **Orgs:** Omega Psi Phi Fraternity Inc. **Honors/Awds:** All-American, 1995; Dick Butkus Award, 1995; All-Pro, 1999; Pro Bowl, 1999. **Special Achievements:** Films: 1996 NFL Draft, 1996; 1999 AFC Championship Game, 2000. **Home Addr:** , Jacksonville, FL. **Business Addr:** Head Coach, Southern Illinois University, 1263 Lincoln Dr, Carbondale, IL 62901, **Business Phone:** (618)453-2121.

## HARDY, MICHAEL LEANDER

Marketing executive, association executive. **Personal:** Born Feb 21, 1945, Petersburg, VA; married Jacqueline; children: Sheila Jacqueline & Michelle Lorraine. **Educ:** Columbia Univ NY, BS, 1966; Rollins Col Winter Park, MCS, 1973. **Career:** Martin-Marietta Corp, Orlando Div, assoc engr, 1966-67, prog plng analyst, 1967-71; Carborundum Co, mgt maint servs & repairs pangborn, Pangborn Div, mgr mkt plng & control, 1973-79. **Orgs:** Bd mem, pres, Bethel Corp, 1973; Citizens Adv Com Wash Co Bd Educ; bd mem, Big Bros Wash Co; past pres, Orange Co Fla Br; Nat Advan Asn Colored People, 1971-73. **Home Addr:** 782 Southland Pass, Stone Mountain, GA 30087-4918. **Business Addr:** President, Principal Officer, Bethel Corp, 356 Henry Ave, Hagerstown, MD 21740-3879, **Business Phone:** (301)733-3350.

## HARDY, TIMOTHY W.

Lawyer, business owner. **Personal:** Born Feb 7, 1952, Shreveport, LA; married Stacia Saizon; children: Nicole Saizon & Amanda Victoria. **Educ:** Southern Univ, BS, chem, 1978; Southern Univ Law Ctr, JD, 1981. **Career:** Pennzoil Res, 1977; Allied Chem, lab techinican, 1978; La Dept Justice, asst atty gen, lands & natural resources div, environ sect, 1982-88; La Dept Environ Qual, asst secy, Off Solid & Hazardous Waste, 1988-92; Gov Environ Affairs, exec asst, 1990-92; Gov Edwin Edwards' Dept Environ Qual Transition Team, chmn, 1991; La Dept Justice, dir pub protection div, 1992-94; Baton Rouge law firm, atty, 1994-; Gov Mike Foster's Environ Qual Transition Team, staff, 1995-96; Shaw Group, exec vpres, 2003; Gov Kathleen Blancos Dept Natural Resources Transition Team, staff, 2004; Lemle & Kelleher, partner & chmn mgt comt, 2004-, chmn, 2008; Transition Adv Coun Gov Bobby Jindal, vice chair environ group, 2007; Shaw E&I, exec vpres; Southern Univ Law Ctr teaching Environ Law, adj prof, currently; Roedel, Parsons, Koch, Blache, Balhoff & McCollister Law Firm, atty & partner, currently. **Orgs:** La Leadership Class, Coun Better La, 1994; La State Bar Asn; Am Heart Asn; pres, E Baton Rouge Div; bd trustee & bd mem, Nature Conservancy La; Baton Rouge C C; Mid City Redevelop Alliance; Nat Orgn Prof Advan Black Chemists Chem Engrs; Phi Alpha Delta Law Fraternity; bd mem, C Charter Sch; Exec leadership Coun; Sigma Pi Phi Fraternity; US Mid & Eastern Dist Courts; Nat Orgn Prof Advan Black Chemists & Chem Engrs; bd Supvr, La Community & Tech Col Syst Found; bd mem, Am Gateway Bank; La Asn Bus & Indust; Rotary Club Baton Rouge; Exec Leadership Coun; bd mem, Friends La Pub Broadcasting; bd mem, La Resource Ctr Educr; bd mem, Pub Affairs Res Coun; Omega Psi Phi Fraternity Inc; Baton Rouge Bar Asn; Nat Bar Asn. **Honors/Awds:** Louisiana Super Lawyers, 2007; Distinguished Alumnus Award, Southern Univ, Dept Chem, 2008; Distinguished Alumnus Award, Southern Univ Law Ctr, 2009. **Special Achievements:** First African-American to elected as Chairman of the Lemle & Kelleher LLP firm's 100-year history. **Home Addr:** 3070 Yorktown Dr, Baton Rouge, LA 70808, **Home Phone:** (225)924-9945. **Business Addr:** Partner, Chairman, Lemle & Kelleher LLP, 301 Main St Suite 1100, Baton Rouge, LA 70825, **Business Phone:** (225)387-5068.

## HARDY-HILL, EDNA MAE

Psychologist, administrator. **Personal:** Born Feb 14, 1943, Thomasville, GA; daughter of Leroy and Hagar Harris; married Davis Vincent; children: Davis Vincent Jr (deceased) & Michael A. **Educ:** Bennett Col, AB, 1965; Howard Univ, MS, 1968. **Career:** Psychologist (retired); Nat Inst Ment Health, res psychologist, 1967-74, health scientist adminr, 1974-83, Behav & Appl Rev Br, Res Develop & Spec Proj Rev Br, chief, 1983-98; Breast Cancer Res Prog, peer reviewer, 2000. **Orgs:** Treas, Asn Black Psychologists, 1983 Nat Conv; Peoples Congregational Church; Bennett Coll Alumnea Asn; Lotts Read Bk Club, 1999-2001; Bethany Congregational Church, bd dir, 2002-. **Honors/Awds:** Honor soc, Beta Kappa Chi; Pi Gamma Mu; Psi Chi; Howard Univ fel, 1966-67; Bennett Col Scholar, 1961-65; Outstanding Work Performance, Nat Inst Ment Health, 1982, 1985, 1987 & 1989-98, Director Award for Significant Achievement, Nat Inst Ment Health, 1989; Special Achievement Award, Nat Inst Ment Health, 1997; Award for Outstanding Accomplishments in Chosen Profession, Bennett Col, 1993; Staff Recognition Award, Nat Inst Ment Health, 1998. **Home Addr:** 64 Pebble Pt Dr, Thomasville, GA 31792-8669, **Home Phone:** (229)226-6288.

## HARDY-WOOLRIDGE, KAREN E.

Manager, public speaker, consultant. **Personal:** Born Oct 29, 1951, Chicopee, MA; daughter of Humphrey Christopher and Janet Elizabeth Chaffin Lee; married Victor; children: James, Matoaca, Kara Jean & Kendra. **Educ:** Springfield Tech Community Col, Springfield, MA, AS, 1971; Univ NC, Elizabeth City, NC, BS, bus admin, 1974; Western New Eng Col, attended 1978. **Career:** Martin Ins Agency, Springfield, Mass, ins sales, 1974-81; Regency Cove Hotel, Barbados, Wi, gen man, 1981-83; Mass Mutual Life Ins Co, Springfield, Mass, sales div consult, recruiting mgr, 1983, assoc dir, IFM Sales, asst supt disability income sales support, dist mgr, staff plans, 1991; Musical Ministry & Motivational speaker youth & women groups, currently. **Orgs:** Partic, Pro-Motion, 1989, 1991-; parent adv, SDA Community Youth, Young Adult Choir, 1989-; prof develop bd vchair, Mass Mutual Life Ins, 1989-90, prof develop bd chairperson, 1990; vol, SDA Community Servs, 1990-; women's div coordr, Seventh-day Adventist, 1991; mentor, I Have a Dream Prog. **Home Addr:** 146 Longhill St, Springfield, MA 01108-1438.

## HARE, DR. JULIA

Educational psychologist, executive director. **Personal:** Born Nov 7, 1939, Tulsa, OK; married Nathan. **Educ:** Langston Univ, OK, BA, music, 1960; Roosevelt Univ, Chicago, MA, music educ, 1962; Calif Coast Univ, PhD, educ, 1987. **Career:** Teacher, executive director, actress; Flims: Mr. Billion, 1977; State of the Black Union: Jamestown-Memorable Moments, 2007; State of the Black Union: Jamestown-The Next 400 Years, 2007; Oakland Mus, dir educ prog; Fed Housing Prog, pub rels dir, 1971-73; Black Think Tank, co-founder, 1979-, nat exec dir, currently; Chicago, Ill, elem sch teacher. **Orgs:** Asn Black Social Workers; Asn African Historians; Int Black Writers & Artists. **Special Achievements:** Named as one of the ten most influential African Americans in the San Francisco Bay Area. **Business Addr:** National Executive Director, Co-Founder, The Black Think Tank, 1801 Bush St Suite 118, San Francisco, CA 94109, **Business Phone:** (415)929-0204.

## HARE, JULIA REED

Journalist, administrator. **Personal:** Born Nov 7, 1942, Tulsa, OK; married Nathan. **Educ:** Langston Univ, BA, music, 1964; Roosevelt Univ Chicago, MA, music educ, 1966; Calif Coast Univ, Santa Ana, PhD, educ; DC Teachers Col, attended 1967. **Career:** Chicago Pub Sch, teacher, 1966; DC Teachers Col, supvr stud teachers, 1967-68; Nat Comt Against Discrimination Housing, pub rels dir, 1969-72; Univ San Francisco, instr, 1969-70; Golden W Broadcasters KSFO radio, dir comm affairs, 1973-; Black Think Tank, exec dir, currently; Oakland Mus, dir educ progs; ABC tv, anchor. **Orgs:** Northern Calif Broadcasters Asn, 1973-; hon bd, Sickle Cell Anemia Develop Res Found, 1976-; bd Afro-Am Cult & Hist Soc, 1978-; bd dir, Bay Area Black United Fund, 1979-; pub rels dir, Local Fed Housing Prog. **Honors/Awds:** Outstanding Educator of the Year, Jr Chamber Com & World Bk Encycl coord with Am Univ; World Book Ency & Am Univ, 1967; Abe Lincoln Award Broadcaster of the Year, 1975; Cert of Appreciation Sickle Cell Anemia Res & Educ, 1976; Meritorious Community Service Award, 1979; Special Service Award, Calif Soc Cert Pub Accountants, 1980; Carter G.Woodson Education Award, The Association of Black Social Workers' Harambee Award; Scholar of the Year Award, Asn African Historians; Lifetime Achievement Award, Int Black Writers & Artists Union; Hall of Fame. **Special Achievements:** The Hare Plan to Overhaul the Public Schools and Educate Every Black Man, Woman and Child, 1991; publ, Black Male/Female Relationships, 1979; co-author: The Endangered Black Family; Bringing the Black Boy to Manhood: The Passage; The Miseducation of The Black Child; Crisis in Black Sexual Politics; How to Find and Keep a BMW; One of the ten most influential African Americans in the San Francisco Bay Area, National Association for Equal Opportunity in Higher Education. **Home Addr:** 1895 Jackson St Apt 606, San Francisco, CA 94109-2881, **Home Phone:** (415)474-1707. **Business Addr:** Executive Director, Black Think Tank, 1801 Bush St Suite 127, San Francisco, CA 94109-5273, **Business Phone:** (415)474-4701.

## HARE, DR. NATHAN

Sociologist, psychologist. **Personal:** Born Apr 9, 1933, Slick, OK; son of Tishia Lee Davis Hare Farmer and Seddie Henry Hare; married Julia Reed. **Educ:** Langston Univ, AB, sociol, 1954; Univ Chicago, MA, 1957, PhD, sociol, 1961; Calif Sch Prof Psychol, PhD, clin psychol, 1975. **Career:** Va State Univ, instr, 1957-58; San Francisco State Col Dept Black Studies, instr, 1957-58 & 1961-63, chmn, coordr black studies, 1968-69; Black Scholar Black World Found, founding pub; Howard Univ, instr & asst prof sociol, 1961-67; Black Scholar, publ, 1969-75; pvt pract & clin psychol, 1977-; Black Male-female Relationships, ed, 1979-82; Black Think Tank, co-founder, chmn bd, 1979-, chief exec officer, currently; pvt pract, clin psychologist, 1979-; San Francisco Stat, lectr part-time, 1984-88. **Orgs:** No Am Zone Second World Black & African Festival Arts & Cult; Black Speakers Club. **Honors/Awds:** Co-editor Contemporary Black Thought, 1973; co-editor Pan-Africanism, 1974; Author: The Black Anglo Saxons, The Endangered Black Family, 1984, Bringing the Black Boy to Manhood, 1985 & various articles in mag & journals; Distinguished Alumni Award Langston Univ, 1975; presidential citation Natl Asn Blacks in Higher Education, 1981; Natl Award Natl Council for Black Studies, 1983; Crisis in Black Sexual Politics, 1989; Fire on Mount Zion, 1990; The Hare Plan: To Educated Every Black Man, Woman and Child, 1991; shared Marcus and Amy Garvey Award, Institute of Pan African Studies, 1990; United Negro Col Fund Distinguished Scholar at Large, 1990; Educator of the Year, Univ Islam, 1992; Joseph Hines Award, Asn Black Sociologists, 2002; Scholar of the Year Award, Asn African Historians; Lifetime Achievement Award, Nat Black Col Alumni Hall Fame; National Council for Black Studies National Award; Joseph Himes Award, Asn Black Sociologists. **Special Achievements:** First person hired to coordinate a black studies program in the United States, 1968. **Home Phone:** (415)929-0204. **Business Addr:** Chief Executive Officer, Co-Founder, The Black Think Tank, 18001 Bush St Suite 118, San Francisco, CA 94109-5273, **Business Phone:** (415)474-1707.

## HARGRAVE, CHARLES WILLIAM

Scientist. **Personal:** Born May 12, 1929, Dandridge, TN; son of Electa Tulip Snapp and Walter Clarence; married Iona Lear Taylor. **Educ:** Johnson C Smith Univ, BS, 1949; Wash Univ St Louis, MA, 1952. **Career:** Scientist (retired); Dept Navy, physicist 1954-55; US Atomic Energy Comn, sci analyst, 1955-62; Nat Aeronaut & Space Admin, tech info, 1962-89. **Orgs:** Adv neighborhood comnr DC Govt, 1979-84, 1991-96; pres, First Dist Police Adv Coun, 1985-88; Mayor's Adv Comm Budget & Resources; SW Neighborhood Assembly; Omega Psi Phi. **Honors/Awds:** Award of Merit, Johnson C Smith Univ Alumni Asn, 1979; Spaceship Earth NASA 1982, 1988; Alumni Award, Univ Wash, 1983. **Home Addr:** 600 3rd St SW, Washington, DC 20024-3102, **Home Phone:** (202)554-8284.

## HARGRAVE, THOMAS BURKHARDT, JR.

Association executive, chief executive officer, executive director. **Personal:** Born Oct 5, 1926, Washington, GA; married Meredith Higgins; children: Kenneth & Anna. **Educ:** Knoxville Col, AB, 1951; Springfield Col, grad study. **Career:** James Welden Johnson Br YMCA FL, exec dir, 1960-64; Pasadena YMCA, asst gen exec, 1964-68, exec dir; YMCA Urban Action LA, assoc gen exec, 1968-71; YMCA, Portsmouth, VA, exec dir; YMCA Univ, asst dir; YMCA col, asst dir; YMCA Metro Wash, Prog Planning & Develop, assoc gen dir, pres, chief exec officer, 1973-92, pres emer, currently. **Orgs:** Rotary Club Int; adv bd, Studio Theatre; adv comt, Tom Sawyer Training Sch; YMCA. **Honors/Awds:** Certificate of Civic Rights, FL NAACP, 1964. **Special Achievements:** Author "Private Differences-General Good, A History of the YMCA of Metropolitan Washington", 1985; First African American to head an Urban Group YMCA. **Business Addr:** President Emeritus, YMCA Metro Washington, 1112 16th St NW 7th Fl, Washington, DC 20036, **Business Phone:** (202)232-6700.

## HARGRAVES, COL. WILLIAM FREDERICK, II

Educator, military pilot. **Personal:** Born Aug 18, 1932, Cincinnati, OH; son of William F and Annie Leona Thomas (deceased); married Maurine Collins; children: William III, Jock & Charles. **Educ:** Miami Univ, BS, educ, 1954, MS, educ, 1961. **Career:** USAF, 1955, res physicist, 1961-65, aircraft comdr, 1965-70, Weapons Res Ctr, air liaison officer res scientist, 1970-71, 22nd Mil Airlift Command, instr pilot; 1st Army Repub Vietnam Div, liaison officer; Miami Univ, asst prof aerospace sci, 1971-74; Wright Patterson AFB, chief flight deck develop, 1978-82; Pentagon, Wash, DC, dep div chief; Cent State Univ, Dept Mathematics, asst prof, 1983, asst dean arts & sci. **Orgs:** Vice comdr, Veteran Foreign Wars, 1986; founder, Alpha Phi Alpha, Miami Univ Chap; leader/founder, Pilgrim Baptist Men's Chorus; Phi Beta Kappa; Omicron Delta Kappa; Kappa Delta Pi; Pi Mu Epsilon; Sigma Pi Sigma, Phi Mu Alpha; charter mem, Phi Kappa Phi; Air Force ROTC. **Honors/Awds:** Black Hall of Fame in Covington, 1992. **Special Achievements:** First Rhodes Scholar Candidate, 1950; comput sci adv, N Cent Eval Team & US Dept Educ Wash, DC; "Magnetic Susceptability of Manganese Compounds", "The Effect of Shock Waves on various Plastic Nose Cone Materials"; Length, Mass, Time, & Motion in One Dimension, software prog, 1986; First African American from Covington to become both a US Air Force pilot. **Home Addr:** 123 W Walnut St, Oxford, OH 45056-1721, **Home Phone:** (513)523-8177. **Business Addr:** Assistant Professor, Assistant Dean, Central State University, 1400 Brush Row Rd, Wilberforce, OH 45384, **Business Phone:** (937)376-6011.

## HARGRETT, JAMES T., JR. (JIM HARGRETT)

State government official, executive. **Personal:** Born Jul 31, 1942, West Tampa, FL; married Berlyn Chatard; children: Crystal Marie & James T III. **Educ:** Morehouse Col, BA, 1964; Atlanta Univ, MBA, 1965. **Career:** US Comptroller Currency, nat bank examr, 1965-67; Aetna Life Ins Co, ins underwriter, 1967-68; Leadership Develop Prog Tampa Urban League, dir, 1968-69; Community Fed Sav & Loan Asn, Tampa, FL, mgr, exec vpres & chief exec officer, 1969-82; Fla State Rep, Dist 63, 1982-92; Fla State, sen, 1992; Bay Area Concessions Inc, chmn & pres, currently; Tampa Hillsborough County Expressway Authority, bd chmn, currently. **Orgs:** Treas, Urban League, 1971-75; cit adv comn, Hillsborough County Sch Bd, 1974-; Dem Exec Comt, 1974; Greater Tampa Chamber Com; bd dir, United Way, Tampa; Fla Housing Adv Comt; Fla Sheriffs Asn; Tampa Bay Area Comt Foreign Rels; Fla Coun Crime & Delinquincy; Gulf Coast Epilepsy Found; Ybor City Chamber Com; Tampa Housing Authority; Fla Trust Hist Preserv. **Home Addr:** 2002 E Emma St, Tampa, FL 33610. **Business Addr:** Chairman, Tampa-Hillsborough County Expressway Authority, 1104 E Twiggs St Suite 300, Tampa, FL 33602, **Business Phone:** (813)396-3908.

## HARGROVE, ELIZABETH RILEY. See HARGROVE, LIZ RILEY.

## HARGROVE, LIZ RILEY (ELIZABETH RILEY HARGROVE)

Executive director. **Personal:** married Marc; children: 2. **Educ:** NC State Univ, BA, commun, 1987, MEd, counr educ, 1995. **Career:** NC State Univ, asst dir undergrad admis, 1987-93; Duke Univ, Fuqua Sch Bus, asst dir admis, 1993-94, assoc dir admis, 1994-98, dir admis, 1998-2003, asst dean & dir admis, 2003-08, assoc dean admis, 2008-. **Orgs:** Exec MBA Coun; Duke Univ Alumni Network; Raleigh Alumnae Chap; Delta Sigma Theta Sorority. **Business Addr:** Associate Dean for Admissions, Duke University, 100 Fuqua Dr, Durham, NC 27708-0120, **Business Phone:** (919)660-7705.

## HARGROVE, DR. TRENT

Lawyer, government official. **Personal:** Born Aug 25, 1955, Harrisburg, PA; son of Odessa Daniels and Willie Clarence; married Eugenia Russell; children: Channing Leah & Tyler Trent. **Educ:** Bucknell Univ, Lewisburg, PA, BA, polit sci & psychol, 1977; Dickinson Law Sch, Carlisle, PA, JD, 1980. **Career:** Off Atty Gen, Harrisburg PA, dep atty, 1979-81; Pa Housing Finance Agency, Harrisburg Pa, asst coun, 1981-86; McNees Wallace & Nurick, assoc, 1987-90; Pa Dept Transp, asst coun charge utilities, 1990-92; Pa Off Atty Gen, chief dep atty gen, Civil Rights Enforcement, 1992-2003; Pa Dept Gen Serv, gen coun, chief coun, 2003-07; Pa Dept, chief diversity officer, 2007-2012. **Orgs:** Harrisburg Jaycees, 1984-; Dauphin County Bar Asn, 1986-; Omega Psi Phi Fraternity, 1986-; pres, Harrisburg Black Attys, 1986-87; bd mem, Vol Ctr, 1986-; external vpres, Harrisburg Jaycees, 1986-87; exec comt, Nat Asn Advan Colored People, 1987-; chmn mgt comn, Vol Ctr, 1988-; bd mem, Harrisburg Sewer & Water Authority, 1988-; chmn, Harrisburg Authority, 1991-2004; chair, Harrisburg City Sch Dist Bd Control, 2000-04; PBA Minority Bar Comt; PBA Govt Lawyers Comt. **Home Addr:** 3018 Green St, Harrisburg, PA 17110-1234, **Home Phone:** (717)238-6301.

## HARKEY, MICHAEL ANTHONY (MIKE HARKEY)

Baseball player. **Personal:** Born Oct 25, 1966, San Diego, CA; married Nikki; children: Michael Jr, Cory & Miani. **Career:** Baseball player (retired), baseball coach; Chicago Cubs, pitcher, 1988, 1990-93; Colo Rockies, 1994; Oakland Athletics, 1995; Calif Angels, 1995; Los Angeles Dodgers, 1997; San Diego Padres, pitching coach, 2000-05; Rancho Cucamonga Quakes, pitching coach, 2000; Ft Wayne Wizards, pitching coach, 2001, 2003; Lake Elsinore Storm, pitching coach, 2002, 2004; Mobile BayBears, pitching coach, 2005; Fla Marlins, bullpen coach, 2006; Iowa Cubs, pitching coach, 2007; New York Yankees, bullpen coach, 2008-13; Ariz Diamondbacks, pitching coach, 2013-15. **Orgs:** Minor League Baseball Alumni Asn. **Home Addr:** 23930 Strange Creek Dr, Diamond Bar, CA 91765. **Business Addr:** Pitching Coach, Arizona Diamondbacks, Chase Field 401 E Jefferson St, Phoenix, AZ 85004, **Business Phone:** (602)462-6500.

## HARKINS-CARTER, DR. ROSEMARY KNIGHTON

Educator, school administrator. **Personal:** Born Aug 5, 1938, Amarillo, TX; daughter of Herbert Curtis and Pauline Cloteal; married Elmer Bud Carter; married Clarence. **Educ:** Amarillo Jr Col, AA, 1957; W Tex State Univ, BS, 1964; Univ Okla, MS, 1971; Univ Okla, Health Sci Ctr, PhD, 1972; Cent State Univ, BS, 1976. **Career:** Veterans Admin Med Ctr, hemat supvr, 1968-70; Advan Studies Ford Found, fel, 1971-72; Univ Okla Col Allied Health, asst prof, 1972-77; Sch Allied Health Prof Univ Okla, dir & assoc prof, 1977-81; Univ Okla Col Allied Health, assoc dean & prof, 1981-88; Howard Univ, Col Allied Health Sci, dean; Langston Univ, Dept Biol, chairperson, fac emer, currently. **Orgs:** Consult, Petrol Training & Tech Serv Workman Inc, 1978; bd dir, Nat Adv Comm Accreditation & Inst Eligibility, 1981-83; nat secy bd dir, Am Soc Allied Health Prof, 1982-84; chmn bd dir, Okla Minority Bus Develop Ctr US Dept Com, 1982-88; consult bd regents, Fla St Univ Syst, 1983; consult, Am Phys Ther Asn, 1983; vice chairperson bd trustee, Okla Inst Child Advocacy, 1983-87; exec coun, Nat Inst Disability & Rehab, US Dept Educ; fel Am Soc Allied Health Prof Wash, 1984. **Home Addr:** 2501 Kingsway Rd, Ft Washington, MD 20744-3324, **Home Phone:** (301)248-2587. **Business Addr:** Faculty Emeritus, Langston University, PO Box 1500, Langston, OK 73050, **Business Phone:** (405)466-2999.

## HARKLESS-WEBB, MILDRED

Educator. **Personal:** Born Aug 17, 1935, Cedar Lake, TX; daughter of Cody Powell and Mayfield; married James E Webb. **Educ:** Prairie View A&M Univ, BS, 1957; San Francisco State Univ, MA, 1976. **Career:** Educator (retired), Webbs Pest Control, vpres, off mgr, 1979-; Everett Mid Sch, teacher, Currently. **Orgs:** Sponsor Scholar Soc, 1968-; NEA; CTA; ISBE; WBEA; CBEA; ABE; 1970-; Nat Asn Advan Colored People1974-; staff rep, ALC SFCTA, 1976-; facilitator, NBEA, 1976-; sponsor Black Stud Club 1983-; Commonwealth Club Calif, 1988-; co-chair, Self-Esteem/Stud Performance Comt; San Francisco Bus Chamber Com Leadership Class, presenter, 1988; Red Cross; Am Cancer Soc; Nat Asn Prof Women. **Home Addr:** 35 Camellia Pl, Oakland, CA 94602, **Home Phone:** (510)531-4815. **Business Addr:** Member, National Association of Professional Women, 1325 Franklin Ave Suite 160, Garden City, NY 11530, **Business Phone:** (516)877-5500.

## HARKNESS, JERRY B.

Basketball player, business owner, association executive. **Personal:** Born May 7, 1940, New York, NY; son of Lucille and Lindsay; married Sarah; children: Jerald, Julie Lyn & Brandon. **Educ:** Loyola Univ, Chicago, IL, BS, sociol, 1963. **Career:** NY Knicks, Nat Basketball League, 1963-64; Am Basketball Asn, Ind Pacers, 1967-69; United Way, campaign assoc, 1969-95; WTHR TV-13, weekend sports caster, 1969-81; Morning sportIndiana Pacers Franchises anchor WTLC Radio; Ind Pacers, Indianapolis, Ind, basketball analyst, 1983; United Way Cent Ind, dir community affairs, beginning, 1985; Sports Channel, Chicago, Ill, basketball analyst, 1988-; Athlete's Foot, co-owner, mgr, currently; Anderson's athletic shoe store, owner, currently; Ind Human Rights Comn; Southern Christian Leadership Conf. **Orgs:** Exec bd dir, Hundred Blackmen Indianapolis, 1986-, exec dir, 1997; bd dirs, Police Athletic League, Indianapolis, 1986-; Coun Black Execs, 1987-; Eastern Star Baptist Church; exec dir, Indianapolis Chap 100 Black Men. **Honors/Awds:** Silver Anniversary Basketball Team, Nat Col Athletic Asn, 1988; 20 Year Volunteer Award, Indiana Black Expo, 1990; Two time All-American; Boy Scouts This is your Life Award; Inducted, Chicagoland Sports Hall of Fame; Inducted, College Basketball Hall of Fame, 2013; Muhammad Ali Athlete Award, 2013. **Special Achievements:** First African-American salesman for Quaker Oats; First African-American fundraiser in United Way of Indianapolis; Indianapolis first African-American sportscaster. **Home Addr:** 8340 Misty Dr, Indianapolis, IN 46236, **Home Phone:** (317)823-9688. **Business Addr:** Co-owner, Manager, Athlete's Foot, 49 W Maryland St Suite C5, Indianapolis, IN 46204-3522, **Business Phone:** (317)226-9596.

## HARLAN, CARMEN

Television journalist. **Personal:** Born Nov 4, 1953, Detroit, MI; married Andrew Henry Jr. **Educ:** Univ Mich. **Career:** WDIV-TV, Channel 4, Detroit, Mich, news anchor, 1978-, sr anchor, currently. **Honors/Awds:** Feted by Nat Coalition 100 Black Women, Detroit, MI; Detroit's top news anchor, Ladies Home Jour Mag, 1991. **Special Achievements:** Carried the Olympic Torch in the summer of 1996 and repeated the honor as the torch again passed through Detroit en route to the 2002 Winter Olympics; one of the most recognizable faces in the Motor City. **Business Addr:** Senior Anchor, WDIV-TV Channel 4, 550 W Lafayette blvd, Detroit, MI 48226-3140, **Business Phone:** (313)222-0444.

## HARLAN, EMERY KING

Lawyer. **Personal:** Born Jan 18, 1965, Gary, IN; son of Wilbert and Bertha. **Educ:** Siena Heights Col, BA, bus admin, 1986; Univ Wisc Law Sch, JD, 1989. **Career:** US Ct Appeals Sixth Circuit, Hon George Edwards, law clerk; US Dist Ct, Northern Dist, Ill, practr; US Ct Appeals Sixth & Seventh Circuits, practr; Ross & Hardies, labor & employ, atty; Gonzalez Saggio & Harlan LLP, chmn, atty & partner, 1994-2016; MWH Law Group LLP, partner, 2016-. **Orgs:** Vice chmn, gen pract sec, Corp Coun Comm, Am Bar Asn; Chicago Bar Asn; Minority Coun Prog Steering Comt; Dem Leadership 21st Century, Steering Comm; co-founder & bd chair, Nat Asn Minority & Women Owned Law Firms; bd mem, Milwaukee Health Serv; bd mem, Urban Day Sch; Alpha Phi Alpha Fraternity; vice chair, State Wis Gaming Bd; Blood Ctr Wis; Sharon Lynne Wilson Ctr Arts; govs coun, Workforce Investment. **Honors/Awds:** Ray & Ethel Brown fel, Univ Wisc Law Sch, 1988; Named Wisconsin Super Lawyer; Community Service Award, Nat Asn Advan Colored People, 2011; Outstanding Member of the Year, Wis Asn African-Am Lawyers, 2012. **Home Addr:** 5337 S Cornell Suite 1, Chicago, IL 60615, **Home Phone:** (312)643-6887. **Business Addr:** Partner, MWH Law Group LLP, 735 N Water St Suite 610, Milwaukee, WI 53202, **Business Phone:** (414)436-0353.

## HARLESTON, BRIGADIER GEN. ROBERT ALONZO

Educator. **Personal:** Born Jan 28, 1936, Hempstead, NY; son of Henry M Sr and Anna Elizabeth Tobin; married Sheila C; children: Robert, Bernice & Paul. **Educ:** Howard Univ, Wash, DC, BA, 1958; Mich State Univ, E Lansing, MS, 1965; Georgetown Univ Law Ctr, Wash, DC, JD, 1984. **Career:** Professor (retired); Univ Md, Eastern Shore, Md, Dept Criminal Justice, chmn & assoc prof. **Orgs:** Omega Psi Phi, 1953-; bd dir, Eastern Shore Red Cross, 1990-93, 2002-; bd dir, Delmarva Boy Scouts, 1990-93; Rotary Club, 1990-93; Black Adv Comt Episcopal Bishop, 1990-93; interview comt, Humanity Habitat, 1995-; sire archon, Gamma Theta Boule, Sigma Pi Phi, 1996; Govenors Educ Coord Comt Correctional Insts, 1997-; Acad Criminal Justice Sci; Am Correctional Asn; vol, Community Found E Shore Inc. **Home Addr:** 30420 Mallard Dr, Delmar, MD 21875-2400, **Home Phone:** (410)219-3510.

## HARLEY, DR. DEBRA A.

College teacher. **Personal:** children: 4. **Educ:** SC State Univ, BS, 1981, MA, 1983; Southern Ill Univ, Carbondale, IL, PhD, 1992. **Career:** SC Employ Security Comn, Beaufort, employ counr, 1984; SC Dept Voc Rehab, Hartsville, rehab counr, 1984-86; Southern Ill Univ, Carbondale, proj coordr, 1990-91, teaching asst, 1991-92, Dept Spec Educ, asst prof, 1992-93; Eastern Ill Univ, Charleston, asst prof, 1992-93; Univ Ky, Lexington, Dept Spec Educ & Rehab Coun, from asst prof to assoc prof, 1993-2003, Dept Early Childhood, Spec Ed & Rehab Coun, 2003-, Dept Chair 2007-11; Grad Prog Rehab Coun, asst dir, 1996-98, coordr, 1998-2000; Rehab Endorsement Curric, coordr, 1996-2003; Infants Young C, reviewer, 1997-; Rehab Psychol, reviewer, 2001-; Jour Coun Psychol, reviewer, 2001-; Jour Rehab Admin, 2002-; Col Arts & Sci, actg dir Gender & Women's Studies, 2002-03, assoc dir, 2003-04, prof & chmn, currently, provosts distinguished serv prof, currently; J Rehab Admin, ed; J Appl Rehab Coun, ed; Rehab Educ Grad Stand Bd, comnr. **Orgs:** Kappa Delta Pi; Chi Sigma Iota. **Home Addr:** 500 Alderbrook Way, Lexington, KY 40515. **Business Addr:** Professor, University of Kentucky, 229 Taylor Educ Bldg, Lexington, KY 40506-0001, **Business Phone:** (859)257-7199.

### HARLEY, LEGRAND

Manager, association executive. **Personal:** Born Jan 19, 1956, Florence, SC; son of Willie Sr and Lela. **Educ:** Francis Marion Col, Florence, SC, BS, polit sci, 1981. **Career:** Red Carpet Inn, Florence, SC, asst mgr, 1973-80; Florence Co Community Alcohol & Drugs, residential mgr, 1981-84; SC Dept Youth Serv, Columbia, SC, youth counr, 1984-86; Lt Gov Mike Daniel, Columbia, SC, field coordr, 1986-87; SC Atty Gen Off, Columbia, SC, admin asst, 1987-92; Merchants Asn Florence, coordr, 1993-95; Florence Co, asst, coordr, 1995; Dem Party, activist. **Orgs:** legal redress comt, leader, Nat Asn Advan Colored People, 1982-; field rep, Florence Jaycees, 1980-82; pres, chmn, emer, SC Young Dem; Black Caucus, admin bd, lay leader, life mem, Salem United Methodist Church. **Honors/Awds:** Young Man of the Year, The Key Inc, 1980; Outstanding Young Men of America, US Jaycees, 1981; Young Democrats of Florence, Florence Young Democrats, 1982; Longest Serving Young Democrat in SC, SC Democratic Party, 1988; Outstanding & Most Loyal Young Democrat, SC Young Democrats, 1989. **Home Addr:** 209 Pearl Cir, Florence, SC 29506-6316, **Home Phone:** (843)230-4123.

### HARLEY, PHILIP A.

Educator. **Personal:** Born Philadelphia, PA; married Ireleen I; children: Anthony, Antoinette, Richard, Michael, Bruce, Annette & Terri. **Educ:** Morgan State Col, BA, 1945; Temple Univ; Univ Cincinnati; Capital Univ Sch Theol; Garrett Theol Sem, Mdiv, 1956. **Career:** Educator (retired); IL, Ind, OH, SDak, Wis, pastor; Garrett Theol Sem, assoc prof; Practical Theol & Field Educ, assoc prof emer. **Orgs:** Chmn, Regional Consultative Com Race; Mayors Com Human Rels; dist dir, Res & Devel Ministries Educ, Ind, SD; prog leadership develop Prog Coun, Northern Ill Conf; vice chmn, Leadership Develop Com N Cent Jurisdictron; regional vpres, Natl Com Black Churchmen; chmn, Chicago Coord Com Black Churchmen; vice chmn, Serv Rev Panel Comm Fund; Ch Fed Met Chicago; Chicago Conf Relig & Race; mem bd dir, Welfare Coun Met Chicago. **Home Addr:** 709 N 40th St, Philadelphia, PA 19104, **Home Phone:** (215)386-5137. **Business Addr:** Associate Professor Emeritus, Garrett-Evangel Theol Sem, 2121 Sheridan Rd, Evanston, IL 60201, **Business Phone:** (847)866-3984.

### HARMON, CLARENCE

Government official. **Personal:** Born Mar 18, 1955, St. Louis, MO; married Janet Kelley; children: 4. **Educ:** Northeast Mo State Univ, BS; Webster Univ, MPA, criminal justice & pub admin. **Career:** St Louis Police Dept, var positions, comdr area I, 1988-90, Bd Police Comnrs, secy, 1991, chief police, 1991-97; City St Louis, mayor, 1997-2001; Southern Ill Univ, Pub Policy Inst, part time lectr, currently; Self-employed, consult, 2001-. **Orgs:** Int Asn Chief Police; Am Mgt Asn; bd trustee, Webster Univ; bd trustee, St Louis Sci Ctr; bd dir, St Louis Symphony; vpres, Fair Found bd dir; bd dir, M Bot Garden; bd dir, United Way St. Louis. **Business Addr:** Part Time Lecturer, Paul Simon Public Policy Institute, PO box 4429, Carbondale, IL 62901, **Business Phone:** (618)453-4009.

### HARMON, JAMES F., SR.

Executive. **Personal:** Born Apr 18, 1932, Savannah, GA; married Clarissa V Poindexter; children: James F Jr, Valerie H Seay, Laurence E & Wendell E. **Educ:** NC Agr & Tech State Univ, BS, 1954; Air Univ, Squad Officer Sch, 1961; Troy State Univ, MS, 1974. **Career:** Atlanta Marriott Hotels, dir personnel, 1975-80; Marriott Hotels, reg dir training, 1980-82; Atlanta Perimeter Ctr Marriott, mgr res, 1982; Marriott Corp, Courtyard Marriott Hotels, mgr prop, 1983. **Orgs:** Alpha Phi Alpha, 1952-; chmn, Ed Comn Nat Hosp Ed Mgr Assoc, 1983; pres, Atlanta Falcon Club Inc, 1983-. **Home Addr:** 3945 Somerled Trl, College Park, GA 30349, **Home Phone:** (404)768-0728.

### HARMON, JESSIE KATE. See PORTIS, KATTIE HARMON.

### HARMON, JOHN H. See Obituaries Section.

### HARPER, DR. ALPHONZA VEALVERT, III

Dentist. **Personal:** Born Feb 5, 1948, Alexander City, AL; son of Alphonza V and Barbara B; married Debra Sanders; children: Niaya A. **Educ:** Tenn State Univ, BS, 1969; Meharry Med Col, DDS, 1975. **Career:** Beverly Hills Dent Off, St Louis, Mo, dentist, currently. **Orgs:** Am Dent Asn; Nat Dent Asn; Greater St Louis Dent Soc; Mound City Dent Soc, 1975-; vpres, Normandy Kiwanis Club, 1979-; Nat Asn Advan Colored People, 1980-. **Home Addr:** 6910 Natural Bridge, St. Louis, MO 63121, **Home Phone:** (314)387-7858. **Business Addr:** Dentist, Beverly Hills Dental Center, 6830 Natural Bridge Rd, St. Louis, MO 63121, **Business Phone:** (314)383-8060.

### HARPER, ARTHUR H.

Marketing executive, founder (originator), executive. **Personal:** Born Dec 3, 1955, Trenton, NJ. **Educ:** Stevens Inst Technol, BS, chem engineering, 1978. **Career:** Conoco Inc, Chem Div, sales rep, 1978-82; DuPont, Polymer Prod Dept, mkt rep, 1983-84; GE Plastics, mkt develop, 1984-87, dist sales mgr, 1987-91, plant mgr, 1991-92, dir crystalline mat, 1992-94, dir lexan, 1994-96, vpres global mfg, 1998-2000; GE Plastics Greater China, pres, 1996-98; GE Plastics Europe, pres & sr managing dir, 2000-02; Gen Elec, sr vpres & Gen Elec Equip Serv, chief exec officer, 2002-05; TEGNA Inc, dir, 2006-13; GenNx360 Capital Partners, founder & managing partner, 2006-. **Orgs:** Dir, Gannett Co Inc, 2006-; bd mem, Monsanto Co, 2006-; bd mem, Yerwood Ctr; exec comt mem, GE's African Am Forum; chmn, Stamford Comn Educ Achievement; bd mem, GE Capital; bd mem, GE's Corp Exec Coun; Bluegrass Comt; dir, VTX Subco Ltd; dir, Schramm Inc; dir & chmn, Vertex Data Sci Ltd. **Honors/Awds:** Career Achievement Award, 1998, Stevens Inst Technol; GE Chairman's Turn Around of the Year Award, 2004; Fairfield County Region National Conference for Community and Justice, Social Justice Hero Award, 2004; Whitney M. Young, Jr. Service Award, 2004, Boy Scouts Am Greater New York Councils; 100 Black Men of Stamford, Connecticut, Professional Achievement Award, 2005; Black Enterprise, 75 Most Powerful African Americans in Corporate America, 2005; Black Enterprise, 75 Most Powerful Blacks on Wall Street, 2011; International Achievement Award, Stevens Inst Technol's, 2015. **Business Addr:** Founder, Managing Partner, GenNx360 Capital Partners, 590 Madison Ave, New York, NY 10022, **Business Phone:** (212)257-6772.

### HARPER, BENJAMIN CHASE

Singer, songwriter. **Personal:** Born Oct 28, 1969, Claremont, CA; son of Leonard and Ellen Chase-Verdries; married Joanna; children: Charles Joseph & Harris; married Laura Dern; children: Ellery Walker & Jaya; married Dern. **Career:** Virgin Rec, rec artist, 1994-2001; Inland Emperor Rec, founder, 2001-; Albums: Pleasure and Pain, 1992; Welcome to the Cruel World, 1994; Fight for your Mind, 1995; The Will to Live, 1997; Burn to Shine, 1999; Live from Mars, 2001; Diamonds on the Inside, 2003; There will be a Light, 2004; Live at the Apollo, 2005; Both Sides of the Gun, 2006; Lifeline, 2007; Live at Twist & Shout, 2007; White Lies for Dark Times, 2009; Give Till It's Gone, 2011; Get Up!, 2013; Childhood Home, 2014. Songs: "Burn to shine", 2000; "Forgiven", 2000; "Steal My Kisses", 2000; "With My Own Two Hands", 2003; "Diamonds on the Inside", 2004; "So High So Low", 2004; "Brown Eyed Blue", 2004; "Better Way", 2006; "Morning Yearning", 2006; "Fight Outta You", 2007; "In the Colors", 2007; "Fool For A Lonesome Train", 2008; "Shimmer & Shine", 2009; "Fly One Time", 2009; Singles: "Like A King / Whipping Boy", 1994; "Ground on Down", 1995; "Excuse Me Mr.", 1996; "Gold to Me", 1996; "Faded", 1997; "Jah Work", 1997; "Glory & Consequence", 1997; "Please Bleed", 1999; "Burn to Shine", 1999; "Forgiven", 2000; "Steal My Kisses", 2000; "With My Own Two Hands", 2003; " "Diamonds On the Inside", 2003; "Brown Eyed Blues", 2004; "Wicked Man", 2004; "There Will Be a Light", 2004; "Better Way", 2006; "Both Sides Of The Gun", 2006; "Morning Yearning", 2006; "Fight Outta You", 2007; "Boa Sorte/Good Luck", 2007; "In The Colors", 2008; "Fool For A Lonesome Train", 2008; "Shimmer & Shine", 2009; "Fly One Time", 2009; "Lay There & Hate Me", 2010; "Skin Thin", 2010; "The Word Suicide", 2010; "Never Tear Us Apart", 2010; "Rock N' Roll Is Free", 2011; "Don't Give Up on Me Now", 2011; Walk Away. Flim: Inland Empire, 2006. **Special Achievements:** Performed on tour with Taj Mahal, 1992; collaborated with Mahal on soundtrack for The Drinking Gourd, a bio of Harriet Tubman; toured US as both solo and warm-up act with his band The Innocent Criminals, 1994-95; toured US, Europe, and New Zealand, 1995-97; headlined at HORDE Festivaland Montreaux Jazz Festival.

### HARPER, DR. BERNICE CATHERINE

Government official. **Personal:** Born Covington, VA; children: Reginald. **Educ:** Va State Col, BS, 1945; Univ So CA, MSW, 1948; Harvard Univ, MSc.PH, 1959; Faith Grant Col, LLD, 1994. **Career:** Childrens Hosp, social worker, 1947-57; City Hope Med Ctr, chief social worker, 1960-74; Dept HEW, chief NH br, 1970-72, dir div ltc, 1973-77, specasst to dir hsqb, 1977-79, med care adv. **Orgs:** Bd Intl Hospice Inst, Bd Intl Coun SW US Community; steering community Nat Asn Social Workers; bd chair, founder, pres, Found Hospices Sub-Saharan Africa, 1999-; bd dir, Nat Asn Social Workers Found. **Home Addr:** 11801 Rockville Pke, Rockville, MD 20852. **Business Addr:** Board of Director, National Association of Social Workers, 750 1st St NE Suite 700, Washington, DC 20002-4241.

### HARPER, CONRAD KENNETH

Association executive, lawyer. **Personal:** Born Dec 2, 1940, Detroit, MI; son of Archibald Leonard and Georgia Florence Hall; married Marsha Louise Wilson; children: Warren & Adam. **Educ:** Howard Univ, BA, 1962; Harvard Law Sch, LLB, 1965. **Career:** Lawyer (retired); NAACP Legal Defense Fund; Nat Asn Advan Colored People, Legal Defense Fund, law clerk, 1965-66, staff lawyer, 1966-70; Rutgers Law Sch, lectr, 1969-70; Simpson Thacher & Bartlett, assoc, 1971-74, partner, 1974-93, 1996-2002, coun, 2003-09; Yale Law Sch, vis lectr, 1977-81; US Dept St, legal advisor, 1993-96; Harvard Corp, 2000-05; U.S. Dept State, legal advisor; New York Bar Asn, pres; Simpson Thacher & Bartlett LLP, partner, currently. **Orgs:** Bd dir, Phi Beta Kappa, 1962, 1992-93; consult, US Dept HEW, 1977; trustee, NY Pub Libr, 1978-93; bd eds, Am Bar Asn Jour, 1980-86; Vestryman St Barnabas Epis Church, 1982-85; Comn Admis & Grievances, US Ct Appeals, 1983-93, chmn, 1987-93; fel Am Bar Found; Coun Foreign Rels; Coun Am Law Inst, 1985-, second vpres, 1998-2000, first vpres, 2000-04-; chancellor, Epis Diocese NY, 1987-92; bd dir, co-chair, Lawyers Comn Civil Rights under Law, 1987-89; trustee, William Nelson Cromwell Found, 1990-; pres, Asn Bar City New York, 1990-92; pres, NY City Bar, 1990-92; dir, Am Arbit Asn, 1990-93, 1997-2001; bd dir, NY Life Ins Co, 1992-93, 1996-; Harvard Club, 1993; trustee, Metrop Mus Art, 1996-; dir, Pub Serv Enterprise Group, 1997-; Am Soc Int Law, 1997-2000, counr, 2000-05; fel Am Acad Arts & Scis; bd dir, Acad Am Poets; bd dir, Acad Polit Sci, 1998; fel Am Col Trial Lawyers; Am Law Inst Coun; Coun Foreign Rels; bd dir, Inst Int Educ; trustee, Lawyers' Comt Civil Rights Under Law; trustee, Metrop Mus Art; vice chmn, NY Pub Libr; Obama Am; Permanent Ct Arbit, 1993-96, 1998-2004; vpres, Am Philos Soc, 2005-10, coun, 2010; Metrop Black Bar Asn; Ny Bar Asn. **Honors/Awds:** LLD, City Univ New York, 1990; LLD, Am Philosophical Soc; Bishop's Cross, Episcopal Diocese of New York, 1992; Alumni Achievement Award, Howard Univ, 1994; LLD, Vt Law Sch, 1994; Whitney North Seymour Award, Fed Bar Coun, 1994; C Francis Stratford Award, Nat Bar Asn, 1999; LLD, Harvard Univ, 2007. **Special Achievements:** New York City Bar Association First African American member; First African American President of the New York City Bar, 1990-92; When he became a partner in 1974, he was one of only two African American partners at a major law firm in New York City; First African American member of the Harvard Corporation, 2000-05. **Business Addr:** Partner, Simpson Thacher & Bartlett LLP, 425 Lexington Ave, New York, NY 10017-3954, **Business Phone:** (212)455-2000.

### HARPER, CURTIS. See Obituaries Section.

### HARPER, DAVID B.

Executive, chief executive officer, president (organization). **Personal:** Born Dec 3, 1933, Indianapolis, IN; married Mae McGee; children: Vicki Clines, Sharon Chaney, Wanda Mosley, Lydia Restivo, Kathleen Bass, Carol, Kyra, David, Daniel & Ralph. **Educ:** Ariz State Univ, BS, 1963; Golden State Univ, MBA, 1968; Eastern Mich Univ, JD, 1970. **Career:** Banker(retired); entrepreneur; Bank Am NT & SA, bank officer & magr, 1963; First Independence Nat Bank Detroit, pres & chief exec officer, 1969-76; Gateway Nat Bank, pres & chief exec officer, 1976-83; County Ford Inc, pres, 1983-88; David B Harper Mgt Inc, pres, 1988-; New Age Financial Bancorporation Inc, pres & chief exec officer, 1989-; Buford, Dickson, Harper & Sparrow Inc, bd dir, chmn, currently. Ford Automobile, owner; Buford Dickson Harper & Sparrow Inc, currently. **Orgs:** Bd dir, Kmart Corp, 1975-; bd dir, Stud Loan Mkt Asn, 1973-; bd dir, Detroit Edison, 1975-83; bd dir, Oper Food Search; bd dir, Cystic Fibrosis Found; bd dir, Cent Inst Deaf; bd dir, St Louis Regional Med Ctr Found; vpres, Fair Found; bd dir, vpres, Confluence St Louis. **Home Addr:** 24 Beaver Dr, St. Louis, MO 63141, **Home Phone:** (314)993-3765. **Business Addr:** Board of Director, Buford, Dickson, Harper & Sparrow Inc, 211 N Broadway Suite 2080, St. Louis, MO 63102, **Business Phone:** (314)725-5445.

### HARPER, DWAYNE ANTHONY

Football player, executive. **Personal:** Born Mar 29, 1966, Orangeburg, SC. **Educ:** SC State Col, BA, mkt, 1988. **Career:** Football player (retired), exec; Seattle Seahawks, corner back & defensive back & left corner back, 1988-93; San Diego Chargers, right corner back & right corner back, 1994-98; Detroit Lions, defensive back, 1999; San Francisco Demons, 2001; ETL Assocs Inc, vpres & dir player develop, currently; Massage Envy Spa, owner, 2011-. **Orgs:** Nat Asn Advan Colored People; bd trustee, Claflin Univ. **Honors/Awds:** Sports Illustrated, All-NFL Team, 1991 & 1995; Unsung Hero Award, 1995; Most Valuable Person, 1995; Almost Hall of Fame. **Home Addr:** 97 Oakbrook Dr, Columbia, SC 29223, **Home Phone:** (803)827-9777. **Business Addr:** Director of Player Development, Vice President, ETL Associates Inc, 100 Pk Ave 20th Fl, New York, NY 10017, **Business Phone:** (212)867-8500.

### HARPER, EARL

Educator. **Personal:** Born Jul 7, 1929, Jackson, MS; married Clara Louise; children: Felicia, Denise, Julie M, Earl Jr, Andre Robinson & Sharmeka Robinson. **Educ:** Grand Rapids Jr Col, AA, voc studies, 1964; Western Mich Univ, BS, indust supv, 1968, MS, mfg engineering & technol, 1971, MBA, mgt, 1973, specialist arts mgt, 1979; Tex Tech Univ, PhD, 1988. **Career:** Doehler-Jarvis, training dir, asst to plant mgr, 1946-71; Grand Valley State Univ, FE Siedman Sch Bus, chair mgt dept, 1981-94, prof mgt, 1994, prof emer, 1994-. **Orgs:** Develop Grand Rapids, Mich Model Cities Career & Acad Coun Ctr, 1971; develop Gen Acad Prog Grand Rapids & Muskegon Inner-City Col Ed Prog Grand Valley State Col, 1971; comt develop Higher Educ Prog Grand Rapids Model Cities, 1972-73; Personal Admin Soc; Delta Mu Delta Epsilon; Die Casting Soc; Indust Mgt Soc; Indust Eng Soc; bd mem, Indust Rel Res Asst; bd mem, Bus Opportunities Soc; Am Legion; Nat Asn Advan Colored People; City Grand Rapids Citizens Adv Compensation Comt; UUS & China Joint Session Indust, Trade & Econ Develop; Sigma Beta Epsilon. **Honors/Awds:** Certificate Appreciation, AM Legion; Management Scholarship Award, State TX; Outstanding EDRs Award, Grand Valley State Univ Alumni Asn, 1993; Excellence in Research Award, Grand Valley State Univ, 1994, Outstanding EDUCATION Award, 1994; Earl Harper Scholarship, named in honor. **Special Achievements:** Publications: "Management the Diversified Workforce: Current Efforts and Future Directions, " Sam Advanced Management Journal, 1993; "An Empirical Examination of the Relationship Between Strategy and Scanning," The Mid Atlantic Journal of Business, 1993; Numerous others. **Home Addr:** 2029 Wolfboro Dr SE, Grand Rapids, MI 49508, **Home Phone:** (616)455-2669. **Business Addr:** Professor Emeritus, Grand Valley State University, 1 Campus Dr, Allendale, MI 49401-9404, **Business Phone:** (616)331-5000.

### HARPER, EUGENE, JR.

School administrator, executive director. **Personal:** Born Feb 1, 1943, Atlanta, GA; son of E Eugene and Sula Mae; married Maryetta; children: Angelia M. **Educ:** Cameron State Col, AA, 1966; Ohio State Univ, BS, 1971; Cent Mich Univ, MS, 1980. **Career:** Cols Recreation Dept, dist supv & dir, 1967-72; Ohio State Univ, assoc dir intramurals, 1972-88; Columbus Pub Schs, dir athletics & stud activ, 1988-. **Orgs:** APA; bd dir, Ohio Spec Olympics; bd dir, Cols Parks & Recreation; consult, Ohio State Univ Nat Youth Sports Prog; chairperson, Ohio Asn Health, Phys Educ, Recreation & Dance; Nat Interscholastic Athletic Asn; Ohio Interscholastic Athletic Asn; Ohio High Sch Athletic Asn; Alpha Phi Alpha, Alpha RHO Lambda Chap; vpres, Recreation & Parks Comn. **Honors/Awds:** Sportsmanship, Ethics & Integrity Award, Ohio High Sch Athletic Asn, 1995-96. **Home Addr:** 208 E Schrock Rd, Westerville, OH 43081-3449, **Home Phone:** (614)898-9875. **Business Addr:** Director, Columbus Public Schools, 270 E State St, Columbus, OH 43215, **Business Phone:** (614)365-5000.

### HARPER, FRANK EUGENE. See HARPER, HILL.

### HARPER, GERALDINE SEAY

Educator. **Personal:** Born Dec 7, 1933, Memphis, TN; daughter of James Edward Seay and Janie Lee Bolden Seay; married Charles N; children: Deborah Brown, Elaine Bell & Charles Terrence. **Educ:** LeMoyne-Owen, Memphis, TN, BS, 1955; Chicago State Univ, Chicago, IL, MS, 1977. **Career:** Educator (retired); Chicago Bd Educ, Chicago, Ill, teacher, 1958-76, teacher & librn, 1976; LeMoyne-Owen Col, nat chap pres. **Orgs:** Chicago Teacher Libr Asn, 1980-, reservation secy, 1987, comt chair, 1986-87; Lilydale First Baptist Church Chicago, 1983-, corresp secy, supt, 1988-; Delta Sigma Theta Sorority; dir, Vacation Bible Sch; chair, Sr Citizens Comt, Top Ladies Distinction Chicago Chap, 1987-89; pres, Manassas High Sch Alumni Asn, Chicago Chap, 1995-; pres, LeMoyne-Owen Col Alumni Asn, Chicago Chap, 2000-. **Home Addr:** 515 W 97th St, Chicago, IL 60628-1115, **Home Phone:** (773)239-0319. **Business Addr:** IL.

### HARPER, HILL (FRANK EUGENE HARPER)
Actor. **Personal:** Born May 17, 1966, Iowa City, IA; son of Harry and Marilyn Hill. **Educ:** Brown Univ, BA, 1988; Harvard Law School,, JD, 1992; Harvard Univ, Kennedy Sch Gov, MPA. **Career:** Boston's Black Folks Theater Co, full time mem; Films: Confessions of a Dog, 1993; Pumpkinhead II, 1994; One Red Rose, 1995; Drifting School, 1995; Get On The Bus, 1996; Steel, 1997; Hav Plenty, 1997; Hoover Park, 1997; He Got Game, 1998; Park Day, 1998; The Nephew, 1998; Beloved, 1998; Slaves of Hollywood, 1999; Loving Jezebel, 1999; In Too Deep, 1999; The Skulls, 2000; The Visit, 2000; Higher Ed, 2001; Crossthe Line, 2002; The Badge, 2002; Love, Sex and Eating the Bones, 2003; Constellation, 2003; Lackawanna Blues, 2005; 30 Days, 2006; Premium, 2006; The Breed, 2006; Max and Josh, writer, 2006; This Is Not a Test, actor & producer, 2008; Lessons from Little Rock: A National Report Card, co executive producer, 2008; A Good Man is Hard To Find, 2008; For Colored Girls, 2010; Shanghai Hotel, 2011; Mama, I Want to Sing!, 2011; Alpha Man: The Brotherhood of MLK, producer, 2011; The Truth, dir, 2011; Miss Dial, 2013; The Volunteer, 2013; 1982, actor & exec producer, 2013; Parts Per Billion, 2014; TV series: "Live Shot", 1995; "City of Angels", 2000; "The Court", 2002; "The Handler", 2003; "CSI: NY", voice, 2004-13; The Sopranos, 2004; Soul Food, 2004; "CSI: Miami", 2004; "The 4400", 2005; "Covert Affairs: Sights Unseen", 2012; "Covert Affairs", 2013-14. TV movies: "Zooman", 1995; "The Dave Chappelle Project", 1998; "Mama Flora's Family", 1998; "Lackawanna Blues", 2005; "Stonehenge Apocalypse", 2010. Writer: One Red Rose, 1995; Max and Josh, 2006; The Game, 2009. **Orgs:** Alpha Phi Alpha Fraternity. **Honors/Awds:** Audience Award, Urban world Film Festival, 2000, 2008; Best Actor, Method Fest, 2000; Emerging Artist Award, Chicago Int Film Festival; John Garfield Best Actor Award, 2001; Image Award, Nat Asn Advan Colored People, 2008-10; Hon Doctorate, Westfield State Col, 2009. **Special Achievements:** First African American practicing anesthesiologists in the United States. **Business Addr:** Actor, c/o Principato-Young Entertainment, 9465 Wilshire Blvd Suite 430, Beverly Hills, CA 90212, **Business Phone:** (310)274-2294.

### HARPER, HOYT H., II
Hotel executive, vice president (organization). **Educ:** Carthage Col, attended 1977. **Career:** Lifeco Serv, vpres & gen mgr; Thomson Vacations Inc, vpres mkt; Avis Rent a Car, dir leisure mkt; Thomson Vacations Chicago, dir opers; ITT Sheraton, vpres & dir mkt progs & partner mkt; Sheraton Hotels & Resorts Group, sr vpres bus develop & mkt progs, sr vpres brand mgt, 2002-; Starwood Hotels & Resorts Worldwide Inc, sr vpres & global brand leader, currently; Four Points, sr vpres. **Orgs:** Bd trustee, Carthage Col Wis, 2006-; Suffolk Univ, Sch Mgt Boston, Mkt Adv Comt; bd mem, ASFONA Inc. **Business Addr:** Senior Vice President, Global Brand Leader, Starwood Hotels & Resorts Worldwide Inc, 1 Star Point, Stamford, CT 06902, **Business Phone:** (203)964-6000.

### HARPER, LAYDELL WOOD
Marketing executive, president (organization), chief executive officer. **Personal:** daughter of R Wood and Felicia; children: Licia Lyn. **Educ:** Wayne State Univ, BA, 1980; Knight Ridder Inst, mgt. **Career:** Detroit Free Press, downtown advert mgr, 1987-89; Detroit Newspaper Agency, features advert gen mgr, 1989-90, co-op advert mgr, 1990-91, community affairs dir, 1991-; Wood & Assocs, pres & chief exec officer, 2004-. **Orgs:** Adv bd, BART, 1991-92; bd dir, Sci & Eng, 1991-93; bd mem, Berat Human Servs, 1992-; mkt comt, Nat Asn Advan Colored People, 1992-, co-chmn; co-chmn, United Negro Col Fund, fashion fair, 1992; bd dir, Proj Pride Chamber, 1992; Hartford Memorial Baptist Church. **Honors/Awds:** Woman of the Year, Friday Women's Club, 1988. **Home Addr:** 1751 Seminole St, Detroit, MI 48214, **Home Phone:** (313)923-1747. **Business Addr:** President, Chief Executive Officer, Wood & Associates, PO Box 14541, Detroit, MI 48214, **Business Phone:** (313)925-4067.

### HARPER, MARY L.
Accountant. **Personal:** Born Feb 24, 1925, Emporia, KS; married Edward J. **Educ:** Lincoln Univ, Jeff City, MO; Emporia State Teacher Col, Emporia, Kans; State Col, LA. **Career:** LA Co Prob Dept Juv Reim Sect, invest, girls coun, 1960-63; Self Employ, acct tax consult, 1965-; Cong Dist Dem Union, spec asst. **Orgs:** Treas, Dem Coal Pomona Valley; treas, Nat Asn Advan Colored People, Southern Calif Area Conf, 1966-71, bd pres, 1971-73; chmn, Pomona Valley, Nat Asn Advan Colored People; comnr, City Pomona; vice chmn, Parks & Recreation Comn; bd dir, YMCA Outreach. **Honors/Awds:** Service Award, Southern Area Conf Nat Asn Advan Colored People, 1969, 1971; Elected Delegate Dem Charter Conf KC, MO 35th Cong Dist, 1974. **Special Achievements:** Only African American candidate in field of 12; One of two female during city council election. **Home Addr:** 1408 W Grand Ave, Pomona, CA 91766, **Home Phone:** (909)622-0076.

### HARPER, MICHAEL STEVEN. See Obituaries Section.

### HARPER, ROBERT LEE
Dentist. **Personal:** Born Oct 3, 1920, Longview, TX; married Eldora; children: Robert Jr & Beverly. **Educ:** Jarvis Christian Col, attended 1942; Wiley Col, BA, 1948; Meharry Med Col, DDS, 1952. **Career:** Dent, pvt prac, 1952-77; Jarvis Christian Col, 1960-77; pvt pract dentist, currently. **Orgs:** Secy, E Tex Med Dent & Pharm Asn; pres, Gulf St Dent Asn, 1962; E Tex Dist Dent Soc; Tex Dent Asn; Am Dent Asn; Nat Dent Asn; Gulf St Dent Asn; Am Soc Dent C; Am Acad Gen Dent; bd dir, Logview C C, 1977; bd, Parks & Rec Prog, 1969-75; Piney Woods Am Red Cross; chmn, adv bd, GoodSamaritan Nursing Home; bd mem, Ment Health Asn Gregg Co; E Tex Area Coun BSA; past mem, bd, Voc Tech Training Longview Ind Sch Dist Hon; Omega Psi Phi Frat; Kappa Sigma Pi Hon Dent Frat. **Honors/Awds:** Recipient Of Clinical of Dentistry, 1952; Silver Beaver Award, Boy Scouts Am, 1966; Omega Man Of the Year, 1967; candidate, City Comnr Longview, 1967. **Home Addr:** 1005 S Martin Luther King Jr Blvd, Longview, TX 75602-2405, **Home Phone:** (903)753-2716. **Business Addr:** Dentist, 1002 S Martin Luther King Jr Blvd, Longview, TX 75602, **Business Phone:** (903)758-4851.

### HARPER, RONALD
Basketball player, basketball coach. **Personal:** Born Jan 20, 1964, Dayton, OH; son of Gloretha. **Educ:** Miami Univ, attended 1986. **Career:** Basketball player (retired), basketball coach; Cleveland Cavaliers, guard, 1986-89; Los Angeles Clippers, 1989-94; Chicago Bulls, 1994-99; Los Angeles Lakers, 1999-2001; Detroit Pistons, asst coach, 2005-07. **Special Achievements:** TV series: "Foul Bull", 1997.

### HARPER, ESQ. RONALD J.
Lawyer, legal consultant. **Personal:** Born Dec 20, 1945, West Palm Beach, FL; married Betty Vance; children: Ronald Jr & Jennifer. **Educ:** Temple Univ, BA, econs, 1968; Temple Law Sch, JD, 1971. **Career:** Metro Life Ins Co, salesman, 1968; New York Life Ins Co, salesman, 1970; Comt Legal Serv Philadelphia, atty, 1971; Opportunities Industrialization Centers Am Inc, house coun, atty; Law Firm Harper & Paul, co-foounder & atty, 1972-. **Orgs:** Bd mgr, Temple Univ, 1974; pres, Barristers Asn, 1977; Nat Bar Asn; Philadelphia Bar Asn; Philadelphia Barristers Asn, 1977-78; Am Bar Asn; Zion Bapt Church; bd mem, Community Legal Serv. **Home Addr:** 336 Pelham Rd, Philadelphia, PA 19119. **Business Addr:** Attorney, The Law Firm Of Harper & Paul, 140 W Maplewood Ave, Philadelphia, PA 19144, **Business Phone:** (215)844-4848.

### HARPER, RUTH B. See Obituaries Section.

### HARPER, SARA J.
Judge, historian. **Personal:** Born Aug 10, 1926, Cleveland, OH; daughter of James Weldon and Leila Smith. **Educ:** Case Western Res Univ, BS; Franklin Thomas Backus Sch Law, Case Western Reserve Univ, LLB. **Career:** Judge (retired); City Cleveland, prosecutor; Cleveland Munic Ct, judge; Eighth Appellate Dist, Cuyahoga, OH, judge; Ohio Supreme Ct, chief justice, 1980, mem, 1992; Ohio Ct Appeals, mem, 1990. **Orgs:** Judicial coun & historian, Nat Bar Asn; Ohio Vet Hall Fame; life mem, Mt Olive Baptist Church; Nat Bar Asns Hall Fame. **Honors/Awds:** Victims Award, OH Ct Claims, 1990; Ohio Women's Hall of Fame, 1991; Ohio Supreme Courts Excellent Judicial Service Award; Unsung Heroine Award; Raymond Pace Alexander Award; Sara J. Harper's Children's Library, 2010. **Special Achievements:** First African American woman to graduate from Case Western Reserve University Law School; first woman to serve on the judiciary of the USMCR; Ohio Supreme Ct first African American woman Judge. **Home Addr:** 13807 Drexmore Rd, Cleveland, OH 44120.

### HARPER, SHARI BELAFONTE. See BELAFONTE, SHARI LYNN.

### HARPER, T. ERROL
President (organization), automotive executive. **Personal:** Born Feb 12, 1947, Birmingham, AL; son of Rev Theophilus E and Callie O; married Elaine Betz; children: Rena Nicole & Zachary Jordan. **Educ:** Morris Brown Col, Atlanta, Ga, BA, 1970. **Career:** Ernst & Ernst, Philadelphia PA, auditor, 1970-73; Philadelphia '76 Inc, Philadelphia, PA, controller, 1973-74; Dupont Co, Wilmington, Del, staff acct, 1974-76; Ford Motor Co, Dearborn, Mich, dealer trainee, 1977-78; Phillips Ford Inc, Conshohocken PA, bus mgr, 1978-79; Harper Pontiac Inc, Upper Darby PA, pres, 1979-82; Heritage Lincoln-Mercury, Hackensack NJ, pres, 1983; Queen City Lincoln-Mercury, pres, currently. **Orgs:** Dir, Com & Indust Asn NJ, 1985-; United Way Bergen Co, 1985-92; Hackensack Lions Club, 1987-; dir & former vpres, Black Ford & Lincoln-Mercury Minority Dealer Asn, 1989-91; bd dir, Better Bus Bur, 2002; Lincoln-Mercury Div Nat Dealer Coun; adv coun, Univ Okla; 100 Black Men in Charlotte; dir & secy, C Aid & Adoption Soc. **Honors/Awds:** Hon Doctor Humanities, Monrova Col, Monrovia, Liberia, 1986. **Home Addr:** 19 Walter St, Old Tappan, NJ 07675, **Home Phone:** (201)358-1651. **Business Addr:** President, Queen City Lincoln-Mercury Inc, 7301 S Blvd, Charlotte, NC 28273-5968, **Business Phone:** (704)553-8300.

### HARPER, TERRY JOE
Baseball player, baseball manager. **Personal:** Born Aug 19, 1955, Douglasville, GA. **Career:** Baseball player (retired), baseball coach; Atlanta Braves, amateur draft, 1973, outfielder, 1980-86; Detroit Tigers, outfielder, 1987; Pittsburgh Pirates, outfielder, 1987; Yakult Swallows, Tokyo, 1988; coach, currently. **Home Addr:** 1685 Dorris Rd, Douglasville, GA 30134.

### HARPER, THELMA MARIE
State government official. **Personal:** Born Dec 2, 1940, Brentwood, TN; daughter of William Claybrooks and Clora Thomas Claybrooks; married Paul Wilson; children: Dylan Wayne & Linda Gail. **Educ:** Tenn State Univ, BS, bus admin & acct, 1978. **Career:** Paul Harpers Convenience Markets, entrepreneur, 1972; county comnr Davidson, Tenn; Foreman 5th Circuit Ct Grand Jury, Tenn, 1977-79; financial analyst, 1978; Dist Dem Exec Comt, 1980; Senate Govt Opers Comt, Vice Chair; Dem Nat Conv, deleg, 1980, 1984, 1988 & 1992; city councilwoman; Tenn Senate, 19th dist, sen, 1991-. **Orgs:** Nat Alumnae Chap; Davidson Co Dem Womens' Club; Cable Inc; vpres, Nat Hook-up Black Women, 1980; state secy, Nashville Women's Polit Caucus, 1980-81; YWCA Adv Comt Links Inc; Delta Sigma Theta Sorority Inc; bd mem, Nashville Downtown Partnership, currently; Schrader Lane Church Christ; bd, Policy Alternative Leader Nashville Symphony Bd WomenGovt; Adv Coun mem, Third Nat Bank Econ Develop; Renewal House Inc. **Honors/Awds:** Business Award, Nat Asn Negro Bus and Prof Womens Club; Woman of the Year Award, Jaycee; June Anderson Leadership Award, MTSU; Frances Williams Preston Award for Breast Cancer Awareness, 1999. **Special Achievements:** First Black female ever elected to Tenn state senate. **Home Addr:** 4955 Clarksville Hwy, Whites Creek, TN 37189, **Home Phone:** (615)876-3466. **Business Addr:** Senator, Tennessee State Senate, 301 6th Ave N Suite 303 War Memorial Bldg, Nashville, TN 37243, **Business Phone:** (615)741-2453.

### HARPER, TOMMY
Baseball player, consultant. **Personal:** Born Oct 14, 1940, Oak Grove, LA; son of Ulysses and Louetta Weir; married Bonnie Jean Williams. **Educ:** San Francisco State Univ. **Career:** Baseball player (retired), baseball coach, consultant; Cincinnati Reds, player, 1962-67; Cleveland Indians, player, 1968; Seattle Pilots, baseball player, 1969; Milwaukee Brewers, player, 1970-71; Boston Red Sox, 1972-74, Calif Angels, player, 1975; Oakland Athletics, 1975; Baltimore Orioles, 1976; New York Yankees, minor league instr, 1977-78; pub rels, spec asst to gen mgr, minor league instr, 1978-79; asst dir, mkt & promotions, 1980; Red Sox, coach, 1980-84 & 2000-02; maj league coach, 1981-84; spec asst to gen mgr, 1985-86; Montreal Expos, minor league instr, 1988-89; maj league coach, 1990; coach, 1990-99; player develop consult, 2013. **Orgs:** Boston Red Sox Hall Fame, 2010. **Special Achievements:** First American League player, 30-30 club, 1970. **Home Addr:** 5 Cow Hill Rd, Sharon, MA 02067-2987. **Business Addr:** Player Development Consultant, Boston Red Sox, 4 Yawkey Way, Boston, MA 02215-3496, **Business Phone:** (617)267-9440.

### HARPER, DR. WALTER EDWARD
Educator. **Personal:** Born Jul 10, 1950, Chicago, IL; son of Walter Edward Sr and Elizabeth Mercer. **Educ:** Loyola Univ, Chicago, IL, BA, hist, 1972, MA, coun psychol, 1978, post grad studies, 1986; State Ill Sec Sch, teaching cert, 1972; Inst Psychoanal, Chicago, IL, cert, teacher educ prog, 1979; Brown Univ, MA, anthrop, 1996, PhD, 2006; Adler Inst, cert, advan coursework. **Career:** Precious Brood Grammar Sch, Chicago, IL, teacher, 1972-74; Loyola Univ, Chicago, IL, fin aid officer, 1974-79; Chicago Pub Sch, substitute teacher; N Pk Col, Chicago, IL, teacher & counr, 1979-86; Brown Univ, Providence RI, asst dir fin aid, 1986-, post doctrol fel, currently, res asst, 2011-12; Urban League RI, health consult, 1996-; Salveregina Univ, vis prof, 2005-07, Family Plng Prog Consult & instr, sociol dept, currently, asst prof, currently; Univ of Ri, adj prof, 2007-10; Ri Tobacco Control Network, dir, 2009-11; Dr. Martha Joukowsky, res asst, 2012-13; Bridgewater State Univ, vis assoc prof, Anthrop, 2013-; The Acad at Harvard Sq, consult, 2013-. **Orgs:** Bd mem, Eisenberg Chicago Boys & Girls Club, 1978; Loyola Univ, UpwardBound Prog, 1978; C G Jung Ctr, 1980; bd mem, Friendship House, Chicago, 1981; Ill Psychol Asn, 1982; Phi Delta Kappa, Loyola Univ Chap, 1982; fel Soc Values Higher Educ, 1982; Asn Black Admis & Fin Aid Admin, IvyLeague & Sister Schs, 1986; workshop leader, High Sch Summer Intern Prog, Philadelphia Daily News, 1987; workshop leader, Atlanta Dream Jamboree, 1988 & 1989; mgt develop prog, teaching fel, Brown Univ, 1988; Eastern Asn Fin Aid Admin; adv, Nat Asn Advan Colored People Stud Chap, 1990; co-chairperson, Campus Ministry Affairs Comm, 1990; pres, Santore Soc, 1990-91; bd mem, AIDs Proj RI; bd mem, Community Prep Sch; bd mem, Providence Black Repertory Co; bd mem, Stone Soup Found; vol, Providence Sch Dept. **Home Addr:** 2 Ternay Garden, Providence, RI 02904-2809, **Home Phone:** (401)751-0319. **Business Addr:** Teacher, College Administrator & Consultant, Salve Regina University, 100 Ochre Pt Ave, Newport, RI 02840-4192, **Business Phone:** (401)847-6650.

### HARPER, WILLIAM THOMAS, III
Psychologist, educator, executive director. **Personal:** Born Sep 10, 1956, Newport News, VA; son of William T Jr and Queen V. **Educ:** Va State Col, Petersburg, BS, psychol, 1978, MEd, coun, 1980; Hampton Univ, Va, attended 1984; Col William & Mary, Williamsburg, Va, attended 1987; Old Dom Univ, PhD, educ & psychol, 1991. **Career:** Hampton Univ, Va, dir stud support servs, 1980-88; USY, Arlington, Va, psychologist & educr, 1986; Olde Hampton Bus Educ Ctr, Va, asst prof, psychologist, vres, 1987-; Norfolk State Univ, Va, dir undeclared students, 1989-; Old Dom Univ, Norfolk, Va, asst prof coun, 1990. **Orgs:** Undergrad adv, Kappa Alpha Psi Fraternity, 1982-88, chmn youth guide right, alumni chap, 1987-89; counr, Peninsula Literacy Coun, 1982-88; comt chmn, Va Asn Black Psychologists, 1987; bd gov, Int Platform Asn, 1990; comt chmn, Va Asn Adminr Higher Educ. **Honors/Awds:** Recognition for Achievement, Christopher Newport College, 1985-86; Certificate of Recognition, William & Mary Col, 1990-91; Black Student Retention Conference Recognition, 1989-90; Volunteer Program Achievement Award, Sarah Bonwell Hudgins Regional Center, 1989-90; Black American Doctoral Research Award, 1991-92; Armed Services Recognition, YMCA, 1990; Roads Recognition, Boys Club of Greater Hampton, 1990; Office of Human Affairs Achievement Award, 1990. **Home Addr:** 204 Dogwood Dr, Newport News, VA 23606, **Home Phone:** (757)599-5362. **Business Addr:** Psychologist, Assistant Professor, Olde Hampton Business & Education Center, 7 E Queens Way Suite 201 202, Hampton, VA 23669, **Business Phone:** (757)722-7900.

### HARRELL, ADAM NELSON, JR.
Lawyer. **Personal:** Born Mar 9, 1957, Norfolk, VA. **Educ:** Univ Va, BA, 1979; Univ Pa Sch Law, JD, 1982. **Career:** Univ Pa Ed, Black Law J, asst ed, 1980-81; Hirshcher & Fleischer, assoc; Harrell & Chambliss LLP, atty, currently, co-managing partner, currently. **Orgs:** Va Bd Asbestos Licensing & Lead Cert, 1994-97; Metrop Bus League, 2002-; bd dir, Richmond Chap Nat Coun Community & Justice, 2001-04; bd dir, Richmond Christian Leadership Inst, 2007-; Exec Comt, Old Dom Bar Asn; Third Dist Comt; Va State Bar; Lawyers Helping Lawyers Comt; bd dir, Greater Richmond Chap Am Red Cross; Va Bar Asn; Exec Comt Venture Richmond. **Business Addr:** Attorney, Co-Managing Partner, Harrell & Chambliss LLP, 8th & Main Bldg, Richmond, VA 23219, **Business Phone:** (804)915-3237.

### HARRELL, ANDRE
Entrepreneur, executive, music producer. **Personal:** Born Sep 26, 1960, Harlem, NY; children: Gianni. **Educ:** Lehman Col, commmuns maj, 1983. **Career:** Rush Mgt, vpres & gen mgr, 1985; Uptown Rec, founder & pres, 1987-92; Uptown Entertainment, pres, 1992-95; "New York Undercover", producer, 1994-96; Motown Rec, pres & chief exec officer, 1995-97; Bad Boy Entertainment, pres, 1999-2001; Nu Am

Music, founder & chief exec officer, 2001-05; Bad Boy TV, producer, 2005-06; Harrell Entertainment, founder; Harrell Rec, chief exec officer; NuAmerica, founder; With Alonzo Brown, formed Dr Jekyll & Mr Hyde (rap duo); consult, currently; Revolt Diddy's Multi-Platform Music Network, vice chmn, currently. **Business Addr:** Consultant, Bad Boy Entertainment, 8-10 W 19th St 9th Fl, New York, NY 10011.

### HARRELL, CHARLES H. (CHUCK HARRELL)

Automotive executive. **Personal:** Born Jan 1, 1945. **Educ:** Cent State Univ, BS, bus admin, 1969. **Career:** Gen Motors, oldsmobile div, dist mgr sales; Harrell Chevrolet-Oldsmobile Inc, Flat Rock, Mich, owner & pres, currently. **Orgs:** Chmn, Nat Automobile Minority Dealers Asn; chair, pres, Gen Motors Minority Dealer Asn, currently; golden life mem, Nat Asn Advan Colored People; pres, Civic Citizen's Asn; life mem, Alpha Phi Alpha Fraternity; pres, Detroit Rotary Club; bd dir Travelers' Aid; mem Detroit Optimist Club; trustee, Hartford Memorial Baptist Church. **Business Addr:** Owner, Harrell Chevrolet-Oldsmobile Inc, 23755 Allen Rd, Trenton, MI 48183, **Business Phone:** (734)782-2421.

### HARRELL, ERNEST JAMES. See Obituaries Section.

### HARRELL, H. STEVE

Automotive executive. **Personal:** Born Apr 25, 1948; son of James and Lula Bell Thomas; children: Shemanthe E Smith & H Steve II. **Career:** H S Harrell Real Estate Invest, Atlanta, Ga, pres, 1978-; Shelby Dodge Inc, Memphis, Tenn, pres, 1987-. **Orgs:** Dist chmn, Boy Scouts Am. **Business Addr:** President, Shelby Dodge Inc, 2691 Mt Moriah Rd, Memphis, TN 38115, **Business Phone:** (901)363-0006.

### HARRELL, OSCAR W., II

Educator, consultant. **Personal:** Born Bristol, VA; son of Oscar Sr and Bernice W; married Sophia M; children: Oscar W III & Stafford B. **Educ:** Va Union Univ, BA, social sci, 1960; Assumption Col, Mass, MA, CAGS, 1974; Northeastern Univ, attended 1990; Brandeis Univ, Heller Sch Social Policy & Mgt, PhD, 1994. **Career:** Leonard Training Sch NC Bd Corr, head counr, 1963-64; Gardner State Hosp, psych Soc Worker, 1964-67; Rutland Heights Hosp, coord rehab, 1967-72; Mt Wachusett Community Col, fac, 1968; Fitchburg State Col, asst dir admis, dir minority affairs/AID, 1974-81; Fitchburg State Col, fac, 1976-80; Tufts Univ, dir african am ctr, 1981-87; Mass Dept Ment Retardation, de passt comn, 1987-90; Assumption Col, Inst Social & Rehab Serv, consult & educr, 1996-2000; Harrell & Harrell Inc, consult, currently. **Orgs:** Mem & bd dir, Mass Ment Health Asn, 1969-89; Am Psychol Asn, 1976-78; Am Personnel Guid Asn, 1976-78; Am Rehab Coun Asn, 1976-78; sec & pres, Soc Organized Against Racism, 1982-; treas, Greater Boston Inter Univ Coun; Alpha Phi Alpha Fraternity; Mass Halfway House Asn; pres, Mass Br Nat Asn Advan Colored People; vpres Mass Asn Ment Health; comt mem, Racial Justice Comn; Nat YWCA; bd dir, Community Chg Inc, Boston MA; bd ordained ministry, United Methodist Church, New Eng Conf; bd mem, Deaconess Abundant Life Communities; social welfare orgn; Northeastern Jurisdiction United Methodist Church; bd mem, New Eng Deaconess Asn. **Honors/Awds:** City Representative, Gardner Massachusetts Opportunity Coun, 1970-72; Citation, Gov Mass, 1981; Citation, Mass Senate, 1987; Citation, Mass House of Rep, 1987; Plaque Appreciation as Dir African Am Ctr, Tufts Black Alumni. **Special Achievements:** Performer (non-professional) in the play "The Man Nobody Saw"; plaque, Outstanding Supporter of Education, Fitchburg Faculty, 1990. **Home Addr:** 15 Bentbrook Rd, Sudbury, MA 01776-2507, **Home Phone:** (978)443-3821. **Business Addr:** Board Member, Deaconess Abundant Life Communities, 80 Deaconess Rd, Concord, MA 01742, **Business Phone:** (978)369-5151.

### HARRELL, DR. PAULA D.

Educator. **Educ:** NC Cent Univ, BA, 1976; Ohio State Univ, MMW, 1977; Univ NC, DMA. **Career:** NC Cent Univ, Dept Music, assoc prof, chairwoman, 2004-. **Orgs:** Int Asn Jazz Educ. **Business Addr:** Chairwoman, North Carolina Central University, 204 1801 Fayetteville St, Durham, NC 27707, **Business Phone:** (919)530-7213.

### HARRELL, WILLIAM EDWIN

Government official. **Personal:** Born Mar 16, 1962, Norfolk, VA; son of Adam Sr and Charity Nix; married Johnna Carson; children: Charity Majette. **Educ:** Univ Va, BS, 1984, MS, Urban & Regional Planning, 1986, MPA, 1986. **Career:** City Suffolk, Suffolk, VA, aide analyst, 1986, sr admin analyst, 1986-87, dir mgt servs, 1987-90, dir pub utilities, 1990-95, asst city mgr, 1995-96; City Greensboro, NC, asst city mgr, 1996-2004; City Richmond, dep city mgr, 1999-2004, interim chief admin officer, 2005-07; Chesapeake City, VA, city mgr, 2007-; Hampton Roads Transit, pres & chief exec officer, currently. **Orgs:** Bd dirs, Suffolk Chamber Com, 1988-; fund distrib comt, United Way-SuffolkDiv, 1988-90; vpres, Great Bridge-Chesapeake Jaycees, 1989; Int City MgrAsn, 1986-89; Am Soc Pub Admin, 1986-88; vice chmn, Com Diversity, AmWaterworks Asn; Conf Minority Pub Adminr; trustee, St John's AME Church. **Honors/Awds:** G Robert House Young Public Administrator Award, Virginia Chapter for the American Society for Public Administration. **Special Achievements:** Fitch Rating Service has assigned the City of Chesapeake the highest bond rating available AAA the first in the City history, 2010. **Home Addr:** 2440 Deerfield Crescent, Chesapeake, VA 23321-2413, **Home Phone:** (804)686-8457. **Business Addr:** President, Chief Executive Officer, Hampton Roads Transit, 3400 Victoria Blvd, Hampton, VA 23661, **Business Phone:** (757)222-6133.

### HARRIGAN, RODNEY EMILE

Administrator. **Personal:** Born Jul 23, 1945, New York, NY; married Elaine Mims; children: Pamela & Sherrice. **Educ:** Paine Col, BS, math, 1967; IBM Syst Res Inst, attended 1969; Howard Univ, MS, comput sci, 1975. **Career:** Royal Globe Ins Co, programmer, 1968; Fed City Col, assoc prof, 1977; Howard Univ, assoc prof, 1977; IBM, systs engr, 1968-72, staff programmer, 1972-75, proj mgr, 1975-76, adv proj mgr, 1976-77, systs eng mgr, 1977-79; Post Col, instr, 1980-81; IBM, employee rels mgr, 1979-81, spec proj mgr, 1981-82, fac loan prof, 1982-92; Discovery Learning Inc, sr consult, 1990-, master trainer, 1991-; Harrigan & Assocs, founder, pres & bus consult, 1997-; NC A&T State Univ, Info Technol & Telecommunications, vice chancellor, chief info officer, 2001-07; SCORE, counr, 2009-; Family Serv Piedmont, proj mgt consult, 2009-; Bennett Col, asst dir acad comput, 2012-.NC A&T Univ, prof, comput sci, currently. **Orgs:** Asn Comput Mach; Data Processing Mgt Asn; Inst Elec Electron Engrs; Compu Soc; Alpha Kappa Mu Hon Soc; Omega Psi Phi Fraternity; exec coach, Guilford Nonprofit Consortium Exec dir Acad, 2008-; itg dir, trainer, exec coach, Ctr Creative Leadership, 1998-2000; mem adv bd, Content Circles, 2010-11. **Home Addr:** 5300 Bancroft Rd, Greensboro, NC 27405-9556, **Home Phone:** (336)621-3460. **Business Addr:** Senior Consultant, Master Trainer, Discovery Learning Inc, 431 Spring Garden St Suite 100, Greensboro, NC 27401, **Business Phone:** (336)272-9530.

### HARRINGTON, DENISE MARION

Consultant, executive. **Personal:** Born Apr 14, 1955, Washington, DC; daughter of Harold Greene and Alma; married Michael; children: Nia. **Educ:** Univ DC, music & voice; Dartmouth Col, Tuck Sch Exec Mgmt. **Career:** Harrington & Assocs, owner, founder & chief exec officer, 1990-; Commcore Consult Group, staff; Blue Dragon Commun, staff; Becomex, staff; DMH Consult Group, chief exec officer & founder, currently. **Orgs:** Bd, Classroom Law Proj; adv bd chair, Boys & Girls Club Portland, 1992-; YWCA. **Special Achievements:** Worked with Tiger Woods, Ken Griffey Jr, Vlade Divac, Michael Johnson, MiaHann, Sheryl Snoopes & many others. **Business Addr:** Founder, Chief Executive Officer, DMH Consulting Group, 11140 Rockville Pke Suite 400, Rockville, MD 20852, **Business Phone:** (301)979-7063.

### HARRINGTON, ELAINE CAROLYN

Educator, association executive, spokesperson. **Personal:** Born Aug 31, 1938, Philadelphia, PA. **Educ:** Tuskegee Inst, BS, elem educ, 1961; NC Agr & Tech State Univ, grad study, 1964; Univ Conn, Storrs, MA, supr admin, 1972; Fairleigh Dickinson Univ, develop educ; EdD. **Career:** Tuskegee Univ, 1961; JC Price Sch, teacher, 1961-71; NC Agr & Tech State Univ, demonstration teacher, 1965; Shiloh Baptist Church, dir cult prog, 1967; NC Agr & Tech State Univ, matls coord mus inst jr high students, 1968; Passaic County Community Col, prof & actg dean stud, 1972-80, prof acad founds, 1980-87, Eng & Math Dept, prof, 1988-2005, prof emer, 2005-; Univ Pittsburgh, Sem fel, 1980. **Orgs:** Soloist, Radio City Music Hall, NY City, 1958; pres, secy, NCEA & NJEA Educ Org, 1961-2005; NEA, 1961-2005; secy, Zeta Phi Beta Sorority Inc, 1963-; Nat Alliance Black Sch Educrs, 1973-; Am Personnel & Guid Asn, 1976-; YWCA; Christ Church United Method; Paterson Bd Educ; chairperson, Reg II, Nat Asn Advan Colored People, pres, Paterson Br, pres, NJ State, 1993-99; layleader, Admin Coun Chair-Christ Church United Methodist, Paterson, NJ; asst parliamentarian, Tuskegee Univ Nat Alumni Asn. **Honors/Awds:** Outstanding Young Educator Award, Greensboro Public Schs, NC, 1968; Participant Leadership Seminar Guilford Co Schs, NC, 1969; Gradute Scholarship, Zeta Phi Beta Sorority Inc, 1971; NEH, 1980. Amelia Boynton Robinson Voting Rights Award, 2009. **Home Addr:** 2712 Gunn Ave, Tuskegee Institute, AL 36088-3019, **Home Phone:** (334)727-5575. **Business Addr:** Professor Emeritus, Passaic County Community College, 1 Col Blvd, Paterson, NJ 07505, **Business Phone:** (973)684-6868.

### HARRINGTON, GERALD E.

Banker. **Personal:** Born Jan 1, 1945, Detroit, MI. **Educ:** Tenn State Univ, BS, 1967; Univ Okla; Rutgers Univ, Sch Banking. **Career:** Better Bus Bur S/E Mich, dir; Recycling Corp, vpres & chief financial officer; Omni Bank, vpres & chief financial officer; Comerica Bank, sr internal auditor; First Independence Nat Bank, sr vpres & cashier, interim pres & exec vpres, chief exec officer, 1974-90; Harrington, Baldwin & Assocs, co-founder, pres & bus financial consult. **Orgs:** Am Inst Banking; Bank Admin Inst. **Business Addr:** Co-Founder & President, Business Financial Consultant, Harrington Baldwin & Associates, 24655 Southfield Rd Suite 205, Southfield, MI 48075, **Business Phone:** (248)443-2857.

### HARRINGTON, JOHN M.

Executive, educator, police chief. **Personal:** Born Jan 1, 1956, Chicago, IL; married Sarah Walker; children: 7. **Educ:** Dartmouth Col, Hanover, Nh, BA, relig; Univ St Thomas, St Paul, MA, pub safety, 1985; Univ Minn, Minneapolis, PhD; Hamline Univ, St Paul, PhD; FBI Nat Acad, Nat Exec Inst, grad; Harvard Sr Mgt Inst, grad. **Career:** St Paul Police Dept, police officer, 1977, sgt, lt, comdr, sr comdr, chief police, 2004-10; Metro Transit Police Minneapolis-St Paul, 1985-97; Metrop State Univ, fac, 1986-, mgr; Western Dist, team comdr; Twin Cities univ, adj fac; Sch Law Enforcement, dir; Minn Senate 67th dist, 2011-12. **Orgs:** Chair, Minn Crime Victims Reparation Bd; pres, Minn Chap Nat Asn Black Law Enforcement Execs; bd dir, Girl Scout Coun, St Croix Valley; bd dir, Neighborhood House; mem state bd, comn & coun, Metro Transit Police Chief; St Paul Police Dept, 1977-2010; Pres, chief exec officer & chair, Ujamaa Pl; bd mem, DeLaSalle High Sch; bd mem, Minn Humanities Comn; bd mem, Upper Midwest Community Policing Inst; YMCA. **Home Addr:** , St Paul, MN. **Business Addr:** Faculty, Metropolitan State University, 700 7th St E, St. Paul, MN 55106, **Business Phone:** (651)793-1300.

### HARRINGTON, OTHELLA

Basketball coach, basketball player. **Personal:** Born Jan 31, 1974, Jackson, MS; married Shannon. **Educ:** Georgetown Univ, attended 1996. **Career:** Basketball player (retired), baseketball coach; Houston Rockets, forward-centre, 1996-99; Vancouver Grizzlies, 1999-2001; New York Knicks, forward-centre, 2001-04; Chicago Bulls, 2004-06; Charlotte Bobcats, power forward-ctr, 2006-08; Los Angeles D-Fenders, 2009; Petrochimi Bandar Imam BC, 2009-10; Georgetown Hoyas, dir, 2011-. **Business Addr:** Director, Georgetown University, McDonough Arena, Washington, DC 20057, **Business Phone:** (202)687-2435.

### HARRINGTON, ZELLA MASON

Administrator, nurse. **Personal:** Born Jan 29, 1940, St. Louis, MO; married Melvyn A; children: Melvyn A Jr & Kevin Mason. **Educ:** Jewish Hosp Sch Nursing, dipl, 1960; Webster Univ, BA, 1976, MA, 1977. **Career:** Nurse (retired), executive; Vis Nurses Asn, sr staff nurse, 1960-65; St Louis Transitional Hope House, exec dir; Nursery Found St Louis, nurse consult, 1963-65; St Luke's Hosp, dir; St Louis, Bd Educ, practical nursing instr, 1966; Cardinal Ritter Inst, chief nurse trainer, 1966-68; Urban League St Louis, health specialist, 1968-69; Nursing & Health Servs ARC, dir, 1969-; St Louis Div Health, chief health prom & educ, 2001-02. **Orgs:** Dir, Community Health Partnership. **Honors/Awds:** Assisted with pub "Handbook for Home Health Aides", Cardinal & Ritter Inst, 1968; listed Outstanding Contributions of Blacks, Health Care Delta Sigma Theta Sorority, 1977; George Washington Carver Award, Sigma Gamma Rho Sorority, 1978; Lifetime Achievers, 2006 Salute to Excellence Health Care Luncheon, 2006. **Business Addr:** Chief, Health Prom & Educ, 634 N Grand Blvd, St. Louis, MO 63178, **Business Phone:** (314)612-5400.

### HARRIS, AL (ALSHINARD HARRIS)

Football coach, football player. **Personal:** Born Dec 7, 1974, Pompano Beach, FL; married Shyla; children: Alshinard Jr & Gavin. **Educ:** Tex A&M Univ, Kingsville, kinesiol. **Career:** Football player (retired), coach; Tampa Bay Buccaneers, Off season/squad mem, 1997; Philadelphia Eagles, defensive back & right defensive back & left defensive back & corner back, 1998-2002; Green Bay Packers, corner back & right corner back & left corner back, 2003-09; Miami Dolphins, 2010, coaching intern, 2012-13; St. Louis Rams, right corner back, 2011-13; Kans City Chiefs, asst defensive backs coach, 2013-14, chiefs defensive asst & sec coach, 2014-. **Honors/Awds:** Pro Bowler Selection Twice, 2007-08; All Pro Selection, 2007. **Business Addr:** Chiefs Defensive Assistant, Secondary Coach, Kansas City Chiefs, 1 Arrowhead Dr, Kansas City, WI 64129, **Business Phone:** (816)920-9300.

### HARRIS, ALFRED CARL, III

Football player, spokesperson, football coach. **Personal:** Born Dec 31, 1956, Bangor, ME; son of Alfred C Jr and Gloria Smith; married Margaret D; children: Emily & Jason. **Educ:** Ariz State Univ, BS, 1982. **Career:** Football player (retired), coach, motivational speaker; Chicago Bears, linebacker, 1979-88; Philadelphia Eagles, 1989-90; San Francisco 49ers, asst coach, 2009-10; Ambassador Speakers Bur & Lit Agency, speaker, currently. **Orgs:** Founder, Faith God Found; served churches, banquets, co, corp & charities, as well as doing chapelsprof baseball & football teams. **Special Achievements:** First unanimous all-American selection in Arizona State University history. **Home Addr:** 12 Stone Ridge Dr, Barrington, IL 60010-9593, **Home Phone:** (847)381-2971. **Business Addr:** Motivational Speaker, Ambassador Speakers Bureau & Literary Agency, 1107 Battlewood St, Franklin, TN 37069, **Business Phone:** (615)370-4700.

### HARRIS, ALONZO

Judge. **Personal:** Born Jul 20, 1961, Opelousas, LA; son of Aaron and Rosa B; married Dawn W; children: Ashley, Lanisha, Valenia, Alonzo Jr & Alexis. **Educ:** Southern Univ, BS, 1983, Law Ctr, JD, 1986. **Career:** Harris & Harris Law Firm, atty law, 1983-87; La Secy State 27th Judicial Dist, dist judge, 1993-. **Orgs:** La Bar Asn, 1987; SW Lawyers Asn, 1990-; La Judicial Col, 1993; Am Asn Juv Judges, 1994; Opelousas Rotary Club, 1994. **Special Achievements:** First Black judge elected in the parish and the youngest District judge in the state of Louisiana. **Home Addr:** 9509 Hwy 103, Washington, LA 70589, **Home Phone:** (318)826-7104. **Business Addr:** District Judge, State of Louisiana District Court, 118 S Ct St St Landry Parish, Opelousas, LA 70571-0478, **Business Phone:** (337)948-0584.

### HARRIS, ANTHONY

Executive. **Personal:** Born Jun 27, 1953, Chicago, IL; son of Roy and Alberta; married Angela C; children: Anthony & Alexander. **Educ:** Purdue Univ, BS, mech engineering, 1975; Harvard Bus Sch, MBA, 1979; Purdue Univ, Deng, 2013. **Career:** Stand Oil Co, Ind, proj engr & design engr, 1975-79; Nat Soc Black Engrs, founding pres, 1975; Ford Motor Co, qual & prod supvr, 1979-81; Eastern Mich Univ, vis lectr, 1980-81; Ford Aerospace & Communs, prog mgr, 1981-86; Anaheim Lincoln Mercury, gen mgr, 1986-87; Sonoma Ford Lincoln Mercury, pres & chief exec officer, 1979-92; Stand Pac Gas Line Inc, pres; Pac Gas & Elec Co, vpres sales & mktg, 1992-99, vpres nat acct servs, 1992-2001 & western region sales; Pac Conserv Corp, chief exec officer, 1995-96, vpres bus customer serv, 1996-2001; Calpine Corp, vpres mkt, 2001-06; Campbell/Harris Security Equip Co, pres & chief exec officer, 2007-. **Orgs:** Vpres, 100 Black Men Am, 1990-92; bd dir, OICW, 1994-; bd dir, Oakland Mus, 1995-; bd dir, Marcus Foster Found, 1996-; pres & adv bd, Sonoma State Col, Purdue Univ; Am Soc Mech Engrs; Soc Automotive Engrs; Exec Leadership Coun; adv bd, One Calif Bank; pres & chief exec officer, Silicon Valley; founder & chair adv bd, Nat Soc Black Eng, 2002-; bd dir, Fuel Systs Solutions Inc, 2013. **Home Addr:** 2809 Sea View Pkwy, Alameda, CA 94502. **Business Addr:** President, Chief Executive Officer, Campbell/Harris Security Equipment Co, 875-A Island Dr Suite 356, Alameda, CA 94502-6768, **Business Phone:** (510)864-8010.

### HARRIS, ARTHUR L., SR.

Association executive, accountant. **Personal:** Born Feb 14, 1935, Texarkana, AR; son of Charlie and Dorthy Johnson; married Martha A; children: Lisa A, Alfred L & Arthur L Jr. **Educ:** San Diego City Col, assoc sci, 1981. **Career:** US Postal Serv, 1976-80; Defense Finance & Acct Serv, Dept Defense, acct tech, 1981-97; CA Veterans Bd, 1991-96; Dept Calif Veterans Foreign Wars, sr vice comdr. **Orgs:** Life mem, Disabled Am Veterans; life mem, Fleet Res Asn; post comdr, 1984-86, dist comdr, 1989-90, state comdr, 2000-01, Veterans Foreign Wars. **Special Achievements:** First African Am Triple Crown Comdr, Veterans Foreign Wars of the USA. **Home Addr:** 8759 Dewsbury Ave, San Diego, CA 92126-2427, **Home Phone:** (858)695-0399. **Business Addr:** CA.

### HARRIS, DR. ARTHUR LEONARD, III

Educator. **Personal:** Born Jul 12, 1949, Pittsburgh, PA; married Wendy; children: Arthur L IV & Wesley P. **Educ:** Community Col Allegheny County, AS, 1971; Temple Univ, BA, 1973; Univ Mass, MEd, 1976, EdD, 1986. **Career:** Univ Mass, grad asst, 1973-74; Bd Educ Springfield, MA, classroom instr, 1974-82; Pa State Schuylkill Campus, prog asst, 1981-84; Penn State Univ Hazleton Campus, Instr, 1981-, dir continuing educ, 1984-, Dept African Am Studies, instr, currently; Penn State Univ, Instr, 2012-. **Orgs:** Bd mem, Hazleton Leadership; master, Mt Nebo 118 Prince Hall Affiliated; Nat Univ Continuing Educ Asn; Hazleton Area Chamber Com; City Coun, Pottsville, PA, 1994-; rep, Schuylkill Campus; dir, Hazleton Campus. **Home Addr:** 319 N 3rd St, Pottsville, PA 17901-2515, **Home Phone:** (570)622-5381. **Business Addr:** Instructor, Pennsylvania State University, 76 Univ Dr 107 Mem Bldg, Hazleton, PA 18202, **Business Phone:** (570)450-3111.

**HARRIS, HON. BARBARA ANN**
Judge. **Personal:** Born Jul 18, 1951, Atlanta, GA; daughter of Thomas Sr. **Educ:** Harvard Univ, AB (cum laude), 1973; Univ Mich Law Sch, JD, 1976; Nat Judicial Col, judicial studies. **Career:** Judge (retired); Ga Supreme Ct, Justice Charles L Weltner, law clerk, 1976-77; Northern Dist Ga, asst US atty, 1977-82; Atlanta Munic Ct, assoc judge, 1982-92, chief judge, criminal Law, 1992. **Orgs:** Bd dir, Am Judicature Soc; Eta Phi Beta, 1980-; State Bar Ga; bd mem, Determine Fitness Bar Applicants Supreme Ct Ga; exec comn, Gate City Bar Asn, 1985-87; co-founder, Ga Asn Black Women Attys; bd mem: Am Bar Asn, Nat Conf Spec Ct Judges; Nat Bar Asn judicial coun; exec comn, Leadership Atlanta, 1987-88; Officer, Atlanta Womens Network; Drifters Inc, Nat parliamentarian, 1990-; bd mem, Lit Vol; Ga Supreme Ct, Comn Race & Ethnic Bias, 1993-95, Comn Equality, 1993-, Comn Substance Abuse, 1995-; bd mem, Salvation Army; bd mem, Metrop Fair Housing; bd mem, Atlanta/Fulton County Drug Ct Task Force; bd mem, Friends Fulton County Jail; bd mem, Domestic Crisis Intervention Ctr; bd mem, Atlanta/Fulton County Justice Ctr Exec Comt; Lawyers Club Atlanta, currently. **Special Achievements:** First woman to serve as Chief Judge of Atlanta Municipal Court. Georgia Association of Black Women Attorneys creation of the Barbara A. Harris Founders Award for exemplary community service, to be awarded annually to an African American lawyer in the state of Georgia committed to community participation, 2006. **Home Addr:** 1301 Avon Ave SW, Atlanta, GA 30310-3955, **Home Phone:** (404)758-9395. **Business Addr:** Member, Lawyers Club of Atlanta, 1230 Peachtree St NE Promenade Bldg Suite 3850, Atlanta, GA 30309, **Business Phone:** (404)815-5250.

**HARRIS, BARBARA CLEMENTINE**
Bishop, clergy, executive. **Personal:** Born Jun 12, 1930, Philadelphia, PA. **Educ:** Charles Morris Price Sch Advert & Jour, cert, 1950; Villanova Univ, attended; Urban Theol Unit, Sheffield, eng, attended 1979; Pa Found Pastoral Coun, grad. **Career:** Episcopal bishop (retired), Assisting Bishop; Joseph V Baker Assocs Inc, Philadelphia, pres, 1968; Sun Oil Co, community rels consult, mgr community & urban affairs, pub rels mgr, 1973-77, sr staff consult; Episcopal Church, ordained priest, 1980; St Augustine Hippo Episcopal Church, Norristown PA, priest-in-charge, 1980-84; Church Advocate, interim rector, 1984-88; Episcopal Church Pub Co, exec dir, 1984-89; Mass Diocese Episcopal Church, Boston, Mass, bishop, 1989-2002; Diocese Wash DC, staff; Episcopal Diocese Wash, assisting bishop, 1989, 2003-. **Orgs:** Union Black Episcopalians; Episcopal Churchs Standing Comn; Int Peace; mem bd trustee, Episcopal Divinity Sch; vpres, Episcopal City Mission; pres, Episcopal Urban Caucus; bd mem, Pa Prison Socs. **Business Addr:** Assisting Bishop, Episcopal Diocese of Washington, Mt St Alban, Washington, DC 20016-5094, **Business Phone:** (202)537-6555.

**HARRIS, DR. BERNARD A., JR.**
Astronaut, physician, association executive. **Personal:** Born Jun 26, 1956, Temple, TX; son of Bernard Sr and Gussie H Burgess; married Sandra Lewis; children: 1. **Educ:** Univ Houston, BS, biol, 1978; Tex Tech Univ Health Sci Ctr, MD, 1982; Univ Tex Med Br, MMS, biomed sci, 1996; Univ Houston, MBA, 1999. **Career:** Univ Tex Speech & Hearing Inst, res asst, 1975-78; Spectrum Emergency Care, pvt pract, 1983-85; Mayo Clinic, internal med, 1985; S Tex Primary Care Group, pvt pract, 1985-86; San Jose Med Group, pvt pract, 1986-87; NASA & Johnson Space Ctr, clin scientist & flight surgeon, 1987-90, proj mgr, 1988-90, astronaut cand, 1990-91, astronaut, 1991-96; Univ Tex Sch Med, clin prof, 1988-96; Baylor Col Med, asst prof, 1988-96; Univ Tex Sch Pub Health, adj prof, 1989-96; Univ Tex Med Br, clin assoc prof, 1993-98; Space Shuttle Columbia, mission specialist, 1993; Space Hab Inc, chief scientist, vpres sci & health servs, 1996-2000; Space Shuttle Discovery, comdr, 1995; Harris Found, founder, chmn, bd mem & pres, 1998-; Space Media Inc, vpres bus develop, 2000; SPACEHAB Inc, vpres & chief scientist; Vesalius Ventures Inc, chief exec officer & managing partner, currently. **Orgs:** Bd regents, Tex Tech Univ; Am Col Physicians Fel; Am Soc Bone & Mineral Res; Asn Space Explorers; Am Astronaut Soc; Aerospace Med Asn; Nat Med Asn; Tex Med Asn; Harris County Med Soc; bd dir, Boys & Girls Club Houston; comt mem, Greater Houston Area Coun Phys Fitness & Sports; bd dir, Manned Space Flight Found; Nat Space Club; chair, Space & Tech Adv Bd; Houston Tech Ctr Comn; Med Informatics & Tech Applications Consortium, NASA Life Sci Comn; NASA Life & Microgravity Sci & Appln Adv Comn; Aircraft Owners & Pilot Asn; vpres, Spacehab Inc; Am Socs Bone & Mineral Res; Phi Kappa Phi Hon Socs; Phi Kappa Phi Hon Socs; Endorsement Microsoft; bd, Nat Math & Sci Initiative; Houston Angel Network; Med Informatics; Houston Technol Ctr; Nat Space Biomed Res Inst; Bd Sci Counors; Coun Nat Inst Health/Nat Inst Deafness; Tex Higher Educ Coalition; Nat Academies Inst Med; Tex Comn Rep Stud Body Commun Dis; fel Am Col Physicians; NASA Biol & Phys Sci Comt; Tex Tech's Univ Bd Regents; Technol & Applications Ctr; sr consult, NASA Aerospace Safety Pane. **Honors/Awds:** University of Houston Achievement Award, 1978; Group Achievement Award, NASA Lyndon B Johnson Space Ctr, 1993; Flight Medal, 1993; NASA Space; Physician of the Year, Nat Tech Asn, 1993; Achiever of the Year, 1993; Achievement Award, Kappa Alpha Psi Fraternity, 1993; NASA Outstanding Performance Rating, 1993; Distinguished Alumnus, Univ Houston Alumni Orgn, 1994; Distinguished Scientist of the Year, ARCS Found, 1994; Space Act Tech Brief Award, 1995; DSc, Morehouse Sch Med, 1996; Medal of Excellence, Golden State Minority Found, 1996; Challenger Award, Ronald McNair Found, 1996; Award Achievement, Asn Black Cardiologist, 1996; Strong Men, Strong Women Award, VA Power, 1997; Civil & Humanitarian Award, Fiesta Inc, 1997; NASA Group Achievement Award, 1997; NASA Team Excellence Award, 1998; Savvy Award Comm Serv, 1999; Candle in Dark Award, Morehouse Col, 2000; Hall Fame, Tex Sci, 2000; Horatio Alger Award, 2000; Hon doctorates, Stony Brook Univ; NASA Space Flight Medal; NASA Award Merit; 2000 Horatio Alger Award; Numerous other honors and awards. **Special Achievements:** First African American to walk in space, 1995; Author & co author of several scientific articles and papers. **Home Addr:** 2327 S Lake Dr, 2327 S Lake Dr, TX 77573-2877. **Business Addr:** President, Founder, The Harris Foundation, 1330 Post Oak Blvd Suite 2550, Houston, TX 77056, **Business Phone:** (713)877-1731.

**HARRIS, BERNARDO JAMAINE**
Football player. **Personal:** Born Oct 15, 1971, Chapel Hill, NC; married Kellie Farrington; children: Bradley. **Educ:** NC State Univ, attended 1994. **Career:** Football player (retired); Green Bay Packers, 1995, mid linebacker, 1997-2001; Baltimore Ravens, right inside linebacker, 2002, 2003. **Honors/Awds:** Rookie of the Year, 1995.

**HARRIS, DR. BETTY WRIGHT**
Educator, administrator, chemist. **Personal:** Born Jul 29, 1940, Monroe, LA; daughter of Henry Jake and Legertha; married Alloyd Sr; children: Selita, Jeffrey (deceased) & Alloyd A II. **Educ:** Southern Univ, Baton Rouge, BS, chem, 1961; Atlanta Univ, MS, chem, 1963; Univ NMex, PhD, 1975. **Career:** Miss Valley State Univ, math, phys sci & chem teacher, 1963; Southern Univ, New Orleans, chem instr, 1964-72; Univ Okla, res asst summer, 1966; Int Bus Mach, vis staff mem summer, 1969; Los Alamos Sci Lab, vis staff mem summers, 1970-72; Los Alamos Nat Lab, Chem & Metall Res/Anal Chem Grp, res chem, 1970-2002; Conn Col, chem teacher, 1974-75; Solar Turbines Inc, chief chem technol, 1982-84; Univ Nmex, adj prof org chem, 1999; US Dept Energy, sr doc reviewer, 2000-; Solar Turbine Inc, chief chem technol. **Orgs:** Delta Sigma Theta Sorority, 1959-; Nat Consortium Black Prof Develop, 1975-; nat mem, Nat Asn Advan Colored People, 1975; Planning Conf Status Women Sci, Washington, DC, 1977; US Dept Labor Women Community Serv, 1978-; Nat Tech Asn, 1979-; Sunday sch, catechism teacher, Lutheran Ch Coun; chmn, bd dir, Self-Help Inc; chmn, Mission Outreach Bd, sec, Multicultural Comn, Rocky Mountain Synod Evangel Lutheran Ch Am; Women UnitedYouth, Albuquerque Pub Sch; outreach prog, Los Alamos Nat Lab; Sigma Xi, 1980-; Nat Asn Parlimentarians, 1989-; chair, Cent NM Sect Am Chem Soc, 1993-94; pres, NMex State, Bus & Prof Women, Los Alamos, 1996-97; bd dir, Lutheran Off Govt Ministry, 1998-; pres, Southern Christian Leadership Conf, Albuquerque, Metrop Chap Inc; 50 yr mem Am Chem Soc. **Home Addr:** 13207 Chalet Pl Suite 101, Germantown, MD 20874. **Business Addr:** Senior Document Reviewer, US Department of Energy, HS-93 Off Doc Rev, Germantown, MD 20874-1290, **Business Phone:** (301)903-1563.

**HARRIS, BILL (WILLIAM ANTHONY HARRIS)**
Educator, poet, writer. **Educ:** Wayne State Univ, BA, MA. **Career:** Poet, playwriter; Yardbird Suite, writer; "Every Goodby Ain't Gone", 1989; Stories About Old Days, 1990; Jazzmobile, prod coord; Wayne State Univ, assoc prof, prof eng, emer, currently, Book: Birth of a Notion; Or, The Half Ain't Never Been Told, A Narrative Account with Entertaining Passages of the State of Minstrelsy & of America & the True Relation Thereof. **Business Addr:** Professor of Emeritus, Wayne State University, 10001 5057 Woodward Suite 9408, Detroit, MI 48202, **Business Phone:** (313)577-3414.

**HARRIS, BRUKLIN. See WRIGHT, N'BUSHE.**

**HARRIS, BURNELL**
Educator, government official. **Personal:** Born Oct 19, 1954, Fayette, MS; son of Levi and Louiza; married Dyann Bell; children: Tomika Tantrice, Tineciaa & Tiaura Tichelle. **Educ:** Alcorn State Univ, BA, hist & polit sci, 1976, MS, polit sci, 1993. **Career:** W Dist Jr High Sch, instr hist & social inst, 1976-77; Adams Jefferson Franklin County, Comn Action Agency, instr ged & consumer educ, 1977-78; Alcorn State Univ, instr hist, 1978-81; Grand Gulf Nuclear Sta, bechtel security supvr, 1981-83; Jefferson Co, circuit clerk, 1982-2007, adj prof hist, 1993-94. **Orgs:** Jefferson Co Nat Advan Asn Colored People; Phi Beta Sigma Fraternity; secy, Mountain Valley Lodge 6; MS Circuit Clerks Asn; potentate Arabia Shrine Temple 29. **Honors/Awds:** Outstanding Leadership Award, Gov Off Job Develop & Training, 1978. **Home Addr:** 217 Hwy 28, PO Box 893, Fayette, MS 39069-4377, **Home Phone:** (601)786-6147.

**HARRIS, CALVIN D.**
School administrator, county government official. **Personal:** Born Aug 27, 1941, Clearwater, FL; son of Augustus and Alberta Beatrice; married Ruth H Owens; children: Randall, Cassandra & Eric. **Educ:** Gibbs Jr Col, St Petersburg, Fla, AA, 1965; Univ S Fla, BA, 1966; Truman State Univ, Kirksville, MA, 1970; Nova Univ, Ft Lauderdale, EdD, 1975. **Career:** Pinellas Co Sch Syst, instr, hist, 1966-70; Seminole High Sch, Social Studies Instr, 1968-70; St Petersburg Jr Col, dean, dir continuing educ, 1970-75, provost, open campus, 1979-94, dir spec prog, 1975-79, dir stud comn & serv, 1970-75; St Petersburg Col, dir stud community serv, 1970-75; dir progs spec students, 1975-79; Pinellas Co Govt, comnr, 1998-. **Orgs:** Chmn, Pinellas Co Arts Coun, 1980; State Employ & Training Coun; Pinellas Co Coord Coun; Pinellas Manpower Planning Consortium; State Fla Standing Comn Continuing Educ; chmn, Ponce de Leon Elem Sch Adv Com; dep comnr Clearwater Babe Ruth Baseball; Deleg White House Conf Families; guest columnist, Eve Ind Newspaper; chmn, Juv Welfare Bd; mem bd dir, Am Red Cross, YMCA; mem adv bd, First Union Bank; mem bd dir, Upper Pinellas Asn Retarded C; Employ & Develop Coun; Fla Asn Counties; chmn, Fla Counties Found, 2000, 2010; Nat Asn Counties; Pres cabinet; Affirmative Action Comt; Friendship Trail Bridge Oversight Comt; Juv Welfare Bd; Pinellas Co Value Adjust Bd; Pinellas Educ Found; chmn, Post-Disaster Redevelop Comt; Salvation Army Community Adv Bd; St. Petersburg Col Appl Ethics Inst Bd; St. Petersburg Col Educ Adv Bd; St. Petersburg Col Hospitality Adv Comt; Fla Asn Counties Bd Dirs; St. Petersburg Col Found; YMCA Suncoast; United Way; Am Heart Asn. **Honors/Awds:** Past-Pres Award, Clearwater Am Little League, 1978; Certificate of Appreciation, Pinellas Co Sch Bd, 1978; David Bilgore Memorial Award, Clearwater Kiwanis Club, 1989. **Home Addr:** 1621 Young Ave, Clearwater, FL 33756, **Home Phone:** (727)581-9731. **Business Addr:** Commissioner, Pinellas County Government, 315 Co St 5th Fl, Clearwater, FL 33756, **Business Phone:** (727)464-3360.

**HARRIS, CARLA**
Executive, executive director, association executive. **Educ:** Harvard Univ, Econs; Harvard Bus Sch, MBA, 1987. **Career:** Morgan Stanley Investment Mgt, managing dir & vice chmn-Global Wealth Mgt & Sr Client Advisor, 1987-. **Orgs:** Chair Bd, Morgan Stanley Found; Food Bank NYC; Exec Leadership Coun; Sponsors Educ Opportunity; A Better Chance Inc; Apollo Theater Found; Mt. Sinai Hosp; chair, Nat Women's Bus Coun, 2013; vice chmn, Wealth Mgt & Sr Client Advisor, Morgan Stanley. **Honors/Awds:** "Black Enterprise," Top 50 African Americans on Wall Street; "Essence," The 50 Women Who are Shaping the World; "Ebony," 15 Corporate Women at The Top; "Fortune," The 50 Most Powerful Black Executives in Corporate America; Harvard University Black Men's Forum, Woman of the Year, 2004; "Fortune," Most Influential List, 2005; The Network Journal," 25 Most Outstanding Women in Business, 2005; U. S. Bankers Top 25 Most Powerful Women in Finance, 2009-12; "Black Enterprise," 75 Most Powerful Blacks on Wall Street, 2011. **Special Achievements:** Author: "Expect To Win". **Business Addr:** Vice Chairman, Morgan Stanley Investment Management Inc, 522 Fifth Ave, New York, NY 10036, **Business Phone:** (212)296-6600.

**HARRIS, CARLA ANN**
Executive, singer. **Personal:** Born Oct 28, 1962, Port Arthur, TX. **Educ:** Harvard Univ, AB, econ; Harvard Bus Sch, MBA. **Career:** Practising Law Inst, fac; Morgan Stanley, investment banker, 1987, Mergers & Acquisitions dept, 1985, managing dir global capital markets, currently, chair Placement Commitment Equity Comt, currently; gospel singer, 2000. Albums: Carla's First Christmas; joy is waiting, 2006. **Orgs:** Bd chair, NY City Food Bank Food Survival; bd chair, Morgan Stanley Found; adv bd, Harvard Univ Bus Sch Alumni Asn; St Charles Borromeo Cath Church; bd coun, Manhattan Coun Boy Scouts Am; Exec Leadership Coun; sr mem, Equity Syndicate desk. **Business Addr:** Managing Director, Morgan Stanley, 1585 Broadway, New York, NY 10036, **Business Phone:** (212)761-4000.

**HARRIS, CAROL R.**
Sales manager, consultant. **Personal:** Born Jun 12, 1954, West Point, MS. **Educ:** Cornell Col, IA, BA, psychol fr, educ, 1976; Keller Grad Sch Bus, MBA, mkt, 1978. **Career:** ADT Security Systs, gen mgr, 1977-97; Pitney Bowes, maj acct exec, 2002-04; Alarm Detection Systs, sr security consult, 2004-. **Orgs:** Co-chmn, Nat Conv NBMBAA, 1981; Nat Black MBA Asn, 1981; treas, 1986-89, vpres, 1991, Young Execs in Politics; co-chmn, Young Execs in Polit Awards Banquet, 1989. **Honors/Awds:** ADT Chicago Sales Rep of the Year, 1982, 1984, 1986; Youth Executive of the Year, Young Exec in Politics, 1986; ADT Career Develop Prog, valedictorian, 1992. **Business Addr:** Senior Security Consultant, Alarm Detection Systems, 1111 Church Rd, Aurora, IL 60505, **Business Phone:** (630)844-5318.

**HARRIS, CASPA L., JR.**
Association executive, accountant, lawyer. **Personal:** Born May 20, 1928, Washington, DC. **Educ:** Am Univ, BA, acct, 1958, Wash Col Law, JD, 1967. **Career:** Auditor, educator (retired); Peat Marwick Mitchell & Co, sr auditor, 1958-62; Howard Univ, vpres bus & fiscal affairs, treas, comptroller, 1965-87, chief internal auditor, 1962-65, prof law sch, 1967-87; US. Cols & Univs, consult. **Orgs:** Comnr, Fairfax Co Redevel & Housing Auth, 1970-73; bd, Common Fund; bd, Connie Lee Ins Co; State Va Debt Mgt Comn; Presidential CommHistorical Black Col & Univ; Columbian Harmony Soc; Nat Harmony Memorial Pk; Supreme Ct Bar; Am, DC, Va Bar Asn; Ar Inst CPA's; Va Soc CPA's; Acad Mgt; Fin Exec Inst; Nat Asn Col & Univ Bus Officers; consult, NIH; bd dir, Morse Enterprises Inc; Edinburgh Centre Carbon Innovation; chmn dir, Col Construct Loan Asn; pres, chmn, Nat Asn Col & Univ Bus Officers; consult, Com Capital Access Prog Corp. **Honors/Awds:** Distinguished Alumni Award, The Am Univ, Sch Bus Admin. **Home Addr:** 39109 John Wolford Rd, Waterford, VA 20197. **Business Addr:** Board Member, Morse Enterprises Inc, 510 Wolf Dr 1st Fl, Silver Spring, MD 20904, **Business Phone:** (301)879-7933.

**HARRIS, CHARLES CORNELIUS**
Manager, financial manager. **Personal:** Born Mar 2, 1951, Arkadelphia, AR; son of Benjamin Franklin (deceased) and Lucy Lois (deceased); married Marva Lee Bradley; children: Charla Nicole. **Educ:** Stanford Univ, BCE, 1973, MCE, 1974. **Career:** Procter & Gamble, cost engr, 1974-75, affirmative action specialist, 1975-76, bldg design engr, 1976-81, proj engr, 1981-84, proj mgr, 1984-91, prog mgr, 1991-94, purchasing mgr, 1994. **Orgs:** Kappa Alpha Frat, 1969; Adv Jr Achievement, 1978-81; Sun Sch teacher, chmn deacon bd, Mt Zion Bapt Chap Woodlawn, 1979, 1983-96; consult, Cincinnati Minorty Contractors Asst Corp, 1981; exec bd mem, Cincinnati Nat Asn Advan Colored People, 1994-96; Black Male Coalition, 1994. **Honors/Awds:** Scholar Stanford Univ, 1968-73; EIT St Ohio, 1976. **Home Addr:** 5766 Chancellor Lane, Morrow, OH 45152, **Home Phone:** (513)779-1655.

**HARRIS, CHARLES F. See Obituaries Section.**

**HARRIS, CHARLES SOMERVILLE**
Educator. **Personal:** Born Aug 22, 1950, Richmond, VA; married Lenora Billings. **Educ:** Hampton Inst, BA & BS, mass media, 1972; Univ Mich, 1973. **Career:** Hampton Inst, audio-vis specialist, 1972-73; Newsweek, staff writer, 1973; Univ Mich, asst athletic dir, 1973-79; Univ Pa, dir athletics, 1979-85; Ariz State Univ, dir athletics, 1985-96; Excel Develop Systs Inc, partner, 1987-; Mid-Eastern Athletic Conf, comnr, 1996-2002; Nc State Univ, dir athletics; Averett Univ, dir athletics, 2004-07, vpres stud servs, 2007-09, exec vpres, currently. **Orgs:** Kappa Alpha Psi, 1971-; Valley Big Bro, 1985-96; Valley Sun YMCA, 1986-96; Sigma Pi Phi, 1987-; Greensboro Sports Comn, 1996-2004; Danville, Pittsylvania Habitat Humanity, 2004; numerous Natcollegiate athletic Asn; bd mem, Nat Asn Col dir Athletics; Nat Col Athletic Asn. **Home Addr:** PO Box 1628, Greensboro, NC 27402-1628.

**Business Addr:** Executive Vice President, Averett University, 420 W Main St, Danville, VA 24541, **Business Phone:** (434)791-5600.

**HARRIS, DR. CHARLES WESLEY**
Dean (education), educator. **Personal:** Born Sep 12, 1929, Auburn, AL; children: Neeka & Angela. **Educ:** Morehouse Col, BA, 1949; Univ Pa, MA, 1950; Univ Wis, PhD, 1959; Harvard Univ, attended 1964; Univ Mich, attended 1966; Johns Hopkins Univ; Georgetown Sch Law. **Career:** Professor, dean (retired), professor emeritus; Tex Col, asst prof polit sci, 1950-53; Tuskegee Inst, asst prof polit sci, 1954-56; Univ Wis, James Found fel, 1956-58; Grambling State Univ, assoc prof polit sci, 1959-61; Coppin State Col, assoc prof polit sci, 1961-70; res assoc, Xerox Corp, 1968; Ford Found, res grant, 1969; Howard Univ, chmn polit sci, assoc dean col arts & sci, 1982-92, prof polit sci, 2002, prof emer, currently, dept polit sci, mentor, Cong Res Serv, sr specialist & chief govt div; US Civil Serv Comn, assoc dir exec insts; Smithsonian Inst, Woodrow Wilson fel, 1992-94. **Orgs:** Pi Gamma Mu Hon Soc, Univ Pa Chap, 1951; div chair & sr specialist, Govt Div Cong Res Serv, 1974-74; Alpha Phi Alpha Frat; Alpha Kappa Mu Hon Soc. **Home Addr:** 13908 Turnmore Rd, Silver Spring, MD 20906, **Home Phone:** (301)460-0285.

**HARRIS, CLIFTON L.**
Businessperson, mayor, business owner. **Personal:** Born Feb 3, 1938, Leland, MS; son of Willie and Gertrude; married Maxine Robinson; children: La'Clitterfer Charisse. **Career:** Harris Construct Co, Arcola, Miss, owner; C&M Realty Co, Arcola, Miss, owner; Town Arcola, Arcola, Miss, mayor, 1986. **Orgs:** Nat Asn Advan Colored People, 1969; Elk Lodge, 1984; Deercreek Nat Gas Dist, 1986-; Salvation Army, 1986; bd mem, Am Red Cross, 1988-; treas, Miss Conf Black Mayors, 1990; bd mem, Nat Asn Advan Colored People; pres, bd mem, Miss Rural Water Asn. **Honors/Awds:** Certificate of Achievement, Delta Jr Col, 1983-84; Certificate of Achievement, Howard Univ, 1988; Certificate of Accomplishment, Clark Atlanta Univ; Meritorious Service Award, Nat Asn Advan Colored People. **Home Addr:** PO Box 383, Arcola, MS 38722-0383, **Home Phone:** (662)827-7347. **Business Addr:** Board Member, Mississippi Rural Water Association, 5400 N Midway Rd, Raymond, MS 39154, **Business Phone:** (601)857-2433.

**HARRIS, COREY**
Singer, guitarist. **Personal:** Born Feb 21, 1969, Denver, CO. **Educ:** Bates Col, BA, anthropol, 1991. **Career:** Musician; Thomas J. Watson, Cameroon, fel; Albums: Between Midnight & Day, 1995; Fish Ain't Bitin', 1997; Greens from the Garden, 1999; Vu-Du Menz, 2000; Live at Starr Hill, 2001; Downhome Sophisticate, 2002; Didn't My Lord Deliver Daniel; Johnny's Blues: A Tribute To Johnny Cash, 2003; Mississippi to Mali, 2003; Daily Bread, 2005; Zion Crossroads, 2007; blu. black, 2009; Father Sun Mother Earth, 2011; Fulton Blues, 2013; Live from Turtle Island, 2015. Labels: Alligator; Rounder; Telarc. TV appearances: The Blues, 2003; Winston fel. **Business Addr:** Musician, Vocalist & Guitarist, Rounder Records, 29 Camp St, Cambridge, MA 02140, **Business Phone:** (617)354-0700.

**HARRIS, COREY LAMONT**
Football player, business owner. **Personal:** Born Oct 25, 1969, Indianapolis, IN; children: Lauren. **Educ:** Vanderbilt Univ, BS, human resources. **Career:** Football player (retired), bus owner; Houston Oilers, 1992; Green Bay Packers, defensive back, kick returner, 1992-94; Seattle Seahawks, right corner back & free safety, 1995-96; Miami Dolphins, free safety, 1997; Primary Kickoff Return Specialist; Wide Receiver; Baltimore Ravens, strong safety & free safety & kick returner, 1998-2001; Detroit Lions, strong safety & free safety, 2002-03; Somethin Live, R&B club owner, currently; Strong Young Black Entrepreneur Rec, prod & dir, currently. **Orgs:** Kappa Alpha Psi Fraternity Inc. **Honors/Awds:** Raven's Ed Block Courage Award, 2001; Joe Schmidt Leadership Award, 2002; Super Bowl Champion Once (XXXV). **Home Addr:** , TX. **Business Addr:** Producer, Director, SYBE Rec, 209 Printers Alley, Nashville, TX 37201, **Business Phone:** (615)254-5483.

**HARRIS, CORNELIA**
Educator. **Personal:** Born Sep 30, 1963, Ennis, TX; daughter of Virgil L Sr and Cleo; married Douglas E. **Educ:** Tex Woman's Univ, BS, social work, 1985; Alternative Cert Prog, Dallas, TX, 1990; MS, educ admin, 1996. **Career:** Big Brothers & Sisters Metro Dallas, caseworker, 1986-90; Dallas Independent Sch Dist, Dallas, Tex, teacher, kindergarten, 1990-. **Orgs:** Young Dem TWU campus, 1982-83; Nat Asn Advan Colored People TWU Campus, 1982-85; Alpha Omega Social Club TWU, 1983-84; Delta Sigma Theta Sorority, 1983-; Social Sci Soc TWU Campus, 1985; Nat Asn Social Workers, 1985-88; Nat Asn Black Social Workers, 1985-90. **Home Addr:** PO Box 2006, Red Oak, TX 75154-1570. **Business Addr:** Teacher, Nancy J Cochran Elementary School, 6000 Keeneland Pkwy, Dallas, TX 75211, **Business Phone:** (972)794-4600.

**HARRIS, CYNTHIA JULIAN**
President (organization), business owner. **Personal:** Born Oct 11, 1953, Burlington, NC. **Educ:** Univ NC, Chapel Hill, BA, psychol, 1975; Univ Va, Charlottesville, MA, counr educ, human serv, 1977. **Career:** Proj AID-SIR, Richmond, VA, rehab counr, 1977-78; NC St Univ, dir Upward Bound, 1978-98; CJH Educ Grant Servs Inc, owner & pres, 1998-; Slender Lady Northridge, owner; pres, One Mission Tree Inc, currently. **Orgs:** Greater Raleigh Chamber Com: SAEOPP; active mem, Delta Sigma Theta Sorority; interim exec dir, pres, Mission tree; active mem, human resources dir, First Baptist Church Raleigh; field reader, US Dept Educ; active mem, Delta Sigma Theta Sorority; pres, Cynthia J Harris; dir, Planned Gifts jr blind am. **Home Addr:** 700 Rawls Dr, Raleigh, NC 27610-2858. **Business Addr:** Owner, President, CJH Educational Grant Services Inc, PO Box 14264, Raleigh, NC 27620-4264, **Business Phone:** (919)832-0306.

**HARRIS, CYNTHIA MARIE**
Educator. **Educ:** Univ Kans, BA, biol, 1978, MA, genetics, 1980; Meharry Med Col, PhD, nutrit biochem, 1984; Harvard Sch Pub Health, postdoctoral, biol/toxicol, 1987. **Career:** Univ Kans, Dept of Cell Biol & Physiology, Masters' Cand, 1978-80; Meharry Med Col, Pre-Doctoral Work, 1980-84; Harvard Sch Pub Health, postdoctoral fel, respiratory biol, 1984-87; Agency Toxic Substances & Dis Registry, Div Health Assessment & Consult, staff toxicologist, 1987-90, br chief, 1990-96; Nat Minority Health Conf, dir, 1995; Fla A&M Univ, Inst Pub Health, dir, 1996-, assoc prof, currently; Fla Disaster Preparedness Initiative, prin investr; Agency Toxic Substances & DisRegistry Bd Sci Counselors, mem; Coun Educ Pub Health, Bd Councilors, mem, 2004-07, Consortium African-Am Pub Health Progs, co chmn, 2007-. **Orgs:** Fla Pregnancy Assoc Mortality Rev Coun; Kid Care Outreach Spec Populations Task Force; Leon County Indigent Health Care Adv Coun; bd mem, NW Fla Chap March Dimes; bd mem, Trust Am's Health; bd mem, Fla Pub Health Asn, 1996-; Nat Acad Scis Inst Med Gulf War & Health Comt; Solvent Toxicity Panel; Cong Black Caucus Homeland Security Adv Comt; Socs Toxicol; Am Pub Health Asn, 1996-; Black Caucus Health Workers, 1998-; Delta Omega Hon Soc, 2004-. **Home Addr:** 2989 N Umberland Dr, Tallahassee, FL 32308, **Home Phone:** (850)668-2662. **Business Addr:** Director, Associate Professor, Florida A&M University, 207E Frederick S Humphries Sci Res Ctr, Tallahassee, FL 32307-3800, **Business Phone:** (850)599-8655.

**HARRIS, DAISY (DAISY GRIFFIN HARRIS WADE)**
Disc jockey, activist. **Personal:** Born Apr 22, 1931, Hattiesburg, MS; daughter of Joseph and Annie B Griffin; married James Harrison; children: James jr, Anthony & Harold; married Willie. **Educ:** Pearl River Jr Col. **Career:** Disc jockey, activist (retired); WDAM-TV, secy & receptionist; WORV Radio, disk jockey & secy; Cong Racial Equality, off work; Stud Non-Violent Coord Comt, off work; activist. **Orgs:** Secy, Forrest Co Br, Nat Asn Advan Colored People; Forrest Co Action Comt; Fifth Dist Loyalist Dem Party; vol, Southern Christian Leadership Conf; Miss Freedom Dem Party. **Honors/Awds:** Vernon Dahmer Community Service Award, Hub City Bus & Prof Men's Club, 1978; Certificate of Special Recognition, Miss Community Found, 1994; Long Distance Runner Award, Forrest Co Br, Nat Asn Advan Colored People, 1996; A Voice & A Vote, Freedom's Foundation Award, Hattiesburg Pub Sch Dist, 1998; Achievement Award, Miss Homemakers Vol Inc & Miss State Univ Exten Serv; Most Popular Disc Jockey. **Home Addr:** 216 Fredna Ave, Hattiesburg, MS 39401, **Home Phone:** (601)582-4917.

**HARRIS, DALE F.**
Chief executive officer. **Career:** Bound Brook Ford Inc, owner & chief exec officer, 1997-. **Business Addr:** Chief Executive Officer, Bound Brook Ford Inc, 427 W Union Ave, Bound Brook, NJ 08805, **Business Phone:** (732)356-2000.

**HARRIS, DAVID ELLSWORTH**
Pilot. **Personal:** Born Dec 22, 1934, Columbus, OH; son of Ruth A Estis (deceased) and Wilbur R (deceased); married Lynne Purdy; children: Camian & Leslie. **Educ:** Ohio State Univ, BS, educ, 1957. **Career:** Pilot (retired); USAF, second lt & capt, 1958-64; Amer Airlines, capt, 1964-94. **Orgs:** Former pres, Org Black Airline Pilots; Negro Airmen Int. **Honors/Awds:** Black Achievement in Industry Award, YMCA, 1971. **Special Achievements:** First African American to hired by American Airline. **Home Addr:** 10 Inlets Blvd, Nokomis, IL 34275-4108.

**HARRIS, DAVID L.**
Chief executive officer. **Educ:** Univ Ark, Little Rock. **Career:** DiverseStaff Inc, pres & owner; Beststaff Servs Inc, pres, chmn & secy, currently. **Orgs:** Houston Minority Bus Coun; Houston Area Urban League; bd mem, Shell Youth Training Acad. **Business Addr:** President, Chairman, Beststaff Services Inc, 3730 Kirby Dr Suite 320, Houston, TX 77098-3986, **Business Phone:** (713)527-8233.

**HARRIS, DERRICK (SIDNEY DERRICK HARRIS)**
Football player. **Personal:** Born Sep 18, 1972, Angleton, TX. **Educ:** Univ Miami. **Career:** Football player (retired); St Louis Rams, 1999, fullback, 1996, 1998; San Diego Chargers, running back, 2000-01; Dallas Cowboys, running back, 2002; Sam Houston bearkats, defencive back. **Honors/Awds:** Defensive Player of the Week, Southland Conference, 2006; Super Bowl champion.

**HARRIS, DEWITT O.**
Government official. **Personal:** Born Aug 10, 1944, Washington, DC; son of DeWitt and Corinne Banks Thomas; married Brenda Bing; children: Rhonda & Tanya. **Educ:** Johnson C Smith Univ, Charlotte, NC, BA, 1966; Southeastern Univ, Wash, DC, MBPA, 1979. **Career:** US Postal Serv, Wa, DC, contact compliance examr, 1968-76, mgr, eeo complaints div, 1976-79, gen mgr affirmative action div, 1979-86; US Postal Serv, Green Bay, WI, msc & mgr postmaster, 1986-90; US Postal Serv, Milwaukee, WI, dir city oper, 1988-90; US Postal Serv, Dayton, Ohio, msc mgr & post master, dist mgr, 1990-92, Employee Resource Mgt, vpres, currently. **Orgs:** Nat Asn Advan Colored People, 1966-. **Home Addr:** 290 Murray Dr Suite B, King of Prussia, PA 19406-3410. **Business Addr:** Vice President, United States Postal Service, 475 Lenfant Plz SW Rm 10407, Washington, DC 20260, **Business Phone:** (202)268-2500.

**HARRIS, DR. DOLORES M.**
Educator, school administrator. **Personal:** Born Aug 5, 1930, Camden, NJ; daughter of Roland H (deceased) and Frances Gatewood (deceased); married Morris E Sr; children: Morris E Jr, Sheila D Davis & Gregory M. **Educ:** Glassboro State Col, BS, 1959, MA, 1966; Rutgers Univ, EdD, 1983. **Career:** School administrator (retired); Glassboro Bd Educ, teacher admin, 1959-70; Camden Welfare Bd, supvr adult ed ctr, 1968; SCOPE Glassboro Ctr, dir headstart, 1969-70; Nat ESL Training Inst Jersey City State Col, assoc dir, 1971; Glassboro State Col, dir cont educ, 1970-, actg vpres acad affairs, 1989, dir continuing educ, 1990-91, Adult Educ Resource Ctr, dir; Pierce Col, adj fac, currently. **Orgs:** Pres & vpres, Gloucester Co United Way, 1968-; pres & vpres, NJ State Fed Colored Women's Clubs Inc, 1972-80; consut, NY Model Cities Right to Read Nat Training Conf, 1973-81; bd dir, Adult Educ Asn USA, 1973-79; chair bd, Glassboro Child Develop Ctr, 1974-82; bd dir, Glassboro State Col Mgt Inst, 1975-; pres, Glassboro State Col Alumni Asn, 1975-77; comm, NJ Task Force Thorough & Efficient Educ, 1976-78; examr, New York Civil Serv, 1976-; chair adv bd, Women's Educ Equity Comm Network Proj, 1977-78, 1980; consult, Temple Univ, 1978-79; deleg, Int Women's Yr Nat Conf, 1978; consult, NJ Gov's Conf Libr & Info Serv, 1979; legis comm, Amer Asn Adult & Continuing Educ, 1982-; vpres, Large N Eastern Fedn Colored Women's Clubs Inc, 1983-; vice chair, 1983-86, chair, 1986-, Commn Status Women Gloucester Co NJ; Gloucester Co Pvt Indust Counc, 1984-; first vpres, 1984-88, pres, 1988-92, Nat Asn Colored Women's Clubs Inc, 1984-; pres, S Jersey Chap Links Inc, 1984-; exec comm & educ chair, Nat Coun Women; founding mem, Societas Docta; bd dir, WomenGreater Philadelphia; Zeta Phi Beta Sorority; Omicron Omicron Zeta Chap; Anti-Basileus, Phylacter; EMC Score chair, sem prog, 2001-. **Home Addr:** 7439 Barclay Rd, Cheltenham, PA 19012, **Home Phone:** (215)782-8509.

**HARRIS, DR. DON NAVARRO**
Biochemist. **Personal:** Born Jun 17, 1929, New York, NY; son of John Henry and Margaret Vivian Berkley; married Regina B; children: Donna Wolfe, John Craig & Scott Anthony. **Educ:** Lincoln Univ PA, BA, 1951; Rutgers Univ, MS, 1959, PhD, 1963. **Career:** Biochemist (retired); Columbia Univ, lab technician; Colgate Palmolive Res Ctr, sr res, 1963-64; Rutgers Univ, asst res specialist, 1964-65, assoc prof, 1975-77; Bristol-Myers Squibb Pharmaceut Res Inst, res fel, 1965, consult human resource; Lincoln Univ, Pa, vis lectr, 1983-; Southern Univ Baton Rouge, LA, lectr, 1987; Squibb, 1993; Temple Univ Sch Med, assoc prof. **Orgs:** AAAS, 1966-; treas, bd dir, Frederick Douglass Liberation Libr, 1970-82; steering comm, 1975-, secy, 1986-, Biochem Pharmacol Discussion Group NY Acad Sci; Philadelphia Physiol Soc, 1978-; Am Soc Pharmacol & Exp Therapeut, 1980-; consult, AUS Sci Bd, 1981-85; reviewer, NSF, 1981-; adv comm Biochem Sec, NY Acad Sci, 1983-; bd trustee, Lincoln Univ, Pa, 2005-; partic Nat Urban League Black Exec Prog; lectr, Tex Southern Univ, 1984; ed bd mem, Jour Enzyme Inhibition, 1985-; Sigma Xi, NY Acad Sci, Am Heart Assoc, Amer Chem Soc, Theta Psi Lambda Chap Alpha Phi Alpha, Mu Boule, Sigma Pi Phi. **Honors/Awds:** Recipient of Harlem YMCA Black Achievers Award, 1984. **Special Achievements:** Author or co-author of 40 scientific papers, 40 scientific abstracts and 4 patents. **Home Addr:** 26 Summerall Rd, Somerset, NJ 08873, **Home Phone:** (732)247-8806.

**HARRIS, PROF. DONALD J.**
Economist, educator. **Personal:** married Shyamala Gopalan; children: Kamala & Maya. **Educ:** Univ Col WI-London Univ, BA, 1961; Univ Calif, Berkeley, PhD, 1966. **Career:** Univ Ill, Urbana-Champaign, asst prof, 1965-67; Univ Wis, Madison, assoc prof, 1968-72; Stanford Univ, dept econs, prof econs, 1972-98, prof emer, 1998-; J Econ Lit, ed bd, 1979-84; Consult. **Orgs:** Am Econ Asn. **Honors/Awds:** Fac fel, Econs, Cambridge Univ, Eng, 1966; Assoc fel, Trinity Col, Cambridge Univ, 1982; Ford Found fel, Nat Res Coun, 1984-85; Fulbright Scholar, Brazil, 1990, 1991, Mexico, 1992. **Special Achievements:** Has published various books & numerous articles in professional journals. Has been a visiting researcher and has delivered lectures in numerous universities & institutions in various countries including: Mexico, Holland, England, Brazil, Italy, India, Africa, the Caribbean. **Business Addr:** Professor Emeritus, Stanford University, Econ Bldg, Stanford, CA 94305-6072, **Business Phone:** (650)725-3266.

**HARRIS, PASTOR DOUGLAS ALLAN**
Public relations executive, clergy. **Personal:** Born Feb 7, 1942, Burlington, NJ; son of Milton and Marvel Clark; married Myrna L Hendricks. **Educ:** Col Nj, BA, Educ, 1964; Rutgers Univ Grad Sch Educ, MEd, 1973; Fordham Univ Grad Sch Bus, MBA, mgt & mkt, 1982. **Career:** NJ Bd Educ, teacher, 1964-69; Webster Div McGraw-Hill Bk Co, dir mkt serv, 1969-76; RR Bowker, mgr Educ Admin bk div, 1976-79; Scott, Foresman & Co, mkt mgr, 1980-86; Am Dent Asn, dir mkt, 1986-88; Silverman's Dent Supplies, mkt mgr; Portfolio Assoc Inc, sr acct exec, 1991-2012, proj mgr, currently; Covenant House Church God, co-pastor, currently. **Orgs:** Coun Concerned Black Exec, 1975-78, Am Asn Adult Continuing Educ, 1980-; founding bd mem, Literacy Vols Chicago, 1982-; vpres bd, Simek Mem Coun Ctr, 1983-; dir, Mid Atlantic Asn Temp Servs, 1989. **Honors/Awds:** Volunteer of the Year, N Shore Mag, 1985; Gold Award/Mkt Training, Am Mkt Asn, 1987; Ordained Baptist Deacon, 1985; Licensed Minister, 1997. **Home Addr:** 10 Drummers Lane, Wayne, PA 19087, **Home Phone:** (610)989-0684. **Business Addr:** Project Manager, Portfolio Associates Inc, 510 Walnut St, Philadelphia, PA 19106, **Business Phone:** (215)627-3660.

**HARRIS, DR. DUCHESS**
Educator, chairperson. **Personal:** daughter of Frank Jr and Miriam Mann. **Educ:** Univ Ibadan, Nigeria, Inst African Studies, 1989; Univ Oxford, Eng, Oxford Ctr African Studies, 1990; Univ Pa, BA, Am hist Afro-Am studies, 1991; Univ Mich, attended 1992; Yale Univ, attended 1994; Lund Univ, Sweden, attended 1996; Univ Minn, PhD, Am studies, 1997; William Mitchell Col Law, St Paul, MN, JD, civil rights law, 2011. **Career:** Univ Pa, instr, 1991; US Sen Paul David Wellstone, constituent advocate, issue liaison, 1993-94; Univ Minn, teaching asst, 1993-94, instr, 1993-95, reader, grader, 1995; Macalester Col, Womens & Gender Studies, instr, 1994-97, Inst Race & Poverty, dir, fel, 1996-97, vis asst prof polit sci & womens & gender studies, 1997-98, Dept African Am Studies & Polit Sci, asst prof, 1998-2004, Dept Am Studies, chmn, 2003-05, assoc prof, 2004-13, prof, 2013-; Univ Ga, fel, 1996; co-ed, Racially Writing Repub: Racists, Race Rebels & Transformations Am Identity; Hubert Humphrey Inst Pub Affairs, policy fel, 1998-99; Woodrow Wilson Career Enhancement fel, 2001-02; Am Bar Asn Sects quart flagship publ, Litigation News, assoc ed; Law Raza J, ed-in-chief, 2010. **Orgs:** Mensa, 1983-; Onyx Sr Hon Soc, 1990-91; Mortar Bd Nat Hon Soc, 1990; bd, secy, Model Cities Family Develop Ctr; chmn, Nominations & Planning, 1994-99; comnr, Minneapolis Comm Civil Rights, co-chmn, Educ & Planning comt, 1996-98; bd mem, vpres, Genesis II Women Inc, 1996-99; Delta Sigma Theta Sorority; Am Studies Asn; chmn, Am Studies Dept, 2003-04. **Home Addr:** . **Business Addr:** Professor and Chairman, Macalester College, Humanities, Old Main 213 1600 Grand Ave Bldg 109, St Paul, MN 55105, **Business Phone:** (651)696-6478.

**HARRIS, PROF. E. NIGEL**
Physician, educator, college administrator. **Personal:** Born Georgetown; married Yvette Williams; children: Zaman, Tamia & Sandhya. **Educ:** Howard Univ, BS, chem, 1968; Yale Univ, MPhil, biochem, 1973; Univ Pa, MD, 1977; Univ Wis, DM, 1981. **Career:** Univ Louisville, Div Rheumatology, chief, prof med, 1987-93; Morehouse Sch Med, dean & sr vpres, acad affairs, 1996-2004; Univ WI, vice chancellor & prof, 2004-; Royal Postgrad Med Sch, Fel in Rheumatology. **Orgs:** Am Med Asn; Nat Med Asn; GA State Med Asn; Asn Am Med Cols; Nat Ctr ResResources; Asn Acad Health Ctrs; pres, Caribbean Asn Univs & Res Insts; Nat Adv Res Resources Coun; dep chmn, Asn Commonwealth Univ. **Home Addr:** 901 Edgewater Dr, Atlanta, GA 30328. **Business Addr:** Vice Chancellor, Professor, University of the West Indies, PO Box 42, Kingston7, **Business Phone:** (876)927-1201.

**HARRIS, REP. EARL L. See Obituaries Section.**

**HARRIS, EDDY LOUIS (EDDY L HARRIS)**
Writer. **Personal:** Born Jan 26, 1956, Indianapolis, IN; son of Samuel and Georgia Louise. **Educ:** Leland Stanford Jr Univ, BA, 1977. **Career:** Wash Univ, St. Louis, MO, writer-in-residence; Goucher Col, fac membe; Auth bks: Miss Solo, 1988; Native Stranger, 1992; Haunted Southern Dream, 1993; Still Life Harlem, 1996; Jupiter et Moi, 2005; Paris en noir et black, 2009. **Honors/Awds:** MVP Award, A World of Difference, & Am Motorcyclist Assn; Missouri Governor's Humanities Award. **Home Addr:** 607 S Elliott Ave, Kirkwood, MO 63122, **Home Phone:** (314)822-7258.

**HARRIS, ELIHU MASON**
College administrator, legislator. **Personal:** Born Aug 15, 1947, Los Angeles, CA; son of Frances and Elihu Sr; married Kathy Neal. **Educ:** Calif State Hayward, BA, polit sci, 1968; Univ Calif, Berkeley, MA, pub policy, 1969; Univ Calif, Davis Sch Law, JD, 1972. **Career:** Congresswoman Yvonne Burke, legis asst, 1974-75; Nat Bar Asn, exec dir, 1975-77; Alexander Millner & McGee, partner, 1979; Calif Uniform Law Comnr, 1981-; City Oakland, Calif, Mayor, 1991-99; Calif State Assembly mem, 1978-91; Peralta Community Col Dist, interim chancellor, chancellor, 2003-10; KDIA radio sta, Vallejo, Calif, co owner. **Orgs:** Chair, Bay Area World Trade Ctr; exec secy, Peralta Col Found. **Special Achievements:** First major party politician to lose a state legislative race to a Green Party candidate in the United States.

**HARRIS, EUGENE EDWARD**
Labor relations manager. **Personal:** Born Feb 10, 1940, Pittsburgh, PA; married Marva Jo. **Educ:** Pa State Univ, BA, labor econ; Univ Pittsburgh, MPA, pub admin, 1969; Duquesne Univ Law Sch, JD, 1980. **Career:** PA State Univ Basketball team, capt, 1962; personnel serv analyst, 1964, labor contract adminr, clairton works, 1965; Gary Proj, labor contract adminr, 1968, prog coordr, 1969; asst mgr & mgr labor rels, 1973-78; US Steel, mgr employ, 1978, dir human resources; Harris Consult, prin, diversity recruitment dir, currently. **Orgs:** Chmn, Gary Concentrated Employ Pgm, 1969-73; chmn, Gary Econ Devel Corp, 1970-73; dir, Gary Urban League, 1970-72; treas, Community Partners Corp, 1975-; Allegheny County Bar Asn; Extra Mile Educ Found, Develop & Mkt Comt. **Honors/Awds:** Hon mention, All-Am, 1962. **Home Addr:** 107 Laurel Oak Dr, Sewickley, PA 15143. **Business Addr:** Principal, Diversity Recruitment Director, Harris Consulting, Dom Tower Ctr, Pittsburgh, PA 15230, **Business Phone:** (412)402-6674.

**HARRIS, FOREST**
Colonial administrator, college teacher, college president. **Educ:** Knoxville Col, BA, 1971; Am Baptist Col, BTh, 1980; Vanderbilt Univ, MDiv, 1983, DMin, 1990. **Career:** Us Energy Res & Develop Admin, facil compliance officer, 1971-77; Robert Shaw Controls Co, employ consult, 1977-78; Oak Valley Baptist Church, pastor, 1979-88; Roane State Community Col, minority prog develop officer & black studies instr, 1987; Pleasant Green Baptist Church, pastor, 1989-90; United Theol Sem, adj prof, 1994-96; Vanderbilt Divinity Sch, dean stud life, 1988-96, asst prof, dir Kelly Miller Smith Inst Black Church Studies & dean Black Church Studies, 1996-2012, assoc prof & dir Kelly Miller Smith Inst Black Church, 2012-; Am Baptist Col, Nashville, TN, pres, 1999-. **Orgs:** Am Acad Relig; Soc Study Black Relig; Black Relig Scholars Group; Nat Asn Independent Cols & Univs; Tenn Col Asn; World Baptist Alliance; NAACP (pres Oak Ridge Br, 1987-89); Delta Epsilon Chi Hon Soc, 1979-; Opportunities Industrialization Ctr, bd 1993-96; United Theol Sem Nat Adv Bd, 1995-97; Ctr Develop Ethical Leadership Nat Adv Bd, 1996-98; Ctr Non-Profit Mgt bd, 2006-08; Pastoral Ctr Healing bd, 2010-; Chicago Theol Sem bd trustees, 2010-; Samuel DeWitt Proctor Conf bd, 2011-; Nat Asn Independent Cols & Univs Bd, 2012-. **Honors/Awds:** Luke/Act Prize, American Baptist College, 1979; Benjamin E. Mays Fellow, The Fund for Theological Education, 1979-81; Florence Conwell Prize in Preaching, Vanderbilt Divinity School, 1981; Alumni Hall of Fame Shelby County Schools, inductee, 2005; OIC Community Achievement Award, 2007; Distinguished Faculty Award, Athletic Department, Vanderbilt University, 2012; Distinguished Faculty Award, Organization of Black Graduate and Professional Studies, Vanderbilt University, 2013; Human Relations Award, Community/Nashville, 2014; Kente Cloth Award, Campbellsville University, 2015. **Special Achievements:** Author, Ministry for Social Crisis: Theology and Praxis in the Black Church Tradition, 1993; What Does It Mean to Be Black and Christian: The Pulpit, Pew, and the Academy in Dialogue, 1996; What Does It Mean to Be Black and Christian: The Meaning of the African American Church, 1998; numerous articles, essays, and sermons. **Business Addr:** Vanderbilt Divinity School, 411 21st Ave South, Nashville, TN 37240, **Business Phone:** (615)343-3981.

**HARRIS, FRAN. See HARRIS, JOHNNIE FRANCES.**

**HARRIS, FRANCIS C.**
Writer, historian. **Personal:** Born Sep 25, 1957, Brooklyn, NY; son of Charles and Sammie. **Educ:** Cambridge Col, MEd, mgt, 1992. **Career:** Senior Researcher for A Hard Road To Glory, The History of the African-American Athlete, 1983-86, summer, 1987, 1992-93; Essay: Paul Robeson: An Athletes Legacy, 1998; co-author: The Amistad Pictorial History of the African American Athlete, Collegiate (1 & 2), 1999-, prof, 2003-. **Orgs:** Nat Black MBA Asn; Soc Am Baseball Res (SABR).

**HARRIS, FRANCO**
Football player, executive, president (organization). **Personal:** Born Mar 7, 1950, Ft. Dix, NJ; son of Cad and Gina Parenti; married Dana Dokmanovich; children: Franco Dokmanovich. **Educ:** Pa State Univ, BS, hotel & restaurant mgt, 1972. **Career:** Football player (retired), president, executive; Pittsburgh Steelers, full back, 1972-83; Seattle Seahawks, full back, 1984; Francos All Natural, pres; Pk Sausages Co, owner, currently; Super Bakery Inc, owner, chief exec officer & pres, 1990, DBA RSuper Foods, 2006-; Pa State Univ, Sch Hospitality Mgt, conti prof, currently; Tv Series: "The NFL on NBC", 1965-97; "NFL Monday Night Football", 1970-; "Super Bowl XIV", 1980. **Business Addr:** Owner, President, Super Bakery Inc, 5700 Corp Dr Suite 455, Pittsburgh, PA 15237-5851, **Business Phone:** (412)367-2518.

**HARRIS, DR. GARY LYNN**
Consultant, educator, vice president (organization). **Personal:** Born Jun 24, 1953, Denver, CO; son of Norman and Gladys Weeams; married Jennifer Dean; children: Jamie. **Educ:** Cornell Univ, Ithaca, NY, BS, elec engineering, 1975, MS, elec engineering, 1976, PhD, elec engineering, 1980. **Career:** Martin Marietta Corp, Littleton, CO, trainee engr, 1972; IBM Corp, jr engr, 1973; Nat Res & Resource Facil Sumicron Struct, Ithaca, NY, asst, assoc, 1977-80; Naval Res Lab, Wash, DC, vis scientist, 1981-82; Lawrence Livermore Nat Lab, consult, 1984-; Inst Elec & Electronics Engrs, Wash Sect Electron Devices Group, chmn, 1984-85; Howard Univ, Wash, DC, assoc prof elec eng, 1980-92, prof elec eng, 1992-, Mat Sci Res Ctr, dir, 1999-, assoc vpres res, 1995-2000; dean grad sch & assoc provost currently; Int Conf Silicon Carbide & Related Mat, chmn; Int Sch of Solid-State Device Res, lectr. **Orgs:** Sigma Xi, Inst Elec & Electronic Engrs; chmn, IEEE Electron Devices, Wash Sec, 1984-86; selection comm, Black Engr yr, 1989; Am Asn Advan Sci; Am Phys Socs; Mat Res Socs; Optical Socs Am; Am Coun Educ Citations; Nat Socs Black Engrs; Wash Apple Pi; Am Ceramic Socs Inst Elec & Electronics; dir, Howard Nanoscale Sci & Engineering Facil & sch's Nat Nanotechnology Infrastructure Network facil; rev panelist, Nsf; consult, Am Educ Coun; Lawrence-Livermore Nat Labs, Naval Res Lab, McDonnell Aircraft Co; Nat Inst Stand &Technol. **Home Addr:** 1724 Allison St NW, Washington, DC 20011, **Home Phone:** (202)722-4194. **Business Addr:** Director, Professor, Howard University, 2300 6th St NW, Washington, DC 20059, **Business Phone:** (202)806-6618.

**HARRIS, DR. GENE THOMAS**
Educator, chief executive officer. **Personal:** Born Apr 4, 1953, Columbus, OH; daughter of William Sr and Thelma Thomas; married Stanley E; children: Wade Thomas. **Educ:** Univ Notre Dame, BA, eng, 1975; Ohio State Univ, MA, educ admin, 1979, PhD, educ, 1999. **Career:** Columbus City Schs, teacher, 1975-79, high sch asst prin, 1980-85, prin, 1985-89, supvr principals, 1989-91, asst supt, curric, 1991-94, dep supt, 1999-2000, supt & chief exec officer, 2001; Ohio Dept Educ, state asst supt, 1995-98. **Orgs:** Bd mem, United Way Cent Ohio, 2001-; bd mem, Columbus Symphony Orchestra, 2001-; bd mem, CAPA, 2003-; trustee bd & sunday sch teacher, Mt Olivet Baptist Church, 2003-; chair, Ohio Univ; bd mem, Action C. **Home Addr:** 6271 Alissa Lane, Columbus, OH 43213, **Home Phone:** (614)866-7993. **Business Addr:** Superintendent, Chief Executive Officer, Columbus City Schools, 270 E State St, Columbus, OH 43215, **Business Phone:** (614)365-5000.

**HARRIS, DR. GERALDINE E.**
Scientist, microbiologist. **Personal:** Born Detroit, MI; children: Reginald & Karen. **Educ:** Wayne State Univ Med Tech, BS, 1956, MS, microbiol, 1969, PhD, microbiol, 1974. **Career:** Detroit Gen Hosp, med tech, 1956-60; Parke Davis & Co, asst res microbiol, 1961-66; Wayne St Univ, Dept Biol, res asst, 1967-68; Wayne St Univ, Col Med, tutor/adv post baccal prog, 1971-73; Drake Inst Sci, consult, 1971-73; Met Hosp Dt, microbiol, 1975; Winston-Salem St Univ, asst prof microbiol, 1975-77; Nat Caucus Black Aged, consult, 1976; Food & Drug Admin, Ctr Food Safety & Appl Nutrit, consumer safety officer, 1980-90, liaison, Off Regulatory Affairs, Div Field Sci, sci coordr; Clin Microbiol Group Health Asn Inc, chief. **Orgs:** Reg Am Soc Clin Pathol MT 28926, 1956-; Am Soc Microbiol, 1967-; fel NIH, 1968-71; Asn Univ Prof, 1968-; Sigma Xi; Asn Advan Sci, 1975-; Educ Comput Minority Inst, 1977; Alpha Kappa Alpha Sorority; Urban League, Orphan Found; fel African Sci Inst; Allied Health Prog Develop, Am Asn State Cols & Univ, Wash, assoc coord. **Home Addr:** 2671 E Hulet Dr, Chandler, AZ 85225-4016, **Home Phone:** (480)963-5135. **Business Addr:** Fellow, African Scientific Institute, PO Box 12161, Oakland, CA 94604, **Business Phone:** (510)653-7027.

**HARRIS, GIL W.**
Educator. **Personal:** Born Dec 9, 1946, Lynchburg, VA; married Paula Bonita Gillespie; children: Deborah Nicole Gillespie & Paul Henry Gillespie. **Educ:** Nat Acad Broadcasting, dipl radio & tv, 1965; Winston-Salem Col, AS, bus admin, 1971; Shaw Univ, BA, radio, tv & film, 1980; NC A&T State Univ, MS, educ media, 1982; Pac Western Univ, PhD, 1986. **Career:** WEAL WQMG Radio Stas, oper dir, 1972-79; Shaw Univ, dir radio broadcasting, 1979-81; Col Telecommun, syst producer, sport dir, 1981-84; SC St Univ, asst prof broadcasting, instr broadcast journalism, 1984-; SC State football, pub add announcer, 1991. **Orgs:** Omega Psi Phi; Prince Hall Mason; Nat Asn Advan Colored People. **Home Addr:** 416 Robinson St NE, Orangeburg, SC 29115, **Home Phone:** (803)531-3827. **Business Addr:** Instructor of Broadcasting, South Carolina State University, Turner Hall A Wing 2nd Fl Rm 258, Orangeburg, SC 29117, **Business Phone:** (803)536-7109.

**HARRIS, GLADYS BAILEY**
Judge. **Personal:** Born Mar 23, 1947, Boykins, VA; daughter of William L and Dorothy R Ferguson; married Stanley Christian Sr; children: Stanley Jr, Chad Gregory & Adrienne Michelle. **Educ:** Va State Univ, Petersburg, BS, biol, 1968; Univ Richmond, Richmond, JD, 1981. **Career:** Sch Bd City Richmond, Richmond, gen coun, 1981-83; Univ Richmond, Richmond, adj prof, 1983-84, 1991-; Law Off Gladys Bailey Harris, solo practicioner, Richmond, 1983-86; Supreme Ct Va, Richmond, hearing officer, ade law judge, 1983-; Clute & Shilling, Richmond, partner, atty, 1986-87; VIR Alcoholic Beverage Control Bd, Richmond, Va, agency head, cbd, 1987-90; VIR Alliance Minority Particip Sci & Eng, VAMPSE, Richmond, Va, exd, 1990-91; Law Off Gladys Bailey Harris, solo practitioner, Richmond, Va, 1990-92; Carpenter & Harris, Richmond, partner, 1992-; pvt pract, atty, currently. **Orgs:** Arbitrator, NY Stock Exchange, 1983-; Alumni bd mem, Univ Richmond, 1988-; bd mem, Va Instr Law & Citizenship Studies, 1988-; bd mem, Commonwealth Girl Scout Coun Va, 1988-; bd mem, Local Community Cols Bd, 1991-; comnr, Circuit Ct City Richmond, 1991-; mbr, VIR State Bar Com Prof, 1991-. **Honors/Awds:** Hon Woodrow Wilson Fel, Woodrow Wilson Found, 1968; Distinguished Serv Award, Richmond Area Prog Minorities Eng, 1988; Citizen of the Year, NAFEO/Va State Univ, 1990; SERWA Award, Nat Coalition of 100 Black Women, 1990. **Special Achievements:** First Black Woman appointed to head the agency & Second Black in the 55 years to serve on the board. **Home Addr:** 4210 Southaven Rd, Richmond, VA 23235-1029, **Home Phone:** (804)320-4611. **Business Addr:** Attorney, Private Practitioner, 4210 Southaven Rd, Richmond, VA 23235-1029, **Business Phone:** (804)560-1786.

**HARRIS, REV. H. FRANKLIN, II**
Clergy. **Personal:** Born Jun 3, 1969, Augusta, GA. **Educ:** Interdenominational Theol Ctr; BS, airway sci admin, 1991; Mdiv, psychol, 1995. **Career:** Liberty Baptist Church, assoc minister; Morehouse Sch Relig, Chaplain, 1994-95; Tried Stone Baptist Church, pastor, currently. **Orgs:** Treas, Community Churches Social Action; secy, Baptist Minister's Union San Antonio & Vicinit; fel Tabernacle Baptist Church; NAACP; Airway Sci Club. **Honors/Awds:** Durwood Cason Award; Robert Penn Memorial Scholarship. **Business Addr:** Pastor, Tried Stone Baptist Church, 2434 E Houston St, San Antonio, TX 78202, **Business Phone:** (210)226-1162.

**HARRIS, DR. HARCOURT GLENTIES**
Physician. **Personal:** Born Apr 16, 1928, New York, NY; married Charlotte L Hill; children: Harcourt Jr, Michael, Brian & Andrea. **Educ:** Fordham Univ, BS, 1948; Howard Univ, MD, 1952. **Career:** Harlem Hosp, intern, 1953; John D. Dingell VA Med Ctr, resident, 1958; pvt pract physician, 1960; United Am Healthcare Corp, staff; Highland Pk Gen Hosp, chief med, dir med educ, 1973-76; Wayne State Univ, clin asst prof, 1975; United Am Healthcare Corp, dir, 1985-98; Omni Care, Mich, bd chmn, 1992-2001. **Orgs:** Life mem, Nat Asn Advan Colored People. **Home Addr:** 15521 W 7 Mile Rd, Detroit, MI 48235, **Home Phone:** (313)836-5800. **Business Addr:** Physician, 1155 Brewery Park Blvd Suite 200, Detroit, MI 48207, **Business Phone:** (313)325-9400.

**HARRIS, HELEN B.**
Educator, president (organization), executive. **Personal:** Born Mar 6, 1925, High Point, NC; daughter of Willie Boulware and Hattie Whitaker; married Wendell B; children: Wendell B Jr, Charles B & Hobart W. **Educ:** Bennett Col, BA, 1945; Univ Iowa, MA, 1952. **Career:** Prismatic Images Inc, exec producer. **Orgs:** Exec dir, YWCA, High Point, NC, 1945-48; prog dir, YWCA, Des Moines, 1948-51; pres, League Women Voters, 1965; pres, Bd Educ, Flint, 1973-74, 75-76; bd mem, NBD Genesee Bank, 1980-89; trustee, Comm Found Greater Flint, 1986-89; bd mem emer, Questar Sch Gifted, 1987-89; pres, Flint Area Educ Found, 1988-89; chair, Endowment Campaign; bd mem, Christ Episcopal Ctr; Policy Comt, Community Found Greater Flint; St Neighborhood Educ Auth; bd mem, Flint Pub Schs; secy, Mayors Adv Comn; charter mem, Flint Chap, Delta Sigma Theta; Jack & Jill; Nat Asn Adv Colored People; Delta Sigma Theta, Urban League, ACLU. **Home Addr:** 1632 Kensington Ave, Flint, MI 48503-2775, **Home Phone:** (810)232-3732. **Business Addr:** Executive Producer, Prismatic Images Inc, 1632 Kensington Ave, Flint, MI 48503, **Business Phone:** (810)232-3732.

**HARRIS, HERNANDO PETROCELLI. See HARRIS, PEP.**

**HARRIS, DR. HORATIO PRESTON**
Dentist, educator, executive. **Personal:** Born Sep 25, 1925, Savannah, GA; son of Horatio and Foustina; married Barbara E Monroe; children: Gary P, Patricia L, Michael M, Conrad W, Nancy E, David M, Cathy C, Roxanne D & Robert H. **Educ:** Howard Univ, BS, 1951, DDS, 1956. **Career:** Dentist (retired); Washington, Va, IBM specialist, 1949; St Elizabeth Hosp, intern oral surg, 1956-57; Wash, pvt prac dent, 1957; Freedman's Hosp, courtesy staff oral surg; Bur Dent Health, dent officer, 1960-65; Howard Univ, instr, 1966-67, asst prof, 1967-71; Jehovah's Witness, minister, 1973-82. **Orgs:** Am Dent Asn; Nat Dent Asn; DC Dent Asn; RT Freeman Soc; Omega Psi Phi; bd dentist, Wash DC Dept Health. **Honors/Awds:** Honored UAU; The Mother Pearl Achievement. **Home Addr:** 1400 Franklin St NE, Washington, DC 20018-3744, **Home Phone:** (202)635-8103.

**HARRIS, J. ROBERT**
Marketing executive. **Personal:** Born Apr 1, 1944, Lake Charles, LA; son of James Robert and Ruth E Boutte; married Nathaleen Stephenson; children: Evan Scott & April Ruth. **Educ:** City Univ NY, Queens Col, BA, psychol, 1966; Berlitz Sch Lang, conversational Span & Fr 1974; NY Univ, cert Span, 1978. **Career:** Equitable Life Ins Co, 1965-66; NBC, mkt res supvr, 1966-69; Gen Foods Corp, group mkt res mgr, 1969-72; PepsiCo Int, res dir, 1972-74; JRH Mkt Serv Inc, pres, 1975-; also NYU Sch Continuing Educ, prof mkt res, 1992-93. **Orgs:** Am Mkt Assn; Europ Soc Opinion & Mkt Res (ESOMAR); founding mem, Qual Res Consults Asn (QRCA); pres, Chair Prof Comt; Explorers Club; Omega Psi Phi Fraternity; chmn, Res Indust Coalition (RIC); Mkt Res Coun. **Honors/Awds:** Scholarship-Franklin & Marsh College; Scholarship-Howard University; Scholarship-New York State Regents; La Llave del Exito/Key of Success, (PepsiCo) Mexico City, 1973; 1000 Most Successful Blacks (Ebony Magazine); Certificate of Merit for Distinguished Service to the Community (Dictionary of International Biography). **Special Achievements:** QRCA Presi-

dent's Award for Distinguished Service, 2002; Market Research Hall of Fame, 2016. **Business Addr:** President, JRH Marketing Services Inc, 8319 141 St Suite 707, New York, NY 11435, **Business Phone:** (718)805-7300.

### HARRIS, JACKIE BERNARD

Business owner, football player. **Personal:** Born Jan 4, 1968, Pine Bluff, AR; married Letrece; children: Jackie Jr. **Educ:** Univ La, Monroe, grad, 1990; Univ Ark Pine Bluff, BA, criminal justice & corrections, 2005; Univ Ark, William H. Bowen Sch Law, Little Rock, JD, 2008. **Career:** Football player (retired), business owner; Green Bay Packers, tight end, 1990-93; Tampa Bay Buccaneers, tight end, 1994-97; KPBA (1270 AM), owner, 1996; Tenn Oilers, tight end, 1998; Tenn Titans, tight end, 1999; Metro Media Group, pres, 1999-2001; Dallas Cowboys, tight end, 2000-01; Univ Ark Pine Bluff, asst football coach, 2003-04; Character Coun Southeast Ark, vpres, 2004-10; McKissic & Assocs PLLC, partner, 2008-; Jefferson County Ark, county atty, 2013. **Honors/Awds:** All-Pro selection, 1992; Small Business Persons of the Year, Greater Pine Bluff Chamber of Com, 2001. **Special Achievements:** Film: Super Bowl XXXIV, 2000. TV Series: "The NFL on NBC", 1992; "ESPN's Sunday Night Football ", 1992-2000; "NFL Monday Night Football" 1993-2000; "NFL on FOX", 1997; "The NFL on CBS", 1998. **Business Addr:** Partner, McKissic & Associates PLLC, 116 W Sixth Ave, Pine Bluff, AR 71601, **Business Phone:** (870)534-6332.

### HARRIS, JAMES ALEXANDER. See Obituaries Section.

### HARRIS, MAJ. JAMES E.

School administrator, educator. **Personal:** Born Sep 24, 1946, Castalia, NC; son of Wilmon and Marie; married Justine Perry; children: Kasheena & Jamillah. **Educ:** Montclair State Col, BA, social studies, 1968, MA, personnel serv & pub admin, 1970; Pub Serv Inst NJ, 1974; Harvard Univ, summer, 1974; NY Univ, PhD, pub admin, 1973-. **Career:** Montclair State Col, asst librn, 1964-67; Camp Weequahic, Lake Como, Pa, porter, 1964, res counr Upward Bound Proj summer, 1966-67; Elko Lake Camp, NY, counr, 1965; Bamberger's, Newark, asst dir community rels, 1968; Montclair State Col, counr, 1969-70, asst dean stud, 1970-, cross country coach, 1975-, assoc dean stud & ombuds person, 1986-. **Orgs:** Pres, NJ Asn Black Educr, 1973-; Montclair Civil Rights Comn, 1979-; pres, Nat Asn Advan Colored People Montclair Br, 1983; chmn, NJ Black Issues invention Educ Task Force, 1986-; consult, Educ Testing Serv, Am Col Testing Inc; Ctr Opportunity & Personnel Efficiency, NJ; Nat Orientation Dir Asn; pres, Montclair State Col Asn Black Fac & Adminr Staff; pres, Educ Opportunity Fund Comt; adv bd, Montclair State Col; No NJ Counr Asn; Nat Asn Personnel Adminr; Am Personnel & Guid Asn; Am Col Personnel Asn; vice chmn, NJ Amateur Athletic Union Women Track & Field Com; bd mgr, NJ Asn Amateur Athletic Union Am; bd trustee, Leaguers Inc; dir, coach, Fed Essex Co Athletic Club Newark; Cross Country Coach Montclair State Col; Legis Aide Com Assemblyman Hawkins; Sigma Pi Fraternity; N Ward Block Asn; cert mem, NJ Track & Field Officials Asn; Amateur Athletic Union Officials; chmn, Press Coun Affirmative Action Univ Med & Dent NJ; Urban League Essex County; Mt Calvary Missionary Baptist Church; vpres, State Conferences NAACP br. **Honors/Awds:** Outstanding Black Educator Award; Student Leadership Award, Montclair State Col; Essex Co Volunteer Award; Athlete of the Year Award for Montclair St Coll; New Jersey Association of Black Educators; New Jersey Black United Fund; New Jersey Alliance of Black Educators; Iota Phi Theta Fraternity Community Leadership Award, National Associations of University Women Community Service Award, Montclair NAACP; The Thursgood Marshall Award & Administration of the year Award, African Unity Montclair State Univ. **Special Achievements:** Has been cited several times in Who's Who among American Educators. **Home Addr:** 9 Pleasant Ave, Montclair, NJ 07042-3111, **Home Phone:** (973)783-4668. **Business Addr:** Associate Dean Students, Ombudsperson, Montclair State University, Rm 400 Stud Ctr, Montclair, NJ 07043, **Business Phone:** (973)655-4118.

### HARRIS, JAMES G., JR.

Executive director. **Personal:** Born Oct 27, 1931, Cuthbert, GA; son of James Sr and Eunice Mitchner; married Roxie Lena Riggs; children: Peter C & Robin Allen. **Educ:** Hillyer Col, attended 1956; Univ Hartford, BS, 1958. **Career:** State Conn, social worker, 1958-59; EJ Korvette, acct payable supvr, 1959-60; State Conn, social worker, 1960-65; State Off Econ Opportunity, asst dir, 1965-66; Gov John Dempsey, spec asst to gov, 1966-70; Greater Hartford Community Renewal Team, exec dir state civil rights coord, 1970-82; Conn Dept Hr, comnr, 1983-87; Data Inst Inc, consult, 1987-89; Bethol Ctr Humane Serv, consult, 1987-89; State Dept Human Resources, comnr. **Orgs:** Pres, life mem, Nat Asn Advan Colored People, Greater Hartford Br, 1962-64; secy, Alpha Phi Alpha, 1964-66; chmn, chmn emer, State Conf Nat Asn Advan Colored People, 1967-70; Pres, legis chmn, Conn Asn Comt Action, 1975-83; vpres & panelist, New Eng Comn Action Assoc, 1977-80; Gov's Task Force Homeless, 1983-; Adult Educ Study Comn, 1984-; Priorities Comm United Way, 1984-; Gov's Designee Femia Distrib Comt, 1984. **Home Addr:** 42 Tower Ave, Hartford, CT 06120, **Home Phone:** (203)278-4855.

### HARRIS, JAMES LARNELL

Football player, football executive, manager. **Personal:** Born Jul 20, 1947, Monroe, GA; married Vickie. **Educ:** Grambling State Univ, educ. **Career:** Football player (retired), football exec; Buffalo Bills, quarterback, 1969-72; Los Angeles Rams, quarterback, 1973-76; San Diego Chargers, quarterback, 1977-81; Tampa Bay Buccaneers, W Coast scout, 1987-92; NY Jets, asst gen mgr, 1993-96; Baltimore Ravens, dir pro personnel, 1997-2003; Jacksonville Jaguars, gen mgr & vpres player personnel, 2003-08; Detroit Lions, personnel exec, sr personnel exec, 2009-. **Orgs:** Subcomt, Nat Football League. **Honors/Awds:** Most Valuable Player, Orange Blossom Classic, 1967; Pittsburgh Courier Player of the Year, 1968; Most Valuable Player, Nat Football League Pro Bowl, 1974; leads the NFC in passing; 36th most influential minority person in sports, Sports Illustrated, 2003; Southwestern Athletic Conference Hall of Fame; Grambling Athletic Hall of Fame; Louisiana Sports Hall of Fame; Atlanta Right & Wrong Hall of Fame. **Special Achievements:** One of the first African American quarterbacks to start in the National Football League; one of the top 50 most influential minorities in sports; First to lead a team to a division title, to play in a conference championship. **Business Addr:** Senior Personnel Executive, Detroit Lions, 222 Republic Dr, Allen Park, MI 48101, **Business Phone:** (313)262-2000.

### HARRIS, JAMES SAMUEL, III. See JAM, JIMMY.

### HARRIS, DR. JASPER WILLIAM

Educator, psychologist. **Personal:** Born Dec 10, 1935, Kansas City, MO; son of Jasper and Mary P; married Joann S Harper; children: Jasper Jr. **Educ:** Rockhurst Col, BS, biol, 1958; Univ Mo, MA, 1961; Univ Kans, EdD, 1971, PhD, 1981. **Career:** Kans City Sch Dist, teacher, 1963-69, assoc supt, 1977-86, supt, 1986-, asst supvr, 1988-91; Univ Kans, res assoc, 1969-77; Blue Springs Sch Dist, Spec Educ, exec dir, 1992-. **Orgs:** Phi Delta Kappa Fraternity; Alpha Phi Alpha Fraternity; Jr Chamber Com; Rockhurst Col Alumni Asn; Univ Mo Alumni Asn; vice chmn, United Negro Col Fund; adv bd & chmn educ & youth incentives comn, Urban League; Sci Teachers Asn; Am Educ Res Asn; Am Psychol Asn; Univ Kans Alumni Asn; life mem, Nat Asn Advan Colored People; Asn Supv & Curric Develop, Personnel Res Forum; theta boule, Sigma Pi Phi Fraternity; consult, Kaw Valley Med Soc Health Careers Prog, 1971-; partic, Pres US Comn Employ Handicapped, White House, Wash, DC, 1980; bd trustee, Pk Col, 1984-94; alumni bd mem, Univ Kans. **Home Addr:** 11945 PA, Kansas City, MO 64145, **Home Phone:** (816)942-6056. **Business Addr:** Executive Director, Blue Springs School District, 1801 NW Vesper, Blue Springs, MO 64015, **Business Phone:** (816)224-1300.

### HARRIS, JAY TERRENCE

Media executive, association executive, writer. **Personal:** Born Dec 3, 1948, Washington, DC; son of Richard James and Margaret Estelle Burr; married Anna Christine; children: Taifa Akida, Jamarah Kai & Shala Marie. **Educ:** Lincoln Univ, BA, 1970. **Career:** Wilmington News-J, gen assignment reporter, 1970, urban affairs reporter, 1970-71, investigative reporter, 1971-73, spec projs ed, 1974-75; Northwestern Univ, instr journ & urban affairs, 1973-75, asst prof journ & urban affairs, 1975-82; Frank E Gannett Urban Journ Ctr, asst dir, 1975-76, assoc dir, 1976-82; Northwestern Univ Medill Sch Journ, asst dean, 1977-82; Gannett News Servs, nat corresp, 1982-84; Gannett Newspapers & USA Today, columnist, 1984-85; Philadelphia Daily News, exec ed, 1985-88, vpres; Knight-Ridder, exec ed, Newspaper Div, asst to pres, vpres opers, 1987-94; San Jose Mercury News, chmn & publ, 1995-2001; Univ Southern Calif, Los Angeles, Calif, prof, currently. **Orgs:** Bd mem, Joint Venture, Silicon Valley Network, Bay Area Coun; bd mem, Am Leadership Forum; bd mem, Community Found Santa Clara C; bd mem, Tech Mus Innovation; bd mem, Santa Clara C Mfg Group; trustee, John S & James L Knight Found; bd mem, Am Press Inst; Pac Coun Int Policy; Coun Foreign Rels; bd dir, Pulitzer Prize; bd, Pac Coun Int Policy; Nat Adv Bd Poynter Inst; Am Socs Newspaper Ed; bd, Fed Res Bank. **Honors/Awds:** Public Serv Awards, Assoc Press Managing Ed Asn & Greater PA Chap Sigma Delta Chi; Spec Citation Investigation Minority Employ Daily Newspapers, Nat Urban Coalition, 1979; Par Excellence Award Distinguished Serv Journ, Oper PUSH, 1984; Ida B Wells Award, National Association of Black Journalists, 1992; Drum Major Justice Award, Southern Christian Leadership Conf, 1985; Siebert Lect, Mich State Univ, 2000. **Special Achievements:** Co-author of a series of articles on heroin trafficking in Wilmington DE, 1972; Author: Minority Employ Daily Newspapers, 1978. **Home Addr:** 19630 Cannon Dr, Los Gatos, CA 95030, **Home Phone:** (408)354-5032. **Business Addr:** Professor, University of Southern California, USC Office of International Services, Los Angeles, CA 90089, **Business Phone:** (213)821-6383.

### HARRIS, DR. JAZMINE A.

Pediatrician. **Educ:** Hahnemann Univ Sch Med, Philadelphia, Pa, MD, 1999. **Career:** Mem Hosp Salem County, pediatrician, currently; pvt pract, currently; Univ Med & Dent, resident physician. **Honors/Awds:** Pediatric Emergency Medicine Award, Univ Med & Dent Nj-Cooper Health Syst, 2000; Sidney J. Sussman Award, Cooper Hosp & Univ Medl Cts, Camden, NJ, 2001-02. **Business Addr:** Physician, 621 Beverly Rancocas Rd Suite 2D, Willingboro, NJ 08046, **Business Phone:** (609)877-6800.

### HARRIS, JEANETTE

Artist, writer, singer. **Personal:** Born Mar 6, 1952, Bridgeport, CT; daughter of Hugo and Rosetta; children: Lonnell Lawson Jr & Lynnette D Lawson. **Educ:** Found Bible Inst, BA, eng, 1998. **Career:** Performance artist, storyteller, writer, composer, singer & 3D Motivational Entertainment, currently; Ethan Allen Furniture, Internal Audit Dept, secy; United Illum Co, acct payable clerk; Northeast Utilities, customer serv rep; Southern Conn Gas Co, customer serv rep; Coun Churches Greater Bridgeport Inc, Evangel Church Am. **Orgs:** Mendelsohn Chorale Conn. **Home Addr:** 715 Pearl Harbor St, Bridgeport, CT 06610-2386, **Home Phone:** (203)366-6778. **Business Addr:** Performance Artist, 3D Motivational Entertainment, 715 Pearl Harbor St, Bridgeport, CT 06601-2386, **Business Phone:** (203)366-6778.

### HARRIS, JEANETTE G.

Executive. **Personal:** Born Jul 18, 1934, Philadelphia, PA. **Educ:** Inst Banking, attended 1970. **Career:** First PA Bank NA, banking officer, bank mgr, dept store bookkeeper, sales clerk. **Orgs:** Urban League; bd dir, YMCA; bd mem, Philadelphia Parent Child Care Ctr; vis prof BEEP, Nat Asn Black Women Inc; Philadelphia Black Bankers Asn; comn orgn dealing sr city; treas, Ch Fed Credit Union; treas, Merchants Asn; Progress Plaza Shopping Ctr.

### HARRIS, JEROME C., JR.

Government official, administrator, president (organization). **Personal:** Born Dec 15, 1947, New York, NY; married Rosemarie Mcqueen; children: Rahsaan & Jamal. **Educ:** Rutgers Univ, BA, 1969, MS, urban planning & pub policy anal, 1971. **Career:** Livingston Col, Rutgers, Dept Community Develop, instr, asst to dean acad affairs, 1969-73; Mayor's Policy & Develop Off, Newark, dir urban inst, 1973-74, urban develop coord, 1974-75; Middlesex County Econ Opportunities Corp, dep exec dir mgt & admin, 1975-77; NJ Educ Opportunities Fund, Dept Higher Educ, asst dir, fiscal affairs, 1977-78, assoc dir budget & fiscal planning, 1978-82; City Plainfield, dir pub works & urban develop, 1982, dep city admin, 1983, city admin, 1983, vpres govt affairs; Essex County, admin; State NJ, asst secy state & asst state treas; Rowan Univ, Urban & Pub Policy Inst, exec dir; Metro Newark Chamber Com, vpres; Polit Sci Dept, adj prof; Harris Orgn, pres, currently. **Orgs:** Pres, NJ Jaycees, 1977; vpres, Nb Nat Asn Advan Colored People, 1978-79; pres, mem bd, NJ Pub Policy Res Inst, 1979-84; chmn, Middlesex City CETA Adv Comt, 1979-83; chmn, NJ Black Issues Conv, 1983-; Int City Mgrs Asn; Am Soc Pub Admin; Conf Minority Pub Admin; Forum Black Pub Admin; NJ Munic Mgrs Asn; bd dir, Plainfield Econ Develop Corp; State NJ, Adv Comt Police Standars; CAM Connect; Capital Corridor CDC; Camden African Am Cult Ctr; chmn, Nj Black Issues Conv Inc; chief operating officer, Shiloh Community Develop Corp; dir, Dept Housing & Econ Develop; Nj Inst Social Justice, Nat Minority Disability Coalition. **Home Addr:** 273 Leland Ave, Plainfield, IL 07062, **Home Phone:** (908)756-4824. **Business Addr:** Chairman, The New Jersey Black Issues Convention Inc, PO Box 1843, Newark, NJ 07101, **Business Phone:** (973)824-7463.

### HARRIS, DR. JOHN, III

Educator. **Personal:** Born Altoona, PA; children: Julie. **Educ:** Highland Park Col, MI; Wayne State Univ, BS; Univ Mich, MS, behavioral sci educ & educ admin & supv, PhD, educ admin & supv. **Career:** Univ Ky, Col Educ, prof & dean; Col Educ Cleveland State Univ, prof & dean; Ind Univ, Sch Educ, Div Educ Leadership & Policy Studies, prof & chmn; Ind Univ Ctr fro Urban & Multi Cultrual Educ, dir, assoc dir off sch prog, spec asst dean; Detroit Pub Schs, asst prin, 1968-73; Pa State Univ, Univ Pk, asst prof, 1973-76; USDA, state urban curric specialist & prog coordr; African Am Studies & Res, prof admin & supv, currently; Comn Diversity Univ Ky, chmn, currently. **Business Addr:** Professor, African-American Studies & Research, 102 Breckinridge Hall, Lexington, KY 40506-0056, **Business Phone:** (859)257-3593.

### HARRIS, JOHN B., JR.

Executive. **Personal:** son of John B and Ruth Coles. **Career:** Deutsche Bank AG, vpres, eTelecare, chief exec officer & pres; Pace Univ, adj prof pub admin, currently. **Orgs:** Bd mem, Manhattan Community. **Home Addr:** 7 E 14th St Apt 1429, New York, NY 10003-3124, **Home Phone:** (212)243-7953. **Business Addr:** Adjunct Professor of Public Administration, Pace University, 1 Pace Plz, New York, NY 10038, **Business Phone:** (212)346-1200.

### HARRIS, JOHN CLIFTON

Surgeon, physician. **Personal:** Born Jan 15, 1935, Greensboro, NC. **Educ:** NY Col Podiatric Med; NC Agr & Tech, BS, 1962; Howard Univ, attended 1965. **Career:** Dr Podiatric Med, self employed; Towers Nursing Home, staff podiatrist, 1970-71; Comm Med Group, 1970-74; Addiction Res & Treat Corp, 1972; Lyndon B Johnson Community Health Ctr, staff podiatrist, 1974-77. **Orgs:** Podiatry Soc St NY; Am Podiatry Asn; Acad Podiatry; NY Co Podiatry Soc; bd dir, Harlem Philharmonic Soc Inc; Nat Bd Podiatry; Nat Asn Advan Colored People; YMCA. **Business Addr:** Podiatrist, 10 W 135th St, New York, NY 10037-2604, **Business Phone:** (212)926-6880.

### HARRIS, JOHN D., II

Vice president (organization), president (organization). **Educ:** Boston Univ, BS, bus admin; Raytheon's Advan Mgt Prog, grad. **Career:** Raytheon Co, vpres, contracts govt & defense businesses, 2003-05, vpres contracts & supply chain 2003-10, exec diversity champion, 2006-08, vpres bus develop, 2013, vpres, 2013, vpres & gen mgr, 2015; Raytheon Serv Co LLC, pres, 2010-; Raytheon Int Inc, chief exec officer, 2013. **Orgs:** Advisor, Aerospace Industs Asn's Procurement & Finance Exec Coun Comt; bd advisor, Asn Aus Coun; bd mem, Exec Leadership Coun; bd mem, Exec Leadership Coun Found; dir, Exostar; bd advisor, Nat Adv Coun Minority Bus Enterprises; bd mem, Nat Contract Mgt Asn; bd advisor, NextGen Adv Comt; Vice Chair, Urban League Eastern Mass; bd dir, Merrimack Col & USO Metrop Wash. **Business Addr:** Vice President, Raytheon Co, 22265 Pacific Blvd, Dulles, VA 20166, **Business Phone:** (571)250-3399.

### HARRIS, DR. JOHN H.

Educator. **Personal:** Born Aug 12, 1940, Memphis, TN. **Educ:** LeMoyne Col, BS, 1962; Atlanta Univ, MA, 1966; Memphis State Univ, PhD, 1990. **Career:** US Peace Corps, pc vol Accra Ghana, 1962-64; LeMoyne-Owen Col, instr, 1967-, div natural sci & math sci, prof, currently, prof math & Comput sci, currently, proj dir. **Orgs:** Nat Asn Math, 1986-; Am Math Soc, 1987-; Math Asn Am, 1996-; bd mem, Memphis Urban Math Colaborative, (MUMC). **Home Addr:** 3348 E Oakside Dr, Memphis, TN 38118-5844, **Home Phone:** (901)794-4813. **Business Addr:** Professor, Campus Project Director, LeMoyne-Owen College, 807 Walker Ave, Memphis, TN 38126-6595, **Business Phone:** (901)435-1381.

### HARRIS, JOHN HENRY

Banker, financial manager, executive. **Personal:** Born Jul 7, 1940, Wynne, AR; married Adele E Lee; children: Cheryl E & Angela M. **Educ:** Southern Ill Univ, BS, 1967; Southwestern Grad Sch Banking, 1974. **Career:** Gateway Nat Bank, vpres, cashier, 1965-74, exec vpres, 1975; Boatmens Nat Bank, opers officer, 1976-77; Sch Dist Univ City, dir finance. **Orgs:** Nat Bankers Asn, 1967-; Am Inst Banking, 1967-77; adv Jr Achievement MS Valley Inc, 1967-77; Bank Admin Inst, 1968-73; dir, treas, St Louis Coun Campfire Girls Inc, 1972-73; Phi Beta Lambda; Nat Asn Black Accts, 1974-75; treas, fund dr, United Negro Col Fund, 1975; bd dir, Inst Black Studies, 1977; Nat Asn Advan Colored People, US Selective Serv Comm; dir, treas, Greely Comm Ctr Waring Sch PTA; dir, King-Fanon Ment Health Ctr, Child Day Care Assoc; supvry comn, Educ Employees Credit Union; treas, Block Unit 1144; dir, Am Cancer Soc. **Home Addr:** 1350 Clay Ave, Springfield, MO 65802.

### HARRIS, JOHN J.

Chief executive officer. **Personal:** Born Sep 18, 1951, Plymouth, NC; son of Jerome; children: 3. **Educ:** Calif State Univ, BA, 1972; Univ Calif, Los Angeles, Grad Sch Mgt, MBA, 1974. **Career:** Carnation Co, mkt mgt trainee, 1974, vpres & gen mgr, 1987-91; Friskies Pet Care Div, vpres & gen mgr, 1991; Nestle SA, sr vpres, 1997; Friskies PetCare Co, pres, 1999; Nestle worldwide, chief exec officer & chief world wide integration officer, 2001; Nestle Purina Europ oper, chief exec officer, top mgr 2002-; Nestle Waters, exec vpres & chmn, 2007-13, chief exec officer, 2008. **Orgs:** Chmn, Pet Food Insts, 1993; bd dir, Lane Col; dir, Anderson Sch Mgt, Univ Calif Los Angeles; mem exec bd, Nestle S.A; dir, Nestle Waters, 2007. **Business Addr:** Chief Executive Officer, Nestle Purina Pet Care, Case postale 352, Vevey1800, **Business Phone:** (412)1924-211.

### HARRIS, JOHNNIE FRANCES (FRAN HARRIS)

Media executive, business owner, basketball player. **Personal:** Born Mar 12, 1965, Dallas, TX. **Educ:** Univ Tex, BA & MA, jour, 1991, PhD, bus admin. **Career:** Basketball player (retired), media exec, bus owner; Procter & Gamble, sls exec, ae, sls mgr, 1991-95; Houston Comets, guard, 1997; ESPN, Color Analyst, Sideline Reporter, Studio Analyst, 1994-2001, Play-by-Play Announcer, 2011; Lifetime TV & FOX Sports, color commentator, 1994-9; Bks: Dream Season; About My Sister's Bus: Black Woman's Rd Map to Successful Entrepreneurship, 1996; Fran Harris Enterprises, exec dir, 1995-; Kabooyow Digital Mkt, chief exec officer, 1998-. **Special Achievements:** First and only NCAA Championship team, 1986; First woman to host her own sports talk radio show in Austin, Texas in 2001; University of Texas at Austin Hall of Honor 2007; Texas Black Sports Hall of Fame, 2009; Most Valuable Player, UT Austin 1985-86; Southwest Conference Player of the Year, 1985. Alumni of the Year Award, Tex Exes Black Alumni Network. **Business Addr:** Executive Director, Fran Harris Enterprises, PO Box 3594, Culver City, CA 90231, **Business Phone:** (310)745-7762.

### HARRIS, JONATHAN CECIL (JON HARRIS)

Football player, executive. **Personal:** Born Jun 9, 1974, Brooklyn, NY. **Educ:** Univ Va, BA, psychol, 1996. **Career:** Football player (retired), executive; Philadelphia Eagles, defensive end, 1997-98; Cleveland Browns, defensive end, 1999; Green Bay Packers, defensive end, 1999; Berlin Thunder, 2001; Oakland Raiders, 2002; Benford Kalu Investments LLC, proj mgr, 2005-07; Prudential Fox & Roach, realtor, 2005-10; Ricoh Bus Solutions, acct exec, 2010-14; True Blue Inc, sales rep, 2014-. **Home Addr:** , Swedesboro, NJ.

### HARRIS, JOSEPH ELLIOT, II

Automotive executive. **Personal:** Born Feb 21, 1945, Boston, MA; son of Joseph E and Muriel K; married Young Ja Chung; children: Joy Electra & Joseph E III. **Educ:** Howard Univ, BSEE, 1968; Rochester Inst Technol, MBA, mkt & finance, 1978; Northeastern Univ, cert advan studies, 1980. **Career:** Stromberg Carlson, elec engr, 1967-74; Xerox Corp, sr mfg engr, 1974-76; Ford Motor Co, buyer, 1976-78; Polaroid Corp, mgr minority bus & minority dealer develop, 1978-91; Chrysler Corp, spec supplier rels exec, 1990-96; Global Team Inc, pres, 2010-; Global Mfg Resources, china exec dir, 2010-; Global Tooling Engineering & Mfg, china opers, 2010-12; Huayuan Group, distribr diversity mgr, 2012; ITM, dir ud opers, 2012-13. **Orgs:** Vice chmn, MNY Enterprise Dev Week, 1988-91; Nat Asn Purchasing Mgt, min bus dev group, 1988-92; Mattapan Co Health, 1989-91; Try-Us, 1992; Nat Minority Supplier Develop, 1992; chmn, Mic Minority bus develop, 1992; Oakland Boy Scout, 1992. **Home Addr:** 345 E Crescent Lane, Detroit, MI 48207, **Home Phone:** (313)567-0107. **Business Addr:** Executive, Chrysler Corp, 12000 Chrysler Dr, Highland Park, MI 48288-1919, **Business Phone:** (313)252-6094.

### HARRIS, JOSEPH JOHN, III

Educator, school administrator. **Personal:** Born Oct 10, 1946, Altoona, PA; son of Joseph John II and Ann M Hart; married Donna Ford; children: Julie Renee & Khyle Lee. **Educ:** Highland Park Col, AS, 1967; Wayne State Univ, BS, 1969; Univ Mich, Ann Arbor, MS, 1971, PhD, 1972. **Career:** Detroit Pub Sch, teacher, asst prin, 1968-73; Highland Pk Pub Sch, consult proj dir, 1972-73; Pa State Univ, asst prof, 1973-76; Ind Univ, assoc prof, 1976-83, co dir & co prin investr, 1979-80, spec asst to dean, 1981-82, dir, 1981-86, assoc dir, 1982-84, prof, chair & ctr dir, 1984-87; Cleveland State Univ, prof & dean, 1987-90; African-Am Studies & Res, scholar residence, currently; Univ Ky, prof & dean, 1990-95, prof admin & supv, 1995-, pres Comn Diversity, chair, advisor, currently. **Orgs:** Bd dir, Marotta Montessori Sch Cleveland, 1987-90; bd trustee, Greater Cleveland Lit Coalition, 1988-; adv bd, Nat Sorority Phi Delta Kappa, 1988-; bd trustee, Nat Pub Radio Affil-WCPNW, 1988-; bd dir, Nat Orgn Legal Probs Educ, 1988-91; ed bd, CSU Mag, 1989-; Lexington Arts & Cult Ctr; Holmes Group Ed Schs, E Lansing. **Home Addr:** 3390 Pepperhill Rd, Lexington, KY 40502, **Home Phone:** (859)266-0644. **Business Addr:** Professor of Administration and Supervision, Scholar in Residence, University Kentucky, 103 Dickey Hall, Lexington, KY 40506-0017, **Business Phone:** (859)257-9000.

### HARRIS, JOSEPH PRESTON

Vice president (organization), teacher, executive. **Personal:** Born Apr 11, 1935, Rome, MS; married Otha L; children: Jacqui & Joe Jr. **Educ:** Chicago Teachers Col, BE, 1956; John Marshall Law Sch, JD, 1964. **Career:** Chicago Bd Educ, teacher, 1956-64; Allstate Ins Co, asst vpres, agent, currently. **Orgs:** Bd dir, Maywood Proviso State Bank, 1973-76; Ill & Chicago Bar Asn; Nat Asn Advan Colored People. **Home Addr:** 2431 W Grand Ave, Detroit, MI 48208. **Business Addr:** Insurance Agent, Allstate Insurance Co, 7895 Hwy 119 Suite 11, Alabaster, AL 35007, **Business Phone:** (205)685-8686.

### HARRIS, JOYCE

Executive, spokesperson. **Educ:** Howard Univ, BA, jour, 1985; Johns Hopkins Univ, Baltimore, MBA, mkt, 2003. **Career:** USAToday.com, asst news ed; US Mint, Web Content Off Appln Develop, exec producer, web dir, div chief & spokeswoman, currently; Govt, US Dept Treas, pub & legis affairs staff, dir, 2006-. **Orgs:** US Dept Treas, 2002. **Business Addr:** Division Chief, US Mint, 801 9th St NW, Washington, DC 20220-0001, **Business Phone:** (202)354-7222.

### HARRIS, JUAN

Government official. **Career:** City Paterson, bus Adminr, currently. **Business Addr:** Business Administrator, City of Paterson, 155 Mkt St City Hall 2nd Fl, Paterson, NJ 07505, **Business Phone:** (973)881-3365.

### HARRIS, KAMALA DEVI, JR.

Lawyer, city planner. **Personal:** Born Oct 20, 1964, Oakland, CA; son of Donald and Shyamala Gopalan; married Douglas Emhoff. **Educ:** Howard Univ, Wash, DC, BA, 1986; Univ Calif, Hastings Col Law, JD, 1989. **Career:** Calif State Off, Alameda County, dep dist atty, 1990-98, Career Criminal Unit, San Francisco Dist Attys Off, atty, 1998-2000, Community & Neighborhood Div, San Francisco City Atty's Off, chief, 2000-03, dist atty, 2003-11, atty gen, 2011-; City & County San Francisco, dist atty, 2004-11; Leakey Found, advisor; San Francisco Mus Mod Art, mentor. **Orgs:** Bd dir, Nat Dist Attorneys Asn; Calif Dist Attorneys Asn; fel Aspen Inst Rodel Fels Pub Leadership; founder, Coalition to End Exploitation Kids; vpres, Nat Dist Attorneys Asn; Alpha Kappa Alpha Sorority; San Francisco Found; bd dir, San Francisco Bar Asn. **Honors/Awds:** Woman of Power, Nat Urban League, 2004; Thurgood Marshall Award, Nat Black Prosecutors Asn, 2005; One of the top 100 lawyers in California, The Daily Journal Calif. **Special Achievements:** First woman District Attorney in San Francisco; First African American to serve as top prosecutor in California; First Indian American to serve as district attorney in the United States. Book: Smart on Crime: A Career Prosecutor's Plan to Make us Safer, 2009. **Business Addr:** Attorney General, State of California Department of Justice, PO Box 944255, Sacramento, CA 94244-2550, **Business Phone:** (916)322-3360.

### HARRIS, KELLY C. (KELLY HARRIS-BRAXTON)

Association executive, executive, government official. **Personal:** married George P; children: 2. **Educ:** Univ Va, BA, 1989. **Career:** Housing & Econ Develop E Dist Initiative, mayor's chief staff & coordr; Off Gov, spec asst policy, 1992-94; Young Men's Christian Asn Metro, Greater Richmond, Va, bd dir, currently. **Orgs:** Va State Bar; Old Dom Bar Asn; bd mem, Richmond Communities Schs; chairperson Downtown YMCA Bd Mgt, 2000; bd assocs, Lewis Ginter Botantical Garden; Leadership Metro Richmond Class, 2001; pres, Richmond Chap Links Inc, currently. **Special Achievements:** The first black president of the YMCA Board in Richmond Virginia. **Business Addr:** Board Director, Young Men's Christian Association Metro, 2 W Franklin St, Richmond, VA 23220, **Business Phone:** (804)649-9622.

### HARRIS, KENNETH G., JR.

Executive, educator, musician. **Personal:** married Pamala Hal; children: Kristi. **Educ:** Univ Ark, Pine Bluff, BS, elem educ; Henderson State Univ, MSE, elem educ; E Tex State Univ, EdD, 1993. **Career:** Chairman, professor (retired), professor emeritus, musician; Henderson State Univ, Dept Curric & Instr, assoc prof, prof & chmn, 1996-2007, prof emer, currently; Arkadelphia Sch Bd, pres. **Orgs:** Pres, Arkadelphia School Bd, 2007; bd vice chair, Arkansas Baptist Col, currently. **Business Addr:** Board Vice Chair, Arkansas Baptist College, 1621 Dr Martin Luther King Jr Dr, Little Rock, AR 72202, **Business Phone:** (501)420-1200.

### HARRIS, LEE

Journalist. **Personal:** Born Dec 30, 1941, Bryan, TX; married Lois. **Educ:** Calif State Univ, attended 1968. **Career:** Riverside Press, 1968-72; San Bernardino Sun Telegra, 1972-73; Los Angeles Times, reporter. **Special Achievements:** L.A. City Hall Turns a Genteel 50", 1978. **Home Addr:** 5719 S Rimpau Blvd, Los Angeles, CA 90043. **Business Addr:** Reporter, Los Angeles Times, Times Mirror Sq, Los Angeles, CA 90053.

### HARRIS, LEODIS

Judge. **Personal:** Born Aug 11, 1934, Pensacola, FL; married Patsy Auzenne; children: Courtney, Monique & Darwin. **Educ:** Cleveland Col Western Res Univ, attended 1957; Cleveland Marshall Law Sch, JD, 1963. **Career:** Pvt prac law, 1963-77; Common Pleas Ct Juv Div, juv ct judge, 1993. **Orgs:** The Greater Cleveland Citizens League, 1961-; Urban Affairs Com Cleveland Bar Asn, 1975-77; hon trustee, Cleveland-Marshall Law Alumni Asn, 2005. **Honors/Awds:** Service award, Cleveland Jr Women's Civic League, 1978; Freedom Award, Cleveland Nat Asn Advan Colored People, 1979; Man of the Year, Cleveland Negro Bus & Prof Women, 1979; Silver Award, OH Prince Hall Knights Templar, 1980; Award for Advocacy for Juveniles, named in his honor. **Home Addr:** 527 Riverview Rd, Gates Mills, OH 44040, **Home Phone:** (440)423-3577. **Business Addr:** 745 Leader Bldg 526 Super Ave, Cleveland, OH 44114.

### HARRIS, LEON L. (LEON HARRIS)

Labor activist. **Personal:** Born Nyack, NY; married Evelyn. **Educ:** Hampton Inst, attended 1950; RI Col Educ, AA, 1956; Harvard Univ, attended 1963. **Career:** John Hope Settlement Providence, athletic instr, 1950-53; Providence New Eng, phys educ instr, 1954-60; Am Fedn State, County & Munic Employee AFL-CIO, int rep, 1960-64; Cable News Network, journalist, 1983. **Orgs:** Dir, Civil Rights Res Educ; Retail Wholesale Dept Store Union & AFL-CIOCLC, 1964-; nat life mem, com Nat Asn Advan Colored People; vice chmn, Manhood Found Inc; adv bd, recruitment training prog, NY Black Trade Union Leadership Com; pres, Greenwich Village Nat Asn Advan Colored People 8 other chaps; pres, New Eng Golf Asn; nat vpres, United Golf Asn; Am Social Club; chmn, CORE Rochester; lectured several univ; A Philip Randolph Inst; Friends Nat Black Theater. **Honors/Awds:** Honor Award Outstanding Athlete, Am Legion, 1947; 16 Letterman; Kans City Monarchs. **Special Achievements:** First African American New England to sign with St Louis Cardinals, 1952. **Home Addr:** 1089 Grand Ave Apt 2H, Englewood, NJ 07631, **Home Phone:** (201)875-3542.

### HARRIS, LEONARD ANTHONY (LENNY HARRIS)

Baseball player, baseball executive. **Personal:** Born Oct 28, 1964, Miami, FL; son of Arthur and Rebecca Clark; married Carnettia Evan Johnson. **Educ:** Miami-Dade Col. **Career:** Baseball player (retired), baseball coach; Cincinnati Reds, 1988-89, 1994-98; Los Angeles Dodgers, infielder, 1989-93; New York Mets, 1998, 2000-01; Colo Rockies, 1999; Ariz Diamondbacks, 1999-2000; Milwaukee Brewers, 2002; Chicago Cubs, 2003; Fla Marlins, infielder, 2003-05; Wash Nationals, infield coordr, interim hitting coach, 2008; Camelback Ranch, hitting instr, 2008; Los Angeles Dodgers, hitting inst, currently; Great Lakes Loons, hitting coach, 2011; Gulf Coast League Marlins, coach; Miami Marlins, asst hitting coach, third base coach, currently. **Orgs:** Optimist Club Miami, 1990-91. **Home Addr:** 17330 NW 63 Pl, Miami, FL 33015. **Business Addr:** Professional Baseball Player, Washington Nationals, RFK Stadium, Washington, DC 20003, **Business Phone:** (202)675-6287.

### HARRIS, HON. LESLIE E.

Judge. **Personal:** Born May 23, 1948, Chicago, IL. **Educ:** Northwestern Univ, attended 1974; Boston Univ, MA, 1974; Boston Col Law Sch, JD, 1984. **Career:** Suffolk County, probation officer, 1998-92; Comt Pub Coun Serv, 1988-92; Suffolk County Dist Attys Off, Juv Div, chief, 1992-94; Suffolk County Juv Ct, Judge, 1994-. **Honors/Awds:** Judge of the Yr Award, Mass Judges Conf; Community Serv Award, Mass Bar Asn; 10-Point Coalition Serv Award; Mary Q Hawkes Serv Award, Crime & Justice Found; Distinguished Alumni Award, Boston Col Law Sch. **Home Addr:** 8 Carlisle St, Boston, MA 02121-1308, **Home Phone:** (617)442-0815. **Business Addr:** Judge, Suffolk County Juvenile Court, Edward W Brooke Courthouse, Boston, MA 02114, **Business Phone:** (617)788-8565.

### HARRIS, LESTER L.

Administrator, association executive. **Personal:** children: Michelle, Ernie, Leon & Lester. **Career:** Econ Opportunity Coun Suffolk Inc, chmn. **Orgs:** Vpres, Deer Pk, Nat Asn Advan Colored People, 1964-70, pres, 1973-74; elected comt man, Babylon Dem Party; Suffolk Co Migrant Bd; Suffolk Co Hansel & Gretal Inc; Deer Pk Civic Asn; Negro Airman Int Inc. **Honors/Awds:** Suffolk Co Humanitarian Award, Suffolk Co Locality Mayor JF Goode & Ossie Davis, 1973. **Home Addr:** 180 Tell Ave, Deer Park, NY 11729-6933.

### HARRIS, LORETTA K.

Librarian. **Personal:** Born Nov 20, 1935, Bryant, MS; daughter of Estella Kelley Parker; married James Joe; children: Sheila Lynne Ragin. **Educ:** S Ill Univ, cert, 1954; Kennedy-King Col, cert, 1971; City Col Chicago-Loop, dip, 1974; Chicago State Univ, BA, 1983, MSLS, 1990. **Career:** Librarian (retired); Univ Il Libr, photog tech, 1957-59; S Ill Univ Libr, libr clerk, 1959-63; Univ Ill Chicago, libr clerk, 1963-68; John Crerar Libr, order librn, 1968-70; Univ Ill Chicago, Libr Health Sci, libr tech asst III, 1970-98; Memphis City Sch Syst, PACE/NCLB coordr, substitute teacher, 2004-. **Orgs:** Health Sci Librn Ill, 1976-98; chairperson, Coun Libr & Media Tech Assts, 1977-80, const chairperson, 1980-84, Med Libr Asn Midwest Chap, 1976-98; Ont Asn Libr Techs, 1977-90; Black women Mid W Proj, 1984, Am Libr Assoc, Standing Comm Libr Ed; Training Libr Supportive Staff Subcomm, 1979-81; Int Fedn Libr & Asn & Insts Printing & Reproduction Comt IFLA ann meeting, 1985; Nat Coun Negro Women, 1986; const chairperson, Coun Libr & Media Tech Assts, 1986-91, chairperson, nominating comt, 1988; Ill Sch Libr Asn, 1990; corresp secy, Nat Assoc Negro Musicians, R Nathaniel Dett Br, 1993-97. **Honors/Awds:** Hatie Beverly Education Award, 1987; Janice Watkins Award Comm; 1994-95, 1997. **Special Achievements:** Listed in Natl Deans List, 1982-83. **Home Addr:** 4011 Lacewood Dr, Memphis, TN 38115, **Home Phone:** (901)366-9092.

### HARRIS, LUCIOUS H., JR.

Basketball player. **Personal:** Born Dec 18, 1970, Los Angeles, CA; children: Lucious III. **Educ:** Calif State Univ, Long Beach, attended 1993. **Career:** Basketball player (retired); Dallas Mavericks, shooting guard, 1993-96; Philadelphia 76ers, shooting guard, 1996-97; NJ Nets, shooting guard, 1997-2003, point guard, 2003-04; Cleveland Cavaliers, shooting guard, 2004-05. **Honors/Awds:** Named MVP of the Big West Tournament, 1993; Long Beach State's Athletic Hall of Fame, 1999; Eastern Conference Player of the Week, 2003; Retired his jersey 30, Long Beach State, 2007. **Home Addr:** 11612 Poema Pl, Chatsworth, CA 91311-1283, **Home Phone:** (661)312-6239.

### HARRIS, M. L. (MICHAEL LEE HARRIS)

Founder (originator), football player, chief executive officer. **Personal:** Born Jan 16, 1954, Columbus, OH; married Linda; children: Michael Lee II & Joshua. **Educ:** Univ Tampa; Kans State Univ. **Career:** Football player (retired); Hamilton Tiger-Cats, tight end, 1976-77; Toronto Argonauts, tight end, 1978-79; Cincinnati Bengals, tight end, 1980-85; ML Harris All Boys Acad, chief exec officer. **Orgs:** Founder, ML Harris Outreach; Sports World Ministries. **Business Addr:** Founder, ML Harris Outreach, PO Box 24143, Columbus, OH 43224-0143.

### HARRIS, MAJOR GEN. MARCELITE J.

Air force officer. **Personal:** Born Jan 16, 1943, Houston, TX; daughter of Cecil Oneal and Marcelite Elizabeth Terrell Jordan; married Maurice Anthony; children: Steven Eric, Tenecia Marcelite & Sherry. **Educ:** Spelman Col, BA, speech & drama, 1964; Squadon Offr Sch, Corresp, Air Univ, attended 1975; Cent Mich Univ, attended 1978; Chapman Col, attended 1980; Air War Col, Sem, Air Univ, attended 1982; Univ Md, Okinawa, Japan, BS, bus mgt, 1986; Sr Offs Nat Security, Harvard Univ, attended 1989; Capstone, Residence, Nat Defense Univ, attended 1990; Nat & Int Security Mgt Course, Harvard Univ, attended 1994, Sr Mgr Govt, 1995. **Career:** Air force officer (retired); Head Start, teacher, 1964-65; Travis Afb, 60th Mil Airlift Wing, asst dir admin, 1965-67; Bitburg Air Base, W Ger, 71st Tactical Missile Squadron, admin offr, 1969-70; Korat Royal Thai Afb, Thailand, 49th Tactical Fighter Squadron, maintenance supvr, 1971-72; Travis Afb, from job control offr to field maintenance supvr, 1972-75; Hq USAF, personnel staff offr & White House social aide, 1975-78; USAF Acad, Cadet Squadron 39, air offr comndg, 1978-80; Mc Connell Afb, Kans, maintenance control offr, 384th Air Refueling Wing, 1980-81, comdr 384th Avionics Maintenance Squadron, 1981-82, comdr 384th Field Maintenance Squadron, 1982; Pac Air Forces Logistic Support Ctr, Kadena Air Base, Japan, dir maintenance, 1982-86; Keesler Afb, Miss, dep comdr maintenance, 1986-88, comdr 3300th Tech Training Wing, 1988-90; Tinker Afb, Okla City Air Logistics Ctr, vice comdr, 1990-93; Hq Air Educ & Training Command, Randolph Afb, dir tech training, 1993-94; Hq USAF, dir maintenance, 1994-97; United Space Alliance, 1997-2002. **Orgs:** Air Force Asn, 1965-; Delta Sigma Theta, 1980-; Miss Gulf Coast Chamber Com, 1987-90; Biloxi Rotary, 1989-90; Tuskegee Airmen, 1990-; bd dir, United Serv Automobile Asn, 1993; Unite States Rep WomenNATO Comm, 1994; treas, Nat Asn Advan Colored People; dir, Bd Peachtree Hope Charter Sch; Bd Visitors USAF Acad, 2010. **Honors/Awds:** White House Social Aide, Pres Carter, 1977-78; First two women cadet squadron commanders, USAF Acad, 1978; Woman Year, New Orleans Chap, Nat Sports Orgn, 1989; Outstanding Young Woman of America, 1990; Women of Distinction Award, Thomas W. Anthony Chapter, Air Force Asn, 1995; Trailblazer Award, Black Girls Rock Found, 2010; Has been received numerous other civilian awards. **Special Achievements:** First Woman Aircraft maintenance officer, USAF, 1969; First woman Avionic sand Field Maintenance Squadron Commander, Strategic Air Command, 1981-82; First woman dir of maintenance in the USAF, 1982; First woman deputy commander of maintenance in the USAF, 1986; Top 100 Afro-American Business & Professional Women, Dollars & Sense Magazine, 1989; First African-American woman brigadier general, USAF, 1990; First African-American woman major general in the United States, 1995. **Home Addr:** 7714 Gingerbread Lane, Fairfax Station, VA 22039-2203, **Home Phone:** (703)562-1515.

## HARRIS, DR. MARION HOPKINS

Educator, vice president (organization). **Personal:** Born Jul 27, 1938, Washington, DC; daughter of Dennis C Hopkins and Georgia Greenleaf; children: Alan Edward. **Educ:** Univ Pittsburgh, MPA, 1971; USC, MPA, 1984; Univ Southern Calif, DPA, pub admin/policy, 1985. **Career:** Westinghouse Corp, Pittsburgh, housing consult, 1970-71; Univ Pittsburgh, Carnegie-Mellon fel, 1970-71; Dept Urban Renewal & Econ Develop, Rochester, NY, dir prog planning; Fairfax City, Redevel & Housing Auth, exec dir, 1971-72; Fairfax County Redevelop & Housing Authority, exec dir, 1972-73; HUD Detroit Area Off, dep dir housing, 1973-75; US Gen Acct Off, Wash, DC, managing auditor, 1979-80; U.S. Dept Housing & Urban Develop, off asst sec, sr field officer housing, 1979-89, dir eval div, off mgt & qual assurance, 1989-91; Bowie State Univ, Grad Prog Admin Mgt, coordr, prof, 1991-93, Master Pub Admin Prog, prog coordr, vpres finance & admin, 2000-, comnr, Howard County Charter Comn, 2002-03, actg vpres finance & admin, 2005-07, Sch Bus, prof mgt & pub admin, chair mgt mkt & pub admin, currently; Univ Md, Grad Sch Mgt & Technol, prof, 1997-; Leo Group Mgt Consult, pres, 2005-. **Orgs:** Fel Ford Found, 1970-71; pres, USC-WPAC Doctoral Asn, DC, 1979; exec bd mem, SW Neighborhood Assembly, DC, 1979-80; Black Womens Agenda, 1980; chmn, Housing Comn, DC League Women Voters, 1980-82; Adv Neighborhood Comnr, 1986; sub cabinet, Citizens Adv Bd, Wash Suburban Sanit Comn, 1989-; steering comt mem, Acad Leadership Inst, Univ Md, 1993; co-chair, bd mem, Gov Workforce Investment Bd, 1996-98; Am Soc Pub Admin; presenter, Acad Bus Admin; Gov Workforce Investment Bd Bus Admin; Am Acad Social & Polit Sci, Am Eval Asn; chmn, Educ Comn, Caribbean Am Inter cult Orgn; ex-off mem, Bowie State Univ Found; chair, Govs Policy Group Workforce Develop, 2004; Am Acad Soc & Polit Sci; Univ Southern Calif Doctoral Asn. **Honors/Awds:** Outstanding Performance Award, US Dept Housing & Urban Develop, 1984, 1987; Secretary's Cert Achievement, 1988; Secretary's Group Award, 1990; Merit Award, 1990; Governor Maryland's Transition Team, 1996; Carnegie-Mellon Mid-career Fel, Univ Pittsburgh. **Home Addr:** 10229 Ruthland Round Rd, Columbia, MD 21044, **Home Phone:** (301)621-4949. **Business Addr:** Professor of Management and Public Administration, Chair of Management Marketing and Public Administration, Bowie State University, Rm 0221 14000 Jericho Pk Rd, Bowie, MD 20715-9465, **Business Phone:** (301)860-4000.

## HARRIS, MARION REX

Chairperson, association executive, chief executive officer. **Personal:** Born Jun 30, 1934, Wayne County, NC; son of Virginia and Eugene; married Aronul Beauford Edwards; children: Amy, Angelique & Anjanette. **Educ:** LaSalle Ext Corres Law Sch, 1970; NC Agr & Tech State Univ, DHH, 1983. **Career:** A&H Cleaners Inc, proprietor & chmn bd, 1965-; A&H Coin-Op Laundromat, proprietor & chmn bd, 1970-; Off Min Bus Enterprise Adv Bd, bd mem, 1970-; NC Dept Trans, bd mem, 1972-76; Custom Molders Inc, bd dir, 1976-83; Int & Domestic Develop Corp, vice chairperson & chief exec officer, 1976-; Rexon Coal Co, chmn bd, 1981-; Vanguard Investment Co, chief exec officer, 1982-84; Cape Fear Reg Bur Community Action Inc, bd dir. **Orgs:** Fayetteville Area Chamber Com, 1965-; NC Coal Inst, 1976-; dir, Nat Bus League, 1980-; chmn, Rexon Coal Co, 1982-; dir, Middle Atlantic Tech Ctr, 1983-; bd trustees, St Augustine's Col, 1983-; bd trustees, A&T State Univ, 1985-. **Honors/Awds:** Recognition Black Hist Sears Roebuck Co, 1969; Letter Recognition & Excellence Business US Dept Com Off Minority Bus Enterprise, 1972; Businessman of the Year, Nat Asn Minority Cert Pub Accts, 1982; "Driven"Business, NC Mag, 1983; Horatio Alger Award, St Augustine's Col, 1983; Par Excellence Operation PUSH, 1983. **Home Addr:** 1815 Gola Dr, Fayetteville, NC 28301-0519, **Home Phone:** (910)339-5160. **Business Addr:** Vice Chairperson, Chief Executive Officer, International Domestic Development Corp, 4511 Bragg Blvd, Fayetteville, NC 28303, **Business Phone:** (910)864-5515.

## HARRIS, DR. MARJORIE ELIZABETH

College administrator, president (organization). **Personal:** Born Dec 8, 1924, Indianapolis, IN; daughter of T Garfield Lewis and Violet T Harrison-Lewis; married Atty Richard Ray; children: Frank L Gillespie, Grant G Gillespie, Gordon L Gillespie & Jason Ray. **Educ:** WVa State Col, Inst WVa, BS, 1946; Univ Mich, Ann Arbor, MA, 1975, PhD, 1981. **Career:** Lewis Col Bus, Detroit, Mich, fac, 1946-60, admin asst, 1960-65, pres, 1968-2006. **Orgs:** Bd trustee, Lewis Col Bus, 1950-, property trustee chair, 2006, bd mem; bd comnrs, Detroit Pub Libr, 1970-86; regional dir, Gamma Phi Delta Sorority, 1989. **Business Addr:** Property Trustee Chair, President, Board Member, Lewis College of Business, 17370 Meyers Rd, Detroit, MI 48235, **Business Phone:** (313)862-6300.

## HARRIS, MARY LORRAINE

Government official. **Personal:** Born Jan 18, 1954, Durham, NC; daughter of Greenville E and Mable Freeland. **Educ:** NC Cent Univ, BA, 1975; Univ Miami, MS, 1980. **Career:** Metro Dade Transp Admin, prog analyst, 1978-80, prog analyst 3, 1980-81, prin planner, 1981-83, chi Conf Minority Transit Officials & chair 1988-; efurban init unit, 1983-84, asst exec dir, 1984-88, asst dep dir, 1988-90; Metro Dade Co, Dept Human Resources, adminr, 1990. **Orgs:** Bd dir, League Women Voters, 1988-; Conf Minority Transit Officials & chair, 1988-; Metro Dade Off Rehabilitative Servs, Miami, Fla, asst dir, 1989; Greater Miami Opera Guild, 1990-; Metro Dade Women's Asn; Nat Forum Black Pub Adminr; Womens Transp Sem; Nat Asn Female Execs; Am Heart Asn Greater Miami; Nat Asn Advan Colored People; chairperson, COMTO Mid Yr Conf; task force Inner City "Say No To Drugs"; Metro Dade County United Way Cabinet. **Honors/Awds:** Gold Award, United Way; Outstanding Black American, State Florida, 1986. **Home Addr:** 1851 NW 170 St, Miami, FL 33056. **Business Addr:** Administrator, Miami Dade County, 111 NW 1st St Suite 220, Miami, FL 33128.

## HARRIS, DR. MARY STYLES

Educator, executive, president (organization). **Personal:** Born Jun 26, 1949, Nashville, TN; daughter of George and Margaret; married Sidney E; children: 1. **Educ:** Lincoln Univ, BA, biol, 1971; Cornell Univ, PhD, molecular genetics, 1975; Robert Wood Johnson Med Sch; Cornell Univ, PhD, molecular virol, 1977; Rutgers Univ. **Career:** Rutgers Med Sch, teacher, 1976-77; Sickle Cell Found GA, exec dir, 1977-79; Morehouse Col Sch Med, asst prof, 1978-; WGTV Channel 8 Univ Ga, scientist residence, 1979-80; Atlanta Univ, asst prof biol, 1980-81; GA Dept Human Resources, dir genetic servs; Harris & Assoc, founder pres & genetics consult, 1987; Biotechnical Communs Inc, founder, pres, currently; CNN Radio, exec producer & host, currently; Journey to Wellness, founder, pres & exec producer, currently. **Orgs:** Bd visitor, CDC; bd visitor, Grady Hosp; bd mem, Families First Atlanta; Women's Forum Ga; bd mem, CDC Found; GA Breast Cancer Alliance; Sickle Cell Found; Cong Black Caucus Health Brain Trust; Govs Adv Coun Alcohol & Drug Abuse; Pub Health Asn, 1977-; Am Soc Human Genetics, 1977-; ga bd regents, Univ Ga, 1979-80. **Honors/Awds:** Doctoral Fel, Ford Found; Outstanding Young women of America, 1977, 1978; Outstanding Working Woman, Glamour Mag, 1980; Outstanding Georgia Business Woman, Ga Trend Mag, 1999; Excellence in Radio Broadcasting, Atlanta Med Asn, 2001, 2002; 10 NIH grants; Woman of Achievement, Young Women Chrisitian Asn, 2002; Distinguished African-American Scientists of the 21 Century; Profiles in Progress Award; Science Residency Award, NSF. **Special Achievements:** Leadership Atlanta, 2000; First African-American to enter Jackson high school in Miami. **Business Addr:** President, Founder, BioTechnical Communications, 227 Sand Springs Pl Suite 103D-190, Atlanta, GA 30328, **Business Phone:** (404)252-9872.

## HARRIS, DR. MARYANN

School administrator, entertainer, consultant. **Personal:** Born Jun 10, 1946, Moultrie, GA; married John W; children: Paul & Justin. **Educ:** Knoxville Col, BS, 1969; Wayne State Univ, MA, 1971; Nova Univ, EdD, 1986; Univ Akron, MA, 1992. **Career:** Case Western Res Univ, geront supvr, 1972-74; Cuyahoga Community Col, geront consult, 1975-80; City Cleveland, geront consult, 1980-81; Proj Rainbow Asn Inc, exec dir & founder, 1980-; E Cleveland City Sch, bd mem; UAW-Ford Develop & Training Prog, reg coord; story teller, currently. **Orgs:** Sch bd E Cleveland City Sch Dist, 1979-; geront consult, Coun Econ Opportunity Greater Cleveland, 1980-84; grants develop, Cleveland Adult Training, 1980-; pres & sr assoc Grantsmanship, Res Coun, 1980-; exec comt mem, Cuyahoga County Demo Party, 1984; chmn, Youth Comn Nat Asn Advan Colored People, 1985; second vpres, Alpha Kappa Alpha, 1985; Nat Sch Bd Asn Fed Rel Network, 1988-; Ohio Northeast Region Bd; pres, Ohio Community Educ Asn; vpres, Cleveland Asn Black Storytellers. **Honors/Awds:** Gerontology Study Grant USA Admin on Aging, 1969-71; Women's Rights, Practices Policies Community Service Award, 1984; Career Mother of the Year, Cleveland Call & Post Newspaper, 1984; Award of Achievement, Ohio School Boards Asn, 1991-94; Award Winning Author, 1997. **Business Addr:** Storyteller, Cleveland Story Tellers, 1326 E 143 St, East Cleveland, OH 44112, **Business Phone:** (216)249-6427.

## HARRIS, MELVIN

Government official. **Personal:** Born Feb 9, 1953, Oxford, NC. **Educ:** NC Cent Univ, BA, 1975; Am Univ, MPA, 1977. **Career:** US Off Personnel Mgt, personnel mgt specialist, 1977; Am Fed State Co & Munic Auth, res analyst, 1977-78; Prince Georges Co Md, personnel & labor rels analyst, 1978-79; Dist Columbia Gov, prin labor rels officer, 1979-88; Howard Univ, dir labor & employees rels, 1988-92; City Baltimore, labor comnr; Nat Asn Air Traffic Specialists, dir labor & employee rels; Off Labor & Employee Rels, Fed Aviation Admin, dir, dir labor & employee rel, 2004; Off Employ & Labor Mgt, exec dir, currently. **Orgs:** Pres, Alpha Phi Omega, NC Cent Univ, 1973-75; Conf Minority Pub Admin, Am Soc Pub Admin, 1978-; round table coordr, Nat Capitol Area Chap, Am Soc Pub Admin, 1980-83; chmn, VA Voter Regis Educ Task Force, 1984; co-founder & treas, Nat Young Prof Forum, Am Soc Pub Admin, 1981-83; bd dir, Nat Coun Asn Policy Sci, 1984-85; bd dir, Nat Capitol Area Chap, Am Soc Pub Admin, 1980-82, 1984-85; Alexandria Forum, 1983-; co-chmn, Young Prof Forum Nat Capitol Area Chap, ASPA; camp dir, Alex Young Dem, 1982, pres, 1983-84; Alex Dem Exec Comn, 1983-84; exec vpres, Va Young Dem, 1984-; Am Univ Title IX Adv Comn, 1984-; chmn, Va Young Dem NVA Fundraiser, 1985. **Business Addr:** Executive Director, Labor Management Relations, US Department of Transportation, 800 Independence Ave SW, Washington, WA 20591, **Business Phone:** (202)267-3456.

## HARRIS, REV. DR. MICHAEL NEELY

Clergy, counselor. **Personal:** Born Feb 5, 1947, Athens, GA; son of William T and Mattie Neely Samuels; married Sylvia Ann Jones; children: Crystal Michele (deceased) & Michael Clayton. **Educ:** Morehouse Col, BA, 1968; Eastern Baptist Theol Sem, DMin, 1984. **Career:** Philadelphia Sch Dist, res intern, 1968-69, admin asst; Off Fedr Eval, day-care prog, 1969-71; First Baptist Church of Passtown, Coatesville, Pennsylvania, pastor, 1971-80; Emmanuel Baptist Church, Brooklyn, NY, pastor, 1980-89; Wheat St Baptist Church, pastor, 1989-. **Orgs:** Bd mem, Roosevelt, NY Bd Educ, 1987-89; chmn, PNBC Home Mission Bd, 1988-90; bd mem, Wheat St Fed Credit Union, 1989-; chmn, Wheat St Charitable Found, 1989-; trustee, Morehouse Sch Religion, 1991-; dir, Sweet Auburn Area Improvement Asn, 1992; mayor's religious adv bd, City of Atlanta, 1992-; convener & adv, Auburn Ave Merchants Asn; Concerned Black Clergy; panelist, Georgia Public Television's Town Hall meeting, Investigating President Clinton. **Honors/Awds:** MDiv, Eastern Baptist Theol Seminary, 1975; Most Outstanding Preacher, Eastern Baptist Sem, 1975; Man of the Year, Coatesville Club Nat Negro & Bus Prof, 1978; Man of the Year, Queens County Nat Negro Bus & Prof Women, 1987; Morehouse Col of Ministers Inductee, 1991; Key to the City, Kansas City, Mo, 1996; Outstanding Achievement in relig, Morehouse Col Atlanta Alumni Chap, 1997; Key to the City, Columbus, Ga, 1997; Key to the City of New Orleans, La, 2001; Ky Col, Gov Commonwealth of Ky, 2003; Key to the City, Mayor of Louisville, Ky, 2003; Many citations in mag like: Who's Who in Black Atlanta, Communicator Magazine, Upscale Magazine, Who's Who in Black America. **Special Achievements:** Publication: "The He, Thee, Me Program: A Stewardship Plan to Undergird a Third World Missilogical Ministry in the Context of the Black Church in the USA", 1984; "Living In Hell", 1996; African American Devotional Bible, 1997; "The Trash Man", 2003. **Home Addr:** 2195 Blvd Granada SW, Atlanta, GA 30311-3311, **Home Phone:** (404)753-0981. **Business Addr:** Pastor, Wheat St Baptist Church, Corner Auburn Ave, Atlanta, GA 30312, **Business Phone:** (404)659-4328.

## HARRIS, MICHAEL WESLEY

Historian, educator. **Personal:** Born Nov 9, 1945, Indianapolis, IN; son of Harold I and Edwina N Bohannon; married Carrol Grier. **Educ:** Ball State Univ, Muncie, IN, attended 1966; Andrews Univ, Berrien Springs, MI, BA, 1967; Bowling Green State Univ, Bowling Green, OH, MM, 1968; Harvard Univ, Cambridge, MA, PhD, 1982. **Career:** Oakwood Col, Huntsville, Ala, instr music & Ger, 1968-71; UnivTenn-Knoxville, Knoxville, Tenn, asst prof relig studies, 1982-87; Temple Univ, Philadelphia, Pa, vis asst prof relig studies, 1987-88; Wesleyan Univ, Middletown, Conn, assoc prof hist, 1988-91; Univ Iowa, assoc prof hist & african-am world studies, currently; Union Theol Sem City NY, prof church hist, currently. **Orgs:** Co-chair, prog comt, Nat Coun Black Studies, 1988-90; coun mem, Am Soc Ch Hist, 1990-93; Am Historical Asn, 1978-; Am Studies asn, 1987-. **Business Addr:** Professor, Union Theological Seminary City of New York, 3041 Broadway 121st St, New York, NY 10027, **Business Phone:** (212)622-7100.

## HARRIS, MICHELE ROLES

Executive. **Personal:** Born Jul 10, 1945, Berkeley, CA; daughter of Mahlon and Marguerite Barber; married Joseph. **Educ:** Univ San Francisco, BS, 1978. **Career:** Ted Bates Advert, asst acct exec, 1979-82; Essence Mag, acct exec, 1982-83; Johnson Publ Co, acct exec, 1983-84; Am Heritage Publ, eastern sales mgr, 1984-86; Gannett Co Inc, acct exec, 1986-. **Orgs:** EDGES Group Inc, co-chair commun comm, 1986-. **Home Addr:** 4 Cedar Lane, Croton on Hudson, NY 10520, **Home Phone:** (914)271-6846. **Business Addr:** Account Executive, Gannett Co Inc, 535 Madison Ave, New York, NY 10022.

## HARRIS, ONA C.

Executive director, media executive, association executive. **Personal:** Born Jun 7, 1943, Detroit, MI; children: Michael. **Educ:** Wayne Co Community Col, AA; Univ Detroit, BS, health care admin; Univ Detroit Mercy, MS, health care & health care admin. **Career:** Carnegie Inst Tech, med asst, 1962-63; Blvd Gen Hosp, Southwest Detroit Hosp, sp chem tech, 1965-77; Qual Clin Lab Inc, suprv sp chem tech, 1977-86; Univ Detroit, tech comput asst, 1986-89; Simon House Inc, vol, 1989-90, asst dir, 1990-92, exec dir, 1992-. **Orgs:** Bd pres, IDS Consortium; adv bd, Crains Nonprofit News; Mich Soc Asn Execs; bd mem, Mich Coalition Against Homelessness; Mich Prof Women's Network; Women's Econ Club; Nat Alliance End Homelessness; coun mem & vice minister, Secular Franciscan Order; bd mem, Wayne Co Neighborhood Leg Serv; bd mem, AIDS Nutrit Servs Alliance. **Honors/Awds:** The Family Award, Sec Franciscan Order, 1994; Crain's Honorary Mention, Crain's Best Managed Nonprofit, 1996; Black Tribute, Messiah Baptist Church, 1997; Drt Excellence, US Dept Housing & Urban Develop, 1997. **Home Addr:** 20527 Hubbell St, Detroit, MI 48235-1640, **Home Phone:** (313)862-3297. **Business Addr:** Executive Director, Simon House Inc, 17300 Burgess, Detroit, MI 48219, **Business Phone:** (313)531-3400.

## HARRIS, PAUL CLINTON, SR.

Lawyer. **Personal:** Born Mar 31, 1964, Charlottesville, VA; son of Pauline Jackson; married Monica Michelle Lamont; children: Paul Jr, Alexandra & Alanah Madison. **Educ:** Hampton Univ, BA, polit sci, 1986; George Washington Univ, JD, 1995. **Career:** VA House Deleg, state legislator, 58th dist rep, 1997-2001; Dept Justice, Civil Div, dep asst atty gen, 2001-02, dep assoc atty gen, 2002-03; Raytheon Co, Enterprise Compliance, sr coun & dir enterprise compliance, 2003-06; Shook, Hardy & Bacon LLP, partner, 2007-08; Ernst & Young, sr mgr, fraud invest & dispute serv, 2008-11; Northrop Grumman Corp, corp coun, 2011-; McGuire, Woods, Battle & Booth, atty; atty, deleg, currently. **Orgs:** Charlottesville-Albemarle C & Youth Comn; exec comn, Albemarle City Republican; legis action comn, Charlottesville-Albemarle C; Thomas Jefferson Inn Ct; Boys & Girls Club; hon mem, DARE; pres, Stud Body, Hampton Univ; cadet battalion com dr, Army ROTC Cadet Corps; Baptist church; Charlottesville-Albemarle & Greene County Chambers Com; Charlottesville-Albemarle Bar Assn; bd trustee, Inst Responsible Citizenship; Hampton Univ Bd Trustees; bd visitor, Mt Vernon; life mem, Alpha Phi Alpha Fraternity Inc. **Honors/Awds:** Outstanding Twenty-Year Alumnus, 2006; Distinguished 20-Year Alumnus Award, Hampton University, 2006; George C Marshall Leadership Award, VA Mil Inst Found. **Special Achievements:** The First African American Republican elected to the House of Delegates since Reconstruction in the 1997 legislative elections; Won Republican primary with 72 percent of the vote, June 10, 1997; Won general election with 63 percent of the vote, 1997; rep Virginia Republicans as a delegate to Republican Nat Conventions,

2000, 2004. **Home Addr:** 162 Larkspur Ct, Charlottesville, VA 22902, **Home Phone:** (804)293-7923. **Business Addr:** Corporate Counsel, Northrop Grumman Corp, 2980 Fairview Pk Dr, Falls Church, DC 22042, **Business Phone:** (703)280-2900.

### HARRIS, PEP (HERNANDO PETROCELLI HARRIS)
Baseball manager, baseball player. **Personal:** Born Sep 23, 1972, Lancaster, SC; children: 2. **Career:** Baseball player (retired), baseball coach; Calif Angels, 1996; Anaheim Angels, pitcher, 1997-98; Los Angels Dodgers, 2004.

### HARRIS, DR. PERCY G.
Physician, surgeon. **Personal:** Born Sep 4, 1927, Durant, MS; son of Norman Henry and Glendora; married Evelyn Lileah Furgerson; children: 12. **Educ:** Howard Univ, BS, 1953, MD, 1957. **Career:** Physician (retired); Health Dept, nurse, 1956-58; Beth Israel Hosp New York, nurse, 1958-60; Pvt Duty, RN, 1960-66; Sydenham Hosp NY, surg, 1977; Met Hosp NY Med Col, clin instr surg, 1979; Sydenham & Hosp NY, dir emergency room, 1980-99; SNFCC Harlem Hosp, surgeon, 1980; Brooklyn Hosp, staff. **Orgs:** Cedar Rapids/Marion Human Rels Coun, 1961-67; founder & pres, Cedar Rapids Negro Civic Orgn, 1961-67; pres, Cedar Rapids Chap, 1964-66; Mayor's Comt, Low Cost Housing, 1967; pres, Jane Boyd Community House, 1967-69; chmn, Mass Immunization Measles, 1968; United Way, Nominating Exec Comt, 1969-72; Oak hill-Jackson Econ Develop Corp, 1972-75; founder & pres, Cedar Rapids Community Cable, 1973-83; vpres, Non-Profit Housing Corp, 1973-; bd mem, Oak Hill Eng, 1973-75; Community Ment Health Ctr, Linn County, 1974-82; vpres, Cedar Rapids Cable Commun, 1976-83; med adv comt, Kirkwood Community Col, 1976-; Iowa Found Med Care, 1977-; Iowa Bd Regents, 1977-89; Iowa Football Coaches Asn, 1980; Mercy Hosp, Med Liaison Comt; St Luke's Hosp, Pub Rels Comt; Linn County Med Soc; Nat Asn Advan Colored People. **Honors/Awds:** Community Service Award, Nat Asn Advan Colored People, 1979; Community Building Award, B'nai B'rith, 1982; Serv High Sch Athletics Award, 1982; Recipient of Gold-Headed Cane, Mercy Med Laureate, 1998. **Special Achievements:** Author: "Prime Guidelines to Good Health: Periodic Checkup, " Cedar Rapids Gazette, Mar 14, 1979; "Room Rates Vary with Hospital Size, Cedar Rapids Under State Norm", Cedar Rapids Gazette, Jan 16, 1979; "Prescription Drug Price Methods Vary", Cedar Rapids Gazette, Nov 22, 1978; "Hospital Room Rate Breakdown in Cedar Rapids Bares Exceptional Deal," Cedar Rapids Gazette, Sept 27, 1978; numerous other articles; First African-American to hold an internship at St. Luke's Hospital; Iowa's first and only medical examiner, 1977. **Home Addr:** 3626 Bever Ave SE, Cedar Rapids, IA 52403-4331, **Home Phone:** (319)365-2473.

### HARRIS, PETER J.
Editor, publisher. **Personal:** Born Apr 26, 1955, Washington, DC. **Educ:** Howard Univ, BA, jour, 1977. **Career:** Publ, journalist, ed & broadcaster; Baltimore Afro-Am, staff reporter/ed, 1977-78, sports & cult, columnist, 1979-84; Pk Heights St Acad, founding dir & instr, 1978-80; AFRO-AM NEWSPAPERS, columnist, 1979-84; NEWS-J NEWSPAPER, Staff Reporter, 1980-81; Genetic Dancers Mag, ed/publ, 1984-91; Dispatcher, Int Longshoremen's & Warehousemen's Union, San Francisco, CA, asst ed, 1983-87; Genetic Dancers, founding publ/ed, 1984-91; Forgotten Lang, Statewide Anthology, Calif Poets Schs, co-ed, 1985; Neighborhood Reinvestment Corp, ed, 1987-91; Black Film Rev, Wash, DC, asst ed, 1989-91; Drumming Between Us, founding publ/ed, 1994-99; Inspiration House, founder & Artistic dir, 1991-; Bks: Wherever Dreams Live, auth, 1982; Hand Me My Griot Clothes, Black Classic Press, Baltimore, auth, 1993; Claremont Grad Sch, asst dir, 1994-96; Claremont Cols, asst & assoc dean, 1996-2001; HeArt Proj, prog dir, 2002-08; Safe Arms, auth, 2004; Johnson Chronicles, auth, 2005; Essays: "Tenderheaded: A Comb-Bending Collection Hair Stories"; "Black Men Speaking"; "Fathersongs"; "I Hear a Symphony: African Americans Celebrate Love"; "What It Means to be a Man". **Orgs:** Pub rels consult Coun, Independent Black Inst, 1983-. **Home Addr:** PO Box 41-1986, Los Angeles, CA 90041, **Home Phone:** (818)415-0420. **Business Addr:** Founder, Artistic Director, Inspiration House, 7102 Lockraven Rd, Temple Hills, MD 20748-5308.

### HARRIS, RAMON
Administrator. **Educ:** Pa State Univ, BS, bus admin & bus, 1971; Univ Pittsburgh, Joseph M Katz Grad Sch Bus, MBA, finance, 1972. **Career:** Xerox Corp, mgr, fin & adminr mgmt, 1978-80, region controller, mid-atlantic region, 1980-85, qual mgr, 1986-87, bus mgr, 1988-95; Educ Alternatives Inc, div pres, 1995-96; Exec Leadership Coun, bus mgr, Technol Transfer Proj, dir, 1997-, Inst Leadership Develop & Res, interim exec dir; Harris Solution Serv Inc, owner, prin, 2008-. **Orgs:** Bd mem, Exec Leadership Found; adv bd mem, Certifi Now LLC. **Business Addr:** Director of Technology Transfer Project, The Executive Leadership Council, 1010 Wis Ave NW Suite 520, Washington, DC 20007, **Business Phone:** (202)298-8235.

### HARRIS, RANDALL OWEN
Automotive executive. **Educ:** Western Mich Univ, BBA, acct, 1978; Univ NC, Chapel Hill; Kenan-Flagler Bus Sch, MBA, 1984. **Career:** Inns golf course, owner; Ultimate Pontiac Buick GMC Subaru, pres & owner, operator, currently. **Orgs:** Adv bd, Spotsylvania Regional Med Ctr. **Business Addr:** President, Owner, Ultimate Pontiac Buick GMC Subaru, 5150 Jefferson Davis Hwy, Fredericksburg, VA 22408, **Business Phone:** (540)898-6200.

### HARRIS, RAYMONT LESHAWN (QUIET STORM)
Executive, football player. **Personal:** Born Dec 23, 1970, Lorain, OH; married Leslie; children: Shakia, Olivia & Elijah. **Educ:** Ohio State Univ, BA, commun, 1994. **Career:** Football player (retired), consultant, executive director; Chicago Bears, full back, 1994, running back, 1995-97; Green Bay Packers, running back, 1998; Denver Broncos, running back, 2000; New Eng Patriots, running back, 2000; WBNS Radio, sports radio broadcaster, 2002-05; Chase Home Finance, mortgage consult, 2004-08; Ohio State Univ, Fisher Col Bus, asst dir develop, 2008-10, Dept Athletics, dir develop, 2010-. **Orgs:** Young Women Christian Asn; Buckeye Club Adv Bd. **Honors/Awds:** Most valuable player, Ohio State Buckeyes Football Season, 1993; Rookie of the year, 1994. **Home Addr:** , New Albany, OH. **Business Addr:** Assistant Director of Development, Director of Development, Fisher College of Business, 2100 Neil Ave, Columbus, OH 43210, **Business Phone:** (614)292-5187.

### HARRIS, REGGIE (REGINALD ALLEN HARRIS)
Baseball player. **Personal:** Born Aug 12, 1968, Waynesboro, VA. **Career:** Baseball player (retired); Oakland Athletics, pitcher, 1990-91; Boston Red Sox, pitcher, 1996; Philadelphia Phillies, pitcher, 1997; Houston Astros, pitcher, free agt, 1998 & 2004; Milwaukee Brewers, pitcher, 1999; Tampa Bay Devil Rays, 2000 & 2002; Atlanta Braves, 2000; Pittsburgh Pirates, 2001; Newark Bears, pitcher, 2004; Sussex County Miners, pitching coach, 2015.

### HARRIS, RHONDA EVA. See VANZANT, REV. DR. IYANLA.

### HARRIS, DR. ROBERT ALLEN
Conductor (music), college teacher, composer. **Personal:** Born Jan 9, 1938, Detroit, MI; son of Major L and Rusha Marshall; married Mary L Pickens; children: Shari Michelle. **Educ:** Wayne State Univ, BA, 1960, MA, 1962; Mich State Univ, PhD, 1971; Aspen Music Sch, post-doctoral, 1974. **Career:** Detroit Pub Schs, music teacher, 1960-64; Wayne State Univ, vis prof, asst prof, 1964-70; Mich State Univ, assoc prof, prof, dir, 1970-77; Univ Tex, Austin, vis prof; Univ S Africa, Pretoria, vis prof; Inchon City Chorale, guest conductor; Choral Festival Youth Chorale, guest conductor; Northwestern Univ, Sch Music, prof conducting & ensembles, 1977-, dir, currently. **Orgs:** Dir music, Trinity Church N Shore, 1978-; co chair, choral panel mem, Nat Endowment Arts; Am Choral dir Asn; Am Socs Composers & Publishers; Chorus Am; Pi Kappa Lambda Nat Hon Music Socs; Phi Mu Alpha Prof Music Fraternity. **Home Addr:** 4550 Grove St, Skokie, IL 60076-1855, **Home Phone:** (847)679-3270. **Business Addr:** Director, Professor of Conducting & Ensembles, Northwestern University, 711 Elgin Rd, Evanston, IL 60208-1200, **Business Phone:** (847)491-3141.

### HARRIS, ROBERT D.
Manager. **Personal:** Born Aug 31, 1941, Burnwell, WV; married Barbara. **Educ:** WVa State Col, BA, 1966; Univ Akron Sch Law, JD. **Career:** Firestone Tire & Rubber Co, indust rel trainee, 1966-67, Akron, indust rel rep plant, 1967-69, mgr labor rel, 1971-73; Firestone Foam Prod Co, mgr indust rel, 1969-71. **Orgs:** Employers & Assn; exec com Summit Co; comnr Civil Serv Comm Akron, 1977; Am OH & Akron Bar Assns; adv bd, YMCA; Nat Alliance Businessmen's Youth Motivation Task Force; W Side Neighbours; Alpha Phi Alpha frat; Akron Barristers Club; OH Bar, 1976. **Honors/Awds:** Black Exec Exch Prog Nat Urban League; Ebony Success Story. **Home Addr:** 797 Nome Ave, Akron, OH 44320.

### HARRIS, ROBERT EUGENE PEYTON
Financial manager. **Personal:** Born Sep 5, 1940, Washington, DC; son of John F and Jane E (deceased); married Yvonne Ramey; children: Lisa & Johanna. **Educ:** Morehouse Col, BA, 1963; Long Island Univ, MBA, 1981. **Career:** Equitable Life Assurance Soc, exp exam; Bronx Community Col Asn Inc, opers mgr. **Orgs:** Vpres, Battle Hill Civic Asn, 1977; 100 Black Men, 1976; Coun Concerned Black Exec New York, 1980; worshipful master Bright Hope Masonic Lodge, 1981; Illustrious Potentiat Elejmal Temple Shrine, 1987; Asn MBA Execs. **Home Addr:** 20 Jefferson Ave, White Plains, NY 10606, **Home Phone:** (914)684-2545.

### HARRIS, ROBERT F.
Teacher, government official. **Personal:** Born May 15, 1941, Knight Station, FL; son of James and Gertrude; children: Roger & Lisa. **Educ:** Fla A&M Univ, BS, 1964. **Career:** Pub Instr Polk Co, teacher & coach, 1966-72; U.S. Sen Lawton Chiles, asst, 1973-88; Bd Comt Govt Affairs, dep dir, 1988; U.S. Sen John Glenn, asst, 1989-94; Subcomt Govt Opers, US Senate, chief clerk, dep staff dir; US Postal Serv, vpres diversity develop, 1994. **Orgs:** Chmn & bd dir, Neighborhood Serv Ctr Inc, Lakeland; Cath Soc Serv Cent Fla; Coun Concerned Citizens Lakeland; Pi Gamma Mu. **Honors/Awds:** All Conf Track & Field; Cleve Abott Award for Track, 1963; various track record awards; inductee, Polk Co Schs Hall of Fame, 1997. **Home Addr:** 3707 Stonesboro, Oxon Hill, MD 20745.

### HARRIS, ROBERT L., JR.
Educator, school administrator. **Personal:** Born Apr 23, 1943, Chicago, IL; son of Robert L and Ruby L Watkins; married Anita B Campbell; children: Lisa Marie, Leslie Susanne & Lauren Yvonne. **Educ:** Roosevelt Univ, Chicago, IL, BA, 1966, MA, 1968; Northwestern Univ, Evanston, IL, PhD, 1974. **Career:** St Rita Elem Sch, Chicago, Ill, 6th grade teacher, 1965-68; Miles Col, Birmingham, AL, instr, 1968-69; Univ Ill, Urbana, Ill, asst prof, 1972-75; Cornell Univ, Ithaca, NY, asst to assoc prof, 1975, dir africana studies & res ctr, 1986-91, assoc prof, currently, vice provost, 2000-08; Asn for the Study African Am Life & Hist, pres, 1991-93. **Orgs:** Ed bd, Jour Negro Hist, 1978-96; mem & bd dir, New York Coun Humanitites, 1983-87; chair & memship comt, Am Hist Asn, 1989-94; ed bd, Western Jour Black Studies, 1990-; pres, Asn study Afro-Am Life & Hist, 1991-92; chair & prog comn, Am Hist Asn, 1995; Nat Adv Bd, Soc Hist Educ, 1996-; Nat Historian, Alpha Phi Alpha Fraternity Inc. **Home Addr:** 102 Burleigh Dr, Ithaca, NY 14850-1710, **Home Phone:** (607)257-4478. **Business Addr:** Associate Professor, Africana Studies & Research Center, Cornell University, 449 Day Hall, Ithaca, NY 14853, **Business Phone:** (607)255-5358.

### HARRIS, ROBERT LEE
Football player. **Personal:** Born Jun 13, 1969, Riviera Beach, FL; married Johnetta. **Educ:** Southern Univ, grad. **Career:** Football player (retired); Minn Vikings, 1992-93, defensive tackle, 1994; New York Giants, right defensive tackle, 1995, left defensive tackle, 1996-99. **Honors/Awds:** Rookie of the Year, 1992. **Home Addr:** , MN.

### HARRIS, ROBERT LEWIS
Executive, vice president (organization). **Personal:** Born Mar 4, 1944, Arkadelphia, AR; son of Benjamin and Lucy; married Glenda Newell; children: Anthony, Regina, Brittany & Phillip. **Educ:** Merritt Col, AA, 1963; San Francisco State Univ, BA, 1965; Univ Calif Sch Law Berkeley, JD, 1972; Harvard Grad Sch Bus, AMP, 1988. **Career:** Vice president (retired); Alameda County Probation Off, dep probation officer, 1965-69; Pac Gas & Elec Co, atty, 1972, cent div mgr, 1989-93, vpres community rels, 1994-98, vpres environ health safety tech & land serv. **Orgs:** Pres, Western Region, Kappa Alpha Psi, 1975-79; founder, Calif Asn Black Lawyers, 1977; pres, Nat Bar Asn, 1979-80; admin mem, Blue Shield Calif, 1979-92; Calif State Bar, 1980-81; lawyer fel, adv comn, RH Smith Comn, Howard Univ Sch Law, 1981-83; pres, Wiley Manuel Law Found, 1982-88; secy, Nat Bar Inst, 1982-87; chmn, Legal Comn Oakland Br, Nat Asn Advan Colored People, 1983-87; grand pole march, Kappa Alpha Psi, 1991-95; bd, Port Oakland, 1996-2000; bd mem, co-chair, San Francisco Lawyers Community, 1998-; chmn, Pub Law Sect; chmn, pres, Charles Houston Bar Asn; Calif Minority Coun Prog. **Home Addr:** 4082 Sequoyah Rd, Oakland, CA 94605, **Home Phone:** (510)638-1331.

### HARRIS, ROOSEVELT, JR.
Government official. **Educ:** Valdosta State Univ, MPA. **Career:** City Brunswick, Ga, exec dir community develop, city mgr, currently. **Orgs:** Int City & Co Mgt Asn; Nat Asn Housing; Redevelop Off; Community Develops Asn; Nat Asn Pub Adminrs; Lambda Beta Sigma Chap; Phi Beta Sigma Fraternity Inc; Coastal Ga Pan-Hellenic Coun; Preserv Technicians Group Inc; Fourteen Black Men Glynn Inc; Brunswick Area Transp Study; Connecting Link Links Inc; Black Panther Party. **Home Addr:** 3504 Darien Hwy, Brunswick, GA 31525-2401, **Home Phone:** (912)267-0552. **Business Addr:** City Manager, City Brunswick, 601 Gloucester St, Brunswick, GA 31520, **Business Phone:** (912)267-5501.

### HARRIS, DR. RUTH COLES
School administrator. **Personal:** Born Sep 26, 1928, Charlottesville, VA; daughter of Bernard A and Ruth Wyatt; married John Benjamin; children: John Benjamin Jr & Vita Michelle. **Educ:** Va State Univ, BS, bus, 1948; NY Univ Grad Sch Bus Admin, MBA, 1949; Col William & Mary, EdD, 1977; Va Union Univ, LHD, 1998. **Career:** Va Union Univ, instr, 1949-64, head com dept, 1956-59, assoc prof com dept, 1964-69, prof, dir div com, 1969-73, Distinguished prof emer, currently; Sydney Lewis Sch Bus Admin, dir, 1973-81; Sydney Lewis Sch Bus Admin, dir, mem mgt team, 1985-87, acct dept chair, 1988-97; Va Union Univ, prof, adminr. **Orgs:** Equal Oppurtunity Comm AACSB, 1975-76; bd dir, Am Assembly Colegiate Schs bus, 1976-79; adv bd, InterColegiate Case Clearing House, 1976-79; St Adv Coun Community Serv Continuing Ed Prog, 1977-80; bd dir, Richmond Urban League, 1979-84; agency eval comm United Way Greater Richmond, 1980-85; Southern Asn Cols & Schs; bd dir, Va Soc Cert Pub Accountants; bd dir, Am Assembly Col Schs Bus; app, 1983-85 by gov Robb Inter departmental Comm Rate Setting Cs Facil; bd, Richmond Va Chap Nat Coaltion 100 Black Women; chairperson, Minority Doctoral FelsComt, Am Inst Cert Pub Accts, 1990-92; bd dir, Va Soc CPA's, 1995-98. **Honors/Awds:** Virginia Power, Strong Men a Delver Womans Club Award for Achievement in Business, 1963; Faculty Fellowship Award United Negro Col Fund, 1976-77; Serwa Award, Virginia Commonwealth Chapter, Nat Coalition of 100 BlackWomen, 1989; Teacher of the Year Award, Va Union University, Sears Roebuck Found, 1990; Outstanding Accounting Educator Award, Virginia Society of CPAs & American Institute of CPAs, 1991; Tenneco Excellence in Teaching Award; Fox TV Networks Black Achievers Award; Virginia State Council of Higher Educations Outstanding Faculty Award; Va Heroes, participant, 1991-94 &1996-97; Outstanding Faculty Award, Va State Coun Higher Educ, 1992; American Institute of Certified Public Accountants; Nissan, HBCU Fellow, 1992; Bell Ringer Richmond, NAUW, 1992; Ebone Images Award, Northern VA Chapter, Nat Coalition of 100 Black Women, 1993; Distinguished Career in Accounting Award, 1997; hon DHL, 1998; Tenneco Excellence in Teaching and Women Honoree, 1998; Business Leadership Award, VABPW Found. **Special Achievements:** First black woman to pass CPA exam in VA, 1962; first female as well as the first black to receive Outstanding Accounting Educator in Virginia; first 100 black CPAs in the nation; first black woman in Virginia to earn a state license as a certified public accountant, 1962. **Home Addr:** 2816 Edgewood Ave, Richmond, VA 23222-3518, **Home Phone:** (804)321-3875. **Business Addr:** Professor Emeritus, Virginia Union University, 1500 N Lombardy St, Richmond, VA 23220, **Business Phone:** (804)257-5600.

### HARRIS, DR. SARAH ELIZABETH
Manager, consultant, executive director. **Personal:** Born Dec 31, 1937, Newnan, GA; daughter of Dan W Gates (deceased) and Sarah L Gates; married Kenneth Eugene; children: Kim Y. **Educ:** Miami Univ, BS, educ, 1959, MEd, 1967, PhD, 1973; Wilberforce Univ, DHL. **Career:** Career Opportunity Prog, univ coor dr, 1970-73; FL Sch Desegregation Expert, consult, 1971-77; Gen Elec Co, mgr sup serv, 1973-75; Urban Rural Joint Task Force, ESAA Proj, proj dir, 1975-76; Sinclair Col, consult, 1976; Inst Educ Leadership George Washington Univ, educ policy fel, 1977-78; Cleveland Sch Desegregation Exp, consult, 1977; Citizens Coun OH Schs, staff assoc, 1978-79; Dayton Power & Light Co, dir community rel, 1985; Dayton & Montgomery County Pub Educ Fund, sr consult, 1986; Montgomery County, treas, 1987-91, comnr, 1991-93; Dayton Urban League Inc, pres, 1991-93; cert sem leader & independent consult; Nat Conf Christians & Jews, exec dir, 1994-99. **Orgs:** Bd dir, bd trustees, YSI Inc; pres, Dayton Found; co-chmn, Dayton Dialogue Race Rel (DDRR); Challenge 95 Network; Criminal Justice Comt; Dayton Women's Network; Self-Sufficiency Task Force; bd trustees, Wright State Univ; bd trustees, Sisters Mercy Health Corp; bd trustees, Parity, 2000; Delta Sigma Theta Inc; Corinthian Baptist Church; Univ Dayton; Franciscan Health Syst Ohio Valley Inc. **Honors/Awds:** C Service Award; Jack & Jill Am Dayton, 1975; Outstanding Woman of the Year, Iota Phi Lamba Dayton, 1978; Salute Career Women, YWCA, 1982; Outstanding Grad Award Dayton Pub Schs, 1983; Top Ten Women, 1983; Induction OH Women's Hall of Fame, 1984; Martin Luther King Nat Holiday Celebration Meritorious Award Community Soc Servs; Bishop Alumni Medal, Miami Univ; Outstanding Community Leader Award, Great Lakes Midwest Reg Blacks Govt, 1986; Dayton Champion Award, Nat

Multiple Sclerosis Society, 1987; Mark Excellence Award, Nat Forum Black Pub Add, 1991. Ohio Women's Hall of Fame. **Business Addr:** Board of Director, YSI Inc, 1700/1725 Brannum Lane, Yellow Springs, OH 45387, **Business Phone:** (937)688-4255.

### HARRIS, SEAN EUGENE
Football player. **Personal:** Born Feb 25, 1972, Tucson, AZ. **Educ:** Univ Ariz, grad. **Career:** Football player (retired); Chicago Bears, 1995-96, linebacker, 1997, 2000, right linebacker, 1998, middle linebacker, 1999; Indianapolis Colts, 2001.

### HARRIS, SHAWNTAE
Rap musician, singer, actor. **Personal:** Born Apr 14, 1974, Chicago, IL. **Educ:** Acad Scholastic Achievement, attended 1992. **Career:** Throwin's Tantrums Rec Label, founder, 2000; Albums: Funkda fied, 1994; Anuthat antrum, 1996; Unrestricted, 2000; Limelite Luv & Niteclubz, 2003; TBC; TV guest appearances: "The Parent Hood", 1997, 1998; "VIP", 2000; TV movie: "Carmen: A Hip Hopera", MTV, 2001; TV series: "Sabrina, the Teenage Witch", 2002; "The Surreal Life", 2005; "Video on Trial", 2005; "Katt Williams: 9 Lives", 2009; Movie compositions: Bad Boys, 1995; Hard Ball, 2001; Like Mike, 2002; Precious, 2009; Films: Kazaam, 1996; Carmen: A Hip Hopera, 2001; Glitter, 2001; Civil Brand, 2002; 30 Days, 2006; Songs: "Funkda fied", 1994; "Fa AllY'all", 1994; "Give It To Ya", 1995; "Sittin' On Top of the World", 1996; "Ghetto Love", 1997; "That's What I'm Looking For", 2000; "Whatch u Like", 2000; "In Love Wit Chu", 2003. **Honors/Awds:** Top Hot Rap Artist, 1994; Top Hot Rap Single, 1994; Best Rap Album, 1995; Top Hot Female Rap Artist, 1995; Best Rap Performance by a Duo or Group, nominated, 1998; Best Female Rap Solo Performance, nominated, 2004. **Business Addr:** Rapper, So So Def Recordings, 685 Lambert Dr NE, Atlanta, GA 30324, **Business Phone:** (404)888-9900.

### HARRIS, SIDNEY DERRICK. See HARRIS, DERRICK.

### HARRIS, SIDNEY E.
Educator. **Personal:** Born Jul 21, 1949, Atlanta, GA; son of Nathaniel and Marion Johnson; married Mary Styles; children: Savaria B. **Educ:** Morehouse Col, BA, 1971; Cornel Univ, Ithaca, NY, MS, opers res, 1975, PhD, opers res, 1976. **Career:** AT&T Bell Tel Labs, Opers Res Ctr, tech staff mem, 1973-78; Ga State Univ, J MackRobinson Col Bus, Atlanta, Ga, assoc prof, 1978-87, dean, 1997-2004, prof comput info systs, dean emer; Claremont Grad Univ, Peter F Drucker Grad Mgt Ctr, Claremont, Calif, prof mgt, 1987-90, chair mgt prog, 1990-91, dean, 1991-96; Inst US-Japan Rels, co founder; Property Secured Investment, Los Angeles, corp dir, 1994-95; GM/Hughes Electronics, consult; Coca-Cola Co, consult; Xerox Corp, consult; IBM, consult; Hewlett Packard, consult; BellSouth Serv, consult; AT&T, consult; Equifax Serv, consult; Lanier Worldwide, consult; AirGate PCS, consult; AMRESCO, consult; AACSB Int, consult; S Bus Admin Asn, consult. **Orgs:** Nat Sci Soc, 1976-; vice chmn, Los Angeles Co Productivity Comn, 1988-91; corp dir, Family Saving Bank, Los Angeles, CA, 1988-; assoc ed, MIS Quart, 1989-92; ed adv bd, Bus Forum, 1989-; bd govs, Peter F Drucker Non-Profit Found, NY, 1991-; Beta Gamma Sigma, Nat Hon Soc Bus Sch, 1994-02; corp dir, Serv Master Co, Chicago, IL, 1995-; bd dir, Trans Am Investors, Los Angeles, CA, 1995-; bd trustee, Menlo Col, 1995-; corp dir, Total Serv Syst Inc, 1999-; corp dir, Air Gate PCS, 2000-02; Soc Int Bus Fel, 2002-; Sigma Xi; bd dir, Ridgeworth Funds; chmn, Technol Comt, TSYS, bd mem, Exec Comt. **Home Addr:** 4800 Paran Oak Ct, Atlanta, GA 30327. **Business Addr:** Professor of Computer Information Systems, Georgia State University, Dept Computer Information Systems, Atlanta, GA 30302, **Business Phone:** (404)413-7017.

### HARRIS, STANLEY EUGENE
Banker. **Personal:** Born May 19, 1953, Columbus, OH; son of Harvey J Sr (deceased) and Julia Ann V; married Gene C Thomas; children: Wade T. **Educ:** Univ Notre Dame, BBA, 1975; Univ Del, Stonier Grad Sch Banking, ABA, 1996; Ohio Univ Del, MBA, mgt & finance, 2004. **Career:** Ohio Nat Bank, banking mgt trainee, 1980-81, supvr credit res, 1981-82, credit banking rep, 1982-84, asst vpres & mgr credit res, 1985-87, mgr community develop, 1988-90; BancOhio Corp, vpres, 1986-95; Nat City Corp, community reinvestment officer, 1991-92; Nat City Bank, Columbus, mgr, vpres-retail admin, 1994-97, vpres-pub funds, 1997-2009; PNC Financial Serv Group, vpres relationship mgr pub finance, 2009-; Mt Olivet Baptist Church, chmn bd trustees, 2011-. **Orgs:** Comnr, Ohio Develop Finance Adv Bd, 1986-94; treas, Columbus Area Community Ment Health Ctr, 1988-91; chair, Columbus Found-Community Arts Fund, 1989-97; Columbus Urban League, treas, 1986-91, first vice chair, 1992-94, chair, 1994-95; trustee, Buckeye Boys Ranch, 1990-94; trustee, I Know I Can Inc, 1990-2002; chair, trustee bd, Mt Olivet Baptist Church, 1993-02; vice chair, Ohio Black Legis Caucus Corp Roundtable, 1999-; comnr, Columbus Metro Housing Auth, 2000-; trustee, Proj Linden Inc, 2000-02; Proj Grad Inc Colo; Urban Financial Serv Coalition, Columbus chap, 2000-; Eastern Union Bible Col, instr develop church trustee, 2011-. **Honors/Awds:** Golden Rule Award, J C Penney Co, 1984; Columbus Jaycees, 10 Outstanding Young Citizens, 1986. **Home Addr:** 1466 Wakefield Ct E, Columbus, OH 43209, **Home Phone:** (614)231-0337. **Business Addr:** Vice President, Relationship Manager Public Finance, PNC Financial Services Group Inc, 1530 W 1st Ave, Columbus, OH 43212, **Business Phone:** (614)297-5420.

### HARRIS, STEVE
Actor. **Personal:** Born Dec 3, 1965, Chicago, IL; son of John and Mattie. **Educ:** Northern Ill Univ, BA, drama; Univ Del, MFA, theater. **Career:** Films: Don't Miss With My Sister, 1985; Seven Hours to Judgment, 1988; Sugar Hill, 1994; The Rock, 1996; Lesse Prophets, 1997; Lovers & Liars, 1998; The Mod Squad, 1999; King of the World, 2000; The Skulls, 2000; Minority Report, 2002; Beyond the City Limits, 2001; Bringing Down the House, 2003; Death & Texas, 2004; Diary of a Mad Black Woman, 2005; The Unseen, 2005; Ball Don't Lie, 2008; Quarantine, 2008; 12 Rounds, 2009; Takers, 2010. TV series: Against the Wall, 1994; "Law & Order", 1994-95; "Homicide", 1994; New York Undercover, 1994-95; "Heaven & Hell: North & South, Book III", 1994; "Ally McBeal", 1997; George Wallace, 1997; "The Practice", 1997-2004; Nightmare Street, 1998; "The Mod Squad", 1999; "The Skulls", 2000; "King of the World", 2000; "Minority Report", 2002; "The Batman", 2004-06; "The Unseen", 2005; "Heist", 2006; "Grey's Anatomy", 2006; "Protect & Serve", 2007; Eli Stone, 2008; "Good Behavior", 2008. **Honors/Awds:** Q Award, Viewers Qual TV, 1998 & 1999; Image Award, 2004. **Business Addr:** Actor, Williams Morris Agency, 1 William Morris Pl, Beverly Hills, CA 90212, **Business Phone:** (310)859-4000.

### HARRIS, STEVE
Vice president (organization), executive. **Personal:** Born OH. **Educ:** Hampton Univ, attended 1974; Cleveland State Univ, attended 1975. **Career:** KRLY, prog dir, 1981-85; WCIN-AM, prog dir; ABC Radio Network, vpres urban programming, 1993-2000; XM Satellite Radio, vpres external programming, 2000-02, vpres music programming, 2003-05; ABC Radio Networks, vpres, multicultural programming, 2005-06; Mainstream/Hip Hop Sta, prog dir; WIZF-FM, prog dir; Urban A/C Sta, prog dir; WMOJ-FM, prog dir; Reach Media, vpres opers, 2006-08; Radio One, opers mgr; ESPN Radio, sr dir audio content, 2008-10; Radio One, pgm dir, 2010-13; radio broadcasting, currently. **Business Addr:** Broadcast Profeesional, Radio Broadcasting, Cincinnati, OH.

### HARRIS, DR. TEREA DONNELLE
Physician. **Personal:** Born Aug 5, 1956, St. Louis, MO; daughter of Samuel Elliott and Dixie Kay Gardner. **Educ:** Fisk Univ, BA, 1978; Meharry Med Col, MD, 1982. **Career:** Henry Ford Hosp, intern, 1983-84, resident internal med, resident infectious disease, 1984-86, fel, 1993-95; Health Alliance Plan, staff physician, 1986-88; Outer Dr Hosp, Lincoln Pk, Mich, internist, 1988-91; Mich Health Care Ctr, urgent care physician, 1991-92; Bi-County Hosp, internist, house physician, 1992-93; Henry Ford Hosp, fel, Div Infectious Dis, 1993-95; Henry Ford Health Syst, Detroit Northwest, staff physician, 1995-. **Orgs:** Nat Med Asn; Links; life ber, Fisk Alumni Asn; Meharry Alumni Asn; Infectious Dis Soc Am; Am Soc Microbiol. **Honors/Awds:** Outstanding Young Women of America, Alpha Kappa Alpha Sor Inc. **Home Addr:** 17181 Alta Vista Dr, Southfield, MI 48075, **Home Phone:** (248)483-4103. **Business Addr:** Physician, Henry Ford Health System, 1 New Ctr 3031 W Grand Blvd Suite, Detroit, MI 48202, **Business Phone:** (800)436-7936.

### HARRIS, THOMAS C. See Obituaries Section.

### HARRIS, THOMAS WALTER
Librarian, playwright. **Personal:** Born Apr 30, 1930, Bronx, NY; son of Melvin and Mary; married Joyce Carter. **Educ:** Howard Univ, BA, 1957; Univ Calif, MA, Los angles, 1959; Univ Southern Calif, MLS, 1962. **Career:** Appeal Printing Co, staff, 1948-49; Voice Am, writer, 1953-55; Bur Internal Rev, Wash DC, staff, 1956-57; Los Angeles Pub Libr, Los Angeles, Calif, librn lit & fiction dept, 1961; Studio W Channel 22, writer & dir; Inner City Cult Ctr, teacher, 1968; Actors Studio, writer, 1967-74; Pasadena Playhouse, playwright; Los Angeles Citizens Co, producer & dir; Univ Calif, Los Angeles, teacher playwriting, 1966, playwright & writer, currently; Plays: Pray for Daniel Adams; A Number One Family; Daddy Hugs & Kisses, 1960; The Relic, 1961; The Selma Maid, 1967; Always with Love, 1970; The Solution, 1970; Mary Queen of Crackers, 1971; Suds, 1973; No Time to Play, 1977; A Streetcar Salad, 1979; Other: Fall of an Iron Horse; All Tigers Are Tame; City Beneath the Skin; Who Killed Sweetie; Beverly Hills Olympics; At Wits End; The Man Handlers; Clothespins & Dreams; Books: The Fall of Archy House, Barnstormer, Flight into the Unknown, 1957; Get Out of My Body, You'll Like It on Mars, Goodbye, Dead Man, 1958; Baby, 1959. **Orgs:** Dramatists Guild; Nat Playwrights Co; Black Theatre Network; Nat Asn Advan Colored People; Am Asn Retired People; Am Fedn State, Co & Munic Employees; Los Angeles Black Playwrights; Alliance Los Angeles Playwright. **Honors/Awds:** Outstanding Contribution to Theatre in Loa Angeles, Citation Los Angeles City Coun, 1967; All CIAA, All Tournament, Howard Univ, 1956. **Special Achievements:** Musical: "Suds as Clothespins & Dreams", Pasadena Civic, 1990; Black Writers, Gale, Detroit, MI, 1989; Contemp Authors, Vol 141, Gale, 1994; writer of several television plays and stage performances; Radio Appearances, Stage Plays. **Home Addr:** 1786 S Fairfax Ave, Los Angeles, CA 90019. **Business Addr:** Playwright, 630 W 5th St, Los Angeles, CA 90071.

### HARRIS, TRICIA R.
Executive. **Personal:** Born Feb 16, 1977, Wiesbaden; daughter of Virginia. **Educ:** DePaul Univ; Oglethorpe Univ; Am Inst Managing Diversity. **Career:** Estate Martin Luther King, Jr Inc, licensing adminr, 1995, licensing operations mgr, 1995-96, dir, licensing & opers; Intellectual Properties Mgt, mgr, 1995-96, dir, 1996-99; King Ctr, dir opers, 1998-99; Intel Online Serv, prog consult, tokyo data ctr rollout, 1999-2000; Tokyo Data Ctr, Rollout, prog consult, 1999-2000; Martin Luther King Jr., Ctr Nonviolent Social Change Inc, managing dir, 2004-04, chief operating officer, chief staff; Political Campaign Mgt, consult, 2004-06; Global Sourcing Off, dir, 2005-07, human resource mgr, 2008-09; Ambassador Andrew J Young, exec aide; Equifax; Dr Bernice A King, exec advisor & writer, 2009; Isaiah Wash, exec advisor, consult & social media strategist, 2011. **Orgs:** Consult, Corp Social Responsibililty & Diversity Mgt, 2004-; dir, Martin L King Mem Found. **Business Addr:** Executive Advisor & Writer, Dr. Bernice A. King.

### HARRIS, DR. TRUDIER
Educator, scholar. **Personal:** Born Feb 27, 1948, Mantua, AL; daughter of Terrell Sr (deceased) and Unareed Burton Moore. **Educ:** Stillman Col, Tuscaloosa, AL, BA, 1969; Ohio State Univ, Columbus, OH, MA, eng, 1972, PhD, Am lit & folklore, 1973. **Career:** Ohio State Univ, Columbus OH, teaching assoc, 1970-73, vis distinguished prof, 1988; Col William & Mary, Williamsburg, VA, asst prof, 1973-79; Univ NC, Chapel Hill, NC, assoc prof, 1979-85, prof, 1985-88, J Carlyle Sitterson, prof Eng, 1988-2009, distinguished prof Eng, 1997-2009, assoc chair, 2005-07, prof emer, 2009-; Univ Ark, Little Rock, AR, William Grant Cooper vis distinguished prof, 1987; Emory Univ, Augustus Baldwin Longstreet, prof Am lit, 1993-96; Univ Ala, Dept Eng, vis prof, 2010-11, prof Eng, 2012-. Author: From Mammies To Militants: Domesticsin Black Am Lit, 1982; Exorcising Blackness: Hist & Lit Lynching & Burning Rituals, 1984; Black Women In The Fiction ofJames Baldwin, 1985; Fiction & Folklore: The Novels of Toni Morrison, 1991; The Power of the Porch: The Storytellers Craft in Zora Neale Hurston, Gloria Naylor & Randall Kenan, 1996; Saints, Sinners, Saviors: Strong Black Women in African Am Lit, 2001; S of Tradition: Essays on African Am Lit, 2002; Summer Snow: Reflections from a Black Daughter of the S, 2003; The Scary Mason-Dixon Line: African American Writers and the South, 2009; Martin Luther King Jr., Heroism and African American Literature, 2014. ed: Afro-Am Writers After, 1955; Afro-Am Poets After, 1955 &1985; Selected Works of Ida B Well Afro-Am Fiction Writers After 1955 in the Dict of Lit Biog Ser, 1984; Dramatists & Prose Writers, 1985; Afro-Am Writers Before The Harlem Renaissance, 1986; Afro-Am Writers From The Harlem Renaissance To 1940, 1987; Afro-Am Writers From 1940 To 1955, 1988; The Oxford Companion to Womens Writing in the Us, 1994; New Essays on Baldwins Go Tell It On the Mountain, 1996 The Oxford Companion to African Am Lit, 1997; Call & Response: The Riverside Anthology of the African Am Lit Tradition, 1998; The Lit of the Am S: A Norton Anthology, 1998; The Concise Oxford Companion to African American Literature, 2001; Reading Contemporary African American Drama: Fragments of History, Fragments of Self, 2007. **Orgs:** Mod Lang Asn Am, 1973-2002; Am Folklore Soc, 1973-; Col Language Asn, 1974-; Langston Hughes Soc, 1982-; Zeta Phi Beta Sorority Inc; fel Nat Res Coun & Ford Found, 1982-83; Rockefeller Fel, Bellagio, Italy, 1994; fel Nat Humanities Ctr, 1996-; Col Lang Asn; Asn African; African Am Folklorists; vpres, S Atlantic Mod Lang Asn, 2009-10; Richard Wright Circle; Toni Morrison Soc; Zora Neale Hurston Soc; Alice Childress Soc; St. George Tucker Soc; founder & pres, George Moses Horton Soc Study African Am Poetry, 1996-2009. **Special Achievements:** Harris is one of the nations top scholars in African-American and Southern literature and cultural theory. **Home Addr:** 2109 Tadley Dr, Chapel Hill, NC 27514, **Home Phone:** (919)933-5677. **Business Addr:** Professor, University of Alabama, Department of English, Tuscaloosa, AL 35487-0244, **Business Phone:** (205)348-5065.

### HARRIS, VERA DIAL
Educator, government official, teacher. **Personal:** Born Nov 10, 1912, Palestine, TX; daughter of Caesar Albert and Estalla Pryor (deceased); married James A. **Educ:** Prairie View A&M Col, BS, home econs, 1935; Tex So Univ, MS, 1950. **Career:** Government official (retired); S Newspaper Feat, Dallas, home econ lectr, 1935-37; Tex Agr Extens, county negro home demonstration agt, Austin County, 1937-41, Harris County, 1941-73. **Orgs:** Secy, Order E Stars, 1945-46; Prairie View Alumni Asn, 1945-47, secy, 1968-72, chmn, const & bylaws, 1969-70, chmn budget comt, Gamma Sigma Chap; pres, 1945-47, secy, 1972-77; Cambridge Village Civic Club; NRTA & AARP; pres, Gardenia Garden Club; Optim 13 Soc Club, 1970-72; life mem, Young Women's Christian Asn, 1973; chmn, Health Comn, Houston Harris Co, Ret Teachers Asn, 1974; hist, Home Econ Homemaking, 1974; Am Home Econ Asn; Prairie View Alumni Club; Sigma Gamma Rho Sorority; Epsilon Sigma Phi Frat; Tex Home Econ Asn; Home Econ Homemaking; Am Home Econ Asn; Houston Harris Co Ret Teachers Asn; Clint Pk Unit Methodist Church; Nat Asn Extn Home Econs & Nat Asn Ret Fed Employ Sec; Houston Negro C C; pres, Tex Negro Home Dem Agts Asn; Pine Crest Home Demo Club; pres, Houston Harris Co Ret Teachers; life mem, Gulfgate Chap No 941, Young Women's Christian Asn, 1973-; Grand Order Ct Calauthe; vpres, Nat Asn Retd Fed Employees; 4-H youth. **Honors/Awds:** Certificate of Recognition, Tex Negro Home Demo Agts Asn, 1947; Certificate of Award, Nat Asn Fash & Access Design, 1957; Distinguished Service Award, Tex Negro Home Demo Agts Asn, 1962; Sigma of the Year Merit Award, 1973; "Palm Branch & Laurel Wreaths" Pal Negro Bus & Prof Wom Club, 1976; 100 Plus Club, Prairie View Develop Fund, 1976-78; Cooperative Extension Program, Prairie Vew A&M Univ, 1986; Houston Harris County Retired Teachers Asn, 1988; Gardenia Garden Club, Plaque, 40 year member, 1994; Certificate of Merit, Asn Retired Black County Agents, 1991; Framed Memories, Family & Friends, 1992; Sigma Gamma Rho, Dedicated Service, 1995; Prairie View A&M Univ, Coop Extension Prog, Certificate of Appreciation, 1997; Houston Harris County Retired Teacher's Awd, 2000; Presented the Hilltopper Award, Prairie View A&M Univ Alumni, 1994. **Special Achievements:** Woman of the Week, The Informer 1954. **Home Addr:** 5110 Trail Lake Dr, Houston, TX 77045-4035, **Home Phone:** (713)433-6870.

### HARRIS, VERNON JOSEPH, JR.
Manager. **Personal:** Born May 18, 1926, Washington, DC; son of Vernon J Sr (deceased) and Beatrice Virginia Robinson; married Georgetta Mae Ross; children: Elliott F, Cassandra Lockwood, Georgette E H Lee, Wayne J, Verna J H Agen & Dolores A (deceased). **Educ:** Cath Univ Am, BE, elec, 1952. **Career:** Manager (retired); Gen Elec AESD, Testing Prog Rotating Assignments, staff, mgr, sr engr, cons, proj engr, design engr, jr engr, 1952-88; GE Aerospace Electronics Systs, mgr, 1988; pvt pilot, 1990; Navy personnel, lect; Frontiers Int, officer; K2UII, radio operator; W3RSE, radio operator. **Orgs:** Pres, lt gov NY dist Kiwanis & Kiwanis Club N Utica, 1962-95; Col Coun SUNY, Col technol Utica, 1968-84; comdr & financial officer, Provost Post Am Legion; past comdr Provost Post Am Legion, 1974-76; treas, Cent NY Chap Amer Heart asn, 1975-80; treas, NY State Affil Am Heart Asn, 1978-80; bd mem & treas, Cornell Coop Exten Oneida County, 1991-97; pres, A Good Old Summer Time, Inc, Utica, NY, 1995-97. **Honors/Awds:** Elfun Territorial Award, Pub Serv Utica Elfun Soc Gen Elec AESD, 1974-75; Elfun Man of Year, Utica Chap, Elfun Soc Gen Elec AESD, 1975; Nominee Phillippe Award for Pub Serv, Gen Elec Co, 1977; Phillippe Award, Gen Elec Co, 1978; Gerald L. Phillippe Award, Gen Elec Found. **Home Addr:** 6014 Glass Factory Rd, Marcy, NY 13403, **Home Phone:** (315)733-8048.

### HARRIS, VIRGINIA R.
Artist. **Personal:** Born Jan 1, 1937, Macon, GA. **Career:** Sonoma State Univ, quilt artist, currently; Exihib: SSU Gallery, 2004. **Honors/Awds:** Honor of Carolyn L. Mazloomi, Smithsonian Am Art Mus. **Business Addr:** Quilt Artist, Sonoma State University, Ives Hall 1801 E Cotati Ave, Rohnert Park, CA 94928-3609, **Business Phone:** (707)664-2880.

**HARRIS, VITA M.**
Executive. **Educ:** Howard Univ, BS, mkt, MBA; Univ Md, doctorate-level courses. **Career:** Draft Direct Worldwide, exec vpres, 2003, chief incite officer, insight serv, exec vpres & dir, currently, chief strategy officer, 2009-; Draftfcb, chmn Educ & Cult awareness team, affinity groups, advisor. **Orgs:** Exec Diversity Coun. **Home Addr:** 1825 Foster Ave Apt 3D, Brooklyn, NY 11230-1831, **Home Phone:** (718)859-6012. **Business Addr:** Executive Vice President, Director of Insight Services,Draft, New York, NY.

**HARRIS, DR. WALTER, JR.**
College administrator. **Personal:** Born Jan 27, 1947, Suttle, AL; son of Walter Sr and Arie L B; married Henrietta Augustus; children: Ayana Kristi & Askala Almaz. **Educ:** Knoxville Col, Knoxville, TN, BS, 1968; Harvard Univ, MDP; Mich State Univ, E Lansing, MI, MS, 1969, PhD, 1979. **Career:** Ariz State Univ, Tempe, AZ, coordr, undergrad studies, music, asst dean, Col Fine Arts, actg dean, assoc dean, interim asst vpres acad affairs, vice provost; NC Cent Univ, Durham, NC, provost & vice chancellor acad affairs, prof music; Loyola Univ New Orleans, prof music, provost, vpres, acad affairs, 2003-. **Orgs:** Univ NC, Chapel Hill, NC, sr exec fel; Pi Kappa Lamda Hon Fraternity, Mich State Univ, 1968; fel NEH, 1974; Luce Fel, Luce Found, 1977; Int Coun Fine Arts Deans, 1985-; regional chairperson, Am Choral Dir Asn, 1987-; bd dir, Phoenix Symphony Orchestra, 1990-; Am Bar Asn, bd trustee, Phoenix Boys Choir, 1990-; pres, Ariz Alliance Arts Educ, 1991-93; Southern Asn Cols & Schs Comn; La Philharmonic Orchestra; Greater New Orleans Youth Orchestra. **Home Addr:** 939 E Gemini Dr, Tempe, AZ 85283-3001, **Home Phone:** (602)897-1159. **Business Addr:** Provost, Vice President, Academic Affairs, Loyola University New Orleans, Marquette Hall 221, New Orleans, LA 70118, **Business Phone:** (504)865-3034.

**HARRIS, WALTER LEE**
Football player. **Personal:** Born Aug 10, 1974, LaGrange, GA; married Trina; children: Courtney, London, Summer & Brandon. **Educ:** Miss State Univ, grad. **Career:** Football player (retired); Chicago Bears, right corner back, 1996-98, left corner back & corner back, 1999-2001; Indianapolis Colts, left corner back, 2002-03; Wash Redskins, right corner back & left corner back, 2004-05; San Francisco 49ers, right corner back & corner back, 2006-09; Baltimore Ravens, 2010. **Honors/Awds:** All-Rookie, 1996; National Football Conference Player of the Month; National Football Conference Defensive Player of the Week; Bill Walsh Award; Interception Co-Leader, Nat Football Conf, 2006; Pro-Bowl, 2006; San Francisco 49ers Team Most valuable Player, 2006. **Business Addr:** Cornerback, San Francisco 49ers, 4949 Centennial Blvd, Santa Clara, CA 95054, **Business Phone:** (408)562-4949.

**HARRIS, DR. WHITNEY G.**
Executive director. **Educ:** McNeese State Univ, BS, 1973; La State Univ, Med, spec educ, psychol, 1976; Univ Ottawa & St Paul Univ, theol; Univ Cincinnati, MS, spec educ; Union Inst, PhD, 1987; Harvard Mgt Develop Prog, cert, 1996. **Career:** Ebolowa Col, teacher & prin, 1983-1988; Spec educ teacher; Union Inst, adj prof; Southern Develop Found, Lafayette, La, youth consult; McNeese State Univ, vpres spec serv & equity, exec dir human rels & social equity, dir, equal opportunity/minority affairs, 1990-2001; La Dept Social Serv, impartial hearing officer, 1995-2001; Burton Col Educ, prof, 1996; Eastern Mich Univ, Dept Diversity & Affirmative Action, dir, 2001-05; Minn State Cols & Univs, chief diversity officer, dir diversity & multiculturalism, 2005-; Women & Gender Studies at Eastern Mich Univ, adj prof; Minneapolis Community & Tech Col, exec dir, diversity, 2013-. Journals: Journal of African American Studies; Journal of Men's Studies and Black Issues in Higher Education. **Orgs:** Am Asn Affirmative Action; Nat Am Asn Affirmative Action; Phi Kappa Pi Hon Soc; Nat Asn Advan Colored People; Am Civil Liberties Union; Phi Delta Kappa; Nat Human Rights Campaign; Sourn Poverty Law Ctr; bd mem, Am Men's Studies Asn; bd mem, Mich Equality & Ruth Ellis Ctr; pres, La Higher Educ; pres, African-Americans La Higher Educ. **Business Addr:** Director of Diversity and Multiculturalism, Minnesota State Colleges and Universities, Wells Fargo Pl 30 7th St E Suite 350, St Paul, MN 55101-7804, **Business Phone:** (651)296-8012.

**HARRIS, DR. WILLA BING**
Educator. **Personal:** Born Mar 12, 1945, Allendale, SC; daughter of Van Bing and Willa M Lofton Bing; married Jake J; children: KeVan Bing. **Educ:** Bennett Col, BA, 1966; Bloomsburg State Col, MEd, 1968; Univ Ill, EdD, educ admin & spec educ admin, 1975. **Career:** White Haven State Sch & Hosp, teacher, 1967-69; Albany State Col, instr, 1969; SC State Col Orangeburg, asst prof & suprv grad practicum stud, 1969-70; Univ Ill, Urbana Champaign, Upward Bound, head counr, 1971, asst to maj adv, 1971-73; Barber-Scotia Col, asst prof educ & psychol, 1975-76; Ala State Univ, Montgomery, prof & coordr, currently; Cent Ala Regional Educ In-Serv Ctr, assoc prof & coordr spec educ, 1976-, coordr, 1985-88, Rural & Minority Spec Educ Personnel Prep, dir, 1988, dir emotional conflict, teacher prep prog, 1990-98, curric & instr, interim chair, 2004-. **Orgs:** USOE Fel, Ford Found Fel, Univ Ill, 1970-73; Consult Head Start, 1977-80, 1984-85; lay deleg ann conf, Ala W Fla Conf United Methodist Church, 1980-90; bd dir, United Methodist C's Home, Selma, AL, 1984-94, 1996; Ala State Univ Credit Union, 1984-87; Nellie Burge Comm Ctr, 1985-91; Am Asn Ment Deficiency-Ment Retardation; Am Asn Univ Professors; Ala Consortium Univ dir Spec Ed; Black Child Devel Inst; Coun Excep C; Coun C Behav Dis; Div C Commun Dis, Div Ment Retardation, Teacher Ed Div; Ill Admin Spec Ed; Kappa Delta Pi; Nat Asn Educ Young C; Nat Asn Retarded Citizens; Montgomery City Asn Retarded Citizens; Phi Delta Kappa; Ala State Univ Grad Fac; Ala State Univ Woman's Club; Montgomery Newcomers Club; Tot n Teens; Peter Crump Elem Sch PTA State & Nat Chapt; active mem, Metrop United Methodist Church, Adult II Sunday Sch Class; comt chmn, Fund Raising Choir Robes; admin, Organizer United Meth Youth Fel; jurisdictional coordr, Black Methodists Southeastern Jurisdiction Church Renewal, 1989-; bd mem, finance chair, Nat Black Methodists Church Renewal, 1989-; pres, bd dir, United Methodist C's Home, 1990-94. **Home Addr:** 2613 Whispering Pines Dr, Montgomery, AL 36120, **Home Phone:** (334)280-0117. **Business Addr:** Professor, Coordinator, Alabama State University, 915 S Jackson St 109 Councill Hall, Montgomery, AL 36104, **Business Phone:** (334)229-4100.

**HARRIS, WILLIAM ALLEN**
Sociologist. **Personal:** Born Aug 3, 1937, Providence, RI; son of William A and Ruth Pell; children: Rebecca Jackson, Kurt R, Trevor & Jimbo S. **Educ:** Univ Calif, Santa Barbara, BA, 1968; Yale Univ, MA, 1970; Stanford Univ, PhD, 1981. **Career:** Sociologist (retired); 6927th Radio Squadron Mobile, Onna Pt, 1958-60; Wesleyan Univ, Ctr Afro-Am Studies asst prof, 1978-82; Univ Vi, res scientist, 1982-87; Clean Sites, res assoc, 1987-90; Univ Iowa, African Am World Studies, vis fac, 1990-92; Boston Col, Dept Sociol, asst prof, 1992-2000. **Orgs:** Am Sociol Asn, 1977-; Asn Black Sociologists, 1990-; Asn Social & Behav Scientist, 1994-. **Honors/Awds:** NCEA Fel, Black Theatre, 1968; UCSB, Asian Studies, Top Grad, 1968. NDFL Fel, Japanese Lang, 1969; Nat Fel Fund, grad study, 1974-79; Fulbright Res Fel, Beijing, China, 2000-01. **Special Achievements:** Author of: Theatrical Performances, CA & Virgin Islands, 1967-86; Films of Spike Lee, 1995; Theory Construction, Socological Theory, Vol 10, 1992; Upward Mobility Among African Americans, 1996. **Home Addr:** 247 Chestnut Hill Ave Suite 31, Brighton, MA 02135, **Home Phone:** (617)254-6136.

**HARRIS, WILLIAM ANTHONY**
Writer, educator. **Personal:** Born Jan 25, 1941, Anniston, AL; son of Edwin and Elizabeth Gay; married Carole McDonald. **Educ:** Wayne State Univ, BA, 1971, MA, 1977. **Career:** Playwright, poet, critic & novelist; JazzMobile, prod coordr, 1981-83; New Fed Theatre, prod coordr, 1983-85; Wayne State Univ, 1985-90, prof, 1993-; Ctr Creative Studies, 1985-90; Mus African-Am Hist, cur, 1990-. **Orgs:** Bd mem, Detroit Coun Arts, 1987-; bd mem, Inside Out, 1997-. **Honors/Awds:** Paul Robeson Cultural Arts Award, State Mich, 1985; Rosa Parks Vis Scholar Fel, Martin Luther King, Jr, 1987; Writer in Residence Grant, Rockefeller Found, 1988; Art Achievement Award for Alumni, Wayne State Univ, 1989; Silver Medal, 1997; Kresge Arts in Detroit Eminent Artist of Award, 2011; Kresge Eminent Artist, 2011; Dr Alain Locke Award, 2015; Atlanta Black Legend Award, 2015. **Special Achievements:** Publ: Stories About the Old Days, 1989; Every Goodbye Ain't Gone, 1989; Robert Johnson: Trick the Devil, 1993; The Ringmaster's Array; Yardbird Suite: Side One; Riffs & Coda, 1998; Birth of a Notion; Booker T & Them; Approximately 80 productions of plays written. "He Who Endures" in anthology African American Literature, edited by Al Young; "Every Goodbye Ain't Gone" in anthology New Plays for the Black Theater, edited by Woodie King, Jr. **Home Addr:** 15 E Kirby Suite 611, Detroit, MI 48202-2708, **Home Phone:** (313)871-2982. **Business Addr:** Emeritus Professor, Wayne State University, Rm 10001 5057 Woodward Eng Dept, Detroit, MI 48202.

**HARRIS, WILLIAM ANTHONY. See HARRIS, BILL.**

**HARRIS, WILLIAM H., JR.**
Lawyer. **Personal:** Born Sep 8, 1942, New Orleans, LA; son of William H and Victoria Fontenette; married Cynthia; children: Alisa Carol & William H III. **Educ:** Xavier Univ, BA, 1965; Howard Univ Sch Law, JD, 1968. **Career:** Dept Housing & Urban Develop, Off Gen Coun, atty, 1968; pvt pract, 1969-; Greenstein Delorme & Luchs PC, shareholder, 1989-, atty-prin, currently; pvt pract, 1969-. **Orgs:** US Ct Appeals Wash, DC; US Dist Ct; US Ct Claims; Nat Asn Advan Colored People; Am, Nat, DC Bar Asn; DC Mayor's Comn Rental Housing Prod; Nat Asn Security Professionals; assoc mem, DC Bldg Indust Asn; Mortgage Bankers Asn Am; Alpha Phi Alpha Fraternity; Am Bar Asn. **Home Addr:** 14012 Northwyn Dr, Silver Spring, MD 20904-5926, **Home Phone:** (301)384-1603. **Business Addr:** Attorney Principal, Greenstein Delorme & Luchs PC, 1620 L St NW Suite 900, Washington, DC 20036-5605, **Business Phone:** (202)452-1400.

**HARRIS, DR. WILLIAM HAMILTON**
Educator, association executive. **Personal:** Born Jul 22, 1944, Fitzgerald, GA; son of Robert and Sallie; married Wanda F; children: Cynthia Maria & William James. **Educ:** Paine Col, AB, 1966; Ind Univ, MA, 1967, PhD, 1973. **Career:** Paine Col, instr hist, 1967-69, pres, 1982-88; Ind Univ, lectr, prof hist, 1972-82, dir cic minorities fel prog, 1977-82; Univ Hamburg, Ger, fulbright prof, vis prof, 1978-79; Tex Southern Univ, pres, 1988-94; Ala State Univ, pres, 1994-2000, interim pres, pres, 2009-12, pres emer, 2012-; Network Instrnl TV Inc, bd dir, 2001-, chmn bd & chair exec comt, 2002-; Ft Valley State Univ, interim pres, 2005-06; Tex Col, interim pres, 2008. **Orgs:** Leadership Augusta/Leadership Ga, 1982-84; bd dir, Augusta Jr Achievement, 1984-88, bd trustees, ETS, 1984-90; bd dir, United Negro Col Fund, 1984-88; Nat Asn Equal Opportunity Com Inter col Athletics, 1984-86; Lilly Endowment Inc, Comn Lilly Open Fel, 1984-87; Boy Scouts Am; bd dir, Nat Asn Equal Opportunity, 1985-88; Ga Comn Bicentennial US Const, 1986-88; Augusta Chamber Com/Augusta Rotary, 1988; bd dir, Montgomery Area United Way, 1995-; bd dir, Montgomery Metrop YMCA, 1995-; bd dir, Montgomery Chamber Com, 1995-; bd visitors, Air Univ, USAF, 1996-; bd dir, Leadership Ala, 1996-; bd dir, City erence (SWAC) Coun Pres, 1996-97; chair, Ala Coun Col & Univ Presidents, 1997-; Ga Asn Cols. **Honors/Awds:** Susan O'Kell Memorial Award, Ind Univ, 1971; Fulbright Fel, Univ Hamburg, 1978-79; Distinguished Alumni Service Award, Ind Univ, 1991; Doctor of Laws, Honoris Causa, Paine Col, 1991; Distinguished Son of Fitzgerald, Ga Centennial Observance, 1996; Doctor of Humanities, Tuskegee Univ. **Special Achievements:** Author: Brotherhood of Sleeping Car Porters, 1977; Keeping the Faith: A Philip Randolph, Milton P Webster, 1978; The Harder We Run, Oxford Univ Press, 1982; Records of the Brotherhood of Sleeping Car Porters, 1996; One of the Fifty Most Influential Black Georgians. Alabama State University's first female president. **Home Addr:** 6 Oyster Landing Rd, Hilton Head Island, SC 29928, **Home Phone:** (843)671-5832. **Business Addr:** President Emeritus, Ala State University, 915 S Jackson St, Montgomery, AL 36101, **Business Phone:** (334)229-4202.

**HARRIS, WILLIAM J.**
Educator, writer. **Personal:** Born Mar 12, 1942, Fairborn, OH; son of William Lee and Camilla Hunter; married Susan Kumin; children: Kate Elizabeth. **Educ:** Cent State Univ, Wilberforce OH, BA, 1968; Stanford Univ, Stanford, CA, MA, 1971, PhD, 1974. **Career:** Educator & Writer; Cornell Univ, Ithaca NY, asst prof, 1972-77; Epoch Mag, poetry ed, 1972-77; Univ Calif, Riverside CA, asst prof, 1977-83; Harvard Univ, Cambridge MA, Andrew W Mellon, fac fel, 1982-83; State Univ New York, Stony Brook NY, assoc prof, 1985-92; Minn Rev, poetry ed, 1988-92; Norton Anthology Afro-Am Lit, adv ed, 1988; Pa State Univ, assoc prof, 1992-2002; Univ Kans, assoc prof, 2002, assoc prof emer, Eng; Publications: Hey Fella Would You Mind Holding This Piano a Moment, 1974; In My Own Dark Way, 1977; The Poetry and Poetics of Amiri Baraka: The Jazz Aesthetic, 1985; The New Jazz Studies, 2004; Every Goodbye Ain't Gone: An Anthology of Innovative Poetry by African Americans Every Goodbye Ain't Gone: An Anthology of Innovative Poetry by African Americans, 2006; Editor: The LeRoi Jones & Amiri Baraka Reader, 1991, second ed, 2000; Call & Response: The Riverside Anthology of the African-American Literary Tradition, co-editor, 1997; a double issue of The African American Review on Amiri Baraka, 2003; The African American Review; mixed blood; the University of Iowa Press Contemporary North American Poetry Series; Penn Sound: Amiri Baraka; Modern American Poetry: Amiri Baraka. **Orgs:** Mod Lang Asn Am, 1971-; Am & Cult Soc; Columbia Univ's Ctr, Jazz Studies Group. **Home Addr:** 5221 Harvard Rd, Lawrence, KS 66049, **Home Phone:** (785)842-6772. **Business Addr:** Associate Professor Emeritus, University of Kansas, 3106 Wescoe Hall rm 3001 1445 Jayhawk Blvd, Lawrence, KS 66045, **Business Phone:** (785)864-2534.

**HARRIS, WILLIAM JOSEPH, II**
Educator, sculptor, association executive. **Personal:** Born Nov 19, 1949, Lansing, MI; son of William and Ella; children: Damon. **Educ:** UCLA. **Career:** Middlebury Col, prof emer; Self-employed, sculptor, currently. **Orgs:** Co-chair, Decatur GA Arts Festival, 1994-95; vol, African Am Parokaine Experience Mus; bd mem, Decatur-Dekalb Arts Alliance. **Honors/Awds:** Works Catalogued Permanetly in the African-American Design Archive at Smithsonian's Cooper-Hewitt Museum Dec Arts, 1994; Earl Pardon Memorial Invitational Award Exhibit, 1994; African Expressions, Spruill Center for the Arts, 1994. **Special Achievements:** Work of Art, which is traveling the US with the Uncommon Beauty in Common Objects, Exhibitions, sponsored by Lila Wallace Readers Digest Fund, National Afro-American Museum; Published 79th Annual Conference of the Association for the Study of Afro-American Life and History, 1994. **Business Addr:** Owner, Sculptured Creations, PO Box 752, Avondale Estates, GA 30002.

**HARRIS, WILLIAM M.**
School administrator. **Personal:** Born Jan 19, 1932, Middletown, OH; married Mary Buchanan; children: William, Walter & Adrienne. **Educ:** Ohio State, BS, 1954; Univ NDak, MS, 1968. **Career:** Essex Co Col, counr, 1968-69; Rutgers Univ, asst dean students, 1969-71, dir camp ctr & stud act, 1971-77; Univ MS Amherst, dir camp ctr. **Orgs:** Asn Col Union Intern, 1971-; help alien youth, E Orange Bd Educ, 1970-74; Vind Soc, 1971-; Comn Minor Prog. **Home Addr:** 25 Maplewood Dr, Amherst, MA 01002, **Home Phone:** (413)549-0529.

**HARRIS, DR. WILLIAM MCKINLEY, SR.**
Consultant, educator. **Personal:** Born Oct 29, 1941, Richmond, VA; son of William and Rosa Minor; children: Rolisa, William Jr, Dana & Melissa. **Educ:** Howard Univ, BS, physics, 1965; Univ Wash, MUP, urban planning, 1972, PhD, urban planning, 1974. **Career:** Western Wash State Col, Ctr Urban Studies, dir, 1973-74; Portland State Univ, Black Studies Dept, chmn, 1974-76; Off Afro Am Affairs, dean, 1976-81; Univ Va, prof city planning, 1987-98; Planning Consult, 1987-; Mass Inst Technol, Martin Luther King Jr vis prof, 2006-08; Jackson State Univ, Sch Policy & Planning, Dept Urban & Regional Planning, chair, prof, assoc dean; Western J Black Studies, ed; Univ Wash, fac; Va State Univ, fac; Cornell Univ, fac; advocate; Ga Regents Univ, adj prof; Augusta State Univ, adj prof, currently. **Orgs:** Nat Asn Advan Colored People, 1964-; Am Planning Asn, 1976-; Am Inst Cert Planners, 1978-; Charlottesville Planning Comn, 1981-98; bd mem, Develop Training Inst, 1988-; bd dir, TJ United Way, 1990-98; Charlottesville Bd Zoning Appeals, 1991-98; fel People People's Citizen Ambassador Prog, 1993-96; fel Am Inst Cert Planners; past mem, AICP Ethics Comt; ACSP Mem Comt; Urban Affairs Asn; Am Col Schs Planning; Asn Study African Am Life & Hist. **Honors/Awds:** Portland Oregon Citizen Year, 1975; Outstanding Service, Community Develop Soc VA, 1984; Teacher of the Year, Monticello Community Action Agency, 1990; Delegation leader to China, Citizen Ambassador Prog, 1992, 1994; Life Time Achievement Award, Planning & Black Community Div Am Planning Asn. **Special Achievements:** He is author of four books & numerous scholarly articles; Black Community Development, 1976; Charlottesville Little League Basketball, coach, championships, 1982, 1988, 1992; "Professional Education of African Americans: A Challenge to Ethical Teaching," Business & Professional Ethics Journal, 1990; "Technology Education for Planners: A Century for African & People of African Descent," African Technology Forum, 1992; "African-American Economic Development in Baltimore," The Urban Design & Planning Magazine, 1993; "Environmental Racism: A Challenge to Community Development," Journal of Black Studies, 1995; "Challenge & Opportunity: Core Cities & Surburbs," 2002; "Urban Segregation in the Deep South: Race, Education, & Planning Ethics in Jackson MS," 2003; First African American elected to the College of Fellows of the American Institute of Certified Planners; University of Virginia's first Dean of African-American. **Home Addr:** 1309 Maple Leaf Ct, Evans, GA 30809-5275, **Home Phone:** (706)868-0280. **Business Addr:** Adjunct Professor, Augusta State University, 2500 Walton Way, Augusta, GA 30904-2200, **Business Phone:** (706)737-1405.

**HARRIS, DR. ZELEMA M.**
Chancellor (education), executive director, association executive. **Personal:** Born Jan 12, 1940, Newton County, TX; daughter of James Robert Marshall and Gertrude Violet; married Manuel Holloway; children: Narissa, Cynthia Bond & James (Jay). **Educ:** Prairie View A&M Col, BS, 1961; Univ Kans, MS, 1972, EdD, higher educ/admin, 1976. **Career:** Asst dir, urban affairs Univ Kans, Lawrence, 1970-72; Centennial Col, asst dir, 1970-72; dir supportive educ serv, 1970-72; Metrop Community Col, coordr curric eval, 1976-77, dir curric eval, 1977-78, dir ed opportunity ctr, 1978-80, dir dist serv, 1980; Nat Ctr Voc Ed, consult, 1978-81; Pioneer Community Col, pres, 1980-

90; Penn Valley Community Col & Pioneer Campus, pres, 1987-90; Parkland Col, pres emer, 1990-2006; St Louis Community Col, chancellor, chancellor, 2007-11; Zelema Harris Consult, life coach, 2013-. **Orgs:** Eval Spec Off Ed, 1976; consult, McMannis Assoc, 1978-80; bd mem, Black Econ Union, 1981-85; Urban League Greater Kans City, 1981-90; pres, Nat Asn Advan Colored People, 1982-86; gen chmn, Greater Kans City, MO United Negro Col Fund Campaign, 1988; Steering Comt, Mayor's Prayer Breakfast; Full Employ Coun; Nat Conf Christians & Jews; Downtown Minority Develop Corp; Pub Bldg Auth; Qual Ed Coalition; co-chair, Kans City's Jazz Comn; United Way Champaign County; Champaign County Chamber Com; Jr League Champaign-Urbana; Rotary Club Champaign; Urban League Champaign County. **Honors/Awds:** Mary McLeod-Bethune, Alpha Phi Alpha, 1983; Recognition for OutstandingParticipation, UNCF Lou Rawls Parade Stars Fund-Raising TV spec, 1983; Jefferson Award, Channel 4 TV NBC, 1984; Recognition for Service, Adv Comt House Select Comt C Youth & Females, 1984; Protestant of the Year Citation-Award, Nat Coun Christians & Jews, 1986; Kansas City Spirit Award, GillisCtr, 1987; Leadership Award, Nat CounBlack Am Affairs, 1994; Wingspread Award, IL Sect, Am Asn Women Community Col, 1995; Woman of Distinction, Green Meadows Girl Scout Coun, 1996; Marie Y Martin ChiefExecutive Officer Award, Asn Comt Col Trustees, 1997; Athena Award forOutstanding Business Professional Woman, Champaign City Chamber Com, 1997; President of the Year, Am Asn Women Community Col, 1997. **Special Achievements:** The Mo Adv Coun Voc Educ, 9th Annual Report, 1978; One of the 60 Women of Achievement, Mid Continent Coun Girl Scouts, 1983; Developed, "Vocational Evaluation Model", One of the 100 Most Influential Women, Globe Newspaper, 1983, 1990; One of the Most Powerful Women in KS City, KS Citian published by Cof C, 1984; One of Nations Most Influential Black Women, Dollars & SenseMag, 1986; One of 30 Women of Conscience, Panel Am Women, 1987; Author: Meeting the Growing Challenges of Ethnic Diversity, Community, Techn & Jr Col Times, 1990; Creating a Climate of Institutional Inclusiveness, Community, Tech & Jr Col Times, 1992; Leadership for Creating CommunityWithin Institutions; Multicultural and International Challenges to the Community College: A Model for Collegewide Proactive Response, ERIC Clearing house Community Cols, 1995; Leadership in Action: LeadingCollectively at Parkland College, Community Col Jour, 1996; Embracing a New Vision in the Information Age, Community Col Week, 1996; From Policyto Action: Implementation of NCA's Statement on Access, Equity, andDiversity, NCA Quarterly, 1997; St. Louis Leader of Distinction, Youth Women's Christian Asn, 2008. **Home Addr:** 2014 Scottsdale Dr, Champaign, IL 61821.

### HARRIS-BRAXTON, KELLY. See HARRIS, KELLY C.

### HARRIS-DIAW, ROSALIND JUANITA

Publisher. **Personal:** Born Mar 19, 1950, Grand Rapids, MI; daughter of Ruth Boyd Smith and Doyle James; children: Lawrence & Donald. **Educ:** Davenport Col Bus, 1970; Patricia Stevens Career Sch, attended 1973; Univ Nebr Omaha, 1981; Metro State Col, African Am Leadership Inst, cert, 1991. **Career:** Omaha Nat Bank, chartographer, 1975-77; Salt & Pepper Art Studios, owner & operator, 1977-80; Rees Printing Co, grapic artist, 1981; Colo Homes & Lifestyles, prod artist, 1981-82; DK Assoc Excel Serv, Lowry AFB graphic artist, 1982-84; Prod Plus/Spectrum Designs, owner & operator, 1984-; Urban Spectrum, publ, art dir & owner, publisher, 1987-. **Orgs:** Pres & publist, Five Points Bus Asn, 1989-; treas, Mothers & Daughters Inc, 1989-; active mem, Colo Black Chamber Com, 1990-97; dir, Rocky Mountain Women's Inst, 1994-97; Metro State Col Press's Community Adv Coun, 1994; Colo Hist Soc African Am Adv Coun, 1994-; Chairs Steering Com, Hiawatha Davis Campaign Better Communities Comt, 1995; Metro State Cols Press Community Adv Coun; app comnr, Mayors Off Art Cult & Film; Co Asn Black Journalists; African-Am Leadership Inst; Nat Coun Negro Women; dir, Girls Scouts Mile Hi Coun; Denver Metro Conv & Visitors Bur; stapleton Redevelop, Citizen Adv Bd; Mayor's Coun Safe City Summit Task Force; Five Points Bus Asn; Rocky Mountain Womens Inst; Five Points Bus Asn; founder, Urban Spectrum Youth Found, 2000; founder, Spectrum Hope, 2005-; bd dir, Blacktie. **Honors/Awds:** Women of Achievement Nominee, YWCA, 1990; Business Award, CBWPA-Co Black Women Polit Action, 1991; Print Journalist of the Year, CABJ-Co Asn Black Journalist, 1994; MLK Jr Humanitarian Award, Major Wellington E Webb, 1995; Community Newspaper Media Award, Am Legion, 1995; Trailblazer Award, Nat Coun Negro Women, 1997; LOC Million Man March Media Award, 1998; Top 100 Media Award, 1999; Women of Distinction, Girl Scouts, 2000; Corp Award, Bus & Prof Women, 2000; Community Diversity Award, Delta Sigma Theta, Denver Alumae chap, 2000; Dr MLK Business Social Responsibility Award, 2003; Burger King Everyday Hero Award, 2003; Overall Excellence Award. **Home Addr:** 5563 Xanadu St, Denver, CO 80239, **Home Phone:** (303)375-1304. **Business Addr:** Publisher, President, Urban Spectrum, 2499 Wash St, Denver, CO 80205, **Business Phone:** (303)292-6446.

### HARRIS-EBOHON, DR. ALTHERIA THYRA

Educator, executive. **Personal:** Born Jun 26, 1948, Miami, FL; daughter of Andrew Sr and Mary White; married John Ikpomwenosa; children: Paul, Samson, Terrian Sheyvonne McNeal-Berry, Marquell Hughes-Berry, LaDarius McNeal-Berry, LaDonte' McNeal-Berry & Nigel Berry. **Educ:** Miami-Dade Community Col, AA, 1968; FL Atlantic Univ, BA, 1970, EdS, 1976; Morgan State Univ, MS, 1972; Nova Univ, EdD, 1981; Barry Univ; Fla Int Univ; Univ Miami. **Career:** Businesswoman, 1988-; Dade Co Pub Schs, educr; Niam Inc dir. **Orgs:** Nat Educ Asn, 1970; Baptist training union directress New Mt Zion Missionary Baptist Church Hialeah, 1980-; bd mem, Fla Baptist Conv Inc, 1986; life fel Int Biog Asn, Cambridge, Eng, 1988-; Am Biog Inst, 1988; Blk Hist Oratorical Comt Sponsor, 1990; New Mt Zion Missionary Baptist Church Hialeah. **Honors/Awds:** Awards Banquet Honoree by Senator Bob Graham, St Augustine, FL, 1986. **Home Addr:** 475 NW 90th St, El Portal, FL 33150-2145, **Home Phone:** (305)759-8082.

### HARRIS-JONES, YVONNE

Consultant, executive, association executive. **Personal:** Born West Palm Beach, FL; daughter of Albert Thomas and Mary G Thomas Simpson. **Educ:** City Col NY, BA, sociol, 1970; New Sch Univ Soc Res, MA, human resource mgt, 1977. **Career:** Fed Res Bank NY, sr training specialist, 1972-76; Am Stock Exchange, Human Resources & Employee Rels, managing dir, 1976-96; Yvonne Harris Jones Enterprises, pres & chief exec officer, 1997-2009; City Univ New York, Medgar Evers Col, adj prof, 1997-2003; Westchester Community Col, adj fac mem, 1998-99; Africa-Am Inst, consult/dir human resources, 1998-2007. **Orgs:** Pres, Zeta Delta Phi Grad Chap, 1970-76; Soc Hum Res Mgt, 1976-; Coalition 100 Black Women, 1977-; adv bd, Murry Bergtraum HS, 1979-96; NY Club, Nat Asn Negro Bus & Prof Women's Club Inc, 1986-; adv bd, Career Opportunity, 1991-03; adv bd, Medgar Evers Sch Bus & Pub Admin, 1998-; Leadership Am, 1998; bd mem, Ny Soc Cert Pub Accountants Inc. **Honors/Awds:** Black Achievers in Industry Award, YMCA Harlem Br, 1979; Corporate Achievement Award, Negro Bus & Prof Women's Clubs Inc, 1985; Mary McCloud Bethune Award, Nat Coun Negro Women, 1991. **Home Addr:** , NY. **Business Addr:** President, Chief Executive Officer, Yvonne Harris Jones Enterprises, PO Box 20, Mohegan Lake, NY 10547.

### HARRIS-PERRY, MELISSA (MELISSA V HARRIS-LACEWELL)

Writer, talk show host. **Personal:** Born Oct 2, 1973, Seattle, WA; married James Perry, Jan 1, 2010?; married Dennis Lacewell, Jan 1, 1999?, (divorced 2005); children: Parker Lacewell. **Educ:** Wake Forest University, B.A. in English; Duke University, Ph.D. in Political Science; Meadville Lombard Theological School, Honorary Doctorate; Union Theological Seminary (New York), Attended. **Career:** University of Chicago, Faculty; Princeton University, Center for African Studies, Associate Professor; MSNBC show "Melissa Harris-Perry," Host; Tulane University, Professor of Political Science, 2011-; "The Nation" Magazine, Monthly Columnist; "The Rachel Maddow Show," Regular Fill-in Host. **Orgs:** Anna Julia Cooper Project, Director; The Century Foundation, Trustee; Chef's Move!, Advisory Board Member. **Honors/Awds:** American Political Science Association, Race and Ethnics Politics Section, Best Book Award for "Barbershops, Bibles, and BET: Everyday Talk and Black Political Thought," 2005; W.E.B. DuBois Book Award for "Barbershops, Bibles, and BET: Everyday Talk and Black Political Thought," 2005. **Special Achievements:** Author of "Barbershops, Bibles, and BET: Everyday Talk and Black Political Thought," Princeton (2004) and "Sister Citizen: Shame, Stereotypes, and Black Women in America," Yale University Press (2011); youngest scholar to deliver W.E.B. DuBois Lectures at Harvard University, 2009; youngest woman to deliver Ware Lecture, 2009.

### HARRISON, DR. A. B.

Physician. **Personal:** Born Jan 1, 1909, Portsmouth, VA. **Educ:** Va State Col, BS; Meharry Med Col, Md, 1930. **Career:** Franklin, Va, pvt pract, 1936-; S Hampton Memorial Hosp, staff mem, 1945, Chief Staff; Franklin, Va, City Coun, 1968-74, vice mayor, 1974-76, mayor, 1976-; Provident Hosp, intern. **Special Achievements:** First Negro admitted into the Organization.

### HARRISON, ALVIN L.

Track and field athlete. **Personal:** Born Jan 20, 1974, Orlando, FL; son of Albert and Juanita; children: Shraee, Shiyah Marie, Dejahna & Anaia. **Educ:** Hartnell Col. **Career:** Athlete (retired); Track & field athlete, Us; Track & field athlete, Dominican Repub, 2009. **Honors/Awds:** Third Place, USA Juniors Competition, 1993; Winner, Bruce Jenner Classic, 1996; Gold Medal, Olympics, 1996; First Place, Nat Indoor Track & Field, 1998; Silver Medal, Olympics, 2000; Second Place, US Olympic Trials, 2000; hon master's degree, exercise sci, Dominican Repub. **Special Achievements:** Co-author, Go to Your Destiny, 2000.

### HARRISON, DR. ANDOLYN B.

Educator, dean (education). **Educ:** Xavier Univ, BA; Valley State Col, MS; Bowling Green State Univ, PhD. **Career:** Grambling State Univ, Dept Educ Leadership, dean, prof; J Develop Educ, bd ed. **Orgs:** La Educ Consortium; chair, Grambling State Univ. **Business Addr:** Professor of Educational Leadership, Grambling State University, 403 Main St, Grambling, LA 71245-3091, **Business Phone:** (318)274-3811.

### HARRISON, ANGELA

Manager. **Educ:** Univ San Diego, BA, 1989; Ind State Univ, MBA, 1999. **Career:** Ind State Univ, help desk mgr info technol, 1995-, interim dir multimedia support, 2000-. **Business Addr:** Help Desk Manager, Interim Director, Indiana State University, 200 N 7th St, Terre Haute, IN 47809-9989, **Business Phone:** (812)237-8264.

### HARRISON, DR. BEVERLY E.

Lawyer. **Personal:** Born Jun 17, 1948, Port Chester, NY. **Educ:** State Univ NY, Oneonta, BA, 1970; Univ Ill, Col Law, JD, 1973. **Career:** Counr Housing & Spec Equal Opport Prog, grad asst, 1970-73; State Univ NY, Oneonta Legal & Affirm Action Affairs, asst pres employ, 1974-81; State Univ NY, Stony Brook, spec asst pres affirm action & equal employ, 1981-83; Nassau Community Col, Human Resources & Labor Rels, assoc vpres, 1983-, adminr emerita. **Orgs:** Fac adv, Varsity Cheerleaders, State Univ NY, 1974-81; bd mem, Am Asn Univ Women, 1978-79; bd mem, Planned Parenthood Otsego & Del County, 1978-80; Am Asn Affirmative Action Nominating Comn, 1979-80; Univ Fac Senate Fair Employ Practices Comn, 1979-81; State Univ Affirmative Action Coun, 1981-83; bd mem, Am Red Cross Suffolk County, 1981-83; Suffold Comm Develop Corp, 1981-83; NY State Pub Employer Labor Rels Asn; Indust Rels Res Asn; Metrop Black Bar Asn; Comt Minority Labor Lawyers; Nat Conf Black Lawyers; Nat Asn Black Women Atty; bd mem, Suffolk County Girl Scout Coun; founder, Asn Black Women Higher Educ; Educ & Assistance Corp. **Honors/Awds:** Public Service Award. **Home Addr:** PO Box 1006, Port Chester, NY 10573-8006. **Business Addr:** Associate Vice President of Personal & Labor Relations, Nassau Community College, Tower 820 8th Fl 1 Educ Dr, Garden City, NY 11530, **Business Phone:** (516)572-7660.

### HARRISON, BOYD G., JR.

Automotive executive. **Personal:** Born Feb 23, 1949, Detroit, MI; son of Boyd G Sr and Jessie Mae Trussel; married Alfreda Rowell; children: Deonne & Devon. **Educ:** Detroit Col Bus, comput sci, 1972. **Career:** Ford Motor Co, Dearborn, Mich, inspector, 1968-72, Minority Dealer Training Prog, Detroit, Mich, dealer cand, 1985-86; Chevrolet Cent Off, Warren, Mich, comput opers, 1972-85; W Covina Lincoln Mercury Inc, W Covina, Calif, dealer prin, owner, 1986-. **Orgs:** Dir, W Covina Chamber Com, 1988-; Ford Lincoln Mercury Minority Dealers Asn Polit Action Comt. **Home Addr:** 2260 Omega Cir, La Verne, CA 91750, **Home Phone:** (714)596-9312. **Business Addr:** Owner, Dealer Principal, West Covina Lincoln Mercury, 2539 E Garvey Ave N, West Covina, CA 91791, **Business Phone:** (818)966-0681.

### HARRISON, DR. C. KEITH

Educator, founder (originator). **Educ:** Cerritos Col, AA; W Tex State Univ, BS; Calif State Univ, Dominguez Hill, MS, phys educ; Univ Southern Calif, PhD, higher & post-sec educ. **Career:** Univ Mich, Ann Arbor, Paul Robeson Res Ctr Acad & Athletic Prowess, founder, 1997-2004; Black Coaches Asn, auth & prin investr, 2003-; Ariz State Univ, fac, 2004-06; Univ Cent Fla, Col Bus Admin, DeVos Sport Bus Mgt Grad Prog, assoc prof, currently; Rush Philanthropic's Hip Hop Summit Action Network, Scholar-in-Residence, currently. **Orgs:** Co-founder, Scholar Baller. **Business Addr:** Associate Professor, Devos Sport Business Management, University of Central Florida, 4000 Cent Fla Blvd, Orlando, FL 32816-1400, **Business Phone:** (407)823-4887.

### HARRISON, CALVIN

Track and field athlete. **Personal:** Born Jan 20, 1974, Orlando, FL; son of Albert and Juanita; children: Jarijah. **Educ:** Hartnell Col, attended 1994. **Career:** USA Track & Field, Nike club, track & field athlete, currently. **Honors/Awds:** USA Juniors competition, first place, 1993; Reno Air Games, won 400-meter, 1996; Nike Perfontaine Classic, won 400-meter, 1996; Natl Indoor Track & Field, 400-meter, second place, 1998; Olympics, 4x400-meter, gold medal, 2000. **Special Achievements:** Co-author: Go to Your Destiny, 2000; The Oprah Winfrey Show in 2001. **Home Addr:** , Salinas, CA. **Business Addr:** Agent, Andre Farr, 9255 Sunset Blvd, Los Angeles, CA 90069, **Business Phone:** (310)858-6565.

### HARRISON, CAROL L.

Educator. **Personal:** Born Nov 15, 1946, Buffalo, NY. **Educ:** State Univ NY, Buffalo, BA, eng psychol, 1968, PhD, 1970. **Career:** Educator (retired); Univ Buffalo, Alumni Asn, 1968-; Am Asn, Univ Prof, 1968-; Medailla Col, Eng Dept, instr, asst prof, chmn, 1970-73, prof, 1999; Acad Com Buffalo Philharmonic, 1971-73; State Univ New York, Buffalo, eng educ colloquim, 1972-; Int Plaform Asn, 1972-74; Media-Commun Medaille Col, actg dir, assoc prof, 1974. **Orgs:** Mod Lang Asn, 1969-; Vol work Buffalo Childrens Hosp, 1972; Western Ny Consortium Eng & Am Lit Prof, 1974; Nomination Am Asn Univ Womens Educ Found.

### HARRISON, CHARLES

Chief executive officer. **Career:** Crown Energy Inc, chief exec officer, 1987-, pres. **Business Addr:** Chief Executive Officer, President, Crown Energy Inc, 1130 E 87th St, Chicago, IL 60619, **Business Phone:** (312)978-7600.

### HARRISON, CHRIS

Football player. **Personal:** Born Feb 25, 1972, Washington, DC. **Educ:** Univ Va, grad. **Career:** Football player (retired); Detroit Lions, guard, 1996-98; Baltimore Ravens, guard, 1999.

### HARRISON, DR. DAPHNE DUVAL (DAPHNE D COMEGYS)

Teacher, consultant, educator. **Personal:** Born Mar 14, 1932, Orlando, FL; daughter of Alexander Chisholm Duval and Daphne Beatrice Alexander Williams; married Daniel L Comegys Jr; children: Michael Alexander & Stephanie Dolores. **Educ:** Talladega Col, BMus, 1953; Northwestern Univ, MMus, 1961; Univ Miami, FL, EdD, 1971. **Career:** Marion & Broward Co, Fla, music teacher, 1953-66; Broward Co, Fla, TV instr, 1966-68; Fla Atlantic Univ, asst prof educ, 1969-70; Univ Miami, southern fel, 1969-70; Hallandale Mid Sch, Fla, dean girls, 1970-71; BenedictCol, assoc prof fine arts, 1971-72, Africana Studies Dept, actg dir, 1974-75; Moton Ctr Independent Studies, Philadelphia, fel, 1976-77; Univ Calif Los Angeles, NEH African humanities fel, 1979, Fulbright fel, 1986; Univ Md, Baltimore, Africana Studies Dept, assoc prof, chairperson, prof, 1981-92, Ctr Study Humanities, founding dir, 1996-99, prof emer, 1999-, assoc ed; Univ pa, assoc prof; Howard Univ, assoc prof, currently. Book: Black Pearls: Blues Queens of the 1920s, 1998. **Orgs:** Chair music dir, St Andrews Church, Hollywood, Fla, 1960-70; bd mem, Fla State Teachers Asn, 1963-65; bd mem, CTD Fla Educrs Asn, 1965-67; consult, Fla Sch Desegregation Consult Ctr, 1965-70; social planner, New Town Harbison, SC, 1971-72; proj dir, Racism Intervention Develop Proj, Univ Md, 1975-77; proj dir, Summer Inst African & African Am Hist Cult & Lit, 1984-85; Nat Asn Negro Bus & Prof Women; Alpha Kappa Alpha; Asn Study Afro-Am Life & Hist; co-chair, Black Family Comt African Am Empowerment Proj; comnr, Md Comn African-Am Hist & Cult; Sonneck Soc; Int Asn Study Popular Music. **Home Addr:** 5560 Shepherdess Ct, Columbia, MD 21045, **Home Phone:** (410)997-5775. **Business Addr:** Professor Emeritus, University Maryland Baltimore, 1000 Hilltop Cir, Baltimore, MD 21250, **Business Phone:** (410)455-1000.

### HARRISON, DELBERT EUGENE

Executive. **Personal:** Born Jan 8, 1951, Flint, MI; son of Eugene and Audrey; married Mary Hill; children: Darren, Whitney & Danielle. **Educ:** Wilberforce Univ, Wilberforce, OH, BA, 1978. **Career:** Kemper Ins Co, Long Grove, Ill, personnel asst II, 1981-82; Allstate Ins Co, S Barrington, Ill, div human resources mgr, 1982-86; Chem Bank NY, Chicago, Ill, vpres human resources, credit card div, dir 1987-88; Navistar Financial Corp, Rolling Meadows, Ill, vpres, human resources, 1988-95; Hewlett-Packard, dir, 1997-2005; Progressive Ins, dir human resources, 2007-11; Independant Consult, human resources prof, 2011-12; Realm Real Estate Professionals, realtor, currently. **Orgs:** Bd trustee, Latino Inst, 1986-90; adv bd mem, Roosevelt Univ, Robin

Campus, 1989-; secy, Black Human Resources Network. **Home Addr:** 5727 Ring Ct, Hanover Park, IL 60103, **Home Phone:** (708)837-6680.

### HARRISON, DON K., SR.

Psychologist, educator, association executive. **Personal:** Born Apr 12, 1933, Nashville, NC; married Algeo O Hale; children: Denise & Don K. **Educ:** NC Cent Univ, BA, lib arts, 1953; Wayne State Univ, MA, rehab coun, 1958; Univ Mich, PhD, coun, 1972. **Career:** Univ Mich, Guid & Coun Prog, asst prof, 1972-76, chmn, 1974-77, Rehab Coun Educ, dir, assoc prof, 1976-82, prof, 1982-97, prof emer, 1997-; Wayne State Univ, Voc Rehab, adj asst prof, 1972-97. **Orgs:** Am Psychol Asn; dir, Prime Inc, Mich, 1970-80; Personnel & Guid Asn Rehab Couns Traineeship Rehab Serv Admin, 1975. **Honors/Awds:** Outstanding Service Award, MI Personel & Guide Asn, 1976. **Home Addr:** 33228 W 12 Mile Rd Suite 371, Farmington Hills, MI 48334-3309, **Home Phone:** (248)851-8139. **Business Addr:** Professor Emeritus, University of Michigan, 500 S State St, Ann Arbor, MI 48109, **Business Phone:** (734)764-1817.

### HARRISON, FAYE VENETIA

Anthropologist, educator. **Personal:** Born Nov 25, 1951, Norfolk, VA; daughter of James and Odelia B Harper; married William Louis Conwill; children: Giles, Mondlane & Justin. **Educ:** Brown Univ, BA, anthrop, 1974; Stanford Univ, MA, anthrop, 1977, PhD, anthrop, 1982. **Career:** Univ Louisville, asst pro anthrop, 1983-89; Univ Tenn, Knoxville, assoc prof anthrop, 1989-97, lindsay young prof, currently; Univ SC, Columbia, prof anthrop & grad dir women's studies, 1997-99; State Univ New York, Dept Anthrop, adj assoc prof, 1996-98; Univ Tenn-Knoxville, prof anthrop, 1999-2004; Univ Tenn, Dept Anthrop, assoc head, 2000-02; Union Inst & Univ, Grad Col, adj prof, 2002-05; Univ Fla, Prof African Am Studies & Anthrop, 2004-, affil fac, Ctr Latin Am Studies & Ctr Women's Studies & Gender Res, 2004-, dir African Am Studies, 2007-10; Univ BC, Vancouver, Centre Cult, Identity & Educ, int assoc, 2007-. **Orgs:** CMS Anthrop Women; pres, 1989-91, secy, 1985-87, ed, 1984-85, Asn Black Anthropologists; KEN Rainbow Coalition, 1988-90; Dem Socialists Am, 1990-; bd mem, Am Anthrop Asn, 1990-91, mem exec prog comt, 2006, mem comn world anthropologies, 2007-10; Union Anthrop & Ethnol Sci, 1993-98; adv bd, Off Justice, Peace, Integrity Creation, Knoxville Roman Cath Diocese, 1994-97; fel Soc Appl Anthrop, 1995; ed bd, Univ Tenn Press, 1995-97; E Tenn Coalition Abolish State Killing, 1995-97; co-chair, chair, 1998-2003, Int chair, Black Fac & Staff Asn, Univ Tenn-Knoxville, 1995-97; treas, Comn Anthrop Women Int Union Anthrop & Ethnol Sci,2009-13; Nat Alliance Against Racist Polit Repression; bd mem, Nat Asn Advan Colored People; Annual Rev Anthrop; ed, bd, Critique Anthrop; assoc ed, Urban Anthrop; ed bd, Identities; ed bd, Womanist Theory & Res; Am Ethnol Soc; Asn Feminist Anthrop; Soc Cult Anthrop; Soc Urban; Nat & Transnational Global Anthrop; Caribbean Studies Asn; Nat Coun Black Studies; Asn Study African; Am Life & Hist. **Honors/Awds:** Samuel T Arnold Fellowship, Brown Univ, 1974-75; Graduate Fellowship, Ford Found, 1976-78; Fulbright Hays Predoctoral Fellowships, US Dept Educ, 1978-79; Dorothy Danforth Compton Fellowship, Danforth Found, 1981-82; Postdoctoral Fellowship, Ford Found, 1987-88; Certficate of Merit for Scholarly Achievement, Phi Beta Kappa, 1993; Knoxville Professional Development Award, Univ Tenn, 1994; Certificate in Recognition & Appreciation for Contributions & Commitment to the American Anthropological Association, 2001; SARIF Small Grants Award, Univ Tenn, 2002-03; Hardy Liston Jr Symbol Hope Award, 2003; Ronald C Foreman Visiting Lecturer Award, 2004; Prize for Distinguished Achievement in the Critical Study of North America, Soc Anthrop N Am, 2004; President's Award, Am Anthrop Asn, 2007; Zora Neale Hurston Award, Serv & Scholar Southern Anthrop Soc, 2007; Outstanding Research Mentoring Award, Ronald McNair Scholars Prog, Univ Fla, 2008; Legacy Scholar Award, Asn Black Anthropologists, 2010; Andrew W Mellon Visiting Fellow, Univ Cape Town, 2011. **Special Achievements:** Editor & Contributor: "WEB DuBois and Anthropology," special issue, Critique of Anthrop, 1992; editor and contributor: Decolonizing Anthropology, Am Anthrop Asn, 1991, Second ed, 1997; editor and contributor: "Black Folks in Cities Here and There: Changing Patterns of Domination & Response," special issue, Urban Anthropology and Cultural Systems in World Economic Development, 1988; "Women in Jamaica's Urban Informal Economy," New West Indian Guide (reprinted in Third World Women and the Politics of Feminism, Indiana UNV Press), 1988 (1991); "Jamaica and the INT Drug Economy," TransAfrica Forum, 1990; performer: "Three Women, One Struggle," Louisville, KY, INT Women's Day Celebration Dayton, OH, 1989, Black Arts Festival, Summer 1990; author: Writing Against The Grain: Cultural Politics of Difference in Alice Walker's Fiction, Critique of Anthropology, 1993; Foreword, Comparative Perspectives on Slavery, 1993; "The Persistent Power of Race in the Cultural and Political Economy of Racism," Annual Review of Anthropology, 1995; "Give Me That Old Time Religion: The Genealogy and Cultural Politics of an Afro-Christian Celebration in Halifa County, NC," Religion in the South, 1995; co-editor, contributor, African AMR Pioneers in Anthropology, Univ of ILL Press, 1998; contributed entries, "The Blackwell Dictionary of Anthropology," 1998; "The Gendered Politics and Violence of Structural Adjustment: A View from Jamaica; "in Situated Lives: Gender and Culture in Everyday Life, 1997; Author & Editor of Numerous Books & Journals. **Home Addr:** 351 S Waccamaw Ave, Columbia, SC 29205, **Home Phone:** (803)779-5906. **Business Addr:** Professor, University of Florida, Rm B129 Turlington Hall, Gainesville, FL 32611-8120, **Business Phone:** (352)392-1020.

### HARRISON, DR. FRED

Dean (education), educator. **Personal:** Born Sep 16, 1949, Edison, GA. **Educ:** Ft Valley State Col, BS, agr educ, 1971; Univ Ga, MEd, agr educ, 1972; Ohio State Univ, PhD, agr educ, 1979. **Career:** Us Dept Agr, civil engineering trainee, 1968; Ft Valley State Col, Housing Dept, resident asst, 1968-70; Ford Motor Co, auto prod line assemblyman, 1969; Us Dept Agr, conserv trainee, 1970; Univ Ga, Housing Dept, grad resident advisor, 1972, county exten agt, 1972-76, interim dept head, 1979-80; asst prof exten educ, 1979-82, exten specialist personnel & staff develop, 1979-82, Ohio State Univ, Col Agr & Natural Resources, grad admin assoc, 1976-79; Ft Valley State Univ, Coop Exten Prog, adminr & dir, 1982-2004, actg dean, 1988-90, interim dean, dep dir small farms, dir, Col Agr, Home Econs & Allied Progs, dean, 1998-2004; Har/Mcc Properties & Enterprises LLC, pres & chief operating officer, currently. **Orgs:** Soc Int Develop; Ga Prof Agr Asn; Ft Valley State Col Agr Alumni Asn; Mid Ga Basketball Officiating Asn; Ga Asn 4-H Agents; Nat Asn 4-H Agents; Ga Asn County Agr Agents; Nat Asn County Agr Agents; FY 89 Nat Asn State Univs & Land-Grant Cols; admin advisor, 4-H Prog & Staff Develop, Exten Comt Orgn & Policy; bd dirs, Ga Stud Health Asn, Med Col Ga; secy & treas, 1984-85, Chmn Elect, 1985-86, chmn, 1986-87, Asn Exten Adminr; bd trustees, Leadership Ga, 1985-89; Ga Agr Econs Bd Dirs, 1986-87; chmn, Southern Rural Development Center Program Advisory Committee, 1987-92; Morehouse Sch Med, Nat Cancer Adv Bd, 1987-91; USDA-Joint Coun Food & Agr Sci, 1989-92; bd dirs, Ohio State Univ Agr Alumni Asn, 1988-90; chmn Exten Comt Orgn & Policy, 1993-94; Ft Valley State Col Regional Univ Task Force, 1993-96; Joint Study Comn Ga Tax & Revenue Struct, 1994-95; Nat Res Coun, Bd Agr Land-Grant Study Comt, 1993-96; Nat Asn State Univs & Land-Grant Cols, Bd on Agr, Steering & Exec Comt, 1994; bd dir, Atlanta Farmers Club, 1996-2005; bd dirs, Ga Develop Authority, 1997-2004; Exten adminr, Asn Res Dirs Inc, currently, dean emer, Ft Valley State Univ; Ga Rural Develop Coun, 2004-; USDA Farm Serv Agency State Comt, 2010-; bd dirs, Ga Farm Bur, 2012-. **Honors/Awds:** Personalities of the South, 1986; Hall of Fame, Int Nat Adult & Continuing Educ, 1996; NAFEO Alumni Hall of Fame, Ft Valley State Univ, 1998; Award of Excellence, Univ Ga, Col Agr & Environ Sci Alumni Asn, 2003. **Business Addr:** President, Chief Operating Officer, HAR/McC Properties & Enterprises LLC, 167 Double Bridges X-ING, Winterville, GA 30683, **Business Phone:** (706)549-6735.

### HARRISON, REV. GEORGE

Clergy. **Career:** First Baptist Church NBC, pastor, currently. **Orgs:** Vpres, Tex Gospel Announcers Guild; St John Missionary Baptist Church, Assoc Minister. **Business Addr:** Pastor, First Baptist Church NBC, 500 Webster Ave, Waco, TX 76706, **Business Phone:** (254)752-3000.

### HARRISON, JAIME

Lobbyist, lawyer, state government official. **Personal:** Born Feb 5, 1976; married Marie Boyd; children: William. **Educ:** Yale Univ, BA, polit sci, 1998; Georgetown Univ Law Ctr, JD, 2004. **Career:** Orangeburg-Wilkinson High Sch, teacher, 1998-99; Col Summit, chief opers officer, 1999-2002; US House Representatives, off rep, vice chair dem caucus, exec dir, 2003-05; US House Representatives, House Dem Caucus, floor dir & coun, 2007-08; Podesta Group, prin, 2008-; Sc Dem Party, chmn, 2013-; Brookings Inst, guest lectr; Cong Black Caucus Polit Educ Leadership Inst's, Polit Training Boot Camp, lectr; Harvard Kennedy Sch, Black Policy Conf, lectr; New York Univ, Brennan Ctr Justice, Wash Semester Progs, lectr. **Honors/Awds:** Politico, Politico Pro; "The Hill" newspaper, 35 Stellar Staffers Under 35; "Roll Call," Fabulous 50 Movers and Shakers Behind the Scenes on Capitol Hill; "National Journal," Hill People of 2007; "The Root" Magazine, The Root 100 Honorees, 2010, 2013; National Bar Association, Top 40 Lawyers Under 40; Impact DC, Top 40 Lawyers Under 40. **Special Achievements:** First African American and the youngest person to serve as chairman of the South Carolina Democratic Party. **Business Addr:** Chairman, South Carolina Democratic Party, 915 Lady St Suite 111, Columbia, SC 29201, **Business Phone:** (803)799-7798.

### HARRISON, JAMES, JR.

Pharmacist. **Personal:** Born Oct 14, 1930, Pittsburgh, PA; married Eunice Kea; children: Wanda, James III & Donna. **Educ:** BS, 1954. **Career:** Harrison Pharm Inc, pres; Berg Pharm, purchased, 1971. **Orgs:** Sunday Sch Teacher; Boy Scout Leader; adv bd, Bloomfield HS; pres, treas, NJ Pharm; bd dir, Essex Co Pharm Soc. **Home Addr:** 36 Dewey St, Bloomfield, NJ 07003, **Home Phone:** (973)338-0902. **Business Addr:** President, Harrison Pharm, 634 Martin Luther King Jr Blvd, Newark, NJ 07102.

### HARRISON, JAMES C.

President (organization). **Career:** Protective Indust Ins Co, pres & chief exec officer, 1923. **Business Addr:** President, Chief Executive Officer, Protective Industrial Insurance Co, 2300 11th Ave N, Birmingham, AL 35234, **Business Phone:** (205)323-5256.

### HARRISON, JAY P.

Executive. **Educ:** Univ Mich, BS, comput engineering; Anna Univ, BS, electronics, MS, comput sci & engineering; Grand Valley State Univ, BS, pub admin. **Career:** Int Olympic Comt, chief technol officer; Deneb Robotics Inc, sr vpres res & develop, prin architect, 1985-98; Quest, prin architect; Internet Opers Ctr Inc, pres & chief technol officer, 1999-2006; Harrison Technol, pres, 2006-; ReallyMake LLC, Co-Founder & Chief Architect, 2014-. **Orgs:** Inst Elec & Electronics Engrs; bd mem, Detroit Charter sch Indust Arts, 1999-2003; pres, Int Olympic Comt; bd mem, Automation Alley. **Honors/Awds:** Forty under Forty Crains Detroit Business, Detroit Charter Sch Indust Arts, 2000; Ernst and Young Entrepreneur of the Year, Detroit Charter Sch Indust Arts, 2001. **Business Addr:** President, Harrison Technologies, 3325 Paces Ferry Rd NW, Atlanta, GA 30327, **Business Phone:** (404)536-1343.

### HARRISON, LISA DARLENE

Basketball player, basketball coach. **Personal:** Born Jan 2, 1971, Louisville, KY; daughter of Cobble and Larry; married Paul Rogers. **Educ:** Univ Tenn, attended 1993. **Career:** Basketball player (retired), basketball coach; Columbus Quest, guard, 1996-97; Portland Power, 1997-99; Phoenix Mercury, 1999-2003, 2005, asst coach, 2004-05; Bike Athletic Co, mkt dir.

### HARRISON, MARVIN DANIEL

Football player. **Personal:** Born Aug 25, 1972, Philadelphia, PA; son of Linda; children: Marvin Jr. **Educ:** Syracuse Univ, BS, retailing, 1995. **Career:** Football player (retired); Indianapolis Colts, punt returner, 1996, wide receiver, 1996-2008. **Orgs:** Colts-Star News Gridiron Geog Prog; Indianapolis Housing Agency Develop. **Honors/Awds:** Maxwell Award; Pro Bowl selection, 1999-06; All-Pro selection, 1999-06; NFL Receiving Yards Leader, 1999, 2002; NFL receptions leader, 2000, 2002; NFL Receiving Touchdowns Co-Leader, 2005; Indianapolis Colts Ring of Honor, 2011; Super Bowl champion XLI. **Special Achievements:** Appeared on "Wheel of Fortune"; became the only player ever in the history of the NFL to have six double digit reception games in one single season in the 2002 regular season.

### HARRISON, DR. MERNOY EDWARD, JR.

School administrator. **Personal:** Born Nov 15, 1947, Denver, CO; son of Doris L Thompson Jackson and Mernoy E; married Frankie Gilliam; children: Dara T & Jelani T. **Educ:** Stanford Univ, Stanford, CA, BS, 1969, MBA, 1975; Univ NC, Chapel Hill, NC, PhD, bus admin, 1988. **Career:** Ravenswood High Sch, E Palo Alto, Calif, teacher; Sequoia Union Sch Dist, Redwood City, Calif, teacher, 1969-70; Kaiser Found, Los Angeles, Calif, teacher, 1970-72; San Mateo County, Redwood City, Calif, analyst, 1973-74; Merrill Intern, 1974; Woodrow Wilson fel, 1974-76; NC Cent Univ, Durham, NC, Controller, 1974-81, asst to vice chancellor acad affairs & undergrad dean, 1974-77, adj fac mem, 1977-81; Calif State Univ, Sacramento, Calif, dir finance & bus affairs, 1981-84, assoc vpres finance, 1984-86, vpres finance, 1986-90, vpres, 1990-97, vice chancellor bus & finance, 1993-94; Ariz State Univ, exec vpres admin & finance, chief financial officer, downtown phoenix campus, exec provost & vpres, 1997-. **Orgs:** Treas, Sacramento-Yolo Camp Fire, 1982-86; pres, 1989-90, vpres, 1990-91, Western Asn Col & Univ Bus Officers; bd dir, Nat Asn Col & Univ Bus Officers, 1988; chair, exec comt, Calif State Univ Bus Officers Asn, 1983-85; Sacramento community tv sta KVIE, 1991-97; bd trustee, Stanford Univ, 1992-97; partic rep, Educause; mem bd dir, Nat Asn State Univs & Land Grant Cols; secy & chmn, Nat Asn Col & Univ Bus Officers; Soc Col & Univ Planning. **Home Addr:** 3823 E Hiddenview Dr, Phoenix, AZ 85048-7371, **Home Phone:** (480)706-4477. **Business Addr:** Vice President, Provost, Arizona State University, PO Box 872303, Tempe, AZ 85287-2303, **Business Phone:** (480)965-3201.

### HARRISON, MYA MARIE

Dancer, singer, actor. **Personal:** Born Oct 10, 1979, Washington, DC; daughter of Sherman and Theresa. **Educ:** Univ Md, College Park. **Career:** Albums: Mya, 1998; Fear of Flying, 2000; Moodring, 2003; Liberation, 2007; Sugar & Spice, 2008; K.I.S.S. (Keep It Sexy & Simple), 2011. Singles: "Movin' On", 1998; "It's All About Me", 1998; Films: Chicago, 2002; In Too Deep, 1999; Volcano High, 2001; Chicago, 2002; Dirty Dancing: Havana Nights, 2004; Shall We Dance, 2004; Cursed, 2005; NCIS, 2005; Swap Meet, 2006; Ways of the Flesh, 2006; The Metrosexual, 2007; Cover, 2007; Love For Sale, 2008; Bottleworld, 2009; Penthouse, 2008; Dancing with the Stars, 2009; The Penthouse, 2010; The Heart Specialist, 2011; TV series: "Haunted", 2002; "1-800-Missing", 2004; "NCIS", 2005; "Video on Trial", 2006; "Bermuda Tentacles", 2014. Music Performer: Bulworth, 1998; Un paso adelante. Historia de una serie, 2001; Legally Blonde, 2001; Un paso adelante, 2002; Chicago, 2002; The Disco Ball, 2003; Barbershop 2: Back in Business, 2004; Fat Albert, 2004; Quelli che... il calcio, 2007; I Love the New Millennium, 2008; EastEnders, 2009. **Honors/Awds:** MTV Music Award, 1998 & 2001; Grammy Award, 1999 & 2002; Lady of Soul, 1999; MVPA Award, 1999; Soul Train Music Award, 1999 & 2001; Radio Music Awards, 2001; Teen Choice Awards, 2001; TMF Awards, 2001; VH1 Music Awards, 2001; ALMA Awards, 2002; ASCAP Pop Music Awards, 2002; BMI Award, 2002; Channel Thailand Music Awards, 2002; Channel Thailand Music Awards, 2002; Billboard Video Awards, 2003; Broadcast Film Critics Association Award, 2003; Phoenix Film Critics Society Award, 2003; Screen Actors Guild Award, 2003; OFTA Film Award, Online Film & Tv Asn, 2003; MTV Movie Award, 2005; Cross Over Award, 2006. **Special Achievements:** Best Video, "Lady Marmalade"; Nominee of Best Frightened Performance for cursed, 2005. **Business Addr:** Vocalist, c/o Interscope Records Inc, 10900 Wilshire Blvd, Los Angeles, CA 90024, **Business Phone:** (310)208-6547.

### HARRISON, NANCY GANNAWAY (NANCY C GANNAWAY)

Dentist. **Personal:** Born Oct 20, 1929, Trinity, NC; married Robert; children: Renee & Susan. **Educ:** Shaw Univ, BS, 1950; Howard Univ, DDS, 1954. **Career:** St Elizabeth Hosp, Wash, DC, intern, 1955; pvt pract dentist, currently. **Orgs:** Acad Gen Dent; treas, Twin City Dent Soc, 1969, 1971; Old N State Dent Soc; NC Dent & Soc; Am Dent Asn Urbn League Guild; Delta Sigma Theta Sorority; secy, Altrusa Ind; vpres & bd dir, Young Women's Christian Asn, 1973-75. **Special Achievements:** First African American dentist in Winston-Salem. **Home Phone:** (336)761-1689. **Business Addr:** Dentist, Private Practice, 3405 New Walkertown Rd, Winston Salem, NC 27105, **Business Phone:** (336)725-7721.

### HARRISON, PAUL CARTER

Educator, writer, television producer. **Personal:** Born Mar 1, 1936, New York, NY; son of Paul and Thelma Carter; married Wanda Malone; children: Fonteyn; married Ria Vroemen. **Educ:** Ind Univ, BA, psychol, 1957; New Sch Soc Res, MA, psychol & phenomenol, 1962. **Career:** Educator, Television Producer (retired), emeritus; NSF fel, 1959-60; Howard Univ, asst prof theatre arts, 1968-70; Kent State Univ, assoc prof afro-am lit, 1969; Calif State Univ, prof theatre arts, 1970-72; Univ Massachusetts, Amherst, prof theatre arts & afro-am studies, 1972-76, prof emer, currently; Choice Mag, cult consult, 1973-83; Elan Mag, contrib edtheatre, 1981-83; Rockefeller Found, fel, 1985; Callaloo Mag, contrib & adv ed, 1985-88; Evergreen Col, curric & cult diversity consult, 1986; Columbia Col, Theatre & Music Dept, artistic producer & chmn, 1976-80, writer-in-residence, 1980-2002, prof emer, 2003-; NEA Playwrights fel, 1995; Director plays: "Junebug Graduates Tonight", 1969; "Lady Day: A Musical Tragedy", 1972; "My Sister, My Sister", 1981; "The River Niger", 1987; "Pavane for a Deadpan Minstrel" & "Tophat"; "The Post Clerks" & "The Experimental Leader"; producer, play: Black Recollections, 1972; conceptualized, directed: "Ain't Supposed to Die a Natural Death", 1970; dir: "In an Upstate Motel", 1981; playwright: "Tabernacle", 1981; "Anchorman", 1988; "The Death of Boogie Woogie", 1980; "Goree Crossing", 1992; developer & producer, television film: playwright, "Leave Em Laughin", CBS-TV, 1981, Stranger On The Square; playwright: "The Experimental Leader", 1965; "The Great Mac Daddy", 1974; author: The Drama of Nommo, Grove Press, NY, 1972; Kuntu Drama: Plays From the African Continuum, 1974; In the Shawdow of the Great White Way, Thunder Mouth Press, 1989; Charles Stewart's Jazz File,

1985; screenwriter: Lord Shango, 1974; Young blood, 1978; Getting' to Know Me, 1980; editor: Kuntu Drama, anthology, Grove Press, NY, 1974; dir, "Food for the GODS", 1994; editor: Totem Voices, Anthology, Grove Press; co-editor: Classic Plays from the Negro Ensemble Co, Univ Pittsburgh Press, 1995; Black Theatre: Ritual Performance in the African Diaspora, Temple Univ Press, 2002; dir: "Trial of One-Short Sighted Black Woman vs Safreeta Mae & Mammy Louise", 1996-2001; CA premiere, "Waiting to Be Invited"; dir, Sty of the Blind Pig, 2002, 2003, 2004; editor: "African American Review Special Issue on Black Theatre", winter, 1997. **Orgs:** Atre panel, Ill Arts Coun, 1976-79; panel, NEA Playwrights, 1992; Meet Composer, Readers Digest Comn, 1992, 1995; exec comm, Nat Black atre Summit Golden Pond, 1998; bd govs, African Grove Inst Arts, 1998. **Business Addr:** Professor Emeritus, University of Massachusetts, 37 Mather Dr, Amherst, MA 01003, **Business Phone:** (413)545-0222.

## HARRISON, PEARL LEWIS

Association executive. **Personal:** Born Jun 8, 1932, East Orange, NJ; married John Arnold; children: Lauren Deborah & Adrianne Carol. **Educ:** Juilliard Sch Music NY, cert, 1952. **Career:** Association executive (retired); Pearl Lewis Harrison Piano Studio, dir, 1953-83; Gov's Task Force Suburban Essex Arts Coun, mem, 1978; City E Orange, coord arts/cult, 1979-80, actg dir pub rels, 1986, Dept Arts & Cult Affairs, dir, 1986-90. **Orgs:** NJ Music Educ Coun, 1960-77; Suburban Essex Arts Coun, 1978-82; Friends NJ Opera, 1982-; Resolution Cult Expertise Essex Co Bd, 1983; Essex Co Arts & Cult Planning Bd, 1983-86; bd trustee, United Way Essex & Hudson Co, 1985-86; Black Composers, 1985-; NJ Motion Picture Comn, 1986-; exec dir, E Orange Arts & Cult, 1986-88; E Orange Libr Bd, 1986-90; Hist Soc E Orange, 1999; Pearl Lewis Harrison Fine Arts Scholar Fund, 1994. **Honors/Awds:** White House Citation, Mrs Nancy Reagan music/comn spirit, 1983; Women of the Year Award, Pride & Heritage Int Year Environ Concerns, 1983; State New Jersey Excellence Award, NJ State Sen, 1983; Certificate of Appreciation, Comn Serv, City E Orange, 1983; Annual Black Heritage Pioneer Family Awards, City E Orange, 1986; United Nations Citation, 1989. **Home Addr:** 287 Beachwood Terr, Orange, NJ 07050-3012, **Home Phone:** (973)675-2812.

## HARRISON, ROBERT

Football coach, scout. **Personal:** Born Sep 9, 1941, Cleveland, OH; married Anna Marie Bradley; children: Lorraine Ellen & Barbara Annette; married Faye. **Educ:** Kent State Univ, BS, 1964, MEd, 1969. **Career:** Coach; John Adams High Sch, Cleveland, asst head football coach, 1964-66, head football coach, 1967-68; Kent State Univ, assoc admis dir, asst football coach, 1969-70; Univ Ia, asst football coach, 1971-73; NC State Univ, asst coach, 1975-76; Univ Tenn, asst coach, 1977-82; Univ Ga, coach, 1988-91; Atlanta Falcons Prof Football Team, asst coach, receivers coach, 1983-86, col scout, 1994-; Pittsburgh Steelers, asst coach, 1992-93; Boston Col, receivers coach, 1994-96. **Orgs:** Offensive coord, Cornell Univ Ithaca, 1974; Nat Asn Advan Colored People, 1982-. **Honors/Awds:** Fritz Pollard Alliance Awards; Scout of the Year Award, Nat Football Conf. **Home Addr:** , Atlanta, GA. **Business Addr:** College Scout, Atlanta Falcons, 4400 Falcon Pkwy, Flowery Branch, GA 30542, **Business Phone:** (770)965-3115.

## HARRISON, DR. ROBERT WALKER, III

Educator, administrator. **Personal:** Born Oct 13, 1941, Natchez, MS; son of Robert and Charlotte; married Gayle Johnson; children: Robert & Seth. **Educ:** Tougaloo SC Col, BS, 1961; Northwestern Univ, MD, 1966. **Career:** Vanderbilt Univ Sch Med, instr, 1972-74, from asst prof to assoc prof, 1974-85; Univ Ark Med Sci, prof, 1985-93; Univ Rochester Med Sch, prof emer, 1993; consult, NIH; Knoll Pharmaceut, consult; Abbott & Roche, consult; Beeslender.com Inc, pres & chief exec officer, currently. **Orgs:** Endocrine Soc; Alpha Phi Alpha. **Business Addr:** President, Chief Executive Officer, beeSlender.com Inc, 91 Berkeley St Suite 3, Rochester, NY 14607, **Business Phone:** (585)271-6878.

## HARRISON, DR. RODERICK J.

Executive, executive director. **Educ:** Harvard Univ, AB, 1971; Princeton Univ, MA, sociol, 1975, PhD, sociol, 1978. **Career:** Univ Calif, La, Afro-Am Studies & Sociol Dept, fac, asst prof, 1976-84; Howard Univ, Dept Sociol & Anthrop, fac, asst prof, 1984-90, sr res scientist, 1998-2012; US Census Bur, Racial Statist Br, chief, 1990-97; Joint Ctr Polit & Econ Studies, Off Res, dir, sr res fel, 1998-2008; DataBank, founding dir; 2M Res Serv LLC, vpres social sci res, 2012-. **Orgs:** Am Statist Soc Asn. **Business Addr:** Director, Senior Research Fellow, Joint Center Political & Economic Studies, 1090 Vt Ave Suite 1100, Washington, DC 20005-4961, **Business Phone:** (202)789-3514.

## HARRISON, RODNEY SCOTT

Football player. **Personal:** Born Dec 15, 1972, Markham, IL; son of Barbara; married Erika; children: Christian, Rodney Jr & Mikala. **Educ:** Western Ill Univ, gen studies. **Career:** Football player (retired), analyst; San Diego Chargers, defensive back & strong safety, 1994-2002; New Eng Patriots, safety & free safety & strong safety, 2003-08; NBC Sports' Football Night Am, analyst, 2009. **Honors/Awds:** San Diego Chargers, Defensive Player of the Year, 1996 & 1997; Chargers Co-Defensive Player of the Year, 1996, 1997, 2000 & 2001; Pro Bowler Twice, 1998, 2001; First-team All-Pro Twice, 1998, 2003; Peter King's Defensive Player of the Year, Associated press, 2003; Ed Block Courage Award, 2006; Super Bowl champion, XXXVIII, XXXIX. **Special Achievements:** Became first player in NFL history to score touchdowns on an interception return, fumble return and kickoff return in same season. TV series: Quite Frankly with Stephen A. Smith, 2005; Who Made You?, 2008; Rome Is Burning, 2009; Mike & Mike, 2011. **Business Addr:** Safety, New England Patriots, Gillette Stadium 1 Patriot Pl, Foxboro, MA 02035, **Business Phone:** (508)543-8200.

## HARRISON, RONALD E. (RON HARRISON)

Executive, vice president (organization). **Personal:** Born Jan 11, 1936, New York, NY; son of Olive DeVaux and Edmund; married Sharon Irving; children: Richard, David & Katherine. **Educ:** City Col NY, BBA, 1958; Boston Col, corp community rels prog, 1987. **Career:** Area Manager, vice president (retired), director; Pepsi Cola Metro Bottling Co NY, vpres, area mgr; Pepsi-Cola Inc, Cincinnati dir spec mkts, 1966, control div Chicago dir training, 1969, mgmt instr Phoenix dir training, 1970, franchise develop NY dir, 1972; Pepsi Bottling Co, area vpres, 1974-78; Pepsi-Cola Co, div vpres, 1979-81; Pepsi-Cola Inc, nat sales dir, 1981-86; PepsiCo syst, vpres, 1986-99; PepsiCo, sr vpres, community affairs & spec asst to chmn, 2000-03; Harrison & Assocs LLC, chief exec officer & managing dir, 2004-; RE/MAX LLC, dir, 2013-. **Orgs:** Nat Asn Mktg Develop; Sales Exec Club NY; bd trustee NY Orphan Asylum Soc; Educ Spl Sch Dist Greenburgh; chair, Bus Policy Rev Coun; bd mem, Westchester Coalition; bd mem, NY State Job Training Partnership Coun; Am Mkt Asn; Exec Leadership Coun; Nat Hisp Corp Coun; Westchester Clubmen; chair, Int Franchise Asn; chair, Int Franchise Asn Ed Found; Int Franchise Asn Minorities Franchising Comn; chair, Bus Consortium Fund; adv bd, Cong Black Caucus; founding chmn, Int Franchise Asn, 1999-. **Home Addr:** 6401 Lake Meadow Dr, Burke, VA 22015, **Home Phone:** (703)250-9527. **Business Addr:** Director, RE/MAX LLC, 5075 S Syracuse St, Denver, CO 80237, **Business Phone:** (303)770-5531.

## HARRISON, ROSCOE CONKLIN, JR.

Publicist. **Personal:** Born Sep 20, 1944, Belton, TX; son of Roscoe Conklin Sr and Georgia Dell Moore; married Sandra K Smitha; children: Corinne Michelle. **Educ:** Temple Jr Col, AA, 1964; Prairie View A&M Univ, BA, 1966; Univ Mary Hardin Baylor, 1967. **Career:** KTEM Radio, announcer, 1960-64; Temple Daily Telegram, reporter, 1966-67; San Antonio Express News, reporter, 1967-68; Jet Mag, assoc ed, 1968-69; KCEN-TV, news bur chief & reporter, 1970-76; Tex Atty Gen John Hill, dep press secy, media liaison & speechwriter, 1976-79; KCEN-TV, pub affairs dir, 1979-93; Scott & White Mem Hosp, assoc dir spec proj; Scott & White Mem Hosp, dir community affairs, 1993-. **Orgs:** Nat Asn Health Servs Execs, 1994-; Am Soc Health Care Mkt & Pub Rels, 1994-; bd mem, Tem Bel Heart Asn, 1994-; Temple Chamber Com, 1994-; pres, Ebony Cult Soc; Legis Adv Comn TX Asn Pub & Nonprofit Hosp; Communities Sch bd; Baylor Univ Col Arts & Sci, adv coun; bd, Belton Christian Youth Ctr; bd, Temple Bus Growing Ctr; TX A&M Univ, Race & Ethnic Studies Nat Corp Adv Bd; Bell County Judge Comnr Ct COM People Disabilities. **Honors/Awds:** Texas Asn Broadcasters, Central Texas Community Service Award; First African-American radio announcer for Temple radio station KTEM; Distinguished Local Programming, 1977; Communicator of the Year, Bell County Communs Prof, 1988; Jefferson Awards Media Award, Outstanding Public Service, 1990; Broadcaster of the Year, Texas Farmers Union, 1993. **Special Achievements:** First black to serve in the upper level of hospital administrative staff. **Home Addr:** 3806 Wendy Oaks Dr, Temple, TX 76502, **Home Phone:** (254)773-0173. **Business Addr:** Director of Community Affairs, Scott & White Memorial Hospital, 2401 S 31st St, Temple, TX 76508, **Business Phone:** (254)724-1929.

## HARRISON, SARAH S.

Vice president (organization), consultant. **Educ:** Southern Univ, Baton Rouge, LA, BS, chem; Univ Houston, Houston, TX, MBA. **Career:** Zeneca Agr Prod, chemist, 1977, prod mgr, 1993-95, mkt strategy & contract opers dir, 1995-98; AstraZeneca Pharmaceut Inc, vpres, healthcare exec, customer strategy integration & exec consult. **Orgs:** Nat Asn Female execs; Healthcare Businesswomen's Asn; Delta Sigma Theta Nat Sorority; Nat Polit Cong Black Women; Nat Coalition 100 Black Women; Int Women's Forum; bd dir, Nat Sales Network Girls Inc; bd dir, Young Women Christian Asn Del; Xavier Col Pharm; Wilmington Women Bus. **Business Addr:** Vice President, AstraZeneca Pharmaceuticals LP, 1800 Concord Pke, Wilmington, DE 19850-5437, **Business Phone:** (302)886-3000.

## HARRISON, SHIRLEY DINDY

Executive, vice president (organization). **Personal:** Born Apr 11, 1951, Syracuse, NY; daughter of Homer Leonard and Eve Uchal. **Educ:** Syracuse Univ, NY, BFA, 1973. **Career:** Artifacts Syst Ltd, Manchester, NH, graphic artist, 1973-74; PEACE Inc, Syracuse, NY, dir, community devel, 1974-77; Miller Brewing Co, Milwaukee, Wis, dir, training & compliance, employee rels & compl, corp mgr, affirmative action & recruitment dept, 1977-92; Philip Morris Co Inc, dir diversity mgt & devel, 1992-96, diversity mgt & devel, vpres, 1997-; Altria Group Inc, vpres. **Orgs:** Bd mem, LEAD National. **Business Addr:** Vice President of Diversity Management, Philip Morris USA Inc, 6604 W Broad St, Richmond, VA 23230-1702, **Business Phone:** (804)274-2000.

## HARRISON, WENDELL RICHARD

Musician. **Personal:** Born Oct 1, 1942, Detroit, MI; son of Walter R and Ossalee Lockett; married Pamela Wise. **Educ:** Highland Pk Community Col; Detroit Inst Arts Conserv Music; Wayne County Community Col, AA, 2012; Spring Arbor Univ, BS, sci & orgn mgt, 2013. **Career:** Musician, clarinetist, saxophonist & composer; Hank Crawford's band, mem; Rebirth Inc, artistic dir, 1978-; Nat Endowment Arts, fel grant, 1978, 1992; Albums: An Eve with Devil, 1972; Message from Tribe: An Anthology Tribe Rec 1973, 2004; Dreams a Love Supreme, 1979; Org Dream, 1981; Birth a Fossil, 1985; Reawakening, 1985; Wait Broke Wagon Down, 1987; Carnivorous Lady, 1988; Fly By Night, 1990; Forever Duke, 1991; Be Boppers Method Bk, 1991; Live Concert, 1992; Something Pops, 1993; Rush & Hustle, 1994; Battle Tenors, 1998; Eighth House, 2002; Riding With Pluto; Urban Expressions, 2004; It's About Damn Time, 2011. **Orgs:** Detroit Fedn Musicians Union, 1970; Nat Jazz Serv Orgn, 1991-93; Chamber Music Am, 2002-. **Honors/Awds:** Distinguished Service Award, Wayne County, 1985; Creative Artist Grant, Arts Found Mich, 1992-97; Proclamation, Congressman John Conyers, 1992; Jazz Masters Award, Arts Midwest, 1993; Proclamation, Barbara Rose Collins; Distinguished Artist Award, Detroit City Coun; Jazz Master Award, Detroit City Coun; Creative Artists Grand Award, 2000; Chamber Music America Doris Duke Creative New Works, 2003; Chamber Music Am Residency, 2005; Art Serve Mich Comn Award; Am Comn Award, Chamber Music; Am Residency Award, Chamber Music; African American Music Festival Award; Commission Award, Art Serve Mich; National Endowment Composer Award. **Business Addr:** Musician, Rebirth Inc, 81 Chandler St, Detroit, MI 48202, **Business Phone:** (313)875-0289.

## HARRISON-HALE, DR. ALGEA OTHELLA

Educator. **Personal:** Born Feb 14, 1936, Winona, WV; children: Denise & Don Jr. **Educ:** Bluefield State Col, BS, Ed, 1956; Univ Mich, MA, Ed, 1959, PhD, psychol, Ed, 1970. **Career:** Detroit Pub Sch Syst, teacher; Inkster Sch Syst, res design, Urban Action Needs Anal, Wayne County Head start Prog, MI, Dept Educ, consult, 1962-66; Highland Pk Sch Syst, sch diagnostician, 1968-69; Oakland Univ, Dept Psychol, prof. **Orgs:** Am Psychol Asn; Mich Psychol Asn; Asn Black Psychol; Soc Res Child Develop; Asn Soc & Behav Sci; bd trustees, New Detroit Inc, Roeper City & City Schs; Founders Soc; Your Heritage House A Black Mus; Nat Org Women; Child Care Coordr Coun. **Honors/Awds:** US Public Health Grants, 1965-68; Fel Horace Rackham Predoctoral, 1969-70; Graduated second highest member class. **Special Achievements:** Editor: Our Children Too: A History of the First 25 years of the Black Caucus of the Society for Research in Child Development, 1973-1997. **Home Addr:** 30273 Rosemond Dr, Franklin, MI 48025-1477, **Home Phone:** (248)851-0816.

## HARRISON-JONES, LOIS

School administrator. **Educ:** Va State Univ, BS; Temple Univ, MA; Va Tech Univ, CAGS, EdD. **Career:** Dallas Pub Schs, assoc supt, 1991; Boston Pub Sch, supt, 1991; Howard Univ, Dept Educ Admin Policy, assoc clin prof, 2000-, interim chair, currently. **Orgs:** Pres, Nat Alliance Black Sch Educrs; dir, Lightspan Inc, 2003-; Unit Adv Bd; Nat Coun Accreditation Teacher Educ. **Business Addr:** Associate Professor, Interim Chair, Howard University, 2441 4th St NW, Washington, DC 20059, **Business Phone:** (202)806-7060.

## HARRISON-SULLIVAN, JEANETTE LAVERNE

Television journalist, executive. **Personal:** Born Dec 4, 1948, Kyoto; married James Michael; children: Katherine & James Brady. **Educ:** Colo State Univ, BA, fr, 1968; Univ Calif, Berkeley, MA, jour, 1973; Babson Col, cert. **Career:** KPIX-TV, San Francisco, Calif, TV news agt, 1973-74; KTVU-TV, Oakland Calif, ed, 1973-74; KQED-TV, San Francisco, Calif, reporter, 1974-75; KGW-TV, Portland, Ore, TV news reporter, 1975-78; WTCN-TV, Minneapolis, Minn, TV news reporter, 1978-; KARE-TV, TV news reporter, 1975-78; Bechtel Parsons/Brickerhoff, media rels dir, 1988-92; Boston Cent Artery/Tunnel Proj, media rels mgr, 1988-92; FleetBoston, Corp Commun, vpres, 1992-98; PNC Financial Serv Group, vpres, media rels mgr, 1998-2007, PFPC Inc, Corp Commun, vpres & managing dir; Eaton Vance Corp, vpres & mgr pub rels, 2007-09; Natixis Global Asset Mgt, vpres Pub Rels, 2009-14. **Orgs:** Ltd Thirty Black Prof Womens Orgn; Nat Hon Phi Sigma Iota, 1970-. **Special Achievements:** Community service at Veteran of foriegn wars, Waite Park, 1984; community service at Gannet Corporation, MN, 1984; wrote & produced 5 TV Series. **Home Addr:** 764 Dayton Ave, Saint Paul, MN 55104.

## HARROLD, REV. AUSTIN LEROY

Government official, clergy, bishop. **Personal:** Born Jan 28, 1942, Omaha, NE; son of Walter W and Madeline Brown; married Gussie; children: Sabrina Butler, Austin Jr & Sophia. **Educ:** Lane Col, TN, BA, sociol, 1964; Interden Theol Ctr & Phillips Sch Theol, Atlanta, MDiv, 1968. **Career:** Mayor Jersey City, exec secy, 1981-85; Interdenominational Christian Community Church, pastor & founder, 1985; US Dept Com, Bur Census, community awareness specialist, 1986-88; Jersey City, Water Dept, dir, 1989-; Barr's Chapel CME Church, Paris, TN, first appointment; St Mary CME Church, pastor; W Mitchell CME Church, Atlanta, asst pastor; Ln Chapel CME Church, pastor; Turner Chapel CME Church, Mt Clemens, pastor; Calvary CME Church, Jersey City, pastor; Phillips Memorial CME Church, pastor; Russell CME Church, pastor; Mt Clemens High Sch, teacher; Detroit Dist CME Church Leadership Trng Sch, dean; Jersey City's King Solomon Lodge, bishop, currently. **Orgs:** Secy, Mich Nat Black Conv, 1972; bd mem, Oper PUSH, 1975-; exec dir, Concerned Clergy Jersey City, 1980-; Dem Nomination Kans House Reps 45th Dist; vpres, Jersey City Br Nat Asn Advan Colored People; secy, Interdenominational Ministerial All Jersey City Br Nat Asn Advan Colored People; secy, Interdenominational Ministerial All Jersey City & Vicinity; chaplin, Topeka Jaycees; co-chmn, Employ Task Force Coord Comn Black Comt; secy, Interdenominational Ministerial Alliance Topeka Vicinity; cent mgr, NE Macomb Act Ctr; bd dir, Macomb County Child Guid Clin; Mt Clemens Ministerial Asn; pres, Macomb County Chap Nat Asn Advan Colored People; pres, Christ Clemens Elem Sch PTA; WM Excelsior Lodge; vpres, Macomb County Community Human Rels Asn; bd pension, Mich-Ill Ann Conf, Third Epopal Dist CME Church; Mich Dept Educ Voc Rehab Serv; coun mem, Mt Clemens Dist Off; chmn, Mt Clemens Chap, Youth Understanding; Mt Clemens City Comn; Macomb County Off Substance Abuse Adv Coun. **Honors/Awds:** Cert of Merit, Third Episcopals Dist, Christ Methodist Episcopal Church, 1960-62; Effective Christ Leadership, 1960-64; Outstanding Young Men of Am, Bd Educ, 1970, 1976; Dept Sociol Award, Dept Relig & Philos. **Special Achievements:** Selected to spend summer 1963 in Sierra Leone W Africa in Operation Crossroads Africa Project, 1963. **Home Addr:** 28 Lexington Ave, Jersey City, NJ 07304-1602, **Home Phone:** (201)432-3622. **Business Addr:** Bishop, King Solomon Lodge, Jersey City, NJ 07304.

## HARROLD, LAWRENCE A.

Teacher, manager. **Personal:** Born Apr 4, 1952, Belle Glade, FL; married Phyllis Lea; children: Lawrence Jr, Lamont & James. **Educ:** Hillsborough Community Col, AA, lib arts, 1974; San Francisco State Univ, BA, 1977, bus mgt, MBA, bus admin, 1979. **Career:** Pac Tel, mkt off supvr, 1979-81; Westvaco Corp, prod mgr, 1981-2005; Ritemade Paper Converters Inc, plant mgr/gen mgr, 1997-2004; Antioch Sch Dist, phys educ teacher, 2004-07; Alan Ritchey Inc, opers mgr, 2007-10; Ritchey Inc, opers mgr, 2007-10. **Orgs:** Black MBA. **Home Addr:** 2150 Glen Canyon Dr, Pittsburg, CA 94565-6456, **Home Phone:** (925)432-1710. **Business Addr:** Operations Manager, Alan Ritchey Inc, 40 S I 35, Valley View, TX 76272, **Business Phone:** (940)726-3276.

## HARRY, JACKEE

Actor. **Personal:** Born Aug 14, 1956, Winston-Salem, NC; daughter of Warren Perry and Flossie Perry; married Elgin Charles Williams; children: Frank. **Educ:** Long Island Univ, Brooklyn Ctr, BA, educ. **Career:** Actress, currently; Brooklyn Tech High Sch, hist teacher. TV series: "Another World", 1983-85; "227", 1985-89; "The Royal Family", 1991; "Sister, Sister", 1994-99; "Twice in a Lifetime", 2000; "7th Heaven", 2003; "The Nick at Nite Holiday Special", 2003; "To Tell the Truth", 2000; "One on One", 2005; "That's So Raven", 2005; "Everybody Hates Drew", 2006; "The Last Day of Summer", 2007; "Knight to D7", 2010; "Friends & Lovers", 2010; "Christmas Cupid", 2010; "The Ideal Husband", 2011; "Let's Stay Together", 2011; "Nurse Jackee", 2011; "Brother White", 2012; "The First Family", 2012; "Celebrity Ghost Stories", 2012; "The Coalition", 2013; "Glee", 2014; "Girl Meets World", 2014. Broadway productions: A Broadway Musical, 1978; Eubie!; The Wiz; One More Time; For Colored Girls Who Have Considered Suicide When the Rainbow is Enuf, 2000; Lady Day at the Emerson Bar & Grill, 2001; The Boys from Syracuse, 2002; A Christmas Carol, 2004; Too Good To Let Go, 2005; Man Of Her Dreams, 2006; Damn Yankees, 2007, U Got Me Bent And Twisted, 2007, The Sunshine Boys, 2008; JD Lawrence's The Clean Up Woman, 2008; Hairspray, 2009; Nurse Jackee, 2011. Films: The Women of Brewster Place, 1989; Ladybugs, 1992; The Reluctant Agent, 1996; The Nick at Nite Holiday Special, 2003; You Got Served, 2004; One on One, 2005; All You've Got, 2006; The Man of Her Dreams, 2009; GED, 2009; Movie; Nurse Jackee, 2011; Knock 'em Dead, 2014; Producer: Ronnie: Cary Grant's Younger Brother, 2016. **Honors/Awds:** Primetime Emmy Award, 1987; Image Award, 1999-2000; Emmy Award, 2004. **Special Achievements:** Golden Globe Nominee for Best Performance by an Actress, Supporting Role Series, Mini Series Motion Picture Made for TV, 1989; First African American actress to win an Emmy award for Outstanding Supporting Actress in a Comedy Series, 2004. **Home Addr:** 1022 S Crescent Heights Blvd, Los Angeles, CA 90035, **Home Phone:** (213)934-4899. **Business Addr:** Actress, PO Box 69248, Los Angeles, CA 90069-0248.

### HARSHAW, KARLA GARRETT

Newspaper editor. **Personal:** Born Jan 23, 1955, Cleveland, OH; daughter of Morgan Garrett and Bertha C Johnson Garrett; married Timothy C; children: Jason D Milton, Vincent V & Alexander M. **Educ:** Wright State Univ, Dayton, OH, BS, sec educ, 1984; Recipient Master Leadership Develop, 2013; Ctr Philanthropy Ind Univ Fund Raising Sch, cert fundraising mgt, 2010. **Career:** Dayton Daily News, Dayton, OH, var positions, 1971-90; Springfield News-Sun, Springfield, OH, ed, 1990-; Cox Ohio Media - Springfield News-Sun, ed & sr ed, 1990-2006, vpres community develop, 2006-10; Cox Career Enhancement Sem, consult. **Orgs:** Chair, Am soc Newspaper Eds Educ Jour Comt; Maynard Inst Jour Educ; Ohio State Univ, Sch Jour Adv Coun; founder, Dayton Asn Black Journalists, 1984; Nat Asn Black Journalists; Nat Asn Minority Media execs; Ohio Newspaper Womens Asn; keynote speaker, Inland Press Asn Conv, 1994; Pulitzer Prize Nominating Juries Jour, 1995-96; John S & James L Knight Found Newspaper Residence Prog, 1997; vchair, Am soc Newspaper Eds, pres, 1998-99, 2004-05; vpres, regional dir develop, Advocates Basic Legal Equality & Legal Aid Western Ohio, Rotary Greater Dayton Wright-Dunbar Inc, 2010-; Asn Fundraising Professionals Greater Dayton Region; Develop Chmn Pres Am Soc Newspaper Ed Healthy People Outcome Team - Montgomery County Mound St Academies Bd Clark County Hist Soc Bd. **Honors/Awds:** Media Award, Montgomery County Ment Health Asn, 1980; Community Service Award, Miami Valley Health Systs, 1982; Honor Religon Writing, Ohio Newspaper Womens Asn, 1981-82; Daytons Up & Comers Award, Price Waterhouse & the Muse Mach, 1989; Springfield Urban Leagues Equal Opportunity Day Award, Career Achievement, 1990; Second Place Award, Ohio Asniated Press, Column Writing, 1995; Third-Place Award, Ohio Asniated Press, Editorial Writing, 1997; Hall of Fame, Nat Asn Black Journalists Region VI, 1997; Best of Cox. **Home Addr:** 582 E Eva Circle, Springfield, OH 45504-3769, **Home Phone:** (937)322-7645. **Business Addr:** Regional Director Development, Wright Dunbar Inc, 1105 W Third St, Dayton, OH 45402, **Business Phone:** (937)443-0249.

### HART, BRENDA G.

Educator. **Personal:** Born Jul 8, 1949, Williamstown, MA; daughter of Thomas A and Adalyne Monroe; children: Patrick & Katheryn. **Educ:** Boston Univ, BA, fr lang & lit, 1970; Univ Louisville, MEd, stud personnel serv-col coun, 1972. **Career:** Community Action Comm, manpower coord, 1973; Univ Louisville, Coop Educ Off, asst dir, 1973-77; Univ Louisville, Gen Eng, asst dir, 1977-81, dir, 1981-94, dir, Minority & Women Engineering Progs, 1994-2001, dir, Stud Affairs, 2001-14. **Orgs:** Ky Asn Blacks Higher Educ; Nat Acad Advising Asn; Nat Asn Minority Engineering Prog Adminr; African Am Alumni Asn, Univ Louisville, 2003-13; bd dir, Univ Louisville Athletic Bd, 2003-14; Women Engineering Progs & Advocates Network, Lincoln Found, Bd trustee, 2010-. **Home Addr:** 3616 Breeland Ave, Louisville, KY 40241-2604, **Home Phone:** (502)429-6172. **Business Addr:** professor emerita, Professor of Engineering Fundamentals, University of Louisville, KY.

### HART, DR. CHRISTOPHER ALVIN

Government official, lawyer. **Personal:** Born Jun 18, 1947, Denver, CO; son of Judson D (deceased) and Margaret Murlee Shaw; married LeeAnn Moore; children: Adam Christopher & Brooke Corinne. **Educ:** Princeton Univ, BSE, 1969, MSE, aerospace engineering, 1971; Harvard Law Sch, JD, 1973. **Career:** Peabody Rivlin & Lambert, assoc, 1973-76; Air Transp Assn, atty, 1976-77; US Dept Transp, dep asst gen coun, 1977-79; Dickstein, Shapiro & Morin, assoc, 1979-81; Hart & Chavers, managing partner, 1981-90; Nat Transp Safety Bd, mem, 1990-93; Nat Hwy Traffic Safety Admin, dep adminr, 1993-95; Fed Aviation Admin, asst adminr syst safety, 1995, dep dir, currently; Nat Transp Safety Bd, mem, pres, vchmn, 2011-, chmn, 2015-. **Orgs:** Fed Wash Bar Asns, 1973-; Aircraft Owners & Pilots Asn, 1973-; Princeton Eng Adv & Resource Coun, 1975-90; Lawyer Pilots Bar Asn, 1975-; dir, pres, Beckman Pl Condo Asn, 1979-83; Fed Communs Bar Asn, 1981-; dir, WPFW-FM, 1983-88; Nat Transp Safety Bd, 1990-93; DC Bar. **Home Addr:** 1612 Crittanden St NW, Washington, DC 20011-4218, **Home Phone:** (202)882-5393. **Business Addr:** Deputy Director, Federal Aviation Administration, 800 Independence Ave SW Rm 1040A, Washington, DC 20591, **Business Phone:** (866)835-5322.

### HART, DR. CLYDE JAMES, JR.

Association executive, administrator, vice president (organization). **Personal:** Born Nov 29, 1946, Jersey City, NJ; son of Clyde J Sr and Audrey E; married Lauralee. **Educ:** St Peters Univ, BS, polit sci & hist, 1972; Catholic Univ Am, JD, law, 1975; George Washington Univ, MPP, pub policy, 1986; Marymount Univ, MA, lit & lang, 2010. **Career:** US Dist Ct, Hon Aubrey E Robinson Jr, law clerk, 1975-77; Akin Gump Strauss Hauer & Feld LLP, atty, 1977-80; Interstate Com Comn, atty, 1980-94; US Senate Com Comt, sr coun, 1994-98; US Dept Transp, Maritime Admin, admin, 1998-2001; Fed Motor Carrier Safety Admin, adminr, 2000-01; Am Bus Asn, from vpres to sr vpres, govt affairs, 2001-2010, sr vpres, govt affairs & policy, 2010-15; George Washingtona Univ, adj prof, 2006-08. **Orgs:** DC Bar Asn, 1976-; WA Bar Asn, 1976-; bd mem, Oper Lifesaver, 2001-; Dc chap, U.S. Comn Civil Rights, 2010; bd regents, St Peter's Col Bd Visitors; Cath Univ Am; Columbus Sch Law Coun trustee; United Seamen's Serv; Wash Govt Rels Group. **Home Addr:** 1475 N Highview Lane, Alexandria, VA 22311.

### HART, EDWARD E., JR.

Physician, ophthalmologist. **Personal:** Born May 8, 1927; married Joycelyn Reed; children: Edward, Janet, Reed, Cynthia & Jonathan. **Educ:** Univ Toledo, BS, 1946; Meharry Med Sch, MD, 1949. **Career:** Ophthalmologist (retired); Am Col Surgeons, FACS fel, 1960; pvt pract ophthalmologist. **Orgs:** Organizer, Ithaca's civil rights actions, 1960; chmn, Cornell Comn Against Segregation, Ithaca Freedom Walk Comt; partner, Family Reading Partnership; fel Am Acad Ophthal & Otolaryngol; advisor, Black Biomed & Tech Asn. **Home Addr:** 311 E Green St, Ithaca, NY 14850-6060, **Home Phone:** (607)272-2943.

### HART, DR. JACQUELYN D.

Educator. **Personal:** Born Gainesville, FL; daughter of Edna M. **Educ:** Lane Col, Jackson, MS, BS, 1959; Ind Univ, Bloomington, IN, attended 1965; Univ Fla, Gainesville, FL, med, 1970, EdS, 1972, PhD, 1985. **Career:** Univ Fla, Equal Opportunity Affirmative Action, vice provost, 2004, asst vpres minority affairs, vice provost emer. **Orgs:** Am Asn Affirmative Action, Nominating Comt; Delta Pi Epsilon; Kappa Delta Pi; bd secy, League Women Voters; legis comt, Comm Status Women, 1983; pres, life mem, Delta Sigma Theta Inc; Am Cancer Soc Bd, 1984-; United Way Alachua Cty, 1985-; Allocation Reviewer Comt; Inst Black Cult Adv Bd, 1988; bd mem, United Nat Asn, Fla Div, 1989. **Home Addr:** 1236 SE 13th Ave, Gainesville, FL 32641-8155, **Home Phone:** (352)372-4741.

### HART, MILDRED

Librarian. **Personal:** Born Wadley, AL; daughter of Ella Mae Underwood and Owen; married Robert Lewis; children: Monica Lynne. **Educ:** Cuyahoga Community Col; Notre Dame Col, S Euclid, OH; Ursline Col, OH. **Career:** Librarian (retired); E Cleveland Pub Libr, E Cleveland, Ohio, br mgr. **Orgs:** Bd, YWCA, N Cent, E Cleveland, Ohio; Bd Coop Exten, Ohio State Univ; Bd Cuyahoga Community Col, Metro Alumni; 4-H Club adv, Coop Exten, Ohio State Univ; moderator Deacon bd, St Marks Pres by Church; E Cleveland Kiwanis Club; Bd Berea C Home & Family Serv; bd, Nebr Ohio Neighborhood Health Serv Inc; Mt Paran Church God; pres, Ohio Franklin County. **Honors/Awds:** Outstanding Service, St Mark's Presby Church; Dedicated & Loyal Service, ECleveland Pub Libr. **Home Addr:** 205 Putting Green Lane, Roswell, GA 30076.

### HART, NOEL A. See Obituaries Section.

### HART, PHYLLIS D.

State government official. **Personal:** Born Aug 8, 1942, Detroit, MI; daughter of James Davidson and Louise Boykin Ransom; married Raymond; children: Darlene Annette. **Career:** Ohio Dept Rehab & Correction, EEO contract compliance adminr, EEO regional prog adminr, currently; Ind Dept Natural Resources Div, dir, blasting specialist, currently. **Orgs:** Dem Nat Comm. **Home Addr:** 1091 Ellsworth Ave, Columbus, OH 43206-1713, **Home Phone:** (614)252-3611. **Business Addr:** Blasting Specialist, Indiana Department of Natural Resources, 14619 W State Rd 48, Jasonville, FL 47438, **Business Phone:** (812)665-2207.

### HART, RONALD O.

Government official, school administrator. **Personal:** Born Jun 9, 1942, Suffolk, VA; married Ethel D; children: Aprill Jenelle & Ryan O. **Educ:** NC Agr & Tech State Univ, BS, biol, 1964; Hampton Inst, MS, biol, 1968; Old Dom Univ, cert admin, 1976. **Career:** John F Kennedy High Sch, 1964-76; Metrop Church Fed C Union, 1966-; Ruffner Jr HS, 1976-; Suffolk City Coun, vmayor, Cypress rep; councilman; Metrop Church Fed Cu, mgr. **Orgs:** Nat Educ Asns, Norfolk, 1976-; Odd FelsLodge, 1978-; adv, Cypress Comn League, 1978-; Metrop Baptist Church; Omega Psi Phi Frat; adv, Stratford Terr Civic League. **Honors/Awds:** Outstanding Educator, Elks Lodge Suffolk, Va, 1975; Man of the Year, Omega PsiPhi Frat Suffolk, 1979; North Carolina A&T Universitys football hall of fame. **Home Addr:** 806 Seminole Dr, Suffolk, VA 23434, **Home Phone:** (757)539-4221. **Business Addr:** Vice Mayor Cypress Representative, Suffolk City County, 129 Co St, Suffolk, VA 23434-4602, **Business Phone:** (757)934-3291.

### HART, REV. TONY

Counselor, educational consultant. **Personal:** Born Jul 27, 1954, Harlem, NY; married Judy Murphy; children: Tonya. **Educ:** State Univ NY, attended 1978, New Paltz, MA, humanistic educ, 1987. **Career:** Highland Educ Occup Ctr Juv Offenders, Orange County Jail, Marist ColHEOP Prog, counr; Green Haven Correctional Facil, correction counr; Marist Col Humanities Dept, part-time col instr, adj prof; Downstate Correctional Facil, counr, 1989-; Beacon Correctional Facil. **Orgs:** NY Coalition Criminal Justice; bd mem, Coalition Peoples Rights; Nat Rainbow Coalition; Newburgh Black Hist Comt. **Honors/Awds:** Spec Acad Award, State Univ NY, 1977; Outstanding Serv Award, Pre Release Ctr, Green Haven Correctional Facil, 1986; Martin Luther King Jr Award, Newburgh Mem Comt, 1987; Black Humanitarian Award, Newburgh Free Acad, 1987; Most Deserving Black Award, Newburgh Black Hist Comt, 1989. **Home Phone:** (914)566-1317. **Business Addr:** Correction Counselor, Downstate Correctional Facility, 122 Red Schoolhouse Rd, Fishkill, NY 12524-0445, **Business Phone:** (845)831-6600.

### HART-HOLIFIELD, EMILY B.

Educator, teacher. **Personal:** Born Oct 29, 1940, St. Joseph, LA; children: Tammylynn & Lynnella. **Educ:** Southern Univ, Baton Rouge, LA, BS, speech & hearing, 1966; Pepperdine Univ, MS, sch mgt & admin, 1974; Univ Calif, Los Angeles. **Career:** NV Cos, speech therapist, 1968-69; Compton Unified Sch Dist, teacher, 1969-80, consult, 1975-78, teacher & speech therapist, 1969-75, sr bd trustee mem, currently; Orleans Parish, New Orleans, teacher, 1978. **Orgs:** Los Angeles County, Trustee Asn, 1977; adv dir, Univ Southern Calif, Acad Educ Mgt, 1978-79; vpres, 1978, pres & bd trustee, 1980, Compton Community Col; Calif Dem Party Affirmative Action, 1979-80; dir, Calif State, Long Beach, Math Engineering & Sci Achievement Bd; accrediation, W Hills Col. **Home Addr:** 515 S Barclay Ave, Compton, CA 90220. **Business Addr:** Senior Board of Trustee Member, Compton Community College, 1111 E Artesia Blvd, Compton, CA 90221, **Business Phone:** (310)900-1600.

### HART-NIBBRIG, HAROLD C.

Lawyer. **Personal:** Born Aug 16, 1938, Los Angeles, CA; married Deanna T McKenzie; children: Nand, Jaunice & Lauren. **Educ:** Univ Calif Law Sch, Los Angeles, polit sci, BA, 1961, JD, 1971. **Career:** Law Off Harold C Hart-Nib brig, atty, 1972-, A Law Corp, owner. **Orgs:** Vpres, La Black Cong, 1968; Western Ctr Law & Poverty, 1968-71; Martin Luther King fel Woodrow Wilson Fel Found, 1968; Community Educ Develop & Referral Serv, 1969-; Black Law Ctr Inc, 1971-73; State Bar Asn Calif, 1972; bd dir, Am Civil Liberties Union, 1973-79; chmn bd, Viewer Spon TV Found KVST-TV, 1973-74; bd dir, Pac Coast Regional Small Bus Develop Corp, 1983-; La Co Bar Asn; John M Langston Law Club chair, Calif Small Bus Roundtable, 1996-99, 2003-05; del, White House Conf Small Bus, 1991-95; chairperson, CSBA, 2004-06; Solomon Leadership Found, 2009. **Honors/Awds:** Order of Golden Bruin, Unic Calif, Los Angeles, 1960; Service Award, Calif Jobs Agents Asn, 1974; W Law & Justice Award, Southern Christian Leadership Conf, 1979; Image Award, Nat Asn Advan Colored People, 1980; State of California Entrepreneurial Spirit Award, Governor Arnold Schwarzenegger, 2007. **Home Addr:** 4820 Escalon Ave, Los Angeles, CA 90043, **Home Phone:** (323)295-1423. **Business Addr:** Attorney, Law Office of Harold C Hart-Nibbrig, 3255 Whilshire Blvd, Los Angeles, CA 90010-1418, **Business Phone:** (213)739-7896.

### HARTAWAY, PASTOR THOMAS N., JR.

Administrator, clergy. **Personal:** Born Mar 28, 1943, Lonoke County, AR; married Arnice Slocum; children: Katina, Carla, Keith, Thomas III & Britt. **Educ:** Henderson St Teachers Col, Ark; Inst Pol Gov Batesville Col, attended 1972; Harding Col, attended 1973. **Career:** Ch Christ, st dir christian educ; Carter Mondale Camp, st dep cam coord, 1976; Hartaway Assoc Adv & Pub Rel, pres, 1974-76; OKY Radio, gen sales mgr, 1972-74; Ch Christ, asst minister, 1968-71; AR Carrier Newspaper, pub, 1975-76; Black Cnsmr Dir, publ, 1976-77; Dixie Ch Christ, pastor, evangelist, minister emer, currently. **Orgs:** Bd mem, No Little Rock Downtown Dev Com; adv bd mem, NLR Comm Dev Agy; bd mem, Cent AR Christian Col; bd mem, consult HOPE Inc No Little Rock AR. **Honors/Awds:** Outstanding Young Men of America Award, 1976; Best Service Award, Pulaski Co Sheriff Dept; Outstanding Leadership Award, Conf CME Chs. **Home Addr:** 7401 Deer Meadow Dr, Little Rock, AR 72209, **Home Phone:** (501)565-8728. **Business Addr:** Pastor, Minister Emeritus, Dixie Church of Christ, 916 H St, North Little Rock, AR 72114-4452, **Business Phone:** (501)945-9748.

### HARTH, RAYMOND EARL

Lawyer. **Personal:** Born Feb 4, 1929, Chicago, IL; son of Daniel W and Helen M; married Fran Byrd; children: Cheryl, Raymond Jr & Douglass. **Educ:** Univ Chicago Law Sch, JD, 1952. **Career:** Pvt pract atty, currently. **Orgs:** Pres, Ill Conf Br, chmn, 1960-62, Nat Asn Advan Colored People, 1962-65; 1966-69, Handled No Civil Rghts Cases, State & Fed Cts, 1960-72. **Business Addr:** Attorney, 188 W Randolph St Suite 1903, Chicago, IL 60601, **Business Phone:** (312)368-1390.

### HARTLEY, FRANK

Football player. **Personal:** Born Dec 15, 1967, Chicago, IL. **Educ:** Ill Univ, grad, 1986. **Career:** Football player (retired); Cleveland Browns, tight end, 1994-95; Baltimore Ravens, tight end, 1996; San Diego Chargers, tight end, 1997-98.

### HARTMAN, HERMENE DEMARIS

Publisher. **Personal:** Born Sep 24, 1948, Chicago, IL; daughter of Herman D and Mildred F Bowden; married David M Wallace. **Educ:** Roosevelt Univ, BFA, 1970, MPh 1974, MA 1974; Univ Ill, MBA, 1994. **Career:** WBBM-TV-CBS, prod & asst mgr comm affairs, 1973-84; Soul publ, columnist, 1978-; Hartman Group, pres, 1978-80; City Col Chicago, assoc prof, 1980-83, dir develop & comm, 1983-88; vice chancellor external affairs, 1988-89; Hartman Publ NDIGO, Chicago, IL, pres & chief exec officer, 1989-, ed-in-chief, currently; Truman Col, assoc prof behav sci; Alliance Bus Leaders & Entrepreneurs, pres. **Orgs:** Am Acad Poets, 1979; adv comm, Arts John F Kennedy Ctr, 1979; adv bd, UnivIll, Sch Art & Design, 1979; exhib com Chicago Pub Libr Cult Ctr, 1979; exec com Nat adv coun, John F Kennedy Ctr, Wash, DC, 1980; bd dir, Boy Scouts Am; vpres, Chicago Asn Black Journalists; founder, NDIGO Found, 1995. **Honors/Awds:** Hartman has received over 300 awards in her areas of expertise; Outstanding Community Service Award, Hydiah Proj Inc, 2000; Community Spirit Award, Black Women Lawyers Asn, 2000; Media Maker honoree, History Makers, 2001; Winnie Mandela Endurance with Dignity Award, 2001; Black Women's Expo Phenomenal Woman in Communications Award, 2001; Trailblazer in Chicago Journalism Award, Chicago Asn Black Journalists; Ebony Magazine/Colgate Palmolive Outstanding Mother Award; Crain's Chicago Business Magazine Top 100 Business Leaders list; America's Top Business/Professional Women, Dollars & Sense Mag. **Home Addr:** 1919 S Prairie Ave, Chicago, IL 60616, **Home Phone:** (312)949-9918. **Business Addr:** Publisher, Chief Executive Officer, NDIGO Foundation Hartman Publishing Group,

1006 S Mich Ave suite 200, Chicago, IL 60605, **Business Phone:** (312)822-0202.

**HARTSFIELD, ARNETT L, JR.** **See Obituaries Section.**

**HARTSFIELD, HON. JUDY A.**
Judge. **Educ:** Univ Mich, grad; Univ San Diego, law degree. **Career:** Highland Pk, asst city atty, 1982-88; Third Judicial Circuit Ct, Family Div, Juv Sect, presiding judge; Mich Dept Atty Gen, staff atty, 1988-2007; Child & Family Serv Bur, bur chief, 2003-04; Wayne State Univ, guest lectr; Wayne Co Probate Ct, judge, 2004-2020. **Orgs:** Nat Col Probate Judges; Asn Black Judges; Cs Aid Soc; Cs Charter Courts Mich. **Business Addr:** Judge, Wayne County Probate Court, 2 Woodward Ave Suite 1306, Detroit, MI 48226-3437, **Business Phone:** (313)224-5708.

**HARTZOG, ERNEST E.**
School administrator, chairperson, business owner. **Personal:** Born Jan 8, 1928, York, PA; married Jeanne Leatrice Shorty; children: Daniel & Sharon; married Marilyn. **Educ:** San Diego State Univ, BA, 1955, MA, 1962; NY Univ, MA, 1964; US Int Univ, PhD, 1969. **Career:** San Diego Pub Sch, teacher, 1956-61, counr, 1961-63; San Diego Urban League, 1964-66; San Diego High Sch, vice prin, 1966-67; Lincoln High Sch San Diego, prin, 1967-69; Detroit Pub Sch, 1969-70; Philadelphia Pub Sch, rockefeller int; San Diego Pub Sch, dir neighborhood youth corps; Govt Studies Syst Philadelphia, prog mgr, 1970-72; Portland Pub Sch, asst supt comm rels staff devel, 1972-92; Portland After Sch Tennis & Educ Inc, founder & chair; NME Assoc LLC, partner, currently. **Orgs:** African Methodist Episcopal church; Nat Asn Advan Colored People; Martin Luther King Scholar Fund; chmn, Ore St; Alliance Black Sch Educr; Ore Sch Activists Asn; United Negro Col Fund; Am Asn Sch Adminr; pres, Nat Alliance Black Sch Educr, 1979-81; vpres, USTA Pac NW Sec; bd dir & chmn, A-MAN; bd dir, Portland After Sch Tennis & Educ; pres, Ore Alliance Black Sch Educr; founder, Bldg Blocks To Success, LEGO Robotics prog; Sigma Pi Phi Boule; bd dir, African Am Male Achievers Network; bd dir, Pac Northwest Sect US Tennis Asn. **Honors/Awds:** Bluey Key Nat Hon Soc. **Home Addr:** 522 SW Mawrcrest Dr, Gresham, OR 97080-6574. **Business Addr:** Partner, NME Associates LLC, 14130 N W Bordeaux Lane, Portland, OR 97201, **Business Phone:** (503)617-4815.

**HARVARD, BEVERLY BAILEY**
Police chief, secretary general. **Personal:** Born Dec 22, 1950, Macon, GA; married Jimmy; children: Christa. **Educ:** Morris Brown Col, BA, 1972; Ga State Univ, MS, 1980; FBI Nat Acad, grad, 1983. **Career:** Atlanta Police Dept, police officer, 1972-79, dep chief police, 1982-94, actg chief police, 1994; police chief; Atlanta Dept Pub Safety, affirmative action spec, 1979-80, dir pub info, 1980-82; Atlanta Harts field Int Airport, asst security dir, currently. **Orgs:** Bd trustee, Mem Leadership Altanta; secy, Comn Accreditation Law Enforcement Agencies; Police Exec Res Forums; Gov's Task Force Police Stress, Nat Org Black Law Enforcement Exec; mem exec comt, Int Asn Chief Police; Delta Sigma Theta Sor Inc, 1979-; bd dir, Ga State Univ Alumni Asn; Ga Asn Chiefs Police; bd dir, Am Red Cross. **Honors/Awds:** Outstanding Atlantan, 1983; Alumni of the Year, Morris Brown Col, 1985; Woman of the Year, 1995; YWCA Woman of the Year; SCLC Drum Major for Justice Award; Trumpet Award, 1998. **Special Achievements:** One of the 100 Most Influential Georgians; First African-American women to hold the rank of chief of police of a Atlanta city. **Home Addr:** 3541 Cumberland Rd, East Point, GA 30344. **Business Addr:** Assistant Security Director, Atlanta Hartsfield International Airport, 6000 N Terminal Pkwy Suite 435, Atlanta, GA 30320, **Business Phone:** (800)897-1910.

**HARVELL, DR. VALERIA GOMEZ**
Librarian. **Personal:** Born Jun 27, 1958, Richmond, VA. **Educ:** Va State Col, BS, 1978; Pittsburgh Theol Sem, Mdiv, 1983; Univ Pittsburgh, MLS, 1983; Temple Univ, PhD. **Career:** Burr Oaks Regional Libr Syst, chief librn, 1984-85; Newark Pub Libr, br mgr, 1985-86; Penn State Univ, head librn, 1986, assoc prof, Africana Res Ctr, fac African Am Studies, currently. **Orgs:** Am Libr Asn; Am Theol Libr Asn; Penn Libr Asn; Black Librn Caucus. **Home Addr:** 900 E Pittsburgh St, Greensburg, PA 15601, **Home Phone:** (412)836-0604. **Business Addr:** Associate Professor African American Studies, The Pennsylvania State University, 305 Sutherland, University Park, PA 16802, **Business Phone:** (215)881-7520.

**HARVEY, ANTONIO**
Basketball player, basketball coach, radio host. **Personal:** Born Jul 6, 1970, Pascagoula, MS; married Kim; children: Aryanna & Kameron. **Educ:** Southern Ill Univ, attended 1989; Connors State Col, attended 1990; Univ Ga, attended 1991; Pfeiffer Univ, NC, BA, sociol, 1993. **Career:** Basketball player (retired), basketball coach, radio analyst; Atlanta Eagles, 1993; Los Angeles Lakers, power forward, 1993-95; Vancouver Grizzlies, power forward, 1995-96; Los Angeles Clippers, power forward, 1995-96; Seattle Supersonics, power forward, 1996-97, 2001-02; Portland Trail Blazers, power forward, 1999-2001; Atlanta Hawks, power forward, 2002-03; Am Basketball Asn, Portland Reign, gen mgr & head coach, 2004; All-Stars Sports Acad, owner; Portland Trail Blazers, radio analyst, 2005-16; Travis Outlaw, 2006. **Orgs:** Founder, LIQUID Sports Found. **Business Addr:** Radio Analyst, Portland Trail Blazers, 1 Ctr Ct Suite 200, Portland, OR 97227, **Business Phone:** (503)234-9291.

**HARVEY, BRODERICK STEVEN.** **See HARVEY, STEVE.**

**HARVEY, DANA COLETTE**
Marketing executive. **Personal:** Born Jan 6, 1971, Detroit, MI; daughter of Vernice Davis Anthony; married Kenneth E Jr; children: Kenneth E III. **Educ:** Mich State Univ, BS, multi-disciplinary health studies, 1993; Wayne State Univ, MBA, mkt, 1999. **Career:** Hermanoff & Assocs, acct exec, 1996-97; Southland Ctr Rouse Co, mkt dir, 1999-2003; City Southfield Cable 15, anchor & reporter, 2001-14; Briarwood Mall, mkt dir, 2003-05; Mills Co, mkt dir, 2003-05; Hotel Assocs, vpres & new bus Mkt mgr, 2006-07; Henry Ford Health Syst, mkt specialist, 2007-09; GlobalHue, acct supvr, 2009-11; Amberworks Mkt & Media, chief exec officer & pres, 2011-; Verve360 Media, pres, 2011-; Detroit Media Partnership, consumer mkt/audience develop dir, 2012-14; Pub Lighting Authority, sr vpres govt & community affairs, 2014-15; MGM Grand Casino Detroit, mkt mgr; Lipstick Lounge TV, producer & host. **Orgs:** Media comt mem, Sojourner Truth Found, 2003-; commun comt mem, Big Bros Big Sisters Metro Detroit, 2007-; event comt mem, Southfield Women's Found, 2008-; mkt comt, Mosaic Youth Theater, 2010; Am Cancer Soc, 2010-; mkt comt, Mosaic Youth Theater, 2010; trustee, Rosa Parks Scholar Found, 2013; bd mem, Mich Bus & Prof Asn, 2013; bd mem, Girl Scouts Southeastern Mich, 2014; Nat Black MBA Asn; AKA Sorority Inc; Detroit Regional Chamber Leadership Detroit; Am Cancer Soc; Big Bros Sisters Metro Detroit. **Special Achievements:** Woman of Excellence, Mich Chronicle, 2013. **Home Addr:** 26808 Cong Ct, Southfield, MI 48034, **Home Phone:** (248)353-7720. **Business Addr:** Account Supervisor, GlobalHue, 4000 Town Ctr Suite 1600, Southfield, MI 48075.

**HARVEY, REV. ERROL ALLEN**
Clergy. **Personal:** Born Aug 5, 1943, Grand Rapids, MI; son of Fred and Elizabeth. **Educ:** Aquinas Col, BA, 1965; Seabury Western Theol Sem, BD, 1969; NY Univ, MPA, 1977; Nat Theol Sem Commonwealth Univ, DDiv, 1991. **Career:** Trinity Cathedral, curate, 1968-70; St Mark's Church, rector, 1970-72; St Andrew's Church, rector, 1972-83; St Augustine's Church, NY, rector, 1983-. **Orgs:** Convener, Episcopal Black Caucus Diocese New York; pres, Lower E Side Needle Exchange; mem bd dir, Housing Works Inc, currently. **Honors/Awds:** Outstanding Service Award, Council Churches City New York, 1998; DeWitt Reformed Church Community Service Award; Leadership Award, Black Caucus Diocese of New York; James H Robinson Jr Award, Henry St Settlement Cadet Corps; Honorary Doctor of Divinity Degree, Nat Theol Seminary Commonwealth Univ. **Home Addr:** 575 Grand St Suite 2005, New York, NY 10002, **Home Phone:** (212)505-5575. **Business Addr:** Rector, St Augustine Church, 333 Madison St, New York, NY 10002, **Business Phone:** (212)673-5300.

**HARVEY, GERALD**
Government official, executive. **Personal:** Born Feb 21, 1950, Macon, GA; married Cotilda Qanterman; children: Marcia & Gerald. **Educ:** Tuskegee Inst, BS, polit sci, 1972; GA Col, MEd, behavior disorder, 1977. **Career:** GA Psycho-Educ Ctr, therapist, 1973-85; City Macon, councilman, 1980-87; City Macon Off Workforce Devel, youth coordr; Self-employed. **Orgs:** Co chmn, founder, Unionville Neighborhood Improv Asn. **Home Addr:** 1255 S Clarotina Rd, Apopka, FL 32703-7062. **Business Addr:** Youth Coordinator, City of Macon, 700 Poplar St, Macon, GA 31201, **Business Phone:** (478)751-7400.

**HARVEY, DR. HAROLD A.**
Educator, physician. **Personal:** Born Oct 24, 1944; married Mary; children: 3. **Educ:** Univ W Indies, MD, BS, 1969. **Career:** Queen Elizabeth Hosp, intern; Lemuel Shattuck Hosp, resident, internal med, 1972, med oncol, 1973; Tufts N Eng Med Ctr, Dept Med, fel med oncol, teaching fel, 1974; Pa State Univ, assoc prof med; New Eng Med Ctr, fel med oncol, 1974; Pa State Univ Milton S Hershey Med Ctr, assoc prof med, medoncologist, cancer res, 1974-, prof med, 2004-, Hemat & Oncol Fel Prog, dir, currently; Hershey Co. **Orgs:** Am Fedn Clin Res; Am Soc Clin Oncol; Am Asn Cancer Res; Am Asn Cancer Educ; Am Cancer Soc; Prev & Res Adv Bd, Pa Cancer Control; Bd Sci Coun, Nat Cancer Inst; Am Bd Intern Med; clin oncol study sect, Nat Inst Health; adv bd mem, Oncology Congress; med adv, PCCAN. **Home Addr:** 68 Woodland Ave, Hershey, PA 17033-2156. **Business Addr:** Professor Medicine, Pennsylvania State University, 500 Univ Dr, Hershey, PA 17033-0850, **Business Phone:** (717)531-8678.

**HARVEY, JACQUELINE V. (JACKIE HARVEY)**
Educator, association executive, executive. **Personal:** Born Jan 21, 1933, Gramercy, LA; daughter of Alexander B Pittman and Selena Robinson Pittman; married Herbert Joseph; children: Cassondra Dominique, Gretchen Young, Herbert & Yolonda. **Educ:** Nat Voc Col, Voc Coun, 1953; Southern Univ New Orleans, soc mkt cert, 1969; Xavier Univ, Spec Training, 1970; Loyola Univ, adv studies, 1978; La State Univ, Baton Rouge, LA, attended 1988; CPM cand. **Career:** Educator (retired); LA Family Planning Prog New Orleans, aux health worker, 1967-68; Family Health Inc, team supvr aux health wroker, 1968-69; LA Family Planning Prog, New Orleans, dir community serv, sec supvr family health counr, 1970-74, family health counr supvr comn active workers, 1974; Ctr Health Training, state training mgr, 1982-2001; La Off Pub Health, Family Planning Prog, dir, community serv, 2001. **Orgs:** Consult, Vol Mgt, 1967-; consult, Outreach Family Planning, 1967-; pres, Easton Community Schs Adv Coun; Am Pub Health Asn; Nat Asn Advan Colored People; pres, Minority Women Progress; adv bd mem, Orleans Parish, Community Sch Prog, 1970-; chair, ad-hoc, ed comn, LA Pub Health Asn, 1984-91; Nat Family Planning & Reproductive Health Asn, 1989-; founding mem, LA Initiative Teen Pregnancy Prev, vpres, secy, treas, state dir; chair, LITPP Tri Regional Task Force. **Honors/Awds:** Community Involvement Plaque, Proj Enable, 1967; Merit Award, Family Health Found, 1971; Community Service, LA Black Women Progress, 1976; Outstanding Achievement, Women Hist No LA, 1976; Service Award, Noteworthy Commun Leaders LA, 1981; Merit Award, No Human Rel, 1982; Out standing Service Award, Nat Asn Neighborhoods, 1987; Service Award, Super Parent Support Network, 1989-90; Community Service Award, North Neighborhood Devt, 1989-90; Outstanding Volunteer Service Award, State LA, 1999; Service Award, Orleans Parish Schs Parental Involvement. **Home Addr:** 4416 Demontluzin St, New Orleans, LA 70122, **Home Phone:** (504)288-1341.

**HARVEY, KENNETH RAY**
Football player, zoologist, executive. **Personal:** Born May 6, 1965, Austin, TX; married Janice; children: Anthony, Marcus & Nathaniel (deceased). **Educ:** Laney Col; Univ Calif. **Career:** Football player (retired); Phoenix Cardinals, linebacker, 1988, right linebacker, 1989, 1993, right outside linebacker, 1990-92; Wash Redskins, left outside linebacker, 1994-99; Ikoya Productions, TV & film prod co, exec producer, currently; Com Cast Sports; Cent Union Homeless Shelter, staff; Leading Authorities Inc, speaker, currently; fitness trainer, currently. **Orgs:** Pres, Wash Redskins NFL Alumni Asn; Cent Union Homeless Shelter. **Honors/Awds:** Pro Bowler, 1994-97; One of the Washington Redskins 70 Greatest Players; Redskins Ring of Fame at Fed Ex Field. **Special Achievements:** Wrote children books; Spokesman for drug awareness programs. **Business Addr:** Speaker, Leading Authorities Inc, 1220 L St NW Suite 850, Washington, DC 20005-4070, **Business Phone:** (202)783-0300.

**HARVEY, LINDA JOY**
Media executive. **Personal:** Born Jun 11, 1957, Detroit, MI; daughter of Charles Edward and Royetta Lavern Phillips; children: Rodgerick Keith Philson & Autumn Joy Philson. **Career:** Booth Broadcasting Inc, promotions asst, 1989-91; Mich Con Gas CPN, boiler operator, 1975-; Fritz Broadcasting Inc, Mix 92.3 WMXD-FM, promotions dir & on-air staff mem, 1991-. **Orgs:** Life mem, NCP. **Business Addr:** Director, Fritz Broadcasting Inc, 15600 W 12 Mile Rd, Southfield, MI 48076, **Business Phone:** (313)569-8000.

**HARVEY, DR. LOUIS-CHARLES**
Educator, theologian. **Personal:** Born May 5, 1945, Memphis, TN; son of Willie Miles and Mary Jones; married Michelle Stevenson; children: Marcus, Melanee & Jared. **Educ:** LeMoyne-Owen Col, BS, 1967; Colgate Rochester Divinity Sch, Mdiv, 1971; Union Theol Sem, MPhil, syst theol, 1977, PhD, syst theol, 1978. **Career:** African Methodist Episcopal Church, life mem; Colgate Rochester-Divinity Sch, prof, 1974-78; Payne Theol Sem, dean, 1978-79, pres, 1989-97; United Theological Sem, prof, 1979-, arthur heck lecturer; Metrop African Methodist Episcopal Church, pres emer, sr minister, 1996-, presiding elder, 2001-; Wesley Chapel, preacher; Wesley Sem, martin luther king jr lectr, preacher, 2001; Howard Univ Divinity Sch, vis prof ethics. **Orgs:** Alpha Phi Alpha Fraternity; Soc Study Black Relig; fac mem, Ebenezer AME Church Bible Inst; Churches Ctr Theol & Pub Policy; bd mem, Georgetown Visitation Prep High Sch, currently. **Special Achievements:** First African Americans to receive a degree in this area of study from this seminary. **Home Addr:** 1354 Tuckerman St NW, Washington, DC 20011, **Home Phone:** (202)723-8731. **Business Addr:** Board Member, Georgetown Visitation Preparatory School, 1524 35th St NW, Washington, WA 20007-2785, **Business Phone:** (202)337-3350.

**HARVEY, MAURICE REGINALD**
Executive. **Personal:** Born Sep 26, 1957, Atlanta, GA; son of Cardia B and Charle E; married Kimberly Kay. **Educ:** Ga State Univ; DeKalb; Atlanta Area Tech. **Career:** Am Presedent Co, MIS dir; Mentis, syst programmer; Thacker, data processing mgr; H J Russell & Co, comput programmer; Concept Technologies Corp, pres, currently. **Orgs:** Common Black Data Processor Asn. **Special Achievements:** Developed customs documentation system for international freight. **Home Addr:** 735 Caron Cir NW, Atlanta, GA 30318-6039, **Home Phone:** (770)722-2583. **Business Addr:** President, Concept Technologies Corp, 5883 Glenridge Dr Suite 160, Atlanta, GA 30328, **Business Phone:** (404)847-0999.

**HARVEY, MICHAEL P.**
Chief executive officer. **Personal:** children: Jason. **Career:** Phatco Beverage Co, chief exec officer; Russell Simmons Beverage Co, chief exec officer, currently. **Business Addr:** Chief Executive Officer, Russell Simmons Beverage Co, 2248 N State Col Blvd, Fullerton, CA 92831, **Business Phone:** (800)251-1877.

**HARVEY, NORMA BAKER**
Educator, counselor, administrator. **Personal:** Born Nov 23, 1943, Martinsville, VA; daughter of Nannie Hobson Baker (deceased) and John T Baker (deceased); married William R; children: Kelly R, Christopher & Leslie D. **Educ:** Va State Univ, BS, educ, 1965; Fisk Univ, MA, educ media, 1976. **Career:** Educator (retired); VA & AL, elem sch teacher, 1965-68; State MA Planning Off, admin asst, 1968-70; Tuskegee Inst, res asst, 1974-78; Hampton Univ, bus counr, 1982; Kelech Real Estate Corp, pres, 1981; Pepsi Bottling CoHoughton Inc, secy & treas; Hampton Univ, dir. **Orgs:** Bd mem, Peninsula Coun Arts, 1978-80; Planning & Res Comt United Way 1978-82; bd dir, United Way, 1978-80; bd dir, Am Heart Asn, 1981-83; panelist Va Community Arts, 1983-84; bd dir, Va Symphony, 1983-86; trustee, United Way, 1985-87; bd trustee, Va Symphony, 1987-91; bd trustee, Peninsula Fine Arts Ctr, 1990-; bd trustee, Va Mus Nat Hist, 1990-91; bd trustee, Col William & Mary, 1991-95; bd trustee, Peninsula Chap Nat Conf Christians & Jews; charter mem, Harbor Bank, Newport News; Hampton Roads Sports Facil Authority, 1996-98. **Home Addr:** 612 Shore Rd, Hampton, VA 23669, **Home Phone:** (804)727-5206.

**HARVEY, DR. PETER C.**
Lawyer, executive. **Educ:** Morgan State Univ, BA, 1979; Columbia Univ Sch Law, JD, human rights law rev, 1982. **Career:** US Dist Judge Dist NJ, law clerk; NJ State Law & Pub Safety Dept, gen law div, asst atty gen, atty gen, 2003-06; Patterson Belknap Webb & Tyler LLP, partner, currently. **Orgs:** NAAG Corp Responsibility & Securities Working Group; Nat Asn Attys Gen; Nat Bar Asn; Am Bar Asn; Pi Sigma Alpha. **Honors/Awds:** Lawyer of the Year, NJ Law Journals, 2003; Top Black Lawyers in America, Black Enterprise Magazine, 2004; 100 Most Influential Black Americans, Ebony Magazine, 2005. **Special Achievements:** First African American to serve as New Jersey Attorney General. **Business Addr:** Partner, Patterson Belknap Webb & Tyler LLP, 1133 Avenue of the Americas, New York, NY 10036, **Business Phone:** (212)336-2810.

**HARVEY, RAYMOND**
Music director. **Personal:** Born Dec 9, 1950, New York, NY; son of Lee and Doris Walwin. **Educ:** Oberlin Conserv Music, Oberlin, OH, BMus & MMus, 1973; Yale Sch Music, New Haven, CT, MMA, 1978, DMA, 1984. **Career:** Northfield Mt Hermon Sch, choral dir, 1973-76; Des Moines Metro Opera, assoc conductor, 1976-80; Tex Opera Theater, music dir, 1979-80; Opera Idaho; Ind Univ Music Theater; Indianapolis Symphony, Exxon, arts endowment conductor, 1980-83; Marion (Ind) Philharmonic, music dir, 1982-86; Buffalo Philharmon-

ic, assoc conductor, 1983-86; Springfield Symphony Orchestra, music dir, 1986-94; Fresno Philharmonic, music dir, 1993-2000; Kalamazoo Symphony Orchestra, music dir, 1999-; El Paso Opera, music dir, 1995-2007, artistic dir, 2007-09; Orchestral perfomances; Detroit Symphony; NY Philharmonic; Buffalo Philharmonic; Indianapolis Symphony; Houston Symphony; Louisville Orchestra; Minn Orchestra; Atlanta Symphony; San Diego Symphony; St Louis Symphony; Utah Symphony. **Special Achievements:** Has conducted opera in US, Canada and Italy; has been featured in Ebony & Symphony magazines and is profiled in the book, Black Conductors. **Home Addr:** 6664 N Baird Ave, Fresno, CA 93710. **Business Addr:** Music Director, Kalamazoo Symphony Orchestra, 359 S Kalamazoo Mall Suite 100, Kalamazoo, MI 49007, **Business Phone:** (269)349-7759.

### HARVEY, RICHARD CLEMONT, JR.
Founder (originator), football player, business owner. **Personal:** Born Sep 11, 1966, Pascagoula, MS; married Regina; children: Richard Jr & Tiffany. **Educ:** Tulane Univ, BS, comput info syst. **Career:** Football player (retired), bus owner; New Eng Patriots, linebacker & left inside linebacker, 1990-91; Buffalo Bills, linebacker, 1992-93; Denver Broncos, linebacker, 1994; New Orleans Saints, linebacker & right linebacker & left linebacker, 1995-97; Oakland Raiders, linebacker & right linebacker & right outside linebacker, 1998-99; San Diego Chargers, linebacker, 2000; businessman, Pleasanton, currently; Eye-Sports Inc, founder, currently. **Orgs:** Player rep, Nat Football League Players Asn. **Special Achievements:** TV appearance: 1989 NFL Draft, 1989; TNT Sunday Night Football, 1997; ESPN's Sunday Night Football, 1998. **Business Addr:** Founder, Eye-Sports Inc, 419 Peterson St, Oakland, CA 94601, **Business Phone:** (510)436-6406.

### HARVEY, RICHARD R.
Executive. **Career:** Tuskegee Fed Savings & Loan Asn, Tuskegee, AL, managing officer. **Business Addr:** Managing Officer, Tuskegee Federal Savings & Loan Association, 301 N Elm St, Tuskegee, AL 36088, **Business Phone:** (205)727-2560.

### HARVEY, SANDI
Sales manager. **Educ:** Norfolk State Univ, BS, mkt, 1983. **Career:** Sands Hotel & Casino, nat sales mgr, 1983-95; Atlantic City Conv & Visitors Authority, nat sales mgr, dir wash, DC, sales, 1995-2014; Meet AC, dir sales, 2014-. **Honors/Awds:** Shawn Corwin-Myland Award, CSPI 2013. **Business Addr:** Director Sales, Meet AC, 1 Conv Blvd, Atlantic City, NJ 08401, **Business Phone:** (609)449-7148.

### HARVEY, STEVE (BRODERICK STEVEN HARVEY)
Actor, entertainer, comedian. **Personal:** Born Jan 17, 1957, Welch, WV; son of Jesse and Eloise Vera; married Marcia, Jan 1, 1980, (divorced 1994); children: Brandy, Charlie & Steve Jr; married Mary Lee Shackleford, Jun 21, 1996, (divorced 2005); children: Wynton; married Marjorie Bridges, Jun 25, 2007. **Educ:** Univ Va. **Career:** Stand up comedian; TV Series: "Me & the Boys", ABC, 1994; "The Steve Harvey Show", WB Network, 1996-2002; "My Wife and Kids", 2002; "Steve Harvey's Big Time", WB, 2003-; "The Parkers", 2003; "2005 BET Comedy Awards", host, 2005; "The 2nd Annual BET Comedy Awards", host, 2005; Films: "The Fighting Temptations, 2003; Love Don't Cost a Thing, 2003; You Got Served, 2004; Johnson Family Vacation, 2004; Crown Royal Kings of Comedy Tour, host; Racing Stripes, 2005; Madea Goes to Jail, 2009; Think Like a Man, 2012; Steve Harvey Foun, founder, currently; Writer: "HBO Comedy Half-Hour", 1995; "The Original Kings of Comedy", 2006; "Before They Were Kings", 2004; "Don't Trip He Ain't Through with Me Yet", 2006; "Celebration of 2008", 2008; Think Like a Man, 2012; Think Like a Man Too, 2014. Producer: "Big Time", 2003; "Pulled Over", 2004; "Mobile Home Disaster", 2005; "Don't Trip He Ain't Through with Me Yet", 2006; "Mobile Home Disaster", 2008; Think Like a Man, 2012; Think Like a Man Too, 2014. **Orgs:** Omega Psi Phi Fraternity Inc. **Honors/Awds:** Image Award, Nat Asn Advan Colored People, 1999-2002, 2014-16; 33rd Annual Award for Entertainer of the Year, 2000; Syndicated Personality/Show of the Year Award, Radio & Rec mag, 2007; Humanitarian Award, BET Award, 2011; People's Choice Award, 2013; Star on the Walk of Fame, 2013; Daytime Emmy Award, 2014; Hall of Fame, NAB Broadcasting, 2014; 30th Annual Award for Outstanding Actor & Outstanding Comedy Series; 31st Annual Award for Outstanding Actor in a Comedy Series; 32rd Annual Award for Outstanding Actor in a Comedy Series; Keeper of the Dream Award, Martin Luher King Jr. **Special Achievements:** Author: Act Like a Lady, Think Like a Man, Amistad, 2009; Straight Talk, No Chaser: How to Find and Keep a Man, Amistad, 2012. **Home Addr:** , New York City, NY. **Business Addr:** Comedian, Premiere Radio Networks, 15260 Ventura Blvd Suite 400, Sherman Oaks, CA 91403, **Business Phone:** (818)377-5300.

### HARVEY, REV. DR. WARDELLE G., SR.
Clergy, business owner, activist. **Personal:** Born Jun 12, 1926, Booneville, IN; married Christine P; children: Marian Jeanette, Wardell, Monica Perirr & Dione. **Educ:** Tri State Baptist Col, attended 1957; Evansville Col, attended 1958; Inter Baptist Theol Sem, attended 1962, BTh, DDiv, 1963, DCL, 1970; Union Theol Sem, DDiv, 1992. **Career:** Paducah Pub Housing, comnr, 1966-67; City Paducah, city comnr, 1968-75, mayor pro-temn, 1970-72; Greater Harrison State Baptist Church, Paducah, pastor; Cosmopolitan Mortuary, founder & owner; WG Harvey Manor, owner; Greater Love Baptist Church, pastor, currently. **Orgs:** Mayors Adv Bd, 1964-66; vpres, Ky Baptists Asn, 1964-66; pres, Baptist Ministers Alliance, Paducah Area, 1965-67; auditor, 1st Dist Asn, 1965; State Voca Ed Bd Chmn Comt Chest, 1965; chmn, RISE Comt, 1995; pres, founder, Non-Partisan League; Inter-Denominational Ministers Alliance, Nat Asn Advan Colored People; Christ Leadership Conf, Ky Col, Duke Paducah; activist, Civil Rights, Non Partisan League, Paducah. **Honors/Awds:** National Association for the Advancement of Colored People Award, 1990; Outstanding Afro-American Man, 1995; Civil Rights Hall of Fame, 2000; Civic Beautification Award; Optimist Club Blue Ribbon Award; Voca Indust Ed Award; Pol Know How, Beta Omega Omega Chap, Alpha Kappa Alpha. **Special Achievements:** First African American to hold public office in Western KY; Only African American in America to attend a KKK meeting; First African American to be appointed to the Paducah City Commission; First African American on Paducah Housing Board; First African American pro-term mayor. **Home Addr:** 1429 Reed Ave, Paducah, KY 42001-2452, **Home Phone:** (270)443-7161. **Business Addr:** Pastor, Greater Love Baptist Church, 1249 N 12th St, Paducah, KY 42001-2309, **Business Phone:** (270)443-7161.

### HARVEY, WILLIAM J.
President (organization). **Educ:** Va Commonwealth Univ, BS, 1972; Univ Va, Colgate W Darden Grad Bus Sch, MBA, 1972; Harvard Bus Sch, grad, 1995. **Career:** DuPont, mkt rep, 1979-82, prod planning mgr, 1982-84, sales mgr, Fluoropolymers, 1984-85, sales mgr, Clysar, 1985-87, mkt mgr, 1987-88; DuPont Tech Serv Labs at Chestnut Run, Wilmington, Del, mgr, 1988-90; DuPont Elastomers-Neoprene, Nordel & Hypalon, bus mgr, 1990-91; FMC Corp, Peroxygen Chem Div, Philadelphia, Pa, gen mgr, 1992-96; DuPont Packaging & Indust Polymers, global bus dir, 1996-1999; DuPont-Kevlar, Richmond, Va, global bus dir, 1999-2002; DuPont Advan Fiber-Kevlar & Nomex, vpres & gen mgr, 2002-07; DuPont Personal Protection, 2003-07; DuPont Corp Opers, vpres, 2007-08 DuPont Corp Plans, vpres, 2008-09; DuPont Packaging & Indust Polymers, pres, 2009-. **Orgs:** Bd dir, Kennametal Inc, 2011-; dir, Salvation Army, Richmond, Va; trustee, Univ Va, Darden Grad Bus Sch, 2003-09; Va Bus Coun; trustee, Del State Univ, 1995-2000; gov, St. Catherine's Sch, Richmond, Va, 2001-08; trustee, Wash Col, 2014-; vis exec Lectr, Darden Grad Sch Bus, Univ Va, 2015-. **Business Addr:** President DuPont Packaging and Industrial Polymers, Member of DuPont Operating Team, DuPont, 1007 Market St, Wilmington, DE 19898.

### HARVEY, REV. DR. WILLIAM JAMES, III
Clergy. **Personal:** Born Jun 18, 1912, Oklahoma City, OK; son of William J Jr and L Mae Johnston; married Betty Jenkins Jean Nelson; children: William J, IV, Janice Faith & Edward Jr. **Educ:** Fisk Univ, BA, 1935; Chicago Theol Sem, MDiv, 1938; Univ Chicago Divinity Sch, PhD. **Career:** Clergy (retired); Philadelphia, pastor, 1939-50; Pinn Mem Baptist Church, Philadelphia, PA, pastor, 1939-50; Va Union Univ, guest preacher, 1946-48; Cheyney St Teachers Col, guest preacher, 1949; Fisk Univ, guest preacher, 1949; Hampton Univ, guest preacher, 1950; Okla City, pastor, 1950-53; Calvary Baptist Church, pastor, l950-54; Mission Herald, assoc ed, 1950-54; Church Hist Sch, prof homiletics relig, 1951-53; PrairieView St Col, guest preacher, 1951-52; Okla St Univ, guest preacher, 1953; Macedonia Baptist Church, pastor, 1954-66. **Orgs:** Auditor, Pa Baptist Conv, 1945-50; mem exec bd foreign mission bd, Nat Baptist Conv, Am Foreign Mission Bd, 1949-50, exec secy, 1961; vpres, Philadelphia Baptist Ministers Conf, 1950; Convening Conv Nat Coun Churches, 1951; pres, Okla City Ministers Alliance, 1953; Nat Baptist Conv World Baptist Alliance, 1955; pre-invested, World Baptist Alliance, 1959; vpres, Pittsburgh Baptist Ministers Conf, 1961; treas, Allegheny Union Baptist Asn, 1961-62; Ministers Conf, 1961; Alpha Phi Alpha; Sigma Pi Phi; bd dir, Nat Baptist Conv, 1961; bd dir, Bread World, 1986; bd dir, Africa News, 1987; bd dir, Philadelphia Urban League; life mem, Nat Asn Advan Colored People. **Home Addr:** 2454 N 59 St, Philadelphia, PA 19131, **Home Phone:** (215)878-2854.

### HARVEY, DR. WILLIAM R.
School administrator. **Personal:** Born Jan 29, 1941, Brewton, AL; son of Willie D C and Mamie Claudis; married Norma Baker; children: Kelly Renee, William Christopher & Leslie Denise. **Educ:** Talladega Col, BA, 1961; Va State Univ, MA, 1966; Harvard Univ, PhD, col admin, 1972. **Career:** Sec sch teacher, 1965-66; Southern Ala Econ Opportunity Agency, dep dir, 1966-68; Harvard Intensive Summer Studies Prog, 1969; Harvard Univ, asst to dean govt affairs, 1969-70; Woodrow Wilson Intern Fel, 1970-72; Fisk Univ, admin asst to pres, 1970-72; Tuskegee Inst, vpres stud affairs, 1972-74, vpres, admin servs, 1974-78; Hampton Univ, pres, 1978-; Pepsi Cola Bottling Co, Houghton, Mich, owner, chmn, pres, 1986-. **Orgs:** Fel Admin, Harvard Univ, 1969; fel Martin L King, Woodrow Wilson Found, 1968-70; bd dir, Newport News S&L, 1980; bd visitors, Univ Va, 1981; bd dir, Nat Merit Scholar Corp, 1981; bd dir, Signet Banking Corp, 1989-97; comt mem, Pres, Adv Bd, 1990-; comt mem, US Dept Comt Min Econ Develop Coun, 1990-; bd, Signet Bank Peninsula; bd dir, Int Guaranty Ins Co, 1990-; bd, AM COUN EDUC, 1992; bd, Trigon Blue Cross Blue Shield, 1992; bd trustee, VIR Mus Fine Arts, 1992; bd trustee, VIR Hist SOC, 1992; AM COUN EDUC CMSGOV Rels; bd, Newport News Shipbuilding, Inc, 1996; bd dir, First Union Nat Bank, 1997; Wachovia Bank; Newport News Savings Bank; Harvard Coop Soc; Va Asn Higher Educ; Peninsula Chamber Com; Coun Independent Cols Va; Omega Psi Phi; Sigma Pi Phi fraternities; Pres's Nat Adv Coun Elem & Sec Educ; Defense Adv Comt Women Serv; chair, Fund Improv Postsecondary Educ; Historically Black Cols; US Dept Com Minority Develop Adv Bd; chair, Southern Univs Res Asn; coun presidents, chair bd, Nat Asn Equal Opportunity Higher Educ; chair, Mid-Eastern Athletic Conf. **Honors/Awds:** Honorary Degrees: LHD, Salisbury State Col, 1983; Medaille Col, PdD, 1987; LHD, Lemoyne-Owens Col, 1988; VIR Cultural Laureate Award, 1992; Phi Delta Kappa, Harvard Chapter Award, 1992. **Special Achievements:** First African American to head the organizations annual drive and raised a record setting $6.6 million. **Home Addr:** 612 Shore Rd, Hampton, VA 23669, **Home Phone:** (757)727-5231. **Business Addr:** President, Hampton University, Rm 200 Admin Bldg, Hampton, VA 23668, **Business Phone:** (757)727-5231.

### HARVEY-SALAAM, DYANE MICHELLE
Dance teacher, choreographer, dancer. **Personal:** Born Nov 16, 1951, Schenectady, NY; daughter of Walter Franklin; married Abdel Rut; children: Khisekh Nekhekh-Naut. **Career:** Forces Nature Dance Theatre Co, founding mem, prin soloist, 1981-, asst to dir; New York Found Arts, artist residence, 1982-97; Bor Manhattan Community Col, adj prof, 1988-97; Lehman Col, adj prof, 1989-97; City Ctr Educ Outreach, dance instr, 1993-97; Hofstra Univ, adj prof, 1996-97, guest artist, adj assoc prof drama & dance, currently; Manhattan E Mid Sch, dance consult, 1997-98; Eleo Pomare Dance Co, prin soloist; Stephen's Col, Dance Dept, dir; Princeton Univ, prof. **Orgs:** Actor's Equity, 1973; Screen Actor's Guild, 1977; Forces Nature Dance Theatre, prinl soloist, founding mem, 1982-; Troupe New York, adv bd, mem, choreographer, 1997-. **Honors/Awds:** Audience Develop Comn, Audelco, 1983; Monarch Merit Award, Nat Coun Arts Achievements, 1991; second Black Theatre Conference, IRA Aldridge Award, 1995; Goddesses and Gurus Award; AUDELCO Award; Black Theatre Award; Dance for Life Award, Better Family Life. **Special Achievements:** Choreographed "Herizon, " 1987, 1996, 1997; "The Women of Plums," 1997; Oiga Mi Voz, 1997; "Ki-Ache Stories From the Belly," collaborated with Peggy Choy and Fred Ito, 1997; "Loves Fire," the Acting Co, evening of plays, 1998; dancer, Fred Benjamin, Eleo Pomare, Alvin Ailey, Ze'eva Cohen, Dianne McIntyre, Your Arms Too Short to Box With God, Timbuktu, TheWiz; Performed and toured with numerous dance companies. **Home Addr:** 14 Mt Morris Pk W Suite 6, New York, NY 10027, **Home Phone:** (212)289-2057. **Business Addr:** Adjunct Associate Professor of Drama and Dance, Hofstra University, 139 Calkins, Hempstead, NY 11549-1000, **Business Phone:** (516)463-5444.

### HARVIN, ALVIN
Executive, journalist. **Personal:** Born Feb 20, 1937, New York, NY; married Norma Ellis; children: A Jamieson, Khary & Demetria. **Educ:** City Col NY, BA, 1967. **Career:** Journalist (retired); NY Post, sports reporter; NY Times, sports reporter. **Orgs:** Baseball Writers Asn Am; pres, Alumini Asn City Col New York. **Home Addr:** 2541 Adam Clayton Powell, New York, NY 10039-3502, **Home Phone:** (212)862-6123.

### HARVIN, REV. DURANT KEVIN, III
Clergy. **Personal:** Born Jul 5, 1966, Baltimore, MD; son of Durant Jr and Cynthia S; married Lisa M Clark; children: Durant K IV & Dairia Kymber. **Educ:** Hampton Univ, BA, Mass Media Arts, 1988; Colgate Rochester Divinity Sch, Mdiv, Theol & Bibilical Interpretation, 1991. **Career:** Hampton Univ, asst dean, 1987-88; Colgate Rochester Divinity Sch, minority recruiter, 1988-91. **Orgs:** Vpres, Interdenominational Ministerial Alliance; Youngstown Cms Social Justice; Forest Pk Sr Ctr; Nat Asn Black Jour, 1987-88; stud minister, Baber African Methodist Episcopal Church, 1988-91; nat officer, Nat Asn Black Seminarians, 1989-91; African Methodist Episcopal Ministerial Alliance, 1991-92; Nat Bd mem, Collective Banking Group; charter mem, CBG's Baltimore Chap; Omega Psi Phi Fraternity; chief exec officer, Kingdom Excellence Ministries; exec asst pastor, Bethel African Methodist Episcopal Church, Baltimore, 1991-92; sr pastor, Emmanuel Christian Community Church, 1995-2012; sr pastor, bishop, Greater Immanuel Faith Temple, 2012-; sr pastor, Richard Brown Church. **Honors/Awds:** Distinguished Serv, Nat Asn Black Seminarians, 1990, 1991; Distinguished Serv, Colgate Rochester Divinity Sch, 1991. **Special Achievements:** Books: Journey From My Dungeon: Confessions of an African Child of Divorce, 1992; First African-American pastor of the Richard Brown Memorial United Methodist Church in Youngstown. **Home Addr:** 509 Timber Springs Ct, Reisterstown, MD 21136-5843, **Home Phone:** (410)429-5134. **Business Addr:** Senior Pastor, Bishop, Greater Immanuel Faith Temple, 9631 Liberty Rd Suite C D E, Randallstown, MD 21133.

### HASAN, AQEEL KHATIB
Labor relations manager. **Personal:** Born Sep 10, 1955, Augusta, GA; married Venita Lejuene Merriweather; children: Aqeel. **Educ:** Augusta Area Tech Sch, dipl, 1978. **Career:** Augusta News Rev, columnist, 1978-79; WRDW Radio, broadcaster, 1978-80; Black Focus Mag, columnist, 1982; Employ Planning Consult Inc, pres, 1985. **Orgs:** Counr, Richmond Co Correction Inst, 1876-80; minister, Am Muslim Mission, 1977-80; Richmond Co Bd Educ, 1982-86, 2005-. pres, 1983-84; Richmond Co Bd Health, 1983-84; Augusta City Coun, 1988-89. **Honors/Awds:** Citizen of the Year, Omega Psi Phi Fraternity, 1983; Citizen of the Year, Augusta News Rev, 1983; Outstanding Young Man America, Jaycees Nat, 1984. **Special Achievements:** First black president of Richmond County Board Education. **Home Addr:** PO Box 1837, Augusta, GA 30903-1837.

### HASKINS, CLEM SMITH
Basketball coach, basketball player. **Personal:** Born Jul 11, 1943, Campbellsville, KY; son of Charles Columbus and Lucy Edna; married Yevette Penick; children: Clemette, Lori & Brent. **Educ:** Western Ky Univ, BS, 1967, MA, 1971. **Career:** Basketball player, basketball coach (retired); Chicago Bulls, prof athlete, 1967-70; Phoenix Suns, prof athlete, 1970-74; Washington Bullets, prof athlete, 1974-76; Western Ky Univ, asst coach, 1977, head basketball coach, 1980-86; Univ Minn, head basketball coach, 1986-99; Olympic Dream Team II, asst basketball coach, 1996; Goodwill Games, head basketball coach, 1998. **Orgs:** NBA Players' Asn, 1971-73; Nat Asn Basketball Coaches, 1977; Sheriff Boys & Girls Ranch, 1980; Sigma Pi Phi, Omicron Boule, 1990. **Home Addr:** 2632 Roberts Rd, Campbellsville, KY 42718, **Home Phone:** (270)465-0014.

### HASKINS, CLEMETTE L.
Basketball coach. **Personal:** Born Nov 28, 1965, Bowling Green, KY; daughter of Clem and Yevette. **Educ:** Western Ky Univ, BS, broadcast jour, 1987; Le Cordon Bleu Culinary Arts degree, Scottsdale Culinary Inst Ariz; Louisville Presby Theol Sem, MS, divinity, 2009. **Career:** Univ Dayton, asst women's basketball coach, women's basketball head coach; Hill topper Sports Satellite Network, commentator; The Fielding Lewis Walker Fellowship, Doctrinal Theol; Lady Toppers, 1984-87. **Orgs:** Nat Col Athletic Asn Final Four All-Tournament team, 1986.

**HASKINS, JAMES W, JR.** See Obituaries Section.

### HASKINS, JOSEPH, JR.
Banker. **Personal:** children: one son. **Educ:** Morgan State Univ, BA, econ; NY Univ, MBA, fin; Johns Hopkins Univ, MLA, econ; Wharton Sch, Univ PA, advan banking studies. **Career:** Chase Manhattan Bank, New York; Chem Bank, New York, loan officer; Midlantic Nat Bank, Nj, loan officer; Coppin State Col, vpres, bus & finance; Prudential-Bache Securities, investment broker; Harbor Bank Md, co-founder, chmn, pres & chief exec officer, 1987-; Harbor Bankshares Corp, chief exec officer, dir, pres, 1992-, chmn, 1995-; New Markets Venture Partners, mem adv bd, currently. **Orgs:** Nat Banker's Asn; Am Banker's Asn; Pres Roundtable; bd mem, Md Banking Sch; Acad

Finance; Better Bus Bur; Greater Baltimore Comt; Villa Julie Col; Assoc Black Charities; Md Indust Devt Financing Authority; mem adv bd, New Markets Venture Partners; dir bd, CareFirst Blue Cross Blue Shield; Morgan State Univ Bus Sch; Security Title, Chairs E Baltimore Bio-Tech Urban Develop Proj; bd mem, Harbor Bank Md, dir, 1980-, chmn, 1995-; chmn, E Baltimore Develop Inc; independent dir, Baltimore Gas & Elec Co, 2008-; Greater Baltimore Comt; chmn, State Md, Dept Bus & Econ Develop. **Honors/Awds:** SBA Financial Advocate of the Year, 1989; Black Outstanding Marylander, 1991; Entrepreneur of the Year, Ernst & Young. **Business Addr:** Chairman, President & Chief Executive Officer, Harbor Bank of Maryland, 25 W Fayette St, Baltimore, MD 21201, **Business Phone:** (410)528-1801.

### HASKINS, MICHAEL KEVIN

Vice president (organization), public relations executive, consultant. **Personal:** Born Mar 30, 1950, Washington, DC; son of Thomas and Frances Datcher. **Educ:** Lincoln Univ, Oxford, PA, BA, econs, 1972; LaSalle Univ, Sch Bus Admin, Philadelphia, PA, MBA, finance, 1980. **Career:** Fidelity Bank, Philadelphia, Pa, asst mgr, 1972-76; First Pa Bank, Philadelphia, Pa, mkt specialist, 1976-77, asst vpres, 1983-89; Greater Philadelphia CDC, Philadelphia, Pa, sr proj mgr, 1977-80; Emerson Elec, Hatfield, Pa, mkt serv mgr, 1980-82; Cabot Med Corp, prod mgr, 1982-83; Crawley Haskins Sloan PR & Advert, Philadelphia, Pa, exec vpres & commun consult, 1989-2006; Strategic Mgt Consults, prin, 2006-; Bankers Life & Causality Co, consult, 2008-09. **Orgs:** Vpres & secy, Greater Philadelphia Venture Capital, 1983-; dir, Pa Minority Bus Develop Authority, 1988-91; pres, Richard Allen Mus Bd, 1989-91; bd dir, Philadelphia Coun Community Advan. **Home Addr:** 6460 Drexel Rd, Philadelphia, PA 19151-2401. **Business Addr:** Board Director, Philadelphia Council Community Advancement, 100 N 17th St, Philadelphia, PA 19103, **Business Phone:** (215)567-7803.

### HASKINS, MORICE LEE, JR.

Financial manager, executive. **Personal:** Born Jun 9, 1947, New Brunswick, NJ; son of Morice L Sr and Mary Toombs; married Jane Segal; children: Rachel. **Educ:** Colgate Univ, BA, 1969; Hofstra Univ Sch Law, JDL, 1978. **Career:** Financial manager (retired), executive; Colony S Settlement House Brooklyn, Soc Studies Curric, coordr, 1969; State Univ NY, assoc dean, dir full opportunity prog, 1969-71; NY State Educ Dept, assoc higher educ, 1971-75, Comn Educ Opporunity, exec secy, 1974-75; First Tenn Bank Corp, vpres & mgr estate admin, 1979. **Orgs:** Asn Equality & Excellence Educ, 1978-82; Nat Bar Asn, Memphis, 1979-; AmInst Banking, Memphis, 1979-; Tau Kappa Epsilon; Mediator Memphis City Ctr Dispute Prog, 1979-81; vice chmn, La Rose Sch Title I, 1979-81; Chicasaw Coun; Boy Scouts Am, 1981-84; bd dir, Memphis Black Arts Alliance, 1982-86; loan comnr, Tenn Valley Ctr Minority Econ Develop, 1984-87; chmn, bd dir, Dixie Homes Boys Club, 1988-90; bd dir, Agri ctr Int, Shelby Co Agricenter Comn, 1994-; sec, bd trustee, Grace-St Luke's Episcopal Sch. **Home Addr:** 1952 Higbee Ave, Memphis, TN 38104-5217. **Business Addr:** Board of Director, Agricenter International, 7777 Walnut Grove Rd Suite B, Memphis, TN 38120, **Business Phone:** (901)757-7777.

### HASKINS, WILLIAM J.

Administrator, executive director, athlete. **Personal:** Born Oct 16, 1930, Binghamton, NY; son of William L and Signora; married Bessie White; children: Billy, Terri & Wendell. **Educ:** Syracuse Univ, BA, 1952; Columbia Univ, MA, sociol, 1953; NY Univ, cert admin, 1954. **Career:** Boys Club Am, Milwaukee, asst dir, 1957-60, Richmond, 1960-62; Nat Urban League, exec dir Eliz NJ, 1962-64, mid eastern reg, 1964-66, deputy dir, 1966-69; Nat Urban League, assoc dir, 1967; Nat Alliance Bus, nat dir comn rel, 1969-72; Arthur D Little, sr staff consult, 1972; Eastern Reg Nat Urban League, dir; Human Resources Social Serv Nat Urban League, nat dir; Urban League Whitney M Young Jr Training Exec Develop & Continuing Educ Ctr, dir, 1986; Nat Urban League Progs, vpres, 1989-94. **Orgs:** Nat Coun Urban League; exec mem, Nat Asn Advan Colored People; pres, Comn Mental Health; pub mem, Pres Strategy Coun Drug Abuse; bd mem, Nat Coun Black Alcoholism; Alpha Phi Alpha Frat; chmn, Human Environment Ctr Wash DC; 100 Black Men New Jersey. **Honors/Awds:** Many Athletic Awards, 1948-53; Athlete Year, 1951; Man of the Year, 1970; Letterman of Distinction, Syracuse Univ, 1978; Pacesetters Award, Syracuse Univ Black Alumni, 1979; inducted into NY State Athletic Hall of Fame, 1982. **Special Achievements:** First Black elected vice president of the Syracuse University. **Home Addr:** 8306 Brookfield Rd, Richmond, VA 23227, **Home Phone:** (804)266-5669.

### HASKINS, ESQ. YVONNE B.

Lawyer. **Personal:** Born Feb 23, 1938, Atlanta, GA; daughter of Joseph H Blakeney and Rozlyn Douthard Blakeney; married Harold J, Mar 15, 1969; children: Randall, Russell & Kristin. **Educ:** Spelman Col, Atlanta, GA, 1956; Temple Univ, Philadelphia, PA, BS, summa cum laude, 1968, James E Beasley Sch Law, JD, 1986. **Career:** Univ Pa, Philadelphia, security specialist, 1972-74; PA Comn Crime & Delinq, Philadelphia, regional dir, 1974-77; PA Bd Probation & Parole, Philadelphia, regional dir, 1977-86; Schnader, Harrison, Segal & Lewis, Philadelphia, Pa, atty, 1986-89; Ballard, Spahr, Andres & Ingersoll, Philadelphia, Pa, assoc atty, 1986-95; Yvonne B Haskins Law Off, atty, entrepreneur & real estate developer, 1986-; Fannie Mae, sr community bus develop mgr & sr underwriter, 1998-2007. **Orgs:** Pres, Big Sisters Philadelphia, 1980-88; pres, Prog Female Offenders Inc, 1987-; bd mem, W Mt Airy Neighbors Inc, 1989-; chair progs comt, Germantown United Community Develop Corp, 2011-14. **Honors/Awds:** Appreciation Award, Black Pre-Law Soc; Outstanding Service, Univ Penn, 1988-89. **Home Addr:** 516 W Queen Lane, Philadelphia, PA 19144-4092, **Home Phone:** (215)991-5711. **Business Addr:** Attorney, Real Estate Developer, Yvonne B Haskins Law Office, 7035 McCallum St, Philadelphia, PA 19119, **Business Phone:** (215)242-3042.

### HASSELBACH, HARALD

Football player. **Personal:** Born Sep 22, 1967, Amsterdam; married Aundrea; children: Terran. **Educ:** Univ Wash. **Career:** Football player (retired); Calgary Stampeders, defensive end, 1990-93; Denver Broncos, right defensive tackle, 1994, left defensive tackle & defensive end, 1995, defensive tackle & defensive end, 1996-2000; Green Bay Packers, 2001. **Honors/Awds:** Super Bowl Champion, XXXII, XXXIII; Grey Cup, 1992; CFL All Star, 1993.

### HASSON, NICOLE DENISE

Business owner, association executive. **Personal:** Born Sep 18, 1963, Chicago, IL; daughter of Willie and Beverly Johnson; married Rueben E Barrett. **Educ:** Western Ill Univ, BA, 1985; Roosevelt Univ, MPA, 1991. **Career:** Western Ill Affirmative Action Off, admin asst, 1985; Nat Opinion Res Co, asst supvr, 1986; Keck, Mahin & Cate, legal asst, 1986; Horwitz, Horwitz & Assoc, legal asst, off mgr, 1986-89; Prairie State Col, assoc prof. **Orgs:** Pres, Nat Asn Advan Colored People, 1984-; secy, Alpha Kappa Alpha Inc, 1985-; spec events chmn, St Phillip Neri Woman's Bd, publicity chmn, 1988-; Alpha Kappa Alpha Educ Found, 1988-; Kiwanis Int, 1991-; prog chair, Top Ladies Distinct, TTA adv, beautification comt, 1991-; Friends Parks, 1991-; Alpha Kappa Alpha Sorority Inc, off opers asst dir, 1989-. **Honors/Awds:** Miss Alpha Phi Alpha, Alpha Phi Alpha, 1983; Alice Motts Scholarship, Alpha Kappa Alpha Educational Foundation, 1990; Woman of Destiny Protege Award, Women of Destiny, 1990; Initiative Award, Friends of the Parks, 1992. **Home Addr:** 2203 E Sauk Trl, Chicago, IL 60411-5152. **Business Addr:** Office Operations Assistant Director, Alpha Kappa Alpha Sorority Inc, 5656 S Stony Island Ave, Chicago, IL 60637, **Business Phone:** (773)684-1284.

### HASTICK, ROY A., SR.

Entrepreneur. **Career:** Caribbean Am Chamber Com & Indust Inc, founder, pres & chief exec officer, 1985-; White House deleg, 1995. **Orgs:** Chase Manhattan Bank Community Develop Bd; Trop Tv Network; NYC Mayor's Small Bus Adv Bd; Brooklyn Ctr Performing Arts Brooklyn Col; DHL, Evers Col; DHL, City Univ New York; chair, Medgar Evers Col Caribbean Res Ctr Adv Bd; Brooklyn Navy Yard Econ Develop Corp; J P Morgan Chase CAB Bd; New York & Co, Inc; bd mem, Brooklyn Empowerment Zone. **Honors/Awds:** Nat Award, U.S. Dept Com; Minority Business Advocate of the Year Award; Immigrant of the Year Award, Brooklyn Borough Pres Hon Howard Golden, 1986; West Indian American Achievers Award; Ron Brown Leadership Award; Goodwill Ambassador Award, Jewish community; Special Award, Caribbean Tourism Orgn, 2008; African American Achievers Award, Ny Atty Gen, 2008. **Home Addr:** 212 Rutland Rd, Brooklyn, NY 11225-5374, **Home Phone:** (718)941-4042. **Business Addr:** President & Chief Executive Officer, Founder, Caribbean American Chamber of Commerce & Industry Inc, Brooklyn Navy Yard 63 Flushing Ave Bldg Suite 5 Unit 239, Brooklyn, NY 11205, **Business Phone:** (718)834-4544.

### HASTINGS, REP. ALCEE LAMAR

Government official, judge. **Personal:** Born Sep 5, 1936, Altamonte Springs, FL; son of Mildred L and Julius C; children: Alcee Lamar II, Chelsea & Leigh. **Educ:** Crooms Acad, Sanford, FL, attended 1953; Fisk Univ, Nashville, TN, BA, 1958; Howard Univ, Wash, DC, Sch Law, attended 1960; Fla A&M Univ, JD, 1964. **Career:** Allen & Hastings, Ft Lauderdale, FL, atty, 1963-66, pvt law pract, 1966-77; Broward County, FL, circuit ct judge, 1977-79; US Dist Ct, judge, 1979-89; Southern Dist Fla, dist judge; House Rules Comt, 2001-; US House Representatives, Fla 23rd Dist, congressman & rep, 1993-, Fla 20th Dist; Parliamentary Assembly Orgn Security & Co-oper, Europe, pres. **Orgs:** Broward County Bar Asn; Fla Bar Asn; Amn Bar Asn; Nat Bar Asn; Am Trial Lawyers Asn; Broward County Trial Lawyers Asn; Broward County Criminal Defense Atty Asn; Am Arbit Asn; Broward County Classroom Teachers Asn; Broward County Coun Human Rels; State Fla Educ Comn; Task Force Crime; bd dir, Urban League Broward County; bd dir, Broward County Sickle Cell Anemia Found; Fla Voters League; vice chmn, House Permanent Select Comt Intelligence; vice chmn, Dem Select Comt on Election Reform; sr mem, House Rules Comt; chmn, Legis & Budget Process Subcomt; AME Church; Nat Asn Adv Coloured People; Miami-Dade Chamber Com; Family Christian Asn; ACLU; Southern Poverty Law Ctr; NOW; Planned Parenthood; Women & C First Inc; Sierra Club; Costeau Soc; Broward County Dem Exec Comm; Dade County Dem Exec Comm; Lauderhill Dem Club; Hollywood Hills Dem Club; Pembroke Pines Dem Club; Urban League; T J Reddick Bar Asn; Natl Conf Black Lawyers; Simon Wisenthal Ctr; Furtivist Soc; Progressive Black Police Officers Club; Intl Black Firefighters Asn; Foreign Affairs Comm; Merchant Marine & Fisheries Comm; Sci Comm; co-chmn, House Dem Caucus; Cong Black Caucus; co-chmn, Cong Everglades Caucus; co-chmn, Fla Deleg. **Special Achievements:** First African Americans elected to Congress from Florida since Reconstruction; First African-American Federal Judge in the State of Florida; First African-American to chair the Helsinki Commission. **Business Addr:** Member, US House of Representatives, 2701 W Oakland Pk Blvd Suite 200, Ft. Lauderdale, FL 33311, **Business Phone:** (954)733-2800.

### HASTINGS, ANDRE ORLANDO

Football player. **Personal:** Born Nov 7, 1971, Atlanta, GA. **Educ:** Univ Ga. **Career:** Football player (retired); Pittsburgh Steelers, 1993, wide receiver, 1994, punt returner, 1995, punt returner & wide receiver, 1996; New Orleans Saints, wide receiver, 1997-99; Tampa Bay Buccaneers, 2000. **Honors/Awds:** USA Today Offensive Player Of the Year Award, 1989. **Home Addr:** 17157 Oriole Rd, Ft Meyers, FL 33912-5111.

### HASTON, DR. RAYMOND CURTISS, JR.

Dentist. **Personal:** Born Jul 24, 1945, Lexington, VA; married Diane Rawls; children: Lisa, Crystal, April & Tasha. **Educ:** Bluefield State, BS, 1967; Howard Univ, DDS, 1977. **Career:** Appomattox Pub Sch Systs, teacher, 1967-68; Milton Sumners HS, teacher, 1969; DC Pub Sch Syst, teacher, 1969-73; Raymond C Haston Jr DDS PC, owner & dentist, currently. **Orgs:** Nat Dent Asn, 1987; Am Dent Asn, 1987, Gen Acad Dent, 1987; Alpha Phi Alpha Frat; Nat Asn Advan Colored People. **Honors/Awds:** Scholars, Nat Sci Found, 1971-72. **Home Addr:** 6425 Battle Rock Dr, Clifton, VA 20124, **Home Phone:** (703)830-5897. **Business Addr:** Dentist, Owner, Raymond C Haston Jr DDS PC, 14393 Hereford Rd, Dale City, VA 22193-2107, **Business Phone:** (703)670-8400.

### HASTY, JAMES EDWARD

Football player, football coach, television show host. **Personal:** Born May 23, 1965, Seattle, WA; children: J R & Tyler. **Educ:** Wash State Univ, BS, commun. **Career:** Football player (retired), football coach, talk show host; New York Jets, right corner back, 1988-94; Kans City Chiefs, right corner back & corner back & free safety, 1995-2000; Oakland Raiders, defensive Back, 2001; Bellevue High Sch, asst defensive coach, 2001-04, defensive back coach, 2010; Entertainment & Sports Programming Network, nat football league analyst, 2006-; Franklin High Sch, head coach, currently. **Orgs:** Found, Jessica Guzman Scholarship Found; Omega Psi Phi Fraternity Inc. **Honors/Awds:** Pro Bowl, 1997 & 1999; NFL Interceptions Co-Leader, 1999. **Business Addr:** Head Coach, Franklin High School, 218 Oak St, Franklin, MA 02038, **Business Phone:** (508)613-1400.

### HASTY, KEITH A.

President (organization), executive. **Educ:** DePaul Univ, BA, acct, 1980. **Career:** Best Foam Fabricators Inc, Chicago, Ill, pres & chief exec officer, 1981-2009; Keystone Advisors Illinios, sr partner, bus develop, 2008-12. **Orgs:** Nat Minority Bus Coun. **Business Addr:** Senior Partner, Keystone Advisors of Illinois, 16000 S Van Drunen, South Holland, IL 60628, **Business Phone:** (708)566-4524.

### HATCHER, BILLY. See HATCHER, WILLIAM AUGUSTUS.

### HATCHER, JEFFREY FRENCH

Sales manager, accountant, manager. **Personal:** Born East Orange, NJ; son of John Cornelius and Cordella Garnes; children: Troy. **Educ:** Tenn State Univ, attended 1969; New Sch Social Res, attended 1978. **Career:** Spot Time Ltd, Nat TV State Reps, sales mgr, 1979-82; MCA TV, acct exec, 1982-84; Channel Syndication Corp, mkt dir, 1984-85; USA Network, regional mgr affil rels, 1985-. **Orgs:** Nat Acad TV Arts & Scis; Int Radio & TV Soc Inc; Nat Asn Minorities Cable, New York Chap. **Business Addr:** Regional Manager, USA Network, 1230 Avenue of the Americas, New York, NY 10020, **Business Phone:** (212)618-6370.

### HATCHER, LIZZIE R.

Lawyer. **Personal:** Born Feb 8, 1954, Houston, TX; daughter of Fred Randall and Azzie Wafer Parker; married Sherman; children: Charmonda, Marcus & Madeira. **Educ:** Grambling State Univ, BA, 1975; Southern Univ, JD, 1982; La Tech Univ; Southwestern Univ. **Career:** Thomas M Burns Ltd, Las Vegas, NV, atty, law clerk, 1980-83; Lizzie RHatcher, Las Vegas, NV, atty, 1983-; Capital Murder Case Defense Panel; Eighth Judicial Dist Ct, paternity referee; Nev Comn Ethics; pvt pract atty at law, currently. **Orgs:** Pres, Las Vegas Chap, NBA, 1985-87; Victory Missionary Baptist Church, 1986-; trustee, Victory Missionary Baptist Church, 1987-88; Nat Asn Advan Colored People, Las Vegas Br, 1988-; regional dir, Nat Bar Asn, 1990-; Nev State Bar CLE Comt; Nev State Ethics Comn; Am Immigration Lawyers Asn Nev Chap; Clark County; Nat Asn Criminal Lawyers. **Special Achievements:** Syst Discriminatory Treat African-Am Capital Cases, Criminal Justice Syst, Howard Univ Criminal Law Symposium, 1990. **Business Addr:** Attorney at Law, Private Practice, 725 S 6th St, Las Vegas, NV 89101, **Business Phone:** (702)386-2988.

### HATCHER, RICHARD GORDON

Politician, college teacher, educator. **Personal:** Born Jul 10, 1933, Michigan City, IN; son of Carlton and Catherine; married Ruthellyn Marie Rowles; children: Ragen Heather, Rachelle Catherine & Renee Camille. **Educ:** Ill Univ, BS, bus & govt, 1956; Valparaiso Univ, JD, 1959. **Career:** E Chicago, Ind, pvt legal pract; Lake County, Ind, dep prosecutor, 1961-63; Gary City Coun, councilman-at-large, 1963-66; Mayor Gary, 1968-87; R Gordon Hatcher & Assocs, founder, 1988-; Roosevelt Univ, polit sci, teacher, 1989; Valparaiso Univ, law prof, 1991, sr res prof & spec asst to dean, currently; Ind Univ Northwest, adj prof african am studies. **Orgs:** Chmn, Human & Resources Develop, 1974; Dem Conf Mayors, 1977; chair, African Am Summit, 1989; Nat League Cities; pres, US Conf Mayors; Nat Conf Black Mayors; Nat Black Polit Conv; vice chair, Nat Dem Comn, 1981-85; fel Harvard Univ's Kennedy Sch Govt, 1988-89; Mikulski Comn; Nat Urban Coalition; nat chmn, bd dir, Oper PUSH; exec bd, Nat Asn Adv Colored People; Nat Dem Comn Deleg Selection; founder, Nat Black Caucus Locally Elected Officials; Nat Black Caucus; Ill State Dem Cent Comn; Asn Coun Arts; chair, Trans Africa Inc; Jesse Jackson Pres Campaign; pres, Nat Civil Rights Mus & Hall Fame; bd dir, Marshall Univ Soc Yeager Scholars; fel Kennedy Sch Govt, Harvard Univ; Ind Bar Asn; Am Bar Asn; Gary Bar Asn; co-founder, Muigwithania social civic club. **Honors/Awds:** Urban Leadership Award, Ind Asn Cities & Towns, 1986; Nat League Cities Press's Award, 1987; Nat Black Caucus Local Elected Officials Liberty Award, 1987; Outstanding Achievement Civil Rights 10 Ann Ovington Award; Life Mem & Leadership Award, Nat Asn Adv Colored People; Man of the Year, Harlem Lawyers Asn; Distinguished Service Award, Capital Press Club; Distinguished Service Award, Jaycees; Employ Benefactors Award, Int Asn Personnel Employ Security; Service Loyalty & Dedication Award, Black Stud Union, Prairie State Col; Outstanding Citation Year Award, United Viscounts, Ind; Inspired Leadership, Ind State Black Caucus. **Special Achievements:** Among 100 Most Influential Black Americans, Ebony Magazine, 1971; Among 200 most outstanding young leaders of US, Time Magazine, 1974; First African-American mayor of Gary, Indiana, 1967. **Home Addr:** 2210 Hayes St, Gary, IN 46404-3432, **Home Phone:** (219)944-9225. **Business Addr:** Senior Research Professor, Assistant to the Dean, Valparaiso University, 1700 Chapel Dr, Valparaiso, IN 46383, **Business Phone:** (219)464-5000.

### HATCHER, ROBERT L.

Automotive executive. **Educ:** Grambling State Univ, attended 1973; Univ Ill, MBA, exec mgt, 1984. **Career:** Gen Motors, dist mgr, exec gen mgr, 1974-93; Chicago Truck Ctr Inc, pres, mgr & gen mgr, 1993-2003; Sears, asst store mgr, 2003-08. **Orgs:** Chmn, Minority Bus Roundtable. **Home Addr:** 7310 Hilda St, Pittsburgh, PA 15235, **Home Phone:** (412)441-0441. **Business Addr:** IL.

**HATCHER, SCHNAVIA SMITH**
College teacher, social worker, college administrator. **Educ:** Spelman Col, BA; Univ Ga, MSW; Univ Kans, PhD. **Career:** Dept Corrections, Atlanta City Jail, psychol serv specialist, 1998-2000; Smith Hatcher Group, owner/eval consult, 1998-; Univ Kans Sch Social Work, res asst, 2000-03; MayaTech Corp, res scientist, 2004-05; Univ Ga Sch Social Work, asst prof, BSW prog dir & assoc prof, 2005-12; Univ Tex at Arlington, dir Ctr African Am Studies, assoc prof Sch Social Work & Dept Criminol & Criminal Justice, 2012-16; Univ N Carolina, Charlotte, dir Sch Social Work, 2016-. **Orgs:** Soc Social Work & Res, 2003-; Coun Social Work Educ, 2003-. **Special Achievements:** Contributor, Journal of Public Child Welfare, Journal of Correctional Health Care, and Social Work in Public Health. The first director of the School of Social Work at the University of North Carolina Charlotte. Research focuses on issues of race, class, and social policy implications for the black community and broader society. **Business Addr:** University of North Carolina Charlotte, School of Social Work, CHHs 496, Charlotte, NC 28223-0001, **Business Phone:** (704)687-7938.

**HATCHER, WILLIAM AUGUSTUS (BILLY HATCHER)**
Baseball player, athletic coach. **Personal:** Born Oct 4, 1960, Williams, AZ; married Karen; children: Derek & Chelsea. **Educ:** Yavapai Community Col, Prescott, Ariz. **Career:** Baseball player (retired), baseball coach; Chicago Cubs, outfielder, 1984-85; Houston Astros, outfielder, 1986-89; Pittsburgh Pirates, 1989; Cincinnati Reds, 1990-92; Boston Red Sox, 1992-94; Philadelphia Phillies, 1994; Tex Rangers, 1995; Tampa Bay Devil Rays, roving minor-league instr, 1996, minor-league coach, 1997, base coach, 1998-99, 2003-05, third base coach, 2000, bench coach, 2001-02; Cincinnati Reds, first base coach, 2006-. **Home Addr:** PO Box 207, Williams, AZ 86046. **Business Addr:** First Base Coach, Cincinnati Reds, 100 Main St, Cincinnati, OH 45202-4109, **Business Phone:** (513)765-7000.

**HATCHETT, ELBERT L.**
Lawyer. **Personal:** Born Jan 24, 1936, Pontiac, MI; married Laurestine; children: 4. **Educ:** Cent St Col OH; Univ MI; Fla A&M Univ, LLD. **Career:** Hatchett Brown Watermont & Campbell, atty, 1969; Circle H Ranch OtterLake MI, owner; Hatchett, DeWalt & Hatchett PLLC, sr & founding partner, atty, 1968-. **Honors/Awds:** Numerous awards from local & state orgs for serv to community & outstanding contribs to the pursuit of human rights; Distinguished Alumni Award, FL A&M Univ. **Business Addr:** Trial Attorney, Senior Partner, Hatchett DeWalt Hatchett PLLC, 485 Orchard Lake Rd, Pontiac, MI 48341, **Business Phone:** (248)334-1587.

**HATCHETT, GLENDA A.**
Judge. **Personal:** Born Dec 14, 1951, Atlanta, GA; children: Charles & Christopher. **Educ:** Mt Holyoke Col, BA, polit sci, 1973; Emory Univ Law Sch, JD, 1977. **Career:** Delta Air Lines, mgr & sr atty, legal & pub rels depts, 1981-90; Fulton Co, Ga Juv Ct, chief presiding judge, 1990-99; Ct App Spec Advocates, nat speaker; Sony Pictures Entertainment Inc, Ct Rm TV Show, judge, 1999-; TV judge, 2000-. **Orgs:** Bd mem, Gap; bd mem, Serv Master; bd mem, Columbia & HCA; Nat Ct App Spec Advocates Asn, 2003; bd dir, Nat Football League Atlanta Falcons & Hosp Corp Am; Nat Bd Gov, Boys & Girls Clubs Am; bd dir, Atlanta Falcons. **Honors/Awds:** Distinguished Alumna, Mount Holyoke Col; Outstanding Alumni of the Year, Emory Univ Law Sch; Honorary degree, Mount Holyoke Col; Outstanding Jurist of the Year, Nat Bar Asn; Pound Award, Outstanding Work in Criminal Justice, Nat Coun Crime & Delinquency; Outstanding Community Service Award, Spelman Col Bd Trustees; Thurgood Marshall Award, Nat Asn Advan Colored People; Prism Award, 2003; Woman of the Year, Nat Orgn 100 Black Men Am. **Special Achievements:** Book: Say What You Mean and Mean What You Say; Ga First African American chief presiding judge state ct; 100 Best and Brightest Women in Corporate America. **Home Addr:** , Atlanta, GA 30301. **Business Addr:** Author, Sony Pictures Entertainment Inc, 10202 W Wash Blvd, Culver City, CA 90232, **Business Phone:** (310)244-4000.

**HATCHETT, JOSEPH WOODROW**
Circuit court judge, lawyer. **Personal:** Born Sep 17, 1932, Clearwater, FL; son of John Arthur and Lula; children: Cheryl Nadine Clark & Brenda Audrey Davis. **Educ:** Fla A&M Univ, BA, polit sci, 1954; Howard Univ Sch Law, LLB, 1959; Naval Justice Sch, cert, 1973; NY Univ, appellate judge course, 1977; Am Acad Jud Educ, appellate judge course, 1978; Harvard Law Sch, prog instr lawyers, 1980, 1990. **Career:** Nat Asn Advan Colored People Legal Defense Fund, coop atty, 1960-66; City Atty, Daytona Beach, spec asst, 1963-66; Mason Fla, gen coun, 1963-66; Daytona Beach Urban Renewal Dept, consult, 1963-66; Mid Dist Fla, asst US atty, 1966-68, conscientious objectors, Dept Justice, spec hearing officer, 1967-68, US Atty Mid Dist Fla, first asst, 1968-71, US magistrate, 1971-75; Supreme Ct Fla, justice, 1975-79; US Ct Appeals Fifth Circuit, US circuit judge, 1979-81; US Ct Appeals 11th Circuit, US circuit judge, 1981-99, chief US circuit judge, 1996-99; Akerman Senterfitt & Eidson, Pa, shareholder, partner, co-chair, 1999-. **Orgs:** Bd dir, Int Acad Trial Lawyers; co-chmn, United Negro Col Fund, 1962; Jacksonville Naval Res Training Corps, 1971; bd dir, Jacksonville Opportunities Industrialization Ctr, 1972-75; Am Judicature Soc; Jacksonville Bar Asn; D W Perkins Bar Asn; adv comt, Appellate Rules Nat Coun Fed Magistrates; Fla Bar Asn; Am Bar Asn; Nat Bar Asn; bd dir, Am Judicature Soc; bd dir, Jacksonville Bar Asn, 1972-75; DW Perkins Bar Asn; Fla Chap, Nat Bar Asn; Phi Delta Phi Legal Frat; Phi Alpha Delta Legal Frat; Omega Psi Phi Frat; bd mem, Sun Trust Bank; chair, Appellate Pract Group; Veterans Foreign Wars; Fed Magistrate Judges Comt, 1984; Judicial Nominating Comn. **Special Achievements:** First African-American elected to the highest court of a state since Reconstruction when Governor Reuben Askew appointed him to the Florida Supreme Court in 1975. **Home Addr:** 106 E Col Ave, PO Box 1877, Tallahassee, FL 32301-7750, **Home Phone:** (850)224-9634. **Business Addr:** Partner, Co-Chair of Appellate Practice, Akerman LLP, Highpoint Ctr 12th Fl, Tallahassee, FL 32301, **Business Phone:** (850)224-9634.

**HATCHETT, PAUL ANDREW**
Banker. **Personal:** Born May 27, 1925, Clearwater, FL; married Pearlie Young; children: Paulette Simms, Pamela Hunnicutt & Paul A II. **Educ:** Hampton Inst, Hampton, Va, BS, 1951; Fla A&M Univ Tlhs, MEd. **Career:** Pinellas Co Sch Syst, Fla, teacher admin, 1951-71; Clearwater Fed Savings & Loan, personnel dir mkt, 1972-78, asst vpres; Clearwater City, comnr, 1981-82. **Orgs:** Dir, Clear water Slvtn Army, 1973-76; pres, Cealr water Kwns Club E, 1974-; chmn, Pinellas Co Housing Auth, 1974-; bd trustee, St Pittersburg Jr Col, 1978-; bd trustee, Med Ctr Hosp, 1978-. **Honors/Awds:** Service award, St Pittersburg Jr Col; Service award, Pinellas Co Housing Auth, 1979. **Home Addr:** 1158 Queen St, Clearwater, FL 33756-3221, **Home Phone:** (727)446-0368.

**HATCHETTE, MATT ISAAC**
Football player, actor. **Personal:** Born May 1, 1974, Cleveland, OH. **Educ:** Langston Univ; Mercyhurst Col. **Career:** Football player (retired), actor; Minn Vikings, 1997-99, wide receiver, 2000; New York Jets, 2001; Oakland Raiders, 2002; Jacksonville Jaguars, wide receiver, 2003; Amsterdam Admirals, 2003. Film: Playas Ball, 2003; Doing Hard Time, 2004; Take, 2007, Wasting Away, 2007; Extra Ordinary Barry, 2008, Working It Out II, 2010; Stonerville, 2011. TV: Doing Hard Time, 2004; Tackling Hollywood, 2006; How I Met Your Mother, 2008; Boston Legal, 2008; Millionaire Matchmaker, 2009, T.O. Show, 2009. Producer: Take, 2007; Cru II, 2013; Cru, 2014.

**HATHAWAY, CYNTHIA GRAY**
Judge. **Personal:** Born Jan 15, 1948, Detroit, MI; married DeWayne R Hayes. **Educ:** Wayne State Univ, BS, bus admin; Univ Detroit, MS, criminal justice; Detroit Col Law, JD. **Career:** Wayne County Circuit Ct, Ct Common Pleas Detroit, Mich, ct clerk & gen clerk, 1971-74; Detroit Recorder's Ct, probation officer, judicial asst, 1974-83; Vandeever, Garzia PC, law clerk, 1984-85; Philip R Sever TitleCo, title examr, 1985-87; Law Offices Cynthia Gray Hathaway, trial practitioner, 1987-94; Third Judicial Circuit Ct, judge, 1994-. **Orgs:** Nat Hon Socs; Amateur Athletic Asn; Mich Bar Asn; Detroit Bar Asn; Am Bar Asn; Straker Bar Asn; Sports Lawyers Bar Asn; Black Judges MI Bar Asn; life mem, Nat Asn Advan Colored People; Detroit Urban League; bd mem, Women's Econ Club; bd mem, Inner City Sub-Ctr; dir, Reggie McKenzie Found; bd mem, Doorsteps; Hist Little Rock Baptist Church; bd mem, Tutor & Dir Reggie McKenzie Found. **Home Addr:** 1300 E Layfayette Suite 2812, Detroit, MI 48207-2926, **Home Phone:** (313)393-3339. **Business Addr:** Judge, Wayne County Circuit Court, Frank Murphy Hall of Justice, Detroit, MI 48226, **Business Phone:** (313)224-2120.

**HATTER, HENRY**
Engineer, president (organization). **Personal:** Born May 21, 1935, Livingston, AL; son of Frank and Isabella McIntyre; married Barbara King; children: Marcus A, Kelly Mays, Henry II & DeAngelo Deloney. **Educ:** Saginaw Valley Col, BS, chem, 1965; Eastern Mich Univ, MS, ecol, 1975. **Career:** Engineer (retired), executive; Chem engr, 1965-69; GM, prod supv, 1970-73, tech, 1971; Buick Mtr Div GMC, engineering supvr, sr engr, 1973-96; MSU, govt educ liasion, 1996; Clio Area Regional Planning Bd, pres, 1999-, Pres Clio Aea Schs, pres, 2006-11, vpres & trustee, currently; Hamilton Community Network, vpres, 2001; Pub Educ State Mich, ambassador. **Orgs:** Secy, Genesee County Republican Party, 1972-76; Clio Bcntnl Comn, 1975; alt deleg, Nat Conv GOP, 1976; Electoral Col, 1976; chmn, Old Nwsbys Black Mtr Div, 1976; 7th dist chmn, GOP, 1977, 1978; comnr, Mich Travel Comn, 1978-87; Gns Co Bicentennial Comn; Flint Riv Beautif Workshop; MI Trvl Commn, 1979; pres, C's Mus, 1979-84; pres, Am Lung Asn, 1980-86; pres, Old Nwsbys Genesee County, 1981; rep, GM Area Wide C C; trustee, Clio Bd Educ, 1990-; indust ber, Environ Licensing Bd, 1991-; pres, Genesee County Asn Sch Bds, 1994-96; vpres, Issues & Resolution Comt, Mich Asn Sch Bd, 1995; adv bd Hurley Hosp N Pointe; fin chair, Genesee County Republican Party, 1996-98; Genesee County co-chair, 1998; bd, Clio; pres, Old Newsboys Flint. **Honors/Awds:** Distinguished Alumnus Award, Saginaw Vly Col, 1978, 1984; Jack Hamady Humanitarian Award, Salvation Army Award, 1999; Board Member of the Year Award, Mich Primary Care Asn, 2002; National Health Care Board member of the Year Award, Nat Asn Clin Healthcare, 2009; Most Distinguished Alumnus Award, Flint Cent High Sch, 2009. **Home Addr:** 1238 E Farrand Rd, Clio, MI 48420, **Home Phone:** (810)686-5748. **Business Addr:** President, Clio Area School District, 430 N Mill St, Clio, MI 48420, **Business Phone:** (810)591-0500.

**HATTER, HON. TERRY J., JR.**
Judge. **Personal:** Born Mar 11, 1933, Chicago, IL; married Trudy Martin; children: Susan, Allison, Terry & Scott. **Educ:** Wesleyan Univ, BA, 1954; Univ Chicago Law Sch, JD, 1960. **Career:** Judge (retired); US Veterans Admin, adjudicator, 1960-61; pvt pract, 1961-62; Cook Co, asst pub defender, 1961-62; Northern Dist Calif, asst US atty, 1962-66; Eastern Dist Calif, spec asst US atty, 1965-66; Off Econ Opportunity, regional legal serv dir, 1967-70; Western Ctr Law & Poverty, exec dir, 1970-73; Univ Southern Calif Law Ctr, assoc clin prof law, 1970-74; Loyola Univ, prof law, 1973-75; Off Mayor, exec asst dir criminal justice planning, 1974-75; Off Mayor, exec asst dir urban develop, 1975-77; Calif Super Ct, judge, 1977-80; Fed Dist Ct, Cent Dist Calif, judge, 1980; US Dist Ct, Ctr Dist Calif, chief judge, 1998-2001, judge, 2005-. **Orgs:** Chief coun, San Francisco Neighborhood Legal Assistance Found, 1966-67; chair & bd Counsilors, Univ S Calif Law Sch; trustee, Mt St Mary's Col; bd mem, Western Justice Ctr Found; bd overseers, Rand Ct Justice Inst. **Business Addr:** Judge, US District Court, US Courthouse 312 N Spring St, Los Angeles, CA 90012-4701, **Business Phone:** (213)894-1565.

**HATTON, DR. BARBARA R.**
Educator. **Personal:** Born Jun 4, 1941, LaGrange, GA; children: Kera. **Educ:** Howard Univ, BS, psychol, 1962; Atlanta Univ, MA, 1966; Stanford Univ, MEA, bus & educ, 1970, PhD, admin & policy anal, 1976. **Career:** Nat Defense Educ Act, fel, 1965-66; Europ Parkinson's Dis Asn, fel, 1969-71; SC State Univ, pres, 1992-95; Tuskegee Inst, dean sch educ; Atlanta Univ, dean educ; Atlanta Pub Sch Syst, teacher; Howard Univ, counr; Federal City Col Wash, asst dir, admis asst, dean stud servs; Stanford Urban Rural Inst; Stanford Univ Sch Educ, prof educ; Ford Found Ed & Cult, dep dir; Knoxville Col, pres, 1997-2005; Ga Prof Stand Comn, chmn. Author: Reinventing black colleges in postethnic America: The case of Knoxville College; A Game Plan for Ending the Minority Teacher Shortage; The Politics of success: an HBCU leadership paradigm. **Orgs:** Co-dir, Iniative Improv Educ Governance, 1973; Community Yearbook, 1974-75; chair & bd trust, Ravenswood City Sch Dist; East Palo Alto; Alpha Kappa Alpha Sor; Psi Chi Hon Soc Psychol; Phi Delta Kappa Hon Soc Educ; founding mem, Nat Bd Prof Teaching Stand. **Special Achievements:** First woman president of South Carolina State University, 1992-95; First African-American woman to serve as professor in the University's School of Education. **Home Addr:** 508 Union Ave, Knoxville, TN 37902, **Home Phone:** (865)971-1046.

**HAUGABOOK, DR. TERRENCE RANDALL**
Lawyer. **Personal:** Born May 16, 1960, Detroit, MI; son of LaVerne; married Maria I; children: Donovan Baker, Terrence Randall II & Tia Rachelle. **Educ:** Univ Mich, BS, psychol & biol, 1982; Mich State Univ Col Law, JD, 1991. **Career:** UAW-Ford Legal Svcs Plan, staff atty, 1991-94; Lewis, White & Clay, asn atty, 1994-95; Wayne County Prosecutor's Off, asst Prosecuting atty, 1995-2003; Univ D Mercy, Personal Injury Law, adj prof, 1998-; US Dept Justice, asst US atty, 2003-. **Orgs:** Alpha Phi Alpha Fraternity, 1979-; Phi Alpha Delta Legal Fraternity, 1990-; Am Bar Asn, 1991-; Mich Bar Asn, 1991-; Wolverine Bar Asn, 1991-; adult mentor, Life Directions, 1993-; Detroit Bar Asn, 1994-. **Honors/Awds:** American Jurisprudence Book Award in Professional Responsibility, Lawyer's Coop Publ, 1991. **Home Addr:** 43852 Stonebridge Dr, Belleville, MI 48111-4486, **Home Phone:** (734)697-5152. **Business Addr:** Assistant US Attorney, United States Department of Justice, 211 W Fort St Suite 2001, Detroit, MI 48226-3220, **Business Phone:** (313)226-9157.

**HAUGHTON, DR. ETHEL NORRIS**
Educator. **Personal:** Born Mar 3, 1956, Petersburg, VA; daughter of Marie Perry and Granville M; married Harold J Sr. **Educ:** E Carolina Univ, BM, 1977; Ohio State Univ, MA, 1978, PhD, 1994; Westminster Choir Col, attended 1986. **Career:** Ohio State Univ, One-Yr Minority fel, 1977-78, grad teaching asst, 1987-88; Ohio State Univ, Presidential fel, 1993-94; Va State Univ, Dept Music Art & Design, assoc prof music, currently. **Orgs:** Ctr Black Music Res; Soc Am Music, 2000; Col Music Soc; Sigma Alpha Iota; PhiKappa Phi; Music fac Va State Univ; Petersburg Symphony Orchestra bd. **Special Achievements:** First National Congress on Women in Music. **Business Addr:** Associate Professor of Music, Virginia State University, Davis Hall 1 Hayden Dr Rm 213, Petersburg, VA 23806, **Business Phone:** (804)524-5018.

**HAUGSTAD, MAY KATHERYN**
Insurance executive, college teacher. **Personal:** Born Oct 18, 1937, Dallas, TX; married Paul; children: Monika Moss, Veronica Moss & Karsten. **Educ:** Southern Univ, BS, 1959; Yale Univ, MS, 1960; Cath Univ, PhD, 1971. **Career:** Howard Univ, res asst, 1961-63, instr, 1963-66; Fed City Col, asst prof, 1968-69; Univ NH, asst prof, 1969-75, dept chmn, 1972-73; Univ Oslo, researcher, 1977-86; Prudential Annuity Serv Ctr, regist rep, agt, 1987-. **Orgs:** Delta Sigma Theta Sor; Sigma Xi; life underwriting, trainer, coun fel, LUTCF. **Special Achievements:** Author, The Effect of Photosynthetic Enhancement on Photorespiration in Sinapis Alba, 1979; Determination of Spectral Responses of Photorespiration in Sinapis Alba by CO2; Burst Effect of O2 & CO2 Compensation Concentrations, Photosynthetica, 1980; author of several publications including: Effect of Abscisic Acid on CO2 Exchange in Lemna Gibba; Yield of Tomato & Maize in Response to Filiar & Root Appl of Triacontanol; Photoinhibition of Photosynthesis: Effect of Light & the Selective Excitation of the Photosystems on Recovery. **Home Addr:** 3901 Crozier St, Dallas, TX 75215-4026, **Home Phone:** (214)288-6886. **Business Addr:** Agent, Prudential Annuity Serv Center, 6805 N Capital Tex Suite 270, Austin, TX 78731-1749, **Business Phone:** (512)345-5056.

**HAVIS, JEFFREY OSCAR**
Executive, manager, accountant. **Personal:** Born Dec 7, 1966, Chicago, IL; son of James and Thelma; married Teterina; children: Alexia Jade. **Educ:** Univ Ill Champaign, BS, mkt & mkt mgt, 1990. **Career:** Northern Telecom, mkt intern, 1985-89; Otis Elevator, acct exec, 1990-94; Rainbow Elevator Corp, gen mgr, 1994-2000; Clear Channel Radio, acct exec, 2001-03; Total Traffic Network, sales mgr, 2003-05; Entercom, gen sales mgr, 2005-06; Clear Channel, gen sales mgr, 2006-09; Radio One, gen sales mgr, 2009-. **Orgs:** Pres, Alpha Phi Alpha Fraternity Inc, 1987-; Minority Com Asn, 1988-90; Inroads Alumni Asn, 1990-; pres, African Am Elevator Prof, 1993-. **Home Addr:** 1032 W 107th Pl, Chicago, IL 60643-3718. **Business Addr:** General Manager, Radio One Inc, 14th Fl 1010 Wayne Ave, Chicago, MD 20910, **Business Phone:** (708)371-7700.

**HAWES, BERNADINE TINNER**
Computer executive. **Personal:** Born Feb 16, 1950, Washington, DC; daughter of Bernard T and Geneva Childs; married William Henry. **Educ:** Lincoln Univ, Pa, BA, sociol & res, 1972; Univ Pa, Philadelphia, Pa, MS, med sociol, 1977, ABD, 1980. **Career:** Lincoln Univ, PA, res asst, 1971-72; Univ City Sci Ctr, Philadelphia, PA, dir info systs, 1975-88, dir res mgt, vpres & dir, 2001; New Millenium Found, consult, 1994-96; Off Pa Rep Curtis Thomas, spec asst technol, 2002-04; Peples Emergency Ctr, interim pres & chief exec officer, 2010; Am Cities Found, prog developer, 2007-11; Community Mkt Concepts Inc, sr res analyst, 2012-; Mfg Exten Prog, nat adv bd, 2014-. **Orgs:** Chairperson, Black Alumni Soc, 1990-91; United Way SE Pa Fund Allocation, 1987-91; Women Tech, 1986; bd mem, Philadelphia Doll Mus, 1988-91; bd mem, Appln Develop Ctr, 1987-91; dir, Am Cities Found; vice chair, PEC Bd, 2000-; chairwoman, DVIRC, 2000-; chair, PECCDC Bd; Phi Beta Kappa; entrepreneurial ctr adv bd, Urban League Philadelphia, 2011-. **Home Addr:** 3301 Baring St Apt 6, Philadelphia, PA 19104-2587, **Home Phone:** (215)387-5720. **Business Addr:** Senior Research Analyst, Community Marketing Concepts Inc, 7300 City Ave Suite 330, Philadelphia, PA 19151, **Business Phone:** (215)871-0900.

### HAWK, CHARLES N., JR.
Educator, school principal. **Personal:** Born Aug 10, 1931, Madison Heights, VA; married Amarylyiss Murphy; children: Charles Nathaniel III, Lloyd Spurgeon & Natalyn Nicole. **Educ:** Evanston Community Col, AAS, educ, 1951; Northwestern Univ, Sch Ed, BS, educ, 1953; Loyola Univ Chicago, MA, counr educ, sch coun & guid serv, 1965; Clark Atlanta Univ, EdD, 1993. **Career:** Chicago Pub Schs, teacher, 1953-56; Hoke Smith High Sch Atlanta, prin, 1957; Atlanta Pub Schs, prin, 1957-2001; Ill State Dept Educ, consult, 1999; educ consult, 2000-; Ga Accreditation Schs, consult, 2003-; Perkerson Elem Sch, prin, currently. **Orgs:** chmn bd deacons, Friendship Baptist Church, 1952-; Alpha Phi Alpha Fraternity Inc, 1957-; Chmn Bd Deacons, Friendship Baptist Church, 1971-77; 1981-83; Am Baptist Churches S, treas, 1975-79, area 3 moderator, 1996-2000, 2008-12; Am Baptist Churches, USA, 1991-94; Nat Urban League; Nat Asn Advan Colored People; Nat Educr Asn; Nat Alliance Black Sch Educr; Am Personnel & Guid Asn; Asn Supv & Curric Develop; Nat Atlanta & GA Elem Prins Asn; Nat Asn Sec Sch Prins, NEA, Atlanta & GA Asn Educ; Phi Delta Kappa, Mason; bd mgrs, YMCA; bd dirs, Ralph C Robinson Boys Club, BSA. **Honors/Awds:** Outstanding Leadership Award, Boy Scouts Atlanta Reg, 1969; Outstanding Leadership Award, YMCA, 1974; Outstanding Leadership Award, Alpha Phi Alpha, 1975. **Home Addr:** 4600 Heatherwood Dr SW, Atlanta, GA 30331-7412, **Home Phone:** (404)349-2362. **Business Addr:** Principal, Perkerson Elementary School, 2895 Lakewood Ave SW, Atlanta, GA 30315-5809, **Business Phone:** (404)756-3990.

### HAWK, CHARLES NATHANIEL, III
Lawyer, school administrator. **Personal:** Born Oct 25, 1957, Atlanta, GA. **Educ:** Morehouse Col, BA, 1979; Georgetown Univ Law Ctr, JD, 1982. **Career:** Cooper & Weintraub PC, assoc, 1982-83; Morehouse Col, dir off alumni affairs; Hawk Law Firm, atty; Global Com Co, vpres, currently. **Orgs:** Sec Deacon Bd Friendship Baptist Church, 1978-; mem Coun Advan & Support Educ, 1983-; chmn, United Way Campaign Morehouse Col, 1983-; GA Bar Asn, 1983-; off coun, Law Firm Cooper & Assoc, 1983-; legal coun, Nat Black Alumni Hall Fame, 1983-; legal coun, Hank Aaron Found Inc, 1984-; legal coun, Coun Nat Alumni Assoc Inc, 1984-. **Home Addr:** 4600 Heatherwood Dr SW, Atlanta, GA 30331-7412, **Home Phone:** (404)349-2362. **Business Addr:** Vice President of Legal Affairs, Global Commerce Co, 400 Colony Sq Suite 200, Atlanta, GA 30361, **Business Phone:** (404)870-9033.

### HAWKINS, ANDRE
School administrator. **Personal:** Born Aug 1, 1953, Jacksonville, FL; son of Sylvester and Emma J; married Annette Campbell; children: Anika, Alicia & Antoinette. **Educ:** Univ Southern Calif, BA, hist, 1975; Fla Atlantic Univ, MEd, admin & super, EdS, admin & super, 1985. **Career:** Fla Sch Boys, occup counr, 1975-76, classroom teacher, 1976-79; Indian River Community Col, acad counr, 1979, dir educ, 1979-82, dir instrnl serv, 1982-86, asst dean instr, 1986-89, assoc dean voc educ, 1989-98, dean voc Educ, 1998-; Ind River State Col, prog dir, 2005-06, dean, NW ctr. **Orgs:** Univ S Calif & Fla Atlantic Univ Alumni Asn, 1976-; New Hope Lodge 450, 1981-; Southern Regional Coun Black Am Affairs, 1981-; Fla Adult Educ Asn, 1981-, 1982-; Am Asn Adult & Continuing Educ FACC, 1982-; Ft Pierce Chamber Com St Luce Leadership, 1983-; bd dir, St Lucie Co Learn Read Lit Prog, 1985-87; Nat Coun Instrnl Adminrs, 1986-; bd dir, NY Mets Booster Club, 1987-; bd dir, chmn, 1987, second vpres, 1988, vpres, 1989, pres elect, 1990, pres, 1991, pres, 1992, Fla Asn Com Cols, Indian River CC Chap; bd dir, Indian River Community Ment Health Asn Inc, 1989-; treas, Martin Luther King Jr Comorative Community, 1989-; SLW Centennial High Sch Adv Coun, 1997-; exe comt bd, Area Agency Aging Palm Beach/Treas Coast; Southern Asn Cols & Schs Accreditation Team; Treasure Coast CNL Collab Agencies; Perkins Reauthorization Comt; ex officio mem, Asn Fla Cols Found Bd. **Home Addr:** 1136 SW Greenbriar Cove, Port St. Lucie, FL 34986, **Home Phone:** (561)340-2224. **Business Addr:** Dean of Northwest Center, Indian River Community College, 3209 Virginia Ave, Ft. Pierce, FL 34981-5596, **Business Phone:** (772)462-4242.

### HAWKINS, ARTRELL, JR.
Radio host, football player. **Personal:** Born Nov 24, 1976, Johnstown, PA; son of Artrell Sr and Althea. **Educ:** Cincinnati Col, grad. **Career:** Football player (retired), executive; Cincinnati Bengals, right ctr back, 1998-2000, 2002, corner back, right corner back, 2001, corner back, left corner back, 2003; Carolina Panthers, corner back, defensive back, line backer, 2004; Wash Redskins, 2005; New Eng Patriots, strong safety, 2005, free safety, 2006; New York Jets, 2008; Cincinnati sportstalk radio, sideline reporter, co host; Bengals Radio Network, weekly contribr; 2 Deep Zone, online radio host, currently. **Honors/Awds:** Univ Cincinnati, scholar. **Home Addr:** , Cincinnati, OH.

### HAWKINS, DR. BENNY FRANK
Educator, dentist. **Personal:** Born Feb 27, 1931, Chattanooga, TN; son of Bennie and Corinne Virginia; married E Marie Harvey; children: Benny F Jr, Christopher Thomas & Rachel M. **Educ:** Morehouse Col, BS, 1952; Meharry Med Col, DDS, 1958; Univ Iowa, MS, 1972, cert periodont, 1972. **Career:** USAF Dent Corps, lt col, 1958-78; dentist, 1958-1978; Univ IA Col Dent, periodont Grad, dir, assoc prof periodont, 1978-93; Univ Iowa, interim assoc provost, 1993-94, spec adv minority affairs provost & vpres health Sci, 1995-97, Periodont Pre Doctoral Prog, dir, assoc prof periodont, assoc prof emer periodont, currently. **Orgs:** Vestry Trinity Episcopal Church Iowa City, 1980-83; bd dir, Iowa City Rotary Club, 1982-84, 1991-93, 1998-2000; Human Rights Comn Iowa City, 1983-86; fel Int Col Dentists, 1984; vpres, Univ Dist Dent Soc, 1984-85; pres, Iowa Soc Periodontology, 1985-86; Am Dent Asn; Am Acad Periodontology; Am Asn DentSchs; Int Asn Dent Res; pres, Omicron Kappa Upsilon Hon Dent Fraternity, Iowa, 1988-89; chmn, Orgn Post-Doctoral Periodont Prog dir; pres, Midwest Soc Periodontology, 1992-93; Grant reviewer, Nat Inst Dent & Craniofacial Res; fel Am Col Dentists. **Home Addr:** 60 Penfro Dr, Iowa City, IA 52246. **Business Addr:** Associate Professor Emeritus, University of Iowa, 450 Dent Sci Bldg S, Iowa City, IA 52242-1001, **Business Phone:** (319)335-7238.

### HAWKINS, DR. CALVIN D.
Lawyer, clergy, government official. **Personal:** Born Jun 14, 1945, Brooklyn, NY; son of Wallace and Azalien; married Lennie E James; children: Alia, Alex & Jason. **Educ:** Huntington Col, BA, 1967; Howard Univ, JD, 1970; Wesley Theol Sem, MDiv, 1974; Univ Nev, MJS. **Career:** US Dept Justice, atty, 1971-74, comm rel specialist, 1971; Am Univ, assoc chaplain, 1971-72; Supreme Ct, Ind, 1971; So Dist Ct, Ind, 1971; DC Ct Appeals, 1973; Dist Ct DC, 1973; Unitd Ct Appeals DC, 1973; Supreme Ct, USA, 1974; First United Presby Church, Gary, interim pastor; Valparaiso Univ Sch Law, adj prof; Shropshire & Allen, Gary, Ind, atty, currently; Nat Judicial Col, fac, 2013-; Lake Super Ct, judge. **Orgs:** Am Bar Asn; Ind State Bar Asn; Gary Bar Asns; DC Bar Unified; Thurgood Marshall Law Asn; Am Bar Asn; Coun Urban State Local Govt Law Sec; bd trustee, Huntington Col; Ind Republican Platform Comn Ind Bd Law Examiners; Ind Bar Found; Bd Legal Servs Northwest Ind; Lake County Bar Asn; trustee, US Bankruptcy Ct, Northern Dist Ind; Gary Police Civil Serv Comn; bd advisor, Multitasking Hearts Corp. **Honors/Awds:** Social Theological Award, Martin Luther King Jr Hood Theol Sem, 1971; Jonathan M Daniels Fellow Award, 1974; Alumnus of the Year Award, Huntington College, 1975; Fellow Award, Chicago Theol Sem, 1976. **Home Addr:** PO Box M630, Gary, IN 46401. **Business Addr:** Faculty, National Judicial College, Judicial Col Bldg MS 358, Reno, NV 89557, **Business Phone:** (775)784-6747.

### HAWKINS, COURTNEY TYRONE, JR.
Football player, football coach. **Personal:** Born Dec 12, 1969, Flint, MI. **Educ:** Mich State Univ, grad. **Career:** Football player (retired), football coach; Tampa Bay Buccaneers, punt returner, wide receiver, 1992, wide receiver, 1993-96; Pittsburgh Steelers, wide receiver & punt returner, 1997-2000; Beecher High Sch, head football coach, athletic dir, currently. **Business Addr:** Head Football Coach, Athletic Director, Beecher High School, 6255 Neff Rd, Mount Morris, MI 48458-2761, **Business Phone:** (810)591-9206.

### HAWKINS, DR. DORISULA WOOTEN
Educator. **Personal:** Born Nov 15, 1941, Mt. Pleasant, TX; daughter of Artesia Ellis Wooten and Wilbur Wooten; married Howard; children: Darrell & Derek; children: Darrell & Derek. **Educ:** Jarvis Christian Col, BS, 1962; E Tex State Univ, attended 1965; Prairie View A&M Univ, MS, 1967; Tex A&M Univ, attended 1970; Univ Houston, EdD, 1975; Univ Minn, attended 1987. **Career:** Jarvis Col, secy & asst pub rels dir, 1962-63; Roxton Sch Dist, instr bus, 1963-66; Prairie View A&M Univ, assoc prof, 1966-96, head gen bus dept, 1976-88, assoc dean, Sch bus; Jarvis christian Col, develop officer, 1996-97, prof bus admin, 1997. **Orgs:** Adv bd, Milady Publ Co; exec bd mem, TX Asn Black Personnel Higher Educ, 1978-83; bd mem, TX Bus Educ Asn, 1978-83; presm Alpha Kappa Alpha, 1982-85; chmn, TX Bus Thcr Educ Coun, 1985-87; Nat Bus Educ Assoc; bd trustee, Jarvis Christian Col, 1986-88; pres, Nat Alumni Assoc, 1986-88, 2005. **Home Addr:** 114 Diane Lane, Mt Pleasant, TX 75455, **Home Phone:** (903)577-0548.

### HAWKINS, EDWIN
Songwriter, composer, conductor (music). **Personal:** Born Aug 18, 1943, Oakland, CA; son of Dan Lee and Mamie. **Career:** Recording artist; He's A Friend Of Mine, 1969; Jesus, Lover Of My Soul, 1969; Hebrew Boys, 1969; worked with: Buddah Records, 1969-74; Polygram Records, 1975-81; Myrrh Records, 1982; Birthright Records, 1983-85; Fixit Records, 1992-93; Harmony Records, 1997-98; World Class Records, 1999-2000; Albums: Let Us Go Into the House of the Lord, 1968; Oh Happy Day, 1969; He brew Boys, 1969; Lord Don't Move That Mountain, 1969; Ain't It Like Him, 1970; Live at the Concertgebouw in Amsterdam, 1970; Lay Down (Candles In The Rain) with Melanie Safka, 1970; Pray For Peace, 1970; More Happy Days, 1971; Peace Is Blowin' In The Wind, 1972; Children Get Together, 1972; I'd Like To Teach the World To Sing, 1973; New World, 1974; Edwin Hawkins Presents the Matthews Sisters, 1975; Wonderful, 1976; The Comforter, 1977; Imagine Heaven, 1982; Love Alive 2, 1993; Music & Arts Seminar Mass Choir, 1983; Angels Will Be Singing with the Music & Arts Seminar Mass Choir, 1984; Have Mercy with the Music & Arts Seminar Mass Choir, 1985; Give Us Peace with the Music & Arts Seminar Mass Choir, 1987; 18 Great Songs, 1989; That Name with the Music & Arts Seminar Mass Choir, 1988; Face to Face, 1990; Love Is the Only Way, 1998; Edwin Hawkins Music & Arts Seminar, founder, 1992; Love Fellowship Mass Choir, 2002-. **Orgs:** Founder & pres, Music & Arts Sem, 1982-. **Honors/Awds:** Grammy Awards, 1970, 1971, 1978 & 1993; Christian Music Hall of Fame, 2007. **Home Addr:** 1555 Lakeside Dr, Oakland, CA 94612. **Business Addr:** Singer, Composer, c/o StreamRing Music Network, 80 Remington Blvd, Ronkonkoma, NY 11779, **Business Phone:** (631)588-6218.

### HAWKINS, ERNESTINE L.
Librarian, executive director. **Personal:** Born Oct 30, 1950, Cleveland, OH; daughter of John Taylor and Odessa; children: Amanda. **Educ:** Miami Univ, BA, 1974; Case Western Res Univ, MLS, 1977. **Career:** Cuyahoga Co Pub Libr, Garfield Libr, ref librn, 1977-87, Mayfield Reg Libr, ref specialist, 1987-88; E Cleveland Pub Libr, bd liaision & dep dir, 1988-, exec dir, 2010-. **Orgs:** Black Caucus ALA, 1978-; Am Librn Asn, 1978-; Pub Libr Asn, 1978-; Ohio Libr Coun, 1988-; bd mem, E Cleveland Neighborhood Ctr, 1988-2003; bd mem, Ohio Libr Coun, 2004-; comt chair, PLA Com-Suc Homeless; bd mem, Black Caucus ALA. **Special Achievements:** Co-author: Stop Talking, Start Doing: Attracting People of Color to the Library Profession. **Home Addr:** 3318 Tullamore Rd, Cleveland Heights, OH 44118, **Home Phone:** (216)371-2630. **Business Addr:** Deputy Director, East Cleveland Public Library, 14101 Euclid Ave, East Cleveland, OH 44112, **Business Phone:** (216)541-4128.

### HAWKINS, DR. GENE
Educator. **Personal:** Born Henderson, NC; son of Argenia Sr and Roxie Smith. **Educ:** Glassboro State, BS, 1955; Temple Univ, MA, 1969; Nova Univ, DEd, 1976. **Career:** Dept Ford Twp Pub Schs, math teacher, 1955-64, chmn, math dept & coun, 1957-67; Gloucester County Col, dir financial aid, 1968-74; The Col Bd, financial aid serv, dir. **Orgs:** Publicity dir, Nat Asn Advan Colored People, 1963-66; consult, Financial Aid Inst, 1968-78; consult, ETS Upward Bound Col Bd, 1970-74; consult, HEW, 1970-76; exec dir, Glou County Econ Develop, 1970-72; treas, Eastern Asn Financial Aid Admin, 1973-75; NJ Asn Col & Univ Presidents, 1982. **Honors/Awds:** Distinguished Alumni Award, Glassboro State, 1971; Black Student Unity Movement Award, Gloucester County Col, 1971; Distinguished Educator, NJFOF Dir Asn, 1979; Spec Recognition NY Bd Educ, 1982; Ten Year Service Award, Col Bd, 1985; Distinguished Service Award, NJ Stud Financial Aid Admin, 1989. **Home Addr:** 2130 Bailey Terr, Philadelphia, PA 19145, **Home Phone:** (215)465-1599. **Business Addr:** Director Financial Aid Services, The College Board, 45 Columbus Ave, New York, NY 10023-6992.

### HAWKINS, HERSEY R., JR.
Basketball player, basketball coach. **Personal:** Born Sep 29, 1966, Chicago, IL; son of Hersey and Laura. **Educ:** Bradley Univ, BA, commun & media studies, 1988. **Career:** Basketball player (retired), basketball coach; Philadelphia 76ers, 1988-93; Charlotte Hornets, 1993-95, 2000-01; Seattle Supersonics, 1995-99; Chicago Bulls, 1999-2000; Estrella Foothills High Sch, asst coach, 2006-07; Hoopfest, 2009; Portland Trail Blazers, player develop dir, 2009-. **Home Addr:** 9410 A Otter Creek Dr, Charlotte, NC 28277. **Business Addr:** Player Develop Dir, 1 Ctr Ct Suite 200, Portland, OR 97227, **Business Phone:** (503)234-9291.

### HAWKINS, DR. JAMES
School administrator, educational consultant, association executive. **Personal:** Born Jul 2, 1939, Sunflower, MS; married Vivian D; children: Lisa & Linda. **Educ:** Western Mich Univ, BS, 1963; Wayne State Univ, MS, guid & coun, 1967; Mich State Univ, PhD, educ admin, 1972. **Career:** School administrator (retired), education consultant; Pontiac Pub Sch, teacher, 1963-67, proj dir, 1967-68, prin, 1968-72; Jackson Mich Pub Sch, asst supt, 1973-75, dept supt, 1975-78; Benton Harbor Area Sch, supt, 1973-78; Ypsilanti Pub Schs, supt, 1984-90; Evanston, Ill, asst supt, 1990-91; Gary Community Schs, interim supt, 1991-97; Pontiac Sch Syst, interim supt, 1997-98; Siebert Brandford Shank & Co, LLC, exec educ liaison, 1999; Oakland Schs, educ consult, 1999; Bd Educ Ypsilanti, interim supt, 2005-06, supt, 2006-09. **Orgs:** Mayors Urban Entrp Com, 1983-84, N Cent Reg Lab, 1984-85; State Partnership Sch Relationship Task Force, 1984-85; Kappa Alpha Psi; Rotary Int; Nat Asn Advan Colored People; pres, Mid Cities Ed Asn, 1984-85; Gamma Rho Boule, 1986; bd dir, United Way; Govs Comn Community Serv, IN, 1994; bd dir, High Scope Educ Res Found; Mayor's Blue Ribbon Comt on City Finances; bd dir, Parents Together; chair, Sigma Pi Phi; chair, Second Baptist Church. **Honors/Awds:** Man of Year, Negro Bus & Prof Womens Club, 1977; Benton Harbor Citizens Award, 1983; Volunteer of the Year, Urban League NW Ind, 1992; Outstanding Community Service Award, Urban League NW Ind, 1993-94; Outstanding K12, Alumni Administrator of Year, Mich State Univ, 1994; Marcus Foster Outstanding Educator of the Year, Nat Alliance Black Sch Educr, 1994; Dr Martin Luther King Jr Humanitarian Award, Eastern Mich Univ; Marcus Foster Distinguished Educator of the Ysar Award, Nat Alliance Black Sch Educr; Col of Education Outstanding Alumni Award, Mich State Univ; Outstanding Communicator Award, Nat Sch Pub rel Asn, 2006; Excellence in Education Leadership Award, Univ Mich, 2007; Golden Apple Award, Western Mich Univ, 2007; Outstanding Leadership Award, Negro Bus & Prof Women's Club; Education Award, Brown Chapel's Brotherhood Banquet; Community Service Award, Jewish Fedn; One Church One School Leadership Award, Midwest Reg Conf One Church One Sch Prog; Educator of the Year Award, INROADS/Northwest Ind; Nat Volunteer Service Award, Nat Urban League Cent Reg Deleg Assembly; Par Excellence Award, 21st Nat Oper Push Ann Conv. **Special Achievements:** Author of numerous articles on educational topics. **Home Addr:** 2144 Collegewood St, Ypsilanti, MI 48197, **Home Phone:** (734)544-5918.

### HAWKINS, JAMES C.
Manager. **Personal:** Born Mar 26, 1932, Apalachicola, FL; son of Prudence and Harold; married Gloria M Edmonds; children: Brian & Cynthia. **Educ:** Univ RI, BSME, 1959; Northeastern Univ, MSEM, 1971; Mass Inst Technol Sloane Sch, attended 1977. **Career:** Rayethon Co & MIT Labs, sr engr, 1966-68; Nat Radio Co, mgr engrs, 1968-70; consult, 1971-77; Polaroid Corp, mgr, 1973-77, sr mgr, 1978-95, div mgr, 1984, corp dir, 1989-95; Barnstable High Sch, teacher. **Orgs:** Int & ext consult various organs; past grand knight K C; Actors Guild, ASME; CCD instructor; Org & coach basketball team, tennis player, tutor, inst Karate, 1985-; trustee, Mount Auburn Hospital, 1987-; bd dir, Chamber Commerce, 1989-; chmn bd, Cambridge Chamber Com, 1989-92; bd trustee, audit comt, East Cambridge Savings Bank; bd dir, Youth Men's Christian Asn. **Honors/Awds:** Scholar LaSalle Acad. **Home Addr:** 8 Indian Spring Rd, Ashland, MA 01721, **Home Phone:** (508)881-1596.

### HAWKINS, MAJOR GEN. JOHN RUSSELL, III
Publicist. **Personal:** Born Sep 7, 1949, Washington, DC; son of John; married Michelle Mary Rector; children: John R IV & Mercedes Nicole. **Educ:** Howard Univ, BA, 1971; Am Univ, MPA, 1976; Am Univ Law Sch, JD, 1979; Univ London Law Fac Eng, independent study. **Career:** Fed Trade Comn & US EEOC, personnel mgt spec, 1972-75; Pentagon Counterintelligence Forces AUS, admin ofcr, 1975-77; Theoseus T Clayton Law Firm, law clerk, 1979-80; US EEOC Pub Affairs, asst dir Pub Affairs, 1981-85; AUS Pub Affairs, maj gen, dep chief staff mobility & res affairs, 1986-. **Orgs:** Phi Delta Phi Int Law Fraternity, 1978-; pres & chief coun, HRH Com Farms Inc NC, 1979-; cub scout leader, Pack 442, 1985-; treas, St John Baptist Home Sch Asn, 1986-; Kappa Alpha Psi. **Honors/Awds:** Sustained Superior Performance, Fed Govt, 1979-85; ed writer, Wash Informer & Wash Afro, 1985-86; Outstanding Young Men of America, 1986. **Home Addr:** 2123 Apple Tree Lane, Silver Spring, MD 20905-4414, **Home Phone:** (301)236-9292. **Business Addr:** Deputy Chief of Staff For Mobility And Reserve Off, US Army, Washington, DC 20310.

### HAWKINS, ESQ. JOHNNY L.
Lawyer. **Educ:** Wayne State Univ, BS, labor rels & human resources, 1992; Mich State Univ Col Law, JD, 1996. **Career:** Law Off J L Hawkins PLLC, owner & atty, 1996-; Mighty Jon-youth Movement, founder & chief exec officer, 2015-; Mighty Jon Entertainment, pres &

chief exec officer, 2015-; Spec Olympics-Southern Calif & San Diego, asst coach, 2011-14. **Orgs:** Comt Mem, State Bar Mich-Law & Media Comt, 2010-11; sustaining mem & exec bd mem, Mich Asn Justice, 2015; Nat Hons Soc; Black Entertainment & Sports Lawyers Asn. **Honors/Awds:** Robert L. Millender Visionary Award, Mich State Univ Col Law - BLSA, 2013. **Special Achievements:** Publication: A Most Humble "THANK YOU" to the Following Men I consider my MENTORS, 2015. **Business Addr:** Owner, Attorney, J L Hawkins & Associates PC, 2000 Town Ctr Suite 1900, Southfield, MI 48075, **Business Phone:** (248)819-2500.

### HAWKINS, LA-VAN
Executive, business owner. **Personal:** Born Jan 1, 1960; married Wendy. **Career:** Pizza Hut, owner; Burger King, owner; Checkers Dr-In, owner; Sweet Ga Brown, owner; McDonalds, gen mgr, dir opers; Wayne County Bd Commissioners, chief operating officer; Ky Fried Chicken, staff mktg, area mgr, dist mgr, regional vpres, 1978-86; Checkers & Bojangles Restaurants, franchise operator, 1986-95; La-Van Hawkins Inner City Foods Corp, chief exec officer, founder & owner, 1995-98; Urban City Foods, chmn, chief exec officer, pres, 1998-; Burger King, owner, 2001; Lineage Group Inc, owner, 2002-; La-Van Hawkins Food Group LLC., chmn & chief exec officer. **Special Achievements:** Black Enterprise's List of Top 100 Industrial/Service Companies, ranked 93, 1994, 14, 1999, 12, 2000. **Business Addr:** Chief Executive Officer, Chairman, La-Van Hawkins Food Group LLC, 607 Shelby St Suite 200, Detroit, MI 48226, **Business Phone:** (313)963-9805.

### HAWKINS, LATROY
Baseball player. **Personal:** Born Dec 21, 1972, Gary, IN; married Anita; children: Dakari & Troi. **Career:** Minn Twins, pitcher, 1995-2003; Chicago Cubs, pitcher, 2004-05; San Francisco Giants, 2005; Baltimore Orioles, 2006; Colo Rockies, 2007, 2014-15; New York Yankees, 2008; Houston Astros, 2008-09; Milwaukee Brewers, relief pitcher, 2010-11; Los Angeles Angels Anaheim, 2012; New York Mets, 2013; Toronto Blue Jays, pitcher, 2015-. **Business Addr:** Pitcher, Rogers Centre 1 Blue Jays Way Suite 3200, Coors Field 2001 Blake St, Toronto, ON M5V1J1, **Business Phone:** (416)341-1000.

### HAWKINS, MARY L.
Counselor, educator, executive. **Personal:** Born Jan 1, 1931, Columbus, GA; daughter of Bruno and Eva Powell Robinson. **Educ:** Meharry Med Col, cert dent hygene, 1961; Western Mich Univ, BS, 1976, MA, 1979. **Career:** Benton Harbor Area Schs, Benton Harbor, Mich, counselor & educator; Link Crisis Intervention Ctr, St Joseph, Mich; drug prevention educr; Priv Prac, dent hygenist, 1961-67; Brrn Co Health Dept, sr dent hygenist, 1967; Brass Found, Chicago, Ill, project co-ord, 1986-87; Mich Rehab, Kalamazoo Mich, substance abuse & voc rehabilitation coun, 1988. **Orgs:** Am Dent Hygenist Asn, 1961; Nat Asn Advan Colored People, 1963; YWCA, 1965; March Dms, 1970; Bus & Prof Women; Am Asn Univ Women; Nat Counr's Asn; Meharry Alumni Asn; Mnority Affairs Co, spec consult, 1973-75; Tri-Co Health Planners Comn, 1970-75; Oper PUSH, 1980; Blossomland United Way, 1983-89; EAP; Mich Asn Alcoholism & Drug Abuse Counrs Inc; NAADAC. **Honors/Awds:** Outstanding Dental Hygienist, Meharry's Alumni, 1974; President's Award, Nat Dent Hygienists Asn, 1975. **Home Addr:** PO Box 320, St Joseph, MI 49085-0826, **Home Phone:** (616)925-0135. **Business Addr:** 8501 S Cottage Grove Ave Suite 23, Chicago, IL 60619, **Business Phone:** (312)874-1223.

### HAWKINS, MICHAEL. See HAWKINS, STEVEN MICHAEL.

### HAWKINS, DR. MURIEL A.
Educator, consultant. **Personal:** Born Apr 22, 1946, Norfolk, VA; daughter of George and Frieda Robinson Mitchell; children: Jamal Scott. **Educ:** Chicago Med Sch Health Sci, BS, radiol sci, 1975; Citadel, MEd, 1979; Loyola Univ Chicago, PhD, 1988. **Career:** Meharry Med Col, radiographer, 1967-69, Matthew Walker Health Ctr, radiol supvr/clin coordr, 1969-71; Cook County Hosp, Sch Radiol Technol, clin instr, 1971-76; Malcolm X Col, adj instr, 1974-76; Med Univ SC, Col Allied Health Scis, instr/clin instr, 1976-78, Dept Psychiat, res asst & instr, 1978-80; Chicago State Univ, Col Allied Health, coordr stud & community affairs, 1981-87, Col Nursing & Allied Health Prof, asst prof radiol sci, 1984-93, Joint Prog Col Allied Health & Arts & Sci, Health Careers Opportunity Prog, prog dir, 1987-90, dir acad support & develop serv, 1990-92, Col Nursing & Allied Health Prof, dir acad enrichment & outreach prog, 1992-93; Numerous agencies, prof consult; Univ Wisc-Oshkosh, Ctr Acad Support & Diversity, Human Serv & Prof Leadership, assoc prof & asst vice chancellor, 1993-; Partnerships & Engagement, assoc provost; Dillard Univ, Campus & Community Rels, asst pres; Div Educ & Psychol. **Orgs:** Kellogg fel, Am Soc Allied Health Prof, 1983-84; ICEOP fel, 1986-87; grants reviewer, Allied Health Spec Proj, Bur Health Prof, 1990, 1991; coordr, Univ Wisc Oshkosh Multicult & Disadvantaged Syst, 1993-; One Oshkosh: Diversity Network, 1993-; UW Oshkosh Multicultural & Disadvantaged Coordr UW Syst, 1993-; Cent Asn Col & Sch, 1994-; peerreviewer, Higher Learning Comn; mentor, Big Bros Big Sisters Fox Valley, 1995-; bd dir, Oshkosh Symphony Orchestra, 1995-; Diversity Coun, 2000-04; Kimberly Clark Diversity Outreach Comt, 2000-; chair, Diversity Innovation Grants Comt, 2001; consult, Multicult Affairs, William Paterson Univ, 2002; bd dir, Tempo Int, 2003-; African Am Studies Comt, 2005-; founding bd mem, Asn Blacks Higher Educ, 2005-; vol mediator, Winnebago Conflict Resolution Ctr, 2006-; Fel Am Coun Educ Fels Prog; Pres's Sr Cabinet; Am Coun Educ; campus diversity officer, Univ Wis; Col Nursing & Allied Health Professions. **Home Addr:** 602 E Irving Ave, Oshkosh, WI 54901, **Home Phone:** (920)233-6009. **Business Addr:** Assistant Vice Chancellor, University of Wisconsin Oshkosh, 800 Algoma Blvd, Oshkosh, WI 54901, **Business Phone:** (920)424-2245.

### HAWKINS, PAULETTE
Executive, consultant, vice president (organization). **Career:** Warner & Chappell Music Inc, vpres licensing, 1983-2008; Paulette Hawkins Prof Music Serv, owner, 2008-; Sync Serv, owner, 2009-; Music Bus Consult, consult, 2009-. **Business Addr:** Owner, Paulette Hawkins Professional Music Services, Los Angeles, CA.

### HAWKINS, ROBERT B.
Manager, salesperson, accountant. **Personal:** Born Mar 13, 1964, Marion, IN; son of David and Margaret; married Michele; children: Lauren N & Kayla A. **Educ:** E Mich Univ, BS, indust distrib, 1988. **Career:** Kimberly-Clark, manufacturers rep, 1988-91; Princeton Pharmaceut, sales rep, 1991-93; Bristol-Myers Squibb, assoc territory mgr, 1993-94; Gannett Outdoor, nat acct mgr, 1994-97, transit mgr, currently. **Orgs:** Prof Develop Comt, Pharmaceut Rep's Detroit Excelling, 1991-94; Adcraft Club Detroit, 1994-. **Honors/Awds:** National Acctountant's Award, 1990; Eagle Award, Kimberly-Clark, 1991; Philip Morris, BOB Award, 1995-98; Advertising Salute, Air Force, 1999. **Home Addr:** 18311 Cherrylawn St, Detroit, MI 48221-2078, **Home Phone:** (313)345-8460. **Business Addr:** Transit Manager, Gannett Outdoor, 88 Custer St, Detroit, MI 48202, **Business Phone:** (313)556-7115.

### HAWKINS, STEVEN MICHAEL (MICHAEL HAWKINS)
Basketball executive, basketball player. **Personal:** Born Oct 28, 1972, Canton, OH; children: 3. **Educ:** Xavier Univ, BS, orgn commun, 1995. **Career:** Basketball player (retired), coach, executive; Rockford Lightning, 1995-97, 1998-99; Boston Celtics, pt guard, 1996-97; Olympiacos, Greece, 1997-98; Sacramento Kings, pt guard, 1998-99; Charlotte Hornets, pt guard, 1999-2000; Cleveland Cavaliers, pt guard, 2000-01; FC Barcelona, Spain, 2001; Slask Wroclaw, Poland, 2001-02; Real Madrid, Spain, 2002; Basketball Club Oostende, 2002-03; Sioux Falls Skyforce, 2003-04; La Palma, Spain, 2004-06; Al Jalaa Aleppo, Syrian basketball league, 2005-06; One Up Basketball, coach, owner & consult, 2013-. **Honors/Awds:** All-Defensive Team, All-League Second Team, CBA, 1996-97; Silver Medal, Pan Am Games, 1999; Bronze Medal, World Championships, 1998. **Business Addr:** Coach, Owner, One Up Basketball, **Business Phone:** (281)271-7090.

### HAWKINS, STEVEN WAYNE
Lawyer, executive director. **Personal:** Born Jul 10, 1962, Peekskill, NY; son of Peter and Ida Marie Boyd. **Educ:** Harvard Univ, BA, econs, 1984; Univ Zimbabwe, attended 1986; NY Univ, JD, 1988. **Career:** Judge A Leon Higgin botham, Philadelphia, Pa, law clerk, 1988-89; Nat Asn Advan Colored People Legal Defense Fund, NY, staff atty, 1989-95; Nat Judicial Col, fac instr; Nat Asn Advan Colored People, exec vpres & chief prog officer, currently; Nat Coalition Abolish Death Penalty, exec dir, 1995-; Justice, Equality, Human dignity & Tolerance Found, sr prog mgr; Atlantic Philanthropies, prog exec; Amnesty Int USA, exec dir, 2013-15; Coalition Pub Safety, pres, 2016-. **Orgs:** Bd trustee, NY Univ, Ctr Int Studies, 1989-; NY State Bar; Bar US Supreme Ct; bd dir, Death Penalty Info Ctr; Criminal Justice Comt; Nat Conf Black Lawyers; Am Bar Asn; US Cts Appeal. **Honors/Awds:** Ames Award, Harvard Univ, 1984; Rockefeller Fellowship, Harvard Univ, Univ of Zimbabwe, 1985; Am Jurisprudence Award, NY Univ Law Sch, 1987; Next Generation Leadership Fellow, Rockefeller Found, 1998-99; Civil Rights Advocacy Awards; Public Interest Advocacy Award, Nat Asn Advan Colored People Legal Defense & Educational Fund; Outstanding Graduate Award, NY Univ Pub Int Law Found; Public Interest Service Award, 2003. **Special Achievements:** Author: "Commentary: The Death Penalty Revisited,"; "Justice in the International System". **Home Addr:** 823 Glass Ave NE, Olympia, WA 98506, **Home Phone:** (360)570-8744. **Business Addr:** .

### HAWKINS, TRAMAINE (TRAMAINE DAVIS)
Gospel singer. **Personal:** Born Oct 11, 1951, San Francisco, CA; married Walter; children: Walter Jr & Trystan; married Tommy Richardson; children: Demar. **Career:** Gospel vocalist; Albums: I Love The Lord; Tramaine Hawkins Live, 1976; Determined, 1983; The Search Is Over, 1986; Freedom, 1987; The Joy That Floods My Soul, 1988; Live, 1990; Tramaine, Tramaine Treasury, 1993; All My Best to You, 1994; A To a Higher Place, 1994; Still Tramaine, 2001; Mega3 Collection, 2002; All My Best to You Vol 2, 2001; Light Records Classic Gold: Determined, Light Records Classic Gold: Tramaine Treasury, 2004; Gospel Goes Gold, 2006; My Everything, Quint essential EMI Gospel, O Happy Day; I Never Lost My Praise, 2007. Singles: "He's Alright" (Music City), 1966; "In The Morning Time", 1986; "Child Of The King", "Fall Down", 1986; "The Rock", 1987; "Do Not Pass Me By", 1992; "I Found The Answer", 1995; "Who's Gonna Carry You", 1995; By His Strength, 2001; "Excellent Lord", 2007; "I never Lost my Praise", 2007. **Honors/Awds:** Gospel Music Excellence Award, Tramaine Hawkins Live, 1991; Grammy Award; Commun Excellence Black Audiences Awards, Nat Asn Adv Colored People Image Award; Stellar Award; Brit Gospel Music Award; Gospel Music Excellence Award; Dove Award; Gospel Music Hall of Fame, 1999. **Business Addr:** Gospel Singer, c/o Sony Record, 1 Sony Dr, Park Ridge, NJ 07656, **Business Phone:** (201)930-1000.

### HAWKINS, WALTER L.
Police officer, military leader, writer. **Personal:** Born Jan 17, 1949, Atlanta, GA; son of Walter and Helen Johnson; married Carol H; children: Winter L, Michael Donta & Whitney L. **Educ:** Atlanta Police Acad, attended 1971; Dekalb Col, attended 1972; Univ Ga, attended 1977. **Career:** Atlanta Police Dept, police officer, 1971-72, detective, 1972-75; Fulton County Police, sgt, 1975-82; Fulton County Sheriff Dept, sheriff, 1985-87; US Postal Inspection Serv, postal police & chair Atlanta div diversity com, 1987-; Hawkins Bks, Owner; Book: African American Biographies: Profiles of 558 Current Men and Women; African American Biographies 2: Profiles of 332 Current Men and Women; African American Generals and Flag officers. **Orgs:** Nat Asn Advan Colored People; Non comn Officer acad; Millennial Lodge #537, MF&AM W; Guiding Light Chap #923; A-Plus. **Home Addr:** 670 Clover St SW, Atlanta, GA 30310-2255, **Home Phone:** (404)758-8356. **Business Addr:** Diversity Chairman, US Postal Inspection Service, 200 Tradeport Blvd Suite 209, Atlanta, GA 30354-2994, **Business Phone:** (404)765-7382.

### HAWKINS, WILLIAM DOUGLAS
Executive, association executive. **Personal:** Born May 14, 1946, Los Angeles, CA; son of William D and Marian Parrish; married Floy Marie Barabino; children: William D, Yonnine, Kellie & Todd. **Educ:** Howard Univ, BA, polit sci, 1968. **Career:** US Congressman Samuel S Stratton, admin asst, 1968-69; Security Pac Nat Bank, banker, com loan officer, 1969-73; Nat Econ Mgt Asn, sr vpres, 1973-76; Korn Ferry Intl, managing assoc, 1976-84; Hawkins Co, founder, pres & chief exec officer, 1984-. **Orgs:** Ed & chair, Black Bus Asn Los Angeles, 1975; bd dir, Boy Scouts Am, Los Angeles Coun, 1979-82; sr mem, Korn Ferry Int; fundraiser, Los Angeles Chap United Negro Col Fund, 1984; Calif Exec Recruiters Asn, 1985; Nat Asn Advan Colored People; chmn, Josephite Lay Adv Bd, 1988-92; vpres, Los Angeles Archdiocese Cath Sch Bd, 1994-97; bd dir, Los Angeles Chap Am Red Cross, 1995-97; bd chair, Col Bound, 1995-98. **Honors/Awds:** Award of Merit, Boy Scouts Am, 1977; Silver Beaver, Boy Scouts Am, 1989. **Business Addr:** President, Chief Executive Officer, The Hawkins Co, 11040 Bollinger Canyon Rd Suite E-216, San Ramon, CA 94582, **Business Phone:** (310)348-8800.

### HAWKINS-RUSSELL, HAZEL M.
Educator, teacher. **Personal:** Born Jun 11, 1924, Cedar Lake, TX; daughter of Nelse and Evelyn Hawkins; married James; children: Beverly Ann & Vicki Rochelle. **Educ:** New State Univ, BA, 1944; Univ Redlands, MA, 1965; US Int Univ, PhD, 1973. **Career:** Casa Blanca Elem Sch, fac; Lubbock Independent Sch Dist, teacher, 1944-46; Riverside Unified Sch Dist, teacher, 1947-65; Pupil Servised Riverside Unified Sch Dist, consult, 1965-74, admin, 1970-82; Emergency Sch Aid Act, coordr, 1974-82; Calif State Univ, assoc prof, 1982-91; Riverside Community Col Dist, adj prof, part time fac, currently; Riverside NAACP Child Develop Centers, interim co-dir. **Orgs:** Nat Coun Negro Women, 1960; Am Asn Univ Women, 1965; Delta Kappa Gamma, 1965; Alpha Kappa Alpha, 1973; Phi Delta Kappa, 1975; Urban League; Nat Asn Advan Colored People; Western Riverside County Ment Health Asn; Atty Gen's Comn Racial, Ethnic, Relig & Minority Violence. **Special Achievements:** First African American teacher at Riverside Unified School District. **Home Addr:** 2094 Carlton Pl, Riverside, CA 92507-5804, **Home Phone:** (909)683-5715. **Business Addr:** Part Time Faculty, Riverside City Community College District, 1533 Spruce St, Riverside, CA 92506, **Business Phone:** (951)222-8000.

### HAWTHORNE, ANGEL L.
Television producer, administrator. **Personal:** Born May 31, 1959, Chicago, IL. **Educ:** Columbia Col, BA, 1981. **Career:** WLS-TV, desk asst, 1980; ABC News, desk asst, 1980-81, assignment ed, 1981-85, field producer, 1985-; Univ Tenn, Ctr Telecommunications & Video; Home & Garden TV, exec producer; WVLT-TV/CBS, exec producer; Turner Broadcasting, dir develop, 2004-06; Cornell Univ, Cornell Media Production Group, asst dir, 2007-08; t.h.g. media, producer, 2006-. **Home Addr:** 68031 So Crandon, Chicago, IL 60649. **Business Addr:** Assistant Director, Cornell University, 410 Thurston Ave, Ithaca, NY 14850-2488, **Business Phone:** (607)255-5241.

### HAWTHORNE, KENNETH L.
Executive. **Personal:** Born Mobile, AL; married Eugenia G; children: Cecilia Patterson, Bruce & Bart. **Educ:** Pac Western Univ, BBA; Univ Pittsburgh, teaching cert, 1956. **Career:** Executive (retired); NY City Dist Gulf Oil Corp, retail consignment representative, 1963, sales representative, 1964, sales mgr, 1971-73, mkt mgr, 1973-76; Gulf Trading Transp Co, vpres, 1976-81; Gulf Tire Supply Co, pres, 1981-83; Gulf Oil Corp, mgr mgt training dev; KLH & Assocs Inc, pres, owner, currently. **Orgs:** Adv bd, Hermann Hosp Soc; bd, Am Cancer Soc; vice chmn, Charter Review Comn; bd comnr, chmn, Housing Authority, W Palm Beach, Fla, 1998-2001; chmn, W Palm Beach Red Cross; Human Resources Comn. **Home Addr:** 2000 Presidential Way Apt 1601, West Palm Beach, FL 33401-1517, **Home Phone:** (561)712-1182.

### HAY, SAMUEL ARTHUR
Educator. **Personal:** Born Mar 26, 1937, Barnwell, SC; son of Thomas Jr and Maebelle Glover H; married Delores Ricks Glover. **Educ:** Bethune Cookman Col, AB, speech & drama & eng, 1959; John Hopkins Univ, AM, 1967; Cornell Univ, PhD, theater hist & criticism, 1971. **Career:** Roosevelt High Sch, instr eng & drama, 1971-74; Univ Md Baltimore County, asst prof eng & African Am studies, 1971-74; Purdue Univ, assoc prof & chmn black studies, 1974-78; Wash Univ St Louis, prof & chmn black studies, 1978-79; Morgan St Univ, prof & chmn theatre, 1979-87; UC Berkeley, vis prof African Am studies, 1987-88; Chicory, guest ed; Ed Bullins Collection, archivist, 1988-2000; NC Agr & Tech St Univ, prof & head theatre, dir, interim chmn, 1993-2002; Ind State Prison, prof lit; W Jupiter Prep Sch, curric adv; Lafayette Col, vis asst prof govt & law, 2002-. **Orgs:** Founder, Nat Conf African Am Theatre, 1980-87; managing dir, Bullins Mem Theatre, 1987-88; founding archi vist, Ed Bullins Collection, 1988-98; artistic dir, Riviera Beach; artistic dir, Bullins Memorial Theater; Founder artistic dir, Cottage Theatre, 1988-93; founder, Nat Symp African Am Theatre, 1989-95; Simon & Schuster Lang Arts, 1992-94; consult, N Carolina Shakespeare Festival, 1994-99; Nat Black Theatre Festival, 1998-; bd dir, Nat Autonomous Syst Networks Schs Theatre, 2000-; Asn Theatre Higher Educ; Black Theatre Network. **Home Addr:** 422 Mccartney St, PO Box 1183, Easton, PA 18044-1183, **Home Phone:** (610)923-8139. **Business Addr:** Visiting Assistant Professor, Government & Law, Lafayette College, 17 Watson Hall, Easton, PA 18042, **Business Phone:** (610)330-5000.

### HAYDEL, JAMES V., SR.
Insurance executive. **Career:** Majestic Life Ins Co Inc, New Orleans, La, chief exec. **Business Addr:** Chief Executive, Majestic Life Insurance Co Inc, 1833 Oretha Castle Haley Blvd, New Orleans, LA 70113, **Business Phone:** (504)523-5872.

### HAYDEN, AARON CHAUTEZZ
Football player. **Personal:** Born Apr 13, 1973, Detroit, MI; married ChaToya Chante. **Educ:** Univ Tenn. **Career:** Football player (retired); San Diego Chargers, running back, 1995-96; Green Bay Packers, running back, 1997; Philadelphia Eagles, running back, 1998. **Honors/**

**Awds:** Champion, Nat Football Conf, 1997. **Home Addr:** 504 Stone Oaks Cv, Collierville, TN 38017-9124, **Home Phone:** (901)853-4542.

### HAYDEN, DR. CARLA DIANE

Library administrator, executive director. **Personal:** Born Tallahassee, FL; daughter of Bruce Kennard Jr and Colleen Dowling. **Educ:** Roosevelt Univ, BA, 1973; Univ Chicago, MA, 1977, PhD, 1987; Univ Baltimore, hon Doctor Humane Lett, 2000; Morgan State Univ, DHL, 2001. **Career:** Chicago Pub Libr, C's librn & libr assoc, 1973-79, young adult serv coordr, 1979-81; Mus Sci & Indust, libr serv coordr, 1982-87; Univ Pittsburgh, Sch Libr & Info Sci, asst prof, 1987-91; Chicago Pub Libr, chief librn & first dep comnr, 1991-93; Am Libr Asn, former pres; Enoch Pratt Free Libr, Baltimore, Md, exec dir to chief exec officer, 1993-. **Orgs:** Pub Libr Asn; bd mem, Comn Md Mus African Am Hist & Cult, 1987; Md African Am Mus Corp, 1988-; bd mem, Franklin & Eleanor Roosevelt Inst & Libr; bd mem, Md Hist Soc; Baltimore City Hist Soc; bd mem, Goucher Col; bd mem, Wash Col; Md Pub Broadcasting Comn; Sinai Hosp; Mercy Hosp Adv Bd; Nat Aquarium Baltimore Adv Bd; bd mem, Univ Pittsburgh Sch Info Sci; chair, Am Libr Asn, Comt Accreditation & Spectrum Initiative; Sinai Hosp; Univ Pittsburgh Sch Info Sci; chair, Mayor's Youth Cabinet; pres, Am Libr Asn, 2003-04. **Honors/Awds:** Librarian of the Year, Libr J, 1995; Carver-Wash Award, Baltimore Tuskegee Alumni Asn, 1995; Legacy of Literacy Award, DuBois Circle, 1996; Maryland's Top 100 Women, Warfield's Bus Rec, 1996; Torch Bearer Award, Coalition of 100 Black Women, 1996; Andrew White Medal, Loyola Col, 1997; President's Medal, Johns Hopkins Univ, 1998; Notable Black American Women, 2000; Women of the Year, Ms Mag, 2003; Maryland's Top 100 Women, Daily Rec, 2003; Pro Urbe Award, College Notre Dame Maryland, 2004; Whitney M. Young, Jr. Award, Greater Baltimore Urban League, 2004; YWCA Leader Award, YWCA, 2004; Barnard College Medal Distinction, 2005. **Special Achievements:** Ed: Venture into Cultures: A Multi-Cultural Bibliography & Resource Book, Am Libr Assn, 1992; Author of numerous chapters & articles; Listed in the publications, Who's Who in America, American Education & Among African Americans; First African American to win Librarian of the Year Award, Library Journal magazine,1995. **Home Addr:** 111 Hamlet Hill Rd, Baltimore, MD 21210. **Business Addr:** Chief Executive Officer, Enoch Pratt Free Library, 400 Cathedral St, Baltimore, MD 21201-4484, **Business Phone:** (410)396-5395.

### HAYDEN, FRANK F.

Government official, college administrator, chairperson. **Personal:** Born Quantico, VA. **Educ:** Wayne County Community Col, AA, polit sci, 1973; Univ Mich, BA, gen studies & polit sci, 1976. **Career:** City Detroit, tree artisan, 1966, Dept Parks & Recreation, jr forester, Dept Water & Sewage, govt analyst, pub affairs mgr & exec ed, pub rels dir, contracts mgr, 1996-2001; Wayne County Community Col, chmn, vice chair, currently. **Orgs:** Bd trustee, Wayne County Community Col, Dist 3; Pub Affairs Coun, Am Water Works Asn; Educ Task Force; Mich Minority Bus Develop Coun; Water People; dir procurement, S Fla Water Mgt Dist, 2001-10; chief exec officer, Sickle Cell Found, 2012-13; procurement off, City W Palm Beach, 2013-. **Business Addr:** Procurement Officer, City of West Palm Beach, 401 Clematis St, West Palm Beach, FL 33401, **Business Phone:** (561)822-2222.

### HAYDEN, REV. DR. JOHN CARLETON

Educator, clergy. **Personal:** Born Dec 30, 1933, Bowling Green, KY; son of Otis Roosevelt and Gladys Gatewood; married Jacqueline Green; children: Jonathan Christopher Janai & Johanna Christina Jamila Whitson. **Educ:** Wayne State, BA, 1955; Univ Detroit, MA, 1962; Col Emmanuel & St Chad, MDiv, LTh, honors, 1963; Howard Univ, PhD, 1972; Col Emmanuel & St Chad, MDiv, 1991. **Career:** St Mary's Sch Indian Girls, teacher, 1955; Detroit Pub Schs, teacher, 1956-59; St Chad's Sec Sch, instr, 1962-64; Univ Regina, Anglican chaplain, 1963-67, instr hist, 1965-68; St Georges Episcopal Church, asst rector, 1968-71, 1973-82, 1986-87 & 1994-, assoc rector, 2002-; Church Atonement, asst, 1971-72; St Monica's Church, priest-in-charge, 1972-73; Howard Univ, asst prof hist, 1971-87, scholar church hist, 1978-79, Episcopal & Anglican chaplain, lectr church hist, 1994-2002; Angus Dunn fel, 1973-74, 1978, 1989, 1995 & 1998-2000; Bd Theol Educ, fel, 1978-79; Robert R Motonfel, 1978-79; Morgan State Univ, Dept Hist & Geog, chmn, 1979-86; Holy Comforter Church, St Andrew's Parish, rector, 1982-86; Frostburg State Univ, prof hist, 1986-87; Univ S Sch Theol, assoc dean, 1987-92; Episcopal Off Black Ministries, consult, 1992-94; St Michael & All Angels Church, Adelphi Parish, priest-in-charge, 1992-94; Montgomery Col, adj lectr hist, 1992-94; Asn Relig & Intellectual Life, Coolidge fel, 1998; Va Theol Sem, adj prof church hist. **Orgs:** Tuxis & Older Boys' Parliament Bd, 1963-68; Anglican chaplain, Sask Correctional Inst, 1963-68; protestant chaplain, Sask Boys' Sch, 1963-68; chmn youth conf, Sask Centennial Corp, 1964-67; founding dir, Wascana Stud Housing Corp, 1965-68; pres, Sask Asn Retarded C, 1966-68; lt-gen Sask, 1967; founding dir, Ranch Ehrlo, 1967-68; chaplain's assoc, Royal Can Mountain Police, Regina; Comn Community Improv; pres, Black Episcopal Clergy, Wash Diocese, 1974-76; lifetime mem, bd dir, Wash Urban League, 1980-87; bd dir, St Patrick's Episcopal Day Sch, 1981-87; Soc Prom Christian Knowledge USA Bd, 1987-92; secy, bd trustee, St Mary's Episcopal Ctr, 1988-92; bd adv, St Andrew's Sewanee Sch, 1989-; prog comt, KANUGA Conf Ctr, 1989-93, bd adv, Diversity Comn, KANUGA Conf Ctr, 1996-2000; bd trustee, bd adv, 2000-; bd dir, Evangel Educ Soc, 1992-98; bd trustee, Wash Episcopal Sch, 1992-; bd, National Council of Churches; Church Hist Soc; bd dir, Asn Study Afro-Am Life & Hist; Am Hist Asn; Southern Hist Asn; lifetime mem, parliamentarian, Union Black Episcopalians; Diocese of Maryland's Commission for Black Ministry; consult, Baltimore Pub Schs; consult, Archdiocese Wash Schs; consult, Nat Sci Found; lifetime mem, Nat Asn Advan Colored People. **Honors/Awds:** Faculty Research in the Social Sciences Award, 1973-74; Spencer Foundation Award, 1975; American Philosophical Society Award, 1976; Commission for Black Minsters Grant, 1976-78; Absalom Jones Award, 1987; Grambling University Award, Grambling State Univ, 1990; Kanuga Conference Center Award, 1991. **Special Achievements:** Publications: The Church and the Civil Rights Movement; Freedom's Matrix; Struggle Strive and Salvation; The Role of Blacks in the Episcopal Church; Afro-Anglicanism Linkages, 1701-1900; Ethiopia Shall Soon Stretch Out Her Hands Unto God. Authored: The biographical sketches in Lesser Feast and Fast of the first three African American Saints: Absalom Jones, Alexander Crummell and Dr. Martin Luther King Jr. **Home Addr:** PO Box 10125, Washington, DC 20018-0125. **Business Addr:** Associate Rector, Saint Georges Episcopal Church, 160 U St NW, Washington, DC 20001, **Business Phone:** (202)387-6421.

### HAYDEN, ROBERT C., JR.

Historian, writer, educator. **Personal:** Born Aug 21, 1937, New Bedford, MA; son of Robert C Sr (deceased) and Josephine Hughes (deceased); children: Deborah Hayden-Hall, Kevin R Esq & Karen E McAdams. **Educ:** Boston Univ, Boston MA, BA, 1959, MED, 1961; Harvard Univ, Cambridge MA, cert, 1966; MA Inst Technol, cert, 1977. **Career:** Newton Pub Sch, sci teacher, 1961-65; Xerox Educ Div, sci ed, 1966-69; Metrop Coun Educ Opportunity, Boston MA, exec dir, 1970-73; Educ Develop Ctr, Newton MA, proj dir, 1974-80; Northeastern Univ, Boston MA, adj fac, 1978; Northeastern Univ, Boston, sr lectr, 1978-2001; MA Inst Technol, dir, Sec Tech Educ Proj, 1980-82; Boston Pub Schs, Boston MA, exec asst, supt, dir proj develop, 1982-86; MA Pre-Engineering Prog, Boston MA, exec dir, 1987-91; Lesley Univ, sr lectr, 1992-2005; Univ MA, Boston, lectr, 1993; Art Inst Boston, lectr, 1994; Schomburg Ctr Res Black Cult, scholar-in-residence, 1994-95; Oak Bluffs Hist Comn, 1998-2000; RCH Assoc, founder & pres, currently; Xerox Corp, ed educ div, solutions exec, sr info risk analyst. **Orgs:** Kappa Alpha Psi Fraternity, 1957; Nat Asn Black Sch Educr, 1976-90; Black Educr Alliance MS, 1980-92; secy, Asn Study Afro-Am Life & Hist, 1995; nat secy, pres, Asn Study African Am Life & Hist. **Home Addr:** PO Box 5453, Boston, MA 02102. **Business Addr:** President, 22 Menahan St, Vineyard Haven, MA 02568, **Business Phone:** (508)693-8714.

### HAYDEN, WILLIAM HUGHES

Investment banker. **Personal:** Born Apr 26, 1940, New Bedford, MA. **Educ:** Southeastern Mass Univ, BS & BA, 1962; New Eng Sch Law, JD, 1967; New Sch Social Res, cert, 1968. **Career:** Atty Gens Off, MA, 1963-67; US Dept, treas, 1966-67; Pres Comn Civil Dis, asst dir cong rels, 1967-; NY State Urban Devel Corp, reg dir, 1968-73; Grapetree Bay Hotels Co, gen partner, 1973-75; E End Resources Corp, pres, 1973-75; Metro Appl Res Ctr, sr fel, 1974-75; JP Morgan & Co, managing dir; First Boston Corp, managing dir, 1974-84; Bear Stearns & Co, sr managing dir & partner, 1984-. **Orgs:** Former dir, Wiltwyck Sch Boys, 1976-78; bd dir, Urban Home Ownership Corp, 1977; bd dir, United Neighborhood Houses NY City, 1977-; former dir, First Women's Bank NY, 1979; Munic Bond Club NY, 1980-; former trustee, vice chmn, Citizen's Budget Comt, City NY, 1981-99; trustee, vice chair, Citizens Budget Comn, City NY, 1983-89; trustee, Nat Asn Advan Colored People Spec Contrib Fund; life mem, Nat Asn Advan Colored People; trustee, African Am Inst, 1985-98; dir, Mus African Art; dir, S African Free Election Fund; chair, Get Ahead Found (S Africa Bus Financing Orgn), 1985-98; trustee, mem exec comt, New Sch Univ, 1990-; past chair exec comt, Nat Asn Securities Prof, 1990-93; dir, Nat Asn Securities Profs; trustee, NY Law Sch, 1995-; SIA, Comt Pub & Munic Finance; trustee, Citizen Union, NY, 1998-; bd trustee, Trooper Found. **Home Addr:** 30 5th Ave, New York, NY 10011, **Home Phone:** (212)677-5605. **Business Addr:** Senior Managing Director, Partner, Bear Stearns & Co Inc, 383 Madison Ave, New York, NY 10179, **Business Phone:** (212)272-2000.

### HAYE, ESQ. CLIFFORD S.

Lawyer. **Personal:** Born Dec 20, 1942, NY; son of Clifford and Sylvia; married Jenelyn; children: Angela & Christopher. **Educ:** Mich State Univ; NC Cent State Univ, BA, 1966; Columbia Law Sch, JD, 1972. **Career:** US Dept Justice, trial atty, 1972-73; NY Stock Exchange, enforcement atty, 1973-74; Teachers Ins & Annuity Asn-Col Retirement Equities Fund, asst gen coun, 1974, minority lawyer, corp coun, sr coun, currently; David M Fleisher PC, strategic advisor; Columbia Univ Law Sch, residence adv; Spencer Partners LLC, partner, consult & atty, currently. **Orgs:** Comn elect Charles Evers Gov, 1971; vol atty, Comm Law Off, 1974-78; atty, Indigent Panel Kings Co, 1975-79. **Home Addr:** 5 Heritage Dr, Pleasantville, NY 10570, **Home Phone:** (914)747-0765. **Business Addr:** Partner, Attorney, Spencer Partners LLC, PO Box 7333, Bloomfield, CT 06002-7333, **Business Phone:** (888)530-5551.

### HAYES, DR. BARBARA E.

Dean (education), educator. **Personal:** married Robert L. **Educ:** Tex Southern Univ, BS, pharm, 1975; Purdue Univ, MS, pharamacol, 1977; Univ Houston, PhD, pharamacol, 1984. **Career:** Tex Southern Univ, Sch Pharm, assoc dean acad affairs, assoc prof pharmacol, 1984-89, assoc prof pharamacol, 1989-2008, Col Pharm & Health Scis, dean, 2001-11, prof pharamacol, 1984-2014 & 2008-, prin investr, 2008-13, prof emer, 2014-; Nat Insts Health, prin; Am Asn Cols Pharm, chair. **Orgs:** Pres, Asn Minority Health Prof Sch, 2005-; Amn Asn Cols Pharm; Amn Diabetes Asn; Amn Asn Pharmaceut Scientists; Food & Drug Admin's Generic Drugs Adv Comt; Nat Inst Diabetes, Digestive & Kidney Dis Adv Coun; Nat Ctr Res Resources Sci & Tech Rev Bd; bd dir, Asn Minority Health Professions Schs. **Business Addr:** Professor, Professor Emeritus, Texas Southern University, Gray Hall 3100 Cleburne St Rm 134, Houston, TX 77004, **Business Phone:** (713)313-7011.

### HAYES, CHARLES

Government official, commissioner, lawyer. **Personal:** Born Oct 14, 1943, Catherine, AL; married Muriel. **Educ:** Mobile Bus Col, dipl, 1970; Selma Univ, assoc, 1971; Wallace Community Col, dipl, 1973; Univ S Ala, attended 1983; Dale Carnegie, attended 1984. **Career:** Government official (retired); Wilcox Co, comnr, currently; 4th Judicial Circuit, spec investr dist atty, indigent def comn. **Orgs:** Alta Comn Health Clin, 1981-84; Asn Co Comnr, 1982-; deacon Salem Baptist Ch, 1982-; dir, Alta Comn Club, 1983-85; dir, Alta Community Fire Dept, 1984-; Wilcox Co Dem Conf; Ala Dem Conf Black Caucus. **Honors/Awds:** Outstanding Leadership Award, Alberta Comn Club-Alberta AL, 1984. **Home Addr:** 300Patterson Rd, Catherine, AL 36728, **Home Phone:** (334)225-4561.

### HAYES, CHARLES DEWAYNE (CHARLIE HAYES)

Baseball player, baseball executive. **Personal:** Born May 29, 1965, Hattiesburg, MS. **Career:** Baseball player (retired), baseball exec; San Francisco Giants, third baseman, 1988-89, 1998-99; Philadelphia Phillies, third baseman, 1989-91, 1995; New York Yankees, third baseman, 1992, 1996-97; Colo Rockies, third baseman, 1993-94; Pittsburgh Pirates, third baseman, 1996; Milwaukee Brewers, third baseman, 2000; Houston Astros, third baseman, 2001; Big League Baseball Acad, owner & operator, currently. **Business Addr:** Owner, Operator, Big League Baseball Academy, 22119 Hufsmith Kohrville, Tomball, TX 77375, **Business Phone:** (281)357-4330.

### HAYES, CHRIS

Football player, executive. **Personal:** Born May 7, 1972, San Bernardino, CA; married Aran; children: Christopher Jr, Isaiah & Jeremiah. **Educ:** Wash State Univ, BA, social sci & mkt, 1995. **Career:** Football player (retired), exec; Green Bay Packers, defensive back, 1996; New York Jets, 1997-2001; New Eng Patriots, 2002; New Century Mortgage Corp, region acct exec, 2004-06; New Century Mortgage, acct exec, 2005-07; Homecomings Financial, GMAC, acct exec, 2006-07, acct exec, 2007; 3030 Productions Inc, founder & chief exec officer, 2007-09; Game Clip LLC, chief exec officer & founder, 2008-09; Its 90 Percent Inc, chief exec officer & founder, 2008-; Eli Lilly & Co, diabetes sales rep, 2014-. **Orgs:** Founder, Chris Hayes Motivational. **Business Addr:** Chief Executive Officer, Founder, My Game Clip LLC, 26500 W Agoura Rd Suite 102-768, Calabasas, CA 91303, **Business Phone:** (818)381-2141.

### HAYES, CURTISS LEO

Educator, clergy. **Personal:** Born Jan 10, 1931, Glasgow, MO; son of Otis and Janie; married Opal Juanita Owens; children: Janice R Almond, Curtiss L Jr & Collin L. **Educ:** Morning Side Col, BA, 1956; Ariz State Univ, MA, 1974; Dallas Theol Sem, ThM, 1980. **Career:** Teacher, pastor (retired); Sec Pub Schs, teacher, 1956-75; Sudan Interior Mission, Christian educ coord, 1980-84; Liberian Baptist Theol Sem, theol instr, 1982-83; Dallas Bible Col, missionary residence, 1984-85; Dallas Independent Sch Dist, substitute teacher; United Methodist Church, pastor. Author: Life Still Goes On. **Orgs:** Nat Asn Advan Colored People, 1956; pres, Desert Sands Teachers Asn, 1972; Stull Bill Steering Comm, 1973; Nat Educ Asn, 1973; lic minister, Mt Zion Baptist Church, 1980; instr, Monrovia Bible Inst, 1982. **Home Addr:** 8451 La Prada Dr E Suite 1082, Dallas, TX 75228. **Business Addr:** Substitute Teacher, Dallas Independent School District, 3807 Ross Ave, Dallas, TX 75204, **Business Phone:** (972)925-3700.

### HAYES, DENNIS COURTLAND

Lawyer, government official. **Personal:** Born Jan 29, 1951, Indianapolis, IN; son of Robert Frederick Sr and Nadine Whitlock. **Educ:** Ind Univ, BS, hist, 1973; Ind Univ, JD, 1977. **Career:** Nat Asn Advan Colored People, atty, 1977-85; Nat Asn Advan Colored People, MD, asst gen coun, 1985-90; Nat Asn Advan Colored People, MD, gen coun, 1990-; Nat Asn Advan Colored People, MD, interim chief exec officer, 1993; Nat Asn Advan Colored People, MD, interim chief exec officer, 2005. **Orgs:** Diversity Comt, vice chair, Am Bar Asn, 1994-; pres, Columbia Sportsmens Asn, 1994-; vpres, Waring-Mitchell Law Soc Columbia, Maryland, 1990-93; bd mem, Am Judicature Soc; Nat Bar Asn. **Business Addr:** General counsel, National Association for the Advancement of Colored People, 4805 Mount Hope Dr, Baltimore, MD 21215, **Business Phone:** (410)580-5777.

### HAYES, DONALD ROSS, JR.

Football player. **Personal:** Born Jul 13, 1975, Century, FL; son of Donald Sr and Diana Thomas; married Takina Alona Wright; children: Ross Emile. **Educ:** Univ Wis, grad. **Career:** Football player (retired); Carolina Panthers, 1998, 2004, left guard, 1999, wide receiver, 2000-01; New Eng Patriots, wide receiver, 2002; Jacksonville Jaguars, 2003; Can Football League, Toronto Argonauts, wide receiver, 2006. **Honors/Awds:** Madison Sports Hall of Fame, 2013.

### HAYES, EDWARD, JR.

Lawyer. **Personal:** Born Jun 19, 1947, Long Branch, NJ; son of Edward and Bessie E Dickerson; married Alice Hall; children: Blair Hall & Kia Hall. **Educ:** Wesleyan Univ, BA, polit sci, 1969; Stanford Law Sch, JD, 1972. **Career:** Commr Mary Gardner Jones FTC, clerk, 1971; Citizens Commun Ctr, atty, 1972-74; Hayes & White, partner atty, 1974-84; Baker & Hostetler, partner atty, 1984-92; US Dept Health & Human Serv, counr to secy, 1993-; MVM Inc, sr vpres admin & gen coun, 2002-; Voxiva Inc, chief legal officer & gen coun; Allied Commun Inc, gen coun; Regulatory Task Force Africa Iridium Satellite Corp, chmn. **Orgs:** Supreme Ct Bar; DC Bar; bd mem, Nat Capital YMCA; adv comm, African Develop Fund; bd mem, Inst Int Trade & Develop; bd mem, DC Chamber Comm; Nat Asn Broadcasters; Nat Asn Black Owned Broadcasters; exec comt, Wash Int Trade Asn, Fed Commun Bar Asn; Wash Foreign Law Soc; Orgn Am States-DC Chamber Joint Comt Int Trade. **Special Achievements:** Published articles in National Bar Association. **Home Addr:** 3206 Morrison St NW, Washington, DC 20015, **Home Phone:** (202)363-8183. **Business Addr:** Senior Vice President, MVM Inc, 8301 Greensboro Dr Suite 300, Mclean, VA 22102, **Business Phone:** (703)790-3138.

### HAYES, ELEANOR MAXINE

Television news anchorperson. **Personal:** Born Feb 9, 1954, Cleveland, OH; daughter of Jimmy and Ruth. **Educ:** El Instituto Tecnologico de Monterrey, Monterrey, mex, 1971; Western Col, Oxford, OH, 1972; Oberlin Col, Oberlin, OH, commun & polit sci, 1976; Miami Univ Oxford. **Career:** WERE Radio, Cleveland, Ohio, anchor & reporter, 1976-79; WTOL-TV, Toledo, Ohio, investigative reporter; WTVF-TV, Nashville, Tenn, anchor; WISN-TV, Milwaukee, Wis, co-anchor, 1983-87; WJW-TV 8, Cleveland, OH, co-anchor, 1987, reporter & anchor; WVIZ-TV, "Women's Health Service", prog host; ACN-TV, anchor; McDonald's Restaurants, owner, 1993-2003; Ohio News Network, anchor & reporter, 2005-; Cleveland Clin, dir commun. **Orgs:** Am Sickle Cell Anemia Asn, 1989-; bd trustee, Cleveland Inst Music. **Honors/Awds:** Numerous awards including Three Emmy Awards, Nat acad TV Arts & Sci; Volunteer Achievement Award, United Black Fund Greater Cleveland, 1991; National NABJ, UPI & AP reporting honors; inductee, Broadcasters Hall of Fame, 2003. **Home Addr:** 4146 Ellison Rd, South Euclid, OH 44121, **Home Phone:** (216)381-3155. **Business Addr:** Reporter, Ohio News Network, 770 Twin Rivers Dr, Columbus, OH 43215, **Business Phone:** (614)280-3600.

### HAYES, ELVIN ERNEST

Executive, baseball player, government official. **Personal:** Born Nov 17, 1945, Rayville, LA; married Erna; children: Elvin Jr, Erna Jr, Erica & Ethan. **Educ:** Univ Houston, attended 1968; Col Md Law Enforcement Acad. **Career:** Basketball player (retired), business owner, government official; SanDiego Rockets, 1968-71, Houston Rockets, 1971-72, 1981-84, 1981-84, Baltimore Bullets, 1972-73, Capital Bullets, 1973-74, Wash Bullets, 1974-81; Greater Cleveland Ford-Mercury Inc, chief exec officer; Elvin Hayes Ford Inc, owner, currently; Liberty Co Sheriff's Off, res dep, 2007-12. Tv Series: "Blank", 2012. **Orgs:** Iota Phi Theta Fraternity; NBA's 50th Anniversary All-Time Team. **Business Addr:** Owner, Elvin Hayes Ford Inc, PO Box 1547, Crosby, TX 77532, **Business Phone:** (281)328-9555.

### HAYES, DR. FLOYD WINDOM, III

Educator. **Personal:** Born Nov 3, 1942, Gary, IN; son of Charles Henry and Thelma Ruth Person; married Charlene Moore; children: Tracy, Keisha, Ndidi & Kia-Lillian. **Educ:** Univ Paris, cert, 1964; NC Cent Univ, BA, fr & polit sci, 1967; Univ Calif, Los Angeles, MA, African area studies, 1969; Univ Md, PhD, govt & polit, 1985; Univ Paris, Certificat d Etudes, fr. **Career:** Univ Calif, Los Angeles, instruction specialist, 1969-70; Princeton Univ, lectr dept polit, exec sec Afro-Amer studies, 1970-71; Swarth more Col, Dept Hist, vis lectr, 1971; Univ Md, asst coord Afro-Amer studies, 1971-73, instr, 1971-77; Cornell Univ, instr Africana studies, 1977-78; Close Up Found, prog instruct, 1979-80; Howard Univ, res asst, res felinst ed policy, 1980-81, 1981-85; US Equal Employment Oppor Com, special asst to chmn, 1985-86; San Diego State Univ, asst prof Africana studies, 1986; NC State Univ, assoc prof; John Hopkins Univ, sr lectr & coord undergrad prog, currently; Author: A Turbulent Voyage: Readings in African American Studies, 2000. **Orgs:** Consultant Union Township Sch System, 1971, Comm Educ Exchange Prog Columbia Univ, 1972, MD State Dept Educ, 1973-75; Early Childhood Educ Sub comm FICE, US Dept Educ, 1986. **Home Addr:** 284 61st St, San Diego, CA 92114, **Home Phone:** (619)263-0444. **Business Addr:** Senior Lecturer, Coordinator of Programs and Undergraduate Studies, John Hopkins University, Greenhouse 107, Baltimore, MD 21218, **Business Phone:** (410)516-7659.

### HAYES, GRAHAM EDMONDSON

Lawyer. **Personal:** Born Nov 2, 1929, Horton, KS; married Juanita (Charles) Hil; children: Sondra, Karen, Graham II (deceased) & Alisa. **Educ:** Washburn Univ, AB, 1956; Washburn Univ, JD, AB, 1957, LLB. **Career:** Sedgwick Co, dep dist atty, 1958-62; KS Comn Civil Rights, atty, 1970-74; Wichita Comn Civil Rights, examr, 1974, atty, 1975-; Pvt pract atty law, currently. **Orgs:** Supreme Ct US; US Ct Claimes; Tax Ct US; US Dist Ct; Circuit Ct US; Supreme Ct Kans; USAF Bd Correction Mil Rec; St Bd Law Examr KS; bd dir, Kans Trial Lawyers Asn; Am Trial Lawyers Asn; Nat Asn Criminal Def Lawyers; pres, Urban League Wichita; Veterans Foreign Wars Post 6888; Kappa Alpha Psi; Kans State Bar. **Honors/Awds:** Appt Exmnr, 1976; Kans State Bd Admis Atty, 1979. **Business Addr:** Attorney, 2459 N Plumthicket Ct, Wichita, KS 67226-1525, **Business Phone:** (316)315-0884.

### HAYES, JACQUELYN

Executive. **Career:** Ford-Employees African Ancestry Network, pres, 2016. **Business Addr:** President, Ford-Employees African Ancestry Network, 3663 Lake Shore Rd, Buffalo, NY 14219.

### HAYES, JAMES HAROLD, JR.

Television journalist. **Personal:** Born Apr 21, 1953, McKeesport, PA; son of J Harold Sr and Gladys Burrell; married Iris Dennis; children: Kristin Heather & Lindsay Victoria. **Educ:** Univ Pittsburgh, Pittsburgh, Pa, BA, speech & commun, 1975. **Career:** Urban League Pittsburgh, "Reading Fundamental" prog, res asst, 1975-76; WSIV-AM, Pekin, Ill, announcer, 1976-77; WRAU-TV, Peoria, Ill, weekend anchor & reporter, 1977-79; KDKA-TV, Pittsburgh, Pa, reporter, 1979-. **Orgs:** Nat Asn Black Journalists, 1987-; trustee, Mt Ararat Baptist Church; spokesman, Negro Educ Emergency Fund. **Honors/Awds:** Recipient of scholarship, Negro Educ Emergency Fund (NEED). **Home Addr:** 1217 S Negley Ave, Pittsburgh, PA 15217-1218, **Home Phone:** (412)422-7965. **Business Addr:** Reporter, KDKA-TV, 1 Gateway Ctr, Pittsburgh, PA 15222, **Business Phone:** (412)575-2200.

### HAYES, JIM (JAMES C HAYES)

Association executive, mayor, clergy. **Personal:** Born May 25, 1946, Sacramento, CA; son of Juanita Hayes Metoyer; married Murilda C; married Chris Parham; children: LaNene Hayes-Pruitt & James Jr. **Educ:** Univ Alaska, BA, 1970. **Career:** Joy Elem Sch, Fairbanks, AK, teacher, 1970-71; President's Coun Youth & Job Opportunity, Juneau, AK, bur dir, 1971; Off Gov, Manpower Planning Div, Juneau, dep dir, 1971-72; Off Consumer Protection, Fairbanks, assoc atty-investr, 1972-90, 1991, investr, 1990-91; City Coun Fairbanks, councilman; State Alaska, Consumer Protection Off, investr; City Fairbanks, mayor, 1992-2001; Univ Alaska Bd Regents, regent, 2003; Lily Valley church, pastor. **Orgs:** Fairbanks City Coun, 1987-92; Fairbanks N Star Bor Sch Bd; bd dir, Love Social Services Ctr, 2001-05. **Home Addr:** Doyon Estates, 2601 Chief Alexander Dr, Fairbanks, AK 99709, **Home Phone:** (907)456-7698. **Business Addr:** AK.

### HAYES, JONATHAN MICHAEL

Football coach, football player. **Personal:** Born Aug 11, 1962, South Fayette, PA; son of Jewett and Florence Joy; married Kristi; children: 4. **Educ:** Univ Iowa, BS, criminol, 1986. **Career:** Football player (retired); football coach; Kans City Chiefs, tight end, 1985-93; Pittsburgh Steelers, tight end, 1994-96; Univ Okla, asst coach, 1999-2002; Okla Sooners, staff, 1999-2002; Cincinnati Bengals, tight ends coach, 2003-. **Special Achievements:** Considered one of the finest blocking tight ends in the NFL. **Business Addr:** Tight Ends Coach, Cincinnati Bengals, 1 Paul Brown Stadium, Cincinnati, OH 45202, **Business Phone:** (513)621-3550.

### HAYES, LAURA

Comedian, actor. **Personal:** Born Oaktown, CA. **Career:** TV series: "Martin", 1992-96; "The Parent Hood", 1997; "That's Life", 2001; "The Hughleys", 2001; "King of Queens", 2001; "Bette", 2001; "For Your Love", 2002; "Kristin"; "Politically Incorrect"; "The Parkers", 2003; Finders Keepers, 2005; "All of Us", 2006; "The Sarah Silverman Program", 2007; "Safety Geeks SVI, 2009; "Meet the Browns", 2010; "Whatcha Cookin", 2013. Stage shows: Bay Area Black Comedy Competition, host, 1988-96; BET's Comic View, co-host, 1996-98 & 2000; Theater performance: Out on a Twig. Films: I Got the Hook-Up; Miss Laura: Felon to Funny; Def Comedy Jam 1, 1993; The Latham Comedy Collection, 2000-03; Comic View All-Stars, 2002; Beauty Shop, 2005; Low, 2006; Virus, actor, dir, exec producer & writer, 2006; Act of Faith, 2014. TV Shows: "Showtime's Queens of Comedy", host; "ABC's Christmas Spec, Sinbad & Friends"; "Health Insurance", 2005; "Neesee's Grave Plot", 2006; The Sea of Dreams, 2011. **Orgs:** Spokesperson, CalWORKS/Behav Health Care Serv. **Honors/Awds:** Comedian of the month. **Business Addr:** Comedian, c/o Shirley Wilson & Associates, 5410 Wilshire Blvd Suite 806, Los Angeles, CA 90036, **Business Phone:** (323)857-6977.

### HAYES, DR. LEOLA G.

Educator, college teacher, chairperson. **Personal:** Born Rocky Mount, NC; married Spurgeon S. **Educ:** PhD, 1973; BS; MA; MS, prof dipl. **Career:** NY Inst Blind, teacher, 1953-54; Fair Lawn NJ, teacher handicapped c; Blind Chicago, consult, 1954-57; Fair Lawn NJ, supv spl educ, 1957-64; William Paterson Col, NJ, Spec Educ Dept, chmn, currently. **Orgs:** Drug Abuse Prog, 1973-; CEC; Voc Rehab Soc; AAMD; NJEA; Young People Coun Session, Alpha Kappa Alpha Sorority. **Home Addr:** 193 Lakeview Ave, Leonia, NJ 07605. **Business Addr:** Professor, William Paterson College, 300 Pompton Rd, Wayne, NJ 07470.

### HAYES, MELVIN ANTHONY

Football player. **Personal:** Born Apr 28, 1973, New Orleans, LA. **Educ:** Miss State Univ, BS. **Career:** Football player (retired); New York Jets, guard, 1995-96; Houston Oilers, 1996; Tennessee Oilers, 1997; Tennessee Titans; Nat Strength and Conditioning Asn, personal trainer.

### HAYES, MERCURY WAYNE

Football player. **Personal:** Born Jan 1, 1973, Houston, TX; son of Richard. **Educ:** Univ Mich, BS, commun. **Career:** Football player (retired); New Orleans Saints, wide receiver, 1996-97; Atlanta Falcons, wide receiver, 1997; Wash Redskins, 1998; Barcelona Dragons, Europe, 1999; Montreal Alouettes, 1999-2000; Norfolk Nighthawks, 2002. **Honors/Awds:** Michigan All-time Record consecutive games with reception, 1995-01. **Home Addr:** Whitney St, Houston, TX 77018.

### HAYES, NORMAN A.

Executive. **Career:** Ind State Univ, dir financial aid. **Orgs:** Enrollment Mgt Team Subcomt. **Business Addr:** Director Financial Aid, Indiana State University, 200 N 7Th St, Terre Haute, IN 47809-1902, **Business Phone:** (812)237-6311.

### HAYES, REGINALD

Actor. **Personal:** Born Jul 15, 1969, Chicago, IL; son of Reginald and Frances. **Educ:** Ill State Univ, BA, theater; N western Mil Naval Acad. **Career:** Films: A Family Thing, 1996; Space Above and Beyond, 1996; Nick Fresno, 1996; Something So Right, 1997; Pretender, 1997; Chicago Cab, 1997; Being John Malkovich, 1999; Grown Ups, 1999; Party of Five, 1999; Charlie's Angels, 2000; Stop Thief!, 2004; Mother's Day, 2014. TV Series: "Getting Personal", 1998; "Roswell", 1999; "Girlfriends", 2000-08; "Will & Grace", 2000; "Then Came You", 2000; "The Twilight Zone", 2003; "Kim Possible", 2003; "Hummingbird Magic", narrator, 2009; "Femme Fatales", 2011; "Criminal Minds", 2012; "Let's Stay Together", 2013; "The First Family", 2013; "The Devon Taylor Show", 2013; "Hart of Dixie", 2013-14. **Orgs:** Ill Shakespeare Festival. **Honors/Awds:** Outstanding Young Alumni Award, Ill State Univ, 2004; Image Awards, Nat Asn Advan Colored People, 2005-07; Sexiest Man Alive, People Mag, 2007; Notable Men of the Academy Award, St John's Northwestern Mil Acad, 2011. **Business Addr:** Actor, c/o United Paramount Network, 11800 Wilshire Blvd, Los Angeles, CA 90025, **Business Phone:** (310)575-7000.

### HAYES, TEDDY (THEODORE HAYES)

Writer, playwright, movie director. **Personal:** Born Oct 20, 1951, Cleveland, OH; son of Evelyn and Ernest; children: Kai. **Educ:** Cleveland State Univ, BA, film & tv, 1974. **Career:** Vindicator, ed, 1970; community action agency, Dayton, Ohio, short filmmaker & commun officer, 1970; Roberta Flack world tour, tour mgr, 1976; Melvin Van Peebles Productions, writing asst & off mgr; freelance writer & music video dir; Waltz of the Stork Boogie, producer, 1980; creative writing teacher, London, Eng, 1990-; Vroom Vroom Vroom, actor, 1995; SKD Productions, owner, currently; DEvil Barnett Detective novels, theatrical producer/writer; Theatre Stream Channel, co-managing dir; Screenwriter: Panther, 1995; Case No. 603, 2003. **Orgs:** Crime Writers Asn; Burry Man Writers Ctr. **Business Addr:** Owner, Teddy Hayes Productions Ltd, 51 Oaklands Ave, London, GL TW7 5PY, **Business Phone:** (208)581-7684.

### HAYES-GILES, JOYCE V.

Executive. **Personal:** Born Jackson, MS; daughter of Isaac and Myrtle Stigger; married Ronald; children: Kristen & Erica. **Educ:** Knoxville Col, BA, psychol, 1970; Univ Detroit, MBA, indust rels & personnel mgt, 1978; Wayne State Law Sch, JD, 1985. **Career:** Chrysler Corp, salary admin analyst supvr, 1971-76; Conn Gen Life Ins Co; Auto Club Mich, compensation adminr, 1976-78; MichCon Gas Co, dir mat mgt & other managerial positions; MCN Energy Group, vpres corp resources, 2001, DTE Energy, sr vpres customer serv, bd mem, asst chmn, sr vpres pub affairs; Detroit Pub Sch, bd dir, 2013-. **Orgs:** Nat Black MBA Asn, 1978-; exec comt, Amer Red Cross; Detroit Bar Asn, Mich Bar Asn; Nat Purchasing Asn; chairperson personnel comt & vpres bd, YWCA; Nat Asn Advan Colored People; Links Inc; Delta Sigma Theta Sor Inc; pres, Metropol YWCA, 1988-89; Jack & Jill Am; bd chair, Detroit Urban League; chair, Marygrove Coll; Wolverine Bar Asn; chair, Oakwood Healthcare Inc; State Mich; Wolverine Bar Asn; Women's Econ Club, Detroit; Leadership Detroit Alumni Asn; bd dir, Am Asn Blacks Energy; bd mem, Health Alliance Plan Mich, 2011-; chmn, Education Achievement Authority, 2014-. **Home Addr:** 19535 Afton, Detroit, MI 48203-1437.

### HAYES-JORDAN, MARGARET

Executive. **Personal:** Born Jan 1, 1943; children: 3. **Educ:** Georgetown Univ, Wash, DC, BSN, 1964; Univ Calif-Berkeley, Berkeley, CA, MPH, 1972; Harvard Univ Sch Bus, advan mgt prog. **Career:** San Bernardino Community Hosp, San Bernardino, Calif, staff nurse, 1964-65; Vis Nurse Asn San Francisco, San Francisco, Calif, pub health nurse, 1966-67, pvt duty nurse, 1967-68; Southern Calif Edison Co, vpres health care & employee serv, 1992-96; Margaret Jordan Group, chief exec officer & pres; OraSure Technologies Inc, dir; Tex Health Harris Methodist Ft Worth Hosp Inc, Tex Health Resources, exec vpres corp affairs; Epitope Inc, dir; Kaiser Found Health Plan, vpres & regional mgr; Comprehensive Child Care Proj, Mt Zion Hosp, San Francisco, Calif, sr pub he; Dallas Med Resource, chief exec officer, pres, 2004-. **Orgs:** Exec bd mem, Am Pub Health Asn; founder & dir, Nat Black Nurses Asn Inc; pres & dir, Bay Area Black Nurses Asn Inc; founder & dir, Bay Area Black Consortium Qual Health Care Inc; Dallas Assembly; Dallas Citizens Coun; adv bd, Dallas Women's Found; bd dir, Greater Dallas Community Churches; bd dir, Tex State Bd Ins High Risk Health Pool; Sch Nursing Adv Coun, Univ Tex, Arlington; adv bd, Women's Ctr Dallas; Dir, Dallas Mus Art, Dir; Pub Health Inst; AT&T Performing Arts Ctr; dir, Colonial Bank; dir, Eckerd Corp, 1995; dir, Tex Region; Dir, Reliant Pharmaceut, 2005; trustee, Am Hosp Asn Inc; dir, Fed Res Bank Dallas; bd dir, Dallas Mus Art; bd dir, Women's Mus; dir, nominating & governance comt, Mentor Worldwide LLC, 2007-; bd dir, Montpelier Found. **Home Addr:** 5919 Tree Shadow Pl, Dallas, TX 75248, **Home Phone:** (214)248-3607. **Business Addr:** Executive Vice President for Corporate Affairs, Dallas Medical Resource, 2911 Turtle Creek Blvd Suite 300, Dallas, TX 75219, **Business Phone:** (214)523-9034.

### HAYGOOD, MARSHA

President (organization), founder (originator). **Educ:** Lehman Col NY, BA; NY Univ, human resource training & develop cert. **Career:** Orion Pictures, human resources exec, 1984-92; New Line Cinema, exec vpres, human resources & admin, 1993-2006; StepWise Assocs LLC, founder & pres, 2006-. **Orgs:** Soc Human Resource Mgt; New York Women Film & Tv; Nat Asn Female Execs; co founder & dd co chair, Black Women Influence; bd dir, YouthBridge NY, 2005-. **Business Addr:** Founder, President, StepWise Associates LLC, 1 Glenwood Ave, Yonkers, NY 10701, **Business Phone:** (914)965-1339.

### HAYGOOD, WIL

Journalist. **Personal:** Born Sep 19, 1954, Columbus, OH; son of Jack and Elvira. **Educ:** Miami Univ, BA, 1976. **Career:** Journalist, writer; Columbus Ohio Call & Post, reporter, 1977-78; Community Info & Referal, hotline operator, 1978-79; Macy's Dept Store NY, exec, 1980-81; The Charleston Gazette, copy ed, 1981-83; The Pittsburgh Post Gazette, reporter, 1984-85; The Boston Globe, feature reporter; Wash Post, Style Sect, writer, currently; Books: Two on the River; King of Cats: The Life and Times of Adam Clayton Powell Jr; The Haygoods of Columbus: A Love Story. **Orgs:** Fel James Thurber Lit; fel Alicia Patterson Found; Yaddo fel. **Honors/Awds:** National Headliner Award, Outstanding Feature Writing, 1986; Editors Award, Sunday Mag; New England Associated Press Award; Nat Headliners Award; Nat Asn Black Journalists Award; Great Lakes Book Award, 1997. **Special Achievements:** Auth: Two on the River, 1986; King of the Cats: The Life and Times of Adam Clayton Powell Jr., 1993; The Haygoods of Columbus: A Family Memoir, 1997; In Black and White: The Life of Sammy Davis Jr., 2003. **Home Addr:** 2801 Que St NW Suite 208, Washington, DC 20008. **Business Addr:** Writer, Washington Post, 1150 15th St NW, Washington, DC 20071, **Business Phone:** (202)334-6000.

### HAYLING, DR. WILLIAM HARTLEY

Gynecologist, obstetrician. **Personal:** Born Dec 7, 1925, Trenton, NJ; son of Dr William Hartley; married Carolyn Anne Mitchem; children: Pamela Hoffman & Patricia Price. **Educ:** Boston Univ, pre-med, 1945; Howard Univ, MD, 1949. **Career:** NJ Col Med & Dent, assoc prof obstet & gynec, 1960-80; King Drew Med Ctr, asst prof obstet & gynec, 1981-87, chief ambulatory obstet & gynec, 1981; Martin Luther King Jr, Hosp, chief ambulatory obstet & gynec, 1981-98; Charles R. Drew Univ Med & Sci, chief ambulatory obstet & gynec & prof, 1981-. **Orgs:** Pres, 100 Black Men NJ, 1975-78; bd mem, Jersey City State Col, NJ, 1975-80; pres, founder, 100 Black Men LA Inc, 1981-83; founder & pres, Nat 100 Black Men Am, 1987; fel Am Col Obstet & Gynec; fel Am Col Surgeons; bd trustee, Ymca; Nj State Med Soc; pres, Howard Univ Alumni Club Nj. **Honors/Awds:** Image Award, 100 Black Men of LA, 1982; LA Sentinel Award LA Sentinel Newspaper, 1983; Presidential Award Alpha Phi Alpha Fraternity, 1984. **Special Achievements:** Written numerous medical papers. **Home Addr:** 4314 Marina City Dr Suite 830S, Marina del Rey, CA 90292, **Home Phone:** (213)827-1049. **Business Addr:** Founder, 100 Black men of Los Angeles Inc, 3701 stocker st suite 309, Los Angeles, CA 90008, **Business Phone:** (323)294-7444.

### HAYMAN, WARREN C.

Consultant, educator. **Personal:** Born Oct 1, 1932, Baltimore, MD; married Jacqueline; children: Warren Jr, Guy & Julia. **Educ:** Coppin State Col, BS, elem educ, 1961; Stanford Univ, MA, math, 1967; Harvard Univ, EdD, 1978. **Career:** Baltimore City Schs, elem teacher, 1961-66; Belle Haven, elem prin, 1968-71; Stanford Univ, fac resident, 1970-73; Ravenswood, asst supt, 1971-73; Coppin State Col, dean educ; San Francisco State Univ, instr, 1971-74; Ravenswood City Sch Dist, supt, 1973-77; US Off Educ, consult, 1968-76; Morgan State Univ, Sch Educ & Urban Studies, asst dean, 2003-04, Coordr Urban Educ Doctoral Prog, currently. **Orgs:** Chmn bd, Nairobi Col, 1970-76; chmn bd, Mid-Peninsula Urban Coalition, 1973-75; reg dir educ, Phi Beta Sigma Frat Inc, 1980; bd trustee, Community Col Baltimore Co, 2007-; 100 Black Men Md; Coun Urban Bd Educ; Am Asn Sch

Adminr; Bd Educ Baltimore County; educ policy fel US Dept Educ; Baltimore Co Pub Schs, bd mem. **Honors/Awds:** Good Conduct Ribbon, AUS, 1955-57; elem math teacher fel, NSF, 1966; exp teacher fel, US Off Educ, 1966; higher educ fel, Rockfeller Found, 1976-78; Distinguished Black Marylander Award; Fullwood Foundation Valued Hours Award; Rotary Club Service Above Self Award; Dr Hayman mem Oxford Univ Round Table, 2006; Phi Beta Sigma Educ Award, 2007; Baltimore County NAACP Excellence Educ Award, 2008; Coppin State Univ Vision Award, 2009. **Home Addr:** 3714 Sylvan Dr, Baltimore, MD 21207. **Business Addr:** Board Trustee, The Community College of Baltimore County, 800 South Rolling Rd, Baltimore, MD 21228-5317, **Business Phone:** (443)840-2222.

### HAYMON, ALAN

Executive. **Personal:** Born Cleveland, OH. **Educ:** Harvard Univ, BA, 1977, MBA, 1980, studying econs. **Career:** Budweiser Superfest, concert series, 1979-99; Haymon Entertainment Inc, founder, chmn, owner currently. **Home Addr:** 247 Country Club Rd, Newton Center, MA 02459-3118. **Business Addr:** Chairman, Owner, Haymon Events LLC, 15 Sevland Rd, Newton, MA 02459-2841, **Business Phone:** (617)332-9680.

### HAYMORE, TYRONE

Curator. **Personal:** Born Mar 12, 1947, Chicago, IL; son of Mildred Ernestine Calhoun and T H. **Educ:** Thornton Jr Col, AA, 1969; Northeastern Ill Univ, BA, educ, 1986; Ill Inst Munic Clerks, munic clerk cert, 1992. **Career:** Chicago Transit Authority, rail clerk, 1968-1997; Village Robbins, IL, village clerk, trustee, 1983-87, village clerk, 1989; Village Robbins, 4 yr term, re-elected, clerk, 1993-2011; Channel 14 Cable TV, first exec producer & dir, 1994-; Robbins Hist Soc Mus, exec dir, cur, 1999-. **Orgs:** Dir, Comn Youth Bremen Twp, 1983; treas, Black Elected Officials Ill, 1984; Ill Civil Air Patrole; Munic Clerks Ill, 1989-93. **Honors/Awds:** Christian Leadership, Christ Crusader Church Robbins, 1965; Music Scholar Summer Music Camp, Eastern Ill Univ, 1965; Achievement Award, Mayor Robbins Ambulance Fund Dr, 1984; Plaque for Outstanding Service as Treasurer, Black Elected Officials Ill, 1990; Commuity Leadership Award; Plaque for Outstanding Historian in Robbins, Robbins Recreation & Training Ctr, 1992; Certificate for Professionalism as a CMC, 1993. **Special Achievements:** History Coloring Book entitled, Robbins, Illinois, co-author, 1994. **Business Addr:** Curator, Robbins Historical Society Museum, 13822 S Cent Pk Ave, Robbins, IL 60472, **Business Phone:** (708)389-5393.

### HAYNES, DR. ALPHONSO WORDEN, JR.

School administrator, educator. **Personal:** Born Brooklyn, NY; married Margaret S Alvarez; children: Thomas, Pia, Mia, Pilar, Alphonso III & Alejandro. **Educ:** Long Island Univ, BA, 1965; Columbia Univ, MS, 1967, MA, 1974, EdD, 1978. **Career:** NY City Dept Welfare, admin & recreation, 1953-67; Harlem Hosp Ctr, pediatsocial worker, 1967-69; Long Island Univ, dean stud, 1969-79; Norfolk State Univ, Sch Social Work, assoc prof & prog dir, 1979-81; Old Dom Univ, stud affairs, asst dean; Grand Valley State Univ, prof, Sch Social Work, prof emer, currently. **Orgs:** Nat Asn Soc Workers, 1967; Acad Cert Soc Workers, 1969; staff training consult, Chesapeake Soc Serv, 1979-80; Res FocusBlack Ed, 1980; admin, Va Asn Stud Personnel, 1981; bd mem, Young Adult & Campus Ministry, 1983; bd mem, Columbia Univ Sch Social Work Alumni Asn. **Honors/Awds:** Pi Gamma Mu Soc Sci Hon Soc, 1962; Karagheusian Memorial Fel, Columbia Univ, 1965-67; Outstanding Educator In America. **Home Addr:** 2132 Paramont Ave, Chesapeake, VA 23320. **Business Addr:** Professor Emeritus, Grand Valley State University, 391C DeVos Ctr, Grand Rapids, MI 49504, **Business Phone:** (616)331-6550.

### HAYNES, BARBARA ASCHE

Association executive, educator, administrator. **Personal:** Born Jun 26, 1935, Rochester, PA; married Donald F. **Educ:** Chatham Col, BS, 1958; Univ Pittsburgh, MS, 1967, PhD, 1985. **Career:** Educator (retired); Allegheny Gen Hosp Sch Nursing Pittsburgh, instr nursing, 1959-67; Allegheny Community Col, asst prof nursing, 1967-70, assoc prof & dept head, 1970-74, dean life sci & dir nursing prog, 1974-79; Col DuPage, instr nursing, 1979-80; Univ Ill Chicago Co Nursing, asst prof gen nursing & dir stud serv. **Orgs:** Secy, Univ Pittsburgh Sch Nursing Alumnae Asn, 1967-69; speaker, Teachers Col Columbia Univ, 1972; bd dir, Pa Nurses Asn, 1973-77; chmn nominating comn, Univ Pittsburgh Sch Nursing Alumnae Asn, 1974; speaker, Nat League Nursing-Coun Asn Degree Progs NY, 1974; bd dir, United Ment Health Allegheny Co, 1975-79; prof adv comn, NW Allegheny Home Care Prog, 1976-79; vice chmn conf group teaching, Pa Nurse's Asn, 1977-79; community nursing educ, Pa Nurses Asn, 1977-79; adv community, BSN Prog LaRoche Col, 1978-79; reg continuing educ adv comn, Duquesne Univ Group, 1978-79; Sigma Theta Tau Alpha Lambda Chapt. **Honors/Awds:** Chancellors Distinguished Public Service Award. **Special Achievements:** Publication: "The Practical Nurse" & "Auto-Education", PA Nurse, 1972. **Home Addr:** 149 Heritage Landing Rd, Williamsburg, VA 23188-7894, **Home Phone:** (757)259-9689.

### HAYNES, DR. BRIAN LEE

School administrator, association executive. **Personal:** Born Jul 20, 1964, Columbus, OH; son of Lewis and Sarah; married Jacquelyn Harris. **Educ:** Ohio State Univ, BA, hist, 1986; Ohio Univ, MS, health, PE, 1987, PhD, higher educ, 1991. **Career:** Ohio Univ, stud activ, asst dir, 1988-89, Health Careers Opportunity Prog, asst coordr, 1989-90, coordr minority stud serv, 1990-91; Gettysburg Col, asst dean, inter cult adv, 1991-92; E Carolina Univ, asst vc stud life, 1992-99; State Univ Syst Fla, dir, stud affairs, 1999-2000; FlaInt Univ, asst vpres stud affairs & state dir, 2000-05; Clayton State Univ, Morrow, Ga, Stud Affairs, vpres, 2005-. **Orgs:** Am Col Personnel Asn; Nat Asn Stud Personnel Adminr; Kappa Alpha Psi Fraternity; bd mem, N Am Scrabble Players Asn. **Home Addr:** 7737 NW 18th St, Hollywood, FL 33024, **Home Phone:** (954)965-3573. **Business Addr:** Vice President of Student Affairs, Clayton State University, 2000 Clayton State Blvd, Morrow, GA 30260, **Business Phone:** (678)466-5444.

### HAYNES, CORNELL IRAL, JR. See NELLY.

### HAYNES, FARNESE N. (FARNESE HAYNES MC-DONALD)

Lawyer, real estate agent. **Personal:** Born Dec 25, 1960, Bluefield, VA; daughter of Jesse Sr and Melda. **Educ:** Am Univ, BA, criminal justice, 1983; Howard Univ Sch Law, JD, 1986. **Career:** Howard Law J, ed-chief, 1984-86; Leftwich Moore & Douglas, staff atty, 1987; US Dept Agr, staff atty, 1987-93; GAO Personnel Appeals Bd, legal technician, 1987; Off Gen Coun, USDA, off gen coun, 1987-93; United Negro Col Fund Inc, asst gen coun, 1993-2000; Law off Farnese H. McDonald, atty, 2000-10; Leftwich & Douglas PLLC, sr atty, 2001-02; Weichert, Realtors, assoc broker, 2003-14; Md Dept Transp, equal opportunity officer, 2011-12; PREEMPT Corp, equal opportunity specialist fed agency, 2012; Transp Security Admin, eeo specialist & case mgr, 2013-14; Dept Defense, sr eeo specialist, 2014-, Dep Dir, Affirmative Employ & Diversity, 2015-16, lead human resources specialist, 2016-; Fairfax Realty Inc, assoc broker, 2014-. **Orgs:** Delta Sigma Theta Sorority Inc, 1980-; Ineffective Assistance Coun, 28, HOWLJ 191, 1985; Supreme Ct PA, 1986; Penn Bar Asn, 1986-93; DC Bar Asn, 1988-; Dist Columbia Ct Appeals, 1988; Md Bar Asn, 1989-; Ct Appeals Md, 1989; US Dist Ct, Dist Md, 1989; J Franklin Bourne Bar Asn, 1990-92; Supreme Ct VA, 1995; US Supreme Ct, 1997; Alfred St Baptist Church, 2014; chair, Fund raising Comt; Nat Asn Advan Colored People. **Special Achievements:** Publication:District of Columbia Court of Appeals Project on Criminal Procedure, Ineffective Assistance of Counsel, 28 How. L.J. 191 (1985), Howard Law Journal, 1985. **Home Addr:** 11685 Newbridge Ct, Reston, VA 20191-3516, **Home Phone:** (703)620-6629. **Business Addr:** Associate Broker, Fairfax Realty Inc, 3190 Fairview Pk Suite 100, Falls Church, VA 22042, **Business Phone:** (703)533-8660.

### HAYNES, ESQ. GALE STEVENS

Educator. **Educ:** Long Island Univ, BA, eng, MA, coun; St Johns Univ Sch Law, JD, 1983. **Career:** Long Island Univ, Higher Educ Opportunity Prog, dir, legal coun, 1983-89, provost, 1989-; chief opers officer, 2013-. **Orgs:** Chairwoman bd educ, Roosevelt Union Free Sch Dist, 2007-10; bd dir, Brooklyn Hosp Ctr, 2008. **Business Addr:** Provost, Long Island University, 1 Univ Plz, Brookville, NY 11201, **Business Phone:** (718)488-1000.

### HAYNES, DR. JAMES H.

School administrator. **Personal:** Born Nov 27, 1953, Pensacola, FL; son of Jap and Annie Sims. **Educ:** Pensacola Jr Col, AA, 1973; Morehouse Col, BA, 1975; Ga State Univ, MEd, 1977; Univ Iowa, PhD, educ admin, 1979. **Career:** Atlanta Pub Sch Syst, teacher, 1975-77; Philadelphia Training Ctr, asst dir, 1979-80; Fla A&M Univ, dir planning, 1980-83; Morgan State Univ, dir inst res, 1983-84, adj prof educ leadership, 1983-, vpres, Planning & Instnl Res, 1984-88, title III dir, title III prog coordr, 1988-; pres, Haynes Properties Inc, 1993-. **Orgs:** Woodrow Wilson Nat Fel Found, 1980; consult, Asn Minority Health Profession Sch, 1982; consult, Title III Prog Bowie State Col, 1984-; supvr admin, NTE, GMAT, 1984-; secy, Alpha Phi Alpha, Baltimore Morehouse Alumni Club; Nat Asn Advan Colored People; Morehouse Col Nat Alumni Asn; bd dir, Baltimore Employ Network; Nat Asn Historically Black Cols & Univs; hon mem, Promethean Kappa Tau; hon mem, Phi Delta Kappa; hon mem, Phi Alpha Theta; pres, Hanlon Improv Asn, 2005-09; mem bd dir, Hanlon Improv Asn. **Home Addr:** 3239 Powhatan Ave, Baltimore, MD 21216-1934, **Home Phone:** (410)462-9619. **Business Addr:** Title III Director, Morgan State University, 1700 Cold Spring Lane & Hillen Rd Rm 305 D, Baltimore, MD 21251, **Business Phone:** (443)885-3573.

### HAYNES, JOE A.

Executive director. **Career:** Jobs Miss Graduates Inc, exec dir, 2001-. **Business Addr:** Executive Director, Jobs for Mississippi Graduates Inc, 6055 Ridgewood Rd Suite A, Jackson, MS 39211, **Business Phone:** (601)978-1711.

### HAYNES, DR. JOHN KERMIT

Educator. **Personal:** Born Oct 30, 1943, Monroe, LA; son of John Kermit Sr and Grace Quanita Ross; married Carolyn Ann Price. **Educ:** Morehouse Col, Atlanta, GA, BS, biol, 1964; Brown Univ, Providence, RI, PhD, post-doctoral, molecular biol, 1971; Mass Inst Technol, Cambridge, MA, post-doctoral, biochem, 1973. **Career:** Brown Univ, Providence, RI, Div Biol, NIH trainee & teaching asst, 1964-70, res fel, 1970-71, vis res prof, sect physiology, 1991-92, adj prof, 1993-2000; Mass Inst Technol, Cambridge, Dept Biol, res assoc & teaching asst, 1971-73; Meharry Med Col, Nashville, TN, asst prof, 1973-78; Morehouse Col, Atlanta, GA, assoc prof & dir off health professions, 1979-81, prof biol & dir off health professions, 1981-90, David Packard prof Sci & chmn, Dept Biol, 1985-01, David Packard prof & dean div Sci & Math, 1999-2015; Clark Atlanta Univ, Atlanta, GA, adj prof, 1980-95; MDI Biol Lab, Saulsbury Cove, ME, res scientist, 1993, 1994, 1995; Univ Paris-SUD, Paris, France, res scientist, 1996. **Orgs:** Aaas; Am Chem Soc; Peer Reviewer Nat Sci Found; chmn, bd dir, Afro Arts Ctr, 1970-72; Sickle Cell Task Force, GA, 1979-84; bd dir, Sickle Cell Found, 1980-2008; bd trustee, Morehouse Col, 1984-87, dir, Self Study, 1986-88; GRE Biochem, Cell & Molecular Biol Comm Exam, 1989-92; minority affairs comm, Am Soc Cell Biol, 1991-2004, chair, 1994-2001, co-chair, 2001-04; chair, Bridges to Future, NIH, 1992-96; comm, Undergrad Sci Ed, NRC, 1994-96, comm, Progs Adv Study Math & Sci, 1999-2001; coun undergrad res, 1994-97; comm, Equal Opp Sci & Math, NSF, 2003-06, biol adv comm, 2005-09; fac Proj Kaleidoscope, 1995-1999, nat adv comm, 2010-13; Phi Beta Kappa, 1999, bd trustee, World Learning, 2004-10; co-chair, bioredesign comm, Col Bd, 2006-07; fac, AACU Workshops, 2010-12; vis & chg, biol, Undergrad Ed Adv Bd, 2012-; coun, Am Soc Cell Biol, 2015-. **Home Addr:** 4155 Morning Trail, College Park, GA 30349. **Business Addr:** David Packard Professor, Morehouse College, 830 Westview Dr SW, Atlanta, GA 30314, **Business Phone:** (404)215-2610.

### HAYNES, DR. LEONARD L.

Government official. **Personal:** Born Jan 26, 1947, Boston, MA; son of Leonard L Jr and Leila Davenport; married Mary Sensley; children: Leonard IV, Eboni Michelle, Bakari Ali, Jabari & Kenyatta. **Educ:** Southern Univ, Baton Rouge, BA, hist, 1968; Carnegie Mellon Univ, Pittsburgh, PA, MA, Am hist, 1969; Ohio State Univ, Columbus, OH, PhD, higher educ admin, 1975. **Career:** Howard Univ, fac; Ohio State Univ, fac; Univ of Md, fac; Brookings Inst, fac; George Wash Univ, fac; Inst Serv Educ, Wash, DC, dir, desegregation unit, 1976-79; Nat Asn State/Land Grant Col, Wash, DC, dir, pub black cols, 1979-82; Southern Univ Syst, Baton Rouge, LA, exec vpres, 1982-85, prof hist, 1985-88; La Dept Educ, Baton Rouge, LA, asst supt, 1988-89, sr asst; US Dept Educ, Wash, DC, asst secy, 1989-9, spec asst secy, 2001-03, Fund Improv Post sec Educ, dir, 2003-07, White House Initiative on Historically Black Col & Univs, exec dir, sr dir, 2007-09, 2010-; Brookings Inst, adj fac, 1991-92; US Info Agency, asst secy, dir acad progs, 1992; sr consult & nat educ goals panel, 1993; Univ Md, visscholar, 1994; Am Univ, sr asst pres, 1994; Fine Host Corp, Greenwich, CT, sr adv, 1995-97; Provost, prof, 1997-99; Grambling State Univ, Grambling, LA, actg pres, 1997-98; DC Pub Schs, sr adv supvr, 1999-2001; commentator, radio & tv. **Orgs:** Omega Psi Phi Frat, 1968-; Jack & Jill Inc, 1988; Rotary Int Wash D.C; Ford Found; Merck Corp. **Home Addr:** 1346 Atwood Rd, Silver Spring, MD 20906. **Business Addr:** Senior Director, Institutional Service Grant Operations, 1990 K St NW 6th Fl, Washington, DC 20006, **Business Phone:** (202)502-7777.

### HAYNES, MICHAEL DAVID

Football player. **Personal:** Born Dec 24, 1965, New Orleans, LA; married Cookie Oubre. **Educ:** Northern Ariz Univ. **Career:** Football player (retired); Atlanta Falcons, wide receiver, 1988-93, 1997; New Orleans Saints, wide receiver, 1994-96. **Special Achievements:** Led NFL in yards per reception in 1991 with 22.4.

### HAYNES, DR. REV. MICHAEL E.

Executive, government official, clergy. **Personal:** Born May 9, 1927, Boston, MA. **Educ:** Berkshire Christian Col; New Eng Sch Theol, ABM, 1949; Shelton Col. **Career:** Senior minister, government official, clergy (retired); Breezy Meadows Camp, prog dir, 1951-62; Robert Gould Shaw House, asst boys worker, 1953-58; Commonwealth MA Youth Serv Div, 1955-57; Norfolk House Ct, soc work staff, 1957-64; 12th Baptist Church, sr minister, 1964-2004; House Representatives Seventh Suffolk Dist, mem, 1965-69; Fair Housing Comn, comnr. **Orgs:** Chmn, Metro Boston Settlement Asn, 1965-67; Mass House Representatives, 1965-68; bd dir, New Eng Baptist Hosp; Citizen Training Group Boston Juv Ct; Cushing Acad; bd dirs, Billy Graham Evangelistic Asn; bd dirs, Christianity Today; bd dirs, Gordon-Conwell Theol Sem; Malone Col; Boys' Club Boston; Roxbury Clubhouse; Mayor's Comt Violence, 1976; New Boston Comt; City Boston Charitable Fund; chmn, gov adv comt State Chaplains; Ministeriall Alliance Greater Boston; Gordon-Conwell Bd Trustees, 1976-; US Bd Daystar Univ, Nairobi; Commonwealth MA State Parole Bd; Commonwealth Mass Parole Bd; Billy Graham Evangelistic Asn; Vision New Eng; Christianity Today; Northeastern Univ, 2009; adj mem ministerial staff, Grace Chapel Lexington. **Honors/Awds:** LLD, Gordon Col, 1969; Doctor of Public Service, Barington Col, 1971; DD, Northeastern Univ, 1978; Intervarsity Press Champion, Urban Challenge, 1979; DDiv, Gordon-Conwell Theol Sem; Hon doctorate, S Hamilton, MA; hon doctor, divinity degree Gordon-Conwell Theol Sem, Gordon Col. **Special Achievements:** Published "Five Minutes Before Midnight", Evang Missions, 1968; "Christian-Secular Coop"Urban Mission, 1974. **Home Addr:** 26 Clifford St, Boston, MA 02119.

### HAYNES, PHILIP R.

Engineer. **Personal:** Born Feb 25, 1946, Beckley, WV; son of James and Pearl. **Educ:** Devry, AEET, 1973; Ohio State Univ, attended 1975. **Career:** AT&T, programming staff mem, 1969-91; Alpha Protection Syst, electronic protection engr, 1991-; Alpha Funding, dir, 2004. **Orgs:** Nat Tech Asn, 1980-92; Main St Bus Asn, 1992-; MATAH, 1999-. **Home Addr:** 1167 Studer Ave, Columbus, OH 43206-3214, **Home Phone:** (614)492-9971. **Business Addr:** President, Alpha Funding, 3000B E Main St Suite 183, Columbus, OH 43209, **Business Phone:** (614)492-9971.

### HAYNES, RICK. See HAYNES, AMBASSADOR ULRIC ST. CLAIR, JR.

### HAYNES, SUE BLOOD

Writer, educational consultant, computer scientist. **Personal:** Born Mar 21, 1939, Pine Bluff, AR; married Joe Willis; children: Rodney & Joe B. **Educ:** Seattle Univ, BA, MA, 1974; Union Inst, PhD, 1978; Bryn Mawr Col, mgt cert, 1979. **Career:** S Seattle Community Col, dir spl prog, 1974-; Seattle Univ, head couns, 1972-74; IBO Data Processing Co Inc, exec officer & owner, 1969-99; The Boeing Co, comput engr, 1965-95, Y2K mgr & consult, 1998-99; Seattle Cult & Ethnic Tours, chief exec officer, currently; Sue Blood-Haynes, owner, currently; Auth: "A Game of Marbles", 2002; "Creative Mavericks: Beacons". **Orgs:** Bd dirs, Educ Talent Search, 1977-; bd dir, New Careers Found, 1978-; ed bd, The Western Jour Black Studies, 1978-; Alpha Kappa Alpha, 1977-; vpres, bd dir, Coun Black Am Affairs, Western Region, 1978-79; chairperson, founder, The Inner-City Health Careers Proj-jack & Jill Am, 1978-79; vpres, The Union Inst Alumni Bd; WA Int Bus Network pres, field reader, US Dept Educ/Technol; Nat Asn Advan Colored People; ex-sec, NW Black Chamber Com Bd, 1997. **Honors/Awds:** Community Service Award, Univ Chicago, 1974; Public School Volunteer Award, Seattle Pub Sch, 1978; Martin Luther King Jr Memorial Award, Blanks Wooten Prod, 1980; Black Education Award, Western Regional Coun Black Am Affairs, 1980; Computer Design Award, Boeing Defense & Space Div, 1988. **Home Addr:** 6207 Hampton Rd S, Seattle, WA 98118-3031, **Home Phone:** (206)721-2262. **Business Addr:** Chief Executive Officer, Seattle Cultural & Ethnic Tours, PO Box 80602, Seattle, WA 98108, **Business Phone:** (206)760-9199.

### HAYNES, AMBASSADOR ULRIC ST. CLAIR, JR. (RICK HAYNES)

Diplomat. **Personal:** Born Jun 8, 1931, Brooklyn, NY; son of Ulric S Sr and Ellaline Gay; married Yolande Toussaint; children: Alexandra & Gregory. **Educ:** Amherst Col, BA, 1952; Yale Law Sch, JD, 1956; Harvard Bus Sch Advan Mgt Prog, 1966. **Career:** US Dept State, foreign serv officer, 1963-64; Nat Security Coun, staff, 1964-66; Mgt Formation Inc, pres, 1966-70; Harvard Bus Sch, vis lectr, 1968-72;

Spencer Stuart Asn, sr vpres, 1970-72; Cummins Engine Co, vpres mgt develop, 1972-75, vpres Mid-E & Africa, 1975-77; Am Embassy-Algeria, ambassador, 1977-81; Cummins Engine Co, vpres int bus planning, 1981-83; Self-Employed, consult, 1984-85; State Univ New York Col, Old Westbury, actg pres, 1985-86; AFS Int, Intercult Prog, pres, 1986-87; Drake Beam Morin, sr vpres, 1988-91; Hofstra Univ Sch Bus, dean, 1991-96, exec dean univ intl rels, 1996-2000, consult to pres, 2000-03; Rollins Col, adj prof, currently; Univ Cent Fla; Drew Univ, int recruiter. **Orgs:** Coun Foreign Rel, 1968-; sel comt, Henry Luce Found Asian Scholars Prog, 1975-; bd dir, Am Broadcasting Co, 1981-84; Rohm & Haas Co, 1981-84; HSBC Bank USA, 1981-; Yale Club NY; chmn, Ind United Negro Col Fund Dr, 1981; bd mem, Environ Prod Corp, 1993-99; US Africa Airways, 1994-96; bd dir, Hemmeter Enterprises Inc, 1994-96; Grand Palais Casino Inc, 1994-96; bd dir, Pall Corp, 1994-; bd mem, Coun Am Ambassador; trustee, Deep Springs Col, 1998-2001; Reliastar Ins Co NY, 1998-2003; NNCOM Int Inc, 1998-2003; Am Acad Dipl Coun, Am Ambassadors & Atlantic Coun US. **Honors/Awds:** Martin Luther King Humanitarian Award; New York City Martin Luther King Award, Black Christian Caucus Riverside Church; Resolutions of Commendation, Ind State Senate & Assembly, Calif State Senate, City Detroit & LA; Alumni Award, Class, 1952; Liberty Bell Award, Ind Young Lawyers Asn; Freedom Award; Ind Black Expo, 1981; Certificate of Appreciation, US Dept State; Honorary LLD, Ind Univ; Honorary LLD, Ala State Univ; Honorary LLD, Fisk Univ; Honorary LLD, John Jay Col; Honorary LLD, Butler Univ, Amherst Col, & Mercy Col. **Home Addr:** 2403 Timothy Lane, Kissimmee, FL 34743-3661, **Home Phone:** (407)348-7441.

## HAYNES, DR. WALTER WESLEY

Dentist. **Personal:** Born Nov 16, 1919, St. Matthews, SC; married Peggy; children: Saundra & Donald. **Educ:** Lincoln Univ, AB, 1943; Howard Univ Col Dent, DDS, 1946. **Career:** Dentist (retired); Queens Gen & Tribro Hosp, 1960-65; 1st Presby Church Hempstead, deacon, 1962-67; Hempstead Sch, dentist, 1962-93. **Orgs:** Pres, Queens Clin Soc, 1961-62; Ethical Dent Soc, 1975-77; Am Dent Asn; Nat Dent Asn; 10th Dist Dent Soc; Beta Kappa Chi; Omega Psi Phi. **Honors/Awds:** Man of the Year, Lincoln Univ, 1967; fel, Acad Gen Dent, 1984; Lincoln Univ Founders Day Award Outstanding Achievement, 1999. H. Alfred Farrell Memorial Alumni Award, 2011. **Home Addr:** 16 Manor Ct, Hempstead, GA 11550-3534, **Home Phone:** (516)483-4551. **Business Addr:** .

## HAYNES, WILLIAM JOSEPH, JR.

Judge. **Personal:** Born Sep 5, 1949, Memphis, TN; son of William J and Martyna Q; married Carol Donaldson; children: Paz, Anthony & Maya. **Educ:** Col St Thomas, BA, 1970; Vanderbilt Sch Law, JD, 1973. **Career:** Tenn State Atty, Gen Off, from atty to dep state atty, 1973-84; asst state atty gen, 1973-77; Sr state asst gen, 1977-78; Tenn State Antitrust & Consumer Protection, dep atty gen, 1978-84, spec dep atty gen spec litigation, 1984; Pvt pract, Nashville, TN, 1984;US Magistrate, US Dist Ct for the Mid Dist of Tenn, 1984-99; Southeastern Paralegal Inst, adj prof, 1986-90; Vanderbilt Sch Law, lectr law, 1987-94, 1997-98, 2000-; US Dist Ct Mid Dist Tenn, magistrate judge, 1984-99, chief judge, 2012-14. **Orgs:** Am Bar Asn, 1978, 1985, 1988-91; vice chair, State Enforcement Comt, Antitrust Section; vpres Nashville Bar Asn, 1980-84; dist atty gen, pro tem Shelby Cty Criminal Ct, 1980; Rotary Int, 1980-90; bd dir, Cumberland Mus Sci Ctr, 1981-87; bd mem, esponsibility Tenn Supreme Ct, 1982-84; bd dir, Napier Lobby Bar Asn, 1983-84; chmn, antitrust planning comn Nat Asn Atty Gen, 1984; bd adv, Corporate Practice Series, Bureau Nat Affairs, 1989-90. **Home Addr:** 3000 Hillsboro Pke Suite 121, Nashville, TN 37215-1331, **Home Phone:** (615)297-3203. **Business Addr:** Chief District Judge, United States Government, Rm A845/Ct Rm A859 801 Broadway, Nashville, TN 37203, **Business Phone:** (615)736-7217.

## HAYNES, WILLIE C., III

School administrator, government official. **Personal:** Born Nov 23, 1951, Opelousas, LA; son of Willie Jr and Watkins Lillie; married Rebecca M Smith; children: Markisha A & Willie C IV. **Educ:** Southern Univ, Baton Rouge, BA, 1973, MA, educ, 1976. **Career:** Clark Lodge No 186, jr deacon, 1975-88; Melville High Sch, asst prin, 1981-90; N Cent High Sch, asst prin, 1990; St Landry Parish Police Jury, 1978-92; Town Melville, 1986-92; Melville Elem Sch, prin, 2009; Melville, mayor. **Orgs:** Nat Asn Advan Colored People, 1981-88; Gov Coun Phys Fitness & Sports, 1984-87; Acidiana Prin's Asn, 1984-88; mem bd dir, St Landry Parish Coun Aging, 1985-88; Concerned Citizens Group. **Home Addr:** 848 Ollie St, PO Box 483, Melville, LA 71353, **Home Phone:** (337)623-4364. **Business Addr:** Principal, Melville Elementary School, 536 Fontenot St, Melville, LA 71353, **Business Phone:** (337)623-4688.

## HAYNES, DR. WORTH EDWARD

School administrator, government official, association executive. **Personal:** Born Apr 20, 1942, Webb, MS; son of Shellie (deceased) and Annie Mae; married Linden C Smith; children: Natasha C & Worth Edward. **Educ:** Alcorn State Univ, Lorman, Miss, BS, 1965; Wis State Univ, River Falls, MST, 1971; Iowa State Univ Am, PhD, 1977. **Career:** Alcorn St Univ, youth camp dir, 1964; Eva H Harris HS Brookhaven Miss, teacher voc agr, 1964-69; Hinds Co AHS Utica, teacher voc agr, 1969-72; Utica Jr Col, dir voc tech educ, 1972-74; Iowa St Univ Ames, instr agr educ dept, 1974-76, grad stud adv, 1976-77; UticaJr Col, dir voc-tech educ, 1977-; Gov Off Job Develop & Training, exec dir, 1985-86; Div Indust Serv & Fed Prog, ast st dir; Off Voc Tech & Adult Educ, Bur Bus & Com & Technol, dir; Miss Dept Educ, Bur Voc Community Develop, dir. **Orgs:** Pres, Utica Comm Develop Assoc, 1978-80; pres, Post Sec Voc Dirs Asn, Missi, 1979; chmn, Post Sec St Eval Comn Voc Educ Missi, 1980; deacon, vpres, laymen asn; New Hope Bapt Church, Jackson, Miss; Sunday sch teacher New Hope Church; pres, Koahoama County Incubator, Clarksdale, Miss; state leader, State Baptist Asn, 1990. **Honors/Awds:** Outstanding Teacher Award, Miss Econ Devel Council Eva Harris High Sch, Brookhaven, Miss, 1967-69; Man of the Year Award, Alpha Phi Alpha FratNatchez, Miss, 1972; Achievement Award, Gamma Sigma Delta Honor Soc Agr Ames, Iowa, 1976; Outstanding Contributions Agr Educ Iowa, Vocational Educ Asn Ames, 1976; Outstanding Serv, Utica Jr Col, 1984; Outstanding Contribution Econ Develop, Gulf Coast Bus Serv Corp, 1986. **Home Addr:** 709 Woodlake Dr, Jackson, MS 39206, **Home Phone:** (601)982-3019. **Business Addr:** Director, Mississippi Department of Education, 359 NW St, Jackson, MS 39201, **Business Phone:** (601)359-3513.

## HAYNIE, SHARON

Biochemist, scientist, college teacher. **Personal:** Born Nov 6, 1955, Baltimore, MD. **Educ:** Univ Pa, BA, biochem, 1976; Mass Inst Technol, PhD, chem, 1981. **Career:** AT&T Bell Laboratories, technical staff member, 1981-84; DuPont, scientist and principal investigator for Company Experimental Station Laboratory and DuPont Central Research and Development, 1984-; Delaware State University and the University of Delaware, adjunct professor. **Orgs:** Bd dir, Am Chem Soc Chem Heritage Found. **Special Achievements:** Author and co-author of numerous patents; student mentor in outreach projects.

## HAYSBERT, DENNIS DEXTER

Actor. **Personal:** Born Jun 2, 1954, San Mateo, CA; son of Charles Whitney Sr and Gladys Minor; married Lynn Griffith; children: Charles & Katharine; married Elena Simms. **Educ:** Am Col Dramatic Arts, Pasadena, Calif; Col San Mateo; Am Acad Dramatic Arts. **Career:** Films: Major League, 1989; Navy Seals, 1990; Mr Baseball, 1992; Love Field, 1992; Suture, 1993; Major League II, 1994; Heat, 1995; Waiting to Exhale, 1995; Amanda, 1996; Insomnia, 1996; Absolute Power, 1997; Major League: Back to the Minors, 1998; How to Make the Cruelest Month, 1998; Standoff, 1998; The Thirteenth Floor, 1999; The Minus Man, 1999; Random Hearts, 1999; Love & Basketball, 2000; What's Cooking?, 2000; Ticker, 2002; Far From Heaven, 2002; Sinbad: Legend of the Seven Seas (voice), 2003; Splinter Cell: Pandora Tomorrow, 2004; Call of Duty: Finest Hour, 2004; Jarhead, 2005; Splinter Cell: Double Agent, 2006; Breach, 2007; Goodbye Bafana, 2007; Cessation, 2008; Kung Fu Panda 2, 2011; Vanilla Gorilla, 2011; LUV, 2012; Welcome to the Jungle, 2013; Life of a King, 2013; Mr. Peabody & Sherman, 2014; Dear White People, 2014; Think Like a Man Too, 2014; Sin City: A Dame to Kill For, 2014; Men, Women & Children, 2014; Sniper: Legacy, 2014; TV series: "The White Shadow", 1979; "Buck Rogers in the 25th Century", 1980-81; "Code Red", 1981; Grambling's White Tiger, 1981; The Return of Marcus Welby MD, 1984; Growing Pains, 1985-88; "Wilder Westen, inclusive", 1988; "Just the Ten of Us", 1988-89; "K-9000", 1991; "Queen", 1993; "Return to Lonesome Dove", 1993; "Halleluja", 1993; "Widow's Kiss", 1996; "The Writing on the Wall", 1996; "Just the Ten of Us", 1988-89; "Now & Again", 1999-2001; "Static Shock", 2001-03; Justice League, 2001-04; 24, 2001-06; "Secrets of Pearl Harbor", 2004; Empire, 2005; "The Unit", 2006-09; "The Color of Freedom", 2007; "Race", 2010; "Details", 2011; "Newsreaders", 2013; "Battledogs", 2013; "Axe Cop", 2013; "Trophy Wife", 2013-14; "The Boondocks", 2014. **Orgs:** NETDAY. **Honors/Awds:** Saturn Award, Acad Sci Fiction, Fantasy & Horror Films, 2000; WAFCA Award, Wash DC Area Film Critics Asn, 2002; Black Reel Award, 2003 & 2013; Golden Satellite Award, 2003; Golden Globe Award nomination, Actor in a Supporting Role in a Series, 24, 2003; Career Achievement Award, Temecula Valley Int Film Festival, 2006. **Business Addr:** Actor, c/o Paradigm Talent Agency, 36 N Cresent Dr, Beverly Hills, CA 90210.

## HAYWARD, ANN STEWART

Television producer, television director, writer. **Personal:** Born Aug 23, 1944, Philadelphia, PA. **Educ:** Simmons Col, AB, 1966; New York Univ, grad, 1970; Am Film Inst, Directing Workshop Women, attended 1978; Stanford Univ, prof jour Knight fel, 1979. **Career:** ABC TV Network, dir res, 1972-73, News Doc Div, assoc producer, producer, dir & writer; KPIX TV, Westinghouse Broadcasting Co, video producer, 1979-80; Group Visionary Prod Inc, writer, reporter & producer, 1980; Healthy DC Found Inc, exec dir, 2000-07; Ann S. Hayward Consult, prin, 2007-; Managed You, managing partner, 2011-. **Orgs:** Dir, Guild Am; Guild Am; Future Starzz Inc. **Home Addr:** 1861 Scott St, San Francisco, CA 94115.

## HAYWARD, GARLAND, SR.

Commissioner, government official. **Educ:** Univ Md Eastern Shore. **Career:** Princess Anne Town Commissioners Off, town comnr, chmn, pres, vpres currently. **Orgs:** Pres, Delmar Educ Asn. **Special Achievements:** First African American to sit on the Princess Anne Town Commission. **Home Addr:** 808 Hancock St, Hayward, CA 94544, **Home Phone:** (510)582-7312. **Business Addr:** President, Princess Anne Town Commissioners Office, 30489 Broad St, Princess Anne, MD 21853-1243, **Business Phone:** (410)651-1818.

## HAYWARD, DR. JACQUELINE C. (J C HAYWARD)

Journalist, television news anchorperson. **Personal:** Born Oct 23, 1944, East Orange, NJ; married Sidney G. **Educ:** Howard Univ, BA, 1966. **Career:** WTOP TV 9, anchorwoman; WAGA TV 5, 1970-72; V Mayor's Ofc, asst to vmayor, 1970; City Miami, dir training, 1969-70; W*USA 9 NEWS NOW, anchor, currently, vpres, media outreach, 2006-; WTOP-TV9; Documentaries: Sahel: The Border of Hell; Somalia: The Silent Tragedy; We Shall Return. **Orgs:** Delta Sigma Theta Sor; Nat Coun Negro Women; Nat Bus & Prof Women; bd mem, Nat Asn Advan Colored People Legal Defense Fund; Nat Asn Social Workers; vpres, Boys & Girls Club Greater Wash; Summer Opera Theatre Co; United Black Fund; Montgomery County, Md's Hospice Caring. **Honors/Awds:** Emmy Award, 1976, 1994; Women of the 70's Capitol Press Club; Bronze Medal, Int Film Festival, New York, 1980; Hon Doctorate, Howard Univ, 1985; Outstanding Woman, Am Asn Univ Women; Woman of Achievement, Nat Mult Sclerosis Soc; Publishing Citizen of the Year, Kiwanis Club, Toastmasters Club; Board of Governors Award, 1995; prestigious Board of Governors Award, 1995; Washingtonian of the Year, Washingtonian Mag; Dr Edward C Mazique Memorial Award, 1995. **Special Achievements:** The first female in the Wash market to anchor a newscast; One of the top news people on Washington television. **Home Addr:** 2208 Parallel Lane, Silver Spring, MD 20904, **Home Phone:** (301)384-0773. **Business Addr:** Anchor, Vice President for Media Outreach, W*USA 9, 4100 Wis Ave NW, Washington, DC 20016, **Business Phone:** (202)895-5999.

## HAYWARD, OLGA LORETTA HINES

Librarian. **Personal:** Born Alexandria, LA; daughter of Samuel James and Lillie Florence George; married Samuel E Jr; children: Ann Elizabeth & Olga Patricia Ryer. **Educ:** Dillard Univ, BA, 1941; Atlanta Univ, BS, libr sci, 1944; Univ Mich, MA, libr sci, 1959; La State Univ, MA, Hist, 1977; La State Univ, further study. **Career:** Librarian (retired); Marksville, La, High Sch, teacher, 1941-42; Grambling Col, head librn, 1944-46; New Orleans Pub Libr, librn, 1947-48; Southern Univ Baton Rouge, head ref dept, 1948-74, collection develop librn, 1984-86, head ref dept, 1986-88; Southern Univ, head bus & social sci collections ref dept, 1974-84. **Orgs:** Episcopal Social Serv Community La Episcopal Diocese, 1972-79; banquet community mem, Baton Rouge Conf Christians & Jews, 1982; vice chair, 1985-86, chair, 1986-87, La Libr Assoc Subject Specialists Sect; steering comt, La Community Develop Libr, 1987-89; secy, treas, vpres, pres, La Chap Special Libraries Asn. **Honors/Awds:** Lucy B Foote Award, Subject Specialists Sect, La Libr Asn, 1990; Roll of Honor Award, La Southern Miss Chap, Spec Libraries Asn, 1995. **Special Achievements:** Introduced and taught the first teacher-librarian courses at Grambling Col, 1945; participated in forming LA Certification standards for teacher-librarians, 1945; First black employed in New Orleans Public Library System as a Branch Libraries, 1947; Publications: "Annotated Bibliography of Works By and About Whitney M Young" Bulletin of Bibliography July/Aug 1974; "Spotlight on Special Libraries in LA" LA Library Asn Bulletin 41 Summer 1979; Author, The influence of humanism on sixteenth century English courtesy texts. **Home Addr:** 1632 Harding Blvd, Baton Rouge, LA 70807, **Home Phone:** (225)775-7317.

## HAYWOOD, DWAYNE A.

Government official. **Educ:** Eastern Mich Univ, BS, criminal justice, 1985, MA, pub admin, 1995; Harvard Univ, John F Kennedy Sch Govt Leadership Prog. **Career:** Wayne County DHS, c's protective serv specialist, 1992-97, personnel, 2000-02, Spectrum Human Serv, child care mgr, 2001-02r; City Detroit, Dept Human Serv, exec dir, 2002-05, Bur Community Action & Econ Opportunity, dir; Dept Human Serv, dir, Currently . **Orgs:** Dir, Detroit Dept Human Serv; dir, Mich Dept Human Serv. **Business Addr:** Director, Bureau of Community Action & Economic Opportunity, 235 S Grand Ave Suite 1314, Lansing, MI 48909, **Business Phone:** (517)241-7911.

## HAYWOOD, GAR ANTHONY

Writer. **Personal:** Born May 22, 1954, Los Angeles, CA; son of Jack and Barbara; married Lynnette; children: Courtney & Erin. **Career:** Comput maintenance technician, 1970-90; Bell Atlantic, field engr, 1976; detective fiction writer, 1987-; tv script writer, 1998-; Novelist, writer, currently; Books: Fear of the Dark, 1987; Not Long for This World, 1990; You Can Die Trying, 1993; Going Nowhere Fast, 1994; Bad News Travels Fast, 1995; Its Not a Pretty Sight, 1996; When Last Seen Alive, 1997; All the Lucky Ones Are Dead, 2000; Man Eater, 2003; Firecracker, 2004; Cemetery Road, 2010; Assume Nothing, 2011. **Orgs:** Pvt Eye Writers Am, 1988; Mystery Writers Am, 1989; Am Crime Writers League, 1989. **Honors/Awds:** Best First Private Eye Novel, Pvt Eye Writers Am, 1988; "Fear of the Dark", Shamus Award, Pvt Eye Writers Am, Best First Novel, 1988. **Home Addr:** 2296 W Earl St, Los Angeles, CA 90039-3650, **Home Phone:** (213)660-0040. **Business Addr:** Author, c/o GP Putnam's Sons, 200 Madison Ave, New York, NY 10016.

## HAYWOOD, GEORGE WEAVER

Executive director, association executive, executive. **Personal:** Born Sep 30, 1952, Washington, DC; son of John Wilfred Jr and Marie Weaver; married Cheryl Lynn Jenkins; children: Allison Marie. **Educ:** Harvard Col, BA, 1974; Harvard Law Sch, 1979. **Career:** Lehman Bros inc, assoc, 1982-84, vpres, 1984-86, sr vpres, 1986-88, exec vpres, 1988-91, managing dir, bond trader, 1991-94; Moore Capital Mgt, dir, 1994-98; pvt investor, 1998-; PingTone Commun Inc, dir; XM Satellite Radio Holdings Inc, dir, 2004-06; Denny's Corp, dir, 2011-. **Orgs:** Bd trustee, Brooklyn Poly Prep Sch, 1992-; bd dir, Advan Bionutrition; bd dir, PingTones; bd trustee, New Sch Univ; mem vis comt, Harvard Col, Cambridge. **Home Addr:** 47 Plz St W, Brooklyn, NY 11217, **Home Phone:** (718)783-1009. **Business Addr:** Director, Denny's Corp, 203 East Main St, Spartanburg, SC 29319, **Business Phone:** (864)597-8000.

## HAYWOOD, DR. L. JULIAN

Educator, physician. **Personal:** Born Reidsville, NC; son of Thomas W Sr and Louise V Hayley; married Virginia Elizabeth Paige; children: Julian Anthony. **Educ:** Hampton Inst, BS, 1948; Howard Univ, MD, 1952. **Career:** St. Mary's Hosp, 1952-53; Univ Rochester; Georgetown Univ; Univ Va, psychiat, 1953; Howard Univ, Freedman's Hosp, internal med, 1953-54; Los Angeles County Hosp, internal med, 1956-58; White Memorial Hospitall, fel, cardiol, 1959-61; Univ Southern Calif, asst prof, 1963-67, LAC/Univ Southern Calif Med Ctr, dir, CCU, 1966-, assoc prof, 1967-76, sr physician, Comprehensive Sickle Cell Ctr, dir, 1972; Keck Sch Med, prof med, 1976-; Loma Linda Univ, clin, prof med, 1978-; ECG, dir, 1996-. **Orgs:** Fel AAAS, 1957-; fel AHA, fel Am Col Cardiol, 1968-; consult, Martin Luther King Jr.Hosp, 1970-; pres, Sickle Cell Dis Res Found, 1978-89; gov comt, Am Col Physics, 1981-; pres, AHA/Greater Los Angeles Aff, 1983; fel Am Heart Assoc, 1983-; fel Arteriosclerosis & Coun Clin Cardiol; fel Med Div, 1990-; master, Am Col Physicians; pres, Asn Physicians LA County Hosp, 1991-2006; consult, Calif State Dept Health Hypertension Ctrl Prog; consult, NHLBI; counr, Asn Acad Minority Physicians, pres elect, 1992-93, pres, 1993-94; Armed Forces Epidemiol Bd, 1996-; HCT Div PHS; pres, Salerni Colegium, USC, 1997-98; pres, Assn Physicians Los Angeles City Hosp, 1997-2007; prog coordr, Steering Comt, 1997-99; Alpha Omega Alpha; Assn Black Cardiologists. **Home Addr:** 3551 Lowry Rd, Los Angeles, CA 90027, **Home Phone:** (323)661-2426. **Business Addr:** Professor Emeritus of Medicine, University of Southern California, 2020 Zonal Avemie IRD Rm 332, Los Angeles, CA 90033, **Business Phone:** (323)226-7116.

## HAYWOOD, SPENCER

Businessperson, basketball player. **Personal:** Born Apr 22, 1949, Silver City, MS; married Iman; children: Zulekha; married Linda; children: Nikiah, Shaakira & Isis. **Educ:** Trinidad Jr Col, attended 1967; Univ Detroit Mercy, 1969. **Career:** Basketball player (retired), business person, motivational speaker; Denver Rockets, 1969-70; Seattle Super Sonics, 1970-75; NY Knicks, 1975-79; New Orleans Jazz, 1979; Los Angeles Lakers, 1979-80; Reyer Venezia Mestre, 1980-81; Wash

Bullets, 1981-83; European League, Italy, 1981-82; Spencer Haywood LLC, pres & chief exec officer, 2005-; PD Entertainment, speaker; Smith Ctr, floor covering, 2011-12. **Orgs:** Am Basketball Asn; founder, Spencer Haywood Found. **Business Addr:** Motivational Speaker, PD Entertainment, 3225 Johnson Ave Suite 5F, Bronx, NY 10463, **Business Phone:** (718)543-2042.

## HAYWOODE, M. DOUGLAS

Lawyer, educator. **Personal:** Born Feb 24, 1938, Brooklyn, NY; children: Alyssa, Arthur, Helene, Drake, Phillip & Edward. **Educ:** Brooklyn Col, BA, 1959; Brooklyn Law Sch, JD, 1962, LLM, 1967; New Sch Social Res, MA, 1970; PhD. **Career:** NY City Br Nat Asn Advan Colored People, coun, 1962-64; City NY, prof polit sci, 1969; Human Resources Admin NYC, assoc gen coun, 1972-74; pvt pract law, currently. **Orgs:** Founding mem, Nat Conf Black Lawyers; NY City Bar Asn; Nat Conf Black Lawyers; Am Soc Int Law; Int African Ctr; dir, Enterprise 9 Invest Agency. **Business Addr:** Lawyer, Private Practice Law, 71 Maple St, Brooklyn, NY 11225-5001, **Business Phone:** (718)940-8800.

## HAZEL, DARRYL B.

President (organization). **Personal:** Born Jul 10, 1948, New York, NY; son of Osborne and Olive; married Sheila McEntee; children: Osborne & Margaret. **Educ:** Wesleyan Univ, BA, econs, 1970; Northwestern Univ, MA, econs, 1972. **Career:** Executive (retired); N Am Automotive Opers Mkt, mkt prog, strategy mgr, educ & training mgr & mkt res dir; N Am Car Prod Develop, bus planning mgr; Lincoln Mercury Mkt, analyst, mkt mgr, bus mgr, field mgr & pres mkt, 1972-2005; Ford Div, gen mkt mgr, 1997; Ford Customer Serv Div, exec dir, 1999, pres, 2006-09; Global Mkt Serv, 2005; Ford Motor Co, vpres, 2005-06, sr vpres, 2006-09; Darryl B. Hazel Consult LLC, prin, 2010-. **Orgs:** Think Detroit Police Athletic League; bd mem, Oakland Family Serv; bd mem, Cong Black Caucus Found; dir, Percepta LLC; dir, Interstate Power & Light Co, 2006-; dir, mem exec comt, Alliant Energy Corp, 2006-; dir, mem audit comt, Wis Power & Light Co, 2006-. **Business Addr:** Director, Member of Executive Committee, Alliant Energy Corp, 4902 N Biltmore Lane, Madison, WI 53718-2148, **Business Phone:** (608)458-3311.

## HAZEL, DARRYL B.

Vice president (organization), president (organization). **Educ:** Wesleyan Univ, BA, econs, 1970; Northwestern Univ, MA, econs, 1972. **Career:** Ford Motor Co, sr vpres, Lincoln Mercury Div, pres, 2002-05, pres mkt, 2005-06, Ford Div, pres, 2005, Ford Customer Serv Div, pres, 2006-09; IPL, dir, 2006-; WPL, dir, 2006-; Darryl B. Hazel Consult LLC, founder, 2010-. **Orgs:** Dir, Alliant Energy Corp, 2006-; bd mem, Think Detroit/Police Athletic League; bd mem, Alliant Energy; bd mem, Oakland Family Serv; bd mem, Cong Black Caucus Found. **Honors/Awds:** Edward Davis African American Executive of the Year, On Wheels Inc, 2003; The 100 Most Powerful Executives in Corporate America, Black Enterprise, 2010. **Business Addr:** Board of Director, Alliant Energy, 4902 N Biltmore Lane Suite 1000, Madison, WI 53718-2148, **Business Phone:** (800)255-4268.

## HAZEL, JANIS D.

Executive. **Personal:** Born Jan 19, 1963, Detroit, MI; daughter of Charlie H and Gladys D. **Educ:** Univ Mich, BA, polit sci, 1985; L'Inst de Touraine, Tours France, intensive fr lang prog, 1985. **Career:** Cong Black Caucus Found Inc, intern, 1982; US Dept Transp, policy planning intern, 1983; Sen Donald W Riegle Jr, legis aide, 1985-87; Bldg Owners & Mngs Assn Int, legis rep, 1987-89; Cong John Conyers Jr, legis dir, 1989-91; Asn Am Pub TV Stas, mgr advocacy progs; Marshall Heights Community Develop Orgn, financial secy. **Orgs:** Alpha Kappa Alpha Sorority, 1982-; secy, Pacifica Found, bd dir, 1988-; chmn adv bd, WPFW FM Radio, 1989-94; Nat Black Prog Consortium, 1991-95; Nat Black Media Coalition, 1991-95; Am Women Radio & TV, 1991-; Am Soc Asn Execs, 1992-; Women Govt Rels, 1994-; Telecommunications Policy Roundtable, 1995; exec dir, Rhythm & Blues Found; Bldg Owners & Managers Asn; Asn Pub Tv Stas; US Dept Com-Bur Census; Dc Dept Motor Vehicles; Howard Univ Tv; Detroit Econ Growth Corp. **Business Addr:** Financial Secretary, Board Director, Marshall Heights Community Development Organization, 3939 Benning Rd NE, Washington, DC 20019, **Business Phone:** (202)396-1200.

## HAZZARD, DR. TERRY LOUIS

School administrator, dean (education). **Personal:** Born Jul 8, 1957, Mobile, AL; son of Milton and Ora D Sheffield; married Tanya Finkley; children: Jared Finkley. **Educ:** Ala A&M Univ, BS, 1979; Univ Ala, MA, higher educ, 1980; Fla State Univ, EDS, 1991, EdD, 1996. **Career:** Univ Ala, financial aid peer counr, 1979-80, residence hall asst dir, 1980, coord & coop educ, 1980-81; Mobile Opera, vocalist; Spring Hill Col, counr & upward bound, 1981-85; Bishop State Community Col, asst dean stud, 1985-91, dean stud, currently. **Orgs:** Alpha Phi Alpha Fraternity; Nat Asn Stud Personal Adminr; Choir Greater Mt Olive Suite 2 Baptist Church; Ala Asn Guid & Coun; Ala Asn Deans Students. **Special Achievements:** Vocalist, Governor's Inauguration, Alabama; Appeared in movie Under Siege; vocalist, Miss USA Pagent, 1989; Publications in the Eric System, "Attitudes of White Students Attending Black Colleges & Universities", 1989; "Affirmative Action & Women in Higher Education", 1989; Publications: Sexual Harassment: What's Good for the Goose is Good for the Gander; Eric System, 1989. **Home Addr:** 6322 Hillcrest Oaks Dr, Mobile, AL 36693-3410, **Home Phone:** (251)660-0788. **Business Addr:** Dean of Students, Bishop State Community College, 351 N Broad St, Mobile, AL 36603-5898, **Business Phone:** (251)405-7087.

## HEACOCK, DR. DON ROLAND

Psychiatrist, educator. **Personal:** Born Jun 2, 1928, Springfield, MA; son of Roland T and Lucile LaCour; married Celia Arce; children: Stephan, Roland & Maria. **Educ:** Colby Col, BS, 1949; Howard Univ Col Med, MD, 1954. **Career:** State Univ NY Health Sci Ctr, Brooklyn, intern, 1954-56, 1958-60; Mt Sinai Hosp, fel; Kings County Hosp Ctr, resident, intern; Mt Sinai Sch Med, resident, 1960-62, Dept Psychiat, clin asst prof psychiat; Knickerbocker Hosp, dir, Dept Psychiat, 1970-72; Bronx Psychiat Ctr, diradolescent serv, 1975-79; pvt psychiat, currently. **Orgs:** Life fel Am Psychiat Asn; NY Dist Br Am Psychol Asn; NY State Med Asn; life fel Am Ortho Psychiat Asn; NY Coun Child Psychiat; Am Acad Child Psychiat. **Honors/Awds:** Diplomate Am Bd Psychiat & Neurology, 1962; diplomate, Am Bd Child Psychiat, 1965. **Special Achievements:** Editor: A Psyco dynamic Approach to Adolescent Psychiatry, 1980; Author: Black Slum Child Problem of Aggression, 1977; Article: Suicidal Behavior in Black and Hispanic Adolescents, Psychiatric Annels, 1990; Chapter on Group Therapy with Adolescents by Paul Kymissis. **Home Addr:** 9 Kingswood Way, Lewisboro, NY 10590-2613. **Business Addr:** Psychiatry, Private Psychiatry, 3333 Henry Hudson Pkwy Suite 1D, Bronx, NY 10463, **Business Phone:** (914)299-0585.

## HEAD, DENA

Basketball player. **Personal:** Born Aug 16, 1970; daughter of James. **Educ:** Univ Tenn, sports mgt, 1992; Baker Col. **Career:** Ancona, Italy, guard, 1992-94; DKSK, Hungary, 1994-95; Mirande, France, 1996-97; Utah Starzz, 1997-98; Phoenix Mercury, 2000; Cent Conn State Univ, asst coach, 2001-2007; Blue Devils, develop guard & recruiting coordr. **Home Addr:** 200 Burlington Woods Suite 121, middle town, CT 48104. **Business Addr:** Assistant Coach, Recruiting Coordinator, Central Connecticut State University, 1615 Stanley St, New Britain, CT 06050, **Business Phone:** (860)832-2278.

## HEAD, EDITH

Government official. **Personal:** Born Nov 16, 1927, Autaugaville, AL; married Toysie Lee; children: Alberta, Patricia A, Timothy L & Robert W. **Educ:** Wilkins Cosmetology Sch, 1955; Mkt Training Inst, grad, 1968; Cuyahoga Community Col. **Career:** Clin Inn Motel, desk clerk, 1969-72; E Cleveland Pub Libr, frnt off aide, 1972-74; Villa Angela Sch, media aide, 1974-75; City E Cleveland, cmser, 1978-; St James Luthern Church, Hunger Ctr, vol, Grand Parents Support Grp, pres, currently. **Orgs:** Pres, Orinoco St Club, 1968-82; pres, Community Action Team, 1975; Cuyahoga Democ Party, 1975; Nat League Cities, 1978; Ohio Munic League, 1978; pres, Comn E Cleveland Black Women, 1983; Omega Baptist Church, correspondance secy, sr usher bd; Helen S Brown Sr Citizens Ctr, choir, sightseers club; Mother's bd, Omega Baptist Church, 2000-. **Honors/Awds:** Honorary Citizen City of Atlanta, 1979; Special Recognition, ECCJC E Cleveland, 1980; Certificate of Appreciation, City E Cleveland, 1984; Outstanding Work, Citizens E Cleveland, 1982; Volunteer of the Year, St James Lutheran Church, Hunger Ctr. **Home Addr:** 12409 Signet Ave, Cleveland, OH 44120, **Home Phone:** (216)751-5271. **Business Addr:** President, The Grand Parents Support Group, 1424 Hayden Ave, East Cleveland, OH 44112, **Business Phone:** (216)541-1665.

## HEAD, HELAINE

Television director, stage manager. **Personal:** Born Jan 17, 1947, Los Angeles, CA. **Educ:** Univ San Francisco, BA, Eng & theatre, 1968. **Career:** Am Conserv Theatre, stage mgr; Univ Southern Calif, Sch Cinema-TV, tv prog head, assoc prof, 2000-; Broadway prod, Porgy & Bess, The Royal Family, Raisin, Ain't Supposed to Die a Natural Death, prod stage mgr; Theatre prod, Second Thoughts, The Yellow Pin, Orrin, The Effect of Gamma Rays on Man-in-the Moon Marigolds, dir; the liar, dir; Ain't Supposed To Die A Natural Death, dir; The Effect of Gamma Rays on Man-In-The-Moon, dir; Remo Williams: The Adventure Begins, asst art dir, 1985; Music: The Color Purple, 1985; The Country Girl, stage mgr, 1982; TV series: "Sidekicks", 1986; "Cagney and Lacey", 1986-87; "St Elsewhere", 1986-87; "Frank's Place", 1987; "LA Law", 1987-88; "Mariah", 1987; "A Year in the Life", 1987-88; "L.A. Law", 1987-89; "Annie McGuire", 1988; "Wiseguy", 1989; "CBS Schoolbreak Special", 1989; "Island Son", 1989; "Tour of Duty", 1989; "Brewster Place", 1990; "Danger Team", 1991; "You Must Remember This", 1992; "My Past Is My Own"; "Jack's Place", 1992-93; "Class of '96", 1993; "Tribeca", 1993; "The American Experience", 1993; "Simple Justice"; "A Perry Mason Mystery: The Case of the Lethal Lifestyle", 1994; "Harts of the West", 1994; "Law and Order", 1994; "Touched By An Angel", 1994; "Sisters", 1994; "New York Undercover", 1994-96; "The Client", 1995; "SeaQuest 2032", 1993; "Lena Horne: The Lady and Her Music"; "The Net", 1998; "Sliders", 1998; "After All", 1999; "Dear America: A Picture of Freedom", 1999; "Dear America: Color Me Dark", 2000; "Soul Food", 2000-01. **Honors/Awds:** Director's Guild Award, 1993; Humanitas Prize. **Home Addr:** 3284 Barham Blvd Suite 305, Los Angeles, CA 90068, **Home Phone:** (213)969-0424. **Business Addr:** Associate Professor, Television Program Head, University of Southern California, 850 W 34th St, Los Angeles, CA 90089-2211, **Business Phone:** (213)740-3317.

## HEAD, RAYMOND J., JR.

Government official, executive. **Personal:** Born Feb 23, 1921, Griffin, GA; son of Raymond Sr and Pauline; married Ceola Johnson; children: Cheryl Johnson, Raylanda Anderson & Raymond III. **Educ:** Tuskegee Inst, BS, 1943. **Career:** Cleanwell Cleaners, partner & tailor, 1956-; Griffin Co, city comnr, 1971, mayor, 1977, 1985, mayor pro team, 1975, 1986, 1989; Head Raymond Pressing Club, owner. **Orgs:** Comdr, qm, 1946-51; Vaughn-Blake VFW Post, 8480; charter mem, Morgan-Brown Am Legion Post 546; Spalding Improv League; Spalding Jr Achievement; C C GA Assoc Retarded C; treas, steward Heck Chapel United Meth Ch, 1948; bd Family & C Serv, 1970; vol worker Am Cancer Soc Inc Spalding Co Unit; Cert Lay Sprark United Meth Ch; chmn, Pastor Parish Rel Heck Chapel Red Oak Charge; Griffin Dist Comn Bldg & Loc; United Meth N Ga Conf Com Ethnic Minority Local Ch; convener, Griffin Spalding Co Comn Human Rels; pres, NAACP; bd dir, Spalding & Convalescent Ctr; mem trustee, bd N Ga Meth Conf; Griffin Spalding Hosp Authority, 1971; Spalding Pike Upson Co Dept Labor, 1972; app by Ga Gov, Carter State Hosp Adv Coun, 1972; Ga Munic Asn 6th Dist Dir, 1974-75; Dem Nat Conv deleg; vice chmn, bd dir State McIntosh Trail Area Plng & l Comn, 1975; del Nat Dem Conv, 1976; GMA Munic Comn; Spalding Co Health Bd. **Honors/Awds:** Outstanding Community Service, Citizens Spalding Co, 1969; Dedicated Service, Laciso Club, 1971; Outstanding Service Awards, 1st Black Elected Official Caballeros Dlub, 1972; Civic Improv League, 1976; Bicentennial Award, Griffin Spalding Bicentennial Comn, 1976; Heck Chapel United Meth Ch, 1977; 8 St Bapt Ch, 1977; Award, 30 yrs dedicated Serv; Disting Service Award, Mayor, Bus, Religious Ldr, & Civic Ldr, 1977; Ft Valley St Col 38th Annual Award; Man of year Award; Griffin Spalding NNBPW Club, 1977; Proclamation, City Griffin; Mayor Raymond Head Jr, lifetime mem, Vauhn-Blake VFW Post 8480; Citation, Locust Grove Masonic Lodge 543; Griffin Branch NAACP citation, 1977, Roy Wilkins Freedom Award, 1985; Tuskegee Univ & Spalding County Athletic Halls of Fame, 1985; Certificates of appreciation, American Heart Asn; Am Len Post 546; General Griffin Chamber of Commerce Award, 1989. **Home Addr:** 438 N 4th St, Griffin, GA 30223-3154, **Home Phone:** (770)227-7149. **Business Addr:** Owner, Head Raymond Pressing Club, 118 N 8th St, Griffin, GA 30223, **Business Phone:** (770)227-2839.

## HEADLEY, HEATHER

Singer, actor. **Personal:** Born Oct 5, 1974, Barataria; daughter of Eric and Hannah; married Brian Musso; children: John David. **Educ:** Northwestern Univ, commun & musical theatre. **Career:** Stage: The Lion King; Aida; Albums: This Is Who I Am, 2002; In My Mind, 2006; Audience of One, 2009; Films: "The Lion King 2: Simba's Pride", 1998; "Elmo's Magic Cookbook", 2001; "Golden Dreams", 2001; Dirty Dancing: Havana Nights, 2004; TV: "The Rosie O'Donnell Show", 2000; "Great Performances", 2001"Walt Disney World Christmas Day Parade", 2002; "Sidewalks Entertainment", 2003; "9th Annual Soul Train Lady of Soul Awards", co-host, 2003"; Sidewalks Entertainment", 2003; "Breakin' All the Rules", 2004; "Diary of a Mad Black Woman", 2005; "An Evening of Stars: Tribute to Stevie Wonder", 2006; "An American Celebration at Ford's Theater", 2006; The Mark Twain Prize: Neil Simon, 2006; An American Celebration at Ford's Theater, 2006; "Getting Played", 2006; "It's Show time at the Apollo", 2006; Episode dated 12 March 2009, 2009; "The Tonight Show with Jay Leno", 2009. **Orgs:** Bd dir, Catalyst Charter Schs. **Honors/Awds:** Tony Award, Aida, 2000; Two Grammy Award, Best Actress in a Musical, Sarah Siddons Award, 2000; Drama Desk Award; R&B/Soul Album of the Year - Solo, 2003; Best R&B/Soul or Rap New Artist - Solo, 2003; Best Contemporary R&B Gospel Album, Grammy Award, 2010; NAACP Image Award. **Special Achievements:** One of People Magazine's 50 Most Beautiful People and Essence Magazine's 30 Women to Watch. **Home Addr:** 3205 Bowser Ave, Ft Wayne, IL 46806, **Home Phone:** (260)456-2753. **Business Addr:** Actress, Disney Corporation, 3205 Bowser Ave, Ft. Wayne, IN 46806, **Business Phone:** (260)456-2753.

## HEADLEY, SHARI

Actor. **Personal:** Born Jul 15, 1964, Queens, NY; married Christopher Martin; children: Skyler. **Career:** Films: Coming to America, 1988; The Preacher's Wife, 1996; A Woman Like That, 1997; Johnson Family Vacation, 2004; Nothing Is Private, 2007; Towelhead, 2007; Belly 2: Millionaire Boyz Club, 2008; Act Like You Love Me, 2013; The Congregation, 2014. TV series: "The Cosby Show", 1985; "Miami Vice ", 1986; "Kojak: Ariana", 1989; "Gideon Oliver", 1989; "Kojak: None So Blind", 1990; "Quantum Leap", 1990; "Matlock", 1990; "Walker", "Texas Ranger", 1993; "All My Children", 1991-2005; "New York Undercover", 1995; "Walker, Texas Ranger", 1996; "Cosby", 1996; "413 Hope St", 1997; "413 Hope St.", 1997; "The Love Boat: The Next Wave", 1998; "Getting Personal", 1998; "Malcolm & Eddie", 1998; "For Your Love", 1998; "The Wayans Bros.", 1999; "The Guiding Light", 2001-02; "Half & Half", 2003; "The Bold & the Beautiful", 2004-05; "One on One", 2004; "House M.D.", 2005; "Veronica Mars", 2005; "Castle", 2009; "10 Things I Hate About You", 2010; "White Collar", 2011; "Love That Girl!", 2014; video: Daytime's Greatest Weddings, 2004. **Honors/Awds:** Image Award nomination, 1992. **Business Addr:** Actress, c/o J Michael Bloom & Associates, 233 Pk Ave S 10th Fl, New York, NY 10003, **Business Phone:** (212)529-6500.

## HEARD, BLANCHE DENISE

Administrator. **Personal:** Born Aug 9, 1951, Washington, DC; daughter of Albert M Winters Sr and Marlene Coley; married Emanuel F Jr; children: Latricia Poole, Michael Poole & Mannikka L. **Educ:** Montgomery Co Jr Col, attended 1969; Univ Col, attended 1976; Tenn State Univ, attended 1972. **Career:** Am Security Bank, supvr, 1974-75, sr ed auditor, 1976-83; Savings Bank Baltimore, sr ed auditor, 1984-85; US Fidelity & Guaranty, info interity admin, 1985-88, supvr, data security, 1988-93; Comput Based Syst Inc. **Orgs:** Chair, Elec Data Process Auditors Asn, 1980-81; int secy, EDPP Conf, 1982; Dp Mgt Asn, 1986; United Black Fund Greater Baltimore, 1986-87; Black Dp Asn; Womens Aux; Baltimore Chap Nat Asn Advan Colored People; Nat Asn Female Exec. **Home Addr:** 2104 Willow Switch Lane, Upper Marlboro, MD 20774-4217.

## HEARD, GAR (GARFIELD HEARD)

Basketball player, basketball coach. **Personal:** Born May 3, 1948, Hogansville, GA; son of Charlie Mae and Preston Martin; married Kathleen Cline; children: Kim, Jaasmeen, Gyasi & Avery. **Educ:** Univ Okla, BS, 1970. **Career:** Basketball player, basketball coach (retired); Seattle Supersonics, forward, 1970-72; Chicago Bulls, 1972-73; Buffalo Braves, 1973-76; Phoenix Suns, 1976-80; San Diego Clippers, 1980-85; Arizona State Univ, vol ast coach, 1982-83; Arzi Phoneix, realtor, 1984-87; Dallas Mavericks, interim head coach, 1992-93; Ind Pacers, asst coach, 1993-97; Philadelphia 76ers, asst coach, 1997-98; Detroit Pistons, asst coach, 1998-99 & 2004-05, asst head coach & interim coach, 2004-05; Wash Wizards, head coach, 1999-2000.

## HEARD, GEOFFREY A.

Chief executive officer. **Career:** SERO/Nat Scholar Serv, pres & chief exec officer, currently. **Orgs:** Bd mem, Henry W Grady Health Syst Found; trustee, Fulton-DeKalb Hosp Authority, Grady Health Syst. **Home Addr:** 3399 Elmtree Dr SW, Atlanta, GA 30311, **Home Phone:** (404)696-0143. **Business Addr:** President, Chief Executive Officer, National Scholarship Service, 230 Peachtree St Suite 230, Atlanta, GA 30303, **Business Phone:** (404)522-7260.

## HEARD, GEORGINA E.

Airline executive, executive, association executive. **Personal:** Born Aug 8, 1952, Chicago, IL; daughter of George and Minnie; married Paul Labonne; children: Marc Labonne. **Educ:** Bradley Univ, BS, psychol, 1974; DePaul Univ, MS, clin psychol, 1978; Inst Family Ther, cert, Behav Family Ther, 1981, cert, coun. **Career:** Comprehensive Care Families, dir, 1980-82; Inwood Community Ment Health Ctr, Wash Heights, unit chief, 1982-83; United Airlines, human resources staff mgr, 1983-86, personnel adminr, 1986-88, benefits commun mgr, 1988-93, human resources mgr, 1993-, dir Govt & Pub Affairs, 2000-

04; Chicagoland Bus Partners, pres & exec dir, 1998-2000; MLG, prin, 2003-05; IDES, dep dir strategic planning, 2004-08; Ill Dept Transp, mgr strategic plng & pub engagement, 2008-; State Ill, assoc dir, currently. **Orgs:** Vpres, bd dir, Youth Guid, 1993-2014; chairperson, Nat Asn Advan Colored People Fair Share Corp, Adv Coun, 1993-; vice chmn, Ann Blackbook Music Awards, 1993; OIC Nat Tech Adv Coun, 1994-; dir, Bottomless Closet, 1998-; vpres, Literacy Chicago, 1998-99; Chicago Workforce Bd, 2002-; bd trustee, Bradley Univ, 2004-, bd secy; bd dir, Africa Int House, 2008-09; chair fund develop, Links Inc; exec dir, Cosmopolitan Chamber Com, 2014-. **Honors/Awds:** Outstanding Young Woman of America, 1984; United Airlines Human Resources Annual Award, 1991; Community Partnership Award, Mutual America, 1999. **Special Achievements:** In-School Consultation: School-based Community Mental Health, Educational Resources, 1981. **Home Addr:** 8832 Gleneagles Lane, Darien, IL 60561. **Business Addr:** Board Trustee, Bradley University, 1501 W Bradley Ave, Peoria, IL 61625, **Business Phone:** (309)676-7611.

### HEARD, HERMAN WILLIE, JR.
Football player, police officer, executive. **Personal:** Born Nov 24, 1961, Denver, CO. **Educ:** Colo State Univ-Pueblo, attended 1984. **Career:** Football player (retired), police officer, partner; Kans City Chiefs, running back & half back, 1984-89; Local City & County Colo, police officer, 2003-; H&A LLC, partner, 2008-. **Business Addr:** Partner, H&A LLC.

### HEARD, LONEAR WINDHAM
Executive. **Personal:** married James T; children: 4. **Educ:** Rust Col, BA, 1964; Atlanta Univ, GA, MBA. **Career:** Rust Col, sec dir pub rels, sec pres, vpres bd trustee; Am Nat Bank Trust, statist sec; James T Heard Mgmt Corp, Cerritos, Calif, co-mgr, owner, pres, 1979; Vt Slauson, mem bd dir. **Orgs:** Nat Asn Advan Colored People. **Business Addr:** Owner, James T Heard Management Corp, 17401 Woodruff Ave, Bellflower, CA 90706-6746, **Business Phone:** (714)521-0660.

### HEARD, MARIAN L.
Association executive, chief executive officer. **Personal:** Born Jan 1, 1940, Canton, GA; daughter of Ural Noble and Indiana Billinglea; married Winlow H; children: Gregory & Derek. **Educ:** Univ Bridgeport, Jr Col, AA, 1963; Univ Mass, Amherst, MA, BA, 1976; Springfield Col, MEd, 1978. **Career:** Inner-City Cs Ctr, exec dir, 1972-74; Housatonic Community Col, instr, 1976-84; WICC Radio, Bridgeport, CT, radio show moderator, 1977-83; United Way, Eastern Fairfield County, CT, dir, opers, 1981-88, assoc exec dir, 1988-89, pres & chief exec officer, 1989-92, United Way, Mass Bay, pres & chief exec officer, 1992-2004; Fleet Boston Financial Corp, dir, 1992-2004; United Way, New Eng, chief exec officer, 1992-2004; New Eng Aquarium, dir, 1993-; Liberty Mutual Holding Co Inc, dir, 1994-; Liberty Financial Co Inc, dir, 1994-; Oxen Hill Partners, pres & chief exec off, 2004-; Sovereign Bank, dir, 2004-; Santander Holdings USA Inc, dir, 2005-15; Biosphere Med Inc, bd dir, 2006-10; Liberty Mutual Ins Co, dir. **Orgs:** Bd mem, Blue Cross & Blue Shield, MA, 1992-, dir, 1994; bd dir, Fleet Bank Mass, 1992-98; trustee, Dana Farber Cancer Inst, 1994-; bd mem, CVS, 1999-2007, dir, 1999-2013; bd mem, CVS Caremark, 2007-13; Obama Victory Fund, 2012-; Am Mgt Asn; Exec Women's Group; Nat Bus & Prof Womens Club; Non-Profit Mgt Group; Women Philanthropy; Women Radio & TV; trustee, Fairfield Univ & Berea Col; Nat Asn Corp Dirs; Boston Athenaeum & Natick Serv Coun; Nat Asn Advan Colored People. **Honors/Awds:** John H Garber Jr Minority Dev Award, United Way Am, 1988; Golden Tee Award, Cardinal Shehan Ctr, 1990; Community Leadership Award, Girl Scouts, Housatonic Coun, 1990; Women Achievement Award, Big Sisters Asn Greater Boston, 1991; Youth Leadership Community Service Award, Walter Memorial Amzion Church, 1992; National Public Citizen of the Year Award; prestigious Warren Bennis Award. **Special Achievements:** Contributor: CRP Bylaws, 1990; Agency Self-Support Policy, 1981; United Way; Allocation/Distribution Policy, 1982; Author of two books: The Complete Leader & Take Time. **Home Addr:** 47 Hopewell Farm Rd, Natick, MA 01760, **Home Phone:** (508)651-0699. **Business Addr:** President, Chief Executive Officer, Oxen Hill Partners, 695 Atlantic Ave 8th Fl, Boston, MA 02111, **Business Phone:** (617)526-7979.

### HEARN, DR. ROSEMARY
School administrator. **Personal:** Born May 1, 1929, Indianapolis, IN; daughter of Oscar Thomas and Mabel Lee Ward. **Educ:** Howard Univ, BA, 1951; Ind Univ, MA, 1958, PhD, 1973. **Career:** Professor(retired); Lincoln Univ, Jefferson City, Mo, eng prof, 1958-62, dir hons prog, 1968-72, exec dean acad affairs, 1982-85, spec asst to pres acad affairs, 1985-87, dean, Col Arts & Sci, 1989, vpres acad affairs, 1997-2000, prof emer, 2000-. **Orgs:** Nat Asn Teachers Eng; Col Lang Asn; reviewer & consult, US Dept HEW, 1977-79; Delta Sigma Theta; secy & bd dir, Jefferson City United Way, 1983; judge, Miss Community Betterment Awards Competition, 1983; Mo State Planning Comm, Am Coun Educ; Nat Identification Prog, 1983-; Planning Comm, Nat Asn State Land Grant Col & Univ, 1985-; Mid-Miss Asn Col & Univ, vice-chair, exec comm mid-Mo; Miss Asn Social Welfare; reviewer & consult, Am Asn Univ Women; adv panel, Mo Coun Arts, 1987-; reviewer, Am Libr Asn; Comn, Urban Agenda, NASVLGC, 1992-; bd dir, Mo Humanities Coun, 1995; pres-elect, bd dir, Coun Col Arts & Sci, 1997-. **Home Addr:** 811 E Dunklin St, Jefferson City, MO 65101, **Home Phone:** (314)636-5527. **Business Addr:** Professor Emeritus, Lincoln University of Missouri, Col Arts & Scis, Jefferson City, MO 65101-3537, **Business Phone:** (573)681-5000.

### HEARNE, EARL
Government official, administrator. **Personal:** Born Aug 2, 1956, Calvert, TX; son of Earlie and Ellen Foster Rosemond; children: Timothy Earl & Tiffany Charisse. **Educ:** Univ Tex, Austin, TX, BBA, finance, 1979; Tex A & M Corpus Christi, Corpus Christi, TX, MBA, mgt, 1982. **Career:** Univ Tex, Austin, Tex, clerk typist I, 1976; Amoco Prod Co, Corpus Christi, Tex, admin analyst, 1979-83; Corpus Christi ISD, Corpus Christi, Tex, paraprofessional aide II, 1984-85; City Corpus Christi, Corpus Christi, Tex, mgt & budget analyst II, 1985-, aso auditor, 1992-; City League TX, internal audit dir, 1995; City Houston TX, Munic Ct, ade supr, 1996; Galveston County Treasurers Off, asst county treas, 1996-; Galveston County, admin servs mgr, 1996-2012. **Orgs:** Tex Asn Assessing Officers, 1985-87; Nat Asn Advan Colored People, 1987; United Way Fin Adv Comt, 1987-92; mem, finance adv bd, 1987-95; Nueces County Ment Health & Retardation Adv Comt, 1988-90; coordr, Leadership Tomorrow, City Corpus Christi, 1988-92; Gov Fin Officer's Asn, 1989-97; middle school mentro Corpus School District, 1990-95; Community Action Agency, Corpus Christi, 1990-95; mem gov finance officers asn. **Home Addr:** 3703 Rosedale St, Houston, TX 77004-6409, **Home Phone:** (713)523-9536. **Business Addr:** Administrative Services Manager, Galveston County, 601 Tremont Suite 306, Galveston, TX 77550, **Business Phone:** (409)766-2300.

### HEARNS, THOMAS
Boxer, boxing promoter. **Personal:** Born Oct 18, 1958, Memphis, TN; son of Lois; married Rena; children: Ronald, Natasha & Thomas Charles K A. **Career:** Boxer (retired), boxing promoter; prof boxer, 1977-2000; Hearns Entertainment Inc, co-owner & boxing promoter, 2000-; res policeman, Detroit Police Dept. **Orgs:** World Boxing Coun. **Business Addr:** Owner, Boxing Promoter, Hearns Entertainment Inc, 19244 Bretton Dr, Sterling Heights, MI 48223.

### HEARST, GERALD GARRISON
Football player. **Personal:** Born Jan 4, 1971, Lincolnton, GA; married Jennifer O Neil; children: 4. **Educ:** Univ Ga, attended 1992. **Career:** Football player (retired); Phoenix Cardinals, running back, 1993; Ariz Cardinals, running back, 1994-95; Cincinnati Bengals, running back, 1996; San Francisco 49ers, running back, 1997-2003, fullback, 2001; Denver Broncos, running back, 2004. **Honors/Awds:** ESPN's ESPY Winner Outstanding Col Athlete; SEC Player of the Year, 1992; Victor Award, 1995; NFL Comeback Player of the Year, Assoc Press, 1995 & 2001; All-Pro selection, 1998; Madden NFL Cover Athlete, 1999; Pro Bowl selection, 1998 & 2001; Doak Walker Award; All-American, 1992; Florida-Georgia Hall of Fame. **Special Achievements:** Film: 1997 NFC Championship Game, 1998. TV Series: "TNT Sunday Night Football", 1995; "NFL on FOX", 1995-2001; "NFL Monday Night Football", 1995-2003; "ESPN's Sunday Night Football", 1998-2004. **Home Addr:** , GA.

### HEATH, DR. JAMES E.
Composer, music arranger or orchestrator. **Personal:** Born Oct 25, 1926, Philadelphia, PA; son of Arlethia and Percy; married Mona Brown; children: James Mtume, Roslyn & Jeffrey. **Educ:** Theodore Presser Sch Music, saxophone. **Career:** Educator (retired), musician; Yale Univ, Duke Ellington, Fel; Afro-Am State Evolution, performer, 1976; Woodwinds, Housatonic Comm Col, Bridgeport, instr; Aaron Copland Sch Music, Queens Col, New York, prof, 1987-98; Louis Armstrong House, adv, 1987-; Jazz Repetory Co; Heath Bros Quartet, Jimmy Heath Quartet; Compositions: "Three Ears", 1988; "Prelude to a Kiss", 1993; "Praise", 1994; "Leadership Suite", 1995; "Sweet Jazz mobile", 1999, "Turn Up Heath", 2008. **Orgs:** Bd trustee, Thelonious Monk Inst, 1990-; adv bd, Int Asn Jazz Educrs, 2000; adv panel, NY State Coun Arts, 2002; Jazzmobile, Louis Armstrong Bd. **Home Addr:** 11315 34th Ave Suite 3D, Corona, NY 11368, **Home Phone:** (718)478-3638.

### HEBERT, STANLEY PAUL, III
Executive, lawyer. **Personal:** Born Jun 18, 1922, Baton Rouge, LA; married Mary Lou Usher; children: 6. **Educ:** Univ Wis, PhB, 1947; Marquette Univ Law Sch, JD, 1950. **Career:** US Govt Off Price Stabilization Milwaukee, investr atty, 1951; Southern Univ Law Sch, asst prof, 1951-52; NC Col Law Sch, assoc prof law, 1952-55; Columbus, Ga, atty pvt pract, 1955-56; atty pvt pract Milwaukee, 1956-58; City Milwaukee, City Atty's Off, asst city atty, 1958-61; State Wisc & Pub Serv Comn Wisc, comnr, 1961-63; US Govt Dept Navy Off Gen Coun Wash DC, dep gen coun, 1963-69; US Equal Employ Opportunity Comn, gen coun, 1969-71; Bank Am, vpres asst secy, 1971-76, coun; Gen Coun, Port Oakland, gen coun, 1976-95; Wendell Rosen Black & Dean LLP, 1996-2001; pvt pratice, currently. **Orgs:** Calif Bar Asn; DC Bar Asn; US Supreme Ct; US Ct Appeals; Ga Bar Asn; Fed Bar Asn; Wisc Bar Asn; chmn, Exec Comt Nat Cath Community Serv; vpres & mem, exec comt & bd dir, United Serv Orgn Inc; chmn, Pastoral Comn Comt Role Church Changing Metro, Diocese, Wash DC; Bd Gov John Carroll Soc & Pastoral Comn, Archdiocese, Wash; Exec Comt Wisc Welfare Coun; Exec Comt Int Inst Milwaukee; Exec Comt Madison Comn Human Rels; Exec Comt Milwaukee & Madison Chaps Nat Asn Advan Colored People; mem bd trustee, Voorhees Col; adv bd, Calif State Univ Hayward; chair, Golf Comt; pres, Nat Cath Conf Interracial Justice; Bay Area Urban League; chmn, Calif Atty Gen's Adv Comn Comt Police Rel; regent, Holy Names Col; mem bd, Wiley Manuel Law Found; nat dir, bd, Marcus Foster Ed Inst; Sigma Pi Phi Frat; Alpha Gamma Boule; Am Asn Port Authorities. **Home Addr:** 100 Bay Pl Suite 511, Oakland, CA 94610-4405, **Home Phone:** (510)891-8100. **Business Addr:** Attorney Private Practice, 2733 Mountaingate Way, Oakland, CA 94611, **Business Phone:** (510)531-8874.

### HECKER, BARRY
Scout, radio director. **Personal:** Born Washington, DC; married Merle; married Terri; children: Monica, Derick & Michela. **Educ:** Frostburg State Col, BS, health, phys educ & recreation; George Washington Univ, WA, DC, MA, educ; Fla State Univ, Tallahassee, PhD, athletic admin. **Career:** John Wooden Basketball Fundamentals Camp, CA, instr, 1971, 1981; B S Leiden Basketball Club, Dutch Prof League, head coach, 1975-76; George Washington Univ, asst coach; George Mason Univ, dir & asst coach, 1973; Westminster Col, Salt Lake City, UT, dir & head basketball coach, 1976-78; Bertka's Views Nat Scouting Serv, scout; Cleveland Cavaliers, player personnel dir, 1984-86; Los Angeles Clippers, dir scouting, 1986-94, asst coach, 1994-88, dir player personnel, 2001-05; Las Vegas Bandits, interim head coach, asst coach & player personnel dir, 1999-2001; Jiangsu Nangang Dragons, asst coach, 2008; Memphis Grizzlies, asst coach, Gen Mgr & vpres, 2009-. **Business Addr:** Assistant Coach, Memphis Grizzlies, 191 Beale St, Memphis, TN 38103, **Business Phone:** (901)888-4667.

### HEDGEPETH, LEONARD
Chief executive officer, president (organization). **Career:** United Nat Bank, Fayetteville, NC, chief exec officer, pres. **Business Addr:** Chief Executive Officer, President, United National Bank, 320 Green St, Fayetteville, NC 28302, **Business Phone:** (919)483-1131.

### HEDGLEY, DR. DAVID RICE, JR.
Mathematician, educator. **Personal:** Born Jan 21, 1937, Chicago, IL; son of David R Sr (deceased) and Christine Kelly (deceased); children: Angela Kay Garber & Andrea Kim. **Educ:** Va Union Univ, BS, biol, 1958; Mich State Univ, BS, math, 1964; Calif State Univ, MS, math, 1970; Somerset Univ, PhD, comput sci, Ill minister, l988. **Career:** So Adhesive Corp, chemist, 1958-59; Ashland Sch Syst, teacher, 1961-65; Richmond Sch Syst, teacher, 1965-66; NASA Dryden Flight Res Facil, mathematician, 1966; AU Col, asst prof, 1975-78; Mfg Tools Inc, consult, 1982-86. **Orgs:** Bd mem, Local Black Adv Group, 1984-87; consult, Univ Wash, 1984; fel African Sci Inst; pastor, First Baptist Church; Urban League; Nat Asn Advan Colored People; Organizing comt. **Home Addr:** PO Box 1674, Lancaster, CA 93539. **Business Addr:** Chief Research Mathematician, NASA Dryden Flight Research Center, PO Box 273, Edwards, CA 93523, **Business Phone:** (661)276-3311.

### HEDGPETH, KIM ROBERTS. See ROBERTS, KIM.

### HEDGSPETH, ADRIENNE CASSANDRA
Journalist. **Personal:** Born Aug 29, 1959, Norfolk, VA; daughter of Beulah Hedgspeth Reid. **Educ:** Norfolk State Univ, Norfolk, VA, BA, jour, 1981; Conn Sch Broadcast, Farmington, CT, attended 1985. **Career:** Cincinnati Enquirer, Cincinnati, Ohio, reporter, summer, 1980; Shoreline Times Inc, Guil ford, CT, reporter, 1981-83; Norwich Bull, Norwich, CT, reporter, 1983-84; Regist, New Haven, Ct, staff writer, 1984, polit columnist, 1989; Aquarion Co, commun dept, mgr pub rels. **Orgs:** Nat Asn Advan Colored People, 1985; Nat Asn Black Journalists, 1989-. **Home Addr:** 596 Newhall St Apt BL, Hamden, CT 06517-3332.

### HEEP, DARLENE DAVIS. See DAVIS, DARLENE ROSE.

### HEFLIN, MARRION
Executive. **Personal:** Born Aug 28, 1963, Akron, OH; son of Lou J and Marion L. **Educ:** Ohio Univ, BBA, acct, 1985, MBA, finance, 1996. **Career:** KPMG LLP, sr mgr, assurance serv, 1986-94, sr mgr, trans serv, 2000-01; Huntington Bancshares Inc, vpres & asst audit dir, 1994-96, vpres, treas group, 1996-97; McDonalds Corp, sr acct mgr, 1997-98; TMP Worldwide, staff; Clark Atlanta Univ, adj prof; Trans Adv Group, sole proprietor, 2001-03; Prestige Design Group Inc, pres & chief exec officer, 2001-, chief operating officer, 2001-03; Nevis Securities LLC, managing prin, 2003-08, chief exec officer, managing dir & chief financial officer, currently; Global United Ltd, actg chief operating officer, 2008; HLB Galanisbain, sr mgr, 2008-10; CMF Assocs, subcontractor, 2011; Cortera Inc, dir financial planning & anal, 2011-. **Orgs:** Nat Asn Black Accts; Am Inst Cert Pub Accts; Fla Inst Cert Pub Accts; pres, Col Bus Ohio Univ; bd trustee, My Own Inc; bd trustee, Neighborhood House Inc; Nat Black MBA Asn; chmn bd, S Fulton Chamber Com; mem bd, dir Ohio Univ Alumni Asn; vol investment comt, Metro Atlanta United Way; bd mem, Trans Serv Group; Clark Atlanta Univ; Nevis Securities LLC. **Home Addr:** 7508 Cole Lane, Atlanta, GA 30349, **Home Phone:** (770)969-2577. **Business Addr:** Director of Financial Planning & Analysis, Cortera Inc, 777 Yamato Rd Suite 500, Boca Raton, FL 33431, **Business Phone:** (877)569-7376.

### HEGAMIN, GEORGE RUSSELL
Football player, football coach, executive. **Personal:** Born Feb 14, 1973, Camden, NJ; married Kimbre. **Educ:** NC State Univ, BA, bus mgt & sociol, 1994; Univ Phoenix, BS, psychol, 2009; Walden Univ, BS, psychol, leadership develop & coaching, 2016. **Career:** Football player (retired), coach, executive; Dallas Cowboys, tackle, 1994-97; Philadelphia Eagles, 1998; Tampa Bay Buccaneers, 1999-2000; Vintage Mortgage Corp, sales mgr, 2002-04; World Savings / Wachovia, wholesale acct exec, 2004-07; Pta Sports, dir truth athletics, 2008-13; Six 9 / Seven 9 Holdings LLC, owner, 2008-; NFLPA, sr mgr, 2015-; Carrollton Christian Acad, coach, currently; Shelton Sch, coach, currently. **Honors/Awds:** Super Bowl XXX Champion. **Business Addr:** Coach, Carrolton Christian Academy, 2205 E Hebron Pkwy, Carrollton, TX 75010, **Business Phone:** (972)242-6688.

### HEGGANS, T. DARRYL
Founder (originator), executive. **Personal:** Born Jan 1, 1921. **Educ:** Brown Univ, AB orgn behav. **Career:** Black Entertainment TV, regional vpres, vpres advert & media; CableTV Ties Inc, founder, pres, 2005-. **Honors/Awds:** BET Star Award. **Business Addr:** President, Cabletv Ties Inc, 1008 Wisconsin Ave, Oak Park, IL 60304.

### HEGGER, WILBER L.
Clergy. **Personal:** Born May 6, 1936, Lemoine, LA; son of Luke and Derotha Sam; married Marlene Mouton; children: Kevin Norbert. **Educ:** Grambling State Univ, Grambling, La, BS, math & sci, 1960; Univ Southwestern, Lafayette, La, post-baccalaureate, 1974; Diocese Lafayette, Lafayette, La, permanent diaconate formation prog. **Career:** Lafayette Parish Sch Bd, Lafayette, La, teacher, 1960-72; Univ Southwestern La, Lafayette, La, asst football coach, 1972-74; Prudential Ins Co, Lafayette, La, dist agt, 1974-80; Chubby's Fantastic Cakes, Lafayette, La, self-employed, 1980-; Diocese Lafayette, Lafayette, La, dir OBCM, 1989-. **Orgs:** Treas, Grambling Alumni Asn-Lafayette Ch, 1960-; jail minister, Diocese Lafayette, 1986-; chairperson, Ministers Black Cath Communities, 1988-90; coordr, Lafayette Civil Parish, currently. **Honors/Awds:** Bishop's Service Award, Diocese Lafayette, 1989. **Home Addr:** 201 Becky Lane, Lafayette, LA 70508, **Home Phone:** (318)984-1672. **Business Addr:** Co-Ordinator, Lafayette Civil Parish, Lafayette, LA 70501.

### HEINEBACK, BARBARA TAYLOR
Hospital administrator, association executive. **Personal:** Born Dec 29, 1944, New York, NY; daughter of John and Robella; children: 1. **Educ:** Howard Univ, Sch Commun, BA, jour, 1971; Univ Stockholm, cert lang arts, 1975. **Career:** CBS TV, asst prod, "Face Nation", 1969-71; Swed Nat Radio Stockholm, freelance journalist, 1972-75; White House, press asst first lady; Commun Satellite Corp, dir pub rels & dir ir, 1976-87; Scripps Mem Hosp, dir develop; Am's Cup, chief & dir, currently. **Orgs:** Dir, Wash Urban League; dir, Chamber Com, Chula Vista Calif; PRSA; Nat Asn Health Developers; Pub Rels Soc Am; Nat Soc Fund Raising Exec; Sunrise Bonita Rotary; Bi-nat Emergency Med Care Comt; San Francisco Libr; bd dir, Frederick County Ment Health Asn; Int Eye Found, San Francisco World Affairs Coun, & San Francisco Foreign Affairs Comt; NAACP; Scripps Healthcare; Silicon Graphics; Biotechs; Bi-nat Emergency Med Care Comt; San Francisco Libr. **Honors/Awds:** Plaques Appreciation, Pres Carter, Pres Tolbert; San Diego Arts Bd; United Negro Col Fund Steering Comm San Diego. **Special Achievements:** First African American woman to serve as a press officer to former First Lady Rosalynn Carter; Articles in Stockholm's major morning daily "Dagens Nyheter". **Home Addr:** PO Box 8604, La Jolla, CA 92038-8604. **Business Addr:** Chief of Protocol, Director of Public Relations, America's Cup, 2044 1st Ave Suite 300, San Diego, CA 92101-2079.

### HEISKELL, MICHAEL PORTER
Lawyer. **Personal:** Born Sep 11, 1951, Ft. Worth, TX; married Gayle Regina Beverly; children: Marian Phenice & James Dewitt II. **Educ:** Baylor Univ, BA, 1972; Baylor Law Sch, JD, 1974. **Career:** Dawson Dawson Smith & Snodd, law clerk, 1974-75; Galveston Co, asst dist atty, 1975-80; Johnson Vaughn & Heiskell, atty; Us Atty, asst atty, 1980-84; Johnson Vaughn & Heiskell, partner, atty & coun at law, 1984-. **Orgs:** Del Phi Alpha Delta Law Frat Conv, 1974; Am Bar Asn, 1976-77 Galveston Co Bar Asn; vpres sec Galveston Co Young Lawyers Asn, 1977-78; Tex State Bar Asn; Tex Dist & Co Attys Asn; bd dir mem, Gulf Coast Legal Found; Disaster Relief Com; Tex Young Lawers Asn; Min Recruit Com Baylor Law Sch; pres, Pi Sigma Alpha Baylor Univ; pres, Agiza Funika Soc Serv Club Baylor Univ; pres, Ft Worth Black Bar Asn; pres, Tarrant County Criminal Defense Lawyers Asn; assoc dir, pres, Tex Criminal Defense Lawyers Asn Nat Bar Asn Bar Asn Fifth Circuit Ct Appeals; fel & dir, Tex Criminal Defense Lawyers Educ Inst Nat Asn Criminal Defense Lawyers San Antonio Criminal Lawyers Asn; mem comt & adv comt, Northern Dist, Tex; adv comt, Second Ct Appeals; fel State bar, Tex; La Asn Criminal Defense Lawyers; Asn Trial Lawyers Am. **Honors/Awds:** Mr Navarro Jr Col Corsicana Tex, 1971; Tex Criminal Defense Lawyers Asn Presidential Award of Excellence 1994, 1995 & 2003; Lawyer of the Year Award, Tarrant Co Black Bar Asn, 1995, 2000. **Special Achievements:** Frequent Author and Lectr: "Confessions in Texas;" "Guilty Pleas; "Cross-Examination of Experts in Federal Fraud Investigations", "GrandJury Practice in Federal Courts", "Opening Statements"; "Fundamentals of Federal Representation"; "Effective Federal Pretrial Motions"; "Litigating Multi-Defendant Cases"; "Handling the Narcotics Case"; "Capital Murder Jury Selection"; First African American president of the Texas Criminal Defense Lawyers Asn; Superlawyer, 2003-04; First black to grad from Baylor Law School; First black asst DA Galveston Co. **Business Addr:** Partner, Senior Attorney, Counselor, Johnson Vaughn & Heiskell, 5601 Bridge St Suite 220, Ft. Worth, TX 76112, **Business Phone:** (817)457-2999.

### HELLER, BRIDGETTE P.
President (organization). **Educ:** Northwestern Univ, BA; JL Kellogg Grad Sch Mgt, MBA. **Career:** Kraft Foods Inc, exec vpres & gen mgr, 1985-02; Chung's Foods Inc, chief exec officer; Heller Assocs, founder & managing partner, 2004-05; Baby, Kids & Wound Care, global pres, 2005-07; Johnson & Johnson's Baby Global Bus Unit, pres, 2007-10; Merck & Co Inc, pres & exec vpres, 2010-. **Orgs:** Dir, Portrait Corp Am, 1998-2005; dir, ADT Corp, 1998-2005. **Honors/Awds:** "Black Enterprise", 75 Most Powerful Women in Business, 2010; "Black Enterprise", 100 Most Powerful Executives in Corporate America, 2009. **Business Addr:** President, Executive Vice President, Merck & Co Inc, 1 Merck Dr, Whitehouse Station, NJ 08889-0100, **Business Phone:** (908)423-1000.

### HELLER, BRIDGETTE P.
President (organization), executive. **Educ:** Northwestern Univ, BA, 1983; Northwestern Univ Kellogg Grad Sch Mgt, MBA, 1985. **Career:** Kraft Foods, exec vpres & gen mgr, 1985-2002; Chung's Foods Inc, chief exec officer, 2003-04; Heller Assocs, founder & managing partner, 2004-05; mkt strategy consult; Johnson & Johnson, Baby, Kids & Wound Care, pres, 2005-07, Baby Global Bus Unit, pres, 2007-10; Merck & Co, exec vpres & pres consumer care, 2010-14; early life nutrition, exec vpres, 2016-. **Orgs:** Bd dir & audit comt, ADT Corp, 2012-; dir, PCA Int Inc, 1998-2005. **Honors/Awds:** Award For Safe Motherhood Un Pop Fund, 2008; Award For Commitment to Philanthrophy and Professional Excellence, Sponsors Educ Opportunities, 2009; Black Enterprise, The 100 Most Powerful Executives in Corporate America 2010; Women of the Year, Healthcare Bus Womens Asn, 2013.

### HEMBY, DOROTHY JEAN
School administrator. **Personal:** Born Aug 21, 1940, Greenville, NC; daughter of Samul Emanuel and Queenie Ester. **Educ:** Essex Co Col, AS, lib arts, 1975; Montclair State Col, sociol & social studies, 1975; Kean Col, NJ, stud personnel serv, 1977. **Career:** Newark Bd Educ, teacher, 1974-76; Kean Col NJ, Col counr, 1976-77; Passaic Co Community Col, counr & admin, 1978-; Planet Earth Comt, chmn, 1986-. **Orgs:** vpres, Econ Consumer's Community Aid, 1971-73; Chmn, HOPE Orgn, 1978-82; NJ EOF Prof Assoc Inc, 1978-; community mem, NJ Assoc Black Educr, 1979-; chmn, Passaic Co Col Stud Life, 1983-84; counr, Love Jesus Ministry, 1983-; NJ Black Issues Assoc, 1984; exec bd & secy, Passaic Co Admin Assoc; advisor & consult, Passaic Co Newman Christian Club, 1983-; exec bd & treas, Passaic County Col Admin Assoc, 1985-88; coordr, Crispus Attucks Scholar Found, 1986-87; Am Assoc Coun& Develop; chmn, mission & goals mid state comt, Passaic County Col; bd mem, Human Serv Prog, Passaic City Community Col; co-chair, Alcohol & Drug Awareness Community, 1993-; NJ Higher Educ Consortium; Spec Needs C; co-chair, fund raiser community, 1994-. **Honors/Awds:** Counselor of the Year Award, 1993; Excellence Awards, NJ Coun Co Cols, 1995. **Home Addr:** PO Box 11, East Orange, NJ 07019-0011. **Business Addr:** Counselor, Passaic County Community College, 1 College Blvd, Paterson, NJ 07505, **Business Phone:** (973)684-6800.

### HEMMINGWAY, DR. BEULAH S.
Educator. **Personal:** Born Mar 11, 1943, Clarksdale, MS; daughter of Willie Smith Jr and Pennie Ree; married Theodore; children: Kofi Patrice & Julius Chaka. **Educ:** Coahoma Jr Col, attended 1962; Alcorn State Univ, BA, 1964; NC Cent Univ, MA, 1965; Fla State Univ, PhD, 1972. **Career:** Southern Univ, teacher, 1965-66; Voorhees Col, teacher, 1966-67; Benedict Col, teacher, 1967-72; Fla A&M Univ, Dept Eng, assoc prof lang & lit, 1972, vpres, Fac Sen, pres, 1995-99, prof eng, currently. **Orgs:** Chmn, Poetry Festival, 1975-82; adv, Lambda Iota Tau, 1975-82; Role& Scope Comt, 1976; Libr Resource Comt, 1977; Jack & Jill Am, 1979-81; bd dir, LeMoyne Art Found, 1980-82; Fla Col, Eng Teachers, Undergrad Coun Col Arts & Sci, 1982-; search comt vpres acad affairs, Fla A&M Univ, 1982; Mothers March Dimes, 1982-; vpres, Nat Coun Negro Women, 1982-; HomecomingComt, 1983; panelist, Fla Div Cult Affairs, 1986; Am Popular Cult Asn, 1988; bd mem, Drifters Inc, 1989; NatCoun Teachers Eng; Col Lang Asn; Curric Comt Lang & Lit; Southern Asn Cols & Schs Editing Comt; Col Level Acad Skills Test Task Force; prog chmn 112th anniv, Bethel Baptist Church; Tallahassee Urban League; Nat Asn Advan Colored People; Am Asn Higher Educ. **Home Addr:** PO Box 6029, Tallahassee, FL 32314-6029. **Business Addr:** Professor of English, Florida A & M University, Rm 410 & 414 422 Tucker Hall, Tallahassee, FL 32307, **Business Phone:** (850)599-3465.

### HEMPHILL, FRANK J.
Educator. **Personal:** Born Nov 16, 1943, Cleveland, OH; married Brenda; children: Tracie, Dawn & Frank John Parker Jr. **Educ:** W Ky Univ, BS, 1968; Ky State Univ, Coun Higher Ed & Sec Schs, MEd, 1975. **Career:** Shaw High Sch, E Cleveland, biol teacher, 1968-71, teaching asst biol, 1971-73, assoc dean students, dir acad asst, 1975; Ravenna Christian Acad, bus adminr, 1978-81; Hiram Col, dir stud acad serv, adj fac. **Orgs:** Minority Educ Serv Asn; vpres, Black Studie Consortium NE OH; Alpha Phi Omega; Nation Tutoring Asn; Ohio Planning & Zoning Bd; Nat Asn Stud Personnel Adminr. **Home Addr:** 11820 Kenyon, PO Box 181, Hiram, OH 44234-0181, **Home Phone:** (330)569-7623. **Business Addr:** Director of Student Academic Services, Hiram College, Hinsdale 105, Hiram, OH 44234, **Business Phone:** (330)569-5415.

### HEMPHILL, REV. DR. MILEY MAE
Educator, school principal, teacher. **Personal:** Born Jan 8, 1914, Gwinnett County, GA; married John R. **Educ:** Morris Brown Col, AB, 1950; Atlanta Univ, MA, 1957; Col New Truth, DD, 1970. **Career:** Teacher, school principal, Educator (retired); teacher & prin; Gwinnett-Jackson Co & Winder City Sch, curric dir; Ga Dept Educ, reading eng specialist; notary pub, 1957; W Hunter St Baptist Church, assoc minister, 1980-. **Orgs:** Life mem, NEA; GEA; GTEA; ACS; pres, Atlanta Ga Jeanes Curric dir; dir, Region IV Fine Arts; pres, Royal Oaks Manor Comm Club; YMCA; pres, Helen A Whiting Soc, 1989-. **Home Addr:** 896 Woodmere Dr NW, Atlanta, GA 30318-6002, **Home Phone:** (404)792-8113. **Business Addr:** Associate Minister, West Hunter Street Baptist Church, 1040 Ralph David Abernathy Blvd SW, Atlanta, GA 30310, **Business Phone:** (678)824-5441.

### HEMPSTEAD, HESSLEY JAMES, II
Football player, scout. **Personal:** Born Jan 29, 1972, Upland, CA. **Educ:** Univ Kans, grad. **Career:** Football player (retired); Detroit Lions, offensive guard, 1995-97, scout, 2000-01; Bing Steel, Consult, 1999-2000; Wash Redskins, area scout, 2001-03; John Wieland Homes & Neighborhoods, signature builder, 2003-12; RJ Leeper Construct, Proj Mgr, 2013-14; M/I Homes Inc, proj mgr, 2015; CMCS L.L.C, pres, 2015-currently. **Orgs:** Vice Pres, NFL Players Asn - Former Player Chapters, 2009-15; Construct Liason, Dem Nat Conv Comt, 2012.

### HEMSLEY, NATE (NATHANIEL RICHARD HEMSLEY)
Football player. **Personal:** Born May 5, 1974, Willingboro, NJ. **Educ:** Syracuse Univ, attended 1996. **Career:** Football player (retired); Dallas Cowboys, linebacker, 1997-99; Houston Oilers, 1997; Carolina Panthers, line backer, 2001; Miami Dolphins, 2001-02.

### HENDERSON, ALAN LYBROOKS
Basketball player, business owner. **Personal:** Born Dec 2, 1972, Morgantown, WV; son of Ray and Annette. **Educ:** Ind Univ, BA, biol; Howard Univ Sch Med, 1995. **Career:** Basketball player (retired), bus owner; Atlanta Hawks, forward, 1995-2004; Dallas Mavericks, 2004-05; Cleveland Cavaliers, forward, 2005-06; Philadelphia 76ers, free agt, 2006-07; Utah Jazz, 2007; Hendu Entertainment, owner, currently. **Orgs:** Kappa Alpha Psi Fraternity.

### HENDERSON, ANGELO B.
Journalist. **Personal:** Born Oct 14, 1962, Louisville, KY; son of Roger L (deceased) and Ruby M (deceased); married Felecia Dixon; children: Grant. **Educ:** Univ KY, BA, jour, 1985; Howard Univ, Wash, DC, mag publ; Harvard Univ, John F Kennedy Sch Govt Bus Sch, leadership; Harvard Divinity Sch; Summer Leadership Inst. **Career:** Walt Disney World, intern & attractions, 1982; WHAS-TV, reporting intern, 1983; Wall St J, Cleveland, OH, intern, 1984; Lexington Herald Leader, intern, 1984-85; Detroit Free Press, intern, 1985; Real Times LLC, assoc ed; St Petersburg Times, staff writer, 1985-86; Courier-J, Louisville, Ky, bus reporter, 1986-89; Detroit News, bus reporter & columist, 1989-93, city desk reporter, 1993-95; Wall St J, staff reporter, 1995-97, dep bur chief, currently, sr spec writer & page one, 1998-2000, dep detroit bur chief; Hope United Methodist Church, Southfield, Mich, assoc pastor worship, vision & emerging ministries, 2004-; AngeloInk LLC, founder, pres & chief exec officer, currently. **Orgs:** Pres, Detroit Chap Nat Asn Black Journalists; Nat Asn Black Journalists, parliamentarian. **Honors/Awds:** Best of Gannett Award for Business/Consumer Reporting, 1991; Nat Asn Black Journalists Award, Outstanding Coverage of the Black Condition for a series of Business Stories, 1992; 1st Place, Detroit Press Club Found, 1993; Unity Award for Excellence in Minority Reporting for Public Affairs/Social Issues, 1993; Pulitzer Prize for Distinguished Feature Writing, 1999; nations best reporters on race & ethnicity in am, 2000. **Special Achievements:** He also is the First African American to win a Pulitzer for The Wall Street Journal, one of the world's most influential newspapers; He also was named one of "39 African-American Achievers to Watch? in the next millennium by Success Guide magazine. **Business Addr:** President, Founder, AngeloInk LLC, 200 Liberty St, New York, NY 10281, **Business Phone:** (212)416-2327.

### HENDERSON, BARRINGTON
Singer. **Personal:** Born Jun 10, 1956, Washington, PA; son of Joyce. **Career:** Albums: "Meet the Temptations"; "The Temptations Sing Smokey"; "The Temptin' Temptation"; "Gettin' Ready"; "The Temptations with a Lot o' Soul"; "The Temptations Wish It Would Rain"; "Cloud Nine"; "Puzzle People"; "Psychedelic Shack"; Sky's the Limit"; "Solid Rock"; "All Directions"; "Masterpiece", 1990; "A Song for You"; "House Party"; "Wings of Love"; "The Temptations Do the Temptations"; " Bare Back"; "Hear to Tempt You"; Power; Bulls-eye; I Wanna Hold Your Hand; "Reunion"; "Surface Thrills"; "Back to Basics"; "Truly for You"; "Touch Me"; "To Be Continued"; "Together Again"; "Special"; "Milestone"; Phoenix Rising, 1998; Ear-Resistible, 2000; "I'm Sorry", writer & singer; The Temptations, 1998; It's All Right to Be Wrong, vocalist; A Little Bit Lonely, vocalist; Awesome, 2001; " Legacy"; "Still Here"; My Baby; Best Kept Secret, 2003; Singles: "My Girl"; "Get Ready"; "Ain't Too Proud to Beg"; "Beauty Is Only Skin Deep"; " I'm Losing You"; "All I Need"; "You're My Everything"; "I Wish It Would Rain"; "When You're Young and in Love"; "I Could Never Love Another"; "Cloud Nine"; "I'm Gonna Make You Love Me"; "Run Away Child, Running Wild"; "I Can't Get Next to You"; "Psychedelic Shack"; "Ball of Confusion"; "Just My Imagination"; "Papa Was a Rollin' Stone"; "Masterpiece"; "Let Your Hair Down"; "Happy People"; "Shakey Ground"; "The Motown Song"; Films: Save the Children; Happy New Year; The Temptations; Walk Hard: The Dewey Cox Story. **Orgs:** The Dramatics. **Honors/Awds:** Grammy Award. **Business Addr:** Singer, William Morris Agency, 9601 Wilshire Blvd, Beverly Hills, CA 90210, **Business Phone:** (310)285-9000.

### HENDERSON, CARL L., JR.
Police officer. **Personal:** Born May 5, 1945, Pelahatchie, MS; son of Carl (deceased) and Mary Sample (deceased); married Eunice; children: Carl Dwaine, Gary Lee & Linette. **Educ:** Prentiss Jr Col, Prentiss, MS, AS, 1966; Univ New Haven, W Haven, CT, BS, 1976. **Career:** Hartford Bd Educ, Hartford, Conn, social worker, 1968-71; Hartford Police Dept, Hartford, Conn, supervr, lt, 1971-76, sgt, 1979-. **Orgs:** Pres, Hartford Guardians, 1988-92; Hartford Police Union, 1971-. **Honors/Awds:** Community Service Award, Hartford Guardians Inc, 1980, 1987, 1995. **Home Addr:** 90 E Burnham St, Bloomfield, CT 06002, **Home Phone:** (203)242-3415. **Business Addr:** Sergeant, Hartford Police Department, 50 Jenning Rd, Hartford, CT 06120, **Business Phone:** (860)757-4440.

### HENDERSON, CEDRIC EARL
Basketball player. **Personal:** Born Mar 11, 1975, Memphis, TN. **Educ:** Univ Memphis, attended 1997. **Career:** Basketball player (retired), free agent; Cleveland Cavaliers, forward, 1997-2001; Golden State Warriors, 2001-02; Mobile Revelers, 2003; Sagesse Beirut, Lebanon, 2003; Sagesse Beirut, Lebanon, 2003; Yakima Sun Kings, 2003; Great Lakes Storm, 2004; Fayetteville Patriots, 2004; Seoul SK Knights, 2004; Huntsville Flight, 2005; Blue Stars, 2005; Khimik, 2006-07, Ukraine; Keravnos, Cyprus, 2007; Milwaukee Bucks, free agt, 2002.

### HENDERSON, CHERI KAYE
Executive director, association executive. **Personal:** Born Feb 3, 1947, Knoxville, TN; daughter of James Noel and Marion Perry. **Educ:** Univ Tenn Knoxville, BS, 1974. **Career:** Knox Co Sch Syst, instr, 1974-76; Metrop Nashville Bd Educ, instr, adult basic educ, 1976-78; Tenn State Dept Econ & Community Develop, asst chief procurement, 1976-78; Minority Bus Opportunity Comt, exec dir, 1978-79; Tenn Minority Supplier Develop Coun Inc, exec dir, 1979-, pres, currently; TriState Minority Supplier Development Council, Pres & chief exec officer, currently. **Orgs:** Citizens Bank Community Adv Coun; bd dir, United Way Mid Tenn; bd dir, Nashville Bus Incubation Ctr; bd mgr, Northwest Young Men's Christian Asn; Leadership Nashville; bd dir, Am Heart Asn; Third Nat Bank Econ Develop External Coun; Hugh OBrien Youth Found; Matthew 25, Nashville Read; chair, United Negro Col Fund, Mid Tenn Campaign, Small & Medium Bus; bd mem, Nashville Area Chamber Com. **Honors/Awds:** Minorities & Women In Business, Women Who Make A Difference, 1992, National Award of Excellence, 1990; Minority Business News USA, Women Who Mean Business, 1992; Woman of the Year, Davidson Co Bus & Prof Women, 1991; Executive Director of the Year, Nat Adv Comt, 1983; Alpha Phi Alpha Fraternity Tau Lamba Chapter Public Service Award, 1999; "The Best of Decade", Minority Business News USA, Dallas, TX, 2002. **Home Addr:** 210 Hickory Dr, Old Hickory, TN 37138-1122, **Home Phone:** (615)758-0114. **Business Addr:** Executive Director, President, Tennessee Minority Supplier Development Council Inc, 220 Athens Way Suite 105 Metro Ctr Plz I Bldg, Nashville, TN 37228, **Business Phone:** (615)259-4699.

### HENDERSON, CHERYL BROWN
Association executive. **Personal:** Born Dec 20, 1950, Topeka, KS; daughter of Oliver L Brown (deceased) and Leola; married Larry; children: Christopher. **Educ:** Baker Univ, BS, elem educ, 1972; Emporia State Univ, MA, guid & coun, 1976; Washburn Univ, DHL. **Career:** Topeka Pub Schs, teacher, 1972-76, counr, 1976-79; KS State, Dept Educ, educ consult, 1979-94; Brown & Brown Asn, owner, 1984-; Brown Found, pres, founding pres, founder & chief exec officer, 1988-; Brown & Assocs, owner; Coming Age/ RSVP Johnson County, coord. **Orgs:** St John AME, 1964-; bd mem, 1982-93, chair, 1990-92, Nat Network Women's Employ; adv, Nat Pk Serv-Brown Bd Educ, 1990-; bd mem, Kans State Hist Soc, 1997-; bd mem, Kans Humanities Coun, 1997-; bd mem, Nat Trust Hist Preserv, 1998-; adv, US Senate Adv Comt-Math & Sci, KS, 1998-; chair, Mayor's Coun

Diversity, 1998-; second vpres, Shounee County Repub Women, 1999-; bd mem, Univ Kans Libr Advocacy Bd; bd mem, Washburn Univ Educ Dept Adv Coun; bd mem, Univ Mo at Kans City Women's Ctr; bd trustee, Kans City Pub Libr Found; Nancy Boydas Mil Acad. **Honors/Awds:** 100 most influential people in Topeka, 1991; Distinguished Alumni Citation, Baker Univ, 1997; Spirit of Topeka, Topeka Convention & Visitors Bur, 1998; Heart-to-Heart Award, Volunteer Ctr, Topeka, 1999; Capitol Citizen Award, Cable TV, 1999; Diversity Council Leadership, City Topeka, Mayor's Office, 1999; Spirit of Amelia Earhart Role Model Award, Amelia Earhart Museum; Kansan of the Year, Topeka Capitol J, 2004; The Friend of Education Award, Nat Educ Asn, 2005; Life Time Achievement Award, Nat Alliance Black Sch Educ; Fight for Justice Award, Southern Univ Law Ctr; Women of Distinction Award, Girl Scouts; Mid-American Education Hall of Fame, 2010; Martin Luther King Jr. Anniversary Award, 2011; Multimedia Cable and Capitol Federal Savings Capitol Citizen Award; Mayor's Award, Mayor's Diversity Coun; Thurgood Marshall Scholarship Fund Award; Outstanding Young Women of America. **Special Achievements:** Developed legislation to establish "Brown v Bd" Natl Park, 1992; Publications: Brownv Bd of Educ: In Pursuit of Freedom & Equality, Teachers Guide; Forty Years After the Brown Decision: Implications, Perspectives and Future Direction, Readings on Equal Educ, vol 13, 1997; "The Brown Foundation Story: Preserving Public History" CRM vol 19, No 2, 1996; one of a group of individuals invited to a reception at the White House in honor of Dr.King and the children of Civil Rights Movement and the 75th Anniv, US Deptof Labor, Women's Bureau, 1994, 1995; "Landmark Decision-Remembering the Struggle for Equal Education", Land and People, The Trust for Public Lands, vol 6, no. 1, 1994; "Schoolhouse Restoration", Preserving Our Recent Past, Historic Preservation Education Foundation, Washington, DC, 1995; First African American woman from Kansas to run for the U. S. House of Representatives, 1996. **Home Addr:** 1500 SW Campbell, Topeka, KS 66604, **Home Phone:** (785)235-9000. **Business Addr:** President, Chief Executive Officer, Brown Foundation, PO Box 2338, Mission, KS 66201-2338, **Business Phone:** (785)235-3939.

### HENDERSON, DR. CORTEZ V.
Educator. **Personal:** Born Jun 8, 1960, Pine Bluff, AR; daughter of Ed and Sue. **Educ:** Univ Ark, Pine Bluff, BS, fashion merchandising/textiles & clothing, 1982; Iowa State Univ, ME, family & consumer sci, 1987, PhD, stud coun & personnel serv, 1992. **Career:** St Community Col, dean students; Univ Cent Ark, Conway, vis prof; NewBirth Youth Difference Prog, educ coordr, grant writer; Univ Md Eastern Shore, Human Ecol Dept, lectr, 1987-88; Iowa State Univ, Col Educ-Prof Studies Dept, Teaching Asst, 1988-92; acad advisor, Col Lib Arts & Sci, 1988-90; Jumpstart Community Mentoring Prog, Iowa State Univ, prog dir, 1990-92; Simpson Col, dir Career Planning & Placement, asst dir minority stud affairs, 1992; State Community Col, Dean Studentaffairs, coun serv, 1992-93; Univ Cent Ark, Col Educ, vis prof, 1993-94, Ronald E McNair Scholars Prog, prin investr & prog dir, 1996-2008; Philander Smith Col, Upward Bound Trio Counr, instr, 1994; VCH Consult Inc, prolific orator, educr, auth, grant writer, workshop facilitator, chief exec officer & founder, 1996-; ELI, Southwest Asn Stud Assistance Progs, founder, 1998; Spiritual Ed & Team Facilitator, Inspire Mag; ILEAD Inst, 2005-; Col Oauchitas, vpres stud affairs, 2008-11. **Orgs:** Bd mem, Coun Opportunity Educ, 1997-2000; pres, SW Asn Students Assistance Prog, 1997-2000; Leadership Pine Bluff, 2002; Alliance Cand Inst, 2002; Pine Bluff Comn C & Youth; Task Force Reinventing Downtown; Nat Asn Advan Colored People; comt mem, Nat TRIO Conf; founder & dir, Ark Mcnair Sr Summer Cam, 2004-; founder, Ark Alliance Grad Educ, 2005-. **Home Addr:** 207 W Martin Pl, Pine Bluff, AR 71601, **Home Phone:** (870)540-0282.

### HENDERSON, DAVID
Writer, poet, educator. **Personal:** Born Jan 1, 1942, Harlem, NY; married Barbara Christian; children: Najuma Ide & Imetai Malik. **Educ:** Bronx Comm Col, attended 1960; Hunter Col, New York, 1961; New Sch Social Res, 1962; E W Inst, MA, 1965; Univ Without Walls, Berkeley, 1972. **Career:** Black Arts Movement, founder; Soc Umbra, co-founder, 1962-; Nat Endowment Arts, consult, 1967-68, 1980; City Col New York, SEEK prog lectr, 1967-69, poet-in-residence, 1969-70; Berkeley Pub Sch Syst, consult, 1968; New York Pub Sch Systs, cosult, 1969; Univ Calif, Berkeley, lectr, 1970-72; fulltime auth, 1973-79; Univ Calif, San Diego, vis prof, 1979-80; Naropa Univ, vis prof, 1981, 1995, 2004; State Univ New York, Stony Brook, vis prof, 1988-89; St. Mark's Poetry Proj, workshop leader, 1995, 2003; New York Found Arts, artist fel, 1999; New Sch, vis prof, 2000; Auth: Felix Silent Forest, 1967; De Mayor Harlem, Dutton, 1970; Jimi Hendrix: Voodoo Child Aquarian Age, 1978; Low E, 1980; Neo-Calif, 1998; Ed: Umbra, from co-ed to ed, 1963-74; Umbra Anthology, 1968; Umbra/Latin Soul, 1975; New York Found Arts, artist fel, 1999. **Orgs:** Int PEN, 1972-; Arts Comn City Berkeley, 1975-77; Afro-Am Third World Writers Union, 1980-; New York's Lower E Side art community. **Honors/Awds:** Great Lakes College Association of New Writers Award, 1971; New Genre Poetry Grant, Calif Arts Coun, 1992; Artist Grant, Found Contemp Performance Arts, 1999. **Special Achievements:** Lyrics to compose love in outer space; Editor: Umbra Anthology, 1968. Author: The Low East, 1980; Neo-California, 1998. **Home Addr:** PO Box 1018, Cooper Station, NY 10276-1018. **Business Addr:** Editor, Umbra Publications, Sather Gate, Berkeley, CA 94704, **Business Phone:** (510)848-6767.

### HENDERSON, EDDIE L.
Engineer. **Personal:** Born Feb 25, 1932, Quincy, FL; son of Ennis and Ruby Green; married Velma Dean Hall; children: Tracy & Dionne. **Career:** Engineer (retired); Freedmens Hosp, 1961-67; Nat Asn Broadcast Employees & Technicians, engr, 1994; Am Broadcasting Co News, DC. **Orgs:** Local 644 Int Alliance Theatrical Stage Employees; Hillcrest Heights Baptist Church. **Honors/Awds:** Amateur Fighter Golden Gloves, NY, 1949-50; So Conf Air Force Japan, 1953. **Home Addr:** 1312 Owens Rd, Oxon Hill, MD 20745, **Home Phone:** (301)873-5630.

### HENDERSON, FRANK S., JR.
Executive director, government official. **Personal:** Born Oct 12, 1958, Oakley, KS; son of Frank S and Meade A Jones; married Lorraine M White; children: Ashley A. **Educ:** Barton County Community Col, Great Bend, KS, AA, 1981; Washburn Univ, Topeka, KS, BA, 1987. **Career:** Kans Dept Social & Rehabilition Serv, Topeka, Kans, ment health activ therapist, 1979-82, social serv admin, 1982-85; Kans Dept Corr, topeka, Kans, corrections specialist, 1985-87; Kans Parole Bd, Topeka, KS, vice-chmn, 1988-89, chmn, 1989-90; Kans Crime Victims Compensation Bd, exec dir, 1995-2012. **Orgs:** Nat Asn Advan Colored People, 1986; vpres, Ment Health Asn, Kans, 1988-90; comnr, Gov's Adv Comn Ment Health & Retardation Servs, 1988-90; Topeka Sunset Optimist Club, 1989-; Nat Asn Blacks Criminal Justice, 1989-; councilman, Kans Criminal Justice Coord Coun, 1989-90; Nat Forum Black Pub Admin, 1990-; prog chmn, Gov's Martin Luther King Commemoration, 1991; pres, Kans Orgn Victim Assistance; Nat Asn Crime Victims Compensation Bd; consult, US Dept Justice. **Home Addr:** 2700 NE 46th, Topeka, KS 66617, **Home Phone:** (913)246-3343. **Business Addr:** Executive Director, Kansas Crime Victims Compensation Board, 120 SW 10th Ave Suite 2, Topeka, KS 66612-1237, **Business Phone:** (785)296-2359.

### HENDERSON, DR. GEORGE
Educator. **Personal:** Born Jun 18, 1932, Hurtsboro, AL; son of Kidd L and Lula Mae Crawford Fisher; married Barbara Beard; children: George Jr, Michele, Lea Murr, Joy, Lisa, Dawn Johnson & Faith Mosley. **Educ:** Mich State Univ, attended 1952; Wayne State Univ, BA, sociol, 1957, MA, sociol, 1959, PhD, educ sociol, 1965. **Career:** Educator (retired), consultant; Church Youth Serv, soc caseworker, 1957-59; Detroit Housing Comn, soc economist, 1960-61; Detroit Urban League, community serv dir, 1961-63; Detroit Mayors Youth Comn, prog dir, 1963-64; Wayne State Univ, Detroit, Delinq Control Training Ctr, asst dir, 1964-65; Detroit Pub Sch, asst dir intercultural rels, 1965-66, asst supt, 1966-67; Univ Okla, assoc prof, sociol & educ, 1967-69, prof, human rels, educ, assoc prof, sociol, 1969-2006, Dept Human Rels, chmn, 1970-82, 1987-95, David Ross Boyd distinguished prof, 1985, Regents distinguished prof, 1989, Col Libr Studies, dean, 1996-2000, prof human rels & dir, Kerr-McGee Presidential prof, 2001, Dept Human Rels Advan Studies Prog, dir, Sylvan N Goldman Prof Emer, David Ross Boyd Prof Emer & Regents Prof Emer, human rels, educ & sociol, currently; Langston Univ, vis prof, sociol, 1969-70; USAF Acad, distinguished vis prof, 1980-81; Fayetteville State Univ, distinguished lectr, 1999; US Dept Def, consult; US Dept Justice, consult; US Comn Civil Rights, consult; Social Sec Admin, consult; Am Red Cross, consult; books: Teachers Should Care, 1970, Foundations of American Education, 1970, America's Other Children: Public Schools Outside Suburbia, 1971, To Live in Freedom: Human Relations Today and Tomorrow, 1972, Education for Peace: Focus on Mankind, 1973, Human Relations: From Theory to Practice, 1974, Human Relations in the Military: Problems and Programs, 1975, A Religious Foundation of Human Relations: Beyond Games, 1977, Introduction to American Education: A Human Relations Approach, 1978, Understanding and Counseling Ethnic Minorities, 1979; Physician-Patient Communication, Transcultural Health Care & Police Human Relations, 1981, The Human Rights of Professional Helpers, 1983, Mending Broken Children: A Parent's Manual & Psychosocial Aspects of Disability, 1984, College Survival for Student-Athletes, 1985, International Business and Cultures: A Human Relations Perspective, 1987, Understanding Indigenous and Foreign Cultures, 1989, Values in Health Care, 1991, Social Work Interventions: Helping People of Color & Cultural Diversity in the Workplace: Issues and Interventions, 1994, Migrants, Immigrants and Slaves: Racial and Ethnic Groups in America & Understanding Indigenous and Foreign Cultures, 1995, Human Relations Issues in Management, 1996, Ethnicity and Substance Abuse: Prevention and Intervention, 2002, Psychosocial Aspects of Disability, 2004, Understanding Indigenous and Foreign Cultures, 2006, Excellence in College Teaching and Learning, 2007, Race and the University: A Memoir, 2010, Psychosocial Aspects of Disability, 2011. **Orgs:** Kappa Alpha Psi Fraternity; Am Sociol Asn; Asn Black Sociologist; Asn Supr & Curric Develop. **Special Achievements:** First African American dean of a degree granting college on the Norman campus. **Home Addr:** 2616 Osborne Dr, Norman, OK 73069, **Home Phone:** (405)329-8614. **Business Addr:** Professor Emeritus, University of Oklahoma, 601 Elm Ave Rm 728, Norman, OK 73019-0315, **Business Phone:** (405)325-1756.

### HENDERSON, GERALD, SR. (JEROME MCKINLEY HENDERSON, SR.)
Television broadcaster, basketball player, business owner. **Personal:** Born Jan 16, 1956, Richmond, VA; married Marie; children: Gerald Jr, Jade & Marie A. **Educ:** Va Commonwealth Univ, 1978. **Career:** Basketball player (retired), tv broadcaster, bus owner; Boston Celtics, guard, 1979-84; Seattle SuperSonics, 1984-86; NY Knicks, 1986-87; Philadelphia 76ers, 1987-89; Milwaukee Bucks, 1989; Detroit Pistons, 1989-91; Houston Rockets, 1991-92; All state Transp Co Inc, owner & pres; Genesis Adv, rep; Pa Merchant Group, vpres investment mgt; Comcast Sports Net, NBA analyst; RE MAX Serv, sales assoc, currently; 76ers post game live, analyst, currently. **Home Addr:** 185 Birkdale Dr, Blue Bell, PA 19422-3276, **Home Phone:** (610)272-8167. **Business Addr:** Sales Associate, RE MAX Services - Blue Bell, 725 Skippack Pke Suite 100, Blue Bell, PA 19422, **Business Phone:** (215)654-6166.

### HENDERSON, HENRY F., JR. (HANK HENDERSON)
Executive, president (organization), athlete. **Personal:** Born Mar 10, 1928, New Jersey, NJ; son of Henry F Sr and Elizabeth (Hamond). **Educ:** State Univ NY Agr & Tech Inst, elec mach & power distrib, 1950; William Paterson Col, attended; William Paterson Univ, attended; Seton Hall Univ, attended; NY Univ, attended; Stevens Inst Technol, attended; Alfred State Col, attended. **Career:** Richardson Scale Co, res & develop dept; Thoreb North America, managing dir; HF Henderson Indust, pres & chief exec officer, 1952-. **Orgs:** Paterson Econ Develop Corp; Comt Common Defense; Regional Plan Asn; Task Force Pub TV; Century Found; NJ State Employ & Training Comn; comnr, Port Authority NY & NJ; chair, Gov Comn Int Trade during admin Gov; Delta Dent Plan NJ; NJ Chamber Com; trustee, Stevens Inst Technol; NY Theol Sem; chair, Audit Comt; head, Essex County Econ Develop Comn. **Business Addr:** President, Chief Executive Officer, HF Henderson Industries, 45 Fairfield Pl, West Caldwell, NJ 07006, **Business Phone:** (973)227-9250.

### HENDERSON, HENRY FAIRFAX, JR. (HANK HENDERSON)
Executive. **Personal:** Born Mar 10, 1928, Paterson, NJ; son of Henry F Sr and Elizabeth Hammond; married Ethel Miller; children: Kathleen Carter, Kenneth, David & Elizabeth. **Educ:** State Univ NY Alfred, attended 1950; William Paterson Col, Seton Hall Univ; NY Univ. **Career:** Thoreb N Am LLC; Howe Richardson Scale Co, engr, 1950-67; HF Henderson Indust, founder, 1954-67, pres & chief exec officer, 1967-. **Orgs:** Comnr, Port Authority NY & NJ; chmn, Gov's Comn Int Trade; dir, NJ State Chamber Com; World Trade Inst Port Authority NY & NJ; adv bd mem curric, State Univ NY Agr & Tech Inst; bd mem, Partnership NJ; bd trustee, Stevens Inst Technol; bd dir, Gen Pub Utilities Corp; bd trustee, Community Found NJ; Pres Comn Exec Exchange; Found NJ Alliance Action; adv comt, Essex County Super Ct; bd mem, NJ State Employ & Training Comn. **Home Addr:** 315 Rifle Camp Rd, Woodland Park, NJ 07424, **Home Phone:** (201)742-4321. **Business Addr:** President, Chief Executive Officer, H F Henderson Indust, 45 Fairfield Pl, West Caldwell, NJ 07006-2630, **Business Phone:** (201)227-9250.

### HENDERSON, HUGH C.
Government official. **Personal:** Born Dec 3, 1930, Poughkeepsie, NY; married Sandra V Bell; children: Hugh III & Denise. **Educ:** Kent Univ; Univ Ind; Univ Ill; Univ Wis. **Career:** Valley Mold & Iron Co, maintenance electrician, 1949-68; United Steel Workers Am, staff rep, 1968-78; State Dept Employ Relat, secy, 1979; State Wis, Labor & Indust Review Comn, comnr, 1986. **Orgs:** Chmn bd, Milwaukee Industrialization Ctr, 1971-; bd dir, Milwaukee Urban League, 1974-79; pres, Milwaukee Frontier Club, 1977-79; nat bd, Nat OIC, 1978-; Int Personnel Mgt Asn, 1979. **Honors/Awds:** Cert of Appreciation, OIC Bd Dir, 1978; Outstanding Community Effort Award, Dane City State Employees Combined Campaign, 1979; Enlightened Leadership, Dedicated Community Service Award, Milwaukee Frontiers Club, 1980. **Home Addr:** 17310 N Galileo Way, Surprise, AZ 85374-6408, **Home Phone:** (623)544-1185.

### HENDERSON, I. D., JR.
Government official. **Personal:** Born Jul 23, 1929, Lufkin, TX; son of I.D. Sr and Willie; married Jerlean Eastland; children: Brenda Kay Heads, Lara Wayne Parker, Gwendolyn Joyce McKinley & Bruce Anthony. **Career:** Commissioner (retired), executive; Lufkin Foundry Inc, mat control, 1971-72; F Home Savings & Loans Asn, bldg supr, 1972-79; Recinct 2 Angelina County, TX, pres & county comnr, 1979; Cedar Grove Community Asn, pres, currently. **Orgs:** Master mason Franfurt Ger, 1962-65; master mason Mistletoe Lodge #31 Lawton OK, 1966-77; master mason Southgate Lodge #42 Lufkin TX, 1978-; pres, Citizens Chamber Com, 1978-84; deacon, Mt Calvary Bapt Ch Lufkin TX; founder, Asn Black County Commissioners. **Honors/Awds:** Recipient KSM w/1 Bronze, SV Stara; NDSM; GMC w/5 Loops; Purple Heart AUS; inducted Hall of Honor in Lufkin, 2010. **Special Achievements:** First African American Commissioner in Agelina County. **Home Addr:** 3086 FM 326, Rt 13 PO Box 750, Lufkin, TX 75901-1822, **Home Phone:** (936)824-2358.

### HENDERSON, JAMES H.
Government official, educator. **Personal:** Born Apr 20, 1937, Lexington, NC; son of Henry and Callie Spindell; married Joan E Woods; children: Tonya L, James H Jr, James, Jennifer, Janet, Jacqueline & Patricia. **Educ:** Pikes Peak Community Col, AA, gen studies, 1978; Univ Southern Colo, BS, 1979; Community Col Air Force, AAS mgt, AAS, educ methodology, 1981; Webster Univ, MA, mgt, 1982; Univ Northern Colo, MA, coun, 1983; Harvard Univ, Grad Sch Educ, Inst Mgt Lifelong Educ. **Career:** USAF, educ supt, 1955-81; Ed Ctr Hurlburt Fla, educ coun, 1982-84, Hq Strategic Air Command, command educ counr, 1984, USAF Civil Serv, HQSAC & DPAE, asst dir educ serv, 1989, educ specialist. **Orgs:** Recorder Kadesia Temple 135, 1975-; Am Asn Adult Continuing Educ, 1978; Am Numis Asn, 1982; Am Asn Coun Develop, 1982; mid w cord, Mili Educr & Coun Asn, 1983; Nat Cert coun, Natl Brd Cert Coun, 1984; USAF Radars-Iceland Asn. **Home Addr:** 4106 Cobia St, Yorktown, VA 32507. **Business Addr:** Chief, Education Development -Retired, Defense Activity for Non-Traditional Educatioon Services, Hampton, VA.

### HENDERSON, JEROME MCKINLEY, SR. See HENDERSON, GERALD, SR.

### HENDERSON, JEROME VIRGIL
Football player, athletic director, football coach. **Personal:** Born Aug 8, 1969, Statesville, NC; married Traci; children: Jazmin, Taylor & Tyler. **Educ:** Clemson Univ. **Career:** Football player (retired), football coach, athletic dir; New Eng Patriots, defensive back, 1991-93, 1996; Buffalo Bills, 1993-94; Philadelphia Eagles, 1995; New York Jets, 1997-98, dir player develop & defensive backs coach, 2006-08; HomeBanc Mortgage Corp, vpres, 2002-05; Cleveland Browns, defensive backs coach, 2009; Dallas Cowboys, sec coach, 2012-.

### HENDERSON, DR. JOHN L.
President (organization), college administrator, executive. **Personal:** Born Apr 10, 1932, Evergreen, AL; married Theresa Crittenden; children: Dana, Nina & John. **Educ:** Hampton Inst, BS, 1955; Univ Cincinnati, MEd, 1967, EdD, 1976; Inst Afro-Am Studies Earlham Col, attended 1971; PhD, 1976. **Career:** Univ Cincinnati, fac, 1957-67, asst dean stud, 1968-69, Dean Pub Serv Div, dean stud develop, 1972-76, consult, vpres Instnl Develop, Cincinnati State Tech & Community Col, 1984, interim pres, 2007-10; Xavier Univ, res asst, 1967-68, asst dean men, asst dean stud, Coordr Univ & Urban Affairs, lectr psychol educ, 1970-72; Raymond Walters Col, instr psychol educ, 1969-70; Wilberforce Univ, pres, 1988-2003; Ayers & Assocs Inc, sr assoc, 2003-; Univ Urban Affairs, dir; Sinclair Community Col, Am Asn Higher Educ, vpres Stud Serv; US Pub Health Serv, res asst. **Orgs:** Cincinnati Br Nat Asn Advan Colored People, 1969; Phi Delta Kappa, 1971; Cincinnati Manpower Planning Coun, 1971-72; Spec Task Force Study Racial Isolation Cincinnati Pub Schs, 1972-73; bd trustee, Cincinnati Sch Found, 1973-75; Cincinnati Pvt Indust Coun, 1973-75; Develop Educ Adv Comt, Ohio Bd Regents, 1974; ed bd, NASPA Jour, 1974; bd dir, Dayton Urban League, 1977-; bd dir, Miami Valley Lung Asn, 1978; bd dir, Miami Valley Educ Oppor Ctr, 1978; bd dir, Miami Val-

ley Coun Aging, 1979; ed bd, Jour Develop & Remedial Educ, 1980; pres, Asn Non-White Concerns; Nat Asn Stud Personnel Adminstrs; Am Col Personnel Asn; comnr, Cincinnati Human Rels Comt; chmn, Educ Comt; chmn & bd comnr, Cincinnati Human Rels Comt; Coun Black Am Affairs; Cincinnati Human Rels Comn, chmn; Historically Black Cols & Univs, Pres's Bd Advisors, 2002; Coun Presidents Asn Gov Boards; boards Proj; Greater Cincinnati Found; Greater Cincinnati Urban League; Greater Cincinnati Chamber Com. **Home Addr:** 1109 Towanda Ter, PO Box 32360, Cincinnati, OH 45216. **Business Addr:** Senior Associate, Ayers & Associates Inc, 2001 Jefferson Davis Hwy Suite 803, Arlington, VA 22202, **Business Phone:** (703)418-2815.

### HENDERSON, JOYCE ANN (JOYCE JOHNSON HENDERSON)

Executive, teacher. **Personal:** Born Jan 12, 1947, Oklahoma City, OK; daughter of Eddie Lee and Fannie M Johnson; married William Gerald; children: Kevin G & Wm Kelly. **Educ:** Langston Univ, OK, BS, 1969; Univ Cent Okla, MEd, 1973; Univ Okla, cert, sec admin. **Career:** Harvard Mid Sch Okla City Sch Syst, asst prin, 1978-80; Life Guthrie Job Corps Ctr, supvr basic educ & dept head ctr, 1976-78; Orchard Park Girls Sch Ok City Sch Syst, counr, 1974-76; Teacher Corps Univ Okla & Okla City Sch Syst, teacher corps supvr, 1972-74; Northeast High Sch, prin; Star Spencer High Sch, prin; Emerson Alternative High Sch, prin; Classen Sch Advan Studies, prin; Okla City Pub Sch, prin, 1980-, exec dir sch & community serv. **Orgs:** Bd mem, vice-pres & secy, YWCA; bd mem, Okla Comn Educ Leadership; Youth Serv Okla County; Sunbeam Family Serv; OKC Chap Am Red Cross; S Okla City Chamber Com; Schs Healthy Lifestyles Prog, 1998-; charter mem, Okla City Metrop Chap Black Educr; Cent Okla Turning Pt Health Initiative; Leadership Okla City Alumni Asn & Nat Sorority Phi Delta Kappa Inc; Gamma Epsilon Chap; lifetime mem, Langston Univ Alumni Asn; lifetime mem, Univ Cent Okla Alumni Asn; lifetime mem, Alpha Kappa Alpha Sorority Inc; Nat Asn Advan Colored People; pianist missionary choir, St. John C.M.E. Church Spencer, Okla, currently. **Home Addr:** 1214 NE 67, Oklahoma City, OK 73111-7857, **Home Phone:** (405)478-1049. **Business Addr:** Executive Director, Oklahoma City Public Schools, 900 N Klein, Oklahoma City, OK 73106, **Business Phone:** (405)587-0407.

### HENDERSON, DR. LENNEAL JOSEPH

Consultant, educator. **Personal:** Born Oct 27, 1946, New Orleans, LA; son of Marcelle and Lenneal; married Joyce E Colon; children: Lenneal C & Lenneal J III. **Educ:** Univ Calif, Berkeley, BA, 1968, MA, 1969, PhD, polit sci, 1977. **Career:** San Jose State Univ, Afro-Amer Studies, lectr, 1973-75; Shepard & Assoc, 1973-74; Morrison & Rowe, sr analyst, 1974; Dukes Dukes & Assocs, San Francisco, assoc consult, 1974-75, prof; Howard Univ, Wash, vis prof polit sci, 1975, prof sch bus & pub admin, 1979-87; Univ Tenn Knoxville, head, prof polit sci, 1988-89, Bur Pub Admin, dir; Fed Exec Inst, Charlottesville Valif, sr fac mem, prof, 1989; Univ Baltimore, William Donald Schaefer Ctr Pub Policy, sr fel & sr res assoc, 1989-, prof, State Md, Henry C Welcome fel, 1989-92, Sch Pub & Int Affairs, distinguished prof emer; Calvert Inst Policy Res, distinguished prof govt & pub admin, currently; NC Ct Univ, Daniel T Blue Endowed Prof Polit Sci, 2001-03; Fielding Grad Inst, part-time fac, 1991-; Ronson Mgt Corp, vpres energy mgt, vpres sci & technol; Dynamic Concepts, consult; Wash Gas Co, consult; City Coun Baltimore, proj mgr; NC Cent Univ, faculty; St Mary's Col, fac; State Dept Africa, Asia, Latin Am & Europe, acad specialist; William Donald Schaefer Ctr, sr fel, currently. **Orgs:** Bd dir, actg pres, C & Youth Serv Agency; pres, San Francisco, African Am Hist & Cult Soc; Campaign Human Devel; co-ed "J on Polit Repression"; affil Joint Ctr Polit Studies, Wash, 1971-; Conf Minority Pub Adminr, 1972-; Am Asn Univ Prof, 1972-; educ bd, The Black Scholar Mag; chmn, Citizens Energy Adv Comn, Wash, 1981-; Natl Res Coun, 1983-84; bd trustee, Pop Ref Bur; bd dir, Decision Demographics, Natl Civic League; bd trustee, Chesapeake Bay Found, 1991-98; bd gov, Citizen's Plng & Housing Asn Baltimore, 1990-; sr fel Hoffberger Ctr Prof Ethics; Ford Found; Postdoctoral Fel, Johns Hopkins Sch Advan Int Studies; fel, Rockefeller Found, 1981-83; fel Kellogg Nat; chair, Mayor's Adv Comn Resources & Budget; Fel The Regionalist J; Fel Pub Admin Rev; Baltimore Neighborhoods Inc; Fel Policy Studies Rev; Fel The J of Mkt; Baltimore Urban League; bd mem, Inst Regional Studies; Regionalist J. **Honors/Awds:** Outstanding Service Award, San Francisco, Afro-Am Hist Soc, 1975; Outstanding Educator of America, 1975; Distinguished Faculty Award, Howard Univ; Kellogg Nat Fel, 1984-87; Distinguished Chair in Teaching, Univ Baltimore, 1992-93; Rockefeller Brothers Fund Mentor, 1999-02. **Special Achievements:** Author: "Black Political Life in the US", 1972; "Diversity Management in the Baltimore-Washington Metropolitan Area," Maryland Policy Issues, Vol. 2, No. 1, Spring 1999; "Energy Policy and Urban Fiscal Management," Public Administration Review, Vol. 41, Jan. 1981; "Managing Human and Natural Disasters in Developing Nations, ", 1994; Administrative Advocacy: Black Administrators in Urban Bureaucracies; Public Policy and Public Administration: A Minority Perspective; The New Black Politics: The Search for Political Power; Energy Management in the Third World; Baltimore and Beyond. **Home Addr:** 4530 Mustering Drum Way, Ellicott City, MD 21042-5949, **Home Phone:** (410)992-8853. **Business Addr:** Distinguished Professor of Government & Public Administration, Calvert Institute for Policy Research, 1304 St Paul St, Baltimore, MD 21202-2786, **Business Phone:** (410)837-6198.

### HENDERSON, LEON C.

School administrator. **Personal:** Born Aug 4, 1947, Cincinnati, OH. **Educ:** Xavier Univ, BA, sociol; Wash Univ, MA, sociol, PhD, sociol. **Career:** Carmele Hall, prin & pres; St Alphonsus Ligouri Parish, pres, Parish Coun, vpres; Xavier Univ, Inst Black Cath Studies, coordr, instr & adminr; Wilberforce Univ, dean stud affairs & develop; Cardinal Ritter Col Prep High Sch, teacher, adminr, pres emer, currently. **Orgs:** St Louis Archdiocesan Pastoral Coun; trustee, Kenrick-Glennon Sem; bd mem, Community Women Against Hardship; St. John Vianney High Sch; N Grand Neighborhood Serv & Inst Peace & Justice. **Business Addr:** President Emeritus, Cardinal Ritter College Preparatory High School, 701 N Spring Ave, St. Louis, MO 63108, **Business Phone:** (314)446-5507.

### HENDERSON, LEROY W., JR.

Photographer, educator, painter (artist). **Personal:** Born May 27, 1936, Richmond, VA; married Helen Foy; children: Kerby F & Keith. **Educ:** Va State Col, BS, 1959; Pratt, MS, 1965; Nat Acad TV Arts & Sci Film & TV Workshop, cert, 1973. **Career:** Richmond Pub Sch Syst, art teacher, 1959; New York Sch Syst, art teacher, 1962-66; freelance photogr, 1967-; Brooklyn Mus Educ Dept, art teacher, 1968; Bedford-Lincoln Neighborhood Mus, Brooklyn, art teacher, 1968-70. **Orgs:** Emergency Cult Coalition, 1968; bd mem, Aunt Len's Doll & Toy Mus, NY; Kappa Alpha Psi Frat; Full Opportunities Com Acad TV Arts & Sci, 1970-73; African Am Photogr Guild. **Honors/Awds:** Commendation for Heroic Performance, High Sch Mus & Art New York, 1968; Recipient Certificate of Excellence, Mead Libr Ideas Mead Paper Co, 1972; One Show Merit Award, Dir Club Inc & Copy Club, NY, 1974; Photo-Graphic Int Annual Award of Outstanding Art & Photog. **Home Addr:** 881 Washington Ave Apt 6C, Brooklyn, NY 11225-1016, **Home Phone:** (718)636-4910.

### HENDERSON, DR. NANNETTE SMITH

Educator, executive director. **Personal:** Born Jun 9, 1946, Washington, DC; daughter of Percival Carlton Smith and Edith Richardson; married Lyman Beecher; children: Kara Michelle & Kristi Bynn. **Educ:** Howard Univ, BS, 1967, MS, 1969; NC State Univ, PhD, plant path, 1973. **Career:** NC St Univ, Raleigh, asst prof plant path; Vance Granville Community Col, dir col transfer prog, Sci Dept, chair, 2003. **Orgs:** NC Asn Educr; Am Asn Jr & Community Col; NC Asn Two-Yr & Community Col Biologists; Nat Sci Teachers Orgn, 1980-; Phi Kappa Phi Hon Soc; Beta Kappa Chi Hon Soc. **Honors/Awds:** Excellence in Teaching, NC Dept Community Col, 1987; CASE Teaching Award, 1988; Tar Heel of the Week, News & Observer Newspaper, 1988; O Harris Award, Nat Sci Teachers Asn, 1990. **Special Achievements:** First Female African-American to be awarded PhD at NC State. **Home Addr:** 516 W Ridgeway St, Warrenton, NC 27589, **Home Phone:** (919)257-2249. **Business Addr:** Chair, Vance Granville Community College, PO Box 917, Henderson, NC 27536, **Business Phone:** (919)492-2061.

### HENDERSON, RAMONA ESTELLE. See PEARSON, RAMONA HENDERSON.

### HENDERSON, REMOND

Government official. **Personal:** Born Sep 21, 1952, Los Angeles, CA; son of Ernestine and Riebert M; married Joann Bukovich; children: Audra Elizabeth & Riebert Sterling. **Educ:** Cent Wash State Univ, BA, acct, 1974; Univ Alaska Southeast, MBA. **Career:** Ernst & Young, Los Angeles, Calif, staff & sr acct & auditor, 1974-77; Laventhol & Horwath, Los Angeles, Calif, sr acct & auditor, 1977-79; Kaufman & Broad Inc, Los Angeles, Calif, internal auditor, 1979-81; Kaufman & Broad Inc, Irvine, Calif, controller, 1981; Dept Community & Regional Affairs, internal auditor III, 1982-84; Dept Community & Regional Affairs, Juneau, AK, dep dir, div admin serv, 1984-; Dept Labor & Workforce Develop, admin serv dir, 2003-. **Orgs:** Pres, Juneau Chap Blacks Govt, 1984-89; treas, Blacks Govt, Region X, 1986-88; pres, Region V, 1994-; Alaska Soc Cert Pub Accountants; Am Inst Cert Pub Accountants; co-founder, First Shiloh Missionary Baptist Church, Juneau; Juneau Rotary Club; emergency interim successor, Juneau Assembly Coun; chair, Dr Martin Luther King Jr Commemorative Comt Juneau, 1986-88; Juneau Arctic Winter Games Comt, 1990. **Home Addr:** PO Box 21506, Juneau, AK 99802, **Home Phone:** (907)789-1707. **Business Addr:** Administrative Services Director, Department Of Labor & Workforce Development, PO Box 21149, Juneau, AK 99802-1149, **Business Phone:** (907)465-2720.

### HENDERSON, RICKEY NELSON HENLEY

Baseball player, baseball manager. **Personal:** Born Dec 25, 1958, Chicago, IL; son of John L (deceased) and Bobbie; married Pamela; children: Angela, Alexis & Adrianna. **Career:** Baseball player (retired), baseball coach; Oakland Athletics, outfielder, 1979-84, 1989-93, 1994-95, 1998; New York Yankees, outfielder, 1985-89; Toronto Blue Jays, 1993; San Diego Padres, 1996-97, 2001; Anaheim Angels, 1997; New York Mets, 1999-2000, spec instr, 2006-07, first base coach, 2007-08; Seattle Mariners, 2000; Boston Red Sox, 2002; Los Angeles Dodgers, 2003; Newark Bears, 2004; San Diego Surf Dawgs, Golden Baseball League, 2005-07. **Home Addr:** 10561 Englewood Dr, Oakland, CA 94621. **Business Addr:** First Base Coach, New York Mets, 123-01 Roosevelt Ave, Flushing, NY 11368, **Business Phone:** (718)507-6387.

### HENDERSON, RONALD, SR.

Law enforcement officer. **Career:** St Louis City Police, Bur Patrol Support, 1970, dep chief, chief police, 1996-2001; US Fed Govt, US marshal eastern dist MO, 2002-, dir adv comt, mem, Judicial Security Working Grp, mem. **Orgs:** Int Asn Chiefs Police; bd dir, cath charities; vice chair, Archdiocese St. Louis; bd mem, BackStoppers Inc. **Business Addr:** US Marshal for the Eastern District of Missouri, US Federal Government, 111 S 10th St Suite 6353, St. Louis, MO 63102-1125, **Business Phone:** (314)539-2212.

### HENDERSON, RUTH FAYNELLA

Educator, composer. **Personal:** Born Jan 1, 1945?, Kansas City, MO; daughter of Isaiah Hilkiah Jr and Ophelia Beatrice. **Educ:** Bishop Col, BS, elem educ, 1965; N Tex State Univ, MEd, early childhood, 1975; La Salle Univ, EdD, 1995. **Career:** Dallas Independent Sch Dist, early childhood educr; First Baptist Church Hamilton Pk, minister music, 1969-89; Dixwell Enterprise Community Mgt, vice chair; Yale Univ, partner; Lighthouse Church God Christ, pianist, 1991-; Willow Grove Baptist Church, minister music, 1992-. **Orgs:** Pres, Christians Action; founder, Christian Dating & Friendship Ministry; producer, Fruit Fest, 1992. **Home Addr:** 1811 Dancliff Dr, Dallas, TX 75224.

### HENDERSON, PROF. STEPHEN MCKINLEY

Educator, actor. **Personal:** Born Aug 31, 1949, Kansas City, MO; son of Elihue Kelley and Ruby Naomi Johnson; married Pamela Reed; children: Jamal Stephen. **Educ:** Lincoln Univ, attended 1968; Juilliard Drama Div, attended 1970; NC Sch Arts, BFA, 1972; Purdue Univ, MA, 1977. **Career:** State Univ NY, Buffalo, NY, dept chairperson, tenured prof; Actor: 6 Broadway productions, 6 off-Broadway productions, Royal Nat Theatre of Great Britain, Dublin Theatre Festival, 3 Kennedy Center productions; Sundance Theatre Lab Co, 2003; Everyday People HBO film, 2004; Tower Heist, 2011; Steven Spielberg's Lincoln; TV series: New Amsterdam, Fox Television, 2006. **Orgs:** AEA, 1976-; SAG, 1982; SSDC, 1992-; Actors Ctr, 2001-; Fox Found fel, 2002-. **Special Achievements:** Nominated for Tony Award, 2010. **Home Addr:** 44 Gunnell Ave, Buffalo, NY 14216, **Home Phone:** (716)875-3455. **Business Addr:** Professor, State University of New York, 189 Alumni Arena, Buffalo, NY 14260-5030, **Business Phone:** (716)645-0576.

### HENDERSON, HON. THELTON EUGENE

Judge, lawyer, association executive. **Personal:** Born Nov 28, 1933, Shreveport, LA; son of Eugene M and Wanzie (Roberts) H; children: Geoffrey A. **Educ:** Univ Calif, Berkeley, BA, polit sci, 1956, Boalt Hall Sch Law, JD, 1962. **Career:** AUS Corporal, 1956-58; Sys Develop Corp, jr res scientist, 1958-89; US Dept Justice, atty, 1962-63; Fitz Simmons & Petris, assoc, 1964-66; San Mateo County Legal Aid Soc, dir atty, 1966-69; Stanford Univ Law Sch, asst dean, 1968-77; Rosen, Remcho & Henderson, pvt pract & partner, 1978-80; Golden Gate Univ, Sch Law, assoc prof, 1978-80; US Dist Ct, 9 Circuit, CA, judge, 1980-90, chief judge, 1990-97, sr judge, 1998; US Dist Ct, Northern Dist Calif, sr dist judge, 1998-; Univ Calif Hastings Col Law, adj fac, currently. **Orgs:** Nat Bar Asn; Charles Houston Law Asn; Ctr Social Justice Adv Coun; Boalt Hall Alumni Community. **Honors/Awds:** Lewis F Powell Jr Award for Professionalism and Ethics, Am Inns Ct, 2003; Pearlstein Civil Rights Award, Anti-Defamation League; Distinguished Service Award, Nat Bar Asn; Judge Learned Hand Award, Am Jewish Comt; Alumnus of the Year Award, Univ Calif Calif Alumni Asn, 2008. **Special Achievements:** A documentary on his life, Soul of Justice by Abby Ginzberg, was released in 2005; Thelton E Henderson Center for Social Justice; Justice Department's first African-American lawyer in the Civil Rights Division. **Business Addr:** Senior District Judge, United States District Court, Phillip Burton Federal Bldg, San Francisco, CA 94102, **Business Phone:** (415)522-2000.

### HENDERSON, THERESA CRITTENDEN

Educator, school principal. **Personal:** Born Nov 11, 1937, Montgomery, AL; daughter of Willie L and Jacob K; married John L; children: Dana, Nina & Brent. **Educ:** Univ Cincinnati, BS, educ & fine arts, 1959, MEd, 1969. **Career:** Educator (retired); Newark, NJ, pub schs, teacher, 1959-60; artist, 1960-; NY City Pub Schs, elem teacher, 1960-64; Cincinnati Pub Schs, art teacher, 1964-83, asst prin, 1983-84, prin, 1984-93, dir, 1992-. **Orgs:** Alpha Kappa Alpha, 1957-; chmn, Urban Arts Comm, Womans City Club; Links Inc, 1971-75, chmn fund raising prog, vpres & secy, 1972-; Delta Kappa Gamma, 1988-; pres, Cincinnati Contemp Arts Ctr, 1980-84; Phi Delta Kappa, 1988-; Nat Alliance Black Sch Educrs, 1988-; regular mem, Cincinnati Opera, 1991-; Playhouse Pk Bd. **Home Addr:** 1109 Towanda Ter, Cincinnati, OH 45216, **Home Phone:** (513)242-3939. **Business Addr:** Regular Members, 1243 Elm St, Cincinnati, OH 45202, **Business Phone:** (513)768-5500.

### HENDERSON, TRACY

Basketball player. **Personal:** Born Dec 31, 1974; daughter of Dorothy Ann; married Robert Edwards; children: 3. **Educ:** Univ Ga, consumer econ, 1997. **Career:** Atlanta Glory, 1997-98; Nashville Noise, 1998-99; Cleveland Rockers, ctr, 1999 & 2002-03.

### HENDERSON, DR. VIRGINIA RUTH MCKINNEY

Psychologist. **Personal:** Born Feb 19, 1932, Cleveland, OH; daughter of Wade Hampton (deceased) and Ruth Berry (deceased); married Perry A; children: Sheryl, Virginia & Perry Jr. **Educ:** Spelman Col, BA, psychol, 1953; Boston Univ, MA, 1955; Univ NMex, PhD, curric & instr & develop psychol, 1974. **Career:** Psychologist (retired); Muscatatuck State Sch, dir nursery educ psychologist, 1955-57; Cleveland Guid Ctr, psychologist, 1957-59; Cleveland Metro Gen Hosp, psychologist, 1963-65; Seattle, sch psychol, 1967-68; Univ NMex, asst prof ped psychiat, 1968-76; Model Cities Day Care Ctr, consult, 1972-74; Mad Metro Sch Dist, sch psychol, 1976-97; Madison Sch Dist, from spec asst to supt equity & diversity, 1993-97. **Orgs:** Am Asn Ment Def, 1964; Am Psychol Asn, 1968-92; bd dir, All Faiths Receiving Home, 1973-76; bd trustee, Mazano Day Sch, 1974-76; Nat Asn Sch Psychologists, 1976-; bd dir, TWCA, 1977; First Baptist Church Mad, WI; bd dir, Wis Nurses Asn; bd dir, Madison Urban League; founder mem, Nat Asn Sch Psychologists; pres, Women Focus; gen bd, Am Baptist Churches USA, 1983-92; bd dir, Green Lake Conf Ctr; Wayland Bd, Univ Wis; chair, Minority Stud Achievement Comn, Madison Sch Dist; United Way Allocation Comt, 1987-91; pres, bd dir, African Am Acad; co chair, Mann Educ Opportunity Fund, 1991; Dane County Econ Summit, 1991-93; Jr League Madison Comn Adv Bd; Madison Civics Club; Dist 4 Carl Perkins, adv comnMATC, Spec Pop; Prog Comt Proj Opportunity; founding mem, pres & bd dir, African-Am Ethnic Acad; bd dir, Madison C Mus, 1998-; bd gov, Madison Community found; grand making comt, 1998-2001, Asset Builders Award comn, 1999; bd develop comt, 2000; Evjue Foun; founding mem, Found Madison Pub Schs Womens Health Initiative Community Adv Bd; African Am Educr Asn; Madison Rotary Found, 2011. **Honors/Awds:** Grand Magna Cum Laude, Spelman Col, 1953; Distinguished Service Award, Madison Sch Dist, 1990; Woman Distinction, Young Women Christian Asn, 1990; Citizen of the Year, Omega Psi Phi Frat, 1991; Madison Mag 50 Most Influential People, 1992, 1997; Nat Cert Sch Psychologist, 1992; Tribute to Black Women, 1994; Woman of the Year Award, Mothers of Simpson St, 1994; African-Am C Festival Award, 1995; Cert Appreciation, Neighborhood Intervention Prog, 1996; Whitney M Young Award, Urban League of Madison, 2000; Community Builder Award, Dane Fund, 2001; Dr.Martin Luther King Jr Award, Dane County, 2003. **Home Addr:** 5888 Schumann Dr, Fitchburg, WI 53711, **Home Phone:** (608)274-5808.

### HENDERSON, ESQ. WADE

Educator, association executive, lawyer. **Personal:** Born Apr 12, 1948. **Educ:** Howard Univ; Rutgers Univ Sch Law, JD; City Univ NY, Queens Col Sch Law, PhD, law. **Career:** Am Civil Liberties Union, legis coun, lobbyist, Wash Nat Off, assoc dir; Univ DC, David A Clarke

Sch Law, Joseph L Rauh Jr Prof Pub Interest Law, currently; Leadership Conf Civil & Human Rights, pres & chief exec officer, currently, Leadership Conf Civil Rights Educ Fund, coun, currently. **Orgs:** Bar Supreme Ct, DC, NJ; bd dir, Nat Qual Forum; bd dir, Ctr Responsible Lending; bd trustee Educ Testing Serv; bur dir, Nat Asn Advan Colored People; adv comt econ inclusion, Fed Deposit Ins Corp; exec dir, coun legal educ opportunity. **Honors/Awds:** Bar's William J Brennan Award, DC, 2002; Everett C Parker Award, Off Commun Inc, United Church Christ, 2002; Congressional Black Caucus Chair's Award, 2003; hon dr, Queens Col Sch Law, City Univ New York; Eleanor Roosevelt Award for Human Rights. **Special Achievements:** Author of numerous articles on civil rights, human rights & pub policy issues. **Business Addr:** President, Chief Executive Officer, Leadership Conference on Civil & Human Rights, 1629 K St NW 10th Fl, Washington, DC 20006-1601, **Business Phone:** (202)466-3311.

### HENDERSON, MAJOR GEN. WILLIAM AVERY

Pilot, military leader. **Personal:** Born Jan 18, 1943, Ann Arbor, MI; son of William and Viola; married Francine; children: Nicole & Justin. **Educ:** Eastern Mich Univ, BS, social & hist, 1964. **Career:** Pilot, commader (retired); Gen Motors Corp, pilot, 1974-93, chief pilot, 1993, dir flight opers, 2000-03; 127th Tactical Fighter Wing, asst chief command post, chief safety, 1977-90; Mich Air Nat Guard Hq, plans officer, dep dir, 1990-93, dep comdr, 1991, comdr, 1992, brig gen, 1993-95, maj gen, 1996. **Orgs:** Kappa Alpha Psi, 1963-; Tuskegee Airmen, 1989-; Nat Guard Asn US, 1977-; Nat Guard Asn Mich, 1977-; bd mem, Oper Never Forgotten. **Honors/Awds:** Michigan Aviation Hall of Fame, 2012. **Special Achievements:** First African American brigadier general in the history of the MichiganAir National Guard; First African American to head Gen Motors corp fleet. **Home Addr:** 5530 Pineview Dr, Ypsilanti, MI 48197, **Home Phone:** (313)942-5620. **Business Addr:** Chair Member, Operation Never Forgotten, PO Box 132, Saline, MI 48176.

### HENDERSON, WILLIAM TERRELLE

Television show host, football player. **Personal:** Born Feb 19, 1971, Richmond, VA; married Brigitta; children: William II & Jayden. **Educ:** Univ Nc, BS, phys educ, 1994. **Career:** Football player (retired); Green Bay Packers, fullback & running back, 1995-2006; Marco Rivera's youth Football Clin, instr; WBAY, co-host, 1996-2006; ESPN's NFL Draft, analyst, 2006. **Orgs:** Am Diabetes Asn; Make-a-Wish Found; Am Red Cross; Big Bros/Big Sisters; Leukemia Soc; Crippled C's Fund. **Honors/Awds:** Green Bay Unsung Hero, 2001; Pro Bowl, 2004. **Special Achievements:** Stands 12th on the franchise's all-time list; Stands 11th on the Packers' all-time receptions list; "Monday Night Kickoff, " WBAY, co-host, 1996; Earned first-team Associated Press All-Pro and NFC Pro Bowl starter accolades, 2004.

### HENDERSON-NOCHO, AUDREY J.

Activist. **Personal:** Born Aug 27, 1959, Sacramento, CA; daughter of Lillian Riccardo; married Kim; children: Antiquia, Serenia & Asheley. **Educ:** Univ ND, Grand Forks, ND, BA, BS, 1991. **Career:** USAFB NCO Club, Grand Forks, ND, cook, 1984-86; Univ NDak, Grand Forks, ND, stud aid, EBT cult ctr, 1986-89, mail sorter, 1989, stud coun, career serv & job placement, 1990-. **Orgs:** Chairperson, Multi-Ethnic Support Asn, Community Housing Resource Bd, 1987-89; chairperson, ND Comt Martin Luther King Jr Holiday, 1988; Mayors Human Needs Com, 1990-; Concerned Citizens Against Prejudice, 1990-; NDak Adv Comt US Civil Rights Comn, 1991-93; deleg, Black mem Dem Comt, N Dakota. **Honors/Awds:** Making of the King Holiday Award, 1991. **Home Addr:** 2303 27th Ave Apt 109, Grand Forks, ND 58201-6493, **Home Phone:** (701)746-4597. **Business Addr:** Student Cousel, University of North Datkota, 250 Centennial Dr, Grand Forks, ND 58202, **Business Phone:** (701)777-2011.

### HENDON, LEA ALPHA

Administrator, manager, consultant. **Personal:** Born Mar 27, 1953, Hartford, CT; daughter of Charles Martin and Willie Mae Wilcox Martin. **Educ:** Boston Col, Chesnut Hill, MA, BA, educ, 1975; Eastern NMex Univ, Portales, NM, MA, psychol, 1979. **Career:** Boston Pub Schs, Boston, teacher, 1975-77; Coord stud reformed progressive Eastern New Mex Univ, 1978-79, All St Ins Co, Farmington CT, off opers supvr, 1979-80; Aetna Ins Co, Hartford CT, bus syst analyst, 1980-83; Hartford Ins Group, Hartford CT, off automation consult, 1983-85; Aetna Life & Casualty, Hartford CT, recruiter, consult, 1986-. **Orgs:** Adv bd, DP, Post Col, 1987-88; Am Soc Personnel Admin, 1988-; Adv Jr Achievement, 1988-89; pres, Black Data Processing Asn, Hartford Chap, 1989-90; sec, ITC-Gavel, 1990-91; Delta Sigma Theta Sorority; NAFE; nat elections chairperson, 1989-90, mem, Nat Asn Female Execs. **Home Addr:** 16 Pk Terr, Hartford, CT 06106, **Home Phone:** (203)528-2653. **Business Addr:** Administrator, Corporate Staffing, Aetna Life & Casualty, 151 Farmington Ave DA09, Hartford, CT 06156, **Business Phone:** (860)273-0123.

### HENDRICKS, BARBARA

Opera singer. **Personal:** Born Nov 20, 1948, Stephens, AR; daughter of M L and Della; married Martin T; children: Sebastian Amadeus & Jennie Victoria. **Educ:** Univ Nebr, BS, math & chem, 1969; Juilliard Sch Music, BMus, 1969. **Career:** Ormindo, San Francisco Spring Opera, 1974; Boston Opera; St Paul Opera; Santa Fe Opera; Deutsche Opera; Berlin; Aix-en-Provence Festival; Houston Opera; De Nederlandse Opera stichting; Glyndebourne Festival Opera; Boston Symphony Orchestra; New York Philharmonic; Los Angeles Philharmonic; Cleveland Symphony Orchestra; Philadelphia Orchestra; Chicago Symphony; Berlin Philharmonic; Vienna Philharmonic; London Symphony Orchestra; Orchestre de Paris; Orchestre National de France. **Orgs:** Spec adv inter culturality to dir gen, UNESCO, 1994; founder, Barbara Hendricks Found, Peace & Reconciliation, 1998; Swed Acad Music; Refugee Educ Trust, 2000-. **Honors/Awds:** Numerous honors & awards including Dmus, Nebr Wesleyan Univ, 1988; Doctorat Honoris Causa, Univ Louvain, Belg, 1990; Chevalier de la Legiond' Honneur, 1992; Doctorat Honoris Causa, Univ Grenoble, France, 1996; DMus, Juilliard Sch Mus, 2000; Prince of Asturias Award for the Arts, 2000; Lions Club International Award, 2001; Premio Internacional Xifra Heras, 2004. **Special Achievements:** Film: Mimi in La Boheme, 1994. **Business Addr:** Opera Singer, c/o Agence Diane du Saillant, 3 rue Gerando, Paris75009, **Business Phone:** (014)281-3821.

### HENDRICKS, BARKLEY L.

Painter (artist), educator. **Personal:** Born Apr 16, 1945, Philadelphia, PA. **Educ:** Pa Acad Fine Arts, cert, 1967; Yale Univ Sch Art, BFA & MFA, 1972. **Career:** Conn Col, artist, asst prof art, prof art studio, 1972-2010, prof emer studio art, currently; Univ Sask, vis artist, 1974; Glassboro State Col, 1974; Pa Acad Fine Arts, instr, 1971, 1972; Offset Lithography Inst, Brandywine Workshop, Philadelphia, PA, artist fel, 1987; People to People, Citizens Ambassador fel, 1991; One Man Exhibs: Conn Col, New London, CT, 1973, 1984 &1993; Benjamin Mangel Gallery, Philadelphia, Pa, 1981, 1993; Walnut St Theater, Philadelphia, Pa, 1983; Brattleboro Mus & Art Ctr, Brattleboro, VT, 1984; Pa Acad Fine Arts, Peale House Gallery, Philadelphia PA, 1985; Housatonic Mus Art, Bridgeport, CT, 1988; Manchester Community Col, Manchester, CT, 1992; Cape May County Art Gallery, Cape May, NJ, 1992; Norwalk Community Col, Norwalk, CT, 1993; Lag-Time Line-up, Mumbo Jumbo Gallery, 2006; lack Panther: Rank & File, Yerba Buena Ctr Arts, San Francisco, Calif, 2006; The Conn Contemp Wadsworth Atheneum Mus Art, 2007; Am Vision, Philips Exeter Acad Lamont Gallery, 2007; Collections: Chrysler Mus, Norfolk, VA; Nat Afro-Am Mus & Cult Ctr, Wilberforce, OH; Conn Comn Arts Collection, Hartford, CT; Forbes Mag Collection, New York, NY; Univ Conn Law Sch, Hartford, CT; Brandywine Offset Inst, Philadelphia, Pa; Nat Ctr Afro-Am Artists, Boston, MA; Philadelphia Mus Art, Philadelphia, Pa; Pa Acad Fine Arts, Philadelphia, Pa; Uris Collection, New York, NY; Exhibitions Group Shows: Philadelphia Art Alliance, Philadelphia, Pa, 1968, 1970, 1973 & 1992; Conn Col, New London, CT, 1972-93; Benjamin Mangel Gallery, Philadelphia, Pa, 1981-93; Erector Sq Gallery, New Haven, CT, 1986; Black Am Art Japan, Tokyo, Japan, 1987; Fine Arts Mus Long Island, Long Island, NY, 1988; Laura Knott Gallery, Bradford Col, Bradford, Mass, 1992-93; Cent Conn State Univ, New Britain, CT, 1992; Hera Art Gallery, Wakefield, RI, 1993. **Honors/Awds:** Childe Hassam Purchase Award, Am Acad Arts & Letters, 1971 & 1977; First Prize, Conn Artist Annual, Slater Mem Mus, 1976; Second Butler Medal, 43rd Annual Midyear Show, Butler Inst Am Art, 1979; Individual Artist Award, 1979; Purchase Award, Conn Comn Arts, 1991; Salute to the Arts Award, Philadelphia, PA, 1984; Joan Mitchell Foundation Award, 2008; Amistad Center for Art & Culture President s Award, 2010; Connecticut Governor s Award for Excellence, 2010; 17th Annual Rappaport Prize, deCordova Sculpture Pk & Mus & Rappaport Found, 2016. **Special Achievements:** Selections from the Studio Museum in Harlem, NY State Museum, Albany, NY, 2007. **Home Addr:** 22 Addison St, New London, CT 06320-5309, **Home Phone:** (860)447-0717. **Business Addr:** Professor Emeritus of Studio Art, Connecticut College, 270 Mohegan Ave, New London, CT 06320, **Business Phone:** (860)447-1911.

### HENDRICKS, BEATRICE E.

Lawyer. **Personal:** Born St. Thomas. **Educ:** Morgan State Col, BS, 1962; Howard Univ Law Sch, JD, 1972. **Career:** William Morris Agency NY, jr acct, 1962-64; IRS, field agt, 1964-69; Ford Motor Co, staff atty, 1972-74; Acacia Mutual Life Ins, atty, 1974-76; Acacia Mutual, asst coun, 1976-79; Dept Housing & Comm Develop, asst corp coun, 1980-85; A&B Household Serv Inc, pres, half-owner, 1979-85, asst corp coun, con affairs sect, asst Corp Coun, Spec Lit Sect, currently. **Orgs:** Nat Bar Asn; Am Bar Asn; DC Bar Asn; Mich Bar Asn; Alpha Kappa Alpha Sor Inc; Inez W Tinsley Cult Soc; Nat Asn Colored Women Clubs Inc; jr warden, St Mary's Episcopal Church, 1990; bd dir, St Mary's Ct. **Home Addr:** 1225 NJ Ave NW, Washington, DC 20001. **Business Addr:** Assistant Corporate Counsel, Special Litigation Section, Enforcement Division, 441 4th St NW, Washington, DC 20001, **Business Phone:** (202)393-0934.

### HENDRICKS, DR. CONSTANCE SMITH (CONSTANCE KASANDRA SMITH-HENDRICKS)

Educator, administrator. **Personal:** Born Aug 25, 1953, Selma, AL; daughter of Henry Daniel Jr and Geneva Cornelia Glover; children: Denisha Lunya. **Educ:** Univ Ala, Birmingham, BSN, 1974, MSN, 1981; Univ Ala, Tuscaloosa, grad cert, geront, 1987; Boston Col, PhD, clin nursing res, 1992. **Career:** Univ Ala, Birmingham, nursing assoc fac, 1975, instr, 1981-82; Roosevelt Area Family Health Ctr, nurse practr, 1975-76; Univ Hosp, staff RN, 1976-78; Good Samaritan Hosp, dir nursing, 1982-83; Tuskegee Univ, asst prof, 1983-85; John Andrew Hosp, nurse adminr, 1985-87; Auburn Univ, Sch Nursing, asst prof, 1987-96, prof, 2007-; Boston Col, grad minority fel, 1989-92; Univ SC, asst prof, 1996-2001; Southern Univ A&M Col, Baton Rouge, assoc prof, chair, 2001-04; Hampton Univ Sch Nursing, dean & prof, 2004-; Ky State Univ, vis presidential scholar, 2014-. **Orgs:** Omicron Delta Kappa, 1981-; SE regional dir, 1985-89, nat second vpres, 1992-97, Chi Eta Phi Sorority; Sigma Theta Tau Int, 1985-; choir mem & Bible instr, Greater St Mark Missionary Baptist Church, 1986-; Asn Black Nurse Fac, 1987-; Nat Sorority Phi Delta Kappa, 1988-; state vpres, Ala State Nurses Asn, 1993-96; bd dir, Nat Z-HOPE, 2002-; bd mem, Kiwanis Int, 2003; Zeta Phi Beta Sorority Inc; pres elect, Theta Delta; NIH Minority Post Doctoral Res Fel, Univ Nc, Chapel Hill. **Home Addr:** 612 Kimberly Cir, Selma, AL 36701, **Home Phone:** (757)753-4506. **Business Addr:** Dean, Associate Professor, Hampton University, Emancipation Dr & Tyler St William Freeman Hall Rm 110, Hampton, VA 23668, **Business Phone:** (757)727-5251.

### HENDRICKS, JON CARL

Musician, president (organization), educator. **Personal:** Born Sep 16, 1921, Newark, OH; son of Rev Alexander Brooks and Willie Carrington; married Judith; children: Aria; married Colleen Moore; children: Jon Jr, Michele, Eric & Colleen. **Educ:** Univ Toledo, attended 1951. **Career:** Lambert, Hendricks & Ross, singer & songwriter, 1957-62; San Francisco Chronicle, jazz instr; Cal St Univ, jazz instr; Sonoma, jazz instr; Univ Calif, Berkeley, jazz instr; Univ Calif, Los Angeles, jazz instr; Stanford, jazz instr; Evolution of the Blues, writer; TV series: "Somewhere to Lay My Weary Head"; "The Steve Allen Plymouth Show", 1958; "NET Playhouse", 1967. Jon Hendricks & Co, singer & songwriter; Hendricks Music Inc, pres; Univ Toledo, distinguished prof jazz studies, 2000-; Films: Jazz Is Our Religion; Hommage a Cole Porter; People I Know; Al Pacino; White Men Can't Jump, 1992; Foreign Student, 1994; Scheherazade, 2003. Music: White Men Can't Jump, 1959; Evolution of the Blues Song, 1959; A Good Git-Together, 1959; iSalud Joao Gilberto, Originator of the Bossa Nova, 1961; Fast Livin Blues, 1962; Jon Hendricks Recorded in Person at the Trident, 1965; Jon Hendricks Live, 1970; Cloudburst, 1972; Times of Love, 1972; Tell Me the Truth, 1975; September Songs, 1975; Love, 1982; Cloudburst, 1982; Freddie Freeloader, 1990; Boppin at the Blue Note, 1994. **Orgs:** Kennedy Center Honors comt; dir & host, Annual San Francisco Jazz Festival. **Honors/Awds:** Number One Jazz Singer in the World, London's Melody Maker, 1969; Emmy Award; Iris Award; Peabody Awards; Seven Grammy Awards; hon doctorate, Univ Toledo. **Special Achievements:** Sang with and wrote for King Pleasure, Count Basie, Duke Ellington, Louis Armstrong, Dave Brubeck, Carmen McRae; first American jazz artist to lecture at the Sorbonne in Paris; His fifteen voice group, the Jon Hendricks Vocalstra at the University of Toledo, performed to a standing ovation at the Sorbonne. **Home Addr:** 375 S End Ave, New York, NY 10280-1025, **Home Phone:** (212)321-9039. **Business Addr:** Distinguished Professor, University of Toledo, 2801 W Bancroft, Toledo, OH 43606-3390, **Business Phone:** (800)586-5336.

### HENDRICKS, LETA

Librarian. **Personal:** Born May 22, 1954, Galesburg, IL; daughter of Mary Martha and Lee B. **Educ:** Western Ill Univ, BA, Afro Am studies, 1977; Clark Atlanta Univ, MA, Afro Am studies, 1979; Univ Ill, Urbana Champaign, MS, libr info sci, 1989. **Career:** Carl Sandburg Col, instr, 1983; Galesburg Pub Libr, spec col libr, 1980-89; Knox Col, ref asst, 1986-89, instr, 1989; Ohio State Univ Libr, minority libr intern, 1989-91, head, Human Ecol Libr, 1991-98, head, EHS Syst/Human Ecol Bibliogr, libr, 2010-, asst prof, 1989-. **Orgs:** Phi Kappa Phi, 1976; Nat Women Studies Asn, 1982-; fel Am Libr Asn, 1989-; Asn Col & Res Libr, 1989-; Black Caucus Am Libr Asn, 1990-. **Home Addr:** 4783 Glaton Ct Suite B, Columbus, OH 43220, **Home Phone:** (614)481-6208. **Business Addr:** Assistant Professor, Ohio State University, 1858 Neil Ave Mall, Columbus, OH 43210-1286, **Business Phone:** (614)688-7478.

### HENDRICKS, DR. MARVIN B.

Molecular biologist. **Personal:** Born Dec 4, 1951, Newnan, GA; son of Jimmie Lee and Margaret Petty; married Helen Porthia Talley; children: Bridget. **Educ:** Mass Inst Technol, Cambridge, MA, BS, 1973; Johns Hopkins Univ, Baltimore, MD, PhD, molecular biol, 1980. **Career:** African Sci Inst, fel; Fred Hutchinson Cancer Res Ctr, Seattle, WA, fel, 1980-84; Integrated Genetics, Framingham, Mass, staff scientist, 1984-87, sr scientist, 1987-89; Repligen Corp, Cambridge, Mass, res scientist, 1989-91; Cambridge Neuro Sci Inc, Cambridge, group leader, 1991-95; Brigham & Women's Hosp, Boston, Mass, res scientist, 1995-97; Millennium Pharmaceut Inc, sr scientist, 1997-. **Orgs:** AAAS, 1976-, NY Acad Sci, 1984-; Am Soc Mech Engrs, 1994-; Am Soc Microbiol. **Honors/Awds:** Scholar, Mass Inst Technol, 1969; Valedictorian, Cent High Sch, Newnan, GA, 1969; Post-doctoral Fel Awards, Am Cancer Soc, 1980, Ann Fuller Fund, Yale Univ, 1980, Nat Inst Health, 1980. **Special Achievements:** Publ 20 Articles in int res Js, 1976-; co-author, articles in two books, 1980-; Featured in Ebony Mag, 1988. **Home Addr:** 21 Perry H Henderson Dr, Framingham, MA 01701-4307. **Business Addr:** Senior Scientist, Millennium Pharmaceuticals Inc, 40 Landsdowne St, Cambridge, MA 02139, **Business Phone:** (617)679-7000.

### HENDRICKS, RICHARD D.

President (organization), executive, executive director. **Personal:** Born May 26, 1937, Glen Cove, NY; son of William Richard and Ruth Delamar; married Madelyn Williams; children: Pamela, Jeannette & Natalie. **Educ:** Hofstra Univ, BBA, 1960. **Career:** Executive (retired); Abraham & Straus Dept Stores NY, dept mgr, 1960-65; Johnson Pub Co, adv sls rep, 1965-66; JC Penney Co, buyer, Island Store, mdse exec, 1966-97; Delamar Mkt Int, consult, 1997; Nichelson Entertainment Grp, vpres, 1999, dir mkt & corp commun, currently. **Orgs:** Founder, bd mem, QNS Asoc Inc; founder, pres, LISA Prodns; spl lectr, Black Exec Exchange Prog; lectr, State Univ NY, 1963-64; Black Artist Asn; Nat Asn Advan Colored People; adv bd, Nichelson Entertainment Grp, currently. **Home Addr:** 9821 Clocktower Ct, Plano, TX 75025-6584, **Home Phone:** (214)495-9537. **Business Addr:** Director-Marketing and Corporate Communications, Nichelson Entertainment Group, 1402 N Corinth St Suite 115, Corinth, TX 76208, **Business Phone:** (214)295-6115.

### HENDRICKS, STEVEN AARON

Public relations executive, executive director. **Personal:** Born Feb 5, 1960, Kansas City, KS. **Educ:** Wichita State Univ, BA, commun, 1982. **Career:** Wichita State Univ Football Team, 1978-82; Wichita Eagle-Beacon Newspaper, adv rep, 1981; Pizza Hut Inc, comn asst, 1982, opers mgr, 1982-83; State Kans, asst, 1983-86; Hallmark Cards, Govt Affairs, mgr, 1987-89; AT&T, Exec Commun, area mgr, 1989-97; Weber Shandwick PR Agency, acct supvr, 1997-99; Xerox, Pub rel, sr mgr, 1999-2000; Motorola, Commun & Pub Affairs, dir, 2000-06; Gerdau Ameristeel Corp, Corp Commun & Pub Affairs, dir, 2007-08; PRtegrity, pub rel consult, 2009-10. **Orgs:** Wichita State Univ Advert & PR Club, 1980-82; Fel Christian Athletes, 1981-82; Advert & PR Club Whichita, 1981-82; Kappa Alpha Psi Fraternity, 1982-; Black Dem Caucus, 1984; Pub Rels Soc Am; Int Asn Bus Communicators; sr commun consult, Blue Cross & Blue Shield Fla Inc, 2010-15; bd mem, Grace Family Church, 2010; bd trustee, Acad Prep Centers Educ, 2012. **Business Addr:** Senior Communications Consultant, Blue Cross & Blue Shield of Florida Inc, PO Box 1798, Jacksonville, FL 32231-0014, **Business Phone:** (813)882-6718.

### HENDRIX, DEBORAH LYNNE

Association executive, consultant. **Personal:** Born Nov 30, 1961, Chicago, IL; daughter of Edward Wright Jr and Donna L Radford Wright; married Charles W; children: Catherine Elizabeth & Danielle Marie. **Educ:** Howard Univ, Wash, DC, BS, consumer econs, 1983; Roosevelt Univ, Lawyers Assistant Program, corp law, 1983, Chicago, Il, paralegal cert; Inst Paralegal Training, Chicago Ill, cert, 1984; Univ Phoenix, MBA, human res mgmt. **Career:** Winston & Strawn Law Firm, corp paralegal, 1984-85; Jr Achievement Chicago, Ill, vpres & ed serv, 1985-88; Jr Achievement S Bend, Ind, pres, 1988-91; Jr Achievement Inc, dir, training & sem, 1991-94, vpres diversity, vpres diversity

& qual assurance, vpres training, diversity & qual, vpres, training & cult chg, vpres orgn develop, 1983-2001; Sch Dist Two Harrison, secy, bd educ, pres, currently; Dale Carnegie, adj instr, 1999-; CD Global Enterprises, owner, 2001-; Restoration Church, treas & event coordr, 2001-; event planner, currently; Alpine Tech, sales rep, currently; Parents Challenge, exec dir, 2014-. **Orgs:** NAFE, 1990-; Urban League Col Springs; Am Soc Training & Develop, 1991-; After 5 Christian Bus & Prof Women, 1992-; Workout Ltd, 1997; Goodwill Indust, 1998; Communities Sch, 1998; secy, Bd Col Springs Early Cols, currently; Jr Achievement; Discover Goodwill; Boys & Girls Club Pikes Peak. **Honors/Awds:** Named most outstanding stud, sch human ecol, Howard Univ, 1983; Outstanding Young Women Am, 1988; Chicago's Up & Coming Bus & Prof Women, Dollars & Sense Mag, 1988; Emerging Black Leaders, 1994. **Home Addr:** 4860 Beechvale Dr, Colorado Springs, CO 80916-2249, **Home Phone:** (719)271-2411. **Business Addr:** Owner, CD Global Enterprises, 3554 W Richwoods Blvd, Peoria, IL 60586, **Business Phone:** (309)685-2950.

### HENDRIX, IDA

Executive, manager. **Personal:** Born Jun 1, 1952. **Educ:** Mich State Univ, BA, commun, 1975. **Career:** Fed-Mogul Corp, prod mgr, 1989-94; Detroit Hist Mus, proj mgr, 1994-96; Taubman Ctr Inc, Great Lakes Crossing, asst mall mgr, 1998-2001; Fairlane Town Ctr, asst gen mgr; Simon Property Group, Briarwood Mall, mall mgr, 2001-2014. **Home Addr:** 14410 Bramell St, Detroit, MI 48223-2564, **Home Phone:** (313)533-0431. **Business Addr:** General Manager, Senior Vice President, Briarwood Mall, 100 Briarwood Cir, Ann Arbor, MI 48108, **Business Phone:** (734)761-9550.

### HENDRIX, MARTHA RAYE

Educator, mayor. **Personal:** Born Aug 17, 1939, Mineral Springs, AR; daughter of Lewis and Flossie Johnson; married Clarence Jr; children: Marcia & Clarisse Renee. **Educ:** Shorter Col, N Little Rock, AR, AA, 1959; Philander Smith, Little Rock, AR, BA, 1961; Henderson State Univ, Arkadelphia, AK, MA. **Career:** Howard County High Sch, Mineral Springs, Ark, teacher, 1961-70; Saratoga Sch, Saratoga, Ark, teacher, 1970-89; Town Tollette, Tollette, Ark, mayor, 1989-; Saratoga Sch Dist, Saratoga, Ark, elem prin, 1990-91; Saratoga Elem Sch, Wyo, prin. **Orgs:** Am Educ Asn, 1961-89; Nat Educ Asn, 1961-89; EHC, 1985-89; Literacy Coun, 1987-89; adv bd, Munic League, 1988-89; Hosp Adv Bd; Ark Munic League, mayor; Rural Develop Comn. **Home Addr:** 301 Peach St, Mineral Springs, AR 71851-9049, **Home Phone:** (870)287-4273. **Business Addr:** WY.

### HENDRY, GLORIA

Actor. **Personal:** Born Mar 3, 1949, Winter Haven, FL; daughter of George C and Lottie Beatrice Sconions. **Educ:** Essex Col Bus; Univ Phoenix, Los Angeles City Col Theatre Acad. **Career:** Los Angeles, legal secy; Films: Live & Let Die, 1973; Black Caesar, 1973; Come Back Charleston Blue; Black Belt Jones, 1974; Hell Up In Harlem; Slaughter's Big Rip-Off; Bare Knuckles; Across 110th Street; Appleman; For Love of Ivy, 1968; Landlord; Pumpkin head II, 1993; South Bureau Homicide, 1996; Lookin' Italian, 1998; Seven Swans, 2005; Savannah's Ghost; Man in the Mirror, 2008; Absolute Evil, 2009; Freaky Deaky, 2012. TV Series: "Women in Law"; "Seeds of Tragedy", 1991; "Law & Order"; "Hunter", 1990; "Doogie Howser"; "Falcon Crest"; "Blue Knight"; "As The World Turns"; "Blooper's & Practical Jokes"; "Another World"; "Love American Style"; "Snoop Sisters"; "Santa Barbara"; "As the World Turns"; "This is The Life"; "Turner Classics"; "Love of a Flunky". **Orgs:** Exec dir, Women Performing Arts Los Angeles, Kwanza Found; Actors' Equity Asn; Am Fedn TV & Radio Artists; Screen Actors Guild; Nat Asn Advan Colored People; Hon Phi Beta Omega Frat Inc Rho Iota Chap. **Honors/Awds:** Black Achiever in US Award; National Association of Tennis Award; After Hours News Award, Newark; I Am Somebody Award; Outstanding Celebrity Award; Key to City Birmingham, Ala Mayor George G Seibels; Key to City, Mayor Kenneth Gibson, Newark, NJ; Kathleen Brown Rice Tennis Award; Buffalo Soldiers Award, 10th Calvary. **Business Addr:** Actor, Castle Hill Enterprises, 1101 S Orlando Ave, Los Angeles, CA 90053, **Business Phone:** (323)653-3535.

### HENLEY, CARL R.

Administrator. **Personal:** Born Jul 4, 1955, Los Angeles, CA; children: 2. **Educ:** Calif State Univ, Los Angeles, BA, psychol, 1977, MS, pub admin, 1980; Whittier Col, Sch Law, JD, 1991. **Career:** Universal Artists, asst spec proj, 1977-, assoc producer; Black Leadership Conf, Calif State Univ, Los Angeles, adv, 1977-; Backyard Prods, vpres, bd dir, 1978-; Los Angels United Sch Dist, coun asst, 1979; Law Offices Carl Henley, owner, 2000-13; Los Angeles Co, community develop analyst asst, 1979-; HME Subsidiaries, vpres, 1982-; pvt pract lawyer; US Supreme Ct Bar, atty, 2006-; Calif State Univ, comnr; Southern Christian Leadership Conf, dir corp giving; Calif Dem Assembly Cand, campaign mgr; Calif Voter Regist Coalition, dir; Congressman Augustus Hawkins' Silver Anniversary Comn, exec dir. **Orgs:** Pres & co-founder, Youth & Col Div, Nat Asn Advan Colored People, Los Angeles, 1977-80, reg dir, 1980-82; Los Angeles Co Dem Cent Comn, 1978-; exec bd mem, S Cent Planning Coun United Way Am, 1979-80; deleg, Calif Dem State Party, 1982-84. **Honors/Awds:** Honorary Life Member Award, Calif State Univ, Los Angeles, 1977; Honarary President Emeritus, Youth & Col Div, Nat Asn Advan Colored People, Los Angeles, 1980; Community Service Resolution, Los Angeles City Coun, 1980; The Mark of Excellence Award, Dan Towler Educ Found; Roy Wilkins Award, Nat Asn Advan Colored People; United Way of America Annual Award Man of the Year, S Cent Planning Coun; Award of Excellence, Los Angeles County Bd Supervisors; Community Service Award Resolution, Los Angeles City Coun; Outstanding Public Service Award, State Calif; U.S. Congressional Award of Merit, Us Congressman Augustus Hawkins. **Business Addr:** Attorney, United States Supreme Court, PO Box 75988, Los Angeles, DC 90075, **Business Phone:** (323)969-1737.

### HENLEY, VERNARD W.

Banker. **Personal:** Born Aug 11, 1929, Richmond, VA; son of Walter A and Mary Crump; married Pheriby Christine Gibson; children: Vernard W Jr, Wade G & Adrienne C. **Educ:** Va State Univ, BS, 1951. **Career:** Banker (retired); Mech & Farmers Bank Durham, NC, asst note teller, 1951-52, cashier & head personal loan dept, 1954-58; Consol Bank & Trust Co, secy & cashier 1958-69, bd dir, 1961, vpres & secy, 1961, vpres, 1969, exec vpres, 1971, pres 1971, & chmn bd, chief exec officer & trust officer, 1984-01; Unity State Bank Dayton, OH, chief exec officer, 1969; Consol Bank & Trust Co, chmn bd, chief exec officer, trust officer, 2001. **Orgs:** Bd trustee, Va Mus Fine Arts, exec exhib & finance comm, 1983; bd dir, exec & finance comn, Richmond Renaissance Inc; vchmn, chmn, Audit Comn City Richmond, 1983-88; bd trustee, J Sargeant Reynolds Col Found, 1984; bd trustee, exec & finance comt, Va Union Univ, 1984; lay mem, bd dir, Old Dom Bar Asn, 1985; bd trustee, Va Coun Econ Ed, 1985; bd dir, Am Bankers Asn; bd trustee, Univ Fund Va Commonwealth Univ, 1986; bd trustee, Hist Richmond Found; bd dir, Retail Merchants Asn Greater Richmond; Kiwanis Club Richmond; Nat Corp Comn United Negro Col Fund; community & econ develop; Arts, Educ, & Health Care; bd dir, Atlantic Rural Expos; adv bd, Arts Coun Richmond Inc; adv coun, bd trustee, Salvation Army Boys Club; bd dir, Va Region, Nat Conf Christians & Jews; Richmond Adv Coun Small Bus Admin, 1989; bd dir, Cities Sch Found Va, 1989; bd dir, vchmn, Va Housing Found, 1989; pres, Va Bankers Asn; bd, Owens & Minor Inc; Audit Com, 1993; Comp & Benefits Com, 1994. **Honors/Awds:** Order of Merit Boy Scouts of America, 1967; Man & Boy Award, Salvation Army Boys Club, 1969; Citizenship Award, Astoria Beneficial Club, 1976; Brotherhood Award, Richmond Chap Nat Conf Christians & Jews, 1979; Order & Citizenship Award, Independent Order St Luke, 1981; The Quest for Success Award, Miller Brewing Co & Philip Morris. **Special Achievements:** First African-American president of the Virginia Bankers Asn, 1993. **Home Addr:** 1728 Hungary Rd, Richmond, VA 23228, **Home Phone:** (804)264-2113.

### HENRY, ALARIC ANTHONY

Lawyer. **Personal:** Born Jan 14, 1963, Detroit, MI; son of Leonard and Marguerite; married Sharon E; children: Ashley E, Jared C & Conner A. **Educ:** Univ Detroit, BS, cum laude, bus admin, 1985; Ga State Univ, JD, 1991. **Career:** K-Mart Corp, asst store mgr, 1985-86; Safeco Ins Co, ins adjuster, 1986-91; Luther-Anderson PLLP, assoc atty, 1991-96, managing partner, 1996-; CEU Inst, fac. **Orgs:** Phi Delta Phi Int Legal Fraternity, 1989-; Am Bar Asn, 1991-; Ga Bar Asn, 1991-; Tenn Bar Asn, 1991-; Chattanooga Bar Asn, 1991-; S L Hutchins Bar Asn, 1991-; bd mem, pres 100 Black Men Chattanooga, 1992-03; Tenn Defense Lawyer Org; Lookout Mountain Bar Asn; bd mem, Give a Hoot Kids, 2001-; St Jude Sch Bd, 2003-06; Defense Res Inst; Coun Litigation Mgt; Fel Litigation Coun Am; Notre Dame Sch Bd, 2008-. **Honors/Awds:** Chapter Development Award, 100 Black Men of America, 1999; Listed in Mid-South Super Lawyers as being in top 5% of Attorneys in TN & some surrounding states. **Home Addr:** 8312 Mitchell Mill Rd, Ooltewah, TN 37421. **Business Addr:** Managing Partner, Luther-Anderson PLLP, 100 W Martin Luther King Blvd, Chattanooga, TN 37401-0151, **Business Phone:** (423)756-5034.

### HENRY, ALICIA

College teacher, artist. **Educ:** Art Inst Chicago, BFA; Yale Univ Sch Art, MFA. **Career:** Artist, 1985-; Fisk Univ, assoc prof art & chair art dept. Exhibitions: "On Target", Zephyr Gallery, Louisville, KY, 1991; "Alicia Henry: Figures", Universal Fine Objects Gallery, Provincetown, MA, 1993; "Alice Henry: Objects", Univ Ill, Urbana-Champaign, 1996; "Alicia Henry: Untitled", Cheekwood Museum, Nashville, TN, 2000; "Alicia Henry: Mostly", One Good Thing, NY, 2000; "Alicia Henry: Black and Blue", Frist Center for the Visual Arts, Nashville, TN, 2003; "Alicia Henry", Rhodes College/Clough-Hanson Gallery, Memphis, TN, 2004; "Alicia Henry", Northeastern Ill Univ Gallery, Chicago, IL, 2005; "Intimacy and Peace", Music City Center, 2012; "Alicia Henry", Zeitgeist, Nashville, TN, 2016. **Honors/Awds:** The School of the Art Institute of Chicago Merit Award, 1986-88; Ford Foundation Fellowship, 1989-91; Fine Arts Work Center Fellowship, 1991-93; Guggenheim Fellowship, 2000-01; Joan Mitchell Foundation Award, 2014; Prize for Contemporary Southern Art, 2016. **Special Achievements:** Served as a Peace Corps volunteer for two years in Ghana; volunteered for a year at the Pine Ridge Reservation in South Dakota. **Business Addr:** Fisk University, Basic College #200, Nashville, TN 37208, **Business Phone:** (615)329-8824.

### HENRY, ANTHONY DANIEL

Executive, football player. **Personal:** Born Nov 3, 1976, Ft. Myers, FL. **Educ:** Univ S Fla, BA, commun. **Career:** Football player (retired), executive; Cleveland Browns, cornerback, defensive back, right corner back, 2001, defensive back, right corner back, left corner back, free safety, 2002, left corner back, 2003-04; Dallas Cowboys, right corner back, 2005-06, 2008, right corner back, cornerback, 2007; Detroit Lions, cornerback, left corner back, right corner back, 2009; First Picks Management, member, 2011-. **Orgs:** Make-A-Wish Found; Spec Olympics; United Way; ambassador, Fel Christian Athletes, currently. **Honors/Awds:** Ranked first in the AFC; Hall of Fame, Univ S Fla, 2011. **Special Achievements:** First University of South Florida football player inducted into the Hall; TV appearance: NBC Sunday Night Football, 2006-07; Kendra, 2009; Collection Fred Vargas, 2010; Films: Once Upon a Time in Brooklyn, 2013. Launched his online music magazine Coool Flame. **Business Addr:** Member, First Picks Management, Janss Marketplace 205 N Moorpark Rd Suite N, Thousand Oaks, CA 91360, **Business Phone:** (805)494-4500.

### HENRY, BRENT LEE

Lawyer, vice president (organization). **Personal:** Born Oct 9, 1947, Philadelphia, PA; son of Wilbur and Minnie Adams; children: Adam & Aisha. **Educ:** Princeton Univ, Woodrow Wilson Sch Pub & Int Affairs, BA, 1969; Yale Law Sch, JD, 1973; Yale Sch Art & Archit, urban studies, 1973. **Career:** New Haven Housing Info Ctr, coun, 1973-74; Yale Univ, Dept Afro-Am Studies, lectr, 1973-74; Jones Day Reavis & Pogue, atty, 1974-82; NY Human Resources Admin, dept admin, 1978-79; Greater Southeast Community Hosp Found, dir bus & govt affairs, 1982-84; Howard Univ Sch Bus Admin, adj prof, 1982-94; Univ Md, prof health adminr; Med Star Health, sr vpres & gen coun, 1985-2002; Partner's Health Care Syst, vpres & gen coun, 2002-. **Orgs:** Alumni trustee, Bd trustee, Princeton Univ, 1969-72, charter trustee, 1999-2009; adv coun, Princeton Univ, Woodrow Wilson Sch Pub & Int Affairs, 1969-72; staff mem, Concerned Citizens Comn Criminal Justice, Cleveland Found, 1975; bd dir, Bazelon Ctr Ment Health Law, 1987-98; bd dir, pres, Nat Health Lawyers Asn, 1988-96, 1994-95; bd dir, Combined Health Appeal, Nat Capital Area, 1989-93; exec comt mem & chair, Alumni Coun, Princeton Univ, 1994-99; bd mem, Pub Welfare Found, 1996-; bd trustee, Princeton Univ, 1999-; bd gov, Nat Insts Health Clin Ctr, 2001-04; Nat Inst Health, Adv Bd Clin Res, 2004-06; Am Bar Asn; Nat Bar Asn; Ohio Bar Asn; DC Bar Asn; bd dir, New Eng Legal Found; bd dir, New Eng Coun; bd dir, Pub Welfare Found, currently; Boston Bar Asn; pres, Am Health Lawyers Asn; trustee, Boston Symphony Orchestra Inc; adv coun, Ctr African Am Studies; Black Princeton Alumni; regional comt mem, Princeton Prize Race Rels; bd dir, Martha's Vineyard Hospital, 2007-; bd dir, Fiduciary Trust Co, 2010-. **Honors/Awds:** Frederick Abramson Award, DC Bar Asn, 1996. **Special Achievements:** Author of "The Provision of Indigent Defense Servs, Greater Cleveland". **Home Addr:** 295 Sayre Dr, Princeton, NJ 08540, **Home Phone:** (609)919-0587. **Business Addr:** Vice President, General Counsel, Partners Health Care System, 800 Boylston St Suite 1150, Boston, MA 02199, **Business Phone:** (617)278-1065.

### HENRY, DR. CHARLES E.

Consultant, educator, entrepreneur. **Personal:** Born Apr 14, 1935, Palestine, TX; son of E W Sr and Ophelia Spencer; married Janice Normandyne OBrien; children: Melvin Wayne & Carolyn Janiece Ross. **Educ:** Tex Col, BS, 1956; Tex Tech Univ, Med, 1971, EdD 1974; Erick sonian psycho ther & psycho neuro immunol, cert, 1980; Continuous Improv Facilitator & Facilitator Inst, cert, 1994; Univ Tex, Total Qual Mgt instr, cert, 1995; Tex Tech Univ, Hr mgt, cert, 1996. **Career:** Coronado High Sch, teacher; Lubbock Sch Dist Sci Inst, 1956-72; Tex Tech Univ Proj Upward Bound, consult/instr, 1968-72; Tex Tech Univ HSC Sch Med, coordr/instr, 1972-76; Wayland Baptist Univ, adj fac, Educ Admn & Supv, 1997-98, adj prof; Henry Enterprises, educ consult, owner & mgr, currently. **Orgs:** Int Platform Asn; Am Soc Prof Consult; Ment Health Asn; Phi Delta Kappa Educ Fraternity; Alpha Phi Alpha Fraternity Inc; Nat Asn Advan Colored People; Tex Ment Health Counr Asn; Phi Delta Kappa; Am Asn Prof Hypno therapists; Soc Human Resource Mgt; Educ Found rep, Theta Kappa Lambda Chap & Alpha Phi Alpha Fraternity; Lubbock Chamber Com; Am Soc Trng & Develop; Lubbock Bd Health; Upward Bound; YMCA; United Way; Lubbock Black Chamber Entrepreneurs. **Honors/Awds:** Citation Excellence, Tex Col Tyler, 1980; Community Service Award, Alpha Kappa Alpha Sorority, 1978; Area 3-G coord, Phi Delta Kappa Educ Fraternity, 1977-78; Presidents Award, Estacado HS PTA, 1975-76; Phi Delta Kappa Int, Service Key Award, 1996, Twenty-Five Year Membership Award, 1997; Thirty year PDK Award, 2002; Inducted, African-American Heroes of Lubbock, Hall of Fame, 2003; Distinguished Alumnus. **Special Achievements:** First African American male to complete doctorate at Texas Tech University; First African American faculty member at Texas Tech University School of Medicine; First African American to serve on Lubbock Chamber of Commerce Board of Directors. **Home Addr:** 9715 Miami Ave, Lubbock, TX 79423-3943, **Home Phone:** (806)794-0741. **Business Addr:** Educator, Management Consultant, Henry Enterprises, 2345 50th St Suite 104, Lubbock, TX 79412-3943, **Business Phone:** (806)799-7322.

### HENRY, DR. CHARLES PATRICK, III

Educator. **Personal:** Born Aug 17, 1947, Newark, OH; son of Charles Patrick II and Ruth Holbert; married Loretta Crenshaw; children: Adia, Wesley & Laura. **Educ:** Denison Univ, Granville, OH, BA, polit sci, 1969; Univ Chicago, Chicago, IL, MA, 1971, PhD, polit sci, 1974. **Career:** Howard Univ, Wash, DC, asst prof, 1973-76; Denison Univ, Granville, OH, asst prof, dir, asst dean, 1976-80; Atlanta Univ, NEH post-doctoral fel, 1979; Univ Calif, Berkeley, CA, assoc prof, 1981, prof African Am Studies, currently; Amenesty Int, chair, 1986-88; Univ Mich, vis prof, 1993; Nat Coun Humanities, 1994; DRL, US State Dept, off dir, 1994-95; Univ Bologna, Distinguished Chair Am Hist & Polit, 2003; African Am Studies, Univ Calif, prof emer. Books: Culture and African American Politics, auth, 1990; Jesse Jackson: The Search for Common Ground, auth, 1990; Ralph J. Bunche: Selected Speeches and Writings, ed, 1996; Foreign Policy and the Black (Inter)national Interest, ed, 2000; Ralph Bunche: Model Negro or American Other?, auth, 2005; Long Overdue: The Politics of Racial Reparations, auth, 2007; The Obama Phenomenon: Toward a Multiracial Democracy, co-ed, 2011. **Orgs:** Cong fel, Am Polit Sci Asn, 1972-73; Nat Coun Black Studies, nat secy, 1981-83, pres, 1992-94; Amnesty Int USA, Int exec comt, 1989-91, chair & bd dir, 1986-88; fel Nat Jr Hon Socs; co founder, black Stud Union; Cong Black Caucus. **Home Addr:** 3015 Wisconsin St, Oakland, CA 94602, **Home Phone:** (510)530-6471. **Business Addr:** Professor, University of California Berkeley, 674 Barrows Hall, Berkeley, CA 94702, **Business Phone:** (510)642-3426.

### HENRY, FOREST T., JR.

Football coach, educator. **Personal:** Born Jan 2, 1937, Houston, TX; son of Forest Sr and Belzora Butler; married Melba J Jennings; children: Felicia Denise & Forest III. **Educ:** Howard Univ, BS, 1958; Tex Southern Univ, MEd, 1971, admins cert, 1972. **Career:** Educator (retired); F T Henry Income Tax & Real Estate Serv, 1958; Carter G Woodson Jr High Sch, Houston, asst football coach, 1959-68, teacher, 1959-68, golf coach, 1960-70, teacher phys educ, head football coach & athletic dir, 1968-70, asst prin, 1971-74, prin, 1974-78; Evan E Worthing Sr High Sch, Houston, prin, 1978-82; Phillis Wheatley Sr High, prin, 1984-89; Houston Independent Sch Dist, asst supt athletics & extracurricular activ, 1982-84, dir opers, 1989-95. **Orgs:** Pres, Greater Fifth Ward Citizens League, 1972-; exec bd, Bhouston Prin Asn, 1972-; Boys Scout Am; YMCA; Tex Asn Sec Sch Prin; Nat Asn Sec Sch Prin; bd dir, N Side Sr Citizens Asn; Houston Asn Supv & Curric Develop; Tex State Teachers Asn; Alpha Phi Alpha; Appraisal Rev Bd mem, Harris County Appraisal Dist. **Honors/Awds:** Worthing Scholarship; Nat Sci Summer Fellowship Biology; Community Service Award, Religious Heritage Am. **Home Addr:** 3317 Binz St, Houston, TX 77004, **Home Phone:** (713)522-3004.

### HENRY, GRACE ANGELA

Management consultant, president (organization). **Educ:** Tufts Univ, BA, child study, dance; Harvard Univ, Med. **Career:** Am Int Sch (Barnako, Mali), mgt consult; Phillips Oppenheim, Bus Developer, prin, 2002-08; Grace Angela Henry Inc, founder, pres & owner, 2006-; Hear Here, pres, 2010-. **Orgs:** Chair bd, Manhattan Country Sch, 1998-2009; co-chair bd, Ethical Cult Fieldston Sch; Am Fedn Tv & Radio Artists; founding exec dir, Early Steps; Empire State Col, 2009; founding bd mem, Black Women Influence, 2006-. **Business Addr:**

President, Grace Angela Henry Inc, PO Box 2028, Hyde Park, NY 12538-8088, **Business Phone:** (917)509-5636.

### HENRY, HERMAN (SKEETER HENRY)
Association executive, basketball player. **Personal:** Born Dec 8, 1967, Dallas, TX. **Educ:** Midland Col, attended 1988; Univ Okland, attended 1990. **Career:** Basketball player (retired); Continental Basketball Asn, Pensacola Tornados, 1990-91; Continental Basketball Asn, Birmingham Bandits, 1991-92; Nat Basketball Asn, Phoenix Suns, shooting guard, 1994-94; Large Rapids Mackers, 1994-95; Real Madrid, Spain, 1994-95; Continental Basketball Asn, Grand Rapids Hoops, 1994-95; Continental Basketball Asn, Sioux Falls Skyforce, 1995-96; Panteras de Miranda, Venezuela, 1995-96; Tuborg Pilsner Spor Kulubu Izmir, 1995-96; Montpellie, 1996-97; Cholet Toulouse Illiabum Clube, Port, 1997-98; Toulouse, 1998-99; Illiaburn Clube, Port, 1999-2000; Dijon, France, 2000-01; Le Havre, France, 2001-02; free agent, currently.

### HENRY, I. PATRICIA (PAT HENRY)
Executive, systems analyst, association executive. **Personal:** Born Aug 20, 1947, Martinsville, VA; daughter of Ida Walker Pinnix; children: Hans & Tiffany. **Educ:** Bennett Col, BS, 1969; Harvard Univ; Siebel Inst Brewing Tech. **Career:** Gen Elect Co Inc, systs analyst, 1970; Norfolk & Western Rwy, systs analyst, 1971; Ethyl Corp, systs analyst, 1972; EI DuPont de Nemours, staff asst to area head, 1973-77; Miller Brewing Co, brewing mgr, 1977-95, plant mgr, dir, 1995-; BB&T Corp, dir, 2013-. **Orgs:** Master Brewers Am, 1983; bd trustee, Carlisle Sch, 1984-86; bd dir, Main St Financial, 1996; bd trustee, Mem Hosp. **Honors/Awds:** Kizzie Award, Black Women Hall of Fame, 1984; Top Black Achiever, NY YMCA, 1984. **Special Achievements:** First African American female to hold a Leading Management post in any major US Brewery, 1995; First female plant manager for miller brewing company. **Home Addr:** 34 Woodshire Rd, Collinsville, VA 24078, **Home Phone:** (276)647-9179. **Business Addr:** Director, BB&T Corp, 200 W Second St, Winston-Salem, NC 27101, **Business Phone:** (336)733-2000.

### HENRY, JO-ANN
Executive. **Educ:** Harvard Univ, Kennedy Sch Govt, MPA, pub admin, 1985. **Career:** US Equal Employ Opportunity Comn, dir human resources; Fed Deposit Ins Corp, dir off diversity & sr exec, 1990-98; Georgetown Univ, vpres & chief human resources, 1999-2005; Re Max Premiere Selections, practr & assoc broker, 2003-. **Orgs:** Nat Asn Realtors; Real Estate Buyer's Agt Coun; Coun Residential Specialists; Habitat Humanity. **Home Phone:** (301)536-7971. **Business Addr:** Associate Broker, Practitioner, RE/MAX Premiere Selections, 822 B Rockville Pke, Rockville, MD 20852, **Business Phone:** (301)299-1000.

### HENRY, JOHN WESLEY, JR.
College president, school administrator, college administrator. **Personal:** Born Jun 3, 1929, Greensboro, NC; son of John Wesley and Carrie Lillian; married Cassandra; children: Dawn Yolanda, John Wesley III, Pamela Michelle, Linda Leverne, BrendaDiane & Robin Karen. **Educ:** NC A&T State Univ, BS, 1955; Chicago State Univ, MEd, 1965; Vet Admin Res Hosp, Chicago, cert personnel mgt, 1964; NY Univ, cert voc testing & eval, 1966; Chicago Cosmopolitan Free Sch, cert bus mgt, 1964. **Career:** School administrator, college president (retired); Vet Admin Hosp, Perry Pt, Md, manual arts therapist, phys med & rehab serv, 1955-58, actg chief, 1958-60; Vet Admin Res Hosp, Chicago, Voc Testing & Eval, chief, 1960-70; Malcolm X Community Col, City Cols Chicago, Tech & Occup Educ, dean, 1970-71, Acad Affairs, vpres, 1971-73; Denmark SC Tech Educ Ctr, assoc dir, 1973-77; Denmark Tech Col, pres, 1977-85. **Orgs:** Bd mem, Chicago W side Planning Comn, 1970-73; vice chmn, Bamberg Co Indust Develop Comn, 1979; SE Regional Coun Black Am Affairs; bd mem, Am Asn Community & Jr Col, 1979-85; hon life mem, Phi Delta Kappa; Phi Theta Kappa; hon life mem, Phi Beta Lambda; Nat Coun Resource Develop; Nat Asn Tech Educ; Coun Advan & Support Educ; Asn Cols & Univs; Am Asn Rehab Ther; Nat Asn Equal Opportunity Higher Educ; Am Legion; Disabled Am Veterans Asn; Asn Supv & Curric Develop; Asn Am Cols; Coun Occup Educ; Nat Comn Coop Educ; Pres Round table; Nat Rehab Asn. **Home Addr:** 168 Cooper St, PO Box 25, Denmark, SC 29042, **Home Phone:** (803)793-5463.

### HENRY, JOSEPH KING
Educator. **Personal:** Born Aug 2, 1948, St. Louis, MO; son of King and Geraldine; married Diana Edwards. **Educ:** Lincoln Univ, BS, 1973; Boston Univ, MA, 1974. **Career:** Humboldt Elem Sch, St Louis, teacher, 1972-73; Metro Coun Educ Opportunity Inc, coordr, 1974-77; Am Lives, instr, grad teaching asst, 1982; Univ Iowa, instr, grad teaching asst, Introd Afro-Am Soc; grad res ast, 1983-85, Spec Servs, acad coun, 1985-86, grad outreach coun, 1986-87, grad outreach coordr, Grad Col, asst dean, 1992, asst dean recruitment & minority affairs, recruitment & outreach coordr, currently; Cornell Col Mt Vernon, IA, lectr hist, 1985. **Orgs:** Coun, Univ Iowa Upward Bound Prog, 1980; pres, Afro-Am Studies Grad StudAsn, 1982-83; Nat Asn Col Admis Counrs Asn & Conf, 1985; Nat Coun Black Studies, 1988; Soc Study Multi-Ethnic Lit US, 1988; Orgn Am Historians, 1988; Joint Ctr Political Studies Assoc Prog; Univ Iowa African Am Coun; patron, St Louis Black Repertory Co; Cote Brilliante Presby Ch; Unitarian Universalist Ch; Nat Asn Grad Admis Prof; bd dir, African-Am Historical Mus & Cultural Ctr. **Home Addr:** 1232 Michelle Ct, Iowa City, IA 52240. **Business Addr:** Assistant to the Dean, University of Iowa, 205 Gilmore Hall, Iowa City, IA 52242-1320, **Business Phone:** (319)335-2138.

### HENRY, KARL H.
Lawyer. **Personal:** Born Jan 21, 1936, Chicago, IL; son of Karl H and Almeta Macintyre; married Dolores Davis; children: Marc & Paula. **Educ:** Southwestern Univ Sch Law, La, JD, 1969; USC Law Shc Prac Aspects Rec Indus; Fisk Univ; La City Col; Northwestern Univ. **Career:** Sys Outlet Shoes, asst mgr, 1962-63; Pabst Brewing Co, merchandising salesman, 1964-68; Green Power Found, mkt sales mgr, 1968; Spartan Missile Proj McDonnel Douglas Corp, sr employee rels rep, 1968-69, sr contracts negotiator, 1969-70; pvt pract atty, 1970-; Juv Ct, referee, 1975-76. **Orgs:** Am Bar Asn; LA Co Bar Asn; Juv Cts Bar; Langston Law Club; LA Trial Lawyers Asn; Engle wood Youth Asn; Nat Police Asn; John F Kennedy Club; bd dir, Green Power Found; adv bd, Step Inc; bd dir, Nat Asn Advan Colored People; pres, Holly pk Home owner Asn; dir, Spec Prog Push. **Home Addr:** 14001 Purche Ave, Gardena, CA 90249-2814, **Home Phone:** (213)804-7268. **Business Addr:** Attorney, Private Practice, 14001 Purche Ave, Gardena, CA 90249-2814, **Business Phone:** (213)804-7268.

### HENRY, LISA JENNIFER
Executive. **Personal:** daughter of Robert C (deceased). **Educ:** Univ Cincinnati, attended 1980. **Career:** Univ Cincinnat Libr, Spec Collections & Arch, collection specialist, 1978-80; Robert C. Henry Funeral Home, bus mgr, 1988-; Henry's Floral Design, owner, designer, 1991-. **Orgs:** Bd Mem, Clark County Bd Trustees; former bd mem, past pres, Springfield Mus Art; former mem, Springfield Chap Links Inc; Am Libr Asn. **Business Addr:** Business Manager, Robert C Henry Funeral, 527 Robert C Henry Way, Springfield, OH 45506, **Business Phone:** (937)322-8520.

### HENRY, LOUIS C., JR.
President (organization). **Educ:** Southern Univ, Baton Rouge, La, BS, mkt. **Career:** Franchise Food Systs Minn, pres. **Orgs:** Bd dirs mem, Friends St Paul Col; bd dirs mem, HealthEast Care Syst. **Special Achievements:** Owns and operates eight McDonald's franchises in St. Paul and at Minneapolis-St. Paul International Airport.

### HENRY, DR. MARCELETT CAMPBELL
Educator. **Personal:** Born Apr 16, 1928, Langston, OK; married Delbert V Jr; children: Jacqueline M, Sharon R, Delbert V III & Andrea D. **Educ:** Langston Univ, BS, 1949; Univ Okla, Norman, ME, 1963; San Fran State Univ, ME, admin, 1969; Walden Univ, PhD, admin, 1973. **Career:** Educator (retired); Anchorage Community Col, AK, Voc Home making Courses, teacher, 1954-55, adult Educ & curric develop, teacher & coordr summer teachers workshops, 1958-59; Anchorage Indep Sch, Dist AK Lang Arts & Soc Stud, teacher, 1956-59, teacher & homemaking, 1960-65; Tamalpais Union High Sch, Dist Mill Valley, Calif, dept chmn, teacher & dir occup training prog, 1966-74; Calif State Dept Educ, mgr summer sch, consplanning, develop, coordr alternative educ, proj mgr, cons sec educ, state staff liaison co supt & dir, 1974-96, chmn, 2002; MC Henry Enterprises, pres, 1997-98; Calif Dept Educ, consult. **Orgs:** Real Estate Training, 1959; AK Dept Educ, 1964; Marin Co Home Educ, 1966-68; Proj FEAST City Col San Francisco, 1968; consult, Pace Ctr Syst Anal Workshop Tamalpais HS Dist, 1969; adv comn & educ, JC Penny Bay Area, 1969-74; consult, Calif State Dept Voc Educ, 1970; consult, Marin Co Supt Off Corte Madera, Calif, 1970; Develop model Tamalpais Union High Sch Dist, 1970; state exec bd, Delta Kappa Gamma Chi, 1971; consult, Proj Breakthrough, Tamalpais High Sch Dist, 1972; Calif State Dept, 1973; rev & eval, Panelist Right Read Prog Higher Educ Wales, 1973; US Senate Select Com Nutrit & Human Needs Wash, DC, 1973; subcom, Calif Attorneys Gen Consumer Educ, 1975; rep, State Supt Pub Instr Select State Century III Leaders, 1976-78; chmn & conf, Adv Bd Phi Delta Kappa, 1976-77; pres, Sacramento Phi Delta Kappa, 1977-78; US Presidential Task Force, 1981; pres, Asn Multicultural Coun & Develop. **Home Addr:** 360 Cedar River Way, PO Box 2256, Sacramento, CA 95812-2256, **Home Phone:** (916)359-7781.

### HENRY, DR. MILDRED M. DALTON (MILDRED DALTON HAMPTON HENRY)
Dean (education), educator. **Personal:** Born Tamo, AR; children: Delano Hampton, Alvia Hampton Turner, Lawrence Hampton & Pamela Hampton Ross. **Educ:** AM&N Col Pine Bluff, BS, music educ, 1971; Southern Ill Univ, Edwardsville, MS, coun educ, 1976; Southern Ill Univ, Carbondale, PhD, counr educ, 1983. **Career:** AM&N Col, sec bus off, 1949-51; St Paul Pub Libr, libr asst, 1956-58; AM&N Col, lib asst & secy, 1968-71; Pine Bluff Sch Dist, music teacher, 1971-75; Southern IL Univ Edwardsville, libr asst, 1975; Watson Chapel Sch Dist, counr, 1976-77; Univ AR Pine Bluff, counr, 1978-80; Southern IL Univ Carbondale, dean's fel, 1980-81, grad asst, 1981; Carbondale Elem SchDist, teacher, 1981-83; CA State Univ, San Bernardino, asst prof, 1983, prof emer, currently. **Orgs:** Adv bd, Creative Educrs Inc Riverside, 1983-; city comnr, Fontanta CA, 1984-; exec bd, Rialto/Fontana Nat Asn Advan Colored People, 1984-; founder, pres, Provisional Educ Servs Inc, 1984-; Am Asn Univ Profs; Nat Educ Asn; CA Fac Asn; CA Teachers Asn; CA Asn Coun Develop; Asn Teacher Educrs; CA Black Fac & Staff Asn; CA State Employees Asn; Inland Empire Peace Officers Asn; Nat Asn Advan Colored People; Nat Coun Negro Women; steering comt San Bernardino Area Black Coc; San Bernardino Pvt Indust Coun; founder & chief exec officer, exec dir, Provisional Accelerated Learning Ctr. **Home Addr:** 15667 Curtis Ave, Fontana, CA 92335. **Business Addr:** Professor Emeritus, California State University, 5500 Univ Pkwy, San Bernardino, CA 92407, **Business Phone:** (909)537-5000.

### HENRY, PAT. See HENRY, I. PATRICIA.

### HENRY, DR. SAMUEL DUDLEY
Educator, executive director, consultant. **Personal:** Born Oct 9, 1947, Washington, DC; son of Shendrine Boyce and Dudley; married Ana Maria Meneses. **Educ:** DC Teachers Col, BS, 1969; Columbia Univ, MA, curric develop, 1974, EdD, 1978. **Career:** Binghamton, teacher, eng & social studies, 1971-73; HMLI Columbia Univ Teachers Col, res assoc, 1975-77; Univ MA, Sch Ed, Amherst, asst prof, 1977-78; Race Desegregation Ctr, NY, NJ, VI & PR, dir, 1978-81; San Jose State Univ, dir Equal Opportunity & Affirmative Action, Sch Social Scis, assoc dean, 1987-88, assist vpres Stud Affairs, 1989-92; CSU Northridge, Northridge, CA, Sch Educ, actg assoc dean, 1988-; Portland State Univ, assoc prof educ, 1992-94, dept chair, Curric & Instr, 2000-03, assoc prof, Curric & Instr, coordr doctoral pgm, currently; Urban Fel, 1994-2000; Univ Massachusetts, fed sch desegregation assistance ctr Region, univ presidential asst, assoc dean, asst vpres stud affairs; De Pauw Univ, chair ed dept, 1998-99; Penn State Univ, Curric & Instr, dept chair; Media Working Group, consult, currently. **Orgs:** Exec bd, Greenfield Sec Sch Comm, 1977-79; sponsor, Harlem Ebonetts Girls Track Team 1980-81; exec bd, Santa Clara Valley Urban League, 1982-83; exec bd, CAAAO, CA Assoc Affirmative Action Off, 1983-84; Prog Comm No CA Fair Employ Round table, 1983-85; ASCD Assoc Supr Curr Ser, 1984-85; bd dir, Campus Christian Ministry, 1984-85; chair-drug prev task force, San Jose Round table; chair, Ore Comm C & Families, 2003-09; Portland Educ Network; City Portland C's Investment Fund, Multnomah County Comn C & Families; Educ Leadership Prog, 2007-; exec dir, Portland Educ Network; urban fel, Portland State Univ Col Urban & Pub Affairs; City Portland C's Investment Fund; Multnomah County Comn C & Families; chair, Ore Comn C & Families, 2003-09; Ore State Bd Educ, 2010, chair, 2013-15; Ore Educ Investment Bd, 2011; Legis Comt Governance & Struct Higher Educ, 2013-14; western states dir, Nat Asn State Boards Educ, 2014; chair, Pub Educ Comt, 2014; Portland State Univ internationalization Coun; Diversity Action Coun; Acad Priorities Comt; adv bd, Rosegarden Turkish-Am Community Ctr. **Home Addr:** 1186 SW 12th Ct, Troutdale, OR 97060, **Home Phone:** (503)666-1202. **Business Addr:** Program Coordinator of Doctor of Education, Associate Professor, Portland State University, SBA 1900 Rm 596 SW Fourth Ave Bldg, Portland, OR 97207-0751, **Business Phone:** (503)725-3304.

### HENRY, SKEETER. See HENRY, HERMAN.

### HENRY, THOMAS
Educator. **Personal:** Born Nov 27, 1934, St. Louis, MO; married Gemalia Blockton. **Educ:** Lincoln Univ, BS, 1957; Harris Teachers Col. **Career:** St Louis Co Transp Community; St Louis Syst, teacher; Free Lance, com artist, 1962; Turner Mid Sch St Louis, head art dept, 1985. **Orgs:** Bd dir, St Louis Co Grand Jury, 1974-77; bd dir, Bicentennial St Louis Co; chmn, Dist Aunts & Uncles Give Needy Kids Shoes; resource dir, Inner City YMCA. **Honors/Awds:** City of Week, KATZ Radio; Honor, Rehab Educ Leavenworth Kans; Outstanding Artist, Sigma Gamma Rho, Mo. **Special Achievements:** Painted Portraits of Many Movie Stars & Celebs. **Home Addr:** 6940 Willow Woods Dr, St Louis, MO 63121-2728, **Home Phone:** (314)862-9400. **Business Addr:** 2815 Pendleton Ave, St. Louis, MO 63113.

### HENRY, WILLIAM ARTHUR, II
Lawyer, manager. **Personal:** Born Feb 11, 1939, Canalou, MO; married Alice Faye Pierce; children: William III & Shawn. **Educ:** Lincoln Univ, BS, 1962; Georgetown Univ Law Ctr, JD, 1972. **Career:** Xerox Corp, patent atty; IBM, rep, 1964-66; US Patent Off, patent examnr, 1966-72; Xerox Corp, prog opers mgr, currently. **Orgs:** DC Bar; DC Bar Asn; Pa Bar; Am Bar Asn; Urban League; Nat Patent Law Asn; Rochester Patent Law Asn; Alpha Phi Alpha Frat. **Home Addr:** 11 Pepperwood Ct, Pittsford, NY 14534-9442, **Home Phone:** (585)385-3798. **Business Addr:** Program Operations Manager, Xerox Corp, 100 Clinton Ave S, Rochester, NY 14604-1801, **Business Phone:** (585)423-4711.

### HENRY J, THELMA PREYER
Educator, association executive. **Personal:** Born Mar 11, 1919, Philadelphia, PA; daughter of Katherine Person Preyer Perry and Bando; married McDonald M. **Educ:** Howard Univ, BA, 1935; Va Sem & Col, LHD; Columbia Univ, MA, 1939; Univ PA, postgrad, 1940; Temple Univ, postgrad, 1955. **Career:** Educator, dean (retired); Bishop Col, Educ Dept, chmn, 1939-40; Dudley High Sch, Eng Dept, chmn, 1940-41; Morgan State Univ, assoc prof, 1942-55, dean, 1942-77, asst dean women, 1996; Va Sem, Lynchburg, asst dean women & head educ. **Orgs:** Pres, Morgan Univ Bredgettes, 1943-; Col Woman's Asn; Alpha Kappa Alpha; nat pres, Chi Delta Mu Wives, 1949-53; Gov's Comn Status Women; pres, Women's Med Auxil, Baltimore, MD; comnr, Baltimore City Comn Women; pres, Philomathian Club; bd mem, Pickersgill, Pk Ave Lodge; comt mem, Baltimore Symphony Orchestra, 1990-. **Honors/Awds:** Received 2 major proclamations in Baltimore, MD; At Morgan Univ founder of Women's Week, Charm Club, Mentor Syst, Col Canteen; City Coun Award; Morgan State Univ Meritorious Award; Morgan Heritage Award, Morgan State Univ, 1991; Recognition Award, Distinguished Serv as Pres of the Phelomathians, 1994; Thelma Preyer Bando Lounge was dedicated in the Harper-Lubman Residence Hall, Morgan State Col, 1994. **Special Achievements:** Author of Handbook for Col Res Hall Dir; Guide for Off Campus Housing; Handbook for Mentors. **Home Addr:** 3506 Callaway Ave, Baltimore, MD 21215, **Home Phone:** (410)466-7432.

### HENRY-FAIRHURST, ELLENAE L.
Executive, business owner, president (organization). **Personal:** Born Jan 6, 1943, Dayton, OH; daughter of Jack J Hart Sr and Ellen Nora. **Educ:** Miami Univ, BS, 1965; Univ Detroit, MA, 1978. **Career:** Ford Motor Co, mgr mkt res, 1968-86; Chrysler Corp, dealer cand, 1986-88; Cumberland Chrysler-Plymouth, pres & gen mgr, 1988-92; Huntsville Dodge Inc, owner, pres & gen mgr, 1991-; Infiniti Huntsville, owner & pres, 1999-. **Orgs:** Secy bd dir, Chrysler Minority Dealer Asn, 1989-; bd dir, Sickle Cell Found, 1989-; bd dir, Dayton Contempory Dance Co, 1993-. **Special Achievements:** First African-American owned infinity dealership in North America. **Business Addr:** President, General Manager, Huntsville Dodge Inc, 6580 Univ Dr NW, Huntsville, AL 35806-1718, **Business Phone:** (256)824-8000.

### HENSLEY, WILLIE L.
Military leader, executive director. **Educ:** La State Univ, BS, social studies; Univ Northern Colo, Greeley, MA, edu; Harvard Univ, John F Kennedy sch govt, VA's SES cand develop prog & sr exec fel prog. **Career:** US Dept Veterans Affairs, Ctr Minority Veterans, head, 1995, exec secy, 2006, dir, currently, dept veterans affairs, prin adv, currently, Oper Enduring Freedom, 2001, Oper Iraqi Freedom, 2003, Human resources & admin, actg asst secy, currently. **Orgs:** Life mem, Rocks Inc; Mil Officers Asn Am. **Honors/Awds:** Army Achievement Medal; The Army Commendation Medal; The Meritorious Service Medal, the Defense Meritorious Service Award; Legion of Merit. **Home Addr:** 7926 Hollington Pl, Fairfax Station, VA 22039-3161, **Home Phone:** (703)643-2786. **Business Addr:** Acting Assistant Secretary, Department of US Veterans Affairs, 810 Vt Ave NW Suite 700, Washington, DC 20420, **Business Phone:** (202)461-6913.

## HENSON, DANIEL PHILLIP, III (DAN HENSON)
Executive, executive director, president (organization). **Personal:** Born Apr 4, 1943, Baltimore, MD; son of Daniel P Jr and Florence Newton; married Delaphine S; children: Darren P & Dana S. **Educ:** Morgan State Univ, BA, 1966; Johns Hopkins Univ, 1970. **Career:** Baltimore City Pub Sch, social studies, teacher, 1966-67; Metrop Life Inst Co, sales agent, assoc mgr, 1967-74; Dan Henson & Assocs, pres, 1973-77; Guardian Life Ins Co Am, gen agt, 1974-77; US Small Bus Admin, reg adm, 1977-79; US Minority Bus Dev Agency, dir, 1979-81; Greater Baltimore Comm, dir, 1981-82; G & M Oil Co Inc, vpres, 1982-84; Struever Bros Eccles & Rouse Inc, vpres, 1984; Housing & Comm Develop, comnr, 1993-99; Housing Authority Baltimore City, exec dir, Commissioner, 1993-99; Henson Develop Co, pres, currently; Univ Md, fac mem. **Orgs:** Bd mem, Home Builders Asn Md, 1981-82; chmn bd, Develop Credit Fund Inc, 1982-; Greater Baltimore Comm, 1982-; bd mem, Baltimore Urban League, 1982-88; bd mem, 1982-, chmn bd, 1990-, Baltimore Sch Arts; chmn bd, Investing Baltimore Inc; bd mem, Johns Hopkins Univ Inst Policy Studies; bd mem, Ctr Ethics & Corp Policy, 1989-; bd mem, Fed Res Bank Richmond, Baltimore Br, 1991-; bd mem, Coun Large Pub Housing Authorities; chmn bd, Nat Org African Am Housing, currently; bd dir, Home Builders Asn Md. **Home Addr:** 5517 Groveland Ave, Baltimore, MD 21215, **Home Phone:** (410)664-9413. **Business Addr:** President, The Henson Development Co, PO Box 26469, Baltimore, MD 21207, **Business Phone:** (443)367-8001.

## HENSON, DARRIN DEWITT
Actor, choreographer. **Personal:** Born May 5, 1972, Bronx, NY. **Career:** Choreographer, dancer, actor, director & producer; TV Series: "Dance Grooves", 2001; "BET Open Mic: HIV Testing Day, Violation", 2003; "Sharon Osbourne Show, Retrosexual: 80's", 2004; "Love Me or Leave Me", 2004; "Take It to the Limit", 2004; "In the Garden", 2004; "Fear Eats the Soul", 2004; "E! True Hollywood Story", 2004; "Don't Think This Hasn't Been Fabulous", 2004; "Soul Food", 2000-04; "Bump & Grind", 2006; "The Feeling That We Have", 2007; "The Cost of a T-Shirt", 2007; "No Way Back", 2007; "Eye for an Eye", 2007; "The Vision", 2007; "Glass House", 2008; "Disarmed", 2008; "Lincoln Heights", 2007-08; "The Mo'Nique Show", 2009-10; "Gillian in Georgia", 2010; "The Ideal Husband", 2011; "Single Ladies", 2011; "Milk & Honey", 2011; "In the Meantime, 2013; "Black Coffee", 2014; "I Really Hate My Ex", 2014; "Silent Cry Aloud", 2014; Choreographer: Britney Spears-Crazy; Britney Spears - Sometimes; Christina Aguilera - Genie in a Bottle; Enrique Iglesias - Bailamos; Jagged Edge - Where the Party at; Jennifer Lopez - Love don't cost a thing; Jennifer Lopez - Play; Jordan Knight - Give It to you; Nsync- Bye Bye Bye; Movies: Double Platinum, 1999; Longshot, 2000; Salon, 2005; The Fabric of a man, Voice, 2005; Last Stand, 2006; April Fools, 2007; Stomp The Yard, 2007; Life Support, 2007; The Hustle, 2008; A Good man is hard to find, Voice, 2008; The Express, 2008; Tekken, 2009; Frat Brothers, exec producer, 2013; Four of Hearts, 2013; Broad way Dance ctr, teacher Hip Hop, currently; Dance & Entertainment Workshop, founder; Darrin's Dance Grooves, choreographer, actor, currently; Broadway Dance Ctr, fac, currently. **Honors/Awds:** MTV Video Music Award, Best Choreography, 2000; Nominee, Image Awards, 2004, 2005. **Special Achievements:** Has choreographed for Christina Aguilara, Brittany Spears, N'Sync, & Jennifer Lopez. **Business Addr:** Faculty, Hip Hop, BroadWay Dance Center, 322 W 45th St, New York, NY 10036, **Business Phone:** (212)582-9304.

## HENSON, TARAJI P. (TARAJI PENDA HENSON)
Television producer, movie producer, actor. **Personal:** Born Sep 11, 1970, Washington, DC; son of Boris and Bernice Gordon; children: Marcel Johnson. **Educ:** Howard Univ, BFA, 1995; NC Agr & Tech State Univ. **Career:** Actress, 1995-; exec producer, 2014-. Television: Smart Guy, The WB, 1997-99; Satan's School for Girls, 2000; Murder, She Wrote: The Last Free Man, 2001; The Division, 2002-04; Boston Legal, 2007-08; Eli Stone, 2008; Taken from Me: The Tiffany Rubin Story, 2011; Person of Interest, 2011-15; Seasons of Love, 2014; Taraji and Terrence's White Hot Holidays, 2015; Empire, Fox, 2015-; Taraji's White Hot Holidays, 2016. Film: Streetwise, 1998; The Adventures of Rocky & Bullwinkle, 2000; All or Nothing, 2001; Baby Boy, 2001; Hair Show, 2004; Hustle and Flow, 2005; Four Brothers, 2005; Something New, 2006; Smokin' Aces, 2006; Talk to Me, 2007; The Family That Prays, 2008; The Curious Case of Benjamin Button, 2008; Not Easily Broken, 2009; I Can Do Bad All by Myself, 2009; Hurricane Season, 2009; Date Night, 2010; Karate Kid, 2010; Once Fallen, 2010; Peep World, 2010; The Good Doctor, 2011; Larry Crowne, 2011; Think Like a Man, 2012; From the Rough, 2013; Think Like a Man Too, 2014; Top Five, 2014; No Good Deed, 2014; Term Life, 2016. Executive producer: No Good Deed (film), 2014; Seasons of Love (TV movie), 2014; executive producer, Taraji and Terrence's White Hot Holidays (TV special) 2015. **Orgs:** Acad TV Arts & Sci. **Honors/Awds:** BET Award, 2006, 2009, 2011, 2015, 2016; Austin Film Critics Association Award, 2008; Image Award, 2009, 2012, 2014, 2015, 2016; Golden Globe Award, 2016. **Special Achievements:** Co-author, "Around the Way Girl", 2016. **Business Addr:** United Talent Agency, 9336 Civic Center Dr, Beverly Hills, CA 90210.

## HENTON, GEORGE
Executive. **Educ:** John Marshall High Cleveland Ohio, acct, 1969; Univ Toledo, BA, acct, 1971; Nat Univ, BS, acct, 1979. **Career:** ShoeBox-Acct, pres, 1979-, owner, chief exec officer, 1980-2011; Oede Investment, partner, 1982-2011; Sidley Austin LLP, paralegal, 1990-92; Am Bar Asn, budget dir & it liaison, gen ledger specialist, financial analyst, 1996-2010; J. Hilburn Men's Clothier, style advisor, 2011-. **Orgs:** African Am Asn Fitness Professionals; Omega Psi Phi Fraternity, 1970-2014. **Home Phone:** (773)297-6419. **Business Addr:** Style Advisor, J Hilburn Men's Clothier, 12700 Pk Cent Dr Suite 2000, Dallas, TX 75251, **Business Phone:** (866)789-5381.

## HERBERT, DR. ADAM W., JR.
School administrator, administrator. **Personal:** Born Dec 1, 1943, Muskogee, OK; son of Addie; married Karen. **Educ:** Univ Southern Calif, BA, polit sci, 1966, MA, pub admin, 1968; Univ Pittsburgh, PhD, urban affairs & pub admin, 1971. **Career:** Va Tech, chair urban affairs prog & assoc prof urban affairs, 1972; Univ N Fla, pres, 1989-98; State Univ Syst Fla, chancellor, 1998-2001, Fla Ctr Pub Policy & Leadership, regents prof & exec dir, 2001-03; AvMed Health Plan, 2001-; Fla Banks Inc, dir, 2002-03; BioCrossroads, dir; Ind Univ, pres, prof emer, 2003-07, Sch Pub & Environ Affairs & Polit Sci, prof; State Farm FlaIns Co, dir, 2004-; St Joe Co, dir, 2004-; Jacksonville ENT Surg, exec dir, currently. **Orgs:** Fel, one 15 White House, 1974; spec asst, US Secy Health, Educ & Welfare; pres, Nat Asn Schs Pub Affairs & Admin; Knight Found Comn; chair, Jacksonville Chamber Com, 1993; co chair, NFL Now; Fla Comnr Educ Comn; Fla Fed Judicial Nominating Comn; chair, Nat Asn Schs Pub Affairs & Admin Comn Peer Rev & Accreditation; br trustee, Nat Acad Pub Admin; bd dir, Joe Corp, 2004-; chmn bd, pres, Ind Univ Found. **Special Achievements:** First African American president of Indiana University. **Business Addr:** Director, St Joe Co, 133 S Watersound Pkwy, Panama City Beach, FL 32413, **Business Phone:** (904)301-4200.

## HERBERT, BOB
Journalist, columnist. **Personal:** Born Mar 7, 1945, Brooklyn, NY. **Educ:** State Univ NY, BS, journalism, 1988. **Career:** Star-Ledger (Nj), reporter & night city ed, 1970-76; "New York Daily News," reporter & ed, 1976-85; Sunday Ed & Hotline, WCBS-TV (New York), panelist, 1990-93; NBC News, Nat corresp, 1991-93; "The New York Times", op-ed writer, 1993-2011; Demos, distinguished sr fel, 2011-. **Honors/Awds:** Meyer Berger Award, recipient; Distinguished Newspaper Writing, Am Soc Newspaper Ed, recipient; David Nyhan Prize, Shorenstein Ctr at Harvard Univ, recipient; Ridenhour Courage Prize, recipient; Pulitzer Prize for National Reporting, nominee. **Special Achievements:** "Promises Betrayed: Waking Up from the American Dream," Author (Times Books, 2005); "Losing Our Way: An Intimate Portrait of a Troubled America," Author (Doubleday, 2014).

## HERBERT, DOUGLAS A.
Sheriff, government official. **Educ:** Henrico Co Sheriff's Off, Spec Law Enforcement Acad. **Career:** Law enforcement sheriff (retired); Henrico Co Sheriff Off, Jail Security Div, from corporal to sergeant, 1980-85, shift sergeant, 1985-87, lt, 1987-88, capt, major, jail W adminr, chief dep sheriff. **Special Achievements:** First African American captain with the Henrico Co Sheriff's Off.

## HERBERT, JOHN TRAVIS, JR.
Lawyer, counselor. **Personal:** Born Feb 17, 1943, Montclair, NJ; married Jean Dolores, Jan 1, 1965; children: Stephanie, Travis III & Suzanne. **Educ:** Howard Univ, BS, polit sci, 1966; Seton Hall Univ Sch Law, JD, law, 1974. **Career:** Allied Chem, mgr labor rels, 1968-72; Rutgers Univ, adj prof, 1973-; Johnson & Johnson, atty, mgr, 1972-74, corp dir, 1974-76, labor rels exec; Pitney Bowes Inc, Stamford, Conn, Corp Facil & Admin, vpres, 1984-96; Pfizer Inc, vpres human resources, 1997-2008, sr coun, 2002-08, Global Res & Develop, lawyer, 2004-08; Cornell Univ, adj instr, 2008-; Herbert Law Group, LLC, managing mem, 2008-; Epstein Becker Green, counr; Cent Jersey OIC, bd atty; Rivera & Colon LLP, coun; Ferreira & Herbert Law Group Llc, partner. **Orgs:** Chmn, BALSA Seton Hall Law Sch, 1973-74; vol, Parole, 1974-; coach, Pop Warner Football, 1975-77; organizer, Franklin Twp Youth Athletic Asn, 1976-77; Middlesex Co Bar Asn, 1979-80; bd secy & gen coun, Rutgers Min Bus Co, 1980; bd mem, Westchester Fairfield City Corp Coun Assoc, 1985-; bd mayors, Transp Mgt Round Table, 1985-; corp liason, Nat Urban League Stamford, 1986-; Franklin Twp Bd Educ; Am Bar Asn; Nat Bar Asn; NJ Bar Asn. **Home Addr:** 2 Tamarack Rd, Somerset, NJ 08873-2923, **Home Phone:** (732)846-6838. **Business Addr:** Partner, Ferreira & Herbert Law Group LLC, 96 Engle St, Englewood, NJ 07631-2948, **Business Phone:** (201)490-4070.

## HERD, REV. JOHN E.
Educator, clergy, air force officer. **Personal:** Born May 29, 1932, Colbert County, AL; married Eleanor; children: Arnold & Garland. **Educ:** BS, MS, 1966, AA cert, 1976. **Career:** Russa Moton High Sch, Tallassee, Ala, instr; Cobb High Sch, Anniston, Ala, instr; Brutonville Jr High Sch, Al, prin; Alexandria High Sch, Ala, prin; New Elam Missionary Baptist Church, pastor; Rocky Zion Baptist Church, Pell City, Ala, pastor, currently. **Orgs:** Alpha Phi Alpha; pres, Calhoun Co Educ Asn, 1972. **Special Achievements:** First African American president of Calhoun County Educational Association. **Home Addr:** 161 Whisenant Rd, Ohatchee, AL 36271-7100, **Home Phone:** (256)892-3474. **Business Addr:** Pastor, Rocky Zion Baptist Church, 1505 10th Ave S, Pell City, AL 35128, **Business Phone:** (205)338-3231.

**HEREFORD, DR. SONNIE WELLINGTON, III. See Obituaries Section.**

## HERENTON, DR. WILLIE WILBERT
Mayor, administrator, association executive. **Personal:** Born Apr 23, 1940, Memphis, TN; married Ida Jones; children: Duke, Rodney & Andrea. **Educ:** LeMoyne-Owen Col, BS, 1963; Memphis State Univ, MA, 1966; Southern Ill Univ, PhD, 1971. **Career:** Memphis City Sch Syst, elem sch teacher, 1963-67, elem sch prin, 1967-73; Rockefeller Found, fel, 1973-74; Memphis City Schs, dept supt, 1974-78, supt schs, 1979-92; City Memphis, mayor, 1991-2009. **Orgs:** bd dir, Nat Urban League; bd dir, Nat Jr Achievement; Am Asn Sch Adminstr, 1969-80; Nat Alliance Black Educr, 1974-; Nat Urban League Educ Adv Coun, 1978; bd dir, Achievement Memphis, 1979-; bd dir, United Way Greatr Memphis, 1979-. **Honors/Awds:** Raymond Foster Scholar Award, So IL Univ, 1970; Alumnus of the Year, LeMoyne Owen Col, 1976; Horatio Alger Award, 1988; Municipal Leader of the Year, Am City & County Mag, 2002; hon doctorates, Rhodes Col, Christian Bros Univ. **Special Achievements:** The first mayor in the hist of the city of Memphis to be elected to a fourth consecutive term as mayor; Named one of Top 100 Sch Adminr in US & Can Exec Educr Journal 1980, 1984. **Home Addr:** 3732 Masonwood, Memphis, TN 38116. **Business Addr:** Board Director, United Way Greater Memphis, 6775 Lenox Center Ct 200, Memphis, TN 38115-4429, **Business Phone:** (901)433-4300.

## HERMAN, ALEXIS MARGARET
Government official, legislator. **Personal:** Born Jul 16, 1947, Mobile, AL; daughter of Alex and Gloria Caponis; married Charles L Franklin Jr. **Educ:** Xavier Univ, BA, sociol, 1969; Cent State Univ, hon doctorate; Lesley Col, hon doctorate. **Career:** Cath Soc Serv, soc worker, 1969-72; Recruitment Training Prog, outreach worker, 1971-72; Black Women Empl Prog Southern Regional Coun, dir, 1972-74; Dept Labor Recruitment Training Prog, consult supvr, 1973-74; Women's Prog Minority Women Empl Atlanta, nat dir, 1974-77; Orgn Econ Coop & Develop, White House rep; Nat Consumer Coop Bank, founding mem; Women's Bur, Dept Labor, dir, 1977-81; Green Herman & Assocs, vpres, 1981-85; A M Herman & Assocs, founder, 1981-, pres, 1985-93; Dem Nat Conv Comt, chief exec officer, 1991; Dem Nat Comt, dep chair & chief staff, 1992; Presidential Transition Off, dep dir, 1992-93; White House Off Pub Liaison, dir, asst to US Pres, 1993-97, secy labor, 1997-2001; New Ventures Inc, chair & chief exec officer, 2001-; Coca-Cola Co, Bias Suit Task Force, chair, 2001-, dir, 2007-; Toyota Motor Corp, N Am Diversity Adv Bd, chair; Cummins Inc, dir; Metro Goldwyn Mayer Mirage Inc, bd mem; Prudential, bd mem; Entergy Corp, bd dir, currently; speaker, currently. **Orgs:** Bd mem, Adams Nat Bank; bd mem, DC Econ Develop Finance Corp; Nat Coun Negro Women; Delta Sigma Theta Sorority Inc; bd mem, One Am Found; chair, Sodexo Adv Bd; co-chair, Bush Clinton Katrina Fund; Mardi Gras Asn; founding mem; Natl Coun Negro Women; Natl Dem Inst; Affiliated with US Conf Social Justice, World Peace Comn. **Honors/Awds:** Dorothy I Height Leadership Award; Sara Lee Frontrunner Award, 1999. **Special Achievements:** First African-American to lead the Department of Labor. **Home Addr:** 700 7th St SW, Washington, DC 20024, **Home Phone:** (202)554-4509. **Business Addr:** Director, Coca-Cola Co, 1 Coca Cola Plz NW, Atlanta, GA 30313, **Business Phone:** (404)676-2121.

## HERMAN, KATHLEEN VIRGIL
Administrator. **Personal:** Born May 17, 1942, Buffalo, NY; children: Jonathan Mark. **Educ:** Goddard Col, BA, 1976; Boston Univ, MS, commun, 1980. **Career:** Pub Info Boston Edison, consult, 1979; Minority Recruitment Big Sister Assoc, coordr, 1980; Coun Battered Women, comt educ dir, 1980; Access Atlanta Inc, dir, 1981; City atlanta, coordr cable commun. **Orgs:** Minorities Cable, Nat Assoc Telecom, Nat Fed Local Programmers, Women Cable; co-chair, Nat Asn Advan Colored People Media Comt; Am Women radio & TV. **Honors/Awds:** Pub, "Minority Participation in the Media", sub comt Telecom Consumer Protection & Finance Comn Energy & Com, US House Reps, Ninety Eighth Congress. **Home Addr:** 875 Oakhill Ave SW, Atlanta, GA 30310.

## HERMANUZ, PROF. GHISLAINE
Educator, architect, dean (education). **Personal:** Born Lausanne; daughter of Max and Manotte Tavernier; children: Dahoud Walker. **Educ:** ETH/Lausanne Switz, arch dipl, 1967; Harvard Grad Sch Design, attended 1969; Columbia Univ, MS, urban planning, 1971. **Career:** Candilis, Josic & Woods, architect, 1964-65; Llewelyn-Davies & Weeks, architects, 1967-68; Abeles & Schwartz, planner, 1969-71; Architects Renewal Co, Harlem, architect, 1970-72; Cornell Univ, lectr, 1971-73; Brooklyn Col, instr, 1973-74; Columbia Univ, assist dean, 1974-79, assoc prof, 1974-86; Urban Design Group City Planning Dept, urban designer, 1972-73; Columbia Univ, Grad Sch Archit, prof archit; Bernard & Anne Spitzer Sch Archit, prof, 1986-; CCAC, dir, 1986-89; City Col NY, prof archit, prof & dir advising, currently; Hermanuz Ltd, prin, 1988-; Taubman Col Archit, charles moore vis prof, urban design, currently. **Orgs:** UN Huairou comn, Women Homes & Community; Nat Orgn Minority Architects; Asn Community Design; Salzburg Cong Urban Planning & Develop; Int Archive Women Archit; Regist Architect, Switz. **Home Addr:** 409 Edgecombe Ave Apt 8A, New York, NY 10032. **Business Addr:** Professor, Director of Advising, The City College of New York, 141 Convent Ave SH 109B, New York, NY 10031, **Business Phone:** (212)650-8731.

## HERNANDEZ, AILEEN CLARKE
Consultant, executive. **Personal:** Born May 23, 1926, Brooklyn, NY; daughter of Charles Henry Clarke Sr and Ethel Louise Hall; married Alfonso Rafael. **Educ:** Howard Univ, BA, polit sci & sociol, 1947; Univ Oslo, postgrad, Int stud exchange prog, 1947; NY Univ, attended 1950; Calif State Univ, MA, gov, 1961; Univ Southern Calif; La State Univ, MA, 1961. **Career:** Int Ladies Garment Workers Union Los Angeles, organizer, asst educ dir, 1951-59, dir pub rel & educ, 1959-61; US State Dept, Ttoured S Am Countries, spec asst labor educ, 1960; Calif Fair Employ Prac Comn, asst chief, dep chief, 1962-65; US Equal Employ Comn, comnr, 1965-66; Aileen C Hernandez Asn, owner & pres, 1967-; San Francisco State Univ, lectr & instr polit sci, 1968-69; Univ Calif Berkeley, instr, urban planning, 1978-79; Univ Calif, San Francisco, Inst Health & Aging, Tish Sommers Lectr, 1993; Howard Univ, Dept Gov, res asst; Sapphire Publ Co, founder; Univ Calif, Santa Barbara, regents scholar residence, 1993. **Orgs:** Western vpres, Nat Orgn Women, 1967-70, nat pres, 1970-71; bd dir, Nat Comn Against Discrimination Housing, 1969; second pres, Nat Orgn Women, 1970-71; co-founding mem, Black Women Organized Act, San Fran & Nat Hookup Black Women, 1973; life trustee, Urban Inst Wash, DC; bd mem, MS Found Women; Am Acad Polit & Soc Sci; Indust Rel Res Asn; Am Civil Liberties Union; comnr, Foreign Policy Study Found; steering & exec comnr & co-chair, Nat Urban Coalition; pres & bd trustee, Working Assets Money Fund; bd overseers, Inst Civil Justice Rand Corp; adv, Nat Inst Women Color; treas, Eleanor R Spikes Mem Fund; adv comt, Prog Res Immigration Policy, Rand & Urban Inst; bd mem & ed, comm chair, Death Penalty Focus; bd mem, Meiklejohn Civil Liberties Union; Calif Community Campaign Financing; Nat Asn Advan Colored People; bd pres, Ctr Common Good; Alpha Kappa Alpha; Bay Area Urban League; co-founder & chair, Coalition Econ Equity; vice chair, San Francisco, 2000; comnr, Bay Vision 2020; chair, Calif Women's Agenda; chair emer, Citizen's Trust; bd, Pesticide Edu Ctr; bd, Garden Proj; bd, Ctr Women Policy Studies; bd & exec comnr, Citizen's Comn Civil Rights; bd & exec comnr, Ctr Govt Studies; bd, Wellesley Ctrs Res Women; bd, San Francisco Workforce Investment; bd, chair Working Group, San Francisco Redevelop Agency; Prog Resources Comt & WISF Bd, 2001-; chair, Calif Women's Agenda; coordr, Black Women Stirring Waters, currently; Northern Calif Am Civil Liberties Found; educ & pub rels dir, Pac Coast Region Union. **Honors/Awds:** Woman of the Year, Community Rels Conf Southern CA, 1961; Postgraduate Achievement Award, Bay Area Alumni Club Distinguished, Howard Univ, 1967; Named one of 10 Most Distinguished Women, Bay Area San Fran Examiner, 1968; Public Service Award, Charter Day Alumni Postgrad Achievement

Labor, 1968; Hon DHL, Southern Vt Col, 1979; Award of Recognition, Equal Rights Advocates, 1981; Women Award, Friends Community Status, 1984; Award Ten Women Who Make a Difference, SF League Women Voters, 1985; Parren J Mitchell Award, SF Black Chamber Community, 1985; Distinguished Service Award, Nat Urban Coalition, 1987; Earl Warren Civil Liberties Award, N Calif ACLU, 1989; Wise Woman Award, Ctr Women Policy Studies, 1989; Silver Spur Award, SF Planning & Urban Res Asn, 1995; Mary Lepper Award, Am Polit Sci Asn, 1996; WAVE Award, Alumnae Resources, 1997; Ella Hill Hutch Award, Black Women Organized Polit Action, 1997; Activist of the Year Award, San Francisco Bay Area 100 Black Women, 2001; Ten Women Campaign Award, Flyaway Productions, 2003. **Special Achievements:** Second National President of the National Organization for Women. **Business Addr:** Owner, President, Aileen C Hernandez Associates, 818 47th Ave, San Francisco, CA 94121-3208, **Business Phone:** (415)752-4506.

### HERNANDEZ, MARY N.

Religious educator. **Personal:** Born Nov 21, 1940, Nashville, TN; daughter of Rafael and Mary DeWees. **Educ:** Fisk Univ, Nashville, Tenn, BA, Span & Fr, 1962; Hunter Col, span lang & lit, 1963; Tenn State Univ, Nashville, Tenn, 1967, 1979, MS, orgn coun, 1985; Peabody Vanderbilt, Nashville, Tenn, MLS, spec libr, 1986. **Career:** Tenn Bot Gardens & Fine Arts Ctr, Nashville, TN, Fine Arts Librn, 1986-88; Univ Tenn, Chattanooga, TN, asst prof, asst librn, 1988-91, head Circ Serv, 1989-91; Univ Ariz Libr, Tuscon, AZ, Fine Arts & African Studies Librn, 1991-98; DC Pub Libr Syst, Watha T. Daniel/Shaw Neighborhood Libr, br mgr, 1999-2007; Fisk Univ, 2008-09; Northeast Neighborhood Libr, br mgr, 2005-06; Georgetown Neighborhood Libr, br mgr, 2006-; John Paul Great Univ, vol recruiter, 2009-10; St. Vincent de Paul Cath Church, Nashville, TN, dir relig educ, 2009-. **Orgs:** Pres, Art Libr Soc, TN-KY, 1989-90; ARLIS/ NA Mem Comt, 1990-91, 1993-95; Arts & Educ Coun, Southern Writers Conf, 1990-91; Black Caucus, Am Libr Asn, 1989-91; pres-elect, ARLIS, Ariz, 1993-94; Tucson Jazz Soc, 1991-98; Coun Black Educrs, Tucson. **Honors/Awds:** Dean's Award, Lupton Libr Univ Tenn Chattanooga, 1990; LoPresti Award, ARLIS, SE, 1990-91; NEH Award, 1992-93. **Special Achievements:** Order of Merit, Archdiocese Wash, 2004. **Home Addr:** 4313 W Hamilton Rd, Nashville, TN 37218, **Home Phone:** (615)876-4207. **Business Addr:** Director of Religious Education, St Vincent de Paul Roman Catholic Church, 1700 Heiman St, Nashville, TN 37208, **Business Phone:** (615)320-0695.

### HERNDON, CRAIG GARRIS

Educator, photographer. **Personal:** Born Jan 23, 1947, Washington, DC; son of Lucy Frances Mills and Garris McClellan; married Valerie Ingrid Naylor; children: Stacey Arlene, Robert Eric, Marcus Vincent, Monica Amber & Maya Violet. **Educ:** Howard Univ, BA, 1970; Md Inst Col Art, MA, 2004, MFA, 2005. **Career:** Potomac Mag, news aide, 1968-72; Wash Post, photojournalist & ed, 1968-2000; PicSmart Inc, founder & chief exec officer, 2000-03; Craig Herndon Photog, sole proprietor, 2001-08; Howard Univ, prof multi-media studies, 2006-14; Creative Edge Studio Collab, Adv Bd, 2013-. **Orgs:** White House News Photogr Asn; Nat Asn Black Journalists, 1989-99. **Home Addr:** 3212 Walnut Dr, Highland Bch, Annapolis, MD 21403, **Home Phone:** (410)263-4028. **Business Addr:** Professor Multi-Media Studies, Howard University, 2400 6th St NW, Washington, DC 20059, **Business Phone:** (202)806-6100.

### HERNDON, GLORIA E.

Executive. **Personal:** Born Aug 9, 1950, St. Louis, MO; married Brent A. **Educ:** Southern Ill Univ, BA, 1970; Johns Hopkins Univ, MA, 1972, PhD, 1978. **Career:** Am Embassy London, financial economist; Ahmadu Bello Univ Nigeria, res, 1978-79; Brooking Inst, res asst; Johns Hopkins, res asst; African-Am Inst, prog asst; Dept State, escort interpreter; Carnegie Endowment Int Peace Coun Foreign Rels, res asst; Equitable Financial Servs, ins co exec, 1984-; GB Herndon & Assoc, chief exec officer & pres, 1989-. **Orgs:** Accomplished Musician; Mu Phi Epsilon; Nat Econ Asn; Am Soc Int Law; Nat Conf Black Polit Scientist; Nat Coun Negro Women; Nigerian-Am C; US Youth Coun Res initial Black Caucus, 1970-71; planner United Minority Arts Coun; Nat Asn Equal Opportunity Higher Educ; Am Asn Community Col; Asn Community Col trustee. **Home Addr:** 9909 Bald Cypress Dr, Rockville, MD 20850, **Home Phone:** (301)762-4199. **Business Addr:** President, Chief Executive Officer, G B Herndon & Association Inc, 601 Pa Ave NW Suite 900, Washington, DC 20004, **Business Phone:** (202)396-1315.

### HERNDON, HAROLD THOMAS, SR.

President (organization), chief executive officer, teacher. **Personal:** Born Oct 28, 1937, Lincolnton, NC; son of John W Jr and Elizabeth; married Catherine Thompson; children: Harold Thomas Jr, Dwayne, LaShawn, Colin & Cynthia. **Educ:** Bluefield State Col, BS, 1959; Univ MAR, MS, 1980. **Career:** St Marys bd educ, music teacher, 1960-70, adr, 1970-80; Compliance Corp, pres & chief exec officer, currently. **Orgs:** Nat Contract mgt asn; pres, Chesapeake Bay Chap; Rotary int; St Mary's County Econ Develop cms; soc enterpreneurs & Scientists; Mer 100; bd mem, St Marys Nursing Home; St Marys Voc Tech educ coun; bd mem, Tri-County Small Bus Develop Ctr; bd mem, Md Chamber Com. **Home Addr:** 25335 3rd Notch Rd, Hollywood, MD 20636, **Home Phone:** (301)373-5016. **Business Addr:** President, Chief Executive Officer, Compliance Corp, 21617 S Essex Dr Suite 34, Lexington Park, MD 20653, **Business Phone:** (301)863-8070.

### HERNDON, LARRY DARNELL

Baseball player, athletic coach. **Personal:** Born Nov 3, 1953, Sunflower, MS; married Faye Hill; children: Latasha, Kamelah, Myia & Larry Jr. **Educ:** Tenn State Univ, doctor nursing pract. **Career:** Baseball player (retired), athletic coach; St Louis Cardinals, outfielder, 1974; San Francisco Giants, outfielder, 1976-81; Detroit Tigers, outfielder, 1982-88, hitting coach; Durham Bulls, pitching coach, 2000-06; Lake land Flying Tigers, batting coach, 2006. **Business Addr:** Batting Coach, Lakeland Flying Tigers, 2125 N Lake Ave, Lakeland, FL 33805, **Business Phone:** (863)686-8075.

### HERNDON, PHILLIP GEORGE

Investment banker. **Personal:** Born Jul 3, 1951, Little Rock, AR; son of James Franklyn and Georgia Mae Byrd. **Educ:** Villanova Univ, Pa. **Career:** Pulaski Co, Ark, survr, co-survr, 1972; KATV Little Rock, news reporter 1972; Just Kicks Inc retail shoe store, owner 1973-74; Kip Walton Productions (TV/Motion Pictures), Hollywood, Calif, prod asst 1974-78; US Assoc Investment Bankers, Little Rock, Ark, investment banker, 1985-87; Blinder, Robinson & Co, Denver, Colo, asst mgr bond dept 1987-88; Colo African/Caribbean Trade Off, consult, 1988-; Anisco Enterprises (import/export), consult, 1988-; Mfg & Distributing Int, sr vpres, 1992-. **Orgs:** Dir Community Rels GYST House, (fund raiser drug rehab prog); dir, vol serv, New Futures Little Rock Youth; Amer Legion Boy's State, 1968; Black Rel Dir Youth Div Gov Winthrop Rockefeller's Re-Election Campaign, 1970. **Honors/Awds:** National HS Track Champ National & state record holder high hurdles, 1968; Million Dollar Club, Blinder, Robinson & Company 1988. **Special Achievements:** First black elected in Amer Legions Boys State, 1968; First Black inducted into Little Rock Central HS Hall of Fame, 1969; Recipient over 200 full scholarship offers from college & Univ nationwide, 1969; First black elected officer, Pulaski Co, 1972. **Home Addr:** 2123 S Pk St, Little Rock, AR 72202-6141, **Home Phone:** (501)376-0790. **Business Addr:** Senior Vice President, Manufacturing and Distributing International Inc, 913 S Hughes St, Little Rock, AR 72202.

### HERRELL, DR. ASTOR YEARY

Chairperson, educator, army officer. **Personal:** Born Feb 13, 1935, Fork Ridge, TN; son of Clarence and Charity; married Doris Vivian Smith; children: Patricia Faye. **Educ:** Berea Col, BA, chem, 1957; Tuskegee Inst, MS Ed, sci educ, 1961; Wayne State Univ, MI, PhD, inorg chem, 1973. **Career:** St Augustines Col, instr, 1961-63; Knoxville Col, prof & chmn, 1963-79; Wayne State Univ, sci fac fel, 1970-72; Winston Salem Forsyth Co Schs, consult, 1983-85; Winston Salem State Univ, chairperson phys sci & adj prof chem, currently. **Orgs:** Am Chem Soc; bd dir, Forsyth Co Environ Affairs Bd; Sigma Xi, 1985-. **Honors/Awds:** Biography display Martin Luther King Libr DC, 1984. **Home Addr:** 1735 Ardmore Rd, Winston-Salem, NC 27127-7508, **Home Phone:** (336)788-0682. **Business Addr:** Adjunct Professor, Winston Salem State University, 601 Martin Luther King Jr Dr W B Atkinson 311, Winston-Salem, NC 27110, **Business Phone:** (336)750-2540.

### HERRING, DR. BERNARD DUANE

Educator, physician. **Personal:** Born Massillon, OH; son of James and Eva; married Odessa Mae Appling; children: Kevin, Duane, Terez & Sean. **Educ:** Kent State Univ, BS, 1952; Univ Cincinnati Med Sch, MD, internal med & geriatrics, 1956; LaSalle Univ, LLB, 1963; Audio Inst Am, dipl, 2003. **Career:** San Fran Gen Hosp, intern, 1956-57; Brooklyn Vet Hosp, resident, 1957-58; Crile Vet Hosp, resident, 1958-59; Merritt Hosp, teaching, 1966-84; Univ CA Med Sch SF, asst clin prof med; gen pract, currently; Alta Bates Summit Med Ctr, Family Med & Geriat Med, physician, currently; William Byron Rumford Med Ctr, W Oakland Health Coun, physician. **Orgs:** Am Bd Family Med; Am Bd Internal Med; Am Col Legal Med; Am Med Writers Asn; Am Diabetes Asn; Am Col Physician; Am Soc Composers & Authors; AMA; Am Heart Asn; pres, Sunshine Vitamin Co; Am Acad Family Physicians, 1983; Am Geriat Soc, 1989; Watchtower Bible & Tract Soc, 1980-89. **Honors/Awds:** Cited by Phi Beta Kappa, Kent State Univ, 1952. **Special Achievements:** Article: "Kaposi Sarcoma in The Negro" 1963 Jama; "Hospital Priviledges", 1965; Cleveland Marshall Law Review; "Pernicious Anemia & The AmericanNegro", Am Practr, 1962; "Hepatoma with Unusual Associations", J. Nat Med Asn, 1973; "Cancer of Prostate in Blacks", J. Nat Med Asn, 1977; Listed Best Doctor Am, 1979; "Unravelling Pathophysiology of Male PatternBaldness", 1985; "Understanding Insulin-Resistance in Type 2 Diaretes", J.National Medical Asn, 2002. **Home Addr:** 712 Longridge Rd, Oakland, CA 94610-2325, **Home Phone:** (510)832-0464. **Business Addr:** Physician, William Byron Rumford Medical Center, 2960 Sacramento St, Berkeley, CA 94702, **Business Phone:** (510)549-3166.

### HERRING, CEDRIC

Educator. **Educ:** Univ Houston-Univ Park, BA, sociol, 1980; Univ Mich, Ann Arbor, MA, sociol, 1982, PhD, sociol, 1985. **Career:** CIC Minorities Fel, 1980-82; Am Sociol Asn Minority Fel, 1982-84; Tex A&M Univ, Dept Sociol, from asst prof to assoc prof, 1985-90; Ford Found, fel, 1987-88; Ind Univ Minority Fac Recruitment fel, 1989; Univ Ill Chicago, Inst Govt & Pub Affairs, Dept Sociol, assoc prof, 1990-95, prof sociol & pub policy, 1991-2012, Great Cities Inst, Great Cities, fel, 1995-96, prof, 1995-, Inst Res Race & Pub Policy, founding dir, 1996-98, Race & Pub Policy Prog, founding dir, 2007-13-, CIC Acad Leadership Prog, fel, 2007-08, Dept Sociol, actg head, 2008-09; Univ Md Baltimore County, prof, 2014-, dir, 2015-. Books: Splitting the Middle: Political Alienation, Acquiescence and Activism Among America's Middle Layers, 1989; African Americans and the Public Agenda: The Paradoxes of Public Policy, ed, 1997; Empowerment in Chicago: Grassroots Participation in Economic Development and Poverty Alleviation, co-ed, 1998; Skin Deep: How Race and Complexion Matter in the Color-Blind Era, co-ed, 2004; The State of the State of Illinois, ed, 2006; Combating Racism and Xenophobia: Transatlantic and International Perspectives, ed, 2011; Reinventing Race, Reinventing Racism, co-ed, 2013; Diversity in Organizations, co-auth, 2014. **Orgs:** Am Sociol Asn; Midwest Sociol Soc; Nat Res Coun Selection Panel Ford Found Minority Fel Prog; pres, Asn Black Sociologis, 1994-95; Am Polit Sci Asn; Midwestern Sociol Soc; Nat Conf Black Polit Scientists. **Business Addr:** Professor, Director, University of Maryland Baltimore County, 620 W Lexington St, Baltimore, MD 21201, **Business Phone:** (410)706-3100.

### HERRING, DR. LARRY WINDELL, SR.

Dentist. **Personal:** Born Jul 8, 1946, Batesville, MS; married Rubbie P; children: Cedric, La Canas Nicole & Yolanda. **Educ:** TN State Univ, BA, 1967; Meharry Med Col, DDS, 1971. **Career:** Pvt pract dentist, currently. **Orgs:** Nat Dent Asn; Am Dent Asn; Pan TN Dent Asn; Tri-Lakes Study Club; Shelby Co Dent Soc; Nat Asn Advan Colored People; Omega Psi Phi; Masonic Lodge; W Camp MB Ch. **Home Addr:** 183 Tillman st, Memphis, TN 38111-2721, **Home Phone:** (901)452-3211. **Business Addr:** Dentist, Larry W Herring DDS Inc, 115 Wood St, Batesville, MS 38606-1826, **Business Phone:** (662)563-5344.

### HERRING, LEONARD, JR.

Public relations executive, chief executive officer. **Personal:** Born Oct 1, 1934, Valdosta, GA; son of Leonard Sr and Gussie; children: Leonard III & Lynne Rene. **Educ:** Univ Cincinnati, BA, 1960, BS, hist, govt & bus admin, 1964. **Career:** Colgate-Palmolive Co NY Co, San Fran, mktg & sales; Cincinnati Bell Tele, acct mgr, mktg staff asst, 1964-66; Armco Steel Corp, asst personnel dir, 1966-67; Leonard Herring Jr. Enterprises, pub rel officer, 1967-, pres & chief exec officer, chmn, 1976-; Celebrity Tennis Tournament Ltd, chmn, 1976-; Pub Rel Consult movies: Amityville Horror; Omen; A Piece Action Part II; Sounder, Cross Creekl; Clarion Jazz, chief exec officer, 2002-; Mgt Ltd, chief exec officer, pres; Celebrity Golf & Tennis Ltd, chief exec officer, producer. **Orgs:** Kappa Alpha Psi, 1960-; Univ Cincinnati Aumni Asn, 1964-; Am Tennis Prof, 1970-; Univ Cincinnati 100 Distinguished Alumni, 1970; Am Tennis Writers Asn, 1970-; Am Tennis Profs, 1970; United Tennis Writers Asn, 1970; Advert Asn Am, 1972-; vpres, Pub Rel Soc Am, 1972-76; vpres, US Lawn Tennis Asn, 1975-76; Men Achievement World, 1976; bd mem, United Way Los Angeles, 1984-; Screen Actor's Guild, 1992-; Prof Tennis Registry, 2001; US Tennis Asn; US Tennis Prof Registry; chmn, Cincinnati Nat Jr Tennis League. **Special Achievements:** Cinci Chap Nat Jr Tennis Leagues Boys & Girls, coach, 1972-74. **Home Addr:** 900 Hammond St Suite 434, West Hollywood, CA 90069, **Home Phone:** (310)855-0172. **Business Addr:** Chairman, Chief Executive Officer, Leonard Herring Jr Enterprises, 900 Hammond St Suite 434, West Hollywood, CA 90069, **Business Phone:** (310)855-0172.

### HERRING, MARSHA K. CHURCH. See Obituaries Section.

### HERRINGTON, PERRY LEE

Executive director, consultant, educational consultant. **Personal:** Born Mar 26, 1951, Waynesboro, GA; son of Theodore and Judy; married Janet Bailey; children: Jeffrey Bailey, Tiese, Kara & Brittany. **Educ:** Univ Chicago, Chicago, IL, cert, urban studies, 1971; Coe Col, Cedar Rapids, IA, BS, sociol, 1973; Lindenwood Col, St Louis, MO, MBA, bus admin & mgt, 1985. **Career:** Lynndale Sch, Augusta, Ga, instr educables, 1973-74; Paine Col, Augusta, Ga, dir recruitment & admis, 1974-76; Voorhees Col, Denmark, SC, dir instnl develop, 1976-78; Voorhees Col, title III coordr; Am Can Co, St Louis, Mo, labor rels assoc, 1978-87; CSRA Bus League & Augusta Minority Bus Develop Ctr, Augusta, Ga, exec dir, 1987; United Healthcare's Medicare, bus mgr, 1993-2000; Miss Valley State Univ, dir sponsored progs & title III, 2002-06; Fla Agr & Mech Univ, exec dir title III, 2006-09; Clark Atlanta Univ, dir title iii & strategic initiatives, 2009-; U.S. Dept Com, Minority Bus Develop Ctr, dir; Voorhees Tri-County Workforce Ctr, exec dir. **Orgs:** Nat Asn Advan Colored People, 1987-; bd dir & exec dir, CSRA Bus League, 1987-; bd dir & treas, Augusta Community Housing Resource Bd, 1987-; Ga Statewide Resource Network Initiative, 1990-; regional vpres, Nat Bus League, 1991-; bd dir, Ga Asn Minority Entrepreneurs, 1991-; bd dir, Augusta Mini Theatre, 1991-; title adminr, Nat Asn Hist Black Col & Univ; pres, Nat Asn HBCU Title III Adminrs, currently. **Honors/Awds:** Meritorious Service Award, Vorhees Col, 1978; Sammy Davis Jr "Yes I Can" Award, St Louis Urban League & Am Can Co, 1979-80; Regional MBDA Advocacy Award, Atlanta Regional Off, MBDA & US Dept Com, 1990; Meritorious Service Award, Lucy C Laney High Sch Voc Ed Prog, 1990. **Home Addr:** 3681 Woodcock Dr, Hephzibah, GA 30815, **Home Phone:** (404)793-9849. **Business Addr:** Director of Title III & Strategic Initiatives, Clark Atlanta University, 223 James P Brawley Dr SW, Atlanta, FL 30314, **Business Phone:** (404)880-8000.

### HERRON, BRUCE WAYNE

Executive, football player, accountant. **Personal:** Born Apr 14, 1954, Victoria, TX; married LaGuina Clay Clark; children: Monica Yvonne, Bruce Wayne Jr, Jordaya & Vance. **Educ:** Univ NMex, BA, 1977. **Career:** Football player (retired), executive; NMex Football, 1975-76; Miami Dolphins, linebacker, 1977-78; Chicago Bears, linebacker, 1978-82; Accurate Air Express, owner, 1982-83; Metro Media TV Channel 32, acct exec, 1984; Chicago State Univ, dir athletics; Waste Mgt Inc, acct exec, currently, sales exec; Invensys Plc, vpres bus develop; Grainger Terry Inc, dir talent serv. **Orgs:** Dir, Big Bros & Big Sisters; vol, Better Boys Found; hon chmn, Sicle Cell Anemia, 1982; pres, NFL Retired Players Asn; pres & bd mem, NFL Retired Players Asn. **Honors/Awds:** Man of the Year, Big Brothers & Big Sisters; Byron Wizzer White, Nat Football League Players Asn. **Home Addr:** 8504 S Calumet Ave, Chicago, IL 60619. **Business Addr:** Accountant Executive, Sale Executive, Waste Management Inc, 1001 Fannin St Suite 4000, Houston, TX 77002-6711, **Business Phone:** (713)512-6200.

### HERRON, DR. CAROLIVIA

Writer, educator, association executive. **Personal:** Born Jul 22, 1947, Washington, DC; daughter of Oscar S and Georgia C J. **Educ:** Eastern Baptist Col, St Davids, PA, BA, Eng lit, 1969; Villanova Univ, MA, eng, 1973; Univ Pa, MA, creative writing, 1985, PhD, comparative lit & lit theory, 1985. **Career:** Harvard Univ, African-Am Studies & Comparative Lit, asst prof, 1986-90; Bunting Inst fel, Radcliffe Col, 1988; Beineke Libr fel, Yale Univ, 1988; Mt Holyoke Col, assoc prof eng, 1990-92; Hebrew Col, vis scholar, 1994-95; Harvard Univ, vis scholar, 1995; Brandeis Univ, vis scholar; Carlton Col, vis scholar; Marien N'Guabi Univ, vis scholar; Hollins Univ, vis scholar; Univ Binghamton, vis scholar; Grinnell Col, vis scholar; Col William & Mary, vis scholar; Ariz State Univ, vis scholar, vis proj humanities distinguished scholar, currently; Calif St Univ, Chicago, eng prof; Random House Inc, writer; Kar-Ben, writer; Epic Ctr Stories, multimedia developer, currently; Books: Thereafter Johnnie, novel, 1991; Selected Works of Angelina Weld Grimke, 1991; Nappy Hair, 1997; Always An Olivia, 2007; Let Freedom Sing; The Story of Marian Anderson (librettist for opera, w composer Bruce Adolphe); Little Georgia and the Apples, 2012. **Orgs:** Classical Asn New Eng, 1986-93; fel Fulbright, Mex; Beinecke to Yale, Folger Shakespeare Libr Scholar; Nat Endowment Humanities Curric Develop African Am Studies; vpres, Takoma Theatre Conservancy; prog dir, Northgate Kiwanis Club; St to St. **Honors/Awds:** Fulbright Post-Doctoral Research Award, US Info Serv, 1985; Visit to Collections Award, Nat Endowment Humanities, 1987; Post-Doctoral Research Award, Folger Shakespeare Libr, 1989. **Special Achievements:** 2010 Exceptional Women in the Arts Award for Outstanding Work in the Field of Operatic Arts, from Washington, DC Councilmember Muriel Bowser. **Business Addr:** President, EpicCenter Stories, 6514 7th St NW, Washington, DC 20012, **Business Phone:** (202)829-2427.

### HERRON, VERNON M.

Consultant, clergy, administrator. **Personal:** Born Oct 7, 1928, Charlotte, NC; children: 3. **Educ:** Shaw Univ, AB, 1951; Johnson C Smith Univ, MDiv, 1958; Pa State Univ, MPA, 1978; Pittsburgh Theol Sem, DMin, 1978. **Career:** Clergy, consultant (retired), administrator; First Baptist Church, Dallas, pastor, 1952-55; Friendship Baptist Church, Pittsburgh, pastor, 1955-62; Harrisburg State Hosp, clin psychol, 1958; Allentown State Hosp, clin psychol, 1959; Hopewell Baptist, Jeannette, Pa, pastor; Second Baptist Church, Joliet, pastor, 1962-68; Mich State Univ, conf planning, 1968; Am Baptist Church HQ, asst sec div soc ministries, 1968-75; Valley Forge, strategic planning, 1969-74; Urban Training Ctr, Chicago, 1970; Valley Forge, planning prog obj, 1973, planning budget obj, 1974; Pub Progs, consult admin mgt, 1975; Shiloh Baptist Church, S Philadelphia, asst minister; St Paul's Baptist Church, W Chester, Pa, interim pastor, 1995-96. **Orgs:** Alpha Phi Alpha Frat; Prince Hall Mason; Comprehensive Geneal Serv, founder, exec dir & chief exec officer. **Special Achievements:** Authored a Book: "The Power of Tithing". **Business Addr:** Founder, Comprehensive Genealogical Services, 2510 Century Oaks Lane, Charlotte, NC 28262, **Business Phone:** (704)599-4914.

### HERRON-BRAGGS, CINDY ANN

Singer, actor. **Personal:** Born Sep 26, 1961, San Francisco, CA; married Glenn Braggs; children: 4. **Career:** En Vogue, founding mem; Albums: Born to Sing, 1990; Funky Diva", 1992; EV3, 1997; Masterpiece Theatre, 2000; The Gift of Christmas, 2002; Soul Flower, 2004; TBA, 2011; TV series: "Johnnie Mae Gibson: FBI", 1986; "Wally & the Valentines", 1989; "Roc", 1993; "On Our Own", 1994-95; "Saturday Night Live", 1992-97; "Malcolm & Eddie", 1999; "Lexie", 2004; "En Vogue Christmas", 2014. Films: Juice, 1992; Batman Forever, 1995; Deadly Rhapsody, 2001. Compilations: Best of En Vogue, 1999; Very Best of En Vogue, 2001; Hold On and Other Hits, 2005; The Essentials, 2005; The Platinum Collection, 2007; Don't Let Go: The Very Best of En Vogue, 2010. Singles: "Hold On"; " Lies"; " You Don't Have to Worry"; " Don't Go"; " Strange"; "My Lovin' (You're Never Gonna Get It)"; "Giving Him Something He Can Feel"; "Yesterday"; "Free Your Mind"; "Give It Up, Turn It Loose"; "Love Don't Love You"; "Runaway Love"; "What Is Love"; "Whatta Man"; "Don't Let Go (Love)"; " Whatever"; "Too Gone, Too Long"; "No Fool No More"; "Hold On"; "Riddle"; "Losin' My Mind"; "Ooh Boy"; Featured singles: "Freedom (Theme from Panther)"; "Free Your Mind"; "So What the Fuss"; "Glamorous". **Honors/Awds:** BillBoard Music Awards, 1990; Soul Train Music Awards, 1991 & 1993; MTV Video Music Awards, 1992-94; American Music Awards, 1993-94; Grammy Awards, Soul Train Lady of Soul Awards, 1997. **Special Achievements:** Miss San Fransisco, 1986; second runner Up in 1986 Miss california; Former Miss Black California. **Business Addr:** Singer, Triad Artists Inc, 10100 Santa Monica Blvd 16 Fl, Los Angeles, CA 90067, **Business Phone:** (213)556-2727.

### HERVEY, BILLY T.

Aerospace engineer. **Personal:** Born Apr 2, 1937, Naples, TX; married Olivia M Gray; children: Jewel, Marcus & Patrick. **Educ:** BS, 1960. **Career:** Aerospace engineer (retired); AUS Corps Engrs Ballistic Missle Off Atlus, mech engr, 1960-62; Gen Dynamics Corp, Atlas F Missile Prog Altus, mech design engr test conductor; NASA/ Johnson Space Ctr Houston; Kennedy Space Ctr Cape Kennedy, NASA & mech engr, 1964-65; Mission Control Ctr Houston Gemini & Apollo Flights, NASA flight controller, 1966-71; phys sch tech mgr; NASA, Space Shuttle Prog Off. **Orgs:** Gulf Coast Soc; Trinity United Meth Chap; Prince Hall Free & Accepted Masonry; Douglas Burrell Consistory No 56; Ancient Accepted Scottist Rite; Ancient Egyptian Arabic Order Noble of Mystic Shrine N & S Am. **Honors/Awds:** Group Achievement Award, Gemini Missions; Group Achievement Flight Oper Award; Presidential Medal Freedom Award; Apollo Xiii Mission Oper Team; Johnson Spacecraft Ctr EEO Award. **Special Achievements:** First minority MOCR flight controller during Apollo 4. **Home Addr:** 2701 Bellefontaine St Apt A30, Houston, TX 77025-1614, **Home Phone:** (713)432-0454. **Business Addr:** .

### HESTER, ARTHUR C.

Automotive executive. **Personal:** Born Mar 5, 1942, Columbus, MS; married Mae J Howard; children: Zina, Karen, Lisa & Arthur III. **Educ:** US Mil Acad, W Pt, BS, engineering, 1965; Stanford Univ, MS, indust engineering, 1970; NY Univ, MBA, finance, 1977. **Career:** Gen Motors, Tarrytown, NY, plant mgr, 1981, Arlington, plant mgr, 1989; ChB Inc, ChB Calibration Serv, exec vpres & chief operating officer, currently. **Orgs:** Trustee, Asn Grads USMA, 1970-73; Ger-Am Coun Fulda, W Ger, 1973-; bd dir, Am Youth Activ Fulda, W Ger, 1974-; Nat Asn Advan Colored People; Asn AUS; Armor Asn; Blackhorse Asn; Master Mason; Asn Black Bus Studs, NYU. **Home Addr:** 728 E 103 Pl, Chicago, IL 60628. **Business Addr:** Executive Vice President, Chief Operating Officer, Main ChB Inc, 4924 Contec Dr, Lansing, MI 48910-7101, **Business Phone:** (517)882-5035.

### HEWAN, CLINTON GEORGE

Educator. **Personal:** Born Dec 22, 1936, Montego Bay; son of Daniel and Emily; married Virginia R; children: Monique. **Educ:** Univ Cincinnati, BA, polit sci & econs, 1969, MA, foreign affairs & int rels, 1971, PhD, polit sci, 1991. **Career:** Jamaica Foreign Serv, dep ambassador, Venezuela, Peru, Columbia, 1974-79, dep ambassador, Ethiopia, Nigeria, Ghana, 1971-73, dep high comnr, 1980-84, counsellor, polit, trade & econ affairs, Protocol & Consular Div, dep dir, ministry foreign affairs; Northern Ky Univ, Polit Sci, assoc prof, 1988-. **Orgs:** Ky Can Round Table Asn, 1986-; Am Polit Sci Asn, 1988-; state bd mem, Am Civil Liberties Union, 1989-; Ky Polit Sci Asn, 1989-; head, Chancery at Jamaica High Comn Can. **Special Achievements:** Book: Jamaica and the United States Caribbean Basin Initiative: Showpiece Or Failure?, 1991. **Home Addr:** 90 Springhouse Dr, Cold Spring, KY 41076, **Home Phone:** (859)466-3238. **Business Addr:** Associate Professor, Northern Kentucky University, Nunn Dr, Highland Heights, KY 41099, **Business Phone:** (859)572-1400.

### HEWETT, HOWARD

Singer, composer. **Personal:** Born Oct 1, 1955, Akron, OH; married Mari Molina; married Angela; children: Anissa; married Nia Peeples; children: Christopher. **Career:** Mem Vocal Group Shalamar; solo artist, 1986-; Albums: I Commit to Love, 1986; Forever And Ever, 1988; Howard Hewett, 1990; Allegiance, 1992; It's Time, 1994; The Journey, 2001; The Journey Live From the Heart, 2002; Intimate, 2005; Enough, 2006; It's Time, 2006; If Only, 2007; Howard Hewett Christmas, 2008; Actor: A Fight for Glory, 2003, Musical Theater of Hope, 2009. **Honors/Awds:** Grammy, Compose for Motion Picture & TV for Beverly Hills Cop, 1985. **Business Addr:** Vocalist, c/o Elektra Records, 75 Rockefeller Plz, New York, NY 10019, **Business Phone:** (212)275-4000.

### HEWING, DR. PERNELL HAYES

Editor, educator, college teacher. **Personal:** Born May 13, 1933, St. Matthews, SC; married Joe B; children: Rita & Johnny. **Educ:** Allen Univ, Columbia, BS, 1961; Temple Univ, MA, bus, 1963; Univ Wis, Madison, PhD, bus, 1974; Int Theol Sem Calif, ThD. **Career:** Palmetto Leader Newspaper, lino typist gen printer, 1952-57; Allen Univ, Dept Printing, supv, 1958-61, instr, 1961-62; Philadelphia Tribune, lino typist, 1962-63; Allen Univ Columbia, asst prof bus, 1963-71; Palmetto Times Newspaper, woman's ed, 1963-64; Palmetto Post, Columbia, SC, mgr ed, 1970-71; Palmetto Post Weekly Newspaper, co-founder, 1970; Univ Wis, prof bus educ, 1971, prof emer, currently; Share-A-Prayer & Word Theol Sch Ministry, founder & pres; Sanctuary, owner & minister; Sanctuary Outreach Ministries, founder & dir; Church Firstborn, founder & sr pastor; Christian Int Apostolic Network Churches, coordr. **Orgs:** Nat Bus Educ, 1950; Sigma Gamma Rho Sorority, 1962; Pi Lambda Theta Nat Hon & Prof Asn Women Educ, 1972; Develop Chap, Univ Wis, Madison, 1973; Wis Coord Coun Women Higher Educ; Delta Pi Epsilon Hon Bus Orgn; Am Bus Commun Asn; founder & dir, Avant-Garde Cult & Develop Orgn; Asn Bus Commun. **Home Addr:** 921 W Main St, Whitewater, WI 53190-1706, **Home Phone:** (262)473-7472. **Business Addr:** Professor Emeritus, University Wisconsin, 800 W Main St, Whitewater, WI 53190-1790, **Business Phone:** (262)472-1234.

### HEWITT, REV. BASIL

Clergy. **Personal:** Born Jan 31, 1926, Colon; married May Shirley; children: Nidia, Gloria & Chris. **Educ:** Kent Southern Col, BA, 1969; Southern Baptist Theol Sem, MDiv, 1973. **Career:** Clergy (retired); Fifth St Baptist Church, asst pastor, 1967-73; Emmanuel Baptist Church, pastor, 1973-91. **Orgs:** Secy, Laurel Clergy Asn, 1974-75; exec comt, Citizen's Adv Coun Pkwy; Evangel Theol Soc; Bethany Baptist Church. **Special Achievements:** Author: The Cosmic Struggle of Redemption of God's Own People, 2002; Revelations of the Divine Plan of the Ages: It's Time to Wake Up, 2007. **Home Addr:** 11299 Laurel Walk Dr, Laurel, MD 20708, **Home Phone:** (301)776-4870.

### HEWITT, CHRISTOPHER HORACE

Football coach, football player. **Personal:** Born Jul 22, 1974, Kingston; married Tanisha La; children: Azia, Briana, Christina & Christopher. **Educ:** Cincinnati Univ, attended 1996. **Career:** Football player (retired) football coach; New Orleans Saints, defensive back, 1997-99; Rutgers Scarlet Knights Football Team, corner back coach, 2008-09, running back coach, 2010-11; Baltimore Ravens, asst coach, 2012-15.

### HEWITT, RONALD JEROME

Executive. **Personal:** Born Oct 31, 1932, Welch, WV; married Deanna Cowan; children: Ronald Jr, Kevin, Robert, Jonathan, Mkonto & Mwanaisha. **Educ:** Fisk Univ, BA, 1955. **Career:** Detroit Housing Comn, supt opers, 1969, asst dir, 1971, dir, 1973; Comm & Econ Develop Detroit, exec dep dir, 1974, dir, 1974-79; Mayor Coleman A Young, exec asst, 1979-; DPT Transp, dir, 1982-85; Detroit Planning Dept, dir, 1985-. **Orgs:** Downtown Dev Authority; Detroit Econ Develop Corp; Ford Councl Urban Econ Develop; CORD; SE MI Coun Govt; Detroit Financial Ctr Task Force; Mus AFA Hist; Greater Detroit Econ Develop Group; bd dir, Detroit Foreign Trade Zone; Detroit Econ Growth Corp; Detroit-Wayne Port Authority liaison; bd mem, Metrop Ctr High Technol, 1985-; bd mem, Local Iniatives Support Corp, 1989-; Detroit Munic Credit Union; Tanahill Soc; Shrine Black Madonna Church; mem bd dir, Charles Wright Mus African Am Hist; Detroit Munic Credit Union; Detroit Area Agency Aging. **Home Addr:** 9340 LaSalle Blvd, Detroit, MI 48206. **Business Addr:** Director, Detroit Planning Department, 2300 Cadillac Twr, Detroit, MI 48226, **Business Phone:** (313)224-6389.

### HEWITT, VIVIAN ANN DAVIDSON

Association executive, librarian. **Personal:** Born Feb 17, 1920, New Castle, PA; daughter of Arthur Robert Davidson and Lela Luvada Mauney Davidson; married John Hamilton Jr; children: John Hamilton III. **Educ:** Geneva Col, BA, 1943; Carnegie Mellon Univ, BS, LS, 1944; Univ Pittsburgh, Grad Stud, 1948. **Career:** Librarian (retired); Carnegie Libr Pittsbgh, sr asst libr, 1943-49; Atlanta Univ Sch Libr Sci, instr & librn, 1949-52; Crowell-Colier Publ Co, researcher asst dir, 1953-55; Rockefeller Found, librn, 1955-63; Mex Agr Prog, Rockefeller Found, librn, 1958; Carnegie Endowment Int Peace Coun Foreign Rels, chief librn, 1963-83; Katharine Gibbs Sch, dir libr info servs, 1984-86; Univ Tex, Grad Sch Libr & Info, fac, 1985; Coun Foreign Rels, ref asst, 1987-88; Hewitt Art Collection, founder. **Orgs:** Librn, Carnegie Endowment Int Peace, 1963-83; exec com & sec bd, Graham-Windham Child Care & Adoption Agency, 1969-87; pres, Spec Libr Asn, 1978-79; exec com & secy, Laymens Club Cathedral St John Divine NY; Order St John Jerusalem; Alpha Kappa Alpha; Tower Soc; Geneva Col; Ctr Bks First Nat Adv Bd. **Honors/Awds:** LHD, Geneva Col, 1978; Distinguished Alumni Award, Carnegie-Mellon Univ, 1979; Distinguished Alumni Award, Univ Pittsburgh, 1979; Distinguished Service Award, Black Caucus Am Libr Asn, 1979; Hall of Fame, Spec Libr Asn, 1984; BCALA Leadership in the Profession Award, 1993; Leadership Award, Black Alumni, Carnegie Mellon, 2001; Black Caucus, Am Libr Asn. **Special Achievements:** Pittsburgh's First African-American librarian; First African-American president of the Special Libraries Association 1979; Author of an autobiographical history of her remarkable life, called The One and Only. First African American librarian to work at the Carnegie Library of Pittsburgh. **Home Addr:** 862 W End Ave, New York, NY 10025, **Home Phone:** (212)865-1256.

### HEWLETT, ANTOINETTE PAYNE

Government official. **Personal:** Born Martinsburg, WV; children: Adora. **Educ:** WVa State Col, BA; Columbia Univ, MA, 1961. **Career:** Jefferson Co, teacher, 1960; San Francisco Redevelop, relocation asst, 1962-66; Oakland Redevelop, planner & reloc supvr, 1967-76, dir; City Oakland, dir community devel, 1976-, asst agency dir, 1997; Off Housing & Neighborhood Devel, dir, 1995. **Orgs:** Oakland Mus Asn; Friends Ethnic Art; Nat Forum Black Pub Admin; Am Soc Pub Admin; Nat Asn Housing & Redevel Officials; Community Club CA; bd dir, Nat Community Devel Asn, 1984-. **Home Addr:** 641 Valle Vista Ave, Oakland, CA 94610, **Home Phone:** (510)763-0932.

### HEWLETT, DR. DIAL, JR.

Physician. **Personal:** Born Jul 26, 1948, Cleveland, OH; son of Dial and Lydia; married Janice M Chance; children: Kwasi, Tiffany, Whitney Joy & Brandon. **Educ:** Univ Wis, Madison; Univ Wis, Sch Med, MD, 1976. **Career:** Harlem Hosp Ctr, internship & resident, 1976-80; Harlem Hosp Ctr, chief med residency, 1979-80; Montefiore Hosp & Albert Einstein Col Med, fel infectious dis, 1980-82; Our Lady Mercy Med Ctr, Bronx, NY, chief infec dis sec, 1984-91; Calvary Hosp, Bronx, NY, consult, 1985-; Lawrence Hosp, Bronxville, NY, consult, 1988-; NY Med Col, assoc prof clin med, 1990-96; Mentor Mag, health ed, 1994-96; Hosp Physicians J, ed bd. **Orgs:** Am Soc Microbiol; Infectious Dis Soc Am; Am Col Physicians; NY Acad Sci; Nat Med Soc. **Honors/Awds:** Physician Humanitarian Award, Nilda Lebron Memorial Found, 1992; Excellence in Teaching Awards, NY Med Col, 1992 & 1993; Distinguished Teaching Award, NY Med Col, 1996. **Home Addr:** 95 Ralph Rd, New Rochelle, NY 10804, **Home Phone:** (914)235-4361. **Business Addr:** Physician, 1740 Eastchester Rd, Bronx, NY 10461-2300, **Business Phone:** (914)330-3747.

### HEWLETT, EVERETT AUGUSTUS, JR.

Lawyer, county commissioner. **Personal:** Born Mar 27, 1943, Richmond, VA; son of Everett A Sr (deceased); married Clothilde. **Educ:** Am Univ, Wash, DC, attended 1964; Dickinson Col, Carlisle, Pa, BA, 1965; Golden Gate Univ Law Sch, San Francisco, Calif, JD, 1975. **Career:** Univ Calif, Berkeley, Calif, writer-ed, 1970-75; Bayview-Hunters Pt Comn Defender, San Francisco, Calif, staff atty, 1976-80; Pvt Law Pract, atty, 1980-86; San Francisco Super Ct, ct comnr, 1986-2011, Juv Ct, 1987-91, Civil Trial Dept, 1996-97, Civil Discovery Dept, 1997-2010, Gen Civil Dept, 2010-, Community Justice Ct, 2011-. **Orgs:** Bd dirs, SF Neighborhood Legal Asst Found, 1979-; hearing officer, SF Residl Rent Stabilization & Arbit Bd, 1980-82; bd dir, Calif Asn Black Lawyers, 1980-; vpres, Couniers W, 1980; parliamentarian, Wm Hastie Bar Asn, 1980-86; Charles Houston Bar Asn, 1981-; State Bar Comn Legal Specialization, 1982; pres, William Hastie Bar Asn, 1984; vchmn, SF Neighborhood Legal Asst Found, 1984; Calif State Bar Legal Serv Trust Fund Comn, 1984-85. **Honors/Awds:** Editor of Best Newspaper in its class, USAF & Nakhon Phanom, 1967, 1968. **Home Addr:** 419 Crestmont Dr, San Francisco, CA 94131-1018, **Home Phone:** (415)566-5237.

### HEYWARD, REV. DR. ISAAC

Media executive, president (organization), executive. **Personal:** Born Apr 30, 1935, Charleston, SC; son of Rev St Julian (deceased) and Chrestina Capers; children: Regina Vermel (deceased) & Bryant Isaac. **Educ:** Radio Broadcast Inst, New York, NY, cert, 1967; Morris Col, Sch Relig, Orangeburg Exten, cert, 1975. **Career:** WHBI Radio, Newark, NJ, prog announcer & sales mgr, 1965-67; WRNW Radio, Mt Kisco, NY, announcer & dir, 1967-71; WQIZ Radio, St George, SC, announcer & sales mgr, 1971-85; Midland Commun Co, pres, WTGH Radio, Cayce, SC, announcer, sales mgr, gen sales, sta mgr & pres, currently. **Orgs:** Assoc ordained minister, St Paul Baptist Church, Orangeburg, SC, 1971; Gospel Music Workshop Am, 1974; Nat Asn Advan Colored People, SC Br, 1974; Baptist Assn, Orangeburg SC, 1985; fel Boy Scouts Am Coun, 1986; bd mem, Savannah Asn Blind, Nat Fed Blind. **Honors/Awds:** Second Runner-up DJ, Gospel of the Year, Lamb Records, 1978; Best Radio Gospel Prog, Lee's Publ, 1979; Gospel Prom, Gospel Workshop Am, 1982; Community Serv, Am Cancer Soc, 1982, 1983; Living Legacy, Nat Coun Negro Women, 1984; Boy Scouts of Am Service, 1986; Honorary Doctor, Christian Ministry, CE Graham Baptist Bible Sem, 1996. **Home Addr:** 1343 Cactus Ave, Columbia, SC 29210, **Home Phone:** (803)776-2387. **Business Addr:** President, Midland Communications Co, 1303 State St, Cayce, SC 29033, **Business Phone:** (803)796-9533.

### HEYWARD, JAMES OLIVER

Educator, army officer, college administrator. **Personal:** Born Jul 17, 1930, Sumter, SC; son of Julian H Sr (deceased) and Lue (deceased); married Willie Mae Thompson; children: James O Jr, Julian & Edward. **Educ:** SC State Univ, BS, 1953; Armed Forces Staff Col, attended 1969; Shippensburg State Univ, MA, 1972. **Career:** Educator (retired), Army Officer (retired); AUS, dep comdr mil comdr, 1974-75; Cmdr Training & Doctrine Command Field Element, 1976-79; Ala A&M Univ, prof mil sci, 1979-83, dir admin. **Orgs:** Am Asn Col Registrars & Admin Officers; Equal Opportunity Comt, 1986-87; Phi Delta Kappa; life mem, Nat Advan Asn Colored People; chap vpres, pres & area dir, Alpha Phi Alpha, 1984-92; Human Rels Coun Huntsville Ala; chmn, Huntsville Citizens Police, qual coun, 1992-94; Steward Bd, secy, St John Am Church. **Home Addr:** 747 Bluewood Dr SE, Huntsville, AL 35802, **Home Phone:** (256)881-7999.

### HEYWARD-GARNER, ILENE PATRICIA

Executive, manager. **Personal:** Born Apr 9, 1948, Plainfield, NJ; daughter of William W Nesbitt Jr and Bonlyn Pitts Nesbitt; children: Eric Eugene. **Educ:** Fairleigh Dickinson Univ, BS, chem & math, 1976; NY Univ, MS, chem, 1988; George Washington Univ, master cert, proj mgt, 1995. **Career:** AT&T Bell Labs, tech assoc, 1976-77, sr tech assoc, 1977-79, assoc mem tech staff, 1979-81, tech mgr, 1981-94, div mgr, 1994-97, gen mgr; Parcel Plus, owner; Univ VI, Community & Personal Develop Unit, dir, Community Engagement & Lifelong Learning Ctr, dir, currently. **Orgs:** AAAS, 1982-; Plainfield Teen Proj, 1989-97; Alliance Black Telecommunications Employees Inc, 1990-

95; adv coun, Nat Black United Fund, 1991-94; bd mem, Big Brors Big Sisters Essex County, 1992-93; bd, treas, Beacon Sch, 1997; Proj Mgt Inst; Am Mgt Asn; Strategic Planning Steering Comt, Univ VI. **Honors/Awds:** Honor, Bell Communications Res, 1985; AT&T Architecture Award, 1992; African American Biography Hall of Fame, 1993. **Special Achievements:** Author and co-author, many articles in technical journals such as ACS and Journal of the Soc Plastic Engrs 1976-; author, chap in ACS Symposium Monograph Series 1985; featured in cover story of Black Enterprise 1985; featured in UnFold, 1999. **Home Phone:** (340)714-1408. **Business Addr:** Director of Community & Personal Development, Principal Investigator, University of the Virgin Islands, 2 John Brewers Bay, St. Thomas00802, **Business Phone:** (340)693-1101.

## HEYWOOD, ANTHONY
Executive. **Orgs:** Exec dir, Mt Hope Child Care Ctr. **Business Addr:** Executive director, Mt Hope Day Care Center, 438 Hope St, Providence, RI 02906, **Business Phone:** (401)521-7252.

## HIATT, DANA SIMS
School administrator, executive director, lawyer. **Personal:** Born Chickasha, OK; daughter of William Edward Sims and Muriel Crowell Sims; married James H. **Educ:** Langston Univ, BA, hist, 1968; Univ Kans Sch Law, JD, 1971. **Career:** RH Smith Community, Chicago, Ill, Okla City, Okla, law fel, 1971-73; City Okla, asst munic atty, 1974; Darrell, Bruce, Johnson & Sims Asn, pvt pract law, 1975-77; Colo State Univ, teaching asst black hist, Off vpres Acad Affairs, info specialist, title IX coordr, cncltn officer, 1979-82, Off Equal Opportunity & Diversity, dir; R H Smith Law fel; Denver Chap, Links Inc. **Orgs:** Am Asn Univ Women; Am Asn Affrim Action; dir, Higher Educ Affirm Action; pub affairs chair, Jr League Ft Collins, 1991-92. **Honors/Awds:** Outstandng Young Woman, Zeta Phi Beta Sorority, Okla City, OK, 1975. **Special Achievements:** First African American to become the assistant municipal attorney for the city of Oklahoma City; One of 100 nationally selected Reginald Heber Smith Community Law Fellows. **Home Addr:** 1701 Collindale Dr, Fort Collins, CO 80525-5724, **Home Phone:** (970)226-3243. **Business Addr:** Director, Colorado State University, 104A Stud Serv Bldg, Fort Collins, CO 80523-1016, **Business Phone:** (970)491-5836.

## HIATT, DIETRAH
Journalist, counselor. **Personal:** Born Sep 23, 1944, Washington, DC; married Robert Terry; children: Stephanie Gail & Benjamin Jesse. **Educ:** Howard Univ, BA, 1965. **Career:** US Peace Corps Vol Rep Panama, 1965-67; DC Dept Pub Assistance, social serv rep caseworker, 1968-70; Pierre-Ft Pierre Head Start Prog, vol teachers asst, 1973-74; Huron SD Daily Plainsman, reporter, 1973-74; Nyoda Girl Scout Coun, brownie ldr resource person, 1976-77; Pierre Indian Learning Ctr, sch counr; Sen George Mc govern, comm rep; Pierre Times, ed columnist, currently. **Orgs:** Am Asn Univ Women, 1972-74; treas, Short Grass Arts Coun, 1974-75; vpres, Nat Orgn Women Cent SD Chap, 1975-; Dem Party Precinct Woman, 1976-; chairperson, Hughes Co Dem Comt; co-chaiperson, Cand Task Force SD Womens Caucus; Nat Abortion Rights Action League; State Prof Pract & Stand Comn, Dept Educ & Cult Affairs; Alpha Kappa Alpha. **Honors/Awds:** Nominated Outstanding Young Woman of Am, 1973, 1977; Cand, Pierre Sch Bd, 1976; Cand, SD State Senate, 1978. **Special Achievements:** Choreographed & performed rev of dance & history for AAUW Cultural Study Group 1973; Performed in modern & native Am dance recital for Arts Festival arts workshop 1973. **Home Addr:** 3833 11th Ave S, Minneapolis, MN 55407-2629, **Home Phone:** (651)822-8686. **Business Addr:** 817 S Illinois Ave 26, Mason City, IA 50401-5487.

## HIBBERT, DOROTHY LASALLE
Educator. **Personal:** Born Sep 17, 1923, New York, NY; daughter of Arthur Hilbert Sr and Lily Roper. **Educ:** Hunter Col, BA, 1945; Teachers Col, Columbia Univ, MA, 1949; City Col, grad div, PD, 1983; Walden Univ, MN, doc, educ, 1991. **Career:** Educator (retired); Bd Educ NY, PS 186, teacher, 1947-59, High Sch 136, math teacher, 1959-68, PS 146 & 36, asst prin, 1969-79, PS 138, actg interim prin, 1979-81, PS 93, asst prin, 1981-85, PS 146, prin, 1985-90; Col New Rochelle, instr, 1990. **Orgs:** Vpres, Int League Human Rights, 1976-86; secy, Int League Human Rights, 1987; planning partic, NY State Conf Status Women; secy, Am Comn Africa 1979-; asst examr, Bd Examrs, 1982; conf chair, Bronx Reading Coun, 1985; Nat Asn Advan Colored People; Asn Black Educrs, NY, 1986. **Home Addr:** 90 Meucci Ave, Copiague, NY 11726-2804, **Home Phone:** (631)842-5764.

## HIBBERT, LAWRENCE M.
Executive, president (organization), business owner. **Personal:** Born Brooklyn, NY; son of George and Melida; married Patrell; children: Caleb Joseph & Joshua Christopher. **Educ:** Rutgers Univ, Sch Engineering, BS, mech engineering, 1995; Rutgers Bus Sch, MBA, finance. **Career:** Merrill Lynch Pvt Client Archit Grp, asst vpres & network servs mgr; Gen Elec, wired area network engr; AMP Inc; Access One Corp, founder & mng partner; MBS Educ Serv & Trng, founder & mng partner; Rutgers African-Am Alumni Alliance, web commun chair; BCT Partners Inc, founder, pres & chief technol officer, currently. **Orgs:** Small Bus Develop Sub comt Econ Develop; bd mem, NJ Pub Policy Res Inst; deacon, technol adv & proud mem, First Baptist Church Lincoln Gardens. **Business Addr:** Founder, President & Chief Technology Officer, BCT Partners Inc, 105 Lock St Suite 203, Newark, NJ 07103, **Business Phone:** (973)622-0900.

## HICKLIN, DR. FANNIE FRAZIER
Educator, administrator, curator. **Personal:** Born Talladega, AL; daughter of Willie Pulliam and Demus; children: Ariel Yvonne Ford. **Educ:** Talladega Col, BA, 1939; Univ Mich, MA; Univ Wis, Madison, PhD. **Career:** Educator (retired); Magnolia Ave HS, Avery Inst, Burke HS, Tuskegee Inst, Ala A & M Col, Univ Wis, Madison, teacher; Univ Wis, Whitewater, fac mem, 1964-88, assoc dean faculties, 1974-88, dir affirmative action, Theatre/Dance Dept, chair. **Orgs:** Pres & mem, State Hist Soc Wis Bd Curs; Cent States Commun Asn; Speech Comm Asn; Alpha Kappa Alpha; Friendship Force Wis; Kappa Psi Omega Chap Alpha Kappa Alpha Socs. **Special Achievements:** First African-American faculty member on University of Wisconsin-Whitewater. **Home Addr:** 3814 Univ Ave, Madison, WI 53705-2145, **Home Phone:** (608)233-5748.

## HICKMAN, ELNOR B. G.
Association executive, secretary (office). **Personal:** Born Jan 31, 1930, Jackson, MS; daughter of Lerone Sr and Alma Reed Bennett; married Caloway; children: Thelma B McDowell, Marshall L Bennett & Shirley L Bennett. **Educ:** Loop Jr Col, AA, 1975. **Career:** Secretary (retired); Legal Assistance Found Metrop Chicago, legal secy, admin supvr & exec secy. **Orgs:** Int dir, Prof Secretaries Int, Great Lakes Dist, 1988-90, int sec, 1990-91, vpres, 1991-92, vpres, 1992-93, int pres, 1994-95; pres, Int Asn Admin Prof, Chicago Lake Chap, Ill-Div, 1987-88; bd dir, Int Asn Admin Prof, Chicago Lake Chap, Ill Div. **Special Achievements:** First Black President of Professional Secretaries International; Cert Prof Secy Rating, 1977; One of 100 Women Making a Difference, Today's Chicago Women, 1995. **Home Addr:** 501 W 24th Pl Apt 907, Chicago, IL 60616-1898, **Home Phone:** (312)225-8045.

## HICKMAN, FREDERICK DOUGLASS (FRED HICKMAN)
Broadcaster. **Personal:** Born Oct 17, 1956, Springfield, IL; son of George Henry (deceased) and Louise Winifred (deceased); married Judith Tillman; children: Mack; married Sheila Bowers; children: 2. **Educ:** Coe Col, Cedar Rapids, Iowa, BA, sociol, 1978. **Career:** KCOE radio Cedar Rapids, Iowa, music dir, 1976; KLWW Radio, Cedar Rapids, Iowa, news anchor, 1977; WFMB-FM Radio, Springfield, Ill, news & sports anchor, 1977-78; WICS-TV, sports dir, 1978-80; CNN Broadcasting, Atlanta, Ga, sports anchor, reporter, 1980-84; WDIV-TV, Detroit, Mich, sportscaster/commentator, beat reporter Detroit Tigers, 1984-86; CNN/Turner Broadcasting, sportscaster/commentator, 1986; WALR-FM, sports dir, 1992; Yes Network; New York Yankees Nets studio host, New York, Stamford, Conn, E Rutherford, Nj, 2001-04; ESPN Sports Ctr Host, reporter, NBA KIA pre-game host, Baseball Tonight host, ESPN Classic host, 2004-09; master ceremonies, speaker & guest panelist; Fox Sports S, Braves Live pre & post game show host, 2009-10; Fred Hickman Commun Inc, founder; WVUE, sports dir, 2011-. **Orgs:** Butkus Awards Voting Comt, 1991-; Ga State Univ Athletic Asn Bd; life mem, Downtown Athletic Club Orlando. **Honors/Awds:** Cable ACE Award Winner, 1989 &1993; "Sexiest Sportscaster", US TV Fan Asn, 1993. **Special Achievements:** Cable ACE award winner, 1989 & 1993; named "sexiest sportscaster", U.S. Television Fan Association, 1993; New York Sports Emmy winner, 2004; Springfield Sports Hall of Fame, 2007; Southeast Regional Emmy Winner, 2011. **Home Addr:** PO Box 18977, Atlanta, GA 31126, **Home Phone:** (404)505-1421. **Business Addr:** Sports Director, Fox 8 WVUE-TV, 1025 S Jefferson Davis Pkwy, New Orleans, LA 70125, **Business Phone:** (504)486-6161.

## HICKMAN, GARRISON M.
Educator. **Personal:** Born Jan 14, 1945, Washington, DC; married Cynthia Burrowes; children: Michael Barrington. **Educ:** Va Union Univ, BA, 1967; Howard Univ, Mdiv, 1971. **Career:** Neighborhood Youth Corps Dept Defense, teacher counr, 1967-68; Wash Concentrated Employ Prog, 1968-70; DC City Govt, counr 1971; Stud Affairs & Affirmative Action Capital Univ & Abiding Saviour Lutheran Church, assoc dean. **Orgs:** Nat Col Hon Soc; coord com, Nat Crises Conf Inner City Ministries; nat sec, Conf Inner City Ministries, 1973-74; Ohio reg chmn Coord Com Nat Crisis 1973-75; Coalition Minority Prof Am Lutheran Ch Col & Univ, 1974-75; Nat Chmn Conf Inner City Ministries, 1975-76; Am Asn Higher Edn; Nat Pres Am Asn Affirmative Action, 1976-77. **Home Addr:** 2633 Mock Rd, Columbus, OH 43219. **Business Addr:** Associate Dean, Capital University Huntington Hall, 2199 E Main St, Columbus, OH 43209, **Business Phone:** (614)236-6011.

## HICKS, DR. ARTHUR JAMES
Educator, association executive, writer. **Personal:** Born Feb 26, 1938, Jackson, MS; son of A R and Julia M; married Pearlie Mae Little; children: Arnetta Renee & Roselyn Marie. **Educ:** Tougaloo Col, BS, 1960; Univ Ill, PhD, 1971; Harvard Univ, attended 1989; Lilly Endowment Lib Arts Workshop, Col, 1992. **Career:** Grenada City Sch, biol & gen sci teacher, chmn sci div, 1960-64; Univ Ga, Bot Dept, asst prof, 1971-77; Mo Bot Gardens, NEA postdoctoral fel, 1976; Nat Sci Found, vis grants officer, 1987; NC Agr & Tech State Univ, Biol Dept, cur, prof & chmn, 1977-88, dean, Col Arts & Scis, Prog dir, 1988-. **Orgs:** Am Inst Biol Sci; Am Soc Plant Taxonomists; Asn SE Biologists; Bot Soc Am; NC Acad Sci; Intern Asn Plant Taxonomists; Miss Acad Sci; Sigma Xi; Torrey Bot Club; past co-pres Gaines Sch PTA Athens, 1973-74; bd dir, NE Girl Scouts Am, 1977; bd trustee, Hill First Bapt Church Athens, 1977; Swim Bd Gov Athens Pk & Rec Dist Athens, 1977; Natural Areas Adv Comt NC Dept Natural Resources & Comt Develop, 1978; adv bd, Guilford Co NC Environ Qual, 1979-87; Nat Inst Health Extramural Asn, 1982; Alpha Phi Alpha; bd trustee, Nat Wildflower Res Ctr, 1991-93; Greensboro Beautiful & Greensboro Bog Garden, 1992-. **Honors/Awds:** Hon mem, Beta Kappa Chi Sci Hon Soc, 1960; senior biology Award, Tougaloo Col, 1960; NSF Summer Fellowship SIU Carbondale, 1961; Univ Illinois Botany Fellowship Urbana, 1968-69; So Fellowship Found Fund fel, Univ Ill Urbana, 1969-71; NEA fel, Missouri Botanical Garden St Louis, 1975-76; Faculty Award, Excellence Sci & Tech, White House Initiative Historically Black Cols & Univs, 1988. **Special Achievements:** Author: "Apomixis in Xanthium?" Watsonia, 1975 "Plant Mounting Problem Overcomewith the Use of Self-Adhesive Plastic Covering" Torreya, 1976; co-auth, A Bibliography Plant Collection & Herbarium Curation. **Home Addr:** 6 Crossfield Ct, Greensboro, NC 27408-6741, **Home Phone:** (336)292-0953. **Business Addr:** Program Director Alliances for Minority Participation, North Carolina Agricultural & Technical State University, 1601 E Market St, Greensboro, NC 27411, **Business Phone:** (919)334-7806.

## HICKS, AUGUSTA M. GALE
Nurse. **Personal:** Born Feb 14, 1941, Ruston, LA; daughter of Perry; children: Byron Barrington Berry. **Educ:** Provident Hosp & Training Sch, attended 1963; Gov State Univ, BSN, 1979; Univ Ill Med Ctr, MPH, 1981. **Career:** Vis Nurse Asn Greater Lynn, dir staff develop, 1991-92; REW Home Health, dir clinical serv, 1992-93; Prof Med Enterprises, clinical dir, 1993-95; Blue Cross/Blue Shield MA, case mgr, 1996. **Orgs:** Am Cancer Soc. **Honors/Awds:** Women of Distinction Award, 1995; She Knows Where She's Going Award, Girls, Inc, 1997; Women of Hope Award, Am Cancer Asn, 1997; Community Service Award, Blue Cross/Blue Shield MA, 1998; Continous Service & The Fight Against Breast Cancer, Am Cancer Society, 1998. **Special Achievements:** Author: "How I Coped With the Number One Killer of Black Women", Ebony, 1979; Published book, Older Than My Mother. **Home Addr:** 66 Fernview Ave, North Andover, MA 01845, **Home Phone:** (978)685-7657. **Business Addr:** Case Manager, Blue Cross Blue Shield MA, 25 Newport Ave Ext, Quincy, MA 02171-1754, **Business Phone:** (800)392-0098.

## HICKS, BRIAN L. See HICKS, SKIP LAVELL.

## HICKS, DR. CLAYTON NATHANIEL
School administrator, association executive, optometrist. **Personal:** Born May 2, 1943, Columbus, OH; son of Amos Nathaniel and Augusta Louvenia; married Patricia Larkins. **Educ:** Ohio State Univ, BS, 1964, OD, 1970. **Career:** Ohio Dept Health, microbiologist, 1965-70; Ohio State Univ, Col Optom, clin instr, 1970-; Driving Pk Vision Ctr, owner, optometrist, 1970-; Ohio Dept Human Servs, optom consult, 1977-; Nat Optom Asn, pres, meeting & conf planner, 1984-, consult, 1989-, exec dir NOF, currently; Outcomes Mgt Group Ltd, partner & vpres mkt, 1995-. **Orgs:** Pres, Columbus Panhellenic Coun, 1975-80; Columbus Inner City Lions Club, 1977-80; bd dir, Neighborhood House Inc, 1979-81; Martin Luther King Holiday Observance Comn, 1981-83; Alpha Phi Alpha Fraternity, 1981-83; Nat Optom Asn, 1983-85; bd dir, meeting planner, Nat Coalition Black Meeting Planners, 1983-2012; Driving Pk Ment Health Comn, 1984; consult, Annette Cosmetiques, 1989-; exec dir, Alpha Rho Lambda Educ Found, 1989-; Livingston Ave Collab Community Develop. **Honors/Awds:** Outstanding Service Award, Alpha Phi Alpha Fraternity, 1981; Optometrist of the Year, Nat Optometric Asn, 1983; Citizen of the Week, WCKX Radio, 1986; Outstanding Alumni Award, Ohio State Univ, 1995; Distinguished Leadership Community Award, Driving Park Area CMS, 1999; Outstanding Service Award, APA, 1999; Human Service Award, AKA, 2002; Community Building Award, Gov Bob Taft, 2003; Political Leadership Award, 29th Dist Citizens Caucus. **Home Addr:** 6283 Alissa Lane, Columbus, OH 43213-3456, **Home Phone:** (614)864-8189. **Business Addr:** Executive Director NOF, National Optometric Association, 1489 Livingston Ave, Columbus, OH 43205-2931, **Business Phone:** (614)253-5593.

## HICKS, D'ATRA
Singer, actor, executive. **Personal:** Born Sep 21, 1974, Bronx, NY; daughter of Edna; married Loren Dawson; children: 1. **Career:** Several commercials, music videos, theatre appearances; Albums: D'Atra Hicks, 1989; This Time, 1997; The Godess is Here, 2003. Singles: "Ooh, Ooh Baby", 1996; "Distant Lover", 1997; "Silly", 1998; "How Can I Get Over You", 1998. Films: A Bronx Tale, 1993; Just Cause, 1995; The Preacher's Wife, 1996; Belly, 1998; The Salon, 2005; Humenetomy, 2007; Aunt Bam's Place, 2012; The Hilltop Barbershop, 2014; The Hills, 2016; TV series: "Educating Matt Waters", 1996; "SUBWAYStories: Tales from the Underground", 1997; "100 Centre Street", 2002; "Soul Food", 2003. **Orgs:** Am Fedn Tv & Radio Artists; Screen Actors Guild; Am Soc Composers, Authors & Publishers. **Honors/Awds:** Toured extensively in Japan; NAACP Image Award Nominee, 1989; New York City Music Award Nominee, 1989. **Special Achievements:** Two Top 10 Records in Japan. **Business Addr:** Actor, Capitol Records Inc, 1750 N Vine St, Hollywood, CA 90028, **Business Phone:** (323)462-6252.

## HICKS, DORIS ASKEW
School administrator, teacher. **Personal:** Born May 24, 1926, Sulphur Springs, TX; married George P; children: Sherra Daunn Chappelle. **Educ:** Butler Col, AA, 1946; Bishop Col, BA, 1948; Univ Tex, MLS, 1959. **Career:** Quit man Independent Sch Dist, teacher, 1950-52; Naples Independent Sch Dist, teacher librn, 1952-54; Bowie Co Common & Independent Sch, multi sch librn, 1654-62; Macedonia Sch Dist Texarkana, sch librn, 1962-69; Rochester City Sch Dist Rochester, sch librn, 1969-73; Rochester City Sch Dist, Rochester, NY, dir learning resources, 1973-81; Largo Community Church, co-chairperson, currently. **Orgs:** Vpres, Sch Libr Media Sect, NY Libr Asn; vpres, Sch Libr Media Sect, NY Libr Asn; pres & unit vice chmn, Am Asn Sch Librn, ALA, 1979-80; Mt Olivet Baptist Church Scholar Com, 1976-; bd mem, Hillside C's Ctr, 1977-81; chair fel Com Rochester Chap Zonta Int, 1979-80; vpres, Prince George's MD Chap Links Inc, 1993-97; chmn, libr comt, Largo Comt Church, 1994-; co chairperson, Mature Singles. **Honors/Awds:** Sch Library & Media Program Year, Am Asn Sch Librarians, 1975. **Home Addr:** 3812 Sunflower Cir, Mitchellville, MD 20721-2467, **Home Phone:** (301)464-1943. **Business Addr:** Co-Chairpersons, Largo Community Church, 1701 Enterprise Rd, Mitchellville, MD 20721, **Business Phone:** (301)249-2255.

## HICKS, DORIS MORRISON
Government official. **Personal:** Born Jun 19, 1933, St. Marys, GA; daughter of Eleazar and Renetta Jenkins; married Samuel; children: Barbara Caughman & Sheryl Stokes. **Educ:** Savannah State Col, Ga, attended 1950, BS, 1954, cert, 1959. **Career:** US Postal Serv, Savannah, Ga, distrib clerk, 1966-72, LSM operator, 1972-74, exam clerk, 1974-77, exam spec, 1977-79; training tech, 1974-79; US Postal Serv, Ridgeland, SC, postmaster, 1979-. **Orgs:** Ed, MSC Newsletter, US Postal Serv, 1975-86; Postal Life Adv Bd, US Postal Serv, 1980-82; chairperson, Women's Prog, US Postal Serv, 1979-83; Rev & Selection Comt, US Postal Serv, 1986-. **Honors/Awds:** Certificate & Award, Savannah Asn Retarded C, 1972, 1974; Letter of Commendation, Equal Employ Coun US Postal Serv, 1972; Letter of Commendation, Southern Region, US Postal Serv, 1976; Certificate& Award, Postal Life US Postal Serv, 1981; Outstanding Achievement, Savannah Women's Prog, US Postal Serv, 1986. **Home Addr:** 510 W 45th St, Savannah, GA 31405, **Home Phone:** (912)236-7979. **Business Addr:** Postmaster, US Postal Service, 406 Main St Fed Bldg, Ridgeland, SC 29936, **Business Phone:** (803)726-5528.

## HICKS, EDITH A.

Government official, school administrator, school principal. **Personal:** Born Sep 6, 1939, Barnwell, SC; married James Adams; children: Ronald, Curtis, Craig, Paul, Paula & Kevin. **Educ:** Antioch Col, BA, 1974, MA, 1976. **Career:** Bd Educ, para prof, 1967-69, asst prin; Morrisania Comn Corp, training specialist, 1969-70; Community Sch Bd, exec asst, 1975-77; Touro Col, adj prof; Col New Rochelle, instr. **Orgs:** Vpres, Community Sch Bd NY; female dist leader, 78th Assembly Dist NY; chairperson, People's Develop Corp, Comn Planning Bd 3; dir, C Circle Day Care, 1970-75. **Honors/Awds:** Sojourner, Truth Black Women Bus & Prof Group, NY City Chap; Woman of the Year, Morrisania Community Coun; Outstanding Community Serv, Bronx Unity Dem Club. **Home Addr:** 575 E 168th St Apt 1, Bronx, NY 10456-3889. **Business Addr:** Assistant Principal, Board of Education, 1265 Boston Rd, Bronx, NY 10456.

## HICKS, ELEANOR

Government official, educational consultant. **Personal:** Born Feb 21, 1943, Columbus, GA; daughter of Carl and Annie Pearl. **Educ:** Univ Cincinnati, BA, 1965; Johns Hopkins Sch Advan Int Studies, MA, int rels, foreign rel, 1967. **Career:** Thailand Dept State, desk officer, 1970-72; US consult to Monaco & Nice Dept State, 1972-75; Dept State, policy analyst, 1975-76; Dept State Cent Am Affairs, dep, 1976-78; Dept State US Embassy Cairo, dep polit sect, 1979-82; Univ Cin, adv int liaison, 1983; Minds Int, pres, 1996-. **Orgs:** Phi Beta Kappa, Univ Cincinnati, 1964-; Mid E Inst; bd, Women's Action Orgn Dept State, 1978; Alpha Kappa Alpha; SW Ohio Transp Authority, 1984-; bd treas, Am Red Cross, 1987-89; Am Assembly, Columbia Univ, 1990; dir, Fed Res Br, Cincinnati Br, 1990-; mkt comn, Cin Conv Ctr & Int Visitors Bur; Golden Key Nat Hon Soc, 1991-. **Honors/Awds:** Honorific Award, Chevalier De Tastevin, 1973; Civic Award in Int Realm, Cavalieri Del Nouvo Europe, 1974; Scholar Award named after her for outstanding arts & sci stud Univ Cincinnati Ann Eleanor Hicks Award, 1974; Legendary Woman Award, St Vincent's, Birmingham, Ala, 1975; Leadership Cincinnati, 1988-; Career Woman of Achievement, YWCA, 1985. **Home Addr:** 3621 Eaton Lane, Cincinnati, OH 45229, **Home Phone:** (513)751-1408. **Business Addr:** President, M I N D S International, 3621 Eaton Lane, Cincinnati, OH 45229, **Business Phone:** (513)281-7770.

## HICKS, ERIC DAVID

Football coach, football player. **Personal:** Born Jun 17, 1976, Erie, PA; son of Cheryl Vaughn and Augustas; married Erica; children: Shayla & Rocco. **Educ:** Univ Md, College Park, BA, criminal justice, 1998, criminol, 2012. **Career:** Kans City Chiefs, defensive end, 1998-2006; New York Jets, defensive end, 2007; Detroit Lions, 2009; Blue Valley Southwest High Sch, defensive line coach, 2010; Lakewood Mid Sch, 8th grade boys basketball coach, 2010-11; Lamar Univ, outside linebackers coach, 2012-; free agt, currently. **Orgs:** co-founder, Hicks Hearts Found, 2002-06; spokesperson, Am heart Asn. **Honors/Awds:** Football Digest All-Pro, 2000; Ed Block Courage Award, 2001; Distinguished Alumni Award, 2006. **Business Addr:** Outside Linebackers Coach, Lamar University, 4400 S M L King Jr Pkwy, Beaumont, TX 77710.

## HICKS, FOSTER

Teacher, basketball coach, high school teacher. **Career:** People's High Sch, teacher; Spartans, head coach; City Vallejo, coun mem & found african am alliance & sch adminr; Hogan High Sch, basketball head coach, teacher, currently. **Orgs:** Solano County Black Chamber Com. **Business Addr:** Teacher, Hogan High School, 850 Rosewood Ave, Vallejo, CA 94591-5647, **Business Phone:** (707)556-3510.

## HICKS, DR. REV. H. BEECHER, JR.

Clergy. **Personal:** Born Jun 17, 1944, Baton Rouge, LA; son of H Beecher Sr (deceased) and Eleanor Frazier (deceased); married Elizabeth Harrison; children: H Beecher III, Rev Ivan Douglas & Kristin Elizabeth. **Educ:** Univ Ark, Pine Bluff, BA, 1964; Colgate Rochester, Mdiv, 1967, Dr Ministry, theol, 1975; Harvard Univ Divinity Sch, Cambridge, MA, PhD, 1994; George Washington Univ, MBA, 1999. **Career:** Colgate Rochester Divinity Sch, rockefeller protestant fel, 1964-65; Second Baptist Church, sr minister, 1965-68; Irondequoit United Church Christ, minister youth, 1965-68; Rochester Urban League, employ counr, 1967; Nat Urban League, training coordr, 1968; Mt Ararat Baptist Church, sr minister, 1968-73; Colgate Rochester, martin luther king fel, 1972-75; Antioch Baptist Church, sr minister, 1973-77; Metrop Baptist Church, sr minister, 1977-2014, sr servant, 2014, pastor emer, currently; Howard Univ Divinity, Adj Prof, 1981, 1987; Harvard Univ, merrill fel, 1994; Colgate Rochester Divinity Sch, vis prof, 1995; Wesley Theol Sem, distinguished vis prof, 1999-; H. Beecher Hicks, Jr. Ministries Inc, pres; Books: Preaching Through A Storm, 1987; My Souls Been Anchored, 1998; Prophetic Business, 2002; Jordans Stormy Banks, 2004. **Orgs:** Chmn bd, funeral dir, 1985; co-chair, Ministers Partnership, 1985; vpres, Eastern Reg Nat Black Pastors Conf; admin, Nat Black Pastors Conf; bd Coun, Ct Excellence; asst secy, Progressive Nat Baptist Conv; co-chair, Am Baptist Ministers Coun DC; pres, Martin Luther King Fels Inc, 1988-; pres, Kerygma Assoc, 1989-; fel Nat Adv Bd Black Church Studies, 1989; fel Mayors Comn Econ Develop, 1989; fel Relig Comt United Negro Col Fund, 1989; A Relig Consult Serv; bd trustee, United Theol Sem, Dayton, OH; fel Nat Bd Advisors Bibl Inst Social Chg, 1990-91; bd trustee, United Theol Sem, 1991-; chair, Comt Strict Liability, 1991-; bd trustee, Richmond Va Sem, 1991-; bd trustee, Church Asn Community Serv, 1992-; treas, Comt Against All Killing, 1992-; bd trustee, Alban Inst, 1993-96; bd trustee, Skinner Farm Inst, 1993-; fel Alumni Coun Colgate Rochester Divinity Sch, 1993-94; fel Orgn New Equality Adv Bd, 1996-; fel D. C. Comt to Promote Wash, 1996-; bd dir, Church Asn Community Serv; bd dir, Tantallon Country Club, 1998. **Home Addr:** 1010 Colln Ct, Ft. Washington, MD 20744, **Home Phone:** (301)292-0923. **Business Addr:** Pastor Emeritus, Metropolitan Baptist Church, 96 Harry S Truman Dr, Largo, MD 20774, **Business Phone:** (202)238-5000.

## HICKS, DR. INGRID DIANN

Educator, writer, psychologist. **Personal:** Born Jun 17, 1958, Flint, MI; daughter of Walter and Barbara Mae; married Thomas E Brooks. **Educ:** Univ Mich, BA, psychol, 1980; Univ Wis-Milwaukee, MS, clin psychol, 1982, PhD, clin psychol, 1985. **Career:** Univ Wisc, Med Sch, from asst prof to assoc prof, 1985-91; Med Col, Wisc, pvt pract & consult, 1991-; Ctr Teaching Entrepreneurship, consult, 1999-2000; Womens Treat Ctr-Chicago, consult, 1999-2000; City Transformation, clin consult, 1999-; African-Am Womens Ctr, 2003-04; CornerStone Achievement Acad, consult, 2003-04; La Casa de Esperanza Inc, consult, 2007-09; A Purpose Life, consult, 2007-; Transformation Serv Inc, clin & exec dir, 2007-; Super Steel, employee assistance serv; Cargill, employee assistance serv; Kohl's, employee assistance serv; Whole Foods, employee assistance serv; Gen Elec, employee assistance serv; IRS, employee assistance serv; Master Lock, employee assistance serv. Author: For Black Women Only: The Complete Guide to a Successful Lifestyle Change-Health, Wealth, Love & Happiness, 1991; For Black Women Only (but don't forget about our men); play & book, 1995; For Black Women Only: Our Lives in the New Millennium, 2001; Black Women Only: Our Relationships; Our Childhood Mother; TV appearance: The Oprah Winfrey Show; Provided numerous seminars & workshops. **Orgs:** Am Psychol Asn, 1985-; Wis Psychol Asn, 1985-; Am Soc clin Hypn, 1985-; Nat Asn Black Psychologists, 1985-; Milwaukee Community; Am Group Psychother Asn; Am Asn Behav Ther; Nat Regist Health Providers. **Business Addr:** Clinical, Executive Director, Transformation Services, 1003 E Lyon St, Milwaukee, WI 53203, **Business Phone:** (414)933-7083.

## HICKS, JESSIE YVETTE

Basketball coach, basketball player. **Personal:** Born Dec 2, 1971, Richmond, VA; children: 2. **Educ:** Univ Md, BA, criminal justice, 1993; Bowie State Univ, MA, guid & coun, 1998. **Career:** Basketball player (retired), basketball coach; Univ Md, asst coach, 1992-93; Juven Saski Baloia, Spain, 1993-94; Md Eastern Shore, asst coach, 1994-95; Bowie State Univ, asst coach, 1995-97; Utah Starzz, forward ctr, 1997; Md Terrapins, asst coach, 2000-01; Orlando Miracle, forward ctr, 2000-02; Conn Sun, guard, 2003; San Antonio Silver Stars, forward ctr, 2003-05; Besiktas, 2004-05.

## HICKS, JIMMIE, JR.

Executive, business owner, consultant. **Personal:** married Lynda Phillips; children: 4. **Educ:** Kent State Univ, BA, gen studies, community develop, 1986; Calvary Bible Inst, Bible/Bibl Studies, 1997; Trinity Col Bible & Trinity Theol Sem, bibl coun, 2004. **Career:** Cleveland Heights, police chaplin, 2001-; City Cleveland Heights, councilman, currently; Hicks Ins Agency, owner, currently; Start Right Church, pastor, 2006-; Non Slip Tablet Grip, creator & distribr, 2014-. **Orgs:** Ordained Elder, Nat Church God Christ; community rels & recreation comt, 1998-2001; munic servs comt coun, 2002-05; Nat Asn Advan Colored People; exec dir, Start Right Community Develop Corp, 2008-. **Home Addr:** 3315 Mayfield Rd, Cleveland, OH 44118-1329, **Home Phone:** (216)812-3642. **Business Addr:** Chief Executive Officer, Hicks Insurance Agency, 13905 Kinsman Rd, Cleveland, OH 44120, **Business Phone:** (216)752-1958.

## HICKS, LEON NATHANIEL

Artist, educator. **Personal:** Born Dec 25, 1933, Deerfield, FL. **Educ:** Kans State Univ, BS, painting & sculpture, 1959; State Univ Iowa, MA, painting, 1961, MFA, printmaking, 1963; Stanford Univ, ancient & mod art hist, 1964; Atlanta La Romita Sch Arts, Ital art hist, 1966; Univ, Afro-Am art hist, 1971. **Career:** Concord Col, art instr, 1965-67; Lincoln Univ, asst prof, 1967; Lehigh Univ, Bethlehem, asst prof, 1970-74; Hicks Etch print, Philadelphia, chmn bd, exec & vpres, 1974; Webster Univ, prof art, 1974-99; Webster Univ, prof emer art, 1999-. **Orgs:** Col Art Asn; Nat Conf Artists; Int Platform Asn; Brandywine Graphic Workshop; Creatadrama Soc; Kappa Alpha Psi. **Honors/Awds:** First prizes for prints & art work, Nat Conf Artists, Mo; Black Artists Art publ, 1969; Am Negro Printmakers, 1966; Directions Afro Am Art, 1974; Engraving Am, 1974; Dict Int Biog, 1974; Mo Arts Award, 2000. **Special Achievements:** Second Prize, Atlanta Univ, Ga, 1965; First Prize, Tuskegee Inst's Ninth Ann Beaux Arts Guild Exhib, 1968; comn winner, Arts and Humanities, St. Louis Ed Portfolio, 1981; Received numerous awards. **Home Addr:** 3424 Old Saint Augustine Rd Lot 105, Tallahassee, FL 32311. **Business Addr:** Professor Emeritus, Webster University, 470 E Lockwood Ave, St. Louis, MO 63119, **Business Phone:** (314)968-7006.

## HICKS, MARYELLEN

Judge, association executive, talk show host. **Personal:** Born Mar 10, 1949, Odessa, TX; daughter of Albert G Whitlock and Kathleen Durham; children: Erin Kathleen. **Educ:** Tex Womans Univ, BA, grad work, 1971; Tex Tech Sch Law, JD, 1974. **Career:** Judge (retired); Bonner & Hicks, atty law, 1975-77; City Ft Worth, munic ct judge, 1977-82; 231st Judicial Dist Ct, dist judge, 1983-85, sr appellate judge; blogtalk radio, talk show host, currently. **Orgs:** Fel Nat Endowment Humanities, 1980; con secy, Nat Women Achievement, 1985; State Bang TX; Nat Bar Asn; vpres, Nat Coun Negro Women; Delta Sigma Theta Sor Jack & Jill Inc; pres, Font Work Black Bar Asn; vpres, Sojourner Truth Community Theatre; pres, Students Asn. **Honors/Awds:** Outstanding Black Women, 1982; Outstanding Black Lawyer, 1982; Female Newsmaker, First Year Press Club, 1982; Citizen Award, Black Pilots Am, 1986; Citizen of the Year, SS Dillow Elem Sch, 1987; Alumna Award, Tex Woman's Univ, 1989. **Special Achievements:** Texas Tech School of Law and was the law schools First female black graduate, 1974. **Home Addr:** PO Box 19165, Ft Worth, TX 76119-1165, **Home Phone:** (713)523-7000.

## HICKS, MICHAEL

Football player. **Personal:** Born Feb 1, 1973, Barnesville, GA. **Educ:** SC State Univ. **Career:** Football player (retired); Chicago Bears, running back, 1996-97.

## HICKS, DR. MICHAEL L.

Physician. **Personal:** Born Apr 8, 1960, Tuskegee, AL; son of Lee Otis and Lillie R; married Rhonda M; children: Michael Leon II & Maya Michelle. **Educ:** Luther Col, BA, 1981; Univ Ala Birmingham, MD, 1986. **Career:** Henry Ford Hosp, resident obstet & gynec; Roswell Pk Cancer Inst, fel gynec oncol, 1990-92; St Joseph Mary Hosp, dir gynec oncologist, 1992-; St Joseph Mercy Oakland, Mich Cancer Inst, physician, currently; pvt pract; Crittenton Hosp Med Ctr, physician; McLaren Macomb, physician. **Orgs:** Nat Med Asn; AMA; Soc Surg Oncologist; Soc Gynec Oncologist; Am Soc Clin Oncologist; Am Col Obstetricians & Gynecologists. **Special Achievements:** Author of numerous medical articles. **Home Addr:** 6019 Carmen Ct, Orchard Lake, MI 48324. **Business Addr:** Gynecologic Oncologist, Michigan Cancer Institute, ASC Bldg 44405 Woodward Ave Suite 202, Pontiac, MI 48341, **Business Phone:** (248)858-2270.

## HICKS, MONIQUE ANGELA. See IMES, MO'NIQUE.

## HICKS, DR. PATRICIA LARKINS

Executive. **Personal:** married Clayton N. **Educ:** Hampton Univ, BA, 1971; Mich State Univ, MA, 1972; Univ Memphis, PhD, speech-lang path, 1980. **Career:** Easter Seals Speech & Hearing Ctr, head & speech pathologist, 1972-75; Armstrong Atlantic State Univ, instr, 1975-77; Howard Univ, asst prof, 1980-84; NIH; NovaCare Inc, vpres prof serv, 1989-93; Outcomes Mgt Group Ltd, founder & pres, 1994-; Hampton Univeristy, Alumni Asn, pres; Publication: Be Your B.E.S.T, 2010; Author of 25 publications and 3 books. **Orgs:** Outcomes Adv Comt, United Way Cent Ohio; Payne Theol Sem Bd; Nat Governance Eval Comt, Links Inc; chmn, Orgn Effectiveness & Technol, Cent Area; chmn, Hampton Univ, BA, 1971; Mich State Univ, Mass, 1972; Univ Memphis, PhD, speech-lang path, 1980, Serv Youth Facet; Delta Sigma Theta Sorority Inc; fel Am Speech-Lang-Hearing Asn, dir, Speech-Lang Path Br, 1984-89; Nat Insts Health; pres, Nat Hampton Alumni Asn Inc; chair, Integration Comt, Columbus Chamber Small Bus Coun; Diversity & Inclusion Comt, United Way Cent Ohio; co chair, Orgn Effectives, Links Inc; Delta Sigma Theta Sorority; vice chair pro tem, Steward Bd, St Paul AME Church. **Business Addr:** Founder, President, Outcomes Management Group Ltd, 786 S Front St, Columbus, OH 43206, **Business Phone:** (614)445-3966.

## HICKS, DR. RAYMOND A.

College administrator, president (organization). **Personal:** Born Jan 1, 1943; married Georgia; children: Shannan, Michael & Jared. **Educ:** Grambling State Univ, BA, 1968; La Tech, MA, 1971; Southern Ill Univ, PhD, educ admin, 1974. **Career:** College administartor (retired); Grambling State Univ, interim pres, 1993-94, pres, 1994-97, prof; Univ La Syst, Bd Supvr, pres, 1995; Hicks Mgt Consults, pres, currently. **Orgs:** Nat Asn Equal Opportunity Higher Educ; la bd trustee, State Cols Univs; vice chancellor, Acad Affairs-Southern Univ-Shreveport. **Business Addr:** President, Hicks Management Consultants, 4305 S Bowen Rd Suite 121, Arlington, TX 76016, **Business Phone:** (817)640-4441.

## HICKS, ROBERT OTIS, JR.

Football coach, football player. **Personal:** Born Nov 17, 1974, Atlanta, GA. **Educ:** Miss State Univ. **Career:** Football player (retired), coach; Buffalo Bills, tackle, 1998, right tackle, tackle, 1999, left tackle, tackle, 2000; Houston Texans, 2000-02; Camp Lineman, coach, currently. **Business Addr:** Coach, Camp Lineman, 5700 Riverview Rd SE, Atlanta, GA 30327.

## HICKS, SAMUEL DAVID. See MOORE, SAMUEL DAVID.

## HICKS, REV. DR. SHERMAN G.

Clergy. **Personal:** Born Jun 22, 1946, Brooklyn, NY; son of Charles and Sarah; married Anna Marie Peck; children: Andrea, Geoffrey & Christopher. **Educ:** Wittenberg Univ, BA, polit sci, DD; Hamma Sch Theol, MDiv; Carthage Col, DD; Elmhurst Col, DD. **Career:** Old Lutheran Church, asst bishop, Ill; Metrop Chicago Synod, bishop; First Trinity Lutheran Church, sr pastor, currently; Lutheran Sch Theol, Gettysburg, adj fac; bishop Metrop Chicago Synod; Evangel Lutheran Church Am, Div Outreach, mission dir, Multicultural Ministries Prog Unit, exec dir, currently. **Orgs:** Bd dir, Nat AIDS Fund; Bethphage Mission Inc; bd dir, Community Family Life Servs; bd dir Lifeline, A Ment Retardation Partnership; bd dir, AIDS Nat Interfaith Network; bd dir, Lutheran Housing Servs Inc; coordr, African Am/Black Outreach Strategy, Div Outreach; pres, Interfaith Coun Homeless; asst bishop Ill Synod, (Lutheran Church Am); co-pastor Holy Trinity Lutheran Church, E Orange, NJ; & pastor Concordia Lutheran Church, Buffalo, NY; bd regents & Diversity Nat Adv Bd, Wartburg Col, Carthage Col, Kenosha Wis; Nat Mosaic Allied Voice; Lutheran Housing Serv; Lutheran Serv Am; Lutheran Social Serv Ill; Bethphage Mission; pres, Interfaith Coun Homeless, Chicago; AIDS Nat Interfaith Network, Wash, DC; Coun Relig Leaders, Chicago; adj fac mem, Lutheran Theol Sem, Gettysburg; bd Comm Renewal Soc; bd, Community Renewal Soc. **Honors/Awds:** Alumni citation, Wittenberg Univ, 1993; Doctor of Divinity, Wittenberg Univ. **Home Addr:** 646 5th St NE, Washington, DC 20002, **Home Phone:** (202)543-2551. **Business Addr:** Mission Director, Executive Director, Evangelical Lutheran Church America, Lutheran Ctr, Baltimore, MD 21230, **Business Phone:** (410)230-2878.

## HICKS, SKIP LAVELL (BRIAN L HICKS)

Football player. **Personal:** Born Oct 13, 1974, Corsicana, TX. **Educ:** Univ Calif, BA, 1998. **Career:** Football player (retired); Wash Redskins, running back, 1998-99, 2000; Tenn Titans, running back, 2001; Carolina Panthers, 2002; Cincinnati Bengals, running back, 2004; Toronto Argonauts, 2004; Sports Scholarships USA, dir sports & compliance, 2011-15; Oaks Christian Sch, asst football coach running back, 2014-. **Honors/Awds:** UCLA All-American. **Business Addr:** Assistant Coach Running Back, Oaks Christian School, 31749 La Tienda Dr, Westlake Village, CA 91362, **Business Phone:** (818)575-9900.

## HICKS, DR. VERONICA ABENA

Executive, manager. **Personal:** Born Feb 22, 1949, Awate; daughter of Stephen Kwani Kokroko and Salone Atawa Dzeble Kokroko; married Anthony M; children: Esi, Gloria & Tania. **Educ:** Univ Ghana, Legon, BSc, 1971, grad dipl, 1972; Iowa State Univ, Ames, MSc, 1976, PhD, 1980. **Career:** Ministry Agri, Accra Ghana, nutrit consult, 1976-77; ISU Dept Biochem & Biophys, Ames, res fel, 1980-81; Kellogg Co,

Battle Creek, nutritionist, 1981-82, mgr nutrit res, 1982-84, dir nutrit, 1984-86, dir, chem & physiol, 1986-. **Orgs:** Infant Health Adv bd, Calhoun County Dept Health, l983-; adv bd, Iowa State Col Consumer & Family Sci, l985-88. **Home Addr:** 275 McNeil St, Memphis, TN 38112, **Home Phone:** (901)672-7623. **Business Addr:** Director, Kellogg Company Science & Technology Center, 235 Porter St, Battle Creek, MI 49017.

## HICKS, WILLIAM JAMES

Educator, physician. **Personal:** Born Jan 3, 1948, Columbus, OH; children: 3. **Educ:** Morehouse Col, BS, 1970; Univ Pittsburgh, Sch Med, MD, 1974; Am Bd Med Examr, dipl, 1974; Am Bd Internal Med, dipl, 1977; Am Bd Med Oncol, dipl, 1981. **Career:** Univ Health Ctr Pittsburgh, Presby-Univ Hosp, internship, 1974-75, resident, 1975-77; Ohio State Univ, Dept Hemat & Oncol, fel, 1977-79, assoc, clin prof med, 1986-02; Grant Med Ctr, Internal Med Dept, chmn, 1989-91, Div Hemat & Oncol, prof clin internal med, 2002-08, resident adv, 2009-; William J Hicks Md, 1979-2002; Grant Med Ctr, Med Oncol, assoc dir, 1979-, attend staff; Columbus Cancer Clin, staff, 1982-86; St Anthony's Med Ctr, attend staff, prof clin med, 2002. **Orgs:** Alpha Phi Alpha Fraternity, 1968-; Southwest Oncol Group, 1979-; ECCO Family Health Ctr, 1979-; Grant Med Ctr, 1979-86; pres, Nat Med Asn, 1982-84; Nat Surg Adjuvant Breast & Bowel Proj, 1982-; pres, Columbus Chap Nat Med Asn, 1982-84; assoc prin investr, Columbus Community Clin Oncol Prog, 1983-, bd trustee, 1983-, inst rev bd, 1983-; Franklin County Acad Med, 1983-; Sigma Pi Phi Phi Fraternity, 1985-; Ohio State Med Asn, 1986-; Am Soc Clin Oncologists, 1986-; State OH Comn Minority Health, 1987-; Planned Parenthood Cent OH, 1989-95; vice chmn, State OH Comn Minority Health, 1993-; chmn, Nat Black Leadership Initiative Cancer Columbus Coalition, 1994-; Comn African-Am Males, 2002-; Cent Ohio Breathing Asn, Blue Ribbon Adv Panel, 2004-; UNCF Adv Comt, 2005-; Ohio State Univ, Master Space Planning Task Force, 2006-; OSU Minority Fac Support & Leadership Group, 2007-; OSU Minority Recruitment & Retention, 2008-; Ohio Dept Health, 2009-; Am Lung Asn, 2010-; Nat Cancer Inst; Scott & White Memorial Hosp; Laser Med Res Found; Yale Cancer Ctr; Comprehensive Cancer Centers Nev; Wayne State Univ; Wash State Univ Pullman; City Hope Nat Med Ctr; Univ Ariz; Univ Hawaii; Univ Ore; Ind Univ Bloomington; Food Innovation Ctr; Health Behav & Health Prom; Col Pub Health; Comprehensive Cancer Ctr-Exp Therapeut. **Home Addr:** 475 Jessing Trl, Columbus, OH 43235, **Home Phone:** (614)885-0269. **Business Addr:** Physician, 904 Morehouse Medical Plaza-Tower, 2050 Kenny Rd, Columbus, OH 43221, **Business Phone:** (614)236-6718.

## HICKS, WILLIAM L.

Engineer, construction manager, business owner. **Personal:** Born Jan 19, 1928, Yoakum, TX. **Educ:** Univ Calif, Col Engr, Berkeley, BS, 1954. **Career:** Corps Engrs La, engr trainee; Daniel Mann Johnson & Mendenhall La, design engr; Ralph M Parsons Co La, design engr; Mackintosh & Mackintosh, La, civil engr; Hick Construct Co, owner. **Orgs:** Am Soc & Civil Engrs. **Home Addr:** 1212 S Ogden Dr, Los Angeles, CA 90019-2430, **Home Phone:** (323)931-9996.

## HICKS-BARTLETT, SHARON THERESA

Social scientist. **Personal:** Born Nov 22, 1951, Chicago, IL; married David Charles; children: Alani Rosa Hicks. **Educ:** Roosevelt Univ, BA, 1976, MA, 1981; Univ Chicago, MA, 1985; Univ Chicago, PhD, sociol, 1994. **Career:** IL Coun Cont Med Educ, prog & activ, sec, 1975-78; Amherst Asn, off mgr, 1978-80; Univ Chicago, convocation coordr, 1980-81; Univ Chicago Urban Family Life Proj, res asst, 1985-; Am Jewish Comt, Hands Across Campus, dir, 1995-98; Terrapin Training Strategies Inc, pres, 1998-. **Orgs:** Instr, Thornton Comm Col, 1982 & 1987; freelance researcher, Better Boys Found, 1985; Vol Ford Heights Comm Serv Ctr, 1986-; literacy tutor, Literacy Vols Am, 1987-; NORC, surv dir II. **Home Addr:** 66 Water St, Park Forest, IL 60466. **Business Addr:** President, Terrapin Training Strategies Inc, PO Box 238, Olympia Fields, IL 60461.

## HICKSON, EUGENE, SR.

Executive. **Personal:** Born Jun 10, 1930, Limestone, FL; married Verlene Deloris Stebbins; children: Eugene Jr (deceased), Vergena Faust & Edward Tyrone. **Educ:** Gupton Jones Col Mortuary Sci, Nashville, TN, MS, mortuary sci, 1952. **Career:** Arcadian newspaper, printer; Arcadia, Fla, mayor, 1971-75, 1981, 1983; Brown's Funeral Home, embalmer & funeral dir; Hickson Funeral Home, owner, 1960-. **Orgs:** Shriner; 32 Degree Mason; deacon, Elizabeth Bapt Ch; chmn C C; second vpres, FA Martician Asn. **Home Addr:** 142 S Orange Ave, Arcadia, FL 34266, **Home Phone:** (863)494-2920. **Business Addr:** Owner, Hickson Funeral Home, 142 S Orange Ave, Arcadia, FL 34266, **Business Phone:** (863)494-2920.

## HICKSON, DR. SHERMAN RUBEN

Dentist, army officer. **Personal:** Born Apr 3, 1950, Ridgeland, SC; son of Glover M Jr (deceased) and Justine Odon; married Eavon Holloway; children: Sherman Jr (deceased), LaTonya, Thurston & Adrienne. **Educ:** SC State Col, BS, 1971; Meharry Med Col Sch Dent, DDS, 1975. **Career:** Pvt pract, gen dentist, 1977-. **Orgs:** SC Dent Asn, 1975; Palmetto Med Dent & Pharm Asn, 1976-87; Nat Dent Asn, 1976-87; Acad Gen Dent, 1978-87; Dickerson Lodge 314 Mason Prince Hall, 1981-87; CC Johnson Consistory 136, 1982-87; Cairo Temple 125 Shriners, 1982-87; Orion Chap 135 Eastern Star, 1986-87; trustee, Friendship Baptist Church; life mem, Nat Asn Advan Colored People; life mem, Omega Psi Phi Fraternity Inc; SC Basketball & Football Off Asn; off, Mid eastern Athletic Col Football. **Honors/Awds:** Dentsply Int Merit Award, Meharry Med Col Sch Dent; Second degree black belt, World Tae Kwon Do Asn, 1982-87; Distinguished alumni award, SC State univ, 1998. **Business Addr:** Dentist, Private Practice, 500 Richland Ave E, Aiken, SC 29801, **Business Phone:** (803)648-0709.

## HICKSON, DR. WILLIAM F., JR.

Dentist, radio host. **Personal:** Born Aug 27, 1936, Aiken, SC; son of William F Sr and Nina; married Charlestine Dawson; children: Nina R, William F, III & G G Oneal. **Educ:** SC State Col, BS, 1956; Meharry, DDS, 1962. **Career:** Pvt pract dentist; WSSB Radio, SC State Col, radio host, 1985. **Orgs:** Am Nat SC Palmetto Dent Asn; cty dent dir, OEO State; pres, Palmetto Dent Asn; reg consult, HEW Dist IV Beta & Kappa Chi; Omega Psi Phi; past basileus Alpha Iota Boule; past sire Archon; Nat Bd Missions United Presby Nat Asn Advan Colored People; Fed Dent Cons; pres, Orangeburg Sickle Cell Found. **Home Addr:** 121 Weybridge Ct, Orangeburg, SC 29115, **Home Phone:** (803)516-9360.

## HIGGINBOTHAM, DR. EVE JULIET

Physician, educator, dean (education). **Personal:** Born Nov 4, 1953, New Orleans, LA; daughter of Luther and Ruby; married Frank C Williams Jr. **Educ:** Mass Inst Technol, SM, chem engineering, 1975, MS, chem engineering, 1975; Harvard Med Sch, MD, 1979. **Career:** Pac Med Ctr, intern, 1979-80; LSU Eye Ctr, resident, 1980-83; Mass Eye & Ear Infirmary, fel, 1983-85; Head Found fel, 1983; EB Durphy fel, 1984; Univ Ill, asst prof, 1985-90; Univ Mich, assoc prof & asst dean, 1990-94; Univ Md Med Sch, Dept Ophthal Visual Sci, prof & chair; Morehouse Sch Med, dean & sr vpres acad affairs, 2006-09; Howard Univ, sr vpres & exec dean, 2010-11. **Orgs:** Bd dir, Women Ophthal, 1980-94; bd dir, Prevent Blindness Am, Chair Publ Comt, 1990-; ed bd, Arch Ophthal Ed bd, 1990-; bd trustee, Am Acad Ophthal, 1992-95; ed bd, Arch Ophthal, 1994-; prof & chair ophthal & visual sci, Univ Md Med Ctr, 1994-06; Inst Med, 2000-; voting mem, Food & Drug Admin Ophthalmic Med Devices Panel, 2001; Nat Med Asn; Nat Eye Health Educ Prog, Nat Eye Inst; Planning Comt, Nat Eye Health Educ Prog, Nat Eye Inst; dir outreach serv, FCGCF; Maryland Soc Eye Physicians & Surgeons; pres, Baltimore City Med Soc; bd dir, Georgia Bio; bd mem, Nat Bd Med Examiners; mem adv group, Spec Med Adv Group to Undersecretary Veteran Affairs; bd mem, Alpha Omega Alpha Hon Soc Bd; bd mem, Defense Health Bd; bd overseers, Harvard Univ, 2008-; bd mem, Naitonal Space Biomedicl Res Inst, 2008-10; Am Acad Arts & Sci, 2009-; corp mem, Massachusetts Inst Technol Corp, 2011-; vis scholar, Asn Am Med Cols, 2011-. **Home Addr:** 2915 Poland Springs Dr, Ellicott City, MD 21042, **Home Phone:** (410)203-9839. **Business Addr:** Dean, Senior Vice President, Association of American Medical Colleges, 2450 N St NW, Washington, DC 20037-1126, **Business Phone:** (202)828-0400.

## HIGGINBOTHAM, EVELYN BROOKS

College administrator, college teacher, writer. **Personal:** Born Jun 4, 1945, Washington, DC; daughter of Albert Neal Dow Brooks and Alma Elaine Campbell. **Educ:** Univ Wis-Milwaukee, BA, hist, 1969; Howard Univ, MA, hist, 1974; U.S. Nat Arch, archival admin & rec mgt; Newberry Libr (Chicago), cert quant methodology social sci, 1977; Univ Rochester, PhD, hist, 1984. **Career:** Dartmouth Col, prof; Univ Md, prof; Univ Pa, prof; Harvard Univ, Dept African & African Am Studies, prof, 1993-2006, chair, 2006-13. **Orgs:** Am Philos Soc, fel; Harvard Univ, Walter Channing fel, 2003. **Honors/Awds:** Association for the Study of African American Life and History (ASAALH), Carter G. Woodson Scholars Medallion, 2008, Living Legacy Award, 2012; American Historical Association, Joan Kelly Memorial Prize in Women's History; Association of Black Women Historians, Letitia Woods Brown Memorial Award; Howard University, Honorary Doctorate of Humane Letters, 2011. **Special Achievements:** Author: "Righteous Discontent: The Women's Movement in the Black Baptist Church, 1880-1920" (Harvard University Press, 1993); editor-in-chief: "The Harvard Guide to African-American History" (Harvard University Press, 2001); co-author: "From Slavery to Freedom: A History of African-Americans" (McGraw-Hill, 2010); co-editor: "African American National Biography" (Oxford University Press, 2013).

## HIGGINBOTHAM, PROF. F. MICHAEL

Educator. **Educ:** Brown Univ, AB, 1979; Yale Univ, JD, 1982; Cambridge Univ, LLM, 1985. **Career:** Law clerk; Pillsbury, Madison & Sutro, assoc, 1981; Us Ct Appeals, law clerk to judge cecil poole, 1982; Davis, Polk & Wardwell, assoc, 1983-84; Univ Pa Law Sch, lectr law, 1986-88, vis prof law, 2011; Univ Baltimore Sch Law, asst prof law, 1988-91, assoc prof law, 1991-95, prof law, 1995, interim dean, 2011-12; New York Univ Law Sch, adj prof law, 1991-2009; Univ Miami Law Sch, vis prof law, 2004. Articles: New York University Law Review; University of Hawaii Law Review; Howard University Law Journal; Columbia University International Law Journal; Boston University International Law Journal; Harvard Blackletter Law Journal; University of Illinois Law Review; Yale Law and Policy Review. Book: Race Law; Ghosts of Jim Crow: Ending Racism in Post-Racial America, NYU Press, 2013. **Orgs:** Chmn, Pub Justice Ctr; Coun Foreign Rels; chairperson, Asn Am Law Schs Comt Recruitment& Retention Minority Fac; DC Bar; chair, Md Atty Gens Task Force Electronic Weapons; co-chair, OMalley/Brown Transition Team Minority Affairs Working Group; vice chair, Civic Frame Inc; Md Appellate Judicial Nominating Comn; life mem, Nat Asn Advan Colored People; Nat Bar Asn; Brown Univ Athletic Coun; pres & chmn, Pub Justice Ctr; co founder, Baltimore Scholars Prog; chair, AALS Comt Recruitment & Retention Minority Fac; Sen Barbara Mikulski's Legal Adv Group; co-founder, Fannie Angelos Prog. **Business Addr:** Professor of Law, University of Baltimore School of Law, 1420 N Charles St, Baltimore, MD 21201-5779, **Business Phone:** (410)837-4649.

## HIGGINBOTHAM-BROOKS, ESQ. RENEE

Lawyer. **Personal:** Born Jan 3, 1952, Martinsville, VA; daughter of Curtis and Charmion; married Clarence Jackson, Jun 20, 1975; children: Leigh & Codie. **Educ:** Howard Univ, BA, polit sci, phi beta kappa, magna cum laude, 1974; Georgetown Univ Sch Law, JD, law, 1977. **Career:** Nat Labor Rels Bd, field atty, 1977-79; US Dept Health Educ & Welfare, civil rights atty, 1979-87; Law Off Renee Higginbotham Brooks, pvt pract law, 1987-; Tex Alcoholic Beverage Comn, chair, 1991-94; Block Capital Equity Fund LP, founder & patner, 2006-08; R B Block Capital LLC, chair & chief exec officer, 2011-; US Dept Health & Human Serv, asst regional atty; Howard Univ, prin, currently; Law Off Renee Higginbotham-Brooks, atty, currently. **Orgs:** State Bar Tex, 1977-; vice chairwoman bd, Howard Univ Hosp, 1997-, vice chmn, 2005-; NBA, 1979-; Links Inc, 1985-; Tarrant County Trial Lawyers Asn, 1989-; Jack & Jill AME, 1990-; Col State Bar Tex, 1992; vice chairwoman, Howard Univ, 2005-14; Tex Trial Lawyers Asn; Tarrant County Bar Asn; Am Trial Lawyers Asn; Dallas/Ft Worth Minority Bus Develop Coun; State Bar Tex Found; bd mem, Ft Worth Transp Authority; bd mem, M D Anderson Cancer Ctr; bd mem, Dallas African Am Mus; Tex Dept Com; Nat Asn Advan Colored People; Womens Polit Forum; United Negro Col Fund. **Honors/Awds:** Quest for Success Award, Dallas Black COC, 1992; Excellence in Law Award, KAP, 1992; Outstanding Woman of the Year Award, City Ft Worth, 1994; Excellence Award, Nat Dent Asn, 2001; Thurgood Marshall Award, Nat Asn Advan Colored People, 2002; Distinguished Alumni Award, Howard Univ, 2003; Wiley A. Branton Award, Nat Bar Asn, 2011. **Special Achievements:** First female and the first African American appointed to the Texas Alcoholic Beverage Commission, 1991; The Peoples Law Show, television host. **Home Addr:** 308 Canyon Creek Trl, Fort Worth, TX 76112-1147. **Business Addr:** Principal, Howard University, 2400 Sixth St NW Suite 440, Washington, TX 20059, **Business Phone:** (202)806-2250.

## HIGGINS, CHESTER ARCHER, JR.

Photojournalist. **Personal:** Born Jan 1, 1946, Lexington, KY; son of Johnny Frank and Varidee Loretta Young; married Renelda Walker; children: Nataki & Chester III; married Betsy Kissam. **Educ:** Tuskegee Inst, BS, bus mgmt, 1970. **Career:** Photogr, auth; Exhibs NY & World Wide Retrospective; USIA, 1975-76; part-time photog instr, NY Univ, instr, 1975-78; NY Times, staff photogr, 1975-; Nat Endowment Arts, grant; Andy Warhol Found, grant; Ford Found, grant; Rockefeller Found, grant; Am Revolution Bicentennial Comn, grant; Int Ctr photog, grant; Bks: Black Woman, 1970; Life, 1974; Some Time Ago: A Hist Portrait Black Americans 1850-1950, 1980; Feeling Spirit: Searching World for-People Africa, 1994; Elder Grace: Nobility Of, 2000; New York Times Co, staff photogr, photojournalist. **Orgs:** Int Ctr Photog; fel, Tuskegee Inst Archive Ford Found, 1972-74. **Honors/Awds:** Works in Mus of Mod Art; Libr Cong; Vassar Col; African Distinguished Lectr, 1975; United Nations Award; American Graphic Design Award; Graphics Magazine Award; Artist Dir Club of New York Award; Publishers Award, NY Times. **Special Achievements:** Author: Black Woman, McCalls, 1970; Drums of Life, Doubleday, 1974; Some Time Ago, Doubleday, 1978; Feeling the Spirit: Searching the World for the People of Africa, Bantam Books, 1994; Elder Grace: The Nobility of Aging, Bull Finch, 2000; Echo of the Spirit: A Visual Journey, Random House/Harlem Books, 2004. Published his works in Newsweek, New York Times Sunday Magazine, Fortune, Art News, Essence and Archeology; One of the original photos provided the basis for the three-story photo mosaic at the new Museum of the African Diaspora in San Francisco. **Home Addr:** 57 S Portland Ave, Brooklyn, NY 11217-1301, **Home Phone:** (718)625-2474. **Business Addr:** Staff Photographer, Photo Journalist, The New York Times, 229 W 43rd St, New York, NY 10036-3959, **Business Phone:** (212)556-1091.

## HIGGINS, CLARENCE R., JR.

Pediatrician. **Personal:** Born Sep 13, 1927, East St. Louis, IL; son of Clarence and Louise; married Edwina Gray; children: Rhonda, Adrienne & Stephen. **Educ:** Fisk Univ, attended 1948; Meharry Med Col, attended 1953; Baylor Univ Col Med, attended 1957. **Career:** Homer Phillips Hosp St Louis, internship, 1953-54, pediat res, 1954-56; Baylor Col Med, res fel, 1956-57, asst clin prof pediats; Peds Sec Nat Med Asn, self employed pediat, chmn, 1973-; St Joseph Hosp, dir; Higgins Clarence R Jr & Assoc, owner & pediatrician, 1985-. **Orgs:** Alpha Phi Alpha Fraternity; Diplomat Am Bd Pediats; fel Am Acad Pediats; Houston Med Forum; founder, Lockwood Community Hosp; secy, Nat Med Asn. **Home Addr:** 3502 S Parkwood, Houston, TX 77021. **Business Addr:** Owner, Pediatrician, Higgins Clarence R Jr & Associates, 4315 Lockwood Dr Suite 9, Houston, TX 77026, **Business Phone:** (713)672-2586.

## HIGGINS, CLEO SURRY

Educator, dean (education), chairperson. **Personal:** Born Aug 25, 1923, Memphis, TN; married William; children: Kyle Everett & Sean Craig. **Educ:** LeMoyne Col, BA, 1944; Univ Wis, MPh, 1945, PhD, 1973; Univ Chicago; NY Univ; Fla A & M Univ; Bryn Mawr Col. **Career:** Bethune-cookman Col, instr, 1945-46, Div Humanities, actg chmn, chmn, 1970-73, Eng Dept, chmn, 1973-76, actg acad dean, 1976, prof emer, currently; W Va St Col, vis prof, 1948; Cent Acad High Sch, instr reading, 1958-60; CollierBlocker Jr Col, dean stud perssonel regist instr, 1960-63; Humanities St Johns & River Jr Col, instr, 1964-70; Univ WI, Dept Eng, scholar, 1971. **Orgs:** Fessenden Acad, instr, 1943-44; chmn, Bethune-cookman Col, 1946-48; chmn, Div Humanities, Bethune-Cookman Col, 1948-56; fed mem, Beta Iota Sigma Sigma Gamma Rho Society, 1948; standing mem, Vis Com S Asn Sec Schs & Cols, 1948-56; chap mem, Daytona Br, Chap Links Inc, 1956; speaker, St Louis George Wash Day Observance, 1959; nat pres, Sigma Sigma Gamma Rho Society, 1962-63; asst chmn, SACS Vis Team, 1962; chmn, Bilingualism WI, 1963; exec bd mem, Putnam County Chap, Nat Found Marchof Dimes, 1964; Bi-Racial Comn, Putnam County, 1964-70; vol secy, Putnam City Comn Action Prog, 1966; consult, In-Serv Ed Meeting, Putnam County Sec Schs, 1966; FlaCitizens Comn Humanities, 1972-73; Am Dialect Soc; Nat Coun Teachers Eng; Nat Coun Col Pub Adv; Am Asn Univ Women; Putnam Co Hist Soc; Emanuel United Methodist Church; Womens Serv League; Distinguished Professor Emeriti, 1988. **Honors/Awds:** Outstanding Educators American, 1970; Recreation, Charles Dana Fac Scholar, Univ NCF, 1972-73; Woman of the Year, Bethune-Cookman Col, 1975; Panelist, Humanities Prog Disadvantaged, 1976; Higher Educ Assistance Award, 2001; Teacher of the Year, 1966. **Special Achievements:** Oratorical contest judge, VFW Voice of Democracy National Program, 1975. **Home Addr:** 1437 Continental Dr, Daytona Beach, FL 32117, **Home Phone:** (386)252-8761. **Business Addr:** Professor Emeritus, Bethune Cookman College, 640 Dr Mary McLeod Bethune Blvd, Daytona Beach, FL 32114, **Business Phone:** (386)481-2000.

## HIGGINS, JENN (JENNIFER HIGGINS)

Political consultant. **Personal:** Born Hillsborough, NC. **Educ:** Davidson Col, BA, 2002; Georgetown Univ, cert legis studies, 2012. **Career:** Centers Medicare & Medicaid Serv, analyst, 2002-03; Adv Bd Co, analyst, 2003-04; Marwood Group, sr assoc, 2004-06; Capitol Health Group, prin, 2006-12; Temple Univ, adj asst prof, 2011-13; Tauzin Consults, prin, 2012-13; Chamber Hills Strategies, partner, 2013-; Govt Affairs Inst at Georgetown Univ, guest lectr, 2013-; To Contrary, PBS, guest panelist, 2015-. **Orgs:** Davidson Athletic Fund, 2012-; RightNOW Women PAC, 2014-; Running Start: Bringing Young Women to Polit, 2015-. **Business Addr:** Chamber Hill Strategies, 700 12th St NW Suite 700, Washington, DC 20005, **Business Phone:** (202)470-4944.

**HIGGINS, RODERICK DWAYNE (ROD HIGGINS)**
Basketball player, basketball coach, executive. **Personal:** Born Jan 31, 1960, Monroe, LA; married Concetta; children: Rick & Cory. **Educ:** Fresno State Univ, attended 1982. **Career:** Basketball player (retired), basketball coach, executive; Chicago Bulls, 1982-85 & 1986; Seattle SuperSonics, 1985; Tampa Bay Thrillers, 1985-86; San Antonio Spurs, 1986; Tampa Bay Thrillers, 1986; NJ Nets, 1986; Golden State Warriors, 1986-92 & 1994, asst coach, 1995-2000, gen mgr, 2004-07; Sacramento Kings, 1992-93; Olympiacos, 1993; Cleveland Cavaliers, 1993-94; Wash Wizards, asst gen mgr, 2000-04; Charlotte Bobcats, from gen mgr to pres basketball opers, 2007-. **Business Addr:** President, Charlotte Bobcats, 333 E Trade St, Charlotte, NC 28202, **Business Phone:** (704)688-8600.

**HIGGINS, SAMMIE L.**
Clergy, educator, teacher. **Personal:** Born May 11, 1923, Ft. Worth, TX; married Elizabeth; children: Pam, Don, Benita, Kim & Garry. **Educ:** Univ Denver, BS, 1954; Western Theol Sem, Bth, 1963; Merritt Col, AA, 1969; Univ Utah; San Francisco State Col. **Career:** Teacher; methodist clergyman; educr. **Orgs:** Nat Asn Advan Colored People; Omega Psi Phi. **Honors/Awds:** Outstanding Citizen, Ogden, 1964; Outstanding Financial Educ Officer, Polytechnic High Sch, 1970; Outstanding Fac Mem & Teacher, 1972. **Home Addr:** 3921 14 Ave, Sacramento, CA 95820.

**HIGGINS, SEAN MARIELLE**
Basketball player, basketball coach, president (organization). **Personal:** Born Dec 30, 1968, Detroit, MI; son of Earle and Lara Anderson. **Educ:** Univ Mich, attended 1990. **Career:** Basketball player (retired), basketball coach; San Antonio Spurs, guard-forward, 1990-91; Orlando Magic, guard-forward, 1992; Los Angeles Lakers, guard-forward, 1992-93; Golden State Warriors, guard-forward, 1993; Nj Nets, guard-forward, 1994-95; Aris Thessaloniki, Greece, 1994-95; Philadelphia 76ers, guard-forward, 1995-96; Ulker SC Istanbul, 1996-97; Ulkerspor, Turkey, 1996-97; Portland Trailblazers, guard-forward, 1997; Grand Rapids Hoops, 1997-98; Iraklio, Greece, 1998; Cocodrilos de Caracas, Venezuela, 1998-99; Ural Great, Russia, 1999-2000; Albany Patroons, guard-forward; Inglewood Cobras, 2005-06; Las Vegas Stars, asst coach, 2006-07; Edmonds Community Col, coach, 2009-12; Nine Sports Int, founder, pres & chief exec officer, currently. **Orgs:** BTB, asstHurricane Katrina victims; exec producer: Let's Play H O R S E; dir & club pro, NineSports Basketball Club. **Business Addr:** President, Chief Executive Officer, Nine Sports International, 410 E Denny Way, Seattle, WA 98122, **Business Phone:** (866)589-2940.

**HIGGINS, STANN**
Arts administrator. **Personal:** Born May 16, 1952, Pittsburgh, PA. **Educ:** Columbia Col Commun Arts, BS, graphics & advt, 1979. **Career:** Jordan Tamraz Caruso Advt, art dir, 1985, prod mgr, 1979; Bentley Barnes & Lynn Advt, asst prod mgr, 1978; Starstruck Productions LLC, creative dir, 1985, pres, chief exec officer, currently; Raddim Intl Musicpaper, art dir, prod mgr, 1986. **Orgs:** Bd dir, chmn graphics Youth Communs, 1985; founder, Roots Rock Soc. **Honors/Awds:** Work selected, recipient 2 honors mentions Art Inst Chicago, 1965; District Art Award, May wood Bd Ed, 1966; Certificate Appreciation, Guest Speaker Advertising Triton Col, 1981; winner of several Chicago Musical Alliance Awards. **Business Addr:** Chief Executive Officer, StarStruck Productions LLC, 8501 S Maryland Ave 1, Chicago, IL 60619-6215, **Business Phone:** (773)994-6756.

**HIGGINSEN, VY**
Music producer, philanthropist, publisher. **Personal:** Born Harlem, NY; married Ken Wydro. **Educ:** Fashion Inst Technol, New York, NY, 1970. **Career:** Ebony mag, sales rep, beginning 1970; Essence mag, ed; WBLS-FM, host; NBC TV, reporter; Metro Channel, reporter; KISS FM, host; WWRL FM, host; Unique NY mag, publ; Joe Turner's Come, co-producer, 1988; Books: 60 Minutes, 1968; Mama I Want to Sing, 1983; This is My Song; The Positive Zone; Harlem Is; Producer: Mama, I Want to Sing; Gospel Is!; This is My Song; Glory, Glory Hallelujah; Mama, I Want to Sing, Part II, 2011. **Orgs:** Mama Found Arts, Harlem, exec dir, founder & chief exec officer, 1998-; exec dir, Emmy Award-winning Mama Found. **Business Addr:** Chief Executive Officer, Executive Director, Mama Foundation for the Arts, 149 W 126th St, New York, NY 10027, **Business Phone:** (212)280-1045.

**HIGGINSON, VY**
Television producer, administrator, writer. **Personal:** Born Harlem, NY; daughter of Geraldine; married Kenneth Wydro; children: Ahmaya Knoelle. **Educ:** Fashion Inst Technol. **Career:** WBLS-FM, disc jockey; WRKS-FM, radio host; WWRL-AM, talkshow host; WNBC-TV, "Positively Black", hostess, reporter; Metro Channel, reporter; Unique NY Mag, publ & ed; Essence mag, contrib ed; Supv Inc, pres & chief exec officer; MAMA Found Arts Inc, chief exec officer & exec dir, 2000-, interfaith minister, 2002, Gospel for Teens, free educ prog, founder, 2006-. Film: Mama I Want to Sing, exec producer, 2011. **Orgs:** Founder, MAMA Found Arts Inc, 1998-. **Business Addr:** Chief Executive Officer, Executive Director, Mama Found Arts Inc, 149 W 126th St, New York, NY 10027, **Business Phone:** (212)280-1045.

**HIGGS, FREDERICK CHARLES**
Executive. **Personal:** Born Jul 3, 1935, Nassau; married Beryl Vanderpool; children: Rory, Linda & Saundra. **Educ:** St John's Col, 1951. **Career:** Bahamas Airways, sta mgr, 1965-70; Charlotte St Prop, properties mgr, 1971-73; Lisaro Enterprises Ltd, pres, 1973; New Providence Div BGA; Bahamas Golf Asn, pres, tournament dir & chmn Southern Div; Caribbean Golf Asn, founding pres. **Orgs:** Vice chmn, tournament dir, New Providence Div BGA; first vpres, Bahamas Confed Amateur Sports; Ment Health Asn Exec; Scout Asn Bahamas; secy, Amateur Boxing Asn Bahamas; Nat Hall Fame, 2010.

**HIGGS, DR. MARY ANN SPICER**
Educator. **Personal:** Born May 10, 1951, South Bend, IN; daughter of Bobby Jr and Willa B Thornton; married Jack Spicer IV; children: Jack V. **Educ:** N Tex State Univ, BA, psychol, 1973; Abilene Christian Univ, MPA, 1975; Drake Univ, MAT, 1992; Univ Phoenix, ABD, 2011. **Career:** Instructor (retired); Veterans Affairs Recruitment Off, Waco Tex, Dallas Tex, Lincoln NE, Knoxville IA, 1973-89; Herbert Hoover Sr High Sch, Eng instr & psychol instr, 1992-2000; Communicator Newspaper, columnist, 1992-2000; Des Moines Sch Dist, Teacher, 1993-2000; Hoover High Drill Team, coach, 1994-; Hoover High Drill Team, Eng Dept, chmn, 1997-99; Iowa Employ Appeal Bd, vice-chair & Mgt Rep, 2000-08; US 2010 Census, Dept Com, Iowa asst mgr, 2008-10; St Louis Univ, dual credit instr, 2010-14. **Orgs:** Stud sen, Drake Univ, 1971-72; Zeta Phi Beta Sorority, 1982-86; Veteran's admin, Nat Civil Rights Adv Coun, 1986-89, eeo counr trainer, Nat Trainer Supvr's EEO; nat parliamentarian; nat vpres, Zeta Phi Beta Sorority, 1986-90, nat dir leadership develop, 1992-96; stud senate comt, Drake Univ, 1990-92; dir non-traditional grad studs & dir multi-cult theatre, Drake Univ, 1991-92; co-chair, Hoover High Mkt Comt, 1992; dir, Performing Arts Imani Players, Hoover High, 1992; sponsor, SADD, Hoover High Br, 1992-94; act so chair, Nat Asn Advan Colored People, 1995-97; Am Inst Parliamentarians, 1996-97; pres, Nat Black Child Develop, 1998-; Polk County Republican Exec Bd, 1998; Polk County Republican Credential Comt, 1998-2000; Cent City Optimist, 1999-; coordr, Partner Econ Progress; pres, Sisters Target, 2000-07; chmn, State Republican Credential, 2000; bd dir, Nat Fed Repub Women, 2008-; pres, Polk County Republican Women, 2008-10; bd mem, Women Pub Policy. **Home Addr:** River Oaks Town Homes, 6001 Creston Ave Unit 8, Des Moines, IA 50321, **Home Phone:** (515)283-1083.

**HIGH, CLAUDE J., JR.**
Executive. **Personal:** Born Nov 5, 1944, Marshall, TX; son of Claude and Lolee Coursey; married Nelda Nadine Spencer; children: Kino, Claude III & Kimberli; married Renee Lea Watkins; children: Danielle & Marissa. **Educ:** Univ Mich, BA, psychol, 1974; Oakland Univ, MA, coun psychol, 1977. **Career:** Western Elec, installer, 1964-73; grocery store owner, 1973-74; Flint Bd Educ, caseworker, 1974-75; Pub Serv Employ Agency, exec dir, 1974-81, employ counr, 1975, employ coordr, 1975-76; Action Mgt Corp, founder, pres & chief exec officer, 1981-2012. **Orgs:** Secy, Burton Neighborhood House Serv Bd, 1980-84; found, chmn, Metrop Chamber Com, 1986, 1989-91; bd mem, chmn, Flint Area Chamber Com, 1987-97, 1995-96; Chairs Personnel Comt, 1989-96; Fair Bankng Coalition, 1990-97; local bd, Fed Emergency Mgt Agency, 1991-; Gen Motors/United Auto Workers Task Force, 1991-92; Sports Found Bd, 1992; treas, Food Bank Eastern Mich, 1992-; vice chmn, Axxon Comput Servs Inc, 1994-2000; vice chair, dir, Insight Bd, 1995-; Genessee Dist Libr Bd, 1995-98; Greater Flint Health Coalition, 1996-2000; chmn, Vines Menswear Inc, 1996-; pres, Flint Inner City Golf Club, 1996; pres, Downtown Kiwanis, 1998-99; comt mem, Buick Open Community Alliance, 2001-; bd mem, Uptown Reinvestment Corp, 2001; chmn, Goodwill Industs Mid-Mich; vice chmn, Uptown Reinvestment Corp; chmn, Food Bank Eastern Mich. **Home Addr:** 6137 Pebbleshire Dr, Grand Blanc, MI 48439. **Business Addr:** President, Founder, Action Management Corp, 915 S Grand Traverse St, Flint, MI 48502, **Business Phone:** (810)234-2828.

**HIGH-TESFAGIORGIS, FREIDA W.**
Historian, educator, artist. **Personal:** Born Oct 21, 1946, Starkville, MS; married Gebre Hewit; children: 2; married Gebre Hewit; children: 2. **Educ:** Graceland Col, AA, 1966; Northern Ill Univ, BS, 1968; Univ Wis, MA, 1970, MFA, 1971; Univ Chicago, PhD. **Career:** Univ Ibadan, res assoc, 1973-74; Univ Wis, dept studies exhibs, 1970-, afro-amer studies, artist-in-residence, 1971-72, asst prof art dept, dept Afro Am Studies, asst prof, 1972-77, assoc prof, 1977-86, prof, 1986-2008, Chairwoman, 1990-93, evjue-bascom prof, 2008-12; Contemp African & Afro-Am Art, researcher; Trad African Art, maj shows cur, 1971, 1972; Prints & Paintings Afro-Am Art, cur, 1972; Wis Acad Arts Lett Sci; Ky State Univ, 1974; Studio Mus, NY, 1976; Ford Found W Africa & Inst Int Educ, consul, 2006-07, consult & educator, 2009. **Orgs:** Nat Conf Artists. **Honors/Awds:** Visual Arts Grant, Wis Arts Bd, 1977; City Arts Grant, Cult Comm Off Mayor, 1977. **Special Achievements:** Numerous exhibitions & publications. **Business Addr:** Professor, University of Wisconsin-Madison, 4141 Helen C White Hall 600 N Pk St, Madison, WI 53706, **Business Phone:** (608)263-2338.

**HIGHSMITH, ALONZO WALTER**
Football player, football coach. **Personal:** Born Feb 26, 1965, Bartow, FL; son of Walter; married Denise; children: Alonzo, A J, Jordan, Jasmine & Brando. **Educ:** Univ Miami, FL, BBA, mkt, 1987. **Career:** Football player (retired), scout, coach, social worker; Houston Oilers, fullback & running back, 1987, fullback, 1988-89; Dallas Cowboys, fullback, 1990-91, Tampa Bay Buccaneers, running back, 1991-92; Kans City Chiefs, 1993; boxer, 1995-99; Univ Ark, linebacker; Tex Southern Univ, head coach; Green Bay Packers, scout, 1998-, sr personnel exec, currently; Natl Recruiting Serv, founder, currently. **Home Addr:** 3703 Valley Dr, Missouri City, TX 77549. **Business Addr:** Scout, Senior Personnel Executive, Green Bay Packers Inc, 1265 Lombardi Ave, Green Bay, WI 54307-0628, **Business Phone:** (920)569-7500.

**HIGHSMITH, CARLTON L.**
Executive, president (organization). **Personal:** Born Greenville, NC; children: Alexis & Jennifer. **Educ:** Univ Wis-Madison, BA, econs & MBA, mkt, 1973; Univ Conn, attended 1980; Duke Univ Fuqua Grad Sch Bus, exec training prog; Dartmouth's Tuck Grad Sch Bus, exec training prog; Harvard Univ Grad Sch Bus, exec training prog. **Career:** Warner Packaging, Mgt Trainee/Sales & Strategic Planning Coordr, 1974-76; I Have A Dream & New Haven, chmn; Rexham Corp, acct mgr, 1974-76; Amstar Corp, mkt & prod develop mgr, 1976-83; Specialized Packaging Group Inc, pres, chief exec officer & co-founder, 1983-; Univ Wis-Madison, l&s bd visitors, 1999-2011; Hamden Parks & Recreation Dept, youth basketball coach; NewAlliance Bank, dir, 2006-; NewAlliance Bank, dir, 2006-; Bridgeport, oper; New Alliance Bancshares Inc, dir, 2006; Fed Res Bank Boston, new eng community econ adv coun, 2009-; Conn Ctr for Arts & Technol, chmn, 2010-; Specialized Packaging Radisson LLC, exec; First Niagara Financial Group Inc, dir, 2011-. **Orgs:** Bd trustee, Quinnipiac Univ, 2006-; Am Mkt Asn; Am Mgt Asn; Soc plastic Engrs; Inst Packaging Profs; Paperboard Packaging Coun; life mem, Nat Asn Advan Colored People; Urban League Greater New Haven; cult curric comn, New Haven Pub Sch Adv Bd; adv bd, Conn Coalition Achievement Now; bd dir, First City Fund Corp; trustee, Yale-New Haven Hosp Inc; dir, Amistad Acad Charter Sch; chmn, Dixwell Ave Congregational Church; dir, Achievement First; dir, Yale-New Haven Health Serv Corp; dir, First Niagara Bank. **Home Addr:** 56 Leatherman Trail, Hamden, CT 06518, **Home Phone:** (203)281-1592. **Business Addr:** President, Chief Executive Officer, Specialized Packaging Group Inc, 3190 Whitney Ave Suite 7-3, Hamden, CT 06518, **Business Phone:** (203)248-3370.

**HIGHTOWER, ANTHONY**
Lawyer, state government official, college teacher. **Personal:** Born Atlanta, GA; son of John Vincent and Erie Beavers. **Educ:** Clark Atlanta Univ, Atlanta Ga, BA, polit sci, 1983; Univ Iowa, Iowa City, IA, JD, 1986; Harvard Univ, MPA, 1996. **Career:** Self-employed, Col Park Ga, atty, 1986-; Clark Col, Atlanta Ga, teacher, 1988-; City Col Park, Col Park, Ga, city councilman, 1986-90; Dallas, asst city atty; Clark Atlanta Univ, Atlanta, Ga, adj prof, 1988-; mayor pro team, 1990; State Ga, Atlanta, Ga, state rep, 1991-92; Univ Wis, Milwaukee, Off Equity & Diversity Serv, dir; Med Col Ga, sr legal adv, 2006-. **Orgs:** Nat Asn Advan Colored People, 1979-; Alpha Phi Alpha Frat, 1980, 1982-83; bd mem, Clark Col, 1982-83; State Bar Ga, 1986-; Nat Bar Asn, 1986-; Am Bar Asn, 1986-; Natl League Cities, 1986-; Nat Black Caucus Local Elected Offs, 1986-; Ga Munic Asn, 1986-; bd mem, Fulton County Pub Safety Training Ctr, 1989-. **Home Addr:** 2210 Ross Ave, College Park, GA 30337. **Business Addr:** Senior Legal Advisor, Medical College of Georgia, AA 211, Augusta, GA 30912, **Business Phone:** (706)721-4018.

**HIGHTOWER, HERMA J.**
Federal government official, teacher. **Personal:** Born Mesa, AZ; daughter of Mae Kemp Harris and Oliver Harris; married Claude George; children: Collette, Yvette, Valerie & Kimberly. **Educ:** Ariz State Univ, BA, 1963, MA, 1966, PhD, 1977. **Career:** Roosevelt Sch Dist, classroom teacher, 1963-70; Ariz State Personnel Comn, training officer, 1970-71; Ariz Dept Educ, educ prog consult, 1971-74, dir, ESEA Title I, 1974-76, dep assoc supt schs, 1976-78; Internal Revenue Serv, asst dir, 1978-79, asst dir, 1980-81, asst dist dir, 1985-, dist dir, 1988; Smithsonian Inst, dir nat progs, currently. **Orgs:** Guest speaker, Challenger Space Ctr, Peoria, 1963; adv bd, Ariz State Univ Model Mobility Women, 1976; ad hoc consult, Nat Inst Educ, Nat Coaltion Title I Parents, Lawyers Comn Civil Rights Under Law, 1976; City Phoenix Human Rels Comn, 1977; bd dir, Phoenix Urban League, 1977-79; adhoc consult, Am Educ Res Asn, 1977; bd dir, Phoenix Opportunities Indust Ctr, 1978-79; Seattle Opportunities Indust Ctr, 1980-81; bd dir, Seattle Urban League, 1980-81; Bus Admin Tech Comt, Seattle Jr Col, 1980-81; Sr Exec Asn, 1980-; exec comt, Resurgens Atlanta, 1983-; bd dir, Young Women's Christian Asn, 1985-; natspeaker, motivation/goal setting; bd dir, United Way Greater Des Moines, 1988-; Rotary Club Greater Des Moines, 1988-; Nexus Breakfast Club; LINKS Inc; Delta Sigma Theta; bd dir, United Way Cent Md. **Honors/Awds:** Distinguished Service Award, Nat Asn Black Accountants, 1982; Key notespeaker, Governor's Salute Black Women Ariz, 1986; Certificate of Merit, City Atlanta, 1988; Partnership in Administration Award, Gen Serv Admin, 1989; Outstanding Performance Rating, 1990; Regional Commissioner's Leadership Award, 1990; Distinguished Performance Rating, 1991; Meritorious Presidential Rank Award; Coalition of 100 Black Women Award, 1992; Outstanding Performance Rating, 1992. **Special Achievements:** First African-American Female in the History of IRS to be Selected for its Executive Program in 1978; First African-American Female Director in History of IRS, 1988; First Female Executive in nine-state region, 1988. **Home Addr:** 3105 Edgewood Rd, Ellicott City, MD 21043, **Home Phone:** (410)461-1577. **Business Addr:** Director of National Programs, Smithsonian Institute, SI Bldg Rm 153 MRC 010, Washington, DC 20013-7012, **Business Phone:** (202)633-1000.

**HIGHTOWER, MICHAEL**
Government official, administrator. **Personal:** Born College Park, GA; son of Erie; married Sandra; children: Evie. **Educ:** Clark Col Atlanta, BA, music, 1979; Ga State Univ. **Career:** Ga State Univ, admin coordr, asst to dir physical plant oper, 1979-; City Hall Col Park, councilman, mayor pro team; Fulton County, comnr; Collaborative Firm, founder & managing partner, 2001-; Barton Malow, dir community develop. **Orgs:** Friendship Baptist Church, 1965-, Eta Lambda Chap Alpha Phi Alpha, 1979-, Ga Munic Assoc, 1980-, Nat League Cities, 1980-; S Fulton Chamber Com, 1980-, Airport Int Jaycees, 1982-, bd dir Jesse Draper Boy's Club, 1983-; pres, Nat Asn Counties; Fulton County Bldg Authority; Fulton County Water Resources Bd; Grady Memorial Hosp Oversight Comt; comnr, Fulton Co Comn; chair, African Am Golf Found; Urban Land Inst; Woodruff Arts Ctr Bd; Ga Regional Transp Authority Policy Comt; Americans Arts; 100 Black Men; Atlanta Urban League Bd; chair, Fulton County Retirement Bd; chmn, S Fulton Community Resource Alliance Inc. **Honors/Awds:** Outstanding Service, HS & Community Atlanta Airport Rotary Club, 1975; Man of the Year Award, Alpha Phi Alpha, 1979; Outstanding Young Men of America Award, Am Jaycees, 1980, 1983; Disting Alumni Award, Men Clark Col, 1980; Outstanding Young People of Atlanta Award, 1980; Disting Community Service Award, Woodward Acad, 1981; Disting Community Service Award, Friendship Baptist Church, 1983; Award of Appreciation, Flipper Temple AME Church, 1984; Professional Man of the Year, 1989; Numerous awards from various organizations including Ga Trend Mag, Clark Atlanta Univ, White House; Received More Than 300 Awards. **Home Addr:** 510 11th St W, Tifton, GA 31794-5103, **Home Phone:** (404)696-4561. **Business Addr:** Founder, Managing Partner, Collaborative Firm, 1514 E Cleveland Ave Suite 82, Atlanta, GA 30344, **Business Phone:** (404)684-7031.

**HIGHTOWER, STEPHEN LAMAR, II**
Executive, petroleum worker. **Personal:** Born Sep 21, 1956, Middletown, OH; son of Elsie and Yudell; married Brenda Ware; children: Quincy, Stephanie, Sabrina & Stephen Jr. **Educ:** Wright State Univ, mgt & commun, 1978. **Career:** Hi-Mark Construct Corp, pres, 1979-; Hightowers Petrol Co, pres & chief exec officer, 1981-; HP Energy, chmn & pres, 2010-; Prudential Environ Technologies Inc, pres; Landmark Bldg Serv Inc, pres; NBCSL CRT, primary rep. **Orgs:** Black Male Coalition, 1992; pres, SOS Community Inc, 1992; Minori-

ty Supplier Develop Coun, 1992; ABC Ohio Contractors, 1992; bd dir, Jr Achievement, 1992; United Missionary Baptist Church, 1992; Nat Parks Found Bd; Cincinnati Zoo Bd; Nat Petrol Coun; Wright State Univ Found Bd; State Ohio Underground Storage Tank Bd; Am Asn Blacks Energy; Soc Independent Gasoline Marketeers Asn; Nat Asso od Convient Stores; Nat Minority Supplier Develop Coun; Nat Caucaus Black State Legislatures; Un Global Compact. **Honors/Awds:** Salesman of the Year, Snyder Realtors, 1979; Top 100 Minority Business, State Ohio, 1981; Toastmaster Int, 1986; Ceco Bldg, Largest Bldg Sold Midwest Region, 1989; Distinguished Service Award, Ohio Young Dem, 2001. **Special Achievements:** Honored as one of Cincinnati's Emerging Leaders for his work Young Professional Circles. **Home Addr:** 4700 Deer Crk, Middletown, OH 45042-5802, **Home Phone:** (513)217-1949. **Business Addr:** President, Chief Executive Officer, Hightowers Petroleum Co, 3577 Com Dr, Franklin, OH 45005, **Business Phone:** (513)423-4272.

### HIGHTOWER, HON. WILLAR H., JR.
Executive, county government official, engineer. **Personal:** Born Aug 8, 1943, Greenville, SC; married Pergetta K Smith; children: Willa J, Terri T & Catrice. **Educ:** SC State Univ, BS, math, 1964; NC Col, Durham, MS, math, 1965; Interdenominational Theol Ctr, M Div, theol, 2010. **Career:** AUS, battery comdr, 1965-67; Du Pont SRP, Westinghouse SRP, lessons learned, engr, 1967-2001; Hightower-enterprize, chief exec officier, 1976, retired; USAR Defense Personnel Support Ctr, logistician, 1981-89; WSRC, comput programmer, 1967-79, buyer, 1979-89, asst purchasing agt, 1980-89; Aiken County, Dist 8, city councilman, 1981-; Lessons Learned, engr, 1989-2000; Church, FBC Aiken, asst minister, 2007-. **Orgs:** Nat Asn Advan Colored People, 1967-; Res Officers Asn, 1968-; bd dir, Aiken Chap Am Red Cross, 2001-. **Honors/Awds:** Presented Key to the City of Aiken, 1986. **Home Addr:** 736 Richland Ave W, Aiken, SC 29801, **Home Phone:** (803)648-3020. **Business Addr:** Associate Minister, Friendship Baptist Church, 515 Richland Ave NE, Aiken, SC 29801, **Business Phone:** (803)221-3240.

### HILDRETH, DR. GLADYS JOHNSON
School administrator, educator. **Personal:** Born Oct 15, 1933, Columbia, MS; married Eddie Jr; children: Bertina, Dwayne, Kathleen & Karen. **Educ:** Southern Univ, Baton Rouge, La, BS, 1953; Univ Wis, Madison, MS, 1955; Mich State Univ, East Lansing, PhD, 1973. **Career:** Southern Univ, assoc prof, 1955-74; La State Univ Sch Human Ecol, chair & prof dept family studies, 1975-89, Sch Human Ecol, prof emer, 1989-; Tex Woman's Univ, Denton, prof dept family studies, 1990-2000; Univ Ky, chair & prof dept family studies, 1998-2005, dept chair, 2000-06; Univ N Tex, Educ Psychol, lectr, 2005, retired. **Orgs:** Delta Sigma Theta, 1970-; consult, Nat Asn Educ Young C, 1974-; Ctr Family Am Home Econ Asn, 1977-79; state chmn aging serv, La Home Econ Asn, 1978-80; chmn, jr div adv coun La State Univ, 1979-80; Phi Upsilon Omicron Southern Univ Home Econ; Omicron Nu Mich State Univ Human Ecol; Nat Coun Family Rels; Sect, TCFR; Tex Consortium Geriat Educ. **Honors/Awds:** Grad Sch Fel, Mich State Univ Human Ecol, 1970; Thelma Porter Fel, Mich State Univ Human Ecol, 1970; Recipient Los Angeles Home Econ Asn Distinguished District & State Service Award, 1986; Nominated Am Coun Educ Fel; Distinguished Faculty Fellowship Award, La State Univ; Distinguished Service Award, SE Coun Family Rels; Nat Coun Family Rel, Marie Peters Ethnic Minority Award. **Home Addr:** 1012 Indian Ridge Dr, Denton, TX 76205, **Home Phone:** (940)320-1991. **Business Addr:** Lecturer, University of North Texas, 1155 Union Circle, Denton, TX 76203-5017, **Business Phone:** (940)369-7046.

### HILDRETH, JAMES (JAMES EARL KING HILDRETH)
Immunologist, educator, dean (education). **Personal:** Born Dec 27, 1956, Camden, AR; son of R J and Lucy; married Phyllis King; children: 2. **Educ:** Harvard Univ, BS, chem, 1979; Oxford Univ, PhD, immunol, 1982; John Hopkins Univ, MD, 1987. **Career:** Johns Hopkins Univ, Sch Med, assoc dean grad stud affairs, 1997-2004, prof pharamacol, 2002-05; Nat Insts Health, chief res; Meharry Med Col, var positions, 2005-11, incl: dir ctr AIDS Health Disparities Res, prog dir Res Centers Minority Insts, dir Meharry Ctr Translational Res, assoc dir, Vanderbilt-Meharry Ctr AIDS Res, prof internal med, microbiol & immunol; Univ Calif-Davis, Col Biol Sci, Dean, 2011-; Meharry Med Col, pres & chief exec officer, 2016-. **Orgs:** American Society of Microbiology, Member; National Academy of Sciences, Institute of Medicine, Member. **Honors/Awds:** Rhodes Scholar; Alpha Omega Alpha; NSF Presidential Young Investigator; NIH Director's Pioneer Award; Arkansas Black Hall of Fame, 2009; Johns Hopkins University Alumni Association Knowledge for the World Award, Johns Hopkins Univ, 2012. **Special Achievements:** First African American Rhodes Scholar from Arkansas; author and co-author of numerous articles published in concerning autoimmune issues; expert in HIV and AIDS research; First African American In 125 Year Of History Of Johns Hopkins To Earn Full Professorship With Tenure In The Basic Sciences, 2012.

### HILL, ANITA FAYE
Educator, lawyer. **Personal:** Born Jul 30, 1956, Lone Tree, OK; daughter of Albert and Erma. **Educ:** Okla State Univ, BS, psychol, 1977; Yale Univ Law Sch, JD, 1980. **Career:** Wash, DC, law firm, 1980-81; US Dept Educ, Asst Secy Clarence Thomas, spec coun, 1981-82; US Equal Employ Opportunity Comn, chmn, 1982-83; Oral Roberts Univ, law prof, 1983-86; Univ Okla, Col Law, prof law, 1986-96; Univ Calif, Inst Study Social Chg, vis scholar, 1997; Brandeis Univ, prof social policy, law & women's studies, 1998-. Books: Race, Gender and Power in America: The Legacy of the Hill-Thomas Hearings, co-ed, 1995; Speaking Truth to Power, 1997; Reimagining Equality: Stories of Gender, Race and Finding Home, 2011. **Orgs:** Antioch Baptist Church; Big Bros Big Sisters, Am Green County, OK; DC Bar, 1980; Nat Women's Law Ctr; Okla Bar Asn; fel Fletcher Found, 2005; bd trustee, Southern Vt Col. **Special Achievements:** Her opening statement to the Senate Judiciary Committee in 1991 is listed as #69 in American Rhetoric's Top 100 Speeches of the 20th Century. **Business Addr:** Professor of Social Policy Law & Womens Studies, Brandeis University, Heller-Brown Bldg 374, Waltham, MA 02453, **Business Phone:** (781)736-3896.

### HILL, ANNETTE TILLMAN
Educator, counselor, elementary school teacher. **Personal:** Born Nov 9, 1937, Copiah County, MS; daughter of Fayette and Martha Coleman; children: Gerri Lavonne Hill-Chance. **Educ:** Tougaloo Col, BS, 1956; Chicago State Univ, MS, educ, 1971; Jackson State Univ; Univ Miss. **Career:** Educator (retired); sci & math teacher, 1956-60; Chicago Pub Sch, sci teacher, 1960-69; Wendell Phillips High Sch, Chicago, counr, 1969-71; Jackson State Univ, counr, 1971-82; Hazlehurst High Sch, counr, 1982; Hazlehurst Mid Sch, substitute counr, 2008-09. **Orgs:** Bd dir, Cent Miss Chap, Am Red Cross, 1978-81, 1985-88; adv comn mem, Juv Justice, State Miss, 1981-89; chmn, Emergency Food & Shelter Adv Comt, Copiah County, 1985-; Copiah County Econ Develop; bd dir, Boys & Girls Club S Cent Miss; Develop Plan Early Childhood Educ Serv, Copiah County; Miss Counr Asn; Am Asn Coun & Develop; Multicultural Asn Coun & Develop; Hazlehurst Pub Schs PTA; vpres, Hazlehurst Br, Nat Asn Advan Colored People. **Home Addr:** 321 N Massengill St, Hazlehurst, MS 39083-2815, **Home Phone:** (601)894-3660.

### HILL, BARBARA A.
Consultant, association executive, chief executive officer. **Educ:** Ky State Univ, BS; Wash Univ, St Louis, MO, MS, social work. **Career:** Mich Womens Found, pres & chief exec officer, 2003; Girl Scouts USA, consult; Nat Off Young Women's Christian Asn, USA, consult; Girl Scouts Mitten Bay, chief exe cofficer; Young Women's Christian Asn, Metropolitan Detroit, chief exec officer; Women Cos Bus Initiative, Milwaukee, WI, chief exec officer; Detroit Empowerment Zone Develop Corp, consult; Marygrove College, Institutional Advancement, vpres, 2007-. **Orgs:** Bd trustee, Grant Allocation Comn; Alliance Women Entrepreneurs; Olivet Col, Olivet, MI; bd trustee, Mich Women's Found. **Business Addr:** Vice President, Marygrove College, 8425 W Mcnichols Rd, Detroit, MI 48221-2546, **Business Phone:** (313)927-1200.

### HILL, BARBARA ANN
Educator. **Personal:** Born Mar 31, 1950, Brooklyn, NY; daughter of Robert Floyd and Delphine Chaplin Floyd; married Larry; children: Vaughn & Kinshasa. **Educ:** Long Island Univ CW Post Ctr, BS, 1974, MS, 1984. **Career:** Howard T Herber Mid Sch, educr; Tyrrell County Pub Schs, parent involvement Coordr, Columbia NC; Columbia HS & MS, Columbia, NC, phys educ teacher. **Orgs:** NY State Pub High Sch Athletic Asn, 1976-92; found, adv, Malverne Girls Varsity Club, 1976-92; track champ Nassau Co HS Girls Track, 1978-84; Nassau Girls Athletic Rep, 1979-92; Black Educr Coalition Malverne HS, 1984-92; found & adv Carter G Woodson Black Studies Club, 1984-92; sec Nassau Co Volleyball Coaches Asn, 1985-87; workshop crd Hempstead Pre-K Reading Workshop, 1984-91; pres, Ludlum PTA, 1985-89; corresp secy, Nassau County High Sch Athletic Asn, 1990-92; rep, Nassau County High Sch Athletic Coun, 1987-92; treas, PTA, 1990-92; Key Women Am, 1986-92, vip, 1990-92; treas, Ludlum PTA, 1989-92; pres, Alta B Gray-Schultz Mid Sch PTA, 1991-92; Tyrell Elem Sch Parents Planning comn, 1992-93; Community Voices, 1992-95; Church Rd Emergency Food Closet, Food Pantry, chair person, 1994; found, adv, Black Hist Club Prog, Columbia HS & MS, 1992-; secy, NC Breast Cancer Screening Prog, Tyrrell County Lay Community Adv Bd, 1994-01; secy, NCP, 1998-. **Home Addr:** 160 Travis Sch Rd, Columbia, NC 27925. **Business Addr:** Physical Education Teacher, Atnletic Director, Columbia High School, PO Box 419, Columbia, NC 27925-0419, **Business Phone:** (252)796-8161.

### HILL, BEATRICE MELBA. See MOORE, MELBA.

### HILL, BOB. See HILL, ROBERT LEWIS.

### HILL, BOBBY L., SR.
Government official. **Educ:** Wayne State Univ, BS, bus admin, 1971, educ specialist cert, 1974; Eastern Mich Univ, MA, educ admin, 1973. **Career:** Mt Clemens Community Schs, teacher admin; Real Estate Investor, 1980-; United Memorial Funeral Home, partner, 1985; Community Cent Bank, bd dir & dir emer, currently; Macomb County, bd comnr; Community Cent Mortgage Co LLC, chmn. **Orgs:** Trustee, N Broadway Church Christ; chmn, Midwestern Christian Inst Bd Dir; Mt Clemens Found; Macomb County Comn Growth Aliance; Macomb County Br Nat Asn Advan Colored People Exec Comn; Macomb County Bd Comnr; N Broadway Church Christ; Midwestern Christian Inst; Mt Clemens Educ Found; Macomb County Community Dispute Resolution Ctr; Salvation Army; Macomb County Br Nat Asn Advan Colored People. **Home Addr:** 37552 Charter Oaks Blvd, Clinton Township, MI 48036, **Home Phone:** (586)463-5947. **Business Addr:** Director Emeritus, Community Central Bank Corp, 120 N Main St, Mount Clemens, MI 48043-5605, **Business Phone:** (586)783-4500.

### HILL, DR. BONNIE GUITON
Foundation executive, president (organization). **Personal:** Born Oct 30, 1941, Springfield, IL; daughter of Zola Elizabeth Newman Brazelton and Henry Frank Brazelton; married Walter Jr; children: 3. **Educ:** Mills Col, BA, psychol, 1974; Calif State Univ, MA, educ psychol, 1975; Univ Calif, Berkeley, EdD, 1985. **Career:** Mills Col, Ethnic Studies Dept, asst dean studs, 1974-76, lectr, interim dir; Marcus Foster Educ Inst, exec dir, 1976-79; Kaiser Ctr Inc, vpres & gen mgr, 1979-84; US Postal Rate Comn, comnr, 1984-87; US Dept Educ Wash, DC, asst secy, 1987-89; US Off Consumer Affairs, Wash, DC, spec adv to pres & dir, 1989-90; Earth Conserv Corps, chief exec officer & pres, 1990-91; State Calif, State & Consumer Servs Agency, secy, 1991-92; Niagara Mohawk Holdings Inc, dir, 1991-; Univ Va, McIntire Sch Com, dean, 1992-96, prof; Hershey Co, dir, mem Comt dir & Corp Governance, mem Governance Comt & mem Compensation & Exec Orgn Comt, 1993-2007; Times Mirror Found, pres & chief exec officer, 1997-2001; Los Angeles Times, Community Rels, sr vpres, 1998-2001; Icon Blue, co-founder, 1998-, dir, chief operating officer; Home Depot Inc, lead dir, chmn Nominating & Corp Governance Comt & mem Leadership Develop & Compensation Comt, 1999-; Choicepoint Inc, dir, 2001; B Hill Enterprises LLC, pres, 2001-; Nat Grid plc, non-exec dir & dir-Nat Grid Transco, 2002-03; New Albertson's Inc, dir, chmn Nominating & Corp Governance Comt & mem Exec Comt, 2002-; Times Mirror Co, vpres; Kaiser Aluminum & Chem Corp, vpres; Gene Juarez Salons, vpres, human resources, currently. **Orgs:** Bd dir, Conf Christians & Jews Asn, 1983-86; Nat Urban Coalition; Nat Asn Regulatory Utility Comrs, 1984-87; Exec Women Govt, 1985-; bd dir, Nat Mus Women Arts, 1988-89; bd dir, Niagara Mohawk Power Corp, 1991; Albertsons, 2002-06; bd dir, Yum! Brands, 2003; independent dir, Calif Water Serv Group, 2003-; Nat Asn Advan Colored People Legal Defense Fund; Urban Land Inst; bd dir, La Pac Corp; Hershey Foods Corp; bd dir, AK Steel Holding Corp; Crestar Financial Corp; bd dir, Home Depot; bd dir, NASD Regulations; fel Investor Educ Found; chair, Consumer Affairs Adv Comt Securities & Exchange Comn; Hershey Foods Corp; RREEF Fundsl dir, AK Steel Holdings Corp; RREEF; Joint Ctr Polit & Econ Studies; Ponoma Col; La Downtown Women's Ctr; Ctr Excellence Educ; trustee, RAND Corp. **Honors/Awds:** Tribute to Women in Int Indust, YWCA, 1981; Outstanding Community Leader & Humanitarian Award, Nat Asn Advan Colored People Legal Defense Fund, 1981; Candace Award, Nat Coalition 100 Black Women, 1982; Equal Rights Advocate Award, 1984; Distinguished Meritorious Award, DC Human Servs, 1987; Hon Doctorate Tougaloo Univ, 1988; Dirs Choice Award; Nat Women's Econ Alliance Coun, 1992; Citation, Marcus Foster Educational Institute. **Business Addr:** Director, Chief Operating Officer, Icon Blue, 5670 Wilshire Blvd Suite 600, Los Angeles, CA 90036, **Business Phone:** (323)634-5301.

### HILL, BRUCE EDWARD
Football player. **Personal:** Born Feb 29, 1964, Ft. Dix, NJ. **Educ:** Ariz State Univ. **Career:** Football player (retired); Tampa Bay Buccaneers, wide receiver, 1987-93. **Honors/Awds:** Most Valuable Player, Tampa Bay Buccaneers, 1988.

### HILL, CALVIN G.
Businessperson, athlete, consultant. **Personal:** Born Jan 2, 1947, Baltimore, MD; son of Henry and Elizabeth; married Janet McDonald; children: Grant. **Educ:** Yale Univ, BA, 1969; Southern Methodist Univ, Perkins Sch Theol, 1971. **Career:** Football running back (retired); Nat Football League, running back, 1969-81; Dallas Cowboys, running back, 1969-74, team consult, currently; Hawaiians WFL, running back, 1975; Wash Redskins, 1976-77; World Football League, 1975; Cleveland Browns, running back, 1978-81; Baltimore Orioles, vpres & admin personnel, 1987, bd dir; Bill Clinton's Coun Phys Fitness, pres, 1993-2000; Peace Corp, spec asst dir; Pepper Co, Pub Rel Rep & Nat Good Will, ambassador; Dallas Bank & Trust, com loan officer & asst vpres; Jarvis Christian Col, develop dir; Bethlehem Steel Co, labor rel rep; NFL Cleveland Browns, consult; Alexander & Assoc Inc, consult, currently; Fleet Financial Serv, consult, currently; Cleveland Browns Football Club, consult, currently. **Orgs:** Yale Club Wash, DC; exec bd, Yale Develop Bd; Yale Univ Coun, 1982-86; adv bd, Rand Corp Drug Policy Res Ctr; Delta Kappa Epsilon Fraternity; Battel Chapel Deacons; St Elmo's Soc; Black Stud Yale; Md Athletic Hall Fame; assoc fel Pierson Col. **Honors/Awds:** Pro Bowl NFL All-Star Game, 1969, 1972-74; NFL Rookie of the Year, 1969; Sporting News NFL Estrn Conf All-Star Team, 1969; All NFL Pro Football Writers America, 1969, 1973; NFL Champ Games, 1970-71; 1000 Yard Club, 1972; Sporting News NFC All-Star, 1973; hon doctorate, Yale Univ, 2016; Jordan Oliver Award; Chester Pla Roche Scholarship; Calvin Hill Day Care Center, New Haven. **Special Achievements:** First Cowboy running back, 1972. **Business Addr:** Consultant, Alexander & Associates Inc, 4400 Jenifer St NW, Washington, DC 20015, **Business Phone:** (202)363-8520.

### HILL, CLARA GRANT
Educator, executive. **Personal:** Born Oct 5, 1928, Hugo, OK. **Educ:** Philander Smith Col, BA, 1952; Memphis State Univ, MA. **Career:** Long view Elem Sch, chairperson, sixth grade teachers, 1963-77, teacher, 1985; Memphis Educ Asn, faculty rep, 1963-; Prof Growth Comt, chairperson, 1973-; acting prin, 1972-77. **Orgs:** Cancer Fund; Birth Defects; teacher Sun Sch, 1964-; dir, Chrian Ed, 1966-67; adv, Jr Usher Bd, 1970-; pres, Les Demonselles Club, 1972; pres, Usher Bd, 1972; Memphis Ed Asn; W TN Ed Asn; TN Ed Asn; Nat Ed Asn; exec bd MEA, 1973-76; chairperson, Birth month Fel, 1973; basileus Sigma Gamma Rho Sor, 1973-75; chairperson, Outstanding Sigma Woman Yr, 1973-74; chairperson, memship comn MEA, 1974-76; exec bd mem, chairperson, Xmas Seals, 1975-76; Credentials Comn TEA, 1976; pres, Dept Classroom Teachers TEA, 1976-78; chairperson, Const Comt, 1976; comt mem, Curric Develop Elem Ed, app St Comn Educ, 1977; chairperson, Status Women Educ MEA, 1977; chairperson, Screening Comt Hiring Staff MEA, 1977-78; chairperson, Black Caucus MEA, 1977; Resultants Comn TEA, 1977; Nat Asn Advan Colored People; mem Comn Reg & Nat Chapters Sor; YWCA; pres, Optimistic Chartable Soc Club, 1r Smith Alum Asn; community weeker Heart Fund; Ada Cir Missionary Soc; pres, Dept Classroom Teacher TEA, 1977. **Honors/Awds:** Five Outstanding Service Awards, MEA, 1974-77; Leadership Training Award, NEA, 1976; Two Community Service Awards, US Congressman Harold Ford TN, 1976-77. **Home Addr:** 1085 Stafford Ave, Memphis, TN 38106, **Home Phone:** (901)946-9504.

### HILL, COLIN C.
Executive, association executive. **Educ:** Va Polytech Inst & State Univ, BS, physics, 1996; McGill Univ, MS, physics; Cornell Univ, MS, physics, 2000. **Career:** Dow Chem Co, engineering co-op, 1993-95; Santa Fe Inst, intern, 1996; Via Sci, chief exec officer & chmn, 2000-; Fina Technologies, chmn, 2008-12; GNS Healthcare, chief exec officer, 2010-; BioTelemetry Healthcare, bd dirs, 2016-. **Orgs:** Bd dir, New York Found Sci Technol & Innovation; bd dir, AesRx, currently; bd dir, Fina Technologies. **Honors/Awds:** Rising Star Award, Black Enterprise, 2004; Alumini Award, Virginia Tech Alumini Asn. **Special Achievements:** Appeared in numerous publications & television segments including The Wall Street Jour, CNBC Morning Call, Nature, Wired, & Economist; named to MIT Technology Review's TR100 list of the top innovators in the world under the age of 35, 2004. **Business Addr:** Chairman & Co-Founder, Chief Executive Officer & President, GNS Healthcare, 1 Charles Pk, Cambridge, MA 02142-1254, **Business Phone:** (617)374-2300.

### HILL, CURTIS T., SR.

Educator, insurance agent, politician. **Personal:** Born Jun 30, 1929, Vernon, OK; son of Curtis L and Virginia; married Teresa; children: Sonya L & Curtis. **Educ:** BS, 1950; Dent Tech, 1953; Adviced Life Ins, 1971. **Career:** St Farm Ins Co, agent; Jr High Sch, teacher. **Orgs:** Nat Asn Life Underwriters; vpres, Elkhart Co Life Underwriters; pres, Nat Asn Advan Colored People Chap; pres, Elkhart Urban League; bd dir, Am Cancer Soc; Nat Black Caucus Sch Bd Mem; former life mem chair, Elkhart Nat Asn Advan Colored People; bd mem, Jaycees; Elkhart Sch Bd; Life Ins Millionaires Club, 1972. **Honors/Awds:** Outstanding Historian Award, Ind Jaycees, 1960; Award for Outstanding Contribution to Education, Ind Sch Bd Asn, 1974. **Special Achievements:** First African American candidate for Mayor of Elkhart. **Home Addr:** 1322 McPherson St, Elkhart, IN 46514, **Home Phone:** (574)264-2502. **Business Addr:** Agent, State Farm Insurance Co, 2408 S Nappanee St, Elkhart, IN 46514.

### HILL, CYNTHIA D.

Lawyer. **Personal:** Born Feb 5, 1952, Bethesda, MD; daughter of Melvin Leroy and Mamie L Landrum. **Educ:** Wellesley Col, BA, polit sci, 1974; Georgetown Univ Law Ctr, JD, 1977. **Career:** DC Off Consumer Protection, law clerk to admin law judge, 1977-78; League Women Voters Educ Fund, staff atty litigation dept, 1978-84, actg dir litigation dept, 1984-85, dir election serv & litigation, 1985-90; DC Bar, asst exec dir progs, 1990-2010, chief progs officer, 2010-. **Orgs:** DC Bar; Women's Div Nat Bar Asn, 1977-; Wash Bar Asn, 1978-; Women's Bar Asn, DC, 1979-; bd dir, Metro Wash Planning & Housing Asn, 1980-89; Wash Coun Lawyers, 1986-2006; Am Soc Asn Execs, 1990-; Nat Asn Bar Execs, 1990-, bd dir, 1998-2000; Asn Continuing Legal Educ, 1991-; bd dir, Friends Nat Parks, Gettysburg Inc, 2001-06; mem comt, Gettysburg Found, 2006-; DC Bar Found. **Home Addr:** 843 20th St NE, Washington, DC 20002, **Home Phone:** (202)396-1070. **Business Addr:** Assistant Executive Director for Programs, District of Columbia Bar, 1101 K St NW Suite 200, Washington, DC 20005-4210, **Business Phone:** (202)737-4700.

### HILL, DEBORAH

Labor relations manager. **Personal:** Born Oct 15, 1944, Long Beach, CA; daughter of David and Eva. **Educ:** Calif State Col Long Beach, BA, 1967; Western State Univ Col Law, JD, 1975. **Career:** Shell Oil Co, analyst, 1968-76, sr emp rel analyst, 1976-78, employee rel rep, 1978-82, employee rel asn, 1982-85, serv mgr, 1985-86, sr employee rel rep, 1986; human resources mgr. **Orgs:** Chmn, personnel commun, Alpha Kappa Alpha Sor Inc, 1982-86; historian, Int Asn Personnel Women, 1983; Top Ladies Distinction, 1980-; trustee, bd Wesley Chapel African Methodist Episcopal Church, 1983; Links, 1986; Leadership Long Beach, 1990; bd dir, Nat Conf Community & Justice, 1990; bd dir, CRI, 1990; bd dir, trust fund comt mem, State Bar, Calif, 1991; bd dir, Bouggess White Scholar Fund, 1990-91; United Way, 1991. **Home Addr:** 590 E Pleasant St, Long Beach, CA 90805-6652.

### HILL, HON. DEIRDRE HUGHES

Judge. **Personal:** daughter of Frank E Staggers and Teresa. **Educ:** Univ Calif, Santa Barbara, CA, BA, polit sci; Loyola Law Sch, JD, 1985. **Career:** Los Angeles Police Dept, inspector gen; Los Angeles Police Comn, pres, 1993-96; Saltzburg, Ray & Bergman LLP, sr assoc, 1990-98; Los Angeles Munic Ct, judge, 1999-2000; Los Angeles Super Ct, judge, 2000-; pvt pract, atty, currently. **Orgs:** Bd dir, State Calif, Calif Sci Ctr; dep dir, Calif Dem Party; adv bd, Judicial Coun; Los Angeles County Super Ct Educ Comt. **Business Addr:** Judge, Los Angeles Superior Court, Stanley Mosk Courthouse, Los Angeles, CA 90012, **Business Phone:** (213)974-5671.

### HILL, DENNIS ODELL

Educator, basketball coach. **Personal:** Born Nov 25, 1953, Kansas City, KS; son of Buster and Yvonne Marie Bennett James; married Kathryn Kinnear; children: Erica Nicole & Anthony Jerome. **Educ:** Southwest Mo State Univ, Springfield, MO, BS, 1976. **Career:** Basketball player, 1973-75; Southwest MO State, Springfield, Mo, asst basketball coach, 1978-89; Pittsburg State Univ, Pittsburg, Kans, head basketball coach, 1989-93. **Home Addr:** 4628 S Scenic, Springfield, MO 65810, **Home Phone:** (417)882-6267. **Business Addr:** Head Coach, Pittsburg State University, 1701 S Broadway, Pittsburg, KS 66762, **Business Phone:** (316)235-4648.

### HILL, DIANNE

Educator. **Personal:** Born Mar 6, 1955, Newark, NJ; children: Tania Regina & Gary Robert. **Educ:** Caldwell Col, BA, 1977; Rutgers Univ, cert, 1982; Jersey City State Col, MA, 1985; Rutgers Univ, urban systs, PhD. **Career:** Newark Bd Educ, teacher, 1976-77; Friendly Fuld Head start Prog, teacher, policy comm mem, 1977-80; Caldwell Col, dir educ oppor fund prog, 1980-88; Educ Opportunity Prof Asn, pub rels officer, 1982-86; Rutgers Univ, Acad Foundations Ctr, asst chancellor, 1988-; Pre Col Educ & Community Outreach, co-founder, co-dir; Tri State Inst, vpres; WBGO Pub Broadcast Radio Sta Bd, currently. **Orgs:** Mem policy coun, Friendly Fuld Head start, 1983-85; bd mem, Irvington Community Develop, 1985-86; Womens Employ Network; pvt sector rep, Asn Independent Cols & Univs NJ; bd mem, St James Prep Sch; founder, Off Campus & Community Rels, 2002; pres, NJ Educ Opportunity Fund Prof Asn; co chair, Global Womens Leadership Collab Summit, 2008; chairperson, Educ Cluster Global Women Leadership Collab NJ; co chair, NJ Global Womens Leadership Collab Summit, 2008; founding bd mem, Marion P Thomas Charter Sch; bd mem, St James Prep Sch; Newark Preschool Coun; NJ Legis Black Caucus Found; pres, Positive Choices Enterprises; Newark Women's Conf Inc, currently. **Honors/Awds:** Outstanding Black Women of the Year, 1985; Outstanding Alumnae Award, Caldwell Coll BSCU & Faculty, 1985; 100 Most Influential persons, NJ; The Tri-State Consortium Award for Excellence and Service to the Community, 2009; Chancellors Community Engagement Award; Rutgers Sch Pub Affairs & Admin Pi Alpha Alpha Soc Induction & Award; Legacy Award, Orgn Black Fac & Staff; Shirley Chisholm Education Award. **Home Addr:** 26 Oak Ave, Irvington, NJ 07111. **Business Addr:** Assistant Chancellor, Rutgers University, 249 Univ Ave, Newark, NJ 07102, **Business Phone:** (973)353-1766.

### HILL, DONNA. See NICHOLAS, DONNA DENISE.

### HILL, DONNA

Writer. **Personal:** Born Aug 6, 1955, Brooklyn, NY; children: Nichole, Dawne & Matthew. **Educ:** Pace Univ. **Career:** Medgar Evers Col, Elders Writing Prog, instr; Brooklyn Bor Pres's off, writer, currently; Author: Rooms of the Heart, 1990; Indiscretions, 1991; Murder Uptown, 1992; Scandalous, 1995; Deception, 1996; Temptation, 1997; Intimate Betrayal, 1997; Charade, 1998; Chances Are, 1998; A Private Affair, 1998; Shipwreck Season, 1998; Quiet Storm, 1998; Interlude, 1999; Pieces of Dreams, 1999; Soul to Soul, 2000; If I Could, 2000; A Scandalous Affairs, 2000; Through the Fire, 2001; Rhythms, 2001; Night Winds Calling, 2001; An Ordinary Woman, 2002; Rockin' Around That Christmas Tree: A Holiday Novel, 2003; Divas Inc, 2004; Dark Thirst: An Anthology, 2004; Say Yes, 2004; Dare to Dream, 2004; In My Bedroom, 2004; Getting Hers, 2005; Interlude, 2006; Long Distance Lover, 2006; Love Becomes Her, 2006; Guilty Pleasures, 2006; Saving All My Lovin', 2006; If I Were Your Woman, 2007; After Dark, 2007; Moments Like This, 2007; Wicked Ways, 2007; Sex and Lies, 2008; Seduction and Lies, 2008; Temptation and Lies, 2009; What Mother Never Told Me, 2010; Longing and Lies, 2010; Heart's Reward, 2010; Private Lessons, 2010; Spend My Life with You, 2011; co-wrote screenplay, Fire, 2000, Steele-Perkins Lit Agency, currently; Novels: Spirit of the Season, 1994; Love Letters, 1997; Winter Nights, 1998; Rosie's Curl and Weave, 1999; Welcome to Leo's, 2000; Della's House of Style, 2000; Midnight Clear, 2000; Going to the Chapel, 2001; Sister, Sister, 2001; Tis the Season, 2001; Rockin' Around That Christmas Tree, 2003; Living Large, 2003; Let's Get It on, 2004; A Whole Lotta Love, 2004; Rockin' Around The Christmas Tree, 2004; Courageous Hearts, 2005; Big Girls Don't Cry, 2005; Destiny's Daughters, 2006; Takin' Chances for the Holidays, 2006. **Orgs:** Dir, Kianga House, 1988-92; exec dir, Brooklyn Teen Pregnancy Network, 1992-94; Black Writers Alliance; Novelist; Romance Writers Am; writing instr, Frederick Douglass Creative Arts Ctr. **Honors/Awds:** Community Service Award, Dept Children's Servs, 1993; Named Hon State Senator, mayor Lake Charles, La, 1999; Career Achievement Award, Romantic Times Mag, 1998, 2000; Trailblazer Award; Zora Neale Hurston Literary Award; Gold Pen Award. **Special Achievements:** Featured in Essence, The Daily News, USA Today, Today's Black Woman, and Black Enterprise magazine. **Home Addr:** 737 Dekalb Ave Apt 1R, Brooklyn, NY 11216-4646, **Home Phone:** (718)782-3074. **Business Addr:** Author, Pattie Steele-Perkins, 26 Island Lane, Canandiagua, NY 14424, **Business Phone:** (716)396-9290.

### HILL, DULE (KARIM DULE HILL)

Actor, dancer. **Personal:** Born May 3, 1975, East Brunswick, NJ; son of Bert and Jennifer; married Nicole Lyn. **Educ:** Seton Hall Univ. **Career:** Stage roles: Bring in 'da Noise, Bringin 'da Funk; Shenandoah; Films: Sugar Hill, 1993; She's All That, 1999; Men of Honor, 2000; Television guest appearances: All My Children, 1995; Cosby; Smart Guy; Whisper, 2007; Remarkable Power, 2007-10; Tv movies: "The Ditchdigger's Daughters", 1997; "Color of Justice", 1997; "Love Songs", 1999; "10.5", 2004; Tv series: "Good Old Boy: A Delta Boyhood", "The River Pirates", 1988; "The More You Know", 1989; "City Kids", "Ghostwriter: To Catch a Creep: Part 1", 1992; American Playhouse, 1993; "Sugar Hill?, 1994; "New York News: New York News", "New York Undercover: CAT", 1995; "Cosby: Shall We Dance?", 1997; "Color of Justice, The Ditchdiggers Daughters", 1997; "Smart Guy: Gotta Dance", 1998; "The West Wing", 1999-; "The West Wing: Mr. Willis of Ohio"; "The West Wing: The Crackpots & These Women", "The West Wing: Five Votes Down", "The West Wing: A Proportional Response", "The West Wing", "Chicken Soup for the Soul: Mother's Day", 1999; Love Songs, Shes All That, 1999; The Jamie Foxx Show, 1999; "The West Wing: Take This Sabbath Day", 2000; Men of Honor, 2000; "The West Wing: Isaac & Ishmael", "Mad TV:", 2001; "The West Wing: 100, 000 Airplanes", "The West Wing: 20 Hours in America: Part 1", 2002; Holes, 2003; "The West Wing: Abuel Banat", "Punk'd:", "The West Wing: Twenty Five", 2003; "The West Wing:No Exit", "The West Wing: The Supremes", "The West Wing: Eppur Si Muove", "The West Wing: The Warfare of Genghis Khan", "The West Wing: The Benign Prerogative", 2004; Sexual Life, Edmond, The Numbers, 2005; Edmond, 2005; "Psych Webisodes", "The West Wing: Welcome to Wherever You Are", 2006-; "Hellion, The Guardian", 2006; WWE Raw, 2010; actor, tap dancer, currently. **Orgs:** Nat Bd Screen Actors Guild, 2009. **Honors/Awds:** Dule Hill Day declared Chicago, 1986; Screen Actors Guild Awards, 2001, 2002. **Home Addr:** 9100 Wilshire Blvd W Twr 6th FL, Beverly Hills, CA 90212, **Home Phone:** (310)248-6117. **Business Addr:** Actor, Warner Bros Studios, 4000 Warner Blvd, Burbank, CA 91505, **Business Phone:** (818)954-6000.

### HILL, ERIC

Football player, president (organization). **Personal:** Born Nov 14, 1966, Blytheville, AR; children: Erica & Arielle. **Educ:** La State Univ. **Career:** Football player (retired), executive; Phoenix Cardinals, mid linebacker, 1989, right inside linebacker, 1990-92, right linebacker, 1992-93, left linebacker, 1993; Ariz Cardinals, mid linebacker, 1994-97; St Louis Rams, mid linebacker, 1998; San Diego Chargers, linebacker, 1999; Eric Hill Nissan, owner & pres, currently. **Business Addr:** Owner, President, Eric Hill Nissan, 13050 Interstate 10 Service Rd, New Orleans, LA 70128, **Business Phone:** (504)245-5900.

### HILL, DR. FREDERICK W.

Educator, president (organization). **Educ:** Univ Pittsburgh, BA, 1975, JD, 1978. **Career:** Rose Schmidt & Dixon, assoc Atty, 1978-90; Univ Pittsburgh, adj prof 1980-91; Westinghouse Elec Corp, exec dir govt affairs, 1990-93, vpres pub affairs, 1990-95; McDonnell Douglas corp, sr vpres commun & community rels, 1995-97; Chase Manhattan Bank, dir corp mkt & commun, 1997-2005; JP Morgan Chase & Co, dir corp mkt & commun, 1997-2005; NYC Teaching Fellows, teaching, 2010; FWHill LLC, pres & owner, currently. **Orgs:** Twelve Person Bd, lawyer Mem, Commonwealth Pa Bd Pardons, 1979-87; Disciplinary Bd Pa Supreme Ct, 1986-88; judicial Conduct Bd, Commonwealth Pa, 1988-90; Bd trustee, Univ Pittsburgh; bd dir, Ad Coun. **Business Addr:** Owner, President, FWHILL LLC, 195 Hudson St, New York, NY 10013.

### HILL, DR. GEORGE C.

Educator. **Personal:** Born Feb 19, 1939, Moorestown, NJ; married Linda; children: Yvette, Kevin, Nicole & Brian. **Educ:** Rutgers Univ, BS, 1961; Howard Univ, MS, 1963; NY Univ, PhD, 1967; Univ Ky Med Ctr; Molteno Inst, Univ Cambridge. **Career:** Univ Ky Med Ctr, NIH post-doctoral fel, 1967-69; Squibb Inst Med Res, res invstr, 1969-71; Univ Cambridge, Eng, NIH spl res fel, 1971-72; Colo State Univ, assoc prof, 1972-83; Fulbright Fel, Univ Nairobi, Nairobi, Kenya, 1982; Meharry Med Col, dir div biomed sci, dean sch grad studies & res, vpres sponsored res, int prog, prof, 1983-2001; Vanderbilt Univ, Sch Med, prof, assoc dean, 2002-12, diversity med educ, Levi Watkins Jr prof diversity med educ, vice chancellor, health affairs, 2002-11, asst vice chancellor, multicultural affairs, spec asst to provost, 2011-12, prof med educ & admin prof, currently, Dept Microbiol & Immunol, prof; Leadership Excellence LLC, founder & pres, 2012-. **Orgs:** Am Inst Bio Sci; Am Soc Protozoologists; Am Soc Parasitologists; Soc Biol Chem; Sigma Xi; Inst Med Nat Acad Sci, 1998; fel Am Acad Microbiol, 2002; pres, Nat Found Infectious Dis, 2007-2009; Fel Am Asn Advan Sci, 2009; Stud Nat Med Asn. **Business Addr:** Associate Dean for Diversity in Medical Education, Professor of Pathology, Microbiology & Immunology Emeritus, Vanderbilt University- School of Medicine, 301 Light Hall, Nashville, TN 37232-0190, **Business Phone:** (615)322-7498.

### HILL, GEORGE HIRAM

Executive. **Personal:** Born Apr 13, 1940, Detroit, MI; married Alma Matney; children: Dylan Foster. **Educ:** Wayne State Univ, BA, polit sci, 1962. **Career:** MI Bell Tel Co, comn consult employ supr & comn supvr, 1963-68; Asst Negro Youth Campaign, exec dir, 1967; Job Oppty Line WJBK-TV, host, 1968-73; Chrysler Corp, labor rel supr & corp personnel staff, 1968-71; Paperworks Inc, chief exec officer; Quaker Chem Corp, treas dir; Diversified Chem Technol, founder & pres, chmn & chief exec officer, 1971-. **Orgs:** Treas, Greater Detroit Chamber Com; bd advs, Univ Detroit Bus Sch; bd mem, Mich Minority Bus Develop Corp, 1976-91; secy, Nat Asn Black Automotive Suppliers, 1990; bd adv, Detroit Literacy Vols Am; Mich Minority Chem Asn; adv bd mem, Kraft Foods MBE; adv bd mem, Procter & Gamble MBE; adv bd mem, Ford Motor Co MBE; chair, Detroit jazz fest; exec mem, Adcraft Club, Detroit; mem bd advisors, Pro-Literacy Detroit; bd advisors, Wayne State Univ; bd trustee, Detroit Music Hall; Vice Chmn, LeadersUp. **Home Addr:** 4003 Autumn Ridge Dr, West Bloomfield, MI 48323, **Home Phone:** (248)681-6547. **Business Addr:** President & Chief Executive Officer, Founder, Diversified Chemical Technologies Inc, 15477 Woodrow Wilson St, Detroit, MI 48238-1586, **Business Phone:** (313)867-5444.

### HILL, GILBERT R.

Government official. **Personal:** Born Nov 5, 1931, Birmingham, AL; married Delores Hooks. **Career:** Detroit Police Dept, Detroit, MI, police detective, police officer comdr, 1959-89; Detroit City Coun, Detroit, MI, city coun mem, 1990, pres; Films: Beverly Hills Cop, actor, 1984; Beverly Hills Cop II, actor, 1987; Beverly Hills Cop III, actor, 1994. **Business Phone:** (313)224-1251.

### HILL, GLENALLEN

Baseball player, baseball manager. **Personal:** Born Mar 22, 1965, Santa Cruz, CA; married Lori; children: Simone, Chanel, Heleyna & Glenallen Jr. **Educ:** Ariz State Univ. **Career:** Baseball player (retired), baseball coach, manager; Toronto Blue Jays, outfielder, 1989-91; Cleveland Indians, 1991-93; Chicago Cubs, 1993-94, 1998-2000; San Francisco Giants, 1995-97; Seattle Mariners, 1998; New York Yankees, 2000; Anaheim Angels, 2001; Calif & Carolina League All-Star Game, coach, 2006; Modesto Nuts, mgr, 2006; Colo Rockies, first base coach, 2007-12, Colo Springs Sky Sox, mgr, 2013-14; Albuquerque Isotopes, mgr, 2015-. **Business Addr:** Manager, Albuquerque Isotopes, Isotopes Pk 2nd Fl, Albuquerque, NM 80106, **Business Phone:** (505)924-2255.

### HILL, GRANT HENRY

Basketball player. **Personal:** Born Oct 5, 1972, Dallas, TX; son of Calvin and Janet; married Tamia; children: Myla Grace & Lael Rose. **Educ:** Duke Univ, BA, hist & polit sci, 1994. **Career:** Basketball player (retired); Detroit Pistons, small forward, 1994-2000; Orlando Magic, small forward, 2000-07, shooting guard, 2006-07; Phoenix Suns, small forward, 2007-12; Los Angeles Clippers, small forward, 2012-13. **Orgs:** Dream Team III, US Olympics, 1996; Co-founder, Dillard Univ, Malcolm McDonald Scholar Fund. **Honors/Awds:** Champion, Nat Col Athletic Asn, 1991, 1992; Henry Iba Award, Best Collegiate Defensive Player, 1992; Defensive Player of the Year, Nat Asn Basketball Coaches, 1993; Player of the Year, Atlantic Coast Conf, 1994; Co-rookie of the Year, Nat Basketball Asn, 1995; All-Rookie First Team, Nat Basketball Asn, 1995; All-Star, Nat Basketball Asn, 1995-98; Gold Medal, US Olympic Basketball Team, 1996; All-NBA First Team, 1997; IBM Award, 1997; Community Service Award; Sportsmanship Award, Nat Basketball Asn, 2005, 2008, 2010. **Special Achievements:** Starting at the Finish Line: The Coach Buehler Story, producer & exec producer, 2012; Duke 91 & 92: Back to Back, exec producer, 2013. Film: With a Kiss, 2016. **Home Addr:** , Phoenix, AZ. **Business Addr:** Professional Basketball Player, Phoenix Suns, US Airway Ctr, Orlando, AZ 85004, **Business Phone:** (602)379-7900.

### HILL, GREGORY LAMONTE (GREG HILL)

Football player. **Personal:** Born Feb 23, 1972, Dallas, TX; children: Jordan. **Educ:** Tex A&M Univ. **Career:** Kans City Chiefs, running back, 1994-97; St Louis Rams, running back, 1998; Detroit Lions, running back, 1999; KRLD-FM 105.3, host, 2009. **Orgs:** Founder, Greg Hill Time Charitable Found. **Honors/Awds:** NCAA freshman debut record. **Special Achievements:** TV Series: Wild On, 1997.

### HILL, HATTIE

Consultant, executive, association executive. **Personal:** Born Jul 6, 1958, Marianna, AR; daughter of Carrie Flowers; married Terry. **Educ:** Ark State Univ, BA, educ, 1977, MA, coun, 1981. **Career:** Tex Rehab Comn, dir training, rehab counr; Hattie Hill Enterprises, owner, founder & chief exec officer, currently; Books: "connect". **Orgs:** Am Bus Women's Asn, 1986-90; co-founder, Vision 100; Dallas

Women Together, 1989-; Nat Asn Women Bus Owners, 1992-; Dallas Women's Convenant, 1993-; bd mem, Leadership Am, 1993-; exec bd mem, Trinity Med Ctr, 1994-97; African Am Women Entrepreneurs Inc, 1994-; adv bd mem, YWCA Dallas Women's Ctr, 1994-; bd, Presby Hosp; Women's Mus; adv bd, YWCA Metrop Dallas; Soc Int Bus Fel; Fed Res Bank Dallas; Goizueta Bus Sch Emory Univ; Nat African Am Women's Leadership Inst; adv bd, Wyndham Int External Diversity; adv bd, Orleans Customer; vice chmn, mktg & chap rels, MPI Found Bd trustee, currently. **Honors/Awds:** Best & Brightest African American Business Woman, Dollars & Sense Mag, 1993, Hall of Fame, 1994; Forty Under Forty, Dallas Bus Jour, 1994; Today's Dallas Woman of the Year, Today's Dallas Woman, 1995; Leading Women of the Future, Mirabella Mag; Entrepreneur of the Year, Quest for Success, 2000; Louise Raggio Pathfinder Award, 2001; 25 Most Influential People in the Meeting's Industry, Meeting News Magazine. **Special Achievements:** Articles: "South Africa: The Good, The Bad & the Ugly, "Sharing Ideas, 1992; "Sensitivity Training: Do it Right!," Texas Banking, 1994; "Tip Off: Diversity," Dallas Business Journal; numerous other article & interviews; author: Women Who Carry Their Men; Smart Women, Smart Choices, Named Hot 25 Speakers by Successful Meetings Magazine; nominee for "Entrepreneurial Excellence"; International Supplier of the Year, Meeting Professionals International. **Business Addr:** Chief Executive Officer, Hattie Hill Enterprises Inc, 5220 Spring Valley St 340, Dallas, TX 75380-2967, **Business Phone:** (972)473-3003.

### HILL, HENRY, JR.

Chief executive officer, banker. **Personal:** Born Mar 19, 1935, Nashville, TN; married Mary E; children: Michael E, Terrill E & Veronica E. **Educ:** Weaver Sch Real Est, cert; Am Inst Banking, dipl, 1981. **Career:** Citizens Savings Bank & Trust Co, br mgr/loan officer, 1963-76, exec vpres, 1976-84, interim pres & chief exec officer, 1984, pres & chief exec officer, 1984-. **Orgs:** Bd dir, Better Bus Bur; bd dir, Am Inst Banking; bd dir, Citizens Savings Bank & Trust Co; bd dir, March Dimes Birth Defectd Found; chmn, bd dir, S St Community Ctr; chmn, trustee & bd, Progressive Bapt Ch; Nat Asn Negro Bus & Prof Women's Club Inc, 1986; Jefferson St, Nashville; bd mem, Nashville area chamber com. **Home Addr:** 926 Lawrence Ave, Nashville, TN 37201, **Home Phone:** (615)876-8922. **Business Addr:** President, Chief Executive Officer, Citizens Savings Bank & Trust Co, 1917 Heiman St, Nashville, TN 37208-2409, **Business Phone:** (615)327-9787.

### HILL, JACQUELINE R.

Lawyer, association executive. **Personal:** Born May 23, 1940, Topeka, KS; daughter of Boyd Alexander and Noblesse Armenta Demoss Lansdowne; children: Dana Alesse Jamison. **Educ:** Univ CA Berkeley, BA, 1962; Univ Southern CA, teachers credential, 1966; Southwestern Univ Sch Law, JD, 1972; Calif State Univ, Long Beach, cert Calligraphy, 1989; W Los Angeles Community Col, cert Med Billing, 1998. **Career:** Univ Calif Lawrence Radiation Lab, admin exec, 1963-66; La Unified Sch Dist, math teacher, 1966-73; La Comm Col Dist, instr, 1972-75; Los Angeles County, dep dist atty, 1973-99; Calif State Univ, Long Beach, instr, 1990-91; Jacque All Trades, pres, 1990; Los Angeles County Dist Atty Off, atty, currently. **Orgs:** Alpha Kappa Alpha Sorority; Calif State Bar; Am Bar Asn; Calif State Adv Group Juvenile Justice & Delinquency Prev, 1983-95. **Honors/Awds:** Legal Book Awards, Southwestern Univ Sch Law, 1969-72. **Home Addr:** 4812 Salem Vlge Ct, Culver City, CA 90230-4320, **Home Phone:** (310)839-2838. **Business Addr:** Attorney, Los Angeles County District Attorney Office, 210 W Temple St Suite 18000, Los Angeles, CA 90012-3210, **Business Phone:** (213)974-3512.

### HILL, JAMES, JR.

Accountant. **Personal:** Born Aug 20, 1941, Baltimore, MD; married Sheree; children: James III & Brian. **Educ:** Central State Col, BS, acct, 1964; Univ Chicago, Booth Sch Bus, MBA, personnel, admin & acct, 1967. **Career:** Union Carbon, cost acct, 1964-65; Alexander Grant & Co, auditor, 1967-69; Chicago Econ Develop Corp, dep dir, 1968-70; Hill Taylor LLC, chmn & chief executive officer, 1972-2009; Mitchell & Titus LLP, accountant, 2009-. **Orgs:** bd dir, Econ Club Chicago; bd dir, Chicago United; bd trustee & lifetime trustee, Ill Inst Technol; mem Coun, lifetime mem, Univ Chicago; mem coun, Univ Ill; bd dir, Chicagol & Chamber Com, Audit Comt, PAC Comt, Taxation Comt; United Way Chicago, Audit Comt; founding mem & past pres, Alliance Bus Leaders & Entrepreneurs; Rainbow Push Coalition; bd dir, Civic Consult Alliance; bd dir, City Chicago Econ Adv Comt; lifetime mem, Kappa Alpha Psi; Exec Club Chicago, Finance Comt; mem coun, Chicago State Univ; Citizen Info Serv; Rotary Int; bd dir, Youth Guid; bd dir, Pkwy Community Ctr; bd dir, Nat Asn Minority CPA firms; bd dir, Regal Theater; bd mem, State Ill Bd Accountancy; adv bd, Nat Asn Black Accountants; pres adv coun, Cent State Univ; United Way Minority Outreach Prog Comt; bd dir, Union Nat Bank; bd dir, Ariel Capital Mgt; bd dir, Chicago Commons Asn; bd dir, Better Govt Asn; Japan Am Soc; bd dir, Nat Conf Community & Justice. **Honors/Awds:** Certificate of Appreciation, Nat Asn Real Estate Brokers; Cert Merit, Central State Univ Alumni Asn; Outstanding Prof Achievement, Central State Univ; Distinguished Service Award, Coun Community Serv; Little Gold Oilcan Award, Chicago Econ Develop Corp; Certificate of Appreciation, Chicago State Univ; Whos Who in the Midwest; Outstanding Young Men Am; Chairman's Award, Nat Asn Minority CPA Firms; Citation, Inst Internal Auditors; Leaders of Color Award, Chicago United; History Makers Award; Alumnus of the Year Award, Cent State Univ, 2010. **Home Addr:** 1350 N Astor, Chicago, IL 60610, **Home Phone:** (312)587-7936. **Business Addr:** Managing Partner, Mitchell & Titus LLP, 333 W Wacker Dr Suite 1600, Chicago, IL 60606, **Business Phone:** (312)332-4964.

### HILL, JAMES A., JR.

Lawyer, financial manager, politician. **Personal:** Born Apr 23, 1947, Atlanta, GA; married CJ Van Pelt; children: Jennifer Joy. **Educ:** Mich State Univ, BA, econs, 1969; Ind Univ, MBA, 1971; Ind Univ Col Law, JD, 1974. **Career:** Bankers Trust Co, 1970; Judge Adv Gen Corp, 1972; State Ore, state rep, 1983-87, senate, 1987-93, treas, 1992-2001; Ore Dept Revenue, hearing officer; Ore Dept Justice, asst atty gen, law clerk; Ind Univ, consortium grad study bus blacks fel; Mentor Graphics Corp, corp accounts mgr latin Am, currently. **Orgs:** Ore State Bar Asn, 1975-; treas, Ore State, 1993-2001; Salem Ore Chap; Nat Asn Advan Colored People; charter mem, Ore Assembly Black Affairs; pres, Western State Treasurers Asn; Employee Retirement Income Security Act Bd; Ore Investment Coun; Multnomah County. **Special Achievements:** First African American elected to statewide office in Oregon, 1992. **Home Addr:** 4584 12th Pl S, PO Box 515, Salem, OR 97302-2302, **Home Phone:** (503)399-7530. **Business Addr:** Corporate Accounts Manager, Mentor Graphics Corp, 8005 SW Boeckman Rd, Wilsonville, OR 97070, **Business Phone:** (503)685-7000.

### HILL, DR. JAMES A., SR.

Educator, clergy. **Personal:** Born Jun 10, 1934, Chicago, IL; son of Robert E Sr and Fannie M Whitney; children: Carl J, Jewell Davis, Fannie M, James A Jr & Robert E. **Educ:** Chicago Baptist Col, Sem Dept, 1959; Blackstone Sch Law, LLB, 1962; Am Bible & Divinity Col, ThM, 1966; Clarksville Sch Theol, BD, 1966, THD, 1979; St John's Univ, BA, 1974; Trinity Col, MS, 1976; Gradelupa Col & Sem, San Antonio, TX, DHum, 1988; Faith Evangel Luthern Sem, Tacoma, WA, DMin, 1989. **Career:** Methodist CME Church, minister, 1950-; Wayne County EOE, dept dir, 1967-69; Wayne County Probation Dept, probation officer, 1969-72; Memphis Urban League, dept dir, 1975-80. **Orgs:** Gov's Comn Human Rights, Fairbanks Human Rels Coun; exec bd, Fairbanks USO, United Fund Comm; chmn, Boy Scouts Am; Fairbanks Ministerial Asn; Anchorage Ministerial Asn; Am Acad Polit & Soc Sci; asst state chaplain, Elks State MI Asn; asst grand chaplainn, Elks Nat Asn IBPOE W; prof mem, Adult Educ Asn USA; life mem, AMVETS; Am Counrs Soc; Am Ministerial Asn; Nat Asn Social Workers Inc. **Home Addr:** 3733 Juneau St, PO Box 18616, Seattle, WA 98118, **Home Phone:** (206)723-6560. **Business Addr:** Minister, Curry Temple CME Church, 172 23rd Ave, Seattle, WA 98122, **Business Phone:** (206)325-9344.

### HILL, JAMES H.

Public relations executive. **Personal:** Born Aug 11, 1947, Toledo, OH; son of James Sr and Cassie; married Cynthia Carter; children: Jasmine Dianae. **Educ:** Ohio Univ, Athens OH, BS, jour & pub rels, 1969; Ohio Univ Grad Sch, Athens, OH. **Career:** Owens-Corning Fiberglas, Toledo OH, merchandise supvr, 1970-75; WGTE-TV FM Pub Broadcasting, Toledo OH, dir pub info, 1975-77, producer/writer, 1977-80; S C Johnson, Racine Wis, mgr opers, pub rels, 1980-82; Sara Lee Corp, Chicago, Ill, dir pub rels & communs, 1982-86; Burrell Pub Rels Inc, Chicago, Ill, pres & chief exec officer, 1986-; Kaiser Found, Health Plan & Hosps, vp commun, 1994-98; Hill Commun, pres, 1988-. **Orgs:** Bd mem, Nat Asn Advan Colored People/Toledo, 1973-75; PCC, 1983-; PRSA, 1983-; co-chmn fundraising, UNCF/Chicago, 1983, mem comt, 1985-; bd mem, C & Adolescent Forum, 1984-86, 1989-; BPRSA, 1985-; Econ Club Chicago, 1986-; bd mem, Travelers & Immigrant Aid, 1989-; pub rels adv comn, Chicago Urban League, 1989-; Oakland Chamber Com; E Bay Community Found; Oakland Mus Calif; Alpha Phi Alpha. **Honors/Awds:** CINE Golden Eagle, 1981; Gold Trumpet, PCC, 1981; Silver Trumpet, PCC, 1981, 1986, 1989; Gold Quil Award of Excellence and Merit, Int Asn Bus Communicator, 1984; Silver Anvil, Pub Rels Soc Am, 1986; Mar-Com Award, 2004, 2005. **Home Addr:** 7006 S Constance, Chicago, IL 60649, **Home Phone:** (312)363-4455. **Business Addr:** President, Hill & Co Communications Inc, 1050 Marina Village Pkwy Suite 105, Alameda, CA 94501, **Business Phone:** (510)521-2200.

### HILL, JAMES L.

Vice president (organization), school administrator. **Personal:** Born Oct 22, 1936, Bowling Green, OH; son of Joe L and Flossie Mae Susan; married Carolyn L; children: Todd Derek & Candace Leah. **Educ:** Ind State Univ, Terre Haute, BS, phys educ, 1965, MS, phys educ, 1966; Cent Mich Univ, Mt Pleasant, MI, specialist educ admin. **Career:** School administrator (retired); Arsenal Tech High Sch, Indianapolis, Ind, teacher/coach, 1966-68; Shortridge High Sch, Indianapolis, Ind, teacher/coach, 1968-70; Cent Mich Univ, Mt Pleasant, Mich, instr, 1970-74; Blue Lake Fine Arts Camp, Muskegon, Mich, dir, summer coun prog, 1972-74, asst prof, 1974-75, actg dean studs, 1975-76, dean studs, 1976-79, vpres, stud affairs, 1970-95; Albany State Univ, Col Arts & Sci, fac & dean, vis prof, 2001. **Orgs:** Phi Kappa Epsilon, 1966-; Mich Stud Affairs Admin, 1976-; Am Coun Educ, 1978-; asst vpres, NASPA Region IV-E, 1980-81; legis comt, Asn Col/Univ Housing Officers, 1980-82; awards comt chair, Nat Asn Stud Personnel Admin, 1989-90. **Home Addr:** 1841 W Pickard St, Mount Pleasant, MI 48858, **Home Phone:** (989)772-1033.

### HILL, DR. JAMES LEE

School administrator, educator. **Personal:** Born Dec 10, 1941, Meigs, GA; son of Willie Lee and Vanilla; married Flo J; children: Deron James & Toussaint LeMarc. **Educ:** Ft Valley St Col, BS, eng, 1963; Atlanta Univ, MA, eng, 1968; Univ Iowa, PhD, Am civil & Afro Am studies, 1976, 1978; Purdue Univ, post doctoral study, 1981; John Carroll Univ, post doctoral study, 1984. **Career:** Winder City Schs, Instr Eng, 1964-65; Hancock Cent HS, eng chair, 1965-68; Paine Col, Instr, 1968-71; Benedict Col, chair, Eng Dept, 1974-77; Albany State Univ, chair eng dept, 1977-96, dean, Arts & Sci, 1981-2000, asst vpres, Acad Affairs, 2000-02, chair, eng dept, 2008-. **Orgs:** NEH Fel Atlanta Univ, 1969, 1971-74; consult, Nat Res Proj Black Women, 1979-81; secy, Albany Urban League Bd, 1979-81; chair, assoc, asst chair, Conf Col Comp & Comm, 1980-83; chair, vice chair, GA Endowment Humanities, 1981-83; exec, Comm NCTE, 1982-83; prof serv dir, NEA Writer Res Prog Asn, 1982-91; dir, NEH Summer Humanities Inst ASC, 1983-84, 1989; pres, Beta Nu Sigma Phi Beta Sigma Fraternity, 1983-; chair, Acad Comm Eng-GA, 1983-84; vpres, S Atlantic Asn Dept Eng, 1984-85; bd dir, Nat Fed State Humanities Couns, 1984-87; asn col, Sect Comm Nat Coun Teachers Eng, 1985-89, chair, 1993-95; Am Reg Dr Southern Region Phi Beta Sigma; Visit Scholar, Nat Humanities Fac; Ga Desoto Comn; Ga Christopher Columbus Comn; dir, NCTE Summer Inst Teachers Lit; Beta Nu Sigma, 2009; adv comm, bd, Regents Univ Syst; Ga Coun Teachers; 100 Black Men Albany. **Home Addr:** 2408 Greenmount Ct, Albany, GA 31705-4311, **Home Phone:** (229)432-9847. **Business Addr:** Chairman, Professor, Albany State University, 504 Col Dr Holley Hall 101, Albany, GA 31705, **Business Phone:** (229)430-4833.

### HILL, JAMES O.

Government official, air force officer. **Personal:** Born Sep 5, 1937, Austin, TX; married Eva Marie Mosby; children: Eva Marie, James O II & Dudley Joseph. **Educ:** Howard Univ, BA, 1964; Nova Univ, MPA, 1975. **Career:** Government official (retired); Boys Clubs Newark, asst dir, 1964-68; Boys Clubs Broward Co, Fla, dir, 1968-71; City Ft Lauderdale, asst city mgr, manpower analyst, admin asst, 1971-99. **Orgs:** KC, 1968; Elks, 1970-; ARC, 1971-; Govts Crime Prev Task Force, 1971-; Ft Lauderdale Chamber Comn, 1971-; Int City Mgrs Asn, 1972-; Am Soc Pub Admin, 1973-; Seminole Hist Soc, 1975. **Honors/Awds:** Three Boys Club Serv Awards, 1964-70; Youth Serv Award, 1970; Exemplary Former City Employee Award, 1999; Trinity Intl Univ, hon doctorate, 2001. **Home Addr:** 450 NW 34th Ave, Lauderhill, FL 33311, **Home Phone:** (954)583-1136.

### HILL, JANICE LYTHCOTT. See LYTHCOTT, JANICE LOGUE.

### HILL, JEFFREY RONALD

Marketing executive. **Personal:** Born Nov 14, 1948, Philadelphia, PA. **Educ:** Cheyney State Col, BS, sci, 1972; Pa State Univ, PA, mkt cert, 1974. **Career:** Philip Morris Tobacco Co, NY, sales mgr, 1972-75; 3rd Jazz Rec Co & Retail Philadelphia, mgr, 1975-76; Second Story/Catacombs Disco Complex Philadelphia, mgr, 1978-79; Hilltop Promotions Philadelphia, dir, 1979-; Nabisco Inc, mkt sales mgr. **Orgs:** Nat Hist Soc, 1968-77; Black Music Asn; Am Film Inst. **Honors/Awds:** Merit Achievement Award, Am Legion Philadelphia Post, 1963. **Home Addr:** 309 N Holliston Ave Apt 11, Pasadena, CA 91106-1551. **Business Addr:** Marketing Sales Manager, Nabisco Inc, 201 Precision Dr, Horsham, PA 19044, **Business Phone:** (215)672-1401.

### HILL, JENNIFER A.

Journalist. **Educ:** Case Western Res Univ, BA, 1974; Columbia Univ Grad Sch Jour, MS, 1978. **Career:** Atlanta J Const, dep bus & tech ed, 1982-2001; Univ Ga Press, ed; Paideia Sch, commun dir, 2001-. **Business Addr:** Communications Director, The Paideia School, 1509 Ponce de Leon Ave, Atlanta, GA 30307, **Business Phone:** (404)377-3491.

### HILL, JIMMY H.

Government official. **Personal:** Born Jun 14, 1948, Macon, GA; son of Harvie and Mertis; married Lucille; children: Chandra, Jamie & Jennifer. **Educ:** Compton Col, AS, 1977. **Career:** Government official (retired); Los Angeles Fire Dept, firefighter, 1973-78, apparatus operator, 1978-79; fire inspector I, 1979-82, fire inspector II, 1982-83, capt I, 1983-85; capt II, 1985-89, battalion chief, 1989-97; fire marshal & dep chief, 1997-2011. **Orgs:** NFPA, 1989-; IFMA, 1999-, bd mem, 2001-; Southern Calif Fire Prev Officers Asn; Western Fire Chief Assn; African Am Firefighter Mus; pres, Int Fire Marshals Asn N Am. **Special Achievements:** He is the highest ranking African American in the history of the Los Angeles City Fire Department. **Home Addr:** 4711 Don Portirio Pl, Los Angeles, CA 90008, **Home Phone:** (323)291-7527.

### HILL, JULIA H.

Educator. **Personal:** Born Jan 1, 1922, Kansas City, MO; daughter of Arthur H Hicks and Ethel Williams; married Quincy T. **Educ:** Lincoln Univ, BS, 1943; Univ Southern Calif, MA, attended 1954; Nova Univ, PhD, 1982. **Career:** Educator (retired); Miss Sch Dist, Kansas City, elem sch teacher, 1943-66, consult urban affairs, 1966-67, coordr title I para prof, 1968-75, elem sch prin, 1975-76; Pioneer Community Col, community serv coordr, 1976-79; Northland Work & Training Unit, coordr, 1980-81; Kans City Skill Ctr, eve coordr, 1982-85, coordr, col rel, 1985-92. **Orgs:** Pres, Miss Nat Asn Adv Colored People Br, Kans City, 1971-80; SW Bell Tele Adv Comn, 1981-94; Miss Sch Bd, Kans City, 1984-96; Kans City Campus Ministers, 1984-94; chair, Miss Nat Asn Adv Colored People Br, Kans City, 1984-99; life mem, Alpha Kappa Alpha Sorority, Beta Omega Chap; heritage life mem, Nat Asn Adv Colored People; Community Comt Social Action; Girl Scouts Am. **Honors/Awds:** Mo Leon M Jordan Memorial Award, Dist Servs, Kans City, 1971; Citizen of the Year, Omega Phi Psi Fraternity, Kans City, MO, 1973; Leadership & Civil Rights, Kans City, Mo Baptist Ministers Union, 1974; SCLC Black Woman on the Move, 1975; Othell G Whitlock Memorial Award, 1976; Nat Association Advancement Colored People Civil Rights Award, 1976; Afro-Am Stud Union Distinguished Comn Leadership, 1977; Outstanding Civil Rights, 1978; Outstanding Community Service, Beacon Light Seventh Day Adventist Church, 1979; Civil Rights Black Archives Award, 1980-81; Harold L Holiday Sr Civil Rights Award, Nat Asn Adv Colored People, 1988; Distinguished Service Award, Lincoln Univ, Mo Nat Alumni Asn, 1990; Zeta Phi Beta Sorority Outstanding Leadership; Greater Kans City Bussiness & Professional Women Sojourner Truth Award; Outstanding Women of the Year Award; Girl Scouts of American Award; Dr Martin Luther King Jr Awards, Oper PUSH; Alpha Kappa Alpha Educational Service Award; the Northeast Kansas National Association of Black School Educators Educators Award; the Phi Delta Kappa Outstanding Community Service Award. **Special Achievements:** One of the 100 Most Influential Blacks of Kans City, 1986-88. **Home Addr:** 5100 Lawn Ave, Kansas City, MO 64130, **Home Phone:** (816)921-0955.

### HILL, KENNETH D.

Executive, association executive. **Personal:** Born Jan 22, 1938, Bryn Mawr, PA; married C Irene Wigington; children: Kimberly Diane. **Educ:** Temple Univ, Assoc Arch Tech, 1958; Univ PA, Indust Mgt, 1972; Harvard Bus Sch, PMD, 1980. **Career:** Sun Co Inc, cent sales trng mgr, 1969-71, dist mgr, 1973-75, proj mgr corp human res, 1975-76, div mgr mkt, 1976-79, mgr corp citizenship, 1979-84, community rels vpres; Sun Refining & Mkt Co, vpres pub affairs, 1984-; Alliance Enterprise, pres, 1971-73. **Orgs:** Chmn, coun trustees Cheyney State Univ, 1981; bd trustee, Comt Leadership Seminar, 1983; pres, Am Asn Blacks Energy, 1984-86; bd dir, Private Industry Coun, 1984; assoc, Temple Univ col Educ; Laura H Carnell. **Honors/Awds:** Ebony Women's Award, Community Serv Womens Res Network, 1982; James McCoy Founder's Award, NAACP, 1982; Centennial Award, Advan & Image Bldg Cheyney Univ, 1983; Community Service Award, Urban League Philadelphia, 1983. **Special Achievements:** First Black Member at Aronimink Golf Club. **Home Addr:** 1476 Hancock Lane, Wayne, PA 19087. **Business Addr:** Vice President Public Affairs,

Sun Refining & Marketing Co, 3144 Passyunk Ave, Philadelphia, PA 19145, **Business Phone:** (215)339-2000.

### HILL, KENNETH WADE

Baseball player. **Personal:** Born Dec 14, 1965, Lynn, MA; married Lorrie Rollin; children: Ken Jr. **Educ:** N Adams State Col; Mass Col Lib Arts. **Career:** Baseball player (retired); Detroit Tigers, free agt, 1985; St Louis Cardinals, pitcher, 1988-91, 1995; Montreal Expos, 1992-94; Cleveland Indians, 1995; Tex Rangers, free agt, 1996-97; Anaheim Angels, 1997-2000; Chicago White Sox, 2000; Tampa Bay Devil Rays, 2001; Cincinnati Reds, free agt, 2001; Boston Red Sox, free agt, 2001. **Home Addr:** 43 Kings Hill Dr, Lynn, MA 01905.

### HILL, LEO

Administrator. **Personal:** Born Mar 27, 1937, Columbus, TX; married Jacquelyne; children: Leo & Stacy. **Educ:** Los Angeles City Col, attended 1958; Los Angeles State Col, BA, 1961, Grad Work, 1962; Calif Inst Technol, attended 1969; Pepperdine Univ, attended 1970; Univ Calif, Los Angeles, cert Indust Rel, 1979, cert personnel mgt, 1979; Inst cert Prof Mgrs, cert mgt, 1984. **Career:** Administrator, director (retired); RCA Serv Co, sr job develop admin; Hughes Aircraft Co, head action prog, 1977-81; Lockheed Martin Aeronaut, Diversity & Equal Opportunity Progs, dir, 1981-2004; Keller Williams Real Estate Assocs Brokerage, sr real estate consult, 2011-; Alston & Assocs, sr real estate consult, 2004-; L & H Enterprise, owner. **Orgs:** Dir, comn prog, Greater LA, Community Action Agency; dir, Prog Monitoring, Neighborhood Youth Corps, Narcotics, 1973; asst eeo, 1972, dir personnel, 1972, Econ & Youth Opp Agency, Greater, Los Angeles; personel dir, 1966-71; actg admin officer, 1968-69; dir, Bethune Co Park; comn Florence-Firestone Coun & Case Conf; Los Angeles Area Ed Comm, Men Tomorrow, Hunters Elite Gun Club, Narcotics Task Force; Am Soc Training & Develop; vpres, 1961, treas, 1960, Los Angeles State Col Inter-Frat Coun; pres, Kappa Psi Frat. **Honors/Awds:** Sam Berry Tournament Most Valuable Player; Broke-Tied 11 Records Jr Coll Career; CCAA best team 3 yrs; Leading Scorer NCAA Most Valuable; Calif State Univ Los Angeles Hall of Fame (Basketball), 1985. **Home Addr:** 1355 Buckhorn Bend Loop R, Los Angeles, CA 71202, **Home Phone:** (318)387-3850. **Business Addr:** Owner, L & H Enterprise, 9181 W Pine St, Lowgap, NC 27024, **Business Phone:** (336)352-4048.

### HILL, MARVIN LEWIS

Executive. **Personal:** Born Aug 19, 1951, Indianapolis, IN; son of Maurice and Luciele Campbell; married Deborah Jill Shaffer; children: Jessica Ashley & Alison Victoria. **Educ:** Ind State Univ, BA, criminal justice, 1974. **Career:** Marriott corp, mgr, 1974-78; Steak & Ale Restaurant, corp trainer, 1978-79; MLH dba Sir Speedy, pres, 1979-86; Shaffer-Hill, Express Press Inc, pres, 1986. **Orgs:** Citizen Participation Org, 1974; pres, Wheeling, 1983-85; coun, Village Hoffman Estates, 1991-94; chmn, Kiwanis Int dist young c, 1992, gov, I-I Dist, 1991. **Honors/Awds:** Distinguish Past Lt Governor, Kiwanis Int, 1992; Outstanding dir, Vill Hoffman Estates, 1991. **Home Addr:** 47 Willow Bay Dr, South Barrington, IL 60010-7117, **Home Phone:** (847)713-2048. **Business Addr:** President, Shaffer-Hill Inc, Hoffman Estates, Schaumburg, IL 60195, **Business Phone:** (847)882-2234.

### HILL, MARY ALICE

Association executive. **Personal:** Born Sep 15, 1938, Marlow, GA; married Elton E. **Educ:** NJ Col Com, pub admin, 1956; Univ Col, urban studies, 1972. **Career:** City Newark, sr budget analyst, 1972-83, mgt info spec, 1985; Nat Coun Negro Women, pres; Rutgers Univ, certified pub mgr, 1986. **Orgs:** chair, Metrop BC Women's Day, 1983; NJ Bethune Recog Team Steering Comt, 1985; chair, NJ Rainbow Coalition; chmn UMDNJ-PCAA, 1987; Am Mgt Assoc; Nat Assoc Black Pub Admin; pres, Newark Sect Nat Coun Negro Women Inc; chmn, US Selective Serv Bd 33; NJ State Univ Med & Dent; bd pres, Coun Affirm Action; officer, Bethany 43, OES PHANewark NJ. **Honors/Awds:** Nominee Mayor's Committee Service Award, 1980; Rainbow Coalition Service Award, 1984. **Home Addr:** 351 Seymour Ave, Newark, NJ 07112, **Home Phone:** (973)923-2918.

### HILL, MERVIN E., JR.

Television producer. **Personal:** Born Jul 12, 1947, St. Louis, MO. **Educ:** Grand Valley State Col, BA; William James Col, Allendale, MI, attended 1974. **Career:** Black Free Form Theatre Co, Grand Rapids, actor & asst dir, 1971-72; Living Arts Proj, Grand Rapids Bd Educ, drama dir, 1971-72; WOTV, Grand Rapids, mgr, 1973; WGVC-TV, Allendale, MI, asst, producer, 1975-; TV Series: "Arbitration Mr Businessman"; "Portrait of African Journey"; "The Neighborhood". **Home Addr:** 1208 Dunham St SE, Grand Rapids, MI 49506. **Business Addr:** Assistant to Producer, WGVC TV 35, Allendale, MI 49401.

### HILL, MICHAEL (MIKE HILL)

Baseball executive. **Personal:** Born Mar 25, 1971; son of Ben Hill and Irene Hill; married Vivian; children: Donovan, Xavier & Baron. **Educ:** Harvard Univ, bachelor, 1993. **Career:** Baseball player (retired), baseball executive; Erie Sailors, New York-Pa League, player, 1993; Hudson Valley Renegades, New York-Pa League, player, 1994; Tampa Ray Devil Rays, front off position, 1995-99; Colo Rockies, front off position, 1999-2001; Fla (later Miami) Marlins, asst gen manger, 2002-07, gen mgr, 2007-13, 2015-, pres baseball opers, 2013-. **Special Achievements:** Drafted by the Texas Rangers in the 31st round of the 1993 June Amateur draft. **Business Addr:** Miami Marlins, 501 Marlins Way, Miami, FL 33125, **Business Phone:** (305)480-1300.

### HILL, DR. OBIE CLEVELAND

School administrator, educator. **Personal:** Born Oct 20, 1949, Enterprise, MS; son of John C and Florine F Nichols; married Lois Charles; children: Demetria & Christina. **Educ:** Nicholls State Univ, BA, lib arts, 1973, teacher cert, 1976, MEd, 1978; Univ New Orleans, PhD, 1993. **Career:** School administrator, educator (retired); LaFourche Parish Sch, teacher, 1976-79; Nicholls State Univ, asst mens basketball coach, 1979-85, asst prof phys ed, 1985-94, dir stud teaching, 1994-98, dean educ, 1999-2006; Dean Stud Life, 2007-08; Southern Univ New Orleans, dean educ, 1998-99; MAX Charter Sch, Prin, 2008-10; Our Lady Holy Cross Col, Coordr Educ Leadership, 2012-. **Orgs:** La Fourche Parish Community & Housing Develop Org, 1995-; La Asn Cols Teacher Educ, pres, 1998-2006; bd commr, Thibodaux Regional Med Ctr, 2002-; La Bd Ethics; Lafourche Educ Found Inc; La Asn Deans Stud Serv, 2007-08; MAX Charter Sch Bd Dirs, 2007-08, 2012-, Greater Grace Charter Acad, 2011-. **Honors/Awds:** Hall of Fame, Nicholls State Univ Athletics, 1981; Hall of Fame, Louisiana Asn Basketball Coaches, 1994; James Lynn Powell Award, Nicholls State Univ Alumni Fed. **Home Addr:** 2130 Hwy 3185, Thibodaux, LA 70301-8402, **Home Phone:** (985)446-8100. **Business Addr:** Coordinator, Educational Leadership, Our Lady of Holy Cross College, 4123 Woodland Dr, New Orleans, LA 70131-7399, **Business Phone:** (504)394-7744.

### HILL, PATRICIA LIGGINS

Educator. **Personal:** Born Sep 18, 1942, Washington, DC; children: Sanya Patrice & Solomon Philip. **Educ:** Howard Univ, BA, 1965; Univ San Francisco, MA, 1970; Stanford Univ, PhD, 1977. **Career:** Univ San Francisco, from instr to assoc prof, 1970-84, dir ethnic studies, 1977-, prof eng, 1984-; gen ed; Urban Inst Human Serv Inc, res consult, 1976-80; Univ Minn, Upper Midwest Tri-Racial Ctr, resource consult, 1977-78; Nat Endowment Humanities fel, 1978. **Orgs:** Bd dir, W side Ment Health Ctr, 1971-78; SF Community Col Bd, 1972-78; Calif Coun Black Educ, 1973-. **Home Addr:** 56 Oceanside Dr, Daly City, CA 94015. **Business Addr:** Professor, University San Francisco, 2130 Fulton St, San Francisco, CA 94117-1080, **Business Phone:** (415)422-6837.

### HILL, PAUL, JR.

Social worker, activist, publisher. **Personal:** Born Nov 6, 1945, Cleveland, OH; son of Paul Sr and Mabel Craig; married Marquita McAlliser; children: 7. **Educ:** Ohio Univ, BS, bus educ; Univ Ky, master's degree, educ policy studies; Univ Wis, MSW; Gestalt Inst Cleveland, OSD cert, 2006. **Career:** Teachers Corp, teacher, 1969-70; E End Neighborhood House, employee, 1971-2011, pres, 2011-14; US Justice Dept, regional educ specialist, 1973-75; US Health, Educ & Welfare Dept, equal opportunity specialist, 1975-77; Soc Nat Bank, human resources consult, 1984-86; Nat Rites Passage Inst, founder & pres, 1993-; W.K. Kellogg Found, consult, 2010-13; Cleveland State Univ, adj fac, 2011-13; "Black Child Journal", co-publisher, 2013-. **Orgs:** Ctr Educ Innovation, Bd trustee; Cleveland State Univ Dept Social Work, Vis Comt. **Special Achievements:** Ohio Licensed Social Worker 1994-; author, "Coming of Age: African Americana Male Rites-of-Passage" (1992; contributor, "African Presence in Black America"; author of journal articles. **Business Addr:** National Rites of Passage Institute, PO Box 301, University Heights, OH 44118.

### HILL, RANDAL THRILL

Football player, federal government official. **Personal:** Born Sep 21, 1969, Miami, FL; married Michelle. **Educ:** Univ Miami, BS, sociol. **Career:** Football player (retired); Miami Dolphins, 1991, 1995, wide receiver, 1996; Phoenix Cardinals, wide receiver, 1992-93; Ariz Cardinals, wide receiver, 1994; New Orleans Saints, wide receiver, 1997; US Dept Homeland Security, agt, currently. **Honors/Awds:** National Champion, 1987, 1989. **Special Achievements:** TV appearance: 30 for 30, 2009; Politics Nation with Al Sharpton, 2014; Fox and Friends, 2014. **Home Addr:** , Davie, FL. **Business Addr:** Agent, U.S. Department of Homeland Security, Washington, DC 20528, **Business Phone:** (202)282-8000.

### HILL, DR. RAY ALLEN

Educator. **Personal:** Born Sep 16, 1942, Houston, TX; son of Ann Stewart and Cal Hill Jr. **Educ:** Howard Univ, Wash, DC, BS, 1964, MS, 1965; Univ Calif, Berkley, PhD, 1977. **Career:** Southern Univ, Baton Rouge, La, instr, 1965-66; Howard Univ, Wash, DC, instr bot, 1966-75; Fisk Univ, Nashville, Tenn, asst prof, 1977-80; EPA, Wash, DC, staff scientist, 1978; NASA, Wash, DC, staff scientist, 1979; Univ Calif, San Francisco, Calif, vis res assoc prof, 1985; Lowell Col Prep Sch, San Francisco, Calif, instr, 1986-; Purdue Univ, W Lafayette Ind, vis prof bot & plant path, 1989, 1990 & 1991; Alpha Distribr, owner, 1989-; Genentech Inc, vis scientist, 1992; DOE fel, staff scientist, 1993; Calif Mentor Teacher, 1993-97; Lowell Col prep, 1995-97. **Orgs:** Nat Inst Sci, 1968-85; Am Asn Advan Sci, 1972-85; Am Soc Cell Biol, 1972-85; Bot Soc Am, 1972-85; Info Vis Ctr, 1975-; Alpha Phi Alpha Fraternity 1980-; bd mem, Big Bros E Bay, 1986-89; E E Worthing fel, E E Worthing Trust, 1960-64; fac fel, Howard Univ, 1972; fel, Ford Found, 1975-77; fac fel, Nat Sci Found, 1975; NASA/ASEE fel, Stanford Univ, 1983-84; IISME fel, genentech Inc, 1992. **Home Addr:** PO Box 785, Cotati, CA 94931, **Home Phone:** (707)664-0106. **Business Addr:** Owner, Alpha Distributors, 4700 N Ronald St, Harwood Heights, IL 60706, **Business Phone:** (708)867-5200.

**HILL, RAYMOND.** See Obituaries Section.

### HILL, REUBEN BENJAMIN

Lawyer. **Personal:** Born Aug 1, 1938, Indianapolis, IN; son of Joe L and Flossie M; married Sheila; children: Philip, Martin & Nicholas. **Educ:** Ind Univ, attended 1969; Ind Univ Law Sch, attended 1971. **Career:** Judge (retired); Ind State Police/Trooper, legal adv, 1964-74; Bingham Summers Welch & Spilman, assoc, 1974-75; Marion Co, pros dep, 1975-; Flanner House Indianapolis, exec dir, 1975; Social Serv Agency, atty, exec dir; Butler Hahn Little & Hill, atty, managing partner; Marion County Super Ct, Criminal Div 18, judge, 2000-12. **Orgs:** Indianapolis Lawyers Comn; bd dir, Ind Lawyers Comn; bd mem, WYFI-Pub Broadcasting Serv; C's Mus; bd dir, Metro Arts Coun; Am Bar Asn; Indianapolis Bar Asn; Ind Bar Asn; Nat Bar Asn Adv Bd; Indianapolis Repertory Theatre; Kiwanis Club; Indianapolis Mus Art Adv comt; adv bd, Indianapolis Urban League; Inner-City Y's Men Club; bd dir, Indianapolis 500 Festival; Ind Univ Law Sch Min Enrollment Adv Comt; Greater Ind Progress Comt; bd dir, Ind State Dept Ment Health; Golden Glove Off Ind; bd mem, Selective Serv Syst; dist appeal bd; Alpha Eta Boule; Sigma Pi Phi Fraternity; pres, Flanner House Found; bd mem, Salvation Army; Indianapolis Zoo bd; Heroes Found. **Honors/Awds:** Outstanding Ind Citizen Ind Black Bi-Centennial; WTLC Indianapolis Citizen of the Day; WTLC Man of the Year, 1978. **Home Addr:** 5125 N Grandview Dr, Indianapolis, IN 46228-2324, **Home Phone:** (317)251-5535. **Business Addr:** Judge, Marion County Superior Court, 200 E Wash St Suite T-1221, Indianapolis, IN 46204, **Business Phone:** (317)327-3237.

### HILL, ROBERT A.

Business owner, association executive. **Career:** Nat Asn Minority Auto Dealers, exec dir, 1991-94; Ford Motor Minority Dealers Asn, exec dir & chief exec officer, 1988-2003; StonePond140, owner; Stone Pond Technol, owner. **Orgs:** Bd mem, exec dir, Nat Asn Minority Auto Dealers; bd mem, Ford Motor Minority Dealers Asn. **Business Addr:** Owner, Stone Pond Technology, 514 Stone Pond Rd, Marlborough, NH 03455, **Business Phone:** (603)876-4953.

### HILL, ROBERT BERNARD

School administrator, educator. **Personal:** Born Sep 7, 1938, Brooklyn, NY; children: Bernard & Renee. **Educ:** City Col NY, BA, sociol, 1961; Columbia Univ, NYC, PhD, sociol, 1969. **Career:** Bur Appl Soc Res, Columbia Univ NY, res assoc, 1964-69; Princeton Univ Fordham U, adj fac, 1969-73; Nat Urban League, Res Dept, dep dir res, 1969-72, dir res, 1972-81; Bur Census, chmn, mem adv comt black pop, 1974; Howard Univ Wash, DC, vis scholar soc dept sch Human ecol, 1975-77; Bur Soc Sci Res, vpres, sr res assoc, 1981-86; White House, adv & consult; Morgan State Univ, res dir, urban res, 1989-98; Westat, sr researcher, 2001-; Univ Md, staff; New York Univ, staff; Univ Pa, staff. **Orgs:** Pres, Washington, DC Sociol Soc, 1975; pres, Nat Asn Advan Colored People Chap. **Honors/Awds:** HHS Adoption Excellence Award, res on family strengths and informal adoption, 2001; hon Doctrate, Sojourner-Douglass Col, 2000, Univ Md, 2002. **Special Achievements:** Author: The Strengths of Black Families, 1972; Informal Adoption Among Black Families NUL, Res Dept Wash, DC, 1977; Research on the African American Family, Auburn House, 1993; The Strengths of African American Families: Twenty-five Years Later, 1997; The Strengths of African American Families: Twenty-Five Years Later, 1999; The Strengths of Black Families: Reprint, 2003; Synthesis of Research on Disproportionality in Child Welfare, 2006. **Home Addr:** 907 6th St SW Apt 216 C, Washington, DC 20024. **Business Addr:** Senior Researcher, Westat Inc, 1650 Res Blvd, Rockville, MD 20850-3129, **Business Phone:** (301)251-1500.

### HILL, ROBERT J., JR.

Architect. **Personal:** Born Feb 23, 1943, Wilmington, NC; married Sheila G. **Educ:** A&T State Univ, BS, 1971. **Career:** Norfolk Naval Shipyard, archit engr pub works, naval architect. **Orgs:** Soc Prof Naval Engr; Kappa Alpha Psi; YMCA; 35th St Karate Club; A&T Alumni Club. **Honors/Awds:** Letter Commendation, Shipyard Comdr, 1974. **Business Addr:** Naval Architect, Norfolk Naval Shipyard, Code 402, Portsmouth, VA 23709.

### HILL, REV. DR. ROBERT LEE

Clergy, counselor. **Personal:** Born Oct 9, 1931, Birmingham; son of Elcano and Zora; children: Robert Rowland Renel, Victoria, Shvone & Peter. **Educ:** Universal Life Church Inc, doctorate, am church law & parliamentary law, 1980; Union Baptist Sem Sch Relig Studies, BS, theol, 1996, MS, theol, 1998. **Career:** Ford Motor Co, roving part inspector; US Postal Serv, clerk; City Det, Zool Dept; Hill Invest & Exterminating Co, pres & chief exec officer; Universal Life Hope, pastor, counr; Community Christian Church, minister. **Orgs:** Detroit Zoo Soc; Detroit Inst Arts; Mayors Clean SweepTeam; United Found Girl Scouts & Boy Scouts; former vice comdr, Veterans Foreign Wars; chair, pres, Universal Life Gospel Prod; Prince Hall, master mason; Notary Pub Org, 1994; NCP. **Honors/Awds:** Certificate of Appreciation, Detroit Police Second Precinct, 1999; Recognition Award, Detroit City Coun, 1984. **Home Addr:** PO Box 27546, Detroit, MI 48227, **Home Phone:** (313)836-2100.

### HILL, ROBERT LEWIS (BOB HILL)

Association executive, air force officer, educator. **Personal:** Born Feb 23, 1934, Spartanburg, SC; son of Modecai and Texanna Hardy; married Marcia Norcott; children: Robin Lindsey & Lisa Beth. **Educ:** Southern Conn State Univ, New Haven, BS, educ, 1960; Fairfield Univ, CT, attended 1967; Brandeis Univ, Waltham, MA, cert human resource mgt, 1980. **Career:** New Haven Bd Educ, New Haven, CT, teacher, 1963-65; Community Progress Inc, New Haven, CT, counr & trainer, 1965-67; Opportunities Indus Ctr, New Haven, CT, exec dir, 1968-69; Nat League Cities, Wash, DC, coord nat urban, fel, 1969-71, nat dir, vets prog, 1971-78, dir, human resources & pub safety, 1978-82; Am Gas Asn, Arlington, Va, vpres consumer & community affairs, 1985-95; Am Asn Blacks Energy, pres, 1992-96 & 1998-2007, exec dir, 2002, immediate past pres & chief operating officer, 2007. **Orgs:** Asn fel Yale Univ, 1970; deacon bd, chancel choir, Peoples Congregational United Church Christ, Wash, DC, 1976-; bd, Am Asn Blacks Energy, 1986-92; Peoples Neighborhood Fed Credit Union; vis prof, Black Exec Exchange Prog Nat Urban League, 1988; founding organizer, Nat Forum Black Pub Adminr; Nat Asn Advan Colored People; Am Asn Affirmative Action. **Honors/Awds:** Outstanding Achievement Award, Am Veterans Comt, 1974; Distinguished Supporter Award Support HBCU's, Dept Interior, 1988; Role Model Achievement Award, Ft Valley State Col, 1989. **Home Addr:** 12426 Herrington Manor Dr, Silver Spring, MD 20904, **Home Phone:** (301)572-4117. **Business Addr:** President & Executive Director, Chief Operating Officer, American Association of Blacks in Energy, 1625 K St NW Suite 405, Washington, DC 20006, **Business Phone:** (202)371-9530.

### HILL, DR. ROSALIE A.

Educator, executive director. **Personal:** Born Dec 30, 1933, Philadelphia, PA; daughter of Joseph Behlin (deceased) and Anna Mae Elliott (deceased); children: Bernadette Hill Amos. **Educ:** Fla A&M Univ, Tallahassee, FL, BS, music educ, 1956, MEd, guid & coun, 1963; FL State Univ, Tallahassee, FL, PhD, 1985. **Career:** Leon Interfaith Child Care Inc, dir; staff dir; Taylor Co Adult Inst, basic educ teacher; Fla A & M, counr; Taylor Co Head Start Prog, dir; Jerkins HS, music teacher & counr; Fla State Univ, res assoc; RA Hill & Assoc, educ consult; Fla A&M Univ, exec asst vpres; Tallahassee Girls Choir CHOICE, exec dir; Bethel AME Church, Tallahassee, Fla, dir music & admin coordr; Univ S Fla, equal opportunity dir; Univ Fla, counr. **Orgs:** Secy, vpres, pres, Taylor Co Educ Asn, 1966-69; Taylor City Teachers Asn, 1961;

pres, 1963-65; vpres, Fla State Teachers Asn, 1965; chairperson Dist iII, 1960-66; chairperson, Fla State Teachers Asn, 1965-66; exec bd mem Dist III, 1963-65; Fla Educ Asn Small Co Prob Comt, 1967-69; chairperson Jerkins High Sch, 1964-79; bd mem, Taylor Co Sch Bd; PK Yonge Lab Sch; Leon City Sch Bd, 1974-75; secy, Fla A & M Univ Alumni Asn, 1974-76; Nat Asn, 1974-; Am Higher Educ Asn; Am Asn Affirmative Action Officers; Zeta Phi Beta Sor; Taylor Co Improv Club Inc; Tri-Co Econ Coun; Taylor Co Bi-racial Com; Region III Drug Abuse Com; Miss Black Am Pageant; Am Cancer Soc; Hills bor County Community Status Women; spec proj coord, Fla A & M Univ Nat Alumni Asn, 1985-; Nat Asn Advan Colored People; Greater Tampa urban League. **Honors/Awds:** Lewis State Scholarship, 1952-56; Teacher of the Year, Jerkins High Sch, 1960; Yearbook Dedication Jerkins High Sch, 1960; founder, Conf Educ Blacks, Tampa, 1982; Tampa Bay Most Influential Blacks, 1983; co-founder, Fla Statewide Alumni Consortium Historically Black Insts, 1985; Outstanding Alumni Hall of Fame, Fla A&M Univ, 1987; Martin Luther King Education Award, Start Together on Progress Inc, 1988. **Home Addr:** 715 Springsax Rd, Tallahassee, FL 32305-6149, **Home Phone:** (850)574-0942. **Business Addr:** Executive Director, Founder, Tallahassee Girls Choir of C.H.O.I.C.E., 501 West Orange Ave, Tallahassee, FL 32310, **Business Phone:** (850)576-7501.

**HILL, SANDRA PATRICIA**
Social worker, manager. **Personal:** Born Nov 1, 1943, Piedmont, AL; daughter of Edith Palmore (deceased) and Theotis Rosenthal. **Educ:** Berea Col Berea, KY, BS, 1966; Southern Baptist Theo Sem, MRE, 1968; Univ Mich, MSW, 1977; Cornell Univ. **Career:** Harvard St Baptist Ctr, Alexandria, Va, assoc dir, 1968-73, dir, 1974-75; Home Mission Bd, S Baptist Conv, consult, 1977-86, res status, 1987; Southern Baptist Theol Sem, Louisville, Ky, vis prof soc work, 1987-88; Empire State Col, Ithaca, NY, mentor, community & human servs, 1989-90; Displaced Homemakers Ctr, peer servs & minority advocacy coord, 1989-98; Dresden House, mgr, currently. **Orgs:** Old, Inc, Alexandria, Va, 1970-75; Asn Black Social Workers, 1974-; secy & treas, Southern Baptist Soc Serv Asn, 1977-82; bd dir, Reach Out Inc Atlanta, 1980; Nat Asn Advan Colored People; Cornell Coop Exten Tompkins Co, 1991-98; bd dir, vice chair, chair, strategic plng comn, Task Battered Women Tompkins Co, 1992-; chair, 1994-97, vice chair, 1997-98, Soc Work Adv Comn, Cornell Univ; Black Women's Empowerment Grp; vpres, Home Econ & Human Ecol Prog Comn. **Home Addr:** 200 S Hanks St SW, Rome, GA 30165-4160, **Home Phone:** (706)232-1793. **Business Addr:** Manager, Dresden House, 18 Albany Villas, HoveBN3 2SA, **Business Phone:** (127)373-2173.

**HILL, SONNY.** See HILL, WILLIAM RANDOLPH.

**HILL, DR. SYLVIA IONE-BENNETT**
Educator, association executive, criminologist. **Personal:** Born Aug 15, 1940, Jacksonville, FL; daughter of Paul Theodore Sr and Evelyn Harker; children: Gloria Angela Davis. **Educ:** Howard Univ, BS, 1963; Univ Ore, MS, 1967, PhD, 1971. **Career:** Univ Ore, Curric & Instr Dept, asst prof, 1969-71; Macalester Col, asst prof, 1972-74; Carleton Col, Dept Educ, adj prof, 1972-73; Univ DC, Dept Criminal Justice, prof criminal justice, 1974-, Dept Urban Affairs, prof, currently, part-time core prof, 1976-, dir, 1994-97, chairperson, 1996-99, co-dir, 1999-; Mich State Univ, Urban Educ Inst, vis prof, 1975-76; Intercultural Open Univ Found, external scholar, 2008. **Orgs:** Sec gen, Sixth Pan African Cong, 1974; founder & co-chairperson, Southern Africa Support Proj, 1978-; founder & mem, Steering Comn Free S Africa Movement, 1984-; treas, bd Trans Africa Forum, 1984-; bd mem, Trans Africa, 1984-90; bd mem, New World Found, 1988-; assoc dir, USA Tour Nelson & Winnie Mandela, 1990. **Honors/Awds:** Nat Certified Councils, 1984-89. **Special Achievements:** Publications: Cabrals Legacies: Challenges for the 21st Century, Univ MA, 2000; Crime & Criminal Justice: The Dilemmas confronting the African American Community, Ctr Res on African-Am Women Vol 2, 2001; The Free South Movement, william scott ed, Light Among Shadows, policy studies, Washington DC, 2001. **Home Addr:** 1823 9th St NW, Washington, DC 20001-4133, **Home Phone:** (202)387-5343. **Business Addr:** Professor of Criminal Justice, Professor of Administration of Justice, University of the District of Columbia, Rm 407-03 Bldg 41 4200 Conn Ave NW, Washington, DC 20008, **Business Phone:** (202)274-5687.

**HILL, TAMIA MARILYN (TAMIA MARILYN WASHINGTON)**
Actor, entrepreneur, singer. **Personal:** Born May 9, 1975, Windsor, ON; married Grant; children: Myla Grace & Lael Rose. **Educ:** Walkerville Col Inst. **Career:** Albums: Tamia, 1997; A Nu Day, 2000; Still, 2003; Officially Missing You, 2003; More, 2004; Between Friends, 2006, A Gift Between Friends, 2007; Greatest Hits, 2009; Beautiful Surprise, 2012; Love Life, 2015. Hit Singles: "Stranger in the House", 2001; Honey, 2003; TV Series: "The Center", 2003; "Almost", 2007; Films: Speed 2: Cruise Control, 1997; Imagination, 1998; The Center, 2003; TV: Kenan & Kel; Beverly Hills 90210; Rock Me Baby; For Your Love. **Business Addr:** Singer, Plus 1 Music Group, 56 W 45th St Suite 1201, New York, NY 10036, **Business Phone:** (212)239-1732.

**HILL, TRENA TRICE.** See TRICE, TRENA.

**HILL, TYRONE**
Basketball player, basketball coach. **Personal:** Born Mar 19, 1968, Cincinnati, OH. **Educ:** Xavier Univ, BA, 1990. **Career:** Basketball player (retired), basketball coach; Golden State Warriors, ctr forward, 1990-93; Cleveland Cavaliers, 1993-97, 2001-03; Naughty Koalas, 1994-95; Hunger Dunkers, 1995-99; Milwaukee Bucks, 1997-99; Philadelphia 76ers, 1999-2001, 2003; Miami Heat, forward, 2003-04, Atlanta Hawks, vol coach, 2006-08, asst coach, 2008-12.

**HILL, VELMA MURPHY**
Association executive, psychotherapist. **Personal:** Born Oct 17, 1938, Chicago, IL; married Norman. **Educ:** N Ill Univ, Dekalb; Roosevelt Univ, Chicago, attended 1960; Harvard Univ, MEd, 1969. **Career:** Chelsea resident; OEO, summer recruit dir, 1964-65; CORE, 1960-64; Am Dem Action Wash, exec dir, 1965-66; United Fedn Teachers, asst to pres, Para prof Chap, coun mem, chairwoman, 1969-79; Community Bd 4 mem; NY City Training Inst, consult, 1967-68; Randolph Inst, pres; Serv Employees Int Union, dir human rights & int affairs; psychotherapist, currently. **Orgs:** Labor Adv Comt, OEO, 1970-71; Trade Union Comt Histadrut Labor Sem Israel, 1969; Commn Status Women, 1975; bd mem, A Philip Randolph Inst; Chelsea Midtown Dem Club, exec vpres; int affairs dir, human rights dir, Serv Employees Int Union; vpres, Bayard Rustin Fund. **Special Achievements:** First Chairwoman of the UFT's paraprofessional chapter from 1969-79. **Home Addr:** 321 W 24 St, New York, NY 10011-1503, **Home Phone:** (212)929-9066.

**HILL, VONCIEL JONES**
Judge. **Personal:** Born Sep 23, 1948, Hattiesburg, MS; married Charles Edward. **Educ:** Univ Tex, BA, hist & eng, 1969, JD, 1979; Atlanta Univ, MA, libr sci, 1971; Rice Univ, MA, hist, 1976; Univ Tex, Austin Sch Law, JD, 1979; Southern Methodist Univ, Mdiv, 1990; Paul Quinn Col, PhD, 2003. **Career:** GA Pub Sch, Atlanta, teacher, 1969-70; Atlanta Univ, Ford Found fel, 1970-71; Prairie View A&M Univ, asst circulations libr, 1971-72; Tex Southern Univ, asst law libr, 1972-76; Rice Univ, fel, 1974-76; Pub Utility Comt TX, staff atty, 1979-80; Dallas, Ft Worth Airport, asst city atty, 1980-86; St Luke Community United Methodist Church, asst pastor, 1985-; Dallas Munic Ct, munic ct judge, 1987-2004; Pvt Pract, atty, 2005-; City Dallas, Dist 5, Councilmember, currently, asst city atty. **Orgs:** Nat Asn Advan Colored People, 1958-; Chmn & bd dir, Methodism's Breadbasket, 1983-85; comt chmn, Dallas Bar Asn, 1985, Libr Comt, 2006; secy, JL Turner Legal Asn, 1985; treas, State Bar TX Women & Law Sec, 1986-87; Col State Bar Tex; Bench Bar Comt, 2006; Dallas City Coun woman; Dallas Black Chamber Com. **Business Addr:** Council Member, Dallas City Council, Rm 5FN 1500 Marilla St, Dallas, TX 75201-6390, **Business Phone:** (214)670-0777.

**HILL, WILLIAM BRADLEY, JR.**
Lawyer, association executive, judge. **Personal:** Born Mar 3, 1952, Atlanta, GA; married Melba Gayle Wynn; children: Kara & Morgan Kristopher. **Educ:** Wash & Lee Univ, Lexington, Va, BA, 1974, JD, 1977. **Career:** St Law Dept Atlanta GA, asst atty gen, 1977-90; Ga Atty Gen's Off, atty gen & dir, Criminal Div, sr asst, 1982-88, head, dep atty gen, 1988-90; State Ct Fulton County, judge, 1990-92; Super Ct Fulton County, judge, 1992-95; Paul Hastings, partner, 1995-2004; Lawrence Ashe & Nancy Rafuse, partner, 2004-13; Rafuse Hill & Hodges LLP, partner, 2004-13; Atlanta, atty, currently; Polsinelli, shareholder, 2014-. **Orgs:** ;St Bar Ga, 1977; exec chmn, Wash & Lee Univ Black Alumni Found, 1980-; Ga Comn Dispute Resolution; State Judicial Nominating Comn; Northern Dist Ga Bar Coun; adv bd dir, Atlanta Bar Asn, 1989-92; Kiwanis Club Atlanta, 1991-97; Ga Chief Justice's Comn, 1994-2002; founding mem bd dir, Ga Drug Abuse Resistance Educ; bd trustee, Wash & Lee Univ, 1999-2009; adj, Emory Univ Sch Law, 2007-. **Honors/Awds:** Listed among 2003 The Best Lawyers in America. **Home Addr:** 600 Peachtree St NE, Atlanta, GA 30308, **Home Phone:** (404)815-2276. **Business Addr:** Partner, Lawyer, Polsinelli P C, 1201 W Peachtree St NW, Atlanta, GA 30309, **Business Phone:** (404)253-6025.

**HILL, WILLIAM RANDOLPH (SONNY HILL)**
Executive director, basketball player. **Personal:** Born Jul 22, 1936, Philadelphia, PA; son of K Brent; married Edith Hughes; children: K Brent, Starr & Leah. **Career:** Basketball player (retired), executive, talk show host; Eastern Basketball League, basketball player, 1958-67; Teamsters Local 169, secy, treas, bus agt & trust, 1960-93; WPEN Lct Sports & Humanitarian, analyst, 1966-; Philadelphia 76ers, broadcast, 1969, exec advisor, exec advisor to pres, 1996-; CBS TV, commentator, 1972-77; Lancaster Red Roses Basketball Team, owner, 1975; Eastern Basketball League, basketball player; Sonny Hill, founder, John Chaney Basketball Camp, co-owner, 1975-, exec dir, currently; WIP Sports Radio Talk Show, host, 1987-; WRIT Radio, Temple Univ Basketball, color analyst, 1993-; First Union Complex, exec advisor to pres & chief exec officer, 1995-. **Orgs:** Pres, Charles Baker Mem Summer League, 1960-; pres & founder, Sonny Hill Community Involvement League Inc, 1968-; adv bd, MacDonald's HS All Am Team, 1978-80; bd dir, Big Bros Asn Nat Comn, Opr PUSH; Nat Asn Advan Colored People; Philadelphia Sports Hall of Fame. **Honors/Awds:** Outstanding Community Service Award, Sports Mag, 1970; Human Rights Award, Comn on Human Rel, 1972; Man of the Year, Nite Owl, 1972-73; good neighbour Award, WDAS Radio, 1973; Oxford Circle JC Award, 1973; Man of the Year Award, Fishtown, 1973; Tribune Charities, 1976; Basketball Weekly Player Develop Award, Toyota Motors, 1977; Mutual Radio Broadcaster NBA Championship, 1980; Mellon Bank Good Neighbour Award, 1985; John B Kelley Award, 1986; City Hope Spirit Life Award; Whitney Young Leadership Award, Urban League of Pa, 1990; Service Award, Leon H Sullivan Charitable Golf Tournament, Zion COT Center, 1992; EDR's Roundtable Dr Wm H Gray Jr COTA Activist Award, 1993; honorary doctorate, Temple Univ, 1998; Clarence Farmer Award, Pa Comn on Human Relations, 2001; One of the 100 most influential minorities in sports, Sports Illustrated, 2004; Mannie Jackson Human Spirit Award, Naismith Memorial Basketball Hall Fame, 2008. **Business Addr:** Founder, Executive Director, Sonny Hill League, 429 S 50th St, Philadelphia, PA 19143, **Business Phone:** (215)474-2801.

**HILL, WINFER L.**
Electrical engineer. **Career:** Infineon Technologies, elec engr. **Business Addr:** Electrical Engineer, Infineon Technologies, 6000 Technology Blvd, Sandston, VA 23150.

**HILL-LUBIN, DR. MILDRED ANDERSON**
Educator, association executive. **Personal:** Born Mar 23, 1933, Russell County, AL; daughter of Luther and Mary; married Maurice A; children: Walter H Hill & Robert T Hill. **Educ:** Paine Col Augusta, BA, Eng, 1961; Western Res Cleveland, MA, Eng, 1962; Ind Univ, attended 1964; Univ Minn, attended 1966; Howard Univ & African Am Inst, 1972; Univ Ill Urbana-Champaign, PhD, Eng, African studies, 1974. **Career:** Paine Col, instr, asst prof, 1962-65, 1966-70; Hamline Univ, exchange prof, 1965-66; Paine Col, asst prof Eng, dir EPDA prog, 1970-72; Univ Ill, teaching asst, instr, 1972-74; Univ Fla, assoc prof eng, dir eng prog spec admit stud, 1974-77, asst dean grad sch, 1977-80, assoc prof eng & african studies, 1982-2004, assoc prof emer, currently. **Orgs:** Exec comm, Col Comp & Comm (CCCC), 1977-80; pres, FOCUS, 1978-79; panel mem Adv Coun Mellon Humanities Grant UNCF Col Fund, 1980-90; proj Asn coun, Chief State Sch Officers, 1981-82; consult, Am Coun Educ, 1981-; discipline comm African Lit Fulbright Awards, 1983-86; exec comm, African Lit Asn, 1983-89; pres, Gainesville Chap Links, 1985-87; bd dir, Gainesville/Alachua Co Ctr Excell, 1985-; Alpha Kappa Alpha Sor; pres, African Lit Asn, 1987-88; dir, Gainesville-Jacmel Haiti Sister Cities Prog, 1987-92; pres, Visionaires, 1988-91; Fla Humanities Coun, 1991-95; Santa Fe Community Col Dist, 1993-. **Honors/Awds:** Alpha Kappa Mu Honor Soc Paine Col, 1960; Travel-Study Grant to W Africa African-Amer Int 19; Trainer of Teachers Fellowship Univ Ill, 1973-74; Leadership and Achievement Award, Nu Eta Lambda Chapter Alpha Phi Alpha Fraternity, 1988; Women of Distinction Award, Gainesville Area, 1992; Teacher of the Year, Univ Fla, 1994; Susan B Anthony Award, Gainesville Comm on the Status of Women, 1994, 2012. **Special Achievements:** Co-editor of "Towards Defining the African Aesthetic" and articles in "Southern Folklore Quarterly", "Coll Lang Assn Journal"; "Presence Africaine"; "Okike"; articles, "The Black Grandmother in Literature," in Ngambika, 1986. **Home Addr:** 6211 NW 23rd Lane, Gainesville, FL 32606-8523, **Home Phone:** (352)373-8331. **Business Addr:** Associate Professor Emeritus, University of Florida, 4008 Turlington Hall, Gainesville, FL 32611-7310, **Business Phone:** (352)392-6650.

**HILL-MARLEY, LAURYN NOELLE**
Actor, rap musician. **Personal:** Born May 26, 1975, South Orange, NJ; daughter of Mal Hill and Valerie Hill; married Rohan Marley; children: Zion David, Selah Louise, Joshua & John. **Educ:** Columbia Univ. **Career:** The Fugees, mem; Albums with the Fugees: Blunted on Reality, 1993, The Score, 1996; Solo Albums: The Miseducation of Lauryn Hill, 1998; MTV Unplugged No 2.0, 2002; Films: Sister Act II, 1993; Rhyme & Reason, 1997; Restaurant, 1997; Hav Plenty, 1998; King of the Hill, 1999; Turn It Up, 2000; Concerning Violence, 2014. TV series: "As the World Turns", 1991; "Here and Now", 1992; "Daddy's Girl", 1996; "ABC Afterschool Specials", 1996; "Mic Check Live: Ms. Lauryn Hill & Tyrese Gibson", exec producer, 2011. Songs: "If I Ruled the World (Imagine That)", 1996; "The Sweetest Thing", 1997; "All My Time", 1997; "The Miseducation of Lauryn Hill", 1998; "Can't Take My Eyes off of You", 1998; "Doo Wop (That Thing)", 1998; "Lost Ones", 1999; "Ex-Factor", 1999; "Everything Is Everything", 1999; "Mr. Intentional", 2002; "Say", 2006; "Lose Myself", 2007; "Africa Unite", 2008. **Orgs:** Founder, Refugee Proj. **Honors/Awds:** NAACP Image Awards; Outstanding New Artist; Outstanding Female Artist; Outstanding Album; American Music Awards; Favorite New Artist; Am Music Award; Favorite R&B/Soul Album; Grammy Award for Album Of The Year, 1998; Grammy Award for Best New Artist, 1998; Grammy Award forR&B Female Vocal, 1998; Grammy Award for R&B Song, 1998; Grammy Award for R&B Album, 1998; Grammy Award for Album Of The Year, 1999; President's Award, 1999; Favorite Female, R&B/Soul Artist, 2000. **Special Achievements:** Nineteen Grammy Nominations; First of only seven female artists awarded five Grammys in one year. **Business Addr:** Singer, Sony Music, 550 Madison Ave, New York, NY 10022-3211, **Business Phone:** (212)833-8000.

**HILLARD, TERRY**
Police officer. **Personal:** Born Aug 11, 1943, South Fulton, TN; married Dorothy; children: Lee & Dana. **Educ:** Chicago State Univ, BS,1976, MS, 1978, corrections; US Secret Serv Dignitary Protection Course. **Career:** Police officer (retired); Chicago Police Dept, Area 2 patrol officer, 1968, wounded line duty, 1975, mayoral bodyguard contingent, 1980; dist comdr, dep chief patrol, 1995, chief detectives, 1995-98, supt, 1998-2003; Hillard Heintze LLC, partner & sr leadership coun, currently; Intelligence Div Sgt, dist comdr; Chicago Terrorist Task Force, coordr; Hillard Heintze, co-founder, partner, 2004-. **Orgs:** NOBLE; Chicago Westside Police Asn; FBI Nat Acad Asn; S Suburban Chiefs Police Asn; Nat Comm Future DNA Evidence; Domestic Violence Advocacy Coord Coun; adv bd, Ill State Police Forensic Sci Ctr, Chicago; architect, Enhanced Drug & Gang Enforcement Prog. **Honors/Awds:** Hon Dr, Lewis Univ; hon dr, St Xavier Univ; hon dr, Calumet Col, St Joseph; Police Awards: Police Medal; Superintendent's Award of Valor, Chicago Police Dept, 1995; Police Blue Star Award; Carter Harrison/Lambert Tree Honorable Mention; Special Service Award, Chicago Community Policing; Special Service Award, Democratic Nat Convention; 3 DPT Commendations; Unit Meritorious Performance Award; Chicago COC Award; The Police Medal; FBI Directors Community Service Award. **Special Achievements:** First African-American chief of detectives in Chicago Police Dept; First African American chief of police in Chicago. **Business Addr:** Partner, Senior Leadership Council, Hillard Heintze LLC, 30 SWacker Dr Suite 1730, Chicago, IL 60606.

**HILLIARD, ALICIA VICTORIA**
Television journalist. **Personal:** Born Jan 4, 1949, Wadesboro, NC; daughter of George Allen and Annie Louise. **Educ:** Morgan State Univ, BA, 1971; Univ Wis, Madison. **Career:** Baltimore City Hosps, nutrit asst & kitchen asst, 1970; State atty's Off, polit sci intern, 1970-71; Morgan State Univ, pub rels asst, 1971-72; Housing Authority Baltimore City, info asst, 1972-75;, reporter & producer, 1977-82; Univ Wis, Madison, teaching asst assoc, 1977-78; WISC TV, exec news producer, 1982-88; WHDH TV, news producer, 1988-. **Orgs:** AKA Sorority, Inc, 1971-; Boston Aan Black Journalists, 1988-; Nat Asn Black Journalists, 1988-; mentor & vol, Black Achievers, YWCA, 1992-. **Honors/Awds:** Sword of Hope Award, Am Cancer Soc, 1990; Unity Award/Education, 1990, Unity Award/AIDS, 1990, Univ MSR-Lincoln; Gabriel Awards for coverage Nelson Mandela visit to Boston, 1990; Special Chair Award, AFTRA-SAG, 1991; American Scene Award, New England AFTRA-SAG, 1991; Best Feature, NAT Asn Black Journalists, 1991; Black Achiever, Boston YWCA, 1992; Community Service Award, Veterans Benefits Clearinghouse, 1992. **Home Addr:** PO Box 8754, Boston, MA 02114-0037, **Home Phone:** (617)899-2804. **Business Addr:** Television News Producer, WHDH TV New 7, 7 Bulfinch Pl News Dept 3rd Fl, Boston, MA 02114-2913, **Business Phone:** (617)725-0864.

**HILLIARD, AMY SHARMANE (AUDREY SHAR-**

**MANE AMY HILLIARD)**
Entrepreneur, marketing executive, chief executive officer. **Personal:** Born Aug 16, 1952, Detroit, MI; daughter of Stratford and Gwendolyn; children: Angelica & Nicholas Jones. **Educ:** Howard Univ, BS, 1974; Harvard Bus Sch, MBA, 1978. **Career:** DePaul Univ's bus sch, adj prof; Univ Chicago, lectr; Univ Calif, lectr; Bloomingdales, NY, buyer; Gillette Inc, Boston, sr prod mgr, 1985, dir mkt, 1987-90; Lustrasilk, mkt exec; Pillsbury Inc, Baked Goods Div, dir mkt develop, 1992; Burrell Communs Group, sr vpres, Integrated Mkt Servs, dir, 1992-95; Hilliard Mkt Group LLC, pres & chief exec officer, 1995-; Soft Sheen Prods & L'Oreal, sr vpres mkt, 1999-2000; DePaul Univ, adj prof; Comfort Cake Co, pres & chief exec officer, 2001-. **Orgs:** Bd dir, Metrop Family Servs; Nat Restaurant Asn; Direct Mkt Asn; Am Advert Found; Black Enterprise Entrepreneurs Conf; Womens Bus Develop Ann Entrepreneurs Conf; United Way Nat Leadership Conf; Int Inst Res; bd trustee, Howard Univ, 2010-; bd dir, Nat Asn Specialty Food Trade; Ethnic Adv Bd Pepsi Co; Clinton Found Econ Initiative/Entrepreneurship Mentor Prog; Chicago Chamber Com; Rainbow Push Coalition. **Special Achievements:** First African American elected to the Board of Directors of the National Association of the Specialty Food Trade (NASFT). **Business Addr:** President, Chief Executive Officer, Comfort Cake Co LLC, 1243 S Wabash Ave Suite 201, Chicago, IL 60605, **Business Phone:** (866)264-2253.

**HILLIARD, BILL.** **See HILLIARD, WILLIAM ARTHUR.**

**HILLIARD, EARL FREDERICK**
Lawyer, politician. **Personal:** Born Apr 9, 1942, Birmingham, AL; son of William and Iola Frazier; married Mary Franklin; children: Alesia & Earl Jr. **Educ:** Morehouse Col, BA, 1964; Howard Univ Sch Law, JD, 1967; Atlanta Univ Sch Bus, MBA, 1970. **Career:** Ala State Univ, asst to pres, 1968-70; Pearson & Hilliard Law Firm, partners, 1972-73; Birmingham Legal Aid Soc, regional heber fel, 1970-72; State Ala, state rep, 1970-72, dem, 1974, 1975-81, state sen, 1981-92; WJLD-AM FM Radio, owner, 1985-87; US House Rep, cong man, 1993-2003; Pvt Pract, lawyer, currently; US state Ala, politician, currently. **Orgs:** Pres, Am Trust Life Ins Co, 1977-90; Nat Bar Asn, 1979; Alpha Phi Alpha Fraternity Inc, 1980; pres, Am Trust Land Co, 1980-; Morehouse Col Nat Alumni Asn, 1983; Nat Asn Advan Colored People, 1984; bd trustee, Miles Law Sch, 1984-92; bdtrustee, Tuskegee Univ, 1986-92; chmn, Ala Black Legis Caucus; bd mem, Cong Black Caucus Inst; vice chmn, 105th Cong, 1997-99. **Home Addr:** 1625 Castleberry Way, Birmingham, AL 35214, **Home Phone:** (205)798-7352. **Business Addr:** Lawyer, 1625 Castleberry Way, Birmingham, AL 35214, **Business Phone:** (205)798-7352.

**HILLIARD, IKE (ISAAC JASON HILLIARD)**
Football player. **Personal:** Born Apr 5, 1976, Patterson, LA; son of Ivory Sr and Doris; married Lourdes; children: Kye, Kalyn, Leila Marie & Ilysa Jade. **Educ:** Univ Fla, BA, sociol. **Career:** Football player (retired), coach; New York Giants, wide receiver, 1997-2004; Tampa Bay Buccaneers, wide receiver, 2005-08; Fla Tuskers, coach, 2009-10; Miami Dolphins, coach, 2011; Wash Redskins, coach, 2012; Buffalo Bills, coach, 2013-. **Home Addr:** 17020 SW 74th Ave, Palmetto Bay, FL 33157-4889. **Business Addr:** Coach, Buffalo Bills, 1 Bills Dr, Orchard Park, NY 14127, **Business Phone:** (716)646-9229.

**HILLIARD, PATSY JO**
Government official. **Personal:** Born Aug 20, 1937, Denver, CO; daughter of Elmer Audley Morrison and Jessie Morrison; married Asa G; children: Asa G IV, Robi Herron, Patricia Nunn & Michael Hakim. **Educ:** San Francisco State Univ, BA, interdisciplinary soc sci, 1976. **Career:** Denver Pub Sch Syst, supvr, 1956-61; Montessori teacher & lectr; E Pt City, Ga, mayor, 1992-2005; Waset Educ Prod Co, co-owner & chief exec officer, currently; Peace Corps, chmn sec educ dept, dean educ & consult. **Orgs:** Atlanta Chap Links; Nat League Cities Human Develop Steering Comt; chair, GMA Munic Govt & Admin Policy Comn; Atlanta Chap, Delta Sigma Theta Sorority Inc; state chair, GMA Unfunded Mundates Day; Ga Munic Asn; vol, Liberian Rural Women Asn; E Pt Bus Asn; Fulton County Sch Dists Superintendents Adv Bd; Atlanta Airport Rotary Club; Atlanta High Mus Art; DeYoung Mus Art; exec bd, Atlanta chap Nat Asn Advan Colored People; pres, Links Inc; Delta Sigma Theta Sorority Inc. **Special Achievements:** In 1975, Hilliard became the first African American and the first woman board member of the South San Francisco Unified School District. She was the first African American elected as mayor of East Point, Georgia. **Home Addr:** 3350 Sir Henry St, East Point, GA 30344. **Business Addr:** Co-owner, Chief Executive Officer, Waset Education Productions, 3350 Sir Henry St, East Point, GA 30344-5832, **Business Phone:** (404)761-4500.

**HILLIARD, RANDY**
Football player. **Personal:** Born Feb 6, 1967, New Orleans, LA; married Lynette. **Educ:** Northwestern State, La. **Career:** Football player (retired); Cleveland Browns, 1999, right cornerback, 1991, defensive back, 1992, left cornerback, 1993; Denver Broncos, 1995, 1997, defensive back, 1994, 1996; Chicago Bears, defensive back, 1998. **Honors/Awds:** N Club Hall of Fame, Northwestern State Univ, 2008.

**HILLIARD, DR. ROBERT LEE MOORE**
Physician, obstetrician, gynecologist. **Personal:** Born Jan 1, 1931, San Antonio, TX; son of Otho Earl and Robbie Moore; married Marilu Moreno; children: Ronald, Bennie Karen Brown, Portia Denise Byas, Robert Jr, Rudyard Lance, Robbie Lesley, Ruby Lucinda & Barbara Felix. **Educ:** Howard Univ, BS, 1951; Univ Tex Med Br, Galveston, MD, 1956. **Career:** Dc Gen Hosp, internship, 1956-57; Univ Tex Health Sci Ctr, San Antonio, resident obstet & gynec, 1960-63; TX Bank, dir, 1975-88; St Mary's Univ, trustee, adv bd, 1983-90; TX State Bd Med Examiners, mem, 1984-91, pres, 1989-90; Northeast Baptist Hosp, pract; St Lukes Baptist Hosp, pract; Southeast Baptist Hosp, pract; Baptist Med Ctr, pract; Metrop Methodist Hosp, pract; Santa Rosa Health Care Corp, staff; Women's Clin San Antonio, obstet & gynec physician, currently; pvt pract physician, currently. **Orgs:** Chmn, San Antonio Housing Authority, 1969-71; vice chmn, United Negro Col Fund, 1971-75; councilman, San Antonio City Coun, 1971-73; trustee, Nat Med Asn, 1975-81, pres, 1982-83; comnr, San Antonio Fire & Police Civil Serv Comn, 1978-80; vice chmn, City Water Bd San Antonio, 1980-85; dir, Nat Med Fels, 1982-; chmn, City Water Bd, 1986-88; chmn, NMA Judicial Coun, 1984-94; fel Am Cong Obstetricians & Gynecologists; fel Am Col Surgeons. **Honors/Awds:** Dedicated Service, United Negro Col Fund, 1973, Distinguished Leadership, 1982; Benefactor de la Communidad, City San Antonio, 1981; Cert of Appreciation, State TX House Reps, 1983; Achievement Award, S Central Region AKA Sorority, 1983; Distinguished Alumnus, Univ Texas Med Branch, 1991; Distinguished Alumnus Award, Howard Univ, 1995. **Business Addr:** Physician, Women's Clinic of San Antonio, 710 Augusta St, San Antonio, TX 78215, **Business Phone:** (210)225-6131.

**HILLIARD, WILLIAM ARTHUR (BILL HILLIARD)**
Journalist, editor. **Personal:** Born May 28, 1927, Chicago, IL; son of Felix Henry and Ruth Little; children: Gregory Stephen, Linda Karen & Sandra Gunder; married Dian. **Educ:** Pac Univ, Forest Grove, Ore, BA, jour, 1952, Hon Law Degree. **Career:** Journalist (retired); Oregonian Publ Co, copy boy, sports clerk, sports reporter, relig & gen assignment reporter, asst city ed, city ed, exec ed, ed, 1952-94. **Orgs:** Bd dir, Nat Urban League, 1973-78; chair, Nat Conf Nat Urban League, 1979-80; chair & bd dir, Fed Res Bank, San Francisco, Portland Br, 1991-93; pres, Am Soc Newspaper Ed, 1993-94; APA Fraternity; Nat Asn Black Journalists; Nat Asn Advan Colored People; adv bd, Alpha Phi Alpha Fraternity, Freedom Forum First Amendment Ctr. **Honors/Awds:** Anti-Defamation League Torch Liberty Award; Publ Serv Award, Univ Ore; named executive editor of the Oregonian, 1982; named editor of the paper, 1987; Amos E Voorhies Award, 1991; Equal Opportunity Award, Urban League Portland; Presidential Award, Nat Asn Black Journalists; Special Recognition Award, Asian Am Journalists Asn; Sculpture Friendship Award, Native Am Journalist Asn; Distinguished Serv Award, Ore State Univ; Distinguished Serv Award, Western Oregon State Col; Oregon Newspaper Hall of Fame Award, Ore Newspaper Publ's Asn, 1998. **Special Achievements:** First African American editor of the Oregonian; First African American to hold that position, president of the American Society of Newspaper Editors, 1993. **Home Addr:** 2315 NW Aspen Ave, Portland, OR 97210-1220, **Home Phone:** (503)222-2057.

**HILLMAN, GRACIA M.**
Association executive, executive. **Personal:** Born Sep 12, 1949, New Bedford, MA; daughter of George (deceased) and Maria DaGraca (deceased); married Robert E Bates Jr; children: Hillman Martin. **Educ:** Univ Mass, Boston, Col Pub & Community Serv, attended 1978. **Career:** Mass Legis Black Caucus, admin, 1975-77; Mass Dept Correction, exec asst to comnr, 1977-79; Mass Port Authority, pub & govt affairs spec, 1979; Joint Ctr Polit & Econ Studies, coor dr, 1979-82; Nat Coalition Black Voter Participation, exec dir, 1982-87; Cong Black Caucus Found, interim exec dir, 1988; Dukakis Pres Campaign, sr advisor cong affairs, 1988; Coun Found, exec consult, 1989-90, exec advisor; League Women Voters US & League Women Voters Educ Fund, exec dir, 1999; US Election Assistance Comn, mem, 2003-, 2005-08, comnr, 2003-10, vice-chair, 2004, chair, 2005; World Space Found, pres & chief exec officer; US Dept State, sr coordr int women's issues; GM Hillman & Assocs Inc, pres & prin consult, currently; Howard Univ, vpres external affairs, currently. **Orgs:** Nat Polit Cong Black Women; secy, United Front Homes Develop Corp, New Bedford, MA, 1972-76; pres, United Front Homes Day Care Ctr, New Bedford, MA, 1973-76; pres, BD Community Action Prog, New Bedford, MA, 1974-76; chairperson, Mass Govt Serv Career Prog, 1977-78; vice chairperson, Ctr Youth Serv, Wash, DC, 1985-; prog devel consult, Cong Black Caucus Found, 1987; sr fel Demos; bd dir, OWL. **Special Achievements:** First Cape Verdean American to hold the position of executive director of the league of women voters of the united states. Autor: "Toward A More Perfect Union: The Congressional Black Caucus & Voting Rights"; "E-Voting and Democracy in America". **Home Addr:** 2710 Unicorn Lane NW, Washington, DC 20015, **Home Phone:** (202)244-0305. **Business Addr:** Vice President, Howard University, 2400 Sixth St NW, Washington, DC 20059, **Business Phone:** (202)806-6100.

**HILLSMAN, GERALD C.**
Association executive. **Personal:** Born Jul 7, 1926, Dayton, OH; married Julia. **Educ:** Marjorie Webster Jr Col, AA, 1975; Nat Inst Drug Progs, cert, 1975. **Career:** Cent City Bricks Kick Proj, founder & prog dir, 1970-; VA Hosp, Brentwood, CA, drug consult, 1971-72; VA Hosp, drug consult, 1972-73; Univ SC Hosp, drug consult. **Orgs:** Pres, Partners Progress; hon mem, bd dir, W Coast Asn Puerto Rican Substance Abuse Workers Inc; adv bd mem, Cent City Substance Abuse Trng LA. **Home Addr:** 10248 6th Ave, Inglewood, CA 90303. **Business Addr:** Program Director, Central City Bricks/Kick Proj, 1925 S Trinity St, Los Angeles, CA 90011.

**HILSON, DR. ARTHUR LEE**
School administrator, clergy. **Personal:** Born Apr 6, 1936, Cincinnati, OH; son of Shepard and Bertha McAdoo Wilburn; married Florine McClary; children: Gabrielle, Antionette & David. **Educ:** Wheaton Col, Springfield Christian Bible Sem, Wheaton, IL, bachelor theol; Andover Newton Theol Sem, Newton Ctr, MA, MDiv; Univ Mass, Amherst, MA, MEd, 1974, EdD, 1979. **Career:** Human Resources Develop Ctr, Newport, RI, human rels consult, 1973; Univ Mass, Amherst, Mass, admin asst to dean Grad affairs, Sch Educ, 1973-75, dept head, Veterans Assistance & Coun Servs, 1976-78, dept head, Univ Placement Servs, 1978-87, exec dir, Pub Safety, 1987-92; Univ NH, fac, dept head, Am studies stud affairs, 1992-94; Portsmouth High Sch, hist teacher, 2000-; New Hope Baptist Church, pastor, sr pastor, sr servant, 1991-; NH Comnr Human Rights; United Baptist Churches MA, RI &NH, pres, 2013-. **Orgs:** Phi Delta Kappa; Am Personnel Officers Asn; Eastern Col Personnel Officers Asn; Col Placement Coun; Nat Asn Advan Colored People; bd mem, Am Veterans Comt; chmn, Nat Asn Minority Veterans Prog Adminr; bd mem, Nat Asn Veterans Prog Adminr; bd mem, interim dir, Veterans Outreach Ctr, Greenfield, MA; Int Asn Campus Law Enforcement Adminr; Int Asn Chiefs Police; chmn, United Christian Found; United Baptist Conv Mass RI, NH; Am Baptist Conv, Vt & NH; charter pres, Amherst Nat Asn Advan Colored People; bd dir, Western Mass Girl Scouts; bd dir, United Way Hampshire County. **Honors/Awds:** Kellogg Fellow, Kellogg Found, 1973-74; Martin Luther King Award, 2000. **Home Addr:** 2 Joffre Terr, Portsmouth, NH 03801-4915, **Home Phone:** (603)433-7343. **Business Addr:** Senior Pastor, New Hope Baptist Church, 263 Peverly Hill Rd, Portsmouth, NH 03801, **Business Phone:** (603)431-7310.

**HILTON, STANLEY WILLIAM, JR.**
Executive. **Personal:** Born Philadelphia, PA; son of Stanley W Sr and Jennie Parsons Cooper; children: Richard H. **Educ:** Fisk Univ, BA, 1959; Temple Univ, attended 1959. **Career:** Mill Run Playhouse Niles IL, treas, 1969-70; Shubert Theatre, co mgr, Hair, 1969-70; Orpheum Theatre San Francisco, mgr, 1970-74; "My Fair Lady", "Jesus Christ Superstar", "No Place to be Somebody", San Francisco, co mgr; Park & Theatre Opers Art Park Lewiston NY, dir, 1974; Evanston Theatre Co IL, bus mgr; Blackstone Theatre Chgo, mgr, 1974-86; Emory & Co, owner, 1990-92; real estate & retail entrepreneur; "Pope Joan", Chicago, gen mgr, 1996; "Hair", Chicago, gen mgr, 1996; Auditorium Theatre, mgr, 1998-99. **Orgs:** Exec asst, sec Bd Pensions Meth Ch Ill, 1965-66; off mgr, Cook Cty Dept Publ Aid Chicago, 1966-70; coordr ed & vocl couns, Concentrated Employ Prog, Comn, Col Dist San Fran, 1971-73; mem assoc, Theatrical Press Agt & Mgr NY; reg soc worker, Ill; cert teacher & voc couns, Calif; comt mem, Artist Chicago. **Home Addr:** 1540 N State Pkwy, Chicago, IL 60610-1678, **Home Phone:** (312)751-1222.

**HILTON, TANYA**
Association executive, executive director. **Personal:** married Steven; children: Taylor & Justin. **Educ:** Univ Minn, BA, bus; postgrad study, Eng. **Career:** Am Asn Univ Women, Educ Found, dir. **Business Addr:** Director, American Association of University Women, 1111 16th St NW, Washington, DC 20036-4873, **Business Phone:** (202)785-7700.

**HINDS, PROF. LENNOX S.**
Educator, lawyer. **Personal:** Born Port-of-Spain; son of Arthur and Dolly Stevens; married Bessie; children: Brent, Yvette & Renee. **Educ:** City Col, NY, BS, chem, 1962; Mass Inst Technol, MS, chem; Univ Minn; Rutgers Sch Law, JD, 1972. **Career:** Director (retired), professor, partner; Charles Pfizer & Co, staff; Cities Serv Res & Develop Co, staff; Citgo Corp, res sect chief, 1964-69; Prisoner's Rights Org Defense, dir, 1971-72; Heritage Found, dir, 1969-72; Nat Conf Black Lawyers, nat dir, 1973-78; City Col New York, Ctr Legal Educ Urban Policy, Charles H Revson Fel, 1979-80; Rutgers Univ, chmn admin justice prog, prof criminal justice, currently; Stevens Hinds & White PC, sr partner, currently; Nat Lawyers Guild, lawyers; Int Criminal Tribunal Rwanda, lead coun. **Orgs:** Vpres & Permanent Rep, pres, Int Asn Dem Lawyers, 1973-; Int Bd Orgn Non-Govt; Nj Bar Asn; Nat Minority Adv Comn Criminal Justice; Nat Adv Coun Child Abuse; bd mem, Soc Mobilization Legal Proj; nat secy, Black-Am Law Students Asn; bd mem, Law Studetns Civil Rights Res Coun. **Home Addr:** 42 Van Doren Ave, Somerset, NJ 08873-2734, **Home Phone:** (908)873-3096. **Business Addr:** Professor, Rutgers University, Lucy Stone Hall Rm A359 Livingston Campus, New Brunswick, NJ 08903, **Business Phone:** (848)445-4267.

**HINE, DARLENE CLARK**
Educator, president (organization), editor. **Personal:** Born Feb 7, 1947, Morley, MO; daughter of Leveste and Lottie Mr; children: Robbie Davine. **Educ:** Roosevelt Univ, Chicago, BA, 1968; Kent State Univ, Kent, OH, MA, 1970, PhD, 1975. **Career:** SC State Col, asst prof, 1972-74; Purdue Univ, asst prof, 1974-79, interim dir, Africana & Res Ctr, 1978-79, assoc prof 1979-81, vice provost, 1981-85, prof hist, 1985-87; Truth, Newsletter ABWH, ed, 1979-80; Mich State Univ, John A Hannah prof Am hist, 1985-2004, dir, adj prof, 2004-; Univ Del, vis distinguished prof women's studies, 1989-90; Historian, assoc ed, 1995-; Univ SC, Robert E McNair vis prof southern studies, 1996; Roosevelt Univ, Harold Washington vis prof, 1996; Northwestern Univ, Avalon distinguished vis prof, 1997, Northwestern Univ, Dept African Am Studies, Chair, 2008-11. **Orgs:** Exec coun mem, Asn Study Afro-Am Life Hist, 1979-81; dir publ, Asn Black Women Historians, 1979; bd dir, Consortium Social Sci Asn, 1987-91; Yale Univ Coun Comt Grad Sch, 1988-93; nominating comt chair, Am Hist Asn, 1988-89; exec coun, Southern Hist Asn, 1990-93; Asn Study African Life & Hist Carter G Woodson Scholar-in-Residence Comn, 1995; exec comt mem, Nat Acad Critical Studies, 1996-; chair, Comn Women, Southern Hist Asn, 1996-98; prog comt mem, Orgn Am Hist, 1998; Delta Sigma Theta Sorority Inc, 2000; Am Acad Arts & Sci, 2006; Phi Beta Kappa; bd trustee, prof African Am studies & prof hist, 2004-; Asn Study African Am Life & Hist; Orgn Am Historians; Southern Asn Women Historians; Southern Hist Asn. **Home Addr:** 2357 Burcham Dr, East Lansing, MI 48823, **Home Phone:** (517)337-1630. **Business Addr:** Professor of History, Professor of African American Studies, Northwestern University, 5-128 Crowe Hall 1860 Campus Dr, Evanston, IL 60208, **Business Phone:** (847)491-5122.

**HINES, ALICE WILLIAMS**
Housing developer. **Personal:** Born Sep 8, 1921, San Antonio, TX; daughter of Earl and Clara Williams; married Henry; children: Henry Nelson & William Earl. **Educ:** Prairie View A&M Univ; St Phillip Jr Col, attended 1940; Samuel Huston Col, BS, 1942. **Career:** Housing developer (retired); San Antonio Sch Syst, substitute teacher; San Antonio, Tex Housing Authority, pub housing mgr. **Orgs:** Pres, treas, Nat Asn Housing & Redevelop Officials, local chapter; pres, treas, vpres, sec, Delta Sigma Theta Sorority; Nat Coalition 100 Black Women. **Honors/Awds:** Delta Woman of the Year, Delta Sigma Theta Sorority, 1982. **Special Achievements:** First African American Woman San Antonio Housing Authority manager in TX, 1965. **Home Addr:** 1028 Dawson St, San Antonio, TX 78202-2339, **Home Phone:** (210)222-0724.

**HINES, CARL R., SR.**
Real estate agent, state government official. **Personal:** Born Mar 23, 1931, Louisville, KY; married Teresa Churchill; children: 4. **Educ:** Univ Louisville, BS; Louisville Sch Law. **Career:** Housing Opportunity Ctr, exec dir, 1974; KY Gen Assembly Louisville, state rep, 1978-86; Housing Opportunity Cts Inc, city dir, exec dir; Carl R Hines Realty Co, owner, currently. **Orgs:** Louisville Bd Educ, 1968 & 1972;

Housing Com Louisville C C, 1985; Housing Task Force Louisville C C; Mayor's Housing Task Force under Mayor Frank Burke; Nat Asn Community Develop; bd dir, State KY Housing Corp; Coun, Nat Ctr Housing Mgt Wash; adv comt, Non-Profit Housing Ctr; vice chmn, Jefferson Co Bd Educ; Dist Lines Subcom Charter Com Merger Louisville & Jefferson Co Schs; mem bd, Louisville Nat Asn Advan Colored People, W Louisville Optimist Club; chmn, Shawnee Dist Boy Scouts Am; pres, Just Men's Civic & Social Club; exec secy, Louisville & Jefferson Co Community Action Comn; vice Chmn bd mgrs, YMCA; chmn, Fifth Region KY Sch Bd Asn; Gov's Adv Coun Educ; Fed Rels Network Nat Sch Bd Asn; dir, chair, Nat Caucus Black Sch, Ky City; Asn Realtors. **Honors/Awds:** Air Force Distinguished Flying Cross. **Special Achievements:** first African American state representative elected from the 43rd House District, 1977. **Home Addr:** 635 S Western Pkwy, Louisville, KY 40211. **Business Addr:** Owner, Carl R Hines Realty, 1300 W Broadway Suite 206, Louisville, KY 40203-2096, **Business Phone:** (502)587-9650.

### HINES, COURTNEY
Publisher, executive, business owner. **Career:** Shades of Color, publ, chief exec officer, co-owner & exec, 1995-. **Business Addr:** Co-Owner, Chief Executive Officer, Shades of Color, 4000 Punta Alta Dr, Los Angeles, CA 90008-1131, **Business Phone:** (323)296-1330.

### HINES, DR. DEBORAH HARMON
Educator. **Personal:** Born Sep 6, 1948, Memphis, TN; daughter of Callie Turner Harmon and Jessie Harmon; children: Christopher Jeffrey & Damion Jesse. **Educ:** LeMoyne-Owen Col, BS, biol, 1970; Univ Tenn, PhD, human anat, 1977. **Career:** Meharry Med Col, asst prof, 1976-89; Univ Mass Med Sch, assoc dean minority progs, 1989-91, assoc dean, Sch Serv, 1991-94, assoc provost, 1994-95, assoc vice chancellor, 1995-, prof cell biol, vice provost sch serv, 2008-; Univ Liberia Dogliotti Sch Med, vis prof, 2012. **Orgs:** NAMME, 1979-; Asn Am Med Col, Minority Affairs Sect, 1989-; trustee, Mech Hall, Mkt Comt, 1996-; pres, Community Adv Comt, Worchester State Col, 1994-; bd dir, Int Ctr Worcester, 1994-97; bd dir, Centro Las Americas, 1995-2005; Visions 2000, 1999-; Ctr AIDS Res; Am Soc Cell Biol; ASCB Minorities Affairs Comt, 2007-15. **Business Addr:** Professor, Associate Vice Chancellor School Services, University of Massachusetts Medical School, 55 Lake Ave N S1-842, North Worcester, MA 01655-0132, **Business Phone:** (508)856-2444.

### HINES, GARRETT
Athlete, military leader. **Personal:** Born Jul 3, 1969, Chicago, IL; married Ileana. **Educ:** Southern Ill Univ, BA, biol sci, MA, educ, 1994. **Career:** Athlete (retired), military leader; US Olympic Comt, bobsledder, 1998-2003; USAR, lt, 1996-. **Orgs:** Olympic Athletes Prog, Home Depot. **Honors/Awds:** World Cup overall and combined champion, 1992-93; Brakeman Push Champion, 1992, 1995; Bronze medals, World Championships, 1993, 1997; Silver medal, World Cup, 1996; Three World Cup medals, Hines, 1996-97; Gold medal, World Cup, 1997; Gold medal, World Cup, 1998; Armed Forces Athlete of the Year, 1998; Silver medal, World Cup, 1999; Brakeman Push Championships, 2000; Brakeman Push Champion, 2000, 2001; Gold medal, World Cup, 2000; Medal Contention, World Cup, 2002; Silver medal, Winter Olympics, Salt Lake City, UT, 2002. Silver medal, 4-man bobsled, Winter Olympics, 2002; Silver medal, World Championships, 2003. **Special Achievements:** With Randy Jones, First African American men to win medals at Winter Olympics, 2002; Fourth in 4-man & sixth in 2-man at 2000 World Championships. **Home Addr:** 1985 Inverness Rd SE, Smyrna, TN 30080.

### HINES, JIMMIE
Automotive executive, manager. **Career:** Edmond Dodge Inc, pres & gen mgr, 1992-96. **Business Addr:** President, General Manager, Edmond Dodge Inc, Edmond, OK.

### HINES, KINGSLEY B. (KINGSLEY BERRISFORD HINES)
Lawyer. **Personal:** Born Mar 27, 1944, Pasadena, CA; married Camille; children: Tiffany & Garrett. **Educ:** Univ SC, BA, 1966; Loyola Univ, JD, 1969. **Career:** Family Law Ctr, leg servs, 1969-71; Eng Sq Law Ctr LA, 1970-71; Southern Calif Edison Co, atty, 1972-. **Orgs:** Calif Bar Asn; Los Angeles County Bar Asn; Langston Law Club. **Business Addr:** Attorney, Southern Calif Edison Co, PO Box 6587, Altadena, CA 91003, **Business Phone:** (626)794-0782.

### HINES, DR. MORGAN B.
Dentist. **Personal:** Born Aug 11, 1946, New York, NY; son of Emmie and Edgar; children: Morgan B Jr. **Educ:** Toledo Univ, attended 1968; Meharry Med Col, DDS, 1973. **Career:** Hubbard Hosp, intern, 1973-74; Maury Co Health Dept, dentist, 1974-75; Columbia, Tenn, pvt pract dentist, 1974-; Meharry Med Col, dept oral path, assoc prof, 1975-76, prof hypn pract, 1976-. **Orgs:** Prof artist pen & ink, sculpture, oils, pencil; Tenn Arts League; TN Performing Arts Ctr; Columbia State Comm Col, Tenn State Univ; chmn Maury Co Fine Arts Exhib, 1983; piece collection art, Mid State TN Regional Libr, 1985; Tenn Art League, Columbia Creative Arts Guild, Columbia; hosp staff, Maury Co Hosp; Am Dent Assoc, Omega Psi Phi Frat Inc, Tenn Sheriff Org, Tenn Black Artist Assoc; bd dir, Nashville Amateur Boxing Assoc; Maury Co Creative Art Guild, Tenn/Ala/Ga Amateur Boxing Hall Fame. **Honors/Awds:** Tenn Special Deputy Sheriff; numerous art awards; Numerous appreciation awards for dedication to youth & boxing; Three articles Amateur Boxing Magazine, 1980-82; Coach of the Year Award Spirit of America, Tournament Decatur Ala, 1981. **Special Achievements:** Poem published in "The World Book of Poetry", 1981. **Business Addr:** Physician, Dentist, Private Practitioner, 418 W 6th St, Columbia, TN 38401-3124, **Business Phone:** (931)388-3336.

### HINES, ROSETTA
Radio host. **Personal:** Born Chattanooga, TN; children: 1. **Career:** WGPR, mid-day announcer & prog dir, 1998-; WDET, staff; WJZZ, prog dir & dr time announcer, mid-day announcer, disc jockey, currently. **Orgs:** Hon mem, Nat Asn Media Women. **Honors/Awds:** Lifetime Achievement Award in Recognition of the lifetime Artistic Works in the field of Music & Entertainment, Motown Alumni Asn. **Special Achievements:** Voted Number One DeeJay in the Metro Area by the Detroit News, 1982; The Michigan Chronicle included her name in a Top DeeJay Poll in 1985; First Black Woman in Michigan to earn a degree in Broadcast Engineering; First Honorary Member of the National Association of Media Women (Detroit Chapter). **Business Addr:** Jockey, Radio One Inc, 3250 Franklin St, Detroit, MI 48207-4219, **Business Phone:** (313)259-2000.

### HINES, DR. WILEY EARL, JR.
Dentist. **Personal:** Born Apr 29, 1942, Greenville, NC; married Gloria D Moore; children: Wandria, Wiley & Derrick. **Educ:** Knoxville Col, BS, 1963; Meharry Med Col, DDS, 1971. **Career:** Oak Ridge Nat Labs, biologist, 1963-65; Melpar, biologist, 1965-67; St NC, pub health dentist, 1971-73; Howard Univ, asst clin prof, 1975; pvt pract dentist, 1973-. **Orgs:** Am Dent Asn; Old N St Dent Asn; E Med Dent Pharm Soc, Alpha Phi Alpha, IBPOE, Prince Hall Mason; NC Dent Soc; Fifth Dist Dent Soc; Greenville Planning & Zoning Comn, 1981-86; Ment Health Asn; New E Bank Greenville, bd dirs, 1989-99; RBC Centura Bank, bd dirs, 1999-2003. **Honors/Awds:** Distinguished Service Award, ANCA, 1984; Presidential Citation, National Association for Equal Opportunity in Higher Educ, 1989; Community Service Award, Eta Nu Chapter of Alpha Phi Alpha, 1991. **Home Addr:** 283 Foxcroft Ln, Winterville, NC 28590-8666, **Home Phone:** (252)756-2647. **Business Addr:** Dentist, Private Practitioner, 1720 W Arlington Blvd, Greenville, NC 27834, **Business Phone:** (252)353-2111.

### HINES, DR. WILLIAM E.
Physician. **Personal:** Born Jun 16, 1958, St. Louis, MO; son of Bessie M. **Educ:** Northwestern Univ, Evanston, Ill, BA, 1980; Univ Mo Columbia, Columbia, Mo, MD, 1984; Ohio State Univ, Columbus, OH, MS, 1988. **Career:** Wayne State Univ, Detroit, Mich, resident family med, 1984-87; Ohio State Univ, Columbus, Ohio, resident family med, fel, clin instr, 1987-88; Howard Univ, Wash, DC, asst prof, 1989-90; Ind Univ, Gary, Ind, dir-family pract & clin asst prof, 1990-92; Hines Family Care Ctr, pres & chmn, currently. **Orgs:** Nat Med Asn, 1985-, trustee, Region V, 2001; Am Acad Family Physicians, 1984-; prof bd mem, Stud Nat Med Asn Bd Dirs, 1986-94; exec comt mem, Stud Nat Med Asn Bd Dirs, 1987-89, 1990-94; Prof Bd Mem Emer, 1994; Soc Teachers Family Med, 1991-. **Honors/Awds:** Nat Medical Fellowship Award, Nat Med Fel, 1980-81, 1981-82; Percy H Lee Award for Outstanding Alumni Achievement, Middlewestern Province, Kappa Alpha Psi Fraternity Inc, 1984, 1996; Recognition Award, Stud Nat Asn, Region II, 1987; Black Stud Leadership Award, Grad Stud, Ohio State Univ, 1988; Grand Polemarch's Appreciation Cert, Grand Chap, Kappa Alpha Psi Fraternity Inc, 1988; Fac Orientation Award, Soc Teachers Family Med, 1991; Hon Life Mem, Stud Nat Med Asn, 1994; HealthGrades Recognized Doctor. **Home Addr:** 6136 Wagner Ave, St. Louis, MO 63133, **Home Phone:** (314)727-0827. **Business Addr:** President, Chairman, Hines Family Care Center, 13300 New Halls Ferry Rd Suite C, Florissant, MO 63033, **Business Phone:** (314)830-1900.

### HINSON, ANN J.
Librarian, executive, educator. **Personal:** Born Mar 13, 1937; married Prince Jr; children: Gerald, Prince L & Terence. **Educ:** Fla A&M Univ, BS; Atlanta Univ, MSLS. **Career:** Fla A&M Univ, fac, 1961-, dept head & librn, Coleman Mem Libr, asst dir pub & info servs, currently. **Home Addr:** 3128 Parkridge Dr, Tallahassee, FL 32305-6837, **Home Phone:** (850)576-3818. **Business Addr:** Assistant Director, Florida A&M University, 1500 Martin Luther King Blvd S, Tallahassee, FL 32307-4700, **Business Phone:** (850)599-3370.

### HINSON, ROY MANUS, JR.
Basketball player. **Personal:** Born May 2, 1961, Trenton, NJ; married Cynthia Chitwood; children: Calvin Chitwood. **Educ:** Rutgers Univ, BA, polit sci, 1983. **Career:** Basketball player (retired); Knights Rutgers Sc, 1979-83; Cleveland Cavaliers, 1983-86; Philadelphia 76ers, 1986-88; NJ Nets, 1988-91; Nat Basketball Players Asn, regional rep, 1993-. **Orgs:** Dir, Jewish Community Center; bd mem, Home Safe. **Business Addr:** Regional Representative, National Basketball Players Association, 310 Lenox Ave, New York, NY 10027, **Business Phone:** (212)655-0880.

### HINTON, ALFRED FONTAINE
Artist, educator, football player. **Personal:** Born Nov 27, 1940, Columbus, GA; son of Eddie H (deceased) and Johnnie Mae Sipp; married Ann Noel Pearlman; children: Adam, Melina & Elizabeth. **Educ:** Univ Iowa, BA, 1967; Univ Cincinnati, MFA, 1970. **Career:** Toronto Argonaurs, prof football player, 1963-67; Khadejha Primitive Prints Toronto, design consult, 1967-68; Dickinson Col, Carlisle, Pa, instr, 1969; Western Mich Univ, asst prof painting & drawing, 1970-77; Univ Mich, Sch Art & Design, assoc prof painting, 1977-82, prof, painting, 1982-2007, prof emer art, 2007-. **Orgs:** Artist Gallery 7, Detroit, 1970-; coordr, Visual Arts Mich Acad Sci Arts & Lett, 1972-74; Visual Arts Adv Panel Mich Coun Arts, 1973-; bd mem, Mich Coun Arts, 1980-84; exec bd mem, Concerned Citizen's Arts Michi, 1983-86; panelist, Ongoing Mich Artist Prog, Detroit Inst Arts, 1986-88; master panel bd, Detroit Coun Arts, 1987-; Urban Landscape Rural Ladscape. **Honors/Awds:** Research grant, Western Mich Univ, 1972-73; Flint Inst of Arts All Mich Exhibition Purchase Award, 1972; 16 one-person shows; 40 invitational & group exhibitions; All-Amer, cocapt; Most Valuable Player, Univ Iowa Football Team, 1961; Creative Artist Grant, Mich Coun for the Arts, 1985; State of Michigan Commission on Art in Public Places, 1986; Distinguished alumni achievement Award, Univ Iowa, 2000. **Home Addr:** 1311 Brooklyn St, Ann Arbor, MI 48104, **Home Phone:** (313)769-4022. **Business Addr:** Professor Emeritus, University of Michigan, 2055 Art & Archit Bldg, Ann Arbor, MI 48109, **Business Phone:** (734)936-0684.

### HINTON, CHRISTOPHER JEROME
Photographer, business owner. **Personal:** Born Sep 23, 1952, Raleigh, NC; son of A M and J D. **Educ:** Winston-Salem State Univ, NC, BA, music, 1975. **Career:** J D Hinton Studio, Raleigh, NC, photogr, owner, 1976-. **Orgs:** Phi Beta Sigma Frat, 1972-; Garner Road Family, YMCA Back A Child Campaign; United Negro Col Fund Campaign, 1989; Nat Asn Advan Colored People. **Honors/Awds:** Phi Beta Sigma Frat Award; Business Award, Raleigh Alumnae Chapter Delta Sigma Theta; photography works featured in natl publications such as: Jet Publication, Black Radio Exclusive, Ohio Historical Soc. **Home Addr:** 120 Colleton Rd, Raleigh, NC 27610, **Home Phone:** (919)833-0086. **Business Addr:** Owner, J D Hinton Studio, 515 S Blount St, Raleigh, NC 27601, **Business Phone:** (919)833-6095.

### HINTON, DR. GREGORY TYRONE
Lawyer. **Personal:** Born Nov 22, 1949, Barrackville, WV; son of Nathan and Amelia; children: Gregory T II, Hamilton H & Carol Princess Jean. **Educ:** Fairmont State Col, AB, hist, 1978; WVa Univ, Col Law, JD, 1981; Kellogg Leadership Develop, cert, 1995. **Career:** Thorofare Markets Inc, stock clerk & carry-out, 1968-69; Hope Nat Gas Co, casual rouster, 1970-71; Mont Power Co, elec clerk, 1972-73; Gibbs & Hill, elec clerk, 1973-75; N Cent Opportunity Indus Ctr, job developer, 1975-78, exec dir, 1978; Fairmont City Coun, coun mem, 1977-86, mayor, 1983-85; Hinton Enterprises, owner, 1981-; WVa Univ Col Law, consult; atty pvt pract; Fairmont State Col, prof, 1989-, sr prof bus law. **Orgs:** Mont Valley Asn Health Centers Inc, 1974-; deacon Good Hope Baptists Church, 1974-; hon mem, Magnificent Souls, 1983; hon mem, Am Soc Nondestructive Testing Fairmont State Col Sect, 1984; corp banking & bus law & minority affairs comt, WV State Bar, 1984-86; vis comt, WV Univ Col Law, 1984-87, consult, 1985-; adv bd, WNPB-TV, 1984-86; bd mem, Fairmont Gen Hosp, 1985-86; WV Adv Comt US Commn Civil Rights, 1985-89; pres, MT State Bar Asn, 1986-88; ethics comn, WV State Bar, 1986-87; Nat Asn Advan Colored People Legal Redress Comt. **Honors/Awds:** Outstanding Young Man of American Jaycees, 1979 & 1984; West Virginia Outstanding Black Attorney, Black Am Law Stud Asn, Morgantown, WV, 1984; West Virginia Outstanding Black Attorney; Special Award as Mayor, WVa State Asn & PER-PDR Tri-State Conf Couns IBPOEW PA-OH-WV, 1984; Special Award as Mayor, Dunbar HS class, 1947 & 1984; Honored, Black Am Law Stud Asn, Morgantown, WV, 1985; Outstanding West Virginia Black Attorney; Wiliam A Boram Award for Teaching Excellence, 1996 & 1997; West Virginia Professor of the Year, Carnegie Found Advancement Teaching, 1997; Alumni of Achievement, Fairmont State Univ, 2000; Student Government Teacher of the Year; Fairmont State Excellence in Advising Award, Fairmont State Univ; Faculty Recognition Award, Fairmont State Univ; Faculty Merit, Found WVa Inc; Excellence in Leadership Award; "Living the Dream" Award, WVa Martin Luther King Jr. Holiday Comn. **Special Achievements:** First African American elected Mayor to a major city, WV, 1983; First faculty member selected by Student Government to present the "Last Lecture". He was nationally recognized among African-American leaders with the Strong Men and Strong Women. **Home Addr:** 700 Locust Ave, Fairmont, WV 26554, **Home Phone:** (304)366-8068. **Business Addr:** Senior Professor of Business Law, Fairmont State University, Rm 215a Jaynes Hall, Fairmont, WV 26554, **Business Phone:** (304)367-4892.

### HINTON, DR. HORTENSE BECK
College administrator. **Personal:** Born Apr 27, 1950, Charlottesville, VA; children: Shani O, Adisa A & Ajamu A. **Educ:** State Univ NY, BA, psychol, 1971; Univ DC, MA, coun, 1977; Univ Va, EdD, counr educ, 1988. **Career:** Univ DC, coordr, sr counr & asst dir spec serv prog, 1971-78; Univ Va, assoc dean & dir summer prep prog off afro-am affairs, 1978-88; Germanna Community Col, dir, stud develop servs, 1988-2000; Northern Va Community Col, Manassas Campus, dean studs develop, 2000-02, interim vpres acad stud serv, 2003-04, actg vpres, provost, 2004-11, spec asst to pres, 2011-, chief admin & acad officer, currently, dean stud develop, currently. **Orgs:** Am Asn Coun & Develop; Nat Asn Women's Deans & Counors; Am Asn Univ Women; Am Asn Affirmative Action; clerk, trustee, youth adv, Free Union Baptist Church; consult, Alcohol & Other Drug Ctr; exed consult, Women in Worship Ministries. **Home Addr:** 21325 Mt Pony Rd, Culpeper, VA 22701. **Business Addr:** Provost, Chief Administrative & Academic Officer, Northern Virginia Community College, AA 228 6901 Sudley Rd Howsmon Hall Rm 317, Manassas, VA 20109-2399, **Business Phone:** (703)257-6664.

### HINTZEN, PERCY CLAUDE
Educator. **Personal:** Born Jan 26, 1947, Georgetown; son of Vera Malfalda Khan and Percival Coppin; married Joan Alicia McIntosh; married Joan Alicia McIntosh; children: Ian, Shawn, Alicia & Candace. **Educ:** Univ Guyana, Georgetown, Guyana, BS, 1973; Yale Univ, New Haven, CT, MA, sociol, 1977, MPhil, comparative sociol, 1977, PhD, comparative polit sociol, 1981; Clark Univ, Worcester, MA, MA, int urbanization & pub policy, 1985. **Career:** Univ Guyana, Guyana, lectr, 1977-78; Yale Univ, New Haven, CT, acting instr, 1978-79; Univ Calif, Berkeley, Calif, assoc prof, 1979-, African Am Studies, assoc prof, chmn, 1994-, Peace & Conflict Studies, dir, 1994-, Ctr Race & Gender, actg dir, 2006-, prof, currently. **Orgs:** Am Sociol Soc, 1979-; Caribbean Studies Asn, 1979, vpres, 2005-06, pres, 2006-; Am Polit Sci Asn, 1979-81; Adv Comt, Diaspora Summer Seminar, Fla Int Univ, 2004-. **Home Addr:** 2765 Acton St, Berkeley, CA 94702, **Home Phone:** (510)649-8272. **Business Addr:** Professor & Chair of African American Studies, University of California, Berkeley, 654 Barrows Hall, Berkeley, CA 94720-2572, **Business Phone:** (510)642-0393.

### HIPKINS, CONRAD
Executive, chief executive officer. **Educ:** Rutgers Univ, BS, 1955. **Career:** Automated Sci Group Inc, owner, chief exec officer, share holder & chmn. **Home Addr:** 1425 Leegate Rd NW, Washington, DC 20012, **Home Phone:** (202)291-7110.

### HITCHCOCK, JIMMY DAVIS, JR.
Football player. **Personal:** Born Nov 9, 1970, Concord, NC. **Educ:** Univ NC, grad. **Career:** Football player (retired); New Eng Patriots, 1995, right cornerback, 1996-97, 2002; Minn Vikings, right cornerback, 1998-99, left cornerback & cornerback, 1999; Carolina Panthers, cornerback, 2000, left cornerback, 2001; Detroit Lions, cornerback, 2002. **Honors/Awds:** AFC champion, 1996; NFL Interception Return Yards Leader, 1998. **Special Achievements:** Film: 1998 NFC Championship Game, 1999. TV Series: "ESPN SportsCentury", 2002.

### HITE, NANCY URSULA

Television producer, public relations executive. **Personal:** Born Aug 1, 1956, White Plains, NY; daughter of Forest Davis and Jesse Davis. **Educ:** Spelman Col, BA, 1978; Iona Col, MS, 1985. **Career:** WOVX-Radio Sta, reporter, 1978-79; Louis-Rowe Enterprises, pub rel exec secy, 1979-; Potpourri WVOX Radio, producer, 1982-; freelance journalist newspapers & mag, US, 1982-; Int Photo News Serv, mng ed; Conversation Rowe, producer; Nat Photo News Serv, producer & managing ed, 1985-. **Orgs:** Assoc ed, vpres, New Rochelle Br, Nat Asn Advan Colored People, 1985-86; adv, New Rochelle Nat Asn Advan Colored People Youth Coun, 1987; Alpha Kappa Alpha Sorority; secy, African Am Guild Performing Artists; co-founder, African Heritage Educ Forum; co-founder, Ki Africa Taalimu Shule. **Home Addr:** 4 Consulate Dr Apt 4J, Tuckahoe, NY 10707-2435. **Business Addr:** Executive Secretary to the Corporation, Louis-Rowe Enterprises, 455 Main St Suite 99, New Rochelle, NY 10801.

### HIXON, MAMIE WEBB

Educator, grammarian, editor. **Personal:** Born Mar 30, 1946, Indianola, MS; daughter of Sam and Rosa Lee. **Educ:** Talladega Col, Talladega, AL, BA, eng, 1967; Univ W Fla, Pensacola, FL, MA, eng, 1978. **Career:** Escambia Co Sch Dist, Eng teacher, 1967-80; Pensacola Jr Col, instr eng, 1980-82; Univ W Fla, Writing Skills Lab, dir & creator, 1982-, Dept Eng, asst prof, currently. Books: Real Good Grammar; Real Good Grammar Too; Grammar Shots; Essentials of English Language. **Orgs:** Pres, Local Chap, Alpha Kappa Alpha Sorority Inc, 1982-; founding pres, Pensacola Chap, Nat Coalition 100 Black Women, 1993-; bd dir, Alzheimer's Family Servs Inc, 1995-; bd dir, African Am Heritage Soc, 1995-; W Fla Lit Fedn, 1996-; secy, Pensacola Chap, Links Inc, 1997-; bd dir, Panhandle Tiger Bay Club, 1998-; W Fla Leadership Acad class, 1999. **Home Addr:** 3075 N 10th Ave, Pensacola, FL 32503, **Home Phone:** (850)433-3324. **Business Addr:** Assistant Professor, University of West Florida, 11000 Univ Pkwy Bldg 51 Rm 157, Pensacola, FL 32514, **Business Phone:** (850)474-2029.

### HOAGLAND, EVERETT H.

Educator, poet. **Personal:** Born Dec 18, 1942, Philadelphia, PA; son of Everett Jr and Estelle; married Darrell Steward Forman; children: Kamal, Nia, Ayan & Reza; married Alice Susan Trimiew. **Educ:** Lincoln Univ, PA, BA, 1964; Brown Univ, MA, 1973. **Career:** Lincoln Univ, asst dir admis, 1967-69; Claremont Col, Black Studies, instr Afro-Am poetry, 1969-71; Brown Univ, univ fel, 1971-73; Univ Mass, prof, Dartmouth Eng, 1973-2003, New Bedford, MA, poet laureate, 1994-1998, prof emer, 2003-; Mass Arts & Humanities Found, creative artists fel, 1975; NEH fel, 1984. **Orgs:** Unitarian Universalist Faith, 1973-; clerk corp & bd mem, New Bedford Foster Grandparents Prog, 1976-82; weekly columnist, New Bedford Stand-Times, 1979-82; contrib ed, Am Poetry Rev, 1984-; poet residence, Wm Carney Acad New Bedford, 1985; Nat Asn Advan Colored People; Black Radical Cong, 1999; First Unitarian Church; liberation poets collective, Black Lives Matter New Bedford, MA. **Home Addr:** PO Box 7463, New Bedford, MA 02742. **Business Addr:** Professor Emeritus, University of Massachusetts Dartmouth, 285 Old Westport Rd, North Dartmouth, MA 02747-2300, **Business Phone:** (508)999-8000.

### HOARD, LEROY J.

Football player. **Personal:** Born May 15, 1968, New Orleans, LA. **Educ:** Univ Mich, educ. **Career:** Football player (retired); Cleveland Browns, running back, 1990-92, 1995, fullback, 1993-94; Baltimore Ravens, running back, 1996; Carolina Panthers, running back, 1996; Minn Vikings, running back, 1996-99. **Honors/Awds:** Rose Bowl Most Valuable Player Award, 1989; Rookie of the Year, 1990; Pro Bowl, 1994. **Home Addr:** 176 Dockside Cir, Ft. Lauderdale, FL 33327.

### HOBBS, DR. ALMA COBB

Administrator. **Personal:** Born Oct 16, 1949, Farmville, NC; daughter of Nathan R Cobb Sr; children: Steven L. **Educ:** Univ NC, BS, 1970; NC State Univ, MS, 1975, PhD, 1981. **Career:** Windsor NC Exten Serv, home ec & 4-h agt, 1970-73; Davidson Co Exten Serv, 4-h agt, 1974-78; USDA, asst exten agt, 1970, nat prog leader, 1988-89, asst dep admin, 1990-94, dep admin, 1994, dep asst secy admin, 2009; Tenn State Univ, adminr, 1981-90; Va State Univ, Sch Agr, dean & adminr, 2006-. **Orgs:** Vpres, Hendersonville Links, 1982-92; Treas, Arlington Chap Links, 1992-93; Alpha Kappa Alpha Sorority; Nat Asn Ext Agt 4-h Agents; Epsilon Sigma Phi; Phi Delta Kappa; Nat Asn Family & Consumer Sci; bd mem, Va Pesticide Control Bd; Pres Coun, Va State Univ Pres Moore; chair, USDA Hon Awards Eval Comt, 2004; NCCU Alumni Chap Baltimore Md; Exten Diversity; ECOP Strategic Planning Coun; Prog Leadership Comt; Nat Futures Task Force; Pres Crime Prev Coun; USDA 1890 Task Force. **Home Addr:** 1506 S Stafford St, Arlington, VA 22204-4065. **Business Addr:** Dean, Administrator, Virginia State University, 1 Hayden Dr, Petersburg, VA 23806-9081, **Business Phone:** (804)524-5961.

### HOBBS, DARYL RAY

Football coach, football player, executive. **Personal:** Born May 23, 1968, Victoria, TX; married Tamiyka. **Educ:** Univ Pac. **Career:** Football player (retired), coach; Los Angeles Raiders, 1993-96; Oakland Raiders, wide receiver, 1995-97; New Orleans Saints, 1997; Seattle Seahawks, 1997; Kans City Chiefs, 1998; Montreal Alouettes, 1999; Sask Roughriders, 2000; Memphis Maniax, 2001; Robert E Lee High Sch Houston, head coach, 2012; Legacy Christian High Sch, head coach; Santa Monica Col, offensive cord; Humble, TX, exec, currently.

### HOBBS, DR. JOSEPH

Educator, physician. **Personal:** Born Aug 5, 1948, Augusta, GA; married Janice Polk. **Educ:** Mercer Univ, BS, 1970; Med Col Ga, MD, 1974. **Career:** Am Acad Family Pract, fel, 1979; Med Col Ga, asst prof family med, 1979, instr family med, 1978, chief resident, 1977, family pract res, 1976, medintern, 1975, prof & chmn family med, currently, GaFP Tollison, distinguished chmn, currently, vice dean primary care & community affairs, Coun Grad Med Educ Health Resources & Servs Admin, currently, sr assoc dean, currently. **Orgs:** Richmond Co Med Soc, 1978; vpres, Stoney Med Dent Pharm Soc, 1979; team physician, T W Josey High Sch; vice chmn, 1993; vpres, Sch Med Alumni Asn, 2009-10, pres elect, 2010-11. **Home Addr:** 3629 Nassau Dr, Augusta, GA 30909. **Business Addr:** Professor and Distinguished Chair, Vice Dean for Primary Care and Community Affairs, Medical College Georgia, 1120 15th St HB-4000, Augusta, GA 30912, **Business Phone:** (706)721-4075.

### HOBSON, CHARLES BLAGROVE

Television producer. **Personal:** Born Jun 23, 1936, Brooklyn, NY; son of Charles Samuel and Cordelia Victoria; married Maren Stange; children: Hallie & Clara. **Educ:** Brooklyn Col, attended 1960; Emory Univ, attended 1976. **Career:** ABC-TV, New York, NY, producer, 1967-71; WETA-TV, Wash, DC, tv producer, 1967-89; Vassar Col, Poughkeepsie, NY, instr, 1969-71; Clark Col, Atlanta, GA, dir mass communs, 1971-76; Visamondo Prod, Montreal, Can, writer, 1988; Jamaica Broadcasting Corp, consult, 1988; WNET-TV, New York, NY, dir mkt plng, 1989-; Medgar Evers Col, City Univ NY, prof, sr res fel; Vanguard Documentaries Inc, founder, artistic head, currently; Producer: "An American Voice"; "Inside Bedford-Stuyvesant"; "Jump Street: The History of Black Music"; "Negroes with Guns"; "Global Links"; "Spaces"; "Like It Is"; "The Africans". **Orgs:** Consult, Nat Endowment Arts, 1976-87, NEH; bd mem, Am Beautiful Fund, 1977-87; Writer's Guild Am; African Studies Asn; consult, Greycom Int; consult, Nat Black Arts Festival; bd mem, Am Beautiful Fund; pres & bd dir, Nat Black Programming Consortium; educ sub comt, Mus Mod art; consult, Am Jazz Mus, Kans City, MO. **Honors/Awds:** Capital Press Club Award, 1968; Emmy Award NATAS, 1968; Governor's Award, Natl Acad Arts & Sci, 1976; WC Hardy Award, 1981; Natl Black Prog Consortium Award, 1985; Ohio State Award, 1987; One of the Leading TV Producers, Millimeter Magazine; The Japan Prize, 1987; Golden Eagle Award, CINE, 1987; Ohio State Award for Excellence in Educational Programming, 1988; Fulbright Scholar, The University of Munich Amerika Institute, 1996-97; Fulbright Scholar in Munich, Germany, 1996-97. **Special Achievements:** Ranked one of the fifty top producers in the film and television industry by Millimeter magazine. **Home Addr:** 293 State St, Brooklyn, NY 11201, **Home Phone:** (917)804-8768. **Business Addr:** Founder, Artistic Head, Vanguard Documentaries Inc, 293 State St, Brooklyn, NY 11201, **Business Phone:** (347)725-1677.

### HOBSON, MELLODY

President (organization). **Personal:** Born Apr 3, 1969, Chicago, IL; daughter of Dorothy Ashley; married George Lucas; children: Everest. **Educ:** Princeton Univ, Woodrow Wilson Sch Int Rels & Pub Policy, AB, 1991; Howard Univ, hon doc; St. Mary's Col, hon doc; Univ Southern Calif, hon doc. **Career:** Ariel Investments LLC, intern, sr vpres dir mkt, 1991-2000, pres, 2000-; ABC, host, 2009; Starbucks Corp, dir; Estee Lauder Cos Inc, dir; Groupon Inc, dir; DreamWorks Animation SKG Inc, chmn bd dir, currently. **Orgs:** bd trustee, Ariel Investment Trust; bd mem, Field Mus; bd mem, Chicago Pub Educ Fund; bd mem, Sundance Inst; bd gov, Investment Co Inst. **Honors/Awds:** "Ebony," 20 Leaders of the Future, 1992; "Working Women," 20 Under 30, 1992; World Economic Forum, Global Leaders of Tomorrow, 2001; "Esquire," America's Best and Brightest, 2002; "The Wall Street Journal," 50 Women to Watch, 2004; "Black Enterprise," 75 Most Powerful Blacks on Wall Street, 2011; DHL, Howard Univ, St. Mary's Col. **Special Achievements:** Regular contributor to ABC television's "Good Morning America"; created and hosted ABC television special "Unbroke: What You Need to Know About Money," 2009. **Business Addr:** President, Ariel Investments LLC, 200 E Randolph St Suite 2900, Chicago, IL 60601, **Business Phone:** (312)726-0140.

### HOBSON, MELLODY L.

Marketing executive. **Personal:** Born Apr 3, 1969, Chicago, IL; daughter of Dorothy Ashley; married George Lucas; children: Everest. **Educ:** Princeton Univ, Woodrow Wilson Sch Int Rels & Pub Policy, BA, int rels & pub policy, 1991. **Career:** Ariel Investments, LLC, Ariel Capital Mgt, Chicago, vpres mkt, 1991-94, sr vpres & dir mkt, 1994-2000, dir & pres, 2000-; Ariel Mutual Funds Bd Trustees, chmn; Starbucks Corp, dir; Princeton Univ, trustee, adminr. **Orgs:** Secy, Princeton Club Chicago, 1991-; chmn bd trustee, Ariel Investment Trust; bd mem, St Ignatius Prep Sch Alumni org, Ariel Capital Mgt, 2000; bd mem, Tellabs, 2002; bd mem, DreamWorks Animation SKG, 2004; bd mem, Estee Lauder, 2004; bd mem, Starbucks, 2005; bd dir, Civic Fedn Chicago; bd dir, Chicago Pub Libr; trustee, Chicago Archit Found; bd dir, Field Mus; bd dir, Do Something; emer trustee, Lucas Mus Narrative Art & Sundance Inst; bd mem, Chicago Pub Educ Fund; George Lucas Educ Found. **Honors/Awds:** Named one of 20 Leaders of the Future, Ebony, 1992; Named one of 20 Under 30, Working Women Magazine, 1992; hon doctorate degree, Howard Univ; hon doctorate degree, St Mary's Col; hon doctorate degree, Univ Southern Calif. **Business Addr:** President, Ariel Investments LLC, 200 E Randolph Dr Suite 2900, Chicago, IL 60601, **Business Phone:** (312)726-0140.

### HOBSON, ROBERT R.

Government official. **Personal:** Born Oct 20, 1930, Memphis, TN; children: Mafara & Alicia. **Educ:** Tenn State Univ, BA, govt, 1952; Howard Univ, attended 1957; Johns Hopkins Univ, attended 1959. **Career:** Pres's Comt Equal Employ Off Fed Contract Compliance, sr compliance adv, 1963-71; Nat Urban Coalition, asst to pres, 1971-73; Off Fed Contract Compliance, sr compliance officer, assoc dir, 1973-82; White House, sr staff mem. Distinguished Serv Career 1974; Gerald Fold, vpres. **Home Addr:** 3305 Highwood Dr SE, Washington, DC 20020, **Home Phone:** (202)583-7730.

**HOBSON-SIMMONS, JOYCE ANN.** **See SIMMONS, JOYCE HOBSON.**

### HODGE, ALETA S.

Writer, financial manager. **Personal:** Born May 15, 1954, Indianapolis, IN; daughter of Frank and Doryce. **Educ:** Stanford Univ, BS, environ sci, 1976; Ind Univ, MBA, finance, 1978; Univ Sci Philadelphia, MS, biomedical writing, 2011. **Career:** Ind Univ, instr; Purdue Univ, Indianapolis, instr; Indianapolis Star, columnist, 2000-; Money Coun Inc, pres, 2003-; Covidien, proj mgr & med writer, 2008-11; Eli Lilly & Co, prog mgr, 2011-12; ASH Consult LLC, chief exec officer, 2012-; Auth: Women & Money Common Sense Handbk, 1995; Value Bk, 2001; Women & Money Common Sense Handbk second ed, 1998. **Orgs:** Financial Planner Asn, 1998-; Inst Cert Financial Planners, Stanford Alumni Asn, 2007; Proj Mgt Inst; Healthcare Bus womens Asn; Soc Clin Res Assocs. **Home Addr:** 709 N Pk Ave Apt 202, Indianapolis, IN 46202, **Home Phone:** (317)634-8049. **Business Addr:** President, Money Counsel Inc, 709 N Pk Ave Suite 202, Indianapolis, IN 46202, **Business Phone:** (317)634-8049.

### HODGE, DR. CHARLES MASON

School administrator. **Personal:** Born Jun 25, 1938, Seguin, TX; son of Clifford D and Goldie M Campbell; married Elizabeth Howze; children: Gwendolyn & Clinton. **Educ:** Univ Ark, Pine Bluff, BA, 1960; Univ N Tex, MEd, 1969; Univ Tex, EdD, 1976. **Career:** Terrell HS Ft Worth, high sch teacher, 1964-69; Jarvis Christian Col, instr social studies educ, 1969-73; AR Desegregation Ctr Pub Sch, assoc dir, 1973-74; Ark Dept Higher Educ, co ordr human res, 1974-76, asst dir res & planning, 1980; Univ Cent Ark, assoc prof & teacher educ, 1976-80, asst vpres acad affairs, 1981-83, dean, col educ, 1983-89; Lamar Univ, Beaumont TX, dean col educ, 1989-92; Bowie State Univ, Sch Educ, assoc provost, Graduare Sch, asst dean, dean, Dept Educ Leadership, interim chmn, 1989-2004; RFTEN Proj, qual assurance consult, currently; Higher Educ, consult, 2004-; Chowan Univ, NC, vis prof educ, 2007-, chmn; Tech Assistance Network, Nat Coun Accreditation Teacher Educ, consult; Western Mich Univ, Col Educ, dean; Univ Cent Arkanasas, dean. **Orgs:** Ford fel 1972; Sch Deseg Monitoring Team, US Dist Ctr, 1980; Unit Accreditation Bd Nat Coun Accred Teacher Educ, 1986-; Ark State Coun EconEduc, 1987-89; bd dir, Tex Com Bank-Beaumont, 1991; bd trustee, Robert Morris Col, Philadelphia, 1992-; ed bd, Teacher Educ & Pract J; Am Asn Col Teacher Educ; Nat Coun Accreditation Teacher Educ; Teacher Educ Coun State Cols & Univs; Asn Teacher Educr. **Home Addr:** 12861 Shumard Pl, Jacksonville, FL 32246, **Home Phone:** (904)641-2695. **Business Addr:** Chair, Visiting Professor of Education, Chowan University, 1 Univ Pl, Murfreesboro, NC 27855, **Business Phone:** (252)398-6500.

### HODGE, DR. CYNTHIA ELOIS

Dentist. **Personal:** Born Feb 23, 1947, Troup, TX; daughter of Robert Spencer and Doris Lydia; children: Delwyn Ray Madkins. **Educ:** Univ Denver, pre dent, 1975; Ore Health & Sci Univ, DMD, dent, 1979; Univ NC, Chapel Hill, MPH, health care admin & mgt, 1983, oral med cert, 1985; Harvard Univ Sch Pub Health, MPA, health mgt admin, 2002; Harvard Univ, MPA, health care mgt, 2002; Harvard Med Sch, minority health policy cert, 2003; Memorial Hosp-UNC, cert oral med. **Career:** US Dept Health & Human Servs Health Resources, res fel Internship; Dent C, assoc dent, 1979-82; Post Grad Training Univ NC, 1982-85; Meharry Med Col, Dept Hosp Dent, chairperson, 1985-90, Sch Dent, dir, gen pract resident prog, 1985-90; pvt pract, gen dentist, 1990-2002; Fairrow Dent Ctr, dentist; Univ Conn Health Ctr, Sch Dent Med, dir, 2003-, assoc dean, Off Community & Outreach Progs, 2003-08, asst prof, 2003-10, proj dir pipeline, profession & pract, currently; DeSti Consult Inc, pres & chief exec officer, 2009-; Nat Dent Asn Found Inc, pres, 2010-. **Orgs:** Mem & pres, Nat Dent Asn, 1979-99; Am Dent Asn, 1979-; dent consult, Multnomah County Health Dept Portland, OR, 1979-81; dent consult, Health Adv Bd, Albina Ministerial Alliance, Headstart Prog, 1980-82; dent coordr regional, Nat Dent Asn, 1981-82; Headstart Prog; Infectious Dis Control Comn; gov, Tenn Dent Asn, 1987-; Health & Educ Facil Bd Metrop Davidson County, 1990-; Am Asn Women Dentists, 1990-; Acad Gen Dent, 1994-; Am Asn Pub Health Dent, 1994-; chairperson, Commt Minority Affairs; exec bd, Nashville Cares Inc; Am Cancer Soc Prof Educ Comn; bd advisor, Natchez Col, MS; Inst Healthcare Poor & Underserved, Meharry Med Col; past gov, Tenn; gov, Ned McWherter. **Honors/Awds:** Certificate of Recognition, Wash Monroe High Sch; Award for Participation in Dental Field Experiences, Wash Monroe High Sch, Portland, OR, 1981; Valuable Contribution to the Scientific Session, Nat Dent Asn, 1988; Award for Scientific Presentation, Nat Dent Asn, 1991, 1992; Distinguished Service Award, US Asst Secy Health. **Home Addr:** 11 Heritage Glen Ct, Madison, TN 37115-5900, **Home Phone:** (615)868-6452. **Business Addr:** Project Director, University of Connecticut School of Dental Medicine, 263 Farmington Ave, Farmington, CT 06030, **Business Phone:** (860)679-4150.

### HODGE, DONALD JEROME

Basketball player. **Personal:** Born Feb 25, 1969, Washington, DC. **Educ:** Temple Univ, 1991. **Career:** Basketball player (retired); Dallas Mavericks, power forward, 1991, ctr, 1992-96; Charlotte Hornets, ctr, 1996; Power Wevelgem, Belgium, 1999. **Honors/Awds:** NBA Draft, 1991.

### HODGE, ERNEST M.

Automotive executive, chief executive officer, business owner. **Career:** March & Hodge Holding Co, chief exec officer, currently; March & Hodge Automotive Group, co-chief exec officer, currently; Heritage Cadillac Inc, chief exec officer & owner, 1991-. **Business Addr:** Chief Executive Officer, Heritage Cadillac Saab, 7134 Jonesboro Rd, Morrow, GA 30260, **Business Phone:** (770)960-0060.

### HODGE, MARGUERITE V.

Executive, social worker, educator. **Personal:** Born May 21, 1920, Avondale, PA; married Dee; children: Dee. **Educ:** Howard Univ, BA, 1943; Univ Chicago, 1947. **Career:** Provident Hosp, med social worker, 1944-46; Provident Hosp, psychiat social worker, 1948-49; Provident Hosp, med social worker, 1947-48; Munic TB Santorium, med social worker, 1949-51; Field Rep, 1953-60; Agency Coordr, 1960-64; UCLA, field instr, 1966-67, 1969-70, prof & vol serv, supr, 1965-68; Info & Referral Serv, supr, 1968-70; Placement Stud, field instr, 1974; Partners Care, prog consult, 2003-05. **Orgs:** Nat Conf Social Welfare; Nat Asn Social Workers; licentiate Royal Acad Health; consult, S Ctr Area Welfare Planning Coun; adv com, LA Urban League Health & Welfare Comt Head start; SEARCH Bd USC Sch Med; discussion leader, Alchololism Conf Welfare Planning Coun, 1962; discussion leader, Conf Home Care Welfare Planning Coun & City Hope, 1962; regist chmn, Pac SW Regional Inst NASW, 1966; serv & rehab comn, Am Cancer Soc Calif Div Cervical Cancer Screening Sub-comt; regional dir, Lung Asn, 1970-; bd dir, Calif Asn Ment Health, 1973; Prog Planning Com So Calif Pub Health Asn; LA Co Inter agy Coun Smoking & Health; Mayor's Adv Coun Handicapped, 1974; adv comt Area IX Regional Med Prog; panel partic TB Asn; Numerous Other Comt; westminster pres; Alpha Kappa Alpha Sor. **Honors/Awds:** Volunteer Service Award, Patton State Hosp, 1965-66; Community Service Award, El Santo Nino Comn Develop Proj Cath Welfare Bur, 1972; Special Recognition Award, S Ctrl Area Planning Coun, 1973; Recipient, Special Recognition Award, Bd Dir Lung Asn 20 yrs Serv, 1974; Special Award King-Drew Sickle Cell Ctr, 1974; Special Award, Kedren Community Mental Health Ctr. **Home Addr:** 1500 S Pt View St, Los Angeles, CA 90035-3912, **Home Phone:** (323)935-7789.

## HODGE, NORRIS

Broker, appraiser. **Personal:** Born Apr 3, 1927, Kingsville, TX; married Ruby Faye; children: Brenda, Theodora & Myrna. **Educ:** BBA, MS, 1964. **Career:** Tex Southern Univ, asst prof; Friends Univ Wichita Kans, asst prof; Hodge & Co Realtors, currently. **Orgs:** Am Econ Asn. **Honors/Awds:** So Econ Asn Recipient Ford Found Fellowship; Western Econ Asn; Gen Elect Fellowship Univ Chicago. **Home Addr:** 3915 Cheryl Lynne, Houston, TX 77045-3415, **Home Phone:** (713)723-5009. **Business Addr:** Real Estate Agent, Hodge & Company Realtors, 13027 Hiram Clarke, Houston, TX 77045-3204, **Business Phone:** (713)729-6212.

## HODGE, WILLIAM ANTHONY

Businessperson. **Personal:** Born Apr 26, 1962, Tuskegee, AL; son of Johnie Albert and Lula Pearl McNair; married Audrey Maria; children: Alani Maria. **Educ:** Tuskegee Univ, Tuskegee Inst, AL, BS, 1985; Auburn Univ, AL, MS, 1989. **Career:** Purdue Univ Dept Agron, W Lafayette, Ind, res asst, 1983; Walt Disney World, Epcot Ctr, Orlando, Fl, agri intern, 1983-84; Tuskegee Univ, Sch Agri, Tuskegee, AL, teaching asst, 1984-85, soil scientist & water qual tech, 1989-, exten specialist & water qual coop exten prog, 1991-; Oak Ridge Nat Labs, Oak Ridge, TN, res asst, 1985; Auburn Univ, Auburn, AL, grad res asst, 1986-89; Carter Funeral Home, mgr, funeral dir, 1992-; US Transp Inc, owner, 1998. **Orgs:** Am Soc Agron, 1983-; Gamma Sigma Delta, 1987; Negro Airmen Int, 1988-; Ala Agri & Forestry Leaders, 1989-; Worshipful master, Prince Hall Masonic Lodge 17, 1990-; Ala Farmers Fedn, 1990-; Ala Funeral Dirs Asn, 1995-; Ala Soil & Water Conserv Soc; bd mem, Bullock Co Hosp, 1997-; Union Springs Housing Authority, 1997-; Southern Region Sustainable Agri Res & Educ. **Honors/Awds:** Outstanding Agronomy Student, Am Soc Agron, 1985; Nat Honarary, Alpha Kappa Mu, 1985. **Home Addr:** PO Box 167, Union Springs, AL 36089-0167, **Home Phone:** (334)738-2543. **Business Addr:** Chair, Extension Specialist/ Water Quality, Tuskegee University, 101-C Vocation Bldg 209 Morrison-Mayberry Hall, Tuskegee, AL 36088, **Business Phone:** (334)724-4450.

## HODGES, DR. CAROLYN RICHARDSON

Educator. **Personal:** Born Nov 25, 1947, Roebling, NJ; daughter of Luther Kendrick and Mary Catherine; married John Oliver; children: Daniel Oliver. **Educ:** Arcadia Univ, BA; Beaver Col, BA, fr, 1969; Univ Chicago, MA, ger lang & lit, 1971, PhD, ger lang & lit, 1974. **Career:** Univ Chicago, trustee fel, 1969-73; Cent YMCA Community Col, instr ger, 1970-72; Kennedy-King Jr Col, asst prof humanities, 1975-82; Univ Tenn, Knoxville, asst prof Ger, 1982-88, assoc prof Ger, 1988-, Col Arts & Sci, Acad Personnel, assoc dean, chmn, prof Ger lang, vice provost, Dept Mod Foreign Lang & Lit, head & prof, 1999-2004, assoc dean acad personnel, dean Grad Sch, 2007-. **Orgs:** Tenn Collab Coun Foreign Lang, 1986-; vpres, Tenn Am Asn Teachers Ger, 1987-89; bd mem, Tenn Foreign Lang Teacher Asn, 1989-92; secy, treas & pres, Southern Comparative Lit Asn, 1990-; ed bd, Comparatist; dean, Am Acad Kinesiology & Phys Educ; vice provost & dean, CSGS institutions. **Home Addr:** 4815 Skyline Dr, Knoxville, TN 37914, **Home Phone:** (615)673-0989. **Business Addr:** Professor of German Language, Department Head, University of Tennessee, 701 McClung Tower, Knoxville, TN 37996-0470, **Business Phone:** (865)974-3694.

## HODGES, CRAIG ANTHONY

Basketball coach, basketball player. **Personal:** Born Jun 27, 1960, Park Forest, IL; son of Jibril; married Allison D Jordan; children: Jibril & Jamaal. **Educ:** Calif State Univ, attended 1982. **Career:** Basketball player (retired), basketball coach, executive; Long Beach State, 1978-82; San Diego Clippers, guard, 1982-84, Milwaukee Bucks, guard, 1984-88; Phoenix Suns, guard, 1988-89; Chicago Bulls, guard, 1989-92; Shampoo Clear Cantu, Italy, 1993; Galatasaray, Turkey, 1994-95; Chicago State Univ, men's basketball coach, 1994-96; Rockford Lightning, 1995-96; Jamtland Ambassadors Ostersund, 1997-98; Wash Congressionals, 1998; Los Angeles Lakers, shooting coach, spec asst coach, 2005-11; RTD Basketball, pres & shooting coach, currently; Westchester Knicks, head coach, 2014. **Orgs:** Pres, Operation Unit; SaveYouth; pres, Three Point Inc. **Business Addr:** President, Shooting Coach, RTD Basketball, **Business Phone:** (562)639-9344.

## HODGES, DR. DAVID JULIAN

Educator, anthropologist. **Personal:** Born Jan 11, 1944, Atlanta, GA. **Educ:** Morris Brown Col, BA, 1965; Emory Univ Ga, attended 1965; Columbia Univ, attended 1966; Sophia Univ Tokyo, post grad study, 1967; NY Univ, MA, 1969, PhD, 1972; Harvard Univ, post doctoral study, 1973; Oxford Univ, post doctoral study, 2005. **Career:** So Educ Found fel, 1965; Woodrow Wilson Fel, 1965; So Fel Fund fel, 1969-71; Educ Action Specialist, NYC Comn Devel Agency, 1969-71; Nassau Comm Col Garden City, instr, 1970; Heritage Mus NY, cur, 1971-73; Hunter Col, prof, 1971-, actg dean, Sch Educ, 2001-03, prof anthrop, currently; Cornerstone Chg Inc, pres & founder, 1974-80. **Orgs:** Sr st club worker, NY City Youth Bd, 1965-69; PGM Serv Com YMCA Greater NY; Aaas; Phi Delta Kappa; Alpha Kappa Delta; Alpha Kappa Mu; Nat Soc Study Educ; Asn Blk Anthro, Am Anthrop Asn. **Home Addr:** 185 Hall St Apt 1001, Atlanta, GA 11205, **Home Phone:** (718)636-1376. **Business Addr:** Professor of Anthropology, Hunter College, Rm 733 HN 695 Pk Ave, New York, NY 10065, **Business Phone:** (212)772-5069.

## HODGES, DR. HELENE

Association executive, executive director. **Personal:** Born Apr 27, 1949, Schwabach; daughter of Joseph J and Eugenie Ann Hellwig. **Educ:** Finch Col, attended 1971; St Johns Univ, Jamaica, NY, attended 1975, prof dipl, 1979, PhD, 1985. **Career:** Vi Dept Educ, teacher, 1970-71; NY Bd Educ, teacher & sch dir, 1971-86; Asn Supv & Curric Develop, Alexandria, Va, dir res & info, 1986-93, dir collab ventures, 1993-. **Orgs:** Educ comn mem, Martin Luther King Jr Fed Holiday Comn, 1986-; steering comt mem, Nat Assessment Educ Progress, 1990; selection comt mem, Can Soc Surg Oncol, Nat Teacher Yr Prog, 1991-; Phi Delta Kappa; Nat Alliance Black Sch Educrs; Mid-Atlantic Equity Consortium. **Home Addr:** 1752 Preston Rd, Alexandria, VA 22302, **Home Phone:** (703)379-7330. **Business Addr:** Director, Association Supervision Curriculum Development, 1703 N Beauregard St, Alexandria, VA 22311-1714, **Business Phone:** (703)578-9600.

## HODGES, DR. JACQUELINE STEWART

Educator. **Personal:** married William A Earnest. **Educ:** Huntingdon Col; MEd. **Career:** Stanhope Elmore High Sch, Mill brook, AL, teacher; Wayne County Community Col Downtown Campus, vice chancellor, dean enrollment mgt & stud serv, pres & chief exec officer, currently. **Orgs:** Bd mem, Huntingdon Col Nat Alumni Asn, 1996-99, vpres, 1999-2000, pres, 2001. **Business Addr:** President, Chief Executive Officer, Wayne County Community College, 10001 W Fort St, Detroit, MI 48226, **Business Phone:** (313)496-2651.

## HODGES, DR. JOHN O.

Educator. **Personal:** Born Jan 26, 1944, Greenwood, MS; son of Tommy James and Samantha Wilson; married Carolyn R Richardson; children: Daniel. **Educ:** Univ Nantes, France, cert fr lang & lit, 1967; Morehouse Col, Atlanta, GA, BA, eng & fr, 1968; Atlanta Univ, Atlanta, GA, MA, eng, 1971; Univ Chicago, IL, MA, relig & lit, 1972, PhD, relig & lit, 1980. **Career:** Professor (retired), associate professor emeritus; Morehouse Col, Atlanta, GA, dir lang lab, 1969-70; Barat Col, Lake Forest, IL, lectr eng, 1970-72, dir, Afro-Am studies, 1972-75, asst prof eng, 1972-75; Univ Chicago, IL, asst to dean univ students, 1977-80, asst dean univ students, 1980-82; Univ Tenn, Knoxville, Dept Relig Studies, asst prof cult studies, 1982-88, assoc prof cult studies, 1988-, actg head, 1989-90, chair, African & African-Am Studies, 1997-2002; assoc prof emer, 2010. Author: DELTA FRAGMENTS: RECOLLECTIONS A SHARECROPPER'S SON, 2013. **Orgs:** Merrill Overseas fel, Morehouse, 1966-67; Rockefeller fel, Rockefeller Found, 1970-71; Ford fel, Ford Found, 1976-78; Mod Lang Asn, 1981-; Am Acad Relig, 1982-; Col Lang Asn, 1982-; S Atlantic Mod Lang Asn, 1983; NEH fel, Nat Endowment Humanities, 1984; Langston Hughes Soc; Richard Wright Circle. **Home Addr:** 6736 Ingleside Lane, Knoxville, TN 37918, **Home Phone:** (865)621-6135. **Business Addr:** Associate Professor Emeritus, University of Tennessee, Knoxville, TN 37996-0450.

## HODGES, LILLIAN BERNICE

Business owner. **Personal:** Born Apr 2, 1939, Rosebud Island Mar, AR; married Alzetl Joe Nathan; children: Lillian L. **Educ:** Shorter Jr Col, N Little Rock, Ark, 1958; Tex Women Univ, Denton, Tex, attended 1965. **Career:** E Cent Econ Corp, outreach person, 1965-66; Univ Ark, nutritionist, 1967; Mr Tax Am, mgr, 1968-74; Beautiful Zion Baptist Church, sunday sch teacher, 1976-80; Local 282, United Furniture Workers Am, rep, 1977-80; countries NAACP, liaison officer, 1985. **Orgs:** Vice chmn, Coalition Better Broadcast, 1968-71; dir, L R Jackson Girls Club Am; vpres, Demo Women Critt Co; ex-sec, Critt Co Improv Asn; pres, Nat Asn Advan Colored People Critt Co, 1972-78; vpres, State Nat Asn Advan Colored People, 1973-75; bd mem, Bd METOG Youth Serv, 1973-75. **Honors/Awds:** Outstanding Participation Univ S Census Bus, 1970; Outstanding Award Minority Bus, Minority Bus Develop, 1975; Outstanding Service Award, NAACP Local, 1976; Outstanding Religious Work Non-Denominational Coun, 1979. **Home Addr:** 710 Purdue ave, WEST MEMPHIS, AZ 72301, **Home Phone:** (870)735-2063.

## HODGES, MELVIN SANCHO

Lawyer. **Personal:** Born Jan 1, 1940, Columbia, SC; son of Hilliard Jr and Aubrey; married Ugertha Birdsong; children: Melvin II. **Educ:** Morehouse Col, attended 1960; Univ Calif, Santa Barbara, Calif, BA, 1965; Univ Calif, Boalt Hall Sch Law, Berkeley, Calif, JD, 1969. **Career:** IBM Corp, atty, 1969-72; Hastings Law Col, prof, 1972-73; St Calif, depatty gen, 1976-78; Chevron USA Inc, atty, 1978-93; pvt pract atty, 1993-; Dianne Williams Law Off, atty, currently. **Orgs:** Financial comt, Bay Area Black United Fund, 1982-84; ast treas, Am Asn Blacks Energy, 1984-86; Calif Bar Asn; San Francisco Bar Asn; Charles Houston Bar Asn; bd trustee, Univ Calif Santa Barbara Found; corresp secy, Morehouse Col Nat Alumni Asn. **Honors/Awds:** Outstanding Legal Service, San Francisco Bar Asn, 1983-84, 1994-97; Outstanding Legal Service, Calif Bar Asn, 1983-84; Distinguished Alumni Award, Univ Calif, Santa Barbara, 1990. **Home Addr:** 610 16th St Suite 503, Oakland, CA 94612, **Home Phone:** (510)839-7711. **Business Addr:** Attorney, Dianne Williams Law Offices, 610 16th St Suite 503, Oakland, CA 94612, **Business Phone:** (510)839-7711.

## HODGES, PATRICIA ANN

Executive. **Personal:** Born Mar 24, 1954, Indianapolis, IN; daughter of Jeremiah McKeage and Betty Ann Brooks. **Career:** Interpreter Community Serv Deaf, Indianapolis, 1968-1969; Ind Sch Deaf, residential asst, 1977-79; Ind Voc Col, interpreter deaf, 1979-83; Ind Nat Guard, file clerk, 1983-85; Tel Interpreter Serv Deaf, Co-founder, 1985-; Specialized Interpreter Serv, pres, 1993-. **Orgs:** Ind Regist Chap Interpreters; Black Deaf Advocate; Indianapolis Resource Ctr Independent; Mem Serota, Indianapolis 1987. **Home Addr:** Shamrock Lakes Ests, Hartford City, IN 47348-0000, **Home Phone:** (765)348-4196. **Business Addr:** President, Specialized Interpreter Service, PO Box 88814, Indianapolis, IN 46208, **Business Phone:** (317)328-1584.

## HODGINS, JAMES WILLIAM

Football player, football coach. **Personal:** Born Apr 30, 1977, San Jose, CA; married Stephanie; children: Isaiah & Isaac. **Educ:** San Jose State Univ, BA, sociol, 1999. **Career:** Football player (retired), coach, free agt; St Louis Rams, running back & fullback, 1999-2002; Ariz Cardinals, fullback, 2003-05; New York Jets, 2006; Fel Christian Athletes, area rep, 2011-; Berean Christian High Sch, head football coach, 2013-; One Way 2 Play, wester region spokesman, 2014-; Bay Area Fel Christian Athletes, motivational speaker & coach, currently; NFL, free agt; Voice Am Talk Radio, "O & Hodge Show", show host, currently. **Orgs:** Cardinals Charities. **Home Addr:** , Oakley, CA. **Business Addr:** Motivational Speaker & Coach, Bay Area Fellowship of Christian Athletes, PO Box 24308, San Jose, AZ 95154, **Business Phone:** (408)300-0744.

## HODGSON-BROOKS, GLORIA J.

Artist, psychotherapist. **Personal:** Born Nov 28, 1942, Hartford, CT; daughter of Marion S Jackson and Charles O; married Peter C. **Educ:** Bennett Col, BA, 1965; Smith Col Sch Social Work, MSW, 1979; Hartford Family Inst, Gestalt-Body Centered Psychother, 1983; Nat Asn Social Workers, cert, 1982; State Conn, cert social work, 1987; Am Bd Examiners Clin Social Work, dipl, 1988. **Career:** Child & Family Serv Inc, social worker, 1974-77; Inter-Agency Serv, social worker, 1974-77; Hartford Family Inst, intern, 1976-78; pvt pract psychother, 1976-78; Child & Family Serv Inc, clin social worker, 1979-80; Dr Isaiah Clark Family & Youth Clin, dir, 1980-81; Hartford Family Inst, assoc, 1978-85; pvt pract, psychother, 1978-85; Psychother & Coun Assocs, psychother & partner, 1985-; Brooks & Brooks Ltd, Hartford, Conn, pres, 1985-; Solitude Visual Arts Studio, Hartford, Conn, partner, 1989-. **Orgs:** Nat Asn Black Social Workers, 1972-; Nat Alliance Against Racist & Polit Repression, 1977-85; Nat Asn Social Workers, 1977-; coun minority stud, Trinity Col, 1982-85; staff training, Directions Unlimited, 1984-85; Conn Caucus Black Women Polit Action, 1984-86; assoc mem, PRO Disabled Entrepreneur, 1985-86; workshop leader goal setting PRO Disabled Entrepreneur Goal Setting Workshops, 1985-86; staff training commun, Sandler Sales Inst, 1986; admin consult, Conn Ctr Human Growth & Develop, 1986; Farmington Valley Arts Ctr, 1986-; adv bd, IAM Cares, 1986-; Int Sculpture Ctr; Am Craft Coun; Am Craft Mus; charter mem, Nat Mus Women Arts; Nat Trust Hist Preserv; comt mem, State CT Judicial Br. **Honors/Awds:** Award, Dr Issiah Clark Family & Youth Clin, 1988. **Special Achievements:** Published "An Exploratory Study of the Diagnostic Process in Gestalt Therapy", Smith College Library 1975; social Worker for Justice Awd Smith College School for Social Work, 1979; art exhibits: International Biographical Centre, 1989, ECKANKAR Creative Art Festival, 1987, 1988, New England Hardweavers, 1987. **Home Addr:** 136 High Path Rd, Windsor, CT 06095-4131. **Business Addr:** Psychotherapist, Partner, Psychotherapy & Counseling Associates, 483 W Middle Tpke W Suite 217, Manchester, CT 06040-3864, **Business Phone:** (860)647-0899.

## HOFFLER, DR. RICHARD WINFRED, JR.

Physician. **Personal:** Born Jun 22, 1944, Lynchburg, VA; son of Richard Winfred Sr and Julia; married Sylvia C; children: Edward & Erika. **Educ:** Hampton Inst, BA, 1966; Meharry Med Col, MD, 1970. **Career:** Southside Med Ctr, intern, 1970, resident, 1971-74, med consult; pvt pract physician, 1974-90; st agency med consult, 1974-; Ambulatory Care VAMC, Hampton, Va, staff physician, 1990-; Tidewater Disability Determination Servs, st agency med consult, 1974-80, chief med consult, 1980-90; Sentera Hosps, consult staff; Veterans Affair Med Ctr, physician; pvt pract, currently. **Orgs:** AMA; Norfolk Acad Med; Norfolk Med Soc; Nat Med Asn. **Honors/Awds:** Scholar, Hampton Inst, 1963-64. **Home Addr:** 4700 Pickle Barn Ct, Virginia Beach, VA 23455, **Home Phone:** (804)490-4485. **Business Addr:** Physician, Veterans Affair Medical Center, 100 Emancipation Dr, Virginia Beach, VA 23455, **Business Phone:** (757)722-9961.

## HOFFMAN, DR. JOSEPH IRVINE, JR.

Physician. **Personal:** Born Apr 14, 1939, Charleston, SC; married Pamela Louise Hayling; children: Kathyrn, Kristen & Kara. **Educ:** Harvard Col, AB, 1960; Howard Univ, MD, 1964. **Career:** Lenox Hill Hosp, internship, 1964-66, resident, gen surg, 1967-68; Hosp Spec Surg, orthop, resident, orthop surg, 1968-72. **Orgs:** Nat Med Asn; AMA; past pres, Atlanta Med Asn; Nat Asn Advan Colored People; Urban League; Atlanta Chamber Com; Omega Psi Phi; fel Am Rheumatism Asn, 1972; cert Am Bd Orthop Surg, 1973; Acad Orthop Surg, 1977; past pres, 100 Black Men Atlanta; pres, Joseph Hoffman MD PC. **Home Addr:** 3400 Kilby Pl NW, Atlanta, GA 30327, **Home Phone:** (404)264-9911. **Business Addr:** President, Joseph Hoffman MD PC, 2950 Stone Hogan Connector Rd SW Suite 3A, Atlanta, GA 30331-2837, **Business Phone:** (404)344-9454.

## HOGAN, BEVERLY WADE

College administrator, government official. **Personal:** Born Jul 5, 1951, Crystal Springs, MS; daughter of W D Wade Sr and Mae Ether Easley Wade; married Marvin; children: Maurice DeShay & Marcellus Wade. **Educ:** Tougaloo Col, Tougaloo, BA, psychol, 1973; Jackson State Univ, Jackson, MS, pub policy & admin, 1990; Fielding Grad Univ, PhD, human & orgn develop; Univ S Miss, clin psychol; Univ Ga, clin psychol. **Career:** Friends C Miss, health serv coordr, 1970-71; Ment Health Ctr, Jackson, Miss, ment health rapist, 1973-74; Hinds County Ment Health Asn, Jackson, Miss, exec dir, 1974-80; Jackson State Univ, leadership & pub policy, adj instr, adj prof; Miss Ment Health Asn, Jackson, Miss, exec dir, 1980-83; Gov Off Fed/State Progs, Jackson, Miss, exec dir, 1984-87; Coun State Govts, Toll fel, 1987; Miss Workers' Compensation Comn, Jackson, Miss, comnr, 1987-97; Tougaloo Col, Health & Wellness Ctr, exec asst to pres & dir, 1997-2000, trustee & col adminr, dir, vpres, Instnl Advan, 2000-02, interim pres, pres, 2002-. **Orgs:** Chairperson & nat deleg, White House Conf Families, Miss, 1980; Southern reg dir, Coun State Plng Agencies, 1985; chairperson, Nat Child Support Implementation Proj, 1986; chairperson, Miss Campaign UNCF Telethon, 1987 &1988; chairperson, Sch Bus Adv Coun, Jackson State Univ, 1988-; pub rels chairperson, Miss Childrens Home Soc, 1990-91; founding mem & pres, nat Coalition 100 Black Women, Cent Miss Chap, 1994-98; bd trustee, Tougaloo Col, 1991-97; Entergy Mississipii, bd mem, 1999-; bd mem, Found Mid-S, 1999-; adv bd, Bancorp S; adv bd, Metro Chamber Com; adv bd, Univ Club; bd visitors, Univ Miss; bd, Reg Comn Bldg Philanthropy; bd dir, United Negro Col Fund; bd dir, Nat Asn Equal Opportunity Higher Educ; bd dir, Brown Univ Leadership Alliance; fel Alpha Kappa Alpha Sorority; fel links; fel Mt. Wade Missionary Baptist Church; founding dir, Owens Health & Wellness Ctr; bd advisor, Historically black cols & univs; Jackson Med Mall Found; RAND's Gulf States Policy Inst; founder, First psychiat halfway house, Miss; Dir, Sanderson Farms, currently. **Home Addr:** 111 Rock Glen Pl, Jackson, MS 39206-3131, **Home Phone:** (601)982-2831. **Business Addr:** President, Tougaloo College, 500 W County Line Rd, Tougaloo, MS 39174, **Business Phone:** (601)977-7730.

**HOGAN, CAROLYN ANN**
Government official, president (organization), consultant. **Personal:** Born Jul 13, 1944, New Orleans, LA; daughter of Elijah Sr (deceased) and Yolanda Getridge Mosley. **Educ:** Dillard Univ, BA, 1966; Fisk Univ, MA, 1969; Southern Ill Univ, attended 1974. **Career:** Dillard Univ, instr, 1969-73; Southern Univ, New Orleans, LA, instr, 1973-75; Orleans Parish Sch Bd, psychologist, 1974-75; City New Orleans, eval specialist, 1976-79; Int consult, 1979; Nat Opinion Res Ctr, opinion researcher, 1980-82; Nat Testing Servs, opinion researcher, 1981; Transit Mgt Southeast La, benefits specialist, 1985-86, workers compensation rep, 1986-. **Orgs:** Consult, Albert Wicker Schs Spec Educ Class Orleans Parish Sch Bd, 1978; Gestalt Inst Psychodrama, 1978-79; New Orleans Neighborhood Police Anti-Crime Coun, 1983-86; scholar comn, Crescent City Chap Conf Minorities Transp, 1986-87; pres adv, Voters Dem Nat Comt; Nat Asn Female Exec. **Home Addr:** 6213 Tennyson Dr, Baton Rouge, LA 70817-2940, **Home Phone:** (225)753-3673.

**HOGAN, EDWIN B.**
Consultant, president (organization). **Personal:** Born Sep 2, 1940, Cleveland, OH; son of Lonnie N and Helen Marie Brock; married Letitia G Jackson; children: Edwina R & Bryan C Jackson; married Tish. **Career:** New Visions Group Inc, pres & chief exec officer, 1996-; Success Group Inc, sr lobbyist, legis specialist, partner & vpres govt affairs, chief liaison, currently. **Orgs:** Exec comt, Columbus Nat Asn Advan Colored People, 1989-; vice chmn, Ballet Met, 1990-; vice chmn & bd mem, Maryhaven, 1991-; COT Connections, 1992-; Fortune 500 clients; Ohio Legis Black Caucus; Nat Black Caucus State Legislators; Nat Black Caucus Local Elected Officials; Alvis House; Muscular Dystrophy Asn; Columbus Metrop Area Community Action Orgn; Ohio Lobbying Asn; adv bd, Ohio Alliance Pub Charter Schs; mentoring prog, 100 Black Men Cent Ohio. **Home Addr:** 2727 Mitzi Dr, Columbus, OH 43209, **Home Phone:** (614)237-4005. **Business Addr:** President, Chief Executive Officer, New Visions Group LLC, 33 N 3rd St Suite 400, Columbus, OH 43215, **Business Phone:** (614)280-1299.

**HOGAN, DR. JAMES CARROLL, JR.**
Biologist. **Personal:** Born Jan 3, 1939, Milledgeville, GA; son of James C Sr and Leanna Johnson; married Izola Stinson; children: Pamela Renita Robertson, Gregory Karl & Jeffrey Darryl. **Educ:** Morehouse Col, BS, 1961; Atlanta Univ, MS, biol, 1968; Brown Univ, PhD, cell biol, 1972. **Career:** Hancock Co Bd Educ, teacher sci dept & chmn, 1961-66; Atlanta Pub Schs, sci teacher, 1967-68; Atlanta Univ, instr, 1967; Yale Univ, Sch Med, res assoc, 1973-76; Howard Univ, asst prof dept anat, 1976-78; Yale Univ, Vis Fac Fel; Howard Univ, asst prof grad sch, 1976-78; Univ Conn, assoc prof Allied health sci, 1979-82, dir minority stud affairs; UCONN Health Ctr, assoc prof & univ dir, 1982-87; Conn Dept Pub Health, Hartford, CT, chief, clin chem & hemat, 1990, Chief Environ, Chem & Biochem, 2001-03, Sect Chief, Biomonitoring, Health Lab sec mgr. **Orgs:** Founder & chmn, Rhode Isl& Community Sickle Cell Disease, 1970-72; founder, UCONN Health Sci Cluster Progs Parents Auxilary, 1979; vpres, CT's Black Health Prof Network, 1982-86; Pres, Nat Assoc Med Minority Educr, 1985-86; Omega Psi Phi Fraternity Inc; bd adv, Sickle Cell Assoc CT Inc; Urban League, Atlanta Univ Hon Soc, Sigma Xi; AAAS; Am Soc Cell Biol; Nat Assoc Med Minority Educr Inc; NY Acad Sci; Alpha Eta Soc; founder & pres, N Haven (CT) Asn Black Citizens, 1988-; N Haven Community Serv Comn, 1990; adv bd, Greater New Haven State Tech Col, 1989-; founder & pres, CT Chap Nat Tech Asn, 1988-; bd dir, A Better Chance Inc; bd dir, Hartford Alliance Sci & Math; life mem, chair, Educ Comt, New Haven Chap, Nat Asn Advan Colored People; bd dir, Conn Pub Health Assoc; bd dir, Nat Tech Asn, 1993-; pres, Immanuel Bapt Ch, Mens Club, 1998-; Conn Acad Sci & Engineering, 2002; mem comm (CASE), 2003, mem chmn, 2004-; Dem Town Comt. **Honors/Awds:** Macy Scholar Marine Biol Lab Woods Hole MA, 1978-80; Research Found Grant, Univ Conn, 1979-80; Cert Clinical Lab Dir, State of CT, 1993; Omega Man of the Year Award, Chi Omicron Chap, 1992; Frederick G Adam Award, Univ CT's, 2001; Certificate of Recognition, CT Dept Pub Health, 2001; Outstanding Citizen's Award, NOH Asn Black Citizen's, 2001; NW Elm City Negro Prof & Bus Women's Man of the Year Award, 2002. **Special Achievements:** Twenty-six publications including "An Ultrastructural Analysis of Cytoplasmic Makers in Germ Cells of Oryzias Laptipes, " J Ultrastruct Res 62, 237-250; "Regeneration of the Caudal Fin in Killfishes (Oryzias laptipes and Fundulus heteroclitus)" J Cell Biol 91(2), pt 2, p110a; numerous presentations; First African American to hold the position of chief of environmental chemistry at the Connecticut Department of Public Health Laboratory. **Home Addr:** 51 Pool Rd, PO Box 146, North Haven, CT 06473-2711, **Home Phone:** (203)239-1805.

**HOGAN, DR. WILLIAM E., II**
Computer executive, executive, association executive. **Personal:** Born Sep 30, 1942, Montgomery, AL; son of William E and D S; married Shadra; children: Shalaun & William E III. **Educ:** Okla State Univ, Stillwater, Okla, BSEE, 1965, PhD, 1973; Southern Methodist Univ, Dallas, Tex, MS, 1969. **Career:** Univ Kans, Lawrence, Kans, from asst dean to assoc exec vice chancellor, 1973-84; AMIC, Lawrence, Kans, pres, 1982-84; Honeywell Inc, Minneapolis, Minn, vpres technol & bus develop, 1984-86, vpres staff exec to pres, 1986, vpres corps TQS, 1987-88; vpres, IIO, 1988-; Medtronic Inc, vpres corp oper; Hogan Co, founder, 1993-, chmn & chief exec officer, 1998-; Wikifamilies, bd dir, chmn, currently. **Orgs:** Chair, Res Adv Bd, Greater Minn Corp, 1989-90; chair, Minn High Technol Coun, 1989-90; chmn, Historically Black Res Univ Found Bd, 1990; bd mem, Bethune-Cookman Univ; chair, Univ Minnesotas bd regents, 1977-99; White House task forces educ. **Honors/Awds:** Outstanding Young Men in America, Chamber Com, 1977; Plaques for Outstanding Contribution to Minority Programs, Univ Kans Students, 1977, 1979; Outstanding Black Engineer of America, Co & All Historically Black Cols, 1989; International Business Fellow, Indust & Col, 1989. **Home Addr:** 18520 Beaverwood Rd, Minnetonka, MN 55345, **Home Phone:** (952)474-8211. **Business Addr:** Founder, Chief Executive Officer, The Hogan Co, 80 S 8th St Suite 4040, Minneapolis, MN 55402, **Business Phone:** (612)470-7457.

**HOGGES, DR. RALPH**
Executive director, educator. **Personal:** Born Aug 3, 1947, Allentown, GA; son of Laura Burnett Rembert; married Lilia N Pardo; children: Genithia L & Alicia I. **Educ:** Tuskegee Inst, BS, 1971, MEd, 1972; Nova Univ, Ft Lauderdale, EdD, 1977; Univ Miami, PhD; Harvard Univ, PhD. **Career:** Fla Int Univ, Miami, prin tech, 1972-73, coordr col work-study prog, 1973-74, admin asst dean, 1974-78, assoc dean stud affairs, 1978-; Ctr Minority Res Inc, Miami, exec dir, 1979-; Fla Mem Col, dir, study abroad prog, assoc dean, prof, 1984-90; Nat Writers Club, pres, chmn; Miami Courier Newspaper, columnist; Nova Southeastern Univ, Fischler Grad Sch, dir, prof, admin, 1991-; Inst Pub Policy & Exec Leadership Higher Educ, founder, exec dir, diversity Advi coun, currently; Poems: American Poetry Anthology; Treasured Poems of America; Windows on the World; The National Library of Poetry; Paths Less Traveled; Anthology of Poetry; Hemispheres; Poetic Voices; Crescendo. **Orgs:** Kappa Delta Pi, 1971-; bd trusee, Am Interdenomi Nat Univ, 1978-; Fla ColStud Affairs Asn, 1978-; Phi Delta Kappa, 1978-; bd dir, Ctr Minority Res Inc, 1979-; S Fla Writers Asn; Writers' Network S Fla. **Home Addr:** 15630 SW 109th Ave, Miami, FL 33157, **Home Phone:** (305)254-6278. **Business Addr:** Executive Director, Diversity Advisory Council, Nova Southeastern University, 1750 NE 167th St, North Miami Beach, FL 33162-3017, **Business Phone:** (954)678-2273.

**HOGU, BARBARA J. JONES**
Educator, artist. **Personal:** Born Apr 17, 1938, Chicago, IL; married Jean Claude; children: Kuumba. **Educ:** Howard Univ, BA, 1959; Sch Art Inst Chicago, BFA, 1964, Gov State Univ, humanities studies, 1995, MS, fil, currently; Ill Inst technol, Inst Design, MS, 1970. **Career:** Chicago Post Off, clerk, 1961-64; Robt Paige Designs, designer, 1968-69, lectr, 1968; Chicago Pub High Schs, Art Inst high schs, 1964-70; Malcolm X Col, asst prof, assoc prof, currently. **Orgs:** Southside Comm Ctr, 1971; Third World Press, staff artist, 1973; Nat Conf Artists, vpres, 1973; Art Hist Sch Art Inst, lect, 1974-79; founding mem, African Commune Black Relevant Artists; Union Black Artists. **Honors/Awds:** First Print Award Black Aesthetics "69" Service Award; Malcolm X Umoja Award, 1973. **Home Addr:** 249 Forest Blvd, Park Forest, IL 60466-1750, **Home Phone:** (708)747-5492. **Business Addr:** Associate Professor, Malcolm X College, 1900 W Van Buren St, Chicago, IL 60612, **Business Phone:** (312)850-7000.

**HOGUE, LESLIE DENISE**
Editor. **Personal:** Born Sep 1, 1966, Detroit, MI; daughter of Dennis O and Katherine F Green; married Earlonzo D; children: Earlonzo Jr. **Educ:** Wayne State Univ, BA, 1992. **Career:** Surreal Mag, ed, pub, 1992-95; Comput Training & Support Corp, ed, 1995-96; Health Care Weekly Rev, ed, 1996. **Orgs:** Treas, Olive Tree Found, 1997; Inst Health Improv Southeast Mich, 1997, Word Faith Int Christian Ctr, writer, 1998. **Home Addr:** 4090 E Outer Dr, Detroit, MI 48234, **Home Phone:** (313)892-6678. **Business Addr:** Editor, Health Care Weekly Review, 24901 Northwestern Hwy Suite 316A, Southfield, MI 48075, **Business Phone:** (248)352-3322.

**HOLBERT, JOANNE**
Mayor, county commissioner, educator. **Personal:** Born Washington, DC; daughter of Lelond. **Educ:** Univ Kans, BS, home econ educ, 1965; Peabody Teachers Col, MA, educ, 1968; Ind Univ, Bloomington, PhD, coun, 1975; Univ Kans, BS, home econ educ, 1965; Peabody Teachers Col, MA, educ, 1968; Ind Univ, Bloomington, PhD, coun, 1975. **Career:** Oakland Univ, asst prof, 1975-77; Wayne St Univ, Col Educ, asst dean, 1977, assoc prof, currently, 1991-, assoc dean curric, 1991-93, Div Theoret & Behav Foundations, asst div, Div Admin & Orgn Studies, 1997-2008, interim dep dean; City Pontiac, dep mayor, 1986-89; OaklandCounty, county comr, 1995-98. **Orgs:** Alpha Kappa Alpha; Oakland County Chap, Links; Nat Asn Advan Colored People; Pontiac Urban League; div admin, class schedules, fac & stud Issues, prog develop, Theoret & Behav Found. **Special Achievements:** First black female Deputy Mayor. **Business Addr:** Associate Professor, Interim Assistant Dean, Wayne State University, 3 S Col Educ Rm 361, Detroit, MI 48202, **Business Phone:** (313)577-1691.

**HOLBERT, RAY ARTHUR, III**
Baseball player. **Personal:** Born Sep 25, 1970, Torrance, CA; married Cecilia. **Career:** Baseball player (retired), baseball coach; San Diego Padres, 1994-95; Montreal Expos, 1998; Atlanta Braves, 1998; Kans City Royals, infielder, 1999-2000; Tampa Bay Devil Rays, 2000; El Camino Col, asst coach, currently. **Business Addr:** Assistant Coach, El Camino College Compton Center, 1111 E Artesia Blvd, Compton, CA 90221, **Business Phone:** (310)900-1600.

**HOLBERT, RAYMOND**
Educator, artist. **Personal:** Born Feb 24, 1945, Berkeley, CA; son of James Albert and Carolyn Bernice Gary; married Susan Demersseman; children: Onika Valentine, Lauren Dakota & Brian Jaymes. **Educ:** Laney Col, AA, 1964; Univ Calif, AB, 1972, MA, 1974, MFA, 1975. **Career:** City Col San Francisco, art dept, chmn, 1996-2000, coordr, 1990-96, prof art, prof emer, currently; Exhibits: San Francisco Art Mus, 1972; Oakland Art Mus, 1973, Berkeley, 1974; Baylor Univ, Waco, Tex, 1975; Studio Mus, Harlem, NY, 1977, 1979; Howard Univ, Washington, DC, 1980; Helen Euphrat Gallery, Calif, 1982, Brockman Gallery, LA, 1982; Grand Oak Gallery, 1983; LA Mus African Am Art Printmakers, 1984; Calif Mus African Am Art, 1986, San Francisco Art Comn Gallery, 1987; City Art Gallery, San Francisco; Memory Bank, comput imaging & dir, 1970-2004. **Orgs:** Artists Books Advocate, Nat Conf Artists. **Business Addr:** Professor Emeritus, City College of San Francisco, 50 Phelan Ave, San Francisco, CA 94112, **Business Phone:** (415)239-3000.

**HOLCOMBE, ROBERT WAYNE**
Football coach, football player. **Personal:** Born Dec 11, 1975, Houston, TX. **Educ:** Univ Ill, LAS, Speech Commun, 1998. **Career:** St Louis Rams, running back & fullback, 1998-2001; Tenn Titans, running back & fullback, 2002-04; Kans City Chiefs, running back, 2005; Pub Broadcasting Serv, Intern, 2008; New Orleans saints, Interim Running Backs Coach, 2008; Washinton Redskins, interim running backs Coach, 2009; Austin Col, asst football coach, 2010; Jimmy John's, franchisee, 2012-. **Honors/Awds:** Super Bowl XXXVI; All-Am & All-Far W hons, Prep Football Report. **Business Addr:** 9490 FM 1960 Bypass Rd W Suite 300, Humble, TX 77338, **Business Phone:** (281)548-0010.

**HOLDEN, KIP.** **See HOLDEN, MELVIN LEE.**

**HOLDEN, MELVIN LEE (KIP HOLDEN)**
State government official, mayor. **Personal:** Born Aug 12, 1952, New Orleans, LA; son of Curtis and Rosa Rogers; married Lois Stevenson; children: Melvin II, Angela, Monique, Myron A & Brian Michael; married Lois Stevenson; children: Melvin II, Angela, Monique, Myron & Brian Michael. **Educ:** La State Univ, BA, jour, 1974; Southern Univ, MA, jour, 1982; Southern Univ Sch Law, JD, 1985; Nat Inst Trial Advocacy, grad, 1998; Oxford Univ Round Table, 2002. **Career:** WXOK Radio, Baton Rouge, La, news dir, 1975-77; WWL Radio, New Orleans, La, reporter, 1977-78; WBRZ Channel 2, Baton Rouge, La, reporter, 1978-79; US Census Bur, Baton Rouge, La, pub rels specialist; Baton Rouge City Police, Baton Rouge, La, pub info officer; La Dept Labor Off Workers Compensation, Baton Rouge, La, law clerk; Baton Rouge Metro Coun Dist 2, councilman, 1984-88; La House Representatives, Dist 63, state rep, sen, 1988-2001; Southern Univ Sch Law, Baton Rouge, La, adj prof law, 1991-; La State, Dist 15, sen; Melvin "Kip", Holden & Assocs, prin, currently; City Baton Rouge, Parish E Baton Rouge, mayor-pres, 2005-; E Baton Rouge Parish Pub Schs; Baton Rouge Area Violence Elimination proj, dist atty, 2012. **Orgs:** Xi Nu Lamba Chap, Alpha Phi Alpha; La Bar Asn; Am Bar Asn; Nat Bar Asn; Greater Baton Rouge Airport Comn; Greater King David Baptist Church; chair, Nat League Cities Coun Youth, 2007-; Green Light Baton Rouge Citizens Coun; bd mem, Pennington Biomed Res Ctr, currently; bd mem, Nat League Cities Adv Coun, currently. **Home Addr:** 234 Rivercrest Ave, Baton Rouge, LA 70807-2543, **Home Phone:** (225)774-8995. **Business Addr:** Mayor-President, Office of the Mayor President, 222 St Louis St 3rd Fl, Baton Rouge, LA 70802, **Business Phone:** (225)389-3100.

**HOLDEN, MICHELLE Y.**
Television journalist. **Personal:** Born Mar 31, 1954, Toledo, OH; daughter of Richard and Ammie Edmond; children: Richard. **Educ:** Univ Toledo, Toledo, OH, 1975. **Career:** Television journalist, actor; WDHO-TV, Toledo, Ohio, reporter, 1976; WBNS-TV, Columbus, Ohio, noon anchor, 1978-82, WHAS-TV, Louisville, Ky, noon anchor, 1982-85; WEWS-TV, Cleveland, Ohio, weekend anchor, 1985-88; WBBM-TV, Chicago, Ill, TV news reporter, 1988-90; KTTV-TV, Los Angeles, Calif, TV news reporter, 1990; Encore Cable Host "Trade Secrets, " 1992; KCAL-TV, Los Angeles, Calif, freelance reporter, 1993; Spec Corresp Conus Satellite Network OJ Simpson Trial, 1994; Films: Stranger by Night, 1994; Speechless, 1994; The Sun, the Moon & the Stars, 1996; TV series: "Real Charlotte", 1990; "SeaQuest DSV", 1994; "Picket Fences", 1994; "The Positively True Adventures of the Alleged Texas Cheerleader-Murdering Mom", 1994; "Without Warning", 1995. **Orgs:** Nat Asn Black Journalists, 1982-; Alpha Kappa Alpha Sorority; First Baptist Church, Jeffersontown, KY. **Honors/Awds:** Female Broadcaster of the Year, Nat Asn Career Women, 1987; Ohio Gen Assembly Commendation, 1982; Greater Cleveland Enterprising Women, 1987; Fred Hampton Communications Award, 1989; Emmy Nomination News Reporting, 1991; Emmy Nomination News Writing, 1992.

**HOLDER, ERIC HIMPTON, JR.**
Lawyer, government official. **Personal:** Born Jan 21, 1951, Bronx, NY; son of Eric Sr and Miriam Holder R Yearwood; married Sharon Malone; children: Maya, Brooke & Eric. **Educ:** Columbia Univ, BA, Am hist, 1973; Columbia Law Sch, JD, 1976. **Career:** Nat Asn Advan Colored People, Legal Defense Fund, clerk, 1974; US Dept Justice, clerk, 1975, Pub Integrity Sect, trial atty, 1976-88; DC Super Ct, assoc judge, 1988-93; US dist atty DC, 1993-97; US dep atty gen, 1997-2001, US atty gen, 2009-14; Covington & Burling, partner, 2001-09, 2015-. **Orgs:** Bd trustee, George Wash Univ, 1996-97; founder, Lawyers One Am; bd, Columbia Univ, Save C Found; Bd dir, Meyer Found; bd dir, See Forever Found; bd dir, I Am Your Child Found; bd dir, Concerned Black Men; trustee, Save C; US Sentencing Comn Ad Hoc Adv Group; chmn, Eastman Kodak External Diversity Adv Panel; bd mem, Microwave Commun Inc; bd dir, Am Const Soc Law & Policy. **Honors/Awds:** The Best Lawyers in America, 2007. **Special Achievements:** First African American to serve as Attorney General for Washington, DC of the United States; First African American to be named deputy attorney general; Named by The Natl Law Journal as one of The Most 50 Influential Minority Lawyers in America; Named one of the Greatest Washington Lawyers of the Past 30 Years by the Legal Times. **Home Addr:** 4246 50th St NW, Washington, DC 20016, **Home Phone:** (202)966-5694. **Business Addr:** Partner, Covington & Burling LLP, 1 City Ctr 850 Tenth St NW, Washington, DC 20001-4956, **Business Phone:** (202)662-6000.

**HOLDER, KAREN ZELIS.** **See ZELIS, KAREN DEE.**

**HOLDER, LAURENCE**
Playwright. **Personal:** Born Feb 26, 1939, Brooklyn, NY; son of Barbadian immigrants; married Andrea; children: 3. **Educ:** City Col NY, degree geol, MA, creative writing, 1975. **Career:** Playwright; TV series: "Watch Your Mouth", WNET NBC TV, 1974-75; hist musical Juba, La Mama Co, 1978; "When the Chickens Came Home to Roost", 1982; plays: Zora Neale Hurston, 1990; M: The Mandela Saga, 1995; Mercy Col; Col New Rochelle & John Jay Col Crim Justice, prof, 1999; Monk, 2000, NY Univ; S Mountain Comm Col. **Orgs:** Mem fac, John Jay Col Criminal Justice. **Honors/Awds:** Three Audelco (Audience Development Comm) Awards; OTTO, Garland Anderson Award, Nat Black Theatre Festival. **Special Achievements:** Is the author of several volumes of poetry and 7 novels; First OTTO Award for political writing. **Home Addr:** 626 Riverside Dr Apt 10 J, New York, NY 10031-7214, **Home Phone:** (212)690-7787.

### HOLDSCLAW, CHAMIQUE SHAUNTA

Basketball player. **Personal:** Born Aug 9, 1977, Astoria, NY; daughter of Willie Johnson and Bonita. **Educ:** Univ Tenn, attended 1999. **Career:** Basketball player (retired); SullivanWash Mystics, forward & guard, 1999-2004; Ros Casares Valencia, 2004-05; Los Angeles Sparks, forward & guard, 2005-07; TS Wisla Can-Pack Krakow, 2006-07; Atlanta Dream, 2009; San Antonio Silver Stars, 2010.TV Series : "Arli$$", 1999; "60 Minutes Wednesday", 1999; "The Tim McCarver Show", 2003; "Dog Bites Man", 2006; "Iyanla, Fix My Life", 2013; "Little Ballers", 2013; "The Unquiet Journey of Chamique Holdsclaw", 2015. **Orgs:** Alpha Kappa Alpha Sorority. **Business Addr:** Professional Basketball Player, San Antonio Silver Stars, 1 AT&T Ctr, San Antonio, TX 78219, **Business Phone:** (210)444-5090.

### HOLLAND, DR. ANTONIO FREDERICK

Educator. **Personal:** Born Dec 5, 1943, Petersburg, VA; son of Garnett G and Carmen T; married Carolyn Turner; children: Bradley Wilkins & Erik G. **Educ:** Northeastern Univ, BA, 1967, MA, 1969; Univ Mo-Columbia, PhD, hist & social sci, 1984. **Career:** Lincoln Univ, div chair, 1970, Dept Psychol, chmn, Dept Social & Behav Sci, chmn, prof hist, chair, 2010; Self Employed, consult, 2010-. Book: Nathan B. Young; Struggle over Black Higher Education. **Orgs:** Alpha Phi Alpha, 1978-; bd mem, Mo Folklore Soc, 1992-; vice chair, fomer chair, Mo Adv Coun Hist Preserv, 1994-2001; vice chair, Mo Ctr Bk, 1996-; fomer vpres, pres, 1997-, Mo Mil Hist Soc; bd mem, treas, 1997-, John William Blind Boone Found. **Home Addr:** 306 W El Cortez Dr, Columbia, MO 65203, **Home Phone:** (573)442-8661. **Business Addr:** Professor of History, Chairman, Lincoln University, 413 Martin Luther King Hall, Jefferson City, MO 65101, **Business Phone:** (573)681-5148.

### HOLLAND, BOB. See HOLLAND, ROBERT, JR.

### HOLLAND, BRIAN

Television producer, songwriter. **Personal:** Born Feb 15, 1941, Detroit, MI; married Sharon; children: 3. **Career:** Satintones, vocalist; Holland Dozier Holland, song writer & producing team, currently; Films: Holiday Heart, 2000; Hollywood Rocks the Movies: The Early Years, 1955-70, 2000; An Extremely Goofy Movie, 2000; Frequency, 2000; Riding in Cars with Boys, 2001; The Martins, 2001; Rat Race, 2001; Standing in the Shadows of Motown, 2002; Sorority Boys, 2002; Boat Trip, 2002; Auto Focus, 2002; Monster, 2003; Gothika, 2003; Matchstick Men, 2003; Reach Out Ill Be There, 2003; Cradle 2 the Grave, 2003; Envy, 2004; Shark Tale, 2004; The 40 Year Old Virgin, 2005; Harsh Times, 2005; Four Brothers, 2005; Glory Road, 2006; Bobby, 2006; Wellkamm to Verona, 2006; Larry the Cable Guy: Health Inspector, 2006; Glory Road, 2006; Larry the Cable Guy: Health Inspector, 2006; Zodiac, 2007; Amazing Journey: The Story of The Who, 2007; License to Wed, 2007; The Nines, 2007; Tv Series: "American Dreams", 2002; "Great Performances", 2005; "Shminiya, Ha", 2006; "The Sopranos", 2007; "TV Land Confidential", 2007; Songs: "Stop In the Name of Love"; "Baby I Need Your Loving"; "Come See About Me"; "Locking Up My Heart"; "Can I Get a Witness"; "How Sweet It Is To Be Loved by You"; "Little Darling"; "Heat Wave"; "Nowhere to Run"; "Jimmy Mack"; "Where Did Our Love Go"; "Baby Love"; "Back in My Arms Again"; "You Can't Hurry Love"; "You Keep Me Hanging On"; "Love Is Here & Now Youre Gone"; "The Happening"; "symphonic soul"; "I Cant Help Myself"; "Its The Same Old Song"; "Dont Leave Me Starvin for Your Love". **Orgs:** The Satintones; The Rayber Voices. **Honors/Awds:** Songwriters Hall of Fame, 1988; Rock & Roll Hall of Fame, 1990; BMI Icon Award, 2003. **Business Addr:** Song Writer, Holland Dozier & Holland Productions, 1800 N Highland Ave Suite 124, Los Angeles, CA 90028, **Business Phone:** (214)783-8354.

### HOLLAND, DARIUS JEROME

Executive, minister (clergy), football player. **Personal:** Born Nov 10, 1973, Petersburg, VA. **Educ:** Univ Colo, Boulder, BA, sociol, 1995; Golden Gate Baptist Theol Sem, Denver Campus, MDiv, pastoral studies & coun, 2013-. **Career:** Football player (retired), exec, pastor; Green Bay Packers, defensive tackle, 1995-97; Kans City Chiefs, 1998; Detroit Lions, 1998; Hard money lending, pres, 1998-2008; Cleveland Browns, defensive tackle & left defensive tackle, 1999, 2001; Minn Vikings, 2002; Denver Broncos, left & right defensive tackle, 2003, 2004; True Life Church, pastor, 2010-; Valor Christian High Sch, enrollment coordr, 2011-13. **Orgs:** Bd mem, Mapleton Pub Schs, 2011-13. **Honors/Awds:** Gatorade Player of the Year; named in hon, Darius Holland Day, State NM, 1997; state's Defensive Player, Albuquerque Journal Super Bowl champion XXXI. **Special Achievements:** Holland earned all-State and all-District honors as a junior and a senior, Champion, Super Bowl XXXI; Films: 1995 NFL Draft, 1995; Super Bowl XXXI, 1997; Super Bowl XXXII, 1998. TV Series: "NFL on FOX", 1995. **Business Addr:** Pastor, True Life Church, 130 Executive Dr Suite 8, Newark, DE 19702, **Business Phone:** (302)983-0483.

### HOLLAND, DORREEN ANTOINETTE

Educator. **Personal:** Born Jul 29, 1968, Charlottesville, VA; daughter of Earl. **Educ:** Va Union Univ, BS, 1990. **Career:** Locust Grove Elem Sch, 5th grade teacher, 1990-93; N side Christian Sch, 1-4 gr teacher, summer sch; Charlottesville Sch Syst, proj yes teacher, 1993-94; Fluvanna County Sch Syst, chap one resource teacher, 1994-. **Orgs:** Secy, Sr Class, 1986-96; freedom funder organizer, Nat Asn Advan Colored People, 1993-; Am Heart Asn, 1993-; Bible Study, art teacher, 1993-; Youth Organizer Church, 1993-. **Home Addr:** 3699 Rising Sun Rd, Palmyra, VA 22963-4022, **Home Phone:** (434)589-8603. **Business Addr:** Teacher, Fluvanna County Public Schools, 14455 James Madison Hwy, Palmyra, VA 22963, **Business Phone:** (434)589-8318.

### HOLLAND, EDWARD, JR.

Television producer, singer, songwriter. **Personal:** Born Oct 30, 1939, Detroit, MI. **Career:** Films: The Martins, 2001; Cradle 2 the Grave, 2003; I'll Be There, 2003; Zodiac, 2007; Albums: The Complete Eddie Holland, Eddie Holland; Songs: "You", 1958; "Merry-Go-Round", 1959; "The Last Laugh", 1960; "Magic Mirror", 1960; "Because I Love Her", 1960; "Jamie", 1961; "Darling I Hum Our Song", 1962; "If It's Love (It's Alright)", 1962; "If Cleopatra Took A Chance", 1962; "You Deserve What You Got", 1962; "Leaving Here", 1963; "Baby Shake", 1963; "I'm on the Outside Looking In", 1963; "Just Ain't Enough Love", 1964; "Candy to Me", 1964; TV series: "Funhouse", 2000; "Hard Cases", 2003; "Michael Buble: Caught in the Act", 2005; Hollad-Dozier-Holland, mem songwriting & producing team, owner, currently. **Honors/Awds:** Inductee, Rock & Roll Hall of Fame, 1990; BMI Icon Award, 2003. **Business Addr:** Owner, Holland-Dozier-Holland, 1800 N Highland Ave Suite 124, Los Angeles, CA 90028, **Business Phone:** (323)463-2391.

### HOLLAND, ETHEL MARIE

Nurse. **Personal:** Born Oct 31, 1946, Washington, DC; married Reginald D Johnson. **Educ:** Immaculate Conception Acad, Wash, DC, HSD, 1964; Mt Mrty Col Ynktn SD, BS, 1968; Nursing Cath Univ Am Wash DC, MS, 1974. **Career:** Walter Reed Army Hosp, Wash, DC, staff nurse, 1968-69; 91st E Vac Hosp Vietnam, asst head nurse, 1969-70; DC Gen Hosp, clin nurse, Dept Pediat, 1970-73; Childrens Hosp Nat Med Ctr, Wash, DC, serv dir, Acute Care, 1974; DC Dept Health, Bur Comm, coord. **Orgs:** DC Nurses Asn, 1968-88; Sigma Theta Tau Kappa Chap, Wash, DC, 1974; vol, Ancst Neighborhood Clin, Wash, DC, 1974; Black Nurses Asn Greater Metro Area, 1978-; Ethnic Nurses Adv Health Care Among Minorities, 1978-80; vpres, Regist Nurse Exam Bd, 1979-88. **Honors/Awds:** Inducted into Nat Hon Soc for Nurses; Army Cmndtn Medal Mrtrs Serv Vietnam, 1970; papers presented Nurse Care of Pts who Fail to Thrive, 1979; Patterns of Elimination, 1976; Nursing Care of Patients with Sickle Cell Anemia, 1975. **Home Addr:** 2128 32nd Pl SE, Washington, DC 20020. **Business Addr:** Coordinator, DC Department of Health, 6323 Ga Ave NW, Washington, DC 20011, **Business Phone:** (202)576-9335.

### HOLLAND, LOUIS A.

Executive. **Personal:** children: Lou Jr. **Educ:** Univ Wis, BS, agr econ, 1965; Loyola Univ, Chicago, Grad Sch Bus. **Career:** Football player; UW football team, Chicago Bears, Brit Columbia Lions; Holland Capital Mgt LP, managing partner & chief investment officer, 1991-, chief exec officer, Founding Partner & Investment Strategist; HCM Investment Inc, Pres & chief exec officer; Lou Holland Growth Fund, pres, prin exec officer & portfolio mgr; Hartford Large Cap Growth Hls Fund, Managing Partner, chief exec officer, founding partner & investment strategist; AG Becker Paribas Inc, vpres; AmerUs Life, dir, managing partner, vice chmn, 2005-, chief investment officer, investment advisor, 2006-; Independent Dir Athene USA, 2005-; Indianapolis Life Ins Co, managing partner, vice chmn, chief investment officer, investment advisor & dir, 2006-; Amerus Annuity Group, managing partner & dir, 2006-; Univ Wis Found, vice chmn; Am Beacon Holland Large Cap Growth Fund, prin exec officer, pres & trustee. **Orgs:** Vice chmn, Univ Wis Found; dir, Assoc Gov Bd Univ; bd dir, Packaging Corp Am; bd dir, McCormick Theol Sem; bd dir, Univ Wis, Madison Col Agr & Life Sci; Kappa Alpha Psi fraternity; founder, Holland Health Emotions Res Fund; bd dir, Nat Asn Securities Professionals, Northwestern Memorial Hosp, Am Gov Bd Cols & Univs & Northwestern Mutual Ser Fund; dir, Index 400 Stock Fund, 2003; dir, Int Equity Fund, 2003; dir, Packaging Corp. Am, 2001; Trustee, Lou Holland Growth Fund; Dir, Asn Gov Boards Univs & Cols; Adv Dir Int Found Employee Benefit Plans; active mem local civic & bus orgn. **Business Addr:** Managing Partner, Chief Investment Officer, Holland Capital Management LP, 1 N Wacker Dr Suite 700, Chicago, IL 60606, **Business Phone:** (312)553-4830.

### HOLLAND, DR. LOYS MARIE

Health services administrator. **Personal:** Born Jun 9, 1950, Carp, MS; daughter of James Lee Flagg and Ora Lee Flagg. **Educ:** Loop City Col, Harold Wash Univ, AA, 1971; Nat Col Educ, BA, 1974. **Career:** Chicago Dept Health, clerical supvr, 1975-95, pub health adminr, 1995-, regional adminr, currently; Robert Taylor Initative, dir, 1996-97. **Orgs:** Adv bd, Can Armament Res & Develop Estab, 1995-; adv bd, Holman Health Ctr, 1995-; Parent-teacher Asn, 1993-, pres, 2000-01, Christ King Luran Sch; Grand Blvd Found, 1995-; bd dir, Chicago Pub Sch, Homeless Educ Prog. **Home Addr:** 431 E 48th Pl, Chicago, IL 60615-1403, **Home Phone:** (773)285-3879. **Business Addr:** Regional Administrator, Chicago Department of Health, 4410 S State St, Chicago, IL 60609, **Business Phone:** (312)747-1020.

### HOLLAND, MAJOR LEONARD

Educator, architect. **Personal:** Born Mar 8, 1941, Tuskegee, AL; son of Soloman M and Emily L; married Sceiva; children: Mark, Michael & John. **Educ:** Howard Univ, BA, 1963. **Career:** Fry & Welch Architects, 1966-69; Tuskegee Univ, assoc prof, 1969-; Maj Holland Architect & Assocs PC, vpres, 1972, pres, owner & prin, chief exec officer, currently. **Orgs:** Bd mem, Tuskegee Univ; fel Am Inst Architects, 1992. **Home Addr:** 801 Ave B, Tuskegee, AL 36088, **Home Phone:** (205)727-4494. **Business Addr:** President & Owner, Principal & Chief Executive Officer, Major L Holland Architect & Associates PC, 111 S Main St Suite B, Tuskegee, AL 36083, **Business Phone:** (334)727-4079.

### HOLLAND, ROBERT, JR. (BOB HOLLAND)

Chief executive officer, executive, executive director. **Personal:** Born Jan 1, 1940, Albion, MI; son of Robert Sr; married Barbara Jean; children: Robert III, Kheri & Jaclyn. **Educ:** Union Col, BS, mech engineering, 1962; Bernard Baruch Col, MBA, 1969. **Career:** Mobil Corp, engr, 1962-68; McKinsey & Co, assoc & partner, 1968-91; Rokher-J Consult Firm & Holding Co, chmn & chief exec officer, 1981-84, 1991-95; City Mkt Inc, chmn & chief exec officer, 1984-87; Gilreath Mfg, sr vpres & chmn, 1987-91; Ben & Jerry's Homemade Inc, pres & chief exec officer, 1995-96; WorkPlace Integraters, pres & chief exec officer, 1997-2001; Cordova, Smart & Williams LLC, advisor, currently; Williams Capital Partners, gen partner & indust specialist, currently; Pepsico, adv bd. **Orgs:** Bd mem, Nat Col Athletic Asn; New York Bd C's Aid Socs; Lincoln Ctr Theater; bd trustee, Spellman Col; bd dir, Neptune Orient Lines LTD; bd dir, YUM! Brands Inc; bd dir, Carver Bancorp Inc; bd mem, Tricon Global Restaurants, 1997-2002; bd dir, Lexmark Int Inc, 1998-; Bill Bradley Pres; bd dir, Res Corp; Sharpton 2004. **Special Achievements:** First African American to head a major corporation. **Business Addr:** Director, Lexmark International Inc, 740 W New Cir Rd, Lexington, KY 40511, **Business Phone:** (859)232-2000.

### HOLLAND, ROBIN W.

Educator, writer. **Personal:** Born May 23, 1953, Columbus, OH; daughter of Robert R Jackson (deceased) and Elizabeth W; married Ralph V Jr. **Educ:** Ohio State Univ, BS, 1974, MA, 1975. **Career:** Columbus Pub Sch, reading teacher, 1975-76, classroom teacher, 1976-86, gifted educ teacher, 1977-80, consult teacher, 1986-89, reading recover yearly literacy teacher, 1990-2002, coach intervention specialist, 2002-, Reading Dept & Title I Dept, coord; Salem Elem Sch, teacher; Columbus Area Writing Proj, co dir, 2005-. **Orgs:** Nat Educ Asn, 1975-; Reading Recovery Coun N Am, 1993-; Order Daughters King, 1996-; St Philip Episcopal Church; Int Reading Asn; Nat Coun Teachers Eng; Nat Writing Proj, 2005-; co-dir, Columbus Area Writing Proj. **Home Addr:** 4991 Lyle Rd, Columbus, OH 43229, **Home Phone:** (614)436-4481.

### HOLLAND, DR. SPENCER H.

Educator, president (organization), psychologist. **Personal:** Born Sep 11, 1939, Suffern, NY. **Educ:** Rowan Univ, BA, sec sci educ, 1965; Columbia Univ, MA, develop psychol, 1968, MPhill, PhD, 1976. **Career:** Burnet Jr HS, teacher, 1965-67; Essex Co Col, asst prof, 1968-73, chmn, psychol dept, 1970-73; Harlem Interfaith Coun Serv, prev ment health teacher, 1974-75; Child Abuse & Neglect Proj Div Pupil Personnel Serv, Wash, DC Pub Sch, coordr, 1976-90; Morgan State Univ, Ctr Educ African-Am Males, dir; Nehemiah Consult Group Inc, vpres, currently; Proj 2000 Inc, pres, founder, 1994-, exec dir, 1994-2005; Morgan State Univ, Ctr Educating African-Am Males, founder. **Orgs:** Am Psychol Asn; Asn Black Psychologists, 1972-. **Honors/Awds:** Nat Fel Fund Fel, 1973-76. **Home Addr:** 2055 36th St SE, Washington, DC 20020. **Business Addr:** President, Founder, Project 2000 Inc, 411 8th St SE, Washington, DC 20003-2833, **Business Phone:** (202)543-2309.

### HOLLAND-CALBERT, MARY ANN

Registered nurse. **Personal:** Born Jul 12, 1941, New York, NY; daughter of James Kirkland and Doris Wiles Vance; married Clarence E; children: Toussaint Michael. **Educ:** Wash Tech Inst, AAS, 1976; Univ Dc, BSN, 1987. **Career:** St Elizabeth Hosp, Washington DC, psychiatric nurse coord, 1970-88; Greater Southeast Community Hosp, Washington DC, psychiatric nurse, 1988-. **Orgs:** Nat Coun Negro Women, 1976-; exec sec, 1983-88, Chi Eta Phi Sorority Inc, 1976-; Top Ladies Distinction, 1986-; St Mark Presbyterian Church. **Home Addr:** 11963 Autumnwood Lane, Fort Washington, MD 20744, **Home Phone:** (301)292-8554. **Business Addr:** Psychiatric Nurse, Greater Southwest Community Hospital, 1310 Southern Ave SE 4-E, Washington, DC 20032-4699, **Business Phone:** (202)574-6716.

### HOLLAND-CORN, KEDRA

Basketball player. **Personal:** Born Nov 5, 1974; married Jesse. **Educ:** Univ Ga, health & phys educ, 1997. **Career:** Basketball player; San Jose Lasers, guard, 1997-99; Sacramento Monarchs, guard, 1999-2002; Detroit Shock, guard, 2003, 2006; Houston Comets, 2004-. **Orgs:** Fel Christian Athletes. **Business Addr:** Professional Basketball Player, Houston Comets, 1510 Polk St, Houston, TX 77002, **Business Phone:** (713)627-9622.

### HOLLEY, REV. JIM

Clergy, administrator. **Personal:** Born Dec 5, 1943, Philadelphia, PA; son of Charles James Sr and Effie Mae King; married Phyllis Dean; children: Tiffani Dionne. **Educ:** Wayne State Univ, PhD, higher educ, Detroit, Mich; Drew Univ, DMin, econ develop; Chicago Theol Sem, BA, divinity old testament, MA, divinity new testament; Tenn State Univ, BS, pre-law, MS, int rels. **Career:** Ashland Theol Sem, dean; Little Rock Baptist Church, Detroit, Mich, pastor, 1972-, sr pastor; Cognos Advert, pres & chief exec officer, Detroit, 1988-; Country Preacher Foods Inc, pres & chief exec officer, currently; E/W Cargo Airlines, founder & pres, currently; Valet Syst, Mich, founder & pres, currently. **Orgs:** Bd mem, Woodward Ave Action Asn; chmn, Budget Personnel & Training Policy& Promotional Appeals; founder & chmn, Detroit Acad Arts & Sci, 1997; Bd Police Commissioners, 2004-. **Honors/Awds:** Michiganian of the Year, Detroit News; One of the top five ministers in Michigan, Detroit Free Press; One of the "Foremost Voices in Detroit", Crain's Business Magazine; Trumpet Awards, 2010. **Special Achievements:** Author of several books. **Home Addr:** 1465 Balmoral Dr, Detroit, MI 48203, **Home Phone:** (313)368-3600. **Business Addr:** Pastor, Little Rock Baptist Church, 9000 Woodward Ave, Detroit, MI 48202, **Business Phone:** (313)872-2900.

### HOLLEY, JOHN CLIFTON

Military leader, association executive. **Personal:** Born Jan 8, 1940, Virginia Beach, VA; son of Edward L and Hazel L; married Harriett N; children: John C & Barbara J Davis Robinson. **Educ:** NC Agr & Tech State Univ, BS, chem, 1961; Am Univ, MS, polit sci & govt, 1977. **Career:** Military leader (retired), association executive; AUS progressive mgr, key leader, comdr Army units from platoon to brigade, staff officer highest level Dept Army, 1961-91; Maynard Jackson Youth Found, pres, 1992-2010. **Orgs:** Am Acad Polit Sci & Social Sci, 1980-; Am Univ Alumni Asn, 1987-; Acad Polit Sci, 1990-; Ben Hill United Methodist Church, treas, Class Benjamin, pres, finance comt, sec, Invest Club, 1991-; pres, NC A&T Alumni Asn, Atlanta chap, 1993-97; lt gov, Kiwanis Int, 1998-99; Asn AUS; Nat Asn Advan Colored People. **Honors/Awds:** NC A&T State Univ, Distinguished Mil Grad, 1961; Leadership Award, 1996; Man of the Yr, Ben Hill United Methodist Church, 1997; Int Civil Rights Ctr & Mus, Sit-in Participants Award, 1998; Mentor of Excellence, Teray Mill Sch, Dekalb County Sch Syst, 1996. **Home Addr:** 100 Creek View Trl, Fayetteville, GA 30214-7228, **Home Phone:** (770)461-3469.

### HOLLEY, KENNETH

Executive. **Educ:** Univ Pa, BS, civil & urban Engineering, 1982, Wharton Sch, MBA, int finance, 1987; Charter Financial Analyst designation, 1995. **Career:** Int Bus Mach, mkt rep, 1982-85; Saloman Bros, fixed-income salesman, 1987-89; Ward & Assocs Asset Mgt, portfolio mgr; African Develop Bank, Abidjan, Cote d'Ivoire, sr finance officer, 1990-93; Morgan Stanley Asset Mgt, co-mgr int equity portfolio, prin, 1993-2002; Atlanta Life Financial Group Inc, investment advisor, chief info officer & prin; Herndon Capital Mgt LLC, chief investment officer, portfolio mgr & prin, 2002-. **Honors/Awds:** "Black Enterprise," 75 Most Powerful Blacks on Wall Street, 2011. **Business Addr:** Principal & Portfolio Manager, Chief Investment Officer, Herndon Capital Management, 191 Peachtree St NE Suite 2500, Atlanta, GA 30303, **Business Phone:** (404)232-8801.

### HOLLEY, DR. SANDRA CAVANAUGH
Educator, pathologist, college administrator. **Personal:** Born Mar 30, 1943, Washington, DC; daughter of Clyde Howard and Rebecca Naomi Arthur; children: David Marshall. **Educ:** George Washington Univ, BA, 1965, MA, 1966; Univ Conn, PhD, 1979. **Career:** Rehab Ctr Eastern Fairfield Co, speech pathologist, supvr, 1966-69; Southern Conn State Univ, speech & lang pathologist, prof, commun dis, 1970-, Sch Grad Studies, dean. **Orgs:** Exec bd, 1971-83, fel, 1980 vpres & admin, 1982-85, pres elect, 1987-88, pres, 1988-, Am Speech-Lang-Hearing Asn; chmn, Humane Comn City New Haven, 1977-87; bd dir, NewHaven Vis Nurse Asn, 1977-79; bd dir, Am Nat Red Cross S Cent Chap, 1979-80; Afro-Am Hist Socs, 1982-83; Nat Black Asn Speech; bd dir, Foote Sch Asn, 1985-89. **Home Addr:** 215 Stimson Rd, New Haven, CT 06511. **Business Addr:** Dean, Southern Connecticut State University, Engleman Hall B018 501 Crescent St, New Haven, CT 06515-1355, **Business Phone:** (203)392-5234.

### HOLLEY, SHARON YVONNE
Librarian, administrator. **Personal:** Born Aug 15, 1949, Gainesville, FL; daughter of Johnnie Jordan and Rebecca Bryant Jordan; married Kenneth; children: Nzinga, Asantewa & Makeda. **Educ:** Santa Fe Community Col, Gainesville, FL, AA, 1968; Fla Atlantic Univ, Boca Raton, FL, BA, eng/educ, 1970; Wayne State Univ, Detroit, MI, MS, libr sci, 1972. **Career:** Librarian (retired), administrator; Juneteenth Buffalo Inc; Buffalo & Erie Co Pub Libr, Buffalo, NY, librn, 1972, coordr urban servs & exten servs adminr, currently; NY Freedom Trail, comnr, 1999; Harambee Bks & Crafts, owner; Cent Libr, C's Dept, head. **Orgs:** Afro-Am Hist Asn Niagara Frontier, 1977-; Kwanzaa Comt Buffalo, 1980-; Nat Asn Black Storytellers, 1986-; Black Caucus Am Libr Asn, 1990-; African-Am Librarians Western NY, 1990-; mgr, Cent Libr's C's Dept, 1997; founding mem, Spin-A-Story Tellers Western NY; coordr, Tradition Keepers; Nat Storytelling Network; comt, African Am Ancestral Heritage Tour; founding mem, Daughters Creative Sound; Buffalo Geneal Soc African Diaspora; Buffalo Quarters Hist Soc; Asn Study Class African Civilizations. **Special Achievements:** First African American Historical Brochure for Western New York. **Home Addr:** 31 St Paul Mall, Buffalo, NY 14209, **Home Phone:** (716)886-1399. **Business Addr:** Extension Services Administrator, Buffalo & Erie County Public Library, 1 Lafayette Sq, Buffalo, NY 14203-1887, **Business Phone:** (716)858-8900.

### HOLLIDAY, BILLIE. See HOLLIDAY-HAYES, WILHELMINA EVELYN.

### HOLLIDAY, DIMETRY GIOVONNI. See HOLLIDAY, VONNIE.

### HOLLIDAY, DR. GAYLE
President (organization), business owner. **Personal:** married Harold Jr. **Educ:** BA; PhD. **Career:** Kans City Transp Authority, dep dir; G&H Consult LLC, owner, pres, currently. **Orgs:** St James Methodist Church; Greater Kans City Health Care Found; Kans City Conv & Visitors Asn, 2011-. **Business Addr:** President, G & H Consulting LLC, 6144 Brooklyn Ave, Kansas City, MO 64130, **Business Phone:** (816)363-8006.

### HOLLIDAY, JENNIFER-YVETTE
Singer, actor. **Personal:** Born Oct 19, 1960, Houston, TX; daughter of Omie Lee and Jennie Thomas; married Rev Andre Woods; married Billy Meadows. **Educ:** Berklee Col Music, Boston, PhD, music, 2000. **Career:** Stage performances: Your Arms Too Short to Box with God, 1979-80; Dreamgirls, 1981; Sing, Mahalia, Sing, 1985. TV series: "Saturday Night Live", 1982; "The Love Boat", 1986; "In Performance at the White House", 1988. Albums: Dreamgirls, 1981; Feel My Soul, 1983; Say You Love Me, 1985; Get Close to My Love, 1987; Im On Your Side, 1991; On & On, 1995; The Best of Jennifer Holliday, 1996; 20th Century Masters - The Millennium Collection: The Best of Jennifer Holliday, 2000; Duet with Najiyah Through The Storm, 2006; Goodness & Mercy, 2011; The Song Is You, 2014. Songs: "And I Am Telling You Im Not Going", 1982; "I Am Changing", 1982; "I Am Love", 1983; "Just Let Me Wait", 1983; "Hard Time for Lovers", 1985; "No Frills Love", 1996; "Heart on the Line", 1987; Im on Your Side", 1991; "Love Stories", 1991; "A Womans Got The Power", 2000; "Think It Over", 2000; "And I Am Telling You Im Not Going, 2001 & 2007; "Givin Up", 2007; "God is Faithful", 2011; "Touch", 2014. **Honors/Awds:** Grammy Award, 1981; Tony Award, 1981; Antoinette Perry Award, Best Actress in a Musical, 1982; Drama Desk Award for Outstanding Featured Actress in a Musical, 1981; Theatre Awards Outstanding Broadway Debut, 1982; Drama Desk Award, Best Lead Actress in a Musical, 1982; Grammy Award, Best R&B Performance-Female, 1983; Grammy Award Best New Artist, 1983; Image Award, Nat Asn Advan Colored People, 1983; Grammy Award, Best Inspirational Performance-Female, 1986; Distinguished Alumni Award, Tex Southern Univ; honorary doctoral degree, Berklee Col Music. **Special Achievements:** Two-time Grammy Award-winning African-American singer & actress. **Home Addr:** Revival Tabernacle Church Christ, 3627 Mt Eliot St, Detroit, MI 48207, **Home Phone:** (313)579-3232. **Business Addr:** Actress, Singer, c/o Jendayi Productions, 1133 Broadway Suite 911, New York, NY 10010.

### HOLLIDAY, VONNIE (DIMETRY GIOVONNI HOLLIDAY)
Football player. **Personal:** Born Dec 11, 1975, Camden, SC; married Eboni; children: Kali & Joey. **Educ:** NC Univ, BCS. **Career:** Football player (retired); Green Bay Packers, right defensive end, 1998-99, left defensive end, 2000-02; Kans City Chiefs, right defensive end, 2003, defensive end, 2004; Miami Dolphins, right defensive tackle, 2005-07, right defensive end, 2008; Denver Broncos, defensive end, 2009; Wash Redskins, defensive end, 2010; Ariz Cardinals, 2011, defensive end, 2012. **Orgs:** Vonnie Holliday Found, 2001-; Kids Co; chmn, United Way Kershaw County, SC, 2003-04; Camden Bulldogs football camp. **Honors/Awds:** South Carolina's Male Professional Athlete of the Year, South Carolina Athletic Hall of Fame, 1999; Defensive Rookie of the Month honor, Nat Football League, 1998; Hall of Fame, San Francisco 49ers. **Special Achievements:** Ranked Third in the League among Defensive Tackles. **Home Addr:** , Camden, SC. **Business Addr:** Founder, Vonnie Holliday Foundation, **Business Phone:** (404)229-8125.

### HOLLIDAY-HAYES, WILHELMINA EVELYN (BILLIE HOLLIDAY)
Government official, executive director, police officer. **Personal:** Born Jacksonville, FL; daughter of John and Leah Ervin; married John; children: Stepson & John W II. **Educ:** NY Univ, BS; Columbia Sch Social Work, grad studies; New Sch Social Res, MA, human resources; Inst Mediation & Conflict Resolution, cert mediator. **Career:** Government Official (retired); New York Dept Social Serv, case worker, 1956-61; New York Off Probation, ct reporting officer, 1961-68; New York Police Dept, asst dir & exec dir, 1968-74; Vera Inst Justice & Pretrial Serv Agency, bor dir, 1974-76; Bd Parole, NY, comnr, 1976-84; New York Police Dept, dep comnr community affairs, 1984-94; Mt Vernon Police Dept, dep police comnr, 1994-95, comnr, 1995-96; NACCP, Manhattan, pres, currently. **Orgs:** Hon pres, Friends N side Ctr Child Develop, 1974-; pres, Mid Manhattan Nat Asn Advan Colored People, 2000-; vpres & bd dir, Wiltwyck Sch Boys; chairperson & bd dir, Wiltwyck Brooklyn Div; bd dir, Exodus House; consult, Equal Opportunity & Womens Career Mag; fel organizer, Harlem Improv Proj; Delta Sigma Theta; pres, Black Resources & Issues Now (BRAIN); adv, Greater New York Coun Boy Scouts Am & Law Enforcement Explorer Scouts; consult, Key Women Am; Manhattan Urban League; Women Criminal Justice. **Honors/Awds:** Humanitarian Award, New York Chap Continental Soc Inc, 1985; So journer Truth Loyalty Award, Coalition Black Trade Unionists, 1986; Achievement Award, Fedn Negro Civil Assocs New York, 1986; Govt & Community Service Award, Nat Coun Negro Women, 1989. **Special Achievements:** AME's Top 100 Black Women, 1985. **Home Addr:** 157-10 Riverside Dr W, New York, NY 10032, **Home Phone:** (212)795-5066. **Business Addr:** President, Mid-Manhattan NAACP, 270 W 96th St, New York, NY 10025, **Business Phone:** (212)749-2323.

### HOLLIE, PAMELA GAIL. See KLUGE, PAMELA HOLLIE.

### HOLLIER, DWIGHT LEON, JR.
Football player, football coach. **Personal:** Born Apr 21, 1969, Hampton, VA; married Chandra; children: Deandre. **Educ:** Univ NC, BS, speech commun & psychol, 1991; Nova Southeastern Univ, MS, men health coun, 2000. **Career:** Football player (retired); football coach; Miami Dolphins, right inside linebacker, 1992, middle linebacker, 1993, right linebacker, 1994-95, left linebacker, 1996, linebacker, 1997, 1998-99; Indianapolis Colts, middle linebacker, 2000; Carolinas Healthcare Syst, psychotherapist, 2001-04; Tony Dungy, Indianapolis, coaching intern, 2004; Frankfurt Galaxy, coach, 2004; Family Ctr, sch based intervention therapist, 2005; Stanly County Schs, sch social worker & asst football coach, 2005-06; Access Family Serv, foster care prog mgr & case mgt supvr, 2006-07; Pt After Transition Coun & Consult, pres & lic prof counr, 2007-13; Southeast Psych, lic prof counr, 2009-13; Mind Over Body Southeast Psych, psychotherapist & sports psychol consult, 2011-13; Nat Bd Cert Counr & Lic Prof Counr, currently. **Orgs:** Dir transition & clin serv, Nat Football League, 2013-15, vpres, wellness & clin serv, 2015-; bd residential & support Serv; vpres, NFL Alumni Carolinas chap; vpres, Charlotte Chap NFL retired players union. **Honors/Awds:** Patterson Metal, Univ NC. **Special Achievements:** Film: 1992 NFL Draft, 1992. TV Special: "1992 AFC Championship Game", 1993. **Home Addr:** 5012 Woodview Lane, Matthews, NC 28104-8057. **Business Addr:** Vice President, Wellness & Clinical Services, National Football League, 345 Pk Ave, New York, NY 10154, **Business Phone:** (212)450-2000.

### HOLLIMAN, DAVID L. See Obituaries Section.

### HOLLIMAN-CHIBUZO, ARGIE N. (ARGIE HOLLIMAN-CHIBUZO)
Association executive, president (organization). **Personal:** Born Jun 8, 1957, Grand Rapids, MI; daughter of John and Mattie M; married James; children: Stephine Bryant, Stephen Bryant Jr & Shawn Bryant. **Educ:** Grand Valley State Univ, commun, 1979; Columbia Sch Broadcasting, BA, commun, 1982. **Career:** WEHB Radio, host & producer, 1980-82; WKWM Radio, news dir, 1982-87; Sarah Allen Family Neighborhood Ctr, tutorial serv dir, 1987-88; S E End Neighborhood Asn, crime prev dir, 1988-92; Creative Commun Ctr, pres; GRTV, channel 25, pres, chief exec off, prod, Time To Talk, host, exec producer, currently; YWCA, vol servs coun ctr coordr, 1990-; WKTV. **Orgs:** Chmn pub rel, PTA, 1988-89; chmn, Govs Task Force Youth Initiatives, 1988-89; co-founder, Burton St Church Christ, 1989; co-chmn, pub relminority affairs, Chamber Com, 1991-92; chmn, Grand Rapids Cable Access Ctr, 1992; co-founder, Oakdale HR Ctr; Coailition Rep Govt; co-chmn, racism rtsk force, YWCA, 1992. **Special Achievements:** Actress, Community Mental Health Theatre Troupe, 1992. **Business Addr:** Producer, GRTV, 711 Bridge St NW, Grand Rapids, MI 49504, **Business Phone:** (616)459-4788.

### HOLLIN, KENNETH RONALD (KEN HOLLIN)
School administrator. **Personal:** Born Nov 6, 1948, Yuma, AZ; son of James T and Cleo E Cook; married Michelle Brown; children: Cheyenne, Kenya, James & Antonio. **Educ:** Ariz Western Col, Yuma, AZ, AA, 1968; Ariz State Univ, Tempe, AZ, BA, educ & polit sci, 1973. **Career:** Phoenix Job Corps Ctr, Phoenix, Ariz, counr, 1973-75; Phoenix Opportunities Industrialization Ctr, Phoenix, Ariz, counr, 1975-80; Educ Opportunity Ctr, Phoenix, Ariz, counr, 1978-80; Abbey Rents, Phoenix, Ariz, truck driver, 1980-82; Educ Opportunity Ctr, Phoenix, Ariz, counr, 1982-85; Ariz State Univ, Tempe, Ariz, asst dir stud recruitment undergrad admis, 1985-2009, asst dir, stud recruitment/off dean students, 2009-12; hons acad advisor, 2012-. **Orgs:** Vpres, Ariz Multicultural Stud Serv Asn, 1987-89; chmn, Chap I Parent Coun, Phoenix Elem Sch Dst 1, 1987-89; pres, Garfield Sch PTO, 1987-90; planning comt mem, Statewide Parent Involvement Conf, Ariz Dept Educ, 1988-89; pres, Citizen's Adv Coun, Phoenix Elem Sch Dst1, 1989-90; educ outreach & stud serv, dir, Ariz State Univ Art Mus. **Home Addr:** 11804 N 111th Pl, Scottsdale, AZ 85259, **Home Phone:** (480)451-1195. **Business Addr:** Honors Academic Advisor, Arizona State University, 1151 S Forest Ave, Tempe, AZ 85281, **Business Phone:** (480)965-0920.

### HOLLINGER, REGINALD J. (REG HOLLINGER)
Executive. **Personal:** children: 2. **Educ:** Williams Col, BA; Harvard Bus Sch, MBA. **Career:** Morgan Stanley & Co, Corp Finance Dept, prin, 1989-97; PaineWebber Inc, managing dir, 1997-99, Telecom Banking, managing dir & group head; Advanced Communications Group Inc; Chase Securities Inc, managing dir, 1999-2000; Archway Broadcasting Group LLC, dir, currently; Advan Commun Group Inc, bd dir, dir; Radiovisa Corp, dir, currently; Quetzal & JP Morgan Partners, co-founder, managing partner, 2000-10; Montclair Art Mus, bd trustee, treas, pres, currently; Radiovisa Corp, dir, currently; SunTrust Robinson Humphrey Inc, managing dir, 2011-12; Fuse Sci Inc, bd dir, 2013-14; CastleOak Securities, managing dir, 2014-. **Orgs:** Bd dir, Advan Commun Group Inc. **Home Addr:** 71 Hathaway Lane, Essex Fells, NJ 07021, **Home Phone:** (973)364-1398. **Business Addr:** Managing Director, CastleOak Securities, L.P., 110 E 59th St 2nd Fl, New York, NY 10022, **Business Phone:** (646)521-6700.

### HOLLINGSWORTH, ALFRED DELANO
Executive. **Personal:** Born Oct 26, 1942, Jackson, MS; married Hattie. **Educ:** Univ Colo, BS, psychol & speech path; Univ Wash, MA. **Career:** Crown Zellarbach, jr exec sales dept, 1965-67; Fiberboard Corp, sales mgr, 1967-68; Sheet Plant Corp, pres, 1968-; Aldelano Packaging Corp, founder, owner, pres & cheif exec officer, 1968-; Alhatti Pvt Christian Resort & Retreat Ctr, owner, founder, 1990-; Squat Corp, pres & owner, 1970-; B.O.S.S. Movement, coach, founder, 1985-; Oral Roberts Univ, cabinet mem, 2001-. Author: Vertical Leap. **Orgs:** Bd dir, Black Bus Asn; LAC C Chmn "Hot Seat" prog; Rotary Club; foundr, Christian Bus Ministries, 1985-; bd trustee, Promise Keepers, 1990-; Youth Bus Prog; Nat Minority Supplier Develop Coun; bd mem, Save Africas C. **Home Addr:** 24021 Lodge Pole Rd, Diamond Bar, CA 91765. **Business Addr:** Owner, Chief Executive Officer, Aldelano Packaging Corp, 3525 Walnut Ave, Chino, CA 91710, **Business Phone:** (909)861-3970.

### HOLLINGSWORTH, JOHN ALEXANDER
Educator, teacher. **Personal:** Born Sep 25, 1925, Owego, NY; son of John Sr (deceased) and Florence Eve Haley (deceased); married Winifred Stoelting; children: 5. **Educ:** NC A&T State Univ, BS, agr, 1950, MS, adult educ, 1985; NC Cent Univ, MS, biol, 1960; Cornell Univ, attended 1963. **Career:** Educator (retired); Fayetteville City Schs, sci teacher, 1959-73, biol instr, 163-64, sci & math coordr, 1968-83; NC A&T State Univ, grad stud, 1983-85, staff develop intern; consult, writer, 1985. **Orgs:** Pres, Fayetteville City Unit NCTA, 1968-71; pres, NC Sci Teachers Asn, 1971-73; Fayetteville Airport Comn, 1973-79; grad stud intern, Maj Int Stress Mgt & Prev Health Care, 1983-85; life mem, NEA; NCAE; NEA-R; Black World Found, Nat Mus Am Indian; Ecol Action/Comn Ground; NC Retired Sch Personnel; Nat Retired Teacher Asn; life mem, Nat Asn Black Veterans; A&T Alumni Asn; NC Retired Govt Employees Asn; Inst Noetic Sci. **Home Addr:** 61 Otalco Dr, Cherokee Village, AR 72529-6407, **Home Phone:** (870)257-3096.

### HOLLINS, PROF. JOSEPH EDWARD
School administrator. **Personal:** Born Dec 14, 1927, Baton Rouge, LA; married Louise T; children: Reginald, Larry, Patrice & Stephanie R. **Educ:** Leland Col, BS, 1952; NMex Styland Univ, attended 1957; Southern Univ, ME, 1969. **Career:** Thomas A Levy, 1950-60; Upper Marengauin, prin, 1960. **Orgs:** Alderman Town Maringouin, 1970. **Home Addr:** 10725 Ctr St, PO Box 156, Maringouin, LA 70757-0156, **Home Phone:** (225)625-2601.

### HOLLINS, LIONEL EUGENE
Basketball player, basketball coach. **Personal:** Born Oct 19, 1953, Arkansas City, KS; married Angela; children: Christopher, Anthony, Jacqueline & Austin. **Educ:** Ariz State Univ, attended 1975. **Career:** Basketball player (retired), basketball coach; Portland Trail blazers, guard, 1975-80; Philadelphia 76ers, 1980-82; San Diego Clippers, 1982-83; Detroit Pistons, 1983-84; Houston Rockets, 1984-85; Ariz State Univ, asst coach, 1985-88; Phoenix Suns, asst coach, 1988-95; Utah, 1993; AZ, 1995; Vancouver Grizzlies, asst coach, 1995-99, head coach, 1999-2000; Memphis Grizzlies, asst coach, 1999-2000, 2002-07, interim head coach, 2004, coach, 2009-13; Las Vegas Silver Bandits, coach, 2000-01; St Louis Skyhawks, coach, 2002; Brooklyn Nets, coach, 2014-. **Orgs:** Nat Basketball Asn Championship Team, 1996-97. **Home Addr:** 1206 1500 Hornby St, Vancouver, BC V6Z 2R1. **Business Addr:** Head Coach, Brooklyn Nets, 15 MetroTech Ctr 11th Fl, Brooklyn, NY 11201, **Business Phone:** (718)933-3000.

### HOLLIS, MARY LEE
Business owner, real estate agent. **Personal:** Born May 15, 1942, Miller, GA; married Albert H; children: Naomi M & Pat Ann. **Educ:** Sacramento City & State Col; Real Estate Sch, cert. **Career:** Hollis Small Family Home CCF, owner, dir & broker, currently. **Orgs:** Adv bd, Sacramento Bd Realtors; Sacramento Asn Artists; Sacramento Asn C; Trinity Church Choir. **Business Addr:** Owner, Director, Hollis Small Family Home CCF, 1297 Valley Brook Ave, Sacramento, CA 95831, **Business Phone:** (916)424-5213.

### HOLLOMAN, J. PHILLIP
President (organization), executive. **Personal:** married Gail. **Educ:** Univ Cincinnati, BS, civil engineering. **Career:** Cintas, vpres engineering & construct, 1996-2000, Distrib/Prod Planning Div, vpres, 2000-03, exec champion six sigma initiatives, 2003-05, sr vpres global supply chain mgt, 2005-08, pres & chief operating officer, 2008-; Rockwell Automation Inc, dir, 2013-. **Orgs:** Adv coun, Fla A&M Sch

Bus & Indust; bd mem, Urban League Greater Cincinnati. **Honors/Awds:** "Black Enterprise," The 100 Most Powerful Executives in Corporate America, 2010. **Business Addr:** President, Chief Operating Officer, Cintas Corp, 6800 Cintas Blvd, Cincinnati, OH 45262, **Business Phone:** (513)459-1200.

### HOLLOMAN, THADDEUS BAILEY, SR.

Banker. **Personal:** Born Jun 30, 1955, Newport News, VA; son of Paul and Elsie; married Renee D Brown; children: Thaddeus Jr & Kelsey. **Educ:** Howard Univ, BBA, 1977; Old Dom Univ, pub admin, 1983; Univ Va, Va Bankers Asn, Sch Bank Mgt, 1992. **Career:** Peat Marwick Mitchell & Co, auditor, 1977-79; Stud Loan Mkt Assoc, acct, 1979; Hampton Univ, acct, 1979-81; City Newport News Va, auditor 1981-85; Community Fed Savings & Loan, 1985-90; Consol Bank, vpres; Old Pt Nat Bank, vpres, com loan officer, sr vpres, currently; Consol Bank & Trust Co, Hampton, asst vpres. **Orgs:** Bd trustee, C Waldo Scott Ctr HOPE; Newport News Educ Found, currently; 100 Black Men Am Inc; Newport News Sch Bd; Phi Beta Sigma Fraternity Inc; Va Bankers Asn, 1990; charter mem, citizens rev bd, Subsidized Housing, 1991-92; Nat Advan Asn Colored People; Newport News Va; Newport News Polit Action Comn, currently; treas, Peninsula Habitat Humanity; chmn, Bd Zoning Appeals, City Newport News, Va; Beta Gamma Sigma Bus Hon Soc; Newport News Econ & Indust Develop Authority, currently; bd dir, Riverside Health Syst, 2006-; Riverside Tappahannock Hosp. **Home Addr:** 323 Woodbrook Run, Newport News, VA 23608-1258, **Home Phone:** (757)930-3012. **Business Addr:** President, Newport News Education Foundation, 12465 Warwick Blvd, Newport News, VA 23606, **Business Phone:** (757)591-4500.

### HOLLOWAY, ARDITH E.

Executive. **Personal:** Born Oct 9, 1958, Youngstown, OH; daughter of James E Matthews (deceased) and J Faye; married Kenneth; children: Steffany & Autumn. **Educ:** Ohio State Univ, BA, speech commun, 1981. **Career:** Gulf Oil, vital source speaker, 1980-82; Metro Page Columbus, sales rep, 1982-84, relief dist mgr, circulation dept, 1984-85; Neighbor News, acct exec, 1985-88; Columbus Dispatch, acct exec, retail advert, 1988-. **Orgs:** United Way Speakers League; Columbus Urban League, resource develop com; Dublin Black Parent Asn, equity com co-chair; Faith Mission, vol; Columbus Metrop Club; bd mem, Dahlberg Learning Ctr; bd mem, YMCA Black Achievers. **Home Addr:** 8619 Roscoe Pl, Dublin, OH 43017, **Home Phone:** (614)791-8822. **Business Addr:** Account Executive, Columbus Dispatch, 34 S 3rd St 5300 Crosswind, Columbus, OH 43215, **Business Phone:** (614)461-8819.

### HOLLOWAY, CECELIA

Executive director. **Educ:** Syracuse Univ, BS, bus admin & human resources, 1979; Utica Col, BS, bus admin & human resources, 1979. **Career:** Viacom, sr vpres, human resources generalist, 1988-97; Spelling Entertainment Group Inc, sr vpres, human resources, 1997-2000; Paramount Pictures, sr vpres, diversity, training & orgn develop, 2000-06; UBS Investment Bank, managing dir, human resources & diversity, americas, 2006-12, co-head, community affairs, cult & inclusion, 2011-12; TheBarnYardGroup, chief human resources & diversity officer, 2012-14; Lincoln Financial Media, AVP, Human Resources, 2014. **Orgs:** Bd trustee, Utica Col; pres, Women Film, 2006-; immediate Treas, Fairfield County CT Chap, 2014; immediate Treas, Jack & Jill Am, Stamford-Norwalk Chap, 2014. **Business Addr:** AVP, Human Resources, Lincoln Financial Media.

### HOLLOWAY, DOUGLAS V.

Executive. **Personal:** Born Jul 3, 1954, Pittsburgh, PA; son of Arnold and Hattie Keys; married L Susan Branche. **Educ:** Emerson Col, BS, mass commun, 1976; Columbia Univ, Grad Sch Bus, MBA, mkt & finance, 1978. **Career:** Gen Foods, asst prod mgr, 1978-79; CBS TV Network, financial anal, 1979-81; CBS Cable, sales rep, 1981-82; TV Cable Week, Time Inc, mgr nat acct, 1982-83; USA Network, dir, nat acct, 1983-85, vpres, affil rels, 1985-87, sr vpres, affil rels, 1987-2000, pres network distrib, 1997-2004; Universal, Pres Distrib & Mkt, 1997-2004; TV, pres, network distrib & affil rels, 2000; Cable Investments NBC Universal Cable, pres, 2004-07; Universal NBC Universal TV Networks Distrib, pres nbc network distrib & affil partnerships & affil mkt, 2008-09; One World Sports, sr bus consult, 2009-11; Am Express, bus develop consult, 2009-11; ValueVision Media Inc, dir, currently; ION Media Networks Inc, pres multichannel distrib, 2011-15. **Orgs:** Pres, Uptown Investment Assoc, 1986-; vpres, Nat Asn Minorities Cable, 1988-90, pres, 1990-93; bd mem, Cable TV Admin & Mkt, 1992-; chmn, Nat Asn Multi-ethnicity Commun; Westchester Clubman Found; bd trustee, Emerson Col. **Business Addr:** President, Cable Investments for NBC Universal Cable, 900 Sylvan Ave 1 Cnbc Plz, Englewood Cliffs, NJ 07632, **Business Phone:** (201)735-3568.

### HOLLOWAY, DR. ERNESTINE

Educator, college teacher. **Personal:** Born May 23, 1930, Clyde, MS. **Educ:** Tougaloo Col, BS; NY Univ, MA; Mich State Univ, NDEA, stud personnel serv higher educ; Univ Miss, MEd; Univ Southern Miss, PhD, educ admin. **Career:** Professor (retired); High Sch, teacher, 1952-53; Greenville Pub Schs Systs, sci teacher, 1952-53; Tougaloo Col, sect pres, admin asst to pres, 1953-63, asst dean, 1963-65, dean stud, 1965-85; NASPA J, ed bd, 1972-75; St Dept Educ, Jackson, Miss, Div Accreditation, accreditation monitor, 1987, Div St wide Testing, educ technologist, 1987-92; Jackson St Univ, Educ Found & Leadership, Sch Educ, asst prof educ admin, 1992-. **Orgs:** Undergrad prog adv mem, Alpha Kappa Alpha Sorority, 1974-78; bd dir, OperaS, 1975-76; charter mem, Opera S Guild, 1976-; Nat Asn Stud Personnel Admin, 1976-78; Reg III Adv Bd, 1978; res comt, Jackson Mun Separate Sch Dist; Col Comt Nat Asn Women Deans & Counors; consult, Workshops & Conf Stud Personnel Serv; Phi Delta Kappa Fraternity; Miss Personnel Guid Asn; Southern Col Personnel Asn; Am Miss Asn; United Church Christ Study, NY Univ Nat Def Ed; Miss Asn Minority Sch Admin; Pi Lambda Theta Nat Hon & Prof Asn Educ; Nat Asn Women Deans Admin & Counr; Am Asn Univ Women; Supvr & Curric Develop; Am Asn Univ Women; Yth Task Group, Hinds Co Asn Mental Health. **Home Addr:** 808 Windward Rd, Jackson, MS 39206-2318.

### HOLLOWAY, GERALD

Executive. **Career:** Essex Co Col, Fashion Entertainment Bd, producer & adv, PEB Opers, supvr, currently. **Business Addr:** Producer, Advisor, Fashion Entertainment Board, 303 Univ Ave PEB 405, Newark, NJ 07102-1798, **Business Phone:** (973)877-3300.

### HOLLOWAY, REV. HARRIS M.

Businessperson, funeral director, clergy. **Personal:** Born Jan 26, 1949, Aiken, SC. **Educ:** Livingston Col, BS, 1971; Hood Theol Sem, attended 1971; Am Acad-Mc Allister Inst Funeral Serv, PMS, 1974. **Career:** NJ Dept Labor Indust, employ interviewer, 1971-73; Carnie P Bragg Funeral Homes Inc, funeral dir, 1972-78; Perry Funeral Home, funeral dir; Pure Light Baptist Church, Newark, NJ, pastor; Gen Motors Accept Corp, field rep, 1974-84, credit rep, 1984-93, customer rels supvr, 1993-94, acquisitions analyst, 1994-. **Orgs:** Paterson Jaycees, 1975-76; Garden State Funeral Dirs, 1977; Rotary Col Paterson, 1977-78; treas, Teacher Corp Community Coun Peterson, 1979; master mason Mt Zion Lodge No 50. **Honors/Awds:** Named best lighting technician, best stage mgr, best Set Designer, most coop thespian Livingston Col, 1966-71. **Home Addr:** 52 Richmond St, Newark, NJ 07103, **Home Phone:** (973)623-0905. **Business Addr:** Director, Perry Funeral Home, 34 Mercer St, Newark, NJ 07103.

### HOLLOWAY, JERRY

Educator. **Personal:** Born May 14, 1941, Chicago, IL; married Mary Bowie. **Educ:** Parson Col, BA, 1963; Univ Nev, MEd, 1971. **Career:** Matt Kelly Elem Sch Las Vegas, teacher, 1963-66; Las Vegas, coordr recprog elem studs, 1965-66; coordr summer work experience prog, 1966; Washoe Co Sch Dist Reno, asstd in planing & supvr disadvantaged studs in work experience prog, 1966; Trainer Jr HS Reno, teacher, 1966-67, teacher, admin asst to prin, vprin, 1968-69, dean studs, 1969-71; Traner Rec Prog City Reno Rec Dept, asst dir, 1970-71; Washoe Co Sch Dist, Reno, intergroup specialist, 1971-72, sch admin, curric coordr, asst supt, Stud Support Serv, Sch Impr Plan, 2007-08. **Orgs:** Reno-Sparks Br Nat Asn Advan Colored People; chmn, Black Coalition Fair Housing Law Com; chmn, Human Rels Com NV State Educ Asn; chmn, comt mem, Cub Scouts Div BSA, Las Vegas; secy treas, Econ Oppor Bd Washoe Co; vice chmn, CETA Manpower Adv Plng Coun; bd dir, YMCA; chmn, sr ctzns vol prog; commn Equal Rights Citizens; NV Asn Adminr; Nat Staff Devel Coun; Family Support Am; Nat Asn Elem Sch Prins; Literate Community Comn; NV Cent Off Admin Asn. **Home Addr:** 2880 Rowland Rd, Reno, NV 89502. **Business Addr:** Assistant Superintendent, School Improvement Plan, Washoe County School District, 425 E 9th St, Reno, NV 89520-3425, **Business Phone:** (775)348-0380.

### HOLLOWAY, DR. JOAQUIN MILLER, JR.

School administrator, librarian, vice president (organization). **Personal:** Born Dec 28, 1937, Mobile, AL; son of Joaquin M Sr and Ariel Williams; married Malvina Murray; children: Monica, Joaquin III & Josef. **Educ:** Talladega Col, AB, 1957; Ind Univ, MS, instrnl media, 1958, EdS, instrnl media, 1960; Univ Ala, PhD, admin higher educ, 1976. **Career:** School administrator (retired); Tex S Univ, instr& fac mem, 1958-61; Cent High Sch, fac mem & instr, 1961-65; Mobile Co Pub Sch Syst, media specialist, 1965-69; Univ S Ala, prof bus, 1969, sr librn & head instrnl media ctr, dir instrnl media ctr; Artistic Photographs, chief exec officer, 2011-. **Orgs:** Host "Holloway House" progressive jazz prog, WKRG AM-WKRG FM Radio, 1969-79; vpres, Cult Black & White, 1969-; bd mem, YMCA Dearborn Br, 1975-86; bd mem, Cine-Tel Comn, 1976-; Consult, Int Paper Co, 1977-80; consult, Necott Devel Co, 1978; consult, Mid States Asn Col & Schs, 1978; coun mem, Ala State Coun Arts, 1979-; co-host local, UNCF Telethon, 1983-84, 1988; chairperson centennial celebration, Omega Psi Phi Frat, 2011-; Asn Educ Comm & Tech; Minorities Media; Phi Delta Kappa; Omicron Delta Kappa; lic lay reader Episcopal Ch. **Honors/Awds:** Fifth Place Award Photog, Allied Arts Coun Competition, 1974; Second Place Award Photog, First Annual Fort Conde Arts Festival, 1979; 3 First Place Awards, Photog Mobile Soc Model Eng 20th SER Conv, 1980; one-man photog shows, including: Percy Whiting Gall, 1985, Tel Fair Peet Gall, Auburn Univ, 1986, Tacon Station Gall, 1986; George Washington Carver Mus, Tuskegee Univ, 1987, Fine Arts Mus S, 1987, Hay Center Art Gall, Stillman Col, 1988, Isabel Comer Mus of Art, 1989; The John L LeFlore Civic Award, 1990; Gladys M Cooper Fine Arts Award, 1991. **Home Addr:** 2206 De Kruif Ct, Mobile, AL 36617-2405, **Home Phone:** (251)479-0295.

### HOLLOWAY, KARLA F.C.

College teacher, writer. **Personal:** Born Sep 29, 1949; married Russell Holloway; children: Ayana & Bem. **Educ:** Talladega Col, BA, eng, 1971; Mich State Univ, MA, eng, 1972, PhD, eng & ling, 1978; Duke Univ Sch Law, MLS, 2005. **Career:** North Carolina State University, educator; Western Michigan University, educator; Old Dominion University, educator; Duke University, visiting professo, 1992-93, professor, 1993-, dean of the faculty of humanities and social sciences, 1999-2004; John Hope Franklin Center for African and African-American Documentation, founding co-director, 1996-; Franklin Humanities Institute, founding co-director. **Orgs:** Bd mem, Greenwall Found Adv Bd Bioethics; bd mem, Duke Univ Ctr Doc Studies; bd mem, Princeton Univ Coun Study Women & Gender. **Special Achievements:** Author, "The Character of the Word: The Texts of Zora Neale Hurston" (Greenwood Press, 1987); "Moorings and Metaphors: Figures of Culture and Gender in Black Women's Literature" (Rutgers University Press, 1992); "Codes of Conduct: Race, Ethics, and the Color of Our Character" (Rutgers University Press, 1995); "Passed On: African American Mourning Stories" (Duke University Press, 2002); "BookMarks: Reading in Black and White-A Memoir" (Rutgers University Press, 2006); "Private Bodies/Public Texts: Race, Gender, and a Cultural Bioethics" (Duke University Press, 2011); "Legal Fictions: Constituting Race, Composing Literature" (2014); "Legal Fictions: Constituting Law, Composing Literature" (Duke University Press, 2014). Coauthor, "Reading of the Novels of Toni Morrison" (Greenwood Press, 1987); "New Dimensions of Spirituality: A Biracial and Bicultural Reading of the Novels of Toni Morrison" (Greenwood Press, 1987). **Business Addr:** Duke University Department of English, 304F Allen Bldg, Durham, NC 27708, **Business Phone:** (919)684-8993.

### HOLLOWELL, JOHNNY LAVERAL

Military leader, child care worker, business owner. **Personal:** Born Sep 13, 1951, New Orleans, LA; married Angie D; children: Chandler A, Ivory D & Alexandria B. **Educ:** Utica Jr Col, AA, 1971; Alcorn State Univ, bus admin, 1972; Columbia Col, BA, bus admin, 1980; Univ Phoenix, pursuing MBA, grad studies. **Career:** Military leader (retired), Child care worker; USCG, exec officer, 1999; Daycare Pvt Sch, owner & adminr; Tex real estate agt; IAC Group, Willowell Develop Ctr Inc, co-owner, dir, pres & chief exec officer, currently. **Orgs:** Big Brothers Am; life mem, Nat Naval Officers Asn; life mem, Omega Psi Phi Frat; Role Models Unlimited; Rotary Club Int; owner, serv disabled veteran owned small bus, Advantage Legal Wheels. **Honors/Awds:** Omega Man of the Yr, 1992, Rho Nu Chap; Roy Wilkins Renown Serv Award, Nat Asn Advan Colored People, 1999. **Home Addr:** 8105 Catalpa St, Texas City, TX 77591-2411, **Home Phone:** (409)955-1579. **Business Addr:** President, Director, Willowell Child Development Center, 909 Med Ctr Blvd, Webster, TX 77598-0000, **Business Phone:** (281)338-2117.

### HOLLOWELL, KENNETH LAWRENCE

Government official. **Personal:** Born Mar 5, 1945, Detroit, MI; son of Herman JDJ Sr and Rachel A Kimble; married Patricia J; children: Terrance L & Rhonda L. **Educ:** Wayne County Community Col, AA, 1979. **Career:** Cook Paint & Varnish Co, rsch tech, 1967-71; Teamsters Local Union No 247, bus rep, 1971-80, trustee & bus rep, 1980-82, rec sec & bus rep, 1982-85, vpres & bus rep, 1985-87, pres & bus rep, 1987-88, secy & treas, prin exec officer, 1988-2001; Detroit Mayor's Off labor, faith based affairs, Liaison, 2003; 107.5 FM WGPR Radio, vpres & sta mgr, currently; Wayne County Airport Authority, secy; Wayne County Comm Col, secy, treas. **Orgs:** Exec comdr, Detroit Police Reserves, 1970-94; Dep imp potentateIntl Shriners, 1975-83; bd mem, Teamsters Nat Black Caucus, 1976-; comnr, Civic Ctr City Detroit, 1976-94; vpres, Mich Assoc Masonic Grand Lodges, 1979-; grand master, Ralph Bunche Grand Lodge Int Masons, 1979-81; bd mem, Mich Coalition Black Trade Unionists, 1980-; bd dir, United Way Southeastern MI, 1980-86; adv comm, Ctr Volunteerism UCS, 1981-87; Metro Agency Retarded Citizens, 1981-94; Indust Rels Res Asn, 1981-2000; Econ Alliance MI, 1982-2002; dep supreme grand master, Int Masons, 1983-86; supreme grandmaster, Int F&AM Masons, 1986-89; Metro Detroit Conv & Visitors Bur, 1986-2002, vice chmn, 1994; bd dir, MI Chap Int Asn Exhib Mgrs, 1987-93; exec bd mem, Metro Detroit AFL-CIO, 1988-2002; bd mem, Metro Detroit Chap, A Phillip Randolph Inst, 1988-; bd dir, Teamsters Credit Union Wayne & Oakland Counties, MI, 1989-; trustee, Mich Teamsters Joint Coun No 43, 1989-95; Nat Asn Advan Colored People, 1989-; bd dir, Robert Holmes Teamsters Retiree Housing Corp, 1990-98; Corp, 1992-2000; bd dir, Metrop Realty Comnr Detroit Police Dept, 1994-98; rec secy, Mich Teamsters Joint Coun No 43, 1995-98; comnr, Youth Sports & Recreation Comn, 2001-; bd dir, Southeast Mich Chap, Am Red Cross, 2002-; bd dir, Barnabas Inc, 2006-; treas, Mich Asn C Emotional Dis; trustee & asst treas, Presbytery Detroit; vice chmn, Presby Villages Mich; bd trustee, New Detroit Inc; Detroit Urban League; Salvation Army; youth Dev Comn; 14th Cong Dist Dem Party org; Broadstreet presby Church; trustee & asst treas, Presbytery Detroit; exec bd mem, Teamsters Local Union No 247; bd mem, United Way Community Serv; Detroit Youth Sports Comn; bd mem, Police Commissioners. **Home Addr:** 15336 Robson, Detroit, MI 48227, **Home Phone:** (313)835-5925. **Business Addr:** Vice Chairman, Presbyterian Villages of Michigan, 26200 Lahser Rd Suite 300, Southfield, MI 48033, **Business Phone:** (248)281-2020.

### HOLLOWELL, ESQ. MELVIN BUTCH

Lawyer. **Personal:** Born Nov 6, 1959; married Desiree Cooper; children: Melvin Jay III & Desiree Rae. **Educ:** Albion Col, BA, 1981; Univ Va Sch Law, JD, 1984. **Career:** Dickinson Wright PLLC, assoc, 1985; Wayne County, Mich, asst wayne county exec, purchasing div, dir, interim dir, human rels div & asst corp coun, 1985-91; Shareholder, Lewis, White & Clay, 1991-94; Shareholder, Butzel Long PC, gen coun, atty, partner, 1995-2004; Allen Bros PLLC, coun, 2004-08; Nat Asn Advan Colored People, corp coun, gen coun, 2005-05, 2011-; State Mich, ins consumer advocate, 2008-09; Nat Asn Ins Commissioners, nat consumer rep, 2010; Melvin Butch Hollowell, ESQ PC, atty, 2011-; Mich Legis Black Caucus, legal coun, 2011-; Mike Duggan Detroit Mayor, chief legal coun, 2013; Mich Dem Party, gen coun, chair; Allen Bros PLLC, lawyer, currently. **Orgs:** Chmn, Freedom Fund Dinner, Nat Asn Advan Colored People, 1995, legal comt mem, 2012-; State Bar Mich; Nat Bar Asn; Wolverine Bar Asn; co-chair, Citizen Advocacy Comt, US Dist Ct; Detroit Music Hall; Am Red Cross; Detroit Cent Bus Dist Asn; Univ Detroit Jesuit High Sch; adv bd, Bank Bloomfield Hills; partner, Kern Woodward Assocs LLC; bd mem, Nature Conservancy; bd mem, Albion Col Gerald Ford Inst Pub Serv; bd mem, Univ Mich Ctr Community Serv; bd mem, Wayne State Univ Med Sch; bd mem, Marygrove Col; bd mem, United Way Southeast Mich; life mem, US Sixth Circuit Ct Appeals Judicial Conf; Interlochen Ctr Arts; Mich State Univ Mich Polit Leadership Prog; Dem Nat Comt; chair, Wayne County Clerk Transition Team; chair, City Detroit City Clerk Transition Team. **Honors/Awds:** First Lifetime Achievement Award, Detroit Chap; President's Award, Wolverine Bar Asn. **Special Achievements:** Columnist, Mich Chronicle & Jewish News. Numerous Publications. **Home Addr:** 100 Riverfront Dr Suite 2011, Detroit, MI 48226, **Home Phone:** (313)207-3890. **Business Addr:** Legal Counsel, National Association for the Advancement of Colored People, 4805 Mt Hope Dr, Baltimore, MD 21215, **Business Phone:** (410)358-8900.

### HOLLOWELL, DR. MELVIN LAVERNE

Surgeon. **Personal:** Born Nov 24, 1930, Detroit, MI; married Sylvia Regina Ports; children: Regina, Dana, Melvin Jr, Danielle, Christopher, Courtney & Sylvia. **Educ:** Wayne State Univ, BS, 1953; Meharry Medical Col, MD, 1959. **Career:** Tripler Army Med Ctr, internship, 1959-60; Harper Hosp, resident, 1963-64, training genral surg; Detroit Receiving Hosp, resident, 1964-67; Hutzel Hosp, vice chmn dept urol, 1980-87; Harper Grace Hosp Detroit, med bd, 1983-85, exec comt, 1983-85; Southeast Mich Surg Soc, pres, 1983-84; NCent Sect Am Urol Asn, exec comt, 1984-86; Samaritan Health Ctr, Sisters Mercy, exec comt, 1985-87, chmn dept surg, 1985-; Wayne State Univ Col Med, Dept Urol, clin asst prof; pvt pract; Urologicargry Adults & C, urologist, pres, currently; Sinai-Grace Hosp; Providence Hosp;

St. John Hosp & Med Ctr. **Orgs:** Life mem, Nat Asn Advan Colored People; Kappa Alpha Psi Frat; GESU Cath Church; pres, Mich Br Am Urol Asn, 1976-77; fel Am Col Surgeons; Am Col Med Dirs Physician Execs; Royal Col Med; Am Bd Urol. **Business Addr:** Urological Surgeon, 20905 Greenfield Rd Suite 507, Southfield, MI 48075, **Business Phone:** (248)559-5640.

### HOLMAN, ALVIN T.
Manager, consultant, executive director. **Personal:** Born Jul 21, 1948, Washington, DC; married Karen. **Educ:** Los Angeles Harbor Col, AA, 1969; Univ Wash, AB, 1970; Mich State Univ, attended 1972. **Career:** Southern Calif Rapid Transit Dist, Planning Dept, planning proj mgr; UHURU Inc, proj dir; City Seattle, comn planning consult; Off Econ & Opportunity Seattle, res consult; State Mich, urban planner, comn planning specialist; Berryman & Assocs, sr planning consult; Gardner & Holman Consult, owner. **Orgs:** Am Inst Planners; Am Soc Planning Officials; Am Soc Planning Consults Nat Asn Housing & Rehab Officials; Nat Asn Planners. **Special Achievements:** Book: "Six-month Evaluation of Service in Mid-Cities". **Home Addr:** 3645 S Muirfield Rd, Los Angeles, CA 90016-5717. **Business Addr:** Research Consultant, Gardner & Holman International Ltd, 3761 Stocker St Suite 103, Los Angeles, CA 90008-5111.

### HOLMAN, DORIS ANN
Educator, association executive. **Personal:** Born Feb 14, 1924, Wetumpka, AL; daughter of Willie G and Mattie Banks; children: DeWayne, Douglas, Desiree & Glenn. **Educ:** Ala State Univ, BS, 1944; Univ San Francisco, MA, 1979. **Career:** Educator (retired); Detroit City Sch; Compton Unified Sch Dist, teacher. **Orgs:** NEA; Phi Delta Kappa Beta Phi; Nat Asn Univ Women; rep, Calif Teachers Asn StCoun, 1960-62; bd dir, ATEB Corp; chmn, Neg Coun Compton Unified Sch Dist, 1971-73; pres, Compton Educ Asn, 1971-74; bd dir, Compton YMCA, 1970-; regional dir, Nat Tots & Teens, 1972-; chmn, Neighborhood GS A; bd dir, BSA; bd dir, Christian Day Sch Comm Lutheran Church; Int Toastmistress Club; pres, Women Church Comn Lutheran Church, 1977, 1992-94; treas, So Bay Conf Am Lutheran Church Women, 1977; secy, Compton Educ Asn, 1976-77; Compton Sch Dist Compens Educ Adv Coun Sch Adv Coun; bd dir, Mid Cities Sch Credit Union, 1998-; pres, 1993; elect bd, Col & Univ Serv Am Lutheran Church, 1982-88; worthy matron, Gethsemane Chap Order Eastern Star, 1994. **Honors/Awds:** Pro Achievement Award, Enterprise Teachers Asn, 1968; Who Award, Calif Teacher Asn, 1970; Teacher in Political Award Theol Bass Mem, 1972; Nat Sorority Phi Delta Kappa, Soror of the Year, 1994; Ala State Univ Alumni Asn, Los Angeles Chap, Alumnus of the Year, 1989. **Home Addr:** 9309 S O Range Blossom Trl Apt 510, Orlando, FL 32837, **Home Phone:** (407)850-4374.

### HOLMAN, KARRIEM MALIK
Association executive, government official. **Personal:** Born Apr 13, 1969, Chicago, IL; son of Forest and Beverly. **Educ:** Howard Univ, BA, 1993. **Career:** Mich Youth Corp, supvr, 1988; Rep John Conyers, D-Mich, legis intern, 1989; Alliance Justice, staff asst, 1992-93; Gov Ann Richards Re-election Campaign, field coordr, 1994; Nat Black Bus Coun, exec asst, legis asst, 1994; DC Coun, legis asst, 1996-99; Brooklyn Acad Music, develop assoc, 2003-04; kpolitics, prin, 2005-; Bill Lynch Assocs, community rels advisor, 2007-08; 99 Solutions LLC, sr commun advisor, 2009-11; Scott Benson State Rep, sr advisor, 2012. **Orgs:** Legis Consult, Summit 1993 Health Care Coalition, 1994; Participation 2000 PAC, 1994. **Special Achievements:** One of 5 African-Americans young people to work on a major gubernatorial campaign. **Home Addr:** 1845 N Capitol St NW, Washington, DC 20002, **Home Phone:** (202)832-1288. **Business Addr:** Legislative Assistant, National Black Business Council, 1010 Wayne Ave Suite 430, Silver Spring, MD 20910, **Business Phone:** (301)585-6222.

### HOLMAN, KWAME KENT ALLAN
Journalist. **Personal:** Born Jul 4, 1953, New Haven, CT; son of M Carl; married Miriam Rudder; children: Kevin Alton & Donovan Joseph. **Educ:** Howard Univ, BS, 1977; Northwestern Univ, MS, jour, 1981. **Career:** Dist Columbia Govt, actg press sec to mayor, 1980; Nat Summit Conf Black Econ Develop, pub rels consult, 1980; C Defense Fund, commun asst, 1980; CBS, reporter & producer; WTOC-TV, reporter, talk show host, 1982-83; Newshour with Jim Lehrer, producer & corresp, 1983-93, cong corresp, 1992-; "By the People: Hard Times, Hard Choices", corresp, 2010. **Orgs:** Nat Asn Black Journalists, occas speaker; Partners Journ, occas ed, 1990-; Journalists Round Table, C-Span, occas panelist, 1993-; Nat Press Club, occas panelist, 1994-. **Honors/Awds:** George Polk Award for Nat TV Reporting, 1984; Nat News & Docu Emmy, 1985; Local News & Doc Emmy, 1991; Joan Shorenstein Barone Award, 1994. **Special Achievements:** Consulting Writer, "AIDS and Race"-The AIDS Quarterly: Fall 1989 with Peter Jennings, 1989. **Home Addr:** 718 15th St SE, Washington, DC 20003-3019, **Home Phone:** (202)543-8028. **Business Addr:** Congressional Correspondent, The Newshour with Jim Lehrer, 3620 S 27th St, Arlington, VA 22206, **Business Phone:** (703)998-2861.

### HOLMES, ALVIN ADOLF
State government official, educator, association executive. **Personal:** Born Oct 26, 1939, Montgomery, AL; son of John H and Willie Ann; married Judy; children: Veronica. **Educ:** Ala State Univ, BS, 1962, MEd, 1972, MA, 1979; Selma Univ, Selma, AL, LLD, 1982; Rochester Bus Inst, attended; Atlanta Univ, attended; Univ Pa, OIC; Univ Ala, attended; Jones Sch Law, LLD. **Career:** Lic real estate broker; Ala State Univ, asst prof hist; State Ala, 78th Dist, state rep, 1974-. **Orgs:** State Dem Exec Comt; Dem Party Ala; Nat Asn Advan Colored People; bd dir, Southern Christian Leadership Conf; Hutchinson Missionary Baptist Church; Kappa Alpha Psi Fraternity; Southern Christian Leadership Conf; Montgomery Improv Asn; chair, Montgomery County Legis. **Home Addr:** 325 Bitford Way, Montgomery, AL 36106, **Home Phone:** (334)281-8637. **Business Addr:** State Representative, State of Alabama, Rm 525-A 11 S Union St, Montgomery, AL 36130, **Business Phone:** (334)242-7706.

### HOLMES, MAJOR GEN. ARTHUR, JR.
Executive, military leader. **Personal:** Born May 12, 1931, Decatur, AL; son of Arthur and Grace L; married Wilma King; children: Deborah H Cook, Rick Fairley-Brown, Sharon H Key & Sharon Fairley-Nickerson. **Educ:** Hampton Univ, BS, chem, 1952; Kent State Univ, MBA, 1967; Naval War Col. **Career:** AUS, 2nd lt, maintenance battalion comdr, exec officer to secy, 1977-79, mat command, dir readiness, 1980-82, Mil Personnel Ctr, chief ord br officer personnel directorate, First Inf Div, Ft Riley, Kans, asst div comdr-support; AUS, dep inspectorgen, 1982-83; AUS Logistics, asst dep chief staff, 1983-84; AUS, AUS Tank-Automotive Command, comndg gen, 1984-87; Automated Sci Group Inc, vpres logistics, 1987-90, exec vpres & chief operating officer, 1990, pres & chief exec officer, 1990; Montgomery County Coun, chmn, comnr & vice-chair, Go Montgomery, Dept PubWorks & Transp, dir, 2002-04. **Orgs:** Omega Psi Phi Fraternity, 1952-; chmn, Nat Asn Advan Colored People, Educ Comm, Montgomery Co, MD, 1993-95; pres, Retired Mil Officers asn, 1994-; comnr, Md Nat Capital Pk & Planning Comn, 1994-. **Honors/Awds:** Businessman of the Year, Omega Psi Phi Fraternity, Mu Nu Chap, 1993; Ordnance Corps Hall of Fame, 1999. **Special Achievements:** First combat service support officer to serve as Executive Officer to the Secretary of the Army, 1977-79. **Home Addr:** 17104 Blossom View Dr, Olney, MD 20832-2409, **Home Phone:** (301)774-1269.

### HOLMES, DR. BARBARA J.
Educator, writer. **Personal:** Born Jun 26, 1934, Chicago, IL; daughter of Wyess Wilhaite and Helyne Wilhaite; married Laurence H Sr; children: Carole, Helyne, Sheryl & Laurence. **Educ:** Talladega Col, attended 1953; Univ Colo, BA, 1973, MA, 1974, PhD, 1978. **Career:** Nat Assessment Educ Progress, writer, 1977-83; State Educ Policy Sem Progco-sponsored Educ Comn States & Inst Educ Leadership, nat coordr; Policy Studies, ECS dir; other educ prof organs, presentations; Consult Recruitment & Retention Minority Teachers, Expertise Teacher Educ, Work Force Literacy; Univ Colo, chairperson sch's commun dept, 1992-93, assoc prof ethics & african am relig studies, 1992-; A Race the Cosmos; An Invitation View the World Differently; Pvt Woman in Pub Spaces; Joy Unspeakable; The Contemplative Practices the Black Church; The Legacy Martin Luther King Jr; The Boundaries Law Polit & Relig. **Orgs:** Delta Sigma Theta Pub Serv Sor; bd dir, Whitney M Young Jr Mem Found, 1974-84; fel Educ Policy Fel Prog, 1982-83. **Honors/Awds:** Phi Beta Kappa Honor Society, 1974; Academic Fellow Whitney M Young, 1973-74. **Special Achievements:** Published over 20 articles & reports. **Home Addr:** 3801 S Spruce St, Denver, CO 80237-2150, **Home Phone:** (303)771-4934. **Business Addr:** Associate Professor Ethics & African American Religious Studies, University of Colorado, PO Box 185, Denver, CO 80217-3364, **Business Phone:** (303)556-2872.

### HOLMES, PROF. CARL
Executive. **Personal:** Born Jan 6, 1929, Oklahoma City, OK; married Marvella; children: Carla D. **Educ:** Drake Univ, MBA, 1951; Univ MD Fire Dept Staff & Command Sch; Motivational Mgt Schs; Okla Univ Equal Opportunity Sem. **Career:** Executive (retired); Okla City Fire Dept, fire chief, 1951-81; Carl Holmes & Assoc, dir, chief exec officer, 1980; Carl Holmes Exec Develop Inst, exec dir, 1990-96; LA State Univ, fire dept; Southern Methodist Univ, fire dept admin. **Orgs:** Consult, City Ft Worth, 1979; City Atlanta, 1980; City San Francisco, 1982; Nat Fire Acad, Wash DC Fire Dept; Int Assoc Fire Instr; assoc mem, Nat Assoc Black Mgrs; fire serv training instr, Okla State Univ; city chmn, Okla Lung Assoc; tTch Adv Training Mag; Instr Motivational Mgt Phycol Chem Corp; Am Airlines; Tex Light & Power Inc; Okla Natural Gas Inc; Continental Oil Inc; Tex Instrument Inc; consult, City Admin Tech Asst Orlando, FL. **Honors/Awds:** Guest lectr, Univ MD. **Home Addr:** 5106 N Lottie Ave Suite 22, Oklahoma City, OK 73111, **Home Phone:** (405)427-9516.

### HOLMES, CARLTON
Marketing executive. **Personal:** Born Apr 1, 1951, New York, NY; married Thelma Dye; children: Kyle & Arianna. **Educ:** Cornell Univ, BA, 1973; Columbia Univ, Grad Sch Bus, MBA, 1975. **Career:** Lever Bros, asst prod mgr, 1975-77; Johnson & Johnson, prod dir, 1977-82; Drake Bakeries, prod mgr, 1982-83; Block Drug Co, dir new bus develop, 1983-89. **Orgs:** Cornell Black Alumni Asn; Nat Black MBA Asn. **Home Addr:** 175 W 87th St Suite 14G, New York, NY 10024-2907, **Home Phone:** (212)799-8644. **Business Addr:** Director New Business Development, Block Drug Co, 257 Cornelison Ave, Jersey City, NJ 07302, **Business Phone:** (201)434-3000.

### HOLMES, CLAYTON ANTWAN
Football player, executive. **Personal:** Born Aug 23, 1969, Florence, SC; son of Phillip Windom and Claudia; children: Dominique, Colton Jackson & Kenya Briana. **Educ:** N Greenville Univ, attended 1990; Carson Newman Univ, attended 1992. **Career:** Football player (retired), executive; Dallas Cowboys, defensive back, 1992, 1994, left cornerback, 1995; Miami Dolphins, 1997; Topeka Knights, 1999; Kans Koyotes, 2003-04; motivational speaker; personal trainer, 2010-. **Honors/Awds:** Defensive Player of the Year Award, S Atlantic Conf, 1991; Little All-American, 1991; Super Bowl Champion, XXVII, XXVIII, XXX. **Business Addr:** Owner, Realize Athletics, 2 5th St, Wenatchee, WA 98801, **Business Phone:** (509)888-5200.

### HOLMES, CLOYD JAMES
Labor activist, president (organization). **Personal:** Born Nov 23, 1939, Houston, TX; son of Haywood and Charlene Cooper; married Madelyn Holmes; children: Reginald B, Patrice, Cloyd J Jr & Anthony E. **Career:** Ramada Inn, fry cook, 1960-63; Howard Johnson Hotel, fry cook, 1964-66; CW Post Col, Automatique Food Serv, chef, shop stewart, 1966-70; USEU Local377, Long Island City, NY, bus rep, 1970-71, fin secy, treas, 1971-72, pres, 1983-1992. **Orgs:** Int Found Employee Benefit Plan, 1970-; exec bd mem, vpres, Retail Wholesale & Dept Store Union, 1978; former sec, treas, The Negro Labor Comn; exec vpres, Huntington Boy's Club; vpres, Nat Asn Advan Colored People, Greenwich Village Br, Huntington Br; A Philip Randolph Inst, 1986, Coalition Black Trade Unionists; Am Cancer Soc, Queen's Br. **Honors/Awds:** Greenwich Village Nat Asn Advan Colored People Br, 1980; The Trade Union Women African Heritage, 1981; NAACP 'Man of the Year', 1983; Negro Labor Comn 'Man of the Year', 1984; Am Cancer Soc Greater Jamaica Unit for Notable Serv in' the Crusade to Conquer Cancer Award', 1984. **Home Addr:** 86-11th Ave, Huntington Station, NY 11746-2226, **Home Phone:** (516)351-9386.

### HOLMES, DARICK LAMON
Football player. **Personal:** Born Jul 1, 1971, Pasadena, CA; son of Gloria. **Educ:** Portland State Univ. **Career:** Football player (retired); Buffalo Bills, running back, 1995-98, kick returner, 1995; Green Bay Packers, running back, 1998-99; Indianapolis Colts, running back, 1999-2000; Pro Way Training, owner, currently. **Honors/Awds:** Pacific League Player of the Year, 1988; San Gabriel Valley Player of the Year, 1988; All-CIF Southern Section All-State, 1988; Football Digest, "Sweet 16" Rookie Team, 1995. **Business Addr:** Owner, Pro Way Training, 23620 Mulholland Hwy, Calabasas, CA 91302, **Business Phone:** (909)452-9462.

### HOLMES, DR. DOROTHY EVANS
Psychologist, psychoanalyst. **Personal:** Born Mar 9, 1943, Chicago, IL; daughter of Major Moten Evans and Queen McGee Evans Pryor; married Raymond L M. **Educ:** Univ Ill, BS, 1963; Southern Ill Univ, MA, psychol, 1966, PhD, clin psychol, 1968. **Career:** Howard Univ Hosp, Dept Psychol, assoc prof; Univ Rochester, instr & postdoctoral fel, 1968-70; Univ Md, Dept Psychol, asst prof, 1970-73; George Wash Univ, Dr Psychol Prog, dir, currently, prof clin psychol, prof emer clin psychol, currently; Baltimore-Wash Psychoanal Inst, training & supvr analyst, training & supvr analyst emer, currently. **Orgs:** Nat Inst Ment Health; fel Am Psych Asn; Sigma Xi; Am Psychoanal Asn; DC Psychol Asn; Baltimore-Wash Inst & Soc Psychoanalysis; bd dir, Prof Exam Serv, 1987-; bd dir, Nat Regist Health Serv Providers Psychol, 1988-; Am Bd Prof Psychol. **Special Achievements:** Published 1 book & 7 science articles and 3 book reviews; First American Psychological Association-accredited internship in a historically black university. **Home Addr:** 11712 Owens Glen Way, Gaithersburg, MD 20878. **Business Addr:** Professor Emeritus of Clinical Psychology, George Washington University, 1922 F St NW Suite 103, Washington, DC 20052, **Business Phone:** (202)994-4929.

### HOLMES, EARL L.
Football player, football coach. **Personal:** Born Apr 28, 1973, Tallahassee, FL; married Tiffany; children: Earl Jr. **Educ:** Fla A&M Univ. **Career:** Football player (retired), coach; Pittsburgh Steelers, linebacker & right inside linebacker & left inside linebacker, 1996-2001; Cleveland Browns, right inside linebacker & left inside linebacker, 2002; Detroit Lions, line backer & mid linebacker, 2003-05; Fla A&M Univ, co-defensive coordr, 2008-10, defensive coordr, 2011-12, head coach, 2012-14. **Orgs:** Kappa Alpha Psi Fraternity, 1994. **Honors/Awds:** Sports Hall of Fame, Fla A&M Univ, 2005. **Business Addr:** Head Coach, Florida A&M University, Lee Hall Suite 400, Tallahassee, MI 32307, **Business Phone:** (850)599-3000.

### HOLMES, EMMA SELEAN
Educator, museum curator, consultant. **Personal:** Born Jul 15, 1954, Cincinnati, OH; daughter of Bert L Sr and Harriet J. **Educ:** Knoxville Col, attended 1973; Univ Cincinnati, BA, 1979, MA, 1983; Yale Univ, prog African lang, 1983. **Career:** Artist & designer; Yale Univ, fel, prog African lang, 1983; Travelers Aid Int Inst, foreign lang coordr, 1985; Nat ARO Mus & Cult Ctr, cur, 1985-89; Smith Col, Mwangi Cult Ctr, dir, 1989-90; Arts Consortium African Am Mus, assoc dir, 1991-; Cincinnati Hist Soc, mus ctr dir African Am prog, 1992-96; Cult Consult, 1996-98; Nat Underground Rr Freedom Ctr, cur, 1999-2001; DuSable Mus African Am Hist, chief cur & dir exhibs & collections, 2001-05; Taft Mus Art, cur; Northwestern Univ, instr, currently; consult, currently; African Am Collection, cur, currently; Cirilos Inc, cur, currently. **Orgs:** Treas, African Am Mus Asn, 1986-89; African Am Studies Asn, 1986-; Mass Asn Women Deans & Adv, 1989-90; dir develop, YWCA, 1990-93; mid w rep, African Am Commentary Mag, 1990; vpres, Univ Cincinnati Friends Womens Studies, 1991-93; Cincinnati Art Mus, 1991-92; bd, Int Visitors Coun, USIA, 1996-99; dir, African-Am Hist, Cincinnati Hist Mus, 1996-; adv bd, Chicago Artists Month, 2005. **Honors/Awds:** Grant for prof develop, Alliance Ohio Comt Arts Agencies, 1988; Philo T Farnsworth Video Award, 1993; Certificateof Appreciation, Ohio Crime Prev Asn, 1994; Applause Mag Image maker Honoree, 1995; Recognized for compiling the Cincinnati Enquirer Black Hist Month Teacher's Guide, Newspaper Asn Am, 1996; Zora Neale Hurston Outstanding Scholar Award, 1999. **Home Addr:** 3830 Washington Ave Suite 3, Cincinnati, OH 45229, **Home Phone:** (513)281-4517. **Business Addr:** Instructor, Consultant, Northwestern University, 339 E Chicago Ave, Chicago, IL 60611-3008, **Business Phone:** (312)503-6950.

**HOLMES, DR. HENRY SIDNEY, III.** **See Obituaries Section.**

### HOLMES, REV. JAMES ARTHUR
Clergy, historian, chaplain. **Personal:** Born May 27, 1954, Charleston, SC; son of James Arthur Sr and Maranda Phillips. **Educ:** Allen Univ, Columbia, SC, BA, 1976; Turner Sem, Interdenominational Theol Ctr, Atlanta, GA, MDiv, 1982; Boston Univ Sch Theol, Boston, MA, MTS, 1989, ThD. **Career:** Shady Grove AMEC, Blythewood, SC, pastor, 1974-75; Rock Hill AMEC, Columbia, SC, pastor, 1975-76; Lagree AMEC, Sumter, SC, pastor, 1976-77; Am Church SC, Columbia, SC, hist consult, 1987-88; Charleston County Substance Abuse Comn, Charleston, SC, community resource person, 1990-; Boston Univ, asst prof church hist; Shaw Univ, asst prof church hist, currently. **Orgs:** SC Hist Soc, 1985-; Res Officers' Asn, 1986-. **Honors/Awds:** Annual Am Fellow, Int African Methodist Episcopal Church, 1989-91; Bishop Fredrick C James Fel, Bishop F C James, 1989. **Special Achievements:** Author: Thirty Bishops South Carolina, 1987; "The Priority Emanuel AME Church: Longest Continuous AME Church in South" AME Review, 1987; contributor, five chaps, African Methodism in South Carolina: A Bicentennial Focus, 1987; Various others. **Home Addr:** 2 Ct St, Charleston, SC 29403, **Home Phone:** (803)723-5891. **Business Addr:** Assistant Professor of Church History, Shaw University Divinity School, 295B Leonard Hall, Raleigh, NC 27602, **Business Phone:** (919)546-8576.

**HOLMES, JAMES FRANKLIN**
Government official. **Personal:** Born Nov 1, 1945, Leesburg, GA; son of Benjamin and Rosa Johnson; married Elaine Durham; children: Marcel J. **Educ:** Albany State Col, Albany, GA, BA, 1967. **Career:** US Cen Sub Bur, Detroit, Mich, surv statistician, 1968-73; US Census Bur, Cetroit, Mich, prog coordr, 1973-79; US Census Bur, Kans City, Md, asst reg dir, 1979-82; US Census Bur, Los Angeles, Calif, asst reg dir, 1982-83; US Census Bur, Philadelphia, Pa, regional dir, 1983-85; US Census Bur, Atlanta, Ga, regional dir, actg dir, 1986. **Orgs:** Atlanta Econs Club, 1986-; US Census Bur Strategic Planning Comt, 1987-89; Southern Demographic Asn, 1988-; vpres, S Cobb Improvement Asn, 1988-; Atlanta chap, Am Stat Asn, 1990-; vpres, Mableton Tigers Youth Baseball Asn, 1988-. **Home Addr:** 4779 Langford Ct SW, Mableton, GA 30126-1473, **Home Phone:** (770)944-3276. **Business Addr:** GA.

**HOLMES, JERRY LEE**
Football player, football coach. **Personal:** Born Dec 22, 1957, Newport News, VA. **Educ:** Chowan jun Col, assoc deg, bus admn, 1977; W Va Univ, BS, 1980; Hampton Univ, MBA; Long Island Univ, MBA. **Career:** Football player (retired), football coach; NY Jets, 1980, right cornerback, 1981-83, left cornerback, 1986-87; Pittsburgh Maulers, 1984; NJ Gen, 1985; Detroit Lions, left cornerback, 1988, right cornerback, 1989; Green Bay Packers, right cornerback, 1990, left cornerback, 1991; Hampton Univ, co-defensive cord & linebacker coach, 1992-94, 2004, defensive cord, linebacker coach, 2005-07, head coach, 2008; W VA, asst football coach, 1994-98; Cleveland Browns, defensive back coach, 1999-2000; Wash Redskins, defensive back coach, 2001; San Diego Chargers, defensive back coach, 2002-03; Hartford Colonials, sec coach, 2010; Morgan State Univ, defensive coordr, linebackers coach, 2013. **Honors/Awds:** Sporting News United States Football League All-Star Team, 1984, 1985; Black Coll Natl Champions Hampton Univ, 1992, 1993; CIAA championships; Ira A Rodgers Award. **Home Addr:** 103 Alderman Dr, Morgantown, WV 26505.

**HOLMES, JUNE T. See THAXTON, JUNE E.**

**HOLMES, KENNY (KENNETH JEROME HOLMES)**
Football coach, football player. **Personal:** Born Oct 24, 1973, Gifford, FL. **Educ:** Univ Miami, BA, lib arts; NMex State Univ, MA, curric & instr; Harvard Sch Bus, cert, bus mgt & entrepreneurship. **Career:** Football player (retired), coach, coordinator; Tenn Oilers, right defensive end, 1997-98; Tenn Titans, defensive end, 1999-2000; NY Giants, 2001-03; Ft Pierce Fire, head coach, defensive coordr & spec teams coordr, 2006-08; Vero Beach High Sch, defensive coordr, spec team coordr, & defensive line coach, 2008-11; New Mex State Univ, defensive tackles coach & grad asst, 2011-12; New Mex Mil Inst, asst head coach, recruitment coordr & defensive line coach, 2012-14; USD Toreros, defensive line asst coach, currently. **Honors/Awds:** ED Block Courage Award, 2000; Titans Man of the Year Award, 2001. **Business Addr:** Assistant Coach, The USD Toreros, 5998 Alcala Pk, San Diego, CA 92110, **Business Phone:** (619)260-4551.

**HOLMES, LARRY**
Boxer, businessperson. **Personal:** Born Nov 3, 1949, Cuthbert, GA; son of John and Flossie Holmes; married Diane; children: Misty, Lisa, Belinda, Kandy & Larry Jr. **Career:** Professional kick boxer (retired), businessperson; boxer, 1968-85; Muhammad Ali, sparring partner; Round 1 Bar & Disco, owner; sports wear store, owner; prof boxer; Larry Holmes Enterprises Inc, owner, 2003-; Ringside Restaurant & Nightclub, 2008. **Honors/Awds:** World Heavyweight Champion, 1978-85; champion, Int Boxing Fed, 1984; undefeated record, 45 professional fights, 31 won by knockouts; One of Ten Outstanding Men in Am, Junior Chamber Com; Inducted into the International Boxing Hall of Fame, 2008. **Special Achievements:** Holmes is mentioned in the Drake song "Miss Me, " 2010; Autobiography: Against the Odds, 1998. **Home Addr:** , Easton, PA 18042. **Business Addr:** Owner, Larry Holmes Enterprises Inc, 91 Larry Holmes Dr Suite 200, Easton, PA 18042, **Business Phone:** (610)253-6905.

**HOLMES, LESTER**
Football player. **Personal:** Born Sep 27, 1969, Tylertown, MS. **Educ:** Jackson State Univ. **Career:** Football player (retired); Philadelphia Eagles, right guard, 1993-94, 1996, guard, 1995; Oakland Raiders, right guard, 1997; Ariz Cardinals, right guard, 1998-2000, guard, 1999. **Honors/Awds:** Rookie of the Year, 1993.

**HOLMES, LOUTELIOUS. See HOLMES, T. J.**

**HOLMES, MICHAEL R.**
Executive. **Personal:** Born St. Louis, MO; married Gail; children: Brooke & Michael. **Educ:** Wash Univ, St. Louis, BA, 1979; Webster Univ, MA, bus, 1993. **Career:** Monsanto, Human Resources Dept, 1980; Arrow Electronics, human resources, 1983-84; Automatic Data Processing Inc, corp vpres, 1986-91; Edward Jones Ltd, prin partner, chief human resources officer, head hr, 1996-2005; Express Scripts, exec vpres human capital, 2005-10; Rx Outreach Inc, founder & pres, 2010-; Mercedes-Benz USA LLC. **Orgs:** United Way; bd trustee, Mary Inst Country Day Sch; adv bd, Webster Univ's Sch Bus & Technol; Harris-Stowe State Univ; bd dir, Mo Baptist Hosp; St Louis Reg Chamber Growth Asn; bd dir, Barnes Jewish Hosp; bd mem, Needy-Meds Inc; bd mem, BJC HealthCare; bd mem, St. Louis Col Pharm; bd mem, United Way Greater St. Louis; secy, bd mem, Good Samaritan Guild; past chmn, Nat Bd Dirs Sickle Cell Dis Asn Am; co-chaired, St Louis Inner City Competitive Alliance Bd. **Business Addr:** President, Founder, Rx Outreach, 3171 Riverport Tech Ctr Dr, Maryland Heights, MO 63043, **Business Phone:** (800)769-3880.

**HOLMES, PRIEST ANTHONY**
Football player, philanthropist. **Personal:** Born Oct 7, 1973, Ft. Smith, AR; son of Herman Morris and Norma; children: DeAndre, Jekovan, Corion & Jaylenn. **Educ:** Univ Tex, Austin, grad, 1996. **Career:** Football player (retired); Baltimore Ravens, running back, 1997-2000; Kansas City Chiefs, running back, 2001-07; philanthropist, currently. **Orgs:** Nat spokesperson, Nat Dairy Coun; fel Christian Athletes; supporter & benefactor, Children's Miracle Network; spokesperson, Chiefs & Price Chopper Most Valuable Player Kid prog, 2002-03; founder, Priest Holmes Found, 2005-. **Honors/Awds:** Offensive Player of the Year, San Antonio Light; Civic Leader Award, Nat Consortium Acad & Sports; Super Bowl Champion XXXV, The Snickers Hungriest Player of the Year, Super Bowl XXXIX; Sportsman of the Year, San Antonio Express-News, 2000; Named to American Football Conference Pro Bowl Team, 2001-03; Special Achievement Award, Kansas City Sports Community, 2002; Chiefs Unsung Hero Award, Nat Football League Players Asn, 2002; Named National Football League Offensive Player of the Year, 2002; National Football League All-Pro, 2002; Father of the Year, Afro-Am Newspapers, 2002; National Football Leagu Alumni Running Back of the Year, 2002; Named Top 100 Good Guys in sports, The Sporting News, 2003; Civic Leader Award, Nat Consortium Academics, 2004; Ed Block Courage Award, 2004; JB Teamwork Award, FOX Sports, 2005; Univ Tex Hall of Honor; Texas High School Sports Hall of Fame, 2007; Most Valuable Person, Sun Bowl; Kansas City Chiefs Hall of Fame. **Business Addr:** Founder, Philanthropist, Priest Holmes Foundation, 5804 Babcock Rd Suite 100, San Antonio, TX 78240, **Business Phone:** (210)541-4642.

**HOLMES, RICHARD BERNARD**
Banker. **Personal:** Born Apr 4, 1951, Chicago, IL; son of Robert B and Florence M; married Marion Turner; children: Reginald B. **Educ:** Chicago City Col, attended 1970; DePaul Univ, attended 1975; Univ Phoenix, BSBA, 1989. **Career:** First Nat Bank Chicago, sr tax acct, 1972-79; Valley Nat Bank, trust tax adminr, 1979-82; Ariz Bank, mgr, trust tax unit, 1982-85; Security Pac Bank, employee benefit trust admin, 1985-89, systs conversion proj consult, 1989-90; Bank Am, mgr, employee benefit acct, 1990-92, vpres, sr trust officer, 1992-2000; Comerica Bank, vpres, 2000-. **Orgs:** Pres, Ariz Asn Urban Bankers, 1988-89; acct dir, United Negro Col Fund, San Diego, Phoenix, 1988-90, 1992-; vpres, Western Region, Nat Asn Urban Bankers, 1989-90, vpres finance, 1991-92, pres, 1996-97; pres, San Diego Urban Bankers, 1993-94. **Honors/Awds:** Man of the Year, Southern Calif Conference of the African Methodist Episcopal Church, 1996. **Home Addr:** 12765 Kestrel St, San Diego, CA 92129, **Home Phone:** (619)484-3243. **Business Addr:** Vice President, 450 B St Suite 1700, San Diego, CA 92101, **Business Phone:** (619)515-5724.

**HOLMES, DR. ROBERT A.**
Government official, executive director, administrator. **Personal:** Born Jul 13, 1943, Shepherdstown, WV; son of Priscilla L and Clarence A; married Gloria C; children: Donna Lee Vaughn, Darlene Marie Jackson & Robert A Jr. **Educ:** Shepherd Col, attended 1964; Columbia Univ, MA, 1966, PhD, political science, 1969. **Career:** Harvard-Yale-Columbia Summer Studies Prog, dir, 1968-69; Southern Univ, assoc prof, 1969-70; City Univ New York, Bernard Baruch Col, dir SEEK, 1970-71; Atlanta Univ, prof, 1971-; Ga Gen Assembly, state rep, 1974-2008; Govt Affairs Comn, chmn; Clark Atlanta Univ, Southern Ctr Studies Pub Policy, dir, 1989, distinguished prof polit sci, 2002-05; N Ga Bank, co-founder; Capitol City Bank, co-founder; Policy Design Corp, co-founder. **Orgs:** Pres, Adams Pk Residents Asn, 1972-73; pres, Nat Conf Black Polit Scientists, 1973-74; pres, Asn Social & Behav Scientists, 1976-77; chmn & bd dir, YMCA SW Atlanta, 1976-78; chmn & bd dir, Res Atlanta, 1978-79; chair, Ga Legis Black Caucus, 1990-91; bd dir, Capitol City Bank, 1995-; chair & bd trustee, Jomandi Theater Co, 1998-; exec coun, Am Polit Sci Asn, 2000-02; Maynard Jackson's Mayoral Transition Team; chair & pres, Alpha Phi Alpha Fraternity; Citywide League Neighborhoods; Grady Hosp Authority; John Harland Boys Club; Jomandi Theater Co; Metrop Atlanata YMCA; Res Atlanta, Sickle Cell Found Ga; S Fulton Running Partners. **Honors/Awds:** Outstanding Young Man of the Year, Atlanta Jaycees, 1975; Outstanding Legislator's Award, Am Asn Adult Educr, 1978; Alumnus of the Year, Shepherd Col, 1978; Layperson of the Year Award, Metrop Atlanta YMCA, 1989; Chmn, Ga Legis Black Caucus, 1990-91; Amoco Foundation Outstanding Professor Award, Clark-Atlanta Univ, 1992; Fannie Lou Hamer Community Service Award, 1993; Torchbearer Award, Sickle Cell Found Ga, 1996; Legislator of the Year, Nat Black Caucus State Legislators, 1999; Bob A Holmes Freeway, named in honor, 1999; Honorary Doctorate in Humanities, Shepherd Col, 2001; Received more than 100 awards for his work in academia, community service and politics. **Special Achievements:** Author & co-author: 25 monographs & books; 75 articles; Editor of two annual publications, The Georgia Legislative Review & the Status of Black Atlanta; Book: Maynard Jackson: A Biography; First African American in the history of the General Assembly to serve on the Budget Subcommittee. Part of Interstate 285 was named in his honor, from Interstate 85 in South Fulton County to Interstate 20. **Home Addr:** 2421 Poole Rd SW, Atlanta, GA 30311. **Business Addr:** Director, Distinguished Professor, Clark-Atlanta University, 223 James P Brawley Dr, Atlanta, GA 30314, **Business Phone:** (404)880-8089.

**HOLMES, ROBERT C.**
Commissioner, lawyer. **Personal:** Born Mar 20, 1945, Elizabeth, NJ; children: 1. **Educ:** Cornell Univ, AB, govt, 1967; Harvard Law Sch, JD, 1971. **Career:** Roxbury, cir assoc, 1969-71; State NJ, atty, 1971; Newark Housing Devel & Rehab Corp Newark, exec dir, 1971-74; Newark Watershed Conserv & Develop Corp, chief exec, 1979-87; Wilentz Goldman & Spitzer, partner, 1987; coun, Medvin & Elberg, 1995; NJ St Dep Comm Affairs, asst commr atty; Rudgers Sch law, clin prof law, currently, dep dir clin progs, Community Law Clin, dir, currently. **Orgs:** NJ Bar Asn; Nat Bar Asn; Am Soc Pub Adm; Garden St Bar Asn; NAHRO; pres, Nj Pub Policy Res Inst; secy, Legal Serv Nj. **Honors/Awds:** Nat hon soc, Cornell Univ; Deans List; 4 yr Teagle Found Scholar; Sr Men's Hon Soc MA NG; Rutgers Human Dignity Award, 2016. **Business Addr:** Clinical Professor, Director, State University of New Jersey, 123 Wash St, Newark, NJ 07102-3094, **Business Phone:** (973)353-3190.

**HOLMES, ESQ. ROBERT ERNEST**
Lawyer, president (organization). **Personal:** Born Jul 24, 1943, New York, NY. **Educ:** Wash Sq Col, BA, 1966; NY Univ Sch Law, JD, 1969; Manhattan Sch Music & Univ Southern Calif, addn study. **Career:** Paul Weiss Rifkind Wharton & Garrison, summer assoc, 1968, part time atty, 1968-69, assoc atty, 1969-71; WA Sq Col Arts & Sci, guest lectr, 1969-70, adj instr am lit, 1970-71; NY Sch Continuing Educ, adj instr black am, 1969-70; Motown Rec Corp, sr coun, 1971, legal coun, 1971; Motown Rec & Filmworks, gen coun; Arista Music Publ Group, vpres; Sony Pictures Entertainment's Music Group, exec vpres; Columbia Pictures, Music Group, sr vpres, gen mgr, Music Publ Div, pres. **Orgs:** Bd dir, Pac Psychother Asn, Calif; bd dir, Nat Asn Advan Colored People; bd dir, Const Rights Found CA; Liberace Found; bd dir, Black Music Asn; pres, Black Entertainment & Sports Lawyers' Asn; assoc couns, Motown Rec, 1971-77; pres, Black Entertainment & Sports Lawyers Asn; co-founder, Black Am Law Students Asn; bd mem, NYU Africa House. **Honors/Awds:** Dean's List, Temple Univ & NY Univ Sch Law; Univ Schlorship NY Univ, NY State Schlorship, NY Univ; Leopold Schepp Fund Schlorship, NY Univ; various debate & pub speking awrads; Am Juris prudence Prize in Copyright; Military History Award, Temple Univ, 1963; recipient Fulbright-Dougherty Travel Grant, 1967; Samuel Rubin Schlorship Carnegie Fund Schlorship; Washington Square College Alumni Distinguished Service Award, 1992. **Special Achievements:** Author of numerous publs; recipient of NYU Alumni Achievement Award, 1998. **Business Addr:** Senior Vice President General Manager, President, Columbia Pictures, Columbia Plz E, Burbank, CA 91505, **Business Phone:** (818)954-2687.

**HOLMES, ROBERT KATHRONE, JR.**
Executive, president (organization), chief executive officer. **Personal:** Born Sep 5, 1952, Louisville, KY; son of Robert K Sr and Cecile E Thompson; married Stephanie A Kennedy; children: Robert K III, Tomika C & Justin C. **Educ:** McKendree Col, Lebanon, IL, bus admin, 1988; Leadership Louisville, attended 1990; Bingham Fellows, attended 1997. **Career:** Ky Fried Chicken, Louisville, Ky, mgr facil, 1979-88; Brown-Forman Corp, Louisville, Ky, vpres, dir corp servs, 1988; Louisville Real Estate Develop Co, pres & chief exec officer; Mardrian Group, chmn & asst vpres, currently; Endeavour Corp Inc, Develop Partner, currently; Corp Serv Consults LLC, pres, chief exec officer, currently-. **Orgs:** Past pres, Int Fac Mgt Asn, 1985-; Nat Asn Corp Real Estate Execs, 1988-; Int Soc Fac Execs, 1989-; prof cert, Certified Com Investment Mem; bd dir, Louisville Real Estate Develop Co. **Home Addr:** 8809 Juniper Springs Pl, Louisville, KY 40242-7659, **Home Phone:** (502)423-0836. **Business Addr:** Development Partner, Endeavour Corp Inc, 770 N Milwaukee St, Milwaukee, WI 53202, **Business Phone:** (414)431-0021.

**HOLMES, T. J. (LOUTELIOUS HOLMES)**
Television journalist. **Personal:** Born Aug 19, 1977, West Memphis, AR; married Marilee Fiebig; children: Sabine; married Amy Ferson; children: Brianna & Jaiden. **Educ:** Univ Ark, BA, broadcast journalism. **Career:** KSNF Channel 16 (Joplin, MO), producer/assignment reporter/weekend anchor; KTHV (Little Rock), gen assignment reporter/weekend anchor, 2000-03; KNTV, NBC O&O Sta (San Francisco), eve anchor, 2003-06; CNN's "Saturday & Sunday Morning", anchor, 2006-11; BET Networks, host/corresp, 2012-13; MSNBC, substitute anchor, 2013; CNN, anchor, 2013; ABC News, anchor, 2014-. **Orgs:** 100 Black Men Atlanta; Nat Asn Black Journalists; chancellor's bd advisors, Univ Ark; bd visitors, Emory Univ Atlanta. **Honors/Awds:** University of Arkansas, Young Alumni Award, 2007; "The Grio", 100 List of History Makers; "The Root", 100 List of Most Influential Black Americans, 2012; Hennessy Privilege Award, Recipient, 2012; NAACP Image Award Nomination, 2013.

**HOLMES, DR. WENDELL P., JR.**
Education reformer, funeral director. **Personal:** Born Feb 10, 1922, Brunswick, GA; married Jacquelyne Spence; children: Wendell P III & Carolyn Nesmith. **Educ:** Hampton Inst, Pres Class, BS, 1943; Eckels Col Mortuary Sci, pres class mortuary sci, 1947. **Career:** Duval Co Sch Bd, chmn, 1980-84; Holmes & W Funeral Home PA, pres, 1956-86; Wendell Holmes Funeral Dirs Inc, funeral dir, pres, 1986-. **Orgs:** Duval Co Sch Bd, 1969-92; chair & bd dir, Century Nat Bank, 1976-85; chmn & bd trustees, Bethune Cookman Col; founding sire archon, Gamma Beta Blvd, Sigma Pi Phi Fraternity; bd trustees, chmn, Hampton Univ; Alpha Phi Alpha Fraternity, bd mem, Hampton Univ; mem community develop coun, First Union Nat Bank; DuPont Community Bldg Fund Adv Comt; Better Jacksonville Plan Finance Admin Comt; chairperson, Coun Bd Chairs Asn Gov Boards Univs & Cols; life mem, Alpha Phi Alpha fraternity; founding Sire Archon, GammaBeta Boule Sigma Pi Phi fraternity. **Honors/Awds:** Received more than 100 awards & recognitions for his support of humanitarian causes & for his community service, including, Hon LLD Degree Bethune-Cookman, 1982; Annual Brotherhood Award, Nat Conf Christians & Jews, 1985; Small Bus man of the Year, Jacksonville Area-Chamber Com; Meritorious Service in Area of Human Relation, Alpha Phi Alpha Fraternity; Silver Bell Award for Significant Contribution to Education, Duval County Classroom Teachers Asn; Distinguished Leadership Award, United Negro College. **Special Achievements:** First African American elected to a school board. **Home Addr:** 12859 Muirfield Blvd S, Jacksonville, FL 32225-4783, **Home Phone:** (904)997-0557. **Business Addr:** President, Wendell Holmes Funeral Directors Inc, 2719 W Edgewood Ave, Jacksonville, FL 32209, **Business Phone:** (904)765-1641.

**HOLMES, WILLIAM**
Executive, minister (clergy). **Personal:** Born Aug 19, 1940, Allendale, SC; married Diane T; children: Renada Irene & Eva Regina. **Educ:** Voorhees Col, BS, math, 1973. **Career:** Mayor, City Allendale, 1976-88; DuPont, sr engr; Westinghouse Savannah River Co, engr, 1997; Allendale Sta Church Christ, radio ministry, currently. **Orgs:** SC Sect Conf Black Mayors;Nat Asn Advan Colored People; Allendale County Indust Develop Bd. **Home Addr:** 241 Bay St E, Allendale, SC 29810-3817, **Home Phone:** (803)584-2707. **Business Addr:** Radio Ministry, Allendale station for the Church of Christ.

**HOLMES, WILLIAM B.**
Law enforcement officer, social worker, teacher. **Personal:** Born Jan 31, 1937, Trenton, NJ; married Helen Vereen; children: Mark William & Allen C. **Educ:** Va Union Univ, BA, 1959. **Career:** Fed Probation Officers Asn, teacher, 1960-61; Dept Pub Welfare, soc caseworker, 1961-62; Mercer Co Welfare Bd, social case worker, 1962-63; State NJ, Div Ment Retardation, social worker, 1963-66, parole officer, 1966-75;

Fed Job Corp, group leader, 1966; E Dist PA, US probation officer, 1975. **Orgs:** Bd dir, Lawrence YMCA, 1968-; pres, vpres, Bd Educ, Lawrence Twp, 1969-, pub safety adv comt; life mem, past polemarch Kappa Alpha Psi Frat, 1970-71; chmn, Mercer Co, Community Col EOF, 1972-; exec bd, Nat Asn Advan Colored People Trenton. **Honors/Awds:** Pioneer Award for Achievement; Polemarch Award, Kappa Alpha Psi Frat; Certificate of recognition, Lawrence Township Recreation Comn; Certificate of recognition, Lawrence Township Non-Profit Housing; Achievement Award, Distinguish Service Kappa Alpha Frat; Achievement Award, Nat Asn Advan Colored People; Recognition Award for Outstanding service, Lawrence Township. **Home Addr:** 47 Altamawr Ave, Lawrenceville, NJ 08648. **Business Addr:** 601 Market St, Philadelphia, PA 19106.

## HOLMES, WILLIE A.
Salesperson, consultant. **Personal:** Born Jul 25, 1928, Warwick, VA; married Addie Smith; children: Audrey, Yolanda & Wendell. **Educ:** Quinn Col, BS, 1961. **Career:** Litton Med Prod, salesman, 1955-68; Equit Life, agt, 1968-82, asst dist sales mgr, 1969, dist sales mgr, 1970; AXA Adv LLC, consult & adv, currently; Barkley travel LLc, pres & owner, 1982-. **Orgs:** Alpha Phi Alpha, 1957; Nat Asn Life Underwriters, 1968-; Career Sales Club, 1974-; Conn Develop Authority, 1976; New Haven Bus & Prof Asn; vpres, Bus Vent; dir, Urbn League Nat Asn Advan Colored People; Quinn Col Alum Asn; pres, Barkley associates, 2011-. **Honors/Awds:** Man of the Year, Alpha Phi Alpha, 1965. **Special Achievements:** First & only black member appointed to Connecticut Development Authority. **Business Addr:** Owner, President, Barkley Travel LLC, 87 Antrim St, West Haven, CT 06516-1843, **Business Phone:** (203)934-7256.

## HOLMES, WILMA K., JR.
Educator. **Personal:** Born Apr 25, 1933, Washington, DC; daughter of Elton F and Edith T; married Arthur Jr; children: Ricki Fairley Brown & Sharon Fairley. **Educ:** DC Teachers Col, Wash, DC, BA, 1956; Stanford Univ, Palo Alto, Calif, MA, 1970. **Career:** Vario Sch Syst, teacher, 1964-70; Montgomery Co Pub Sch, teacher, 1964-70, lang arts teacher specialist, 1969-70, dir human rels, 1970-84, human rels training coordr, 1970-71, supvr instr, 1987-92, prin retired; Flower Valley Elem Sch, elem prin, 1992. **Orgs:** Nat Alliance Black Sch Educ; Am Asn Sch Adminr; Montgomery Co Alumni Chap; Delta Sigma Theta Soreity; Phi Delta Kappa Sorority; Pi Lambda Theta Hon Educ Soreity; Family Justice Fund Raising Comt; Nat Coun Negro Women; conf chair, Elem Sch Admin Asn, 2001; Nat Asn Elem Prin; Nat Asn Advan Colored People, Montgomery County Br; pres & gospel choir class leader, Clinton AME Zion Church; Silver Spring mem & bd dirs, Community Concerts Olrey Links Inc. **Honors/Awds:** Back to Basics & Multiculturalism are not Mutually Exclusive, NEA Human Rights Conf; Creative Solutions to Staff Reduction, Am Asn Sch Adminrs; Woman of the Year, Montgomery County, 1979; Design & Implemented Multiethnic Conv Educ & Consult-Sexism; Community Service Award, 2013; Shining Star Award, Montgomery Women. **Home Addr:** 17104 Blossom View Dr, Olney, MD 20832-2409, **Home Phone:** (301)774-1393. **Business Addr:** Principal, Montgomery County Public Schools, 4615 Sunflower Dr, Rockville, MD 20853, **Business Phone:** (301)924-3135.

## HOLMES, REV. ZAN W., JR.
Clergy, educator, association executive. **Personal:** Born Feb 1, 1935, San Angelo, TX; married Carrie Collins. **Educ:** Huston-Tillotson Col, BA, 1956; Southern Methodist Univ, BD, 1959, STM, 1968. **Career:** Educator, pastor (retired); Hamilton Pk UMC, pastor, 1958-68; Tex St rep, 1968-72; Dallas Cent Dist, N Tex Conf, 1968-74; Intern Prog, Southern Methodist Univ, assoc dir, 1974-78; St Luke Community United Methodist Church, sr pastor, 1974-2002; Perkins Sch Theol, Southern Methodist Univ, assoc prof preaching, 1978-2002. **Orgs:** Judicial Coun United Methodist Church; Bd Regents, Univ Tex Syst, regent; Greater Dallas Community Churches, past pres, bd dirs; Comerica Bank, bd dirs; State Fair Tex, bd dirs; Dallas Found, bd dirs; Soc Study Black Relig; Black Methodist Church Renewal; life mem, Nat Asn Advan Colored People; Alpha Phi Alpha Fraternity; pres, Dallas Pastor's Asn, 1963; Tri-Ethnic Comt, chair, 1971; Legis Comt Tex Const Rev Comn, chair, 1974; United Methodist Publ House, bd dirs; CDF, Tex adv bd; Chase Bank, ministerial adv bd; Am Acad Homiletics; co chairperson, World Difference; Task Force Educ ExcellenceDallas Independent Sch Dist. **Honors/Awds:** Jr Black Acad Arts & Letters, Living Legend Award, 1991; Huston-Tillotson Col, Humanitarian Award, 1991; Linz Jewelers & Dallas Morning News, LinzAward, 1991; Peace Maker Award, Dallas Peace Ctr, 1990; Peace Maker Award, Dallas Peace Ctr, 1991; Linz Award, Line Jewelers & Dallas Morning News, 1991; Humanitarian Award, Houston-Tillotson Col, 1991; Living LegendAward, Jr Black Acad Arts & Letters, 1991; Dillard Univ, honorary doctors of laws, 1993; honorary degrees Huston-Tillotson Col, DDiv, 1970; RustCol, Honorary Doctor of Laws, 2002; Tom Unis Diversity Award, GreaterDallas, Human Rels Comn, 2002. **Special Achievements:** First African American to hold the position of president of Dallas Pastor's Assn, 1963; "Black and United Methodist," in Our Time Under Godis Now, Abingdon Press, 1993; author: Reaching for Renewal, 1991, Encountering Jesus, Abingdon Press, 1992; When Trouble Comes, CSS Press, 1996; "Enabling the Word to Happen", "in Power in the Pulpit: How America's Most Effective Black Preachers Prepare Their Sermons, 2002; narrator: "Disciple" Bible Study Video, Cokesbury/Graded Press Video, 1987/1992; first African American to serve on the Board of Regents of the University of Texas System, 1991; published entitled Songs of Zion, Abingdon Press, 1981; Come Sunday-The Liturgy Zion, Companion to SZO-Abingdon Press, 1990; When Trouble Comes, CSS Publishing Co, Inc, 1996. **Home Addr:** 6910 Robin Rd, Dallas, TX 75209-4815, **Home Phone:** (214)358-0467. **Business Addr:** Educator, Los Angeles, CA 90009.

## HOLSENDOLPH, ERNEST
Journalist. **Personal:** Born Oct 31, 1935, Quitman, GA; son of Wallace (deceased) and Ethel; married Linda Shelby; children: Nora & Joseph. **Educ:** Columbia Col, BA, 1958. **Career:** Journalist (retired); Cleveland Press, reporter, 1961-65; E Ohio Gas Co, ed, 1965-67; Wash Star, reporter, 1967-69; Fortune Mag, assoc ed, 1969-71; NY Times, reporter, 1972-83; Plain Dealer, Cleveland, OH, bus ed, 1983-89; Atlanta J Const, city ed, 1989-91, bus columnist, 1991. **Orgs:** Bd dir, Alumni Asn Columbia Col. **Honors/Awds:** SABEW Distinguished Achievement Award, 2000. **Home Addr:** 4248 Autumn Woods Ct, Stone Mountain, GA 30083-5247, **Home Phone:** (404)299-1060.

## HOLSEY, BERNARD (LEONARD BERNARD HOLSEY)
Football player, football coach. **Personal:** Born Dec 10, 1973, Rome, GA. **Educ:** Duke Univ. **Career:** Football player (retired), coach; New York Giants, defensive end, 1996-99, defensive tackle, 1997; Indianapolis Colts, defensive end, 2000; New Eng Patriots, 2002; Wash Redskins, left & right defensive tackle, 2003; St Louis Rams, 2004; Utah Blaze, 2006; Austin Wranglers, 2006; Orlando Predators, 2007; Wittenberg-Birnamwood High Sch, head football coach, currently. **Business Addr:** Head Football Coach, Wittenberg-Birnamwood High School, 300 S Prouty St, Wittenberg, UT 54499, **Business Phone:** (715)253-2221.

## HOLSEY, LEONARD BERNARD. See HOLSEY, BERNARD.

## HOLSEY, DR. LILLA GWENDOLYN
Educator. **Personal:** Born Aug 20, 1941, San Mateo, FL; children: Linita. **Educ:** Hampton Univ, BS, 1963; Fla State Univ, MS, 1971, PhD, 1974. **Career:** Lincoln High Sch, 1964-70; Gainesville High Sch, home econ teacher, 1970-72; Fla State Univ, grad res asst, 1971 & 1973; E Carolina Univ, adv & assoc prof home econs, 1974-, Dept Bus, Carrer & Tech Educ, assoc prof & grad prog dir, assoc prof, prof emer, 2008-. **Orgs:** Nat & Am Home Econ Assn; Am & Voc Assn; NC Consumer Assn; Bethel AME Church; bd trustee, Alpha Kappa Alpha; Kappa Delta Pi & Omicron Nu Hon Soc; Phi Kappa Delta. **Home Addr:** 1021 W Wright Rd, Greenville, NC 27834. **Business Addr:** Professor Emerita, East Carolina University, 2309 Bate Bldg, Greenville, NC 27858, **Business Phone:** (252)328-6762.

## HOLT, DELORIS LENETTE
Educator, writer, teacher. **Personal:** Born East Chicago, IN; daughter of Willis Adams and Pearl; married Chester A. **Educ:** Ball State Univ, BSEd, 1956; Pepperdine Univ, credential, 1969; Univ SanFrancisco, MSEd, 1978. **Career:** Los Angeles City Schs, parent involvement coordr; Cleveland Pub Schs, teacher; Los Angeles City Schs, Follow Through, adv proj; Bk: Heritage, 2007; Los Angeles Unified Sch Dist, teacher & auth, currently. **Orgs:** Alpha Kappa Alpha; Kinderpress, 1991. **Honors/Awds:** Resolution of Commendation, Los Angles City Coun, 1972; Merit Award, Calif Asn Teachers Eng, 1973; Early Childhood Educ Instrnl Guides Teachers Kinderpress, 1991. **Special Achievements:** Author of books published by Ward Ritchie Press 1971, Childrens Press1973, LA Unified School Dist 1987; Publications: Black Hist Playing Card Deck US Games Systems Inc, 1978. **Home Addr:** 3943 Degnan Blvd, Los Angeles, CA 90008-2615, **Home Phone:** (323)291-9935. **Business Addr:** Teacher, Author, Los Angeles Unified School District, 419 W 98th St, Los Angeles, CA 90003, **Business Phone:** (213)756-1419.

## HOLT, DONALD H.
Executive, lawyer. **Personal:** Born Jan 22, 1941, Cleveland, OH; married Dianne Williford. **Educ:** J Carroll Univ, BS & BA, 1964; Case Western Res Univ, MBA, 1971; Univ Akron, JD, 1976. **Career:** Prmr Indus Corp, asst vpres corp prsnl admin; spec asst to pres, 1968-69; cst anlyst, 1967-68; E OH Gas Co, asst to pres, 1969-; atty, Holt Legal Serv LLC, currently. **Orgs:** Test Urban Leag Greater Cleveland; City Club Cleveland; United Way Serv; Rotary Club, Cleveland; Blacks Mgt;Nat Asn Advan Colored People; Alpha Phi Alpha; Nat Urban Affairs Coun; OH State Bar Asn. **Home Addr:** 23512 Cedar Rd, Beachwood, OH 44122, **Home Phone:** (216)381-6728. **Business Addr:** Attorney, Holt Legal Services LLC, 13940 Cedar Rd 255, University Heights, OH 44118, **Business Phone:** (216)453-2666.

## HOLT, DR. DOROTHY L. THOMAS
Educator, administrator. **Personal:** Born Nov 11, 1930, Shreveport, LA; married James S III; children: James IV, Jonathan Lamar & Roderick Lenard. **Educ:** Wiley Col Marshall Tex, BS, 1962; La Tech Univ Ruston, MS, 1973; Northwestern State Univ, attended 1975; E Tex State Univ Com, EdD, 1978. **Career:** Administrator, educator (retired); Caddo Parish Educ Sec Assoc, pres & founder, 1954-62; Caddo Teachers Assoc, sec, 1973-74; La Distrib Educ Assoc, from treas to pres, 1979-81; League Women Voters, Shreveport, from treas to vpres, 1979-83; Cent High Alumni Assoc, treas, 1980-93; Nat Assoc Adv Black Am, sec & bd mem, 1983-85; Caddo Asn Educrs, vpres, 1984-85; La Assoc Dist Educ Teachers Awards Comm, chairperson, 1984-85; Caddo Parish Sch Syst, coord; Mayor's Women's Comn, bd mem, 2014-15. **Orgs:** Chmn, Alpha Kappa Alpha Sorority Inc, 1983-85; vpres, Caddo Asn Educr, 1984-85; Phi Delta Kappa, Kappa Delta Pi, Nat Assoc DE Teachers, Am Voc Ed Assoc, La Assoc DE Teachers NEA, YMCA, YWCA; bd trustee, MDEA/AV Dist Ed Prof Develop Award; chmn, Caddo Parish Textbk Comm Dist Educ Teachers; planner & presenter, CPSB Prof Improv In-Serv Prog; pres, Ave BC Jr Mission; Allendale Br YWCA Bd Mgt, Caddo Parish Teachers Fed Union, Ed Comm Ave Bapt Church Fed Credit Union; pres, Allendale Br YWCA, 1988-91; Shreveport Reg Arts CNL; vip, Civic Club, 1993; pres, Sigma Rho Omego Chap, Alpha Kappa Alpha Sorority Inc, 1997-98; bd dir, David Raines Med Ctr. **Home Addr:** 306 Holcomb Dr, Shreveport, LA 71103-2030, **Home Phone:** (318)424-7915. **Business Addr:** Board Member, City of Shreveport, 505 Travis St, Shreveport, LA 71101.

## HOLT, DR. EDWIN J.
Educator, counselor, college teacher. **Personal:** Born Shreveport, LA; son of James S and Sammie Lee Draper (deceased); married Essie W; children: Lisa Michele & Rachelle Justine. **Educ:** Cent State Univ, BA, 1958; Ind Univ, MS, 1962; Univ Ariz, EdD, 1971; Univ Tenn, attended 1977. **Career:** Caddo Parish Sch Bd, teacher, 1959-67, guid coun, 1967-68, from asst prin to sch prin, 1968-74, instr dir, 1974-80, asst supt, 1980-90; La State Univ, adj prof, 1972; La Tech Univ, 1973-75; Northeast La Univ, 1973-75; NE La Univ, 1973; Southern Univ, 1976-79; Grambling St Univ, 1980-84; H Enterprises, founder & cochmn, 1980-81; La State Univ, assoc prof Holt sch, 1990. **Orgs:** Bd dir, Rutherford House, 1980-84; Trinity Baptist Church, 1980-; co-dir, Afro Am Hist Actvists, Trinity Baptist Church, 1980-; pres, La Alpha Phi Alpha Frat, 1981-83; Shreveport Clean Community, 1981-86; bd mem, Caddo Dist PTA, 1981-90; bd dir, Norwela Coun BSA, 1981-86; appeal bd mem, Selective Serv Syst, 1981-89; bd dir, Coun Aging, 1982-84; bd mgt, Carver Br, YMCA, 1982-87; Youth Involvement Prog, 1986-89; Shreveport Proj Sel Sufficiency Task Force, 1984-87; bd dir, Am Heart Asn, 1991-; pres, Delta Kappa Boule; Sigma Pi Phi Fraternity, 1997; prof mem, Nat Educ Asn; LEA; CAE; Phi Delta Kappa; Caddo Jt Adm Org; Kappa Delta Pi; Hon Soc; auditor, Shreveport Nat Coun Negro Women; dir, Summer Youth Work Study Prog; lic La prof counr. **Honors/Awds:** John Hay Fel Williams Col, 1964; Caddo Parish Educatorof the Year, 1966; NDEA Fel State Col, Ariz, 1968; Southern Fel Fund, Univ Ariz, 1970-71; Man of the Year, Alpha Phi Alpha Fraternity, 1972. **Home Addr:** 208 Plano St, Shreveport, LA 71103-2057, **Home Phone:** (318)221-1795.

## HOLT, DR. ESSIE W.
Educator, association executive. **Personal:** Born Sicily Island, LA; married Edwin J; children: Lisa Michelle & Rachelle Justine. **Educ:** Grambling State Univ, BS; Univ Ark, Fayetteville, MEd, Educ Specialist; Univ Tenn, Knoxville, EdD. **Career:** Educator (retired); LSU-Shreveport, Caddo Parish Sch Bd, classroom teacher, guid counr, psychologist, elem prin, elem instrnl supvr, asst supt curric & instrn, asst supt; La Lic Prof Counr Bd Examiners, counr; Judson Fundamental Magnet Sch, prin. **Orgs:** Alpha Kappa Alpha Delta Lambda Omega Chap; Links Inc; NAESP; PTA; bd dir, United Way; bd dir, Rutherford House; bd dir, Juv Justice Prog; Vol, Sickle Cell Anemia Dr; bd dir, YWCA; bd dirs; Child Care Serv Bd; bd dir, Goodwill Indust; bd dir, LSU Med Ctr Instnl Rev Bd Protection Human Res Subjects, secy trustee bd, Trinity Baptist Church; Women's Auxiliary Orgn. **Honors/Awds:** Zeta Phi Beta Educator Award; Leadership Shreveport Grad CAE Educator of the Year Award; LA Gov Comm Women life mem PTA recipient; Women Who Have made a Difference Award, LA PTA Service Scroll; Athena Award Recipient, 1998. **Home Addr:** 208 Plano St, Shreveport, LA 71103-2057, **Home Phone:** (318)221-1795. **Business Addr:** Professor, La Prof Counr Bd of Examiners, 8631 Summa Ave, Baton Rouge, LA 70809, **Business Phone:** (225)765-2515.

## HOLT, REV. FRED D.
Clergy. **Personal:** Born Feb 7, 1931, Macon, GA; married Nancy Smith; children: Larry, Kenny, Tim, Tony & Clevetta Rogers. **Educ:** Chapaman Col, BA, sociol, 1982; Goldengate Univ, masters, pub admin, 1984. **Career:** M & H Restaurant, owner, 1973-76; Salinas City Coun, candid, 1979-83; Nadon Enterprise, owner, 1981-85; St James Christian Methodist Episcopal, Steward Bd, chmn, 1983, preacher, 1991, emer pastor, currently. **Orgs:** Sr deacon, Fremont Masonic Lodge No 13, 1958-82; Salinas Chamber Com, 1972-83; pres, Salinas Nat Asn Advan Colored People, 1974-75, chm, 1983-85; Salinas City Affirm Active Action Bd Chap, 1980-82; Sal Rent Mediation Bd, 1981-83; life mem, Nat Asn Advan Colored People, 1984; KRS Omega Psi Phi Omicron Nu, 1984-85, basilius, 1994-96; legal redress officer Salinas Br, Nat Asn Advan Colored People, 1995-; vpres, Holts Rec Co. **Honors/Awds:** Thalheimer Award Class I, Nat Asn Advan Colored People, 1975-76; Man Of the Year Award, Nat Asn Advan Colored People, 1979; Achievement Award, Nat Asn Advan Colored People, 1984; Omicron-Nu Omega Psi Phi Man of the Year, 1990, 1995; Lay Leader Award, 1997. **Home Addr:** 1433 Shawnee Way, Salinas, CA 93906-2605, **Home Phone:** (831)422-4504. **Business Addr:** Emeritus Pastor, St James Christian Methodist Episcopal, 285 Calle Cebu St, Salinas, CA 93901, **Business Phone:** (831)422-3741.

## HOLT, DR. JAMES STOKES, III
Executive, real estate agent, educator. **Personal:** Born Sep 23, 1927, Shreveport, LA; son of James and Sammie Lee Draper; married Dorothy L Thomas; children: James IV, Jonathan Lamar & Roderick Lenard. **Educ:** Cent State Univ, BS, 1949; La State Univ, MEd, 1956; Univ Ar, Fayetteville, PhD, 1973; Lincoln Grad Ctr, San Antoine, Tex, MSA, 1989. **Career:** Educator (retired); Caddo Parish Sch Bd, math bio chem instr, 1950-66; State Dept LA, coun mem state drug abuse, 1972-74; Grad Sch S Univ, fac mem, 1972-79; Southern Univ, div chmn, 1972-79; HHH Real Estate Investments Co, pres, 1981; MRA Nat Asn Master Appraisers, 1982; Holt Real Estate Appraisal Co, Shreveport, owner, 1987; LA Ins Comn, lic salesman, 1991; Cert Real Estate Property Inspector, 1999; Ruben Real Estate Co, Shreveport, LA, salesman; Southern Univ, prof biol. **Orgs:** Xi Chap, 1947; Alpha Phi Alpha Frat, 1947-; Beta Kappa Chi Hon Soc, 1948-; life mem, LEA Teacher orgn, 1955-; life mem, NEA Teacher Orgn, 1960-; pres, Lakeside Acres Civic Asn, 1968-; Supt Sunday Sch Ave Baptist Church, 1969-92; 3rd Degree Mason AF & AM, 1970-; secy, Shreveport Metro Bd Appeals, 1975-; LA Home Mgrs Asn, 1987-; Nat Orgn Black County Officials, 1988-; Shreveport Black Chamber Com, 1988; Nat Soc Environ Consult, 1995; Boy Scouts Am, Cherokee Dist, Norweia Coun Dist comnr, 2002-; YMCA, Nat Asn Advan Colored People, LA Coun Human Rights; co-chmn, Biol Scholar Award Comt, 1992; charter mem, EAC; mem 20 yr Celebration Steering CommSU-Shreveport. **Honors/Awds:** Univ Texas, Academic Year Grant, Nat Sci Found, 1960; Nat Sci Fel Biol Stud, TSU, 1958, Dillard Univ, 1962; Shreveport Times Award, 1962; Fla State Univ Radiation Biology Award, 1963; Phi Delta Kappa, Univ Ark, 1971; Southern Fellow Higher Education Award, Univ AR, 1972-74; Fourth District Distinguished Achievement Award, La Educ Asn, 1974; recipient of Scout Leaders Regional Tr Cert & Scout masters key; Sprit of Scouting Award, Boy Scouts of Am (BSA), 1999; Silver Beaver Award, BSA, 1999; Woodbadge Training Award, BSA, 1999; Whitney Young Award, BSA, 2001; Small Business Man of the Year, Minority Bus Coun, 2002; Educator of the Year, Caddo Educ Asn; Wall of Honor, Norwela. **Home Addr:** 306 Holcomb Dr, Shreveport, LA 71103, **Home Phone:** (318)425-1908.

## HOLT, DR. JONATHAN LAMAR
Physician. **Personal:** son of James S and Dorothy. **Educ:** BS; MS. **Career:** Schumpert Med Ctr, respiratory therapist, neonatal pediat specialist, currently. **Business Addr:** Respiratory Therapist, Neonatal Pediatric Specialist, Schumpert Medical Center, 5646 S Lakseshore Dr Unit 3, Shreveport, LA 71118-4027, **Business Phone:** (318)636-7608.

**HOLT, KENNETH CHARLES**
School administrator. **Personal:** Born Feb 9, 1948, Pine Bluff, AR; son of Curtis Sr and Velma Lovell; married Helen N Reed; children: Byron Kieth, Derrick Vaughn & Briana Dashon. **Educ:** Univ Ark, Pine Bluff, AR, BS, 1970; Univ Wis, Milwaukee, WI, MS, 1978; supt prog, 1988. **Career:** Milwaukee Pub Schs, teacher, 1970-80, asst prin, 1980-88, prin, 1988-, stud serv div, dir, currently; Parkman Mid Sch, prin. **Orgs:** Educ Employment Coun Milwaukee Pub Sch, 1988-; chairperson, WI Dept PubInstn-Prog Rev Panel AIDS Educ Prog, 1989-; co-chairperson, African Am Male Youth Task Force-Milwaukee Pub Sch, 1989-; exec comm, WI Black Historical Soc, 1989-91; Nat Asn Sec Sch Prin, 1989-; Nat Middle Sch Asn, 1991-; co-chair, African-Am Immersion Schs Implementation Comt. **Home Addr:** 7258 N 97th St, Milwaukee, WI 53224, **Home Phone:** (414)543-6756. **Business Addr:** Director, Milwaukee Public Schools, 5225 W Vliet St, Milwaukee, WI 53208, **Business Phone:** (414)475-8393.

**HOLT, HON. LEO E.**
Judge. **Personal:** Born Jul 2, 1927, Chicago, IL; son of Pullman porter Miller and Laverne Hamilton; married Dorothy Considine; children: Pamela L & Paula. **Educ:** Wilson Jr Col, AA, 1949; Roosevelt Univ, acct & bus law; John Marshall Law Sch, LLB, 1959. **Career:** Judge (retired); Circuit County Cook Co, judge. **Orgs:** Cook Co Bar Asn; Kappa Alpha Psi Fraternity. **Honors/Awds:** Kappa Alpha Psi Achievement Award, 1971; Richard Westbrook Award, Cook Co Bar Asn, 1975; Robert R Ming Award, 1981; Operation PUSH Community Service Award, 1981; South Suburban Leadership Council Community Service Award, 1985; Charles E Freeman Award, Ill Judicial Coun, 2003. **Home Addr:** 3211 S Rhodes Ave, Chicago, IL 60616-4039, **Home Phone:** (312)842-5886.

**HOLT, LEROY**
Football player. **Personal:** Born Mar 16, 1967, Carson, CA. **Educ:** Univ Southern Calif, BA, hist, 1990. **Career:** Football player (retired); Miami Dolphins, running back, 1990. **Special Achievements:** Honorable mention All-America, junior year; Honorable mention All-Pac 10, sophomore year. **Home Addr:** 1204 E Radbard St, Carson, CA 90746.

**HOLT, MAUDE R.**
Health services administrator. **Personal:** Born Aug 3, 1949, Thomaston, AL; daughter of Henry J and Naomi Levert; children: Andre & DeNeal Madry. **Educ:** Ala A&M Univ, BS, 1976; Univ Miami, MBA & HA, 1983. **Career:** Rochester Tel, acct clerk, 1972-76; Allstate Ins, supvr, 1976-77; Jackson Memorial Hosp, asst adminr, 1978-89; Metro-Dade, adminr; Alcohol & Drug Abuse Servs Admin, adminr, state dir; Dist Columbia, Dept Human Serv, Medicaid Managed Care Med Assistance Admin, adminr & chief; Off Health Care Ombudsman & Bill Rights, Dept Health Care Finance, assoc dir, 2009-. **Orgs:** Delta Sigma Theta Sorority; Eta Phi Beta Sorority; Nat Asn Advan Colored People; Urban League; Coalition Homeless; Black Pub Adminrs; Nat Asn Coalition Bus & Prof Women; Am Bus Women; Fla Voters League; pres, Greater Miami Chap AL A&M Univ Metro-Action Plan. **Home Addr:** 100 Mich Ave NE A41, Washington, DC 20017. **Business Addr:** Associate Director, Office of Health Care Ombudsman & Bill of Rights, 441 4th St NW Suite 360 N, Washington, DC 20001, **Business Phone:** (202)727-6860.

**HOLT, MELONIE R.**
Television journalist. **Personal:** Born Hartford, CT; daughter of Joseph and Jo. **Educ:** Pa State Univ, BA, jour, 1993. **Career:** WCVB-TV, Leo L Beranek fel, 1993-94; WLEX-TV, health reporter & weekend anchor, 1994-96; WSOC-TV, anchor, gen assignment reporter & pub affairs host, 1996-2004; WAXN-TV, producer & host; WFTV, gen assignment reporter, 2004-. **Orgs:** Muscular Dystrophy Asn. **Honors/Awds:** Outstanding Achievement in Newscast Daytime, 16th Annual Midsouth Regional Emmy Awards. **Special Achievements:** Was recognized by the Muscular Dystrophy Association three times for raising awareness of neuromuscular diseases. **Business Addr:** General Assignment Reporter, WFTV, 490 E S St, Orlando, FL 32801, **Business Phone:** (407)841-9000.

**HOLT, MIKEL**
Editor. **Personal:** Born Mar 12, 1952, Milwaukee, WI. **Educ:** Univ Wis Milwaukee. **Career:** Milwaukee Sentinel, intern, 1968-69; Naval AP & Group Vietnam, hist writer 1971-72; Stringer Jet Mag, 1971-72; Comnine Great Lakes IL, media rel officer, 1972-73; Milwaukee Star Times, managing ed, 1975-76, sports ed photo journ, 1974-75; Seabreeze Mag, Milwaukee ed; DJ WCLG, asst prog dir; Milwaukee Community Journ, ed & assoc publ, 1976-; Malik Commun Inc, prin acct exec, owner, assoc publ, 1976-, pres, 1984-2013; Miller Brewing Co, chief acct exec; Sunday Insight, WTMJ-TV, panelist, 2005-. **Orgs:** Founder, Wis Black Media Asn; bd dir, Messmer High Sch; Nat Asn Advan Colored People Youth Coun; co-chmn, Black Awareness Study Group; Milwaukee Black Photo-Journ; WI Black Press; TUJU; vpres, Asn Stud Afro-Am Life & Hist; founder, Black Res Orgn; Wis Donor Network. **Honors/Awds:** Letter appreciation for broadcasting, 1972; Two-time winner Best Column Award, NNPA; Braggs & Brooks Sports Serv Award, 1974; Community Service Award, NNPA; Senate Award, State Wis; Black Achievement Award, 1976; Community Serv Award, Univ Wis, 1977; Community Service Award, Black Studio Union, 1977; Messner Impact Award, 1993; Men Who Dare Award, 1994; A Phillip Randolph Award, Recipient, 1994; NNPA Award for Best Feature Story, Mayoral Citation, 1996; Peace Achiever Award, 2000; A Philip Randolph Messenger Award, 2000; NNPA Best Columnist Award, 2000; Messmer Award, 2002; Christ The King Achievement Award, 2003; President's Diversity Award, Med Col Wis. **Special Achievements:** Author, Not Yet Free at Last, 2000. **Home Addr:** 4551 N 22 St, Milwaukee, WI 53209. **Business Addr:** Owner & Associate Publisher, Principal Accounts Executive, Malik Communications Inc, 3612 N King Dr, Milwaukee, WI 53212, **Business Phone:** (414)372-8600.

**HOLT, DR. RODERICK LENARD**
Cardiologist. **Career:** Schunpnet Med Ctr, cardiologist. **Orgs:** Cardiovasc Serv La LLC. **Home Addr:** 1917 Weinstock St, Shreveport, LA 71103, **Home Phone:** (318)674-8520. **Business Addr:** Member, Cardiovascular Services Of Louisiana LLC, 306 Halcomb Dr, Shreveport, LA 71103, **Business Phone:** (318)424-7915.

**HOLT, RONALD WAYNE, JR.**
President (organization), chief executive officer. **Educ:** Neosho County Community Col, AS, chem, 1988; Columbia Univ, BA, econs, 1991; NY Univ Stern Sch Bus, MBA, finance, gen, 1996. **Career:** Merrill Lynch, 1991-97; Hansberger Global Investors Inc, global instnl money mgr, pres, chief exec officer & chief investment officer, 1997-2014; PREMIS Capital Partners Inc, owner, pres & chief exec officer, 2014-. **Orgs:** Charter holder & CFA Inst mem, Chartered Financial Analyst (CFA); Black Stud Orgn. **Honors/Awds:** "Black Enterprise", 75 Most Powerful Blacks on Wall Street, 2006. **Business Addr:** President, Chief Executive Officer, PREMIS Capital Partners Inc, 101 NE 3rd Ave Suite 320, Fort Lauderdale, FL 33301, **Business Phone:** (954)522-5150.

**HOLT, TORRY JABAR**
Administrator, football player. **Personal:** Born Jun 5, 1976, Greensboro, NC; son of Ojetta V Holt-Shoffner (deceased); married Carla; children: 3. **Educ:** NC State Univ, sociol. **Career:** Football player (retired), analyst, executive; St Louis Rams, wide receiver, 1999-2008; Jacksonville Jaguars, wide receiver, 2009; New Eng Patriots, 2010; NFL Network, analyst, 2010; ESPN, analyst; Fox, analyst; Holt Bros Inc, vpres, currently. **Orgs:** Founder, Holt Found. **Honors/Awds:** Rookie of the Year, St Louis Rams, 1999; Super Bowl Champion, 1999-2000; ACC Player of the Year; Offensive Back of the Year; Fred Biletnik off Award; Wide Receiver of the Year, Nat Football League Alumni, 2003; Most Valuable Palyer, St Louis Rams, 2003 & 2005. **Special Achievements:** Producer: The Hip-Hop Fellow, 2014. **Business Addr:** Vice President, Holt Brothers Inc, 8801 Fast Park Dr Suite 105 & 107, Raleigh, FL 27617, **Business Phone:** (919)787-1981.

**HOLTE-EDWARDS, PATRICIA LOUISE.** **See LABELLE, PATTI.**

**HOLTON, MICHAEL DAVID (MIKE HOLTON)**
Basketball player, basketball coach, broadcaster. **Personal:** Born Aug 4, 1961, Seattle, WA. **Educ:** Univ Calif, Los Angeles, attended 1983. **Career:** Basketball player (retired), basketball coach, tv Analyst; Pr Coquis, 1983-84; Phoenix Suns, 1984-86; Fla Stingers, 1985-86; Chicago Bulls, 1986; Portland Trail Blazers, 1986-88; Charlotte Hornets, 1988-90; Tulsa Fast Breakers, 1990-91; Tri-City Chinook, 1991-92; Pasadena City Col, asst coach, 1993-94; Portland Pilots, Univ Portland, asst coach, 1994-95, head coach, 2001-06; Comcast SportsNet, currently. **Business Addr:** Studio Analyst, Sideline Reporter, 1 Ctr Ct Suite 200, Portland, OR 97227, **Business Phone:** (503)234-9291.

**HOLYFIELD, EVANDER**
Boxer, founder (originator). **Personal:** Born Oct 19, 1969, Atmore, AL; son of Annie Laura; married Paulette Bowen, May 17, 1985, (divorced 1991); children: 3; married Candi Calvana Smith, Jul 1, 20032012); children: 2; married Janice Itson, Oct 4, 1996, (divorced 2000); children: 1. **Career:** Prof boxer (retired); Evander Holyfield Buick & Subaru, Atlanta, Ga, partner, currently; Real Deal Rec, founder; Black Family Channel, partner; trainer, currently. Films: "Holyfield vs. Tyson II ", 1997; "Grudge Watch", 2013; "Champs", 2015. **Orgs:** Founder, Holyfield Found. **Home Addr:** 6865 Jonesboro Rd, Morrow, GA 30260. **Business Addr:** Owner, Holyfield Management, 794 Evander Holyfield Hwy, Fairburn, GA 30213, **Business Phone:** (770)460-6807.

**HONABLUE, DR. RICHARD RIDDICK, JR.**
Physician. **Personal:** Born Apr 1, 1948, Staten Island, NY; children: Richard III, Xavier & Michael. **Educ:** Long Island Univ, AA, 1968; Wagner Col, Grymes Hill, BS, 1970; Meharry Med Col, MD, 1974. **Career:** Pildes Opticians NY, optical dispenser, 1968-70; CBS Radio News, ed desk asst, 1969; United Negro Col Fund Pre-Med Prog Fisk Univ, tutor, 1971; Meharry Col, GW Hubbard Hosp, resident, 1974-77; Dede Wallace Community Ment Health Serv, consult, 1976; Med Exam Ctr, med dir, 1977; George Wash Univ Sch Allied Health Sci, asst clin prof, 1979; Duke Univ Dept Family Pract, asst clin prof, 1981-87; Suffolk Community Health Ctr, med dir; Tidewater Regional Jail, physician dir; Family Health Care Ltd, owner, physician, currently. **Orgs:** Buffalo Boyz Motorcycle Club, Williamsburg chap; pres, Resident's Asn, Mehary, 1976; dipl, Am Bd Family Pract, 1980; med examr, Comm Va; Lord Chamberlain Soc; Tidewater TV Adv Comt; Tau Kappa Epsilon; AMA; Am Asn Family Physicians; VAFP; chmn, Reg II Nat Med Asn, 1984-85; pres, Williamsburg Men's Club, 1984; Asn Mil Surgeons US; Nat Naval Officers Asn; Frontiers Int; life mem, Nat Asn Advan Colored People; Nat Comn Cert Physician Assts, 1990-98. **Honors/Awds:** Eagle Scout Award, 1966; Order of the Arrow. **Home Addr:** Hwy 616, PO Box 1566, Gloucester, VA 23061, **Home Phone:** (804)693-5528. **Business Addr:** Owner, Family Health Care Limited, 8025 Belroi Rd, Gloucester, VA 23061, **Business Phone:** (804)693-5528.

**HONEYCUTT, ANDREW E.**
Educator. **Personal:** Born Jan 28, 1942, Humboldt, KS; son of Ed Lee and Thelma; married Pamela Hatchett; children: Michael, Andrea, Andrew Jr & Aaron. **Educ:** Ottawa Univ, BA, 1964; Boston Univ, MBA, 1970; Harvard Bus Sch, DBA, 1975. **Career:** Fla A&M Univ, Fla Region II Housing Ctr, co-dir, 1974-75, mgt scis div, chair, 1974-77; Tex Southern univ, Ctr Int Develop, assoc dir, 1979-81, interim dept head, 1979-80; Nat Ctr Housing Mgt, coordr organ develop, 1983-89, strategic planning, 1990-91; Savannah State Col, Sch Bus, dean, 1991, Univ Ark, Pine Bluff, Sch Bus, dean; Argosy Univ, dean; Anaheim Univ, dean, currently. **Orgs:** Chair, Savannah Regional Minority Purchasing coun, 1991-92; bd, First Union Bank, 1991-92; bd, United Way, 1991-92; bd, Savannah Econ Develop Authority, 1991-92; bd, hospice Savannah, 1991-92; bd, Small bus Asst corp, 1991-92; bd, W Broad YMCA, 1991-92; bd, Pvt Indust coun, 1991-92; bd dir, Ewing Marion Kauffman Found; Nat Bd dir, SCORE; nissan fel Northwestern Univ; distinguished Fel, Shorter Univ; vice chmn & sr partner, Edgenics Inc. **Home Addr:** 38 Monterey Ave, Savannah, GA 31405, **Home Phone:** (912)352-9586. **Business Addr:** Dean, Anaheim University, 1240 S State College Blvd Rm 110, Anaheim, CA 92806-5150, **Business Phone:** (714)772-3330.

**HONEYCUTT, JERALD DEWAYNE**
Basketball player. **Personal:** Born Oct 20, 1974, Shreveport, LA. **Educ:** Tulane Univ. **Career:** Milwaukee Bucks, forward-guard, 1997-99; Philadelphia 76ers, 1998-99; Idaho Stampede, 1999-2000, 2003; Gallitos de Isabela, 2000, 2002; Avtodor Saratov, 2000-01, 2003-04; Nea Filadelfia, 2001; Phoenix Eclipse, 2001-02; Talk 'N Text, 2002, 2004, 2005; Grand Rapids Hoops, 2002-03; Guaros de Lara, 2002; Changwon Sakers, 2004-05; OSG Phoenix, 2005-06; Diamond Dolphins, 2006-08; Blue Stars Beirut, 2007; Panasonic Trians, 2008-11; Toyota Alvark, 2011-13; Mamamatsu-Higashi Mikawa; Japanese Super league; Toyota Tsusho Fighting Eagles, Japan Basketball League, currently. **Business Addr:** Professional Basketball Player, Toyota Tsusho Fighting Eagles.

**HONORE, STEPHAN LEROY**
Lawyer. **Personal:** Born May 14, 1938, Urbana, OH; son of Albert R and Lulu May Dolby; married Flor A Chico; children: Francis, Andrew & Stephanie. **Educ:** Capital Univ, BS, 1960; Univ Toledo Col Law, JD, 1974. **Career:** Peace Corps Columbia, dominican rep, 1961-63, 1978-81, assoc dir, 1963-66; US State Dept, youth develop advisor, 1966-68; Trans Century Corp, 1968-69; Model Cities Prog Toledo, organizer, 1970-71; Thurgood Marshall Sch Law, law prof, 1974-84; Houston, Tex, self-employed atty law import & export bus & real estate, 1984-; Telecommunications, 1994-. **Orgs:** Stud body pres, Capital Univ, 1960-69; presiding justice, Stud Hon Ct, Univ Toledo Col Law, 1973-74; law rev, case note ed, Univ Toledo Law, 1973-74; bd dir, Immigration Coun Ctr, 1976-78; Tex State Bar, 1977-; pres, Parochial Sch Bd, 1983-88; bd educ, Galueston-Houston Cath Diocesan, 1988-94, pres bd, 1991-93; State Bar Tex; Nat Bar Asn; Houston Bar Asn; Am Immigration Lawyers Asn; treas, Braeswood Dem. **Special Achievements:** Articles on criminal & labor law published in Univ of Toledo Law Review, 1973-74. **Business Addr:** Attorney, Private Practice, 4131 Levonshire Dr, Houston, TX 77025-3914, **Business Phone:** (713)664-3208.

**HOOD, DR. ARETHA DIONNE**
Dentist. **Educ:** Univ Detroit Mercy, DDS, 1996. **Career:** Paradise Dental Ctr, dentist, 1997-. **Business Addr:** Dentist, Paradise Dental Center, 20755 Greenfield Rd Suite 500, Southfield, MI 48075-5408, **Business Phone:** (248)559-3800.

**HOOD, CHARLES MCKINLEY, JR.**
Government official. **Personal:** Born Aug 9, 1936, Richmond, VA; son of Charles M Sr and Ethel Saunders; married Marion Elaine Overton; children: Charles III, Brian M & Cheryl E. **Educ:** Hampton Inst, BS, math, 1959; Univ Richmond; Univ Okla, MA, 1974; Command & Gen Staff Col, Ft Leavenworth; Army War Col. **Career:** Government official & military (retired); AUS, 1960; AUS War Col, fac mem, 1983-84; AUS Europe, Herzogenaurach, Ger, comdr, 1984-86; AUS Army Forces Command, Atlanta, Ga, chief war plans, 1986-87; US Forces Command, Atlanta, Ga, dep J5, 1987-88; US Second Army, Atlanta, Ga, chief opers, 1988-90; US Vi, St Thomas, VI, adj gen, 1990; US Vi Nat Guard, adj gen; Fulton County Airport; Metro Atlanta Kiwanis Club, pres, 2002-03 & 2004-05; Atlanta Chap Tuskegee Airmen Inc, torchbearer & vpres; Eagle Group Int Corp, proj mgr, 2002-04; 6th Battalion, battery comdr; 27th Field Artillery, div artil; 7th Div Vietnam, g3 adv; Emergency Mgt, exec dir; Grad Sch Univ Vi, adj prof; Dep Chief Staff Opers; Second United Sates Army; War Plans Div; J5, dep dir; US. Forces Command, comdr; Ft McPherson, comdr; 210th Field Artil Brigade VII Corps; Legion Merit, two oak leaf clusters, Bronze Star, two oak leaf clusters, Meritorious Serv Medal, two oak leaf clusters, Air Medal, Army Commendation Medal & Humanitarian Serv Medal, US Vi' Distinguished Serv & Repub Vietnam Hon Medal, First Class. **Orgs:** APA, 1973-; Asn USY, 1960-; Alumni Asn War Col, 1983-; Adj Gen Asn, 1990-; Nat Guard Asn, 1990-; Family Tree at Therrell High Sch; Common Ground Coalition; Campbellton Rd Coalition; ministerial mentoring group corp exec, Leaders' Legacy Group; chmn, Fulton County Community Zoning Bd; chmn, Key Leader Prog; secy-treas & gov, Ga Dist Kiwanis. **Home Addr:** 5155 Dublin Dr SW, Atlanta, GA 30331-7875, **Home Phone:** (404)349-7568.

**HOOD, DENISE PAGE**
Judge. **Personal:** Born Feb 21, 1952, Columbus, OH; married Nicholas III; children: Nathan & Noah. **Educ:** Yale Col, BA, 1974; Columbia Univ Law Sch, JD, 1977. **Career:** City Detroit, lawyer, city atty, 1977-82; Detroit's 36th Dist Ct, judge, 1983-89; Recorder's Ct, judge, 1989-92; Wayne Co Circuit Ct, judge, 1993-94; Eastern Dist Mich, US Dist Ct, judge, 1994-. **Orgs:** Bd dir, Detroit Bar Asn, 1983-, pres, 1993; pres, Asn Black Judges Mich, 1991-92; chair, Exec Coun, United Church Christ, 1991-93; Detroit Metrop Bar Asn Found Bd; Asn Black Judges Mich; vpres, Olivet Col Bd trustee; bd trustee, Harper-Hutzel Hosp; Inside Out Lit Arts Proj Bd; chair, Mich State Planning Bd legal serv; State Bar Pro Bono Initiatives Comt; & Detroit Metrop Bar Asn Found Bd. **Business Addr:** Judge, Eastern District Michigan, 231 W Lafayette Blvd Suite 238 Rm 251, Detroit, MI 48201, **Business Phone:** (313)234-5165.

**HOOD, HON. HAROLD.** **See Obituaries Section.**

**HOOD, REV. DR. NICHOLAS**
Government official, president (organization), founder (originator). **Personal:** Born Jun 21, 1923, Terre Haute, IN; married Elizabeth Flemister; children: Nicholas III, Stephen, Victor Irvine III, Emory (deceased) & Sarah Cyprian (deceased); married Doris Chenault; married Daisy. **Educ:** Purdue Univ, BS, 1945; N Cent Col, BA, 1946; Yale Univ, BA, divinity, 1949. **Career:** Government official (retired); City Detroit, city councilman, 1963-92; Plymouth Church, sr minister; Dixwell Cong Church, asst minister; Cent Cong Church, minister; Cong Churches US, vice mod; Non-Profit Housing Ctr, pres; Fed Nat

Mortgage Asn, Cyprian Ctr, founder & adv comm; Cent Congregational Church, New Orleans, La, pastor. **Orgs:** Bd mem, Ministers Life & Casualty Union Bd; mem bd trustee, Hutzel Hosp; Indust Housing Study Tour Europe, 1971; US rep World Conf Non-Profit Housing, 1972. **Honors/Awds:** Outstanding mem 1949 class, Yale Divinity Sch, 1974; Olivet Col, hon DD, 1966; Divinity Sch Univ Chicago, hon LittD, LLD, 1966; N Cent Col, hon DD, 1966; Amistad Award, Outstanding Serv to Am, 1977. **Special Achievements:** First African-American graduate of North Central College; Second Black to be elected to the Detroit City Council in the history of modern Detroit. **Business Addr:** Retired Councilman, Detroit City Council, 2 Woodward Ave Rm 1340, Detroit, MI 48226-3413.

## HOOKER, DR. BILLIE J.

Educator, college administrator. **Educ:** Albany State Col, Eng; Atlanta Univ, libr serv; Ohio State Univ, PhD, educ admin, 1982. **Career:** Interdenominational Theol Ctr, Dir Instititional Advan, 1986-90; Bennett Col, vpres develop; Del State Univ, vpres univ advan, 1999-2003; United Negro Col Fund, dir educ servs; TMT Group Inc, sr trainer, currently; Wiley Col, assoc vpres Develop & Alumni Affairs, 2004-05. **Business Addr:** Senior Trainer, TMT Group Inc, 415A Church St Suite 100, Huntsville, AL 35801, **Business Phone:** (256)536-9717.

## HOOKER, DOUGLAS RANDOLF

Executive, government official, vice president (organization). **Personal:** Born Mar 31, 1954, Moultrie, GA; son of Odessa R Walker and H Randolph; married Patrise M Perkins; children: Douglas Patrick & Randi Michelle. **Educ:** Ga Inst Technol, Atlanta, GA, BS, mech engineering, 1978, MS, technol & sci policy, 1985; Emory Univ, Atlanta, GA, MBA, 1987. **Career:** Ga Power Co, Atlanta, Ga, design engr, proj mgr, design sect supvr & technol policy analyst, 1979-85; Bio-Lab Inc, Decatur, Ga, dir finance & admin, 1987-91; City Atlanta, from dep comnr to comnr pub works, 1991-97; Randolph Group, chief exec off & pres, 1997-; SL King & Assocs, vpres opers, 1999-2001; HDR Eng Inc, vpres & dept mgr, 2001-03; State Rd & Tollway Authority, exec dir & chief exec officer, 2003-05; PBS&J, vpres & southern states dist dir, 2005-10; Atkins, vpres bus develop & mkt & southern states dir, 2010-11; Atlanta Regional Comn, exec dir, 2011-. **Orgs:** Vpres, Ga Tech Minority Alumni Comt, 1982-85; vpres, Nat Soc Black Engrs-Alumni Exten, 1991-; Leadership Georgias Class, 1996; Leadership Atlantas Class, 2003; bd mem, Metro Atlanta Chamber; bd mem, Coun Qual Growth; bd visitors, Emory Univ; co-founder, bd mem & chmn, Civic League Regional Atlanta; bd mem, CHRIS Kids; inaugural bd, Govs Adv Coun ACT; inaugural bd, ACF River Basin Compacts; inaugural bd, Metrop N Ga Water Planning Dist; bd mem, Pk Pride; bd mem, Inst Ga Environ Leadership; bd mem, Georgians Passenger Rail; bd mem, Atlanta Opera; bd mem, Ga Conservancy; Am Coun Eng Co; Am Pub ransp Asn; Am Pub Works Asn; Nat Soc Black Engrs; bd dir, Regional Leadership Forum. **Home Addr:** 335 Glenhurst Lane SW, Atlanta, GA 30331-2080, **Home Phone:** (404)696-9163. **Business Addr:** Executive Director, Atlanta Regional Commission, 40 Courtland Suite NE, Atlanta, GA 30303, **Business Phone:** (404)463-3100.

## HOOKER, ODESSA WALKER

School administrator. **Personal:** Born Sep 21, 1930, Moultrie, GA; daughter of Anderson Walker and Pauline Walker; married Homer; children: Douglas R, Melanie Ann, David A, Margaret P & Darrell W. **Educ:** Paine Col, BA, 1951; Atlanta Univ, cert, 1951; Univ Cincinnati, MEd, supv & admin, 1967. **Career:** Barnesville HS, eng teacher, 1951-53; Whittemore High Sch, eng teacher, 1954-55; Cincinnati Pub Sch, elem teacher, 1961-83, elem asst prin, 1983-90; Fund Independent Sch Cincinnati Inc, coord, 1990; Summerbridge Cincinnati Inc, founder; Breakthrough Cincinnati, bd trustee mem, bd trustee emer; Bk: With Heads Held High: Legacy My Southern Parents, 2003; Premier African Am Role Models Cincinnati. **Orgs:** Co-choir dir & organist, Peoples Tabernacle Bapt Church, 1955-; bible class teacher, Peoples Tabernacle Bapt Church, 1977-; vol organist, Chapel Serv Bethesda Oak Hosp, 1983-. **Home Addr:** 132 Cottsford Dr SW, Atlanta, GA 30331, **Home Phone:** (404)699-2247. **Business Addr:** Board Trustee Emeritus, Breakthrough Cincinnati, 6905 Given Rd, Cincinnati, OH 45243, **Business Phone:** (513)979-0345.

## HOOKER, DR. OLIVIA J.

Psychologist. **Personal:** Born Feb 12, 1915, Muskogee, OK; daughter of Samuel D and Anita J. **Educ:** Ohio State Univ, BS, 1937; Columbia Univ Teachers Col, MA, psychol, 1947; Univ Rochester, PhD, clin psychol, 1962; Am Acad Forensic Psychol, dipl, 2001. **Career:** Psychologist (retired); NY Dept Ment Health, psychologist, 1947-57; Univ Rochester, grad fel, 1955-57; Kennedy Child Study Ctr, dir psychol & assoc adminr, 1961-83; Fordham Univ, assoc prof clin psychol, 1963-83; Fred S Keller Sch Behav Anal, consult, 1988-2000. **Orgs:** Nat Asn Advan Colored People, 1945-2001; chair const comt, Am Asn Ment Retardation, 1949-2001; fel Am Psychol Asn, 1958-2001; bd mem, Terenee Cardinal Cooke Servs, 1970-96; bd mem, Kennedy Child Study Ctr, 1986-01; admin coun, Trinity United Methodist Church; Sigma Xi. **Honors/Awds:** New State Senate Veterans Hall of Fame. **Special Achievements:** First African-American woman to enlist and go on active duty in the Coast Guard during World War II; Co-author: Comparative Study of Intelligence Variability; read papers at conferences in Bologna, Italy and Cairo, Egypt; first black woman toenlist in the SPARs. **Home Addr:** 42 Juniper Hill Rd, White Plains, NY 10607-2104, **Home Phone:** (914)949-2981.

## HOOKS, BRIAN

Actor. **Personal:** Born Jul 27, 1973, Bakersfield, CA. **Career:** Actor, producer, writer; Films: Bulworth, 1998; Thursday, 1998; Beloved, 1998; Q: The Movie, exec producer, 1999; Phat Beach, 1996; High Sch High, 1996; Austin Powers: The Spy Who Shagged Me, 1999; Obstacles, 2000; 3 Strikes, 2000; Nothin' 2 Lose, exec producer, 2000; The Luau, exec producer, 2001; The Chat room, exec producer, 2002; The Entrepreneurs, 2003; Soul Plane, 2004; All Starz Live, exec producer, 2005; Malibooty, exec producer, 2003; Wifey, exec producer, 2005; 7eventy 5ive, dir, writer & producer, 2007; Dead Tone, dir, writer, music supvr & producer, 2007; Cutlass, 2007; Fool's Gold, 2008; Coming & Going, 2011; Laughing to the Bank, exec producer, 2011; I Do I Did, exec producer, 2009; Basketball 3:16, 2012; The Trace, 2012; The Love Section, assoc producer, 2013. TV series: Runaway Car, 1997; "Cracker", 1998; "The Parkers", 1999-2000; "The Proud Family", 2003; "Eve", 2003-06; "Cold Case", 2009; "The Ropes", 2012; "LA Live the Show", 2013; "Marked", producer, 2013; "According to Him & Her Live at the Improv!", 2014. **Honors/Awds:** Nominee, Video Premiere Award, 2001. **Business Addr:** Actor, c/o Michael Greenwald, 6500 Wilshire Blvd Suite 2200, Los Angeles, CA 90048, **Business Phone:** (323)655-7400.

## HOOKS, FRANCES DANCY

Educator, teacher, secretary general. **Personal:** Born Feb 23, 1927, Memphis, TN; daughter of Andrew Jackson and Georgia Harriet Graves; married Benjamin Lawson; children: Patricia Louise & Gray. **Educ:** Fisk Univ, BS, 1949; Tenn State Univ, MS, 1968. **Career:** Shelby County Sch, Tenn, teacher, 1949-51; Memphis City Sch, teacher, counr, 1951-59, high sch counr admin, 1959-73, counr-pregnant girls, 1976-77; Benjamin L Hooks Inst Social Chg, Univ Memphis, secy & mentor, currently; Memphis Vol Placement Prog, People Power Proj, co-founder. **Orgs:** Organizer People Power Proj, 1968; pres, Memphis Chap, Links Inc, 1968; pres & co-founder, Riverview, Kans Community & Day Care Ctr, 1969-73; diryouth activ, Mt Monah Baptist Church, 1973-75; dir, Youth Activ MidBaptist Church, 1973-75; co-chair, Nat Civil Rights Award Affair, 1999; Women Achievement; Women's Found; adv bd, YWCA; bd mem, Memphis CancerFound; bd mem, Memphis Col Art; Nat Asn Adv Colored People; adv bd, Rhodes Col & Memphis Symphony League. **Home Addr:** 200 Wagner Pl Suite 408, Memphis, TN 38103, **Home Phone:** (901)578-3904. **Business Addr:** Secretary, Mentor, Benjamin L Hooks Institute for Social Change, 107 Scates Hall, Memphis, TN 38152-3530, **Business Phone:** (901)678-3974.

## HOOKS, DR. JAMES BYRON, JR.

Educator, business owner. **Personal:** Born Sep 23, 1933, Birmingham, AL; son of James Byron Sr and Bessie Ardis; married Marcell Elizabeth; children: Angelique L, James Byron III, Kimberly M, Jamal B, Joffrey B & Keisha M. **Educ:** Ind Univ, BS, 1955; Roosevelt Univ, MA, 1969; Northwestern Univ, PhD, 1975. **Career:** Educator (retired); J M Harlan High, asst prin, 1969-75; Talent Inc, exec dir, 1971; Skiles Mid Sch, prin, 1975; Haven Mid Sch, prin, 1976; Whitney Young, teacher & dean, 1980-92; Hooks & Co Real Estate Investments, owner, 1989; "Ritual Without Reality" & "Thread The Needle", cable TV producer. **Orgs:** Bd dir, Sullivan House Local Serv Syst, 1984-89. **Home Addr:** 7937 S Clyde Ave, Chicago, IL 60617-1111, **Home Phone:** (773)721-1130.

## HOOKS, KEVIN (KING ROYAL)

Movie director, actor. **Personal:** Born Sep 19, 1958, Philadelphia, PA; son of Robert Brooks and Yvonne; married Cheryl; children: 3; married Regina Hooks. **Career:** Films: Sounder, actor, 1972; Aaron Loves Angela, actor, 1975; A Hero Ain't Nothin' But a Sandwich, actor, 1978; Take Down, actor, 1979; Innerspace, actor, 1987; Strictly Business, dir & actor, 1991; Passenger 57, 1992; Fled, 1996; Black Dog, 1998; Lie Detector, 1999; Shallow Hal, actor, 2001; TV series: "J.T.", actor, 1969; "Just an Old Sweet Song", actor, "The Rookies", actor, 1976; The Greatest Thing That Almost Happened, actor, 1977; "The White Shadow", actor, 1978-81; "Lou Grant", actor, A Hero Ain't Nothin' But a Sandwich, 1978; CanYou Hear the Laughter? The Story of Freddie Prinze, actor, FriendlyFire, actor, "Backstairs at the White House", actor, 1979; St. Elsewhere, 1983-84; For Members Only, actor, "The Powers of Matthew Star", actor, 1983; Fame, Hotel, 1984; V, 1984-85; "ABC Afterschool Specials", 1986-87; "He's the Mayor", actor, 1986; "Vietnam War Story", "21 Jump Street", "Once a Hero", Mariah", 1987; "Midnight Caller", 1988-89; Roots: The Gift, China Beach", "CBS Schoolbreak Special", "Probe", 1988; "Alien Nation", 1989; HeatWave, "Doogie Howser, M.D.", 1990; Murder Without Motive: The Edmund Perry Story, "I'll Fly Away", 1992; "Tales from the Crypt", Irresistible Force, 1993; To My Daughter with Love, 1994; "Homicide: Lifeon the Street", 1996; "Profiler", 1997; Glory & Honor, dir & actor, 1998; "The Hoop Life", Mutiny, "Rescue 77", 1999; The Color of Friendship, dir & producer, "City of Angels", dir & exec producer, ER, 2000; "Soul Food", 2000-04; "Philly", dir & exec producer, 2001-02; NYPD Blue, 2001-04; "Without a Trace", 2003-04; "Las Vegas", "Dragnet", dir & co-exec producer, 2003; "Sounder", dir & producer, 2003; "Cold Case", "Line of Fire", 2004; North Shore, 2004; "24", 2004-05; "Lost", 2004-05; "Ghost Whisperer", 2005; "Alias", 2005; "The Inside", 2005; "Prison Break", dir, 2006-08, co-exec producer, 2006, exec producer, 2006-08; "Lincoln Heights", dir & exec producer, 2007; "Bones", 2009-13; "Monk", 2009; "Detroit 1-8-7", exec producer, 2010-11; "Human Target", exec producer, 2010; "Drop Dead Diva", 2011-12; "Alphas", 2011; "Necessary Roughness", 2011-13; "Intercept", dir, 2012; "The Finder", dir, 2012; "The Mentalist", dir, 2012; "Castle", dir, 2012-14; "Last Resort", producer & dir, 2012; "Supernatural", dir, 2013; "The Good Wife", dir, 2013; "Agents of S.H.I.E.L.D.", dir, 2014; "Person of Interest", dir, 2014. **Honors/Awds:** Emmy Award, 2001. **Business Addr:** Actor, c/o United Talent Agency, 9560 Wilshire Blvd Fl 5, Beverly Hills, CA 90212, **Business Phone:** (310)273-6700.

## HOOKS, MICHAEL ANTHONY, SR.

Educator, state government official. **Personal:** Born Oct 13, 1950, Memphis, TN; married Janet Dean Perry; children: Michael Jr & Kristian Nichole. **Educ:** Lane Col, attended 1969; Memphis State Univ, attended 1969. **Career:** Shelby County Assessor's Off, dep tax assessor, 1972-77; Gilliam Communs Inc, acct exec; State Tech Inst, lectr & instr; Michael Hooks & Assocs, pres; Memphis, city councilman; Shelby County, property assessor, 1988-92; Shelby County Bd Comnrs, comnr, 1994-98, 1998; Memphis Sch, vpres, 2001; Div Pub Serv & Neighborhoods, mgr multicultural & relig affairs, 2005. **Orgs:** Deleg Tenn Const Conv, 1977; Councilman, Memphis, TN, 1979-81; Nat Asn Advan Colored People; PUSH Inc; Knights Pythion; Commitment Memphis; Omega Psi Phi Fraternity; Prince Hall Masonic Lodge; Memphis Downtown Photog Soc Inc; State Bd Equalization; bd mem, Memphis Sch. **Honors/Awds:** Tenn Asn Assessing Officers; Assessor of the Year, Int Asn Assessing Officers; Soc Real Estate Appraisers; Nat Asn Real Estate Brokers; Memphis Bd Realtors; One of 50 Outstanding Leaders of the Future, Ebony Mag, 1978. **Home Addr:** 2143 Pkwy, Memphis, TN 38114, **Home Phone:** (901)458-1457.

## HOOPER, MICHELE J.

Executive, chief executive officer, president (organization). **Personal:** Born Jul 16, 1951, Uniontown, PA; daughter of Percy and Beatrice Eley; married Lemuel Seabrook III. **Educ:** Univ Pa, Philadelphia, BA, econs, 1973; Univ Chicago, MBA, 1975; State Ill, CPA, 1981. **Career:** Baxter Corp, Chicago, parenterals div, 1976-83, dir, coverage & reimbursement, 1983-85, vpres, corp planning, 1985-88, Can, pres, 1988-92; Int Bus Group, Caremark Int Inc, corp vpres, 1984-, pres, 1992-98; TLContact, dir; Target Corp, dir, 1990-2005; PPG Industs, dir, 1995-; Seagram Co Ltd, dir, 1997-; Stadtlander Drug Co Inc, pres & chief exec officer, 1998-99; Voyager Expanded Learning, pres & chief exec officer, 1999-2000; MJH Consult LLC, pres, 2001-; AstraZeneca plc, non-exec dir, 2003-, sr independent non-exec dir, 2007-; DaVita Inc, dir, 2003-05; Dayton Hudson Corp, dir; Dir's Coun, co-founder, managing partner, pres, chief exec officer, 2003-; Warner Music Group Corp, dir, 2006-; Joseph E Seagram & Sons Inc, exec officer. **Orgs:** Chmn, Baxter Credit Union dir, 1981-88; bd dir, 1985-89, bd chmn, 1988, Joseph Holmes Dance Theatre; Econ Club Chicago, 1986-; bd dir, Lake Forest Grad Sch Mgt, 1987-88, bd, Med Dev Can, 1988-; Young Pres Org, 1989-; Com 200, 1989-; pres, Nat Asn Corp Dir Chicago Chapter, currently; adv bd, Am Telecare; adv bd, LEK Consult; adv bd, Equis Corp; bd mem, Seagram & Sons, 1996; Ctr Dis Control Found; Joffrey Ballet & Evanston Northwestern Healthcare; bd dir, Nat Asn Corp dir, 2000-; comnr, Nat Asn Corp dir Blue Ribbon Comns, 2004, 2005; bd mem, UnitedHealth Group, 2007-; Econ Club Chicago; Exec Leadership Coun; bd dir, Nat Asn Corp dir; World Presidents Orgn; dir, NorthShore Univ Health Syst; vice chair, Ctr Audit Qual, 2007-. **Home Addr:** 58 Hazelton Ave, Toronto, ON M5R 2E2, **Home Phone:** (416)929-5493. **Business Addr:** Managing Partner, Founder, The Directors Council, 825 Green Bay Rd Suite 230, Wilmette, IL 60091, **Business Phone:** (847)251-3776.

## HOOVER, JESSE

Government official. **Personal:** Born Sep 6, 1918, Tamo, AR; son of William and Magonila Martin; married Dorothy Franks. **Educ:** Wayne State Univ, 1952. **Career:** US Postal Serv, personnel action & rec supvr, 1946-77; Detroit Postal Employees Union, vpres, 1946-77, bd dir; City of Detroit, Detroit, Mich, councilman Hood, admin asst, 1978-90. **Orgs:** NAACP; Freedom Fund; The Moors; 1st Nighters; Sagicornians; bd deacons & trustee, Plymouth Cong Ch; Pilot Club Cert Merit, Mens Club, 1968. **Honors/Awds:** US Postal Service Bicentennial Award, 1976; Certificate Appreciation, NAACP, 1976; Co-chmn, Annual Easter Teas; Pilot Club Cert Merit; Certificate Appreciation, Easter Tea. **Special Achievements:** First black in the Detroit Postal Employees Union to be appointed as Board of Director. **Home Addr:** 16825 Normandy St, Detroit, MI 48221, **Home Phone:** (313)862-7203.

## HOPE, REV. JULIUS CAESAR

Clergy, activist, executive director. **Personal:** Born Sep 6, 1932, Mobile, AL; son of Robert and Zeola King; married Louise Portis; children: Julius Escous & Tonya Louise. **Educ:** Ala State Col, BS, 1958; Interdenominational Theol Ctr, MST, 1961. **Career:** Zion Baptist Church, Brunswick, Ga, pastor, 1961-70; Polit Action Chair, Brunswick, Ga, br Nat Asn Adv Colored People, 1961-78; Ga State Conf Nat Asn Adv Colored People Br, pres, 1967-78; First Baptist Church, Macon, Ga, pastor, 1970-78; Nat Asn Advan Colored People, Midwest Region III, nat dir relig affairs, 1978-; New Grace Missionary Baptist Church, Highland Pk, Mich, pastor, 1979-; Nat Asn Advan Colored People, Midwest Region III, Relig Affairs Dept, dir, 1988-. **Orgs:** Bd mem, Nat Asn Advan Colored People; Pres Comn Civil Rights, 1977-81; bd dir, Proj Smile, 1974-76; pres, Ga State Church Sch & Baptist Training Union Cong, 1974-78; dir, Neighbourhood Youth Corps, Coastal Area, GA, 1967-78; Alpha Phi Alpha; dir, Nat Asn Advan Colored People Nat Dept Relig Affairs. **Home Addr:** 14377 Grandmont Rd, Detroit, MI 48227, **Home Phone:** (313)838-3030. **Business Addr:** Director, National Association for the Advancement of Colored People, 4805 Mt Hope Dr, Baltimore, MD 21215, **Business Phone:** (410)580-5777.

## HOPE, MARIE H. SAUNDERS

Educator. **Personal:** Born Mar 6, 1927, Detroit, MI; daughter of Leander C Holley and Elvine P Holley; children: John Jerry Saunders Jr. **Educ:** Bennett Col, BA, elem educ, 1948; Ohio State Univ, MA, elem educ, 1954. **Career:** Educator (retired); Tazewell Co Va Sch bd, elem teacher, 1951-54; Cols Pub Schs, substitute elem schs, 1954-55; elem teacher, Milo elem Prek-K-1, 1955-73; Columbus schs, teacher; chap I reading teacher, John XVIII Cath Sch, 1973-75; parent coordr chap I elem Sch, 1975-87; Life Care Alliance, part time substitutes dining ctr coordr, 1987-94. **Orgs:** Alpha Kappa Alpha Sorority Inc; Alpha Sigma Omega; Aesthetics Social Club, pres, 1992; Cols S Dist United Methodist Church, assoc lay mem, 1992; United Methodist Church, lay speaker S Dist & W Ohio Conf, 1992. **Home Addr:** 3988 Karl Rd Suite 37, Columbus, OH 43224, **Home Phone:** (614)267-4674.

## HOPE, DR. RICHARD OLIVER

Educator, sociologist. **Personal:** Born Apr 1, 1939, Atlanta, GA; married Alice Anderson; children: Leah & Richard Jr. **Educ:** Morehouse Col, BA, 1961; Syracuse Univ, MA, 1964, PhD, 1969. **Career:** Metro Appl Res Ctr, res assoc, 1960-72; Brooklyn Col, asst prof sociol, 1968-72; Dept Defense, dir res, 1972-74; Morgan State Univ, chmn & prof, 1974-82; Goddard Space Flight Ctr, res fel, 1976-78; Ind Univ, Indianapolis, Dept Sociol, chmn & prof; Mass Inst Technol, exec dir, 1988-. **Orgs:** Assoc ed, J Inter-cult Rels, 1976-; vis lectr, Univ Wi Mona Jamaica, 1977; mem bd dir, Moton Found, 1978-; mem bd dir, Urban League, Flanner House Indianapolis, 1982-; Corp Vis Comt, Mass Inst Technol, 1982-; bd mem, WEB DuBois Scholars Inst; sr advisor, bd mem, MMUF Dissertation Grants; vpres & dir prog int affairs,, Woodrow Wilson Nat Fel Found, Thomas R Pickering Foreign Affairs Fel Progs, currently. **Home Addr:** 2 Jamesway, Cambridge, MA 02141, **Home Phone:** (617)864-5977. **Business Addr:** Vice President, Director, Programs in International Affairs, Woodrow Wilson National Fellowship Foundation, 5 Vaughn Dr Suite 300, Princeton, NJ 08540-6313, **Business Phone:** (609)452-7007.

**HOPKINS, BERNARD**
Boxer. **Personal:** Born Jan 15, 1965, Philadelphia, PA; son of Bernard Sr and Shirley; married Jeanette; children: Latrice. **Career:** Penn tower hotel, Philadelphia, cook; prof boxer, currently; Golden Boy Promotions, partner, currently. **Honors/Awds:** USBA, world middleweight champion, 1992-94; IBF, middleweight title, 1995; IBF, world middleweight champion, 1995-05; WBC, middleweight title, 2001; Fighter of the Year, World Boxing Hall of Fame, 2001; WBA, middleweight title, 2001; WBC, world middleweight champion, 2001vJuly 16, 2005; WBA, world middleweight champion, 2001-05; WBO, world middleweight champion, 2004v05; pound for pound first boxer, 2004-05; The ring world light, heavyweight champion, 2006-07; Total fights 58, Wins 51. **Business Addr:** Professional Boxer, c/o Norman Horton, 5780 W Centinela Ave Suite 409, Los Angeles, CA 90071, **Business Phone:** (323)418-0850.

**HOPKINS, BRADLEY DONNELL**
Football player, media executive. **Personal:** Born Sep 5, 1970, Columbia, SC; married Kellie. **Educ:** Univ Ill, BS, speech communs. **Career:** Football player (retired), sports reporter; Houston Oilers, left tackle, 1993-96; Tenn Oilers, left tackle, 1997-98; Tenn Titans, left tackle, 1999-2005, ctr, 1999, tackle, 2000; WSMV, sports reporter, 2006-; SiruisXM's Bleacher Report Radio, analyst, currently. **Honors/Awds:** Pro Bowl, 2000, 2003; All-Pro, 2000. **Special Achievements:** Films: 1999 AFC Championship Game, 2000; Super Bowl XXXIV, 2000; Glazer Palooza: Big Game Kick Off Live on Torio.Tv, 2016. TV Series: "30 for 30", 2012; "A Football Life", 2013. **Business Addr:** Sports Reporter, WSMV-TV, 5700 Knob Rd, Nashville, TN 37209, **Business Phone:** (615)353-4444.

**HOPKINS, DR. DIANNE MCAFEE**
Educator. **Personal:** Born Dec 30, 1944, Houston, TX; daughter of DeWitt Talmadge and Valda Lois McAfee; married Dale William; children: Scott McAfee & Brent William. **Educ:** Fisk Univ, BA, 1966; Atlanta Univ, Med Sci Liaison Soc, 1967; Western Mich Univ, educ specialist, 1973; Univ Wis-Madison, PhD, 1981. **Career:** Houston Independent Sch Dist, librn, 1967-71; Dept Educ Mich, Lansing, MI, sch librn specialist, 1972-73; W Bloomfield Sch, high sch librn media specialist, 1973-74; Univ Mich, Ann Arbor, MI, sch librn consult, 1974-77; Wis Dept Pub Instr, Madison, dir, sch librn, 1977-87; Univ Wisc-Madison, from asst prof to assoc prof, 1987-99, prof & asst dir, 1999, Sch Lib & info Sci, asst dir, prof emer, currently, Nat Libr Power Prog, co-prin investr. **Orgs:** Beta Phi Mu Int Libr Fraternity, 1967; Phi Delta Kappa, 1980; Delta Sigma Theta; chmn, AASL White House Conf Libr & Info Serv Planning & Implementation Comt, 1986-92; ed bd, Sch Libr Media Quart, AASL, 1988-91; chair, Educr Sch Lib Media Specialists Sect, AASL, 1989-90; AASL Rep, White House Conf Lib & Info Serv, 1991-; Intellectual Freedom Comn, Ala, 1991-95; Vision Comn Nat Sch Lib Media Stand, AASL, 1994-98; trustee, bd dir, FTRF, 1997-99; bd mem large, Libr Res Round Table, AL, 1997-2000; exec comt, bd dir, Freedom Read Found, 1998-99; ed bd, Sch Libr Media Online J, Am Asn Sch Librns, 1999-2002; Wis Sch Libr; Jack & Jill Am; External Rev Panel Pool mem, Off Accr, Am Libr Asn. **Home Addr:** 501 Meadowlark Dr, Madison, WI 53714-3303, **Home Phone:** (608)221-1300. **Business Addr:** Professor Emeritus, Former Assistant Director, University of Wisconsin-Madison, 600 N Pk St, Madison, WI 53706, **Business Phone:** (608)263-2955.

**HOPKINS, DONALD RAY**
Lawyer, government official. **Personal:** Born Nov 14, 1936, Tulsa, OK; son of Stacey E and Carolyn McGlory; children: Yvonne Ann-Marie. **Educ:** Univ Kans, BA, polit sci, 1958; Yale Univ, MA, polit sci, 1961; Univ Calif, Berkeley, JD, 1965; Harvard Law Sch, LLM, 1970. **Career:** Govt offical (retired), lawyer; Univ Calif Berkeley, teaching asst, 1960-63, asst dean students, 1965-67, asst exec vice chancellor, 1967-68; Nat Asn Advan Colored People, Legal Defense Fund Inc, staff atty, 1969-70; Pac Cons, exec vpres, 1970-71; Us Cong 8th Calif Cong Dist, dist admin, 1971-92; atty, pvt pract, 1981-. **Orgs:** Estate tax examr, US Treas Dept, 1965; Acad Polit Sci; Arbit Asn Bd Arbitrators; bd dir, Am Civil Liberties Union, No Calif, 1969-71; bd dir, Univ Calif Alumni Asn, 1976-79; bd dir, African Film Soc; bd dir, Travelers Aid Soc; Univ Calif Alumni Asn; Calif State, Nat, Am, Fed, Alameda County Bar Asn; bd dir, Chas Houston Bar Asn; Am Trial Lawyers Asn; Nat Conf Black Lawyers; Nat Lawyers Guild; Calif Asn Black Lawyers; bd dir, Vol Parole; adv bd, Afro Sports hall; fel Woodrow Wilson; Nat Polit Sci Hon Soc. **Honors/Awds:** Various achievement awards; Phi Beta Kappa; PiSigma Alpha. **Special Achievements:** Contributing author of "Politics & Change in Berkeley", Nathan & Scott 1979; contributing author to numerous periodicals. **Home Addr:** 18050 Broadway Terr, Oakland, CA 94611-1036, **Home Phone:** (510)594-2578. **Business Addr:** Attorney, 4606 S Garnett Suite 310, Tulsa, OK 74146, **Business Phone:** (918)622-6613.

**HOPKINS, DR. DONALD ROSWELL**
Physician. **Personal:** Born Sep 25, 1941, Miami, FL; son of J Leonard and Iva Major; married Ernestine M. **Educ:** Morehouse Col, BS, 1962; Univ Chicago Med Sch, MD, 1966; Harvard Sch Pub Health, MPH, 1970; Univ Vienna, Inst Europ Studies. **Career:** San Francisco Gen Hosp, intern, 1966-67; Harvard Sch Pub Health, asst prof, 1974-77; Smallpox Eradication/Measles Control Prog, dir; Carter Ctr, Ctr Dis-Control & Prev, asst dir, int health, 1978-84, dep dir, 1984-87, actg dir, 1985; Carter Ctr, sr consult, 1987-97, assoc exec dir, 1997, vpres, health prog, currently. **Orgs:** Am Soc Trop Med & Hyg, 1965; Inst Med, 1987; fel, bd dir, MacArthur Found, currently; fel Am Acad Arts & Sci; Nat Acad Sci, Inst Med. **Honors/Awds:** CDC Medal of Excellence; Distinguished Service Medal, US Pub Health Serv, 1986; DSc, Morehouse Col, 1988; DSc, Emory Univ, 1994; Honorary chief in three traditional areas of Nigeria: Akoko South, 1994, Aninri, 1998 & Ikwo, 1998; DHL, Univ Mass-Lowell, 1997; Nat Order Mali, 1998; Knight of the National Order of Mali, 1998; DSc, Morehouse Sch Med, 1999; Medal of Honor of Public Health (Gold), Niger, 2004; Champion of Public Health, Tulane Univ, 2005; Mectizan Award, Merck & Co, 2007; James F. & Sarah T. Fries Foundation Prize; Pumphandle Award, Coun State & Territorial Epidemiologists, 2012; DSc, Harvard Univ, 2013. **Special Achievements:** Directed: "Smallpox Eradication Prog", Sierra Leone, 1967-69; Directed: "Guinea Worm Eradication Initiative at CDC", 1980-87; Author: "Princes & Peasants: Smallpox in Hist", 1983; "At Carter Ctr", 1987; led the Guinea worm eradication initiative, which has brought down the no of Guinea worm cases from an estimated 3.5 million in 1986 to approx 15, 500 cases in 2004. **Home Addr:** 1840 N Hudson Ave, Chicago, IL 60614, **Home Phone:** (312)337-1955. **Business Addr:** Vice President, The Carter Center, 1 Copenhill 453 Freedom Pkwy, Atlanta, GA 30307, **Business Phone:** (404)420-5100.

**HOPKINS, EDNA J.**
Educator. **Personal:** Born Sep 29, 1924, Weatherford, TX; married Fritizer; children: Stephen. **Educ:** Tex Col, BA, 1952; Columbia Univ, MA. **Career:** LA Co Schs, teacher, 1955; Enterprise Sch Dist, teacher, 1958; Educ Workshops, 1965-67, Task Force New Ling Prog, supvr teacher; Task Force Early Childhood Educ, 1970; Compton Unified Sch Dist, Task Force PIRAMID, coordr, 1974. **Orgs:** Chair, PR&R Community Educ Asn, 1965-68; nat corp bd, Women Community Serv Inc, 1968-; White House Conf Food, Hunger & Nutrit, 1969-; vpres, Nat Coun Negro Women, 1970-; chairperson, Greater LA WIGS Bd, 1970-; Calif Teacher Asn; Nat Educ Asn; Compton Educ Asn; Int Asn Chlidhood Educ; Delta Sigma Theta; Dir Christian Educ LA Dist Christian Meth Epis Church; dir, Christian Educ Philllip Tem CME Church, 1970; secy & chmn, C Care & Dev Ser Inc; Int Asn Vol Eds; bd dir, LA Coun Chs, 1970-72; bd dir, Womn Coal Com Comn Actg, 1970-73; bd dir, Teen Age & Mothers, Harriet Tubman Sch, 1970-74; Educ Adv Comt PUSH; Bd Advs Am Youth Actg Org Inc, 1974-. **Honors/Awds:** Apple Grammy Teacher of the Year, 1968; Award Women, 1972; Woman of the Year, Christian Methodist Episcopal Church Womens Miss Soc, 1972. **Home Addr:** 2940 Farmdale Ave, Los Angeles, CA 90016-2944, **Home Phone:** (323)708-6457.

**HOPKINS, EDWARD CHARLES, JR.**
Business owner, air force officer. **Personal:** Born Jan 1, 1973. **Educ:** USAF Acad, 1995; Univ Ariz, Col Social & Behav Sci; Univ Ariz, James E. Rogers Col Law alumnus, 2010. **Career:** USAF Acad, CO, cadet, admis adv & officer; 366th Air Expeditionary Wing, Mountain Home, ID, acct & finance officer; 366th Air Expeditionary Wing Comptroller, Mountain Home, ID, budget officer & cost analyst; USAF Southern Command & 12th Air Force, dep comptroller & staff officer; Criterion Mgt Consult, pres, founder & owner; Slutes, Sakrison & Rogers PC, law clerk, currently. **Orgs:** Pres, Davis-Monthan Afb Black Heritage Asn; mem bd dir, Ariz Black Bd Dir Proj; chairperson, African Am Adv Coun, Univ Ariz; dir, bd dir, PRIME Sch Music & PRIME Found; dir, bd dir, Tucson Urban League; pres, Black Law Students Asn; pres, Oral Advocacy Orgn. **Special Achievements:** Young Leader of the Future, Ebony Mag, 2003. **Business Addr:** Law Clerk, Slutes, Sakrison & Rogers PC, 4801 E Broadway Blvd Suite 301, Tucson, AZ 85711, **Business Phone:** (520)624-6691.

**HOPKINS, DR. ESTHER ARVILLA HARRISON**
Lawyer, scientist. **Personal:** Born Sep 18, 1926, Stamford, CT; married T Ewell; children: Ewell Jr. **Educ:** Boston Univ, BA, chem, 1947; Howard Univ, MS, chem, 1949; Yale Univ, MS, chem, 1962, PhD, chem, 1967; Suffolk Univ Law Sch, JD, 1976. **Career:** Va State Col, fac, 1949-52; New Eng Inst Med Res, asst researcher biophys, 1955-59; Am Cyanamid's Stamford Res Lab, res chemist, 1959-61; Polaroid Corp, scientist, 1967-73, patent atty, 1973-78, sr proj adminr, 1979, emulsion coating & anal lab; Mass Dept Environ Protection, dep gen coun, 1989; Boston Univ, dir, 1998-. **Orgs:** Bd govs, Asn Yale Alumni; chair, Yale Medal Comt; nat bd, YMCA USA; former chair, pres & bd selectman, Gen Alumni Asn, Boston Univ; Fin Comt, Town Framingham, Mass; corp mem, Cambridge Family, YMCA; hon mem, Boston Univ Women's GradClub; bd dir & pres, Framingham Region, YMCA; Alpha Kappa Alpha Sorority; Soc Promoting Theol Educ; dean, Stamfort Chap Am Guild Organists; natscholar, Nat Asn Col Women, 1963; distinguished alumni, Boston Univ Col Liberal Arts, 1975; Phi Beta Kappa; Sigma Xi; Sigma Pi Sigma; Beta Kappa Chi; Sci Res Soc Am. **Honors/Awds:** Training Grant, USPHS, 1962-66; First Parish Award, 1977; Women of Achievement, Mass Fedn Bus & Prof Women's Club, 1979; Woman of the Year, Framingham Bus & Prof Women's Club, 1979; Woman of the Year, Regional Family YMCA, Framingham, 1984. **Special Achievements:** First African American to be elected to the Framingham Board, 1999. **Home Addr:** 1550 Worcester Rd Rm 524, Framingham, MA 01701, **Home Phone:** (508)872-8148. **Business Addr:** Director, Boston University, 1 Silber Way, Boston, MA 02215, **Business Phone:** (617)353-2000.

**HOPKINS, DR. GAYLE P.**
Athletic director. **Personal:** Born Nov 7, 1941, Tulsa, OK; son of Elbert and Sophia Jackson; married Patricia Cartwright; children: Alissa & Christopher. **Educ:** Univ Ariz, Tucson, AZ, BA, 1965; San Francisco State, San Francisco, CA, MA, 1972; Claremont Grad Sch, Claremont, CA, PhD, 1978. **Career:** Athletic staff (retired); San Francisco State, San Francisco, Calif, phys educ coach, 1969-75; Claremont Col, track coach & dir phys educ; Claremont-McKenna, Claremont, Calif, assoc prof, 1975-83; US Dept Agr, Wash, DC, EEO specialist, 1979-80; Univ Ariz, Tucson, Ariz, asst athletic dir, assoc to dir athletics, community & alumni rels, 1983. **Orgs:** Fel Lyndon Johnson Cong, 1978; pres, Nat Asn Athletic Advs Acads, 1983-; pres, Univ Ariz Black Alumni Asn, 1987-; chmn, Black Studies, Tucson Unified Sch Dist; Ariz C Asn; Quad Cities Sports; Iowa prep hist; charter mem, Ariz Sports Hall Fame; NCAA Track & Field Comt; Urban League Caucus; Nat Asn Advan Colored People; Urban League, Ariz C Asn; Carondelet Health Network Pub Policy Coun; UAs Sports Hall Fame selection comt. **Honors/Awds:** Hall of Fame, Drake Univ, Univ Ariz, 1967; Coach of the Year, San Francisco State Univ, 1974; University of Arizona Sports Hall of Fame, 1976. **Special Achievements:** Represented the United States in the 1964 Tokyo Olympics as a long jumper; Wildcats' first NCAA champion. **Home Addr:** 3333 N Nambe Dr, Tucson, AZ 85749-9598, **Home Phone:** (520)749-9394.

**HOPKINS, DR. JOHN DAVID**
Educator, association executive, radiologist. **Personal:** Born Mar 6, 1933, Trenton, NJ; son of John P Sr and Edith Harvey; married Lillian L Henry; children: John III, Kay & Lisa. **Educ:** Lincoln Univ, AB, 1954; Meharry Med Col, MD, 1958; Ohio State Univ, residency, 1963; Vanderbilt Univ, Fellowship, 1970. **Career:** Educator (retired); Meharry Med Col, from assoc prof to dir, 1963-75; Tuskegee VA Hosp, consult, 1965-68; Riverside Hosp, dir, 1972-75; VA Hosp, chief radiol, 1973-75; Norfolk Community Hosp, radiologist, 1975-98, pres staff, 1983-85, chief radiologist; Lake Taylor Hosp, consult radiologist, 1985. **Orgs:** Am Col Radiol; fel Am Col Nuclear Physicians; Soc Nuclear Med; adv bd, Community Ment Health Ctr; Aeolian Club; Clin Serv Comn, E VA Sch Med; bd dir, United Givers Fund; bd trustees, Eastern VA Med Sch; Nat Med Asn; AMA; comnr, Norfolk Pub Health Dept, 1983-. **Honors/Awds:** Guest lecturer; 8 publications; Alpha Omega, Honor Medical Society; Sigma Pi Phi; examiner, Am Bd Radiology, 1983-90; case report, "Adrenal Tumors, "Journal Computed Tomography, 1988. **Home Addr:** 5312 Halter Lane, Norfolk, VA 23502-4435, **Home Phone:** (757)461-1788.

**HOPKINS, LEROY TAFT, II**
Educator. **Personal:** Born Aug 19, 1942, Lancaster, PA; son of Leroy T and Mary E. **Educ:** Millersville State Col, BA, ger & russ, 1966; Harvard Univ, PhD, ger lang & literatures, 1974. **Career:** NE Univ, instr Ger, 1971-72; Hedwig-Heyle-Schule, W Ger, instr Eng, 1974-76; Urban League Lancaster Co Inc, assoc dir, 1976-79, actg exec dir, 1979; Millersville State Col, asst prof Ger, 1979, prof Ger(retired), Dept Foreign Lang, chmn, 1998-; Av Media Lab Study Cultures Soc, res assoc. **Orgs:** Bd mem, Lancaster County Libr & Lancaster Neighborhood Health Ctr, 1977-; chmn, Pa Deleg White House Conf Libr, 1978-79; founding mem. adv comt, Black Hist Pa Hist & Mus Comn, 1979-; Pa Humanities Coun, 1988-94; com person, City Lancasters Overall Econ Develop Prog; first vpres, 1989, pres, 1991-94, Lancaster Hist Soc; bd dir, DAAD Alumni Asn US; Lancaster Urban League; bd mem & trustee, LancasterHistory.org. **Honors/Awds:** Travelling Fellow, Harvard Univ, 1969-70; Study & Visit Grant for Research, German Acad Exchange Serv, 1989 & 1994; Hon Mem, Phi Kappa Phi, 1991. **Home Addr:** 531 Church St, Lancaster, PA 17602-4415. **Business Addr:** Professor of German, Millersville University, McComsey 252 1 S George St, Millersville, PA 17551-0302, **Business Phone:** (717)872-3525.

**HOPKINS, NOVELLETE O.**
Taxonomist. **Career:** City Atlantic City, dep tax assessor, 2009, tax assessor, Munic Assessor, 2009-13. **Business Addr:** Municipal Assessor, City of Atlantic City, 1301 Bacharach Blvd Suite 606, Atlantic City, NJ 08401, **Business Phone:** (609)347-5380.

**HOPKINS, PEREA M.**
Meeting planner. **Personal:** Born Apr 13, 1931, Marshall, TX; daughter of Charles A McCane and Margaret Perea McCane; married Milton M Hopkins Jr; children: Christina Elizabeth. **Educ:** Seton Hill Col, BA, math, 1953. **Career:** Ballistic Res Lab, Aberdeen Proving Ground, MD, mathematician, 1954-60; Spacetrack Syst Div LG Hanscom Field MA, mathematician, 1960-68; Dynatrend Inc, Woburn, MA, staff acct, 1972-81; IOCS Inc, finance asst, 1981-83; Heritage Meetings & Incentives Inc, acct mgr, 1983-; Krikorian Miller Assoc, Bedford, MA, opers mgr, 1987-93; ECNE, meeting planner. **Orgs:** Am Asn Univ Women, 1953-; Am Math Asn, 1953-68; League Women Voters Bedford, 1969-; chmn human resources, League Women Voters Bedford, 1970-76; bd dir, Boston C's Serv; pres bd dirs, Roxbury C's Serv, 1973-79; charter mem, Middlesex County Chap Links Inc, 1976-; pres, Middlesex County Chap Links, 1976-77; secy, Middlesex County Chap Links, 1978-80; Gov Adv Comt, Am Col Phys, Wash, DC, 1980; chairperson, Middlesex County Chap Links, 1986-88, rec secy, 1988-90; chmn, Bedford-Lexington Br, Am Asn Univ Women, 1986-88; vpres, Bedford-Lexington Br, Am Asn Univ Women, 1994-96; treas, Rho Epsilon Omega, Alpha Kappa Alpha Sorority Inc, 1994-96; secy, Bedford-Lexington Br, Am Asn Univ Women, 2006. **Home Addr:** 8 Hilltop Dr, Bedford, MA 01730, **Home Phone:** (781)275-8563.

**HOPKINS, TELMA LOUISE**
Actor, singer. **Personal:** Born Oct 28, 1948, Louisville, KY; married Donald B Allen; children: 1. **Career:** Tony Orlando and Dawn, singer; Isaac Hayes, backup singer; Roots: The Next Generations, 1979; Films: The Kid with the Broken Halo, 1982; Future Cop, 1985; Trancers, 1985; Vital Signs, 1990; Trancers II, 1991; Trancers III, 1992; The Wood, 1999; The Love Guru, 2008; The Clean Up Woman, 2010. TV series: "Love Boat", 1979; "A New Kind Of Family", 1980"; "Bosom Buddies", 1980; "Dance Fever", 1981; "Fantasy Island"; "Gimme A Break", 1983-87; "Circus of the Stars", 1985; "Getting By", 1994; "Family Matters", 1989-97; "Half & Half", 2002-06; "Psych", 2008; "Are We There Yet?", 2010-12; "JD Lawrence's the Clean Up Woman", 2012; "Lab Rats", 2012-13; "LA Live the Show", 2013; "Getting On", 2013; "Partners", 2014. **Honors/Awds:** BET Comedy Award, 2005. **Special Achievements:** Four times Image Award nominee. **Business Addr:** Actress, c/o ABC Productions, 2020 Ave of the Stars 5th Fl, Los Angeles, CA 90067, **Business Phone:** (310)557-6860.

**HOPKINS, THOMAS FRANKLIN**
Educator, research scientist. **Personal:** Born Culpepper, VA; son of Thomas and Dorothy L Atkins Brown; children: Winifred Louise, Thomas M, Charles M, Michael & Arthur G. **Educ:** Calvin Coolidge Col, Boston, BS, 1955; Mich State Univ, MS, 1961; Boston Univ, PhD, 1970. **Career:** Educator (retired); Worcester Found Exp Biol, res asst, 1949-60, scientist, 1960-70; Univ Conn, assoc prof biol, 1970-75; Univ Md Eastern Shore, Dept Natural Sci, chmn, 1975-86, prof biol, 1986-94. **Orgs:** Am Physiol Soc, 1970-; Nat Sci Teachers Asn. **Special Achievements:** Published many journals and articles. **Home Addr:** 159 North St, Salem, MA 01970, **Home Phone:** (978)825-9222.

**HOPKINS, DR. VASHTI EDYTHE JOHNSON**
Educator, president (organization). **Personal:** Born Aug 22, 1924, VA; daughter of Louis Tenner and Matilda Ann Robinson; married Haywood Sr; children: Haywood Jr, Yvonne Andrews & Sharon. **Educ:** Va Sem & Col, BS, 1963; St Pauls Col, BS, elem educ, 1967; Univ Va, MEd, 1969; S western Univ, PhD, educ, 1984. **Career:** Educator (retired); Amherst City Pub Schs, teacher, 1963-67; Lynchburg Pub Schs, teacher, 1967-74; Sandusky Mid Sch, teacher, 1974-82; Va Sem & Col, prof eng, 1991-97. **Orgs:** Dep organizer, Order Eastern Star Prince Hall Affiliated, 1967-91; pres, vpres, Lynchburg Retired Teachers, 1989-90; pres, Dist F Retired Teachers, 1990-92; Eastern Theol Ctr;

Zeta Chap Zeta Phi Beta Sorority; life mem, Univ Va Alumni Asn; life mem, Century Club St Paul's Col; life mem, Nat Educ Asn; life mem, Va Educ Asn; life mem, Lutheran Educ Asn; Daughter Isis, Golden Circle Past LL Ruler; pres, Episcopal Church Women; pres, Amity Soc; Bridgette Soc; Nat Sor Phi Delta Kappa Inc; Alpha Tau Chap; Lynchburg Va Chap; Phi Delta Kappa Fraternity. **Honors/Awds:** Achievement Award, Order of Eastern Star Chap 40, 1984; Outstanding Achievement Grand Chap, Va Order of the Eastern Star Prince Hall Affiliated, 1984; Golden Poet Award, World of Poetry, 1989-96. **Special Achievements:** Published poetry in Century Mag, 1960; published poems in 1989, 1992. **Home Addr:** RR 5, PO Box 630, Lynchburg, VA 24501.

### HOPKINS, WESLEY CARL

Football player, actor. **Personal:** Born Sep 26, 1961, Birmingham, AL. **Educ:** Southern Methodist Univ, grad. **Career:** Football player (retired), actor; Philadelphia Eagles, free safety, defensive back, strong safety, 1983-93. **Honors/Awds:** Most Valuable Defensive Player, Cotton Bowl; Defensive Player of the Week, Sports Illustrated; Defensive Player of the Week, Nat Football League; National Football Conference Defensive Player of the Month; Eagles Defensive Most Valuable Player; Pro Bowl selection, 1985; Ed Block Courage Award, 1988. **Special Achievements:** Films: The Complete History of the Philadelphia Eagles, 2004; Minister of Defense: The Reggie White Story, 2006.

### HOPKINS, WILLIAM A.

Government official. **Personal:** Born May 27, 1943, Americus, GA; married Desi Page; children: Ellen, Ryan, Christopher P & Leslee. **Educ:** Albany State Col, BA, 1968; Ga State Univ, MPA, 1984. **Career:** St Regis Paper Co, asst indust rels, 1967-69; Sentry Ins, dist mgr, 1969-72; Ins Multi Line, territory mgr, 1972-77; Piedmont Ins Agency, pres, 1977-82; State Ga, Dir Small Bus Affairs, spec asst to comdr, currently. **Orgs:** Vpres, Atlanta Alumni KAY, 1976-78; pres, Albany State Alumni, 1980-82; bd mem, Morris Brown Col. **Home Addr:** 3975 Old Fairburn Rd SW, Atlanta, GA 30331, **Home Phone:** (404)346-3965. **Business Addr:** Special Assistant to the Commander, State of Georgia Director Small Business Affairs, 200 Piedmont Ave Suite 1416, Atlanta, GA 30334.

### HOPKINSON, MARK I.

Chief executive officer. **Career:** Brit Info Serv, Brit Embassy, New York, Radio & tv div, vice consul; Brit Gov, US media strategist; Brit Broadcasting Corp, trained journalist; NewsMark Pub Rels Inc, founder & chief exec officer, currently. **Home Addr:** , FL. **Business Addr:** Chief Executive Officer, Founder, NewsMark Public Relations Inc, 10750 Hayden Dr, Boca Raton, FL 33498, **Business Phone:** (561)852-5767.

### HOPPER, DR. CORNELIUS LENARD

School administrator, vice president (organization), neurologist. **Personal:** Born Aug 30, 1934, Hartshorne, OK; son of Claude and Hazel Pugh; married Barbara M Johnson; children: Adriane, Brian & Michael. **Educ:** Ohio Univ, AB, 1956; Univ Cincinnati Col, MEd & MD, 1960; Marquette Univ, attended 1963; Univ Wis. **Career:** Univ WI, instr neurol, 1967-68, Mult Sclerosis Clinics, founding dir, asst prof neurol, 1968-71; Tuskegee Inst, John A. Andrew Memorial Hosp, med dir, 1971-79, vpres health affairs; Univ Ala Sch Med, asst clin prof, 1971-79; Univ Calif, spec asst health affairs, pres, 1979-83, vpres health affairs, 1983-2000, sr admin officer, univ health sci syst, emer vpres health affairs, currently; State Calif Health, manpower policy comnr, 1981-2002; Nat Health Serv Corps, founder. **Orgs:** Consult, Off Spec Progs Bur Health Manpower Educ, NIH, 1972-79; consult, Am Pub Health Asn Div Int Health Prog, 1974-; pres, Ala, St Med Asn, 1974-79; DHEW Nat Adv Coun Prof Stand Rev Org, 1974-78; Nat Adv Comt Robert Wood Johnson Found Comn Hosp-Med Staff Sponsored Primary Care Group Pract Prog, 1974-82; Va Med Sch Asst Rev Comt, 1975-76; Nat Adv Comm Robert Wood Johnson Found Nurse Fac Fels Prog, 1976-82; Calif Health Manpower Policy Comm, 1981-2001; Epilepsy Found Am, Nat Info & Resource Ctr Adv Comt, 1982-; vpres, Calif Asn HMOs Found, 1994-; chair, Univ Oakland, Bd Regents Samuel Merritt, chmn, 2000-11; chair, King./Drew Med Ctr, 2004-05; vice chmn, Kaiser Arbit Oversight Bd; assoc mem, Am Acad Neurol Nat Med Asn; Am Asn Advan Sci; Asn Acad Health Ctrs; Golden St Med Asn; Meharry Med Col; E Bay Reg Bd Sutter Health Syst; consult, Nat Insts Health; consult, DHEW; Am Int Health Alliance. **Honors/Awds:** Special Research Fellow, Demyelinating Dis Nat Inst Neurol Dis & Blindness, 1967-68; CS Cleeland and CG Matthews, MMPI Profiles in Exacerbation & Remission of Multiple Sclerosis Psychol Reports 27, 343, 1970; The Health Care Delivery System, A Rural Perspective Contact '72 - Proceedings of the Governor's Health manpower Conference, 174, 1972; CG Matthews & CS Cleeland, Symptom Instability & Thermo regulation in Multiple Sclerosis Neurology 22, 142, 1972; publ including, PSRO, A Current Status Report Proceedings of Sixth Annual Conf on the Southern Region Conf on the Humanities and Public Policy May, 1976; Alumnus of the Year, Ohio Univ, 1985; Medal of Merit, Ohio Univ, 1985; First Recipient Of National Medical Fellowships Founder's Award, 2001; Drake Medal, Univ Cincinnati Col Med, Robert Wood Johnson Foundation Medallion; Distinguished Service Awards, Regional Medical Program Services & the Veterans Administration; Resolutions of Appreciation, California State Senate; Resolutions of Appreciation, Univ Calif Bd Regents. Annual Hopper Lectureships and Research Awards in Breast Cancer, AIDS, and Tobacco were created by the University in his honor. **Home Addr:** 1420l Skyline Blvd, Oakland, CA 94619-3625, **Home Phone:** (510)635-4839. **Business Addr:** Vice President Emeritus for Health Affairs, University of California, 1111 Franklin St 11th Fl, Oakland, CA 94607-5200, **Business Phone:** (510)987-9220.

### HOPSON, CYNTHIA A. BOND

Writer, educator. **Personal:** children: 2. **Educ:** Clark Atlanta Univ, BA, 1985; Murray State Univ, MS, 1989; Southern Ill Univ, Carbondale, PhD, 2000. **Career:** Lane Col, instr & newspaper coordr, 1989-91; Murray State Univ, vis lectr, 1991-95; Univ Memphis, prof journalism, 1995-2005; Touched by Grace Ministry, auth, educr, speaker, workshop/retreat leader & chief inspiration officer, 2002-; Gen Bd Higher Educ & Ministry, asst gen secy-Black Col Fund & Ethnic Concerns, 2005-. **Orgs:** Delta Sigma Theta Sorority; Nat Asn Black Journalists; NAACP. **Honors/Awds:** Jackson, Tennessee Daughters of the American Revolution for Excellence in Print Media; University of Tennessee Award for Outstanding Civil Rights Contributions to West Tennessee; Wiley College Woman of Excellence; Black College Fund Award of Excellence; Thurston Group of Washington State Excellence in Education Award. **Special Achievements:** Author, Bad Hair Days, Rainy Days and Mondays: Wisdom and Encouragement to Life a Woman's Spirit, 2006; Too Many Irons in the Fire, 2008; I Do Every Day: Words of Wisdom for Newlyweds and Not So Newlyweds, 2011; The Women of Haywood: Their Lives, Our Legacy, 2012. **Business Phone:** (615)340-7378.

### HOPSON, HAROLD THEODORE, JR. (SONNY HOPSON)

Executive, entertainer. **Personal:** Born Jan 24, 1937, Abington, PA; son of Harold and Christine; children: Ronald, Lynette, Regina, Lisa-Shelia, Harold III, Kelley LynetteWashington, Ashley Lorraine Stanley, Ronald John II & Barry. **Educ:** Philadelphia Wireless Sch, 3 post grad courses, 3rd class Radio Tel Operators License, 1965. **Career:** Harold Randolph & Harvey Schmidt, div Ins Investr, 1958-65; Philadelphia Tribune, writer, reporter, 1965-66; Pepsi Generation Come Alive Radio Personality, 1965-66; Radio sta WHAT 1340-AM Philadelphia, communicator & radio personality, 1965-71, 1980-86; Scene Philadelphia Tribune, entertainment critic & reviewer, 1966-67; Sonny Hopson's Celebrity Lounge Germantown, proprietor & mgr, 1969-73; Astro Disc Club, proprietor; WDAS AM-FM Radio Sta, asst to pres, 1978; WHTH-FM Radio, owner, 1986-; Megastarr Entertainment WHTH Music com, chmn & chief exec officer, 1999-; WKBS-TV, Astro Disc Tv Show, exec producer. **Orgs:** Nat Asn Advan Colored People, 1957-; SCLC, 1965; Nat Asn Radio & TV Announcers, 1965; Jazz Home Club, 1968-; pres, founder, new chmn, Concerned Communicators, 1971-; organizer, People United Save Humanity, 1971-; co-founder, Nat Black Media Coalition. **Business Addr:** Chairman, Chief Executive Officer, Megastarr Entertainment WHTH Music, 4936 Wynnefield Ave, Philadelphia, PA 19131, **Business Phone:** (215)879-2624.

### HOPSON, KEVIN M.

Scientist, health services administrator. **Personal:** Born May 11, 1959, Roanoke, VA; son of James M; married Deborah. **Educ:** Va Tech, BS, biochem & biol, 1983; Hood Col, MBA, 2003. **Career:** Hercules Inc, prod develop mgr, 1983-84, process engr, 1984-87, res chemist, 1987-90; FDA, chemist, 1990-94, consumer safety officer, staff, bio res monitoring, currently. **Business Addr:** Consumer Safety Officer, Food & Drug Administration, 10903 Nh Ave, Silver Spring, MD 20993, **Business Phone:** (888)463-6332.

### HOPSON, MELVIN CLARENCE

Executive, administrator. **Personal:** Born Jun 29, 1937, Sawyerville, AL; son of Lovell Sr and Irene; children: Steven, Wayne & Myra. **Educ:** Roosevelt Univ, BA, eng, 1966. **Career:** Administrator, executive (retired); Montgomery Ward, store Mgr, 1968, dir EEO, 1969-80; McDonalds Corp, dir, asst vpres diversity develop, 1994. **Orgs:** Bd mem & life trustee, Chicago Urban League, 1971-; officer, Rat Pac Inc, 1980-; pres, Chicago Urban Affairs Coun, 1983; bd mem, Chicago Nat Asn Advan Colored People, 1984; Kappa Alpha Psi Fraternity Inc, 1984-86; bd dir, YMCA, 1985-. **Home Addr:** 4510 S Mich Ave, Chicago, IL 60653, **Home Phone:** (773)667-9204. **Business Phone:** (773)667-9204.

### HOPSON, SONNY. See HOPSON, HAROLD THEODORE, JR.

### HORAD, SEWELL D., SR.

Educator, army officer. **Personal:** Born Jan 26, 1922, Washington, DC; married Ella Garnett; children: Sewell D Jr & Denise H. **Educ:** Howard Univ, BS, 1942; George Washington Univ, MA, 1973. **Career:** Real estate salesman & bus owner, 1946-; Wash DC Pub Schs, admin officer spec educ, currently, teacher math, sci physically handicapped, 1958-72. **Orgs:** Lodge Masonic Temple; vpres, What Good Are We Club; Oldest Black Clubs DC; founding mem, Pro-Duffers Golf Club DC. **Special Achievements:** Instrumental in developing new techniques for teaching handicapped children, some have been copyrighted; Author "Fraction Computer", math book designed to solve fractional problems without finding least common denominator; invented an info retrieval system. **Home Addr:** 2118 Univ Blvd W, Silver Spring, MD 20902-4426, **Home Phone:** (301)942-8363.

### HORD, DR. FREDERICK LEE (FRED L HORD)

Educator, writer. **Personal:** Born Nov 7, 1941, Kokomo, IN; son of Noel E and Jessie Tyler; children: Teresa D Hord-Owens, F Mark & Laurel E. **Educ:** Ind State Univ, BS, speech & hist, 1963, MS, speech & educ, 1965; Union Grad Sch, PhD, black studies lit & hist, 1987. **Career:** Educator, Auth: Wabash Col, prof black studies, 1972-76; bk poems After h(ours), Third World Press, 1974; Ind Univ, guest lectr black studies, 1976; Frostburg State Univ, asst dir minority affairs, 1980-84; PANFRE, lectr, 1981-; Howard Univ, prof afro-am studies, 1984-87; W Va Univ, dir Ctr Black Cult, 1987-88; Knox Col, prof black studies & chmn, black studies prog, 1988-; lead article, W Va Law Rev Black Cult Centers, Summer, 1989; bk: Reconstruction Memory, Third World Press, 1991; Life Sentences: Freeing Black Relationships; co-ed: I Am Because We Are: Readings Black Philos, 1995; Black Cult Centers: Inside Out. **Orgs:** Consult ed, Nightsun; regional consult, NAMSE; consult, black studies Afro Am Enterprises; founder, pres & exec dir, Asn Black Cult Ctrs, 1994-; pres, Nat Asn Black Cult Ctr; bd mem, Nat Coun Black Studies; ed bd, J Black Studies; bd mem, Ill Comt Black Concerns Higher Educ. **Home Addr:** 203 Lombard St, Galesburg, IL 61401, **Home Phone:** (309)341-7714. **Business Addr:** Professor of Africana Studies, Chairman, Knox College, 2 E S St, Galesburg, IL 61401-4999, **Business Phone:** (309)341-7224.

### HORD, NOEL EDWARD

Executive. **Personal:** Born Jul 10, 1946, Kokomo, IN; son of Noel Ernest and Jessie Mae Tyler; married Tamar; children: Michelle Denise & Noel Daniel. **Educ:** Ind State Univ, Terre Haute, IN, 1967. **Career:** Wohl Shoe Co, Clayton, Mo, var responsibilities, 1967-84; Nine W Grp, vpres opers, 1984-86, sr vpres, gen mgr, 1986, exec vpres, gen mgr, 1987; group pres, 1991, pres & chief operating officer, 1995-98; Enzol Angiolini Div, pres, 1988-91, group pres, 1991-93, pres & chief financial officer, 1995-98; US Shoe Corp, Footwear Group, pres & chief exec officer, 1993; Dunk Inc, pres, chief exec officer, 1999; BCBG Max Azria, pres & chief operating officer, 2002-; New York Transit Inc, pres & chief operating officer, 2003-; LF USA Footwear Group, pres, 2009-; Donald J Pliner Inc, pres, chief operating officer, 2011-. **Orgs:** Urban Leagues Nat Black Exec Exchange Prog; co-founder, pres, Concerned Black Man Action Youth Danbury, Conn; co-founder, Hord Found, Danbury, Conn. **Home Addr:** 51 Mid River Rd, Danbury, CT 06811-4315. **Business Addr:** President, DONALD J PLINER, INC, 10800 NW 97th St Suite 103, Miami, FL 33178, **Business Phone:** (888)307-1630.

### HORN, JOSEPH (JOE HORN)

Football player, football coach. **Personal:** Born Jan 16, 1972, Tupelo, MS; married Lacreshia; children: 6. **Educ:** Itawamba Community Col, attended. **Career:** Football player (retired), coach; Shreveport Pirates, 1995; Memphis Mad Dogs, 1995; Kans City Chiefs, 1996-97, wide receiver, 1998, split end, 1999; New Orleans Saints, wide receiver, 2000-06; Atlanta Falcons, wide receiver, 2007-08, New Orleans Saints, 2010; Bayou 87, owner; Northeast Miss Community Col, asst coach, currently, wide receivers coach, 2015-. **Honors/Awds:** Saints Offensive Player of the Year, 2000; Pro Bowl, 2000, 2001, 2002, 2004; New Orleans Saints Hall of Fame, 2010. **Business Addr:** Wide Receivers Coach, Northeast Mississippi Community College, 101 Cunningham Blvd, Booneville, MS 38829.

### HORN, LAURETTA FREEMAN. See FREEMAN, LAURETTA.

### HORN, SHALLEY JONES. See JONES, SHALLEY A.

### HORNBUCKLE, NAPOLEON

Executive. **Personal:** Born Feb 16, 1942, Birmingham, AL; son of Lee E and Louisa Coleman; married Dorothy Jeanne Sadler; children: Scott & Vance. **Educ:** Tenn State Univ, Nashville, TN, BA, elec electronics engineering, 1964; Ariz State Univ, postgrad course, 1968. **Career:** Executive (retired); Motorola Space & Systs Technol Group, Diversified Technologies Div, Ariz, develop engr mgr, proj engr mgr, proj leader mgr, mkt develop mgr, vpres & dir, vpres & gen mgr, SED, 1990-95; Worldwide Mkt Systs Solutions Group, corp vpres & dir, 1995. **Orgs:** Omega Psi Phi Fraternity, 1964; Armed Forces Commun Asn, 1976-; Electronics Indust Asn, 1976-; Nat Security Indust Asn, 1984-; life mem, Nat Asn Advan Colored People, 1987-; Boule, 1988-; Sigma Pi Phi Fraternity; fel African Sci Inst; Providence Missionary Baptist Church; bd mem, Greater Phoenix Urban League; bd mem, Maricopa Community Col Found; treas, Bill Dickey Golf Scholar Found, currently. **Home Addr:** 1441 E Los Arboles, Tempe, AZ 85284, **Home Phone:** (480)838-8126. **Business Addr:** Treasurer, Bill Dickey Scholarship Association, 1140 E Wash St Suite 103, Phoenix, AZ 85034, **Business Phone:** (602)258-7851.

### HORNBURGER, JANE M.

Educator. **Personal:** Born Aug 26, 1928, Fayetteville, AR; daughter of Ella Carter Melvin and Roy D Melvin. **Educ:** Fayetteville State Univ, BS, 1948; NY Univ, MA, 1950, EdD, 1970. **Career:** Kinston, NCA Pub Schs, teacher, 1948-53; Wilmington, Del Pub Schs, teacher, 1954-66, suv reading/lang arts, 1966-69, dir teacher training, 1969-72, Boston Univ, asst prof, 1972-77; City Univ NY, Brooklyn Col, assoc prof educ serv, 1978-. **Orgs:** Dir, Mass Asn Reading Educrs, 1976-77; NYC Reading Coun; NY State Eng Coun; New Eng Asn Teachers Eng; Int Reading Asn, policy guidelines comt, 1981-83, exec search comn, 1983, bd mem, 1987-90, chap, hq comt, 1989-90; Nat Coun Teachers Eng, comn classroom pract, 1983, 1978-81 & 1985-88, comn mem communicating res, 1989-92, ed bd, 1981-84; NY State Reading Asn, chair, 1990-; Bronx Reading Coun, pres, IRA hon coun, 1987-89; Am Asn Univ Profs; Phi Delta Kappa; Pi Lambda Theta; Kappa Delta Pi Episcopalian. **Home Addr:** 1001 Grand Concourse, Bronx, NY 10452, **Home Phone:** (718)992-9223. **Business Addr:** NY.

### HORNE, DR. AARON, SR.

Educator, college administrator. **Personal:** Born Dec 3, 1941, Chipley, FL; son of Albert and Laura; married Myrtle; children: Ericka, Michelle & Aaron Jr. **Educ:** Tenn State Univ, BS, 1968; Roosevelt Univ, MM, 1972; Univ Iowa, MFA, 1973, doctorate musical arts, 1976; Univ NH Inst Enrollment, mgt dipl, 1990; Harvard Univ, Grad Sch Educ, dipl, 1993. **Career:** College administrator, educator (retired); Fla A & M Univ, asst prof, 1968-72; Univ Iowa, lectr, 1973-76; Tex Southern Univ, assoc prof, 1976-77; Northeastern Ill Univ, prof & dir jazz studies, 1977-89, Ctr Inner City Studies, prof music, 1996-97, actng dir, 1998-2001; Northwestern Univ, sr lectr, 1982-89; Bd Govs Univs, asst vice chancellor acad affairs, 1990-2001; Winston-Salem State Univ, Col Arts & Scis, dean & prof music, assoc vice chancellor acad affairs enrollment mgt, 2001-07. **Orgs:** Exec bd, Int Asn Jazz Educrs, 1970-; Nat Asn Col Wind & Percussion Instrs, 1972-; Music Educrs Nat Conf, 1977-; bd mem, Duke Ellington Soc, 1988-; Am Asn Higher Educ, 1989-; Black Music Caucus, 1989-; Ill Comm Black Concerns Higher Educ, 1989-; Arts-in-Educ; advisor, Alpha Kappa Mu hon Socs; bd mem, Winston-Salem Symphony Inc; bd mem, Arts Coun Inc. **Home Addr:** 122 Scottsdale Dr, Advance, NC 27006, **Home Phone:** (336)998-8095.

### HORNE, ANTONIO TREMAINE

Football player, football coach. **Personal:** Born Mar 21, 1976, Queens, NC. **Educ:** Clemson Univ, grad, 1998. **Career:** Football player (retired), football coach; St Louis Rams, kick returner, 1998-2000; Kans City Chiefs, 2001; D1 Sports Training, head strength & speed coach, currently. **Honors/Awds:** Super Bowl champion, XXXIV. **Business Addr:** Head Strength Coach, Speed Coach, D1 Sports Holdings LLC, 7115 South Springs Dr, Franklin, TN 37067, **Business Phone:** (615)778-1893.

**HORNE, DEBORAH JEAN (DEBORAH HORNE)**
Television journalist. **Personal:** Born Jul 26, 1953, Newport News, VA; daughter of Willie Edward and Daisy Mae Pellman. **Educ:** Hampton Univ, Hampton, VA, BA, 1975; Ohio State Univ, Columbus, OH, MA, 1976. **Career:** Providennce Jour, Providence, RI, gen assignment reporter, 1976-81; KIRO TV, reporter, 1991-; WPRI-TV, E Providence, RI, chief reporter, 1981; KIRO 7 Eyewitness News, gen assignment reporter, 1991-, KIRO InColor, exec producer, creator, 1994, KIRO Backstage, creator, 2004. **Orgs:** Pres, Delta Sigma Theta Inc, 1974-; bd mem, Vol League Ri, 1981-82; vol, Shelter Battered Women, 1983-86; bd mem, Big Sister Asn RI, 1986-90; Archit preserv, bd mem, Elmwood Found, 1989-; Seattle Domestic Violence Coun; bd mem, Seattle Emergency Housing Serv; bd Urban League RI; Nat Conf Women's Bar Asns, secy, 2003-04, bd dir, 2002-03; pres, 2008-09. **Honors/Awds:** Massachusetts Asniated Press Highest Award, "A Question of Rape", special TV program, 1985; Four Emmy awards; 1st place, features, "Chatham Houses: Washed Away", New England United Press InterNat, 1989; 1st place, continuing coverage, "Ocean Dumping", lead reporter, 1989, 2nd place, spot news, "Coventry Chemical Fire", 1989, Massachusetts Asniated Press Broadcasters Award. **Home Addr:** 24 Wesleyon Ave, Providence, RI 02907-1233, **Home Phone:** (401)861-9444. **Business Addr:** General Assignment Reporter, KIRO 7 Eyewitness News, 2807 3rd Ave, Seattle, WA 98121, **Business Phone:** (206)728-7777.

**HORNE, DR. EDWIN CLAY. See Obituaries Section.**

**HORNE, GERALD CHARLES**
Executive, government official, college teacher. **Personal:** Born Jan 3, 1949, St. Louis, MO; son of Jerry and Flora; married Savenda. **Educ:** Princeton Univ, BA, 1970; Univ Calif-Berkeley, JD, 1973; Columbia Univ, MA, 1978, PhD, 1982, Revson fel. **Career:** Affirmative Action Coordr Ctr, dir coun, 1979-82; Sarah Lawrence Col, prof, 1982-88; Nat Conf Black Lawyers, exec dir, 1985-86; Local 1199 Health & Hosp Workers Union AFL-CIO, spec coun, 1986-88; Univ Houston, John J. & Rebecca Moores chair hist & African Am studies, currently; Univ Calif, Santa Barbara, prof, 1988, chmn, black studies dept, 1989; Univ NC, prof chem, currently, prof commun studies, African & Afro-Am Studies, currently. **Orgs:** Secy & treas, Am Fedn Teachers, Local 2274, 1976-78; chair, Nat Conf Black Lawyers, Int Comt, 1982-85, nat dir; chair, Nat Lawyers Guild, Int Comn, 1988-92; chair, Pears & Freedom Party, 1991-92. **Honors/Awds:** Hope Stevens Award, Nat Conf Black Lawyers, 1983; Getman Service to Students Award, Univ Calif, Santa Barbara, 1990; Carter G Woodson fellow, Univ Va, 1991-92; City Univ NY, Belle Zeller Visiting Prof, 1993-94; Coun Intl Exchange Scholars, Full bright Scholar & Univ Zimbabwe, 1995. **Special Achievements:** Black and Red: W E B DuBois & Afro-Am Response Cold War, 1944-63, State Univ NY Press, 1986; Communist Front? Civil Rights Cong, London: Assoc Univ Presses, 1988; Thinking and Re-thinking US Hist, Coun Intl Books C, 1989; Reversing Discrimination: The Case Affirmative Action, Intl Publ, 1992; Pub include: Black Liberation & Red Scare: Ben Davis and the Communist Party, London: Assocs Univ Presses, 1994. Published numerous books. **Home Addr:** 106 Cameron Glen Dr, Chapel Hill, NC 27516-2333, **Home Phone:** (919)967-6878. **Business Addr:** Professor, University North Carolina, Communication Studies, Chapel Hill, NC 27599-3195, **Business Phone:** (919)967-6878.

**HORNE, JUNE C.**
Buyer. **Personal:** Born Sep 3, 1953, New York, NY; daughter of Samuel and Ceceill Sledge; married Frank. **Educ:** Lab Inst Merchandising, BS, 1971. **Career:** Saks Fifth Ave, exec trainee, 1971-72, asst buyer swimwear, sportswear, 1976-78, buyer swimwear, 1977-79, buyer designer sportswear, 1978-82, assoc div merch mgr, designer sportswear, 1985-92, dir, designer sportswear, 1986-, sr buyer designer sportswear & ready-to-wear, 1993-; Saks Garden City Br, store gen mgr, 1982-84. **Orgs:** YMCA Greater NY, Black Achievers, Black Retail Action Group; Fashion Outreach; Fashion Group Int. **Honors/Awds:** Black Achievers in Industry Award, YMCA Greater NY, 1979; Interviewed for NY Times Article "A Buyer's View of the Busy World of Fashion", 1980; "The Shadow Designer", 1999; Buyer Achievement Award, Black Retail Action Group, 1982; Lab Inst Merchandising, Adv Bd Alumnae Award, 1998; Pioneer Award, 100 Black Men of America Inc, & the Magic Johnson Found, 1998; Brag Business Achievement Award, 2003. **Special Achievements:** First black female store gen mgr, Saks Garden City Br, 1982. **Home Addr:** 71 W 85th St, New York, NY 10024. **Business Addr:** Senior Buyer, Saks Fifth Avenue, 3108 PGA Blvd, Palm Beach Gardens, FL 33410.

**HORNE, JUNE MERIDETH**
Technician. **Personal:** Born Feb 23, 1936, Chicago, IL; daughter of William and Elizabeth Neal; married Brazell; children: Brazell Rodney. **Educ:** Kennedy King Jr Col, attended 1975. **Career:** Technician (retired); Veterans Admin, psychiat tech, 1964-94. **Orgs:** Pres, Browder & Watts Inc, 1985; Int Biog Ctr; Int Order Merit, 1990; Womens Inner Circle Achievement, Am Biog Inst, 1990; Int Parliament Safety & Peace, 1991-92. **Honors/Awds:** Knighthood, Lofsensic Ursinius Order, Found Ethiopia Netherland, 1991, 1992. **Special Achievements:** Emergency Escape Apparatus, US Patent; Order Souberain Et Militaire De La Milice Du Saint Sepuulcre Confederation Chivalry, Australia. **Home Addr:** 1713 W 90th St, Chicago, IL 60620, **Home Phone:** (312)881-7832.

**HORNE, MARVIN L. R., JR.**
Manager. **Personal:** Born Mar 5, 1936, Richmond, VA; married Vernell Bell; children: Marvin III, Tracy R, Carl E & Kelly M. **Educ:** Va State Col, BS, physics, 1957; Howard Univ, physics, 1960; Univ Rochester, MBA, 1975. **Career:** US Naval Weapons Lab, math & physicist, 1960-61; Gen Elec Co, physicist, 1961-63; US Naval Weapons Lab, math & physicist, 1963-65; Eastman Kodak Co, Eng mgr. **Orgs:** Alpha Phi Alpha Frat, 1954-; Kappa Mu Epsilon, 1954-57; Sigma Pi Sigma, 1954-57; Amer Inst Aero & Astronaut, 1963-67; Beta Gamma Sigma, 1975-; chmn, Rochester City Planning comn, 1977-82; Tech Mkt Soc Am, 1978-. **Home Addr:** 280 Newcastle Rd, Rochester, NY 14610, **Home Phone:** (585)288-3993.

**HORNSBY, DR. ALTON, JR.**
Educator, editor, college teacher. **Personal:** Born Sep 3, 1940, Atlanta, GA; married Anne R; children: Alton III & Angela. **Educ:** Morehouse Col, BA, hist, 1961; Univ Tex, MA, hist, 1962, PhD, hist, 1969. **Career:** Univ Tex, Woodrow Wilson fel, 1961-62; Tuskegee Inst, instr hist, 1962-65; Southern Educ Found fel, 1966-68; Morehouse Col, Dept Hist, asst prof, actg chmn, 1968-71, assoc prof, 1971-74, chmn, 1971-98, prof, 1974, Fuller E Callaway prof, hist, 1989-2001, prof emer, 2010; Univ fel; independent ed, 1975; Rockefeller Humanities fel, 1977-78; Publications: Journal of Negro History, editor; The Papers of John and Lugenia Burns Hope, editor. **Orgs:** Chmn, St Comt Life & Hist Black Georgians, 1968-; Exec comt mem, Asn Study Afro-Am Life & Hist, 1977-; Danforth Found Assoc, 1978-81; pres & adv comt mem, Southern Conf Afro-Am Studies, 1979-; exec coun, pres & prog comt chair, Asn Soc & Behav Scientists, 1984-85; int comt mem & exec comt mem, Southern Hist Asn, 1988-; Conf Ed Hist J; Plantation Socs Am; Nat CounBlack Studies; Orgn Am Historians; Ga Asn Historians; Phi Alpha Theta; PhiBeta Kappa; Ed bd, Atlanta Hist J; ed bd, Western J Black Studies; ed, JNegro Hist; chair, Benjamin E. Mays Lect Comt. **Home Addr:** 424 Cativo Dr SW, Atlanta, GA 30311.

**HORRY, ROBERT KEITH, JR.**
Basketball player, broadcaster. **Personal:** Born Aug 25, 1970, Hartford, MD; son of Robert Sr and Leila; married Keva Develle; children: Ashlyn (deceased) & Cameron. **Educ:** Univ Ala, attended 1992. **Career:** Basketball player (retired), commentator; Houston Rockets, forward, 1992-96; Phoenix Suns, 1996-97; Los Angeles Lakers, forward, 1997-2003; San Antonio Spurs, forward-ctr, 2003-08; Time Warner Cable SportsNet, commentator, currently. **Business Addr:** Commentator, Time Warner Cable SportsNet, 2345 Alaska Ave, El Segundo, CA 90245, **Business Phone:** (424)247-0663.

**HORSFORD, ANNA MARIA**
Television producer, actor. **Personal:** Born Mar 6, 1948, New York, NY; daughter of Victor A and Lillian Agatha Richardson. **Educ:** Inter-Am Univ Puerto Rico, attended 1967; Manhattan's Sch Performing Arts. **Career:** Stage appearances: Coriolanus, 1965; In the Well of the House, 1972; Perfection in Black, 1973; Les Femmes Noires, 1974; Sweet Talk, 1975; For Colored Girls Who Have Considered Suicide/When the Rainbow Is Enuf, 1978; Peep, 1981. Films: An Almost Perfect Affair, 1979; Times Square, 1980; The Fan, 1981; Love Child, 1982; Class, 1983; Crackers, 1984; Presumed Innocent, 1990; Mr. Jones, 1993; Once Upon a Time When We Were Colored, 1995; One Fine Day, 1996; Set It Off, 1996; Dear God, 1996; Kiss the Girls, 1997; At Face Value, 1999; Dancing in September, 2000; Nutty Professor II: The Klumps, 2000; Jacked, 2001; Along Came a Spider, 2001; How High, 2001; Minority Report, 2002; Friday After Next, 2002; Justice, 2004; Guarding Eddy, 2004; My Big Phat Hip Hop Family, 2005; Ganked, 2005; Angel from Montgomery, 2006; Broken Bridges, 2006; Gridiron Gang, 2006; Trade, 2007; I Tried, 2007; Pretty Ugly People, 2008; Our Family Wedding, 2010; Wigger, 2010; C'mon Man, 2012; Tyler Perry's A Madea Christmas, 2013; Gladys Brown, 2016. TV series: "The Good News", 1978; "Watch Your Mouth", producer, 1978; "An Almost Perfect Affair", 1978; "The Guiding Light", 1979; "Times Square", 1979; "Love Child", 1981; "Bill", 1981; "Crackers", 1982; "Benny's Place", 1982; "A Doctor's Story", 1984; "Nobody's Child"; "Amen", 1986-91; "Rhythm & Blues", 1992; "The Wayans Bros"; "The Chronicle", 2002; "The Bernie Mac Show", 2004; "Entourage", 2005-06; "The Shield", 2005-08; "Entourage", 2005; "Heist", 2006; "Grey's Anatomy", 2005-07; "Everybody Hates Chris", 2008; "Las Vegas", 2008; "Everybody Hates Chris", 2008; "Cold Case", 2009; "Funny or Die Presents", 2011; "Let's Stay Together", 2011; "Reed Between the Lines", 2011; "Living Loaded", 2012; "Key and Peele", 2012; "New Girl", 2012; "The League", 2012. **Orgs:** Variety Club Am; pres, Black Women Theatre, 1983-84; Screen Actors Guild, Am Fedn TV & Radio Artists; Actor's Equity; Sigma Gamma Rho Sorority. **Honors/Awds:** Best Comedy Actress, Brooklyn Links, 1963; Outstanding Leadership Award, Nat Asn Advan Colored People, 1973. **Business Addr:** Actor, 2121 Ave of the Stars Suite 950, Los Angeles, CA 90067.

**HORSFORD, STEVEN**
State government official, chief executive officer. **Personal:** Born Apr 29, 1973, Las Vegas, NV; married Sonya; children: Benjamin, Ella & Bryson. **Educ:** Univ Nev, Reno. **Career:** Culinary Training Acad, chief exec officer, 2001-12; Nev State Senate, sen, 2004-12; majority floor leader, 2009-12; US rep Nev, 2013-15; R&R Partners. **Orgs:** Nat Asn Advan Colored People (NAACP), Las Vegas Chap, Mem; Nat Network Sector Partners, Mem; Southern Nev Workforce Investment Bd, Mem; Southern Nev Workforce Investment Bd (later Workforce Connections), Bd Mem, 2000-04; Comt Homeland Security, Mem; Comt Oversight & Govt Reform, Mem; Comt Natural Resources, Mem; Dem Legis Campaign Comt, Nat Vice Chmn; House Progressive Caucus; Dem Nat Comt's Chg Comn; DNC's Rules & Bylaws Comt; Alpha Phi Alpha fraternity. **Honors/Awds:** "Business Las Vegas," Top 40 Under 40; AFL-CIO, Friend to Working Families Award; Dr. Martin Luther King Jr. Committee, Distinguished Man of Southern Nevada; TheGrio.com, 100 Making History Today, 2012. **Special Achievements:** First African American congressperson ever from the state of Nevada. **Business Addr:** R&R Partners, 900 S Pavilion Center Dr, Las Vegas, NV 89144, **Business Phone:** (702)228-0222.

**HORTON, ANDRE (ANDREANA SUK HORTON)**
Skier. **Personal:** Born Oct 4, 1979, Anchorage, AK. **Educ:** Univ Alaska, BBA, mkt & mgt & discourse studies, 2008, MBA, entrepreneurship & finance, 2010. **Career:** Skier (retired), executive; Stewart Sports, skier; US Ski Team, prof athlete, 1988-2004; Alaska Serv Grp LLC, prin, 2004-12; Andre Horton Photog, prin artist, 2004-; Arthrex, Small Joint Consult, 2009-10; Cimbiant Inc, founder & chief exec officer, 2009-11; Sockeye Bus Solutions, dir bus develop, 2010-13; Haka, prin consult, 2012-; Yuit LLC, prin, dir finance & client rels, 2013-; TruVim LLC, bus develop, 2015; Lottsfeldt, strategy & opers consult, 2016-. **Orgs:** US Ski & Snow Bd Asn, athlete bd rep, currently; nat youth dir & competition dir, Nat Brotherhood Skiers; bd mem, US Ski Asn, 2004-06; bd mem, AMA Alaska Chap, 2012-; Supvry Comt bd dirs, Credit Union 1, 2015. **Honors/Awds:** AK state champion, 1998; First place, Mt Bachelor's NW Cup Finals, 2001. 4th place, NorAm Competition, 2001; 9th place overall finish in the U.S. Alpine National Championships, 2001. **Special Achievements:** First African American selected to US Ski Team Develop Prog, 2000; First African American to win an FIS race in Europe, 2001. **Business Addr:** Principal, Director of Finance & Client Relations, Yuit LLC, 1407 W 31st Ave Suite 800, Anchorage, AK 99503, **Business Phone:** (907)222-6300.

**HORTON, ANDREANA SUKI (SUKI HORTON)**
Skier. **Personal:** Born May 3, 1982, Anchorage, AK; daughter of Garry and Elsena. **Educ:** Univ Alaska Anchorage, BS, jour & pub rels, currently. **Career:** Nat Brotherhood Skiers, Western Region Elite Ski Team, mem & competition dir, currently. **Orgs:** Nat Brotherhood Skiers Ski Club. **Honors/Awds:** US Ski Teams Junior Development Croup, 1997; AK State Champion, 1998; Athlete of the Year, NBS, 2001; second pl, Western Region Downhill FIS series, 2001; ranked No 1 in Age Group; Compete in the U.S. Alpine National Championships three years in a row. **Special Achievements:** Andre & Suki Horton became top-ranked African American ski racers in the country, 2002; Fifth American at Snow Basin Nor Ams; First African American to Win International Ski Federation Contest; First African Americanto ve on the US Ski Team. **Home Addr:** 21542 Green Hill Rd, Farmington Hills, MI 48335, **Home Phone:** (248)957-8423. **Business Addr:** Competition Director, National Brotherhood of Skiers, 1525 E 53rd St Suite 418, Chicago, IL 60615, **Business Phone:** (773)955-4100.

**HORTON, CARL E. See Obituaries Section.**

**HORTON, DR. CARRELL PETERSON**
Educator, college teacher. **Personal:** Born Nov 28, 1928, Daytona Beach, FL; daughter of Preston S Peterson and Mildred Adams; married Richard G; children: Richard Preston. **Educ:** Fisk Univ, BA, 1949; Cornell Univ, MA, 1950; Univ Chicago, PhD, 1972. **Career:** Cornell Univ, grad asst, 1949-50; Fisk Univ, instr & res assoc, 1950-55; Meharry Med Col, stat anal, 1955-66; Fisk Univ, prof psychol & admin, 1966, Div Social Sci, dir, dean acad affairs, 1996-99, Dept Psychol, chair, emer prof, currently; Ford Found, IBM, fac fel, 1969-71; Health Serv Res, consult, 1977-80; NSF, consult, 1979; Nat Res Coun, consult, 1979. **Orgs:** Bd dir, Rochelle Training Ctr, 1968-72, 1978-85; adv comt mem, Nashville Voc & Technol Sch, 1970-72; bd dir, Wesley Found, 1977-86; bd dir, Samaritan Pastoral Coun Ctr, 1983; Bd Higher Educ & Campus Ministry, UM Church, 1983-89; bd mem, 18th Ave Family Enrichment Ctr, 2000-; Am Psychol Asn. **Honors/Awds:** Urban League Award, Jacksonville, FL, 1949; article in professional journals. **Special Achievements:** Co-editor: Statistical Record of Black America, 1990, 1992. **Home Addr:** 2410 Buchanan St, Nashville, TN 37208-1937, **Home Phone:** (615)244-6310. **Business Addr:** Emeritus Professor, Fisk University, 1000 17th Ave N, Nashville, TN 37208-3051, **Business Phone:** (615)329-8500.

**HORTON, CLARENCE MICHAEL**
Executive. **Personal:** Born Chicago, IL. **Career:** Capital Rec; Interscope Rec; Universal Rec, sr vpres prom. **Business Addr:** NY.

**HORTON, DOLLIE BEA DIXON**
Executive. **Personal:** Born Apr 19, 1942, Ft. Valley, GA; daughter of Lillian Byrd Dixon and Hezzie Dixon; married Cornelious Jr; children: Alre Giovanni & Roderick Cornelious. **Educ:** Ft Valley State Col, Ft Valley, GA, BS, 1964, MS, 1974; Atlanta Univ, cert, fr, 1966; Univ Mich, Ann Arbor, MI, cert, 1975; Thomason Real Estate Sch cert, 1978; Phelps-Stokes, Wash, DC, cert, 1978; Am Asn Community & Jr Cols, Kiawah Island, SC, cert, 1982; Ga Ins Pre-lic Sch, cert, 1988. **Career:** Educator, executive (retired); Pearl Stephens High Sch, Warner Robins, Ga, teacher, 1964-67; Ft Valley State Col, admin asst, 1967-74, asst dir develop & placement, 1974-76, actg dir col & community rels, 1976-77, dir col & community rels, 1977-80, dir, 1999-2010; HA Hunt High Sch, Ft Valley, Ga, teacher, Span, 1968-69; Peach County Bd Educ, Ft Valley, Ga, adult educ teacher, 1969-71; Warner Robins Air Logistics Ctr, Robins Afb, Ga, personnel staffing specialist, 1980-82; Valmedia Inc, owner, 1982; City Ft Valley, Utility Bd Comnrs, 1995-. **Orgs:** Bd dir, Peach County Ft Valley Chamber Com; Int Toastmistress Clubs Am; vpres, Gia Coalition Black Women; Ga Asn Broadcasters; Nat Asn Broadcasters; Mid Ga Minority Media Asn; Vogue Socialite Club. **Home Addr:** 201 Col St, Fort Valley, GA 31030, **Home Phone:** (912)825-2087.

**HORTON, EARLE CHICO, III**
Lawyer, association executive. **Personal:** Born Mar 9, 1943, Tampa, FL; son of Earle and Helen Belton; children: Brett & Earle III. **Educ:** Morehouse Col, BA, polit sci, 1964; Howard Univ Sch Law, JD, 1968. **Career:** Blue Sky Housing LLC, Owner & prin; Thunder Bay Community, pres; Graves & Horton LLC, atty & managing partner, 1997-. **Orgs:** Nat Asn Bond Lawyers; DC Bar Asn; Md Bar Asn, Nat Bar Asn, Nat Asn Securities Professionals; bd dir, Metrop Community Develop Corp; DC Morehouse Alumni chap; Howard Univ Law Sch Alumni Chap; First Black Law Firm OH; spec coun, Atty Gen OH; Am Bar Asn; Ohio State Bar Asn; Cleveland Bar Asn; John Harlan Law Club; Cleveland Fisk Univ Club; Nat Asn Advan Colored People; Urban League; Norman Minor Bar Asns; coun, Dc Housing Finance Agency; co-founder, Graves Horton Askew & Johns LLC. **Honors/Awds:** Recipient Meritorious Service Award, Cleveland Bar Asn, 1971; District Service Award, John Harlan Law Club, 1973. **Home Addr:** 15 Oakshore Dr, Cleveland, OH 44108, **Home Phone:** (216)681-8833. **Business Addr:** Attorney, Graves & Horton LLC, 1750 K St Suite 200, Washington, DC 20006, **Business Phone:** (202)872-6483.

**HORTON, DR. JOANN**
College administrator, executive, consultant. **Personal:** Born Lenoir, NC. **Educ:** Appalachian State Univ, BS, fr, 1970, MA, fr, 1971; Ohio State Univ, PhD, higher educ admin, 1977. **Career:** Olive-Harvey Col, curric coordr, acad vpres, provost; Tenn Dept Gen Serv, asst comnr; Iowa Community Col Syst, state adminr; Tex Southern Univ, pres, 1993-95; Am Coun Educ, sr fel, 1995-; Kennedy-King Col, Chicago, pres, 1998; Baltimore City Community Coll, exec vpres, 2004-06, interim vpres acad affairs, chief acad officer; Team Masters Inc, founder & pres, 2000-; Pac Crest, chief oper officer, inst facilitator, 2007-11.

**Business Addr:** President, Team Masters Inc, 360 E Randolph St Suite1208, Chicago, IL 60532-5069, **Business Phone:** (312)819-0549.

## HORTON, LARKIN J., JR.

Government official, executive, association executive. **Personal:** Born Feb 18, 1939, Lenoir, NC; married Patricia Richardson; children: Larkin III & Gregory Derwin. **Educ:** Catawba Valley Tech Inst, assoc elect, 1960; Gen Elec Control Sch, master controls, 1961; Clever-Brooks Pressure Vessels, cert pressure vessels, 1961; Caldwell Community Col, cert powder activated Tools, 1972, cert massage ther, 1998. **Career:** Executive (retired); E Finley Auto Laundry, owner; City Lenoir, councilman, 1979-91; Horton's Elec Co, owner & contractor; prof photogr; Elec Consult & Safety Specialist, ANSI, NIOSHA & UL, instr. **Orgs:** Trustee, St Paul AME Ch; bd mem, Nat Cancer Soc, 1983, bd dir; Caldwell Friends Inc, 1984-85; Gov Crime Prev Comn; inspector, Int Asn Elect Inspectors. **Honors/Awds:** Value Analysis Award, Burlington Ind, 1980-82; Man of the Year, Am Legion, 1984; Lenoir Police Explorer Post 246, Appreciation Plaque, 1990; Volunteer Service Award, 1986; Resolution Appreciation, City Lenoir, Lenoir City coun, Key City, 1991; Dr Martin Luther King Jr Award, 1991; Richard Allen Humanitarian Award, St Paul Am Chap, 2003. **Home Addr:** 445 Arlington Cir NW, PO Box 1256, Lenoir, NC 28645-4206, **Home Phone:** (828)754-4267.

## HORTON, PASTOR LARNIE G., SR.

Government official, clergy, business owner. **Personal:** married Katrena B; children: Larnie Glenn Jr & Langston Garvey. **Educ:** Morris Brown Col, AB; Univ NC, Chapel Hill; Duke Univ, MDiv; Nat Theo Sem& Col. **Career:** Saxapaw, NC, pastor, 1960-64; Kittrell Col, NC, acad dean, 1961-62, pres, 1966-73; Emanuel African Methodist Episcopal Church, Durham, pastor, 1964-66; Gov Minority Affairs, spec asst to NC Gov James E. Holshouser Jr., 1973-77; Horton & Horton Enterprises Inc, owner, pres. **Orgs:** Bd trustees, Vance County Tech Inst, 1968; bd dir, Soul City Found, 1968; bd dir, Nat Lab Higher Educ, 1970; consult, Am Asn Jr Col, 1970-72; Nat Asn Advan Colored People; Merchants Asn Chapel Hill; Alpha Phi Alpha Fraternity; C C, Henderson, NC; fel Woodrow Wilson & Rockefeller; bd giv, Univ NC Sixteen Constituent Insts; Assoc Presiding Elder, womenministry, African Methodist Episcopal Church. **Honors/Awds:** National Alumni Association Award, Stillman Col, 1970; Civic Achievement Award, Morris Brown Col, National Alumni Association. **Home Addr:** 1301 Granada Dr, Raleigh, NC 27612-5120, **Home Phone:** (919)782-4803. **Business Addr:** Owner, President, Horton & Horton Enterprises Incorporation, 116 W Jones St, Raleigh, NC 27611, **Business Phone:** (910)864-5515.

## HORTON, LEMUEL LEONARD

Executive, manager, association executive. **Personal:** Born Jun 29, 1936, Ft. Valley, GA; married Yvonne Felton; children: Lorna Y Hill. **Educ:** Ft Valley State Univ, BS, bus admin, 1972; Atlanta Univ, bus admin; Ga State Univ, exec mgt prog; Emory Univ, employee rels, labor rels & assessment centers admin. **Career:** Civil Serv Robins AFB, Ga, warehouseman, 1958-65; State Ga, community serv consult, 1965-68; Ft Valley State Col, dir stud union, 1968-71; Res Group, assoc, 1971-73; New York Life, field underwriter, 1973; Gold Kist Inc, mgr employee rels; Israel Missionary Baptist Church, deacon; Nat African-Am RV'ers Asn Inc, pres, 2013-. **Orgs:** RVing, 1973-; Pres, Resurgens Int Asn Qual Circles, IRRA, 1980-81; pres, vpres & bd mem, Ga Chap Epilepsy Found; pres, TAPS Epilepsy Found; Int Mentoring Asn; bus rep, Toomer Elemenatary Sch; treas Phi Beta Sigma Fraternity Inc, 1928; Nat African-Am RV'ers Asn Inc, 1996-; treas, Lambda Sigma Chap; pres, Monterey Community Coun Inc; DeKalb County's 5th Dist Community Coun; Sigma-Zeta Found Boarcd; Ft Valley State Univ Alumni Asn; Resurgence Atlanta. **Honors/Awds:** Presidential Citation, Nat Asn Equal Opportunities Higher Educ, 1983. **Home Addr:** 2275 Tarian Dr, Decatur, GA 30034-2939, **Home Phone:** (404)381-3055. **Business Addr:** President, National African-American RV'ers Association Inc, 614 Chipley Ave, Charlotte, NC 28205, **Business Phone:** (704)333-3070.

## HORTON, OSCAR J.

Executive, chief executive officer, president (organization), chief executive officer, president (organization), chief executive officer, president (organization). **Personal:** Born Jul 22, 1952, Camden, AR; married Miriam; children: Kelli & Alisan. **Educ:** Univ Ark, psychol, 1974. **Career:** Int Truck & Engine: Navistar's Engine, Credit Co, oper mgr Mfg, vpres Labor Rels, vpres & gen mgr; Int Harvester Co, vpres & gen mgr; Sun State Int Trucks, pres & chief exec officer, owner, currently. **Orgs:** TTampa Chamber Com, 1999; Tampa Urban League, 2000; USF Stavros Ctr, 2002; In-Roads, 2002; bd mem, Tampa Mus Art, 2002; bd mem, Goodwill Ind, Sun Coast, 2002; bd trustee, USF Found, 2003; bd mem, Bank Tampa, 2004; bd dir, Boys & Girls Club Tampa; bd mem, Fed Res Bank Atlanta; bd mem, Ogline Design; bd dir, bd trustee mem, Acad Prep Ctr Tampa; bd dir, Navistar Diversity. **Business Addr:** President, Chief Executive Officer, Sun State International Trucks LLC, 6020 Adamo Dr, Tampa, FL 33619, **Business Phone:** (813)621-1331.

## HORTON, RAYMOND ANTHONY

Football player, football coach. **Personal:** Born Apr 12, 1960, Tacoma, WA; married Leslie; children: Taylor. **Educ:** Univ Wash, BA, soc, 1983. **Career:** Football player (retired), football coach; Cincinnati Bengals, corner back, nickel back & safety, 1983-88, coach, 1997-2001; Dallas Cowboys, safety, 1989-92; Long Shots, driving range, Seattle, WA, owner; Wash Redskins, asst defensive backs coach, 1994-96; Detroit Lions, sec coach, 2002-03; Pittsburgh Steelers, asst defensive backs coach, 2004-07, defensive backs coach, 2007-10; Ariz Cardinals, defensive coordr, 2011-12; Tenn Titans, defensive coordr, 2014-15; Cleveland Browns, defensive coordr, 2013, 2016-. **Orgs:** Organizer, Ray Hope Food Dr, Dallas, Tex. **Business Addr:** Defensive Coordinator, Cleveland Browns, 100 Alfred Lerner Way, Cleveland, OH 44114, **Business Phone:** (440)891-5001.

## HORTON, DR. STELLA JEAN

Management consultant, teacher, executive director. **Personal:** Born Aug 16, 1944, Durham, NC; daughter of Charlie and Stella Ruth; children: Braheim Knight. **Educ:** St Augustine's Col, attended 1964; NC Agr & Tech State Univ, BS, hist, 1966; State Univ Rutgers, MEd, 1976, EdD, anthrop, 1986. **Career:** Orange County Bd Educ, teacher, 1966-69; Rutgers State Univ, assoc prof, 1970-76; Alternative Sch, Camden Bd Educ, teacher & prin, 1976-80; Camden Ctr Youth Develop, exec dir, 1980-; Juv Resource Ctr, Exec dir, 1985; Univ NC, Chapel Hill, NC; NJ Sch Syst, prin; Rutgers State Univ; Educ Training & Enterprise Ctr, sr mgt consult & sr training specialist, currently. **Orgs:** Consult, NJ Dept Educ, 1980-84; Urban League Camden Co, 1981-83; vpres, Camden City Bd Educ, 1983-84, 1980-; 5th Legilsative Dist, NJ Sch Bds, 1983-. **Honors/Awds:** Serv Young People, Juvenile Resource Ctr Inc, 1979; Community Serv, NJ Asn Black Social Workers, 1982. **Home Addr:** 1412 Van Hook St, Camden, NJ 08104. **Business Addr:** Senior Management Consultant, Senior Training Specialist, Education Training & Enterprise Center, 200 Fed St Suite 244, Camden, NJ 08103, **Business Phone:** (800)963-9361.

## HORTON, SUKI. See HORTON, ANDREANA SUKI.

## HORTON, WILLIE WATTISON (WILLIAM WATTISON HORTON)

Baseball player, baseball executive. **Personal:** Born Oct 18, 1942, Arno, VA; son of James and Lillian; married Gloria; children: 7. **Career:** Baseball player (retired), baseball executive; Detroit Tigers, out fielder, 1963-77, comt mem, 2000, spec asst to pres, 2003-; Tex Rangers, outfielder, 1977; Cleveland Indians, outfielder, 1978; Oakland Athletics, outfielder, 1978; Toronto Blue Jays, outfielder, 1978; Seattle Mariners, outfielder, 1979-80. **Special Achievements:** First athlete to receive The Order of Saint Maurice award, the highest military honor to be given to civilians, 2006. **Home Addr:** 9813 Nottingham Rd, Detroit, MI 48224-2552, **Home Phone:** (313)839-3416. **Business Addr:** Special Assistant to the President, Detroit Tigers, Comerica Pk 2100 Woodward Ave, Detroit, MI 48201-3470, **Business Phone:** (313)962-4000.

## HOSKINS, DR. MICHELE

Executive. **Personal:** children: 3. **Career:** Michele Foods Inc, owner, founder & chief exec officer, 1984-. **Honors/Awds:** The Entrepreneurial Women Award, 1998; Madam Walker Entrepreneurial Award, 1999; Phenomenal Women Award, 2000; Entrepreneur of the Year, Womens Food services Forum, 2002; Honorary Doctorate, Wales Univ; Top 100 Professional Women, Dollars & Sense Mag; Emerging Company of the Year Award, Black Enterprise Mag; Lifetime Achiever Award, Sigma Gamma Rho Sorority Inc; honorary doctorate degree, Johnson & Wales Univ. **Special Achievements:** Author: Sweet Expectations: Michele Hoskins Recipe for Success, 2004; First African American vendor with Costco!. **Business Addr:** Owner, Chief Executive Officer, Michele Foods Inc, 16117 Lasalle St, South Holland, IL 60473, **Business Phone:** (708)331-7316.

## HOSTEN, DR. ADRIAN OLIVER

Physician, educator. **Personal:** Born Grenada, WI; married Claire C; children: Karen & Lester. **Educ:** Atlantic Union Col, BA, 1958; Howard Univ, MD, 1962. **Career:** Bates Memorial High Sch, prin, 1954-55, instr to assoc prof, 1966-82; Fel Wash Va Hosp, 1967; Howard Univ, chief nephrology div, 1967-87, prof med, 1982-, chmn dept med, 1988-, Renal Div, chief, physician asst, currently; Howard Univ Hosp, Med Intensive Care Unit, dir, 1968-75. **Orgs:** Nat Med Asn, 1968-; Am Soc Nephrology, 1971-; Int Soc Nephrology, 1973-; fel Am Col Physicians. **Home Addr:** 10808 Barnwood Lane, Potomac, MD 20854-1328, **Home Phone:** (301)469-0653. **Business Addr:** Chairman, Howard University Hospital, 2041 Georgia Ave NW, Washington, DC 20060, **Business Phone:** (202)865-6100.

## HOUSE, JAMES E.

Executive, consultant. **Personal:** Born Goldsboro, NC; son of Edward AE and Cleo Peoples. **Educ:** Howard Univ, BS, mech engineering, 1963. **Career:** McDonnell Douglas Corp, St Louis, test & struct engr, 1963-67; Fairchild Hiller Corp, stress analyst, 1967-68, res engr; Boeing Co Seattle, res engr, 1968-72; Eckenberge Group, Wash, DC, pres, 1970-; WIPCO Inc St Croix, vpres treas, 1972-77; Nat Asn Minority CPA Firms, Govt DC, Jones & Artis Co Wash, DC, consult, 1981-86; JBH Assocs, consult, 1986-87; US Dept of State Archieve, Off Small & Disadvantaged Bus Utilization, sr exec serv, dir, 1991-93, Dep Agr, dir, currently; Dept of Minority Bus Enterprise, Va, spec asst to gov, dir, 1994-96. **Orgs:** Pres, Stud Govt Sch Eng & Arch, Howard Univ, 1962; secy, Republican Cent Comn Prince Georges Co, MD, 1982-84; chmn, Md Frederick Douglass Scholar Fund, 1984-; chmn, Va Black Republican Coun, 1984-96; VI C C Econ Develop Comn; VI Businessmens Asn; Minority Bus Develop Org; St Croix Howard Univ Alumni Asn; Alpha Phi Omega; chmn, Black Republican Coun Prince Georges Co, MD, 1984-85; co-chmn, Reagan-Bush, 1984; vice chmn, Md State Republican Party, 1986-90; bd mem, Nat Coun 100, 1986-; pres, Nat Asn African Am Bus Owners, 1989-; Comt Purchase From People Who Are Blind or Severley Disabled, Ability One. **Home Addr:** 14011 Old Stage Rd Suite A, Bowie, MD 20720, **Home Phone:** (301)262-7714. **Business Addr:** Director, Office of Small and Disadvantaged Business Utilization, 14th & Independence Ave SW 1566 S Bldg, Washington, DC 20250-9501, **Business Phone:** (202)720-7117.

## HOUSE, KYLA N.

Administrator. **Educ:** Univ Okla, BA, commun gen, 1996. **Career:** Boeing, sr human resource rep, 1996-99; TV Guide, human resource staffing consult, 1999-2001; Am Elec Power, col rels coordr & sr human resources consult 2001-12; Time Warner Cable, human resources mgr, 2013-. **Orgs:** Leadership Tulsa Class 29; bd mem, YMCA; Human Res & Diversity Taskforce comt; Alpha Kappa Alpha Sorority. **Business Addr:** Human Resources Manager, Time Warner Cable, 60 Columbus Cir, New york, NY 10023, **Business Phone:** (800)892-4357.

## HOUSE, MICHAEL A.

Journalist. **Personal:** Born Jul 13, 1941, Louisville, KY; son of William T Hodges and Jamesetta; married Doris J; children: Robert, Margoit & William. **Educ:** Howard Univ, attended 1965; Baruch Col, City Univ NY, MBA, 1974. **Career:** Ford Motor Co, staff; Mobil Oil Corp, staff; Rockwell Int; Amalgamated Pub Inc, pres; Call & Post Newspapers Inc, pres & chief operating officer; Mayor Frank G Jackson, Cleveland, OH, press secy & spokesman; Cleveland's Cable TV Pub Access Channel, gen mgr, 2006-08; Chicago Defender, pres, 2008-13. **Orgs:** Pres, Nat Asn Mkt Developers; 100 Black Men Nj; Urban League Greater Cleveland; Hunger Network; Minority Organ Transplant Educ Prog. **Honors/Awds:** Publisher of the Year, Natl Newspaper Publ Asn, 2003. Publisher of the Year, Philadelphia Tribune; John B. Russwurm Award, Natl Newspaper Publ Asn, 2009. **Business Addr:** President, Executive Director, Chicago Defender, 4445 S King Dr, Chicago, IL 60653, **Business Phone:** (312)225-2400.

## HOUSE, MILLARD L., II

Educator, founder (originator), school administrator. **Personal:** Born Jan 28, 1944, Langston, OK; married Anna Shumate; children: Milton, Signee & Millard II. **Educ:** Langston Univ, BA, 1966; Northeastern St Col, MA, 1971. **Career:** Gilcrease Jr HS, soc sci instr, 1966-70; Dept Human Rel Tulsa Pub Sch, dir, 1970-, prin, 1999-2004, assoc supt, 2008-11, dep supt, 2011-12; Marian Anderson Elem Sch, asst prin to prin; KIPP Tulsa Col Prep, founder & prin, 2004-08; Charlotte-Mecklenberg Schs, Charlotte, chief operating officer, 2012-13; New Leaders, exec dir, 2013-15. **Orgs:** NEA OK Educ Asn; supvrs & dir, Tulsa Asn Curric; Tulsa Pub Sch Affirmative Action Com; Urban League; Nat Asn Advan Colored People; Langston Univ Alumni Asn; YMCA; Kappa Alpha Psi; Phi Delta Kappa; Royal Housa Club; StJohn's Bapt Ch; Mayor's Comn Comt Rels. **Home Addr:** 1726 W Woodrow, Tulsa, OK 74127, **Home Phone:** (918)584-7667. **Business Addr:** Founder, Principal, KIPP Tulsa College Preparatory, 1661 E Virgin St, Tulsa, OK 74106, **Business Phone:** (918)925-1580.

## HOUSE, N. GERRY (GERALDINE HAGWOOD)

School administrator. **Personal:** Born Jan 1, 1947?; married Lee A Jr; children: Jennifer & Lee A III. **Educ:** NC A&T State Univ, BA, eng; Southern Ill Univ, MA, coun; Univ NC, Chapel Hill, NC, PhD, educ admin. **Career:** Teacher; Jr & Sr High Sch Guid Coun, prin & asst suptd; NC State Off Supt Schs, Chapel Hill, 1985-92; Tenn State Off Supt Schs, 1992-2000; Memphis City Schs, supt; Inst Stud Achievement, pres, chief exec officer, 2000-. **Orgs:** Asn Supv & Curric Develop; Am Asn Sch Admin; Phi Delta Kappa Soc; Nat Asn Black Sch Educrs; AutoZone, 1996-; Girls Inc Memphis; bd dir, Woodrow Wilson Found; bd dir, Nat Civil Rights Mus; nat adv bd, Nat Ctr Study Privatization Educ; Wallace Found Educ Leadership Adv; bd dir, New Am Schs; bd dir, New Teacher Proj; George W. Bush Pres; bd trustee, Adelphi Univ; bd dir & chmn, Educ Testing Serv, 2002-05; bd dir, Alliance Excellent Educ. **Business Addr:** President, Chief Executive Officer, Institute for Student Achievement, 1 Old Country Rd Suite 250, Carle Place, NY 11514, **Business Phone:** (516)812-6700.

## HOUSTON, ALICE K.

Executive. **Educ:** Baldwin Wallace Col, Berea, OH, attended 1968; Vanderbilt Univ, attended 1969; Univ Louisville, MEd, personnel serv, 1975. **Career:** Univ Louisville, asst & assoc dir financial aid; Johnson-Houston Corp, dir admin & finance, 1985; Houston-Johnson Inc, exec vpres, pres & owner, currently; Active Transp Co, pres; Automotive Carrier Serv, chief exec officer, chmn bd; Louisville Arena Authority Inc, dir, 2013-. **Orgs:** Nat Urban League; African Am Venture Capital Fund; Muhammad Ali Ctr; Reg Leadership Coalition; Community Partnership Bd; Jewish Hosp Health Care Serv Bd; W Louisville Econ Alliance Adv Comt; Louisville Community Develop Bank; trustee, St Mary's HealthCare Inc. **Business Addr:** President, Owner, Houston Johnson Inc, 13200 Complete CT, Louisville, KY 40223, **Business Phone:** (502)638-8033.

## HOUSTON, DR. ALICE VIVIAN

Educator, association executive, executive director. **Personal:** Born Baton Rouge, LA. **Educ:** S Univ, BA, 1953; La State Univ, MEd, 1956; Univ Tex, PhD, 1974. **Career:** Educator (retired); teacher, 1953-68; S Greenville Elem Sch, Baton Rouge, prin, 1968-69; Beechwood Elem Sch, E Baton Rouge Parish Sch Bd, prin, 1969-75, supr res & prog eval, 1976-77, supr eval state & fed progs, 1976; Okla City Pub Schs, dir curric serv, 1977-82; Seattle Pub Schs, asst supt, 1982-91, Human Resources Recruitment & Develop, dir, 1991-96, Early Childhood Educ, dir, 1996-98. **Orgs:** Exec bd, Nat Alliance Black Sch Educr, 1975-79; exec coun, asn supvr & Curric Develop, 1979-81; Phi Delta Kappa; Kappa Delta Pi; Nat Advan Asn Colored People; Zeta Phi Beta; bd dir, United Way King Co. **Honors/Awds:** Award, Plaque Girl Scouts, 1964; Award, Plaque Zeta Phi Zeta, 1970; Award, Doctoral Fed Univ Tex, 1972-73; Outstanding Serv, Nat Alliance Black Sch Educrs Recognition, 1974-77, 1977-79; Outstanding Prin of the Year, 1975; Outstanding Contrib Area Educ, 1977; Citizen of the Year, Omega Psi Phi Recognition, 1981; Award, All Stud Okla City Okla Black Liberated Arts Ctr, 1982; Award providing Excellence in Educ, Benefit Guild Asn Martin Luther King Jr, 1985; Award of Merit for Community, Serv Alpha Phi Alpha, 1986. **Home Addr:** 1802 17th Ave, Seattle, WA 98122.

## HOUSTON, ALLAN WADE, SR.

Business owner, basketball coach. **Personal:** Born Oct 9, 1944, Alcoa, TN; married Alice Kean; children: Allan, Lynn & Natalie. **Educ:** Univ Louisville, BS, 1966, MS, educ psychol. **Career:** Basketball coach (retired), businessman; Univ Louisville, asst coach, 1976-89; Univ Tenn, head coach, 1989-94; Active Transp Co, partner; Automotive Carrier Serv, partner; Old Nat Bank, dir; Dallas & Mavis Specialized Carriers, partner; ATC Leasing Co, partner; JHT Holdings, pres & chief exec officer, 2001; Johnson-Houston Travel Agency, exec vpres, owner, currently. **Orgs:** Univ Louisvilles Athletic Hall Fame; KY Athletic Hall Fame; bd dir, Univ Louisville Athletic; co chair, Gov Steve Beshears Inauguration Comt; chair, Ryder Cup Community Rels Comt; First Tee Louisville; Kentuckiana Minority Bus Coun. **Special Achievements:** First African-American basketball player to earn a scholarship at the University of Louisville. **Home Addr:** 7506 Chestnut Hill Dr, Prospect, KY 40059-9484, **Home Phone:** (502)228-3877. **Business Addr:** Owner, Johnson-Houston Travel Agency, 13200 Complete Ct, Louisville, KY 40223-2283, **Business Phone:** (502)638-8020.

### HOUSTON, ALLAN WADE
Executive, basketball player. **Personal:** Born Apr 20, 1971, Louisville, KY; son of Wade and Alice; married Tamara; children: Remie, Allan III, Rowan, Asher, Jodi Jean, Truth Grace & Jade. **Educ:** Univ Tenn, BA, African Am studies, 1993. **Career:** Basketball player (retired), executive; Detroit Pistons, guard & shooting guard, 1993-96; New York Knicks, guard & shooting guard, 1996-2005, Basketball Opers, asst gen mgr, currently; ESPN Radio, broadcaster; Top Gun Leather, founder, currently; Allan Houston Enterprises Inc, pres & chief exec officer, currently; H2O Prods, founder & pres, currently; UNK NBA. co found, currently. **Orgs:** Founder & pres, Allan Houston Found, currently; fel Kappa Alpha Psi Inc. **Honors/Awds:** Gold Medal, FIBA Americas U18 Championship, 1990; Gold Medal, FIBA Americas Championship, 1999; Gold Medal, Olympic Games, 2000; All-Star team, NBA, 2000 & 2001; Haier Shooting Stars Champion, 2012. **Special Achievements:** First round, 11th pick, NBA Draft, 1993; Flim: Laws of Attraction, 2004. **Business Addr:** Assistant General Manager, New York Knicks, Madison Sq Garden 2 Pa Plz, New York, NY 10121-0091, **Business Phone:** (212)465-6471.

### HOUSTON, BOBBY DARIN (ROBERT DARIN HOUSTON)
Football player. **Personal:** Born Oct 26, 1967, Washington, DC; children: Taylor. **Educ:** NC State Univ, grad. **Career:** Football player (retired); Green Bay Packers, linebacker, 1990; NY Jets, 1991, left linebacker, 1992-96; Kans City Chiefs, left linebacker, 1997; San Diego Chargers, 1997-98; Minn Vikings, linebacker, 1998. **Special Achievements:** Film: "1990 NFL Draft", 1990.

### HOUSTON, CISSY (EMILY CISSY DRINKARD HOUSTON)
Gospel singer. **Personal:** Born Sep 30, 1933, Newark, NJ; daughter of Nicholas (deceased) and Delia (deceased); married John Russell Jr; children: Whitney (deceased) & Michael; married Freddie Garland; children: Gary. **Career:** Drinkard Singers, mem; Sweet Inspirations, gospel group singer, 1963-69; Albums: Sweet Inspiration, 1968; What the World Needs Now is Love, 1968; Cissy Houston, 1971; Private Stock, 1977; Think It Over, 1978; Warning Danger, 1979; Step Aside for a Lady, 1980; (with Chuck Jackson) I'll Take Care of You, 1992; Face to Face, 1996; He Leadeth Me, 1997; Love Is Holding You, 2001; Walk on By Faith, 2012; Presenting Cissy Houston; The Long & Winding Road; Atlantic Rec; Muscle Shoals; New York; night club singer, currently; New Hope Baptist Church, Radio Choir, dir, currently; TV series: "Taking My Turn", 1984; "Whitney Houston: This is My Life", producer, 1999; "Vernon John's Story", 1994; "Killing Me Softly: The Roberta Flack Story", 2014. Film: The Wiz, 1978; The Preachers Wife, 1996; Daddy's Little Girls, 2007. **Orgs:** Chief exec officer & pres, Whitney Houston Found, 1988-. **Honors/Awds:** Medal for Distinguished Humanitarian Leadership, Univ Med & Dent, NJ, 1992; Pioneer Award, Rhythm & Blues Found, 1995; Grammy Award for Best Traditional Soul Gospel Album, 1996 & 1998; Third annual BET Honors, 2010. **Special Achievements:** Film: T Author: How Sweet the Sound: My Life with God & Gospel, 1998. she recorded the song "Family First" for the soundtrack to the movie Daddy's Little Girls in 2006. **Home Addr:** 2160 N Central Rd, Ft Lee, NY 07024. **Business Addr:** Singer, c/o House of Blues Music, 8439 Sunset Blvd Suite 404, West Hollywood, CA 90069, **Business Phone:** (323)848-5100.

### HOUSTON, EMILY CISSY DRINKARD. See HOUSTON, CISSY.

### HOUSTON, IVAN J.
Insurance executive. **Personal:** Born Jun 15, 1925, Los Angeles, CA; son of Norman O and Doris Talbot Young; married Philippa Jones; children: Pamela, Kathi & Ivan A. **Educ:** Univ Calif, Berkeley, CA, BS, 1948; Univ Man, actuarial sci. **Career:** Insurance executive (retired); Life Off Mgt Inst, fel; Am Col Life Underwriters, charter life underwriter; Actuary, 1948; Golden State Mutual Life Ins Co, Actuarial & Policy Owners Serv Div, acct, 1948-50, supr, 1950-52, admin asst charge, 1952-54, asst sec actuarial, 1954-56, actuary, 1956-59, bd dir exec com mem, 1959-62, vpres actuary, 1962-66, sr vpres, actuary, 1966-70, pres & chief exec officer, 1970-80, chmn bd & chief exec officer, 1980-90, chmn bd, 1991-99. **Orgs:** Asn Conf Consult Actuaries; Am Acad Actuaries; Am Soc Pension Actuaries; Int Actuarial Asn; pres, Los Angeles Actuarial Club; Kappa Alpha Psi Frat; Sigma Pi Phi Frat; bd, Regents Loyola Marymount Univ; corp bd, United Way Los Angeles Inc; bd dir, Calif C C; past chmn bd dir, Los Angeles Urban League; past bd dir, Pac Indemnity Co; former chmn bd dir, M&M Asn; former bd dir, Los Angeles C C; former chmn bd, Life Off Mgt Asn, 1979-80; bd dir, First Interstate Bank CA, Pac Thesis Grp; former bd, Kaiser Alum & Chem Corp, Metromedia, Family Savings & Loan; comnr, Los Angeles Human Rels Comm; bd dir, Am Coun Life Ins; Chartered Life Underwriter; Conf Actuaries; Int Asn Actuaries; fel Life Mgt Inst; chair, bd dir, Life Off Mgt Asn; bd dir, Nat Ins Asn; founding mem, bd dir, Black Agenda Inc; pres, bd dir, Golden State Minority Found; chair, bd dir, Merchants Manufacturers Asn; life mem, Nat Asn Advan Colored People; co-chair, Nat Conf Christians & Jews; bd trustee, Nat Urban League, 1980-86; bd dir, Young Mens Christian Asn Metrop; bd dir, Am Col; bd, Cath Univ Am; bd fel Claremont Univ Ctr; bd dir, Kaiser Aluminum Chem Corp; bd regents, Loyola Marymount Univ; bd dir, Pac Bell; bd dir, Pac Telesis Grp; Stand Res Inst, adv coun; bd dir, Pac Indemnity; bd visitor, UCLA Grad Sch Mgt. **Special Achievements:** First African-American elected bd dir Am Life Ins Asn; Appointed Knight, Order of St Gregory the Great, by Pope John Paul II, 1993. **Home Addr:** 5111 S Holt Ave, Los Angeles, CA 90056-1117, **Home Phone:** (310)645-5200.

### HOUSTON, DR. JOHNNY L.
Administrator, mathematician, computer scientist. **Personal:** Born Nov 19, 1941, Sandersville, GA; son of Bobby Lee Harris and Catherine Vinson; married Virginia Lawrence; children: Mave Lawrence & Kaiulani Michelle. **Educ:** Morehouse Col, BA, math, 1964; Atlanta Univ, MS, math, 1966; Purdue Univ, PhD, math, 1974. **Career:** Atlanta Univ, chmn, math & comput sci, 1975-81; Lawrence Livermore Nat Lab, vis scientist, 1979, 1983; Ft Valley State Col, coord comput sci, 1981-83, Callaway prof comput sci, 1983-84; Elizabeth City State Univ, vice chancellor acad affairs, 1984-88, Dept Math & Comput Sci, prof, 1984-88, sr res prof, 1988-08, coordr comput Sci, 1988-96, Computational Sci & Sci Visualization Ctr, dir, 1996-2008, African Studies Prog, dir, 2002-08, Text bks & Learning Mat Prog, 2002-08, prof emer, 2010; NASA Langley Res Ctr, vis scientist, 1989. **Orgs:** Dir, Black Cult Ctr, Purdue Univ, 1972-73; founder, exec secy, Nat Asn Mathematicians, 1975-2000, exec secy emer; vis scientist, Nat Ctr Atom Res, 1976; co-dir, Nat Conf Math & Phys Sci, Boulder, 1979; pres, chmn bd, Int Trade & Develop Corp, 1979-86; consult, Math, Comput Sci Spec Nih's-MARC Rev Comn, 1980-86; Am Math Soc; Asn Comput Mach; Asn Comput & Info Sci/Engineering Depts at Minority Insts, 1990-94; Bd Gov Math Asn Am, 1992-95; Human Resource Adv Group, Math Sci Res Inst, 1993-98; Soc Indian Automobile Manufacturers; NSF; Southern Asn Cols & Sec Schs. **Home Addr:** 602 W Main St, Elizabeth City, NC 27909, **Home Phone:** (919)338-0068. **Business Addr:** Professor Emeritus, Elizabeth City State University, 129 Lane Hall 1704 Weeksville Rd, Elizabeth City, NC 27909, **Business Phone:** (252)335-3361.

### HOUSTON, KAREN GRAY. See GRAY, KAREN G.

### HOUSTON, KENNETH RAY
Football player, football coach, counselor. **Personal:** Born Nov 12, 1944, Lufkin, TX; son of Herod; married Gustie Marie Rice; children: Kenneth Christian & Kene. **Educ:** Prairie View A&M Univ, BSM, guid coun, 1967. **Career:** Football player (retired), coach, counselor; Am Football League, Houston Oilers, defensive back & left safety & strong safety & punt returner, 1967-72; Nat Football League, Wash Redskins, defensive back & strong safety, 1973-80; Wheatley High Sch, head football coach; Westbury High Sch, head football coach; Houston Oilers, defensive backfield coach, 1982-85; Univ Houston, defensive backfield coach, 1986-90; Houston Independent Sch Dist, guid counr, 1990-. **Orgs:** Bd trustee, Prairie View A&M Found. **Honors/Awds:** NFL Record for Touchdowns On Interceptions (9), Houston, 1967-71; Pro Bowl, 1968-79; American Football League All-Star, 1968-69; Byron Whizzer White Award for Humanitarian Service, NFL Players Asn, 1980; Pro Football Hall of Fame, 1986. **Special Achievements:** Listed in 100 Greatest Football Players by Sporting News, 1999; Named one of the 70 Greatest Redskins. **Home Addr:** 511 Glenburnie Dr, Houston, TX 77339, **Home Phone:** (713)697-2688. **Business Addr:** Guidance Counselor, Houston Independent School District, 4400 W 18th St Level 2SE, Houston, TX 77092-8501, **Business Phone:** (713)556-7025.

### HOUSTON, LILLIAN S.
Educator. **Personal:** Born Oct 24, 1946, Tyler, TX; married David. **Educ:** Tex Col, BA, 1966; E TX State Univ, MS, sociol, 1975. **Career:** Nursing Home Admin Wiley Col, instr, prog dir. **Orgs:** Tex Nursing Home Asn; Nat Caucus Black Aged; Am Asn Retired Persons; Cole Hill CME Church, Tyler, TX; Local CYF Christian Youth Fel; dir, Cole Hill CME Church; bd dir, Tyler City Libr, Tyler, TX; Am Col Nursing. **Home Addr:** 1435 N Bois D Arc Ave, Tyler, TX 75702-4563, **Home Phone:** (903)592-2008.

### HOUSTON, ROBERT DARIN. See HOUSTON, BOBBY DARIN.

### HOUSTON, SEAWADON L. (HOUSTON SEA)
Banker, vice president (organization). **Personal:** Born Aug 29, 1942, Liberty, MO; son of Samuel and Thelma Merical; married Carole L Floyd; children: Brenda, Toni, George & Michael. **Educ:** Golden Gate Univ, BA, bus; Univ Wash, Banking Sch; Stanford Sloan Prog, grad. **Career:** Wells Fargo Bank, trainee, 1965-66, several mgt positions, 1966-84, sr vpres, 1984-90, exec vpres, 1990-. **Orgs:** Bay Area Urban Bankers Asn; bd mem, Consumer Bankers Asn; bd mem, Golden Gate Univ; adv bd, Nat Asn Urban Bankers; adv bd, Stanford Sloan. **Home Addr:** 8 Pelican Ct, Pittsburg, CA 94565, **Home Phone:** (925)432-7940. **Business Addr:** Executive Vice President, Wells Fargo Bank, 2 Grant Ave, San Francisco, CA 94108, **Business Phone:** (415)396-2404.

### HOUSTON, WILLIAM DEBOISE
School administrator, president (organization). **Personal:** Born Mar 10, 1940, Quincy, FL; son of Albert and Ada; married Elizabeth Shorter; children: William Carril, Kendra, Karli & Kylean. **Educ:** SC State Col, BSEd, 1963; NC Agr & Tech State Univ, MEd, 1972; Lehigh Univ, admin cert, 1975. **Career:** School administrator (retired); Easton Area Sch dist, teacher, adminr, 1964-74; Shawnee Intermediate Sch, asst prin, 1975, prin; Channel 39 Black Exposure TV Show, co-host; Easton City Coun. **Orgs:** Vpres Easton City Coun; chairperson, Easton Econ Develop, Police Fire & Health Bd City Easton; Pa State Ed Asn; Am Asn Health Phys Ed & Recreation, Women's League Voters, Nat Asn Advan Colored People, exec bd; bd mem, Easton Boys Club, pvt indust coun; pres, Pride & Joy Ed Nursery Inc, S Side Civic Asn; bd trustee, Union AME Church; pres, Easton City Coun. **Honors/Awds:** Certificate of Appreciation, Nat Asn Advan Colored People, 1967, 1982, First Black Councilman City of Easton Pa Certificate; Rainbow Festival Award, Bahai, 1981; Easton City Counc, 1985-87, 1988-90. **Special Achievements:** First African American to be elected in Easton City Council. **Home Addr:** 201 Reese St, Easton, PA 18042, **Home Phone:** (610)559-7608.

### HOUSTON, WILLIE LEWIS
Museum director. **Personal:** Born Aug 21, 1948, Pensacola, FL. **Educ:** Adelphi Univ, BA, 1978. **Career:** African Am hist Mus nassau co, mus dir, 1981-2004, musician cur, currently. **Orgs:** Pres, United Fed Tribal Chiefs, 1995; Civil Serv Employees Asn Nassau County, NY; co-chair, Unity Comn. **Honors/Awds:** Community Service Award, Concerned Citizens for Roslyn's Youth, 1991; Community Serv Award, NY State Assembly 18th Dist, 1994; Community Service Award, Nassau County exec, 1996 & 1998; Community Serv Award, Nassau County Legislator, 1997 & 1999; Community Serv Award, Nat Asn Univ Women, 1998; Man of the Year Award, Hempstead Community, 2002.

### HOUZE, JENEICE CARMEL WONG
Educator. **Personal:** Born New Orleans, LA; married Harold Emmanuel; children: Harold Emanuel Jr & Miles Peter. **Educ:** Xavier Univ, New Orleans, LA, BA, 1959; Univ San Francisco, MA, 1980; Calif State Univ, LDS. **Career:** Chicago Sch Dist, teacher, 1959-65; Torrance Unified Sch Dist, teacher, 1965-, mentor teacher, 1991-; staff, develop clin teaching Rowland Heights, Calif, 1983-84; Hawthrone Sch Dist, consult, 1998. **Orgs:** CA Teachers Asn, 1966-; Nat Educ Asn, 1966-; Torrance Teachers Asn, 1966-; Parent Teachers Asn, 1966-; Dist Sci Workshop on Sci Framework, 1982-83; coord, Career Awareness Prog, Lincoln Sch, 1982-84; vpres, Xavier Univ Nat Alumni Asn, secy, 1983-93; proj writing team mem, Lincoln Elem Sch, 1983-84; Olympic Field Day chairperson, budgeting asst, coord ECT Musical Holiday Presentation, 1983-84; facilitator Workshops, Lincoln Elem Sch, 1983-87; curric writer Gifted & Talented Prog, Lincoln Elem Sch, 1983-86; Univ St Francis Alumni, 1986-87; mentor, Beginning Teacher Support Assessment, 1992-2000; Sci Leadership, team mem, 1993-; Lang Arts Steering Comt, 1995-; Rdg Task Force, site mentor & lead teacher, 1995-97; lead teacher, 1990-00, trainer Peer Qual Rev, 1996-98; comt mem, St. Katharine Drexel Mass. **Home Addr:** 6150 Wooster Ave, Los Angeles, CA 90056, **Home Phone:** (213)776-8969. **Business Addr:** Mentor Teacher, Elementary Mentor Teacher, Torrance Unified School District, 2335 Plz del Amo, Torrance, CA 90504, **Business Phone:** (310)972-6500.

### HOVELL, YVONNE
Automotive executive, president (organization), chief executive officer. **Personal:** married Larry. **Educ:** Howard Univ, BS, pharmaceut sci; Univ Ill Med Ctr, MD, MS, pub health. **Career:** Univ Chicago, Hosp Pharm; Univ Ill, Int Health & Pub Health, fac; Univ Ill, Chicago, fac; prof football Packers, community leader; Chrysler Corp; E Tulsa Dodge dealership; Dodge Chrysler Jeep Tulsa, owner & gen mgr; E Tulsa Dodge, pres & chief exec officer, gen mgr, 2001-. **Orgs:** Bd dir, Tulsa Metro Chamber; Founders Asn, Univ Wis; Nat Automobile Dealers Asn; Ment Health Asn; Jr League Tulsa; Ok Work Force; Found Schs. **Home Addr:** 235 Waverly Dr, Tulsa, OK 74104-2129. **Business Addr:** President, Chief Executive Officer, E Tulsa Dodge, 4627 S Mem Dr, Tulsa, OK 74145, **Business Phone:** (918)663-6343.

### HOWARD, ANICA
Chief executive officer, association executive. **Educ:** Duke Univ Fuqua Sch Bus, BS, eng; Duke Univ Fuqua Sch Bus, BS, indust eng; Duke Univ Fuqua Sch Bus, MBA. **Career:** Xantus Corp, exec dir & dir oper, 1994-99; Christianseeds.com, pres & cheif exec officer, 1999-2000; nat black mba asn inc, exec vpres, chief operating officer, southern regional dir; Miragent Communs, cheif exec officer, currently; Career Commun Group Inc, MBA mgr. **Orgs:** Southern regional dir, Nat Black MBA Asn, 1998-99; bd dir, Nat Black MBA Asn, 1998-2001; Nat Black MBA Asn; chair, Bethlehem Ctr Nashville; bd dir, Nashville Ballet. **Business Addr:** Chief Executive Officer, Miragent Communications, 216 Ctrview Dr Suite 330, Brentwood, TN 37027, **Business Phone:** (615)377-1334.

### HOWARD, AUBREY J.
Executive. **Personal:** Born Mar 23, 1945, Memphis, TN; married Patricia Claxton; children: Adrian K. **Educ:** Rhodes Col, BA, 1972. **Career:** Prev Med Ctr, actg dir, 1972; Proj Aging, asst dir, 1973; Intergovernmental Coord Dept Shelby County Govt, assoc dir res, 1974; Beale St Nat Hist Found, exec dir, 1975; Doyen Asn Inc, pres, 1977-83; TESCO Develop, dir develop, 1983-85; Belz/Curits Outdoor Opers, mgr real estate opers, 1985-; Belz Enterprises, proj dir new hotels & com develop, 1986-; Ment Health Serv, dep dir, 1992; Midtown Ment Health Ctr, chief exec officer, 1992-. **Orgs:** Fel Nat Endowment Humanities, 1977; chmn, Midtown Memphis Ment Health Ctr, 1980-82; pres, Ballet S Inc, 1980-82; Mason, Nat Asn Advan Colored People; bd mem, Memphis Oral Sch Deaf, 1985; Memphis Crisis Stabilization Ctr, 1985; State Tenn Dept Ment Health & Ment Retardation, 1986-94; Tenn Asn Ment Health Orgs. **Home Addr:** 1858 S Rainbow Dr, Memphis, TN 38107, **Home Phone:** (901)725-7508. **Business Addr:** Midtown Mental Health Center, City of Memphis, 2714 Union Extended, Memphis, TN 38112.

### HOWARD, BRIAN EUGENE
Baseball executive, basketball player. **Personal:** Born Oct 19, 1967, Winston-Salem, NC. **Educ:** NC State Univ. **Career:** Basketball player (retired), owner; Omaha Racers, 1990-92; Dallas Mavericks, small forward, 1992-93; Francorosso Torino, 1993-94; Sioux Falls Sky force, 1994-95; ASVEL Villeurbanne, 1995-97; Efes Pilsen, 1997-98; Olympique Antibes, 1998-99; Paris Basket Racing, 1999-2000, 2002-03; Strasbourg IG, 2000-01; ES Chalon-sur-Saone, 2001-02; CB Bilbao Berri, 2003-04; Mlekarna Kunin, 2004-05; Brian Howard's Basketball Acad, owner, currently. **Business Addr:** Owner, Brian Howards Basketball Academy, PO Box 461012, Glendale, CO 80246.

### HOWARD, CALVIN JOHNSON
Law enforcement officer. **Personal:** Born Oct 17, 1947, Miami, FL; son of Norman and Mary Magdalene Johnson Ferguson; children: Tara Evette, Calvin Deon, Arlethia Michelle, LaTonya Linnell, CortenayDeMaun, LaToya Linnett, Troy Everett, Jabari Deon & Christian Jerrod Jameel. **Educ:** Tarrant County Jr Col, Hurst, TX, AA, law enforcement; Univ Tex, Arlington, TX; Abilene Christian Univ, Garland, TX, BS, criminal justice. **Career:** Law enforcement officer (retired); Dade County Seriff's Off, Miami FL, dep Sheriff, 1969-70; Tarrant County Sheriff's Off, Ft Worth TX, dep Sheriff, 1970-72; Dallas Police Dept, Dallas TX, police officer, 1972, retired sr corporal, 1993; sr spec adv Minister Interior. **Orgs:** Founder, Tex Peace Officers Asn, Dallas Chap, 1975-77, First state vpres, 1977-82; vice chmn, Southern Region, Nat Black Police Asn, 1980-84, chmn, 1984-92, nat chmn, 1988-90; Nat Asn Advan Colored People, Cong Task Force, Dallas Chap, 1987; Inspiring Body Christ, Dallas, TX, 1992; Dallas & Grand Prairie Tex Nat Asn Advan Colored People, 1989. **Home Addr:** 1818 Dodge Trl, Grand Prairie, TX 75052-1726, **Home Phone:** (972)522-2227.

### HOWARD, DALTON J., JR.
Lawyer. **Personal:** Born Vicksburg, MS; married Marian Hill. **Educ:** Parsons Clge, BS, 1964; Howard Univ Sch Law, JD, 1974. **Career:**

Gary Sch City, teachr, 1968-69; Mutual NY, field underwriter, 1968-69; Wash Tech Inst, instr, 1974-75; Neighborhood Legal Serv Prog, managing atty, 1975-. **Orgs:** Vpres & dir, Movin' Inc, 1974-; Nat Bar Asn; Am Bar Asn; Asn Trial Lawyers Am; DC Bar Asn; Sigma Delta Tau Legal Frat; Recreation Assistance Bd, OBC, 2005. **Special Achievements:** First licensed to practice law in Washington DC. **Home Addr:** 4020 Lee St NE, Washington, DC 20019, **Home Phone:** (202)399-1876. **Business Addr:** Attorney, 4020 Lee St NE, Washington, DC 20019, **Business Phone:** (703)399-1876.

### HOWARD, DESMOND KEVIN

Football player, television talk show host. **Personal:** Born May 15, 1970, Cleveland, OH; son of James D and Hattie V Dawkins Shockley; married Rebkah; children: Sydney, Desmond Jr & Dhamir. **Educ:** Univ Mich, BA, commun, 1992. **Career:** Football player (retired), TV analyst; Wash Redskins, wide receiver, 1992-94; Jacksonville Jaguars, 1995; Green Bay Packers, 1996, 1999; Oakland Raiders, 1997-98; Detroit Lions, wide receiver, 2000-02; ESPN Inc, col football analyst, currently; Detroit Lions TV Network, color commentator, currently; Actor: Michigan vs. Ohio State: The Rivalry, 2007. **Orgs:** Peer facilitator & prog adv, Beale Harden Beale Inc, 1990; employee, Habari Gani, 1992; chmn, Nat Consortium Acad & Sports, 1992; chmn, NCAA Found, 1992; spokes person, Spec Olympics, 1992; Green Bay Packers; bd mem, USA Football Inc; at-large mem, Miami-Dade Sports Comn. **Home Addr:** 6622 Villa Sonrisa Suite 820, Boca Raton, FL 33433, **Home Phone:** (407)561-0707. **Business Addr:** College Football Analyst, ESPN Inc, ESPN Plz 935 Middle St, Bristol, CT 06010, **Business Phone:** (860)766-2000.

### HOWARD, DONALD R.

Engineer. **Personal:** Born Oct 13, 1928, Wightman, VA; married Virdie M Hubbard; children: Jada Marni & Donald Jr. **Educ:** BS, 1959. **Career:** IITRI, 1956-64; Mobil Oil Corp, 1964-68; Commonwealth Edison Co, prin chem engr, 1968. **Orgs:** Am Inst Chem Engrs; Am Chem Soc; Prof Black Chemists & Chem Engrs; Carter Temple CME Church. **Home Addr:** 9218 S Dunbar Ave, Chicago, IL 60619-7323. **Business Addr:** 72 W Adams, Chicago, IL 60603.

### HOWARD, DR. ELIZABETH FITZGERALD

College teacher, librarian, writer. **Personal:** Born Dec 28, 1927, Baltimore, MD; daughter of John MacFarland Fitzgerald and Bertha McKinley James; married Lawrence Cabot; children: Jane Martin, Susan C & Laura L. **Educ:** Harvard Univ, Radcliffe Col, AB, 1948; Univ Pittsburgh, MLS, 1971, PhD, 1988. **Career:** Boston Pub Libr, catalogue asst, c librn, 1952-56; Episcopal Diocese Pittsburgh, resource librn, 1972-74; Pittsburgh Theol Sem, librn, 1974-77; Univ Pittsburgh, vis lectr, 1976-78; WVA Univ, asst prof, 1978-85, leave sr librn, prof emer, 1993-; Radcliffe Col, prof; Univ Maiduguri, Nigeria, fac, 1981-82, assoc prof, 1985-89, prof, 1989-93; catalogue asst, Boston Pub Libr. Books: Papa Tells Chita a Story; America As Story: Historical Fiction for Secondary Schools, 1988; Chita's Christmas Tree, 1989; Mac & Marie & the Train Toss Surprise; Aunt Flossie's Hats, 1995; Virgie Goes to School with Us Boys, 2000. **Orgs:** Dir, Radcliffe Alumnae Asn, 1969-72; bd trustee, Ellis Sch, Pittsburgh, 1970-75; trustee & bd mem, Magee Women's Hosp, 1980-94; Episcopal Diocese Pittsburgh Cathedral Chap, 1984-86; bd mem, QED Commun, 1987-94, chair ethics Comt; bd mem, Beginning With Bks, 1987-93; cand bd dir, Harvard Alumni Asn, 1987; bd mem, US Bd Bks Youth, 2000-02; Pittsburgh chap, LINKS Inc; Am Libr Asn; C's Lit Asn; Soc C Bk Writers; Pa Sch Librn's Asn; C's Lit Asn; Socs C's Bk Writers; Caldecott Comt; Hans Christian Andersen Comt; Teachers C's Lit Discussion Group. **Home Addr:** 825 Morewood Ave, Pittsburgh, PA 15213, **Home Phone:** (412)605-0293. **Business Addr:** Professor Emeritus, West Virginia University, 1550 Univ Ave, Morgantown, WV 26506, **Business Phone:** (304)293-0111.

### HOWARD, ELLEN D.

Association executive, executive director. **Personal:** Born Apr 8, 1929, Baltimore, MD; daughter of Lucious Norman Dolvey and Louise Tignor; children: Harold H Jr & Larry K. **Educ:** Morgan State Col, BS, higher educ & higher educ admin, 1951; Johns Hopkins Univ, MEd, admin & coun, 1968. **Career:** Educ Talent Search US Off Educ, exec dir; MD Educ Opportunity Ctr, exec dir, dir, 1968-. **Orgs:** Bd trustee, Col Entrance Exam Bd; DE DC Md Asn Financial Aid Admin; 4thDist Dem Orgn, Baltimore City; Nat Asn Stud Financial Aid Admin; Nat Coun Negro Women; Md Personnel & Guid Asn; Nat Educ Asn; YWCA; Nat Asn Advan Colored People; Baltimore Pub Sch Teachers Asn; Delta Sigma Theta Inc; Baltimore Continental Soc Underprivileged C Inc; Town & Country Set; Baltimore Chap Moles Inc; Girl Scouts Cent, Md Nominating Coun; Nat Vol Planning Prog Mgt & Audits Girl Scouts, USA; Phi Delta Gamma, Gamma Chap Nat Hon Fraternity Grad Women; Phi Lambda Theta Chi Chap Nat Hon & Prof Asn Women Educ; Enon Baptist Church; Girl Scouts Cent Md; Md Personnel & Guid Asn; Baltimore Urban League & League Women Voters; Pub Sch Adminr & Supvr Asn. **Honors/Awds:** Certificate of Appreciation, Am Biog Inst, 1975; Community Servive Certificate, 1974; Certificate of Achievement, Morgan Col, ROTC, 1974; Am Legion Award; Inter Nat Women's Year Award; Outstanding Woman in Youth Development, Baltimore Alumni Chap Delta Sigma Theta Inc; Hall of Fame, MECEO; Maryland State Award for Outstanding Services. **Special Achievements:** Author: Financial Aid for Higher Education. **Home Addr:** 3220 Yosemite Ave, Baltimore, MD 21215-7513. **Business Addr:** Executive Director, Maryland Educational Opportunity Center, 2641 Md Ave, Baltimore, MD 21218, **Business Phone:** (410)728-3400.

### HOWARD, GLEN

Clergy. **Personal:** Born May 20, 1956, Oakland, CA; married Marian Byrd. **Educ:** La Tech Univ, BS, psychol, 1980; Gammon Theol Sem, Mdiv, 1984. **Career:** Marc Paul Inc, mgt, 1976-79; Xerox Corp, sales & mkt, 1980-81; United Methodist Church Iowa Conf, pastor, 1984-. **Orgs:** Sec, Ankeny Ministerial Asn, 1985. **Home Addr:** 52 Country Hill Rd, PO Box 2171, St. Peters, MO 63376, **Home Phone:** (636)397-7730. **Business Addr:** Pastor, United Methodist Church, 206 SW Walnut, Ankeny, IA 50021.

### HOWARD, GLEN L.

Executive. **Personal:** Born Sep 12, 1942, Detroit, MI; son of Green (deceased) and Rebecca Hall (deceased); married Sheila Perkins; children: Sheryce & Glen Jr. **Educ:** Wayne County Community Col, attended 1973. **Career:** A & P Tea Co, asst mgr, 1960-67; Detroit Edison, meter reader, 1967-68; The Drackett Co, sales rep, 1968-70; United Beverage Co, area mgr, 1970-76; Great Lakes Beverage Co, area mgr, 1976-85; Coors Brewing Co, community rels field mgr, 1986-. **Orgs:** Nat Asn Advan Colored People, 1973-; bd dir, Food Indust Coun; bd dir, Detroit Chamber Com, 1989-; adv coun mem, Detroit Chap, Southern Christian Leadership Conf, 1990-. **Home Addr:** 15766 Monte Vista St, Detroit, MI 48238-1010, **Home Phone:** (313)861-8942. **Business Addr:** Community Relations Field Manager, Coors Brewing Co, 8420 W Bryn Mawr Ave Suite 420, Chicago, IL 60631-3495.

### HOWARD, GREGORY ALLEN

Screenwriter, playwright. **Personal:** Born Jan 1, 1962, Norfolk, VA. **Educ:** Princeton Univ, Am hist. **Career:** Playwright, screenwriter & author; CBS, story ed; guest lectr, Howard Univ; Screenwriter: "True Color", 1990; Fox, "True Colors", 1988; "Where I Live", 1993; Christmas Eve, "Tinseltown Trilogy"; CBS, "The Royal Family"; CBS, "Teach"; ABC, "Where I live", story ed; "21 Jump Street"; "Ali", 2001; Remember The Titans, 2000; Drummer Boy; We Are A Chain; Baptism In Fire; first black armored unit to see combat in World War II, currently; Night Witches, 2014; Producer: Night Witches. **Orgs:** Kennedy Ctr Circles; founder & creator, Howard Lonsdale Scholar; Alvin Ailey Partner; bd mem, Ctr Creative Community; Guest Lectr Howard Univ; bd mem, Ctr Creative Voices. **Business Addr:** Screenwriter310-859-4462, William Morris Agency, 151 El Camino Dr, Beverly Hills, CA 90212, **Business Phone:** (310)274-7451.

### HOWARD, GWENDOLYN JULIUS

Educator, president (organization). **Personal:** Born Nov 15, 1932, Brooklyn, NY; children: Calvin & Lisa C. **Educ:** Bethune Cookman Col, BS, 1956; Univ Northern Colo, MS, 1974, EdD, 1976. **Career:** Sunlight Beauty Acad-Kingston Jam Cri Deliq Task Force Mod Cities, assoc, 1968-70; SE Reg NANB & PW Clubs, gov, 1970-73; Gala Travel Inc, Miami, co-owner; Dade Co Pub Sch, sch liaison juv justice support prog. **Orgs:** Sigma Gamma Rho, 1967-; pres, Epsilon Chap Gamma Phi Sigma Gamma Rho; pres, Epsilon Chap Gamma Phi Delta, 1978-81; pres, Sigma Gamma Rho, Gamma Delta Sigma Chap, 1980-82; pres, Miami Chap Top Ladies Distinction Inc, 1983-87; exec bd, YWCA NW; adv coun, Miami Dade Community Col, 1984. **Home Addr:** 7956 NW 18 Ave, Miami, FL 33147, **Home Phone:** (305)836-0850. **Business Addr:** School Liaison Education Specialist, Dade Co Public School, 3300 NW 27th Ave, Miami, FL 33142, **Business Phone:** (305)633-4955.

### HOWARD, ESQ. JOHN MILTON

Lawyer. **Educ:** Tufts Univ, BA, 1966; Cath Univ Sch Educ, MA, 1969; Cath Univ, MS, 1971; Cath Univ Am, JD, 1979; Columbus Sch Law. **Career:** DC Ment Health Advocacy Trust, ment health lawyer; Pvt pract, currently. **Business Addr:** Lawyer, Private Practice, 1532 Upshur St NW, Washington, DC 20011-7008, **Business Phone:** (202)723-5919.

### HOWARD, DR. JOHN ROBERT

Educator, lawyer. **Personal:** Born Jan 24, 1933, Boston, MA; married Mary Doris Adams; children: Leigh Humphrey. **Educ:** Brandeis Univ, BA, 1955; NY Univ, MA, 1961; Stanford Univ, PhD, 1965; J Du Pace Univ, attended 1985. **Career:** Univ Ore, asst prof, 1965-68; Rutgers Univ, assoc prof, 1969-71; State Univ NY, dean & prof, 1971-80, prof sociol, 1971-, Div Social Sci, distinguished serv prof emer sociol, currently; Pvt Pract, atty, 1986-. **Orgs:** United Way Westchester, 1976-78; bd adv, Inst Urban Design, 1978-; vpres, Soc Study Social Prob, 1978-79; St Theater Inc, 1978-80; Friends Nueberger Mus, 1982-85. **Home Addr:** 445 Gramatan Ave Apt HB1, Mt Vernon, NY 10552-2958, **Home Phone:** (914)664-2963. **Business Addr:** Attorney, 271 N Ave, New Rochelle, NY 10801-5104, **Business Phone:** (914)235-2235.

### HOWARD, JULES JOSEPH, JR.

Executive. **Personal:** Born Aug 24, 1943, New Orleans, LA; son of Jules J Sr and Ophelia; children: Gwendolyn. **Educ:** Calif State Univ, BA, bus admin, 1975, MBA, 1977. **Career:** City Carson, exec asst, 1973-79; Comput Careers Corp, mgr, 1979-81; Great 400 Group Int, exec dir, 1981, sr recruiter & sr proj leader currenlty. **Orgs:** Vpres, Carson Lions Club; Kappa Alpha Psi Fraternity; Carson Br Nat Asn Advan Colored People; Calif Inst Employ Coun; Calif Asn Personnel Consults. **Business Addr:** Executive Director, Senior Recruiter, Great 400 Group Intl, 500 E Carson St Suite 105, Carson, CA 90745, **Business Phone:** (310)518-9627.

### HOWARD, JUWAN ANTONIO

Basketball player, basketball coach. **Personal:** Born Feb 7, 1973, Chicago, IL; son of Leroy Watson Jr and Helena; married Jenine Wardally; children: Jace & Jett. **Educ:** Univ Mich, BA, commun, 1995. **Career:** Basketball player (retired), coach; Wash Wizards, power forward, 1994-2001, small forward, 1996-99; Dallas Mavericks, power forward, 2001-02, 2007-08; Denver Nuggets, power forward, 2002-03, 2008; Orlando Magic, power forward, 2003-04; Houston Rockets, power forward, 2004-07; Charlotte Bobcats, small forward, 2008-09; Portland Trail Blazers, ctr, 2009-10; Miami Heat, power forward, 2010-13, asst coach, 2013-. **Orgs:** Fab Five, Univ Mich, 1991-94; nat spokesman, Nat Basketball Asn; founder, Juwan Howard Found. **Honors/Awds:** NBA All-Star, 1996; Good Guys in Sports, The Sporting News; Chopper Travaglini Award; Champion, Nat Basketball Asn, 2012-13. **Special Achievements:** Film: Hoop Dreams, 1994; Series: "Hang Time", 1995; "The West Wing", 1999; " Arli$$", 1999; "The Crackpots and These Women". **Home Addr:** 848 Brickell Key Dr Apt 4603, Miami, FL 33131-3730. **Business Addr:** Assistant Coach, Miami Heat, 601 Biscayne Blvd, Miami, FL 33132, **Business Phone:** (786)777-1000.

### HOWARD, DR. KEITH L.

Optometrist. **Personal:** Born Feb 27, 1940, Buffalo, NY; son of Robert B Sr and Annie C; married Patricia; children: Jennifer & Kristopher. **Educ:** AA, BS & OD, 1966. **Career:** Optical Corp, partner, 1968; pvt pract, 1969; Melnick, Howard, Grzankowski Opt, prof corp formed, 1974; Southern Tier Optom Ctr, vpres, partner, 1979-; Coun Optom Ctr, optometrist, currently. **Orgs:** Dir, Nat & Am Optom Asn; Nat Eye Res Found Optom Exten Prog, Olean YMCA; Olean Community Chest; EGO Health Studios Inc; bd mem, State Bd Optom, 1985-89, 1989-93; bd mem, regional dir, Nat Optom Asn, 1988-89; pres, Nat Optom Asn, 2000. **Honors/Awds:** Olean YMCA Man Year, 1970; One of Two Black Optometrists, NY State; Founders Award, Nat Optom Asn, 2000; President Medal Honor, Illinois Col Optom, 2000. **Home Addr:** 25 Hamilton Ave, Olean, NY 14760-1732, **Home Phone:** (716)373-0528. **Business Addr:** Optometrist, Council for Optometric Center, 168 N Union St, Olean, NY 14760, **Business Phone:** (716)372-9464.

### HOWARD, DR. LAWRENCE CABOT

Consultant, educator. **Personal:** Born Apr 16, 1925, Des Moines, IA; son of Charles Preston and Louisa Maude Lewis; married Elizabeth Fitzgerald; children: Jane, Susan & Laura. **Educ:** Drake Univ, BA, 1949; Wayne State Univ, MA, 1950; Harvard Univ, PhD, 1956. **Career:** Hofstra Univ, instr & asst prof, 1956-58; Brandeis Univ, asst prof, 1958-63; Peace Corps, Phillippines, assoc dir, 1961-63; Ctr Innovation NY St Dept Educ, assoc dir, 1964; Univ Wis-Milwaukee, dir human rel inst, 1964-67; Danforth Found, vpres, 1967-69; Univ Pittsburgh, dean, Grad Sch Pub & Int Affairs, 1969-73, prof, 1973-94, prof emer, 1994-; Govt Bahamas, mgt consult, 1986-94; Chatham Col, distinguished vis prof, 1995-98; Pub Policy Assoc, pres, currently. **Orgs:** Nat Adv Comn Tchr Corps, 1967-69; Pgh World Affrs Coun, 1969-; mem exec Coun, Nat Asn Sch Pub Affrs Admin, 1971-73; Am Soc Pub Admin, 1972-; bd mem, Episcopal Relief & Develop Fund, 2001-; trustee, Ch Soc Col Work, Drake Univ, St Augustine Col, Seabury Western Theol Sem, Epis Diocese Pgh; Harvard Grad Soc Advan Study & Res; Dep Epis Diocesan Conv; Consult US Off Edn State Dept Bur Extnl Res; mem res & adv bd, Comn Econ Develop; Pgh Hist & Landmarks Found. **Honors/Awds:** Man of the Year, Alpha Phi Alpha, 1949; Distinguishing Alumnus Award, Drake Univ, 1971; natl pres, COMPA, 1979-80; Full bright Prof, Univ Maiduguri, Nigeria, 1981-82; Phi Beta Kappa; Lawrence Cabot Howard Doctoral Research Award, Univ Pittsburgh, named in honor. **Special Achievements:** Authored "American Involvement in Africa South of the Sahara 1800-1860 (Harvard Dissertations in American History and Political Science)"; Lawrence Cabot Howard Doctoral Research Award; co-author, "Public Administration, Balancing Power & Accountability"; contributing articles to professional journals; first black dean of University of Pittsburgh Graduate School of Public and International Affairs. **Home Addr:** 825 Morewood Ave Apt M, Pittsburgh, PA 15213, **Home Phone:** (412)606-9094. **Business Addr:** Professor Emeritus, University of Pittsburgh, 3601 Posvar Hall, Pittsburgh, PA 15260, **Business Phone:** (412)648-7640.

### HOWARD, DR. LEON

Educator. **Personal:** Born Jan 1, 1958. **Career:** Ala State Univ, Dean Col Sci & Humanities, prof, 1976, interim pres, 1983, pres, 1984-91. **Home Addr:** 2724 Tremont St, Montgomery, AL 36110, **Home Phone:** (334)262-8526. **Business Addr:** President, Alabama State University, 915 S Jackson St, Montgomery, AL 36104-5732.

### HOWARD, LEON W., JR.

Insurance agent. **Personal:** Born May 3, 1935, Pittsburgh, PA. **Educ:** Pa State Univ, attended 1968; Univ Pgh, attended 1974. **Career:** Robt C Golden, real estate, 1956-57; Surety Underwriters Inc, vpres, 1970-73; lic broker, 1971; Nationwide Ins Co, agency agreement, 1972-; Leon W Howard Jr Ins, broker, currently. **Orgs:** Chmn, Labor & Indus Com Pgh National Association for the Advancement of Colored People, 1974; pres, Pgh Br National Association for the Advancement of Colored People, 1975; pres, COPP; vpres, PABU; bd dir, Black Cath Ministries & Laymen's Coun; exec bd mem, Pgh Chap National Association for the Advancement of Colored People; exec bd mem, Homewood-Brushton YMCA; commr, City Pgh, Dept City Planning; nat Assn, Sec Dealers; Pgh Life Underwriters Asn Inc; Nat Asn, Life Underwriters; Ins Club Pgh Inc. **Honors/Awds:** Outstanding Contribution to the Struggle for Human Rights Award, Western PA Black Polit Assembly. **Home Addr:** 564 Forbes Ave 810, Pittsburgh, PA 15233, **Home Phone:** (412)281-9500. **Business Addr:** Insurance Broker, Agent, Leon W Howard Jr Insurance, 564 Forbes Ave Suite 810, Pittsburgh, PA 15233, **Business Phone:** (412)281-9500.

### HOWARD, LESLIE CARL

Administrator, lawyer. **Personal:** Born Jun 18, 1950, Aberdeen, MD; son of Willis C and Ethel B; married Corrine Felder; children: Kevin, Keith & Kenneth. **Educ:** Community Col, Baltimore, AA, 1971, cert electronics, 1982; Howard Univ, BA, 1980; Baruch Col, MPA, 1984; Johns Hopkins Univ, cert, 1990; Univ Baltimore, Sch Law, JD, 1997. **Career:** MD Dept Human Resources, caseworker II, 1975-77; Mayor Baltimore, spec asst, 1979-82; Neighborhood Housing Serv Baltimore, prog dir, 1982-83; Mayor Baltimore, spec asst, 1983-84; Neighborhood Housing Serv, Baltimore, neighborhood coord asst dir to neighborhood dir, 1985-87; Hartford County, Md, housing coordr, 1987-89; City Baltimore Develop Corp, develop dir, 1989-96; Eubie Blake Nat Jazz Inst & Cult Ctr, exec dir, 1996-2000; Priv Pract, atty, 2000-. **Orgs:** Pres, atty law & bd dir, Coppin Heights Community Corp; Nat Urban fel Class, 1983-84; organizer & pres, Alliance Rosemont Community Orgn Inc, 1987-91; founding pres, MD Low Income Housing Coalition, 1989-91; steering comt mem, Baltimore Neighborhood Resource Ctr, 1990-92; vpres, bd govs, MD Am Civil Liberties Union, 1999-. **Home Addr:** 2322 Harlem Ave, Baltimore, MD 21216, **Home Phone:** (410)566-0146. **Business Addr:** Attorney, Law Offices of Leslie Carl Howard, 441 E 22nd St, Baltimore, MD 21218, **Business Phone:** (410)566-5223.

### HOWARD, DR. LILLIE PEARL

Educator, school administrator. **Personal:** Born Oct 4, 1949, Gadsden, AL; daughter of Walter Moody and Zola Mae; married Willie D Kendricks; children: Kimberly Denise & Benjamin Richard. **Educ:**

Univ S Ala, Mobile, BA, eng, 1971; Univ NMex, Albuquerque, NM, MA, eng, 1972, PhD, eng, 1975; Harvard Univ, Cambridge, grad inst educ mgt, 1988. **Career:** Ford Found, fel, 1971-75; Wright State Univ, Dayton, Ohio, asst prof, assoc prof eng, 1980-85, Col Lib Arts, from asst dean to assoc dean, 1982-87, prof eng, 1985-, asst vpres acad affairs, 1987-88, assoc vpres acad affairs, 1988-99, undergrad educ & acad affairs, assoc provost, 1994-99, assoc provost acad affairs, dean univ, vpres res, prof Eng & sr vpres curric & instr, currently, co-chair, Wright State Semesters Transition Team, currently. Books: Alice Walker and Zora Neale Hurston: The Common Bond. **Orgs:** Am Asn Higher Educ; Ohio Bd Regents Comn Enhancement Undergrad Educ; Ohio Bd Regents Comn Articulation & Transfer; Nat Asn Women Deans, Adminr & Counrs; Nat Asn Acad Affairs Admin; consult & evaluator, NCA Rev Coun; Zora Neale Hurston Socs; Acad Assemby Col Bd. **Home Addr:** 3908 Valley Brook Dr S, Englewood, OH 45322-3628. **Business Addr:** Senior Vice President for Curriculum & Instruction, Professor of English, Wright State University, 3640 Col Glenn Hwy, Dayton, OH 45435, **Business Phone:** (937)775-2097.

## HOWARD, LINWOOD E.

Banker, manager. **Personal:** Born Mar 12, 1954, Roanoke Rapids, NC; son of Alexander M and Norma; married Denise Laws; children: Marcellus & Jeniene. **Educ:** Livingstone Col, BS, bus & acct, 1976; Univ NC, Chapel Hill, Advan Sch Banking, attended 1984. **Career:** First Union Nat Bank, br mgr, 1976-86, consumer banking br mgr & vpres, 1986-93; Crestar Bank, mkt mgr, sr vpres, 1993; Downtown Norfolk, bd dir, currently; SunTrust Bank, area mgr, sr vpres, currently; PNC Bank, regional mgr, 2008-. **Orgs:** Dir, United Neighborhood Econ Devel Corp, 1991; bd mem, Greenville Chamber Comt, 1992; bd mem, Greenville Area Coun, 1992; bd dir, Downtown Norfolk Coun; Norfolk State Univ Sch Bus; bd mem, Bon Secours Hampton Roads Health Syst. **Home Addr:** 1801 Duke York Quay, Virginia Beach, VA 23454-1107, **Home Phone:** (757)496-3432. **Business Addr:** Senior Vice President, SunTrust Banks, 25 Pk Pl NE, Atlanta, GA 30303, **Business Phone:** (404)588-7610.

## HOWARD, DR. MAMIE R. (MAMIE HOWARD GOLLADAY)

School administrator, president (organization). **Personal:** Born Nov 24, 1946, Pascagoula, MS; daughter of E; married Golladay. **Educ:** Pensacola Jr Col, AS, 1971, BS, 1976; Univ Ala, MS, 1979, PhD, admin & higher educ, 1988. **Career:** DW McMillan Hosp, gen duty rn, 1967-71, supvr, 1971-76; Jefferson Davis JrCol, instr, 1976-78; Pensacola Jr Col, dept chmn allied health ed, 1978-90; CS Mott Community Col, Flint, Mich; Montgomery Col, dean, 1990-93; dean bus, sci, mathematics, technol; Sullivan County Community Col, pres, 1998-2011. **Orgs:** Am Nurses Asn, 1971-, USA Alumni Asn; consult, Escambia Sickle CellDisease Found, 1979-82; UAB Alumni Asn, 1979-, ComtAllied HealthEduc, 1981-, AAWCGC, 1982-; chief execofficer, State Mgmt Ltd, 1985-86; bd dir, Fla Lung Asn, 1983-90; dir, large Lung Asn, 1986-90; AlphaKappa Alpha; chair, PRIDE Comt Am Lung Asn, 1989-90; Am Lung Asn Bd, Genesse County, Mich, 1991-. **Honors/Awds:** Honor Award, Kappa Delta Pi Grad Honor Soc, 1981-; Selected as a Leader of the 80's, FIPSE, 1982; hon by the gov as an Outstanding BlackAmerican, 1988; Leadership Award, Pensacola Chamber Com, 1990; OutstandingEducr, Alpha Kappa Alpha Sor, 1990. **Home Addr:** 432 Chandler Ave, Flint, MI 48503, **Home Phone:** (313)239-1513. **Business Addr:** President, Sullivan County Community College, 112 College Rd, Loch Sheldrake, NY 12759-4002, **Business Phone:** (845)434-5750.

## HOWARD, MICHELLE

Naval officer. **Personal:** Born Jan 1, 1964; daughter of Nick and Phillipa; married Wayne K Cowles. **Educ:** US Naval Acad, BS, 1982; USY Command & Gen Staff Col, MA, mil arts & sci, 1998. **Career:** USS Tortuga, exec officer, 1996; Expeditionary Warfare Div, dep dir; Amphibious Squadron Seven, comdr, 2004-05; OPNAV, 2006; USn, secy navy sr mil asst, dep chief naval opers for opers, plans & strategy, currently; Expeditionary Strike Group, comdr, 2009-10; BALTOPS, Maritime Task Force, comdr, 2010. **Honors/Awds:** Captain Winifred Collins Award, Secy Navy & Navy League, 1987; Meretorious Serv Medal; Navy Commendation Medal; Navy Achievement Medal; Nat Defense Medal; Armed Forces Expeditionary Medal; Armed Forces Serv Medal; Southwest Asia Serv Medal; NATO Medal; Kuwaiti Liberation Medal; Kuwaiti Liberation Medal; Meretorious Serv Medal; Navy Commendation Medal; Navy Achievement Medal; Nat Defense Serv Medal; Armed Forces Expeditionary Medal; SW Asia Serv Medal; Armed Forces Serv Medal; NATO Medal; Kuwait Liberation Medal; Kuwait Liberation Medal. **Special Achievements:** First African American woman to command a ship in the U.S. Navy; First admiral selected from the United States Naval Academy class of 1982 & the First woman graduate of the United States Naval Academy selected for Admiral. **Business Addr:** Deputy Chief of Naval Operations for Operations Plans & Strategy, United States Navy, 701 Pa Ave NW Suite 123, Washington, DC 20004, **Business Phone:** (202)737-2300.

**HOWARD, MILTON L.** See Obituaries Section.

## HOWARD, REV. MOSES WILLIAM, JR.

Clergy, school administrator, executive director. **Personal:** Born Mar 3, 1946, Americus, GA; son of Moses William Sr and Laura Turner; married Barbara Jean Wright; children: Matthew Weldon, Adam Turner & Maisha Wright. **Educ:** Morehouse Col, BA, 1968; Princeton Theol Sem, MDiv, 1972. **Career:** Reformed Church AM, exec dir Black Coun, 1972-92; New York Theol Sem, pres, 1992-99; Bethany Baptist Church, pastor, 2000-. **Orgs:** Ordained minister Am Baptist Churches, 1974; moderator, Prog Combat Racism World Coun Churches, 1976-78; pres, Nat Coun Churches, 1979-81; provided X-mas serv US Hostages Iran, 1979; bd trustee, Nat Urban League, 1981-88; bd trustee, Independent Sector, 1981-86; trustee, C's Defense Fund, 1981-86; pres, Am Comn Africa; chair, NJ Death Penalty Study Comn; founding mem, Newark Community Found; Sigma Pi Phi Fraternity; human rights adv group, World Coun Churches, 1989; chair, relig comn, Welcome Nelson Mandela to New York, 1990; chair, Rutgers Univ Bd Gov; exec comt, Asn Theol Schs, 1994-2000; Coun Foreign Rels, 1997-; founder, Bethany Cares, Inc, 2000-. **Honors/Awds:** Hon Dr of Divinity Degree, Miles Col & Central Col, 1979-80; Citations Mayors of Philadelphia, PA & Americus, Ga, 1981-84; Distinguished Alumnus Award, Princeton Sem, 1982; Hon Dr of Humane Letters Morehouse Col, 1984; Citations from the NJ ST Assembly; The City of Waterloo, Iowa; The Township of Lawrence, NJ; The Toussant Loverture Freedom Award, NY Haitian Community; Chaired the Seminar against bank loans to South Africain Zurich, Switzerland, 1982; The Measure of A Man Award; Bennie Award for Achievement. **Home Addr:** 10 Paddock Dr, Lawrence, NJ 08648-1567. **Business Addr:** Pastor, Bethany Baptist Church, 275 W Mkt St, Newark, NJ 07103, **Business Phone:** (973)623-8161.

## HOWARD, NORMAN H., JR.

Administrator, executive, manager. **Personal:** Born Jan 30, 1947, Johnson City, TN; married Nancy Goines; children: Erick, Nicole & Nichelle. **Educ:** Georgetown Univ Inst Comparative Polit & Econ Syst, dipl, 1972; Benedict Col, BS, bus admin, 1974; Univ Detroit, MBA, 1979. **Career:** Ford Motor Co, Casting Div & Transmission & Chassis Div, salary admin, 1974-81, sales opers staff, affirmative action prog coordr, 1981-82, supvr sales pers & training, 1982-83, ford world hq, personnel & orgn staff, ind rels analyst, 1983-85, dearborn glass plant, mgr ind rels dept, 1985-99; Greektown Casino, vpres human resources. **Orgs:** Pres, Phi Bet Lambda, 1973-74; Delta Mu Delta, 1973-74; chmn, Gesu Boy Scout Troop 191 Comt, 1982-85; pres, Detroit Chap Bendict Col Alumni Club, 1984-; Greater Detroit Area Health Coun; dir human resource, W.K. Kellogg Found; Boy Scouts, Greater Detroit; Big Bro & Big sister Metrop Detroit; bd dir, Battle Creek Health Syst. **Honors/Awds:** Outstanding Service Recognition Award, Gesu Boy Scout Troop 191 Detroit, 1983, 1984, 1985; Distinguished Alumni Citation, Nat Asn Equal Opportunity Higher Educ, 1986. **Home Addr:** 24635 Ridgeview Dr, Farmington Hills, MI 48336-1906, **Home Phone:** (248)476-1619. **Business Addr:** Vice President of Human Resources, Greektown Casino, 555 E Lafayette St, Detroit, MI 48226, **Business Phone:** (313)223-2999.

## HOWARD, NORMAN LEROY

Administrator, army officer, law enforcement officer. **Personal:** Born May 22, 1930, New York, NY; married Barbara; children: Karen, Dale & Steven. **Career:** Consol Edison Co NY Inc, equal employ oppurtunity coordr; New York Dept Parks, playground dir, 1948-51; New York Police Dept, detective, 1952-72; Inst Mediation & Conflict Resol, consult, 1972-73. **Orgs:** Boys Yesteryr; 100 Black Men Inc; 369th Vet Asn; K C St Patricks Coun; Retired Guardians New York Police Dept; Int Black Police Asn; Welterweight boxing champion amatuer, NY City Dept Parks, 1943-44; Middleweight Champion Amatuer Met AAU, 1945; Air Force Mem Found; Air Force Asn. **Honors/Awds:** Combat Cross for Bravery, New York Police Dept, 1955. **Special Achievements:** Won 15 awards for Bravery & Excellent Police Work, New York Police Dept; First black detective assigned to 40th squad Bronx, 1954. **Home Addr:** 444 E 86th St, New York, NY 10028. **Business Addr:** 4 Irving Pl, New York, NY 10003.

## HOWARD, OSBIE L., JR.

Executive. **Personal:** Born Feb 9, 1943, Memphis, TN; son of Osbie L Sr and Bertha S; married Rose O Ollie; children: John, Kendra & Nathan. **Educ:** Memphis State Univ, BBA, 1967; Wash Univ, MBA, 1971. **Career:** Exxon Co, finan analyst, 1971-72; Memphis Bus Resource Ctr, finan specialist, 1972-74; Tenn State Bd Accountacy, CPA, 1973; Banks Findley White & Co CPA's, tax mgr, 1974-78; Shelby Cty Govt, asst chief admins officer, 1978-79; Tenn Valley Ctr Minority Econ Devel, exec vpres, 1979-88; Secured Capital Developers, partner, 1988-91; City Memphis, Treas Div, treas & dir; OmniCare Health Plan Inc, exec dir, 1995-; United Am Healthcare Corp, sr vpres, 1995-, dir, 2003-, Health Plan Tenn Inc, pres & chief exec officer. **Orgs:** Grad Bus Sch fel, Consortium Grad Study Mgt, 1969; Treas & co-founder, New Memphis Develop Corp, 1976; treas, Ind Develop Corp Memphis & Shelby Co, 1980-91; bd dir, W Tenn Venture Capital Corp, 1981. **Home Addr:** 648 Riverside Dr Apt 312, Memphis, TN 38103-4622, **Home Phone:** (901)523-1801. **Business Addr:** Director, United American Healthcare Corp, 303 E Wacker Dr, Chicago, IL 60601, **Business Phone:** (313)393-4571.

## HOWARD, PAUL LAWRENCE, JR.

Lawyer. **Personal:** Born Sep 22, 1951, Waynesboro, GA; son of Paul L Sr and Gussie P; married Petrina M Moody; children: Jamila, Paul L III & Simone. **Educ:** Morehouse Col, BA, polit sci, 1972; Emory Univ Sch Law, JD, 1976. **Career:** City Atlanta, Munic Ct, dep solicitor; Fulton Co, Dist Atty's Off, asst dist atty, 1977-80; Thomas, Kennedy, Sampson & Patterson, assoc; Off Local Child Fatality Rev, Ga Dept Human Resources, chairperson, currently; Fulton Co, State Ct, solicitor, dist atty, 1997-. **Orgs:** Bench & bar comt, Gate City Bar; pres, Black Am Law Students Asn; vpres, Stud Bar Asn; Nat Bar Asn; Atlanta Bar Asn; Ga Bar Asn; Ga Solicitors Asn; Ga Supreme Ct Bar; Providence Baptist Church Law, 1992; Ga Asn Black Women Atty, 1992; Nat Asn Advan Colored People; Urban League. **Special Achievements:** First African-American to be elected district attorney in the history of the State of Georgia. **Home Addr:** 1280 Regency Ctr Dr SW, Atlanta, GA 30331-2081, **Home Phone:** (404)696-3960. **Business Addr:** District Attorney, Fulton County, 136 Pryor St SW 3rd Fl Rm 301, Atlanta, GA 30303, **Business Phone:** (404)612-4982.

## HOWARD, RAY F.

Government official, executive director. **Personal:** Born Oct 5, 1945, Troy, AL; son of Arthur (deceased) and Maudie L Bennett (deceased); married Sharon G Harvey; children: Leslie R & Joy R. **Educ:** Cleveland State Univ, BBA, 1970; Case Western Res Univ Sch Mgt, Cleveland, OH, MBA, 1972. **Career:** Bausch & Lomb & UCO, Rochester, NY, mgr, planning & prod, customer serv, 1973-81; CIBA Vision Care, Atlanta, Ga, nat customer serv mgr, 1981-85; GMD, Dunwoody, Ga, prod mkt dir, 1985-87; Proj Mkt Group, Atlanta, Ga, pres, 1987-89; US Treas Dept, Internal Rev Serv Div, San Jose, Calif, asst dist dir, 1989-, dir, currently. **Orgs:** Am Mgt Asn, 1975-81; Sales & Mkt Execs Club, 1983-89; Am Soc Training & Develop, 1987-89; Sr Execs Asn, 1989-; Rotary Club Int, 1994-; Prod Develop & Mgt Asn. **Honors/Awds:** Sales & Mkt Awards, Bausch & Lomb & CIBA Vision, 1976-85; Achievement Award, United Way, 1989; Excellence Award, Atlanta Dist, IRS, 1990; Commissioners Award, 2000. **Home Addr:** 1721 Healey Walk SE, Smyrna, GA 30080, **Home Phone:** (770)431-4953. **Business Addr:** Director, US Treasury Department, 68 Sewall St, Augusta, ME 30308, **Business Phone:** (207)622-1508.

## HOWARD, RAYMOND

Lawyer, government official. **Personal:** Born Mar 13, 1935, St. Louis, MO; married Dorothy J; children: Raymond III, Monica, Heather & Angelique; married Sharon Cecile Enoex; children: 2. **Educ:** Univ Wis, BA; St Louis Univ, Sch Law, JD. **Career:** MO State Senate, sen; Mo House, representatives, 1964-68; St Louis Munic judge; Howard Law Firm, atty, personal injury, family law, malpractice, real estate & bus law, currently. **Orgs:** St Louis Christian Ctr; bd dirs & bd mem, St Louis Urban League; bd dir, atty, bd mem, Nat Asn Advan Colored People, St Louis; bd dir, bd mem, Metrop Young Men Christian Asn; bd dir, bd mem, Gateway Nat Bank; Nat Bar Asn; Am Bar Asn; St Louis Bar Asn; Am Trial Lawyers Asn; pres, St Louis Cong Racial Equality; Mt City Bar Asn; bd mem, St Louis Symphony Orchestra, chmn, Higher Educ Comt. **Honors/Awds:** Outstanding Man of America, Jr Chamber Com; St Louis Argus Newspaper Award; Outstanding Man of Kappa Alpha Psi, Outstanding Professional Achievement, Polemarch, Kappa Alpha Psi; Distinguished Service Award, St Louis Bar Asn; Distinguished Service Award, Lawyers Asn; Vashon High School Hall of Fame; Distinguish Service Award, St Louis Univ; Distinguished Service Award; NAACP's one of 100 Distinguished Citizens of St Louis; Outstanding Young Man Award, Jr Chamber Com; Legends Award, Mound City Bar Asn; Hall of Fame, Nat Bar Asn, 2014. **Special Achievements:** Second African American elected to the MO Senate; author of MO's Fair Employment Law, Fair Housing Law, Public Accommodation's Law, State Scholarship Law, Missouri's Equal Opportunity Employment Law; Won over 200 cases; Tried cases before US Supreme Court; Youngest Senator at Age 33. **Home Addr:** . **Business Addr:** Attorney, Private Practice, 225 S Meramec Suite 820, St Louis, MO 63105, **Business Phone:** (314)721-6622.

## HOWARD, SAMUEL HOUSTON

Executive. **Personal:** Born May 8, 1939, Marietta, OK; son of Nellie Gaines and Houston; married Karan A Wilson; children: Anica Lynne & Samuel II. **Educ:** Okla State Univ, BS, bus, 1961; Stanford Univ, MA, econs, 1963. **Career:** Gen Elec Co, fin analyst, 1963-66; White House, spec asst fel, 1966-67; Howard Univ, dir, 1967-68; HEW, consult secy, 1967-69; TAW Int Leasing Corp, vpres fin, secy, treas, 1968-72; HAI, vpres & treas; Phoenix Community Grp Inc, founder, pres, 1971-98; Meharry Med Col, vpres fin, 1973-77; Hosp Affil Int Inc, vpres, 1977-79, vpres & treas, 1980-81; INA Health Care Grp, vpres; Hosp Corp Am, vpres & treas, 1981-88, sr vpres pub affairs, 1988-89; Phoenix Holdings, founder, chmn, pres, chief exec oficer, 1989-; Xantus Corp, chmn & chief exec officer, 1993-2007; O'Charley's Inc, dir. **Orgs:** Phi Kappa Phi; Blue Key; Beta Gamma Sigma; Delta Sigma Pi; Alpha Phi Alpha; Human Rels Coun; Cordell Hall Coun; Lariats; Sigma Epsilon Sigma; Fed Am Hosp; Fin Exec Inst, Bd Nashville Br, Nat Asn Advan Colored People; Utah Sch Bus Adv Bd; TSU Presidents Adv Bd; St Thomas Hosp Bd Counors; Am Hosp Asn; chmn, Nashville Chamber Com; dir, Corp Child Care; dir, Genesis Health Ventures; dir, Potomac Group; dir, Nashville Elec Serv; nat chmn, Easter Seals Inc, 2000-03, vice chmn, 1995, nat dir, 1997-99; Nat Bipartisan Comn Future Medicare; trustee, Fisk Univ, 1984-96; Tenn Indust & Agr Develop Comn, 1985-1988; chmn, Nashville Conv Ctr Comn1986-87; founder & dir, 100 Black Men Mid Tenn; chmn, bd mem, Urban League Mid Tennl; bd mem, dir, Southeast Community Capital Corp; co-chmn, Nat Conf Christians & Jews Inc, 1993-94, 1986-87, comn chmn, 1988-92; chmn, Fin Comt, Metrop Nashville Conv Ctr; trustee, Leadership Nashville Found. **Special Achievements:** Book: The Flight of the Phoenix: Thoughts on Work and Life, 2007. **Home Addr:** 5320 Cherry Blossom Trail, Nashville, TN 37215, **Home Phone:** (615)373-5691. **Business Addr:** Owner, Chairman & Chief Executive Officer, Phoenix Holdings Inc, 216 Centerview Dr Suite 300, Brentwood, TN 37027-3227, **Business Phone:** (615)377-9480.

## HOWARD, SHERRI

Fashion model, athlete, actor. **Personal:** Born Jun 1, 1962, Sherman, TX; daughter of Eugene and Barbara. **Educ:** Calif State Univ, Los Angeles, BS, elec engineering. **Career:** Athlete, actress, fashion model, coach; Olympic athlete, 1984-88; The Scorpion King, actor, 2002; TV appearances: "Profiler", 1996; "Beverly Hills 90210", 1990; "Diagnosis Murder", 1993; "X-files", 1993; "Martial Law", 2000; "No Fare", 2000; "Criminal Minds", 2007; Head Girls/Sprints Coach. **Orgs:** Screen Actor's Guild; Am Fedn Tv & Radio Artists. **Honors/Awds:** First gold medal in the 200 meter, Arco Jesse Owens Games; runGold Medal, 4x400 meter relay, Olympics, 1984; National Collegiate Athletic Association, I Track & Field Championship titles 400 meters; Silver Medal, 4x400 meter relay, Olympics, 1988; Athlete of the Year. **Special Achievements:** Appeared in numerous commercials. **Business Addr:** Actor, c/o Ross Stephens Artist Management, 3760 Cahuenga Blvd Suite 209, Studio City, CA 91604, **Business Phone:** (818)760-0801.

## HOWARD, SHIRLEY M.

Educator, college teacher. **Personal:** Born Dec 15, 1935, Chicago, IL; married Johnnie; children: Patrice, Paula & Christopher. **Educ:** Cook Col Sch Nursing, dipl, 1960; DePaul Univ, BSN, 1969, MSN, 1972; Univ Iowa, PhD, 1972. **Career:** Gov's State Univ, res grant, 1972-75; Village Nursing Serv, co-owner, nursing admin, instr, publ health nurse, prof health sci; HEW Proj, nursing educ & res, auth & proj dir; Health Sci Instrnl Prog, coord. **Orgs:** Nat League Nursing; Asn Rehab Nurses; Deans & Dirs Coun Baccalaureate & Higher Degree Progs; consult, Robbins Human Resource Ctr; Independent Peoples Party; PTA; bd mem, Family Health Ctr; adv bd, Kennedy-King Col Nursing Alumni; bd mem, Comprehensive Comn Health Planning & Develop Coun. **Honors/Awds:** Cert Merit, Youth Motivation Comn & Chicago Merit Employ Comn, 1971-72. **Home Addr:** 13407 S Monticello Ave, Robbins, IL 60472-1122, **Home Phone:** (708)710-5132.

## HOWARD, STEPHEN (STEPHEN CHRISTOPHER HOWARD)

Basketball player, broadcaster. **Personal:** Born Jul 15, 1970, Dallas, TX. **Educ:** DePaul Univ, attended 1992. **Career:** Basketball player (retired), basketball executive, speaker; Utah Jazz, forward, shooting forward, 1992-94, 1997; San Antonio Spurs, 1996-97; Seattle Supersonics, power forward, 1997-98; Acappella Juice, owner, 1999-2001; Al Hilal, 2006; Papa Murphy's Int, owner, 2002-03; Howard Group, chief exec officer, pres, 2007-16; Proj Basketball, chief exec officer & founder, 2007-; ESPN, Col Basketball Commentator, 2007-, col basketball studio analyst, 2011-; Nat Consortium Acad & Sport & Ctr Study Sport & Soc, 2008-; Stephen Howard's Experience, speaker, 2009-; Longhorn Network, studio analyst, 2011-13; Fox Sports, studio analyst, 2012-. **Honors/Awds:** Wendell Smith Award of Excellence, 1990; Honorable Mention Anson Mount Scholar Athlete, 1991; Chicago Amateur Athlete of the Year, 1991; Anson Mount Scholar Athlete of the Year, 1992; Great Midwest Conference Award of Excellence, 1992; DePaul's All-time leader in Free Throw's, 1992; Inducted, DePaul University's Hall of Fame, 2009. **Business Addr:** Motivational Speaker, Stephen Howard's Experience, 3941 Legacy Dr Suite 204, Plano, TX 75023.

## HOWARD, SUSAN E.

Writer, lecturer. **Personal:** Born Apr 9, 1961, Ft. Wayne, IN; daughter of John Sr and Ferdie A Webster. **Educ:** Syracuse Univ, Syracuse, NY, BS, 1983. **Career:** Frost Illustrated, Fort Wayne, Ind, intern, 1978; Jour-Gazette, Fort Wayne, Ind, intern, 1978-79; Daily Orange (campus paper), Syracuse, NY, ed ed, 1982; Courier-Jour, Louisville, KY, intern, 1982; Atlanta Jour-Const, Atlanta, Ga, sports writer, mag writer, 1983-88; Newsday, Melville, NY, news reporter, feature writer, 1988; Ind Univ-Purdue Univ Fort Wayne, lectr, currently. **Orgs:** Nat Asn Black Journalists, 1983-; Nat Black Women's Health Proj, 1988-. **Home Addr:** 4 Lawrence Hill Rd, Huntington, NY 11743-3114, **Home Phone:** (516)549-1593. **Business Addr:** Lecturer, Indiana University-Purdue University Fort Wayne, Classroom-Med Bldg Rm 143, Melville, NY 11747-4250, **Business Phone:** (260)481-6100.

## HOWARD, TANYA MILLICENT

Computer engineer. **Personal:** Born May 4, 1968, Chapel Hill, NC; daughter of Charlie Edward and Sadie Ann Graves. **Educ:** Howard Univ, Wash, DC, BS, engineering, 1991. **Career:** Close-Up Found, Alexandria, Va, transp clerk, 1989-; Dept Defense, Wash, DC, tech clerk, 1989-; Martin Marietta, Air Traffic Systs, systs engr, 1991-. **Orgs:** Secy, Howard Univ Sch Engineering, 1989-90; news ed, Howard Engr Mag, 1989-91; Region II secy, Nat Soc Black Engrs, 1990-91; chairperson, Inst Elec & Electronics Engrs, 1990-91; comt chair, Springfield Baptist Church, 1990-91; Toastmasters Inc, 1991-92; Nat Asn Female Execs, 1991-92. **Honors/Awds:** Academic Award, Nat Soc Black Engrs, 1990. **Home Addr:** 4613 Sargent Rd, Washington, DC 20017. **Business Addr:** Systems Engineer, Martin Marietta - Air Traffic Systems, 400 Va Ave SW, Washington, DC 20024.

## HOWARD, TERRENCE

Actor. **Personal:** Born Mar 11, 1969, Chicago, IL; son of Tyrone and Anita Jeanine Williams; married Miranda, Jan 1, 2013?; children: 1; married Michelle Ghent, Jan 1, 2010?, (divorced 2011); married Lori McCommas, Jan 1, 1989?, (divorced 2001; remarried and divorced 2005-08); children: Aubrey, Hunter & Heavenly. **Educ:** Pratt Inst, chem engineering, attended. **Career:** Actor: Highlights--ABC Miniseries "The Jacksons: An American Dream", 1992; TV Movie "The O.J. Simpson Story", 1995; theatrical movie "Mr. Holland's Opus", 1995; TV series "Sparks" (as lead Greg Sparks), 1996-98; theatrical movie "The Players Club", 1998; TV series "NYPD Blue", 1998-99; theatrical release "The Best Man, 1999. TV movie "King of the World" (as Cassius Clay), 2000; theatrical release "Big Momma's House", 2000; "Love Beat the Hell Out of Me", 2000; "Angel Eyes", 2001; "Glitter", 2001. TV series "Street Time", 2003; "Soul Food", 2002-03. Theatrical release "Crash", 2004; "Ray", 2004; "Hustle & Flow", 2005; "Four Brothers", 2005; "Iron Man", 2008; "The Princess and the Frog", 2009. TV series "Law & Order: LA", 2010-11. Theatrical release "Winnie Mandela", 2011; "Red Tails", 2012; "Movie 43", 2013; "Lee Daniels' The Butler", 2013; "The Best Man Holiday", 2013. TV series "Wayward Pines", 2015-; "Empire", 2015-. **Orgs:** Dramatic jury mem, Sundance Film Festival, 2006. **Honors/Awds:** NAACP Image Award, Independent Spirit Award nomination, and a Chicago Film Critics nomination for "The Best Man" (1999), Academy Award for Best Actor, "Hustle & Flow", 2006.

## HOWARD, TY L.

Football player. **Personal:** Born Nov 30, 1973, Columbus, OH. **Educ:** Ohio State Univ, BA, Eng, 1996. **Career:** Football player (retired), mgr; Ariz Cardinals, defensive back, 1997-98, Cincinnati Bengals, defensive back & corner back & left corner back & right corner back, 1999; Tenn Titans, defensive back, 2000; Worthington Steel, territory mgr, 2000-08; CR Bard, territory mgr, 2008-10; St Jude Med, struct heart territory mgr, 2010-, Regional Sales Dir, 2016-. **Business Addr:** Regional Sales Director, St. Jude Medical, 1 St Jude Med Dr, St. Paul, MN 55117-9983, **Business Phone:** (651)756-2000.

## HOWARD, VERA GOUKE

Educator. **Personal:** Born Brooklyn, NY. **Educ:** Baruch Col, BBA, 1958; NY Univ, MA, 1969. **Career:** NY City Bd Educ, 1963-71; Brooklyn Col, adj instr, prog lectr; Manpower Develop Training, teacher; NY Dept Welfare, social worker investr; NY Inst Technol, counr, 1971-. **Orgs:** NY City Personnel Guid Asn; Black Alliance Educrs; vol counr, Long Island Asn Black Counr. **Business Addr:** 1303 Pk Pl, Brooklyn, NY 11213.

## HOWARD, WARDELL MACK

Opera singer. **Personal:** Born Apr 11, 1934, Shreveport, LA; son of Arthur Mitchell and Lubertha Williams; married Shirley Rollins; children: Merlin W. **Educ:** NY Univ, attended 1976; Univ Calif, Los Angeles, music; Prof Theater Inst, Los Angeles, Civic Light Opera. **Career:** The Roger Wagner Choral, soloist, 1980-85; The Los Angeles Master Choral, 1980-85; The Los Angeles Cult Affairs, choral-conductor, 1985-; Opera Roles Performed: La Boheme, Colline, Puccini; Cavalleria- Rusticano; Porgy and Bess; Don Giovanni, Leporello, Mozart; Tremonisha, Parson Alltalk, Scott Joplin; Univ Calif Opera Theatre, mem; Album: Mostly Broadway, 2005; honored classic: "Show Boat"; "Ole Man River"; singer, currently. **Orgs:** Los Angeles Master Choral; Roger Wagner Choral; City Los Angeles Cultural Affairs. **Honors/Awds:** Southern Calif Motion Picture Coun Contribution to The Entertainment Industry, 1986; Saints & Sinners, Great Artist Award, 1986, 1988; Women's American ORT, Golden Names For Israel, 1980. **Business Addr:** Singer, 8746 Tobias Ave Suite 7, Panorama City, CA 91402-2307, **Business Phone:** (818)891-4226.

## HOWARD-COLEMAN, BILLIE JEAN

Educator, nurse. **Personal:** Born Jul 31, 1950, Chicago, IL. **Educ:** Univ Ill, Chicago, BSN, 1973; Loyola Univ, MSN, 1976. **Career:** Univ Ill Hosp, staff nurse, 1973-76; Univ Ill Col Nursing, instr, 1976-77; Michael Reese Hosp, clin specialist, 1977-78; Univ Ill Col Nursing, asst prof, 1978-81; Univ Chicago Hosp, supvr, 1981-83; Nursing Provident Med Ctr, assoc dir, 1983-84; Chicago St Univ, asst prof nursing, 1984-; Chicago St Univ, asst prof nursing, 1987; Chicago Bd Educ, sch nurse, teacher, 1987; Chicago Pub High Sch, teacher, currently. **Orgs:** Ill Sch Health Asn; past mem, Sigma Theta Tau, March Dimes Perinatal Nursing Adv Coun; Chicago Teachers Union. **Honors/Awds:** School Nurse of the Year, Chicago, 2001. **Home Addr:** 5925 Throop St, Chicago, IL 60425, **Home Phone:** (708)758-8280. **Business Addr:** Teacher, Chicago Public Schools, 125 S Clark, Chicago, IL 60628, **Business Phone:** (773)553-2688.

## HOWE, PROF. RUTH-ARLENE W.

Educator. **Personal:** Born Nov 21, 1933, Scotch Plains, NJ; daughter of Grace-Louise Randolph Wood and Curtis Alexander; married Theodore Holmes; children: Marian, Curtis, Helen & Edgar. **Educ:** Wellesley Col, AB, 1955; Simmons Col, MSW, 1957; Boston Col, JD, 1974. **Career:** Nat Inst Ment Health, fel, 1956-57; Cleveland Ohio Cath Youth Serv Bur, case worker, 1957-61; Tufts Delta Health Ctr, Mound Bayou, Miss, housing develop consult, 1969-70; Simmons Col Sch Social Work, instr soc pol, 1970-78; Law & Child Develop Proj, DHEW/ACYF Funded B C Law Sch, asst dir, 1977-79; Boston Col Law Sch, from asst prof law to prof law, 1977-2008, prof emer, 2009; Mary Ingraham Bunting Inst, Radcliffe Col, Hermon Dunlap Smith fel law & social/pub policy, 1994-95; Third World Law J, fac advisor. **Orgs:** Bd mem, Boston League Women Voters, 1963-68; clerk, Grimes-King Found Elderly Inc, 1972-; guardian adv litem, Mass Family & Probate Ct, 1979-; ABA Tech NCCUSL Uniform Adoption & Marital Property Acts, 1980-83; Mass Gov St Comn Child Support Enforcement, 1985; Mass Adv Comn Child Support Guidelines, 1986-89; Mass Gov/MBA Comn Legal Needs C, 1986-87; NCCUSL Uniform Putative & Unknown Fathers Act Reporter, 1986-88; ed bd, Family Advocate, ABA sect Family Law, 1989-95, 2001-; Mass Supreme Judicial Ct Comn, Study Racial & Ethnic Bias Courts, 1990-94; US State Dept, Study Group Inter country Adoption, 1991-97; adv, Black Law Stud Asn; treas, Black Alumni Network. **Home Addr:** 19 Akron St, Roxbury, MA 02119-3409, **Home Phone:** (617)445-2344. **Business Addr:** Professor Emeritus, Boston College, 885 Centre St EW322, Newton Center, MA 02459-1163, **Business Phone:** (617)552-4377.

## HOWELL, AMAZIAH, III

Executive. **Personal:** Born Oct 12, 1948, Goldsboro, NC; son of Amaziah Jr and Theresa Reid; married Jessica McCoy; children: Joy Elizabeth & Aimee Denise. **Educ:** Johnson C Smith Univ, Charlotte, NC, attended 1968; NY Inst Credit, attended 1970; Amos Tuck Sch Bus, Dartmouth Univ, minority bus exec prog. **Career:** Manufacturers Hanover Trust Co, credit investr, 1968-72; Off US Sen James L Buckley, spec asst, 1973-76; Wallace & Wallace Fuel Oil Co, mkt mgr, 1978-79; Asn Minority Enterprises NY Inc, exec dir, 1976-77, 1979-81; Las Energy Corp, Roosevelt NY, vpres, 1981-85; Howell Petrol Prod Inc, Brooklyn, NY, pres & chief exec officer, 1985-. **Orgs:** Am Asn Blacks Energy; Brooklyn Chamber Com; exec bd, Brooklyn Sports Found; Comn Students African Descent NY City Bd Educ; Comt Econ Develop; bus adv coun, Dist Community Sch; adv bd & oversight comt, chmn, Downtown Brooklyn Community; Environ Action Coalition; vpres, Halsey St Black Asn; Helen Keller Servs Blind; Latimer Woods Econ Develop Corp; exec adv coun, Long Island Univ; adv coun, Metrop Transit Authority; New York & NJ Minority Purchasing Coun; planning comt, vpres, chmn, Pub Sch 282; adv comt, US Courthouse Foley Sq; Cornerstone Baptist Church; New York Water Bd. **Home Addr:** 317 Halsey St Apt A, Brooklyn, NY 11216-2411, **Home Phone:** (718)453-0770. **Business Addr:** President, Chief Executive Officer, Howell Petrol Prod Inc, 499 Van Brunt St Suite 9, Brooklyn, NY 11231, **Business Phone:** (718)855-4400.

## HOWELL, REV. CHESTER THOMAS

Clergy, executive. **Personal:** Born Mar 23, 1937, Tarentum, PA; son of Hunter Lee and Jessie Leona Sharp; married Loretta J Lewis; children: Tracey Lynn, Jennifer Lynne & Hunter Lee II. **Educ:** Allegheny Tech Inst, indust electronics technol/technician, 1971, assoc's degree, electronics, 1972; Third Dist African Methodist Episcopal Theol Inst, 1994; Payne Theol Sem. **Career:** Executive (retired), superintendent; Veterans Admin Hosp, nursing asst, 1961-68; Atlantic Design Corp, elec engr, 1968-72; Xerox Corp, Pittsburgh, dist bus mgr, chief financial officer, 1988-90; Nat City Bank, customer serv rep, 1999-2002; Penn State Univ, security officer, 2005-; Bethel AME Church, church sch supt, currently. **Orgs:** Free & Accepted Masons, Prince Hall, 1970-79; pres, Metrop Area Minority Employees, Xerox, 1979; deacon, E End Baptist Tabernacle, Bridgeport, 1981-88; Cent Baptist, Syracuse, 1988-90; Human Rights Comn, Harrison Twp Sch Dist; Habitat Humanities, Family Nurture Comt; EdRev Bd, Valley Daily News Dispatch. **Honors/Awds:** Black Achievers Award, Young Mens Christian Asn, 1980; ordained African Methodist Episcopal minister, local deacon, Bethel AMEC, 1992; ordained local elder, Bethel AMEC, Tarentum, Pa 15084, 1996. **Home Addr:** 1308 Montana Ave, Natrona Heights, PA 15065, **Home Phone:** (724)224-9866. **Business Addr:** Superintendent, Bethel AME Church, 250 W 7th Ave, Tarentum, PA 15084, **Business Phone:** (724)224-2417.

## HOWELL, GERALD T.

Insurance executive. **Educ:** Tenn State Univ, BS, 1936. **Career:** Universal Life Ins Co, agt & other offices, 1941-61, agency dir, 1961-66, dir agencies, 1967, vpres & dir agencies, 1968-79, sr vpres & dir field opers, 1980-85, first vpres & secy & chief exec officer, 1986-89, pres & chief operating officer, 1990-95, chmn bd, 1995, exec vpres, Memphis, Tenn. **Orgs:** Nat Ins Asn; Nat Asn Advan Colored People; Emmanuel Epis Ch Alpha Phi & Alpha; Mason; Shriner. **Honors/Awds:** Sports-men's Club Special Serv Award, Nat Ins Asn, 1974; Blount Award, Nat Ins Asn, 1974. **Home Addr:** 655 Riverside Dr Apt S502, Memphis, TN 38103-4623.

## HOWELL, MALQUEEN

Educator. **Personal:** Born Apr 3, 1949, Calhoun County, SC. **Educ:** Benedict Col, BA, 1971; Univ Nebr, MA, 1972. **Career:** Benedict Col, eng instr. **Orgs:** Founding pres, Calhoun County Jr Improv League, 1966; Nat Asn Advan Colored People; adv panel, St Human Affairs Comn; Study & Preserv Black Hist; Art & Folklore Simons-Mann Col, 1973; voter educ proj, Heart Fund Campaign; United Way; Alpha Kappa Alpha. **Home Addr:** 4900 Katy St, Columbia, SC 29203. **Business Addr:** Instructor, Benedict College, 1600 Harden St, Columbia, SC 29204, **Business Phone:** (803)253-5000.

## HOWELL, RACHEL

Human services worker. **Personal:** Born May 28, 1961, Detroit, MI; daughter of Carmen Perry and L C; children: Bruce & Ariana. **Educ:** Franklin, basic emergency med technician, 1987; Detroit EMS Training Acad, EMT-S, 1990; Detroit Receiving Hosp, advan cardiac life support, 1996; Super Med Educ, paramedic, 1997. **Career:** E Jefferson Mkt, Detroit, Mich, cashier, lottery, 1980-84; Barnes & Noble (WCCC), Detroit, Mich, cashier, clerk, 1984-87; Detroit Fire Dept, Detroit, Mich, EMT, 1987-90, specialist, 1990-97, paramedic, 1997-; Int Union Operating Engrs, Local 547, from Union steward to chief steward, 1998-2003, bus agt, EMMTTA rep, 2005-. **Orgs:** Exec bd mem & trustee, Detroit Asn Educ Off Employees. **Honors/Awds:** Life Saver of the Year, Detroit E Medl Control, 1990-91; Life Saver of the Year, 100 Club, 1990-91. **Home Addr:** 3011 Harding, Detroit, MI 48214. **Business Addr:** EMMTTA Representative, International Union of Operating Engineers Local 547, 24270 W 7th Mile Rd, Detroit, MI 48219, **Business Phone:** (202)429-9100.

## HOWELL, ROBERT J., JR.

Executive. **Personal:** Born Feb 24, 1935, New York, NY; married Elestine. **Educ:** New Sch, MA; NY Univ, PhD. **Career:** Prof Recruitment & Replacement, spl asst dir personnel, 1967-68, chief, 1968-72; Cornell Grad Sch & Indust Labor Rel, consult, 1970-71; Div Employ, dep dir, 1972-74; NY State Civil Serv Commision Prof Cand Internal Pub Personnel Asn, oral examr; Human Resources Admin; Personnel Admin. **Orgs:** Hundred Black Men. **Home Addr:** 19 3rd Ave, Westbury, NY 11590-2523, **Home Phone:** (516)333-9549. **Business Addr:** 271 Church St, New York, NY 10013.

## HOWELL, ROBERT L.

Educator. **Personal:** Born Oct 29, 1950, Paterson, NJ; son of David Sr and Sarah Alice; married Yolanda Feliciano; children: Roberto M Jr, Danielle Elsie Sarah & Reynaldo Pressly. **Educ:** William Patterson Col, BA, elem educ & teaching, 1971, ME, 1974. **Career:** Prin (retired); Paterson Pub Sch, teacher, 1971-88, vice prin, 1988-89, prin, 1990, Eastside High Sch, prin, No 29 Elem Sch, prin, 2007-. **Orgs:** Nat Educ Asn, 1971-; Nat Asn Sec Sch Principals, 1973-, 2000-; Psi Kappa Nu Fraternity; Nat Asn Elem Sch Principals, 1990-; bd dir, Positive Impact, 1992-. **Home Addr:** 310 E 38th St, Paterson, NJ 07504-1312, **Home Phone:** (973)523-8278. **Business Addr:** Principal, Paterson High Schools, 88 Danforth Ave, Paterson, NJ 07501, **Business Phone:** (973)321-0290.

## HOWELL, SHARON MARIE, SR.

Executive, dean (education). **Personal:** Born Dec 6, 1950, Minneapolis, MN; daughter of Tyler Jackson Jr and Juanita Olivia Marino. **Educ:** Xavier Univ La, BS, 1972; Univ St Thomas, St Paul, MA, 1985; Midwest Canon Law Soc Inst, Mundelein, IL, attended 1985; St Paul Sem, St Paul, MN, attended 1986. **Career:** Acad Natural Sci Philadelphia, Avondale, Pa, res asst, 1972-74; 3M Co, St Paul, MN, anal chemist, 1974-76; Control Data Corp, Bloomington, MN, chemist, 1976-78; Minneapolis Inst Art, asst coordr exhibs, 1978-79; Minn State Dept Agr, St Paul, MN, anal chemist, 1979-80; Home Good Shepherd, St Paul, MN youth worker, 1980-83; Church St Leonard Port Maurice, pastoral minister, 1983-84; Univ St Thomas, St Paul, MN, dir multicultural & stud serv, dir diversity initiatives; Archdiocese St Paul & Minneapolis, St Paul, MN, intern, 1984-86, Black Cath Concerns, liaison, 1986; Archdiocesan Cms Black Cath, exec secy, 1986; Univ St Thomas, dir, asst dean & stud reconciliation & ombudsperson, currently. **Orgs:** Bd mem, Comn Evangelization, 1983-86; Asn Pastoral Ministers, 1984; assoc mem, Canon Law Soc Am, 1984; bd mem, Comn Ministry, 1985-89; chair, Comn Ministry, 1987-89; Minn Interfaith Coun Affordable Housing, 1988-90; bd dir, Greater Minneapolis Coun Churches, 1989-91; Leadership St Paul, 1989-90; Sisters St Joseph, Carondelet, St Paul Prov; bd dir, Cath Charities, 1990-95; bd trustee, Col St Catherine, St Paul, 1994; Coalition Ministerial Asn. **Home Addr:** 2129 Grand Ave Suite 2, St. Paul, MN 55105, **Home Phone:** (612)699-5286. **Business Addr:** Assistant Dean, University of St Thomas, 2115 Summit Ave, St. Paul, MN 55105, **Business Phone:** (651)962-6076.

## HOWLETT, WALTER, JR.

Chairperson, president (organization). **Educ:** Univ Ala, BS, acct, 1981, CPA, 1983. **Career:** Booker T Wash Ins Co Inc, chmn, pres & chief exec officer, currently; A G Gaston Construct Co Inc, chmn, pres & chief exec officer, currently; TBD Creative Inc, corp partner. **Orgs:** Am South Bank Birmingham; Bus Coun Ala; Birmingham Chamber Com; Univ Ala Birmingham Sch Bus Adv Bd; United Way Cent Ala; Jr Achievement Ala; Boy Scouts Am; Associated Builders & Contractors. **Business Addr:** Chief Executive Officer, A G Gaston Construction Co Inc, 310 18th St N Suite 500, Birmingham, AL 35203-0697, **Business Phone:** (205)328-0376.

## HOWROYD, JANICE BRYANT

Entrepreneur. **Personal:** Born Sep 1, 1952, Tarboro, NC; married Bernard; children: Katharyn & Brett. **Educ:** NC Agr & Tech State Univ, BS, eng; Univ Md, MS; NC State Univ, PhD. **Career:** Am Red Cross; Nat Acad Sci; Billboard mag, temp secy, 1976-77; ACT*1 Personnel Servs, founder & pres, 1978-, chmn, currently; NC A&T, chair. **Orgs:** Nat Asn Women Bus Owners; bd dir, Urban League Los Angeles; bd dir, Greater LA Dept African Am Chamber Comn; bd mem, Econ Develop Corp County Los Angeles; bd mem, Los Angeles Urban League; bd mem, Loyola Marymount Univ; bd mem, Northrop-Rice Aviation Inst Technol; Int Women's Coun; bd mem, Women's Leadership Bd, Harvard Univ. **Honors/Awds:** Minority Enterprise Develop Week Achievement Award, US Dept of Com, 1992; Entrepreneur of the Year, AT&T Univ, 1994; Spirit of Am Enterprise Presidential Award, 2005; Entrepreneur of The Year, BET cable tv network, 2008. **Special Achievements:** Numerous television shows: "The Oprah Winfrey Show" and "The Tavis Smiley Show"; Been twice named by the Star Group as one of the 50 Leading Women Entrepreneurs of the World, the First African-American woman honored. **Business Addr:** Founder & Chairman, Chief Executive Officer, ACT*1 Personnel Services, 1999 W 190th St, Torrance, CA 90504-6202, **Business Phone:** (310)370-5939.

### HOWZE, REV. JOSEPH LAWSON

Clergy. **Personal:** Born Aug 30, 1923, Daphne, AL; son of Albert Otis and Helen Artamesa (deceased). **Educ:** Ala State Jr Col; AL State Univ, BA, 1948; St Bonaventure Univ, DD, 1959; Phillips Col, bus mgt, 1980. **Career:** Mobile Cent High Sch, teacher, 1952; Cath Sch, St Monic, teacher, 1952; Roman Catholic Church, ordained priest, 1959; pastor in various churches including: Charlotte, Southern Pines, Durham, Sanford, Asheville, 1959-72; Natchez-Jackson, aux bishop, 1972-77; Diocese Biloxi, bishop, 1977-2001, bishop emer, 2001-. **Orgs:** Trustee, Xavier Univ, New Orleans; MS Health Care Comn; Nat Coun Cath Bishops & USCC; educ comt, USCC; Social Develop & World Peace Comt; liaison comt, Off Black Catholics, Nat Coun Cath Bishops; bd dir, Biloxi Reg Med Ctr; Dem; KC Knights St Peter Claver; Nat Coun Cath Bishops; Biloxi Regional Health Ctr Bd; bd dir, Gulf Pines Girl Scout Coun; bd dir, Knights Columbus; bd dir, Knights Peter Claver; bd dir, Nat Coun Cath Bishops Interreligious Ecumenical Affairs Comt. **Honors/Awds:** Received many honorary degrees from various universities including: Univ Portland, 1974; Sacred Heart Col, 1977; St Bonaventure Univ, 1977; Manhattan Col, 1979; Bible Crusade Col, 1987; Belmont Abbey Col, 1999. **Special Achievements:** Became one of few Black bishops in history of Catholic Church in US; first Bishop of the New Diocese of Biloxi MS 1977; first Black Catholic bishop to head a Catholic Diocese in the USA since 1900. **Home Addr:** PO Box 1189, Biloxi, MS 39532, **Home Phone:** (228)396-1825. **Business Addr:** Bishop Emeritus, Diocese Biloxi, 1790 Popps Ferry Rd, Biloxi, MS 39532-1189, **Business Phone:** (228)702-2111.

### HOWZE, KAREN AILEEN

Lawyer, consultant, editor. **Personal:** Born Dec 8, 1950, Detroit, MI; daughter of Manuel and Dorothy June Smith; children: Charlene, Karie JoAnn & Lucinda Gloria Patrice. **Educ:** Univ Southern Calif, BS, jour, 1972; Hastings Col Law, JD, 1977. **Career:** Detroit Free Press, reporter, 1971; San Francisco Chronicle, reporter, ed, 1972-78; News day, Long Island, asst ed, 1978-79; Gannett Newspapers, asst managing ed, sunday features ed, 1979-80, dir corp news systs newspaper div, ed; Rochester Times Union, asst managing ed, 1979-80; Rochester Dem & Chronicle, Sunday features ed, 1980-81; USA Today, founding ed, 1981, managing ed systs, 1982-86, managing ed int ed, 1986-88; Gannett Co Inc, Corp News Systs, ed, 1988-91, news exec, 1989; mgt consult, 1990-; Howze & Assocs, diversity Consult, 1990-2002; Howard Univ, Sch Communs, lectr, 1990-92; Adoption Support Inst, pres & founder, 1990-; Am Univ Sch Commun, lectr, prof, 1991-94; DC Super Ct, Family Div, Remedial Proj, spec master, 2000-01; Girl Scout Coun Nation's Capital, bd dir; Am Bar Asn, Ctr C & Law, dir, Adolescent Health Props, 2001-02; DC Super Ct Family Ct, magistrate judge, 2002-; Am Press Inst, presenter; Poynter Inst Media Studies, presenter; Maynard Inst Journalism Educ, presenter. **Orgs:** Nat Asn Black Journal Sigma Delta Chi Women-Commun Alameda Co Comm Hlth Adv Bd; guest lect local comm col Amer Society Newspaper Editors; vice-chair, Minority Opportunities Comm, Amer Newspaper Publisher's Asn; bd dir, North AMR CN Lon Adoptable Children; bd mem, IST; bd mem, Chelsea School; chap mayor'saCOM on Placement ChildrenFamily Homes; Am Bar Asn, 1993-, Probate Educ Comt; Girl Scouts Womens Adv Bd; chmn, Super Ct DC Adoption Rules Advisory; chmn, Wash Bar Asn, 2007-08. **Honors/Awds:** Business Woman of the Year, Spellman Alumni, Wash, DC, 1986; Sr Ed, And Still We Rise, interviews with 50 Black Americans by Barbara Reynolds, 1987. **Special Achievements:** Publications: And Still We Rise, Interviews with 50 Black Americans by Barbara Reynolds, 1987; Making Differences Work: Cultural Context in Abuse and Neglect Practice for Judges and Attorneys, 1997; Health for Teens in Care : A Judges Guide and Making Differences Work :Cultural Context in Abuse and Neglect Practice, 2002; She was selected as the first Congressional Coalition on Adoption Angel in Adoption for the District of Columbia. **Home Addr:** 1905 Tulip St NW, Washington, DC 20012, **Home Phone:** (202)291-2290. **Business Addr:** Family Court Magistrate Judge, District of Columbia Superior Court, 4450 Moultrie Courthouse, Washington, DC 20001, **Business Phone:** (202)879-1061.

### HOXBY, CAROLINE M.

Economist, education reformer, college teacher. **Personal:** Born Apr 16, 1966; married Blair. **Educ:** Harvard Univ, AB, 1988; Univ Oxford, MPhil, 1990; Mass Inst Technol, PhD, 1994. **Career:** Harvard Univ, asst prof, 1994-97, Morris Khan Assoc Prof Econs, 1997-2000, Allie S. Freed Prof Econs, 2001-07, Harvard Col prof, 2005-07; Paris Sch Econs, vis prof, 2006-07; Stanford Univ, Scott & Donya Bommer Prof Econs, 2007-; Nat Bur Econ Res, dir Econs Educ Prog; Hoover Inst, sr fel; Stanford Inst Econ Policy Res, sr fel. **Orgs:** Nat Bd Educ Sci (presidential appointee), Brookings Inst; Hoover Koret Task Force. **Special Achievements:** Rhodes Scholarship, 1988; National Science Foundation Graduate Fellowship, 1990-93; Ford Foundation Fellowship, 1993; National Tax Association Award, 1994; Bunting Institute Fellow, 1996; MacArthur Foundation Fellowship, 1997-2004; Alfred P. Sloan Research Fellowship in Economics, 1999; Carnegie Scholar, 2000; Global Leader of Tomorrow, World Economic Forum, 2002, 2003, 2008; Phi Beta Kappa Prize, 2006; Thomas B. Fordham Prize, 2006; Stanford Economics Department Teacher of the Year, 2013; Smithsonian Institution Ingenuity Award, 2013; John and Lydia Pearce Mitchell University Fellow, 2014. **Business Addr:** Stanford University, 246 Landau Econs Bldg, Stanford, CA 94305, **Business Phone:** (650)725-8719.

### HOYE, CHERRON. See JOYCE, ELLA.

### HOYLE, DR. CLASSIE G.

Educator, college teacher, dean (education). **Personal:** Born Mar 26, 1936, Annapolis, MD; daughter of Nathaniel Daniel Gillis and Truma Lawson Elliott; married Daniel C; children: Dennis James & Lynne Valarie Jones. **Educ:** Morgan State Univ, BS, 1958, MS, 1968; Univ Iowa, PhD, 1977. **Career:** Lab scientist, 1958-59; sci teacher, 1960-68; Morgan State Univ, sci teacher, 1968-73; grad teaching asst, 1974-76; Coop Educ, coordr, 1976-77; Career Serv Placement Ctr, asst dir, 1977-78; Univ Iowa, dir affirmative action, 1978-82; Clarke Col, vpres acad affairs, 1982-85; Univ Iowa, Iowa City, IA, asst dean, 1985-90; NIH/NIGMS, Bethesda, MD, health scientist admin, 1990-; City Annapolis Coun, Ward 3, alderwoman, 2013. **Orgs:** Sen Scholar, 1954-58; Beta Kappa Chi, 1957; Alpha Kappa Mu, 1957; Kappa Delta Pi, 1958; Nat Sci Teachers Asn; Asn Educ Teachers Sci; Nat Asn Biol Teachers; Nat Sci Fel, 1965-68; den mother Cub Scouts, 1968-74; chairperson, courtesy comm Morgan St Univ, 1969-72; admin asst, Mt Lebanon Bapist Church, 1970-73; secy treas, Fed Credit Union, 1970-73; secy, Morgan St Univ, 1972-73; Higher Educ Title III Grant, 1973-75; SoFel Fund, 1975-76; Iowa pres Am Coun Educ Nat Identification Prog, 1979-81; pres, Phi Delta Kappa, 1980. **Home Addr:** 2089 Forest Dr, Annapolis, MD 21401, **Home Phone:** (443)949-7755. **Business Addr:** Alderwoman, City of Annapolis Council, 160 Duke Gloucester St, Annapolis, MD 21401, **Business Phone:** (410)263-7942.

### HOYT, HON. KENNETH M.

Judge. **Personal:** Born Mar 2, 1948, San Augustine, TX; son of Earl and Fannie; married Veola Johnson; children: Michael, Stacy & Justin. **Educ:** Tex Southern Univ, AB, 1969, Thurgood Marshall Sch Law, JD, 1972. **Career:** Judge; Pvt pract, 1972-85; city atty, 1975-81; 125th Civil Dist Ct, State Tex, presiding judge, 1981-82; State Tex Col Trial Advocacy Prog, fac, 1981-82; 125th Civil Dist Ct, State Tex, presiding judge, 1981-82; Tex Southern Univ, Thurgood Marshall Sch Law, adj prof, 1983-84; First Dist Ct Appeals Tex, justice, 1985-88; US Dist Ct, CJA Comt, chair, judge, currently. **Business Addr:** Federation Judge, US District Judge, 515 Rusk St, Houston, TX 77002, **Business Phone:** (713)250-5500.

### HOYTE, DR. ARTHUR HAMILTON

Educator, physician. **Personal:** Born Mar 22, 1938, Boston, MA; married Stephanie Hebron; children: Jacques. **Educ:** Harvard Col, BA, 1960; Columbia Univ Col Physicians & Surgeons, MD, 1964; San Francisco Gen Hosp, internship, 1965; Pres Hosp, resident, 1968. **Career:** Kaiser Found Hosp, 1968-70; E Palo Alto Neighbourhood Health Ctr, 1969-70; Off Econ Opportunity, med officer, 1970-71; Health Care Serv, consult, 1971-; Georgetown Univ Sch Med, asst prof ob-gyn & community med, 1971-99, exec dir, off minority stud develop, 1972-98, Georgetown Exp Med Studies Prog, founder, 1976, vice chancellor med ctr. **Orgs:** Medico-Chirurgical Soc DC, 1974-; Coalition Health Adv, 1975-; Boys Club Wash, 1975-; pres, DC Sci Fair Asn, 1976-77; Presidential Task Force, 1976; DC United Way. **Honors/Awds:** Civil Service Award, Wash Region Med Prog, 1975; The Arthur Hoyte MD Award, Named in Honor. **Home Addr:** 1425 4th St SW, Washington, DC 20024, **Home Phone:** (301)309-3864. **Business Addr:** Assistant Professor of Ob-Gyn & Community Medicine, Georgetown University, 3900 Reservoir Rd NW, Washington, DC 20007, **Business Phone:** (202)687-1602.

### HOYTE, JAMES STERLING

Lawyer, college administrator. **Personal:** Born Apr 21, 1944, Boston, MA; son of Patti Ridley and Oscar H; married Norma Dinnall; children: Keith Sterling & Kirsten Dinnall. **Educ:** Harvard Univ, BA, 1965, Law Sch, JD, 1968; Grad Sch Bus, Mass, PMD cert, 1971; Kennedy Sch Govt, 1986. **Career:** Arthur D Little Inc, sr staff, 1969-74, 1979-82; Mass Sec State, Boston, Mass, dep secy, 1975-76; Mass Port Authority, secy-treas, dir admin, 1976-79; Commonwealth Mass, cabinet secy, secy Environ Affairs, 1983-88; Coate, Hall & Stewart, partner, 1989-91; Mass Hort Soc, interimexec dir, consult, 1991-92; Atty; Harvard Univ, assoc vpres & asst to pres, 1992-, adj lect pub policy & title IX coordr, currently; Earthwatch Inst, dir emer. **Orgs:** Am Bar Asn; secy, Mass Black Lawyers Asn; bd dir, Opportunities Indusrialization Ctr Greater Boston, 1976-83; Nat Bar Asn, 1978-, Long Range Planning Comm, United Way Mass Bay, 1978; bd dir, Roxbury Multi Serv Ctr, 1979-87; chmn bd, Mass Water Resources Authority, 1985-88; chmn, bd trustee, Environ Comm, Boston Harbor Asn, 1989-; exec comm, bd dir, 1, 000 Friends Mass, 1989-; bd trustee, Univ Hosp, 1989; bd trustee, Mass Environ Trust; bd trustee, Union Concerned Scientists; bd trustee, Posse Found; bd trustee, Wheaton Col; bd trustee, Cambridge Col; bd trustee, Mus Afro-Am Hist; dir, Trust Pub Land; sr adv comt, Alliance a Healthy Tomorrow; coun mem, Mass Audubon Soc; nonres fel W.E.B. Du Bois Inst African & African Am Res, Harvard Univ, currently; chmn, New Eng Comt. **Honors/Awds:** Ten Outstanding Young Leaders, Greater Boston Jaycees, 1967; Black Achiever Award, Greater Boston YMCA, 1978; Alpha Man of the Year, Epsilon Gamma Lambda Chap Alpha Phi Alpha Frat, 1984; Governor Francis Sargent Award, Boston Harbor Asn, 1986; Frederick Douglass Award, Greater Boston YMCA, 1987. **Home Addr:** 565 Marrett Rd, Lexington, MA 02421, **Home Phone:** (781)862-3545. **Business Addr:** Assistant to the President, Associate Vice President & Title IX Coordinator, Harvard University, John F Kennedy Sch Gov, Cambridge, MA 02138, **Business Phone:** (617)495-1548.

### HRABOWSKI, DR. FREEMAN ALPHONSA, III

Writer, educator, association executive. **Personal:** Born Aug 13, 1950, Birmingham, AL; son of Freeman and Maggie; married Jacqueline Coleman; children: Eric. **Educ:** Hampton Inst, BA, 1970; Univ Ill, Urbana-Champaign, MA, math, 1971, PhD, higher educ admin & statist, 1975. **Career:** Univ Ill Urbana-Champaign, math instr, 1972-73, admin intern, 1973-74, asst dean, 1974-76; Alab A&M Univ Norm, assoc dean, 1976-77; Coppin State Col, Baltimore, dean arts & scis div, 1977-81, vpres, acad affairs, 1981-87; Univ Md, Baltimore County, vice provost, 1987-90, exec vpres, 1990-92, interim pres, 1992-93; Univ Md, Catonville, pres, 1992-; Bks: Beating Odds & Overcoming Odds; Focusing parenting & high-achieving African Am males & females sci; chmn, Press Adv Comn Educ Excellence African Americans. **Orgs:** Alpha Phi Alpha; sr class pres, Hampton Inst, 1969-70; Baltimore City Life Mus; adv coun, Florence Crittenton Servs Inc; Peabody Inst, Johns Hopkins Univ; evaluator, Mid States Asn Col & Sch; bd, Baltimore Equitable Soc; Unity Md Med Sys; Am Coun Educ, Constellation Energy, Baltimore Comm Found; Ctr Stage, Greater Baltimore Comm; Joint Ctr Polit & Econ Develop, bd, McCormick & Co; Mercantile Safe Deposit & Trust Co; bd, Merrick & France Found; Suburban Md High-Technol Coun; Asn Am Col & Univ; CarnegieInst; Marguerite Casey Found; Corvis Corp; consult, Nat Sci Found; NIH; Univs & Sch Systs; bd, Alfred P. Sloan Found; bd, T. Rowe Price Group, bd, Urban Inst; chmn, Carnegie Found Advan Teaching & Md Humanities Coun; Elected, Am Acad Arts & Sci & Am Philos Soc, fel AAAS; co-founder, Meyerhoff Scholars Prog, 1988; Sigma Pi Phi fraternity. **Honors/Awds:** Outstanding Alumni Award, Phi Delta Kappa, Hampton Univ; Outstanding Community Service Award, Tuskegee Univ; Marylander of the Yr, ed Baltimore Sun; USM Frederick Doughlas Award; Mc Graw Prize; BETA Award; NSF EDR Achievement Award; Edward Bouchet Leadership Award, MNY Grad Educ, Yale Univ; honorary degree, Princeton Univ; hon degrees, Duke Univ; hon degrees, Univ Ill; hon degree, Univ Ala-Birmingham; hon degree, Gallaudet Univ; hon degree, Goucher Col; hondegree, Med Univ SC & Binghamton Univ; Americas Best Leaders, US News & World Report, 2008; Theodore M Hesburgh Award for Leadership Excellence, 2011; Carnegie Corporation of New York's Academic Leadership Award, 2011; Seven Top American Leaders, Wash Post & Harvard Kennedy Sch's Ctr Pub Leadership, 2011; Heinz Award, 2012; McGraw Prize in Education, 2001; U.S. Presidential Award for Excellence in Science, Mathematics, and Engineering Mentoring; Teachers College Medal for Distinguished Service, Columbia Univ; African American Forum ICON Lifetime Achievement Award; Distinguished Public Service Award, Am Educ Res Asn's; William D. Carey Award, AAAS; Black Engineer of the Year, BEYA STEM Global Competitiveness Conf; Educator of the Year, World Affairs Coun Wash, DC; Lifetime Achievement Award, Technol Coun Md; Honorary degrees from more than 20 institutions. **Special Achievements:** Co-author, Oxford Univ Press, beating odds, raising academically successful African Am Males, 1998, overcoming odds, 2002. **Home Addr:** 18 Aston Ct, Owings Mills, MD 21117-1439, **Home Phone:** (410)581-2235. **Business Addr:** President, University of Maryland-Baltimore County, 1000 Hilltop Circle, Baltimore, MD 21250, **Business Phone:** (410)455-1000.

### HUBBARD, AMOS B., II

Educator. **Personal:** Born May 11, 1930, Dora, AL; son of A B; married Irene Windham; children: Melicent Concetta. **Educ:** Ala State Univ, BS, 1955; Ind Univ, MS, 1960; Univ Tenn; Univ Ala, Tuscaloosa; Mich State Univ; Univ Tulsa, Okla. **Career:** Educator (retired); Carver HS Union Springs, AL, teacher & coach, 1955-58; Riverside HS Northport, AL, teacher, 1958-68; Col Educ Ach Prog, Stillman Col, dir, 1968-72, dir educ develop prog, 1972-74, athl dir, 1972-79, dir spec serv prog, 1976, coord instr, teaching-learning, 1975, dir spec progs, 1977-87, dean studs, 1988-95. **Orgs:** Kappa Alpha Psi; Brown Presby Church; comn mgt, Barnes Br Young Men's Christian Asn, 1965-68; Tuscaloosa Civic Ctr Comn, 1971; Kappa Delta Pi, 1973; Phi Delta Kappa, 1973; Family Coun Serv, 1974; Kiwanis Tuscaloosa; Ment Health Bd; Narashino City Sister City Comn; Tuscaloosa Co Community Housing Resources Bd. **Honors/Awds:** Certificate of Achievement Award, Educ Improv Proj Soc Asn Col & Sch, 1973; Distinguished Service Award, United Fund Tuscaloosa City, 1973. **Home Addr:** 4020 19th St, Tuscaloosa, AL 35401-3914, **Home Phone:** (205)345-3367.

### HUBBARD, HON. ARNETTE RHINEHART

Lawyer. **Personal:** Born Stephens, AR; children: Gregory. **Educ:** John Marshall Law Sch, JD, 1969; Southern Ill Univ, BS, chem & math. **Career:** Lawyers Comn Civil Rights Under Law, staff atty, 1970-72; pvt pract, 1972-; Chicago Cable Comn, Chicago, Ill, comnr, 1985-89; Chicago Bd Election Comnrs, Chicago, Ill, comnr, 1989-97; State Ill Circuit Ct, Cook Co Judicial Circuit, judge, 1997-. **Orgs:** Nat Bar Asn, 1975-, pres, 1981-82; Nat Asn Advan Colored People; pres, Cook Co Bar Asn; pres, Asn Election Comn Off Ill; adv comm, Election Authority, St Bd Elections, State Ill; exec bd, Ill Asn Co Off; exec comm, Int Asn Clerks, Recorders, Election Officials & Treas; bd dir, Alpha Kappa Alpha Sorority; pres, Southern Ill Univ Alumni Asn, 1994-; Chicago Network; Women's Bar Asn Ill; vice chair, Ill Comn Brown V. Bd Educ; African Am bar asn. **Honors/Awds:** Obelisk Award for Education & Community Service, 2000; Scroll of Disting Women Lawyers, Nat Bar Asn, 2001; Distinguished Achievement Honor, Aug 2; Margaret Brent Distinguished Achievement Award, Am Bar Asn, 2009; Clarence Darrow Award. **Special Achievements:** First female president of the National Bar Association, 1981-82; First female president of the Cook County Bar Association; First African American commissioner elected president of the Association of Election Commissioners of Illinois. **Business Addr:** Judge, State of Illinois Circuit Court, Daley Ctr, Chicago, IL 60602, **Business Phone:** (312)603-5910.

### HUBBARD, CALVIN L.

Artist, educator. **Personal:** Born Jul 23, 1940, Dallas, TX; son of Ressie and CrinerMildred; married Evelyn McAfee; children: Katrina, Tyletha & Yuressa. **Educ:** Aspen Sch Contemp Art, CO, attended 1963; Tex Southern Univ, Houston, BAE, contemp art, 1966; Rochester Inst Technol, MA, 1971. **Career:** Educator (retired), business owner; Houston Independent Sch Dist, teacher, 1969-70; City Sch Dist, Rochester, NY, teacher, 1970-96; Nazareth Col, coordr art show, 1986-87; Turtle Pottery Studio & Gallery, owner & dir, 1987-. **Orgs:** Bd mem, Woodward Health Ctr, 1988; Eureka Lodge#36, jr warden, 1990-91; Eureka Lodge #36, worshipful master, 1995-96; Nat conf artists. **Home Addr:** 279 Corwin Rd, Rochester, NY 14610, **Home Phone:** (585)288-3252. **Business Addr:** Owner, Turtle Pottery Studio & Gallery, 29 Sherwood Ave, Rochester, NY 14619, **Business Phone:** (585)328-7060.

### HUBBARD, JOSEPHINE BRODIE

Executive. **Personal:** Born May 11, 1938, Tampa, FL; married Ronald C; children: Ronald Charles & Valerie Alicia. **Educ:** Fl A&M Univ, BS hon, sec educ span, 1958; Univ S Fla, MA, hon, guid coun, 1968. **Career:** Howard W Blake H S, teacher, 1958-63; Chicopee H S, teacher, 1965-66; NB Young Jr H S, guid counr, 1968-69; Univ S Fla, proj upward bound counr coordr, 1969-71, spec serv dir & acad adv; Wright

State Univ, acad advisor, 1973; Edwards Afb, sub teacher, 1974-75, guid counr, 1978-80; Dept Army W Ger, guid counr, 1978-80, collateral duty assignment, ed serv officer, 1980-81; Nellis Afb, guid counr, 1981-83; Family Support Ctr, chief prog, 1983-87, asst educ serv officer, 1987-, dir, currently; MacDill Afb Family Support Ctr, dir, 1989-98; Hubbard Family Ministries Inc, pres, dir, owner, currently. **Orgs:** Rep, Family Support Ctr; dir, Vol Agencies Orgn, 1983-; Southern NV Chap Federally Employed Women Inc, 1983-; Fed Women's Prog Interagency Coun, 1983-; scholar chmn, Nellis Noncommissioned Officers Wives' Club, 1985. **Honors/Awds:** Sustained Superior Performance Award, Family Support Ctr, Chief Prog, 1985-86; Tactical Air Command Certificate Recognition Special Achievement, 1985; Notable Achievement Award, Dept Air Force, 1985; Sustained Superior Performance Award, Family Support Ctr, 1990-92. **Special Achievements:** author: Heal Addictions By Using God Word, Healing Relationships, Lord, Heal and Transform My Life, & Ten Steps To Triumph Through Prayer. **Business Addr:** President, Director, Hubbard Family Ministries Inc, 4633 W El Prado Blvd, Tampa, FL 33629-8305, **Business Phone:** (813)831-5114.

### HUBBARD, LAWRENCE RAY

Orator, interior designer. **Personal:** Born Oct 23, 1965, Pittsburgh, PA; son of Sylvia; children: John Perez & Hassan Perez. **Educ:** NY Univ, BA & BS, 1986; Dominican Am Univ, latin cult & span, 2005. **Career:** Residential interiors, freelance designer; Detroit Police Off, 1987-94; Viggiano Interiors, pres & owner, founder, 1988-; Life Style TV prog:"On The Town with Lorenzo", star & exec producer, 2009. **Orgs:** Optimist Club; Am Soc Interior Designers; missionary work, prof Eng & Span, Int stud body; bd dir, Boston Arden Pk Hist Soc; Boston Edison Secret Garden Soc; Chamber Com; Coalition Interior Design; D.P.O.A; Dallas Art Dist Friends; E Boston-Arden Pk Hist Soc; treas, Human Rights Campaign; mem bd dir, chmn adv bd, Lambda Legal Defense & Educ Fund; O.B.D; R.P.C. Midwest Region; Wayne State Univ Racial Diversity Lectr. **Honors/Awds:** Proclamation of Excellence, Congress Woman Barbara Rose Collins ; Outstanding Business Person of the Year, Native Detroiter; Outstanding Business Person 3 years, Mich Dept Com; Proclamation of Excellence, Mayor Dennis Archer; Outstanding Community Service 6 years, Detroit Pub Schs; Outstanding Business Person of the Year, Dallas Friends; Outstanding Person of the Year, Affirmations; Person of the Year, Men of Color; Person of the Year, Triangle Found; Living Legend Award, Legacy Success; Pride Award; Employer's Award, A. Philip Randolph Career & Tech Inst Practicum Prog; Communicator Gold Award, Silver, Bronze awards, 2010; Educator of Excellence Award; Humorous Speech Winner 2009 Area, Toastmasters Int. **Special Achievements:** Appearances & articles: Detroit News; Detroit Free Press; WDIV-TV; "That's Got To Go!"; Michigan Chronicle; Author, Where I Was, Where I Am, Where I'm Going, 2003. **Home Addr:** 1005 Phinney Ave, Dallas, TX 75211-4948, **Home Phone:** (214)331-2536. **Business Addr:** President, Viggiano Interiors, 351 E Boston Blvd, Detroit, MI 48202, **Business Phone:** (313)869-2523.

### HUBBARD, PAUL LEONARD

Government official, businessperson, president (organization). **Personal:** Born Oct 31, 1942, Cincinnati, OH; son of Paul and Sylvia; married Georgia; children: Paul Anthony & Melissa (stepdaughter). **Educ:** Ohio Univ, BS, bus ed, 1961-65; Wayne State Univ, Detroit, MI, MSW, 1971; IBM Exec Mgt Training, cert, 1980; AMA, Exec Training Pres, cert, 1982. **Career:** Stowe Adult Ed, instr, 1965; Detroit Pub Sch, teacher, 1965-71; Wayne County CC, consult, 1971-74; Downriver Family Neighborhood Serv, assoc dir, 1971-74; New Detroit Inc, sr vpres, pres; DHT transp, 1979-89, pres, 1989-93; Western Wayne County, Family & Neighborhood Serv, dep dir; City Toledo, dir neighborhoods & housing, 1993-; Capt D's LLC, franchisee, 2005-; Detroit Haven Group Proj, advisor. **Orgs:** Nat vpres, Nat Assoc Black Social Workers, 1982-86; chmn, Metro Youth Prog Inc, 1983-87; chmn, Mich Bell Consumer Adv Group, 1984-89; US Selective Serv Bd, 1985-87; Inter Nat Exchange Bd Dirs, 1985-; chmn, Mich Supreme CtSubcomt, 1986-; pres, Detroit Chap Nat Asn Black Social Workers; Coun Polit Educ; bd dir, Goodwill Industs Greater Detroit; bd dir, Grand Valley Univ; bd dir, Mary grove Col; bd dir, Southwest Hosp; bd dir, Channel 56; Fed Home Loan bank; life mem, Nat Asn Advan Colored People; Nat Urban League; YMCA; Univ Detroit Sch Social Work; St. Vincent Hosp Found; Alpha Phi Alpha Fraternity; trustee, Hartford Church; Diversified Youth; Franklin Wright Settlement; Goodwill Industs; Goodwill Industs; Marygrove Col; WTVS Channel 56; exec bd, Boy Scouts Am. **Honors/Awds:** Outstanding Service Award, Det chap, Nat Asn Black Social Workers, 1975; Lafayette Allen Sr Distinguished Service Award, 1979; Detroit City Coun Testimonial Resolution for Community Servs, 1980; NABSW Alumni Year Award, 1981; Gentlemen Wall St Service Award, 1984; Am Cancer Soc Service Award, 1985; Black Enterprise Magazine Service Award, 1987; Nat Welfare Rights Service Award, 1988. **Home Addr:** 4337 Woodbriar, Toledo, OH 43623-1539, **Home Phone:** (419)471-9719. **Business Addr:** Franchisee, Captain D, 2060 W Laskey Rd, Toledo, OH 43613, **Business Phone:** (419)473-0227.

### HUBBARD, PHILIP GREGORY (PHIL HUBBARD)

Basketball player, basketball coach. **Personal:** Born Dec 13, 1956, Canton, OH; married Jackie Williams; children: Whitney & Maurice. **Educ:** Univ Mich, BA, educ, spec educ & teaching, 1979. **Career:** Basketball player (retired), basketball coach; Detroit Pistons, 1979-82, Cleveland Cavaliers, 1982-89; New York Knicks, scouting coordr; 1993-94; Atlanta Hawks, asst coach, 1997-2000; Golden State Warriors, asst coach, 2000-03; Wash Wizards, asst coach, 2003-09; Caneros de La Romana, asst coach, 2012; Los Angeles D-Fenders, asst coach, 2011-13; Santa Cruz Warriors, asst coach, 2013-14; Los Angeles D-Fenders, coach, 2014-15; Jeonju KCC Egis, asst coach, 2015-. **Orgs:** Cavalier's rep & hon coach, OhioSpec Olympics. **Home Addr:** 5130 Pleasant Forest Dr, Centreville, VA 20120-1248.

### HUBBARD, REGINALD T.

Automotive executive, chief executive officer. **Educ:** Univ S Fla, 1975. **Career:** Charlotte-based Hubbard Automotive LLC, chief exec officer, 1986; Metrolina Dodge Inc, pres & chief exec officer, owner, 2005-; Hubbard Automotive Group, owner; Metro Sch, pres. **Orgs:** Secy, Found Carolinas; chair, Personnel Policy Comt; bd dir, Found Carolinas & Nc Blumenthal Performing Arts Ctr; vice chair, Bldg Bridges, 2000; bd mem, bd advisors mem, POST. **Home Addr:** 14022 Grand Traverse Dr, Charlotte, NC 28278, **Home Phone:** (704)576-3218. **Business Addr:** Owner, President, Chief Executive Officer, Metrolina Dodge Inc, 7725 S Blvd, Charlotte, NC 28273, **Business Phone:** (704)553-1988.

### HUBBARD, TRENT (TRENIDAD AVIEL HUBBARD)

Baseball player. **Personal:** Born May 11, 1964, Chicago, IL; married Angela; children: Jaylen. **Educ:** Southern Univ. **Career:** Baseball player (retired); Colo Rockies, outfielder, 1994-96; San Francisco Giants, 1996; Cleveland Indians, 1997; Los Angeles Dodgers, 1998-99; Atlanta Braves, 2000; Baltimore Orioles, 2000; Kans City Royals, 2001; San Diego Padres, 2002-03; Chicago Cubs, 2003; Durham Bulls, Round Rock Express & Iowa Cubs, 2005. TV Series: "Sunday Night Baseball", 1998-2001. **Home Addr:** 4206 Clearwater Ct, Missouri City, TX 77459-1668.

### HUBERT, JANET LOUISE (JANET HUBERT WHITTEN)

Actor. **Personal:** Born Jan 13, 1956, Chicago, IL; married James Whitten; children: Elijah Issac; married Larry Kraft. **Educ:** Juilliard Sch; Loyola Unic, acct. **Career:** Alvin Ailey dance co; TV series: "The Fresh Prince of Bel Air", 1990-93; "New Eden", 1994; "What About Your Friends", 1995; "All My Children", 1999; "The Job", 2001-02; "The Bernie Mac Show", 2000-04; "Christmas at Water's Edge", 2004; "One Life to Live", 2005-10; "House of Payne", 2011. Films: Agent on Ice, 1986; White Man's Burden, 1995; California Myth, 1999; 30 Years to Life, 2001; Neurotica, 2004; Proud, 2004; Mom, 2013. Stage credits include: Sophisticated Ladies; Cats, Broadway. **Business Addr:** Actress, Michael Slessinger & Associates, 8730 Sunset Blvd Suite 270-W, West Hollywood, CA 90069, **Business Phone:** (310)657-7113.

### HUCKABY, MALCOLM J.

Basketball player, banker. **Personal:** Born Apr 7, 1972, Burlington, MA. **Educ:** Boston Col, attended 1994. **Career:** Basketball player (retired), executive; Miami Heat, guard, 1997; Fileni JE, 1997; US Trust Bank, vpres; Bank Am, fin adv, vpres; Merrill Lynch, financial advisor, 2004-08; BofA Merrill Lynch, advisor, 2009-12; IMG, color analyst, 2010-; Capitol Securities Mgt, vpres investments, 2012-; ESPN, col basketball analyst, 2012-. **Orgs:** Bd mem, Big Brothers Big Sisters Mass Bay; athlete adv bd, Sports Legacy Inst, 2008; bd trustee, NEXT STEP, 2011-; bd trustee, Boston Col Alumni Asn, 2011-; bd trustee, Crossroads Kids, 2011-; bd overseers, Boys & Girls Club Boston, 2011-; bd trustee, Nativity Prep Sch, 2011-. **Business Addr:** Financial Advisor, Bank of America, 25 Burlington Mall Rd, Burlington, MA 01803.

### HUDGEONS, LOUISE TAYLOR

School administrator, dean (education), association executive. **Personal:** Born May 31, 1931, Canton, OH; married Denton Russell. **Educ:** Roosevelt Univ, Chicago, BS, 1952; Univ Chicago, AM, 1958; Ill Univ, EdD, 1974; Govs State Univ, MBA, 1977. **Career:** School administrator, dean (retired); Mich Blvd Garden Apts, acct, 1952-55; Chicago Pub Schs, teacher, 1955-67; State Ill, Bus Off Educ, supvr, 1967-69; Chicago State Univ, asst prof, assoc prof, chmn, asst dean, actg dean, 1969-78; Eastern NMex Univ, Col Bus, dean, 1978; Cent State Univ, Sch Bus Admin, dean. **Orgs:** Consult, Va Polytech Inst, 1966; N Cent Asn Evaluating Teams, 1968-74; chmn, Col & Univ Div, Ill Bus Educ Asn, 1970; consult, Ill State Univ, 1971; chmn, Eval Supt Pub Schs, Ill, 1972; consult, Cent Syst Res, 1973; consult, US Off Educ, 1975; consult, Minn Bus Opportunities Comn, 1976-78; consult, Jwl Osco Co, 1977-78; consult, Govs State Univ, 1978; fel Am & Assembly Col Schs Bus, 1978. **Special Achievements:** Co-author, Your Career in Marketing, McGraw Hill, 1976; numerous speaking; published numerous articles. **Business Addr:** Dean, Central State University, 1400 Brush Row Rd, Wilberforce, OH 45384, **Business Phone:** (937)376-6011.

### HUDLIN, REGINALD ALAN

Movie producer, movie director, administrator. **Personal:** Born Dec 15, 1961, Centerville, IL; son of Warrington W Sr and Helen Cason; married Chrisette Suter. **Educ:** Harvard Univ, BA, 1983. **Career:** Film dir, writer; Films: House Party, 1983; The Kold Waves, 1984; Reggie's World of Soul, 1985; BeBe's Kids, 1992; Boomerang, 1992; The Great White Hype, 1996; The Ladies Man, 2000; Servicing Sara, 2002; TV Series: "Cosmic Slop", HBO, 1994; "The Last Days of Russell", ABC, 1995; "The Ride", 1998; "Richard Pryor: The Funniest Man Dead or Alive", 2005; "Bring That Year Back 2006: Laugh Now, Cry Later", 2006; Ill State Arts Coun, artist-in-residence, 1984-85; Ogilvy & Mather Advert Agency, NY, copywriter, 1986; Univ Wisc, Milwaukee, vis lectr film, 1985-86; Black Panther, writer, 2004; Hudlin Bros Inc, producer, screenwriter & film maker, currently; Black Entertainment TV network, pres entertainment & chief prog exec, 2005-08; Quentin Tarantinos Django Unchained, producer, currently. Producer: "The Bernie Mac Show", producer, 2004-05; "The Boondocks", 2005-08; "Richard Pryor: The Funniest Man Dead or Alive", exec producer, doc, 2005; "Bring That Year Back 2006: Laugh Now, Cry Later", network exec producer, 2006; "Django Unchained", producer, 2012; "44th NAACP Image Awards", exec producer, 2013; 45th NAACP Image Awards, exec producer, 2014; "The 46th Annual NAACP Image Awards", exec producer, 2015; "Critters", forthcoming, 2015; "The 88th Annual Academy Awards", producer, 2016. Director: "The Bernie Mac Show", 2002-05; "Richard Pryor: The Funniest Man Dead or Alive", 2005; Robin Harris: Live from the Comedy Act Theater, screenplay writer, 2006; "Wifey", 2007; "Untitled Burr and Hart Project", 2010; "Are We There Yet?", 2012; "Murder in the First", 2014-15. Crew: Somebodies, exec, 2006; "BET Hip-Hop Awards", prod, 2006; "The BET Honors", prod, 2008; "Brothers to Brutha", network exec, 2008; "BET's Comicview", pres entertainment, 2008-13. Actor: Ni de jintian he wo de mingtian, 2013. Black Entertainment Tv, chief programming exec, 2005. **Orgs:** Co-founder, Black Filmmakers Found, 1978; Phi Beta Sigma fraternity. **Business Addr:** Producer, Filmmaker, Hudlin Bros Inc, Tribeca Film Ctr, New York, NY 10013.

### HUDSON, ANNE ASHMORE. See POUSSAINT-HUDSON, DR. ANN ASHMORE.

### HUDSON, CHARLES LYNN

Baseball player. **Personal:** Born Mar 16, 1959, Ennis, TX; married Nikki. **Educ:** Prairie View A&M Univ, BA, 1981. **Career:** Baseball player (retired); Philadelphia Phillies, pitcher, 1983-86; New York Yankees, pitcher, 1987-88; Detroit Tigers, pitcher, 1989. **Home Addr:** 2124 Heather Glen, Dallas, TX 75232.

### HUDSON, CHERYL WILLIS

Publisher, book designer. **Personal:** Born Apr 7, 1948, Portsmouth, VA; daughter of Hayes Elijah III and Lillian Watson; married Wade; children: Katura J & Stephan J. **Educ:** Oberlin Col, BA, cum laude, 1970; Ratcliffe Col, publ procedures course, 1970; Northeastern Univ, graphic arts mgt courses, 1972; Parsons Sch Design, attended 1976. **Career:** Houghton Mifflin Co, art ed & sr art ed, 1970-73; Macmillan Publ Co, designer, design mgr, 1973-78; Arete Publ Co, asst art dir, 1978-82; freelance designer spec projs, 1979, 1985-88; Paper Wing Press & Angel Entertainment, art dir, freelance design consult, 1982-87; Just Us Bks, vpres, co-founder & ed dir, 1988-; Books: Bright Eyes, Brown Skin; Many Colors of Mother Goose; Come By Here, Lord: Everyday Prayers for C; Hold Christmas In Your Heart, 1995; How Sweet the Sound, 1995; What Do You Know, Snow!; What a Baby!, 2004; Hands Can & Construct Zone, 2003; Author: Afro-Bets ABC Book, 1987; Afro-Bets 123 Book, 1988; Multiculturalism in Children's Books, 1990; co-author of Bright Eyes, Brown Skin, 1990; Selection In The Multicolored Mirror: Cultural Substance in Literature for Children & Young Adults, 1991; Good Morning, Baby, 1992; Good Night, Baby, 1992; Kwanzaa Sticker Activity Book, Scholastic Inc & Just Us Books, 1994; Glo Goes Shopping, 1998; Come by Here Lord, 2001; Langston's Legacy, 2002; The Harlem Renaissance, 2002; articles have appeared in Edited by Violet Harris, Teaching Multicultural Literature in Grades K-8; "Creating Good Books for Children". Editor: Kids Book of Wisdom, 1996, In Praise of Our Fathers and Our Mothers, 1997. **Orgs:** Soc C's Bk Writers & Illus, 1989-; Nat Asn Black Bk Publ, 1990-92; bd dir, Multicult Publ Exchange, 1990-98; Black Women Publ, 1990-92; adv bd, Small Press Ctr, 1999-; Langston Hughes Libr; Auth's Guild. **Business Addr:** Co-Founder, Editorial Director & Vice President, Just Us Books Inc, 356 Glenwood Ave Suite 3, East Orange, NJ 07017, **Business Phone:** (973)672-7701.

### HUDSON, CHRISTOPHER RESHARD (CHRIS HUDSON)

Football player. **Personal:** Born Oct 6, 1971, Houston, TX. **Educ:** Univ Colo, bus, 1995. **Career:** Football player (retired); Jacksonville Jaguars, defensive back & Punt returner & free safety, 1995-98; Chicago Bears, free safety, 1999; Atlanta Falcons, free safety, 2001. **Orgs:** Colorado Buffaloes. **Honors/Awds:** Jim Thorpe Award, 1994; All-American, 1994.

### HUDSON, CYNTHIA

Lawyer, government official. **Educ:** Va Commonwealth Univ, BS; Col William & Mary, JD. **Career:** McGuireWoods LLP, atty, 1988-96; Va Dept Personnel & Training, dir personnel policy & progs; Col William & Mary, adj law fac; City Hampton, Va, Dept Law, City Atty's Off, 1996-, city atty, 2006-14, Off Atty Gen, chief dep atty gen, 2014-. **Orgs:** Pres, Local Govt Attorneys Va; bd dirs, Va Law Found. **Honors/Awds:** Virginia Lawyers Weekly, Influential Women of Virginia, 2012. **Business Addr:** Chief Deputy Attorney General, Office of the Attorney General, 202 N 9th St, Richmond, VA 23219, **Business Phone:** (804)786-2071.

### HUDSON, DIANNE ATKINSON

Television producer, journalist. **Educ:** Ohio Univ, BA, broadcast journ. **Career:** Assoc Press, broadcast news writer, 1976; TV Series: "The Oprah Winfrey Show", exec producer & producer, 1986, 1994-2003; "I Hate the Way I Look", sr producer, 1994; "ABC Afterschool Specials", sr producer, 1994; "Oprah Visits American Idol", exec producer, 2003; Oprah Winfrey, spec adv; Harpo Productions, vpres; Oprah Winfrey Found & Oprah's Angel Network, pres. **Orgs:** Bd trustee, Howard Univ Hosp, 2005-. **Honors/Awds:** Outstanding Talk Show, 1986; Received nine Emmy Awards. **Special Achievements:** Establishing Oprahs Book Club; Nominee, Daytime Emmy Award. **Business Addr:** Executive Producer, Harpo Productions The Oprah Winfrey Show, 110 N Carpenter St, Chicago, IL 60607, **Business Phone:** (312)633-0808.

### HUDSON, DON R..

Editor. **Personal:** Born Sep 9, 1962, Shreveport, LA; son of David Sr and Gladies; married Miriam Caston. **Educ:** Northwestern State Univ, attended 1980; Northeast La Univ, BA, broadcast jour, 1983. **Career:** Monroe News-Star world, sports writer, ed, 1981; News-Star, sports ed, 1988; Northeast La Univ, asst sports info dir; Atlanta J-Const, asst sports ed, sports news ed, 1989; Ark Gazette, sports ed; Orlando Sentinel, orange county ed, 1991, Sunday sports ed; Jackson Sun, managing ed, 1997; Lansing State J, managing ed, 1999; Jackson Clarion-Ledger, sports writer, managing ed, 2003-10; Decatur Daily, exec ed, 2010-. **Orgs:** Nat Asn Black Journalists; Assoc Press Sports Eds; Orlando Black Achievers Prog. **Honors/Awds:** Orlando YMCA, The Orlando Sentinel's Black Achiever, 1991-92. **Home Addr:** 121 Windy Hill Rd, Jackson, TN 38305. **Business Addr:** Executive Editor, The Decatur Daily, 201 1st Ave SE, Decatur, AL 35609, **Business Phone:** (256)340-2410.

### HUDSON, ELBERT T.

Executive. **Personal:** son of Claude; children: Paul C. **Educ:** Loyola Law Sch, LLB, 1953. **Career:** Chairman & chief executive officer (retired); Broadway Fed Bank, Los Angeles, Calif, pres & chief exec officer, 1972-92, chmn emer, 2007-. **Orgs:** Bd, Calif Bar asn; mem exec comt & chmn audit comt, Golden State Mutual Life Ins Co; chair bd trustee, Angeles Funeral Home pre-need Fund; mem bd, La Trade Tech Col Found; bd dir, Brotherhood Crusade; fel Nat Asn Advan Colored People. **Business Addr:** Chairman Emeritus, Broadway

Federal Bank, 4800 Wilshire Blvd, Los Angeles, CA 90010, **Business Phone:** (323)634-1700.

## HUDSON, ERNIE (EARNEST LEE HUDSON, SR.)

Actor. **Personal:** Born Dec 17, 1945, Benton Harbor, MI; son of Maggie Donald (deceased); married Linda Kingsberg; children: Andrew & Ross; married Jeannie Moore; children: Ernest Jr & Rahi. **Educ:** Wayne State Univ, BA; Yale Univ Sch Drama, MFA; Univ Minn, PhD. **Career:** Janitor; Chrysler Corp, machine operator; MI Bell, customer rep, Actor, currently; TV series: "Mad Bull", 1977; "King", 1978; "Last of the Good Guys", 1978; "The Next Generations", 1979; "High cliffe Manor", 1979; "White Mama", 1980; "Love on the Run", 1985; "The Last Precinct", 1986; "Broken Badges", 1990; "Angel Street", 1992; "Wild Palms", 1993; "The Cherokee Kid", 1996; "Oz", 1997-2003; "Clover", 1997; "Michael Jordan: An American Hero", 1999; "Nowhere to Land", 2000; "A Town Without Christmas", 2001; "HRT", 2001; "10-8: Officers on Duty", 2003; "Fighting the Odds: The Marilyn Gambrell Story", 2005; "Everwood", 2005; "Desperate Housewives", 2006; "Certifiably Jonathan", 2007; "Final Approach", 2007; "Las Vegas", 2007; "Gus's Dad May Have Killed an Old Guy", 2007; "Psych", 2007; "Private Practice", 2008; "Meteor", 2009; "Heroes", 2009; "Criminal Minds", 2010; "Childrens Hospital", 2010; "Smokin' Aces 2", 2010; "STASIS", 2010; "Torchwood", 2011; "Transformers", 2011; "Rizzoli & Isles", 2011;-14; "Franklin & Bash", 2012-14; "The Lottery", 2014; "Scorpion", 2014; "Key and Peele", 2014; "Living the Dream", 2014. "guest appearances on various tv shows; Films: Lead belly, 1976; The Human Tornado, 1976; The Main Event, 1979; The Octagon, 1980; The Jazz Singer, 1980; Penitentiary II, 1982; Going Berserk, 1983; Two of a Kind, 1983; Joy of Sex, 1984; Ghostbusters, 1984; Weeds, 1986; Leviathan, 1989; Trapper County War, 1989; Ghostbusters II, 1989; The Hand That Rocks the Cradle, 1992; Sugar Hill, 1993; No Escape, 1993; The Cowboy Way, 1994; Airheads, 1994; The Crow, 1994; Congo, 1995; The Substitute, 1996; For Which He Stands, 1996; Mr Magoo, 1997; Operation Delta Force, 1997; Leviathan, 1997; Fakin' Da Funk, 1997; October 22, 1998; Stranger in the Kingdom, 1998; Butter, 1998; Shark Attack, 1999; Stealth Fighter, 1999; Paper Bullets, 1999; Lillie, 1999; Interceptors, 1999; Hijack, 1999; Everything's Jake, actor & co-producer, 2000; Red Letters, 2000; The Watcher, 2000; Miss Congeniality, 2000; Anne B Real, 2002; The Ron Clark Story, 2005; Sledge: The Untold Story, 2005; Marilyn Hotchkiss' Ballroom Dancing & Charm Sch, 2005; Miss Congeniality 2: Armed & Fabulous, 2005; Halfway Decent, 2005; Hood of Horror, 2006; Nobel Son, 2006;21 Guns, 2006; Balancing the Books, 2008; Pastor Brown, 2009; Lonely Street, 2009; Dragonball Evolution, 2009; Machete Joe, 2010; Game of Death, 2010; The Adventures of Mickey Matson and the Copperhead Treasure, 2012; Deer Crossing, 2012; The Man in the Silo, 2012; Ambush at Dark Canyon, 2012; Turning Point, 2012; Doonby, 2013; You're Not You, 2014; Merry ExMas, 2014; Gallows Road, 2015; Batman: Bad Blood, 2016; God's Not Dead 2, 2016; Ghostbusters, 2016; Spaceman, 2016; The Deaf Kid, exec producer & producer, 2017-. **Honors/Awds:** Universe Readers Choice Award, Best Supporting Actor Genre Motion Picture, 1995; Golden Satellite Award, Best Performance Actor in a Television Series, Drama, 1999; Career Achievement Award, Ft. Lauderdale Int Film Festival, 2006; AOF/WAB Award, Action Film Int Film Festival, 2011. **Business Addr:** Actor, Innovative Artists, 1505 10th St, Santa Monica, CA 90401, **Business Phone:** (310)656-0400.

## HUDSON, FREDERICK BERNARD

Writer, television producer, management consultant. **Personal:** Born Oct 29, 1947, Chicago, IL; son of Joseph T and Nellie Parham; married Yvonne. **Educ:** Wayne State Univ, BA, 1969; Yale Law Sch, attended 1970; New Sch Social Res, MA, 1975; Am Inst Planners, regist city planner cert, 1979. **Career:** Odyssey House, NJ, adminr, 1971-73; Afarm Assocs, res assoc, 1975; City Univ NY, fac mem, 1975-76; City Univ Res, prog consult, 1975-76; Elon Mickels & Assocs, proj dir, 1976-78; Detroit City Coun, staff analyst, 1978-79; Southern Ill Univ, vis asst prof & coordr, 1979-80; Frederick Douglass Creative Arts Ctr, dir pub rels, 1981-82; Centaur Consult, pres, owner, 1983-; Col New Rochelle, 1986-87; Am Bus Inst, educ officer, 1986-89; A Good Black Man, columnist; Producer TV Movies: Take it to Hill, 1995-99; Things We Take & Undercover Man. **Orgs:** Spec prog asst, Nat Urban League, 1973-75; Am Mgmt Asn; community consult, AT&T, 1974; community consult, Coro Found, 1980; community consult, Reality House, 1982; instr, Dist Coun 37, 1989-; organizer, Nat Action Network, 1995-; October 22 Movement, 2000-; Int Action Ctr, 2000-; Asn Independent Video & Filmmakers; Am Planning Asn; Mensa, Film Video Arts, Am Mgt Asn. **Honors/Awds:** Citation of Merit, 1969, 1973-74; Mayors Commendation for the City of Newark, New Jersey Certificate of Merit, 1974; New Writers Citation, PEN, 1984; Service Award, DC 37, 2000. **Special Achievements:** Author of What's In a Number? An Eval of a Title I Prog, 1975, poems: Black Scholar, Obsedian, 1980, Can't Breathe; Anthology of Magazine Verse, short story, "The Peach Tree," 1982, play, The Indenture of Simon Hastings, 1988, has published in many literary magazines, including the Massachusetts Review and The Black Scholar. **Business Addr:** President, Centaur Consult, 1510 E 172 St Apt 4, Bronx, NY 10472, **Business Phone:** (718)378-7109.

## HUDSON, HEATHER MCTEER

Mayor. **Personal:** Born Greenville, MS; daughter of Charles V; married Abe M Jr. **Educ:** Spelman Col, BA, sociol, 1998; Tulane Univ, Tulane Law Sch, JD. **Career:** McTeer & Assocs Law Firm, atty; Lennys Sub Shop, co-owner; City Greenville, mayor, 2003-; McTeer-Hudson Firm PLLC, owner, currently. **Orgs:** Teen ministry leader, Agape Storge Christian Ctr; co-founder, Proj Give Back; exec dir, McTeer Found; Mission Miss; Alpha Kappa Alpha Sorority Inc; Miss Bar Asn; Am Trial Lawyers Asn; Wash County Bar Asn; Magnolia Bar Asn; Spelman Col Alumnae Asn; Rotary Club; Miss Munic League; Young Elected Officials Network; Miss Munic League; Agape Storage Christian Ctr. **Home Addr:** PO Box, Greenville, MS 38702-1254. **Business Addr:** Mayor, City of Greenville, 340 Main St, Greenville, MS 38701, **Business Phone:** (662)378-1500.

## HUDSON, DR. JEROME WILLIAM

Educator. **Personal:** Born May 9, 1953, Washington, DC. **Educ:** Univ Md, BA, 1975; George Washington Univ, grad cert, 1980; Am Inst Hypnotherapy, PhD, 1986. **Career:** YMCA, asst phys dir, 1977-78; Wesley Early Childhood Ctr, dir, 1978-79; Shore Up Inc, dir training employ, 1979-; Rome joy Inc, Salisbury, MD, chief exec officer, 1986-. **Orgs:** Adj fac mem, Salisbury State Col, 1978-80; gov state adv coun, Off C &Youth, 1978-; dir training & employ, Shore Up Inc, 1979-87; state adv comt mem, Off C & Youth, 1980-; selection comt mem, Foster Care Rev Bd, 1980-87; selection comt mem, Foster Care Rev Bd, 1980-; bd dir, Heart Asn, 1980-81; vpres, Wicomico County Coun Social Serv, 1980-81; Afro-Am Hist Week Phi Delta Kappa, 1982; bd dir, Md Pub Broadcasting-Chem People Adv Bd; bd dir, March Dimes, 1983, YMCA 1984-90; Salisbury Chap Jaycees, 1986-; founder, Rural Opportunity Minority Enterprise Scholar, 1990-. **Home Addr:** PO Box 3305, Salisbury, MD 21802, **Home Phone:** (443)783-1353. **Business Addr:** Chief Executive Officer, Romejoy Inc, 1115 Tuscola Ave Suite 1A, Salisbury, MD 21801, **Business Phone:** (410)543-0713.

## HUDSON, KATE. See BRYANT, JOY.

## HUDSON, LESTER DARNELL

Lawyer. **Personal:** Born Mar 4, 1949, Detroit, MI; married Vivian Ann Johnson. **Educ:** Fisk Univ, BA, 1971; Boston Col, Law Degree; Law Sch Brighton, MA, 1974. **Career:** Bell & Hudson, atty & sr partner; City Boston Law Dept, intern, 1972-73; Boston Legal & Asst Proj, legal intern, 1972; Boston Col, legal internlegal asst, 1973-74. **Orgs:** Detroit Bar Asn; NBA; ABA Young Lawyers sect; Urban League; PUSH Detroit; Nat Asn Advan Colored People Crime Task Force comt. **Honors/Awds:** Award for Leadership & Scholarship, Scott Paper Co Found, 1971; Martin Luther King Award, Leadership & Comn Involvement, 1974. **Home Addr:** 3065 Iroquois St, Detroit, MI 48214, **Home Phone:** (313)571-8080.

## HUDSON, MERRY C.

Government official, law enforcement officer. **Personal:** Born Dec 25, 1943, Baltimore, MD; married Robert L; children: Alicia & Stephen. **Educ:** Howard Univ, BA, 1965, JD, 1968; George Washington Univ, LLM, 1972. **Career:** Howard Univ, acad scholar, 1961-68; Equal Employ Opportunity Comn, supvry atty, 1971-72; Univ Md, affirmative action officer, 1975-76; pvt pract law, 1976-78; Univ Md, consult, 1976; State Md, Comn Human Rels, chief hearing examr, 1978-. **Orgs:** Treas, DC Links Inc, 1985-; Nat Asn Admin Law Judges; Nat Bar Asn; Alpha Kappa Alpha. **Home Addr:** 1216 Edgevale Rd, Silver Spring, MD 20910-1611, **Home Phone:** (301)587-2358. **Business Addr:** Chief Hearing Examiner, Commission on Human Relation, 6 St Paul St Suite 900, Baltimore, MD 21202-1631, **Business Phone:** (800)705-3493.

## HUDSON, PAUL C.

Banker, entrepreneur. **Educ:** Univ Calif, Berkeley, BA, polit sci; Boalt Hall Sch Law, JD, corp, 1973. **Career:** WilmerHale, Assoc Atty, 1973-75; Broadway Fed Bank Savings & Loan, exec chmn, bd dir, 1985, pres & chief exec officer, 1992-2011, chmn, 1997-2012; Paul C. Hudson Consult, founder, 2013-. **Orgs:** Los Angeles Nat Asn Advan Colored People; Boy Scouts Am; chmn, Community Redevelop Agency, 2004-06; State Calif & Dist Columbia bars; chmn, Community Build Inc, 1992-2013; chair bd, Los Angeles Community Redevelop Agency, 2002-04; Bd Orthop Hosp Found; Southern Calif Coun Ctr; dir, Calif Housing Finance Agency; bd mem, Tuskegee Airmen Scholar Found, 2009-; chmn, Ebony Repertory Theatre, 2009-; chmn, Ctr Social Inclusion, 2009-; chmn, Ctr Social Inclusion, 2010-; bd mem, AfrIcan Am Bd Leadership Inst, 2012-; comnr, Housing Authority City Los Angeles, 2013-. **Honors/Awds:** Local Community Heroes, 2007. **Special Achievements:** Company ranked 13 Black Enterprise Top Financial Companies List, 1992. **Business Addr:** Founder, Paul C Hudson Consulting, 8467 S Van Ness, Los Angeles, CA 90305, **Business Phone:** (323)455-0071.

## HUDSON, DR. ROBERT LEE

Educator, physician. **Personal:** Born Oct 30, 1939, Mobile, AL; son of Robert L and Claudia M Jackson Graham; married Merry Brock; children: Alicia & Stephen. **Educ:** Lincoln Univ, BA, 1962; Howard Univ Col Med, MD, 1966. **Career:** C's Nat Med Ctr, fel, 1969-71; Howard Univ Ctr Sickle Cell Disease, physician coord, 1971-72, dep dir, 1972-75; Howard Univ, asst prof, 1971-75; pvt pract, physician, currently; C's Nat Med Ctr, C's Pediatricians & Assocs, physician, currently. **Orgs:** Columbia Hosp Women; DC Gen Hosp; mem bd dir, Capital Head Start, 1971-75; med cons Capital Head start, 1971-76; Med Soc DC; Am Acad Pediat; Medico Chirurgical Soc DC; Am Heart Asn. **Business Addr:** Physician, Children's National Medical Center, 2600 Naylor Rd SE, Washington, DC 20020, **Business Phone:** (202)582-6800.

## HUDSON, DR. ROY DAVAGE

Medical researcher, educator, zoologist. **Personal:** Born Jun 30, 1930, Chattanooga, TN; son of James Roy and Everence Wilkerson; married Constance Joan Taylor; children: Hollye Goler & David K. **Educ:** Livingstone Col, BS, 1955; Univ Mich, MS, 1957, PhD, 1962. **Career:** Danforth Grad, fel, 1962-78; Univ Mich Med Sch, asst prof, 1961-66; Brown Univ Med Sch, assoc prof, 1966-70; Brown Univ Grad Sch, assoc dean, 1966-69; Hampton Univ, pres, 1970-76; Univ VA Med Sch, vis prof, 1974-76; Warner Lambert, Parke-Davis, vpres, pharmaceut res planning, 1977-79; Upjohn Co, sc liaison mgr. 1979-81, Pharmaceut Res & Develop, Europe, vpres, 1987-90, corp vpres pub rels, 1990-92; CNS dis res, mgr, Pharmaceut Res, dir, 1981-87; Univ Mich, ML King/C Chavez/R Parks vis prof, 1989; Guid Clin, interim exec dir & chief exec officer, 1994; Livingstone Col, interim pres, 1995-96. **Orgs:** Danforth fel Danforth Found, 1972-79; bd dir, Peninsula Chamber Com, 1970-76; bd dir, United Va Bankshares, 1971-76; bd dir, Chesapeake & Potomac Tel Co, 1972-76; chmn, Va State Comn Selection Rhodes Scholars, 1973; bd dir, Am Coun Educ, 1972-76; bd dir, Parke-Davis Co, 1974-76; Dept HEW, Adv Com to Dir NIH, 1974-77; bd trustee, Nat Med fel 1990-92; bd dir, Comerica Bank, 1990-95; adv bd, Kalamazoo Math & Sci Ctr, 1990-92. **Honors/Awds:** Scholarship Award, Omega Psi Phi Fraternity, 1954-55; Distinguished Alumni Medallion, Livingstone Col, 1969; Outstanding Civilian Service Award, US Army, 1972; Award of Merit for Continuous Service to Humanity, Omega Psi Phi Fraternity, 1974; Lehigh Univ, LLD, 1974; Princeton Univ, LLD, 1975; Award for Exemplary Leadership, Omega Psi Phi Fraternity, 1978. **Home Addr:** 201 Brookview Pl, Woodstock, GA 30188, **Home Phone:** (770)591-6689.

## HUDSON, STERLING HENRY, III

Educator, college administrator. **Personal:** Born Jul 6, 1950, Hot Springs, VA; son of Sterling H Jr; married Cheryl White; children: Tara L. **Educ:** Hampton Univ, BA, 1973, MA, 1979; Ga State Univ, admin higher educ, pub admin, 1993; Capella Univ. **Career:** Hampton Univ, admissions counr, 1973-77, asst dean admis, 1977-82; Elizabeth City State Univ, dir admis & recruitment, 1982-83; Morehouse Col, dir admis, 1983-2010, asst vpres acad affairs & dir admis, dean freshmen, 1991-96, Admis & Enrollment Mgt, vice provost, 1996-98, Admis & Rec, dean, 1998-10, dir PSP, currently. **Orgs:** Nat Asn Col Admis Counr, 1973-; Am Asn Col Deans Registr Admis Officers, 1973-; Delta Pi Kappa Hon Soc, 1979-; Atlanta Urban League, 1984-; rep, Univ Ctr Ga, 1984-86; coun col level serv, Col Bd, 1985-88; Golden Key Hon Soc, 1999-; Iota Phi Theta Fraternity Inc; SAT Comt; pres & chief exec officer, Child First USA, 2010-. **Home Addr:** 2974 Dodson Dr, East Point, GA 30344, **Home Phone:** (404)349-4415. **Business Addr:** President, Chief Executive Officer, Child First USA, 1230 Peachtree St NE Suite 1900, Atlanta, GA 30306, **Business Phone:** (404)942-2700.

## HUDSON, DR. THEODORE R.

Educator, writer, college teacher. **Personal:** Born Washington, DC; married Geneva Bess; children: Eric & Vicki. **Educ:** Miner Teachers Col, BS; NY Univ, MA; Howard Univ, MA, PhD. **Career:** Educator (retired); Univ DC, prof eng, 1964-77; Am Univ, adj prof lit, 1968-69, 1991; Howard Univ, grad prof eng, 1977-91, consult, prin, 1991. **Orgs:** Vpres, Duke Ellington Soc; ed, Ellingtonia; behind-scenes vol, Smithsonian Inst; pres, Highland Beach City Asn. **Honors/Awds:** Most Distinguished Literature Scholar Award, Col Lang Asn, 1974. **Special Achievements:** From LeRoi Jones to Amiri Baraka, Lit Works, Duke Univ Press, 1973; Numart in periodicals and books; Officer Brother, The Venerable Order of St John. **Home Addr:** 1336 Douglass Ave, Highland Beach, MD 21403-4647, **Home Phone:** (410)268-0045.

## HUDSON, TROY

Basketball player, singer. **Personal:** Born Mar 13, 1976, Carbondale, IL. **Educ:** Univ Mo, attended 1995; Southern Ill Univ, attended 1997. **Career:** Basketball player (retired), singer; Yakima Sun Kings, 1997-98; Utah Jazz, 1998; Los Angeles Clippers, guard, 1997, 1999-2000; Sioux Falls Skyforce, 1998-99; Orlando Magic, 2000-02; Minn Timberwolves, guard, 2002-07; Golden State Warriors, guard, 2007-08; Sioux Falls Skyforce, 2012-13; Albums: Undrafted, 2007.

## HUDSON, WILLIAM THOMAS. See Obituaries Section.

## HUDSON-WARD, ALEXIA

Marketing executive, librarian. **Educ:** Temple Univ, BA, Eng lit & African Am studies, 1993; Univ Pittsburgh, MLIS, 2005; Simmons Col, PhD, managerial leadership info professions, 2013-. **Career:** Coca-Cola Co, customer mkt mgr, 1999-2003; W Chester Univ, frederick douglass librn, 2005-06; Pa State Univ Libr, ref & instr librn, 2006-08; assoc librn, 2008-16; Oberlin Col & Conserv Libr, dir libr, currently. **Orgs:** Pres, Pa African-Am Libr Asn, 2008-09; nat exec bd mem, Am Libr Asn; bd dir, Pa Libr Asn; prog fel CIC Acad Leadership, 2014-15; Alpha Kappa Alpha Sorority Inc; Links Inc; Jr League Philadelphia. **Honors/Awds:** Emerging Leader, Am Libr Asn, 2007; New Librarian of the Year, Pa Libr Asn, 2007; Mover and Shaker, Libr J, 2008; Young Alumni Award, Univ Pittsburgh Sch Info Sci, 2013. **Business Addr:** Director of Libraries, Oberlin College & Conservatory Libraries, 148 W Col St, Oberlin, OH 44074-1545, **Business Phone:** (440)775-5024.

## HUDSON-WEEMS, DR. CLENORA F.

Educator. **Personal:** Born Jul 23, 1945, Oxford, MS; daughter of Matthew Pearson and Mary Cohran Pearson; married Robert E Weems Jr; children: Sharifa Zakiya. **Educ:** LeMoyne Col, BA, 1967; L Univ Dijon, France, cert, 1969; Atlanta Univ, MA, 1971; Univ Iowa, PhD, 1988; L'Universite de Dijon, France, cert, fr studies. **Career:** Ford & Nat Endowment, humanities fels; CIC, internship; Del State Col, asst prof, 1972-73; Southern Univ New Orleans, asst prof eng, 1976-77; Del State Col, dir black studies, asst prof eng, 1980-85; Ford Doctoral Fel, 1986-87; Grad Col Fel, Univ Iowa, 1986-87; Ford Dissertation Fel, 1987-88; Banneker Hons Col, assoc prof eng, 1988-90; Univ Mo, Columbia, assoc prof, 1990, prof Eng, currently; Africana Womanism Socs, chief exec officer; Author: Africana Womanism Trilogy, Africana Womanism: Reclaiming Ourselves, 1993, Africana Womanist Literary Theory, 2004; Africana Womanism & Race & Gender, 2008 & 2009; Emmett Till Trilogy, Till's lynching as the catalyst of the CRM, 1994, Emmett Till: The Sacrificial Lamb of the Civil Rights Movement, 2006; The Definitive Emmett Till: Passion & Battle of a Woman, Truth & Intellectual Justice, 2006; Till Trilogy, Plagiarism Physical & Intellectual Lynchings: An Emmett Till Continuum, editor, 2007; Toni Morrison, co author, 1990; Contemporary Africana Theory, Thought & Action: A Guide to Africana Studies, editor, 2007; artical, "Africana Womanism: The Flip Side of the Coin", guest editor, 2001; Publications: The Western Journal of Black Studies; The Journal of Black Studies; College Language Journal. **Orgs:** Ed bd mem, Western Jour Black Studies, Wash State Univ; Col Lang Asn, 1970-; African Heritage Studies Asn, 1985-; Ford Doctoral fel, 1986-87; Grad Col fel, Univ Iowa, 1986-87, 1987-88; Ford Dissertation fel, 1987-88; Asn Study African-Am Life & Hist, 1992-; Womens Intl League Peace & Freedom; pres, Africana Womanism Socs; ed bd mem, Western J Black Studies; adv bd mem, African Am Lit & Cult Socs. **Special Achievements:** In 2001, she initiated the Nation's First Graduate Degree (MA and PhD) in English Degree with an Africana Concentration at MU. **Home Addr:** 916 W Stewart Rd, Columbia, MO 60637-1908, **Home Phone:** (573)449-5198. **Business Addr:** Professor, University of Missouri, 52 McReynolds Hall, Columbia, MO 65211, **Business Phone:** (573)882-2783.

## HUDSPETH, GREGORY CHARLES

College teacher, dean (education), educator. **Personal:** Born Oct 1, 1947, San Antonio, TX; son of Charles and Louise Menefee; married Dollie Rivers; children: Gregory Jr & Brandon. **Educ:** Huston-Tillotson Col, BA, 1970; St Marys Univ, MA, 1975; Our Lady Lake Univ, PhD. **Career:** Northside Independent Sch Dist, San Antonio, Tex, teacher & coach, 1971-78; St Philips Col, San Antonio, Tex, assoc prof, 1978, Arts & Sci, prof & dean, 2002-. **Orgs:** Alpha Phi Alpha Fraternity Inc, 1968; chmn, Dem Party, 1980; pres, Fac Senate, 1983-86, 1988; trustee, Target 90/ Goals, San Antonio, 1985-89; Deacon, Mt Zion First Baptist Church, 1987; vpres, Huston-Tillotson Col Alumni Asn, San Antonio, 1990; bd trustee, St. Philip's Col. **Home Addr:** 1707 Palmer Vw, San Antonio, TX 78260-7279, **Home Phone:** (830)980-5834. **Business Addr:** Dean of Arts and Sciences, St Philip's College, 142 E Lambert St, San Antonio, TX 78204, **Business Phone:** (210)486-2383.

## HUESTON, DR. OLIVER DAVID

Psychiatrist. **Personal:** Born Oct 23, 1941, New York, NY; children: Michael & David. **Educ:** Hunter Col, BS, 1963; Meharry Med Col, MD, 1968. **Career:** Physician (retired); Harlem Hosp, chief resident pediat, 1970-71; Columbia Univ Col Physicians & Surgeons, attend pediatrician, 1971-72; Harlem Hosp, gen psychiat resident, 1972-74, fel child psychiat, 1974-75; self employed, 1985; NY State Drug Abuse Control Com, clin physician. **Orgs:** Pediatrician Flower 5 Ave Hosp Martin L King Eve Clin, 1971; Josiah Macy Fel 1971-72; Ambulatory Drug Unit 13 Harlem Hops; St Albans Martyr Episcopal Church. **Home Addr:** 114 44 179 St, Jamaica, NY 11434. **Business Addr:** Physician, 843 Barbara Dr, Teaneck, NJ 07666, **Business Phone:** (201)837-4780.

## HUFF, JANICE WAGES

Meteorologist. **Personal:** Born Sep 1, 1960, New York, NY; daughter of Dorothy L Wages; married Kenneth E; married Warren Dowdy. **Educ:** Fla State Univ, Tallahassee, FL, BS, meteorol, 1982. **Career:** Nat Serv, Columbia, SC, weather trainee, 1978-80; WCTV-TV, Tallahassee, FL, weather intern, 1982; WTVC-TV, Chattanooga, Tenn, meteorol, 1982-83; WRBL-TV, Columbus, GA, meteorol, 1983-87; KSDK-TV, St Louis, MO, meteorol, 1987-90; KRON-TV, San Francisco, Calif, meteorol, 1990-95; WNBC 4, chief meteorol, 1995-. **Orgs:** Nat Hon Soc, Secy Stud Coun, Varsity Cheerleader, & Miss Shamrock, 1978; Am Meteorol Soc, 1981-; Nat Asn Black Journalists, 1986-; Alpha Kappa Alpha Sorority, 1986-; Nat Acad TV Arts & Scis; Am Meteorol Socs; Nat Asn Black Journalists; Friars Club. **Honors/Awds:** Weathercasting, Seal Approval, Am Meteorol Soc, 1985; TV Emmy Best Weathercaster, Nat Asn TV Arts & Scis, 1988; St Louis Emmy Award, 1988; Kaleidoscope Award, Bronx Community College, 1995; Woman of the Year Award, 2002; Golden Heart Award, 2004; Miracle Makers Media Award, 2004; Golden Apple Award, American Women in Radio & Television, 2006; Laura Parsons Pratt Award, 2006; Community Service Award, 2007; Spirit of Life Award; Black Media Legends Award, McDonalds, 2011. **Business Addr:** Chief Meteorologist, WNBC-TV, 30 Rockefeller Plz 7th Fl, New York, NY 10112, **Business Phone:** (212)664-2903.

## HUFF, LEON ALEXANDER

Composer, musician, television producer. **Personal:** Born Apr 8, 1942, Camden, NJ; married Regina; children: Inga, Bilail, Erika, Leon Jr, Debra & Dietra. **Career:** Atlantic Rec, songwriter; Excel Rec, founder, 1966; Philadelphia Intl Rec, co-founder & vice chmn, 1971-; Mighty Three Publishing Co, founder; songwriter & producer; Soundtrack: "Great Performances", 2005; Silence Is Golden, 2006; Songwriter: "Only The Strong Survive", Little Manhattan, 2005; "I Wanna Know Your Name", Roll Bounce, 2005; "You'll Never Find Another Love Like Mine", Guess Who, 2005; "Love Train" & "Now That We Found Love", Hitch, 2005; Composer: Mean Johnny Barrows, 1976; The Out-of-Towners, 1999; The Honeymooners, 2005; Nineteenth Ave Baptist Church; I'm Gonna Make You Love Me, co-writer; Album: Here To Create Music, 2008. **Honors/Awds:** Key to City of Camden; Record World Producer-Writer of Decade Award; Best Rhythm & Blues Producers Award, Nat Asn TV & Recording Artists, 1968-69; numerous Grammy nominations and awards; The Number 1 Song Publishing Award; The Number 1 Record Company Award; The Soul of America Music Award, 1992; Philadelphia Music Alliance Walk of Fame Award, 1993; inducted into Songwriters Hall of Fame, 1995; Impact Award of Excellence, 1996; Grammy Lifetime Achievement Award, 1999; Trustees Award, Nat Acad Rec Arts & Sci, Hall of Fame and the Rock and Roll Hall of Fame, 1999; Inaugural Lifetime Achievement Award, Philadelphia Music Conf, 2000; Dance Music Hall of Fame, 2005; Ahmet Ertegnn Award by the Rock and Roll Hall of Fame, 2008; Mulford Street renamed as Leon Huff Way in Camden, NJ, 2009; Top R and B/soul Music Publishers in the Industry, Billboard Mag; Johnny Mercer Award. **Special Achievements:** Over 300 gold and platinum singles & albums. **Business Addr:** Co-Founder, Vice Chairman, Philadelphia International Records, 309 S Broad St, Philadelphia, PA 19107, **Business Phone:** (215)985-0900.

## HUFF, LORETTA LOVE (LORETTA L BOOKER)

Executive, president (organization). **Personal:** Born May 16, 1951, Chicago, IL; daughter of Andrew E and Lois Orr. **Educ:** Howard Univ, BS, psychol, 1972; Univ Chicago, MBA, finance, 1983; New Ventures W Coaching Inst, Prof Effectiveness Coach, cert, 1998. **Career:** Sears Roebuck & Co, programmer, 1972-74, off mgr, 1974-78, consumer res serv mgr, 1978-80, surv consult, 1980-81; Continental Bank, com lending, 1981-83, col rels, 1983-84; Apple Comput Inc, Cupertino, Calif, staffing consult, 1988-89, col rels consult, 1989-90, compensation specialist, 1990-93, prog mgr, 1993-94; Sega Am, hr mgr, 1994-95; Softbank Forums, hr dir, 1995-97; Merlin Consult, pres, 1997-; Sagent Technol Inc, vpres human resources, 1999-2000; PDI/Dreamworks, head human resources, 2001; Univ Phoenix, fac; Kraft Inc, corp recruiter; Merlin Venture Partners LLC, pres; Emerald Harvest Consult LLC, pres & prin consult, 2003-; The Whale Hunters, partner, currently. **Orgs:** Nat Black MBA Asn, 1980-94; sem dir, Werner Erhard & Asn, 1985-87; bd dir, Northern Cook Co Pvt Ind Coun, 1986-89, 1989-, pres, 1990-91; secy, treas & vpres, Career Mgmt Comm, Univ Chicago Women's Bus Group, 1987; personnel bd mem, City Sunnyvale, 1999-2003; Int Mgt Consults, 1999-2000; Nat Speakers Asn; Black Profs Coaches Alliance; Int Coach Fed; Delta Sigma Theta Sorority Inc; Palo Alto/Bay Area Alumnae; pres & bd mem, Gabriels Angels; bd mem, Ariz Parkinson Network; Nat Asn Women Bus Owners; Fraser Net Power Networking; Nat Minority Supplier Develop Coun; Black Prof Coaches Alliance. **Home Addr:** 2606 W Estes Way, Phoenix, AZ 85041-9535, **Home Phone:** (877)436-4278. **Business Addr:** President, Principal Consultant, Emerald Harvest Consulting LLC, 2030 Baseline Rd Suite 182-128, Phoenix, AZ 85041, **Business Phone:** (602)535-1290.

## HUFF, LOUIS ANDREW

Educator, consultant. **Personal:** Born Jan 1, 1949, New Haven, CT; married Suzanne Elaine Cooke; children: Elaine Kai. **Educ:** Howard Univ, BA, econ bus fin, 1971, MA, econ, 1974, PhD, econ, 1981. **Career:** Fed Res Bd, economist, 1971-74; Lincoln Univ, asst prof, 1977-80; CBC ResInst, pres, 1980-82; Univ New Haven, asst prof, 1980-82; 1st Buffalo Corp, economist & stockbroker, 1983-; PA State Univ, asst prof econ; Wilmington col, adj fac; Alliance Consult LLC, financial adv, currently. **Orgs:** Bd mem, CBC Inc, 1982-; Western Econ Soc, 1983-; econ consult, RIE Ltd, 1983-; host & producer, Economist Corner, 1984-; chairperson housing, Nat Asn Advan Colored People Reading Chap, 1984-; Atlantic Econ Soc, 1984-. **Honors/Awds:** Research Study Award, Nat Chap Eastern States, 1979; Outstanding Young Man in America, 1981. **Special Achievements:** Presented papers at numnat econ confs including Montreal Canada, 1983; Article published Atlantic Economic Journal 1985; Rome Italy, 1985. **Home Addr:** 611 W 37th St, Wilmington, DE 19802, **Home Phone:** (302)762-2532. **Business Addr:** Financial Advisor, Alliance Consulting LLC, 4 Daniels Farm Rd Suite 248, Trumbull, CT 06611-3900, **Business Phone:** (203)257-3606.

## HUFF, LULA LUNSFORD

Executive. **Personal:** Born Jul 5, 1949, Columbus, GA; daughter of Walter T (deceased) and Sally M; married Charles E Jr; children: Tamara Nicole. **Educ:** Howard Univ, WA, BA, 1971; Atlanta Univ, Atlanta, MBA, 1973; State Ga, CPA, 1978. **Career:** Ernst & Young, CPA Firm, Columbus, Ga, acct & auditor, 1973-76; Consol Govt Columbus, Columbus, Ga, chief internal auditor, 1976-84; Troy State Univ, Phoenix City, Ala, Acct Dept, instr, 1979-89, chmn, 1980-87, dir personnel mgt grad prog, 1984-85; Pratt & Whitney, UTC, Columbus, Ga, sr fin officer & cost analyst, 1984-85, fin supvr, 1985-89, controller, 1989-96; Precision Components Int, chief financial officer, 1995; Columbus Consol Govt Tag & Tax Off, Muscogee County tax comnr, 1997-. **Orgs:** YMCA, Ga Soc CPA; Urban League; PUSH; Nat Asn Advan Colored People; Howard Univ Alumni Asn; Nat Coun Negro Women; Jack & Jill Am Inc; Links Inc; Delta Sigma Theta Sorority Inc; bd mem, Girl Scouts; Am Inst CPA's; Leadership Columbus, Ga; Uptown Columbus; Dale Carnegie; St Anne Cath Church; Delta Mu Delta Nat Bus Hon Soc; Iota Phi Lambda Sorority Inc; Holy Family Cath Church; Mother Mary Sch Bd; Chattahoochee Valley Community Found Bd/Moving Forward Together; Links Inc; Ga Socs CPAs; Columbus Mus; Liberty Theater Hist Preserv Bd; Delta Life Develop Found Bd; County Officers Asn Ga; Ga Asn Tax Officials; Tax Commissioners Technol Bd. **Home Addr:** 3630 Willow Bend Run, Columbus, GA 31907. **Business Addr:** Muscogee County Tax Commissioner, Columbus Consolidated Government Tag & Tax Office, 100 10th St E Wing, Columbus, GA 31901, **Business Phone:** (706)653-4208.

## HUGER, RAYMOND A.

Executive. **Educ:** Bernard Baruch Col, BA, bus admin, mgt & opers, 1974; Fordham Univ, MBA, mkt mgt, 1976. **Career:** Regional manager (retired), chairman, chief executive officer; Int Bus Mach, field engr, sales & mkt & exec mgt positions, regional mgr, 1966-91; Paradigm Solutions Int Inc, founder, chmn, 1991-2007, pres & chief exec officer, 2006-; Paradigm Holdings, chmn bd & actg chief financial officer, 1991-2004, chief exec officer, 2004-06; Cheyenne Resources Inc, chief exec officer, 2004. **Special Achievements:** Listed in "Top Entrepreneurs" by US Black Engr & Info Technol, 2004. **Business Addr:** President, Chief Executive Officer, Paradigm Solutions International Inc, 6701 Democracy Blvd Suite 300, Bethesda, MD 20817, **Business Phone:** (301)571-9309.

## HUGGINS, DR. CLARENCE L.

Physician, surgeon general. **Personal:** Born Apr 25, 1926, Birmingham, AL; son of Clarence and Lucille; married Carolyn King; children: Patricia, Clarence III & Daphne. **Educ:** Morgan St Col, BS, 1950; Meharry Med Col, Md, 1958; Am Bd Surg, dipl, 1964. **Career:** Huron Rd Hosp, intern, 1959, Surg Res, 1963; Cleveland Transit Syst, med dir, 1969-72; Cleveland Acad Med, bd dir, 1974-76; Medic-Screen Health Ctr, pres, 1974-84; Shaker Med Ctr Hosp, chief surg, 1982-84; Metrohealth Hosp Women, chief surg, 1989-; City E Cleveland, Ohio, dir health, 1990; pvt pract gen surgeon, currently. **Orgs:** Fel Am Col Surgeons, 1966; pres med staff, Forest City Hosp, 1970-73; pres, Hough-Norwood Family Health Ctr, 1974-78; dir, First Bank Nat Asn, 1974-85; mem adv bd, Robert Wood Johnson Found Nat Health Serv Prog, 1977-83; dir, Ohio Motorist Asn, AAA, 1979-85; Seventy Second Am Assembly, Columbia Univ, 1986. **Home Addr:** 124 Colonial St Suite SE, Port Charlotte, FL 33952. **Business Addr:** General Surgeon, 13944 Euclid Ave, Cleveland, OH 44112, **Business Phone:** (216)451-1600.

## HUGGINS, HOSIAH, JR.

Management consultant. **Personal:** Born Aug 17, 1950, Chicago, IL. **Educ:** Univ Akron, BA, commun, speech commun & mass media, 1974; Newport Univ, MPA, 1988. **Career:** Amalgamated Stationers, vpres sales, 1974-80; Sears Xerox Corp, mkt exec & sales assoc, 1980-83; Insight & Attitudes Inc, pres; Huggins Commun, managing partner, 2015-; Zebraa Commun, founder, chmn & chief exec officer, currently. **Orgs:** Bd dir, Urban League Cleveland, 1978-80; bd dir, YMCA, 1979-85; nat pres, Nat Asn Mgt Consult, 1985-; Inst Mgt Consult. **Honors/Awds:** Outstanding Scholastic, Phi Beta Sigma, 1974; Outstanding Young Man of Am, 1982; Man of the Year, Bel-Aire Civic Club, 1983; "1983 Most Interesting People" Cleveland Mag. **Home Addr:** 10930 Wade Pk, Cleveland, OH 44106, **Home Phone:** (216)721-1010. **Business Addr:** Chairman, Chief Executive Officer, Zebraa Communications, 3530 Warrensville Ctr Rd Suite 126, Cleveland, OH 44122, **Business Phone:** (216)491-4600.

## HUGGINS, LINDA JOHNSON

Real estate agent. **Personal:** Born Nov 15, 1950, Oklahoma City, OK; daughter of Wallace C Johnson (deceased) and Wanda Fleming Johnson; married Howard III; children: Andrea Yvette & Valerie Diane. **Educ:** Langston Univ, Langston, Okla, BS, math educ, 1972; Webster Univ, St Louis, Mo, MA, bus admin & mgt, 1977. **Career:** Real estate agent (retired); Southwestern Bell Telephone Co, Kans City, Mo, engr, 1972-75, area mgr, 1976-2000; Century 21-Suburban, real estate agent, 1981; First Class Connections Travel Agency, owner, currently. **Orgs:** Pres, St Louis Chap, 1980-; St Louis Real Estate Bd, 1981-; Mo Real Estate Asn, 1981-; Nat Asn Advan Colored People, 1988-; publicity chair, 1990-91, parliamentarian, 1996-98, vpres, 1999-00, pres, 2001-02, Alpha Kappa Alpha Sorority; YWCA, 1988-; Greater Mt Carmel Baptist Church, St Louis, Mo; Community Network SBC; Langston Univ Nat Alumni Asn. **Honors/Awds:** Distinguished Alumni, Nat Asn Equal Opportunity, 1988; Mother of Merit, Nat Benevolent Asn; Unsung Heroine Community Service Award, Top Ladies Distinction. **Business Addr:** Owner, First Class Connections Travel Agency, 610 Brookstone Dr, Florissant, MO 63033-3927, **Business Phone:** (314)838-5386.

## HUGGINS-WILLIAMS, DR. NEDRA

Educator, businessperson. **Educ:** Fisk Univ; Howard Univ, MS, int affairs; Nat Defense Univ, MS; Univ Utah, PhD, commun. **Career:** Educator (retired), business person, executive; Univ Md, Col Pk, Md, prof; Nat Defense Univ, Wash, DC, prof; USAID, foreign serv prog officer; Global Training Solutions, sr partner, 2003-, pres, currently. **Orgs:** African Studies Asn; bd visitor, Bennett Col Women; bd mem, Big Bros Big Sisters Mid Tenn; bd mem, Nat Bar Asn; Alpha Kappa Alpha Sorority; bd dir, Nashville Conflict Resolution Ctr; trainer & mediator, Tenn Asn Prof Mediators. **Home Addr:** 12357 Herrington Dr, Silver Spring, MD 20904. **Business Addr:** Board Director, Nashville Conflict Resolution Center, 4732 W Longdale Dr, Nashville, TN 37211, **Business Phone:** (615)333-8400.

## HUGHES, ALBERT

Movie director. **Personal:** Born Apr 1, 1972, Detroit, MI; son of Albert and Aida; children: 1. **Career:** Director, producer, writer & cinematographer; Films: Menace II Society, co-producer, writer & dir, 1993; Dead Presidents, producer, writer & dir, 1995; American Pimp, cinematographer, producer & dir, 1999; Scratch, exec producer, 2001; From Hell, exec producer & dir, 2001; The Book of Eli, dir, 2010; TV: "Touching Evil", exec producer, 2004. **Special Achievements:** Nominated in Independent Spirit Awards(1994), Karlovy Vary International Film Festival(1996), Sundance Film Festival(1999), Black Reel Awards(2001 & 2002), Image Awards(2011). **Business Addr:** Film Director, Executive Producer, International Creative Management, 8942 Wilshire Blvd, Beverly Hills, CA 90211, **Business Phone:** (310)550-4000.

## HUGHES, ALLEN

Movie director, movie producer. **Personal:** Born Apr 1, 1972, Detroit, MI; son of Aida. **Career:** Film/TV dir, screenwriter & producer; Films: Menace II Society, story writer & co-producer, 1993; Dead Presidents, producer & story writer, 1995; Clutch, 1998; American Pimp, dir & producer, 2000; From Hell, dir & exec producer, 2001; Knights of the South Bronx, 2005; Broken City, producer, 2013. TV series: Touching Evil, exec producer, 2004; New York, I Love You, 2009; The Book of Eli, dir, 2010; Int Creative Mgt Inc, film director. **Business Addr:** Film Director, 8942 Wilshire Blvd, Beverly Hills, CA 90211, **Business Phone:** (310)550-4000.

## HUGHES, BERNICE ANN

Educator. **Personal:** Born Apr 10, 1959, Medina, TN; daughter of Rena L. **Educ:** Mid Tenn State Univ, BSW, 1982 & MA, 1991. **Career:** Mid Tenn State Univ, phys plant supvr, 1982-88, housing area coordr, 1988-92, housing assoc dir, personnel & develop, 1992, assoc dir judicial & leadership, 1982-1998; Abraham Baldwin Agr Col, dean, 1998-, proj dir, currently. **Orgs:** Exec bd, Tenn Asn Col & Univ Housing Officers, 1988-92; Alpha Kappa Alpha, 1992-. **Home Addr:** PO Box 265, Murfreesboro, TN 37132, **Home Phone:** (615)898-4210. **Business Addr:** Director of Student Life & Housing, Dean, Abraham Baldwin Agr Col, Rm 1 2802 Moore Hwy, Tifton, GA 31793, **Business Phone:** (229)391-5130.

## HUGHES, REV. CARL D.

Minister (clergy), clergy, educator. **Personal:** Born Indianapolis, IN; married Louise; children: 4. **Educ:** WVa State Col Inst, BS, 1942; Wharton Sch Finance Univ PA, MA, 1943; Christian Theol Sem, BD, 1957, MA, 1958; Christian Theol Sem, MDiv, 1972; Cent Baptist Theol Sem, DD, 1975; Ind Univ Sch Law Wayne State Univ & Univ Detroit, Post Grad Studies. **Career:** Mt Zion Baptist Church Indianapolis, ministers asst, 1952; Second Baptist Church Lafayette, 1952-56; St John Missionary Baptist Church, 1956-60; Christian Educ Methodist Baptist Church, Detroit, dir, 1960-61; Bethel Baptist Church E Detroit, pastor, 1961; Hughes Enterprise Inc, vpres treas; Detroit Christian Training Ctr, dean; Bus Educ Detroit Pub Sch, teacher; Church Builder & Bus Educ Detroit Pub Sch, dept head; Calvary Dist Asn Detroit, instr; Wolverine State Conv SS & BTU Cong MI, instr; Nat Baptist SS & BTU Cong, instr; Cent Bible Sem, instr. **Orgs:** Comt YMCA; Comt Nat Asn Advan Colored People; Grand Bd Dir Kappa Alpha Psi Nat Col Frat; Mason; budget comt Nat Negro Bus League; treas, St Emma Mil Acad Parent Asn Detroit; chmn, bd trustees, Todd-Phillips C Home Wolverine State Missionary Baptist Conv Inc; chmn, Finance Pastors' Div Nat Baptist Cong Christian Educ. **Honors/Awds:** Received First John L Webb Award, Nat Baptist Conv, 1948; Auth "The Church Organized For Meaning Ministry" & "Financing Local Church Property". **Home Addr:** 258 Trowbridge, Detroit, MI 48202. **Business Addr:** Vice President Treasurer, Hughes Enterprises Inc, 258 Trowbridge, Detroit, MI 48202.

## HUGHES, CATHERINE LIGGINS (CATHERINE ELIZABETH WOODS)

Radio broadcaster, radio host, media executive. **Personal:** Born Apr 22, 1947, Omaha, NE; daughter of William Alfred Woods and Helen E Jones Woods; married Dewey; married Alfred Liggins; children:

Alfred Charles Liggins III. **Educ:** Creighton Univ, Omaha, Nebr, acct, 1969; Univ Nebr, Omaha, Nebr, attended 1971; Harvard Univ, Cambridge, MA, attended 1975. **Career:** Omaha Star, staff; Howard Univ, Sch Commun, lectr; KOWH, 1969; WYCB-AM, pres & gen mgr, 1970; Howard Univ, sch commun & admin asst, 1971-73; WHUR-FM col radio sta, sales dir, asst, 1973-75, vpres & gen mgr; Radio One Inc, founder, 1980-97; WOL-AM, owner; WOL-AM, owner; WMMJ-FM, owner; WWIN-AM/FM, owner; WERQ-FM/WOLB-AM, owner; WKYS-FM, owner; WJZZ-FM, owner; WCHB-AM/WCHB-FM, owner; BET industs, minority owner. **Orgs:** Bd mem, United Black Fund, 1978-88; bd mem, DC Boys Girls Club, 1983-86; chmn, Community Comm Corp, 1985-87; Wash Post Recall Comn, 1987; fel Alpha Kappa Alpha Sorority. **Honors/Awds:** Woman of the Year, Wash Woman, 1987; People's Champion Award, Nat Black Media Coalition, 1988; Kool Achiever Communications, 1988; Woman of the Year, Women at Work of the Nat Capital Area, 1989; The Cathy Hughes TV Show, 1989; Honorary deg, Sojourner Douglass Col, Baltimore, 1995; Lifetime Achievement Award, Wash Area Broadcasters; Distinguished Service Award, Nat Asn Broadcasters, 2001; Madam CJ Walker Award, Ebony Mag, 2002; Golden Mike Award, Broadcasters Found; Lifetime Achievement Award, Nat Asn Black Owned Broadcasters; Essence Magazine Award, 2002; Entrepreneur of the Year, Ernst & Young, 2007. **Special Achievements:** First African-American woman to head a publicly traded company; Created a radio format called the Quiet Storm; First African-American to attend Duchesne Academy of the Sacred Heart, a prestigious Catholic girls' school in Omaha; Selected as 100 Who Have Changed the World by Ebony Mag; 100 Most Powerful & Influential Person; 20 Most Influential Women in Radio, Radio Ink; 10 most Powerful Women in Black America, Ebony; First African-American to earn an accounting degree from Creighton University. **Home Addr:** 6437 14th St NW, Washington, DC 20009. **Business Addr:** Chairperson & Founder, Radio One Inc, 14th Fl 1010 Wayne Ave, Silver Spring, MD 20910.

### HUGHES, COQUIE

Founder (originator), movie director. **Personal:** Born Nov 7, 1970, Chicago, IL; children: Peacejourney & Truth. **Educ:** Columbia Col. **Career:** GirlCrushTV.com, producer, director, writer and editor; SeeTruePeaceEntertainment, founder; Lights Camera Youth Action, founder and lead instructor; UrbanLesbianWebseries.com, founder and chief exec officer; theater and acting teacher, Chicago; set designer and builder. Films: producer, writer, director, "If I Wuz Yo Gyrl: An Experimental Work in Progress", 2003; executive producer, producer, writer, director, editor, cinematographer, narrator, "My Mama Said Yo Mama's Dyke", 2010; consulting producer, writer, director, editor, cinematographer, "The Lies We Tell But the Secrets We Keep", 2011; co-producer, writer, director, editor, "If I Was Your Girl", 2012; writer, "Girls Like Us! Part 1", 2012; "Last Call", assoc producer, 2015. **Special Achievements:** First African-American woman to direct three features; first African-American to ever write, produce, and direct a digital feature; producer of urban lesbian web series and films for GirlCrushTV.com; films have appeared in film festivals in the United States; written and produced numerous feature and short films; playwright and stage director who has produced over 12 stage plays; appeared in documentary "Sisters in Cinema".

### HUGHES, FRANKIE D.

Founder (originator), president (organization). **Educ:** Howard Univ, BS, math & bus admin, 1975; Stanford Univ, MBA, finance, 1979. **Career:** LF Rothschild; Saloman Bros; Citibank, officer; Exxon Corp, employee benefit fixed income assets mgr; WR Lazard & Co, Investment Policy Comt, dir asset mgt, portfolio mgr, mem Investment Policy Comt; Hughes Capital Mgt Inc, founder, pres & chief investment officer, 1993-; Pacholder High Yield Fund Inc, dir, 2009-. **Orgs:** Bd mem, Victory Funds, 2000-; bd trustee, Va Retirement Syst; bd trustee, JPMorgan Funds. **Honors/Awds:** 75 Most Powerful Women in Business, "Black Enterprise", 2010. **Business Addr:** President, Chief Investment Officer, Hughes Capital Management Inc, 916 Prince St 3 Fl, Alexandria, VA 22314, **Business Phone:** (703)684-7222.

### HUGHES, GEORGE MELVIN

Educator. **Personal:** Born Aug 26, 1938, Charlotte, TN; married Evelyn Benson; children: Vickie L & George M Jr. **Educ:** Tenn State Univ, BS, 1961, MEd, 1963; Univ Wis Milwaukee, post grad studies, 1968; Cardinal Stritch Col, post grad studies, 1983; Ind Univ, post grad studies, 1986. **Career:** Lafollette Elem Sch, teacher, 1963-68; Parkman Mid Sch, asst prin, 1968-71; Garfield Elem Sch, asst prin, 1971-74; Lee Elem Sch, prin. **Orgs:** Bd dir, Carter Child Develop Ctr, 1981, Girl Scouts Am, 1987, Phi Delta Kappa Milwaukee Chap, 1987; panelist US Dept Educ Ctr Systs & Prog Develop Inc, 1987; consult Indianapolis Sch Syst, 1987, Muscogee County Sch Dist Columbus GA, 1987; life mem, Nat Asn Advan Colored People; consult, Southwest Educ Develop Lab TX. **Home Addr:** 831 W Sierra Lane, Mequon, WI 53092, **Home Phone:** (414)241-5613. **Business Addr:** Principal, Lee Elementary School, 921 W Meinecke Ave, Milwaukee, WI 53206, **Business Phone:** (414)267-1700.

### HUGHES, GEORGE VINCENT

Automotive executive, president (organization). **Personal:** Born Apr 8, 1930, New York, NY; son of Lewis and Marion; children: Deirdre & Vincent. **Educ:** City Col NY, MBA, 1954. **Career:** George Hughes Chevrolet, pres, currently. **Orgs:** Alpha Phi Alpha, 1950-. **Business Addr:** President, George Hughes Chevrolet, 3712 Rte 9, Freehold, NJ 07728-6697, **Business Phone:** (732)462-1324.

### HUGHES, HARVEY L.

Lawyer. **Personal:** Born May 7, 1909, Port DePosit, MD; married Ethel C. **Educ:** Univ Pittsburgh Terrell Law Sch, LLB, 1944. **Career:** Off VA, Accredited Present Claims, 1955; Harris & Hughes Law Firm, partner; N Capitol Corp, gen coun. **Orgs:** Wash Bar Asn, 1946; Legal Fraternity Sigm Delta Tau, 1946; Nat Bar Asn, 1954; DC Bar Asn, 1972; counr, St Martin's Boys Club, 1972; Alpha Phi Alpha Fraternity; Fairmount Heights Civic Club. **Home Addr:** 1104 D St SE, Washington, DC 20003. **Business Addr:** 1840 N Capitol St, Washington, DC 20002.

### HUGHES, HOLLIS EUGENE, JR.

Executive. **Personal:** Born Mar 14, 1943, Tulsa, OK; son of Hollis Eugene Sr and Suzan Marie Brummell; married Lavera Ruth Knight. **Educ:** Ball State Univ, BS, soc sci, 1965, MA, sociol, 1972. **Career:** S Bend Community Sch Corp, teacher & coach, 1965-69; Model Cities Prog & City S Bend, exec dir, 1969-74. **Orgs:** Am Planning Asn, 1975; Nat Asn Housing & Redevelop Officials, 1978-; Am Mgt Asn, 1979-89; Alpha Phi Alpha Frat Inc, 1966-; Alpha Phi Omega Serv Frat, 1967-; pres, Ball State Univ Alumni Coun, 1974-; pres & bd mem, Family & C Ctr, 1978-79; trustee, S Bend Community Sch Corp & Pub Libr; vpres, 1978, 1980-81, pres, 1981-82, 1984-85; life mem, Nat Asn Advan Colored People; Adv Comt US Comn Civil Rights; bd trustee, Art Ctr Inc S Bend; trustee, Mem Hosp; bd trustee, Mem Hosp Found, 1987-90; bd mem, Youth Servs Bur; bd mem, Community Educ Round Table dir, S Bend-Mishka Chamber Com, 1987-; dir, Proj Future St Joseph County, 1987-; trustee, Ball State Univ, nominee Alumni Coun, 1989-, bd secy, 2006-11, bd dir, Black Alumni Asn, 1989-; vpres, Visions Progress, 1986-; bd dir, St Joseph County Minority Bus Develop Coun, 1991; dir, S Bend's bur housing; dir, St Joseph County Housing Allowance Off; pres, chief exec officer, United Way St Joseph County, S Bend, Ind; dir, Housing Assistance Off Inc; exec dir, St. Joseph County Housing Authority; secy, Ball State Bd trustee, 2006-11, pres, 2011-12. **Home Addr:** 6126 Miami St, South Bend, IN 46614-6147, **Home Phone:** (574)291-2228.

### HUGHES, ISAAC SUNNY

Mathematician. **Personal:** Born Jun 29, 1944, Zachary, LA; married Anna Ceaser; children: Timothy, Troy & Jessica. **Educ:** Grambling Univ, BA, 1966; Univ NC, pub admin, 1974. **Career:** Naval Surface Weapons Ctr, mathematician, 1967-; King George Co, VA, supvr, 1984-87; Co Sch Bd, 1989-90, 1993-95, Cupel LLC, founder, currently. **Orgs:** Worshipful Master KG Masonic Lodge No 314, 1978; cub master, Boy Scouts Am, 1978-81; bd mem, Zoning Appeals KG, 1981; Wetland Bd KG, 1982; tie breaker, Bd Supervisors KG, 1983; bd trustee-chair, Antioch Baptist Church KG; Worthy Patron Guiding Star Chap No 216; Fredericksburg Consistory No 346; Magnus Temple No 3; asst dist dep grand master, United Supreme Coun, 33rd Degree Masons. **Home Addr:** 10325 Oak Tree Dr, King George, VA 22485-4823, **Home Phone:** (540)775-7977. **Business Addr:** Founder, CUPEL LLC, 10325 Oak Tree Dr, King George, VA 22485-4823, **Business Phone:** (540)775-7977.

### HUGHES, JIMMY FRANKLIN, SR.

Law enforcement officer. **Personal:** Born Apr 10, 1952, Tuscaloosa, AL; son of Lee Marvin Sr and Mary Ann Stanley; married Juanita Price; children: Trina Woodberry, Jimmy Jr & Jared. **Educ:** Ohio Peace Officers Training Acad, police instrs cert, 1985; Northwestern Univ, Acad Police Staff & Comdr, SPSC-22, 1986; Youngstown State Univ, AAS, police technol, 1989, BS, police mgt, 1992, MS, police admin, 1997; FBI Nat Acad, Sect, 193, grad, addn educ, training law enforcement. **Career:** Law enforcement officer (retired); Youngstown Police Dept, patrol officer, 1977-81, detective sgt, 1981-87, lt, 1987-97, capt, 1997-2006, chief police, 2006-11. **Orgs:** Mid-Am Teakwon Do Asn; Nat Black Police Asn; pres, Black Knights Police Asn; Mahoning County Drug & Alcohol Addiction Bd; Mahoning County United Way Distrib Comt; Youngstown Urgan League; Nat Asn Advan Colored People Youngstown; assoc mem, Buckeye Elks Lodge No73 IBPOE. **Home Addr:** 3239 Oak St, Youngstown, OH 44505, **Home Phone:** (330)743-6335.

### HUGHES, JOHNNIE LEE

Miner. **Personal:** Born Nov 18, 1924, Coalwood, WV; son of George and Florine Westbrooke; married Sarah Etta Gibson; children: Leonard C Jones, Jacqueline Lee Jones & Moseley. **Career:** Miner (retired); Osage W Va, mayor, 1959-61, 1968-70; Off Am Asian Free Labor Inst Wash DC Turkey, instr mine safety, 1979; Consol Coal Co, mine worker, 1995. **Orgs:** Pres, UMWA 2122, 1978-80; Mine Com/Safety Com; Coal Miners Polit Action Community. **Honors/Awds:** Miner to Mayor publ Ebony Edition, 1972; consult to Turkey Publ Miner's Jour, 1980. **Special Achievements:** First African American chief of police Monongalia Co WV; First Black mayor State of WV. **Home Addr:** 1210 Milton St, Morgantown, WV 26505, **Home Phone:** (304)291-6241.

### HUGHES, DR. JOYCE A.

Lawyer, college teacher, educator. **Personal:** Born Feb 7, 1940, Gadsden, AL; daughter of Solomon Sr and Bessie Cunningham. **Educ:** Carleton Col, Northfield, MN, BA, 1961; Univ Madrid, Spain, cert, 1962; Univ Minn Law Sch, JD, 1965. **Career:** John Hay Whitney fel, 1962-63; Hamilton & Pearson, atty, 1967-71; Univ Minn, assoc prof law, 1971-75; Northwestern Univ, vis assoc prof law, 1975-76, assoc prof law, 1976-79, prof law, 1979-; Continental Ill Nat Bank, sr atty, 1982-84; Univ Calif, Hastings Col Law, vis prof law, 1991; US Dist Ct Minn, law clerk. **Orgs:** Phi Beta Kappa, 1961; dir, Leadership Coun Metrop Open Communities Chicago, Ill, 1996-2002; trustee, Carleton Col, 1969-94; trustee, Carleton Col Northfield, Minn, 1969-94; dir, First Plymouth Bank, 1971-82; dir, First Plymouth Nat Bank, Minneapolis, Minn, 1971-82; trustee, Nat Urban League, 1972-78; trustee, Nat Urban League, vchair, 1976-78; dir, Chicago Forum, pres, 1978-79; dir, Community Renewal Soc, Chicago, Ill, 1978-86; dir, Chicago Bd Educ, 1980-82; dir, Fed Home Loan Bank Chicago, 1980-84; adv bd, C & Family Justice Ctr, Chicago, Ill, 1981-97; dir, Leadership Greater Chicago, 1983-87; adv bd mem, Refugee & Citizenship Law Abstracts, 2000-; adv comt, Am Const Soc, 2009-; Am Bar asn; Nat Bar Asn; Ill Bar Asn; Cook County Bar Asn; Black Women Lawyers Greater Chicago. **Honors/Awds:** Fulbright Scholar, 1961-62; Alumni Achievement Award, Carleton Col Northfield, Minn, 1969; Achievement, Minn Afro-American Lawyers, 1972; Service Award, Black Law Stud Asn, Univ Minn Law Sch, 1974; Kizzy Award, Black Women Hall Fame Found, 1979; Woman of the Year, Zeta Phi Beta Sorority Inc, Chicago, 1982; Service Award, Nat Alliance Black Sch Educr, 1982; Woman of the Year, Coalition United Community Action, Chicago, 1983; Achievement, Minn Minority Lawyers Asn, 1983; 100 Top Bus & Prof Women, Dollars & Sense Magazine, 1986; Superior Public Service, Cook County Bar Asn, 1987; Distinguished Service, Black Women Lawyers Asn Greater Chicago, 1993; Woman of Achievement & Role Model Day, Bennett Col Founder's, 1993; Honorary Doctor of Laws, Carleton Col Northfield, Minn, 2001; Leno O Smith Award, Black Women Minn Aty, 2002; Clyde Ferguson Award, Asn Am Law Sch, Minority Groups Sect, 2002; Ida B Platt Award, Cook County Bar Asn, 2006; Hall of Fame, Cook County Bar Asn, 2007. **Special Achievements:** First Black female tenure-track law professor at a majority school, 20 years after such a person was a professor at a predominantly Black law school; First woman & the First African American General Counsel of the Chicago Transit Authority; First African American female tenured full professor in any department at Northwestern University. Published numerous Books. **Home Addr:** 680 Lake Shore Dr Apt 1008, Chicago, IL 60615, **Home Phone:** (312)280-7683. **Business Addr:** Professor of Law, Northwestern University School of Law, 357 E Chicago Ave, Chicago, IL 60611, **Business Phone:** (312)503-8373.

### HUGHES, KORI

Public relations executive. **Personal:** married Marc. **Educ:** Hampton Univ. **Career:** Law Off Willie E Gary, pub rels dir, currently. **Home Addr:** , Royal Palm Beach, FL 33411. **Business Addr:** Director of Public Relations, Law Off of Willie E Gary, 221 E Osceola St, Stuart, FL 34994, **Business Phone:** (772)288-0771.

### HUGHES, LARRY

Basketball player. **Personal:** Born Jan 23, 1979, St. Louis, MO. **Educ:** St Louis Univ, attended 1998. **Career:** Basketball player (retired); Philadelphia 76ers, pt guard, 1998-2000; Golden State Warriors, shooting guard, 2000-02; Wash Wizards, pt guard & shooting guard, 2002-05; Cleveland Cavaliers, shooting guard, 2005-08; Chicago Bulls, 2008-09, New York Knicks, 2009-10; Orlando Magic, 2011-12. **Honors/Awds:** USBWA National Freshman of the Year, 1998; NBA Steals Leader, 2005. **Home Addr:** 13034 Autumn Fields Ct, Saint Louis, MO 63146-1806. **Business Addr:** Professional Basketball Player, New York Knicks, 2 Pa Plz, New York, NY 10121.

### HUGHES, MAMIE F.

Civil rights activist, community activist, teacher. **Personal:** Born May 3, 1929, Jacksonville, FL; married Judge Leonard; children: Leonard III, Kevin, Stefan, Patrick & Amy. **Educ:** Fisk Univ, BA, 1949; Univ Mo, attended 1951. **Career:** Community activist (retired); Mo Pub Sch Syst, teacher, 1951-52, 1957-62; Greenville, teacher, 1954-56; St Joseph Cath Sch, vol teacher, 1962-63; Head Start, vol, 1968-69; Jackson Co Legis, charter mem, 1972-78; Fed Agency Reg Dir Action, 1985; Carver Neighborhood Ctr, mem adv comn, 1985; New Metzl Ad Touts Support, civil rights leader; Samuel Univ, Rodgers Community Health Ctr, bd chmn, dir emer. **Orgs:** Cath Interracial Coun, 1959-63; bd mem, HPEED, 1965-66; founding comn, Vol Serv Bur; bd mem, United Campaign Vol, 1964-68; vol, Martin Luther King Jr HS; Greater KS Coord Comn Int Women's Yr; Jackson Co Child Welfare Adv Com; Panel Am Women; chmn, Comn Aging; chmn, Fed Exec Bd; past chmn, Health & Welfare Comn; KC Mo Fair Housing Comn; vol, parent, 1965-66; foster, Parent, 1966-67; St Joseph Sch PTA; pres, Greater KC Minority Women's Coalition Human Rights; rec secy, Greater KC Hearing & Speech Ctr; bd mem, Truman Med Ctr; vchmn, Mid-Am Regional Coun, 1972-78; Parker Sq Housing Corp; Lincoln Black Arch; KC Crime Comn; YMCA Urban Servs; Manpower Adv Mem, Nat Coun Negro Women; Nat Advan Asn Colored People; Jack & Jill Am Inc; Greater KC Links Inc Serv Urban Youth De La Salle Edu Ctr; Beautiful Activists Vol Serv Woolf Bros & Germaine Monteil; exec dir, Black Econ Union, 1981-86; ombudsman, advocate, Bruce R. Watkins Dr proj, 1987-2001; Mo Holocaust Educ & Awareness Comn; Women's Pub Serv Network; adv boards, Friendship House; adv boards, Catherine's Pl; adv boards, Hist Jazz Found. **Honors/Awds:** Community Service Award; Service Award, Nat Advan Asn Colored People; Freedom Fund Dinner Com; National Award, Kansas City, 2009. ATHENA Award Recipient, 2009. **Home Addr:** 1763 Woodland, Kansas City, MO 64108.

### HUGHES, MARK

Executive, basketball player, basketball coach. **Personal:** Born Oct 5, 1966, Muskegon, MI; married Ronna; children: Mark Jr, Madelyn & Jackson. **Educ:** Mich State Univ, grad, sociol, 1989. **Career:** Basketball player (retired), basketball coach, executive; Nat Col Athletic Asn Championship team, co-capt, 1989; Detroit Pistons, 1991; Scaini Venezia, 1991-93; Grand Rapids Hoops, 1995-98, head coach, 1997-2002; Toronto Raptors, 1996; Orlando Magic, asst coach, 2002-04; San Diego State Univ, asst coach, 2004-06; Sacramento Kings, asst coach, 2006-07; New York Knicks, scout, 2007-08, dir w coast scouting, 2007-11, dir pro personnel, 2011-. **Honors/Awds:** Muskegon Area Sports Hall of Fame, 2004. **Home Addr:** , Roseville, CA. **Business Addr:** Director of Pro Personnel, New York Knicks, Madison Sq Garden 2 Pa Plz, New York, CA 10121-0091, **Business Phone:** (212)465-6471.

### HUGHES, ROBERT DANAN

Football player, banker. **Personal:** Born Dec 11, 1970, Bayonne, NJ; married Tifanni; children: Jessicah Briana, Joseph Alan, Taurin Isaiah & Savana Rienne. **Educ:** Univ Iowa, commun. **Career:** Football player (retired), banker; Milwaukee Brewers, wide receiver, 1991-92; Kans City Chiefs, wide receiver, 1993-98; Bank Am, 1999; Metro Sports, TV Analyst; Big Ten Network, col football analyst, 2008-; US Bancorp, US Bank Home Mortgage, mortgage loan originator, loan officer, currently. **Orgs:** Danan Hughes Ann Give Back Benefit. **Home Addr:** 1412 E 97th St Apt D, Kansas City, MO 64131-3483. **Business Addr:** Home Mortgage Originator, US Bancorp, 10401 Holmes Rd, Kansas City, MO 64131, **Business Phone:** (816)668-9992.

### HUGHES, TYRONE CHRISTOPHER

Executive, football player. **Personal:** Born Jan 14, 1970, New Orleans, LA. **Educ:** Univ Nebr, BS, human develop & family studies, 1992. **Career:** Football player (retired); New Orleans Saints, corner back & kick returner & punt returner & right corner back, 1993-96; Chicago Bears, kick returner & punt returner, 1997; Dallas Cowboys, kick returner, 1998; TY33 Consultants LLC, pres, 2010-currently. **Honors/Awds:** Pro Bowls, 1993; NFL Kickoff Return Yards Leader, 1994-96; New Orleans Saints Hall of Fame, 2015. **Special Achievements:** TV Series: "NFL Monday Night Football" 1993-94; "TNT Sunday Night Football", 1993-97; "NFL on FOX ", 1994-96; "ESPN's Sunday Night

Football", 1994-96. **Business Addr:** President, TY33 Consultants LLC, 10231 E Deer Park Blvd, New Orleans, LA 70127-2759.

### HUGHES, SEN. VINCENT J.

State government official. **Personal:** Born Oct 26, 1956, Philadelphia, PA; son of James and Ann; married Sheryl Lee Ralph; children: 4. **Educ:** Temple Univ. **Career:** Univ Pa, libr adminr; Pa St Senate, House Representatives, St rep, Dist 190, 1987-94, Dist 7, sen, 1994-, Dep Minority Whip, 2005-06, Minority Caucus, secy, 2007-08, Minority Caucus, chair, 2009-10; Penn Legis Black Caucus, chmn, 1991-94; 44th Ward Pa Dem Party, Philadelphia County, leader, currently. **Orgs:** Chmn, Pa Legis Black Caucus; chmn, Health & Welfare Comt; St Gov & Labor Rels Comt; bd dir, Penn Higher Educ Assistance Agency; coun, St Govt's Eastern Regional Conf Comt Health & Human Serv; founding mem, Dem Study Group; bd mem, Philadelphia Com Develop Corp; Philadelphia Welfare Pride & Blacks Educating Blacks About Sexual Health Issues; co-founder; dem chair, C First; Senate Pub Health & Welfare Comn; Appropriations, Educ & Policy; Am Fed St Co & Munic Employees Union; Prince Hall Grand Lodge Free & Accepted Masons; Phildelphia Int Airport Adv Bd; Fathers Day Rally Comn; Dep Minority Whip, 2005-06; trustee, Mt Carmel Baptist Church; chair, Senate Dem Caucus, 2008-10; chair, Minority Caucus, 2009-10; fel Am Fedn State, County & Munic Employees Union; trustee, Cheyney Univ Coun trustee; vice chair, Nat Citizens Action Consumer Orgn; bd mem, Ctr Human Advan; bd mem, fel Community Serv Adv Bd; Fathers Day Rally Comt; bd mem, Pa Higher Educ Assistance Agency Bd; Pa Minority Bus Develop Agency; Philadelphia Int Airport Adv Bd; chair, Minority Senate Appropriations Comt, 2011-; chair, Senate Dem Deleg, Philadelphia; Judiciary Comt, Commonwealth Pa Senate. **Home Addr:** 4950 Parkside Ave Suite 300, Philadelphia, PA 19131, **Home Phone:** (215)879-7777. **Business Addr:** State Senator, Pennsylvania General Assembly, 545 Main Capitol Bldg, Harrisburg, PA 17120-3007, **Business Phone:** (717)787-7112.

### HUGHLEY, DARRYL LYNN

Comedian, actor. **Personal:** Born Mar 6, 1963, Los Angeles, CA; son of Charles and Audrey; married LaDonna; children: Tyler, Ryan & Kyle. **Career:** Stand-up comedian, actor; Appeared on Def Comedy Jam, HBO; Comic View, BET, host, 1992; NBC, Jay Leno Show, corresp; CNN's D. L. Hughley Breaks News, host. TV series: "Double Rush", 1995; "The Hughleys", actor, writer, co-producer, 1998; "Studio 60 on the Sunset Strip", 2006-07; Hawaii Five-0, 2010; Who Wants to Be a Millionaire, 2011; DL Hughley: The Endangered List, 2012; Match Game, 2012; Trust Me, I'm a Game Show Host, 2013; Heartbeat, 2016. Films: Inspector Gadget, 1999; DL Hughley Goin' Home, 1999; The Orgininal Kings of Comedy, 2000; The Brothers, 2001; VH1 Big in 03, 2003; Scary Movie 3, 2003; Chasing Papi, 2003; Soul Plane, 2004; Shackles, 2005; Cloud 9, 2006; The Adventures of Brer Rabbit, 2006; K&R: Part 1, 2 & 3, 2007; What Kind of Day Has It Been, 2007; Studio 60 on the Sunset Strip, 2007; Doubting Thomas, 2008; Spy School, 2008; Cat Run, 2011. **Orgs:** Omega Psi Phi Fraternity. **Special Achievements:** Book: "I Want You to Shut the Fuck Up: How the Audacity of Dopes Is Ruining America", 2012. **Business Addr:** Actor, Barash & Altman Inc, 9100 Wilshire Blvd Suite 1000 W, Beverly Hills, CA 90212-3413, **Business Phone:** (310)288-6200.

### HUGHLEY, STEPHANIE S.

Chief executive officer, dancer. **Personal:** Born Oct 16, 1948, Canton, OH; daughter of Robert Lee Sr and Lillie Mae. **Educ:** Kent State Univ, BS, 1969; Antioch Col, Harvard Univ, MEd, 1972. **Career:** Smith Col, dance instr, 1971; Negro Ensemble Co, gen mgr, 1982-86; Atlanta Cult Community, 1987-92; Nat Black Arts Festival, artistic dir, 1987-92, founding artistic dir, chief exec officer, bd dirs, exec producer, 1999-2011; Atlanta Comt, Olympic Games Cult Olympiad, theatre & dance producer, 1992-96; NJ Performing Arts Ctr, vpres programming, 1995-99, 2009-11; Dance Theater Boston, dancer; Elma Lewis Sch Fine Arts, dancer; African & Caribbean & Ballet Co, dancer; Alvin Ailey Am Dance Theater, consult; Pittsburgh Symphony Orchestra, consult; Nat Music Ctr Wash, consult; Brooklyn Acad Music, vpres, currently. **Orgs:** Bd Metro Atlanta Arts & Cult Coalition; Atlanta Conv Ctr & Visitors Bur; Asn Theatrical Press Agts & Mgrs, 1977-. **Business Addr:** Vice President, Brooklyn Academy of Music, 30 Lafayette Ave, Brooklyn, NY 11217, **Business Phone:** (718)636-4100.

### HUGINE, DR. ANDREW, JR.

Educator, president (organization). **Personal:** Born Green Pond, SC; son of Andrew Sr and Irene S; married Abbiegail Hamilton; children: Andrew III & Akilah (Quincy Elmore). **Educ:** SC State Univ, BS, math, MEd, math; Mich State Univ, PhD, philos, higher educ & instnl res. **Career:** Beaufort High Sch, instr, mathematics; Mich State Univ, grad teaching asst & asst prof, instnl res; Southern Asn Col & Schs Self-Study, asst dir & dir; Acad Affairs, asst vpres; SC State Univ, dir spec serv prog, dir univ yr action prog, res fel, asst & dir instnl self-study, asst vpres acad affairs, prof mathematics, interim exec vpres & chief operating officer, pres, 2003-08; Ala A&M Univ, pres, 2009-. **Orgs:** Williams Chapel AME Church, Orangeburg, SC; life mem, Omega Psi Phi Fraternity; Edisto Masonic Lodge; bd dir, Edisto United Way; chmn bd trustee, Orange burg Consol Sch Dist Five; White Hall African Methodist Episcopal Church; St John African Methodist Episcopal Church; Huntsville Rotary; bd dir, Huntsville/Madison Chamber Com; life mem, SC State Univ Nat Alumni Asn; 100 Black Men Am; life mem, Nat Asn Advan Colored People; bd dir, Ala Sch Sci & Mathematics; Sigma Pi Phi Fraternity; Ala Coun Presidents. **Business Addr:** President, Alabama A&M University, 4900 Meridian St N, Huntsville, AL 35810-1015, **Business Phone:** (256)372-5000.

### HULETT, ROSEMARY D. (ROSEMARY D HULETT-PORTER)

School administrator. **Personal:** Born Sep 17, 1954, Chicago, IL; married Melvin D. **Educ:** Chicago State Univ, BSEd, spec educ, 1975; MSEd, spec educ, 1980. **Career:** Archdiocese Chicago Cath Sch Bd, head teacher, 1975-77, headstart dir, 1977-78; Chicago Bd Educ, Spec Educ, teacher, 1978-80; Chicago State Univ, dir alumni affairs, 1980-91; Gov State Univ, assoc dir alumni rels, 1991-93, dir alumni rels, 1997-2004, interim assoc vpres, instnl advan & alumni rels, 2004-, adj fac mem, 2006-; Roosevelt Univ, Chicago, Ill, assoc dir alumni rels & ann giving, 1996-97; CASE Dist Five, bd dir, coun advan & support. **Orgs:** Nat Asn Educ Young C, 1975-77; Coun Excep Educ, 1978-79; exec secy & treas, Chicago State Univ Alumni Asn, 1980-; chmn, CASE V Career Advan Women & Minorities Comn, 1985-88; CASE Dist Five Bd dir, 1986-88 & 1991-92; CASE Nat Bd trustee, 1989-92; CASE Dist Five Conf Comt, 1999; Girls Scouts S Cook County Bd dir, 1998-2003; Coun Treas, 2003-08; CASE Comn Alumni Rels, 2003-06; cheif exec officer, Alumini Asn, Gov State Univ; River Oaks Coop Towne House Memorial Comn; River Oaks Coop Towne House Fin Comn; chair, Comn Career Advan Women & Minorities. **Honors/Awds:** Teacher of the Year Award, Nat Asn Educ Young C, 1976; Special Education Teaching Certificate, Chicago Bd Educ, 1979; Certificate of Recognition for Alumni, Admin Coun Advan Sec Educ, 1980; Outstanding Young Professional Award, Chicago Coalition Urban Prof, 1986. **Home Addr:** 54 Dogwood Ct, Calumet City, IL 60409. **Business Addr:** Associate Vice President, Director of Alumni Relations, Governors State University, 1 Univ Pkwy, University Park, IL 60484-0975, **Business Phone:** (708)534-7892.

### HULETT-PORTER, ROSEMARY D. See HULETT, ROSEMARY D.

### HULL, AKASHA GLORIA

Poet, writer, educator. **Personal:** Born Dec 6, 1944, Shreveport, LA; daughter of Robert T and Jimmie; married Prentice Roy; children: Adrian L Prentice. **Educ:** Southern Univ, BA, eng, 1966; Univ Ill, attended 1966; Purdue Univ, MA, eng lit, 1968, PhD, eng lit, 1972. **Career:** Univ Del, Newark, instr, 1971, from asst prof to prof eng, 1972-88; Black Am Lit Forum, adv ed, 1978-86; Stanford Univ, vis scholar, 1987-88; Univ Calif-SantaCruz, prof womens studies & lit, 1988-2000, chair women's studies dept, 1989-91, prof emerita, womens studies & lit, 2000-; fel Nat Endowment Humanities. Author: Soul Talk: The New Spirituality of African American Women; Give Us Each Day: The Diary of Alice Dunbar-Nelson, 1986; Color, Sex and Poetry: Three Women of the Harlem Renaissance, 1987; Healing Heart, 1989. **Orgs:** Rockefeller Found Fel, 1979-80; co-proj dir, Black Women's Studies proj, 1982-84; Mellon Scholar, Wellesley Ctr Res Women, 1983; Ford Found Fel, 1987-88; comn co-chair, Mod Lang Asn; Nat Women's Studies Asn; adv & consult, Black Am Lit Forum, Feminist Studies; Col Lang Asn; Mod Lang Asn Am; Nat Asn Advan Colored People; Alpha Kappa Alpha; Am Humanities Div Fac Fel, Asn Univ Women, 1990-91; Nat Humanities Ctr, 1994-95; Combahee River Collective. **Home Addr:** 3501 Mission Dr, Santa Cruz, CA 95065. **Business Addr:** Professor Emerita of Literature and Feminist Studies, University of California Santa Cruz, Humanities 1 Suite 503, Santa Cruz, CA 95064-1016, **Business Phone:** (831)459-2696.

### HULL, BERNARD S., SR.

Engineer. **Personal:** Born Aug 1, 1929, Wetipquin, MD; married Marion Hayes; children: Karla L & Bernard S II. **Educ:** Howard Univ, BS, 1951; Univ Md. **Career:** Engineer (retired); Tamarach Triangle Civic Asn, exec bd; Bernard Hull, 1965; White Oak Fed Credit Union, vpres, 1972-77; Naval Mat Command, Wash, DC, corp planning div hq, 1985; Naval Surf Weapons Ctr, Silver Spring, Md, res mech engr adv planning staff, 1987; Naval Surf Weapons Ctr, White Oaks, Md, Col rela rep. **Orgs:** Life mem, Nat Asn Advan Colored People. **Honors/Awds:** Distinguished Able Toastmaster Award, 1974. **Home Addr:** 900 E Randolph Rd, Silver Spring, MD 20904, **Home Phone:** (301)384-9262. **Business Addr:** Owner, Bernard Hull, 900 E Randolph Rd, Silver Spring, MD 20904, **Business Phone:** (301)384-9262.

### HULL, DR. EVERSON WARREN, JR.

Economist, government official. **Personal:** Born Oct 14, 1943; son of Samuel E and Violette (Brown) H; married Melverlynn Surilina Spears; children: Randolph E & Cecilia A. **Educ:** Howard Univ, BA, econs & math, 1970, MA, economet, 1971, PhD, economet, 1977; Univ Md, MA, econs & money, 1974. **Career:** Fed Nat Mort Assoc, economist, 1973-76; Am Petrol Inst, sr economist, 1976-78; TRW Inc, sr economist, 1978-79; Cong Res Servs, head money & banking quant econs, 1979-83; US Dept Labor, dep asst secy policy, 1983-87; Fed Home Loan Bank, dir res, 1987-. **Home Addr:** 811 Quaint Acres Dr, Silver Spring, MD 20904-2727, **Home Phone:** (301)622-4054.

### HULL, DR. STEPHANIE J.

School principal, educator. **Educ:** Wellesley Col, BA, Fr lit, 1987; Harvard Univ, MA, romance lang & literatures, 1988, PhD, romance lang & literatures, 1992. **Career:** Dartmouth Col, asst prof Fr, 1992-96, asst dean col, 1995-98, adj asst prof Fr, 1996-98; Mt Holyoke Col, asst to pres, secy col, 1998-2003; Brearley Sch, head, 2003-11; Wellesley Col, asst to pres & sec & adj asst prof. **Orgs:** Exec vpres & chief operating officer, Woodrow Wilson Nat Fel Found, 2012-. **Honors/Awds:** First African American to lead New York's Brearley School. **Home Addr:** , Easton, CT. **Business Addr:** Executive Vice President, Chief Operating Officer, Woodrow Wilson National Fellowship Foundation, 5 Vaughn Dr Suite 300, Princeton, NJ 08540-6313, **Business Phone:** (609)452-7007.

### HUMMINGS, ARMENTA ADAMS. See ADAMS, ARMENTA ESTELLA.

### HUMPHERY, BOBBY. See HUMPHREY, ROBERT CHARLES.

### HUMPHREY, HOWARD JOHN

Engineer. **Personal:** Born Nov 5, 1940; son of Easton; married Bernadette Barker; children: Hayden & Lynette. **Educ:** NY Univ, BE, 1969; Univ Mich, Am Elec Power Spons Mgt Training Prog, 1976. **Career:** Am Elec Power Serv Corp, engr technol, 1967-99, mgr mat handling div, 1983-88, group mgr civil eng div, 1988-, sect head mat handling div, asst sect head, sr engr, engr, assoc engr; Cl Ford Power Plant Solid Waste Disposal, specialist. **Orgs:** Reg Prof Engr NJ, OH & WV; Am Soc Civ Engr; chmn, hon mem, Am Coal Ash Asn. **Special Achievements:** First Black Department Head in the American Electrical Power Service Corporation. **Home Addr:** 1090 Clubview Blvd N, Columbus, OH 43235-1222, **Home Phone:** (614)846-1726. **Business Addr:** Group Manager, American Electric Power Service Corp, 30 S Nev Ave Suite 602, Columbus, OH 43216, **Business Phone:** (614)223-2980.

### HUMPHREY, MARGO

Educator, writer, artist. **Personal:** Born Jun 25, 1942, Oakland, CA; daughter of James Dudley and Dorothy Reed; married Thais Valentine Nysus. **Educ:** Merritt City Col, attended 1963; Calif State Univ, Hayward, CA, attended 1968; Calif Col Arts & Crafts, fine & studio arts, 1973; Stanford Univ, Palo Alto, CA, MFA, printmaking, 1973. **Career:** Golden State Mutual Life Ins Co, purchase, 1968; Stanford Univ, teaching asst, 1972-74; Ford Found fel, 1980-81; Univ S Pac, Suva, vis fac; Univ Calif, Santa Cruz, asst prof art, 1985; Univ Tex, San Antonio, vis assoc, 1987; Margaret Trowell Sch Fine Art, Kampala, Uganda, 1987; Univ Benin, Benin, Nigeria, artistic specialist, 1987; Nat Endowment Arts, fel, 1988; Yaba TecInst, Nigeria, artistic specialist; Art Inst Chicago, vis assoc, 1987-89; Tiffany fel, 1988; Univ Md, fac, 1989-, grad dir, 1991-93, dept head printmaking, currently; NEA grant; Nat Gallery, Harare, Zimbabwe, vis fac; Univ Md, Dept Printmaking, dept head, currently. **Orgs:** Nat Asn Advan Colored People; "Eight" Inst Contemp Art Va Mus Richmond, 1980; design costume & stage sets comn, Oakland Ballet Co, 1990; US Info Agency Arts Am Prog. **Honors/Awds:** State Honor Proclamation, Mayor Henry Cisneros; Marcus Foster Award forTeaching Excellence, Oakland Pub Sch, 1986; Louis Comfort Tiffany Award; The James D Pheland Award, World Print Coun. **Special Achievements:** Honored as first American to open the American Section, National Gallery of Art, Lagos, Nigeria; author and illustrator of the children's book, "The River That Gave Gifts", 1987; work was selected by the Stanford Committee for the Arts, to be presented to Duke Ellington in an Honorary Degree Ceremony. **Home Addr:** 4310 Notre Dame St, Hyattsville, MD 20783-1909. **Business Addr:** Head of Printmaking, Faculty, University of Maryland, m2324 Art/Soc Bldg, College Park, MD 20742, **Business Phone:** (301)405-1453.

### HUMPHREY, MARIAN J.

Banker. **Career:** Med Ctr State Bank, Okla City, Okla, chief exec. **Business Addr:** Chief Executive, Medical Center State Bank, 1300 N Lottie, Oklahoma City, OK 73117, **Business Phone:** (405)424-5271.

### HUMPHREY, MARION ANDREW

Judge, clergy. **Personal:** Born Nov 2, 1949, Pine Bluff, AR; son of Doris L Pendleton; married Vernita Gloria Thomas; children: Marion Andrew Jr. **Educ:** Princeton Univ, BA, 1972; Harvard Divinity Sch, MDiv, 1978; Univ Aak Law Sch, JD, 1979. **Career:** Attorney (retired), judge, pastor; State Ark, asst atty gen, 1981, circuit ct judge, 1993-2010; self-employed, law pract, 1982-86, 1987-89; Allison Mem Presby Church, pastor, 1984-; City Little Rock, asst city atty, 1986, munic judge, 1989-92; Pine Bluff Com, reporter & ed; Pleasant Hill Baptist Church, assoc minister; Pulaski Co Courthouse, circuit judge, currently; Sprinkle Firm, coun, currently. **Orgs:** Bd, Ark C Hosp, 1992-; bd dir, Lyon Col; Little Rock Rotary Club, 1991-; NCP; NBA, judicial coun, 1989-; Princeton Alumni Asn Ark; fel Ark Bar Asn; Pulaski County Bar Asn; Nat Bar Asn; W Harold Flowers Law Socs; bd, Ark Childrens Hosp Little Rock; bd, Johnson C Smith Sem; fel Lyons adv bd; Nat Asn Advan Colored People; chaplain, Judicial Coun Nat Bar Asn; Ark Judicial Coun. **Home Addr:** 2115 S Arch St, Little Rock, AR 72206, **Home Phone:** (501)375-3345. **Business Addr:** Circuit Judge, Pulaski County Courthouse, 401 W Markham St Suite 420, Little Rock, AR 72201, **Business Phone:** (501)340-8590.

### HUMPHREY, ROBERT CHARLES (BOBBY HUMPHERY)

Football player. **Personal:** Born Aug 23, 1961, Lubbock, TX. **Educ:** NMex State Univ. **Career:** Football player (retired); New York Jets, defensive back, 1984, kick returner, 1985-87, left cornerback, 1988-98; Los Angeles Rams, right corner back, kick returner, 1990-91; San Diego Chargers, defensive back, 1991; San Antonio Riders, 1992; Sacramento Gold Miners, 1993-94; San Antonio Texans, 1995.

### HUMPHREY, SONNIE

Manager. **Educ:** Hunter Col, New York, NY, BA, 1976. **Career:** Hunter Col News, reporter, 1974-76; Arts Bull, ed, 1981; Souvenir, jr ed, 1985-88; Jackie Robinson Found, 1991-96; Black Hist Makers Award, presenter, 1991; talent coordr, Motown Returns Apollo; Ed Newsletter, Zeta Delta Phi Sorority, currently. **Orgs:** Bd mem, YGB Leadership Training, 1971-; coordr, Luncheon & Fashion Event, 1980-89; award coordr, Nat Coalition 100 Black Women Candace Awards, 1982-89; United Negro Col Fund Auxiliary Comn, 1984-; vpres, New York Coalition 100 Black Women, 1986-; pres, Zeta Delta Phi Sorority, 1987-; spec events coordr, UNCF Michael Jackson Benefit, 1988; vol, New York Host Comn Grammys, 1991; New York Women's Agenda, 1993-. **Honors/Awds:** Outstanding Service, Zeta Delta Phi Sorority, 1974, 1977 & 1986; Service To Youth Award, Kennedy Community Ctr, 1975, 1978; Outstanding Young Women, 1982; Achievement Award, New York Coalition 100 Black Women, 1984; Community Service, Joseph P Kennedy Community Ctr, 1985; CBS-TV Adv Comn Black Hist Month Moments, 1995-. **Special Achievements:** Poems, "Black Women", 1977; "Young, Gifted and Black", 1980. **Home Addr:** 3531 Bronxwood Ave, Bronx, NY 10469, **Home Phone:** (212)231-7439. **Business Addr:** Newsletter Editor, Zeta Delta Phi Sorority Inc Corp, 7715 Aquatic Dr, Arverne, NY 11692-2001.

### HUMPHRIES, DR. CHARLES, JR. (DR. CHARLIE HUMPHRIES, JR.)

Obstetrician, gynecologist. **Personal:** Born Apr 14, 1943, Dawson, GA; married Monica Tulio; children: Charlie Christopher. **Educ:** Fisk Univ, BA, 1966; Meharry Med Col, MD, 1972. **Career:** Mercy Hosp & Med Ctr, internship, 1972-73, resident, 1973-75; Phoebe N; pvt pract physician, currently. **Orgs:** Omega Psi Phi Fraternity; Dougherty Co Med Soc; Ga State Med Asn; Med Asn Ga; asst treas, Ga State Affil Univ Ill, 1972-73; Southwest GA Black Health Care Providers. **Home Addr:** 3520 Wexford Dr, Albany, GA 31707, **Home Phone:** (912)999-

0926. **Business Addr:** Physician, 802 N Jefferson St, Albany, GA 31701, **Business Phone:** (229)883-8602.

## HUMPHRIES, DR. FREDERICK S., SR.

College administrator. **Personal:** Born Dec 26, 1935, Apalachicola, FL; son of Thornton Sr and Minnie Henry; married Antoinette McTurner; children: Frederick S Jr, Robin Tanya & Laurence Anthony. **Educ:** Fla A&M Univ, Tallahassee, FL, BS (magna cum laude), 1957; Univ Pittsburgh, Pittsburgh, PA, PhD, phys chem, 1964. **Career:** Pvt tutor sci & math, 1959-64; Fla A&M Univ, Tallahassee Fla, assoc prof, 1964-66, prof chem, 1968-74, Col Curric Prog, prog dir, 1967-68, pres, 1985-01, regent prof, currently; Univ Minn, asst prof chem, 1966-67; Inst Servs Educ, Washington, DC, prog dir summer conf & thirteen-col curric prog, 1968-74, three-univs grad prog humanities, 1970-74, innovative instnl res consortium, 1972-73, study sci capability black col, 1972-74, interdisciplinary prog, 1973-74, two-univ grad prog sci, 1973-74; Tenn State Univ, Nashville, Tenn, pres, 1974-85, pres emer, 1985-; Fla A&M Univ, pres, 1985-01, prof, 2003. **Orgs:** Am Asn Higher Educ; AAAS; Am Asn Univ Profs; Am Chem Soc; Am Asn MinorityRes Univs; Nat Asn Advan Colored People; bd dir, Am Cancer Soc; bd, Barnett Bank; bd, Pride; bd dir, YMCA, 1987; Vis comt, Mass Inst Technol, 1982; Joint Comt Agr Develop, 1982; chmn, Adv Comt Off Advan Pub Negro Col, 1982; secy, Am Coun Educ, 1978; Int Platform Asn; Nat Merit Scholar Corp; chmn, Nat Asn State Univs & Land Grant Cols; bd dir, Walmart Corp; bd dir, Brinker Int; Pres Bill Clinton, White House Adv Comt Historically Black Cols & Univs; trustee, Univ Pittsburgh, 1992-96; pres & chief exec officer, Nat Asn Equal Opportunity Higher Educ, 2001-03; Alpha Phi Alpha fraternity; Sigma Pi Phi fraternity. **Special Achievements:** First African American to receive a PhD in this discipline from the University. **Home Addr:** 8754 Southern Breeze Dr, Orlando, FL 32836-5064. **Business Addr:** President Emeritus, Tennessee State University, 3500 John A Merritt Blvd, Nashville, TN 37209, **Business Phone:** (615)963-5000.

## HUMPHRIES, ESQ. JAMES NATHAN

Lawyer. **Personal:** Born Feb 15, 1958, Detroit, MI; son of Andrew John and Mary Jane; married Diane D Rogers; children: Charneise N Newton, Keyontay S, Karlea T & Kalon J. **Educ:** Univ Mich, BGS, 1980, JD, 1984. **Career:** Mich State Univ, Cooper Exten Prog, 4H youth agt, 1985-87; Detroit City Coun Res Div, anal, 1987-89; City Dearborn, Legal Dept, asst corp coun, 1989-95; Detroit Bd Educ, asst gen coun, 1995; Dept Fed State & Local Grant Develop & Prog Compliance, interim exec dir; pvt pract atty, currently. **Orgs:** Mich Bar Asn, 1986-; Wolverine Bar Asn, 1986-; Detroit Bar Asn, 1986-; Detroit Officials Asn; chmn, Victory Opportunity Trust Polit Action Comt, 1986-. **Home Addr:** 23317 Grayson Dr, Southfield, MI 48075-3694, **Home Phone:** (248)809-9790. **Business Addr:** Attorney, Humphries & Brooks, 1025 Vermont Ave NW 910, Washington, DC 20005, **Business Phone:** (248)569-9007.

## HUMPHRIES, JAY (JOHN JAY HUMPHRIES)

Basketball player, basketball coach. **Personal:** Born Oct 17, 1962, Los Angeles, CA; married Angelica; children: Britni, Courtni, Jden & Xavier. **Educ:** Univ Colo, attended 1984. **Career:** Basketball player (retired), basketball coach; Phoenix Suns, guard, shooting guard, pt guard, 1984-88; Milwaukee Bucks, guard, pt guard, 1988-92; Utah Jazz, shooting guard, 1992-95; Boston Celtics, guard, 1994-95; Chinese CBA, assoc head coach, 2001; Inchon ET Land Black Slamer, asst coach; Wonju TG Xers, assoc head coach; Phoenix Suns, head coach, 2002-07; Reno Bighorns, head coach, 2008-10; Foshan Dralions, head coach, 2010-11; brooklyn nets, asst coach, currently. **Honors/Awds:** Big Eight All-Conf Team; All-Am & Big Eight All-Defensive Team; BigEight's All-Freshman team. **Home Addr:** N 20th Terr, Phoenix, AZ 80138-8736.

## HUMPHRIES, HON. PAULA G.

Judge. **Educ:** Univ Mich, attended 1976; Wayne State Univ Law Sch, JD, 1979. **Career:** Judge (retired); State Mich, asst state atty, 1979-84; Mich Senate, minority coun, 1984-87; 36th Dist Ct, ct magistrate; Mich 36th Dist Ct, judge, 1988-2013. **Business Addr:** Judge, Michigan 36th District Court, 421 Madison Ave, Detroit, MI 48226, **Business Phone:** (313)965-8622.

## HUNDON, JAMES HENRY

Football player. **Personal:** Born Apr 9, 1971, San Francisco, CA. **Educ:** Portland State Univ. **Career:** Football player (retired); Cincinnati Bengals, 1996-97, 1999, wide receiver, 1998; SanJose Sabercats, 2001-04; Calgary Stampeders, 2004; Toronto Argonauts, 2003.

## HUNIGAN, EARL

Executive, army officer, administrator. **Personal:** Born Jul 29, 1929, Omaha, NE; married Lazell Phillips; children: Kirk & Kris. **Educ:** Univ Mich, BBA, 1952. **Career:** Civil Serv Comn, investr, 1956-60, personnel specialist, 1962-63; USAF, mgt analyst, 1960-62; FAA, personnel specialist, 1963-68; USCG, dep dir civil personnel, 1968-69; Dept Transp, spec asst, asst secy admin, 1969-71; S Region FAA, exec officer, 1971-73; Food & Nutrit Serv US Dept Agri, dep admin mgt, 1973-78; Smithsonian Inst, dir personel training, 1985; E&L Assocs, mgt consult; Ebenezer African Methodist Episcopal Church, Ft Wash, Md, adminr, 1990. **Orgs:** Alpha Phi Alpha; Nat Asn Advan Colored People; Urban League; Phalanx; Am Soc Pub Admin. **Honors/Awds:** Sustained Super Performer, 1957-58, 1961 & 1971; Spec Act, 1963-73; Quality Step Increase, 1968; Distinguished Mil Instr Award, 1969-71. **Home Addr:** 46875 Grissom St, Sterling, VA 20165-3575, **Home Phone:** (703)406-2601.

## HUNIGAN, KIRK

Accountant. **Home Addr:** 8713 Mary Lee Lane, Annandale, VA 22003, **Home Phone:** (703)403-0526.

## HUNN, MYRON VERNON

Dentist. **Personal:** Born Aug 9, 1926, Sequndo, CO; married Dorothy Louise; children: Myron Jr, Jonathan & William J. **Educ:** La State Col, BA, 1954; Howard Univ, DDS, 1958. **Career:** Pvt practice, dentist. **Orgs:** Compton Optimist Club; Comn, Redev Agency; personnel bd, City Compton, 1967-70; bd dir, YMCA, 1970-73; pres, trustee bd, United Methodist Church, 1970-73; Nat Dent Asn; Am Dent Asn. **Home Addr:** 820 Clemmer Dr, Compton, CA 90221. **Business Addr:** Dentist, Private Practice, 1315 N Bullis Rd 4, Compton, CA 90221.

## HUNT, BETTY SYBLE

Government official. **Personal:** Born Mar 13, 1919, Forest, MS; married IP; children: Irvin, Vera H Jennings, Garland & Vernon. **Educ:** Jackson State Univ, BS, 1964; Univ Miss, Reading, attended 1969; Miss Col, attended 1979. **Career:** Jackson State Bookstore, asst mgr, 1950-65; Canton Pub Sch, teacher, 1968-73; Packard Elec, assembler, 1973-85; Hinds Co, Miss, election comnr. **Orgs:** Founder, JSU Campus Ministry Methodist Students, 1957; chairperson, United Givers Fund, 1968-69; Election Comn Asn Miss, 1980; 100 Black Women Coalition, 1982; deleg, Co Dem Conv, 1984; pres, Women Progress Miss Inc, 1983-85; pres, pres emer, Miss Chap Nat Coalition 100 Black Women. **Honors/Awds:** Community Excellence Award, Gen Motors, 1974; Award, Pin United Methodist Women, 1984. **Home Addr:** 11517 Evelake Ct, North Potomac, MD 20878-2592. **Business Addr:** Election Commissioner, Hinds Co Dist 5, Hines Co Court House, Jackson, MS 39215, **Business Phone:** (601)968-6555.

## HUNT, CHARLES AMOES

Librarian. **Personal:** Born Jan 21, 1950, Montclair, NJ; son of William Henry and Juliet Adele Carter Bey. **Educ:** Doane Col, Crete, Nebr, BA, 1973; Doane Col, Omaha, Nebr, teaching cert, 1973; Syracuse Univ, Syracuse, NY, MSLS, 1975; Univ Pac, Stockton, Calif, pub mgt, 1996; Calif State Univ-Stanislaus, Turlock, Calif, law, 1999; Humphreys Col, Stockton, Calif, law, 2000. **Career:** MTI Bus Col, Newark, NJ, comput programmer, 1968; Chicago Pub Libr, Chicago, Ill, br librn, 1975-78; Atlantic Richfield Co, Los Angeles, Calif, technical librn, 1978-79; Calif State Univ-Fullerton, Fullerton, Calif, ref librn, 1979; Kiddy Col Eng Sch, Mishima City, Japan, eng instr, 1979-81; Stockton-San Joaquin County Pub Libr, Stockton, Calif, adult serv librn, 1981-91, supervising librn, 1991-98; Univ Pac, Stockton, Calif, ref librn, 2001; San Joaquin Delta Col, Stockton, Calif, adj facility, 2001-. **Orgs:** Guest reviewer, Ref Bks Bull Edl Bd, Am Libr Asn, 1975-79; Black Caucus Am Libr Asn, 1975-78, 1981-; reviewer, Booklist mag, Am Libr Asn, 1976-79; Yelland Mem Scholar Minority Students Comt, Calif Libr Asn, 1987-88; vpres/pres-elect, 1990-91, pres, 1991-92, Community Info Sect, Pub Libr Asn Ala; chair, CIS Nominating Comt, 1993 & 1994; Off Literacy & Outreach Serv Adv Comn, Ala, 1998-2000. **Honors/Awds:** Undergrad Scholar, Turrell Fund, E Orange, NJ, 1969-73; Jr Semester Abroad Prog, Doane Col, 1972; Grad fel, Syracuse Univ, 1974-75; Gold Award for Best Newsletter, Manteca, Calif, Kiwanis, 1988; United Way San Joaquin Co, Recertification Team, Stockton, Calif, 1994 & 1995; City-paid tuition, Univ Pac, Stockton, Calif, 1996. **Special Achievements:** Role of the Public Manager in a Changing Environment, 1996. **Home Addr:** 1209 W Downs St, Stockton, CA 95207, **Home Phone:** (209)951-5385.

## HUNT, CLETIDUS MARQUELL

Football player. **Personal:** Born Jan 2, 1976, Memphis, TN. **Educ:** Ky State Univ, grad. **Career:** Football player (retired); Green Bay Packers, defensive end, 1999, 2001, defensive tackle, 2000, 2002-04, right defensive tackle, 2003, nose tackle, 2004; New York Dragons, 2007.

## HUNT, EDWARD

Executive. **Career:** Stop Shop Save Food Markets, chief exec officer, co-owner, 1978; E & S Mkt, pres, currently. **Business Addr:** President, E & S Markets Inc, 1401 Bloomfield Ave, Baltimore, MD 21227, **Business Phone:** (410)233-7152.

## HUNT, EUGENE

Banker, vice president (organization). **Personal:** Born Jul 19, 1948, Augusta, GA; son of Alfred Sr and Mabel Williams; children: Brian. **Educ:** Augusta Col, BBA, 1971, post-baccalaureate study, 1979. **Career:** Citizen & Soc Nat Bank, Nations Bank, mgr, 1975, dir, 1976, asst banking officer, 1977, banking officer & br mgr, 1980-; Govt Banking Div, asst vpres in-chg, 1984. **Orgs:** Treas, Good Shepherd Baptist Church Inc, 1971-; sec, Cent Savannah River Area Bus League, 1976; pres, Cent Savannah River Area Bus League, 1979; tech adv bd, Opportunity Indus Ctr, 1977-80; bd dir, Augusta Sickle Cell Ctr, 1977; loan exec, Nat Alliance Businessmen, 1979-80; Gov's Educ Rev Comn, l983-84; past chmn, Ga Dept Tech & Adult Educ, l985-. **Honors/Awds:** Service Award, Nat Alliance Businessmen, 1977; Service Award Good Shepherd Baptist Church Inc, 1978; Appreciation Award Cent Savannah River Area Youth Employment Opportunity Inc, 1979; Businessman of the Year, Augusta Black Historical Soc, 1983; Businessman of the Year, Augusta Chap Delta Sigma Theta, 1984. **Home Addr:** 3024 Clinton Rd, Augusta, GA 30906, **Home Phone:** (404)790-0206. **Business Addr:** Staff, Bank Am, 2870 Cent Ave, Augusta, GA 30909-3905, **Business Phone:** (404)828-8249.

## HUNT, ISAAC COSBY, JR.

School administrator, lawyer, commissioner. **Personal:** Born Aug 1, 1937, Danville, VA; married Elizabeth Raucnell; children: Isaac III. **Educ:** Fisk Univ, BA, 1957; Univ Va, Law Sch, LLB, 1962. **Career:** Lawyer, school administrator, commissioner, (retired); Securities & Exchange Comn, staff atty, 1962-67; Nat Adv Comn Civil Dis, team leader, 1967-68; Employ Opportunity Comn, Exec asst, 1968; RAND Corp, res staff, 1968-71; Ford Found, Consult, 1971; Cath Univ Am, asst prof Law, 1971-77; Jones Day Renvis Pogue, assoc, 1977-79; Dept Army, prin dep gen coun, 1979-81; Antioch Sch Law, dean; Akron Sch Law, dean & prof, 1987-95; US Securities & Exchange Comn, comnr, 1996. **Orgs:** Co-chair, DC Consumer Goods Bd, 1974-76; bd gov, Soc Am Law Teachers, 1976-79; troop comt mem, Boy Scouts Am Troop 52, 1982; chair, Sasha Bruce Youthwork Inc, 1987. **Honors/Awds:** Outstanding Civilian Service Award, Dept Army, 1981. **Home Addr:** 6808 32nd St NW, Washington, DC 20015-2202.

## HUNT, JEFFREY C.

Government official. **Personal:** Born Oct 30, 1968, Detroit, MI; son of Clyde Cleveland and Anne Ruth Ellis. **Educ:** Howard Univ, BA, econs, 1991; Mich State Univ, Inst Pub Policy & Social Res, Mich Poverty Law prog, 1997. **Career:** US House Reps, legis asst, 1991; New World Technol Inc, chmn & chief exec officer, 1995; Detroit City Coun, staff analyst; Dartmouth Community Col, caretaker & technician; Detroit Regional Chamber, sr policy analyst, regional lobbyist, sr dir regional pub policy, 2000-04; City Detroit Cable Commun Comn, Dept Elections, sr training specialist, chmn, 2000-10, comnr, Greater Spring Lake Chamber Com, pres & chief exec officer, 2011-. **Orgs:** Founder, Ambitious Students Involved in Community Serv, 1987-; master mason, Mt Pavan Price Hall Affiliated, 1992-; heath allocation comn mem, United Way Community Servs, 1995; Million Man March Asn, 1995-; bd mem, Am Heart Asn, 1995-; Detroit Dem Club, 1996-; chmn, founder, Tomorrow's Leadership Today, PAC, 1996-; Detroit City Coun Substance Abuse Task Force. **Honors/Awds:** Presidential Fellowship, Lyndon Baines Johnson Found, 1991. **Special Achievements:** Conducted Excel Leadership Prog, 1994; MI Political Leadership Prog, 1995; Greater Detroit Chamber of Commerce, Leadership Detroit, 1996. **Business Addr:** Chairman, Commissioner, Detroit City Office, Cable Communications Commission, 243 W Congr Suite 1000 Fl 10, Detroit, MI 48226, **Business Phone:** (313)224-2100.

## HUNT, MAURICE

Football coach, educator. **Personal:** Born Dec 16, 1943, Birmingham, AL; son of Percy Benjamin Sr and Ora Lee Lawson; married Mary Elizabeth Sain; children: Michael Phillip. **Educ:** Ky St Col, BS, 1966; Iowa Univ, attended 1971; Drake Univ, MSE, 1975. **Career:** Football coach (retired); Good Shepherd High Sch, coach, 1965-66; Glen Pk Ambridge Elem Schs, instr, 1967-69; Tolleston High Sch, instr & coach, 1967-69; Grinnell Col, instr & coach, 1969-77; Cent St Univ, asst prof & coach, 1977-78; Morehouse Col, instr & coach, 1979-89, 1995-96; Ky State Univ, 1992-94; Lane Col, coach, 1997. **Orgs:** Grinnell, IA Youth Comn, 1969-71; Am Football Coaches Asn, 1970-; Wrestling Fedn, 1970-73; Iowa Lions Club, 1972-77; Drake Relays Comn, 1973-77; Iowa Human Rights Comn, 1976-77; Rater, NAIA, 1978; Sheridan Black Col Pollster. **Honors/Awds:** Athletics Hall of Fame, Ky State Univ, 1991; Phyllis Wheatley Award, Women's Federated Clubs, 1991. **Special Achievements:** Coach of Year Atlanta Daily World Newspaper, Atlanta Constitution Journal, SIAC, 100 Percent Wreatling Club 1979, Atlanta Extra Point Club 1980-83, 1987-88. **Home Addr:** 4463 John Wesley Dr, Decatur, GA 30035, **Home Phone:** (404)987-2847. **Business Addr:** Physical Education Instructor, Morehouse College, 830 Wview Dr, Atlanta, GA 30314, **Business Phone:** (404)681-2800.

## HUNT, DR. PORTIA L.

Consultant, educator, psychologist. **Personal:** Born Feb 12, 1947, East St. Louis, IL; daughter of Luches and Ethel. **Educ:** Southern Ill Univ, Edwardsville, BS, sec educ & psychol, 1971, MS, counr educ, 1972; Ind State Univ, Terre Haute, IN, PhD, coun & psychol servs, 1975. **Career:** State Comm Col, counr, 1971-73; Portia Hunt & Assocs, psychologist, 1979-; Survivors Move Bombing Philadelphia & W Philadelphia Consortium Ment Health Ctr, consult, 1985-86; Eclipse Mgt Consult Group, pres & founder, 1986-; Temple Univ, prof coun psychol, 1975, emer fac; Bradley Coun Psychol Clin, prog coordr & dir, currently; exec dir, Nat Ctr Family Recover, Philadelphia, PA. **Orgs:** Del Valley Assoc Black Psychologists, 1976-; Nat prog chair, Assoc Black Psychologists, 1979; adv bd pres, Eastern Col Cushing Coun Act 101, 1980-86; bd mem, Ch World Inst, Temple Univ, 1980-86; Philadelphia Desegration Sch Dist; bd mem, ABRAXAS Found, 1985-. **Business Addr:** Professor Counseling Psychology, Temple University, Ritter Annex 228, Philadelphia, PA 19122-6085, **Business Phone:** (215)204-1586.

## HUNT, RICHARD HOWARD

Sculptor. **Personal:** Born Sep 12, 1935, Chicago, IL; son of Howard and Inez Henderson. **Educ:** Art Inst Chicago, BA, 1957; Belli Bare; Univ Chicago, attended 1955. **Career:** Advant-Grade Sculptures, sculptor, creator; Sch Art Inst Chicago, teacher, 1961; Univ Ill, Chicago, dept arch & art, 1962; Yale Univ, vis prof; Purdue Univ, vis prof, 1965; Northwestern Univ, vis prof, 1968; Mich State Univ, E Lansing, Mich, vis prof, 1997. **Orgs:** Perm col art, Mus Chicago, Cleveland, Houston, NY, Buffalo, Milwaukee, Israel; work was exhibited in Artists of Chicago & Vicinity Exhbtn, 1955-56; 62nd, 63rd, 64th Am Exhib of Art Inst of Chicago; Carnegie Intrnat Exhib in Pitts, 1958; Mus of Mod New York City, 1959; one-man Exhib in NYC, Chicago; participated in exhib Ten Negro Artists from US; First World Festival of Negro Arts, Dakar, Senegal, 1966; nat bd dir, Smithsonian Inst's. **Honors/Awds:** Recip 6 Major Awards & Flwshps; Lifetime Achievement Award, Int Sculpture Ctr, 2009; Legacy Award, United Negro Col Fund, 2010. **Special Achievements:** First African-American sculptor to be honored with a retrospective exhibition at the Museum of Modern Art, New York, 1969. **Home Addr:** 1017 W Lill Ave, Chicago, IL 60614-2205, **Home Phone:** (773)929-6161.

## HUNT, RONALD JOSEPH

School administrator, athletic coach. **Personal:** Born Dec 19, 1951, Uniontown, PA; married Karen Elaine Hill; children: Lynnette, Ronald Jr (deceased) & Angela. **Educ:** Slippery Rock St Col, BS, health, phys educ, 1973, MEd, admin & curric, 1975; Pa State Univ, MBA, mkt & finance, 1982. **Career:** Slippery Rock State Col, grad asst, 1973, actg co-ord spec serv, 1974, asst football coach, 1973-77, asst basketball coach, 1978-79, asst dir admis, 1979-, temp instr phys ed, 1979; National City Bank, vpres, Regional Commercial Lending, 2008; First Niagara Bank, vpres, 2009; Fifth Third Bank, vpres, 2014; S&T Bank, vpres, 2014-. **Orgs:** Bd dir, Connie Hawkins Basketball Inc, 1978-80; bd dir, W Side Comn Act Ctr, 1979-80; bd dir, Lawrence County Coun Comn Ctrs, 1979-80. **Honors/Awds:** Outstanding Athletic Am, 1973; Outstanding Man Comn, Jaycees, 1979. **Home Addr:** 210 Willard Ave, New Castle, PA 16101. **Business Addr:** Vice President, S&T Bank, PO Box 190, Indiana, PA 15701, **Business Phone:** (724)349-1800.

### HUNTER, BRIAN LEE

Baseball player. **Personal:** Born Mar 5, 1971, Portland, OR. **Career:** Baseball player (retired); Houston Astros, outfielder, 1994-96, 2002-03; Detroit Tigers, 1997-99; Seattle Mariners, 1999; Colo Rockies, 2000; Cincinnati Reds, 2000; Philadelphia Phillies, free agt, 2001-03; Houston Astros, free agt, 2002-03; San Diego Padres, free agt, 2003-04; Kans City Royals, free agt, 2005; Seattle Mariners, Hitting coach, currently. **Business Addr:** Hiting coach, Everett Aqua Sox, 3802 Broadway, WA 98201, **Business Phone:** (425)258-3673.

### HUNTER, BRIAN RONALD

Baseball player, scout. **Personal:** Born Mar 4, 1968, Torrance, CA; married Stephanie; children: Zachary. **Career:** Baseball player (retired), scout; Atlanta Braves, 1991-93, 1999-2000, scout, currently; Pittsburgh Pirates, 1994; Cincinnati Reds, 1994-95; Seattle Mariners, 1996; St Louis Cardinals, 1998; Philadelphia Phillies, 2000; New York Mets, scouts; Wash Nationals, scout. **Business Addr:** Scout, Atlanta Braves, 755 Hank Aaron Dr, Atlanta, GA 30315, **Business Phone:** (404)522-7630.

### HUNTER, BRYAN C.

Financial manager, president (organization). **Personal:** Born Oct 24, 1961, Kingston; son of Calvin and Monica Chong; married Kimberly A; children: Christopher & Nicole. **Educ:** Harvard Univ, BA, govt, 1983; Univ Chicago, Grad Sch Bus, MBA, finance, 1988; Univ Chicago, Booth Sch Bus, exec prog corp strategy, 2003. **Career:** Arthur Andersen & Co, sr consult, 1984-85; First Nat Bank Chicago, profit planner, 1985-87, sr trader, vpres, 1987-94; ABN AMRO Bank, trading mgr, vpres, 1994-99; Chicago Mercantile Exchange, dir currency prod, foreign exchange, dir, 2000-06, FX MarketSpace, chief operating officer, 2006-07; prin & owner, Asteri Capital Mgt LLC, prin, 2007-09; Fifth Third Bank, managing dir forex futures & options, 2009-11, managing dir, ecommerce, 2012-13; Interactive Data Corp, head foreign exchange, 2014-15; Asteri Consult LLC, managing dir, 2014-. **Orgs:** Alumni interviewer, Harvard Club Chicago. **Home Addr:** 906 W Webster Ave, Chicago, IL 60614, **Home Phone:** (773)772-3742. **Business Addr:** Managing Director, Asteri Consulting LLC, 906 W Webster Ave, Chicago, IL 60614, **Business Phone:** (312)404-2139.

### HUNTER, CECELIA CORBIN

Chief executive officer, president (organization), executive director. **Personal:** Born Jul 8, 1945, Jersey City, NJ; daughter of Leander M and Margaret Nelson; children: Alicia Stacey. **Educ:** Harvard Univ, John F Kennedy Sch Govt, MPA, 1982. **Career:** Atlanta Off Mayor Maynard Jackson, dir fed rels, 1974-81, chief staff, 1990-91, dir olympic coord, 1991-94; ICMA Retirement Corp, mgr, eastern region, 1982-90; 1996 Atlanta Paralympic Organizing Comt, vpres opers & serv, 1994; Teachers's Retirement Syst, exec dir, 2001-05; City Atlanta, Audit Comt & Atlanta Pub Safety Authority, exec, currently; Corbin & Assocs Inc, pres & chief exec officer, currently; Airport Retail Mgt, managing partner & secy. **Orgs:** Bd mem, Atlanta Area Coun Campfire Girls, 1976-80; W End Neighborhood Develop Corp, 1980-; asst secy, bd dir, ICMA Retirement Corp, 1983-88; charter mem, 100 Black Women Metro Atlanta, 1987; trustee, Catalyst Mag, 1989-; bd dir, Atlanta Bus League, 1991-; bd dir, Zoo Atlanta, 1991-; bd dir, chair eeo comt, Atlanta Comt Olympic Games, 1991-94. **Home Addr:** 675 Lawton St SW, Atlanta, GA 30310-2648, **Home Phone:** (404)758-6194. **Business Addr:** President, Chief Executive Officer, Corbin & Associates Inc, 3752 Half Moon Dr, Orlando, FL 32812, **Business Phone:** (407)851-5058.

### HUNTER, CECIL THOMAS

Educator. **Personal:** Born Feb 5, 1925, Greenup, KY; married Gloria James; children: Mildred C, Charlene James, Rosalind H Levy, Roderick & Gloria. **Educ:** Wash Jr Col; FL A&M Univ. **Career:** Brownsville Mid Sch, teacher math. **Orgs:** Chmn, Cath Soc Serv; chmn, Govt Ctr Auth; chmn, Escambia Co Health Facil Auth; comt mem bd dir, Sacred Heart Found; secy, Saenger Mgt; Finance Comt & Gen Govt Comt City Coun; past mem, Hospice NW Fla Area Agency Aging; St Anthony's Cath Church; Knights Columbus; Jack & Jill Am; Kappa Alpha Psi Fraternity; Nat Asn Advan Colored People. **Honors/Awds:** Diocesan Medal of Honor; Secular Franciscan Peace Award. **Home Addr:** 1330 E Scott St, Pensacola, FL 32503-4657, **Home Phone:** (850)433-4137. **Business Addr:** Teacher Mathematics, Brownsville Middle School, 4899 NW 24th Ave, Pensacola, FL 33142, **Business Phone:** (305)633-1481.

### HUNTER, CLARENCE HENRY

Public relations executive. **Personal:** Born Nov 1, 1925, Raleigh, NC; son of Wade H and Katie L; married Mary Ransom; children: Karen, Beverly, Katherine & Andrew. **Educ:** NY Univ, BS, 1950. **Career:** Journ & Guide Norfolk Va, reporter, bur mgr, 1950-53; Ebony Mag Chicago Ill, assoc ed, 1953-55; Post-Tribune Gary Ind, reporter, 1955-62; WA Eve Star WADC, reporter, 1962-65; US Comn Civil Rights WA DC, dir info, 1965-69; WA Journ Ctr WA DC, assoc dir, 1969-71; Howard Univ, dir univ rel & publ, 1971-73; Gen Motors Pub rel, staff asst, 1973-78, Rochester Prod Div, dir communs & pub rel, 1978-88, AC Rochester Div, gm spokesman, mgr pub affairs commun, 1988-. **Orgs:** Pub rel Socs Am; Austin Steward Prof Socs; United Way Greater Rochester; Martin Luther King Jr Festival Comn; GM Civic Involvement Prog. **Honors/Awds:** Howard Coles Community Award, Asn Black Communicators, Rochester Chap, 1984; Distinguished Achievement Award, Black Bus Asn Greater Rochester, 1991; Kathryn B Terrell Award for Distinguished Volunteer Serv, Urban League Rochester, 1991. **Home Addr:** 380 Garnsey Rd, Pittsford, NY 14534-4542, **Home Phone:** (919)933-2119. **Business Addr:** Manager Public Affairs, Communications, Gen Motors Corp, PO Box 92700, Rochester, NY 14692.

### HUNTER, COTTRELL JAMES, III

Athlete, athletic coach. **Personal:** Born Dec 14, 1968, Washington, DC; married Marion Lois Jones; children: Ahny & Coryatt. **Educ:** Pa State Univ, BA, polit sci, 1991. **Career:** Athlete (retired), Athlete coach; world shot-put champion; Cardinal Gibbons High Sch, asst coach, currently. **Business Addr:** Assistant Coach, Cardinal Gibbons High School, 1401 Edwards Mill Rd, Raleigh, NC 27607, **Business Phone:** (919)834-1625.

### HUNTER, REV. DAVID

Educator, clergy. **Personal:** Born Aug 3, 1941, Enterprise, MS; son of Sandy (deceased) and Laura; married Mary Williams; children: David Cornell & Christopher Dante. **Educ:** Alcorn State Univ, BS, 1964; Cleveland State Univ, MEd, 1974; Cent Bible Col, BA, 1976; Trinity Theol Sem, Newburgh, IN, doctoral cand, currently. **Career:** E Cleveland Schs, teacher, 1969-82; Bright Star Missionary Baptist Church, pastor, 1972; Bright Star Missionary Baptist Church, sr pastor, currently; Alcorn State Univ, pres, currently. **Orgs:** Life mem, Alpha Phi Alpha, 1965-; Oper PUSH; Nat Asn Advan Colored People; pres, E Cleveland Bd Educ, 1988-89, 1991; pres, E Ministerial Alliance, 1994-95. **Home Addr:** 157 16th Oak Hill Rd, Cleveland Heights, OH 44112, **Home Phone:** (216)541-8737. **Business Addr:** Pastor, Bright Star Missionary Baptist Church, 13028 Shaw Ave, Cleveland, OH 44108, **Business Phone:** (216)249-5213.

### HUNTER, DR. DAVID LEE

Mathematician. **Personal:** Born Sep 10, 1933, Charlotte, NC; son of Annie L Boulware; married Margaret Plair; children: Karen Leslie & Jocelyn Jeanine. **Educ:** Johnson C Smith Univ, BS, 1955; Atlanta Univ, MS, 1964; Nova Univ, EdD, 1979. **Career:** Carver Col & Mecklenburg Col, instr math, 1957-63; Cent Piedmont Community Col, instr math, 1963-71, coordr col transfer prog, 1971-73, dir, personnel, 1973-75, vpres, dean, gen studies, 1975, dean arts & sci. **Orgs:** Fin sec bd trustee, Little Rock AME Zion Church, 1973; Am Soc Pub Admin, 1974-; admin, NC Asn Community Col Instnl, 1975-; bd dir, Charlotte Rehab Homes Inc, 1978; rep, CPCC League Innovation Community Col, 1979-; bd dir, ARC, 1979; bd dir, Southern Reg Coun Black Am Affairs; NC SRCBAA. **Home Addr:** 4415 Garvin DR, Charlotte, NC 28269.

### HUNTER, DOROTHY

College teacher. **Educ:** Huston-Tillotson Univ, BS, MS, math. **Career:** Huston Tillotson Univ, instr, currently. **Business Addr:** Assistant Professor, Huston Tillotson University, 900 Chicon St, Austin, TX 78702, **Business Phone:** (512)505-3000.

### HUNTER, EDWINA EARLE

Educator, business owner. **Personal:** Born Dec 29, 1943, Caswell County, NC; daughter of Edgar Earl Palmer and Bessie Catherine Brown; married James Weldon Sr; children: James W Jr, Anika Z & Isaac Earl. **Educ:** Spelman Col, BA, music, fr & educ, 1964; Smith Col, MAT, music hist & lit, 1965. **Career:** Music teacher (retired), musician; Vint Hill Farms Sta, post chapel choir dir, 1967-68; Edwina E Hunter Piano Studio, owner, 1968-; Prince Georges County Pub Sch, music teacher, 1968-2006, dir vocal music, 1979; El Paso Community Col, instr music, 1975-76; Kinder Musik with Miss Winnie, owner, currently; Publications: Songs for Children's Games from Africa, 1979; Madison Brown Family Commemorative Calander, Family in the Military-Spanish-America WAR-WWII, Careers in the Military. **Orgs:** Secy, Columbia Chap Nat Alumnae Asn Spelman Col, 1984-, pres, 1986-90; pres, Columbia Chap Nat Alumnae Asn Spelman Col, 1987-; secy & treas, NE Region, Nat Alumnae Asn Spelman Col, 1992-; MSTA Greater Laurel Music Teachers Asn; NEA; Nat Asn Music Educ; MMENC; Suzuki Asn; Nat Asn Advan Colored People; Spelman Glee Club; Stud Govt Asn; Suzuki Asn Americas; Music Teachers Nat Asn; Md Music Teachers Asn; Greater Laurel Music Teachers Asn; corresp secy, Nat Alumnae Asn Spelman Col, 2010-. **Home Addr:** 7192 Sanner Rd, Clarksville, MD 21029-1803, **Home Phone:** (301)490-3874. **Business Addr:** Owner, Edwina E Hunter Piano Studio, 10721 Graeloch Rd, Laurel, MD 20723-1122, **Business Phone:** (240)535-3070.

### HUNTER, DR. FREDERICK DOUGLAS, SR.

Lawyer. **Personal:** Born Jan 30, 1940, Pittsburgh, PA; son of Charlie and Elizabeth; married Rosie M Kirkland; children: Frederick D & Deborah R. **Educ:** Univ Pittsburgh, BS, 1961, PhD, 1967; Univ Md, JD, 1974. **Career:** W R Grace & Co, sr res chem, 1967-72; EI Dupont DeNemours & Co, corp coun, 1972-89; Lubrizol Corp, assoc gen coun, chief patent coun, currently. **Orgs:** Am Bar Asn; Delaware Bar Asn; Dist Columbia Bar Asn; AOA Fraternity; Am Intellectual Property Law Asn; Chem Mfrs Asn. **Honors/Awds:** Published 5 papers on various sci jour. **Home Addr:** 17310 Bittersweet Trail, Chagrin Falls, OH 44023-5700, **Home Phone:** (440)543-5232. **Business Addr:** Chief Patent Counsel, The Lubrizol Corp, 29400 Lakeland Blvd, Wickliffe, OH 44092, **Business Phone:** (216)943-4200.

### HUNTER, GIGI

Actor, dancer, fashion designer. **Personal:** Born Jun 26, 1960, Washington, DC. **Educ:** Duke Ellington Sch Arts, Wash, DC. **Career:** Danced for TV shows: "Fame"; "Broadway musical: The Wiz"; "Solid Gold", 1987-88. "Cold Case", 2006; "VH1: All Access", 2008; "I Know My Kid's a Star", actress, 2008. Danced for the Films: Coming to America, 1988; Mac & Me, 1988; Lambada, 1990; Rent, 2005; Dark Streets, 2008. Gigi Hunter Collection, owner & designer, currently. **Honors/Awds:** Magic Johnson Salute to African-American Designers, 1999. **Business Addr:** Owner, Fashion Designer, GiGi Hunter Collection, 719 S Los Angeles St Suite 332, Los Angeles, CA 90014, **Business Phone:** (213)624-6898.

### HUNTER, DR. IRBY B.

Dentist, educator, teacher. **Personal:** Born Jul 12, 1940, Longview, TX; married Staphalene Johnson; children: Constance A & Irby B Jr. **Educ:** Tex Col Tyler, BS, chem, 1961; Tuskegee Inst Ala, MS, chem, 1963; Univ Tex, Houston, DDS, 1968. **Career:** Atlantic & Richfield Houston, chem, 1964-68; Houston Independent Sch Dist, teacher & ed, 1965-68; Dr WA Hembry Dallas, dentist gen, 1968-70; E Ill Clin, dentist, 1971-. **Orgs:** Am Dent Asn, 1965-; pres, MC Cooper Dent Soc Dallas, 1974-78; pres, Golf St Dent Asn Tex, 1978-; Steering Comt, Small Sch Task Force Dallas ISD, 1979-; mem bd, Community Health Ctrs Dallas Inc, 1979-; Sir Orchun, Sigma Pi Phi Frat Dallas, 1979. **Honors/Awds:** Special Alumni Award, Tex Col Tyler, 1980. **Home Addr:** 4316 Twin Post Rd, Dallas, TX 75244-6743, **Home Phone:** (972)991-2223. **Business Addr:** Dentist, East Illinois Clinic, 2826 E Ill Ave, Dallas, TX 75216-3422, **Business Phone:** (214)372-4621.

### HUNTER, JAMES MACKIELL

Lawyer. **Personal:** Born Feb 7, 1946, Macon, GA; son of Elton and Odessa; married Lorraine Dunlap; children: Adrienne, Michelle & Hillary. **Educ:** Fort Valley State Univ, BA, 1968; Howard Univ, JD, 1973; Harvard Univ, Pract Inst Lawyers, 1991. **Career:** US Equal Employ Opportunity Comn, trial atty, 1973-76, suprv trial atty, 1976-78; M James Hunter & Assoc, prin partner, 1978-81; M&M Prod Co, vpres & gen coun, chief legal officer, 1981-90; Hunt, Richardson, Garner, Todd & Cadenhead, partner, 1990-93; Schnader, Harrison, Segal & Lewis, partner, 1993-2000; Holland & Knight LLP, partner, 2000-; Morris, Manning & Martin, LLP, partner, 2005-; U.S. Equal Employ Opportunity Comn, sr trial atty. **Orgs:** Bd mem, Atlanta Judicial Comn, 1978-; bd visitors, Grady Hosp, 1983-; Clayton Jr Col, 1984-; Atlanta Jr Col Bd, 1986; gen coun, 100 Black Men Atlanta, Inc, 1986-2000; nat gen coun, 100 Black Men Am, 1987-2001; bd mem, Nat Alliance Bus SE Region, 1987-2001; gen coun, Leadership Atlanta, 1988-93; nat coun, Nat Black Col Hall Fame Found Inc, 1988-2001; mem & chmn, Good willI DS N GA Inc, 1999-2001; Corp Dept; co chair, Employ Law Dept; State Bar Ga; Bar Dc; State Bar Iowa; Am Bar Asn; Nat Bar Asn; Atlanta Bar Asn; Gate City Bar Asn; gen coun, First Congregational Church Atlanta; Southeast Region Nat Alliance Bus; Atlanta Guardsmen Inc; Omega Psi Phi Fraternity Inc; chmn, Schnaders Atlanta offices Labor Employ Group & Mkt Group; trustee, Lawyers Comt Civil Rights Under Law; bd mem & chmn, Goodwill Industs N Ga Inc. **Honors/Awds:** Knox Award, Ft Valley State, 1968; Omega Psi Phi Award, 1968; Outstanding Atlantans, 1978; Outstanding Gans, 1984; Georgia Super Lawyer, Atlanta magazine. **Home Addr:** 4610 Orkney Lane, Atlanta, GA 30331, **Home Phone:** (404)229-0029. **Business Addr:** Partner, Morris Manning & Martin LLP, 1600 Atlanta Financial Ctr 3343 Peachtree Rd NE, Atlanta, GA 30326, **Business Phone:** (404)504-7756.

### HUNTER, REV. JAMES NATHANIEL, II

Clergy. **Personal:** Born Aug 16, 1943, Glasgow, VA; son of James N Sr and Helen Louise Strawbridge; married Sharron Joy Condon. **Educ:** St Paul's Col, BA, 1966; Bexley Hall, BD, 1969; State Univ NY, Geneseo, MA, 1970. **Career:** Sch Dist Rochester, teacher, 1970-72; DEP Interior, prin, counr, teacher, 1972-83; Kila, Inc, employ counr, 1983-85; Fairbanks Resource Agency, suv & homeliving specialist, 1985-88; St Jude's Episcopal Church, vicar, 1988-, Jubilee Ctr, exd, 1992-; Univ Alaska, Fairbanks, adj prof. **Orgs:** Secy, Breadline Inc, 1985; Tanana Conf Churches, 1985; Union Black Episcopalians, 1988; chair, Alaska Interfaith Impact, 1988; secy, Comn Ministry-Episcopal, 1990-94; dean, Tanana Interior Deanery, 1990-92; secy, pres, 1989, Kiwanis Club N Pole; consult, Food Bank Fairbanks; elected city coun, Mayor Pro Temp, 1998; Diocese Alaska Standing Comt. **Honors/Awds:** COT Leader Award, Martin Luther King Jr, 1988; Outstanding Board Member, Breadline Inc, 1989; Memorial Award for Outstanding Leadership, Fairbanks Resource Agency, 1988; Bexley Hall, Rossister Fellowships, 1988, 1991; Award to study in Israel, Episcopal Church USA Domestic & Foreign Ministry, 1990; Citizen of the Year, North Pole Chamber of Commerce, 1996; Vice Mayor, 1996. **Special Achievements:** First African American to serve on city cnl of North Pole; First African American priest to serve in Diocese of Alaska; First African American to work as principal of elementary school system in Yukon-Kuskovian area. **Home Addr:** 322 Crossway, North Pole, AK 99705-6047, **Home Phone:** (907)488-4282. **Business Addr:** Vicar, Executive Director, St Jude's Jubilee Center, 1 2 Mile Laurance Rd, North Pole, AK 99705, **Business Phone:** (907)488-9329.

### HUNTER, JERRY L.

Lawyer. **Personal:** Born Sep 1, 1942, Mt. Holly, NC; son of Samuel and Annie B. **Educ:** NC Agr & Tech State Univ, BS, 1964; Howard Univ Sch Law, JD, 1967. **Career:** Roundtree, Knox, Hunter & Parker, atty, partner law firm. **Orgs:** Bar Admissions: DC, 1968; U.S. Dist Ct DC, 1968; U.S. Ct Appeals DC, 1968; U.S. Dist Ct Dist Md, 1970; U.S. Supreme Ct, 1971; DC Ct Appeals, 1972; U.S. Ct Claims, 1981; DC Occup Safety Bd, 1994-97; US Supreme Ct Bar; US Dist Ct (MD & DC); US Ct Appeals; DC Ct Appeals; US Ct Claims; Nat Bar Asn; Am Bar Asn; DC Bar Asn; Asn Plaintiffs Trial Atty; Sigma Delta Tau Legal Frat; Alpha Kappa Mu Hon Soc; Kappa Pi Int Hon Art Soc; Asn Trial Lawyers Am; DC Super Ct Probate Panel; Howard Univ Law J. **Honors/Awds:** American Jurisprudence Award for Academic Achievement in Legal Methods & History. **Special Achievements:** Co-author article, "Current Racial Legal Developments", 12 How-L J 299, Spring 1966. **Home Addr:** 1655 N Portal Dr NW, Washington, DC 20012-1053, **Home Phone:** (202)234-1723. **Business Addr:** Partner, Roundtree Knox Hunter & Parker, 1822 11th St NW, Washington, DC 20001-5015, **Business Phone:** (202)234-1723.

### HUNTER, REV. JOHN DAVIDSON

Insurance executive, president (organization), minister (clergy). **Personal:** married Lucille Chandler; children: Louise, John D Jr, Joshua, Phillip & Jackie Owens. **Educ:** Selma Univ, HS, grad opelika. **Career:** Protective Indust Ins Co, rep, 1962-81; Pilgrim Health Life Ins Co, rep, 1981-. **Orgs:** Tabernacle Baptist Church, 1941-; pres, Nat Asn Advan Colored People, 1950-; Dallas City Voters League, 1975-; Selma City Coun, 1976-84; Pres's Dem Club Ala, 1977-85; Selma Black Leadership Coun, 1979-85; exec comt, Southwest Ala Sickle Cell Anemia Asn, 1984-85; minister, Rocky Br Baptist Church. **Honors/Awds:** Received twenty prof achievement awards & four community service awards. **Home Addr:** 1818 Martin Luther King St, Selma, AL 36703, **Home Phone:** (334)875-7383.

### HUNTER, JOHN W.

Government official, commissioner. **Personal:** Born Apr 18, 1934, Union, MS; son of Frank and Estella; married RoseMary White; children: Eric & Shawn. **Educ:** CS Mott Comm Jr Col, bus arts, 1969. **Career:** Government official (retired); 7th Dist Cong Black Caucus Polit Action Comt No 659, chmn; Genesee County Bd Health, bd dir; Genesee County Bd Comn, county comn, 1974-86; Genesee County Rd Comn, comnr. **Orgs:** Bd dir, Nat Asn County Welfare & Soc Serv Comn, Genesee Memorial Hosp, 1975-84, Model Cities Econ

Develop Corp; chairperson, Genesee County Human Serv Comn; precinct deleg, former deleg, State Dem Conv; Urban League, Nat Asn Advan Colored People, Elks Vehicle City Lodge 1036. **Honors/Awds:** Leadership Award, Black Bus & Professor Womens Organization, 1978; Frederick Douglass Award, National Association Black Bus & Professor Women Organization, 1987; A Philip Randolph Civic Right Award, 1989; National Media Womens Award, 1991. **Special Achievements:** First African American to be named to road commission, 5th black to serve in the State of Michigan as road commissioner; Ambulatory Wing at Genesee memorial Hospital in Flint MI was named The John W Hunter Wing, 1984. **Home Addr:** 5344 Mapletree Dr, Flint, MI 48532, **Home Phone:** (810)230-8398.

### HUNTER, KIM L.

Executive, chief executive officer. **Personal:** Born Jun 30, 1961, Philadelphia, PA; son of Talmadge Edward Milton and Alberta May. **Educ:** Univ Wash, Seattle, BA, bus admin, 1982; Univ St Thomas, MA, int mgt, 1988; Dartmouth Col, cert minority bus exec prog, 1992, cert advan minority bus exec prog, 1993; Northwestern Univ, cert advan mgt educ prog, 2000. **Career:** Pharmaseal, Div Baxter Corp, sales rep, 1982-86, mkt mgr, 1986-89; Calif State Univ, Northridge, Sch Journalism, adj prof, 1993-95; SCAN Health Plan, corp dir; Int Commun & Advert Network, exec vpres & gen mgr, 1989-90; Nat Colllege Resources Found/Black Col Expo, chmn 7chief exec officer, 1990-; Pac Coast Regional, staff instr, 1992-95; Kim Lagrant Hunter Scholar, 1995-98; Am Cancer Soc, vp/mkt commun. 1995-98; Lagrant Commun, founder, chmn, pres & chief exec officer, 1990-. **Orgs:** Pres, Black PR Soc Calif Inc, 1991-94; vpres pub rels, Mus Art Contemporaries, 1993-94; vice chair, Great Beginning Black Babies Task Force, 1993-95; vice chair, Los Angeles County Task Force, 1993-95; Bus Partners Comt, 1994-95; KCET Bus Partners Comt, 1994-95; bd mem, Next Wave Learning, 1995; comnr, City Los Angeles Animal Regulation Dept, 1996-99; chmn, founder & pres, 1998-, Lagrant Found; vpres, Am Cancer Soc, Cent Los Angeles Unit, 1995-98, pres, 1998-2000; bd secy, Planned Parenthood Los Angeles, 1999-2000; vpres & comnr, City Los Angeles Cult Affairs Dept, 1999-2003; bd mem, Calif Coun Humanities, 2000-. **Business Addr:** President, Chief Executive Officer, Lagrant Communications, 600 Wilshire Blvd Suite 1520, Los Angeles, CA 90017-3247, **Business Phone:** (323)469-8680.

### HUNTER, KIMBERLY ALICE

Executive. **Personal:** Born Jan 31, 1962, Chicago, IL; daughter of Eric Earl Graham and Eleanor Lucille Graham; married Bryan Charles; children: Christopher Elliot & Nicole Evelyn. **Educ:** Harvard & Radcliffe Col, AB, 1983; Univ Chicago, Grad Sch Bus, MBA, 1988. **Career:** First Nat Bank Chicago, vpres, 1983-89; Bank One, Capital Markets, vpres, 1992-97, Investment Grade Securities, managing dir, 1997-2000; Corn Prod Int Inc, corp Treas, dir, 2001-04; Ingredion, corp treasr, 2004-. **Orgs:** Bd dir, Nat Asn Corp Treas; Harvard Club Chicago Alumni Interviewer; co-treas YWCA Circle Friends. **Home Addr:** 906 W Webster Ave, Chicago, IL 60614. **Business Addr:** Corporate Treasurer, Ingredion Inc, 5 Westbrook Corp Ctr, Westchester, IL 60154, **Business Phone:** (708)551-2600.

### HUNTER, LINDSEY BENSON, JR.

Basketball coach, basketball player. **Personal:** Born Dec 3, 1970, Utica, MS; married Ivy; children: 2. **Educ:** Alcorn State Univ, attended 1989; Jackson State Univ, attended 1993. **Career:** Basketball player (retired), coach; Detroit Pistons, pt guard, 1993-2000, small guard, 2003-05, pt guard, 2005-08; Milwaukee Bucks, pt guard, 2000-01; Los Angeles Lakers, pt guard, 2001-02; Toronto Raptors, pt guard, 2002-03; Detroit Pistons, 2003-08; Chicago Bulls, pt guard, 2008-10; Phoenix Suns, interim head coach, 2012-13; Golden State Warriors, asst coach, 2013-14; Buffalo Bulls, asst coach, 2016-; Bulls, player develop asst. **Orgs:** Nat Basketball Asn; bd dir, Daybreak Homeless Shelter. **Honors/Awds:** Player of the Year, Southwestern Athletic Conf, 1993; All-Rookie Second Team, Nat Basketball Asn, 1994; Champion, Nat Basketball Asn, 2002, 2004. **Home Addr:** , MI. **Business Addr:** Assistant Coach, Buffalo Bulls, 102 Alumni Arena, Buffalo, NY 14260, **Business Phone:** (716)645-3142.

### HUNTER, DR. LLOYD THOMAS

Physician, pediatrician. **Personal:** Born Feb 6, 1936, Des Moines, IA; married Janice; children: Cynthia, Laura & Elizabeth. **Educ:** Univ Nebr, AB, 1957, MD, 1962. **Career:** Univ Southern Calif, staff; Univ Calif Los Angeles, assoc prof; pvt pract physician, currently; Cedars-Sinai Med Ctr, physician; Childrens Hosp Los Angeles, physician; Brotman Med Ctr, physician. **Orgs:** Dipl Am Bd Pediat; fel Am Acad Pediat; La Pediat Soc; Charles R Drew Med Soc; AMA; Nat Med & Asn; Golden St Med Asn; Calif Med Asn; La Pediat Soc; Kappa Alpha Psi Frat; Nat Asn Advan Colored People; Los Angeles Urban League; Alpha Omega Alpha Med Hon Soc. **Honors/Awds:** Merit Award Army Commendation Medal, 1962; Univ Nebr Regents Scholarship, 1961-62. **Home Addr:** 4050 Kenway Ave, Los Angeles, CA 90008, **Home Phone:** (323)290-9405. **Business Addr:** Physician, 3756 Santa Rosalia Dr Suite 600, Los Angeles, CA 90008, **Business Phone:** (323)299-3200.

**HUNTER, PATRICK J, SR.** See Obituaries Section.

### HUNTER, RHONDA F.

Lawyer. **Educ:** Univ Tex, Austin, BA; Southern Methodist Univ, JD, 1980. **Career:** Law Off Rhonda Hunter, atty, currently; Farrow-Gillespie & Heath, LLP, partner, 2012-. **Orgs:** Pres, Dallas Bar Asn, 2004-05, life fel bd dir, Nat Conf Bar; pres, bd dir, J L Turner Legal Asn; bd dir, State Bar Tex; Dallas Bar Family Law Sect; bd dir, Child & Family Guid Centers; bd dir, Young Audiences Greater Dallas; bd dir, N Tex Food Bank; Chair, Comt Qualified Judiciary, 2016-17; DBA Community Serv Fund; bd life fel, Dallas Bar Found. **Honors/Awds:** Distinguished Alumni Award, Southern Methodist Univ's Dedman Sch Law, 2003; Hon. Sam A. Lindsay Professionalism & Ethics Award, JL Turner Legal Asn, 2012; Outstanding Female Partner in a Mid-Sized Law Firm, Dallas Women Lawyers Asn, 2015. **Special Achievements:** Published in Texas Super Lawyers, 2003-09. **Business Addr:** Attorney, Law Office of Rhonda Hunter, 1700 Pacific Suite 3700, Dallas, TX 75201, **Business Phone:** (214)698-5900.

### HUNTER, RICHARD C.

School administrator, association executive. **Personal:** Born May 4, 1939, Omaha, NE. **Educ:** Univ Omaha, BA, elem educ, 1961; San Francisco State Col, MA, elem sch admin, 1967; Univ Calif, Berkeley, EdD, sch admin, 1971. **Career:** Berkeley, Calif, sch teacher, asst prin, prin; Richmond, Va, Pub Sch, supt; Dayton, Ohio, supt; Tokyo, Japan, teacher; Richmond, Va, prin; Seattle, asst dep supvr; Richmond, Va, Bd Educ, assoc supvr; Valentine Mus Dom Nat Bank, staff; Richmond Chamber Comn, staff; St Paul Col, fac; Baltimore City Pub Schs, Baltimore, Md, supt; Dept Defense Educ Activ, US Govt, Arlington, Va, assoc dir educ, 1998; Univ NC, Sch Educ, Chapel Hill, prof educ leadership, 1999-2000; Univ Ill, Urbana-Champaign, Dept Educ Orgn & Leadership, dept head, 2000-03, prof, 2000-, fac adv, 2000-08; Wash Pub Schs, regional asst supt. **Orgs:** Inst rep, Am Asn Col Teacher Educ, 2002-05; Ill Coun Profs Educ Admin, 2005; Ill Asn Sch Adminr, 2005; Educ Admin Alumni Asn, Champaign, Ill, 2005; Nat Alliance Black Sch Educr, Wash, DC, 2005; Chapel Hill, NC, Urban Rev, 2005; Kappa Alpha Psi; Phi Delta Kappa; ill asn sch adminr, 2001-07; ed bd, Urban Rev, 2003; Chicago, Ill, El Valor Policy & Advocacy Comt, 2004; ed bd, Asn Sch Bus Officials Internation, Reston, Va, Sch Bus Affairs, 2006-10; ed bd, col educ, J Educ Finance, 2008-10; res asn, Am Educ, 2005-10; bd trustee, St Paul Col; bd trustee, Durham County Bd Educ. **Honors/Awds:** Good Government Award, Richmond First Club; Univ Richmond, Hon Doctorate; Scholarship, Southern Hist Asn, 2006; This competitive Cash Award, United Dept State, 2010-11; Top 20 Most Influential Education Professor, 2010. **Special Achievements:** Numerous publications including All things to all people, special circumstances influencing the performance of African-American superintendents. Education and Urban Society, 2005; Tettegah, Sharon and Hunter, Richard C Education and Technology: Issues in Applications of Policy and Administration in K-12 Schools, Advances in Educational Administration, Volume 8, Oxford, England: JAI-Elsevier Science. **Business Addr:** Professor, Faculty Advisor, University of Illinois at Urbana-Champaign, 337 Educ Bldg 1310 S 6th St MC 708, Champaign, IL 61820, **Business Phone:** (217)333-1261.

### HUNTER, REV. SYLVESTER

Clergy. **Personal:** Born Mar 28, 1949, Pensacola, FL; married Janice; children: Sylvester & Chole. **Educ:** Wiley Col, BS, 1975; Houston Bible Inst, 1984; Concordia Theol Sem, 1987; Garrett Theol Sem, Master Theol Studies, 1991; Univ Oxford, attended 2004; St Thomas Christian Col, DDiv. **Career:** Ford Aerospace & Comn Corp, financial cost analyst, 1980-84, sr property coord, 1984-86; Magnavox Electronics Sys, sr contract property analyst, 1986-89; One Church One Offender Inc, exec dir, 1991-92; Union Baptist Church, asst to pastor, 1992-98, sr minister, 1998-, sr pastor & sr minister, currently. **Orgs:** Alpha Phi Alpha; Kappa Tau Delta; vpres, Nat Asn Advan Colored People; chmn, bd dir, Ft Wayne Urban League; bd dir, Ind Minority Consortium; bd dir, Aids Task Force; chmn, InterdenomiNat Ministrial Alliance; fac mem, Cong Christian Educ, Gen Ind State, cong pres, 2000-. **Honors/Awds:** Young Black Achiever, 1986; Honorary Doctorate of Divinity Degree, St Thomas Christian Col. **Home Addr:** 2525 Palisade Dr, Fort Wayne, IN 46806, **Home Phone:** (260)447-5060. **Business Addr:** Senior Pastor, Union Baptist Church, 2200 Smith St, Fort Wayne, IN 46803-2590, **Business Phone:** (260)456-3421.

### HUNTER, TEOLA P.

Government official, association executive, consultant. **Personal:** Born Feb 5, 1933, Detroit, MI; daughter of T P and Olivia Cranon; children: Denise Hughes Ciccel, Jeffrey & Anthony. **Educ:** Univ Detroit, BS, 1958; Wayne State Univ, MEd, 1971. **Career:** Detroit Pub Sch Syst, teacher, 1958-72; Buttons & Bows Nurseries & Prep Schs, founder, owner & operator, 1971-85; Mich House Reps, mem, 1980-82; Pro Tempore, elected speaker, 1989; Wayne County, Health Community Serv, dep dir, 1992-93, co clerk, 1993; Sloan/Hunter Group, founding partner, consult, currently; Blue Care Network Mich Inc, dir, currently. **Orgs:** Intern exec dir, Coleman A Young Found, 2001; vpres, Womens Equity Action League; Pi Lamda Theta; Links, Greater Wayne County Chap; bd dir, Downriver Community; chair, bd dir, Diversified Youth Servs; Delta Sigma Theta Sorority; Citizens Adv Comt, Wayne County Youth; adv bd mem, Childrens Aid Soc; bd mem, Omni Care, Qual Assurance Comt; bd dir, Detroit Urban League; Nat Asn Advan Colored People; founder, Resource Endowment Aiding C Together Love; Nat Asn County Recorders, Election Officials & Clerks; Univ Detroit Mercy, Presidents Cabinet; Womens Econ Club; bd dir, Blue Cross Blue Shield Mich. **Honors/Awds:** Path Finders Award, Black Students Oakland Univ, 1982; Citizen of the Year Award, Detroit Medical Soc, 1985; Outstanding Citizen Award, Gentleman Wall St, 1985; Black Legis Hon Black Hist Month, Blue Cross & Blue Shield, 1986; Award of Merit for Outstanding Achievement & Leadership Develop & Community Rels, Core City Neighborhoods Inc, City of Detroit, 1986; Outstanding Public Service, Wayne Co Comm Col, 1991; Image Maker Award, 1992; Annual Millie Award, Women Pol Caucus, 1995; Outstanding Public Leadership Award, Mich State Univ, 1996; US Point of Lich Rec Award, 1997; YWCA Women of Achievement, 1998; Heritage Award, Ford Motor Co, 1999. **Special Achievements:** First female speaker pro tempore in Michigan; First female to be elected Wayne County Clerk; Michigan's first African American chosen to run as the Democratic candidate for Lieutenant Governor. **Home Addr:** 8120 E Jefferson Condo 2M, Detroit, MI 48214, **Home Phone:** (313)331-8790. **Business Addr:** Director, Blue Care Network of Michigan, 20500 Civic Ctr Dr, Southfield, MI 48086, **Business Phone:** (248)799-6400.

### HUNTER, TONY WAYNE

Football player. **Personal:** Born May 22, 1960, Cincinnati, OH. **Educ:** Univ Notre Dame, BS, econ, 1984. **Career:** Football player (retired); Buffalo Bills, tight end, 1983-84; Los Angeles Rams, tight end, 1985-86; Tribune Publ, chief exec officer; Social Serv Agency, chmn. **Honors/Awds:** Playboy All-Am, NEA All-American Sr; All-American; OH Player of the Year.

### HUNTER, TORII KEDAR

Baseball player. **Personal:** Born Jul 18, 1975, Pine Bluff, AR; son of Theotis and Shirley; married Katrina Hall; children: Cameron, Torii Jr & Monshadrick. **Career:** Gulf Coast League Twins, ctr fielder, 1992-96; New Brit Rock Cats, ctr fielder, 1996-98; Minn Twins, outfielder, 1997-2007, right fielder, 2015-; Los Angeles Anaheim, 2008-12; Detroit Tigers, 2013-14. **Business Addr:** Professional Baseball Player, Minnesota Twins, 1 Twins Way, Minneapolis, MN 55403, **Business Phone:** (612)659-3400.

### HUNTER HAYES, TRACEY JOEL

Librarian. **Personal:** Born Jan 20, 1966, Philadelphia, PA; son of William and Osalee Barbara Jenkins; married Kathleen Jean Butler; children: Tracey Joel, Jalaal Aqil & Makkah Imani. **Educ:** Lincoln Univ, BS, philos, 1987; Univ Pittsburgh, Sch Libr & Info Sci, MLS, 1989; Va Union Univ, Sch Theol, Divinity, 2004. **Career:** Univ Pittsburgh, SLIS, libr asst, 1988, resident asst, 1988; Free Libr Philadelphia, C librn, 1989-92; Lincoln Univ, spec collections librn, 1992; Am Libr Asn, Ala minority fel, 1992-; Ky State Univ, asst dir, libr, 1993-95; Southern IL Univ Carbondale, asst undergrad librn, 1995-96; Temple Univ, ref & CD librn, 1996-98; Hampton Univ Libr, asst dir, 1998; Lincoln Univ, dir, alumni rel, 2000-02 & 2005, Langston Hughes Mem Libr, dir, currenly, assoc prof, currently, Alumini Asn, pres, currently. **Orgs:** Groove Phi Groove, 1985; bd trustee, Concerned Black Men Inc; Nat Deleg, 1987; Black Caucus Am Libr Asn, 1989; Am Libr Asn, 1990-; chmn, Mayors Adv Comt Homeless, 1990; Free & Accepted Masons, PHA, Hiram 5 Philadelphia, 1991; vpres, Lincoln Univ Alumni Asn, 1992-93, pres, 1997-2011; Ky Asn Blacks Higher Educ, 1994-95; Rotary Int, 1994-96; trustee, Lincoln Univ, 2000-02; dir, libr, McGuire Afb; bd trustee, Tree House Bks. **Honors/Awds:** W Fales Prize in Philosophy, Lincoln Univ, 1987; Univ Pittsburgh, State Libr Scholar, 1988-89; Outstanding Young Man of the Year, 1989-90; Community Service Award, Philadelphia Mayors Office, 1990; Hon Delegate, White House Conf Librs, 1991; US Voting Delegate, Int Fed Libr Asn, 1991; participant, Snowbird Leadership Inst, 1993; Achievement Award, Black Caucus Am Library Asn, 1994-95; Alumni Achievement Award, Lincoln Univ, 1998; Men Making a Difference Award, Congressman Chaka Fattah, Model Cities Am, 1998; Leaders & Legends Award; Alumnus Award, 2007; Walter Fales Memorial Prize in Philosophy; Distinguished Alumnus Award; Trustee Award for Distinguished Service; Alumni Founders Day Award; Leaders & Legends Award, 2007; National Association for Equal Opportunity in Higher Education (NAFEO) Alumnus Award, 2007. **Special Achievements:** Workshop & lecture, Sixth Annual Virginia Hamilton Conference, 1990; Storytelling, Free Library of Philadelphia, 1991; lecture & publication, PA Black Conference on Higher Education, 1992; ALA Fellowship Report, "Not New Just Different"; Lecture, Shepherd College, 1992; Lecture, Villanova University, 1992; Association of Research Libraries Leadership and Career Development Program Inaugural Group, 1997-98. **Home Addr:** 1635 W Diamond St, Philadelphia, PA 19121, **Home Phone:** (215)232-4262. **Business Addr:** President, Lincoln University, 1570 Baltimore Pke, Lincoln University, PA 19352, **Business Phone:** (484)365-8000.

### HUNTER-GAULT, CHARLAYNE

Journalist. **Personal:** Born Feb 27, 1942, Due West, SC; daughter of Charles and Althea; married Ronald; children: Chuma; married Walter Stovall; children: Susan Stovall. **Educ:** Wayne State Univ, attended 1961; Univ Ga, BA, 1963; Wash Univ, Russell Sage fel, 1968. **Career:** New Yorker, reporter, 1964-67; New York Times, reporter, 1968-77; MacNeil Lehrer Newshour, reporter & nat affairs corresp, 1978-97; Nat Pub Radio, chief corresp Africa, 1997-99, foreign corresp, currently; CNN, Johannesburg Bur Chief, 1999-05. **Honors/Awds:** New York Times Publisher Awards, 1970, 1974 & 1976; George Foster Peabody Broadcasting Award, 1986; named Journalist of the Year, Nat Asn Black Journalists, 1986; Good Housekeeping Broadcast Personality of the Year Award; American Women in Radio & Television Award; Woman of Achievement Award, New York Chap Am Socs Univ Women; Front Page Award, Newswomen's Club; two National News & Documentary Emmy Awards; National Urban Coalition Award; Lincoln University Unity Award; Peabody Award, 1999; Lifetime Achievement Award, Annenberg Sch Commun, Univ Southern Calif, 2000; Sidney Hillman Award. **Special Achievements:** First African American woman to graduate from the University of Georgia in 1962, reported on Apartheid in 1985, is author of In My Place 1992, is the recipient of more than two dozen honorary degrees; One of two black students who first broke the color barrier in higher education in Georgia. **Business Addr:** Chief Correspondent, National Public Radio, 635 Mass Ave NW, Washington, DC 20001, **Business Phone:** (202)513-2300.

**HUNTLEY, LYNN JONES.** See Obituaries Section.

### HURD, BRIDGET G.

Government official. **Educ:** Univ Mich, BA, commun, 1991; Wayne State Univ, MBA, mkt, 1995; Boston Col, Wallace E Carroll Grad Sch Mgt, cert corp citizenship leadership, 2014. **Career:** St John Health, Warren, corp community rels coordr, 1998-2002; Greater Detroit Area Health Coun, Communs & Corp Affairs, dir, vpres, 2002-10; Detroit Med Ctr, corp dir/press secy, 2006-07; Southfield Community Found, interim exec dir, 2010; Blue Cross Blue Shield Mich, dir, community responsibility, vpres, 2010-. **Orgs:** Bd mem, Spec Olympics Mich Inc, Detroit Acad Arts & Sci, Lebanese Am Heritage Club, Southfield Community Found, Communicating Arts Credit Union; Mich Women's Found. **Business Addr:** Director of Community Responsibility, Blue Cross Blue Shield of Michigan, 600 Lafayette E, Detroit, MI 48226, **Business Phone:** (877)790-2583.

### HURD, DAVID JAMES

Musician, educator. **Personal:** Born Jan 27, 1950, Brooklyn, NY; son of David and Cecile. **Educ:** Juilliard Sch, attended 1967; Oberlin Col, BMus, 1971; Univ NC Chapel Hill, attended 1974; Berkeley Divinity Sch Yale, BMus; Church Divinity Sch Pac, DMus; Seabury Western Theol Sem, LHD. **Career:** Trinity Church, asst organist, 1971-72; St. Paul's Chapel; Duke Univ, asst dir choral activ, asst chapel organist, 1972-73; Church Intercession NYC, organist & music dir, 1973-79; composer; Gen Theol Sem, prof church music, dir chapel music, organist, 1979-2015; Yale Inst Sacred Music, vis lectr, 1982-83; All Saints Church music, dir, 1985; Church Holy Apostles, music dir, 2013. **Orgs:** New York Chap Am Guild Organists, 1966-; Theta Chap Pi Kappa Lambda, 1971-; vice chmn, Standing Comn Church Music, 1976-85; concert organist, Phillip Trucken Brod Artist Rep,

1977-; aristic adv comt, Boys Choir Harlem, 1978-80; Asn Anglican Musicians, 1979-; organ recitalist, AGO Biennial Nat Conv Minneapolis, 1980; Liturgical Comm Episcopal Diocese NY, 1982-86; organ recitalist, AGO Biennial Nat Conv, 1986, 2000. **Honors/Awds:** First Prize Organ Playing, Int Cong Organists, 1977; First Prize Organ Improvisation, Int Cong Organists, Philadelphia, 1977, premiered in Ljubljana, Slovenia at the International Saxophone Congress, 2006; AGO Distinguished Composer Award, 2010; The African Diaspora Sacred Music Living Legend Award, Calif State Univ, 2011; hon doctorate, Berkeley Divinity Sch; hon doctorate, Church Divinity Sch Pac; Recipient of Many Awards. **Special Achievements:** Diploma in improvision Stitching Intl Orgelconcours Goud The Netherlands, 1981. **Home Addr:** 175 Ninth Ave, New York, NY 10011, **Home Phone:** (212)924-4963. **Business Addr:** Music Director, Church of the Holy Apostles, 296 9th Ave 28th St, New York, NY 10001, **Business Phone:** (212)807-6799.

## HURD, DR. JAMES L. P.

Musician, educator, organist. **Personal:** Born Aug 2, 1945, Bonham, TX. **Educ:** Washburn Univ, BA, music, 1967; Am Conserv Music, MMus, 1968; Univ Southern Calif, MusD, 1973. **Career:** Calvary Baptist Church, Topeka, Kans, organist dir, 1962-69; Protestant Chapel, Kans Boys Sch, Topeka, organist choir dir, 1964-67, 1968-69; Cult Arts Div Topeka Recreation Comn, head music, 1965-67; Lawndale Presby Church Chicago, choir dir, 1967-68; Blessed Sacrament Cath Church, Chicago, Ill, organist, 1967-68; Ward African Methodist Episcopal Church Los Angeles, Calif, organist dir, 1969-73; Orgn & Mgt Analyst State Hwy, Comn Kans, 1969-70; El Camino Col, prof music, 1973-; First Pres Church Inglewood, organist & dir Music, 1973-96; Long Beach City Col, organ instr, 1973; St Andrew's Presby Church, Redondo Beach, Calif, organist & dir music, currently; First Baptist Church Palos Verdes, Calif, organist & dir, currently; Calif State Univ, organ prof; Dominguez Hills, organ prof. **Orgs:** Bd dir, pres, Airport Marina Coun Serv, 1995-2005; Am Guild Organists; Kappa Alpha Psi; Phi Mu Alpha; Adjudicator Music Teachers Assn Calif; bd dir, Westchester YMCA. **Honors/Awds:** Outstanding Young Men of America, US Jaycees, 1980; City of Los Angeles Mayor's Certificate of Appreciation, Music Contributions to the Community. **Special Achievements:** Featured organ recitalist for several chapters of the American Guild of Organists, and presented in organ concerts across the united States and Europe. **Home Addr:** 8001 Alverstone Ave, Los Angeles, CA 90045-1447, **Home Phone:** (310)645-0424. **Business Addr:** Professor, El Camino College, 16007 Crenshaw Blvd, Torrance, CA 90506, **Business Phone:** (310)532-3670.

## HURD, DR. JOSEPH KINDALL, JR.

Gynecologist. **Personal:** Born Feb 12, 1938, Hoisington, KS; son of Joseph Sr and Mildred Mae Ramsey; married Jean Elizabeth Challenger; children: Joseph Kindall III & Jason Hansen. **Educ:** Harvard Col, AB, 1960, MD, 1964. **Career:** Harvard Med Sch, clin instr surg, 1972-; Lahey Clin Found, gynecologist, 1972-, dept gynec, chmn, 1988-2000, chm emer, 2000-; Coun Dept, chmn, 1991-99; Tufts Med Sch, asst clin prof obstet & gynec, 1996. **Orgs:** Soc Boston; bd dir, Freedom House Inc; bd dir, Crispus Attucks Day Care Ctr; bd dir, Roxbury Med Dent Group; Am Fertil Soc; Charles River Med Soc; AMA; Nat Med Asn; coun, Mass Med Soc; Am Uro-Gynecol Soc; Am Asn Gynecol Laporoscopy; Alpha Chap, Phi Beta Kappa; bd govs & bd trustees, Lahey Clin, 1977-91, finance & exec comt, 1987-90; pres, New Eng Med Soc, 1980; counr, Harvard Med Alumni Asn, 1990-93, dir, 1990-93, pres, 2004; Iota Chi Chap, Omega Psi Phi; Sigma Pi Phi Fratrernity, 1991-; Mass Sect Am Col Obstet, gynec, 1993-96; Sire Archon, Beta BetaBoule, Sigma Pi Phi Fraternity, 2006-08; Ezekiel hersey coun. **Honors/Awds:** Spencer B Lewis Award, Coleus Soc, Harvard Med Sch, 1990; Harvard Alumni Association Award, 2013. **Home Addr:** 18 Emerson Rd, Wellesley, MA 02481-3419, **Home Phone:** (781)235-5912. **Business Addr:** Chairman Emeritus, Lahey Clinic Medical Center, 41 Mall Rd, Burlington, MA 01805, **Business Phone:** (781)744-8560.

## HURD, DR. WILLIAM CHARLES

Physician, ophthalmologist. **Personal:** Born May 17, 1947, Memphis, TN; son of Leon (deceased) and Doris; married Rhynette Northcross; children: Bill Jr & Ryan. **Educ:** Univ Notre Dame, BS, 1969; Mass Inst Technol, MS, 1972; Meharry Med Col, MD, 1980. **Career:** Gen Elect Corp, systs engr, 1969-70; Tenn State Univ, asst prof, 1972-76; Univ Tenn, intern, 1980-81, resident physician, 1982-85; Memphis Health Ctr, med consult, 1981; Memphis Emergency Specialists, consult physician, 1982-84; Methodist Hosp, staff physician, 1985-; pvt pract, physician, ophthalmologist, currently. **Orgs:** Bd dir, Vis Nurse Asn, 1985-. **Honors/Awds:** All Am Track Athlete at Nortre Dame, 1697-69; Athlete of the Year, Notre Dame Univ, 1968; World Record Holder at 300 yard Dash Indoors, 1968-72; Rhodes Scholar Semi Finalist, 1969; Prof Musician & Winner, Nat Jazz Fest Competition; Harvey G Foster Award, Univ Notre Dame, 1992; Holds US Patent on a Medical Instrument; Silver Anniversary Award, NCAA, 1994. **Business Addr:** Physician, Ophthalmologist, Private Practice, 220 S Claybrook St Suite 101, Memphis, TN 38104, **Business Phone:** (901)276-4844.

## HURDLE, HORTENSE O'MCNEIL

School principal, school administrator, government official. **Personal:** Born May 20, 1925, Marlin, TX; daughter of Leroy McNeil and Annie Mae Williams McNeil-Wade; married Clarence; children: Clarence II & Gaile Evonne. **Educ:** Prairie View Univ, BS, 1947; Sacramento State Univ, MA, 1973, MS, 1974. **Career:** School administrator (retired); Fed Govt, employee, 1947-57, elem teacher vpres, 1957-64; Compensatory Educ, dir, 1964-68; Del Paso & Heights Sch Dist, dir Compensatory Educ, elem sch prin, 1968-86. **Orgs:** Co-founder, Concerned Citizens Greater Sacramento, 1976; Les Belles Artes Club, 1985-90; asst regional dir, FWR Iota Phi Lambda Sorority, 1989-93, western regional dir, 1997-; Sacramento Iota Phi Lambda Sorority, Beta Tau Chap; Calif Admin Asn CTA; ed, Young Child; Nat Alliance Black Educr; Sacramento Black Educr; Women Div Dem Women; Nat Asn Advan Colored People; Phi Beta Delta Frat; XI Field Chap; Negro Coun Women; trustee, Shiloh Baptist Church. **Honors/Awds:** B'nai B'rith Outstanding Award, 1966; Distinguished Community Service Award, Sacramento Chamber Com, 1967; Outstanding Sorority, Far Western Region, Iota Phi Lambda Sorority, 1980; Outstanding Service Award, Beta Tau Chap, Iota Phi Lambda, 1989; Outstanding Service Award, Western Region, Nat Alliance Black School Educr, 1991. **Special Achievements:** Resolution 53 Assembly Dist & Progressive 12, 1970. **Home Addr:** 1370 40th Ave, Sacramento, CA 95822-2954, **Home Phone:** (916)422-7845.

## HURST, ROBERT (BOB HURST III)

Musician. **Personal:** Born Oct 4, 1964, Detroit, MI. **Career:** Out of the Blue, 1985; Wynton Marsalis, 1986-91; Woody Shaw's, 1986; Bemsha Swing; Wynton Marsalis band, 1986-91; J Mood, 1986; Live at Blues Alley, 1987; Standard Time Vol 1 ,1987; Bebob Music Inc, The Tonight Show, directing, arranging, & composing, currently; Do the Right Thing, musician, 1989; Standard Time Vol 2 Intimacy Calling, 1990; Mo Better Blues,1990; Branford Marsalis: The Music Tells You, musician, 1992; Robert Hurst, 1992; One for Namesake, 1993; Tonight Show Band,1995; Mommy's Day, lightning designer, 1997; The Wood, composer, 1999; Brown Sugar, composer & conductor, 2002; Unrehurst Vol 1, 2002; Diana Krall: Live at the Montreal Jazz Festival, actor, 2004; Ocean's Twelve, musician, 2004; Ocean's Eleven, musician; Ocean's Thirteen, musician; Good Night, musician; Good Luck, musician; Burned, writer & dir, 2006; TV ser: "Great Performances", musician, 2007; Unrehurst Vol 2, 2010; Bob Ya Head, 2010; Univ Mich Sch Music, Theatre, & Dance, assoc prof, currently. **Orgs:** Bd dir, John Coltrane Found. **Honors/Awds:** Four Emmy Awards; Five Grammy Awards; Presidential Scholarship, 1980. **Special Achievements:** Received Top Ten & Five Star recognition. **Business Addr:** Associate Professor, University of Michigan, EV Moore Bldg, Ann Arbor, MI 48109-2085, **Business Phone:** (734)615-1265.

## HURST, RODNEY LAWRENCE, SR.

Government official, executive director. **Personal:** Born Mar 2, 1944, Jacksonville, FL; married Ann; children: Rodney II & Todd. **Educ:** Fla Jr Col; Edward Waters Col. **Career:** Corp Pub Broadcasting, fel, 1969-70; Greater Jacksonville Econ Opportunity, proj dir, 1971-73; City Jacksonville, proj dir, 1973-75; Self Employed, ins salesman, 1975-; CILB, exec dir, 1996; Edward Waters Col, Community Develop Corp, dir, Capital Improv, dir, currently. **Orgs:** Ins & underwriter, Prudential, 1965-69; Welfare & Soc Serv Policy Steering Comt; Nat Asn County; Jacksonville Coun Citizen Involvement; City Coun Financial & Rules Comn; Cable TV Comn; chmn, Agr & Recreation Comn; Nat Asn Advan Colored People; Urban League; bd mem, Boy's Club; adv coun mem, Ribault Sr High Sch; Prudential, Consortium Aid Neglected & Abused C Ins & underwriter, 1965-69; Welfare & Soc Serv Policy Steering Comt; Nat Asn County; Jacksonville Coun Citizen Involvement; City Coun Financial & Rules Comn; Cable TV Comn; chmn, Agr & Recreation Comn; Nat Asn Advan Colored People; Urban League; bd mem, Boy's Club; adv coun mem, Ribault Sr High Sch; Consortium Aid Neglected & Abused C. **Honors/Awds:** Man of Year, Jacksonville Club, 1960; Clanzel T Brown Award, Jacksonville Urban league; James Genwright Sr Humanitarian Award, Lincoln-Douglas Memorial Emancipation Proclamation Asn Inc; Dr Mary McLeod Bethune Visionary Award, Bethune-Cookman Univ Nat Alumni Asn. **Special Achievements:** Co-host Feedback WJCT-TV, 1969-71; First thirteen national recipients of the Corporation for Public Broadcasting Television Fellowships; First Black to co-host a television talk show in Jacksonville on PBS Channel WJCT; First Black male hired at the Prudential South Central Home Office in Jacksonville, Florida; First Black to serve as the Executive Director of the State of Florida's Construction Industry Licensing Board. **Home Addr:** 5863 Carver Pines Ct, Jacksonville, FL 32219, **Home Phone:** (904)764-9038. **Business Addr:** Director, Edward Waters College, 1658 Kings Rd, Jacksonville, FL 32209-6199, **Business Phone:** (904)470-8258.

## HURT, PATRICIA A.

Lawyer. **Career:** Essex County, dep admin, prosecutor. **Special Achievements:** First African American and First Woman to serve as prosecutor in Essex County. **Business Addr:** Prosecutor, 480 Valley Rd Apt A6, Upper Montclair, NJ 07043, **Business Phone:** (973)495-0670.

## HUSKEY, BUTCH (ROBERT LEON HUSKEY)

Baseball player, athletic coach. **Personal:** Born Nov 10, 1971, Anadarko, OK. **Career:** Baseball player (retired); Athletic coach; New York Mets, infielder, 1993-98; Seattle Mariners, 1999; Boston Red Sox, 1999; Minn Twins, 2000; Colo Rockies, 2000; Cleveland Indians, 2001; Cameron Univ, asst coach.

## HUSKEY, ROBERT LEON. See HUSKEY, BUTCH.

## HUTCHERSON, DR. HILDA

Educator, writer, gynecologist. **Personal:** Born Jan 21, 1955, Tuskegee, AL; daughter of John F (deceased) and Bernice; married Frederic Fabiano; children: Lauren, Steven, Andrew & Freddie. **Educ:** Stanford Univ, BA, human biol, 1976; Harvard Med Sch, MD, gynec, 1980. **Career:** Vanderbilt Clin Ambulatory Serv, New York, NY, med dir, 1986-89; Columbia Presby Med Ctr, New York, NY, dir, 1986-89; Columbia Col Physicians & Surgeons, New York, NY, asst prof, 1986, dir, 1988, admis comt mem, 1998, asst prof obstet & gynec & assoc dean, off diversity & minority affairs, 2002-; Columbia Presby Med Ctr, New York, NY, asst attend, 1987-& co-dir, 1997, 2001-; AOL, love & sex coach, currently. Books: Having Your Baby: A guide African Am Women, 1997; What Your Mother Never Told You About Sex & Pleasure: A Woman's Guide to Getting Sex You Want, 2002; Need & Deserve. **Orgs:** Fel Am Col Obstet & Gynecol; assoc mem, Am Fertil Soc; Am Med Asn; Nat Med Asn; pres & co-dir, Women's Sexual Health Found. **Business Addr:** Associate Dean Office of Diversity & Minority Affairs, Columbia University, 16 E 60th St Suite 480, New York, NY 10022, **Business Phone:** (212)305-4157.

## HUTCHINS, DR. FRANCIS L., JR. (MICKEY HUTCHINS)

Educator, physician. **Personal:** Born Jul 8, 1943, Ridley Park, PA; son of Francis L and Mercedes; married Sandra; children: Keisha & Francis L. **Educ:** Duquesne Univ, BS, biol, 1965; Howard Univ, Med Wash Col, MD, 1969. **Career:** Lankenau Hosp, intern, 1969-70, residency, 1970-73; Portsmouth Naval Regional Med Ctr, 1973-75; Temple Univ Hosp, Dept Obstet & Gynec, asst prof & dir family planning, 1975-77; Thomas Jefferson Univ, Dept Obstet & Gynec, asst prof, 1977-81, clin assoc prof, 1991-98; Lankenau Hosp, Dept Obstet & Gynec, dir res & educ & dir family planning, 1977-81; Commonwealth Pa, Dept Health, consul to obstet, gynec & family planning adolescents, 1980; Hahnemann Univ, Dept Obstet & Gynec, asst prof, 1981-84, dir family planning, dir ambulatory affairs & community med, 1981-84, dir Maternal/Infant Care Proj, dir, Div Obstet, 1983-84, Dept Obstet, actg chmn, 1984, assoc prof clin obstet & gynec, 1984-98, clin assoc pres, 1985, chmn, 2000-01, prof, 2000-02, 2004-; Booth Maternity Ctr, med dir, 1985-86; Plan Parenthood Pa, med dir, 1985; City Philadelphia, Dept Maternal & Child Health, med dir, 1985-86; TJUH-Jefferson Pk Hosp, 1990-94; Grad Hosp, dir gynec & womens servs, 1992, Dept Gynec, vice chmn, 1993-95, chmn, 1995-98, clin prof, 1998-2000; PCOM-Allegheny Univ Hosp City Line Ave, 1994-98; Roxborough Memorial Hosp, fac, 1998-2000; Howard Univ Col Med, Dept Obstet Gynec, chmn, 2000-01, prof, 2000-02; Fibroid Ctr, dir, currently; consult obstet & gynec, 2001-02; Tap Pharmaceut Prod Inc, med dir, 2002-03; Drexel Univ, adj prof obstet & gynec, 2004-; consult, 2004-; Obstet & Gynec Womens Health, consult, 2004-; pvt pract, 2005-. Books: Adolescent Pregnancy Among Black Philadelphians, The State of Black Philadelphia, 1981; Pre-Test National Board Examination Part II, contrib ed, 1986; Federation Licensing Examination, contrib ed, 1986; Pre-Test Foreign Medical Graduate Examination In The Medical Science, contrib ed, 1987; The Fibroid Book, auth, 1998; Uterine Artery Embolization for the Treatment of Leiomyomata Uteri, In: Gynecological Endoscopy, 2001; The Fibroid Book 2nd Edition, auth, 2004. **Orgs:** Nat Med Asn, 1973-; Obstet Soc Philadelphia, 1973-; fel Am Col Obstetrics/Gynecology, 1976; Am Soc Colposcopy & Colpamicroscopy, 1977-; Philadelphia Col Surgeons, 1978-; Am Asn Gynec Laparoscopists, 1987-; Am Fertil Soc, 1989-; bd dir, Marriage Coun Philadelphia, 1991; bd dir, Family Planning Coun SE Pa, 1992; Int Soc Gynec Endoscopy; Philadelphia Col Physicians; Am Fertil Soc; Hope fibroids inc, 2005; Am Acad Cosmetic Gynecologists; bd dir, Covenant House; bd dir, Community Serv Planning Coun Southeastern Pa; phys adv bd, Childbirth Educ; Family Planning Med Task Force, Commonwealth Pa; Coord Coun Adolescent Pregnancy, Prev, Philadelphia, PA. **Business Addr:** Adjunct Professor, Drexel University College of Medicine, 2900 W Queen Lane, Philadelphia, PA 19129, **Business Phone:** (215)991-8100.

## HUTCHINS, JAN DARWIN

Businessperson, president (organization). **Personal:** Born Feb 11, 1949, Danville, IL; married Teri A Hope. **Educ:** Yale Col, BA, hist, 1971. **Career:** KRON-TV, sports dir; AT&T Long Lines, sales supvr, 1971-72; WIIC-TV Cox Broadcasting, sports journalist, 1972-74; News anchor, sports dir, sports anchor, reporter & tv host, 1972-91; KPIX-TV Westinghouse, sports, anchor & reporter, 1974-80; KNBR 68, producer & host, 1991-93; San Francisco Giants Baseball, community develop dir, 1993-95; Golf Pro Intl, dir commun, 1994-95; City Coun Los Gatos, vice mayor & mayor, 1996-99; Am Champion, pres, 1997-2000; media consult, currently. **Orgs:** Mem, Health & Wisdom; bd dir, Am Champion Entertainment Inc. **Honors/Awds:** Los Gatos Town Council. **Home Addr:** 212 Bella Vista Ave, Los Gatos, CA 95032. **Business Addr:** Board Director, American Champion Entertainment Inc, 26203 Prod Ave Suite 5, Hayward, CA 94545.

## HUTCHINS, LAWRENCE G., SR.

Association executive, vice president (organization). **Personal:** Born Sep 13, 1931, Danville, VA; son of James E Sr (deceased) and Alfrezia Mimms (deceased); married Rebbie Jacobs; children: Karen H Watts, Lawrence Jr, Gary & Gerald. **Educ:** Va State Col, Petersburg, VA, attended 1957; Va Commonwealth Univ, Richmond, VA, attended 1974. **Career:** Nat Asn Lett Carriers, exec vpres 496, 1962-69, pres, Richmond Br 496, 1969-78; VA State Asn, pres, 1970-78; asst, Nat bus agt, 1978-82; Nat bus agt, 1982-87; vpres, 1987-. **Orgs:** Pres, Richmond Br A Philip Randolph Inst; chmn, const comn, Crusade Voters, Richmond; co-founder, Black Metro Little League, Richmond; trustee, Second Baptist Church, S Richmond; adv bd, United Way; co-chair, Richmond Chap MDA. **Home Addr:** 8600 Western Oak Dr, Springfield, VA 22153, **Home Phone:** (703)440-9384. **Business Addr:** Vice President, National Association of Letter Carriers, 100 Indiana Ave NW, Washington, DC 20001-2144, **Business Phone:** (202)393-4695.

## HUTCHINS, REV. MARKEL

Civil rights activist, consultant, clergy. **Personal:** Born Mar 29, 1977, Decatur, GA; son of Leon and Dorothy. **Educ:** DDiv. **Career:** African Methodist Episcopal Church, minister; methodist pastor; Nat Youth Connection, founder, 1995, nat pres & chief exec officer; MRH LLC, managing prin & chief exec officer, currently. **Orgs:** DeKalb County Bd Educ; Rainbow/PUSH Coalition. **Home Addr:** 3065 Mclendon Cir NW, Atlanta, GA 30318, **Home Phone:** (404)794-4445. **Business Addr:** Managing Principal, Chief Executive Officer, MRH LLC, 3330 Cumberland Blvd Suite 500, Atlanta, GA 30339, **Business Phone:** (610)864-1008.

## HUTCHINS, MICKEY. See HUTCHINS, DR. FRANCIS L, JR.

## HUTCHINSON, EARL OFARI

Writer, columnist. **Personal:** Born Oct 8, 1945, Chicago, IL; son of Earl and Nina; married Barbara; children: Sikivu & Fanon. **Educ:** Calif State Univ, Los Angeles, BA, 1969; Pac Western Univ, PhD, 1992. **Career:** Books: The Myth of Black Capitalism, 1970; The Mugging of Black America, 1990; Black Fatherhood I, 1992, vol II, 1993; Black Fatherhood: The Guide to Male Parenting, 1994; Black Fatherhood II: Black Women Talk About Their Men, 1994; The Assassination of the Black Male Image, 1994; Blacks & Reds: Race & Class in Conflict, 1919-90, 1995; Betrayed: A History of Presidential Failure to Protect Black Lives, 1996; Beyond OJ: Race, Sex, & Class Lessons for Americans, 1996; The Assassination of the Black Male Image, 1997; The Crisis in Black & Black, 1998; The Disappearance of Black Leadership, 2000; A Colored Man's Journey Through 20th Century Segregated America, 2000; he Emerging Black GOP Majority, 2006; The Emerging Black Primates, 2006; The Latino Challenge to Black America: Towards a Conversation Between African Americans and

Hispanics, 2007; The Ethnic Presidency: How Race Decides the Race to the White House, 2008; How the GOP Can Keep the White House, How the Democrats Can Take it Back, 2008; How Obama Won, 2009; columnist, currently. **Orgs:** Writers Guild; pres, Nat Alliance Positive Action. **Honors/Awds:** The Gustavus Myers Award; Outstanding Book Award, 1995; Nat Black Journalist Award. **Business Addr:** Author, Journalist, Hutchinson Communications, 5517 Secrest Dr, Los Angeles, CA 90043, **Business Phone:** (323)383-6145.

### HUTCHINSON, DR. GEORGE

School administrator, educator. **Personal:** Born Dec 19, 1938, Albuquerque, NM; son of John and Leona; married Gwen Pierce. **Educ:** Calif State Univ Los Angeles, BS, 1969, MS, 1971; United States Int Univ, PhD, 1977; Nat Univ, San Diego, CA, post doctoral law, 1988. **Career:** Calif State Univ, assoc dean educ support serv, 1986-94; San Diego State Univ, asst prof dept of recreation, 1973-79, asst dean, 1974-77, assoc dean, 1978-81, col prof studies & fine arts, assoc prof dept recreation, 1979-94, dir stud outreach serv dir 1981, assoc prof emer, 1994. **Orgs:** Adv Counc Minority Officer Recruiting US Navy, 1977-; mem at largeIndustry Educ Coun Greater San Diego 1980-; Phi Kappa Phi; mem bd dir; Am Cancer Soci, 1984-; Athletic Adv Comm, 1985-; Senate Comm Minority; Calif Acad Partnership Prog, 1985-; Naval Reserve Officers Asn, NavyLeague US; San Diego Chap, Urban League; State Bar Calif, 1988-; pres, Boy Scouts Am Explorers Division, 1988-. **Home Addr:** 318 Gravilla St, La Jolla, CA 92037. **Business Addr:** CA.

### HUTCHINSON, JAMES J., JR.

Executive. **Personal:** Born Sep 22, 1947, Chicago, IL; children: Kelley & Jimmy. **Educ:** Dartmouth Col, BA, 1969; Amos Tuck Sch Bus Admin, MBA, 1971. **Career:** First Nat Bank Chicago, coop loan off, 1971-74; S Side Bank, exec vpres, 1974-80; Inter-Urban Broadcasting Co, vpres, 1977-81, pres, 1984; Inter-Urban Broadcasting New Orleans Partnership, exec vpres, gen partner, 1980-86; Inter-Urban Rental Systs, pres, 1985; Savannah Cardinals Baseball Club, secy, 1986; Inter-Urban Broadcasting Group, pres, 1986-; Family Advocacy & Neighborhood Serv, exec dir, currently. **Orgs:** Adv bd mem, New Orleans Reg Vo-Tech Inst, 1982-; exec comt mem, Chambers Small Bus Coun, 1984; radio vpres, Greater New Orleans Broadcasters Asn, 1984-85; Comn New Orleans Exhibs Hall Auth, 1986-; chmn, Urban League Greater New Orleans, 1986-; YMCA Greater New Orleans; United Way; Metrop Area Comt; LA Calif Mus Pvt Indust Coun; Greater NO Tourist & Conv Comn; Mayor Morials Superbowl Task Force; AP Tureaud Comn; Mayor Morials Bus Devel Coun; Bus Task Force Educ. **Home Addr:** 6930 Thor Ct, New Orleans, LA 70126, **Home Phone:** (504)241-5538. **Business Addr:** Executive Director, Family Advocacy & Neighborhood Serv, 5700 Read Blvd, New Orleans, LA 70150-0157, **Business Phone:** (504)343-7173.

### HUTCHINSON, LOUISE DANIEL

Historian. **Personal:** Born Jun 3, 1928, Ridge, MD; daughter of Constance Eleanor Hazel; married Ellsworth W Jr; children: 6. **Educ:** Miner Teacher Col; Prairie View A&M Univ; Howard Univ, attended 1952; Am Hist & Afro-Am Studies, Grad Hons, Sociol. **Career:** Historian (retired); Nat Portrait Gallery SI, res harmon collection, 1971, educ res spec, 1972-73; Nat Capitol Parks E Wash, educ res spec, 1973-74; Anacostia Mus Smithsonian Inst, hist, dir res, 1974-86. **Orgs:** Bd mem, SE Neighbor House, 1968-70; bd dir, Wash Urban League, 1968-70; mem bd, SE Unit Am Cancer Soc, 1969-; chmn supt, Coun Arts Educ, DC Pub Sch, 1972-74; Nat Asn Negro Bus & Prof Women's Club Inc, 1973-; exec comt bd, DC Citizens Better Pub Educ, 1974-76; Frederick Douglass Mem & Hist Asn, 1974-, Douglass ad hoc community, Nat Capitol Parks E; planning comn bicent Smithsonian Inst; Anacostia Hist Soc. **Honors/Awds:** Author: "The Anacostia Story, 1608-30", 1977", Out of Africa, From Kingdoms to Colonization", Smithsonian Press, 1979", Anna J Cooper, A Voice from the South", Smithsonian Press, 1981; Exhibit Black Women, Achievements Against the Odds Smithsonian Traveling Exhib Service. **Home Addr:** 2415 18 St SE, Washington, DC 20020-6313.

### HUTCHISON, DR. HARRY GREENE

College teacher, educator. **Personal:** Born Apr 12, 1948, Detroit, MI; son of Harry and Mary Robinson. **Educ:** Wayne State Univ, Col Lib Arts, Detroit, MI, BA, econ, 1969, MA, econ, 1975; Univ Mich, Ann Arbor, MBA, 1977; Wayne State Univ Law Sch, JD, 1986; Univ Bristol, PGCE, 1999; Univ Oxford, dipl, 2000. **Career:** Detroit Edison, Detroit, MI, bus analyst, 1971-74; Ford Motor Co, Troy, MI, financial analyst, 1977-80; Lawrence Technol Univ, Southfield, MI, asst prof econ & law, 1981-89; Lathrup Village, Mich, atty & counr, 1987-89; Univ Detroit, Detroit, MI, from asst prof law to prof law, 1989-97, fac dir london law prog & prof law, 1998-2000, prof, 1997-2001; First Am Bank, bd dir, 1991-94; Univ San Diego Law Sch, vis prof law, 1992; Univ Bristol, fac law, 1998-99; Wayne State Univ, fractional time prof, 2000, vis prof, 2001-02, prof & dir grad studies, 2003-04, law prof, 2002-06; George Mason Univ Sch Law, vis prof, 2005-06, prof law, 2006-; Belmont Univ, Col Law, prof, 2011-13; Harris Manchester Col, Univ Oxford, vis fel, 2014-. **Orgs:** Bd Scholar, sr policy analyst, Mackinac Ctr, 1987-; chair, arbitrator, Nat Asn Securities Dealers arbit panels, 1990-98; AAA Securities Arbit Panels; bd adv, Heartland Inst, 1990-; Mich Civil Rights Comn, 1991-93; bd dir, First Am Bank, 1991-94. **Home Addr:** 27600 Rackham, Lathrup Village, MI 48076, **Home Phone:** (313)559-4206. **Business Addr:** Professor of Law, George Mason University School of Law, 3301 Fairfax Dr Rm 321 Arlington Campus, Arlington, VA 22201, **Business Phone:** (703)993-8980.

### HUTCHISON, DR. PEYTON S.

School administrator, consultant. **Personal:** Born Mar 24, 1925, Detroit, MI; son of Gladys Palace Smith and Harry Greene; married Betty L Sweeney; children: Peyton Jr, Allison Leigh & Jonathan Alan. **Educ:** Wayne State Univ, BS, educ, 1950, MEd, 1955; Northern Ill Univ, attended 1969; Mich State Univ, PhD, 1975. **Career:** Detroit Pub Schs, admin asst, 1966-73, asst prin, 1964-65, dir, proj READ; City Col Chicago, supv dir, 1973-75; Chicago Urban Skills Inst, vpres, 1974-75, pres, 1975-84, exec dean; Roosevelt Univ, adj prof, 1984-94; Hutchison Assoc (consult bus) currently; Richard J. Daly Col, exec dean & dir; Knoxville Col, interim pres. **Orgs:** Teacher, Detroit Pub Sch, 1950-54; dir, Green Pastures Camp Detroit Urban League, 1959-65; asst prin, Detroit Pub Sch, 1964-65; matl develop suprv Detroit Pub Sch, 1965-67; sr level res assoc, Mich State Univ, 1968-69; chmn, bd dir, Classic Chorales Inc, 1983-; chmn, Col Univ Unit Am Assoc Adult Cont Educ, 1983-; trustee, Knoxville Col, 1984-; mem Alpha Phi Alpha; div dir, pres, 1992-93, pres, Am Asn Adult/Continuing Educ; exec comt, chmn pub educ, Am Cancer Soc. **Honors/Awds:** Pres, Phi Delta Kappa, Wayne State Univ, 1963; Mott Doctoral fel, Charles Stewart Mott Found, 1968; Carl Sandburg Award, Friends Chicago Pub Libr, 1984; Community Service Award, Univ Chicago Int Kiwanis, 1985; Phi Kappa Phi Nat Hon Soc; Phi Beta Sigma Hon Soc; Listed in Who's Who in American Education & Who's Who in Black America; Hall of Fame, Am Asn Adult/Continuing Educ. **Home Addr:** 688 Old Elm Rd, Lake Forest, IL 60045, **Home Phone:** (312)234-3392. **Business Addr:** Executive Dean, Director, Richard J Daly College, 7500 S Pulaski Rd Suite 100, Chicago, IL 60652, **Business Phone:** (773)838-0300.

### HUTSON, TONY

Football player. **Personal:** Born Mar 13, 1974, Houston, TX. **Educ:** Northeastern Okla A&M Col. **Career:** Football player (retired); Dallas Cowboys, guard, 1997-98, right guard & tight end, 1999; Wash Redskins, 2000; Oakland Raiders, 2001. **Home Addr:** 5308 Carnaby Suite 224, Irving, TX 75063.

### HUTTON, GERALD L.

Educator, consultant. **Personal:** Born Pittsburg, KS; married Marjorie. **Career:** Lincoln & HP Study Schs, teacher; Springfield Pub Schs, pub info rep; St Louis NW HS, athletic dir & bus educ instr; St Louis Educ TV, Zoning Pk Bd, community comnr, pub tv-utilization consult; Ancient Egyptian Arabic Order Nobles Mystic Shrine N & S Am, officer. **Orgs:** Am Guild Variety Artists; Anerucah Fed TV & Radio Artists; Am Equity Asn; Royal Vagabonds St Louis Mens Civic Club; St Louis Area Bus Teachers Asn; Kiwanis Club; Nat Advan Asn Colored People; St Louis Br; hon past, potentate PHA Shriners; United Supreme Coun, PHA So Jurisdiction 33rd deg, Soloist World Ser Games, St Louis, 1967, 1968; life mem, Kappa Alpha Psi. **Honors/Awds:** Festival Appreciation Award, Sigma Gamma Rho Sorority Inc & Zeta Sigma chap Afro-am Arts. **Special Achievements:** Book: "High School & College Typewriting". **Home Addr:** 11893 Branridge Rd, Florissant, MO 63033, **Home Phone:** (314)741-1962.

### HUTTON, MARILYN ADELE

Lawyer. **Personal:** Born Jul 21, 1950, Cincinnati, OH. **Educ:** Fisk Univ, BA, 1972; Harvard Law Sch, JD, 1975; Hague Acad Int Law, cert, 1983. **Career:** US Sen Lloyd M Bentsen, legis aide, 1975-76; Procter & Gamble Co, corp coun, 1976-81; Cincinnati Queen City Bowling Senate, corp secy, 1980-82; Nat Asn Advan Colored People, legis coun, 1986-87; Arlington Co, Va, Human Rights Comn, 1992-; Va State Coal & Energy Comn, 1994-; Nat Educ Asn Staff Org, atty human & civil rights spec, currently. **Orgs:** Legal adv comm, Nat Bowling Assoc, 1978-80; Int Bar Assoc; Am Soc Int Law; Am & Fed Bar Assocs; Dist Columbia Bar Assoc; Am Assoc Art Mus; Corcoran Gallery Art; US Ct Mil Appeals; US Ct Appeals Fed Circuit; US Ct Appeals Dist Columbia Circuit; Dist Columbia Courts Appeals. **Special Achievements:** Author American Soc of Int Law 1986, annual meeting report 1987. **Home Addr:** 1011 Arlington Blvd Suite 829 S, Arlington, VA 22209-3925, **Home Phone:** (703)516-4977. **Business Addr:** Attorney, National Education Association Staff Organization, 1201 16th St NW Level B2, Washington, DC 20036, **Business Phone:** (202)822-7739.

### HUTTON, DR. RONALD IRVING

Dentist. **Personal:** Born Jul 23, 1949, High Point, NC; son of Joseph E (deceased). **Educ:** Hampton Inst, BS, biol, 1971; Howard Univ Col Dent, DDS, 1975. **Career:** Winston-Salem Dent Care, dentist; Kimbrough Army Hosp, gen pract residency, 1975-76; Army Dent Corp, dentist, 1975-78; USAR, col, 1978-2003; pvt pract, currently. **Orgs:** Am Col Dent; Asn Mil Surgeons US; Old N St Dent & Soc; NC 2nd Dist Dent Soc; Am & Nat Dent Asns; Acad Gen Dent; Zoning Bd Adjustments, Town Lewisville; bd trustee, Big Bros-Big Sisters; bd trustee, Summit Sch Winston-Salem, NC; exec bd, Old Hickory Boy Scout Coun; bd dir, Big Bros-Big Sisters; bd dir, Boy Scouts Am; sedation evaluator, NC State Bd Dent Examiners, Greensboro Chap Nat Hampton Alumni Asn. **Honors/Awds:** Organized society fel Campus of Hampton Inst, 1969; Mastership, Acad Gen Dent; Outstanding Alumnus at Large Award, Hampton Univ, 2010. **Home Addr:** 1220 Brook Acres Trail, Clemmons, NC 27012. **Business Addr:** Dentist, Private Practitioner, 201 Charlois Blvd, Winston-Salem, NC 27103-1507, **Business Phone:** (336)718-1800.

### HUYGHUE, MICHAEL L.

Football executive, association executive. **Personal:** Born Sep 21, 1961, Ponte Vedra Beach, FL; son of Bruce and Joan; married Kimberly; children: 3. **Educ:** Cornell Univ, BS, commun & media studies, 1983; Univ Mich, JD, law, 1987. **Career:** Birmingham Fire, gen mgr; World League Am Football; Detroit Lions, gen coun, vpres admin, 1993-94; Jacksonville Jaguars, sr vpres football opers; Axcess Sports & Entertainment LLC, chief exec officer; Nat Football League labor standoff, 2011; United Football League, comnr, 2007-12; Michael Huyghue & Assocs, pres, 2012-. **Orgs:** Sports Lawyers Assoc; bd trustee, alma mater; MPS Group; Nat Football League Players Asn. **Business Addr:** President, Michael Huyghue & Associates LLC, 841 Prudential Dr Suite 1200, Jacksonville, FL 32207, **Business Phone:** (904)371-6532.

### HYDE, DR. MAXINE DEBORRAH

Neurosurgeon, physician. **Personal:** Born Jan 18, 1949, Laurel, MS; daughter of Sellus and Ann McDonald. **Educ:** Tougaloo Col, BS, biol, 1970; Cleveland State Univ, MS, biol, 1973; Case Western Res Univ, MD, 1977; Am Bd Neurol Surg, dipl. **Career:** Univ Hosp, internship gen surg, 1977-78, resident neuro surg, 1978-82; Guthrie Clin, neuro surg staff, 1982-87; Canoga Pk, Calif, pvt pract neurosurg, 1987-; Northridge Hosp MedCtr. **Orgs:** Cong Neurol Surgeons; Alpha Omega Alpha Hon Med Soc, 1977; Calif Neuro surg Soc; Am Asn Neurol Surgeons; Neuro Surg Today; founder, Beacon Hope Scholar Found Inc; Am Osteop Asn. **Honors/Awds:** Black Women Who Make It Happen, Nat Coun Negro Women, 1989; Strong Men & Women Excellence Leadership Award, 1996; DHL, Tongaloo Col, Tongaloo, Miss. **Special Achievements:** Second woman to become a neurosurgeon in the US; Publications:"5-Hydroxytryptophan decarboxylase & monoamine oxidase in the maturingmouse eye", 1973; "The Maturation of 5-hydroxytryptophan decarboxylase in regions of the mouse brain", 1973; "The maturation of indoleamine metabolism in the lateral eye of the mouse", 1974; "The maturation of monoamine oxidase and 5-hydroxyindole acetic acid in regions of the mouse brain", 1974; "Re-expansion of previously collapsed ventricles", 1982; Featured Story, Ebony, 1983; Featured in first edition of Medica, 1983; Featured story Am Med News, 1984; First Register as one of "the best of the new generation-those who exemplify in their professional lives the qualities of courage, originality, ingenuity, vision and selfless service", Esquire mag, 1984; Patients Choice Award, 2009. **Business Addr:** Founder, Beacon of Hope Scholarship Foundation, 7230 Med Ctr Dr Suite 300, West Hills, CA 91307, **Business Phone:** (818)716-7003.

### HYLER, LORA LEE

Radio journalist, president (organization). **Personal:** Born Oct 4, 1959, Racine, WI; daughter of Leona McGee and Haward. **Educ:** Univ Wis Milwaukee, BA, mass commun, 1981. **Career:** WISN Radio, an ABC Affil, news reporter, 1980-84; Wis Natural Gas Co, commun writer, 1984-88; J Commun, corp commun mgr, 1988-91; We Energies, actg media rels mgr, 1991-95, resource coordr, 1995-99, info technol dept, commun mgr, 1999-2001,; Wis Elec Power Co, Milwaukee, pub info rep, 1991-2001; Hyler Commun, founder, 2001-, pres & chief exec officer, 2004-; Northwestern Mutual, commun consult, 2012-13, consult, 2015-. **Orgs:** Pub Rels Soc Am, 1990-; Wis Black Media Asn. **Home Addr:** 1331 E Randolph Ct B, Milwaukee, WI 53212, **Home Phone:** (414)964-6858. **Business Addr:** President, Chief Executive Officer, Hyler Communications, 11512 N Port Washington Rd Suite 201A, Mequon, WI 53092, **Business Phone:** (414)520-0019.

### HYLTON, ANDREA LAMARR

Librarian. **Personal:** Born Dec 12, 1965, Martinsville, VA; daughter of Gloria Mae Hodge and Vallie Walker. **Educ:** James Madison Univ, Harrisonburg, BS, 1988; NC Cent Univ, Durham, MLS, 1990; Va Polytech Inst & State Univ, EdS, Instrnl Technol, 2010. **Career:** Blue Ridge Regional Libr, Martinsville, Va, libr asst, 1987; Spotsylvania Co Sch Bd, Spotsylvania, Va, librn, 1988-89; NC Cent Univ, Durham, NC, grad asst, 1989-90; Family Health Int, Res Triangle Pk, NC, intern, 1990; Advan Sci Inc, careirs librn, 1992-93; Freddie Mac, ref librn, 1995; Nat Econ Res Assocs, libr mgr, 1995-98; Wachovia Securities, res librn, 1999-2000; First Union Securities; Duke Energy Co, asst librn, 2000-03; James B. Duke Memorial Libr, Johnson C. Smith Univ, info syst librn, currently; IL Buddy Mentorship Prog; Online Prog Coordr. **Orgs:** Va Educ Media Asn, 1986-90; pres, NC Cent Univ Stud Chap Am Libr Asn, 1989-90; treas, NC Cent Univ Stud Chap Spec Libr Asn, 1989-90; NC Cent Univ Sch Libr & Info Sci Curric Comt, 1990; stud staff mem, Am Libr Asn, Nat Conf, 1990; Nuclear Energy Inst, libr mgr, 1993-95; JMU Alumni Asn. **Honors/Awds:** Special Talent Award, NC Cent Univ, 1989; Jenkins-Moore Scholar, Sch Libr & Info Sci, NC Cent Univ, 1990. **Home Addr:** 850 N Randolph St Apt 1510, Arlington, VA 22203-4020. **Business Addr:** Information System Librarian, Johnson C Smith University, Libr 216 100 Beatties Ford Rd, Charlotte, NC 28216, **Business Phone:** (704)371-6747.

### HYLTON, TAFT H.

Manager. **Personal:** Born Jun 22, 1936, Washington, DC. **Educ:** Wash Conserv Music; Wash Inst Music. **Career:** Dept Human Serv DC Govt, chief & payments br; Ofc Budget & Mgmt Sys DC Govt, budget & acct analyst; choral conductor; tcht pvt piano; Voices of Expression Inc, dir. **Orgs:** Am Choral Dir Asn; dir of sr choir New Bethel Bapt Ch; Dir Anthem Choir Allen AME Ch; Cosmopolitan Choral Ensemble; Am Light OperaCo; Negro Oratorio Soc; 12th St Christian Ch; Univ Soc Piano Tchrs; corresp, Nat Negro Opera Co Collection. **Honors/Awds:** Work Performance Award; Pub Health Serv NIH, 1963; Eligible Bachelor featured, Ebony Mag, 1974. **Home Addr:** 6503 Knollbrook Dr, Hyattsville, MD 20783.

### HYMAN, EARLE

Actor. **Personal:** Born Oct 11, 1926, Rocky Mount, NC; son of Zachariah and Maria Lilly Plummer. **Educ:** Amer Theatre Wing; Actors Studio. **Career:** New York State Am Negro Theatre, performer, 1943; Films: The Lost Weekend, 1945; The Bamboo Prison, 1954; John Brown's Raid, 1960; Macbeth, 1968; The Possession of Joel Delaney, 1972; House Party Playhouse, various roles, 1974; The Green Pastures, Coriolanus, 1979; Julius Caesar, 1979; The Ivory Ape, 1980; Fighting Back, 1982; Long Day's Journey Into Night, 1982; Thundercats, 1985; The Life & Adventures of Santa Claus, 1985; Gandahar, 1988, Light Years, 1988; Hijacked: Flight 285, 1996; The Moving of Sophia Myles, 2000. TV series: "Love of Life", 1951; "Look Up and Live", 1954; "Camera Three", 1955; "Hallmark Hall of Fame", 1957; "The United States Steel Hour", 1957; "Play of the Week", 1959-60; "Espionage", 1963; "East Side/West Side", 1963; "The Doctors and the Nurses", 1964; "Playdate", 1964; "The Defenders", 1964; "Seaway", 1965; "Afrikaneren", 1966; "The Cosby Show", 1984-92; "The Edge of Night", 1984; "Thundercats", 1985-86; "A Different World", 1987; "Gandahar ", 1988; "A Man Called Hawk", 1989; "All My Children", 1995; "Cosby", 1997; "Moonshine Over Harlem", 2001; "Twice in a Lifetime", 2001; "A Look Back", 2002; "Recovering the Life of Canada Lee", 2006; "Saturday Night Live", 2015. **Orgs:** Reader, Am Found Blind. **Honors/Awds:** Show Business Award, 1953; Seagram Vanguard Award, 1955; Theatre World Award, 1956; GRY Award, Norwegian, Oslo, Norway, 1965; ACE CableACE Award, Cable Tv, 1983; Norwegian State Award, 1984. **Special Achievements:** Nominated for an Emmy Award in 1986. **Home Addr:** 484 W 43rd St Suite 33E, New York, NY 10036-6319, **Home Phone:** (212)594-8663.

### HYMAN, DR. MARK J.

Executive. **Personal:** Born Apr 25, 1916, Rocky Mount, NC; son of Joshua and Eliza Vick; married Mable V; children: Beverley & Linda. **Educ:** NY Univ, BA, MA; Temple Univ, PhD, 1992. **Career:** Way Publ Co, chmn & owner; Mark Hyman Assocs Inc, pres. **Orgs:** Chmn, pres, Philadelphia Urban League; chmn, Howard Univ Alumni Club Philadelphia; chmn, Philadelphia Press Club; chair, Edythe Ingraham Hist Club; Omega Psi Phi Fraternity; dir, Nat Pub Rels; vpres, Philadelphia Am Cancer Soc; founder & bd mem, Aro Hist & Cult Mus, Philadelphia. **Honors/Awds:** Mary McLeod Bethune Medallion, Bethune Cookman Univ; Philadelphia Tribune Front Page Award; ASOd Press Broadcast Award; Afro American Historical Museum Award; Pennsylvania State Legislature Award. **Special Achievements:** Books: "Blacks Before America, Vol I, II, III", 1979; "Blacks Who Died for Jesus, A History Book", 1983; "Black Shogun of Japan", 1986; "The America that killed King: Fact & Fiction", 1991; "The Survival of Kwame". **Home Addr:** 5070 Parkside Ave Suite 1122, PO Box 36, Philadelphia, PA 19131.

### HYMES, JESSE
President (organization), executive, real estate executive. **Personal:** Born Feb 13, 1939, St. Joseph, LA; married Addie B; children: Kenneth, Tracey & Trina. **Educ:** Univ Chicago, MBA, 1972; Purdue Univ, AAS, 1970. **Career:** Meade Elec Co, draftsman estimator, 1969; financial analyst, 1972; plant acct, 1974; control syst adminr, 1975; Joseph Schlitz Brewing Co, plant controller, asst controller, 1975; Winston-Salem Black Chamber Com, pres; Hymes Appraisals & Realty Group, residential real estate appraiser & pres, 2000-, owner, currently. **Orgs:** Nat Asn Advan Colored People; jr advr Achievement, 1975-76; art coun, 1975-76; bd dir, Urban Arts, 1976; pres, Nat Parent Teacher Asn, 1977; adv dom, Boy Scouts Am, 1977; bd mem, Downtown Winston-Salem Partnership. **Home Addr:** 280 Stanaford Rd, Winston-Salem, NC 27104-2723, **Home Phone:** (336)765-8374. **Business Addr:** Owner, Residential Real Estate Appraiser, Hymes Appraisals & Realty Group, 1001 S Marshall St, Winston-Salem, NC 27101-5852, **Business Phone:** (336)777-8222.

### HYNSON, CARROLL HENRY, JR.
State government official. **Personal:** Born Dec 28, 1936, Washington, DC; son of Adel and Carroll; children: Michelle Hynson Green, Lejuene Tarra, Marcus Carroll & Brandee Carol. **Educ:** Pa State Univ, sociol & polit sci, 1959; Am Univ, summer course, sociol; Morgan State Univ, BA, 1960. **Career:** Sonderling Broadcasting Co, chief announcer & actg prog dir, 1965-75; Hynsons Real Estate, off mgr, 1975-76; Ceda Corp, pub affairs specialist, 1976-77; Provident Hosp Inc, asst vpres, develop & pub rels, 1978-80; Balt/Wash Int Airport, dir off trade develop, 1980-84; MD State Lottery Agency, dep dir sales, 1984-88, dep dir pub affairs, 1984-. **Orgs:** Life mem, Phi Beta Pi Com Frat, 1973; bd dir, Epilepsy Found MD, 1982; adv bd, Baltimore Conv Bur, 1982; vpres, Scholar Scholars Comn, 1984; Kappa Alpha Psi Fraternity; vice chmn, Anne Arundel Co/Annap Bicentennial Comm. **Home Addr:** 95 W St, Annapolis, MD 21401, **Home Phone:** (410)269-6862. **Business Addr:** Deputy Director Public Affairs, MD State Lottery Agency, Plz Off Ctr Suite 204, Baltimore, MD 21214, **Business Phone:** (410)764-5739.

### HYPOLITE, DR. CHRISTINE
Educator. **Personal:** Born Nov 20, 1956, New Orleans, LA; daughter of Harold and Shirley; married Shelby J. **Educ:** Nicholls State Univ, BA, 1978, MEd, 1980; La State Univ, PhD, 2003. **Career:** Lafourche Parish Schs, teacher, 1979-94; Nicholls State Univ, asst prof, 1994, Dept Teacher Educ Initial Progs, chair, Praxis, coordr, Dept Teacher Educ, assoc prof; Our Lady Holy Cross Col, assoc prof, currently. **Orgs:** Nat Sci Teacher Asn, 1995-; Nat Coun Teachers Math, 1995-; Asn Curric Develop, 1995-; bd chair, Bayonland Families Helping Families, 1997-; chair, Univ Disciplinary Comt, Nicholls State Univ; chair, Col Educ Diversity Comt, NCATE Stand 4. **Home Addr:** 212 Midway St, Thibodaux, LA 70301, **Home Phone:** (985)227-7448. **Business Addr:** Associate Professor of Education, Our Lady of Holy Cross College, 4123 Woodland Hwy, New Orleans, LA 70131, **Business Phone:** (504)398-2159.

### HYSAW, GUILLERMO LARK
Chief executive officer, manager, automotive executive. **Personal:** Born Dec 19, 1948, Bakersfield, CA; son of Guillermo and Georgia; married Kimberly; children: S Jamal, Immari A & Megan Ashley. **Educ:** Oakland Univ, BA, psychol, 1972; Claremont Grad Univ, Peter F Drucker & Masatoshi Ito Grad Sch Mgt, MA, mkt, 1991, MBA, finance, 1993, AMBA, strategic mgt, 1996; EMBA, finance & econ; Kellogg Marshall Anderson Bus Mgt Schs, cert; Nat Asn Corp Dirs, cert. **Career:** Gen Motors Corp, staff, 1971-87; Toyota Motor Sales USA Inc, Lexus Div, sr mkt rep admin, 1987-88, venture capital planning mgr, 1988-89, nat advert mgr, 1989-91, nat bus develop mgr, 1991-92, nat mkt develop mgr, 1992-93, nat fleet mkt opers mgr, 1993-97, corp mgr used vehicle dept, 1997-2000, corp mgr, mkt rep, 2000-02, vpres diversity, 2002-05; Hysaw Enterprises Llc, prin owner, 2005-; Calif State Univ, vpres, chief exec officer, 2009-12; Garrison-Walker Financial Group LLC, chief exec officer, managing partner; Mach-1 Autogroup, partner, chief exec officer, currently. **Orgs:** Exec mgt, Gen Motors Inst Bd Regents, 1990; pres, 100 Black Men Los Angeles Inc, 1999-2001; vpres, life mem, Nat Asn Black MBA, Los Angeles; life mem, Nat Comm, Nat Asn Adv Colored People; Nat External Fundraiser; life mem, Alpha Phi Alpha Frat; bd dir & pres, Compton Comm Col Found; bd dir, Drew Med Hosp; nat co-chairperson mkt, 100 Black Men Am Inc; strategic planning mem, Nat Econ Develop; Beta Psi Lambda Chap Los Angeles; life mem, Nat Black Master; bd mem, Los Angeles Automotive Training Ctr; pres, chief exec officer, bd chmn, First Tee S LA; life mem, Nat Asn Advan Colored People; exec dir, chief operating officer, Nat Asn Black Accountants, 2012-13; bd mem, Diversity & Inclusion Comnr, AICPA; Beta Gamma Sigma, Southern Univ & AM Chap; Orange County Black Chamber Com; bd mem, Greater Los Angeles African Am Chamber Com; bd mem, Nat Environ Educ & Transp Found; Exec Leadership Coun; nat external fundraiser chmn, Martin Luther King Jr Memorial Found Inc; bd mem, Cong Black Caucus, currently. **Home Addr:** , Irvine, CA 92602. **Business Addr:** Partner, Mach 1 Autogroup, 1001 Avenido Pico Suite C 258, San Clemente, CA 92673, **Business Phone:** (949)677-3683.

# I

### IBEKWE, LAWRENCE ANENE
Educator, school administrator. **Personal:** Born Apr 17, 1952, Onitsha; son of Eusebius and Marcelina Ibekwe Ozumba; married Theresa Ibekwe Nwabunie; children: Lynn, Lawren & Lawrence Jr. **Educ:** Philander Smith Col, Little Rock, AR, BA, bus admin, 1981; Univ Ark, Fayetteville, AR, MS, mgt, 1983; Capella Univ, PhD, orgn & mgt, 2007. **Career:** State Sch Bd, Holy Rosary Teachers Col, Nigeria, libr asst, 1975-78; Ark Commemorative Comt, Old State House, security officer, 1983-84; Philander Smith Col, instr, 1984-91, adj prof, social sceince dept, 2009-; Shorter Col, assoc prof, 1984-2009, Dept Bus & Appl Sci, head, 1987-88, 1991, acad dean, 1997-2010; Ark Dept Heritage, Mgt Proj Anal, 1992-93; Labekson Eval Serv, chief evaluator, consult, 2008-; Univ Riverside, fac, currently. **Orgs:** Hospitality to African Dignitaries, 1985-; Adv, Phi Beta Lambda, Philander Smith Col, 1986-; chmn, Ark Asn Nigerians, Supv Coun, 1986; chmn, Const Rev, 1986, 1989, 1992; adv, Ark Asn Nigerian Studs, 1986-88; adv, Const Rev, 1987; treas, Elite Social Club, 1987-; Knight Columbus, 1987-; bd adv, Little Rock Job Corp Prog, 1989-90, 2000-07; Southwest Int Studies Consortium, 1989-; campus coordr, Fed Funded Int Studies Prog, 1990-93; treas, Nigerian Professionals Ark, 1991-92; chair, African Cult Heritage Comn, 1995-2001; managing dir, African Professionals Ark, 1997-2003; Asn Col Adminr Professionals, 1997-; Nat Substance Abuse Consortium, 1998-; Southwest Bus Deans Asn, 2000-; Am Mgt Asn, 2000-; adv bd, Little Rock Afb Ark, 2001-; Nigerians Diaspora, 2005-; Bus Deans Asn, 2006-. **Home Addr:** 6812 W 33rd St, Little Rock, AR 72204. **Business Addr:** FACULTY, Univeristy of Riverside, 11840 Pierce St Suite 200, Riverside, CA 92505, **Business Phone:** (951)637-0100.

### IBELEMA, DR. MINABERE
Educator. **Personal:** Born Dec 9, 1954, Bonny; son of Ebenezer Tamunoibelema and Violet Eredappa; children: Danielle Boma & Ibim. **Educ:** Wilberforce Univ, BA, 1979; Ohio State Univ, MA, 1980, PhD, 1984. **Career:** Cent State Univ, Wilberforce, Ohio, assoc prof, 1984-91; Eastern Ill Univ, Charleston, Ill, assoc prof, 1991-95; Univ Ala, Birmingham, assoc prof commun studies, 1995-; Books: The African Press; Civic Cynicism; Democracy; ournalism & Communication Monographs; Free Speech Yearbook; Journal of Development Communication; Newspaper Research Journal; Journal of Radio Studies; Journalism & Mass Communication Educator; Current History; Readings in Popular Culture for Writers, 1994; Afro-Optimism: Perspectives on Africa's Advances, co-auth; The Birmingham News, copy ed or reporter; The (Birmingham) Post-Herald, copy ed or reporter; The (Topeka) Capital-Journal, copy ed or reporter; Dayton (Ohio) Daily News, copy ed or reporter. **Orgs:** Asn Educ Jour & Mass Commun, 1987-; African Studies Asn, 1992-; adv dept commun studies, Nashville Asn Black Journalists; comt chair, dept commun studies, Univ Ala Birmingham. **Home Addr:** PO Box 550173, Birmingham, AL 35255, **Home Phone:** (205)951-7501. **Business Addr:** Associate Professor, University of Alabama, 15 St Office Bldg 901 S, Birmingham, AL 35294-2060, **Business Phone:** (205)934-6907.

### IBN MCDANIELS-NOEL, MUHIYYALDIN MALAK ABD AL MUTA'ALI
Naval officer. **Personal:** Born Salem, NJ; children: 3. **Educ:** BBA, bus admin; MBA, indust rels & arbit, personnel mgt; MDiv, Islamic studies law; DMin, Islamic studies & muslim-christian rels. **Career:** USN, chaplain, Lt, 1996-. **Orgs:** NCP; APA; Black Ministers Conf; consult, The Ctr Study Relig Freedom; VIR Wesleyan Col; Nat Conf Cot Justice; Am Muslim Coun; Muslim Mil Mbr Asn; Alpha Eta Pho Aviation; Nat Naval Officers Asn; Mil Chaplains Asn; Alumni Asn; Salem Comn Col; Wilmington Col; Am Islamic Col; Lutheran Sch Theol Chi; Muslim Stud Asn; Univ Chi; Old Dom Univ; dir, Islamic Charities Hampton Rds. **Honors/Awds:** Joint Silver Commenation Medal, Joint Silver Achievement Medal, Navy & Marine Corporations Achievement Medal, Combat Action Ribbon; Joint Meritorious Unit Award; Navy Unit Commendation; Meritorious Unit Commendation; Battle "E" Ribbon; Good Conduct Medal; Naval Res Meritorious Silver Medal; Navy Expeditionary Medal; Nat Defense Silver Medal; SW Asia Silver Medal; Humanitarian Silver Medal; Sea Silver Deployment Ribbon; Navy & Marine Corps Overseas Silver Ribbon; Kuwait Liberation Medal Kingdom of Saudi Arabia; Kuwait Liberation Medal, Kuwait; Rifle Sharpshooter Medal; Pistol Expert Medal; Vol Medal; Armed Forces Service Medal. **Special Achievements:** First Muslim chaplain in the history of the US Navy, 1996. **Home Addr:** PSC 557, PO Box 1283, FPO, AP 96379-1200. **Business Addr:** Chaplain, Commander, Carrier Air Wing EIGHT, Suite 60109, FPO, AE 09504-4406, **Business Phone:** (757)433-2089.

### IBRAHIM, ABDULLAH (ADOLPH JOHANNES DOLLAR BRAND)
Pianist, composer. **Personal:** Born Oct 9, 1934, Cape Town; married Sathima Bea Benjamin; children: Tsakwe, Jean Grae & Tsidi. **Educ:** Univ Cape Town. **Career:** Jazz Epistles, pianist & composer, 1949-61; Tuxedo Slickers, pianist & composer, 1949-61; Willie Max Big Band, pianist & composer, 1949-61; Dollar Brand Trio, band leader, 1962-65; Liberation Opera, Kalahari, composer, 1978; Marimba Mus Ctr & Ekapa Rec, dir; AS-Shams Rec Co; Cape Town, S Africa, karate instr; Ekaya, band leader, 1983-; M7 Acad S African Musicians, founder; Chocolat. Albums: Jazz Epistle Verse 1, 1960; The Dream, 1965; Anatomy of a South African Village (Black Lion Records, 1965; This is Dollar Brand (Black Lion), 1965; African Sketchbook, 1969; African Piano, 1969; Good News from Africa, 1973; African Space Program, 1973; Ancient Africa, 1974; Confluence, 1975; Banyana-Children of Africa, 1976; The Journey, 1977; Streams of Consciousness, 1977; Buddy Tate Meets Dollar Brand (Chiaroscuro Records), 1977; Anthem for the New Nations, 1978; Autobiography, 1978; Soweto, 1978; Echoes from Africa, 1979; African Marketplace, 1979; Africa Tears and Laughter, 1979; Dollar Brand at Montreux, 1980; African Dawn, 1982; Ekaya, 1983; Zimbabwe, 1983; Water From an Ancient Well, 1985; South Africa, 1986; Mindif, 1988; Blues for a Hip King, 1989; African River, 1989; The Mountain[3], 1989; No Fear, No Die, 1990; Mantra Mode, 1991; xnysna Blue, 1993; African Sun, 1994; Yarona, 1995; Cape Town Flowers, 1997; African Suite, 1999; Cape Town Revisited, 2000; Ekapa Lodumo, 2001; African Magic, 2002; Senzo, 2008; Bombella, 2009; Sotho Blue (& Ekaya), 2010; Mukashi: Once Upon a Time, 2013. **Orgs:** Nat Endowment Arts. **Honors/Awds:** Rockefeller Grant, 1968; Silver Award, 1973; Grand Prix Award, 1973; Talent Deserving Wider Recognition, Downbeat Mag, 1975; Gresham Col, London, UK, guest lectr, 2000. **Business Addr:** Composer, Hotel Chelsea, 222 W 23rd St, New York, NY 10011.

### ICE, DR. ANNE-MARE
Pediatrician, educator. **Personal:** Born Mar 16, 1945, Detroit, MI; daughter of Lois Tabor and Garnet Terry. **Educ:** Fisk Univ, BA, chem, 1966; Howard Univ Col Med, MD, 1970; Madonna Univ, MSBA, 1996. **Career:** Wayne State Univ Col Med, clin asst prof; Internal Med Ctr, pediat physician; Milwaukee C Hosp, intern & resident pediat, 1973; pvt pract pediat, 1973-. **Orgs:** Am Bd Pediat; Nat Med Asn; Links Inc; Delta Sigma Theta Inc. **Honors/Awds:** Community Pediatrician Award, Coalition Reduce Infant Mortality, 1997; Sojourner Truth Humanitarian Award, Nat Asn Negro Bus & Prof Women Detroit Chap, 1998. **Home Addr:** 17120 E Goldwin Dr, Southfield, MI 48075-7003, **Home Phone:** (248)569-7549. **Business Addr:** Pediatrics Physician, Private Practice, 22341 W 8 Mile Rd, Detroit, MI 48219-1217, **Business Phone:** (313)255-2209.

### ICE CUBE (O'SHEA JACKSON, SR.)
Actor, rap musician. **Personal:** Born Jun 15, 1969, Los Angeles, CA; son of Hosea and Doris; married Kimberly Woodruff; children: Darrell, O'Shea Jr, Shareef & Kareema. **Educ:** Phoenix Inst Technol, cert archit design, 1988. **Career:** Rap musician; actor; NWA, mem, 1988-90; albums: AmeriKKKa's Most Wanted, 1990; Death Cert, 1991; The Predator, 1993; Lethal Injection, 1993; War & Peace Vol 1, 1999; War & Peace Vol 2, 2000; Next Friday, 2000; Gone in Sixty Seconds, 2000; Save the Last Dance, 2001; Jay & Silent Bob Strike Back, 2001; How High, 2001; Ali G Indahouse, 2002; Friday After Next, 2002; The Hot Chick, 2002; BladeII, 2002; All About the Benjamins, 2002; Hollywood Homicide, 2003; Grand Theft Auto: San Andreas, 2004; Harsh Times, 2005; Beerfest, 2006; Waist Deep, 2006; Laugh now Cry later, 2006; Raw footage, 2008; I Am the West, 2010; Everything's Corrupt, 2012. Actor: Next Friday, 2000; Ghosts of Mars, 2001; All About the Benjamins, 2002; Barbershop, 2002; Friday After Next, 2002; WC: Bandana Swang in-All That Glitters Ain't Gold, 2003; Torque, 2004; Barbershop 2: Back in Business, 2004; XXX: State of the Union, 2005; Are We Done Yet?, 2007; First Sunday, actor & producer, 2008; The Longshots, producer, 2008; Lottery Ticket, 2010; Rampart, 2011; Ride Along, 2012; 21 Jump Street, 2012; 22 Jump Street, 2014; The Book of Life, 2014; Straight Outta Compton, producer, 2015. TV Series: 'BarberShop: The Series", producer, 2005; "WrestleMania 21", 2005; "Black. White.", producer, 2006; "Friday: The Animated Series", producer & writer, 2007; "30 for 30", dir, 2010; "Are We There Yet?", producer & actor, 2010-13; "The Rebels", 2014. **Business Addr:** Actor, Creative Artists Agency, 2000 Avenue of the Stars, Los Angeles, CA 90067, **Business Phone:** (424)288-2000.

### IDEWU, OLAWALE OLUSOJI
Physician, educator. **Personal:** Born Abeokuta Ogun; son of George B and Rali; married Linda; children: Ayodele & Olanrewaju. **Educ:** Blackburn Col, BA, 1959; Heidelberg Univ; Freidburg Univ, W Ger, MD, 1961; Am Bd Otolaryngol, head & neck surg. **Career:** John H. Stroger Hosp Cook County, internship, 1967-68; Harlem Hosp Ctr, 1968-70; St. Louis Univ Hosp, 1971-73; Am Col Surgeons, Chicago, fel, 1977-78; Fawcett Memorial Hosp; Gulf Coast Med Ctr; Peace River Regional Med Ctr; Ear, Nose & Throat Health Ctr, physician & owner, currently; NW Univ, Dept Otolaryngol & Maxillofacial Surg, Chicago, Ill, instr. **Orgs:** AMA; Iowa Med Soc; fel Am Acad Otolaryngol; fel Am Col Surgeons; fel Int Col Surgeons; Am Acad Otolaryngol, Allergy; fel Rotary Club Int, Harris; Am Cancer Soc. **Honors/Awds:** Distinguished Person, Nigerian-Am Forum, 1990. **Special Achievements:** Scholar to study Med, Heidelberg Univ, 1960; Nigerian Folk Tales. **Home Addr:** 103 W Marion Ave Suite 111, Punta Gorda, FL 33950, **Home Phone:** (941)205-5555. **Business Addr:** Physician, Ear Nose & Throat Health Center, 2400 Harbor Blvd Suite 14, Port Charlotte, FL 33952, **Business Phone:** (941)235-2131.

### IFALASE, DR. OLUSEGEN (ERLIN BAIN)
Clinical psychologist. **Personal:** Born Sep 25, 1949, Nassau; son of Clifford Bain and Jennie Bain; children: Akilah-Halima, Kwasi Rashidi & Jamila Rashida. **Educ:** Univ Miami, BA, 1980, PhD, 1986. **Career:** Ctr Child Devel, psychologist, 1979-82; Miami Ment Health Ctr, dir substance abuse, 1982-84; Dept Youth & Family Devel, clin psychologist, 1985-92; Ujima Assocs Inc, exec dir, 1986-. **Orgs:** Ment Health Asn Dade Co, 1982-, Chiumba Imani African Dance Co, 1983-, Nat Black Alcoholism Coun, 1984-; pres, S Fla Asn Black Psychologists, 1986-; consult, Informed Families, 1986, Switch Bd Miami, 1986; Kuumba Artists Asn, 1986; consult, Family Health Ctr Miami, 1987. **Honors/Awds:** Nat Minority fel grant, 1978-83; Community Service Award, Welfare Mothers Dade, 1982; Appreciation Award Dade Co Sch Bd, 1986; Inner City Task Force, 1986. **Home Addr:** PO Box 598, Bronx, NY 10461.

### IFILL, GWEN (GWENDOLYN L IFILL)
Journalist. **Personal:** Born Sep 29, 1955, Queens, NY; daughter of O Urcille (deceased) and Eleanor (deceased). **Educ:** Simmons Col, Boston, MA, BA, commun, 1977. **Career:** Boston Herald-Am, reporter, 1977-80; Baltimore Eve Sun, reporter, 1981-84; Wash Post, polit reporter, 1984-91; New York Times, Cong & White House corresp, 1991-94; NBC News, Wash, DC bur, chief Cong & polit corresp, 1994-99; Wash Week, panelist & guest moderator, 1992-99, moderator & managing ed, 1999-; PBS Newshour With Jim Lehrer, sr polit corresp, 1999-; Funeral: Tim Russert, 2008; Pub Broadcasting Serv, moderator & managing ed, 2013-. **Orgs:** Nat Assoc Black Journalists; chair, Robert F Kennedy Memorial Jour Awards; bd mem, Univ Md's Philip Merrill Col Jour; bd mem, Harvard Inst Polit; Am Acad Arts & Scis, 2006; bd dir, Comt Protect Journalists.

**Special Achievements:** Book: The Breakthrough: Politics and Race in the Age of Obama, 2009. **Business Addr:** Senior Correspondent, PBS NewsHour with Jim Lehrer, PO Box 473, Warsaw, MO 65355, **Business Phone:** (866)678-6397.

### IFILL, SHERRILYN
Lawyer, college teacher, president (organization). **Personal:** daughter of Lester and Myrtle; married Ivo Knobloch, Jan 1, 1988; children: 3. **Educ:** Vassar Col, BA, 1984; NY Univ, JD, 1987. **Career:** Am Civil Liberties Union, fel; NAACP Legal Defense & Educ Fund Inc, New York Off, asst coun; Univ Md Law Sch, fac, 1993-, 7th pres & dir-coun, 2012-. **Orgs:** Chair bd, Open Soc Group, US Progs; bd mem, Enoch Pratt Free Libr (Baltimore); co-dir, Mt Calvary African Methodist Episcopal Church (Towson, MD), C's Choir. **Special Achievements:** Author, "On the Courthouse Lawn: Confronting the Legacy of Lynching in the 21st Century," (Beacon Press, 2007); appearances on NBC Nightly News, CNN, ABC World News Tonight, C-Span, and Baltimore's WYPR "The Marc Steiner Show"; op-ed articles in the "Baltimore Sun," "Jurist," and "AFRO American" newspapers. FIrst fellow at the American Civil Liberties Union. **Business Addr:** President, Director Counsel, NAACP Legal Defense and Educational Fund Inc, 40 Rector St 5th Fl, New York, NY 10006, **Business Phone:** (212)965-2200.

### IGE, DR. DOROTHY W. (DEE DEE IGE)
Educator. **Personal:** Born Parma, MO; daughter of Rufus and Florida Belle. **Educ:** Southeast Mo State Col, BS, speech educ, 1971; Cent Mo State Univ, MA, commun, 1973; Ohio State Univ, PhD, speech commun, 1980. **Career:** Bowling Green State Univ; Ind Univ Northwest, Gary, Ind, Dept Commun, prof commun, 1985-, Col Arts & Sci, dean, 2002-08, interim vice chancellor acad affairs, 2004-05, rotating dept chmn, 2005-, speaker & auth, 2005-, Orgn Fac, chmn, Fac Sen Equivalency, pres. **Orgs:** Fel Am Coun Educ, 2002; Mayor's Cult, Arts, & Recreation Task Force, Gary, Ind; bd mem, Lake Area Arts Alliance; bd mem, Gary Neighborhood Serv; bd mem, Ind Humanities Coun; speech consult, Sen Michael Schwarzwalder Ohio; Nat Commun Asn; pres & elected legis coun mem, Nat Speakers Asn Ill; Cent States Commun Asn; Phi Delta Kappa Hon Soc; Alpha Kappa Alpha. **Business Addr:** Speaker, Author, Indiana University Northwest, Hawthorn Hall Rm 238 3400 Broadway, Gary, IN 46408-1197, **Business Phone:** (219)980-6500.

### IGE, DR. DOROTHY W. K.
Educator. **Personal:** Born Apr 18, 1950, Parma, MO; daughter of Rufus A and Florida B Madden; married Adewole A; children: Olufolajimi Wm. **Educ:** Southeast Mo State Univ, BS, speech, 1971; Cent Mo State Univ, MA, speech commun, 1973; Ohio State Univ, PhD, speech educ, 1980. **Career:** Webster Grove Schs, speech & drama teacher, 1971-77; DOD Dependents Schs, drama teacher, 1977-78; Bowling Green State Univ, fac & field exp cord, 1980-84; Ind Univ, Dept Commun, fac, internship supvr, 1985-2013, dean arts & sci, 2002-, dept chair, currently, adj prof Afro-Am Studies & Women's & Gender Studies, interim vice chancellor acad affairs & tenured prof commun, currently. **Orgs:** Pub adv brd, Bowling Green State Univ, 1980-83; assoc, Ohio State Univ Black Alumni, 1980-; Phi Delta Kappa, 1980-; speech commun mem & assoc black caucus pres, legis coun, Black Opportunities Task Force, 1981-87; State Ohio Brd Redesign Educ Progs, 1982; pres & prog chairperson, Women Investing Together, Human Rels Comn, Bowling Green State Univ, 1984; fel Am Coun Educ, 2002. **Home Addr:** 9006 King Pl, Crown Point, IN 46307. **Business Addr:** Chair & Dean of Arts & Sciences, Tenured Professor of Communication, Indiana University Northwest, 3400 Broadway Tamarack 54, Gary, IN 46408-1197, **Business Phone:** (219)980-6730.

### IGHNER, BENARD T.
Musician, singer. **Personal:** Born Jan 18, 1945, Houston, TX. **Career:** Almo Publ Co, staff writer; Alamo Music Corp, singer; singer, music arranger, rec engineer; Single: Con Alma, 1967; Never Again, 1967; Album: Rock Requiem, 1971; Nobody Does It Like Me, 1974; Body Heat, 1975; Magic Lady, 1975; Who Is This Bitch Anyway, 1975; Little Dreamer, 1979; The Planet Is Alive, Let It Live, 1984; Sum Serious Blues, 1993. **Special Achievements:** Received $ Gold & Platinum Awards for his classic "Everythinh must Change" in 1974; Appeared in Jack Nicholson film "The Two Jakes" & also in "227" for TV. **Home Addr:** 4565 Don Milagro, Los Angeles, CA 90008. **Business Addr:** Singer, Alamo Music Corp, 1416 N La Brea, Los Angeles, CA 90028.

### IGINLA, JAROME (JAROME ARTHUR-LEIGH ADEKUNLE TIG JUNIOR ELVIS IGINLA)
Hockey player. **Personal:** Born Jul 1, 1977, Edmonton, AB; son of Elvis and Susan Schucard; married Kara Kirkland; children: 3. **Career:** St Albert Raiders, 1991-93; Kamloops Blazers, Western Hockey League, 1993-96; Dallas Stars, Natl Hockey League, prof hockey player, 1995; Calgary Flames, Natl Hockey League, right wing, 1995-2002, capt, 2003-.13; Pittsburgh Penguins, 2012-13; Boston Bruins, 2013-14; Colo Avalanche, 2014-16. **Honors/Awds:** Memorial Cup Championship team, 1994-95; George Parsons Trophy, 1995; Four Broncos Mem Trophy, 1996; All-Star First Team, Canadian Hockey League, 1996; All-Star First Team, Western Hockey League, 1996; gold medal, World Junior Championships, 1996; All Rookie Team, Natl Hockey League, 1996-97; gold medal, World Championships, 1997; Molson Cup, 2001-04; 2008; Ralph T Scurfield Humanitarian Award, 2001-02; Team Canada Gold Medal, Olympics, 2002; Maurice Richard Award, 2002, 2004; Art Ross Trophy, 2002; Lester B. Pearson Award, 2002; Scurfield Humanitarian Award, 2002; ESPY Best NHL Player, 2002, 2004; gold medal, Winter Olympics, 2002; World Cup of Hockey Championship, 2004; Memorial Cups; King Clancy Memorial Trophy, 2004; J. R. McCaig Award, 2008; Mark Messier Leadership Award, 2009. **Special Achievements:** First African American captain in NHL history. Film: "Gold Rush 2002", 2002; "It's Our Game: Team Canada's Victory at the 2004 World Cup of Hockey", 2004. TV Series: "The 2004 Stanley Cup Finals", 2004. **Business Addr:** Professional Hockey Player, Calgary Flames, Canadian Airlines Saddledome, Calgary, AB T2P 3B9, **Business Phone:** (403)777-4646.

### IKE, ALICE DENISE
Lawyer. **Personal:** Born Mar 25, 1955, Washington, DC; daughter of William Howard Jr and Allyre Owens. **Educ:** Univ Md, Baltimore County, BA, psychol, early childhood educ, 1977; Univ Md, Sch Law, JD, 1981. **Career:** Legal Servs Inst, legal intern, 1980-81; Legal Aid Md Inc, staff atty, 1981-82; City Baltimore, Off State's Atty, asst states atty, 1983-85; Morgan State Univ, part-time inr, 1984, 1985; Md Off Atty Gen, Dept Health & Ment Hyg, Off Atty Gen, asst atty gen, 1985-2011; Univ Md, Baltimore County, part-time inr, 1990-; Motor Vehicle Admin, Md Dept Transp, com drivers lic coordr, 2012-. **Orgs:** State Md Bar Asn, 1981-; DC Bar Asn, 1982-; Alliance Black Women Attys, 1982-; chap bd, Foster Care Rev Bd Baltimore City, 1986- . **Home Addr:** 233 W Lafayette Ave, Baltimore, MD 21217-4216, **Home Phone:** (410)342-8420. **Business Addr:** Coordinator Commercial Drivers License, Motor Vehicle Administration, 6601 Ritchie Hwy, Glen Burnie, MD 21062, **Business Phone:** (410)768-7000.

### ILOANI, GWENDOLYN SMITH
Businessperson. **Personal:** children: Brandon, Bryan & Corey. **Educ:** Colgate Univ, BA, sociol, 1976; Univ Hartford, MBA. **Career:** New York Life, math analyst; Conn Mutual, mgt trainee; Aetna Inc, investment analyst, managing dir, 1980-94; Smith Whiley & Co, chairwoman, pres, chief investment officer & chief exec officer, 1994-. **Orgs:** Trustee, Univ Conn Found; emer trustee, Colgate Univ; treas, Greater Hartford Chap Jack & Jill Am; charter mem, Marathon Club, Nat Assoc Securities Professionals, & Nat Assoc Investment Co; mem, Epsilon Omicron Omega Chap Alpha Kappa Alpha Sorority; Farmington Valley ChapLinks Inc; First Congregational Church Bloomfield; life mem Nat Asn Advan Colored People; bd mem, Nat Asn Advan Colored People Spec Contrib Fund; bd dir, Nat Asn Small Bus Investment Co. **Honors/Awds:** Chase Medallion from Eastern Connecticut State Univ; numerous Community Service & Business Leadership Awards. **Special Achievements:** Named one of the Eight Remarkable Women of 2008 by the Hartford Business Journal; named one of the "75 Most Powerful Blacks on Wall Street" and one of the "50 Most Powerful Black Women in Business" by Black Enterprise Magazine. **Business Addr:** Chairwoman, President, Smith Whiley & Co, 242 Trumbull St 8th Fl, Hartford, CT 06103-1213, **Business Phone:** (860)548-2513.

### IMES, MO'NIQUE (MONIQUE ANGELA HICKS)
Actor. **Personal:** Born Dec 11, 1967, Woodlawn, MD; daughter of Steven Jr and Alice; married Mark Jackson; children: Mark Jr & Shalon; married Sidney Hicks; children: Jonathan & David. **Educ:** Morgan State Univ. **Career:** Films: 3 Strikes, 2000; Baby Boy, 2001; Two Can Play That Game, 2001; Half Past Dead, 2002; Good Fences, 2003; Soul Plane, 2004; Hair Show, 2004; Garfield: The Movie, 2004; Shadowboxer, 2005; Domino, 2005; Phat Girlz, exec producer, 2006; Beerfest, 2006; Farce of the Penguins, voice, 2006; Welcome Home, Roscoe Jenkins, 2008; Precious: Based on the novel push by Sapphire, 2009; Steppin: The Movie, 2009; Blackbird, 2014. TVseries: "Moesha", 1999-2000; "The Parkers", 1999-2004; "The Queens of Comedy", 2001; Platinum Comedy Series: Roasting Shaquille O'Neal, 2002; "Good Fences", 2003; "Heroes of Comedy: Women on Top", 2003; 3rd Annual BET Awards, 2003; Shaq's All Star Comedy Roast 2, 2003; TV in Black: The First Fifty Years, 2004; Pryor Offenses, 2004; "The Bernie MacShow", 2004; "Mo'Nique's Fat Chance", , exec producer, 2005; "Mo's House", 2006; Entertainment Tonight, 2006-08; Mo'Nique's F.A.T. Chance: The Road to Paris, 2007; Flavor of Love Girls: Charm School, producer, 2007; "Celebrity Family Feud", 2008; The Mo'Nique Show, exec producer, 2009. **Honors/Awds:** Image Award, 2001, 2002, 2004, 2005, 2010; Black Reel Award, 2004, 2010; AAFCA Award, African-Am Film Critics Asn, 2009; BSFC Award, 2009; EDA Award, 2009; DFWFCA Award, Dallas-Ft Worth Film Critics Asn, 2009; FFCC Award, Fla Film Critics Circle, 2009; DFCS Award, Denver Film Critics Soc, 2009; EDA Special Mention Award, 2009; Sierra Award, Las Vegas Film Critics Soc, 2009; KCFCC Award, Kansas City Film Critics Circle, 2009; NYFCC Award, New York Film Critics Circle, 2009; LAFCA Award, Los Angeles Film Critics Asn, 2009; IFJA Award, Ind Film Journalists Asn, 2009; CFCA Award, Chicago Film Critics Asn, 2009; PFCS Award, Phoenix Film Critics Soc, 2009; SFFCC Award, San Francisco Film Critics Circle, 2009; Satellite Award, 2009; Special Jury Prize, Sundance Film Festival, 2009; Best Actress Award, Stockholm Film Festival, 2009; VVFP Award, Village Voice Film Poll, 2009; UFCA Award, Utah Film Critics Asn, 2009; SLFCA Award, St. Louis Film Critics Asn, 2009; SEFCA Award, Southeastern Film Critics Asn Awards, 2009; WAFCA Award, Wash DC Area Film Critics Asn, 2009; Golden Globe, 2010; IFC Award, Iowa Film Critics, 2010; Oscar Awards, 2010; BAFTA Film Award, 2010; BET Award, 2010; Independent Spirit Award, 2010; Critics Choice Award, 2010; Screen Actors Guild Award, 2010; COFCA Award, Cent Ohio Film Critics Asn, 2010; ALFS Award, London Critics Circle Film, 2010; OFCS Award, Online Film Critics Soc, 2010; OFCC Award, Oklahoma Film Critics Circle, 2010; Chlotrudis Awards, 2010; NSFC Award, Nat Soc Film Critics, 2010; CinEuphoria Awards, 2011. **Special Achievements:** Author of Skinny Women Are Evil, 2003. **Business Addr:** Actor, Anderson & Smith PC, 7322 S W Freeway Suite 2010, Houston, TX 77074, **Business Phone:** (713)621-5522.

### IMHOTEP, AKBAR
Artist. **Personal:** Born Dec 22, 1951, Perry, GA; son of Carrie L Ridley and Robert Hart; children: Akilah, Garvey & Sara-Maat. **Educ:** Paine Col, BA. **Career:** Proposition Theater, actor, 1977-79; Ctr Puppetry Arts, puppeteer, 1979-86; Wren's Nest, storyteller residence, 1986-; self-employed storyteller & puppeteer, 1986-; Arts Mach, puppetry & storytelling; Kuumba Storytellers Ga, pres, founder, storyteller & puppeteer, currently. **Orgs:** Founder & exec dir, Kawanda & Kwanzaa Network, 1993-94; chmn, Metro-Atlanta Kwanzaa Asn, 1986-92; Asn Black Storytellers, 1991-; Puppeteers Am, 1986-; Omega Psi Phi, 1971-; Nat Asn Advan Colored People, 1989-; Nation Islam, 1975-78. **Honors/Awds:** Performances in three consecutive Nat Black Arts Festival, 1988, 1990, 1992; WACP, Kwumba Award, 1990; Metro-Atlanta Kwanzaa Asn, Mzee Olutunji Award, 1992; performances in Jazz and Heritage Festival, 1994. **Special Achievements:** Publ three vols of poetry, 1982, 1988, 1994. **Home Addr:** 880 Rock St NW Apt D5, Atlanta, GA 30314-3319, **Home Phone:** (404)688-3376. **Business Addr:** Storyteller, Kuumba Storytellers of Georgia, PO Box 91568, East Point, GA 30364, **Business Phone:** (404)468-3392.

### INCE, DR. HAROLD SEALY
Dentist. **Personal:** Born Jan 7, 1930, Brooklyn, NY; married Mary Ann Jackson; children: Nancy & Harold Jr. **Educ:** BS, 1951; Howard Univ Col Dent, DDS, dent, 1956. **Career:** Pvt pract dentist, currently. **Orgs:** Am Dent Asn; Conn Dent Asn; New Haven Dent Asn; First New Haven Nat Bank; Urban League; Bias Stanley Fund; Alpha Phi Alpha. **Business Addr:** Dentist, Private Practice, 226 Dixwell Ave Suite 206, New Haven, CT 06511-3456, **Business Phone:** (203)776-9391.

### INGRAM, HON. EDITH J.
Judge, teacher. **Personal:** Born Jan 16, 1942, Sparta, GA; daughter of Robert T and Katherine Hunt. **Educ:** Ft Valley State Col, BS, elem educ, 1963. **Career:** Judge (retired); Moore Elem Sch, Griffin, Ga, teacher, 1963-67; Hancock Cent Elem, Sparta, Ga, teacher, 1967-68; Hancock County Probate Ct, judge, 1968-2004. **Orgs:** Macedonia Baptist Church Choir, 1951-; Hancock County Womens Club, 1964-; State Nat & Int Asn Probate Judges, 1969; State Dem Exec Comt; Sparta community; comt chairwoman, Ga Coalition Black Women, 1980-; Ga Asn Probate Judges; Ga Gen Assembly; Ga Coalition Black Women; Nat Col Probate Judges; Hancock County NAACP & Dem Club; Hancock Womens Club; Delta Sigma Theta Sorority Inc. **Honors/Awds:** Achievement Award, Nat Asn Advan Colored People, 1969; Cert of Merit, Booker T, Wash, 1973; Outstanding Citizen's, Fulton County, 1978; Outstanding Courage Southern Polit Arena, Atlanta Br Nat Asn Advan Colored People, 1979. **Special Achievements:** First African-American elected probate judge of Hancock County. **Home Addr:** 503 Augusta Hwy, Sparta, GA 31087, **Home Phone:** (706)444-6134.

### INGRAM, GAREY LAMAR
Baseball player, athletic coach. **Personal:** Born Jul 25, 1970, Columbus, GA. **Career:** Baseball player (retired), baseball coach; Los Angeles Dodgers, outfielder, 1994-95, 1997; Columbus Catfish, hitting coach, 2003-06; Great lakes loons, hitting coach, 2007-08; Conn Defenders, hitting coach, currently; Dodgers Farm Syst, hitting coach; Atlanta Braves; Miss Braves, hitting coach, currently. **Business Addr:** hitting coach, Atlanta Braves, Turner Field, Atlanta, GA 30315, **Business Phone:** (404)522-7630.

### INGRAM, GREGORY LAMONT
Artist. **Personal:** Born Apr 10, 1961, Greensboro, NC; son of Bradley and Mary L. **Educ:** NY Col Technol, graphic design & fine arts, 1981; New York Dept Cult Affairs, cert, 1985. **Career:** Gallery Henoch, art handler, 1982-; New York Housing Asn, artist consult, 1994-95; Harmony Visions Gallery, dir, 1994; Gli Graphics & Consults, owner, 1978-, pres, 1995-; Gregory's Garden, 1998-; Disco Fundraiser, photog, 2012-13. **Orgs:** Consult, Rush Philanthropic Arts Found, 1998-; New York Green thumb Proj, Brooklyn, NY; vol, Comm Bd 5 Brooklyn NY, 1996-99; St Paul Comm Chap, 1997; Americorps, Black Chap Educ, 1997-99; vol, Brooklyn Parks, 1997-98; United Comm Ctrs Residency; Americorps: Blacks Chap Educ. **Honors/Awds:** Citizens Week Awards. **Business Addr:** Consultant, Rush Philanthropic Arts Foundation, 334 Grand Ave, Brooklyn, NY 11238, **Business Phone:** (718)230-5002.

### INGRAM, JAMES EDWARD
Songwriter, musician. **Personal:** Born Feb 16, 1952, Akron, OH; married Debbie Robinson; children: 6. **Career:** Musician, songwriter, currently. Albums: Yah Mo Be There, 1983; It's Your Night, 1983; Never Felt So Good, 1988; It's Real, 1989; The Power of Great Music, 1991; Always You, 1993; Forever More: The Best of James Ingram, 1999; Stand In The Light, 2008. Singles: "Just Once", 1981; "One Hundred Ways", 1981; "Baby, Come to Me", 1982; "How Do You Keep the Music Playing", 1983; "She Loves Me (The Best That I Can Be)", 1984; There's No Easy Way, 1984; What About Me, 1984; "Always", 1986; "Never Felt So Good", 1986; "Somewhere Out There", 1987; "Better Way", 1987; "A Natural Man (You Make Me Feel Like)", 1989; "It's Real", 1989; "I Wanna Come Back", 1989; "I Don't Have The Heart", 1990; "Secret Garden", 1990; "Get Ready", 1991; "When Was The Last Time The Music Made You Cry?", 1991; "Where Did My Heart Go", 1991; "The Day I Fall In Love", 1994; "When You Love Someone", 1995; "Give Me Forever I Do", 1998; "Forever More (I'll Be the One)", 1999; "Lean On Me", 2001; "My People", 2008; "Don't Let Go", 2009. **Honors/Awds:** Grammy Award, Best Male R&B Vocal Performance, 1982; Grammy Award, Best R&B Performance by a Duo or Group with Vocals, 1985. **Special Achievements:** First artist in the history of pop music to win a Grammy Award without having released his own album; guest vocalist, Michael McDonald's In The Spirit holiday album, 2001; His 1994 composition "The Day I Fell in Love", from the movie Beethoven's Second (on which he dueted with Dolly Parton) was nominated for an Oscar. **Business Addr:** Musician.

### INGRAM, KEVIN
Executive. **Personal:** Born Philadelphia, PA; married Deann. **Educ:** Mass Inst Technol, BS, chem engineering, 1980; Stanford Univ, MBA, 1984. **Career:** Goldman Sachs & Co, jr assoc, 1985, Collateralized Mortgage Obligations Derivatives, desk head, 1992, US Treas Debt & Options Trading, global responsibility, founding mem & dir, 1995; Deutsche Bank, managing dir, 1996; Lehman Bros, assoc; Deutsche Morgan Grenfell, managing dir; TruMarkets Inc, founder; consult, currently. **Special Achievements:** Listed as one of 25 "Hottest Blacks on Wall Street", Black Enterprise, 1992. Author of several books.

### INGRAM, DR. LAVERNE
Physician. **Personal:** Born Mar 1, 1955, Lawrenceville, VA; daughter of James and Lydia House; married Robert Dean. **Educ:** Va Union Univ, Richmond, Va, BS, biol, 1977; Harvard Univ, Cambridge, MA, attended 1975; Va Commonwealth Univ, Richmond, VA, attended 1978; Eastern Va Med Sch, Norfolk, VA, MD, 1981. **Career:** Med Col Va, Richmond, Va, lab asst, 1972-73, lab specialist, 1973-78; Howard Univ Hosp, Washington, DC, med intern, 1981-82, radiol res, 1982-85; USn, Norfolk, Va, head, radio dept, 1985-87; USn, Portsmouth, Va, staff radiologist, 1987-90; Univ Tex Health Sci Ctr, Houston, Tex, staff radiol, 1990-, chief mammography, asst prof, currently; LBJ Hosp, Asst chief diag imaging serv, currently. **Orgs:** Life mem, Nat

Naval Officers Asn; Soc Aid Sickle Cell Anemia; Big Bro Big Sister, 1986-; Nat Med Asn; vice chair, Am Red Cross, NE Houston, 1998; Alpha Kappa Alpha, Am Roentgen Ray Soc. **Honors/Awds:** Distinguished Service Award, Nat Naval Officers Asn, 1988; Deans Excellence Award, UTHSC, 1997-98, 2000-01; Physician of the Year, Lyndon B. Johnson General, Hospital, Harris County Hospital District, 2001. **Special Achievements:** Publications: How to Diagnose and Stage Primary Breast Cancer with Scintimammography and SPECT, 1995; Uptake in Various Breast Conditions Benign and Malignant. Society of Nuclear Medicine, 1999. **Home Addr:** 7419 Naremore Dr, Spring, TX 77379, **Home Phone:** (713)376-4662. **Business Addr:** Assistant Chief of Diagnostic Imaging Services, Assistant Professor, University of Texas, MSB 2 130B 6431 Fannin St, Houston, TX 77030, **Business Phone:** (713)566-5440.

## INGRAM, PHILLIP M.

Computer executive. **Personal:** Born Nov 14, 1945, Detroit, MI; son of Henry and Marion Martin Lewis; children: Marc J. **Educ:** Wayne State Univ, Detroit, Mich, BFA, indust design, 1971, MBA, 1978. **Career:** Gen Motors Eng, Warren, Mich, proj engr, 1964-78; Am Motors Corp, Detroit, Mich, prin engr, 1978-79; Systemation Corp, Detroit, Mich, pres, 1979-80; Detroit Inst Technol, Detroit, Mich, assoc prof, 1980-81; Gen Automation, Detroit, Mich, dist sales mgr, 1980-82; The Comput Group Inc, Novi, Mich, pres & founder, 1982-. **Orgs:** Engineering Soc Detroit, 1975. **Honors/Awds:** Reviewer, Nat Sci Found Cause Grant Progs, 1980. **Home Addr:** 29673 White Hall Dr, Farmington Hills, MI 48331, **Home Phone:** (248)788-9072. **Business Addr:** President, Founder, The Computer Group Inc, 41252 Vincenti Ct, Novi, MI 48375-1925, **Business Phone:** (248)888-6900.

## INGRAM, STEPHEN ANTHONY (STEVE INGRAM)

Football player. **Personal:** Born May 8, 1971, Cheverly, MD; married Robyn. **Educ:** Univ Md, BS, criminal justice. **Career:** Football player (retired); Tampa Bay Buccaneers, tackle & guard & offensive tackle, 1995-97; Jacksonville Jaguars, offensive tackle & offensive guard, 1999-2000.

## INGRAM, VALERIE J.

Television journalist, television producer. **Personal:** Born Dec 5, 1959, Chicago, IL; daughter of Bettie J Rushing and Archie R. **Educ:** Columbia Col, Chicago, Il, BA, radio, writing, 1979; Loyola Univ, Chicago, IL, MBA, 1996. **Career:** WUSN Radio US99, Chicago, Ill, sr sales asst, 1984-85; CBS Radio Network, Chicago, Ill, off mgr, 1985-87; WBBM-AM Radio, Chicago, Ill, assoc producer, prodn dir; WFLA, reporter, 1995-2005; Univ Tampa, adj prof, 2004-; WUSF Pub Broadcasting, reporter, 2005-06; Metro Networks, anchor & producer, 2007-08. **Orgs:** Radio ad hoc comt, Int Lutheran Layman's League, 1990-; Nat Asn Black Journalists, 1990-; Lutheran Women's Missionary League, 1989-; secy, Minority Employees Asn, CBS Inc, 1985-90; Leader, Gospel Choir, 1989-, youth group officer, St Paul Lutheran Church Austin, 1986-88; Sunday sch teacher, HS, 1988-90. **Honors/Awds:** Outstanding Volunteer, Aid Asn Lutherans Branch No 385, 1989; First Chuck Stone Award, Nat Asn Black Journalists, 2005. **Home Addr:** 806 Woodlawn St, Clearwater, FL 33756-2164, **Home Phone:** (727)449-1678. **Business Addr:** Reporter, WFLA, 4585 140th Ave N, Clearwater, FL 33760, **Business Phone:** (727)536-8443.

## INGRAM-SAMPSON, JOHNSON

Manager. **Personal:** Born Apr 25, 1962, Omaha, NE; daughter of Robert Lewis and Lillian Reech Ingram; married Aaron L; children: Alyse Nicole. **Educ:** Iowa State Univ, BA, archit, 1985; Metrop Tech Inst; Univ Calif, Los Angeles, archit, 1991. **Career:** Archit freelance consult, 1991-92; Harold Williams Assoc, Design Team, 1992-93; Am Stores Properties Inc, CADD planner, 1993-95; Valentine Crane Brunjes Onyon Architects, proj coordr, 1995-; Univ Utah, archit design studio juror, 1995-; Sr High, youth mentor, 1996. **Orgs:** Chair mem, youth comt counsr, Calvary Baptist Church, 1993-. **Honors/Awds:** Dean Award, Alpha Chi Omega, Grad Sch Archit & Planning, Univ Calif Los Angeles, 1991; SNW Thesis Award, 1991. **Special Achievements:** Created water color Dod, 1984; UCLA, Grad School of Architecture and Planning, The Next Generation Thesis Exhibit, 1991, The Architectural Forum, developer, organizer, 1990, Women in Environmental Design Conference, San Francisco, representative, 1991. **Home Addr:** 6974 S Boulder Dr Apt 11, Salt Lake City, UT 84121, **Home Phone:** (801)944-1330.

## INGRUM, ADRIENNE G.

Publishing executive. **Personal:** Born Mar 21, 1954, St. Louis, MO; daughter of Clister Jack and Leontine Yvonne Pulliam; married Arn Reginald Ashwood. **Educ:** Georgetown Univ, Wash, DC, BS, intl econs. **Career:** Publisher; Harvard Univ, Boston, Mass, staff asst, 1977-79; Grosset & Dunlap, New York, NY, assoc ed, 1980-82; Putnam Berkley Group, New York, NY, vpres & exec ed, 1982-90; Waldenbooks, Stamford, Conn, publ & vpres, Longmeadow Press, 1990-94; Crown Publishers, vpres & dir of trade paperback publ, 1994-96; HarperCollins Publishers, publ & consult, currently; Adrienne Ingrum, LLC, chief exec officer & pres, currently; Bks: Black Issues Bk, assoc publ; Black Issues Bk Rev; The African Am Pavilion, founder, 2004; Pavilion, co founder. **Orgs:** Women's Media Group; Go On Girl! Book Club. **Special Achievements:** The African American Pavilion Awards, BookExpo Am. **Home Addr:** 43 St Nicholas Pl, New York, NY 10031-1244, **Home Phone:** (212)283-6632. **Business Addr:** Publisher, President, Adrienne Ingrum LLC.

## INNIS, ROY EMILE ALFREDO

Executive, association executive, association executive. **Personal:** Born Jun 6, 1934, St. Croix, VI; son of Alexander and Georgianna Thomas; married Doris Funnye; children: Roy Jr (deceased), Alexander (deceased), Cedric, Patricia, Corinne, Kwame, Niger, Kimathi & Mugabe. **Educ:** City Col NY, attended 1956. **Career:** Vick Chem Co, res chemist, 1958-63; Montefiore Hosp, res chemist, 1963-67; Harlem Commonwealth Coun, dir, 1967-68; Metrop Appl Res Ctr, New York, res fel, 1967; Cong Racial Equality, assoc dir, 1968, nat dir, 1968-81; Cong Racial Equality, nat chmn, 1981-; Cong Racial Equality, chmn, 1968-, Second Nat vice chmn, chief exec officer, currently; Manhattan Tribune, co-ed. **Orgs:** Mem bd, New York Urban Coalition, Haryou Act, Harlem Commonwealth Coun, exec dir; Coalition Fairness Africa; bd mem, Hudson Inst; bd mem, Daemen Col; Am Alliance Better Sch; Landmark Legal Found; Nat Ethnic Coalition Orgn; Nat Rifle Asn; African Am Fund Higher Educ; assoc mem, Fraternal Order Police; fel Ford Found. **Honors/Awds:** Life membership of CORE. **Special Achievements:** First American to attend the Organization of African Unity (OAU) in an official capacity. Book: The Little Black Book, 1971. **Home Addr:** , NY. **Business Addr:** National Chairman, Chief Executive Officer, Congress of Racial Equality, 817 Broadway Fl 3, New York, NY 10003, **Business Phone:** (212)598-4000.

## IONE, CAROLE

Clergy, psychotherapist. **Personal:** Born May 28, 1937, Washington, DC; daughter of Hylan Garnet Lewis and Leighla Whipper; married Salvatore J Bovoso; children: Alessandro, Santiago & Antonio. **Educ:** Bennington Col, attended 1959; Helix Training Prog, psychother & Healing Arts, 1986; Chinese Healing Arts Ctr, Qi Gong Therapist, 1993; Nat Guild Hypnotists, Advan Clin Hypnotherapist, 1994. **Career:** Renaissance Poets Ser, co-founder, 1960; Renaissance House, Inc, artistic dir, 1960; Dream, J & Notebook Workshops, instr, 1980-; Essence Mag, contrib ed, 1980-82; Manhatten Theatre Club, dir, writers performance, 1980-82; Women's Mysteries, dir, 1987-; Live Lett, artistic dir, 1974-; The Pauline Oliveros Found, founder, 1985-, vpres, co-artistic dir; Deep Listening Inst, artistic dir, currently. **Orgs:** Poets & Writers, Inc, 1979-; Nat Writers Union, 1988-; The Inl Womens Writing Guild, 1988-; The Author's Guild, Inc, 1991-. **Honors/Awds:** New York State Council on the Arts and Poets and Writers, Inc, for Live Letters Presentation, 1979-; Rockefeller Foundation & Nat Endowment for the Arts, for Njinga, The Queen-King, a play w/music and pageantry, 1987-91; South Carolina Comm for the Humanities, for A Diary of Reconstruction, 1985; Fellowships to the Macdowell Colony, Yaddo, Edward; Albee Foundation, The Writers Room; Tele-conference, Woman of Spirit, 2012. **Special Achievements:** Scripts: Njinga the Queen-King; A Diary of Reconstruction; Mirage, A Friend; New York City, Evidence; Script devel for Rizzoli Productions, NYC; Publications: This is a Dream, Mom Press, 2000; Pride of Family, 4 generations of Amer Women of Color, Summit Books, 1991, Avon Books, 1992; The Coffee Table Lover, The Country Press, 1973; Unsealed Lips, Capra Press, 1990; Piramada Negra, The Country Press, 1973, Live Letters, Press, 1991; Contemporary Literary Criticism, 1989; Fiction, Reviews and Articles in: The Village Voice, New Dawn, Oui, Ms American Film Ambassador, Working Women; Oggi; Vogue; Christian Science; Monitor; Essence; Arcadie; Revue Literature; Readings and Presentations: Skidmore College, New School for Social Research, Teachers and Writers Collaborative, City College of New York, Columbia Green Comm Coll, Seattle Douglass-The Truth Library, The College of Charleston, Avery Institute, The New York Public Library, The Actors Institute, Manhattan Theatre Club, Natl Public Radio, CBS Nightwatch, The Open Center, SUNY, New Paltz, Omega Institute, Esalen Institute, New York Geneological Society, Shomburg Center, NY Public Library and Others. **Home Addr:** 156 Hunter St, Kingston, NY 12401-6620, **Home Phone:** (914)339-5776. **Business Addr:** Artistic Director, Deep Listening Institute, 77 Cornell St, Kingston, NY 12401, **Business Phone:** (845)338-5984.

## IRBY, GALVEN

Government official. **Personal:** Born Sep 29, 1921, Laurens, SC; son of Henry D and Grace L; married Delores Virginia Odden (deceased); children: Barbara J, Grace M, Kelley R Garrett, Vickie L Strickland, Sandra MGarrett, Galven C & Craig R. **Educ:** Youngstown Univ, AB, 1949; Howard Univ, LLB, 1952. **Career:** Government official (retired); Republic Iron & Steel Mills & Fabrication, 1940-49; US Postal Serv, part time postal clerk, 1950-63; State Ore, dept Employ Security, claims supvr, 1954-63; Veterans Admin, legal disability rating supt, 1972-86. **Orgs:** Bd controls, Pacific Lutheran Univ; bd controls, adv, Concordia Col, 1973-75; dept admis, exec & nat bd, Am Lutheran, 1978-79; sre, N Pacific Dist, Portland Conf, 1965-67; Alpha Phi Alpha Fraternity; bd controls, Pacific Lutheran Univ, 1988-94; Alpha Phi Alpha & Nat Asn Advan Colored People Sch Mentoring Project, 1989-. **Home Addr:** 14343 NE Alton St, Portland, OR 97230-3633, **Home Phone:** (503)255-8324.

## IRBY, MARY

Automotive executive. **Personal:** Born Oct 19, 1944, Columbus, MS; daughter of Robert and Lettie B Swopes; children: Cassandra Delk, Robert Smallwood & Joseph Smallwood. **Educ:** Bowling Green State Univ, BLS, 1989; Cent Mich Univ. **Career:** Gen Motors Corp, spokeswoman, Metal Fabricating Div, dir commun, 1968-. **Orgs:** Second vpres, Girl Scouts USA, 1987-89; bd mem, Leadership Saginaw Alumni, 1994-; bd mem, Reuben Daniels Found, 1994-; bd mem, Big Bros Big Sisters, 1994-; Pub Rel SocAm White Pines Chap, 1994-; Saginaw Community Found, Distrib Comn, 1995; Alpha Kappa Alpha Sorority. **Business Addr:** Director of Communications, General Motors Corp, 1450 Stephenson Hwy, Troy, MI 48083, **Business Phone:** (248)696-2054.

## IRELAND, HON. RODERICK LOUIS

Supreme court justice, association executive, lawyer. **Personal:** Born Dec 3, 1944, Springfield, MA; children: Helen Elizabeth & Michael Alexander. **Educ:** Lincoln Univ, BA, 1966; Columbia Univ Law Sch, JD, 1969; Harvard Law Sch, LLM, 1975, N eastern Univ, PhD, law, policy & soc prog, 1998. **Career:** Neighborhood Legal Serv atty, 1969; Harvard Ctr Law & Educ, staff atty, 1970-71; Roxbury Defenders Comt, chief atty, dep & exec dir, 1971-73; Harvard Law Sch, teaching fel, 1972-78, adj fac, 1978-; Mass Civil Serv Comn, hearing officer, 1973-75; Roxbury Dist Ct Clin, legal coun, 1974-77; Burnham, Stern & Shapiro, assoc, 1973-75; Mass Exec Off Admin & Fin, asst secy & chief legal coun, 1975-77; Boston Juv Ct, judge, 1977-90; Bd Appeal Motor Vehicle Liability Policies & Bonds, chmn, 1977; Col Criminal Justice, N eastern Univ, adj fac, 1978-; Mass Appeals Ct, judge, 1990-97; Judicial Youth Corps, adv & teacher, 1990-; Mass Supreme Judicial Ct, assoc justice, 1997-, sr assoc justice, 2008, chief justice, 2010-14; New York Univ Law Sch, fac mem Appellate Judges Sem, 2001-, Col Social Sci & Humanities, distinguished prof criminol & political justice, currently. **Orgs:** bd dir, Columbia Law Sch Alumni Asn; Mass Bar Asn; Boston Bar Asn; ABA; Mass Black Lawyers Asn; NY Bar Asn Bd Dirs Proj Aim; bd dir, First Inc; bd dir, Roxbury YMCA; bd dir, Mass Minority Coun Alcoholism; Omega Psi Phi; Lincoln Alumni. **Honors/Awds:** St. Thomas More Award, Boston Col Law Sch; Recipient, 10 Outstanding young leaders of Boston Award, Boston Jaycees, 1979; 10 Outstanding Men of America Award, US Jaycees, 1980; Boston Covenant Peace Prize, 1982; Haskell Cohn Distinguished Judicial Service Award, Boston Bar Asn; 1990; Judicial Excellence Award, Mass Judges Conference, 1996; The Judicial Excellence Award, Mass Bar Asn, Lawyers Weekly Newspaper, 2001; several honorary Doctor of Law degrees; Friend of Justice Award; Massachusetts Bar Found; 2008. **Special Achievements:** First African American justice On Massachusetts Supreme Court in its over three hundred year history & First African-American Chief Justice; Author of Massachusetts Juvenile Law, 2d edition, published by West Publishing, 2006. **Business Addr:** Distinguished Professor, Northeastern University, 360 Huntington Ave, Boston, MA 02115, **Business Phone:** (617)373-2000.

## IRMAGEAN, U.

Artist. **Personal:** Born Apr 9, 1947, Detroit, MI; daughter of Theodore Curry and Mamie Lee Sago Curry; children: Sundjata T Kone. **Educ:** Wayne State Univ Monteith Col, attended 1966; Grove Str Col, AA, 1974; Calif Col Arts & Crafts, BFA, 1976. **Career:** Isabelle Percy W Gallery CA Col Arts & Crafts Oakland, exhibit, 1979; NY Carlsberg Glyptotek Mus Copenhagen Denmark, rep, 1980; Los Medanos Col Pittsburg, CA, exhibit artist, 1980; Berkeley Art Ctr CA, exhibit, 1981; Galerie Franz Mehring Berlin, Germany, exhibit, 1981; SF Mus Modern Art, exhibit, 1981; Ctr Visual Arts Oakland CA, exhibit, 1985; Spanish Speaking Citizens Found, Oakland, CA, guest art instr, 1989; E Oakland Youth Develop Ctr, Oakland, CA, mural instr, 1989; City Sites, CA Col Arts & Crafts, artist mentor, 1989; Berkeley Art Ctr, exhibitor, 1988; San Francisco State Univ, exhibitor, 1989; Koncepts Cult Gallery, Oakland, CA, art instr, 1989; Ebony Mus, Oakland, CA, exhibitor coord, 1989-90; Hatley Martin Gallery, CA, exhibit, 1990; Capp St Gallery, San Francisco, CA, pubart installation, 1991; Ebony Mus, cur, 1994-95; artist, currently. **Orgs:** Juror Vida Gallery SF, CA, 1981; coordr, US participation 11 Bienal del Grabado De Am Maracaibo, Venezuela, 1982; juror, Festival at lake, Craft/Art Mkt, Oakland, CA, l989; Berkeley Juneteenth Asn Inc, 1992; Art & Creative Writing Youth Competition Prog, Golden State Life Ins. **Honors/Awds:** Amer Artist Today in Black & White Vol 11 1980 author Dr H L Williams; exhibit Dept De Bellas Artes Guadaljara, Mexico, 1982; exhibit Brockman Gallery Prod LA, CA, 1982; Hon mem Sigma Gamma Rho Sor, 1986; Daniel Mendelowitz "A Guide to Drawing" 3rd ed Holt Rinehart and Winston, 1982, 4th ed revised by Duane Wakeham, 1988; Outstanding Women of the Twentieth Century, Sigma Gamma Rho Sorority, 1986; Certificiate of Appreciation, St Augustine's Church, 1988; feature, The Aurora, 1987, Sigma Gamma Rho Sorority, l987; The CA Art Review, 2nd edition Amer Reference Inc, 1988; Amer artist, 2nd edition, References, 1989; 1st Place, Best of Show, Ebony Museum, Expo 89-90, 1990; Black Scholar, vol 20, no 3 & 4, Black World Foundation (cover), 1990; Feature, Eugene White's Kujionia Magazine, 1990. **Special Achievements:** Selected publications: Anthology of Contemporary African-American Women Artists, 1992, A Guide to Drawing, 1993, Poetry: An American Heritage, 1993; Smell This 2, UC Berkeley, 1991; exhibitions: Prague, Czechoslovakia, Art of Ecology: Recycling the Collective Spirit, 1991, Richmond Art Center, Looking Out Looking In, 1992, Bomani Gallery, 1992; Voices of the Dream; African American Women Speak, Venice Johnson, Chronicle Books. **Home Addr:** PO Box 5602, Berkeley, CA 94705. **Business Addr:** Artist, 832 37th Ave, Berkeley, CA 94608-3911, **Business Phone:** (510)428-1932.

## IROGBE, KEMA

Educator, college administrator. **Personal:** Born Mar 30, 1956, EBU; son of Onwuanukwu and Eunice Iyanwa; married Helen; children: Kumama. **Educ:** Instituto Allende, Mex, BA, 1978; Jackson State Univ, BA, 1980, MPPA, 1982; Atlanta Univ, PhD, 1987. **Career:** Bridge water State Univ, instr, 1987-90; Curry Col, adj prof, 1988-90; Ga Southern Univ, asst prof, 1990-91; MIT, MIT Summer fel, MIT, 1990; Claflin Univ, int prog, dir int progs, 1991-, prof polit sci, currently; SC State Univ, adj prof, 1993-; Harvard Univ, NEH Summer fel, 1995. Book: The Roots of the United States Foreign Policy Toward Apartheid South Africa: 1969-85. **Orgs:** Campus coordr, Pi Sigma Alpha; campus coordr, Pi Gmama Mu; Am Soc Pub Admin; Nat Conf Black Polit Scientists; Am Politicial Sci Asn; dir, Afro fest; fel, Harvard Univ, Oxford Univ, Massachusetts Inst Technol. **Home Addr:** 1600 Columbia Rd Apt E-3, Orangeburg, SC 29115, **Home Phone:** (803)534-6883. **Business Addr:** Professor of Political Science, Director of International Programs, Claflin University, Rm 6 Trustee Hall 400 Magnolia St, Orangeburg, SC 29115-9970, **Business Phone:** (803)535-5000.

## IRONS, DR. EDWARD DAVIS

President (organization), educator, college administrator. **Personal:** Born Aug 29, 1923, Hulbert, OK. **Educ:** Wilburforce Univ, BS, bus admin; Univ Minn, MA, hosp admin, 1951; Harvard Univ, PhD. **Career:** Riverside Nat Bank, Houston, Tex, partner, 1964, prin organizer, pres; Fla A&M Univ, fac; Howard Univs bus sch, founding dean; Atlanta Univ ctr, Altanta, GA, prof; City Wash, DC, Off Banking & Financial Inst DC, supt; Irons & Assocs, pres; consol State Inst, adminr; Investment Surv Div, Agency Int Develop, chief; Fla A&M Univ, asst bus mgr; Clark-Atlanta Univ Sch Bus Admin, econ prof, dean emer, finance prof, 1975-. **Orgs:** Atlanta Life Ins Corp; Lincoln Nat Life Corp; BE Bd Economists. **Business Addr:** Dean Emeritus, Clark Atlanta University, 223 James P Brawley Dr SW 200A Wright Hall Rm 101, Atlanta, GA 30314, **Business Phone:** (404)880-8454.

## IRONS, HON. PAULETTE R.

Judge. **Personal:** Born Jun 19, 1952, New Orleans, LA; married Alvin L; children: Marseah & Paul. **Educ:** Loyola Univ, BBA; Tulane Univ, JD. **Career:** Systs engr, 1976-83; construct estimator, 1984-92; atty, small bus consult, 1992-93; Paulette Irons Law Firm, sole practr, 1992-; La State, Dist 95, rep, 1992-94; La State Dist 4, sen, 1994-2004; Civil Dist Ct Parish Orleans, Judge, 2004-. **Orgs:** La Women's Caucus; La Legis Black Caucus; Women's Network Nat Conf State Legislatures; League Women's Voters; Am Asn Univ Women; Nat Order Black Elected Legislators; sen vice chair, La Legis Women's Caucus; Pub Interest Law Found; Tulane Law Women; Parent-Teacher Orgn; La League Women Voters; New Orleans Oncol Nurses Breast Cancer Prev, La Initiative Teen Pregnancy Prev; New Orleans Area Literacy

Coalition. **Honors/Awds:** Alliance for Good Government, Legislator of the Year, 1995; Women For a Better Louisiana; Good Housekeeping Award for Women in Government. **Home Addr:** 4819 Bancroft Dr, New Orleans, LA 70122, **Home Phone:** (504)286-0846. **Business Addr:** Judge, Civil District Court for the Parish of Orleans, 421 Loyola Ave Rm 303, New Orleans, LA 70112, **Business Phone:** (504)592-9250.

### IRVIN, KENNETH PERNELL

Football coach, football player. **Personal:** Born Jul 11, 1972, Rome, GA; married Shay; children: Joshua & Ava. **Educ:** Univ Memphis, BS, edu; Univ Ga, MS, early childhood edu. **Career:** Football player (retired), coach; Buffalo Bills, 1997, defensive back, 1995-96, left cornerback, 1998, left cornerback, cornerback, 1999, right cornerback, 2000-01; New Orleans Saints, defensive back, left cornerback, right cornerback, cornerback, 2002; Minn Vikings, right cornerback, free safety, left cornerback, 2003, free safety, 2004; Pepperell High Sch, defensive back coach; Greater Atlanta Christian Sch, coach, currently. **Honors/Awds:** NCAA: Most blocked punts (four) in one game, 1992; Action Award, 2002; Byron Wizzard Humanitarian Award, 2004. **Business Addr:** Head Coach, Greater Atlanta Christian School, 1575 Indian Trail Rd, Norcross, GA 30093, **Business Phone:** (770)243-2000.

### IRVIN, MICHAEL JEROME

Executive, football player, entertainer. **Personal:** Born Mar 5, 1966, Ft. Lauderdale, FL; son of Walter (deceased) and Pearl; married Felicia Walker; children: Myesha Beyonca; married Sandi Harrell; children: Chelsea, Michael & Elijah. **Educ:** Univ Miami, BA, bus mgt, 1988. **Career:** Football player (retired), analyst, executie; Dallas Cowboys, wide receiver, 1988-2000; Entertainment & Sports Programming Network, Nat Football League, analyst, 2003-07; Nat Football League Network, 2009; TMI Group, prin & co-founder; Spike TV, host; Elite Football League India, investors & adv, 2011. **Honors/Awds:** First-Team All-Pro selection, 1991; NFL Alumni, Wide Receiver of the Year, 1991; Pro Bowl, 1991, 1992, 1993, 1994, 1995; University of Miami Sports Hall of Fame, 2000; Pro Football Hall of Fame, 2005; Professional Football Hall of Fame, 2007; Super Bowl champion XXVII, XXVIII, XXX; Dallas Cowboys Ring of Honor; NFL 1990s All-Decade Team. **Special Achievements:** Film Appearances: The Year of the Yao, 2004; The Longest Yard, 2005; TheComebacks, 2007. **Home Addr:** 11498 Luna Rd Suite 102, Dallas, TX 75234.

### IRVIN, MILTON M.

Executive. **Personal:** Born East Orange, NJ. **Educ:** US Merchant Marine Acad, BA; Univ Pa, Wharton Sch Bus & Finance, MBA, finance, 1974. **Career:** Chase Manhattan Bank, corp lending officer, asst treas, 1974-77; Salomon Bros Inc, managing dir, 1977-88, 1990-98; Paine Webber, managing dir, 1988-90; Blaylock & Partners LP, pres, chief operating officer, 1988-2000; Imbot.com, pres, chief operating officer, 2000-02; UBS, managing dir, 2002-12; NexTier Capital Solutions LLC, non-exec chmn, 2013-. **Orgs:** Founding mem, found bd mem, Exec Leadership Coun, 1986-; Bd mem, Wharton Grad Exec Adv Bd, 1994-; adv comt, Pension Benefit Guaranty Corp, 1995-98; bd mem, Harlem Sch Arts, 1999-; NJ Bd Recreation; trustee, Kent Pl Sch & Essex Cath High Sch; bd gov, Baltusrol Golf Club; bd gov, YMCA; chmn adv bd, CastleOak Securities LP, 2012-. **Special Achievements:** Listed as one of 25 "Hottest Blacks on Wall Street", Black Enterprise, 1992. **Business Addr:** Non-Executive Chairman, Nextier Capital Solutions LLC, 515 N State St Suite 2640, Chicago, IL 60654-4843.

### IRVIN, REGINA LYNETTE

State government official. **Personal:** Born Sep 13, 1963, Columbia, MS; daughter of Eugene and Carolyn J Barnes. **Educ:** Alcorn State Univ, BA, 1985; Thurgood Marshall Sch Law, JD, pub admin, 1988. **Career:** Magistrate Karen K Brown, law clerk, 1988; Dept Navy, Naval Sea Syst Command, atty, 1988-89; Atty S Ralph Martin Jr & Benjamin W Spaulding Jr, law clerk, 1989; Atty Raymond Regist, law clerk, 1989-90; Secret & ASC, law clerk, 1989-90; Dept Veterans Affairs, claims examr, 1991; Miss Dept Human Servs, child support enforcement officer, 1992-93, admin hearings officer, 1993-2000; Miss State Dept Health, br dir, 2000-. **Orgs:** Basileus & anti basileus, Grammateus, 1983-84, Alpha Kappa Alpha Sorority; secy, Polit Sci Soc, 1983-84; pres, Social Sci Soc, 1984-85; gen mem, Am Bar Asn, 1985-88; vpres, Phi Alpha Delta Law Fraternity Int, 1985-88; vpres, NBA, Black Law Studs Asn, 1985-88; State Bar Tex, Studs Div, 1985-88; staff mem, Thurgood Marshall Law Rev, 1985-88. **Home Addr:** 1212 Maxwell Ave, Columbia, MS 39429-2326, **Home Phone:** (601)736-4336. **Business Addr:** Branch Director, Mississippi State Department of Health, 570 E Woodrow Wilson Dr, Jackson, MS 39216, **Business Phone:** (601)576-7751.

### IRVIN, SEDRICK

Football player, football coach. **Personal:** Born Mar 30, 1978, Miami, FL; children: Sedrick Jr & Amarri. **Educ:** Mich State Univ, polit sci & govt, 1999. **Career:** Football player (retired), football coach; Detroit Lions, running back, 1999-2000; NFL Miami Dolphins, squad mem, 2003; NFLE Berlin Thunder, 2003; AFL Columbus Destroyers, 2005; Gulliver Prep Sch, asst coach, 2006-08; Univ Ala, asst coach, 2008-09; Univ Memphis, Memphis Tigers, running backs coach, 2010; Westminster Christian Sch, head football coach, 2011. **Orgs:** Founder, Smile Found, 2015. **Honors/Awds:** Sporting News National Player of the Year, 2009; National Championship Offensive MVP honor. **Special Achievements:** USA Today All-American, 1995. **Business Addr:** Football Coach, Westminster Christian Sch, 6855 SW 152nd St, Miami, FL 33157, **Business Phone:** (305)233-2030.

### IRVINE, DR. CAROLYN LENETTE

Educator. **Personal:** Born Mar 7, 1947, Quincy, FL; daughter of Robert L Green and Jessie M Jones McCloud; married Freeman R Jr; children: Fredreka R & Freeman R III. **Educ:** Fla A&M Univ, Tallahassee, FL, BS, 1970; Univ Fla, Gainesville, FL, MEd, 1975; Fla State Univ, Tallahassee, FL, PhD, 1984. **Career:** Shanks High Sch, Quincy, Fla, speech & eng teacher, 1976-77; Fla A&M Univ, Tallahassee, Fla, speech teacher, 1975-76, 1983-, eng teacher, 1978-83, dept Eng, assoc prof speech commun, currently. **Orgs:** Jack & Jill Am, 1988-90; Asn Teachers Am, 1989-90; Fla Speech Commun Asn, 1984-91; Phi Delta Kappa, 1984-91; Fac Senate Rep Comt, 1999-2000. **Home Addr:** 618 Brookridge Dr, Tallahassee, FL 32304, **Home Phone:** (904)576-4081. **Business Addr:** Associate Professor of Speech Communication, Florida A&M University, 304 Tucker Hall Rm 410, Tallahassee, FL 32307, **Business Phone:** (850)599-3799.

### IRVING, DR. CLARENCE LARRY, JR.

Executive director, lawyer. **Personal:** Born Jul 7, 1955, Brooklyn, NY. **Educ:** Northwestern Univ, BA, 1976; Stanford Univ Law Sch, JD, 1979. **Career:** Kirkland E Ellis, summer assoc, 1977; Breed Abbott & Morgan, summer assoc, 1978; Hogan & Hartson, assoc, 1979-83; US Rep Mickey Leland, legis dir & coun, 1983-87; US House Rep Subcomn Telecomm & Finance, sr coun, 1987-92; Nat Telecommunications & Info Admin, asst secy com & dir, 1993-99; U.S. Dept Com, Nat Telecommunications & Info Admin, asst secy, 1993-99; Irving Info Group, prin, pres & chief exec officer, currently; US House Representatives, sr coun; Privacy Coun Inc, consult & chief strategy officer, 2001-03; Hewlett-Packard Co, Global Govt Affairs & vpres, 2009-11; Mobile Alliance Global Good, co-founder, 2012-. **Orgs:** Nat Bar Asn, 1980-; Precinct capt Wash DC Dem Party, 1983-84; Nat Conf Black Lawyers Comn Task Force, 1983-; Variety Club Greater Wash, 1985-; chair, House Rep Fair Employ Practices Comt, 1985-87; bd vis, Stanford Law Sch; bd mem, House Rep Child Care Ctr; co-chair, Am Bar Asn, Electronic Media Div, Comt Commun Law; bd dir, Covad Commun; bd dir, WorldGate Commun; bd dir, Internews Network; bd dir, Reliability First Corp, 2005-; bd dir, Pub Broadcasting Serv, 2009-. **Honors/Awds:** Pres, Stanford Law Sch Class of 1979; Outstanding Young Man Am, Jaycees, 1979; 50 most influential persons in the Year of the Internet, Newsweek Mag, 1994. **Home Addr:** 1050 Conn Ave NW, Suite 1000, Washington, DC 20036. **Business Addr:** President, Chief Executive Officer, Irving Information Group, 1634 I St NW Suite 1100, Washington, DC 20006, **Business Phone:** (202)638-4370.

### IRVING, OPHELIA MCALPIN

Librarian. **Personal:** Born Apr 4, 1929, Gadsden, AL; daughter of Jerry and Lamae Prater; married Charles G Jr; children: Cyretha G Jr. **Educ:** Clarks Col, AB, 1951; Atlanta Univ, attended 1958; Syracuse Univ, MLS, 1958, 1972; Drexel Inst Tech, geneal cert, 1976, mgt cert, 1977; NC Cent Univ, attended 1984. **Career:** Ctr High Sch Waycross, librn, 1951-54; Spencer Jr High Sch Columbus, librn, 1954-55; St Augustine's Col Raleigh, librn, 1955-68; fel, Study Librariesin Europe, 1964; NC State Libr Raleigh, asst chief info ser sect, 1968-91; Shaw Univ, Raleigh, resource librn p/t, 1992-. **Orgs:** Alpha Kappa Alpha Sor, 1954-; NC Libr Asn, 1955-; Jack & Jill Am Inc, 1961-73; Am Libr Asn, 1963-; YWCA, 1965-; NC Line Users Grp, 1982-; Microcomput Users Grp NC, 1983-; Top Ladies Distinction; Continental Soc Inc, 1990; Links Inc, 1991; Alpha Theta Omega Chap. **Honors/Awds:** Faculty Fellowship, St Augustine Col Raleigh, NC, 1964; NC Road Builders Award, 1991; Order of the Long Leaf Pine Award, 1991; Appointed to the NC State Library Commission, 1992; BCALA Distinguished Award, 1992; NCLA Life Membership Award, 1997; Docent Emeritus Award, NC Mus Hist, 2002. **Home Addr:** 533 E Lenoir St, Raleigh, NC 27601-2484, **Home Phone:** (919)833-3658. **Business Addr:** Librarian, Shaw University, 118 E S St, Raleigh, NC 27601, **Business Phone:** (919)546-8200.

### IRVING, TERRY DUANE

Football player. **Personal:** Born Jul 3, 1971, Galveston, TX; married Frankie; children: Breana. **Educ:** McNeese State Univ, BS, elec eng. **Career:** Football player (retired); Ariz Cardinals, 1994, 1996, left linebacker & right linebacker, 1995, right linebacker, 1997, linebacker, 1998. **Home Addr:** 3033 Bardin Rd Apt 1205, Grand Prairie, TX 75052-3879.

### ISAAC, BRIAN WAYNE

Administrator, president (organization). **Educ:** NY Univ, BA, 1976, MA, pub admin, 1984. **Career:** Long Island Lighting Co, training & educ coordr, 1977-79, EEO admin, 1979-84, employ serv admin, 1984-. **Orgs:** Pres, Manhattan Spokesman Club, 1977-78; Edges Group Inc. **Home Addr:** 326 E 92nd St, Brooklyn, NY 11212.

### ISAAC, HON. EARLEAN

Judge. **Personal:** Born Feb 11, 1950, Forkland, AL; daughter of Robert Percy and Mary Virginia Smith; married Johnny L; children: Johnny L Jr, Jamaine L & Janetha L. **Career:** Greene County Judge Probate, Eutaw, Ala, license clerk, 1971-75, chief clerk, 75-89, judge, 1989-. **Orgs:** St Paul United Methodist Church, 1988; Ala Probate Judges Asn. **Honors/Awds:** Citizen of the Yr Award, Kappa Alpha Psi Fraternity, 1989. **Special Achievements:** First Black Woman Probate Judge in Alabama. **Home Addr:** 288 Lloyd Chapel Rd, Forkland, AL 36740, **Home Phone:** (205)289-3866. **Business Addr:** Judge, Greene County Judge of Probate, 400 Morrow Ave, Eutaw, AL 35462, **Business Phone:** (205)372-3340.

### ISAAC, DR. EPHRAIM

Historian, scholar, educator. **Personal:** Born May 29, 1936, Nedjio; son of Ruth and Yishaq; married Sherry Rosen; children: Devorah Esther, Raphael Samuel & Yael Ruth. **Educ:** Concordia Col, BA, philosophy, chemistry, 1958; Harvard Divinity Sch, BA, philos, chem & music, M Div, 1963; Harvard Univ, PhD, near eastern lang, 1969; Calif Univ, New York, DHL; LittD. **Career:** Harvard Univ, instr to lectr, 1969-71, assoc prof to prof, 1971-77, Divinity Sch, vis prof; Hebrew Univ, lect, 1977-79; Bard Col, vis prof, 1981-83; Inst Semitic Studies, dir, 1985-2009; Princeton Univ, vis prof, Relig & African Am Studies, 1995-2001; Inst Relig & Pub Policy, dir, currently. **Orgs:** Pres, Ethiopian Stud Asn N Am, 1959-62; chorale dir, Harvard Grad Chorale, 1962-64; treas, Harvard Grad Stud Asn, 1962-65; chmn, Comn Ethiopian Literacy, 1963-68; dir gen, Nat Literacy Campaign Ethiopia, 1966-72, exec dir, 1967-74; bd mem, African Studies Heritage Asn, 1969-73; bd mem, Am Asn Ethiopian Jews, 1973-; vice chmn, Ethiopian Famine Relief Comn, 1984-; fel Harvard Univ, Dubois Inst, 1985-86; fel Princeton Univ, Ctr Theol Inquiry,1989-92; fel Butler Col; fel Dead Sea Scrolls Found; chair, Ethiopian Peace & Develop Ctr; chair, Africa Bd Peace & Develop Orgn; ed bd, J Afroasiatic Lang; ed bd, Second Temple Jewish Lit; Temple Understanding; Inst Relig & Pub Policy; Tanenbaum Ctr Inter-relig Understanding; Princeton Fel Prayer; Inst Jewish Community Res, & Oxford Forum; Harvard-Radcliff Alumni Asn; Nat Comt Am Foreign Policy; Peacemakers Action Tanenbaum Ctr Interreligious Understanding, 2002; pres, Yemenite Jewish Fedn Am, currently. **Honors/Awds:** Ethiopian National Prize for literacy, 1967; NEH Research Grant, 1976; fel, Endowment for the Humanities, 1979; fel, Am Philos Soc, 1980-81; Faculty Fund Research Grants, Harvard Univ; United Nations Associations of Ethiopia Peace Award; Best teacher of the Year; Hon degree, DHL, John J. Col CUNY, 1993; Ephraim Isaac Prize in African Studies in honor, named in honor, 1999; Society of Ethiopian Established in Diaspora Education Award, 2002; Peacemaker Award, Rabbi Tanenbaum Ctr, 2002; Hon degree, Litt D, Addis Ababa Univ, Ethiopia, 2004; Interfaith Peace-Building Initiative Decree of Merit, 2004; Morton Deutsch Conflict Resolution Award, Am Psychol Asn, 2013; NEH Fellowship. **Special Achievements:** Outstanding Educators of America, 1972; Author of numerous articles on Ethiopian and Jewish studies; Author of Ethiopic book of Enoch, Doubleday, 1983, a history of religions in Africa; First professor hired in Afro-American Studies at Harvard Univ; The Ethiopian Orthodox Tawahido Church, 2012; From Abraham to Obama, A History of Jews, Africans, and Africanamericans, 2015. **Business Addr:** Director, Institute on Religion and Public Policy, 1620 I St NW Suite LL10, Washington, DC 20006, **Business Phone:** (202)835-8760.

### ISAAC, DR. JOSEPH WILLIAM ALEXANDER

Physician, obstetrician, gynecologist. **Personal:** Born Jan 1, 1935; son of Agatha Henry and Timothy; married Gertrude Harris; children: Charles, Zoe & Joseph A. **Educ:** City Col, BS, biol, 1967; Howard Univ, MD, 1971; Am Bd Obstet & Gynec, dipl. **Career:** Howard Univ Hosp, Wash, DC, med intern, 1971-72; Howard Univ, resident obstet & gynec, 1972-76; Norfolk Health Dept, family planning phys, 1976-77; Norfolk & Portsmouth, pvt pract obstet & gynec, 1977-; Portsmouth Gen Hosp, Dept Obstet & Gynec, chmn, 1985-88; Norflk Comm Hosp, chmn dept obstet & gynec, 1991-98; Portsmouth Gen Hosp, pres med staff, 1993; Harvard Univ Hosp, obstet & gynec; Eastern Va Med Sch, asst prof. **Orgs:** Am Med Asn, 1975-; Nat Med Asn; Norfolk Med Soc, 1976; Norfolk Acad Med, 1977-99; Portsmouth Chamber Com, 1978; Med Adv Comt Tidewater March Dimes, 1979; fel Am Col obstet & gynec, 1979, vpres, 1986-90, pres, 1990-92; pres, Old Dom Med Soc; pres, Norfolk Med Soc, 1985-87; Cent Tex Med Found; treas, W Indian Students Asn. **Home Addr:** 712 Elderberry Ct, Chesapeake, VA 23320, **Home Phone:** (757)436-4776. **Business Addr:** Physician, 549 E Brambleton Ave Suite 4, Norfolk, VA 23510, **Business Phone:** (757)627-0222.

### ISAAC, TELESFORO ALEXANDER

Clergy. **Personal:** Born Jan 1, 1928?, San Pedro de Macoris; son of Simon and Violet Francis; married Juana Maria Rosa Zorrilla; children: Juan Alexander, Marcos Alexander & Miriam Elizabeth. **Educ:** Instituto Vazquez, 1950; Sem Haiti, 1958; Univ Antonoma de Santo Domingo, lang, 1970; Seminario Episcopal del Caribe, MDiv, 1971. **Career:** Clergy (retired); Morey Hardware Store, Porvenir Sugar Mill, clerk, 1950-54; San Gabriel Episcopal Church, vicar, 1958-61; Jesus Nazarene Episcopal Church, vicar, 1961-65; San Andres Episcopal Church, vicar, 1965-69; San Esteban Episcopal Church, vicar, 1971-72; Dominican Repub Diocese, diocesan bishop, 1972-90; Diocese Southwest Fla, asst bishop, 1991-2000; VI, Interim Bishop. **Orgs:** Founder, prin, San Gabriel & Jesus Nazarene Schs, 1959-62; co-founder, Dominican-Am Lang Inst, 1964-; bd trustee, Church World Serv, 1966-91; founder & prin, San Marcos & San Andres High Schs, 1966-70; chair & bd Caribbean Episcopal Sem, 1975-76; founder, pres & bd dir, Ctr Theol Sch, 1975-91; pres & bd dir Ctr Rehab, Handicapped, 1985-91; chair & bd dir, Asn Human Rights, 1991. **Honors/Awds:** DDiv, City Univ Los Angeles, 1977; Distinguished Citizen, San Pedro de Macoris, 1983. **Special Achievements:** La Labor Educativa de la Iglesia Episcopal Dominicana, 1971; First Dominican-born deacon; Author of books on spirituality. **Home Addr:** 503 St Tropez Cir NE, Saint Petersburg, FL 33703, **Home Phone:** (813)526-0177.

### ISAACS, CHERYL BOONE

Marketing executive, public relations executive. **Personal:** Born Jan 1, 1949?, Springfield, MA; married Stanley; children: Cooper. **Educ:** Whittier Col, BA, polit sci, 1971. **Career:** Columbia Pictures, staff publicist; Melvin Simon Productions, campaign promotions; Ladd Co, campaign promotions; Paramount Pictures, exec vpres worldwide publicity; New Line Cinema, pres theatrical mkt, 1997-99; CBI Enterprises Inc, founder & pres. **Orgs:** Gov pub rels, Acad Motion Picture Arts & Sci (AMPAS), 1992-13, first vpres, pres, 2013-; Gov Awards, producer, 2012. **Honors/Awds:** Essence Magazine s Trailblazer Award, 2013; African-American Film Critics Association (AAFCA) Horizon Award, 2014; NAACP Image Awards Hall of Fame, 2014. **Special Achievements:** First African American woman to lead a major studio's marketing operation (New Line Cinema, 1997); first African American and third woman to hold the office of President of AMPAS. **Business Addr:** Founder, President, Cbi Enterprises Inc, 203 N Irving Blvd, Los Angeles, CA 90004, **Business Phone:** (323)462-9920.

### ISAACS, JESSICA C.

President (organization). **Educ:** Spelman Col, lib arts; Ga State Univ, BA, polit sci & sociol; John Marshall Law Sch, Ga, law degree; Northwestern Univ, Kellogg Sch Mgt, grad level studies, 1992. **Career:** Allstate Ins Co., var mgt positions; Am Int Group Inc, asst vpres & vpres Personal Lines Div, sr vpres Field Opers, global reinsurance officer, Chartis Int Personal Lines, 2005-11; Marsh & McLennan Co, managing dir, 2011-12; AJI Group, pres, 2013-. **Orgs:** Bd mem, Wash Regional Prog; chmn bd, Exec Leadership Coun; bd mem, Next Generation Network; bd mem, Urban Tech. **Honors/Awds:** "The Network Journal: Black Professionals & Small Business Magazine", 25 Influential Black Women in Business, 2006; "Black Enterprise", 100 Most Powerful Executives in Corporate America, 2009; "Black Enterprise", 75 Most Powerful Women in Business, 2010. **Business Addr:** Senior Vice President, American International Group Inc, 175 Water St, New York, NY 10038, **Business Phone:** (212)770-7000.

**ISAACS, STEPHEN D.**
Safety engineer. **Personal:** Born Feb 22, 1944, Boston, MA; children: Athelia & Stephanie. **Educ:** Howard Univ, Wash, BMech, engr, 1969, MBA, 1973. **Career:** Off Mgmt & Budget, Opers Res Analyst, 1973-75, exec off pres; US Nuclear Reg Comn, prog analyst, 1975-77; US Nuclear Reg Comn, FOIA officer, 1977-86; Fed Aviation Admin, aviation safety inspector, 1986-89; Wash Flight Stand Dist Off, Wash Dulles Airport, Aviation Safety Inspector, 1989-. **Orgs:** Am Soc Mech Engrs, 1973-; Am Soc Access Profs, 1980-86; bd dir, Spec Air Serv Inc, 1983-85; acct exec, Int Monetary Founding Grp Inc, 1984-86; Wash Soc Engrs, 1985-; Nat Asn Flight Instrs. **Home Addr:** 1907 2nd St NW, Washington, DC 20001-1624, **Home Phone:** (202)462-5605. **Business Addr:** Aviation Safety Inspector, Washington Flight Standards District Office, Washington, DC 20041, **Business Phone:** (703)572-2700.

**ISAACS-GREENE, PATRICIA**
Executive, executive director. **Personal:** Born May 6, 1949, Georgetown; daughter of Violet; married Morty Greene; children: Krystal Louise. **Educ:** DC Teachers Col; S Eastern Univ. **Career:** McDonalds Corp, Mich Region, dir opers, 1975-91, regional vpres, 1991-96, McDonald's Restaurant, Jamaica, managing dir, chief exec officer, 1996-; Three Rivers Mgt, managing dir, chief exec officer, prin; Green Produce Farm Ltd, prin; Jam Rock Sports Bar & Grill, owner. **Orgs:** Detroit Chamber Com; bd mem, Homes Black C; Black Owners Asn. **Home Addr:** 7570 Whithorn Ct, West Bloomfield, MI 48322. **Business Addr:** Managing Director, Chief Executive Officer, McDonalds Corp, 2111 McDonald, Oak Brook, IL 60523, **Business Phone:** (630)623-3000.

**ISAACS-LOWE, ARLENE ELIZABETH**
Financial manager. **Personal:** Born Oct 17, 1959, Kingston; daughter of Lawrence G and Barbara C Davis; married Walter J IV; children: Walter J V. **Educ:** Howard Univ, Wash, DC, BBA, acct, 1981; Fordham Univ, New York, NY, MBA, finance, 1990. **Career:** VSE Corp, Alexandria, VA, staff acct, 1981-84; W World Holding Inc, New York, NY, financial mgr, 1984-86, sr acct, 1984-87, acct mgr, 1987-; Metrop Life, New York, NY, financial analyst, 1986-88, mgr, 1988-89, controller, 1989-92, portfolio mgr, 1992-94; Equinox Realty Advisors LLC, prin & chief financial officer, 1994-98; Moody's Investors Servs, sr analyst, lead analyst, 1998-2004, Financial Insts Group, sr vpres, 2004-10, Com Group, sr vpres, 2010-12, Head Relationship Mgt Financial Insts & PPIF, sr vpres, assoc managing dir, 2012-15, Head Relationship Mgt EMEA, managing dir, 2016-. **Orgs:** Nat Urban League, 1988-; Nat Asn Black Accts, 1989-; Nat Black MBA, 1990-; Beta Gamma Sigma Hon Soc, Fordham Univ, 1990; bd mem, Rheedlen Found, 1991-; BEEP; bd dir, Enterprise Community Investment Inc; chair, Ny Soc; Exec Leadership Found; New York Soc Security Analysts; Ny Soc CPAs; dir, Enterprise Social Investment Corp, 2000-; treas, Exec Leadership Coun, 2004-; bd visitor, Howard Univ Sch Bus, 2012-; bd dir, Moody's Shared Serv UK Ltd, 2016-. **Honors/Awds:** 25 Influential Black Women, Network J, 2010; Samuel Traum Award, Ny Soc CPA's Nassau County Chap, 2012. **Special Achievements:** America's Best & Brightest, Dollars & Sense Mag, 1991; 100 Most Promising Black Women in Corporate America, Ebony Mag, 1991. **Home Addr:** 219-21 144th Ave, Jamaica, NY 11413, **Home Phone:** (718)712-5565. **Business Addr:** Senior Vice President, Moody's Investors Services, 99 Church St, New York, NY 10007, **Business Phone:** (212)553-7841.

**ISADORE, DR. HAROLD W.**
Lawyer, librarian. **Personal:** Born Alexandria, LA. **Educ:** Southern Univ, BS, 1967; Southern Univ Sch Law, JD, 1970; State Univ NY, Buffalo Law Sch, cert, 1978. **Career:** US Dept Labor Off Solicitor, atty, 1970-73; Baton Rouge Legal Aid Soc, atty, 1973-74; Pub Defender Baton Rouge, atty, 1974-75; Southern Univ Sch Law, sr ref librn, interim dir, currently; pvt pract, currently. **Orgs:** Am Bar Asn, Nat Bar Asn, Delta Theta Phi Law Frat, Am Asn Law Librs, Kappa Alpha Psi Frat, Inc. **Honors/Awds:** Service Award, Student Bar Asn, Southern Univ Law Sch, 1970; Hypotext Security Devices, Southern Univ Publisher, 1979; Hypo text Civil Procedure, Vols 1 & 11 S Univ Publisher, 1980-81; Humanitarian Award, Louis AMartinet Legal Soc; Staff Award, Southern Univ Law Ctr, 1980-81, 1985-87, 1990-94. **Home Addr:** 8008 Bluebonnet Blvd Apt 10-13, Baton Rouge, LA 70806, **Home Phone:** (225)216-2301. **Business Addr:** Senior Reference Librarian, Southern University Law Center, 2 Roosevelt Steptoe Dr, Baton Rouge, LA 70813, **Business Phone:** (225)771-2669.

**ISHMAN, DR. SYBIL RAY**
Educator. **Personal:** Born Jul 25, 1946, Durham, NC; married Reginald E. **Educ:** Univ NC, Greensboro, BA, Eng, 1968; Univ NC, Chapel Hill, MA, AM lit, 1971, PhD, appl ling, 1983. **Career:** Educator (retired); NC Cent Univ, grad asst, 1969-71, instr, 1970-72; NC State Univ, eng instr, 1972-76, asst prof, 1979-85; Howard Univ, eng instr, 1976-77; Nazareth Col, adj prof, 1985-86, eng instr, 1986, 1988, 1990, 1992; Rochester Inst Technol, Nat Tech Inst Deaf, Eng Dept, chair, 1986-91, Dept Lib Arts Support, asst prof, assoc prof, prof. **Orgs:** Am Asn Univ Women; Mod Lang Asn; Nat Coun Teachers Eng; TESOL; Nat Smart Set Durham Chap; N Carolina State Univ; Harley Sch Bd Trustees; Rochester Contemp Arts Coun; Livingston County Wadsworth Libr; Wilson Commencement Ctr Women; Livingston Community Bd Literacy. **Honors/Awds:** Who's Who Among Outstanding Black Collegians, 1972; Teaching Effectiveness Recognition Student Award, NC State Univ, 1984. **Home Addr:** 43 Westview Cres, Geneseo, NY 14454-1011. **Business Addr:** Professor, Rochester Institute of Technology, 1 Lomb Mem Dr HLC-2214, Rochester, NY 14623-5603, **Business Phone:** (585)475-2444.

**ISIBOR, EDWARD IROGUEHI**
Dean (education), educator, engineer. **Personal:** Born Jun 9, 1940, Benin City; married Edwina Williams; children: Ekinadose & Emwanta. **Educ:** Howard Univ, BSc, civil engineering, 1965; Mass Inst Technol, MSc, transp engineering, 1967; Purdue Univ, PhD, transp engineering, 1970. **Career:** Mass Inst Technol, res asst, 1965-67; Purdue Univ, res asst, 1967-69; Cleveland State Univ, Afro-Am Cult Ctr, dir, 1970-71; NE Ohio Areawide Coord Agency, Cleveland, transp engr, 1972; Fla Int Univ, Dept Civil Eng, assoc prof & head urban syst prog, 1973-75; Tenn State Univ, Sch Eng & Tech, dean, 1975, assoc prof, Sch Engineering & Technol, prof civil & environ eng, currently; Claret Ctr, dir; Univ Notre Dame Scott Malpass, exec vpres finances bus opers. **Orgs:** Tau Beta Pi Hon Soc, 1964; Sigma Xi Hon Soc, 1970; Am Soc Eng Educ; Transp Res Bd, WA, DC; Ohio Soc Prof Engrs; C C Reg Engr, OH; Am Soc Civil Engrs; dir, Retreats Int; dir, Univ Ndak; dir, Claret Ctr; exec vpres finances, Bus Opers, Univ Notre Dame Scott Malpass; bd Regents, State Univ & Community Col Syst; dir, Retreats Int & UND. **Home Addr:** 8220 Frontier Lane, Brentwood, TN 37027-7318, **Home Phone:** (615)370-3036. **Business Addr:** Professor, Tennessee State University, 3500 John A Merritt Blvd, Nashville, TN 37203, **Business Phone:** (615)963-5432.

**ISLER, MARSHALL A., III**
Real estate developer, vice president (organization), executive. **Personal:** Born Jan 9, 1939, Kinston, NC; son of Marshall A Jr and Louise Douglas; married Verna Harmon Bradford; children: Bryan C, Christi Johnson & Regan Sales. **Educ:** Howard Univ, BSEE, 1962; George Washington Univ, MEA, opers res, 1968; Harvard Bus Sch, PMD, bus, 1975. **Career:** Johns Hopkins Univ Appl Physics Lab, space sys officer, 1967; Naval Air Sys Command, satellite proj engr, 1971; Nat Bur Stand Law Enforcement Stand, security syst prog mgr, 1973; Sen John Tunney, sci adv, 1974; Nat Bur Stand Dept Com Ctr Consult Prod Tech, dep dir, 1978; Parametric Inc, pres, 1978-91; Parametric Garage Assocs, Managing Partner, 1983; Isler Assoc, pres, owner, 1979-95; Isler Consults LLC, prin, 2008-; Nat Engineering Lab, assoc dir; Ctr Consumer Prod Technol, dep dir. **Orgs:** Howard Univ Alumni Assoc; Omega Psi Phi Frat; SBF Credit Union; assoc Urban Land Ins; Durham Bus & Prof Chain; Durham Chamber Com; Nat Home Builders Assoc; Mayor's Downtown Redevelop Comt Durham; pres, Abiding Savior Lutheran Church, Durham, NC, 1989-91; vpres, Bus & Prof Chain Durham, NC, 1989-90; Bd dir, Dispute Settlement Ctr, Durham, NC, 1989-90; Human Rels Comt, Durham NC Chamber Com, 1990-91; Churches Action, Durham, NC, 1990-; exec vpres, Downtown Develop Corp; Covenant Love Church; Fayetteville-Cumberland County Chamber Com. **Honors/Awds:** Congressional Fellowship, 1973-74; John T. Gibson Business and Economic Award, Kappa Alpha Psi Fraternity; Professional Service Award, Cumberland Regional Improv Corp. **Special Achievements:** Author of An Unwitting Pioneer, 2011. **Home Addr:** 309 E Lochhaven Dr, Fayetteville, NC 28314, **Home Phone:** (910)488-2480. **Business Addr:** Principal, Isler Consultants LLC, 309 E Lochhaven Dr, Fayetteville, NC 28314, **Business Phone:** (910)488-2480.

**ISLEY, ERNIE (ERNEST BERNARD ISLEY)**
Musician, singer. **Personal:** Born Mar 7, 1952, Cincinnati, OH; married Tracy. **Career:** The Isley Brothers, music band mem, 1973-; guitarist, drummer, singer & songwriter, currently; Albums: Shout!, 1959; Twist & Shout, 1962; Twisting& Shouting, 1963; This Old Heart of Mine, 1966; Soul on the Rocks, 1967; It's Our Thing, 1969; The Brothers Isley, 1969; Live at Yankee Stadium, 1969; Get Into Something, 1970; In the Beginning, 1971; Givin' It Back, 1971; Brother, Brother, Brother, 1972; 3+3, 1973; Live It Up, 1974; The Heat Is On, 1975; Harvest for the World, 1976; Go for Your Guns, 1977; Showdown, 1978; Timeless, 1978; Winner Takes All, 1979; Go All the Way, 1980; Grand Slam, 1981; Inside You, 1981; The Real Deal, 1982; Between the Sheets, 1983; Greatest Hits, Vol 1, 1984; Masterpiece, 1985; Smooth Sailin', 1987; Spend the Night, 1989; High Wire, solo album, 1990; Tracks of Life, 1992; Live, 1993; Beautiful Ballads, 1994; For The Love of You, 1995; The Isley Brothers Live, 1996; Mission to Please, 1996; Shake it Up Baby: Shout, Twist & Shout, 2000; Eternal, 2000; Love Songs, 2001; 20thCentury Masters - The Millenium Collection: The Best of the Isley Brothers, 2001; Body Kiss, 2003; Here I Am: Isley Meets Bacharach, 2003; Live It Up, 2004; Rebound, 2005; # Karaoke Revolution Party, 2005; The Sentinel, 2006; Code Name: The Cleaner, 2007; Superbad, 2007; Pineapple Express, 2008. TV series: Summer Breeze: The Isley Brothers Greatest Hits Live, 2005. **Honors/Awds:** Rock & Roll Hall of Fame, 1992. **Business Addr:** Musician, c/o Varese Sarabande Records Inc, 11846 Ventura Blvd Suite 130, Studio City, CA 91604, **Business Phone:** (818)753-4143.

**ISMAIL, QADRY RAHMADAN**
Football player, football coach. **Personal:** Born Nov 8, 1970, Newark, NJ; married Holly G; children: Qalea, Qadry & Qadir. **Educ:** Syracuse Univ, speech commun, 1992. **Career:** Football player (retired), football coach, analyst; Minn Vikings, wide receiver & kick returner, 1993-96; Miami Dolphins, 1997; Green Bay Packers, 1997; New Orleans Saints, 1998; Baltimore Ravens, wide receiver & tight end, 1999-2001; Indianapolis Colts, wide receiver, 2002; W Boca Raton Community High Sch, coach, currently; Comcast Sports Net, analyst; BET Black Col Football, analyst; Entertainment & Sports Programming Network, analyst; Rave TV, analyst; WBAL, analyst; Patterson Mill High Sch, coach, currently. **Orgs:** Spokesperson, Drug Abuse Resistance Educ. **Honors/Awds:** Track Athlete-of-the-Year; All-Am hons, Track & Field News; Martin Luther King Citizenship Award; Offensive Player of the Week, AFC, 1999. **Home Addr:** 1506 Sunningdale Way, Bel Air, MD 21015-2101, **Home Phone:** (410)420-0958. **Business Addr:** Coach, West Boca Raton Community High School, 1501 NW 15th Ct, Boca Raton, FL 33486, **Business Phone:** (561)338-1400.

**ISMAIL, RAGHIB RAMADIAN**
Football player. **Personal:** Born Nov 18, 1969, Elizabeth, NJ; son of Ibrahim (deceased) and Fatma; married Melani; children: 4. **Educ:** Univ Notre Dame. **Career:** Football player (retired); Toronto Argonauts, Can Football League, running back, 1991-92; Los Angeles Raiders, Kick returner, 1993-94; Oakland Raiders, Kick returner & Wide receiver, 1995; Carolina Panthers, wide receiver, 1996-98; Dallas Cowboys, wide receiver, 1999-2001. **Honors/Awds:** All-American, 1989, 1990; Walter Camp Award, 1990; CFL All-Star, 1991; Most Valuable Player, Grey Cup, 1991; Sprint Runner, NCAA Indoor Championships.

**ISMIAL, SALAAM IBN**
Association executive, founder (originator), business owner. **Personal:** Born Jersey City, NJ. **Educ:** Robert Walsh Sch Bus, 1979; Kean Col, NJ, 1982; Union County Col, 1983. **Career:** EYC After Sch Prog Rec Dept, coordr, 1984-85; Salaam Ismial Communs, owner. **Orgs:** Youth leader Local Chap, CORE, 1973; chmn, Kean Col Black Stud Union, 1982; pres, Elizabeth Youth Coun, 1982-85; vpres, Union County Col, 1983; pres, Nat Asn Advan Colored People, youth, 1984; Black Issue Conv, Southern Christian Leadership, 1984, Progressive Rainbow Alliance NJ, 1985; coordr, Union African Stud Orgs, Col Org Statewide; bd, Urban League Essex Co Pediats Aid Foster Care, 1989; founder, pres & dir, Nat United Youth Coun Inc. **Honors/Awds:** Medal of Honor Elizabeth Boys Scouts, 1972; Outstanding Service Award, Kean Black Stud Union, 1982; Comm Serv Elizabeth Youth Coun, 1983; Life Time Membership, NAACP, 1984. **Business Addr:** Chairman, Founder, National United Youth Council Inc, 513 Richmond St, Elizabeth, NJ 07202, **Business Phone:** (215)316-7952.

**ISOM, EDDIE L.**
Hotel executive, manager. **Educ:** Livingstone Col, Salisbury, NC. **Career:** Marriott Corp, food & beverage dir; Howard Univ Hotel, dir food, gen mgr, currently. **Business Addr:** General Manager, Howard University Inc, 2225 Ga Ave NW, Washington, DC 20059-1014, **Business Phone:** (202)462-5400.

**ISRAEL, MAE H.**
Journalist. **Personal:** Born Apr 8, 1953, Robeson County, NC; daughter of Samuel L and Mae C. **Educ:** Univ NC, Chapel Hill, BA, jour, 1975. **Career:** Greensboro Daily News, reporter, 1975-80; Charlotte Observer, reporter, assignment ed, 1980-89, asst metro ed, 1989-2008; Wash Post, ed, 1989-; Montgomery Co, ed; Independent Commun Specialist, writer & ed, 2008-. **Orgs:** Women Communs, 1977-79; Southeastern Black Press Inst, 1977-79; Nat Asn Black Journalists, 1978-; pres, Charlotte Area Asn Black Journalists, 1985-89; Wash Area Asn Black Journalists, 1989-; Delta Sigma Theta. **Honors/Awds:** Press Award, Feature Writing, NC Press Asn, 1977; Excellence in Writing, Landmark Commun, 1978; News Writing, Feature Writing, Black Media Asn, 1985 & 1986. **Home Addr:** 717 Streamside Dr, Mitchellville, MD 20721, **Home Phone:** (301)336-3091. **Business Addr:** Editor, The Washington Post Montgomery Edition, 51 Monroe St Suite 500, Rockville, MD 20850, **Business Phone:** (301)738-1565.

**ISRAEL, STEVEN DOUGLAS**
Football player, broadcaster, executive. **Personal:** Born Mar 16, 1969, Lawnside, NJ; married Lorae; children: Averi Lorae & Ashley Shardae. **Educ:** Univ Pittsburgh, BA, econs; Stanford Grad Sch Bus, cert, bus; Harvard Bus Sch, cert, bus. **Career:** Football player (retired), analyst; Los Angeles Rams, defensive back, 1992-94; San Francisco 49ers, defensive back, 1995-96; New Eng Patriots, defensive back, 1997-99; New Orleans Saints, defensive back, 2000-01; Nat Football League, chapel speaker; sunday sch teacher; ESPNU TV, col football studio & color analyst, currently. **Orgs:** Founder, EndZone Luncheon Ser; founder, Gridiron Luncheon Ser; bd trustees, Charlotte Christian Sch; bd trustees, Men Who Care Global; bd dir, March Dimes-Charlotte. **Honors/Awds:** NJ Hall Of Fame; South Jersey Coaches Hall of Fame; AT&T Long Distance Award winner; East-West Shriners All-Star Game player; Defensive Most Valuable Person, Hula Bowl. **Home Addr:** 4039 Lissadell Cir, Charlotte, NC 28277-3141, **Home Phone:** (704)544-0095. **Business Addr:** College Football studio & Color Analyst, ESPNU TV, 11001 Rushmore Dr, Charlotte, NC 28277-3434, **Business Phone:** (704)973-5000.

**ITA, LAWRENCE EYO**
Educator. **Personal:** Born Dec 1, 1939, Calabar; married Autumn Dean; children: Eyo & Ekanem. **Educ:** London Univ, BS, 1962; Univ Mich, MSE, PhD, 1970. **Career:** Commonwealth Assoc, eng consult, 1970-72; Bur Assoc Serv, dir, 1974-77; Univ Nev, assoc prof, 1978; Col Southern Nev, prof, currently. Book: "Life's Experiences, Science & The Name of God". **Orgs:** Am Soc Eng Educ, 1974-; Int Soc Solar Energy, 1975-; Am Soc Heat Refrig & Air-Cond Engrs, 1976-. **Home Addr:** 1941 Ophir Dr, Las Vegas, NV 89106, **Home Phone:** (702)631-1100. **Business Addr:** Professor, College of Southern Nevada, 6375 W Charleston Blvd, Las Vegas, NV 89146, **Business Phone:** (702)651-5000.

**IVERSON, ALLEN EZAIL**
Basketball player. **Personal:** Born Jun 7, 1975, Hampton, VA; son of Allen Broughton and Ann; married Tawanna Turner; children: 5. **Educ:** Georgetown Univ, attended 1996. **Career:** Basketball player (retired); Philadelphia 76ers, pt guard, 1996-98, 2004-06, shooting guard, 1998-2004, 2009-10; Denver Nuggets, shooting guard, 2006-08; Detroit Pistons, shooting guard, 2008-09; Memphis Grizzlies, pt guard, 2009; Besiktas, 2010-11. **Honors/Awds:** NBA Draft, First round pick, 1996; Player of the Week, Nat Basketball Asn, 1997; Rookie Challenge Most Valuable Player, Nat Basketball Asn, 1997; Schick Rookie of the Year Award, 1997; Scoring champion, Nat Basketball Asn, 1999, 2001-02, 2005; All-Star, Nat Basketball Asn, 2000-10; Steals leader, Nat Basketball Asn, 2001-03; All-Star Game Most Valuable Player, Nat Basketball Asn, 2001, 2005; bronze medal, Summer Olympics, 2004; Hall of Fame, Naismith Memorial Basketball, 2016; Big East Defensive Player of the Year Award. **Special Achievements:** First rookie in history to score 40 points or more in four consecutive games. Film: Like Mike, 2002; 1 Love , 2003; Imagine That, 2009; My Other Home, 2016. **Business Addr:** Professional Basketball Player, Philadelphia 76ers, 3601 S Broad St, Philadelphia, PA 19148.

**IVERSON, JOHNATHAN LEE**
Circus performer. **Personal:** Born Jan 30, 1976; son of Sylvia. **Educ:** Univ Hartfords, Hartt Sch, voice performance, 1998. **Career:** Ringling Bros Barnum & Bailey, circus ringmaster, 1999-2004, 2010-. **Orgs:** Charismatic Goodwill Ambassador; vpres, Boys & Girls Choir Harlem Alumni Asn Inc. **Honors/Awds:** Virtuoso tenor. **Special Achievements:** First African American ringmaster of a major US circus in 1999 at the age of 22. Named Johnathan one of the ten most fascinating people, 1999; Seeing Placido Domingo perform in Japan, 1989; Singing at the intermission for Luciano Pavarotti's Concert in Cent Park; Performed in a live show on Broadway for two weeks, 1993; Won second place in the Lena Horne Vocal Jazz Scholarship; Won Ringling Brothers and Barnum and Bailey Circus. **Business Addr:** Ringmaster Red Unit, Ringling Bros & Barnum & Bailey Circus, 8607 Westwood Ctr Dr, Vienna, VA 22182, **Business Phone:** (703)448-4000.

**IVERY, DR. CURTIS L.**
College administrator, chancellor (education), chief executive officer. **Educ:** Tex A&M Univ, BS, polit sci & jour; West Texas St, MA, psychol; Univ Ark, doc, educ admin. **Career:** State Ark, commissioner Hum Serv, 1985; El Centro Col, vpres; Mt View Col Of Dallas County Community Col Dist, vpres & act pres; Wayne County Community Col Dist, chief exec officer; Wayne County Community Col, chancellor & chief exec officer, 1995-. **Orgs:** Bd dir, Detroit Comm Bank; New Detroit Inc; Detroit Urban League; bd dir, Am Asn Community Cols; Schs 21st Century. **Special Achievements:** First African American and youngest cabinet member in Arkansas state history. **Business Addr:** Chancellor, Chief Executive Officer, Wayne County Community College, 801 W Fort St, Detroit, MI 48226, **Business Phone:** (313)496-2600.

**IVERY, EDDIE LEE**
Football player, football coach. **Personal:** Born Jul 30, 1957, McDuffie County, GA; married Anna; children: Tauvia Edana & Eddie Lee Jr; married Antoinette; children: Gabriella. **Educ:** Ga Tech, BS, indust mgt, 1992. **Career:** Football player (retired), player develop assistant; Ga Tech Yellow Jackets football team, 1975-78; Green Bay Packers, running back, 1979-86; Thomson High Sch, coach, 1988-90, running backs coach, currently; Ga Tech athletics staff, asst strength & conditioning coach, 2000-08; Ga Tech Athletic Asn, player develop asst, currently; Outreach Inc, resource coordr; McDuffie Achievement Ctr, activ coordr, currently. **Home Addr:** 342 Heckle St, Thomson, GA 30824-8285, **Home Phone:** (706)361-0887. **Business Addr:** Player Development Assistant, Georgia Tech Athletic Association, 150 Bobby Dodd Way NW, Atlanta, GA 30332-0455, **Business Phone:** (404)894-3961.

**IVERY, JAMES A.**
Federal government official. **Personal:** Born Jan 5, 1950, Zebulon, NC; son of Eugene Copeland and Dorothy; children: Jacinda D I & Toshiba I. **Educ:** Fayetteville State Univ, Fayetteville, NC, BS, health & phys educ, 1972; Bucknell Univ, Lewisburg, PA, MPA, 1982. **Career:** Wake County Pub Schs, Raleigh, NC, instr & coach, 1972-74; Internal Revenue Serv, Raleigh, NC, revenue officer, 1974-76; US Dept Health & Human Serv, Wash, DC, spec asst dir, Off Intergovernmental Affairs, asst dep undersecretary, policy analyst, 1976-2008. **Orgs:** Life mem, Alpha Phi Alpha Fraternity, 1977; Nat Forum Black Pub Admin, 1986; Mt Zion Baptist Church, Arlington, VA, 1986; bd dir, Potomac Massage Training Inst, 1995. **Home Addr:** 6563 Zoysia Ct, Alexandria, VA 22312, **Home Phone:** (703)256-1651.

**IVEY, ARTIS LEON, JR.**
Actor, rap musician. **Personal:** Born Aug 1, 1963, Compton, CA; son of Jackie Jones and Artis; married Josefa Salinas; children: 4. **Career:** Albums: It Takes a Thief, 1994; Gangsta's Paradise, 1995; My Soul, 1997; Fantastic Voyage: The Greatest Hits, 2001; El Cool Magnifico, 2002; The Return of the Gangsta, 2006; Three Days to Vegas, 2007; Chinaman's Chance, 2008; Steal Hear, 2008; The Lost Archives of Quincy Taylor, 2009; From the Bottom 2 the Top, 2009. Songs: "County Line", 1993; "Gangsta Paradise", 1995; "1, 2, 3, 4", 1996; "Fantastic Voyage", 1994; "Mama, I'm in Love'"; TV series: "Sabrina, the Teenage Witch", 1996; "Hitz", 1997; "Muppets Tonight", 1997; "The Nanny", 1998; "Malcolm & Eddie", 1999; "18 Wheels of Justice", 2000; "Futurama", 2001-10; "Robbery Homicide Division", 2002; Red Water, 2003; Dracula 3000, 2004; "Cookin' with Coolio", writer, 2008; "Star-ving", 2009; "Gravity Falls", 2012; "Get Rich", 2013; "Sleepless with Coolio", 2013; "Alternative Press Music Award Show", 2014; "Black Jesus", 2014. Films: Dear God, 1996; Batman & Robin, 1997; An Alan Smithee Film: Burn Hollywood Burn, 1997; Tyrone, 1999; Midnight Mass, 1999; The Convent, 2000; Submerged, 2000; China Strike Force, 2000; Perfume, 2001; Gangland, 2001; Storm Watch, 2002; The Beat, 2003; Daredevil, 2003; Stealing Candy, 2003; Exposed, 2003; Tapped Out, 2003; A Wonderful Night in Split, 2004; Gang Warz, 2004; Pterodactyl, 2005; Grad Night, 2006; Three Days to Vegas, 2007; Chinaman's Chance: America's Other Slaves, 2008; Sides, 2008; Two Hundred Thousand Dirty, 2012; Inertia, 2012. **Honors/Awds:** Billboard Music Award, 1994, 1996; American Music Award, 1996; Nominated for Grammy Award, 1994-96; MTV Video Music Award, 1996, 1997; won ASCAP Award, 1997. **Special Achievements:** Co-hosted the MOBO Awards in the UK in 2005; nominated several times for MTV Music Awards and Grammy Awards. **Business Addr:** Rap Artist, Record Producer, Dragonrider Inc, PO Box 5147, Culver City, CA 90231-5147.

**IVEY, HORACE SPENCER**
Social worker, educator. **Personal:** Born Nov 13, 1931, DeLand, FL; married Barbara Edwards; children: Lawrence, Derek, Chandra, Allegra & Elliot. **Educ:** Univ Conn, MSW, 1956; Syracuse Univ, attended 1962; Smith Col Sch Soc Work. **Career:** State Univ Hosp, social worker, 1956-61, case worker, 1958-60, supvr, 1961-62; State Univ NY Upstate Med Ctr, assoc prof, dir, social worker serv. **Orgs:** Nat Asn Social Workers; Acad Cert Soc Workers; Med Social Work Sec; Healther Serv Comn Coun Aging; Am Hosp Asn Coun Vols; Syracuse Univ Rehab Coun. **Honors/Awds:** Social Worker of the Year. **Special Achievements:** Publications: "Factors in Selection of Patients for Home Chemo-Therapy", 1956; "Hospital Abortion Program Implication for Social Work Planning & Serv Delivery", 1971; numerous others. **Home Addr:** 8718 Radburn Dr, Baldwinsville, NY 13027-0715, **Home Phone:** (315)635-9077. **Business Addr:** Associate Professor, State University of New York Upstate Medical Center, 750 E Adams St, Syracuse, NY 13210, **Business Phone:** (315)464-5175.

**IVEY, PHIL**
Philanthropist, gambler. **Personal:** Born Feb 1, 1976, Riverside, CA; son of Phil Ivey Sr. and Pamela Ivey; married Luciaetta Ivey, Jan 1, 2002?, (divorced 2009). **Career:** World Series of Poker, three bracelets, 2002, nine career bracelets as of 2013; European Poker Tour, Second Place, September 2006; European Poker Masters, Seventh Place, 2006; World Poker Tour, Winner, February 2008 (prize of nearly $1.6 million), nine final-table appearances in career as of 2013; Aussie Millions, High-Roller Event, Winner, January 2012; World Series of Poker: Asia Pacific, Winner, April 2013. **Orgs:** Budding Ivey Foundation, Founder, 2008-. **Honors/Awds:** "Bluff" Magazine, Player of the Year, 2005; ESPN: Poker, Five Players to Watch, 2014. **Special Achievements:** At 37, he became the youngest poker player to win nine bracelets and in the shortest time span (13 years) at the World Series of Poker; tied a record at the 2002 World Series of Poker when he won three bracelets in a single series; as of 2013, ranked sixth on the all-time money list.

**IVY, JAMES E.**
Police officer. **Personal:** Born Sep 13, 1937, Memphis, TN; son of John and Mary Wells Coleman; married Sally Gibbs; children: Jacqueline, Pamela & Gwendolyn & Bridgette. **Educ:** Memphis State Univ; Univ N Fla; Nat Exec Inst, Nat FBI Acad. **Career:** Police officer (retired); Memphis Police Dept, Memphis, Tenn, police officer, 1963-73, lt, 1973-79, capt, 1979-81, inspector, 1981-83, chief inspector, 1983-84, dep chief, 1984-88, dir, 1988-95. **Orgs:** Int Asns Chiefs Police; Memphis Metrop Asn Chiefs Police; Nat Exec Inst Alumni Asn. **Honors/Awds:** Outstanding Achievement, Governor Ned McWherter, 1988; Dedicated Community Serv, Breath Life SD A Church, 1990; Outstanding Religious Serv, Gospel Temple Baptist Church, 1991; Dedicated Community Serv, Moolah Temple 54. **Special Achievements:** First Black Director to Memphis Police Dept, 1988. **Home Addr:** 6304 Briergate Dr, Bartlett, TN 38134.

**IZELL, BOOKER T.**
Newspaper executive, consultant, association executive. **Personal:** Born Feb 14, 1940, Auburn, AL; son of Davis Walker; married Birdie M Carpenter; children: Gwendolyn R. **Educ:** Wright State Univ, acct, 1970. **Career:** Dayton Newspaper, circulation mgr, 1965-78; Springfield Newspaper, circulation dir, 1978-84; Cox Enterprises Inc, mgr human resources develop, 1987-93; Atlanta Jour & Const, single copy mgr, 1984-87, vpres community affairs / workplace diversity, 1993; Coca-Cola, consult; Delta Airlines; consult; US Postal Serv; consult; Spelman Col, consult; Morehouse Col, consult; Clayton Col, consult; Red Cross, consult; United Way, consult; Ga Power, consult; Booker T Izell Assoc, pres, currently. **Orgs:** Nat Asn Advan Colored People, 1975; Nat Asn Black Journalists, 1986; bd mem, Atlanta Bus Forum, 1991; bd mem, Atlanta Art & Bus, 1992; Atlanta Chamber Com, 1992; Southern Circulation Mgr Asn, 1992-95; bd mem, Alliance Theatre Arts, 1993; Regional Leadership Found, 1993; Newspaper Asn Am, 1994; trustee, Clayton State Univ, 1996; Southern Co, Diversity Adv Coun. **Honors/Awds:** Glenn L Cox Award, Dayton Newspaper, 1975; Ohio President Award, 1983. **Home Addr:** 3019 Duke of Gloucester, Atlanta, GA 30344-5808, **Home Phone:** (404)768-5423. **Business Addr:** Member, Southern Co, 96 Annex, Atlanta, GA 30396.

**IZRAEL, JIMI**
Journalist. **Personal:** married Teshima walker. **Educ:** Cleveland State Univ, BA, commun; Spalding Univ, MFA. **Career:** E Cleveland, Ohio, writer & journalist; New Times, staff writer; What It Iz, writer; AOL BlackVoices.com, commenter; Africana.com, columnist, 1999-; Cuyahoga Community Col, artist residence, teacher film & media courses, 2009; Cleveland State Univ, teacher, 2010; Nat Pub Radio, contribr, "Day Day", commenter, "Tell Me More with Michel Martin", "The Barbershop", co-moderator; Cable News Network, commentary contribr; Cable-Satellite Pub Affairs Network, commentary contribr; Fox News, commentary contribr; Al Jazeera, commentary contribr; Brit Broadcasting Corp, commentary contribr; Current TV, commentary contribr; Am Broadcasting Co, "Nightline", commentary contribr. **Orgs:** Presidential fel, Case Western Res Univ; Ataff writer, United Church Christ, 1999-2003. **Home Phone:** (216)236-3975. **Business Addr:** Presidential Fellow, Case Western Reserve University, 1422 W 81st St, Cleveland, OH 44102, **Business Phone:** (216)255-2025.

# J

**J., RAY (WILLIE RAYMOND NORWOOD, JR.)**
Singer, executive, actor. **Personal:** Born Jan 17, 1981, McComb, MS; son of Willie Norwood and Sonja Bates-Norwood. **Career:** Singer, record producer, rapper & actor; Albums: Everything You Want, 1997; This Ain't a Game, 2001; Raydiation, 2005; All I Feel, 2008; Raydiation 2, 2010; Tv: "Television Ads", 1989-93; "The Sinbad Show", 1993-94; "The Enemy Within", 1994; "Aftershock: Earthquake in New York", 1999; "Moesha", 1999-2001; "Source Sound Lab", 2000; "The Proud Family", 2001; "Black Sash", 2003; "Christmas at Water's Edge", 2004; "One on One", 2005-06; "Love Triangle", 2006; "BET Countdown"; "All That", guest singer; "Wild N Out"; "For the Love of Ray J", 2009-10; "Brandy and Ray J: A Family Business", 2010-; "The Rickey Smiley Show", 2012-; "Bad Girls All-Star Battle.", hosting currently, "Ridiculousnes", 2013; "Love & Hip Hop: Hollywood", 2014-; Films: Once Upon a Time...When We Were Colored, 1996; Mars Attacks!, 1996; Steel, 1997; Superstar, 2007; Christmas at Water's Edge, 2003; Envy, 2008; A Day in the Life, 2009; Labels: Atlantic; Knockout/Deja 34; E1; Koch Entertainment; Elektra; KnockOut Entertainment, Los Angeles, Calif, prin, chief exec officer, currently. **Business Addr:** Chief Executive Officer, KnockOut Entertainment, 10960 Wilshire Blvd Suite 2150, Los Angeles, CA 90024-3807, **Business Phone:** (818)716-7047.

**JA RULE (JEFFREY ATKINS)**
Rap musician. **Personal:** Born Feb 29, 1976, Queens, NY; married Aisha Murray; children: Britney, Jeffrey & Jordan. **Career:** American rapper, singer & actor; Albums: Venni Vetti Vecci, 1999; Rule 3:36, 2000; Pain Is Love, 2001; The Last Temptation, 2002; Blood in my Eye, 2003; R.U.L.E, 2004; Caught Up, 2005; Exodus, 2005; The Mirror, 2009; The Renaissance Project, 2010; Welcome to Rule York, 2009 Films: Turn It Up, 2000; The Fast & the Furious, 2001; Half Dead, 2003; Pauly Shore Is Dead, 2003; "Inked", 2005; "South Beach", 2006; Films: Turn It Up, 2000; The Fast & the Furious, 2001; Half Dead; 2002; Scary Movie3, 2003; The Cookout, 2004; Shall We Dance, 2004; Back in the Day, 2005; Assault on Precinct 13, 2005; Furnace, 2006; Half Dead 2, 2007; Don't Fade Away, 2009; Wrong Side of Town, 2010; The Cookout 2, 2011; The INC Records, co-owner, 1999; Pain Is Love 2, 2012-. **Orgs:** Founder, LIFE Camp. **Business Addr:** Rap Musician, A & M Records, 825 Eigth Ave Fl 23, New York, NY 10019, **Business Phone:** (212)333-8000.

**JACKET, BARBARA JEAN**
Athletic director, educator. **Personal:** Born Dec 26, 1936, Port Arthur, TX; daughter of Raymond and Eva Mae Getwood-Pickney. **Educ:** Tuskegee Inst, BS, 1958; Prairie View A&M Univ, MS, 1968; Univ Houston, advan studies, 1976. **Career:** Head coach (retired); US World Championships, head coach, 1986; US Olympic, Women's Track Team, head coach, 1992; Van Buren High Sch, phys educ teacher; Lincoln High Sch, phys educ teacher; Prairie View A&M Univ, womens track & field, head coach, dir athletics, prof phys educ, currently. **Orgs:** Nat Col Athletic Asn; Nat Asn Intercollegiate Athletics; Southwestern Athletic Conf. **Honors/Awds:** Joe Robercher Award; Presidents TAC Award; twice received the Yellow Rose of Texas Award; Texas Womens Hall of Fame, 1993. **Special Achievements:** Second Black female to coach an Olympic team. **Home Addr:** PO Box 875, Prairie View, TX 77446, **Home Phone:** (409)857-3576. **Business Addr:** Professor of Physical Education, Prairie View A&M University, New Athletic Bldg T R Soloman O J Thomas St, Prairie View, TX 77446, **Business Phone:** (936)261-9100.

**JACKS, ULYSSES**
Counselor, lawyer. **Personal:** Born Jan 15, 1937, Coatesville, PA; son of Fred Douglas and Mable; married Esterlene A Gibson; children: Marcus U & Eric D. **Educ:** Va Union Univ, BS, 1959; La Salle Col, acct, 1967; Howard Univ Law Sch, JD, 1970. **Career:** Philadelphia Pub Schs, teacher, 1964-67; Equal Employ Opportunity Comn, decision writer, 1969-70; Howard Law Sch, admin asst univ coun; Csaplar & Bok, assoc, 1970-77; Mass Hwy Dept, dep chief coun, 1977-. **Orgs:** Teaching fel Howard Univ Law Sch, 1969-70; Mass Black Lawyers; Mass Bar Asn, 1971-; Am Bar Asn; dir, Opportunities Indust Ctrs Greater Boston, 1982-88; dir, Codman Sq Housing Corp, 1988-90; dir, Commonwealth Coop Bank, 1991-. **Special Achievements:** Development Editor for Howard University Law Journal, 1968-69. **Home Addr:** 167 Wilmington Ave, Dorchester, MA 02124. **Business Addr:** Deputy Chief Counsel, Massachusetts Highway Department, Rm 3542 10 Pk Plz, Boston, MA 02116, **Business Phone:** (617)973-7810.

**JACKSON, DR. ADA JEAN WORK**
President (organization), educator. **Personal:** Born Nashville, TN; daughter of Lucuis Work Jr and Josephine Wilson; children: Andrea Eva Fitzpatrick Collins. **Educ:** Tenn State Univ, BS, 1959, ME, 1965; George Peabody Col Teachers, EdS, guid & couns, 1975; Vanderbilt Univ, PhD, educ admin, 1981. **Career:** Educator (retired), President; Metro Pub Sch, reading specialist, 1964-76, careers spec, 1976-77, guid counsr, 1977-79, asst prin, 1979-83, coordr stud referrals, 1983-85, admin, Comprehensive High Sch, 1985-95, US Dept Educ, reviewer, 1989-200; United Methodist Church, Black Col Fund, asst gen secy, 1995-97, prin; J'S Serv Concept, owner. **Orgs:** Alpha Delta Omega; Alpha Kappa Alpha; 1957-; Miss Nat Educ Asn; TEA; Nat Educ Asn, 1959-; Phi Delta Kappa 1972-; Nat Asn Sec Sch Prin, 1978-; nat pres, Nat Pan-Hellenic Coun, 1985-89; interim asst gen secy, United Methodist Church Black Col Fund, 1995, dir, 1996; Coalition 100 Black Prof Women; Urban League; Urban League Guild; life mem, Nat Asn Advan Colored People; Nashville Dem Women Soc; Top Ladies Distinction; pres, Nashville Chap, 1996-00; Leadership Brentwood, 1999-2000; scholar bd, Am Baptist Col; nat pres, Tenn State Univ Alumni Asn, currently. **Home Addr:** 6616 Valley Dr, Brentwood, TN 37027-5408, **Home Phone:** (615)371-1393. **Business Addr:** National President, Tennessee State University, 3500 John A Merritt Blvd, Nashville, TN 37209, **Business Phone:** (615)963-5000.

**JACKSON, AGNES MORELAND**
Educator. **Personal:** Born Dec 2, 1930, Pine Bluff, AR; daughter of Nathaniel Edmund Moreland and Rosa Lorenda Mae; married Harold Andrew Jr; children: Barbara R Arnwine & Lucretia D Peebles. **Educ:** Univ Redlands, BA, eng, 1952; Univ Wash, MA, eng lit, 1953; Columbia Univ, PhD, philos, 1960. **Career:** Spelman Col, instr, 1953-55; Boston Univ, Col Basic Studies, Lib Arts, instr, asst prof, 1959-63; Calif State Univ, Los Angeles, from asst prof to assoc prof, 1963-69; Claremont Sch Theol, Univ Redlands, vis fac, 1969-; world lit & black studies Claremont Calif Col, eng prof, 1963-69; Pitzer Col, Intercollegiate Dept Black Studies, founder, chair, eng prof, 1969, Peter S & Gloria Gold prof, 1992-97, prof emer, 1997-; Claremont McKenna Col, Sojourner Truth Lectr, 2000-01. **Orgs:** Soc Values Higher Educ Cent Comt, 1971-74; Danforth Asn Prog, 1971-; bd trustee, pres, Pomona Unified Sch Dist, 1981-89; nominating comt bd dir, Girl Scouts Am, 1980-84, 1986-88; Phi Beta Kappa, Univ Redlands, 1982-; Pomona Sch Bd; bd dir, Mod Lang Asn, 1993-95; Am Asn Univ Professors; Am Asn Univ Women. **Home Addr:** 1234 Douglass Dr, Pomona, CA 91768. **Business Addr:** Professor Emerita, Pitzer College, 1050 N Mills Ave, Claremont, CA 91711, **Business Phone:** (909)621-8129.

**JACKSON, ALFRED THOMAS**
Athletic coach, executive, executive director. **Personal:** Born May 30, 1937, Issue, MD; married Clarice Cecelia Brooks; children: Michael, Karen & Damien. **Educ:** Fisk Univ, BS, 1964. **Career:** Grand Union Co, Elmwood Pk, NJ, 1965-69, mgr training & develop, 1974-75, admin Training & develop, 1975; NBC NY, admin training & devel, 1976, mgr & org Develop, 1976, dir & org Develop, 1978, dir training, 1979-80, employee devel & coun, 1980, emp coun & develop & AA, dir, 1986-91; Nat Broadcasting Corp, Develop & Affirmative Action, diversity & employee coun, dir, 1991-92; Diversity & Strategic Planning Scholastic Inc, dir, 1992-96; ATJ Enterprises, LLC, founder & pres, diversity consult, 1996-. **Orgs:** Pres, Better Human Rels Coun, Bloomfield, NJ, 1973-78; chmn comt, Adv Bd Bloomfield Col, 1973-77; bd trustee, Bloomfield Col NJ, 1977-78; Am Red Cross Metro NJ. **Honors/Awds:** Black Achievers Award, Harlem Ymca NY, 1971. **Home Addr:** 214 Elmwynd Dr, Orange, NJ 07050, **Home Phone:** (973)678-2613. **Business Addr:** President, Founder, ATJ Enterprises LLC, PO Box 826, South Orange, NJ 07051, **Business Phone:** (973)678-9888.

### JACKSON, ALPHONSO ROY
Government official. **Personal:** Born Sep 9, 1945, Marshall, TX; son of Arthur and Henrietta; married Marcia A Clark; children: Annette & Lesley. **Educ:** Turman State Univ, BA, polit sci, 1968, MA, educ admin, 1969; Wash Univ Sch Law, JD, 1973. **Career:** Mo State Off, dir pub safety, 1977-81, dir st louis housing authority, 1981-83; City St Louis, dir pub safety, 1977; St Louis Housing Authority, exec dir; Laventhol & Horwath, St Louis, Mo, dir consult serv; Univ Mo, spec asst chancellor & asst prof; Dept Pub & Assisted Housing, WA, DC, dir; Tex State Off, Dallas Housing Authority, pres & chief exec officer, 1989-96; Am Elec Power-Tex, Austin, Tex, pres, 1996-2001; US Housing & Urban Develop Dept, dir pub & assisted housing, 1987-89, dep secy & chief operating officer, 2001-04, secy, 2004-08; Hampton Univ, Hampton, Va, prof & dir, 2008-12; JPMorgan Chase, New York, NY, vice-chmn retail financial serv, 2012-. **Orgs:** Fel Apsen Inst, 1995; Chairperson, DC Redevelop Land Agency Bd; chmn, Gen Serv Comn, State Tex; Nat Comn Am's Urban Families; Nat Comn Severely Distressed Pub Housing; Kappa Alpha Psi Fraternity; bd mem, JP Morgan Chase; Boy Scouts Am; bd dir, US Chamber Com. **Special Achievements:** First African American to lead the formerly troubled agency. **Business Addr:** Vice Chairman, JPMorgan Chase, 270 Pk Ave, New York, NY 10017, **Business Phone:** (212)270-6000.

### JACKSON, ALTERMAN
Educator, administrator, association executive. **Personal:** Born Feb 28, 1948, Bronx, NY. **Educ:** Lincoln Univ, BA, 1970; Millersville State Col, ME, 1973. **Career:** City Lancaster, personnel asst, 1970-71; Sch Dist Lancaster, dir, 1971-72; Millersville Univ, asst dir & counr, 1972-76; Lancaster Rec Comn, supvr, 1974-76; Hahnemann Univ Sch Med, dir & admis, 1976; Harrisburg Area Community Col, vpres stud affairs & enrollment mgt, dir admis & mkt, 2004. **Orgs:** Pres, 307-Acad Fel 1968-69; Lancaster City Co Human Rel Comn, 1971; comn mem, King-Clemente Memorial Scholar Fund Trinity Luth Church, 1972-77; regist rep, Pa State Ed Asn, 1972-77; Pa Black Conf Higher Educ, 1973-76; NE Med Schs, 1976-77; bd dir, Nat Asn Med Minority Educ, 1976-77; registrep, Asn Am Med Col, 1977; Omega Psi Phi. **Honors/Awds:** Outstanding Young Men of America, 1976. **Home Addr:** 7933 Woolston Ave, Philadelphia, PA 19150.

### JACKSON, DR. ALVIN B., JR.
Government official. **Personal:** Born Mar 21, 1961, Miami, FL; son of Gussye M Bartley; married Dorothea U; children: Alvin Bernard III, Carla, Desarae, Doreen, Kavell, Nicola, Sharonette & Tiffini. **Educ:** Univ Md, College Park, MD, BA, govt & polit, 1982; Thomas Brown Bible Col, DMin, philos ministry, MA, ministry & leadership, 2010. **Career:** Urban Resources Consul, Wash DC, admin aide, 1979-81; Birch & Davis Asn, Silver Spring MD, govt conf coordr, 1982-83; Ft Lauderdale Col, Miami, fla, dir admin, 1984; Real Estate Data Inc, Miami FL, county coordr, 1985-88; Opa-Locka Com Develop Corp, pastor, Church Kingdom God, 1984-97; Opa-Locka FL, com revitalization specialist, 1988; City Eatonville, City Adminr, 1988-90; City Eustis, dir human servs, leisure serv dir, 1990-93; Econ Develop Comn Mid-Fla, Lake County Govt, econ develop dir, 1993-96, dep county mgr, 1996-2001; S Fla Water Mgt Dist, dep exec dir, govt & pub affairs, 2001-05; Nova Consult Engineering Inc, outreach mgr, 2005-07; Quantum Leadership Group Inc, prin officer, 2007-11; City Hallandale Beach, exec dir, 2011-13; Jackson-Vaughans Group Inc, vpres, 2013-14; Suwannee County Econ Develop Off, econ develop dir, 2014-. **Orgs:** Am Soc Pub Admin, 1985; secy, King Clubs Greater Miami, 1987-88; chmn, Day Care Comt, 1987-88, area pres, Dade County PTA/PTSA; chair, Fla State Comt African Am Hist, 1988; Fla League Cities Black Elected, 1988; Preserve Eatonville Community, 1988-; Zora Neale Hurston Ad Hoc, 1988-90; state chmn, Progress; coun mem, Fla State Hist Preserv Coun, 1988-94; bd dir, Ctr Drug Free Living, 1989-91; bd dir, Lake Sumter Ment Health & Hosp, 1990-93; vpres, Golden Triangle Kiwanis; Lake County Urban Network; HRS Health & Human Serv Local Bd; Fla Dept Educ Tech Comn Mkg Educ; bd dir, Fla Waterman Hosp Found, 1994-96; bd regents, Leadership Lake, 1994. **Special Achievements:** Author of It Is Another Great Day: An Inspiring Guide to Effective Leadership, 2009. **Home Addr:** PO Box 124, Eustis, FL 32727-0124, **Home Phone:** (352)357-6668. **Business Addr:** Economic Development Director, Suwannee County Economic Development Office, 13302 80th Terr, Live Oak, FL 32060, **Business Phone:** (386)364-1700.

### JACKSON, ANDREA R.
Archivist, curator. **Educ:** Spelman Univ, BA, hist; NY Univ, MA, U.S. hist. **Career:** Fisk Univ, proj archivist; Atlanta Univ Ctr, Robert Woodruff Libr, cur, dir Arch Res Ctr. **Orgs:** Curatorial team mem, Ctr Civil & Human Rights; archivist, Soc Ga Archivists, 2012. **Special Achievements:** "Archives and Archivists of Color Roundtable" newsletter, Editor. **Business Addr:** Director, Atlanta University Center, 111 James P Brawley Dr SW, Atlanta, GA 30314, **Business Phone:** (404)978-2115.

### JACKSON, DR. ANDREW
Educator, sociologist. **Personal:** Born Feb 2, 1945, Montgomery, AL; married Hazel Ogilvie; children: Yasmine Nefertiti. **Educ:** Yale Univ, study prog, 1966; Alabama State Univ, BA, 1967; Univ Nairobi Kenya, Ed, 1970; Univ Calif, Santa Barbara, MA Ed, psych, 1970, MA, 1972, PhD, soc, 1974. **Career:** Tenn St Univ, prof soc, 1973-, Dept Africana Studies, head, prof; Desegregation Inst Emergency Sch Aid Act, consult, 1977; Fisk Univ, adj prof, 1978-; Nat Assoc Equal Oppty Higher Ed, consult, 1981. **Orgs:** HBC fac fel US Dept Labor, 1980; pres, Assoc Social & Behav Scientists Inc, 1983-84; Ed Bd Jour Soc & Behav Sci, 1984-; chairperson, bd dir, Sank a Dance Theatre, 1984-; Am Soc Assoc; Am Acad Polit & Soc Sci; Southern Soc Assoc; Am Assoc Univ Prof; Kappa Alpha Psi; Islamic Ctr Inc; life mem, Asn Social & Behav Scientists Inc. **Honors/Awds:** Delegate Crisis Black Family Summit, NAACP, 1984; Article "Illuminating the Path to Community Self-Reliance" Journal of Soc & Behavioral Sci, 1984; Textbook Sci of Soc, 1985; article "Apart he id, the Great Debate and Martin Luther King Jr" The AME Church Review, 1985. **Home Addr:** 209 Hodge Cir, Nashville, TN 37218, **Home Phone:** (615)942-7791. **Business Addr:** Professor, Tennessee State University, 3500 John A Merritt Blvd, Nashville, TN 37203, **Business Phone:** (615)963-5000.

### JACKSON, ANDREW PRESTON (SEKOU MOLEFI BAAKO)
Library administrator. **Personal:** Born Jan 28, 1947, Brooklyn, NY; son of Walter L Sr and Bessie Lindsay. **Educ:** City Univ NY, York Col, Jamaica, NY, BS, bus admin, 1990, MLS, libr sci; Queens Col, City Univ NY, Flushing, NY, MLS, 1996; Univ State New York Educ, pub librarians prof cert, 1996. **Career:** NY Agency Child Develop, coordr personnel serv, 1971-76; Robinson Chevrolet, Novato, Calif, customer rels mgr, 1976-78; Langston Hughes Community Libr & Cult Ctr, Corona, NY, exec dir, 1980-; York Col, City Univ NY, adj prof, 2001-; Roosevelt Pub Libr, Trng, Develop & Opers, consult, 2005-. **Orgs:** Bd mem, Elmhurst Hosp Ctr, 1983-97; life mem, Nat Asn Adavn Colored People; NY Black Librarians Caucus; York Col Alumni, Inc; adv coun, York Col; exec bd, Am Lib Asn; community adv bd, Louis Armstrong House & Arch, 1998-; bd dir, Dollars Scholars, Corona-E Elmhurst chap, 1998-; bd educ, People African Ancestry, 1999-; Poet Laureate Queens Selection Comt, 1999-; NY State Freedom Trial Community, 1999-2002; NY Libr Asn; bd trustee, Renaissance Charter Sch, 2000-; bd mem, Queens Col; Queens Bor Pres's Community Coun, 2002; pres, Black Caucus Am Libr Asn, 2004-06; pres, Black Caucus Am Libr Asn. **Honors/Awds:** Queens Library Lamplighter Award, 1999; BCALA Library Advocacy Award, 1999; BCALA Professional Achievement Award, 2007; Excellence in Librarianship Award, New York State Library Association, 2011. **Special Achievements:** Contributing Author-Foreword, African American Almanac, 9th and 10th Editions, 2003, 2008; "If You Want to Know the Secrets of the World, Read a Book!", Turn The Page and You Don't Stop Sharing Successful Chapters in Our Lives With Youth, 2006; "In the Tradition: The Legacy of Culture Messengers From Langston Hughes to Tupac Shakur", 2006. **Home Addr:** 9424 30th Ave, East Elmhurst, NY 11369-1723, **Home Phone:** (718)397-9261. **Business Addr:** Executive Director, Queens Library, 100 01 Northern Blvd, Corona, NY 11368, **Business Phone:** (718)651-1100.

### JACKSON, ANGELA
Poet, playwright, writer. **Personal:** Born Jul 25, 1951, Greenville, MS; daughter of George Sr and Angeline Robinson. **Educ:** Northwestern Univ, BA, eng & am lit, 1977; Univ Chicago, MA, humanities, 1995. **Career:** Ill Arts Coun, poets-in-the-Sch prog, 1974-76, 1979-83; Stephens Col, writer residence, 1983-86; Columbia Col, 1986-88, writer residence, 1988-92; Framingham State Col, writer residence, 1994; Howard Univ, lectr, 1995-97; Sch Art Inst, fac, creative writing prog, 1998; freelance writer & ed, 1998-; Poems: Voodoo Love Magic, 1974; he Greenville Club, 1977; Solo in the Boxcar Third Floor E. Oba House, 1985; The Man with the White Liver, 1987; Dark Legs and Silk Kisses: The Beatitudes of the Spinners, 1993; All These Roads Be Luminous, 1997.Plays: Witness, 1970; Shango Diaspora, An African American Myth of Womanhood and Love, 1980; When the Wind Blows, 1984; Lightfoot: The Crystal Stair; Novels: Treemont Stone; Lightfoot. **Orgs:** OBAC Writers Workshop, 1970-90; Ebony Talent Found Aux, 1977; Black Am Cult; First World, 1977-78; Ill Arts Coun Lit Panel, 1979-81, 1992; fel, Coord Coun Lit Mag, 1981-85, secy, 1983, pres, 1984, treas, 1985; ETA Playwright Discovery Iniative, 1991-98. **Honors/Awds:** Conrad Kent Rivers Memorial Award, 1973; Academy of American Poets Award, Northwestern University, 1974; NEA Creative Writing Fellowship, 1980; Hoyt W. Fuller Award, 1984; America Book Award, 1985; ETA Gala Award, 1989; Book of the Year Award, 1994; Carl Sandburg Award, Chicago Pub Libr, 1994; Illinois Authors Literary Heritage Award, 1996; The Carl Sandburg Award; Chicago Sun-Times Friends of Literature Book of the Year Award; Daniel Curley Award, IAC Arts Coun, 1997; Creative Writing Fellowship, Ill Arts Coun, 2000; Shelley Memorial Award, Poetry Society of America, 2002. **Special Achievements:** Author, Dark Legs & Silk Kisses: The Beatitudes of the Spinners, 1992; "Shango Diaspora," 1980; "Comfort Stew," 1997; And All These Roads Be Luminous: Poems Selected & New, 1998. **Home Addr:** 5527 S Wentworth Ave, Chicago, IL 60621, **Home Phone:** (773)324-8480.

### JACKSON, DR. ANNA MAE
Educator. **Personal:** Born Apr 10, 1934, Wetumpka, AL; daughter of Moses E and Alice M; married Lawrence W; children: Stevan & Sean. **Educ:** Bowling Green State Univ, BA, 1959; Univ Denver, MA, 1960; Colo State Univ, PhD, 1967. **Career:** State Home & Training Sch, Lapeer, Mich, staff psych, 1960-61; State Home & Training Sch, Wheat ridge, Colo, chief psych, 1962-68; Univ Colo Health Sci Ctr, assoc prof psych, assoc prof, assoc dean. **Orgs:** Vis lectr, Afro-Am Studies Dept, 1971-73; consult, US Homes Inc, 1975-78; adv bd, Sch Comn & Human Serv; Nat Advan Asn Colored People Pk Hill Br, 1982-83; pres, Assoc Black Psych, Denver Rocky Mountain Chap, 1993-94; Denver Urban League. **Honors/Awds:** Woman of Achievement, Denver Alumnae Chap Delta Sigma Theta Sor, 1976; Woman of the Year, Regina's Soc and Civic Club, 1977; Founders Award, Asn Black Psychologists, 1987; Distinguished Chapter Service Award, Denver-Rocky Mountain Chapter Asn Black Psychologists, 1987; Distinguished Psychologist, Assoc Black Psychologists. **Home Addr:** 6533 Westfall Dr, Nashville, TN 37221-6544, **Home Phone:** (615)646-6192.

### JACKSON, ARTHUR D., JR.
Judge, legal consultant. **Personal:** Born Oct 31, 1942; married Suellen Kay Shea; children: Christopher Daniel, Kyle Joseph & Courtney Kathleen. **Educ:** Ohio Northern Univ, BS & BMusEd, 1964, JD, 1968. **Career:** City Dayton Dept Law, negotiator & asst city atty, 1968-70; Jackson & Austin, atty law, 1969-71; City Dayton, asst city prosecutor, 1970-71; Dept Justice S Dist Oh, asst US atty, 1971-74; Dayton/Mont Co Crim Justice Ctr, legal spec/instr, 1974-75; Skilken & Jackson, atty, 1975-77; Dayton Munic Ct, judge; Costco Wholesale, vpres gen admin, currently. **Orgs:** Choir dir, Epworth Meth Church, 1964-67; dep dir, Pub Defender Asn, 1975-76; instr, Sinclair Comn Col, 1975-; hearing officer, Ohio Civil Rights Comn, 1975-76; exec comn, Mont Co Emergency Serv Coun; Dayton Performing Arts Fund Bd; pres, Dayton Ballet Co Bd; adj prof law, Univ Dayton Col Law, 1977-; bd dir, Thurgood Marshall Scholar Fund; Chmn, Costco's Charitable Contrib Comt; bd dir, Am Red Cross; bd dir, Schs Wash State; FBI Citizens Acad. **Honors/Awds:** Outstanding Actor-Musical Dayton Co, 1980; State Certified EMT Paramedic, 1981 & 1984. **Home Addr:** 2812 161st Ave SE, Bellevue, WA 98008-5611, **Home Phone:** (425)746-9582. **Business Addr:** Vice President of General Administration, Costco Wholesale, 999 Lake Dr, Issaquah, WA 98027-5367.

### JACKSON, ARTHUR HOWARD
Executive. **Personal:** Born Mar 27, 1956, Bronx, NY; son of Arthur H and Minnie Belle McChaney. **Educ:** Am Col, BA, MA, bus & technol, PhD, bus & ethics; Joint Ctr Polit Studies, cert govt mgt; Prince George Washington Univ, paralegal studies; John Hopkins Univ, community planning. **Career:** DC Govt, contracting engr, 1990-99; AHJ Group, pres & chief exec officer, 2000-10; Arthur Jackson Global AHJ Group, chief exec officer, 2000-09; Pesident Barack Obama Inaugural Transition Comt, team leader Security & Logistics Planning, 2008-09; Certify Your Bus.com, dem cand State Deleg Advocating tax Cuts Small Biz, 2010-. **Orgs:** Mayor's Task Force Govt Finance, 1994-98; adv Mayor Wash DC, MB Focus Group, 1994-98; nat vpres, Fighting 54th Inc, 1994-; precinct coordr, Unify Beautify Campaign, 1995; bd dir, Stuard Mc Guire Corp, 1998-99; bd consumer adv, Giant Foods Stores, 1998-2000; adv bus develop, Southwest Hill Asn, 1999-; bus consult, Fundraising Network Inc, 1999-; planning comt, Mayor's Neighborhood Action Proj, 1999-2000; aids benefit planning Comt, Race Cure, 2000. **Home Addr:** 4660 Martin L King Jr Ave SW B-607, Washington, DC 20032, **Home Phone:** (202)563-6769. **Business Addr:** President, Chief Executive Officer, The AHJ Group, 1101 Pa Ave NW, Washington, DC 20004, **Business Phone:** (202)271-5522.

### JACKSON, DR. ARTHUR JAMES
Educator. **Personal:** Born Jan 11, 1943, Union Springs, AL; married Beverly Fennoy; children: Monica D. **Educ:** Wayne State Univ, BS, psychol, 1972, MS, anat, 1976, PhD, anat, 1979, postdoctorate, anat. **Career:** Wayne St Univ, grad asst, 1974-76, grad asst, 1976-79; Tenn State Univ, Dept Phys Sci, adj fac, currently; Meharry Med Col, teaching asst, Dept Biomed Sci, Dept Prof Educ, assoc prof anat & vice chair, currently. **Orgs:** Treas, Alpha Omega Alpha Hon Med Socs; Black Med Asn; advisor, Am Med Students Asn. **Home Addr:** 205 Augusta Nat Ct, Franklin, TN 37069, **Home Phone:** (615)646-8881. **Business Addr:** Associate Professor of Anatomy, Vice Chair, Meharry Medical College, WBS B116 1005 Dr DB Todd Blvd, Nashville, TN 37208, **Business Phone:** (615)327-6712.

### JACKSON, DR. ARTHUR ROSZELL
School administrator. **Personal:** Born Aug 16, 1949, Ft. Dix, NJ; son of Arthur and Elouise Fussell; married Celeste Budd; children: Kyle Arthur & Tamara Sheree. **Educ:** State Univ NY, BA, polit sci, 1971, MA, sociol, 1977; Univ Mass, Amherst, MA, EdD, higher educ admin, 1988. **Career:** Educ Opportunity Prog, State Univ NY, acad counr, 1971-72; State Univ NY Binghamton, asst dir stud financial aide, 1972-77; Univ Mass, assoc dir, Financial Aid Serv, dir, 1977-82; Financial Aid Serv Univ Mass Amherst, dir, 1982-90; Norfolk State Univ, assoc prof, vpres stud affairs, 1997-2000; Univ NC, Charlotte, vice chancellor stud affairs, 2007-, adj assoc prof educ, currently; Eastern Conn State Univ, assoc dean stud affairs; W fied State Col, vpres stud affairs. **Orgs:** Vice chmn New Eng Col Bd, 1984-86; liaison/consult, Nat Consortium Educ Access, 1985-87; vpres, Eastern Asn Stud Financial Aid Admins, 1986; pole march, pres, Hartford Alumni Chap Kappa Alpha Psi, 1986-87; Nat Conf Black Retention, 1986, Col Bd Nat Forum, 1986; bd dir, Mass Higher Educ Assistance Corp, 1988-; pres, Eastern Asn Stud Financial Aid Admin, 1989; Conn state dir, Nat Asn Stud Personnel Admin, 1993-95; chmn, Educ Resource Inst, 1994-96; Sigma Pi Phi Fraternity, 1994; Minority Undergrad Fels Prog, NASPa, 1997-2000; adv Bd, Norfolk Acad, 1998-2000; adv bd, White Oak Sch, 2000; Rotary Club Int; dir, Nat Asn Stud Personnel Adminr; Golden Key Hon Soc; Kappa Alpha Psi Fraternity. **Honors/Awds:** Network on Equity & Excellence Award, Nat Asn Stud Personnel Admin, 1992; Speaker Nat Asn Student Personnel Adminrs, 1995; Golden Key Honor Soc, 1997; Found Excellence, Asn Col & Univ Housing Org, 1999; Distinguished Accomplishment Award, Nat Asn Stud Personnel Adminr, Pillar of the Profession. **Special Achievements:** President Clinton Post Secondary Education Transition Task Force, 1992-93. **Home Addr:** 161 Tallyho Dr, Springfield, MA 01118. **Business Addr:** Vice Chancellor of Student Affairs, The University of North Carolina at Charlotte, 9201 Univ City Blvd, Charlotte, NC 28223-0001, **Business Phone:** (704)687-0350.

### JACKSON, DR. AUBREY NATHANIEL
Dentist. **Personal:** Born Feb 11, 1926, Lynchburg, VA; married Laura Thompson; children: Aubrey, Kelly & Carl. **Educ:** Bluefield State Col, BS, 1949; Howard Univ, attended 1950; Meharry Med Col, DDS, 1954. **Career:** Keystone, pvt pract dentist, 1961-; Dent Clin, Salem, pvt pract, currently. **Orgs:** NDA; Am Dent Asn; past pres, WVa Med Soc; WVa State Dent Soc; pres, Mercer-Mcdowell Dent Soc; Mcdowell Co Health Coun; Chas Payne Dent Study Club; Bluefield Study Club; chmn exec comn, Nat Advan Asn Colored People; polit coun, Coun Southern Mountains; treas, Alpha Zeta Lambda Chap Alpha Phi Alpha; treas, Upsilon Boule Sigma Pi Phi. **Business Addr:** Dentist, 107 Main St, Keystone, WV 24852-0671, **Business Phone:** (304)862-3338.

### JACKSON, AUDREY NABORS
Executive. **Personal:** Born Jul 10, 1926, New Orleans, LA; daughter of Raymond Nabors Sr and Beluah Carney; married Freddie Sr; children: Claudia J Fisher, Beverly J Franklin, Freddie Jr (deceased), Sharyll Muri Curley-Etuk, Antria Curley Wilson & Zefron Curley. **Educ:** Southern Univ, Lab Sch, Baton Rouge, LA; Southern Univ & A&M Col, Baton Rouge, LA, BA, 1951, MEd, 1966; Chicago Teachers Col, attended 1959. **Career:** Librarian (retired); JS Dawson High Sch, librn, 1951-54; Southdown HS, librn, 1954-55; Chaneyville High Sch Zachary La, librn, 1955-81; La Legis Bur, secy, 1979 & 1980; Baton Rouge Sch, 1981; Clerk Ct's Off, abstractor, 1982; La Senate Docket, legis session, 1982, 1983 & 1984; census taker, 1990; Nabors Bid Tabulation Serv, pres/owner. **Orgs:** Pres, lib dept, La Asn Educr, 1967-69, 1977-78; treas, 1973, vpres, 1973-74, Rural Prog Adv Bd; Usher, Greater PhiLa delphia Baptist Church; golden life mem, treas, DST Sorority Inc, 1971-75 & 1979; exec bd LLA, sch librn, 1977-79; secy, Human Resource & Develop CRP, 1978-80; YWCA Auth Comm; life mem, Southern Univ Alumni Fed; charter mem, Women Mainstream; treas, Friends Int, 1982-; Mayor Press Comn Needs Women, 1982-85; fin chair, La Womens Pol Caucus, 1984-85, treas, 1985; 1st vice chair, Baton Rouge Womens Pol Caucus, 1984-85, treas, 1985-; La Retired Teachers Asn; La Dem Fin Coun; Nat Retired Teachers Asn; Nat Educ Asn; treas, Baton Rouge Women's Polit, 1986-; treas, La Women Polit,

1986-; bd dir, Doug Williams Found, 1988; life mem, Southern Univ Alumni Fed; Am Asn Retired Persons; life mem, Am Lib Asn; adv comt, Am Asn Sch Librarians; Centroplex, 1991-; vol, Baton Rouge City Ct; La Dem State Cent Comt, Dist 64, elect unopposed, 1992-96, 1997-2002; secy, treas, Sixth Cong Dist La, 1993-; Woman Greater Baton Rouge Coun, 1998-2004; vpres, 1999-2000, pres-elect, 2000-01, pres, 2001-02, treas, 2003-, Kiwanis; Angela Proctor, Cur Spec Collections; City-Parish Planning & Zoning Comn, 2001-04; vol, Florissant Area Athletic Asn; chair, City Planning & Zoning Comn, 2003-04; comnr & chmn, Recreation & Pk Comn Parish E Baton Rouge, 2005-. **Home Addr:** 24004 Reames Rd, Zachary, LA 70791-6606, **Home Phone:** (225)654-5491.

### JACKSON, HON. AVA NICOLA

Lawyer. **Personal:** Born Nov 10, 1957, Preston, MS; daughter of Enos and Alma; married Charles G Woodall, Nov 13, 1981; children: Raphael Kenzell Woodall & Amanda Nicola Woodall. **Educ:** Univ Miss, BS, social work & pub admin, 1979, Sch Law, JD, 1981. **Career:** Morris & Jackson, assoc atty, 1981-82; N Miss Rural Legal Serv, managing atty, 1983-90, exec dir, 1990-99, exec asst, bd dir, currently. **Orgs:** Magnolia Bar Asn, 1981-; Miss Bar Asn, 1981-; pres, Zeta Phi Beta Sorority, 1985-. **Honors/Awds:** Service Award, NCP, Kemper County Br, 1986; Leadership Award, NMRLS, 1991; Legal Services Lawyer of the Year, Miss Bar Asn, 1992; Zeta of the Year, Zeta Phi Beta, 1993. **Special Achievements:** First female executive director of the North Mississippi Rural Legal Services. **Home Addr:** 807 Hwy 6 W, PO Box 545A, Oxford, MS 38655, **Home Phone:** (662)234-3351. **Business Addr:** Board of Director, North Mississippi Rural Legal Service, 5 County Rd 1014, Oxford, MS 38655, **Business Phone:** (662)234-2918.

### JACKSON, DR. BENITA MARIE (BENITA MARIE JACKSON-SMOOT)

Physician. **Personal:** Born Aug 14, 1956, Englewood, NJ; daughter of Benjamin and Gloria. **Educ:** Mt Holyoke Col, BA, 1978; Howard Univ, Col Med, MD, 1982; Emory Univ, MPH, 1989. **Career:** Prev med residency prog, Ctrs Dis Control, dir; Dc Gen Hosp, resident internal med, 1982-83; George Wash Univ, internship, 1983-84; Howard Univ Hosp, resident internal med, epidemic intelligence officer & prev, 1984-86; Group Health Asn, HMO staff, 1986-87; Geo Wash Univ Hosp, resident anat & clin path; Morehouse Sch Med, Internal Med, 1987-89; Neighborhood Health Ctr/Pub Health Clin, ambulatory care, 1990-92; USpHs Comn Corp Assignee, epidemic intelligence officer, 1990-92; Group Health Prev Pub Health, Emergency Med, staff physician; Ohio State Univ, Col Pub Health, dir & asst prof, 1995-2005, asst prof, 1997-2005, asoc dean, 2000-02; Q2Administrators, assoc med dir, 2005-07; Am Health Holding, med dir, 2007-12, assoc med dir, 2009-11; Bur Disability Determination, med consult, 2009-11; BJSSAAB LLC, physician, 2012-; Quantum Health, med dir, 2013-14; Aetna, med dir, 2014-. **Orgs:** Nat Med Asn; Am Pub Health Asn; Natural Med Asn; Am CLG Prev Med; Am Pub Health Asn; Asn Teachers Prev Med. **Honors/Awds:** Nat Achievement Scholarship Finalist for Outstanding Negro Students, 1974. **Business Addr:** Medical Director, Aetna, 151 Farmington Ave, Hartford, CT 06156, **Business Phone:** (860)273-6382.

### JACKSON, BEVERLY ANNE

Executive, television director, television producer. **Personal:** Born Nov 29, 1947, Philadelphia, PA; daughter of Frank E Sr and Alice M McConico; children: Michelle Marie. **Educ:** Pa State Univ, BA, speech, broadcasting, commun, 1969; Chas Morris Price Sch Advert & Jour, advert cert, 1972. **Career:** Sch Dist Philadelphia, substitute teacher, 1969-70; US Cencus Bur, ade clerk, 1970-71; RCA Serv CPN, spec proj inr, 1971-72; KATZ-TV Tv, advert sales, sales asst, 1972; KYW-TV, Westinghouse Broadcasting CPN, prod asst, 1972-74, assoc producer, 1974-76, dir, 1976-91; Nationally Syndicated Joan Rivers Show, tv broadcast dir, 1991-93; "Gossip, Gossip, Gossip with Joan Rivers", dir, 1992-; US Dept Com, Bur Census 2000, media specialist, 1999-2000; Asn Retarded Citizens, Gloucester County, interim dir pub affairs, 2000; United Way Southeastern Pa, media & pub rels mgr, 2001-03; Community Col Philadelphia, commun consult, 2005; United Way Int, commun consult, 2005; Comcast SportsNet, freelance dir, 2003-06; VerVe Graphix video, pres, owner, currently; "Biz Whiz", media & pub rels consult, currently. **Orgs:** DRRs Guild Am; AMR Women Radio & TV; DST; vol, Big Sister, Big Sisters Philadelphia, 1980; Intl TV Asn; Nat Acad TV Arts & Sci; SOC Motion Picture & TV ENRs; Intl Brotherhood Elec Workers; Nat Black Media Coalition; Nat Asn Female EXEs; Cherry Hill MNY Civic Asn; media & pub rels mgr, United Way Southeastern Pa, 2001-03; interim dir pub affairs, Asn Retarded Citizens, Gloucester County, NJ; media & pub rels consult, Founds Inc, 2005-09; media & pub rels consult, Child Welfare League Am, 2007-. **Home Addr:** 21 N Green Acre Dr, Cherry Hill, NJ 08003, **Home Phone:** (609)424-7899. **Business Addr:** Media & Public Relations Consultant, The Biz Whiz, **Business Phone:** (856)504-6656.

### JACKSON, BEVERLY JOYCE

Television producer, educator. **Personal:** Born May 17, 1955, Detroit, MI; daughter of Samuel and Laura Grogan. **Educ:** Univ Mich, Ann Arbor, MI, BA, 1977. **Career:** WTOL-TV, Toledo, Ohio, news reporter, 1977-79; WGBH-TV, Boston, Mass, news reporter, 1982-83; WCVB-TV, Boston, Mass, producer, 1983-85; CBS News, New York, NY, producer, 1985-88; ABC News, New York, NY, producer, World News Tonight, 1988-93; NBC News, sr producer; Columbia Univ, adj prof. **Orgs:** NAB; Delta Sigma Theta Sorority Inc; vpres, Nat Asn Black Journalists, 1984-85. **Home Addr:** 3969 Tall Pine Dr, Marietta, GA 30062.

### JACKSON, BO (VINCENT EDWARD JACKSON)

Football player, baseball player, actor. **Personal:** Born Nov 30, 1962, Bessemer, AL; son of A D Adams and Florence Bond; married Linda Garrett; children: Morgan, Garrett & Nicholas. **Educ:** Auburn Univ Sch, BS, family & child develop, 1995. **Career:** Football player, baseball player (retired), actor; Kansas City Royals, baseball player, 1986-90; Los Angeles Raiders, football player, 1987-90; Chicago White Sox, baseball player, 1991, 1993; Calif Angels, baseball player, 1994; Bo Jackson Elite Sports Complex, co-owner & chief exec off, currently; Films: The Chamber, 1996; Fakin' Da Funk, 1997; Pandora Project, 1998. **Orgs:** Pres, Health South Sports Med Coun. **Home Addr:** PO Box 380488, Birmingham, AL 35238. **Business Addr:** Owner, Chief Executive Officer, Bo Jackson Elite Sports Complex, 167th St & New I-355 Exten, Lockport, IL 60441, **Business Phone:** (815)221-6001.

### JACKSON, BOBBY

Basketball player. **Personal:** Born Mar 13, 1973, East Spencer, NC; son of Sarah (deceased). **Educ:** Western Nebr Community Col, attended 1995; Univ Minn, sports mgt, 1997. **Career:** Basketball player (retired); Seattle SuperSonics, 1997; Denver Nuggets, guard, 1997-98; Minn Timber wolves, 1998-2000; Sacramento Kings, guard, 2000-05; Memphis Grizzlies, pt guard, 2005-06; NO Okla City New Orleans Hornets, guard, 2006-08; Houston Rockets, 2008; Sacramento Kings, 2008-09; Minn Timberwolves, player develop coach, 2013-. **Business Addr:** player development coach, Minnesota Timberwolves, 600 1st Ave N, Minneapolis, MN 55403, **Business Phone:** (612)673-1600.

### JACKSON, BRENDA

Executive. **Personal:** Born Oct 27, 1950, Aberdeen, MD. **Educ:** Prairie View A&M Univ, BS, home econs, 1972. **Career:** Dallas Power & Light Co, home serv adv, 1973-78, supvr consumer serv, 1978-81, community prog mgr, 1981; TXU Bus Serv, exec vpres, 2002; Oncor Elec Delivery Co, sr vpres elec asset ownership, 2003; TXU Elec Delivery, sr vpres customer, community serv, 2004-. **Orgs:** Vol, Tom Paukins Campaign Cong, 1978; bd dir, Dallas Co Chap, Am Heart Asn; bd visitor, Bishop Col, Mus Afro-Am Life & Cult, 1979-; Dallas Black C C; Am Home Econs Asn; Tex Home Econs Asn; N Tex Home Economist Bus Am Asn; Blacks Energy; trustee, Teacher Retirement Syst Tex; Baylor Col Dent; Dallas Mus Art; Metrop YWCA; N Tex Comn; Dallas Opera; Presby Hosp; Dallas Symphony; trustee, Dallas Women's Found; bd mem, Dallas Regional Chamber; adv bd mem, Tex Women Ventures Fund LP; bd, Presby Hosp. **Home Addr:** 5539 McCommas Blvd, Dallas, TX 75206. **Business Addr:** Senior Vice President, TXU Electric Delivery, 1601 Bryan St, Dallas, TX 75201-3411, **Business Phone:** (214)486-2534.

### JACKSON, DR. BURNETT LAMAR, JR.

Dentist. **Personal:** Born Jan 31, 1928, Athens, GA; married Dorian Sara Gant; children: Burnett Lamar & Stephen Mouzon. **Educ:** Ky State Col, BS, 1950; Meharry Med Col, DDS, 1960. **Career:** Dent Tuskegee, AL, pvt pract, 1961-68, Philadelphia, 1969-; John A Andrew Hosp, Tuskegee Inst, chief dent serv, 1961-68; Temple Univ Philadelphia, pub health dentist, 1968-70; W Nice Town-Fioga Neighbourhood Health Ctr, chief dent serv, 1970-. **Orgs:** Secy, John A Andrew Clin Soc, 1965-68; Macon Co Action Com, 1965-68; Acad Gen Dent; Com Greater Tuskegee, AL, 1966-68; secy, Philadelphia County Dent Asn, Jackson, 1969-70, New Era Dent Soc, 1972; Ala Dent Soc. **Home Addr:** 6043 Germantown Ave, Philadelphia, PA 19144-2111, **Home Phone:** (215)848-2232. **Business Addr:** Physician, 7009 Emlen St, Philadelphia, PA 19119-2557, **Business Phone:** (215)843-7387.

### JACKSON, MAJ. CARLOS

Administrator. **Career:** Denver Sheriffs Dept, Dep, capt, maj, currently. **Special Achievements:** First black to hold the post as major of Denver Sheriff's Department. **Business Addr:** Major, Denver Sheriffs Department, PO Box 1108, Denver, CO 80201, **Business Phone:** (303)375-5690.

### JACKSON, CAROL E.

Judge. **Personal:** Born Aug 9, 1952, St. Louis, MO. **Educ:** Wellesley Col, BA, 1973; Univ Mich Law Sch, JD, 1976. **Career:** Thompson & Mitchell, atty, 1976-83; Mallinckrodt Inc, coun, 1983-85; US Dist Ct, Eastern Dist Mo, magistrate judge, 1986-92, dist judge, 1992, chief judge, 1992-; Wash Univ, adj prof law, 1989-92; US District Court, chief judge, 1992-; Dist ct, chief judge, 2002-2009. **Orgs:** Trustee, St Louis Art Mus, 1987-91; Nat Asn Womens Judges; Fed Magistrate Judges Asn; Miss Bar Asn; St Louis Co Bar Asn; Metro St Louis; Mound City Bar Asn; St Louis Lawyers Asn; Mo Bar; Bar Asn Metro St Louis; Lawyers Asn St Louis. **Special Achievements:** First African-American to serve as chief judge of the district court, 2002. **Business Addr:** Chief United States District Judge, US District Court, Thomas F Eagleton US Courthouse 111 S 10th St Suite 14-148, St. Louis, MO 63102, **Business Phone:** (314)244-7540.

### JACKSON, CHARLES N., II

Association executive. **Personal:** Born Mar 16, 1931, Richmond, VA; son of Miles M and Thelma Manning; married Marlene Mills; children: Renata, Andrea & Charles III. **Educ:** Va Union Univ, BS, 1958; Temple Univ, Post Grad, 1976; Miss Southeastern Univ, Post Grad, 1976. **Career:** Soc Am Foresters, Bethesda, Md, dir, finance & admin, 1991, sr dir & chief forest officer; Nat Urban Coalition, vpres admin & finance; Agency Int Devl, sr auditor, chief acct; IRS Intell Div, spec agt; Phila, auditor & treas vol tech. **Orgs:** Asst bd mem, Wash Hosp Nat Asn Accts; nat Soc Pub Accts Am Acctg Asn; Am Mgmt Asn Accredited; Accreditation Coun Acctg. **Home Addr:** 14424 Bakersfield Ct, Silver Spring, MD 20906-1952, **Home Phone:** (240)604-8428.

### JACKSON, CHERYLE ROBINSON

Association executive, president (organization), chief executive officer. **Personal:** Born Jul 20, 1965, Chicago, IL; married Charles. **Educ:** Northwestern Univ, attended 1988. **Career:** Regional vpres gov & pub affairs; Nat Pub Radio, vpres communs & brand mgt, 1997-2000, dir corp communs & dir corp identity & info; nat dir state & local gov affairs; Amtrak, sr-level gov affairs positions, vpres commun & govt affairs, 2000-02, spokesperson; Ill Gov, dir communs, 2003-06, dep chief commun & chief press secy; Chicago Urban League, pres & chief exec officer, 2006-; US Senate, cand, 2009-10; AAR Corp, vpres govt affairs & corp develop, 2010-. **Orgs:** Bd dir, Metrop Planning Coun; Chicagoland Chamber Com; Chicago Mfg Renaissance Coun; Field Mus; trustee, Northwestern Univ; trustee, Chicago Symphony Orchestra; Daniel Burnham Anniversary Planning Comt; Chicago Olympics Comt, 2016; Exec Club Chicago & White House Proj, currently; Aerospace Indust Asn. **Home Addr:** 6723 S Constance Ave, Chicago, IL 60649-1015. **Business Addr:** Vice President of Government Affairs & Corporate Development, ARR Corp, 1100 N Wood Dale Rd, Wood Dale, IL 60191, **Business Phone:** (630)227-2000.

### JACKSON, CHRIS WAYNE. See ABDUL-RAUF, MAHMOUD.

### JACKSON, CLARENCE A.

Automotive executive, chief executive officer. **Career:** Royal Dodge Inc, chief exec officer, 1989-. **Honors/Awds:** Co is listed No 88 on list of top 100 auto dealers, Black Enterprise, 1994. **Business Addr:** Chief Executive Officer, Royal Dodge Inc, 555 Mantua Ave, Woodbury, NJ 08096, **Business Phone:** (609)848-5008.

### JACKSON, CURTIS JAMES, III. See FIFTY CENT.

### JACKSON, DAMIAN JACQUES

Baseball player. **Personal:** Born Aug 16, 1973, Los Angeles, CA. **Educ:** Laney Jr Col. **Career:** Cleveland Indians, infielder, 1996-97; Cincinnati Reds, 1997-98; San Diego Padres, infielder, 1998-2001, 2005; Detroit Tigers, 2002; Boston Red Sox, 2003; Chicago Cubs, 2004; Kans City Royals, 2004; Wash Nationals, 2006; Los Angeles Dodgers, 2007; Fullerton Flyers, currently. **Business Addr:** Baseball Player, Fullerton Flyers, 1549 W Embasy St, Anaheim, CA 92802, **Business Phone:** (714)526-8326.

### JACKSON, HON. DARNELL

State government official, judge. **Personal:** Born Feb 2, 1955, Saginaw, MI; son of Roosevelt and Annie L; married Yvonne K Givens; children: Brandon D & Elliott S. **Educ:** Wayne State Univ, BA, 1977; Sch Law, JD, 1981; Kalamazoo Valley Community Col, AS, law enforcement, 1993. **Career:** Wayne State Univ, Free Legal Aid Clin, stud atty, 1979-81; Allan & Jackson PC, atty at law, 1983-85; Motivational speaker, 1983-; City Saginaw, Attys Off, atty, 1985-86; County Saginaw, Prosecutors Off, asst prosecutor, 1986-89, dep chief asst, 1990-93; Braun Kendrick, atty law, 1989-90; Delta Col Univ Ctr Mich, criminal justice instr, 1990-96; City Saginaw Police Dept, dep chief police, 1993-96; State Mich, Off Drug Control Policy, dir, 1996-01; Saginaw County, 70th Judicial Dist Ct, judge, 2001-06, 10th Judicial Circuit Ct, Saginaw, Mich, judge, 2006-. **Orgs:** Bd dir, Mr Rogers Say No to Drugs Prog, 1991-95; Multicultural Adv Comn, Saginaw Valley State Univ, 1991-96; bd dir, Saginaw Cty Child Abuse & Neglect Coun, 1994-96; bd dir, Westchester Village Essex Manor, 1994-96; chmn, State Mich, Drug Educ Adv Comn, 1996-01; Dare Adv Bd, State Mich, 1996-01; bd dir, United Way Saginaw County, 1996-; Mich Youth Gang & Violence Task Force, 1997-01; co chmn, State Mich, African Am Male Health Initiative Steering Comt, 1997-01; exec comn, Southeast Mich High Intensity Drug Trafficking Area, HIDTA, 1997-01; co chmn, Partnership A Drug-Free Mich Steering Comn, 1997-. **Honors/Awds:** Award Prof Excellence, FBI, Saginaw County Gang Crime Task Force, 1995; Frederick Douglass Award for Community Serv, Mich State Legis, 1991; Award for Effort in War on Drugs, Saginaw Police Dept, Special Operations Unit, 1989; Special Tribute for Community Serv, Mich State Legis, 1985; Community Service Award, Free Legal Aid Clinic, Wayne State Univ, 1980, 1981. **Home Addr:** 1863 Glendale Ave, PO Box 1342, Saginaw, MI 48605, **Home Phone:** (517)791-1981. **Business Addr:** Judge, Saginaw County Governmental Center, 111 S Mich Ave, Saginaw, MI 48602, **Business Phone:** (989)790-5471.

### JACKSON, DARRELL DUANE (DARRELL D JACKSON)

Lawyer, colonial administrator. **Personal:** Born Aug 7, 1965, Cleveland, OH; son of William L Sr and Mary D. **Educ:** Col William & Mary, BA, 1987; Univ Madrid Sch Law, 1988; George Mason Univ Sch Law, JD, 1990; Univ Colo, Boulder, PhD, 2011. **Career:** Fairfax County Pub Sch, substitute teacher, 1985-92; Jay B Myerson Esquire, law clerk, 1988-89; Krooth & Altman, summer assoc, 1989; Hon Leonie M Brinkema, judicial law clerk, 1990-91; Hon Marcus D Williams, judicial law clerk, 1991-92; Hon LM Brinkema, judicial law clerk; DC, asst us atty; County Fairfax, asst county atty, 1992-2000; Marymount Univ, adj prof, 1994; Fairfax County, Va, asst county atty; Off US Atty, asst US atty, 2000-04; Nat Advocacy Ctr, fac mem, 2003; George Mason Univ Sch Law, Pub Sector & Diversity Outreach, dir diversity serv, dir, asst dean & dir minority affairs, 2004-07; Univ Colo Law Sch, grad asst, 2007-09; grad instr, 2010-11. **Orgs:** Va State Bar, 1991-; Northern Va Black Attorneys Asn, treas, 1992, Co Chmn, 1993-95; bd dirs, George Mason Univ Sch Law Alumni Asn, 1992-95; Fairfax County Bar, 1993-; co-founded, George Mason Univ Civil Rights Law J; Chantilly High Pyramid Minority Stud Achievement Comt; historically marginalized communities; Marymount Univ Paralegal Adv Comt, 1993-; Nat Inst Trial Advocacy, Georgetown Univ Law Ctr; Judicial Clerkship Comt, 2002-; master bench mem, 2004-07, barrister mem, 1995-98, George Mason Am Inn Ct; Pub Serv Prog Comt, 2011-. **Special Achievements:** Author, The Sunset of Affirmative Action?: The City of Richmond vs JA Cronson Co, 1990; speeches: "Survival in Law School," 1990; "Judicial Clerkship," 1992. **Home Addr:** 11311 Myrtle Lane, Reston, VA 20191, **Home Phone:** (703)620-9047.

### JACKSON, DR. DEBORAH BYARD CAMPBELL

Association executive, manager, chief executive officer. **Personal:** Born Oct 23, 1947, Bluefield, WV. **Educ:** Bluefield State Col, BA, bus admin, 1968; Union Grad Sch, PhD, human resource develop, 1978. **Career:** Ctr Human Rel, prof asst; Univ Md Eastern Shore, workshop mgr, conf mgr, currently; Crimson Group LLC, assoc, 2006-; Prince George's County, city coun, resident, 2009-; D Byard Int LLC, owner & chief exec officer, currently; Mountain State Univ, adj prof, 2009-. **Orgs:** Coordr, Minority Involvement Prog, Nat Educ Asn, mgr, 1991-2004; pres, Asn Fed Credit Union; pres, Conn Educ Asn; WV Educ Asn; Delta Sigma Theta; Nat Coun Negro Women; Nat Educ Asn; Nat Asn Advan Colored People; Zonta Int; bd mem, F3B Scholar Athlete Prog, vpres prof develop, 2001-12. **Special Achievements:** First African American president of Association Fedral Credit Union; first African American executive director of CT Education Association. **Home Addr:** 7901 Prentice Ct, Ft Washington, MD 20744-4449.

**Business Addr:** Adjunct Professor, Mountain State University, 410 Neville St, Beckley, WV 25801, **Business Phone:** (304)253-7351.

## JACKSON, DR. DENNIS LEE

Educator, teacher. **Personal:** Born Feb 18, 1937, Pachuta, MS; married Althea Yvonne Tucker; children: China; married Annie Earl Anderson; children: Donna, Danna, DeAnna & Dennis II. **Educ:** Alcorn A&M Col, BS, 1959; Univ Miami, MEd, 1969, EdD, 1977. **Career:** Oakley Training Sch, teacher, 1959-64; Utica High Sch, teacher, 1964-65, prin, 1965-68; Orange County Pub Schs, sr admin, 1971-91, dir, 1991-. **Orgs:** Nat Asn Advan Colored People, 1960-; Am Educ Res Asn, 1968-; Fla Assoc Sch Admin, 1971-; Leadership Orlando, 1980-; supporter, Urban League, 1980-. **Honors/Awds:** Scholar 4-H Club, 1955; NDEA fel, Univ Miami, 1968. **Home Addr:** 6000 Pk Hamilton Blvd, Orlando, FL 32808-8204. **Business Addr:** Director, Orange County Public Schools, 445 W Amelia St, Orlando, FL 32801-1127, **Business Phone:** (407)317-3200.

## JACKSON, DERRICK ZANE

Journalist. **Personal:** Born Jul 31, 1955, Milwaukee, WI; son of Samuel T and Doris; married Michelle D Holmes; children: Marjani Lisa, Omar Holmes & Tano Holmes. **Educ:** Univ Wis, Milwaukee, BA, jour, 1976. **Career:** Milwaukee Courier, Wis, reporter, 1970-72; Milwaukee J, Wis, sportswriter, 1972-76; Kans City Star, Mo, sportswriter, 1976-78; Newsday, Melville, sportswriter, NY city, reporter, 1978-85, New Eng, bur chief, 1985-88; Harvard Univ, nieman fel journalism, 1984; Boston Globe, Mass, columnist, assoc ed, 1988-; Simmons Col, part time fac journalism, currently; Grace United Methodist Church, scoutmaster & adv. **Orgs:** Nat Asn Black Journ, 1977-; Boston Asn Black Journ, 1985-; Nieman fel journalism, Harvard Univ; advisor& scoutmaster, Boyscout Troop. **Honors/Awds:** First Place, Newsday Annual Award, Sportswriting, 1984; First Place, Newsday Annual Award, Deadline News, 1985; Meyer Berger Award, Columbia Univ, 1985; First Place, Meyer Berger Award for NY City Reporting, Columbia Univ, 1986; Best New Columnist, Boston Mag, 1989; Political & Sports Commentary, Nat Asn Black Journ; Unity Journalism Awards, Lincoln Univ; Five-time winner, Nat Asn Black Journalists; Sword of Hope Commentary Award, New England Div Am Cancer Soc; Human Rights Award, Curry Col; Honorary Degree, Episcopal Divinity Sch, Salem State Col, Cambridge, Mass; Let's Do It Better commentary awards, Columbia University; Commentary, National Lesbian & Gay Journalists Association; Award for Feature Writing, Professional Basketball Writers Association, 1979. **Home Addr:** 12 William St, Cambridge, MA 02139-3916. **Business Addr:** Columnist, Associate Editor, Boston Globe, 135 Morrissey Blvd, Boston, MA 02107, **Business Phone:** (617)929-3088.

## JACKSON, DEXTER LAMAR

Administrator, football coach, football player. **Personal:** Born Jul 28, 1977, Quincy, FL; married Tina; children: Jazmine, Daisia, Meah & Taylor. **Educ:** Fla State Univ, BS, human & family sci, 2001. **Career:** Football player (retired), coach, radio host, exec; Tampa Bay Buccaneers, defensive back & safety & free safety, 1999-2002, 2004-05; Ariz Cardinals, free safety, 2003; Cincinnati Bengals, strong safety & free safety, 2006-08; Va Destroyers, 2009; Tan talk, radio host, 2011-12; Mhc, counr/ activ therapist, 2012-13; Directions Living, c case mgr, 2013-; 98.7 Fan, radio personality, 2013-; Ala State Univ, asst football coach, 2014-. **Orgs:** Buccaneer Stud Adv Bd, 2002; Mental Health Care Inc. **Honors/Awds:** Tallahassee Democrats Big Bend Offensive Player of the Year; Super Bowl MVP (XXXVII); Super Bowl champion (XXXVII). **Business Addr:** Assistant Football Coach, Alabama State University, 915 S Jackson St, Montgomery, OH 36104, **Business Phone:** (334)229-4100.

## JACKSON, DONALD J.

Television producer, marketing executive, executive. **Personal:** Born Sep 18, 1943, Chicago, IL; son of John Wesley and Lillian Peachy; married Rosemary; children: Rhonda & Dana. **Educ:** Northwestern Univ, BS, radio, TV & film, 1965. **Career:** RH Donnelly, salesman, 1965-66; WBEE-RAD, acct exec, 1966-67; WVON-RADIO, sales mgr, 1967-70; Cent City Prods, founder, 1970, pres, 1984, chief exec officer, currently. **Orgs:** Bd trustee, DuSable Mus African-Am Hist; bd mem, Chicago Transit Authority; bd mem, Gateway Found; bd mem, Chicago Jr Achievement; bd mem, Columbia Col; Chicago Minority Bus Develop Coun Inc; Nat Asn Tv Prod Execs; Nat Asn Mkt Developers; Chicago Asn Com & Indust; founder, Alliance Bus Leaders & Entrepreneurs. **Honors/Awds:** Sickle Cell Anemia Award, 1972; Chic Jaycees Award, 1974; Community Service Award, Ill Nurs Asn & Nat Med Asn, 1975; Blackbook's Ten Outstand Black Bus People, 1976; Numerous awards for service from the Chicago Minority Business Development Council Inc; Cosmopolitan Chamber of Commerce; Truman College; Gateway Foundation; Kizzy Foundation; National Association of Black Construction Workers. **Special Achievements:** TV programs include: programs include: The Bud Billiken Back-to-School Parade, the first and only televised black parade; MBR: Minority Business Report, the first nationally syndicated business show highlighting minorities; The Stellar Gospel Music Awards, which Jackson began, 1985; and Know Your Heritage, the first televised quiz show featuring African American students. **Home Addr:** 4740 S Kimbark, Chicago, IL 60615. **Business Addr:** Founder & Chairman, Chief Executive Officer, Central City Productions Inc, 212 E Ohio St Suite 300, Chicago, IL 60611-3244, **Business Phone:** (312)654-1100.

## JACKSON, DOROTHY R.

Vice president (government), teacher, government official. **Personal:** Born Brooklyn, NY; daughter of Ollie (deceased) and Willamina Belton; married William W Ellis; children: Samantha Dorian Smith. **Educ:** Lincoln Univ, BA, 1971; Seton Hall Univ Law Sch, JD, 1978; Harvard Uni, John F Kennedy Sch Govt, SMG, 1989, fel; Jackson State Univ, cert, criminal justice admin, 1990; John C Stennis Ctr Pub Serv Wash, DC, fel; Am League Lobbyists, cert, prof lobbying. **Career:** Judicial Deleg Fifty Seventh assembly dist, Brooklyn, NY, elective off; NewYork City Bd Educ, teacher Eng, 1971-84, educ adminr, 1984-85; Vincent L Johnson ESQ, law asst, 1985-86; Congressman Edolphus Towns, chief staff, 1986-89; Samdor Enterprises LTD, pres, chief exec officer, 1989-91; Congresswoman Barbara-Rose Collins, chief staff, 1991-92; US House Reps, Speaker Thomas S Foley, spec coun, 1992; Tom Foley, sr prof adv; Congresswoman Eddie Bernice Johnson, chief staff; legis coun congressman Donald M Payne. **Orgs:** Elected deleg Judicial, 1985-87; pres, New York Urban League, Brooklyn Br, 1986-88; pres, Bridge St AME Church Legal Soc, 1987-88; fel Harvard Univ John F Kennedy Sch Govt, 1989; by-laws comt, legis rep, Alpha Kappa Alpha Sorority; Stuyvesant Heights Lions Club; adv bd, Kings County Hosp Develop Proj; bd dirs, Young Techocrats; Women's Campaign Network; Nat Asn Negro Bus & Prof Women's Clubs; League Women Voters; Joint Ctr Polit & Econ Studies. York State State United Teachers; United Fedn Teachers; liason, Nat Asn Advan Colored People; dir voter participation, Dem Cong Campaign Comt; spec asst, liason & legis coun, Cong Black Caucus; chmn, Donald M. Payne; Am League Lobbyists; Wash Govt Rels Group; Women Govt Rels Inc; bd bdir, Nat Coalition Black Civic Participation; vpres govt affairs, Am Gaming Asn, currently. **Honors/Awds:** Woman on the Move Award, Concerned Women of Brooklyn, 1988; Public Affairs Award, Mid-Brooklyn Civic Asn, 1989; Civil Rights Award, Nat Black Police Asn, 1990; Spirit of Democracy Award, Nat Coalition. **Home Addr:** 1504 Red Oak Dr, Silver Spring, MD 20910-1549, **Home Phone:** (301)588-2289. **Business Addr:** Vice President of Government Affairs, The American Gaming Association, 555 13th St NW Suite 1010 E, Washington, DC 20004, **Business Phone:** (202)637-6500.

## JACKSON, DUANE MYRON

Educator, zoo keeper. **Personal:** Born Jan 6, 1948, Chicago, IL; son of A P and Harriet; married Fleda M; children: Kimya & Kari. **Educ:** Morehouse Col, BA, psychol, 1974; Univ Ill, MA, biol psychol, 1976, PhD, comparative psychol & behav-genetics, 1990. **Career:** Univ Ill, teaching asst, 1976-80, coordr, 1980-81, instr, 1981; Clark Col, asst prof, 1981-87; Morehouse col, prof, 1987-, dir Math & Sci Upward Bound Prog, 1991, curr coord, 1992-98, actg chair dept psychol, 1992-94, chair, 1994-95, 2008-13; Zoo Atlanta, vis scientist, 1992, cur insects & res scientist, 1993-2003. **Orgs:** Animal Behav Soc, 1977-; Atlanta Univ Ctr Instnl Animal Care & use Comt, 1984-86; Conserv & Res Comt, 1984-89; Fac Eval Comt, 1985-86; Comt Assessment, 1988-92; Mentorship Task Force, 1991; Tech Adv Bd, 1991-93; Am Asn Zoo & Aquariums, 1992-; bd gov, Nat Conf Undergrad Res, 1993-99; counr, Coun Undergrad Res, 1994-97; McIntosh Comn, 1994; chair, Fac Sem Ser, 1995-98; Fac Coun, 1997-2003; secy, Am Zoo & Aquarium Asn Terrestrial Invert Taxon Adv Group, 1998-2002; Am Zoo & Aquarium Asn Task Force, 1999-2002; chair, Stud Affairs Div Sci & Mathematics, 2001-07; Libr Comt, 2002-03; Zoo Atlanta Bd dir, 2004-; Ad hoc Comt, 2007; chair educ comt, Ctr Behav Neuroscience, 2006-09. **Home Addr:** 2076 Highland Rd SW, Atlanta, GA 30311, **Home Phone:** (404)753-2336. **Business Addr:** Associate Professor, Morehouse College, Nabrit-Mapp-McBay Hall 2nd Fl 830 Westview Dr SW, Atlanta, GA 30314, **Business Phone:** (404)681-2800.

## JACKSON, DWAYNE ADRIAN

Insurance executive, executive, association executive. **Personal:** Born Aug 3, 1955, New York, NY; son of George and Ina Stockton; married Cheryl; children: David & Courtney. **Educ:** Westfield State Col, BA, 1977. **Career:** Crawford & Co Ins Adjusters, adjuster, 1977-79; Mass Mutual, second vpres, 1979-98; Hamilton Sun strand Div United Technologies, 1998-2000; United Technologies, Leadership Progs, mgr, 1998-2000; Sikorsky Aircraft, sr mgr & human resources, 2001-10. **Orgs:** Chartered life underwriter, Am Soc CLU/CHFC, 1990-; bd dir, Jr Achievement, 1993-96; bd dir, Dunbar Community Ctr, 1993-; bd dir, NAACP, Springfield Chap, 1993-96; bd dir, Goodwill Industs, 1994-96; bd dir, Vis Nurses Asn, 1995-96; pres, bd dir, Dunbar Community Ctr, 1996. **Home Addr:** 178 Sen St, Springfield, MA 01129, **Home Phone:** (413)782-7905. **Business Addr:** Manager, United Technologies, 1 Financial Plz, Hartford, CT 06101, **Business Phone:** (860)728-7000.

## JACKSON, EARL, JR.

Microbiologist. **Personal:** Born Sep 4, 1938, Paris, KY; son of Earl Sr and Margaret Elizabeth Cummins. **Educ:** Ky State Univ, BS, 1960; Univ Conn; Northeastern Univ; Univ Paris; Northeastern Univ, Boston, MA & MS, 1986. **Career:** Microbiologist (retired); Hydra Power Corp, chem analyst, 1964-68; Mass Gen Hosp, sr res analyst dept anesthesia, 1968-81, microbiologist dept med, 1981-95. **Orgs:** Am Soc Microbiol; Am Assoc Advan Sci; Ky State Univ Alumni Assoc; NE Asn Clin Microbiol & Infectious Disease; Am Asn Clin Chem; NY Acad Sci. **Honors/Awds:** Outstanding & Distinguished Community Leaders & Noteworthy, Am Citation, 1977; Distinguished Alumni of the Year, Nat Asn Equal Opportunity Citation, 1986; Hall of Fame, Ky State Univ, 1986, 1988; Hall of Fame Distinguished Alumni, Ky State Univ, 1988; Who's Who in Science & Engineering, 1992-2007; Who's Who in Medicine & Healthcare, 1998-2007; Who's Who in the World, 1998, 2000, 2002 & 2006. **Special Achievements:** Spec articles publ "Hemoglobin-O2 Affinity Regulation", 1977 J Applied Physiology, "Measurement of Levels of Aminoglycosides & Vancomycin in Serum", May 1984 pp 707-709 J Clinical Microbiol. **Home Addr:** 501 Fenwick Dr, San Antonio, TX 78239, **Home Phone:** (210)946-0048.

## JACKSON, DR. REV. EARL J.

Clergy. **Personal:** Born Mar 11, 1943, Chattanooga, TN; son of James C (deceased) and Kathryn C; married Barbara Faye Anderson; children: Earl Darelwin & Roderick Lamar. **Educ:** Tenn A&I State Univ, attended 1965; Am Baptist Theol Sem, attended 1966; Detroit Baptist Sem, DD, 1969; Emmanuel Bible Col, MDiv, 1978. **Career:** New Bethel Baptist Church, pastor, 1968-, radio ministry, 1969; KY Dept Human Resources, sr employ interviewer, 1970-. **Orgs:** Bowling Green Warren Co Chap, Nat Asn Advan Colored People; IAPES Employ Serv Organ; Bowling Green Alumni Kappa Alpha Psi Fraternity Bowling Green Noon Kiwanis Club; Bowling Green Warren Co Jaycees, 1971-73; asst chmn bd, Bowling Green Human Rights Comn, 1976-79; Worshipful master House Solomon Ancient & Accepted Scottish Rite MasonsWorld, 1981-90; bd dir, Bowling Green War Memorial Boy's Club, 1979-; bd dir, Bowling Green Noon Kiwanis Club; grand dep inspector gen, House Solomon 767 Ancient & Accepted Scottish Rite MasonsWorld; pres, Ky State Missionary, Baptist Missionary & Educ conv. **Home Addr:** 804 Gilbert St, Bowling Green, KY 42101, **Home Phone:** (270)842-3613. **Business Addr:** Radio Minister, Pastor, New Bethel Baptist Church, 801 Church St, Bowling Green, KY 42101, **Business Phone:** (270)842-5221.

## JACKSON, EARL W

Artist. **Personal:** Born Nov 12, 1948, Ann Arbor, MI; children: Daniel. **Educ:** Washtenaw Community Col; Eastern Mich Univ. **Career:** Artist; Exhibition: African Am Mus Hist, Detroit Washtenaw Community Col; Univ Mich Mus Art; Chicago's Mus Sci & Indust; Nat Gallery Art, Dakar, Senegal; Borders Bk Shop, picture framer, 1974-89; Jackson Studio, owner & prof picture framer. **Orgs:** Nat Conf Artists, 1983-; Ann Arbor Art Asn; founding mem, African Am Cult & Hist Mus. Ann Arbor, MI; Apex Mus, Atlanta, GA; Marietta & Cobb Mus Art; Ga Registry Artist. **Honors/Awds:** Best Miniature Paintings, African World Festival, Detroit, MI, 1983; The Willow Run High School Hall of Fame, Ypsilanti, MI, 1998. **Business Addr:** Owner, Professional Picture Framer, Jackson Studio, 1063 7 Springs Cir, Marietta, GA 30068-2660, **Business Phone:** (770)321-6842.

## JACKSON, EARLINE

School administrator. **Personal:** Born Mar 26, 1943, Columbia, SC; children: Tanyl Lea & Tamara P Newsome. **Educ:** Molloy Col, BA, psych & sociol, 1982. **Career:** Cornell Univ, FDC Pilot Prog, exec bd mem educ planning, assessment, 1974-77; LI Minority Alliance Inc, educ, remedial serv prog coordr, 1978-82; ABWA Pandora Chap, chairperson educ comn, 1983; Molloy Col, assoc dir st thomas aquinas prog, currently. **Orgs:** Founder & exec dir, FDC Asn Nassau Co Inc, 1972-79; exec bd mem, Nassau Co Rep Lic FDC Asn NYS Inc, 1973-78; bd mem, Daycare Coun Nassau Co Inc, 1974-78; bd mem Comm, Adv Bd Roosevelt NY, 1976-78; Nassau Co Rep, Cornell Univ, FDC Prog Planning Comm, 1978; chmn emer, FDC Asn Nassau Co Inc, 1979. **Home Addr:** 107 Maxwell Ave, Greenville, SC 29605-3244, **Home Phone:** (864)283-0305. **Business Addr:** Associate Director Of Saint Thomas Aquinas Program, Molloy College, Rockville Ctr, Rockville Centre, NY 11570-5002, **Business Phone:** (516)678-5000.

## JACKSON, DR. EDGAR NEWTON, JR.

Educator. **Personal:** Born Apr 20, 1959, Washington, DC; son of Joan F J Clement and Edgar Newton Sr. **Educ:** Univ DC, WA, DC, BS, 1987; Grambling State Univ, Grambling, LA, MS, 1989; Howard Univ, WA, DC, postgrad studies, 1990; Univ NMex, Albuquerque, NM, PhD, 1995. **Career:** Warner Theatre, WA, DC, box off mgr, 1979-81; Howard Univ, WA, DC, aquatic mgr, 1981-, instr, 1989-, asst prof, head swim coach, 1991-98; Univ DC, WA, DC, adj instr, 1987-88; Grambling State Univ, Grambling, La, instr, 1988-89; Univ NMex, Albuquerque, NMex, teaching asst, 1990-91, athletic dept intern, 1991; Fla State Univ, asst prof, 1998-2003, assoc prof & dept chmn, 2003, Sport Mgt Rctrn Mgt & Phys Educ dept, instr, currently. Theses: Facility Matters: The Perception Of Academic Deans Regarding The Role Of Facilities in Higher Education, third advisor. **Orgs:** Am Alliance Health, Phys Educ, Rctrn & Dance, 1983-; Coun Nat Coop Aquatics, 1984-; chair, Aquatic Safety Comm, Am Red Cross, 1985-; Nat Rctrn & Pk asn, 1985-; Nat Org Athletic Develop, 1987-; N Am Soc Sociol Sport, 1987-; life mem, Omega Psi Phi; life mem, Nat Asn Advan Colored People; Grambling State Univ Alumni asn, Univ DC Alumni asn; Kappa Delta Pi; life mem, Wash Urban League; Phi Delta Kappa; pres, FL Ahperd, 2001-02. **Home Addr:** 2626 E Pk Ave Suite 6201, Tallahassee, FL 32301, **Home Phone:** (850)942-4569. **Business Addr:** Instructor, Florida State University, Tallahassee, FL 32301, **Business Phone:** (850)644-4813.

## JACKSON, DR. EDISON O.

College administrator. **Personal:** Born Oct 1, 1942, Heathsville, VA; married Florence; children: 2. **Educ:** Howard Univ, BS, zool, 1965, MA, coun, 1968; Union Theol Sem NY, MA, theol; NY Theol Sem, Mdiv; Rutgers State Univ, NJ, DEd, 1983. **Career:** Legal Aid Agency Dist Columbia, offender rehab proj, 1967-68; Fed City Col, sr coun instr, 1968-69; Essex County Col, Newark, NJ, dean stud affairs, 1969-74, vpres stud affairs, 1974-80, exec vpres & chief acad officer, 1983-85; Upsala Col E Orange, adj fac; Compton Community Col, pres & supt, 1985-89; Bridge St African Wesleyan Methodist Episcopal Church, ministerial staff; City Univ New York, Medgar Evers Col, New York, pres, pres emer, 1989-2009; Bethune-Cookman Univ, interim pres, 2012-, pres, 2013-. **Orgs:** Crown Heights Coalition; Cath Interracial Coun New York Inc; bd dir, Prospect Pk Alliance; bd dir, Brooklyn C's Mus; bd overseer, New York Univ Grad Prog; bd trustee, Brooklyn Bot Gardens; chmn bd dir, Bridge St Develop Corp; Brooklyn Prospect Pk Coalition; New York Comn Human Rights New York Bd Educ; Am Asn Higher Educ; Am Asn Col Deans & Advisors Students; Nat Asn Univ Personnel; Nat Asn Black Col Presidents & Chancellors; Asn Gov Boards Univs & Cols; Nat Alliance Black Sch Educr; Am Personnel & Guid Asn; Am Col Personnel Asn; Am Asn State Cols & Univs; bd dir, Nat Asn Equal Opportunity Higher Educ; Press's Round Table; Nat Coun Crime & Delinq; mentor, Am Asn State Cols & Univs Millennium Leadership Inst; Comn Educ Credit & Credentials Am Coun Educ; Mid States Asn Cols & Schs Personnel Comt; Urban & Metrop Mission Focus Group; Phi Beta Sigma Fraternity Inc; Sigma Pi Phi Fraternity; Team Volusia Econ Develop Corp, currently; Daytona Regional Chamber Com, currently; HBCU-ETS Steering Comt, currently; Young Men's Christian Asn, currently; Nat Asn Schs & Cols United Methodist Church, currently; Fla Coun Social Status Black Men & Boys, currently; Volusia & Flagler YMCA, currently; New York Theol Sem, currently; Allen Chapel AME Church. **Home Addr:** 231 Riverside Dr Unit 401, Daytona Beach, FL 32117-4972, **Home Phone:** (804)580-8028. **Business Addr:** President, Interim President, Bethune-Cookman University, 640 Mary McLeod Bethune Blvd, Daytona Beach, FL 32114, **Business Phone:** (386)481-2001.

## JACKSON, DR. EDWARD R.

Educator, administrator. **Personal:** Born May 24, 1942, New Iberia, LA; son of Leona Strauss and Oliver; married Nedra Clem; children: Chris, Corey, Robert, Edward II & Camy. **Educ:** Univ Southwestern La, Lafayette, LA, BA, polit sci, 1963; Marquette Univ, Milwaukee, WI, MA, polit sci, 1965; Univ Iowa, Iowa City, IA, PhD, polit sci, 1968. **Career:** Southern Univ A & M Col, Baton Rouge, La, from asst prof polit sci to dept chmn, 1968-70, chancellor, 1998-2008; Fisk Univ, Nashville, Tenn, assoc prof polit sci, 1970-76; Howard Univ, Wash, DC, assoc prof polit sci, 1976-79; Natl Aeronaut & Space Admin, Admin & Support dirate, admin officer; SC State Col, Orangeburg, SC, Dept polit sci, chmn, 1979-86, vice provost & vpres acad affairs, 1986. **Home Addr:** 3185 Landing Way, Orangeburg, SC 29115, **Home**

**Phone:** (803)533-0917. **Business Addr:** Chancellor, Southern University A&M Col, PO Box 9374, Baton Rouge, LA 70813, **Business Phone:** (225)771-5020.

## JACKSON, ELIJAH
Executive, president (organization). **Personal:** Born Feb 9, 1947; married Mary. **Career:** Paradise Airways, pres & chief exec officer, 1994; Navcom Aviation, pres; Navcom Systs Inc, pres & chief exec officer, currently. **Orgs:** Inst Navig; LORAN Working Group; Wildgoose Asn. **Business Addr:** President, Chief Executive Officer, NAVCOM Systems Inc, 9815 Godwin Dr, Manassas, VA 20110-4156, **Business Phone:** (703)361-0884.

## JACKSON, EMORY NAPOLEON
Association executive, consultant, president (organization). **Personal:** Born Oct 29, 1937, Magnolia, MS; son of Aaron Napoleon and Juanita Gordon; married Adrea Perry; children: Lisa A & Charles L. **Educ:** Newark St Col, MA counselling; Morehouse Col, BA, 1961; Adler Inst Psychother, 1974; Ariz State Univ. **Career:** UN Int Sch, teacher, 1962; NY Urban League, comm org, 1967; Nat Med Asn, consult; Int Asn Off Human Rights Agencies, consult; Econ Develop Nat Urban League, dep dir; Off Manpower Dev & Training Nat Urban League, nat dir; US Dept Housing Urban Develop, spec & asst to secy, 1976-77; Urban League Eastern MS, pres, 1977-80; Dept Energy, New York, human resources admin, dep comnr, 1980; City NY, Dept Sanit, dep comnr, 1983-86; We Care About NY Inc, pres & chief operating officer, 1986; St NY, Dormitory Auth, dir exec proj, 1997-2008, Off Opportunity Progs, dir, currently. **Orgs:** Vpres, US Team Handball Fed & Olympic Com Chmn Community Housing Resources Bd Boston; bd dir, Boston Pvt Inc; bd dir, Boston Metro Nab Nat Urban League fel; Nat Urban League, 1969; pres & coo, We Care about New York Inc. **Honors/Awds:** Highest scorer team handball N Am, 1965-70; Outstanding achievement, Boston City Coun Resolution, 1980; Community Serv Boy Scouts-Brooklyn Dist, 1987, 88 & 89; Community Service Girl Scout, Coun Greater NY, 1988. **Home Addr:** 1333 President St, Brooklyn, NY 11213. **Business Addr:** Director, Dormitory Authority of the State of New York, Fl 52 1 Penn Plz, New York, NY 11545, **Business Phone:** (212)273-5000.

## JACKSON, ERIC SCOTT
School administrator, educator, athletic coach. **Personal:** Born Jan 26, 1964, Ann Arbor, MI; son of Geraldine and Lionel; children: Davis & Brooks. **Educ:** Eastern Mich Univ, BS, hist, 1987; Univ Cincinnati, Masters Prog, coun educ, 1989. **Career:** Football player (retired), football coach; Eastern Mich Univ, defensive back, 1982-84; Ypsilanti High Sch, sec & defensive line freshman coach football, 1984-87; Univ Cincinnati, grad asst football, 1987-89, head grad asst football, 1988; Cornell Univ, freshman defensive coordr & sec coach football, 1989-91, sec coach, 1997-98; Alma Col, head track coach, asst football coach, 1991, defensive coordr, 1991-93, PE supvr, field coach; Las Vegas Aces, prof spring football league, asst football coach, 1992; Idaho, sec coach, 1993; Univ Idaho, coach, 1993-94; Calif Polytech State Univ, defensive coordr, spec teams coordr & sec coach, 1994-97; Ithaca Col, defensive coordr & sec coach, 1998-2000; Princeton Univ, Dept Athletics, defensive backs coach, sec coach & spec teams coordr, 2000-09; Portland State Univ, defensive coordr & safeties coach, 2010-12; Coach J, acad coach, founder, pres, 2013-; Lewis & Clark Col, Defensive Coordr, 2014-. **Orgs:** Track, Athletic Cong, 1991-; Am Football Coaches Asn, 1991-; network comn, Black Coaches Asn, 1992; Off Publ Princeton Football Asn. **Home Addr:** 530 Wright Ave Suite 3, Alma, MI 48801, **Home Phone:** (517)463-1359. **Business Addr:** Defensive Coordinator, Lewis & Clark College, 0615 SW Palatine Hill Rd, Portland, OR 97219-7889, **Business Phone:** (503)768-7064.

## JACKSON, ESTHER COOPER
Editor, social worker, activist. **Personal:** Born Aug 21, 1917, Arlington, VA; daughter of George Posea and Esther Irving; married James Edward; children: Harriet Jackson Scarupa & Kathryn Jackson Seeman. **Educ:** Oberlin Col, AB, 1938; Fisk Univ, MA, 1940. **Career:** Southern Negro Youth Cong, exec secy, 1940-50; Nat Urban League, educ dir, 1952-54; Nat Bd Girls Scouts Am, social worker, 1954-; Freedomways Mag, founding, managing ed, 1961-85; WEB Du Bois, co-ed; Black Titan & Paul Robeson, co-ed; Great Forerunner, co-ed; Voting Proj, staff. **Orgs:** Parents Teachers Asn. **Honors/Awds:** Rosenwald Fel, 1940-41; Rabinowitz Fund Grant, 1962-63; William L Patterson Foundation Award, 1978; Nat Alliance of Third World Journalists, 1981; Harlem School of the Arts Award, 1987; Lifetime Achievement Award, New York Asn Black Journalists, 1989. **Home Addr:** 21 St James Pl Apt 15m, Brooklyn, NY 11205-5030, **Home Phone:** (718)857-3744.

## JACKSON, EUGENE D.
Executive. **Personal:** Born Sep 5, 1943, Waukomis, OK; son of Joseph Gordon and Queen Esther Royal; married Brenda; children: 3. **Educ:** Univ Mo-Rolla, elec engineering, 1964; Columbia Univ, MS, 1971. **Career:** Colgate Palmolive NYC, indust engr, 1967-68; Black Econ Union NYC, prod, proj engr, 1968-69; Interracial Coun Bus Opportunity NYC, dir maj indust prog, 1969-71; Unity Broadcasting Network, founder, pres & chmn, 1993; Queens Inner-Unity Cable Syst, vice chair; Int Coun Bus Opportunity, dir; Urban Laegue; Nat Black Network, founder; World Af Network, chair, chief exec officer, currently. **Orgs:** Founder, Nat Asn Black-Owned Broadcasters; Coun Foreign Rels, Nat Action Coun Minorities Engineering; Miami/Dade County Chamber Com; Howard Univ Intl Sponsors Coun; Alpha Phi Alpha Fraternity, bd, Lincoln UNIV, Pa; founding mem, Nat Asn Black Owned Bus; founding mem, Cong Black Caucus; founder, CEBA awards. **Business Addr:** Chief Executive Officer, World African Network, 510 Whitehall St SW, Atlanta, GA 30303, **Business Phone:** (404)521-6120.

## JACKSON, FELIX W.
Physician. **Personal:** Born Sep 6, 1928, Woodville, MS. **Educ:** Ill Col, optom. **Career:** Am Sch, self instr opthamologist; Strip Founders Inc, purchasing agent; USPOe, carrier; FW Jackson Enterprises, owner. **Orgs:** Bd exec vpres, Forsyth Century Art, 1964-68; Pres, Nat Asn Advan Colored People, 1965-67; vice chmn, Model Cities Bd, 1968-70; Winston-Salem Redevel Comn, 1974. **Honors/Awds:** Rep All Am City Event, 1965. **Special Achievements:** First African American opth of NC state. **Home Addr:** 533 N Liberty St, Winston Salem, NC 27101, **Home Phone:** (336)725-9653.

## JACKSON, FRANK
President (organization), educator. **Personal:** Born Jan 1, 1929?, Mound City, IL; married Hope Turk; children: Wallace Turk, Michael Turk, Diane Brooks & Bonnie Alexis. **Career:** Educator (retired); USN, instr; Solano Community Col. **Orgs:** Community Develop Comm, 1989-93; pres, Nat Asn Advan Colored People, Vallejo Br, 1991-2002, sect dir, 1999-; Fighting Back Partnership, 1992-93; Human Rels Comm, 1993-99; chair, Am Red Cross, Solano Co Chap, 1994-98; Civil Serv Comm, 2000-; Affirmative action comt. **Home Addr:** 39 Darlington Pl, Vallejo, CA 94591, **Home Phone:** (707)647-3244.

## JACKSON, FRANK DONALD
Government official, mayor, administrator. **Personal:** Born Jul 25, 1951, Luling, TX; son of Willie Louise Smith and Robbie Sr; married Marian Elaine Jones; children: Tracy, Ayanna, Chelkh & Okofo. **Educ:** Prairie View A&M Univ, BA, geog, 1973. **Career:** Govt affairs officer, currently; A&M Univ, asst prof, 1982, assoc counr admis, asst dir univ centers, dir auxiliary serv, 1987-; Craft Opportunity 2215 Galveston Tex, Comndg Officer, 1988-; mayor, Prairie View, Tex, 2002-. **Orgs:** Prince Hall Mason, 1970; Alpha Phi Alpha, 1971; Gamma Theta Upsilon, 1972; city Counman, City Prairie View, 1982-92; dir, Prairie View A&M Univ, Memorial Stud Ctr, 1982-87; Phi Alpha Theta, 1983; Nat Naval Officers Asn, 1985; Waller County Hist Comn & Soc, 1989-; County Comner Waller County, 1991-96, reelected, 1996-2000; Chamber Com; pres, Prairie View Vol Fire Fighting Asn Inc. **Honors/Awds:** Man of the Year, Memorial Stud Ctr Adv Bd, 1985; publ, Prairie View Messenger, 1984-88; Staff Member of The Year, Prairie View A&M Univ, 1988-89. **Home Addr:** PO Box 475, Prairie View, TX 77446-0475, **Home Phone:** (936)857-5550. **Business Addr:** Mayor, City of Prairie View, 44500 Bus Hwy 290, Prairie View, TX 77446, **Business Phone:** (936)857-3711.

## JACKSON, DR. FRANKLIN D. B.
Executive. **Personal:** Born Mar 21, 1934, Cypress, AL; son of J H and Mary; children: Franklin K, Debra R, Sabrina F, Delilah E & Jacquelyn R. **Educ:** Univ N Colo, Greeley, BS, bus admin, 1976, MS, pub admin, 1977; Webster Col, St Louis, MS, health & hosp admin, 1978, LaSalle Univ, PhD, health serv admin, 2002. **Career:** Executive (retired); EEOC, employ opportunity specialist, 1976-78; HUD, fair housing & EO spec, 1978; Jackson's Enter Ltd, pres & owner, 1980; Entrepreneur Mentor Society, chief exec officer, 1995-. **Orgs:** Publicity chmn, Univ Colo, 1972; historian, Kappa Alpha Psi Fratenity, 1975; band leader, Happy Jacks Combo & Dance Band; Am Soc Pub Admin, 1976; bd dir, Occup Industrialization Ctr, 1977; res chmn, Police Comn Denver, 1977-78; Nat Asn Black Veterans Inc; founder, Colo State Command Coun. **Home Addr:** 9931 E Ohio Ave, Denver, CO 80247, **Home Phone:** (303)482-0654.

## JACKSON, FRED H.
Pilot. **Personal:** Born Mar 12, 1933, Bridgeton, NJ; son of Fred H Sr and Hortence P Steward; married Linda Lee Brokaski; children: Pamela, Antionette, Cheri, Fred, II, Courtney Page, Heather Schulte, Holly Schulte & Lisa Pullan. **Career:** Pilot (retired); Eastern Air Lines, pilot, 1967-91. **Orgs:** Negro Airman Int; asst scout master, Troop 254, 1969-74; Black Airline Pilot's Asn; NJ Bd Real Estate Salesman; Nanticoks - Lenni - Lenape Native Am Tribe. **Home Addr:** 5 Deland Pk B, Fairport, NY 14450-1405, **Home Phone:** (585)388-0717.

## JACKSON, FRED JAMES, SR.
Administrator. **Personal:** Born Jun 11, 1950, High Point, NC; son of Mary Jane Walker (deceased); children: Marrian Ann, Fred James Jr & Patrice M. **Educ:** Monterey Peninsula Col; Sacramento State Univ, BA, relig educ, 1977; Univ Md; Armed Forces Inst, cert; Univ San Diego; Hartnell Col; Harvard Univ Grad Sch Educ. **Career:** Boulder Col, veterans affairs officer, 1978-79; Hiram Johnaosn High Sch, head golf coach; McClellan AFB Logistic Ctr, procurement mgr, 1975-87; Black Rose Enterprise Publ, pres, chief exec officer, 1986-; Drug Intervention Network Inc, exec dir, 1987-92; USDA, procurement officer, 1992-94; Grant Joint Union Sch Dist, eng teacher, dept chair, 1994-96; Sacramento Unified Sch Dist, Hiram Johnson High, lead teacher, comput educ, 1995-; Hole One Jr Golf Club Inc, dir, currently. **Orgs:** City Sacramento, Mayors Drug Gang Task Force, 1987-93; AAAS, Black Church Proj, 1992-95; Nat Educ Asn, 1994-; Calif Teachers Asn, 1994-; Nat Asn Black Sch Educr, 1995-; peer coun, leadership coordr, tobacco drugand alcohol prog coord, 1996-, State Calif; Harvard Univ Prin Ctr; Am Writers Asn; Small Publishers Asn N Am. **Home Addr:** 5370 Kevinberg Dr Suite 1, Sacramento, CA 95823, **Home Phone:** (916)422-7730. **Business Addr:** Director, The Hole In One Jr Golf Club Inc, PO Box 5283, Sacramento, CA 95817, **Business Phone:** (916)705-4653.

## JACKSON, FREDDIE ANTHONY
Actor, singer, composer. **Personal:** Born Oct 2, 1956, Harlem, NY. **Career:** Night club performer; back-up vocalist/cameo soloist with Melba Moore, 1984; Mystic Merlin, singer. Albums: Rock Me Tonight, 1985; Just Like The First Time, 1986; Don't Let Love Slip Away, 1988; Do Me Again, 1990; Time For Love, 1992; Here It Is, 1994; At Christmas, 1994; Private Party, 1995; For Old Times Sake: The Freddie Jackson Story, 1996; Anthology, 1998; Life After 30, 1999; Live In Concert, 2000; On Tour, 2001; It's Your Move, 2004; Personal Reflections, 2005; Transitions, 2006; Greatest Hits, 2007; For You, 2010; Climax Entertainment, "Love & Satisfaction", 2014; composer with Paul Laurence, currently. Tv series: The Golden Girls, 1989. TV series documentary: Soul Train, actor, writer, 1986-2004. **Honors/Awds:** Am Black Gold Award, Outstanding Male Artist, 1986; American Music Award, 1988. **Special Achievements:** Grammy nomination for Best New Artist, 1985; American Music Award, 1986; Film: King of New York. **Home Addr:** , New York, NY. **Business Addr:** Singer, Capitol Records, 1750 N Vine St, Los Angeles, CA 90028.

## JACKSON, FREDERICK LEON
Educator. **Personal:** Born Aug 15, 1934, Albany, NY; married Mildred Helen Hagood; children: Leon K & Anthony W. **Educ:** Ore State Univ, BS, 1976; Portland State Univ, MS, 1977. **Career:** Portland Pub Schs, handicapped teacher, 1976-81, sixth grade teacher, 1981-84, integration coordr, 1984-86, stud transfer coord, 1986-. **Orgs:** Dir, Portland Asn Teachers, 1978-86; KRS, 1983-85; basileaus, 1985-86; Omega Psi Phi; chmn minority proj, Ore Educ As, 1984-85; Ore Alliance Black Sch Ed, 1985-87. **Home Addr:** 2804 NE 25th Ave, Portland, OR 97212-3423, **Home Phone:** (503)284-4268. **Business Addr:** Coordinator, Portland Pub Schs, 8020 NE Tillamook, Portland, OR 97213, **Business Phone:** (503)916-5747.

## JACKSON, GARNET NELSON
Writer, columnist, educator. **Personal:** Born May 27, 1944, New Orleans, LA; daughter of Carrie Brent Sherman; married Anthony; children: Damon. **Educ:** Dillard Univ, BA, 1968; Eastern Mich Univ, attended 1972. **Career:** Flint Bd Educ, teacher; Self Employed, publ, auth, 1989-; Flint Ed, columnist, 1989-90; Flint J, columnist, 1990-94; Mod Curric Press, Simon & Schuster, auth, pioneer Biographies Concept, 1990-94; Author: Phillis Wheatley, Poet; Benjamin Banneker, Scientist, 1992; Phillis Wheatley, Poet, 1993; Rosa Parks-Hero Our Time, 1993; Begining Biographies Garrett Morgan, 1993; Toni Morrison: Autora, 1995; Garrett Morgan Inventor: Beginning Biographies/6 Hardcover Books & Teaching Companion, 1993; Phillis Wheatley: Poet; Beginning Biographies : African Americans-Maggie Walker; Frederick Douglass Freedom Fighter; Thurgood Marshall, Supreme Ct Justice, 1994; Mae Jemison Astronaut, 1994; Maggie Walker: Bus Leader, 1994; Charles Drew Doctor, 1994. **Orgs:** Nat Asn Advan Colored People, 1987-; Sylvester Broome Bk Club, 1990-; Greater Flint Optimist Club, 1993-; Int Reading Asn, 1996; Am Libr Asn, 1996. **Honors/Awds:** Rejoti Publ, Honorable Mention for Outstanding Poetry, 1987; Educator of the Year Award, Nat Asn Advan Colored People, 1991; Harambee Medal, Nat Asn Advan Colored People, 1991; Dorothy Duke Evans Educator of the Year, 1991; Award for Children's Lit, Mt Zion Church, 1991; City Flint, Off Mayor, Proclamation of Outstanding Citizenship, 1992; State Mich, Gov Engler, Letter of Commendation, 1992; Christa McAuliffe Special Tribute Award, State Mich, 1992; Congressional Record, Proclamation of Outstanding Citizenship, US Cong, 1992; Certificate of Special Recognition, US Senator, Don Reigle, 1992; Special Tribute Award, Civil Park Sch, 1992; Zeta Phi Beta Finer Womanhood Hall of Fame, Zeta Phi Beta Sorority, 1993. **Business Addr:** Writer, 3519 Applewood Lane, Grand Blanc, MI 48439, **Business Phone:** (810)695-9157.

## JACKSON, GARY MONROE
Lawyer. **Personal:** Born Nov 10, 1945, Denver, CO; son of Floyd M Jr and Nancelia Elizabeth; married Regina Lee; children: Michael Mascotti & Tara Mascotti. **Educ:** Univ Colo, BA, 1967, Sch Law, JD, 1970. **Career:** Denver Dist Atty Off, chief trial dep, 1970-74; US Atty Off, asst US atty, 1974-76; Di Manna, Eklund, Ciancio & Jackson, partner, 1976-82; Di Manna & Jackson LLP, partner, lawyer, 1976-; Denver County Ct, atty, 2012-13. **Orgs:** Founder, pres, Sam Cary Bar Asn; bd dirs, Col Trial Lawyers Asn; bd trustees, Denver Bar Asn, 1980-81; chair, Comt Conduct, 1982-86; Am Col Trial Lawyers; Am Bd Trial Advocates; vpres, Colo Bar Asn; Best Lawyers Am; chair & mem, US Dist Ct; chair & mem, Colo Supreme Ct; AfricanAmerican legal asn; Colo Criminal Defense Bar; pres, Am Bd Trial Advocates, 2010; bd trustee, Dbas; chair, Colo & Denver Bar joint Minorities; Profession Comt; chair, Colo Law Alumni Bd; Lowry Redevelop Authority Bd; Colo Black Chamber Com; James P. Beckwourth Mountain Club; Diversity Legal Profession Comt; mem Peer Prof Assistance Group; Sixth May Found; Colo Bar Found Fel. **Honors/Awds:** Special Commendation, US Dept Justice, 1976; Wiley A Branton Award, Nat Bar Asn, 2001; Lifetime Achievement Award, Sam Cary Bar Asn; Order of the Coif, Univ Colo; George Norlin Award, 2003; Order Coif Award, 2003; Norlin Award, 2008; The Best Lawyers in America, 2006; King Trimble Life Time Achievement Award, Sam Cary Bar Asn, 2006; Hon, 2011 CBA Award of Merit, Colo Bar Asn; Hon, William Lee Knous Award, law schs highest hon, 2010; George Norlin Award; chair, Delta Eta Boule Found; Northeast Denver Youth Serv; Urban League Metrop Denver; United Negro Col Fund; Cleo Parker Robinson Dance Ensemble; 100 Black Men Denver Inc; Beckwourth Outdoors; Sixteenth May Found. **Home Addr:** 330 Garfield St, Denver, CO 80206, **Home Phone:** (303)322-2528. **Business Addr:** Lawyer, Partner, DiManna & Jackson LLP, 1741 N High St, Denver, CO 80218, **Business Phone:** (303)320-4848.

## JACKSON, GEORGE W., JR.
Chief executive officer, president (organization). **Educ:** Oakland Univ, BS, human resource develop; Cent Mich Univ, MA, bus mgt. **Career:** Lawrence Tech Univ Sch Mgt, adj fac; Detroit Edison Energy Co, dir customer mkt; United States Navy, personnel & human rel; Mich Consol Gas Co, Econ Develop Exec, Detroit City, City Planning & Develop Dept, interim dir; Detroit Econ Growth Corp, pres & chief exec officer, 2002-; City Detroit, chief develop officer, 2006; GWJ Group LLC, chair person, pres & chief exec officer. **Orgs:** City Detroit Econ Develop Orgn; Detroit Regional Chamber; Greater Detroit Foreign Trade Zone; Am Arab Chamber Com Mich; chmn, bd mem, Next Energy Corp; exec bd dir, Mich Econ Develop Corp; bd dir, Mich Strategic Fund; bd dir, State Mich Land Bank Fast Track Authority; bd dir, Downtown Detroit Partnership; bd dir, Am Arab Chamber Com Mich; chmn bd dir, Eastern Mkt Corp; bd trustee, Oakwood Healthcare Syst; exec bd, Greater Wayne County Econ Develop Corp; Detroit Regional Chamber Econ Develop Partnership; chmn bd gov, Renaissance Club; CoreNet Global Inc; Am Econ Develop Asn; Mich Econ Develop Asn; Nat Coun Urban Econ Develop; Automation Alley Exec Bd; chmn, Mich Utility Econ Develop Consortium; vice chmn & bd dir, Detroit Empowerment Zone; bd dir, Detroit RiverFront Conservancy. **Business Addr:** President, Chief Executive Officer, Detroit Economic Growth Corp, 500 Griswold St Suite 2200, Detroit, MI 48226, **Business Phone:** (313)963-2940.

## JACKSON, GERALD E.
Executive, chief executive officer, president (organization). **Personal:** Born Apr 13, 1949, Chicago, IL; son of Bruce and Hazel; married Denorsia; children: Gerald Jr, Gavin & Syreeta. **Educ:** Olive Harvey

Col, attended 1972; Roosevelt Univ, BBA, 1975. **Career:** Lic pvt investr; cert real estate broker; Chicago Police Dept, Chicago, Ill, police officer; GEJ Security, chief exec officer & pres, 1982-. **Orgs:** Chicago Asn Com & Indust, 1986; Chatham Bus Asn, 1989; bd mem, Rosenblum Boys & Girls Club, 1989; Nat Org Black Law Enforcement Execs; Kappa Alpha Psi; Nat Burglar Alarm Asn; Am Soc Indus Security Assoc. **Home Addr:** 2000 W 91st St, Chicago, IL 60620. **Business Addr:** President, GEJ Security Services Inc, 719 E 79th St, Chicago, IL 60619, **Business Phone:** (312)994-0516.

## JACKSON, GERALD MILTON

Lawyer, consultant. **Personal:** Born Jan 8, 1943, Cleveland, OH; son of Albert and Mary L; children: Alisa, Carmen & Jason A. **Educ:** Ky State Univ, BA, 1967; Univ Colo Sch Law, post grad legal training, 1968; Case Western Res Univ Sch Law, JD, 1971. **Career:** Jackson Law Cuyahoga Co Juv Detention Home, supvr, 1965; Cuyahoga Co, Dept Welfare, case worker, 1967-68; Univ Colo, Minority Students Enrichment & Scholar Prog, dir, 1968; Cleveland Trust Co, acct, 1969; EEO Comn US Govt, case anal, 1970; E Cleveland, asst law dir, 1971; Ohio Gen Assembly, legis advocate, 1971-72; Reginald Heber Smith Community Lawyer fel, 1971-73; Lawyers Housing ABA & Cleveland Bar, asst dir, 1972-75; John M Harlan Law Club Inc, vpres, 1975-76; Alexander Jackson & Buchman, atty partner law firm; Jackson Law Co, owner, atty & legal serv consult, currently, sr partner, mgr, 2007-; Gen Coun Strategic Bus Links, LLC, sr mgr; Shaker Heights Munic Ct, vis judge. **Orgs:** Organizer chmn, Black Am Law Stud Asn, Case Western Univ Sch Law, 1970-71, Induction Soc Benchers, 2001; vice chmn, Cleveland Chap, Nat Conf Black Lawyers, 1974-75; NBA Host Civic; dist rep, Ohio Asn Black Atty, 1974-75; Am Bar Asn; NH Bar Asn; Ohio Bar Asn; Bar Asn Great Cleveland; Cleveland Lawyers Asn; S African ClubChicago, Ill; Nat Asn Advan Colored People; Citizens League Cleveland; Legal Aid Soc; vpres, Case Western Res Law Sch Alumni Asn, 2004-06; Shaker Heights Human Rels Comn; pres, Shaker One Hundred, currently; mem bd dir, Shaker Works; bd commissioners, Grievances & Discipline Ohio Supreme Ct found. **Honors/Awds:** Recipient MLK & Award, Baccus Law Sch, 1970-71; Co-designer for BALSA Emblem, 1971; Certificate of Appreciation, Bar Asn Greater Cleveland, 1973-75. **Home Addr:** 15925 Van Aken Blvd, Cleveland, OH 44120, **Home Phone:** (216)561-1160. **Business Addr:** Owner & Attorney, Senior Partner, Jackson Law Co, 15925 Van Aken Blvd Suite 205, Shaker Heights, OH 44120-5108, **Business Phone:** (216)752-8000.

## JACKSON, GILES B.

Judge. **Personal:** Born Mar 1, 1924, Richmond, VA; son of Bessie A and Roscoe C; married Gwendolyn Lackey Battle; children: Mignon W Carter, Yvette L Townsend & Yvonne Ruth Jackson. **Educ:** Va State Univ, BA, 1948; Southwestern Univ, JD, 1953; Univ Southern Calif, attended 1968; Univ Calif Berkeley, Judicial Col, attended 1977. **Career:** Judge (retired); Pvt pract, atty, 1954-66; Los Angeles Co Super Ct, comn, judge pro tem, 1966-77; Los Angeles Judicial Dist, judge, 1977-86. **Orgs:** Los Angeles Co Bar Asn; life mem, Nat Asn Advan Colored People; life mem, DAV. **Home Addr:** 5625 Cambridge Way Suite 303, Culver City, CA 90230, **Home Phone:** (310)641-0281.

## JACKSON, GORDON MARTIN, JR.

Journalist, writer, manager. **Personal:** Born Jul 3, 1954, Portsmouth, VA; son of Melveen Sr and Gordon; children: Gordon III & Gregory. **Career:** Album:Don't close door our lives, 1978; Minority Opportunity News, sr ed, 1993-94; Dallas Weekly, actg mgr ed, 2009-13; Healthy Living, dir mkt/commun, 1997-98; Urban Press Syndicate, owner & pres, 2011-; Denver Weekly News, ed-in-chief, 1998-99, managing ed, 2009-13. **Orgs:** Parlimentarian, Dallas/Ft Worth Asn Black Communicators, 1994-97; Nat Asn Black Journalists, 1996-; Colo Asn Black Journalists, 1997-; Colo Press Asn, 1997-; Am Psychiat Asn, 1997; Colo Black Chamber Com, 2000-; 100 Black Men, Colo Chap, 2000-. **Honors/Awds:** A Phillip Randolph Messenger Award Educ, Nat Newspaper Publ Asn, 1998; A Phillip Randolph Messenger Award Civil Rights, 1997; Colorado Black Roundtable President's Award, 1990. **Special Achievements:** Featured in Colorado Black Leadership Profiles, 2000. **Home Addr:** , Dallas, TX, **Home Phone:** (214)421-8045. **Business Addr:** Owner, President, Urban Press Syndicate.

## JACKSON, GOVERNOR EUGENE, JR.

Administrator. **Personal:** Born May 5, 1951, Linden, TX; son of Mary Catherine Cato; married Linda Kay Sueing; children: Governor Eugene III; married Nicole Farmer; children: Elise Gabrielle. **Educ:** E Tex State Univ, BS, 1973; N Tex State Univ, MEd, 1978. **Career:** E Tex State Univ, Sam Rayburn Memorial Stud Ctr, bldg serv supr, 1969-73; DeVry Inst Tech, assoc dean students, 1974-76; Tex Woman's Univ, dir financial aid, 1977-2015, exec dir, 1977-. **Orgs:** Nat Asn Stud Fin Aid Adminstr, 1973-; SW Asn Stud Financial Aid Admin, 1973-; admin coun, Tex Woman's Univ, 1977-80; Voter Regist Com Dallas, 1978-80; admin bd, St Luke Methodist Church, 1978-80; nominating co, Tex Stud Financial Aid Adminr, 1979; mem bd dir, Denton State Sch Vol Serv Coun, 1983-2007; pres, N Tex Higher Educ Authority, 1986-; mem bd dir, Higher Educ Servicing Corp, 1986-2010; pres, bd dir, Denton State Sch Vol Serv Coun, 1986-92; chmn, Tex Prof Nursing Stud Adv Comt, 1989-; Lender/Sch Adv Comt Tex Guaranteed Stud Loan Corp, 1999-2007; Enrollment Serv Comt Coun Pub Univ Presidents & Chancellors, 2011-; Nat Asn Stud Fin Aid Adminstr Higher Educ Task Force, 2012-13. **Honors/Awds:** Leadership Award, E Tex State Univ, 1969-70, 1970-71; Outstanding Young Man of America, Jaycees, 1979, 1983; Outstanding Educator, St Phillips School, 1983; Leadership denton, 1998; Alumni Ambassador, Tex A & M Com Dept Math, 2001; Commitment to Student Success Award Council for the Management of Educational Finance, 2004; Outstanding Service for Innovation, Community Colleges, 2008; National Administrator Role Model Award, 2009. **Home Addr:** 202 Charlotte, Linden, TX 75563. **Business Addr:** Executive Director, Texas Woman's University, 304 Admin Dr, Denton, TX 76204-5408, **Business Phone:** (940)898-3051.

## JACKSON, GRADY O'NEAL

Football player. **Personal:** Born Jan 21, 1973, Greensboro, AL; children: 5. **Educ:** Knoxville Col, Bus & Phys Educ. **Career:** Football player (retired); Oakland Raiders, 1997, 1999, defensive tackle, 1998, defensive tackle, 2000-01, right defensive tackle, 2001; New Orleans Saints, defensive tackle & right defensive tackle, 2002-03; Green Bay Packers, nose tackle, 2003-04, defensive tackle & left defensive tackle, 2005; Atlanta Falcons, nose tackle, 2006-07, defensive tackle, 2006, 2007-08, right defensive tackle, 2008; Jacksonville Jaguars, 2007; Detroit Lions, defensive tackle & left defensive tackle, 2009; Fla Tuskers, 2010.

## JACKSON, GRANT DWIGHT

Baseball player, athletic coach. **Personal:** Born Sep 28, 1942, Fostoria, OH; married Millie; children: Gayron, Debbie, Yolanda & Grant II. **Educ:** Bowling Green State Univ, Bowling Green, Ohio. **Career:** Baseball player (retired), baseball coach; Philadelphia Phillies, pitcher, 1965-70; Baltimore Orioles, pitcher, 1971-76; New York Yankees, pitcher, 1976; Pittsburgh Pirates, pitcher, 1977-81 & 1982, pitching coach, 1983; Montreal Expos pitcher, 1981; Kans City Royals, pitcher, 1982; Gold Coast Suns, 1989; Pittsburgh Pirates, coach, 1983-85; Cincinnati Reds, pitching coach, 1994-95; Indianapolis Indians, pitching coach, 1996-97, 1999; Durham Bulls Baseball Club, coach, 2000; Louisville RiverBats, pitching coach, 2001; Rochester Red Wings, pitching coach, 2002-05. **Orgs:** Baltimore Orioles. **Home Addr:** 212 Mesa Cir, Upper St Clair, PA 15241, **Home Phone:** (724)941-1396.

## JACKSON, GREG ALLEN

Football player, football coach. **Personal:** Born Sep 20, 1966, Hialeah, FL; married Dina; children: Greg Jr & Jayden. **Educ:** Fairleigh Dickinson Univ, commun, 2004. **Career:** Football player (retired), football coach; New York Giants, defensive back, 1989-93; Philadelphia Eagles, 1994-95; New Orleans Saints, 1996; San Diego Chargers, 1997-2000; Idaho Vandals football, defensive back coach, 2003; La-Monroe Warhawks, defensive back coach, 2004-06; Tulane Univ, defensive back coach, 2007, safeties & kick off coach, 2008, lineback & kick off coach, 2009; Wis Badgers, nickleback, linebackers asst coach, 2010; San Francisco 49ers, asst defensive back coach, asst sec coach, 2011-14; Univ Mich, defensive back coach, 2015, sec coach; Dallas Cowboys, safeties coach, 2016-, defensive backs coach, currently. **Business Addr:** Assistant Secondary Coach, San Francisco 49ers, 4949 Marie P DeBartolo Way, Santa Clara, LA 95054, **Business Phone:** (408)562-4949.

## JACKSON, GREGORY

Automotive executive. **Personal:** Born Jul 12, 1957, Detroit, MI; son of Roy and Doris; married Jackie B; children: Anika S & Gregory J. **Educ:** Atlanta Univ, Grad Sch Bus, MBA, finance & mkt, 1979; Morris Brown Col, BS, acct. **Career:** Arthur Andersen & Co, sr acct, 1981-84; Stroh Brewery Co, controller, 1982-84; Kastleton Co, pres, 1984-91; Jackson Automotive Mgt LLC, chmn, pres & chief exec officer; Harvard Univ, guest lectr; Atlanta Univ, guest lectr; Prestige Auto Group, founder & pres, currently. **Orgs:** Lifetime mem, Kappa Alpha Psi Fraternity, 1977-; pres, Gen Motors Minority Dealers Asn, 2002; Nat Automobile Dealers Asn; Mich Auto Dealers Asn; bd dir, Nat Asn Minority Auto Dealers; lifetime mem, Nat Asn Advan Colored People; bd dir, Automotive Hall Fame; Rainbow PUSH Coalition; bd trustee, Morris Brown Col; Music Hall Bd Dirs; Henry Ford Health Syst Found trustee. **Honors/Awds:** Ranked No 20, Black Enterprise 100, 1999; Ranked No 3, Black Enterprise 100, 2000; Ranked No 1, Black Enterprise 100, 2001; Named Auto Dealer of the Yr, Black Enterprise, 2005. **Special Achievements:** First African American to lead an auto dealership group. **Home Addr:** 8180 Stanley Rd, Flushing, MI 48433-1110. **Business Addr:** Founder, President, Prestige Auto Group, 20200 E 9 Mile Rd, St. Clair Shores, MI 48080, **Business Phone:** (586)773-2369.

## JACKSON, HAROLD BARON, JR. See Obituaries Section.

## JACKSON, HAROLD JEROME

Journalist. **Personal:** Born Aug 14, 1953, Birmingham, AL; married Denise Estell Pledger; children: Annette Michelle & Dennis Jerome. **Educ:** Baker Univ, Baldwin, KS, BA, jour, polit sci, 1975. **Career:** Birmingham Post-Herald, Birmingham, Ala, reporter, 1975-80; United Press Int, Birmingham, Ala, reporter, 1980-83, state news ed, 1983-85; Philadelphia Inquirer, Philadelphia, Pa, asst nat ed, 1985-87; United Press Int & Birmingham Post-Herald; Birmingham News, Birmingham, Ala, ed writer, 1987-94; Baltimore Sun, ed bd, Baltimore, Md, 1994; Philadelphia Inquirer, Ed Page, coordr, 1999-2004, dep ed, 2004-07, Philadelphia Newspapers Inc, inquirer ed page ed, 2007-; ed page ed, 2007-. **Orgs:** Nat Asn Black Journalists, 1980-; Westminster Presby Church, 1964-. **Honors/Awds:** Achievement Award, Writing, Asniated Press, 1978; Merit Award, UPI, 1987; Green Eyeshade, Soc Prof Journalists, 1989; Hector Award, Troy State Univ, 1990; American Psychological Association Award, Ala Press Asn, 1990; Journalist of the Year, Nat Asn Black Journalists, 1991; Pulitzer Prize, Columbia Univ, 1991; Alumnus of the Year, Baker Univ, 1992; Citizenship Award, Birmingham Emancipation Asn, 1993. **Home Addr:** 57 Fox Hollow Lane, Sewell, NJ 08080-3139, **Home Phone:** (856)401-9589. **Business Addr:** Editorial Page Editor, The Philadelphia Inquirer, PO Box 8263, Philadelphia, PA 19101, **Business Phone:** (215)854-4975.

## JACKSON, HAROLD LEONARD, JR. See Obituaries Section.

## JACKSON, REV. HENRY RALPH, SR.

Clergy, founder (originator). **Personal:** Born Aug 22, 1915, Birmingham, AL; married Cheri J Harrell; children: Zita J. **Educ:** Daniel Payne Col, BA; Jackson Theol Sem, BD; Wilberforce Univ, LlD; Campbell Col, DD; Allen Univ, HHD; Monrovia Col. **Career:** N Memphis Dist AME Church, presiding elder; Bethal AME Church, Minimum Salary Dept, founder & dir, pastor, sr pastor, currently. **Orgs:** Gen conf, AME Church, 1944-80; founder & pres, Brotherhood AME Church; gen bd, AME Church; pres, Christian Brotherhood Homes Inc; cochmn, Comn Move Equality; Thirty Second Degree Mason; State Dem Exec Comt; hon mem, State County Munic Employees AFL-CIO; founding father, Memphis Goodwill Boys Club; Goodwill Boys Club; Mallory Knights Charitable Orgn; Memphis Welfare Rights Orgn; JUGS Inc; Co-Ettes Inc Congressman Harold Ford. **Honors/Awds:** National Association Advance Colored People Meritorious Service Awards, Brotherhood AME Church; Man of the Year, IBPOE; Citizens Award, Local 1733, AFSCME; Outstanding Tennesse Award, Gov Ray Blanton; Julius Montgomery Pioneer Award. **Home Addr:** 1443 South Pkwy E, Memphis, TN 38106. **Business Addr:** Pastor, Bethel AME Chuch, 405 3rd Ave, Pompano Beach, FL 33060, **Business Phone:** (954)657-8770.

## JACKSON, DR. HERMOINE PRESTINE

Psychologist. **Personal:** Born Mar 11, 1945, Wilmington, DE; daughter of Herman Sr and Ella B Roane. **Educ:** Elizabeth town Col, BA, 1967; Ohio State Univ, MA, 1979, PhD, psychol, 1991. **Career:** Wilmington Pub Sch, teacher, 1967-68; Philadelphia Pub Sch Syst, teacher, 1968-74; Cent Mich Univ, instr, 1979-81; State NY W Seneca Develop Ctr, psych, 1981-90; NY State Div Youth, Buffalo Residential Ctr, psychologist, 1990-94; Va State Dept Juv Justice, Bon Air Juv Correctional Ctr, psychologist; Bermuda Corrections Ctr. **Orgs:** Am Psych Assoc; Am Assoc Ment Retardation; Coalition 100 Black Women. **Honors/Awds:** Outstanding Instr, Cent Mich Univ, 1981; Treatment Practitioner of the Year, Va Dept Juv Justice. **Home Addr:** 4501 Briarwick Dr, Richmond, VA 23236-1021, **Home Phone:** (804)276-5241. **Business Addr:** Psychologist, Bon Air Juvenile Correctional Center, 1900 Chatsworth Ave, Bon Air, VA 23235, **Business Phone:** (804)323-2550.

## JACKSON, HIRAM

Executive. **Personal:** Born Jan 1, 1965?, Highland Park, MI; son of Hiram Sr and Naomi. **Educ:** Cornell Univ, BS, indust & labor rels, 1987. **Career:** DMC Technologies, pres & chief exec officer; GlobalView Technologies, pres & chief exec officer, 1998; Genesis Energy Solutions LLC, pres & chief operating officer, 1998-; Real Times Media, co-owner & chief exec officer, 2006-; Mich Chronicle, publ, 2012. **Orgs:** Founder, ACCESS Am; exec bd mem, Nat Asn Advan Colored People, Detroit Br; chair, Freedom Fund Dinner; Charles H Wright Mus African Am Hist; Freedom Inst; bd dir, Real Times Media, 2011; mem, Gov Rick Snyders Off Urban & Metrop Initiatives Adv Group; First Independence Bank CDC, Detroit BrNat Asn Advan Colored People. **Home Addr:** 271 Arden Pk Blvd, Detroit, MI 48202, **Home Phone:** (313)867-2565. **Business Addr:** President, Chief Operating Officer, Genesis Energy Solutions LLC, 407 E Ft Suite 410, Detroit, MI 48226, **Business Phone:** (313)962-9060.

## JACKSON, DR. HORACE

Association executive, executive. **Personal:** Born Feb 19, 1935, Opelika, AL; son of Howard Taft and Emma Lee; children: David, Michael & Karen M Stewart. **Educ:** Tenn A & I State Univ, BS, 1957; Wash Univ, MA, educ, 1969; Wash Univ, PhD, 1976. **Career:** Chattanooga Pub Schs, curric resource teacher, 1957-68; Rutgers Col, lectr, 1973-74; Va Polytech Inst, asst prof, 1974-75; E St Louis Ctr, coordr acad progs, 1976-77; Magnet Sch Enrich Prog, St Louis Univ, lead instr, 1978-80; St Louis Pub Schs, div asst, 1980-83; Mika Bus Serv Inc, pres, 1983-89; Chattanooga Area Urban League, dir progs, 1989-90; Partners Econ Progress, mgr minority bus develop; Southeast Indust Develop Asn, spec proj coordr, asst dir. **Orgs:** Kappa Alpha Psi, 1954-; Kappa Delta Pi, 1970-; Phi Delta Kappa, 1970-; Chattanooga African Am Chamber Com, currently; coordr proj, Southeast Indust Develop Asn. **Home Addr:** 5240 Polk St, Chattanooga, TN 37410, **Home Phone:** (423)400-4830. **Business Addr:** Assistant Director, Southeast Industrial Development Association, 535 Chestnut St, Chattanooga, TN 37402, **Business Phone:** (423)424-4245.

## JACKSON, INEZ AUSTIN

Executive. **Personal:** married Raymond. **Educ:** Int Sch Design, attended 1964. **Career:** Design Innerphase Inc, Silver Spring, MD, pres, currently. **Orgs:** Camellia Soc Potomac Valley. **Business Addr:** President, Design Innerphase Inc, 1732 Overlook Dr, Silver Spring, MD 20903-1409, **Business Phone:** (301)439-8400.

## JACKSON, ISAIAH ALLEN

Conductor (music). **Personal:** Born Jan 22, 1945, Richmond, VA; son of Isaiah and Alma Alverta Norris; married Helen Caroline Tuntland; children: Benjamin, Katharine & Caroline. **Educ:** Harvard Univ, BA, 1966; Stanford Univ, MA, music, 1967; Juilliard Sch, MS, 1969, DMA, 1973; Univ Dayton, DM, 1999. **Career:** Bach Soc Orchestra, music dir, 1965-66; Juilliard String Ensemble NYC, founder & conductor, 1970-71; Am Sym Orchestra, asst conductor, 1970-71; Baltimore Sym Orchestra, asst conductor, 1971-73; Rochester Philharmonic Orchestra, assoc conductor, 1973-87; Flint Sym Orchestra, MI, music dir & conductor 1982-87; Royal Ballet London Eng, prin conductor, 1986, music dir, 1987-90; Dayton Philharmonic Orchestra, music dir, 1987-95; Queensland Sym Orchestra, Australia, prin guest conductor, 1993-95; Youngstown Sym, music dir, 1996-; Canberra Sym Orchestra, prin guest conductor, 1996-97; Pro Arte Chamber Orchestra Boston, mus dir, 2000-05, conductor emer, currently; Belvedere Productions, chief exec officer & creative dir; pres, Rhythm Rhyme Results; Harvard Univ, Memorial Church, musician; Berklee Col Music, assoc prof; Harvard Exten Sch; Longy Sch Music; Songs: "Music Nigel Butterley", "Music William Grant Still", "My First Concert", "New Yr's Eve Concert", "Piano Quintets Schumann & Dohnanyi", "Romeo & Juliet", "Twentieth Century Harp". **Orgs:** Bd dir, Ralph Bunche Scholar Fund, 1974-87; music panel, NY Coun Arts, 1978; guest conductor, NY Philharmonic, 1978; guest conductor, Boston Pops, 1983, 1990-94; Detroit Sym Orchestra, 1983, 1985; Cleveland Orchestra, 1983-84, 1986-87, 1989-92; guest conductor, San Francisco Sym, 1984; Toronto Sym, 1984, 1990, 2002; Orchestre de la Suisse Romande, 1985, 1988; BBC Concert Orchestra, 1987; guest conductor, Berlin Sym, 1989-95; Signet Soc Medal Arts, Harvard Univ, 1991; Dallas Sym, 1993; Houston Sym, 1995; Royal Liverpool Phil, 1995; trustee, Boston Athenaeum, 2001-; Hochstein Sch Music & Dance; fel W E B Du Bois Inst, Harvard Univ. **Business Addr:** Conductor Emeritus, Pro Arte Chamber Orchestra of Boston, 107 Brighton Ave Suite 1, Boston, MA 02134, **Business Phone:** (617)779-0900.

**JACKSON, JAMES ARTHUR**
Basketball player, basketball executive. **Personal:** Born Oct 14, 1970, Toledo, OH; children: Traevon. **Educ:** OH State Univ, attended 1992. **Career:** Basketball player (retired), analyst; Dallas Mavericks, guard & shooting guard, 1992-97; NJ Nets, 1996-97; Philadelphia 76ers, 1997-98; Golden State Warriors, 1998; Portland Blazers, shooting guard, 1998-99; Atlanta Hawks, small forward, 1999-2001; Cleveland Cavaliers, 2000-01; Miami Heat, small forward, 2001-02; Sacramento Kings, small forward, 2002-03; Houston Rockets, small forward, 2003-04; Phoenix Suns, forward-guard, 2005-06; Los Angeles Lakers, 2006; Big Ten Network, analyst, currently. **Orgs:** Founder, James Arthur Jackson Found. **Honors/Awds:** Bronze, Pan Am Games, 1991; Big Ten Player of the Year, 1991, 1992; Player of the Year, UPI Col Basketball, 1992. **Business Addr:** Analyst, Big Ten Network, 600 W Chicago Ave Suite 875, Chicago, IL 60610, **Business Phone:** (312)665-0700.

**JACKSON, JAMES E., SR.**
Insurance executive, president (organization). **Personal:** Born Feb 4, 1943, Roberta, GA; son of J B Wornum C and Dollie; children: James Jr, Nsombi, Jawara, Brandon & Barenda. **Career:** Allstate Ins Co, agency owner, 1971-; Dunhill Staffing Systs, chief exec officer akland & Macomb franchise's, 1996-; Poole & Jackson Ins Agency, owner & chief exec officer, 2001-. **Orgs:** Nat Asn Advan Colored People, 1978; Optimist Club Detroit, 1991, pres, 1998. **Honors/Awds:** Michigan Sales Leader, Allstate Ins, Auto Ins, Territory 3, 1998; FLPI Production, Territory 3, 1998; Life Ins, Territory 3, 1998; Personal Property, Territory 3, 1998; Motor Club, 1998. **Special Achievements:** First minority chief exec officer & owner of a Dunhill Staffing Systs Franchise. **Home Addr:** 454 Wishbone Dr, Bloomfield Hills, MI 48304-2351, **Home Phone:** (248)723-6682. **Business Addr:** Senior Account Agent, Allstate Insurance Co, 17051 W 10 Mile Rd, Southfield, MI 48075-2946, **Business Phone:** (248)443-0000.

**JACKSON, JAMES GARFIELD**
Law enforcement officer. **Personal:** Born Oct 24, 1933, Columbus, OH; son of George and Sarah; married Mary; children: James II & Jason. **Educ:** FBI Nat Inst; Harvard Univ, John F Kennedy Sch Gov; Ohio State Univ; Northwestern Univ. **Career:** Columbus Div Police, officer, 1958-67, sgt, 1967-71, dep chief, 1977, lt, 1971-74, capt, 1974-77, dep chief, 1977-90, chief police, 1990-. **Orgs:** Major City Chiefs Asn; Int Asn Chiefs Police; Ohio Asn Chiefs Police; Nat Black Law Enforcement Execs. **Home Addr:** 1349 Bryden Rd, Columbus, OH 43205, **Home Phone:** (614)645-6003. **Business Addr:** Chief of Police, Columbus Division of Police, 120 Marconi Blvd, Columbus, OH 43215, **Business Phone:** (614)645-4760.

**JACKSON, JAMES HOLMEN**
Executive. **Personal:** Born Oct 5, 1949, Newark, NJ; married Lynda P Valrie; children: Lamarr. **Educ:** ICBO Rutgers Univ, bus mgt, 1974; Bloomfield Col, BA, 1979. **Career:** Moldcast Lighting Div, asst mgr qc, 1972-79; Condor Int Corp, treas, 1979-80; Internal Revenue Serv, revenue officer, 1980-83; Jacmin Inc, pres; JS Minor Corp, consult. **Orgs:** Treas, Citizens Improv League, 1979-82; pres, Montgomery Ave Block Asn, Irv, NJ, 1979-83; chmn bd, Sugar Bear Prods; bd dir, People's Comn Corp; Budget Construct Co; chmn, Tenant Asn, Orange, NJ. **Home Addr:** 111 S Harrison St, East Orange, NJ 07018, **Home Phone:** (201)676-4847. **Business Addr:** Owner, President, Jacmin Inc, 210 Pinehurst Ave, Scotch Plains, NJ 07076, **Business Phone:** (201)642-7019.

**JACKSON, DR. JAMES SIDNEY**
Educator, behavioral scientist. **Personal:** Born Jul 30, 1944, Detroit, MI; son of Pete James and Johnnie Mae Wilson Taylor; married Toni C Antonucci; children: Ariana Marie & Kendra Rose. **Educ:** Mich State Univ, BS, psychol, 1966; Univ Toledo, MA, psychol, 1970; Wayne State Univ, PhD, social psychol, 1972. **Career:** Inst Social Res, res scientist, 1986-; Fogarty Sr Postdoctoral Int, fel, 1993-94; Daniel Katz Distinguished Univ, prof psychol, 1995-; Res Ctr Group Dynamics, Inst Social Res, dir; Health Behav & Health Educ, Sch Pub Health, prof; Inst Social Res. **Orgs:** Fac assoc, Inst Soc Res, 1971-85; chmn, Nat Asn Black Psychologists, 1972-73; chmn, Asn Adv Psychol, 1978-80; bd dir, Pub Comt Ment Health, 1978-83; chair, Social Psychol Training Prog, Univ Mich, 1980-86; fac assoc, Ctr Afro-Am & African Studies, 1982-; mem comt status black, Am Nat Res Coun, 1985-; mem bd trustee, Asn Adv Psychol, 1986-; chmn, Task Force, Geront Soc Am, 1989; Nat Adv Ment Health Coun, NIMH, 1989-; Data Anal Res Network, Nat Col Athletic Asn, 1989-, chair, 1994-; Grad Rec Exam Comn, 1990-93; prog comn, Am Psychol Soc, 1990-91; adv bd, Brookdale Nat Fel Prog, Humanities, Behav & Social Sci, 1990-; bd dir, Ronald McDonald House, 1993-99; Fed Behav, Psychol & Cognitive Sci, 1994-; US Census Bur, Adv Comm African Am, 1994-2004; bd trustee, Greenhills Sch, 1997-; nat adv comn mem, Boston Mus Sci Traveling Exhib Aging, 1998-2000; Nat Inst Aging, Bd Sci Counrs, 2000-04; Nat Res Coun, Comm Pop, Panel Race, Ethnicity & Health Later Life, 2001-02; Nat Occup Res Agenda, 2001; Am Psychol Asn, Deleg UN World Conf Race, 2001; chmn-elect, AAAS, 2002-03, chmn, 2003-04; Nat Acad Sci, Inst Med, 2002; dir, Ctr Afroamerican & African Studies; pres, Black Students Psychol Asn; fel Am Psychol Asn. **Home Addr:** 340 Orchard Hill Dr, Ann Arbor, MI 48104. **Business Addr:** Professor, Director, University of Michigan, 426 Thompson St, Ann Arbor, MI 48106-1248, **Business Phone:** (734)615-0380.

**JACKSON, JANET DAMITA JO**
Actor, entertainer, singer. **Personal:** Born May 16, 1966, Gary, IN; daughter of Joseph and Katherine Walter; married James Debarge, Sep 7, 1984, (divorced 1985); married Rene Elizondo, Mar 31, 1991, (divorced 2000); married Wissam Al Mana, Jan 1, 2012. **Career:** Studio Albums: Janet Jackson, 1982; Dream Street, 1984; Control, 1986; Janet Jackson's Rhythm Nation, 1989; Janet, 1993; Design of a Decade, 1995; The Velvet ope, 1997; All For You, 2001; Damita Jo, 2004; 20 YO, 2006; Discipline, 2008; DVD: The Rhythm Nation Compilation, 1997; Design of a Decade, 1997; The Velvet Rope Tour-Live In Concert, 1999; All For You special edition, 2001; Live in Hawaii, 2002; From Janet. To Damita Jo, 2004. TV Series: "Good Times", 1977-79; "A New Kind of Family", 1979-80; "Different Strokes", 1980-84; "Fame", 1984-85. Films: Poetic Justice, 1993; Nutty Professor II: The Klumps, 2000; "Why Did I Get Married", 2007; Why Did I Get Married Too?, 2010; For Colored Girls, 2010. Music Videos: Dream Street, 1984; What ave You Done For Me Lately, 1986; Nasty, 1986; When I Think Of You, 1986; Control, 1986; Let's Wait A while, 1987; The Pleasure Principle, 1987; Diamonds, 1988; 2300 Jackson Street, 1989; Miss You Much, 1989; The Knowledge, 1989; Rhythm Nation, 1989; Escapade, 1989; Alright, 1990; Come Back To Me, 1990; Black Cat, 1990; Love Will Never Do (Without You), 1990; The Best things in life re free (Janet & Luther aren't in the video), 1992; That's The Way Love Goes, 1993; If, 1993; Again, 1993; Because of Love, 1993; Any Time, Any Place, 1994; Throb (Saturday Night live performance), 1994; You Want This, 1994; Whoops Now, 1995; What 'll I Do, 1995; Scream, 1995; Runaway, 1995; Twenty Foreplay, 1996; Got 'Til It's Gone, 1997; Together Again, 1997; Together Again (Deeper Remix), 1997; I Get Lonely, 1998; Go Deep, 1998; You, 1998; Luv Me (Janet Doesn't appear in the video), 1998; Every Time, 1998; Boyfiend/Girlfriend, 1999; Whats it gonna be, 1999; Doesn't Really Matter, 2000; All for You, 2001; Someone To Call My Lover, 2001; Son Of A Gun, 2001; Feel It Boy, 2002; Just A Little While, 2004; I Want You, 2004; All Nite (Don't Stop), 2004; R&B Junkie (not released), 2004; Gotta Getcha, 2005; Call On Me feat, 2006; So Excited Feat, 2006; With U, 2007. **Honors/Awds:** American Music Awards, Favorite R&B Female Artist; World Music Awards, Outstanding Contribution to Rhythm and Blues; American Society of Composers, Authors and Publishers Award, 1995; American Music Awards, Award of Merit, 2000; Entertainer of the Year, Nat Asn Black Owned Broadcasters, 2002; Essence Award, 2002; Governor's Award, Recording Academy, 2002; Touching a Life Award, Behind the Bench, 2004; received more than 150 awards including Grammy Awards; American Music Awards; MTV Video Music Awards; MTV Movie Awards; MTV Japan Video Music Awards; Billboard Music Awards; Soul Train Music Awards; MTV Europe Awards; Nickelodeon Kids' Choice Awards; Radio Music Awards; BMI Pop Awards; NBA / Touching a Life Awards; World Music Awards; VH Fashion Awards; Blockbuster Entertainment Awards; Golden Globes; Essence Awards; Japan Gold Disc Awards; Rolling Stone Readers Choice Awards; Oscar Awards (Academy Awards); AIDS Project Los Angeles (APLA); Hollywood Walk of Fame; Ebony Magazine Awards; IFPI Platinum Europe Awards; Source Awards; Dutch Grammys TMF Awards; BPI UK Sales Awards; GLAAD Media Awards; Playboy Magazine Entertainment Awards; Inter Nat Dance Music Awards; ACE (American Cinema Awards); ARIA Awards (Australian Sales Awards); Emmy Awards (Academy of Television Arts & Sciences); Dutch Edison Awards; Narm Awards (Nat Asn Recording Merchandisers); Nat Alumnae Asn Of Spelman Awards; Nat Asn Advan Colored People Image Awards; CORE (Congress of Racial Equality); Starlight Foundation Awards; Ctr for Population Options; Channel V Awards; Dansk Grammy Awards (Danish Music Awards); Brazilian TVZ Video Awards; Bravo Awards; Swiss Sales Awards (Switzerland Sales); Radioscope Awards; BMG Music Club Sales Award; DMC DJ Awards; Performance Magazine Awards; LEAP Awards. **Special Achievements:** The only performer male or female to be nominated for Grammy Awards in Pop, Rock, Dance, Rap and R&B, and the first female recording artist of color to be nominated for a Producer Of The Year Grammy; only woman singer in the history of Rock & Roll to score 5 back to back #1 studio albums on the Billboard Album's chart; nominated for Oscar Award Best Music, Original Song for: Poetic Justice (1993) in 1994; one of the richest women in entertainment by Forbes Magazine; Author, "La Toya:, 1991. **Home Addr:** 4641 Hayvenhurst Ave, Encino, CA 91436. **Business Addr:** Entertainer, Grabow & Associates Inc, 4219 Creekmeadow Dr, Dallas, TX 75287-6806, **Business Phone:** (972)250-1162.

**JACKSON, JANET E.**
Judge, president (organization), chief executive officer. **Personal:** children: Harrison. **Educ:** Wittenberg Univ, BA, 1975; George Washington Univ, Nat Law Ctr, JD, 1978. **Career:** Ohio Atty Gen Off, asst atty gen, 1978-80, asst chief civil rights sect, 1980-82, chief crime victims compensation sect, 1982, chief work comp sect, 1983-87; Sindell, Sindell & Rubenstein, atty, 1982-83; Franklin County Munic Ct, judge, 1987-97, admin & presiding judge, 1992; Columbus City, atty, 1997-2003; United Way Cent Ohio, pres & chief exec officer, 2003-; Wittenberg Univ, bd mem; Franklin Univ, bd mem. **Orgs:** Columbus Bar Asn; Nat Conf Black Lawyers; Women Lawyers Franklin County; Ohio State Bar Asn; bd dir, Action C; bd trustee, Wittenberg Univ; Columbus Mortar Brd Alumni Club; pres, Col Metrop Club; bd mem, Leadership Colombus; bd mem, Marty's Kids Foundn; vice chair, Cent Ohio Workforce Investment Bd; Ctr Child & Family Advocacy; Capitol Club; Columbus Coalition Against Family Violence; Leadership Columbus; YWCA Columbus; Twin Rivers Chap Links Inc; Nat Coalition 100 Black Women; Columbus Found; bd dir, Grant/Riverside Methodist Hosp. **Honors/Awds:** Distinguished Barrister Award, Natl Conf Black Lawyers, 1988; Outstanding Accomplishments Award, Franklin County Dem Women, 1988; Community Service Award, Metrop Dem Women's Club, 1989; Warren Jennings Award, Franklin County Ment Health Brd, 1989; Dr Martin Luther King Jr Humanitarian Award, Columbus Educ Asn, 1991; Allies of Equality Award, Equality Ohio; Woman of Achievement Award, YWCA, 1992; Citizen's Award, Columbus Asn Educ Young C, 1993; Citations Award, Pi Lambda Theta, 1993; John Mercer Langston Award, Natl Conf Black Lawyers & Robert B Elliot Law Club, 1994; Peacemaker Award, Choices; Ohio Women's Hall of Fame in 2001; Professional Woman of the Year, Women Color Found & Woman Yr by Niagara Found, 2013. **Special Achievements:** Blue Chip Profile, 1992; Jackson is the first woman and the First African American to lead the United Way of Central Ohio in its 80-year history; First woman elected Columbus City Attorney; First African-American judge in Franklin County, where she served from 1987-1996. **Business Addr:** Chief Executive Officer, President, United Way Central Ohio, 360 S 3rd St, Columbus, OH 43215, **Business Phone:** (614)227-2700.

**JACKSON, JANINE MICHELE**
Journalist. **Personal:** Born Jan 30, 1965, Wilmington, DE; daughter of Wagner and Arva Marshall; married Jim Naureckas; children: 1. **Educ:** Sarah Lawrence Col, BA, 1985; New Sch Social Res, MA, sociol, 1992; Univ Col London. **Career:** FAIR, res dir, prof dir, co-producer, CounterSpin & co-host, currently; FAIR Mag, An Extra, contrib; Labor at Crossroads, host, 1994-. **Orgs:** Labor at Crossroads, 1994-. **Honors/Awds:** Communicator of the Year, Metro NY Labor Press Coun, 1996. **Home Addr:** 432 E 11th St Apt 4R, New York, NY 10009, **Home Phone:** (212)598-4436. **Business Addr:** Program Director, Co-producer of CounterSpin & Co-Host, FAIR (Fairness & Accuracy In Reporting), 130 W 25th St, New York, NY 10001, **Business Phone:** (212)633-6700.

**JACKSON, JAREN**
Basketball player, basketball coach. **Personal:** Born Oct 27, 1967, New Orleans, LA; married Terri; children: Jaren Jr. **Educ:** Georgetown Univ, BA, finance, 1989. **Career:** Basketball player (retired), basketball coach; NJ Nets, shooting guard, 1989-90; Wichita Falls Texans, Continental Basketball Asn, 1990-91; Dayton Wings, WBL, 1991; La Crosse Catbirds, Continental Basketball Asn, 1991-92, 1993-94; Golden State Warriors, shooting guard, 1992; Los Angeles Clippers, shooting guard, 1992-93; Portland Trailblazers, shooting guard, 1993-94; Philadelphia 76ers, shooting guard, 1994-95; Pittsburgh Piranhas, Continental Basketball Asn, 1995; ASVEL Lyon-Villeurbanne, France, 1995-96; Ft Wayne Fury, Continental Basketball Asn, 1995-96; Houston Rockets, shooting guard, 1996; Wash Wizards, shooting guard, 1996-97; San Antonio Spurs, shooting guard, 1997-2001; Orlando Magic, shooting guard, 2001-02; Continental Basketball Asn, GarySteel heads, coach; Pittsburgh Xplosion, head coach, 2007; Ft Wayne Mad Ants, asst coach, 2007, asst coach, 2007-09, 2014-15; St John Mill Rats, head coach, 2011-12; Ottawa SkyHawks, head coach, 2013-14. **Orgs:** Founder, New Orleans Youth Org; founder, Back Block Found. **Honors/Awds:** NBA World Champion San Antonio Spurs, 1999; Spalding 3-Point Champion, McDonald's Championship-Milan, Italy, 1999. **Home Addr:** 2109 Dante St, New Orleans, LA 70118.

**JACKSON, REV. JESSE LOUIS, SR.**
Clergy, civil rights activist, government official. **Personal:** Born Oct 8, 1941, Greenville, SC; son of Noah Robinson (deceased) and Helen Burns; married Jacqueline Lavinia Brown; children: Sanitita, Jesse Louis Jr, Jonathan Luther, Yusef DuBois J Esq & Jacqueline Lavinia Jr. **Educ:** Univ Ill, attended 1960; NC Agr & Tech State Univ, BA, 1964; Chicago Theol Sem, DD, MDiv, 2000; Pepperdine Univ; Oberlin Univ; Oral Roberts Univ; Howard Univ; Georgetown Univ; Univ RI. **Career:** Greenville, SC Civil Rights Movement, leader, 1960; Serv Statewide TV Prog, dir, 1962; Oper PUSH, founder, exec dir, 1971-96, nat pres, 1972-83; Greensboro, NC Civil Rights Movement, mem, 1963; NC Intercoll Coun Human Rights, pres; Gov Stanford's Off, liaison officer; Cong Racial Equality, field rep S Eastern region, 1965; Baptist Church, ordained minister, 1968; Nat Rainbow Coalition, founder & pres, 1984-96; US Senate, shadow sen, 1991-96; CNN Network, "Both Sides With Jesse Jackson", host, 1992-2000; Rainbow PUSH Coalition, founder & pres, 1996-; founder, Wall St. Proj, 1997; US Dept State, Prom Democracy Africa, pres & sec, 1997-2000; Edge Hill Univ, hon fel. **Orgs:** Assoc minister, Fel Missionary Baptist Church; nat dir, SCLC Oper Breadbasket, 1967-71; Nat dir, Coord Coun Community Orgn, 1966-71; Active Black Coalition United Comt Action; founder, PUSH-Excel, 1977-96; fel Oxford Univ, 2007. **Honors/Awds:** Greensboro Citizen of the Year, 1964; Chicago Club Frontier's Intl Man of the Year, 1968; Presidential Award, Nat Med Asn, 1969; Humanitarian Father of the Year, Nat Father's Day Community, 1971; Third Most Admired Man, 1985; Presidential Medal of Freedom, 2000; 100 Most Influential Black Americans, Ebony Mag, 2006; Global Diversity and Inclusion Award, 2009. Received numerous honors; honorary doctorate, University of KwaZulu-Natal, 2010. **Special Achievements:** Second African American to mount a nationwide campaign for President of the US; author, Straight From The Heart, Fortress Press, 1987; author, Keep Hope Alive, 1989; Appointed by President Clinton as the Special Envoy to Africa, 1997; co-author, Legal Lynching: Racism, Injustice, and the Death Penalty, 1996; co-author, It's About Money, 2000. **Home Addr:** 6101 16th St NW, Washington, DC 20011. **Business Addr:** President, Founder, National Rainbow Coalition Inc, 30 W Washington, Chicago, IL 60602, **Business Phone:** (773)373-3366.

**JACKSON, JESSE LOUIS, JR.**
**Personal:** Born Mar 11, 1965, Greenville, SC; son of Jesse Louis Sr and Jacqueline; married Sandi; children: Jessica Donatella & Jesse L III. **Educ:** NC A&T State Univ, BS, 1987; Chicago Theol Seminary, MA, 1990; Univ Ill Law Sch, JD, 1993. **Career:** Nat Rainbow Coalition, nat outreach field dir; US House Rep, Sec Dist, Ill, congressman, 1995-2013. **Orgs:** Pres, "Keep Hope Alive" Polit Action Comt; Democratic Nat Comt; Oper PUSH, vpres-at-large; House Appropriations Comt; sr dem, Subcomt Labor, Health & Human Serv, Educ, & Related Agencies; vice-chair, Subcomt State, Foreign Opers, & Related Progs; Subcomt Agr, Rural Develop, Food & Drug Admin & Related Agencies.sr adv bd, Harvard Univ John F. Kennedy Sch Govt's Inst Polit, 2000-; Dem Party; Rainbow/PUSH Coalition; Cong Black Caucus; Apollo Alliance; mem, Omega Psi Phi. **Home Addr:** 2559 E 72nd St, Chicago, IL 60649. **Business Addr:** Congressman, US House of Representatives, 2419 Rayburn House Off Bldg, Washington, DC 20515-1302, **Business Phone:** (202)225-0773.

**JACKSON, JOHN, III**
Landscape architect, chief executive officer. **Personal:** Born Aug 14, 1961, New York, NY; son of John Jr and Lucille; children: John IV. **Educ:** Miss State Univ, BS, landscape archit, 1983. **Career:** Pickering Firm, landscape architect, 1983-87; Toles Assocs, dirlandscape archit, land planning & chief operating officer, 1987-90; Jackson Person & Assocs Inc, pres & chief exec officer, 1991-. **Orgs:** Am Planning Asn, 1984-; comt chmn, 1991-, Am Soc Landscape Architects, 1986-; vice chmn, Coun Fed Procurement Architects & Engrs, 1995-.Am Planning Asn, 1984-; comt chmn, 1991-, Am Soc Landscape Architects, 1986-; vice chmn, Coun Fed Procurement Architects & Engrs, 1995-. **Home Addr:** 5400 Pk Ave Suite 321, Memphis, TN 38119. **Business Addr:** President, Owner, Jackson Person & Assocs Inc, 44 N 2nd St Suite 502, Memphis, TN 38103-2263, **Business Phone:** (901)579-4605.

**JACKSON, JOHN**
Football player. **Personal:** Born Jan 4, 1965, Camp Kwe; married Joan; children: Josh & Jordan. **Educ:** Eastern Ky Univ, BA, police admin, 1988. **Career:** Football player (retired); Pittsburgh Steelers, left tackle, 1988-97; San Diego Chargers, left tackle, 1998-99; Cincinnati Bengals, left tackle, 2000-01. **Orgs:** John & Joan Jackson Found. **Honors/Awds:** Kentucky Pro Football Hall of Fame, 2009. **Special**

Achievements: Films: 1994 AFC Championship Game, 1995; 1995 AFC Championship Game, 1996; Super Bowl XXX, 1996; 1997 AFC Championship Game, 1998.

### JACKSON, JOHN H.

Engineer, civil engineer. **Personal:** Born Jun 8, 1943, Boonville, MO; son of Louis R and Elnora Smith Campbell; married Mae Jones. **Educ:** Univ Mo, BS, civil engineering, 1968; Univ Houston, MBA, finance, 1975. **Career:** Dow Chem, design engr, 1968-72, proj engr, 1974-83; J F Pritchard & Co, design engr, 1972-74; City Miami, asst dir pub works. **Orgs:** Am Soc Pub Admin, 1983-; Nat Forum Black Pub Admin, 1984-; Nat Asn Advan Colored People. **Home Addr:** 8506 SW 103rd Ave, Miami, FL 33173-3957, **Home Phone:** (305)271-9039. **Business Addr:** Director of Public Works, City of Miami, 444 SW 2nd Ave, Miami, FL 33130.

### JACKSON, JOHNNY, JR.

Executive director, legislator, association executive. **Personal:** Born Sep 19, 1943, New Orleans, LA; married Ara Jean; children: Kenyatta Shabazz. **Educ:** Southern Univ, BA, 1965; Univ New Orleans, attended 1966. **Career:** Logan Cab Co, dispatcher, 1958-61; Sears Gentilly, porter, 1961-65; Desire Community Ctr, exec dir, 1963-73; Social Welfare Planning Coun, comt orgn, 1965-68; Dist 101, state rep, 1973-77; State La, coun mem, 1986-94; La Legis Black Caucus, founding mem, currently. **Orgs:** Munic & Prochial Gov't Comn, 1972-77; Health & Welfare Comn House, 1972-77; Joint Comn Health & Welfare, 1972-77; subcomt mem, Career & Sec Educ, 1972-77; House Comn Educ, 1972-77; subcomt mem, Health & Ment Dis, 1972-77; joint comt mem, Spec Educ, 1972-76; Gov Blue Ribbon Comn, Southern Univ Crisis, 1972; New Orleans Community Schs, 1973-77; spec comt mem, Stud Concerns, 1974-76; Gov Comn St Rev Sharing, 1974; Gov Comn Adv Valorem Taxes, 1975; Desire Credit Union, 1975-77; pres, OSEI Day Care, 1975-77; LA Legis Gov Food Stamps Adv Comt, 1977; House Comn Ways & Means, 1977; Joint Comn Legis Coun, 1977; New Orleans Jazz & Heritage Found; St Roch Comn Improv Asn; Nat Black Found; Desire Comt Housing Corp Affiliated; Desire Area Comt Coun Affiliated; Desire/FL Sr Citizens Prog; Boy Scouts Am; Urban League; Nat Asn Advan Colored People; Free Southern Theatre; Desire Community Ctr; bd mem, Northern Sickle Cell Anemia Found; bd mem, Greater Northern Asn Retarded Citizens; La House Representatives, 1972-86; New Orleans City Coun, 1986-94; vice chmn, House Comt Labor & Indust Rels. **Home Addr:** 3201 St Ferdinand, New Orleans, LA 70126. **Business Addr:** Founding Member, Louisiana Legislative Black Caucus, PO Box 44003, Baton Rouge, LA 70804, **Business Phone:** (225)342-7342.

### JACKSON, JONATHAN LUTHER

Association executive, president (organization). **Personal:** Born Jan 7, 1966, Chicago, IL; daughter of Jesse and Jacqueline; married Marilyn Ann Richards; children: Jonathan T, Jackson, Leah & Noah. **Educ:** NC A & T Univ, bus; Northwestern Univ, MBA. **Career:** Consult & developer pvt pract; PUSH-Excel, pres bd, currently; Jesse L Jackson Sr Productions, secy, currently; Jacqueline Inc, pres, currently; River N Sales & Serv LLC, vpres; Chicago State Univ, bus prof, currently. **Orgs:** Pres, Citizenship Educ Fund. **Business Addr:** National spokesman, PUSH-Excel, 930 E 50th St, Chicago, IL 60615, **Business Phone:** (773)373-3366.

### JACKSON, DR. JULIUS HAMILTON

Scientist, educator. **Personal:** Born Jan 6, 1944, Kansas City, MO; son of Virgil Lawrence Sr and Julia Esther Jones; married Patricia Ann Herring; children: Rahsaan Hamil, Sajida Lazelle & Ajani Josef. **Educ:** Univ Kans, Lawrence, KS, AB, microbiol, 1966, PhD, microbiol, 1969. **Career:** Purdue Univ, W Lafayette, NIH res fel, 1969-71, postdoctoral res assoc, 1971-72; Meharry Med Col, Nashville, TN, asst prof microbiol, 1972-76, assoc prof, chmn microbiol, 1981-85, dir, hybridoma res support facil, 1985-87; Mich State Univ, E Lansing, Grad Stud Affairs, asst dean, Dept Microbiol & Molecular Genetics, assoc prof microbiol, 1987, prof microbiol, currently; Nat Sci Found, Div Molecular & Cellular Biosciences, dir, 1995-97. **Orgs:** Am Soc Biol Chemists, 1982-; chmn, Comt Equal Opportunities Minority Groups, Am Soc Biochem & Molecular Biol, 1992; Am Acad Microbiol; Am Soc Microbiol; Nat Inst Health; Am Soc Biochem & Molecular Biol. **Honors/Awds:** William A Hinton Research Training Award, Am Soc Microbiol, 2000. **Special Achievements:** Author of numerous articles. **Home Addr:** 2512 Capeside Dr, Okemos, MI 48864, **Home Phone:** (517)337-3935. **Business Addr:** Professor, Michigan State University, 6178 Biomed & Phys Sci Bldg, East Lansing, MI 48824, **Business Phone:** (517)884-5398.

### JACKSON, KAREN DENISE

Engineer. **Personal:** Born Jan 14, 1947, Chicago, IL; daughter of William Jesse and Kathryn; married Raymond; children: Cheo Oronde Diallobe & Ahkil Asaad Diallobe. **Educ:** Elmira Col, BS, math & chem, 1976; Mich State Univ, BS, elec engineering, 1984. **Career:** Gen Motors, foreman, 1977-82; Motorola Govt Electronics Group, Tactical secure commun div, software engr, 1984-. **Orgs:** Vpres, comput camp chmn, Ariz Coun Black Engrs & Scientists, 1986-; charter secy-treas, Word Wizards Toast Masters, 1987-; chmn, ACBES Summer Comput Camp, 1989-92; co-founder bus group black women, Strictly Bus. **Honors/Awds:** Black Engineer of the Year for Community Service, US Black Engr Magazine, 1992; The Career Communications Group; ACBES, High Five Award, 1991. **Special Achievements:** First Black history radio program in Corning NY, 1974; created KomputerEd-Tools, 1996. **Home Addr:** 7748 S Rita Lane, Tempe, AZ 85284-1502, **Home Phone:** (602)820-2788. **Business Addr:** Software Engineer, Motorola Government Electronics Group, 8201 E McDowell Rd Hayden Bldg, Scottsdale, AZ 85257-3893, **Business Phone:** (602)441-1197.

### JACKSON, KAREN EUBANKS

Association executive. **Personal:** married Kyle Scott; children: Caleen. **Educ:** Morgan State Univ, BA, sociol, 1963. **Career:** YWCA, Houston Health Initiative, prog mgr; Newark Dept Welfare, social worker; Sisters Network Inc, partner, founder & chief exec officer, 1994-. **Orgs:** Int Breast Cancer Res Found; Ctr Res Minority Health; Am Soc Breast Dis; Consumers Liaison Group; Nat Breast Cancer Coalition; Susan G Komen Breast Cancer Found, African Am Nat Adv Comt; Baylor Methodist Breast Care Ctr Adv Coun; Am Cancer Soc. **Honors/Awds:** Certificate, Nat Breast Cancer Coalition Proj Lead; Certificate, Encoreplus Breast Health Educr; Certificate, Am Cancer Soc Spec Touch Breast Health & Look Good-Feel Better; Breast Cancer Hero, Lifetime TV; TNT Dramatic Difference Award; Champion of Change, JC Penney; The Jefferson Award, ABC; Lance Armstrong Voice of Survivorship Award; Status Women Award; Nat Coun Negro Women; Vanderbilt-Ingram Cancer Ctr Award. **Special Achievements:** Co-author, Breast Cancer in African American Women: The Evolution of the Sisters Network Inc, Breast Diseases: A Year Book Quarterly, 2003; Her story has also been included in an HBO special: Cancer: Evolution to Revolution and in several breast cancer related books: Breast Cancer Black Women, My Mother's Breast & Celebrating Life. **Business Addr:** Founder, Chief Executive Officer, Sisters Network Inc, 2922 Rosedale St, Houston, TX 77004, **Business Phone:** (713)781-0255.

### JACKSON, DR. KEITH HUNTER

Physicist. **Personal:** Born Sep 24, 1953, Columbus, OH; children: Kamilah & Akil. **Educ:** Morehouse Col, BS, physics, 1974; Ga Tech Univ, BSEE, 1976; Stanford Univ, MS, physics, 1979, PhD, physics, 1982. **Career:** Hewlett Packard Labs, tech staff, 1981-83; Howard Univ, asst prof, 1983-88; Rockwell Int, Rocket dyne Div, tech staff, 1988-91; Lawrence Berkeley Nat Lab, staff scientist, 1992-2005, Ctr X-Ray Optics, dir; Fla A&M Univ, vpres res, 2005-08, prof physics; Morgan State Univ, Dept Physics, prof & chair physics, 2010-13, interim provost & vpres acad affairs, 2013-. **Orgs:** Fel Nat Soc Black Physicists, pres, 2001-06; founding dir, Nat Asn Equal Opportunity Higher Educ, 2002-03; Am Phys Soc; Optical Soc Am; Army Res Lab Tech Assessment Bd; exec comt mem, Advan Light Source; fel African Sci Inst. **Honors/Awds:** The 50 Most Important African Americans in Technology, US Black Engr & Info Technol. **Business Addr:** Interim Provost, Vice President, Morgan State University, Calloway Hall Rm G-22, Baltimore, MD 21251, **Business Phone:** (443)885-3350.

### JACKSON, KEITH JEROME

Football player, broadcaster. **Personal:** Born Apr 19, 1965, Little Rock, AR; son of Gladys; married Melanie; children: 3. **Educ:** Okla Univ, BS, communs, 1988. **Career:** Football player (retired), radio broadcaster; Philadelphia Eagles, tightend, 1988-91; Miami Dolphins, tight end, 1992-94; Green Bay Packers, tightend, 1995-96; Ark Razorback Sports Network, color commentator, currently; Univ Ark, radio broadcast color analyst, currently. **Orgs:** Omega Psi Phi; founder, Positive Atmosphere Reaches Kids Prog, 1993. **Honors/Awds:** Rookie of the Year, Sporting News, 1988; Top VI Award, Nat Col Athletic Asn, 1988; Champion, Super Bowl, XXXI; College Football Hall of Fame, 2001; Silver Anniversary Award, Nat Col Athletic Asn, 2013. **Special Achievements:** Six Pro Bowl selection, 1988, 1989, 1990, 1992, 1993, 1996; Five All-Pro selection, 1988, 1989, 1990, 1992, 1996; TV Series: "The Complete History of the Philadelphia Eagles", 2004; "Jimmy Kimmel Live!", 2005; "The Top 5 Reasons You Can't Blame", 2005; "Minister of Defense: The Reggie White Story", 2005; "Year of the Quarterback", 2011. **Home Addr:** , Little Rock, AR. **Business Addr:** Color Commentator, Arkansas Razorback Sports Network, PO Box 77, Little Rock, AR 72203, **Business Phone:** (501)324-7562.

### JACKSON, KEITH M.

Executive. **Personal:** Born Nov 22, 1948, Springfield, IL. **Educ:** Dartmouth Col, BA, 1971; Columbia Univ, MS, 1975. **Career:** Sahara Energy Corp, pres; Trans Urban E Orgn Inc NYC, consult econ dev & mkt anal, 1971-73; Rep Charles B Rangel US House Reps Wash, legis asst, 1973-74; Cong Black Caucus Inc, exec dir. **Home Addr:** 316 W 93rd St Apt 5D, New York, NY 10025.

### JACKSON, KENYA LOVE

Executive. **Personal:** Born Nov 25, 1963, Flushing, NY; daughter of James G Newman II and Gladys Maria Knight; married Jimmy. **Educ:** Univ San Diego, BA, 1986. **Career:** Cedar Sinai Hosp, Los Angeles, Calif, lab res technician, 1982-84; Jeremiah's Steak House, Dallas Tex, asst mgr, head cashier, 1984-85; Marquee Entertainment, Los Angeles, Calif, asst exec vpres, 1986-87; Shakeji Inc, Las Vegas, Nev, pres & exec adminr, 1987-; Kenya's Cakes Stars, Las Vegas, Nev, owner, 1994-. **Orgs:** Secy & treas, Newman Mgt Inc, 1987-; corp dir, KNS Prod Inc, 1987-; corp dir, Knight Hair Care Inc, 1988-; secy & treas, Ms G Inc, 1988-; pres, Kenya's Kitchen Inc, 1993; bd dir, Saints Unified Voices; founder, Elizabeth Knight Fund with Am Diabetes Asn; pres, Relief Soc orgn. **Business Addr:** Owner, Kenya's Cakes of the Stars, 1301 E Sunset Rd, Las Vegas, NV 89120, **Business Phone:** (702)450-7661.

### JACKSON, KEVIN ALLEN

Executive, government official. **Personal:** Born Aug 27, 1962, Chicago, IL; son of Allen JacksonUS Dept Labor and Elizabeth; married Paula; children: Ryann Elizabeth. **Educ:** Northeastern Ill Univ, BA, pre-law, 1986; Roosevelt Univ, Grad Div, 1988; Columbia Col, Grad Div, 1990. **Career:** Var Firms, Law clerk, paralegal, var firms, 1982-86; US Off Personnel Mgt, personnel mgt specialist, 1986-90; JEG Inc, pres, chief financial officer, 1989-; US DOL/Occup Safety & Health Admin, mgt analyst, 1990-97, regional training officer, 1997-. **Orgs:** United Negro Col Fund, Fund Raising Bd mem; Oper Push, mem, vol; InterNat Film & Video Festival, panel mem; Midwest Radio & Music asn; asst, chair, exec bd mem, Rat Pack InterNat; Am Soc Pub Adminr; Chicago Metro Staffing Coun; InterNat Personnel Mgt asn. **Home Addr:** 8005 S Fairfield, Chicago, IL 60652, **Home Phone:** (312)497-0295. **Business Addr:** Regional Training Officer, US Department Labor & OSHA, 230 So Dearborn Suite 3244, Chicago, IL 60604, **Business Phone:** (312)353-6628.

### JACKSON, KEVIN ANDRE

Athlete, athletic coach. **Personal:** Born Nov 25, 1964, Phoenix, AZ; married Robin; children: Cole, Trinity, Bailee, Kira & Brynn. **Educ:** Iowa State Univ; Univ Am & US Sports Acad, BA, sports sci, 2005. **Career:** Wrestler (retired), coach; US Olympic Athlete, freestyle wrestler, 1992; USA Wrestling, freestyle wrestling coach, 2001-08; AUS team, head coach, 1998-2001; Iowa State univ, head wrestling coach, 2009-; Olympic Training Center, freestyle coach; Sunkist youth develop prog, head coach. **Orgs:** Cyclone Wrestling Club, 1989-92; FILA Int Wrestling Hall Fame; US Nat Wrestling Hall Fame; Iowa State Univ Athletics Hall Fame. **Honors/Awds:** USOC Wrestler of the Year, 1991; Gold Medalist, World Championships, 1991, 1995; Gold Medalist, Pan Am Games, 1991, 1995; Gold Medalist, Olympic Games, Barcelona, Spain, 1992; National Freestyle Wrestler of the Year, 1992; Gold medal in Freestyle wrestling, Summer Olympics, 1992; Amateur Wrestling News Man of the Year, 1992; John Smith Award, USA Wrestling Freestyle Wrestler of the Year, 1995; US Nat Wrestling Hall of Fame. **Special Achievements:** One of only five U.S. wrestlers to claim three career World-level titles; First American to win the prestigious Takhti Cup 1998. **Business Addr:** Head Wrestling Coach, Iowa State University, Jacobson Athletic Bldg 1800 S 4th St, Ames, IA 50011-1140, **Business Phone:** (515)294-3662.

### JACKSON, KEVIN L.

Executive. **Personal:** Born Mar 23, 1956, Washington, DC; son of Thomas and Dorothy; married Michelle; children: Bruce & Kevin Nolan. **Educ:** Lehigh Univ, Col Bus & Econs, BS, mkt, 1978; Univ Minn, mgt principles; Defense Syst Mgt Col, defense contractor finance. **Career:** NCR Corp, acct mgr, 1978-82, customer engr; Honeywell Fed Syst, acct mgr, 1982-87; HFSI, mkt mgr, 1984-88; Honeywell Inc, mkt develop mgr, 1987-90; Alliant Techsystems, mgr, AF Prog, 1990-98, dir bus develop, 1998-; Sports Enhancements Inc, bd mem, 1997-; AT&T Inc, proj mgr; Alliant Techsystems Inc, dir bus develop, 2004-12; Saab N Am, vpres support & serv, 2012-. **Orgs:** Vpres, AFA-DW Steele Chap, 1995-; dir, ATK Inc. **Home Addr:** 4714 W Estrella St, Tampa, FL 33629-5518. **Business Addr:** Vice President Air Warfare Systems, Saab Defense and Security, 2101 L St NW, Washington, DC 20037, **Business Phone:** (703)406-7900.

### JACKSON, LA TOYA YVONNE (LA TOYA JACKSON)

Entertainer, actor, singer. **Personal:** Born May 29, 1956, Gary, IN; daughter of Joseph and Katherine; married Jack Gordon. **Career:** Singer, dancer, television star, exec currently; Albums: You're Gonna Get Rocked, 1988; Imagination, 1986; TV series: "We Are the World", 1985; "Late Night with David Letterman", 1989; "Hola Raffaella!", 1993; "Howard Stern", 1994-95; "So Graham Norton", 1999; "Larry King Live", 2003; "V Graham Norton", 2003; "Show de Cristina, El", 2004; "Michael Jackson's Boys", 2005; "Airport", 2005; "Armed & Famous", 2007; Ja-Tail Enterprises LLC & Ja-Tail Records, owner, currently; Studio Albums: La Toya Jackson, 1980; My Special Love, 1981; Heart Don't Lie, 1984; Imagination, 1986; La Toya, 1988; Bad Girl, 1989; No Relations, 1991; Formidable, 1992; From Nashville to You, 1994; Stop in the Name of Love, 1995; Lady Blues, 2008, Startin' Over, 2009. **Honors/Awds:** Outstanding Song Awards, 1985. **Special Achievements:** Worked with Nancy Reagan's Just-Say-No Anti Drug campaign, 1987; Geraldo, guest appearance; Posed for Playboy mag, 1989; Bob Hope's Easter Vacation in the Bahamas, tv special, participant, 1989; La Toya: Growing Up in the Jackson Family, autobiography, co-author with Patricia Romanowski, Dutton, 1991; She received a Grammy nomination for Best Reggae Recording; One of five Outstanding Song Awards at the 1985 World Popular Song Festival in Japan, for her single "Baby Sister"; She was one of the recipients of a Grammy Award for Record of the Year as a vocalist for "We Are the World"; She is the spokeswoman for "Star Ice"; First Jackson girl to have a solo career. **Home Addr:** 2151 5th Ave, New York, NY 10037, **Home Phone:** (917)507-2417. **Business Addr:** Singer, Owner, Ja Tail Records, 8306 Wilshire Blvd Suite 528, Beverly Hills, CA 90211, **Business Phone:** (323)934-9268.

### JACKSON, LARRON DEONNE

Accountant, football player. **Personal:** Born Aug 26, 1949, St. Louis, MO; children: Laresa, Temple & Larron Jr. **Educ:** Mo Univ, BS, 1971. **Career:** Football player (retired), exec; Denver Broncos, 1971-74; Atlanta Falcons, 1975-76; Monsanto Chem, mgt trainee, 1970; Touch-Ross, jr & sr staff acct, 1972-74; Jackson & Montgomery Tax & Acct Serv, 1975; Jackson & Assocs Fin Serv, acct, 1975. **Orgs:** Hon bd mem, Mathew-Dickeys Boys Club, 1971. **Home Addr:** 4205A E Maffitt Ave, St. Louis, MO 63113.

### JACKSON, LARRY EUGENE

Engineer. **Personal:** Born Feb 18, 1943, Chicago, IL; married Roberta O Staples; children: Crystal, Robyn & Larry Jr. **Educ:** Purdue Univ, BSME, 1967. **Career:** Inland Steel Co, sr engr, 1967-75; Kaiser Eng Inc, proj eng, 1977. **Orgs:** Front Int Gary Chap Art Pub AISE, 1970; Am Inst Stl Engr Mem; Lake Area United Way Budget Comn; racing chmn, INSki Coun; pres bd dir, Gary & Bldg; Alpha Phi Alpha. **Home Addr:** 7117 E 1st Ave, Gary, IN 46403. **Business Addr:** 35 E Wacker Dr, Chicago, IL 60601.

### JACKSON, LEE ARTHUR

Government official. **Personal:** Born Apr 14, 1950, Lynch, KY; son of Sylmon James and Marie Stokes; married Carolyn Bates; children: Michelle Tarese. **Educ:** Univ Ky, BA, polit sci, sociol, 1973; Ky State Univ, CPM, 1990. **Career:** Manager & supervisor (retired); Dept Employ Servs, Lexington, KY, field off mgr & prog supvr; Peterson Arts & Educ Fund Inc, financial secy; Lyman T. Johnson African-Am Alumni Group, pres. **Orgs:** Dist dir, Alpha Phi Alpha, 1972; St Luke Lodge Suite 123, 1972; pres, Ky Asn State Employees, 1990-; vice chmn, Am Fed Teachers; Fed Pub Employees, 1992; chmn, Community Action Coun Bros Policy Bd; Ky Am Water Co Consumer Adv Coun; pres, AFT-Ky; vpres, Ky State AFL-CIO, 1999-2003; bd mem, Lexington Pub Libr, KY; UK Black Stud Union & Black Voices; vice chmn, Evergreen Brucetown Inc; coordr, Martin Luther King Jr. **Home Addr:** 2804 Mt McKinley Way, Lexington, KY 40517-3814, **Home Phone:** (606)272-4305. **Business Addr:** President, Kentucky Association of State Employees, 207 Holmes St, Frankfort, KY 40604-4110, **Business Phone:** (502)875-2273.

**JACKSON, LESLIE ELAINE.** See SOUTH, LESLIE ELAINE.

### JACKSON, LILLIAN
Association executive. **Personal:** Born Montgomery, AL. **Educ:** Troy State Univ, AA; Ala State Univ, BA, MA. **Career:** Nat Asn Advan Colored People, Metro Montgomery Br, dir, pres; Ala State Nat Asn Advan Colored People, pres. **Business Addr:** President, Ala State Nat Asn Advan Colored People, PO Box 9581, Dothan, AL 36304, **Business Phone:** (334)714-4128.

### JACKSON, LISA P.
Executive, government official. **Personal:** Born Feb 8, 1962, Philadelphia, PA; married Kenny; children: Marcus & Brian. **Educ:** Tulane Univ Sch Engineering, BS, chem engineering, 1983; Princeton Univ, MS, chem engineering, 1986. **Career:** Asst Comnr Land Use Mgt; Asst Comnr Compliance & Enforcement, worked 16 yrs an employee US EPA; Dept Environ Protection (DEP), asst comnr, 2002; US Environ Protection NJ, asst comnr compliance & enforcement & asst comnr land use mgt, 2006-08, state's comnr, chief staff to Gov Jon S. Corzine, 2008-09; US Environ Protection Agency, 12th Adminr, 2009-13; Apple Inc, vpres environ, policy & social initiatives, 2013-. **Orgs:** Hon mem, Delta Sigma Theta sorority, 2013. **Special Achievements:** First African American to serve as the Administrator of the EPA, 2009-. **Business Addr:** Vice President, Environment Policy & Social Initiatives, Apple Inc, 1 Infinite Loop, Cupertino, CA 95014, **Business Phone:** (408)996-1010.

### JACKSON, LURLINE BRADLEY
Executive, executive director. **Personal:** Born Dallas, TX; daughter of Henry (deceased) and Alice Young (deceased). **Educ:** N Tex State Univ, attended 1956; El Centro Jr Col, attended 1974; Richland Col, 1978; Respiratory Ther Sch, attended 1980; Tarrant Co Jr Col, nursing home admin, 1983. **Career:** Presby Hosp, Dallas, respiratory ther; Caring Med Supply Co, founder, owner, pres, chief exec officer; Bradley Home Assisted Living Inc, dir. **Orgs:** Nat vpres, Lincoln Alumni Asn, Dallas, 1990-92; Dallas Chap, Nat Asn Advan Colored People; vpres, NCW; Nat Caucus & Ctr Black Aged; speaker, Altzheimer, Dallas Chap. **Honors/Awds:** Iota Phi Lambda, Psi Chap, 1968; Welcome House Inc, Nat Coun Negro Women Inc, Oak Cliff Sect, 1983; Dallas Metro Club, Nat Asn Negro Bus & Prof Women, 1989; Wash-Lincoln Alumni Asn Dallas, 1989; FDR Award, She-Roes & He-Roes, 1990. **Special Achievements:** Lurline Bradley Jackson is the first black students to attend North Texas State College, 1956. **Home Addr:** 8932 Clearwater Dr, Dallas, TX 75243. **Business Addr:** Director, The Bradley Home For Assisted Living Inc, 2700 N Stemmons Fwy, Dallas, TX 75207-2209.

### JACKSON, MANNIE L.
Executive, baseball executive. **Personal:** Born May 4, 1939, Illmo, MO; son of Emmett and Margaret; married Cathy; children: Cassandra & Candace. **Educ:** Univ Ill Urbana-Champaign, BS, educ, 1960; Univ Detroit, mkt & econ, 1968. **Career:** Gen Motors, 1964-68; Honeywell Inc, var positions, 1968-93, Commun Serv Div, vpres & gen mgr, 1981-87, Corp Mkt, vpres; Harlem Globetrotters Int Inc, owner, 1993-, chmn & chief exec officer, 1993-2007, bd dir, currently; Boxcar Financial Holdings, chmn, currently. **Orgs:** Founding mem, Exec Leadership Coun, pres; bd gov, Am Red Cross, 2000-; trustee, Univ Ill Found; mem bd, Ashland, 1994-; mem bd, Jostens Corp; mem bd, Reebok, 1996-; mem bd, Stanley Work, 1995-; chmn, Basketball Hall Fame. **Honors/Awds:** Naismith Memorial Basketball Hall of Fame, 2006; Basketballs Human Spirit Award; One of Americas "40 Most Powerful Black Executives", Black Enterprise Mag, 1988, 1993; Theodore Roosevelt Award, 2015. **Special Achievements:** First African American owner of a major international sports organist ration; first African American to start the University of Illinois varsity basketball team. **Business Addr:** Board Director, Harlem Globetrotters International Inc, 400 E Van Buren St Suite 300, Phoenix, AZ 85004, **Business Phone:** (602)258-0000.

### JACKSON, MARCUS
Consultant. **Educ:** Southern Ill Univ, BS, mech engineering technol; Rockhurst Univ, MBA; Univ Mo, nuclear engineering. **Career:** Kan City Power & Light Co, engr, 1974-80, asst dir power supply, sr dir power supply, vpres power prod, sr vpres power supply, exec vpres, chief operating officer, 1996-99, exec vpres, chief financial officer, 1999-2000, pres power; Provo Arabia Ltd, Saudi Arabia, proj engr, 1980-83; SEMCO Energy Corp, chmn, pres & chief exec officer, 2001-03; Gibbs & Hill Engineering Inc, proj engr; KLT Power Inc, pres & chmn; Accion Group, consult, sr consult, currently. **Business Addr:** Senior Consultant, Accion Group, 244 N Main St, Concord, NH 03301, **Business Phone:** (603)229-1644.

### JACKSON, HON. MARIE OLIVER
Judge. **Personal:** Born Aug 14, 1947, Pittsburgh, PA; daughter of Warren Joseph Oliver and Nettie Marie Wall; children: Toney, Vincent, Alphonso & Ana. **Educ:** Mt Holyoke Col, BA, 1969; Harvard Law Sch, JD, 1972. **Career:** Cambridge & Somerville Legal Servs, gen trial work, 1972-74; Tufts Univ, vis lectr, 1973-74; Mass Comn Against Discrimination, staff dir, 1974-76; Div Hearing Officers, admin justice, 1976-77, Exec Off Admin & Finance, gen coun, 1977-80; Dist Ct, Dept Trial Ct Cambridge Div, justice, 1980-97; Dist Woburn, presiding justice, 1997-98; Cambridge Dist Ct, judge, 1998-. **Orgs:** Bd & regional dir, Nat Asn Women Judges, 1981-84; Nat Coun Juv & Family Ct Judges, 1981-89; Greater Boston Youth Symphony Orchestra, 1985-87; Nat Conf Christians & Jews, 1985-87; Alpha Kappa Alpha Sor Psi Omega Chap; Middlesex Co Dist Atty's Child Sexual Abuse Task Force, 1985-86; Gov's Task Force Correction Alternatives, 1985-86, Foster Care, 1986-87; bd Judge, Baker Guid Ctr, 1987-94; Dist Ct Stand Comn Care & Protection & CHINS cases, 1990; bd dir, Adolescent Consult Servs, 1996; PRS, MAS Black Judges Conf, 1998-; Racial & Ethnic Access & Fairness Adv Bd, 2000-; Comn Pub Trust & Confidence, 2001-03; Boston Inn Ct, 2002-. **Honors/Awds:** Outstanding Young Leader Boston Jaycees, 1981; Leadership Massachusetts Black Lawyers, 1981; Community Justice Award, MA Justice Resource Inst, 1985; Achievement Award, Cambridge YWCA, 1985; Sojourner Truth Award, Nat Asn Negro Bus & Prof Women, 1986; Leadership Achievement & Service Awards; Sesquicentennial Alumnae Award, Mt Holyoke Alumnae Asn, 1988. **Special Achievements:** First Justice of the Woburn District Court. **Home Addr:** 18B Buttaro Rd, Woburm, MA 01801, **Home Phone:** (781)935-3650. **Business Addr:** Justice, Cambridge District Court, 40 Thorndike St, Cambridge, MA 02141, **Business Phone:** (617)494-4350.

### JACKSON, MARK A.
Executive, basketball player, basketball coach. **Personal:** Born Apr 1, 1965, Brooklyn, NY; married Desiree Coleman; children: Mark II, Christian, Micah & Heavyn. **Educ:** St John's Univ, St Vincents Col, Jamaica, NY, commun arts, 1987. **Career:** Basket player (retired), analyst, coach; New York Knicks, guard, 1987-92, 2001-02; Los Angeles Clippers, 1992-94; Indiana Pacers, 1994-96, 1997-2000; Ordained Minister, 1996; Denver Nuggets, 1996-97; Toronto Raptors, 2000-01; Utah Jazz, 2002-03; Players Wear Int, co-owner, currently; Houston Rockets, 2003-04; Yankees Entertainment & Sports network, NJ Nets, analyst; ABC, broadcast commentator; ABC studio show; Golden State Warr, head coach, 2011-2014; ESPN, broadcast commentator, game analyst, 2014-. **Orgs:** United Negro Col Fund Wheelchair Charities. **Home Addr:** , Los Angeles, CA. **Business Addr:** Game Analyst, ESPN, ESPN Plz, Bristol, CT 06010.

### JACKSON, MARY
Financial manager, executive. **Personal:** Born Jan 7, 1932, Lumpkin, GA; daughter of Adie Beauford Jr and Ida B Robinson; married Arthur L; children: Richard L George III & Cynthia A George. **Educ:** Albany St Col, BEd, 1953; Anchorage Ak Community Col, ABus, 1980; Columbia State Univ, BS, 1997. **Career:** Sheraton Hotel, Wash DC, payroll supvr, 1963-66; Westover AFB MA, procurement clerk, 1966-68; Edwards AFB CA, procurement clerk, 1968-71; Elmendorf ABF AK, purchasing agt, 1971-75; Automotive Parts, Anchorage AK, purchasing agt, 1975-78; Alaska Village Elec Coop, Anchorage AK, purchasing mgr, 1978-95; EMJ Travel, 1995. **Orgs:** Delta Sigma Theta Sorority, 1952; educ adv, Anchorage Community Col, 1977-79; comt mem, Kimo News Adv Coun Prog, 1978-80; Alpha Delta Zeta, Phi Theta Kappa Hon Soc, 1978; illustrious commandress, Daughter Isis, 1980-81; St Grand Loyal Lady Ruler, Order Golden Circle, 1982-89; st pres, Alaska St Fedn BPW/USA, 1983-84; dir, Int Affairs Purchasing Mgt, 1983-84; past sec, Soroptimist Int, 1984; chmn, Job Serv Exec Comt, 1985; chmn, Anchorage Community Block Grant Develop (HUD), 1986-95; grand worthy matron, Prince Hall GC Order Eastern Star, 1987-90; strategic long range comt, Links, Ak Chap, 1992; Imp Ct Daughters Isis, chmn Imp DirectressYr, 2003-04; Nat Coun Negro Women; local 100 Black Women. **Honors/Awds:** Outstanding Service Award, purchasing mgt, 1983-84; Woman of the Year, Nat Bus Women, 1984; Outstanding Achievement Leadership, Prince Hall Masons F&AM, 1988; Community Service Award, Alaska Black Caucus, 1988; Imperial Deputy of the Desert, Isiserettes, 1988-; Community Service Award, Zeta Phi Beta Sorority, 1989; Outstanding Service Award Public Relations, Imperial Ct, Daughters Isis, 1990; Employee of the Quarter, Alaska Village Electric, 1992; Outstanding Accomplishment, North Future Bus & Prof Women's Club, 1992; Outstanding Letters Recognition, Gov Alaska, Outstanding Commission Service, 1995. **Home Addr:** 8539 Crosspointe Ct, Antelope, CA 95843, **Home Phone:** (916)728-3872.

### JACKSON, MEL (MELTON JACKSON)
Actor. **Personal:** Born Oct 13, 1970, Chicago, IL. **Career:** Actor, Producer, Spoken word, Artist & R&B musician; Films: Scenes for the Soul, 1995; Soul Food, 1997; Carmin's Choice, 1997; An Invited Guest, 1999; The List, 1999; Dancing in September, 2000; Dirty Hearts, 2000; Dancing in September, 2000; Automatic, 2001; Deliver Us From Eva, 2003; Motives, 2004; Friends and Lovers, 2005; Love on Layaway, 2005; Where Is Love Waiting, 2006; Motives 2, 2007; Stick Up Kids, The, 2008; A Good Man Is Hard to Find, 2008; Dreams, 2013; Four Seasons, 2014; TV movies: "To Sir With Love 2", 1996; "George Wallace", 1997; "Temptations", 1998; "Little Richard", 2000; "Playing With Fire", 2000; "The Making of Motives", 2004; "Flip the Script", 2005; "The Black Man's Guide to Understanding Black Women", 2006; "Abduction of Jesse Bookman", producer, 2008; The Marriage Chronicles, 2012; Tv series: "The Division", 1994; "Midnight Ma", 1995; "The Parent Hood", 1996; "Hitz", 1997; "NYPD Blue", 1997; "In the House", 1997-99; "Living Single", 1997-98; "The Jamie Foxx Show", 1999; "Vengeance Unlimited", 1999; "DAG", 2000; "The Steve Harvey Show", 2000; "For Your Love", 2002; "The Parkers", 2004; "Love Inc", 2005; "Half & Half", 2005; "Reed Between the Lines", 2011; "If You Really Love Me", 2012; "To Love and to Cherish", 2012; Am Majic Entertainment, owner, currently; Stone Manners Agency, owner, currently. **Honors/Awds:** Best Performance by an Actor, 2008. **Business Addr:** Owner, Stone Manners Agency, 6500 Wilshire Blvd Suite 550, Los Angeles, CA 90048, **Business Phone:** (323)655-1313.

### JACKSON, MICHAEL W.
Judge, district attorney. **Personal:** Born Nov 18, 1963, Fayetteville, TN. **Educ:** Centre Col, Danville, KY; Fla State Col Law, JD, 1988. **Career:** Selma Muni Ct, munic judge, 1995-98; Ala 4th Judicial Circuit, asst dist atty, dist atty, currently; pvt pract atty, currently. **Orgs:** State Dem Exec Comt. **Business Addr:** District Attorney, 4th Judicial Circuit, 105 Lauderdale St, Selma, AL 36702-0000, **Business Phone:** (334)874-2540.

### JACKSON, MIKE (MICHAEL RAY JACKSON)
Baseball player. **Personal:** Born Dec 22, 1964, Houston, TX; married Tammy; children: Lindsey, Ryan, Amber & Michael. **Educ:** Hill Col. **Career:** Baseball player (retired); Philadelphia Phillies, pitcher, 1986-87; Seattle Mariners, pitcher, 1988-91, 1996; San Francisco Giants, pitcher, 1992-94; Cincinnati Reds, pitcher, 1995; Cleveland Indians, pitcher, 1997-99; Houston Astros, pitcher, 2001; Minn Twins, pitcher, 2002; Chicago White Sox, pitcher, 2004.

### JACKSON, MILES M.
School administrator, educator. **Personal:** Born Apr 28, 1929, Richmond, VA; son of Miles M Sr and Thelma; married Bernice R; children: Milles III, Marsha Bethards, Muriel & Melia Phifer. **Educ:** Va Union Univ, BA, 1955; Drexel Univ, Col Info Sci, MS, libr & info sci, 1956; Syracuse Univ, Newhouse Sch Commun, PhD, 1974. **Career:** Free Libr, Philadelphia, ref res librn, 1956-58; Hampton Univ, head librn, 1958-62; Am Samoa, territorial librn, 1962-64; Atlanta Univ, Trevor Arnett Libr, dir, 1964-67; Tehran Univ, prof, 1968-69; State Univ NY, assoc prof, 1969-75; Univ Hawaii, prof libr info studies, 1975-95, dean sch libr & info studies, 1982-95, prof & dean emer, 1975-95. **Orgs:** Am Libr Asn, 1958-; Asn Libr & Info Sci Edu, 1969, pres, 1969-70; bd mem, Hawaii Libr, 1984-92, pres, 1984-86; bd mem, Cent YMCA, 1986; Winward Y's Men, 1996-; Hawaii State Libr Adv Coun, 1996-98; Hawaii Coun Humanities, 2000. **Honors/Awds:** Sr Fulbright Award, Lectr Tehran, Iran, 1968-69; Harold Han cour Travel Award, S Pac, 1978; Outstanding Achievement Award, Nat Asn Advan Colored People, 2010; Citizen of the Year Award, Lambda Beta Beta Chapter, 2010; Civil Rights ML King Jr Award, 2011. **Special Achievements:** Editor: "Pacific Island Studies:, 1986; "International Handbook of Contemp Develop in Librarianship", 1981, Author: "Comparative & Int Librarianship", 1970; "Linkages Over Space & Time", 1991; "And They Came", 2001; "They Followed the Trade Winds", 2005; Documentary Film: "Holding Fast the Dream: Hawaii's African American Experience", co-producer. **Home Addr:** 47-106 Pulama Rd, PO Box 1602, Kaneohe, HI 96744, **Home Phone:** (808)239-8943. **Business Addr:** Professor, Dean Emeritus, University of Hawaii, 303A POST Bldg 1680 E W Rd, Honolulu, HI 96822, **Business Phone:** (808)956-7321.

### JACKSON, MILLIE (MILDRED JACKSON)
Singer, actor. **Personal:** Born Jul 15, 1944, Thompson, GA; children: Keisha & Jerroll. **Career:** Albums: Millie Jackson, 1972; Hurts So Good, 1973; I Got To Try It Once, 1974; Caught Up, 1974; Still Caught Up, 1975; Free & In Love, 1976; Feelin' Bitchy, 1977; Lovingly Yours, 1977; Get It Out'cha Syst, 1978; A Moment's Pleasure, 1979; Royal Rappin's, 1979; Live & Uncensored, 1979; For Men Only, 1980; I Had To Say It, 1980; Live, 1980; Just a Li'l BitCountry, 1981; Hard Times, 1982; Millie Jackson "Live & Outrageous", 1982; E.S.P. (Extra Sexual Persuasion), 1983; Imitation of Love, 1986; The Tidels Turning, 1988; Back To The Shit, 1989; Young Man, Older Woman, 1991; Young Man, Older Woman: Cast Album, 1993; Rock N' Soul, 1994; It's Over, 1995; The Sequel, It Ain't Over, 1997; Not for Church Folk!, 2001; Singles:; "An Imitation of Love"; "Living With A Stranger"; "Taking My Life Back"; "Love Quake"; "Chocolate Brown Eyes"; "Breaking Up Somebody's Home"; "The Lies That We Live"; "I Miss You Baby"; "Ask Me What You Want", 1971; "A Child of God (It's Hard to Believe)", 1971; "My Man, A Sweet Man", 1972; "It Hurts So Good", 1973; "Breakaway", 1973; "How Do You Feel the Morning After", 1974; "The Rap", 1975; "Loving Arms", 1975; "Leftovers", 1975; "(If Loving You Is Wrong) I Don't Want to Be Right", 1975; "Kiss You All Over", "I'm Through Trying To Prove My Love To You"; "There You Are", 1976; "Feel Like Making Love", 1976; "Bad Risk", 1976; "If You're Not Back in Love By Monday"; "I Can't Say Goodbye", 1977; "Do You Wanna Make Love", 1979; "A Moment's Pleasure", 1979; "We Got To Hit It Off", 1979; "Never Chg Lovers In The Mid of The Night"; "Keep The Home Fire Burnin"; "Sweet Music Man"; "All The Way Lover"; "A Love of Your Own"; "You Never Cross My Mind", 1980; "This Is It ", 1980; "Despair", 1980; "I Can't Stop Loving You", 1981; "Spec Occasion", 1982; "I Feel Like Walkin' In The Rain", 1983; "Act of War", 1985; "Hot! Wild! Unrestricted! Crazy Love", 1986; "Did You Think I Wouldn't Cry"; "Butt-A-Cize"; "Leave Me Alone"; "Love Quake"; "Taking My Life Back"; "Living With A Stranger"; "Something You Can Feel"; "An Imitation of Love", 1987; "Love Is A Dangerous Game", 1987; "It's A Thang", 1987; "Something You Can Feel", 1988; "Will You Love Me Tom", 1989; "Young Man Older Woman", 1991, "Check in the Mail, 1994"; Compilations: Pimps, Players & Pvt Eyes, 1992, Wild Women Do Get the Blues, 1996; Films: Cleopatra Jones; Wigstock; Spring Rec, rec artist; Jive/Zomba Rec, rec artist; soul singer, currently; KKDA, radio show host, Dallas, Tex; Weird Wreckuds, owner, currently; actress, currently; documentary; "Unsung - The Story of Mildred 'Millie' Jackson", 2012. **Orgs:** Whodini; Facts Life. **Honors/Awds:** Best Female R&B Vocalist, Cash Box Magazine. **Business Addr:** Owner, Weird Wreckuds, PO Box 491000, College Park, GA 30349.

### JACKSON, NORMAN A. (NORMAN A SHOT JACKSON)
Association executive, basketball coach. **Personal:** Born Nov 16, 1932, New York, NY; married Nellie; children: Deborah, Norma & Leona. **Educ:** Tuskegee Univ, attended 1955. **Career:** Asn exec (retired); Gibbs Jr Col, Fla, athletic dir & dept chmn; St Petersburg, Fla, chmn dept phys educ & athletic dir, 1959-65; Fla Comn Human Rels Comn, exec dir; Stud Comt Serv St Petersburg Jr Col, dir, 1965-70; Minority Affairs Fla State Univ, dir, 1970-72; Col Entrance Exam Bd So Regional Off Atlanta, asst dir, 1972-74; Univ AR, instr; Res Devel Fla Jr Col, asst dir. **Orgs:** Pres So Asn Black Admin, 1973-74; cons, lectr & writer, Fla Equal Access; Nat Coun Measurement Edn; Phi Delta Kappa; Nat Asn Fin Asst Minority Students; Nat Alliance Black Sch Educr; AACJC; Am Pers & Guid Asn; Fla Asn Comt Col; Fla Asn Fin Aid Admins; So Asn Financial Aid Admins; Fa Educ Res Asn; Nat Voc Guid Asn; Fla Coaches Asn; Fla Community Cols Mens Basketball Coaches. **Home Addr:** 2035 29 St S, St Petersburg, FL 33712.

**JACKSON, O'SHEA, SR.** See ICE CUBE.

### JACKSON, OLIVER L.
Educator, artist, painter (artist). **Personal:** Born Jun 23, 1935, St. Louis, MO; son of Oliver Lee and Mae Nell. **Educ:** Ill Wesleyan Univ, Bloomington, IL, BFA, 1958; Univ Iowa, Iowa City, IA, MFA, 1963. **Career:** Educator (retired), artist; St Louis Comm Col, St Louis, Mo, art instr, 1964-67; Washington Univ, St Louis, Mo, art instr, 1967-69; Southern Ill Univ, E St Louis, Ill, instr, 1967-69; Oberlin Col, Oberlin OH, Dept Afro American Studies, assoc prof, 1969-70; California State Univ, Sacramento, prof of art, 1971-03; Sch Art Inst Chicago, Chicago, Ill. Vis artist, 1979; Southeastern Ctr Contemp Art, Wake Forest Univ, artist residence, 1980; NC Sch of the Arts, Winston-Salem, NC, artist residence, 1980; Univ of Calif, Santa Barbara, vis artist, 1985; Univ of Wash, Seattle. Vis artist, 1985; Univ of Iowa, Iowa City. Vis artist, 1985; Humboldt State Univ, Arcata, CA. vis artist, 1986; Univ of Ill, Champaign, vis artist, 1988; Univ of Calif, Berkeley, vis artist, 1989; San Francisco Art Inst, San Francisco, Calif, vis artist, 1993; Calif State Univ Summer Arts Prog, Arcata. Vis artist, 1994; Calif Col of Arts & Crafts Summer Inst, Aix-en-Provence, France, vis artist, 1999; Harvard Univ, Fogg Art Mus, Cambridge, Mass, artist residence, 2000; Calif Col of Arts & Crafts Summer Inst, Paris, vis artist, 2000; Univ Hawaii, Hilo, vis artist, 1993, 2001 & 2005; Pan African

Studies, curric consult. **Orgs:** Black Artists Group; consult & collabr, African Am community.

### JACKSON, OSCAR JEROME

Physician, surgeon. **Personal:** Born Dec 17, 1929, Fairfield, AL; son of William and Lillian. **Educ:** Howard Univ, BS, MD. **Career:** Gen surg internship & residency; Homer G Phillips Hosp, internship, resident, gen surg; pvt pract physician, 1963-; Univ Calif, clin instr surg; Mt Zion Hosp, attend surgeon; John Hale Med Soc, pres, currently. **Orgs:** Am Bd Surg, 1963; fel Am Col Surg, 1967; dir, John Hale Med Plan; chmn, United Health Alliance; pres, Bus & Prof Asn; Nat Med Asn; Omega PhiPsi Fraternity. **Honors/Awds:** Professor of Chemistry Prize, Howard Univ. **Home Addr:** PO Box 170039, San Francisco, CA 94117. **Business Addr:** President, John Hale Medical Society, 1342 Haight St, San Francisco, CA 94117, **Business Phone:** (415)552-0916.

### JACKSON, PAMELA J.

Sales manager, government official. **Personal:** Born Jun 9, 1967, Louisville, KY; daughter of Philip M and Donna W. **Educ:** Univ Pa, BA, econ, 1988; Wayne State Univ, MA, econ, 1993. **Career:** Univ Pa Tutoring Ctr, counr, adv, 1985-88; Pryor, Govan & Counts, investment banking assoc, 1986-87; Black, Bus Bus Pubation, sales mgr, 1987-88; City Detroit, asst Mayor, 1988. **Orgs:** Coordr, Census 1990 Complete Count Comt, pub rels sub-com crd, fund raising sub-comcrd, 1990-91; Amandla Mandela Detroit Comt, logistics-opers crd, 1990; Wayne State Univ-City Detroit Consortium, steering comn, co-chair, 1991-; Colman A Young Found, Scholar com crd, recipient liaison, 1992-. **Home Addr:** 2112 John R 10, Detroit, MI 48201. **Business Addr:** MI.

### JACKSON, PAZEL G., JR.

Banker, executive. **Personal:** Born Feb 21, 1932, Brooklyn, NY; son of Pazel and Adalite; children: Karen, Pazel, Peter & Allyson. **Educ:** City Col NY, BCE, 1954, MCE, 1959; Columbia Univ, MBA, 1972; Pace Univ, PhD, bus policy studies. **Career:** Vice president (retired); NYC, civil engr, 1956-62; Worlds Fair Corp NYC, chief design, 1962-66; NY City Dept Pub Works, dep gen mgr, 1966-67; New York Dept Bldgs, asst comn, 1967-69; Bowery Savings Bank, NY, sr vpres, 1969-86; Chem Bank NY, Residential Mortgage Div, sr credit officer, 1986-95; JPMorgan Chase, sr vpres, 1995-2000; Carver Bancorp Inc, dir, 1997-. **Orgs:** Dir, Nat Housing Partnership Corp; NY State Urban Develop Corp; New York Housing Develop Corp, Battery Park City Authority, Bedford Stuyvesant Restoration Corp; bd dir Community Serv Soc, Citizens Housing & Planning Coun; NY Prof Engrs Soc, Am Soc Civil Engrs; NY Bldg Cong, City Col Alumni Asn; Lambda Alpha; Columbia Univ Alumni. **Honors/Awds:** Man of the Year, Brooklyn Civic Asn, 1967; Special Award, Paragon Fed Credit Union, 1968. **Home Addr:** 135 Rutland Rd, Brooklyn, NY 11225-5370, **Home Phone:** (718)856-5145. **Business Addr:** Director, Carver Bancorp Inc, 75 W 125th St, New York, NY 10027-4512, **Business Phone:** (718)230-2900.

### JACKSON, RANDELL

Basketball player. **Personal:** Born Jan 16, 1976, Boston, MA. **Educ:** Fla State Univ, attended 1998. **Career:** Ft Wayne Fury, 1998-2000; Wash Wizards, Dallas Mavericks, 1999; Conn Pride, 2000-01; Hapoel Galil Elyon, Titanes de Morovis, 2001; Trotamundos de Carabobo, 2001, 2003; Panionios B.C., 2001-02; Gallitos de Isabela, 2002; Bnei Herzliya, 2002-03; Maccabi Givat Shmuel, 2004-05; Cocodrilos de Caracas, 2005; Xinjiang Flying Tigers, 2005-06, Panteras de Aguascalientes, 2006-08; Cent E. Gualeguaychu, 2007; Alba Fehervar, 2008. **Business Addr:** Professional Basketball Player, Tokyo Apache.

### JACKSON, HON. RANDOLPH

Judge. **Personal:** Born Oct 10, 1943, Brooklyn, NY; son of James Titler and Rathenia McCollum; children: 2. **Educ:** NY Univ, BA, 1965; Brooklyn Law Sch, JD, 1969. **Career:** Ny Guard, lt col; Mudge Rose Guthrie & Alexander, assoc atty, 1969-70; Pvt Pract Law, 1971-81; New York Family Ct, hearing examr, 1981; Civil Ct City New York, Housing Ct, judge, 1981-87; Civil Ct, judge, 1987-88; Supreme Ct Brooklyn NY, justice, 1988-2002; Supreme Ct, Kings County, judge, 2003-10; Okun, Oddo & Babat, PC, of coun, 2011-. **Orgs:** Life mem, Nat Bar Asn, 1971-; Brooklyn Bar Asn, 1971-; pres, Bedford-Stuyvesant Lawyers Asn, 1974; Crown Hgts Lions Club, 1980-; Sigma Pi Phi, 1986-; life mem, Nat Asn Advan Colored People, 1990-; co founder, Metrop Black Bar Asn. **Special Achievements:** Book, "How to Get a Fair Trial By Jury", 1978; "Black People in the Bible," 2002; "Picking the Jury in a Criminal Case", 2003. **Business Addr:** Of Counsel, Okun Oddo & Babat PC, 8 W 38th St, New York, NY 10018, **Business Phone:** (212)642-0950.

### JACKSON, RANDY (RANDALL DARIUS JACKSON)

Music producer, actor, broadcaster. **Personal:** Born Jun 23, 1956, Baton Rouge, LA; son of Herman and Julia; married Elizabeth; children: Taylor; married Erika Riker; children: Zoe & Jordan. **Educ:** Southern Univ, BA, music, 1979. **Career:** Music producer & speaker, currently; played bass & keyboards on over 1000 records; Columbia Rec, vpres; MCA Rec, sr vpres; Univ Calif, Los Angeles, teacher, rec ind classes; TV series: "Bubblegum Babylon", 2002; "American Idol: The Search for a Superstar", judge, 2002-08; "E! True Hollywood Story", 2003-04; "Late Night with Conan O'Brien", 2004-08; "General Hospital", 2004; "Jimmy Kimmel Live!", 2004-08; "Dr. Vegas", 2004; "The Tonight Show with Jay Leno", 2004-07; "Tavis Smiley", 2004; "The Bernie Mac Show", 2004; Kevin Hill, 2005; "Randy Jackson", 2005; "What Did ITV Do for Me?", 2005; "The View", 2005-07; "The Late Late Show with Craig Ferguson", 2005-07; "Late Show with David Letterman", 2006-08; "Ellen: The Ellen De Generes Show", 2006-08; "Entertainment Tonight", 2007-08; "Family Guy", 2007; "Stax Records 50th Anniversary Concert", 2008; "Randy Jackson Presents America's Best Dance Crew", exec producer, 2008-10; The Simpsons, 2010; "R U There?", producer, 2010; "Mariah Carey: Merry Christmas to You", exec producer, 2010; "A Fairly Odd Movie: Grow Up, Timmy Turner!", 2011. Album: Randy Jackson's Music Club, Vol. 1, 2008; Singles:"Dance Like There's No Tomorrow", 2008; "Real Love", 2008. **Business Addr:** Actor, PMK & HBH, 8500 Wilshire Blvd Suite 700, Los Angeles, CA 90211, **Business Phone:** (310)289-6200.

### JACKSON, RAYMOND DEWAYNE

Executive, football player. **Personal:** Born Feb 17, 1973, East Chicago, IL; married Natalie; children: Raymond Jr & Alissa. **Educ:** Colo State Univ, BS, social work, 1995; Wharton Sch Bus, attended 2012. **Career:** Football player (retired); Buffalo Bills, defensive back, 1996-98; Cleveland Browns, defensive back, 1999-2001; Cleveland Browns, player develop; Pittsburgh Steelers, dir player develop, 2004-. **Business Addr:** Director of Player Development, Pittsburgh Steelers, 3400 S Water St, Pittsburgh, PA 15203-2349, **Business Phone:** (412)432-7800.

### JACKSON, DR. RAYMOND THOMPSON

Educator. **Personal:** Born Dec 11, 1933, Providence, RI; son of Raymond T and Beulah B; married Inez Austin; children: Andrea C & Yewande K. **Educ:** New Eng Conserv Music, BMus, 1955; Juilliard Sch Music, BS, 1957, MS, 1959, DMA, 1973; Am Conserv Music Fontainebleau, France, dipl, 1961. **Career:** Univ RI, asst prof music, 1968-75; Cath Univ, adj prof; Mannes Col Music, NY, instr, 1970-77; Concordia Col, Bronxville, NY, asst prof music, 1970-77; Howard Univ, prof music, 1977-, chmn piano div & appl music studies, 1986-88, chmn, Dept Music, 1989-92, coordr stud & fac concerts, 1990-; Thursday Stud Recital Ser Weekly, coordr, currently. **Orgs:** Organist & choir dir, Congdon St Baptist Church, 1948-57; concert pianist US, Europe, S Am, 1951; organist & choir dir, Trinity Lutheran Church, Tenafly, NJ, 1957-60; fel Eliza & George Howard Found, 1960 & 1963; lect & recitalist, Class Piano Music composer, Africandecent Adjudicator Col & Univ Piano Master Classes, 1963; fel John Hay Whitney Found, 1965; organist & choir dir, Trinity Lutheran Ch Bogota, NJ, 1961-72; fel Ford Found, 1971-73; fel Roothbert Fund, 1971-73; organist second, Church Christ Scientist, NY, 1972-77; organist First Church Christ Scientist Chevy Chase, Md, 1978-; piano rec artist, Performance Rec Black Artist Ser, 1982; substitute organist, First Church Christ Scientist, 1993; pres, Raymond Jackson Music Forum; Baldwin Piano Roster Distinguished Performing Artists; honarary mem, Chopin Club Providence, RI, 1966; founder & dir, Jackson Class Piano Found Inc, 1999. **Honors/Awds:** George W Chadwick Medal, New Eng Conserv Music, Boston, 1955; Prize Winner, Nat Asn Negro Musicians, 1957; New York Town Hall Debut Award, 1959; Prize Winner, Int Piano Competition Rio De Janeiro, 1965; Prize Winner, Marguerite Long Int Piano Competition, Paris, 1965; Prize Winner, Jugg Inc; Outstanding Faculty Award, Howard Univ, 1998; lifetime achievements, Alumni Award, 2005; Outstanding Alumni Award, 2005; Thomas and Birdie C. Smith Arts Foundation Award, 2005. **Special Achievements:** First African American Musician To Be Inducted Into Rhode Island Heritage Hall of Fame. **Home Addr:** 1732 Overlook Dr, Silver Spring, MD 20903-1409, **Home Phone:** (301)439-4978. **Business Addr:** Professor of Music, Pianist, Howard University, 2455 6th St NW, Washington, DC 20059, **Business Phone:** (202)806-7091.

### JACKSON, REBBIE (MAUREEN REILETTE BROWN)

Musician, dancer, singer. **Personal:** Born May 29, 1950, Gary, IN; daughter of Joseph and Katherine; married Nathaniel Brown; children: Stacee, Yashi & Austin. **Career:** Albums: Centipede, 1984; Reaction, 1986; You Send the Rain Away, 2300 Jackson Street, 1987; Plaything, R U Tuff Enuff, 1988; Rebbie Jackson Collection, 1996; Yours Faithfully, 1998; Fly Away. **Honors/Awds:** Hollywood Walk of Fame for Recording. **Business Addr:** Singer, MJJ, 550 Madison Ave, New York, NY 10022, **Business Phone:** (212)833-8500.

### JACKSON, REGGIE MARTINEZ (REGINALD MARTINEZ JACKSON)

Executive, sports manager, baseball player. **Personal:** Born May 18, 1946, Wyncote, PA; son of Martinez and Clara; married Jennie Campos. **Educ:** Ariz State Univ. **Career:** Baseball player (retired), executive, actor; Kans City Athletics, outfielder, 1967; Oakland Athletics, outfielder, 1968-75; Baltimore Orioles, outfielder, 1976; NY Yankees, outfielder, 1977-81; Calif Angels, outfielder, 1982-86; Oakland Athletics, outfielder, 1987, hitting coach, part-time, 1991; ABC Sports, field reporter & color commentator; NY Yankees, spec adv to gen partner, 1993-; Viking Components, dir new bus develop; Yankees, spec advisor, currently. Films: The Naked Gun: From The Files of Police Squad!, Summer of Sam & BASEketball; Tv Series: "The Bronx is Burning". **Orgs:** Nat chmn, Amyotrophic Lateral Sclerosis; pres, Mr October Found Kids. **Home Addr:** 305 Amador Ave, Seaside, CA 93955. **Business Addr:** Special Advisor, Yankees.

### JACKSON, DR. REGINALD LEO

Artist, educator. **Personal:** Born Jan 10, 1945, Springfield, MA; son of Leo and Katharine Edwards; married Christle Rawlins; children: Ashe Cook. **Educ:** RIT, AAS, graphic arts & printing; Yale Univ Sch Art & Archit, BFA & MFA, 1970; State Univ NY, Stony Brook, NY, MSW, 1977; Union Inst Cincinnati, OH, PhD, commun, visual anthrop, 1979. **Career:** Yale Univ Sch Art & Archit, instr, 1970; Northeastern Univ Boston, African Am Master Artists Resident, 1979; Biomed Comn, asst media prod, dir, 1972-74; Quinnipiac Col, asst prof, film making, 1972; Simmons Col, resident, tenured prof photo commun, prof commun, 1974-95, prof emer, 1999-; Olaleye Commun Inc, founder & pres, 1986-; Photog Collective Community Chg, coordr, 1995-97; African Univ Col Commun, Accra Ghana, W Africa, assoc dean, vpres dean int rels, 2008-12, prof visual commun & vpres. **Orgs:** Founding mem, Heightened Black Awareness, 1973; consult, Ny HEOP Higher Educ Opportunity Prog, 1975; Poetry Lives Ser, Mc Dougal Littel & Co, 1976; African Heritage Inst Simmons Rev Photo & Essay-Ghana Simmons Col, 1976; co-chmn & legis Comn, METCO-MA Coun Educ Opportunity, 1977-; consult, Eng High Sch, 1977-; consult, Charles E Mackey Mid Sch Photo, 1979-; Ford Found Post Doctorate fel Mass Inst Technol, 1980; Comn fel Mass Inst Technol, 1980; Smithsonian Res fel Mus Nat Hist, 1981; FATE, 1989; Nat Conf Artists; pres, Community Chg Inc, 1992-93; Mass Asn; pres, United Neighbors Lower Roxbury; proj rev comt co-chair Parcel 3; Roxbury Strategic Master Plan Oversight Comt; Black Community Info Ctr; Massachusetts Asn Ment Health; WGBH Community Adv Bd; Fulbright fel 2000-01. **Honors/Awds:** Mass Arts & Humanities Grant, 1979; James D Parks Spec Award, Nat Conf Artists, 1979; Crystal Stair Award, African Am Alumni Asn, Simmons Col; Man of the Year Award, Simmons Col, 2007. **Business Addr:** President, Founder, Olaleye Communications Inc, 71 Windsor St, Boston, MA 02120, **Business Phone:** (617)442-1464.

### JACKSON, RICARDO C.

Judge. **Personal:** Born Aug 27, 1935, Philadelphia, PA. **Educ:** Va Union Univ, Richmond, VA, BA, 1962; Howard Univ Sch Law, WA, DC, JD, 1965; Howard Univ Sch Law, WA, DC, Juris Dr, 1969. **Career:** Co Ct Philadelphia Co, Clerk, 1955-56; Pa Dept Pub Asst, caseworker, 1962; Nix & Nix, Philadelphia, Pa, 1966-69; Danford Builders Inc, Philadelphia, Pa, gen coun, 1966-70; pvt pract, 1969; Nat Dir OEO, spec consult, 1970; Redevelop Authority City Philadelphia, Legal Staff Gen Coun, contract atty, 1970-77; Munic Ct Philadelphia, judge, 1977-81; US Dept Labor, secy rep, 2000-02; Philadelphia Ct, judge, currently. **Orgs:** Co-chmn, vice chmn, Philadelphia Bar Asn; 1969; pres, Barristers' Asn Philadelphia, 1970-74; chmn, Philadelphia Urban Coalition, 1970-71; Nat Bar Asn; Am Bar Asn; Pa Bar Asn; Pa Trial Lawyers Asn; Am Arbit Asn; Am Judicature Soc; Pa Conf State Trial Judges; Comt 1000, Pa Comn Sentencing, 1992. **Honors/Awds:** Certificate of Appreciation, Disciplinary Bd Supreme Ct Pa, 1976; Community Service Award, Veterans Foreign Wars, 1979; Legion of Honor Membership, Chapel Four Chaplains, 1980; Award for Dedication, Dept Legal & Real Estate Studies, Temple Univ, 1989. **Special Achievements:** Co-Author of Report of the Philadelphia Bar Association's Special Committee on Pennsylvania Bar Admission Procedures - Racial Discrimination In Administration of the Pennsylvania Bar Examination, Temple Law Quarterly, Vol. 44, No. 2, Winter, 1971; Handling Death Penalty Cases, Benchbook (Chapter), March, 1993. **Business Addr:** Judge, Philadelphia Courts, Rm 143 City Hall 800 Spring Garden St, Philadelphia, PA 19107, **Business Phone:** (215)686-9560.

### JACKSON, RICHARD ERNEST, JR.

Government official, educator, politician. **Personal:** Born Jul 18, 1945, Peekskill, NY; married Ruth Sokolinsky; children: Tara, Alice, Abigail & William. **Educ:** Univ Bridgeport, BA, math, 1968. **Career:** Peekskill City Sch, math teacher, 1968; dir, Neighborhood Youth Corps Community Action Prog, 1968; United Way Westchester, bd dirs, 1969; Peekskill Field Libr, bd dir, 1974; Westchester Co Republican Comt, co committeeman, 1975; Peekskill City Republican Comt, vice chmn, 1976; City Peekskill, councilman, 1979-84, mayor, 1984-91, dep mayor, 1993; Peekskill Housing Authority, bd mem, 1982; City Peekskill, dep mayor, 1982-84, mayor, 1985-91; NY Dept Motor Vehicles, comnr, 1995-2000. **Orgs:** Educ Comt, Nat Asn Advan Colored People, 1981-83; Westchester Co Bd Ethics, 1984; chmn, Peekskill Indust Develop Corp, 1985-91; Gov Patakis Gubernatorial cabinet, 1995; pres, Region I, Am Asn Motor Vehicles Admin, 1997; chmn & adv bd mem, Govt Technol Conf, 1997; NY State Auto-Theft & Ins Fraud Bd, 1997. **Honors/Awds:** National Science Foundation Award. **Special Achievements:** First African American Mayor in New York State. **Home Addr:** 1818 Carhart Ave, Peekskill, NY 10566. **Business Addr:** Commissioner, NY Department Motor Vehicles, Swan St Bldg Empire State Plz, Albany, NY 12228, **Business Phone:** (212)645-5550.

### JACKSON, RICKEY ANDERSON

Football player, executive. **Personal:** Born Mar 20, 1958, Pahokee, FL; married Norma; children: Rickeyah. **Educ:** Univ Pittsburgh. **Career:** Football player (retired); New Orleans Saints, linebacker, left outside linebacker, 1981-93; SanFrancisco 49ers, linebacker, right defensive end, 1994-95. **Orgs:** Founder, Rickey Jackson Friends Forever Found; founder, Rickey Jackson Community Hope Ctr, currently. **Honors/Awds:** Defensive Most Valuable Player, E-W Shrine Game; ABC Player of the Game vs Penn St, 1980; pro bowl, 1983- New Orleans Saints Hall Fame; All-Century Team, Fla High Sch Asn, 2007; Pro Football Hall of Fame, 2010. **Business Addr:** Founder, Rickey Jackson Friends Forever Foundation, PO Box 2111, Metairie, LA 70001, **Business Phone:** (504)344-8947.

### JACKSON, ROBERT, JR.

Journalist, columnist. **Personal:** Born Jan 15, 1936, Chicago, IL; son of Robert and Lucille; children: Dawn, Robert III & Randall. **Educ:** Colo State Col, BA, 1957; Northwestern Univ, Columbia Col, addn study. **Career:** Int News Serv, reporter, 1958; Chicago Am Chicago Today, reporter, 1958-69; WBEE Radio Chicago, reporter, 1964; Chicago Bull, ed-writer, 1965; Chicago Urban League, writer-producer, 1966; CCUO, dir pub info, 1969-70; Argonne Nat Lab, dir pub info, 1970-73; Provident Hosp & Training Sch, dir publ rel; Reg Alcoholism Info Prog Nat Coun Alcoholism, field dir, 1975-; Rocky Mountain News, news staff writer, currently. **Orgs:** Chicago Newspaper Reporters Asn; Sigma Delta Chi, 1965; United Black Journalist, 1968; Coun Advan Sci Writing, 1971; Atomic Indust Form, 1971; publ rel Soc Am, 1971; bd dir, S Shore YMCA, 1972; Hosp Publ Rel Soc, 1974. **Honors/Awds:** Community Service Award, Urban League Metropolitan Denver; Community Service Award, Natl Asn Advan Colored People; Malcolm X Award, Black Student Alliance at Metro State Col; Coors, Distinguished Citizen Award; Public Service Award, United Negro Col Fund; Five Points Business Asn, Award; Distinguished Service Award, The Hispanics Colorado; Outstanding Journalist in Print Award, Colo Asn Blacks Journ, 1993; Lifetime Achievement Award, 1999; Awards from the American Legion, The Denver District Attorney's Office & several Denver area Schools. **Home Addr:** 460 S Marion Pkwy, Denver, CO 80209, **Home Phone:** (303)778-7611. **Business Addr:** News Staff Writer, Denver Rocky Mountain News, 400 W Colfax Ave, Denver, CO 80204, **Business Phone:** (303)892-5399.

### JACKSON, ROBERT ANDREW

Advertising executive, vice president (organization), executive director. **Personal:** Born May 16, 1959, Reedville, VA; son of Robert Albert and Lucy; married Felicia Lynn Willis; children: Robert Andrew II. **Educ:** Fla A&M Univ, Tallahassee, BS, 1981, MBA, 1983. **Career:** Leo Burnett Advert, Chicago, Ill, asst acct exec, 1983-85; Bozell Advert, Chicago, Ill, 1985; Burrell Commun Group, Chicago, Ill, sr vp, 1986-2002 & client serv dir, 1986-; McDonald's USA, mkt dir, 2002-, Experienced Mkt Prof with passion results via innovation & accountability, 2015-. **Orgs:** Alpha Phi Alpha; FAMU Alumni Asn; Targeted Advert Prof; Chicago Advert Fedn, Ctrs New Horizon; bd mem, Hyde Pk AYSO soccer; bd mem, Centers New Horizons, 1995-; bd mem, Chicago Youth Progs; bd mem, Southside Ronald McDonald House.

**Home Addr:** 4944 S Wash Pk Ct, Chicago, IL 60615, **Home Phone:** (773)548-8517. **Business Addr:** Director of Marketing, McDonald's USA, 2111 McDonalds Dr, Oak Brook, IL 60523, **Business Phone:** (800)244-6227.

### JACKSON, ROBERT E.

Association executive. **Personal:** Born Feb 10, 1937, Reading, PA; married Carol A Norman; children: Robert E Jr, Jeannine, Monique & Gregory. **Career:** Food Serv Albright Col, dir, 1971; Schuylkill Valley Restaurant Asn, pres, 1974-76. **Orgs:** pres, secy, Berks Co Asn Blind, 1967-; Bd trustee, Pa Asn Blind, 1971, exec comt, 1972-, second vpres, 1974-; bd dirs, Camp Conrad Weiser; NACUFS; charter pres, Reading Pagoda Lions Club. **Home Addr:** 341 Linden Lane, Reading, PA 19611, **Home Phone:** (610)375-3857.

### JACKSON, RONALD G., JR.

Manager, executive, executive director. **Personal:** Born Sep 7, 1952, New Orleans, LA; married Brenda J Bellamy; children: Ronald Jr, Tiffany & Joseph C. **Educ:** Jackson State Univ, BA, sociol & social work, 1974; Howard Univ, MSW, social work, 1975; Antioch Sch Law, JD, 1985. **Career:** City Councilman Douglas Shanks, admin asst, 1973-74; Sen/Congressman Thad Cochran, staff asst & asst press secy, 1974-77; Southern Miss Legal Serv, paralegal & adminr, 1977-78; Miss Gulf Coast Jr Col, instr, 1978-79; Harrison Co Head Start Prog, exec dir, 1978-79; Univ Southern Miss, asst prof, 1979-83; Nat Urban League, lobbyist & policy analyst, 1986-91; US Cath Conf Bishops, policy advisor, 1991-95; US Cath Conf, policy adv; Nat Asn Social Workers, gov rels assoc, lobbyist, 1995-96; DC Cath Conf, dir, exec dir, 1996-2011; Cath Charities USA, Govt Affairs, sr dir, 2011-. **Orgs:** Nat Asn Advan Colored People, 1979-84; Omega Psi Phi Inc, 1981-; Midtown Montessori Sch, 1985-; St Ann's Infant & Maternity Home, 1989-; Covenant House, Wash DC; Policy Comm Cath; bd mem, Charities. **Honors/Awds:** Benemerenti Award, 2006; Servus Pro Christo Award, Nat Black Cath Cong, 2012. **Special Achievements:** First African-American staff assistant for Senator Thad Cochran, 1974-77. **Home Addr:** 5611 Leon St, Suitland, MD 20746-4590, **Home Phone:** (301)702-0180. **Business Addr:** Senior Director, Catholic Charities USA, 2050 Ballenger Ave Suite 400, Alexandria, VA 22314, **Business Phone:** (703)549-1390.

### JACKSON, RONALD LEE

Educator, government official. **Personal:** Born Jul 13, 1943, Kansas City, MO; married Hattie Robinson; children: Taj & Yasmira. **Educ:** Harris Jr Col, AA, 1963; Wash Univ, AB, 1965; Southern Ill Univ, attended 1976. **Career:** Ill State Univ, admis coun, 1969-70; Wash Univ, asst dir admis, 1970-73, asst dean, Col Arts & Sci, Wash Univ, 1973-; Higher Educ Coord Coun, Admis Comn, 1970-73; St Louis Comn Africa, 1975-76; US Sen John Danforth, asst; Nat Conf Community & Justice, exec dir. **Orgs:** Coun Black Affairs, Ill State Univ, 1969-70; fel CORD, 1973; Leadership St Louis, 1982-83; bd mem, New City Sch, 1984-86; Urban League, Educ Comt, 1984-; chmn, United Way Comn Wide Youth Panel, 1986-87; Minority Bus Advocate Eastern MO, 1986; bd mem, Cardinal Ritter Col Prep HS, 1987-; vpres, Westlake Scholar Comn, St Louis, exec dir, (retired). **Home Addr:** 4453 Laclede Ave, St. Louis, MO 63108.

### JACKSON, DR. ROY JOSEPH, JR.

Chemist, educator, writer. **Personal:** Born Feb 8, 1944, Cotton Port, LA. **Educ:** Southern Univ, Baton Rouge, LA, BS, 1965, MS, 1969; Univ Calif, San Diego, PhD, chem, 1975. **Career:** Dow Chem Co, res chemist, 1968; Southern Univ, grad asst, 1967-69, instr, 1969-70; Univ Calif, teaching asst, 1970-75; Shell Develop Co, res chemist, 1975-. **Orgs:** Am Chem Soc; Kappa Delta Pi; Alpha Phi Alpha; Black Action Comt. **Special Achievements:** Numerous contributions to the study of photochemistry. **Home Addr:** 12707 Havant Cir, Houston, TX 77077-2226, **Home Phone:** (281)497-6730. **Business Addr:** Senior Research Chemist, Shell Development Co, Hwy 6 S, Houston, TX 77077.

### JACKSON, ROY LEE

Baseball player, athlete. **Personal:** Born May 1, 1954, Opelika, AL; married Mary. **Educ:** Tuskegee Inst, Tuskegee, AL. **Career:** Baseball player (retired), instructor; New York Mets, pitcher, 1977-80, Toronto Blue Jays, pitcher, 1981-84, San Diego Padres, pitcher, 1985; Minn Twins, pitcher, 1986; Ala base ball instr, currently. **Honors/Awds:** Voted Most Valuable Player Award, baseball Tuskegee Inst, 1974 & 1975; Appalachian All-Star Team. **Special Achievements:** The first native-born Opelikian to make it to the major leagues. **Home Addr:** 8269 Lee Rd 54, Auburn, AL 36830-8222, **Home Phone:** (334)741-9953.

### JACKSON, DR. RUDOLPH ELLSWORTH

Educator, physician. **Personal:** Born May 31, 1935, Richmond, VA; son of Samuel and Jennie; married Janice Diane Ayer; children: Kimberley R, Kelley J, Rudolph E Jr & Alison D Ligon. **Educ:** Morehouse Col, BS, 1957; Meharry Med Col, MD, 1961. **Career:** Educator (retired), physician; St Jude Childrens Res Hosp, asst mem hemat, 1969-72; Nat Heart Lung & Blood Inst, chief sickle cell disbr, 1972-77; Howard Univ Sch Med, assoc prof, dept pediat, 1977-79; MeharryMed Col, chmn dept pediat, 1979-83; Morehouse Sch Med, act chr dept pediat, 1984-90, prof pediat, AIDS Res Consortium, dir; Asn Minority Health Professions Schs AIDS Res Consortium, dir; Off Int Health Progs, assoc dir. **Orgs:** AMA; Nat Med Asn; Am Soc Hemat; adv comt, DHEW sickle cell disease, 1971-72; Sigma Xi Sci Soc, Howard Univ, 1978-; Nat Adv Coun Nat Inst Arthritis Diabetes Digestive Kidney Dis NIH DHEW, 1979-83; AsnMed Sch Pediat, 1980-89; Alpha Omega Alpha Med Soc, Meharry Med Col, 1980-; adv comt mem, DHEW lead poisoning, 1984; Pediat Task Force, Ageny Health Care Policy Res, 1991-96; adv comt, Ctr DisControl, DHHS, 1991-2003; Am Acad Pediat, 1991-95; Pediat Task Force, Am Acad Pediat, 1992-96; adv bd, Parents Kids with Infectious Dis. **Home Addr:** 893 Woodmere Dr NW, Atlanta, GA 30318, **Home Phone:** (404)794-8379. **Business Addr:** Advisory Board, Parents of Kids with Infectious Diseases, PO Box 5666, Vancouver, WA 98668, **Business Phone:** (360)695-0293.

### JACKSON, DR. RUSSELL A., JR.

School principal. **Personal:** Born Feb 26, 1934, Philadelphia, PA; married Elois; children: Cheryll Renne & Charles Russell. **Educ:** Cheyney State Col, BA, 1956; Temple Univ, MA, 1962, EdD, 1970. **Career:** Philadelphia Pub Sch, teacher, asst prin & elem prin; Chester, Pa, asst supt; E Orange Pub Sch, supt, 1968-72; Roosevelt Sch Dist No 66, supt; Howard Univ, Dept Educ Admin & Policy, asst prof. **Orgs:** Am Asn Sch Adminr; Ariz Sch Admin Inc; Phi Delta Kappa Fraternity; pres, Nat Alliance Black Sch Educ, 1970-72; pres, Greater Phoenix Supr Asn, 1974-75; exec comn, Ariz Found Blind. **Special Achievements:** First Black East Orange Public School, superintendent. **Home Addr:** 155 N Harbor Dr, Chicago, IL 60601, **Home Phone:** (312)861-1717. **Business Addr:** Assistant Professor, Howard University, Rm 207 Acad Support A 2441 4th St NW, Washington, DC 20059, **Business Phone:** (202)806-9178.

### JACKSON, DR. RUSSELL H.

President (organization). **Educ:** Univ Mich, BA, psychol, MA, social psychol, PhD, urban technol, & environ planning; Univ Houston, African Am Studies Prog, Inst African Am Policy Res, 1993. **Career:** City Houston's Human Resources Dept, dir, res & data mgt; Math Policy Res, vpres; Decision Info Resources Inc, founder, 1984-, pres, 2005-08; Am Leadership Forum, pres, 2008. **Orgs:** Bd mem, Upper Kirby Dist Found; bd mem, Am Leadership Forum; bd mem, Upper Coastal Plain Coun Governments. **Business Addr:** Founder, President, Decision Information Resources Inc, 2600 SW Fwy Suite 900, Houston, TX 77098, **Business Phone:** (713)650-1425.

### JACKSON, RUSTY

Executive. **Personal:** Born Greenville, SC; daughter of James Russell and Georgia. **Career:** Trans World Airlines, New York, NY, flight attend; IBM Corp, Columbia, SC, mkt support rep; Lanier Bus Prod, Atlanta, Ga, mkt support mgr; Lexitron Corp, Wash, DC, territory mgr; Wash Conv Ctr, Wash, DC, spec asst gen mgr, 1981-84; Coors Brewing Co, Wash, DC, community rel field mgr & Nat group mgr, 1984; Resolutions Inc, pres; Henderson Event Mgt, vpres & managing dir, 2004-09; HelmsBriscoe, mgr global accounts, currently. **Orgs:** Bd mem, Nat Kidney Found, 1988-91; bd mem, Leukemia Soc, 1990-91; bd mem, DC Chamber Comm, 1990-95; bd mem, Metro Wash YMCA, 1990-92; bd mem, Wash Women League; bd chmn, United Negro Col Fund; Comns adv bd, Ladies Prof Golf asn. **Home Addr:** 1502 Fairlakes Pl, Mitchellville, MD 20721. **Business Addr:** Vice President, Managing Director, Henderson Event Management, 84 Villa Rd, Greenville, SC 29615, **Business Phone:** (864)298-1342.

### JACKSON, DR. RUTH MOORE

Library administrator. **Personal:** Born Sep 27, 1938, Potecasi, NC; daughter of Jesse Thomas Sr and Ruth Estelle Futrell; married Roderick Earle; children: Eric Roderick. **Educ:** Hampton Inst, Hampton, VA, BS, bus, 1960; Atlanta Univ, Atlanta, GA, MSLS, 1965; Ind Univ, Bloomington, IN, PhD, 1976. **Career:** Va State Univ, Petersburg, Va, librn, 1965-69; Ind Univ, Bloomington, Ind, teaching fel/vis lectr; Va State Univ, Petersburg, Va, assoc prof, 1976-84; Univ N Fla, Jacksonville, Fla, asst dir libr, 1984-88; WVa Univ, Morgantown, Wva, dean, univ libr, 1988-98, spec asst to provost, 1999; Wichita State Univ Libr, dean, 1999; Univ Calif, Riverside, univ librn, currently; Ind Univ, fel; Southern Fel Found, fel; Nat Fac Fels for Minority Res, fel; U.S. Off of Educ, fel. **Orgs:** Am Libr Asn, 1976-; Am Mgt Asn, 1976-84; Asn Col & Res Libr, 1984-; chair, WVa Higher Educ Libr Resources Adv Coun, 1988-98; chair, WVa Acad Libr Dir's Group, 1989-97; Coalition for Networked Info, 1990-99; chair, WVa Acad Libr Consortium, 1991-98; Fel Res Librn's deleg, 1992; WVa Libr Asn, 1991-99; WVa Legis Comt, 1994-99; Addison-Wesley Higher Educ, tech bd, 1996-97; HW Wilson Adv Bd, 1999-; CODDL, Kans Regent's Univs, 1999-; Fel Beta Phi Mu; Fel Pi Lambda Theta. **Honors/Awds:** US Off Educ Fel, US Off Educ, 1969-71; Competitive Research Award, Ind Univ, 1973; Southern Fel Found Fel, SFF, 1973-74; Nat Fac Minorities Res Fel, 1979-80; Outstanding Alumni Award, Hampton Inst, 1980; Distinguished West Virginian Award, 1992; Non-Italian Woman of the Year, 1992. **Special Achievements:** Jackson is the First African American university librarian in all of the University of California campuses, and is one of only a few African Americans nationally who lead an Association of Research Libraries (ARL) library. **Home Addr:** 8703 E Boston St, Wichita, KS 67207, **Home Phone:** (316)618-0711. **Business Addr:** University Librarian, University Of California Riverside, 900 Univ Ave Rivera Libr 1st Fl, Riverside, CA 92521, **Business Phone:** (951)827-3221.

### JACKSON, SAMUEL LEROY

Actor. **Personal:** Born Dec 21, 1948, Washington, DC; son of Roy Henry (deceased) and Elizabeth; married LaTanya Richardson; children: Zoe. **Educ:** Morehouse Col, dramatic arts. **Career:** Actor, currently; Stage productions: A Soldiers Play, 1981; The Piano Lesson, 1987; Sally & Prince, 1989; The District Line, 1990; Two Trains Running, 1990; Home; Fences, Seattle Repertory Theater; Distant Fires, Coast Playhouse, 1993. Films: Together for Days; Ragtime, 1981; Raw, 1987; Sch Daze, 1988; Sea of Love, 1989; Do the Right Thing, 1989; Mo' Better Blues, 1990; Def by Temptation, 1990; Goodfellas, 1991; Jungle Fever, 1991; Jumpin' at the Boneyard, 1992; White Sands, 1992; Patriot Games, 1992; True Romance, 1993; Menace II Society, 1993; National Lampoon's Loaded Weapon I, 1993; Amos & Andrew, 1993; Jurassic Park, 1993; Against the Wall, 1994; Assault at West Point, 1994; The Court Martial of Johnson Whittaker, 1994; Fresh, 1994; Pulp Fiction, 1994; Kiss of Death, 1995; DieHard With A Vengeance, 1995; A Time to Kill, 1996; The Long Kiss Goodnight, 1997; Eve's Bayou, 1997; 187, 1997; Jackie Brown, 1998; The Negotiator, 1998; Sphere, 1998; Deep Blue Sea, 1999; Star Wars Episode I, 1999; Any Given Wednesday, 2000; Rules of Engagement, 2000; Shaft, 2000; Unbreakable, 2000; The Caveman's Valentine, 2001; The 51st State, 2001; Changing Lanes, 2002; Die Hard with a Vengeance; Star Wars Episode II, 2002; XXX, 2002; The House on Turk Street, 2002; Basic, 2003; SWAT, 2003; Blackout, 2003; HBO movie, Unchained Memories: Readings from the Slave Narratives, reader, 2003; XXX2, 2004; Twisted, 2004; Kill Bill Vol 2, 2004; Home of the Brave, 2006; Black Snake Moan, 2006; Snakes on a Plane, 2006; Resurrecting the Champ, 2007; Jumper, 2008; Lakeview Terrace, 2008; Soul Men, 2008; The Other Guys; Mother & Child, 2009; The Other Guys, 2010; The Sunset Limited, 2011; African Cats, 2011; Captain America: The First Avenger, 2011; Arena, 2011; The Samaritan, 2012; Meeting Evil, 2012; The Avengers, 2012; Zambezia, 2012; Django Unchained, 2012; Turbo, 2013; Oldboy, 2013; Robocop, 2014; Captain America: The Winter Soldier, 2014; Kite, 2014; The Hateful Eight, 2015; Avengers: Age of Ultron, 2015; Kong: Skull Island, 2017. TV series: "The Displaced Person", 1976; "The Trial of the Moke", 1978; "Uncle Tom's Cabin", 1987; "Dead Man Out", 1989; "Dead & Alive: The Race for Gus Farace", 1991; "Simple Justice", 1993; "Agains the Wall", 1994; "ESPY Awards", 2002, 2004; "A Light Knight's Odyssey", 2004 (voice); "The Boondocks", 2006; "Freedom land", 2006; "Afro Samurai", 2007. **Orgs:** Just Us Theater Co, cofounder; Negro Ensemble Co. **Honors/Awds:** Best Supporting Actor, Jungle Fever, Cannes Film Fest, 1991; Best Supporting Actor, Cannes film Festival, 1991; New York Film Critics Award, Jungle Fever, 1991; BAFTA Film Award, 1995; nominated, Academy Award, Best Supporting Actor, Pulp Fiction, 1995; Independent Spirit Award, 1995, 1998; Image Award, 1997, 2006; Blockbuster Entertainment Award, 1997; Outstanding Supporting Actor in a Motion Picture, 1997; Silver Berlin Bear, Berlin International film festival, 1998; Black Film Award, 1998; Artists of Vision Award, 1999; Man of the Year, Hasty pudding Theatricals, 1999; Career Achievement Award, Acapulco Black Film Fest, 1999; received a star on the Hollywood Walk of Fame, 2000; Essence Awards, honoree, 2001; BET Comedy Award, 2005; Outstanding Actor in a Motion Picture, 2006; Bambi Award, 2006; Television Arts Award; Lifetime Achievement Award; Received more than awards. **Business Addr:** Actor, International Creative Management, 8942 Wilshire Blvd, Beverly Hills, CA 90211.

### JACKSON, SAMUEL S., JR.

Educator, association executive, dean (education). **Personal:** Born Nov 8, 1934, Natchez, MS; married Margaret Atkins; children: Sharon, Orlando, Sheila & Samuel III. **Educ:** Alcorn State Univ, BS, agr educ & gen sci; Antioch Col, MS, educ admin, 1970. **Career:** Lincoln Attendance Ctr, high sch teacher, 1957-66, sch prin, 1967-68; Wilberforce Univ, assoc dir coop educ, 1968-70, dean stud, 1970-78; Cent St Univ, assoc dean stud, 1978-83, vpres stud affairs, 1983-96, spec asst pres, 1995-96. **Orgs:** Phi Delta Kappa; Am Personal Guid Asn; Nat Asn Stud Personnel Adminr; Am Col Union Asn; Nat Col Housing Asn; Admis & Fin St & Nat Orgn; Ohio Stud Personnel Asn; Omega Psi Phi Fraternity; Nat Asn Advan Colored People; Am Personnel Guid Asn. **Honors/Awds:** Scholar, NSF, 1966-67; Omega Man of the Year, Omega Psi Phi fraternity, 1972; S GA Award, Wilberforce Univ, 1980-85; Hall of Honor, Alcorn St Univ, 1995. **Home Addr:** 1615 Spillan Rd, Yellow Springs, OH 45387-1232, **Home Phone:** (937)767-1112. **Business Addr:** Educator, Wilberforce University, 1055 N Bickett Rd, Wilberforce, OH 45384-1001, **Business Phone:** (937)376-2911.

### JACKSON, SANDRA STEVENS

Government official, banker. **Personal:** Born Sep 14, 1963; daughter of Robert Stevens and Sarah Stevens; married Jesse Jr; children: Jessica Donatella & Jesse Louis. **Educ:** Bowling Green State Univ, BA, 1985; Univ Ill Col Law, JD, 1992. **Career:** Us Congressman Mickey Leland, press secy, US Info Agency, Pub Dipl Prog, former sr coordr; Export-Import Bank, Off Cong & External Affairs, vpres. **Home Addr:** 313 16th St NE, Washington, DC 20002, **Home Phone:** (202)399-4861.

### JACKSON, DR. SHIRLEY ANN

Government official. **Personal:** Born Aug 5, 1946, Washington, DC; married Morris A Washington; children: Alan. **Educ:** Mass Inst Technol, SB, physics, 1968, PhD, theoret elem particle physics, 1973. **Career:** Fermi Nat Accelerator Lab, resident assoc theoret physicist, 1973-76; Europ Orgn Nuclear Res, vis sci assoc, 1974-75; Bell Tel Labs, technol staff, 1976-92; Rutgers Univ, prof physics, 1991-95; Nuclear Regulatory Comn, chair, 1995-99; Rensselaer Polytech Inst, pres, 1999-; Nat Soc Black Physicists, pres. **Orgs:** Amn Physicists Soc; New York Acad Sci; Sigma Xi; Nat Inst Sci; ComtEducating & Employing Women Scientists & Engrs; MichT Corp, bd trustees, 1975-85; Lincoln Univ, 1980-; Nat Acad Sci, 1981-82; Nat Acad Eng; pres, AAAS, 2004; chmn, AAAS Bd Dirs, 2005; Am Philos Soc, 2007; Nj Comn Sci & Technol; Int Nuclear Regulators Asn. **Honors/Awds:** Ford Foundation, Advanced Study Fellowship, 1971-73, Grant, 1974-75; Martin Marietta Corp, Fellowship, 1972-73; First African American female to receive PhD from MIT and the first in the nation to get doctoral degree in physics; Thomas Alva Edison Award, 1993; inducted National Women's Hall of Fame, 1998; Golden Torch Award, National Society Black Engs, 2000; 100 Women of Excellence Award, Albany-Colonie, 2000; Immortal Award, Associated Black Charities, 2001; Richtmyer Memorial Lecture Award, American Association Physics Teachers, 2001; Community Citizenship Award, Troy Rehabilitation & Improvement Program, 2006. **Special Achievements:** The first woman to win the Black Engineer of the Year Award by US Black Engineer & Information Technology magazine; First African-American to become a Commissioner of the U.S. Nuclear Regulatory Commission; First African American students to attend MIT; First woman to receive a Ph.D. in physics in MIT. **Home Addr:** 3 Compton Way, Bridgewater, NJ 08807-1482, **Home Phone:** (908)704-1808. **Business Addr:** President, Rensselaer Polytechnic Institute, 110 8th St, Troy, NY 12180, **Business Phone:** (518)276-6000.

### JACKSON, STANLEY LEON

Basketball player. **Personal:** Born Oct 10, 1970, Tuskegee, AL. **Educ:** Univ Ala, Birmingham. **Career:** Basketball player (retired); Minn Timber wolves, guard, 1993-94; Fla Beach dogs, guard, 1995-96; Caceres, guard, 1996-97; Sevilla, guard, 1997-98; Quad City Thunder, guard, 1998-99; Dijon, guard, 1999-2000; ES Chalon-Sur-Saone, guard, 2000-05; Strasbourg, guard, 2006.

### JACKSON, STEVEN WAYNE

Football player, football coach. **Personal:** Born Apr 8, 1969, Houston, TX; children: Dominique & Stephen. **Educ:** Purdue Univ, grad. **Career:** Football player (retired), football coach; Houston Oilers, defensive back & right defensive back, 1991-96; Tenn Oilers, defensive back & left defensive back, 1997-99; Washington Redskins, safeties coach, 2004-11. **Honors/Awds:** Ed Block Courage Award, 1998. **Spe-**

**cial Achievements:** Films: 1999 AFC Championship Game, 2000; Super Bowl XXXIV, 2000. **Business Addr:** VA.

### JACKSON, STUART WAYNE (STU JACKSON)
Vice president (organization), sports manager, athletic coach. **Personal:** Born Dec 11, 1955, Reading, PA; son of Harold Russell and Pauline Virginia Artist; married Susan Taylor; children: Lauren, Taylor, Erin & Yanna. **Educ:** Univ Ore; Seattle Univ, WA, BA, bus mgt, 1978. **Career:** Basketball player, basketball coach, basketball executive (retired); Univ Ore, basketball player, 1970; IBM, Los Angeles, Calif, Mict Rep DPD, 1978-81; Univ Ore, Eugene, Ore, asst coach, 1981-83; Wash State Univ, Pullman, Wash, asst coach, 1983-85; Providence Col, Providence, RI, assoc coach & head recruiting coordr, 1985-87; NY Knicks, asst coach, 1987-89, head coach, 1989-90; Nat Basketball Asn, dir basketball oper, 1991, exec vpres basketball opers, 2007; Univ Wis Badgers, head basketball coach, 1992-93, 1993-94; Orca Bay Sports & Entertainment, pres & gen mgr, 1994-2006; Vancouver Grizzlies, pres & gen mgr, 1994, head coach, 1997. **Orgs:** Nat Asn Basketball Coaches. **Home Addr:** , NY. **Business Addr:** Executive Vice President Basketball Operations, National Basketball Association, 645 5th Ave, New York, NY 10022, **Business Phone:** (212)223-5159.

### JACKSON, SUZANNE FITZALLEN
Artist, painter (artist). **Personal:** Born Jan 30, 1944, St. Louis, MO; daughter of Roy Dedrick and Ann Marie (Butler); children: Rafiki Casey Dedrick Smith-Mhunzi. **Educ:** SF State Univ, BA, art, 1966; Otis Art Inst, 1968; Yale Univ, Sch Drama, MFA, theatre design, 1990. **Career:** Painter, poet, 1960-; Desert Sun Sch, fac, 1982-85, currently; Freelance scenic & costume designer, 1987-94; St Mary's Col Md, stenographer, asst prof, 1994-96; Savannah Col Art & Design, prof painting, 1996-; SCAD Presidential, fel, artist resident, 2002. **Orgs:** United Scenic Artists, Local 829, 1990-; Costume Soc Am, 1990-; fel Cave Canem African-Am Poets, 1996-. **Special Achievements:** Nomination for the First Nat Award in the Visual Arts, 1981. **Home Addr:** 15 W 41st St, Savannah, GA 31401-8984, **Home Phone:** (912)220-5921. **Business Addr:** Artist, Suzanne F Jackson Fine Arts, 15 W 41st St, Savannah, GA 31401-8984, **Business Phone:** (912)220-5921.

### JACKSON, TAMMY ELOISE
Basketball coach, basketball player. **Personal:** Born Dec 3, 1962, Gainesville, FL. **Educ:** Univ Fla, attended 1985. **Career:** Basketball player (retired), basketball coach; Fla Gators women's basketball team, 1982-85; Houston Comets, forward-ctr, 1997-98, 1999-2002; Wash Mystics, 1998; Santa Fe Community Col, asst coach, 2004. **Home Addr:** 5118 SW 57th Ave, Gainesville, FL 32608-4867, **Home Phone:** (352)373-2127.

### JACKSON, TERRY (TERRANCE BERNARD JACKSON)
Football executive, football player. **Personal:** Born Jan 10, 1976, Gainesville, FL; son of Willie Sr. **Educ:** Fla Univ, BA, bus & mkt, 1998. **Career:** Football player (retired), exec; San Francisco 49ers, 1999, 2002-05, fullback & running back, 2000-01; Gators Football, dir player & community rels, 2008; Univ Fla, col football adminr, currently. **Honors/Awds:** Championship, Southeastern Conf, 1995, 1996; Bowl Alliance National Championship, 1996; Leadership Award; All-SEC Award; Spec Teams Player of the Week, Nat Football Conf, 2003. **Business Addr:** College Football Administrator, University of Florida, 1600 SW Archer Rd, Gainesville, FL 32610-3001, **Business Phone:** (352)265-0111.

### JACKSON, TIA
Basketball player, basketball coach. **Personal:** Born Apr 21, 1972, Salisbury, MD; daughter of Barbara and David Gates. **Educ:** Univ Iowa, BA, media studies film, 1995. **Career:** Iowa Hawkeyes, guard, forward; Va Commonwealth Univ, asst coach, 1996-99; Phoenix Mercury, guard, forward, 1997; Stanford Univ, asst coach, 1999; Univ Calif, Los Angeles, Calif, Bruin, recruiting coordr, asst coach, 2000-05; Duke Women's Basketball, coaching staff, 2005-07; Univ WA women's basketball, head coach, 2007-11. **Orgs:** Women's Basketball Hall Fame. **Business Addr:** Coach, University of Washington Women's Basketball, 3910 Montlake Blvd Graves Bldg Rm 101, Seattle, WA 98195-4070, **Business Phone:** (206)543-2200.

### JACKSON, TOM (THOMAS LOUIE JACKSON)
Football player, broadcaster. **Personal:** Born Apr 4, 1951, Cleveland, OH; married Jennifer; children: Taylor, Morgan & Andrea (deceased); married Diana Maria Hill. **Educ:** Louisville Univ, bus. **Career:** Football player (retired), analyst; Denver Broncos, linebacker, 1973-86; ESPN Inc, host, color commentator, Nat Football League studio analyst, 1987-2016. **Honors/Awds:** Conference Player of the Year, Mo Valley, 1970, 1972; Most Valuable Player, Denvers Broncos, 1974, 1976-77; Champion, Asian Football Confederation, 1977, 1986; Pro Bowl, 1977, 1978, 1979; Blue-Gray Game; Broncos Ring of Fame, 1992. **Special Achievements:** All-Pro Bowl, 1977, 1978, 1979, 1984; Published Blitz: An Autobiography in 1987. **Home Addr:** 7475 Brill Rd, Cincinnati, OH 45243-3525. **Business Addr:** NFL Studio Analyst, ESPN Inc, 935 Mid St, Bristol, CT 06010-1001, **Business Phone:** (203)585-2000.

### JACKSON, TOMI L.
Broadcaster, association executive, television show host. **Personal:** Born Nov 28, 1923, Dallas, TX; daughter of Thomas Stephens and Ida Stephens; children: Joanne Ragan & Linda Marlane Craft. **Educ:** Wayne State Univ, BA, 1940. **Career:** WPON Radio, host; Channel WCHB, tv host; Channel 2 TV, 1950; Channel 7 TV, 1965; Det Water & Sewerage Dept, 1979; Tomi Jackson & Assoc, pub rel; WCHB Radio, jockey. **Orgs:** Pres, Am Women Radio & TV, 1965, regional vpres, 1966; bd mem, Women's Advert Club Detroit; bd mem, United Found; Travelers Aid Soc. **Honors/Awds:** Demmy Award, United Found, 1981. **Special Achievements:** First black women to be regional vice president of Detroit Chapter of AWRT. **Home Addr:** 11424 E Rembrandt Ave, Mesa, AZ 85212-4169.

### JACKSON, TONYA CHARISSE
Executive, administrator. **Personal:** Born Feb 28, 1959, Indianapolis, IN; daughter of Fred and Loretta; married Jerry L Smallwood; children: Eddie Jackosn & Justin Smallwood. **Educ:** Purdue Univ, BS, comput tech, 1981; George Mason Univ, MS, mgt info systems, 1987; Univ Va, exec training prog, 2000. **Career:** Thomas & Skinner, mgr systs develop, 1977-84; Planning Res Corp, mgr, financial systs, 1984-87; Freddie Mac, exec, 1987-2006; Freddie Mac, mgr, prod develop, 1987-89, dir, strategic systs planning, 1989-90, dir, corp bus re-engineering, 1990-91, dir, mgt & control systs, 1991-92, dir, nat & distressed acct, 1992-93, dir, customer & mkt interface, 1993-94, dir, nat revenue acct, 1994-95, dept head, trans processing, 1996-97, vp, trans processing, 1997-2001; TC Visions LLC, owner, 2006-09; vpres customer care; Family Matters Greater Wash, chief exec officer, 2009-. **Orgs:** Chair & pres, Sisters Son Found, 1997-; bd leader & vice chair, Phillips Progs C & Families, 1998-; chair, Women's Mortgage Indust Network, 2002-. **Home Addr:** 2200 Roark Dr, Reston, VA 20191, **Home Phone:** (703)709-0848. **Business Addr:** President, Sisters Of The Son Foundation, PO Box 2376, Reston, VA 22553.

### JACKSON, TYOKA
Broadcaster, football player. **Personal:** Born Nov 22, 1971, Washington, DC; married Tenique; children: 2. **Educ:** Pa State Univ, BA, labor & indust rels, 1994. **Career:** Football player (retired), analyst; Miami Dolphins, defensive end, 1994; Jackson Investment Co, founder, 1995-currently; Tampa Bay Buccaneers, defensive end & left defensive end & defensive tackle, 1996-2000; St Louis Rams, defensive end, 2001-05; Detroit lions, 2006-07; Int House Pancakes, franchisee, 2008-; CBS Radio, nat football league analyst, 2013-14; Big Ten Network, col football studio analyst, 2014-15; ESPN, Col Football Analyst, 2015-currently. **Orgs:** Get IntoGame; Rams Reader Team; Bowl-a-RAM-a; Make a Wish Found; founder, Tyoka's Troops with Am Red Cross; bd mem, YMCA, 2009-. **Honors/Awds:** Go to Guy Award, St Louis Ram, 2004. **Special Achievements:** Nominee for the Walter Payton Man of the Year award. **Business Addr:** Founder, Jackson Investment Co, 125 Yuma St SE Suite 101, Washington, DC 20032, **Business Phone:** (202)562-4446.

### JACKSON, VINCENT EDWARD. See JACKSON, BO.

### JACKSON, W. SHERMAN
Educator, college teacher. **Personal:** Born May 21, 1939, Crowley, LA; married Frances P McIntyre; children: Sherlyn, Sherrese & W Sherman II. **Educ:** Southern Univ, BA, 1962; NC Cent Univ, MA, 1963; Ohio State Univ, PhD, 1969. **Career:** Alcorn Col, Lorman, MS, instr, 1963-64; Cent State Univ, instr, 1966-68; Univ Lagos, Nigeria, sr fulbright lectr, 1972-73; Miami Univ, assoc prof am const hist & law, 1969-; Proj title Supreme Ct & Judicial Emasculation. **Orgs:** Pres & founder, Asn Acad Advan, 1969; pres, Oxford Nat Asn Advan Colored People, 1979; consult, NEH; ed consult, Pentagon Ed Testing Serv; Nat Underground Rr Mus; hist consult, Nat Pk Serv. **Home Addr:** 114 Country Club, Oxford, OH 45056. **Business Addr:** Emeritus Professor of History, Miami University, Rm 272 Upham Hall Oxford Campus, Miami, OH 45056, **Business Phone:** (513)529-5137.

### JACKSON, WARREN GARRISON
Executive. **Personal:** Born Yonkers, NY; son of Charles R and Ethel R Garrison; married Christina; children: Tenley Ann, W Garrison & Terrance V. **Educ:** Manhattan Col, Riverdale, NY, BS, 1952. **Career:** NY Times, New York, NY, circulation inspector, asst circulation mgr; Amsterdam News, New York, NY, circulation dir; Circulation Experti, Hartsdale, NY, founder, pres & chief exec officer, 1968-. **Orgs:** Vice chair, Jackie Robinson Found, 1989-; trustee, Jackie Joyner Kersee Found, 1989-; trustee, White Plains Hosp, 1990-. **Home Addr:** 7 Brookdell Dr, Hartsdale, NY 10530. **Business Addr:** President, Chief Executive Officer, Circulation Experti, 707 Westchester Ave Suite 309, White Plains, NY 10604, **Business Phone:** (914)948-8144.

### JACKSON, WAVERLY ARTHUR, JR.
Football player, football coach. **Personal:** Born Dec 19, 1972, South Hill, VA. **Educ:** Va Polytech Inst & State Univ, attended 1996. **Career:** Football player (retired), free agent, coach; Carolina Panthers, defensive tackle, 1997-98; Indianapolis Colts, 2000-01, guard, 1998, right guard, right tackle & tight end, 1999, left guard, right tackle, 2002, free agt, currently; Bluestone High Sch, teacher & coach, currently. **Business Addr:** Teacher, Coach, Bluestone High School, 6825 Skipwith Rd, Skipwith, VA 23968, **Business Phone:** (434)372-5177.

### JACKSON, BISHOP WILEY, JR.
Clergy. **Personal:** Born Jan 16, 1953, Atlanta, GA; son of Wiley Sr; married Mary Ann; children: Wiley III & Paul Emerson. **Educ:** S Ga Col; Dekalb Cent Col, AD; Beulah Heights Bible Col, BA. **Career:** Frito-Lay Inc, 1971-81; Gospel Tabernacle, pastor & founder, chief exec officer, 1982-, sr pastor. **Orgs:** Nat Relig Broadcasters; Churches Uniting Global Mission; fel Inner City Word Faith Churches; fel Pentecostal, N Am; bd preachers, Morehouse Col; founder & presiding bishop, Word Action Fel Pastors; bd dir, Fel Inner City Word Faith Ministires. **Honors/Awds:** Hon DDiv, Shiloh Theol Sem, Stafford, Va; Hon DDiv, Beulah Heights Bible Colleg, Atlanta, Ga. **Special Achievements:** Book: Born to Overcome, 2002; Uncommon Faith. **Business Addr:** Chief Executive Officer, Pastor & Founder, Gospel Tabernacle, 277 Clifton St, Atlanta, GA 30317-2122, **Business Phone:** (404)370-3800.

### JACKSON, WILLIAM ALVIN
Automotive executive. **Personal:** Born Sep 20, 1950, Chicago, IL; son of James and Elnora; married Rita F; children: Richard A, Alyssa B & Danielle L. **Educ:** Loyola Univ, BSBA, 1975. **Career:** L-M Div Ford Motor Co, zone mgr, 1975-79; Volkswagen Am Inc, dist sales mgr, 1979-82, advert productions super, 1982-84, shows & exhibs mgr, 1984-87; Jones Transfer Co, vpres sales & mkt, 1987-89; Chrysler Int Corp, merchandising mgr, 1989-93, France & Spain, regional sales & mkt mgr, 1993-96, int fleet sales mgr, 1996. **Orgs:** Mentor, Detroit Big Bro Prog, 1990-93; founder, bd dir, Tia Nedd Organ Donor Found. **Home Addr:** 3283 Springbrook Ct, West Bloomfield, MI 48324-3252, **Home Phone:** (248)366-0045.

### JACKSON, WILLIAM E.
Educator. **Personal:** Born Dec 1, 1936, Creedmoor, NC; married Janet. **Educ:** NC Cent Univ, BA, 1958; NY Univ, MA, 1961; Univ Pa, PhD, 1972. **Career:** City Co, NY, 1961-64; Univ Pa, instr, 1967-70; Yale Univ, asst prof ger; Univ Va, fac, 1981-2005, chmn; Univ Va, Dept Ger, assoc prof emer, 2005-. **Orgs:** Am Asn Teachers Ger; NC Cent Alumni. **Honors/Awds:** Outstanding Faculty Award, African-Am Affairs, 1999; Univ Teaching Award, Univ Va, 2005. **Special Achievements:** Author: Reinmar's Women, Amsterdam benjamins, 1980; publs in "Neophilologus" "Colloquia Germanica" & "Germanica Studies in Honor of Otto Springer". **Business Addr:** Associate Professor Emeritus, University of Virginia, New Cabell Hall 2nd Fl, Charlottesville, VA 22904-4125, **Business Phone:** (434)924-3530.

### JACKSON, WILLIAM R.
Psychotherapist, businessperson. **Personal:** Born Aug 28, 1945, Sioux Falls, SD; son of Juanita R Clardy; married Jacqualine; children: Felicia & Kimberly. **Educ:** Washburn Univ, BEd, 1968; Ball St Univ, MA, coun psychol, 1975. **Career:** Great Clips Inc, owner, 1989-; Dr Bayless & Assoc, pvt pract, psychotherapist, 1989-2003. **Honors/Awds:** Million Dollar Club, Great Clips Inc, 1998. **Home Addr:** 6121 W Corrine Dr, Glendale, AZ 85304, **Home Phone:** (602)486-2192. **Business Addr:** Owner, 12228 N Cave Creek Rd Suite 115, 3620 N 3rd St, Phoenix, AZ 85022-6519, **Business Phone:** (602)230-7373.

### JACKSON, WILLIE BERNARD, JR.
Football player, executive. **Personal:** Born Aug 16, 1971, Gainesville, FL; son of Willie Sr. **Educ:** Univ Fla, BS, telecommun, 1993. **Career:** Football player (retired); Dallas Cowboys, 1994; Jacksonville Jaguars, wide receiver, 1995-96, kick returner, 1997; Cincinnati Bengals, 1998, wide receiver, 1999; New Orleans Saints, wide receiver, 2000-01; Atlanta Falcons, wide receiver, 2002; Wash Redskins, tight end, 2002; Denver Broncos, 2004; AAFL, 2008-; Edward Waters Col, athletic dir, 2015-. **Honors/Awds:** SEC Championship, 1991; 1993; First team All SEC, 1992; Honorable mention All American, 1991; 1992; 1993; University of Florida Athletic Hall of Fame; Georgia Hall of Fame. **Business Addr:** Athletic Director, Edward Waters College, 1658 Kings Rd, Jacksonville, FL 32209, **Business Phone:** (904)470-8000.

### JACKSON, WILLIS RANDELL, II
Athletic director, educator, athletic coach. **Personal:** Born Sep 11, 1945, Memphis, TN; son of Willis Randell and Louise Hallbert; married Patricia F Crisp; children: Ericka, Hasani & Jamila. **Educ:** Rochester Jr Col, cert, 1965; ND State Univ, BS, 1967; SIU Edwardsville, MS & admin cert, 1980. **Career:** Rochester Lourdes High Sch, head wrestling coach, 1967-68; Soldan High Sch, head wrestling coach, 1969-71; Lincoln Sr High Sch, head wrestling coach, 1971-74, athletic dir, 1973-74; E St Louis Sr High Sch, head wrestling coach, 1974-84, athletic dir, 1974-81; Hughes Quinn Jr High Sch, head girls track coach, 1985-91, teacher, currently; Dr Jack's Sports Ltd, chief exec officer & owner, currently. **Orgs:** Ill Wrestling Coaches & Off Assoc, 1974-; NWCOA Wrestling Coaches & Off Assoc, 1974-; Nat Basketball Coaches Assoc, 1985-; Nat Athletic dir Assoc, 1974-; pres, Grandmaster Athletic Asn; Southern Cross 112 Prince Hall Mason, 1975-. **Home Addr:** 410 Suite 18th St, East St. Louis, IL 62205, **Home Phone:** (618)271-4108. **Business Addr:** Chief Executive Officer, Owner, Dr Jack's Sports Ltd, 1000 St Louis Ave, East St. Louis, IL 62201-1734, **Business Phone:** (618)271-8860.

### JACKSON, YVONNE RUTH
Vice president (organization). **Personal:** Born Jun 30, 1949, Los Angeles, CA; daughter of Giles and Gwendolyn Lackey Battle; married Frederick Jr; children: Cortney & Douglass. **Educ:** Spelman Col, BA, hist, 1970; Harvard Bus Sch, PMD, mgt develop cert, 1985. **Career:** Avon Prod, vpres-hr, 1979-93; Sears; Roebuck & Co; Burger King, human resource head, 1993-99; Compaq Comp Corp, human resource head, 1999-2002; Pfizer Inc, human resource head, 2002-05; Corp Human Resources, leadership team & sr vpres, 2004; BeecherJackson, Pres & Prin, 2006-. **Orgs:** Dir, Best Buy, 1988-99; Vice chmn, chmn, Bd trustee Spelman Col, 2004; Bd Inst Women's Policy Res; Adv Bd Catalyst; dir, Winn-Dixie, 2006-12; dir, AGB Consulting, 2014-; dir, Spartan Stores. **Business Addr:** Chair of the Board of Trustees, Chairman, Spelman College, 350 Spelman Lane S W Atlanta, Atlanta, GA 30314, **Business Phone:** (404)681-3643.

### JACKSON-BENNETT, ROSALIND
Executive director. **Career:** US Off Diversity & Inclusion Avon Prod Inc, dir, currently. **Business Addr:** Director, US Office of Diversity & Inclusion for Avon Products Inc, 1345 Avenue of the Americas, New York, NY 10105-0196, **Business Phone:** (212)282-5000.

### JACKSON-CRAWFORD, VANELLA ALISE
Association executive, consultant, social worker. **Personal:** Born Nov 25, 1947, Washington, DC; daughter of James Vance Jackson Jr and Dorothy Samella Raiford Patton; married William Alexander; children: Kahina B. **Educ:** Fed City Col, BA, 1973; Howard Univ, MSW, admin, 1975, cert, short term anxiety provoking psychother, 1978; Wash Sch Psychiat, cert, c's & adolescent psycotherapy, 1978; Fisk Univ, sociol. **Career:** Urban Prof Assoc, dir outpatient serv, 1975-79; Lt Joseph P Kennedy Inst, counr, 1977-79; Howard Univ Hosp, psy chiat social worker, 1980-86; Cong Nat Black Churches Inc, proj dir black families progs, 1986-92; Decades Inc, Body Shaping Shoppe, co-owner, 1992-; Vanella Group, motivational trainer/facilitator, 1989-. **Orgs:** Georgetown Univ, Child Develop Dept, 1978; United Way Am, 1978; Nat Asn Social Workers, 1979; dir, Christian Educ N Brent wood AME Zion Church, 1982-85; Young People's Proj 15-24 Clin, 1985-88; pvt productions/co-owner, Psychol Resource Ctr, 1985-87; trainer, DCPC, 1985; CNBC, 1985; Nat Asn Black Social Workers, 1985; consult, Cong Nat Black Churches, 1986; DC Coalition Social Work Health Care Providers; adv bd, Am Red Cross Adolescent Prog; exec bd/co-chairperson, Duke Ellington Sch Performing Arts. **Honors/Awds:** Alpha Delta Mu Nat Work Honor Soc. **Special**

**Achievements:** Designed nationally acclaimed parent education program, PRAISE: Parents Reclaiming African Information for Spiritual Enhancement, 1980-93. **Business Addr:** Motivational Trainer, Facilitator, The Vanella Group, 1109 Mich Ave NE, Washington, DC 20017, **Business Phone:** (202)529-1561.

### JACKSON-FOY, LUCY MAYE

Educator. **Personal:** Born Sep 28, 1919, Forney, TX; daughter of Louise and L J; married Joseph Daniel. **Educ:** A&T Col; Ohio State Univ; Prairie View Col; Tex Woman's Univ; N Tex State Col; Kans State Teachers Col; Kans Univ; Kans Cent Mo State Univ; Univ Mo. **Career:** Educator (retired); Veteran admin, 1946-50; A&T Col, 1950-54; Hamilton Pk High Sch, 1954-62; Kans City Mo Sch Dist, voc coordr, 1963-84. **Orgs:** Eta Phi Beta, 1968-74; Nat Rehab Asn; Counc Except C; Mo State Teachers Asn; Disabled Am Veterans; Nat Coun Teachers Math; Nat Asn Advan Colored People; Nat Coun Negro Women; Eta Phi Beta Sor; exec bd dir, Kans City Asn Ment Retarded C; Comt Davis Brickle Report; Spec Educ Adv Com; Community Serv Greater Kans City; co-founder Shelly Sch Ment Retarded; vol, Adult Basic Educ Prog; Health Care AARP Bd Kans City; pres, Wash-Lincoln High Sch Club, 1987-88; bd, Women's Chamber Com Kans City. **Honors/Awds:** Outstanding Sec Educ Am, 1974-75; Cert, Nat Wis Law Alumni Asn, 1987-88. **Home Addr:** 1414 E 28 St, Kansas City, MO 64109-1214.

### JACKSON-GILLISON, ESQ. HELEN L.

Lawyer. **Personal:** Born Jul 9, 1944, Colliers, WV; daughter of George W Sr and Helen L; married Edward L Gillison Sr; children: Edward L II. **Educ:** W Liberty State Col, BS, 1977; WVa Univ Col Law, JD, 1981. **Career:** Helen L Jackson-Gillison Law Off, owner, atty, 1981-, sr partner, currently. **Orgs:** WVa State Bar Found, currently; WVa Trial Lawyers Asn; Mountain State Bar Asn; Hancock Co Bar Asn; Am Bar Ass; Nat Bar Asn; Am Trial Lawyers Asn; Weirton Bus; Prof Womens Club; Wva All Black Schs Sports & Acad Hall Fame. **Honors/Awds:** Black Attorney of the Year Award, WVa Col Law, 1986. **Special Achievements:** First African American female to began her own private law practice in Weirton, WVa; First African American female to serve on the Audit & Budget Committee and the Unlawful Practice of Law Committee, WVa State Bar; First African American appointed to the WVa North Community College Board of Trustees. **Home Addr:** 264 Lakeview Dr, Weirton, WV 26062-9614. **Business Addr:** Attorney, Senior Partner, Helen L Jackson-Gillison Law Offices, 3139 W St, Weirton, WV 26062, **Business Phone:** (304)748-7116.

### JACKSON-HAMMOND, CYNTHIA

College president. **Personal:** married James Eric Sr; children: James Eric Jr, Christopher Adam & Erin Jenea. **Educ:** Grambling State Univ, bachelor's degree, PhD, educ; Univ La-Monroe, master's, commun, master, coun educ. **Career:** High sch teacher LA; Univ La, Monroe, instr, 1987, asst prof, dir Develop Educ, dir Stud Develop; Calif State Univ Dominguez Hills, educr; Del State Univ, fac mem, asst dean, dir Ctr Sch Chg, founding dean Sch Educ & Human Performance; Univ Nc, Charlotte, asst dean Col Educ; Winston-Salem State Univ, prof & dean Sch Educ & Human Performance; Coppin State Univ, provost & vpres acad affairs; H&H Educ Consults, lead consult, 2011-12; Cent State Univ, pres, 2012-. **Orgs:** Nat Coun Accreditation Teacher Educ, Mem Bd Examiners; comt mem, Southern Asn Cols & Schs; comt mem, Mid States Asn Cols & Schs. **Special Achievements:** First female president of Central State University; speaker on issues of cultural competency and global education. **Business Addr:** Office of the President, 1400 Brush Row Rd, Wilberforce, OH 45384.

### JACKSON-LEE, SHEILA

Congressperson (U.S. federal government). **Personal:** Born Jan 12, 1950, Queens, NY; married Elwyn C; children: Erica & Jason. **Educ:** Yale Univ, BA, polit sci, 1972; Univ Va, Law Sch, JD, 1975. **Career:** Houston City Coun, atty, 1990-94; US House Reps, congresswoman, 1995-; Homeland Security Subcomt on Transp Security & Infrastructure Protection, chairwoman. **Orgs:** Founder, mem & co-chair, Cong C's Caucus; founder, mem & co-chair, Afghan Caucus; founder, mem & co-chair, Pakistan Caucus; founder, mem & co-chair, Algerian Caucus; Foreign Affairs; ranking mem, Border and Maritime Subcomt; sr mem, House Judiciary Comt; ranking mem, Subcomt on Crime, Terrorism, Homeland Security and Invests; Dem Caucus Health Care Task Force; vice chair, chair, Energy Task Force, Cong Black Caucus; co-chair, Redistricting Task Force. **Home Addr:** 4428 N Roseneath, Houston, TX 77021, **Home Phone:** (713)741-1822. **Business Addr:** Congresswoman, United States House of Representatives, 2160 Rayburn Bldg, Washington, DC 20515, **Business Phone:** (202)225-3816.

### JACKSON-RANSOM, BUNNIE

Business owner, executive. **Personal:** Born Nov 16, 1940, Louisburg, NC; daughter of Burnal James Hayes and Elizabeth Day Hayes; married Raymond; married Maynard Jackson; children: Elizabeth, Brooke, Maynard H III & Rae Yvonne. **Educ:** NC Col, BS, bus, 1961, cert, Com, 1962; NC Cent Univ, MS, bus & econs, 1969, MS, bus, 1970. **Career:** NC Col, instr bus & supvr secretarial serv, 1962-63; Bennett Col, instr bus & supvr secretarial serv, 1963-64; N Carolina Fund, admin asst, 1965-68; Econ Opportunity Atlanta Inc, contract specialist, prog coordr, dir planning & prog develop, 1968-70; Pvt Consult Serv, 1972-76; firstClass Inc, founder, 1975; Co Art, pvt consult serv, 1973-74; First Class Inc, admin asst, 1965-, pres & founder, 1975-; Atlanta Arts Alliance, pvt consult serv, 1975-76; BJT Inc, owner & operator, airport amusement concessions, 1979-83; conglomerate co, chief admin officer, 1978-88; OS Band Inc, mgt serv, 1980-84; Atlanta Artists Mgt Inc, pres, 1980-89, mgt serv, 1980-89; Ga State Univ, instr, 1981-90, 1995. **Orgs:** Dir planning & prog develop, NC Fund, 1968-70; exec comt mem, Nat Asn Advan Colored People; active mem, Delta Sigma Theta Sorority; Link Inc; pres, 100 Black Women; Atlanta Asn Black Journalists; nat commun, pub rels comt, Links Inc; adv bd, Univ Community Acad; Black Methodist Church Renewal; bd dir, Atlanta Bus League; Rainbow PUSH; NC Col Alumni Asn; active mem, Cascade United Methodist Church; Atlanta League Women Voters; Nat Coun Negro Women; chmn, Nat Proj Comt; pres, Atlanta Chap Jack & Jill; Bd Dirs Partnership Against Domestic Violence. **Honors/Awds:** Outstanding Young Women in America, 1970-80; Certificate Appreciation, Atlanta Pub Schs, 1974; Nat Media Women, Atlanta Chap, Community Leader Int Scope, 1975; Bronze Jubilee Award, 1984; President Award, Atlanta Asn Black Journalists, 1984, 1991, 1993; Community Service Award, SCLC, 2008; Business Award, Atlanta Chap Delta Sigma Theta Sorority; Millennium Award, Atlanta Bus League. **Special Achievements:** One of the Top 100 Black Bus & Prof Women, Dollar & Sense Magazine, 1985; Top 100 Women of Influence, Atlanta Business Magazines, 1997-05. **Home Addr:** 450 Hickory Glen, Atlanta, GA 30311, **Home Phone:** (404)226-8000. **Business Addr:** President, Founder, First Class Inc, PO Box 110090, Atlanta, GA 30311, **Business Phone:** (404)505-8188.

### JACKSON-SMOOT, BENITA MARIE. See JACKSON, DR. BENITA MARIE.

### JACKSON-TEAL, RITA F.

Educator. **Personal:** Born Apr 26, 1949, Memphis, TN; children: Rashel, Janette & Teal. **Educ:** Tenn State Univ, BS, 1971; Univ Mich, MA, 1973; EdD; Memphis State Univ, 1989. **Career:** Argonne Lab Argonne IL, stud trainee, 1971; Rust Col Holly Springs, Miss, math instr, tutor, 1973-75; Lincoln Lab Lexington MA, vis scientist, 1974; LeMoyne-Owen Col Memphis, math instr, 1975-78; Upward Bound & Learning Resource Ctr, dir spec serv; SC State Univ, Instnl Effectiveness, exec dir, currently, interim vpres admin, currently. **Orgs:** Coord, Dual-Degree Eng Prog, 1977-80; chairperson, Greek Lett Comn, 1978-80; Cult & Ath Comm Rust Col; Freshman Comt, Orientation Comt, Acad Standing Comt, Acad Task Force Cluster Coop Ed Delta Sigma Theta; Delta Sigma Theta; Alpha Kappa Mu, Beta Kappa Chi; Kappa Delta Pi; vpres, Tenn Assoc Spec Prog, 1983-85, pres, 1985-87; chairperson, Delta Sigma Theta Scholar Comt, 1984-85; reg chairperson, Southeastern Assoc Ed Opportunity Prog Personnel (SAEOPP) Ann Conf, 1985, chmn, 1985-87, secy, 1987; chmn, SAEOPP Scholar Comt, 1986-87. **Home Addr:** 892 E Dr, Memphis, TN 38108. **Business Addr:** Executive Director of Institutional Effectiveness, Interim Vice President for Administration, South Carolina State University, 300 Col St NE, Orangeburg, SC 29117-0001, **Business Phone:** (803)516-4586.

### JACOB, JOHN EDWARD

Executive director, association executive. **Personal:** Born Dec 16, 1934, Trout, LA; son of Emory and Claudia Sadler; married Barbara May Singleton; children: Sheryl Rene. **Educ:** Howard Univ, BA, 1957, MSW, 1963. **Career:** US Post off, parcel post sorting mach oper, 1958-60; Baltimore City Dept Pub Welfare, caseworker, 1960-63, child welfare case work suprv, 1963-65; Wash Urban League, dir ed & youth incentives, 1965-66, br off dir, 1966-67, assoc exec dir admin, 1967-68, actg exec dir, 1968-70, spec lectr, 1968-69, San Diego, pres, 1975-79; Howard Univ Sch Social Work, spec lectr, 1968-69; Wash Urban League, dir soc work field work stud unit, 1968-70; Eastern Reg Nat Urban League, dir com org training, 1970; San Diego Urban League, exec dir, 1970-75; Nat Urban League, exec vpres, 1979-81, pres & chief exec officer, 1982-94; Anheuser-Busch Cos Inc, bd dir, 1990-2006, exec vpres global commun & chief communs officer, 1994-2006; Morgan Stanley, bd dir; Coca-Cola Enterprises Inc, bd dir; LTV Corp, bd dir; NY NEX New York, bd dir; Continental Corp, bd dir; Nat Westminster Bancorp, bd dir; Howard Univ, chmn emer; US Civil Rights, leader; Edward Jones, mem investment policy adv comt, currently. **Orgs:** Kappa Alpha Psi, 1954; Nat Assoc Social Workers, 1961-; consult, Nat Coun Negro Women, 1967-69, Nat Urban League, 1968-69; chmn, bd trustee, Howard Univ, 1971-78, chmn, 1988; consult, Timely Investment Club, 1972-75; Judicial Nominating Comt DC, 1976-79; dir, Local Initiatives Support Corp, 1980-; Advert Rev Bd, 1980-83; adv comt mem, NY Hosp, 1980-83; dir A Better Chance, 1980-83; dir, NY Found, 1982-85; corp dir, NY Tel Co, 1983-; dir, Nat Conf Christians & Jews, 1983-88; Rockefeller Univ Coun, 1983-88; chmn, emer bd trustee, Howard Univ; bd dir, Legal Aid Soc; bd dir, Drucker Found; Nat Conf Bd; Econ Policy Inst; bd dir, Nat Parks Found; bd dir, Local Initiatives Support Corp; bd mem, NYNEX. **Honors/Awds:** Whitney M Young Award, Wash Urban League Inc, 1979; Special Citation Atlanta Club Howard Univ Alumni Asn, 1980; Atty Hudson L Lavell Soc Action Award, Phi Beta Sigma, 1982; Exemplary Service Award, Alumni Club Long Island Howard Univ, 1983; Achievement Award, Zeta Phi Beta, 1984, Cleveland Alumni Chap Kappa Alpha Psi, 1984; Alumni Achievement Award, Alpha Psi Atlanta Club Howard Univ, 1984; Nat Kappaman Achievement Durham Alumni Chapter Kappa, 1984; Black book's Bus & Professional Award, Dollars & Sense Mag, 1985; Achievement Award, Peoria Alumni Chap Kappa Alpha Psi, 1985; Forrester B Washington Award, Atlanta Univ Sch Social Work, 1986; United Way of America's National Professional Leadership Award, 1989. **Home Addr:** 2409 Wexford Woods Ct, St Louis, MO 63131. **Business Addr:** Member Investment Policy Advisory Committee, Edward Jones, 12555 Manchester Rd, St. Louis, MO 63131, **Business Phone:** (314)515-2000.

### JACOBS, DR. REV. DANIEL WESLEY, SR.

Clergy, administrator. **Personal:** Born Aug 26, 1933, Aragon, NM; son of Daniel Lott (deceased) and Fannie Lou Cosby Jacobs Pannell (deceased); married Mary Louise Jenkins; children: Daniel Jr, Reginald Eugene & Dana Michelle. **Educ:** Morris Brown Col, BA, 1955; Turner Theol Seminary, Mdiv, 1962; Emory Univ, PhD, 1967; Columbia Theol Seminary, 1987. **Career:** Clergy, administrator (retired); E Atlanta Dist, AME Church, presiding elder, 1971-72; Allen Temple, AME Church, pastor, 1972-77; St James AME Church, pastor, 1977-80; Steward Chapel AME Church, pastor, 1980-82; St Mark AME Church, pastor, 1982-85; Turner Theol Sem, dean, pres, 1985-08. **Orgs:** Pres, Atlanta AME Ministers Union, 1970; pres, Deans coun, Interdenominational Theol Ctr; prs, Columbus Phenix City Ministers Alliance, 1978-80; housing comn chmn, Atlanta Nat Asn Advan Colored People, 1973-77; sec, Christian Coun Metrop Atlanta, 1977. **Home Addr:** 2760 The Fontainebleau SW, Atlanta, GA 30331-2722, **Home Phone:** (404)629-2804.

### JACOBS, DANNY ODELL

Educator, chairperson, physician. **Personal:** Born Sep 7, 1954, Camden, AR; son of Felix and Helen; children: Nia & Daniel. **Educ:** Harvard Univ, AB, biol, 1975; Wash Univ, MD, 1979; Harvard Sch Pub Health, MPH, biostatistics, 1989. **Career:** Hosp Univ Pa, Intern Surg, 1979-80, Gen Surg, 1980-85, chief resident, 1985-86; Univ Pa Sch Med, Philadelphia, PA, Asst Instr Surg, 1980-85, Instr Surg, 1985-86; Harvard Med Sch, asst prof surg, 1989-93, assoc prof surg, 1993-99; Brigham & Women's Hosp, physician mem, nutrit support, 1992-95, sr surgeon, 1993-, assoc prog dir, clin res, 1995-98, dir, metab support svcs, 1995-2000, dir, lab surg metab, 1995-2000; Creighton Univ Sch Med, Omaha, NE, prof & chmn, 2000-03, Arnold W Lempka Distinguished Prof Surg, 2001-03, dir, 2001-03; Durham Veteran's Admin, attend surgeon, 2003-12; Duke Univ Health Syst, Dept Surg, managing dir, chair, 2003-12, David C Sabiston Jr prof, 2007-12. **Orgs:** Fel Harrison Dept Surg Res, Hosp Univ Pa Philadelphia, Pa, 1982-84; res fel Surg Nutrit & Metab, sci adv comt, gen clin res ctr, 1998-2000, Brigham & Women's Hosp, Boston, Mass, 1986-88; Am Soc Parenteral & Enteral Nutrit, 1987-; Soc Univ Surgeons, 1990-; Asn Acad Surg, 1991-; Am Col Sugeons, fel 1992-; Soc Black Acad Surgeons, 1992-; Soc Surg Alimentary Tract, 1994-; Alpha Omega Alpha Hon Med Socs; New Eng J Med Surg, 1994-; World J Surg; Soc Critical Care Med, 1994-; dir, St Joseph Hosp, Omaha, NE, 2000-03; bd dir, exec comt, Creighton Med Assocs, 2000-03; Am Surg Asn; Am Physiol Soc; Soc Black Acad Surgeons; Southern Surg Asn; Am Soc Nutrit Sci; Europ Acad Sci; Inst Med Nat Acad Sci, 2001. **Home Addr:** 126 Independence Dr, Chestnut Hill, MA 02467. **Business Addr:** Chair, David C Sabiston Jr Professor, Duke University Health System, DUMC 3704, Durham, NC 27710, **Business Phone:** (919)681-3445.

### JACOBS, ENNIS LEON, JR.

Lawyer. **Personal:** Born Jan 19, 1954, Tampa, FL; son of Ennis Sr and Vetta; married Ruth; children: Bron & Jasmine. **Educ:** Fla A&M Univ, BS, data processing, 1976; Fla State Univ Col Law, JD, 1986. **Career:** Eastman Kodak Co, syst analyst, 1976-80; RCA Corp, syst rep, 1980-82; Fla Pub Serv Comn, staff atty, 1986-89, comnr & chmn, 1998-2002; Fla Atty Gen, staff atty, 1989-91; Fla Sen, staff coun, 1991-93; Fla Legis House, legis coun, 1993-98; Fla A&M Univ, exec asst to pres, 2002-03; Kerry Election Campaign, volunteer, 2004; Track Life Solutions, outside legal advisor, 2005-11; Sierra Club, consult, 2007-08; Nat Resources Defense Coun, consult, 2007-09; Southern Alliance Clean Energy, consult, 2007-13; Fla Elections Comn, 2009-12; Quantum Broadband Solutions, LLC, spec coun & advisor, 2011-13; Williams Jacobs & Assoc LLC, partner & atty, currently. **Orgs:** Bd dir, Child Advocates II Inc; Fla Bar, 1987-; Pres bd, Tallahassee Habitat Humanity; Nat Bar Asn; Am Bar Asn; Leon County Guardian Ad Litem; former comnr, chair, Nat Asn Regulatory Utility Commissioners; Natural Resources Defense Coun; Sierra Club; bd dir, Southern Alliance Clean Energy; chairperson, bd dir, Visions Manhood Inc; Alpha Phi Alpha Marching; Tallahassee Southside Rotary. **Special Achievements:** Author, "State Regulation of Information Services", Barrister, ABA Young Lawyers Division, Spring 1991; "The State Public Service Commission Response to Y2K", National Regulatory Research Institute, 2000. **Business Addr:** Attorney, Partner, Williams Jacobs & Associates LLC, 2510 Miccosukee Rd Suite 104, Tallahassee, FL 32308, **Business Phone:** (850)222-1246.

### JACOBS, REV. GREGORY ALEXANDER

Clergy, lawyer. **Personal:** Born Mar 10, 1952, Bilwaskarma; son of Solomon N and Lynette G; married Beverly C; children: Charlotte Elizabeth & Stephanie Nicole; married Sheila Abdus-Salaam. **Educ:** Princeton Univ, AB, 1974; Columbia Univ Sch Law, JD, 1977; Bexley Hall Divinity Sch, MDiv, 1995. **Career:** Thompson Hine & Flory, partner; St Philip's Episcopal Church, vicar; Diocese Ohio, priest, 1995, bishop's asst, 2002-06; Trinity Episcopal Cathedral, Canon Mission & Ministry, partner, currently; Urban Ministry Develop in the Diocese Massachusetts, staff officer, 2008; Diocese Newark, chief staff, 2009-. **Orgs:** Bd dir, Minority Contractors Assistance Prog, 1985-97; bd dir, trustee, Diocese Ohio, Episcopal, 1989-94; African-Am Arch Auxiliary, 1990-95; area bd dir, Socs Bank, 1990-95; convenor, Black Episcopal Seminarians, 1991-95; chair, United Negro Col Fund Founds, 1991-95; Diocesan Coun, 1996-99; bd dir, Inter Act Cleveland, 1999-; adv bd, W Side Ecumenical Ministry, 2001-. **Home Addr:** 3330 Elsmere Rd, Shaker Heights, OH 44120, **Home Phone:** (216)991-5176. **Business Addr:** Partner, Trinity Episcopal Cathedral, 2230 Euclid Ave, Cleveland, OH 44115, **Business Phone:** (216)774-0409.

### JACOBS, HAZEL A.

Manager, government official. **Personal:** Born Sep 25, 1948, Blakely, GA; daughter of Leamon and Pearlia Jewell; married Claude. **Educ:** Ga State Univ, BS, 1982, MPA, 1986. **Career:** City Atlanta, Ga, admin asst, 1970-71, Atlanta Charter Comn, 1971-73, off mgr, 1974-78, legis policy analyst, 1978-, Res & Policy, dir, 1990-2007; Fulton county, County rep BeltLine Affordable Housing Adv Bd, mem, currently. **Orgs:** Am Asn Pub Admin, 1984-; Nat Asn Prof Women, 1985-; Nat Forum Black Pub Admin, 1985-. **Home Addr:** 3474 Mt Gilead Rd SW, Atlanta, GA 30331, **Home Phone:** (404)346-7452.

### JACOBS, REV. LARRY BEN

Chemical engineer, clergy. **Personal:** Born Dec 15, 1959, Arlington, GA; son of Mattie C Jackson and Tommy L; married Carolyn Laverne Malone; children: Matthew, Leah & Christopher. **Educ:** Tuskegee Inst, cert, 1980, BS, chem, 1984. **Career:** Int Paper Co, co-op engr, 1980; Procter & Gamble, co-op engr, 1982; Weyerhaeuser Co, prof intern, 1984-86; Hercules Inc, process engr, 1986-88; Gen Elect Co, Burkville, AL, prod engr 1988-91; Hoechst Celanese Corp, Salisbury, NC, develop engr, 1991-; Charlotte, NC, bus reengr, 1992-96, activ base cost coordr, 1996-97; BP, sr chem engr, 1997-; First Decatur AME Zion Church, pastor, 1998-. **Orgs:** AICHE, 1980-86; assoc mem, Tech Asn Pulp & Paper Indus, 1980-86; steward & choir pres Turner Chapel AME Church, 1984-86; educ chmn, Columbus MS Coalition Black Orgn, 1985-86; corresp, Jackson Advocate, 1986; toastmaster, Toastmasters Int, 1986-; math tutor, Asbury UM Church, 1987; secy, Tuskegee Univ Eng Alumni Asn, 1988-; Soldiers Memorial AMEZ Church Steward, 1991-; sch adv chair, Salisbury, NC, 1992-93; bd dir, Rowan Co, NC Red Cross, 1994-; adv bd, City Salisbury, 1994-; vpres, Leadership Roman, 1997; secy, Decatur Many Develop Asn, 1999-; pres, Decatur Ministerial Network, 2001. **Home Addr:** 811 Longbow Dr SW, Decatur, AL 35603, **Home Phone:** (256)584-7069. **Business Addr:** Pastor, First Decatur A M E Zion Church, 106 11th Ave NW 303D Beltline Pl, Decatur, AL 35601, **Business Phone:** (256)340-9100.

### JACOBS, PATRICIA DIANNE
Executive, lawyer. **Personal:** Born Jan 27, 1950, Camden, AR; daughter of Felix H and Helen M Tate; children: Branden Kemiah, Brittne Katelyn-Helen & Bradley Kareem-Felix. **Educ:** Lincoln Univ, BA, 1970; Harvard Law Sch, JD, 1973. **Career:** Lincoln Univ, asst dir financial aid, 1970; Exxon Corp, legal assoc, 1973-75; John Jay Col Criminal Justice, adj prof, 1974-75; Lincoln Univ, dir & trustee, 1983-; K-Com Micrographics Inc, pres; Am Asn Minority Enterprise Small Bus Investment Co, pres, 1983-97; GreenLeaf Assocs, owner, currently. **Orgs:** Asst min coun, US Senate Small Bus Comt, 1975-77; dir, Wider Opportunities Women, 1983-; dir, Coop Assistance Fund, 1983-; pres, Nat Assoc Investment Co. **Home Addr:** 215 Sheridan St NW, Washington, DC 20011, **Home Phone:** (202)291-8387. **Business Addr:** Owner, Greenleaf Associates, 114 Sheridan St NW Suite 200, Washington, DC 20011, **Business Phone:** (202)291-8387.

### JACOBS, REGINA
Track and field athlete, real estate agent. **Personal:** Born Sep 28, 1963, Los Angeles, CA; daughter of Cecilia; married Tom Craig. **Educ:** Stanford Univ, BA, eng & commun, 1990; Univ Calif, Berkeley, MBA, 1992; Grad Realtor Inst, GRI designation. **Career:** Track & field athlete (retired); Mid & long-distance track athlete; Oakland, real estate agt; E Bay Sotheby's Int Realty, producer. **Orgs:** Inst Study Sport & Soc. **Honors/Awds:** 1500 champion, U.S. Olympic Trials, 1992 & 1996; Sixth World Championships Athletics, Athens, silvermedal, 1997; 1,500 silver medal, 1999; US Indoor 1500 & 5000 champion; World Championships, Sevilla, silvermedal, 1999. **Special Achievements:** First woman to break the 4-minute barrier, 2003; Set a world record in the indoor 1500 m with a time of 3:59.58, becoming the first woman to break 4minutes in the event. **Business Addr:** East Bay Sothebys International Realty, 1986 Mountain Blvd, Oakland, CA 94611, **Business Phone:** (510)693-7973.

### JACOBS, TIMOTHY, JR.
Football player. **Personal:** Born Apr 5, 1970, Washington, DC; married Valerie; children: Taylor Arden. **Educ:** Delaware Univ. **Career:** Football player (retired); Cleveland Browns, corner back & defensive back, 1993-95; Miami Dolphins, defensive back, 1996-97.

### JACOX, KENDYL (KENDYL LEMARC JACOX)
Football player. **Personal:** Born Jun 10, 1975, Dallas, TX. **Educ:** Kans State Univ, soc sci. **Career:** San Diego Chargers, right guard & ctr, 1998-2001; New Orleans Saints, left guard, 2002-05; Miami Dolphins, left guard, 2006; free agt, currently. **Orgs:** Mem, K-State Alumni Asn. **Honors/Awds:** All-Big 12 hons, 1997. **Special Achievements:** Selected to play in E W Shrine All-Star game, 1998.

### JACQUES, CORNELL
Executive. **Personal:** Born Jul 12, 1949, Detroit, MI; son of Hernando and Hazel J; married Elaine Tribble; children: Monique S. **Educ:** Mich State Univ, attended 1968; Mercer Univ, BBA, bus admin & mgt, 1980. **Career:** USaF, 1969-74; Fed Aviation Admin, Journeyman Air Traffic Controller, 1974-81; Cent Vending Co, rte supvr, 1983-85; Lockheed IMS, resident parking consult, 1985-86; City Detroit, parking comn coordr, 1986-88; Lockheed Martin IMS, consult, asst vpres, 1989-91, munic serv vpres, 1991-94, regional vpres, 1995-2010; ACS State & Local Solutions Inc, regional vp, currently; Cornell Jacques Consult LLC, Prin, 2011-; Parking Mgt Consult, 2011-; Duncan Solutions, consult, 2013-. **Orgs:** Int Parking Inst, 1985-; Nat Forum Black Pub Admin, 1992-; Kappa Alpha Psi Fraternity, 1968-. **Home Addr:** 3520 E 139th Ave, Thornton, CO 80602, **Home Phone:** (303)452-4163. **Business Addr:** Regional Vice President, ACS State & Local Solutions Inc, 2828 N Haskell, Dallas, TX 75204, **Business Phone:** (214)841-6111.

### JACQUET, NATE (NATHANIEL MARTIN JACQUET)
Football player. **Personal:** Born Sep 2, 1975, Duarte, CA. **Educ:** Mt San Antonio Col; San Diego State Univ. **Career:** Football player (retired); Indianapolis Colts, wide receiver, 1997; Miami Dolphins, wide receiver, 1998-2000; San Diego Chargers, wide receiver, 2000; Minn Vikings, wide receiver, 2000-01; Carolina Panthers, wide receiver, 2002; Chicago Bears, wide receiver. **Honors/Awds:** Rookie of the Year, 1997.

### JAGGERS, GARLAND
Social worker, writer. **Personal:** Born Mar 24, 1933, Detroit, MI; son of Bennie and Garland; children: Howard Robinson, Leslie Moorer, Dr Kim & Melanie. **Educ:** Wayne State Univ, BA, 1957, MSW, 1962. **Career:** Creative Strategies Inc, dir & chief exec officer, 1968-; Univ Detroit, adj prof, 1973-78; Nat Black United Fund, exec dir, 1982-84; Community Case Mgt, interim dir; Proctor Publ LLC, auth, currently. Auth: Black Arts Mag, 1967; To The Poet in You, 1981; Activate Your Leadership, 1981; Fog: An Anal of Cath Dogma, 1999. **Orgs:** Co-Founder, Asn Black Social Workers Detroit, 1967; chmn bd, Mich Black United Fund, 1972-83; dir, Off Black Cath Affairs Am; founder, Nat Asn Black Social Workers, 2000. **Home Addr:** 1739 Canton St, Detroit, MI 48207-3603, **Home Phone:** (313)923-5085. **Business Addr:** Author, c/o Proctor Publ LLC, Ypsilanti, MI 48197-4422, **Business Phone:** (734)480-9900.

### JAKES, BISHOP THOMAS DEXTER, SR.
Clergy, playwright, writer. **Personal:** Born Jun 9, 1957, South Charleston, WV; son of Ernest Sr and Odith; married Elder Serita Ann Jamison; children: Jamar, Jermaine, Cora, Sarah & Thomas Dexter Jr. **Educ:** Ctr Bus Col, attended 1972; W Va State Col, attended 1976; Friends Univ, BA, MA, 1990, DMin, 1995. **Career:** Greater Emmanuel Temple Faith, founder & pastor, 1979-96; radio ministry, "The Master's Plan", 1982-85; TD Jakes Ministries, 1994-; Potter's House, pastor, 1998-; Potter's House Dallas Inc, founding pastor, chief exec officer & sr pastor, 2002-; auth, T D Jakes Ministries Inc, owner, currently; TDJ Enterprises, founder, currently. **Home Addr:** , Dallas, TX 75201. **Business Addr:** Owner, T D Jakes Ministries Inc, PO Box 5390, Dallas, TX 75208-5208, **Business Phone:** (214)333-6400.

### JAM, JIMMY (JAMES SAMUEL HARRIS, III)
Music producer, songwriter, executive. **Personal:** Born Jun 6, 1959, Minneapolis, MN; son of Cornbread Harris; married Lisa Padilla; children: Tyler James, Maximillian Lee & Isabella B. **Career:** Tv Series: "Fresh Off the Boat", 2016. Flyte Tyme Prods Inc, co-producer & songwriter, currently. **Orgs:** Chmn bd, Nat Acad Rec Arts & Sci. **Honors/Awds:** American Music Award, Best R&B Single, 1986; Grammy Award, Producer of the Year, 1987; Academy Award, 1993; Grammy Award, Best R&B Song, 1994; Grammy Award, Best Dance Recording, 2001; Grammy Award, Best Dance Recording, 2002; Essence Award, 2002; Grammy Award, Best Gospel Song, 2006; Grammy Award, Best R&B Album, 2008; The SoulMusic Hall of Fame, 2012. **Business Addr:** Co-Producer, Flyte Tyme Productions Inc, 4100 W 76th St, Edina, MN 55435, **Business Phone:** (952)897-3901.

### JAMAL, AHMAD (FREDERICK RUSSELL JONES)
Artist, composer, pianist. **Personal:** Born Jul 2, 1930, Pittsburgh, PA; children: Sumayah. **Career:** George Hudson Orchestra touring 1940s, jazz pianist; Four Strings, player, 1950; Cald wells, accompanist, 1951; Okeh Recs, Cadet Recs, rec contract; performer: Jazz Alley Downtown Seattle; Georges Chicago; Joe Segals Jazz Showcase; Voyager West St Louis; Ethyl's Place; Fairmont Hotels; Cricket Theater Hennepin Ctr; Apollo Theatre Town Hall; Rainbow Grill (Waldorf Astoria); The Embers; Village Gate; Iridium; The Village Vanguard; "Digital Works", "Rossiter Rd", "Live at the Montreal Jazz Festival", Atlantic Recs; Ellora Mgt, musician, currently; Albums: All of You; Jamal Plays Jamal; At The Penthouse; Extension; The Awakening; Freelight; Naked City Theme; One; Digital Works; Crystal; Pittsburgh, 1989; Chicago Revisited, 1993; Live in Paris '92; Ahmad's Blues; Poinciana; Telarc Recording Artist; I Remember Duke, Hoagy & Stray horn, 1995; Chicago Revisited, 1994; Birdology Distributed by Polygram, "Live In Paris", 1994; The Essence, Part 1, 1996; The Essence, Part 2, 1997; Nature, The Essence Part III, 1998 Atlantic; Birdology, "Olympia 2000", 2000; Recordings: "Waltz for Debby", 1980; Birdology: "Live in Paris", 1992, 1996; "Big Byrd", 1996; " In Search Of", 2003; "After Fajar", 2005; It's Magic, 2008; Poinciana - One Night Only, 2008; A Quiet Time, 2009; Blue Moon, 2012; Saturday Morning, 2013; Ahmad Jamal featuring Yusef Lateef, 2014. **Honors/Awds:** Entertainment Award, Pittsburgh Jr Chamber of Com, 1959; Who's Who In America, 1960; Distinguished Service Award, Anacostia Neighborhood Mus, Smithsonian Inst, 1980; Merit Award, The Art Dirs Club, 1986; Honorary Membership, Philippines Jazz Foundation, 1987; American Jazz Masters Award, NEA, 1994; Duke Ellington Fellow Award, Yale Univ, 1994; CHOC De L'annee Jazzman Award, 1995; Djangod 'Or Award, 1996; Arts & Culture Recognition Award, 2001; American Jazz Hall of Fame, NJ Jazz Soc, 2003; Gold Medallion, 2004; Named Officer, French Order of Arts and Letters, 2007; Living Legends Award, The Kennedy Ctr for the Performing Arts, 2007; The French Jazz Academy Award, 2011; Inducted, Poll Hall of Fame, 2011. **Special Achievements:** Only artist to have an LP in the album top ten of nat charts for 108 consecutive weeks But Not For Me, performed 2 years with Philip Morris Tour around the world; published: The Ahmad Jamal Collection of a collection of piano transcriptions. **Home Addr:** 820 Hunns Lake Rd, Stanfordville, NJ 12581. **Business Addr:** Musician, Ellora Management, 11 Brook St, Lakeville, CT 06039, **Business Phone:** (860)435-1305.

### JAMAR, LORD (LORENZO DECHALUS)
Actor, rap musician. **Personal:** Born Sep 17, 1968, New Rochelle, NY; children: Jamar Allah. **Career:** Brand Nubian, rap group, member, 1989-; actor, 2000-; solo artist, 2006-. Television: Oz, HBO, 2000-01; 100 Centre Street, 2001; Law & Order, 2002; Law & Order: Special Victims Unit, 2003; Third Watch, 2004-05; The Sopranos, 2006; Wifey, 2007; Rescue Me, 2011; Elementary, 2012; Person of Interest, 2013; The Night Of, 2016; Money.Power.Respect, 2016. Film: Morning Breath, 2002; L-o-v-e, 2004; Funny Valentine, 2005; They're Just My Friends, 2006; Father's Day, 2009; Buffalo Bushido, 2009; Drugs 101, 2010. **Special Achievements:** Albums (with Brand Nubian): One for All, 1990, In God We Trust, 1993, Everything Is Everything, 1994, Foundation, 1998, Fire in the Hole, 2004. Solo albums: The 5% Album, 2006. **Business Addr:** Sweet180, 141 West 28th St Suite 300, New York, NY 10001.

### JAMERSON, DR. JOHN W., III
Dentist. **Personal:** Born Apr 26, 1951, Savannah, GA; son of JW Jr and Dorothy Breaux; married Shearon Brown; children: Desiree Maria, Elizabeth Rene, Amanda Louise, JW IV, Charles Martin Breaux & Amelia Morgan. **Educ:** Morris Brown Col; Savannah State Univ, BS, 1974; Howard Univ, DDS, 1980. **Career:** Westside Comprehensive Health Ctr, dentist, 1980-82; pvt pract dentist, 1982-. **Orgs:** Vpres, bd dir, King-Tisdell Found, 1987-89, 1991-93; Dept Family & C Serv, 1994-, vpres, bd dir, 1997-2000, pres, 1999-; Ga Dent Asn, 1996-; pres, Southeast Dist Dent Soc, 1999-; fel Acad Dent Int, 1999; St Matthews Episcopal Church, 1999-; fel Int Col Dent, 2000; hon fel Ga Dent Asn, 2000. **Honors/Awds:** Man of The Year, Alpha Phi Alpha Fraternity Inc, 1974, 1986, 1993. **Special Achievements:** First African American president of the South East District Dental Society of the Georgia Dental Association. **Business Addr:** Dentist, John W Jamerson III, 315 E Henry St, Savannah, GA 31401, **Business Phone:** (912)232-6171.

### JAMES, ADVERGUS DELL
School administrator. **Personal:** Born Sep 24, 1944, Garden City, KS; son of Advergus D Sr and Helen Lee; married Anna Flave Glenn; children: Anthony David & Adam Glen (deceased). **Educ:** Langston Univ, BS, 1966; Okla State Univ, MS, 1969. **Career:** Langston Univ, asst registr, 1966-69, dir admis & rec, 1969-70; Prairie View A&M Univ, dir, 1970-85, dir admis & financial aid, 1986-88, dir financial aid, 1988-98, Stud Financial Serv, exec dir financial serv, 1998; Tuskegee Univ, Stud Financial Serv, exec dir, currently. **Orgs:** Consult, State Stud Financial Asst Training, 1979-80; pres, Tex Asn Stud Financial Aid Admin, 1981-82; Tex Guaranteed Stud Loan Adv Bd, 1984-86; Nat Coun Stud Financial Aid Admin, 1985-86; bd dir, Depelcin Ctr, 1986; adv bd, Outstanding Rural Scholars, 1990-; bd dir, Adv Comt, Greater E Tex Higher Educ Authority, 1995-; bd dir, Tex Asn Stud Financial Aid Admin; bd dir, Greater Tex Found; Tex Higher Educ Coord; Alpha Phi Alpha Fraternity; charter mem, Prairie View Optimist Club. **Home Addr:** 7611 Hertfordshire Dr, Spring, TX 77379, **Home Phone:** (281)251-4856. **Business Addr:** Executive Director, Tuskegee University, 1200 W Montgomery Rd, Tuskegee, AL 36088, **Business Phone:** (334)727-8011.

### JAMES, ALEXANDER, JR.
Engineer, manager, executive. **Personal:** Born Nov 2, 1933, Branchville, SC; married Dorothy L Jones; children: Audrey D, Gregory A & Kevin ES. **Educ:** City Col NY, BE, 1961; NY Univ, Grad Eng, MSEE, 1963, Grad Bus Admin, MBA, 1986. **Career:** Bell Tele Lab, engr, 1961-68; Mkt Monitor Data Inc, oper mgr, 1968-69; EF Shelley & Co, Mgt Cons, sr vpres, 1969-75; Citibank NA, vpres, 1975-82; Group 88 Inc, sr vpres, 1982-. **Orgs:** Inst Elec & Electronics Engr; Am Mgt Asn; bd dir, Group 88 Inc Consult; bd dir, Urban Home Ownership Corp; chmn trustees, Pilgrim Baptist Church; commnr, Middletown Twp Human Rights Comm, 1976-80; Nat Black MBA Assoc, 1984. **Honors/Awds:** Community Achievement Award, Nat Asn Negro Bus & Prof Women's Clubs, 1978. **Home Addr:** 11 Sir Paul Ct, Middletown, NJ 07748-3542, **Home Phone:** (732)671-5409. **Business Addr:** Senior Vice President, Group 88 Systems Inc, 1099 Wall St W, Lyndhurst, NJ 07071, **Business Phone:** (201)507-8815.

### JAMES, ANTHONY R.
Executive. **Personal:** Born Lake Alfred, FL. **Educ:** Polk Community Col, AA, eng, 1970; Univ S Fla, BS, elec engineering, 1973. **Career:** Executive (retired); Procter & Gamble Co, elec instrumentation mgr, prod dept mgr, resident engr; NASA Kennedy Space Ctr, eng asst; Southern Co, Ga Power Co, maintenance supt, cent cluster mgr, safety health supvr, 1978, Plant Scherer, plant mgr, 1996-2000, cent cluster mgr, 2000-01, Southern Co Servs, safety health supvr, bd mem, African Am, chief exec officer, exec vpres; Savannah Elec & Power, vpres power generation sr prod officer, 2000-01, dir, pres, chief exec officer, 2001-05, chmn, 2005-06; Southern Co, exec vpres, 2005-08; Shared Servs Group, pres, 2005-08; SunTrust Bank Savannah, dir; Ala Power Co, dir; Gulf Power Co. **Orgs:** Bd mem, Southeastern Elec Exchange; Rotary Club Savannah; Am Asn Blacks; Ash Tree Orgn; Ga Chamber Com; Prof Asn Ga Educr; Savannah Econ Develop Authority; Boy Scouts Am, Coastal Empire Coun Inc; Asn Edison Illum Co Chambers Com; Edison Elec Inst Chambers Com; bd mem, Prof Asn Ga Educr; Am Asn Blacks Energy; adv bd, Savannah State Presidential; adv bd, Ga Tech Regional Engineering Prog; 100 Black Men Savannah; Sigma Pi Phi Fraternity; Omega Psi Phi Fraternity; USF Alumni Asn; bd mem, Univ S Fla Found; Nat Asn Guardsmen. **Honors/Awds:** Black Engineer of the Year, 2004, 100 Most Important Blacks in Technology, 2005, 2006, US Black Engr Mag & Career Commun. **Special Achievements:** Co-author, The Shoulders of Giants, 2005; Only black CEO in the Southern network; One of the "50 Most Important Blacks in Technology, " Career Commun, 2005.

### JAMES, DR. BETTY HARRIS
Educator, executive, association executive. **Personal:** Born Jun 21, 1932, Gadsden, AL; daughter of William and Mary Etta Wacasey; married Joseph E; children: Cecilia Denise James Joyce, Tyrone Michael & Tyshaun Michele. **Educ:** Univ Pitts, BS Educ, MEd, 1971, PhD, 1974; Marshall Univ, MA, 1976. **Career:** WV St Col, prof educ, 1974-84, spec asst pres, 1981-84; Livingstone Col, assoc vpres, acad affairs, 1984-86; Appalachia Educ Lab, dir, regional liaison ctr, 1986-. **Orgs:** Pres, Charleston Br Nat Asn Advan Colored People, 1979-81; Comm Coun Job Corps, 1979-; consult, WV Human Rights Comm, 1980-; Phi Lambda Theta Hon Soc, Kappa Delta Phi. **Honors/Awds:** Danforth Asn, 1976; Fac Meritorious Service Award, WVa St Col, 1977; Meritorious Service Livingstone Col Stud Govt, 1985. **Special Achievements:** Author: Organizing Communities for Educational Improvement: The Brownsville Site Interim Report, 1993. **Home Addr:** 1005 2nd Ave, Charleston, WV 25302, **Home Phone:** (304)344-4907. **Business Addr:** Director, Appalachia Educational Laboratory, 1031 Quarrier St Atlas Bldg, Charleston, WV 25301, **Business Phone:** (304)347-0400.

### JAMES, DR. BETTY NOWLIN
Executive director, administrator. **Personal:** Born Feb 16, 1936, Athens, GA; married Lewis Francis; children: Beth Marie Morris & Dewey Douglas Morris III. **Educ:** Fisk Univ, BA, 1956; Univ Houston, MEd, 1969, EdD, admin & supv, 1975. **Career:** Administrator, executive director (retired); Houston Ind Sch Dist, teacher & music specialist, 1958-71, fed prog asst, 1972-74, assoc dir res & eval, 1975-76; Univ Houston, Downtown, coord instr planning & eval, 1976-80, dir inst res, 1980-83, dir inst serv, 1983; Tex Higher Educ Coord Bd, Access & Equity Div, asst comnr, 1999. **Orgs:** Phi Delta Kappa Res Fraternity, 1976-; allocations rev panel, United Way, 1983-; worksite coordr, Tenneci Inc Cities Sch Pro, 1984; top black achiever award comt mem, Human Enrichment Life Prog, 1985-; Black Achiever Selection Comt Chair, Riverside Gen Hosp, 1986; exec bd, Houston YWCA, UNCF, Patterson Awards Comt UNCF; active mem, Beta Psi Omega; exec dir, Alpha Kappa Alpha Sorority, 1999-2009. **Home Addr:** 3301 Oakdale, Houston, TX 77004.

### JAMES, CARRIE HOUSER
Educator. **Personal:** Born Nov 6, 1949, Orangeburg, SC; daughter of Alfred Houser Sr and Lula Bell Riley; children: Gabrielle DeAnna, Claudia Michelle & Louis Maxx. **Educ:** Univ SC, Columbia, SC, BSN, 1971; Cath Univ Am, Wash, DC, MSN, 1974; SC State Col, Orangeburg, SC, 1990; Univ SC, Columbia, SC. **Career:** C Hosp Nat Med Ctr, Wash, DC, clin specialist, 1974-76; Univ SC-Col Nursing, Columbia, SC, instr, 1976-78; Richland Memorial Hosp, Columbia, SC, dir nursing, C Hosp, 1977-84; SC State Univ, Orangeburg, SC, asst prof, 1984-; Edisto Health Dist, Orangeburg, SC, consult, child birth educr, 1986-89; Reg Med Ctr, Orangeburg, SC, relief staff nurse-pt, 1988-96, child birth educ & LCHS health educ, 2000-; Low Country Healthy Start & TRMC, perinatal health educr, 2003-04; Low Country Healthy Start, perinatal health educr, 2004-. **Orgs:** Sec, Orangeburg County, Ambulance Comt, 1987-; recorder, SACS steering comt, SC State Col, 1988-90; treas, SC Nurses Found, 1988-93; pres, SC Nurses Asn, 1990-94; Cong Econ, Am Nurses Asn, 1990-94; Maternal, Infant, Child Health Coun SC, 1990-98; Alliance 2020 Leadership Team, 1992-; chair, Constituent Assembly, ANA, 1994-96; ANA; ANA'S Ctr Ethics &Human Rights, 1994-97; pioneer nurse, Tri County Black

Nurses Asn, 1995; Delta Sigma Theta Inc 1999-; bd dir, Orangeburg County First Steps, 2000-; Tri-County Comn Alcohol & Drug Abuse, 2000-04; LLR Bd Nursing, 2004-07; pres, Ctr Am Nurses; moderator, Community Adv Panel Albemarle Coop-Orange burg Plant, 2004; Am Cancer Soc, Community Action Team & Relay Life Planning Comt Orange burg County. **Home Addr:** 462 Meadowlark Dr NE, Orangeburg, SC 29118-2104, **Home Phone:** (803)534-7936. **Business Addr:** Assistant Professor of Nursing, South Carolina State University, 1890 Res & Exten 300 Col St NE, Orangeburg, SC 29117, **Business Phone:** (803)536-8465.

## JAMES, CHARLES L.

Educator, teacher. **Personal:** Born Apr 12, 1934, Poughkeepsie, NY; son of Stanley and Romaine; married Rose Jane Fisher; children: Sheilah Ellen & Terri Lynn. **Educ:** State Univ NY, New Paltz, BS, 1961; State Univ NY, Albany, MA, 1969; Yale Univ, attended 1971. **Career:** Spackenkill Sch Poughkeepsie NY, elem teacher eng, 1961-67; Dutchess CommCol Poughkeepsie NY, instr eng, 1967-69; State Univ New York Oneonta, NY, asst prof & assoc prof, 1969-73; post grad fel Yale Univ Danforth Found, 1971-72; Swarthmore col, assoc prof, 1973, prof & chmn, prof emer, currently, Sara Lawrence Lightfoot prof emer eng lit, 1997; Clare Hall Col, Eng, vis assoc prof, 1981; Eugene M Lang Fac, fel, 1984-85; George Becker Fac, fel, 1992-93. **Orgs:** Am Asn Univ Prof; Mod Lang Asn; Col Lang Asn. **Honors/Awds:** Summer seminar National Endowment for the Humanities, 1978; National Endowment for Humanities, 1990. **Special Achievements:** Author: "The Black Writer in Am" Albany State University New york 1969; From the Roots: Short Stories by Black Americans; Harper and Row, 1975. **Home Addr:** 402 Laurel Lane, Wallingford, PA 19086-6818, **Home Phone:** (610)566-3605. **Business Addr:** Professor Emeritus, Swarthmore College, 500 College Ave, Swarthmore, PA 19081, **Business Phone:** (610)328-8000.

## JAMES, CHARLES LESLIE

Insurance executive. **Personal:** Born Sep 23, 1939, Monticello, AR; son of Mamie; married Elaine. **Educ:** Am Col Life Underwriters, CLU, 1969; Sacramento City Col, AA, 1970; San Francisco State Univ, BS, 1981. **Career:** Golden State Mutual Life Ins Co, vpres & gen agency dir, 1961-; Mirador Diversified Servs Inc, bd dir. **Orgs:** Life Underwriters Asn Los Angeles, 1981-; Soc Fel Lime Mgt, 1981-; Soc Chartered Life Underwriters, 1989; vpres, Black Agenda, 1989; YMCA Los Angeles, 1989; Hugh O'Brian Youth Found, adv bd, 1990; Los Angeles County Sheriff Found, 1989 & 1993. **Honors/Awds:** Certificate of Appreciation, County Los Angeles, 1990; Appreciation & Recognition, Los Angeles County Sheriff's Dept, 1992. **Special Achievements:** Hall of Fame, John C Fremont High School, 1993. **Home Addr:** 3652 Kensley Dr, Inglewood, CA 90305, **Home Phone:** (310)677-4017. **Business Addr:** Vice President, General Agency Director, Golden State Mutual Life Ins Co, 1999 W Adams Blvd, Los Angeles, CA 90018, **Business Phone:** (213)731-1131.

## JAMES, CHERYL R.

Rap musician, actor. **Personal:** Born Mar 28, 1966, Brooklyn, NY; married Gavin Wray; children: Chapele & Corin. **Educ:** Queensborough Community Col. **Career:** Films: Stay Tuned, 1992; Who's the Man?, 1993; Raw Nerve, 1999; Queen of Media, 2011. TV series: "Sisters in the Name of Rap", 1992; "Saturday Night Live", 1994; "The John Larroquette Show", 1994; "Happily Ever After: Fairy Tales for Every Child", 1997; "3rd Annual VH1 Hip-Hop Honors", 2006; "The Salt-N-Pepa Show", exec producer, 2007; "Fashion News Live", 2008; "Let's Talk About Pep", exec producer & writer, 2010; Sears Roebuck & Co, telephone customer-serv rep, 1985; Salt-N-Pepa, mem group, 1985-; Albums: Hot, Cool & Vicious, 1986; A Salt with a Deadly Pepa, 1989; Blacks' Magic, 1990; A Blitz of Salt-N-Pepa, 1991; Juice, 1992; Brand New, 1998; For Our Children; Concert, contributor, 1993; GavFam Music Inc, owner; Compilation: The Greatest Hits, 1990; The Best of Salt-n-Pepa, 2000; 20th Century Masters: The Millennium Collection, 2008; Icon, 2011. **Honors/Awds:** Ablum "Push It, " gold single, 1988; A Salt with a Deadly Pepa, gold, 1988; Hot, Cool & Vicious, platinum, 1988; Nat Acad Rec Arts & Sci, Grammy Award nomination, rap category, 1989. **Special Achievements:** Ranked No 83 on VH1's 100 Greatest Women of Rock N Roll.

## JAMES, DANIEL, III

Air force officer. **Personal:** son of Daniel (deceased) and Dorothy Watkins (deceased); married Dana. **Educ:** Univ Ariz, Tucson, BA, psychol, 1968; Air Command & Staff Col, attended 1981; Nat Security Mgt Course, attended 1992. **Career:** Airforce officer (retired); Cam Ranh Bay Air Base, S Vietnam, forward air controller, 1969-70; Williams AFB, Ariz, squadron instr pilot, 1970-72, squadron flight training class comdr, 1972-73; Hq USAF, Wash, DC, air opers staff officer, 1973; Udorn Royal Thai Afb, Thailand, squadron asst flight comdr, 1974-75; Nellis Afb, Nev, squadron pilot, 1975-76, squadron flight comdr, 1976-78; Kelly Afb, 149th Tactical Fighter Group, Tex, weapons tactics officer, 1978-79, 182nd Tactical Fighter Squadron, Kelly AFB, Tex, group pilot & unit pilot, 1979-82, unit comdr, 1982-83, comdr, 1983-88, C flight, pilot, 1988-89, 149th Tactical Fighter Group, command post asst officer-in-charge, command post officer-in-charge, 1989-92, 149th Tactical Fighter Wing, vice comdr, 1992-94, 149th Opers Group, comdr, 1994-95; Hq Tex Nat Guard, Austin, adj gen, 1995-2002; Air Nat Guard, Arlington, Va, dir, 2002-06. **Orgs:** Chmn, Greater Austin Qual Coun, 1998-99; bd dir, Greater Austin Chamber Com. **Honors/Awds:** Garvey-Woodson Award, Black United Fund Tex, 1995; Outstanding Service Award, Texas STARBASE Exec Adv Bd, 1995-96; Benjamin D. Foulois First Flight Award, Air Force Asn, Tex, 1997; Central Texas Combined Federal Campaign Community Service Award, 1997-98; Honored Patriot Award, Selective Serv Syst, 1998 & 1999; Commendation for Military Service, Joint Session Tex Legislature, 1999; The Palmetto Patriot Award, SC, 1999. Distinguished Achievement Award, Tuskegee Airmen Nat Hist Mus, 2003. **Special Achievements:** Military-State Partnerships: A Winning Relationship for All, National Guard Review, 1997; First African-American to hold the post of Director of the Air National Guard.

## JAMES, REV. DARRYL FARRAR

Clergy. **Personal:** Born Jul 3, 1954, Bridgeport, CT; son of Laurayne and Anthony Francis Sr. **Educ:** Howard Univ, BA, 1976; Interdominational Theol Ctr, MA, 1977; Yale Divinity Sch, MDiv, 1979. **Career:** Trinity Cathedral, lay asst to dean, 1979-81; St Matthew's & St Joseph's, asst priest, 1981-85; Messiah-St Bartholomew Episcopal Church, rector; Grace Episcopal Church, rector, currently. **Orgs:** Nat bd mem, Proj Equality Inc; African Male Cms; Aids Task Force; Cms Ministry, 1988-91; pres, Howard Univ Alumni, Chicago Chap, 1990; Chicago Bd Educ, 1990-95; Cathedral Shelter, 1986-90; Urban Strategy Cms, 1989; Interfaith Coun Homeless, 1979; Kappa Alpha Psi, Chicago Alumni Chap; nominating comt, Selecting Alumni Trustees; bd mem, Community Renewal Socs; nat pres, Union Black Episcopalians; bd manager, Investment Comt & Episcopal Health Serv. **Honors/Awds:** Scholar, Yale Divinity Sch, 1977; Alpha Kappa Alpha Monarch Award, 1994; Distinguished Alumni Award for Howard Univ, Nat Asn Equal Opportunity Higher Educ, 1996; Chicago Alumni Achievement Award, Kappa Alpha Psi. **Special Achievements:** First African American diocesan bishop in the Episcopal Church, to attend Yale University. **Home Addr:** 3312 S Ind Ave, Chicago, IL 60616, **Home Phone:** (312)791-1699. **Business Addr:** Rector, Grace Episcopal Church, 155-24 90th Ave, Jamaica, NY 11432, **Business Phone:** (718)291-4901.

## JAMES, DAVA PAULETTE

School administrator, counselor. **Personal:** Born Sharon, PA; daughter of David Sr and Pauline (deceased). **Educ:** Westminster Col, BA, 1974; Hampton Inst, MA, 1978; Iowa State Univ, PhD, 1992. **Career:** Hampton Inst, grad asst women's div, 1976-78; Slippery Rock State Col, asst dir admis, 1978-79; Youngstown State Univ, acad adv, 1980-85; Marshalltown Community Col, Iowa Valley Community Col Dist, prof, counr & adv, 1989-2001. **Orgs:** Nat Acad Advising Asn; vpres, Nat Asn Negro Bus & Prof Women's Clubs Ohio Valley Club; bd mem, Nat Asn Advan Colored People; Urban League; social science fac, Marshalltown Buena Vista Extention, 2000-01. **Home Addr:** 1137 Cedar Ave, Sharon, PA 16146. **Business Addr:** Professor, Counselor, Advisor, Marshalltown Community College, 3702 S Ctr St, Marshalltown, IA 50158, **Business Phone:** (641)752-4643.

## JAMES, DR. DAVID PHILLIP

Educator, consultant. **Personal:** Born Sep 2, 1940, Greenville, NC; son of John Oscar and Lula Forbes; married Janie Russell; children: Lauren Nicole & Joi Melissa. **Educ:** Elizabeth City State Univ, NC, BS, social sci, 1962; Georgetown Univ, Wash, DC, MA, world hist, 1971; Nova Univ, Ft Lauderdale, FL, EdD, retention & supporting fields, 1978. **Career:** Pittsburgh County, NC, teacher & coach, 1962-63; Clarke Col, Va, social sci teacher & coach, 1963-67; Pub Schs, Wash, DC, social sci teacher & coach, 1967-71; Prince George's Community Col, educ admin, 1971-2008, educ develop degree & exten centers & spec progs, dean, 1988-2008; part-time consult, self-employed, 1978-; DPJ Mentoring, prin consult, 2008-; Robert Wood Johnson Found, training & mentoring consult. **Orgs:** Nat Coun Community Serv & Continued Educ, 1973-; Adult Educ Asn, 1978-; Am Asn Higher Educ, 1982; pres, Int Mentoring Asn, 1989-2000, pres emer; Student Retention. **Home Addr:** 5007 Southern Star Terr, Columbia, MD 21044, **Home Phone:** (410)740-8572. **Business Addr:** Principal Consultant, DPJ Mentoring, 6238 Satin Wood Dr, Columbia, MD 21044, **Business Phone:** (410)997-0585.

## JAMES, DION

Baseball player. **Personal:** Born Nov 9, 1962, Philadelphia, PA; children: Justin, Jared & Jarvis. **Career:** Baseball player (retired); Milwaukee Brewers, outfielder, 1983-85; Atlanta Braves, outfielder, 1987-89; Cleveland Indians, 1989-90; New York Yankees, outfielder, 1992-93, 1995-96; Chunichi Dragons, outfielder, 1994. **Home Addr:** 804 9th Ave, Sacramento, CA 95818.

## JAMES, DONNA ANITA

Executive, president (organization). **Personal:** Born Jun 30, 1957; married Larry; children: Christopher Michael & Justin Michael. **Educ:** NC A&T, acct, 1979. **Career:** Executive (retired); Coopers & Lybrand, Columbus, OH, auditor, 1979-81; Nationwide, Columbus, OH, var acct positions, 1981-90, Opers & Treas Servs, dir, 1990-93, exec asst to Nationwide chief exec officer & chmn, 1993-96, Human Resources Div, vpres, 1996-98, sr vpres, chief human resources officer, 1998-2000, exec vpres, chief admin officer, 2000-03; Ltd Brands Inc, dir, 2003-; Nationwide Strategic Investments, Columbus, OH, pres, 2003-06; Coca-Cola Enterprises, dir, 2005-; Lardon Assocs, consult, bus advisor, managing dir, 2006-; Nationwide Life, investment prod admin & dir treas; Time Warner Cable Inc, dir, 2009-; Marathon Petrol Corp, dir, 2011-. **Orgs:** NC A&T, exec adv coun; bd mem, Am Foreign Servs; bd mem, Intimate Brands Inc; bd mem, Ohio Col Access Network; Columbus Chapt Links; AICPA; bd gov, United Way Am; bd trustee, Bennett Col Women; chair, YWCA Columbus; bd trustee; I Know I Can; Bd Comnr, Ohio Supreme Ct Grievances & Discipline; Client Security Fund Comn; bd dir, Nationwide Fed Credit Union; Ohio State Univ Coun Women; bd trustee; Cent State Univ; Wexner Ctr Arts. **Business Addr:** Managing Director, Lardon & Associates LLC, 500 S Front St, Columbus, OH 43215, **Business Phone:** (614)222-0810.

## JAMES, ELDRIDGE M.

Educator. **Personal:** Born Mar 23, 1942, Eunice, LA; married Betty Lea Stewart; children: Rona La Ne & Heath Elridge Floront. **Educ:** Grambling State Univ, BS, 1966; Wayne State Univ, MEd, 1969; Mich State Univ, PhD, 1973. **Career:** Ford Motor Co, supvr, 1966-68; Great Lakes Steel Corp, dir educ, 1968-70; Ecorse HS, teacher, 1968-70; Great Lakes Steel Corp, indus instr, 1969-70; Mich State Univ, grad asst, 1972; Grambling State Univ, assoc prof, 1973-74; Quachia Parish Bd Educ, asst prof & clin prof, 1974-; NE LA Univ, mem grad fac, asst prof sec & coun educ, 1975-76; CJ Miller Elem Sch; Richwood High Sch. **Orgs:** La Indust Arts Asn; Am Vocat Asn; La Asn Pub Sch Adult Edn; So Asn Counr Educ & Supv; La State Reading Coun; Asn Supv & Curric Develop; Phi Delta Kappa; Scottish Rite Mason King Solomon's Lodge; Omega Psi Phi. **Special Achievements:** Wrote numerous articles & books for Grambling Col; Dean's list of outstanding graduates, Mich State University. **Home Addr:** 7400 Farwood Dr, New Orleans, LA 70126, **Home Phone:** (504)242-4368. **Business Addr:** Assistant Professor, Northeast Louisiana University, 1407 Martin Luther King Dr, Monroe, LA 71202, **Business Phone:** (318)410-1005.

## JAMES, EUGENIA H.

Government official. **Personal:** Born Feb 23, 1954, Chicago, IL; daughter of John and Gladys Ward; children: Jeneena Eugenia. **Educ:** Worsham Col Mortuary Sci, cert, 1974. **Career:** AA Rayner & Sons Funeral Home, mortician, 1974-77; City Dallas, ct opers, 1983-88, jail opers mgr, 1988-90, purchasing agt, 1990-96, asst dir human serv, 1996. **Orgs:** Chair, Nat Inst Govt Purchasing, 1993-95; bd mem, Ex-Offico, Dallas Youth Servs Corp, 1996; Nat Forum Black Pub Adminrs; Nat Asn Purchasing Mgrs; Am Pub Works Asn. **Home Addr:** 1906 Shoreline Dr, Mesquite, TX 75149. **Business Addr:** TX.

## JAMES, DR. FELIX. See Obituaries Section.

## JAMES, FRANK SAMUEL, III

Lawyer, writer, army officer. **Personal:** Born Aug 10, 1945, Mobile, AL; son of Frank Jr and Ermatine; married Jothany Dianne Williams; children: David RF, Jothany Michelle & Julia Dianne. **Educ:** Campbell Col, BS, 1973; Univ Ala, JD, 1978; AUs War Col, grad, 1990. **Career:** Fed Judge Virgil Pittman, law clerk, 1978-80; US Dept Justice, asst us atty, 1980-86; Univ Ala Sch Law, prof, asst dean, 1986-90; Berkowitz, Lefkovits, Isom & Kushner, partner, atty, 1990-. **Orgs:** Am Bar Asn, 1978-, AL State Bar, 1978-, Birmingham Bar Asn, 1980-; coun Synod Mid S, 1985-86; moderator, mem coun Birmingham Presbytery, 1986; pres bd, 1988-90, chmn bd, 1991-, Ala Capital Representation Resource Ctr, 1991-; trustee, Farrah Law Soc, 1990-; trustee, Presbytery Sheppards & Lapsley, 1990-98; dir, Columbia Theol Sem, 1991-99; Bd YMCA Metro Birmingham, 1996-; Am Arbit Asn Nat Roster Neutrals; charter Mmmber, Ala Asn Atty-Mediators; Alexis de Tocqueville SocUnited Way; dir, Mountain Retreat Asn. **Honors/Awds:** Author Contingent Fees Domestic Relations Actions, 3 Jour Legal Prof 209, 1978; elected to bench & bar, Legal Hon Soc, 1978; Distinguished Alumnus, Campbell Univ, 1987; author with Charles W.Gamble, Perspectives on the Evidence Law of Alabama: A Decade Evolution, 1977-87, 40 Alabama Law Review 95, 1988; author, "Protecting Final Judgments: A Critical Overview Provisional In Junctive Relief Alabama", 20 Cumberland Law Review 227, 1990; Sam W. Pipes Distinguished Alumnus Award, University of Alabama School of Law, 2011. **Home Addr:** 1576 Woodridge Pl, Birmingham, AL 35216, **Home Phone:** (205)822-8959. **Business Addr:** Attorney, Partner, Berkowitz Lefkovits Isom & Kushner, SouthTrust Tower 420 N 20th St Suite 1600, Birmingham, AL 35203-5202, **Business Phone:** (205)250-8317.

## JAMES, FREDERICK C.

Bishop. **Personal:** Born Apr 7, 1922, Prosperity, SC; married Theressa Gregg. **Educ:** Allen Univ, BA, 1943; Howard Univ, MDiv, 1947. **Career:** Bishop (retired); AME Episcopal Church, ordained ministry; Friendship AME Church Irmo SC, pastor, 1945; Mem AME Church Columbia SC, bishop, 1946; Wayman AME Church Winnsboro SC, bishop, 1947-50; Chappelle Mem AME Church Columbia SC, bishop, 1950-53; Mt Pisgah AME Church Sumter SC, bishop, 1953-72; AME Church Dallas, bishop, 1972-. **Orgs:** Bd dir, Greater Little Rock Urban League; chmn bd, Shorter Col; founder, Mt Pisgah Apts, Sumter, James Ctr; maseru, Lesotho; Nat Interfaith Comt Fund Open Soc Dem Clubs; Odd Fels, Masons, Shriners; dean, Dickerson Theol Sem, 1949-53; pres, Sumter; br National Association for the Advancement of Colored People, 1959-72; World Conf Church & Soc Geneva, 1966; chmn, Wateree Community Actions Agency, 1969-72; bishop, Botswana, Lesotho, Swaziland, Mozambique, SafricA, Namibia, 1972-76; presiding bishop, AR OK, 1976-; chmn, Comn Missions AME Church, 1976-; Nat Coun Church Christ USA, 1979-; hon consult, gen representing Lesotho AR & OK, 1979-; deleg, World Meth Coun Honolulu, 1981; secy, AME Coun Bishops, 1981; bd trustee, Allen Univ. **Honors/Awds:** The 93rd elected Bishop, African Methodist Episcopal Church. **Business Addr:** Bishop, African Methodist Episcopal Church, 604 Locust St, North Little Rock, AR 72114, **Business Phone:** (501)375-4310.

## JAMES, FREDERICK JOHN

Auditor, lawyer. **Personal:** Born Sep 1, 1938, Chicago, IL; son of John Henry and Frances Harris; married Barbara L Penny; children: Frederick J & Edward A. **Educ:** Univ Chicago, attended 1958; San Francisco State Col, BA, 1968; Univ Calif, Berkeley, Grad Sch Bus, MBA, 1972; Univ Calif, Berkeley, Boalt Hall Sch Law, JD, 1973. **Career:** Wells Fargo Bank, field auditor, 1964-66; Del Monte Corp, mgt trainee, 1966-68; Ctr Real Estate & Urban Econs, res asst, 1970; Law Off Hiawatha Roberts, law clerk, atty, 1972-74; Law Off Frederick J James, atty, 1974-; Calif State Univ, lectr, 1976; sole practr, currently. **Orgs:** Treas, Black MBA Asn, 1973; bd mem, Men Tomorrow, 1977; bd mem & legal coun, Northern Calif Black C C & Oakland Alameda Co Black Chamber Com, 1978-; bd mem, Comnrs Oakland Housing Authority, 1983-89; pres, Alameda Co Dem Lawyers, 1986; Charles Houston Bar Asn; Nat Bar Asn; Am Bar Asn. **Honors/Awds:** Academic Scholarship, Univ Chicago, 1955-58; Certificate of Recognition for Legal Services to Poor, Charles Houston Bar Asn, 1979; Certificate of Appreciation for Writing Judicare, Grant Proposal, 1979. **Home Addr:** 2468 60th Ave, Oakland, CA 94605-1402. **Business Addr:** Attorney, Law Office of Frederick James, 7750 Pardee Lane Suite 130, Oakland, CA 94621, **Business Phone:** (510)430-8243.

## JAMES, GERRY M.

Executive. **Personal:** Born Mar 15, 1959, Little Rock, AR; son of Cleo Charles; married Darlene; children: LaTasha, Gerry III & Danielle. **Educ:** Univ Ark, Pine Bluff; Chicago State Univ, Chicago, IL, BS, bus mgt, 1979. **Career:** Johnson Prods Co, asst off mgr, 1978-83, distribr spec markets, sales mgr, 1983-86; New York Life Ins Co, field underwriter, financial planner, 1986-89; Gillette Co, Lustrasilk, territory acct mgr, 1989-93; JM Prod Inc, regional sales mgr retail & prof, 1993-95; Ecoco Inc, nat sales mgr, vpres sales mkt & chief operating officer, 1995-. **Orgs:** Bd mem, Campaign for a Drug Free Westside. **Home Addr:** 11426 S Longwood Dr, Chicago, IL 60643, **Home Phone:** (773)239-0879. **Business Addr:** President, Chief Operating Officer,

Ecoco Inc, 1830 N Lamon Ave, Chicago, IL 60639-4512, **Business Phone:** (773)745-7700.

**JAMES, DR. GILLETTE ORIEL**
Clergy, president (organization). **Personal:** Born May 5, 1935, Dominica; son of Samuel and Ethlyn; married Rosa Vernita Ferguson; children: Jennifer. **Educ:** Univ San Francisco, BA, 1968; Am Baptist Sem W, MDiv, 1970, DMin, 1976; Univ Calif-Berkeley, MSW; Nova Southeastern Univ Fla, EdD. **Career:** Christian Union Church, WI, pastor, 1959-60; Western Union, tel rec, 1962-65; Grace Baptist Church, San Francisco, organizer & pastor, 1963-69; Beth Eden Baptist Church, Oak land, Calif, asst pastor & minister Christian educ, 1970-71, sr pastor, 1971-. **Orgs:** Dean, Baptist Ministers Union Oakland, 1971-85; pres, bd dir, Social Serv Bur Oakland, 1976-79; vpres, Northern Calif Credit Union, 1976-79; pres, Black Am Baptists Northern Calif, 1977-84; vpres, Black Am Baptists, 1985-90; exec secy, Calif State Baptist Conv, 1985-86; vpres, Baptist Ministers Union Oakland, 1986-; chmn, Community Earthquake Disaster Comt, 1989-91; Mayor's Earthquake Relief Fund, 1989-91; pres, Black Am Baptist, 1991-; exec comt mem, Western Comn Ministry, 1992-; trustee, Am Baptist Sem W, 1992-; Beth Eden church Women's Ministries, currently. **Honors/Awds:** Caliborne Hill Award, Am Baptist Sem W, 1970; Outstanding Immigrant Award, Int Inst E Bay, 1977; Distinguished Service Award, Baptist Ministers Union Oakland, 1985; 4th Ann Black Clergy Award, Bay view Multipurpose Sr Serv. **Home Addr:** 2400 Havenscourt Blvd, Oakland, CA 94605, **Home Phone:** (510)636-1044. **Business Addr:** Senior Pastor, Beth Eden Baptist Church, 1183 10th St, Oakland, CA 94607, **Business Phone:** (510)444-1625.

**JAMES, HAWTHORNE**
Entertainer, actor. **Personal:** Born Chicago, IL; son of Robert and A M Alene. **Educ:** Univ Notre Dame, BA, 1974; Univ Mich, MA, 1975. **Career:** Films: Disco Godfather, 1979; Penitentiary II, 1982; The Color Purple, 1985; I'm Gonna Git You Sucka, 1988; Patty Hearst, 1988; Ricky 1, 1988; Othello, 1989; The Color Purple; The Doors, 1991; The Five Heartbeats, 1991; The Fresh Prince of Bel-Air, 1992; The Water Engine, 1992; TheHabitation of Dragons, 1992; Caroline at Midnight, 1994; I'm Gonna Get YouSucka; Speed, 1994; Se7en, 1995; Heaven's Prisoners, 1996; Sparks, 1997; Campfire Tales, 1997; Amistad, 1997; The Art of a Bullet, 1999; AuggieRose, 2000; Code Blue, 2000; Past Present, 2002; The Dist, 2003; Plant Oneon Me, 2004; Boss'n Up, 2005; Today You Die, 2005; The System Within, 2006; Hood of Horror, 2006; The Stick Up Kids, dir, 2008; A Christmas Wedding, 2013. TV Series: "Hill Street Blues", 1984-86; "What's Happening Now!", 1985-86; "Amazing Stories", 1986; "Cheers", 1987; "Police Story: The Freeway Killings", 1987; "The Water Engine", 1992; "The Fresh Prince of Bel-Air", 1992; "The Habitation of Dragons", 1992; "The Heart of Justice", 1992; "Frasier", 1993; "The Adventures of Brisco County Jr.", 1994; "Martin", 1994; "The Good News", 1997; "Sparks", 1997; "NYPD Blue", 1998; "City of Angels", 2000; "Roswell", 2001; "Charmed", 2002-04; "The District", 2003; "ER", 2004; "Carnivale", 2005; "Stargate SG-1", 2006; "Workaholics", 2012-13. **Honors/Awds:** Los Angeles Drama-Logue Award, 1982, 1989; Los Angeles Weekly Award, 1987; Jury Prize, Barcelona Cinema Festival, 2005; Winner, Ted Lange Ira Aldridge Actg Competition. **Business Addr:** Actor, c/o Select Artists Agency, 3900 W Alameda Ave Suite 1700, Burbank, CA 91505-4316, **Business Phone:** (818)972-1747.

**JAMES, HENRY CHARLES**
Basketball player. **Personal:** Born Jul 29, 1965, Centerville, AL; married Carmen; children: 6. **Educ:** St Mary's Univ, BS, comput sci. **Career:** Basketball player (retired); Span League, forward, 1988-89; Continental Basketball Asn, Wichita Falls Texans, 1989-90, 1993; Cleveland Cavaliers, power forward, 1990-91, 1997-98, small forward, 1991-92; Scavolini Pesaro, Italy, 1992-93; Utah Jazz, 1992-93; Sacramento Kings, power forward, 1993; Los Angeles Clippers, power forward, 1993-94; Sioux Falls Skyforce, Continental Basketball Asn, 1994-96, 1988-99; Houston Rockets, power forward, 1995-96; Atlanta Hawks, power forward, 1996-97; Philippine Basketball Asn. **Honors/Awds:** All-League second team, CBA, 1993, 1996; All-League first team, CBA, 1994; Most Valuable Player, CBA Playoffs, 1996; CBA Championship, 1996.

**JAMES, DR. HERBERT I.**
Scientist, manager. **Personal:** Born Mar 30, 1933, St. Thomas; son of Henry O and Frances Smith; married Christine M Stolz; children: Herbert Jr & Robyn. **Educ:** Hampton Inst, BS math, chem & physics, 1955; Clark Univ, MA nuclear radiation chem, 1958, PhD, phys chem; DB Hill Train Cs, ins broker; DB Hill Train Cs, investment broker; LaSalle Ext Univ, bus mgt. **Career:** DB Hill & Co, br mgr; DB Hill & Assoc, br mgr; Clark Univ, teacher asst; St Thomas HS, teacher; Exp Col VI, teacher; Hampton Inst, teacher; Elec Storage Battery Co Inc, res sci, 1965-76; Xerox Corp, res scientist, 1976-80, mgr minority rels; personnel mgr, 1980, human resource mgt, currently. **Orgs:** Electrochem Soc; AAAS; Instrument Soc Am; Beta Kappa Chi; Alpha Kappa Mu; NY Acad Sci; exec bd, Bucks Co Boy Scouts; bd dir, Freedom Valley Coun Girl Scouts; Nat Asn Advan Colored People; scholar, Hampton Inst; Episcopal Church. **Honors/Awds:** JF Kennedy Library Award; VI Public Affairs Award, 1965 Presidential Recommendation Award; Chairperson Award, Nat Alliance Bus. **Home Addr:** 49 Cumberland Dr, Mississauga, CAN L5G 3N1, **Home Phone:** (416)278-6722. **Business Addr:** Manager, Xerox Corp, Bldg 128 800 Phillips Rd, Webster, NY 14580, **Business Phone:** (585)423-5090.

**JAMES, DR. HERMAN DELANO.** **See Obituaries Section.**

**JAMES, JEROME KEITH**
Basketball player. **Personal:** Born Nov 17, 1975, Tampa, FL; son of Jessie; children: Jamarcus; married Caciques de Humacao. **Educ:** Fla A&M Univ, pre law, 1998. **Career:** Harlem Globetrotters, 1998, 1999-2000; Sacramento Kings, ctr, 1999; KK Buducnost Podgorica, Yugoslavia, 2000-01; Seattle SuperSonics, ctr, 2001-05; ASVEL Villeurbanne, 2001; New York Knickerbockers, 2005-09; Chicago Bulls, 2009-10; Caciques de Humacao, 2012; Atenienses de Manati, 2015.

**JAMES, DR. JIMMIE, JR.**
College administrator. **Personal:** Born Jul 5, 1938, Hattiesburg, MS; son of Jimmie Sr and Annie M Rogers; married Carrie Green; children: Michael Renwick. **Educ:** Jackson State Univ, BME, 1960; Roosevelt Univ, Chicago Musical Col, attended 1960; Univ Wis, MS, 1966; Univ Southern Miss, PhD, 1973. **Career:** AME Church, connectional dir Music, dir music emer & historiographer; Earl Travillion Attendance Ctr, Hattiesburg, band dir & jr high sch eng teacher, 1959-66; Jackson State Univ, music prof, Brass Ensemble, asst band dir & dir, 1966-80, Grad Music Prog, coordr, Concert Band, dir, dir musical activ, 1980-83, chmn & prof, dept music, 1983-2009; Jacksonville State Univ, teacher, band dir, music dept chmn, 2009. **Orgs:** Phi Delta Kappa, 1980-2002; minister music, dir sanctuary choir, steward bd, Pearl St AME Church, 1980-2002; dir, Nat Talent Hunt, Omega Psi Phi, 1990-94; connectional dir music, AME Church, 1992-2000; Gamma Boule, 1998-2000; sire archon elect, sire archon, 2001-02, Sigma Pi Phi; bd dir, Jour Black Sacred Music; bd commissioners, Jackson Redevelop; gen bd, AME Church; nat talent hunt dir, Omega Psi Phi Fraternity; dir, Fste comn workship & liturgy; Nat Asn Schs Art & Design. **Special Achievements:** First African-American graduate from the University of Southern Mississippi in music. **Home Addr:** 2815 Hemingway Cir, Jackson, MS 39209-7304, **Home Phone:** (601)969-3328. **Business Addr:** Chairman, Professor of Music, Jackson State University, 1400 J R Lynch St, Jackson, MS 39217, **Business Phone:** (601)979-8804.

**JAMES, JOHN A.**
Executive, administrator. **Personal:** Born Starkville, MS; married Sharon Nicks; children: John, Lorron & Keri. **Educ:** Miss Valley State Univ, BS, sociol; Univ Toledo, guid, MS, 1964; Wayne State Univ, bus admin, 1972. **Career:** Chrysler Corp, Personnel & Labor Rels, 1969-78; James Group Int, founder, chmn & chief exec officer, 1971-. **Orgs:** Alpha Phi Alpha; Booker T Wash Bus Asn; 100 Black Men Greater Detroit; bd dir, Charles H Wright Mus African Am Hist; Dept Transp Adv Comn; Detroit, MI; bd dir, Detroit Econ Growth Corp; bd dir, Detroit-Wayne CoPort Authority; Econ Club Detroit; life mem, Nat Asn Advan Colored People; trustee, Hartford Baptist Church; Renaissance Club Detroit; bd mem, Wayne Co Econ Develop Corp; Minority Bus Develop Coun; Boys & Girls Clubs SEMich; Detroit Regional Chamber; Nat Asn Black Automotive Suppliers; World Trade Club; Gen Motors, Toyota & McKesson Pharmaceut Corp. **Special Achievements:** First African American nationally to be granted such authority by the interstate Commerce Commission; First African American whose company was issued broad operating authority to transport automotive parts and other commodities in the State of Michigan. **Business Addr:** Founder & Chairman, Chief Executive Officer, James Group Intl, 4335 W Fort St, Detroit, MI 48209-3221, **Business Phone:** (313)841-0070.

**JAMES, JOSEPH J.**
Executive. **Personal:** Born Glen Ridge, NJ. **Educ:** Union Col, Schenectady, NY, BS, sci; NY Univ, law & bus admin. **Career:** Prince George's County Econ Develop Corp, pres & chief exec officer; Mainstream Bus Enterprises LLC, mng mem, currently; SC Sci Inc, pres & chief exec officer, currently; Agri-Tech Producers LLC, founder, pres, 2005-. **Orgs:** Am Asn Enterprise Zones; Int Econ Develop Coun; founding bd mem, vice chmn, Southern Asn Utilization Biomass Resources; Fed Biomass R&D Tech Adv Comt; founding mem, vice chmn, Sc Biomass Coun; Int Coun Shopping Ctr; Nat Capitol Minority Bus Opportunity Comt; bd dir, Chicago Conv & Tourism Bur; Prince Georges County Visitors & Tourism Bd; Gov Tourism Adv Roundtable; Sc Econ Developers Asn; S Carolinas Workforce Investment Bd; bd mem, Social Venture Network, 1994-98; educ constituent roundtable, Nat Oceanic & Atmospheric Admin; life mem, Am Tennis Asn; pub affairs comt, Us Tennis Asn; Southeast Agr & Forestry Energy Resources Alliance; pres & chief exec officer, Corp Econ Opportunity, 2004-; Charleston & Columbia Angel Partners. **Business Addr:** President, Founder, Agri-Tech Producers LLC, 116 Wildewood Club Ct, Columbia, SC 29223, **Business Phone:** (803)462-0153.

**JAMES, JUANITA T.**
Publishing executive, executive, president (organization). **Personal:** Born Oct 1, 1952, Brooklyn, NY; daughter of Compton Carew and Nora Corlette; married Dudley Norman Williams Jr; children: Dudley Norman III. **Educ:** Princeton Univ, BA, 1974; Columbia Univ Grad Sch Bus, MS, bus policy, 1982. **Career:** Thomson-CSF Inc, pur agt, 1974-76; Time Life Bks Inc, ed res, 1976-78, ed admin, 1978-81, vpres hr, 1983-86; Time Inc, fin analyst, 1981-83; Time Life Libr Inc, pres & chief exec officer, 1987-90; Bk Month Club Inc, vpres & dir specialty clubs, 1990-92, sr vpres, ed, 1992-; Rouse Co, dir; Doubleday Direct Inc, Sr VP Finance and Opers, exec vpres mkt & ed; Pitney Bowes Inc, gen mgr, 1999-2007, vpres & proj leader, 2002-04, vpres direct mkt Strategy & bus develop, 2004-06, chief mkt & commun officer, 2007-10; Fairfield County Community Found, pres & chief financial officer, 2011-. **Orgs:** Nat Black MBA Asn, 1982-; Nat Urban League, 1982-; bd mem, Green Door, 1984-88; trustee, Princeton Univ, 1984-; Nat Coalition 100 Black Women, 1986-; Black Women Publ; Women's Media Grp; Nat Asn Advan Colored People; bd mem, Asbury Automotive Grp, 2007-; bd mem, Rouse Co; trustee, Lesley Univ; trustee emerita, Princeton Univ; dir, Reading Fundamental. **Home Addr:** 101 Doewodd Lane, Stamford, CT 06903-4532, **Home Phone:** (203)329-9907. **Business Addr:** Chief Executive Officer, President, Fairfield County Community Foundation, 383 Main Ave, Norwalk, CT 06851-1543, **Business Phone:** (203)750-3200.

**JAMES, KAY COLES**
State government official, executive director. **Personal:** Born Jun 1, 1949, Portsmouth, VA; married Charles E; children: 3. **Educ:** Hampton Inst, Hampton, Va, BS, 1971; Pepperdine Univ, Doctor Law. **Career:** NRLC, Wash, DC, dir pub affairs, White House Task Force Black Family, 1986-88; Nat Comn C, comnr, 1987; US Dept HHS, Wash, DC, asst secy pub affairs, 1989; Family Res Coun, sr vpres; One to One, Wash, DC, exec vpres, 1990, sr vpres & chief operating officer, 1991; White House Off Nat Drug Control Policy, assoc dir, 1991; Commonwealth Va, secy health & human resource, 1993; One to One Partnership, a nat umbrella orgn mentoring progs, exec vice-pres & chief operating officer; Family Res Coun, sr vpres, 1993; Regent Univ, Sch Govt, dean; bd dir, Amerigroup Corp; Heritage Found, Citizenship Proj, dir; US Off Personnel Mgt, dir, 2001-05; Joint Financial Mgt Improv Prog, chmn, 2004-; NASA Adv Coun, mem, currently; Gloucester Inst, pres & founder, currently. **Orgs:** Dir publ, Nat Right Life Comt, 1985; bd mem, Nat Comn C, 1988; chair, Chief Human Capital Officers Coun. **Honors/Awds:** Publius Award, Univ Va; Spirit of Democracy Award, Nat Coalition Black Civic Participation; Dr Laws, Pepperdine Univ; Numerous hon degrees. **Special Achievements:** Publishes, Never Forget, Transforming America, 1993; From the Inside Out, 1995. **Business Addr:** President, Founder, Gloucester Institute, 6496 Allmondsville Rd, Gloucester, VA 23061.

**JAMES, KEVIN PORTER**
Administrator. **Personal:** Born Aug 2, 1964, Wichita, KS; son of James Jr and Alice Jean Jr. **Educ:** Dodge City Community Col, AA, gen studies, commun technol, 1984; Univ Ariz, BA, radio tv, pub rels, 1988. **Career:** Univ Ariz, Luke Olson, men's basketball mgr, 1984-88; vpres event mgt serv, asst mgr, southwest region, 1988-90; Orlando Magic, Brian C Williams, mgr, 1991-; Fred L Slaughter, NBA scout, recruiter, 1992-. **Business Addr:** 1616 14th St Suite D1, Denver, CO 80202-1340, **Business Phone:** (303)256-0020.

**JAMES, LAWRENCE W. (LARRY JAMES)**
Executive, chief executive officer. **Personal:** Born May 15, 1956, Columbus, OH; son of Lois Belton and Elijah Larry; married Adrienne C; children: Aaron Vincent & Brandon Michael. **Educ:** Wittenberg Univ, BA, bus admin & mgt, 1978; Northwestern Univ, MA, mkt & finance, 1980. **Career:** Proctor & Gamble, asst brand mgr, 1980-83; Borden, prod mgr, 1983-85; Ross Labs, mkt mgr, 1985-88; Lens Crafters, dir mkt, 1988-92; Primetime Mgt Inc, pres, 1992-94; Choice Care, dir spec health plan, 1994-96; Middletown Reg Health Syst, vpres, 1996; Atrium Med enter, vpres, chief mkt officer, 1996-2004; Lenscrafters, dir mkt serv, 1988-92; ChoiceCare/Humana Health Plans, dir, 1994-96; Atrium Med Ctr, vpres, chief mkt, diversity officer, 1996-2004; CMCHO LLC/LW James & Assocs LLC, pres, chief exec officer, 2004-11; Cincinnat C's Hosp Med Ctr, sr dir, community rels, 2010-12; Ctr Multicultural Competence Healthcare Orgns pres, chief exec officer; Mercy Health, Cath Health Partners, vpres, Multicultural Competence & Inclusion, 2012-. **Orgs:** Middletown Action, 1996-2000; bd, Arts Middletown, 1997-99; Middletown Int, 1997-99; bd, Middletown Adolescent Leaders Achieve, 1998-; bd, Middletown YMCA, 1998-; bd, Middletown Social Health Ctr, 1999-; steering comn, Middletown Ownership Coun, 2000-; comt mem, United Way Greater Cincinnati, 2012; bd mem, Gabriel's Pl, 2012-; bd mem, Alzheimer's Asn, 2014. **Home Addr:** 8079 Trotterstrail Ct, Cincinnati, OH 45249, **Home Phone:** (513)489-7134. **Business Addr:** President, Chief Executive Officer, The Center for Multicultural Competence in Healthcare Organizations, 4555 Lake Forest Dr Suite 650, Cincinnati, OH 45242, **Business Phone:** (513)563-3004.

**JAMES, LEBRON RAYMONE**
Basketball player. **Personal:** Born Dec 30, 1984, Akron, OH; son of Gloria; married Savannah Brinson; children: LeBron Jr & Bryce Maximus. **Career:** Cleveland Cavaliers, star guard, 2003-10; Miami Heat, small forward, 2010-.Tv Series :"Entourage", 2009; "SpongeBob SquarePants", 2009; "The LeBrons", 2011; "Trainwreck", 2015; "Survivor's Remorse", 2015, actor; Tv Series Producer :"The LeBrons", 2011; "Survivor's Remorse", 2014-15; "NBA All Star All Style", 2015. **Business Addr:** Small Forward, Miami Heat, AmericanAirlines Arena 601 Biscayne Blvd, Miami, FL 33132, **Business Phone:** (786)777-1615.

**JAMES, LETITIA (LETITIA TISH JAMES)**
City council member. **Personal:** Born Oct 17, 1962, Brooklyn, NY. **Educ:** City Univ NY, Lehman Col, BA, 1983; Howard Univ, Wash, DC, law sch educ, JD, 1986; Columbia Univ, Grad Sch Intl & Pub Affairs, MPA, 2003. **Career:** Legal Aid Soc, pub defender; Brooklyn Regional Off, asst atty gen; New York Coun, city councilwoman, 2003, comt chair, currently, coun mem, 35th Dist. **Orgs:** Founder, Urban Network; Contracts Comt; chair, Econ Develop Comt; Housing & Buildings Comt; chair, Sanit & Solid Waste Mgt Comt; Small Bus Comt. **Special Achievements:** First asst atty gen in Charge of the Brooklyn Regional Off. **Business Addr:** City Councilman, New York City Council, 250 Broadway Suite 1792, New York, NY 10007, **Business Phone:** (212)788-7081.

**JAMES, MARILYN.** **See MOSBY, MARILYN.**

**JAMES, MARQUITA L.**
Educator, association executive. **Personal:** Born Nov 9, 1932, Philadelphia, PA. **Educ:** Wilberforce Univ, BA, 1955; Seton Hall Univ, S Orange, NJ, MA, 1966; Candidacy NY Univ, PhD, 1974. **Career:** Wyandanch Schs, Wydandanch, NY, chmn, 1964-68; Freeport New York, Afro-Am Hist curr coor, 1968-69; Nassau Comm Col, Garden City, Long Island NY, assoc prof hist, prof hist polit sci & geog, currently. **Orgs:** Asn Univ Profs; Asn Afro-Am Educ; Am Hist Asn; Afro-Am Black Heritage Asn; Cong Racial Equal; Coun Interracial Bks Child; Alpha Kappa Alpha Sor; Nat Black Feminist Org; pres, Nassau-Suffolk Br Asn Study Afro-Am Life & Hist; Soc Cath Soc Scientist, 2007. **Honors/Awds:** Listed among black Elders in Black History Museum Hempstead LI NY; Nat Defense Educational Award, Teachers Col, Columbia Univ, NY; Martin LutherKing Jr Graduage Fellow Award, NY Univ, 1968-71; Inter Nat Education Award, Univ Ghana, Legon, W Africa, 1969; Chancellors Award, State Univ NY, 1981. **Special Achievements:** Published a book: "The State of African American Catholicism Today". **Home Addr:** PO Box 216, Uniondale, NY 11553-0216. **Business Addr:** Professor, Nassau Community College, 1 Education Dr Bldg G-G224, Garden City, NY 11530, **Business Phone:** (516)572-7422.

**JAMES, MELISSA E.**
Manager, executive. **Personal:** children: 3. **Educ:** Yale Col, BA, 1985; Harvard Bus Sch, MBA, 1989. **Career:** Morgan Stanley & Co, financial analyst, 1985, managing dir, 1989-, global head loan prod. **Honors/Awds:** "Black Enterprise", 75 Most Powerful Women in Business, 2010. **Business Addr:** Managing Director, Morgan Stanley & Co,

1585 Broadway, New York, NY 10036, **Business Phone:** (212)761-4000.

### JAMES, OLIVE C. R.
Library administrator. **Personal:** Born Dec 4, 1929, New York, NY; daughter of Audley C Roach and Edith E Brown Roach; married Edmond Austin; children: Alan E, Karen Straughn, Jeffrey A & Christopher E. **Educ:** City Col New York, New York, NY, BS, 1950, grad work, 1952; Rutgers Univ, MLS, 1965, NY Univ, grad work, 1976. **Career:** Queens Col, CUNY, New York, NY, ref librn & dept head, 1966-76; Stanford Univ, Stanford, Calif, libr dept chief, 1976-80; Libr Cong, Wash DC, div chief, 1980-87; Yale Univ, New Haven, Conn, consult, 1985-86; San Francisco State Univ, San Francisco, Calif, libr dir, 1987-92, librn emer. **Orgs:** Exec bd, ASO Col & Resource Librs; exec comt bibliog instr sect, Univ librs sect, prog & lang plng Comn; bd, Friends San Francisco Pub Libr, 1988-; pres, Ocean Beach Homeowners Asn, 1991-; pres, Stanford Univ Librns Assembly, 1979-80. **Honors/Awds:** Dept Educ, France, Assistante de Langue Anglais, 1952-53; Member four National Honor Societies: French, Spanish, Education, Librarianship; USS Dept Educ, UNIV Maryland, Fellowship libr Admin Develop Prog, 1973; UCLA Senior Fellow, Coun Res Librs, 1987; Fellowship Consultants Program, ASN Res Librs, 1982. **Home Addr:** 1860 Tice Creek Dr Apt 1424, Walnut Creek, CA 94595-2452, **Home Phone:** (925)947-2122.

### JAMES, PATRICIA REA COLEMAN
Lawyer. **Personal:** Born Jun 22, 1959, Tachikawa. **Educ:** Univ Calif, Los Angeles, CA, BS, chem engineering, 1982; George Washington Univ, JD, 1990. **Career:** Fliesler Dubb Meyer & Lovejoy, 1990-94; Limbach & Limbach LLP, assoc, 1994-98; Limbach & Limbach, LLP, Life Sci Pract, partner, 1994-2001; McCutchen Doyle Brown & Enersen LLP, Life Sci Pract, partner, 2001-02; Abbott Labs co, patent coun, 2002-09, div coun, 2009-12, corp liaison; Prairie State Legal Serv Inc, vol atty, 2003-; Chicago Botanic Garden, 2008-; AbbVie Inc, div coun, 2013-; Ctr Disability & Elder Law, vol atty, 2015. **Orgs:** Exec coun, Nat Biotechnology & Pharmaceut Asn, 2015; United Way Lake County, Women's Leadership Coun, 2015; mem pro pono comt, Abbott Labs; mem exec comt, Nat Bar Asn; San Francisco bar asn; Am Intellectual Property Law Asn Bar; Calif State Bar. **Honors/Awds:** Life Cycle Management Program Award, R&D President, 2004; President's Award, Abbott Labs Legal Div, 2012; R&D President's Award, AbbVie Inc, 2015. **Business Addr:** Division Counsel, AbbVie Inc, Dept V0377 Bldg AP6A 1 1 N Waukegan Rd, Abbott Park, IL 60064-6008, **Business Phone:** (847)937-4558.

### JAMES, DR. ROBERT D.
School administrator, consultant. **Personal:** Born Aug 24, 1950, New Rochelle, NY; son of Shirley Clark and Everett Lanier; married Cheryl D Holley; children: Ayanna Laura, Anika Laren & Jamaal Malik. **Educ:** State Univ NY, Brockport, BS, 1972, MS, 1975; State Univ NY, Albany, EdD. **Career:** Administrator (retired); Baden St Settlement Coun Ctr, asst dir, 1973-74; State Univ NY, Brockport, counr, 1974-77, educ opprtunity prog, dir, 1977-79, EOC, exec dir, 1979-87, Off Spec Prog, actg sr assoc, 1987-91, State Univ NY Cent Off, assoc vice chancellor off spec progs, 1991-99, assoc provost, 1995-, assoc vice provost opportunity progs, currently, syst admin, 2012; Pub Employ Rels Bd, mediator & fact finder, 1985-; NY State Martin Luther King Jr Inst Non Violence, interim dir, 1991; Hunter Col, consult, 2001; Millersville Univ, consult, 2003; US Dept Educ, consult. **Orgs:** Consult, Univ Rochester Ct Ment Health Team, 1974-79; consult, Ctr Urban Ethnic Affairs, 1975-77; bd mem, Cath Youth Orgn, 1979-87; bd mem, YMCA, Rochester, 1979-85; bd mem, Urban League, Rochester, 1984-88; bd mem, Legal Aid Soc, 1984-86; bd mem, Am Diabetes Asn, 1984-86; mediator & factfinder, NY State Pub Employ Rel Bd, 1985-; former dir & pres, Tri-State Consortium Opportunity Progs, 1988-; bd dir, Nat Guard Challenge Prog, 1997-; consult, Montclair St, 2000; bd gov, Finger Lakes Occup Educ Ctr. **Honors/Awds:** Outstanding Service Award, State Univ NY, 1988; Arthur A Schomburg Distinguished Service Award, Asn Equality & Excellence Educ Inc, 1989; Distinguished Service Award, State Univ NY, 1990; Distinguished Service Award, Tri State Consortium, 1991; Man of the Year Award, Tri-State Consortium, 2001; Governors Award Outstanding Service in Education; Outstanding Alumni Award, State Univ NY. **Home Addr:** 206 Exec Dr, Guilderland, NY 12084. **Business Addr:** Associate Vice Provost for Opportunity Programs, State University of New York College, 350 New Campus Dr, Brockport, NY 14420-2914, **Business Phone:** (585)395-2796.

### JAMES, DR. ROBERT EARL
Banker. **Personal:** Born Nov 21, 1946, Hattiesburg, MS; son of Jimmie Sr and Annie Mae; married Shirley B; children: Robert II, Anne & Rachelle. **Educ:** Morris Brown Col, Atlanta, Ga, BA, acct, 1968; Harvard Univ, MBA, 1970. **Career:** Armco Steel Corp, Middletown, OH, acct trainee, 1967; C & S Natl Bank, Atlanta, Ga, mgt trainee, 1969; Savannah Tribune, Savannah, Ga, publ; Carver State Bank, Savannah, Ga, pres & chief exec officer, 1971-; Ft Valley Herald, owner & publ, 1989-. **Orgs:** Gen partner, Atlantic Investors; trustee mem, Morris Brown Col; White House Conf Small Bus; chmn bd, Nat Bankers Asn, 1978, 1990-92; dir, Ga Telecommunications Comn, 1981-2002; fel Int Bus, 1983. **Honors/Awds:** Distinguished Service Award, Nat Bankers Asn, 2003. **Special Achievements:** First African Americans to be accepted into Harvard Business School; One of the 100 Most Influential Black Americans, Ebony Magazine, 2003. **Home Addr:** 4761 Sylvan Dr, Savannah, GA 31405-5133, **Home Phone:** (912)352-2286. **Business Addr:** President, Chief Executive Officer, Carver State Bank, 701 Martin Luther King Jr Blvd, Savannah, GA 31402, **Business Phone:** (912)233-9971.

### JAMES, RONALD
Executive, president (organization), chief executive officer. **Personal:** Born Dec 3, 1950, Port Arthur, TX; married Renee; children: Joshua & Jordan. **Educ:** Doane Col, Crete, NE, BBA, 1971; Creighton Univ, Omaha, NE, 1977. **Career:** US W Commun, Minneapolis, Minn, exec officer & vpres, 1971-96; Ceridian Corp, Human Resources Group, pres & chief exec officer, 1996-98; Us Sentencing Comn, 2002-04; Ctr for Ethical Bus Cultures, pres & chief exec officer, currently. **Orgs:** Dir, St Paul Co; dir, Automotive Indust Holding Inc; co-chair, Action CComunity, 1991-; bd mem, Guthrie Theater, 1992-94; chair, United Way Minneapolis, 1998; dir, Ceridan Corp; dir, Great Hall Investment Funds Inc; bd dir, Tamarack Funds; bd dir, Travelers Found; bd dir, Bremer Fin Corp; bd dir, Allina Hosps & Clins; bd dir, Best Buy Co Inc, 2004-; bd mem, Guthrie Theater Speak Word Church Int; bd mem, RBC Funds. **Business Addr:** President, Chief Executive Officer, Center for Ethical Business Cultures, 1000 LaSalle Ave TMH 331, Minneapolis, MN 55403-2005, **Business Phone:** (651)962-4120.

### JAMES, RONALD J.
Lawyer, executive director. **Personal:** Born Apr 8, 1937, Centerville, IA; son of Raymond B and Jennie M Smith; married Vivian Thelma; married Patricia ODonnell; children: Catlin, Kelly, Shannon, Ronald Jr & Kevin. **Educ:** Univ Mo, BA, polit sci, 1959; Am Univ Wash Col Law, JD, 1966; Southern Ill Univ, MA, econs & polit sci, 1972. **Career:** US Dept Transp, atty; Equal Employ Opportunity Comn, asst gen coun; EEO Comn, regional atty, 1972-75; Waterloo IA Comn Human Rights, exec dir, 1967; Waterloo IA, asst Co atty, 1967-69; OEO, spec asst to dir, 1970-71; spec atty to con to pres, 1971-72; Congressman James Bromwell, staff asst, 1963-64; US Dept Labor, admin wage & hour div, 1975-77; Squire Sanders & Dempsey, partner, 1977-2003; US Dept Homeland Security, chief human capital officer, Secy Homeland Security, sr advisor; US Senate; US Dept Army, Off Asst Secy, Manpower & Res Affairs, asst secy army, 2006-09. **Orgs:** Am Bar Asn; Nat Bar Asn; IA Bar Assn; Supreme Ct Bar; Urban League; Ohio Bar Asn. **Honors/Awds:** Nat speech honorary Delta Sigma Rho. **Home Addr:** 10923 Magnolia Dr A, Cleveland, OH 44106, **Home Phone:** (216)721-7529. **Business Addr:** Assistant Secretary of the Army, US Department of the Army Office of the Assistant Secretary, Rm 2E460 Pentagon, Washington, DC 20310.

### JAMES, SHARPE
Politician, mayor, government official. **Personal:** Born Feb 20, 1936, Jacksonville, FL; married Mary Mattison; children: John, Elliott & Kevin. **Educ:** Montclair State Col, BA, educ, 1988; Springfield Col, MA, phys educ; Wash State Univ; Columbia Univ; Rutgers Univ. **Career:** Pub off, S ward councilman; Newark Pub Schs, teacher; Essex Co Col, prof, 1968-86; City Newark, NJ, coun mem, 1970-86, coun man-at-large, 1982-86, mayor, 1986-2006; NJ State Sen, 29th Legis Dist, sen, 1999-2008; Am Dem Party, politician. **Orgs:** Founder, Little City Hall Inc; charter mem & pres, Org Negro Educrs; exec, Scholar Assistance Guid Asn; bd mem, Nat League Cities; US Conf Mayors; exec comt, Newark Collab Group; Nj League Munic, Bd Dir. **Honors/Awds:** Distinguished Alumni Award, Hon Doctor Law, 1991, Montclair State Col; NJ State Tennis Asn Champion; Newark Sr Tennis Champion; City Livability Award, 1991; Top 100 influential black Americans, Ebony, 1991; Honorary Doctorate, Drew Univ, 1991, 1992; Most Valuable Public Official Award, City & State, 1992; inducted, NJ Elected Officials Hall of Fame, 1999; Arts Leader sr, Little City Hall Inc; charter mem & pres, Org Negro Educrs; hip Award, US Conf Mayors & Am Arts, 2002; Mayor of the Year, NJ Conf Mayors, 2003; Hon Doctorate, Drew Univ. **Special Achievements:** Second African American Mayor of Newark, NJ; First Newark mayor to run unopposed when he sought re-election, 1990; Book: A Sharpe View.

### JAMES, SHERRI GWENDOLYN
Lawyer. **Personal:** Born Columbus, GA; daughter of Johnny and Zelma; children: Johnny & Zelma. **Educ:** Georgetown Univ, BA, 1984; Univ Ga Law Sch, JD, 1988. **Career:** Attorney (retired); Dist Atty Off, asst regional coun. **Orgs:** State Bar Ga; Am Bar Asn; Nat Bar Asn; Ga Asn Black Women Atty; Ga State Bar. **Home Addr:** PO Box 3414, Atlanta, GA 30302-3414. **Business Addr:** Assistant Regional Counsel, District Attorney, PO Box 1827, Albany, GA 31707, **Business Phone:** (912)562-1083.

### JAMES, DR. STEPHEN ELISHA
Government official. **Personal:** Born May 19, 1942, Montgomery, AL; son of Hazel Todd and Elisha; married Janie; children: Lydia Yvonne Boseman & Stephen Christopher. **Educ:** Case Western Res Univ, Cleveland, BA, 1970, MSLS, 1971; Univ Wis, Madison, PhD, 1983. **Career:** Cleveland Pub Libr, Cleveland, librn, 1969-73; Atlanta Univ, Atlanta, prof, 1976-87; Pub Libr Saginaw, Saginaw, asst dir, 1987-90; Libr Mich, Lansing, div dir, 1990-. **Orgs:** Intellectual freedom comt, Mich Libr Asn, 1988-92; accreditation comt, Am Libr Asn, 1990-92; Kappa Delta Lambda chap, Alpha Phi Alpha, 1991-. **Honors/Awds:** Beta-Phi-Mu, Am Libr Asn, 1984. **Home Addr:** 2174 Regency Dr, East Lansing, MI 48823, **Home Phone:** (517)351-5708. **Business Addr:** Director of Statewide Library Programs, Library of Michigan, 717 W Allegan, Lansing, MI 48909, **Business Phone:** (517)373-1580.

### JAMES, DR. SYNTHIA SAINT
Painter (artist), writer, educator. **Personal:** Born Feb 11, 1949, Los Angeles, CA. **Educ:** Los Angeles Valley Col; Dutchess Community Col, Inner City Cult Ctr. **Career:** Prof visual artist, 1969-; auth, artist-in-residence, speaker & workshop facilitator; Atelier Synthia ST JAMES, owner. **Orgs:** Paul Getty Trust Fund Visual Arts, 1992; Screen Actors Guild, Am Fedn Tv & Radio Artists; BMI. **Special Achievements:** Image Award Nominee for Outstanding Literary Work: Instructional, National Association for the Advancement of Colored People, 2012. **Home Addr:** PO Box 27683, Los Angeles, CA 90027, **Home Phone:** (323)993-5722. **Business Addr:** Owner, Atelier Synthia SAINT JAMES, PO Box 27683, Los Angeles, CA 90027, **Business Phone:** (323)993-5722.

### JAMES, TONI-LESLIE
Costume designer. **Personal:** Born Jun 11, 1957, McKeesport, PA; daughter of Leslie Burrell and Alice B; married David Higham; children: Cosima B. **Educ:** Ohio State Univ, BFA, theatre, 1979. **Career:** Theatre Arts, costume designer, currently; Va Commonwealth Univ, prof costume designer, dir costumes, 2007-. **Orgs:** United Scenic Artists Local 829; Sokka Gakki Int. **Honors/Awds:** Audelio Awards, Audelio Award Nominations, 1990, 1991; Drama-Logue Award, Drama-Logue, 1991; Drama Desk Nominations, Drama Desk, 1991, 1992; Am Theatre Wine Award, 1992; Tony Nomination, 1992. **Home Addr:** 254 Vanderbilt Ave No 4R, Brooklyn, NY 11205, **Home Phone:** (718)857-2890. **Business Addr:** Professional Costume Designer, Director of Costumes, Virginia Commonwealth University, 821 W Franklin St, Richmond, VA 23284, **Business Phone:** (804)828-0100.

### JAMES, TORY STEVEN
Football player. **Personal:** Born May 18, 1973, New Orleans, LA; married Angela; children: T'yanna. **Educ:** La State Univ, grad. **Career:** Football player (retired); Denver Broncos, defensive back, 1996, 1998, cornerback, right cornerback & mid linebacker, 1999; Oakland Raiders, cornerback, 2000-02, linebacker, 2001, right cornerback, 2002; Cincinnati Bengals, corner back & right cornerback, 2003, 2005, right cornerback, 2004, 2006; New Eng Patriots, defensive back, 2007. **Honors/Awds:** AFC champion, 1998, 2002; Super Bowl champion XXXIII; Pro Bowl, 2004. **Special Achievements:** Films: 1996 NFL Draft, 1996; Super Bowl XXXIII, 1999; Super Bowl XXXVII, 2003. **Business Addr:** MA.

### JAMES, VENITA HAWTHORNE
Journalist, editor. **Personal:** Born Jul 8, 1955, Des Moines, IA; daughter of Peter and Frances; married Daryl; children: Jahara & Akil. **Educ:** Lincoln Univ, BA, 1977. **Career:** Ariz Repub, asst city ed, 1991-94, dep metro ed, 1994-97, sr ed, 1997-, W Valley, gen mgr & sr ed, 2005-08; Repub Media, w valley communities ed, 2009-12, communities dir, 2012-. **Orgs:** Nat Asn Black Journalists, 1985; pres, Ariz Asn Black Journalists, 1998-. **Home Addr:** 17235 N 75th Ave Suite A-100, Glendale, AZ 85308, **Home Phone:** (602)444-6932. **Business Addr:** Communities Director, Republic Media, 200 E Van Buren St 9th Fl, Phoenix, AZ 85004, **Business Phone:** (602)444-8443.

### JAMES, WIL (WILBERT W JAMES, JR.)
Executive. **Personal:** son of Wilbert W. **Educ:** Old Dom Univ, BS, 1978. **Career:** Olin Corp, prod, maintenance & proj engineering; Toyota, supvr, 1987; Toyota Motor Mfg Ky, vpres mfg, 2003-05, pres, 2010-; Toyota, pres TABC, Long Beach, CA, 2006-09; Toyota Motor Mfg Ind, sr vpres, 2009-10; Toyota Motor Engineering & Mfg N Am, sr vpres, 2009-12. **Orgs:** Exec Leadership Coun, Kappa Alpha Psi; Ky Chamber Com, chmn, 2014-16; Bluegrass Econ Advan Movement, Cent Bank & Trust; Nat Urban League; Nat Soc Black Engrs; Ky State Univ & Acad UpRise. **Honors/Awds:** Univ Ky, honorary doctorate of engineering, 2013; Univ Pikeville, honorary degree, 2015; named one of the Top 100 Most Influential Blacks in Corporate America. **Business Addr:** Toyota Motor Manufacturing Kentucky, 1001 Cherry Blossom Way, Georgetown, KY 40324, **Business Phone:** (502)868-2000.

### JAMES, WILBERT W., JR.
Automotive executive, president (organization). **Personal:** married Michaelene; children: 3. **Educ:** Old Dom Univ, AAS, 1976, BS, mech engineering technol, 1978. **Career:** Olin Corp, prod, maintenance, proj engr; Toyota Motor Mfg, Ky Inc, 1987-03, vpres mfg, 2003-06; TABC, sr vpres opers, 2006-07, pres, 2007-08; Toyota Motor Mfg, Evansville, Ind, sr vpres mfg & qual, 2008-10; Toyota Motor Mfg, Ky Inc, pres, 2010-. **Orgs:** Bd dir, Ky Chamber Com; Toyota's Diversity Champion TEMA; Exec Leadership Conf; Kappa Alpha Psi Fraternity; bd affil, Nat Soc Black Engrs; bd mem, Ky State Univ; Acad UpRise, currently; Urban League, Louisville, Ky; Ky Humanities Coun; Partnership Youth Orgn. **Home Addr:** , Lexington, KY. **Business Addr:** Chairman of Board of Director, National Society of Black Engineers.

### JAMES, PROF. WILLIAM
Educator, lawyer. **Personal:** Born May 10, 1945, Augusta, GA; son of Harriet Martin and Hinton; married Avis Cooper; children: Kevyn & William. **Educ:** Morehouse Col, BA, 1967; Howard Univ, JD, 1972; Atlanta Univ, MSLS, 1973. **Career:** Fed City Col, lectr, 1972; Fed Trade Comn, law clerk, 1972; Atlanta Univ, grad asst, 1972-73; Univ Tenn, asst prof & asst librn, 1973-77; Univ Ky, from asst prof law librn to dir law libr, 1977-88; Villanova Univ, prof law & dir law libr, 1988-, assoc dean info serv, 1995-. **Orgs:** Chair, Minorities Comn, 1985-87; AALS; LSAC; Asn Am Law Sch Comn Libr; bd adv, Legal Ref Serv Quart; Am Asn Law Libr; Comn Placement, Educ, Minorities, Scholar & Grants; chair, Scholar & Nomination Comn, S eastern Asn Law Librn. **Special Achievements:** Numerous publications including Law Libraries Which Offer Service to Prisoners, 1975; Recommended Collections for Prison Law Libraries, 1975; Legal Reference Materials and Law Library Services, 1976; written annotated bibliographies for Law and Psychiatry, 1979. **Home Addr:** 15 Cypress Lane, Berwyn, PA 19312-1004, **Home Phone:** (610)296-8894. **Business Addr:** Professor of Law & Director of the Law Library, Associate Dean for Information Services, Villanova University, 299 N Spring Mill Rd Libr Garey Hall, Villanova, PA 19085-1597, **Business Phone:** (610)519-7000.

### JAMES, WYNONA YVONNE
Consultant. **Personal:** Born Dec 7, 1953, Sacramento, CA; daughter of Robert and Estelle. **Educ:** Allan Hancock Col, Assocs Degree, sociol, 1975; San Jose State Univ, sociol, 1976; Mid Tenn State Univ, BS, sociol & anthrop, 1978; Univ Colo, attended 1995; Fuller Theol Sem, MA, theol, 1997; Abraham Lincoln Univ Sch Law, JD, 2008; Abilene Christian Univ, MA, conflict resolution & reconciliation, 2010; Nova Southeastern Univ, PhD, conflict resolution & reconciliation, 2010-. **Career:** USAF, mgt engineering manpower analyst, 1985-2009; chief, Air Force suggestion prog, 1992-95, human resources dir, 1995-96, qual consult, 1996-97, mgt analyst & consult, 1997-2009, productivity-idea prog mgr, 2004-09, spec emphasis prog & diversity mgr, 2007-, alternative dispute resolution installation mgr & equal opportunity advisor, 2009-; Franklin Covey, consult, 1994-2000; Abilene Christian Univ, master's prog online fac facilitator, 2014; I G Brown Air Nat Guard Training & Educ Ctr, vis consult. **Orgs:** Nat Asn Suggestion Syst, 1987-95; pres, Rocky Mountain Employee Involvement Asn Chap, 1993-94; Employee Involvement Nat Task Force, DOD Rep Awards Comt, 1993-94; vpres, Rocky Mountain Employee Involvement Asn, 1994-95; secy & mem chair, Toastmasters Int, 1995-96; bd mem, Girl Scout Wagon Wheel Coun, 1995-96; Am Cancer Soc, 1995-96; mem comt, Employee Involvement Asn, 1996-97; Knoxville Lace Soc, 2000-01; team leader, Pikes Peak Habitat Humanity, 2000; Nat Quilt Asn, 2001-02; E Tenn Hist Soc, 2002-; Knoxville Quilters Guild, 2002-03; Beck Cult Mus, 2002-03; Philanthropic Educ

Orgn (P.E.O.) Int, 2015; Colo Mediators Asn; Asn Conflict Resolution. **Honors/Awds:** Civilian of the Year Award, Twenty first Space Wing-Space Command, 1991; Competant Toastmaster Award, 1995; Outstanding Civilian of the Quarter, Twenty first Space Wing-Space Command, 1996; Air Force Commendation Medal, 1999; Air Force Commendation Medal Civilian Award, 2000; Special Emphasis Program Manager Award for Disability, 2010; Alternative Dispute Resolution Individual Achievement Award, USAF Gen Coun, 2011; Air Force Space Command Alternative Dispute Resolution Manager Award, 2011. **Special Achievements:** Movie extra in film Switchback, 1997. **Home Addr:** 4909 Black Vulture Grv, PO Box 5573, Colorado Springs, CO 80916-5761, **Home Phone:** (719)579-0261. **Business Addr:** Visiting Consultant, I G Brown Air National Guard Training & Education Center, 400 IG Brown Dr, Louisville, TN 37777, **Business Phone:** (865)336-3872.

## JAMES-FOSTER, JOY LYNNE

Administrator, educator. **Personal:** Born Jul 31, 1967, Knoxville, TN; daughter of Joseph and Joyce; married Jerry; children: Kennedy. **Educ:** Univ Tenn, Knoxville, BS, criminal justice & sociol, 1990, MS, curric develop & instr, 1994, EdS, holistic teaching, 1996, admin, 1999, doctorate, educ, 2004; Univ St Mary Leavenworth, MBA, 2015. **Career:** Tenn Dept Educ, admin & educ mgt, 1993-2015; Knox Co Sch, Powell Elem Sch, teacher, 1994-2003, W View, teacher asst, 1987-94, curric facilitator, 2003-04, adminr, currently; Univ Tenn & Dept Health, vis scholar asst ship, 1997-98; Univ Tenn Knoxville, grad res asst, 2000-04; Univ Tenn, black grad opportunity fel, 2000-03; Beaumont Magnet Sch, asst prin, 2004-05; Blue Grass Elem Sch, asst prin, 2005-08; Teacher Yr Prog Tenn Dept Educ, judge, 2005-; FBC, contractor, 2015-. **Orgs:** Phi Delta Kappa, 2000; Kappa Delta Pi, 2000; Knoxville Area Chamber Partnership, 2000; panel mem, Educ Testing Serv, 2000; bd mem, Weekend Acad; bd mem, Linking Librarians with At Risk Kids; bd mem, Shannondale Elem Sch Found; Jr League Knoxville; vpres educ, Toast Masters Int Energy Club, 2013-15. **Home Addr:** 1124 Ferncliff Way, Knoxville, TN 37923, **Home Phone:** (865)470-3165. **Business Addr:** Assistant Principal, Blue Grass Elementary School, 8901 Blue Grass Rd, Knoxville, TN 37922, **Business Phone:** (865)539-7864.

## JAMISON, ANTAWN CORTEZ

Basketball player. **Personal:** Born Jun 12, 1976, Shreveport, LA; son of Albert and Kathy; married Ione Rucker; children: Alexis, Kathryn Elizabeth, Antawn Jr & Rucker. **Educ:** Univ NC, attended 1998. **Career:** Basketball player (retired); Golden State Warriors, forward & small forward, 1998-2003; Dallas Mavericks, small forward, 2003-04; Wash Wizards, forward & power forward, 2004, 2006-10, small forward, 2005; Cleveland Cavaliers, forward & small forward, 2010-12; Los Angeles Lakers, forward & small forward, 2012-13; Los Angeles Clippers, forward & small forward, 2013-14; free agent, currently; Time Warner Cable SportsNet, TV analyst, 2014-. **Honors/Awds:** North Carolina Mr. Basketball, 1995; Wooden Award, 1998; Oscar Robertson Trophy, 1998; Adolph Rupp Trophy, 1998; Naismith College Player of the Year, 1998; AP National Player of the Year, 1998; ACC Player of the Year, 1998; ACC Tournament MVP, 1998; Sixth Man of the Year, Nat Basketball Asn, 2003-04; NBA All-Star, Nat Basketball Asn, 2005, 2008; Bronze Medal, FIBA World Championship, US Nat Team, 2006. **Special Achievements:** Films: Duke-Carolina: The Blue Blood Rivalry, 2013. TV Series: Dennis Miller, 2004. **Business Addr:** Broadcaster, Time Warner Cable SportsNet, **Business Phone:** (310)531-156.

## JAMISON, BIRDIE HAIRSTON

Judge. **Personal:** Born Jul 1, 1957, Martinsville, VA; daughter of Irvin Spencer Sr and Ida Dalton; married Calvin D Sr; children: Calvin D Jr. **Educ:** Col William & Mary, Williamsburg, VA, BBA, 1979; Marshall Wythe Sch Law, Col William & Mary, Williamsburg, VA, JD, 1982. **Career:** George W Harris, Jr & Assoc, Roanoke, Va, assoc atty, 1982-84; Roanoke Commonwealth Atty, Roanoke, Va, asst commonwealth atty, 1984-88; Va Polytech Inst, Blacksburg, Va, adj instr, 1983-88; Va Atty Gen, Richmond, Va, asst atty gen, 1988-90; Richmond Commonwealth Atty, Richmond, Va, dep commonwealth atty, 1990-91; Gen Dist Ct, Richmond, Va, judge, currently. **Orgs:** Delta Sigma Theta, Inc, 1978-; Old Dom Bar Asn, 1982-; Corresp secy, Girlfriends, Inc, 1984-; pres, Roanoke Chap Old Dom Bar Asn, 1985-87; bd mem, Big Bro & Big Sister, 1990-; bd mem, Garfield Memorial Fund, 1990-; pres, Jack & Jill, Inc, 1990; chair, James River Chap links Inc. **Honors/Awds:** SERWA Award, Coalition 200 Black Women, 1992; Virginia Heroes Award, 1992; Alumini Achievement Award, Richmond Alumini chapter; Influential Women of Virginia, Virginia Lawyers Media, 2010. **Home Addr:** 2801 Skipton Rd, Richmond, VA 23225, **Home Phone:** (804)323-7144. **Business Addr:** Judge, General District Court, 400 N 9th St John Marshall Courts Bldg, Richmond, VA 23219, **Business Phone:** (804)780-6437.

## JAMISON, GEORGE R., JR.

Football player. **Personal:** Born Sep 30, 1962, Bridgeton, NJ; married Arnella; children: 1. **Educ:** Univ Detroit, BA, hum res develop, 1990; Univ Cincinnati. **Career:** Football player (retired); Philadelphia Stars, linebacker, 1984; Baltimore Stars, 1984-85; Detroit Lions, 1987, left outside linebacker, 1988, 1991-93, 1997, right outside linebacker, 1989, hon capt, 1997-98; Kans City Chiefs, left linebacker, 1994, left outside linebacker, 1995, 1996; Ford Field, hon capt. **Honors/Awds:** Most Valuable player, Detroit Lions, 1991; Lions' Block Award, 1998. **Home Addr:** , Rochester, MI. **Business Addr:** Honorable Captain, Detroit Lions, 222 Republic Dr, Allen Park, MI 48101.

## JAMISON, ISAAC TERRELL

Executive. **Personal:** Born Jun 30, 1969, Baltimore, MD; son of Joan Jenkins and Issac; married Aticha M. **Educ:** Tuskegee Univ, BBA, mkt mgt gen, 1993. **Career:** Morton Int Salt Co, sales rep, Jackson, Miss, 1993-96, Pittsburgh, 1994-97, nat sales, accounts mgr, 2001-03, region sales admin mgr, 2004-06, mkt bus segment mgr, 2007-09, Alberto Culver, sr. bus mgr-wm team, 2009-10; LOreal SA, bus mgr, 2009-13, field sales vpres, nat accounts, 2013-. **Orgs:** Nat Life mem, Kappa Alpha Psi Fraternity, 1996-, Fayetteville, AR Alumni Chap Polemarch, 2008-2009, Mid Western Prov Life Mem, 2010; bd mem, African Am Comt, Nat Kidney Found, 1995; bd trustee, Tuskegee Univ, 1994. **Home Addr:** 12928 Bradford Lane, Plainfield, IL 60585, **Home Phone:** (815)609-3380. **Business Addr:** Regional Sales Administration Manager, Morton International Salt Co, 11111 Houze Rd Suite 105, Roswell, GA 30076.

## JAMISON, JUDITH ANN

Executive, dancer, artistic director. **Personal:** Born May 10, 1943, Philadelphia, PA; daughter of John Sr and Tessie B; married Miguel Godreau. **Educ:** Fisk Univ, attended 1962; Univ Arts, Philadelphia, PA, attended 1964; Judimar Sch Dance. **Career:** Alvin Ailey Am Dance Theater, prin, 1964-80, dancer & choreographer, 1980-89, artistic dir, 1989-2011; guest appearances in var orgn incl: Am Ballet Theatre, 1964; Harkness Ballet; San Francisco Ballet; Dallas Ballet; Vienna State Opera; Munich State Opera; Hamburg State Opera; choreographer: Divining, 1984; Forgotten Time, 1989; Rift, 1991; Hymn, 1993; Riverside, 1995; Sweet Release, 1996; Echo: Far From Home, 1998; Mefistofele, Judith Jamison: The Dance maker; Double Exposure, 2000; Here Now, 2002; Love Stories, 2004; Reminiscin, 2005; Among Us, 2009. The Jamison Proj, dir, 1988-89; TV Ser: "The Cosby Show", actor, 1985; "A Tribute to Alvin Ailey", actor, 1990. **Orgs:** Bd mem, Coun Arts; Harper Festival Chicago, 1965; Festival Negro Arts Dakar Senegal, 1966; Edinburgh Festival, 1968; Women's Choreography Initiative; founder, BFA Prog, Ailey Sch & Fordham Univ. **Honors/Awds:** Dance Magazine Award, 1972; Key to City of New York, 1976; Distinguished Service Award, Harvard Univ, 1982; Distinguished Service Award, Mayor of New York City, 1982; Philadelphia Arts Alliance Award; The Franklin Mint Award; Candace Award, Nat Coalition 100 Black Women; received honorary doctorates from various universities including: Univ Arts; Mary mount Col; Middlebury Col; The Dance USA Award, 1998; Manhattanville Col; Outstanding Choreography for "Dance in America: A Hymn For Alvin Ailey, ", Prime time Emmy Awards, 1999; Kennedy Center Honoree, 1999; Emmy Award; American Choreography Award for Outstanding Choreography; Algur H Meadows Award, Southern Methodist Univ, 2001; National Medal of Arts, Pres George Bush, 2001; Honored by the National Theater of Ghana, 2002; "Making a Difference" Award, Nat Asn Advan Colored People ACT-SO, 2003; Paul Robeson Award, Actors Equity Asn, 2004; Bessie Award, 2007; BET Honors Award, 2009; The World's Most Influential People, TIME 100, 2009; Congressional Black Caucus Phoenix Award, 2010; The Handel Medallion, 2010. **Special Achievements:** Co-author, Dancing Spirit, 1993. **Business Addr:** Artistic Director, Alvin Ailey American Dance Theater, 405 W 55th St, New York, NY 10019, **Business Phone:** (212)405-9000.

## JARREAU, ALWYN LOPEZ

Actor, singer, songwriter. **Personal:** Born Mar 12, 1940, Milwaukee, WI; son of Emile and Pearl; married Phyllis Hall; children: Ryan; married Susan Player; children: Ryan. **Educ:** Ripon Col, BS, psychol, 1962; Univ IA, MS, voc rehab, 1964. **Career:** Singer & songwriter; Albums: We Got By, 1975; Glow, 1976; Look to theRainbow, 1977; All Fly Home, 1978; This Time, 1980; Breaking Away, 1981; Lis for Lover, 1986; Heart's Horizon, 1989; Al Jarreau, 1992; Tenderness, 1994; Best of Al Jarreau, 1996; Tomorrow Today, All I Got, 2000; Accentuate the Positive, 2004; Al & Lou, 2004; Lean on Me, 2004; R&B Soul, 2005; Givin' It Up, 2006; Look To The Rainbow: Live in Europe, 2008; Love Songs (Rhino), 2008; Christmas (Rhino), 2008; Singles: "Rainbow In Your Eyes", 1976; "Take Five", 1977; "Thinkin' About It Too", 1978; "Distracted", 1980; "Gimme What You Got", 1980; "Never Givin' Up", 1980; "We're In This Love Together", 1981; "Breakin' Away", 1982; "Teach Me Tonight", 1982; "Your Precious Love", 1982; "Boogie Down", 1983; "Mornin'", 1983; "Trouble In Paradise", 1983; "After All", 1984; "Raging Waters", 1985; "L Is For Lover", 1986; "Tell Me What I Gotta Do", 1986; "The Music Of Goodbye", 1986; "Moonlighting", 1987; "So Good", 1988; "All of My Love", 1989; "All or Nothing At All", 1989; "Blue Angel", 1992; "It's Not Hard to Love You", 1992; "In My Music", 2001. TV series: "The Billy Crystal Comedy Hour", 1982; "Touched by an Angel", 1997; "Promised Land", 1997; "Night of the Proms", 2013. **Honors/Awds:** Italian Music Critics Award, 1977; Grammy Award, 1978 & 1981 & 1992 & 2006; winner, Readers'Poll Down Beat Mag, 1977-79; Distinguished Alumni Award, Ripon College, 1928; honored with a star on the Hollywood Walk of Fame, 2001; Literacy Champion Award, 2002; French Music Academy Awards; Ford Freedom Award Scholar, 2005. **Special Achievements:** Film: Touched by an Angel, 1997; A Taste of Us: The Movie, 2007; Soundtrack: Warner Bros, Girls Know How, 1982; Universal pictures, Moonlighting, 1984; Motown, Never Explain Love, 1989; The Fighting Temptations, 2003; Against the Ropes, 2004. **Business Addr:** Singer, 1954 First St, Highland Park, IL 60035, **Business Phone:** (847)716-6336.

## JARRETT, GERALD I., SR.

Educator, lawyer. **Personal:** Born Jul 18, 1947, Newark, NJ; son of Nelson and Zelma; married Karen Jordan; children: Laini, Gerald Jr, Brandon & Michael. **Educ:** Western New Mex Univ; Youngstown State Univ, BA, 1971; Seton Hall Sch Law, JD, 1974. **Career:** State NJ Labor Dept, hearings officer, 1977-79; State NJ ade law judge, 1979-81; pvt pract atty, 1981-85; NJ Assembly Majority Leader Off, legal asst, 1985-86; NJ Pub Defender Off, pub defender, 1986-97; Essex County Col, adj prof, 1996; St Augustine Col, asst prof, 1997; E Carolina univ, Teaching Inst, 2007-08. **Orgs:** Treas, 1983-84, pres, 1984-85, Garden State Bar Asn; chair ade law sect, Nat Bar Asn, 1979-81; Kappa Alpha Psi, 1968-; bd & exec secy, Essex Newark Legal Serv, 1981-85. **Home Addr:** 10913 Bexhill Dr, Cary, NC 27518-1512, **Home Phone:** (919)363-2662.

## JARRETT, DR. VALERIE B.

Government official. **Personal:** Born Nov 14, 1956, Shiraz; daughter of James E Bowman and Barbara Taylor Bowman; married William Robert; children: Laura. **Educ:** Stanford Univ, BA, psychol, 1978; Univ Mich Law Sch, JD, 1981. **Career:** Pope Ballard Shepard & Fowle Ltd, assoc, cre banking; Sonnenschein, Carlin, Nath & Rosenthal, Real Estate Dept, assoc; City Chicago, Dept Law, dep corp coun finance & develop, Off Mayor, dep chief staff, Dept Planning, actg comnr, Dept Planning & Develop, comnr; Chicago Stock Exchange, chmn, 2004-; Habitat Co, exec vpres & managing dir, chief exec officer, 1995-2002; pres Obama & asst to pres pub engagement & intergovernmental affairs, sr adv, currently. **Orgs:** Lambda Alpha Int; Ctr Int Bus Educ & Res; pres, SE Chicago Comn; Ncp Legal Defense & Educ-Chicago Fund, dir; Local Initiatives Support Corp; Econ Club Chicago; Nat Coun Urban Econ Develop; dir, Leadership Greater Chicago, 1988-89; chmn bd dir, Chicago Transit Authority; bd dir, Navigating Consult; chmn Univ Chicago Hosp; exec coun, Metropolis 2020; bd dir, USG Corp; dir, Harris Insight Funds; dir, Joyce Found; chair, White House Coun; co chair, Obama Biden Presidential Transition Team; sr advisor, Obamas presidential campaign; chmn, Chicago Transit Bd, Comnr Planning & Develop City Chicago, dep chief, Staff Mayor Richard M Daley, Dep Corp Coun Finance & Develop; dir, Fed Res Bank Chicago, chmn, Univ Chicago Med Ctr Bd trustee, vice chair, Univ Chicago Bd trustee, dir, Local Initiative Support Corp, Joyce Found, trustee, Mus Sci & Indust; bd trustee, Univ Chicago Med Ctr, 1996-2009, vice chmn, 2002, chmn, 2006; bd mem, Chicago Stock Exchange, 2000-07, chmn, 2004-07; vice chmn bd trustee, Univ Chicago;trustee, Chicago's Mus Sci & Indust. **Home Addr:** 4950 S Chicago Beach Dr, Chicago, IL 60615. **Business Addr:** Assistant to the President, Public Engagement & Intergovernmental Affairs, 1600 Pennsylvania Ave NW, Washington, DC 20500.

## JARRETT-JACKSON, MARY FRANCIS

Executive. **Personal:** Born Feb 15, 1931, Nickolasville, KY; daughter of Bronaugh and Gladys Bridges; married Clarence; children: Ernest L Jarrett & Ruth E Jarrett-Cooper. **Educ:** Howard Univ, BS, 1952; Atlanta Univ, MA, 1988. **Career:** Executive (retired); Detroit Police Dept, police exec, dep chief western oper, 1958-94; Wayne County Juv Detention Facil, chief asst dir, 1995-2000, Crime Lab; Wayne County Sheriff's Dept, dep admin, 2000. **Home Addr:** 20006 Robson St, Detroit, MI 48235, **Home Phone:** (313)342-2139.

## JARVIS, CHARLENE DREW (CHARLENE ROSELLA DREW)

School administrator, president (organization). **Personal:** Born Jul 31, 1941, Washington, DC; daughter of Charles R Drew and Minnie Lenore Drew; married Ernest; children: Ernest Drew & Peter. **Educ:** Roosevelt High Sch, attended 1958; Oberlin Col, BA, 1962; Howard Univ, MS, 1964; Univ Md, PhD, neuro psychol, 1971; Amherst Col, DHL, 1994; George Washington Univ, Doctor Pub Serv. **Career:** Howard Univ, instr psychol, 1965, prof; Nat Inst Ment Health, pre-doctoral fel, res scientist, 1978; DC City Coun, coun woman, 1979-2000; Southeastern Univ, pres, 1996-2009; Montgomery Col, prof. **Orgs:** Chair, Coun Govts; chairperson, pres, DC Chamber Com; Greater Wash Bd Trade; chair, Community Bus Partnership Comn; bd dir, BB & T Bank; bd dir, Nat Asn Independent Col & Univ; chair, DC City Coun, Comt Econ Develop; exec comt mem, Fed City Coun; Wash Chap, Am Red Cross; Breast Cancer Task Force Dept Health & Human Serv; Womens Health Initiative, NIH; Nat Mus Health; Nat Bone Marrow Prog; mem, Coun DC; chair bd, Wash Metrop Coun Governments; Greater Wash Soc Cert Pub Accountants; Am Asn Univ Women; dir, Nat Womens Bus Ctr Inc, currently. **Special Achievements:** First woman to hold the position as president of Southeastern University in Washington, DC, 1996. **Business Addr:** Director, National Women's Business Center Inc, 1001 Connecticut Ave NW, Washington, DC 20036, **Business Phone:** (202)785-4922.

**JASON, JEANNE. See WRIGHT, JEANNE JASON.**

## JASPER, EDWARD VIDEL

Football player. **Personal:** Born Jan 18, 1973, Tyler, TX. **Educ:** Tex A&M Univ, agr. **Career:** Football player (retired); Philadelphia Eagles, defensive tackle, 1997, 1998; Atlanta Falcons, 1999, right offensive tackle, 2000-01, 2004, left defensive tackle, 2000, nose tackle, 2002-04, defensive end, 2002, defensive tackle, 2003; Oakland Raiders, defensive tackle, 2005.

## JASPER, KENJI NATHANIEL

Writer. **Personal:** Born Jan 1, 1976; son of Melvin and Angela. **Educ:** Morehouse Col, attended 1997. **Career:** Inst Preserv & Study African Am Writing, instr; WTTG, Fox 5's Newsbag, on-air personality, 1986-87; Black Entertainment TV Teen Summit, founding cast mem, 1989-93; Bks: Dark, 2001; Dakota Grand, 2002; Seeking Salamanca Mitchell, 2004; House Childress St, 2006; Beats, Rhymes & Life, 2007; Snow, 2007; Armory, 2007; What We Love & Hate About Hip Hop; Armory Press, chief exec officer & ed. **Business Addr:** Author, c/o Random House Inc, 1745 Broadway Suite 3, New York, NY 10019, **Business Phone:** (212)782-9000.

## JASPER, LAWRENCE E.

Insurance executive. **Personal:** Born Oct 25, 1946, Philadelphia, PA; son of Lawrence (deceased) and Geraldine (deceased); married Diana Lundy; children: Laurette & Dawn. **Educ:** ICA; LUTC. **Career:** Debit Agt, 1968-69; Supr, 1969-71; Serv Asst Spectrum Arena, supr, 1971-74; Pilgrim Life Ins Co, asst vpres, 1974, vpres, currently. **Orgs:** Nat Asn Advan Colored People; Young Great Soc, 19 St Bapt Ch Youth Dept; Interest Bus Trng Black & Youth. **Honors/Awds:** Man of Year, Pilgrim Life Ins, 1970, 1972. **Special Achievements:** First Black in mgmt Pilgrim Life; first man to receive Man of Year Award twice; youngest man & only black on bd dir at Pilgrim Life. **Home Addr:** 8545 Forrest Ave, Philadelphia, PA 19150-2303, **Home Phone:** (215)247-9282. **Business Addr:** Vice President, Pilgrim Life Insurance Co (Pilgrim Mutual Insurance Co), 8049 Westchester Pke, Upper Darby, PA 19082.

## JAYCOX, MARY IRINE

Public relations executive. **Personal:** Born Aug 19, 1939, Camp Hill, PA; daughter of Eddie B Knight and Betty Busby; married James Curtis; children: James Jr, Sharon, Mary & Thomas P. **Educ:** Univ Northern Iowa, BA, 1984, MA, 1986. **Career:** Har-lin Pre-Sch Erie Pa, parent coordr, 1966-67; Sears Roebuck & Co, div mgr, 1973-80; KBBG-FM Waterloo Iowa, talk show host, 1981-84; Dubuque City Festivals, prom dir, pub info coordr. **Orgs:** Freelance feature writer Waterloo Courier, Tel Herald Dubuque; housing analyst, Comn Housing Resource Bd; mem & publicity comn, Waterloo, Young Mens Christian Asn, 1985-86; comnr, Cable Comn Teleprogramming. **Home Addr:** 1600 Shelby Dr, Dyersburg, TN 38024-3439, **Home Phone:** (731)285-0054. **Business Addr:** Public Information Coordinator, City Dubuque, 50 W 13th St, Dubuque, IA 52001, **Business Phone:** (563)589-4100.

### JAYNES, DR. GERALD DAVID

Educator. **Personal:** Born Jan 30, 1947, Streator, IL; son of Homer and Lorraine Greenwood; married Patricia Hall; children: Vechel & Hillary. **Educ:** Univ Ill-Urbana, BA, 1971, MA, 1974, PhD, 1976; Yale Univ, MA, 1984. **Career:** Univ Penn, asst prof econ, 1975-77; Yale Univ, asst prof econ, dir & chair, 1977-81, assoc prof econ, 1981-84, prof econ & African Am Studies, 1984-; Nat Res Coun, Wash, DC, study dir Comm Status Black Am, 1985-89, chair, African & Afro-Am Studies, 1990-96. **Home Addr:** 28 Hillhouse Ave, New Haven, CT 06511. **Business Addr:** Professor of Economics & African American Studies, Director, Yale Univ, 81 Wall St Rm 205, New Haven, CT 06511-6606, **Business Phone:** (203)432-3586.

### JEAN, KYMBERLY

Business owner, founder (originator), president (organization). **Personal:** Born Dec 31, 1963, Chicago, IL. **Educ:** Los Angeles City Col, AA, 1985. **Career:** Opposites Attract, owner, pres & founder, 1989-. **Orgs:** Toastmaster; Womens Referral Ser; Nat Asn Women bus owners; BLK Women's Network. **Special Achievements:** The Oprah Winfrey Show, 1991; Jet Magazine, 1992; The Phil Donahue Show, 1992; Essence Magazine, 1993; KABC's City View; A.M. Los Angeles; The Montel Williams; People Are Talking in San Francisco.

### JEAN, NELUST WYCLEF (WYCLEF JEAN)

Rap musician, guitarist. **Personal:** Born Oct 17, 1969, Croix-des-Bouquets; son of Gesner and Nazarene preacher; married Marie Claudinette; children: Angelina Claudinelle. **Career:** Rapper, guitarist, recording artist & producer, 1993-; Albums: The Carnival, 1997; The Ecleftic: 2 Sides II a Book, 2000; Masquerade, 2002; The Preacher's Son, 2003; Greatest Hits, 2003; Welcome to Haiti: Killing Me Softly, Ready or Not & No Woman, No Cry, We Trying to Stay Alive, Secret Lover; Gone Till November, Creole 101, 2004; The Carnival II: Memoirs of an Immigrant, 2007; From the Hut, To the Projects, To the Mansion, 2009; Wyclef Jean, 2010; If I Were President: My Haitian Experience, 2010; TV series: "Postcards from Buster", 2004; "Rock the Paint", 2005; "The Apprentice (US Season 4)", 2005; "Film: Life", 1999; "Chappelle's Show"; "Jimmy Kimmel Live"; Flim: Dirty, 2005; Shottas, 2006; Ghosts of Cite Soleil, 2007; TBA, The Carnival Returns; Suicide Love, 2009. **Honors/Awds:** 3 times Grammy Awards winner. **Special Achievements:** Nominated for two Grammy Awards, including Best Rap Album for the Carnival, 1998; Nominated for Best Hip-Hop Act at the 2000 MTV Europe Music Awards; In 2005, he earned a Golden Globe nomination for his track entitled "Million Voices" featured on the soundtrack to the film Hotel Rwanda. **Business Addr:** Composer, Actor, Ruffhouse/Columbia Records, 515 Madison Ave, New York, NY 10022, **Business Phone:** (212)833-8000.

### JEFF, D J JAZZY (JEFFREY ALLAN TOWNES)

Singer, chief executive officer. **Personal:** Born Jan 22, 1965, Philadelphia, PA; married Lynette Jackson. **Career:** Albums: Rock House, 1987; He's DJ, I'm Rapper, 1988; Greatest Hits, 1988; And in This Corner, 1989; Homebase, 1991; Code Red, 1993; Boom Shake Room, 1993; Before Willennium, 1999; Magnificent, 2002; Magnificent EP, 2002; Platinum & Gold Collection, 2003; House, 2004; Very Best DJ Jazzy Jeff & Fresh Prince, 2006; Return Magnificent, 2007; Singles: I'm Looking One (To Be with Me), 2005; We Live Philly, 2005; How I Do, 2005; Cobbs Creek, 2005; Girls Ain't Nuthin' But Trouble, 2006; Da Love Da Game, 2006; Break It Down, 2006; My Peoples, 2006; Return Magnificent EP, 2007; Return Hip Hop EP, 2007; He's King...I'm DJ, 2009; DJ Jazzy Jeff & Mick Summertime Vol 1, 2010; DJ Jazzy Jeff & Ayah Back for More, 2011; DJ Jazzy Jeff & Mick Summertime Vol 2, 2011; Shorti Bomb, 2011; Mayer Hawthorne No Strings DJ Jazzy Jeff Roller Boogie Remix, 2011; DJ Jazzy Jeff & Mick Summertime Vol 3, 2012; 92 Til Infinity with Mac Miller, 2012; Girl of My Life by Mint Condition, 2012; DJ Jazzy Jeff & Mick Summertime Vol 4, 2013; DJ Jazzy Jeff & Mick Summertime Vol 5, 2014; DJ Vice World is Out Playground, 2014; Terry Hunter featuring Jay Adams We Are One, 2014; song: "Fresh Prince Bel Air"; A Touch Jazz Inc, founder & chief exec officer, 1990-. **Business Addr:** Founder, Chief Executive Officer, A Touch of Jazz Inc, 444 N 3rd St Suite C9, Philadelphia, PA 19123, **Business Phone:** (215)928-9192.

### JEFF, GLORIA JEAN

State government official. **Personal:** Born Apr 8, 1952, Detroit, MI; daughter of Doris Lee and Harriette Virginia Davis. **Educ:** Univ Mich, Ann Arbor, MI, BSE, civil engineering, 1974, MSE, civil engineering, 1976, MUP, 1976; Carnegie-Mellon Univ, Prof Prog Urban Transp, cert; Ind Univ, cert; Purdue Univ, cert; Am Asn State Hwy Transp Off Mgt Inst, cert. **Career:** S Eastern Mich Transp Authority, prin planner, prog analyst, equip engr, 1976-81; Mich Dept Transp, Multi-Regional Planning Div, Lansing, Mich, div adminr, 1981-84, Urban Transp Planning Div, div adminr, 1984-85, Bur Transp Planning, asst dep dir, 1985-90, dep dir, 1990, dir, 2003-06; Univ Mich, Col Archit & Urban Planning, Ann Arbor, Mich, adj prof, 1988; Fed Hwy Admin, dep adminr, 1998-2003; Los Angeles Dept Transp, gen mgr, 2006-08; Gloria J Jeff, Consult, prin, 2008-10; Dc Dept Transp, assoc dir, 2010-. **Orgs:** Am Planning Asn, Transp Planning Div; bd dir, 1988, vpres, 1989-90, pres, 1990, Am Planning Asn, Mich Chap; Mich Soc Planning Off; Am Inst Cert Planners; bd dir, Univ Mich Alumni Asn; Women's Transp Sem; bd dir, Univ Mich Col Archit & Urban Planning Alumni Soc; chair, Univ Mich Col Engineering; Transp Res Bd, Statewide Multi-modal Transp Planning Comt; Delta Sigma Theta Sorority; vice chair, Intermodal Issues Comt, Am Asn State Hwy & Transp Off; vice chair, Miss Valley Conf, Strategic Issues Comt, 1990-; Transp Res Bd Exec Comt, 2005. **Home Addr:** 5283 E Hidden Lake, East Lansing, MI 48823. **Business Addr:** MI.

### JEFFCOAT, JAMES WILSON, JR.

Football player, football coach. **Personal:** Born Apr 1, 1961, Long Branch, NJ; married Tammy; children: Jaren, Jackson, Jacqoline & Jasmine. **Educ:** Ariz State Univ, BA, commun, 1983, MBA. **Career:** Football player (retired), football coach; Dallas Cowboys, defensive end & right defensive end, 1983-94, asst coach, 1998-2000, defensive ends coach, 2000-04; Buffalo Bills, defensive end, 1995-97; Univ Houston, defensive line coach; Plano W High Sch, defensive end coach, 2008-10; Bally Total Fitness, partner; All state ins agency, owner, currently; Houston Cougars football team, defensive line coach, 2008-10; San Jose State Spartans football team, defensive line coach, 2011-12; Colo Buffaloes football, defensive line coach, 2013-. **Orgs:** Boys Clubs; Leukemia Soc; Make-A-Wish Found; Sickle Cell Anemia Found; Spec Olympics. **Honors/Awds:** All-American, 1982; Unsung Hero Award, NJ Sportswriter's Asn, 1991; Super Bowl Champion. **Special Achievements:** Dallas Cowboys' Man of the Year nominee, 1990; Arizona State Hall of Fame, 1994; Fiesta Bowl Hall of Fame. **Business Addr:** Defensive End Coach, University of Colorado Athletics, 368 UCB, Boulder, CO 80309-0372, **Business Phone:** (303)492-5331.

### JEFFERIES, CHARLOTTE S.

Educator, lawyer. **Personal:** Born Mar 8, 1944, McKeesport, PA. **Educ:** Howard Univ, BS, 1966; Rollins Col, attended 1967; Duquesne Univ Sch Law, JD, 1980. **Career:** Seminole Co FL, teacher, 1966-67; OIC Erie, dir coun, 1967-70; Urban Coalition RI, health planner, 1970-71; Stud Serv Oic RI, dir, 1971-72; Career Devel Brown Univ, assoc dir, 1973-77; Neighborhood Legal Serv Mckeesport, legal intern, 1978-79; Off US aty Dept Justice, law clerk, 1979-80; Hon Donald E Ziegler Judge US Dist Ct & Western Dist Pa Off US Atty, law clerk, 1980-81; Horty Springer & Mattern PC, partner, 1981, sr partner & atty, currently; Horty Springer Publ, res ed, currently. **Orgs:** Appellate moot ct bd, Duquesne Univ, 1979-80; chmn, Merit Selection Panel US Magistrates Western Dist Pa, 1987-88; Delta Sigma Theta Inc; judiciary comt, Allegheny Co Bar Asn; Pa Bar Asn; Am bar Asn; Nat Bar Asn; Homer S Brown Law Asn; Soc Hosp Atty Western Pa; city counperson, City Duquesne; YWCA Mc Keesport; Nat Asn Advan Colored People; Howard Univ Alumni Club; Allegheny Co Air Pollution Adv Comt; munic Adv comt; Nat Health Lawyers Asn; Am Health Lawyers Asn; adv bd, Study Women's Health Across Nation; sr fel Estes Pk Inst; US Bankruptcy Judge Merit Selection Panel; exec comt, Nat Practr Data Bank; fel Allegheny Co Bar Found. **Honors/Awds:** Richard Allen Award, Outstanding Civic contrib, 1980. **Special Achievements:** Outstanding Student of the Year, Black Amer Law Student Asn, Duquesne Univ Chap, 1980. **Home Addr:** 113 Parise Rd, Pittsburgh, PA 15221-4107, **Home Phone:** (412)241-4445. **Business Addr:** Attorney, Senior Partner, Horty Springer & Mattern PC, 4614 5th Ave, Pittsburgh, PA 15213, **Business Phone:** (412)687-7677.

### JEFFERIES, MARY T.

Executive. **Career:** Community Action Orgn Erie County Inc, Wage Subsidy Program, employ coordr & dir. **Business Addr:** Director, Wage Subsidy Employment Program, Community Action Organization of Erie County Inc, 99 Harvard Pl, Buffalo, NY 14209, **Business Phone:** (716)881-6277.

### JEFFERS, BEN L.

Government official, business owner, editor. **Personal:** Born Jun 18, 1944, Lake City, FL; married Salomia Lawson; children: Ben II. **Educ:** Southern Univ, BS, mgt; Mt State Univ; A&T U; McNeese State Univ. **Career:** Politician, business owner, editor & publisher; LA Health & Human Res Admin, dir div mgt; LA Health & Human Resources Admin, dir; LA Comn Human Rels Rights & Responsibilities, dir; Gov Edwin Edwards, cong aide; LA Dem Party, chair, 1997-2003; Dem Natl Conv, LA, deleg, 2000, 2004, 2008; State La, Gov's chief of staff; Lake Charles Times, ed & pub; La Dem Party Exec Comt, 6th Cong Dist, DNC at-large, 2004-; Ben Jeffers Inc, prin, chief exec officer, currently; City of Baton Rouge, personnel administrator; Vanderbilt Consult LLC, sr advisor, currently. **Orgs:** Chmn, LA Coalition Social Serv Prog; state adv bd Comprehensive Health Planning; Develop Disabilities Coun; Nat Rehab asn; LA Rehab Asn; Am Soc Training & Devel; Am Pub Welfare Asn; LA Health Asn; Kiwanis Club Lake Charles; Am Legion; Prince Hall Masons; bd dir, Advert & Press Clubg SW LA; bd mem, Foreman-reynaud Br YMCA; gen mgr, Lake Charles Newsleader; exec asst to pub newsleader, Newspapers LA & MS; State Manpower Planning Coun; Nat Asn Adv Coloured People; bd mem, Regents Adv Coun, Post Sec Educ; bd mem, Grambling State Univ Found; chmn, Dem Nat Comt, 2001-03; chmn, La Dem State Cent Comt; undersecretary, La Dept Health; chief exec officer, Charity Hosp, New Orleans; dir mgt & finance, La Health & Human Resources Admin; dir, Div Human Serv; actg dir, Aging Serv; prin regional off, Region VI, US Dept Health & Human Serv Dept; super deleg 2008 presidental election nomination, 2008; pres, Arts Coun Greater Baton Rouge; chmn, Downtown Develop Dist; Baton Rouge Chamber Com; Vols Am; chmn, La Leadership Inst. **Home Addr:** 922 Mayflower St, Baton Rouge, LA 70802, **Home Phone:** (225)383-9724. **Business Addr:** Chairman, The Louisiana Leadership Institute, 5763 Hooper Rd, Baton Rouge, LA 70811, **Business Phone:** (225)358-6700.

### JEFFERS, CLIFTON R. See Obituaries Section.

### JEFFERS, EVE JIHAN

Rap musician, actor. **Personal:** Born Nov 10, 1978, Philadelphia, PA; daughter of Jerry and Julie Wilcher; married Maximillion Cooper. **Career:** Albums: Let There Be Eve: Ruff Ryders' First Lady, 1999; Scorpion, 2001; Eve-Olution, 2002; Flirt, 2009; Films: Barbershop, 2002; XXX, 2002; Charlie's Angels: Full Throttle, 2003; Barbershop 2: Back in Business, 2004; The Cookout, 2004; Dark Moon, 2010; 4321 The Countdown Begins, 2010; All Wifed Out, 2012; Bounty Killer, 2013; Animal, 2014; TV Series: "Eve", 2003-06; "Spider-Man", 2003; "Third Watch", 2003; "XIII", voice, 2003; "Spider-Man: The New Animated Series", 2003; "The Woodsman", 2004; "One on One", 2004; "Red Nose Day", 2005; "Saturday Night Live", 2005; "The Apprentice", 2005; "Flashbacks of a Fool", 2008; "Whip It!", 2009; "Glee", 2009; "Good Hair", 2009; "Double Exposure", 2012; "Single Ladies", 2012; "Whitney", 2012; "With This Ring", 2015. **Business Addr:** Rapper, Actress, Interscope Records, 2220 Colorado Ave, Santa Monica, CA 90404, **Business Phone:** (310)865-1000.

### JEFFERS, GRADY ROMMEL

Executive. **Personal:** Born Jul 11, 1943, New York, NY; son of Robert and Alberta; married Maryann P; children: Anna, Debbie, Michael & Alberta. **Educ:** Bernard Baruch Col; Manhattan Community Col, AA, 1973. **Career:** Franklin Nat Bank, mgr, 1969-74; Repub Nat Bank, 1974, asst vpres, vpres & mgr, 1980-; Bankers Trust Co, asst vpres com loan group. **Orgs:** Secy, exec bd, Pvt Indust Coun, 1989-; Nat Bankers Asn Masons; 100 Black Men; Minority Bus & Develop; Nat Asn Acct; Urban Bankers Coalition. **Honors/Awds:** Nom White house Fellowship. **Home Addr:** 762 Hartwell St, Teaneck, NJ 07666, **Home Phone:** (201)833-1410.

### JEFFERS, ESQ. JACK

Executive, college teacher. **Personal:** Born Dec 10, 1928; son of George William and Rose Elizabeth Bosfield; married Cynthia Rogers; children: Laura & Lee. **Educ:** Northeastern Univ, BS, 1951; NY Univ Sch Law, JD, 1982. **Career:** State Univ NY, prof emer music, 1985-94; Duke Ellington Orchestra, dir; Freelance Conductor; Composer; Instrumentalist. **Orgs:** Chmn, 7 Arts Chap CORE, 1964-66. **Home Addr:** 119 Manhattan Ave, New York, NY 10025-4044, **Home Phone:** (212)222-3245.

### JEFFERS, DR. SHEILA B.

Educator. **Personal:** Born Dec 4, 1954, New York, NY; daughter of Carl H Sr; children: Clifton Lamar & Terri Anika Prudhomme. **Educ:** State Univ NY, Oneonta, NY, BS, speech/theater & psychol, 1975; Nat Hosp Col Speech Sci, speech path, 1975; Webster Univ, MA, 1985; Syracuse Univ, MSW, health care admin, 1992; Univ Fla, PhD, appl & cult anthrop, 2003. **Career:** Beneficial Finance Las Vegas Nev, asst mgr, 1978-79; Los Angeles Temps, Temp employee Cedars Sinai Med Ctr, 1978-79; USAF, squadron cmdr, 1980-89; Salvation Army New York, dir infant mortality, 1990-92; Syracuse Community Health Ctr, dir CMCM, 1991-92; Fla A&M Univ, exten specialist, 1992-, asst prof agr sci & coop exten serv, 2004-; Inst African Am Health, grant & res advisor, 2003-; City Univ New York at Hunter Col, assoc dean Schs Health Professions, 2006-07. **Orgs:** Life mem, Int Black Womens Cong; Am Asn Anthropologists; secy-treas, Asn Black Anthropologists; Nat Asn Advan Colored People, 1992-; Nat Asn Behav Sci, 1999-; Soc Med Anthropologists, 1999-; Inst African Am Health, 2000-; dir, Proj HEALTH, Fla A&M Univ. **Home Addr:** 2877 Alexis Lane, Tallahassee, FL 32308, **Home Phone:** (850)656-2889. **Business Addr:** Assistant Professor, Florida A&M University, Perry Paige Bldg Rm 306C S, Tallahassee, FL 32308-5596, **Business Phone:** (850)599-3383.

### JEFFERSON, ALPHINE WADE

Educator. **Personal:** Born Dec 31, 1950, Caroline County, VA; son of Horace Douglas and Ellie Mae Lewis. **Educ:** Univ Chicago, AB, 1973; Duke Univ, MA, 1975, PhD, 1979. **Career:** Duke Univ, Oral Hist Inst, instr, 1974, Inst Policy Sci Res, assoc & coordr oral interviews, 1974, instr social sci, 1976; Northern Ill Univ, Dept Hist, instr, 1978-79, Ctr Black Studies, fac assoc, 1978-85, asst prof dept hist, 1979-85; Harvard Univ, Andrew W Mellon post doctoral fel, 1982-83; Southern Methodist Univ, vis asst prof hist & interim dir African-Am studies, 1984-85, asst prof hist, 1984-89; Col Wooster, OH, assoc prof hist, 1989-96, prof & chair, 1996-99, Dept Hist, prof, First VPres, 2006-; Randolph-Macon Col, prof hist & black studies. **Orgs:** Reader, Nat Endowment Humanities, 1980-; consult, Dwight Correctional Ctr Humanities Proj, 1980-81; reader, Newberry Libr Inst, Chicago, 1984-; reader, Scott Foresman & Co, 1984-; adv bd, Int Jour Oral Hist, 1986-; bd dir, African Heritage Cult Arts League, 1986-; bd dir, Int Theatrical Arts Soc, 1988-; bd dir, Huang Int Inc, 1988-; African-Am Adv Bd, Dallas Independent Sch Dist, 1988-; Am Hist Asn; Asn Study Afro-Am Life & Hist; first vpres, Oral Hist Asn, vpres & pres, 2006-07; Org Am Historians; Nat Coun Black Studies; Ill Coun Black Studies; Du Sable Mus African Am Hist. **Home Addr:** 530 Forest Creek Dr Apt 6993A, Wooster, OH 44691-1779, **Home Phone:** (330)264-8680. **Business Addr:** Professor, The College of Wooster, 1189 Beall Ave, Wooster, OH 44691, **Business Phone:** (330)263-2455.

### JEFFERSON, DR. ANDREA GREEN

Marketing executive. **Personal:** Born Oct 9, 1946, New Orleans, LA; daughter of Herman and Bernice Johnson; married William J; children: Jamila, Jalila, Jelani, Nailah & Akilah. **Educ:** Southern Univ, BA, 1969; Rutgers Univ, MEd, 1970; Univ New Orleans, EdD, 1979; Harvard Grad Sch Educ Mgt, 1989. **Career:** Southern Univ New Orleans, dir financial aid, 1980-81, vice chancellor stud affairs, 1988-92, asst vpres develop, vpres acad affairs; New Orleans Pub Schs, admin intern, 1982-83, supvr math, 1983-84, instrnl specialist, 1985-86, dir instr/staff develop, 1986-87, dir area I schs, 1987-88; Grambling State Univ, coordr/doctoral prog, 1992-94. **Orgs:** Bd mem, Nat Cou Negro Women, 1984-88; secy, fundraising chair, Links New Orleans Chap, 1986-; Pres's Coun Tulane Univ, 1991-; Women's Nat Dem Club, 1991-; bd mem, Cong Black Caucus Found, 1992-; chair/issue forum chair, Cong Black Caucus Spouses, 1992-95; Stanley S Scott Cancer Res Ctr, 1993; pres, chmn, bd dir, Amistad Res Ctr, 1994-; bd supvr, Southern Univ, 1995-; La State Univ Med Ctr; chair, Baton Rouge Community Col Bd. **Honors/Awds:** Role Model, YWCA, 1993. **Special Achievements:** Publication Board, Initiatives, scholarly journal of the National Assn of Women in Education, 1990-93; The College Student Affairs Journal, 1991-93; Ethnic Women Newsletters, editor, 1992-93; The Changing Faces of Aids, 1993; Congressional Black Caucus Spouses Publication. **Home Addr:** 1922 Marengo St, New Orleans, LA 70115-5416, **Home Phone:** (504)895-1339. **Business Addr:** Chairman, President, Amistad Research Center Inc, 6823 St Charles Ave, New Orleans, LA 70118, **Business Phone:** (504)862-3222.

### JEFFERSON, DR. ARTHUR

School administrator. **Personal:** Born Dec 1, 1938, AL; children: Mark & Michael. **Educ:** Wayne State Univ, BS, 1960, MA, polit sci, 1963, EdD, 1973. **Career:** Detroit Pub Schs, asst regional supt, 1970-71, regional supt, 1971-75, interim gen supt, 1975, gen supt, 1975-90, supt emer, currently; Univ Mich, distinguished vis prof, 1990-95. **Orgs:** Chmn bd, African Am Mus, 1965; Nat Polit Sci Hon Soc; Pi Sigma Alpha; Nat & Mich Couns Soc Studies; Am Mich Asn Sch Adminr; Coun Basic Educ; Metrop Detroit Soc Black Educ Adminr; Nat Alliance Black Sch Educr; Nat Rev Panel Study Sch Desegregation; bd trustee, Wayne State Univ Alumni Asn, 1968-71; Am Civil Lib Union; trustee, Rosa L Parks Scholar Found; Nat Asn Advan Colored People; bd dir, Coun Great City Sch; bd trustee, Detroit Econ Growth Corp; bd dir, Detroit Educ TV Found; bd adv, Detroit Pre-Employ Training Ctr; bd dir, Detroit Teachers Credit Union; Econ Club Detroit; bd dir, United Found; PTA Urban Adv Task Force; chair, bd trustee, Mus African Hist; bd dir, Col Bound Kids Learning Ctr. **Honors/Awds:** DHL, Univ Detroit, 1986. **Special Achievements:** First African American Superintendent of Detroit Public Schools, 1974. **Home Addr:** 8267 Parkstone Pl Suite 202, Naples, FL 34120, **Home Phone:** (239)348-3485. **Business Addr:** Superintendent Emeritus, Detroit Public Schools, 250 E Harbortown Dr Apt 701, Detroit, MI 48207-5016, **Business Phone:** (313)567-1826.

## JEFFERSON, DR. REV. AUSTIN, JR.
Clergy. **Personal:** Born Aiken, SC; married Evelyn Griffin; children: Leonard A, Harry P, Evelyn L & Gene A. **Educ:** Temple Sch Theol, attended 1953; Moody Bible Inst; New Era Sem; Eastern Sem; Univrsal Bible Inst, bible study, 1974. **Career:** Pastor (retired); Abyssinian Baptist Church, interim pastor, 1948-49, pastor, 1948, emer pastor, 1988. **Orgs:** Bd Foreign Missions; chmn, Bd St Home; Nat Baptist Conv; Methodist Christian Coun; adv bd, Eastern Sem; vpres, New Eng MS Conv, 1971. **Business Addr:** Pastor Emeritus, Abyssinian Baptist Church, 4210 Germantown Ave, Philadelphia, PA 19140, **Business Phone:** (215)324-1981.

## JEFFERSON, DR. FREDERICK CARL, JR.
School administrator. **Personal:** Born Dec 30, 1934, New Orleans, LA; married June Greene; children: Crystal, Frederick & Christian. **Educ:** Hunter Col, BS, music, 1957, MA, music, 1959, MA, guid, 1967; Univ Mass, Amherst, MA, EdD, 1981. **Career:** Suny Albany, prog assoc, 1971-73; Univ Rochester, dir educ oppor prog, 1973-76, dir minority stud affairs & assoc dean stud, 1976-85, asst prof, pres, univ & community affairs, dir, urban sch & educ, 1996-99, prof emer, currently; New Perspectives Inc, consult. **Orgs:** Action a Better Community, 1976-; United Way, 1978-; vice chmn & bd dir, PRIS2M, 1978-84; Nat Training Labs; William Warfield Scholar Fund; Primary Ment Health Proj; Austin Steward Prof Soc, 1985-; Round table Educ Chg, 1987-; Urban League Rochester; bd dir, Am Red cross. **Home Addr:** 461 Bonnie Brae Ave, Rochester, NY 14618, **Home Phone:** (716)461-5619. **Business Addr:** Professor Emeritus, University Rochester, 252 Elmwood Ave, Rochester, NY 14611, **Business Phone:** (585)275-2121.

## JEFFERSON, GARY SCOTT
Airline executive, educator. **Personal:** Born Nov 4, 1945, Pittsburgh, PA; son of Willard M; married Beverly J Allen; children: Gary S & Kelly J. **Educ:** Ind Univ Pa, Ind, BA, 1967. **Career:** United Airlines Corp, asst to pres, chief exec officer, Northeast Region, vpres, govt affairs; Golf Mgt Solutions Inc, lead instr, 2008-. **Orgs:** Chicago Urban League; Nat Asn Advan Colored People; Chicago Econ Club; pres, Clinton's Welfare Work Reform Prog; Chicago Coun Race Rels; bd dir, Chicago Coun Urban Affairs, 1999-2000. **Honors/Awds:** Distinguished Alumni Award. **Special Achievements:** Listed as 50 top black executives in corporate America. **Home Addr:** 4 Gregory Lane, Barrington, IL 60010, **Home Phone:** (312)382-6904.

## JEFFERSON, GREG BENTON
Football player, teacher, football coach. **Personal:** Born Aug 31, 1971, Orlando, FL; married Twana; children: Victoria & Samantha. **Educ:** Univ Cent Fla, BS, criminal justice. **Career:** Football player (retired); Philadelphia Eagles, defensive end, 1995-2000; Evans High Sch, teacher, 2006; Orlando Predators, 2006-07; Cypress Creek High Sch; hist teacher & football coach; currently. **Home Addr:** 1673 Glenhaven Cir, PO Box 69, Ocoee, FL 34761-4033. **Business Addr:** Teacher & football coach, Cypress Creek High School, 1101 Bear Crossing Dr, Orlando, FL 32824, **Business Phone:** (407)852-3400.

## JEFFERSON, DR. HORACE LEE
Dentist. **Personal:** Born Oct 10, 1924, Detroit, MI; son of John Lee and Mattie Louis; married Betty Lou Brown; children: Linda, Eric, Judith & Michael. **Educ:** Highland Pk Jr Col, pre dent prog, 1948; Univ Mich Dent Sch Dent, DDS, 1952. **Career:** Dentist (retired); Ford Motor Co, staff, 1946; dentist, 1948-53; Lincoln Motor Car Co, 1952; Herman Keifer City Hosp Detroit, staff sr dentist, 1954-70; pvt pract dentist, 1954-99. **Orgs:** Detroit Dist Dent Soc; Mich Dent Asn; Am Dent Asn, 1953; former pres, Wolverine Dent Soc; Afro-Am Mus Detroit; Alpha Phi Alpha Fraternity; life mem, Nat Asn Advan Colored People; life mem, Detroit Int Afro-Am Mus; life mem, Charles H Wright Mus African Am Hist; bd dir, Delta Dent Plans Mich, 1977-82; Acad Gen Dent. **Honors/Awds:** Clinical Presentation 15th Review, Detroit Dist Dental Soc, 1957; forum presentation Gamma Lambda Chap AOA, 1973. **Home Addr:** , MI.

## JEFFERSON, DR. JOSEPH L. (STEVEN LEVOID JEFFERSON)
Counselor, educator. **Personal:** Born Nov 8, 1940, Pensacola, FL; married Ida C Wedgeworth; children: Eric, Clynita & Steven. **Educ:** Tex Southern Univ, BS, econs, 1968, MA, coun, 1971; Ohio State Univ, PhD, educ develop & counr, 1974. **Career:** Tex Southern Univ, grad fel, 1970-71; Voc Guid Houston, counsr, 1971; Tex Southern Univ, admin asst dean col arts & sci, assoc dir, Off Inst Res, prof coun & asst prof educ currently, prof & chairperson, 1971-2002, Dept counr educ, prof, currently, founder & dir, 1982-; Ohio State Univ, fel. **Orgs:** Am Educ & Res Asn; Phi Delta Kappa; Asn Inst Res; Am Coun Asn; Tex Couns Asn; Kappa Alpha Psi Fraternity; Houston Jr club; Houston Lions Club. **Honors/Awds:** Directory of Distinguished Americans; Community Leaders & Noteworthy Americans. **Special Achievements:** Who's Who Among Black Americans; Who's Who in the South and Southwest, 16th Edition; 12 Publications. **Home Addr:** 13534 Schumann Trl, Sugar Land, TX 77498, **Home Phone:** (281)240-0606. **Business Addr:** Professor of Counseling, Texas Southern University, 3100 Cleburne St, Houston, TX 77004, **Business Phone:** (713)313-7389.

## JEFFERSON, KAREN L.
Librarian. **Personal:** Born Oct 30, 1952, Eglin AFB, FL; daughter of Henry S and Agnes McLean. **Educ:** Howard Univ, Wash, DC, BA, 1974; Atlanta Univ, Atlanta, GA, MSLS, 1975. **Career:** Moorland-Spingarn Res Ctr, Howard Univ, Wash, DC, manuscript librn, 1976-80, sr manuscript librn, 1980-87, cur, 1987-93; Nat Endowment Humanities, Wash, DC, humanities adminr; Robert W Woodruff Libr, Atlanta Univ Ctr, Head Arch & Spec Collections, rec mgr, currently. **Orgs:** Black Caucus ALA, 1972-; Mid Atlantic Region Arch Conf, 1982-; Soc Am Archivists, 1983-; Co-ed, African Am & Third World Archivist Roundtable Newsletter, 1987-93; bd mem, African-Am Educ Arch Proj, 1989-93; Acad Cert Archivists, 1989-. **Home Addr:** 254 Madison St NW, Washington, DC 20011, **Home Phone:** (202)726-5003. **Business Addr:** Head of Archives & Special Collections, Records Manager, Robert W Woodruff Library, 111 James P Brawley Dr SW, Atlanta, GA 30314, **Business Phone:** (404)978-2045.

## JEFFERSON, LINDA
President (organization). **Career:** Burrell Communs Group LLC, sr vpres & dir media serv, 2004-. **Orgs:** Arbitron Inc. **Business Addr:** Senior Vice President, Director of Media Services, Burrell Communications Group LLC, 233 N Michigan Ave Suite 2900, Chicago, IL 60601, **Business Phone:** (312)297-9600.

## JEFFERSON, MARCIA D.
Librarian, educator. **Personal:** Born Jan 2, 1935; daughter of Jacob A Dyer (deceased) and Marjorie Lewis (deceased); married Eugene; children: Denise (Marc Nolan Casper) & Darryl. **Educ:** Brooklyn Col, Brooklyn, NY, BA, 1957; Rutgers Univ Sch Libr Sci, NB, NJ, MLS, 1959; State Univ NY, Stony Brook, NY, MALS, 1987. **Career:** Brooklyn Pub Libr, NY, page & librn trainee, 1954-63; Bayshore & Bright waters Pub Libr, NY, ref librn, 1963-66; Staff-Libr & UST, NY Worlds Fair, 1965; Patchogue-Medford Schs, NY, sch librn, 1966-67; Bayshore & Brightwaters Pub Libr, ref librn, 1969; Suffolk County Community Col, Selden, periodicals librn, 1978, prof, 2001. **Orgs:** SC Libr Asn, 1978; bd trustee, Patchogue-Medford Libr, 1989; Black Caucus & ALA, 1989; vpres, acad div SC Libr Asn; vpres, Data & Story Libr, 1990. **Home Addr:** PO Box 129, Medford, NY 11763.

## JEFFERSON, MARGO
Journalist. **Personal:** Born Oct 17, 1947, Chicago, IL; daughter of Ron and Irma. **Educ:** Univ Chicago Lab Sch; Brandeis Univ, BA; Columbia Univ, MS, jour. **Career:** Rockefeller & Theater Commun Group, fel, 1984; Columbia Univ, instr; NY Univ, instr; Vogue Mag, ed; News week Mag, ed; NY Times, critic, 1993, 2003; Ianna Deveare Smith's Inst Arts & Civic Dialogue, artist-in-residence, 2001; New Sch, assoc prof, writing, currently.Book: Negroland: A Memoir; On Michael Jackson; Roots of Time: a Portrait of African Life and Culture. **Orgs:** Sr fel Nat Arts Journalism Prog, 2002-03. **Business Addr:** Associate Professor, The New School, 72 5th Ave, New York, NY 10011, **Business Phone:** (212)229-5155.

## JEFFERSON, PATRICIA ANN (PAT JEFFERSON)
Appraiser. **Personal:** Born Nov 26, 1951, Richmond County, NC. **Educ:** Augusta Col, BBA, 1973. **Career:** GA Power Co, customer serv rep, 1969-73; Black Stud Union Augusta Col, secy, organizer, 1971-73; Augusta/Richmond Co Human Rels Comn, from admin asst to dir, 1974-81; Augusta Focus Newspaper, gen mgr, 1982-87; Pat Jefferson Realty, Appraisals, cert residential appraiser, 1987-; Jefferson Appraisal Co, cert residential appraiser, currently. **Orgs:** Founder, Eta Theta Zeta Sorority; dir, Spiritualettes, 1974-; Spirit Creek Bapt Ch; bd, Am Red Cross; bd, Cent Savannah River Area BUS League; Nat Asn Real Estate Appraiser; affil, Appraisal Inst; bd mem, Ga Real Estate Appraisers Bd; bd mem, Oper Self Help. **Home Addr:** 3814 Carmichael Rd, Augusta, GA 30906, **Home Phone:** (706)793-7144. **Business Addr:** Certified Residential Appraiser, Jefferson Appraisal Co, 1126 11th St, Augusta, GA 30901, **Business Phone:** (706)722-8430.

## JEFFERSON, REGGIE (REGINALD JIROD JEFFERSON)
Baseball player, athletic coach. **Personal:** Born Sep 25, 1968, Tallahassee, FL; married Kay; children: Shayna, R J, Jannay & Jalen. **Educ:** Univ S Fla, BA, bus admin, 2003. **Career:** Baseball player (retired), athletic coach, executive; Cincinnati Reds, infielder, 1991; Cleveland Indians, 1991-93; Seattle Mariners, 1994; Boston Red Sox, 1995-99; Seibu Lions, 2000; Japanese league, 2000; Tampa Bay Devil Rays, spring training camp, guest instr, 2004; Albuquerque Isotopes, Fla Marlins, hitting coach; Univ S Fla, asst coach, 2005, hitting coach, 2006; Reynolds Sports mgt, dir e coast opers, 2013-. **Special Achievements:** Eighth in American League in Batting Average (.319), 1997. **Business Addr:** Hitting Coach, University of South Florida, 4202 E Fowler Ave, Tampa, FL 33620, **Business Phone:** (813)974-2011.

## JEFFERSON, ROBERT R.
Manager, government official. **Personal:** Born Sep 21, 1932, Lexington, KY; married Katie E Scott; children: Robert Jr & Stanley. **Educ:** Ky State Col, BA, hist, polit sci, biol, 1967, MPA, mgt & equal opportunity, 1973; Nat Judicial Col, Reno Nev, cert, adminstrative law, fair hearing gen session, 1984. **Career:** Government official (retired); US Pub Health Hosp, var positions, 1957-74; IBM, assembler, 1959; US Bur Prisons, sr case mgr, 1974-83; Jefferson Affirmative Action Consultancy, consult, 1974-88; Lexington Fayette Human Rights Comn, actg exec dir, 1986-87; Lexington Fayette Urban County, coun mem, 1988-2000. **Orgs:** Chmn, Human Rights Comn, 1969-83; comt organizer, Whitney Young Sickle Cell Ctr, 1973-74; actg exec dir, Urban Co Human Rights Comn, Lexington, 1974; past dist rep & mem, Supreme Coun; Black & Williams Community Ctr; Nat Conf Christians & Jews; LFUC Urban League, CORE, Bluegrass Black Bus Asn, Agency Exec Forum; bd mem, KY League Cities, 1990-2000; bd mem, Nat League Cities, 1993-95. **Honors/Awds:** Minority Affairs Community Distinguished Services, 1973; Honorary Doctorate Degree, Micro City Univ, 1975; Brotherhood Award, NCCJ, 1979; Outstanding Service Award, Lima Dirve Seventh Day Adventist Church, 1981; Distinguished Service Award, KY State Univ, 1981; Outstanding Service Award, LFUCG Human Rights Comn, 1985; Distinguished Service Award, Micro City Govt, 1985; Several Omega Psi Phi Fraternal Awards; Outstanding Achievement in Fair Housing Award for individual, 2007. **Home Addr:** 955 Effie Rd, Lexington, KY 40511, **Home Phone:** (859)252-1203.

## JEFFERSON, ROLAND SPRATLIN
Physician, writer. **Personal:** Born May 16, 1939, Washington, DC; son of Bernard S and Devonia H Spratlin; married Melanie L Moore; children: Roland Jr, Rodney Earl, Shannon Devonia & Royce Bernard. **Educ:** Univ S CA, BA, anthrop, 1961; Howard Univ, MD, 1965; GA State Med Lic, 1965-; CA State Med Lic, 1966-. **Career:** Metrop State Hosp, intern, 1965-66; Camarillo State Hosp, resident, Psychiat, 1967-69; Martin L King, Jr Hosp, assoc prof, 1972-75; Dept Rehab, consult, 1972-78; Watts Health Found, staff psychiatrist, 1973-80; Asn Black Motion Picture & TV Producers, pres/founding mem, 1980-81; pvt pract physician. **Orgs:** Writers Guild Am W; Nat Med Asn; bd dir, Am Sickle Cell Found, 1973-76; bd adv Brockman Gallery, 1976-78. **Honors/Awds:** Grassroots Award, Sons Watts, 1977; Golden Quill Award, Abffriham Found, 1977; Nat Asn Advan Colored People Image Award, 13th Annual, Nat Asn Advan Colored People Image Awards, 1980; Award Merit Black Am Cinema Soc, 1989; Special DRRs Award, 24th Annual Nat Asn Advan Colored People Image Awards, 1992; Producer, Writer, Dir, Feature Film "Perfume", 1989. **Special Achievements:** First Place, Film Drama Black Filmmakers Hall of Fame 1980; author of 4 novels, The School on 103rd Street (1976), A Card for the Players (1978), 559 to Damascus (1985), Damaged Goods (2003), One Night Stand (2006), White Coat Fever (2009). **Business Addr:** Physician, Private Practitioner, 3870 Crenshaw Blvd Suite 215, Los Angeles, CA 90008-1828, **Business Phone:** (323)299-4508.

## JEFFERSON, SHAWN (VANCHI LASHAWN JEFFERSON)
Football player, football coach, business owner. **Personal:** Born Feb 22, 1969, Jacksonville, FL. **Educ:** Univ Cent Fla, bus admin. **Career:** Football player (retired), football coach, adminr; San Diego Chargers, wide receiver, 1991-95; New Eng Patriots, wide receiver, 1996-99; Mellon Bank, internship, 1998; Atlanta Falcons, wide receiver, 2000-02; Detroit Lions, wide receiver, 2003, coaching intern, 2005-06, offensive asst coach, 2006-07, asst wide receivers coach, 2007, wide receivers coach, 2008-; Tenn Titans, coach, 2013-; Any Occasion Catering, co-owner, currently; Miami Dolphins, wide receivers coach, currently. **Orgs:** Ducks Unlimited. **Honors/Awds:** Super Bowl. **Business Addr:** Co-Owner, Any Occasion Catering, 1275 Powers Ferry Rd Suite 260, Marietta, GA 30067, **Business Phone:** (770)952-8050.

## JEFFERSON, STEVEN LEVOID. See JEFFERSON, DR. JOSEPH L.

## JEFFERSON, VANCHI LASHAWN. See JEFFERSON, SHAWN.

## JEFFERSON, HON. WALLACE BERNARD
Lawyer, judge. **Personal:** Born Jul 22, 1963; son of William D and Joyce; married Rhonda J; children: William Douglas, Samuel Lewis & Michael Andrew. **Educ:** Univ Mich, BA, polit philos, 1985; Univ Tex Sch Law, JD, 1988; Tex Bd Legal Specialization, cert, civil appellate law. **Career:** Justice (retired); Groce, Locke & Hebdon Inc, atty, 1988-91, appelate sect, 1989; Tom Crofts & Sharon Callaway, owner, 1991; Am Law Inst, 2001; Waco City Coun, fel; Supreme Ct, Austin TX, US atty gen, 2001-03, chief justice, 2004-13; ALI coun, 2011; Alexander Dubose Jefferson Townsend LLP, partner, 2013-. **Orgs:** Pres, San Antonio Bar Asn, 1998-99; pres, William S Sessions Am Inn Ct, 1999; advs comm, Supreme Ct Tex; Tex State Comn Judicial Conduct; dir, San Antonio Pub Libr Found; Am Bar Asn; chair, host comm, Fifth Circuit Judicial Conf, 2000; vpres, pres, Asn Chief Justices, 2008-; Pillars Found, N Side Independent Sch; Am Law Inst; San Antonio Young Lawyers Asn; bd trustee, Univ Tex Sch Law, Law Sch Found, 2012-; pres, Conf Chief Justices. **Honors/Awds:** Forty Under 40 Rising Star, San Antonio Bus Jour, 1996; Outstanding Young Lawyer, San Antonio Young Lawyers Asn, 1997; 40 Under 40 Rising Star, Tex Lawyer, 2001; Distinguished Alumnus Award, James Madison College, 2002; Outstanding Alumnus Award, Univ Tex Sch Law, 2005; Outstanding Alumnus Award, Mich State Univ, 2007; Robert L. Hainsworth Outstanding Service Award, Houston Lawyer's Asn, 2007; Morton A. Brody Distinguished Judicial Service Award, 2012. **Special Achievements:** National recognition for his speech celebrating Law Day, American Bar Association, 2001; First African American Chief Justice of the Supreme Court of Texas, 2004. **Business Addr:** Board of Trustee, University of Texas, Law School Foundation, Austin, TX 78705, **Business Phone:** (512)471-5151.

## JEFFERSON, HON. WILLIAM JENNINGS
**Personal:** Born Mar 14, 1947, Lake Providence, LA; son of Mose and Angeline Harris; married Andrea Green; children: Jamila Efuru, Jalila Eshe, Jelani, Nailah & Akilah. **Educ:** Southern Univ A& M Col, Baton Rouge, LA, BA, eng & polit sci, 1969; Harvard Univ, Cambridge, MA, JD, 1972; Georgetown Law Ctr, LLM, 1996. **Career:** US Ct Appeals, 5th Circuit, Judge Alvin B Rubin, judicial clerk, 1972-73; US Sen J Bennett Johnston, Wash, DC, legis asst, 1973-75; Jefferson, Bryan & Gray, New Orleans, La, founding partner, 1976; La State Senate, mem, 1979-90; Baton Rouge, La, mem, 1980-90; US House Reps, Wash, DC, Second Dist La, mem, 1991-2009, Cong 102nd, 1991-93, Cong 103rd, 1993-95, Cong 104th, 1995-97, Cong 105th, 1997-99, Cong 106th, 1999-2001, Cong 107th, 2001-03, Cong 108th, 2003-05, Cong 109th, 2005-07, Cong 110th, 2007-09. **Orgs:** La Bar Asn; Am Bar Asn; Nat Bar Asn; DC Bar Asn; chair, Cong Black Caucus Found, 2001-; sr mem, Ways & Means Comt; House Comt Budget; co chair, Africa Trade & Investment Caucus; Cong Caucus Brazil & Nigeria; trustee, Greater St Stephen Full Gospel Church; Southern Univ Found Bd; Urban League Greater New Orleans. **Home Addr:** 1922 Marengo St, New Orleans, LA 70115-5416, **Home Phone:** (504)895-4339.

## JEFFERSON-BULLOCK, JALILA ESHE
Lawyer, association executive. **Personal:** Born Jan 1, 1975, New Orleans, LA; daughter of William J; married Torey; children: Torey Jr. **Educ:** Harvard Col, BA, Eng; Univ Chicago, MA, humanities; Harvard Law, JD. **Career:** LA Dist 91, atty & state rep, 2004-07; Murray Law Firm, Atty, currently; Phoenix Sch Law, asst prof; Ariz Summit Law Sch, asst prof, 2011-. **Orgs:** LA State Bar Asn; Am Bar Asn; Nat Bar Asn; New Orleans Bar Asn; bd dir, REAL; vpres, CHESS; bd dir,

Lindy's Pl; bd dir, CASA; bd dir, Bks You; bd dir, New Orleans Jazz Orchestra; Adv Comt, Dress Success; Adv Comt, WOW Home Ownership Prog; Stud Nat Community. **Honors/Awds:** Servant of the Year, Nat Coun Negro Women. **Home Addr:** 3423 E Desert Trumpet Rd, Phoenix, AZ 85044-7032, **Home Phone:** (504)457-2798. **Business Addr:** Assistant Professor, Arizona Summit Law School, 1 N Central Ave, Phoenix, AZ 85004, **Business Phone:** (602)682-6904.

### JEFFERSON-FORD, CHARMAIN
Law enforcement officer. **Personal:** Born Oct 2, 1963, Detroit, MI; daughter of Walter L Patton and Hercules; children: Krysten N. **Educ:** Wayne State Univ, Detroit, MI, attended 1987. **Career:** Detroit Pub Schs, Detroit, Mich, clerk, 1978-81; Hudsons Dept Store, Cetroit, Mich, model, 1979-81; Grand Value Pharm, Detroit, Mich, pharm teacher, 1981-88; City Southfield, Southfield, Mich, police officer, 1988-; Drug Abuse Resistance Educ, officer, 1991-. **Orgs:** Pres, Future Homemakers Am, 1980-81. **Home Addr:** 27070 Pebblebrook St, Southfield, MI 48034, **Home Phone:** (248)350-2354. **Business Addr:** Police Officer, City of Southfield Police Department, 26000 Evergreen Rd, Southfield, MI 48037-2055, **Business Phone:** (248)796-5500.

### JEFFERSON-JENKINS, DR. CAROLYN
High school principal, president (government), administrator. **Personal:** Born Sep 19, 1952, Cleveland, OH; daughter of James and Ruby; married Kenneth B Jenkins Sr. **Educ:** Western Col Women, BA, social sci & educ, 1974; John Carroll Univ, MEd, admin & supv, 1981; Kent State Univ, EdS, 1985; Cleveland State Univ, PhD, urban educ & admin, 1991. **Career:** Publi sch, teacher & adminr, 1974; Cleveland Heights, Univ Heights Schs, prin, 1993-95; Jr Achievement Inc, vpres, 1996-98; League Women Voters, chair & pres, 1998-2002; Hunt Inst, dir prog & commun. **Orgs:** Pres, Bus & Prof Women Pikes Peak Region, 1997-98; Phi Delta Kappa; Asn Supv & Curric Develop; Nat Asn Sec Sch Prin; Nat Coun Social Studies; Adv Comn, Citizens Proj Colo Springs; Aspen Inst, Democracy & Citizenship Proj; bd, Howard Univ, Women Ambassadors Prog; Colo Judicial Inst; sr assoc, Nat Ctr Educ & Econ; prof develop coordr, Nat Inst Urban Sch Improv; Nat Ctr Culturally Responsive Educ Systs. **Honors/Awds:** Ivy Young Willis Award, Cabrini Col, 1999; BPW Woman of the Year, Pikes Peak, 1998; Good Gonernment Volunteer Award, Carrie Chapman Catt, 1995; Whos Who Among Successful African-Americans; Whos Who in American Education; Outstanding Young Woman in America Award; Civic Leadership Award, Nat Coalition Black Civic Participation; Distinguished Alumni Award, Civic Leadership Cleveland State Univ; Good Housekeeping Award for Women in Government; National Women's Hall of Fame. **Special Achievements:** Author: The Road to Black Suffrage and One Man One Vote: The History of the African-American Vote in the United States; Current Issues in Global Education; First African American woman to head the League of Women Voters of the United States. **Home Addr:** 95 Woodbridge Dr, Colorado Springs, CO 80908, **Home Phone:** (719)527-9890.

### JEFFERSON-MOSS, CAROLYN
Government official. **Personal:** Born Sep 20, 1945, Washington, DC; married Alfred Jeffrey Moss. **Educ:** Howard Univ, BA, polit sci, 1970, MA, pub admin, 1974. **Career:** Reps C Diggs & A Hawkins, cong Black caucus legis dir, 1970-71; Exotech Systs Inc, sr asso, proj dir, 1971-74; Black Group Inc, sr assoc, dir surv res, 1974-75; Mark Battle Assoc Inc, sr assoc dir mkt, surv res div, 1975-78; Dept Com, dep to asst secy cong affairs, 1978; Va Secy Admin; Fairfax County, dir State & Local Affairs; Common Wealth Va, Dom Resources, dir corp pub policy, 2005-; Capitol Sq Preserv Coun, legis, gov, currently. **Orgs:** Alpha Kappa Alpha Inc, 1968; fel Advan Studies Polit Sci Ford Found Joint Ctr Polit Studies, 1970-71; Met Dem Women's Club, 1974; Va Pub Buildings Bd. **Home Addr:** 1800 Old Meadow Rd, Mc Lean, VA 22102. **Business Addr:** Director of Corporate Public Policy, Common Wealth of Virgnia, 1111 E Main St Suite 901, Richmond, VA 23219, **Business Phone:** (804)786-4718.

**JEFFERY, VONETTA.** See FLOWERS, VONETTA.

### JEFFREY, RONNALD JAMES
Writer, lecturer. **Personal:** Born Mar 11, 1949, Cheyenne, WY; son of John Thomas and Lillian Leola Carter; married Marilyn Mansell; children: Keeya & Kaylee. **Educ:** Chadron State Col, BA, sociol & anthrop, 1972; Univ Northern Colo, MA, communs, 1976. **Career:** Off Youth Alternatives, dir, Ct Serv, 1971-; Laramie County Community Col, instr, 1980; Univ Wyo, instr; Cheyenne Munic Ct, Juv Ct, judge, currently. **Orgs:** Lect, 1975-; consult, 1975-; bd mem, Cheyenne Child Care Ctrs, Nat Asn Advan Colored People, 1984; bd mem, Juv Justice Adv Bd, 1984-; pres, Wy Asn Marriage & Family Therapist, 1986-88; dir Rocky Mountain Fed Bank, 1988-89; clin mem, Am Asn Marriage & family Ther. **Honors/Awds:** George Washington Honor Medal, Freedom Found, 1977; Distinguished Service Award, Cheyenne Jaycees, 1978; Jefferson Award, Am Ins Pub Serv, 1980; Phi Delta Kappa Award, Serv Educ, 1986; Craig & Susan Thomas Foundation Leadership Award, 2011. **Special Achievements:** Co-author: "A Guide for the Family Therapist"; "COT Hero"; Torch bearer for Olympic Games, 1996. **Home Addr:** 8812 Cowpoke Rd, Cheyenne, WY 82009-1254, **Home Phone:** (307)634-6515. **Business Addr:** Director, Office of Youth Alternatives, 1328 Talbot Ct, Cheyenne, WY 82001, **Business Phone:** (307)637-6480.

### JEFFREYS, JOHN H.
Management consultant. **Personal:** Born Mar 27, 1940, Youngsville, NC; married Constance Little; children: Gregory & Alvin. **Educ:** Shaw Univ, AB, sociol, 1962; Univ Ga, MA, pub admin, 1975, ABD, DPA, 1985. **Career:** Rowan County, Salisbury, NC, Anti Poverty Prog, Neighborhood Serv Ctr, dir, 1964-67; City Hickory, dir human resources, 1967-70; US Adv Comn Intergovernmental Rels, intern, 1969-70; Clarke County, comnr, 1982-90; Univ Carl Vinson Inst; Univ Ga, Fanning Inst Leadership, instr, leadership develop specialist, 1994, sr pub serv assoc & sr fanning fel emer. **Orgs:** Consult, Int Asn City Mgrs, 1983; Pub Safety Personnel, St Croix, 1984; Am Soc Training & Develop, 1984; parliamentarian, Ga Asn Black Elected Off, 1984; Athens Clarke County, chief elected officer, 1994.pub safety & criminal justice comn, Nat Asn Counties; charter mem, Nat Asn Blacks Criminal Justice; chmn, Clarke County Dem Comt; pres, Asn County Commissioners Ga; life mem, Univ Ga; coun mem, Univ Ga Retirees Asn; Ebenezer Baptist Church W; facilitator, Nat Asn Community Leadership USA; nat adv bd, Nat Leadership Forum, Colo chap. **Honors/Awds:** Man of the Year, Phi Beta Sigma Delta Mu Sigma Chap, 1977, 1981 & 1983; Outstanding Management Instructor, Ga Clerks Asn, 1983; Walter Barnard Hill Award, 1998-99. **Special Achievements:** First Black elected in the Clarke County commissioner, Ga, 1982; First Black intern in US Advisory Commisson Intergovernmental Relations. **Home Addr:** 140 Jones Dr, Athens, GA 30606-3251, **Home Phone:** (706)549-6033. **Business Addr:** Life Member, University of Georgia, 286 Oconee St Suite 200N, Athens, GA 30602-1999, **Business Phone:** (706)542-3000.

### JEFFRIES, FRAN M.
Journalist. **Personal:** Born Jul 21, 1959, Yanceyville, NC; daughter of William and Elizabeth; married Lawrence Muhammed. **Educ:** Am Univ, BA, 1982; Ind Univ, MA, 1984. **Career:** Post-Tribune, Gary Ind, reporter, 1984-87; Louisville Courier-J, suburban ed, 1994-; Courier-Jour, copy ed, reporter, asst city ed, neighborhoods ed, suburbun ed, 1996-; USA TODAY, loaner to businesssection, 1998; Sun-Sentinel, S Fl, educ ed, 1998-2005; Atlanta J Const, features ed, 2005-, digital producer, 2008-. **Orgs:** Nat Asn Black Journalist; Soc Prof Journalists; Louisville Asn Black Journalist. **Home Addr:** 7929 Kismet St, Miramar, FL 33023-5814, **Home Phone:** (954)961-6863. **Business Addr:** Features Editor, Atlanta Journal-Constitution, 72 Marietta St NW, Atlanta, GA 30303, **Business Phone:** (404)526-5384.

### JEFFRIES, REAR ADM. FREDDIE L.
Engineer, executive director. **Personal:** Born Apr 12, 1939, Gates, TN; son of Freddie R and Lora (deceased); married Helen A Ginn; children: Elizabeth, Terri, Joyce, Ivy & Lee. **Educ:** Tenn State Univ, BSCE, 1961; Univ Mich, MSE, 1970; Indust Col Armed Forces, dipl, 1984; George Washington Univ, MPA, 1984. **Career:** Nat Oceanic & Atmospheric Admin, Rear Admin; United S Dept Com, Coast & Geod Surv, engr, environ sci serv admin engr; Soc Am Mil Engrs, dir, 1970; Nat Oceanic & Atmospheric Admin, Atlantic Marine Ctr, dir, 1999. **Orgs:** Am Cong Surv & Mapping; Am Soc Photogram, 1961-73. **Honors/Awds:** Unit Citations, 1974, 1988; Karo Award, 1979; Special Achievement Awards, 1986, 1987; Distinguished Grad Award, Tenn State Univ, 1991. **Home Addr:** 4101 Taunton Dr, Beltsville, MD 20705-2857, **Home Phone:** (301)595-3825.

### JEFFRIES, GREG (GREGORY LEMONT JEFFRIES)
Executive, football player. **Personal:** Born Oct 16, 1971, High Point, NC. **Educ:** Univ Va, commun, 1993. **Career:** Football player (retired); Detroit Lions, defensive back, 1993-99; Miami Dolphins, defensive back, 1999-2001; Miami Dolphins, col scout, 2001-03; Legg Mason, financial advisor, 2003-05; Wachovia, A Wells Fargo Co, Personal Banker, 2005-07; UBS, Financial Advisor, 2007-09; Edward Jones, Financial Advisor, 2009-11; WSFS Bank, Advisor-PBIII LRA, 2011-14; PNC Financial Serv, 2014-. **Special Achievements:** Film: 1993 NFL Draft, 1993. **Home Addr:** 160 Bonaventure Blvd Apt 202, Weston, FL 33326-1417. **Business Addr:** 300 Fifth Ave, Pittsburgh, PA 15222, **Business Phone:** (412)762-2000.

### JEFFRIES, HAKEEM
State government official, lawyer. **Personal:** Born Aug 4, 1970, Crown Heights, NY; married Kennisandra Arciniegas; children: Jeremiah & Joshua. **Educ:** State Univ NY, Binghamton, BS, polit Sci, 1992; Georgetown Univ, MA, pub policy, 1994; NY Univ Sch Law, JD, 1997. **Career:** Paul, Weiss, Rifkind, Wharton & Garrison LLP, asst litigator, atty-at-Law, 1997-2004; US Dist Ct Southern Dist New York, law clerk, 1997-98; CBS/Viacom, litigation coun, 2004-06; NY Assembly 57th Dist, assembly mem, 2007-12; US House Representatives NY 8th dist, congressman, 2013-. **Orgs:** Mem, Progressive Asn Polit Action (PAPA); NY Bar Asn, Mem; Budget Comt; Judiciary Comt; Subcomt Courts, Intellectual Property & Internet Comt; Subcomt Regulatory Reform, Com & Antitrust Law Comt. **Honors/Awds:** "The Root" Magazine, The Root 100 Honorees, 2013. **Business Addr:** Congressman, US House Representatives New York 8th District, 1607 Longworth House Office Bldg, Washington, DC 20515, **Business Phone:** (202)225-5936.

### JEFFRIES, DR. LEONARD, JR.
Educator. **Personal:** Born Jan 19, 1937, Newark, NJ; son of Leonard and Neola J; married Rosalind Robinson. **Educ:** Lafayette Col, BA, 1959; Columbia Univ, MA, 1965, PhD, 1971. **Career:** Oper Crossroads Africa, Community Develop Proj, group leader, 1962-65; W Africa, prog coordr, 1965-69; NY State Comn Educ, Task Force Deficiency Correction Curric Regarding People Color, consult & mem; City Col City Univ New York, instr polit sci, 1969-71, Dept African Am Studies, chmn, 1972-92, prof black studies, currently; San Jose State Col, prof black studies, 1971-72. **Orgs:** African Heritage Studies Asn; Nat Black United Front; founding dir, Nat Coun Black Studies, 1975-76; int exec dir, Orgn Afro-Am Unity; founding dir, vpres & pres, Asn Study Class African Civilizations; int pres, World African Diaspora Union, currently. **Business Addr:** Professor of Black Studies, City College of the City University of New York, 160 Convent Ave, New York, NY 10031, **Business Phone:** (212)650-8651.

### JEFFRIES, DR. ROSALIND ROBINSON (NANA ESSIE ABIBIO)
Sculptor, artist, educator. **Personal:** Born Jun 24, 1936, New York, NY; daughter of Edmond Felix Robinson and Mary Gibson; married Leonard Jr. **Educ:** Hunter Col, BA, 1963; Columbia Univ, MA, 1968; Yale Univ, PhD, 1990. **Career:** US Govt USIS, Abidjan & Ivory Coast, W Africa, dir exhib, 1965-66, Group Seminars, Africa, co-leader, 1966-72; Brooklyn Mus, lectr, 1969; San Jose St Univ, asst prof, 1969-72; City Univ New York, art hist, artist & prof, 1972-; African Am Hist & Cult Mus, cur; Bishop's Bible Col Church God Christ, New York, NY, asst prof, 1991; Jersey City Univ, Jersey City, asst prof, currently; Sch Visual Arts, New York, NY, teaching fac, currently; Metrop Mus Art, New York; Ramapo Col, Arthur Schomburg fac. **Orgs:** Col Arts Asn; Calif St Art Historians; Nat Conf Artists; bd dir, Kem-Were Sci Consortium, 1986-; dir art & cult, Asn Study African Class Civilizations, 1986-; Blacklight fel Black Presence Bible, 1991-; Nat Coun Black Studies. **Honors/Awds:** Negro Music & Art Award, 1969; Arts Achievement Award, Pres Senegal, 1986; Paramount Chief Nana Conduah VI, 1986; Enstooled Queen Mother, Ashantehene Traditional Govt Ghana, 1988; Q Kingdom Award, United Nations, 1998; International Black Women Congress Award, 1999. **Special Achievements:** Essays appear in books Black Women in Antiquity & African American History, 2001; Instrumental in Production of Class Room Textbook "African History: A Journey of Liberation", Peoples Publishing Group, Saddle Brook, NJ, 2001. **Home Addr:** 96 Schoonmaker Rd, Teaneck, NJ 07666-6013, **Home Phone:** (201)837-1355. **Business Addr:** Teaching Faculty, School of Visual Arts, 209 E 23rd St, New York, NY 10010-3994, **Business Phone:** (212)592-2000.

### JELLS, DIETRICH DAVIS
Football player. **Personal:** Born Apr 11, 1972, Brooklyn, NY. **Educ:** Univ Pittsburgh, grad. **Career:** Football player (retired); New Eng Patriots, 1997, wide receiver, 1996; Philadelphia Eagles, 1998, wide receiver, 1999.

### JEMISON, AJ D. (AJ JEMISON COFFEE)
Executive. **Educ:** Univ Tulsa; Univ Phoenix, BA, mkt; Booker T Wash High Sch, dipl bus & mkt, 1975; Tulsa Community Col, AA, mkt, 1983; Davenport Univ, mgt, 1998. **Career:** Fairlane Town Ctr, gen mgr; Tampa, Fla mall, mgr; Dillard's Dept Store, sales assoc, 1972-80; Tulsa Urban League, admin asst, 1980-82; Richardson Realty Inc, sales admin asst, 1982; Williams Realty Corp, admin asst, 1982-83, property mgr, 1983-86; The Portman Co, Peachtree Ctr, construct coordr, 1987-89; Intershop Real Estate Serv, property mgr, 1989-91; Corp Property Investors, gen mgr, 1991-93; The Taubman Co, gen mgr, 1993-2007; Beverly Ctr, gen mgr, 2005-07; Simon Property Group-Phipps Plaza, mall mgr, 2007-08, Town Ctr at Aurora, gen mgr, 2008-10, Cottonwood Mall & ABQ Uptown, area mall mgr, 2010-12, Oak Ct Mall, gen mgr, 2012-14; Fed Realty Investment Trust, gen mgr, 2014-. **Orgs:** Vol, Hillborough Comn Status Women; bd mem, Girl Scouts Suncoast Coun; HARC; bd mem, Fla State Fair Authority; Tampa Org Black Affairs; Tampa Bay Conv & Visitors Bur; Int Coun Shopping Centers, 1984-2010; Leadership Tulsa, 1986; W End Com Develop Assn, 1990-91; Aurora Gang Task Force, City Aurora, Co, 1992-93; Leadership Aurora, 1992-93; Leadership Detroit, 1996-2000; Westshore Alliance, 2000-05; Leadership Westshore, 2001; Wedu Fla W Coast Pub Broadcasting, 2002-03; Girl Scouts Suncoast Coun, 2002-04; Lowry Pk Zoo, 2002-04; Tampa Bay Cvb, 2002-04; C's Home, 2002-05; Tampa Orgn Black Affairs, 2002-05; Tampa Chamber Com, 2002-06; Buffalo Soldiers Motorcycle Club, 2003-; Hillsborough City Comn Status Women, 2003-05; Tampa Bay Illus, 2004; Leadership Tampa, 2004-05; nat vpres, Divas A Cure, 2006-; Aurora Chamber Com, 2008-10; Buffalo Soldiers Rocky Mountains Horse Cavalry, 2009; Albuquerque Chamber Com, 2010-. **Business Addr:** General Manager, Simon Property Group, 225 W Wash St, Indianapolis, IN 46204, **Business Phone:** (317)636-1600.

### JEMISON, DR. MAE CAROL
Astronaut, physician, educator. **Personal:** Born Oct 17, 1956, Decatur, AL; daughter of Charlie and Dorothy Green. **Educ:** Stanford Univ CA, BChE, African & African Am studies, 1977; Cornell Univ, MD, 1981. **Career:** Univ SC Med Ctr, Los Angeles, intern, 1982; Peace Corps W Africa, staff doctor, 1983-85; CIGNA Health Plans CA, gen practr, 1985-87; Nat Aeronaut & Space Admin, astronaut, 1987-93; Dartmouth Col, Montgomery fel, 1993, adj prof, currently; Jemison Group, founder & pres, 1993-; Discovery Channel, World Wonder ser, host & tech consult, 1994-95; Jemison Inst Advan Technol, dir, 1995-2002; Cornell Univ, prof; Dartmouth Col, prof, 1995-2002; BioSentient Corp, founder, chief exec officer & pres, 1999-; Earth We Share, founder. **Orgs:** Bd dir, Scholastic Inc; bd dir, Keystone Ctr; bd dir, Nat Urban League; bd dir, Gen-Probe Inc; AAAS; Houston's UNICEF; Aspen Inst; dir, Valspar Corp; Am Chem Soc; Asn Space Explorers; Alpha Kappa Alpha Sorority; World Sickle Cell Found; founder & chair, 1990-92; Dorothy Jemison Found Excellence; Nat Inst Sci Inst Med. **Honors/Awds:** Essence Award, Essence Mag, 1988; Gamma Sigma Gamma Woman of the Year, 1990; ScD, Lincoln Univ, 1991; DHL, Winston Salem Col, NC, 1991; Du Sable Museum Award, 1992; Mae C Jemison Academy, named in honor, 1992; Johnson Publications Black Achievement Trailblazers Award, 1992; National Women's Hall of Fame, 1993; Kilby Science Award, 1993; Turner Trumpet Award, 1993; selected as one of the top seven women leaders in a Presidential Ballot Nat straw poll conducted by The White House Project, 1999; Tribute to a African American Award, Nat Conf Black Mayors, 2003; Ford Freedom Award Scholar, 2003; Intrepid Award, Nat Orgn girls, 2003; International Space Hall of Fame, 2004; Rotary Club Chicago's ROTARY/One Award; Doctor Humanities, Princeton Univ, 2000; Doctor of Science, Wilson Col, 2005; Doctor of Science, Dartmouth Col, 2006; Doctor of Engineering, Harvey Mudd Col, 2007; Doctor of Engineering, Rensselaer Polytech Inst, 2007; Doctor of Humanities, DePaul Univ, 2008; Doctor of Engineering, Polytech Inst New York Univ, 2009; NASA Space Flight Medal; Rachel Carson Award, Nat Audubon Soc, 2005. **Special Achievements:** First African American female to enter into space, September 12, 1992; listed in "50 Most Beautiful People in the World" by People magazine, 1993; appeared in the PBS documentary, "African American Lives", 2006; Television: Star Trek: The Next Generation, actress. **Home Addr:** , Houston, TX. **Business Addr:** President, Founder, The Jemison Group, PO Box 591455, Houston, TX 77259-1455, **Business Phone:** (281)486-7918.

### JEMMOTT, HENSLEY B.
Manager, executive. **Personal:** Born Mar 14, 1947, New York, NY; son of Hensley Barton and Alice Lucille Lee; married Lynn Hooper; children: Hensley & Dara. **Educ:** Syracuse Univ, BA, 1968; Columbia Univ, MBA, 1973. **Career:** Squibb Corp, financial analyst, 1973-78; Lederle, prod mgr, 1975-80; Am Stand, sr financial anal, 1978-79; Am Cyanamid Co, Am Far E Div, mgr planning, 1979-81; Lederle Int, mgr mkt res, 1981-91; Wm Douglas McAdams Inc, vpres, acct supvr, 1991-93; Torre Lazur McCann, vpres, supvr, 1993-94; UniWorld Group Inc, mgt supv, mgt supvr, 1994-2003; DiversityInc Advert, prin, 2003-04; Am Cyanamid Co, prod mgr; H. B. Jemmott Assocs, consult, 2004-07; VanguardComm, Client Serv, sr vpres, 2007-. **Orgs:** Bd dir, Urban

League Manhattan, 1977-79; bd dir, Am Lung Asn, NJ, 1983-85, dir, 1984-87; Omega Psi Phi. **Home Addr:** 947 Columbus Dr, Teaneck, NJ 07666, **Home Phone:** (201)833-9209. **Business Addr:** Senior Vice President, VanguardComm, 2 Disbrow Ct 3rd Fl, East Brunswick, NJ 08816, **Business Phone:** (732)246-0340.

## JENIFER, DR. FRANKLYN GREEN

Executive, college president. **Personal:** Born Mar 26, 1939, Washington, DC; son of Joseph and Mary Green; married Alfleda; children: Brenda, Tracey & Ivan. **Educ:** Howard Univ, BS, biol, 1962, MS, microbiol, 1965; Univ Md, PhD, microbiol, 1970. **Career:** Educator, executive (retired); Libr Cong, messenger, 1957-58; U.S. Dept Agr, MD, plant pathologist, 1963-70; Livingston Col, Rutgers Univ, asst prof biol, 1970, 1976-79, Biol Dept, chairperson, 1974-77; Rutgers Univ, Newark, NJ, prof biol, 1970-79, assoc provost, 1977-79; NJ Dept Higher Ed, Trenton, NJ, vice chancellor, 1979-86; Mass Bd Regents Higher Ed, chancellor, 1986-90; Howard Univ, pres, 1990-94; Univ Tex, pres, 1994-2005. **Orgs:** Texaco, 1993-2000; Bd dir, Chevron Texaco Inc, 2000-05; Chevron, 2005-11; bd dir, United Way Metrop Dallas; monitoring comt mem, La Desegregation Settlement; bd trustee, Univ Res Asn Inc; Dallas Citizens Coun; bd dir, N Tex Comn; bd trustee, Tex Health Res Inst; Dallas Citizens Coun, Greater Dallas Chamber Com; Adv Coun Jacob's Ladder; Dallas Ctr Performing Arts Pres Adv Coun; Monitoring Comn La Desegregation Agreement; chair, Am Coun Educ; Am AsnAdvan Sci; Am Socs Microbiol; Greater Dallas Chamber Com; Boy Scouts Am; bd trustee, Fairleigh Dickinson Univ, 2011-14. **Honors/Awds:** Honary LLD, Babson Col, 1990; Honary LLD, Mount Holyoke Col, 1990; Honary DHL, Univ Med & Dentistry NJ, 1989; Honary Doctor of Education, Wheelock Col, 1990; Honorary Doctor of Science, Bowdoin Col, 1992; LLD, Univ Mass, Amherst, 1992; DHL, Kean Col, NJ, 1992; Honorary Doctor Science, Essex County Community Col, 1992. **Home Addr:** 6809 Briar Cove Dr, Dallas, TX 75240.

## JENKINS, ADAM, JR.

Executive, manager. **Personal:** Born Sep 9, 1942, North Carrollton, MS; married Margaree Gordon; children: Veronica, Randolph & Darryl. **Educ:** Alcorn A&M Col, BS, 1967; Univ Omaha, attended 1968; Miss State Univ, attended 1969; Miss Col, MBA, 1975. **Career:** Utica Jr Col, cashier, 1967-68, bus mgr, 1969-; Hinds Jr Col, bd dir, Utica Campus, bus mgr, Raymond Campus, dist vpres bus affairs. **Orgs:** Consult Natchez Jr Col; Miss Jr Col Bus Mgrs Assoc; Nat Asn Cols & Univs Bus Officers; Nat Educ Asn; Miss Teachers Asn; Nat Asn Advan Colored People; secy treas, Phi Beta Sigma, 1971-72; develop found bd mem, Hinds Jr Col, Raymond Campus. **Home Addr:** , North Carrollton, MS. **Business Addr:** Development Foundation Board Member, Raymond Campus, PO Box 1100, Raymond, MS 39154-1100, **Business Phone:** (800)446-3722.

## JENKINS, DR. ADELBERT

Educator. **Personal:** Born Dec 10, 1934, St. Louis, OH; son of Helen Howard and Herbert; married Betty Lanier; children: Christopher. **Educ:** Antioch Col, BA, psychol, 1957; Univ Mich, MA, psychol, 1958, PhD, clin psychol, 1963; dipl clin psychol, ABPP. **Career:** Training consult, Veterans Admin Med Centers, Bronx, Brooklyn; A Einstein Med Col, post doctoral fel, 1962-64, asst instr, instr, 1964-67; New York Univ Med Ctr, asst prof, 1967-71; New York Univ, New York, assoc prof, 1971, dir, undergrad studies psychol, 1982-86 & 1989-93, assoc prof emer, currently. **Orgs:** Fel Am Psychol Asn, 1964-; NY State Psychol Asn, 1966-; Nat Asn Black Psychol, 1968-; fel Soc Personality Assessment, 1974-; pres, Soc Theoret & Philos Psychol, 2003-04. **Home Addr:** 196 Kendal Dr, Oberlin, OH 44074, **Home Phone:** (440)774-4591. **Business Addr:** Associate Professor Emeritus, New York University, New York, NY 10003.

## JENKINS, DR. ALTHEA H.

Librarian, educator. **Personal:** Born Sep 11, 1941, Tallahassee, FL; daughter of Samuel and Florence Brown; children: James C II. **Educ:** Fla A&M Univ, BSLS, 1963; FL Atlantic Univ, LD, cert, 1970; Fla State Univ, MSLS, 1972; Nova Univ, EdD, educ admin, 1977. **Career:** Educator, librarian (retired); Indian River Sch Bd, sch media specialist, 1963-71; Fla State Univ, grad asst, 1971-72; Miami-Dade Community Col, libr dir, 1972-80, prof; Univ S Fla Sarasota, libr dir, 1980-91; Am Libr Asn, Chicago, IL, exec dir, 1991-2001; Fla State Univ, dir univ libr. **Orgs:** Pres, Fla Asn Col & Res Libr, 1983-85; Eckerd Col Bd Trustees, 1984-; First vpres, Delta Kappa Gamma, 1986-; Phi Delta Kappa, 1987-; Sarasota Co United Way Bd, 1987-; pres, Fla Libr Asn, 1988-89; Sarasota Co Hist Comn, 1988-; Sarasota Co Community Found, 1988-; Sarasota Chamber Com, 1989; Delta Sigma Theta, 1990-; Am Asn Higher Educ, 1997-2001; assoc exec dir, Am Libr Asn; chmn, Asn Col & Res Libr; Nat Sci Digital Libr; Asn Col Res Libr; Southeastern Libr Network; bd mem, TLT Group; NSF. **Honors/Awds:** Certificate of Appreciation, Newtown Libr Planning Bd, 1981; Certificate of Appreciation, Sarasota-Manatee Phi Delta Kappa, 1984; "She Knows WhereShe is Going", Girls Clubs of America Award, 1989. **Special Achievements:** First African American executive director of the Association of College & Research Libraries. **Home Addr:** 5638 Florence Oak Trl, Tallahassee, FL 32309, **Home Phone:** (850)894-9122. **Business Addr:** Board of Director, The TLT Group, PO Box 5643, Takoma Park, MD 20913, **Business Phone:** (301)270-8312.

## JENKINS, ANDREW JAMES

Government official, educator. **Personal:** Born Jun 27, 1941, Brooklyn, NY; married Michelle Rios; children: Andrew Jr & Alexandra. **Educ:** Fordham Univ, Soc Sci, 1969; Fordham Univ Law Sch, JD, 1972. **Career:** City Univ New York Col, adj prof, admin; Jenkins Aings & Johnson Law Firm, atty; NY Assembly, 1979-82; NY State Senate, sen, 1983-90. **Orgs:** Parliamentarian Guy R Brewer Dem Club; Knights Pythia. **Honors/Awds:** Nat Hon Soc. **Home Addr:** 17410 Adelaine Rd, Jamaica, NY 11433, **Home Phone:** (718)658-1933.

## JENKINS, ANDREW M., JR.

Administrator, activist. **Personal:** Born Jul 20, 1936, Philadelphia, PA; son of William and Madeline Green; married Patricia A Green; children: Eric, Denise, Andrea & Andrew. **Educ:** Antioch Univ, BA, human servs, 1982; Jamerson's Sch Ministry, ordained minister. **Career:** Mantva Comt Planners, pres, 1967-85; City Philadelphia, Liaison Officer Anti-Poverty Agency, 1971-79; City Philadelphia, Chmn Mayor's Citizen, Adv Comt, 1977-79; Mt Vernon Manor Apts, pres, 1978-85; Mantva Primary Health Ctr, pres, 1984-85; First United Baptist Church Male Chorus, vpres, 1984-85; Mantva Comt Develop Corp, vpres, 1984-85; Philadelphia Redevelop Authority, dir relocation & prop mgt, exec dir, head, 1990-92; City Philadelphia, dep mayor. **Orgs:** Pres, Mantua Community Planners, 1967-79; dir, Univ PA Commun Develop, 1969-71; Community Organizer Univ PA, 1969-71; liaison officer, Philadelphia Ant Pov Action Comt, 1971-79; pres, Mt Vernon Apt, 1978-; exec bd, W Philadelphia Partnership Inc, 1983-89; Am Legion George J Cornish Post, 1983-85, Nat Forum Black Admin, 1984-85; Mayor Wilson Goode's Labor Std Bd, 1985, Philadelphia Redevelop Authority Labor Mgt Comt; real estate comt bd mem, Martin Luther King Village Comt Asn Inc; bd mem, Stinger Sq Corp; Young Great Soc. **Home Addr:** 3609 Spring Garden St, Philadelphia, PA 19104-2351, **Home Phone:** (215)222-0345.

## JENKINS, AUGUSTUS G., JR.

Funeral director. **Personal:** Born Aug 24, 1943, New York, NY; son of Augustus G Sr and W Louise Johnson; married Nellie Kirkland; children: Natalie & Ashley. **Educ:** Cent State Univ, Wilberforce, Ohio, BS, 1965; Ohio State Univ, Columbus, Ohio, MS, 1966. **Career:** Jenkins Funeral Chapel, New York, NY, owner, funeral dir & operator, 1970-; Black Tennis & Sports Found, New York, NY, founder & vice chair, 1977-; prof pilot & flight instr, 1985-; Nat Cash Regist, systems engr; Int Bus Mach, systems engr. **Orgs:** Founder, Nat Asn Advan Colored People Bergen County, NJ; bd mem, Lions Club; bd mem, Harlem YMCA; Nat Negro Golf Asn; Omega Psi Phi Frat; Englewood Social Club; pres Church Coun, St Mark's United Methodist Church. **Home Addr:** 144 Lake St, Englewood, NJ 07631, **Home Phone:** (201)567-8905. **Business Addr:** Owner, Operator, Jenkins Funeral Chapel, 1893 Amsterdam Ave, New York, NY 10032, **Business Phone:** (212)926-5979.

## JENKINS, BARBARA WILLIAMS

Librarian. **Personal:** Born Aug 17, 1934, Union, SC; daughter of Johncie Sartor Williams and Ernest N Williams; married Robert A; children: Ronald & Pamela. **Educ:** Bennett Col, BA; Univ Ill, MSLS; Rutgers Univ, PhD, libr & info serv, 1980. **Career:** Head Librarian (retired), dean Emeritus: Circulation libr; ref & doc libr; SC State Col, Whittaker Libr, libr, 1957-62, libr dir, 1962-87, head librn, 1963-71, dean libr & info serv, 1974-97, dean emer libr & info serv, 2000-. **Orgs:** SC Lib Asn; SE Lib Asn; Am Lib Asn; Am Soc Info Sci; Alpha Kappa Mu Hon Soc; Am Asn Univ & Profs; lib consult instr; coadj fac, Rutgers Univ; assoc dir, Inst Libr Correction Inst; NAACP; Delta Sigma Theta Inc; S Atlantic Reg dir, 1968-70; Nat Comn Const by-laws, 1971-75; Links Inc; pres, Orangeburg Chap, 1975-77; treas, Black Caucus Am Libr Asn, 1976-78; adv com, SC Mus Comn; vice area dir, Southern Area Links Inc, 1979-83; Land Grant Libr Dirs Asn, 1979-85; Concerned Citizens Black Higher Educ Sc, bd mem, 1981-85; chmn, Ala Black Caucus, 1984-86; pres, SC Libr Asn, 1986-87; bd dir, SOLINET Southeastern Libr Network, 1989-; bd dir, SC African Am Heritage Coun; bd dir, chmn, currently; Harvin Clarendon County Libr; bd dir, SC Arch & Hist Found; bd dir, Ellorec Heritage Mus; Palmetto Trust, Hist Preserv; NAACP, life mem; African-Am Heritage Coun; Alpha Kappa Mu Hon Soc; Journalistic Bd Coastal Times newspaper, chairwomen; Sc African-Am Heritage Coun. **Honors/Awds:** John Cotton Dana Award; Design & Planning Award, MF Whittaker Libr; Boss of the Year Award, Orangeburg Chap Prof Secretaries Asn, 1980; Service Award, 1980; Land Grant, Libr Dir Asn, 1984; President's Award, SC Libr Asn, 1987, Sc State Univ, 1997; ALA Black Caucus Recognition Award, 1991 Distinguished Service Award, SC State Col, 1991; Culture Keeper Award, Black Caucus Ala, 1999; Clarendon County Nat Coun Negro Women Hall of Fame, 2001; inducted SC State Univ Hall Fame, 2004. **Special Achievements:** Author of eight books. **Home Addr:** 102 S Boundary St, Manning, SC 29102, **Home Phone:** (803)435-2406. **Business Addr:** Dean Emeritus, South Carolina State University, 300 Col St NE, Orangeburg, SC 29117, **Business Phone:** (803)536-7000.

## JENKINS, BILLY LEON, JR.

Football coach, football player. **Personal:** Born Jul 8, 1974, Los Angeles, CA; married Tiffany; children: Khalil & Jaden. **Educ:** Howard Univ, BS, biol. **Career:** Football player (retired), coach; St Louis Rams, defensive back, 1997, strong safety, 1998, strong safety, safety, 1999; Denver Broncos, strong safety, 2000-01; Green Bay Packers, 2001; Buffalo Bills, strong safety, 2002; Howard Univ, defensive back coach, currently. **Business Addr:** Defensive Back Coach, Howard University, Burr Gymnasium, Washington, DC 20059, **Business Phone:** (202)806-7141.

## JENKINS, CARLTON J.

Banker, president (organization). **Educ:** Dartmouth Col, BA; Univ Calif, Los Angeles, exec mgt prog. **Career:** Los Angeles Local Develop Corp, bd dirs & mayoral appointee; Los Angeles Develop Reform Comn, mem; Founders Nat Bank Los Angeles, chief exec officer, pres & chmn, 1990-2000; OneNetNow.com LLC, prin & chief exec officer, 1999-2001; Dryades Savings Bank, founder, dir & prin; Yucaipa Co & Yucaipa Corp Initiatives Fund, partner, 2000-. **Orgs:** Calif State Bd Educ; Univ Calif Los Angeles Med Ctr; trustee, Univ W Los Angeles Sch Law; dir, The Fred Meyer Co, 1998-; dir, Kroger Co; dir, Hawthorne Fin Corp, 2002-. **Special Achievements:** Company is ranked No 14 on Black Enterprise's list of Top 100 financial companies, 1994. **Home Addr:** 4272 Hillcrest Dr, Los Angeles, CA 90008, **Home Phone:** (323)299-8490. **Business Addr:** Partner, The Yucaipa Companies LLC, 9130 W Sunset Blvd, Los Angeles, CA 90069, **Business Phone:** (310)789-7200.

## JENKINS, CAROL ANN

Journalist. **Personal:** Born Nov 30, 1944, Montgomery, AL; married Carlos Hines. **Educ:** Boston Univ, BS, 1966; NY Univ, MA, 1968. **Career:** WOR-TV, co-anchor reporter, 1970-71; Straight Talk WOR- TV, moderator, 1971-72, new reporter; ABC-TVREASONOR/SMITH Report Eyewitness News, corr, 1972-73; WNBC-TV, news corr, 1973-96; Greenstone Media, bd chair; Women's Media Ctr, pres & founding mem bd dir, currently; media & polit analyst. **Orgs:** Am Fedn TV & Radio Artists; Writers Guild Am E; Nat Acad Arts & Scis; Int Radio & TV Soc; Am Women Radio & TV; Nat Asn Media Women; US bd, African Med & Res Found; bd, Ms Found Women & Feminist Press. **Honors/Awds:** Service Award, Harlem Prep Sch, 1971; Outstanding Achievement Award, Ophelia DeVore Sch, 1972; Outstanding Achievement Award, Ala State Univ, 1972; Outstanding Achievement Award, Jour Alpha Wives, 1974; hon doctorate, Col New Rochelle; hon doctorate, Marymount Manhattan Col; Lifetime & InterNat Reporting Achievement Award, Asn Black Journalist, NY Chapt; Front Page Award, Daily News; Mother of the Year, Nat Mothers Day Comt; Woman of the Year, Police Athletic League; Humanitarian of the Year, Abbot House; Distinguished Alumna, NY Univ. **Special Achievements:** Co-Author: Black Titan: A.G. Gaston and the Making of a Black American Millionaire; A frequently sought speaker and moderator, she also conducts media training seminars and private sessions for women across the country; executive producer of the PBS documentary, What I Want My Words To Do To You, which won the Freedom of Expression Award at the Sundance Film Festival in 2003; The WMC bestows The Carol Jenkins Young Journalist Award to an accomplished media professional each year; Lifetime Achievement and International Reporting awards from the National Association of Black Journalists NY. **Business Addr:** President, Women Media Center, 350 5th Ave Suite 901, New York, NY 10118, **Business Phone:** (212)563-0680.

## JENKINS, DR. CHIP, JR. (CHARLES LAMONT JENKINS, JR.)

Real estate agent, athlete, lawyer. **Personal:** Born Apr 9, 1964, New York, NY; son of Charles L Sr. **Educ:** Villanova Sch Law, JD. **Career:** Athlete (retired), lawyer, real estate agent; US Olympic Team, Mens Track & Field, 1992; athlete; US Patent Off, atty, currently; real estate investor, currently. **Honors/Awds:** Gold Medalist, Olymic Games, Barcelona, US Mens Track & Field, 4x400 relay, 1992. **Home Addr:** 2200 N Chambliss St Suite 1521, Alexandria, VA 71301. **Business Addr:** Attorney, United States Patent and Trademark Office, 600 Dulany St, Alexandria, VA 22314, **Business Phone:** (571)272-0095.

## JENKINS, DERON CHARLES

Football player. **Personal:** Born Nov 14, 1973, St. Louis, MO; children: Syrus. **Educ:** Univ Tenn, degree, psychol. **Career:** Football player (retired); Baltimore Ravens, defensive back, 1996, right cornerback, 1997-99, left cornerback & cornerback, 1999; San Diego Chargers, cornerback & right cornerback, 2000; Tenn Titans, cornerback & right cornerback, 2001; Carolina Panthers, defensive panthers, 2002; Austin Wranglers, 2004; Nashville Kats, 2005-06. **Honors/Awds:** All-Rookie Team, 2004.

## JENKINS, ELIZABETH AMETA

Counselor, educator. **Personal:** Born Mar 11, 1929, Brooklyn, NY; daughter of Lionel A Hunte and Ameta A Hackett-Hunte; children: Roland, Roderick, Howard, Rebecca & Leah. **Educ:** Molloy Col, BA, social psychol, 1977; Hofstra Univ, MA, 1985. **Career:** Nassau Co Dept Social Serv, social work aid, 1965-68; Econ Opportunity Coun Roosevelt, NY, summer youth dir & community organizer, 1970-72; Alliance MNY Group Leaders Inc, activ planner & parent coord, 1972-77; Molloy Col, St Thomas Aquinas Prog, prog counr. **Orgs:** Pres, Roosevelt Scholar Asn, 1958-75; founding secy, Nassau & Suffolk Health Syst Agency, 1976-78; Am Asn Univ Women, 1977; Higher Educ Opportunity Prog, Prof Orgn Long Island Region, 1978; Nassau Co Task Force Status Women, 1977-79; Asn Black Women Higher Educ, 1977-; Asn Equality & Excellence Educ, 1979; Long Island Coun Stud Perspective Admin, 1981-; Am Bus Womens Asn, 1984. **Honors/Awds:** Ten Year Plaque for Dedicated Service, Molloy Col, 1987; Ten Year Pin for Dedicated Service to Higher Education Opportunity Program Professional Organization, State Educ Dept Higher Educ Opportunity Prog, 1990; Distinguished Service Medal, Molloy Col, 2001; 25-Year Service Medal, Molloy Col, 2002. **Home Addr:** 50 Holloway St, Freeport, NY 11520-1215, **Home Phone:** (516)445-4169. **Business Addr:** Program Counselor, Molloy College, Kellenberg 001 1000 Hempstead Ave, Rockville Centre, NY 11570, **Business Phone:** (516)678-5000.

## JENKINS, ELLA LOUISE

Musician, singer. **Personal:** Born Aug 6, 1924, St. Louis, MO. **Educ:** Wilson Jr Col, attended 1947; Roosevelt Col, attended 1948; San Francisco St Col, BA, sociol, 1951. **Career:** Freelance musician, singer & rec artist; Smithsonian Folkways Rec, rec artist. **Orgs:** Prog dir, YWCA, 1952, camp counr; Music Educ Nat Conf; Int Platform Asn; Am Soc Composers. **Honors/Awds:** Pioneer in Early Television Citation, Natl Mus Am Hist; Parent's Choice Award; Lifetime Achievement Award, KOHL Educ Found; Service to Young Children Award, Chicago Metrop Asn Educ Young C; Headstart Award, KOHL Educ Found; Best Variety Performer Award, Am Acad C Entertainment; American Library Association Award; Keepers of the Culture Award, Natl Asn Black Storytellers; Lifetime Achievement Award, Am Soc Composers, Authors & Publishers Found; Nominee, Grammy for Best Musical Album for Children for Ella Jenkins and a Union of Friends, 1999; Nominee, Grammy for Best Best Musical Album for Children for Ella Jenkins and a Union of Friends Pulling Together, 2000; Meritorious Service Award, Cook County C's Hosp; Grammy Lifetime Achievement Award, 2004; Nominee, Grammy Best Musical Album for Children for Sharing Cultures with Ella Jenkins, 2005; Grammy Award for Best Musical Album for Children for celebration: A Tribute to Ella Jenkins, 2005; Chicagoan of the Year, Chicago Magazine, 2005. **Special Achievements:** Called as the First Lady of Children's Folk Song; Received a salute from the Ravinia Festival; Served as a US delegate to Hong Kong, China and the former Soviet Union with the John F. Kennedy Center for the Performing Arts. **Business Addr:** Musician, 1844 N Mohawk St, Chicago, IL 60614, **Business Phone:** (312)337-5014.

## JENKINS, EMMANUEL LEE

School administrator, association executive, naval officer. **Personal:** Born Aug 7, 1934, Greenville, NC; children: Darel, Gregory, Jerome & Tamara. **Educ:** Howard Univ, BA, pharm, 1956; Long Island Univ, MS, educ, 1974. **Career:** School administrator (retired); Rhodes Med, pharm, 1956; Moore-Schley Cameron & Co, customers broker, 1960-70; US Merchant Marine Acad, dir admis, 1970-95. **Orgs:** Officer, Lakeview Educ Comn, 1968-73; rep, Col Bd, 1973-; rep, Nat Asn Col Admis Officers, 1974-; Col Bd Coun, 1982-83. **Honors/Awds:** Special Achievement Award, USMM Acad, 1975; Special Achievement Award, 1983. **Home Addr:** 26 S Woods Rd, Syosset, NY 11791, **Home Phone:** (516)364-2994.

### JENKINS, FERGUSON ARTHUR, JR.

Baseball executive, baseball player, baseball commissioner. **Personal:** Born Dec 13, 1942, Chatham, ON; son of Ferguson Sr and Delores; married Kathy Williams; children: Kelly, Delores & Kimberly; married Maryanne; children: Raymond & Samantha (deceased); married Lydia. **Career:** Baseball player(retired), association executive, pitcher; Philadelphia Phillies, 1965-66; Chicago Cubs, 1966-73 & 1982-83; Tex Rangers, 1974-75 & 1978-81; Boston Red Sox, 1976-77; Team Can, pitching coach Pan-Am Games, 1987; Tex Rangers, Okla City, pitching coach, 1988-89; Cincinnati Reds, pitching coach, 1992-93, roving pitching instr; Chicago Cubs, minor league coach, 1995-96; Can Baseball League, comnr, 2003-. **Orgs:** Harlem Globetrotters; Order Can, 1987; Maj League Baseball Players Alumni Asn; chmn, Fergie Jenkins Found Inc, 1999-. **Honors/Awds:** Canadian Athlete of the Year, 1967, 1968, 1971 & 1974; 20-game winner, six straight years; Nat League All-Star Team, 1967, 1971 &1972; Cy Young Memorial Award, Nat League, 1971; National League Pitcher of the Year, Sporting News, 1971; Lou Marsh Trophy, 1971; AL Comeback Player of the Year, 1974; Canada's best-known major-league baseball player, 1979; inducted to Canadian Baseball Hall of Fame, 1987; inducted to Baseball Hall of Fame, 1991; Major League Baseball All-Star Game, 1991; baseball's ultimate honour, 1991; commissioner of the now-defunct Canadian Baseball League, 2003; inducted to Texas Rangers Hall of Fame, 2004; inducted into Canada's Walk of Fame; Chicago Cubs #31. **Special Achievements:** The only Canadian honored & elected in the National Baseball Hall of Fame in Coopers town, New York; most strike outs than any other pitcher in Cubs history with 2038; First baseball player to win the Lou Marsh Trophy. **Business Addr:** Chairman, Fergie Jenkins Foundation Inc, 67 Com Pl Suite 3, St. Catharines, ON L2R 6P7, **Business Phone:** (905)688-9418.

### JENKINS, HARRY LANCASTER

Dentist. **Personal:** Born Apr 22, 1932, Columbus, GA; married Janie R; children: Harry, Timothy, Anthony & Gary. **Educ:** Morehouse Col, AB, 1955; Meharry Med Col, DDS, 1962. **Career:** Tuskegee Vet Admin Hosp, internship, 1963; Maryview Hosp Portsmouth, Va, staff; Portsmouth Gen Hosp; Norfolk Community Hosp, staff mem; self-employed dent surgeon, currently; Jenkins Dent Group, pres. **Orgs:** Am Cancer Soc; Am Youth Orgn; Eureka Bus & Prof Club; adv bd, Va State Civil Rights Comn McGriff Dent Soc. **Home Addr:** 1220 Greenbrier Pkwy Suite 120, Chesapeake, VA 23320-1611, **Home Phone:** (757)547-9616. **Business Addr:** Dentist, Jenkins Dental Group Incorporation, 3349 Portsmouth Blvd, Portsmouth, VA 23701, **Business Phone:** (757)393-4361.

### JENKINS, DR. HERMAN LEE

School administrator. **Personal:** Born May 7, 1940, Montgomery, AL; son of William and Betty (Holmes); married Margaret Stephenson; children: Gloria Denise & Herman Jr. **Educ:** Clark Univ, BA, 1974, PhD, 1983. **Career:** Self-employed, artist mapmaker, 1961-; Southern Christian Leadership Conf, comt organizer civil rights activist, 1965-69; Metrop Appl Res Ctr, fel, pres, 1967-68; Clark Univ, dir community rels, 1972; Am Int Col lectr, 1976; Queens Col, exec asst to pres, 1978-80, asst vpres, 1980-, vpres; HL Jenkins Geog Anal Inc, pres & chief exec officer, 1978-; citys personnel comnr, 1992. **Orgs:** Nat Asn Advan Colored People; 100 Black Men Inc; Asn Am Geogr; bd dir, Queens Col Found, 1980; trustee, Queens County Overall Econ Develop Corp, 1980; regional coordr, US Comn Proposals Nat Acad Peace & Conflict Resolution, 1980-81; bd dir, Community Cult Queens Inc, 1993. **Honors/Awds:** Jonas Clark Scholar, Clark Univ, 1977. **Home Addr:** 24120 Northern Blvd Apt 2K, Little Neck, NY 11362-1009, **Home Phone:** (718)225-7140.

### JENKINS, JAMES

Football coach, football player, executive. **Personal:** Born Aug 17, 1967, Staten Island, NY; children: 3. **Educ:** Rutgers Univ, grad. **Career:** Football player (retired), football coach, offensive coordr; Wash Redskins, tight end, 1991-2000; Lifetime Fitness Alpharetta, personal training mgr; Cologne Falcons, head coach; VA State Police, state trooper; Dusseldorf Panthers, head coach; Nat Football League, strength & conditioning coach; New York Giants, tight ends coach; Franken Knights, head coach, offensive coordr, currently. **Honors/Awds:** Super Bowl XXVI, 1991; Ed Block Courage Award, 1997. **Business Addr:** Head Coach, Offensive Coordinator, Franken Knights, 270 Friedrich Karl St, Koln50735, **Business Phone:** (221)168-8320.

### JENKINS, JIM (JAMES B JENKINS, JR.)

Chief executive officer, president (organization). **Personal:** Born Detroit, MI; children: Nicole & Rodney. **Educ:** Tenn State Univ, BSEE. **Career:** Turner Construct Co, purchasing mgr; Jenkins Construct Inc, pres & chief exec officer, 1989-; Walbridge Aldinger Co; Skanska USA. Bldg Inc. **Orgs:** Bd dir, Detroit Regional Chamber; Greater Grace Church & Fel Chapel; Jefferson N Park develop; Queen Lillian med off bldg; Wayne State Univ's Dept Psychiat. **Home Addr:** 15861 Woodingham Dr, Detroit, MI 48201, **Home Phone:** (313)864-5688. **Business Addr:** President, Chief Executive Officer, Jenkins Construct Inc, 985 E Jefferson Ave Suite 300, Detroit, MI 48207-3127, **Business Phone:** (313)625-7200.

### JENKINS, DR. JIMMY RAYMOND, SR.

School administrator, college president. **Personal:** Born Mar 18, 1943, Selma, NC; married Faleese Moore; children: Lisa Lopez, Ginger Cartwright & Jimmy Jr. **Educ:** Elizabeth City State Univ, BS, biol, 1965; Purdue Univ, MS, 1969, biol educ, PhD, 1972. **Career:** Elizabeth City State Univ, asst prof biol, 1972, asst acad dean, 1972, assoc prof biol, 1973, vice chancellor acad affairs, 1977, chancellor, 1977-95, chancellor emer, 1995, chief exec officer; Edward Waters Col, Jacksonville, Fla, pres, 1997-2005; Livingstone Col, Salisbury, NC, pres, chief exec officer, 2006-. **Orgs:** NC Humanities Comt, 1980; Gov Oversight Comt, Nat Caucus Black Aged; Elizabeth City Chap Kiwanis Int; NC Bd Sci & Tech; Am Asn Higher Ed. **Special Achievements:** First alumnus to become the CEO of Elizabeth City State. **Home Addr:** 1304 Parkview Dr, Elizabeth City, NC 27909. **Business Addr:** President, Chief Executive Officer, Livingstone College, 701 W Monroe St, Salisbury, NC 28144, **Business Phone:** (704)216-6153.

### JENKINS, JO ANN

Executive, chairperson, chief executive officer. **Educ:** Spring Hill Col, Mobile, Ala, BA. **Career:** Dept Housing & Urban Develop, exec, 1981-85; Dept Transp, exec, 1985; U.S. Dept Agr, Off Advocacy & Enterprise, dir, 1990-93; Libr Cong, chief operating officer, 1995-2010; Am Asn Retired Persons (AARP) Found, pres, 2010; AARP, chief operating officer & exec vpres, chief exec officer, 2014-. **Orgs:** Bd dir mem, 2004-, chair, 2008-10, AARP Serv Inc; Deleg & Founding fel U.S. Japan Leadership Prog; Cong Hunger Ctr; Colonial Williamsburg Found; US Small Bus Admin Coun Underserved Communities Living Cities; Caring Mil Families. **Honors/Awds:** Malcolm Baldrige fellow, 2013; Black Women's Agenda Economic Development Award, Recipient, 2013; NonProfit Times' Power and Influence Top 50, Recipient, 2013-16; Peace Corps Director's Award, 2014; Washington'ss Most Influential People, 2015-16; Women in Technology Leadership Award for Library of Congress Experience; Library of Congress Distinguished Service Award, Recipient; DHL, Spring Hill Col; DHL, Wash Col. **Special Achievements:** First permanent female chief executive in AARP's history. Book: "Disrupt Aging: A Bold New Path to Living Your Best Life at Every Age". **Business Addr:** Chief Executive Officer, AARP, 3200 E Carson St, Lakewood, CA 90712, **Business Phone:** (888)687-2277.

### JENKINS, JOHN

Mayor, president (organization), chief executive officer. **Personal:** Born May 29, 1952. **Educ:** Bates Col, Lewiston, Maine, BA, psychol. **Career:** Peptalk, pres & chief exec officer, 1970-; John Jenkins Acad Personal Develop, owner, 1970-74; John Jenkins PepTalk com, owner & chief exec officer, 1975-; Inspired To Be Great, Educ & Life Skills Coordr, 1985-; Bates Col, dir housing, 1986-88; Dirigo Corp, pres, 1988-97; Strategic Community Solutions, pres & chief exec officer, 1993-; City Lewiston, mayor, 1993-95; Notary Nuptials, owner & Operator, 1994-; State Senator, ME, 1996-98; City Auburn Maine, mayor, 2008-; John Jenkins, 2009-; Franklin County Adult & Community Educ, Educ & Work Readiness Coordr, 2011-; CBS News, wellness consult; Maine Criminal Justice Acad, critical skills instr trainer; Multi-Cultural Develop, UNUM, dir, currently. **Orgs:** Maine Health care Proj; Muskie Sch Pub Serv; Partners Ending Hunger; Maine Conserv Sch; Maine Sports Legends; Boy Scouts-Pine Tree Coun; Bates Dance Festival; comnr, US Dept Labor; bd trustee, New Eng Asn Schs & Cols. **Special Achievements:** First person in Maine history to serve as Mayor of two municipalities and win a Mayoral write-in campaign; First non-attorney to win the states highest leadership award. **Business Addr:** Founder, Chief Executive Officer, Peptalk.com, PO Box 7205, Lewiston, ME 04243-7205, **Business Phone:** (207)783-3413.

### JENKINS, JOSEPH WALTER

Management consultant. **Personal:** Born Jan 28, 1941, East Orange, NJ; son of Joseph and Annabelle Clarke; married F Louise Diaz; children: Khalil & Medinah (deceased). **Educ:** Tenn State Univ, BBA, 1963; Farleigh Dickinson Univ, MBA, mgmt, 1979. **Career:** Gen Motors, prod control coordr, 1963; Ford Motor Co, engrg analyst, 1966; Travelers Ins Co, asst mgr, personnel admin, 1968; Chubb Corp, eeo mgr, 1974, asst vpres, hr; City E Orange, bus adminr, 1986-90, city admin, 1998; J W Jenkins & Co, pres, 1990; Neward Bd Educ, Pensions & Benefits mgr, 1991-96; Chase Manhattan Bank, benefit consult, 1996-98. **Orgs:** Ams Sailing Asn; pres, Community Day Nursery, 1992; Omega Psi Phi Fraternity; pres, Surry County African Am Heritage Soc. **Honors/Awds:** Black Achievers Award, Harlem Br, YMCA, 1976; Outstanding Serv Optimist Club Orange, E Orange, 1979; Outstanding Citizen Award, Eagle Flight New Jersey, 1988. **Home Addr:** 7 Mountain Dr, West Orange, NJ 07052. **Business Addr:** President, Surry County African American Heritage Society, 205 Enos Farm Dr, Dendron, VA 23839, **Business Phone:** (757)866-0174.

### JENKINS, DR. JULIUS

Educator, chancellor (education), college president. **Personal:** married Mary (deceased); children: Pamela & Christopher. **Educ:** Concordia Col, AA; Concordia Univ, BS, 1968, MS, 1971; Ala State Univ, MEd, 1972; Nebraska Univ, PhD, 1976. **Career:** President (retired), president emeritus; St. Paul Lutheran Church, lay minister; St. Philip's Lutheran Sch, instr; Concordia Col, registr, actg dean students, dir financial aid & asst prof, 1969-73, asst prof, supvr, 1973-75, acad dean & admin asst, 1976-79, interim pres, 1979-80, pres, 1980-2007, pres emer, 2007-; AAL Br 7355, chmn; Selma Econ Develop Bd, bd mem, currently; Blanton Agency Adv Bd Lutheran Brotherhood, bd mem, currently. **Home Addr:** , Selma, AL. **Business Addr:** President Emeritus, Concordia College, 901 8th St S, Moorhead, MN 56562, **Business Phone:** (218)299-4000.

### JENKINS, PASTOR KENNETH JOE

Clergy, educator. **Personal:** Born Sep 8, 1954, Detroit, MI; son of Roger and Lucy; married Karen L; children: Joel D, Jessica D, Jaimi D & Jonathan K. **Educ:** Eastern Mich Univ, BS, 1977, MA, 1983; Cent Bible Col Assemblies God. **Career:** Ypsilanti Pub Sch, sub-teacher, com educ person, 1975-78; Detroit Pub Schs, teacher, 1978-; sch staff adminr, 2001; sch asst prin, 2002; charter pastor, SW MI AGAPE, 2002; Redemption Love Christian Ctr, pastor, currently. **Orgs:** Minister, Church God Christ, 1974-91; Phys Educ Adv Comt, Phys Fitness Comt, 1984-98, Detroit Pub Sch, 1985-98, High Sch Coaches, 1985-93. **Honors/Awds:** Educator's Achievement Award, Booker T Washington Bus Asn, 1998. **Special Achievements:** Detroit Public Schools, physical education, fitness accountability test, 1993-95. **Business Addr:** Pastor, Redemptive Love Christian Center, 12190 Conant Ave, Detroit, MI 48212, **Business Phone:** (313)893-6275.

### JENKINS, DR. KENNETH VINCENT

Administrator, college teacher. **Personal:** Born Elizabeth, NJ; son of Thomas Augustus and Rebecca Meredith Williams; children: 4; children: 5. **Educ:** Columbia Col, NY, BA; Columbia Univ, Teachers Col, NY, MA. **Career:** S Side High Sch, Rockville Ctr, NY, chmn eng dept, 1965-72; NYS Dept Educ, Albany, consult eng, 1965-72; Regents Question Comt Eng, Albany, 1966-71; Nassau Community Col, supvr adj fac, prof eng & afro-am lit, Dept Afro-Am studies, chmn, 1974-. **Orgs:** Afro-Am Inst, NY; Mensa, dv bd mem, Radio Sta WBAI-FM NY, 1972-85; Consult Eng, convener, chmn bd dir, Target Youth Ctrs Inc, NY, 1973-75; chmn, pres, Nat Bd Pac Found, 1973-80; chmn, Nassau County Youth Bd, 1979-98; Phi Delta Kappa; Asn Study Afro-Am Life & Hist; Coun Black Am Affairs; exec bd, NY African Studies Asn; African Heritage Studies Asn; Gov 's NY State Coun Youth, 1986-93; Schomburg Corp, 1989-93; bd mem, Long Island Community Found, 1989-98; bd mem, NY State Youth Support Inc, 1990-93. **Honors/Awds:** Baker Award, Columbia Univ; Martin Luther King Jr Award, Nassau County, 1989; MLK Award, Celebration Com Nassau County, 1990; 100 Black Men Special Service Award, 1994; David K Kadane Family Serv Award; LI Award, Nat Coun Negro Women, 2002; Nat Coun Negro Women Award, 2003; Community Award. **Special Achievements:** Author of essays, short stories, reviews, "Last Day in Church."; owner" Black Books and Artifacts". **Home Addr:** 549 W 123rd St, New York, NY 10027-5041, **Home Phone:** (212)222-3264. **Business Addr:** Professor of English, Chairperson, Nassau Community College, 1 Educ Dr Bldg H 124, Garden City, NY 11530, **Business Phone:** (516)572-7157.

### JENKINS, DR. LOUIS E.

Clinical psychologist, educator. **Personal:** Born Dec 20, 1931, Staten Island, NY; married Althea L; children: Le Toia M. **Educ:** Union Col, BS, 1954; Univ Nebr, MA, 1959; Pepperdine Univ, MA, psychol, 1970; Pa State Univ, PhD, clin psychol, 1973; ABPP. **Career:** LA Union SDA Sch, teacher, 1959-64; LA City Sch, teacher, 1964-65, counr, 1965-66, sch psychologist, 1966-69; Pepperdine Univ, assoc prof psychol, 1970-75; Martin Luther King Jr Gen Hosp LA, Dept Psychol & Human Behav, staff psychologist; CA Fam Study Cent Downey, Calif, pvt pract; Loma Linda Univ, Dept Psychol, dept chair, prof emer, currently. **Orgs:** Nat Asn Advan Colored People; Soc Clin Psychol; Psychol Relig; Am Psychol Law; Family Psychol; Soc Psychol Study Ethnic Minority Issues; Am Psychol Soc; Am Asn Christian Counr; Acad Clin Psychol; Am Bd Prof Psychol; Coun Grad Dept Psychol. **Business Addr:** Professor Emeritus, Loma Linda University, 102 Central Bldg, Loma Linda, CA 92350, **Business Phone:** (909)558-8577.

### JENKINS, LUTHER NEAL

Aerospace engineer. **Personal:** Born Mar 21, 1968, Newport News, VA. **Educ:** Brown Univ, BS, mech engineering; George Washington Univ, MS, engineering. **Career:** NASA Langley Res Ctr, aerospace engr, 1990-, Subsonic Rotary Wing Proj, assoc prin investr. **Orgs:** Omega Psi Phi Fraternity. **Honors/Awds:** Ebony, 50 Leaders of Tomorrow, 1992. **Business Addr:** Aerospace Engineer, NASA Langley Research Center, 8 Lindbergh Way, Hampton, VA 23681, **Business Phone:** (757)864-1000.

### JENKINS, MELVIN

Football player. **Personal:** Born Mar 16, 1962, Jackson, MS; married Javoni. **Educ:** Univ Cincinnati, grad. **Career:** Football player (retired); Can Football League, Calgary, 1984-86; Seattle Seahawks, defensive back, 1987, 1989-90, right center back, left center back, 1988-89; Detroit Lions; cornerback, right center back, 1991-93; Atlanta Falcons, defensive back, 1993. **Special Achievements:** Film: 1991 NFC Championship Game, 1992.

**JENKINS, DR. MELVIN E, JR.** **See Obituaries Section.**

### JENKINS, DR. MELVIN LEMUEL

Lawyer, executive. **Personal:** Born Oct 15, 1947, Halifax, NC; son of Solomon Green and Minerva; married Wanda Joyce Holly; children: Shelley, Melvin Jr, Dawn & Holly Rae-Ann. **Educ:** NC Agr & Tech State Univ, BS, 1969; Univ Kans Sch Law, JD, 1972. **Career:** Legal Aid Soc Kans City, Mo, staff atty, 1972; US Dept Housing & Urban Develop, staff atty, 1972-73; US Commun Civil Rights, reg atty, 1973-79, regional dir, 1979-2002; Stennis & Assocs, atty, 2002; US Comn Civil Rights, Cent Reg Off, dir, currently; Univ Kans Sch Law, Benton fel. **Orgs:** Bd dir, Joan Davis Spec Sch, 1984-; Nat Bar Asn; NE Bar Asn; Mayors Human Rel Comn Kans City, Mo; Alpha Phi Omega Serv Fraternity; Omega Psi Phi Fraternity; Smith fel Legal Aid Soc; Fed Bar Asn. **Honors/Awds:** Civil Rights Award, Blue Valley Lodge Masons. **Home Addr:** 2505 N 24th St Suite 314, Omaha, NE 68110, **Home Phone:** (816)761-2416. **Business Addr:** Regional Director, US Commission on Civil Rights, 400 State Ave Suite 908, Kansas City, KS 66101, **Business Phone:** (913)551-1400.

### JENKINS, MONICA

Salesperson, manager, executive. **Personal:** Born Apr 7, 1961, San Francisco, CA; daughter of James and Marie Taylor; children: 1. **Educ:** Univ Santa Clara, CA, BS, 1983. **Career:** First Nationwide Bank, San Francisco, Calif, customer serv rep, 1983-85, state sales trainer, 1985-90; Nordstrom, San Francisco, Calif, sales assoc, 1989-90; Pacific Gas & Elec Co, San Francisco, Calif, human resources assoc, 1989-90, human resources rep, EEO & diversity unit, 1990-94; Genentech, sr recruiter, 1994-96; Amgen, sr mgr human resources, 1996-2000; Monogram Bioscience, assoc dir, 2003-06; Bill & Melinda Gates Found, human resources bus partner, 2006-08. **Orgs:** CHOCS, 1990-; ACHRC, 1990-; BEA, 1990-. **Home Addr:** 401 Shields St, San Francisco, CA 94132, **Home Phone:** (415)239-5149.

### JENKINS, NEDRA

Lawyer. **Personal:** Born Jan 1, 1969; daughter of John. **Educ:** Univ Chicago, BA, hist, MA, social sci, 1991; Univ Calif, Los Angeles, Sch Law, JD, 1994. **Career:** City Compton, Off City atty, 1994; Wilson & Becks, assocs, 1995-96; Off County Coun, sr coun, 1996-2011, prin dep county coun, currently; Ethics Comn, city controller laura chick, 2008-; Supvr Mark Ridley-Thomas-Los Angeles County, Second Dist, chief dep, 2011-15; Los Angeles County, Off Dist Atty, Los Angeles County Ment Health Diversion, exec dir, 2015; County Los Angeles, sr coun, 2015-; Ill Atty Gens Off; Los Angeles Dist Attys Off. **Orgs:** State Bar CA, 9th Circuit Ct Appeal & US Dist Ct, Cent Dist, 1994-; pres, Black Women Lawyers Asn Los Angeles, 1994; adv bd, Hollywood Black Film Festival, 1999-; bd mem, Calif Asn Black Lawyers, 2003-04; State Bench Bar Coalition, 2004; Local Bench Bar Coalition, 2005; U.S. Supreme Ct, 2005-; Bar Leaders Conf Comt, 2005; Am Bar Asn; Nat Bar Asn; Calif Asn Black Lawyers; Calif Women Lawyers; Los Angeles County Bar Asn; Univ Calif Los Angeles Black Alumni Asn; Pasadena Tournament Roses; Lanterns Comt; Mt Wash Homeowners Alliance; Harriett Buhai Ctr Family Law. **Honors/Awds:** Distinguished Woman Award, Top Ladies Distinction, Pasadena Chap, 2005. **Special Achievements:** Southern California Super Lawyers Rising Star- Employment Law by Law & Politics Magazine and the publishers of Los Angeles Magazine, 2005, 2006, 2007, 2008, 2009. **Business Addr:** Principal Deputy County Counsel, Office of Counsel, 1 Gateway Pl 24th Fl, Los Angeles, CA 90012, **Business Phone:** (213)922-2526.

## JENKINS, OZELLA
Executive, manager. **Personal:** Born Aug 13, 1945, Roanoke Rapids, NC. **Educ:** NC Cent Univ, attended 1964; Howard Univ, attended 1965; Cornell Univ, attended 1974. **Career:** C&P Tel Co, customer serv rep, 1964-71; Pitts Motor Hotel, restaurant mgr, 1964-72; Sheraton Wash Hotel, conv mgr. **Orgs:** Nat Coun Negro Women, 1962-; Nat Asn Catering Execs; Nat Coalition Black Mtg Planners, 1984-; bus mgr Wash Chap JUGS Inc, 1984; vpres, Bonaire Homes Asn, 1985; asn dir, Nat Asn Health Serv Exec, currently. **Honors/Awds:** Cert Daughters Am Revolution, 1979; Recognition Excellence Successful Meeting Mag 1982, 1984, 1986; Cert/plaque Meeting Planners Int, 1984; Plaque Nat Urban League, 1985; US Marshal Service, 1985; Metro Police Dept Wash DC, 1985. **Home Addr:** 8112 Bonaire Ct, Silver Spring, MD 20910. **Business Addr:** Association Director, National Association of Health Services Executives, 8630 Fenton St Suite 126, Silver Spring, MD 20910, **Business Phone:** (202)628-3953.

## JENKINS, WANDA JOYCE
Health services administrator. **Personal:** Born Jun 20, 1946, Kansas City, MO; daughter of S J Holly Sr; married Melvin L Sr; children: Dawn, Shelley, Melvin Jr & Holly. **Educ:** Kans State Col, Pittsburg, CA, BSW, 1969; Univ KS, MSW, 1974. **Career:** YMCA, asst dir, 1974-75; Rainbow Ment Health Ctr, social worker, 1975-80; Community Support, Res Health, coordr, 1980-86; Andrews Way Group Home, dir, 1986-89; Swope Pkwy Health Ctr, 1989-; Univ KS, Sch Social Work, field instr, 1990-94; Washburn Univ, Sch Social Work, field instr, 1992-97. **Orgs:** Leadership prog, Greater Kans City COC, 1985; Nat Asn Black Social Workers; Mo Asn Social Workers; AKA; chair, Ward Chapel Am Church, Steward Bd. **Home Addr:** 8015 Sunset Cir, Grandview, MO 64030-1461, **Home Phone:** (816)763-6754. **Business Addr:** Coordinator of Community Support Services, Swope Parkway Health Center, Bldg B Behav Health Dept 2nd fl 3801 Blue Pkwy, Kansas City, MO 64130, **Business Phone:** (816)923-5800.

## JENKINS, WOODIE R., JR.
Executive, consultant, government official. **Personal:** Born Jun 18, 1940, Washington, DC; son of Rev Woodie R Sr and Laura B Berry Washington; married Ramona M Hernandez; children: Tammy Monique. **Educ:** Howard Univ, BS, physics, 1964; NMex State Univ, MS, mech & indust engineering, 1972. **Career:** Government official (retired), consultant, executive; Nat Range Opers, WSMR, NMex, physicist, 1964-70; Qual Assurance Off, WSMR, gen engr, 1970-77; Qual Eval Div, WSMR, chief, 1977-82; AUS Training & Doctrine Command's Syst Anal Activ, WSMR, spec staff asst tech dir, 1980; Las Cruces, NM, city counr, 1980-85, mayor protem, 1982-85; High Energy Laser Prog Off, WSMR, assoc prog mgr plans & opers, 1982-84; High Energy Laser Systs Test Facil, White Sands Missile Range, chief test opers, 1984-93; S Cent Coun Govts Inc, transp planner, 1993-96; Jenkins Consult Serv, chief exec officer, 1996-. **Orgs:** AUS Tech Liaison Rep Am Defense Preparedness Asn, 1975-; Regist Prof Engr, 1979-96; WSMR Speaker's Bur, 1979-82; Polit Action Comn Dona Ana County Nat Asn Advan Colored People Br, 1979-85; bd dir, White Sands FedCredit Union, 1979-85; WSMR Comdrs Comt Hisp & Black Employ, 1980-85; Transp Communs & Pub Safety Policy Comn Nat League Cities, 1980-83; Dep Activ Career Prog Mgr Engrs & Scientists WSMR, 1981-93; lect circuit, NMex Jr Col; vchmn bd dir, Southern NMex Human Develop Inc, 1985-97; NMex Statewide Health Coord Coun, 1985-86; chmn, Las Cruces Extra Territorial Zoning Comn, 1987-92; vpres bd dir, Las Cruces YMCA, 1988-89. **Honors/Awds:** Certificate of Nobility, NMex Secy State, 1982; WSMR Commander's Award, 1983; Certificate of Appreciation for Public Service, State NMex, 1989; NMex Distinguished Public Service Award, State NMex, 1990. **Business Addr:** Chief Executive Officer, Jenkins Consult Service, 700 Turner Ave, Las Cruces, NM 88005-1327, **Business Phone:** (505)524-1726.

## JENKINS-SCOTT, JACKIE
Health services administrator, college president. **Personal:** Born Aug 18, 1949, Damascus, AR; married James M; children: Amal James & Amber Dawn. **Educ:** Eastern Mich Univ, BS, 1971; Boston Univ Sch Social Work, MSW, 1973; Radcliffe Col, Post Grad Res Prog, 1975. **Career:** Commonwealth, Mass, Dept Pub Health, dir treat serv reg mgr, 1973-77; Roxbury Ct Clin, exec dir, 1977-83; Dimock Community Health Ctr, pres & chief exec officer, 1983-2004; City Boston Pub Health Comn, Comnr, 1998; Wheelock Col, pres, 2004-; Dimock Community Realty Corp, pres. **Orgs:** Trustee, Cousens Fund, 1985-92; pres, Newton Chap Jack & Jill Am, 1985, Delta Sigma Theta; vpres, MA League Health Ctrs, 1987; secy, Mass Pub Health Asn, 1987-88, Consortium Black Health Ctr Direct, 1987; bd mem, NAT Coop Bank, 1997-; bd dir, Boston Found; Kennedy Libr Found & Mus; Boston Plan Excellence; WGBH; Nat Bd Jumpstart; Coun Social Work Educ; bd dir, Century Bank & Trust Co, 2006-; Tufts Health Plan; bd dir, Asset Liability Comt, 2006-. **Home Addr:** 1063 Commonwealth Ave, Newton, MA 02459, **Home Phone:** (617)965-0957. **Business Addr:** President, Wheelock College, 200 The Riverway, Boston, MA 02215, **Business Phone:** (617)879-2000.

## JENNINGS, BENNIE ALFRED
Executive director. **Personal:** Born Nov 21, 1933, Port Gibson, MS; married Mildred B Blackburn; children: Sharon, Marion & Brenda. **Educ:** Alcorn Univ, attended 1957; Grambling State Univ, BS, sec educ, 1960. **Career:** Executive director (retired); Chesebrough-Ponds Inc, mach adjustor, 1960-63; Gen Dynamics, Elec Boat Div, draftsman & apprentice trang admin, 1963-70; Opportunities Industrialization Ctr, New London County Inc, Conn, exec dir, 1970-2006. **Orgs:** Nat Asn Advan Colored People; Nat Coun Negro Women; Blacks In Govt; Opportunities Industrialization Ctr Comt.

## JENNINGS, BERNARD WAYLON-HANDEL
Activist, scholar, chairperson. **Personal:** Born Jun 21, 1968, Bronx, NY; son of Allan Winston and Louise Aiken. **Educ:** Fla Memorial Col, Miami, Fla, BA, pub admin, 1991; Fla Int Univ, Inst Govt Sch Pub Affairs & Serv, code enforcement cert, 1991; Fla A&M Univ, MS, appl social sci & pub admin, 1993. **Career:** City N Miami Mayor's Econ Task Force, intern, 1987; State Rep Elaine Gordon, campaign coordr, 1988, 1990; Fla Memorial Col, intern vpres stud develop, 1990, stud govt asn pres, 1990-91; Metro-Dade County Comn, comnaide comnr Charles Dusseau, 1991-92; Fla A&M Univ, Sch Grad Studies Res & Continuing Educ, grad asst dean grad studies, 1992-92, Campus Alcohol & Drug Res Cent, dir, 1992-93; Gulf Atlantic Indust Supply Inc, 1993; Animation Concepts Inc, chief exec officer & shareholder, 1993-; Fla Memorial Cole, Social Sci Div, prof, 1994-; Metro-Dade County Comn, comn aide chmn bd Arthur E Teele, Jr, 1994; Metro-Dade Transit Agency, transp customer rep, 1994-; IJK govt affais, cheif exec officer & consult, 1994-; BMJ Community Develop Inc, mediator, arbitrator, negotiator & ct app receiver, 2000-; Miami-Dade Dem Party, exec di; Fla Memorial Univ, Social Sci Dept, adj prof. **Orgs:** Founder, pres, United Stud Against Drugs, 1987; Stud Govt Asn, 1987-; pres, Fla Memorial Col Stud Govt Asn, 1990-; Comput Sci Asn; Big Bro, Big Sister, Proj Initiative; Kappa Alpha Psi Fraternity Inc; Kiwanis Club; Fla Memorial Col Bd Trustees, 1990, 1991; Nat Asn Advan Colored People; Citizens Crime Watch Community Comt; chmn adv bd, URGENT Inc; Mod Free & Accepted Masons, Loyal Patterson No 373; Biscayne Gardens Civic Asn; co-founder, nat coordr, & parliamentarian, Nat Stud's Support Coun Africa; nat coord, Second African-Am Summit Liberville, Gabon, Cent Africa, 1993; chmn & pres, Northwest Dade Optimist Club Inc; co-chair, N Miami Sr High Sch Class 87 Reunion Inc; bd mem, BMJ Community Develop Inc. **Honors/Awds:** Police Explorer, N Miami Police Dept, N Miami, Fla, 1986; Awarded Key to the City, 1986; Acad Deans List, 1987; Award of Appreciation, United Stud Against Drugs, 1987; Acad Award Cert, 1988; Plaque, Appreciation for Efforts, Prospect 89; Certificateof Acad Excellence, Alpha Phi Alpha Fraternity Inc, Delta Psi Chapter, 1988; Certificateof Appreciation, TF-101 City Miami, 1988; Volunteer of the Yr Dade County, Certificateof Appreciation, Flagler Fed Dir Vol Agency's, 1988; Acad Hon Roll, 1989, 1990, Fla Memorial Col. **Special Achievements:** Culture Fest 92 in Cote d Ivorie, West Africa, seminar host & keynote speaker, 1992; First African/African-American Summit in Abidjan, Cote d'Ivorie, West Africa, national delegate, 1991; Campaign coordinator for numerous public officials. **Home Addr:** 14910 S River Dr, Miami, FL 33167-1033, **Home Phone:** (305)953-4153. **Business Addr:** Chief Executive Officer, Consultant, IKJ Governmental Affairs Consulting Services, 1320 NW135 St, North Miami, FL 33167-1703, **Business Phone:** (786)486-7217.

## JENNINGS, DEVOYD
Executive. **Personal:** Born Sep 10, 1947, Los Angeles, CA; son of William and Margaret; married Gwendolyn Barbee; children: Shawn, Mark & Demeka. **Educ:** Tex Wesleyan Univ, BS, mkt, 1971. **Career:** Tex Univ, staff asst, 1973-77, customer rep, 1977-85, sr rep, 1985-95, ct affairs specialists, staff asst; Oncor Elec Delivery Co, Sr Staff, 1973-2001. **Orgs:** Pres, Ft Worth Minority Leaders, 1981-88; chmn, Ft Worth Metro Bl Ch, 1986-93; Ft Worth United Way, 1987-93; trustee, Tex Wesleyan Univ, 1987-; N Tex Commn, 1992-; chmn, Tex Asn A A Chambers, 1993-97; US African Am Chambers, 1993-, vice chmn, 1993-95; pres, chief exec officer, Ft Worth Metrop Black Chamber Com, 2001-. **Home Addr:** 4551 Parkwood Dr, Forest Hills, TX 76140, **Home Phone:** (817)478-8464. **Business Addr:** President, Chief Executive Officer, Fort Worth Metropolitan Black Chamber of Commerce, 1150 S Freeway Suite 211, Ft. Worth, TX 76104, **Business Phone:** (817)871-6538.

## JENNINGS, DOMINIQUE
Actor. **Personal:** Born Oct 30, 1965, Stockholm; daughter of Richard and Anchelo; married Lonnie Brandon. **Career:** Films: Sesame Street, 1969; Bad Influence, 1990; Die Hard 2, 1990; A Low Down Dirty Shame, 1994; Sketch Artist II: Hands That See, 1995; Se7en, 1995. TV Series: "Knots Landing", 1991; "Living Single", 1993; "Martin", 1995; "The Fresh Prince of Bel-Air", 1995; "Hang Time", 1995; "Bay watch Nights", 1996; "The Wayans Bros", 1996; "Life with Roger", 1997; "Spawn", 1997-99; "Sunset Beach", 1997-99; "The Jamie Foxx Show", 1999; "Angel", 1999; "Dead Last", 2001; "The Zeta Project", 2001-03; "That's Life", 2002; "44 Minutes: The North Hollywood Shoot-Out", 2003; "50 Cent: Bulletproof", 2005; "Luke 11:17", 2008; "Body of Proof", 2011. **Business Addr:** Actor, Arlene Thornton & Associates, 12711 Ventura Blvd Suite 490, Studio City, CA 91604, **Business Phone:** (818)760-6688.

## JENNINGS, EVERETT JOSEPH
Engineer, executive, president (organization). **Personal:** Born Oct 9, 1938, Shelby, NC; son of Everett and Ardietha M C; children: Sharon B & Carl E. **Educ:** Cath Univ, attended 1952; St Mary's Univ, BBA, 1959, BSIE, 1961; Univ Iowa, attended 1963; Univ Okla, attended 1967. **Career:** San Antonio Fair Inc, dir, planning & scheduling, 1964; Meridian Engineering, proj dir, 1968; Branson Ultra Sonics, sr engr, 1976; Evanbow Construct, dir construct mgt, 1986; State NJ, Dept Transp, asst comnr, 1990; Tish Inc, vpres, oper, 1991; Jennings & Assoc Inc, owner, pres, currently. **Orgs:** Vpres, Am Inst Engr, 1965-68; pres, Am Asn Cost Engr, 1985-88; lt gov, Kiwanis Int, 1988-91; vpres, Habitat NJ, 1990; secy, Goodwill Indust Am, 1992; vpres, Newark Boys Chorus Sch; treas, SHARE Inc; treas, Newark Improv Prog; pres, Montclair Soc Engr; pres, United Hosp Med Ctr Found; bd mem, Metrop YMCA; E Orange Bd Educ; founder, chmn, African Am stud Engr Fund. **Home Addr:** 1610 Corcoran St NW, Washington, DC 20009-3004, **Home Phone:** (202)232-1736. **Business Addr:** President, Owner, Jennings & Associates Inc, 333 Dodd St Suite 3, East Orange, NJ 07017-1700, **Business Phone:** (973)672-1562.

## JENNINGS, DR. LILLIAN PEGUES
Psychologist, writer. **Personal:** Born Youngstown, OH; daughter of Paul and Jessie; children: Dan & Kim. **Educ:** Youngstown State Univ, BSEd, 1954; Univ Pittsburgh, MEd, 1967, PhD, 1971; Univ MD, post-doctoral study. **Career:** Warren Schs, teacher, 1954-57; Youngstown Schs, teacher, prog dir, 1957-66, ed consult, 1966-67; Edinboro State Col, coordr black studies, prof ed & reading clin, 1968-71, affirm action officer, 1972; Youngstown Pub Sch, head start prog dir, res staff assoc, mult ed res teams; James Madison Univ, Col Ed & Human Serv, assoc dean emer, currently; Hosp Corp Am, clin psychologist, prog supvr, currently. **Orgs:** Alpha Kappa Alpha, Va Asn Sch Psychol, Int Reading Asn; served mayors comn Human Resources Pittsburgh, 1966-67; bd dir, Dr Barber's CtrExceptional C Erie; Phi Delta Kappa, Delta Kappa Gamma; chmn, Nat Coun Accreditation Teacher Educ, Dept Ed Accred Teams; Harrisonburg Sch Bd, Va Arts Comn, Nat Alliance Black Sch Ed; lic Prof Counr; vchair, Harrisonburg Sch Bd, Va; chaired mult Accreditation teams WIB. **Honors/Awds:** Res grants, Ford Found, Erie Found, NSF. **Special Achievements:** Multiple Pubs, 1986-87; Author of multiple pubs & monographs; Books: "Reflections of a Native Daughter", 2000; "Damaged Goods: Once Molested, Then a Predator", 2003. **Home Addr:** 4333 Kraft Ave, Studio City, CA 91604. **Business Addr:** Associate Dean Emeritus, James Madison University, 800 S Main St, Harrisonburg, VA 22807-0001, **Business Phone:** (540)568-6211.

## JENNINGS, MARGARET ELAINE
Consultant. **Personal:** Born May 22, 1943, Gadsden, AL; daughter of Izora Torbert Jones and Spencer Small Jr; married Jarvis C; children: Terrence A Hall, Regina Lynn Hall Clay & Jason D. **Educ:** Bowie State Col, Bowie, MD, 1977; Univ Southern Calif, WA, DC, MPA, 1980; Cuyahoga Community Col, Cleveland, OH, AS, regist nurse, 1981. **Career:** Value Engineering Alexandria, Va, programer & analyst, 1975-77; Fed Res Bd, Wash, DC, data base admin, 1977-79; Booz Allen & Hamilton, Bethesda, Md, data base designer, 1979-86, sr systs analyst & asst prog mgr, 1990-; Advan Technol, Reston, Va, sr systs analyst, 1986-89; Perot Systs, Herndon, Va, sr systs analyst, 1989-90; Parma Hospital, 1990-97; Nationwide Ins, assoc agt. **Orgs:** Local Conf Coord, 1984, fund raising, 1985, pub rels, 1986, vpres, 1986-87, pres, 1987-91, nat exec dir, 1991-, Black Data Processing Asn. **Honors/Awds:** Conducted Work Related Sem, 1987-90, Outstanding Leadership Award, 1988, 1990, Managed Nat Conf, 1991, Solicited & Acquired Corp Sponsorship, Increased Chap Mem, Black Data Processing Asn. **Home Addr:** 7102 Good Luck Rd, Lanham, MD 20706-3711. **Business Addr:** Associate Government Systems Division, Booz Allen & Hamilton Inc, 4330 EW Hwy, Bethesda, MD 20814, **Business Phone:** (301)951-2200.

## JENNINGS, DR. ROBERT RAY
Educator, executive. **Personal:** Born Nov 15, 1950, Atlanta, GA; son of Forrest Sr and Mary Beeman. **Educ:** Morehouse Col, BA, sociol, 1972; cert gifted educ, 1975; Univ Ga, cert adult basic educ, 1978; Clark Atlanta Univ, MA, educ psychol, 1974, EdS, educ specialist interrelated learning, 1979, EdD, educ admin & policy studies, 1982; Ga State Univ Sch Educ. **Career:** Atlanta Univ, asst to dir pub rels, 1973; Atlanta Pub Sch, Hoffman reading coordr, 1973-76; Literacy Action Inc Atlanta, reading consult, 1974-75; Reading Learning Ctr Inc E Pt, dir, 1975-79; Atlanta Pub Schs, teacher gifted, 1976-79; Atlanta Univ, consult dean's grant proj, 1979-80; Atlanta Area Tech Sch, part-time prof, 1979-84; Equal Employ Comm US Govt, equal opportunity specialist, 1979-82; Morris Brown Col Atlanta, assoc prof, 1982-84; US Equal Employ Oppor Comn, Atlanta Dist, off common rep off dir, 1982-84, Wash, employee develop specialist, 1984-85; Atlanta Univ, asst vpres, develop & placement, 1985-88; Norfolk State Univ, vpres, develop, 1988-91; Albany State Univ, vp instnl advan, 1991-97; NC Agr & Tech State Univ Found, vice chancellor Develop & Univ Rels & chief exec officer, 1997-98; Wake Forest Univ, Babcock Grad Sch Mgt, Futur Focus 2020, exec vpres & chief opers officer; Kigali Inst Sci, Technol & Mgt, consult, 2001; Ala A&M Univ, pres, 2006-08; Univ Va's Coun, bd dir; White House Fel; Lincoln Univ, pres, 2012-14; Clark Atlanta Univ, Instnl Develop & Alumni Affairs, exec vpres, pres; US Customs & Border Patrol Serv, consult; US Dept Treas, consult; US Equal Employ Opportunity Comn, lead trainer; Gems Loving Care, owner; US Dept State, consult; Macon County Sch Syst, chief consult, currently; Kellogg Grant, chief facilitator, currently, Garrett Theol Sem, consult. **Orgs:** Pres, Atlanta Univ Nat Alumni Asn, 1979-81; bd dir, Exodus Right-to-Read Prog Adult Literacy Prog, 1980; bd adv, Vol Atlanta, 1980-84; parlimentarian Coun Except C Atlanta Area Chap, 1980-81; bd dir, Parents Anonymous Ga, 1981-84; bd trustee, Atlanta Univ, 1981-85; founder& ed-in-chief Alumni Update Leadership Atlanta, 1982-; Self-Study Eval Comt, Morris Brown Col, 1983-84; bd dir, Planned Parenthood, 1983-87; exec bd, Leadership Atlanta, 1986-87; vpres, Coun Advan Pub Black Cols & Univ, 1989-; Naacp Educ Legal Adv bd, chair, 1987-; Leadership Albany, 1992-93; SW Ga Comprehensive Health Ist bd, 1992-; Cot Rels Coun & TurnerJob Corp Inc, Albany Ga, bd, 1996-98; Am Lung Asn, Albany Chap, bd, 1994-; W End Church Christ; Am Asn Higher Educ, 1988-; Am Biog Inst, hon mem, bd adv, 1987-; Coun Advan & Support Educ, 1984-; Phi Delta Kappa, 1982-. **Home Addr:** 2005 King George Lane SW, Atlanta, GA 30331-4917. **Business Addr:** President, Lincoln University of the Commonwealth of Pennsylvania, 1570 Baltimore Pke, Lincoln University, PA 19352, **Business Phone:** (484)365-7400.

## JENNINGS, SYLVESTA LEE
Banker. **Personal:** Born Jan 30, 1933, Halifax, VT; son of Anthony and Luella Freeman; married Lillie Flippen; children: Mitchell. **Educ:** NC A&T State Univ, Greensboro, NC, BS, 1958; Univ Va, Sch Consumer Banking, cert, 1968; Rutgers Univ, Stonier Grad Sch Banking, MS, 1972. **Career:** First State Bank, Danville, VA, chmn, chief exec officer & pres, 1958-2001. **Orgs:** Danville Chamber Com, 1989; Nat Bankers Asn, 1989; Prince Hall Masons Va; Va Sch Bd, Danville; Southside Va Bus & Educ Comt; Kappa Alpha Psi Fraternity; Danville Community Col Educ Found; adv bd mem, Danville Life Saving Crew. **Honors/Awds:** National Association for Equal Opportunity in Higher Education Award, 1989. **Special Achievements:** Research se-

lected for library at Rutgers University, Harvard University, and ABA, 1972. **Home Addr:** 113 Cambridge Cir, Danville, VA 24541-5237, **Home Phone:** (434)793-3882. **Business Addr:** Chairman, Chief Executive Officer, First State Bank, 445 Mt Cross Rd, Danville, VA 24543-6400, **Business Phone:** (804)793-4611.

### JENSEN, MARCUS CHRISTIAN
Baseball player, athletic coach. **Personal:** Born Dec 14, 1972, Oakland, CA; children: Marcus Proctor. **Career:** Baseball player (retired), baseball coach; San Francisco Giants, catcher, 1990-97; Detroit Tigers, catcher, 1997; Milwaukee Brewers, catcher, 1998 & 2002; St Louis Cardinals, catcher, 1999; Minn Twins, catcher, 2000; Boston Red Sox, catcher, 2001; Tex Rangers, catcher, 2001; New York Yankees, catcher, 2003; Reno Silver Sox, catcher; Golden Baseball League, 2005-06; Ariz Athletics, mgr, 2009-13; Oakland Athletics, hitting coach, 2007-, coach, 2015-. **Business Addr:** Coach, Oakland Athletics, Oakland-Alameda County Coliseum 7000 Coliseum Way, Oakland, CA 94621, **Business Phone:** (510)638-4900.

### JENSEN, DR. RENALDO MARIO
Automotive executive, air force officer, association executive. **Personal:** Born Jun 6, 1934, New York, NY; son of Octave and Doris Davis; married Alicia Clark; children: Renaldo M & Malinda L. **Educ:** Howard Univ, Wash, DC, BS, mech engineering, 1958; USAF Inst Technol, Dayton, OH, MS, aerospace engineering, 1966; Purdue Univ, West Lafayette, Ind, PhD, aerospace engineering, 1970. **Career:** Air force officer (retired), executive; NC Agr & Tech State Univ, res officer training corps; Minuteman missile crew; USAF, officer, 1958-78; Malstrom Afb, Mont; Wright Patterson AFB, Air Force Sch Technol, asst prof aerospace-mech engineering, 1967-74; Ford Motor Co, Dearborn, Mich, aerospace engr advan concepts aerodynamics, 1978-86, dir minority supplier develop, 1987-2005; Innovision Technologies Inc, chmn & chief exec officer, 2005-. **Orgs:** New Detroit Inc, 1987-; Greater Detroit Chamber Com, 1987-; bd dir, Minority Bus Dir, Try Us, 1987-; bd dir, Nat Minority Bus Develop Coun, 1988-; bd dir, Plum Hollow Country Club, 1995-; Am Soc Mech Engrs; Am Inst Aeronaut & Astronaut; Combustion Inst; Mil Opers Res Soc; Alpha Phi Alpha Fraternity; Tau Beta Pi Eng Hon Soc; Billion Dollar Roundtable; bd mem, Diversity Info Resources Inc. **Honors/Awds:** Missile Combat Crew Award, 1970; Air Force Commendation Medal; Distinguished Service Award, Wis Minority Purchasing Coun, 1988; MBE Coordinator of the Year Award, Nat Minority Supplier Develop Coun, 1992; Distinguished Service Award, Nat Minority Supplier Develop Coun, 1994; Investor in Education Award, Tuck Sch Bus Dartmouth, 2003; Tuck Lifetime Achievement Award, Tuck Sch Bus Dartmouth, 2004; AMEP Alumni Award, NMSDC Kellogg, 2005; President's Award, Mich Minority Bus Develop Coun, 2005; Outstanding Leadership Award, Nat Minority Supplier Develop Coun, 2005; Impact Award, Billion Dollar Roundtable, 2005; National Director's Appreciation Award, Minority Bus Develop Agency, 2005; Minority Business Hall of Fame & Museum, Minority Bus Hall Fame Inc, 2005; Fifty Influential Entrepreneurs in Business Award, Minority Enterprise Exec Coun, 2006. **Special Achievements:** First African Americans to earn M.S. degrees in aerospace engineering from the US Air Force School of Technology; Minority Suppliers Hall of Fame. **Home Addr:** 26510 Rose Hill Dr, Farmington Hills, MI 48334, **Home Phone:** (248)477-7928. **Business Addr:** Chairman, Chief Executive Officer, Innovision Technologies Inc, 28175 Haggerty Rd, Novi, MI 48377, **Business Phone:** (248)987-6990.

### JERKINS, REV. JERRY GAINES
Clergy. **Personal:** Born Loxley, AL; married Naomi Donald; children: Cntr, Gerald, Jennifer & Jacqueline. **Educ:** Austin Peay Univ, BS, 1972; N Tenn Bible Inst. **Career:** St John Baptist Church, Clarksville, pastor, 1967, pastor emer, currently; Haynes Chapel Baptist Church, pastor. **Orgs:** Clarksville Ministerial Asn; ministerial rep, C C; corres secy, Pastor's Conf Nat & Baptist Conv Am; PTA; bd, C Ctr Hilldale Methodist Church; pres, Missionary Baptist St Conv; bd, United Givers Fund; adv bd, Montgomery Co Welfare Dept; adv bd, Youth Challenge Ctr; pres, Dist Pastor's Conf; bd, Salvation Army; Nat AsnAdvan Colored People; gospel Programmer, Radio Sta WJZM. **Home Addr:** 1113 W Young St, Pensacola, FL 32501. **Business Addr:** Pastor Emeritus, St John Missionary Baptist Church, 662 South 52Nd St, Richmond, CA 94804, **Business Phone:** (510)233-1779.

### JERKINS, RODNEY (RJ DARKCHILD)
Music producer, songwriter, musician. **Personal:** Born Sep 16, 1977, Pleasantville, NJ; son of Frederick and Sylvia; married Joy Enriquez; children: David & Heavenly. **Career:** Many albums including "Gina Thompson - Nobody Does It Better", 1996; "No Authority - Keep On", 1997; "Brandy - Never Say Never", 1998; "Coko - Hot Coko", 1999; "Spice Girls - Forever", 2000; "Rhona - Rhona", 2001; "Brandy - Full Moon", 2002; "Blaque - Torch", 2004; "Joy Enriquez - Atmosphere Of Heaven", 2005; "Janet Jackson - Discipline", 2008; "Natasha Uncontrollable", 2009; Guest raps: Hodge - "Head Nod" (Darkchild Remix), 1995; AZ - "Something About You" (Darkchild Remix), 1996; Tasha Holiday "Just The Way You Like It (Darkchild Remix)" w/ Lil' Cease, Peter Gunz and Mike Nitty, MQ3 - "Everyday", Immature - "I Can't Wait" with Mike Nitty, Mary J. Blige - "Everything (Darkchild Remix)", K-Ball - "On The Weekend", "Love Matters", 1997; Kirk Franklin & The Nu Nation Project - "Revolution", Keith Washington - "Bring It On (Darkchild Remix)", 1998; Brandy - "Top of the World" (Darkchild Remix) with Fat Joe and Big Pun, 1999; Natalie Wilson & The S.O.P. Chorale - "Act Like You Know" with LaShawn Daniels, 2000; Rhona - "Satisfied (Another Darkchild Remix)" with Fats, So Plush - "What You Do To Me" with 50 Cent and Fats, "Ain't My Fault", 2001; Jay Mathis "Kiss" with Pain and Fats, Mary Mary - "He Said" with Fats, K-Young - "Ballinest Player" with Lil' Zal, K-Young - "Ooh Wee", 2002; Shawn Desman - "Sexy" Natalie Wilson & The S.O.P. Chorale - "Good Life", 2003 Kierra "Kiki" Sheard - "You Don't Know", 2004; Joy Enriquez - "Don't You Let Go", Anesha Birchett - "Get Ready" with Mase, 2005; The Darkchild Allstars - "We Are Family", 2006; The Pussycat Dolls With Diddy, Lil Wayne, & Fatman Scoop - When I Grow Up (Darkchild Remix)", 2008; "Angel", 2008; "Right Here (Departed)", 2008; "Long Distance", 2008; "The Definition", 2008; "I Look So Good (Without You)", 2009; "Girls", 2009; "Make Me", 2009; "Telephone", 2009; "The One", 2009; "Shake My", 2010; "Perfect Nightmare", 2010; "I Hate That You Love Me", 2010; "Target Practice", 2010; "Taking His Girl", 2011; "What Are Words", 2011; "Just Can't Get Enough", 2011; "Stitch by Stitch", 2011; "I Forgive You", 2011; "Turn the Lights Out", 2011; "Big Hoops (Bigger the Better)", 2012; "Spirit Indestructible", 2012; "Parking Lot", 2012; "Got Me Good", 2012; "Die in Your Arms", 2012; "As Long as You Love Me", 2012; "Waiting for the Night", 2013; "Bucket List", 2013; "The Art of Letting Go", 2013; "Perfect World", 2013; "Lease My Love", 2013; "Xscape", 2014; Darkchild Inc, chief exec officer, currently. **Honors/Awds:** Dove Award; Grammy Award. **Business Addr:** Chief Executive Officer, Darkchild Inc, 550 Madison Ave, New York, NY 10022-3211, **Business Phone:** (212)833-7442.

### JEROME, CURTIS
Educator. **Personal:** Born Nov 16, 1949, Kansas City, MO; married Valerie Joy Smith. **Educ:** USAF Acad, BS, humanities, 1971; Mich State Univ, MA, eng, 1976. **Career:** USAF Acad CO, asst ftbll coach, 1971-72; Lowry Afb Denver, dir drug/alcohol abuse prgm, 1972-75; USAF Acad, asst prof Eng, 1976-80; USAF Acad Activties Grp, chief congr liaison br, 1980-. **Orgs:** Alcohol Abuse Rehab Coun, SW Denver Ment Health Ctr, 1973-74; Drug Alcohol Abuse Coun, 1973-75; Speakers Bur, Lowry AFB, 1973-75; Nat Coun Teachers Eng, 1975-; acad liaison officer mem, USAF Acad Way Life Com, 1976-80; Speakers Bur USAF Acad, 1976-80; course dir, Black Lit, Minority Lit, African Lit USAF Acad Eng Dept, 1978-80. **Home Addr:** 2944 Lockridge, Kansas City, MO 64128. **Business Addr:** HQ USA MPPA Pentagon, Washington, DC 20330.

### JEROME, REV. JOSEPH D.
Clergy. **Personal:** Born Oct 17, 1951, Port-au-Prince; son of Thelamon and Marie K. **Educ:** Suffolk Co Community Col, attended 1983; Long Island Univ, CW, BS, mgt, 1987; Seabury-Western Theol Sem, MDiv, 1991. **Career:** Family Consult Serv, 1984-86; Suffolk Child Develop, 1985-87; US Legalization & Naturalization Serv, 1987-89; St John's Episcopal Hosp; Interfaith Med Ctr; Diocese Long Island, Church St Luke & St Matthew, priest; St Philips Episcopal Church; Prov Coun, clergy rep; St Gabriel's Episcopal Church, Hollis, NY, interim rector; All Saints' Episcopal Church, rector, currently. **Orgs:** Union Black Episcopalian, 1983-; La Union Hispanica, 1983-87; African People Org, 1985-87; trustee, Diocesan Trustees; Diocesan Youth Ministry, search comt, calling Bishop Provenzano; Diocesan Coun; Dep to last Gen Conv, Long Island; chair, Latino Comn Diocese Long Island; clergy, Asn Episcopal Black, 1989-; Am Bible Lit, 1991-; Alban Inst, 1991-; Diocesan AIDS Comn, 1991-; Nat Asn Advan Colored People, Long Island, 1991-; Boy Scouts. **Home Addr:** 288 Lowell Ave, Islip Terrace, NY 11752, **Home Phone:** (516)224-5116. **Business Addr:** Rector, All Saints' Episcopal Church, 43-12 46th St, Sunnyside, NY 11104, **Business Phone:** (718)784-8031.

### JEROME, DR. NORGE WINIFRED
Educator. **Personal:** Born Nov 3, 1930, Grenada; daughter of McManus Israel and Evelyn Mary Grant. **Educ:** Howard Univ, BS, nutrit & dietetics, 1960; Univ Wis, MS, exp food & human nutrit, 1962, PhD, human nutrit, 1967; Univ Wis, Madison & Milwaukee, post doctoral training, 1967. **Career:** Elem Classes & Domestic Sci, teacher, 1947-56; Univ Wis, Dept Foods & Nutrit, res asst, 1960-62, Sch Home Econ & Nat Inst Res Poverty, Howard Univ, instr food & nutrit, 1962-63; res assoc, 1966-67; Kans Univ Med Ctr, Dept Diet & Nutrit, asst prof, 1967-69, Dept Human Ecol, assoc prof, 1969-72, Dept Prev Med & Community Health, asst prof nutrit, 1969-70, Dept Human Ecol, from asst prof to assoc prof, 1970-74, Dept Human Ecol, prof, 1972-74, Dept Community Health, assoc prof, 1974-78, Dept Prev Med, prof, 1978-95, Community Nutrit Div, dir, 1981-95, Sch Med, nutritionist, anthrop, interim assoc & dean minority affairs, 1996-98, 1996-98, Prev Med & Pub Health, prof emer, 1996-; Univ Mo, lectr, 1968; Tuskegee Inst, Dept Home Econs & Food Admin, vis lectr, 1969; Nutrit Anthrop Communicator, ed, 1974-77; Ed Resources Ctr, dir, 1974-77; Univ Tenn, vis prof, 1977; Campbell Soup Co, res adv, 1979-81; Task Force Animal Agr Res, 1980-82; Nutrit Adv Bd, 1980-82; Bristol Myers Co, media rep, 1981-82; Comt Nutrit Educ, 1983-85; AID, Bur Sci & Technol, Off Nutrit, dir, 1988-91, sr res fel, 1991-92; Solar Cookers Int, bd dir, 1992-2000, pres, 1998-2000; Community Health Scholars Prog, W K Kellogg Found, prog evaluator, 1998-. **Orgs:** Am Dietetic Asn, 1968-70; Panelist, White House Conf Food Nutrit & Health, 1969; bd dir, Urban League, 1969-77; Task Force Comt, 1969-71; Health Welfare Comt, 1970-75; Am Pub Health Asn, 1970-71; C Media Merchandising Coun, 1970-77; acad adv, C's Advert Rev Unit, 1974-78; founder & chairperson, Coun Nutrit Anthrop, 1974-77; World Food & Nutrit Study Nat Acad Sci, 1976; chmn, Soc Nutrit Educ, 1976; Cancer & Nutrit Sci Rev Comt, 1976-79; fel AmAnthrop Asn; fel Soc Appl Anthrop; Soc Med Anthrop; Soc Behav Med; adv bd, J Nutrit Planning, 1977-84; founder & chmn, Comn Nutrit Anthrop, 1978-79; fel Am Soc Nutrit Scis, 1978-; Am Soc Clin Nutrit, 1978-; US Assoc Club Rome, 1980-97; Mayor's Task Force Food & Hunger, 1983-88; bd mem, Urban League, Greater Kans City; fel Am Col Nutrit, 1986-; Ariz DisControl Res Comn, 1986; pres, Asn Women Develop, 1991-93; Black Health Care Coalition, 1992-2002; bd dir, Coop Develop Found; bd trustee, Univ Bridgeport; bd trustee, Child Health Found; Soc Epidemiol Res; AAAS; NY Acad Sci; Inst Food Technologists; Sigma Delta Epsilon; Am Soc Nutrit Sci, 1998-2000; Beta Kappa Chi Unicorn Theatre, 2001-04; bd dir, Maternal & Child Health Coalition Greater Kans City, 2002-03; chair, Northeast Johnson County Nat AsnAdvan Colored People, 2002; Johnson County Libr Found, 2003-; bd dir, Health Care Found Greater Kans City, 2004-09. **Honors/Awds:** Tuition Scholarships & Dean's Honor Roll, Howard Univ, 1956-60, Pepperidge Farm Inc Award, Outstanding Jr, 1958-59, Beta Kappa Chi, Sci Honor Soc, 1959; Omicron Nu, 1961; Matrix Award, Women Commun Inc, 1976; Dairy Council Merit Award, Greater Kans City, 1977, 1988; First Higuchi & Irvin Young berg Research Achievement Award, Univ Kans, 1982; Spotlight Award, Women's Bur, US Dept Labor, 1990; Prev Med Excellence Award, Univ of Kans Sch of Med, 1999; Life time Achievement Award, Excellence in Academia, Inst Caribbean Studies, 2002. **Special Achievements:** Numerous professional articles, technical reports and professional abstracts. **Home Addr:** 14402 W 68th St, Shawnee, KS 66216-2149, **Home Phone:** (913)962-9020. **Business Addr:** Professor Emerita Preventive Medicine & Public Health, University of Kansas Medical Center, 3901 Rainbow Blvd, Kansas City, KS 66160-7313, **Business Phone:** (913)588-2770.

### JERRARD, PAUL (PAUL C JERRARD)
Hockey coach, hockey player. **Personal:** Born Apr 20, 1965, Winnipeg, MB; married Cheryl; children: Meaghan & Catherine. **Educ:** Lake Super State Col, BA, sports mgt; Athol Murray Col Notre Dame, 1983. **Career:** Ice hockey defenceman (retired); Lake Super State Univ, defenceman, 1983-87, asst coach, 1997-98 & 1999-2002; Colo Rangers, defenceman, 1987-88; Kalamazoo Wings, defenceman, 1988-89; Minn N Stars, defenceman, 1988-89; Denver Rangers, defenceman, 1988-89; Kalamazoo Wings, defenceman, 1989-94; Albany Choppers, defenceman, 1990-91; Milwaukee Admirals, defenceman, 1993-94; Hershey Bears, defenceman, 1994-97, asst coach, 2003-05; Ft Wayne Komets, defenceman, 1995-96; Lowell Lock Monsters, asst coach, 1998-99; Colo Avalanche, asst coach, 2002-03; Iowa Stars, asst coach, 2005-06 & 2007-08; Iowa Chops, asst coach, 2008-09; Tex Stars, asst coach, 2009-11; Dallas Stars, coach, 2011-13; Jerrardsport-hockey, coach, 2013; Utica Comets, Vancouver Am Hockey League affil, asst coach, 2013-16; Calgary Flames, asst coach, 2016-. **Orgs:** Nat Strength & Conditioning Soc. **Honors/Awds:** Calder Cup winning Hershey Bears, 1997. **Special Achievements:** 10 years Professional Hockey playing experience; Four years experience coaching National Collegiate Athletic Association; Nine years experience coaching in the American Hockey League (AHL); Three years coaching in the National Hockey League. **Business Addr:** Coach, Jerrard Sport Hockey, 3170 Birchridge Dr, Frisco, TX 75033, **Business Phone:** (515)707-2035.

### JERVAY, DR. MARION WHITE
Lawyer, executive, association executive. **Personal:** Born Mar 26, 1948, Mt. Olive, NC; married Thomas; children: 1. **Educ:** Univ NC, Wilmington, BA, hist, 1971; George Washington Univ, Nat Law Ctr, Wash, DC, attended 1974; Sch Law Duke Univ, Durham, NC, JD, 1976. **Career:** New Hanover County Bd Educ Wilmington, eng teacher, 1972; Norfolk City Schs, teacher, 1972-73; Wade & Roger Smith Attys, Law Raleigh, res asst, 1975; Hon Earl W Vaughn, NC Ct Appeals Raleigh, res asst, 1976-77; Liggett Group Inc Durham, NC, corp atty, 1977; Am Med Int Inc, senoir corp coun, 1983-89; Marken Co, prin, 1993-96; MedPartners Inc, vpres, bus develop & opers, 1997-98; Duke Clin Res Inst, dir, strategic develop, 2000, dir, contracts mgt, 2000-08, dir, strategic develop & contracts mgt, 2000-08; atty pvt practr, currently. **Orgs:** NC State Bar; NC Bar Asn; Wake Co Bar Asn; bd mem, NC Asn Black Lawyers; ABA; Am Bus Women's Asn Delta sigma Theta sorority. **Business Addr:** Lawyer, Private Practitioner, 3631 Stoneybrook Dr, Durham, NC 27705-2428.

### JERVAY, PAUL REGINALD, JR.
Newspaper executive, association executive. **Personal:** Born Oct 25, 1949, Atlanta, GA; son of Paul Reginald Sr (deceased) and Brenda Yancey (deceased); married Evelyn Harrison; children: Jeneea, Adria, Shenay Dunston & Kelvin Dunston. **Educ:** NC Cent Univ, Raleigh, NC, BS, acct, 1971. **Career:** The Carolinian Newspaper, Raleigh, NC, publ, owner, 1971-; Advantage Advert, consult. **Orgs:** Owner, treas, Nay-Kel Educ Ctr; bd chairperson, Triangle Opportunities Industrialization Ctr Raleigh Inc. **Honors/Awds:** Service Award, St Augustines Col, 1983. **Home Addr:** PO Box 28204, Raleigh, NC 27611, **Home Phone:** (919)828-1483. **Business Addr:** Publisher, Owner, The Carolinian Newspaper, 501 E Davie St, Raleigh, NC 27611, **Business Phone:** (919)834-5558.

### JERVAY-PENDERGRASS, DR. DEBRA
Educator. **Educ:** Emerson Col, BS, commun disorder, 1973; Univ Pittsburgh, MA, speech-lang path; Georgetown Univ, PhD, ling. **Career:** Speech-lang pathologist; Lt Joseph P Kennedy Inst, Dept Educ, Off Spec Educ Progs, co-dir, 1997-2001; Childrens Inst; Howard Univ, Dept Commun Dis researcher, adj asst prof; poet; Montgomery County Pub Schs, Div Early Childhood Progs & Servs, speech-lang pathologist & Linguist, storytellers123, currently; Watkins Mill High Sch Parent Teacher Associations, secy, currently. **Business Addr:** Speech-Language Pathologist & Linguist, Founder, Storytellers123, PO Box 15114, Chevy Chase, MD 20825, **Business Phone:** (301)807-0779.

### JESSUP, GAYLE LOUISE (GAYLE JESSUP FRANKLIN)
Executive, journalist. **Personal:** Born Jul 26, 1957, Washington, DC; daughter of Cedric B and Theresa W; married Charles L Jr; children: Charles. **Educ:** Howard Univ, BAJ, commun, 1978; Northwestern Univ, MSJ, broadcasting, 1982. **Career:** WTOC-TV, Savannah, Ga, reporter, educ reporter, hostess, 1982-84; WGXA-TV, Macon, Ga, news co-anchor, anchor, reporter, 1984-86; WSB-TV, Atlanta, Ga, assoc producer, 1986-87; WHUT-TV, Wash, DC, producer, hostess, 1987-; In-Focus Productions, pres, 1991-. **Orgs:** Am Fedn Tv & Radio Artists, 1988-; Montgomery CountyNat Asn Advan Colored People, 1989-; scholar comt head, Doug Wiliams Found, 1989-91; mentor, Mentors Inc, 1989-; Natl Assn Black Journalists, 1990-. **Home Addr:** 8053 Cobble Creek Cir, Potomac, MD 20854, **Home Phone:** (301)299-8696. **Business Addr:** Producer, Hostess, WHUT-TV, 2222 4th St NW, Washington, DC 20059, **Business Phone:** (202)806-3200.

### JESSUP, MARSHA EDWINA
College teacher, educator, executive director. **Personal:** Born Nov 8, 1944, Washington, DC. **Educ:** Howard Univ, BS, 1967; Univ Mich, MS, 1971; Cath Univ, attended 1973; Temple Univ, attended 1978. **Career:** Smithsonian Inst, free-lance sci illus, 1967-68; Howard Univ Col Med, asst med illus, 1968-69; US Dept Agr Grad Sch, fac mem, 1971-74; Armed Forces Inst Path, med illus, 1972; NIH, med illus, 1972-74; Univ Med & Dent NJ, Robert Wood Johnson Med Sch, Dept Media Resources, chief med illus, dir, Surg Dept, adj assoc prof, dir media resources, currently, customized training & indust out reach, dir, currently. **Orgs:** NE region bd gov rep, Asn Biomed Commun dir, 1982-84; chmn, Asn Med Illustrators, 1986-87. **Home Addr:** 80 Ross Hall Blvd S, Piscataway, NJ 08854, **Home Phone:** (732)249-1182. **Business Addr:** Director & Chief Medical Illustrator, Adjunct Associate Professor, University of Medicine & Dentistry of New Jersey, Dept Media Resources, Piscataway, NJ 08854-5635, **Business Phone:** (732)235-4127.

**JETER, CLIFTON B.**
Chairperson, vice president (organization), executive. **Personal:** Born Feb 22, 1944, Martinsville, VA; son of Clifton B Sr and Naomi Winston; married Diane R Bates; children: Sheree, Amani & Aja. **Educ:** Howard Univ, BA, 1967; Am Univ, MBA, 1970, MD, CPA, 1972; Harvard Univ, advan mgt prog, 1991. **Career:** Executive (retired); Peoples Involvement Corp, controller, 1967-69; Peoples Develop Corp, finance vpres, 1969-74; Howard Univ, internal auditor, 1974-75; Wolf & CO, CPA's, mgr, 1975-77; John F Kennedy Ctr Performing Arts, controller, 1977-84, dir finance, 1985-91, chief financial officer, vpres facil. **Orgs:** Treas Qual Construct Co, 1974-77; Nat Inst Tennis Develop, 1975-77; Alpha Phi Alpha; Am Inst CPA'S; MD Asn CPA'S DC Inst CPA'S; Nat Black MBA Asn; Nat Asn Black Accts; Am Mgt Asn; Asn Practicing CPA'S; Harvard Club Wash; Inst Mgt Accountant; chmn bd, Agr Fed Credit Union, currently. **Home Addr:** 1801 Queensguard Rd, Silver Spring, MD 20906-2027, **Home Phone:** (301)460-8669.

**JETER, DELORES DEANN**
Pharmacist. **Personal:** Born Mar 11, 1949, Union, SC. **Educ:** Univ SC, Col Pharm, 1973, PhD, pharm admin. **Career:** Funderburks Drug, intern, 1972; Moncrief Army Hosp, intern, 1973; Richland Memorial Hosp, clin pharm, 1973; Millers Pharm, reg pharmacist & mgr, 1974. **Orgs:** Am Pharmaceut Asn; Palmetto & Med Dent Pharmaceut Asn; Alcoholic & Drug Abuse Coun; organist, Calvary Baptist Church; Islam Grand Ct Daughters Isis. **Honors/Awds:** Cit day, Columbia, SC. **Home Addr:** 153 Ashford St, Chester, SC 29706. **Business Addr:** 827 N Main St, Lancaster, SC 29720, **Business Phone:** (803)285-2066.

**JETER, DEREK SANDERSON**
Baseball player. **Personal:** Born Jun 26, 1974, Pequannock, NJ; son of Sanderson Charles and Dorothy. **Educ:** Univ Mich. **Career:** NY Yankees, infielder, 1995-, capt, 2003-; Saturday Night Live, host. **Orgs:** Turn 2 Found. **Business Addr:** Professional Baseball Player, NewYork Yankees, 880 River Ave, Bronx, NY 10452, **Business Phone:** (718)293-4300.

**JETER, JOSEPH C., JR.**
Engineer, executive, association executive. **Personal:** Born Aug 16, 1961, Philadelphia, PA. **Educ:** Taylor Univ, BA, commun, 1983, BS, syst anal & polit sci, 1983. **Career:** Taylor Univ, minority recruitment coord, 1980-83, minority fund raising & planner, 1982-83; Appl Energy Servs, intern, 1982; Bell Pa, asst mgr network engineering; sem writer & career plng, self-employed, 1983-; minority recruitment writer & consult, self-employed, 1983-; career plng writer & consult, self-employed, 1983-; Unisys, vpres, global outsourcing & infrastructure serv, 2000-08; Bus One Consult, vpres; Asigra Inc, sls officer. **Orgs:** Vpres, Black Cult Soc, 1980-82; ed writer, Taylor Univ, 1982-83; pres Adv Comn, Minority Recruitment Taylor Univ, 1982-83; Stud & Econ Leadership Forum, 1982-83. **Home Addr:** 528 E Church Lane, Philadelphia, PA 19144-1422, **Home Phone:** (215)438-6308. **Business Addr:** Assistant Manager Network Engineering, Bell of Pennsylvania, 2 INA Plz Suite 450, Philadelphia, PA 19103.

**JETER-JOHNSON, SHEILA ANN (KAFI IMA)**
Writer, publisher. **Personal:** Born Mar 4, 1952, Indianapolis, IN; daughter of Helen L and Linzie E Jeter; married Lawrence E; children: Shelette Veal. **Educ:** Ind Univ-Purdue Univ Indianapolis, 1973; Draughons Bus Col, 1982; Martin Univ, BA, communs, 1991. **Career:** LS Ayres & Co, PBX operator, 1970-73; Gen Motors Corp, 1973-96; Twelve Gates Publ, former publ, 1986-88; Indianapolis Star, reporter, 1988. **Orgs:** Founding pres, Intl Black Writers, Indianapolis Chap, 1988; vpres, Midtown Writers Assn, 1989-. **Honors/Awds:** Outstanding Black Women of Indianapolis, NCNW, 1990. **Special Achievements:** Author: Before It's Too Late, Twelve Gates Publ, 1986. **Home Addr:** 5749 Covey Ridge Trl, Loves Park, IL 61111, **Home Phone:** (815)633-5483. **Business Addr:** Publisher, Twelve Gates Publications, PO Box 19869, Indianapolis, IN 46219, **Business Phone:** (317)357-9093.

**JETT, ARTHUR VICTOR, SR.**
Executive, building inspector. **Personal:** Born Dec 16, 1906, Union Springs, AL; married Katie; children: Kay Baker A. **Educ:** Morehouse Acad, attended 1928; Chicago Tech Sch. **Career:** Bankhead W Contractors & Develop Inc, pres; Masonry Trades & Utica Inst, instr, 1932-34; Bricklayers Union Local 9 AFL, bus agt, 1940-44; Masonary Trades, apprent com, 1946-50; Atlanta Bd Educ Estimating & Plan Reading, instr masonry trades, 1948-51; bldg contractor, 1952-; Dept Labor, adv Com, 1967-69. **Orgs:** Atlanta Urban League, 1944-74; YMCA; bd dir, bd mem & treas, Atlanta Br, Nat Asn Advan Colored People; bd, Nat Child Welfare League Am; United Way; pres bd, Gate City Day Nursery Asn; bd mem treas, Consol Mortgage & Investment Co; Atlantic Chamber Com; Nat Conf Social Welfare; first Congregations Chap; UCC; vice chmn, Deacon Bd Morehouse Col Alumni Asn; life mem, Nat Asn Advan Colored People. **Home Addr:** 1158 Fountain Dr SW, Atlanta, GA 30314, **Home Phone:** (404)758-3878. **Business Addr:** 825 Cascade Ave SW, Atlanta, GA 30311.

**JETT, JAMES**
Athlete, football player. **Personal:** Born Dec 28, 1970, Charlestown, WV; children: James Jr & Jordan. **Educ:** WVa Univ. **Career:** Football player (retired); Los Angeles Raiders, 1993-94; Oakland Raiders, wide receiver, 1995-2002.

**JEWELL, CURTIS T.**
Executive, president (organization). **Personal:** Born Sep 8, 1943, Richmond, VA; son of Thelma and Fletcher; married Beverly Ann Cheeks; children: Neonu Allen, Nia, Curtis II, Sisi, Clay Johnson & Leah Johnson. **Educ:** Park Col, social psychol & econs, 1975; Univ Southern Calif, MBA; Case Western Res Univ, BA. **Career:** Rubicon, admin dir, 1967-72; U Hurer Drug Prog, exec dir, 1972-75; Int Inc, pres, 1975-79; State Ohio, chief off human serv, 1978-79; Nationwide Ins Co, automated sales agt, 1979-85; Praxis Consult Group Inc, pres & chief exec officer, 1987-89; Excel Mgt Systs Inc, founder, pres & chief exec officer, owner, 1989-; Accenture LTD, technol consult; MyCypher.com, pres & chief exec officer. **Orgs:** Bd trustee, Spec Ties, 1994-; bd trustee, Community Shelter Bd, 1996-97; bd trustee, Greater Columbus Arts Coun, 1996-97; bd trustee, Young Men Destiny, 1997; bd trustee, Nat Border Patrol Coun, 1998-; bd trustee, COSI, 1998-; bd trustee, Short N Bus Asn, 2000; bd, Franklin County Workforce Policy, 2000; bd chair, pres & chief exec officer Excel Mgt, Nat Black Programming Consortium. **Home Addr:** 2445 Brookwood Rd, Columbus, OH 43209, **Home Phone:** (614)236-4858. **Business Addr:** President, Chairman, Chief Executive Officer, Founder, Excel Management Systems Inc, 691 N High St 2nd Fl, Columbus, OH 43215, **Business Phone:** (614)224-4007.

**JEWELL, TOMMY EDWARD, III**
Judge. **Personal:** Born Jun 30, 1954, Tucson, AZ; son of Bobbie L and Tommie E Jr; married Angela Juzang; children: Taja Marie & Thomas IV. **Educ:** NMex State Univ, BA, 1976; Univ NMex Sch Law, JD, 1979. **Career:** Judge (retired); Soc Albuquerque Inc, staff atty legal aid, 1979; Rocky Mountain, regional dir; Jewell Kelly & Kitson, Albuquerque, NMex, partner, 1981-84; State NMex, Albuquerque, NMex, metrop ct judge, 1983-91, Second Judicial Dist Ct, dist ct judge, 1991-2005. **Orgs:** Omega Psi Phi Fraternity Inc, 1974-; Black Am Law Stud Asn, 1977-79; Adv comt, Juv Justice, 1978-; comt mem, Gov Juv Code Task Force, 1979-; fel Reginald Heber Smith, Howard Univ Sch Law, 1980-81; Nat Bar Asn, 1980-; bd dir, State Justice Inst, 1995. **Honors/Awds:** Dean's Award, Univ NMex Sch Law, 1978-79; Outstanding Young New Mexican, NMex Jaycees, 1986. **Home Addr:** 905 Wash St SE, Albuquerque, NM 87108-4445.

**JEWETT, KATRINA ANN**
President (organization). **Educ:** Clark Atlanta Univ, BA, polit sci, 1995; Emory Univ Sch Law, JD, 1998. **Career:** Miller Martin PLLC, atty, 1998-2002; YKK Corp Am, corp atty, 2002-05; Self Employ Loan Fund, dir, 2006-07; Eeh Mgt Consult, sales mgr, chief exec officer & pres, 2007-. **Business Addr:** Chief Executive Officer, President, Eeh Consulting Inc, 235 SW 136th St, Newberry, FL 32669-3024, **Business Phone:** (352)331-4371.

**JIGGETTS, DANNY MARCELLUS**
Businessperson, broadcaster. **Personal:** Born Mar 10, 1954, Brooklyn, NY; son of Floyd and Hattie Campbell; married Karen; children: Lauren & Kristan. **Educ:** Harvard, BS; MBA; Northwestern Univ. **Career:** Football player (retired), broadcaster: Chicago Bears, 1976-82; Nat 1st Bank Chicago; Proctor & Gamble, sales rep; Bd Urban Affairs NY, field rep; USFL, NBC-WMAQ TV; CBS Sports, co-host, currently; ABN & LaSalle Bank, asst vpres; CSN, sportscaster & co-host; WBBM TV Chicago, sports broadcaster; WSCR Radio; Fox TV; WFLD, broadcaster, currently; Comcast SportsNet Chicago, broadcaster, currently. **Orgs:** Better Boys Found; Nat Hemophilia Found; Spec Olympics; Nat Sudden Infant Death Syndrome Found; Midwest Assoc SickleCell Anemia; March Dimes; Harvard Alumni Assoc. **Honors/Awds:** Leadership Award, BPO Elks Youth; Football 3 times All Ivy New England; Track 2 times All Ivy; Football All Am, 1976; Inducted, Harvard Varsity Hall Fame. **Special Achievements:** Danny Marcellus Jiggetts was named to the Ivys Silver Anniversary All-Star Team. **Home Addr:** 4751 Rfd, Long Grove, IL 60047-6923. **Business Addr:** Broadcaster, Comcast SportsNet Chicago, 350 N Orleans St Suite S1 100, Chicago, IL 60654, **Business Phone:** (312)222-6000.

**JOBE, BEN W.**
Educator, basketball coach. **Personal:** Born Mar 1, 1933, Nashville, TN; son of Arthur and Mary B; married Regina W; children: Bryan A & Gina B. **Educ:** Fisk Univ, BS, 1956; Tenn State Univ, MS, 1963; Univ Tenn, attended 1963; Southern Univ, attended 1966. **Career:** Educator, basketball coach (retired); Cameron High Sch, coach, 1958; Talladega Col, head basketball coach, 1964-67; AL State Univ, head coach, 1967-68; SC State Univ, head coach, 1968-73; Univ SC, asst coach, 1973-78; Univ Denver, head coach, 1978-80; Nat Basketball Asns Denver Nuggets, asst coach, dir, 1980-81; GA Tech Univ, asst coach, 1981-82; AL A&M Univ, head coach, 1982-86; Southern Univ, head coach, 1986-96; Tuskegee Univ, head coach, 1996-2000; Southern Univ, head coach, 2001-03; Southern Univ Jaguars, head coach. **Orgs:** Kappa Alpha Psi, 1954-2000; Tenn Ed Cong, 1956-60; Nat Ed Asn, 1956-60; Health, Phys Ed & Recreation Asn, 1958-60; NAIA Coaches Asn, 1964-73; NatAsn Basketball Coaches, 1973-2000; Los Angles Asn Basketball Coaches, 1986-96. **Home Addr:** 1311 Old Montgomery Rd, Montgomery, AL 36088, **Home Phone:** (334)724-0308.

**JOBE, SHIRLEY A.**
Librarian. **Personal:** Born Oct 10, 1946, San Bernardino, CA; daughter of Fines and Luejeannia; children: Robyn. **Educ:** Texarkana Col, AA, 1966; E Tex State Univ, AB, 1968; Simmons Col, MSLS, 1971. **Career:** John F Kennedy presial Libr, head librn, 1971-84; Boston Globe Newspaper Co, head librn, currently. **Orgs:** Vpres, Mass Black Librns Network, 1984-86; volunteer, Soup Kitchens feed homeless; volunteer visit incarcerated persons Ma prisons. **Honors/Awds:** Educ Prof Developop, Act Grant, 1970; Black Achiever's Award, Boston, 1987. **Home Addr:** 54 Mt Pleasant St, Cambridge, MA 02140, **Home Phone:** (617)868-0079. **Business Addr:** Library Director, The Boston Globe, 135 Morrissey Blvd, Boston, MA 02205-5819, **Business Phone:** (617)929-8803.

**JOE, DR. LONNIE, JR.**
Physician, association executive. **Personal:** married Anne. **Educ:** Univ Mich Sch Med, MD, 1978; John Hopkins Bus Med Prog, resident, internal med, fel. **Career:** Providence Hosp, resident, internal med, 1978-81, fel pulmonary disease, 1981-83; pvt pract physician intern almed & pulmonary pract, 1984-; Detroit Med Soc, pres, pres emer; Mich State Med Soc, dir, currently. **Orgs:** bd trustee, Nat Med Asn, currently, House Delegates, secy; Comt Fed Legis, Mich State Med Soc; bd mem, Awards & Nominating Comt, Off Med Develop & Alumni Rels; bd trustee mem, Wayne County Med Soc; trustee, New Bright Star Church; Univ Mich Med Alumni Asn; Novo Nordis Adv Bd; Southfield Instnl Rev Bd; Am Col Physician Execs; Greater Detroit Health Coun; Health Care Coalition. **Honors/Awds:** Physician of the Year, Nat Med Asn, 2008. **Home Addr:** 23077 Greenfield Rd Suite 190, Southfield, MI 48075-3741, **Home Phone:** (248)557-5227. **Business Addr:** President, Detroit Medical Society, 580 Frederick Douglas, Detroit, MI 48202, **Business Phone:** (313)832-7800.

**JOE, WILLIAM (BILLY)**
Football player, football coach. **Personal:** Born Oct 14, 1940, Aynor, SC. **Educ:** Villanova Univ, BA, econ; Cheyney State Univ, BA, hist; Antioch Col, MA, sec educ. **Career:** Football player (retired), football coach; Denver Broncos, football player, fullback, 1963-64; Buffalo Bills, fullback, 1965; Miami Dolphins, fullback, 1966-67; New York Jets, 1968-69; Stoke broker; Univ MD, asst, 1970-71; Cheyney Univ Pa, head coach, 1972-78; Philadelphia Eagles, running backs coach, 1979-80; Cent State Univ, OH, head coach, 1981-93; Fla A&M Univ, head coach, 1994-2004; Miles Col, Div II, head football coach, 2007-10. **Orgs:** Kappa Alpha Psi Fraternity; pres, Am Football Coaches Asn, 1995. **Honors/Awds:** All-Am hons; Most Valuable Player Award, 1962; American Football League Rookie of the Year, 1963; Silver Medal, Shot put, Pan Am Games, 1963; PA State Conf Coach of the Year, 1978; NAIA Nat Championship, 1990, 1992; Nat Coach of the Year, Pigskin Club; Nat Coach of the Year, 100 Percent Wrong Club of Atlanta; Mid-Eastern Athletic Conf Coach of the Year, 1995, 1996; Florida A&M University Hall of Fame; National Football Foundation's College Football Hall of Fame, 2007; Black college football national championships. **Business Addr:** Football Coach, Miles Col, 5500 Myron Massey Blvd, Fairfield, AL 35064, **Business Phone:** (205)929-1000.

**JOHN, ANTHONY**
Computer operator, executive. **Personal:** Born Feb 19, 1950, New York, NY; son of Alfred S and Maggie Seriven; married Elmira Cooper; children: Genean Corrinda Jessica. **Educ:** Ohio State Univ, Columbus, OH, BS, comput sci, 1977; Fairleigh Dickinson Univ, Paterson, NJ, MBA, 1981. **Career:** AT&T, Piscataway, NJ, comput programmer, 1978-80, self-employed comput programmer, 1981-90; Dow Jones, S Brunswick, NJ, systs proj mgr. **Orgs:** Nat treas, BDPA, 1982-84; pres, NJ Chap, Black Data Processing Asn, 1983-84; pres, S Jersey Black Data Processing Asn, 1987; Burlington Co Concerned Black Men, 1989-; treas & bd trustee, Rossville AMEZ Church, 1989-. **Home Addr:** 16 Crosswick Pl, Willingboro, NJ 08046, **Home Phone:** (609)877-4824.

**JOHN, DAYMOND (DAYMOND GARFIELD JOHN)**
Business owner, businessperson, entrepreneur. **Personal:** Born Feb 23, 1969, Brooklyn, NY; son of Garfield John and Margot John; children: Yasmeen John & Destiny John. **Career:** FUBU, founder and chief exec officer, 1992-; The Shark Group, chief exec officer, pres and branding expert, 2009-; "Shark Tank", ABC, television personality, 2009-; motivational speaker on branding and business-related topics. **Honors/Awds:** Brandweek Marketer of the Year; Advertising Age Marketing 1000 Award for Outstanding Ad Campaign; New York Entrepreneur of the Year, Ernst & Young. **Special Achievements:** Appointed by the White House as Global Ambassador of Entrepreneurship, PAGE Program, 2015. Author, Display of Power, 2007; The Brand Within: The Power of Branding from Birth to the Boardroom, 2010; The Power of Broke, 2016. **Business Addr:** The Shark Group, 214 West 39th Suite 1001, New York, NY 10018, **Business Phone:** (646)930-1400.

**JOHN, DAYMOND G.**
President (organization). **Personal:** Born Feb 23, 1969, Brooklyn, NY; daughter of Margot. **Career:** Branding Expert, Business Strategist, Venture Capitalist & Investor, 1992-2011; Red Lobster, waiter; FUBU Found, founder, 1997; FUBU Entertainment, founder, 2000; Fubu Collection, pres, founder & chief exec officer, currently; Shark Branding, chief exec officer & Pres, 2009-; ABC Tv, TV Personality, 2009-,TV Series:"Sharknado 2: Second One", 2014. **Business Addr:** Chief Executive Officer, Founder, Fubu The Collection, 350 5th Ave Suite 6617, New York, NY 10118, **Business Phone:** (212)273-3300.

**JOHN, DR. MABLE**
Association executive, clergy, singer. **Personal:** Born Nov 3, 1930, Bastrop, LA; daughter of Mertis and Lillie John; children: Jesse P, Joel D, Otis D & Limuel C. **Educ:** Wayne State Univ, RN; Crenshaw Christian Ctr Sch Ministry, divinity degree, 1986; DDiv, 1993. **Career:** Motown Rec, rec artist & mgr, 1956-60; Stax Rec, rec artist, 1966; Ray Charles Raelettes, lead singer & mgr, 1969-; Otis Music Group, owner/publ, 1971-; Joy In Jesus Ministries, founder, 1986-. Album:Stay Out of the Kitchen, 1996; My Name Is Mable: The Complete Collection. Movie: Time of Fear, 2002; Honeydripper, 2007. **Orgs:** Nat Asn Sickle Cell Dis, 1979; founder, Joy Community Outreach, 1986-; Urban League, Los Angeles Chap, Welfare Work, 1997. **Business Addr:** Founder, Joy in Jesus Ministry, 5730 W Manchester Ave, Westchester, CA 90045, **Business Phone:** (323)939-5808.

**JOHNS, DAVID J.**
Educational consultant, founder (originator), government official. **Personal:** Born Los Angeles, CA. **Educ:** Columbia Univ, BA, Eng, creative writing, & African Am studies, 2004; Columbia Univ, Teacher's Col, MA, sociol & educ policy, 2006. **Career:** Obama Am-Nev, policy & res dir; Am Univ, adj prof; Sen Edward M. Kennedy, served under leadership of; Senate Comt Health, Educ, Labor & Pensions, sr educ policy advisor; DJJ Consult, founder, US Senate, policy advisor & educ policy advisor, 2007-; White House Initiative Educ Excellence African Americans, exec dir, 2013-. **Orgs:** Cong Black Caucus, Found Fel; Andrew W. Mellon, Fel; Magic Johnson Taylor Michael's Scholar Prog, Comt Mem; IMPACT, Dir Develop, 2007-13; Plan Success, Bd Mem. **Honors/Awds:** "Ebony" Magazine, 30 Top Leaders Under 30, 2007; EnVest Fund, 40 Under 40; National Association for the Advancement of Colored People (NAACP), Power 40; "The Root" Magazine, The Root 100 Honorees, 2013. **Business Addr:** Founder, Djj Consulting Inc, 428 W 46th St Apt 1c, New York, NY 10036.

**JOHNS, DR. JACKIE C.**
Dentist. **Personal:** Born Jul 14, 1953, Belle Glade, FL; son of Mattie M and Gonte. **Educ:** Tex Col, BS (Cum Laude) 1976; Prairie View

A&M Univ, MS, 1977; Col Med & Dent NJ, DMD, 1981. **Career:** Dr Ford, dent, 1981-82; Dr CJ Beck, dentist, 1981; Dr RL Levine, dent, 1982-83; US Vets Admin Outpatient, dent, 1983-84; Dr Thomas Scholpler, dent, 1983-84; Jackie C Johns & Assoc, dent, currently. **Orgs:** Am FL Dent Asn; NE Regional Bd Palm Beach Co Dent Asn; Acad Gen Dent; Alpha Omega Frat; Westboro Bus & Prof Women Orgn; Family & Comprehensive Dent, Boynton Bch, FL; Family & Comprehensive Dent, Belle Glade, FL; Int Cong Oral Implantologist; Family & Comprehensive Dent WPB Ft Pierce FL; Appalachian Ministries Educ Resource Ctr. **Honors/Awds:** Nationally recognized in Journal of the Nat Dental Asn for active participation in the 1978 Health Fair at NJ Dental School; Comm Serv Citations for work on voters registration drives; Pinacle Award by Being Single Magazine Chicago Ill, 1989; Professional Achievement Award, Black Achievement, Glades Alumnae Chapter, Delta Sigma Theta Sorority Inc, 1991. **Home Addr:** 1417 NW Ave L, Belle Glade, FL 33430-1780, **Home Phone:** (561)996-1010. **Business Addr:** Dentist, Jackie C Johns & Assoc, 2100 45th St Suite A8, West Palm Beach, FL 33407, **Business Phone:** (561)842-5619.

### JOHNS, JAMIE
Association executive. **Personal:** married William. **Career:** Notary Signing Agt & Instr, 1997-; Notary Access Asn, founder, pres, chief exec officer & owner, 1999-, notary; INat Notary Asn, notary, 2004; ic life ins agt, 2006-. **Orgs:** Ambassador, Carson Chamber Com; bd mem, Fed Employees W Credit Union; Nat Adv Coun, GoGet Notary.com & GoGetLoan.com, 2005; J & E Guest Care. **Honors/Awds:** Nat Notary of the Year, Nat Notary Asn, 2004; Martin Luther King Jr Drum Major Award, CAL-State Dominquez, 2004. **Special Achievements:** Ebony Magazine, Speaking of People, March, 2004. **Home Addr:** , Carson, CA. **Business Addr:** Owner, President & Chief Executive Officer, Notary Access Association LLC, 2286 E Carson St Suite 312, Long Beach, CA 90807, **Business Phone:** (562)290-7978.

### JOHNS, HON. MARIE C.
President (organization), vice president (organization), executive. **Personal:** Born Aug 19, 1951, Indianapolis, DC; daughter of Richard D Collins and Freida Delight Casey; married Wendell L; children: Richard. **Educ:** Ind Univ, John F Kennedy Sch Govt, BS, urban studies & pub policy anal, 1979 & MS, mgt, pub policy anal & budgeting; Harvard Univ, attended; Univ Va, Darden Grad Sch Bus Admin. **Career:** L & L Consult LLC, founder, pres, managing mem, 2000-; Verizon Wash, pres, 2004; DC, Dem Primary, mayoral cand, 2006, US Small Bus Admin, telecommunications chief exec & dep adminr, 2010-13; Bell Atlantic Wash, fcc dir, vpres external affairs, pres & chief exec officer; Landmark Systs Corp, dir; Verizon DC, pres & chief exec officer; Ind Legis Serv Agency, fiscal analyst; C & P Tel Co. **Orgs:** Past chair, YMCA Metrop Wash Bd dir, 2005; Wash Performing Arts Soc; dir, Greater Wash Bd Trace; Helen Hayes Awards; Fed City Coun; founding chair, bd, Wash DC Technol Coun; dir, Greater Wash Bd Trade; dir, Econ Club Wash; Int Womens Forum, Wash, DC; Howard Univ & Howard Univ Hosp; Mid-Atlantic Permanente Med Group; founding chair, Howard Univ Mid Sch Mathand Sci; Enlightened Inc; Girl Scouts USA; Sr Bd Stewards Metrop Af Methodist Episcopal Church; Ga Ave Bus Resource Ctr; past pres, DC Chamber Com; past chair, Leadership Wash; trustee, Howard Univ; alumna Ind Univ; dir, Nat Capital Revitalization Corp; adv coun, US Black Chambers Inc. **Honors/Awds:** Honor doctorate, Trinity Col, 1999; Twenty-Five Most Influential Black Women in Business, Network Journal, 2003; Recipient, numerous awards bus & civic leadership. **Special Achievements:** Named by the Washingtonian Magazine as one of the 100 Most Powerful Women in 1999 & 2001; Twenty-five Most Influential Black Women in Business, Network J, 2003.

### JOHNS, POLLYANNA (POLLYANNA CASANGA JOHNS KIMBROUGH)
Basketball player. **Personal:** Born Nov 6, 1975, Nassau. **Educ:** Univ Mich, attended 1998. **Career:** Basketball player (retired), basketball coach; Mich Wolverines Women's Basketball, 1996-98; Charlotte Sting, 1998; Cleveland Rockers, 2000-01, 2003; Miami Sol, ctr, 2001-02; Cleveland Rockers, ctr, 2003; Houston Comets, ctr, 2004; Southern Tech Wild Cats, asst coach, currently. **Business Addr:** Assistant Coach, Southern Tech Wild Cats, 818 Tyvola Rd Suite 101, Charlotte, NC 28217, **Business Phone:** (800)839-4490.

### JOHNS, DR. SONJA MARIA
Surgeon. **Personal:** Born May 13, 1953, Washington, DC; daughter of Ralph L E and Jannie Austin; children: George Wheeler Jr, Ashante, Chiquita & Maria Wheeler. **Educ:** Howard Univ Col Lib Arts, BS, 1976; Howard Univ Col Med, MD, 1978. **Career:** Nat Health Plan Inc, physician attendance, 1981-82; Women's Med Ctr, family practr, 1983; DC Air Nat Guard, chief hosp serv; Warsaw Med Ctr, family physician, 1983-91; Med Squadron, Andrews Afb, Md, comdr, 1991-96; Westmoreland Health Serv, family practr, founder, owner, 1991-; state air surgeon & inspector gen, dean, 1996; Beaumont Juv Ctr, med dir, 1991-97; Northern Neck Regional Jail, med dir, 1996-99; Hanover Juv Correctional Ctr Barrett Juv Correctional, med dir, 1997-99; Am Red Cross, dir, staff. **Orgs:** Am Acad Family Physicians; Nat Med Assoc; Am Med Assoc; Nat Advan Asn Colored People; Assoc Military Surgeons; Northern Neck Med Soc; vpres, Tapp Hosp; co-founder, Black Bus & Prof Coalition; bd mem, Richmond Co Comn Serv Assoc Inc; soloist soprano, Comn Chorus; Northern Neck Convention Choir; Northern Neck Choral Soc; adv, 4-H Club Richmond Co; pres, Tappahannock Kiwanis Club. **Honors/Awds:** Physician's Recognition Award, Am Med Assoc, 1981-88. **Home Addr:** 1383 Stokes Sta Rd, PO Box 179, Goochland, VA 23063-0179, **Home Phone:** (804)457-4307. **Business Addr:** Owner, Founder, Westmoreland Health, PO Box 1120, Warsaw, VA 22572-0640, **Business Phone:** (804)333-3629.

**JOHNS, STEPHEN ARNOLD.** **See Obituaries Section.**

### JOHNSON, ADDIE COLLINS
Educator. **Personal:** Born Jan 1, 1928, Evansville, IN; daughter of Stewart Collins and Willa Shamell Collins; married John Q; children: Parker Collins. **Educ:** Howard Univ, BS, 1956; Framingham State Col, MEd, 1968. **Career:** PBB Hosp, dietetic internship, RD, 1957; Boston Lying In Hosp, therapeut dietitian, 1957-61; Harvard Sch Pub Health Res, dietitian, 1963-64; Hour Glass Newspaper Kwajakin MI, ed, 1965-66; Foxborough Pub Sch, teacher, 1968-00; Mercy Hosp Pittsburgh, intern resident, 1970-72; Meharry Med Col, resident, 1973; Univ Mass, Harbor Campus Dept Nursing, nutritionist, 1980-88; Bridgewater State Col, asst prof, 1982-94; Foxborough High, teacher consumer & family sci, 1994-2000; Century 21 Florence Kates, Sharon, Mass, real estate sales assoc, 2001-. **Orgs:** Bd dir, Fin chmn, Mass Home Econ Asn; Am Dietics Asn; Soc Nutrit Educ; Am Home Econ Asn; Circle Lets Inc; Delta Sigma Theta Sorority Inc; Mass Teachers Asn; Links Inc; pres, Boston Chap Links Inc; nominating comt, Nat Links Inc, 1978-79; Am Asn Univ Women; chairperson, pres, Iota Chap, Delta Kappa Gamma, 1989-; Nat Sci Found, Proj Seed, 1992; Nat Asn Advan Colored People. **Home Addr:** 92 Morse St, Sharon, MA 02067, **Home Phone:** (781)784-5327. **Business Addr:** Real Estate Sales Associate, Century 21 Florence Kates, 21 S Main St, Sharon, MA 02067-1917, **Business Phone:** (781)784-6771.

### JOHNSON, ADRIENNE
Basketball player. **Personal:** Born Feb 5, 1974. **Educ:** Ohio State Univ, BS, exercise physiol, 1996. **Career:** Cleveland Rockers, guard, 1997-98; Orlando Miracle, 1999-2002; Conn Sun, guard, 2003-04; Seattle Storm, 2005; La Tech Lady Techsters, 2007-08.

### JOHNSON, ALBERT JAMES
Golfer. **Personal:** Born Aug 20, 1943, Phoenix, AZ; son of Eddie and Albert; married Beverly; children: Kevin A. **Educ:** Univ Ariz, BS, mgt, 1965. **Career:** Golf player (retired); Harlem Globletrotters, player, 1965-67; Univ AZ, asst coach, 1968-72; Matthew Chevrolet & Orielly Chevrolet, Tucson, Ariz, salesman, 1972-84; City Tucson, Parks & Recreation, Starter II supvr. **Orgs:** Active 20-30 Serv Club, 1970-72; Randolph Mens Golf Club, 1976-; Desert Trails Mens Club, 1969-74; Univ AZ & Alumni Club, 1970-73; deacon & elder Trinity Presb Ch, 1969-73; Saguaro Mens Club, 1984-91. **Honors/Awds:** All Western Athletic Conference, Basketball, 1963, 1964-65; City Tucson, Tom Price Memorial Golf Tournament Winner, 1990. **Special Achievements:** The first black assistant basketball coach in the Western Athletic Conference, 1972. **Home Addr:** 7534 E 31st St, Tucson, AZ 85710, **Home Phone:** (602)299-9652.

### JOHNSON, ALEXANDER HAMILTON (ALEX JOHNSON)
Banker. **Personal:** Born Oct 3, 1924, Greensboro, AL; son of Alexander and Erma; married Delores Mitzie Russel; children: Alexander III. **Educ:** Calif Pac Univ, BA, pub admin, 1978, MA, mgt, 1980. **Career:** Banker (retired); Fed Aviation Admin, personnel staffing spec, 1968-70, chief civil rights staff, 1970-74; US Equal Employ Opportunity Comn, compliance suprv, 1974-81; Ariz Bank, mgr, asst vpres, affirmative action officer human resources, vpres, 1992. **Orgs:** Pres, Am Fed Govt Empl, 1968; clerk session, Southminster Presby Church, 1980-84; chmn bd, Southminster Social Serv Agency, 1981; pres, Southwest Area Conf, Nat Asn Advan Colored People, 1982-84; chmn, Reg I Nat Asn Advan Colored People, 1984-85; keeper rec, Phoenix Alumni Kappa Alpha Psi, 1984-86; Sigma Pi Phi, Gamma Mu Boule, 1988; Maricopa County Comn Trial Ct Appointments, 1989. **Home Addr:** 1225 W Wood Dr, Phoenix, AZ 85029.

### JOHNSON, ALMETA ANN
Lawyer. **Personal:** Born Mar 11, 1947, Rockingham, NC; daughter of V Louise Noel; children: Cesseli A & Harry E IV. **Educ:** Johnson C Smith Univ, BA, 1968; Ohio State Univ, JD, 1971. **Career:** Metzenbaum Gaines Finley & Stern, law clerk, 1969-70; Ohio State Univ, res asst, 1970-71; Bene sch Fried lander Mendelson & Coplan, pro bono assoc, assoc atty, 1971-75; City Cleveland, chief police prosecutor, 1975-80; Sindell, Lowe & Guidubaldi, Coun, 1982-86; Village Woodmere, law dir, 1983-86; pvt pract atty, 1986-2005; Almeta A. Johnson, sr atty, founder, 1986-2005; E Cleveland City Coun, law dir, 2006-09; Cuyahoga County Ct Common Pleas, Juv Div, judge; City Of, dir law, 2006-10; Practising Atty at Almeta Johnson & Assocs, atty, currently. **Orgs:** Chmn, E Cleveland Citizens Adv Comn, 1973-75, 1988-; chmn, E Cleveland Charter Rev Comn, 1976; bd mem secy treas, Ohio Law Opportunity Fund; Am Bar Asn; Bar Asn Greater Cleveland; Ohio State Bar Asn; Black Women Lawyers Asn; Alpha Kappa Alpha; E Cleveland City Coun. **Honors/Awds:** Lett Civil Liberties Award, Ohio State Univ Col Laws, 1971; One of Ten Most Influential Women in greater Cleveland, The Plain Dealer, 1975; Nat Asn Advan Colored People Outstanding Young Citizen Cleveland Jaycees, 1976. **Home Addr:** 26241 Lakeshore Blvd Apt 1557, Euclid, OH 44132, **Home Phone:** (216)261-8944. **Business Addr:** Attorney, Almeta Johnson & Associates, 16000 Ter Rd Apt 1102, East Cleveland, OH 44112-2070, **Business Phone:** (216)451-1462.

### JOHNSON, ALVIN ROSCOE
Executive. **Personal:** Born Oct 15, 1942, Alton, IL; son of Cyrus L and Jennie C Keen; married Thelma Marie Hart; children: Brent Alvin & Dirk Cyrus. **Educ:** Univ Edwardsville, Southern Ill, BS, bus admin, 1972, MBA, 1982. **Career:** Olin Corp, mgr train & develop, 1962-77, mgr personnel, 1977-80; Babcock Industs Inc, sr vpres human res & admin, 1980-93; Yale New Haven Hosp, vpres employee rels, 1994-2007. **Orgs:** Dir, Am Red Cross, Girl Scouts, Urban League, Acct Babcock Inc, 1982-; treas & golden life mem, Nat Asn Advan Colored People; bd dir, Alumni Assoc Ex; chair, deacons, Immanuel Baptist Church; Sigma Pi Phi; hr coun, Manufactures Alliance Prod Innovation, 1982-; life mem, SIUE Alumni Assoc, exec bd dir, 1975-77. **Home Addr:** 47 Upper State St, North Haven, CT 06473, **Home Phone:** (203)239-4310.

### JOHNSON, ANDREW L., JR.
Judge, lawyer. **Personal:** Born Oct 4, 1931, Youngstown, OH; married Joan Carol Phillips; children: Andrew III & Paul. **Educ:** Northwestern Univ, BS, 1953; Cleveland St Univ, Sch Law, JD, 1960. **Career:** Pvt pract atty, 1960-; real estate ownership, 1962-; Shaker Heights Munic Ct, actg judge, 1971-83. **Orgs:** Trustee, Bar Asn Greater Cleveland, 1970-73; chmn bd, trustee, Forest City Hosp Cleveland, 1970-76; Trust Shaker Lakes Regional Native Ctr, 1977-; pres, Bar Asn Greater Cleveland, 1978-79; Panel Expedited Arbit Prog United Steelworkers Am & Steel Co, 1978-81; labor arbitrator, Maj Steel Co NE, OH; hearing examr, Ohio Civil Rights Comn; founding mem & first pres, Cleveland Lawyers Asn Inc; Cleveland Coun Human Rels; pres, Home Owners Title Corp Cleveland; vpres, Northwestern Univ Alumni Club Cleveland; life mem, Alpha Phi Alpha Fraternity; charter mem, Judicial Coun, Nat Bar Asn; charter mem, Eighth Judicial Conf; pres, bd trustee, Forest City Hosp; managing partner, Tower Mgt Co, chmn, Adv Comt; Forest City Hosp Found; life mem, Nat Asn Advan Colored People; Nat Urban League; Sigma Pi Phi Fraternity. **Honors/Awds:** Law Day Award, Cleveland Lawyers Asn, 1969; Meritorious Service Award, Cleveland Bar Asn, 1970; Merit Award, Northwestern Univ Col Arts & Sci, 1979; Alumnus of the Year Award, Northeastern Univ, Col Arts & Sci, 1979. **Special Achievements:** Defending the Defense, author, 1980. **Business Addr:** Attorney, 1205 W 110th St Apt 16, Cleveland, OH 44102-1561, **Business Phone:** (216)651-6000.

### JOHNSON, ANNE-MARIE
Actor, vice president (organization). **Personal:** Born Jul 18, 1960, Los Angeles, CA; married Martin Grey. **Educ:** Univ Calif, Los Angeles, theatre. **Career:** Actress, currently; TV Series: "In the Heat of the Night", 1988-93; "In Living Color", 1993-94; "Spiderman", 1994; "Melrose Place", 1995-96; "Smart Guy", 1997; "JAG", 1997-2002; "The X Files", 2000; "Strong Medicine", 2001; "The Parkers", 2001; "The District", 2001-03; "Dharma & Greg", 2002; "What I Like About You", 2003; "The System", 2003; "Girlfriends", 2003-04; "The Division", 2003; "Rock Me, Baby", 2004; "That's So Raven", 2006; "Adventures in Boss Sitting", 2006; "Navy NCIS: Naval Criminal Investigative Service", 2007; "Bones", 2007; "House of Payne", 2007-09; "CSI: Crime Scene Investigation", 2007; "Boston Legal", 2008; "The Secret Life of the American Teenager", 2009; "I'm in the Band", 2010; "Leverage", 2011; "Fairly Legal", 2011. TV movies: "His Mistress", 1984; "Dream Date", 1989; "Lucky & Chances", 1990; "Steroid", 1997; "Through the Fire", 2002; "Days of Our Lives", 2012; "Murder in the First ", 2014; "Chasing Life", 2014; "See Dad Run", 2014; "Sister Code", 2014-. Films: I'm Gonna Git You Sucka, 1988; The Five Heartbeats, 1991; Strictly Business, 1991; Down in the Delta, 1998; Pursuit of Happiness, 2001; Life & Drawing, 2001; Uncorked, 2009; About Fifty, 2011; Freeloaders, 2012; Knock 'em Dead, 2014; Double Daddy, 2015; Sister Code, 2015. **Orgs:** Nat vpres, Screen Actors Guild, 2005-10. **Business Addr:** National Vice President, Screen Actors Guild, 5757 Wilshire Blvd 7 Flr, Los Angeles, CA 90036, **Business Phone:** (323)954-1600.

### JOHNSON, ANTHONY MARK
Basketball player. **Personal:** Born Oct 2, 1974, Charleston, SC. **Educ:** Col Charleston, BBA, 1997. **Career:** Basketball player (retired), free agt; Sacramento Kings, guard, 1997-98, 2007-08; Atlanta Hawks, guard, 1998-2001, 2006-08; Orlando Magic, 1999-2000, 2008-10; Cleveland Cavaliers, 2000-01; Mobile Revelers, 2001-02; New Jersey Nets, guard, 2001-03; Ind Pacers, guard, 2003-06; Dallas Mavericks, 2006-07; free agt, currently. **Orgs:** Owner, AJ Custom Doors & Windows. **Home Addr:** 5162 Inwood Pl, Mableton, GA 30126-7612. **Business Addr:** Professional Basketball Player, Orlando Magic, 8701 Maitland Summit Blvd, Orlando, FL 32810, **Business Phone:** (407)916-2400.

### JOHNSON, DR. ANTHONY MICHAEL
Physicist, educator. **Personal:** Born May 23, 1954, Brooklyn, NY; son of James W and Helen Weaver; married Adrienne Steplight; children: Kimberly, Justin & Brandon. **Educ:** Polytech Inst NY, BS (magna cum laude), physics, 1975; City Univ, NY Col, PhD, physics, 1981. **Career:** AT&T Bell Labs, sr tech assoc, 1974-77, doctoral can, 1978-81, Quantum Physics & Electronics Res Dept, from mem tech staff to distinguished mem tech staff, 1981-95; NJ Inst Tech, chairperson & distinguished prof appl phys & prof, Elect & Comput Eng, 1995-2003; found prof, optics & photonics & disting prof physics, 2001-03; NJIT, Beijing/Harbin, China, Dept Physics, Int Students, recruiter; Winter Col Optics, Dakar, Senegal, vis lectr; Indian Inst Technol, Kanpur, India, vis lectr; Univ MD Baltimore County, Ctr Advan Studies Photonics Res, dir, 2003-, prof phys & prof comp sci & elect eng, 2004-, Wilson H. Elkins professorship, Univ Syst Md, 2004-. **Orgs:** Fel Am Phys Soc, 1977-; pres, Optical Soc Am, 1982-; Ann Mtg Optical Soc Am, 1985; symp organizer Ultrashort Pulses Optical Fibers, 1985, vice chmn, Tech Prog Com, Ultrafast Optical Phenomena, 1985, symp organizer Ultrashort Non linear Pulse Propagation Optical Fibers, 1988; chmn, Tech Group on Ultrafast Optical Phenomena, 1986-87; tech prog comm, Ultrafast Optics & Electronics for Conf Lasers & Electro-Optics, 1986, 1987; tech prog comm Ann Meeting Optical Soc Am, 1986, 1987, 1988; tech coun, Optical Soc Am; chmn, Tech Prog Subcom Conf on Lasers & Electro-Optics, 1988, 1989, tech prog co-chair, 1990; co-founder, OSA Ad Hoc Comt Women & Minorities Optics, 1988-93; R W Wood Prize Comm, Optical Soc Am, 1989, chair, 1990; topical ed, Optics Lett, 1989-91; Optics News adv comm, 1989-91; sci & tech adv bd, J Nat Tech Asn, 1989-; tech prog co-chair, 1989, charter fel, 1992, Nat Soc Black Physicists; Laser Focus World Ed Adv Comt, 1990-; fel, 1991, vpres, 2000-, Optical Soc Am; fel Optical Socs Am, 1991; fel Am Asn Advan Sci, 1992; gen councillor, 1994-97 & mem exec bd 1996-97, APS; fel AAAS, 1996-; fel Inst Elec & Electron Engrs, 2000-; Basic Energy Scis Adv Comt, Dept Energy; adv bd, Int Centre Theoret Physics (ICTP), Trieste, Italy, 2002-13; Gov Bd Am Inst Physics, 2002-06; African Sci Inst; C E K Mees Medal Comt OSA, 2004-06; AAAS Comt Opportunities Sci, 2004-07; Md Mathematics Engineering & Sci Achievement Adv Bd, 2005-07; IEEE Lasers & Electro-Optics Socs Fels Eval Comt, 2005-06; NRC Comt AMO2010, Assessment & Oulook Atomic, Molecular & Optical Sci, 2005-06; NRC Bd Assessment NIST Progs, 2005-07; APS Nominating Comt, 2006-08; Am Asn Physics Teachers. **Special Achievements:** First African American to serve as president of the Optical Society of America, 2002. **Home Addr:** 170 Sherwood Dr, Freehold, NJ 07728. **Business Addr:** Director, University of Maryland, Rm 029 TRC Bldg 1000 Hilltop Cir, Baltimore, MD 21228, **Business Phone:** (410)455-8440.

### JOHNSON, ANTHONY SCOTT
Football player, chaplain. **Personal:** Born Oct 25, 1967, Indianapolis, IN; married Shelly; children: Taylor, Kylie, Gabriel, Sierra & Elijah. **Educ:** Univ Notre Dame, attended 1990. **Career:** Football player (retired), Chaplin; Indianapolis Colts, running back, 1990-93; New York Jets, 1994; Chicago Bears, 1995; Carolina Panthers, 1995-99;

Jacksonville Jaguars, 2000, chaplain, currently. **Business Addr:** Chaplin, Jacksonville Jaguars, 1 Everbank Field Dr, Jacksonville, FL 32202, **Business Phone:** (904)633-6000.

## JOHNSON, ARGIE K.

School administrator. **Personal:** Born Jan 1, 1939. **Educ:** John C Smith Col, Charlotte, NC, BS, biol, chem; Long Island Univ, Brooklyn, NY, MS, 1995; City Univ NY, Baruch Col, MS. **Career:** Veterans Admin Hosp, Brooklyn, NY, res biochemist; New York Sch Syst, teacher, prin, dep community supt & dep chancellor instr; Chicago Pub Schs, supt, 1993-95; Long Island Univ, adj prof. **Orgs:** Nat Coun Negro Women; Nat Alliance Black Sch Educr; Phi Delta Kappa Hon Soc; Delta Sigma Theta Sorority; community supt, Commmunity Sch Dist 13. **Home Addr:** 5201 S Cornell Ave Apt 26E, Chicago, IL 60615, **Home Phone:** (773)324-6842.

## JOHNSON, ARTHUR E.

Executive, vice president (organization), president (organization). **Personal:** Born Jan 1, 1946?. **Educ:** Morehouse Col, BA, 1968; Univ Calif, Los Angeles, CA, attended 1984; Mass Inst Technol, attended 1987. **Career:** IBM Fed Systs Div, software engr, 1969, gen mgr div, exec asst, pres & chief operating officer, 1992; Loral Corp Fed Systs Group, pres, 1994-96; Lockheed Martin Corp, LM Fed Systs, pres, 1996-97, Info & Serv, pres & chief operating officer, 1997-99, Corp Strategic Develop, vpres, 1999-2001, Corp Strategic Develop, sr vpres, 2001; Eaton Corp, dir, 2009-; Booz Allen Hamilton Holding Corp, dir, 2011-. **Orgs:** Bd mem, Calcomp Technol Inc, 1997; bd mem, IKON Off Solutions Corp, 1999-; lead dir, AGL Resources Inc, 2002-; bd mem, Delta Airlines Inc, 2005-07; independent trustee, mem audit & mem opers comt, Fidelity Sch St Trust, 2008-. **Business Addr:** Director, Booz Allen Hamilton Holding Corp, 8283 Greensboro Dr, McLean, VA 22102, **Business Phone:** (703)902-5000.

**JOHNSON, DR. ARTHUR J.** **See Obituaries Section.**

## JOHNSON, ARTHUR T.

Government official. **Personal:** Born Oct 29, 1947, Earlington, KY; married Dorothy Radford; children: Belinda & Joy. **Educ:** Earlington HS, 1967; Austin Peay State Col, 1968. **Career:** City Earlington, councilman, 1972-83, mayor; Goodyear Tire & Rubber Co, jr adv & mem, 1983-84. **Orgs:** Earlington Vol Fire & Rescue Squad, 1967-; Earlington Civic Club, 1972-, pres, Earlington Jaycees, 1982; bd dir, Pennyrile Area Develop Dist Pennyrile Housing Corp. **Honors/Awds:** Citzen of the Year, Hopkins Countains Progress, 1976; Man of the Year, Hopkins Countians Progress, 1985; Black Man of the Year, Black Award Coun, 1985. **Home Addr:** 112 S Atkinson, Earlington, KY 42410.

## JOHNSON, AVERY

Basketball player, basketball coach. **Personal:** Born Mar 25, 1965, New Orleans, LA; married Cassandra; children: Christianne & Avery Jr. **Educ:** NMex Jr Col, Hobbs, NM, attended 1984; Cameron Univ, Lawton, OK, 1985; Southern Univ, Baton Rouge, LA, 1988. **Career:** Basketball player (retired), basketball coach; Seattle SuperSonics, guard, 1988-90; Denver Nuggets, 1990, 2001-02; San Antonio Spurs, 1991-93, 1994-2001; Houston Rockets, 1992; Golden State Warriors, 1993-94, 2003-04; Dallas Mavericks, 2002-03, asst coach, 2004-05, head coach, 2005-08; Katrina Rescue Ride, co-host, 2005; ESPN/ABC, studio analyst, 2008; NJ Nets, head coach, 2010-12. **Orgs:** Bd dir, Proj Turn Around; bd dir, Hunger Busters. **Business Addr:** Head Coach, Dallas Mavericks, 2909 Taylor St, Dallas, TX 75226, **Business Phone:** (214)747-6287.

## JOHNSON, BEN E.

Executive, manager. **Personal:** Born Jan 31, 1937, Ashley County, AR; married Marlene; children: Jan, Paula & Jay. **Educ:** Univ Wis Milwaukee, BS, 1975, cert pub admin, 1987. **Career:** Milwaukee Enterprise Ctr N, small bus coordr, bus adv, 1989; sr specialist, 2003; Alderman Dist, alderman; Milwaukee Common Coun, pres; City Milwaukee, city clerk. **Orgs:** Black Caucus, Nat League Cities; dist vpres, WI League Munic Exec Comn; joint cong state senate co supv & alderman; legis serv ctr, Nat League Cities Human Resources Comn; Milwaukee Area Manpower Coun; Mil Urban Oserv; bd chmn, Milwaukee Soc Develop Comn; Milwaukee Econ Develop Comm; corp mem, Milwaukee Urban League; bd dir, CHPASW; adv com, SE WI Reg Plan Comn; Nat Asn Advan Colored People; bd, Greater Milwaukee Coun Arts Child; Milwaukee Rec Task Force; Sch Breakfast Coalition Bd; Milwaukee Pabst Theater Bd; Milwaukee Hear Soc Bd; Milwaukee Youth Serv Bur Plan Com; Milwaukee House Task Force; adv bd, Sickle Cell Anemia Found; adv bd, Harambee Revit Proj; Milwaukee Repretory Theatre Bd; Milwaukee Perf Arts Ctr Bd; Milwaukee Caucus Aging; Milwaukee Forum; N Side Bus Asn Fed; N Side Pol Action Ctr Found. **Honors/Awds:** Recog & Appreciation Milwaukee Sch Engr Scholar Univ WI Milwaukee, 1955; Cent City Business Federal Civic Award, 1975; Walnut Improvement Council Civic Award, 1975; Commission Service Award, First Baptist Church; Community Award, CC Rider; Commission Service Award, Milwaukee Little League; Commission Service Award, Upper Third St Merchants; Legis Award, Comm Pride Expo; Commission Service Award, Youth Develop Ctr; Commission Service Award, Milwaukee Theol Inst; Bicen Award, Cent City. **Special Achievements:** First African American Common Council President for Milwaukee. **Home Addr:** 2225 N Lindsay St, Milwaukee, WI 53205-1326, **Home Phone:** (414)263-5025.

## JOHNSON, BENNETT J.

Publisher, exhibition designer, diplomat. **Personal:** Born May 15, 1929, Evanston, IL; son of Bennett J Sr and Kathryn Burnice Hill Samples; married Kathleen H Lucas; children: Bennett J III. **Educ:** Paine Col, GA, 1948; Roosevelt Univ, chem, math, 1950; Univ Calif, Los Angeles, eng sci, 1955, grad degree, 1956; Real Estate Inst Chicago, mortgage banking, 1973. **Career:** Path Assoc, salesman; Fuller Prod Co, salesman; Chicago Courier Newspaper, salesman; PF Collier, salesman; Chicago Pub Schs, high sch teacher, 1957-60; Los Angeles County Probation Dept, probation counr; Ill State Employ Serv, methods & procedures advr, 1961-66; US Dept Defense, Chicago, personnel mgt specialist, 1966-68; Talent Assistance Prog, dir, 1969-71; UCI Group Inc, chmn, 1970-; US Dept Com, regional dir, 1971-72; Merit Trust, dept dir, 1972-73; Ill Govs Off Human Resources, asst dir, 1973-74; Path Press Inc, pres; Third World Press, vpres, currently; Repub Uganda, hon consul gen, 2008-. **Orgs:** Vpres, Nat Asn Advan Colored People, Evanston Br, 1965-66, pres, 1979-83, 1989-91, 1995-2002; regional coordr, Nat Youth Work Comt, 1956-58, Ill State Conf Brs, exec comm; Greater State St Coun, bd, 1972-97; founder, N Cook County Off Econ Opportunity. **Home Addr:** 708 Wash St, Evanston, IL 60202-2215, **Home Phone:** (847)475-5574. **Business Addr:** Vice President, Third World Press Inc, 7822 S Dobson Ave, Chicago, IL 60619, **Business Phone:** (773)651-0700.

## JOHNSON, BERNETTE JOSHUA

Judge. **Personal:** Born Jun 17, 1943, Donaldsonville, LA; daughter of Frank Joshua Jr and Olivia Wire; children: David Kirk & Rachael Denise. **Educ:** Spelman Col, Atlanta, BA, 1964; La State Univ, Law Sch, JD, 1969. **Career:** US Dept Justice, summer intern, 1967; New Orleans Legal Assistance Corp, legal serv atty, 1969-73; self-employed, lawyer, 1973-77; City New Orleans, dep city atty, 1981-84; State La, Civil Dist Ct, judge, 1984-94, chief judge, 1994; La Supreme Ct, assoc justice, 1994-, Chief Justice, 2013-; Adj Fac, Tulane Univ Law Sch; Adj Prof, Southern Univ. **Orgs:** Community organizer, Nat Asn Advan Colored People, Legal Defense Fund, 1964-66; dir, AFNA Nat Educ Found, 1977-81; secy, Nat Bar Asn, judicial coun, 1992-96; pres, exec comt mem, Spelman Col Alumnae Asn, 1991-94; fin secy, Omicron Nu Zeta Chap, Zeta Phi Beta Sorority, 1992-94; pres, chmn, Southern Christian Leadership Conf, 1989-94; dist dir, Nat Asn Women Judges, 1992-94; bd mem, YWCA, 1992-94; bd pres, managing atty, City New Orleans Legal Assistance Corp, 1994-96; Martinet Legal Soc, 1995; chair-elect, Nat Bar Asn, judicial coun, 1996-97; trustee bd, Greater St Stephen Full Gospel Baptist Church; New Orleans Chap, Links Inc; Am Bar Asn; Coun La State Law Inst; Ct's Legal Serv Task Force; Nat Campaign Best Practices area Racial & Ethnic Fairness; Legal Defense & Educ Fund; Martin Luther King Nat Holiday Planning Comt; life mem, NAACP; New Orleans Bar Asn, Fleur De Lis; La State Bar Asn; La Bar Found; pres, AP Tureaud Chap Am Inns Ct. **Honors/Awds:** Ernest N Morial Award, New Orleans Legal Assistance Corp, 1992; Role Model Award, YWCA, 1992; Citizenship Award, Nat Asn Advan Colored People, 1996; President's Award, Louis A Martinet Legal Society, 1997, 2008; AP Tureaud Citizenship Award, La State Conf, Nat Asn Advan Colored People; Outstanding Community Service Award, Imp Ct Daughters Isis, 1998; Margaret Brent Women Lawyers of Achievement Award, Am Bar Asn's, 1998; Outstanding Service Award, Int Law Sect Nat Bar Asn, 1998; Martin Luther King, Jr Torch Bearer Award, 1999; Women of Wonder Award, Nat Coun Negro Women, 2000; Medal of Honor, Mayor of the City of New Orleans, 2000; hon doctorate laws, 2001; National Nobel Woman Award, Orgn Black Elected Legis Women, 2005; Judicial Public Service Award, Ancient Egyptian Arabic Order Nobles Mystic Shrine, 2005; Distinguished Jurist Award, La Bar Found, 2009; President's Award for Exceptional Service, La Bar Asn; Thurgood Marshall College Fund Community Leadership Award, 2009; Distinguished Civil Rights Advocate Award, Lawyers Comt Civil Rights Under Law, 2010; Louisiana Justice Hall of Fame Award, 2010; Spirit of Excellence Award, Am Bar Asn, 2010; Pioneer Award, La Asn Black Women Attorneys, 2011; President's Award, Nat Urban League, Int Asn Off Human Rights Agencies, 2012; Exceptional Contributor Award, Nat Black Prosecutors Asn, 2012; National Association for the Advancement of Colored People Award, 2012; Exceptional Leadership Award, La Bar Asn Comt, 2012; Diversity Law Center's Hall of Fame; Unsung Hero Award, LSU, 2013. **Special Achievements:** First African-American women to attend the Law School at Louisiana State University; First woman elected to the Civil District Court in New Orleans; First African-American Chief Justice of the Louisiana Supreme Court. **Home Addr:** 6 Pk Timbers Dr, New Orleans, LA 70131-8616, **Home Phone:** (504)393-0902. **Business Addr:** Associate Justice, Chief Justice, Louisiana Supreme Court, 400 Royal St, New Orleans, LA 70130, **Business Phone:** (504)310-2300.

## JOHNSON, DR. BETTY JO

Educator. **Personal:** Born Aug 14, 1940, Rankin City, MS; daughter of Louise Hayes and Louis. **Educ:** Piney Woods Sch, AA, 1960; Tougaloo Col, BA, 1964; Jackson State Univ, MS, 1971; Memphis State Univ, Memphis, EdD, 1975. **Career:** Jackson Pub Sch Syst, Miss, teacher, 1964-67; Lawyers Comn Civil Rights Under Law Jackson, Miss, legal secy, 1967-69; City Health Improv Proj, Univ Miss Med Ctr, fiscal spec, 1970; Miss Dept Pub Welfare Title IV, planning & eval specialist, 1972-73; Comn Ed Exten Jackson, Miss, curricspec Headstart, 1972; Alcorn State Univ, vis instr, 1973; Memphis State Univ, grad asst, 1973-76; Ariz State Univ, assoc prof, 1976-78; Shelby State Community Col, head dept, gen & early childhood educ, prof, 1978-89; LeMoyne-Owen Col, coordr, prof, early childhood educ, 1989-96; SW Tenn Community Col, dept chair educ, 1996-, prof educ, currently. **Orgs:** Kappa Delta Pi, 1976-; Nat Asn Educ Young C, 1976; Phi Delta Kappa, 1978-; Asn Childhood Educ; Tenn Asn Young C; Memphis Urban League; Delta Sigma Theta; Memphis May Ed Com; Memphis Asn Young C; Tenn Asn Supv & Curric Develop, 1988-; bd examiners, Tenn Dept Educ. **Home Addr:** 6107 Selkirk, Memphis, TN 38103, **Home Phone:** (901)794-1857. **Business Addr:** Professor of Education, Southwest Tennessee Community College, Rm 220 A Bldg Union Ave Campus, Memphis, TN 38101-0780, **Business Phone:** (901)333-5345.

## JOHNSON, BEVERLEY ERNESTINE

Government official, business owner, president (organization). **Personal:** Born May 16, 1953, Cheverly, MD; daughter of Joanne Juanita Scott and Ernest Charles Lane; married Allen; children: Allen II. **Educ:** Univ Md, College Park, Md, BS, 1985. **Career:** Dept Housing & Urban Develop, Wash, DC, housing mgt officer, 1980-87; Boston Redevelop Authority, Boston, MA, asst dir community & econ devlop, 1987; Bevco Assoc Inc, founder, pres, currently. **Orgs:** Progs Comt, WTS Advancing Women Transp. **Home Addr:** 25 Goodrich Rd Suite 2, Jamaica Plain, MA 02130, **Home Phone:** (617)522-8404. **Business Addr:** President, Founder, Bevco Associates Inc, 25 Goodrich Rd Suite 2, Jamaica Plain, MA 02130, **Business Phone:** (617)522-7003.

## JOHNSON, BEVERLY

Singer, actor, fashion model. **Personal:** Born Oct 13, 1952, Buffalo, NY; married Billy Potter; married Danny Sims; children: Anansa. **Educ:** Northeastern Univ; Brooklyn Col. **Career:** Glamour Mag, prof fashion model, 1971; Halston, runway model; Nat Airlines, television ad singer; Vogue Mag, cover model, 1974; Elle Mag, cover model; Revlon Cosmetics, prof model; Phil Anastasia, singer; Don't Lose the Feeling, solo singer; Films: Land of Negritude, 1975; Ashanti, 1979; National Lampoon's Loaded Weapon 1, 1992; Meteor Man, 1992; How to Be a Player, 1997; 54, 1998; Down n Dirty, 2001; Crossroads, 2002; Red Shoe Diaries 15: Forbidden Zone, 2002; Tyler Perry's Meet The Browns, 2010; Beverly's Full House, producer, 2012; Good Deeds, 2012. TV series: "She's Got the Look", 2008; shows: Oprah Winfrey Show, guest appearance; Arsenio Hall Show, guest appearances; JC Penney Portrait Studio/Wilhelmina Modeling Agency, promotional tour nat young model search promoter, 1992. **Orgs:** Africare; Atlanta Black Educ Fund; AIDS Awareness Campaign; Resident & Mem, PGA West Golf Club, 2011. **Special Achievements:** Amoekar Industries is selling wigs and cosmetics under the brand name Beverly Johnson. First African-American model to appear on the cover of American Vogue in 1974. First African-American woman to appear on the cover of the French edition of Elle magazine. Author, Guide to a Life of Beauty, Times Books, 1981. **Home Addr:** 767 5th Ave, New York, NY 10022. **Business Addr:** Model/Actress, c/o Prima Modeling Agency, 6855 Santa Monica Blvd Suite 406, Los Angeles, CA 90038-1143, **Business Phone:** (213)882-6900.

## JOHNSON, BILL WADE

Executive. **Personal:** Born May 9, 1943, Idabel, OK; married Barbara. **Educ:** Cent Okla State Univ, BA, 1965. **Career:** Night Training Okla City OIC, supvr, 1965-68; Okla City, OIC, dir, 1968-70; OIC Int, field specialist, 1970-71; OIC Pittsburgh, Pa, exec dir, 1970-71; OIC Chicago IL, exec dir, 1976. **Orgs:** Chmn, Frederick Douglass HA, 1965-68; City Chicago Manpower Planning Coun; Convenor Region III OIC's Am; chmn bd dir, Career Develop Inc; chmn bd, Hill Dist Fed Credit Union, 1975-76; mem bd dir, Ozanam Strings; Kappa Alpha Psi Frat; Chicago Assembly. **Home Addr:** 219 S Walnut St, Glenwood, IL 60425-1880, **Home Phone:** (708)758-1228.

**JOHNSON, BILLY.** **See JOHNSON, WILLIAM ARTHUR.**

## JOHNSON, BRENT E.

School administrator, consultant. **Personal:** Born Jan 17, 1947, Springfield, MA; son of Alvin and Matilda Edmonds; children: Jacye Arnee. **Educ:** Hampton Inst, BA, mkt, 1968; W Ga State Univ, MA, 1975; Clark Atlanta Univ. **Career:** Presbyterian Church, USA, dir Mkt & Recruitment & dir Human Resources, 1974-78; AMTAR Inc, vpres, 1977-80; Atlanta Univ, dir admis, 1980-86; Consortium for Grad Study Mgt, St Louis, Mo, dir mkt & recruiting, 1986-89; The Success Factor, Atlanta, Ga, managing prin, 1989-; Clark Atlanta Univ, Sch Bus Admin, Atlanta, Ga, asst dean & dir MBA prog, 1991-2002; Stuart Compton Group, sr exec search consult, 2007-12; Int Bus Mach Corp, human resources; Avon, human resources; BellSouth Corp, human resources. **Orgs:** Nat Hampton Alumni Asn, 1972-; pres & bd mem, NW YMCA, 1975-78; pres, Atlanta Univ Staff Assembly, 1981-84; chmn & founder Minority Admis Recruitment Network, 1981-86; consult, Grad Mgt Admis Coun, 1984; chmn, Minority Affairs Adv Comm, Grad Mgt Admis Coun, 1986-89. **Honors/Awds:** Contributor Black Collegian Mag, 1980-; Developed Destination MBA Prog, Natl Black MBA Asn, 1987; recognized for work with minorities in MBA progs, African-Am MBA Asn, Univ of Chicago, 1990. **Home Addr:** 5739 N Castlegate Dr, College Park, GA 30349, **Home Phone:** (404)767-5556. **Business Addr:** Sr Executive Search Consultant, Stuart Compton Group, 1201 Peachtree St 400 Colony Sq Suite 200, Atlanta, GA 30361, **Business Phone:** (404)872-7600.

## JOHNSON, BRIAN L.

College president, writer. **Personal:** married Shemeka Barnes; children: Brian Asa & Nathan Morgan Qodesh. **Educ:** Johnson C Smith Univ, BA, Eng, 1995; Univ Wis-Madison, MA, Eng, 1998; Univ SC, Columbia, PhD, Am lit, 2003. **Career:** Univ SC, Ronald McNair Post Baccalaureate Achievement Prog, coordr, 2002-03; Gordon Col, asst prof Eng, 2003-06; Claflin Univ, Jonathan Jasper Wright Inst African Am, dir, assoc prof eng, 2005-07; Johnson C. Smith Univ, assoc vpres acad affairs & chief staff/assoc prof Eng, 2007-10; Tenn Higher Educ Comn, Maxine Smith fel, 2011; Ind Univ-Purdue Univ Indianapolis, A.C.E. Fel, 2012-13; Austin Peay State Univ, asst provost, asst vpres acad affairs & chair univ diversity task, 2010-13, interim vpres strategic planning & instnl effectiveness, 2013-14; Tuskegee Univ, pres, 2014-. **Orgs:** Greenville Col Bd Trustees. **Honors/Awds:** Excellence in Academics and Service Award, USC Black Fac & Staff Asn, 2001-02; Andrew W. Mellon/Benjamin Mays Postdoctoral Fellowship, 2003-; Research Fellow W.E.B. Du Bois Institute for African and African American Research, Harvard University (non-resident), 2004-05; Lilly-funded/Center for Faith and Inquiry Fellow, Gordon College, 2005-07; Woodrow Wilson National Fellowship Foundation/Career Enhancement Sabbatical Fellowship, 2006-07; Excellence in Teaching and Scholarship Award (Claflin University), 2006-07; "The Civic Engagement Scholar" at the J. McDonald Williams Institute, research-arm of the Foundation for Community Empowerment (Dallas, Texas), 2006-08; Maxine Smith Administrators' Fellowship (Tennessee Board of Regents), 2011-12; American Association of State Colleges and Universities (AASCU) Millennium Leadership Initiative (MLI), 2012-13; American Council of Education (A.C.E.) Fellowship, 2012-13. **Special Achievements:** Editor of "Du Bois on Reform: Periodical-Based Leadership for African Americans" (Rowman and Littlefield, 2005), author of "The Yancy Years: Age of Infrastructure, Technology and Restoration" (Johnson C. Smith University, 2008), "W.E.B Du Bois: Toward Agnosticism (1868-1934)" (Rowman and Littlefield, 2008), and writer of various journal articles and encyclopedia entries.

## JOHNSON, C. CHRISTINE

Air force officer, administrator, association executive. **Personal:** Born Jun 19, 1928, Jackson, MS; daughter of Cornelius and Simon; children: Edward. **Educ:** Univ Md, Munich, MS, 1960. **Career:** NY

St Div Human Rights, field rep, 1971; Hamilton Col, Clinton, NY, trustee, 1971-, dir higher educ opportunity prog, 1971-2014. **Orgs:** Air Force Asn; Retired Officers Asn; pres, NY St Higher Educ Oppor Prof Orgn; pres, Am Asn Non-White Concerns; NY St Health Sys Agency; bd visitor, Cent NY Psychiat Ctr; NY State's only Forensic Psychiat Ctr; Prof Bus Women's Asn; Nat Asn Advan Colored People; Nat & NY State Asn Human Rights Workers; Opera Guild; rep, Urban Renewal Prog Dayton, OH, 1958; Joint Protestant & Cath Choir; City Planning; Tri-State Ment Health Bd; pres, Rome Day Care Ctr; Black Women Higher Educ; NY State Higher Educ Opportunity Prog & Prof Orgn; bd visitor, Cent NY Psychiat Ctr; pres, Frontiers Inst; Tri-State Consortium Opportunity Progs Higher Edu; founder, C Christine Johnson Higher Educ Opportunity Prog & Scholars Fund, 2001. **Honors/Awds:** Nom Female Heroine of the Year, Pac Air Force, 1969; NOW Unsung Heroine Special Award Honor for Achievement Working, Young Col Women, 1978; Bell Ringer Award for Outstanding Achievement Meritorious Service, Hamilton Col Alumni Coun, 1991; African Americans Distinction Award, NY governor Mario Como, 1994. **Home Addr:** 6548 Fairview Lane, Rome, NY 13440, **Home Phone:** (315)336-5713. **Business Addr:** Director of the Higher Education Opportunity Program, Trustee, Hamilton College, 198 Col Hill Rd, Clinton, NY 13323, **Business Phone:** (315)859-4398.

### JOHNSON, DR. CAGE SAUL
Educator, scientist. **Personal:** Born Mar 31, 1941, New Orleans, LA; son of Cage Spooner and Esther Georgiana Saul; married Shirley; children: Stephanie & Michelle. **Educ:** Creighton Univ Col Med, MD, 1965. **Career:** Univ Southern Calif, instr med, 1971-74, from asst prof med to assoc prof med, 1974-88, prof med, 1988-, Comprehensive Sickle Cell Ctr Southern Calif, dir, currently. **Orgs:** Chmn, Adv Comt, Genetically Handicaped Persons Prog, Calif Dept Health Serv, 1978-; vice chmn & bd dir, Sickle Cell Self-Help Asn Inc, 1983-88; secy, EE Just Soc, 1985-93, pres, 1993-95; secy & bd dir, Sickle Cell Dis Res Found, 1986-94; rev comm chmn, Nat Heart Lung & Blood Inst, 1989-91; Alpha Omega Alpha. **Home Addr:** 5440 Harcross Dr, Los Angeles, CA 90043. **Business Addr:** Professor of Medicine, Director, Sickle Cell Center, University of Southern California, 1200 N State St GNH 3824, Los Angeles, CA 90033, **Business Phone:** (323)226-7564.

### JOHNSON, CALIPH
Lawyer, educator, executive director. **Personal:** Born Oct 3, 1938, St. Joseph, LA; married Cheryl Helena Chapman. **Educ:** Univ Md, BA, polit sci, 1964; San Jose State Univ, MA, pub admin, 1968; Univ San Francisco Sch Law, JD, 1972; Georgetown Univ Law Ctr, LLM, 1973. **Career:** Professor (retired) City Oakland, Calif, admin analyst, 1970-72; Oakland Citizens Comn, Urban Renewal, exec dir, 1970-72; Georgetown Univ Law Ctr, Inst Pub Int Rep, grad fel, 1972-73, atty, 1972-73; Off Gen Coun Equal Employ Opportunity Comn, appellate atty, 1973-75; Thurgood Marshall Sch Law, SW Inst Equal Employ, Tex Southern Univ, asst prof, dir, 1975-78, tenured prof law, assoc dean, interim dean & gen coun, hearing officer, 1990-95; Univ Miaduguri, Nigeria, consult, 1978-80; Off Lawyer Training Legal Serv Corp, advocacy trainer, 1978-80; Equal Employ Opportunity Comn, hearing examr, 1979-80, Off Gen Coun, appellate atty; US Naval War Col, Oceans Law Dept, researcher, 1993; Title VII Proj, Nat Bar Asn, Bd Dir Gulf Coast Legal Found, fac; Bd Trustees, Episcopal Found of Tex; A A White Dispute Resolution Inst, fac; Gen Coun the EEOC, appellate atty; State Bar Tex ADR Sect, chair elect, 1999-2000; SW Inst Dispute Resolution, founder & dir, atty mediator, currently; Usn Res, comn officer. **Orgs:** Contract hearing officer, Equal Employ Opportunity Comn, 1970; Am Arbit Asn, 1880-90; chair, City Houston Ethics Comt, 1997-99; chair, State Bar Tex, ADR Sect & Coun, 1999-00; Comn Law Off Exon, Am Bar Asn; labor law sect, Nat Bar Asn; civil litigation comt mem, Fed Bar Asn; Civil Procedure & Clin Sect Asn Am Law Schs; bd dir, Houston Neighborhood Justice Prog; Task force Law Prof Teaching ADR; adv bd & bd dir, A A White Dispute Resolution Inst; Houston Better Bus Bur. **Special Achievements:** A response to crises of enforcing fair employment, Houston Lawyer, 1975; course material on fair employment literature, Tex Southern Univ, 1976; integrated clinical current module, Texas Southern Univ & HEW, 1978-80; teamsters US Impact on Seniority Relief TX So NBA Law Rev, 1979; Book review, Let Them Be Judges, Howard Univ Law Journal, 1980. **Home Addr:** 3330 Parkwood Dr, Houston, TX 77002-1139, **Home Phone:** (713)412-1559. **Business Addr:** Director, Founder, SouthWest Institute for Dispute Resolution, 5330 Griggs Rd, Houston, TX 77004, **Business Phone:** (713)747-9688.

### JOHNSON, CARL EARLD
Executive. **Personal:** Born Dec 3, 1936, New York, NY; son of Francis Alexander and Gwendolyn Vera; married Mozelle Baker; children: Brian A & Carla D. **Educ:** City Univ NY, BS, 1958, MBA, 1963. **Career:** Western Elec, human resources assoc, 1963-68; Black Exchange Prog, vis prof, 1970-; Mobil Oil Corp, mgr spec proj, 1981-85; Campbell Soup Co, actg dir gov compliance, 1985-90; Philip Morris Co, credit mgr, affirmative action, 1990-91; Summit Bank, vpres employee rels compliance prog, 1991-; United Jersey Bank, vpres, 1991-. **Orgs:** Vpres, Task Force Youth Motivation, 1969-75; Medgar Evers Col Curric Develop Comn, 1974-76; Soc Human Resources Mgt, 1976-; Inst Mgt Consult, 1986-; EDGES Group, 1990-; chair employ coun, Nat Urban Affairs Coun, NJ, 1991-; Lions Club, 1992-; fed, Hisp Bankers Asn NJ; NJ Urban Bankers Asn; bd dir, W Windsor Zone Adjust, 1984-89. **Home Addr:** 9 Allister Lane, Columbus, NJ 08022, **Home Phone:** (609)291-5550. **Business Addr:** Vice President of Employee Relations & Compliance Programs, Summit Bank, 301 Carnegie Ctr, Princeton, NJ 08540, **Business Phone:** (609)987-3200.

### JOHNSON, CARL ELLIOTT
Mechanical engineer. **Personal:** Born Oct 4, 1956, Houston, TX; married Mary Ann Jean; children: Patric, Cristina & Carren. **Educ:** Prairie View A&M Univ, BSME, 1979. **Career:** Union Carbide, maintenance engr, 1979-83; Monsanto Chem Co, sr process engr, 1984-85, process supvr, 1985-, utilities supvr. **Orgs:** Corp solicitor United Way, 1985-; youth basketball, YMCA, 1987; Speakers Bur. **Business Addr:** Process Supervisor, Senior Engineer, Monsanto Chemical Co, Monsanto Rd Suite 1, Nitro, WV 25143.

**JOHNSON, CAROL DIAHANN.** **See CARROLL, DIAHANN.**

### JOHNSON, DR. CARRIE CLEMENTS
Educator. **Personal:** Born Jan 2, 1931, Atlanta, GA; daughter of Lucile Clements and Emanuel Clements; married Alfred James; children: Alfia Katherine. **Educ:** Morris Brown Col, Atlanta, GA, BS, 1951; Columbia Univ, NY, MA, 1954; State Univ NY, Buffalo, EdD, 1978. **Career:** Educator (retired); Fulton County Bd Educ, Atlanta, Ga, high sch teacher, 1951-61; Morris Brown Col, Atlanta, Ga, dir career planning & placement, asst prof, 1961-67; State Univ Col, Buffalo, counr, 1967-71, dir couns, 1971-83, assoc dir, 1977-78, asst prof bus studies, 1981-1983, dir coun & assoc dean, 1983-1986; Taught Bus Commun, Univ Akron, Fall, 1970; Fulton County Schs, dir, classified staff develop, 1986-1988; Fulton County Bd Educ, Atlanta, Ga, exec dir, 1988-1995; Johnson & Johnson, pres. **Orgs:** Nat Urban League Sorority, 1966-67; assoc dir, VISTA Training; Am Personnel & Guid Asn, 1967-; vpres Jack & Jill Am Inc, 1974; HEW fel US Govt Dept HEW, 1979-81; bd dir, Buffalo Area Engineering Awareness Minorities, 1982; bd dir, Child Develop Inst Buffalo, 1983; scholar comn, Buffalo Urban League, 1984; Zeta Phi Beta; Links Inc; adv coun, Atlanta Tech Inst, 1995-98; bd dir, Nat Asn Advan Colored People, 1996; personnel bd, Fulton County Bd Ethics, 2002-15. **Special Achievements:** Elected by the Atlanta Business League as one of Atlanta's 100 Women of Influence, 2005. **Home Addr:** 3965 Old Fairburn Rd SW, Atlanta, GA 30331, **Home Phone:** (404)349-7750.

### JOHNSON, CARROLL JONES
Mayor, school administrator. **Personal:** Born Mar 1, 1948, Blackville, SC; daughter of Louise Felder and Rufus; children: F Kelvin, Herman N & Wayne. **Educ:** Voorhees Col, Denmark, SC, BS, 1978; Univ SC. **Career:** Barnwell Sch Dist 19, Macedonia Elem Sch, Blackville SC, literacy coordr, 1980-; Blackville, SC, mayor. **Orgs:** Barnwell County Help Line; Barnwell County Community Improv Bd; Nat Asn Advan Colored People. **Home Addr:** 37 Broadleaf Dr, Blackville, SC 29817-3750, **Home Phone:** (803)284-4706. **Business Addr:** Literacy Co-ordinator, Barnwell School District 19, 297 Pascallas St, Blackville, SC 29817, **Business Phone:** (803)284-5605.

### JOHNSON, CARROLL RANDOLPH, JR.
Executive, clergy. **Personal:** Born Jun 13, 1951, Baltimore, MD; son of Carroll R Sr (deceased) and Delores Patricia; married Muriel Minor; children: Duane, Sherry Grant & Keith. **Educ:** Baltimore City Col, bus & indust mgt; Johns Hopkins Univ, BA, 1972. **Career:** C & P Tel, bus off asst mgr, 1972-77; Praise Rec Co, prs, 1977-79; Bell Atlantic Corp, comput consult, mgr & Instr, 1979-87; Evergreen CPN, 1987-; Maximum Life Christian Church, founder, sr pastor, bishop, currently; Zamar Music Group Inc. **Orgs:** Baltimore Coun self-esteem curricula & self-empowerment progs; Mid-Atlantic Diocese-Bibleway Churches; bd chmn, Potential Unlimited; vpres, Bd Baltimore Cable Access Corp; Am Solar Energy Soc; fel GreenFaith Fel Prog. **Home Addr:** 1928 Woodlawn Dr, Baltimore, MD 21207, **Home Phone:** (410)298-1238. **Business Addr:** President, Zamar Music Group, 1928 Woodlawn Dr, Baltimore, MD 21207, **Business Phone:** (410)597-9925.

**JOHNSON, CARYN ELAINE.** **See GOLDBERG, WHOOPI.**

### JOHNSON, CATO, II
Vice president (organization), executive. **Personal:** Born Aug 26, 1947, Memphis, TN; son of Cato and Frankie Scales; married Georgette Alexander; children: Cato III. **Educ:** Memphis State Univ, BS, educ, 1970, MS, educ, 1971; Tenn Sch Banking, Vanderbilt Univ. **Career:** Memphis State Univ, manpower specialist, 1971-73, asst dir, 1981-83; Gen Motors Acceptance Corp, field rep, 1971-74; First Tenn Bank, personnel asst, 1974-75; First Tenn Nat Corp, affirmative action coordr, 1975-78, personnel adminr & affirmative action coordr, 1978-80, mgr personnel, 1980-81; Regional Med Ctr, vpres corp affairs, 1983-85; Methodist Health Systs, sr vpres corp affairs, 1985-. **Orgs:** Memphis Conv & Visitors Bur; Kiwanis; Gov's Coun Health & Phys Fitness; Tenn Human Servs Adv Coun; Jr League Memphis Bd; pres's coun, LeMoyne-Owen Col; bd dir, Tenn Comprehensive Health Ins Pool; adv comn, Sr Citizen's Servs; pres coun, LeMoyne-Owen Col; Arts Pk, Memphis Arts Festival; co chair, Mayor WW Herenton Transition Team, Parks & Facitities Comn; exec comt, Memphis & Shelby Co Sports Authority Bd; Goals Memphis Race Rels Comn; Mayor's Mud Island Task Force; Memphis & Shelby Co Med Soc; pres, Univ Memphis Nat Alumni Asn; Jim Rout, Shelby Co Mayor-elect, transition team, Don Sundquist; Gov Tenn, transition team; chair, Southwest Tenn Community Col Bd Advisors; vice chair, Needs Assessment Comt; Tenn Hosp Asn Coun Govt Affairs; Univ Memphis Tigers Club; Coalition Better Memphis & Generations Inc; pres, Univ Memphis Alumni Asn; bd advisor, MIAA Athletic Develop Comt; vice chair, Shelby County Schs Needs Assessment Comt; chmn, Shelby County Schs Athletic Comt; vice chmn, Shelby Schs Found; vice chmn, Youth Educ Through Sports; pres's coun, Shelby County Pub Bldg Authority; pres's coun, Tenn Hosp Asn Bylaws Comt, Tenn Hosp Asn Coun Diversity; pres's coun, Sports Entertainment Recreation Venue Rev Comt; original Gov's TennCare Roundtable; vice chmn, State Health Planning; adv bd & chmn, TennCare Med Care Adv Comt;Thespian Club; State Bd Educ. **Home Addr:** 9155 Hillman Way Dr, Memphis, TN 38133, **Home Phone:** (901)377-2164. **Business Addr:** Senior Vice President of Corporate Affairs, Methodist Health Systems, 1211 Union Ave, Memphis, TN 38104, **Business Phone:** (901)516-7000.

### JOHNSON, CHARLES
Educator, physician. **Personal:** Born Jul 28, 1927, Acmar, AL; married Carol Ann; children: Carla & Charles. **Educ:** Howard Univ, BS, 1953, MD, 1963. **Career:** Lincoln Hosp, pvt pract, 1967-70; Duke Univ Med Ctr, Durham, NC, from asst prof med to prof med, 1970-96, prof emer med, 1996, spec adv chancellor, health affairs, 1997; physician, currently. **Orgs:** Durham Acad Med; Kappa Alpha Psi, 1950-; Am Soc Int Med; Am Col Physicians; Am Diabetes Asn; adv comn, Minority Students NC; fel endocrinol, Duke; s Sch Med, 1967; pres, Old N State Med Soc, 1973-75; chmn, Reg III Nat Med Asn, 1975-78; secy, House Delegates Nat Med Asn, 1975-77; dir, Nat Med Asn, Africa Health Proj, 1975-80; bd admis, Duke Univ Col Med, 1976-81; vis speaker, House Delegates Nat Med Asn, 1977-79; speaker, House Delegates Nat Med Asn, 1980-81; bd trustee, Nat Med Asn, 1982-88, secy bd trustee, 1984-86, chmn, bd trustee, 1986-88, pres-elect, 1989-90, pres, 1990-91; Doric Lodge 28, Durham Consistory 218, Shriner, Zafa Temple 176, 33rd Deg Mason, St Titus Epis Church. **Home Addr:** 1209 E Pointe Dr, Durham, NC 27712, **Home Phone:** (919)620-9107. **Business Addr:** Physician, 1209 E Pointe Dr, Durham, NC 27712-9488, **Business Phone:** (919)575-2532.

### JOHNSON, CHARLES BERNARD
Journalist. **Personal:** Born Mar 9, 1954, Detroit, MI; son of Bessie Mae Gayden and Ira B; married Tara Halsey; children: Janay & Julius. **Educ:** Mich State Univ, E Lansing, MI, BA, journ, 1975. **Career:** Flint J, Flint, Mich, sports columnist, 1975-88; Black Entertainment TV Sports Report, Wash, DC, panelist, 1988-; USA Today, Wash DC, sports writer, 1988-. Films: DVD Bd Game, 2006; City Teacher, 2007. **Orgs:** Pres, Nat Asn Black Jour Mid Mich Chap, 1986-87; Sports task force steering comt, Nat Asn Black Journalists, 1989-. **Honors/Awds:** Man of the Year, Flint Golden Gloves, 1982; In Appreciation for Effort, Greater Flint Wrestling Coaches Asn, 1984; Central Flint Optimists Club, 1985; Honored for Community Serv, Nat Asn Media Women Inc, 1987; Hon Inductee, Greater Flint Afro-Am Hall of Fame, 1988; 'Sports Journalist for the Year', Nat Asn Black Journalists, 2000. **Special Achievements:** Made his movie debut in 2006, portraying himself as a boxing writer in "Rocky Balboa". **Home Addr:** 5131 Temple Hill Rd, Temple Hills, MD 20748, **Home Phone:** (301)630-5804. **Business Addr:** Sports Writer, USA Today, 7950 Jones Br Dr 7th Fl, McLean, VA 22108-0605, **Business Phone:** (703)854-5944.

### JOHNSON, CHARLES E.
Administrator, educator. **Personal:** Born Jul 1, 1946, Woodville, MS; married Bessie M Hudson; children: Vanessa Lashea, Adrianne Monique, Andrea Melita & Krystal Charlese. **Educ:** Alcorn State Univ, BS, 1968; Southern Univ, MEd, 1971. **Career:** Bay St Louis Sch Dist, teacher, 1967-69; Wilkinson County Sch Dist, teacher, 1969-71, supt educ, 1976-97; Brookhaven Sch Dist, teacher, 1972-73; Amite County Sch Dist, teacher, 1974-75. **Orgs:** Nat Asn Advan Colored People; Miss Teachers Asn; Miss Asn Sch Superintendents; Miss Cattlesmen Asn; Nat Cattlesmen Asn. **Honors/Awds:** Charles E Johnson Classroom Bldg, Centreville, Miss, 1980; Charles E Johnson Admin Bldg, Woodville, Miss, 1997. **Home Addr:** 852 W St, Woodville, MS 39669, **Home Phone:** (601)888-7346.

### JOHNSON, DR. CHARLES EDWARD
Scientist. **Personal:** Born Feb 24, 1938, Dallas, NC; son of Lydia D and Ira G; married Gladys E Hawkins; children: Nikolas, Andre, Sean, Markus & Karari. **Educ:** Morgan State Univ, BS, 1960; Univ Cincinnati, PhD, 1966. **Career:** Morgan State Univ, prof biol, 1973-74; Community Col Baltimore, lectr, 1974; Union Cincinnati, adj prof, 1980-81; Procter & Gamble Co, sect head, 1981-88; Clairol Inc, Stamford, CT, mgr & dir, 1988-. **Orgs:** AAAS, 1980-83; Am Soc Microbiol; bd trustee, W End Health Clin, 1980-82. **Home Addr:** 35 High Rock Rd, Sandy Hook, CT 06482, **Home Phone:** (203)426-1389. **Business Addr:** Director, Technical Support, Clairol Inc, 1 Blachley Rd, Stamford, CT 06902, **Business Phone:** (203)357-5000.

### JOHNSON, CHARLES EDWARD, JR.
Baseball player, athletic coach. **Personal:** Born Jul 20, 1971, Ft. Pierce, FL; married Rhonda Thompson; children: Brandon & Beau. **Educ:** Univ Miami. **Career:** Baseball player (retired); Fla Marlins, catcher, 1994-98, 2001-02; Los Angeles Dodgers, catcher, 1998; Baltimore Orioles, catcher, 1999-2000; Chicago White Sox, catcher, 2000; Colo Rockies, catcher, 2003-04; Tampa Bay Devil Rays, catcher, 2005; Am League. **Orgs:** Portland Sea Dogs Hall Fame.

### JOHNSON, CHARLES EVERETT
Football player. **Personal:** Born Jan 3, 1972, San Bernardino, CA; married Tanisha; children: Charles III. **Educ:** Univ Colo, BA, mkt. **Career:** Football player (retired); Pittsburgh Steelers, kick returner, wide receiver, 1994-98; Philadelphia Eagles, 1999-2000; New Eng Patriots, 2001; Buffalo Bills, 2002. **Honors/Awds:** Ed Black Courage Award, 1994; All-Big Eight Offensive Player of the Year; Super Bowl Champion (XXXVI). **Special Achievements:** The first Colorado player to ever surpass the 2000-yard career. Films: 1994 AFC Championship Game, 1995; 1997 AFC Championship Game, 1998; 2001 AFC Championship Game, 2002.

### JOHNSON, DR. CHARLES FLOYD (JAZZ FLOYD JOHNSON)
Lawyer, television producer, television writer. **Personal:** Born Feb 12, 1942, Camden, NJ; son of Orange Maull and Bertha Ellen Seagers; married Anne Burford; children: Kristin Suzanne; married Sandra Brashears. **Educ:** Univ Del, 1961; Howard Univ, BA, 1962; Howard Univ Sch Law, JD, 1965. **Career:** Howard Berg Law Off, atty, 1965; Libr Cong; US Copyright Off, atty, 1967-70; copyright lawyer; Howard Univ's radio sta; Swed Ministry Justice, Stockholm, Sweden, atty, 1970; Universal TV, prod coordr, 1971-74, assoc prod, 1974-76, producer, 1976-82, supv producer, 1982-86, exec producer, 1985; TV ser: "Six Million Dollar Man", actor, 1974; "Toma", actor, 1974; "Kojak", actor, 1975; "Black Sheep Squadron ", assoc producer, 1976; "Rockford Files", producer, 1975-80, supv producer, 1977-79, assoc producer, 1975-76; Hellinger's Law, 1981; "Simon & Simon", 1981; "Bret Maverick", 1981-82; "Magnum, P.I.", producer, 1983, supv producer, 1984-86, co-exec producer, 1980-88; "B.L. Stryker", co-exec producer, 1989-90; Revealing Evidence: Stalking Honolulu Strangler, exec producer, 1990; "Quantum Leap", co-exec producer, 1993; Rockford Files: A Blessing Disguise, exec producer, 1995; Rockford Files: If It Bleeds... It Leads, producer, 1999; "First Monday", co-exec producer, 2002; "JAG", co-exec producer, 1997-2004, actor, 1999-2005; "Navy NCIS: Naval Criminal Investigative Serv", co-exec producer, 2004-07 & 2007-08, exec producer, 2007-09; Films: Silver fox, writer & exec producer, 1991; Red Tails, producer, 2012; A Private Act, producer, 2013; Get Way: Journey John Lewis, producer, 2015. **Orgs:** Vice chmn, Media Forum, 1980-85; Asn Black Motion Picture & TV Producers, 1980-82; bd dir, Comm Bridge, 1981-89; bd, Kwanza Found, 1985; bd, Am

Independent Video Filmmakers, 1985-90; Caucus Producers, Dirs & Writers, 1990-; Crossroads Theatre Arts Acad, 1990; Screen Actors Guild Am; bd, Producers Guild Am; Writers Guild Am; Nat Acad TV Arts & Sci; Am Film Inst; OPP. **Honors/Awds:** Numerous awards including Emmy Award, Rockford Files, Best TV Drama, 1978; 3 Emmy Nominations for: Rockford Files, 1978-79, 1979-80, Los Angeles Area Emmy Award Winner for producing and performing in a KCET/PBS Special "Voices of Our People, A Celebration of Black Poetry", 1981; Alumni Achievement Award, Stony Brook Col Prep, 1979; Commendations, City Los Angeles, 1982, 1993; Commendation, Calif State Senate, 1982; Magnum PI, 1982-83 & 1983-84; Outstanding Alumnus, Howard Univ Alumni Club So Calif, 1982; Commendation, Calif State Legis, 1982; Outstanding Alumnus Award, Howard Univ, 1985; Commendation, Hawaii State Senate, 1988; Commendation, Hawaii House Rep, 1988; Commendation, City Honolulu, 1988; The Primetime Emmy Award. **Special Achievements:** Books: "The Origins of the Stockholm Protocol", 1970; co-author, "Black Women in Television", 1990. **Home Addr:** 2561 Astral Dr, Los Angeles, CA 90046, **Home Phone:** (213)876-5507.

**JOHNSON, CHARLES H. See Obituaries Section.**

### JOHNSON, DR. CHARLES HENRY

Lawyer. **Personal:** Born May 24, 1946, New Haven, CT; son of Charles H and Helen Taylor. **Educ:** Hotchkiss Sch, Lakeville, CT, dipl, 1964; Yale Univ, BA, hist & sociol, 1968; Yale Law Sch, JD, com law, 1972. **Career:** US Peace Corps, in-country vol, 1968-69; Montgomery McCracken Walker & Rhoads, assoc, 1972-75; US Food & Drug Admin, asst chief coun enforcement, 1975-79; US Equal Employ Opportunity Comn, supvry trial atty, 1978-79; Conn Gen Life Ins Co, atty, 1979-82; New Eng Mutual Life Ins Co, coun & asst secy, 1982-93; Clark, Brown & Clark, law off mgr, 1993-99; atty, pvt pract, 1993-99; Whittier Law Sch, Los Angeles, Calif, adj prof, 1997-98; Los Angeles Super Ct, contracts analyst, 1999-2003, mgt analyst, e los angeles courthouse, 2002-03, grant writer & financial analyst, grants admin, 2003-07; New Eng Life Ins Co. **Orgs:** Nat Bar Asn; grant writer & consult, The Clark-Johnson Group, 2007-. **Business Addr:** New Eng Life Ins Co, 699 Boylston St Suite 1400, Boston, MA 02116, **Business Phone:** (617)585-4574.

### JOHNSON, CHARLES RICHARD

Cartoonist or animator, educator, writer. **Personal:** Born Apr 23, 1948, Evanston, IL; son of Benjamin Lee and Ruby Elizabeth Jackson; married Joan New; children: Malik & Elizabeth. **Educ:** Southern Ill Univ, BA, 1971, MA, 1973; State Univ NY, Stony Brook, PhD, phenomenol & lit aesthet, 1988. **Career:** Educator (retired), writer, cartoonist; Chicago Tribune, cartoonist, reporter, 1969-70; St Louis Proud, art staff, 1971-72; Univ Wash, asst prof, 1976-79, assoc prof, 1979-82, prof eng, 1982, endowed chair humanities, 1991, writer & cartoonist, currently; Seattle Rev, fiction ed, 1978-; Author: Charlies Pad, 1970; Black Humor, 1970; Being & Race: Black Writing Since 1970; Half Nation Time, 1972; Faith & Good Thing, Viking, 1974; Chrlie Smith & Fritter Tree, 1978; Oxherding Tale, 1982; Booker, 1983; The Sorcerers Apprentice, 1986; Ind Univ Press, 1988; Pieces of Eight, 1989; Middle Passage, 1990; Rites of Passage: Stories about Growing up by Black Writers from around the World, 1993; On Writers & Writing, 1994; Black Men Speaking, 1997; Still I Rise; A Cartoon Hist African Ams, 1997; Dreamer, 1998; Africans in America: Americas Journey through Slavery, 1998; I Call Myself an Artist: Writings by & about Charles Johnson, 1999; A Treas of N Am Folktales, 1999; Was B a Slave: An Anthology of Classic Slave Narratives, 1999; Sacred Fire: The QBR 100 Essential Black Bks, 2000; King: The Photobiography of Martin Luther King Jr, co-author, 2000; Soulcatcher & Other Stories, 2001; Turning the Wheel: Essays on Buddhism & Writing, 2003; Dr. Kings Refrigerator Other Bedtime Stories, 2005; Mine Eyes Have Seen: Bearing Witness to the Struggle for Civil Rights, co-author, 2007; Remembering Martin Luther King, Jr: 40 Years Later, His Life and Crusade in Pictures, 2008; The Writers Brush: Paintings, Drawings and Sculpture by Writers; An Innovative Introduction: Fiction Narrative, Primary Texts and Responsive Writing, co-author, 2010; Taming the Ox: Buddhist Stories and Reflections on Politics, Race, Culture and Spiritual Practice, 2014; 672 page Words and Wisdom of Charles Johnson, 2015; The Hard Problem, 2015. **Orgs:** Bd mem, dir, Assoc Writing Prog Awards Ser Short Fiction; co-dir, Blue Phoenix Kung Fu Club; MacArthur fel, 1998; trustee, Wash Comn Humanities; bd mem, Seattle Repertory Theater. **Business Addr:** Professor, University of Washington, PO Box 354330, Seattle, WA 98195-4330, **Business Phone:** (206)543-9865.

### JOHNSON, CHARLES V.

Judge. **Personal:** Born Jun 11, 1928, Malvern, AR; son of Charlie and Laura Miller; married Lazelle S; children: James W Brown, Tracy L & Terri Lynn. **Educ:** Ark Agri Mech & Norm Col, Pine Bluff, BA, 1954; Univ Wash, Sch Law, Seattle, LLB, 1957. **Career:** Judge (retired); atty pvt pract, 1958-69; Munic Ct Seattle, judge, 1969-80, presiding judge 1971-72; State Wash King County Super Ct, judge, 1981-98; Presiding Judge King County Super Ct, 1989-93. **Orgs:** Bd dir, WA State Mag Asn; charter mem, Judicial Coun, Nat Bar Asn; Seattle-King County Br-Bar Liaison Comt; Am Judicial Soc; Phi Alpha Delta; nat pres, Sigma Rho Hon Soc, 1954-55; pres, Seattle Br, NAACP, 1959-64; First AME Church, 1960-; treas, Cent Area Comn Civil Rights, 1963-70; chmn bd mgmt, E Madison Br, 1964-69, bd dir; YMCA; pres, NW Area Conf, 1965-70; Nat Legal Comn; chmn, Seattle Model Cities Adv Coun, 1967-72; bd dir, NAACP, 1968-95; Seattle Lawyers Comt Civil Rights, 1968-69; pres, Metro Br, 1972-73; adv comt, US Comn Civil Rights; pres, Am Judges Asn, 1981-82; Bd mem, Nat Ctr State Courts, 1985-90. **Honors/Awds:** Distinguished Citizens Award, Model Cities Seattle, 1973; First Citizens Award, Seattle, 1973; Man of the Year Award, Alpha Phi Alpha, 1973; Distinguished Community Award for United Way; YMCA Serv Youth Award; Benefit Guilds Martin Luther King Community Serv Award; Links Human Rights Award; Award for Distinguished Serv, Seattle-King County Bar Asn, 1991; Distinguished Serv Award, Nat Ctr State Courts; Distinguished Alumnus, Univ Wash, Sch Law, 1992; Municipal League King County, Distinguished Service Award, 1994; King County, Public Official of the Year Award, 1994; Wash State Bar Asn, Outstanding Judge Award, 1994; Edwin T Pratt Award, 1995; Nordstrom's Cultural Diversity Award, 1998. **Home Addr:** 3513 SW Hanford St, Seattle, WA 98126, **Home Phone:** (206)932-8848.

### JOHNSON, CHERYL P.

Chief executive officer. **Educ:** Kalamazoo Col, BA, psychol, 1983. **Career:** Coalition Temp Shelter (COTS), chief exec officer, 1990-, dep dir, 1994-98, shelter dir; CPJ Consult Group, cert integral life coach, 2007-. **Orgs:** Fel Black Stud Orgn; bd mem, New Detroit Inc; chair, Life EmPOWERment Ctr. **Home Addr:** 19361 Ashton Ave, Detroit, MI 48219, **Home Phone:** (313)362-7788. **Business Addr:** Chief Executive Officer, COTS (Coalition on Temporary Shelter), 26 Peterboro st, Detroit, MI 48201, **Business Phone:** (313)831-3777.

### JOHNSON, CLARK W.

Aerospace engineer. **Educ:** Grambling State Univ, BS, chem; Univ Denver, MS, chem; Pepperdine Univ, MA, bus admin; Univ Calif Anderson Sch Bus, exec mgt course. **Career:** SAMPE Foundation, int exec vpres, 1973, int sr vpres, int vpres, int treas, int pres, 2003-04, chmn, currently; Lockheed Martin Corp, staff; Nat Sec Prog Orgn Satellite Syst Div, El Segundo, Calif, syst engineering proj mgr, currently. **Orgs:** NASA Space Sta Mat & Processes Control Bd. **Honors/Awds:** Pioneer of the Year Award, Nat Soc Black Engrs, 2004. **Special Achievements:** First African American President of the Society for the Advancement of Material & Process Engineering (SAMPE). **Home Addr:** 5847 Stonecrest Dr, Agoura Hills, CA 91301-4626, **Home Phone:** (818)991-9169. **Business Addr:** Chairman, SAMPE Foundation, PO Box 3072, Glendale, CA 91221, **Business Phone:** (818)599-8586.

### JOHNSON, CLINISSON ANTHONY (TONY JOHNSON)

Judge. **Personal:** Born Nov 15, 1947, Memphis, TN; son of Ollie Bernard and Emma Tom; married Sharon; children: Collin Anthony, Terrence Galen & Attorney Tiffany Gayle. **Educ:** Fisk Univ Nashville, BA, hist, 1969; Univ Tenn Law Sch Knoxville, JD, 1972. **Career:** City Atty's Ofc Memphis, part-time pub defender 1972-74; Ratner Sugarmon Lucas & Salky Law Ofc Memphi, asso assy, 1972-76; Shelby Co Pub Defenders Ofc Memphis, asst pub defender 1974-75; Memphis Munic Ct Syst, city ct judge div IV 1976-. **Orgs:** Tenn Bar Asn; Memphis & Shelby Co Bar Asn; Nat Bar Asn; Nat Bar Asn & Am Bar Asn; Nat Advan Asn Colored People, 1985. **Special Achievements:** Youngest African American Judge in the entire United States; First African Americans to be admitted to the University of Tennessee College of law. **Home Addr:** 655 Riverside Dr Suite 806A, Memphis, TN 38103-4617. **Business Addr:** Judge, City Memphis Munic Court, 128 Adams Ave, Memphis, TN 38103.

### JOHNSON, REV. CLINTON LEE

Clergy, manager, government official. **Personal:** Born Mar 16, 1947, Mobile, AL; son of Alfred F and Clara Chapman; married Barbara Gibson; children: Ginnessa L, Ashley T & Clinton Jr. **Educ:** Ala A&M Univ, Mobile, Ala, BA, gov & soc, 1969; Univ Southern Ala, Mobile, Ala, MA, hons rehab cons, 1973; Mobile Col, Mobile, Ala, BA, hons, 1982. **Career:** Manager (retired), pastor, councilman; State Ala Voc Rehab Serv, supvr; Bethlehem Baptist Church, Citronelle, pastro; Mobile City Coun, Mobile, Ala, vpres, 1985-; Shiloh Baptist Church, Mobile, Ala, pastor, 1988-; Mobile City Coun, Dist 3, coun pres, councilman, currently. **Orgs:** Ala State Employees Asn; Nat Rehab Asn; Ala Rehab Asn; Nat Rehab Coun Asn; Nat Rehab Asn Supvr; past bd mem, Goodwill Indust; past bd mem, Mobile Asn Blind; bd mem, Independent Living Ctr; Mobile Regional Planning Comn; SCLC; Nat Asn Advan Colored People; Alpha Phi Alpha Fraternity; Boys Club Am; past mem, Leadership Ala; chmn, Ala A&M Univ Bd Trustees; Nat Baptist Conv USA Inc; Ala State Baptist Conv; Mobile Baptist Sunlight Dist Asn; Baptist Ministers Conf InterdenomiNat Ministerial Alliance; asst dir, Cong Christian Educ. **Honors/Awds:** Citizen of the Year, Alpha Phi Alpha Fraternity, 1985; Citizen of the Year, Palestine Temple 16, 1985; Service Award, InterdenomiNat Ministers Alliance, 1986; Service Award, Boys Club Am, 1987; Two Honorary Doctorate degree in Religion; Outstanding Young Man in America; Certified Rehabilitation Counselor. **Special Achievements:** Outstanding Young Man in America. **Home Addr:** 1101 Dunaway Dr, Mobile, AL 36605-3649, **Home Phone:** (251)476-0831. **Business Addr:** Councilman, Mobile City, 1655 Eagle Dr, Mobile, AL 36605, **Business Phone:** (251)470-1728.

### JOHNSON, COLLIS, JR.

Dentist. **Personal:** Born Nov 17, 1946, OK; son of Collis and Ruby; married Marsha Michele Jones; children: Jonathan Ashley, Rachael Christine & Laura Michelle May. **Educ:** Langston Univ Okla, BS, 1969; Meharry Med Col, DDS, 1973. **Career:** Martin Luther King Gen hosp, family pract residency, 1974; Pilot City Health Ctr, chief dent dir, 1974-77; Denver, pvt pract gen dent, 1977-. **Orgs:** life mem, Am Dent Asn; life mem, Nat Dent Asn, 1977-; asst treas, Alpha Phi Alpha Inc; Denver Urban League; pres, Clarence T Holmes Dent Soc, 1986; bd dent examiners, State Colo, 1997-2001; Colo Dent Bd; life mem, Meharry Med Col. **Honors/Awds:** Board of DRRs, Concorde Career CLG. **Business Addr:** Physician, 1756 Vine St, Denver, CO 80206, **Business Phone:** (303)322-1177.

### JOHNSON, COSTELLO O.

Executive, president (organization), chief executive officer. **Personal:** Born Feb 14, 1938, Chicago, IL; son of Adrian and Dorothy; married Eunita Flemings; children: Gina Perry, Pamela Eatman & Darin. **Educ:** Chicago Acad Fine Arts, BA, interior design & space planning, 1962; Ill Inst Technol; Univ Ill. **Career:** Montgomery Wards, designer, space planner, 1968-68; Contract Interiors, designer, space planner, 1968-70; Desks Inc, sales assoc, 1970-73; Haworth Chicago, pres, 1973-79; Costello Johnson & Assocs, pres, 1979-89; Corp Off Syst Inc, chief exec officer & pres, 1989-2003; ClearPath Signage Systs, owner, Currently; . **Orgs:** Dir, Urban Gateways; dir, Metrop Family Serv; Friends Comt, Jesse Owens Found; exec bd mem, Chicago Minority Bus Develop Coun; co-chmn & fundraiser, Marcy Newberry Asn; Alpha Phi Fraternity. **Home Addr:** 1475 E So Ind Ave, Chicago, IL 60605, **Home Phone:** (312)945-3559. **Business Addr:** President, Chief Executive Officer, Corporate Office Systems Inc, 833 W Jackson Blvd Fl 6, Chicago, IL 60607, **Business Phone:** (312)421-7200.

### JOHNSON, CYNTHIA ANN

Association executive, consultant. **Personal:** Born Aug 19, 1958, Detroit, MI; daughter of Willie Louis (deceased) and Beverly (deceased); married Wallace F Hoskins Jr; children: Wallace Franklin Hoskins III, Tyhecia Laverne & Henry Levin. **Educ:** Wayne County Community Col, AA, 1988; Walsh Col, BBA, 1992. **Career:** Wayne County Neighborhood Legal Ctr, prog consult, 1992-94; Inkster Schs, crisis intervention consult, 1994-95; Wayne Co Govt, intern, 1994-95, victim's witness asst, 1995; Mich Dept Corrections, corrections officer, 1999-2009, Parole & Probation, field agt, 2001; Credit Acceptance Corp, bill collector; Morton Sr Citizen's Bldg/Village Green Mgt, asst apt mgr; Legal Aid & Defender's Off, paralegal. **Orgs:** Founder & dir, Giving Our Girls Incentive Real Life Situations, 1995-; Mich House Representatives; Coalition Labor Union Women; Community Rels Coun; Kiwanis Club 1 Detroit; Nat Orgn Black Law Enforcement; New Hope Community Asn; WestSiders. **Home Addr:** 18634 W Chicago, Detroit, MI 48228, **Home Phone:** (313)837-1284. **Business Addr:** Executive Director, Giving Our Girls Incentive for Real Life Situations (GOGIRLS), 1150 Griswold 2350 David Stott Bldg, Detroit, MI 48226.

### JOHNSON, CYNTHIA L. M.

Lawyer, educator, executive. **Personal:** Born Mar 1, 1952, Detroit, MI; daughter of Robert Alexander (deceased) and Frances E (deceased); children: Alexandra, Lauren & Joshua. **Educ:** Univ Mich, BA, psychol & sec educ, 1973, MPH, health econs & health educ, 1975; Mich State Univ Col Law, JD, 1984. **Career:** Detroit Med Found & Mich HMO Plans Inc, dep dir, 1975-76; New York Health Hosp Corp, sr health analyst, 1976-77; United Autoworker shealthcare, consult, 1977-84; Mich Ct Appeals, judicial law clerk, 1984-89; Mich Supreme Ct, judicial law clerk, 1986-87; Clark Hill PLC, partner & atty shareholder, 1987-2000; Couzens, Lansky, Fealk, Ellis, Roeder & Lazar PC, atty shareholder, 2000-14; Wayne County Community Col, Bus Dept, adj fac, 2007-; Henry Ford Community Col, adj fac, 2007-; Community Living Serv Inc, vpres corp affairs & gen coun, 2014-; State Bar Mich, secy, 2014-; HIPAA security, CLS HIPAA privacy officer. **Orgs:** State Bar Mich; Wolverine Bar Asn; Nat Asn Advan Colored People; Am Bar Asn, 1992-; finance comt, Mercy Health Care Corp, 1993-98; Delta Sigma Theta Sorority, 2004-; bd dir, Lula Belle Stewart, 1994-98; bd dir, Ronald McDonald House Detroit, 1996; Detroit Bar Asn; Nat Bar Asn; arbitrator, Am Arbit Asn-Neutral. **Home Addr:** 3201 Cambridge Ave, Detroit, MI 48221, **Home Phone:** (313)345-2440. **Business Addr:** Vice President Corporate Affairs, General Counsel, Community Living Services Inc, 35425 W Michigan Ave, Wayne, MI 48184, **Business Phone:** (734)467-7600.

### JOHNSON, DARRIUS DASHOME

Football player. **Personal:** Born May 18, 1973, Terrell, TX. **Educ:** Univ Okla, grad. **Career:** Football player (retired); Denver Broncos, cornerback & safety & fullback & defensive back, 1996-99; Kans City Chiefs, cornerback, 2003. **Honors/Awds:** Super Bowl XXXIII championship; Broncos Super Bowl.

### JOHNSON, DAVE M.

Basketball player. **Personal:** Born Nov 16, 1970, Morgan City, LA. **Educ:** Syracuse Univ, attended 1992. **Career:** Basketball player (retired); Portland Trail Blazers, shooting guard & forward, 1992-93; Chicago Bulls, shooting guard, 1993-94; NatWest Zaragoza, Spain, 1994; Continental Basketball Asn, Grand Rapids Mackers, 1994-95; Continental Basketball Asn, Rapid City Thrillers, 1995; JDA Dijon, France, 1995-96; Continental Basketball Asn, Fla Beachdogs, 1996-97; Pasta Baronia Napoli, Italy, 1997-98; Cangrejeros de Santurce, Pr, 1998; Continental Basketball Asn, Rockford Lightning, 1998-99; Continental Basketball Asn, Idaho Stampede, 1999; Cangrejeros de Santurce, Pr, 1999, 2000-01; Mets de Guaynabo, Pr, 2000. **Honors/Awds:** All-Big East Second Team, 1991; NBA draft, 1992; Big East All-Tournament Team, 1992.

### JOHNSON, DAVID E.

Banker. **Personal:** Born Aug 4, 1960, Jackson, MS; son of Earnest; married Doris Martin; children: D. **Educ:** Jackson State Univ, BS, bus mgt, 1982; Am Inst Banking, attended 1987; Hinds Community Col, AA, 1987; La State Univ Sch Banking, attended 1992; Pepperdine Univ; Univ NC, Charlotte, attended 2002. **Career:** Deposit Guaranty Nat Bank, rec mgt clerk, 1979-82, mgt trainee, 1982-84, vpres & retail loan officer, 1984-93; vpres & community affairs officer, 1993-2000; Am S Bank, vpres & retirement plan adminr, 2001-03; Trustmark Nat Bank, vpres & dir community develop, 2004-05; BankPlus, sr vpres & dir community develop, 2005-. **Orgs:** Choir pres & musician, 1972-, Nat Asn Urban Bankers; Sunday sch supt, 1987-; bd trustee, Zion Chapel Church God Christ, 1989-, asst pastor, 2014-; charter mem, treas, Jackson Chap, 1992; pres, Youth Act Coun, 1994-; chmn, Bldg FundComt, 1994-; adv bd, Jackson State Univ Continuing Educ Learning Ctr, 1998; bd dir, Minority Capital Fund, 1999; United Way, donor investmentcomt, 1999; bd dir, Miss Coun Econ Educ, 2014-. **Honors/Awds:** Professional Black Achiever of the Year, YMCA, 1984; Bus ManagementAcademic Award, 1982, Pre's List Scholar, 1982, National Dean's ListScholar, 1981, Jackson State Univ; Leadership Jackson, 1998; OutstandingYoung Men of America, 1984, 1989, 1996, 1998; Leadership Mississippi, 2001. **Business Addr:** Assitant Pastor, Zion Chapel Church of God, 1221 Hawes St, San Francisco, CA 94124, **Business Phone:** (415)822-9066.

### JOHNSON, DAVIS

Executive. **Personal:** Born Feb 23, 1932, Detroit, MI; son of Hubert and Carrie (Lee); married Alphia Bymun; children: Cheryl Rene. **Educ:** Wayne State Univ; Harvard Univ, BS, 1954; Mich State Univ; Investment Sem; Notre Dame. **Career:** Investors Diversified Serv Inc, sales rep, 1966-69, dist sales mgr, 1969-72, div sales mgr, 1972; Johnsons Financial Serv Inc, chief exec officer; Diversified Finance Serv, chmn & chief exec officer, 1983. **Orgs:** Nat Asn Securities Dealers; Nat Asn Advan Colored People; Booker T Washington Bus Asn; Cotillion Club; Big Ten Alumni Asn; Metro Contractors; Jugs African

Med Asn. **Home Addr:** 19160 Parkside St, Detroit, MI 48221, **Home Phone:** (313)893-5161.

### JOHNSON, DENNIS
Executive, president (organization). **Career:** NBC TV Networks, mgr, dir, comedy & variety prg; ABC TV Networks, vpres & exec producer; Osmond TV; Showtime Entertainment Group, Showtime Networks Inc, sr vpres, 1985-98; Omni Broadcasting Network Inc, pres & gen mgr, 2003-; Dennis Johnson Prods, film & television prod co; Chengdu Shengang Lutong Tech Ltd, dir & pres, 2003-. **Business Addr:** President, General Manager, Omni Broadcasting Network Inc, 8275 S Eastern Ave Suite 200, Las Vegas, NV 89123, **Business Phone:** (702)938-0467.

### JOHNSON, DENNIS A.
Manager, vice president (organization). **Educ:** Va Mil Inst, BA, econs, 1981; Va Commonwealth Univ, MS, finance, 1985; CFA Inst, cert, chartered financial analyst, 1989. **Career:** SunTrust Bank, portfolio mgr; Citigroup, managing dir, 1994-2004; Calif Pub Employees Retirement Syst, sr portfolio mgr, 2004-08; Shamrock Capital Advisors (Burbank, CA), small cap portfolio mgr, managing dir, 2008-10; Comerica Bank, Comerica Asset Mgt Group, sr vpres, chief mkt strategist, chief investment officer, 2010-. **Orgs:** Chartered Financial Analyst (CFA). **Honors/Awds:** "Black Enterprise," 75 Most Powerful Blacks on Wall Street, 2011. **Business Addr:** Chief Investment Officer, Comerica Bank, 500 Woodward Ave, Detroit, MI 48226, **Business Phone:** (313)222-4000.

### JOHNSON, DINAH (DIANNE JOHNSON-FEELINGS)
Writer, educator. **Personal:** Born Charleston, SC; daughter of Douglas Sr and Beatrice Taylor. **Educ:** Princeton Univ, AB, Eng & creative writing, 1982; Yale Univ, MA, Afro-Am studies, 1984, PhD, 1988. **Career:** Univ SC, prof eng, 1990-; NEH Summer Inst Black Film, Univ Cent Fla, fel, 1999; Books: black Magic; Hair Dance; Sitting Pretty; Quinnie Blue; Sitting Pretty; Sunday Week; All around Town; African Am Review; The Best of the Brownies' Book; Splash; Telling Tales; In Daddy's Arms I am Tall; Presenting Laurence Yep; Nobody's Brat: Life Through the Eyes of Military Kids; Beautiful by Design: The Story of African American Children's Literature, co-producer; edited various publications including: The Collected Works of Langston Hughes, Volume 11:The Works for Children; African American Review, Vol. 32, no.1; The Best of The Brownies' Book; Presenting Laurence Yep; Telling Tales: The Pedagogy & Promise of African Am Literature for Youth. **Orgs:** Chair adv bd, Cs Defense Fund's Langston Hughes Libr; adv bd mem, Int Res Cs Lit; adv ed, Oxford Encycl Cs Lit. **Honors/Awds:** The Best of The Brownies' Book Award, Children's Book Council/NCSS, 1997; Univ SC Black Faculty & Staff Association Award, 2000; Mortar Board Award, Univ SC. **Home Addr:** PO Box 782, Santee, SC 29142. **Business Addr:** Professor, University of South Carolina, 513 Humanities Off Bldg, Columbia, SC 29208, **Business Phone:** (803)777-2345.

### JOHNSON, DONN S.
Journalist. **Personal:** Born May 9, 1947, St. Louis, MO; son of Ivory M Dodd (deceased) and Clyde E Sr; married Earlene Beverly Breedlove; children: Lauren Beverly. **Educ:** St Louis Comm Col Florissant Valley, AA, 1976; Webster Col, BA, media studies, 1977. **Career:** Homer G. Hosp, clerk; City hosp, clerk; Fed Res Bank, clerk & vault keeper; KWK Radio St Louis, newsman & disc jockey, 1970-72; WIL Radio St Louis, newsman & dir comm rel, 1972-78; KTVI Channel 2 St Louis, anchor & reporter, 1978-98; TV ser; Miss, 1980; St Louis Am Newspaper, columnist. **Orgs:** Mem adv bd, Mass Commun Forest Pk Comm Col, 1972-; Greater St Louis Black Journalists Asn, 1979-; St Louis Press Club, 1980; vpres, St Louis Chap, Am Fedn Radio & TV Artists; bd, St Louis Gateway Classic Fund; Nat Asn Adv Color People; Dir, Mo Hist Mus. **Honors/Awds:** Howard B Woods Mem Award, Jour Black Stud Asn, Webster Col, 1977; Best News Story of the Year Award, Greater St Louis Black Journalists Assoc, 1978; Black Excellence in Journalism Award, Greater St Louis Black Journalism Asn, 1978, 1984, 1986, 1988-89; Unity Awards in Media, Lincoln Univ, 1985; Media Award, Gifted Asn, MO, 1987; Emmy (local), Acad TV Arts & Sci, 1978, 1989, 2004, 2006; Media Award of Excellence, Mo Asn Community & Jr Col, 1990; Telly Award, 2005; Outstanding Alumnus, Webster Univ Sch Commun, 2003; GSABJ Award, 2004, 2005. **Home Addr:** 16500 Centerpointe Dr, Grover, MO 63040-1608, **Home Phone:** (636)458-1919. **Business Addr:** Director of Communications, Missouri History Museum, 5700 Lindell Blvd, St Louis, MO 63112, **Business Phone:** (314)454-3150.

### JOHNSON, DONNA ALLIGOOD
Executive. **Personal:** Born Oct 25, 1956, Detroit, MI; daughter of Douglas Lacy and Cynthia Elvira Vincent; married Curtis Charles. **Educ:** Tufts Univ, BS, social psychol, 1978; Manhattanville Col, MS, strategic mgt & leadership, 2012. **Career:** BBDO, acct coordr, 1978-79, asst acct exec, 1980-82, acct exec, 1983-85, sr acct exec, 1985-88; Citicorp POS Info Servs, mktg mgr, 1988-90, sr prod mgr, 1988-92; TSS, vpres, 1992-95; MasterCard Int, vpres acceptance develop, 1995-2002, vpres new mkts, 2002-05, US Customer Mkt, sr bus leader, 2005-10, chief diversity officer, 2010-. **Orgs:** Bd mem, Am Red Cross, 1996-2002, 2004-06; Muscular Dystrophy Found, 2001-02; Nat Asn Advan Colored People; bd mem, Inner City Found Fairfield County, 2003-; bd mem, Urban League Southern Conn, 2007-. **Honors/Awds:** YMCA Black Achievers, 2002; named Top 100 Executives in America, Uptown Prof mag; 25 Influential Black Women, Net work J, 2013; CFO Award, MasterCard Worldwide, 2014. **Home Addr:** 668 Glenbrook Rd Apt 9, Stamford, CT 06906-1433, **Home Phone:** (203)964-1853. **Business Addr:** Chief Diversity Officer, MasterCard Intl, 2000 Purchase St, Purchase, NY 10577, **Business Phone:** (914)249-2000.

### JOHNSON, DORIS ELAYNE
Educator, librarian. **Personal:** Born Jul 13, 1954, Orangeburg, SC; daughter of Angie Pearl Glover and Roscoe Sr; children: LaTroy Damon. **Educ:** SC State Col, Orangeburg, BA, sociol, 1976; Clark Atlanta Univ, Atlanta, GA, MSLS, 1990. **Career:** SC State Univ, Orangeburg, SC, libr tech asst, 1982-89, librn, ref & info specialist, instr, 1982-, Interim Coordr Collection Develop, currently. **Orgs:** Atlanta Law Libr Asn, 1989-; Am Libr Asn, 1989-; SC Libr Asn, 1991-; Delta Sigma Theta Sorority. **Home Addr:** 820 Corona Dr, Orangeburg, SC 29115-6307, **Home Phone:** (803)534-4695. **Business Addr:** Interim Coordinator of Collection Development, South Carolina State University, 300 College Ave NE, Orangeburg, SC 29117, **Business Phone:** (803)536-8642.

### JOHNSON, DOROTHY M.
Nurse. **Personal:** Born Aug 18, 1922, Indianapolis, IN; daughter of Gilbert Hooks and Leola; children: Arlene J Beesing. **Educ:** Mohawk Valley Community Col, AASN, 1972; State Univ NY, Utica, BSN, 1982. **Career:** Nurse (retired); Registered nurse. **Orgs:** Nat Black Leadership Initiative Cancer; chair, Las Vegas Coalition, 1994; chair, Health Comm, Theta Theta Omega Sorority, 1994; Women's Health Coalition, Las Vegas, 1997; Am Cancer Soc, Regional Coun; Witness Proj Sponsoring Org, 2000; Prince Hall Masonic Family, NY Chap; founder, Las Vegas Coalition; United Assembly 72. **Home Addr:** 5324 W Rancher Ave, Las Vegas, NV 89108, **Home Phone:** (702)655-3752.

### JOHNSON, DOUGLAS H., JR.
Educator. **Personal:** Born May 1, 1943, Bolivia, NC; married Shirley L. **Educ:** Cheyney St Col, Cheyne, PA, BA, 1969; Univ RI, Kingston, community planning, 1971; Mass Inst Technol, PhD. **Career:** Univ Ri, Grad Curric Community Planning & Area Develop, asst prof community planning; Wilmington Metro Area Planning Coun, Wilmington, DE, summer intern, 1970; Inst, community planning, 1974-; Community Planning CPAD, asst prof, 1974-; State Ri, Providence, consult Off Continuing Educ, 1974. **Orgs:** Am Asn Univ Profs; United Work-Study Fel US Dept Housing & Urban Develop, 1969-71; Prin, vpres, Community Found, 1973-; ed, Nat Asn Planners, Newsletter, 1973-75; Am Soc Planning Off; Nat Asn Planning. **Honors/Awds:** Award, Am Inst Planning, 1971; National Fellowship Fund Award; Academician of the Year, Mass Inst Technol, 1976-77. **Home Addr:** 15 Walker St, Seekonk, MA 02771-2901, **Home Phone:** (508)336-5843. **Business Addr:** Assistant Professor, University of Rhode Island, Kingston, RI 02881, **Business Phone:** (401)874-1000.

### JOHNSON, DWAYNE
Wrestler, actor. **Personal:** Born May 2, 1972, Hayward, CA; son of Rocky and Ata Maivia; married Dany Garcia; children: Simone Alexandra; children: Jasmine. **Educ:** Univ Miami, 1995. **Career:** Calgary Stampede (Canadian Football League), professional football player, 1995; WWE/WWF, professional wrestler as Rocky Maivia and The Rock, 1996-2004, 2011, 2013-; Actor, 1999-. TV series: "WWF Superstars", 1996-99; "WWF Raw", 1996-; "That '70s Show", 1999; "The Net", 1999; "DAG", 2000; "Hannah Montana", 2007; "Saturday Night Live", NBC, 2009; "Family Guy", Fox, 2010; "Cubed", 2010; "Transformers Prime", 2010; "Clash Time", 2011-12; "America's Book of Secrets", 2013; "WrestleMania", 2015; "Ballers", 2015. Films: "The Mummy Returns", 2001; "Longshot", 2001; "The Scorpion King", 2002; "The Rundown", 2003; "Walking Tall", 2004; "Be Cool", 2005; "Doom", 2005; "Southland Tales", 2006; "Gridiron Gang", 2006; "Reno 911!: Miami", 2007; "The Game Plan", 2007; "Get Smart", 2008; "Race to Witch Mountain", 2009; "Planet 51", 2009; "Tooth Fairy", 2010; "The Other Guys", 2010; "Faster", 2010; "Fast Five", 2011; "Journey 2: The Mysterious Island", 2012; "Snitch", 2013; "G.I. Joe: Retaliation", 2013; "Empire State", 2013; "Pain & Gain", 2013; "Fast & Furious 6", 2013; "Hercules", 2015; "Furious 7", 2015; "San Andreas", 2015; "Jem and the Holograms", 2015. **Special Achievements:** Grandson of professional wrestler Peter "High Chief" Fanene Maivia; 7 time WWE/WWF World Heavyweight Champion; WWF Intercontinental Champion; WWF Tag Team Champion; WWE Tag Team Champion; WWF Royal Rumble Champion; WCW Heavyweight Champion; USWA Tag Team Champion.

### JOHNSON, DWAYNE DOUGLAS
Actor, wrestler. **Personal:** Born May 2, 1972, Hayward, CA; son of Ata Maivia and Rocky; married Dany Garcia; children: Simone Alexandra. **Educ:** Univ Miami, Coral Gables, Fla, BGS, criminol & physiol, 1995. **Career:** Wrestler (retired), actor; Can Football League, Calgary Stampeders, pract team, 1995; World Wrestling Entertainment, prof wrestler, 1996-2001, 2011-13, 2014-; World Wrestling Federation, wrestler, 1996-2004. Films: Beyond the Mat, 1999; Longshot, 2000; The Mummy Returns, 2001; The Scorpion King, 2002; The Rundown, 2003; Walking Tall, 2004; Be Cool, 2005; Doom, 2005; Johnny Bravo, 2006; Southland Tales, 2006; Spy Hunter, 2006; Reno 911!: Miami, 2007; The Game Plan, 2007; Get Smart, 2008; Race to Witch Mountain, 2009; Planet 51, 2009; Tooth Fairy, 2010; Why Did I Get Married Too?, 2010; Faster, 2010; The Other Guys, 2010; You Again, 2010; Fast Five, 2011; Journey 2: The Mysterious Island, 2012; G.I. Joe: Retaliation, 2013; Fast Six, 2013; Pain & Gain, 2013; Snitch, 2013; Empire State, 2013; Hercules, 2014; Furious 7, 2015; San Andreas, 2015; Central Intelligence, 2016; Fast 8, 2017; Baywatch, 2017. TV guest appearances: "That '70s Show", 1999; "Star Trek Voyager", 2000; "DAG", 2000; "Saturday Night Live", 2002; "Cory in the House", 2007; "Hannah Montana", 2007; "Wizards of Waverly Place", 2009; "Saturday Night Live", 2009; "Transformers: Prime", 2010; "Family Guy", 2010; "The Hero", host & producer. **Orgs:** Founder, The Dwayne Johnson Rock Found, 2007. **Honors/Awds:** NCAA National Championship, 1991; Teen Choice Award, 2001; Razzie Award, 2006; Wrestling Observer Newsletter Hall of Fame, 2007; CinemaCon Action Star of the Year, 2012; Blimp Award, 2013; Kids Choice Awards, 2013; People's Choice Award, 2016; Star on the Hollywood Walk of Fame, 2017. **Special Achievements:** Featured in the 2007 Guinness Book of World Records for having the highest salary as an actor in his first starring role; Autobiography: The Rock Says The Most Electrifying Man in Sports Entertainment, 2000.

### JOHNSON, EARL
Engineer, executive. **Personal:** Born Jun 25, 1943, Gilmer, TX; son of Lunnie and Ella; married Pamela G Huddleston; children: Marla A. **Educ:** Electronic Tech Inst, attended 1968; Mesa Jr Col, attended 1976. **Career:** Conic Corp, electronic assembly, 1967-68; Ryan Aeronical, electronic assembly, 1968-69; Ketema Aerospace & Electronics, jr engr, 1969-90; John Sound Lab, pres, owner, 1990-. **Business Addr:** President, Owner, John Sound Laboratory, 9243 Fairlawn St, Santee, CA 92071, **Business Phone:** (619)258-8342.

### JOHNSON, EARTHA JEAN
President (organization), chief executive officer. **Educ:** BS, bus admin; MS, energy, environ & nat resource law; JD; assoc degree, criminal justice. **Career:** Fortune 5 Co, practicing lawer; Legal Watch Inc, owner, pres & chief exec officer, 1998-. **Orgs:** Bd govs, Nat Bar Asn, Womens Lawyers Div, chmn, vice chmn; bd dir, Houston Minority Bus Coun; bd dir, Houston Womens Bus Coun; Women's Bus Enterprise Nat Coun's Nat Leadership Forum; pres, Houston Lawyers Asn; Houston Bar Asn; State Bar Tex; bd dir, Women Impacting Pub Policy, bd dir, Nat Inst Severely Disabled; Avance; chmn, African Am Law Sect, State Bar Tex; Nat Bar Asn Corp Coun, 1990-2013; WBEA, 1997-2011; Corp Coun Women Color, 2004-11; Fountain praise, 2006-10; WIPP, 2007-10; MD/DC Minority Bus Coun, owner, 2009-11; GWAC, 2010-11. **Business Addr:** President, Chief Executive Officer & Owner, LegalWatch Inc, 9800 NW Fwy Suite 600, Houston, TX 77092, **Business Phone:** (713)864-9997.

### JOHNSON, EARVIN, JR. (MAGIC JOHNSON)
Executive, basketball player, basketball coach. **Personal:** Born Aug 14, 1959, Lansing, MI; son of Earvin Sr and Christine; married Cookie; children: Andre, Earvin III & Elisa. **Educ:** Mich State Univ, 1979. **Career:** Basketball player, coach (retired), executive; La Lakers, guard, 1979-92, 1996, head coach, 1994, minority owner, 1996-; Magic Johnson Enterprises, owner & chief exec officer, 1992, chmn & chief exec officer, currently; Johnson Develop Corp, chmn & chief exec officer, currently; Magic Hour, Fox, host, 1998. Books: Magic, 1983; Magic's Touch, 1989; What You Can Do to Avoid AIDS, 1992; My Life, 1992; When the Game Was Ours, 2009. **Orgs:** Magic Johnson Found; AOL; Am Express; Farmers Ins; Fortune Mag; Wash Mutual; Rochester Inst Technol; Samsung; Best Buy; Sun Microsystems; Univ Calif, Irvine; Choice Hotels; Arden Realty, Glaxo SmithKline Pharma; TheCoca-Cola Co; Muscular Dystrophy Asn; co-chair, UN Day; bd trustee, Am Cancer Soc Found; co-chair, VP Al Gore's White House Community Empowerment Bd. **Business Addr:** Chairman, Chief Executive Officer, Johnson Develop Corp, 5005 Riverway Suite 500, Houston, TX 77056, **Business Phone:** (713)960-9977.

### JOHNSON, REP. EDDIE BERNICE
**Personal:** Born Dec 3, 1935, Waco, TX; children: Dawrence Kirk Jr. **Educ:** Univ Notre Dame, St Marys Col, nursing cert, 1955; Tex Christian Univ, Ft Worth, TX, BS, nursing, 1967; Southern Methodist Univ, Dallas, TX, MPA, 1976. **Career:** Dallas Veterans Admin Hosp, Dallas, Tex, chief psychiat nurse; Tex State House Rep, mem, 1972-77; Dept Health, Educ & Welfare, regional dir, 1977; US Dept Health, Educ & Welfare, adminr, 1977-81; Sammons Enterprises Inc, asst to pres, 1981-87; Vis Nurse Asn, vpres, govt affairs, 1981-87; Eddie Bernice Johnson & Assocs, founder; Tex State Senate, 1987-93; US House Rep, 30th Cong Dist Tex, congresswoman, 1993-; Tex Dem Deleg, sr dem dep whip & chmn, currently. **Orgs:** Am Nurses Asn; Links Inc, Dallas chap; Dallas Black Chamber Com; Nat Asn Advan Colored People; Girlfriends Inc; Alpha Kappa Alpha Sorority; pres, Nat Coun Negro Women; vpres & secy, Nat Order Women Legislators; bd dir, Sunbelt Nat Bank; chair, Cong Black Caucus, 2001-; House Comt Sci & Technol; United Way; Urban League; Womens Int League Peace & Freedom; League Women Voters; chair, House Metro Congestion Coalition; Close Up Found; co-chair, TEX-21 Cong Caucus; Delta Kappa Gamma Soc; Cong Arts Caucus; founder, Cong Tri Caucus; LGBT Equality Caucus; Cong Progressive Caucus; Rare DisCong Caucus; Cong Cement Caucus; House Transp & Infrastructure Comt, currently; Aviation Subcomt, currently; Highways & Transit Subcomt, currently; Water Resources & Environ Subcomt, currently; ranking mem, Subcomt Res & Sci Educ, 2000-2002. **Special Achievements:** First woman in Texas history to lead a major Texas House committee, the Labor Committee; Elected as the first African-American and the first female Ranking Member of the House Committee on Science, Space and Technology, 2010. **Home Addr:** 3102 Maple Ave Suite 600, Dallas, TX 75201, **Home Phone:** (214)922-8885. **Business Addr:** Congresswoman, US House of Representative, 1211 Longworth House Office Bldg, Washington, DC 20515, **Business Phone:** (202)225-8885.

### JOHNSON, EDMOND R., JR. (ED JOHSNON, JR.)
Lawyer. **Personal:** Born Jun 26, 1937, Plymouth, NC; married Thelma Crosby; children: Edrenna Renee & Erica Ronelle. **Educ:** NC Cent Univ, BA, 1959; Howard Univ, JD, 1968. **Career:** DE Tech Comm Col, teacher law clerk, 1968-69; pvt pract law, 1970-; Edmond R Johnson & Assoc, atty, currently. **Orgs:** NC Acad Trial Lawyers; NC State Bar; Nat & Am Bar Asns; NC Black Lawyer sAsn; Nat Asn Advan Colored People; Alpha Phi Alpha. **Home Addr:** 916 W 5th St Suite 202, PO Box 31642, Charlotte, NC 28202-1209, **Home Phone:** (704)332-1256. **Business Addr:** Attorney, Edmond R Johnson & Associates, 916 W 5th St Suite 202, Charlotte, NC 28202-1209, **Business Phone:** (704)332-1256.

### JOHNSON, EDWARD ARNET (EDDIE JOHNSON)
Basketball player, radio host, president (organization). **Personal:** Born May 1, 1959, Chicago, IL; married Joy; children: Jade Alexis & Justin Edward. **Educ:** Univ Ill, BA, hist, 1981. **Career:** Basketball player (retired), color commentator, executive; Kans City Kings, forward & guard, 1981-85; Sacramento Kings, 1985-87; Phoenix Suns, 1987-90, color analyst, currently; Seattle SuperSonics, 1990-93; Charlotte Hornets, 1993-94; Olympiacos BC, 1994-95; Ind Pacers, 1995-97; Houston Rockets, forward, 1997-99; Ariz State Univ men's basketball team, color commentator; WNBAs Phoenix Mercury, color analyst, 1997-; HoopsHype, staff; Teamfone Inc, pres & co-founder, currently. **Business Addr:** President, Co-founder, Teamfone Inc, 7904 E Chaparral Rd, Scottsdale, AZ 85250-7210.

### JOHNSON, EDWARD C. (EDDIE C JOHNSON)
Judge. **Personal:** Born Jun 1, 1920, Chicago, IL; married Olivia; children: Edward & Ella. **Educ:** Roosevelt Univ, AB; John Marshall Law Sch, JD; Loyola Univ. **Career:** Attorney, Judge (retired); pvt pract, atty, 1952-65; Brooks, Rhett & Johnson, 1953-55; Gayles, Johnson & Handy, 1957-61; Ellis, Westbrook & Holman, Gillen & Owens, 1961-65; Jones, Ware & Greaud, off coun; Circuit Ct, Cook County, Ill, judge, 1965-91. **Orgs:** Cook Co & Nat Bar Asn, Judical Coun NBA. **Honors/Awds:** Distinguished Service & Alumnus Award, John

Mouskell Law Sch; The PushFoundation Award; Meritorious Service Award & Judicial Career ServiceAward, Ill Judicial Coun. **Home Addr:** 7246 Blair Dr, Orlando, FL 32818, **Home Phone:** (773)233-1192.

### JOHNSON, EDWARD E., JR.
Executive. **Educ:** Rutgers Univ. **Career:** Merrill Lynch, global sales mgr, vpres, managing dir, 1990-2005; Advent Capital Mgt LLC, partner, chief operating officer, 2005-12; Aperio Capital Mgt LLC, partner & hedge fund exec, 2013-; Salomon Bros, dir; Virtual Health Care Solutions Llc, dir. **Orgs:** Trustee, Juilliard Sch. **Honors/Awds:** "Black Enterprise," 75 Most Powerful Blacks on Wall Street, 2011. **Special Achievements:** First African American Vice President at Merrill Lynch. **Business Addr:** Chief Operating Officer, Advent Capital Management LLC, 1271 Avenue of the Americas 45th Fl, New York, NY 10020, **Business Phone:** (212)482-1600.

### JOHNSON, DR. EDWARD ELEMUEL
Educator. **Personal:** Born Crooked River; son of Edward E and Mary Elizabeth Blake; married Beverley Jean Morris; children: Edward E, Lawrence P, Robin Jeannine, Nathan J & Cyril U. **Educ:** Howard Univ, BS, 1947, MS, 1948; Univ Colo, PhD, 1952. **Career:** Educator Southern Univ, Baton Rouge, LA, prof & assoc dean univ, 1955-72; Los Angeles State Univ Med Sch, clin prof psychiat, 1969-72; United Bd Col Develop, dir, 1972-74; NJ Robert Wood Johnson Med Sch, prof psychiat, 1974. **Orgs:** Panelist, Sci Fac Develop Nat Sci Found, 1978-82; site visitor, NIH, 1978-; consult, Bell Lab, Holmdel, NJ, 1982-85; bd trustee, Cross roads atre Co, 1983-; bd dir, PSI Assoc Inc, 1984-; fel AAAS; life mem, Soc Sigma Xi; Sigma Pi Phi Fraternity; Alpha Phi Alpha Fraternity. **Home Addr:** PO Box 597, East Brunswick, NJ 08816, **Home Phone:** (732)257-4885. **Business Addr:** NJ.

### JOHNSON, EDWARD M.
President (organization), executive. **Personal:** Born Jan 15, 1943, Washington, DC. **Educ:** Howard Univ, BArch, city planning, archit & urban planning, 1967, MArch, city planning, archit & urban planning, 1970. **Career:** Architects & Urban Planners, 1969-; JJ Lord Construct Co, pres; Edward M Johnson & Assoc PC, owner & pres, 1993-. **Orgs:** Am Inst Architects; Design Rev Panel DC; Dept Housing & Community Develop; fel Am Soc Landscape Architects; fel Am Planning Asn; fel Nat Coun Archit Regist Boards; fel Nat Orgn Minority Architects; bd mem, YMCA; fel Rotary Club Wash; fel Wallace Johnson Found; fel Greater Brookland Bus Asn; fel Howard Univ Sch Archit Alumna Asn. **Home Addr:** 4881 Queens Chapel Ter NE, Washington, DC 20017, **Home Phone:** (202)248-8980. **Business Addr:** Owner, President, Edward M Johnson & Assoc PC, 3612 12th St NE, Washington, DC 20017-2546, **Business Phone:** (202)526-3610.

### JOHNSON, EDWARD STANTON. See JOHNSON, TRE, III.

### JOHNSON, EDWIN T.
College teacher, commissioner, archivist. **Educ:** Morgan State Univ, BA, MA, PhD; Towson Univ, MA. **Career:** Morgan State Univ, admis dir, 2000-08, acad advisor, 2008-10, interim asst dean, 2010-14, sr coordr disability serv, 2014-16, asst univ archivist, 2016-; Baltimore City Community Col, adj fac, 2004-12; Univ Md Univ Col, adj asst prof, 2009-16, adj assoc prof, 2016-; Woodbourne Ctr, direct care prof, 2014-15; Md Comn African Am Hist & Cult, comnr, 2016-. **Orgs:** Morgan State Nat Alumni Asn, Omega Psi Phi Fraternity, Int Hist Comt (vice chair), Nat Eagle Scout Asn. **Honors/Awds:** Pi Kappa Delta National Forensics Honor Society; Ford Foundation Scholar. **Business Addr:** Morgan State University, 1700 East Cold Spring Lane, Baltimore, MD 21251, **Business Phone:** (443)885-4768.

### JOHNSON, DR. ELAINE MCDOWELL
Government official. **Personal:** Born Jun 28, 1942, Baltimore, MD; daughter of McKinley and Lena Blue; married Walter A; children: Nathan Jr & Michael; married Walter A. **Educ:** Morgan State Univ, BA, 1965; Univ Md, MSW, 1971, PhD, 1988. **Career:** Government official (retired); State MD, actg regional dir, 1971-72; Nat Inst Drug Abuse, pub health adv, 1972-76, Div Community Asst, dep dir & dir, 1976-82, Div Prev & Communs, dir, 1982-85; Alcohol, Drug Abuse & Ment Health Admin, exec asst to admin, 1985, actg admin, 1990-92; Nat Inst Drug Abuse, dep dir, 1985-88, dir, Off Substance Abuse Prev, 1988-90; Substance Abuse Ment Health Serv Admin, actg admin, 1990-92; Ctr Substance Abuse Prev, dir, 1992; Friends Res Inst, Prin Investr. **Orgs:** Ordained officer, Presby Church 1981-84; nat dir, drug abuse prev prog, Zeta Phi Beta Sor, 1986-92; consult, US Info Agency, US State Dept; Links Inc. **Home Addr:** 6631 Hunters Wood Cir, Baltimore, MD 21228, **Home Phone:** (410)744-4318.

### JOHNSON, ELLIS BERNARD
Football player. **Personal:** Born Oct 30, 1973, Wildwood, FL; married Simone; children: Nichole & Ellis Bernard Jr. **Educ:** Univ Fla, grad. **Career:** Football player (retired); Indianapolis Colts, defensive tackle, 1995, left defensive end, 1996, right defensive tackle, 1997-2001; Atlanta Falcons, nose tackle, line backer, defensive tackle, 2002-03; Denver Broncos, 2004. **Honors/Awds:** SEC Championship, 1991. 1993, 1994; Defensive Player of the Year, Cable News Network, 1994; Honorable mention All-American, 1994; Most Valuable Player; Hall of Fame as a Gator Great, Univ Fla, 2007.

### JOHNSON, ERIC G.
Executive, entrepreneur. **Personal:** Born Mar 29, 1951, Chicago, IL; son of George Eillis and Joan Betty; married Pamela; children: Lecretia, Erin, Cara & John. **Educ:** Babson Col, BAS, finance & mgt, 1972; Univ Chicago, MBA, 1977. **Career:** Proctor & Gamble, staff, 1972-75; Johnson's Hair Prod, pres & chief exec officer, 1988-92; Baldwin Ice Cream Co, pres & chief exec officer, 1992; Baldwin Richardson Foods Co, pres & chief exec officer, 1997-. **Orgs:** Young Presidents Orgn; bd dir, Dr Martin Luther King Ctr; bd dir, Chicago State Univ; bd trustee, Babson Col; Flossmoor Country Club; Cobblestone Creek Country Club; Olympia Fields Country Club; bd trustee, Glenwood Sch Boys; Comn Econ Develop; bd dir, Nat Asn Advan Colored People; bd trustee, Rochester Inst Technol, 2000-; chmn, Develop Comt; Securities Comt; mem bd dir, Lincoln Nat Corp; mem bd dir, Urban League Rochester. **Business Addr:** President, Chief Executive Officer, Baldwin Richardson Foods Co, 20201 S LaGrange Rd Suite 200, Frankfort, IL 60423, **Business Phone:** (866)644-2732.

### JOHNSON, ERMA CHANSLER. See Obituaries Section.

### JOHNSON, DR. ERNEST KAYE, III
Surgeon. **Personal:** Born Feb 7, 1950, Ocala, FL; son of E K and Delores; married Clara Perry; children: Ernest IV & Clara Delores. **Educ:** Univ Fla, attended 1971; Meharry Med Col, MD, 1975. **Career:** Stud Nat Med Asn, vpres, 1973-74; G W Hubbard Hosp, resident, 1975-80; Meharry House Staff Assoc, vpres, 1975-76; Hubbard Hosp Meharry Med Col, Gen Surg, 1980; Infinity III Inc, vpres, 1983-85; Baptist Hosp, physician, currently; Centennial Med Ctr, physician; Metro Gen Hosp, physician; Nashville, TN, pvt pract, currently. **Orgs:** Matthew Walker Surg Soc, 1975-87; RF Boyd Med Soc, 1975-87; Nashville Acad Med, 1980-83; Tenn Med Asn, 1980-83; Alpha Phi Alpha; Apollo Club, 1990-91. **Honors/Awds:** Hon mem US House of Reps, 1983; Hon Dep Sheriff Nashville Davidson Co, 1984. **Home Addr:** 1705 Windover Dr, Nashville, TN 37218, **Home Phone:** (615)276-4825. **Business Addr:** Physician, Private Practice, 3803 Hydes Ferry Rd, Nashville, TN 37218, **Business Phone:** (615)244-7985.

### JOHNSON, ERNEST L.
Banker, lawyer. **Personal:** Born Aug 24, 1950, Ferriday, LA; son of Evans Sr and Florence; married Pamela Taylor; children: Emanuel, Louisa & Ernest II. **Educ:** Grambling State Univ, BS, polit sci, 1973; Southern Univ Sch Law, JD, 1976. **Career:** Ed, Grambling Tiger Yr bk, 1972-73; Criminal Ct Judges, law clerk, 1974-76; La Dept Justice, staff atty, 1976-77; Southern Univ Law Sch Aging Prog, dir, 1976-80; Johnson, Taylor & Thomas, managing sr partner, 1976-90; pvt pract, atty, 1976-; La Secy State Jim Brown, legal coun, 1980-81; Southern Univ Law Ctr, adj prof, 1984-; City-Parish Govt, asst parish atty, 1984; Success Motivation Personal Prof Develop, consult, 1985-87; Capital Organizing Task Force Group, chief exec officer, 1987-90; NDC AM, Baton Rouge, co-founder, 1988; WNDC AM Baton Rouge, co-founder, 1988; KCLF AM New Roads, 1990; Life Savings Bank, chair bd, pres & chief exec officer, 1990-93; Midwest Life Ins Co, lead coun/managing atty, 1995-96; Educ Systs Inc, chief exec officer, 1995-97; KVTZ-LPFM, Breaux Bridge, gen coun, 2002-; WTQT-LPFM, Baton Rouge, 2003; KOUS-LPFM, Monroe; KTJZ-FM; WTQT-LPFM, founder & gen mgr, 2003-; Mid S Commun Co, pres & chief exec officer; Arthur R. Thomas & Assocs, assoc, 2005-. **Orgs:** Pres, Sophomore Mens Dormitory, 1969-70; parliamentarian, Stud Govt Asn, 1970-71; vpres, Omega Psi Phi Fraternity, 1972-73; chmn, Pi Gamma Mu Social Sci Hon Socs, 1972-73; pres, Southern Univ Law Sch Stud Bar Asn, 1975-76; La State Bar Asn, 1976-; Louis A Martinet Legal Soc, 1986-; exec vpres. La NCP, 1991-; Proj Invest Blk, bd; Church Pt Ministries Feed Family, bd; bd dir, Nat Asn Advan Colored People, 1996; chmn, Nat Asn Advan Colored People Nat Nominating Comt, Units Comt, 2008; pres & ceo, la community develop capital fund, 1996-; vice chmn, Govs Blue Ribbon Comt, Grambling State Univ; Diversity Off Coordr, Pres George W. Bushs Inaugural Comt, 2001; chief exec officer, Capital Organizing Task Force Group. **Honors/Awds:** Alexander Pierre Tureaud Award, Louisiana State Nat Asn Advan Colored People, 1971; Earl Warren Legal Fellowship Award, Southern Univ Law Ctr, 1973-76; Baker-Voorhis Award, 1976; Scotlandville Man of the Year Award, Scotlandville Jaycees, 1990; The Prestigious Service Award, JK Haynes Edu Fund, 1990; Leadership Award, Louis A Martinet Legal Soc, 1991; NCP, NAT PRS Leadership Award, 1992; Medgar Evers Award, 1997; The Kelly M. Alexander Award, 1997 & 2008; Thalheimer Award, 1998, 1999; Human Rights Leadership Award, Freedom Mags, 2000; pres, La State Conf, 1995; NAACPs Nat Resolutions Comt; Alumni Hall Fame, Southern Univ Law Ctr, 2007; Pillar Award, 2016. **Special Achievements:** Lead counsel, Clark v Roemer, restructuring La judicial system; general counsel, La state conference of NCP, First VIP, 1991; co-host, Legally Speaking Program; Inventor of "The RediWash". **Home Addr:** 12124 Sullivan Rd, Baton Rouge, LA 70818, **Home Phone:** (225)261-6469.

### JOHNSON, ERVIN, JR.
Basketball player, ambassador. **Personal:** Born Dec 21, 1967, New Orleans, LA; married Renee; children: Ezekia & Erin. **Educ:** Univ New Orleans, gen studies, 1997. **Career:** Basketball player (retired), ambassador; Seattle SuperSonics, ctr, 1993-96; Denver Nuggets, 1996-97, community ambassador, currently; Milwaukee Bucks, 1997-2003, 2005-06; Minn Timberwolves, ctr, 2003-05; Ervin Johnson Fitness Ctr. **Home Addr:** , Denver, CO. **Business Addr:** Community Ambassador, Denver Nuggets, Pepsi Ctr 1000 Chopper Cir, Denver, CO 80204, **Business Phone:** (303)405-1100.

### JOHNSON, EUNITA E.
Executive, trader. **Personal:** Born Jul 21, 1939, Chicago, IL; daughter of Ella Peters and Amos; married Costello; children: Gina Perry, Pamela Eatman & Darin. **Educ:** Wilson City Col, attended 1959; Chicago Acad Fine Arts, BA, interior design & space planning, 1963; Nat Col Educ, attended 1977. **Career:** Eucos Mfg, owner, 1970-74; Costello Johnson & Assocs, vpres, 1979-89; Corp Off Systs Inc, vpres, 1989-2003, secy, co-chief exec officer, currently; ClearPath Signage Systs, owner, currently. **Orgs:** Chair, Chicago Community, Jessee Owens Found; Chicago Regional Purchasing Coun; pres, Dempster & Chicago Ave Merchants Asn, 1971-74; chap pres, N Shore Chap Jack & Jill Am, 1978-92; Chicago Urban League, 1989-. **Honors/Awds:** Outstanding Business Women of the Year, Southside County Ctr, 1988. **Home Addr:** 3 Ventura Lane, Hilton Head Island, SC 29926, **Home Phone:** (847)945-3559. **Business Addr:** Co-Chief Executive Officer, Secretary, Corporate Office Systems Inc, 833 W Jackson Blvd 6th Fl, Chicago, IL 60607, **Business Phone:** (312)421-7200.

### JOHNSON, EZRA RAY
Football player, football coach. **Personal:** Born Oct 2, 1955, Shreveport, LA; married Carman Sparks; children: 4. **Educ:** Morris Brown Col, grad. **Career:** Football player (retired), coach; Green Bay Packers, defensive end, 1977-87; Indianapolis Colts, defensive end, 1988-89; Houston Oilers, defensive end, 1990-91; Morehouse Col, coach, currently; Morris Brown Col, coach, currently. **Honors/Awds:** Ranked among NFC leaders with 14 1/2 quarterback sacks, 1983; Hall of Fame, Green Bay Packers, 1997. **Home Addr:** , Atlanta, GA. **Business Addr:** Coach, Morehouse Col, 830 Westview Dr SW, Atlanta, GA 30314, **Business Phone:** (404)681-2800.

### JOHNSON, FRAN (RAGLIN JOHNSON)
Executive. **Personal:** Born Jan 5, 1939, Chicago, IL; daughter of Ernestine Conway and Leon Covington; children: Humont Berry II, Derek C Berry, T David, Mark E & Maria L. **Educ:** Chicago State Univ, BS, 1973, MSed, 1975; Univ Cincinnati, EdD, 1981. **Career:** Chicago State Univ, dir, spec train unit, 1973-77; Kennedy King Col, prof, 1977-80; Greater Cincinnati Chamber Com, dir, YES Prog, 1980-83; Univ Cincinnati, 1981-; Elite Travel Serv, founder & owner, 1983-; Chicago Bd Educ, Michael Reese Hosp; Job Opportunity Better Skills, asst dir; Ctrl YMCA Col, dir, secretarial training. **Orgs:** African Travel Asn, 1977-; Pvt Indust Coun, 1983-89; Int Am Travel Agency Soc, 1983-; trustee, United Way, 1989-; Withrow Local Sch Coun Bd, 1989-; trustee, Cincinnati Local Develop Coun, 1990-; Xonta Int, 1992-; Greater Cincinnati Bus Owners Bd, 1992-; Nat Asn Advan Colored People. **Home Addr:** 820 Red Bud Ave, Cincinnati, OH 45229-1521. **Business Addr:** Founder, Owner, Elite Travel Services Inc, PO Box 3492, Cincinnati, OH 45201-3492, **Business Phone:** (513)861-8555.

### JOHNSON, FRANK (FRANKLIN LENARD JOHNSON)
Basketball player, basketball coach. **Personal:** Born Nov 23, 1958, Weirsdale, FL; married Amy; children: Lindsay & Natalie. **Educ:** Wake Forest Univ, BS, 1981. **Career:** Basketball player (retired), basketball coach; Wash Bullets, 1981-88; Houston Rockets, 1988-89; A Ranger Varese, 1989-91; Marr Rimini, 1991; Olympique Antibes, 1991-92; NIKE Desert Classic, asst coach, 1996; Phoenix Suns, 1992-94, asst coach, 1997-2000, head coach, 2002-03; spokesman, Suns community rels dept. **Orgs:** Nat Basketball Asn.

### JOHNSON, FRANK J., SR.
Publisher, chief executive officer, educator. **Personal:** Born Sep 1, 1939, Hope, AR; son of Odell Sr and Jettie Irene Wingfield; married Betty J Logan; children: Troy & Frank Jr. **Educ:** Calif State Univ Fresno, BA, Educ, 1963. **Career:** Fresno Colony Sch Dist, teacher, 1963-69; Grapevine Mag, publ & edn, 1969-84; W Fresno Sch Dist, prin & counr, 1970-74, dist supt, 1975-79; Who's Who Black Millionaires Inc, chief exec officer & publ, currently; Students Group Home. **Orgs:** Phi Beta Sigma Fraternity, 1959-; W Coast Black Publs Asn, 1979-; exec dir, Non-Profit Housing Asn Inc (NOAH), 1995-. **Honors/Awds:** Outstanding Teacher, West Fresno Sch Dist, 1969, Admin, 1977; First Black Sch Dist Supt in Central Calif, 1975-79; Civil Service Brd Fresno Calif, 1977-81; Outstanding Achievement Education & Publisher, Alpha Phi Alpha Fraternity, 1978; Outstanding Educator, Calif Black Sch Brd Asn, 1989. **Special Achievements:** Author, Who's Who of Black Millionaires, 1984. **Home Addr:** 2890 E Huntington Blvd Suite 121, Fresno, CA 93721-2358. **Business Addr:** Chief Executive Officer, Publisher, Who's Who Black Millionaires Inc, PO Box 12092, Fresno, CA 93776, **Business Phone:** (209)233-3944.

### JOHNSON, DR. FRED D.
Educator, consultant, association executive. **Personal:** Born Mar 7, 1933, Fayetteville, TN; married Dorothy G; children: Fredna & Sheraldine. **Educ:** Tenn State Univ, BS; Univ Memphis, MEd; Univ Tenn, PhD, admin & leadership, 1974. **Career:** Educator (retired), consultant; Shelby County Schs, from sci teacher to sci supvr, 1954-68, asst supt instr, 1968-77; Shelby County Bd Educ, interim supt, 1977-99, exec dir; La Bd Regents, consult, 1994-97; Christian Bros Univ, adj prof; NSF, prog officer; NSTA, pres; Memphis Area Teachers Credit Union, bd; McKenzie Group, sr consult, currently; Univ Memphis, Col Educs Ctr, adj prof, educr, asst supt. **Orgs:** BSCS; Nat Conv Prog, 1972; Area Conv, chmn, 1974; NSTA, 1985; NEA, 1985; ASCD, 1985; AAAS, 1985; NASS, 1985; KDP, 1985; AASA, 1985; Optimist, 1985; Nat Asn Advan Colored People, 1985; Nat Asn Advan Colored People; Nat Sci Found, NSF, prog officer, 1986-87; Memphis Symphony, 1998-01; Memphis Zoo, 2001; Facing Hist & Our Selves, 2001; Nominations Comt, chair, 2002-; Nat Sci Teachers Asn, 1971-, pres, 1997-98. **Honors/Awds:** Outstanding Teacher Award, Tenn Acad Sci, 1971; District Service Award, NAACP, 1983; District Role Model, NABSE, 1994; Educator of the Year, Univ Memphis, 1999; Science Teacher of the Year; Distinguished Science Educator Award; Distinguished Service Award, Nat Sci Teachers Asn; National Conference of Community & Justices Humanitarian Award; Robert H. Carleton Award, Nat Sci Teachers Asn, 2009. **Business Addr:** Technical Assistance Consultant, The McKenzie Group, 8890 Bridlewood Lane, Cordova, TN 38018-3534, **Business Phone:** (901)751-4005.

### JOHNSON, FREDERICK DOUGLASS
Educator. **Personal:** Born Mar 28, 1946, Chattanooga, TN; married Jacqueline Faith Jones; children: Kyle. **Educ:** Oakwood Col, Huntsville, attended 1966; Union Col Lincoln, NE, attended 1968; Nebr Weslyan Univ, BA, 1972; Univ Nebr, MA, 1980. **Career:** Randolph Sch, Lincoln NE, teacher, 1972-75, team leader, 1976-83; Belmont Sch, Lincoln NE, asst prin curric coord, 1983-86; asst prin, Pk Elem Sch, Lincoln, NE. **Orgs:** Phi Delta Kappa, Nat Ed Asn; Nebr State Educ; Lincoln Educ Asn; Lincoln Pub Sch Minority Connection; Guid Study Comt; Personnel Recruitment Comt; Allan Chapel Seventh-Day-Adventist Church; Am Legion, Kiwanis, Malone Community Ctr; bd mem, Allan Chapel Church, Child Guide Ctr Lincoln; Nebr Weslyan Career Ctr. **Home Addr:** 383 Serenity Lane, Hedgesville, WV 25427, **Home Phone:** (304)754-6140. **Business Addr:** Assistant Principal, Park Elementary School, 714 F St, Lincoln, NE 68521.

### JOHNSON, FREDERICK E., SR.
Engineer. **Personal:** Born Jun 24, 1941, Detroit, MI; son of Tommie L and Naomi H; married Sandra A; children: Frederick II & Seth. **Educ:** Wayne State Univ, BEE, 1964; Syracuse Univ, MEE, 1969. **Career:** Engineer (retired); IBM Endicott Lab, line printer test mgr, instru-

mentation & mech anal, mgr prod develop, engr mgr proj off, mgr RAS design, instr, develop; WUCI Radio Sta, pres; FESAJ Enterprises, TQM Specialist, pres; Binghamton Univ, adj instr. **Orgs:** Buddy Camp Assoc, 1970; pres, Iota Theta Lambda Chap Alpha Phi Alpha, 1977-79; Exec comm New York, Pa Health Systs Agency; adv engr, tech asst, engr, Int Bus Mach; pres, bd dir, Broome Ct Urban League; treas, bd dir, New York, Pa Health Systs Agency; trustee, Trinity AME Zion Church; pub chmn, Broome Cty Nat Asn Advan Colored People; Alpha Phi Alpha; Iota Theta Lambda; chmn, Minority Bus Adv Comn, Broome City; Inst Elec & Electronics Engrs. **Home Addr:** 313 Patio Dr, PO Box 232, Endicott, NY 13760-1581, **Home Phone:** (607)748-0519.

### JOHNSON, GENEVA B.
Executive director, association executive. **Personal:** Born Jan 1, 1930, Aiken, SC; daughter of Pierce Bolton and Lillie Mae. **Educ:** Albright Col, BS, 1951; Case Western Res Univ, MS, social admin, 1957; Harvard Sch Bus, cert exec mgt. **Career:** Berks County C's Serv, supr, 1959-64; United Way Berks Co, asst exec dir, 1964-69; United Way Greater Rochester, assoc exec dir, 1969-72; United Way Am, sr vpres, 1978-83; Family Serv Am, pres & chief exec officer, 1983-2004; VistaCare Inc, dir, 2004-; Mt Mary Col, Women's Leadership Inst, exec dir, 2001-04, chmn bd dir, 2005-; YWCA Houston, prog dir; Wernersville State Hosp PA, psychiat socialworker; Childrens Aid Soc, supvr; United Way DE, dir. **Orgs:** Consult, Coun Jewish Feds; consult, YWCA; Nat Fel Prog, WK Kellogg Found; Nat Urban League; Big Bros & Big Sisters Am; Nat Asn Advan Colored People; bd dir, Nat Ctr Learning Disabilities; Found Ctr; Ind Univ Ctr Philanthropy; Case Western Res Univ, Mandel Ctr Nonprofit Orgs; Salzburg Sem; Nat Ctr Nonprofit Bd; Wis Energy Corp & Wis Elect & Power Co; fel Nat Acad Pub Admin; trustee, Nat Coun Aging; trustee, Med Col Wis; trustee, Froedtert Lutheran Memorial Hosp; trustee, Adv Bd Harvard Sch Bus; trustee, Berea Col; Peter F. Drucker Found; Nat Ctr Nonprofit Boards; Nat Asn Social Workers Found. **Honors/Awds:** Recipient Alumni Award, Albright College, 1979; Hon Doctor Humanities, Albright Col, 1983; DHL, Alvernia Col, 2002; Distinguished Service Award, Case Western Reserve Univ, 1983; F Ritter& Hettie L Shumway DistinguishedService Award, 1986; Award for Outstanding Service, Nat Urban LeagueMovement. **Special Achievements:** One of the top 12 nonprofit executive women in America, Savvy magazine, 1985; Top 100 Black Business & Professional Women of America, Dollars & Sense Mag, 1986; One of twenty women selected to attend the Jerusalem Women Seminar held in Israel and Egypt. **Home Addr:** 16745 Mary Cliff Ct, Brookfield, WI 53005, **Home Phone:** (262)781-3583. **Business Addr:** Director, VistaCare Inc, 4800 N Scottsdale Rd Suite 5000, Scottsdale, AZ 85251, **Business Phone:** (480)648-4545.

### JOHNSON, GEORGE ELLIS, SR.
Executive, consultant, association executive. **Personal:** Born Jun 12, 1927, Richton, MS; son of Charles and Priscilla; married Joan B Henderson; children: Eric, John, George E Jr & Joan Marie. **Career:** SB Fuller, 1944; Johnson Prod Co Inc, founder, 1954-, pres, chief exec officer, 1954-89, consult, 1989-. **Orgs:** Independence Bank Chicago; bd dir, Commonwealth Edison Co; Indecorp Inc; Am Health & Beauty Aids Inst; George E Johnson Educ Fund; George E Johnson Found; Babson Col; Boy Scouts Am; Chicago Orchestral Asn; Chicago Sunday Eve Club; Chicago Urban League; Dearborn Pk Corp; nat adv comt, Interracial Coun Bus Opportunity; vpres, Jr Achievement Chicago; Lyric Opera Chicago; Chicago United; Econ Club Chicago; Com Club; Nat Asn Advan Colored People; Nat Asthma Ctr, Northwestern Mem Hosp; Protestant Found Greater Chicago; Northwestern Univ; Hundred Club Cook; Greater Chicago; chmn, Indecorp. **Honors/Awds:** Abraham Lincoln Center Humanitarian Service Award, 1972; D of Bus Admin, Xavier Univ, 1973; D of Humanities, Clark Col, 1974; D of Com Sci, The Col of the Holy Cross, 1975; DL Babson Col, 1976; DHL Chicago State Univ, 1977; DLFisk Univ, 1977; DL Tuskegee Inst, 1978; American Black Achievement Award, EbonyMag, 1978; DHL Lemoyne-Owen Col, 1979; Harvard Club Chicago Public Service Award, 1979; DL Lake Forest Col, 1979; Horatio Alger Award, 1980; Babson Medal, 1983; Hall of Fame, JA Chicago Bus, 1985. **Special Achievements:** First African American to have a company to be listed on the American Stock Exchange in 1971; First African-American to be elected a director on the board of Commonwealth Edison. **Home Addr:** 180 E Pearson St, Chicago, IL 60611, **Home Phone:** (312)587-1692. **Business Addr:** Consultant, 100 E Huron St Apt 4802, Chicago, IL 60611-2940.

### JOHNSON, DR. GEORGIA ANNA LEWIS
Physician, publisher, writer. **Personal:** Born Feb 1, 1930, Chicago, IL; daughter of Robert L Lewis and Sarah Lewis Scoggins; children: Barbara, Ruth & Mary. **Educ:** West Mich Univ, attended 1951; Univ Mich Med Sch, MD, 1955. **Career:** Evanston Hosp, IL, intern, med staff, 1955-56; Detroit Receiving Hosp, resident intern med, 1956-58; Wayne County Hosp, chief resident intern med, 1958-60; Ypsilanti St Hosp, physician, 1960-65; Ingham Co Health Dept, physician, 1967-69; Mich State Univ, Internal Med Dept, fac, dir adolescent serv, Int Med Col, asst prof, 1969-75, co-founder women sci course; Olin Health Ctr, staff physician, 1969-87; Ga A Johnson Publ Co, publ, currently. **Orgs:** Nat Asn Advan Colored People; AMA; MSMS; Ingham Co Med Soc; Alpha Kappa Alpha Sorority; AEI Women's Med Fraternity; Kappa Rho Sigma Hon Sci Fraternity; Sickle Cell Anemia Found; bd trust, Capital Area Comp Health Plan Asn; chmn adv Comt, Health Serv Agency; bd dir, Comp Family Health Proj; hospitality comn, Mich Publishers Asn, 1989-; Great Lakes Booksellers Asn, 1990-; Mich Women's Hist Ctr & Hall Fame. **Honors/Awds:** Scholarship, Jessie Smith Noyes Sch, 1951-55; District Alumna Award, West Mich Univ, 1972; Michigan Women's Hall of Fame, 2005; First African American Physician; Gold Medal, Mich Sr Olympics; Bronze Medal. **Special Achievements:** Publications: Towpath to Freedom, 1989; Webster's Gold, 1990; published by Georgia A Johnson Publishing Company, The Baby Who Knew Too Much, 1993; Black Med Graduates of the Univ of Michigan & Selected Black Michigan Physicians, 1995; Facts, Artifacts and Lies, or the Shackling of Women (comments on the socialization of women); MIC Senior Olympian, track, 1996-; USA Track & Field, 1997-; Natl Sports Classic, 1997-; XIII World Veterans Athletic Championship, 1999; MI State Champion, USA Power Lifting. **Business Addr:** Publisher, Georgia A Johnson Publishing Co, 2608 Darien Dr, Lansing, MI 48912-4538, **Business Phone:** (517)372-9642.

### JOHNSON, GEORGIANNA
Administrator. **Personal:** Born Dec 13, 1930, Asheville, NC; daughter of Amelia Starks and William Fisher; married Eugene W Smith; children: Eugenia Smith Sykes. **Educ:** Empire State Univ, NY, 1976; Long Island Univ, NY, BA, sociol, 1976; Hunter Col, NY, MA, sociol. **Career:** New York State Employ Off, New York, claims examr, 1950-63; Sherman Thursby, New York, ins adjuster, 1963-68; Hosp Joint Diseases, New York, case aide, 1968-79; Orthop Inst, New York, social work asst, 1979-86; Drug, Hosp & Health Care Employees Union, Local 1199, New York, pres, 1986; Quest Serv Inc, facil dir, currently; Local 1199 hosp workers' union, pres. **Orgs:** Alpha Kappa Alpha Sorority, 1986; Black Trade Unionists, 1986; Coalition Union Women, 1986; bd mem, Nat Alliance Party, 1989; Nat Asn Advan Colored People. **Home Addr:** 2722 W Montgomery Ave, Philadelphia, PA 19121-2625, **Home Phone:** (215)236-1915. **Business Addr:** Facility Director, Quest Services Inc, 1169 Philipsburg-Bigler Hwy, Philipsburg, PA 16866, **Business Phone:** (814)342-1515.

### JOHNSON, GERALDINE ROSS
Lawyer. **Personal:** Born May 13, 1946, Moline, IL; married John T; children: Christine E, Glenda R & John T Jr. **Educ:** Augustana Col, BA, 1968; Univ Pa Sch Social Work, MSW, 1974; Univ Iowa Col Law, JD, 1982. **Career:** Linn Co IA Dept Social Servs, caseworker, 1968-69; C's Serv City St Louis, intake case worker, 1969-70; Get Set Day Care, pre sch teacher, 1970-72; Franciscan Ment Health Ctr, social worker, 1974-78; Davenport Civil Rights Comn, atty, 1984-86; City Davenport Legal Dept, atty, 1986-. **Orgs:** Iowa State Bar Asn, Scott Co Bar Asn; Sounds Peace Choral Group, 1981-86; Davenport Civil Rights Comn, 1982-84; bd dir, Family Resources Inc, 1982-; Delta Sigma Theta Pub Serv Sor, 1984-; vol, United Way, 1986; Tabernacle Baptist Church Moline Ill; Pulpit Community, 1986. **Special Achievements:** Survey of sex educ literature on file in the British Library by request, 1984. **Home Addr:** 1221 W 57th St, Davenport, IA 52806, **Home Phone:** (319)391-3665.

### JOHNSON, HANK, JR. (HENRY C JOHNSON)
**Personal:** Born Oct 2, 1954, Washington, DC; married Mereda Davis; children: Randi & Alex. **Educ:** Clark Atlanta Univ, BA, 1976; Tex Southern Univ's Thurgood Marshall Sch Law, JD, 1979. **Career:** Magistrate Ct DeKalb County, assoc judge; Johnson & Johnson Law Group LLC, criminal & civil litigation; Ga Supreme Ct, spec master; DeKalb County Comn, comnr, 2000-05; Ga's 4th cong dist, US rep, 2007-; US House Representatives, Regional Whip, 2009. **Orgs:** House Armed Servs Comt; House Comt Judiciary; House Comt Small Bus; Dem Party; Cong Black Caucus; State Bar Ga; Omega Psi Phi Fraternity; Ga Lawyers Found; Ga Asn Criminal Defense Attorneys; DeKalb County Law Libr; bd dir, Antioch Urban Ministries Inc; Chair, DeKalb County Budget Comt, 2002-05. **Business Addr:** US Representative, Georgia's 4th congressional district, 5700 Hillandale Dr Suite 120, Lithonia, GA 30058, **Business Phone:** (770)987-2291.

### JOHNSON, HAROLD R.
Educator. **Personal:** Born Jan 9, 1926, Windsor, ON; son of Catherine and Lee; married Marion; children: Robert Harold, Karen Elizabeth & Alan Douglas. **Educ:** Patterson Collegiate Inst, Windsor; Univ Western Ont, BA, 1950; Wayne State Univ, Detroit, MI, MSW, 1957. **Career:** Windsor Labor Comn Human Rights, exec dir, 1951-57; Int Union United Brewery Soft Drink & Distillery Workers Am; United Comm Serv Met Detroit, planning consult, 1957-61; Neighborhood Serv Orgn Detroit, assoc dir, 1961-69; Univ MI, Sch Social Work, prof social work, 1969-95, Health Behav & Health Educ, prof, 1976-95, dean, 1981-93, spec coun pres, 1993-94, secy, 1994-95, prof emer social work, 1996-, dean emer, 1995-; Off Youth Serv State MI, dir, 1970; Inst Geront, dir, 1975-81, dean, 1993; Univ Regina, 1978; Univ Toronto, vis fac, 1978-84; Temple Univ, fac, 1978; Community Pract Prog, head & div coordr, 1981; Univ MI Senate, chmn; Geront Soc Am fel; Sch Pub Health, prof. **Orgs:** Nat Asn Social Workers; chmn, Met Detroit Chap, 1963-64; Mayor's Develop Team Detroit, 1967; Wayne Co Planning Comn, 1968-69; Ctr Urban Studies Wayne State Univ, 1969; City Detroit-Charter Rev Comn, 1971; consult, Mich Comn Corrections, 1972; US Dept Justice, 1972; Famiy Neighborhood Serv So Wayne Co, 1972; Met Fund, 1971; pres, Asn Geront Higher Educ, 1979; consult, Prov Alta, 1979; fel, Geront Soc; Acad Cert Social Workers; Asn Black Soc Workers; chmn, Blue Ribbon City Comt Wayne Co; vpres & chmn, Prog Com Northeastern Wayne Co Child Guid Clin; Detroit Pub Sch Res Panel; vice chmn, Mich Comm Criminal Justice; comnr, Am Bar Asn, 1985-91 & 1993-98; consult, Yeungnam Univ, Repub Korea, 1984-; consult, Univ IA, 1987; consult, Chicago COT Trust, 1992-97; chair, SACUA; White House Conf Aging; chair, Nimh Rev Panel Geriat Ment Health Training Grants; consult, Nimh & Nat Inst Aging; chair, Geriat Ment Health Training Grants; consult, Nat Inst Ment Health & Nat Inst. **Home Addr:** 3000 Glazier Way Apt 120, Ann Arbor, MI 48105-2589, **Home Phone:** (734)761-4735. **Business Addr:** Professor Emeritus, Dean Emeritus, University of Michigan, Rm 3768 SSWB 1080 S Univ, Ann Arbor, MI 48109, **Business Phone:** (734)763-5971.

### JOHNSON, ESQ. HARRY E., SR.
Lawyer, educator, association executive. **Personal:** Born Sep 29, 1954, St. Louis, MO; married Karen; children: Jennifer, Harry Jr & Nicholas. **Educ:** Xavier Univ, BS, polit sci, 1986; Wash Univ, pub admin; Thurgood Marshall Sch Law & Sch Pub Affairs, JD, 1986. **Career:** City Atty Kendelton, Tex, 1996-99; Alpha Phi Alpha Fraternity Inc, nat pres, 2001-04; Wash, DC Martin Luther King Jr Nat Memorial Proj Found Inc, pres & chief exec officer, 2002-13; Tex Southern Univ, Thurgood Marshall Sch Law, adj prof. **Orgs:** Nat Bd dir, Big Bros Big Sisters Am, 2001; coun pres, Nat Pan Hellenic Coun; Nat Bar Asn; Am Bar Asn; Nat Asn Advan Colored People; Boy Scouts Am; 100 Black Men; Thurgood Marshall Stud Bar Asn; pres, Phi Alpha Delta; Tex Trial Lawyers Asn; Houston Trial Lawyers Asn; pres & ceo, Memorial Found, currently. **Home Addr:** , TX. **Business Addr:** President, Chief Executive Officer, The Memorial Foundation, 633 Pennsylvania Ave, Washington, DC 20004, **Business Phone:** (202)737-5420.

### JOHNSON, HARVEY, JR.
Government official, mayor. **Personal:** Born Dec 21, 1946, Vicksburg, MS; married Kathy Ezell; children: Harvey III & Sharla. **Educ:** Tenn State Univ, BS, polit sci; Univ Cincinnati, MS, polit sci; Univ Southern Calif, PhD, pub admin. **Career:** Miss Gaming Bd, comnr; City Jackson MS, mayor, 1997-2009-; Jackson Univ, asst prof, polit sci, Ctr Univ-Based Develop, founder, exec dir. **Orgs:** Bd dir, Miss Munic League; bd dir, Metro Jackson Chamber Com; bd dir, Nat Urban Fel Inc; Comn Cols Southern Asn Cols & Schs; bd dir, Union Planters Bank Cent MS; bd dir, Smith Robertson Mus & Cult Ctr; bd dir, Am Red Cross Cent MS; bd dir, Metrop YMCA; Sigma Pi Phi Fraternity; char mem, 100 Black Men Jackson; life mem, Nat Asn Advan Colored People; founder, Miss Inst Small Towns; Alpha Phi Alpha; Hope Spring Missionary Baptist Church; Miss State Tax Comn & Miss Gaming Comn; Am Legion Tyner-Ford, bd dir, Gulf Coast Housing Partnership; Cols Southern Asn Cols & Schs; US Conf Mayors Adv Coun. pres, Nat Conf Black Mayors; Nat Conf Dem Mayors. **Home Addr:** 1141 Hallmark Dr, Jackson, MS 39206-2113, **Home Phone:** (601)366-2903. **Business Addr:** Mayor, The City of Jackson Government, 219 S President St, Jackson, MA 39205-0017, **Business Phone:** (601)960-1084.

### JOHNSON, DR. HENDERSON A., III
Executive, school administrator, dentist. **Personal:** Born Dec 19, 1929, Nashville, TN; son of Henderson A and Minerva Hatcher; married Gwendolyn Gregory; children: Gregory Paul, Andrea Lynn & H Andrew IV. **Educ:** Fisk Univ, BS, 1950; Springfield Col, MA & MS, 1951; Med Col Va, RPT, 1952; Western Res Univ Sch Dent, DDS, 1959. **Career:** School administrator (retired), dentist; H Andrew Johnson DDS Inc, pres, 1959-89; Western Res Sch Dent, clin instr, 1966-69; Highland View Hosp, staff, 1985; pvt pract dentist, 1988-; Mgt Off Design Inc, pres, 1982-86; Cuyahoga Community Col, Enhancement Proj, Dent Prog leader, Chmn, dir, 1985-89, dist dir, 1986-94. **Orgs:** Chmn, Cuyahoga Community Col Found, 1971-84, chmn emer, 1991; pres, Shaker Heights Pub Libr, 1978-83; dir, Cleveland Pub Radio WCPN, 1983-89; Int Col Dentists, 1986; vpres, Ctr Human Rels, 1984-88; vpres, Cleveland Pub Radio WCPN, 1986-89; Ohio Educ Broadcast Network Comn, 1988-91; bd, Ohio Educ Broadcast Network Comn, 1992; vice chair, Ohio Educ Broadcast Network Comn, 1995-; consult, Metro Heights Hosp Found; Comn Accreditation Am Phys Ther Asn. **Home Addr:** 20876 Fairmount Blvd, Cleveland, OH 44118-4840, **Home Phone:** (216)397-7540. **Business Addr:** Dentist, H A Johnson DDS Inc, 2475 E 22nd St Suite 204, Cleveland, OH 44115, **Business Phone:** (216)566-7770.

### JOHNSON, HENRY
Vice president (organization), educator. **Personal:** Born Mar 15, 1937, Atlanta, GA; son of K M; children: Eric, Ian, Stephanie & Rhonda. **Educ:** Morehouse Col, BA, 1958; Atlanta Univ, MSW, 1960; Harvard Univ, Inst Higher Educ, cert, 1984. **Career:** Educator(retired); Ft Wayne State Sch, psychiat social worker, 1960-62; Menninger Clin Kans, trainee post-grad psyciat social work, 1962-63; WJ Maxey Boys Trng Sch, Mich, dir grp care & coun div, 1964-70; Northville State Hosp Soc Serv Dept, conx grp serv, 1966-69; Opportunity Sch Educ, Univ Mich, assoc dir prog educ, 1970-72; Univ Mich, vpres stud serv, 1972-90, vpres community affairs, 1990, Alumni Assn, sr consult, 1992, vpres stud affairs, vpres stud affairs emer, currently; Paul Harris Fel, Rotary Int. **Orgs:** Trustee, Ann Arbor Sch Dist, 1968-74; atty gen adv bd, State Mich, 1972; United Fund chmn, Univ Mich, 1973; reg vpres, NASPA IV-E, 1976-78; consult evaluator, NCent Asn, 1984; sire archon, Sigma Pi Phi Frat, 1986-88; trust adv bd Charitable Trust; state bd Mich Assn emotionally Disturbed C; chmn, Washtenaw United Way; sr consult, Univ Mich, Alumni assn, 1992-; Henry Johnson Assoc Urban Ministry, Presbytery Detroit; chairperson, Presby Villages Mich Bd dir; Strategic Plng Comt; consult, Nat Ctr & Caucus Black Aged; southeast Mich; bd mem, Mich Eval Resource Ctr, Child & Family Serv Washtenaw County, Univ Mich United Way Campaign, Ann Arbor Symphony & Ann Arbor Leaders, Prev Substance Abuse. **Home Addr:** 1250 Westport Rd, Ann Arbor, MI 48103-2572. **Business Addr:** Vice President for Student Affairs Emeritus, University of Michigan, 911 N Univ Ave, Ann Arbor, MI 48109, **Business Phone:** (734)763-4003.

### JOHNSON, HENRY WADE
Media executive, writer. **Personal:** Born Jun 13, 1947, Boston, MA; son of Henry and Helen Wade; married Naja Griffin; children: Shavi Kharim Uhuru & Damani Kharim Ode. **Educ:** Harvard Col, BA, 1970. **Career:** PBS-Boston, WGBH-TV, filmmaker, 1970-79; editor: "Say Brother", 1970; Blackside Inc, producer, developer, 1979; Rainbow TV Workshop, vpres prod, 1979-84; TV ser prod, 1985-89; Warner Bros TV, vpres prod, currently; Producer: "Two of Hearts", 1979; "The Children Shall Lead", 1979; developer/producer: "Eyes on the Prize", 1979; "Righteous Apples", 1980, "The Young Landlords", "The Grand Baby", 1985; TV series: "Growing Pains", 1985-90; "Just the Ten of US", 1987-90; writer: "The Big One: The Truth About the San Andreas", 1996. **Orgs:** African-Am Entertainment Coalition; bd dir, Westside Prep; Black Filmmakers Found; dir Guild Am; Asn Producers & Assoc Producers. **Honors/Awds:** Man of the Year, Am Soc Lighting Designers, 1991; Sandra Eves Manly Team Player Award, Nat Asn Advan Colored People, 1993. **Home Addr:** 920 S Genesee Ave, Los Angeles, CA 90036-4615, **Home Phone:** (323)954-1102. **Business Addr:** Vice President, Warner Bros TV, 3400 Riverside Dr, Burbank, CA 91522, **Business Phone:** (818)846-1403.

### JOHNSON, HERMON M., SR.
Executive, government official, insurance agent. **Personal:** Born May 5, 1929, Gilbert, LA; son of Samuel Vanora and Comay Anderson; married Alfreta Thompson; children: Hermon Jr, Cheryl Lynn, Darryl & Josef. **Educ:** Southern Univ, Baton Rouge, BS, 1955; Miss Valley State Col, elem teacher cert, 1959. **Career:** Magnolia Mutual Life Ins Co, off mgr, 1955-59; Myrtle Hall Sch, teacher, 1964-66; community & action specialist, 1966-68; Tufts Delta Health Ctr, econ develop specialist, 1967-73; Community Health Educ, dir, 1973; Dept Patient Health Serv & Resource Coord, dir, 1973-; Paul Revere Life Ins Co, sales rep; Poultry Farms Inc, stock agt; Hermon Johnson Ins, ins agent. **Orgs:** Dir, Mound Bayou Credit Union, 1960-71; vice-mayor, Alderman Mound Bayou, 1961; pres, Mound Bayou Develop Corp,

1961-63; asst ctr dir, Delta Health Ctr, 1975-77; pres, Delta Housing Develop Corp; Am Legion Post 220; Mound Bayour Civic Club; Mound Bayou Conversation & Recreation League; trustee, Bethel AME Church. **Home Addr:** PO Box 262, Mound Bayou, MS 38762, **Home Phone:** (601)741-2463. **Business Addr:** Insurance Agent, Hermon Johnson Insurance, 201 NW Main Ave, Mound Bayou, MS 38762-7800, **Business Phone:** (662)741-2463.

## JOHNSON, HESTER
Automotive executive. **Personal:** married Samuel Jr. **Career:** Metro Lincoln-Mercury Inc, vpres, gen mgr.

## JOHNSON, I. S. LEEVY
Executive, president (organization), funeral director. **Personal:** Born May 16, 1942, Columbia, SC; married Doris Wright; children: George C & Christopher. **Educ:** Univ Minn, assoc mortuary sci, 1962; Benedict Col, SC, BS, 1965, JD, 1972; Univ SC Sch Law, JD, 1968. **Career:** SC Gen Assembly; Benedict Col, instr; Funeral Dir, lic embalmer; Columbia Develop Corp, dir; First Union Bank Carolinas, dir; First Union Nat Bank SC & Southern Bank & Trust Co, dir; Victory Savings Bank, dir; Bank & Trust Co, dir; Johnson Toal & Battiste PA, pres, founder & atty, 1976-; Leevy Johnson Funeral Home Inc, owner, dir, currently. **Orgs:** Fel Am Bar Asn; fel Am Col Trial Lawyers; chmn bd trustee, SC State Col; mem exec comt & bd dir, First Union Nat Bank SC; pres, SC Bar Asn; Nat Bar Asn; SC Asn Justice; Am Bd Trial Advocates; Fourth Circuit Judicial Conf; Alpha Phi Alpha Fraternity; Sigma Pi Phi Fraternity; Nat Asn Advan Colored People; pres, Am Bar Endowment; Am Bar Asn; chmn, Univ S Carolina Community Adv Coun. **Special Achievements:** First black president of the South Carolina Bar Association; First African-Americans elected to the South Carolina General Assembly since Reconstruction, 1970. **Home Addr:** 3134 Windwood Pl, Columbia, SC 29204. **Business Addr:** Attorney, Johnson Toal & Battiste PA, 1615 Barnwell St, Columbia, SC 29201, **Business Phone:** (803)252-9700.

## JOHNSON, IOLA VIVIAN
Journalist. **Personal:** Born Oct 10, 1950, Texarkana, AR. **Educ:** Univ Ariz, polit sci & jour, 1971. **Career:** Wash Post DC, summer intern, 1969; AR Daily Wildcat Univ Ala, staff writer, 1971; KVOA TV Tucson, reporter, anchor/photogr, 1971-73; Periscope Tucson, managing ed, 1972-73; WFAA TV Dallas, anchor, reporter & talk show host, 1973-85; KKDA radio sta, news anchor; KTVT-TV CBS 11, Dallas-Ft, reporter, currently. **Orgs:** Wigma Delta Chi, 1968; Am Women Radio & TV; Nat Asn Black Journ; chmn pub comt, Dallas Chap Links Inc; Am Quarter Horse Asn; Tex Palimino Horse Breeders Asn; Links Inc; Tucson Urban League;Nat Asn Advan Colored People. **Special Achievements:** First African-American news anchor for a Dallas television station; She was Miss Tan Tucson, 1st runner-up, and Miss Sweetheart for Alpha Kappa Alpha, First runner-up. **Business Addr:** Reporter, KTVT-TV CBS 11, 5233 Bridge St, Ft. Worth, TX 76103, **Business Phone:** (817)451-1111.

## JOHNSON, DR. IVORY
College teacher, school principal, executive director. **Personal:** Born Jun 11, 1938, Oakland, MS. **Educ:** Harris Teachers Col, St Louis, AA, 1960; BA, 1962; St Louis Univ, MEd, 1969; PhD, 1974. **Career:** St Louis Bd Educ, teacher, 1962-69; NDEA fel, 1968; Urban Rural Teacher Renewal Inst, St Louis Pub Sch Syst, consult, 1974; Berkeley Sch Dist, St.Louis, elem sch prin; St Louis Univ, instr; Ferguson-Florissant Reorganized Sch Dist, Title I, prog dir, Fed Progs, exec dir & coordr, currently. **Orgs:** Mo State Teachers Asn; St Louis Suburban Prin Asn; Mo Asn Elem Sch Prin; White House Conf Educ; Nat Asn Elem Sch Prin; Urban League; YMCA; Mo PTA; bd dir, Metroplex; Kappa Alpha Psi; northeast coordr, Learn & Serv. **Home Addr:** 22 Friese Dr, Olivette, MO 63132-3108, **Home Phone:** (314)997-3084. **Business Addr:** Executive Director, Coordinator, Ferguson-Florissant R-II School District, 1005 Waterford Dr, Florissant, MO 63033, **Business Phone:** (314)506-9089.

## JOHNSON, HON. J. LEON
Lawyer. **Personal:** Born Aug 22, 1961, Searcy, AR; married Tamara; children: James & Bowman. **Educ:** Philander Smith Col, BA, 1983; Univ Ark, Sch Law, JD, 1988; Harding Univ, MPA. **Career:** Wilson & Assoc, assoc partner, 1991-2001; Pulaski County Circuit Ct, sixth judicial circuit judge, 2000; atty, 2001-; Ark Atty Gen, 2003. **Orgs:** Parliamentarian, Ark Bar Asn, 2006-09; pres, W Harold Flowers Law Soc; bd dir, Ronald McDonald House; Am Studies Bd, Harding Univ; Ark Access to Justice Found bd dirs; bd mem, Ark Access to Justice Comn; pres, Woods Inns Ct; vpres, Ronald McDonald House Bd Dirs. **Honors/Awds:** Alumni of Year, Harding Univ, 2003. **Special Achievements:** The only African-American Attorney General of Ark. **Home Addr:** 3802 Sierra Forest, Little Rock, AR 72221, **Home Phone:** (501)221-1228. **Business Addr:** Judge, Pulaski County First Division Circuit Court, Rm 420 401 W Markham, Little Rock, AR 72201, **Business Phone:** (501)340-8590.

## JOHNSON, DR. JAMES EDWARD
School administrator. **Personal:** Born Sep 1, 1931, Cuthbert, GA; married Mable Lumpkin; children: James Jr, Meryl & Joni. **Educ:** Morehouse Col, BS, 1956; Atlanta Univ, MA, educ admin, 1971, EdD, Ed Adm, 1980. **Career:** School administrator (retired); DeKalb County Schs, teacher, 1956-57; Atlanta Pub Schs, teacher, 1957-60; Herff Jones Co, mfr rep, 1961-69; Atlanta Pub Sch, coordr personnel, 1969-71, prin, 1971-73, dir personnel, 1973-74, dir employee rels & personnel, 1976, assoc supt, 1994. **Orgs:** Secy chmn, Scholarship Comn Alpha Phi Alpha Frat, 1955-; del, Nat Educ Asn Atlanta Teacher Asn & Ga Asn Educs, 1956-; committeeman Radcliffe PresbyCh, 1956-; committeeman scoutmaster BSA, 1957-; Worker YMCA, 1961-; Official Quarterback Club, 1957-; Jr C C, 1962-64; Atlanta C C, 1963-64; bd dir, Grady Homes Boys Club, 1965-; del, Am Asn Sch Personal Admins, 1970-71; consult Ga Sch Bd Asn, 1975; consult Ga C C, 1976; Asn Educ Neg, 1976-; consult, Miss Educ Serv Ctr, 1976; consult, Ga Asn EducLeaders, 1976; consult, Ga Asn Educs, 1976; consult, Prof Asn Ga Educrs, 1977. **Honors/Awds:** Deans List Morehouse Col; Beta Kappa Chi Sci Hon Soc; Top Salesman Award, Herff Jones Co; Dist Service Award, Morehouse Col; EPDA; fel Doctoral Cand, Atlanta Univ. **Home Addr:** 425 Fielding Lane SW, Atlanta, GA 30311, **Home Phone:** (404)691-5266.

## JOHNSON, PASTOR JAMES H.
Labor activist. **Personal:** Born Aug 5, 1932, Mohobe, MS; son of Eugene G and Leesie Sowell; married Carrie B Miller; children: Carrie Arlena, Michele Francine, Yolanda Clarice & Vivian Jamie. **Educ:** Wells HS, Chicago, IL. **Career:** Labor activist (retired); Kentile Flrs Inc, Chicago, Ill, prod worker, 1956-69; URW Akron, Ohio, field rep, 1969-77, dist dir, 1977-96; Cent Church God, assoc pastor, 1973-84, pastor, 1984-87; Johnson Memorial Church God, pastor, 1987, pres. **Orgs:** Organizer & first pres, Bellwood Community, 1976-79; bd dir & adv, Philip Randolph, 1980-83; Nat Asn Advan Colored People, 1980; bd dirs, IPAC, 1983-. **Honors/Awds:** Korean Serv Medal, Nat Defense Serv; UN Service Medal, Nat Defense Serv. **Home Addr:** 1011 23rd Ave, Bellwood, IL 60104. **Business Addr:** President, Johnson Memorial Church Of God, 1022 S 14Tt Ave, Maywood, IL 60153, **Business Phone:** (708)343-5800.

## JOHNSON, DR. JAMES KENNETH
Surgeon, physician. **Personal:** Born Oct 9, 1942, Detroit, MI; son of William R and Frances C Brantley; married Jean E Hayes; children: Kalyn J & Kendell J. **Educ:** Wayne State Univ, Detroit, MI, BS, 1964; Meharry Med Col, Nashville, TN, MD, 1969; Yale Univ, New Haven, CT, attended 1976. **Career:** Detroit Rec Hosp, resident; Yale New Haven Hosp, resident; Strong & Johnson MD, PC, Detroit, Mich, physician, surgeon, 1976-; Southwest Detroit Hosp, Detroit, Mich, med dir, vpres med affairs, 1986-. **Orgs:** Pres, Detroit Med Soc, 1988-; Am Acad Otolaryngol; Am Acad Otolaryngol; Am Col Surgeons. **Honors/Awds:** Distinguished teacher, Dept Family Practice, Wayne State Univ Med Sch, 1983. **Home Addr:** 6506 Spruce Dr, Birmingham, MI 48009, **Home Phone:** (313)626-4193. **Business Addr:** Vice President of Medical Affairs, Southwest Detroit Hospital, 2401 20th St, Detroit, MI 48226, **Business Phone:** (313)496-7700.

## JOHNSON, JAMES WALTER (JIM JOHNSON)
Lawyer. **Personal:** Born May 12, 1941, Washington, DC; married Eva M Murdock; children: Kimberely, Stephanie & Christopher. **Educ:** Howard Univ, BS, 1963; George Washington Univ, MS, 1969, JD, 1971. **Career:** Lockheed Missile & Space Co, assoc engr, 1963-64; US Patent Off, examr, 1965-66; Mitre Corp, staff, 1968-71; Commun Satellite Corp, patent atty, 1971-74; GE Co, div patent consult, 1974-78; Intel sat, patent consult. **Orgs:** DC Bar Asn; Pa Bar Asn; Nat Bar Asn; Am Patent Lawyers Asn; reg, US Patent Atty; Kappa Alpha Psi; VA Bar Asn; Air Line Pilots Asn, managing atty, Legal Dept, sr managing atty. **Home Addr:** 535 Herndon Pkwy, PO Box 1169, Herndon, VA 20172-1169, **Home Phone:** (703)689-4323. **Business Addr:** Managing Attorney, Air Line Pilots Association, 1625 Mass Ave NW, Washington, DC 20036, **Business Phone:** (703)689-2270.

## JOHNSON, JARED MODELL
Executive, school administrator. **Personal:** Born Oct 31, 1960, Milwaukee, WI; son of Wilbert David and Florence J. **Educ:** Milwaukee Area Tech Col, 1980; Univ Wis, Milwaukee, BS, educ policy & community studies engineering, 1984. **Career:** Wis Construct Corp, proj mgr, 1980-84; Property Assoc Investors Inc, vpres, 1985-90; Aspii Contracting & Develop Corp, pres, 1985-90; ACM Construct Serv LLC, proj mgr & managing mem, 1988-2008; Holladay Valley View LLC, proj mgr, 2005-; Johnson Assocs LLC, proj mgr, 2009-. **Orgs:** Bd dir, Milwaukee Pub Sch, 1989-97; vol, Trans Ctr Youth; Econ dir, 100 Black Men, 1989-1991; Wis Voc Technol & Adult Educ Appt Comt, 1990-92; Nat Asn Christians & Jews; Men Move Investment Club; Ebony Ice Ski Club; Nat Brotherhood Skiers. **Home Addr:** 5404 N Iroquois Ave, Milwaukee, WI 53217, **Home Phone:** (414)963-9484.

## JOHNSON, JAY
Radio broadcaster. **Personal:** Born Apr 2, 1947, Louisville, KY; married Arneda Moncure; children: Jason Troy & Tiffany Faye. **Educ:** Triton Col. **Career:** WGRT Radio, announcer, 1968-71; WJPC, chicago; WVON Radio, announcer, 1971-75; WBBM-TV, announcer, 1974-75; WTLC-FM, prog dir, 1975-93; WISH-TV, reporter & host, 1978-85; "Solid Gold Soul", ABC Radio, host, currently; Jay Johnson Ent, pres. **Orgs:** Bd mem, Am Lung Asn; consult, Ind Black Expo, Ctr Leadership Develop; comt mem, PAXI 10th Pan Am Games, 1986-87. **Honors/Awds:** Air Personality, Prog Director of the Year, Billboard mag, 1974, 80, 82; Air Personality, Prog Director of the Year, Black Radio Exclusive, 1977-79, 1985-86; Super Jay Johnson Day City of Indianapolis, 1977; Outstanding Serv as Host, UNCF, 1978-85; Excellence Award Oper PUSH, 1981; Success Award, Black Woman Hall of Fame Foundation, 1984; 6 times Black Radio Exclusive award. **Home Addr:** 440 Wellington Rd, Indianapolis, IN 46260, **Home Phone:** (317)876-1377. **Business Addr:** Host, ABC Radio Networks, Dallas, TX 75201.

**JOHNSON, JAZZ FLOYD. See JOHNSON, DR. CHARLES FLOYD.**

## JOHNSON, HON. JEH CHARLES
Lawyer. **Personal:** Born Sep 11, 1957, New York, NY; son of Jeh Vincent and Norma Edelin; married Susan Maureen DiMarco; children: Jeh Charles Jr & Natalie M. **Educ:** Morehouse Col, BA, 1979; Columbia Law Sch, JD, 1982. **Career:** Paul Weiss Rifkind Wharton & Garrison LLP, assoc, 1984-88, partner, 1992-98, atty, 2001-, partner, currently; Southern Dist New York, asst US atty, 1989-91; USaF, gen coun, 1998-2001; Dept Defense, gen coun, 2009-12; Homeland Security, secy, 2013-. **Orgs:** Dir, Legal Aid Soc, 1994-98; dir, New York Hall Sci, 1998; dir, FilmSoc Lincoln Ctr, 1995-98; trustee, Adelphi Univ, 2001-; Am Law Inst; vice chair, Asn Bar city; Ny bar; Dist Columbia bar; fel Am Col Trial Lawyers, 2004; New York Bar; Dc Bar. **Honors/Awds:** Benjamin E Mays Service Award, More house Col, 2003; Secretary's Award for Valor, 2014-15; Milton S Gould Award, NY Univ Law Sch. **Special Achievements:** First African American to be elected to Paul, Weiss, Rifkind, Wharton & Garrison LLP. **Home Addr:** 30 Porter Pl, Montclair, NJ 07042, **Home Phone:** (973)655-9725. **Business Addr:** Secretary, Homeland Security, 12th & C St SW, Washington, DC 20528, **Business Phone:** (202)282-8000.

## JOHNSON, JEH VINCENT, SR.
Architect, lecturer, designer. **Personal:** Born Jul 8, 1931, Nashville, TN; son of Charles Spurgeon and Marie Burgette; married Norma Edelin; children: Jeh Charles & Marguerite Marie. **Educ:** Columbia Col, AB, 1953; Columbia Univ, MArch, 1958. **Career:** Paul R Williams, architect, designer & draftsman, 1956; Adams & Woodbridge Architects, architect & designer, 1958-62; Gindele & Johnson PC, architect, designer & pres, 1962-80; Vassar Col, lectr art & design, 1964-2001; LeGendre Johnson McNeil Architects, partner, 1980-90; Jeh V Johnson, FAIA, architect, 1990-. **Orgs:** Am Inst Arch, 1963-; co-founder, Nat Org Minority Arch, 1971-; New York St Arch Regist Bd, 1973-84; dir, Bank Hudson, 1977-2001; consult, Dutchess County Planning Bd, 1984-; Sigma Pi Phi; dir, Scenic Hudson Inc, 1996-. **Honors/Awds:** Students Medal AIA, NY, 1958; William Kinne Fel Traveling Fel, Europe, 1959; elected Fel, Am Inst Arch, 1977; Spec Citation, New York chap Am Inst Architects, 1997. **Special Achievements:** Designed over 300 major projects & 4300 housing units 1963-02. **Home Addr:** 14 Edge Hill Rd, Wappingers Falls, NY 12590-1228, **Home Phone:** (845)297-5309. **Business Addr:** Professor, Vassar College, 202B New Eng Bldg, Poughkeepsie, NY 12604, **Business Phone:** (914)437-5472.

## JOHNSON, JERRY CALVIN
Athletic coach, educator, athletic director. **Personal:** Born Jun 20, 1920, Tulsa, OK; married Vaster M; children: Jerry C Jr, Wandra Haywood & Oliver. **Educ:** Fayetteville State Univ, BS, 1950; Columbia Univ, MA, 1951. **Career:** Educator, basketball coach (retired); Ridgeview High Sch, teacher, coach, 1951-58; LeMoyne Owen Col, athletic dir & coach, prof health phys educ & recreation, 1959, head coach & adj prof educ, 1959-2005. **Orgs:** Vol, Am Red Cross, 1959; consult, Nat Youth Sports Prog, 1972-82; bd dir, Memphis Shelby City Old Age, 1975-80; adv coun, Tenn State Bd Educ, 1984; vpres, Southern Intercollegiate Conf, 1984; Memphis Sports Authority; Tenn Gov Adv Coun C Disabilities; Boys Club Memphis; Amateur Athletic Union; Black Coaches Asn; Memphis Black Bus Asn. **Special Achievements:** LeMoyne-Owen gymnasium renamed to Jerry C. Johnson Gymnasium. **Home Addr:** 1985 Prospect St, Memphis, TN 38106-7647, **Home Phone:** (901)942-1485.

## JOHNSON, JERRY L.
Executive, president (organization). **Personal:** Born Dec 4, 1947, Freeport, IL; son of Charles W and Katherine Moseley; married Raye Sandford; children: Jeri Lynne & Jonathan Wellesley. **Educ:** Northeast Mo State Univ, BS, educ & psychol, 1969; Northern Ill Univ, DeKalb, Ill, MS, psychol, coun & educ, 1973; Western Ill Univ, educ specialist cert; Mass Inst Technol, MS, mgt, 1983; Truman State Univ, BA. **Career:** Galesburg Pub Sch Dist, 205, prin, 1972-76; NWB Tel Co, mgt asst, 1976-81, dist plant mgr, 1981-82; Northwestern Bell Info Technologies, pres, chief exec officer, 1983-85, pres & chief exec officer, 1985; US W Inc, vpres residence planning, 1986-87; US W Home & Personal Serv, vpres & gen mgr, 1987-90; US W Commun Inc, Western Region, Network & Technol Serv, vpres, 1976-95; Safeguard Sci, sr vpres, 1995-98, exec vpres, 1998-2002; eMoney Adv Inc, pres, 2002-; eMoney Advisor LLC, pres, 2002-06; Bryn Mawr Bank Corp, dir, 2011-; Episcopal Acad, dir; Philadelphia Orchestra Asn, dir; Wistar Inst, dir; Dynegy Inc, dir; Educ Mgt LLC, dir; Educ Mgt Corp, dir; eMoney Advisor LLC, dir; Axum Partners, founder; Pupil Personnel Serv, dir; KBL Acquisition Corp, spec advisor, currently; ESmith Legacy Inc, co-chmn, co-founder, currently; Axum Advisors LLC, chief exec officer & pres, currently. **Orgs:** Pac-W Telecomm Inc, chmn, 1998-2001; Int Soc Sloan; Vis Comt, Sloan Sch Mgt, Mass Inst Technol; Sigma Pi Phi Boule; Kappa Alpha Psi; bd trustee, Southeastern Regional Med Ctr; chmn, Radnor Trust Co; vice chmn & dir, PRWT Serv Inc; Axum Financial LLC; Decis Inc; Penn Liberty Bank; mem adv bd, EnerTech Capital; trustee, Elite Co Found. **Honors/Awds:** One of Top 25 Most Powerful Black Executives in Corporate America, 1988, 40 Most Powerful Black Executives, Black Enterprise Mag, 1993. **Home Addr:** 5435 154 Ave SE, Bellevue, WA 98006. **Business Addr:** President, Chief Executive Officer, Axum Advisors LLC, 1515 Mkt St Suite 1700, Philadelphia, PA 19102, **Business Phone:** (215)972-5054.

## JOHNSON, JIMMIE OLDEN, JR.
Football player, football coach. **Personal:** Born Oct 6, 1966, Augusta, GA. **Educ:** Howard Univ, BS, consumer studies, 1989. **Career:** Football player (retired), coach; Wash Redskins, 1989, 1991, tight end, 1990; Detroit Lions, tight end, 1992-93; Kans City Chiefs, tight end, 1994; Philadelphia Eagles, tight end, 1995-98; Sc State Univ, running backs coach, 2001-02; Shaw Univ, running backs & tight end coach, 2002-03, off cord, 2003-04; Tex Southern Univ, offensive coordr & quarterbacks coach, 2004-05; Minn Vikings, tight ends coach, 2006-13; New York Jets, tight end coach, 2016-. **Special Achievements:** TV Special: "1996 Clio Awards ", 1995. **Business Addr:** Tight Ends Coach, New York Jets, 1 Jets Dr, Florham Park, NJ 07932, **Business Phone:** (973)549-4800.

## JOHNSON, JOAN B.
Executive, chairperson, chief executive officer. **Personal:** Born Jan 1, 1929; married George E; children: Eric. **Career:** Johnson Prod Co, Chicago, Ill, 1954, vpres, 1965-75, treas & dir, 1975-89, chairwomen & chief exec officer, 1989-98.

## JOHNSON, JOHN
Writer, insurance executive. **Personal:** Born Jun 20, 1938, New York, NY; son of John and Irene; married Ann Yih. **Educ:** Ciyt Col NY, BA, 1961, masters, 1963; St Thomas Aquinas Col, DLit, 1991. **Career:** NYC Bd Educ, teacher & asst prin, 1960-67; Lincoln Univ, assoc prof, fine arts, 1967-68; Ind Univ, assoc prof; ABC News, NY, producer, dir, writer & doc unit, 1968-71; ABC Eve News, NY, corresp, 1971-72; WABC-TV, NY, reporter, 1972-85, anchor, 1985-95; WCBS-TV, NY, co-anchor, 1995-96; WNBC-TV News, NY, anchor, sr corresp, 1996-97; Auth: Black Power Revolt, 1968; Only Son: A Memoir, 2002; One Man Art Show: John Johnson: Bridges (Recent Paintings), 2003; Walter Wickiser Gallery, Soho, NY, 2003; John Johnson: Am Portraits: Recent Paintings, 2004; Group Art Show: Walter Wickiser Gallery, Chelsea, NY, 2005; Artist, self employed, 1968-2012; Welfare Game and Strangers in Their Own Land: The Puerto Ricans; ins exec, currently. **Orgs:** AFTRA; DGA. **Honors/Awds:** Best Enterprise Re-

porting Award, AP, 1977; Emmy, Best Sports Progamming, 1978; Best Documentary Award, AP, 1979; Emmy, Best Spot News, 1982; Emmy, Best Service News, 1982; Nat Broadcast Award for Outstanding Spot News, VPI, 1982; Emmy, Best Investigating Reporting, 1983; Lifetime Achievement Award, NY Asn Black Journalists, 1997; Communications Hall of Fame, City Col NY, 2000; CCNY President's Award, 2015. **Special Achievements:** First African American filmmakers in the prestigious Directors Guild of America; First African American documentary producer, director and writer at a broadcast network. **Home Addr:** PO Box 547, New York, NY 10963, **Home Phone:** (914)638-2898.

### JOHNSON, JOHN E., JR.

Executive director, association executive. **Educ:** Howard Univ, BA, polit sci, jour, hist, 1974; Valparaiso Univ Sch Law, JD, 1978. **Career:** Wayne County Neighborhood Legal Servs, staff atty, supv atty, dep dir; Nat Consumer Law Ctr, staff atty; UAW Legal Serv Plans, managing atty; City Detroit, corp coun, 2006-08; Dimara Group LLC, pres & chief exec officer, 2008-; State Mich, Mich tax tribunal hearing officer, 2010-11; Mich Legis Black Caucus, exec dir, 2013-; Law Off John E Johnson Jr, owner, currently. **Orgs:** Pres, Wolverine Bar Asn; Detroit Water Bd; dep exec dir, Legal Aid & Defender Asn, 1999-2005; exec dir exec comt, gen coun & first vpres, Nat Asn Advan Colored People, Detroit Br, 2009-10. **Home Addr:** 343 S Crown Hill Rd, Orrville, OH 44667, **Home Phone:** (330)683-0015. **Business Addr:** First Vice President, General Counsel, National Association for the Advancement of Colored People, 8220 2nd Ave, Detroit, MI 48202, **Business Phone:** (313)871-2087.

### JOHNSON, JOHN J.

Association executive. **Personal:** Born Feb 10, 1945, Louisville, KY; married Courtrina; children: 7. **Educ:** Sojourner-Douglass Col, BS, community develop & pub admin. **Career:** Ky Inst Community Dept, trainer, 1968-69, coordr; Southern Ky Econ Opportunity Coun, dir field opers & training, equal opportunity officer, 1969-70; Louisville-Jefferson County, Community Action Comm, supv, 1971-75; Louisville-Jefferson County, Human Rels Comm, assoc dir, 1975-77; Ky Comm Human Rights, dir community serv, 1977-84, exec dir, 2007-; Community Action Agency, exec dir, 1984-86; Nat Asn Advan Colored People, Voter Educ Dept, staff, nat dir, 1986-89, Labor Dept, nat dir, 1988-, dir prog, currently, chief progs off, currently; Armed Serv & Veteran Affairs Dept, from exec asst to exec dir, 1989, nat dir, 1990-; Louisville Forum. **Orgs:** Bd dir, Nat Asn Advan Colored People, chief progs officer, chief exec opers, Youth Coun, Life & Golden Heritage, Ky chap, 1963-, state pres; Lampton Baptist Church; Nat Urban League, local chap; nat bd dir, A Philip Randolph Inst; nat bd dir, Nat Coalition Black Voter Participation; alt comnr, Martin Luther King Jr Fed Holiday Comn; bd dir, Nat Comt Pay Equity; numerous other mem, 1972-; nat bd dir, Nat Coalition Black Civic Participation; chair adv bd, Nat Great Blacks Wax Mus Inc; chair, Ky Coalition Conscience; Urban League; Southern Christian Leadership Conf; Nat Asn Human Rights Workers. **Honors/Awds:** Human Service Award, Mae St Kidd Auxiliary, 1984; Distinguished Service in Social Action Nat Award, Phi Beta Sigma Fraternity, 1985; Award of Merit, Ky Conf, Nat Asn Advan Colored People, 1986; Award of Appreciation, 1986; Golden Apple Leadership Award, Ky Dept Educ, 1987; Ambassador of Goodwill Award, City Franklin, KY, 1989; Nat Services Program Award, US Bur Census, 1990; US Dept of Defense Award, 1991; Whitney M Young Jr Award; John J Johnson Avenue, named in honor, 1993; Hon Doctrate Degree, Simmons Univ; Distinguished Service Award, Ky State Univ; Civil Rights Leadership Award, Ky SCLC; Medgar Evers Award, Nat Asn Advan Colored People. **Business Addr:** Executive Director, Kentucky Commission on Human Rights, 332 W Broadway 7th Fl, Louisville, KY 40202, **Business Phone:** (502)595-4024.

### JOHNSON, DR. JOHN THOMAS

Physician. **Personal:** Born Feb 8, 1942, St. Louis, MO; married Geraldine Ross; children: Christine E, Glenda R & John T Jr. **Educ:** Parsons Col, BS, 1967; Philadelphia Col Osteop Med, DO, 1974. **Career:** Davenport Med Ctr, intern, 1974-75, resident, 1975-76; Community Health Care Inc, physician, 1976-. **Orgs:** Am Osteop Asn, 1976-; Iowa Osteop Med Asn, 1976-; Scott County Med Soc, 1976-; bd dirs, Davenport Med Ctr; vol physician Silver Gloves, Boy Scouts, 1985. **Honors/Awds:** Roast Sepia Guild, 1977; Certificate of Appreciation, The Honor Community, 1982; Recognition Award, Christian Community Serv, 1982; Calvary SDA Church, 1983; Certificate of Appreciation, Sr Citizens, 1985; Recognition Award, Davenport Med Ctr, 1986. **Home Addr:** 1221 W 57th St, Davenport, IA 52806, **Home Phone:** (319)391-3665. **Business Addr:** Physician Assistant, Community Health Care Inc, 500 W River Dr, Davenport, IA 52801, **Business Phone:** (563)336-3000.

### JOHNSON, JOHN WILL

Lawyer, college teacher. **Personal:** Born Nov 6, 1934, Claiborne Parish, LA; children: John Jr, Julian & Juan. **Educ:** Southern Univ, Baton Rouge, BA, 1957; Howard Univ Sch Law, JD, 1962; Georgetown Univ Law Ctr, LLM, 1964. **Career:** US Dept Justice Wash, trial lawyer, 1964-68; Ohio Bell Tel & Co Cleveland Corp ABA, gen atty, 1968-72; AT & T, atty, 1972; NY Law Sch, adj law prof, 1978-. **Orgs:** Nat Bar Asn; NY Bar Asn, 1975-; Ohio Bar Asn; DC Bar Asn; LA Bar Asn. **Honors/Awds:** Distinguished Service Award, Excellence Law Sch & Prof, New York Law Sch. **Business Addr:** Attorney, 2 5th Ave Suite 53, New York, NY 10022, **Business Phone:** (212)777-2068.

### JOHNSON, ESQ. JOHNNIE LOUIS, III

Lawyer. **Personal:** Born Nov 1, 1946, Nesbit, MS; son of Johnnie Louis II and Beulah M Merriweather; married Bethiness Theodocia Walker; children: Johnnie L IV, Gregory Lloyd, Justice Millsaps & Ahmad Nakeill. **Educ:** Morris Brown Col, BA, 1967; Ohio Northern Univ, JD, 1970. **Career:** US Dept Justice, asst atty, 1970-73; US Equal Employ Opportunity Comn, asst reg atty, 1973-75, spec asst to comnr, 1975-78, dir trial team II, 1978-81, asst gen coun, 1981-83, Legal & Spec Polit Div, dir, 1983-84, dir spec proj, 1984-85, sr trial coun, 2003-; Law Offices of Johnnie Louis JohsnonIII LLC, owner, sr trial atty. **Orgs:** Pres, BF Jones Bar Asn, 1970-73; pres, bd dir, Memphis & Shelby City, Legal Serv Asn, 1972-74; vpres, Memphis Chap, Fed Bar Asn, 1972-74; pres, Morris Brown Col Alumni Asn, 1985-92; pres, Mediter Villa Cluster Asn, 1986-; bd dir, Ohio Northern Univ Law Alumni Asn, 1988-; mediator, DC Mediation Serv, 1989-; mediator, Multi-Door Disput Resolution Ctr, 1990-; pres, Nat Coun EEOC Locals 216, 1998-; pres, AFGE Local 2667, 1998-2007. **Honors/Awds:** Donnie Delaney Commission Defense Award, 1974; Outstanding Young Man of America, 1979. **Special Achievements:** Participant in Old Dominion 100 Mile Endurance Run, 1979; Empire State Run Up 1979, 1980; New York City Marathon, 1979, 1980; Marine Corp Marathon, 1979, 1980, 1981; JFK 50 Miler 1980. **Business Addr:** Manager, Senior Trial Attorney, Law Offices of Johnnie Louis Johnson III LLC, 11644 Mediter Ct, Reston, VA 20190-3401, **Business Phone:** (703)471-0848.

### JOHNSON, JON D.

Chairperson, state government official. **Personal:** Born Aug 17, 1948; married Angela Barthe; children: Hannah. **Educ:** Southern Univ, BS; Loyola Univ, MBA. **Career:** Teacher, 1969-71; City New Orleans, Mayor's Human Rights Comn, mem, 1974-80, District E coun mem, 2010-; La State House Reps, state rep, 1980-85; La State Senate, state senator, 1985-2003; commodity broker; New Orleans Health Corp, chmn, currently; St Maria Goretti Church, eucharistic minister & usher; Ninth Ward Housing Develop Corp, 2006. **Orgs:** Nat Asn MBA Execs; assoc dir, Urban League Greater New Orleans, 1972-79; St David's Church. **Special Achievements:** First African American in the history of New Orleans to serve as a State Representative and State Senator; First African American in the history of Louisiana to serve as chairman of the Senate Revenue and Fiscal Affairs Committee. **Business Addr:** Chairman, New Orleans Health Corp, 1008 Jourdan Ave 2nd Fl, New Orleans, LA 70117, **Business Phone:** (504)947-7775.

### JOHNSON, JONATHAN F.

Business owner, chief executive officer, executive. **Career:** Community Pride Food Stores Inc, chief exec officer, 1992; Mkt Pl Holdings Inc, pres & chief exec officer, currently; Rack & Sack stores. **Orgs:** Bd visitors, Va Union Univ; bd dir, Richmond Community Hosp; Gov's Comn, Citizen Empowerment. **Business Addr:** President, Chief Executive Officer, Market Place Holdings Inc, 1301 W Broad St, Richmond, VA 23220, **Business Phone:** (804)353-7760.

### JOHNSON, JOSEPH A.

Educator. **Personal:** Born Jun 9, 1925, Columbus, OH; married Olivia Scott. **Educ:** Allen Univ, BS; Columbia Univ, MBA; NY Univ, MA. **Career:** Bus mgr, 1950-56; Allen Univ, Columbia, SC, asst prof bus, 1968-70, spec servs dir, 1970-73, dir gen studies, 1973-, fed proj dir, 1973-. **Orgs:** Phi Delta Kappa; Prov Pole march; Kappa Alpha Psi; chmn, Jacks Columbia Jack & Jill; Bethel AME Church. **Home Addr:** 3907 Pearl St, Columbia, SC 29203-5465, **Home Phone:** (803)771-2828. **Business Addr:** Director, Allen University, 1530 Harden St, Columbia, SC 29204, **Business Phone:** (803)376-5700.

### JOHNSON, DR. JOSEPH B.

School administrator, association executive. **Personal:** Born Sep 16, 1934, New Orleans, LA; son of Sidney T and Lillie Mickens; married Lula Young; children: Yolanda Dixson, Joseph III, Juliete & Julie. **Educ:** Grambling State Univ, BS, 1957; Univ Colo, Boulder, MS, 1967, EdD, 1973; Harvard Univ, cert, 1976. **Career:** Booker T Wash High Sch, Shreveport, teacher, 1962-63; postdoctoral work, Harvard Univ; Greenville Pk High Sch, teacher, 1963-69; Univ Colo, Boulder, exec asst to pres, 1969-77; Grambling State Univ, pres, 1977-91; Talladega Col, pres, 1991-98; Univ Colo, Nat Alumni Asn, bd dir. **Orgs:** Nat AsnEqual Opportunity, Amer Coun Educ, Amer Asn Univ Admins; Officer, YMCA, 1977; Kappa Alpha Psi Fraternity, AME Church; bd trustee, State Colls & Univ State La, chmn, Pres' Coun, 1982-83; chmn Press's Coun, S western Athletic Conf, 1982-84; Gov's Econ Devel Comm, 1984, comm cols Southern Asn Cols Schs, 1985; chmn, La deleg SACS, 1985; Steering CommHistorically Black Cols; adv Off Educ Res Improv, US Dept Educ, 1987; mem bd advisors, Who's WhoS & Southwest; bd dir, Univ CO Alumni Asn, Boulder, 1989-92; Nat Col Athletic Asn, Pres Comn, 1989-93; Am Asn State Cols & Univs Comm on Humanities; United Negro College Fund, The Commission On Leadership Development Of The American Council Of Education. **Honors/Awds:** National Alliance of Business Leadership Award, 1984; Honorary Doctors Law, Western Mich Univ, 'Jewish National Fund Tree of Life Award', 1985; 'Distinguished Service to Education Award', Harris-Stowe State Col, 1987; Distinguished Alumni Achievement Award, Univ of Colo; Thur good Marshall Educ Achievement Award, 1988; Asn Social & Behavioral Scientists Inc, WEB Dubois Award, 1988; 'Honorary Doctor of Philosophy', Gandhigram Rural Univ, India, 1988; named to La Black History Hall of Fame, 1991. **Home Addr:** PO Box 607, Grambling, LA 71245.

### JOHNSON, JOSEPH DAVID

Executive, president (organization), chief executive officer. **Personal:** Born Oct 26, 1945, Poplar Bluff, MO; son of Archie (deceased) and Curley; married Julie Hamilton; children: Joy Laurice & Joelle Devon. **Educ:** Lincoln Univ, BS, educ, 1968, ROTC Prog, mil grad, 1968, MS, educ admin, 1969. **Career:** Gen Mills Inc, comp per mgt, 1969-72; Dayton Hudson Corp, sr comp specialist, 1972-73; Int Multifoods Corp, div per mgr, 1973-75; Xerox Corp, group vpres personnel orgn, 1975-83, vpres human resources, 1983-88; Telein Group Inc, founder, pres & chief exec officer, 1988-. **Orgs:** Life mem, Alpha Phi Alpha Fraternity, 1965-; co-founder, Exchange Inc, Prof Asn, 1973-74; bd dir, Eltrex Indust, 1982-83; pres adv bd, Eltrex Ind, 1984-; bd dir, Us Acad Decathalon, 1986-; Am Comput Asn; Nat Asn Corp Black Profs; Nat Asn Advan Colored People; SCLC; Urban League; PUSH; Lincoln Univ Alumni Asn; bd adv, Univ S Calif Ctr Orgn Effectiveness; exec exchange prog, Nat Urban League; Exec Leadership Coun; coun advisor, Youth United Ministries, currently. **Home Addr:** 3711 Wisteria St, Seal Beach, CA 90740. **Business Addr:** President, Chief Executive Officer, The Telein Group Inc, 4281 Katella Ave Suite 109, Los Alamitos, CA 90720, **Business Phone:** (714)952-4444.

### JOHNSON, DR. JOSEPH EDWARD, JR.

Executive, educator. **Personal:** Born Aug 7, 1934, Wilmington, DE; son of Joseph E Sr (deceased) and Dorothy Dean (deceased); married Karen E Denton; children: Kevin. **Educ:** Cent State Univ, BS, biol, 1957; Seton Hall Univ, MA, 1965; Univ Mass, EdD, 1976. **Career:** Educator, superintendent (retired), executive; Burnett J High Sch, teacher, 1959-66; Wilm Pub Sch, from vprin to prin, 1966-71, dir personnel & employee rel, 1971-75, from asst supt to supt, 1975-78; PS du Pont High Sch, prin, 1968-70; New Castle Co Sch, dep supt instr, 1978-81; Red Clay Coun Sch Dist, supt, 1981-90; Warner Jr High Sch, vice prin; YMCA, bd vice chair, currently. **Orgs:** bd dir, Boys Club Del, 1985-98; past chmn, bd dir, Del Div Am Cancer Soc, 1987-98; Am Asn Sch Admin; Phi Delta Kappa Educ Frat; Nat Alliance Black Sch Educs; Kappa Alpha Psi Frat; Sigma Pi Phi Boule; bd dir, Del Futures; Hist Soc Del; bd dir, YMCA Del. **Honors/Awds:** Superintendent of the Year, Del Chief Sch Officers, 1989. **Home Addr:** 211 Dakota Ave, Wilmington, DE 19803-3217, **Home Phone:** (302)765-2218. **Business Addr:** Board Vice Chair, YMCA, 101 N Wacker Dr, Chicago, IL 60606-1784, **Business Phone:** (800)872-9622.

### JOHNSON, DR. JOSEPH F.

College teacher, administrator. **Personal:** married Rowena Peterson; children: Katrina. **Educ:** Fayetteville State Univ, BS, biol educ, 1968; Va State Univ, MEd, sci educ, 1973; Va Polytech Inst & State Univ, CAGS, educ admin, 1981, EdD, educ admin, 1981. **Career:** Richmond Pub Schs, supvr opers & serv; Durham County Schs, asst supt; New Hanover County Schs, assoc supt; Univ NC Wilmington, assoc prof educ; Winston-Salem/Forsyth County Schs, assoc supt admin & support serv, 1968-92; Fayetteville State Univ, Sch Educ, dean & prof educ leadership, 1997-2002, 2004-06, prof educ leadership & coordr master sch admin prog, 2002-04, vice chair, Grad Coun, 2003-04, dir & prof educ leadership prog, 2006-07, prof educ leadership prog, 2006-, HRRC/IRB Comt chair, 2007-, senate chmn, 2009-; Va Union Univ, sr vpres. **Orgs:** Cumberland County Libr & Info Ctr Bd trustee, 1997-2003, chair, 2001-03; Cumberland County Schs Qual Coun, 1999-; chair, NC Comn Raising Achievement & Closing Gaps, 2006-; NC State Libr Comn, 2006-. **Business Addr:** Senate Chairman, Professor of Educational Leadership Program, Fayetteville State University, 1200 Murchison Rd, Fayetteville, NC 28301-4298, **Business Phone:** (910)672-1700.

### JOHNSON, JOSEPH KEYSHAWN (KEYSHAWN JOHNSON)

Football player. **Personal:** Born Jul 22, 1972, Los Angeles, CA; son of Vivien Jessie (deceased); married Shikiri Hightower; children: Maia & Keyshawn Jr; married Jennifer Conrad. **Educ:** Univ SC. **Career:** Football player (retired), TV broadcaster; New York Jets, wide receiver, 1996-99; Tampa Bay Buccaneers, wide receiver, 2000-03; Dallas Cowboys, wide receiver, 2004-05; First Picks Mgt, co-founder, 2005; Carolina Panthers, wide receiver, 2006; Entertainment & Sports Programming Network, TV broadcaster, currently. **Honors/Awds:** First team All-American, The Sporting News, 1995; First player selected in the NFL Draft, 1996; Pro Bowl, 1998, 1999, 2001; Rose Bowl Hall of Fame, 2007; Super Bowl champion XXXVII. **Special Achievements:** Author, Just Give me the Damn Ball!: The Fast Times & Hard Knocks of an NFL Rookie, 1997; First player in NFL history to score a touchdown on MNF with four different teams; Hosts a weekly show on SIRIUS Satellite Radio's NFL Radio titled "Taking it to the House". **Business Addr:** Television Broadcaster, Entertainment and Sports Programming Network, ESPN Plz 935 Middle St, Bristol, CT 06010, **Business Phone:** (860)766-2000.

### JOHNSON, JOSEPH T.

Football player. **Personal:** Born Jul 11, 1972, Cleveland, OH. **Educ:** Univ Louisville. **Career:** Football player (retired); New Orleans Saints, right defensive end, 1994, 1996-98, left defensive end, 1995, defensive end, 2000-01; Green Bay Packers, defensive end, 2002-03. **Honors/Awds:** Rookie of the Year, 1994; Pro Bowl, 1998, 1999, 2000; Comeback Player of the Year, Assoc Press, Nat Football League, 2000; Comeback Player of the Year, Pro Football Writers Asn, Nat football league, 2000; All-Pro, 2000.

### JOHNSON, JOSHUA

Photographer. **Personal:** Born Dec 30, 1949, Sumpter, SC; son of William and Marjorie; married Phyllis Graham; children: Terrence & Derrick. **Educ:** Rochester Inst Tech, attended 1977; Eastman Kodak Co Rochester NY, Photogr Courses, 1976; Rutgers Univ Col, BS, Mgt; NY Micros Soc, attended 1981. **Career:** NJ Med Sch & CMDNJ, asst med photogr, 1968-70; NJ Dent Sch, prin bio meddent photogr, 1970-; Univ Med & Dent NJ, biomed photogr & mgr photogr serv, 1984-. **Orgs:** Biol Photogr Asn; NY Micros Soc; Lectr Dentists & Cental Stud Intra Oral Photog; illusr, Many Articles Highly Recognized Nat & Int Dent J; co-founder & first black dent photogr, Educ Commun Ctr NJ Dent Sch; Am Bus Mgt Assoc. **Honors/Awds:** Male Role Model Award, Nat Asn Negro Bus & Prof Women's Club, 1998. **Special Achievements:** Illusr dent textbooks dentists & asst, Four Handed Dentistry Dentists & Asst, 1974; 2nd Book Clinical Mgt Head Neck & TMJ Pain & Dysfunctions, 1977; Artical "Clinical Cameraman" Bio med Commun J, 1980. **Home Addr:** 1200 New World cir, Raleigh, NC 27615.

### JOHNSON, JOYCE COLLEEN

Government official. **Personal:** Born Oct 24, 1939, Terre Haute, IN; married Ronald E. **Educ:** Ind State Univ, BS, 1961. **Career:** Government official (retired); US Dept Housing & Urban Develop, equal opportunity specialist, 1973-78, multifamily housing rep, 1978-83, dir, fair housing, complaints & compliance, 1983-91, housing consult, real estate owned br, 1991. **Orgs:** Tutor Boy's Club, 1968-71; bot mgr, Deco-Plants, 1980-82; educ coordr, Int Toastmistress, 1980-83; consult, Am Cancer Soc, 1982-; regional secy, Alpha Pi Chi Sorority, 1983-; housing adv, Nat Asn Advan Colored People, 1984-85. **Home Addr:** 9662 Cypress Pine St, Orlando, FL 32827-6852.

### JOHNSON, JULIA L.

Government official. **Personal:** Born Jan 18, 1963, Clermont, FL; daughter of Abraham and Gloria. **Educ:** Univ Fla, BS, bus admin, 1985, Sch Law, JD, 1988. **Career:** Maguire, Voorhis & Wells, assoc, 1988-90; Dept Community Affairs, asst gen coun, 1990-92, legis affairs dir, 1991-92; Fla Pub Serv Comn, comnr, 1992-99, chmn, 1997-99; Fla Power & Light, pres, 1995-03; Internet Task Force, chmn,

1999-2001; Milcom Technologies, sr vpres communs & mkt, 2000-01; Ponderosa Lumber Inc, dir; Netcommunications LLC, founder, atty & pres, 2001-; MasTec Inc, dir, 2002-; Allegheny Energy Inc, dir, 2003-; NorthWestern Corp, dir, 2004-; Am Water Works Co Inc, dir, 2008-. **Orgs:** Nat Asn Regulatory Utility Comnrs, commun's comn; Govs State Energy Adv Coun; State Fla Women's Polit Caucus; Leon Co Govt Mgt Efficiency Coun; bd dir, chmn, Boys & Girls Club Big Bend; bd mem, Women Execs State Govt; bd mem, Univ Fla Nat Black Alumni Asn; Women's Polit Caucus; Tallahassee Women Lawyers; Tallahassee Barristers Asn; Nat Bar Asn; Tallahassee Urban League; Dept Energy, Nat Asn Regulatory Utility Comnrs Energy Mkt Access Bd; Fl bd educ; Dept Energy/Nat Asn Regulatory Utility Comnr Energy Mkt Access Bd; nat spokeperson, Net Compete Now Coalition; state chair, Fed State Joint Bd Universal Serv; Audit & Nominating & Governance Comts; chairperson, Emerging Issues Policy Forum; chairperson, Fla African Am Educ Alliance. **Honors/Awds:** Hall of Fame, Univ Fla; Fla Blue Key; Human Relations Award, City Gainesville; Most Outstanding Minority Graduate Award, Univ Fla. **Special Achievements:** Young Leaders of the Future, Ebony Magazines, 1993; Twelve Great Women Of Florida, 1994; Americas Best & Brightest Business & Professional Men and Women, 1994; Consumer Bulletin, Column featured in 12 Florida African-American Newspapers. **Home Addr:** 501 Blairstone Rd Suite 3403, Tallahassee, FL 32301, **Home Phone:** (904)877-8824. **Business Addr:** Director, Allegheny Energy Inc, 800 Cabin Hill Dr, Greensburg, PA 15601-1689, **Business Phone:** (724)838-6196.

## JOHNSON, JULIANA CORNISH

Manager, founder (originator), president (organization). **Personal:** Born Jun 26, 1957, Salisbury, MD; daughter of Jerome and Julia; married Douglas K. **Educ:** Cornell Univ, BA, govt, 1978; Harvard Grad Sch Bus, MBA, finan, 1982. **Career:** Chase Manhattan Bank, intern, 1978; Huntington Nat Bank, sr analyst, 1979-80; World Bank, intern, 1980; Am Tel & Tel Co, mgr, 1982-89; AMACAR Group, founder, dir & officer, currently. **Orgs:** Harvard Alumni Asn, 1982-89, Harvard Grad Sch Bus Black Alumni Asn, 1982-89; Nat Black MBA Asn, 1983-89; sponsor, Oakland Ensemble Theatre, 1984-89; bd dir, Bay Area Black United Fund, 1985-89. **Honors/Awds:** Woodford Memorial Public Speaking Award. **Special Achievements:** Top 50 Fast Track Young Executives Business Week Magazine, 1987. **Home Addr:** 45 Cobane Terr, West Orange, NJ 07052. **Business Addr:** Founder, Director, AMACAR Group, 6525 Morrison Blvd Suite 318, Charlotte, NC 28211, **Business Phone:** (704)365-0569.

## JOHNSON, JUSTIN MORRIS

Judge. **Personal:** Born Aug 19, 1933, Wilkinsburg, PA; son of Oliver Livingstone and Irene Olive Morris (deceased); married Florence Elizabeth Lester; children: William Oliver, Justin Llewellyn & Elizabeth Irene. **Educ:** Univ Chicago, BA, lib arts, 1954, Law Sch, JD, 1962; Univ Va, grad prog judges, 1983. **Career:** Partner & sole proprietor, Johnson, Johnson & Johnson, 1962-77; Bd Educ, Sch Dist Pittsburgh & Pittsburgh-Mt Oliver Intermediate Unit, asst solicitor, 1964-70, solicitor & asst secy, 1970-78; Berkman Ruslander Pohl Lieber & Engel, partner, 1978-80; Super Ct PA, judge, 1980-2007; Duquesne Univ Sch Law, adj prof, 1985-90; Allegheny County Human Rels Comn, Comissioner, 2011-. **Orgs:** Active elder E Liberty Presby Ch; Nat Conf Bar Examiners, 1969-83; Pa Bd Law Examiners, 1969-89, vice chmn, 1975-83, chmn, 1983-89; bd trustee, Mercy Hosp, 1976-93; bd trustee, Southside Hosp, 1978-88 bd trustee, United Way Allegheny Co, 1979-90; bd trustee, Pittsburgh Theol Sem, 1985-93; life trustee, Carnegie Mellon Univ, 1988-93, 1995-; Princeton Theol Sem, 1992-; Urban League Pittsburgh; hearing comn, Pa Supreme Ct Disciplinary Bd; pres & dir, Neighborhood Legal Serv Asn; Am Bar Asn, Nat Bar Asn, Pa Bar Asn, Homer S Brown Law Asn; fel Am Bar Found; adv comt, Nat Consortium Violence Res. **Honors/Awds:** Bond Medal, Univ Chicago, 1954; Dr Martin Luther King Jr Citizen's Medal, 1973; Top Hat Award, 1981; Homer S Brown Service Award, 1982; Man of the Year, Bethesda Presbyterian Church, 1983; President's Award, PA Trial Lawyers Asn, 1983; Award of Merit, Pittsburgh Young Adult Club, 1983; St Thomas More Award, 1985; Public Service Award, Pittsburgh chapter, ASPA, 1986. **Special Achievements:** Second African-American to serve in Pennsylvania Superior Court. **Home Addr:** 4911 Ellsworth Ave, Pittsburgh, PA 15213-2806, **Home Phone:** (412)683-7424.

## JOHNSON, KALANOS VONTELL

Manager. **Personal:** Born Sep 23, 1971, Toccoa, GA; son of Reginald and Rosilyn. **Educ:** Ft Valley State Univ, BS, social work, 1995; Univ Akron, MA, urban planning, 1997; Strayer Univ, MBA, 2013. **Career:** Ga Ctr Youth, prog specialist, 1995; Univ Akron, res asst, 1995-96; summit County Bd MR/DD, intern, 1996-97; Macon-Bibb County Planning & Zoning Comn, city planner, 1997-98; Fulton County Dept Pub Works, transp planner, 1998-2000; Atlanta Regional Comn, prin planner, 2000-; B&E Jackson & Assoc, proj mgr, 2002-04; Wilbur Smith Assocs, 2004-06; Delon Hampton & Assocs, Chartered, vpres bus develop, currently; Jacobs, sr transp planner, 2010-. **Orgs:** Omega Psi Phi Fraternity, Inc, 1994-; Ft Valley State Univ Alumni Asn, 1995-, pres, Southern Crescent Chap, 2002-04; Am Planning Asn, 1996-; Inst Transp Engrs, 1999-; bd dir, Arts Clayton, 2012-; vice chmn & exec dir, Clayton County Develop Authority, 2009-; treas, Commitment Excellence Found Inc, 2009-. **Honors/Awds:** SIAC All Conf Acad Football Team, 1992; sr scholar, Omega Psi Phi Fraternity, Inc, 1994; Outstanding Young Man of America, 1998. **Home Addr:** 8606 Collins Dr, Jonesboro, GA 30236-5000, **Home Phone:** (770)471-1952. **Business Addr:** Business Development Manager, Southern Region, Delon Hampton & Associates Chartered, 229 Peachtree St NE Suite 1510 Int Towers, Atlanta, GA 30303, **Business Phone:** (404)524-8030.

## JOHNSON, KELLEY ANTONIO

Football player. **Personal:** Born Jun 3, 1962, Carlsbad, NM; children: Shaun, Shei, Melanie & Johnson Jr. **Educ:** Los Angeles Valley Col, grad; Univ Colo, grad. **Career:** Football player (retired); Denver Gold, wide receiver, 1985; Canadian Football League, Ottawa Rough Riders, 1986; Indianapolis Colts, 1987; Detroit Lions, 1989.

## JOHNSON, KENNETH L.

Teacher, association executive. **Personal:** Born Feb 19, 1965, Jacksonville, FL; son of Theodore J and Minnie R. **Educ:** Bethune Cookman Col, BS, 1988. **Career:** Daniel Webster Elem Sch, teacher, 1990-92; Drug Enforcement Admin, Chicago Field Div, intelligence analyst, minority affairs coordr, 1992-95; Family Rescue Inc, dir devel & commun, 1995-97; Fund Raising Prog, devel consult, 1997-2000; Chicago Youth Ctr, dir devel; Nat Alumni Coun, United Negro Col Fund, pres; Nat Chicago Inter-Alumni Coun, nat pres; Col Summit, exec dir. **Orgs:** UNCF Bd Insts & Mem; UNCF Adv Bd, Chicago; bd dir, Kaboomes Track Club, Lawndale Community Church; bd dir, Nat Black Col Hall Fame; adv coun, Am Med Asn, Stop Am's Violence Everywhere; Interfaith Coun Homeless; bd dir, Boy Scouts Am DuSable Dist, Chicago Area Coun; judge, Cook C Election; Chicago Pub Sch Sci Fair Symp, Officers Asn; vpres & trustee, Lay Coun, J Claude Allen Christian Methodist Episcopal Church; Asn Fundraising Professionals. **Honors/Awds:** Exemplary Performance Award, Dept Army, Ill Nat Guard Counter-Drug Support Prog, 1992; Commemorative Plagues Outstanding Contributions Field Drug Law Enforcement, DEA, 1993-95; Outstanding Service Award, Chicago Inter-Alumni Council/UNCF, 1994; Outstanding Alumni of the Year Award, Chicago Inter-Alumni Council/UNCF, 1994; Special Recognition Award, Exec Off Pres, Off Nat Drug Control Policy. **Special Achievements:** Chicago Marathon, 1998. **Home Addr:** 3627 S Cottage Grove, Chicago, IL 60653-0012. **Business Addr:** Executive Director, College Summit, 1763 Columbia Rd NW 2nd Fl, Washington, DC 20009, **Business Phone:** (202)319-1763.

JOHNSON, KENNETH LANCE. See JOHNSON, LANCE.

## JOHNSON, KENNETH LAVON

Judge. **Personal:** Born Jul 26, 1937, Columbia, MS; son of Geylon and Minnie O; married Carolyn Elizabeth Dischert; children: Sara Elizabeth & Jennifer Lorraine. **Educ:** Southern Univ & A&M Col, BA, 1959; Howard Univ Law Sch, JD, 1962. **Career:** Judge (retired); US Dept Justice, trial atty, 1967-69; Baltimore Lawyers Comn Civil Rights Under Law, exec dir, 1969-70; pvt law pract, 1970-82; Baltimore City Circuit Ct, 8th Judicial Circuit, assoc judge, 1982-2001; Univ Baltimore Sch Law, prof, 1988; Villa Julia Col, prof, 1988; Md Judicial Conf, Child Support Enforcement Comt, mem, 1997-2000. **Orgs:** Nat Asn Advan Colored People; Monumental City Bar Asn; Am Bar Asn; La State Bar Asn; Dc Bar Asn. **Honors/Awds:** Distinguished Community Service, Baltimore Frontier Club, 1974; Md 7th Cong Dist Award, Congressman Parren J Mitchell, 1981; Outstanding Community Service, Vanguard Justice Soc, 1982; Maryland 7th Congressional District Award for community service; J S Clark Memorial Award for high academic achievement; Leadership Award, Criminal Justice & Law Enforcement Association Anne Arundel Community College, 1998. **Home Addr:** 533 N Calhoun St, Baltimore, MD 21223, **Home Phone:** (410)383-7093.

## JOHNSON, KENYA

Lawyer. **Educ:** Clark Atlanta Univ, BA, polit sci & govt, 1995; S Tex Col Law, JD, 1997; Ga State Univ Col Law, JD, juris prudence, 1998. **Career:** City Atlanta, asst solicitor, 2000-03; Fulton County Ct, GA, sr asst dist atty, 2003-, prog dir. **Orgs:** exec bd, S Atlanta Community Tennis Asn, 2012; exec comt, Ga Asn Black Women Attorneys, 2012; Gate City Bar Asn; exec bd mem, Greater Atlanta Black Prosecutors Association, 2014; exec comt, Links Inc, Buckhead & Cascade City Chap, 2015. **Honors/Awds:** Trailblazer Award, Fulton County Schs Syst, 2013; Community Prosecutor of the Year, Fulton County Dist Attys Off, 2014; Community Service Award, Fulton County Police Dept, 2015; Outstanding Community Service Award, Sally Yates, US Atty, Northern Dist Ga, 2015. **Business Addr:** Program Director, Assistant District Attorney, South Fulton Community Prosecutor, Fulton County Georgia, 136 Pryor St SW Fl 3, Atlanta, GA 30303, **Business Phone:** (404)612-4206.

## JOHNSON, KERRY GERARD (KERRY KRAFT)

Graphic artist, cartoonist or animator. **Personal:** Born Sep 30, 1966, Nashville, TN; son of Dorothy; married Tawanda Williams; children: Deandria & Autumn. **Educ:** Columbus Col Art & Design, BFA, 1989; Ohio State Univ, attended 1989. **Career:** Art dir, Caricaturist, Cartoonist & Graphic designer; Opryland Entertainment Pk, paid illusr; Ohio State Univ, cartoonist, 1988-89; Purpose Mag cartoonist, 1991; This Week, graphic artist, 1990-92; N Hills News Rec, graphic artist, 1992-; Kerry Kraft Studios, owner & operator, currently; Pittsburgh Post-Gazette, graphic journalist & graphic reporter, 1994-; Knight-Ridder Tribune Graphics Network, ed, illustr; Pittsburgh Tribune Rev, dep graphics ed; Baltimore Sun newspaper, graphics dir; Am Phys Socs news, art dir & dir spec subl mgr, currently; art & spec publ at Am Phys Soc Col Pk, dir. **Orgs:** Quill & Scroll Hon Soc, 1984; Publicity dir, Alpha Phi Alpha Fraternity, 1988-89; Martin Luther King Jr Scholar Breakfast Comt; NAB; Pittsburgh Black Media Fed; NCP; Soc Newspaper Design; Pa Publishers Asn, 1995; Nat Asn Black Journalists, 1996; Soc Prof Journalists; Asn Am Ed Cartoonists; Am Inst Graphic Arts; Socs News Design; Assoc Ed to Sphinx; Socs Nat Assoc Publ; Nat Caricaturist Network. **Honors/Awds:** The Black Greek Coun Award, 1989; Citizen of the Week, Communicator News, 1991; Top 25 Under-Thirty Finalist, Urban Profile, 1992; Pittsburgh Black Media Found Award, 1993-96; Feature Illustration, Pa Publishers Asn, 1995-96; Nat Asn Black Journalists, Feature Illustration, 1996; Golden Quill Award, 1996; Society for News Design Award, 2002; First place: Pennsylvania Newspaper Publishers Associations Award for Graphic Illustration, 1994; First place: National Association of Black Journalists (NABJ) Award for Art & Design, 1996; First place: Press Club of Western Pennsylvanias Golden Quill Award for News Illustration, 2002, 2001, 1996; First place: the National Arts Program for Illustration, 2008. **Special Achievements:** Youth Page, Youth Purpose, 1992; Driving Park Libr, Art Exhibition, 1991; North Hills News Record, Communicator News, various illustrations; Kerry Kards & Kerry Klothes. **Home Addr:** 5476 Ring Dove Lane, Columbia, MD 21044, **Home Phone:** (410)997-1892. **Business Addr:** Owner, Operator, Kerry Kraft Studios Inc, 715 Deerfield Circle, Wexford, PA 15090, **Business Phone:** (724)934-6630.

## JOHNSON, KEVIN MAURICE

Mayor, basketball player, executive. **Personal:** Born Mar 4, 1966, Sacramento, CA; son of Lawrence and Georgia West; married Michelle Rhee. **Educ:** Univ Calif, Berkeley, CA, BA, polit sci, 1987; Harvard Divinity Sch, Summer Leadership Inst, attended 2000. **Career:** Basketball player (retired), executive, Mayor; Cleveland Cavaliers, guard, 1987-88; Phoenix Suns, 1988-98, 2000; NBC, "The NBA", studio commentator, 2000-01; The Kevin Johnson Corp, owner, pres & chief exec officer, currently; Mayor of Sacramento, Currently. **Orgs:** Founder, St HOPE Corp. **Business Addr:** President, Chief Executive Officer, The Kevin Johnson Corp, 915 I St 5th Fl, Sacramento, CA 95814, **Business Phone:** (916)808-5300.

## JOHNSON, KEVIN N.

Basketball coach. **Personal:** Born Indianapolis, IN; married Sheila Marie; children: Mitchell Edward & Jai. **Educ:** Ind State Univ, BS, phys educ, 1989. **Career:** Nat Football League, Indianapolis Colts, asst athletic trainer; Ind Pacers, asst athletic trainer, 1990-91, 1993-94; Wash Wizards, head athletic trainer, 1994-95, 2000-01; NBA All-Star Team, eastern Conf athletic trainer, 2001; Philadelphia 76ers, head athletic trainer, currently. **Orgs:** Nat Athletic Trainers Asn; Big Bros Am. **Business Addr:** Head Athletic Trainer, Philadelphia 76ers, 3601 S Broad St, Philadelphia, PA 19148, **Business Phone:** (215)339-7676.

JOHNSON, KEYSHAWN. See JOHNSON, JOSEPH KEYSHAWN.

## JOHNSON, KIMBERLY LYNN (KIMBERLY L THOMAS)

Association executive. **Personal:** married Dermond Edwin Thomas. **Educ:** Univ Toledo, BA, pub rels, broadcast jour, 1993; Wayne State Univ, BA, pub rels, 1998; NY Univ Sch Continuing & Prof Studies, cert, meeting & event mgt, 2009. **Career:** Ford Motor Co, corp meeting planner, 1996-98; Henry Ford Mus & Greenfield Village, publicist, 1998-2003; Talented Youth Develop Inc, founder, exec dir & pres, 2000-; Bear Stearns, corp meeting planning consult, 2003-04; Time Warner Inc, consult, 2004-05, exec asst to pres, 2005-06; Dermond Thomas NY Assembly Campaign, commun dir, 2010; ValleyStream-Mom.com, ed & blogger, 2011-. **Orgs:** Epic Group plc; bd mem, Talented Youth Develop Inc; Jack and Jill of America; founding mem & pub rels chair, Long Island Mocha Moms; exec dir, Miss Brooklyn Scholar Prog. **Honors/Awds:** Community Service Award Recipient, Valley Stream Chamber Com, 2014. **Business Addr:** Founder & Executive Director, President, Talented Youth Development Inc, PO Box 293, Valley Stream, NY 11582, **Business Phone:** (516)531-3823.

## JOHNSON, LANCE (KENNETH LANCE JOHNSON)

Baseball player. **Personal:** Born Jul 6, 1963, Cincinnati, OH. **Educ:** Univ S Ala. **Career:** Baseball player (retired); St Louis Cardinals, outfielder, 1987; Chicago White Sox, outfielder, 1988-95; NY Mets, outfielder, 1996-97; Chicago Cubs, outfielder, 1997-99; NY Yankees, outfielder, 2000.

## JOHNSON, LARRY DEMETRIC

Business owner, basketball player. **Personal:** Born Mar 14, 1969, Tyler, TX; married Celeste Wingfield; children: Larry Jr, Lance & Lasani. **Educ:** Odessa Jr Col, attended 1989; Univ Nevada, Las Vegas, Nev, attended 1991. **Career:** Boxer, basketball player (retired), business owner; Police Athletic Boxing League, boxer, 1978-82; Charlotte Hornets, power forward, 1991-96; NY Knicks, small forward, 1996-98, power forward, 1999-2001; 6001 Hair Studios, owner, currently. **Orgs:** United Way. **Honors/Awds:** Silver Medal, FIBA U19 World Championship, 1987; NJCAA Division I Player of the Year, 1988-89; Gold Medal, Summer Universiade, 1989; Big West Conference Player of the Year, 1990-91; NCAA Men's Basketball Champion, 1990; John R. Wooden Award, 1991; Naismith College Player of the Year, 1991; USBWA College Player of the Year, 1991; Sporting News College Player of the Year, 1991; NBA Rookie of the Year, 1992; NBA All-Rookie first team, 1992; NBA All-Star, 1993, 1995; Gold Medal, World Championships, 1994; Olympic Dream Team II, 1996; Met life Community Assist of the Month Award; Metlife Community Assist of the Month Award. **Special Achievements:** NBA Draft, first round pick, 1991. Films: Eddie, 1996; Space Jam, Eddie. TV Program: Family Matters, 1993; The Garden's Defining Moments, 2015. **Business Addr:** Owner, 6001 Hair Studios, 6001 The Plz, Charlotte, NC 28215, **Business Phone:** (704)535-2722.

## JOHNSON, LATONYA

Basketball player, basketball coach. **Personal:** Born Aug 17, 1975, Winchester, TN; daughter of Jesse and Helen. **Educ:** Univ Memphis, BPhEd, 1998. **Career:** Basketball player (retired), basketball coach; Utah Starzz, forward, 1998-2002; San Antonio Silver Stars, forward, 2003; FIBA Europe Cup Women, Cajacanarias, Spain, 2003-04; Houston Comets, forward, 2004; Chicago Blaze, forward, 2003-04, 2005; Memphis Athletics, asst dir basketball opers, 2007-08. **Orgs:** Olympic Festival S Team, 1994; spokesperson, Breast Health Awareness.

## JOHNSON, LAVERA

Executive. **Personal:** Born St. Louis, MO; married Arthur C. **Educ:** Northwestern Mo State Univ, Maryville, educ; NY Univ, fr; New Sch Univ, New York, NY, MS, human resources & orgn develop, 1997. **Career:** Teacher; Univ Wis, Danforth fel; Brooklyn Hosp; Amalgamated Life Ins Co; c TV Workshop; Nichols Sch, bd mem; Sheehan Mem Hosp, bd mem; human resources consult; Advan Refractory Technologies Inc, vpres human resource; NanoDynamics, S Buffalo, human resources dir, 2002-09, vpres human resources, 2002-09; Workforce Investment Bd Inc, Buffalo & Erie County, bd dir, currently. **Orgs:** Soc Human Resources Profs. **Business Addr:** Human Resources Director, NanoDynamics, 901 Fuhrmann Blvd, Buffalo, NY 14203-3134, **Business Phone:** (716)853-4900.

## JOHNSON, LAWRENCE E.

Lawyer, city council member. **Personal:** Born Sep 22, 1948, Waco, TX; children: Daphne, Lawrence Jr, Demitria & LaShunia. **Educ:** Prairie View A&M Univ, BS, elect engineering, 1971; George Washington Univ, JD, 1975. **Career:** Ins salesman, 1969; Int Bus Mach, design engr, 1970; Gen Elec Corp, sales engr, 1971-72, patent engr, 1972-76; City Waco, city coun mem, 1990-98; Lawrence Johnson Assoc, atty, currently. **Orgs:** Pres bd, Legal Serv Corp, 1983; pres bd, Mitchell Funeral Home, 1982-85; dir, HOT Legal Serv, 1981-85; secy, pres bd, 1990, McLennan Community Col Bd Trustees; Cen-Tex African Am Chamber Com. **Honors/Awds:** City of Waco May Pro-Tem, 1991-92, 1996-97. **Home Addr:** PO Box 423, Corvallis, OR 97339-0423, **Home Phone:** (541)752-1711. **Business Addr:** Attorney, Lawrence Johnson Associate, 801 Washington Ave Suite 400, Waco, TX 76701-1260, **Business Phone:** (254)756-7041.

### JOHNSON, DR. LECTOY TARLINGTON
Physician, surgeon. **Personal:** Born Nov 28, 1931, Tyler, TX; married Helen Collier; children: Lectoy Tarlington III & Lynelle Teresa. **Educ:** Tex Col, BS, chem, 1952; Howard Univ Col Med, MD, 1956; Wash Univ, anesthesiol, 1960; Am Bd Anesthesiol, dipl, 1963. **Career:** Homer G Phillips Hosp, internship, 1956-57, resident, anesthesiol, 1958-60, resident, gen surg, 1957-58; Riverside Gen Hosp, Houston, chmn dept anesthesiol, 1960-68; St Joseph Hosp, Houston, chmn dept anesthesiol, 1970-80, acad chief anesthesiol, 1970-80; Univ Tex Med Sch, Houston, act chmn dept anesthsiol, 1973; pvt pract physician, currently. **Orgs:** Harris County Med Soc; Tex Med Soc; Nat Med Soc; Int Anesthesia Res Soc; Undersea Med Soc; fel Am Col Anesthesiol, 1963-; Houston Surgical Soc; med dir, Ocean Corp Houston, 1970-78; chmn & bd dir, Asn Anesthetists Houston, 1970-80; comm chmn, Boy Scouts Am WL Davis Dist, 1974-75; pres, Gulf coast Anesthesia Soc, 1979-80; bd dir, Stand Saving & Loan, 1984-; life mem, Kappa Alpha Psi Frat. **Honors/Awds:** Certificate of Excellence, Gulf Coast Chap Inhalation Therapists; Outstanding Instructor Award, St Joseph Hosp Surgical Dept. **Home Addr:** 3612 Parkwood Dr, Houston, TX 77021, **Home Phone:** (713)440-9543. **Business Addr:** Physician, Private Practitioner, Houston, TX 77096, **Business Phone:** (713)981-5167.

### JOHNSON, LENA MAE. See MCLIN, REV. LENA JOHNSON.

### JOHNSON, LEON
College administrator, chairperson. **Personal:** Born Jul 14, 1930, Aiken, SC; married Janie L; children: Leon Jr & Lisa J. **Educ:** SC State Col, BS, 1955, MS, 1959; Mich State Univ, MD; State Col Univ, MD. **Career:** Chairperson, college administrator (retired); Clemson Univ, asst count agt, 1955-62; Univ Md, exten agt com & resource Develop; Gov comn on migratory & seasonal farm labour, chair, 1997-2003. **Orgs:** Md Asn County Agr Agents; Teamwork Planning Comn; charter founding mem, Community Develop Soc; Community Resource Develop Task Force; SEMIS Work Group Com; Task Force Community Develop Prog; pres, Somerset County Comn Action Agency; Tri-county Migrant Co; vpres, Somerset County Civic Asn; Delmarva Adv Coun Migrat Com; Princess Anne Area Chamber Com; bd dir, Coston Recreation Coun; Somerset County Civil Defense bd; community orgn, Progress Inc; bd dir, Somerset County Head Start; Propress Inc; Zion Hill Baptist Church; Omega Psi Phi Frat; Epsilon Sigma Phi Frat; Delmarva Ecmenical Agency Rural Coalition; bd dir, Md Churches United Bd Recognitions Countys Head & Start Prog; Migrant Prog; Community Action Agency.

### JOHNSON, REV. DR. LEROY
College president, clergy. **Personal:** married Simmie Mae; children: Leana & Leroy Jr (deceased). **Educ:** Chapman Univ, MA; Kans State Univ, PhD. **Career:** Miles Col, Birmingham, AL, pres & chancellor, 1986-89; Missionary Temple Christian Methodist Episcopal Church, pastor, 1989-. **Special Achievements:** First African American to receive a line officer's commission under the Navy Reserve Officer Candidate Program. **Business Addr:** Pastor, Missionary Temple Christian Methodist Episcopal Church, 1455 Golden Gate Ave, San Francisco, CA 94115, **Business Phone:** (415)921-3324.

### JOHNSON, LESLIE
Basketball player. **Personal:** Born Jan 12, 1975, Ft. Wayne, IN. **Educ:** Western Ky Univ, attended 1998. **Career:** Wash Mystics, forward, 1998.

### JOHNSON, LESTER B., III
Lawyer. **Personal:** Born Dec 4, 1953, Savannah, GA; son of Lester B Jr and Constance M; married Salyon H; children: Ayesha K, Khalil A & Faisal B. **Educ:** Col Holy Cross, AB, 1975; Univ Miami, JD, 1978. **Career:** Community Lawyers Inc, law clerk, 1976-77; Ga Legal Serv Progs Inc, staff atty, 1978-80; Martin, Thomas & Bass, PC, assoc, 1980-82; Martin & Johnson, PC, partner, 1983-86; Lester B Johnson III PC, owner, 1986-; Savannah-Chatham County Pub Sch Syst, Bd Ed, sch bd atty, 1991-2016; City Savannah, asst city atty. **Orgs:** Nat Bar Asn, 1979; pres, Savannah Bar Asn, 1980; State Bar Ga, 1980-; bd mem, Masjid Jihad, 1980-; bd mem, Hist Savannah, 1988-; pres & secy, Mont golfier Soc, 1992-; Hospice Savannah Found, 1995-; gram mateus, Alpha Lambda Mu Boule, 1996-. **Honors/Awds:** Annual Award, Masjid Jihad, 1986; Citizen of the Yr, Omega Psi Phi, 1999. **Home Addr:** 1 Bridgeport Rd, Savannah, GA 31419, **Home Phone:** (912)925-8353. **Business Addr:** Associate Attorney, Lester B Johnson III PC, 216 W Broughton St Suite 201, Savannah, GA 31401-8285, **Business Phone:** (912)238-5100.

### JOHNSON, LILLIAN MANN
Educator, administrator. **Personal:** Born Dec 18, 1948, Springfield, MA; daughter of Donald and Ruth Freeman; married Thornton B Jr; children: Joshua & Zachary. **Educ:** Cent State Univ, BS, 1970; Cent Mich Univ, MSA, 1985. **Career:** JC Penney Co, merchandise presentation supvr, 1980-83; Cent Mich Univ, prog coordr, ctr rep, 1983-87; Wright State Univ, acad adv univ div, 1987-89, career servs, asst dir, 1989, Bolinga Ctr, asst dir, 1989-92, Bolinga Ctr, dir, 1992-2000, adj instr, 2001, asst dean, 2001, coordr mentoring progs, 2001. **Orgs:** Vpres, Am Asn Univ Women, WSU Br, 1996-; pres, Alpha Kappa Alpha Sorority, 1996-; corres secy, Alpha Kappa Alpha Sorority, 1994-96; pres, Orgn Black Fac & Staff, 1996-97; vpres, Wright State Univ, 1995-96; bd mem, Dayton Art Inst Outreach, 1993-; Phi Delta Kappa Fraternity, 1985-88; Nat Asn Advan Colored People; Dayton Urban League; bd mem, Buckeye Trails Girl Scouts; bd mem, Montgomery County Arts Coun. **Home Addr:** 5697 Firegate Ct, Huber Heights, OH 45424, **Home Phone:** (937)667-0604. **Business Addr:** Assistant Dean, Coordinator, Wright State University, 3640 Colonel Glenn Hwy, Fairborn, OH 45435, **Business Phone:** (937)775-3333.

### JOHNSON, DR. LINDA DIANNE
Optometrist. **Personal:** Born Feb 5, 1954, Richland, MS; daughter of Adam and Gertrude; married James Walter Carson Jr; children: James Walter III. **Educ:** Jackson State Univ, BS, 1974; Ind Univ Sch Optom, OD, 1978. **Career:** Univ Miss Med Ctr, physician; Cent Miss Med Ctr, physician; Baptist Med Ctr, physician; Jackson Hinds Comprehensive Health Ctr, dir optom clin, 1978-. **Orgs:** Nat Optom Asn, pres, 1997-99; sec, treas, Miss Optom Asn; Southern Coun Optometrists; Am Red Cross; chair, Cent Miss Chap, 1995-97; Jackson State Univ; bd mem, Nat Alumni Asn; pres, Miss Optom Asn, 2003-04; Jackson Eye Inst Adv Bd. **Honors/Awds:** Outstanding Professional Achievement Award, Jackson State Univ Nat Alumni Asn, 1980; Distinguished Service Award, Jackson State Univ, Hinds Alumni Chapter, 1982; Optometrist of the Year, Nat Optom Asn, 1993; Am Red Cross Cent Miss Chap, 1994; Employer of the Year, Jackson Hinds Comprehensive Health Ctr, 1997; Optometrist of the Year, Am Optom Asn, 2008. **Special Achievements:** First African American female optometrist in the state of Mississippi. **Home Addr:** 5420 I 55 N Suite D, Jackson, MS 39211, **Home Phone:** (601)956-7412. **Business Addr:** Director, Jackson-Hinds Comprehensive Health Center, 3502 W Northside Dr, Jackson, MS 39213, **Business Phone:** (601)362-5321.

### JOHNSON, ESQ. LIVINGSTONE M.
Judge. **Personal:** Born Dec 27, 1927, Wilkinsburg, PA; married Leeburn; children: Lee Carol, Oliver Morris II, Judith Lee, Livingstone James & Patricia Lee. **Educ:** Howard Univ WA, DC, AB, 1949; Univ Mich Law Sch, JD, 1957; Col St Judiciary, Grad Nat, 1973. **Career:** Judge (retired); Allegheny County Ct Common Pleas, judge, 1982-07. **Orgs:** Panel Judges; bd mem, Nat Asn Advan Colored People, 1962-68; Urban League, 1963-68; Am Bar Asn; Am Bar Found; Am Judicature Soc; PA Bar Asn; Allegheny County Bar Asn; bd gov, 1967-74, Pub Serv Comn, 1965-; asn trial lawyres crime; Crt Allegheny County Bar Asn; PA Conf St Trail Judges; bd Dir St Peters Child Develop Ctrs Inc; ARC; Boys Club Western PA; Ile Elegba Inc; Bus & Job Develop Corp Comt Rel Agency; Azanan Strongs Inc; Greater Pittsburg Civic League; BS Am; Omega Psi Phi; Nat Asn Advan Colored People. **Home Addr:** 1161 Calmwood Rd, Glenshaw, PA 15116-3201, **Home Phone:** (412)486-2828.

### JOHNSON, LLOYD A.
Government official. **Personal:** Born Aug 5, 1932, Boston, MA; son of Clarence Lionel and Louise Amelia Dixon; married Constance Riley; children: Scott A & Alison E. **Educ:** Howard Univ, BA, sociol & psychol, 1954; Aldephi Univ, MSW, psychiat social work, 1957; Georgetown Univ Law Ctr, JD, 1984. **Career:** Worked troubled indust & families under pub & pvt auspices, 1954-66; Local Community Corps, exec dir, 1966-69; Community Develop Agency, dir evalutation & res, 1966-69; Urban Ctr Columbia Univ, dir, 1969-74; US House Representatives, coun, sub comt staff dir & serv, labor coun subcomt labor, chmn, 1974-88; Lloyd & Connie Johnson, owner, currently; Prince George's County State's Atty's Off, asst state's atty, 1989-2005; 100 Black Men of Savannah Inc, pres, 2010-11, treas, 2012-13; Savannah 100 Found Inc, pres, 2012-. **Orgs:** Acad Cert Social Workers; Nat Bar Asn; Nat Asn Social Workers; bd dir, Am Orthopsychiatric Asn; sr prosecutor, Prince Georges Co, 1989-2005; vestry, St Lukes Episcopal Church; Nat Dist Attorneys Asn. **Home Addr:** 1121 Holton Lane, Takoma Park, MD 20912-7536, **Home Phone:** (301)431-4568. **Business Addr:** Owner, Lloyd & Connie Johnson, 1121 Holton Lane, Takoma Park, MD 20912-7536, **Business Phone:** (301)431-4568.

### JOHNSON, LONNIE DEMETRIUS
Teacher, football player, football coach. **Personal:** Born Feb 14, 1971, Miami, FL; married Ushanda; children: Tyrone & Summer. **Educ:** Fla State Univ. **Career:** Football player (retired), coach; Buffalo Bills, tight end, 1994-98; Kans City Chiefs, tight end, 1999; Sanford Church Christ, assoc minister; Mt Dora Christian Home, coach, 2005; Bible sch teacher. **Home Addr:** , Mount Dora, FL.

### JOHNSON, LONNIE G.
Inventor. **Personal:** Born Oct 6, 1949, Mobile, AL. **Educ:** Tuskegee Univ, BS, mech engineering, 1973, MS, nuclear engineering, 1976, PhD. **Career:** Oak Ridge Nat Lab, res engr; USF Weapons Lab, actg chief Space Nuclear Power Safety sect, 1978-79; Jet Propulsion Lab, sr systs engr, Galileo Proj, 1979-82; engr, Mariner Mark II Spacecraft ser Comet Rendezvous & Saturn Orbiter Probe missions, 1987-91; USF, advan space systs req mgr non nuclear strategic weapons tech, 1982-85; Strategic Air Command, chief data mgt br, 1985-87, Advan Space Systs Req Officer; Johnson Res Develop Co Inc, founder & pres, 1991-. **Orgs:** Georgia Alliance Children; Hank Aaron "Chasing the Dream" Found; bd dir, Commonwealth Nat Bank. **Honors/Awds:** Pi Tau Sigma National Engineering Honor Society, 1973; USF Commendation Medal, 1984; Air Force Achievement Medal; Inducted, Inventor's Hall of Fame, 2000; Golden Torch Award, Nat Soc Black Engineers, 2001; National Award. **Special Achievements:** Inventor of Super Soaker water gun; Author of several publications on spacecraft power systems; First place, University of Alabama Junior Engineering Technical Society Exposition, 1968. **Business Addr:** President, Founder, Johnson Research & Development Inc, 263 Decatur St, Atlanta, GA 30312, **Business Phone:** (404)584-2475.

### JOHNSON, DR. LORRETTA
Executive. **Personal:** Born Oct 29, 1938, Baltimore, MD; married Leonard; children: Leonard Jr, Jeffrey & Kevin. **Educ:** Coppin State Univ, Baltimore, MD, BS, 1976. **Career:** Baltimore City Pub Schs, paraprofessional, 1966-70; Baltimore Teachers Union, chief negotiator, paraprofessional chmn, 1970-76, pres paraprofessional chap, 1975-2010; Am Fedn Teachers, intl vpres, 1978; Md Am Fedn Teachers, 1997-2009; Am Fedn Teachers, AFL-CIO, exec vpres, 2008-11, secy & treas, 2011-; Metrop Baltimore Coun, AFL-CIO Unions, vpres; Nat Alliance Black Sch Educr, corp rep; Personal Choice Benefits Inc, adv bd, currently. **Orgs:** Exec bd, Met AFL-CIO, 1978; cons res Better Schs, 1980; treas nat bd, A. Philip Randolph Inst, 2008; asst treas, Baltimore County chap Nat Asn Advan Colored People; bd dir, Blue-Green Alliance; bd dir, Union Privilege & Union Label & Serv Trades Dept; co-chair, Citizens Tax Justice; co-chair, Child Labor Coalition; bd dir, Faith & Polit Inst; bd dir, Inst Women's Policy Res; Am Income Life Labor Adv Bd; bd dir, Albert Shanker Inst, bd dir, AFL-CIO's Union Privilege orgn, bd dir, AFL-CIO Transp Trades Dept; treas, AFT Educ Found; chair, AFT Benefit Trust; bd dir, Munic Employees Credit Union, Baltimore; trustee, Md State & DC AFL-CIO; Master Your Card African Am Adv Bd. **Honors/Awds:** Community Service Award, United Way campaigh, 1976; Volunteer Service Award, MD State AFL-CIO COPE, 1977; Meritous Achievemnt Award, United Teachers New Orleans, 1977; Meritous Achievement Award, A Philip Randolph Inst, 1978; Labor Leader of the Year, Md Dem Party, 2005; Albert Shanker PSRP Pioneer Award; Service Award, Baltimore Teachers Unions paraprofessional chap; Hon Dr, Coppin state. **Special Achievements:** Ebony magazine featured her in an article titled "Blacks of Influence in Unions". **Home Addr:** 3207 Greenmeade Rd, Baltimore, MD 21244-1135, **Home Phone:** (410)655-3991. **Business Addr:** Secretary, Treasurer, American Federation of Teachers AFL-CIO, 555 NJ Ave NW, Washington, DC 20001, **Business Phone:** (202)879-4400.

### JOHNSON, DR. LUCIEN LOVE
Physician, cardiologist. **Personal:** Born Dec 26, 1941, New Orleans, LA; children: Lucien III, Kimberly & Yewande. **Educ:** Purdue Univ, BS, 1962; Howard Univ, MD, 1966. **Career:** Howard Univ, Internship, 1966-67; VA Long Beach Healthcare Syst, resident, 1969-73; Los Angeles Metrop Med Ctr, physician; Centinela Hosp Med Ctr; Brotman Med Ctr; pvt pract physician cardiologist, currently. **Orgs:** AMA; Nat Med Asn; Calif Med Asn; exec secy, Orgn Harmonisation Bus Law Africa. **Special Achievements:** Has written and published two articles in medical journals. **Business Addr:** Cardiologist, 3756 Santa Rosalia Dr Suite 424, Los Angeles, CA 90008, **Business Phone:** (323)292-0211.

### JOHNSON, LUTHER E.
Executive, graphic artist. **Personal:** Born Feb 23, 1966, Warrensville Heights, OH; son of Luther and Ann; married Althea; children: Brandon & Stephen. **Educ:** Ohio State Univ, 1986; African Am & African studies, 1987; Columbus Col Arts & Design, BFA, illus & fine art, 1989; Wayne State Univ, MA, 1998; Univ Phoenix, MBA, 2003. **Career:** Alexander Enterprises, art dir, 1989-91; Modeworks Inc, mural artist, 1992-94; Columbus Pub Schs, art instr, 1994-96; Art shows & accomplishments: Ohio State Univ, Columbus, OH, 1993-95; Columbus Christian Acad, Columbus, OH, 1995; Martin Luther King Ctr, Columbus, OH, 1995; 1 X-Design, mural artist, 1995-96; Wayne State Univ Tv, art dir, sr video & audio technician, 1996-2000; Malcolm Brown Gallery, Cleveland, OH, 1996; Chocolate Barbie Prods, Detroit, Mich, co-owner multi-media specialist, 1998; Compuware Corp, art dir, 2000-04; Elec Lizard, proj Mgr, UX designer, 2005-12; Chocolate Caramel Music LLC, dir mkt & prom, 2005-07; WhiteBlox Inc, IT Proj Mgr, 2005-08; Consol Graphics, tech proj mgr, 2008-10; Rovia Travel, independent rep, 2010; Earth Integrate, proj mgr, 2010; TEK Systs, user experience architect, 2012-13; United Services Automobile Association (USAA), user interface creative producer, 2013, currently. **Orgs:** Alpha Phi Alpha Fraternity, 1986; Great Lakes Info Archit Asn; Ohio State African-Am Alumni Network; Houston Bayou City Dance Assoc; San Antonio Pekiti-Tirsia Kali Club; Distinguished Gentlemen Houston; Bushido Kai Karate-Team Focus; Houston Bayou City Dance Assoc. **Home Phone:** (248)358-8789. **Business Addr:** User Interface Producer, United Services Automobile Association, 9800 Fredericksburg Rd, San Antonio, TX 78288, **Business Phone:** (210)531-8722.

### JOHNSON, MAGIC. See JOHNSON, EARVIN, JR.

### JOHNSON, MAMIE PEANUT
Baseball player, nurse, manager. **Personal:** Born Sep 27, 1935, Ridgeway, SC; daughter of Gentry Harrison and Della Belton Havelow; married Charles; children: Charlie. **Educ:** NC A&T Univ, nursing. **Career:** Baseball player (retired), manager, baseball coach; Wash Recreational Baseball League, St Cyrians team, 1940-50; Negro Leagues, Indianapolis Clowns, pitcher, 1953-55; nurse, 1950-90; Negro Baseball League's Memorabilia Shop, mgr, 1990-; All-star baseball teams, coach, currently. **Orgs:** Founder, They Played Baseball Found, 1999-. **Business Addr:** Founder, They Played Baseball Foundation, PO Box 1622, Mitchellville, MD 20717.

### JOHNSON, MARCO
College president, college administrator. **Personal:** married Sandra. **Educ:** Univ Hawaii, BS, polit sci & mkt; Aspen Univ, MEd. **Career:** Firefighter (retired), adminr; Los Angeles, City Fire Dept, firefighter, paramedic; EMT Prog, dir; Paramedic Prog, dir; CSA PrepStar, scouting dir; Antelope Valley Med Col, founder, pres & chief exec officer, currently. **Orgs:** Bd dir, bd mem, Antelope Valley Col Found; pres, Accrediting Bur Health Educ Schs; founder, Marco & Sandra Johnson Found. **Business Addr:** President, Director, Antelope Valley Medical College, 44201 10th St W, Lancaster, CA 93534, **Business Phone:** (661)726-1911.

### JOHNSON, MARGIE N.
Educator, dean (education). **Personal:** Born Aug 21, 1938, Jacksonville, TX; daughter of E J (deceased) and Vivian. **Educ:** Prairie View A&M Univ, RN/BS, 1960; Ind Univ, MS, 1963; Tex Woman's Univ, PhD, 1977. **Career:** Educator (retired); Jarvis Christian Col, Col nurse, 1960-61; Univ Calif, Los Angeles, Neuropsychiatric Div, staff nurse, 1961-62; Fort Dodge Col, intern, 1962-64; Wayne State Univ, asst prof, 1965-72; Dept Nursing, Univ Ibadan, Nigeria, dep dir, 1974-77; Nat Inst Ment Health, Doctoral Fel, 1975-77; Tex Woman's Univ, assoc prof, 1987-88; Tuskegee Univ, Sch Nursing& Allied Health, dean & prof, 1988-98. **Orgs:** Am Asn Cols Nursing; alt delegate Tex, Am Nurses Asn, 1962-; Nat League Nursing, 1968-; Sigma Theta Tau, 1976-; Phi Lambda Theta, 1978-88; Nat Black Nurses Asn, 1982-; Am Nurses Found, 1982-; Asn Black Nursing Fac Higher Educ, 1988-. **Home Addr:** PO Box 617 Rte 3, Jacksonville, TX 75766, **Home Phone:** (903)589-8190.

## JOHNSON, DR. MARGUERITE M. (MARGUERITE A JOHNSON)
School administrator. **Personal:** Born Sep 23, 1948, Wilmington, DE; daughter of Norris R Milburn (deceased) and Elizabeth; married George Stephen; children: Stephanie M & Stephen M. **Educ:** Morgan State Univ, Baltimore, BA, 1970; Ind Univ, Pa, MA, 1976; Temple Univ, Philadelphia, Pa, EdD, 1987. **Career:** Del Tech & Community Col, Northern Br, gen educ develop, instr, co-ordr, 1970-73, Stanton Campus, actg asst dir, continuing educ, 1973-75, asst dir continuing educ, 1975-79, Stanton Wilmington Campuses, actg dir continuing educ, dir continuing educ, 1979, off pres, exec dean instr & stud servs, 1992, Terry Campus, vpres, campus dir, 1994, sr adminr, contribr. **Orgs:** Am Asn Women Community Col; Am Asn Univ Women, Dover Chap; Nat NE Region, AACC Rotary Downtown Club, Dover; DE Cent Del Econ Develop Coun. **Honors/Awds:** Distinguished Kellog Fel, 1989-90; Outstanding Service Award, Nat Coun Black Am Affairs, Northeast Region, 1991; Special Service Award, Brandywine Prof Asn, 1991; Leadership Award, Asn Black Women Higher Educ, 1993; People To Watch, Delaware Today Mag, 1995. **Home Addr:** 1022 Quail Run, Wyoming, DE 19934-9509, **Home Phone:** (302)698-1626.

**JOHNSON, DR. MARIE LOVE. See Obituaries Section.**

## JOHNSON, MARJORIE LYNN
Association executive, lecturer, writer. **Personal:** Born Oct 26, 1961, Beloit, WI; married Dale B; children: Dale Austin. **Educ:** Spelman Col; Long Island Univ, JD. **Career:** Prudential-Bache Securities; Life Underwriters Training Coun; Stay At Home Mothers, founder & pres, 1994-. **Orgs:** Am Bar Asn. **Business Addr:** Founder, President, Stay At Home Mothers, 331 W 57th St Suite 313, New York, NY 10019, **Business Phone:** (212)501-6479.

## JOHNSON, MARK A.
Executive, president (organization). **Personal:** Born Aug 10, 1950, Washington, DC; son of Walter R and Charlotte M; married Vera Marie; children: Maya & Marci. **Educ:** Bowie State Univ, BS, 1972; Univ Md, MBA, 1979. **Career:** Suburban Trust Bank, employ mgr, 1972-75; Cent Intelligence Agency, personnel officer, 1975-77; AT & T Long Lines, acct supvr, 1977-80; Sallie Mae, vpres bus develop, 1980-97; Mark Johnson & Assocs, bus adv serv, pres, 1992-. **Orgs:** Kappa Alpha Psi Fraternity Inc, 1970-; bd dir, Black Ski, DC, 1984-; Nat Brotherhood Skiers, 1984-; Nat Black MBA Asn, 1990-; bd dir, Kappa Alpha Psi Found Md, 1991-; US Ski Coaches Asn, 1992-; US Ski Asn, 1992-; Nat Asn Advan Colored People, 1994-; Leadership Montgomery, 2008-. **Home Addr:** 12605 Pleasant Prospect Rd, Bowie, MD 20721, **Home Phone:** (301)218-8552. **Business Addr:** Member, Leadership Montgomery, 5910 Executive Blvd Suite 200, Rockville, MD 20852, **Business Phone:** (301)881-3333.

## JOHNSON, DR. MARK S.
Chairperson, medical researcher. **Personal:** Born Jun 3, 1951, Newark, NJ; son of Jay Robert and Ann Stevenson; married Marlyn; children: Asha Harare, Kwende Aaron, Zuri Anne & Maia. **Educ:** Coe Col, BA, black lit, 1974; Univ Md, NJ, Med Sch, Md, 1979; Univ NC Sch Pub Health, Chapel Hill, NC, MPH, 1984. **Career:** Univ S Ala Med Ctr, resident; Univ NC, Dept Family Med, Chapel Hill, Robert Wood Johnson clin scholar, clin instr, 1982-84; Meharry Med Sch, residency dir, 1984-86; Univ S Ala, asst dean, 1986-91; NJ Med Sch, Dept Family Med, fac, 1991-, clin prof & chair, currently; Howard Univ Col Med, dean, currently. **Orgs:** Nat Med Asn; Southwest Ala Sickle Cell, 1981-82, 1987-91; Am Acad Family Physicians, Am Pub Health Asn; NJ Acad Family Physicians; Asn Black Cardiologists; Int Soc Hypertension Blacks; Soc Teachers Family Med; CAS rep, AAMC; Nj Med Sch's Steering Comt; Nj Task Force Prev Obesity, 2002-06; Am Soc Hypertension; pres, Asn Depts Family Med, 2003-05. **Honors/ Awds:** America's Best Family Physicians; Top Docs in America; Mead Johnson Competitive Award, Nat Med Asn. **Special Achievements:** Author of numerous health articles, book chapters, and reviews; United States Preventive Services Task Force, member. **Home Addr:** 144 Liberty Corner Rd, Warren, NJ 07059, **Home Phone:** (908)604-6843. **Business Addr:** Chairman, Professor, New Jersey Medical School, 185 S Orange Ave, Newark, NJ 07103, **Business Phone:** (973)972-2111.

## JOHNSON, MARLENE E.
Government official, broadcaster. **Personal:** Born Jul 1, 1936, Milwaukee, WI; daughter of Edward Jay and Elizabeth Leher; married John Odom; children: Jan, Paula & Jay. **Educ:** Univ Wis, BS, 1979. **Career:** Boston Store, sales woman, 1954-64; WXIX-TV Channel 18 Milwaukee, TV hostess, 1962; Milwaukee Pub Sch Syst, social improv instr, 1966-70; First WI Natl Bank, teller, 1973-75; City Milwaukee, alderman, 1980-, alderwoman, 1980; WFOX AM; WAWA-AM. **Orgs:** Century mem, Boy Scouts Am Milwaukee Banner E Div, 1974-75; pres, Women's Aux Milwaukee Courier, 1975-76; bd dir, Bk fellows-Friends Milwaukee Pub Lib, 1976-80; div leader, Youth Womens Christian Asn Leader Luncheon, 1977; bd dir, Milwaukee Symphony Orches, 1977-80; life mem, Nat Asn Advan Colored People, 1980; Milwaukee Redevelop Auth, 1980-92; chair woman, 1980-92; bd dir vchmn, MECCA, 1988-92; vpres bd dir, Milwaukee United Way, 1988; bd dir, Milwaukee Conv & Vis Bur; OIC-GM; bd dir, Pabst Theater; Nat League Cities Comn & Econ Develop Steering Comn; vpres, WI League Munic Sixth Senate Dist; Milwaukee Area Tecnical Col Bd, 1990-92; bd dir, Pvt Indust Coun, 1990-91; comn, Milwaukee Metrop Sewerage Dist, 1994-95. **Honors/Awds:** Quota Buster Award, Youth Womens Christian Asn, 1975; Women in Our Lives, 1978; Milwaukee Women Today, 1979; Mayoral Proclamation, 1985; Milwaukee Realist Presidential Award, 1986; Citation by the Senate State of WI, 1987; Award of Excellence in Community Serv, CYD, 1990; Outstanding Public Service Award, Gamma Phi Delta, 1992; Inducted into African-American Biographies Hall of Fame, 1994. **Home Addr:** 2200 N Martin Luther King Jr Dr Apt B 55, Milwaukee, WI 53217, **Home Phone:** (414)264-0991.

## JOHNSON, DR. MARTIN LEROY
Educator, association executive. **Personal:** Born Dec 31, 1941, Westminster, SC; son of James Courtney and Beatrice Williams; married Jo Ann Clinkscales; children: Yolandra & Martin II. **Educ:** Morris Col Sumter, SC, BS, chem, 1962; Univ Ga, Athens, Ga, MEd, math, 1968, EdD, math, 1971. **Career:** Anderson, SC, math teacher & chmn, 1962-67; Univ Ga, grad asst, 1967-71; Rutgers Univ, asst prof math educ, 1971-72; Univ Md, asst prof, assoc prof, 1972-86, dir, Minorities Sci & Engineering Prog, 1979-80, dir, Dept Curric & Instr, 1980-85, prof educ, 1986-, Dept Curric & Inst, chair, 1994-2001, prof math, currently, Col Educ, Urban & Minority Educ, assoc dean, 2001, Md Inst Minority Achievement & Urban Educ, dir, founder, currently, Dept Curric & Instr, prof emer math educ, 2008. **Orgs:** Vpres, Res Coun Diag & Prescriptive Math, 1978-80; consult, Nat Sci Found, 1984-85, prog dir, 1985-87; pres, MD Coun Teachers Math, 1985-86; chair, Res Adv Comm, Nat Coun Teachers Math, 1988-89; ed bd mem, J Res Math Educ, 1991-94, chair, 1993-94; pres, Res CNL Diag & Prescriptive Math, 1993-95; Am Educ Res Asn; Benjamin Banneker Asn, 1997-99; Nat Asn Math; Asn Math Teacher Educr; MD Asn Teacher Educr; Nat Bd Dir, Sch Sci & Math Asn, 1998-2000; Campus Model Excellence, Univ MD, 2005. **Honors/Awds:** Mathematics Educator of the Year, MD Coun Teachers Math, 1989; Excellence Award, Black Fac & staff Asn, Univ MD, Col Park. **Special Achievements:** Author: Guiding Each Child's Learning of Math - Char Merill, 1983; co-author: A Diagnostic Approach to Instruction, K-8 elementary school mathematics textbooks, Mathematics In Action; "How Primary Children Think and Learn"; Changing the Faces of Mathematics: Perspectives on African Americans, has been recognized as a campus model of excellence by the Office of Multi-Ethnic Student Education (OMSE) Division of the University of Maryland in 2005; has edited numerous articles- Journal for Research in Mathematics Education, The Arithmetic Teacher, and NCTM publications. **Home Addr:** 12832 Forest Creek Ct, Sykesville, MD 21784-5526, **Home Phone:** (410)489-7135. **Business Addr:** Founder, University of Maryland College of Education, 0108AA Cole Stud Activ Bldg, College Park, MD 20742, **Business Phone:** (301)405-5211.

## JOHNSON, MARVIN R., JR.
Chief executive officer, president (organization). **Educ:** Univ Fla, BSc, mat engineering; Ga State Univ, MBA, decision sci. **Career:** Indus Int Inc, prod develop mgr; CipherLink Inc, pres & chief exec officer; Ikobo, pres & chief exec officer. **Business Addr:** President, Chief Executive Officer, CipherLink Inc, Bldg J 1827 Powers Ferry Rd, Atlanta, GA 30339-0000, **Business Phone:** (678)360-8701.

## JOHNSON, MARVIN R.
Chief executive officer, marine corps officer. **Educ:** Univ Fla, BS, mat eng; Ga State Univ, MBA, decision sci. **Career:** Nuclear submarine officer (retired), chmn & chief exec officer; USN, nuclear submarine officer, 1991-97; The Tenn Valley Authority; Brit Energy & Southern Calif; Edison; Cipher Link, co-founder & chief exec officer, 1999-2002; ikobo Inc, chief exec officer & co-founder, 2002-05; Nutrit Systs Inc, founder, chmn & chief exec officer, 2005-. **Business Addr:** Chief Executive Officer, Chairman, Nutrition Systems Inc, Bldg 100 2255 Cumberland Pkwy SE Suite 100, Atlanta, GA 30339, **Business Phone:** (678)360-8701.

## JOHNSON, MARYANN
Executive. **Personal:** Born Oct 11, 1948, Memphis, TN; daughter of William Edward and Maryann. **Educ:** Griggs Bus Col, attended 1968. **Career:** Jerry Butler Prods Inc, exec asst, pres; A&M Rec Inc, off mgr, Nat tour coordr, 1975-79; MJB Mgt Consult, pres, 1980; Lorimar TV Prods, exec asst, pres music; Twentieth Century Fox Film Corp, exec asst, off mgr, 1987-95, mgr, TV music admin, assoc dir, TV music admin, 1997, dir, TV music admin, 1998-. **Orgs:** Jr Achievement, sponsor, 1972-73; secy, Wilshire United Methodist Church, Coun Ministries, 1975-77; United Methodist Women, rep, 1978-; Nat Asn Advan Colored People, 1979-80; Nat Asn Female Exec, 1980; Nat Acad Rec Arts & Scis, 1985-; secy, Wilshire United Methodist Church, Coun Ministries, 1975-77; rep, United Methodist Women; Nat Asn Advan Colored People, 1979-80; Nat Asn Female Exec; Nat Acad Rec Arts & Scis; hon mem, Sigma Gamma Rho Sorority, 2008. **Home Addr:** 7111 Ramsgate Ave Apt 112, Westchester, CA 90045-2279. **Business Addr:** Director of TV Music Administration, Twentieth Century Fox Film Corp, 10201 W Pico Blvd Bldg 19/131, Los Angeles, CA 90035, **Business Phone:** (310)369-1000.

## JOHNSON, MATHEW
Educator, writer. **Personal:** Born Aug 19, 1970, Philadelphia, PA. **Educ:** Earlham Col, BA; Columbia Univ, MFA. **Career:** Writer, educator; MTV, copywriter; Temple Univ; Rutgers Univ; Roosevelt Univ; Columbia Univ; Bard Col, asst prof lit prog, writer, currently; Univ Houston, Dept Eng, Creative Writing Prog, asst prof, currently; Time Out mag, columnist, "Utter Matness"; Novels: Drop, 2000; Hunting in Harlem, 2003; John Constantine Hellblazer: Papa Midnite, 2006; The Great Negro Plot: A Tale of Conspiracy & Murder in Eighteenth-century New York, 2007; Incognegro, 2008; Dark Rain: A New Orleans Story, 2010; Pym, 2011; Right State, 2012; Anthologies: Gumbo: Anthology of African American Literature, 2002; Not Guilty: Twelve Black Men Speak Out on Law, Justice & Life, 2002; Mixed: An Anthology of Short Fiction on the Multiracial Experience, 2006; Black Cool: One Thousand Streams of Blackness, 2012. **Business Addr:** Assistant Professor, University of Houston, 205 Roy Cullen Bldg 4800 Calhoun Rd, Houston, TX 77004, **Business Phone:** (713)743-3004.

## JOHNSON, MELVIN CARLTON, III
**Personal:** Born Apr 15, 1972, Cincinnati, OH; children: Adonis. **Educ:** Univ Ky, grad. **Career:** Football player (retired); Tampa Bay Buccaneers, defensive back, 1995-97; Kans City Chiefs, defensive back, 1998.

## JOHNSON, DR. MELVIN RUSSELL
Physician, executive. **Personal:** Born Aug 26, 1946, Courtland, VA; married Joyce. **Educ:** Hampton Inst, BA, chem, 1968; Meharry Med Col, MD, 1972. **Career:** San Antonio Uniformed Serv Health Educ Consortium, resident internal med, 1972-75, fel pulmonary disease, 1978-80; Brooke Army Med Ctr, res internal med, 1972-73, residency hosp, 1975, fel, 1980; Cape Fear Valley Hosp, assoc staff internist, 1975-77; Womack Army Hosp, staff intern, 1976, chief pulmonary dis, 1976-77, chief dept med, 1977-80; Wm Beaumont Army Med Ctr, staff pulmonologist, asst ch pulmonary dis, 1980; pvt pract physician, currently; Sentara Healthcare, internal med physicians, currently. **Orgs:** Omega Psi Phi Frat, 1971; Nat Asn Resd & Interns, 1972; Am Col Physicians, 1973; C A Whittier Med Soc, 1973; Nat Med Asn, 1974; Am Med Asn, 1975. **Honors/Awds:** National Defense Ribbon, 1972; Fel, Pulmonary Dis Brooke AMC, 1978-80; Patients Choice Award, 2008. **Business Addr:** Physician, Private Practitioner, 3451 Victoria Blvd, Hampton, VA 23661-1545, **Business Phone:** (757)723-9380.

## JOHNSON, MERTHA RUTH
Educator. **Personal:** Born Jackson, MS; children: Victoria M. **Educ:** Jackson State Univ, BS, 1956; Univ San Francisco, MEd, 1977, MPA, 1983. **Career:** Chicago Sch Syst, educr, 1960-66; E Chicago Sch Syst, educr, 1967-70; Manpower Training Prog, adminr & teacher, 1966; OICW, adminr & teacher; San Mateo Sch Dist, educ, 1970-81; Neighborhood Housing Servs, exec dir, 1982-83; Atlanta Sch Syst, instr, currently. **Orgs:** Parlimentarian, Nat Coun Negro Women; Bus & Prof Women's Club; Atlanta Fedn Teachers; Nat Asn Advan Colored People; SCIC; consult, Lit Proj Black Cacus, Ga State Legis; Atlanta's Ministry Int Stud. **Home Addr:** 1445 Monroe Dr NE SF16, Atlanta, GA 30324. **Business Addr:** Instructor, Atlanta School System, 45 Whitehouse Dr SW, Atlanta, GA 30314, **Business Phone:** (404)802-4600.

## JOHNSON, MERVIL V.
Executive. **Personal:** Born Dec 20, 1953, Ft. Worth, TX. **Educ:** Tex Chritian Univ, BA, Span & Fr, 1976, MPA, polit sci & govt, 1982; Universite de Nice, cert, d'Attestation sur la gestion des entreprises, int bus studies, 1977. **Career:** Intl Teleph & Teleg, fel, 1976-77; City Ft Worth, admin asst, 1978-79; City Ft Worth Libr, span & fr instr, 1980-83; N Cent TX Coun Govts, reg clearing house coordr, 1980-84; N Cent TX Coun Govts, NCTCOG Urban fel, 1980-82; ICMA Retirement Corp, serv rep, 1984; Tarrant County Col, asst dean, 1988-89; Challenge Inc, proj dir, 1995-98; Tarrant County Fatherhood Coalition, Workforce Solutions, vice chmn, workforce collab mgr, 1998-, fact proj dir, 2011-, chmn, 2016-. **Orgs:** Phi Sigma Iota Soc Lang, 1975-; Intl City Mgt Asn, 1981-; Am Soc Pub Admin, 1981; chmn, Univ Liaison Urban Mgt Assts N TX, 1982-84; chmn, newsletter Conf Minority Pub Admin, 1983-84. **Honors/Awds:** Clarence E Ridley Scholar, TX City Mgt Asn, 1980-81; ICMA scholar, Intl City Mgt Asn, 1981. **Business Addr:** Vice Chairman, Project Director, Tarrant County Fatherhood Coalition, 1320 S University Dr Suite 600, Ft. Worth, TX 76107, **Business Phone:** (817)413-4438.

## JOHNSON, MICHAEL
Automotive executive, president (organization), chief executive officer. **Personal:** Born Sep 8, 1959, Detroit, MI; son of Ernestine and Eural; married Cheryl R Batchelor; children: Michael Byron. **Educ:** Wayne State Univ, BA, psychol, 1982; Univ Detroit Sch Law, JD, 1986. **Career:** Dreisbach Cadillac, serv rep, 1977-87; UAW, staff atty, 1987-89; Gen Motors, dealer cand, trainee, 1989-90; Durand Chevrolet Geo Pontiac Olds Inc, pres & chief exec officer, 1990-99; Rightway Mgt Consults, pres & owner, 1992-2003; Michael Chevrolet, pres & owner, 1999-2009; Mars Bar Detroit, pres & owner, 2010-15; Prestige Cadillac, used car mgr, 2015-. **Orgs:** State Bar Mich. **Business Addr:** Used Car Manager, Prestige Cadillac, 8333 E 11 Mile Rd, Warren, MI 48093, **Business Phone:** (586)782-4147.

## JOHNSON, MICHAEL ANTHONY
Educator. **Personal:** Born Jan 15, 1951, New York, NY; children: Dieynaba. **Educ:** NY City Tech Col, AA, 1971; City Col NY, premed, 1973; Empire State Col, BS, sci educ, 1985. **Career:** Sci Skills Ctr Inc, exec dir, 1980, prin, 1996; DMC Energy, consult, 1981-84; Energy Task Force, sci writer, 1982-83; NY City Tech Col, res proj, 1983-84. **Orgs:** Pres, Stud Alumni Asn, Empire State Col, 1982-86; NY Acad Scis; AAAS. **Home Addr:** 345 Lincoln Pl, Brooklyn, NY 11238, **Home Phone:** (718)789-7105. **Business Addr:** NY.

## JOHNSON, MICHAEL DUANE
Athlete, journalist, executive. **Personal:** Born Sep 13, 1967, Dallas, TX; son of Paul Sr and Ruby; married Kerry Doyen; children: Sebastian. **Educ:** Baylor Univ, BA, mkt, bus, 1990. **Career:** Athlete (retired), journalist, executive; US Olympic Team, track & field, 1992 & 1996, athlete, 2000; Baylor Track & Field, consult; BBC, UK, tv athletics pundit; Daily Tel, column writer; Ultimate Performance, founder, currently; Michael Johnson Performance, pres, founder, 2007-. **Special Achievements:** Acted in a film The Master of Disguise, 2002. **Business Addr:** President, Michael Johnson Performance, 6051 Alma Dr, McKinney, TX 75070, **Business Phone:** (469)424-6572.

## JOHNSON, MICHAEL L.
Lawyer, executive. **Personal:** Born Aug 1, 1958, Bonn; son of Martinus and Barbara; married Andrea H; children: Christopher M, Carl M & Alyse M. **Educ:** Berklee Col, BS, music educ, 1979; Wayne St Univ, MEd, 1981; Univ Mich, Law Sch, JD, 1986. **Career:** Dickinson Wright, Law Firm, atty assoc, 1986-89; Ameritech, Advert Serv, atty, 1989-92; Ameritech-Mich, regulatory atty, 1993-94, Tel Indust Serv, vpres gen coun, 1994; Pay Phone Serv, vpres gen coun, 1994; Gen Elec Co, sales person; NYNEX Corp, regional sales vpres; Satellite Imaging Corp, vpres sales & bus develop, 2006-. **Orgs:** Mich St Bar, 1986-; Am Bar Asn, 1987-; Detroit Bar Asn, 1987-94; Wolverine Bar Asn, 1987-93; Ill St Bar, 1994-; Chicago Bar Asn, 1995-. **Home Addr:** 1757 Tanager Way, Long Grove, IL 60047-5158, **Home Phone:** (847)540-1115. **Business Addr:** Vice President of Sales & Business Development, Satellite Imaging Corp, 12777 Jones Rd, Houston, TX 77070-4671, **Business Phone:** (832)237-2900.

## JOHNSON, MICHELE
Salesperson. **Personal:** Born Aug 12, 1959, Brooklyn, NY. **Educ:** Boston Univ, BS, 1981; Fordham Univ. **Career:** CBS Inc, clippings coord, 1981-82, admin asst, 1982-83, sr sales asst, 1983-86; JP Martin Assoc Inc, exec asst, 1986-87; Taylor Made Press, sales rep. **Orgs:** CBS Black Employ Assoc, 1981-86; Nat Assoc Black MBA's, 1986-; Assoc MBA Execs, 1986-; Advantage Club NY, 1986-; dir, Union Bapt Church Youth Comn, 1986-; volunteer Roosevelt Ctr Comn Growth,

1987-. **Home Addr:** 148 Elmwood Ave, Roosevelt, NY 11575, **Home Phone:** (516)623-1677. **Business Addr:** Sales Representative, Taylor Made Press, 100 Water St, Brooklyn, NY 11201, **Business Phone:** (718)858-1668.

### JOHNSON, MILDRED H.

Educator. **Personal:** Born Cleveland, OH; daughter of Owena Bradshaw; married John B. **Educ:** WVa State Col, BA; Wayne State Univ, MA; Univ Detroit, MA. **Career:** Detroit Metrop Mutual Ins Co, off mgr, 1948-63; Detroit Pub Schs, teacher, 1963-76, learning disability teacher, 1976-80, teacher consult, 1980-89; Educ Guid Tutoring Ctr, dir & owner, 1986-. **Orgs:** Phi Delta Kappa Hons Fraternity; Nat Asn Negro Bus & Prof Women; Gamma Phi Delta Sorority; Womens Div, United Negro Col Fund. **Home Addr:** 19167 Sorrento St, Detroit, MI 48235-1231, **Home Phone:** (313)342-8156. **Business Addr:** Owner, Director, Education Guidance Tutoring Center Inc, 17500 W McNichols St, Detroit, MI 48235.

### JOHNSON, MILTON D.

Executive. **Personal:** Born May 27, 1928, Sour Lake, TX; married Robbie Russell; children: Paula & Pamela. **Educ:** Paul Quinn Col, BBA, 1951. **Career:** Victoria, TX, teacher, 1956-64; Union Carbide Corp, employee rels assoc, 1964-. **Orgs:** Bd educ, La Marque Ind Schs, 1972-; pres, C C, 1974; chmn adv bd, First State Bank Hitchcock, TX. **Home Addr:** 7309 Mockingbird Lane, Texas City, TX 77591-3528, **Home Phone:** (409)363-9377. **Business Addr:** PO Box 471, Texas City, TX 77590.

### JOHNSON, MIRIAM B.

Businessperson. **Personal:** Born Washington, DC; married Norman B. **Educ:** Miner Teachers Col, Wash, DC; Brooklyn Col, attended 1972. **Career:** Black Music makers Inc, exec dir; Husband's Law Off, off mgr. **Orgs:** Vol secy, Nat Asn Advan Colored People, Brooklyn Br; bd dir, Brooklyn Asn Ment Health; exec bd, Brooklyn Bur Comn Serv; chairperson, Ment Health Comt Health Syst Agency Dist Bd; Urban Comn Episcopal Diocese, Long Island; parliamentarian historian, Brooklyn Lawyers Wives; prog chairperson, Greater NY Links Inc; former mem, Rels Comt Cent YWCA; exec bd, Stuyvesant Comm Ctr; community coun, Medgar Evers Col; New York Community Bd No 8; gen chmn, City Wide Com Looking Glass Ball a fund raising play ballconstruct & devel Mac Donough St Comm Ctr, Bedford-Stuyvesant. **Honors/Awds:** Community Service Award, Berean Baptist Church, 1950 & 1974; NY Amsterdam News; Mac Donough St Comm Ctr, 1963; Awarded Baccalaureate Degree in Sociology Cum Laude. **Home Addr:** 46 Hampton Pl 2 Fl, Brooklyn, NY 11213, **Home Phone:** (718)778-3769.

### JOHNSON, MITCHELL ALLEN (MITCH JOHNSON)

College teacher, football player, executive director. **Personal:** Born Mar 1, 1942, Chicago, IL; son of Mitchell and Marcella; children: Mitchell Matthew & Margo K. **Educ:** Univ Calif Los Angeles, BA, 1965. **Career:** Football player, school administrator (retired), executive director; Wash Redskins, prof football player, 1973; Stud Loan Mkt Asn, sr vpres, 1973-94; MAJ Capital Mgt Inc, pres, 1994-; Eldorado Bankshares Inc, dir; Fed Agr Mortgage Corp, dir, financial consult, 1997-. **Orgs:** Founding pres, Wash Asn Money Managers, 1982-; bd dir, Arena Stage, 1987-; bd dir, Mentors Inc, 1990-; bd dir, Nat Rehab Hosp; trustee, Citizen Investment Trust; trustee, Citizens Funds; trustee, Advisors' Inner Circle Fund; trustee, Nat Capital Region; trustee, Dc Retirement Bd; trustee, FBR Fund, 2001-. **Business Addr:** Director, Federal Agricultural Mortgage Corp, 1999 K St NW 4th Fl, Washington, DC 20006, **Business Phone:** (800)879-3276.

### JOHNSON, NANCY ALINE FLAKE

Television producer, educator, artistic director. **Personal:** Born Jul 23, 1956, Detroit, MI; daughter of Thomas M and Margaret E. **Educ:** Howard Univ, BBA, acct, 1977; DePaul Univ, MS, taxation, 1981. **Career:** Arthur Andersen & Co, sr tax acct, 1977-80; pub acct, 1979-; Laventhol & Horwath, tax acct supvr, 1980-81; Coopers & Lybrand, tax acct mgr, 1981-84; Howard Univ, assoc prof taxation, Small Bus Develop Ctr, dir, exec dir, 1984-94; Small Bus Mag, exec producer & co-host, 1987-; NAFJ & Assocs Llc, 1994-2008; Detroit Urban League Inc, vpres, 2006-08; Urban League Greater Atlanta, pres & chief exec officer, 2008-. **Orgs:** Adv, Jr Achievement, 1979-86; treas, Nat Black MBA Asn, 1983; pres, Nat Asn Black Accts, 1984-85; bd mem, Nat Asn Negro Bus & Prof Womens Clubs; Econ Develop Corp, 1984-87; chairwoman, Bus Comm DC Chamber Com, 1986-87; bd mem, DC Chamber Com, 1987-; coun mem, Mayor Barry's Coord Coun Self Sufficiency, 1985-; comnr, DC Comn Women, 1987-90; Nat Asn Black Accts; Delta Sigma Pi Frat, 1988-; chair, Alternatives Welfare Comt, 1989-; exec dir, Howard Univ Small Bus Develop Ctr; bd mem, City Atlanta Workforce Develop Bd, 2010-; Howard Univ Entrepreneurship Inst. **Home Addr:** 201 Bates St NW, Washington, DC 20001, **Home Phone:** (202)462-4654. **Business Addr:** President, Chief Executive Officer, Urban League of Greater Atlanta, 229 Peachtree St NE Suite 300, Atlanta, GA 30303-1600, **Business Phone:** (404)659-1150.

### JOHNSON, NATHANIEL J., SR. (NATE J JOHNSON)

Educator. **Personal:** Born Oct 1, 1940, Philadelphia, PA; son of Lucius James and Violet Beatrice Branch; married Fannie Mary Long. **Educ:** LaSalle Univ, Philadelphia, PA, BA, comp & info sci, 1990; Univ Tex, Austin, TX, MBA, 1993; Mass Inst Technol, MA; Brooklyn Polytech Univ, NY, Exec Masters Prog, MS, telecommunications & info mgt, 1999. **Career:** Kirk Eng Corp, math technician, 1965-67; Sch Dist Philadelphia, programmer, 1967-68; RCA Corp, New York, NY, sr systs, 1968-70; Electronic Data Systs, New York, NY, systs engr, 1970-72; Hertz Corp, New York, NY, New York Data Ctr, mgr, 1973-80; Amerada Hess Corp, Woodbridge, NJ, mgr comput servs, 1980-83; SCT Resource Mgt Corp, Malvern, Pa, exec dir, comput serv, 1983-87; Milwaukee County, Milwaukee, WI, Info Mgt Serv Div, mgr, 1987-88; Prairie View Agr & Mech Univ, exec dir info systs, 1990-94; Law Sch Admis Coun, chief info officer, 1994-95; Info Systs Group, dir, 1994-95; Nat Exchange Carrier Asn, chief technol officer, 1997-98; Mass Inst Technol, dir IT telecommunications & network servs, 2000-03, chief network officer, 2001-04; Miami Univ, Comput & Commun Serv, exec dir, sr dir, 2004-05; NJJ Assoc, owner, pres, 2006-12. **Orgs:** Fin Aide Adv Comt, Wayne County Community Col, 1984-85; Asn Comput Mach, 1987-88; Soc Info Mgt, 1987-88; Govt Mgt Info Systs, 1987-88; Plant Mgt Asn, 1987-88; Minorities Comput Related Occup, 1987-88; MIS Curric Adv Bd, Marquette Univ, 1987-88; bd dir, Tex Asn State Supported Comput & Commun, 1992-; Asn Comput Mach, 1994-95; Marquette Univ, Comput Sci Curric Comt, 1994-95; Soc Info Mgt, 1995; Info Technol Client Coun, 1995; Diversity Team, Nat Exchange Carrier Asn, 1997-98; Int Facil Mgt Asn, 1998-99; Asn Col & Univ Adminrs, 2000-05; Info Technol Fin Mgt Asn, 2000-05; Steering Comt, Common Solutions Group, 2002-03. **Home Addr:** 12638 Rifleman Trl, Cypress, TX 77429-2630, **Home Phone:** (713)890-4286. **Business Addr:** Owner, NJJ Associates, 4524 Lakes Edge Apt 24, West Chester, OH 45069-8678, **Business Phone:** (617)201-4322.

### JOHNSON, NIESA EVETT

Basketball player, basketball coach. **Personal:** Born Feb 7, 1973, Clinton, MS. **Educ:** Univ Ala, BA, human health serv, 1995. **Career:** Basketball player (retired), basketball coach; USBWA, from jr guard to sr guard, 1994-95; WBB News Serv, sr guard, 1995; Long Beach Stingrays, guard, 1996-98; Seattle Reign, 1998; Charlotte Sting, guard, 1999-2001; Detroit Shock, guard, 2001; N ridge Matadors, Calif State Univ, asst coach.

### JOHNSON, NORMAN B.

Lawyer. **Personal:** Born Lake Charles, LA; married Julius A. **Educ:** DC Teachers Col, BS, 1955; Georgetown Univ Law Ctr, JD, 1962. **Career:** Dept Justice, trial atty, 1963-67; DC, asst corp coun, 1967-70; Super Ct DC, judge, 1970-. **Orgs:** Dir, Am Judicature Soc; dir, Nat Asn Women Judges; Nat Asn Black Women Attys; Nat Bar Asn; Wash Bar Asn; Am Bar Asn. **Home Addr:** 46 Hampton Pl, Brooklyn, NY 11213, **Home Phone:** (718)778-3769. **Business Addr:** 79 Decatur St, Brooklyn, NY 11216.

### JOHNSON, DR. NORRIS BROCK

College teacher, educator. **Personal:** Born Apr 29, 1942, Chicago, IL. **Educ:** Mich State Univ, BA, eng & art, 1965, MA, am lit, 1967, MA, anthrop, 1972, PhD, anthrop, 1976. **Career:** Univ NC, Chapel Hill, Dept Anthrop, fac mem, 1977, from asst prof to assoc prof, 1979-91, prof, 1992-; Univ Tokyo & Waseda Univ, Tokyo, Japan, Fulbright Hays lectr, 1985-86; 13th Century Zen Buddhist Temples & Temple Gardens, res, 1985-86; NC State Univ, Sch Archit, Dept Landscape Design, vis assoc prof, 1988; Spencer Found grant, 1990; Zen Buddhist Temple Gardens, Kyoto, Japan, res, 1992, 1998; Inst Res Social Sci, Univ NC, res grant & curric technol enhancement grant, 2000; Penland Sch Crafts, resident scholar, 2003-, prof, currently; Pilgrimage Press Inc, contribr. **Orgs:** Fac assoc, Nat Humanities Fac, 1980-; fel Am Anthrop Asn, 1980-; fel Inst Arts & Humanities, Univ NC, 1989, 1997; fel Landscape Archit Dumbarton Oaks, Wash, DC, 1990-91; Chapman fel, Inst Arts & Humanities, Univ NC, 1994; Asn Black Anthropologists; bd mem, Soc Humanistic Anthrop. **Home Addr:** 5716 Hideaway Dr, Chapel Hill, NC 27516, **Home Phone:** (919)929-2319.

### JOHNSON, OLRICK

Singer, football player, executive. **Personal:** Born Aug 20, 1977, Miami, FL; son of Lena; married Amirah Brown. **Educ:** Fla A&M Univ, theater educ. **Career:** Football player (retired), singer, executive; Minn Vikings, linebacker, 1999; NY Jets, linebacker, 1999; New Eng Patriots, linebacker, 2000; Olyric Ent, pres, 2003-10, chief exec officer, 2004-; Video appearances: "Brighter Day"; "Shook"; "Happy & You Know It"; "NFL Super Bowl XXXVI & XXXVII Gospel Fest", Word Network, BET; "NFL Kick Off Bash"; "Deco Drive"; Albums: Bless My Soul, 2004; How Did We Get Here; Guest host, Champs Sports Tv; Nat Football League Choir, music dir, currently; Pro Image sports Franchise, owner, 2012-. **Honors/Awds:** Miami Herald Scholar Athlete; Miami Herald All-Dade County; Knight Award, Miami Herald; Miami Times Scholar Athlete Award; Hall of Fame, FAMU Sports, 2010. **Business Addr:** Owner, Singer, Olyric Entertainment, 5925 NE 80 Ave, Portland, OR 97218-2891, **Business Phone:** (503)595-3000.

### JOHNSON, HON. OTIS SAMUEL

School administrator, mayor. **Personal:** Born Mar 26, 1942, Savannah, GA; son of Lillian Brown Spencer and Otis. **Educ:** Armstrong State Col, AA, 1964; Univ Ga, AB, 1967; Clark Atlanta Univ, MSW, 1969; Brandeis Univ, Heller Sch Social Policy & Mgt, PhD, 1980. **Career:** City Savannah Model Cities Prog, dep dir, 1969-71; Simmons Col Social Work, spec instr, 1975-76; Savannah State Col, asst prof, 1976-80, assoc prof, 1981-87, prof, 1987-91, Dept Soc Sci, head, 1980-84, Dept Social Work, 1985-88, prof social work & sociol, 1987-91, Sch Social Sci & Lib Arts, 1998; City Savannah, alderman, 1982-88; Housing Authority Savannah, comnr, 1989; Chatham Savannah Youth Futures Authority, exec dir, 1988-98; Savannah City, mayor, 2004-12; Savannah State, dean Sch Social Work. **Orgs:** Acad Cert Social Workers, 1971-; secy, Ga Chap, Nat Asn Social Workers, 1984-86; bd dir, Nat Coun Community Ment Health Ctr, 1988-91; Am Legion; Black Community Crusade C; C's Defense Fund; Nat Community Bldg Network; chair, bd mem, Mary Reynolds Babcock Found, 1996-; Asn Study Afro-Am Life & Hist; Cent Baptist Church Trustee; Alpha Kappa Delta Socio Hon Soc; Pi Gamma Mu Social Sci Hon Fraternity; Aspen Roundtable Comprehensive Community Chg; chair, MDC. **Honors/Awds:** Social Worker of the Year, SEGA, Nat Asn Social Workers, 1984; Social Worker of the Year, Ga Chap, Nat Asn Social Workers, 1995; Named Healthy Hero by Amerigroup Community Care, 2008. **Special Achievements:** First African American to graduate from A.E. Beach High School. **Home Addr:** 816 Maupas Ave, Savannah, GA 31401, **Home Phone:** (912)232-7735. **Business Addr:** Mayor, Savannah City, Civic Ctr, Savannah, GA 31401, **Business Phone:** (912)651-6550.

### JOHNSON, PAMELA. See ROSHELL, PAMELA P.

### JOHNSON, PARKER COLLINS

School administrator. **Personal:** Born Oct 17, 1961, Boston, MA; son of John Quincy III and Addie Collins. **Educ:** Williams Col, BA, sociol & African Am studies, 1984; Harvard Univ, Cambridge, MA, MEd, 1990. **Career:** Fitchburg State Col, asst dir admis, 1984-85; Bentley Col, asst dir admis, 1985-87; Tufts Univ, Medford, Mass, asst dir admis, 1987-89; Harvard Univ, Cambridge, Mass, grad stud, 1989-90; Am Coun Educ, Wash, DC, researcher, 1990; Calif State Univ, Northridge, Calif, counr, 1990-92; Gettysburg Col, Cult Advan, dean, 1992-96, teacher; Asn Am Cols & Univs, assoc dir curric, 1996-; Univ Southern Calif, Ctr Higher Educ Policy Anal, res asst, 1998; Univ Brit Columbia, coordr, 2002-04, teacher, stud develop officer; Soc Intercultural Educ Training & Res, secy, currently; The Neutral Zone Consult Serv Inc, consult; SIETAR BC, vpres; Vancouver, Equal Employ Opportunity Off; Inst for Am Cultures at Univ of Calif, coordr; Royal Roads Univ; Pac Oaks Col; Summer Inst for Intercultural Commun; Antioch Univ, intercultural commun. **Orgs:** Nat Asn Col Admis Counselors, 1984-89; Greater Boston Inter Univ Coun, 1985-89; vpres, bd dir, Fitchburg Comt Action Ctr, 1985; mem-at-large, New Eng Consortium Black Admis counselors, 1985-89; vol, Boston Youth Risk, 1986-89; external co-chair, New Eng Consortium Black Admis Counselors, 1987-89; Am Asn Higher Educ, 1987-; Trans Africa Boston Chap, 1987-90; bd mem, Mass Pre-Engineering Prog, 1988-90; YMCA; comt mem, Int Progs Comt, 1989-94; exec adv, SIETAR BC; sr res fel, Asn Am Cols & Univs; adv, Vancouver; adv comt, African Am Studies. **Home Addr:** PO Box 341439, Los Angeles, CA 90034, **Home Phone:** (213)287-2849. **Business Addr:** Secretary, The University of British Columbia, 410 - 5950 University Blvd, Vancouver, BC V6T 1Z3, **Business Phone:** (604)822-1444.

### JOHNSON, PATRICE DOREEN

Journalist, editor. **Personal:** Born Jul 17, 1952, New York, NY; daughter of Irma Levy and Wilbourne. **Educ:** Barnard Col, BA, eng, 1974; Columbia Univ Grad Sch Jour, MSJ, 1976. **Career:** Encore Am & Worldwide News, assoc ed, 1976-80; Black News Mag; Newsweek Mag, researcher & reporter, 1981-96; Money Mag, reporter, 1997-2001; NYC Dept Educ, sec Eng & journalism, teacher, 2005-2007; Kaplan K12 Learning Serv, copy editing & proofreading, 2008-2010; independent contractor, freelance journalist, currently. **Home Addr:** 355 W 85 St, New York, NY 10024, **Home Phone:** (212)595-0683.

### JOHNSON, PATRICIA ANITA (PAT JOHNSON)

School administrator, administrator, executive director. **Personal:** Born Mar 17, 1944, Chicago, IL; children: David & Todd. **Educ:** Oberlin Col, BA, 1961; US Int Univ, MFA, 1985. **Career:** Am art adminr; Brockman Gallery Prods, cur, 1976-78; New Visions Gallery, owner, 1978-82; Multicultural Arts Inst, cur, 1982-83; San Diego Community Col Dist, cult affairs coordr, 1982-85; Grad Sch Community Devel, fel, 1983; Chicago Dept of Cult Affairs, chicago Artists Int Prog, comnr & dir, 1983-93; S Dallas Cult Ctr City Arts Prog, dir, 1985-, mgr, 1986; Jamaica Ctr Arts, exec dir, 1988-92; UNESCO & US Dept State, arts & cult orgn, consult; Mus African Diaspora, dir. **Orgs:** Exhib consult, Multicultural Arts Inst, 1981-83; grant recipient, CA Arts Coun, 1983-85; Catfish Club San Diego, 1983-85; adv comt, San Diego Arts Festival Bd, 1985; bd mem, City San Diego Pub Arts Adv Bd, 1985; founder, INROADS an organ Black Prof Singles, 1985. **Home Addr:** 4340 Williamsburg Rd, Dallas, TX 75220-1932, **Home Phone:** (903)223-9202. **Business Addr:** Executive Director, South Dallas Cultural Center, 1925 Elm St, Dallas, TX 75201, **Business Phone:** (214)670-3687.

### JOHNSON, PATRICIA DUREN

Government official, executive. **Personal:** Born Oct 22, 1943, Columbus, OH; daughter of James and Rosetta J; married Harold H Jr; children: Jill. **Educ:** Ohio State Univ, Columbus, BS, educ, 1965; Univ Mich, Grad Sch Mgt, Ann Arbor, MI, attended 1984. **Career:** Teacher, 1966-72; ITT Hartford, Portland, Ore, sales rep, 1972-73; UHP Healthcare, Managed Healthcare Servs, vpres; Wellpoint Health Networks, gen mgr & sr vpres govt serv; Blue Cross Calif, Woodland Hills, Calif, sr vpres govt serv, 1975-1992, nat mkt officer, gen mgr; P Johnson & Assocs, pres, currently; Qual & Productivity Comn, Los Angeles, Calif, comnr, 1977-. **Orgs:** Pres, Delta Sigma Theta Sorority, 1964-65; Am Hosp Asn, 1976-; Women Health Admin, 1979-; bd dir, Am Cancer Soc, 1988-92; trustee, Calif Hosp Found; community adv bd KCET. **Home Addr:** 2916 Oakhurst Ave, Los Angeles, CA 90034, **Home Phone:** (310)559-2143. **Business Addr:** Commissioner, Quality & Productivity Commission, 565 Kenneth Hahn Hall Admin, Los Angeles, CA 90012, **Business Phone:** (213)974-1431.

### JOHNSON, PATRICIA L.

Educator, lawyer. **Personal:** Born Jan 29, 1956, New York, NY; daughter of Mamie. **Educ:** John Jay Col, BA, 1977, MA, 1979; Cornel Univ Sch Law, pre-law prog, 1978; Rutgers Sch Law Newark, JD, 1985; Off Ct Admin NY Frontline Leadership, cert, 1988. **Career:** Bur Alcohol Tobacco & Firearms, stud aide, 1977; US Res Serv, br mgr, 1979-82; Bronx Family Ct, notifications supvr, 1982-83; Bronx Dist Attys Off, legal asst, 1983-85; Judicial Friends, law intern, 1985, asst dist atty, 1985-86; Bronx Pub Admin Off, assoc coun, 1986-88; John Jay Col Criminal Justice, New York, NY, adj prof, 1986; Lex Newspaper, Bus Mgr; Bronx Surrogate's Ct, Bronx, NY, dep chief clerk, 1988-. **Orgs:** Black Women Attys, 1981-; Nat Bar Asn, 1983-; Phi Alpha Delta Law Frat Int, 1983-; Prof Bus Women, 1985-; Nat Asn Advan Colored People, 1985-; Nat Women's Polit Caucus, 1985-; Asn Black Law Students Serv Black Comn, 1985; Black Entertainment & Sports Lawyers Asn, 1986-; rec sec, Black Bar Asn Bronx Co, 1986-; corresp sec chair prog bd, Black Bar Bronx, 1987-89; exec dir, founder, Black Entertainment &, Sports Tribune, 1989-; Big Sister, Big Sisters Inc, 1989; chairperson, Entertainment & Sports Law Comm Metrop Black Bar Asn, 1989-; SEEK Soc; Black Star. **Home Addr:** PO Box 813, Bronx, NY 10451-0813, **Home Phone:** (212)874-5300. **Business Addr:** Professor, John Jay College of Criminal Justice, Rm 422T 899 10th Ave, New York, NY 10019, **Business Phone:** (212)237-8000.

### JOHNSON, REV. DR. PAUL EDWIN

Psychologist. **Personal:** Born Dec 27, 1933, Buffalo, NY; son of Maggie J; married Shirley Ann Williams; children: Paula Rene & Darryl Edwin. **Educ:** Talladega Col, AB, Psychol, 1955; Harvard Univ, MS,

Psychol, 1957; Hartford Sem Fed, MDiv, 1958; Auburn Univ, MEd, Couns Psychol, 1974, EdD, Counc Psychol, 1980. **Career:** Psychologist (retired); N congregational Church, assoc minister, 1958-62, assoc pastor, 1958-61; AUs, chaplain (ltc, ret) 1962-82; AL Dept MH & MR, MR Div, consult II, 1972-79, dir qual assurance, 1979-94; pvt pract psychologist & minister; Congregational-Christian Church, Montgomery, Ala, 1980-94; Ala Dept Pub Safety-Acad, consult, 1983-85; Ala Coun Higher Educ, consult, 1984-85; Montgomery Bd Edn, consult, 1986-88. **Orgs:** Bd dir, Montgomery Coun Aging, 1982-84; chmn, Legis Strike Force Am Ment Health Coun Asn, 1983-84; pres, Ala Ment Health Coun Asn, 1983-84; exec comn, Montgomery Area United Way, 1984-86; chair, Ala Bd Examiners Coun, 1986-91; Delta Phi Kappa; Alpha Phi Alpha. **Home Addr:** 1211 S Que Way Apt 12-108, Denver, CO 80231-8031.

### JOHNSON, PAUL LAWRENCE
Photojournalist. **Personal:** Born Oct 27, 1943, Savannah, GA; married Angelyne Russell; children: Monifa Ife & Ayeola Binta. **Educ:** Matriculated Savannah State Col; Univ Ghana; Univ S Ill; Univ Fla. **Career:** Acad Black Cult Inc, co-founder, dir Savannah Model Cities Cult Ctr, 1969-72; profthree free TV pub serv progs, 1971-72; KTUL-TV, news photogr; Pafala LLC. **Orgs:** Bd dir, Inner City Community Ctr, 1970-72; art instr, local cap agency, EOA, 1970; slide lect, Savannah State Col, pub schs & libr; PUSH; Asn Study African Am Life & Hist; Nat Asn Advan Colored People. **Home Addr:** PO Box 10243, Savannah, GA 31412. **Business Addr:** News Photographer, KTUL-TV, PO Box 8, Tulsa, OK 74101-0008, **Business Phone:** (918)445-8888.

### JOHNSON, PAUL LAWRENCE
Judge. **Personal:** Born Sep 23, 1931, Coatesville, PA; married Dorothy Elizabeth Flowers; children: Bruce Michael & Darryl Lawrence. **Educ:** St Paul's Col, attended 1953. **Career:** Judge (retired); Lukens Steel Co, shearman, 1957-63; estimator, 1963-70; Timestudy Tech, 1970-84; Coatesville City Coun, pres, 1980-85; Supreme Ct Pa, dist justice, 1985-93. **Orgs:** Bd mem, Citadel Fed Credit Union, 1972-; pres & trustee, Hutchinson Church, 1972; bd, 1983-88, 1996-, pres, 1998-2000, Coatesville Sr Citizens Ctr; pres, Lancaster Co Chap Credit Unions, 1984-87; United Way, 1987-90; City Coatesville Authority, 1998-; exec bd, Brandyville YMCA, 1999-; pres, Coatesville Area Sch Dist. **Honors/Awds:** Outstanding Community Service Award J Frederic Wiese, 1984. **Home Addr:** 514 Elm St, Coatesville, PA 19320-3216, **Home Phone:** (610)384-8326.

### JOHNSON, PEPPER (THOMAS PEPPER JOHNSON)
Football player, football coach, executive. **Personal:** Born Jul 29, 1964, Detroit, MI; married Shanna; children: Dionte & Aanjeya. **Educ:** Ohio State Univ, coun & phys educ. **Career:** Football player (retired), football coach, exec; New York Giants, linebacker & left inside linebacker & right inside linebacker, 1986-92; Cleveland Browns, left linebacker & mid linebacker, 1993-95; Detroit Lions, mid linebacker, 1996; New York Jets, left inside linebacker & mid linebacker, 1997-98; New Eng Patriots, asst coach, 2000, inside linebackers coach, 2001-03, defensive line coach, 2004-11, linebackers coach, 2012-13; Pepper Johnson Enterprises, founder; Buffalo Bills, defensive line coach, 2014-. **Orgs:** March Dimes; Make a Wish Found; C's Leukemia Found; Pepper Johnsons Youth Found; Michael Landon Found; Carol M Baldwin Breast Cancer Res Found; Dylan MalaMala Cystic Fibrosis Found; Trey Whitfield Found. **Honors/Awds:** Pro Bowl selection, 1990, 1994; Super Bowl champion; Ohio State Hall of Fame, 2001. **Home Addr:** , Providence, RI. **Business Addr:** Defensive Line Coach, Buffalo Bills, 1 Bills Dr, Orchard Park, MA 14127, **Business Phone:** (716)648-1800.

### JOHNSON, PHYLLIS CAMPBELL
Government official, administrator. **Personal:** Born Jul 21, 1954, Ft. Worth, TX; daughter of Mira G and Ann Miller. **Educ:** Univ Tex, BA, commun, 1979, MA, urban affairs, 1984. **Career:** Tex Instruments, mfg supvr, 1979-82; N Cent Tex Coun Govts, urban fel, 1984; City Ft Worth, Tex, human serv coordr, 1984-87, admin asst, 1987-88, fiscal serv admin, 1988-; City Ft Worth, Police Dept, asst pub safety support mgr. **Orgs:** Kappa Delta Pi Hon Soc, Univ Tex, Arlington, 1979-; Neighborhood Adv Coun, 1983-; Urban Mgt Asst N Tex, 1984-; Tex Munic League, 1985-; Network Exec Women, 1985-; secy, N Tex Conf Minority Pub Admins, 1986-87; vpres, Nat Forum Black Pub Admins, 1987-88; Tarrant County League Women Voters, 1987-88; Nat Asn Advan Colored People; Ft Worth Metrop Black Chamber Com; Minority Leaders & Citizens Coun. **Home Addr:** 3536 Bonnell Ave, Ft. Worth, TX 76107, **Home Phone:** (817)763-8350. **Business Addr:** Fiscal Services Administrator, City Fort Worth, 100 N Univ Suite 239, Ft. Worth, TX 76107, **Business Phone:** (817)392-7353.

### JOHNSON, DR. POMPIE LOUIS, JR.
Banker. **Personal:** Born Dec 19, 1926, Pocatello, ID; son of Pompie L Sr and Nellie B; married Marylynn T Hughes; children: Tamara & Karen. **Educ:** Ind State Univ, BA, 1950; Boston Univ Sch Law, JD, 1952; Am Savings & Loan Inst, dipl, 1967; Am Inst Banking, dipl, 1971. **Career:** Boston MA, atty, 1952-55; Mutual Omaha Ins Co, sales & claims, 1956-60; Golden State Mutual Life Ins Co, planning specialist, 1960-62; Safety Savings & Loan Asn, vpres-mgr, 1963-66; Security Pac Nat Bank, vpres-mgr, 1967-72; Calif Fed Savings & Loan Asn, vpres corp savings, 1973. **Orgs:** Bd dir, Watts Ca Econ Dev Comn, 1973-76; asst treas, Calif State Rep Control Comn, 1974-78; bd dir, Inglewood Calif Chamber Comn, 1975-78; bd dir, Inglewood Calif Merchants Asn, 1975-78; pres, SW Los Angeles Rotary Club, 1979-80; bd dir, Gardena Calif Econ Dev Comm, 1983-; Rotary Int, Dist 5280, Gov Rep, 1994-95; Rotary Int, Dist 5280, chmn Club Serv, 1995-96. **Honors/Awds:** Deleg, Perm Org Comn Rep Nat Conv, 1972; Unsung Hero Award LA Newspaper, 1972; del, Rotary Int Conv Rome, Italy, 1979; Rotarian of the Year, Los Angeles Rotary, 1982. **Home Addr:** 13120 Spinning Ave, Gardena, CA 90249-1721.

### JOHNSON, R. BENJAMIN
Government official. **Personal:** Born Jul 14, 1944, Marion, AR; son of Robert Lee and Willie B Clay; married Jacqueline Vassar; children: Nancy, Rahman, Endesha, Jua & Sekou. **Educ:** Ind Univ; Antioch Col; Tufts Univ; Prince George's Community Col Mgt Inst. **Career:** WSBT TV, news reporter & host afternoon talk show; Action Inc, dir employ; Manpower Assistance Prog, manpower specialist; Youth Advocacy Prog, dir, 1971-73; St Joseph County Credit Union, mgr & treas, 1975-77; Credit Union Inst Nat Ctr Urban Ethnic Affairs, dir, 1977-79; White House Off Consumer Affairs, dir consumer progs & spec asst consumer adv pres, 1979-81; Nat Credit Union Admin, spec asst chmn bd, 1981-82; Black Resource Guide Inc, pres, 1981-; Dept Consumer & Regulatory Affairs, Wash, adminr bus regulation admin, 1983-87, adminr housing & environ regulation admin, 1987-88; spec asst mayor, 1988-89; Dept Pub & Assisted Housing, dir, 1989-91; White House Off Pub Liaison, dep asst pres, 1993-01; BICO Inc, exec vpres & dir, 2001-; Rapid HIV Detection Corp, officer & dir. **Orgs:** Chmn, S Bend Black Voters Asn; vpres, Valley Chap Credit Unions; chmn, St Joseph County CETA Adv Bd; publ, Black Resource Guide; mem bd, AFLAC. **Honors/Awds:** Distinguished Government Service Award, 1987 & 1990; Outstanding Professionals Award, Bus Exchange Network, 1987; Hon doctorate, Morgan State Univ, 1998; Hon doctorate, Ark Baptist Church, 1999. **Special Achievements:** Numerous publications including in New Credit Union Management Systems, 1969, The Community Development Credit Union, 1977 & 1979; The Black Resource Guide, 1981-91. **Home Addr:** 501 Oneida Pl NW, Washington, DC 20011, **Home Phone:** (202)291-4373. **Business Addr:** Executive Vice President, Director, BICO Inc, 3116 Valhalla Dr, Burbank, CA 91505, **Business Phone:** (818)842-7179.

### JOHNSON, R. M.
Writer. **Personal:** Born Apr 1, 1968. **Educ:** Columbia Col; Howard Univ, radiation therapist cert, 1994; Nebr La Univ, BS, 1995; Chicago State Univ, MFA, creative writing. **Career:** Little Co Mary Hosp, radiation therapist, 1995; The Harris Men, 1999; Father Found, 2000; The Harris Family, 2001; Deceit & Devotion; RM Johnson Million Dollar Series E-Book Box Set; Dating Games, 2002; Novels: Father found, 2000; The Harris Men, 2000; The Harris Family, 2002; No One in the World; Love Frustration, 2003; Dating Games, 2004; The Million Dollar Divorce, 2005; Do You Take This Woman?, 2008; The Million Dollar Deception, 2008; Why Men Fear Marriage, 2009; The Million Dollar Demise, 2009. **Home Addr:** 7600 N Bosworth Ave, Chicago, IL 60626, **Home Phone:** (773)262-0356. **Business Addr:** Writer, c/o Simon & Schuster, 1230 Avenue of the Americas, New York, NY 10020-1586, **Business Phone:** (212)698-7000.

### JOHNSON, RAFER LEWIS
Athlete, television sportscaster, sports promoter. **Personal:** Born Aug 18, 1935, Hillsboro, TX; son of Jenny Johnson-Jordan; married Betsy Thorsen; children: Jennifer & Josh. **Educ:** Univ Calif, Los Angeles. **Career:** Decathalon athlete; People to People Intl; sports broadcaster; Peace Corps recruiter; Special Olympics Southern Ca, chmn bd governor, currently; Univ Calif, Los Angeles, dir athletics, currently. **Orgs:** CA Spec Olympics, co-founder, gov's bd chair, 1992-; Calif State Recreation Comn; Fair Housing Cong; Fel Christian Athletes; Campus Crusade; Dept Health, Edu & Welfare, Comt Ment Retardation Pigskin Club Wash. **Business Addr:** Chairman, Special Olympics Southern California, 5875 Green Valley Cir, Culver City, CA 90230, **Business Phone:** (310)215-8380.

### JOHNSON, RAGLIN. See JOHNSON, FRAN.

### JOHNSON, RALPH C.
Chief executive officer, president (organization). **Personal:** Born Dec 4, 1941, Pittsburg, TX; married Nadine; children: Stacie. **Educ:** Oakwood Col, BS, bus admin, 1964; Wichita State Univ, MS, acct, 1967. **Career:** Wichita State Univ, asst prof acct; Fox & Co, Kans City, staff acct, 1964-71; Ala A&M Col, assoc prof & bus adminr, 1967-68; Ralph C Johnson & Co PC, founder, 1971-, pres & chief exec officer, currently. **Orgs:** Lic Cert Pub Acct, KS, 1966, MO, 1971; Am Inst Cert Pub Acct; comt mem, Kans State Bd Accountancy; bd dir & chair, Samuel U Rodgers Health Ctr. **Business Addr:** President, Chief Executive Officer, Ralph C Johnson & Co PC, 106 W 11th St Suite 1530, Kansas City, MO 64105-1817, **Business Phone:** (816)472-8900.

### JOHNSON, RAY
Executive. **Personal:** Born Dec 13, 1935, Port Gibson, MS; son of Norah; children: Raymond Bradle & Fredrick Norman. **Career:** Executive (retired); Ray Johnson Enterprises Inc, pres & chief exec officer, 1982-96; McDonald's Corp, nat oper adv bd, owner; McDonald's Restaurants, owner-operator 10 stores. **Orgs:** Chmn-comnr, Ariz State Athletic Comm, 1981-83; pres, Round-One Prod, 1983-86; chmn, Ariz State Liquor Community, 1983-; comnr, City Phoenix Civil Serv Community, 1986-; dept rev bd, Phoenix Police Dept, 1990. **Honors/Awds:** Phoenix AZ Human Resource Businessman of the Year, 1980; AZ & US Small Businessman of the Year, 1984; hon doctorate, Alcorn State Univ, 1997. **Home Addr:** 100 E Huron St Apt 3001, Chicago, IL 60611-5910, **Home Phone:** (312)642-2675.

### JOHNSON, RAYLEE TERRELL
Football player. **Personal:** Born Jun 1, 1970, Chicago, IL; married Diann; children: Brooke, Brecena, Brandy & Bryce. **Educ:** Univ Ark, bus educ. **Career:** Football player (retired); San Diego Chargers, defensive end, 1993-2003; Denver Broncos, defensive end, 2004.

### JOHNSON, RAYMOND L.
Police chief. **Personal:** Born Apr 20, 1936, AR; son of Grady and Lucy; children: Ava. **Educ:** Calif State Univ, Sacramento, BA. **Career:** Bakersfield, Calif, police dept; Calif Hwy Patrol, chief southern div; City Inglewood, Police Dept, Defendants-Appellees, chief police; Off Criminal Justice Planning, exec dir, currently. **Orgs:** Pres, Peace Officers Asn, Los Angeles Co; CA Peace officers Asn; CA Police Chiefs; Inter-Agency Chief officers; Int Asn Police Chiefs; Los Angeles Co Police Chiefs Asn; S Bay Police Chiefs; Am Mgmt Asn; Nat Org Black Law Enforcement Exec; Los Angeles-Lusaka Zambia Sister City Comn; Sen Task Force Child Abuse; Nat Criminal Justice Asn; Asn Black Law Enforcement Exec; CA Dist Atty Asn; bd dir, Oscar Joel Bryant Asn; dir, Homer Garrott Scholar Found; bd adv, Los Angeles Child Passenger Safety Asn; hon bd, Am Cancer Soc; Asn Black Law Enforcement Exec; Am Mgt Asn; Automobile Club S Calif; Traffic Safety Advisors Prog; Boy Scouts Am Task Force; State Task Force Ga & Drugs; CA Coun Criminal Justice; CA Dist Atty Asn; rep/accreditation task force, CA Peace officers Asn; CA Police Chiefs Asn Inc; dir, Scholar Found; Independent Cities Asn, LA Co; Inglewood Coalition Alcohol & Drugs; Inter-Agency Chief Officers; Int Asn Police Chiefs Narcotics & Dangerous Drugs Comt; bd mem, Loved Ones Homicide Victims; bd mem, LA Child Passenger Safety Asn; LA Co Police Chiefs Asn; Nat Asn Blacks Criminal Justice; Nat Criminal Justice Asn; chmn, Awards Comt, Nat Org Black Law Enforcement Exec, 1989; bd dir, Oscar Joel Bryant Asn; pres, current bd, LA Co; chmn, Uniform Reporting Comt Gangs; Police Found; Police Mgt Asn; Sen Task Force Child Abuse; S Bay Police Chiefs/Criminal Justice Admin Asn; hon mem, Spec People Involved Community Endeavors. **Honors/Awds:** Los Angeles highest-ranking California Highway Patrol officer. **Business Addr:** Executive Director, Office of Criminal Justice Planning, 1130 K St Suite 300, Sacramento, CA 95814, **Business Phone:** (916)324-9140.

### JOHNSON, DR. RAYMOND LEWIS
Educator. **Personal:** Born Jun 25, 1943, Alice, TX; son of Johnny Virginia. **Educ:** Univ Tex, BA, math, 1963; Rice Univ, PhD, math, 1970. **Career:** Univ Md, asst prof, assoc prof, 1968-80, prof math, 1980-, chair, 1987-90, 1991-96, prof appl math & sci comput, currently; Inst Mittag-Leffler, vis mem, 1974-75; Howard Univ, prof, 1976-78; Mc Master Univ, vis prof, 1983-84. **Orgs:** Bd gov, Inst Math & Its Appln, 1993-96; sci adv comt, Math Sci Res Inst, 1994-98, trustee, 1998-; bd dir, Nat Asn Mathematicians, 1994-96; MichE adv bd, Spelman Col, 1994-; bd gov, Math Asn Am, 1998-. **Honors/Awds:** Lifetime Mentor Award, AAAS; Distinguished Minority Faculty Award, 2007. **Home Addr:** 3385 Bellefontaine, Houston, TX 77025. **Business Addr:** Professor of Mathematics, Rice University, Rm 410 Herman Brown Hall MS-136, Houston, TX 77005, **Business Phone:** (713)348-4053.

### JOHNSON, REBECCA M.
Educator, teacher. **Personal:** Born Jul 10, 1905, Springfield, MA; daughter of William D and Harriet B. **Educ:** Fisk Univ, BA, 1927; Northwestern Univ, attended 1934; Springfield Col, attended 1943; Columbia Univ, MA, 1948. **Career:** Educator (retired), adminr; Columbia SC Pub Sch Dept, elem teacher, 1927-35, jr high math teacher, 1935-43; Charleston SC Educ 24 Hr Camp Unemployed, dir, 1935; Springfield MA Pub Sch Dept, jr high math teacher, 1943-46, prin, 1947-75; Mt Holyoke Col, vis lectr; Springfield Col, vis lectr; Am Int Col, vis lectr; Rebecca M Johnson Elem Magnet Sch, founder. **Orgs:** Springfield, Nat Asn Advan Colored People, 1960-89; bd mem, Springfield Child Guid Clin Inc, 1985-89; co-chair, Scholar & Educ Resource Network Urban League, 1985-89; Alpha Kappa Alpha Sorority; Delta Kappa Gamma Hon Soc Women Educ; chmn scholar comt mem, St John's Congregational Church; Black-Jewish Dialogue Community; John Brown Archives Community, St John's Church; bd dir, Springfield Tech Community Col. **Home Addr:** 55 Catherine St, Springfield, MA 01109, **Home Phone:** (413)787-6687. **Business Addr:** Founder, Rebecca M Johnson Elem Magnet School, 55 Catherine St, Springfield, MA 01109, **Business Phone:** (413)787-6687.

### JOHNSON, RENARD U.
President (organization), chief executive officer. **Personal:** Born Chicago, IL. **Educ:** Univ Tex, El Paso, BA, bus admin. **Career:** Mgt Assistance Co Am, sr vpres oper, 1984-94; Mgt & Eng Technologies Int Inc, founder, pres & chief exec officer, 1994-. **Orgs:** Paso del Norte Group; bd mem, El Paso Hisp Chamber Com; bd mem, Boys & Girls Club El Paso; El Paso Asn Performing Arts; Dallas Fed Bd dir; Univ Tex at El Paso Col Engineering Adv Bd. **Business Addr:** President, Chief Executive Officer, Management & Engineering Technologies International Inc, 8600 Boeing Dr, El Paso, TX 79925-1226, **Business Phone:** (915)772-4975.

### JOHNSON, DR. RHODA E.
Educator. **Personal:** Born Nov 14, 1946, Bessemer, AL; daughter of Foy Barge Sr and Peacolia Dancy Barge; married Ruffer R; children: Ryan & Robert E. **Educ:** Tuskegee Inst, Tuskegee, BS, 1968; Univ Mich, Ann Arbor, MI, MA, sociol, 1970; Univ Ala, Tuscaloosa, AL, PhD, sociol, 1980. **Career:** Univ Mich, Ann Arbor, Mich, Horace H Rackham fel, 1968-69, stud res asst, 1969-70; Tuskegee Inst, Tuskegee, AL, instr, 1970-74, asst prof, 1977-81, assoc prof & dir MARC, 1981-86; Ford Found fel, Southern Educ Found, 1975-77; Univ Ala, Tuscaloosa, AL, instr, 1975, asst prof sociol, prof, 1977-81, assoc prof sociol & dir minority access res careers prog, 1981-86, vis prof & actg dir, 1985-86, chair, 1986-91, assoc prof women's studies, 1986-. **Orgs:** Poverty & Ment Health Rural S, CSRS & USDA, Carver Found, 1978-83; steering comm, 21st Century Leadership Proj, 1989-; bd mem, Nat Voting Rights Mus, 1994-; bd mem, Nat Rev Bd, Ala Hist Comn; Univ Ala Grad Coun fel, Univ Ala, 1974-75; Horace H Rackham fel Univ Mich, 1968-69. **Home Addr:** 14 Southmont Dr, Tuscaloosa, AL 35405-4131, **Home Phone:** (205)759-1935. **Business Addr:** Associate Professor, University of Alabama, PO Box 870272, Tuscaloosa, AL 35487-0272, **Business Phone:** (205)348-5782.

### JOHNSON, RHONDA DAVENPORT
Executive. **Personal:** daughter of Rufus and Annie; married Chris. **Educ:** Western Mich Univ, Haworth Col Bus, BBA, bus & mkt, 1984, MBA, bus, 1988. **Career:** Comerica Bank, Detroit, MI, 1987-, regional mgr, 2002-12, sr vpres, 2002-, dir comerica loan ctr, 2012-, exec vpres & nat dir retail sales & serv, 2014-. **Orgs:** Bd dir, Hospice Mich Found; bd trustee, Garden City hosp; Am Cancer Soc; Am Heart Asn; United Negro Col Fund; United Way Washtenaw County; bd dir, Mich Abolitionist Proj. **Special Achievements:** First African American woman appointed to the position of retail regional manager for Comerica Bank; First vice president who directs the operations for 20 Comerica banking centers in Oakland County. **Business Addr:** Senior Vice President, National Director of Retail Sales and Service, Comerica Bank, Comerica Bank Twr, Dallas, TX 75201, **Business Phone:** (214)462-4000.

### JOHNSON, RICHARD HOWARD
Government official. **Personal:** Born Jan 7, 1931, Jersey City, NJ; son of Richard S and Della H; married D Winona; children: Sandra J Harris & Richard Nicholas. **Educ:** Va Union Univ, BA, sociol, 1953; Boston Univ Sch Social Work, MA, 1955. **Career:** Government official (retired); Camp Downingtown, dir, 1953-55; AUS Hosp, chief psychiat sw 1955-57; Hawthornden State Hosp, psychiat social worker, 1957-59; Cuyahoga Co Ct Common Pleas, marriage counr, 1959-65; Maternal & Child Health, coord neighborhood serv 1965-68; Hough Parent-Child Ctr, dir, 1968-72; Parent & Child Ctrs Head Start Bur OCD-DHEW, chief 1972-96; Parent Involvement Br HSB, ACYF, DHHS, chief social serv, 1975-91. **Orgs:** Kappa Alpha Psi Frat; Boule-Sigma Pi Phi Frat; Nat 30-Yr Oldtimers; COSPICS; NAEYC; NASW; NCBCD. **Home Addr:** 13721 Lockdale Rd, Silver Spring, MD 20906, **Home Phone:** (301)460-0208.

### JOHNSON, RITA FALKENER
Interior designer. **Personal:** Born Arlington, VA; married Waldo C Falkener. **Educ:** Academie Julien Paris, 1965; Grande Chaumi re Paris, 1967; Pratt Inst, BFA, 1964. **Career:** Esq residential & com interior design; Essence Mag, home ed, 1975-77. **Orgs:** Allied Bd Trade; Nat Home Fashions League Inc Prof showcase; YWCA Designers' Show house, 1976; Designers' Show house, 1977; YWCA Show house, 1977. **Home Addr:** 50 Pierrepont St Suite 3, Brooklyn, NY 11201-2458, **Home Phone:** (718)624-4718. **Business Addr:** 50 Pierrepont St, Brooklyn, NY 11201.

### JOHNSON, ROBERT B.
Educator. **Personal:** Born Aug 19, 1928, Fair Bluff, NC; married Virginia J; children: Ronald Hal & Jacquelyn Foster. **Educ:** NC Agr & Tech State Univ, BS, 1950, MS, 1959. **Career:** HS Loris, SC, sci teacher, 1955-63; Coastal Jr Col, chem instr, 1959-61; Pleasant Grove Elem Sch Rains, SC, prin, 1963-67; Mullins Sch Dist, SC, elem sch prin, 1968-; Lower Marion County, supt. **Orgs:** Mullins City Coun, 1970-82; Pee Dee Reg Develop Coun; Human Resource Develop Coun. **Home Addr:** 901 Gapway St, Mullins, SC 29574-3823, **Home Phone:** (843)464-8850. **Business Addr:** Superintendent, Lower Marion County, Sch District Suite 3, Rains, SC 29589.

### JOHNSON, ROBERT B.
Health services administrator, chief executive officer. **Personal:** married Geri. **Educ:** Tenn State Univ, BS, biol, 1963; Univ Mich Sch Pub Health, MS, hosp admin, 1971. **Career:** Kings County Hosp Ctr, Brooklyn, from asst dir to assoc exec dir, 1971-74, actg exec dir, 1974-76; Gen Hosp, Wash, DC, chief exec officer, exec dir, 1976-86; St Louis Regional Health Care Corp, pres & chief exec officer, 1986-89; St Louis Regional Med Ctr, chief exec officer, 1986-89; Grady Health Syst, pres & chief exec officer, 1989-93; Grady Memorial Hosp, chief exec officer, 1989-93; Detroit Med Ctr, exec vpres, vpres & chief operating officer, 1993-2000; Robert B Johnson & Assocs, pres, 2000-; RBJ Enterprises LLC, chmn & chief exec officer, 2006-. **Orgs:** Bd dir, Abayomi Community Develop Corp; bd dir, Circle Hope Found; chmn & mem adv bd, 4C Child Care Coord Coun, bd dir, Family Rd Care Ctrs Inc; chmn bd dir, Tried Stone Econ Develop Corp; Greater Detroit Area Health Coun; vpres, 100 Black Men Greater Detroit; co chair, Safe Night Comt; co chair, Health & Wellness Comt; bd trustee, Am Hosp Asn; founder & chmn, Nat Asn Pub Hosps; trustee bd, Cath Health Initiative; fel King Edwards Int Hosp; bd, Am Cancer Soc; Boy Scouts Urban Adv Comt; bd, Southeastern Mich Hosp Coun; secy, Detroit Urban League Bd dir; vpres, 100 Black Men Greater Detroit an orgn; Southern Oakland CountyNat Asn Advan Colored People Exec Comt; Southern Oakland Nat Asn Advan Colored People Health & Econ Develop Comts; Detroit Area Pre-Col Engineering Prog's; bd dir, Abayomi Community Develop Corp; bd dir, Circle Hope Found; bd dir, 4C Child Care Coord Coun; adv bd, Family Rd Care Centers Inc; chmn bd dir Tried Stone Econ Develop Corp; Greater Detroit Area Health Coun; Plymouth United Church Christ, Safe Night Comt Chair. **Business Addr:** Chairman, Chief Executive Officer, RBJ Enterprises LLC, 33228 W Twelve Mile Rd Suite 153, Farmington Hills, MI 48334-3309, **Business Phone:** (248)888-0949.

### JOHNSON, ROBERT E.
Administrator, executive director, president (organization). **Personal:** Born Detroit, MI; married Michelle Jones; children: Jasmine & Alexander. **Educ:** Morehouse Col, BS, econs; Univ Cincinnati, MS, educ admin; Touro Univ Int, PhD, higher educ admin. **Career:** Cent State Univ, exec dir mkt & enrollment mgt; Sinclair Community Col, sr vpres; Univ Dayton, Ohio, vpres enrollment mgt, 2004; Oakland Univ, vice provost; Becker Col, Worcester, MA, pres, currently. **Orgs:** Bd dir, Cols Worcester Consortium; bd dir, Worcester Educ Collab; bd dir, Worcester Regional Chamber Com; bd dir, Worcester Regional Res Bur; Massachusetts Technol Collab. **Business Addr:** President, Becker College, 61 Sever St, Worcester, MA 01609, **Business Phone:** (508)373-9531.

### JOHNSON, ROBERT H.
Educator, association executive. **Personal:** Born Nov 24, 1938, New York, NY; children: Vietta. **Educ:** Smith Univ, BS, 1960; Long Island Univ, MS, 1964; St John's Univ, PhD, 1970. **Career:** Pharma-Verona Chem Co, chemist, 1961-62; Long Island Univ, teacher, 1964-75; Human Affairs Res Ctr, consult, 1970-72; R H Clark & Assoc, partner, 1974-; Medgar Evers Col City Univ NY, teacher, 1975-76, dean students, 1977-84, prof chem, 1984-99, prof emer, currently. **Orgs:** Am Chem Soc; AAAS; NY Acad Sci; Asn Black Chemists & Engr; bd trustee, Nat Black Sci Stds Org, 1972-74; chair, Crown Hts Youth Collective, 1979; Fed Drug Addict Prog. **Honors/Awds:** Outstanding Young Men of America, 1971; Outstanding Educators of America, 1973. **Home Addr:** 5900 Arlington Ave, Riverdale, NY 10471. **Business Addr:** Professor Emeritus, Medgar Evers College, City University of New York, 1650 Bedford Ave, Brooklyn, NY 11225, **Business Phone:** (718)270-4900.

### JOHNSON, ROBERT JUNIUS
Executive. **Personal:** Born Mar 19, 1929, Richton, MS; son of Charles Davis and Priscilla Dean; married Patricia Sutton; children: Robert II & Kemberly Nicole. **Career:** Johnson Prod Co Inc, dir distrib. **Home Addr:** 20740 London Dr, Olympia Fields, IL 60461, **Home Phone:** (708)481-4871.

### JOHNSON, ROBERT L.
Educator, physician. **Personal:** Born Aug 7, 1946, Spartanburg, SC; son of Robert and Clalice Brewton; married Maxine Gilchrist. **Educ:** Alfred Univ, BA, 1968; Col Med & Dent NJ, MD, 1972. **Career:** Martland Hosp, pediat intern, 1972-73, pediat resident, 1973-74, dir adolescent Med, 1976-78; St Michael's Med Ctr, dir adolescent medclin; C Hosp NJ, dir adolescent med, 1976-98; New York Med Sch, asst attend physician, 1976-84; Univ Med & Dent NJ, from asst prof to assoc prof clin pediat, 1976-89, prof clin pediat, 1989-, NJ Med Sch, prof pediatand psychiat, 1995-, Dept Pediat, vice chair, 1996-2001, interim chmn, 2001-05 chmn pediat, 2004-05 & currently; Univ Hosp, dir adolescent Med, 1976-; Sharon & Joseph L Muscarelle Endowed, interim dean, 2005-11, dean, 2011-, Adolescent & Young Adult Med, dir, 1976-; Books: The Race Trap; Strength for Their Journey. **Orgs:** Fel Am Acad Pediat, 1974-; fel Sect Adolescent Health Care, 1974-; Comn Adolescence; Soc Adolescent Med; Comn Sports Med & Accident Prev, 1976-78; bd mem, Adolescent Health Ctr Door, 1977; bd trustee, Frost Valley YMCA; chair & bd deacons, Union Baptist Church, 1978-; bd trustee, Day Care Coord Coun, 1980-81; vpres Health Affairs, Int Ctr Integrative Studies, 1980-; bd dir, Inst Develop Youth Progs, 1983-; bd trustee, Newark Boy's Clubs, 1984-; bd dir, Sex Info & Educ Coun US, 1988-; Carnegie Corp, Substance Abuse Adv Comn, 1989-; credentials comt, chair, 1990-, treas, 1990-91, secy, 1991-; NJ State Bd Med Examrs; AAP, Comt Careers & Opportunities; chair, Nat Task Force Access Minority C Health Care, 1991-; Ore Health Plan Bd Med Examrs, adv comt, 1992; ed bd, Pediat Rev; chair, US Dept Health & Human Serv Coun; adv comt, fel Nat Res Coun's Nat Acad Sci; fel Community Prev Task Force US Centers DisControl & Prev; chair, NJ Gov's Adv Coun; Newark Ryan White Plng Coun; fel, Nat Coun Nat Inst Ment Healt; fel Nat Insts Health Acquired Immune Deficiency Syndrome Res Coun; Inst Med Health Care Serv Bd; fel Inst Med Comt Unintended Pregnancy; chair, Nat Comn Adolescent Sexuality; pres, NJ State Bd Med Examiners; chair, Bd Advocates Youth. **Home Addr:** 732 Berkeley Ave, Orange, NJ 07050, **Home Phone:** (973)672-1654. **Business Addr:** Sharon & Joseph L Muscarelle Endowed Dean, Chair & Professor Pediatrics & Psychiatry, University of Medicine and Dentistry of New Jersey, 185 S Orange Ave MSB Rm C671, Newark, NJ 07101-1709, **Business Phone:** (973)972-5277.

### JOHNSON, ROBERT LOUIS
Founder (originator), executive. **Personal:** Born Apr 8, 1946, Hickory, MS; son of Edna and Archie; married Lauren Wooden; married Sheila; children: Paige & Brett. **Educ:** Ill Univ, BA, social studies, 1968; Princeton Univ, Woodrow Wilson Sch Pub & Int Affairs, MA, int affairs, 1972. **Career:** Black Entertainment Tv (BET), founder, 1980-2001, chmn & chief exec officer, 1980-2005; Charlotte Bobcats, majority owner, 2004-10, minority owner, 2010-; RLJ Equity Partners LLC, founder & chmn, 2006-; Our Stories Films, founder, 2006-; RLJ Credit Opportunity Fund, founder; RLJ Financial LLC, founder; RLJ Entertainment Inc, bd dir, currently; Think Finance Inc, bd dir; RLJ Fixed Income LLC, 2011-; Corp Pub Broadcasting, pub affairs dir; Congressman Walter E. Fauntroy, press secy; Nat Cable & Tv Asn, vpres govt rels; Nat Urban League, dir commun Wash; RLJ Lodging Trust, currently, bd dir; KB Home, bd dir, currently; Lowe's Co Inc, bd dir, currently; Strayer Educ, bd dir, currently; Elevate Credit Inc, bd dir, currently; RLJ Kendeja Resort & Villas; Alright TV; Caribbean CAGE LLC, founder, currently; Charlotte Hornets; RML Automotive, founder, currently; Retirement Clearinghouse, founder, currently. **Orgs:** Bd mem, Gen Mills; Kappa Alpha Psi fraternity; mem bd dir, United Negro Col Fund; mem bd dir, Deutsche Bank's Americas Adv Bd; bd dir,, Bus Coun, currently; bd dir, Nat Mus African Am Hist & Cult, currently. **Honors/Awds:** Junior Achievement's US Business Hall of Fame; "Black Enterprise," 75 Most Powerful Blacks on Wall Street, 2011. **Special Achievements:** Black Entertainment Television (BET) became in 1991 the first African-American-controlled company on the New York Stock Exchange; became the first African-American billionaire in 2001; first African-American listed on any "Forbes" world's rich list. **Business Addr:** Founder, Chairman, RLJ Companies, 3 Bethesda Metro Ctr Suite 1000, Bethesda, MD 20814, **Business Phone:** (301)280-7700.

### JOHNSON, ROBERT T.
District attorney. **Personal:** Born Feb 18, 1948, Bronx, NY; son of Robert and Olga; married Dianne Renwick; children: 4. **Educ:** City Col NY, BA, philos, 1972; NY Univ Sch Law, JD, 1975. **Career:** Legal Aid Soc, criminal defense atty, 1975-78; New York Criminal Ct, judge, 1986; NY Supreme Ct, judge & actg justice, 1986-88, judge, 2016-; Bronx Co, NY, dist atty, 1978-86, 1989-2015. **Orgs:** Pres, bd dir, Ny Dist Atty Asn; adv bd, Bronx Sch Law; Bronx Co Bar Asn; Black Bar Asn Bronx Co; Puerto Rican Bar Asn; bd mem, Bronx Urban League; New York Motor Vehicle Theft & Ins Fraud Prev Bd. **Honors/Awds:** David S Michaels Memorial Award, New York State Bar Asn, 1997. **Special Achievements:** Johnsons District Attorneys office was officially recognized by President George Bush & selected as one of the "Thousand Points of Light" programs, 1991; First African-American District Attorney in New York state; Longest serving District Attorney in Bronx history, 2005. **Business Addr:** Judge, New York Supreme Court, 400 Carleton Ave, Central Islip, NY 11722, **Business Phone:** (631)852-2345.

### JOHNSON, RONALD A.
College president, college teacher. **Personal:** Born Brooklyn, NY; married Irene. **Educ:** Adelphi Univ, BA, econ, MBA, finance; Stanford Univ, MA, econ, PhD, econ. **Career:** Fed Res Syst Bd Gov, Wash, DC, economist; Int Monetary Fund, economist; Fed Res Bank, New York, div chief; Americas Trust Bank, chief strategist & chmn investment comt; Templeton Worldwide Inc, Ft Lauderdale, FL, dir fixed income res & sr portfolio mgr; Smith Graham & Co, Houston, TX, pres & chief investment officer; Howard Univ, vis asst prof; Northeastern Univ, fac mem; Fla A&M Univ, vis assoc prof; Western Carolina Univ, fac mem, 2007-10, BB&T Distinguished Prof Capitalism, 2010-11; Tex Southern Univ, prof & dean Jesse H. Jones Sch Bus, 2011-15; Clark Atlanta Univ, pres, 2015-. **Orgs:** Sigma Pi Phi Boule. **Special Achievements:** Managed more than $3 billion in assets for Smith Graham & Company; managed more than $2 billion in assets for Templeton Worldwide. **Business Addr:** Office of the President, 223 James P Brawley Dr SW, Atlanta, GA 30314.

### JOHNSON, RONALD CORNELIUS
Administrator, clergy. **Personal:** Born Oct 2, 1946, Amelia County, VA; son of Rebecca; married Bessie; children: Aisha. **Educ:** Va State Col, BA, 1969, HL.D; Univ Cincinnati, MA, 1973; Xavier Univ, MEd, bus educ, 1978. **Career:** Ronson Mgmt Corp, pres; US Housing & Urban Dev, specialist asst, mgt analyst; Univ DC, dir instin comm & pub serv; Model Cities Prog, admin; Jewish Hosp, first coordr employee rels; Ronald C Johnson Assoc Inc, pres; Va State Univ, rector, currently; Ronson Network Serv Corp, owner & chief exec officer, currently. **Orgs:** Bd dir, Bushido Inc; servs nat panel Am AcadEd Dev; nat chmn, Conf Minor Pub Admin, 1975-76; Nat Cncl Am Soc-Pub Adminstrn, 1975-76; chmn, Fairfax Cty Urban Leag; secy, Fairfax County Econ Develop Authority, 2001; Rural Am Inc; Nat Asn Hous & Rehab Off; Nat Asn Advan Colored People; Nat Com Responsive Philantropy; Minority Media & Telecommunications Coun; bd trustee, Alfred St Baptist Church; gov appointee, Va Dept Agr & Consumer Serv; gov Alliance, Drug Free Va. **Honors/Awds:** ASPA Appreciation Award; Jewish War Vet Award; Urban League Service Award; Conf of Min Pub Administrator Award; Danforth Fellow; Virginia Outstanding Businessman, 2001; Top 25 Blacks in Technology, Black Enterprise Mags; Excellence in Business; DHL, Virginia State Univ; Best of the Best, Commonwealth of Virginia; Doctor of Humane Letters, Virginia State Univ. **Home Addr:** 4711 Ferry Landing Rd, Alexandria, VA 22309, **Home Phone:** (703)780-2526. **Business Addr:** Chief Executive Officer, Owner, Ronson Network Services Corp, 6911 Richmond Hwy Suite 290, Alexandria, VA 22306, **Business Phone:** (703)660-1200.

### JOHNSON, RONALD J.
Football player, executive. **Personal:** Born Sep 21, 1958, Monterey, CA; son of Mae; married Lynn; children: Wesley & Evan. **Educ:** Long Beach State Univ, Bus Mgt, 1981; Calif State Univ; Monterey Peninsula Col. **Career:** Football player (retired); Hamilton Tiger-Cats (Can Football League), 1982-84; Portland Breakers (USFL), 1985; Philadelphia Eagles, wide receiver, 1985-89; Prudential Securities, investment advisor. **Orgs:** Vpres opers, risk mgt & compliance, Boys & Girls Clubs Monterey County, 1992; bd dir, Pathways Found; bd mem, United Way Monterey County, 1997-99, pres, 2000. **Business Addr:** Vice President of Operations, Boys & Girls Clubs of Monterey County, 1332 La Salle Ave, Seaside, CA 93955-3219, **Business Phone:** (831)394-5171.

### JOHNSON, ROY LEE
Executive, vice president (organization). **Personal:** Born Jun 30, 1955, Charleston, MS; son of James and Viola Sayles; married Vicki Jo Williams. **Educ:** Fisk Univ, Nashville, TN, BS, 1977; Mich State Univ, E Lansing, MBA, 1990. **Career:** Ford Motor Co, Detroit, Mich, financial analyst, 1977-83; Stroh Brewery, Detroit, Mich, mgr financial planning, 1983-91, dir financial planning, 1991-97, vpres financial planning, 1998-99; Handleman Co, vpres budgeting & forecasting, vpres bus support & anal, 2000-08; Roy L Johnson Consult LLC, pres, 2010-11; NCH Corp, dir, financial planning & anal, 2011-. **Orgs:** Nat Black MBA Asn. **Home Addr:** 18820 Jeanette, Southfield, MI 48075, **Home Phone:** (248)569-8340. **Business Addr:** Director, Financial Planning & Analysis, NCH Corp, 2727 Chemsearch Blvd, Irving, TX 75062, **Business Phone:** (972)438-0211.

### JOHNSON, ROY STEVEN
Journalist, columnist, television sportscaster. **Personal:** Born Mar 19, 1956, Tulsa, OK; son of Roy and Ida Mae Brooks Jenkins; married Barbara Y; children: Edwyn Lawrence & Anna Brooks. **Educ:** Stanford Univ, CA, BA, polit sci & Commun, 1978. **Career:** Sports Illus, writer, reporter, 1978-81, sr ed, 1989-94, asst managing ed spec projs, 2002-05; New York Times, sportswriter, 1982-89; Atlanta J-Const, columnist, 1987-89; Money Mag, sr ed, 1994-; Vanguard Media, ed dir; Fortune, ed; Savoy mag, founding ed-in-chief, 2000-02; Vanguarde Media, ed dir; sportswriter, currently; AOL Black Voices, columnist, currently; RSJ Media Solutions, founder & pres, 2006-; Men's Fitness mag, ed-in-chief, 2007, vpres; Fit! Live! Win! LLC, founder & chief exec officer, 2011-; Write Essays, founder & chief exec officer, 2012-; Ala Media Group, dir sports, 2014-, Ed & Birmingham mag, 2015-; Hist Channel Club, exec dir. **Orgs:** Nat Asn Black Journalists, 1985-; Int Amateur Athletic Asn; bd dir, Arthur Ashe Athletic Asn; founder & pres, Roy S Johnson Found; bd dir, Homeboy Golf Tournament. **Honors/Awds:** Service Award, NY Asn Black Journalists, 1996; Communicator of The Year, Nat Black MBA Asn, 1997. **Special Achievements:** Author: Magic's Touch, Addison-Wesley, 1990; Outrageous, Simon-Schuster, 1992. **Home Addr:** 15 Cortlandt Ave, New Rochelle, NY 10801-2005, **Home Phone:** (843)342-5219. **Business Addr:** Columnist, AOL Black Voices, New York, NY 10020.

### JOHNSON, SAM
Automotive executive. **Career:** Metro Lincoln Mercury Inc, Charlotte, NC, chief exec; Universal Ford Inc, Richmond, Va, chief exec; Metro Ford Sales Inc, Tupelo, Miss, chief exec, pres; Cross Creek Lincoln Mercury Subaru Inc, Fayetteville, NC, chief exec, pres; Sam Johnson Lincoln Mercury Inc, chief exec officer & pres, currently. **Orgs:** Am Int Automobile Dealers Asn; Nat Congress. **Business Addr:** Chief Executive Officer, President, Sam Johnson Lincoln Mercury Inc, 5201 E Independence Blvd, Charlotte, NC 28212, **Business Phone:** (704)535-7810.

### JOHNSON, SARAH YVONNE
School administrator. **Personal:** Born Aug 17, 1950, Los Angeles, CA; married Frank Sr; children: Frank Jr & Ingrid Yvette. **Educ:** Tuskegee Inst, BS, 1972; Harvard Univ, EdM, 1973. **Career:** Penn Cult Ctr, assoc dir, 1973-75; Beaufort City Bd Educ, spec educ teacher, 1975-76; Renaissance Wives Headstart Prog, educ dir, 1976; Ala Youth Serv, Vacca Campus State Sch Delinq Youth, prin, 1976-. **Orgs:** Ala Juv Justice Asn, 1979-, Harvard Club Birmingham, Positive Maturity Adv Bd, 1981-85. **Home Addr:** 2019 Trailridge Sq, Birmingham, AL 35214-1716, **Home Phone:** (205)798-5192. **Business Addr:** Princi-

pal, Alabama Youth Service, Vacca Campus, Birmingham, AL 35206, **Business Phone:** (205)838-4900.

### JOHNSON, SHANNON REGINA
Basketball player. **Personal:** Born Aug 18, 1974, Hartsville, SC; daughter of Robert Brockington and Jo-Ann Bennett. **Educ:** Univ SC, BS, retailing, 1996. **Career:** Columbus Quest, guard, 1997-98; Orlando Miracle, 1999-2002; Conn Sun, guard, 1999-2003; Fenerbache, Turkey, 1999-2000; Ros Casares, Valencia, Spain, 2001-02; All-FIBA World Championship Team, mem, 2002; San Antonio Silver Stars, guard, 2004-06; Detroit shocks, free agt, 2007; Houston Comets, free agt, 2008; Seattle Storm, 2009. **Orgs:** USA Basketball team. **Business Addr:** Professional Basketball Player, Seattle Storm, 3421 Thorndyke Ave W, Seattle, WA 98119, **Business Phone:** (206)217-9622.

### JOHNSON, SHARON REED. See Obituaries Section.

### JOHNSON, SHEILA
Entrepreneur, president (organization), chief executive officer. **Personal:** Born Jan 25, 1949, PA; married Robert L; children: Paige & Brett; married Robert L. **Educ:** Univ Ill. **Career:** BET, co-founder, 1980-97, vpres corp affairs; WNBA, Wash Mystics, team pres, managing partner & gov, 2005-; Salamander Hospity, founder & chief exec officer, 2005-; Lincoln Holdings LLC, partner, currently; Films: Kicking It, 2008; exec producer, A Powerful Noise, 2008; "Teen Summit", producer; violin instr, Sidwell Friends Sch. **Orgs:** Bd dir, Univ Va, Sorensen Inst Polit Leadership; Parsons New Sch Design; Sheila C Johnson Performing Arts Ctr; bd mem, AmericansArts; Jackie Robinson Found; Univ Ill Found; Tiger Woods Found. **Business Addr:** Founder, Chief Executive Officer, Salamander Hospitality, 100 W Washington St, Middleburg, VA 20118, **Business Phone:** (540)687-3710.

### JOHNSON, SHEILA ANN
Librarian. **Personal:** Born Apr 11, 1955; daughter of Edna; married Fadhilika Atiba; children: Onaje & Thandiwe. **Educ:** Spelman Col, BA, pre-law hist, 1976; Atlanta Univ, MSLS, 1978; Touro Col Jacob D Fuchsberg Law Ctr, Juris Doctorate, Govt Affairs Specialist, Health Law, Alternative Dispute Resolution, Rights C, 2004. **Career:** Lawrence Livermore Lab, tech info specialist, 1977-78; US Environ Protection Agency Region V, 1978-79; Amherst Col, Sci Libr, head, 1979-80; Brooklyn Pub Libr, Sci & Indust Div, div chief, 1980-93, 1997-; Off Congressman Maj R Owens, dep dir, 1995-96; Nassau Suffolk Law Serv, Govt Affairs Coordr, Dir Develop & Govt Affairs, 2008-09. **Orgs:** New York Black Librarians Caucus, 1999-; Am Libr Asn, 1999-; Am Libr Asn; NY Bar Asn; Black Law Stud Asn; Am Civil Liberties Union. **Honors/Awds:** Merit Award, Spelman Col Nat Alumnae Asn; Volunteers Service Award, Kings City Juvenile Offenders Prog; Distinguished Service Awd, Nat Asn Equal Opp Higher Educ; Women of Achievement Award, New York City Coun. **Home Addr:** 25 Spruce Rd, Amityville, NY 11701. **Business Addr:** Division Chief, Brooklyn Public Library, Grand Army Plz, Brooklyn, NY 11238, **Business Phone:** (718)230-2100.

### JOHNSON, SHEILA CRUMP
Chief executive officer, founder (originator). **Personal:** Born Jan 25, 1949, McKeesport, PA; married Robert L; children: Paige & Brett; married William T Newman Jr. **Educ:** Univ Ill, BA, music. **Career:** Black Entertainment Tv (BET), founding partner; Monumental Sports & Entertainment, vice chmn; Salamander Hospitality, chief exec officer & founder, 2005-; NHL's Wash Capitals, part-owner; NBA's Wash Wizards, part-owner; WNBA's Wash Mystics, pres, part-owner, managing partner & gov; Salamander Hotels & Resorts, chief exec officer, founder; Mistral, partner; ProJet Aviation, partner. Producer: Kicking It, 2008; A Powerful Noise, 2008; She Is the Matador; The Other City, 2010. **Orgs:** Chair bd, Gov Parsons New Sch Design New York; bd mem, Americans Arts; bd mem, Jackie Robinson Found; bd mem, Tiger Woods Found; bd mem, Univ Va Curry Sch Educ; bd mem, Howard Univ; bd mem, Univ Ill Found; global ambassador, CARE, 2006-; Pres's Comt Arts & Humanities, app by Pres Barack Obama; strategic advisor, AOL Huffington Post Media Group; bd mem, Sundance Inst; bd mem, ANNIKA Found; founder, chair, Middleburg Film Festival; Accordia Global Health Foundations Int Coun, 2011-. **Business Addr:** Chief Executive Officer, Salamander Hotels & Resorts, 10 N Pendleton St, Middleburg, VA 20117-0769, **Business Phone:** (540)687-3710.

### JOHNSON, SHEILA MONROE
Librarian. **Personal:** Born Nov 27, 1957, Southern Pines, NC; daughter of Esther M Monroe; married Michael Leon; children: Jade Taylor. **Educ:** Winston-Salem State Univ, Winston-Salem, BA, 1980; Univ NC, Greensboro, MLS, 1987. **Career:** Carpenter Libr Bowman Gray Sch Med, Winston-Salem, circulation supvr, 1982-85; Forsyth Co Pub Libr, Winston-Salem, head, periodicals & docs, librn, 1985-98; ProQuest Dialog, info consult, 1998-. **Orgs:** NC Libr Asn, 1986-; newsletter co-ed, Remco NCLA, 1986-; New Roundtable NCLA, 1986-; Am Libr Asn, 1988-; pres, Alumni Asn UNC, Greensboro Dept Libr & Info Studies, 1989-90. **Honors/Awds:** MLA Scholarship, Medical Libr Asn, 1985; Young Careerist Award, New Members Roundtable, NCLA, 1989. **Home Addr:** 1113 Cutters Creek Dr, Pfafftown, NC 27040, **Home Phone:** (919)945-3488. **Business Addr:** Head Periodicals, Documents, Forsyth County Public Library Business Science, 660 W 5th St, Winston-Salem, NC 27101, **Business Phone:** (919)727-2220.

### JOHNSON, SHIRLEY
Librarian. **Personal:** Born Baltimore, MD; daughter of George Marshall and Virginia Williams; married Edward. **Career:** Enoch Pratt Free Libr, Baltimore, MD, librn, 1989-, br mgr, currently. **Orgs:** Md Libr Asn, 1985-; Univ Baltimore Alumni Asn, 1987-; Am Libr Asn, 1988-; Black Caucus Am Libr Asn, 1988-; Univ Pittsburgh Alumni Asn, 1989-; Am Lib Asn Off Literacy & Outreach Serv, OLOS, 1996-98; SSRT Coretta Scott King Task Force, 1998-99; Black Caucus Am Libr Asn, 2000-; Pub Libr Asn, 2003-. **Honors/Awds:** Esther J Piercy Award, Enoch Pratt Free Libr, 1994; Metropolitan United Methodist Ch Book Lovers Award, 2003. **Business Addr:** Branch Manager, Enoch Pratt Free Library, Edmondson Ave Br 4330, Baltimore, MD 21201, **Business Phone:** (410)396-0946.

### JOHNSON, DR. SHIRLEY BAILEY
Association executive, teacher. **Personal:** children: 2. **Career:** Miami Dade County Fla Pub Schs, teacher, 1970-88; United Teachers Dade Co, secy-treas, chief staff, 2001, interim pres, 2003-04; Miami Dade Pub Sch, supvr curric & instr, currntly. **Orgs:** Pres, Am Fed Teachers, Vienna Chap; pres, Nat Asn Advan Colored People, Jackson, Miss, vpres, Miami-Dade; Delta Sigma Theta Sorority; bd dir, New Way Fel Int Church, elder sunday sch teacher. **Business Addr:** Vice President, National Association for the Advancement of Colored People, 13230 NW 7th Ave, North Miami, FL 33168, **Business Phone:** (305)685-8694.

### JOHNSON, SIDNEY
Vice president (organization), automotive executive. **Educ:** Cent State Univ, Wilberforce, OH, BS, indust eng & technol, 1984; Wesleyan Univ, Indianapolis, IN, MS, indust mgt, 1993; Ctr Creative Leadership-Exec Develop, attended 2005. **Career:** Gen Motors, Allison Transmission Div, Indianapolis, Ind, 1988-94; Saturn, Spring Hill, Tenn, 1994-95; Delphi Harrison Thermal Systs, Dayton, Oh, 1995; Delphi Interior Systs, Warren, Mich, supplier qual mgr, 1998-99, mgr chem, 1999-2000; Delphi Packard Elec, Warren, Oh, dir, N Am purchasing, 2000-02; Delphi Elec/Electronic Archit, dir, 2002-06; Delphi, sr vpres global supply mgt, 2006-, exec champion global supply mgt task team; DGSM Task Team, exec champion. **Orgs:** Bd dir, Nat Minority Supplier Develop Comt; chair, Inst Supply Mgt; adv bd mem, Focus: HOPE; adv bd mem, Mich State Univ, Supply Chain Mgt; bd dir, Mich Minority Supplier Develop Coun.

### JOHNSON, PROF. STEPHANIE ANNE
Educator. **Personal:** Born Aug 19, 1952, Harrisburg, PA; daughter of Lawrence J and Virginia E. **Educ:** Emerson Col, Boston, MA, BFA, theater, 1974; San Francisco State Univ, MA, interdisciplinary studies, 1994; Univ Calif, Berkeley, MFA, 1999; Union Inst & Univ, PhD, interdisciplinary studies, pub policy, 2008. **Career:** Black Filmmakers Hall Fame, lighting designer, 1980-90; Five Heartbeats, film electrician; prod asst; Design Arts, Nat Endowment Fel, 1983; Visions Spirit: Alice Walker, film gaffer & many other films, videos & industrials; guest lectr: Univ Calif, Berkeley, Atlanta, San Fran State Univ, De Melkweg, Amsterdam; Headlands Ctr Arts, artist resident, 1995; Wallace Gerbode, Design Fel, 1999; Lighting Designer: NY, Calif, Paris, Bombay; Visual & Pub Art Dept, Calif State Univ, Monterey Bay, prof, 1994-, co-chmn, 2006-; One person show-Sargent Johnson Gallery, SF, 2006; Johnson Crawford Consults, community & policy consult, 2010-. **Orgs:** Int Asn Stagehands & Theatical Employees, Int Asn Theatrical & Stage Employees, 1993-; Int Asn Lighting Designers, Int Asn Lighting Designers, Col Art Asn; Am Asn Mus; Solar Cookers Int. **Home Addr:** 2740 Mabel St, Berkeley, CA 94702-2345, **Home Phone:** (510)549-1187. **Business Addr:** Professor, California State University Monterey Bay, 100 Campus Ctr, Seaside, CA 93955-8001, **Business Phone:** (831)582-3693.

### JOHNSON, STEPHEN A.
Lawyer. **Educ:** Baruch Col, BBA, acct, 1983; Wayne State Univ, JD, 1987. **Career:** Gen Motors Corp, finance analyst, 1983-87; Pricewaterhouse Cooper LLP, tax partner, 1987-. **Orgs:** One Hundred Black Men, 1997-. **Business Addr:** Tax Partner, Price Waterhouse Coopers LLP, 300 Madison Ave, New York, NY 10017-6204, **Business Phone:** (203)539-3581.

### JOHNSON, STEPHEN L.
Executive. **Personal:** Born Dec 14, 1944, Denver, CO; son of Mary Helen Bess; children: Chemaine D, Scott S & Matthew R. **Educ:** Univ Denver, BS, Eng lang & lit, gen, 1966; Univ San Francisco, BS, mgt, 1989. **Career:** Denver Post, reporter/ed, 1970-74; Bank Am, sr pub info officer, 1975-79; First Interstate Bank, vpres pub rels, Denver Post, reporter/ed, 1970-74; Bank Am, sr pub info officer, 1974-77; Bechtel Corp, pub affairs mgr, 1978-81; First Interstate Bank, vpres pub rels, 1979-83; First Nationwide Financial Corp, subsid Ford Motor Co, sr vpres, pub affairs, 1982-91, vpres, dir corp communs, appt First vpres subsid, 1987, app sr vpres, 1988; Union Bank Calif, sr vpres & dir, corp commun, 1992-2010; Johnson Consult & Commun, prin, 2011-. **Orgs:** Trustee, Calif Neighborhood Housing Found, 1980-85; dir, Communs Bridge (Los Angeles), 1984-87, finance chair mayor's Comt Housing Homeless; conf bd, Pub Affair Exec Comt, 1987-92; adv bd, San Jose State Univ, 1987-90; bd trustee, Fine Arts Mus San Francisco, 1999-2005; bd mem, KQED Pub Tv & Radio, 2002-08; Sigma Pi Phi Fraternity; bd mem, Mus African Diaspora. **Honors/Awds:** Directors Award for Public Service, Calif Neighborhood Housing Found, 1980; Honoree, JFK Sch Govt, Harvard Univ Housing Scholar, 1988. **Home Addr:** 16 Woodleaf Ct, Novato, CA 94945-1325, **Home Phone:** (415)320-2295. **Business Addr:** Senior Vice President, Union Bank California, 400 California St First Fl, San Francisco, CA 94104, **Business Phone:** (415)765-3252.

### JOHNSON, STERLING, JR.
Judge. **Personal:** Born May 14, 1934, Brooklyn, NY; married Barbara; children: Sterling III, Alicia Daniels & Jennifer. **Educ:** Brooklyn Col, BA, 1963; Brooklyn Law Sch, LLB, 1966. **Career:** US Marine Corps, 1952-55; New York Police Dept, officer, 1956-67; Southern Dist, asst US atty, 1967-70; Eastern Dist of New York, asst Us atty, 1967-70; Civil Complaint Rev Bd, exec dir, 1970-74; DEA, exec liaison officer, 1974-75; Drug Enforcement Admin, exec liaison officer, 1974-75; Spec Narcotics Prosecutor's Off, spec narcotics prosecutor, 1974-91; Us Naval Res, Capt, 1974-91; Judge Advocate Gen, Capt, 1974-91; US Dist Ct, fed judge, 1991-; Us Sentencing Comn, comnr, 1999-2002. **Orgs:** Bd dir, Police Athletic League, 1975-; chmn, Drug Adv Task Force Nat Adv Comt CDR USNR Annapolis, 1975-; US Sentencing Comn, comnr, 1999-; Founding Mem, Noble; African Am police officer. **Home Addr:** 146 04 225th St, Jamaica, NY 11413. **Business Addr:** Federal Judge, US District Court for the Eastern District of New York, 225 Cadman Plz E, Brooklyn, NY 11201, **Business Phone:** (718)613-2465.

### JOHNSON, T. J.
Automotive executive. **Career:** Team Ford-Mercury Inc, Tarboro, NC, dealership, owner, pres, currently; Crossroads Ford-Mercury Inc, Jesup, Ga, dealership, owner, currently; Summerville Ford-Mercury Inc, Summerville, SC, dealership, owner, currently. **Orgs:** Bd First Fed Charleston. **Home Addr:** 114 Ruffin Rd, Summerville, SC 29483-1947. **Business Addr:** Owner, Summerville Ford Mercury, 103 Old Trolley Rd, Summerville, SC 29485, **Business Phone:** (843)873-3550.

### JOHNSON, TALIB. See SOULCHILD, MUSIQ.

### JOHNSON, THEODORE, SR.
Military leader. **Personal:** Born Aug 23, 1920, Ft. Mitchell, AL; married Mattie E Butler; children: Theodore Jr, Winfred O, Frederick L, Larry E, Welton C, James C & Jeffrey M. **Educ:** Stockton State Col, Pomona, NJ, BS, 1978, MA, 1982; Kean Col, NJ, Union, NJ, MA, coun, 1982; Univ Md; Brookdale Community Col, community ment health. **Career:** Military leader (retired); AUS, Field Artil Brigade Battery, 829 Tank Destroyer Batallion Shipped, Southampton, Eng, basic training, 1941; Le-Harve France Siefried Line Ger, 1944; SW Pac, 1945, stateside, 1946-50, Korea, 1950; Ger Occup, duty, 1952-55, Signal Corp & Res & Develop Lab, 1955-64; Va Blind Ctr Hines Hosp, rehab, 1965. **Orgs:** Exec dir & nat pres, Nat Asn Advan Colored People, 1973; Red Bank Community Ctr Inc; Title I Adv Comt & Adv Comt Proj Seed; exec comt mem & vpres, chmn, Vet Affairs; pres, Red Bank Br Nat Asn Advan Colored People; VFW 438; Disabled Vet Orgn; Prince Hall Masonic Lodge; Oswitchee Lodge 785. **Honors/Awds:** President Award, Greater Red Bank Br, Nat Asn Advan Colored People, 1980; Am Theater Oper Medal; Asiatic Pacific Theater Oper Medal, European African Mediter & Europe Theater. **Special Achievements:** Motion Picture Photog. **Home Addr:** 248 Leighton Ave, Red Bank, NJ 07701-1459, **Home Phone:** (732)842-1318.

### JOHNSON, THOMAS H.
Evangelist, clergy. **Personal:** Born Aug 5, 1932, Longview, TX; son of Allen Groggs Sr and Gladys Johnson Morrison; married Maggie L Stewart; children: Crystal Louise, Johnson Turner & Cathi Lynn Wilson. **Educ:** Southwestern Christian Col, Terrill, Tex, BA, relig, 1955. **Career:** Madison Ave Ch Christ, minister & evangelist, 1955-. **Orgs:** Nat Asn Advan Colored People, 1975-; chmn, Jamie Harris Livertransplant Fund, 1987; Christian Question & Answer Panelist. **Business Addr:** Evangelist, Minister, Madison Avenue Church of Christ, 1740 N Madison Ave, Wichita, KS 67214, **Business Phone:** (316)265-0583.

### JOHNSON, THOMAS PEPPER. See JOHNSON, PEPPER.

### JOHNSON, TIFFANI TAMARA
Executive, basketball player. **Personal:** Born Dec 27, 1975, Charlotte, NC. **Educ:** Univ Tenn, BS, sociol, 1998. **Career:** Basketball player (retired), executive; US Nat Select Team, 1996; Sacramento Monarchs, 1998; Phoenix Suns, 1998; Turkey, 2000-01; Reyer Venezia, 2000-01; Houston Comets, ctr, 2000-05; Italy with Venezia, 2001-02; Kumho Falcons Womens Korea Basketball League, 2002-03; FIBA Womens World Cup, 2003; Russ Womens Superleague Div, 2003-04; TU Kazan, 2003-04; Sao Paulo FC, 2003; Houston Stealth, 2004; Fenerbahce, 2004-05; K Cero ICP & Wisla Can-Pack Krakow, 2005-06; Wisla Cracovia, 2006; Seattle Storm, 2006; FIBA Euro League Women, 2005-08; Fundamentally Sound Sch Hoops, dir & chif exec officer, currently. **Business Addr:** Chief Executive Officer, Director, Fundamentally Sound School of Hoops, 422 E Union Grove Cir, Auburn, GA 30011, **Business Phone:** (704)980-9726.

### JOHNSON, TIMOTHY JULIUS, JR.
Artist. **Personal:** Born Dec 30, 1935, Chester, VA; son of Timothy J Sr and Lois Peay; married Patricia B Hoye; children: Darryl Julius & Dianne Patrice. **Educ:** Mich State Univ, attended 1956. **Career:** Visual Display Arts Chanute AFB IL, supvr, 1979-82; US Govt Air Force, illusr. **Orgs:** Leader & comm B mem, Boy & Girl Scouts Am, 1964-70; Alpha Phi Alpha, 1955-; libr bd mem, Village Rantoul, IL, 1979-82; River Art Group, 1983-84. **Honors/Awds:** First place, Chanute Fine Arts Festival; Second place, paintings, Third place, sculptures in Urbana, St Fair; First place & Best of Show in the Danville Fine Arts Festival; First & Best of Show, Tech Exhibit Peoria; Best of Show, Black Heritage week Chanute AFB, 1982. **Home Addr:** 2526 Sequoia Height, San Antonio, TX 78251, **Home Phone:** (210)509-6002.

### JOHNSON, DR. TOBE, JR.
Educator, chairperson. **Personal:** Born Sep 16, 1929, Birmingham, AL; son of Evelyn and Tobe; married Goldie Culpepper; children: Tobe III & Cheryl. **Educ:** Morehouse Col, BA, 1954; Columbia Univ, PhD, 1963. **Career:** Ealeton Inst Polit & Nat Ctr Educ polit fac fel, Dem Pres Nom Conv, 1954; Columbia Univ, fel, 1954-55; Prairie View A&M, instr, 1956-57; Prairie View, asst prof, 1961-62; Univ Pittsburgh, vis assoc prof, 1956-66; John Hay Whitney fel, 1959-60; Carleton Col, prof, 1968; Morehouse Col, Dept Polit Sci, distinguished chair, from asst prof to assoc prof, 1958-66, prof, 1967-, Avalon prof polit sci, currently, Div Humanities & Social Scis, interim dean, currently, HUD Mgt Planning Seminars, dir; Ford Found, res fel, 1968-69. **Orgs:** Dir, Urban Studies Prog Former Coun; Am Polit Sci Asn; Bd Examrs Educ Testing Serv, Grad Rec Exam Polit Sci, 1972-76; Am Soc Pub Admin; Conf Ministry Pub Admin Bd, United Way Atlanta; S Ed Found; Nat Asn Reg Coun; Atlanta Reg Comm Hons, Phi Beta Kappa; Nat Acad Pub Admin, 1981Interuniversity Consortium Polit & Social Res, 1988-90. **Honors/Awds:** United Negro Col Fund, distinguished fel, 1981-82. **Special Achievements:** First African American to earn a Ph.D degree in Political Science from Columbia University; Numerous publications including "The Nature and Status of Black Studies", 1965; "The Black College as System", 1974; "Black Metropolitanization", "Joint Center for Political Studies,", 1974; The Atlanta Regional Metropolitan Transit System. **Home Addr:** 3405 Lynfield Dr SW, Atlanta, GA 30311-2915, **Home Phone:** (404)696-6296. **Business Addr:** Professor, Interim Dean of Humanities and

Social Science, Morehouse College, 830 Westview Dr SW, Atlanta, GA 30314, **Business Phone:** (404)681-2800.

### JOHNSON, DR. TOMMIE ULMER MAE
Educator. **Personal:** Born Jun 23, 1925, Gary, IN; daughter of Abraham Ulmer and Mosell Sadler Ulmer; married Walter H. **Educ:** Wayne State Univ, BS, 1961, MEd, 1964, EdD, 1971. **Career:** City Detroit, sr stenographer, 1948-59; Detroit Pub Schs, teacher, 1961-68; Ford Found fel, 1971; Wayne State Univ, asst prof, 1971-76; Wayne State Univ, assoc prof, 1976-; vis prof, Norfolk State Univ, 1978; Wayne State Univ, asst provost, 1985-.Wayne State Univ, BS, 1961, MEd, 1964, EdD, 1971. **Orgs:** Sponsor, Delta Pi Epsilon Wayne State Univ Grad Chap, 1980-; Mich Occup Teacher Educ Asn, 1982-; Alpha Kappa Alpha Sororoty; life mem, Nat Asn Advan Colored People; asst treas & trustee, Second Baptist Church Detroit; Am Educ Res Asn; Am Voc Asn; Mich Bus Educ, Nat Bus Educ Asn; Women's Econ Club; vpres, Iota Phi Lambda, 1974-91. **Home Addr:** 5655 Greenway, Detroit, MI 48204-2176. **Business Addr:** Assistant Provost for Affirmative Action, Wayne State University, 4129 Fac Admin Bldg, Detroit, MI 48202.

### JOHNSON, TONY. See JOHNSON, CLINISSON ANTHONY.

### JOHNSON, TRE, III (EDWARD STANTON JOHNSON)
Football coach, football player. **Personal:** Born Aug 30, 1971, Manhattan, NY. **Educ:** Temple Univ, social admin, 1993, MSW. **Career:** Football player (retired), coach; Washington Redskins, guard & right guard & left guard, 1994-2000, right guard, 2002; Cleveland Browns, guard & right guard, 2001; Landon Sch, history teacher, coach & cult transition counr, currently. **Honors/Awds:** Pro Bowl, 1999. **Business Addr:** History Teacher, Coach, Landon School, 6101 Wilson Lane, Bethesda, MD 20817-3199, **Business Phone:** (301)320-3200.

### JOHNSON, TROY DWAN
Football player. **Personal:** Born Oct 20, 1962, New Orleans, LA. **Educ:** Southeastern LA Univ; Southern Univ. **Career:** Denver Gold, wide receiver, 1985; St Louis Cardinals, wide receiver, 1986-87; Pittsburgh Steelers, 1988; Detroit Lions, wide receiver, 1989.

### JOHNSON, ULYSSES JOHANN, III
Educator, teacher, counselor. **Personal:** Born Aug 11, 1929, Winter Haven, FL; son of Ulysses Johann Sr and Hattle Thomas; married Thelma Mae Simmons; children: Marcus Antonious & Melanie Aida. **Educ:** Fisk Univ, BS, 1951; Univ Denver, MS, stud personnel serv, 1955; Tenn Tech Univ, EdS, 1973. **Career:** Educator, teacher, counselor (retired); Rochelle Jr Sr High Sch, teacher, counr, coach, 1951-69; Polk Community Col, counr, 1969-71, DSS Spec, dir 1971-73, couns dir, 1973-92. **Orgs:** Pres, Cent Fla Guid Asn, 1972-73; master, Samson Lodge 142 F & A M Masons, 1980-84; charter mem, FSC Chap, Phi Delta Kappa, 1983-86; century Soc, Mid-Fla Med Serv Found, Winter Haven Hosp; pres, Fla Asn Community Col; Am Asn Coun Devel; Nat Asn Advan Colored People; Kappa Delta Pi; Kappa Alpha Psi. **Home Addr:** 560 Sears Ave NE, Winter Haven, FL 33881, **Home Phone:** (863)293-1966.

### JOHNSON, VALERIE ANN
College teacher, college administrator. **Educ:** Spelman Col, BA, sociol & urban studies concentration; Atlanta Univ, MA; Univ Calif, Berkeley, PhD, med anthrop. **Career:** Bennett Col Women, Mott Distriguished Prof Women's Studies/Dir Africana Women's Studies. **Orgs:** N Carolina African Am Heritage Comm, chair; Our C's Pl, bd mem; Scarritt Bennett Ctr, bd mem; N Carolina Environ Justice Network. **Special Achievements:** Investigates gender, bioethics, disability, and environmental justice in countries like Costa Rica, Zimbabwe, Tanzania, and the Seychelles Islands; also conducts foodways research on the African-American church supper. **Business Addr:** Bennett College, 900 E Washington St, Greensboro, NC 27401, **Business Phone:** (336)517-2259.

### JOHNSON, VANEESE
Entrepreneur, consultant, public speaker. **Educ:** Vista Jr Col, AA; Univ Calif, Los Angeles, mgt develop entrepreneurs, 2003; Kellogg Sch Mgt, advan mgt educ prog, 2003; Univ Ill & Kellogg Sch Mgt, adult migrant eng prog, 2003; Univ Calif, Los Angeles, MDE cert, 2003; Harvard Bus Sch, entrepreneurial training, 2004. **Career:** Serv coordr; serv supvr; acct mgr; regional sales mgr; speaker; bus teacher & trainer; On The Move Staffing Serv LLC, founder & pres, 1998-. **Orgs:** African Am Bus Summit; San Francisco Black Chamber Com; Jobs 4 Youth; Jewish Voc Serv; bd mem, Northern Calif Supplier Develop Coun; bd mem, Calif Staffing Professionals; Nat Coalition 100 Black Women Inc; instr, Renaissance Entrepreneurship Ctr. **Business Addr:** Founder, President, On the Move Staffing Services LLC, 275 5th St, San Francisco, CA 94103, **Business Phone:** (800)804-3871.

### JOHNSON, DR. VANNETTE WILLIAM
School administrator, educator. **Personal:** Born May 27, 1930, Little Rock, AR; son of Charlie and Laura Delorius Miller; married Delois V Davis; children: Juliette Laureen Lewis, Alberta Lynnette Shelton, Melanie Annette Dumas & Leontyne Delois Howard. **Educ:** Ark AM&N Col, BS, 1952; Univ Ark, MEd, 1961, DEd, 1970. **Career:** Little Rock, swimming pool mgr; Wash, recreation supvr; UAPB, proj adminr & activ dir; Nat Youth Sports Prog, head track coach & recreation dir; Dept Health, chmn, athletic dir & head football coach; Merrill HS, teacher, asst coach, 1952-57; Ark AM&N Col, asst coach & instr, 1957-62, head football coach, 1962-72; Southern Educ Found, fel, 1967-70; Univ Ark, Pine Bluff, head football coach, athletic dir, 1974-75, actg dept chmn & athletic dir, 1980-83, dept chmn & athletic dir, 1983-84, dept chmn, prof, 1984-, Sch Educ & Compliance Coordr, prof, currently; Golden Lions All-Am Quarterback, football coach & athletic dir. **Orgs:** Comnr, Ark Comn Human Rels, 1977-81; justice peace Jefferson County, 1977-; Pine Bluff Conv Ctr Community, fin community, 1977-; pres, Jefferson Cty Black Caucus, 1978-; vpres, Ark Black Caucus, 1981-; corp bd, Jefferson Comprehensive Care Ctr, 1981-; educ community, Pine Bluff Chamber Com, 1982-; Comn Pine Bluff Transp Comn, 1982-; long range plng, Pine Bluff Chamber Com, 1985; NAACP; Pine Bluff/Jefferson County Clean & Beautiful Community, 1982-85 & 1992-; adv bd, Literacy Coun Jefferson County, 1987; fin comt chmn, Jefferson County Quorum Ct, 1989-; secy, Jefferson County Dem Cent Comt, 1990-; pres, Jefferson County Black Elected officials Asn, 1990-; Dem State Comt, 1990-; Nat Asn Col Dir Athletics; secy-treas, Ark Dem Party. **Honors/Awds:** Inductee Legends Hall of Fame, Southwestern Athletic Conf, 2007. **Special Achievements:** Publication: Eval of the Admin of Intercollegiate Athletics in Selected Cols & Univs. **Home Addr:** 8545 Highton Ct, Cincinnati, OH 45236, **Home Phone:** (870)534-3835. **Business Addr:** Compliance Coordinator, Professor, University of Arkansas, 2604 W Pullen, Pine Bluff, AR 71601, **Business Phone:** (870)534-3835.

### JOHNSON, VERDIA EARLINE
President (organization), founder (originator), executive. **Personal:** Born Jul 14, 1950, Ft. Worth, TX; married Everett N Jr. **Educ:** Howard Univ, BA, mkt, 1972; NY Univ, MBA, mkt, 1974. **Career:** Colgate Palmolive, NY, asst prod mgr, 1974-77; Stand Brands, NY, sr prod mgr, 1977-81; Nabisco Brands, NJ, sr prod mgr, 1981-84; BCI Mkt Inc, NY, dir mkt, 1984-85; Black Enterprise Mag, NY, advert dir, 1985-86; JEM Group Inc, pres; Gannett Outdoor Co, vpres sales, 1988-96; Graham Gregory Bozell Inc, managing dir; MOBE, pres, vpres, gen mgr; Stedman Graham & Partners, vpres & gen mgr, 1996-99; Footsteps, pres & co-founder, 1999-. **Orgs:** Nat Asn Mkt Developers; Faith Love Christian Ctr's Jack & Jill Am; Am Asn Adv Agencies; bd mem, dir, African Am Med Network, 2004. **Home Addr:** 3 Marion Dr, Mahwah, NJ 07430-2402, **Home Phone:** (201)854-7841. **Business Addr:** President, Co- Founder, Footsteps LLC, 200 Vanick St Suite 610, New York, NY 10014, **Business Phone:** (212)336-9747.

### JOHNSON, DR. VERMELLE JAMISON
School administrator. **Personal:** Born Aug 2, 1933, Islandton, SC; married Charles Harry; children: Charles H Jr & Temple Odessa. **Educ:** SC State Col, BS, 1955, MEd, 1969; Univ SC, PhD, 1976. **Career:** Ala State Col, 1956-57; Fed Employee, 1957-62; Pub Sch SC, teacher, 1962-68; SC State Col, asst prof bus educ, 1969, provost, dir, chair, Comt Acad Affairs & Licensing, exec vpres, currently; SC, Comnr Higher Educ, 2001-06; Claflin Col, prof, chairperson, dept bus admin & vpres, sr vpres, 1985; Univ NDak, instr; Univ RI, instr. **Orgs:** State secy, SC Bus Ed Asn; Alpha Kappa Mu Hon Soc; Delta Mu Delta Nat Bus Frat; Phi Delta kappa Hon Soc; Iota Phi Lambda Bus Sor; Nat Bus Ed Asn; SC State Bus Ed Asn; Alpha Kappa Alpha Sorority; Daughter Elk; IBPOE W; Sunday sch teacher Trinity United Methodist Church; pres, Conf Chief Acad Officers Southern States, 1991-; chmn, Acad Affairs & Licensing; comnr, SC Higher Educ; Vpres, Acad Affairs. **Special Achievements:** First minority female president of the conference of chief Academic officers of the southern states. **Home Addr:** 691 Bramble Lane, Orangeburg, SC 29115-2640, **Home Phone:** (803)534-8783. **Business Addr:** Chair, South Carolina State College, 300 Col St NE, Orangeburg, SC 29117, **Business Phone:** (803)536-7190.

### JOHNSON, VICKIE ANNETTE
Basketball coach, basketball player. **Personal:** Born Apr 15, 1972, Coushatta, LA; daughter of Susie. **Educ:** La Tech, sociol & psychol, 1996. **Career:** Basketball player (retired), basketball coach; New York Liberty, forward & guard, 1997-2006; San Antonio Silver Stars, forward & guard, 2006-09; San Antonio Silver Stars, asst coach, 2011-. **Home Addr:** PO Box 667, Coushatta, LA 71019. **Business Addr:** Assistant Coach, San Antonio Silver Stars, 1 AT T Ctr, San Antonio, TX 78219, **Business Phone:** (210)444-5090.

### JOHNSON, VINNIE (VINCENT JOHNSON)
Basketball player, radio host, executive. **Personal:** Born Sep 1, 1956, Brooklyn, NY. **Educ:** McLennan Community Col, attended 1977; Baylor Univ, phys educ, 1979. **Career:** Basketball player (retired), business executive; Seattle SuperSonics, 1979-81; Detroit Pistons, player, 1981-94, radio analyst, currently; San Antonio Spurs, 1991-92; Piston Modules LLC, chmn bd, currently; Airea Inc, dir, chmn & chief exec officer; Piston Automotive, founder, chmn & chief exec officer, 1995-; Piston Group, chmn, 1995-. **Orgs:** Detroit Chamber Com; Mich Minority Bus Develop Coun; NBA championship teams, 1989-90. **Home Addr:** , Brooklyn, NY 11256. **Business Addr:** Chairman, Piston Group & Piston Automotive, 12723 Tel Rd, Redford, MI 48239, **Business Phone:** (313)541-8674.

### JOHNSON, VIRGINIA ALMA FAIRFAX
Dancer. **Personal:** Born Jan 25, 1950, Washington, DC; daughter of James Lee and Madeline Murray. **Educ:** Wash Sch Ballet; NY Univ, dance, 1969; Fordham Univ. **Career:** Dancer (retired); Guest appearances: Capitol Ballet, Chicago Opera Ballet, Wash Ballet, Baltimore Civic Youth Ballet, Stars World Ballet, Australia, Detroit Symphony, Nat Symphony, Eugene Ballet; Film: A Piece Action, 1977; TV appearances: "Dance Am"; "Ancient Songs C"; "Night 100 Stars"; Maymount Col White House appearances Pres Carter & Reagan, solo concert; Blanche duBois a Streetcar Named Desire PBS Great Performances, 1952; Les Biches; Giselle; Serenade, Allegro Brillante; Swan Lake (Act II); Othello; Greening; Footprints Dressed Red; Toccata E Due Canzoni; Forces Rhythm; Voluntaries; Designs With Strings; Fall River Legend, 1948; A Creole Giselle, NBC; Dance Theatre Harlem, prin dancer, 1969-97; Wash Ballet, Nutcracker; Alicia Alonso's Ballet de Cuba, Giselle; Chicago Opera Ballet, 1975; Stars World Ballet Australian tour, 1979; Ballet Nacional de Cuba, 1988; Baltimore Civic Youth Ballet, Detroit Symphony & Cleveland Ballet, all 1991; Royal Ballet, Giselle, 1992. **Orgs:** Hon mem, Alpha Kappa Alpha Sorority. **Honors/Awds:** Young Achiever Award, Nat Coun Women United States, 1985; Outstanding Young Woman of America, Nat Coun Women, 1985; Dance Magazine Award, 1991.

### JOHNSON, WALDO EMERSON, JR.
Research scientist, educator. **Personal:** Born Mar 13, 1955, Americus, GA; son of Waldo Emerson Sr and Addie Ben. **Educ:** Mercer Univ, Macon, GA, BA, sociol & eng, 1977; Univ Mich, Ann Arbor, MI, MSW, community develop & admin, 1979; Univ Chicago, PhD, social welfare policy & admin, 1993. **Career:** Ga Sw Col, Upward Bound, proj coordr, 1979-82; Alpha Phi Alpha Frat Inc, asst exec dir, progs, 1982-85, develop consult, 1985-; Firman Community Servs, Chicago, Ill, dir, youth & family servs, 1987-90; Loyola Univ Chicago, Chicago, Ill, vis asst prof, sch social work, 1991-96; Northwestern Univ, Univ Chicago Joint Ctr Poverty Res, fac affil; Princeton Univ, Fragile Families & Child Well-Being Study, Network scholar, investr, 1995-; Univ Chicago, Sch Social Serv Admin, asst prof, assoc prof, 1996-, Ctr Race, Polit & Cult, dir, 2005-. **Orgs:** Chicago Chap, Black Social Workers; Task Force Effective Progs & Res, Nat Campaign Prevent Teen Pregnancy; Working Group Male Family Formation &Fertil, Fed Inter agency Forum Child & Family Statist; secy, bd dir, Proj IMAGE, 1985-91; Southside Br, Nat Asn Advan Colored People; founding mem, Arts Forum Urban Gateways, Chicago; Ill Chap, Nat Asn Social Workers; Coun Social Work Educ; Nat Coun Family Rels; Asn Pub Policy Anal & Mgmt; Metropol bd, Chicago Urban League; Paternal Involvement Proj, adv bd; AIDS Walk Chicago; bd dir, Tulane Univ, Sch Social Work, Porter-Cason Inst Advan Family Pract; Ford Found Scholars Network; 2025 Campaign Black Men & Boys; Phi Beta Kappa; African Am Stud Asn; Nat Asn Black Social Workers; Blue Key Hon Soc. **Home Addr:** 1642 E 56th St Suite 1018, Chicago, IL 60637, **Home Phone:** (773)643-5515. **Business Addr:** Director, Associate Professor, University of Chicago, Ctr Study Race Polit & Cult, Chicago, IL 60637, **Business Phone:** (773)702-1250.

### JOHNSON, WALLACE DARNELL
Administrator, baseball player. **Personal:** Born Dec 25, 1956, Gary, IN; son of Roy and Myrtle Moody. **Educ:** Ind State Univ, acct, 1979. **Career:** Baseball player (retired), baseball coach, administrator; Peat Marwick, staff acct, 1983-84; Interstate Develop & Supply Corp, Indianapolis, Ind, treas, 1985-88; Montreal Expos, baseball player, 1981-83, 1984, 1986-90; San Fransisco Giants, baseball player, 1983; Atlanta Braves, coach, 1995-97; Chicago White Sox, base coach, 1998-2002; W D Johnson & Assoc, pres, currently. **Orgs:** Gamma Gent Alumni Asn, 1977-; treas, Main St Gary, 1991-. **Honors/Awds:** Academic All-American, COSIDA, 1979; McMillan Award for Leadership, Ind St Univ, 1979, Athletic Hall of Fame, 1985; Post-Graduate Scholarship Recipient, Natl Col Athletic Asn, 1979; Most Valuable Player, Fla State League, 1980; American Assoc All Star Team, 1985; Most Valuable player, MVC conf tournament. **Home Addr:** PO Box M618, Gary, IN 46401, **Home Phone:** (219)938-1824. **Business Addr:** President, W D Johnson & Associates, 4629 Wash St, Gary, IN 46408, **Business Phone:** (219)980-0070.

### JOHNSON, WALTER LOUIS, SR.
Government official. **Personal:** Born Jan 2, 1949, Bastrop, LA; son of Samuel and Dorothy Williams Bolden; married Esther Robinson; children: Walter II & Erik. **Educ:** San Francisco City Col, San Francisco, CA, AA, 1969; St Mary's Col, Moraga, CA, BA, 1984. **Career:** City Oakland, Oakland, Calif, dir retirement systs, 1972-93, 2004; City Oakland, dir retirement risk mgt, 1993-99; City Oakland, dir human resources, 1999-2003; Police & Fire Retirement Bd, mem, currently. **Orgs:** Nat Forum Black Pub Adminr; Am Soc Pub Adminr; Nat Conf Pub Employees Retirement Systs; Calif Asn Pub Retirement Systs; trustee, Police & Fire Retirement Syst Bd Admin. **Home Addr:** 4108 Fairway Ave, Oakland, CA 94605, **Home Phone:** (510)562-5467. **Business Addr:** Member, City of Oakland, 1 Frank H Ogawa Plz, Oakland, CA 94612.

### JOHNSON, WALTER THANIEL, JR.
Lawyer, association executive, army officer. **Personal:** Born May 18, 1940, Greensboro, NC; son of Walter T Sr and Gertrude Alexander; married Yvonne Jeffries; children: Walter T III, Vernon K, Lisa Yvonne & Shannon Tamara. **Educ:** NC Agr & Tech State Univ, BS, 1961; Duke Univ Sch Law, JD, 1964; Univ NC, Govt Execs Inst, Chapel Hill, attended 1981, Justice Exec Prog, 1984. **Career:** Frye & Johnson, atty; Redevel Com Greensboro, relocation adv, 1962-63; Law Off Elreta Alexander, assoc, 1964-65; USAF, judge adv, 1965-68; Guilford Co Super Ct, asst dist atty, 1968-69; Pub Storage & Warehousing Inc, secy, exec comnr, 1971-76; Barjo Inc, secy, exec comnr, 1973-; Duke Univ Law Sch, adj prof law, 1975-; NC Cent Sch Law, adj prof, 1985-87; Barbee & Johnson, partner, 1987-88; Barbee Johnson & Glenn, partner, 1988-. **Orgs:** Vpres planning, United Way Greensboro, 1969-71; chmn, Greensboro County Bd Educ, 1970-; bd mem, Eastern Music Festival, 1972-76; chmn bd trustee, Univ NC, 1974-; bd govs, NC Bar Asn, 1975-; chmn, NC Inmate Grievance County Com, 1975-; Greensboro Bd Dirs NC Nat Bank, 1976-; chmn, NC Parole Comt, 1981-85; Citizens Comt Alternatives Inceration, 1981-83; vpres, Asn Paroling Authorities, 1982-85; vice chmn, Greensboro Vision, 1985-; bd mem, Greensboro Econ Develop Coun, 1988-. **Honors/Awds:** Outstanding Young Men of NC, 1970, Freedom Guard Award, NC Jaycees, 1970-71; Distinguish Service Award, Greensboro Jaycees, 1970; Peacemaker Award, Carolina Peacemaker Newspaper. **Special Achievements:** First black student to enroll in the law school, 1961. **Home Addr:** 1306 W Wendover Ave, Greensboro, NC 27408, **Home Phone:** (336)279-8312. **Business Addr:** Partner, Barbee Johnson & Glenn, 102 N Elm St, Greensboro, NC 27401, **Business Phone:** (336)379-1630.

### JOHNSON, WARREN S.
Executive. **Personal:** Born Apr 7, 1947, Philadelphia, PA; married Peggie A Parham; children: Warren S. **Educ:** Hampton Inst, BA, econs, 1969; Temple Univ, MA, 1975. **Career:** Executive (retired); PA Bell & Tele, mgt dev trainee, 1969-70; PA Hosp, training specialist personnel, generalist, 1970-73; Fischer & Porter Co, dir comp, 1973-84; Acts Lifecare, sr vpres human resources, 1993; ACTS Retirement-Life Communities Inc, sr vpres, human resources, 2013; Pa Dept Aging, apprise volunter, 2014; CIGNA Ins Co, dir human resource; Betz Labs, dir human resource. **Orgs:** Am Compensation Asn, 1976; exec, large Philadelphia Surv Grp, 1976-; Am Soc Personal Admin, 1977-; consult, YMFT Workshop, Alliance Bus; bd mem, Impact Thrift Stores, 2014-. **Home Addr:** 8 Edinboro Cir, Chalfont, PA 18914, **Home Phone:** (215)822-2249.

## JOHNSON, WAYNE ALAN

Consultant. **Personal:** Born May 22, 1961, Springfield, MA; son of Karl Anthony Sr and Beverly May Riley; married Terri Clara Colbert; children: Brent W & Alana S. **Educ:** George Washington Univ, BBA, mkt, 1983; Univ Wis-Madison, MBA, mkt, 1984; Georgetown Univ, JD, credits, 1989. **Career:** Freedom Fed Savings, rec dept mgr, 1976-79; US House Reps Hon Edward Poland, staff asst, 1980-83; IBM, mktg rep, 1985-88, mktg progs mgr, 1989-90, mkt mgr, 1990, solution mgr, 2008-09, channel client mgr, 2010-; consult, 1992-. **Orgs:** Consult & Partic IBM Adopt-A-Sch, 1985-86; Nat Black MBA Asn, 1986-88; Nat Asn Advan Colored People, 1989; Montgomery Co Church Christ, 1999-. **Honors/Awds:** College Scholarship Award, Emhart Corp, 1979; MBA Fellow Award, Consortium Grad Study, 1983; IBM 100% Club, 1986, 1987 & 1991. **Home Addr:** 2 Marigold Ct, Silver Spring, MD 20906-3334, **Home Phone:** (301)942-6524. **Business Addr:** Consultant, IBM, Bldg 183 800 N Frederick Ave, Gaithersburg, MD 20879, **Business Phone:** (301)240-2458.

## JOHNSON, WAYNE J.

Lawyer. **Personal:** Born Mar 21, 1958, Oakland, CA; son of Benjamin Francis and Juanita; married Miriamne; children: Kisha M, Afiya Tanzania, Zuberi Ogbonna & Jelani Bakari. **Educ:** Univ Calif, Berkeley, AB, 1979; Univ Calif, San Francisco, Hastings Col Law, JD, 1983. **Career:** Off US Congressman Ronald V Dellums, adm aide, 1979-85; Off Coun Nat Asn Advan Colored People, San Francisco Region, assoc, 1985-86; Castlemont High Sch, asst wrestling coach, 1986-89; Law Off Moore & Moore, coun, 1987; Oakland High Sch, head wrestling coach, 1989-92; Law Off Wayne Johnson, chief coun, 1992-. **Orgs:** Exec bd, Congressman Ronald V Dellums, 1984-98; adv bd, Alameda Co Econ Develop, Urban Revitalization Comn, 1993-97; Econ Develop Alliance Bus, 1998; exec bd, Congresswoman Barbara Lee, 1998. **Special Achievements:** Largest settlement in Oakland, CA history for excessive police force, 2001. **Business Addr:** Chief Counsel, Law Offices of Wayne Johnson, 445 Bellevue Ave Suite 2, Oakland, CA 94619, **Business Phone:** (510)451-1166.

## JOHNSON, WAYNE LEE

Consultant. **Personal:** Born Oct 28, 1953, Hartford, CT; son of Hubert L and Betty Hawthorne; married Bertha J; children: Jamaal Trumaine, Marquis Jawaan & Brittnee Nicole. **Educ:** Grambling State Univ, BA, 1975; Univ Hartford Grad, Sch Bus, attended. **Career:** Hartford Ins Group, work measurement analyst, 1975-77, sr work measurement analyst, 1977-79, mgt consult, 1979-86; City trust, vpres & mgr, 1986-89; Hartford Neighborhood Housing Servs, exec dir, 1990-91; Fox Mid Sch, teacher, 1991-93; State Conn, social worker, 1993-97, childrens servs consult, 1997-. **Orgs:** Asn Internal Mgt Consults, 1981-89; Toastmasters Int, 1982-84; bd dir, IMPACT, 1985-89; Blue Hills Child Care Ctr Hartford, 1986-91; bd dir, Hartford Proud & Beautiful, 1990-91; pres, Windsor Giants, 1994-96; CT Childrens Alliance, 2000-02; Child Fatality Rev Panel, 2001-01; instr, Police Officer Stands & Training Coun, 2001-03. **Honors/Awds:** Honor, Grambling State Univ, 1973; Dean's List, Grambling State Univ, 1974-75. **Special Achievements:** Wrote article: Starting Up a New Internal Management Consulting Department AIMC Forum, 1988. **Home Addr:** 20 Donna Lane, Windsor, CT 06095-3201, **Home Phone:** (860)683-1264. **Business Addr:** Children's Services Consultant, State Connecticut, 250 Hamilton St, Hartford, CT 06106, **Business Phone:** (860)418-8231.

## JOHNSON, WENDY ROBIN

Buyer. **Personal:** Born Dec 26, 1956, New York, NY; daughter of Clarence Woodson Jr (deceased) and Dolores Elizabeth Dominguez; married Keith Andrew Hill. **Educ:** Elizabeth Seton Col, AAS, lib arts, 1980; Marymount Manhattan Col, BBA, finance, 1982; Manhattan Col, Bronx, MBA, 1987. **Career:** RCA Rec, buyer specialist, 1976-85; Poly Gram Rec Inc, mgr purchasing, 1983-85; Kraft Foods Corp, assoc buyer, 1985-86, buyer, 1987-95, sr buyer, 1995-96; Pepsi-Co, mgr, 1996-97; Verizon, sourcing process leader, 1997-99; United Distillers, mgr, 1999-2001; Allied Domecq, regional dir, 2002-04; Columbia Univ, dir, bus serv, 2010-. **Orgs:** Delta Sigma Theta Sorority Inc, 1979-; troop leader, Girl Scout Coun Greater NY, 1983-; Nat Asn Female Execs, 1984-; founder, We Buy, 1988-; asst dean, Learning Ctr Canaan Baptist Church, 1988-; instr, Jr Achievement Proj Bus, 1989-; Co-founder Nuff Said!, 1992; mgr, Brooklyn Pub Libr, 2005-09. **Honors/Awds:** Outstanding Young Women of America, 1984. **Special Achievements:** Crossroads, 1993. **Home Addr:** 2027 Pacific St Apt 7E, Brooklyn, NY 11233, **Home Phone:** (718)342-1785. **Business Addr:** Director, Columbia University, 615 W 131st St 3rd Fl, New York, NY 10027, **Business Phone:** (212)851-2746.

## JOHNSON, WILBUR EUGENE

Lawyer. **Personal:** Born Mar 1, 1954, Columbia, SC. **Educ:** Augusta State Univ GA, BA, hist, 1976; Univ SC Sch Law, JD, 1979. **Career:** Earl Warren Legal Training Prog fel, 1976-79; Richland Co Pub Def Agy, lawclerk, 1977-79; Palmetto Legal Serv, staff atty, 1979-; Charleston Sch Law, adj prof; Off Atty Gen SC, asst atty gen, 1979-94; Young Clement Rivers LLP, atty, managing partner, currently. **Orgs:** Sc Bar Asn, 1979-; Urban League Guild; Kwanza Comn, 1979-; Sc Bar Circuit Rep, Young Lawyers Div, 1986-87, Employ & Labor Law Sect; S Carolina Bar Circuit Rep, Young Lawyers Div, 1986-87; S Carolina Bar Law Related Educ Comt, 1994-2000; Trust Pub Land SC Adv Coun, 2005-; Fedn Defense & Corp Coun, 2006-; SC Bar Comt; SC Bar Law Related Educ Comt; Am Bar Asn; chmn, bd mem, Charleston Metro Chamber Com; bd mem, Community Found; bd dir, bd mem, Roper & St Francis Health Found; bd mem, SC State Chamber Com; bd dir, Charleston County Disabilities Bd; ed bd, ABA/BNA Lawyers Manual Prof Conduct; Fed Bar Asn; Nat Asn Col & Univ Attorneys; bd dir, Fed Res Bank Richmond; Int Asn Defense Coun; bd dir, Sc Aquarium; bd dir, New Morning Found; bd trustee, Hist Charleston Found; bd dir, Int African Am Mus; bd dir, Charleston Regional Develop Alliance; bd dir, Carolina Youth Develop Ctr; Sc Defense Trial Attorneys' Asn; Fourth Circuit Judicial Conf; chmn, bd dir, Coastal Community Found Sc; adv bd, Charleston County Greenbelt Bank; Charleston Stage. **Honors/Awds:** Outstanding College Athelete American, 1973-74; Prestigious Joseph P. Riley Leadership Award, 2013. Listed as Best Lawyers in America. **Special Achievements:** Articles: Leading Charleston's Business Community In Support Of The Port Of Charleston by Betsy Harter, Port Charleston, January and February, 2009; Special Problems Relating to Race Discrimination co-Author, Labor and Employment Law for South Carolina Lawyers, Second Edition. **Home Addr:** 3534 Truman St, Columbia, SC 29204-1642. **Business Addr:** Managing Partner, Young Clement Rivers LLP, 25 Calhoun St Suite 400, Charleston, SC 29401, **Business Phone:** (843)724-6659.

## JOHNSON, WILHELMINA LASHAUN

Executive, financial manager. **Personal:** Born Aug 13, 1950, Ft. Worth, TX. **Educ:** Tex Christian Univ, BS, 1983; Univ Tex, Arlington, 1987. **Career:** City Ft Worth, admin intern, 1979, admin asst, 1979-83, admin analyst, 1983. **Orgs:** Conf Minorities Assoc, 1979-; Urban Mgt Asn N Tex, 1979-; Am Soc Pub Admin, 1980; Int City Mgt Assoc, 1980-; legacy mem, Nat Forum Black Pub Admin, 1984-. **Home Addr:** 7810 Quiet Waters Dr, Arlington, TX 76104.

## JOHNSON, DR. WILLARD RAYMOND

Educator, association executive. **Personal:** Born Nov 22, 1935, St. Louis, MO; son of Willard and Dorothy Neoma Stovall; married Vivian Robinson; children: Caryn L & Kimberly E. **Educ:** Pasadena City Col, AA, 1955; Univ Calif, Los Angeles, BA, int rels, 1957; Johns Hopkins Sch Advan Int Studies, MA, African studies, 1961; Harvard Univ, PhD, 1965. **Career:** Ford Found Foreign Area Training fels, 1959, 1960, 1963 & 1964; John Hay Whitney Found Oppurtunity, fel, 1961; Mass Inst Technol, Dept Polit Sci, from asst prof to prof, 1964-96, prof emer polit sci, 1996-; Rockefeller Ctr Belagio, Italy, resident fel, 1987, fulbright fel, 1987. **Orgs:** Vpres, African Heritage Studies Asn, 1978; Am Polit Sci Asn, 1965-; Nat Econ Asn, 1971-82; Nat Conf Black Polit Scientists, 1971; US Nat Comt, UNESCO, 1960-66; bd mem, Boston New Urban League, 1967-72; bd mem, Nat Scholar Fund Negro Stud, 1958-59; New Eng Polit Sci Asn, 1966-69; Coun Foreign Rels, 1973-97; Black Forum Foreign Affairs, 1976-78; Asn Study Afro-Am Life & Hist, 1968-72; bd mem, Asn Concerned African Scholars, 1977; nat co-chmn, Asn Concerned African Scholars, 1983-89; bd mem, World Univ Serv, 1958-60; exec dir, Circle Inc, 1968-70; bd mem, Interfaith Housing corp, 1970; chmn bd, Circle Complex, Roxbury, 1970-72; dir, Africa Policy Task Force McGovern Pres Campaign, 1972; Dem Party Adv Coun Foreign Affairs Study, 1976; pres, Trans Africa Inc, Boston Chap, 1981-90; bd mem, Trans Africa Inc Nat, 1977-95; dir, Bus Mgt Econ Develop Res Proj, 1973-95; dir, Communs Component African Am Issues Ctr & Mass Inst Technol Ctr Int Studies, 1982-91; founder & sr adv, Boston Pan-African Forum, 1996-; founder, Kans Inst African Am & Native Am Family Hist, 1991-; pres, Kans Inst African Am & Native Am Family Hist, 1997-; UNESCO; founding mem, Nat Asn Advan Colored People. **Honors/Awds:** Research Grant, Ctr Int Studies, Mass Inst Technol, 1971; Research Grant, Technol Adaptation Proj, Mass Inst Technol, 1973-74; Black Achievers Award, Boston Young Men Christian Asn, 1899; Black Men of Vision Award, Boston Mus African Am Hist, 1992; Fulbright Seminar, Indonesia, 1991. **Special Achievements:** Publications Articles & Book chapters on issues of African development & foreign relations, & economic & political development of American inner-city areas; Book: The Cameroon Federation, Princeton University Press, 1996; Co-authored with his wife: West African Governments and Volunteer Development Organizations: Priorities for Partnership. **Home Addr:** 44 Norwood Ave, Newton Center, MA 02459, **Home Phone:** (941)952-3244. **Business Addr:** Professor Emeritus of Political Science, Massachusetts Institute of Technology, MIT E53-367, Cambridge, MA 02139-4307, **Business Phone:** (617)253-2952.

## JOHNSON, WILLIAM A., JR.

Government official, college teacher, association executive. **Personal:** Born Aug 22, 1942, Lynchburg, VA; son of William A Sr and Roberta Davis; married Sylvia M; children: Kelley M, Kristin R, Wynde A & Sylvia McCoy. **Educ:** Howard Univ, BA, polit sci, 1965, MA, polit sci, 1967. **Career:** US Supreme Ct, stud aide, 1966; Nat Hwy Users Conf Wash, legis analyst, 1966-67; Genesee Community Col Flint, instr polit sci, 1967-71; Mott Community Col, Mich, prof polit sci, 1967-71; Urban League, Flint, Mich, dep exec dir, 1971-72; Nat Urban League, dir; Urban League Rochester, pres & chief exec officer, 1972-93; Rochester Dem & Chronicle, columnist; Time Mag, columnist, 1975-90; City Rochester, civil serv comnr, 1980-90, mayor, 1994-2005; Rochester Inst Technol, minett prof, 1996-97, distinguished prof pub policy, 2006-13; Strategic Community Intervention LLC, founder, chief exec officer, 2013-. **Orgs:** Co-founder, Com More Rep Govt; organist, New Bethel CME Church, 1975-91; co-founder, Black Leadership Study Group; trustee, Monroe Community Col, Rochester, NY, 1976-82; NY St Employ & Training Coun, 1977-83; vice chmn, Urban League Rochester Econ Develop Corp, 1978-79, chmn, 1979-83, pres, 1985-93; bd dir, Eltrex Indust Inc, 1982-93; co-founder, Austin Steward Prof Soc, 1985-90; mediator, Fact finder, NYS Pub Employ Rels Bd, 1985-93; Sigma Pi Phi Fraternity; sire archon, Gamma Iota Boule, 1987-; Gamma Iota Boule, 1994-96; chairperson, Gamma Iota Boule, 1992-93; bd dir & vice chairperson, New Futures Initiative Inc, 1988-91; NY State Bd Social Work, 1988-93; trustee, Univ Rochester Grad Sch Educ, Vis Comt, 1991-; grapter, 1996-98; Nat Conf Black Mayors, 1994-2005; trustee, Rochester Philharmonic Orchestra, 1996-; trustee, Partners Livable Community, 1997-; chmn, Partners Livable Community, 2002-; US Conf Mayors, Adv bd, 1998-; trustee, US Conf Mayors, 2001-; Eureka Lodge No 36, Free & Accepted Masons, Prince Hall, 1998-; exec comnr, Ny Conf Mayors, 1999-2005; chair, Nat League Cities, Com & Regional Develop Task Force, 2002-03; dir & bd chairperson, Ctr Community Progress, 2008-; bd trustee, Nat Indusis Blind, 2006-14; trustee, Colgate Rochester Crozer Divinity Sch. **Honors/Awds:** Received more than 200 awards including: Honor, Pi Sigma Alpha, 1967; Jefferson Award for Outstanding Public Service, Am Inst Pub Serv, 1986; Doctor of Humane Letters, KeuKa Col, 1990; DHL, St John Fisher Col, 1998; DHL, Rochester Inst Technol, 1999; One of 10 US Public Officials of the Year, Governing Mag, 1999; Distinguished Alumni Award, Howard Univ, 2003; DHL, Univ Rochester, 2006. **Special Achievements:** First African-American elected mayor of the City of Rochester, New York; Delivered more than 200 speeches to universities, associations & civic groups across the United States since 1973. **Home Addr:** 165 Castlebar Rd, Rochester, NY 14610-2910, **Home Phone:** (585)242-4884. **Business Addr:** Distinguished Professor Public Policy, Rochester Institute Technology, 132 Lomb Memorial Dr Bldg 86, Rochester, NY 14263-5603, **Business Phone:** (585)475-5064.

## JOHNSON, WILLIAM ARTHUR (BILLY JOHNSON)

Football player, football coach. **Personal:** Born Jan 27, 1952, Bouthwyn, TX; married Barbara; children: Marcia, Kendra, Jared & Jazmyn. **Educ:** Widener Univ. **Career:** Football player (retired), football coach; Houston Oilers, 1978-79, Kick returner, Punt returner, 1974, 1977, wide receiver, Kick returner, Punt returner, 1975-76, wide receiver, 1980; Montreal Alouettes, wide receiver, 1981; Atlanta Falcons, 1986, Punt returner, 1982-84, wide receiver, 1985; Wash Redskins, wide receiver, 1988; Morehouse Col, coach; Atlanta Falcons, dir player prog, 1994-2005, asst strength & conditioning coach, 2005-; Duluth High Sch, asst varsity, currently. **Orgs:** Alpha Sigma Phi Fraternity. **Honors/Awds:** Falcon's Top Punt Returner of All-Time; Pro Bowl, 1975, 1977, 1983; Comeback Player of the Year, Nat Football League, 1983; Col Football Hall of Fame, 2000; Pennsylvania Sports Hall of Fame, 2000. **Home Addr:** , TX. **Business Addr:** Assistant Strength, Conditioning Coach, Atlanta Falcons, 4400 Falcon Pkwy, Flowery Branch, TX 30542, **Business Phone:** (770)965-3115.

## JOHNSON, WILLIAM EDWARD

Football player, football coach. **Personal:** Born Dec 9, 1968, Chicago, IL. **Educ:** Mich State Univ. **Career:** Football player (retired), football coach; Cleveland Browns, defensive tackle & left defensive tackle, 1992-94; Pittsburgh Steelers, left defensive tackle, 1995-96; St Louis Rams, defensive tackle & left defensive tackle, 1997; Philadelphia Eagles, right defensive tackle, 1998-99; McKinley high sch, coach, currently. **Honors/Awds:** Football Coach of the Week, Buffalo Bills High Sch, 2007. **Business Addr:** Football Coach, McKinley High School, 2323 17th St NW, Canton, OH 44708, **Business Phone:** (330)438-2750.

## JOHNSON, WILLIAM LEON (WALTER LEON JOHNSON)

Football player, football coach. **Personal:** Born Jul 13, 1974, Morganton, NC; son of William and Shirley; married Vanessa; children: Jaylen. **Educ:** Univ NC. **Career:** Football player (retired), coach; New York Jets, punt returner, 1997-98, 1999-2000; Chicago Bears, 2001, running back, 2002; San Diego Chargers, 2003-04; Dibble High Sch, asst football coach, currently.. **Business Addr:** Assistant Football Coach, Dibble High School, Old Town Main St, Blanchard, OK 73010, **Business Phone:** (405)344-6380.

## JOHNSON, WILLIAM PAUL

Executive director, consultant. **Personal:** Born Jul 17, 1963, Washington, DC; son of William Paul and Elizabeth Ann. **Educ:** Univ Wash, Wash DC, BBA, 1988; Syracuse Univ, attended 1983; Howard Univ, Wash, MEd, 1993. **Career:** Harry Diamond Labs, Adelphi MD, comput specialist, 1981-87; US Treas, Bur Engraving & Printing, Wash, DC, comput specialist, 1987-89; Comput Info & Support Servs, consult, co-owner, 1987-91; Nat High Sch Comput Competition Team, coach, 1988-95; Comp-U-Staff, Silver Springs MD, comput analyst, progr, 1989-90; McDonald-Bradley Inc, McLean, sr progr, analyst, 1989-94, consult; Tonya Inc, sr consult, 1994-99; US Dept Housing & Urban Develop, mgt info specialist, dep adminr, Off Training Serv, Training & Employee Develop Div, dir, currently. **Orgs:** Pres, Univ Wash DC Data Processing Mgt Asn, 1986-87; educ chairperson, Black Data Processing Asn, 1987-91; founder & pres, Univ Wash Black Data Processing Asn, 1987-88; chairperson, Univ Wash DC Col Bus Stud Adv Coun, 1988; pres, Black Date Processing Asn, Wash DC Chap, 1991-95. **Honors/Awds:** Syracuse Univ Academic Scholarship Award, 1981-83; Marion S Barry Scholarship Award, Univ Wash DC, 1987; Member of the Year, Washington DC Chapter Black Data Processing Asn, 1988-91; Nat member of the Year, Black Data Processing Asn, 1991; Numerous Leadership Awards, 1991-95. **Home Addr:** 849 Venable Pl NW, Washington, DC 20012, **Home Phone:** (202)723-3279. **Business Addr:** Director, US Department of Housing & Urban Development, Rm 2278 451 7th St SW, Washington, DC 20410, **Business Phone:** (202)708-1420.

## JOHNSON, DR. WILLIAM RANDOLPH, JR.

Chemist. **Personal:** Born Jul 25, 1930, Oxford, NC; son of William R Sr and Marina Townes; married Wendolyn; children: Wendolyn, Pamela & William III. **Educ:** NC Cent Univ, BS, chem, 1950; Univ Notre Dame, MS, org chem, 1952; Univ Pa, PhD, org chem, 1958. **Career:** Chemist (retired); Prairie View Agr & Mech Col, fac, 1952-53; Fla Agr & Mech Univ, prof chem, 1958-61; W R Grace & Co, res chem, 1961-63; Philip Morris Res Ctr, sr scientist, 1963-66; Va Union Univ, adj prof, chem, 1963-81. **Orgs:** Mem bd trustees, Cath Charities Inc; bd dirs, St Joseph's Villa; sch bd, Richmond Pub Schs; pres bd trustees, Richmond Area Scholar Prog; bd mem, Black Mus & Cult Ctr; bd mem, New Va Rev; bd mem, N Richmond Family Br Young Men's Christian Asn; bd mem, Maymont Found; bd mem, Stuart Circle Adult Day Care Ctr; bd mem, Nat Conf Artists; bd mem, Va Capital Chap Am Red Cross; bd mem, Cent Richmond Asn; City Richmond's Human Rels Comn; mem adv bd, Task Force Hist Preserv & Minority Community; vice chmn, Richmond's City Planning Comn; mem adv bd, Human Ecol Dept, Va State Univ; Nat Asn Guardsmen. **Special Achievements:** Publ: Jour Polymer Sci, 1960; 9 US pat, publ Jour of Org Chem 1971; 3 publ Tobac Sci 1973; 2 publ Nature 1973; 3 publ Chem & Ind 1973, 1975, 1979. **Home Addr:** 1001 Spottswood Rd, Richmond, VA 23220, **Home Phone:** (804)359-2576.

## JOHNSON, REV. WILLIAM SMITH

Clergy, executive. **Personal:** Born Apr 24, 1941, Salisbury, MD; son of Alonzo Lester and Delcie Mae Markland; married Jacqueline Andrea Dennis; children: William Jr & Andrea. **Educ:** Univ Md, Eastern Shore, BS, 1963; Eastern Bible Inst, dipl pastoral min, 1985; Salisbury State Univ, grad study; Howard Univ Divinity Sch, grad study; Capitol Bible Sem, grad study. **Career:** Wicomico Co Bd Educ, teacher, 1963-64; US Govt, comput programmer, 1964-65; Detroit Lions, prof football player, 1965; Sussex Co Bd Educ, teacher, 1965-66; EI duPont De Nemours Co Inc, syst specialist, 1966; Wallace Temple African Methodist Episcopal Zion Church, pastor, 1991-96; Mt Hope AME Zion Church, pastor, 1996-99; St James AME Zion Church, asst pastor. **Orgs:** Adv bd mem, Wicomico Co Housing Authority, 1983-84; adv bd mem, Wicomico Co Sch Rezoning Community; Nat Asn

Advan Colored People; Prince Hall Mason; life mem, Salisbury High Asn. **Home Addr:** 28952 Jacqueline Dr, PO Box 1225, Salisbury, MD 21801, **Home Phone:** (410)742-3504.

### JOHNSON, WILLIAM T.
Banker, chief executive officer. **Career:** OmniBanc Corp, chmn, chief exec officer.

### JOHNSON, WILLIAM THEOLIOUS
Lawyer, chief executive officer. **Personal:** Born Dec 24, 1943, Columbus, OH; son of Andrew and Thelma; married Gloria Kindle, Jun 12, 1966; children: Michael & Michelle. **Educ:** Capital Univ, AB, 1968; Capital Univ, Ohio State Univ, JD, 1972. **Career:** Dunbar Kienzle & Murphey Law Firm, atty, 1972-75; KBLE Ohio Inc, Columbus, cheif exec officer & founder, 1974, producer, dir, 1978-81; Johnson & Ransier Co LPA, managing partner, 1975-79; pvt pract atty, 1979-; KBLE-Am Inc, cheif exec officer & founder, 1979, consult, 1979-89; MedTrans Options, chief exec officer, 2011-; Telemedicine Centers USA, chief exec officer & pres, 2011-; KBLE OH Inc, pres. **Orgs:** Vice Chmn, Franklin County Ment Health Bd, 1972-75; chmn, Black Am Law Stud Asn; chmn, Law Day; Phi Alpha Delta Law Fraternity; vpres, Stud Bar Asn; nat chmn, Elections Comn Am Bar Asn Law Stud Div; pres, Franklin Co Legal Aid & Defender Soc; vice chmn, Franklin Co Ment Health & Retardation Bd; bd mem, spec coun Columbus Urban League; trustee, Columbus Zoo; trustee, Ohio Found Independent Col; nat chmn, Minority Affairs Comn Nat Cable TV Asn; legis comn, NCTA; trustee, Franklin Co Pub Defender Comn; ruling elder, Bethany Presby Church; Columbus, Am Nat Bar Asns; hearing officer, Ohio Civil Rights Comn; hearing officer, Ohio Dept Educ; arbitrator, United Steelworkers; Nat Cable TV Asn; Ohio Cable TV Asn; pract, Supreme Ct US, US Ct Appeals, US Dist Ct & US Tax Ct. **Honors/Awds:** Outstanding Young Man in Columbus, Columbus Jr C C, 1972; Outstanding Community Service Award, Columbus Bar Asn, 1978; Gold Key Award; Lutheran Brotherhood Scholar; Hugh H Huntington Award; American Jurisprudence Book Award; Law Book Award, W Publ Co Const; Community Service Award, Columbus Bar Asn. **Special Achievements:** Publication: Implementing Telemedicine Technology, 2013. **Home Addr:** 22 Watertree Cir, The Woodlands, TX 77380, **Home Phone:** (713)363-0939. **Business Addr:** President, Chief Executive Officer, Telemedicine Centers USA LLC, 1111 SW 1st Ave Suite 1424, Miami, FL 33130, **Business Phone:** (614)638-8526.

### JOHNSON, WILLIE
Government official, musician. **Personal:** Born May 26, 1925, Florence, SC; son of Luther and Evelener Richardson; married Fredericka Helen Gadsden; children: Franklin Lewis. **Educ:** Wayne State Univ, attended 1970; Cass Tech HS, cert accomplish, 1971; Mich Career Inst, cert grad, 1974. **Career:** Government official (retired); Ford Motor Co; Wayne County Gen Hosp, Wayne County guard, 1951-78; Wayne County, dep sheriff, 1961-68; Kaufman & Broad Homes, supvr, 1961-69; State Mich, asst chief fire & safety officer, 1978; Personal Accomplishment, songwriter, 1955; c, city councilman, 1990; minister music, vocalist, 1992. **Orgs:** Inkster, Nat Asn Advan Colored People, 1974-; Cent Wayne County Sanit Authority, 1975-77; Inkster Civil Defense Policy Bd, 1975-; comn mem, Nankin Transit Comn, 1977-; Broadcast Music Inc, 1984-; publ, Wiljoe MusicBMI, 1984-; producer, Inkster's New Sounds "Inkster's New Sound" label, 1984-; Nashville Songwriters Asn Int, 1990; Broadcast Music Inc, 1984-; Nat Black Caucus; bd mem, Mich Asn Govt Employees, 1991. **Honors/Awds:** Certificate of appreciation, Wayne County Bd Comn, 1978; special tribute, State Mich, Sen Plawecki & Rep Wm Keith, 1978; Distinguished Employee of the Year, Walter P Reuther Psychol Hosp, 1981; First Place Trophy at Sumpter Township Rodeo for compositions & vocalist, 1988; Inducted into Inkster Hall Fame. **Special Achievements:** Won lawsuit as private citizen in state supreme ct to return money to citizens Home Owners' Org, 1971-78; First black ambulance driver in Michigan. **Home Addr:** 4066 Durand Ct, Inkster, MI 48141, **Home Phone:** (734)729-0641. **Business Addr:** PO Box 262, Inkster, MI 48141.

### JOHNSON, WILLIE F.
Executive, commissioner, founder (originator). **Personal:** Born Sep 27, 1939, Jacksonville, FL; children: Thandeka. **Educ:** Allen Univ, BA, sociol, 1961; Univ Pa, MSW, 1970. **Career:** SC Pub Sch, teacher, 1961-64; Nat Biscuit Co, foreman, 1965-66; Youth Develop Ctr S Philadelphia, counr, 1966-68; Youth Develop Ctr Philadelphia, counr, 1961-64, exec dir, 1972-74; Commonwealth Pa Dept Pub Welfare, Southern Reg, comnr, off youth serv; Fidelity Systs Inc, owner, pres & chief exec officer; PRWT Servs Inc, co-founded, 1988, chmn & founder, currently; Commonwealth Pa, Off Social Serv, regional comnr; City Philadelphia, Off Employ & Training, Off Mayor, exec dir. **Orgs:** Urban League Philadelphia; bd mem, Philadelphia Tribune; African-Am Chamber Com; Am Heart Asn; bd mem, Cheyney Univ Found; United Way Southeastern Pa; Am Red Cross; Philadelphia Zool Soc; bd mem, Girard Col; W Ins; Del River Port Authority Blue Ribbon Panel; Philadelphia Workforce Invest Bd; Community Serv Develop Corp; chmn bd dir, Transitional Work Corp Inc; Perkiomen Sch; bd mem, African-Am Chamber Com. **Home Addr:** 25475 Marsh Landing Pkwy, Ponte Vedra Beach, FL 32082, **Home Phone:** (904)273-6132. **Business Addr:** Chairman, Founder, PRWT Services Inc, 1835 Mkt St Suite 800, Philadelphia, PA 19103, **Business Phone:** (215)569-8810.

### JOHNSON, WILLIE F.
Commissioner, chief executive officer. **Educ:** Allen Univ, Columbia, SC, BA, sociol; Univ Pa, MSW. **Career:** State Pa, Off Social Servs, regional comnr; City Philadelphia, off mayor, off employ & training, exec dir; Fidelity Systs Inc, owner, pres & chief exec officer; PRWT Servs Inc, founder & chmn, currently; Transitional Work Corp Inc, chmn bd dir, currently. **Orgs:** Urban League Philadelphia; Philadelphia Tribune; African-Am Chamber Com; Am Heart Asn; Philadelphia-based Berean Inst; Cheyney Univ Found; UnitedWay Southeastern Pa; Am Red Cross; Philadelphia Zool Soc; Girard Col; W Ins; Del River Port Authority Blue Ribbon Panel; Philadelphia Workforce Investment Bd; Community Serv Develop Corp; bd, Perkiomen Sch. **Business Addr:** Founder, Chairman, PRWT Services Inc, 1835 Market St Suite 800, Philadelphia, PA 19103, **Business Phone:** (215)569-8810.

### JOHNSON, WYNEVA
Lawyer. **Personal:** Born Oct 28, 1948, Greenwood, MS. **Educ:** Wheaton Col, BA, 1971; Univ PA, JD, 1974; Georgetown Univ Law Ctr, LLM, 1977. **Career:** Howard Jenkins Fr Nat Labor Rel Bd, coun to bd mem; US Atty's Off, asst US atty, currently. **Orgs:** Pa Bar, 1974; MS Bar, 1976; exec bd Wheaton Col Alumnae Asn; chmn, Comn Black Alumnae. **Honors/Awds:** Hon DHL, Wheaton College, 1971; Nominee, Outstanding Young Women Am, 1976. **Home Addr:** 800 4th St SW 805 S, Washington, DC 20024. **Business Addr:** Assistant United States Attorney, US Attorney's Office, 555 4th St NW Suite E 4106, Washington, DC 20530, **Business Phone:** (202)514-7224.

### JOHNSON-BLOUNT, THERESA
Librarian. **Personal:** Born Jan 11, 1952, Lafayette, LA; daughter of Willie and Rosella Veazie; married William III; children: Tyaisha Alyce, Wilicia Ellen & Remus Allen. **Educ:** Southern Univ, Baton Rouge, La, BS, mkt, 1973; Grad Sch, La State Univ, Baton Rouge, La, attended 1989; Tex Woman's Univ, Denton, Tex, MLS, 1990. **Career:** Mid-County Dirt Pit, Port Arthur, Tex, asst Mgr, 1973-75; UScG, Baton Rouge, La, storekeeper, 1975-78; Wilson's Jewelers, Baton Rouge, La, invoice clerk, 1976-77; La State Univ, Troy H Middleton Libr, libr assoc II, 1979-90, librn, 1990-91, soc sci Un specist librn, 1991-95; Woman's Hosp Neonatology Unit, acquisitions librn, consult, 1985-; Tulane Med Ctr Neonatology Unit, acquisitions librn, consult, 1985-; Rehab Hosp Baton Rouge, Vol Servs Dept, librn, res librn, 1996-99; Southern Univ A&M Col, Off Grants & Sponsored Progs, res info assoc, 1999-. **Orgs:** Libr Staff Asn, 1980-; Black Fac & Black Staff Caucus, 1985-; Black Studs Support Group, 1985-89; Am Libr Asn, 1988-; Spec Libr Asn, 1988-, bull ed, 1992-94; LSU, Int Hospity Found, host family, 1988-; RHA rep, TWU, Mary Hufford Hall, 1989-90; Ala Black Caucus, Govt Round Table, 1990-; libr consult, AMR Therapeut Recreation Asn; elected vice chair, LLA GODORT, 1995-96, chair, 1996-97. **Honors/Awds:** Scholarship, Beta Phi Mu; Acad scholar, Tex Woman's Univ; Donna Jean Billington Scholar; Graduate Assistant Award Library/LRC, Tex Woman's Univ; Certificate of Appreciation, Tex Woman's Univ & Nat Alumnae Asn; Service Award, La State Univ; author, "Pull a String for Results: Strings Used as Therapeutic Activities, " Sch Libr Media Activities Monthly, June, 1991; author, "Making Sausages: Old Fashioned Boudin, " Southern Living, November, 1983; author, Cooking from Bayou Courtableau, 1984; author, Lagniappe Cookbook, 1984; Outstanding Family Award, Family Serv Greater Baton Rouge; ASPECT Host Family, 1996-97. **Special Achievements:** Making Sausages: Old Fashioned Boudin, Southern Living, 1983; "Nutty Popcorn Balls," Southern Living, 1988; Special Libraries Assn, LA/Southern Mississippi Chapter, bulletin editor; TWU, Booking Binding Workshop, organizer, 1990; "Pull a String for Results: Strings Used as Therapeutic Activities," School Library Media Activities Monthly, 8(2), p 31-33, Oct 1991; "United Nations Depository Collection at Troy H Middleton Library," Louisiana Library Assn, LLA Bulletin, 1992; "Characteristics of Automated Acquisitions Systems in Organizations Belonging to the Assn For Higher Education of North Texas," Texas Woman's Univ, ERIC, 1992; "A Selected List of Basic Health Science Reference Sources," American Therapeutic Recreation Assn, Newsletter, 1992; "A Selected List of Basic Health Science Reference Sources," American Therapeutic Recreation Assn Newsletter, 8(1), p 8, Jan/Feb 1992; Characteristics of Automated Acquisitions Systems in Organizations Belong to the Assn of Higher Education," ERIC Clearinghouse, Syracuse Univ, 1992; Southern University Recreation Dept, banquet organizer, 1992; Author of articles including "International Year of the Family: Libraries Can Be a Family Educational Affair," Documents to the People, 1994. **Home Addr:** 8926 High Pt Rd, Baton Rouge, LA 70810, **Home Phone:** (504)766-8577. **Business Addr:** Information Associate, Southern University A&M College, 730 Harding Blvd, Baton Rouge, LA 70813, **Business Phone:** (225)771-3890.

### JOHNSON-CARSON, DR. LINDA D.
Health services administrator, optometrist. **Personal:** Born Feb 5, 1954, Richland, MS; daughter of Adam and Gertrude; children: James III. **Educ:** Jackson State Univ, BS, biol & chem, 1974; Ind State Univ, Sch Optom, Dr Optom, 1978. **Career:** Jackson Hinds Comprehensive Health Ctr, Dept Optom, head, 1978-, dir optom. **Orgs:** Pres, Miss Optom Asn; Southern County Optometrists, 1974-; bd dir, Nat Optom Asn, 1974-; Miss Optom Asn, 1978-; Am Optom Asn, 1978-80, 1989-; asst to grad & undergrad comn, Miss Optom Asn, 1979-81; trustee large, Nat Optom Asn, 1981-83; region III trustee, Nat Optom Asn, 1983-85; hon mem, Beta Beta Beta Biol Hon Soc, 1984; bd dir, cent Miss chap Am Red Cross, 1988-; chap chair vol servs, Am Red Cross Cent MS, 1988-91, second vchair & bd dirs, 1991-93, vchair & bd dirs, 1993-95, chair & bd dirs, 1995-97; exec bd, Am Red Cross Cent Miss Chap, 1989-; legis comn, Miss Optom Asn, 1989-; pub rels co-chair, Miss Optom Asn, 1989-90; vpres, Nat Optom Asn, secy, 1989-93, vpres, 1993-95, pres, 1995-97; chmn, Miss Optom Asn, 1991-93; exec comn, AOA Community Ctr, 1992-96; develop & retention chair, Miss Optom Asn, 1993-. **Honors/Awds:** Professional Achievement, Jackson State Univ, Nat Alumni Asn, 1980; Distinguished Service, Jackson Hinds Alumni Chap, Jackson State Nat Alumni Asn, 1982; Certificate of Appreciation, Ms Optometric Asn, 1990; Volunteer of the Month, Am Red Cross Central Ms Chap, 1990; Certificate of Appreciation, Jackson State Univ, Dean Libr, 1991; Optometrist of the Year, Nat Optometric Asn, 1993; J Tate Thigpen Award, Am Red Cross, Central MS Chap, 1994; JC Penney Golden-Rule Award, Top 10 Finalist Award, 1997; You've Made a Difference Award, Comt Working to Unite Youth Org, Rawkin County, 1997; MS Comnr, Volunteer Serv Commendation, 1996-97; Optometrist of the Year, AM Optometric Asn, 2008. **Special Achievements:** First African American female optometrist in Mississippi, 1978. **Home Addr:** 2400 Ladd St, Jackson, MS 39209. **Business Addr:** Department Head of Optometry, Director, Jackson Hinds Comprehensive Health Center, 3502 W Northside Dr, Jackson, MS 39213, **Business Phone:** (601)362-5321.

### JOHNSON-CROCKETT, DR. MARY ALICE
Physician. **Personal:** Born May 6, 1937, Anderson, SC; daughter of William P and Bernice McAlister; married Edward D Crockett Jr; children: Edward D III, Alison V & Sharon P. **Educ:** Howard Univ, Col Lib Arts, BS, 1958; Howard Univ, Col Med, MD, 1962. **Career:** Freedman Hosp, intern, 1963; DC Gen Hosp, Vet Admin, Howard Univ, resident internal med, 1963-66; Walter Reed Army Med Ctr, med officer, 1966-67; Vet Admin Hosp Downey, Ill, staff physician, 1967-69; Community Group Health Found Inc, staff physician & actg med dir, 1969-72; JB Johnson Nursing Ctr, med dir; Home Care Serv Bur, med officer, med dir, 1972-; Hospice Care DC, med dir, 1979-82; pvt prac, internal med & geriatrics. **Orgs:** Consult, Income Maintenance Admin, 1971-86; health physician, Law Enforcement Agency Admin & Consumer Prod Safety Comn, 1975, 1976-77; mem exec comn, Potomac PTA, 1976-81; track physician, Bowie Race Track, 1977-81; prof adv comt, Hospice Care DC, 1983-; Up John, 1985-; steering comt, Sidwell Friends Sch, 1984-85; parent, Support Group Youth Choir Plymouth Congregation UCC; consult, Nat Health Serv, 1972-82; pres, WHenry Greene Friends Music Soc, 1988-; bd mem, rep, Metrop DC Geriatrics Soc; bd mem, Am Geriatrics Soc. **Honors/Awds:** Lucy Moten Fellowship Award, Howard Univ, 1957; Intern of the Year, Howard Univ, 1963; Hospice Award, Hospice Care DC, 1983; Ronald C Newman Award, Jackson-Newman Found Inc, 1987; Clinician of the Year Award, Am Geriatrics Soc, 1995. **Home Addr:** 10700 Alloway Dr, Potomac, MD 20854-1601, **Home Phone:** (301)299-3152. **Business Addr:** Representative, Metropolitan DC Geriatrics Society, 4125 Albemarle St NW Suite 217, Washington, DC 20016, **Business Phone:** (202)895-0327.

### JOHNSON-CROSBY, DEBORAH A.
Executive. **Personal:** Born Jan 15, 1951, Chicago, IL; children: Malik Fanon. **Educ:** Univ Wis, BA, 1974. **Career:** Mt Sinai Hosp, staff worker bus off, 1969; N side Comn Credit Union, loan clerk, community rels, 1970-71; Oper Breadbasket, pub rels dir, 1972-73; Milwaukee Times, reporter, 1973-74; Milwaukee Star Times, managing ed, 1974-75; Milwaukee Bus Fedn, dir; Free-Lance Journalist; Communs Consult; Concentrated Employ Prog, staff worker. **Orgs:** Info officer, Black Comt Stud Alliance, 1972-73; Milwaukee Asn; bd dir, Peck ham Jr HS, 1974; Black Media Alliance WI; Pub Rels Comt. **Home Addr:** 3019 N 18th St, Milwaukee, WI 53206-2202, **Home Phone:** (414)372-7261.

### JOHNSON-FEELINGS, DIANNE. See JOHNSON, DINAH.

### JOHNSON-HELTON, KAREN
College administrator. **Personal:** Born May 20, 1947, Cincinnati, OH; daughter of James C Payne and Ruth Lee; married Malcolm. **Educ:** Ohio Univ, Athens, OH, BA, 1969; Atlanta Univ, Atlanta, GA, MSW, 1976; Univ Mich, Ann Arbor, MI, attended 1978; Tex A&M Univ, attended 1992. **Career:** LeMoyne-Owen Col, Memphis, TN, dir planning, 1976-82; Mary Holmes Col, W Pt, Miss, fed progs coordr, 1982-86; Rust Col, Holly Springs, Miss, proposal writer, 1986-87; Wiley Col, Marshall, Tex, assoc vpres, 1987-88, asst pres, 1988-99, dir sponsored progs, 1999-2005, vpres instnl advan, 2005-15, dir sponsored progs, 2015-, spec asst to pres. **Orgs:** Dist comn, Cub Scouts Am, 1986-87; steering comt mem, Top Ladies Distinction, 1989-; pub rels comt mem, Zonta Int, 1989-; Third Anti-Basileus, 1990-93; State Tex Dem Party, 1992-; Zeta Phi Beta Sorority, 1992-96; bd mem, Harrison Co United Way, 1997-2004; bd mem, Links Inc, 2003-; Marshall Rotary Club, 2003-; Nat Rep UNCF. **Special Achievements:** Experienced proposal writer, 39 years of uninterrupted grantsmanship services for historically black colleges and universities. **Home Addr:** 4807 S Wash St, Marshall, TX 75672, **Home Phone:** (903)938-4539. **Business Addr:** Special Assistant to the President, Director of Sponsored Programs, Wiley College, Rm 116 Willis King Admin Bldg, Marshall, TX 75670-5151, **Business Phone:** (903)927-3283.

### JOHNSON-ODIM, DR. CHERYL
Dean (education), vice president (organization), educator. **Personal:** Born Apr 30, 1948, Youngstown, OH; daughter of Elayne Jeffries; married Carlton Odim; children: Chaka Malik, Rashid Jamil & Maya Ruth. **Educ:** Youngstown State Univ, BA, 1972; Northwestern Univ, MA, 1975, PhD, hist, 1978. **Career:** Fulbright Hays Dissertation Yr fel, 1976; Univ Ibadan, Nigeria, resaffil, 1976; Loyola Univ, Chicago, Afro-Am Studies, dir, 1978-, asst prof, 1978-80, Hist Dept, chmn, prof, 1995-2000; Northwestern Univ, African Studies, asst dir, 1980; Monti cellofel, 1990; Univ Wis, Madison; Columbia Col, Lib Arts & Sci, prof hist, dean, 2000-06; Dominican Univ, Acad Affairs, dean provost & vpres, currently. **Orgs:** Co-chmn, Ill Coun Black Studies, 1979-; co-chmn, memship Asn Black Women Historians, 1979-; bd mem, Chiaravalle Montessori Sch, 1980; bd dir, Black Press Inst, 1987; co-chair elected bd, Women's Caucus, African Studies Asn, 1988-; bd dir, Chicago Comt Solidarity Southern Africa, 1989; ed bd, Nat Women's Studies Asn Jour, 1992; chair, Joan Kelly Prize Comt, Am Hist Asn; bd dir, Am Coun Learned Soc; bd dir, African Studies Asn; head, TransAfrica Support Comt Chicago; adv bd, Ctr Womens & Gender Studies, Rutgers Univ; founding ed bd, Jour Womens Hist; founding mem, Vivian G Harsh Soc; assoc ed, Encycl Twentieth-Century African Hist, 2003, Women Bldg Chicago 1790-1900; vice chmn, Ill Humanities Coun; co-chmn, Coalition Ill Divestment from SafricA; adv comt, Tell Story: Chicago SNCC Hist Proj, 1960-1965; founding mem, Free S Africa Movement. **Home Addr:** 1612 Wash St Apt 1, Evanston, IL 60202-1630. **Business Addr:** Dean Provost, Vice President of Academic Affairs, Dominican University, 7900 W Div St, River Forest, IL 60305, **Business Phone:** (708)366-2490.

### JOHNSTON, ANNA KATHERINE. See TAYLOR, ANNA DIGGS.

### JOHNSTON, CHARLENE B.
Educator. **Personal:** Born Mar 6, 1933, New York, NY; daughter of Louis and Rosenda Batson; married Wallace O; children: Leana Wilkerson, Cunningham Wilkerson & Glen Batson Cunningham. **Educ:** NY Community Col, AAS, dent hyg, 1953; NY Univ, BS, dent health educ, 1974, MA, community health educ, 1977; Va Poly Tech, EDD, higher educ admin, 1990. **Career:** Clin dent hyg pvt pract; Hostos Community Col, prof dent hyg, 1974-75; NYC Community Col, prof dent hyg, 1975-80; Northern Va Community Col, dean, denthyg prog, 1990. **Orgs:** Delta Sigma Theta Sorority, 1978-; Am Dent Hyg Asn,

1980-; Afro-Am Mus Art, Tampa, FL, 1996-; dir pub rels, Afro-Am Club Hernando City, FL, 1997-; pres, Hernando Performing Arts Ctr Guild; United Arts Coun Greater Greensboro. **Home Addr:** 11250 Riddle Dr, Spring Hill, FL 34609-3438, **Home Phone:** (352)666-4867.

## JOHNSTON, ERNEST

Broadcaster, journalist. **Personal:** Born Nov 25, 1938, Roanoke Rapids, NC; son of Bessie W (deceased) and Ernest Sr (deceased); children: Tanya White & Rhonda Cox. **Educ:** NC A&T State Univ, BS, 1960; Columbia Univ, interracial reporting fel, 1972. **Career:** Star-Ledger, reporter, 1964-68; New York Post, reporter, 1968-73; Long Island Press, reporter, 1973-75; Herald News, copy ed, 1975-77; New York Amsterdam News, managing ed, 1977-81, prog coordr, pub info, tech writer, seniors Comm Serv prog, currently; freelance writer, 1981-87; Nat Urban League, commun specialist, pub rels & commun dept, 1987-95; Crossroads Theatre, dir pub rels, 1996-97; LeJay Assoc, pres, currently. **Orgs:** Vpres, New York Press Club, 1968-69; Nat vpres, chmn, pub rels comm & ed, NC A&T State Univ Nat Alumni Asn, A & T Today, Aggie Pride; pres, Northern Nj chap, 1978-83, pres, Nj shore chap, NC A&T State Alumni Asn, 1990-93; Men's Club, Elmwood Presby Church, 1985-90; co-chmn, Pastor Nominating Comm, Bethel Presby Church, pres, Men's Club; regional dir, NE region, A&T Alumni Asn, 1993-95; mem adv bd, Breast Cancer Ctr Harlem. **Honors/Awds:** Service Award, Black Spectrum Theatre Co, 1979; Contribution to Mankind Award, Caribbean Am Designers & Models, 1980; World Service Award, Harlem YMCA, 1981; Special Recognition Award, northern New Jersey chap, 1982, NAFEO Award, 1995, NC A&T State Alumni Asn; First Place Black & White Photo Award, New Jersey Chamber Com, East Orange, 1985; Alumni Achiever, 1991. **Special Achievements:** Managing editor of The Negro Almanac, a reference work African Americans, 1981, 1990, first black reporter at the Star Ledger. **Home Addr:** 66-3A Winding Wood Dr Suite 3A, Sayreville, NJ 08872, **Home Phone:** (732)238-0036.

## JOHNSTON, DR. GLADYS STYLES

School administrator, college administrator. **Personal:** Born Dec 23, 1942, St. Petersburg, FL; daughter of John Edward and Rosa Moses; married Hubert Seward. **Educ:** Cheyney Univ, BS, social sci, 1963; Temple Univ, MEd, educ admin, 1969; Cornell Univ, PhD, 1974. **Career:** College administrator (retired); Chester Sch Dist, Chester, Pa, teacher, 1963-66; W Chester Sch Dist, Pa, teacher, 1966-67, asst prin, 1968-69, dir summer sch & prin, 1969-71; Chester Co Bd Educ, Chester, Pa, dir head start, 1967-69; Cornell Univ, teaching asst, 1971-72, res asst, 1972-74; Rutgers Univ, educ admin & supv, asst prof, 1974-79, chairperson, 1979-83, assoc prof, 1979-83, chairperson dept mgt, 1983-85; Col William & Mary, Williamsburg, Va, vis prof, 1982-83; Ariz St Univ, Col Educ, Temple, Ariz, dean & prof, 1985-91; DePaul Univ, Chicago, Ill, provost & exec vpres; Univ Nebr Kearney, chancellor, 1993-2002, chancellor emer; Am Asn State Cols & Univs, dir MLI, asst to pres & spec asst, currently. **Orgs:** Bd dir, Found Sr Living, 1990-91; bd dir, KAET TV; bd dir, Educ Law Ctr, 1979-86; adv coun bd trustee, Cornell Univ, 1981-86; bd trustee, Middlesex Gen Univ Hosp, 1983-86; Am Educ Res Asn; Asn Supv & Curric Develop; Am Asn Col Teacher Educ; Nat Conf Prof Educ Admin; exec comt mem, Nat Col Athletic Asn; chair div II, chair bd dir, Am Asn St Col & Univ; mem bd dir, Am Coun Educ; chair, Omaha Br Fed Res Bank Kans City; co chair, dir, Millennium Leadership Initiative; bd mem, Fed Res. **Honors/Awds:** Outstanding Alumni, Temple Univ; Andrew D. White Fellowship, Cornell Univ; Phi Kappa Phi Honor Soc; Alpha Phi Sigma National Honorary Scholastic Fraternity, Cheyney State Col. **Special Achievements:** Book: "The Emerging Redefinition of Federal Educational Policy: Implications for Educational Excellence", Journal of Educational Evaluation and Policy Analysis; "The Carnegie Report: A Retrospective, Journal of Arizona School Board Association", Fall 1986; "Rule Administration and Hierarchical Influence of the Principal: A Study of Teacher Loyalty to the Principal", Educational Administrative Quarterly, Fall 1986; "Research and Thought in Administration Theory: Developments in the Field of Educational Administration", 1986. **Business Addr:** Director, Assistant to the President, American Association of State Colleges and Universities, 1307 New York Ave NW 5th Fl, Washington, DC 20005, **Business Phone:** (202)293-7070.

## JOHNSTON, HENRY BRUCE

Administrator. **Personal:** Born Jul 4, 1927; married Cora Virginia Jackson; children: Geraldine, Mark, Lisa & Steven. **Educ:** State Univ Farmingdale, NY, AAS; State Univ Stoney Brook, NY, MA, BS. **Career:** Suffolk Co Hum Rights Comn, exec dir, 1985, county police officer, in-chg community rels br; State Univ Farmingdale, instr criminal justice; Suffolk Community Col, instr criminal justice; Police Acad Suffolk Co Police Dept, instr; Globe-Trotters Prof Basketball Org, mem. **Orgs:** Bd dir, LI Sickle Cell Proj Nassau & Suffolk; bd dir, Suffolk Rehab Ctr; bd dir & adv bd, Suffolk Co Youth Servs; bd dir, Diocesan Task Force Poverty & Racism Nassau & Suffolk; bd dir, Crime Control Coun, Suffolk Co; bd dir educ, NCCJ; bd dir Awards Comt SCPD; bd dir, Boy Scouts Am Suffolk Co; bd dir, Phi Beta Sigma Frat; bd dir, Econ Opportunity Coun Suffolk Co; bd dir, Urban League Suffolk Co; bd dir, Alcoholism Adv Comn Suffolk Co; NYCPD Youth Squad PAL Div; Nat Asn Advan Colored People; Lions Club, Hauppauge, NY; bd ed Grievance Comt Hauppauge High Sch. **Honors/Awds:** Hunting PaL Award, 1958; Top Basketball Official, 1960-61, 1969; Police Youth Award, SCPD, 1961-62; Medal for Bravery, SCPD, 1964; Outstanding Basketball Official, 1966; Meritorious Service, SCPD, 1967; Masons Recognition Award, King Tyre Lodge, 1967; Professionalization Award, SCPD, 1969; Man of the Year, NANBPW, 1974; Black Standard Union, SU Farmingdale, 1975. **Home Addr:** 368 Mac Arthur Blvd, Smithtown, NY 11787.

## JOHNSTON, JULIA MAYO. See MAYO, DR. JULIA A.

## JOHNSTONE, LANCE

Football player. **Personal:** Born Jun 11, 1973, Philadelphia, PA. **Educ:** Temple Univ. **Career:** Football player (retired); Oakland Raiders, left defensive end, 1996-97 & 2006, right defensive end, 1998, defensive end, 1999-2000; Bill Pickett Riding Acad Inc, pres, 1996-2013; pres, 2013-; Minn Vikings, defensive end, 2001-06; Original Printing Serv, pres, 2006-07; Merrill Lynch, financial advisor, 2008-14; STAR Angel Network, dir, 2012-. **Orgs:** Founder, Urban Renaissance Youth Found.

## JOHSNON, ED, JR. See JOHNSON, EDMOND R, JR.

## JOINER, DR. BURNETT

College administrator, educator. **Personal:** Born Nov 10, 1941, Raymond, MS; son of Burnett Sr and Arcine; married Inez Dixon; children: Michael & Christopher. **Educ:** Utica Jr Col, AA, 1962; Alcorn State Univ, BS, 1964; Bradley Univ, MA, 1968; Univ SC, PhD, 1975. **Career:** Oliver Sch Clarksdale, prin, 1968-71; York Sch Dist 1, asst supt sch, 1971-73; SC Col, asst prof, 1974-75; Atlanta Univ, exec dir & assoc prof, 1975-80; Livingstone Col, pres, 1977-2000; Grambling State Univ, exec acad dean & prof, 1984-91; LeMoyne-Owens Col, pres, 1991; Benedict Col, Acad Affairs, sr vpres, currently. **Orgs:** Ouachita Valley Boy Scouts, 1982-; charter mem, Grambling Lions Club, 1983-; consult, US Dept Educ, 1983-85; comnr, La Learning Adv Comn, 1984-85; comnr, La Internship Comn, 1984-85; Nat Inst Educ Study Group Teacher Educ; chair, Col Educ Univ SC Stud Adv; Curric Comt Sch Educ, SC State Col; Ruston-Lincoln C C; vice chairperson, Comt Social Concerns Lewis Temple Church; bd dir, Teacher Educ Coun, State Col & Univ; Am Asn Col Teacher Educ; Gov Internship Comn & Learning Adv Comn. **Home Addr:** 2708 Hwy 563, Grambling, LA 71275, **Home Phone:** (318)247-8926. **Business Addr:** Senior Vice President for Academic Affairs, Advisory Council, Benedict College, 1600 Harden St, Columbia, SC 29204, **Business Phone:** (803)253-4752.

## JOINER, CHARLES, JR.

Football coach, football player. **Personal:** Born Oct 14, 1947, Many, LA; married Dianne; children: Jynayna & Kori. **Educ:** Grambling State Univ, BS, bus admin, 1969. **Career:** Football Player, coach (retired); Houston Oilers, wide receiver, 1969-72; Gulf Oil Co, mgt trainee, 1971; Cincinnati Bengals, wide receiver, 1972-75; San Diego Chargers, wide receiver, 1976-86, coach, 1987-91, wide receivers coach, 2008-12; Buffalo Bills, 1992-2000; Kans City Chiefs, asst coach, coach, 2001-07. **Honors/Awds:** Four varsity letters Grambling; named All Pro & All AFC second team, AP and UPI, 1980; MVP and Most Inspirational Player, San Diego Chargers, 1983; established NFL record for most pass receptions (716); played in Pro Bowl, 1976, 1979, 1980; testimonial in Lake Charles on "Charlie Joiner Day", 1982 & 1986; Pro Football Hall of Fame, 1996; San Diego Chargers Hall of Fame. **Home Addr:** 9223 Petersham Dr, Houston, TX 77031. **Business Addr:** Wide Receivers Coach, San Diego Chargers, PO Box 609609, San Diego, CA 92160-9609, **Business Phone:** (619)280-2121.

## JOLIVET, LINDA CATHERINE

Librarian. **Personal:** Born Mar 5, 1950, New Orleans, LA; daughter of Fred Douglas and Nancy Evans; children: Shakira N Scott. **Educ:** Univ Southwestern La, Lafayette, La, BA, 1974; Univ Calif, Berkeley, Berkeley, Calif, MLIS, 1988; San Francisco State Univ, San Francisco, Calif. **Career:** Lafayette Parish Sch Bd, Layfayette, La, teacher, 1975-80; Oakland Post Newspaper Group, Oakland, Calif, advert asst, 1980-81; Berkeley Pub Libr, Berkeley, Calif, libr asst, 1982; Univ Calif, Berkeley, Berkeley, Calif, clerical asst, 1982-83, libr asst, 1983-84; Oakland Pub Libr, Oakland, Calif, libr asst, 1984-86, ref libr, currently; E Bay Negro Hist Soc Mus-Libr, Oakland, Calif, cur-librn, 1986-87; Stanford Univ, Palo Alto, Calif, asst librn, 1989-90; Col Alameda, Alameda, Calif, librn, 1990; African Am Mus & Libr, ref libr; City El Cerrito, Calif, Crime Prev Comt, member. **Orgs:** Founder, dir, bd Adesua Bea Learning Ctr & Educ Servs, 1982; Am Libr Asn, 1985-91; secy, 1990, coord, scholar comt, 1991, Calif Librn Black Caucus, Northern Chap; program asst, Nat Black Child Develop Inst, East Bay Area Affiliate, 1990-91; Northern Calif Ctr Study of Afro-Am Life & Cult, 1991. **Honors/Awds:** Graduate Minority Fellowship, Univ Calif-Berkeley, 1984-85; Graduate Equity Fellowship Award, San Francisco State Univ, 1990-91. **Special Achievements:** Author: Preparations of Librarians to Serve a Multicultural World, Women Library Workers Journal, 1988; African and African American Audiovisual Materials: A Selected Bibliography, Stanford University Libraries, 1990; Composed Dramas like "Any Given Day". **Home Addr:** 2451 Calif St, Berkeley, CA 94703, **Home Phone:** (510)843-3440. **Business Addr:** Librarian, College of Alameda, 555 Atlantic Ave, Alameda, CA 94501, **Business Phone:** (510)522-7221.

## JOLLEY, DR. SAMUEL DELANOR, JR.

College administrator, school administrator, college president. **Personal:** Born Feb 1, 1941, Ft. Valley, GA; son of Samuel and Mary; married Jimmye Hambry; children: Terena J Washington & Samuel D III. **Educ:** Ft Valley State Col, BS, 1962; Atlanta Univ, MS, 1965; Ind Univ, EdD, 1974. **Career:** College President, Educator (retired); High sch math teacher; Ft Valley State Col, instr math, 1967-70, from asst prof math to assoc prof math, 1970-82, Div Educ, chmn, 1983-85, Sch Arts & Sci, dean, 1985-93; Morris Brown Col, pres, 1993-97, 2004-06; Atlanta Univ Ctr Inc, exec dir, chief exec officer & chief operating officer, 1998-2004. **Orgs:** Omega Psi Phi Fraternity, 1960-; Sigma Pi Phi Fraternity, 1991-; Atlanta Univ Ctr, 1993-; bd mem, Univ Ctr Ga, 1993-; bd mem, Univ Community Develop Corp, 1993-; Am Coun Educ, 1993-; bd dir, Atlanta Paralympics Org Comt, 1994-; adv bd, Salvation Army, 1995-; 100 Black Men Atlanta, 1995-; Alpha Kappa Mu Hon Soc; Phi Delta Kappa Educ Fraternity; Beta Kappa Chi Sci Hon Soc; Math Asn Am; Golden Key Nat Hon Soc; NCP; Atlanta Chamber Com; adv coun, Atlanta Systemic Initiative; stewards bd, Allen Temple African Methodist Episcopal Church, Comm Finance; Nat Alumn Asn, Ft Valley State Col; Upsilon Sigma. **Home Addr:** 4410 Pk Ctr Dr SW, Atlanta, GA 30331, **Home Phone:** (404)505-9298. **Business Addr:** GA.

## JOLLEY, WILLIE

Singer. **Personal:** Born Sep 3, 1956, Washington, DC; married Dee Taylor; children: William & LaToya. **Educ:** Am Univ, BA, psychol & sociol, 1978; Wesley Theol Sem, MA, 1983. **Career:** Jingle singer & jazz vocalist, 1974-90; Wash, DC, pub Schs, drug & violence prev coordr, 1990-91; Willie Jolley Worldwide & Inspir Tainment Plus, full-time motivational speaker, pres & chief exec officer, 1991-; Am Pub TV, pgm host, 2009-; "The Magnificent Motivational Minute". **Orgs:** Nat Speakers Assoc, 1991-; pres, Nat Capital Speakers Assoc, 1995-96; founder, Try Love. **Honors/Awds:** Best Male Jazz Vocalist Washington Area Music Asn Award, 1986, 1989 & 1990; Best Male Inspirational Vocalist Washington Area Music Asn Award, 1991 & 1992; Outstanding Motivational & Inspirational Speaker of the Year, Toastmasters Int, 1999; Hall of Fame; Black Enterprise Mag. **Special Achievements:** Author of two international best selling books: It Only Takes A Minute To Change Your Life, 1997; A Setback Is A Setup For A Comeback, 1999. **Home Addr:** 5711 13th St NW, Washington, DC 20011-3547, **Home Phone:** (202)723-8863. **Business Addr:** President, Owner, Willie Jolley Worldwide InspirTainment Plus, PO Box 55459, Washington, DC 20040, **Business Phone:** (202)723-8863.

## JOLLY, ELTON S., SR.

Educator, association executive. **Personal:** Born Oct 15, 1931, Claymont, DE; son of Ozella Jones and Elton; married Rowena Mozelle Anderson (deceased); children: Elton, Brett & William David. **Educ:** Cheyney Univ, Cheyney, PA, BS, elem educ, 1954; Temple Univ, Philadelphia, PA, MS, educ admin, 1964. **Career:** Educator, associate executive (retired); Philadelphia Bd Educ, Philadelphia, Pa, teacher & adminr, 1954-65; Opportunities Industrialization Centers Am, Philadelphia, Pa, exec vice chmn, 1965, dep exec dir, 1971-72, exec dir, 1973-78, pres & chief exec officer, 1989-90. **Orgs:** Nat Asn Advan Colored People, 1960-; Black Leadership Forum, 1978-; Nat Alliance Bus, 1984-; founder & chmn, Nat Youth Advocacy, 1980-; Nat Assessment Governing Bd, 1987-90; founding chmn, Nat Youth Employ Coalition; pres, Opportunities Industrialization Ctr. **Home Addr:** 6001 Drexel Rd, Philadelphia, PA 19131-1217, **Home Phone:** (215)879-0630.

## JOLLY, MARY B.

School administrator, personal trainer. **Personal:** Born Oct 23, 1940, New Orleans, LA; daughter of Oliver and Audrey Leufroy; married Herbert Nicholas; children: Helaina, Nyla & Chanelle. **Educ:** Loyola Univ, BS, 1975; Univ New Orleans, MS, 1982. **Career:** Jefferson Parish Sheriff's Off, personnel dir, 1976-80; Loyola Univ, personnel dir, personnel coordr, 1980-88; New Orleans Pub Sch Syst, personnel admin, 1988-. **Orgs:** Consult Human Resources, EEO, Policies & Procedure; Col & Univ Personnel Admin; La Equal Opportunity Asn; exec bd mem, Int Info Asn Personnel & Payroll Syst Users Group; regional conf prog chair, Am Asn Affirmative Action, 1986; pres bd, Personnel Mgt Asn; New Orleans Metro Chap, Am Soc Personnel Admin, 1986-87; Cross Keys Hon Serv Soc Loyola Univ; Rels Community United Way Greater New Orleans. **Home Addr:** 7121 Read Blvd, New Orleans, LA 70127-2223, **Home Phone:** (504)241-8373. **Business Addr:** Personnel Administrator, New Orleans Public School Systems, 4100 Touro St, New Orleans, LA 70122, **Business Phone:** (504)286-2861.

## JONAS, DR. ERNESTO A.

Educator, physician, executive. **Personal:** Born Nov 13, 1939, Panama, PA; son of Harold L and Laura Maria Anderson de; married Mary E Cullen; children: Jorge A & Clarissa M. **Educ:** Univ Nueva Leon, Monterrey, Mex, MD, 1966. **Career:** Nassau Univ Med Ctr, internal med, resident, div emergency med, chief, 1973-76, coronary care unit, dir, 1976-79, div cardiol, chief, cardiovasc training prog, dir; St Elizabeth Os Med Ctr, Boston, Mass, cardiovasc training; St Univ NY, Stony Brook, asst prof med, 1973-88, assoc prof med, currently; pvt pract, currently. **Orgs:** Fel Am Col Physicians, 1977-; fel Am Col Cardiol, 1981-; mem & exec comt, Dept Med, St Univ NY, Stony Brook; mem & bd dirs, Nassau Chap, Am Heart Asn; Physician Educ Comn, Am Heart Asn. **Honors/Awds:** Excellence in Teaching Award, St Univ NY, Stony Brook, 1980; D'istinguished Service Award', Asn Black Cardiologists, 1987; Distinguished Leadership Award, Am Heart Asn, 1992. **Special Achievements:** Author of articles in medical journals. **Home Addr:** 8 Villas Cir, Melville, NY 11747. **Business Addr:** Physician, Private Practitioner, 510 Hicksville Rd, Massapequa, NY 11758, **Business Phone:** (516)572-8784.

## JONES, A. LORRAINE

Executive, business owner. **Personal:** daughter of Benjamin (deceased). **Career:** Kleenize-Benje Carpet Specialists, Asbury Pk, NJ, pres & owner, 1977-. **Orgs:** Past pres, atlantic region dir & state pres, Nat Asn Women Bus Owners, NJ Chap; chair, Asbury Park Zoning Bd; Nat Asn Bd. **Business Addr:** Owner, President, Kleenize-Benje Carpet Specialists, 613 Prospect Ave, Asbury Park, NJ 07712-6327, **Business Phone:** (732)774-1314.

## JONES, AARON DELMAS, II

Football player, president (organization). **Personal:** Born Dec 18, 1966, Orlando, FL; children: Mike. **Educ:** Eastern Ky Univ, attended 1988. **Career:** Football player (retire), pres; Pittsburgh Steelers, defensive end, 1988-92; New England Patriots, 1993-95; Miami Dolphins, 1996; Gold Mech Servs Inc, pres, currently; Excel Speed & Fitness Training LLC, pres, currently. **Orgs:** Pres & comnr, S Cent Athletic Asn. **Home Addr:** 3715 Pompano Ct, Gotha, FL 34734-5111. **Business Addr:** Vice President, Excel Speed & Fitness Training LLC, 5327 Cruzan Ct, Orlando, FL 32818-8339, **Business Phone:** (407)466-5637.

## JONES, ALBERT ALLEN

Educator. **Personal:** Born Apr 2, 1913, New Orleans, LA; married Beaulah Mae Houston. **Educ:** Xavier Univ, PhB, AB, 1952. **Career:** Pub Sch, teacher; Bapt Training Union Asn Ministers Alliance, teacher; Union Bapt Theol Sem LA, instr. **Orgs:** Ast dir, Dept Christian Ed 1st Dist Missionary Bapt Asn; dir, Bapt Training Union LA Bapt St Conv S & Region; mem bd trustee, 1st Dist Missionary Bapt Asn; pres, Mem Ponchartrain Pk Improvement Asn DD, conferred Inter-bapt Theol Ctr. **Home Addr:** 4900 Mithra St, New Orleans, LA 70126.

## JONES, ALBERT C.

Educator, executive. **Personal:** Born May 20, 1946, Ft. Lauderdale, FL; son of Milton L and Rhodie; married Carolyn W; children: Alison C. **Educ:** Edward Waters Col, BS, health, phys educ & fitness, 1968; Univ Northern Colo, MA, curric & instr, 1974. **Career:** McArthur High Sch, teacher, 1968, chair phys educ; Sch Bd Broward County, educr, 1968-, supvr, 1995; City Hollywood, recreation supvr, 1968-; Realty 2000 Realtors, realtor, 1979-88; Broward Community Col, prof, 1981-93; City Dania Beach, comnr, 1993-97, vice mayor, 2012-; Memorial Healthcare Syst, S Broward Hosp Dist, chmn bd, comnr, 1999-; Quest Ctr, Hollywood, Fla, teacher, 2001; Everglades High Sch, asst athletic dir & dean; Broward County Comnr, broward county bd comnr, 2010-11; Classic Properties Realtors, broker-salesman, 2011-. **Orgs:** Fla Alliance & Health, Phys Educ, Recreation Dance, 1979-96; Broward County Asn Phys Educ, 1979-96; Omega Psi Phi; Zeta Chi Chap, 1988-; fel Nat League Cities, 1993-97; founding mem, vpres, Col Gardens Neighborhood Asn Inc, 1995-; fel Black Elected Officials Broward County, 1997-; pres, New Republican Club Broward County, 1999-; chmn, Diversity & Cult Outreach Comt, 1999-; S Broward Hosp Dist Bd, 1999, secy treas, 2000-; pres, Jerome E Gray Republican Club; outreach chmn, Broward Republican Exec Comt; bd, Broward County Metrop Plng Orgn; Nat Asn Counties; Fla Asn Counties; Fla League Cities; Broward League Cities; Coordr, Broward County Haitian Relief Effort; fel Leadership Comt; Broward County Haitian Relief Task Force; fel Broward Sheriff's Off Diversity & Equal Opportunity Coun. **Home Addr:** 722 Southwest 3rd St, PO Box 1242, Dania Beach, FL 33004, **Home Phone:** (954)920-0727. **Business Addr:** Commissioner, South Broward Hospital District, 3501 Johnson St, Hollywood, FL 33021-5421, **Business Phone:** (954)987-2000.

### JONES, ALEXANDER R.
Public relations executive, association executive. **Personal:** Born Jan 21, 1952, Washington, DC. **Educ:** Mass Inst Tech, BS, 1974. **Career:** Nat Comn Law Enforcement & Soc Justice, Ch Scientology, assoc dir, 1985. **Orgs:** Ed, Unequal Justice-Under Law, 1979-80; exec dir, Citizens Comn Community Involvement, 1985. **Honors/Awds:** Author, newspaper column, Law & Social Justice, 1980. **Home Addr:** 1708 S St NW, Washington, DC 20009-6116, **Home Phone:** (202)438-4463.

### JONES, ALFREDEAN
Teacher, school administrator, baseball player. **Personal:** Born Sep 30, 1940, Jonesville, SC; son of Bob and Lillian; married Betty Jean Smith; children: Pamela, Shelia & Dean. **Educ:** SC State Col, BS, 1963; NC Agr & Tech State Univ, MS, 1972; Lehigh Univ, cert, 1975. **Career:** Baseball player, teacher, school administrator (retired); Wenatchee Chiefs, player, 1963-65; Chicago Cubs Minors, player, 1963-67; NJ Correctional Syst, supvr recreation, 1964-67; Easton Area High Sch Dist, teacher, 1967-75, adminr, 1975-87, asst prin, 1978, interim prin, 1981, prin, 2000-02; Boys & Girls Club, Easton; Easton Housing Authority, bd chmn. **Orgs:** Bd dirs, Educ Day Care Ctr; C Home Easton; vpres, Easton Br Nat Asn Advan Colored People; deacon, Grace Baptist Church, Phillipsburg; Lehigh Valley Christian High Sch Adv Bd. **Honors/Awds:** Certificates of Appreciation Graduating Class, 1984, Children Home of Easton, 1985, Easton Branch Nat Asn Advan Colored People, 1986; The fourth annual Thomas W. Bright Young Ambassador Community Service Award, 2005. **Home Addr:** 155 Reese St, Easton, PA 18042, **Home Phone:** (610)258-3135.

### JONES, ALICE ELEY
Historian, writer. **Personal:** Born Jan 7, 1949, Murfreesboro, NC; daughter of Fred and Iris D. **Educ:** NC Cent Univ, BA, 1973, MA, 1986. **Career:** NC Cent Univ, prof hist, 1987-92, asst prof, human scis, 2003; Historically Speaking, owner, 1992-; Minnie Troy Publ, owner, 2002-; Books: Hertford County, North Carolina, 2002; The Builders & Architecture of Historic Murfreesboro, North Carolina, 2003; A maritime history of Murfreesboro, North Carolina, 1585-1800, 2004; Within the Hope Plantation household, 2004; Woodworking tools of historic Murfreesboro, North Carolina, 2006. **Orgs:** Bd mem, Preserv-NC, 1992-94. **Honors/Awds:** Stagville Fellowship, NC Dept Cultural Resources, 1985-86; Educator of the Year, NC Cent Univ, 1992; Gertrude S Carraway Award, Preserv-NC, 1997; Minnie Fuller Memorial Scholarship, VISTA volunteer. **Special Achievements:** Publication, "Sacred Places and Holy Ground: West African Spiritualism at Historic Stagville Plantation", 1998; curator "African American Builders and Architects in NC 1526-1998", 1998; "Africans in NC", UNC-Center for TV, 1998; African American Heritage Trail, Duke Univ, 1999. **Home Addr:** 309 Union St, Murfreesboro, NC 27855-2025, **Home Phone:** (252)398-5098. **Business Addr:** Owner, Historically Speaking, 23 Poinciana Dr, Durham, NC 27707, **Business Phone:** (919)688-8736.

### JONES, ALMA WYATT
Educator, vice president (organization). **Personal:** Born Nov 19, 1939, Montgomery, AL; married Melvin O. **Educ:** Ala State Univ, MEd, 1966; Eastern Ky Univ; Purdue Univ; Univ Ala, post grad study. **Career:** Teacher (retired); Tuscaloosa City Schs, teacher, 1959-93; Links Inc, Tuscaloosa Chap. **Orgs:** AARP, State Legis Comn, 1997-; bd dir, Ala Educrs Asn, 1998-99; pres, Ala Retired Teachers Asn, 1999-2000; bd dir, McDonald Hughes Community Ctr; Zeta Phi Beta Sorority; Beta Eta Zeta Chap; second vpres, AARP, Tuscaloosa County Chap Unit 146; Ala Educ Retirees Asn; bd dir, vpres, Ala Educ Retirees Found Bd. **Home Addr:** 1605 Montrose Dr S, Tuscaloosa, AL 35405-3627, **Home Phone:** (205)345-5514. **Business Addr:** Area Coordinator - Area II, Alabama Education Retirees Association Inc, 828 Wash Ave, Montgomery, AL 36104, **Business Phone:** (334)262-4177.

### JONES, AMMIA W.
Clergy. **Personal:** Born Jan 31, 1910, Mesic, NC; children: 4. **Career:** Town Mesic, comnr; clergyman, currently. **Orgs:** Pres, Mesic Branch, Nat Asn Advan Colored People. **Home Addr:** 8276 NC Hwy 304, Bayboro, NC 28515, **Home Phone:** (252)745-3208.

### JONES, ANDRUW RUDOLF
Baseball player. **Personal:** Born Apr 23, 1977, Willemstad; son of Henry and Carmen; married Nicole Derick; children: Druw & Madison. **Career:** Baseball player; Atlanta Braves, outfielder, 1996-2007; Los Angeles Dodgers, 2008; Texas Rangers, 2009; Chicago White Sox, 2010; New York Yankees, 2011-12; Tohoku Rakuten Golden Eagles, 2013-14. **Business Addr:** Professional Baseball Player, Tohoku Rakuten Golden Eagles, 2-11-6 Miyagino, Sendai983-0045.

### JONES, DR. ANNE R.
Educator. **Personal:** Born Jul 5, 1921, New Castle, PA; married Paul L; children: Connie E Rose. **Educ:** Livingstone Col, BA, 1944; Univ Pittsburgh, MSW, 1964, PhD, 1978. **Career:** Educator (retired); Irene Kaufmann Ctr, prog dir, 1952-60; Anna Heldman Ctr, prog dir, 1960-64; Action Housing, dir training, 1964-66; Community Action, dir training, 1966-70; Univ Pittsburgh, Univ Senate, vpres, 1974-75; Univ Pittsburgh, Univ Senate, secy, 1987-88; Univ Pittsburgh, prof emer, interim diraffirmative action, 1989-91. **Orgs:** Provost adv comn, Womens Concerns; dir, Soc Work Field Educ; nom comn, Nat Coun Soc Work; site visitor, Nat Coun Social Educ Work; adv, comn, Allegheny C Youth Serv; pres, Hazel wood Neighborhood Coun; bd dir, Three Rivers Adoption Coun; vpres, Univ Senate, Univ Pittsburgh, 1974-75, secy, 1987-88. **Home Addr:** 144 N Dithridge St Suite 815, Pittsburgh, PA 15213-2616, **Home Phone:** (412)683-2950.

### JONES, ANNETTE MERRITT. See CUMMINGS, ANNETTE MERRITT.

### JONES, ANNIE LEE
Clinical psychologist, educator. **Personal:** Born Apr 10, 1949, Augusta, GA; daughter of Thelma Holliday and Lester; married William James Drislane. **Educ:** Augusta Col, BA, 1971; Univ Tenn, PhD, clin psychol, 1976; NY Univ, Grad Sch Arts & Sci, postdoctoral study. **Career:** Boston Veteran's Admin Med Ctr, intern, 1975; Knoxville Bd Educ Handicapped C's Serv & Headstart Psychologist, citywide coordr, 1975-76; Dillard Univ, asst prof psychol, 1976-77; Harbor Dept Veterans Affairs, clin psychologist, 1977-; HIP Ment Health Serv, clin psychologist, 1990-93; pvt pract, currently; Harlem Family Inst, fac; Us Dept Veterans Affairs, mil sexual trauma coordr, currently. **Orgs:** Am Psychol Asn; Asn Black Psychologists; Nat Alliance Black Educr; Am Col Forensic Examiners. **Home Addr:** 86-75 Midland Pkwy Apt 5J, Jamaica, NY 11432, **Home Phone:** (718)297-4883. **Business Addr:** Military Sexual Trauma Coordinator, United States Department of Veterans Affairs, 810 Vermont Ave NW, Washington, DC 20420, **Business Phone:** (718)526-1000.

### JONES, ANTHONY, JR.
Government official. **Personal:** Born Sep 21, 1933, New York, NY; son of Anthony and Pearl; married Arnoline Whitten; children: Leslie Ann & Anthony Arnold. **Educ:** NY Univ, BS, 1958, MS, 1964. **Career:** Government official (retired); Bd Educ NYC, sci teacher, 1959-69; Bedford Stuyvesant Restoration Corp, dir employ, 1969-79; OIC NY, div mgr, 1979-81; So Bronx Develop Orgn Inc, proj dir, 1981-87, dir Employ & Training; NY City Police Dept, dir victim & vol serv, 1987-95. **Orgs:** Kappa Alpa Psi New York Chap, 1956-65; comt mem, Mayors Comt Adoption, 1973-75; comt mem, Alexander's Dept Store Affirmative Action Comt, 1973-75; Rotary Club Brooklyn, NY, 1975-79; Exec comn, Manpower Planning Coun NY City, 1975-79. **Honors/Awds:** Nat Sci Alfred Univ, 1964; Foundation, Univ Puerto Rico, 1966. **Home Addr:** 8611 Great Meadow Dr, Sarasota, FL 34238, **Home Phone:** (941)924-1492.

### JONES, ANTHONY EDWARD. See JONES, TONY EDWARD.

### JONES, ANTHONY WARD
Executive, manager. **Personal:** Born Aug 15, 1947, Wilmington, NC; son of William Sr and Mary Elizabeth Frasier; married Linda; children: Marilouise Elizabeth. **Educ:** Hampton Univ, BS, mkt, 1969; Univ Calif, Los Angeles, MBA. **Career:** Warner Bros, dir, 1975-88; Munch-A-Million, dir mkt & sales, vpres mkt, 1988-91; Surface Protection Industs Inc, mgr corp sales, 1991-92; Universal Paints & Coatings, pres & chief exec officer, 1992-97; Tony Jones Inc, mkt consult, 1997-2001; Front Row Mgt Corp, mgr, currently; Correction Enterprises, Dir sales & mkt, 2001-. **Business Addr:** Sales Manager, Correction Enterprises, 2020 Yonkers Rd, Raleigh, NC 27604, **Business Phone:** (919)716-3600.

### JONES, DR. ARNOLD PEARSON
School administrator, chancellor (education), army officer. **Personal:** Born Chicago, IL; son of Arnold and Tommie; married Joan L; children: Victoria, Arnold & Douglas. **Educ:** Western Mich Univ, BS, 1950; DePaul Univ, MEd, 1955; Univ Ill, Urbana-Champaign, PhD, 1972. **Career:** Teacher, principal (retired); Chicago Pub Schs, teacher, sch psychologist, prin, 1965, asst supt schs, 1967-69; Malcolm X Col, vpres acad, 1969-70; Northeastern Ill Univ, prof psychol, spec asst to pres, 1971-78; City Cols Chicago, exec vice chancellor human resources & labor rels, prof emer. **Orgs:** Comm Human Rights Comn, 1981-83; bd dir, ACLU; educ task force, Chicago Urban League; life mem, Nat Asn Advan Colored People Educ Core Comn Chicago United; Alpha Phi Alpha; nat pres, Am Bridge Assoc; nat assoc, Affirm Action; sch bd, Nominating Comn City Chicago. **Honors/Awds:** Phi Beta Kappa. **Home Addr:** 6700 S Crandon Ave, Chicago, IL 60649, **Home Phone:** (773)324-2123.

### JONES, ARTHUR L.
Law enforcement officer, radio host. **Personal:** Born Jun 12, 1946, Milwaukee, WI; son of Robert and Addie; married Orelia; children: Derrick & Terrence. **Educ:** Northwestern Univ, dipl, police admin; Univ Wis Milwaukee, BS, social welfare & criminal justice; Marquette Univ, AA, law enforcement. **Career:** Law enforcement officer (retired), radio host; Milwaukee Police Dept, police officer, police patrolman, dep inspector police, 1976-78, detective, 1978-87, lt detectives, 1987-89, capt police, 1989-92, dep inspector police, 1992-96, chief police, 1996-2003; 1290 WMCS, talk radio staff guest host, 2003-. **Orgs:** Am Police Asn; Maj Cities Chiefs Asn; Milwaukee Co Law Enforcement Exec; Nat Org Black Law Enforcement Execs; Police Exec Res Forum; Wis Chiefs Police Asn. **Home Addr:** 6820 N 112th Ct, Milwaukee, WI 53224, **Home Phone:** (414)935-7200. **Business Addr:** Staff Guest Host, 1290 WMCS, 4222 W Capitol Dr, Milwaukee, WI 53216, **Business Phone:** (414)444-1290.

### JONES, DR. BARBARA ANN POSEY
School administrator, educator. **Personal:** Born Jun 23, 1943, Oklahoma City, OK; daughter of Alma Vertena Inglemon and Weldon Burnett; married Mack H; children: Patrice Lumumba, Tayari A & Bomani B. **Educ:** Univ Okla, BA, govt, econs, & math, 1963; Univ Ill, MA, 1966; Ga State Univ, PhD, 1973. **Career:** Univ Ill, Champaign-Urbana, IL, teaching & res asst, 1963-66; Tex Southern Univ, Dept Sociol & Econs, instr, 1966-67; Atlanta Univ, Dept Econs, instr, 1968-69; Clark Col, Dept Bus Admin & Econ, from asst prof econ to prof econs, 1971-87, chairperson, 1971-80, Southern Ctr Studies Pub Policy, sr res assoc, 1981-87; Ahmadu Bello Univ, Dept Econ, Zaria, Nigeria, sr lectr, 1983-84; Prairie View A&M Univ, Dept Econs & Finance, head, 1987-89, Sch Bus, dean, 1989-97; Ala A&M Univ, Sch Bus, dean, 1997-, prof, currently. **Orgs:** Bd dir, 1971-2000, secy & treas, 1975-80, pres, 1987, Nat Econ Asn; bd trustee, 1973-74 & 1975-79; bd ed adv, Rev Black Polit Econ, 1975-, Clark Col; hon mem, Alpha Kappa Mu Hon Soc, 1978; hon mem, Delta Mu Delta Hon Soc, 1991; bd dir, 1993-2004, secy & treas, 1996-2000, pres, 2003, Southern Bus Admin Asn; bd dir, 1994-97, exec comt mem, 1995-97, candidacy comt mem, 1992-95, accreditation task force implementation comt mem, 1992-94, Int Asn Mgt Educ; Southwestern Bus Deans Asn, 1993-97; bd dir, 1994-97, exec comt mem, 1995-97; bd dir, HBCU, Bus Deans Round table, 2002-, pres, 2005-06, Am Assembly Col Schs Bus; vpres, 2002, pres, 2003, chair, 2005, WEDC Found Bd, AACSB. **Home Addr:** 4926 7 Pine Cir, Huntsville, AL 35816, **Home Phone:** (256)372-5092. **Business Addr:** Professor, Alabama A&M University, PO Box 429, Normal, AL 35762, **Business Phone:** (256)372-5092.

### JONES, BEN F.
Educator, artist. **Personal:** Born May 26, 1941, Paterson, NJ; son of Ormsby Sr and Elise North. **Educ:** William Paterson Univ, Wayne, NJ, BA, art, 1963; NY Univ, MA, painting & art educ, 1966; Pratt Inst, Brooklyn, NY, MFA, painting & printmaking, 1983. **Career:** Nat Endowment Arts, fel grant, 1974-75; NJ State Coun Arts, fel grant, 1977-78 & 1983-84; Nat Conf Art, pres, 1978-80, vpres, 1981-84; Sulaimaan Dance Co, chmn bd, 1981-83; NJ City Univ, Fine Arts Dept, prof art, currently. **Orgs:** NJ Printmaking Coun, 1979-; World Printmaking Coun, 1980-; Nat Conf Artists; bd mem, Friends Music & Art Hudson Co, 1985; mem bd adv, Woodson Found NJ; Montclair Art Mus; African-Am Community. **Honors/Awds:** First Place & Second Place in Art Competition, Atlanta Life Ins, 1982-83; Grant, Jersey City State Col, 1982-83; Career Development Award, Passaic Co Community Col, Patterson, NJ, 1984; Excellence in the Arts, Delta Sigma Theta Sorority, 1985; Distinguished Artist, William Paterson Univ, 2001. **Home Addr:** 117 Kensington Ave Apt 206, Jersey City, NJ 07304, **Home Phone:** (201)433-6458. **Business Addr:** Professor of Art, Artist, New Jersey City University, Rm 120 Visual Arts Bldg, Jersey City, NJ 07305-1597, **Business Phone:** (201)200-2000.

### JONES, BENJAMIN A.
Association executive, clergy. **Personal:** Born Mobile, AL; son of Margaret. **Educ:** Col Lifelong Learning, attended 1994; Univ Mich, MSW, 1995, Capella Univ, PhD, 2013. **Career:** Pentecostal Churches Apostolic Faith, assoc minister, asst to pastor, ordained elder, currently; Drug Strategies, bd mem; Nat Coun Alcoholism & Drug Dependence, Greater Detroit Area, exec dir, pres & chief exec officer, 1996-; Nehemiah's Temple Apostolic Faith, senior pastor, 2009-. **Business Addr:** President, Chief Executive Officer, National Council on Alcoholism & Drug Dependence Inc, 4777 E Outer Dr, Detroit, MI 48234, **Business Phone:** (313)369-5400.

### JONES, BENJAMIN E.
Executive, business owner. **Personal:** Born Sep 8, 1935, New York, NY; married Delcenia R; children: Leslie & Delcenia. **Educ:** Brooklyn Col, BA, econs, 1971; Pace Univ, MBA, mgt, 1974. **Career:** Radio Recepter Co, admin, 1959-60; ESX Div Paal Corp, acct, 1962-66; Gen Precision Inc, sr contract admin, negotiator & signer, 1966-71; Capital Formation Inc, Econ Develop Found, New York, pres, 1971-; Interracial Coun Bus Opportunity NY, prog dir, 1971; MBA Mgt Consult Inst, Columbia Univ, dir, 1973; Lightning Supply Inc, pres & owner, 1996-. **Orgs:** Fed Exec Bd, Minority Bus Opportunity Community, 1972-; bd dir, Upper Park Ave Community Asn, Day Care Ctr, 1974-; Am Mgt Asn; Nat Bus League; Coun Concerned Black Execs; Nat Asn Black Mfrs; Asn MBA Execs; Nat Asn Advan Colored People; One Hundred Black Men Inc; Uptown Chamber Community; NY Urban League; Am Asn MESBICS; chmn, Nat Minority Bus Coun, 2009-14, bd dir, currently. **Home Addr:** 87 Chadwick Rd, Teaneck, NJ 07666, **Home Phone:** (201)692-3622. **Business Addr:** President, Owner, Lighting Supply Inc, 87 Chadwick Rd Unit 200, Teaneck, NJ 07666, **Business Phone:** (800)724-9976.

### JONES, BERNIE
Journalist. **Personal:** Born Jun 21, 1952, Baltimore, MD; son of Sumoria Clacks and Newbern L; married Beverly Harvey; children: Linsay Morgan. **Educ:** Univ NC, Chapel Hill, NC, BA, 1974. **Career:** Baltimore News Am, asst news ed, 1980-81, night news ed, 1981-82; Northwestern Univ, fel; San Diego Union, Calif, asst news ed, 1984-92, polit ed, 1985-86, news ed, 1992-96; Copley Newspapers, Opinion Page Ed, 1996-2009; Opinion Pages, San Diego Union-Tribune, ed, 1996-2009. **Home Addr:** 3635 7th Ave, San Diego, CA 92103. **Business Addr:** Editor, San Diego Union-Tribune Opinion Pages, 350 Camino de la Reina, San Diego, CA 92112-0191, **Business Phone:** (619)293-1208.

### JONES, BERTHA DIGGS
Social worker, administrator. **Personal:** Born Richland, GA; children: Betty Jean. **Educ:** Cent Sch Bus, Buffalo, attended 1968. **Career:** Diggs Assoc Urban Affairs, pres; FEPC, consult, 1945; EEA-WDP, supvr. **Orgs:** Consult to chmn, Buffalo Housing Auth, 1942; organizer, Jr Club Nat Asn; Negro Bus & Prof Women, NY, 1945; statewide organizer & exec dir, State Baptist Cong, 1956-69; adv comt, NY Div Housing, 1961-69; pres, Adv Coun Pace Univ NY, 1966-77; adv coun, Corsi Labor/Mgt Inst Pace Univ, 1966-77; bus consult, New York Dept Com, 1970-71; secy, State Labor Dept, 1973-75; Urban League; Nat Asn Advan Colored People; bd dir, Brooklyn Chap Am Red Cross; Am Acad Polit & Soc Sci Ctr; nat hon mem, Lambda Kappa Mu Sor. **Honors/Awds:** Silver Cup, Nat Rep Coun, 1948; Sojourner Truth

Award, 1964; Meritorious Service Award, State Am Legion Unit; Service Award, Vis Nurse Asn Brooklyn, 1967-69; Certificate of Service, NY Labor Dept, 1975; Community Service Award, Woman of the Year, Philadelphia Church Universal Brotherhood, 1977. **Special Achievements:** Author of Home & Family Seminars, 1956; Continuous published newsletters, 1935-77. **Home Addr:** 818 Lincoln Pl, Brooklyn, NY 11216.

### JONES, BERTHA H.

Educator. **Personal:** Born Oct 30, 1918, Earle, AR; married Joseph R; children: Malcolm. **Educ:** Ill State Univ, BE; Ball State Univ, MA; Northwestern Univ; Mich Univ; Loyola Univ; Ind Univ; NW & Purdue Univ. **Career:** Speech teacher, 1951-56; eng teacher, 1956-59; guid counr, 1959-69; Gary Pub Sch Educ Talent Search, dir, 1969-2014. **Orgs:** Chmn, vice chmn, proj dir & assoc; Pers & Guid Assoc; Am Personneland Guid Asn Dele Ind; adv bd, Ind Univ NW Campus; spec serv, Mid W Assoc Stu Fin Aid Admin; bd dir, Upward Bound adv bd Metro Corps OEO Deleg Agency; Delta Sigma Theta; bd dir, Young Women Christian Asn Teen Comm; Van Buren Bapt Church; Urban League, Consumer Ed Task Force Ind Univ. **Honors/Awds:** Pi Lambda Theta; Hon Soc for Women Ed, 1961; Ind Personnel & Guid Asn Merit Award, 1973; Award serv to stud, 1974. **Special Achievements:** Elected Supreme first Anti-basileus Nat Sorority Phi Delta Kappa 1969, 1971. **Home Addr:** 7645 Lake Shore Dr, Gary, IN 46403-1335.

### JONES, DR. BETTY B.

Educator. **Personal:** Born May 4, 1935, Columbia, SC; daughter of William A and Minnie M Brown; married Samuel Preston; children: Allen Preston & Anthony Paul. **Educ:** Hampton Univ, BS, 1956; Cath Univ Am, MSW, 1965; Univ Mich, PhD, 1981. **Career:** Educator (retired); Campfire Girls, Wash, DC, staff, 1960-68; Bay City Pub Schs, social worker & admin, 1969-77; US Patent Off Wash, DC, patent examr; Delta Col, vice pres instr & learning serv, 1977-2001. **Orgs:** Am Asn Univ Profs, 1977-; Am Sociol Soc, 1980-; Midland Hist Soc, 1995-; Nat Orgn Bibl Storytellers, 2002-. **Home Addr:** 2504 Georgetown Dr, Midland, MI 48642-3918, **Home Phone:** (989)631-6774.

### JONES, DR. BETTY JEAN TOLBERT

Educator. **Personal:** Born Jul 14, 1943, Charleston, SC; daughter of Helen Grant Tolbert and Fred W Tolbert; married Donald W; children: Tracey. **Educ:** Hampton Inst Va, BS, 1965; Fairfield Univ, CT, MA, 1970; Univ Va, EdD, 1990; Princeton Univ, post-doctoral study. **Career:** Dolan Jr High Sch, Conn, sci teacher, 1965-68; Fairfield Univ, grad study, 1968-69; Lane High Sch, teacher, 1973-74; Charlottesville High Sch, Va, biol teacher, 1974-, Sci Dept, chairperson, 1994-; Univ Va, Charlottesville, Va, clin instr, 1986; Univ Va Ctr Biol Timing, biol researcher, 1993-2001; bd dir, Links Inc, pres, Charlottesville Chap; Martin Luther King fel; NASA, Goddard Space Flight Ctr, fel, Woods Hole, Mass Marine Biol Lab, fel; Hope Col Nat Biol Linking Prog, fel; Woodrow Wilson fel; Howard Hughes fel; Univ Calif, Berkeley, Nat Bio tech Forum, fel; Univ Kans, Med Ctr Human Genome Proj, fel; Tufts Univ, Wright Sci Ctr, fel; Fulbright Memorial Fund Scholar to Japan, 2001. **Orgs:** Nat Asn Biol Teachers, 1965-; Am Asn Univ Women, 1970-; Va Asn Sci Teachers, 1973-; treas, Barret Day Care Ctr Bd, 1973-; Am Asn Higher Educ, 1973-; Am Asn Higher Educ Black Caucus, 1973-; bd dir, Charlottesville Educ Asn, 1974-; Nat Educ Asn; participant Parent-Edn Conf Univ Va; Alpha Kappa Mu; Beta Kappa Chi Nat Honor Soc; Delta Sigma Theta Sorority; Kappa Delta Pi; Friends Within; Jr League Charlottesville; Family Serv Bd Charlottesville; Va Sci Leadership Asn; bd Emergency Food Bank Charlottesville; bd dir, Va Fund Humanities & Pub Policy; Am Mus Sci & Energy; vpres, Charlottesville chap; vpres & bd dir, Gordonsville Friends Libr; fel Nat Sci Found. **Home Addr:** PO Box 6429, Charlottesville, VA 22906, **Home Phone:** (540)832-2809. **Business Addr:** President, Links Inc, 1200 Massachusetts Ave NW, Washington, DC 20005, **Business Phone:** (202)842-8686.

### JONES, BILL. See JONES, WILLIAM JAMES.

### JONES, DR. BILLY EMANUEL

Government official, physician. **Personal:** Born Jun 11, 1938, Dayton, OH; son of Callie and Paul; children: Alexander. **Educ:** Howard Univ, BS, 1960; Meharry Med Col, MD, 1965; NY Med Col, residency psychiat, 1969; NY Univ, Robert Wagner Grad Sch Pub Serv, MS, 1990. **Career:** Metrop Hosp CMHC, asst dir, 1971-73; Coney Island Hosp Dept Psy chiat, assoc dir, 1973-74; Fordham Hosp, Dept Psy chiat, dir, 1974-77; New York Med Col, Dept Psychiat & Behav Sci, dir, 1977-90, clin prof, currently, Med & Ment Health Ctr, adminr, Dept Psy chiat, 1977-88, med dir, sr assoc dean, 1988-90; NY City, Dept Ment Health, Ment Retardation & Alcoholism Servs, comnr, 1990-; Health & Hosps Corp, pres & chief exec officer, 1992-94; Magellan Behav Health Serv, sr vpres & chief med officer pub solutions Div, 1997-2002; City Col New York, adj med prof; B Jones Consult Serv, chief exec officer & pres, owner, currently; Dept of Veterans Affairs, sr adv to asst secy, 2010-; Care Mgt Technologies, vpres & chief med dir, 2003-06; Lincoln Med and Ment Health Ctr, med dir; Sophie Davis Sch, lect. **Orgs:** Dip, Am Bd Psychiat & Neurol, 1977-; pres, Black Psychiatrists Am, 1978-80; community serv bd, New York, 1980-90; fel Am Psychiat Asn, 1983-; NYS Alcohol Drug Abuse & Ment Health Block Grant Community, 1983-90; 100 Black Men; New York Acad Med; Nat Med Asn; Am Pub Health Asn; chair, Black Equity Alliance Bd; Kellogg Fel, New York Univ's Robert Wagner Grad Sch Pub Serv. **Business Addr:** President, Chief Executive Officer, B Jones Consulting Services, 56 Hamilton Terr Suite 1, New York, NY 10031, **Business Phone:** (212)234-5649.

### JONES, REV. BISHOP SPENCER

Clergy, vice president (organization). **Personal:** Born Mar 24, 1946, Poplar Bluff, MO; son of Frank and Evelina; married Kathy AE Drake; children: Daliz E, Trayon D, Shemen A & Melinet MB. **Educ:** Cent Bible Col, BA, relig, 1972. **Career:** Southside Worship Center, Pastor; Southside Tabernacle, sr pastor, currently; elected Bishop, 1999. **Orgs:** Exec Presbyter, Assemblies God; vpres, Stud Govt; Nat Inner-City Workers Conf; bd mem, Chicago Teen Challenge; block club pres, 1986-; Decade Harvest Comt; pres, Local Sch Coun, 1988-; Speaker Gen Coun, 1989; community rep, 1990-; Black Rep Assemblies God; Beat Rep Chicago Police Dept; founder, Nat Black Fel; bd dir, Evangel Col; Home Missions Bd; bd dir, Africas C; founder & pres, People United to Reach. **Home Addr:** 11751 S Campbell Ave, Chicago, IL 60655, **Home Phone:** (773)233-2609. **Business Addr:** Senior Pastor, Southside Tabernacle, 7724 S Racine Ave, Chicago, IL 60620-2926, **Business Phone:** (773)488-3443.

### JONES, BOBBY M. (ROBERT MITCHELL JONES)

Athletic coach, baseball player. **Personal:** Born Apr 11, 1972, Orange, NJ. **Educ:** Chipola Col, Marianna, FL. **Career:** Baseball player (retired), baseball coach; Colo Rockies, pitcher, 1997-99; New York Mets, pitcher, 2000, 2002; San Diego Padres, pitcher, 2002; Norfolk Tides, 2002; Richmond Braves, 2003; Omaha Royals, 2003; Boston Red Sox, pitcher, 2004; Chicago White Sox, 2005; Charlotte Knights, pitcher, 2005; Detroit Tigers, pitcher, 2006; Rockland Boulders, pitching coach, currently. **Business Addr:** Pitching Coach, Rockland Boulders, 1 Provident Bank Pk Dr, Pomona, NY 10970, **Business Phone:** (845)364-0009.

### JONES, HON. BONNIE LOUISE

Lawyer, judge. **Personal:** Born Feb 3, 1952, Philadelphia, PA; daughter of William Smith and Thelma Mills. **Educ:** Lincoln Univ, BA, 1970; NC Cent Univ Sch Law, JD, 1982. **Career:** VA Legal Aid Soc, law clerk, 1982-83; Newport News Police Dept, permits examnr, 1983-85; Hampton Roads Regional Acad Criminal Justice, training/eval specialist 1985-86; Blayton Allen & Assocs, assoc atty, 1986-88; self-employed atty, Hampton VA, 1988-; McDermott, Roe & Sons, atty, 1992-96; Col William & Mary, Sch Law, adj prof, 1994-97; City Hampton Gen Dist Court, judge, 1996-2002, chief judge, currently. **Orgs:** Phi Alpha Delta Law Fraternity, 1982-; Big Brother/Big Sisters Peninsula, 1985; Am Bar Asn, 1986; VA Bar Asn, 1986; Asn Trial Atty Am; Penn Bar Asn, 1987-; Hampton Bar Asn, 1988-92; coun vpres, Int Training Commun Coun II, 1988-89; Comn Chancery Hampton Circuit Ct; pres, bd dir, Girls Inc Greater Peninsula. **Home Addr:** 24 Fields Dr, Hampton, VA 23664. **Business Addr:** Chief Judge, City of Hampton General District Court, 236 N King St, Hampton, VA 23669, **Business Phone:** (757)727-6480.

### JONES, BOOKER TEE, SR.

Association executive, executive director, executive. **Personal:** Born Jun 30, 1939, Mesic, NC; son of Hezekiah and Mary; married Loretta Johnson; children: Hilda Davis, Booker T Jr, Marietta & Coretta. **Educ:** LaSalle Ext Univ, AA, acct, 1959; Cent Appraiser Soc, real estate appr designation, 1971; Nat Ctr Housing Mgt, housing mgt cert, 1981. **Career:** Executive (retired); Kingsborough Realty Inc, real estate salesman, 1963-67; One Stop Home Sales Co, owner, broker, appraiser, 1967-74; BookerT Jones Real Estate Brokers, pres, real estate broker, 1972-; DPT HUD, real estate appraiser, 1972-73; Costal Progress Inc, coordr, adminr, 1977-80; Twin Rivers Opportunity Inc, housing dir, 1980-85, exec dir, 1985. **Orgs:** Pres, United Communities Asn Net Inc, 1975-85; bd dir, Craven County Fed Credit Union, 1979-82; vice chmn bd, Pamlico County Bd Ed, 1980-85; chmn bd dir, NC Sect 8 Housing Asn Inc, 1984-85, bd mem, 1985-; appointee, Pamlico County Planning Bd, 1991; appointee, Low Income Housing Task Force, New Bern, NC, 1991; bd dir, chmn, Costal COT Develop Corp, 1991; bd dir, NC Housing Fin Agency, 1994-; bd dir, App NC Gov mem NC Housing Fin Agency, 1994-; bd trustees, Pamlico Community Col, 2000-04. **Honors/Awds:** Outstanding Service, United Way, 1977; Leadership Training, Nat Citizen Participation Coun Inc, 1979; NC Gov's Appointment Pamlico Cty Transp Efficiency, 1982; Exemplarary Serv, NC Sect 8 Housing Asn Inc, 1984; appointed local adv comt, 1988-; adv bd, NC Dept HUD, 1988-; Outstanding Service Award, 1989-90, 15 Year Employment Longevity Honor, 1992, Twin Rivers Opportunities Inc; Distinguished Guest Honors, Cong woman Eve Clayton, Cong man Mel Watts, & NC Gov Jim Hunt, 1991. **Home Addr:** PO Box 68, Grantsboro, NC 28529. **Business Addr:** Executive Director, Twin Rivers Opportunities Inc, 318 Craven St, New Bern, NC 28563-1482, **Business Phone:** (252)637-3599.

### JONES, BRENT M.

Photographer, educator, journalist. **Personal:** Born Feb 11, 1946, Chicago, IL; son of Willie Clarence and Madge Alberta; married Ingrid Claire Brister; children: Lauren M & Christopher. **Educ:** Columbia Col, BA, jour, 1969. **Career:** Brent Jones Photojournalist, Chicago, owner, 1969; Opportunity Industrialization Training Ctr, eng instr & asst dir pub rels, 1969-70; Columbia Col, instr creative writing, 1969-70; Black Asn Enterprises, chief photog, 1970-73; Sch Art Inst, Chicago, instr, 1976-79; Chicago Art Inst, teacher; One-man exhibs; US Rep; Second World Black & African Festival Arts & Cult, freelance photogr & writer, currently. **Orgs:** Founding mem, Chicago Alliance African Am Photogr; Southside Community Art Ctr, 1986-; Urban League, 1986; Schomburg Soc, NY, 1988; Mus Sci & Indust, 1988-; US rep 2nd World Black & African Festival Art, 1977; Featured artist Black Esthetic, Mus Sci & Indust, 1978; vpres, American Society Picture Professionals, 1988-89. **Special Achievements:** US rep 2nd World Black and African Festival of Art, Nigeria, 1977; featured artist Black Esthetic, Mus Sci & Indust, 1978; Southside Community Art Ctr, 1986; Urban League, 1986; Mus Sci and Indust, 1988. **Business Addr:** Photographer, 9121 S Merrill Ave, Chicago, IL 60617-3830, **Business Phone:** (773)933-1174.

### JONES, BRIAN KEITH

Executive, radio host, football player. **Personal:** Born Jan 22, 1968, Iowa City, IA. **Educ:** Univ Calif, Los Angeles, BS, commun, 1988; Univ Tex, Austin, BS, corp commun, 2000. **Career:** Football player (retired), host; Indianapolis Colts, linebacker, 1991; Miami Dolphins, 1992; Los Angeles Raiders, 1994; Scottish Claymores, 1995; New Orleans Saints, mid linebacker, 1995, linebacker, 1998; Fox Sports Southwest, col football analyst, 2004-06, Univ Tex football games, reporter; Pro Clubworld Sports, vpres bus develop; KVET (AM), host; CBS Sports Radio, col football analyst, co host, 2013-. **Business Addr:** Co Host, CBS Sports Radio, 1271 Avenue of the Americas 44th Fl, New York, NY 10020, **Business Phone:** (212)649-9600.

### JONES, CARL

Executive, business owner. **Personal:** Born Jan 1, 1955, TN. **Educ:** El Camino Col. **Career:** Business Owner, Licensing; Designers Screen Printing, founder, 1982-85; Surf Fetish, founder, 1985-90; Cross Colours Clothing, pres, 1990-94, creative dir, 1990-95, 2015-; Calif Vintage, creative dir, 2005-07; Pvt Label Develop Jr Mkt, creative dir, 2000-08; BLEULAB-Reversible Collection, creative, 2008-15; pvt lic apparels. **Honors/Awds:** California Mart Design Award, 1987-88; California Mart Marty Award, 1987; Waiter P Chrysler Award, 1992. **Home Addr:** 1370 1/2 Laveta Terr, Los Angeles, CA 90026, **Home Phone:** (213)482-0718. **Business Addr:** Creative Director, Cross Colours, 228 Manhattan Beach Blvd, Manhattan Beach, CA 90266-5347.

### JONES, CAROLYN G.

Consultant, president (organization). **Personal:** Born Aug 5, 1943, Chattanooga, TN; daughter of Clyde Goolsby and Paralee Johnson Goolsby; married Edward G; children: Larketta, Harry Charles, Arthur & Edward Lee. **Educ:** Emory Univ, Atlanta, GA, BS, 1976. **Career:** Metro Hosp W, dir med rec, 1972-74; Erlanger Alton Pk Health Ctr, admin asst, 1974-76; Med Rec Technol Prog, Chattanooga State Community Col, prog dir, 1976-81; regist health info adminr; CJ Health Rec Consult Serv, founder, 1980; CJ Enterprises Inc, pres & chief exec officer, currently. **Orgs:** Chairperson, Ed Comt Chattanooga Area Med Rec Coun, 1984-85; chairperson, Pub Rel CAMRC, 1983-84; By-Laws Comt TMRA, 1983-84; co-dir, Nursing Guild Hawkinsville Baptist Church, 1984-85; Chattanooga Minority Bus Develop, 1984; bd mem, Tenn Multicultural Chamber Com; Polit Action Comt; Minority Health Coalition-Econ Develop Comt; Nat Coalition 100 Black Women Chattanooga Chap; Chattanooga Area Urban League; Chattanooga Leadership Grad; Nat Asn Community Health Ctr; adv bd mem, Women's Leadership Inst; Hawkinsville Missionary Baptist Church; chairperson, Mother & Missionary Ministry. **Home Addr:** 324 Willow Glen Rd, Chattanooga, TN 37421. **Business Addr:** President, Chief Executive Officer, CJ Enterprises Inc, 7010 Lee Hwy Suite 214, Chattanooga, TN 37421, **Business Phone:** (423)899-1770.

### JONES, CEDRIC LEWIS

Football player, football coach. **Personal:** Born Apr 30, 1974, Houston, TX; son of Annette; married Susi; children: Cailey, Cameron & Cash. **Educ:** Univ Okla, grad. **Career:** Football player (retired); NY Giants, defensive end & line backer, 1996-2000; St. Louis Rams, 2000-01; Montclair Prep High, offensive line coach, 2005; Carolina Panthers; Southern Nazarene Univ, coach, currently. **Honors/Awds:** All-Am first team, The Sporting News, 1995. **Special Achievements:** Films: 1996 NFL Draft, 1996; Super Bowl XXXV, 2001. **Business Addr:** Coach, Southern Nazarene University, 6729 NW 39th Expressway, Bethany, OK 73008-2605, **Business Phone:** (405)789-6400.

### JONES, CHARISSE MONSIO

Journalist. **Personal:** Born Sep 2, 1965, San Francisco, CA; daughter of Charles Milton and Jean Stephanie Laing. **Educ:** Univ Southern Calif, Los Angeles, CA, BA, jour, 1987. **Career:** Wave Newspaper, Los Angeles, Calif, intern, 1985; Los Angeles Herald Examr, Los Angeles, Calif, reporter, 1986-88; Los Angeles Times, Los Angeles, Calif, reporter, staff writer, 1989-93; NY Times, staff writer, 1993-97; USA Today, reporter, bus travel corresp, 1997-; Nat Pub Radio, commentator, 1997-98; Essence mag, contrib writer, 1998-2005; Rutgers Univ, Adj Prof, 2009-11; The Greene Space, guest moderator, 2013. **Orgs:** Bd mem, Black Journalists Asn Southern Calif, 1989-93; Nat Asn Black Journalists, 1986-; Golden Key Hon Soc, 1984-; USC Mentor Prog, 1990-93. **Honors/Awds:** Los Angeles Press Club Award, 1992; Pulitzer Prize, Columbia Univ. **Special Achievements:** Shifting: the story of Black women, HarperCollins Publ. **Home Addr:** 800 Glenway Dr Suite 111, Inglewood, CA 90302, **Home Phone:** (213)664-4922. **Business Addr:** Reporter & New York Correspondent, USA Today, 7950 Jones Br Dr, McLean, VA 22102, **Business Phone:** (703)854-3400.

### JONES, CHARLES

Basketball coach, educator. **Personal:** Born May 12, 1946, Bronx, NY; son of Charles and Mae; married Linda Marie Coggshall. **Educ:** Cent Conn State Univ, BS, 1969; MS, educ, 1972; Columbia Univ, PhD. **Career:** Educator retired; Cent Conn State Univ, grad asst, 1970-72, dir educ opportunity prog & asst basketball coach, 1970-95, dir, educ support serv, dir athletics & dir intercollegiate athletics, 1995-2009; Cashman & Katz Integrated Commun, athletics dir, 2007-12. **Orgs:** Hartford Bd Approved Umpires, 1969; Kappa Delta Pi, 1970; coordr, Ann Thanksgiving Food Dr Deprived Families New Brit Area, 1970-; Nat Asn Basketball Coaches, 1970-; CT State Employees Asn, 1970-; bd mem, CT Commn Higher Educ Accrediting Team, 1972; fac adv, Ebony Choral Ensemble, 1974-; pres, Black Admin Staff Inst Cent; field reader, govt grants; Phi DeltaKappa Sect Conn Assoc Educ Opportunities Prog; coordr, Minority Youth BusConf; bd dir, Cent Conn State Univ Alumni; pres, CT Asn Educ Opportunity Prog, 1991-92; treas, New Eng Asn Educ Opportunity Prog Personnel, 1992; trustee, Friendship Ctr; trustee, New Britian Found; Nat Col Athletic Asn, Men's Basketball Rules COM; originator, Endowed Scholar Fund Disadvantaged Stud; Northeast Conf, 1998-2009. **Home Addr:** 4 Tory Xing, Terryville, CT 06786-4911, **Home Phone:** (860)589-7115. **Business Addr:** Director Intercollegiate Athletics, Central Connecticut State University, 1615 Stanley St Harrison J Kaiser 131, New Britain, CT 06053, **Business Phone:** (860)832-3087.

### JONES, CHARLES, III. See DARA, OLU.

### JONES, CHARLES D.

State government official, lawyer. **Personal:** Born Mar 25, 1950; married Ann Sims. **Educ:** Southern Univ, BA, JD; Univ Ill, MA, LLM; Northwestern Univ Dist Atty Sch. **Career:** Asst dist atty, 1976-79; La State Senate, atty, Dist 17, state rep, 1980-92, atty, Dist 34, state sen, 1992-2007; La House Representatives, rep, currently. **Orgs:** La Bar Asn; Northern La Legal Assistance Corp; bd dir, La Sickle Cell Anemia Asn, currently. **Home Addr:** 1803 Medra Dr, Monroe, LA 71202. **Business Addr:** Representative, Louisiana House of Representatives, LA.

### JONES, CHARLES GADGET
Basketball player. **Personal:** Born Apr 3, 1957, McGehee, AR. **Educ:** Albany State Univ, attended 1979. **Career:** Basketball player (retired); Maine Lumberjacks, 1979-80, 1982-85; Nice BC, France, 1980-81; San Bennedetto Gorizia, Italy, 1981-82; Bay State Bombardiers, 1983-84; Philadelphia 76ers, 1983-84; San Antonio Spurs, 1984; Tampa Bay Thrillers, 1984-85; Chicago Bulls, 1984-85; Wash Bullets, 1984-93; Detroit Pistons, 1993-94; Houston Rockets, 1995-98.

### JONES, CHARLES RAHMEL
Basketball player. **Personal:** Born Jul 17, 1975, Brooklyn, NY; son of Charles and Cathy. **Educ:** Rutgers Univ, attended 1995; Long Island Univ, attended 1998; Albany State Univ, attended. **Career:** Basketball player (retired); Chicago Bulls, guard, 1998-99; Los Angeles Clippers, free agt, 1999-2000; BingoSNAI Montecatini, Italy, 2000-01; Ionikos Egnatia Bank, Greece, 2001-02; Ionikos NF Thessaloniki, 2001-02; Brooklyn Kings, 2003; Maccabi Rishon Le-Zion, 2003-04; Libertad de Sunchales, 2003-04; PBC Lukoil Acad, 2004-05; Albany Patroons, 2005; Strong Island Sound, 2005; Albany Patrons, 2005; Gimnasia Esgrima Comodoro Rivadavia, Arg, guard, 2005-06; Long Island Primetime, 2006; Gimnasia y Esgrima de Comodoro Rivadavia, Arg, 2006-08, 2010; Ciclista Olimpico, Arg, 2008; BC Levski Sofia, Bulgaria, 2009.

### JONES, CHARLIE EDWARD
Football player, football coach. **Personal:** Born Dec 1, 1972, Hanford, CA. **Educ:** Fresno State Univ, BA, speech communs major. **Career:** Football player (retired), football coach; San Diego Chargers, wide receiver & tight end, 1996-99; New Orleans Saints, wide receiver; Fresno City Col, coaching staff, currently. **Business Addr:** Coaching Staff, Fresno City College, 1101 E Univ Ave, Fresno, CA 93741, **Business Phone:** (559)442-4600.

### JONES, CHERYL ARLEEN
Television producer, manager, consultant. **Personal:** Born Sep 2, 1963, Portsmouth, VA; daughter of Donna R and Maxwell. **Educ:** Va Polytech Inst & State Univ, BA, commun & broadcasting, 1986. **Career:** Discovery Commun Inc; Discovery Productions, sr mgr develop & co-prod; Discovery Networks, mgr, daytime programming, 1986-91, sr acct mgr, 1991-93; Discovery Pictures, sr acct mgr, 1993-96; Discovery Channel Pictures, dir prog mgt, 1996-99; Pub Broadcasting Serv, vpres programming, prog develop & independent film, sr dir, 2000-05; Grantmakers Film + Electronic Media, consult, prog mgr, 2009-11; OBXtek, consult, 2012-; Primescape Solutions Inc, media consult, 2012-. **Orgs:** Nat Acad Cable Programming, 1986-; Nat Acad TV Arts & Sci, 1988-; Int Doc Asn, 1990-; Mus Broadcasting, 1992-; Am Women Radio & Tv, 1991-92; Women Cable, 1987-92; Big sister, Big Sister Wash, Metrop Area, 1992-. **Business Addr:** Media Consultant, Primescape Solutions Inc, 13221 Woodland Pk Rd, Herndon, VA 20171, **Business Phone:** (703)650-1900.

### JONES, CHESTER RAY
Government official, lawyer. **Personal:** Born Nov 9, 1946, Jackson, MS; son of William Sr and River Lee Clark; married Queen Jackson; children: Jaala & Heddie Rabekah. **Educ:** Tougaloo Col, BA, sociol, 1968; Miss Col Sch Law, JD, 1978. **Career:** Abbott House Irvington-on-Hudson NY, child care worker, 1968; Repub Philippines, peace corps vol, 1968-70; Govrs Off Job Develop & Training, equal employ opportunity, 1978-85; Miss State Dept Pub Welfare, staff atty, 1988-89; Miss State Dept Human Serv, sr atty, 1989-; Sanders Law Firm, atty, currently. **Orgs:** Alpha Phi Alpha Frat Inc, 1965; Miss State Bar Asn, 1979; Hinds County Bar Asn, 1979; Am Trial Lawyers Asn, 1979; Nat Inst Employ Equity, 1982; Am Legion (Post 214), 1984; Nat Urban League, 1984; Magnolia Bar Asn 1985-. **Home Addr:** 133 S Commerce St, Natchez, MS 39120-3307, **Home Phone:** (601)445-5570. **Business Addr:** Attorney, Sanders Law Firm, 126 S Commerce St Suite 103, Natchez, MS 39120-3307, **Business Phone:** (601)445-5570.

### JONES, CHRIS (CHRISTOPHER CARLOS JONES)
Baseball player, baseball manager. **Personal:** Born Dec 16, 1965, Utica, NY; married Cystal; children: Christopher & Crishana. **Career:** Baseball player (retired), executive; Cincinnati Reds, outfielder, 1991; Houston Astros, outfielder, 1992; Colo Rockies, outfielder, 1993-94; New York Mets, outfielder, 1995-96; San Diego Padres, outfielder, 1997; Ariz Diamond backs, outfielder, 1998; San Francisco Giants, outfielder, 1998; Milwaukee Brewers, outfielder, 2000; Newark Bears, 2004, mgr, 2005-06; Kannapolis Intimidators, mgr, 2007-. **Business Addr:** Manager, Kannapolis Intimidators, 2888 Moose Rd, Kannapolis, NC 28083, **Business Phone:** (704)932-3267.

### JONES, CHRISTOPHER TODD
Football player. **Personal:** Born Aug 7, 1971, West Palm Beach, FL. **Educ:** Univ Miami, BA, criminal justice. **Career:** Football player (retired); Philadelphia Eagles, 1995, wide receiver, 1996-97; Oakland Raiders, 1999. **Special Achievements:** TV Movie - NFL Draft, FedEx Orange Bowl, 1995.

### JONES, CLARENCE J., JR.
Government official, president (organization). **Personal:** Born Apr 17, 1933, Boston, MA; son of Clarence J and Elizabeth Middleton; married Wanda Hale; children: Meta, Nadine, Mark, Michael, Melissa, Kenneth & Mark Duane. **Educ:** Winston-Salem State NC, BS, educ, 1955; Goddard Col, MA. **Career:** City Boston, youth worker, 1960-65, dir youth activ comn, 1968-72, dirhuman rights, 1972-76, dep mayor, 1976-81; Boston Juv Ct, probation officer, 1965-68; Boston Redevelop Authority, chmn & bd dir, 1989-; Bostons Roxbury community, resident, currently. **Orgs:** Pres, Winston-Salem State Alumni; bd mem, Boston Redevelop Authority, 1981-; vpres, Winston-Salem State Univ, 1984-; chmn trustee, 12th Baptist Church; bd mem, Girls & Boys Clubs; bd dir, Citizenship Training Groups, Boston Juv Ct. **Honors/Awds:** Outstanding Citizen, Afro-Am Police, 1980; Outstanding Alumnus, Winston-Salem State Univ, 1983; Martin Luther King Jr Drum Major for Peace, 1986. **Home Addr:** 2809 Washington St, Roxbury, MA 02119-1449, **Home Phone:** (617)541-8088. **Business Addr:** Chairman, Board of Director, Boston Redevelopment Authority, 1 City Hall Sq Suite 9, Boston, MA 02201, **Business Phone:** (617)722-4300.

### JONES, CLARENCE THOMAS
Football player. **Personal:** Born May 6, 1968, Brooklyn, NY; married Shari; children: Clarence III. **Educ:** Univ Md. **Career:** Football player (retired); New York Giants, tackle, 1991-93; St Louis Rams, left tackle, 1994-95; New Orleans Saints, tackle & right tackle, 1996-98; Carolina Panthers, tackle & left tackle, 1998-2000. **Home Addr:** 6909 Hillcroft Dr, Austin, TX 78724-3626, **Home Phone:** (512)926-3182.

### JONES, CLYDE EUGENE
Lawyer. **Personal:** Born Dec 5, 1954, Birmingham, AL; son of Bennie and Clyde M; married Janine McCoy; children: Jakarra Jenise & Jasmine Jekesha. **Educ:** Knoxville Col, BA, psychol, 1976; Samford Univ, Cumberland Sch Law, JD, 1979. **Career:** Univ Miss, Pre Law Cleo fel, 1976; Jefferson County Family Ct, law clerk, baliff, 1979-80; 10th Judicial Circuit, Ala, dep dist atty, 1980; 5th Judicial Circuit Ala, asst dist atty, 1980-85; Penick, Williams & Jones, atty partner, 1985-87; Clyde E. Jones PC, 1987-; 10th Judicial Circuit, St Ala, circuit judge, 2002-; 6th Circuit Judges, fel, 2016. **Orgs:** Vpres, Nat Pan Hellenic Coun, 1975-76; undergrad dist rep, Omega Psi Phi Fraternity Inc, 1975-76; Sen Jr Law Class Cumberland Sch Law, 1977-78; law clerk, Shores & Larkin, 1978; stud prosecutor, law clerk, Jefferson County Off, 1978-79; hon mem, Atty Gen Staff State Ala, 1979; pres, Young Dem Macon County, 1981-84; Ancient Egyptian Arabic Order Nobles Mystic Shrine, 1984-; Shriner, Mizraim Temple 119, 1984-; bd dir, Magic City Bar Asn, 1985-86; vpres, Magic City Bar Asn, 1987, pres, 1989, bd dir, 1991; Vestavia-Hoover Kiwanis Club; leadership, Birmingham Alumni Asn, 1990-; chmn, Criminal Justice & Procedures Comt, 1994-95; Birmingham Bar Found, 1996-97; Grievance Comt, 1997-98; chmn, Munic Courts Comt, Mem Fee Arbit Comt, 1998-99; bd dir, Ala Symphonic Asn, 2006; bd dir, Boys & Girls Clubs Cent Ala, 2006; Shades Valley Rotary Club, 2004; Paul Harris Fel, 2006; bd mem, At Large, 2008; Greater Birmingham Criminal Defense Lawyers Asn; Magic City Jaycees; Alpha Phi Chap; deacon, 6th Ave Baptist Church; Birmingham Alumni Asn; Birmingham Bar Asn; adv bd, Cumberland Sch Law; Am Judicature Soc; Ala Law Inst; chmn, Jefferson County Criminal Justice Coord Comt, 2016; Ala Sentencing Comn. **Honors/Awds:** Basileus, Omega Psi Phi, 1974-76; Proclamation, Clyde E Jones Day, Mayor Tuskegee, Ala, 1984; Leadership Birmingham, 1989 Class; 101 Black Men of Birmingham, 1990; Elected Official of the Year Award, Metro Birmingham Branch NAACP. **Home Addr:** 1009 Willowbrook Rd, Birmingham, AL 35215. **Business Addr:** Attorney, PO Box 10005, Birmingham, AL 35203, **Business Phone:** (205)531-3503.

### JONES, COBI N'GAI
Soccer player, athletic coach. **Personal:** Born Jun 16, 1970, Detroit, MI; married Kim Reese. **Educ:** Univ Calif, Los Angeles. **Career:** Soccer player (retired); Athletic Coach; UCLA Bruins, 1988-91; Us, Nat team, 1992-2004, FIFA world cups, 1994, 1998, 2002; Coventry City, midfielder, 1994-95; US Nat Soccer Team, midfielder, 1992-2004; Vasco da Gama, brazel, midfielder, 1995-96; Los Angeles Galaxy, midfielder, 1996-2007; Los Angeles Galaxy, asst coach, 2008, interim, 2008-10; Maj League Soccer, asst coach, currently; New York Cosmos, Assoc Dir Soccer, currently. **Orgs:** Lambda Chi Alpha. **Honors/Awds:** Summer Olympics, Barcelona, 1992; World Cup Soccer Team, 1994; CONCACAF Champions' Cup Winner, 2000; MLS Supporters' Shield Winner, 1998, 2002; U.S. Soccer Athlete of the Year, 1998; Inducted into UCLA Hall of Fame, 2002; CONCACAF Gold Cup, 2002; U.S. Open Cup Winner, 2001, 2005; MLS Cup Winner, 2002, 2005; Major League Soccer Western Conference Champions, 1996, 1999, 2001-02, 2005; Player of the Year Award, Galaxy supporters group, 2006; National Soccer Hall of Fame. **Special Achievements:** One of only two USA players to have played every minute in both the 1994 and 1998 FIFA World Cups; Films: "Jakers! The Adventures of Piggley Winks", 2003, "Sweat", 2002; TV Series: "Access Sportsnet: Los Angeles", 2012. **Home Addr:** 501 N Edinburgh Ave, Los Angeles, CA 90048-2309, **Home Phone:** (323)852-9209. **Business Addr:** Interim Coach, Los Angeles Galaxy, Home Depot Ctr 18400 Avalon Blvd Suite 200, Carson, CA 90746, **Business Phone:** (310)630-2200.

### JONES, CULLEN
Swimmer. **Personal:** Born Feb 29, 1984, Bronx, NY; son of Ronald and Debra. **Educ:** NC State Univ, BA, eng/psychol. **Career:** Competitive swimmer, 2003-; North Carolina State University swim team, member, 2003-06; signed endorsement deal with Nike, 2006. **Orgs:** SwimMAC Carolina. **Special Achievements:** First African American swimmer to break a long-course world record (50m pool); second African American to win an Olympic Gold Medal in swimming; American record holder in the 50m freestyle; competed in U.S. Olympic Trials, 2004, 2008, 2012; competed in Olympics, 2008, 2012; competed in Pan Pacific Swimming Championships, 2006, 2010; competed in World Championships, 2007, 2009; competed in Pan American Games, 2015; does charitable work with the Ronald Jones Foundation; Cullen Jones Diversity Invitational, founder.

### JONES, CYNTHIA R.
Chief executive officer. **Personal:** married Kenneth Parks. **Educ:** Ga State Univ, BA, visual arts. **Career:** Jones Worley Graphic Design Consults, owner, chief exec officer & pres, 1990-. **Orgs:** Vice chmn, bd dir, Atlanta Bus League, 2009; bd Advisors, Metro Atlanta Chamber Com & Atlanta Chap Conf Minority Transp Officials (COMTO); bd dir, Ga State Alumni Asn & Small Bus, Agr; labor adv bd, Fed Res Bank Atlanta; 1997 class Leadership Atlanta. **Business Addr:** President, Chief Executive Officer, Jones Worley Graphic Design Consultants, 723 Piedmont Ave NE, Atlanta, GA 30365-0701, **Business Phone:** (404)876-9272.

### JONES, DAMON DARRON
Basketball player. **Personal:** Born Aug 25, 1976, Galveston, TX; son of Renee Lee and Willie; married Tina Thompson; children: 1. **Educ:** Univ Houston, sociol, 1997. **Career:** Black Hills Posse, 1997-98; Jacksonville Barracudas, 1998; Idaho Stampede, 1998-99; NJ nets, 1998-99; Boston Celtics, guard, 1999; Golden State Warriors, 1999-2000; Dallas Mavericks, 1999-2000; Continental Basketball Asn, Idaho; Vancouver Grizzlies, 2000-01; Detroit Pistons, guard, 2001-02; Sacramento Kings, guard, 2002-03; Milwaukee Bucks, guard, 2003-04; Miami Heat, guard, 2004-05; Cleveland Cavaliers, point guard & shooting guard, 2005-08; Milwaukee Bucks, 2008-09; NSB Napoli, 2009; Piratas de Quebradillas, Puerto Rico Basketball League, 2010; Bucaneros de La Guaira, Venezuela, 2011; Aliaga Petkim, 2011; Reno Bighorns, D-League, 2012. **Orgs:** Contribr, Pistons' Fannie Mae Found partnership.

### JONES, DAMON S.
Football player, football coach. **Personal:** Born Sep 18, 1974, Evanston, IL. **Educ:** Univ Mich; Univ Southern Ill. **Career:** Football player (retired), football coach; Jacksonville Jaguars, tight end, 1997-98, tight end & wide receivers, 1999, 2000, tight end, 2001; Seacoast Christian Acad, head football coach, currently. **Business Addr:** Football Coach, 861 Townsend Blvd, Jacksonville, FL 32211, **Business Phone:** (904)421-3900.

### JONES, DARYL L.
State government official, air force officer, president (organization). **Personal:** Born Aug 31, 1955. **Educ:** Baylor Univ, BS, MS; USaF Acad, Colo Springs, Colo, BS, math, 1977; Univ Miami Sch Law, Miami, Fla, JD, 1987. **Career:** USAF, phantom pilot, 1977-84; 11th Circuit US Ct, Judge Peter T Fav, fed judicial clerk, 1987-88; PR Nat Guard, pilot, 1988-89; Dade County Atty's Off, aviation div, 1988-90; Fla House, rep, 1990-92; Fla Sen, sen, 1992-2002; USAF Acad, bd visitors, presidential appointee, 1995-02; Gov Comn Sustainable S Fla, mem, 1995-97; Dallas Baptist Univ, Bus Sch, adj prof, 1997-2002; St Edwards Univ, Grad Sch Mgt, adj prof, 2004-; Dept Air Force, secy designate; Leadership Fla Bd Regents, exec comt; Air War Col, Air Univ, mobilization asst; pvt pract atty; Maxwell AFB, col, currently; Tex Instruments, prog mgr, bus develop mgr; EquiVest, Inc, pres; D L Jones & Assocs Inc, pres, 2002-; Independent Assoc Legal Shield Serv Inc, assoc, 2005-; Great Fla Bank, dir, 2005-; Law Offices Daryl L Jones, PA, pres, 2008-. **Orgs:** Adv bd, Martin Luther King Jr Inst Nonviolence, 1994-2000; bd dir, Am Bankers Ins Group Inc, 1994-99; Orange Bowl Comt, 1990-; bd govs, Fla Chamber Com; adv bd, Dade Community, AvMed Miami, 2006-; Gov Select Task Force Election Procedures Stand & Technol, 2000-01; Proj Mgt Inst; pres, Nat Stud Bar Asn, Univ Miami. **Honors/Awds:** Iron Arrow Award, Univ Miami. **Special Achievements:** First African American civilian secretary of US Air Force. **Business Addr:** President, D L Jones & Associates Inc, 1542 County Rd 451, Coupland, TX 78615, **Business Phone:** (512)914-5063.

### JONES, DAVID L.
Executive, vice president (organization). **Personal:** Born Dec 30, 1950, Charles City, VA; son of Joseph H Sr and Vernell; married Pauline R; children: Eric Anthony & Christopher David. **Educ:** Williams Col, BA, 1974; Univ NC Sch Bus, attended 1985; Kellogg Sch Bus, Northwestern Univ, attended 1987, 1996; Duke Univ, Fugua Sch Bus, attended 1998. **Career:** Gen Motors Acceptance Corp, vpres consumer credit, 1975-2008; credit mgr, 1983-85, sales mgr, 1985, asst control br mgr, 1985-87, bus develop mgr, 1987-88, control br mgr, 1988-90, asst mgr-plans, 1991-93, vp-plans, 1993. **Orgs:** Adv bd, Credit Res Ctr, Purdue Univ, 1993-; adv bd, Highland Pk Comn, High Sch, 1994-; diversity comt, Farmington Pub Schs, 1996; bd mem, Jr Achievement SE Mich, 1996. **Home Addr:** 29764 Harrow Dr, Farmington Hills, MI 48331, **Home Phone:** (248)788-9789. **Business Addr:** Vice President of Consumer Credit, General Motors Acceptance Corp, 300 Galleria OffiCtr, Southfield, MI 48034.

### JONES, DAVID R.
Executive, lawyer. **Personal:** Born Apr 30, 1948, Brooklyn, NY; son of Thomas R (deceased) and Bertha (deceased); married Valerie King; children: Russell & Vanessa. **Educ:** Wesleyan Univ, BA, 1970, MA, 1982; Yale Law Sch, JD, 1974. **Career:** US Sen Robert Kennedy, senate intern, 1967; Fed Dist Judge Constance Baker Motley, law clerk, 1974-75; Cravath Swaine & Moore, assoc litigation, 1975-79; NY City Mayor Koch, spec adv, 1979-83; NY City Youth Bur, exec dir, 1983-86; Community Serv Soc NY, pres & chief exec officer, 1986-; Carver Fed Savings Bank, chmn, 1996-2000; Nat Comt Responsive Philanthropy, chmn. **Orgs:** Bd mem, Metrop Transp Authority; Fel Thomas J Watson Found, 1970; bd trustee, Wesleyan Univ, 1984-96, trustee emer, 1996-; pres, Black Agency Execs New York, 1988-94; bd mem, Carver Fed Savings & Loan Asn, 1989-95; vice chair, Primary Health Care Develop Corp, 1993-95; bd mem, NY City Health & Hosp Corp, 1993-98; bd dir, Puerto Rican Legal Defense Educ Fund, 1993-98; trustee, NY Hist Soc, 1994; founding mem, Capital & Phys Develop Comt, Upper Manhattan Empowerment Zone, 1996-00; vice chmn, New York Independent Budget Off; adv bd, New York Independent Budget Off; vice chair, Nat Comn Responsive Philanthropy, 1998; bd mem, Prospect Pk Alliance; adv bed meme, Ny Senate Medicaid Reform Task Force; adv bd mem, Sch Pub Affairs, Baruch Col; bd mem, New York Found, 1998-03; fel NY State Fed Bars; chmn bd, Nation Inst; mem adv coun, New York Dept Health & Ment Hyg; Scherman Found; vice chmn, Primary Care Develop Corp; bd trustee, Wildlife Conserv Soc; chmn bd, Nation Institute. **Honors/Awds:** Wesleyan Univ, hon master arts, 1982; City Univ New York, DHL, 1999. **Home Addr:** 530 E 76th St Apt 25H, New York, NY 10021. **Business Addr:** President, Chief Executive Officer, Community Service Society of New York, 633 3rd Ave 10th Fl, New York, NY 10017, **Business Phone:** (212)254-8900.

### JONES, DEACON. See JONES, GROVER WILLIAM, JR.

### JONES, DELISHA MILTON (DELISHA LACHELL MILTON)
Basketball coach, basketball player. **Personal:** Born Sep 11, 1974, Riceboro, GA; daughter of Beverly; married Roland; children: Beverly. **Educ:** Univ Fla, sports mgt & minor commun, 1997. **Career:** Basketball Player, basketball coach; Portland Power, 1998; Los Angeles Sparks, ctr, 1999-2004, forward, 2008-12; Lavezzini Basket Parma, coach, 2001-02; UMMC Ekaterinburg, coach, 2002-04; Gambrinus Brno, coach, 2005-06; Wash Mystics, forward, 2005-07; Ros Casares

Valencia, coach, 2007-09; San Antonio Silver Stars, forward, 2013; New York Liberty, 2013-14; Atlanta Dream, 2014-. **Business Addr:** Professional Basketball Player, San Antonio Silver Stars, 1 AT&T Ctr, San Antonio, TX 78219, **Business Phone:** (210)444-5090.

## JONES, DELORES

Public relations executive. **Personal:** Born Apr 4, 1954, Chicago, IL; daughter of Josephine Walls and Rufus Charles. **Educ:** Kent State Univ, Kent, Ohio, BA, jour & pub rels, 1976; Ohio State Univ, MA, jour & pub rels, 1980; Boston Col, cert corp community rel, 2001. **Career:** Burns Pub Rels, Cleveland, Ohio, commun specialist, 1976; Tribue Chronicle, Warren, Ohio, asst ed & reporter, 1976-79; Ohio Edison Co, Akron, Ohio, sr info rep, 1980-97; Kent State Univ Sch Jour, part-time instr, 1989; FirstEnergy Corp, community initiatives dir, 1997-. **Orgs:** Akron Area Chap, Pub Rels Soc Am, 1981-, pres, 1988, secy, 1987, bd dir, 1983-89; Nat Sci Teachers Asn, 1983-09; Corp Vol Coun, Vol Ctr Summit County, 1987-; bd trustee, Summit County Victim Assistance Prog, 1990-2004, secy, 1991, chair pub rels comt, 1993-2004; ed, Around House Newsletter, House Lord, 2002-08; Muticul Prog Coun, Akron Civic Theatre, 2002-; pub relssequence adv & sem judge, Kent State Univ Sch Jour & Mass Commun, 2003-; co-chair, Summit County Social Servs Adv Bd, Fin Forum, 2005-08; bd trustee, Habitat Humanity Ohio, 2008-, vice chair, 2012-; co-chair community/faith capital campaign comt, Habitat Humanity Summit County, 2009-11; dist rep & exec bd mem, Habitat Humanity; bd mem, Ohio Energy Proj; bd mem, Environ Educ Coun Ohio. **Honors/Awds:** Leadership Ohio Class V, 1998; Governor's Award for Excellence in Energy Efficiency, 2005. **Special Achievements:** Coord, Academic Challenge, a high school quiz program on WEWS-TV5; First African American reporter and assistant editor with The Tribune Chronicle, Warren, Ohio; first African American pres of the Public Relations Society of Am, Akron Chapter; Expanded First Energy's Harvest for Hunger Food Drive across three states, which was recognized by Second Harvest Foodbank for raising more than 4 million pounds of food since 2000; chair, Akron Reads Business Partnership with Akron Public Schools, which helpedraise student reading scores and is recognized by Gov. Taft as a model for Ohio, 1999-; established First Energy's partnership with Habitat for Humanity, providing over $19 million since 2001 to build 410 Energy Star certified homes in Ohio; In 2011, published "A Family Built on Banks and Walls: A History of the Ancestors and Descendants of Tilla Banks and Mack & Anna Wall of Holmes and Carroll Counties, Mississippi", the book represents 17 years of family study, interviews and genealogical research. **Home Addr:** 3718 Northview Dr, Stow, OH 44224-3310, **Home Phone:** (330)686-0835. **Business Addr:** Community Initiatives Director, FirstEnergy Corp, Akron Ctr 76 S Main St, Akron, OH 44308, **Business Phone:** (800)633-4766.

## JONES, DR. DENEESE LAKAY

School administrator, educator. **Personal:** Born Aug 9, 1952, Dallas, VA; daughter of Ben and Theresa Robinson; married Stephen Clyde; children: Stephanie Roberts & Monica Martin. **Educ:** Tex Woman's Univ, BS, educ, 1974; Tex A&M Univ, MEd, educ, 1989, PhD, educ, 1991. **Career:** Univ KY, asst prof, 1991-97, prof literacy educ, 1991-2005, Grad Sch, assoc dean, 1998-2002, Pres's Comn Diversity, chair, 2003-05; Study Acad Achievement Learning Environs Ctr, co-founder & dir, 1994-; Univ Ky, prof literacy educ, 1991-2005, assoc prof, 1997-, assoc dean, 1998-2002, Am Coun Educ fel, 2002-03, Pres's Comn Diversity, chair, 2003-05; Univ Kans, chancellor, Longwood Univ, Col Educ & Human Serv, prof & dean, 2005-12; Drake Univ, provost, 2012-15; Trinity Univ, vpres acad affairs, 2016-. **Orgs:** Am Educ Res Asn, prog chair, Renaissance Group, Col Reading Asn, 1989-; Int Reading Asn, 1989-; spec study group chair multicultural edu, Am Asn Cols Teacher Educrs, 1992-, chair comt multicultural educ, 2001-03; Am Educ Res Asn, 1992-; Nat Reading Conf, 1992-; Nat Asn Multicultural Educ, 1993-; felsadvisory bd, Am Coun Educ, 2012-16; Chrysalis Found, 2012-16; Asbury Univ, 2014. **Honors/Awds:** Notable Alumni for TAMU, 1998; LU Chi Award, 2008, LU Citizen Leader Award, 2008, LU Athletic Training Appreciation Award, 2008, President's Award, Asn Teacher Educrs, 1998, 2000; Most Notable Alumna, Tex A&M Univ, 1999; Mildred M Bailey Award Outstanding Faculty, Phi Beta Sigma, 2000; Exceptional Achievement Award Teaching & Advising, Univ Ky, Col Educ, 2000; Literacy Research Award, 2002; Torch of Excellence Award, 2003; Teacher Who Made A Difference, 2003, Outstanding Alumni, College of Education, TAMU, 2006; Two Outstanding Service Award, American Association Colleges; Outstanding Recognition Award, Association Teacher Educators; Outstanding Researcher Award, Kentucky Reading Association; Torch of Excellence Award, University Kentucky Alumni Association. **Special Achievements:** Publications: "An Exploration of Prospective Teachers' Literacy Instructional Practices: Expectations vs Actual Usage," in Balanced Reading Instruction; Reading Diagnosis and Remediation: Instructors Manual; "Meeting the Faith Challenge of Rearing Sons and Daughters," in Women to Women: Perspectives of Fifteen Afro-Amer Christian Women, 1996; Preparing Student Teachers for Pluralistic Classrooms, 1998; Publications in Black Issues in Higher Education, 2003; invited speaker at Int Learning Conf, London, England, 2003. **Home Addr:** 1523 Woodland Ct, Farmville, VA 23901, **Home Phone:** (434)392-8914. **Business Addr:** Professor & Dean, Longwood University, Hull Bldg Hull Educ Ctr, Farmville, VA 23901, **Business Phone:** (434)395-2051.

## JONES, DEREK K.

Executive, executive director, association executive. **Educ:** Am Univ, BA, econs, BS; NY Univ, MBA, finance. **Career:** Oncore Capital, managing partner; Provender Capital, founding partner; Credit Suisse AG, Asset Mgt Div, managing dir, 2007-. **Orgs:** Bd dir, Diversity Channel Inc; bd mem, Le Gourmet Chef Inc; bd dir, Prestige Brands Int Inc; bd mem, Urban Studios Inc; bd dir, Vanguarde Media Inc; bd dir, Walking Co Inc; founder, former bd mem, Marathon Club; dir, former treas, Nat Asn Investment Co (NAIC); bd dir, Venture Investors Asn New York; bd dir, Partsearch Technologies Inc. **Honors/Awds:** "Black Enterprise," 75 Most Powerful Blacks on Wall Street, 2011. **Business Addr:** Managing Director, Eleven Madison Ave, New York, NY 10010, **Business Phone:** (212)325-2000.

## JONES, DONALD W.

Educator, association executive. **Personal:** Born Dec 7, 1959, Trenton, NC; married Betty Jean Tolbert; children: Tracey La Verne. **Educ:** Hampton Inst Va, BS, bus mgt, 1962; Fairfield Univ Conn, MA, corp & polit commun, 1969; Ohio Univ, PhD, interpersonal commun & higher educ admin, 1973. **Career:** Educator (retired); Carnegie Mellon Univ, post doctoral; Princeton Univ, post doctoral; NY City Dept Labor, labor mgt prac adj, 1965-66; Urban League Westchester Co Inc, assoc dir in-chg econ develop & employ, training adv, field rep, 1966; Norwalk Job Orientation Prog, instr, 1967-68; New Haven Redevel Agency, housing develop officer, 1968-70; Univ Va, Charlottesville, post doctoral, asst prof, Minority Affairs, asst pres, prof, Off Minority Procurement Prog, dir, 1990-2005, Darden Minority Bus Exec Prog, founder, 1998. **Orgs:** Chmn, Time & Pl Comn; Mid Atlantic Reg; Nat Hampton Alumni Asn; Panel Disc Nat Hampton Alumni Asn; part Invit, Sem Deseg Pub Higher Educ; vpres, pres, Nat Black Caucus; Speech Commun Asn; Int Commun Asn; S Asn Black Admin Personal; Am Asn High Educ; Nat Educ Asn US; Int Platform Asn; LibComn Ohio Univ, 1971-72; exec sec, Inst Self-Study Proj Univ Va; Community Col Admin Comn Univ Va; Afro-Am Std Com Univ Va; exec secy, Presidential Admin Comn Comm Col Univ Va, 1972-74, chmn, 1974; Presidential Admin Comn Educ & Employ Opportunity; Oblig & Rights Univ Va, 1975; past pres, NC 4-H Clubs; New York Hampton Alumni Club; pres, Interfrat Coun Unit Negro Col Fund, 1973; chmn, Plan Comn Univ Va Comn Col Artic Conf; Va Community Col Conf Univ Va, 1974; Nat Hampton Alumni Asn, Mid Atlantic Prog; Kiwans Club. **Honors/Awds:** Outstanding Service in University Area for Human Relations, Black Stud Univ Va, 1976; Queen Elizabeth of England Medal, Charlottesville Albermarle Bicent Community, 1976; United Negro Col Fund Vol Leadership Award, United Negro Col Fund, 1977; Thomas Jefferson Area United Way Award, 1977. **Special Achievements:** First Director of the OMPP. **Home Addr:** PO Box 6429, Charlottesville, VA 22906-6429, **Home Phone:** (540)832-2809. **Business Addr:** Director, University of Virginia, 1001 North Emmet St, Charlottesville, VA 22906, **Business Phone:** (804)924-6246.

## JONES, DONELL

Songwriter, television producer, singer. **Personal:** Born May 22, 1973, Chicago, IL; son of Bobby; children: 4. **Career:** Singer, currently; Vocal arrangements for Madonnas Bedtime Stories, 1994; Albums: My Heart, 1996; Where I Want to Be, 1999; Scary Movie 2, 2001; Life Goes On, 2002; Journey Of A Gemini, 2006; Best of Donell Jones, 2007; The Lost Files, 2009; Lyrics, 2009; Forever, 2013. **Orgs:** Kappa Alpha Psi Fraternity Inc. **Home Addr:** , NY. **Business Addr:** Artist, LaFace Rec, 6 W 57th St, New York, NY 10026.

## JONES, DONNA L. (DONNA ROSS-JONES)

Music publisher. **Personal:** Born Apr 18, 1959, Detroit, MI; daughter of Fred Ross and Carol; married David; children: Evyn & Nicholas. **Educ:** Univ Southern Calif, Marshall Sch Bus, bus entrepreneur prog, 1995. **Career:** Int Serv, owner, 1980-82; Creative Entertainment Music, pres, 1985-90; Transition Music Corp, owner, founder & pres, 1993-; Calif Dept Disability Serv, N Los Angeles County Regional Ctr, bd dir, 2006-09; What's Your Lunch Box, bd mem, 2008-10. **Orgs:** Nat Acad Rec Arts & Sci, 1982-; NMPA, 1982; Asn Independent Music Publ, 1996; bd mem, N Los Angeles County Regional Ctr; co founder, Spec Needs Network, 2005-08. **Honors/Awds:** Entrepreneur of the Year, EMBOL-La, 1996; Certificate of Achievement; TEmerging Entrepreneur Award; Emmy Award. **Special Achievements:** One of the Top 50 Most Powerful Women, Hollywood Reporter, 1996, recognized by Black Enterprise as One of 17 Top Rising Stars in Entertainment, 1996, USC Business Enterprise Network. **Business Addr:** President, Founder, Transition Music Corp, 11288 Ventura Blvd 709, Studio City, CA 91604, **Business Phone:** (323)860-7074.

## JONES, DONTAE' ANTIJUAINE

Basketball player. **Personal:** Born Jun 2, 1975, Nashville, TN. **Educ:** NE Miss Community Col, attended 1995; Miss State Univ, attended 1996. **Career:** NY Knicks, forward, 1996-97; Boston Celtics, small forward, 1997-98; La Crosse Bobcats, 1999-2000; Memphis Houn Dawgs, forward, 2000-01; Toros de Aragua, 2001; Pompea Napoli, 2001-03; Vaqueros de Bayamon, Pr, 2003; Apollon Patras, 2003-04; Anyang KGC, 2004-07; Beijing Ducks, 2005-07; Halcones UV Xalapa, 2009-10; free agt, currently. **Business Addr:** Wasserman Media Group LLC, 10960 Wilshire Blvd, Los Angeles, CA 90024, **Business Phone:** (310)407-0200.

## JONES, EDDIE CHARLES

Basketball player. **Personal:** Born Oct 20, 1971, Pompano Beach, FL; married Trina; children: Alexis, Chelsie & Noah. **Educ:** Temple Univ, attended 1994. **Career:** Basketball player (retired); Los Angeles Lakers, shooting guard, 1994-99; Charlotte Hornets, small forward, 1999, shooting guard, 1999-2000; Miami Heat, shooting guard, 2000-05, 2007; Memphis Grizzlies, shooting guard, 2005-07; Dallas Mavericks, shooting guard, 2007-08; Ind Pacers, shooting guard, 2008. **Orgs:** Founder, Eddie Jones Found. **Honors/Awds:** Robert V. Geasey Trophy, 1994; Men's Basketball Player of the Year, Atlantic 10 Conf, 1994; NBA All-Rookie First Team, 1995; Schick Rookie Game, All-Star Weekend, Nat Basketball Asn, 1995, 1997-98; Most Valuable Player, Nat Basketball Asn, 1995; Ranked 1st in the NBA in Steals Per Game, 1999-2000. **Business Addr:** Professional Basketball Player, Dallas Mavericks, 2909 Taylor St, Dallas, TX 75226, **Business Phone:** (214)747-6287.

## JONES, DR. EDITH IRBY

Physician. **Personal:** Born Dec 23, 1927, Conway, AR; daughter of Robert (deceased) and Mattie Buice; married James Beauregard; children: Gary Ivan, Myra Vonceil Jones Romain & Keith Irby. **Educ:** Northwestern Univ, clin psychol, 1948; Knoxville Col, BSM, chem, biol & physics, 1952; Univ Ark Sch Med, MD. **Career:** Univ Hosp, intern, 1952-53; gen pract, Ark, 1953-59; Baylor Affiliated Hosps, res, 1959-62; Tex, pvt pract physician, currently; Baylor Col, asst prof clin med; pvt prac, 1962; Univ Tex, asst prof clin med; Riverside Hosp, chief med staff, 2006, exec comn, secy staff; Houston Coun Alcoholism, adv bd; Comn Revising Justice Code Harris Co; Mercy Hosp Comp Health Care Group, co-founder, secy, bd dir; Jones Coleman & Whitfield, partner; Universal Healthplan Inc, med dir; Jones Properties, co-owner, chief exec officer; Thomas Care Ctr, staff; St. Joseph Hosp, staff; St. Anthony Ctr, staff; St. Elizabeth Hosp, staff; Hermann Hosp, staff; Calanthe Jurisdiction, med examr; Methodist Hosp, staff; Social Security Agency, consult; Tex Dept Pub Welfare. **Orgs:** Admin comn, Univ TeX Sch Med; pres, Nat Med Asn; Houston Am Revolution Bicentennial Comn; pres, Ark Med, Dent & Pharmaceut Asn; chmn, Internal Med Comn, St Eliz Hosp; med adv, Selective Bd 60; bd dir & chmn, Comn Homemakers Serv Family Serv Ctr; chmn, first pres, Delta Res & Educ Found; bd dir, Houston Coun Human Rels; Comn Hypertension, chmn, Sci Coun; bd dir, Nat Med Asn; bd, Third Bank Control Grp; Tex Health Asn; comn Drug Abuse, Houston ISD; adv med bd, Vis Nurses Asn; bd dir, Sudan Corp; bd dir, Afro Am Bk Distribr; med adv bd, Planned Parenthood Houston; chmn, SW Vols Delta one Am; Questions & Answers Health Care, KCOH Monthly Radio; bd trustees, past chmn, Knoxville Col; Links Inc; Delta Sigma Theta; pres, Gamma Mu chp; Drug Use Bd, Mutual Asn Prof Serv; Minority Health Resource Ctr; Resource Person Network Off; chmn, HELP Inc; bd dir, Std Savs Asn; Am Task Force Health Haiti; dir, Prospect Med Lab; Voc Rehab Asn; Alpha Kappa Mu; founding mem, Asn Black Cardiologists Inc. **Honors/Awds:** Golden Anniversary Award, Zeta Phi Beta, 1970; Distinguished Service Award, Houston Sect Nat Coun Negro Women, 1972; service to promote the efficient administration of justice, Am Judicature Soc, 1973; Woman of the Year, Kato Models Woman of the Year Award, 1974; Lois Allen Humanitarian Award, 1975; Cert Recognition, contribution field med, Antioch Baptist Church, 1975; life mem, Nat Coun Negro Women; Houston League of Business & Professional Women Achievement Award, 1977; citation for volunteer service, Eta Phi Beta, 1978; President's Distinguished Service Award, Knoxville Col Nat Alumni Asn, 1979; Exemplary Serv & Support Prof Educ, 1979; one of 30 Most Influential Black Women Houston, 1984; Nat Black Col Alumni Hall of Fame, 1985; Dr. Edith Irby Jones Day in her Honor, State Ark, 1986; Edith Irby Jones Day, City Houston, 1986; Mayor of Houston, 1986; Most Influential People of 1986, Ebony Mag; Internist of the Year, Am Soc Internal Med, 1988; Recognition for Leadership Support, 1992; Special Award, Asn Black Cardiologists, 1994; Cert Appreciation, City Houston, 1995; Outstanding Accomplishment & Performance, Stud Nat Med Asn, 1995; Award for Promotion Improved Econ, Houston Urban League, 1995; Award for Great Contribution Field Med Area Gerontology, Am Gerontology Soc, 1996; Special Recognition for Promotion of Positive Lifestyles, Houston Parks, 1996; Nobel Peace Prize, 1997; Award for Outstanding Accomplishments, Delta Sigma Theta, 1998; Southeast Memorial Hosp, Ambulatory Ctr, named in honor, 1998; Eagle Award, 1999; Award for Contribution to Health of Haiti, UNCF, 2000; Member of the Year, Asn Black Cardiologists, 2000; Volunteerism and Community Service Award, Tex Acad internal Med, 2000; Scroll of Merit Award, Nat Med Asn, 2001; 100 Leading Black Physicians, Black Enterprise Mag, 2001; Living Legend, Joseph Henry Tyler Br Nat Med Asn; UAMS Hall of Fame, 2004; National Achievement Award, Sinkler Miller Med Asn; Pioneer Award, Stud Nat Med Asn; Mickey Leland Certificate of Congressional Award; Bennett College Belle Ringer Image Award; Oscar E Edwards Memorial Award; Distinguished Alumna, J. William Fulbright Col Arts Sci, 2005; Silas Hunt Legacy Award, Univ Ark, 2006. **Special Achievements:** First African American admitted to University of Arkansas School of Med; numerous publ; First Woman to be elected president of the National Medical Association; First African-American woman resident at Baylor College of Medicine Affiliated Hospitals in Houston; Only female founding member of the Association of Black Cardiologists. **Home Addr:** 3402 S Parkwood Dr, Houston, TX 77021, **Home Phone:** (713)747-5116. **Business Addr:** Physician, Internal Medicine, 2601 Prospect St, Houston, TX 77004, **Business Phone:** (713)529-3145.

## JONES, DR. EDWARD L. (LARRY JONES)

Optometrist. **Personal:** Born Aug 12, 1957, Seattle, WA; son of Edward Louis and Dorothy M Bond; married Maxine S. **Educ:** Univ WA, BA, 1981; Pac Univ, OD, 1985. **Career:** Eyes Rite Optical, 1986-2008, 1989-96; JC Penney Optical, 1992-96; Vista Optical, 1985-2000; Dr Edward Lawrence Jones & Asn Inc, optometrist, currently. **Orgs:** Hon co-chair, PI Omicron Sigma, 1978; bd mem, Nat Optom Asn, 1981-2000, 1995-98. **Special Achievements:** Dyslexia is Complexia, 1986-87. **Home Addr:** 13530 SE 181st Pl, Renton, WA 98058, **Home Phone:** (206)941-1191. **Business Addr:** Optometrist, Dr Edward Lawrence Jones & Association Inc, 603 W Gowe St, Kent, WA 98058, **Business Phone:** (253)854-2028.

## JONES, EDWARD LEE (ED JONES)

Football player, boxer, actor. **Personal:** Born Feb 23, 1951, Jackson, TN. **Educ:** Tenn State Univ, BS, health & phys educ. **Career:** Football player, boxer (retired), actor; Dallas Cowboys, defensive end, 1974-78, 1980-89; prof boxer, 1979; Imp Investors, partner; Films: Semi-Tough, 1977; The Double McGuffin, 1979; Necessary Roughness, 1991; TV series: "Different Strokes", guest appearance. **Orgs:** Omega Psi Phi fraternity.

## JONES, ELAINE R.

Association executive. **Personal:** Born Mar 2, 1944, Norfolk, VA. **Educ:** Howard Univ, BA, polit sci, 1965; Univ Va, LLB, law, 1970. **Career:** Peace Corps, eng teacher, 1965-67; NAACP Legal Defense & Educ Fund, pres, dir-coun, 1993-2004, pres & dir-coun emer, 2004. **Orgs:** Nat Bar Asn; Old Dom Bar Asn; Va Trial Lawyers Asn; Int Fedn Women Lawyers; bd gov, Am Bar Asn; Rights orgn; Nat Asn Advan Colored People; Southern Christian Leadership Conf; Cong Racial Equality; Stud Nonviolent Coord Comt; Nat Urban League; Asn Study African Am Life & Hist; United Negro Col Fund; Thurgood Marshall Col Fund; Nat Black Chamber Com; Nat Pan-Hellenic Coun; Nat Coun Negro Women; TransAfrica Forum. **Home Addr:** 1417 Whittier St NW, Washington, DC 20012-2839, **Home Phone:** (202)291-6540.

**JONES, DR. ELNETTA GRIFFIN.** **See Obituaries Section.**

## JONES, ELVIN R.

Teacher, educator. **Personal:** Born Oct 7, 1945, Mobile, AL; son of Johnny M; married Sondra L; children: Beverly R. **Educ:** BA, 1966; MEd, admin, 1972. **Career:** Cleveland Pub Sch, teacher, 1966-72; E Cleveland City Schs, teacher, 1972-74, home sch liaison, 1975-77, prin, 1977-96; dir, pupil serv, 1996-99, supt, 1999. **Orgs:** Nat Asn Elem Sch Principals; Nat Asn Black Sch Educr; Kappa Alpha Psi; Phi Delta Kappa Prof Educ Asn; life mem, Nat Asn Advan Colored People; Inter City Yacht Club; St Andrews Episcopal Church. **Home Addr:** 19436 Scottsdale Blvd, Shaker Heights, OH 44122-6420, **Home Phone:** (216)991-3177. **Business Addr:** Superintendent, East Cleveland City Schools, 15305 Euclid Ave, East Cleveland, OH 44112, **Business Phone:** (216)268-6570.

### JONES, SEN. EMANUEL DAVIE

Automotive executive. **Personal:** Born Apr 1, 1959, Atlanta, GA; son of Leroy and Ethlyn; married Gloria; children: Emanuel II, Elam D & Emani. **Educ:** Univ Pa, BSEE, 1981; Columbia Univ, MBA, finance & acct, 1986. **Career:** Int Bus Mach Corp, prod engr, 1981-84; Arthur Anderson, consult, 1986-88; Ford Motor Co, dealer cand, 1988-92; Legacy Ford Mcdonough, founder, 1992; Legacy Goodyear Tire Co McDonough, pres, 1995-; Legacy Toyota Union City, founder & pres, 1998; Legendary Ford-Mercury Marion, 1998; Ansa Automotive, founder & pres, 2002-; Interstate Coop Comt, sec, currently; Ga State Senate, Dist 10, sen, 2004-; Legacy Chevrolet Cadillac Saab Columbus, pres & owner. **Orgs:** Leadership Henry, 1993-; dir, Henry County Chamber Com, 1994-96, 2000; dir, Henry County Rotary Club, 1994; dir, Henry County High Sch Scholar Found, 1994-; adv bd, United Way Henry County, 1995-; Ga Dept Labor, Adv Bd, 1994-; chmn & stewardship ministry, Shiloh Baptist Church, 1994-95; trustee, Henry Med Ctr, 2000; chair, Henry County Young Mens Christian Asn, 2004; deacon, Shiloh Baptist Church; bd mem, Univ Pa; chair, Henry Countys United Way Campaign; bd mem, James Bristor Socs; chmn, Ga Legis Black Caucus; chmn, Martin Luther King Jr. Adv Coun. **Honors/Awds:** Businessman of the Year, Henry County High Sch, 1993; Businessman of the Year, Henry County Police Dept, 1993; Distinguished Service Award, Shiloh Baptist Church, 1994; Top Profit Dealer, Ford Motor Co, 1994; Atlanta Regional Entrepreneur of the Year, US Dept Com, 1996; Atlanta Minority Service Firm of the Year; Businessman of the Year, Alonzo Crim High Sch, 1996; Freshman Legislator of the year, 2005; Global Peace Festival Award, Atlanta Tribune Mag; 50th Most Influential Award, Atlanta Bus League, 2008; Morris Brown College Pacesetter Award, 2008; Metro Atlanta YMCA Volunteer of the Year; Ford Motor Minority Dealer Exec Dir Award; Governors Proclamation Entrepreneur of the Year. **Home Addr:** 195 14th St NE Unit 2601, Atlanta, GA 30309-2678, **Home Phone:** (404)873-1970. **Business Addr:** Senator, The Georgia State Senate, 302B Coverdell Off Bldg 420-D State Capitol, Atlanta, GA 30334, **Business Phone:** (404)656-0502.

### JONES, EMIL, JR.

Executive director, state government official, politician. **Personal:** Born Oct 18, 1935, Chicago, IL; son of Emil Sr and Marilla Mims; married Lorrie Stone; children: Debra Ann, Renee L, John M & Emil III; married Patricia; children: 4. **Educ:** Loop Jr Col, AA; Roosevelt Univ, bus admin, 1955. **Career:** Senate retired (retired); Lic sanit engr; Dem Orgn 21st Ward Regular, precinct capt, 1962-70; Southern Dist Water Filtration Plant, mem exec bd orgn & chlorine engr, 1964-67; Chicago City Coun, sec to alderman, 1967-73; Dem Orgn 34th Ward Regular, precinct capt, 1971, exec secy, 1971, pub rels, 1972; Ill House Representatives, state rep, chmn, asst dem leader, 1973-83; Ill State Senate, 14th Dist, state sen, 1983-2009, Ill Senate, pres, 2003-09. **Orgs:** Morgan Pk Civic League; Nat Conf State Legis; Nat Black Caucus State Legis; bd dir, Forum Sen Pres; bd dir, State Legis Leaders Found; State Legis Leaders Found's; Forum Senate Presidents bd dir. **Honors/Awds:** Friend of Education Award, Ill State Bd Educ; Illinois Delta Kappa Appreciation; Leadership Award, Coalition to Save Chicago Schs; Civil Rights Award, Ill Dept Human Rights; Award for Assisting Disadvantaged Youth, Chicago Urban League; Hall of Fame, Tilden Tech Inst, 2004; DHL, Roosevelt Univ, 2004; Paul Simon Public Service Award, Ill Hunger Coalition, 2004; Man of the Year Award, Best Buddies, 2005; Let Talent Shine Award, Col Summit, 2005; JohnR. Hammell Award, Chicago Chap ACLU, 2005; Dave Peteron Award, Chicago Teacher Union, 2006; Lifeline Award, Community Mental Health Coun, 2006; One of 100 Most Influential Black Americans, Ebony Mag, 2006; DHL, Chicago State Univ. **Home Addr:** 11357 S Lowe Ave, Chicago, IL 60628-4714.

### JONES, EMMA PETTWAY

Educator, legal consultant. **Personal:** Born Jul 29, 1945, Boykin, AL; daughter of Allie and John B; married J; children: James, John, Tracy & Malik. **Educ:** Albertus Magnus Col, attended 1980; NH Col, Manchester, BS, 1981, MBA, 1985; City Univ NY, Law Sch Queens, JD, 1988. **Career:** New Haven Fed Credit Union, organizer & mgr, 1979-81; Jones Turner & Wright, legal asst, 1986-87; Williams & Wise, legal intern, 1987; Yale Univ, Provost Dept, researcher; Malik Orgn, New Haven, founder, currently; independent consult. **Orgs:** Exec dir, People Actg Chg New Haven, CT; pres, Enterprise Mgt Assocs, consult & trainer, 1980-86; Legal Assistance New Haven, CT; Pub Housing Prog Tenant Rep Coun; NH Col, Orgn Develop Inst; Cheyney State Col, Fair Haven Mediation Prog; exec dir, Conn Afro-Am Hist Soc; chairperson, Nat Econ Develop & Law Ctr; vpres, YWCA, New Haven. **Home Addr:** 286 James St, New Haven, CT 06513-3527, **Home Phone:** (203)624-5760. **Business Addr:** Founder, Malik Organization, 286 James St, New Haven, CT 06513, **Business Phone:** (203)752-1214.

### JONES, ESQ. ERNEST EDWARD

Lawyer, association executive, chief executive officer. **Personal:** Born Nov 21, 1944, Savannah, GA; son of Orlando and Luella Williams; married Denise Rae Scott; children: Jamal & Kahlil. **Educ:** Dickinson Col, BA, econs, 1966; Temple Univ Sch Law, JD, 1972. **Career:** Pres & chief exec officer (retired); Dist Atty Off, Philadelphia, Pa, asst dist atty, 1972-74; Temple Univ Sch Law, gen coun, 1974-77; Community Legal Serv Inc, dep dir, 1977-79, exec dir, 1979-83; Greater Philadelphia Urban Affairs Coalition, exec dir, 1983-98; Philadelphia Workforce Develop Corp, pres & chief exec officer, 1998-2010; EJones Consult LLC, pres, 2010-. **Orgs:** Bd mem, Corp dir, First Union Corp, 1987; Nat Bar Asn, 1988; chmn, Philadelphia Housing Authority, 1991-92; Devereux Found, 1993; Philadelphia Bar Asn; chair, Black Alliance Educ Options; trustee, Thomas Jefferson Univ; mem bd, Core States Financial; bd mem, Universal Group Insts, 2002-; bd mem, Vector Security Inc; trustee, African Am Mus, Philadelphia; bd dir, Life Sci Career Alliance; Obama Am; bd dir, Philadelphia Contributionship; United Way Southeastern Pa Bd; bd mem, CoreStates Financial Corp; corp dir, UGI Corp; corp dir, Philadelphia Nat Bank; Ctr City Dist; Redevelop Authority Philadelphia. **Home Addr:** 2405 N 52nd St, Philadelphia, PA 19131-1408, **Home Phone:** (215)879-5279. **Business Addr:** PA.

### JONES, ERNEST LEE

Football player. **Personal:** Born Apr 1, 1971, Utica, NY; married Maria; children: Andrea & Deja. **Educ:** Ore Univ, grad. **Career:** Football player (retired); Los Angeles Rams, 1994; New Orleans Saints, defensive end, 1995; Denver Broncos, defensive end & defensive tackle, 1996-98; Carolina Panthers, linebacker, 1998-99.

### JONES, ERVIN EDWARD

Physician. **Personal:** Born Oct 4, 1938, Lake City, SC; married Pauline; children: Vincent, Yvette & Michael. **Educ:** Morris Col, attended 1957; Franklin Sch, Sci & Arts, attended 1959. **Career:** Philadelphia Col Osteop Med, med tech, 1973; Norristown, Pa, coun bd, 1974. **Orgs:** Chmn, Opportunity Coun, 1968-69; past mem, Norristown Adv Comn, 1968-70; past mem, Norristown Jaycees, 1970-72; chmn, Pub Safety Pa Police & Dept, 1974-; chmn negot comm Boro, 1976-77; chmn, Norristown House Comn, 1977; Mt Zion Am Methodist Church. **Honors/Awds:** Won state supreme ct dec subpoena power of Boro Coun, 1976; hon mem young Dem, Montg Cnty, 1976. **Special Achievements:** First black Chairman Public Safety Boro, 1974; Second black elected council Boro, 1974. **Home Addr:** 209 Brookside Rd, East Norriton, PA 19401-1303, **Home Phone:** (610)279-8544.

### JONES, DR. FERDINAND TAYLOR

Psychologist, educator. **Personal:** Born May 15, 1932, New York, NY; son of Ferdinand Taylor and Esther Lillian Harris Haggie; married Myra Jean Rogers; children: Joanne Esther Jones Rizzi & Terrie Lynn. **Educ:** Drew Univ, AB, 1953; Univ Vienna, PhD, 1959. **Career:** Riverside Hosp, NY, staff psychologist, 1959-62; Westchester County Community Ment Health Bd, chief psychologist, 1962-67; Lincoln Hosp Ment Health Serv, NY, trng consult, 1967-69; Sarah Lawrence Col, Bronxville, NY, psychol fac, 1968-72; Brown Univ, dir psychol serv, 1972-92, prof psychol & lectr psychiat human behav, 1972-97, prof emer psychol, 1997-, dir emer psychol serv; Schomburg Ctr Res Black Cult, scholar residence, 1987; Univ Dar es Salaam, vis prof, 1993-94; Oberlin Col, vis prof, 1997-98; Univ Cape Town, vis prof, 1999; Sarah Lawrence Col, guest fac. **Orgs:** Pres, Westchester Cnty Psychol Assoc, 1967-69; bd dir, Women & Infants Hosp, 1983-89; bd dir, Am Orthopsychiatric Assoc, 1984-87; pres, Am Orthopsychiatric Asn, 1989-90; ed, Intl Asn Jazz, 1997-; Am Psychol Asn; Assoc Black Psychologist; Am Assoc Univ Profs Soc Psych Study Social Issues. **Home Addr:** 229 Medway St, Providence, RI 02906-5300, **Home Phone:** (401)331-1039. **Business Addr:** Professor Emeritus of Psychology, Brown Univerity, 190 Thayer St, Providence, RI 02912, **Business Phone:** (401)863-7586.

### JONES, FLORESTA DELORIS

Educator, journalist. **Personal:** Born Dec 14, 1950, Hopewell, VA. **Educ:** Berry Col, BA, 1972; Mich State Univ, MA, 1975. **Career:** State J Lansing, MI, Detroit Free Press, staff writer intern, 1974; Richmond Afro-Am, staff writer, reporter, 1975-76; State Off Min Bus Enterprise, prog info off, ed spec, 1976-78; Va State Univ, adj fac, 1977-78; Georgian Ct Col, dir & adj fac educ opport fund prog, 1978-82; Brookdale Community Col, prof, writing team fac, 1982-. **Orgs:** NJ Educ Opport Fund Prof Asn; Am Asn Univ Women; Women Commun; Int Commun Asn; Nat Asn Advan Colored People; Soc Prof J; Asn Equality & Excellence Educ; Young Women's Christian Asn, Ann Womens Conf Comn; Goodwill Chorus Petersburg, VA. **Honors/Awds:** Scholarship Award; Nat Scholar Serv & Fund Negro Studies, 1969; Sigma Tau Delta English Honorary Fraternity, Berry Col, 1970-72; Alpha Chi Beta Georgia College Honour, Berry Col, 1971-72; Graduate Fellowships & Grad Assistantships, Mich State Univ, 1972-74. **Special Achievements:** Published articles in Detroit Free Press, Lansing State Journal, Richmond AFRO, US Info Agency & other newspapers. **Home Addr:** 32 Chelsea Rd, Jackson, NJ 08527. **Business Addr:** Writing Team Faculty, Professor, Brookdale Community College, Applied Humanities Inst, Lincroft, NJ 07738-1543, **Business Phone:** (732)224-2345.

### JONES, FRANCIS R.

Association executive, restaurateur. **Career:** United Airlines, supvr stewardess servs, personnel adv; McDonald's, owner & operator, currently. **Orgs:** Pres, Nat Black McDonald's Operators Asn; bd mem, Ronald McDonald's C's Charities; bd mem, Austin Metrop Bus Resource Ctr; People Assisting Homeless African Am community. **Honors/Awds:** Economic Justice Award; 365Black Award, McDonald's Corp. **Special Achievements:** First African American woman to serve as president of the National Black McDonald's Operators Association; United Airlines first African-American Supervisor of Stewardess Services & Personnel Advisor. **Business Addr:** Owner & Chief Executive Officer, Operator, McDonald's, 6363 W Sunset Blvd Suite 809, Hollywood, CA 90028-7330, **Business Phone:** (323)962-2806.

### JONES, GEN. FRANK

Mayor, police chief, security guard. **Personal:** Born Oct 25, 1950, Sellers, SC; son of John and Pearl Melton; married Sylvia G; children: Dennis, Tyrone & Deon. **Educ:** Marion-Mullins Voc, agr mech, 1970; State SC Law Enforcement, basic law enforcement, 1974; Francis Marion Col, Sci & Law, 1976; Florence Darlington Tech, Jail Removal Initiative, 1983. **Career:** Hargrove Groceries, Sellers, SC, clerk; Latta Police Dept, Latta, SC, policeman, 1971-73; Marion Police Dept, Marion, SC, lt policeman, 1973-87; SC Criminal Justice Acad, Columbia, SC, First Line Supvr, 1983-85, Traffic Radar Operator, 1987-88; Jones Groceries, Marion, SC, owner; McLeod Hosp, Florence SC, security guard; Town Sellers SC, mayor & chief policeman, 1988-99. **Orgs:** Adv, Sellers Jr Policeman Dept; bd dir, community develop corp inc.

### JONES, FRANK BENSON

Clergy, pilot. **Personal:** Born Aug 21, 1938, Kansas City, MO; son of Benson and Frankie Helen Boyd; married Mary S McClendon; children: Eleanor, Angela, Gregory & Mia. **Educ:** Calif State Univ, Dominguez Hills, BA, 1995. **Career:** Jones Comput Syst, pres, 1983-; United Air Lines, pilot, 1966-86; Pentecostal Temple, pastor, 1992-. **Orgs:** Ed, Black Panther Newspaper, 1969; dir, Contra Costa County Emergency Food & Med Serv, 1972-73; pres, PPCP Fed Credit Union, 1971-72; ed, Richmond Crusader Newspaper, 1973-75; secy & treas, Comm Developers Inc, 1973-76; ecumenical dir, Church Acts, 1977-78; pastor, Church Acts, 1977-83. **Home Addr:** 2727 Lantana St, Compton, CA 90220. **Business Addr:** Pastor, Pentecostal Temple, 1717 N Bullis Rd, Compton, CA 90221, **Business Phone:** (310)631-7764.

### JONES, FREDDIE RAY, JR.

Football player, football coach. **Personal:** Born Sep 16, 1974, Cheverly, MD. **Educ:** NC State Univ, BA, polit sci & govt, 1997. **Career:** Football player (retired); San Diego Chargers, tight end, 1997-2001; Ariz Cardinals, tight end, 2002-04; Carolina Panthers, tight end, 2004-05; SportsWorx, Col Recruiting Coordr, 2007-10; Carrollton Christian Acad, Asst Football Coach, 2009-10; Shelton Sch Dallas, Coach & Athletic Admin, 2010-; Carrollton Christian Acad, Head Athletic Dir, 2015-. **Honors/Awds:** Rookie of the Year, Col & Pro Football Weekly, 1997. **Business Addr:** Coach, Athletic Administrator, Shelton School, 15720 Hillcrest Rd, Dallas, TX 75248, **Business Phone:** (972)774-1772.

### JONES, FREDERICK RUSSELL. See JAMAL, AHMAD.

### JONES, FREDRICK E.

Automotive executive. **Career:** Fred Jones Pontiac-GMC Truck Inc, Brookfield, chief exec officer, 1984-; IHOP Corp, owner, currently. **Orgs:** Chmn, trustee bd, Canaan Baptist Church; life time mem, Nat Asn Advan Colored People officer; Wis Auto & Truck Dealers Asn. **Business Addr:** Owner, Chief Executive Officer, Fred Jones Pontiac & GMC Trucks Inc, 13000 W Capital Dr, Brookfield, WI 53005-2438, **Business Phone:** (262)781-1300.

### JONES, REV. G. DANIEL

Clergy. **Personal:** Born Norfolk, VA; son of George Raymond (deceased) and Estelle Campbell (deceased); married Geraldine E Saunders; children: Bryant Daniel. **Educ:** Va Union Univ, BS, 1962; Andover Newton Theol Sch, MDiv, 1966; Howard Univ's Divinity Sch, DMin, 1978. **Career:** Ministry St John Baptist Church Woburn, Mass, pastor, 1965-67; Messiah Baptist Church Brockton, Mass, pastor, 1967-73; Zion Baptist Church Portsmouth, Va, pastor, 1973-82; Norfolk State Univ, Norfolk, Va, undergrad instr, philos relig, 1973-82; Sch Theol, Va Union Univ, grad adj, 1979-82; Grace Baptist Church, Philadelphia, Pa, sr pastor, 1982, pastor emer, currently; Geneva Col, Ctr Urban Theol Studies, adj prof; Lutheran Theol Sem, Philadelphia, adj prof. **Orgs:** Hampton Inst Minister's Conf, 1973; ministers coun, Am Bapt Churches S, 1974-76, vpres, 1981-82, pres, 1998-2002; bd mem, Lutheran Home Germantown, 1986-94; pres, Ministers Coun, Philadelphia Baptist Asn, 1987-90; Philadelphia Baptist Asn, 1996-98; adv bd chair, chair emer, Urban Theol Inst; gen bd, Am Baptist Churches, USA; exec comt bd, LottCarey Baptist Foreign Mission Com; chair, Centennial Comn, 1997; pres, Nat Black Caucus Am Baptist Churches; chair, Conventions Scholar Endowment Campaign; vpres, African Am Interdenominational Ministries; founding pres, ABC S; founding pres, ABC Metrop Philadelphia; exec bd mem, Pa Baptist State Conv; chair, Urban Theol Inst Advising Comt, chair emer, currently; Omega Psi Phi Fraternity Inc. **Honors/Awds:** Human Relations Award, Omega Psi Phi Frat Portsmouth, VA, 1979 & 1982; Citations from City of Portsmouth, Va & Sch Bd, 1980 & 1982; Key to City of Brockton, MA, 1983; First Place Sermon Contest, Am Baptist Churches, PA & DE, 1984; The Jubilee Service Award, Philadelphia Fisk Alumni Club, 1988; Man of the Year, Grace Baptist Church, Germantown, 1989; Citations from City of Philadelphia & House of Representatives, Commonwealth Penn, 1996; Metrop Christian Coun Philadelphia; Honoris Causa, Lutheran Theol Sem Philadelphia, 2011; Va Union Univ, Hon DD. **Special Achievements:** Doctoral Thesis, "Educational Ministries in the Black Baptist Churches of Norfolk and Portsmouth Virginia". **Home Addr:** 25 W Johnson St, Philadelphia, PA 19144. **Business Addr:** Pastor Emeritus, Grace Baptist Church of Germantown, 25 W Johnson St, Philadelphia, PA 19144-1909, **Business Phone:** (215)438-3215.

### JONES, GAIL HORNE. See BUCKLEY, GAIL LUMET.

### JONES, GARY

Theatrical director. **Personal:** Born Jun 29, 1942, Chicago, IL; son of Leonard and Jessie Tolbert. **Educ:** Ill Inst Tech Inst Design, attended 1964. **Career:** Kungsholm Min Grand Opera Chicago, scenic designer & prin puppeteer, 1967-71; Blackstreet USA Puppet Theatre, dir, founder, 1975-; Int Heart Expo, Takamatsu, Japan, 2004; Apejay Schs, New Delhi, India, artist residence, 2004. **Orgs:** UNIMA-USA Union InterNate de la Marionnette, Puppeteers Am; Los Angeles Arts Recovery Grant, 1992. **Honors/Awds:** Designed exec prods Porgy & Bess, Carmen, The King & I, My Fair Lady, Gypsy, 1969-71; Los Angeles Arts Recovery Grant, 1992; Disney KJLH Crystal Castle Award; Outstanding Achievement, 1997. **Special Achievements:** Five week sold out engagement at the Smithsonian Inst Div of Performing Arts, 1980, 1982. **Business Addr:** Director, Founder, Blackstreet USA Puppet Theatre, 4718 West Washington Blvd, Los Angeles, CA 90016, **Business Phone:** (213)308-4805.

### JONES, GARY DEWAYNE

Football player, football coach, teacher. **Personal:** Born Nov 30, 1967, San Augustine, TX; married Tina Haskins. **Educ:** Tex A&M Univ, grad. **Career:** Football player (retired); Pittsburgh Steelers, safety, defensive back, 1990-91, 1993-94; New York Jets, free safety, 1995-96; S Grand Prairie High Sch, defensive backs coach & leadership teacher, currently. **Business Addr:** Leadership Teacher, S Grand Prairie High Sch, 301 W Warrior Trail, Grand Prairie, TX 75052, **Business Phone:** (972)343-1500.

## JONES, GAYL

Writer, educator. **Personal:** Born Nov 23, 1949, Lexington, KY; daughter of Franklin and Lucille Wilson (deceased); married Robert. **Educ:** Conn Col, BA, Eng, 1971; Brown Univ, MA, 1973, DA, 1975. **Career:** Univ Mich, Ann Arbor, MI, prof eng, 1975-83; Wellesley Col; writer, currently. Author: Chile Woman, 1974; BOP, Blacks on paper, 1975; Corregidora, 1975; Eva's Man, 1976; White Rat: Short Stories, 1977; Song for Anninho, 1981; The Hermit-Woman, 1983; Xarque & Other Poems, 1985; A Life Distilled: Gwendolyn Brooks, Her Poetry & Fiction, 1987; Presence Africaine: Revue Culturelle du Monde Noir/Cultural Review of the Negro World, 1987; The Graywolf Annual Seven: Stories From the American Mosaic, 1990; Black-Eyed Susans/Midnight Birds: Stories By & About Black Women, 1990; Liberating Voices: Oral Tradition in African American Literature, 1991; Callaloo: A Journal of African-American & African Arts & Letters, 1994; The Healing, 1998; Mosquito, 1999. **Orgs:** Fel Nat Endowment Arts; fel Mich Soc Fellows. **Honors/Awds:** Award, Howard Found, 1975; Fiction Award, Mademoiselle, 1975; National Endowment for the Arts grant, 1976; Henry Russell Award, Univ Mich, 1981. **Business Addr:** Writer, Beacon Press, 24 Farnsworth St, Boston, MA 02210-1409, **Business Phone:** (617)742-2110.

## JONES, GENEVIEVE

Socialite, designer. **Personal:** Born Jan 1, 1975. **Educ:** McKinley High Sch, Baton Rouge, La. **Career:** Socialite & designer fine jewelry, handbags & luxury accessories (New York). **Special Achievements:** Featured in the "Wall Street Journal" (September 2006), "Vogue" (2006), along with numerous other publications.

## JONES, GEORGE H.

Educator. **Personal:** Born Feb 21, 1942, Muskogee, OK; son of George H and Bernice Weaver. **Educ:** Harvard Col, BS, biochem sci, 1963; Univ Calif, Berkeley, CA, PhD, biochem, 1968. **Career:** Nat Insts Health, vis scientist, 1968-70; Univ Geneva, Switz, postdoctoral fel, 1971; Univ Mich, asst prof zool, 1971-75, from assoc prof biol to prof biol, 1975-89, chmn, dept cellular & molecular biol, div biol sci, 1980-82, assoc chmn, space & facil, 1984, Horace H Rackham Sch Grad Studies, assoc dean; Emory Univ, Atlanta, Ga, prof biol, 1989, grad sch arts & sci, dean, 1989, vpres, res & grad studies, 1990, actg dean, 1990, Goodrich C White prof biol, 1996-, chmn dept biol, currently. **Orgs:** Fel Helen Hay Whitney Found; fel Ford Found, 1982; NY Acad Sci; Am Soc Micro biol; Am Soc Bio chem & Molecular Biol. **Business Addr:** Professor, Chairman of Biology, Emory University, O Wayne Rollins Res Ctr, Atlanta, GA 30322, **Business Phone:** (404)727-0712.

## JONES, GERALD WINFIELD

Government official, lawyer. **Personal:** Born Jun 27, 1931, Jetersville, VA; son of Emmett Jr and Daisy Peachy L (deceased); married Ann H; children: Crenshaw, Cassandra Coleman, Lessie & Eric. **Educ:** Va State Col, BA, 1952; Howard Univ, LLB, 1960. **Career:** Dept Justice, Civil Rights Div, atty, 1960-65, supv atty chief voting & pub accommodations, 1965-, actg dep asst atty gen, 1994. **Orgs:** Mem bd dir, Melwood Hort Training Ctr, 1975-83; Nat Bar Asn; Govt Lawyers Sect Nat Bar Asn. **Honors/Awds:** Superior Performance Award, 1964; Special Commendation Award, Dept Justice, 1972; Attorney General Distinguished Service Award, 1973, 1983; Attorney General Award for Upward Mobility, 1978; Senior Executive Service Meritorious Award, 1982, 1985-89; Presidential Rank Meritorious Executive Award, 1990. **Home Addr:** 5705 Rayburn Dr, Camp Springs, MD 20748. **Business Addr:** Acting Deputy Assistant Attorney General, PO Box 66128, Washington, DC 20035-6128, **Business Phone:** (202)307-2767.

## JONES, GERALDINE J.

Writer, educator, teacher. **Personal:** Born Jul 30, 1939, Seaford, DE; daughter of Thomas and Marion; children: Monica. **Educ:** Del State Col, BS, 1961; Cent MI, MA, bus admin, 1977; Temple Univ, attended 1986; Capella Univ, PhD; Palmer Theol Sem, Mdiv, 1999. **Career:** Div Social Servs, social worker, 1962-64; Head Start Camden Summer, social worker, 1965, dir, 1971; Migrant Prog Summer, home coord, 1974; Parent Early Educ Ctr; Capital Sch Dist, vis teacher, 1975-; pub speaker; soloist; free-lance writer; parent educr, 1990-; Books: From Our Hearts To yours. **Orgs:** Nat Educ Asn; Del State Educ Asn; DE Asn Vis Teachers; Capital Asn; Tri-Co Investment & Savings Asn; Int Asn Pupil Personnel Workers; vol teacher Black Studies DE Youth Servs, 1980-; adv coun, DE Adolescent Prog, 1985-89; Delta Sigma Theta; Nat Coun Negro Women; Whatc oat United Methodist Church; DE State Col Alumni Asn; Kent Co Alumni Asn; Kent County Chap DE State Col Alumni; treas, Wm C Jason Alumni; Del Asn Cert Vis Teachers; Miss Alumni 1986-87; pres, Del State Col, Nat Alumni Asn; JH Wms Ensemble, Yesterday's Youth, Gospel ensemble; UMW, Peninsula Del Conf, pres, 1990-; United Methodist Church, Ann Conf, deleg, 1990-; Gen Conf, deleg, 1992, Penisula Del Conf, deleg, NE Jurisdictional Conf, deleg, 1992; NE Jurisdiction, UM Church; Delta Sigma Theta; treas, Sussex Co Alumni Asn. **Home Addr:** 368 Post Blvd, Dover, DE 19904-4844, **Home Phone:** (302)674-2742. **Business Addr:** Visiting Teacher, Capital School District, 945 Forest St, Dover, DE 19904, **Business Phone:** (302)672-1932.

## JONES, GERI DUNCAN

Association executive, executive director. **Personal:** Born Nov 28, 1958, Chicago, IL; daughter of Grandee and Carrie Gates; married Michael A; children: Michael A II, Marlon G & Marcus E. **Educ:** Eastern Ill Univ, Charleston, IL, BA, jour, 1979; Keller Grad Sch Bus Mgt, Chicago, IL, attended 1982. **Career:** Charles A Davis & Assoc, Chicago, Ill, acct exec, 1979-83; Debbies Sch Beauty Cult, Chicago, Ill, pub rels dir, 1983-84; Am Health Beauty Aids Inst, Chicago, Ill, acct exec, 1984-88, exec dir, 1988-. **Orgs:** Zeta Phi Beta Sorority, 1976-; Chicago Soc Asn Exec, 1985-; bd dir, Heritage Afro Am Beauty Indust, 1988-; Am Soc Asn Exec; nat adv comm, Madame C J Walker Spirit Awards; adv bd, Urban Call; Trade Mag Unbran Retailers; bus admin, St Titus Missionary Baptist Church, 1999-. **Honors/Awds:** Excellence Award, Universal Col Beauty, 1988; Outstanding Business & Professional African American Women, Blackbook, 1990; One of the top 25 Black Women in Black, Enterprise Magazine, 1994. **Home Addr:** 9227 S Woodlawn Ave, Chicago, IL 60619-8011, **Home Phone:** (773)933-7863. **Business Addr:** Executive Director, American Health & Beauty Aids Institute, 16335 Harlem Ave Suite 400, Chicago, IL 60619-0510, **Business Phone:** (708)633-6328.

## JONES, GRACE (GRACE MENDOZA)

Songwriter, singer, actor. **Personal:** Born May 19, 1948, Spanish Town; daughter of Robert W and Marjorie; married Atila Altaunbay; children: Paulo; married Chris Stanley. **Educ:** Syracuse Univ, theater. **Career:** model; actress, singer & peformance artist, currently. Films: Conant he Destroyer; Gordon's War, 1973; Let's Make a Dirty Movie, 1976; Army of Lovers or Revolution of the Perverts, 1979; Deadly Vengeance, 1981; Grace Jones-One Man Show; Grace Jones-State of Grace; Made in France, 1984; Conan the Destroyer, 1984; A View to a Kill, 1985; Vamp, 1986; Siesta, 1987; Straight to Hell, 1987; Boomerang, 1992; Cyber Bandits, 1995; Palmer's Pick Up, 1999. Albums include: Portfolio, 1977; Warm Leatherette; Fame; Portfolio; Living My Life; Nightclubbing; Inside Story; No Place Like Home, 2006; Falco, 2008; Chelsea On The Rocks, 2008. TV: "Stryx", 1978; "A One Man Show", 1982; "A Reggae Session", 1988; "Bellezasal agua", 1993; "Beast Master", 1999; "Wolf Girl", 2001; "Shaka Zulu: The Citadel", 2001; No Place Like Home, 2006; "Falco-Verdammt, wir leben noch, 2006; Chelsea on the Rocks, 2008; Gutterdammerung, 2015. **Honors/Awds:** Q Idol, 2008. **Special Achievements:** Ranked No 82 on VH1's 100 Greatest Women of Rock N Roll; ranked No 19 in Channel 5's World's greatest supermodel; Top model for fashion magazines Vogue and Elle, numerous appearances in Stern. **Business Addr:** Model-Actress, PO Box 82, Great Neck, NY 11021.

## JONES, GREG PHILLIP

Football player. **Personal:** Born May 22, 1974, Denver, CO. **Educ:** Colo Univ, grad. **Career:** Football player (retired); Wash Redskins, linebacker, 1997, 1999-2000, left linebacker, 1998; Chicago Bears, linebacker, 2001; Ariz Cardinals, linebacker, 2002; Houston Texans, 2002.

## JONES, GREGORY ALLAN

Insurance executive, vice president (organization), vice president (organization). **Personal:** Born Aug 15, 1955, New York, NY; son of Alline and Willie; married Sharon; children: Kimberly & Gregory Jr. **Educ:** Lehman Col, BA, 1977; Insu Inst Am, ARM, 1989. **Career:** Am Int Group, underwriter, 1977-79; INA special risk, jr underwriter, 1979-82; Chubb & Son, sr underwriter, 1982-86; Albert G Ruben & Corp, vpres, 1986-90; Near North Brokerage, sr vpres, 1990-95; USI Entertainment Ins Servs / Max Behm, sr vpres, 1995-2005; C M Meiers Co Inc, vpres prod ins, managing dir, 2005-. **Orgs:** Black Filmmakers Found, 1990-; Am Filmmakers Inst, 1992-. **Honors/Awds:** Athelete of the year, Lehman Col, 1977. **Home Addr:** 23741 Del Cerro Cr, West Hills, CA 91304-5338. **Business Addr:** Vice President, Managing Director, C M Meiers Co Inc, 21045 Calif St Suite 100, Woodland Hills, CA 91367-5104, **Business Phone:** (818)224-6145.

## JONES, GREGORY WAYNE

Insurance executive. **Personal:** Born Dec 29, 1948, Newark, OH; son of Gordon and Mildred; married Helen; children: Brian & Derek. **Educ:** Franklin Univ, BA, bus, 1975; Hood Col, MA, 1981; Univ Pa Wharton Sch, MBA, 1984. **Career:** State Farm Ins's Pa Region, underwriter, 1969-75, personnel rep, 1975-81, div mgr, 1981-85, exec asst, 1985-88; Chartered Property Casualty Underwriter, 1986; S Coast Region, reg vpres, 1993-, vpres, 1998-2001, pres, sr vpres & chief exec officer, 2001-; Northern Calif Region, dep reg vpres, 1998; State Farm Gen Co, vpres, pres, 1998; State Farm Mutual Ins Co, sr vp, 2001; State Farm Gen Ins Co, pres & chief exec officer, 2001. **Orgs:** Founder, 100 Black Men Sonoma Co, 1989-93; bd trustee, Calif State Univ Northridge, 1993-; bd, Los Angeles Jr Achievement, 1993-; bd trustee, Wellness Community, 1994; bd mem, Los Angeles Chamber Com, 1995-; 100 Black Men La, 1996-; bd adv, Los Angeles Minority Devel-op Grp, 1996-; chmn, Nat Asn Advan Colored People; chmn, Los Angeles Urban League; bd trustee, Nat Urban League; bd trustee, Franklin Univ; bd dir, State Farm Gen Ins Co; Calif Educ Excellence Found; Los Angeles Sports Coun & Oper Hope; past chmn, Jr Achievement Southern Calif. **Honors/Awds:** Empowerment Achievement Award, 1995; Credit Innovator Award, 1995; Bronze Leadership Award, Jr Achievement Am, 1996; Corporate Trailblazer Award, Dollars & Sense Mag, 1998; Anti-Defamation League world difference Award, 1999; Executive of the Year, Los Angeles African Am Chamber Com, 2006; hon doctorate degree, Franklin Univ. **Special Achievements:** First African American president and CEO in State Farm Insurance's history. 2000 honoree of the Insurance Industry Charitable Fund. **Home Addr:** 29165 Laso Dr, Agoura Hills, CA 91301, **Home Phone:** (818)991-6435. **Business Addr:** President & Chief Executive Officer, Senior Vice President, State Farm Insurance Co, 1 State Farm Plz, Bloomington, IL 61710, **Business Phone:** (309)663-5111.

## JONES, GROVER WILLIAM, JR. (DEACON JONES)

Football player, football coach, executive. **Personal:** Born Apr 18, 1934, White Plains, NY; son of Rita; married Virginia; children: Monica. **Educ:** Ithaca Col, BS, physiotherapy. **Career:** Football player (retired), football coach, executive, scout; Chicago White Sox, mid linebacker, 1962-63, 1966, scout, instr, minor league mgr, 1955-75; Houston Astros, hitting coach, 1976-82; New York Yankees, scout, 1983; San Diego Padres, hitting coach, 1984-87; Baltimore Orioles Minor League, hitting coach, advan scout, 1987; Sugar Land Skeeters, spec asst, currently. **Honors/Awds:** Westchester Co & Ithaca Col Hall of fame; Appleton WI Baseball Hall offame; Nations Top Am League Player, 1951; Silver Bat Award Winner, 1956. **Special Achievements:** First African American Man Recog Hall of Fame Cooperstown; First African-American ballplayer. **Home Addr:** PO Box 135, White Plains, NY 10602-0505.

## JONES, GUS

Association executive. **Career:** Mich Black Horsemen's Asn, pres. **Home Addr:** 8736 Gilmore Ave, Las Vegas, NV 89129-6330. **Business Addr:** President, Michigan Black Horsemen, 29716 Briarbank Ct, Southfield, MI 48034, **Business Phone:** (810)438-0812.

## JONES, GWENDOLYN J.

Librarian. **Personal:** Born Oct 31, 1953, Holly Springs, MS; daughter of Willie Payton and Mary E Johnson; married Willie Frank; children: Anthony Tyrone & Clarissa Danyell. **Educ:** Northwest Jr Col, Senotobia, MS, AS, 1978; Rust Col, Holly Springs, BS, 1984. **Career:** Rust Col, Leontyne Price Libr, Holly Springs, MS, tech serv asst, 1979-. **Orgs:** Jones Grove Missionary Baptist Church, 1983-; pres, Pastor's Aid, 1985-; 11th Reunion Reunions comt, Rust Col. **Honors/Awds:** Agency Parent Year Award, ICS Headstart Inc, 1979-80; Certificate of Appreciation, Rust Col Int Alumni Asn, 1986; Certificate of Appreciation, Jones Grove MB Church, 1987; Certificate of Appreciation, Holly Springs/Marshall Co, Rust Club, 1992; Certificate of Post Matron's Jurisdiction Miss, 1994. **Home Addr:** 123 Old Hwy 7 S, Holly Springs, MS 38635, **Home Phone:** (601)252-6518. **Business Addr:** Technical Service Assistant, Rust College, 150 Rust Ave Libr 201, Holly Springs, MS 38635, **Business Phone:** (601)252-8000.

## JONES, H. THOMAS, II

President (organization), executive. **Personal:** Born Sep 28, 1944, Maxton, NC; son of Henry Thomas Sr and Nannie Ruth Webb; married Joyce McDougald; children: Thomasia Elva. **Educ:** Amarillo Jr Col, Amarillo, TX, 1964; Pembroke State Univ, Pembroke, NC, BS, acct, 1972; Cent Mich Univ, Mt Pleasant, MI, MA, bus, 1979. **Career:** Carolina Power & Light Co, Raleigh, NC, mgr, 1972; Southeastern Utilities Develop Inc, pres & chief exec officer, currently. **Orgs:** Rotary Club, 1988-91; bd mem, Am Cancer Soc, 1989-91; vice chmn, Columbus County Minority Bus Coun, 1989-90; chmn, Columbus County Youth Enrichment Coun, 1990-91; bd mem, United Carolina Bank, 1990-91; bd mem, Columbus County Hosp, 1990-91; former bd trustee, Univ Nc Pembroke; Sybil Collins Pembroke. **Honors/Awds:** Alpha Man of the Year, Alpha Phi Alpha Fraternity, 1982. **Home Addr:** 314 Edgewood Cir, Whiteville, NC 28472-3611, **Home Phone:** (919)642-9788. **Business Addr:** President, Chief Executive Officer, Southeastern Utilities Development Inc, 605 E 4th Ave, Red Springs, NC 28377, **Business Phone:** (910)843-7963.

## JONES, HARDI LIDDELL

Federal government official. **Personal:** Born Nov 2, 1942, St. Louis, MO; son of Thomas H E and Jamesetta B; married Yvonne A Thompson; children: Miriam Yvette & Sandra Lynnette. **Educ:** St Paul's Col, BS, 1962; Univ Md, College Park, attended 1963; George Washington Univ, attended 1965. **Career:** US Naval Oceanog Off, phys oceanogr, 1962-63, 1965-67, equal opportunity officer, 1971-74; US Fish & Wildlife Serv, phys oceanogr, 1963-65; Underwater Syst Inc, oceanogr, 1967-71; Bur Reclamation US Dept Interior, dir off equal opportunity, 1974-81; US Dept Treas IRS, asst to comnr, 1981-89; IRS, Off Chief Coun, Finance & Mgt, spec asst to assoc chief coun, 1989, dir, Equal Employ, currently. **Orgs:** Pres, Prince George's County Club Frontiers Int, 1980-82; chmn bd dir, Combined Comns Action Prince George's County MD, 1981-; Sigma Pi Phi Frat Beta Mu Boule, 1981-; chmn, labor & indust comn & pres, Prince George's Co MD Nat Asn Advan Colored People, 1983-; chmn bd trustee, St Paul's Col Lawrenceville VA, 1985-88; life mem, Kappa Alpha Psi Frat Inc; vpres, Prince George's Nat Asn Advan Colored People, 1990-; pres, Prince George's Country Club Frontiers Int, 1991-; pres, Prince George's County Br NCP, 1991-; Beta Mu Boule, Sigma Pi Phi Fraternity, Sire Archon, 1993-. **Home Addr:** 10215 Buena Vista Ave, Lanham, MD 20706, **Home Phone:** (301)459-5532. **Business Addr:** Special Assistant to the Associate Chief Counsel, Office Chief Counsel, 1111 Const Ave NW Rm 2512, Washington, DC 20224, **Business Phone:** (202)317-3300.

**JONES, HAROLD M.** See Obituaries Section.

## JONES, HELEN HAMPTON

Librarian. **Personal:** Born Jun 9, 1941, Portsmouth, VA; daughter of George Livingston Sr (deceased) and Helen Bowen; married James W Jr; children: Ginger R & Jewell W. **Educ:** Livingstone Col, Salisbury, NC, BS, 1962; Syracuse Univ, Syracuse, NY, MS, 1975. **Career:** Norfolk State Univ, Norfolk, Va, clerk, stenographer & typist, 1963-75, actg libr dir, 1976, asst acq librn, 1976-79, acq librn, 1979-88, actg asst dir personnel, 1989-90, collection mgt librn, 1988-91; Elizabeth City State Univ, GR Little Libr, acq librn, 1997-. **Orgs:** Chmn, Portsmouth Pan Hellenic Coun, 1966-67; charter appointee, Portsmouth Munic Fin Comt, 1972-74, 1978-80; vice chair, Portsmouth Parking Authority, 1979-80; chmn, Portsmouth Pub Sch Bd, 1982-86; Va Libr Asn; SE Libr Asn, Am Libr Asn. **Honors/Awds:** Citizen of the Year, Eureka Club, Inc, 1984; Medallion Award, Brighton Rock AME Zion Church, 1984; Most Valuable Employee, Va Govt Employees Asn, 1986. **Home Addr:** 1006 Robinson Rd, Portsmouth, VA 23701, **Home Phone:** (757)487-9526. **Business Addr:** Acquisitions Librarian, Elizabeth City State University, Elizabeth City, NC 27909.

## JONES, HENRY LOUIS

Football player. **Personal:** Born Dec 29, 1967, St. Louis, MO. **Educ:** Univ Ill, Urbana-Champaign, BS, psychol, 1991. **Career:** Football player (retired); Buffalo Bills, defensive back & safety & strong safety, 1991-2000; Minn Vikings, strong safety, 2001; Atlanta Falcons, 2001-02; personal trainer & strength & conditioning coach, 2010-. **Honors/Awds:** Pro Bowl selection, 1992; All-Pro selection, 1992.

## JONES, DR. HERBERT C.

Physician, otolaryngologist. **Personal:** Born Aug 1, 1936, Demopolis, AL; son of Tom Allen Jr and Bettie Mae Young; married Bessie Chapman; children: Sandra Jo, Nancy Gayle, Herbert Chapman & Lisa Carol. **Educ:** Talladega Col, AL, attended 1956; Ind Univ, Bloomington, IN, AB, 1957, MD, 1961; Univ Mich Med Sch, attended 1988. **Career:** Univ Ill Med Ctr, Chicago, Ill, residency, 1965-68; Brook Gen Hosp, internship; self-employed surg, Atlanta, Ga, physician, 1968-; Cascade Med Ctr, physician, currently. **Orgs:** Chmn, Otolaryngol Sec, Nat Medl Asn, 1969-; fel Am Acad Otolaryngol, 1969-; Am Col Surgeons, 1972-; Ga State Med Asn; Nat Asn Advan Colored People; dir, Am Acad Otolaryngol, 1993-; dir, Am Bd Otolaryngol, 1994-. **Honors/Awds:** Alpha Omega Alpha Hon Soc, 1961; Father Yr, Concerned Black Clergy Atlanta, 1987; Outstanding Physician Otolaryngol, Black Enterprise Mag, 1988; Physician Yr, Atlanta Med Asn, 1990. **Home**

**Addr:** 285 NE Blvd Suite 415, Atlanta, GA 30311, **Home Phone:** (404)521-0108. **Business Addr:** Physician, Cascade Medical Center, 2600 Martin Luther King Jr Dr Suite 302 SW, Atlanta, GA 30311, **Business Phone:** (404)691-7460.

### JONES, DR. HORACE F.
Executive, army officer, chief executive officer. **Educ:** Southern Univ, Baton Rouge, LA, BS, educ, 1963, MA, counr educ, 1973; Univ Denver, EdD, guid & coun, 1979. **Career:** AUS, artil staff officer, comdrtroops, Training Ctr, training unit comdr, staff officer, N Am Aerospace Defense Command, sr intelligence dir, Defense Intelligence Col, vice dean, lt col, 1983. Betac Rosly, 1983-84; Technol Applications Inc, 1984-85; Automation Res Systs Ltd, 1985-86; Advan Resource Technologies Inc, founder, 1986-, pres, chief exec officer, currently. **Honors/Awds:** Northern Viriginia Urban League Corp Award, 1994-96; Fast 50 Award, Wash Technol Newspaper; Fantastic 50, Va Chamber Com, 1997; Fast 50 Award, Va Technol, 1997; Fast-Track Enterprise Award for Best Bus Practices, 1997; Top 100 African American-owned companies in the US, Black Enterprise Mag, 1998; Top Black Technol Entrepreneurs, US Black Engr & Info Technol mag, 2004. **Business Addr:** Chief Executive Officer, Founder, Advanced Resource Technologies Inc, 1555 King St Suite 400, Alexandria, VA 22314-2738, **Business Phone:** (703)682-4740.

### JONES, DR. HOWARD JAMES
President (organization), educator, writer. **Personal:** Born Jun 19, 1944, Benton, LA; son of Elnora Morris and Woodrow; married Joyce Kemp; children: Jonora Kinshasa & Howard James III. **Educ:** C H Irion H S Benton, LA, dipl, 1962; Southern Univ, Baton Rouge, LA, BA, 1966; Howard Univ, Wash, DC, MA, 1968; Wash State Univ, Pullman, WA, PhD, 1975. **Career:** Educator (retired); Grambling State Univ, Grambling, LA, instr, 1967-70; Univ S Miss, Hattiesburg, MS, asst prof, 1974-76; Prairie View A&M Univ, Prairie View, TX, instr, 1976-78, assoc prof, 1985-1992, hist prog coordr, 1992-2000, prof, 1992-2002, freelance writer; Tex Southern Univ, Houston, TX, asst prof, 1978-82; Griot Calendar, ed & proj dir; Digital Console Rental Inc, pres & owner; Humanities Tex, writer, currently. **Orgs:** Fel Southern Fel Fund, 1970-75; secy & treas, founder, Southern Conf Afro-Am Studies Inc, 1979-, treas; vpres, Asn Caribbean Studies, 1988-92; Asn Study Afro-Am Life & Hist; E Tex Hist Asn; La Hist Asn; N La Hist Asn; Southern Conf Mrican Am Studies; Southern Hist Asn; Tex African Am Heritage Orgn; Tex Oral Hist Asn; Am Cowboy Mus. **Home Addr:** 6747 Ridgeway, Houston, TX 77087, **Home Phone:** (713)641-9738. **Business Addr:** Writer, Humanities Texas, PO Box 330163, Houston, TX 77233-0163, **Business Phone:** (713)641-9711.

### JONES, DR. I. GENE
School administrator, vice president (organization), association executive. **Educ:** Jarvis Christian Col, BA, 1942; Ball State Univ, MA, 1963; Univ Mich, PhD, 1974. **Career:** Denver Pub Schs, teacher & admin asst, 1954-62; Ball State Univ, asst prof, 1962-64; Cent Community Col, instr, Inglewood, Calif, 1964-66; Unified Sch Dist, reading resource & curric devel spec, 1966-68; Eastern Mich Univ, asst prof educ, 1969-73; Albany State Col, asst dean acad affairs, 1973-78; GA State Univ, adj fac, 1975-78; St Paul's Col, vpres acad affairs, 1978-, provost, 1988. **Orgs:** Bd dirs, YWCA, Denver, 1960-62; bd dir, United Way Dougherty City, 1975-78; team capt, Ga Heart Fund Asn, 1977-78; N Mex First; adv comt, N Mex Off African Am Affairs. **Honors/Awds:** Am Book Co textbooks publ, 1967; Exxon Fel Am Coun Educ Educ Leadership Devel, 1975; Distinguished Alumni Award, Jarvis Christian Col, 1985; Presidential Citation, Nat Asn Equal Opportunity Higher Educ, 1986. **Home Addr:** 1601 Penn St NE Winrock Villas H 10, Albuquerque, NM 87110, **Home Phone:** (505)884-4049.

### JONES, IDA M.
Teacher, business owner, lawyer. **Personal:** Born Aug 18, 1953, Omaha, NE; daughter of Jonathan and Mary; married Curtis Darrell Bryant; children: Kenneth, Eugene, Kamali & Jamilla. **Educ:** Creighton Univ, Omaha, NE, BA, sociol, 1974; NY Univ, JD, 1977; Univ Calif, Los Angeles, cert, online educ, 2004. **Career:** Legal Aid-Criminal Appeals, New York, NY, assoc appellate coun, 1977-79; Legal Aid Soc, Omaha, NE, assoc atty, 1979-81; Univ Nebr, Omaha, NE, assoc prof, 1981-87; Calif State Univ, Fresno, CA, prof, 1987-, Ctr Scholarly Advan Learning & Teaching, dir, 2012-; spec asst, 2010-12; Verna Mae Brooks & Wayne D Brooks prof bus law, 1996-99. **Orgs:** Alpha Sigma Nu, 1974-; NY Bar Asn, 1978-; Nebr Bar Asn, 1982-95; Am Bus Law Asn, 1985-; Beta Gamma Sigma, 1985-; vpres, Western Bus Law Asn, 1988, pres, 1990; Calif Bar Asn, 1990-; vpres, Fresno Cert Develop Corp. **Honors/Awds:** Research Awards, Calif State Univ, Fresno, 1987-91; Research Awards, UNO, 1987; Meritorious Performance, Calif State Univ, Fresno, 1988, 1990; Craig School Business Award, Educ Innovation, 1990; First recipient, Verna Mae & Wayne A Brooks Professor of Business Law, 1996-99, 2011-13; Excellence in Teaching Award, 1999; Manco-Abbot Faculty Award, 1999 & 2008; Technology in Education, Provost Awards, 2006; Outstanding Educator Award, Acad Educ Leadership, 2008; Fresno Outstanding Fac Award, Fac Womens Asn Calif State Univ, 2013-14. **Home Addr:** 5382 N Angus St, Fresno, CA 93710-7015, **Home Phone:** (559)451-7459. **Business Addr:** Professor, California State University, Finance & Bus Law Dept, Fresno, CA 93740-8001, **Business Phone:** (559)278-2151.

### JONES, INGRID SAUNDERS
Executive. **Personal:** Born Dec 27, 1945, Detroit, MI; daughter of Homer Leon and Georgia Ann Lyles. **Educ:** Mich State Univ, BS, educ, 1969; Eastern Mich Univ, MA, educ, 1973. **Career:** Pub Sch Systs, sch teacher, 1969-73; Detroit Wayne County Child Care, Coord Coun, Detroit, Mich, exec dir, 1974-77; Atlanta City Coun, Atlanta Urban fel, Atlanta, Ga, spec asst, 1977-78; City Atlanta, Atlanta, Ga, legis analyst, atlanta city coun pres, 1978-79, exec asst mayor, 1979-81; Coca-Cola Co, Atlanta, Ga, dir urban affairs, 1982-88, asst vpres urban & govt affairs, 1988-92, vpres, corp external affairs, 1992, sr vpres global community connections, 2003-13. **Orgs:** Bd dir, UNICE; bd dir, Atlanta Neighborhood Develop Corp; bd dir, Cent Atlanta Progress, Cong Black Caucus Found; bd dir, Nat Minority Supplier Develop Coun; bd dir, Exec Leadership Coun Found; bd mem, Woodruff Arts Ctr; Ga Dept Indust, Trade Tourism; bd dir, Just Us Theater Co; bd dir, United Way Metro Atlanta; Metrop Community Found; Atlanta Empowerment Zone Corp; Atlanta Bus League; Links; bd dir, Delta Sigma Theta Sor; bd mem, Soc Int Bus Fel; Atlanta Womens Network; Int Womens Forum; bd dir, Nat Forum Black Pub Admin; bd mem, Apollo Theatre Found; bd mem, Clark Atlanta Univ; bd mem, Cong Black Caucus Found; bd mem, Girls Inc; bd mem, Ohio State Univ Pres Coun Women; bd mem, Andrew Young Sch Policy Studies at Ga State Univ; Coca-Cola Found, chmn, 1992-; bd mem, Nat Bd dir Girl Scouts USA; nat chairperson, Nat Coun Negro Women, 2012-. **Home Addr:** 1639 Stokes Ave SW, Atlanta, GA 30301. **Business Addr:** National Chairperson, National Council Of Negro Women Inc, 633 Pennsylvania Ave NW, Washington, DC 20004, **Business Phone:** (202)737-0120.

### JONES, IRMA RENAE
Police officer. **Personal:** Born Feb 20, 1942, Uriah, AL; daughter of Willie Virginia Harris and Lamb Virginia; married Robert Lloyd; children: Lisa White, Tiffany Dotson & Robin. **Educ:** Wayne County Community Col, AA, 1973; Wayne State Univ, BS, 1982; Eastern Mich Univ, MLS, 1989. **Career:** NY Univ, clerk typist, 1960-64; Columbia Univ, clerk typist, 1965-68; Pac Bell Tel, operator, 1968; Bethlehem Steel, typist, 1968-71; WXYZ-TV, typist clerk, 1971-72; Detroit Partition Co, secy, 1972-77; Detroit Police Dept, police officer, 1977-. **Orgs:** Adv, DPD Law Enforcement Explorers, 1988-; bd mem, BUOY 13, 1988-; National Association for the Advancement of Colored People, 1991-; adv comt, C Ctr Outpatient, 1991-93; adv comt, Burton Detention Ctr, 1991-94. **Honors/Awds:** Officer of the Year, Detroit Police, 1994; Plymouth United Church Christ Community Serv, 1994; Dedication to Exploring, Detroit Police Law Enforcement Explorers, 1994; Devoted & Untiring Work to Detroit Police Law Enforcement Explorer Post 1313, Boy Scouts Am, 1994. **Home Addr:** 5245 Avery, Detroit, MI 48208, **Home Phone:** (313)895-5608. **Business Addr:** Community Relations Officer, Detroit Police Department 13th Precinct, 4747 Woodward, Detroit, MI 48201, **Business Phone:** (313)596-1364.

### JONES, JACQUE DEWAYNE
Baseball player, athletic coach. **Personal:** Born Apr 25, 1975, San Diego, CA; married Krista; children: Jacque Jr & Jourdyn. **Educ:** Univ Southern Calif; Kennesaw State Univ. **Career:** Baseball player (retired), baseball coach; Minn Twins, outfielder, 1999-2005; Chicago cubs, outfielder, 2006-07; Detroit Tigers, 2008; Fla Marlins, 2008; Newark Bears, 2009-; free agt, currently; Ft Wayne TinCaps, hitting coach, 2012-13; San Antonio Missions, 2013-. **Business Addr:** Hitting Coach, San Antonio Missions, 5757 W Old Us Hwy 90, San Antonio, TX 78227, **Business Phone:** (210)675-7275.

### JONES, JACQUELINE VALARIE
Journalist. **Personal:** Born Aug 7, 1954, Washington, DC; daughter of Melvin C and Alice; children: Tony. **Educ:** George Washington Univ, BA, jour, 1976; Cleveland State Univ, eng, 1980; Penn State Univ, attended 2005. **Career:** Mutual Broadcasting & Mutual Black Network, tape ed, 1975-77; UPI, Atlanta, reporter, 1977-78; Cleveland Plain Dealer, reporter, 1978-80; Balt Eve Sun, reporter, 1980-81; Wash Star, reporter, 1981; Detroit Free Press, reporter, copy ed, 1981-84; Mpls Star Tribune, copy ed, 1984-87; NY Newsday, adm ed, night city ed, asst city ed & copy ed, 1987-92; Phila Daily News, city ed, 1992-95; Milwaukee Jour Sentinel, sr ed, local news, 1995-97; Wash Post, asst city ed, 1997-2003; Howard Univ, Instr Freedom Forum Prog, copy ed, 2000-02; Pa State Univ, Col Commun, sr lectr, 2003-05; Reach Media Inc, corresp, 2006-; Jones Coaching LLC, founder & dir, 2006-; Va Commonwealth Univ, virginius dabney prof, 2007; Howard Univ, adj journalism instr. **Orgs:** Vpres print, Nat Asn Black Journalists Parliamentarian, 1989-95; Accrediting Coun Educ Jour & Mass Commun, 1993-2009; George Wash Alumni Asn; Freelance Editing Network. **Home Addr:** 6500 7th Pl NW, Washington, DC 20012, **Home Phone:** (202)291-5959. **Business Addr:** Senior Lecturer, Pennsylvania State University, 217 Carnegie Bldg Suite 217, University Park, PA 16802, **Business Phone:** (814)865-9582.

### JONES, JAKE
Automotive executive. **Personal:** Born Aug 9, 1967, Hollandale, MS; married Veronica Nyhan; children: Savannah & Delaney. **Educ:** Carleton Col, BA, 1989; Miss Delta State Univ, attended 1990; Carnegie-Mellon Univ, MS, 1992. **Career:** US Dept Hamilton Health Sci, health policy analyst, 1992-95; Health Care Financing Admin, sr health policy analyst, 1995-96; CMS Off Legis & Policy, sr legis analyst, Dept Health & Human Serv, analyst; US Sen Carol Moseley-Braun, sr legis asst, 1996-99; AFL-CIO, legis rep, 1999-2000; Daimler Chrysler Corp, External Affairs & Pub Policy, exec dir, 2007-, sr mgr, Legis Affairs; Fed City Coun, vpres legis affairs, 2007-. **Orgs:** Black MBA Asn, 1990-92; pres, Black Grad Stud Orgn, Carnegie Mellon Univ, 1991-92; bd mem, Bright Beginning Inc, 2002-05; exec comt, mercedes-benz; exec comt, Alliance Automobile Manufacturers, currently; exec comt, Daimler Trucks; Fed Polit Action Comt; vice chair, Palisades Community Church; bd dir, Ger Am Bus Coun; bd mem, Wash Performing Arts Soc, 2007-; Nat Acad Social Ins, 2003-; Orgn Int Investment; Ger-Am Bus Coun; co chair, Nat Acad Sci; Econ Club, Carlton Club. **Home Addr:** 5333 Sherier Pl NW, Washington, DC 20016. **Business Addr:** Executive Director, DaimlerChrysler Corp, 1401 H St NW, Washington, DC 20005, **Business Phone:** (202)414-6700.

### JONES, JAMES ALFIE
Football player, executive. **Personal:** Born Feb 6, 1969, Davenport, IA. **Educ:** Northern Iowa Univ, BS, 1992. **Career:** Football player (retired), exec; Cleveland Browns, left defensive tackle, 1991-94; Denver Broncos, left defensive tackle, 1995; Baltimore Ravens, nose tackle, 1996, left defensive tackle, 1997-98; Detroit Lions, defensive tackle, left defensive tackle, nose tackle, 1999-2000; Jones' Tire Serv, co-owner, currently. **Orgs:** Spokespeople, First Family Pledge. **Honors/Awds:** Edge Nat Football League Man of the Year, Cleveland Browns, 1993; Humanitarian Award, Cleveland Touchdown Club, 1993; Ed Block Courage Award, Detroit Lions, 2000; Unsung Heroes Award, Detroit Lions, 2000. **Business Addr:** Co-Owner, Jones Tire Service Inc, 13529 110th Ave, Davenport, IA 52804, **Business Phone:** (563)381-1188.

### JONES, JAMES B.
Automotive executive. **Career:** Macon Chrysler-Plymouth Inc, pres, chief exec officer, 1978. **Honors/Awds:** Co is ranked No 20 on the list of Top 100 auto dealers, Black Enterprise, 1994. **Business Addr:** Chief Executive Officer, President, Macon Chrysler Plymouth Inc, 2110 Eisenhower Pkwy, Macon, GA 31206-3188, **Business Phone:** (478)781-0760.

### JONES, JAMES EARL
Actor. **Personal:** Born Jan 17, 1931, Arkabutla, MS; son of Robert (deceased) and Ruth Williams; married Cecilia Hart; children: Flynn; married Julienne Marie Hendricks. **Educ:** Univ Mich, BA, 1953; Am Theatre Wing, dipl, 1957. **Career:** Plays: Romeo & Juliet; Wedding in Japan; Sunrise in Campobello; Much Ado About Nothing; The Sleep of Prisoners; The Birds; The Caine Mutiny; Velvet Gloves; The Tender Trap; Arsenic & Old Lace; The Desperate Hours; The Pretender; The Cool World; King Henry V; Measure for Measure; The Blacks; A summer Nights Dream; The Apple; Moon on a Rainbow Shawl; Infidel Caesar; The Merchant of Venice; The Tempest; Toys in the Attic; PS 193; Macbeth; The Love Nest; The Last Minstrel; Othello; The Winter's Tale; Mr Johnson; Next Time I'll Sing to You; Blood knot; King Lear; Of Mice & Men; Paul Robeson; Master Harold & The Boys; Fences, 1987-88; Films: Dr Strangelove; The Comedians; The Man; The River Niger; Swashbuckler; BingoLong Traveling All-Stars & Motor Kings; Exorcist II, The Heretic; The Greatest; The Last Remake of Beau Geste; A Piece of the Action; Allan Quartermain & the Lost City of Gold; The Bushido Blade; Conan the Barbarian; Blood Tide; Gardens of Stone; Matewan; Conan the Barbarian; Coming to America; Field of Dreams; Three Fugitives; Into Thin Air; The Grand Tour; Scorchers; I Can't Lose; The Hunt for Red October; Sommersby; Excessive Force; Meteor Man; Patriot Games; Sneakers; Clear & Present Danger; Clean Slate; Sandlot; Confessions: Two Faces of Evil; Cry the Beloved Country; Looking for Richard; Gang Related; The Annihilation of Fish; Undercover Angel; Finder's Fee; The Papp Project; voice of King Mufasa in The Lion King; voice of Darth Vader in the Star Wars Trilogy; Clear & Present Danger, 1994; Jefferson in Paris, 1995; The Beloved Country Cry, 1995; A Family Thing, 1996; Gang Related, 1997; Casper: ASpirited, voice, 1997; The Lion King II: Simba's Pride, 1998; The Annihilation of Fish, 1999; Martin: Our Friend, 1999; Fantasia 2000, 1999; On the QT, 1999; Undercover Angel, 2000; Finder's Fee, 2001; Star Wars Episode III Revenge of the Sith, voice, 2005; The Sandlot 2, voice, 2005; Robots, voice, 2005; Scary Movie 4, narrator, 2006; Click, vioce, 2006; The Benchwarmers, 2006; Welcome Home, Roscoe Jenkins, 2008; Jack and the Beanstalk, 2010; Quantum Quest: A Cassini Space Odyssey, 2010; Gimme Shelter, 2013; The Angriest Man in Brooklyn, 2014. TV series: "The Defenders; East Side/WestSide"; "Camera 3"; "Look Up & Give"; "The Cay; King Lear"; "Big Joe & Kansas"; "UFO Incident"; "Jesus of Nazarath"; "The Greatest Thing That Almost Happened"; "Guyana Tragedy, The Story of Jim Jones"; "Me & Mom"; "Paris"; "The Golden Movement, An Olympic Love Story"; "Sojourner"; "A DayWithout Sunshine"; "Gabriel's Fire"; "Pros & Cons"; "Under One Roof"; "Homicide", 1997; "What The Deaf Man Heard", 1997; "Alone", 1997; "Merlin", voice, 1998; "Anatomy of a "Homicide: Life on the Street", 1998; "Summer's End", 1999; "Santa & Pete", 1999; "The Washington Monument: It Stands for All", 2000; "Feast of All Saints", 2001; TV: "Three Miners from Everwood", 2003; "The L Word", 2004; "A Light Knight's Odyssey", voice, 2004, 2006; "The Tipping Point", 2004; "The Reading Room", 2005; "The Magic 7", 2006; "The Trail of Tears: Cherokee Legacy", 2006; "Tim and Eric's Billion Dollar Movie ", 2012; "The Big Bang Theory", 2014; "Star Wars Rebels", 2014-16; Producer: Rogue One: A Star Wars Story, 2016. **Orgs:** Screen Actors Guild, Actors Equity Asn; Am Fedn TV & Radio Artists; Nat Coun Arts; bd dir, Theatre Commun Group; Nat Rifle Asn Am. **Honors/Awds:** The Village Voice Off-Broadway Awards, 1962; Theatre World Award, 1962; Drama Desk Award, 1964, 1967, 1969, 1970; Obie Award, 1965; Tony Award for Best Actor, Great White Hope, 1969; Golden Globe, 1971; Best Actor, Fences; Golden Gate Award, 1975; Image Award, Nat Asn Advan Colored People, 1975, 1993; Golden Hugo Award, 1975; Gabriel Award, 1975; Grammy Award, 1976; Medal for Spoken Language, Am Acad Arts & Letters, 1981; inducted into Theatre Hall of Fame, 1985; Antoinette Perry Award, 1987; Outer Critics Circle Award, 1987; Emmy Award, Soldier Boys, 1987; ACE Award, 1991; Emmy Award, Heatwave, 1990; Jean Renoir Award, Los Angeles Film Teachers, 1990; Commonwealth Award, Bank DE, 1991; Primetime Emmy Award, Gabriel's Fire, 1991; Hall of Fame Image Award, Nat Asn Advan Colored People, 1992; Nat Medal of the Arts, 1992; Joseph Plateau Life Achievement Award, 1995; KCFCC Award, Kans City Film Critics Circle, 1995; US Nat Board of Review Career Achievement Award, 1995; Method Fest Lifetime Achievement Award, 2001; John F Kennedy Centre Honour, 2002; DVDX Award, 2003, 2006; Camie Award, 2006; Eugene O'Neill Theater Center Monte Cristo Award, 2011; Oscar Micheaux Award, Chicago Film Critics Asn, 2011; Honorary Academy Award, 2012. **Special Achievements:** First African American actor to play the "President of the United States" on film in The Man, 1972. Golden Globe Nominee for Best Performance by an Actor in a TV-Series-Drama, 1992. **Business Addr:** Actor, Horatio Productions, PO Box 610, Pawling, NY 12564-0610.

### JONES, JAMES F.
Basketball coach. **Personal:** Born Feb 20, 1964, Long Island, NY; son of Herman and Edna Davis; married Rebecka; children: Rachel. **Educ:** Univ Albany, BA, commun, 1986, MA, educ admin, 1995. **Career:** Basketball player (retired); NCR Corp, exec acct mgr; Univ Albany, basketball player, 1982-86, asst coach, 1990-95; Yale Univ, asst coach, 1995-97, Head Coach, 1999-; Ohio Univ, asst coach, 1997-99; Yale Univ, Villanova Univ, asst coach, 1999-. **Orgs:** Nat Asn Basketball Coaches; Ny Basketball Coaches Asn; Black Coaches Asn. **Home Addr:** 20 Tower Pkwy, New Haven, CT 06520, **Home Phone:** (203)432-1485. **Business Addr:** Joel E Smilow Head Coach, Yale University, 20 Tower Pkwy, New Haven, CT 06520-8216, **Business Phone:** (203)432-1485.

### JONES, JAMES MCCOY
Educator. **Personal:** Born Apr 5, 1941, Detroit, MI; son of Arthur McCoy and Marcella Hayes; married Olaive Burrowes; children: Shelly & Itenash. **Educ:** Oberlin Col, BA, psychol, 1963; Temple Univ, MA, 1967; Yale Univ, PhD, 1970. **Career:** Franklin Inst, Philadelphia, psychol res, 1964-66; Harvard Univ, asst prof soc psychol, 1970-74,

assoc prof soc psychol, 1974-76, vis prof, 1978; Educ Develop Ctr, Exploring Childhood Proj, sr scholar, 1973-74; Guggenheim Fel, 1973; Boston Off Lawrence Johnson & Assocs, dir, 1974-76; Nat Inst Adv Studies, staff dir, 1976-77; APA MNY Fel Prog, dir, 1977; Am Psychol Asn, dir, 1977-, affirmative action officer, 1986-, exec dir, 1987-91; APA Pub Interest Directorate, Inaugural dir; Univ Del, prof psychol, 1982-, vis distinguished prof, 1981-82, prof & dir, Black Am Studies, 2005-. **Orgs:** Exec dir, Pub Int Am Psychol Asn, 1987-91; Asn Black Psychologists; pres, Soc Psychol Study Soc Issues; educ consult, J Personality & Soc Psychol; J Clin Psychol; Psychol Bull; NIMH Small Grant Rev Comt; assembly Behav Sci, 1973-77; adv bd, WEB Dubois Res Inst; Comt Res Rev Comn, Roxbury, MA, 1970-74; Am Psychol Asn; Am Psychol Soc; Soc Personality & Social Psychol; Soc Psychol Study Ethnic Minority Issues; Soc Exp Social Psychol; Am Educ Res Asn; Asn Behav Scientists Med Educ; DC Psychol Asn; Am Sociol Asn; AAAS; chairperson, Nat Psychol Orgn Prog Comt, 1980. **Home Addr:** 705 Quaint Acres Dr, Silver Spring, MD 20904, **Home Phone:** (301)622-9248. **Business Addr:** Professor, Director, University of Delaware, 224 McKinly Lab, Newark, DE 19716, **Business Phone:** (302)831-2489.

## JONES, JAMES R., III (JIMMY JONES)
Executive, business owner, consultant. **Personal:** Born Apr 1, 1944, Morristown, NJ; son of James E and Elizabeth B; married Janet Watkins; children: Jill, Jackie & Jimmy. **Educ:** Univ Nebr, BS, sec educ & libr sci, 1966; Cent Mich Univ, MA, mgt personnel, 1979. **Career:** Prof football player & teacher, 1966-70; New York Jets Prof Football Club, asst dir personnel, 1970-72; Jersey Cent Power & Light Co, mgr employ & asst to vpres human resources, 1972-80; Gannett Co Inc, dir affirmative action & employee rels, 1980-84, vpres employee rels, 1984-91, pres, chief exec officer & exec coaching; John Hopkins Univ, vpres human resources, 1991-95; Franciscan Health Syst, sr vpres human resources, 1995-96; Inova Health Syst, vpres human resources, 1996-97; Reebok Int Inc, Reebok Div, admin officer, sr vpres human resources & chief human resources officer, 1997; Jimmy Jones & Assocs, chief exec officer, pres, founder & owner, currently; Lululemon Athletic inc, exec vpres, chief human resources & admin officer & exec consult; PRM Consult Inc, prin; United Air Lines Inc, mgr. **Orgs:** Kappa Alpha Phi; bd trustee & chmn, Exec Leadership Coun; Black Human Resources Network; Edges; Soc Human Resources Mgt; sr vpres, Human Resources Round table; trustee, Reebok Found; Conf Bd's Chief Adminr Officer's Coun. **Home Addr:** 14 Washington Valley Rd, Morristown, NJ 07960-3412, **Home Phone:** (973)538-5783. **Business Addr:** Founder, Owner, Jimmy Jones & Associates, 45 Pk Pl S 102, Morristown, NJ 07960, **Business Phone:** (973)605-8301.

## JONES, JAMES V.
Automotive executive. **Personal:** Born May 16, 1942, Jackson, NC; son of James and Viola M Brown; children: James III. **Educ:** NC Cent Univ, Durham, NC, law degree, 1976. **Career:** Ozone Ford Ltd, Ozone Pk, NY, pres, 1987-. **Business Addr:** President, Ozone Ford Ltd, 235 Glen Cove Rd, Greenvale, NY 11548, **Business Phone:** (718)296-2222.

## JONES, JENNIE Y.
Educator, teacher, executive director. **Personal:** Born May 26, 1921, Woodlawn, IL; children: Johnetta, Harry, Jerry & Danny. **Educ:** Southern Ill Univ, Carbondale, BEd, 1942; Univ Ill, MA, 1949. **Career:** Carbonate Sch Dist 95, teacher, 1948-70; Head Start SIU, regional training officer, 1970-74, prog dir, 1973; Southern Ill Univ, Carbondale, Child Develop Lab, asst prof & dir minority affairs, 1975-. **Orgs:** Bd dir, Ill Asn Educ Young C; Delta Kappa Gamma; adv comt mem, Training & Tech Asst Model Cities; bd dir, State Comn Coord Child Care; adv comt mem, Lincoln land Community Col. **Home Addr:** 605 N Marion, Carbondale, IL 62901, **Home Phone:** (618)457-6453. **Business Addr:** Director, Southern Illinois University, 1168 SIU, Carbondale, IL 62901.

## JONES, JENNIFER
Opera singer. **Personal:** Born Wilmington, DE; children: 3. **Educ:** Curtis Inst Music, BM, 1975. **Career:** Grant Martha Baird Rockefeller & Found Philadelphia Orchestra Competition, soloist, 1973; Philadelphia Orchestra, soloist, 1973; Los Angeles Philharmonic, soloist, 1976, 1978 & 1980; Israeli Philharmonic, soloist, 1976 & 1980; New York Philharmonic, soloist, 1979; Houston Grand Opera, alto soloist, 1980; Montreal Symphony, soloist, 1980; opera singer, currently. **Home Addr:** 400 W 43rd St Apt 11T, New York, NY 10036, **Home Phone:** (212)244-2393.

## JONES, DR. JESSE W.
College administrator. **Personal:** Born Jan 16, 1931, Troup, TX; married LaBelle; children: Penola Washington, Tacora Ballums, Phelisha, Jesse Jr, David, Stephen & Lilla. **Educ:** Tex Col, BS, 1954; Univ Utah, advan work, attended 1956; NMex Highlands Univ, MS, 1956; Ariz State Univ, PhD, 1963, DSc, 1993. **Career:** Tex Col, instr chem, 1956-58; Ariz St, rsch assoc, 1958-63; Tex Col, chmn/prof, 1963-68; Bishop Col, chmn & prof, 1968-; Baylor Univ, prof, chem, 1988-. **Orgs:** Pres, Bishop Col Fed Credit Union, 1969-85; vice chmn, City Dallas Bd Adjust, 1977-82; pres, Dallas City Dem Progressive Voters League, 1977-85; vice chmn, Dallas Environ Health Comn, 1983-; Am Chem Soc; fel, Am Sci Soc; sec, Searcy's Youth Found; fel, Am Inst Chemists; rep, Tex State House Representatives, 1992-2006. **Business Addr:** Professor, Baylor University, Baylor Sci Bldg E 211 1 Bear Pl Suite 97348, Waco, TX 76798-7348, **Business Phone:** (254)710-6842.

## JONES, JILL MARIE
Actor, television show host. **Personal:** Born Jan 4, 1975, Dallas, TX. **Educ:** Tex Women's Univ. **Career:** Dallas Cowboys, cheer leader; Dallas Mavericks, dancer; TV Series: "Girlfriends", 2000-06; "City Guys", 2000; "American Dream"; "The Sharon Osbourne Show", 2004; "35th NAACP Image Awards", co-host, 2004; "BET Comedy Awards", 2004; "106 & Park Top 10 Live", 2005; "All Shades of Fine: 25 Hottest Women of the Past 25 Years", 2005; "Gillian In Georgia", 2010; "The Hot 10", 2011; "American Horror Story", 2013; "Sleepy Hollow", 2013-14. Films: City Guys, 2000; Girlfriends, 2000-06; Redrum, 2007; Universal Remote, 2007; The Perfect Holiday, 2007; Major Movie Star, 2008; Private Valentine, 2008; The Longshots, 2008; Drool, 2009; Meeting Spencer, 2010; 35 and Ticking, 2011; Men, Money & Gold Diggers, 2014; Hear No Evil, 2014. **Orgs:** Alpha Kappa Alpha Sorority. **Honors/Awds:** FilmOut Audience Award, FilmOut San Diego, 2010. **Special Achievements:** Featured in King magazine, 2002; first woman to host "2004 NAACP Image Awards" program. **Business Addr:** Actress, United Paramount Network, 11800 Wilshire Blvd, Los Angeles, CA 90025, **Business Phone:** (310)575-7000.

## JONES, JIMMIE DENE, II
Consultant. **Personal:** Born Feb 26, 1939, Childress, TX; married Thelma Wilkerson; children: Vickie Harris, Jimmie D Jr, Amanda Lene Scott & Darryl Bryan. **Educ:** St Mary's Col, BS & BA, 1973; George Washington Univ, MBA, 1978; Col Financial Planning, cert, 1984. **Career:** Law Engineering, personnel dir, 1979-86; bus consult, 1982-; J&L Financial Serv, owner, 1986-. **Orgs:** Northern Va Minority & Prof Bus Assocs, 1984; chmn, exec, president, L B Bailey Found Inc, 2001-. **Honors/Awds:** Proclamation for Volunteer as Financial Counselor, County Exten Off, 1986. **Home Addr:** 14271 Wilderness Lane Apt 15, Woodbridge, VA 22193-5677. **Business Addr:** Consultant, Chairman, L B Bailey Foundation Inc, 14760 Independent Lane, Manassas, VA 20112-3927, **Business Phone:** (703)347-2422.

## JONES, JIMMIE SIMS
Football player. **Personal:** Born Jan 9, 1966, Lakeland, FL; children: Jimmeria & Jimmie Jr. **Educ:** Univ Miami, grad. **Career:** Football player (retired); Dallas Cowboys, left defensive tackle, 1990, right defensive tackle, 1991, defensive tackle, 1992-93; Los Angeles Rams, left defensive tackle, 1994; St Louis Rams, left defensive tackle, 1995-96; Philadelphia Eagles, 1997. **Honors/Awds:** Extra Effort Award, Nat Football League, 1995; True Value Hardware Man of the Year Award, St Louis Rams, 1995; Super Bowl champion, XXVII, XXVIII. **Special Achievements:** Films: 1990 NFL Draft, 1990; Super Bowl XXVII , 1993. Shares the Super Bowl record for Most Fumble Recoveries in a game with two in Super Bowl XXVII vs the Buffalo Bills.

## JONES, JOHNNIE ANDERSON, SR.
Lawyer. **Personal:** Born Nov 30, 1919, Laurel Hill, LA; son of Henry E and Sarah Ann Coats; married Sebell Elizabeth Chase; children: Johnnie Jr (Deceased), Adair Darnell, Adal Dalcho & Ann Sarah Bythelda. **Educ:** Southern Univ, BS, psychol, 1949; Southern Univ Law Sch, JD, law, 1953. **Career:** Universal Life Ins Co, ins agt, 1947-48; US Post Off, ltr carrier, 1948-50; Southern Univ Law Sch, law sch stud, 1950-53; LA State Bar Asn, lawyer, 1953-; Jones & Jones, sr lawyer, 1975. **Orgs:** Nat Asn Advan Colored People, 1936-; founder, Martinet Soc, 1957; asst parish atty, City Parish Govt, 1969-72; Frontiers Club Int, 1962-; Alpha Phi Alpha Frat, 1972-; state rep, La House rep, 1972-76; Southern Univ Bd Supervisors. **Honors/Awds:** Frontier Man of the Year, Frontiers Col Int, 1962; Cert of appreciation, LB Johnson & HH Humphrey, 1964; plaque Alpha Kappa Alpha Sorority, 1972; Most Outstanding Mount, Zion First Bapt Church, 1970; Lifetime Achievement Award, 2009; Hall of Fame, Southern Univ Sch Law Hall. **Special Achievements:** Jones was one of the first graduates of the Southern University Law Center in 1953; He became one of five African American members of the state House of Representatives, 1972; First African American Assistant Parish Attorney for East Baton Rouge Parish. **Home Addr:** 363 3rd St Suite 702, Baton Rouge, LA 70801, **Home Phone:** (225)383-8573. **Business Addr:** Attorney, Jones & Jones Attorneys-at-Law, 263 3rd St Suite 702, Baton Rouge, LA 70801-1703, **Business Phone:** (225)383-8573.

## JONES, DR. JOSEPH, JR.
Dean (education), vice president (organization), educator. **Personal:** Born Jun 3, 1928, Albany, GA; son of Joseph and Hattie Turner; married Etta M; children: Josetta I & Robyn M Thomas. **Educ:** Morris Brown Col, BS, 1950; Northwestern Univ, MSC, 1952; Ohio State Univ, PhD, 1960. **Career:** St Augustine's Col, Dept Biol, head, 1952-57, acad dean, 1966-69, Acad Affairs, vpres, 1969-72, Title III Proj, coordr; United Negro Col Fund fel, 1959; Univ Sci & Technol, Ghana, W Africa, Fulbright-Hayes prof, 1972-73; Tex Southern Univ, dean grad sch, prof biol, assoc vpres res & grad studies, currently; consult strategy planning & educ. **Orgs:** Dir, teacher sci, Nat Sci Found & Atomic Energy Comn Inst; fel Ohio Acad Sci; Sigma Xi Sci Hon Soc; Alpha Mu Hon Soc; Ohio Acad Sci; Am Soc Parasitologists; Nat Sci Teacher Asn; Am Mus Nat Hist; Alpha Phi Alpha Frat. **Home Addr:** 11307 Sandstone, Houston, TX 77072. **Business Addr:** Associate Vice President for Research & Graduate S, Dean of the Graduate School, Texas Southern University, 3100 Cleburne Ave, Houston, TX 77004, **Business Phone:** (713)313-7233.

## JONES, K. C.
Basketball coach, basketball player, executive. **Personal:** Born May 25, 1932, Taylor, TX; son of K C Sr and Eula Daniels; children: 6. **Educ:** Univ San Francisco, attended 1956. **Career:** Basketball player, basketball coach (retired), executive; Boston Celtics, 1958-67, 1983-88, asst coach, 1978-79, 1982-83, 1996-97, head coach, 1983-88, vpres basketball opers, 1988-89; Brandeis Univ, head coach, 1967-70; Harvard Univ, asst coach, 1970-71; Los Angeles Lakers, asst coach, 1971-72; Am Basketball Asn, San Diego Conquistadors, head coach, 1972-73; Capital Bullets/Wash Bullets, head coach, 1973-76; Milwaukee Bucks, asst coach, 1976-77; Seattle Supersonics, asst coach, 1989-90, head coach, 1990-92; Detroit Pistons, asst coach, 1994-95; Am Basketball League, coach, 1996-98; Am Basketball League New Eng Blizzard, 1997-99; Univ Hartford, spl asst to dir athletics & commentator, currently. TV Series: "NBA All-Star Game", 1984-86; "The NBA on CBS", 1985; "NBA All-Star Saturday", 1994; "Bill Russell: My Life, My Way", 2000; "ESPN SportsCentury", 2000-01; "ESPN 25: Who's, 2007. **Orgs:** Kappa Alpha Fraternity. **Home Addr:** 379 Boston Post Rd Suite 302, Sudbury, MA 01776. **Business Addr:** Special Assistant to the Director of Athletics, University of Hartford, 200 Bloomfield Ave, West Hartford, CT 06117, **Business Phone:** (860)768-4100.

## JONES, K. MAURICES (MEJEKE K MAURICE JONES)
Writer. **Career:** Author: Say It Loud! The Story of Rap Music, 1994; Say it Loud, Trd, 1994; Spike Lee & the African American Filmmakers: A Choice of Colors, 1996. **Home Addr:** 44 Madison St Apt 13, Eugene, OR 97402-5062.

## JONES, DR. KATHERINE ELIZABETH BUTLER
Educational consultant, writer. **Personal:** Born Mar 19, 1936, New York, NY; daughter of Theodore Harold Butler (deceased) and Meme Elgitha Clark Butler (deceased); married Hubert; children: Karen, Lauren, Harlan, Renee, Lisa, Hamilton, Cheryl & Tanya. **Educ:** Mt Holyoke Col, BA, econ & sociol, 1957; Simmons Col, MA, urban educ, 1967; Harvard Univ, EdD, admin & social policy, 1980. **Career:** Boston Pub Schs, teacher, 1958-59; Civil Rights Movement Newton, 1960-80, 2002; Newton Pub Schs, coord ed prog, 1966-76; Simmons Col, instr, 1967-69; Newton Pub Schs Metrop Coun Educ Opportunities Prog, dir & founder, 1967-76; Sch Systs Pub & Independent MA, consult, 1968-; Wheelock Col, instr, 1976; Cambridge Pub Schs, supvr staff & prog, 1977-81; self-employed educ consult; Boston Univ, Afro-Am Studies Prog, instr, 1993-95; Deeper Roots Publs, auth, currently; Books: Garnets, Diamonds & Other Black Jewels, Am Visions, 1998; They Called It Timbukto, Orion Mag, 1998; Civil Rights Movement in Newton, 1960-80, 2002; Baseball & Madame St Clair, 2003; Deeper Roots: An American Odyssey. **Orgs:** Bd dir, founding mem, METCO, 1966-73; bd trustee, Mt Holyoke Col, 1973-78; Newton Sch Comt, 1978-85; minority affairs comt, Nat AssocSchs, 1984-89; bd, Boston C's Serv, 1985-; bd, Family Serv Asn, 1986-, vice chairperson, 1989-91; Mass Coalition Homeless, 1989-99; Newton Fair Housing; Equal Rights Comt. **Honors/Awds:** Service Above Self Newton Chamber Com, 1974; Educator Excellence Scholarship to Student Black Citizens of Newton, 1976; Service METCO City of Newton, 1976; Contrib to Integrated Ed METCO Boston Staff, 1976; Doctoral Dissertation Sch Consolidation in Newton, 1980; Citizens Who Make a Difference ContribMental Health MA Assoc Mental Health, 1982; Tribute to 350 years Black Presence in Massachusetts Honoree, Museum Afro-Am History, 1988; Nominating Com for Alumnae Trustees Mt Holyoke Col, 1990-92; Schomberg Scholar in Black Culture NYK Pub Libr, 1991-92; Award Black Alumnae Conference, Mt Holyoke Col, 1994; Newton Citizen Recognition of Distinction, 1994; Family History Exhibitor Museum our Nat Heritage, Lexington, MA, 1995; Discovery Author Non-Fiction, New England PEN Discovery Author Award, 1996; Recipient of Human Rights Award, 2003; Women of Courage and Conviction Award, Nat Coun Negro Women, 2005; Teen Voices Intergeneration Award, 2008. **Special Achievements:** Served as first African American member in Newton School Committee from 1978 to 1985. **Home Addr:** 1087 Commonwealth Ave, Newton Center, MA 02459, **Home Phone:** (617)332-8183. **Business Addr:** Author, Deeper Roots Publications, 2100 Red Gate Rd, Orlando, FL 32818-4718, **Business Phone:** (407)797-8557.

## JONES, DR. KELSEY A.
Educator, association executive, executive. **Personal:** Born Jul 15, 1933, Holly Springs, MD; married Virginia Bethel Ford; children: Kelsey Jr, Cheryl Darlene Campbell-Smith, Eric Andre & Claude Anthony. **Educ:** Miss Indust Col, AB, 1955, DD, 1969; Garrett Theol Sem NW Univ, MDiv, 1959; Univ Mich Med Ctr, clin pastoral care & coun, 1960; Wesley Med Ctr, post grad cert, 1967; Nat Parole Inst, Nat Coun Crime & Deliquency-State Univ NY, Albany, Sch Criminal Justice-Inst Man & Sci, cert, 1970; Gerоge Mason Univ, cert, 1984. **Career:** Fed City Col (UDC Mt Vernon Campus), vis lectr, Black hist, 1973-75; INTER/MET, dir Bacc & Liason consult, 1973-77; Univ DC, Van Ness Campus, prof social sci, 1972-77, chmn dept soc/behav sci, 1977-78, prof, Dept Criminal Justice, 1978-94, chmn, 1979-91, pres, spec asst environ health; Occup Safety & Inst Security, 1984-86; Think Tank Emer Manor, resident faclitator. **Orgs:** Sec NY/WA Ann Conf Vis Chpl Meth Pop Cook County Jail, 1956-58; aptd staff Recep-Diag Cntr Mich Correct Comn, 1961; sec KS/MO Ann Conf, 1962-70; deleg Gen Conf Christ Meth Epis Ch, 1966; chmn, St Bd Probation & Parole, 1967; deleg Centennial Session Gen Conf, 1970; Dean Leadership Educ ea 3 confs 3rd Episcopal Dist; Acad Criminal Justice Scientists; N Atlan Conf Criminal Justice Educr; Inst Criminal Justice Ethics; Nat Criminal Justice Asn, Northeastern Asn Criminal Justice Educr; Am Soc Indust Security; Nat Asn Chiefs Police, Am Soc Pub Admin; Am Asn Higher Educ; Phi Alpha Frat Mu Lamda Chap DC; first vpres Wichita Urban League; bd dirs Bros Inc; LEAP com deseg pub schs, Wichita; Cur Soc. **Honors/Awds:** Presidential Citation, Nat Asn Equal Opportunities Higher Educ; Alumnus of the Year; Distinguished Service Award, Howard Univ; Distinguished Service Award, Univ DC; Lorton Stud Govt Asn contribution to the Lorton Prison Proj; Awarded certificate for workshop on Crime Prevention for Collegesand Universities, Campus Crime Prevention Programs, 1985. **Special Achievements:** Public speaker; written and published many papers and articles. **Home Addr:** 5427 Kansas Ave NW, Washington, DC 20011, **Home Phone:** (202)723-1378. **Business Addr:** Resident Facilitator, Think Tank at Emeritus Manor Takoma Pk, Washington, DC 20039-0379.

## JONES, DR. KENNETH LEROY
Physician. **Personal:** Born Kinston, NC; children: Kathryn, Amber & Jonathan. **Educ:** Amherst Col, BS, 1973; Howard Univ Col Med, MD, 1978. **Career:** US Pub Health Serv Johns Hopkins Hosp, gen surg resident, 1978-83; Advan Indust Med Inc, vpres & med dir; E Coast Health Org Inc, pres & med dir. **Home Addr:** 8 Retinae Ct 202, Baltimore, MD 21207. **Business Addr:** Physician, 10000 S Mayo Trail, Paintsville, KY 41240.

## JONES, KIM HARRIS
Vice president (organization), controller. **Educ:** Univ Mich, BBA, acct, MBA. **Career:** Chrysler Group LLC, vpres & chief controller, vpres prod, procurement & cost mgt finance, vpres prod finance, sr vpres corp controller & auditor, 1992-09; Kraft Foods Inc, sr vpres corp planning & anal, 2009, sr vpres & corp controller, 2009-12; Mondelez Int Inc, sr vpres & corp controller, 2012-. **Honors/Awds:** "Black Enterprise", 75 Most Powerful Women in Business, 2010; "Automotive News", Top 100 Women in Automotive Industry; Professional Achievement Award, Women of Color Mag. **Business Addr:** Mondelez International Inc, 3 Pkwy N Suite 300, Deerfield, IL 60015, **Business Phone:** (847)943-4000.

**JONES, KIMBERLY DENISE (QUEEN BEE)**
Actor, rap musician. **Personal:** Born Jul 11, 1975, Brooklyn, NY; daughter of Linwood and Ruby Mae. **Career:** Albums: Hard Core, 1996; Notorious KIM, 2000; La Belle Mafia, 2003; The Naked Truth, 2005; The Dance Remixes, 2006; The G.O.A.T Mixtape, 2007; Vintage, 2009; Films: Gangstresses, 1997; She's All That, 1999; Long shot, 2000; Zoolander, 2001; Juwanna Mann, 2002; Those Who Walk in Darkness, 2003; Gang of Roses, 2003; You Got Served, 2004; Nora's Hair Salon, 2004; Lil' Pimp, 2005; There's a God on the Mic, 2005; Trick Daddy Feat. Cee-Lo Green and Lil' Kim: Sugar, writer, 2005; Superhero Movie, 2008; Superhero Movie, 2008; TV Series: Fuse's Summer Jam X, 2003; American Dreams, 2003; Lil Kim: Countdown to Lock down, exec producer, 2006; The Game, 2007; Singles: Chillin' Tonight; Queen Bee Records, chief exec officer, 1999-. **Orgs:** Lil' Kim Cares. **Honors/Awds:** Grammy Awards, 2002; MTV Video Music Awards, 1998; 2001; 2001; My VH1 Awards, 2001; 2001; Soul Train Lady of Soul Awards, 1997; 1999; Source Awards, 2003; 2003; Teen Choice Awards, 2001; MOBO Awards, 2003; Radio Music Awards, 2001; TMF Awards-Belgium, 2001; TMF Awards-Netherlands, 2001; ALMA Awards, 2002; ASCAP Music Awards, 2002; MTV Japan Awards, 2002; MVPA Video Awards, 2002; American Music Awards, 2003. **Special Achievements:** Ranked 34 on VH1's 50 Greatest Hip Hop Artists; Ranked 71 on VH1's 100 Sexiest Artists. **Business Addr:** Singer, c/o Atlantic Records, 1290 Ave of the Americas 28 Fl, New York, NY 10104-0101, **Business Phone:** (212)707-2000.

**JONES, KIRK.** See FINGAZ, STICKY.

**JONES, LAFAYETTE GLENN**
Marketing executive. **Personal:** Born Feb 17, 1944, Cincinnati, OH; married Sandra Miller; children: Bridgette, Kevin, Keith, Melanie, Glenn & Tara. **Educ:** Fisk Univ, BA, hist & govt, 1965; Dartmouth Col's Amos Tuck Sch Bus, exec mgt progs; Howard Univ Law Sch, attended 1966; Stanford Univ, cert mktg mgt, 1976. **Career:** Job Corps, ABT Assoc, Westinghouse Learning Corp YMCA, dir prg acct, 1965-67; State WOL, Sonderling Brdcst Co, dir pub rels, 1967-69; Imp Margs Food Div, Lever Bros Co, Golden Glow, prod mdse asst, 1969-70; Pillsbury Co, Refrig Foods Div, prod mgr; Birds Eye Div, Gen Foods Corp, Orange Plus, assoc prod mgr, 1970-72; Procter & Gamble; Pillsbury Co; Kraft Foods, mkt exec; Unilever, sales & mkt exec; Hunt Wesson Foods Div, Norton Simon Inc, Hunts Manwich & Tomato Pastem, mkt mgr, 1974-79; Johnson Publ Co, vpres & gen mgr; Johnson Prod Co, Chicago, gen mgr, vpres mkt & sls, 1979-; Am Health & Beauty Aids Inst, exec dir, 1981-; Supreme Beauty Prod, Chicago, IL, vpres & gen mgr, 1988-; SMSi's Shades Beauty Mag, publ, 1998; Victory Masonic Mutual Credit Union, chmn; Urban Call Mkt Inc, publ, pres & chief exec officer SMSi-Urban; ConAgra Foods; Segmented Mkt Serv Inc, owner, founding chair, exec vpres, pres & chief exec officer, currently. **Orgs:** Bd dir, hon Am Youth Fedn, 1972-74; vpres, bd trustee, Mardan Educ Ctr; Nat Asn Mkt Develop; Urban League; bd mem, Truliant, 2003; assoc dir, Truliant Fed Credit Union; Smith-Jones & Assocs; founder, Goler Community Develop Corp; vice chmn, Downtown Winston-Salem Partnership. **Honors/Awds:** Frederick Douglas Patterson Award, Nat Bus League, 1987; Man of the Year, inston-Salem Chronicle newspaper, 2007. **Special Achievements:** Lectured in Harvard University, Dartmouth College, Duke University, Wake Forest University, & Howard University. **Business Addr:** President, Chief Executive Officer, Segmented Marketing Service Inc, 4265 Brownsboro Rd Suite 225, Winston Salem, NC 27106-3425, **Business Phone:** (336)759-7477.

**JONES, LARRY.** See JONES, DR. EDWARD L.

**JONES, LARRY W.**
Executive. **Personal:** Born Jul 8, 1950, Mt. Pleasant, TX. **Educ:** US Naval Acad, Annapolis, MD, BS, engineering, 1973; US Dept Defense, Defense Systs Mgt Col, Ft Belvoir, VA, 1985; Purdue Univ, MS, mgt, 1997. **Career:** Executive (retired); United Technologies Corp, Pratt & Whitney, dir customer support prog, vpres, serv intergration, 1979, Mil Customer Support, vpres, 2012; Publications: Sustainment of Legacy Propulsion Systems, author. **Orgs:** Us Naval Acad Alumni Asn. **Home Addr:** . **Business Addr:** Vice President, PW 4000 Product Line Management, Pratt & Whitney, 400 Main St, East Hartford, CT 06108, **Business Phone:** (860)557-0430.

**JONES, LAWRENCE W.**
Educator. **Personal:** Born Feb 6, 1942, Newport News, VA; married Lolita Diane Grey; children: Lawrence W Jr & Leonard W. **Educ:** Hampton Inst, VA, attended 1964; State Teachers Col Bowie, BS, educ, 1967; Univ Mass, Amherst, EdD, 1973. **Career:** Bd Educ NYC, teacher, 1967-73; Univ Mass, teaching asst, 1970-73; Univ Mass Brooklyn, COP Prog supvr stud teaching, 1971-73; Youth Action Neighborhood Youth Corp, remedial coord, 1973; Univ NY, Medgar Evers Col, asst prof educ, 1974-77; Bd Educ NY, teacher reading specialist, 1977-; Community Sch, Newark, consult educ, 1978; Mayor Newark, spec asst educ prog, 1979. **Orgs:** Omega Psi Phi Fraternity, 1972-; consult wedn, Pro Day Care Ctrs Pvt Sch NY, 1975-; One Hundered Black Men, 1978-. **Honors/Awds:** Innovation in Teaching Dissertation, Univ Mass, 1973; Pub Classroom Mgt Ind Instn, 1973-74; Community Service Awards, Brooklyn COP & Community Life Ctr, 1974-78; Measuring Children's Growth Reading Expanding Reading Exp, 1978. **Home Addr:** 10425 164th St, Jamaica, NY 11433-2100, **Home Phone:** (917)603-8276.

**JONES, LEANDER CORBIN**
Educator. **Personal:** Born Jul 16, 1934, Vincent, AR; son of Lander Corbin and Una Bell; married Lethonee Angela Hendricks; children: Angela Lynne & Leander Corbin. **Educ:** Univ Ariz, Pine Bluff, BA, speech & drama, 1956; Univ Ill, MS, radio tv, 1968; Union Grad Inst, PhD, commun, 1973. **Career:** Educator (retired); Chicago Pub Sch, eng teacher, 1956-68; 7 art workshop Am Negro Emancipation Centennial Authority, dir, Chicago, 1960-63; Peace Corps Vol, Eng teacher, 1964-66; TV producer City Col Chicago, 1968-73; Meharry Med Col, commun media specialist, 1973-75; Western Mich Univ, Black Americana studies, from assoc prof to prof, 1975-03, African studies prog, chmn, 1980-81, Black caucus, co-chmn, 1983-84; Corbin 22 Ltd, pres, 1986; Mich Black Repertory Theatre, dir dramaturg, 1987-90; Ransom St Playhouse, Kalamazoo, exec prod, 1993. **Orgs:** Kappa Alpha Psi, 1953-; mem exec comt, DuSable Mus African Am Hist, 1970-; pres, TABS Ctr 1972-; Am Asn Univ Professors, 1973-; Nat Coun Black Studies, 1977-; chmn, Kalamazoo Community Rels Bd, 1977-79; Prisoners Progress Asn, 1977-82; Popular Cult Asn, 1978-; pres, Black Theater Kalamazoo, 1978-85; chmn, Comn Against Apartheid, 1977-90; Mich Coun Black Studies, 1977-96; SAfrica Solidarity Orgn, 1978-90; Mich Orgn African Studies, 1980-97; bd dir, Kalamazoo Civic Players, 1981-83; comdr, Vets Peace Kalamazoo, 1980-91; pres, Black Theatre Group Kalamazoo Civic Players, 1980-83; bd dir, Kalamazoo Civic Players, 1981-83, Mich Community Crime & Delinq, 1981-83; pres, Corbin 22 Ltd, 1986-; secy bd, Lester Lake Corp, 1992-; designer progs theatre & TV hard educate; adv bd, Western Mich Univ. **Home Addr:** 2226 S Westnedge Ave Suite 222, Kalamazoo, MI 49008-1939, **Home Phone:** (269)216-6089.

**JONES, DR. LEE**
Educator, school administrator. **Personal:** Born Jul 4, 1965, Newark, NJ; son of Levi and Carrie (deceased). **Educ:** Del State Univ, BA, speech commun, 1987; Ohio State Univ, MA, 1989, MBA, 1992, PhD, speech commun, org develop, 1995. **Career:** Ohio State Univ, resident life dir, 1988-90, dir retention, 1990-93, asstto vpres, 1993-95; Wash State Univ, dir & asst prof, 1995-97; Fla State Univ, assoc dean & assoc prof, 1997-2004; Univ Wis, Whitewater, dean sch grad studies & prof educ found, dean, currently; InSpire Mag, pres, chief exec officer, prof & exec ed, currently; InSpire ILEAD Inst, exec dir, currently; Acad Affairs & Instr Col Educ, assoc dean; dir, Div Multicultural Stud Serv & Asst Prof Educ Leadership, Wash State Univ; VIP Inc, founder & chief exec officer. **Orgs:** Acad Human Resource Develop; Am Asn Higher Educ; Nat Asn Equal Opportunity; Am Soc Training & Develop; Am Soc Qual; founder, Future Univ Orgn, 1993-; founder, bros Acad; Kappa Alpha Psi Fraternity Inc; bd trustee, Keystone Col. **Home Addr:** PO Box 682, Sun Prairie, WI 53590, **Home Phone:** (608)472-1100. **Business Addr:** President, Chief Executive Officer, Inspire Magazine, 3200 Commonwealth Blvd, Tallahassee, FL 32303, **Business Phone:** (904)322-8363.

**JONES, LENOY**
Football player, football coach, teacher. **Personal:** Born Sep 25, 1974, Marlin, TX; married LaJuana; children: Lenoy Jr, Landon, Lance, Lawyer & Lane. **Educ:** Tex Christian Univ, grad. **Career:** Football player (retired), teacher, football coach; Houston Oilers, linebacker, 1996; Tenn Oilers, 1997-98; Cleveland Browns, 2002, linebacker & mid linebacker, 1999-2001; Midway high sch, hist teacher; Midway high sch Cent Tex, football coach. **Business Addr:** Football Coach, Midway High School, 13885 Woodway Dr Woodway, Woodway, TX 76712, **Business Phone:** (254)761-5600.

**JONES, LEONARD WARREN**
Lawyer. **Personal:** Born Sep 20, 1965, Washington, DC; son of Lawrence and Lolita. **Educ:** Norfolk State Univ, BS, acct, 1988; Col Ins, MBA, ins, 1992; Thomas M Cooley Law Sch, JD, 1992; John Marshall Law Sch, Chicago, Ill, LLM, 2004. **Career:** Judge Advocate Gen's Corps, transp officer; Pvt pract, currently. **Orgs:** Omega Psi Phi Fraternity Inc; 100 Black Men Inc; Norfolk State Univ Mil Alumni Asn; Norfolk State Univ Found Inc; Scabbard & Blade Nat Mil Hon Socs; Nat Black MBA Asn; Nat Asn Black Accountants; Nat Asn Bond Lawyers; Bankruptcy Bar Asn; Delta Theta Phi Law Fraternity Inc. **Home Addr:** 5827 Allentown Rd Camp, Springs, NY 20735, **Home Phone:** (301)423-0111. **Business Addr:** Attorney, Private Practice, 16 Ct St Suite 1112, Brooklyn, NY 11241, **Business Phone:** (718)643-1114.

**JONES, LEORA SAM (LEORA SAMUELA)**
Athlete. **Personal:** Born Nov 18, 1960, Mt. Olive, NC; daughter of Ernest Ruthie and Mae. **Educ:** Louisburg Jr Col, attended 1980; E Carolina Univ, attended 1982. **Career:** Athlete (retired); administrator; Lady Pirates, 1980-82; Bayer Pharmaceuticals, mkt asst, 1985-86; First Citizens Bank, phillipsburg machine operator, 1989-90, 1992-; Natl Olympic Handball Team, 1992; United Parcel Serv, currently. **Orgs:** Colorado Team Handball, ASN, vip, 1992-; Us Womens Team Handball Olympic squad. **Home Addr:** 110 Elmore St, Mt Olive, NC 28365, **Home Phone:** (919)658-4081.

**JONES, LESLIE**
Comedian, television comedy writer, actor. **Personal:** Born Sep 7, 1967, Memphis, TN. **Educ:** Chapman Univ; Colo State Univ. **Career:** Comedian, 1986-; cook, cashier, waitress, salesperson, asst to a judge, justice peace & UPS employee; actress, 1998-. Tv: Mermaid, 2000; Girlfriends, 2004; Daddy Knows Best, 2012; Sullivan & Son, 2013; League, 2013; Workaholics, 2014; Saturday Night Live, NBC, 2014-; Awesomes, 2015; Blacklist, 2016; New York's Funniest, 2016. Film: Nat Security, 2003; A Guy Thing, 2003; Gangsta Rap: Glockumentary, 2007; Something Like a Bus, 2010; Lottery Ticket, 2010; Co We Keep, 2010; House Arrest, 2012; Top Five, 2014; Trainwreck, 2015; Ghostbusters, 2016; Sing, 2016; Masterminds, 2016. Tv writer: Saturday Night Live, NBC, 2014-. **Special Achievements:** Performed at the Just for Laughs Montreal Comedy Festival, Aspen Comedy Festival, and Laffapalooza; commentator for NBC, Summer Olympics, 2016. **Business Addr:** Saturday Night Live, 30 Rockefeller Ctr, New York, NY 10112.

**JONES, DR. LESLIE FAYE**
Educator. **Personal:** Born Oct 5, 1970, Napoleonville, LA; married Johnny Hamilton. **Educ:** Nicholls State Univ, BS, math educ, 1991, MEd, curric & instr, 1992; La State Univ, PhD, admin, 1996. **Career:** St James Parish Sch Dist, teacher, 1992-97; Lafourche Sch Dist, asst prin, 1997-98; Assumption Sch Dist, prin, 1998-2000; Nicholls State Univ, asst prof, 2000-06, assoc prof & minor cheramie endowed prof, prof & dean, currently. **Orgs:** Huel Perkins fel La State Univ, 1995; Am Educ Res Asn, 1996-2000; La Educ Res Asn, 1996-2000; La Asn Prinicpals, 1998-2000; Nicholls State Univ Alumni Federation, 1999-; La Prof Educ Admin, 2002-. **Home Addr:** PO Box 176, Napoleonville, LA 70390, **Home Phone:** (985)369-8544. **Business Addr:** Dean, Professor of Education, Nicholls State University, 220 Polk Hall, Thibodaux, LA 70310, **Business Phone:** (985)448-4325.

**JONES, LESTER C.**
Automotive executive, consultant. **Career:** Pasadena Lincoln-Mercury Sales Inc, chief exec officer & owner; Econ Opportunity Ctr, financial serv consult, currently. **Orgs:** Adv bd mem, Econ Opportunity Ctr. **Business Addr:** Financial Services Consultant, Economic Opportunity Center, 18 Technol Way Pine St, Nashua, NH 03060, **Business Phone:** (603)594-8513.

**JONES, DR. LEWIS ARNOLD**
Consultant, physician. **Personal:** Born Sep 16, 1950, Detroit, MI; son of Lewis Arnold Sr and Berlene J; married Pamela D Jennings; children: Jennifer Tiffany, Alicia Dawn & Lewis Alexander. **Educ:** Wayne State Univ, attended 1972; Univ Mich Med Sch, MD, 1978; Diag Radiol Residency, Providence Hosp, 1982. **Career:** Tri-County Radiol PC, radiologist, 1983-84; Harper Hosp, radiologist, 1984, dir gastrointestinal radiol div, 1984; Wayne State Univ Sch Med, clin instr, 1985-92, asst prof radiol, 1992-97; Karmanos Cancer Inst, 1992, dir breast imaging, 2004-06; Mich Dept Community Health, physician consult, 1997-2000; Henry Ford Health Syst, Dept Diag Radiol, staff radiologist, 2000-02; Genesys Physicians Integrated Diagnostics, diag radiologist, 2002-; McLaren Greater Lansing, dir breast imaging, 2006-; Advan Radiol Serv, breast radiologist, 2008-; pvt pract, physician, currently; Ingham Reg Med Ctr, radiologist & dir breast imaging, currently; Eaton Rapids Med Ctr, radiologist, currently. **Orgs:** Radiol Soc N Am, 1979-; bd dir, Am Cancer Soc, Oakland City Mich Div, 1988-; Am Col Radiol, 1989-; Asn Univ Radiologists, 1993-; Am Med Asn, 1994-; community adv & mem, Karmanos Cancer Inst, 1994; co-investr, NIH Women's Health Initiative, Detroit Clin Ctr, 1996-97. **Honors/Awds:** Outstanding Radiol Resident Award, Providence Hosp, 1982; Vol Leadership Award, Am Cancer Soc, 1988; Life Service Award, Am Cancer Soc, 1990; Frederick Douglass Award, New Metropolitan Detroit Club Nat Asn Negro Bus & Prof Women's Clubs Inc, 1996. **Special Achievements:** First winner of the Essence Magazine/Preferred Stock Cologne "What a Man Contest," 1995; Named co-chair of the "Year of the Women's Health" steering comt state of Mich(Michigan Department of Community Health), 1996; "Partners for Life" a woman's health seminar, created and presented by Lewis A Jones, MD & Florine Mark, chief exec officer, Weight WatchersInt, 1996; Creator & mem, "Women's Health: A Lifetime of Care" planning comt, 2000. **Home Addr:** 4951 Champlain Cir, West Bloomfield, MI 48323-3529, **Home Phone:** (248)851-3583. **Business Addr:** Radiologist, Director of Breast Imaging, Ingham Regional Medical Center, 401 W Greenlawn Ave, Lansing, MI 48910, **Business Phone:** (517)975-6382.

**JONES, LISA PAYNE**
School administrator. **Personal:** Born Dec 30, 1958, Camp Zama; daughter of Charles Benjamin Payne Jr and Eleanor Towns Hamilton; married Peter Lawson; children: Ryan Charles, Leah Danielle & Evan Cooke. **Educ:** Eastern Mich Univ, BBA, mkt, 1980; Case Western Res Univ, MBA, 1985. **Career:** Ameri Trust Co NA, gen analyst I, 1980-82, II, 1982-85, III, 1985-86; Cuyahoga Metro Housing Authority, mkt mgr, 1986-88, leasing & mkt mgr, 1989, leasing & transfer mgr, 1990-91, mkt coordr, 1992-94; Shaker Heights Bd Educ, dir, 1994-98, registr, 1994-2003; Independent Consults, Warm Spirit, 2007-09; US Census Bur, partnership asst, 2009-10; Mkt, Commun & Events, consult, 2011-. **Orgs:** Delta Sigma Theta Sor Inc, 1978-; proj bus consult, Jr Achievement, 1982-83; Cleveland Br, Nat Asn Advan Colored People, 1982-; chairperson, 1983, treas, 1984-85, Oper Greater Cleveland: Big Vote, 1983-85; Urban League Greater Cleveland, 1985-; Nat Black MBA Asn Inc, 1986; League Women Voters, 1987; Am Mkt Asn, 1987-89; trustee, Shaker Hts Alumni Asn, 1988-95; bd mem, Shaker Schs Found, 1990-94; second vpres, Shaker Hts PTO, 1995-96; Co-chairperson, PTO Strategic Planning Comt, 1997-99; Shaker Heights Alumni Assoc, exec dir, 1995-98; Dem Precinct, rep, 1998-; Jr League Greater Cleveland, 1998-99. **Home Addr:** 3532 Norwood Rd, Shaker Heights, OH 44122, **Home Phone:** (216)561-8988.

**JONES, LOREAN ELECTA**
Government official. **Personal:** Born Jun 29, 1938, Arlington, TN; daughter of Earnest and Alcorna Harris; married Jimmie; children: Gale Carson, Dale J, Elna Brunetti, Ervin C, Denise Jimenez, Dennis R, Teresa Y & Terry O (deceased). **Educ:** Owen Col, AA, 1968; Le Moyne-Owen Col, BA, 1970; Memphis State Univ, MS, 1977. **Career:** Government official (retired); State TN Dept Ment Health, social worker, 1970-75; State TN Dept Corrections, parole officer, 1975-78; US Dist Cts Western Dist TN, probation officer, 1978-84, fed drug treat specialist, 1984-90, supv probation officer, 1990-92, dep chief probation officer, 1992-98. **Orgs:** Bd trustees, Gov TN Arlington Develop Ctr, 1972-73; Comt mem, Black on Black Crime Task Force, 1979-; Fed Probation Officers Asn; PUSH, 1980; life mem, Nat Asn Advan Colored People, 1980; historian, Nat Coun Negro Women, 1983; TN Selective Serv Local Bd 38; secy, Le Moyne Owen Alumni Asn; Am Probation & Parole Asn; Am Asn Coun & Develop; Nat Alliance Bus Youth Motivating Task Force, 1982-83; secy, treas, Seast Region Fed Probation Officers Asn, 1983-85. **Honors/Awds:** Citizen of the Week Award, WLOK Radio Station, 1978; Distinguished Leadership Award; Outstanding Serv to the Human Serv Profession, 1987; Nat Cert Counrs Cert. **Special Achievements:** First female probation & parole officer, WD TN, 1978. **Home Addr:** 1520 Netherwood Ave, Memphis, TN 38106, **Home Phone:** (901)278-0830.

**JONES, MABLE VENEIDA**
Insurance executive. **Personal:** Born Sep 20, 1950, Detroit, MI; daughter of James U and Fannie. **Educ:** Eastern Mich Univ, BS, spec educ, 1972; Iowa State Univ, MS, guid & coun, 1973; Wayne State Univ, attended 1978; Lasalle Univ, PhD, bus admin. **Career:** Wayne State Univ, Upward Bound, dir, 1973-76; Ford Motor Corp, indust rels prog dir, 1976-80; AAA Mich, employee rels area mgr, employee servs area mgr, training & develop area mgr, exec loan, Detroit strategic planning proj, crime task force, sales admin area mgr, group servs area mgr, br mgr, dir sales adminr, dir pub affairs, dir community rels & corp contrib, 1980-; AAA Ins, dir corp contrib, 1980-; AAA Mich, community rels & corp contrib, dir, 2009-. **Orgs:** Women's Econ Club; bd mem, Neighborhood Servs Orgn; bd mem, Booker T Wash Bus Asn; ARO Mus; UNF; youth develop bd, Urban League; bd mem, Ennis; Nat Asn Advan Colored People; bd vpres & bd mem,

Starr Detroit Acad; secy, dir & sales admin, YWCA; bd mem, Crime Stoppers; bd trustee, C's Hosp Mich Found; bd mem, Elite Meetings Int Inc. **Honors/Awds:** Miss Teamwalk, March Dimes, 1984; Minority Achiever Award, YWCA, 1985; Volunteer of the Year, AAA Mich, 1986; Outstanding Service Award, AAA Mich, 1990-93; Silver Anniversary Achievement, Upward Bound, 1992; Ossawa Sweet Award, Wolverine Bar, 1994; Leadership Award, UNCF, 1997; Community Service Award, BTWBA, 1998. **Home Addr:** 35479 Heritage Lane, Farmington, MI 48335-3135, **Home Phone:** (248)471-5293. **Business Addr:** Director Community Relations & Corporate Contributions, AAA of Michigan, 1 Auto Club Dr, Dearborn, MI 48126, **Business Phone:** (313)336-1234.

## JONES, DR. MARCUS EARL

Educator. **Personal:** Born Jan 7, 1943, Decatur, IL; son of George and Bernetta Mayweather; married Diann; married Valerie Daniel; children: Anthony, Malik, Omar, Taisha, Samira, Malaika, Naël, Amina, Jamia & Punch. **Educ:** Southern Ill Univ, Carbondale, BA, geog, 1965, PhD, geog, 1978; Chicago State Univ, MA, geog, 1969; Univ Ghana, cert, 1968. **Career:** Southern Ill Univ Carbondale, ombudsman, 1972-73; FL A & M Univ, asst prof geog, 1973-76; Univ So FL Tampa, vis prof geog, 1976-77; Morris Brown Col, chair & prof geog, 1978-85; Valdosta State Col, prof geog, 1986-87; Chicago Pub Schs, teacher, 1988-89; SC State Univ, adj prof, 1991-2002; Univ NM, vis prof, 2002; Claflin Univ, Orangeburg, SC, assoc prof, 1990-2003, prof, currently. **Orgs:** Asn Am Geogrs; Southeastern Asn Geogrs; Asn Social & Behav Scientists Inc; African Studies Asn; W African Res Asn, 1991-92; Nat Asn African-Am Studies, area coordr, 1998; Asn Study Class African Civilizations; SC Coun Social Studies, Claflin Univ, 1999-2002. **Home Addr:** 664 Stanley St, Orangeburg, SC 29115. **Business Addr:** Associate Professor, Claflin University, 400 Magnolia St, Orangeburg, SC 29115-6815, **Business Phone:** (803)535-5000.

## JONES, MARCUS EDMUND

Television journalist. **Personal:** Born Feb 12, 1960, Washington, DC; son of Clarance and Lillie Brown; married Janice Lyons; children: Nathan Aaron Alexander. **Educ:** Boston Univ, Boston, MA, BS, broadcast jour, 1982; Temple Univ. **Career:** Daily Evening Item Lynn, Mass, columnist, 1976-78; Boston Globe, Boston, Mass, corresp, 1977-78; WILD-AM, Boston, Mass, news anchor & reporter, 1977-82; WQTV, "Boston Live!, " Boston, Mass, producer & host, 1980-81; Satellite News Channel, Stamford, Conn, news assoc, 1982-83; WEZN-FM, Bridgeport, Conn, news reporter, 1984; WUSA-TV, "Eyewitness News, " Wash, DC, reporter trainee, 1984-85; WGBH-TV, "Ten O'Clock News, " Boston, Mass, news reporter, 1986-91, "The Group", videotape ed, 1991-92; WBZ-TV, "News 4, " Boston, Mass, freelance reporter, 1993; Lowell Cable TV, "News Ctr 6, " Lowell, Mass, news dir, 1992-94; Northeastern Univ, Boston, Mass, jour dept, lectr, 1991-94; New England Cable News, Newton, Mass, freelance reporter, 1994-95; WFXT "Fox 25 News Ten, " Dedham, Mass, freelance reporter, 1995; Newschannel 8, Springfield, Va, Wash, DC reporter, 1995-96; Prince George's County "CTV News, " Channel 15, Largo, Md, freelance reporter & video tape ed, 1996; Fairfax Network, "School Scene, " Channel 21, Annandale, Va, freelance reporter & videographer video tape ed, 1996-98; Arlington Co Info Channel 31, Arlington, Va, freelance, videographer & video tape ed, 1997; Fairfax Co Govt Channel 16, Fairfax, Va, freelance videographer & video tape ed, 1998; FBI Acad, FBI Training Network, Quantico, Va, assoc producer, 1999; ABR Serv Incorporate, Spec Asst, 2006-. **Orgs:** Nat Asn Black Journalists, 1989-; Nat Asn Advan Colored People, 1970-82; Boston Asn Black Journalists, 1989-95; Wash Asn Black Journalists, 1995-. **Honors/Awds:** Emmy Award nominee, two categories, feature & spec reporting, Boston, New England Chapter Nat Acad TV Arts & Scis, 1990; Outstanding Anti-Smoking Report, Am Lung Asn, 1990; Emmy Award nominee, one category, news event, Boston, NE Chapter, NATAS, 1991. **Home Addr:** 5549 Hobsons Choice Loop, Manassas, VA 20112-5465. **Business Addr:** Special Assistant, ABR Services, 14849 Persistence Dr, Woodbridge, VA 22191, **Business Phone:** (703)490-5559.

## JONES, MARCUS EDWARD

Football player, wrestler. **Personal:** Born Aug 15, 1973, Jacksonville, NC; married Bethany. **Educ:** Univ NC, grad. **Career:** Football player, wrestler (retired); Tampa Bay Buccaneers, 1998, defensive end, 1996-97, 1999, right defensive end, 2000, left defensive end, 2001; Buffalo Bills, 2002; Gracie Tampa, wrestler, 2007-09. **Honors/Awds:** Consensus All-American, 1995. **Special Achievements:** Appearances on "Bubba the Love Sponge Show"on Howard 101-SiriusXMRadio & "Talking Sports with Randy Harris".

## JONES, MARGARET B.

Library administrator. **Personal:** Born Mar 11, 1932, Haines City, FL; daughter of John and Elizabeth Byrd; married Glover E; children: Edmond D, Glover E Jr, Lisa Landers, Cedric A & Leslie Wil son. **Educ:** Fla A&M Univ, BS, 1953; Atlanta Univ, MSLS, 1969; Fla A&M Univ, MEd, 1985. **Career:** Wash Jr Col & High Sch, librn, 1955-60; Fla A&M Univ, librn & asst prof, 1960-78; NC Cent Univ, adj prof, 1978-80; Fla A&M Univ, librn, 1981-95, assoc dir libr, 1996-99, develop officer, 2001-, pres, currently. **Orgs:** Consult, FAMU-Libr; Am Libr Asn; Phi Delta Kappa; N Fla Libr Asn; Kappa Delta, Pi Nominee, 1985; Fla Assoc Media Educ, 1975. **Honors/Awds:** Superior Accomplishment Award, Fla A&M Univ, 1990-91; Service Award, 1993-94, 1997-98; Cert Achievement, Panhandle Library Access Network, 1996; Black Achievement Award, Jefferson County Fla, 1997. **Special Achievements:** Six Decades of Research, Fla A&M Univ, 1995; co-author, School Media Specialization Undergraduate Library Science Program, Fla A&M Univ, Journal of Media & Library Service, Vol 24, p 2, 1987; Spanish language proficiency. **Home Addr:** 273 Martin Rd, Monticello, FL 32344, **Home Phone:** (850)997-3827. **Business Addr:** President, Florida A&M University, 315 Coleman Libr, Tallahassee, FL 32307-4700, **Business Phone:** (850)599-8576.

## JONES, MARILYN ELAINE

Government official. **Personal:** Born Waco, TX; children: Spencer. **Educ:** Tex Woman's Univ, MA, 1970, BS, 1972, PhD, 1978. **Career:** Early Childhood Educ Tex Woman's Univ, consult, 1970-74; Tex Woman's Univ, prof/lab instr, 1972-74; Paul Quinn Col, counr/placement dir, 1974-83; Prairie View A&M Univ, instr, 1980-84; Gen Land Off State Tex, field rep; City Coun mem, 1980-84; Heart Tex Coun Govs, vpres, 1982-84; Pro-Tem Waco City Coun, mayor, 1983-84. **Orgs:** Delta Sigma Theta Sor; Nat Asn Advan Colored People; Nat Asn Young C; APGA; Tex Coalition Black Democrats; Eastern Star. **Special Achievements:** First woman and the first black woman to serve on the Waco City Council. **Home Addr:** 1604 Harrison Ave, Waco, TX 76704. **Business Addr:** Field Representative, General Land Office-State of Texas, 1700 N Congress Ave, Austin, TX 78701-1495.

## JONES, MARION (MARION JONES-THOMPSON)

Athlete. **Personal:** Born Oct 12, 1975, Los Angeles, CA; daughter of George and Marion; married CJ Hunter; children: 1; married Obadele Thompson; children: Monty, Amir & Eva-Marie; married Tim Montgomery; children: Tim Jr. **Educ:** Univ NC, attended 1997. **Career:** Athlete (retired), basketball player; USA track & field inc, track & field athlete, 2003; Tulsa Shock, 2010-11.

## JONES, MARKEYSIA DONTA

Football player, football coach. **Personal:** Born Aug 27, 1972, Washington, DC; son of Thomas; children: Tavia Moore. **Educ:** Univ Nebr, BA, acct & bus admin, 1994. **Career:** Football player (retired), football coach, coordinator; Pittsburgh Steelers, 1995, linebacker, 1996-98; Carolina Panthers, 1999-2000; New Orleans Saints, 2000-01; Chicago Bears, 2005; Skyhawks, coach; Providence High Sch, coach; Golden Bulls, defensive backs & spec teams coordr, 2009-. **Honors/Awds:** First-Team All-Big Eight, AP, Coaches, 1994; Nebr co-weight lifter of the Year, 1993; Nebr Lifter of the Year, 1994; Nebraska Football Hall of Fame Inductee, 2007. **Business Addr:** Special Teams Coordinator, Golden Bulls, 100 Beatties Ford Rd, Charlotte, NC 28216, **Business Phone:** (704)378-1000.

## JONES, MARSHA REGINA

Journalist. **Personal:** Born Jan 26, 1962, Brooklyn, NY; daughter of Iona Louisa Williams and Eudolphin; married Donald Collins; children: Hollis Danielle. **Educ:** Nazareth Col, Advan Placement Courses Span, 1980; Purdue Univ, BA, jour/span, 1984. **Career:** Purdue Exponent Newspaper, reporter, 1981-83; Purdue Reports Mag, reporter, 1983-84; Black Cult Ctr Newspaper, reporter, 1983-84; About Time Mag, ed asst/reporter 1984-88, asst ed, 1988-89; Proj KID, commun consult, 1988-90; SUNY Brockport, NY, mktg commun mgr, 1989-93; Rochester Bus Mag, Rochester, NY, contrib ed, 1989-93; Roc Live/After Dark, host/producer, 1991; Rochester Metro Challenger, contrib ed, columnist, 1991-; Rochester Mus & Sci News, contrib ed, 1992; Communicator, Rochester Assn Black Communicators, ed, 1993; Hillside C's Ctr, pub rels coordr, 1993-95; Scene Entertainment Weekly, contrib ed, 1995-97; Camp Good Days & Spec Times, dir commun, 1995-96; Planned Parenthood, mktg commun coord, 1997-. **Orgs:** Soc Prof Journalists, 1980-, Nat Asn Black Journalists, 1988-, E HS Ebony Cult Club; Black Scholars Mentor Prog Urban League Rochester NY Inc, 1985-89; Black Scholars Alumni Comm Urban League Rochester Inc, 1985-89; Amer Red Cross Minority Screening Campaign Comm, 1985-88; Village Gate Theater, 1985-88; 1986, sec, 1991, Rochester Assoc Black Communicators; Rochester Purdue Alumni Assoc; bd mem, R Nelson Mandela Scholar Fund, 1989-93; SUNY Brockport Fac Senate, 1990-91; City Newspaper Ed Adv Bd, 1990-93; vpres, Montgomery Neighborhood Ctr Youth Adv Bd, 1990-93; Rochester Asn Black Communicators Film Festival, 1991; Rochester asn Black Communicators, pres, 1992-94; Guyanese Am Asn, 1992; United Negro Col Fund Commn, 1992; Boys & Girls Club Rochester, bd dir, 1994-, Bowl-a-thon Commt, 1993-95; Hillside's Working Together Team, 1993-95; Bill Klein's 13th Ann Acad Awards Comt, publicity chair, 1995-; Hillside Art Diversity Proj, co-chair, 1995; Asn Women Commun. **Home Addr:** 97 Culver Pkwy, Rochester, NY 14609-4548, **Home Phone:** (716)288-6661.

## JONES, MARVIN MAURICE

Football player. **Personal:** Born Jun 28, 1972, Miami, FL; married Alexsandra; children: Maya, Daryl & Marvin M Jr. **Educ:** Charter Oak State Col, BS & AS; Inst Natural Healing, dipl coun & dipl herbal med; Fla State Univ, BS, psychol. **Career:** Football player (retired); New York Jets, linebacker, 1993, mid linebacker, 1994-96, 2001-03, right inside line backer, 1997-2000, linebacker, 2000. **Orgs:** Founder, Marvin Jones Charitable Found. **Honors/Awds:** Rotary-Lombardi Award, 1992; Dick Butkus Award, 1992; College Football Player of the Year, 1992; Florida State Hall of Fame, 2000; First team All-Pro selection, 2000. **Home Addr:** , Fort Myers, FL.

## JONES, MAXINE

Singer, songwriter, actor. **Personal:** Born Jan 16, 1962, Paterson, NJ; children: Maya. **Career:** En Vogue, mem group, 1988-2001, 2004-; Albums: Born to Sing, 1990; Remix to Sing, 1991; Funky Divas, 1992; Run away love, 1993; Give It Up, Turn It Loose, 1993; Whatta Man, 1994; Don't Let Go (Love) 1996; Whatever, 1997; Too Gone, Too Long, 1997; Riddle, 2000; Greatest Hits, 1998; EV3, 1997; Gift Of Xmas, 2002; Soul Flower, 2004; Essentials, 2005; Hold On & Other Hits, 2005, TBA, 2009; Do You See Me Now, 2014. Singles: "Hold On"; "Lies"; "Free Your Mind"; "This Is Your Life"; "My Lovin' (You're Never Gonna Get It)"; "Desire"; "Yesterday"; "Didn't I", 2014. Films: Batman Forever, 1995; TV: "A Different World", 1993; "Roc", 1993; "Saturday Night Live", 1997. **Orgs:** R&b Group En Vague. **Honors/Awds:** Born to Sing, platinum, 1990.

**JONES, MEJEKE K MAURICE. See JONES, K. MAURICES.**

## JONES, DR. MEREDITH J.

Government official. **Personal:** Born Mar 24, 1948, Hartford, CT; daughter of Cyril J and Rose Randolph. **Educ:** Swarthmore Col, BA, 1968; Yale Law Sch, JD, 1974. **Career:** Chickering & Gregory, partner, 1983-86; Bechtel Financing Serv Inc, srcoun, 1986-93; Nat Oceanic & Atmospheric Admin, gen coun, 1993-94; Fed Community Comn, Cable Serv Bur Fed Commun Comn, chief, 1994; New York Econ Develop Corp, exec vpres & gen coun, currently. **Orgs:** Asn Bar City NY; Fed Commun Bar Asn; Nat Asn Minorities Cable. **Business Addr:** General Counsel, New York City Economic Development Corporation, 110 William St, New York, NY 10038, **Business Phone:** (212)227-5500.

## JONES, MERLAKIA KENYATTA

Basketball player. **Personal:** Born Jul 21, 1973, Montgomery, AL; daughter of George and Jacqueline. **Educ:** Univ Fla, attended 1995; Old Dom Univ, attended 1996. **Career:** Basketball player (retired); Santaram, Port, 1996-97; Cleveland Rockers, guard, 1997-2003; Detroit Shock, guard, 2004. **Orgs:** Prof Women's Sports Orgn. **Home Addr:** 5001 Paddock Club Ct Apt N, Montgomery, AL 36116-4231.

## JONES, DR. MICHAEL ANDREA

Clergy. **Personal:** Born Aug 6, 1937, Atlanta, GA; married Linda; children: Gattie. **Educ:** Ga State Univ, BA; Atlanta Univ, MA; Am Univ, ED. **Career:** Morris Brown Col, dir; Mitchell Chapel Church, pastor. **Orgs:** Soc Christian Leadership, 1959-; Am Christian Atlanta Asn Educrs; GA Asn Educrs; Atlanta Christian Coun, 1975-; GA Coun Christians, 1977-; Soc Christian Leadership Conf; United Youth Adult Conf; Nat Asn Advan Colored People. **Home Addr:** 1461 Ezra Church Dr NW, Atlanta, GA 30314-2103, **Home Phone:** (770)987-5728. **Business Addr:** Pastor, Fayetteville Parish AME, PO Box 430, Fayetteville, GA 30214.

## JONES, MICHAEL ANTHONY

Football player, football coach. **Personal:** Born Apr 15, 1969, Kansas City, MO; married Leslie; children: Taelor, Moriah & Ashley. **Educ:** Univ Mo, attended 1991. **Career:** Football player (retired), football coach; Los Angeles Raiders, 1991-92; linebacker, 1993-94; Oakland Raiders, right linebacker, 1995-96, 2002; St Louis Rams, left linebacker, 1997-98, linebacker, 1999-2000; Pittsburgh Steelers, linebacker, 2001-02; Growth Play Bk, speaker, 2005-06; Michael Jones Enterprises, owner, 2003-07; Hazelwood E High Sch, coach, head coach, 2008; Southern Univ, linebackers coach, 2010; Lincoln Univ, Jefferson City, Mo, head football coach, currently; JRDKS, owner. **Orgs:** Founder, Michael Jones Found, 1995; pres, Fundraiser Not-for-Profits, 2005-07. **Honors/Awds:** Carl Ekern Award; Ed Block Courage Award; Super Bowl XXXIV Champion; World Bowl II Champion. **Business Addr:** Head Football Coach, Lincoln University, 202 Jason Gym, Jefferson City, MO 65102, **Business Phone:** (573)681-5957.

## JONES, DR. MICHAEL BOZELLY

Physician. **Personal:** Born Aug 17, 1969, Reynolds, GA; son of Leroy and Minnie. **Educ:** Morris Brown Col, BS, 1992; Med Col Ga Sch Med, MD, 1996. **Career:** Emory Univ, resident psychiat, 1996-97; Mercer Univ, resident internalmed, 1997-2000; La State Univ, fel, 2005-08. **Orgs:** Am Med Asn, 1999-; Nat Med Asn, 1999-; APA, 1991-. **Honors/Awds:** US Achievement Academy Natural Sciences Honor Award, 1991. **Home Addr:** 2010 Oak Creek Rd Apt 344, New Orleans, LA 70123, **Home Phone:** (504)733-5769. **Business Addr:** Associate, Doctor Care Llc, 3840 St Bernard Ave, New Orleans, LA 70122, **Business Phone:** (504)283-4182.

## JONES, MICHAEL DAVID

Football player. **Personal:** Born Aug 25, 1969, Columbia, SC; married Javonda Floyd; children: Steven, Courtney, Mike Jr & Aja. **Educ:** NC State Univ, grad, 1991. **Career:** Football (retired); Phoenix Cardinals, defensive end, 1991, 1993, left defensive end, right defensive end, 1992; New Eng Patriots, right defensive end, 1994, defensive end, 1995, left defensive end, 1996-97; St Louis Rams, right defensive end, 1998; Tenn Titans, left defensive tackle, 1999. **Special Achievements:** TV Special: "1991 NFL Draft", 1991.

## JONES, MAJ. MICHELE S.

Army officer. **Personal:** Born Nov 24, 1962, Randallstown, MD; children: 2. **Educ:** Milford Mill Acad, grad; Fayetteville State Univ, BS, bus admin, MA, mgt & intl rels. **Career:** Command sgt major (retired), spec asst; USAR, staff, 1982, chief adv, squad leader, sect leader, platoon sgt, first sgt, nineth command sgt maj, 2002-07; Secy Defense, spec asst, 2009-. **Honors/Awds:** Meritorious Service Award, Nat Asn Advan Colored People, 2003; Legion of Merit; Army Commendation Medal; Army Achievement Medal; Good Conduct Medal; National Defense Service Medal; Armed Forces Reserve Medal; Spirit of Democracy Award, Nat Coalition Black Civic Participation, 2009. **Special Achievements:** First female selected as class president at the US Sergeants Major Academy; First Female to serve as a division CSM; First Woman to serve as the CSM of any of the Armys Components, Active or Reserve. **Business Addr:** Command Sergeant Major, US Army Reserve, 2400 Army Pentagon Suite 2B548, Washington, DC 20310-2400, **Business Phone:** (703)697-1784.

## JONES, MICHELE WOODS

School administrator, consultant. **Personal:** Born Oct 3, 1945, Los Angeles, CA; daughter of David A Francis and Mary Ellen Harris; married Reginald L; children: Sjaun & Leasa. **Educ:** Phoenix Col, AA, 1965; Univ Calif, Berkeley, BA, hist, 1969, grad study, hist, 1970; Calif State Univ, Hayward, MS, educ psychol, 1979. **Career:** School adminstrator (retired), consultant; Univ Calif, Berkeley, co-dir spec summer proj, 1968, Educ Opportunity Prog, counr, 1968-70, tutorial staff coordr, 1970-72, counr coordr, 1972-73, Stud Info Ctr, asst dir, 1973-77, Stud Learning Ctr, asst dir, 1977-81, prin stud affairs officer, 1981-83, dir stud activ & servs, 1983-89, asst to vice chancellor & staffombuds person, 1989-91; Newport News Sch Dist, consult; City Hampton Social Servs Multicultural Comun & Prob Solving, consult; Cobb & Henry Publishers, pres; Transp, Sentara Hampton Gen Hosp, consult; Va Dept Transp, Hampton Rd region, fical tech, sr, sr consult, currently. **Orgs:** Pres, sec, Alpha Kappa Alpha sorority, 1967-; campus liaison, Black Alumni Club, Univ Calif, Berkeley, 1969-; bd dir, Calif Alumni Asn, Univ Calif; Asn Black Psychologists; Educ Res Coun, 1979-; adv bd, Ctr Study, Educ & Advan Women, Univ Calif, Berkeley; hon mem, Golden Key Nat Hon Soc, 1985; hon mem, Delta Delta Delta sorority, 1986; Nat Asn Stud Personnel Admin; Nat Orientation Dir Asn; Soroptomist Int; Univ & Col Ombudsman Asn, 1989-; bd dir, Nat Asn Black Pub Sch Admin, 1990-; prog dir, Hampton Chap, Jack & Jill Am; Int Personnel Mgt Asn; Nat Conf Dialogue & Deliberation;

Peninsula Aids Found; Red Cross; Contact Response, Rape Coun Ctr; Hampton Ecumenical Lodgings & Provisions; bd dir, Calif Alumni Asn; Jr League Hampton Roads. **Home Addr:** 13685 Campus Dr, Oakland, CA 94605, **Home Phone:** (510)562-9962. **Business Addr:** Senior Consultant, Virginia Department of Transportation, 1401 E Broad St, Richmond, VA 23219, **Business Phone:** (804)786-5128.

### JONES, MICHELLE
Financial manager, secretary (government). **Personal:** Born May 10, 1954, Columbus, OH; daughter of Ralph and Ora. **Educ:** Ohio State Univ, attended 1975; Columbus State County Col, attended 1983. **Career:** Columbus Pub Sch, secy, 1974-83; United Way Franklin County, secy, 1983-85, commun coord, 1985-. **Orgs:** Women Commun Inc, 1985-87; Youth Advocate Serv, 1988-91. **Home Addr:** 1450 Forest St, Columbus, OH 43206, **Home Phone:** (614)258-4075. **Business Addr:** Communications Coordinator, United Way Franklin County, 360 S 3rd St, Columbus, OH 43215, **Business Phone:** (614)227-2784.

### JONES, MILTON H., JR.
Executive, chief financial officer. **Personal:** Born Jul 25, 1952, Atlanta, GA; son of Milton H Sr and Helen E; married Shelia Pitts; children: Milton C & Tiffany M. **Educ:** Univ Notre Dame, BBA, acct & admin, 1974. **Career:** Peat, Marwick, Mitchell & Co, 1974-77; Citizens & Southern Nat Bank, 1977-91; Nat Bank, exec vpres, 1991-, Dealer Financial Serv Group, pres, 1997; Techwood Pk Inc, chmn; Bank Am, chief financial officer, chief oper officer, global qual & productivity exec, 2003-06, pres, mid s region, 2000-03, global qual & productivity exec, 2003-06, global financial serv group exec, 2006-09, ga mkt pres, 2007-09; Blue Ridge Holdings, CertusBank, pres, chmn & chief exec officer, 2009-12, exec chmn, 2012-14. **Orgs:** Exec com, Leadership Atalanta; Leadership GEO, Class, 1992; chair, Tech wood Pk Inc; Metrop Atlanta YMCA; exec com, Southwest Atlanta YMCA; Atlanta Urban Bankers Asn; Salvation Army Boys & Girls Club, advcoun; adv bd, GEO Coun Child Abuse; chmn, bd, Atlanta Econ Dev Corp; bd, Atlanta Local Dev Corp; 100 Black Men Atlanta, 2003-, chmn, 2008-; Ga Coun Econ Educ Exec Comt; chmn, Bank Am Atlanta Football Classic; bd trustee, Meharry Med Col; United Negro Col Fund; Com Club Bd; Woodruff Arts Ctr Bd; Ga Res Alliance. **Home Addr:** 1353 High Falls Ct, Atlanta, GA 30311, **Home Phone:** (404)699-9182.

### JONES, MONIQUE
Administrator, association executive, executive. **Educ:** Georgetown Univ, BS, finance, 1987; Univ Calif, Anderson Sch Mgt, Los Angeles, CA, MBA, strategy & entertainment mgt, 1993. **Career:** Bankers Trust, staff auditor, 1987-89; Paine Webber, sr auditor, 1989-91; Poly Gram Filmed Entertainment, Bus Planning & Develop, dir, 1996-99; Myriad Pictures, Finance & Admin, vpres, 2000-03; Icon Entertainment Int, Finance & Admin, sr vpres, 2003-04; Sony Pictures Tv Int, exec dir finance, 2004-05; Sidney Kimmel Entertainment, vpres finance, controller, 2005-. **Business Addr:** Vice President, Controller, Sidney Kimmel Entertainment, 9460 Wilshire Blvd Fl 5, Beverly Hills, CA 90212-2711, **Business Phone:** (310)777-8818.

### JONES, NANCY REED
President (organization), executive, chief executive officer. **Personal:** Born Jun 15, 1928, Bamberg, SC; daughter of Aaron and Josie Bell; children: Pat Jernan Jones Hagood & Wendy. **Educ:** Temple Univ, attended 1956; Claflin Col, BS, 1958; SC State Col, MS, 1961; Univ SC, 1964. **Career:** Bamberg Co Bd Educ, 1948-80; Nat Testing Serv, 1977-78; Ga Bd Educ, Augusta, 1979-89; Victoria Slipper Retail & Mfg Co, pres, founder & chief exec officer, 1985-. **Orgs:** Union Baptist Chruch; Am Educ Asn; Am Guid Asn; dir guid, Bamberg Ehrhardt High Sch; pres, Pastors Aid Club. **Home Addr:** 6112 Carolina Hwy, Denmark, SC 29042, **Home Phone:** (803)793-4850. **Business Addr:** Chief Executive Officer, President, Victoria Slipper Retail & Manufacturing Co, 119 Palmelto Ave, Denmark, SC 29042, **Business Phone:** (803)793-5719.

### JONES, NASIR (NASIR BIN OLU DARA JONES)
Rap musician. **Personal:** Born Sep 14, 1973, Queensbridge, NY; son of Olu Dara and Fannie Ann (deceased); married Kelis; children: Knight. **Career:** Albums: Illmatic, 1994; It Was Written, 1996; The Firm: The Album, 1997; I Am, Nastradamus, 1999; QB's Finest, 2000; Stillmatic, 2001; From Illmatic to Stillmatic: The Remixes, The Lost Tapes, 2002; Street's Disciple, 2004; Hip Hop Is Dead, 2006; Greatest Hits, 2007; Untitled, 2008; Distant Relatives, 2009; Life Is Good, 2011; Season of Nasir, 2014. Films: Belly, actor & writer, 1998; In Too Deep, 1999, Ticker, Sacred Is the Flesh, actor, writer & exec producer, 2001; God's Son, 2002; Uptown Girls, 2003; Vapors, 2009; Black Nativity, 2010. TV series: "Me and Mr. Jones", exec producer, 2007; "Hawaii Five-0", 2010. Songs: "Halftime", 1992; "It Ain't Hard to Tell", "The WorldIs Yours", 1994; "If I Ruled the World", 1996; "Nas Is Like", "Hate Me Now", 1999; "One Mic", "Made You Look", 2002; "I Can", 2003; "Thief's Theme", 2004; "Just a Moment", 2005; "Hip Hop Is Dead", 2006; "Can't Forget About You", 2007; Ill Will Rec, founder. **Honors/Awds:** Youth Summit Award, Hip Hop Youth Summit, 2002; I Am Hip-Hop Icon Award, 2006. **Special Achievements:** Launched clothing line Esco. **Business Addr:** Rap Artist, c/o Sony Music Entertainment, 550 Madison Ave, New York, NY 10022, **Business Phone:** (212)833-8000.

### JONES, NATHANIEL, SR.
Government official. **Personal:** Born Oct 3, 1948, New Orleans, LA; married Brenda; children: Natalie, Nathaniel & Natash. **Educ:** Southern Univ, BA, archit, 1973. **Career:** King Triumph BC, mem, 1969; Southern Univ Recreation Club, vpres, 1970-72; Prince Hall Masons, mem, 1973; Lutcher & Gramercy Jaycees, mem, 1984; Am Drafting Serv, owner, 1994-. **Orgs:** Rive Parishes Improv League, 1972; chmn, Bldg & Planning Comn, 1975 & 1981; bd dirs, La Black Music Asn Caucus, 1982, 1983; United Steel Workers Am; La Munic Asn; Nat League Cities, 1983; Lutcher - Gramercy Jaycees, 1984; dist coordr, Nat Black Caucus LEO, 1984; Nat Asn Advan Colored People. **Honors/Awds:** Worked Summer Youth in Drug Prog, 1985; Nat Asn Minority Architects. **Home Addr:** 2596 N Courseault St, PO Box 172 275, Lutcher, LA 70071. **Business Addr:** Owner, American Drafting Service, 2902 St Roch St, New Orleans, LA 70122, **Business Phone:** (504)259-6302.

### JONES, NATHANIEL JAMAL
Executive. **Personal:** Born Jan 14, 1967, Memphis, TN; son of Fred and Naomi; married Jeanette. **Educ:** Tenn State Univ, BS, bus admin. **Career:** Int Paper, acct, 1992-94; Mid-S Coliseum, acct, 1994-96; Summitt Mgt, prod mgr, currently; Star Entertainment, pres, currently. **Honors/Awds:** Tenn State Univ, Alumni Award, 1998. **Business Addr:** Manager, Summitt Management, 4466 Elvis Presley Blvd, Memphis, TN 38116, **Business Phone:** (901)398-6655.

### JONES, NATHANIEL R.
Administrator, judge, lawyer. **Personal:** Born May 13, 1926, Youngstown, OH; married Lillian Graham Hawthorne; children: Stephanie J, William L Hawthorne, Ricky B Hawthorne, Marc D Hawthorne & Pamela L Velez. **Educ:** Youngstown Univ, BA, 1951, LLB, 1956. **Career:** Judge (retired), sr coun; Fair Employ Prac Comn, Ohio, exec dir, 1956-59; pvt pract atty, 1959-60; US Atty Northern Dist, Ohio, asst, 1960-67; Nat Asn Advan Colored People, gen coun, 1969-79; US Attny No Dist OH, asst attny; US Ct Appeals Sixth Circuit, judge, 1979-2002; Blank Rome LLP, sr coun, sr partner, currently; Univ Cinn, adj prof, currently; Case Western Res Sch Law, adj prof, currently; Cleveland State Univ Sch Law, adj prof, currently. **Orgs:** Asst gen coun, Comt Civil Dis, 1967-68; co-chmn, Civilian-Mil Task Force Mil Justice, 1972; co-chair, Cincinnati Bar Asn/Black Lawyers Asn Cincinnati Round Table; adv Comt mem, Urban Morgan Int Human Rights Inst; Potter Stewart Inn Ct; Am Bar Asn; chair, Am Bar Asn Africa Law Initiative; Comn Opportunities Minorities Profession; Am Arbit Asn; Nat Bar Asn; Fed Bar Asn; Ohio State Bar Asn; Cincinnati Bar Asn; Mahoning County Bar Asn; Alpha Delta Boule, Sigma Pi Phi Fraternity; Buckeye Lodge IBPOE; 33rd Degree United Supreme Coun; Kappa Alpha Psi Fraternity; Metrop Club, Covington, KY; bd dir, Am Const Soc; hon co-chair, Nat Underground Rr Freedom Ctr; exec dir, Fair Employ Practices Comn; bd dir, Cincinnati Youth Collab; bd dirs, KnowledgeWorks Found; Bd Trustees, Legal Aid Soc Greater Cincinnati; bd trustees, Southern Africa Legal Serv Found. **Honors/Awds:** Named a "Great Living Cincinnatian", 1997; Inducted, Nat Bar Asn Hall of Fame, 2002; Ohio Bar Medal Award, Ohio State Bar Asn, 2003; Award of Excellence, Thurgood Marshall Scholarship, 2004; Headed three-man team which investigated grievances of black servicemen in W Ger; Metropolitan Club Award, 2005; Annual Fellows Award, Am Bar Asn Young Lawyers Div, 2005. **Special Achievements:** First African American appointed as assistant US Attorney for the Northern District of Ohio, Cleveland, 1962. **Home Addr:** 201 E 5th St, Cincinnati, OH 45202, **Home Phone:** (513)362-8700. **Business Addr:** Senior Counsel, Chief Diversity and Inclusion Officer, Blank Rome LLP, 1700 PNC Ctr 201 E 5th St, Cincinnati, OH 45202, **Business Phone:** (513)362-8772.

### JONES, NATHANIEL R.
Judge, college teacher, lawyer. **Personal:** Born May 12, 1926, Youngstown, OH; son of Nathaniel Beacon and Lillian Brown; married Lillian Hawthorne; children: 4. **Educ:** Youngstown State Univ, AB, 1951, LLB, 1956. **Career:** Pvt law pract, 1957-60; Fair Employ Practices Comn, lawyer, 1960; U.S. Atty Northeastern Dist Ohio, 1960-67; Nat Adv Comn Civil Dis, asst gen coun, 1967; NAACP gen coun, 1969-79; U.S. Ct Appeals, sr judge, 1979-2002; Blank & Rome LLP, partner, 2003-; taught law at Univ Cincinnati Col Law, N Carolina Cent Univ Col Law & Harvard Univ Law Sch. **Orgs:** ABA Coalition Racial & Ethnic Justice, Am Bar Asn, Am Inns Ct, Black Lawyers Asn Cincinnati, BRIDGES a Just Community, Fed Bar Asn, KnowledgeWorks Found, Legal Aid Soc Cincinnati, Marvin Lewis Community Fund, Nat Bar Asn, Ohio State Bar Asn, Soteni Int, Cincinnati Bar Asn, & Cincinnati Youth Collab; mem bd, Knowledge Works Found; mem bd, Marvin Lewis Community Fund; mem bd, Metrop Club; mem bd, Nat Underground Rr Freedom Ctr; mem bd, Cincinnati Mus Ctr Found; adv bd mem, Soteni Int; adv bd mem, Urban Morgan Inst Human Rights; adv bd mem, Toyota Motor Mfg N Am, Inc, diversity bd, 2002-14. **Honors/Awds:** National Bar Association Hall of Fame, inductee, 2002; Ohio Bar Medal Award, Ohio State Bar Association, 2003; Award of Excellence, Thurgood Marshall Scholarship Fund, 2005; Annual Fellows Award, American Bar Association's Young Lawyers Division, 2005; Trailblazer Award, Just the Beginning Foundation, 2006; Lifetime Achievement Award, The American Lawyer, 2007; Laurel Wreath Award, Kappa Alpha Psi Fraternity, 2009; Ohio Civil Rights Hall of Fame, inductee, 2010; Charles Hamilton Houston Medallion of Merit, Washington Bar Association, 2011; Ohio Civil Rights Hall of Fame, inductee, 2011; Changing the Odds Award, Children's Defense Fund, 2012; Pillar of Justice Award, Federal Bar Association, 2014; Spingarn Medal, 2016; International Freedom Conductor Award, National Underground Railroad Freedom Center, 2016. 19 honorary degrees. **Special Achievements:** Led national efforts to end school segregation and defend affirmative action; observer of first democratic elections in South Africa, 1993; Congress renamed H.J. Res. 2 the Nathaniel R. Jones Federal Building and U.S. Courthouse, Youngstown, OH, 2003. Author, Answering the Call: A Memoir of the Modern Struggle to End Racial Discrimination in America, 2016. **Business Addr:** Blank and Rome LLP, 1700 PNC Ctr, Cincinnati, OH 45202, **Business Phone:** (513)362-8772.

### JONES, NETTIE PEARL
Writer, school administrator, educator. **Personal:** Born Jan 1, 1941, Arlington, GA; daughter of Delonia Mears Whorton and Benjamin Delonia Mears Whorton; children: Lynne Cheryl Harris. **Educ:** Wayne State Univ, Detroit, MI, BS, sec educ, 1963; Marygrove Col, Detroit, MI, MEd, reading, 1972; Fashion Inst Technol, New York, NY, advert & communs, 1976. **Career:** Detroit Bd Educ, Detroit, Mich, teacher sec social studies, eng, reading, 1963-72; Royal George Sch, Greenfield Pk, Que, teacher sec eng, 1966-68; Martin Luther King Sch, New York, NY, teacher reading, 1971-72; Wayne State Univ, Detroit, Mich, lectr, vis writer, 1986-87; Chmn Wayne Co Comnr, Detroit, Mich, writer, 1988; Wayne Co Community Col, Detroit, Mich, teacher devel reading, 1988; Mich Technol Univ, Houghton, Mich, asst prof, writer residence, 1988-89, minority affairs asst vpres, 1989; NY Univ, Gallatin Sch Individualized Study, fac, currently; Boricua Col, fac; Montclair State Univ, fac; Essex Co Col, fac; City Univ New Yorks Medgar Evers Col, fac. Novels: Fish Tales, 1984; Mischief Makers, 1989 & 1991. **Orgs:** Detroit Women Writers, 1985; Am Asn Univ Prof, 1986. **Home Addr:** 62 Moss, Highland Park, MI 48203, **Home Phone:** (313)869-0221. **Business Addr:** Faculty, Gallatin School of Individualized Study, 22 Wash Sq N, New York, NY 10003, **Business Phone:** (212)998-7370.

### JONES, DR. NINA F.
School administrator. **Personal:** Born Jul 30, 1918, Madison, GA; daughter of Hallie (Hall) and Sumner L; married William M; children: William M Jr & Steven L. **Educ:** Cent Youth Men's Christian Asn Col, AB, 1938; Chicago Teachers Col, MEd, 1942; Loyola Univ, Chicago, EdD, 1975. **Career:** School administrator (retired); Chicago Public Schs, teacher, 1942, asst prin, 1959-65, prin, 1966-69, dist supt, 1969-75, asst supt personnel, 1975-83, sec bd examrs, 1983-88. **Orgs:** Alpha Kappa Alpha Sorority, 1940; Alpha Gamma Pi Sorority, 1967; Pi Lambda Theta. **Home Addr:** 9156 S Constance, Chicago, IL 60617, **Home Phone:** (773)768-3544.

### JONES, NOLAN E.
Educator, government official. **Personal:** Born Dec 11, 1944, Houston, TX; son of Ernest and Hester Neal Ross. **Educ:** Tex Southern Univ, Houston, BA, 1968; Swarthmore Col, PA, post baccalaureate, 1969; Wash Univ, St Louis, MO, MA, 1973, PhD, polit sci, 1975. **Career:** Univ Mich, Ann Arbor, Mich, asst prof, polit sci, 1973-80; NCLS, Human Resources Comt, Wash, DC, comt dir, 1978-, group dir, 1995-2003, Nat Govs Asn, dep dir, off fed rels, currently. **Orgs:** Secy, Nat Conf Black Polit Scientist, 1976-78; dep dir, Nat Gov Asn, 1978-2008; secy, Allen Adams Fed Credit Union, 1989-92; coun mem, Am Polit Sci Asn, 1990-92; Nat Guard Youth Found, 1999-; Nat Ctr State Courts Res Adv Coun; Nat Crime Prev Coun; Nat Capitol Area Polit Sci; chmn, Ctr Child Protection & Family Support; Human resource group, group dir; staff dir, Nat Gov Asn Force Alchol & Drug Abuse; gov coun, Am Polit Sci. **Home Addr:** 1033 Michigan Ave NE, Washington, DC 20017-1848, **Home Phone:** (202)529-9089. **Business Addr:** Deputy Director, National Governors Association, 444 N Capitol St NW Suite 267, Washington, DC 20001-1512, **Business Phone:** (202)624-5360.

### JONES, ORLANDO
Actor, writer, television producer. **Personal:** Born Apr 10, 1968, Mobile, AL; married Jacqueline Staph; children: 1. **Educ:** Col Charleston, attended 1990. **Career:** Actor, writer, currently; A Different World, writer & actor, 1987-88; RocLive, exec story editor, 1993; The Sinbad Show, producer, 1993; Sound fx, host, 1994; Mad TV, actor & segment writer, 1995-97. Actor: Herman's Head, 1991; King of the Hill, 1997; In Harm's Way, 1997; Sour Grapes, 1998; Woo, 1998; Office Space, 1999; Liberty Heights, 1999; Magnolia, 1999; Waterproof, 1999; New Jersey Turnpikes, 1999; From Dusk Till Dawn 3: The Hangman's Daughter, 2000; The Replacements, 2000; Bedazzled, 2000; Double Take, 2001; Say It Isn't So, 2001; Evolution, 2001; Tortoise Vs Hare, 2002; The Time Machine, 2002; Drumline, 2002; Biker Boyz, 2003; The Runaway Jury, 2003; House of D, 2004; LA Rush, 2005; Looking for Sunday, 2006; Looking for Sunday, 2006; Primeval, 2007; Meridian, 2012; Enemies Closer, 2013; The Devil and the Deep Blue Sea, forthcoming, 2016. TV Series: "Girlfriends", 2003; "Father of the Pride", 2004-05; "The Evidence", 2006; "The Adventures of Chico & Guapo", 2006; "Everybody Hates Chris", 2007; "Men in Trees", 2007; "Ghost Whisperer", 2007; "Everybody Hates Chris", 2007-08; "Untitled Victoria Pile Project", 2008; "New Amsterdam", 2008; "Misconceptions", 2008; "Black Poker Stars Invitational", 2008; "Pushing Daisies", 2008; "Rules of Engagement", 2009; "House M.D", 2010; "CSI: Miami", 2011; "Necessary Roughness", 2011; "Identity", 2011; "Sleepy Hollow", 2013-15. Writer: "A Different World", 1991; Roc, 1992; "The Sinbad Show", 1994; "Mad TV", 1995; "The Orlando Jones Show", 2003; "The Adventures of Chico & Guapo", 2006; "Bufu", 2007; Primeval, 2007; I Think I Love My Wife, 2007; Beyond a Reasonable Doubt, 2009; Cirque du Freak: The Vampire's Assistant, 2009; Producer: "The Sinbad Show", 1994; "The Orlando Jones Show", 2003; The Music Lesson, 2009; Seconds Apart, 2011; The Chicago 8, 2011; United Talent Agency, owner, currently. **Business Addr:** Owner, Actor, United Talent Agency, 9560 Wilshire Blvd 5th Fl, Beverly Hills, CA 90212, **Business Phone:** (310)273-6700.

### JONES, PATRICIA KAY SPEARS
Arts administrator, educator, poet. **Personal:** Born Feb 11, 1951, Forrest City, AR; daughter of Lee and Lillie B Dodd. **Educ:** Rhodes Col, BA, commun, 1973; Vt Col, MFA, 1992. **Career:** Poet & writer, 1974-; Millay Colony, the Va Ctr for the Creative Arts, Bread Loaf & Squaw Valley Community Writers, fel; Samuel Fr Inc, mgr amateur leasing, 1974-77; Heliotrope Lit Mag, contrib ed, 1975-2000; WB Mag, ed, 1975; Coord Coun Lit Mag, grants progs dir, 1977-81; Freelance journalist: Essence, Village Voice, Poetry Proj Newsletter, 1978-; Heresies Colctive Inc, managing coordr, 1982-83; Poetry Proj St Mark's Church, prog coordr, 1984-86; Mass Coun Arts & Humanities, prog specialist, 1987-89; Film News Now Educ, prog dir, 1990-91; New Mus Contemp Art, develop assoc, 1992-94, dir planning develop, 1994-96; Auth Read Aloud, proj dir & consult, 1996-98; Breadloaf, fel, 1996; VIR Ctr Creative Arts, resident, 1996; Millay Colony Arts, resident, 1998; Local Initiatives Support Corp, develop officer, 1998-; Cent Harlem Br, New York Pub Libr, fac; Naropa Univ, fac; New Sch Univ, Sarah Lawrence Col, fac; BOMB mag, ed; LaGuardia Community Col; Queens Col; New Sch; Col New Rochelle; Parsons Sch Design & Poetry, teacher, currently. Poems: The Weather That Kills, 1995; Best American Poetry, 2000; Femme du Monde, 2006; Black Nature: Four Centuries of African American Nature Poetry, 2009; Painkiller, 2010; Angles of Ascent: A Norton Anthology of Contemporary African American Poetry, 2013. **Orgs:** Vpres, Nat Asn Third World Writers, 1979-82; consult, CCLM, 1981; dir, Mabou Mines, 1984-86; Poetry Soc Am, 1984-, NY Asn Black Journalists, 1985-86; panelist, New York Found Arts, 1986, 1993 & 2003; bd dir, Poetry Proj, 1991; juror, Judith's Room Emerging & Outstanding Women Poets Ser, 1991; fel poetry, Nat Endowment Arts, 1994; Found Contemp Performance Arts, 1996; PEN Am Ctr; Authors Guild; Poets House Friends Comm; panelist, Lit Prog, NY Coun Arts, 1993-94; judge, Pen Poetry Transl Prize, 2002; St. Mark's Church, prog coordr; sr fel, Black Earth Inst; grants, Nat Endowment Arts & New York Found Arts; New York Community Trust. **Home Addr:** 216 Macon St Apt 9, Brooklyn, NY 11216-2425, **Home Phone:** (718)399-2356. **Business Addr:** Devel-

opment Officer, Local Initiatives Support Corp (LISC), 501 7th Ave, New York, NY 10018, **Business Phone:** (212)455-9800.

### JONES, PATRICIA YVONNE
President (organization), government official. **Personal:** Born Oct 22, 1956, Muskegon, MI; daughter of Theo and Juanita Henry; children: Dwayne. **Educ:** Muskegon Community Col, practical nursing dipl, 1978, AS, 1978; Grand Valley State Col. **Career:** Hackley Hosp & Med Ctr, lic prac nurse II, 1978-; City Muskegon Heights, council woman; Muskegon County Brd Commissioners. **Orgs:** Mich Lic Practical Nurse Asn, 1978; Nat Asn Advan Colored People, 1981; bd mem, Muskegon Community Col Adv Bd, 1982; Harriet J Cole Order EasternStars, 1983; gen mem, Nat Black Caucus Local Elected Off, 1983; gen mem, Muskegon Heights Bd Com, 1984; vpres, Muskegon Black Women Polit Caucus, treas, 1990-, vpres, 1992; pres, Mich Women Munic Govt, 1990, pres-elect, 1993; pres, 2400 Reynolds Block Club 1990-; Muskegon Heights Econ Develop, 1990-; Muskegon County Black Womens Caucus. **Home Addr:** 3004 Sanford St, Muskegon Heights, MI 49444, **Home Phone:** (616)739-5370.

### JONES, PAUL E.
College administrator, dean (education). **Educ:** MBA. **Career:** Durham Tech Community Col, dean corp educ & coordr continuing educ, currently. **Business Addr:** Dean of Corporate Education, Coordinator, Durham Technical Community College, 1637 E Lawson St, Durham, NC 27703-5023, **Business Phone:** (919)969-3032.

### JONES, DR. PERCY ELWOOD
Physician, pathologist. **Personal:** Born Jun 25, 1940, Richmond, VA; married Nora; children: Sabrina & Christopher. **Educ:** Va Union Univ, attended 1961; Meharry Med Col, MD, 1968; Am Bd Path, dipl. **Career:** Va Commonwealth Univ Health Syst, resident, anat & clin path, 1968-73; L Richardson Memorial Hosp, chief staff, pathologist; Path Lab Kindred Hosp, med dir; pvt pract physician, currently. **Orgs:** Am Soc Clin Pathologists; Old N St Med Soc; Nat Med Asn; Kappa Alpha Psi Fraternity; Greensboro Med Soc; Guilford Co Med Soc; Hayes-Taylor YMCA; fel Col Am Pathologists; fel Am Soc Clin Pathologists; life mem, Nat Asn Advan Colored People; vchmn, Guilford County Bd Health; Am Bd Path. **Business Addr:** Physician, Private Practitioner, 1807 W Market St, Greensboro, NC 27403, **Business Phone:** (336)379-9816.

### JONES, PETER LAWSON
Lawyer, state government official, executive. **Personal:** Born Dec 23, 1952, Cleveland, OH; son of Charles Whitman and Margaret Diane Hoiston; married Lisa Payne; children: Ryan Charles, Leah Danielle & Evan Cooke. **Educ:** Harvard Col, BA, 1975; Harvard Law Sch, JD, 1980. **Career:** Hon Yvonne B Burke US House Rep, pres & leg aide, 1975-76; Carter-Mondale Pres Campaign, writer & spokesman, 1976; Carter-Mondale Transition Planning Group, transition officer, 1976-77; Off Intergovt Rels & Congional Affairs HUD, liaison officer, 1977; Dyke Col Cleveland Ohio, instr, 1980, 1983; Supreme Ct Ohio, law clerk, 1982-83; Ohio Works Co, pres, 1984-85; Shaker Heights, Ohio, vice mayor & councilman, 1984-91; grad, Leadership Cleveland Prog, 1985; Roetzel & Andress, partner & atty, currently; Cuyahoga County, comnr, 2002-. **Orgs:** Pres, bd trustee, Metrop Strategy Group; treas, Harvard Law Sch Asn Cleveland, 1986-, co-gen coun, 1995-; exec comn, Cuyahoga County Dem Party, 1986-; bd trustee, Ct Community Serv Agency; State Cent & Exec Comts, Ohio Dem Party; life mem, Cleveland Br Nat Asn Advan Colored People; bd trustee, Shaker Youth Baseball League; Mt Zion Congregational Church, UCC; adv bd, Shoes & Clothes Kids; adv bd, Sr Corps Retired Execs; Ohio State Bar Asn; Cleveland Bar Asn; Bd County Commissioners. **Honors/Awds:** Harvard Rhodes Scholar Nom; Harvard Nat Scholar; Paul Revere Frothingham Scholar; Currier House Sr Creativity Award; Meritorious Achievement Award, US Dept HUD, 1977, PUSH Excel Prog, 1981; Eastside Coalition Community Service Award, 1986; Inductee, Shaker Heights Alumni Asn Hall Fame, 1987; Outstanding Young Clevelander Pub Serv Jaycees, 1989; Black Hist Month Community Service Award, East Ohio Gas Co WZAK-FM, 1992; Good Neighbor Cert Appreciation, United Area Citizens Agency, 1992; Dem Year Award, Shaker Heights Dem Club, 1996; Emerging Polit Leaders Prog, 1997; Proj Interchange Israel Sem, 1998; Legislator of the Year Award, Ohio Sch Counrs Asn, 2000; Ohio Hunger Hero Award, Asn Second Harvest Food bank, 2000; Comn Award, Ctr Families & C Fathers & Families Together, 2000; Families First Award, Ctr Families & C, 2000; Cert Recognition, Northeast Ohio Breast Cancer Coalition, 2001; Greater Cleveland Lodging Council Politician of the Year Award, 2003; The American Association Bikur Cholim Hospital of Jerusalem International Brotherhood Award, 2004; Ohio Super Lawyer, Law & Politics Mag, 2004-06; National Organization of African-Americans in Housing Chairmans Award for Outstanding Public Service, 2005; National Black MBA Association, Cleveland/Northeast Ohio Chapter Community Impact Award, 2006; A Cultural Exchanges Louis Stokes Champion of Literacy Award, 2006; The Garrett Square Economic Development Corporation Outstanding Leadership Award, 2006; Association of Black Psychologists Community Service Award, 2006; Phi Beta Sigma Fraternity Inc, Gamma Alpha Sigma Chapter Black Male Image Award, 2007; The Blacks United in Local Government Leadership Award, 2007; Co-recipient of the Dominion, Strong Men and Women: Excellence in Leadership Program, Award, 2008; Liberian Association of Cleveland Distinguished Humanitarian Award, 2008. **Special Achievements:** First African-American nominated to run for lieutenant governor of the State of Ohio; "The Family Line" a full length play produced at Harvard Col 1975, Ohio Univ, 1976; staged reading at the E Cleveland Community Theater 1985; The only African American county commissioner in Ohio. **Home Addr:** 3532 Norwood Rd, Shaker Heights, OH 44122-4968, **Home Phone:** (216)561-8988. **Business Addr:** Commissioner, Cuyahoga County, 1219 Ont St 4th Fl, Cleveland, OH 44113, **Business Phone:** (216)443-7182.

### JONES, DR. PHILLIP ERSKINE
Educator. **Personal:** Born Oct 26, 1940, Chicago, IL; son of Dorothy R; married Jo Lavera Kennedy; children: Phyllis & Joel. **Educ:** Univ Iowa, BS, phys educ, 1963, MA, phys educ, 1967, PhD, stud develop & higher educ, 1975. **Career:** Flint Community Sch, Phys Educ & Psychol, teacher, 1967-79; Univ Iowa, coord educ opportunities prog, 1968-70, dir spec support serv, 1970-75, asst vpres & dir affirmative action, 1975-78, adj asst prof educ, 1975-78, assoc dean stud serv & adj asst prof educ, 1978-83, dean stud serv & adj asst prof educ, 1983-89, assoc vpres acad affairs & dean stud, 1989-97, vpres stud serv & dean students; US Ethnic Prof Exchange Prog W Ger, rep; Sister Cities Int; Carl Duisberg-Ges; Inst Auslandsbeziehungen. **Orgs:** Iowa City Human Relations Comn, 1972-74; chair, Iowa City Human Relations Comn, 1974-75; field reader, Grad & Prof Opportunity Prog US Off Educ, 1978; field reader, Spec Prog US Off Educ, 1980-87; consult, US Dept Housing & Urban; Univ Iowa's Off Support Serv Progs; consult redevelop training prog educr, HOSE; Nat Asn State Univs & Land-Grant Cols. **Honors/Awds:** Access Award, Introspect Youth Serv, Chicago, 2004; Honored, Comn Human Rights & Social Chg Nat Asn State Univs & Land-Grant Cols. **Special Achievements:** Numerous publications including "Special Education & Socioeconomic Retardation", J Spec Educators Vol 19 No 4 1983; Commentary: "Student Decision Making, When & How", "College & Career Choice, Right Student Right Time Right Place"; proceedings 1972. **Home Addr:** 3201 Muscatine Ave Suite 1, Iowa City, IA 52240, **Home Phone:** (319)351-1333. **Business Addr:** Vice President Student Services, Dean of Students, University of Iowa, 114 Jessup Hall 249 Iowa Memorial Union, Iowa City, IA 52242-1317, **Business Phone:** (319)335-3557.

### JONES, PHILLIP MADISON
Executive. **Personal:** Born Jul 1, 1958?, New York, NY. **Career:** Intellectual Properties Mgt Inc, chmn, chief exec officer; de Passe Jones Entertainment Group, chief exec officer, co-chmn, tv exec & producer. **Special Achievements:** Nominated for an Emmy as Executive Producer of Our Friend Martin with DIC/Disney. **Business Addr:** Chairman, Chief Executive Officer, Intellectual Properties Management Inc, 449 Auburn Ave NE, Atlanta, GA 30324, **Business Phone:** (404)814-0080.

### JONES, POPEYE (RONALD JEROME JONES)
Basketball player, basketball coach. **Personal:** Born Jun 17, 1970?, Dresden, TN; married Amy; children: Justin, Seth & Caleb. **Educ:** Murray State Univ, attended 1992. **Career:** Basketball player (retired), basketball coach; Aresium Milano, Italy, 1992-93; Dallas Mavericks, forward, 1993-96, 2002-03, player develop coach, 2007-10; Toronto Raptors, ctr, 1996-98; Boston Celtics, ctr, 1998-99; Denver Nuggets, forward, 1999-2000; Wash Wizards, forward, 2000-02; Golden State Warriors, forward, 2003-04; NJ Nets, asst coach, currently; Brooklyn Nets, asst coach, 2010-13; Ind Pacers, asst coach, 2013-. **Business Addr:** Assistant Coach, Indiana Pacers, 1 Conseco Ct 125 S Pa St, Indianapolis, IN 46204, **Business Phone:** (317)917-2500.

### JONES, QUINCY DELIGHT, JR.
Composer, music arranger or orchestrator, television producer. **Personal:** Born Mar 14, 1933, Chicago, IL; son of Quincy Delight Sr and Sarah J Frances Wells; married Jeri Caldwell, Jan 1, 1957, (divorced 1966); children: Jolie Jones Levine; married Ulla Andersson, Jan 1, 1967, (divorced 1974); children: Martina & Quincy III; married Peggy Lipton, Jan 1, 1974, (divorced 1990); children: Kidada & Rashida. **Educ:** Berklee Sch Music; Seattle Univ; Boston Conserv. **Career:** Rock Band, founder; Lionel Hampton band, mem; Dept State tour of Near East, Middle East & South Am, Dizzy Gillespie Orchestra, co-organizer, 1956; Barchlay Disques, Paris, music dir, 1956-60; music arranger & composer; music dir, 1961; Mercury Rec, vpres, 1961; Films: The Wiz; In Cold Blood, 1967; In the Heat of the Night; Blues for Trumpet & Koto; The Color Purple, exec producer; The Making of The Italian Job, 2003; Get Rich or Die Tryin, 2005; music producer: Off the Wall; Thriller; Qwest Recs, owner & founder, 1981-; independent composer, conductor, 1965-; works include: Brand New Bag, Sounds Stuff Like That, Walking in Space, This is How I Feel about Jazz, Back on the Block, producer, 1990; Quincy Jones Entertainment, founder, 1990; Vibe magazine, founder, 1993; Qwest Rec, owner; Quincy Jones Media Group, founder, 1997; Q west Broadcasting, chmn & chief exec officer, currently. Album producer: Off the Wall, 1979; Thriller, 1982; Bad, 1987; "We Are the World", 1985. **Orgs:** Founder, Quincy Jones Listen Up Found; hon memBd Dirs, Jazz Found Am, 2001. **Honors/Awds:** Big Band and Jazz Hall of Fame, 1988; received 27 Grammy Awards and over 50 Grammy nominations; 1979 production of Off the Wall sold over 8 million copies and at that time a record breaking four top-10 singles; album, The Dude received an unprecedented 12 Grammy nominations in 1981 and won 5Grammy Awards; 8 Grammy nominations in 1983 (most by one person in a year); Polar Music Prize, 1994; ABAA Music Award for efforts to aid African famine victims, and for conceiving and giving leadership to USA for Africa, producing the album, We Are the World; numerous others including honorary degrees from Loyola Univ, Seattle Univ, Howard Univ, the Berklee Col Music, Seattle Univ, Wesleyan Univ, Brandeis Univ, Loyola Univ (New Orleans), Clark Atlanta Univ, Claremont Univ Grad Sch, the Univ Connecticut & Harvard Univ; Frederick D Patterson Award, 1999; John F Kennedy Center Honors, 2001; French LTgiond' Honneur medal, 2001; Jean Hersholt Humanitarian Award, Acad Motion Picture Arts & Sci; NAACP Image Award; Prestigious Trustees Award; The Grammy Living Legend Award; Kennedy Center Honoree, 2001. Quincy added in Best Selling Author List in 2001; hon doctorate, Univ Pa; Los Angeles Press Club Visionary Award, 2014. **Special Achievements:** Author: The Autobiography of Quincy Jones, 2002; nominated for Oscar Awards for four film scores; First high-level African American executive of an established Mercury record company; Film: Listen Up: The Lives of Quincy Jones, 1990; First African American to be named as the musical director and conductor of the Academy Awards ceremony. **Business Addr:** Owner, Qwest Records, 3300 Warner Blvd, Burbank, CA 91505-4694.

### JONES, QUINCY DELIGHT, III
Music producer, songwriter, actor. **Personal:** Born Dec 23, 1968, London; son of Quincy D Jr and Ulla Anderson; married Koa; children: 2; married Ulla Andersson; children: Martina & Quincy III; married Jeri Caldwell; children: Jolie Jones Levine. **Educ:** Berklee Col Music. **Career:** Actor, music producer & writer; LL Cool J's album, co-producer & co-writer, 1993; YoYo's album, co-producer & co-writer, 1993; music: Fresh Prince of Bel-Aire; Out All Night; NBC-TV, Menace II SOC, Hughes Bros Prod, 1993; Q D III Sound Lab, owner, currently; Album: Soundlab, 1991; Films: Wiz on Down the Road, 1978; We Are the World, 1985; Michael Jackson: History on Film-Volume II, 1997; Fantasia 2000, 1999; Austin Powers in Goldmember, 2002. **Honors/Awds:** Twenty Seven Grammy Awards & Grammy Legend Award. **Special Achievements:** Numerous honors including 79 Grammy Award Nominations. **Business Addr:** Owner, Q.D. III Soundlab, 10880 Wilshire Blvd Suite 2110, Los Angeles, CA 90024.

### JONES, R R. See JONES, TAMALA R.

### JONES, RANDY (RANDAL JONES)
Athlete. **Personal:** Born Jun 24, 1969, Winston-Salem, NC; married Cheri Alou; children: Roman & Marissa. **Educ:** Duke Univ, BA, mech engineering, 1991. **Career:** Sun Trust Bank, Atlanta, Ga, comput technician; US Olympic Comt, bobsledder, currently; Omnicom Media Group, IT support engr, currently. **Honors/Awds:** World Cup and Overall Championship, 1992, 1993; Nat Brakeman & Side Push Championships, 1992 & 1995; Bronze Medal, FIBT World Championships, 1993, 1997; Silver Medal 4-man Bobsled, Winter Olympics, 2002; Silver Medal 4-man Bobsled, Salt Lake City, 2002; Silver Medal 4-man Bobsled Lake Placid, FIBT World Championships, 2003. **Special Achievements:** With Garrett Hines, first African Am men to win medal in Winter Olympics, 2002. **Home Addr:** , Atlanta, GA. **Business Addr:** Bobsledder, US Olympic Committee, 1 Olympic Plz, Colorado Springs, CO 80909, **Business Phone:** (719)632-5551.

### JONES, RANDY KANE
Lawyer. **Personal:** Born Oct 25, 1957, Jacksonville, NC; son of Henry and Julia Mae Saunders; children: Randy. **Educ:** Univ NC, Chapel Hill, BA, polit sci, 1979, Sch Law JD, 1982. **Career:** US Dept Navy, judge advocate gen's corps, 1982-2011; US Atty, Dept Justice, asst, 1987-; Nat Bar Asn, pres, 1997-98. **Orgs:** Fed Bar Asn, 1984-, Am Bar Asn, 1985-, Christian Fel Cong Church, 1985, BE SLA, 1986-; Parlimentarian Earl B Gilliam Bar Asn, 1988-; mem bd, Calif Asn Black Lawyers, 1989-92; chmn, Veterans Affairs Nat Asn Advan Colored People San Diego Br, 1989-; Nat Bar Asn, 1989-, regional dir, 1991-93, pres, 1997-98; pres, Earl BGilliam Bar Asn, 1990-91, mem bd, 1987-; Chmn Bd Dirs, Neighborhood House Asn, 1990-99; bd mem, San Diego County CrimeVictims, 1991-94; Leadership, Educ, Awareness, Develop, grad, 1991; NC St & Ca St Bar Asn; San Diego County Bar Asn; vpres, Urban LeagueSan Diego Chap; bd mem, Voices C, 1993-; pres & bd dir, Nat Ct App Spec Advocates Asn, 1998-2000; chmn & mem bd managers, Jackie Robinson Family YMCA, 1999-; chmn bd dir, UNC-Gen Alumni Asn, 2008-09; chmn bd gov, YMCA San Diego County, 2009-10; mem bd trustee, Francis Parker Sch, 2011-; chmn bd trustee, Thomas Jefferson Sch Law, 2011-. **Honors/Awds:** Hon Doctor Laws, Claflin Col; 100 Most Influential Leaders, Ebony Mag, 1998; Harvey E Beech Award, 2006. **Home Addr:** 6736 Wunderlin Ave, San Diego, CA 92114-2942, **Home Phone:** (619)262-7529. **Business Addr:** Coordinator, Assistant Attorney, United States Attorney's Office, PO Box 66078, Washington, DC 20035-6078, **Business Phone:** (202)514-4706.

### JONES, HON. RAYMOND DEAN
Judge. **Personal:** Born Nov 30, 1945, Pueblo, CO; married Carolyn S; children: Latoya Bryant, Ruth Marie & Raymond Dean II. **Educ:** Colo Col, BA, polit sci, 1967; Harvard Univ Sch Law, JD, 1971. **Career:** Judge (retired); Colo Supreme Ct, from clerk to chief justice, 1971-72; Holme Roberts & Owen, assoc atty, 1972-74; Consumer Off, coun to metrop dist attorneys, 1974-76; Met Denver Dist Atty Consumer Off Prosec Consumer Defrauders, chief coun, 1974-77; Denver County Ct, judge, 1977-78, 1979-87; Colo Ct Appeals, assoc judge, 1988-2004; Colo Munic Ct, Aurora, Colo, chief judge, 2003-04; Colorado Col, vis prof polit sci; Metrop State Col, Sch Bus, Mgt Dept, asst prof, 2006-07; Brokers Choice Am Inc, sr vpres & corp coun, 2007-08; Holt Group LLC, coun, 2004-. Books: A Search for Better Police Serv & An End Police-Community Tensions Black Urban Neighborhoods & An Examination of Community Control Police, 1971; Whither Arbitration? What Can Be Done to Improve Arbitration and Keep Out Litigations IllAffects?, co-auth, 2009; Expectations of An Expert Witness-The Judges Perspective, American Council of Engineering Companies, auth, 2011; A Report On The Health Status of Residents of Denver, co-auth & ed, 2012. **Orgs:** Bd dir, New Dance Theatre Inc, 1972-, CO State Bd Law Exam, 1973-; vpres, bd dir, Denver Oppurtunity Inc, 1974-; St Bd CO Humanities Prog, 1977, Gov Task Force Labor Legis, 1976, Gov Task Force Employ Agencies, 1976; founder & pres, Sam Cary Bar Assoc, 1986 2012-; founder, Sam Cary Bar Asn; bd trustee, Denver Bar Asn; Denver Bar Asn; CO Bar Asn; Am Bar Asn; bd gov, Nat Bar Asn; Nat Bar Asn; nat bd dir, Nat Bar Asn; reg dir, Nat Bar Asn; secy, CO Dem Party; chmn, CO Black Caucus, 1973-74; deleg, Dem nat Conv, 1976; Am Judges Asn, CO Assoc Dist Judges, Bar State CO, Fed Dist CO, 10th Fed Circuit, US Supreme Ct; fac Nat Judicial Col Reno NV; nat bd dir, Nat Judicial Coun; reg dir, Nat Judicial Coun; bd trustee, Colo Col Colo Springs; Colo Coun Arts; numerous community bd; Am Arbit Asn; fel Am Bar Found; Fel Colo Bar Found; bd dir & founder, Cleo Parker Robinson Dance; nat bd dir, Am Judicature Socs; Colo Trial Judges Asn; founder, emer mem, Colo Coun State Trial Judges; pres, Colo Coun State Trial Judges; Colo Bar Asn; emer mem, Colo Coun State Trial Judges; Cent City Press Club; bd dir, Am Asn Retired Persons, 2012-; bd dir, Denver Consumer Credit Coun Serv, currently. **Special Achievements:** While at Colorado College, Jones was the first African-American president of the Beta Theta Pi fraternity, 1963; First African-American appellate judge in Colorado, 1988. **Business Addr:** Of Counsel, The Holt Group LLC, 1675 Broadway Suite 2100, Denver, CO 80202, **Business Phone:** (303)225-8500.

### JONES, REGGIE (REGINALD LEE JONES)
Football player. **Personal:** Born May 8, 1971, Kansas City, KS. **Educ:** La State Univ, grad. **Career:** Football player (retired); Carolina Panthers, wide receiver, 1995-96; Kansas City Chiefs, 1997-98, 2001; San Diego Chargers, wide receiver, 2000-01; Ottawa Renegades Can Football League, 2002. **Honors/Awds:** All-America honors, seven times, La State Univ. **Home Addr:** , Overland Park, KS.

**JONES, DR. RENA TALLEY**
Educator, college teacher. **Personal:** Born Aug 3, 1937, Pine Mountain, GA. **Educ:** Morris Brown Col, BA, zool, 1960; Atlanta Univ, MS, bot, 1967; Wayne State Univ, PhD, microbiol, 1974. **Career:** Educator (retired); Lee Co Bd Educ, instr, 1960-61; Fulton Community Bd Educ, instr, 1961-66; NSF grant, 1966-67; Wayne State Univ, grad asst, 1967-73; Spelman Col, from asst prof biol to prof biol, 1973-2006, chair biol, dir; Macy Summer Inst Premed Educ, 1977; Chautauqua-type Prog Rnat Sci Found, reviewer, Health Careers Off, dir; Wash, DC, partic, pre-med health careers advs & conf. **Orgs:** Health Careers Comn; adv, Atlanta Univ Ctr, Vio Hon Soc; AAAS; Am Soc Microbiol; Ga Acad Sci; assoc mem, Sigma Xi; Beta Kappa Chi; Nat Sci Hon Soc; dir, Spec Health Careers Opportunity Grant; judge, Sci Fair Sec Schs. **Honors/Awds:** Teaching Assitantship, Wayne State Univ, 1967-73; Tenneco Excellence in Teaching Award, United Nego Col Fund, 1989-90. **Special Achievements:** Books: "General Biology Laboratory Manual", Burgess Publishing Company, Minneapolis, MN, 1977 & 1978; "Life in the Laboratory", 1980; "Article: Experiments in General Biology", 1987; "Effect of Growth Temperature on Folding of Cabamoylphosphate Synthetases of Salmonella typhimurium & a Cold-Sensitive Derivative: J Bacteriology 172: 5089-5096"; "Research: Cephalosporium salvinia sp.nov, A Pathogen of Salvinia rotundifolia. Mycopathologia Mycologia Applicata 43: 195-200", 1971. **Home Addr:** 2148 Springdale Rd SW, Atlanta, GA 30315-6116, **Home Phone:** (404)768-6903.

**JONES, RICHARD JULIUS**
Association executive. **Educ:** Cent State Univ, attended 1966; Toledo Univ, attended 1974; Upsala Col, attended mgt, 1980; Bradley Univ, attended 1982. **Career:** Executive (retired); Lodi Boys & Girls Club Inc, Toledo, unit dir, NY, guid dir, Newark, unit dir, Peoria, exec dir, Am, nat staff, Stockton, asst exec dir, pres, chief exec officer, 1993-2011. **Orgs:** Chmn bd, Peoria Housing Authority, 1980-90; Human Rel Comn, 1982-87; Bradley Univ Chief Club, 1984; vpres, Kiwanis Club, 1985; Ill Coun Aging, 1985; pres, United Way Exec Dir Asn, 1987; pres, Optimist Club, 1987; bd mem, Rotary Club, 1989; trustee, Lodi Unified Sch Dist. **Honors/Awds:** Man of the Year, Boys & Girls Club Toledo, 1974; Staff Award Man/Boy, Boys & Girls Club of Newark, 1977; Nat Keystone Adv, Boys & Girls Club Am, 1984; Community Services of the Year, Peoria Housing Authority, 1985, 1987-88; Citizen of the Year Award, 1987-88; Outstanding Community Leader, 1987; Outstanding Leader, Peoria Action Agency, Peoria Inter City Youth Coun, 1987; Community Leader Award, Peoria Sch Dist, 1987; Citizen of the Year, Peoria Christian Leadership Coun, 1988; Outstanding Staff Award, Boys & Girls Club Peoria, 1990. **Home Addr:** 1032 Coach St, Stockton, CA 95209, **Home Phone:** (209)478-3854.

**JONES, RICHARD TIMOTHY**
Actor. **Personal:** Born Jan 16, 1972, Kobe; son of Clarence and Lorene; married Nancy; children: Aubrey, Sydney & Elijah. **Career:** Films: Helicopter, 1993; What's Love Got to Do with It, 1993; Renaissance Man, 1994; Jury Duty, 1995; Johns, 1996; Black Rose of Harlem, 1996; The Trigger Effect, 1996; Kiss the Girls, 1997; Event Horizon, 1997; Goodbye Lover, 1998; The Wood, 1999; Dirty Down Under... Up Here, 1999; AuggieRose, 2000; Lockdown, 2000; Book of Love, 2002; G, 2002; Moonlight Mile, 2002; Phone Booth, 2002; Twisted, 2004; Collateral, 2004; Finding Neo, co-producer, 2004; Breach, co-producer, 2004; Soul Plane, 2004; Time Bomb, 2005; Traci Townsend, 2005; Guess Who, 2005; Cutting Room, 2006; The Package, 2006; Why Did I Get Married?, 2007; Vantage Point, 2008; 15 Minutes of Fame, 2008; Why Did I Get Married Too?, 2010; Caught in the Crossfire, 2010; Forgiveness, 2011; Super 8, 2011; Note to Self, 2012; The Great Divide, 2012; Atlas Shrugged II: The Strike, 2012; Life of a King, 2013; The Last Letter, 2013; Godzilla, 2014; Hear No Evil, 2014; Cru, 2014; TV series: "In the Heat of the Night: Who Was Geli Bendl", 1994; Brooklyn South, 1997-98; Incognito, 1999; "Judging Amy", 1999-2005; The Extinction of the Dinosaurs, 2002; The Cook of the Money Pot, 2002; Second String, 2002; Full-Court Miracle, 2003; Paradise, 2004; Sex, Love & Secrets, 2005; Riding the Bus with My Sister, 2005; Talk Show Diaries, 2005; Dream a Little Dream, 2005; "Sex, Love & Secrets", 2005; Time Bomb, 2006; Girlfriends, 2007; "Terminator: The Sarah Connor Chronicles", 2008; "Bones", 2010; "Grey's Anatomy", 2010; "Super 8", 2011; "Hawaii Five-0", 2011; "Satisfaction", 2014; "Law & Order: Special Victims Unit", 2014; "Lyfe's Journey", 2014; "Work in Progress", 2014. **Honors/Awds:** Nomination, Image Award, 2000. **Home Addr:** 2 Peter Cooper Rd Apt 11a, New York, NY 10010-6725, **Home Phone:** (212)228-2122. **Business Addr:** Actor, c/o Innovative Artists, 1505 10th St, Santa Monica, CA 90401, **Business Phone:** (310)656-0400.

**JONES, RICHMOND ADDISON**
Graphic artist, watercolorist, painter (artist). **Personal:** Born Jul 9, 1937, Chicago, IL; son of Silas Philip and Mabel Betty Crouse; married Christine Ann Osada; children: Philip Frederick. **Educ:** Univ Ill, attended 1957; Am Acad Art, AA, 1959; Sch Visual Arts, 1961; Lill St Ceramic Studio; Univ Ill; Palette & Chisel Acad Fine Arts, Chicago. **Career:** Batten Barton Durstine & Osborn, asst & assoc art dir, 1961-66; J Walter Thompson Co, art dir, 1966-68; Jones James & Jameson Inc, pres, 1968-69; Fuller Smith & Ross, art dir, 1969-70; Richmond A Jones Graphics, owner & designer, 1970-2000; watercolor painter, currently. **Orgs:** Int House Asn, 1959-62; dir & mem, Sponsors Educ Opportunities, 1965-70; founder, vp, mem Group Advert Progress, Devel Minority Opportunities, 1966-70; dir, mem Ill Epilepsy League, 1972-74; dir, mem, Soc Typographic Arts, 1972-; Am Inst Graphic Arts, 1975-; Chicago Press Club, 1980; Chicago Assoc Com & Indust, 1986; Miss Watercolor Soc; NE Watercolor Soc; Ill Watercolor Soc; Nat Watercolor Soc; Mo Watercolor Soc; Palette & Chisel Acad Fine Arts; Univ Ill Pres Coun; Am Watercolor Soc. **Honors/Awds:** Highest Readership (2 awards) Design News, 1966; Published Art Direction Mag, 1968; Selected Top Creative Visual Talent Amer Showcas, 1978-; Max Award for brochure produced for Underwriters Labs Inc, TCR Graphics, 1985; judge for Typographers Int Awd Prog, 1985; judge for awards prog Acad for Health Serv Mkt, Am Mkt Assoc, 1986; American Corporate Identity Award, 1997. **Home Phone:** (773)588-8221. **Business Addr:** Painter, 2530 W Eastwood Ave, Chicago, IL 60625, **Business Phone:** (773)588-4900.

**JONES, ROBERT ALTON**
Lawyer. **Personal:** Born Jan 30, 1944, Houston, TX; son of Robert J (deceased) and Gloria C; married Velma Chester; children: Jessica Elizabeth. **Educ:** Tex Southern Univ, BA, 1969; Thurgood Marshall Sch Law, Houston, Tex, JD, 1972. **Career:** Univ Houston, part-time prof; Teamster's Local 968, off, 1969-73; Anderson Hodge Jones & Hoyt Inc, stockholder & vpres, 1974-; pvt pract atty, 1983-; Robert A Jones & Assocs, criminal defense atty, currently. **Orgs:** Houston Lawyer's Asn; State Bar TX; ABA; Tex Crim Defense Lawyer's Asn; Bus & Prof Mens Orgn; Phi Alpha Delta; US Dist Ct, So & Eastern Dist TX; partic, Am Bar Asn Sem Criminal Defense Litigation; bd mem, Ensemble Theatre; Trial Advocacy Inst; TDCLA; Sam Houston Univ, Huntsville, TX, 1997. **Honors/Awds:** Recipient achievement awards from Stud Govt & Stud Bar Asn; Am Jurisprudence Awards, Debtors & Creditors Rights & Oil & Gas; Alumnus of the Year, Tex Southern Univ. **Home Addr:** 3340 Parkwood Dr, Houston, TX 77021, **Home Phone:** (713)741-1787. **Business Addr:** Criminal Defense Attorney, Robert A Jones & Associates, 2211 Norfolk St Suite 600, Houston, TX 77098-4055, **Business Phone:** (713)526-1171.

**JONES, REV. ROBERT BERNARD**
Educator, musician. **Personal:** Born Oct 2, 1956, Detroit, MI; son of Evelyn and Jimmie Fletcher; married Bernice; children: Robert Bernard II & Arnesia Nicole. **Educ:** Wayne State Univ, Detroit, MI, BA, eng & near eastern studies, 1979. **Career:** Wayne State Univ, stud asst, 1974-79, affil fac; Detroit Pub Sch, broadcast technician, 1979-86; WDET-FM, dir, Detroit Radio Info Serv, 1986-94, broadcast sales mgr, 1994; Monroe County Libr Syst, musical consult & performer, 1988-; Henry Ford Mus & Greenfield Village, Dearborn, 1993-2007; Detroit Hist Mus, 1993-, "Storyliving", prog, dir, 2002-04; Self-employed, blues musician, educr, 1994-15; Univ Mich, Ann Arbor, presenter, 2004-; Albums: Blues From The Lowlands, 1997; The Time Of The Preacher, 2005; At The Crossroads, 2007; Gasoline, The Detroit Legacy Sessions, 2009; In The Tradition, 2008; Guitar Evangelists, 2010. **Orgs:** Founding mem, Detroit Blues Soc, 1986-; adv bd, Friends Sch Music Festival, 1993-; adv bd, Detroit Radio Info Serv, 1994-. **Home Addr:** 18645 Gainsborough Rd, PO Box 231244, Detroit, MI 48223-1339, **Home Phone:** (313)838-0507.

**JONES, REV. DR. ROBERT EARL**
Clergy. **Personal:** Born Feb 11, 1942, Franklinton, NC; married Karen J; children: Darrell J. **Educ:** Houston-Tillotson Col, BA, 1965; Yale Univ Div Sch, MDiv, 1969, STM, 1970; United Theol Sem, DMin, 1994. **Career:** Clergy (retired); Fair Haven Parents Ministry, exec dir, 1967-74; Quinnipiac Col, sem instr, 1968-69; Yale Divine Sch, asst prof, 1970-74; Southern Conn State Col, adj prof, 1974-75; New Haven Anti-Poverty Agency, dep dir, 1974-75; Grand Ave United Church Christ, asst pastor, 1974-77; Col Hill Community Church, assoc pastor, assoc minister & sr pastor, 1977. **Orgs:** Adv bd, Conn Ment Health Ctr, 1974-77; bd pres, Black Coalition New Haven, 1970-75; vpres & pres, Nat Coalition Econ Justice; consult, Nat Acad Churches Transition, 1970-75; Nat Alliance Bus New Haven, 1970-72. **Honors/Awds:** Richard Allen Achievement Award, 1970; Albert B Beebe Award, 1970; Foundation Nation Service Award, Wash Times, 1996. **Home Addr:** 5339 Sportscraft Dr, Dayton, OH 45414-3655, **Home Phone:** (937)235-2829. **Business Addr:** Senior Pastor, College Hill Community Church, 1547 Philadelphia Dr, Dayton, OH 45406, **Business Phone:** (937)278-4203.

**JONES, ROBERT LEE**
Football player. **Personal:** Born Sep 27, 1969, Blackstone, VA; married Maneesha; children: Cayleb, Levi & Isaiah. **Educ:** E Carolina Univ. **Career:** Football player (retired); Dallas Cowboys, mid linebacker, 1992-95, linebacker, 1993; St Louis Rams, mid linebacker, 1996-97; Miami Dolphins, right linebacker, 1998, linebacker, 1999-2000, mid linebacker, 2000; Wash Redskins, linebacker & mid linebacker, 2001. **Orgs:** Champions Christ Ministry. **Honors/Awds:** Defensive Rookie of the Year, United Press Int, Nat Football League, 1992; All-Pro, USA Today, 1994; Defensive Player of the Week, Am Football League; East Carolina University Hall of Fame, 2004; Super Bowl Champion, XXVII, XXVIII, XXX. **Special Achievements:** First Pirate to be selected in the first round of the NFL Draft. **Home Addr:** 7500 SW 30th St, Davie, FL 33314.

**JONES, ROBERT MITCHELL.** **See JONES, BOBBY M.**

**JONES, ROBERT WESLEY.** **See Obituaries Section.**

**JONES, RODREK EDWARD**
Football coach, football player. **Personal:** Born Jan 11, 1974, Detroit, MI. **Educ:** Univ Kans, human develop & family living. **Career:** Football player (retired), football coach; Cincinnati Bengals, tackle, left tackle, 1996-2000; St Louis Rams, tackle, right tackle, 2001; Wash Redskins, 2002; Ann Arbor Skyline High Sch Eagles, head coach. **Business Addr:** Head Coach, Skyline High School, 2552 N Maple, Ann Arbor, MI 48103, **Business Phone:** (734)994-6515.

**JONES, ROGER CARVER**
Football coach, football player. **Personal:** Born Apr 22, 1969, Cleveland, OH; married Angela; children: Donovan. **Educ:** Tenn State Univ. **Career:** Football player (retired), coach; Tampa Bay Buccaneers, defensive back, 1991-93; Cincinnati Bengals, 1994-97; Tenn Oilers, 1997; Pope John Paul II High Sch, Hendersonville, head track coach, asst football coach & asst athletic dir, 2002-. **Home Addr:** , Goodlettsville, TN. **Business Addr:** Assistant Athletic Director, Head Track Coach, Pope John Paul II High School, 117 Caldwell Dr, Hendersonville, TN 37075, **Business Phone:** (615)822-2375.

**JONES, RONALD JEROME.** **See JONES, POPEYE.**

**JONES, RONALD LYMAN (RON JONES)**
Administrator. **Personal:** Born Mar 29, 1945, Dayton, OH; son of Major E and Cecile E; children: Dana L Bullock, David & Aubre. **Educ:** Cent State Univ; Fisk Univ. **Career:** Battelle Memorial Inst, trainer, 1974-88, personnel mgr, BPMD, 1980-88; Online Comput Libr Ctr Inc, mgr, employee rel & develop, 1988-91, mgr human resources, 1991-93, dir admin serv, 1993-, ed asst, dir human resources, currently. **Orgs:** Am Soc Training & Develop; pres, Cent Ohio Chap; Palo Alto Chamber Orchestra; Black Caucus. **Home Addr:** 1021 Barberry Lane, Columbus, OH 43213-3312, **Home Phone:** (614)501-7079. **Business Addr:** Editorial Assistant, Online Computer Library Center Inc, 6565 Kilgour Pl, Dublin, OH 43017-3395, **Business Phone:** (614)764-6000.

**JONES, RONDELL TONY**
Football player. **Personal:** Born May 7, 1971, Sunderland, MD. **Educ:** Univ NC, grad. **Career:** Football player (retired); Denver Broncos, defensive back, 1993-96; Baltimore Ravens, free safety, 1997.

**JONES, ESQ. ROSALYN EVELYN**
Lawyer. **Personal:** Born Apr 26, 1961, Frankfurt; daughter of Harry T. **Educ:** Harvard Raddiffe Col, AB, hist sci, 1983; Oxford Univ, St John's Col, attended 1984; Harvard Law Sch, JD, 1987. **Career:** Gibson, Dunn & Crutcher, atty, 1987-89; Rosenfed, Meyer & Susman, atty, 1989-91; Manatt, Phelps & Phillips, assoc, 1991-93, partner, atty, 1993-97; Rosalyn E Jones Esq, atty, 1997-; Smithsonian Inst, off gen coun, 2010-12. **Orgs:** Bd dir, Black Entertainment & Sports Lawyers Asn; Am Bar Asn, 1993-; Calif Bar, 1987-; Dist Columbia Bar, 1988; Phi Beta Kappa, Harvard Radcliffe Col; Harvard Knox fel St John's Col, Oxford Univ; State Bar Calif; bd dir, Woolly Mammoth Theatre. **Home Addr:** 1801 Century Pk E Suite 2400, Los Angeles, CA 90067, **Home Phone:** (310)286-9826. **Business Addr:** Attorney, Rosalyn E Jones Esq, 1801 Century Pk E, Los Angeles, CA 90067, **Business Phone:** (310)286-9826.

**JONES, DR. ROSCOE T., JR.**
Dentist. **Personal:** Born Jan 25, 1935, Washington, DC; married Marva A J; children: Nancy Ellen. **Educ:** Howard Univ, BS, 1958, DDS, 1965. **Career:** AUS Dent Corp, Dent Clin Ft Belvoir, actg chief, 1966; pvt pract, dentist, 1968-. **Orgs:** Robert T Freeman Dent Soc, 1970; Sunday Sch teacher All Souls Unitarian Church, 1970-77; Acad Gen Dent, 1973-; treas, Metro Dent Asn Chartered, 1978-; DC Dent Soc. **Honors/Awds:** Outstanding Cadet, Howard Univ. **Home Addr:** 1100 La Grande Rd, Silver Spring, MD 20903-1324. **Business Addr:** Dentist, Private Practice, 1238 Monroe St NE, Washington, DC 20017-2507, **Business Phone:** (202)526-9071.

**JONES, ROSEMARY M.**
Consultant, executive. **Educ:** NY Univ, BS, bus admin & mkt, 1974. **Career:** IBM, Supplier Div Prog, SE region, small bus develop strategist, sr prog mgr & consult, 1970-2002; Turner Broadcasting Syst Inc, Supplier Div Prog, dir, 2002-. **Orgs:** Chair, Ga Women Bus Coun Bd Dirs, 2004-05; Asian-Am Chamber Com Ga; Am Hotel & Lodging Multicultural Adv Bd; CP Plasma Adv Bd; Ga Minority Supplier Develop Coun; Asian-Am Heritage Found; Edge Connection, Asian-Am Chamber Com; Int Women's Think Tank; advisor, Beulah Heights Univ. **Honors/Awds:** Ladies guest prize; Valuable Contribution Award, 2003; Dialogue of Diversity Corporation of the Year Award, 2004. **Business Addr:** Director of Supplier Diversity, Turner Broadcasting System Inc, 1 CNN Ctr 14th Fl S Twr, Atlanta, GA 30303, **Business Phone:** (404)827-1700.

**JONES, ROY LEVESTA, JR.**
Boxer, basketball player, rap musician. **Personal:** Born Jan 16, 1969, Pensacola, FL; son of Roy Sr and Carol; children: DeShaun, DeAndre & Roy III. **Career:** Boxer, rap musician, basketball player; Brevard Blue Ducks, currently; Singles: "Y'all Must've Forgot", 2001; "And Still", 2001; "I Smoke, I Drank", 2004; "Can't Be Touched", 2004; "Battle of the super powers", 2009; Album: Round One, The Album 2002; Release the Beast, 2006; Body Head Bangerz, Volume One. Films: The Matrix Reloaded, 2003; Roy Jones Jr's Greatest Knockouts, 2005; Grudge Match, 2013.TV Series: The Wayans Bros, 1999; The Sentinel, 1998; Arliss, 2000-02. **Home Addr:** 3165 Spreading Oak Dr SW, Atlanta, GA 30311, **Home Phone:** (404)696-0099. **Business Addr:** Rap Musician, 3165 Spreading Oak Dr SW, Atlanta, GA 30311, **Business Phone:** (404)696-0099.

**JONES, SAMUEL**
Basketball player, basketball coach. **Personal:** Born Jun 24, 1933, Wilmington, NC; son of Samuel and Louise K; married Gladys Chavis; children: Aubrey, Phyllis, Michael, Terri & Ashley. **Educ:** NC Cent Univ, BS, 1957. **Career:** Basketball player (retired), basketball coach; Boston Celtics, 1957-69; NC Cent Univ, head basketball coach; New Orleans Jazz Basketball Team, La, asst coach; Fed City Col, Wash, dir athletics, 1969-77; Blue Ribbon Sports, NIKE Shoe Div, head prom; DC Pub Sch, athletic dir, 1989; Montgomery Blair High Sch, substitute teacher, currently. **Orgs:** Kappa Alpha Psi; Naismith Memorial Basketball Hall Fame. **Home Addr:** 15417 Tierra Dr, Wheaton, MD 20906. **Business Addr:** Substitute Teacher, Montgomery Blair High School, 51 Univ Blvd E, Silver Spring, MD 20901-2451, **Business Phone:** (301)649-2800.

**JONES, SANDRA MILLER.** **See MILLER, JONES SANDY.**

**JONES, SARAH**
Poet, playwright, actor. **Personal:** Born Nov 29, 1973, Baltimore, MD; married Steve Colman. **Educ:** Bryn Mawr Univ. **Career:** Bryn Mawr Col, Mellon Minority fel; Van Lier Lit fel, 1998; Plays: Surface Transit, 2000; Bamboozled, 2000; Famous, 2000; Women Can't Wait, 2000; Waking the Am Dream, 2002; I Am Ali, 2002; Bridge and Tunnel, 2005; Hip-Hop: Beyond Beats & Rhymes, 2006; Good Hair, 2009. Films: Lisa Picard Is Famous, 2000; Bamboozled, 2000; TV series: The Sarah Jones Show, 2005. **Honors/Awds:** Grand Slam Championship, 1997; Best One Person Show, HBO Apen Comedy Arts Festival; Tony Award; Obie Award; Helen Hayes Award; Calloway Award, New York Civil Liberties Union; Brendan Gill Prize, 2007. **Special Achievements:** Two Drama Desk nominations; first artist in history to sue

the Federal Communications Commission for censorship; made numerous TV appearances on HBO, NBC, ABC, CBS, PBS, CNN. First Lady Michelle Obama to perform at the White House in celebration of Women's History Month. **Business Addr:** Actor, 302A W 12 St Suite 121, New York, NY 10014.

### JONES, SELWYN ALDRIDGE

Football player. **Personal:** Born May 13, 1970, Houston, TX. **Educ:** Colo State Univ, grad. **Career:** Football player (retired); Cleveland Browns, 1992, 1994, defensive back, 1993; New Orleans Saints, defensive back, 1994; Seattle Seahawks, 1995, defensive back, 1996; Denver Broncos, defensive back, 1997-98.

### JONES, SETH

Hockey player. **Personal:** Born Oct 3, 1994, Arlington, TX; son of Ronald and Amy. **Educ:** Murray State Univ. **Career:** Hockey player; US Nat Team Develop Prog-USHL, Under 17 & Under 18, defenseman, 2010-11; US Nat Team Develop Prog USHL & Under 18, defenseman, 2011-12; Murray State Univ, defenseman; Portland Winterhawks (WHL), defenseman, 2012-13; Team USA, defenseman at World Jr Championships, 2013, World Championships, 2014; Nat Hockey League, Nashville Predators, defenseman, 2013-16; Columbus Blue Jackets, defenseman, 2016-. **Special Achievements:** Son of Ronald "Popeye" Jones, a professional basketball player and assistant coach for the Indiana Pacers; drafted in the first round (fourth pick) of the NHL Entry Draft by the Nashville Predators, 2013; youngest player on the 2014 Team USA at the World Championships. **Business Addr:** Columbus Blue Jackets, 200 W Nationwide Blvd Suite Level, Columbus, TN 43215, **Business Phone:** (614)246-4625.

### JONES, SHALLEY A. (SHALLEY JONES HORN)

Banker, vice president (organization). **Personal:** Born Sep 17, 1954, Moorehead, MS; daughter of Robert Lee and Rosie Lee; children: Shantea K & Ernest J II. **Educ:** Univ Miami, BA, 1975; Fla Int Univ, MSM, 1983, Col Urban & Pub Affairs, PhD, pub admin. **Career:** First Union NAT Bank, asst vpres, loan processing mgr, 1976-84, asst vpres, regional mgr, 1984-85; Chase Fed Bank, vpres, 1985; Sun Bank Miami, NA, CRA & Consumer Compliance, vpres, 1994-95; Fannie Mae, dir community investment; S Fla Partnership Off, dir, 1994-2003; Fannie Mae, housing & community develop Midwest region, vpres; Miami Dade County, Housing & Community Develop, dir, currently. **Orgs:** AKA Sorority Inc, 1974-; pres, Miami Dade Urban Bankers Asn, 1987-89; Nat Black MBA Asn, S Fla chap, 1990-; exec pres, Nat Asn Urban Bankers, 1991-92; Metro-Miami Action Plan, 1991-94; adv bd mem, UNF, 1991-93; dir, Eastern Fin Credit Union, 1993-94; bd, NCP, Miami Dade chap, 1992-94; life mem, bd mem, Dade County Housing Finance Authority, 1996-; bd mem, Miami Parking Authority. **Honors/Awds:** S Fla Bus Jour, Up & Comers Award/Banking, 1989; Dollars & Sense Magazine, Am Best & Brightest, 1991; Am Banker Newspaper, Top 40 Banker Under 40, 1992; Banker of the Year, Miami Dade Urban Bankers ASN, 1992; Unsung Hero Award, City Miami, 1992. **Business Addr:** Director- Housing and Community Development, Miami-Dade County.

### JONES, SHERMAN J.

School administrator, consultant, chief executive officer. **Personal:** Born Jan 12, 1946, Newport News, VA; son of Sherman E and Leola Mae; married J Janice; children: Kimberely & Sherman E. **Educ:** Williams Col Am Studies, BA, 1968; Harvard Univ Gen Mgt, Finance & Orgn Behav, MBA, admin, planning & policy anal, 1970, EdD, 1978. **Career:** Raymond James Financial Serv, independent advisor, 1966-; Cresap, McCormic & Padget Inc, mgt consult, 1972-75; Acad Educ Develo Inc, mgt consult, 1975-77; Harvard Grad Sch, teaching fel, 1976-77; Fisk Univ, vpres admin, 1977-82, vpres & actg dean univ, 1980-82; Tuskegee Univ, exec vpres & prof mgt, 1982-91; Clark Atlanta Univ, provost vpres acad affairs prof bus admin, 1991-93; Southern Norm Sch, pres, headmaster, chief exec officer, 1993-96; Jones Financial Serv, pres & owner, 1996-2014; Emerald Connect Inc, financial advisor; Knoxville Col, vpres, Develop & Finance, chief financial officer, 2000-03; Tenn Wesleyan Col, assoc prof bus admin, 2005-06; Univ Tenn, lectr, 2010-14; Personal Bus Advisors LLC, sr advisor, 2013-; Lincoln Memorial Univ, dean, 2014-; Registry Col & Univ Presidents, mgt consult, 2015-. **Orgs:** Asst pres, Woodrow Wilson Admin Intern, Cent State Univ, Ohio, 1970-71; bd dir, Better Bus Bur Nashville Mid Tenn Inc, 1978-82; mgt comt, John A Andrew Community Hosp, 1982; adv coun, Am Inst Managing Diversity Inc, 1984-; bd adv, 1986-92, bd trustee, St Andrews Sewanee Sch; bd dir, YMCA, Brewton; bd dir, Harvard Alumni Asn, 1991-93; chmn, Havard Grad Sch Educ, 1990-91; Nashville Comn Foreign Affairs; bd trustee, Southern Norm Sch; Kiwanis; Sigma Pi Phi Fraternity; bd mem, Colored Rock Found, Knox Heritage; dir develop, chief operating officer, Knoxville Area Urban League, 2007-10. **Home Addr:** 1151 Briarcliff Pl NE, Atlanta, GA 30306. **Business Addr:** Independent Financial Advisor, Raymond James Financial Services, 6555 Chapman Hwy Suite B, Knoxville, TN 37920, **Business Phone:** (865)579-2776.

### JONES, PROF. SHIRLEY JOAN (SHIRLEY J JONES)

School administrator, educator. **Personal:** Born Nov 26, 1931, New York, NY; children: Susan & Sande Jr. **Educ:** NY Univ, MA, 1954, MSW, 1964; Columbia Univ, PhD, 1977. **Career:** New York Univ Sch Social Work, asst prof, 1967-70; State Univ New York Stony Brook, assoc prof, 1972-78; New York Univ Metro Studies, adj prof, 1973-77; Univ Southern Miss, dean prof, 1978-89; Rockefeller Col Press, ed, 1992; State Univ NY, Albany, Sch Social Welfare, prof, distinguished serv prof & prof emer, 2002-; Sociocultural & Serv Issues Working, ural Clients, ed; Book:"Generalizing from the Rural Experience", co-ed; US African Partnership, emer dir. **Orgs:** Adv bd, US Census Bur, 1980-90; bd dir, Nat Alliance Bus, 1982-85; Comn Child Support Enforcement, 1985; bd dir, Gov Off Vol Citizen Partic, 1985; Nat Asn Black Soc Workers; women & minorities develop; Nat Asn Social Workers; Coun Social Work Educ; Int Asn Social Work; implications social work, social & econ develop; State Const Chg Comt, 1986-87; Nat Adv Comt, 1988-91; Int Comn Nat Asn Social Workers; US African Partnership Bldg Stronger Communities; comnr, Accrediation Coun Social Work Educ; US Census Bur, Minority Adv Comt, 2000; expert panelist, Nat Head Start Dept Health & Human Serv. **Honors/Awds:** Woman of the Year, Hattiesbg City Business mens Club, 1981; National Association of Black Social Workers Distinguished Social Worker of the Year Award, 1988; Waldoffs Achievement, 1983; Social Worker of the Year, MS Chap, Nat Asn Black Social Workers, 1983, Dedicated Service Award, 1986; Collins Fellow Award; Award for distinguished service to the National Advisory Committee; Ruth Hoeflin Forum Scholar Award; Distinguished Service Award, Gov Off Vol Citizen Part, 1983; Certificate of Appreciation DHHS, OHDS, AFCYF, 1986; Martin Luther King Award, State Univ NY, Albany, 1993; City of Albany Award, Human Rights, 1994; Governors Award, Nigeria; National Association for the Advancement of Colored People Award, 2002. **Special Achievements:** Co-editor: Preparing Helping Professionals to Meet Community Needs: Generalizing from the Rural Experience, 2003. **Home Addr:** 170 Kans Rd, Rhinebeck, NY 12572. **Business Addr:** Distinguished Service Professor, Professor Emeritus, University at Albany State University of New York, Rm RI 111 1400 Washington Ave, Albany, NY 12222, **Business Phone:** (518)442-5330.

### JONES, SONDRA MICHELLE

Educator, vice president (organization). **Personal:** Born Sep 7, 1948, Norfolk, VA. **Educ:** Morgan State, BA, 1970; Temple Univ, attended 1977; Harvard Univ Grad Sch Educ; Univ Pa, Sch Edn, grad wor. **Career:** Health & Welfare Coun, social work trainee, 1966; STOP Prog, Norfolk, Va, rec counr, 1967; Health & Welfare Coun, Baltimore, social work trainee, 1968; St Martin's Day Care Ctr, Baltimore, teacher, 1971-72; Develop Disabilities Day Care Ctr, Pa, educ dir comn coord teacher, 1972-73; Buck Lane Mem Community Day Care Ctr, Haverford, Pa, dir, 1976-; Ctr Families & C, head start dir, C Youth & Family Serv, vpres, currently. **Orgs:** Alliance Black Soc Workers; Ivy Club Alpha Kappa Sor; Nat Asn Educ YoungvC; Phil Asn Retarded C; Child Welfare League Am; Phil Coord Child Care Coun 4 C; Nat Coun Black Child Develop; Black Child Develop Inst Vesta Corp. **Home Addr:** 19436 Scottsdale Blvd, Shaker Heights, OH 44122-6420, **Home Phone:** (216)991-3177. **Business Addr:** Vice President of Children Youth & Family Services, Head Start Director, Center for Families and Children, 4500 Euclid Ave, Cleveland, OH 44103, **Business Phone:** (216)431-5800.

### JONES, STACEY FRANKLIN

College administrator. **Personal:** children: 2. **Educ:** Howard Univ, BS, math, 1982; Johns Hopkins Univ, MS, numerical sci, 1986, master, tech mgt, 1991; George Washington Univ, PhD, comput sci, 1997. **Career:** Northrop Grumman, defense & electronic systs software engr & prod develop mgr, 1982-93; engineering mgr & syst architect, 1993-97; Johns Hopkins Univ, res scientist & adj fac mem, 1997-2000; Benedict Col,, SC, chair Mathand Comput Sci Dept, 2000-02, dean Sch Sci, Technol, Engineering & Mathematics, 2002-08, vpres Sponsored Progs & Res (later known vpres Instnl Effectiveness & Sponsored Progs), 2007-09, sr vpres, 2009-10; Bowie State Univ, provost & vpres, 2010; Univ Syst Md, spec asst, 2010-11; sr consult exec mgt, technol partnerships & corp develop, Wash, D.C., 2011-14; Elizabeth City State Univ, chancellor, 2014-. **Special Achievements:** First female chancellor of Elizabeth City State University; served on numerous review panels for federal agencies; speaker and writer on computer and engineering management topics. **Business Addr:** Elizabeth City State University, 1704 Weeksville Rd, Elizabeth City, NC 27909, **Business Phone:** (252)335-3228.

### JONES, STANLEY BERNARD

College administrator, administrator. **Personal:** Born Mar 18, 1961, Greenwood, SC; son of Herbert C Jr and Maggie P. **Educ:** Radford Univ, BS, 1984, MS, educ, 1987; Va Polytech Inst & State Univ, EdD, 2011. **Career:** Radford Univ, asst dir admis, dir, spec stud serv; Hanover Co, educ adminr, hon chmn, 2002; Lee-Davis High Sch, prin; King & Queen County Pub Schs, Supt Schs, 2013-15; Danville Pub Schs, Supt Schs, 2015-. **Orgs:** VA Admin Coun Black Concerns; treas, EEO; Nat Asn Advan Colored People; Nat Asn Student Personnel Adminr; Assoc Handicapped Student Serv Prog Post-sec Educ; Omega Psi Phi Fraternity. **Home Addr:** 1711 Franwill Ave NW, Roanoke, VA 24017-3617, **Home Phone:** (703)731-4255. **Business Addr:** Superintendent of Schools, Danville Public Schools, 341 Main St, Danville, VA 24541, **Business Phone:** (434)799-6400.

### JONES, STAR (STARLET MARIE JONES)

Television talk show host, journalist, lawyer. **Personal:** Born Mar 24, 1962, NC; daughter of James Byard and Shirley; married Al Reynolds. **Educ:** Am Univ, BA, admin justice, 1984; Univ Houston Law Ctr, JD, 1986. **Career:** Kings Co (NY) Dist Att's Off, prosecution staff mem, 1986-91, sr asst dist atty, 1991-92; Ct TV, corresp, 1991; NBC-TV, legal corresp, 1992-93; Jones & Jury, host & co-owner, 1994-; Inside Edition, sr corresp & chief legal analyst, 1995; ABC-TV, The View, host, 1997-2006, legal expert, 2008-; HGTV, House Hunters, host; Star Jones, exec ed, 2007; Payless Shoes, spokesperson. Author: You Have to Stand for Something, or You'll Fall for Anything, 1998; Shine: A Physical, Emotional & Spiritual Journey to Finding Love, 2006; work of fiction, 2011. **Orgs:** Nat vpres, Alpha Kappa Alpha Sorority; bd dir & trustee, E Harlem Sch; G&P Found Cancer Res; God's Love We Deliver; int adv bd, Girls Inc; founder, Starlet Fund; pres, Nat Asn Prof Women; nat vol, Breast Cancer Res Found. **Business Addr:** Legal Expert, International Creative Management Talent Agency, 40 W 57th St, New York, NY 10019, **Business Phone:** (212)556-5600.

### JONES, TAMALA R. (R R JONES)

Actor. **Personal:** Born Nov 12, 1974, Pasadena, CA. **Educ:** Pasadena City Col, Pasadena, CA. **Career:** Film appearances: How to Make an American Quilt, 1995; Booty Call, 1997; Can't Hardly Wait, 1998; The Wood, 1999; Blue Streak, 1999; Next Friday, 2000; Turn It Up, 2000; How to Kill Your Neighbor's Dog, 2000; The Ladies Man, 2000; Kingdom Come, 2001; The Brothers, 2001; Two Can Play That Game, 2001; On the Line, 2001; Head of State, 2003; Nora's Hair Salon, 2004; Long Distance, 2005; Who's Your Caddy?, 2007; American Dreams, 2007; Daddy Day Camp, 2007; Janky Promoters, 2009; Busted, 2009; Janky Promoters, 2009; Up in the Air, 2009; 35 & Ticking, 2011; Things Never Said, 2013; Yellow Ribbon, 2013; Act of Faith, 2014; The Box, 2014; Shaker Pointe, 2014. TV guest appearances: "ER", 1995; "JAG", 1996. TV series: "Dangerous Minds", 1996; "Veronica's Closet", 1997-99; "For Your Love", 1998; "One on One", 2001; "Couples", 2002; "The Tracy Morgan Show", 2003; "Accidental Love", 2005; "Ghost Whisperer", 2006; "CSI: Miami", 2006; "Short Circuitz", 2007; "Studio 60 on the Sunset Strip", 2007; Castle, 2009; "Everybody Hates Chris", 2009; "Everybody Hates Chris", 2009; "Castle", 2009-14; "Party Down", 2010; "The Soul Man", 2012; "King Bachelor's Pad", 2014; "Megachurch Murder", 2015. **Honors/Awds:** One of "The 10 Sexiest Women of the Year", Black Mag, 2000, 2001. **Home Addr:** , CA. **Business Addr:** Actress, Innovative Artists, 1505 10th St, Santa Monica, CA 90401, **Business Phone:** (310)656-0400.

### JONES, TEBUCKY SHERMAIN

Football coach, football player. **Personal:** Born Oct 6, 1974, New Britain, CT; children: Tebucky Jr. **Educ:** Syracuse Univ, child & family studies, 1998. **Career:** Football player (retired), coach; New Eng Patriots, 1998, right cornerback, 1999, free safety, 2000-02; New Orleans Saints, free safety, 2003-04; Miami Dolphins, strong safety, 2005; New Eng Patriots, 2006; New Brit Golden Hurricanes, head coach, currently. **Orgs:** Founder, Tebucky Jones Found. **Honors/Awds:** United States of America Today Connecticut Player of the Year, 1993; Super Bowl Champion, XXXVI. **Home Addr:** 77 Ely Rd, Farmington, CT 06032. **Business Addr:** 76 Adams St, New Britain, CT 06052-1222.

### JONES, TERRY L.

Executive. **Educ:** Trinity Col, BS, elec engineering; George Washington Univ, MS, elec engineering; Harvard Univ Grad Sch Bus Admin, MBA, 1972. **Career:** Syncom Venture Partners, co founder, vpres, managing partner, 1978-; Westinghouse Aerospace & Litton Industs, sr elec engr; Syndicated Commun Inc, pres, 1990-; Citigroup Global Investment Mgt, chief exec officer & chmn, 1999-; Citigroup Asset Mgt, chmn & chief exec officer; Fortiaa-CREF, exec vpres finance & planning & chief financial officer, 1989-93, pres & chief operating officer, 1993-97, vice chmn & dir, 1995-97; Travelers Group, vice chmn & dir; Iridium Commun Inc, dir; Cyber Digital Inc, dir, 1997-; Fox Entertainment Group Inc, dir, 2001-; Univ Nairobi, lectr; bd drs, Syncom portfolio co. **Orgs:** Bd mem, V-me Media; bd mem, Weather Decisions Inc; bd mem, TV One LLC; bd mem, Robert Toigo Found; bd mem, Howard Univ Entrepreneurial Leadership & Innovation Inst; chmn, Nat Asn Investment Co; Iridium Satellite LLC; Southern African Enterprise Develop Fund; bd dir, Radio One Inc, 1995-; Delta Capital Corp; Sun Delta Capital Access Ctr; bd dir, Fed Home Loan Mortgage Corp; bd dir, Philip Morris Co Inc; bd trustee, Cornell Univ; bd trustee, Spellman Col; Robert Toigo Found. **Honors/Awds:** "Black Enterprise," 75 Most Powerful Blacks on Wall Street, 2011; New America Alliance Award of Excellence. **Business Addr:** Managing Partner, Syncom Venture Partners, 8515 Ga Ave Suite 725, Silver Spring, MD 20910, **Business Phone:** (301)608-3203.

### JONES, THERESA C.

Automotive executive, business owner, chief executive officer. **Personal:** children: Michelle, Jason & Joseph. **Educ:** St Marys Col, BA; Wayne State Univ, MS. **Career:** Northwestern Dodge Inc, owner, pres & chief exec officer, 1984-; Henry Ford Hosp, dir. **Orgs:** Pres, Daimler Chrysler Minority Dealer Asn, 1994; bd dir, Automotive Hall Fame; Nat Automobile Dealers Asn. **Special Achievements:** First African American dir of Nursing Education. **Business Addr:** Owner, Chief Executive Officer & President, Northwestern Dodge Inc, 10500 W 8 Mile Rd, Ferndale, MI 48220, **Business Phone:** (248)399-6700.

### JONES, THERESA DIANE

Government official. **Personal:** Born Jun 7, 1953, Erie, PA; daughter of Parker P and Mable R. **Educ:** Edinboro State Col, BA, 1976. **Career:** Pinellas Oppor Coun Inc, sr outreach worker 1976-77; Info & Referral, suicide intervention spec, 1977; City St Petersburg, relocation officer, 1977-80, admin serv officer, 1980-86, MBE coord, 1986-93; Tampa Gen Healthcare, MBE coord, 1993-96; City St. Petersburg, MBE, coord, 1996-98; bus assistance mgr, 1998-2002; community affairs dir, 2002-. **Orgs:** Bd dir Pinellas Oppor Coun Inc, 1984-89; bd govs, St Petersburg Area Chamber Com 1985; co-chair, Community Alliance, 1985; real estate assoc, LouBrown Realty & Mortgage Inc, 1985-88; secy, Nat Forum Black Pub Adminrs, Tampa Bay Chap, 1986-88; pres, Fla Asn MBD Offs, 1996; pres, W Coast Chap, Nat Minority Supplier Develop Coun FL, 1990, 1994; chair, Midtown Wealth Bldg Task Force; bd dir, R Club Child Care Inc, 2003-; guide, Police Civilian Rev Comt; Leadership St Pete; bd mem, Fla Asn Community Rels Prof. **Home Addr:** PO Box 3986, St. Petersburg, FL 33731-3986, **Home Phone:** (727)823-4209. **Business Addr:** Community Affairs Director, City of St Petersburg, PO Box 2842, St. Petersburg, FL 33731, **Business Phone:** (727)893-7345.

### JONES, THOMAS L.

Executive, lawyer. **Personal:** Born Jan 12, 1941, Greenwood, MS; married Nettie Byrd; children: Martilla R, Nicole L, LaTanya Dionne & Thomas II. **Educ:** Tougaloo Col, BS, chem, 1963; Howard Univ Law Sch, JD, 1971. **Career:** US Peace Corps, Philippines, 1963-65; Cook Co Circuit Ct, probationofficer, 1965-66; Neighborhood Consumer Info Ctr, Wash, Hward Univ, prog dir, 1970-71; Fed Hwy Admin, Wash, spl asst chief coun, 1971-73; Continental Tel Co Va Inc, asst vpres & legal atty, 1973-85; McFadden, Evans & Sill, partner. **Orgs:** Am Bar Asn; Nat Bar Asn; DC Bar Asn, 1972; Practicing Law Instr; Phi AlphaDelta; adv couns Fed City Col Psychol Dept; Urban League. **Home Addr:** 4405 Cadillac Lane, Beaumont, TX 77705, **Home Phone:** (409)840-5652. **Business Addr:** Partner, McFadden & Shoreman PC, 1050 Connecticut Ave, Washington, DC 20036, **Business Phone:** (202)772-3188.

### JONES, THOMAS WADE

Chief executive officer, executive. **Personal:** Born Jan 1, 1949, Philadelphia, PA; children: Nigel; married Adelaide Knox; children: Evonne, Michael & Victoria. **Educ:** Cornell Univ, BA, govt, 1969, MS, regional planning, 1972; Boston Univ, MBA; Howard Univ, hon degree; Pepperdine Univ, hon degree; Col New Rochelle, hon degree. **Career:** Athur Young & Co, prin, 1978-82; John Hancock Mutual Life Ins Co, sr vpres & treas, 1982-89; TIAA Cref, chief financial officer & exec vpres fin & plng, 1989-93, vice chmn & dir, 1989-95, pres & chief operating officer, 1993-97; Travelers Grp, vice chmn & dir, 1997-98;

Citigroup Asset Mgt, chmn & chief exec officer, 1997-2004; Travelers Group, vice chmn, 1997; Salomon Smith Barney Asset Mgt, chmn & chief exec officer, 1998; Citigroup, Global Investment Mgt, chmn & chief exec officer, 1999-2004; Citigroup Inc, chmn & chief exec officer, 1999-2004; Fox Entertainment Grp Inc, dir, 2001-04; TWJ Capital LLC, prin, bd dir & sr partner, 2011-. **Orgs:** Bd dir, Fed Home Loan Mortgage Corp; bd dir, Philip Morris; trustee, Cornell Univ; bd overseers, Cornell Med Col; bd dir, Altria Grp, 2002-; trustee emer, Cornell Univ; bd dir, investment portfolio co Floor & Decor Outlets Am; dir, KoolSpan; Acoustic Technologies; bd observer, NetNumber; vice chmn, Fed Res Bank New York; vice chmn, Freddie Mac; Fox Entertainment Grp; Investment Co Inst & Econ Club New York; dir & vice chmn, Pepsi Bottling Grp; vice chair, dir, Teachers Ins & Annuity Asn Col Retirement Equities Fund; dir, KeySpan New Eng LLC; dir, Thomas & Betts Corp; dir, Wooziness Inc; dir, Citigroup Found; vice chmn, TIAA-CREF, 1995-97; vice chmn, Eastern Enterprises; trustee, Econ Club New York. **Business Addr:** Board of Director, Founder & Senior Partner, TWJ Capital LLC, 6 Landmark Sq Suite 404, Stamford, CT 06901, **Business Phone:** (203)359-5610.

### JONES, DR. TONI STOKES
Educator. **Personal:** Born Jul 25, 1954, Detroit, MI; daughter of LeRoy and Hermalene; married Louis E; children: Emmanuel Stokes. **Educ:** Wayne State Univ, BS, 1978, MEd, 1988, PhD, 1998. **Career:** Volkswagen Am Inc, sr training develop specialist, 1986-94; Emdicium Group Inc, instrnl designer, 1994-99; Detroit Col Bus, lectr, 1995; Univ Phoenix, lectr, 1997-99; Univ Mich, Dearborn, Mich, lectr, 1998-99; Eastern Mich Univ, prof, 1999-, dept teacher educ, educ media & technol prog, currently. **Orgs:** Mich Assn Comput Users Learning, 1999-, bd dir, 2000-; Int Soc Tech Educ, 1999-, secy, 2000-; bd examr, Nat Coun Accreditation Teacher Educ, 2004-15. **Home Addr:** 9600 N Canton Ctr Rd, Plymouth, MI 48170, **Home Phone:** (734)254-0222. **Business Addr:** Professor, Eastern Michigan University, 315 John W Porter Bldg, Ypsilanti, MI 48197, **Business Phone:** (734)487-3260.

### JONES, TONY EDWARD (ANTHONY EDWARD JONES)
Football player. **Personal:** Born May 24, 1966, Royston, GA; married Kamilla Orr; children: 3. **Educ:** Western Carolina Univ, BS, mgt, 1989. **Career:** Football player (retired); Cleveland Browns, tackle & right tackle & left tackle, 1988-95; Baltimore Ravens, left tackle, 1996; Denver Broncos, left tackle & right tackle, 1997-2000. **Orgs:** Charter mem, Ty Cobb Museum. **Honors/Awds:** Pro Bowl, 1998. **Special Achievements:** Films: 1989 AFC Championship Game, 1990; 1997 AFC Championship Game, 1998; Super Bowl XXXII, 1998; 1998 AFC Championship Game, 1999; Super Bowl XXXIII, 1999.

### JONES, VAN (ANTHONY KAPEL JONES)
Environmental activist, talk show host, civil rights activist. **Personal:** Born Sep 20, 1968, Jackson, TN; married Jana Carter; children: Two children. **Educ:** University of Tennessee at Martin, B.S. in Communication and Political Science; Yale Law School, J.D., 1993. **Career:** White House Council on Environmental Quality, Special Advisor for Green Jobs, Enterprise and Innovation, 2009; Center for American Progress, Senior Fellow; Green for All, Senior Policy Advisor; Princeton University, Distinguished Visiting Fellow in Center for African American Studies; Woodrow Wilson School of Public and International Affairs, Distinguished Visiting Fellow in Science, Technology and Environmental Policy Program; CNN news program "Crossfire," Co-host, 2013-. **Orgs:** Ella Baker Center for Human Rights, Founder, 1996; Color of Change, Co-founder, 2005; Green for All, Founder, 2007; Rebuild the Dream, Founder, 2011; Presidio, Board Member; Campaign for America's Future, Board Member; Demos, Board Member; Million Hoodies Movement for Justice, Board Member; AFRON African Robotics Network, Board Member. **Honors/Awds:** World Economic Forum, Young Global Leader, 2005; Nautilus Book Award for "The Green Collar Economy," 2008; "Fast Company," 12 Most Creative Minds of 2008; "Essence," 25 Most Inspiring African Americans; "Time" Magazine, "Heroes of the Environment," 2008, 100 Most Influential People, 2009; Hubert H. Humphrey Civil Rights Awards, 2009; NAACP Image Awards, NAACP President's Award, 2010; "Ebony" Magazine, Power 150, 2011; "Rolling Stone" Magazine, 12 Leaders Who Get Things Done, 2012; "The Root" Magazine, The Root 100 Honorees, 2013; "Ebony" Magazine, Power 100, 2013. **Special Achievements:** Bestselling author of "The Green Collar Economy," HarperOne (2008) and "Rebuild the Dream," Nation Books (2012); appointed to White House special advisor position by President Barack Obama.

### JONES, VELMA LOIS
Educator. **Personal:** Born Sep 7, 1930; daughter of Eddie Lee and Ethel Crotie. **Educ:** Lemoyne-Owen Col, BA, 1952; Columbia Univ, MA, 1957; Memphis State Univ, Mich State Univ, grad study. **Career:** Educator (retired); Cypress Jr HS, Memphis, instr math, 1967-96; Hyde Pk Elem Sch Memphis, instr; LeMoyne Owen Col, Mich Col & Memphis Univ, master teacher stud teachers. **Orgs:** Del, TN Educ Asn Rep Assembly, 1970-79; del, Nat Educ Asn Rep Assembly, 1971-79; Memphis Br Nat Asn Advan Colored People, 1972-76; vpres, Tenn Educ Asn, 1994-96, pres, 1996; trustee, LeMoyne-Owen Col, 1987-2001; exec bd, pres, Memphis Educ Asn; parliamentarian co-founder mem chairperson, Memphis chap Nat Educ Asn Black Caucus; pres, W TN Educ Asn; bd dir, TN Educ Asn; Nat Coun Teachers Math; TN Coun Teachers Math; Memphis area Teachers Math; NEA concerns Com; TN Educ Asn; vpres, Memphis Dist Laymen's Coun CME Ch; secy, Soc Rel Missionary Soc W TN Ann Conf CME Ch; asst secy, W TN Ann Conf & chairperson com soc concerns; parliamentarian, TN Conf Nat Asn Advan Colored People Br; Women's Missionary Coun CME Ch; Compilation com revise Chap Discipline; staff, Leadership Fel Prog & Pre-Boule Workshop Alpha Kappa Alpha Sor; S Eastern Reg Dir; Memphis Chap Am Inst parliamentarians; N Memphis Area Adv Coun; Nat Coun Negro Women; TN State Educ Asn; vice chair person, Shelby Co Housing Auth; Am Inst Parliamentarians; dir, Christian Educ Trinity Christian Meth Epis Ch; llife mem, Trinity Christian Methodist Episcopal Church; co-founder, Community Youth & Bus Partnership Proj; pres's adv coun, Rhodes Col; Greater Memphis YMCA; supreme parliamentarian, Alpha Kappa Alpha Sorority Serv Orgn. **Honors/Awds:** Commission Service Award, 1958, 1978; Excellent Leadership & Outstanding Service Awards, Alpha Kappa Alpha, 1966-70; Women of the Year, 1970, 1974; Cert Merit Award, Nat Asn Advan Colored People, 1972; Missionary of the Year, 1975; Twenty Most Prominent Memphians, 1975; Women Making Hist, 1976; Brotherhood Award, 1977; Outstanding Woman of the Year Award, Nat Asn Advan Colored People, Women's Nat Conf, 1980; Outstanding Woman S Eastern Reg; first woman pres memphis Br, Nat Asn Advan Colored People; Numerous other civic awards. **Special Achievements:** First African American Classroom Teacher to Serve of the 44000 Member Tennessee Education Association. **Home Addr:** 1969 Edward Ave, Memphis, TN 38107-3124, **Home Phone:** (901)272-1823.

### JONES, HON. VERA MASSEY
Judge. **Personal:** Born Jan 1, 1943. **Educ:** Fisk Univ, BA, hist, 1965; Univ Detroit Law Sch, JD, 1969. **Career:** Univ Detroit Urban Law Prog, clin div, 1967, res div, 1968-69; Pvt Pract, atty, 1969-70; Legal Aid & Defender Asn Detroit, dep defender, 1970-73; Detroit Recorders Ct, Traffic & Ordinance Div, referee, 1973-79, judge, chief judge; State Mich, Third Circuit Ct, Criminal Div, Judge, currently. **Orgs:** Founding mem, Nat Asn Women Judges, secy, 1982-83; Mich Black Judges Asn; Nat Asn Advan Colored People, Womens Comn; Delta Sigma Theta; State Bar Mich, Judicial Conf; founding mem, Farm. **Honors/Awds:** Rated Outstanding, Detroit Bar Asn, 1990. **Special Achievements:** Rated preferred & well-qualified, Civic Searchlight, 1990. **Business Addr:** Judge, State of Michigan, Frank Murphy Hall Justice 1441 St Antoine, Detroit, MI 48226, **Business Phone:** (313)224-5261.

### JONES, REV. VERNON ALGIE, JR. See Obituaries Section.

### JONES, VICTORIA C.
Television producer, television journalist. **Personal:** Born Dec 30, 1947, Denver, CO; daughter of Marvin K Dillard and Pearl E Reagor; children: Lisa A Camille. **Educ:** Western Univ, BA, BS, 1972; Harvard Univ, EDM, 1979. **Career:** WB2-TV, "People Are Talking", co-creator, 1979-80, "Coming Together", creator, 1980-81, producer, 1980; WHDH-TV, producer, 1982-95, exec producer & sr producer; Strand Theatre, exec dir, 2002-; Special Projects: "Journey of Courage, " 1988; "Mandela's visit to Boston, " 1990; "Save Our Children.Save Our Neighborhood, " 1992; "Million Man March, " 1995; "Voices of Violence, " 1996. **Orgs:** Bd visitors, Bunker Hill Community Col; bd mem, Nat Mus Am Indian; bd mem, Nat Asn Black Journalists; co-founder, Coalition 100 Black Women, Boston Chap; pres, Boston Asn Black Journalists. **Honors/Awds:** Emmy, New Eng Emmys, 1977-96; Nat NAACP Special Image Award, 1983; Iris Award, 1984, 1989, 1990; Outstanding Award for Excellence, Ohio State, 1986; Tribute to Excellence, YWCA, 1990. **Business Addr:** Executive Director, Strand Theatre, 543 Columbia Rd, Dorchester, MA 02125, **Business Phone:** (617)635-1403.

### JONES, VICTORIA GENE
Public relations executive, executive, association executive. **Personal:** Born Jan 30, 1948, Oakland, CA; daughter of Eugene Leocadio Balugo and Lottie Emelda Charbonnet; children: Brandon Wells. **Educ:** Pepperdine Univ, Malibu, CA, BS, bus mgt, 1983; Golden Gate Univ, MBA, 1999. **Career:** Southern Calif Gas Co, pub affairs ref ctr supvr, 1973-74, community rels rep, 1974-79, prof employ adminr, 1979-80, pub affairs rep, 1980-82, acct exec, 1982-84, community involvement energy progs adminr, 1984-85, mkt servs mgr, 1985-88, state affairs mgr; Pac Enterprises Corp, state govt affairs mgr & lobbyist, 1988-95; Clorox Co, mgr govt rels, 1995, dir, Clorox Co Found, currently; Clorox Co, vpres, Global Gov't Affairs & Comm Rel, 1995-. **Orgs:** Los Angeles Urban League, 1980-88; Inst Govt Advocates, 1988-95; Women Advocacy, 1988-95; Calif Elected Womens Asn Educ & Res, 1988-95; Am Asn Blacks Energy, 1988-95; Sacramento Urban League, 1989-95 chmn bd, Oakland Metrop Chamber Com; founding mem & vice chair, Oakland African-Am Chamber Com, currently; Pres, Capitol Network, 1992. **Honors/Awds:** Black Woman of Achievement, Nat Asn Advan Colored People Legal Defense & Educ Fund, 1990; Mayor's Cert Appreciation Community Involvement, City Los Angeles, 1990; Cert Recognition, Calif State Assembly, 1990; Woman of Distinction, East Bay Business Times, 2005. **Home Addr:** 6 Kingwood Rd, Oakland, CA 94619-2346, **Home Phone:** (510)530-7579. **Business Addr:** Manager of Government Relations, Community Relations, The Clorox Co, 1221 Broadway, Oakland, CA 94619, **Business Phone:** (510)271-2971.

### JONES, DR. VIDA YVONNE
School administrator. **Personal:** Born Aug 30, 1946, Collinston, LA; daughter of Willie L and Helen Taylor; married Abdul LaBrie; children: Ghania. **Educ:** San Francisco State Univ, San Francisco, CA, BA, 1969; Univ Calif, Berkeley, CA, MA, city planning, 1972; Univ Calif, San Francisco, CA, PhD, 1986. **Career:** Univ Calif, San Francisco, Calif, from asst planner to assoc planner, 1972-75, sr planner, 1975-77, prin analyst, 1977-87, Inst Health & Aging, asst dir, training & admin, 1987, Acad Geriat Resource Prog, adminr, currently. **Orgs:** Chair, bd dir, Bay Area Lupus Found, 1987-88; chair, Minority Outreach Comn, 1985-87; Nat Forum Black Pub Adminr; Am Sociologist Asn; Am Planners Asn; Am Geriatrics Soc. **Home Addr:** 32726 Bass Lake St, Fremont, CA 94536. **Business Addr:** Administrator of Academic Geriatric Resource Program, University of California, 1111 Franklin St 11th Fl, Oakland, CA 94607-5200, **Business Phone:** (510)987-9706.

### JONES, VIOLA W.
Government official, mayor. **Personal:** Born Apr 27, 1933, Goodnight, OK; daughter of John W and Jeanette Hardimon; married Charles H II; children: Charlesetta, Carolyn, Cynethia & Charles III. **Educ:** Langston Univ, Langston, OK, BS, 1973. **Career:** Langston Univ, Langston, OK, youth specialist community dev, 1972-82; City Langston, OK, mayor. **Orgs:** Langston Beautiful Federated Club, 1972-; chairperson, Okla Baptist State Missionary Pres's Inc, 1981-; missionary pres, St Mark Dist, 1987-; Bus Prof Women, 1988-. **Home Addr:** 316 S Tolson Ave, Coyle, OK 73027, **Home Phone:** (405)466-2596.

### JONES, DR. VIVIAN R.
Executive, president (organization), chief executive officer. **Personal:** Born Sep 4, 1948, AR; daughter of German and Annie B (Deceased); children: 2. **Educ:** Kennedy-King Col, AA, social serv, 1980; Chicago State Univ, BA, 1986, MEd, 1988. **Career:** Ada S McKinley, caseworker, 1986-88; Dept C & Family Serv, childprotective investr, 1989-91; PSI, adminr, 1990-92; Lifelink, foster care supvr, 1992-94; African Am Family Comn, comnr, 1996-2001. **Orgs:** Nat Asn Black Social Workers, Chicago Chap, 1992-; ABJ Community Servs Inc, founder, pres & chief exec officer, 1992-; Child Welfare League Am, 1995-; Child Care Asn Ill, 1995-; Nat Asn Advan Colored People, Chicago Chap, 1998-; Nat Polit Cong Black Women, 1998-; Nat League Negro Women, 1998-; Rainbow Coalition, Oper Push, 1999-; comnr, African Am Family Comn, 2000-01; bd dir, Ill African Am Coalition Prev, 2007-; Urban Sustainability Asn, 2009; vpres & bd dir, S Shore Chamber Com. **Home Addr:** 18A 6700 S Shore, Chicago, IL 60649, **Home Phone:** (773)363-6800. **Business Addr:** Chief Executive Officer, President, ABJ Community Services Inc, 1818 E 71st St, Chicago, IL 60649, **Business Phone:** (773)667-2100.

### JONES, WALTER, JR.
Football player. **Personal:** Born Jan 19, 1974, Aliceville, AL; married Valeria; children: Rafael, Waleria & Walterius. **Educ:** Holmes Community Col; Fla State Univ, BS, criminol. **Career:** Football player (retired); Seattle Seahawks, left tackle, 1997-2009, right tackle, 2002. **Honors/Awds:** Pro Bowl, 1999, 2001, 2002, 2003, 2004, 2005, 2006, 2007, 2008; All-Pro, 2001, 2002, 2004, 2005, 2006, 2007; Alumni Offensive Lineman of the Year, Nat Football League, 2005; Champion, Nat Football Conf, 2005; Pro Football Hall of Fame, 2014. **Special Achievements:** First round pick No 6, NFL Draft, 1997; first off Lineman in Seahawks history to go to Pro Bowl; Bldg Blocks for Kids prog to Evergreen Hosp, Kirkland for a new pediat playroom. **Home Addr:** 11115 123rd Lane NE Apt F-42, Woodinville, WA 98033.

### JONES, DR. WALTER, JR.
Lawyer, executive, association executive. **Personal:** Born Oct 7, 1946, Chicago, IL; son of Walter and Ruby. **Educ:** Univ Ill, Urbana-Champaign, BA, 1969, Col Law, JD, 1972. **Career:** Household Finance Corp, in-house corp coun, 1972-73; Northern Dist Ill, asst US atty, 1973-77; US Attys Off, Criminal Div, dep chief, 1977-80, chief, 1980-83, spec litigation coun, 1983-86; Curiel & Jones, partner, 1986-91; Pugh Jones Johnson & Quandt PC, share holder, dir, vpres & partner, 1991-. **Orgs:** Chair, Am Bar Asn, Prosecution Function Comn, 1981-84; Ill State Bar Asn; Cook County Bar Asn; chair, Seventh Circuit Litigation Rev Comn; Ill chair, Seventh Circuit Bar Asn, Comn Criminal Law & Procedure; Chicago BarAsn; fel Am Bd Criminal Lawyers; fel & chair, Am Col Trial Lawyers; fel Int Acad Trial Lawyers; Chicago Bar Asn. **Honors/Awds:** Leading Lawyers, Leading Lawyers Network. 2009. **Special Achievements:** Am Bar Asn, Criminal Justice Mag, ed, 1986-96. **Business Addr:** Vice President, Partner, Pugh Jones Johnson & Quandt PC, 180 N LaSalle St Suite 3400, Chicago, IL 60601-2807, **Business Phone:** (312)768-7800.

### JONES, WILBERT
Food consultant. **Personal:** Born Mar 14, 1964, Clarksdale, MS. **Educ:** Loyola Univ, Chicago, IL, BS, chem, 1986. **Career:** Kraft Foods, prod dev mgr, 1985-93; Healthy Concepts, pres, 1993-11; Wilbert Jones Co Inc, pres, 2012-. **Orgs:** Adv bd mem, Common Threads Found, 2001-06; Les Amis d'Escoffier Soc Chicago, 2002-; Gold Coast Neighbors Asn, 2006-08. **Business Addr:** President, Wilbert Jones Co Inc, 1400 N Lake Shore Dr Suite 4F, Chicago, IL 60610, **Business Phone:** (312)335-0031.

### JONES, WILLIAM ALLEN
Executive, lawyer. **Personal:** Born Dec 13, 1941, Philadelphia, PA; son of Roland E and Gloria T; married Dorothea S Whitson; children: Zoey, Rebecca, Gloria & David; married Margaret Smith. **Educ:** Temple Univ, BA, 1967; Harvard Bus Sch, MBA, 1972; Harvard Law Sch, JD, 1972. **Career:** Walt Disney Prod, atty, 1973-77, asst treas, 1977-79, treas, 1979-81; Wyman Bautzer Rothman Kuchel Silbert, atty, 1981-83; United Artists Corp, sr vpres, corp gen coun, 1986-91; Metro Goldwyn-Mayer Inc, gen coun, 1983-95, secy, exec vpres, 1991-95, exec vpres, Corp Affairs, 1995-97, sr exec vpres & secy, 1997-; MGM-Pathe, dir, 1991-92; MGM UA Entertainment Co, vpres, gen coun corp & sec. **Orgs:** Hist Hon Soc, 1967; Ger Hon Soc, 1967; Polit Sci Hon Soc, 1967; bus mgr, Los Angeles Bar Jour, 1974-76; Am Bar Asn, 1974-; State Bar, CA, 1974-; Los Angeles City Bar Asn, 1974-; bd dir, Harvard Bus Sch Asn, S CA, 1985-88; bd gov, Inst Corp Coun, 1991-94; bd dir, Nostalgia Network Inc, 1990-94; bd dir, Metro-Goldwyn-Mayer Pathe Commun Corp, 1991-92; bd dir, Metro-Goldwyn-Mayer Inc, 1991-92; bd trustee, Flintridge Prep Sch, 1993-96; Motion Picture Asn Am, 1995-; bd dir, Santa Monica Chamber Com, 1996-98; bd dir, Calif Chamber Com, 2001-04; vice chmn, bd visitor, Temple Univ, 2003-; bd dir, Motion Picture & TV Fund Corp, 2003-; bd trustee, Marlborough Sch. **Honors/Awds:** President Scholar, Temple Univ, 1967; Diamond Achievement Award, 2001. **Home Addr:** 1557 Colina Dr, Glendale, CA 91201, **Home Phone:** (818)240-1337. **Business Addr:** Senior Executive Vice President, Secretary, Metro-Goldwyn-Mayer Inc, 10250 Constellation Blvd, Los Angeles, CA 90067, **Business Phone:** (310)449-3000.

### JONES, WILLIAM BARNARD
Executive. **Personal:** Born Nov 20, 1957, St. Louis, MO; son of Alice Narvelle Dunn; married Phyllis; children: Tanya Nichole, William Barnard II, Ryan Laroy Willard & Ciara Alice Hope. **Educ:** Wash Univ, St Louis, BA, 1980; St Peters Col, BS, bus mgt. **Career:** Anheuser-Busch, sr consult, develop, 1989-90, Nat budget adr, 1990-92, exe asst to vpres, 1992-93, nat mgr, field sales, 1993-95, sales dir Mich, 1994-95, vpres region sales, 1995-99, Bus Develop Group, vpres, corp off, 1999-, Nat Retail Sales Off-Premise Chain Sales, vpres, 2005-07, Anheuser-Busch Inbev, vpres, Midwest Region, 2007-11. **Orgs:** Inroads Inc, 1980-. **Home Addr:** PO Box 138, Chesterfield, MO 63005. **Business Addr:** Chairman, St. Louis chapter of INROADS..

**JONES, DR. WILLIAM BOWDOIN**
Lawyer, diplomat, foreign minister. **Personal:** Born May 2, 1928, Los Angeles, CA; son of William T and LaVelle Bowdoin; married Joanne Fairchild Garland; children: Lisa Jamison, Stephanie A Marioneaux & Walter C. **Educ:** Univ Calif, Los Angeles, CA, BA, polit sci, 1949; Univ Southampton, eng, postgrad, 1949; Univ Southern Calif, JD, 1952; Univ Southern Calif, postgrad sch int rels, 1960. **Career:** Educator, ambassador, lawyer, diplomat (retired); Pvt Prac, atty-at-law, 1953-62; US Foreign Serv Officer, dipl, 1962-84; US Dept State Wash, dep asst secy state, 1969-73; US Dept State, Paris, France, chief, US mission to UNESCO, 1973-77; US Dept State chmn US-Japan Cult Conf, Hawaii, 1973; US Dept State, ambassador to Haiti, 1977-80; Hampton Univ, diplomat-in-residence, 1980-81; Bur Intelligence & Res, State Dept, staff, 1981-82; Univ Va, ambassador-in-residence, 1983-84; US House Rep Sub-Comt Western Affairs, staff dir, 1987; Int Bus Law Firm, partner, 1988-91; Hampden Sydney Col, adj prof, 1991; Pepperdine Univ, distinguished vis prof, 1993-2004, Johns prof Polit Sci, Malcolm R Myers Distinguished chmn, 1999-2000, ambassador-in-residence & William A Johns prof polit sci, 2001-07. **Orgs:** Sigma Pi Phi-Boule; Pi Sigma Alpha; Kappa Alpha Psi; Wash Int Club; Am Acad Polit & Social Sci; Calif Bar; Dist Columbia, US Sup Ct; fel Woodrow Wilson Found, 1986-87; BarUS Ct Int Trade, 1988; press adv coun, St. Marys Col, 1988-94; bd trustee, Hampden Sydney Col, 1992-; bd dir, Asn Black Am Ambassadors, 1995; bd dir, Am Asn UN, Nat Capital Region, 1996-; James Madison Soc, Hampden-Sydney Col, 1996-; US Coun, UN Univ, 1998-; bd dir, Ctr Leadership Pub Affairs, Hampdon-Sydney Col, 1998-; bd dir, Nat Capitol Asn UN; US Coun UN Univ, Tokyo; bd trustee, Hampdon-Sydney Col, 2000-. **Home Addr:** 4807 17th St NW, Washington, DC 20011, **Home Phone:** (310)395-2894.

**JONES, DR. WILLIAM C.**
Obstetrician, gynecologist. **Personal:** Born Oct 22, 1933, Richmond, VA; married Evora Williams; children: Lisa, Mark, Lori, Michael, David & Lydia. **Educ:** Va State Col, BS, 1953; Howard Univ, attended 1959; Meharry Med Col, MD, 1963; Duke Univ Med Ctr, attended 1968. **Career:** GW Hubbard Hosp, Meharry Med Col, resident & internship, 1963-67; Duke Univ & Affil Hosp, Durham, NC, fel endocrinol, 1967-68; Richmond, Va, pvt pract, obstet & gynec, 1968-. **Orgs:** Am Col Obstet & Gynec; Richmond Acad Med; Richmond Med Soc; Old Dom Med Soc; Am Bd Obstet & Gynec; Kappa Alpha Psi Frat. **Home Addr:** 11120 Buckhead Ter, Midlothian, VA 23113-1344. **Business Addr:** Physician Obstetrics & Gynecology, Private Practice, 2809 N Ave Suite 200, Richmond, VA 23222, **Business Phone:** (804)321-2403.

**JONES, WILLIAM EDWARD**
Educator. **Personal:** Born Jul 4, 1930, Indianapolis, IN; married Janet; children: Leslye. **Educ:** Butler Univ, BS, 1956; Ind Univ, MS, 1960. **Career:** Crispus Attucks High Sch, teacher, 1957-61; Ind State Univ, counr, instr, vice prin & dean, 1964-68; Broad Ripple High Sch, prin, 1970-79. **Orgs:** Consult, HEW; Urban Sch Affairs, Ohio State Univ; Midwest Equal Opportunity Ctr; Desegregation Nat Asn; Sec Sch Prin; Phi Delta Kappa; Ind Sec Sch Adminr; adv coun, Danforth Found; elder, Witherspoon United Presb Church; Greater Indianapolis Progress Com; Kappa Alp Psi; Nat Asn Advan Colored People; Urban League; Danforth Sch Adminr, 1975-76; Broad Ripple Merchants Asn. **Home Addr:** 5505 Woodside Dr, Indianapolis, IN 46208. **Business Addr:** Principal, Broad Ripple High School, 1115 E Broad Ripple Ave, Indianapolis, IN 46220.

**JONES, WILLIAM JAMES (BILL JONES)**
Designer, educator. **Personal:** Born Aug 6, 1969, Brooklyn, NY; son of William and Arlene. **Educ:** Kans City Art Inst, Kans City, MO, BFA, graphic design, 1992; Pratt Inst, MPS, design mgt, 1998. **Career:** Kans City Art Inst, sr exhib, 1992; New York, Dept Personnel, art dir & opers specialist, 1993-94, graphic arts, 1995-96; Times Custom Publ, Essence, Black Enterprise, graphic designer & freelance, 1993-96; IV Design, art dir, 1996-2000; New York Bd Educ, Rikers Island Educ, 1997-99; Bd Educ City New York, educr, 1998-2000; Univ Col Educ Winneba, lectr, 2000-01; Col New Rochelle, Sch New Resources, instr, 2001-03; Latina Connections/Urban Frontier Indust, Wash, design mgr, 2001-03; Medgar Evers Col, adj instr; Col New Rochelle, Sch New Resources, instr, 2002-; Univ Calif, vis researcher, vis postgrad researcher, 2003-04. **Orgs:** Nat Asn Graphic Artists; Soc Pubation Designers; Am Inst Graphic Artists; Design Mgt Inst; Graphic Artists Guild. **Home Addr:** 1720 Bedford Ave Suite 11A, Brooklyn, NY 11225, **Home Phone:** (718)771-3007.

**JONES, DR. WILLIAM O.**
Clergy. **Personal:** Born Covington, TN; married Helen Crombie; children: 4. **Educ:** Moody Bible Inst; Ky State, BS; Gammon Theol Sem, BD; Murrys Theol Sem, DD. **Career:** Chattanooga Bible Ctr, dean & dir; Home Mission Bd Soc Baptist Conv, 1975-; pastorates, TN, KY. **Orgs:** Chaplain, CCC Camp, 1935-37; asst secy, Nat BYPU Bd, 1947-54; ed, Intermed Nat BYPU Quartly; precinct chmn, 12 5 Dist. **Home Addr:** 2310 E 5 St, Chattanooga, TN 37404.

**JONES, YVONNE DE MARR**
School administrator, civil rights activist, president (organization). **Personal:** Born Dayton, OH; children: Diane R Singh, Bercenia & Shelley Smith. **Educ:** Hunter Col, BA, 1947, MA, 1955. **Career:** School administrator (retired), civil rights activist; Elmsford Pub Schs, 1955-84; Westchester Conn Col. **Orgs:** Bd, Greenburgh Neighborhood Ctr; chair Westchester, Martin Luther King Jr Inst; pres, St Francis Episcopal Church, ECW; pres, Westchester Asn Study Am Life & Hist; br pres, White Plains Greensburgh, Nat Asn Advan Colored People. **Honors/Awds:** Comm Merit Award, Operation PUSH Westchester, 1976; Achievement Award, Westchester Co Club BPW, 1978; Key Women of Westchester Award, 1987; Connecticut Service Award, NCW, Westchester Section, 1989; Appreciation Award, Woodburn Correctional, 1989; Appreciation Award, Sing-Sing Prison, 1990; Connecticut Enhancement Award, Nat Asn Black Social Workers, 1991; Community College Awards, Mercy Col Westchester, 1995. **Home Addr:** 118 N Evarts Ave, Elmsford, NY 10523, **Home Phone:** (914)592-6425.

**JONES, DR. YVONNE VIVIAN**
Educator, association executive. **Personal:** Born Jul 29, 1946, New York, NY; daughter of Ernest and Irene Washington; married Sylvester Singleton; children: Michael Kenneth. **Educ:** Am Univ, BA, 1971, PhD, 1975. **Career:** Eugene & Agnes E Meyer Found, assoc dir, 1971-74; Univ Louisville, asst prof, 1975-81, assoc prof anthrop, 1981-, Dept Pan African Studies, assoc prof, currently. **Orgs:** Pres bd, Planned Parenthood, Louisville Inc, 1977-81; chair, Minority Group Ment Health Prog Rev Comn, Nat Inst Ment Health, 1979-82. **Honors/Awds:** Outstanding Scholar Graduate Level, Am Univ, 1976; Outstanding Young Woman of America, 1978. **Home Addr:** 4335 River Park Dr, Louisville, KY 40211-3147, **Home Phone:** (502)778-0740. **Business Addr:** Associate Professor, University of Louisville, 430 Strickler Hall 4th Fl E Wing, Louisville, KY 40292, **Business Phone:** (502)852-2428.

**JONES, ZOIA L.**
Educator, president (organization), association executive. **Personal:** Born Oct 2, 1926, Iota, LA; daughter of Elena Laws (deceased) and Joseph (deceased); married Everette M; children: Zoia Sylvia Jones-Blake. **Educ:** TX Southern Univ, BS, home econ, 1960, MEd, guid, 1976; cert elem educ, 1963; Prairie View A&M Univ, cert spec educ, 1981. **Career:** Educator (retired); Evangeline Parish, Rougeau, LA, teacher, 1944-47; Tex Southern Univ, asst instr, 1960-61; HISD, Houston, TX, teacher, 1961-90; Houston-Harris County Proj, vol coord, 1967; Magnet Sch, ade task team, 1975; Globe Advocate, past columnist; Houston Informer, past columnist; KCOH Radio Sta, past moderator; Nat Coun Negro Women Inc, Dorothy I Height Sect, pres, nat exec comm-at-large mem, currently; New Pleasant Grove BC, minister, 2003-; HISD, Task Team Magnet Schs, pub rels admin. **Orgs:** VISTA; Houston COC; Women COT Serv, 1968-70; Nat Asn Advan Colored People; Black Art Ctr; Black Art Mus; RGM Rose Mary Grand Chap OES TX; UNF; golden life mem, DST, Houston Metrop Alumnae Chap, charter officer; May Week Comm; charter bd mem, Adopt Black C Comm; Eta Phi Beta Sor Inc; life mem, Asn study Negro Life & Hist; past activ, Houston Teachers Asn; Tex Classroom Teachers Asn; Tex State Teachers Asn; NEA; All Nations Rescue Mission; charter officer, McGregor Pk Women, pres; past columist, Forward Times; Tex Southern Univ, Nat Alumni Asn; comnr, Civil Ct 3 Harris County; New Pleasant Grove Baptist Church, Sr Mission II; pres, Sunday Sch, teacher, youth supvr, Young Women's Auxiliary; exec nat comm & local pres, Nat Coun Negro Women, 2000-; chair, Delta Dear Task Force, Delta Sigma Theta Sorority Inc. **Honors/Awds:** Distinguished Service Award, Houston Classroom Teachers Asn; Letter of Commendation, President George Bush, 1990; Letter of Commendation, Sen Lloyd Bentsen, 1990; Letter of Commendation, Sen Phil Graham, 1990; Resolutions of Commendation, TEX Senate & House Rep, 1990; Distinguished Service Award, Humanitarian Civil Rights, 1994, Houston-Harris County Retired Teachers Asn; Human Relations Award, Tex State Teachers Asn, Houston Ed Asn, 1994; Distinguished Award, Young Women's Alliance, 1997; Women of Wonder, Nat Gala, Wash, DC; Mary McLeod Bethune Award, Comm Leaders Pacesetter, 2003. **Special Achievements:** Attended the White House Briefing for Afr Amer Leaders; attended 45thCelebration of Civil Rights Movement, Eta Phi Beta Soroity Inc, Xi Chapter, Founders Day Speaker, 1994, Mt Lebanon Baptist Church, Women's Day Speaker, 1994, first "Hall of Fame" inductee, National Council of Negro Women, Dorothy I Height Sect, 1994-95. **Business Addr:** President, National Council of Negro Women Inc, 3417 Charleston St, Houston, TX 77021, **Business Phone:** (713)747-3727.

**JONES-BRADLEY, HON. VANESA F.**
Judge. **Personal:** married Avery J; children: Andrea J. **Career:** Judge (retired); State Mich, 36th Dist Ct, judge.

**JONES-DEWEEVER, AVIS**
Foundation executive, research administrator, founder (originator). **Personal:** Born Jan 1, 1969?. **Educ:** Va State Univ, BA, 1990; Univ Md, College Park, PhD, 2000. **Career:** Joint Ctr Polit & Econ Studies, res asst, 1993-94; Cong Black Caucus Found, res analyst, 1994-95; Md House Delegates, Ph.D. legis fel, 1996-97; Macro Int, res inst/surv mgr, 1997-2000; Univ Richmond, asst prof, 2000-02; Inst Women's Policy Res, employee, 2002-05, dir poverty & social justice progs, 2005-07; Nat Coun Negro Women, dir Res, Pub Policy & Info Ctr, 2007-10, exec dir, 2010-13; Focus Pt with Avis Jones-DeWeever, host, 2013-14; Incite Unlimited, LLC, pres & chief exec officer, 2013-; Except Leadership Inst Women, founder, 2015-. **Orgs:** Women of Color Policy Network Affiliate Scholar; Institute for Women's Policy Research. **Special Achievements:** Youngest ever executive director of the National Council of Negro Women. Co-author, Black Women in the United States, National Coalition on Black Civic Participation, 2015. Author, How Exceptional Black Women Lead. Regular contributor to The Huffington Post, 2010-; contributor to NewsOne Now with Roland Martin, To the Contrary, and The Agenda. **Business Addr:** Exceptional Leadership Institute for Women, PO Box 131, Woodbridge, VA 22194, **Business Phone:** (800)321-1456.

**JONES-GRIMES, DR. MABLE CHRISTINE**
Educator, home economist. **Personal:** Born Dec 6, 1943, Malden, MO; daughter of Albert Jones and Anna Mae Turner Jones; married James Robert Grimes; children: Ori Brandon Jones Grimes. **Educ:** Univ Mo-Columbia, BS, 1965, MS, 1968, PhD, 1976. **Career:** Educator (retired); Univ Mo, Coop exten Serv, home economist, 1965-68, 4-H Prog, youth specialist & asst prof, Human Develop & Family Studies, AA & EEO Off & dir diversity, Univ Outreach & Ext; Delta Head start Prog, home economist, 1968-69; ParentLink, vol, currently. **Orgs:** Black Alumni Orgn; Mizzou Alumni Asn; Am Home Econ Asn, 1965-; Nat Coun Family Rels, 1980-; fac adv, Delta Tau Chap, Alpha Kappa Alpha Sorority, 1983-; bd mem, Planned Parenthood Inc, 1985-; pres, Kappa Chi Omega Chap, Alpha Kappa Alpha Sorority Inc, 1986-87; Chamber Com, Women's Network, 1986; pres, bd dir, Planned Parenthood Cent Mo, 1988-90. **Home Addr:** 522 Huntridge Dr, Columbia, MO 65201, **Home Phone:** (573)449-9937.

**JONES-HENDERSON, NAPOLEON**
Educator, artist. **Personal:** Born Nov 23, 1943, Chicago, IL; son of Maxine Unger and Woodrow; children: Mamemaeli Di & Lylana Von. **Educ:** Sorbonne Stud Continum, Paris, France, attended 1963; Sch Art Inst Chicago, BFA, 1971; Northern Ill Univ, MA, DeKalb, IL, 1971; Md Inst Col Art, MFA, 2005. **Career:** Mus Nat Ctr Afro-Am Artists, Roxbury, Mass, dir educ, 1975-76; Res Inst African & African Diaspora Arts Inc, Roxbury, Mass, founder & exec dir, 1979-; Vt Col Norwich Univ, Montpelier, VT, adj prof, 1989-; Benedict Col, Columbia, SC, 1999-2000; artist, currently; Harriet Wilson Proj, art dir, currently. **Orgs:** Bd mem, Mass Health Comn, 1983-87; African Am Assoc Mus World Craft Coun; Am Craft Coun; Soc Am Goldsmiths; Enamelist Soc; Col Art Assoc; founding mem, Africobra; bd dir, Artists Found, 1986-92; bd dir, Unitarian Unversalist, 1986-; bd dir, Celebration Black Cinema, 1987-92; pres, Nat Conf Artists Inc, 1997-99; bd mem, Bauen Camp; African Commune Bad Relevant Artists. **Business Addr:** Art Director, The Harriet Wilson Project, 614 Nashua St Suite 121, Milford, NH 03055-4917.

**JONES-SMITH, JACQUELINE**
Executive. **Personal:** Born Nov 5, 1952, New York, NY; married Joshua; children: Joshua Smith Jr. **Educ:** Swarthmore Col, BA, 1974; Syracuse Univ, MLS, 1978; Am Univ Sch Law, JD, 1984. **Career:** MAXIMA Corp, syst librn, 1979-85, dir clearing house oper, 1980-81, sr libr syst consult, 1981-84, div mgr, 1984-85, exec vpres & bd mem, 1995-96, pres & chief oper officer; Montgomery County, asst county atty, 1985-87; Fed Election Comn, staff atty, off gen coun, 1987-89; Consumer Prod Safety Comn, chmn, 1989-94; Good Hope Union United methodist Church, pastor. **Orgs:** Am Bar Asn; Nat Bar Asn; MAR State Bar Asn.

**JONES-THOMPSON, MARION.** See JONES, MARION.

**JONES-TRENT, BERNICE R.**
Librarian. **Personal:** Born Apr 22, 1946, Michie, TN; daughter of E C Ray and Ellen Hodge; married Julius. **Educ:** Jackson State Univ, Jackson, MS, BA, 1968; Rutgers Univ, Nb, NJ, MLS, 1969; Rutgers Univ, SCILS, Nb, NJ, PhD cand, 1984-. **Career:** Newark Bus Libr, Newark, NJ, jr librn, 1969-70; Rutgers-Dana Libr, Newark, NJ, bus librn, 1970-82; Rutgers Univ, Libr Sch, Nb, NJ, actg dir, prof, develop studies, 1982-83; Rutgers Univ Libr, Nb, NJ, staff develop librn, 1983-84; Rutgers-Kilmer Libr, Nb, NY, pub servs librn, 1984-85; Old Dom Univ Libr, Norfolk, Va, head, ref dept, 1985-87; Norfolk State Univ, Norfolk, Va, libr, 1987-89; Montclair State Col, Upper Montclair, NJ, Sprague Libr, dir libr serv, 1989-. **Orgs:** Alpha Kappa Alpha Sorority Inc, 1965-; Black Caucus ALA, 1974-; Am Libr Asn, 1975-; charter mem, Nj Black Librarians Network, 1975-; Asn Col & Res Librs, 1975-; Libr Admin & Mgmt Asn, 1978; chair, Leadership Discussion Group & Women Admin Discussion Group, 1988-90. **Honors/Awds:** Acad Scholar, Jackson State Univ, 1964-68; Scholar, Spec Librs Asn, 1968; Title II B Scholar, Rutgers Univ, 1968-69; County Comt Woman, East Orange, NJ, 1984-85. **Special Achievements:** Article, 'Keeping Pace with Changes in the Curriculum and in the Student Body', The American Mosaic Public & Access Services, Quarterly Volume 1, Number 3. **Home Addr:** 2217 Crossing Way, Wayne, NJ 07470, **Home Phone:** (404)284-4521. **Business Addr:** Director of Library Services, Montclair State University, Upper Montclair, NJ 07043, **Business Phone:** (201)893-4301.

**JONES-WILSON, FAUSTINE CLARISSE**
Educator. **Personal:** Born Dec 3, 1927, Little Rock, AR; daughter of James Edward Thomas and Perrine Marie Childress Thomas; married James T Jones; children: Yvonne Dianne Jones & Brian Vincent Jones; married Edwin L Wilson Sr. **Educ:** Dunbar Jr Col, dipl, 1946; Univ Ark, AB, 1948; Univ Ill, AM, 1951, EdD, 1967. **Career:** Gary, Ind Pub Schs, teacher, 1955-62, librn, 1964-67; Univ Ill, Urbana, teaching asst, grad stud, 1962-64, Univ Ill, Chicago, Col Educ, asst prof, 1967-69; Fed City Col, assoc prof, adult educ, 1969-70; Howard Univ, Dept Educ, asst prof, 1969-93, prof educ, actg dean, 1991-92, prof emer, 1993-; J Negro Educ, actg ed-in-chief, 1992-93, ed-in-chief emerita, 1993-. **Orgs:** Am Educ Studies Asn, Nominating Comt, 1974-75, Prog Comt, 1975-76, ExeCoun, 1976-79, 1985-86, Butts lect com, 1978-79, nominating comt chair, 1981-82, pres, 1984-85; John Dewey Soc NBA79, exec bd, 1988-90, nominating comt chair, 1992; Soc Profs Educ, exec bd, 1981-87, nominating comt chair, 1979; Howard Univ Chap, Phi Delta Kappa, pres, 1986-87, Exec Comt, 1986-87; Nat Coun Educating Black C, chair, E Coast Steering Comt, 1986-88, 1990-92, bd dir, 1986-98, third vpres, 1992-94; Adv Coun, Charlotte Hawkins Brown Hist Found Inc. **Home Addr:** 6605 Allview Dr, Columbia, MD 21046-1005, **Home Phone:** (301)596-5328. **Business Addr:** Professor Emeritus of Education, Howard University, 2441 4th St NW, Washington, DC 20059, **Business Phone:** (202)806-7340.

**JOR'DAN, DR. JAMILAH R.**
Executive, business owner. **Educ:** Erikson Inst, MEd, early childhood educ & infant studies, 1993; Loyola Univ Chicago, PhD, res methodology & human develop, 2003. **Career:** Partnership Qual Child Care, founder & pres, 1999-2007; Jordan Consult Group Inc, owner & pres, 2000-. **Orgs:** Vpres, Nat Asn Educ Young C; exec dir, Chicago Accreditation Partnership; accreditation proj dir & interim exec dir Chicago Metro Asn Educ Young C, 1994-98. **Honors/Awds:** James B. Blanton Head Start Center Leadership Award, 1987; Ralph H. Metcalfe Magnet School Local School Council Service Award, 1991; Friends of Lutheran General Children's Day Care Appreciation Award, 1995; Illinois ChildCorps Appreciation Award, Americorps Nat Serv, 1995; Center for Communication Resources Award, 1998; Ecumenical Child Care Network Award, 2003; Woman of the Year, Am Biog Inst Inc, 2004; Ruby Brunson Community Advocacy Award, Nat Asn Family Child Care, 2007. **Business Addr:** Owner, President, Jordan Consulting Group Inc, 12225 S Harvard Ave, Chicago, IL 60628-6511, **Business Phone:** (312)480-6894.

**JORDAN, DR. ABBIE H. (ABIGAIL JORDAN)**
Educator. **Personal:** Born Wilcox County, GA; daughter of Samuel Williams and Leah Jones Williams; married J Wesley; children: W Kenneth. **Educ:** Albany St Col, BS, 1949; Atlanta Univ, MA, 1953; Univ Ga, PhD, 1980. **Career:** Savannah St Col, from dir to asst prof, 1965-79; founder, dir, Chatham County, grand jury foreman, 1987; Consortium Doctors Ltd, founder, 1991-; Tuskegee Inst, instr; Atlanta

Univ Complex, instr reading; Jr HS Ben Hill County, prin; Veterans Sch, prin & instr; GA-SC Read Conf, org & dir; Savannah Morning News, ed-op columnist; Savannah St Col Reading Inst, founder. **Orgs:** Adv Comn IRA Resol Comn, 1974-; Adv Comn Ga Hist Found, 1974-80; exec sec & treas, Savannah Hosp Authority, 1975-; Telfair Art Acad, 1975-80; Basic Ed & Reading, 1977-78; exec bd, Nat Asn Advan Colored People, 1977-83; coord & founder, Soc Doctors Inc, 1986-; founder & dir, Consortium Doctors Ltd, 1991, chair, YMCA; pres, Am Asn Univ Professors. **Honors/Awds:** Outstanding Teacher of the Year, 1973; National Alumni Association Hall of Fame, Albany State Univ. **Special Achievements:** Featured in Essence Mag, 1976; Novelet "Ms Lily", 1977; authored numerous articles; featured in Atlanta Constitution Journal, June 1988; Jet, Sept28, 1992, Oct 5, 1992; First African American Family Monument In America; Declared Dr. Abigail Jordan Day In Savannah, Georgia, July 30, 2005. **Home Addr:** 2207 Glynnwood Dr, Savannah, GA 31404, **Home Phone:** (912)354-4634. **Business Addr:** Founder, Director, The Consortium of Doctors Ltd, PO Box 2040, Savannah, GA 31404, **Business Phone:** (912)238-1234.

### JORDAN, ANDREW, JR.

Football player. **Personal:** Born Jun 21, 1972, Charlotte, NC. **Educ:** W Carolina. **Career:** Football player (retired); Minn Vikings, tight end, 1994-97; Tampa Bay Buccaneers, 1997; Philadelphia Eagles, 1998; Minn Vikings, tight end, 1999-2001, fullback, 2001; W Charlotte, head football coach. **Home Addr:** 7413 Newmans Lane, Charlotte, NC 28270. **Business Addr:** Head Football Coach, West Charlotte, 2219 Senior Dr, Charlotte, NC 28216, **Business Phone:** (980)343-6060.

### JORDAN, B. DELANO

Lawyer. **Personal:** Born Jan 23, 1970, Nashville, TN; son of Dr George L Jr; married Toupazer; children: Alexis, Alayna & Selene. **Educ:** Va Polytech Inst & State Univ, BSEE, 1994; William & Mary Sch Law, JD, 1999. **Career:** Litton Poly-Sci, qual assurance engr, 1994; Canon Va Inc, elec engr, 1994-96; NASA Langley Res Ctr, intern, law clerk & patent contractor, 1997-98; Harness, Dickey & Pierce Assocs, 1999-2001; Kenyon & Kenyon LLP, assoc atty, 2001-03, 2005-08; Intel, sr patent atty, 2003-05; Alston & Bird LLP, coun, 2008-09; Jordan IP Law LLC, founding prin, 2009-. **Orgs:** Inst Elec & Electronic Engrs, 1994 & 1999-; bd dir, Coop Hampton Roads Orgn Minority Engrs, 1995-96; Omega Psi Phi Inc, 1995-; State Bar Mich, 1999-; US Ct Appeals Fed Circuit. **Honors/Awds:** CALI Excellence Award in Patent Law, Williams & Mary Sch Law, 1998; Legal Skills Hon, 1997 & 1998; Moot Court Bar, 1998. **Special Achievements:** Publications: Unfair Competition and the ITC: Actions Before the International Trade Commission Uelec engineering, under Section 337 of the Tariff Act of 1930, 2003; IP Strategies for a Green Economy, Patent Strategy and Management, 2009. **Home Addr:** 14621 Carona Dr, Silver Spring, MD 20905, **Home Phone:** (301)384-3571. **Business Addr:** Founding Principal, Associate Attorney, Jordan IP Law PC, 1701 Pennsylvania Ave NW Suite 300, Washington, DC 20006, **Business Phone:** (202)683-9317.

### JORDAN, BETTYE DAVIS

Entrepreneur. **Personal:** Born Sep 14, 1946, Tampa, FL; daughter of Lee and Ethel; children: Lisa Darlene Walker & Christopher Charles White II. **Educ:** Univ Tampa, BS, med technol, 1968. **Career:** B Davis Enterprises, owner; Harambee Enterprises, pres. **Orgs:** Bd mem, Fla Med Technol Asn, 1979-; exec bd mem, Nat Asn Advan Colored People, 1980-86; bd mem, Womens Survival Ctr, 1981-83; vpres, Pride Joy Enterprises, 1982-85; Movie Guild, 1984-86; vpres, Nat Asn Adbvan Colored People, 1986-; Civic Rev Bd, Tampa Urban League, 1987; bd mem, Col Hill Develop & Comm Cv Org, 1987; vpres, Nat Asn Advan Colored People, 1989-91. **Honors/Awds:** Medical Technologist Award, Univ Community Hosp, 1982. **Business Addr:** President, Harambee Enterprises, 3525 N 22nd St, Tampa, FL 33605.

### JORDAN, BRIAN O'NEIL

Baseball player, television director. **Personal:** Born Mar 29, 1967, Baltimore, MD; married Pam; children: Briana & Bryson. **Educ:** Richmond Univ. **Career:** Baseball player (retired), Atlanta Falcons, safety, 1989-91; St Louis Cardinals, outfielder, 1992-98; Atlanta Braves, 1999-2001, 2005-06, TV pre game analyst, currently; Los Angeles Dodgers, outfielder, 2002-03; Tex Rangers, outfielder, 2004; Gwinnett Braves, TV commentator, 2009-. **Orgs:** Brian Jordan Found. **Business Addr:** TV pre-game analyst, Atlanta Braves, Turner Field 755 Hank Aaron Dr, Atlanta, GA 30315, **Business Phone:** (404)522-7630.

### JORDAN, CAROLYN D.

Investment banker, lawyer. **Personal:** Born Mar 7, 1941, Ft. Worth, TX. **Educ:** Fisk Univ, BA, 1963; Howard Univ, JD, 1966; Dallas County Community Col, arts & sci, bus, 1981; Tex A&M Univ, BS, bus admin, 2011; Southern Methodist Univ, exec educ prog, 2012; Eastfield Col. **Career:** Libr Cong, copyright examr, 1966-68; Va Regional Los Angeles, veterans claims adjudicator, 1968-69; Econ & Youth Opportunities Agency, Los Angeles, prog mgt specialist, 1969-70; Compton Calif, dep city atty, 1970-71; Herman A Eng, atty, 1971-72; Senate Majority Whip Alan Cranston, legis asst, 1971-73; US ie, Banking, Housing & Urban Affairs Comn, coun, 1974-92; Pryor, McClendon, Counts & Co Inc, Investment Bankers, sr vpres, 1992-97; Nat Credit Union Admin, exec dir, 1997-2001, Neighborhood Credit Union, loan receptionist, 1979-83, loan officer, 1983-88, sr mortgage loan officer, 1988-91, vpres lending, 1991-95, vpres retail opers, 1995-2001, coun exec comt mem & sr vpres retail opers, 2001-11, sr vpres retail serv, 2011-13, sr vpres, remote serv, 2013-, vice chmn; chair, CUNA Opers, Sales & Serv Coun. **Orgs:** Delta Sigma Theta Sorority, 1975-78; bd mem, Links Inc; State Bar Calif; Nat Bar Asn; Bar Dist Columbia; Nominating Comt, Tex Opers Coun; dir, 2001, vice chairperson & bd dir, 2003, Independence Fed Savings Bank; dir, Independence Financial Corp. **Business Addr:** Senior Vice President of Remote Services, Neighborhood Credit Union, 13651 Montfort Dr, Dallas, TX 75240-3476, **Business Phone:** (214)748-9393.

### JORDAN, DR. CAROLYNE LAMAR

School administrator. **Personal:** Born Augusta, GA; daughter of Peter and Serena James; married Lawrence M; children: Lara Gayle & Samuel Lamar (deceased). **Educ:** Fisk Univ, BA, music, 1960; New Eng Univ, MMus, 1970; Harvard Univ, Eed, 1977; Leadership Memphis, 1991. **Career:** Hamilton Cent Sch, dir music, 1962-67; Lexington Pub Sch, supvr music, 1967-70; Salem St Col, prof psychol, music, 1971-83; Suffolk Univ, asst pres, 1983-88; Fell Smith Col, pres, 1986-87; Le Moyne Owen Col, vpres acad affairs, 1988-90; Harvard Univ, vis scholar, 1990-91; Maryville Univ, assoc dean grad studies, 1992-93; Fed Express Corp, corp trainer, 1993-95; Cape Cod Comm Col, dean acad affairs, 1995-99; Lamar-Jordan Assoc Inc, pres, educ leadership consult, 1999-. **Orgs:** Friends Nat Ctr Afro Am, 1971-73; Am Psychol Asn, 1977-; trustee, Cambridge Friends Sch, 1980-84; exec brd, Natl Am Friends Serv Comt, 1983-; chairperson, Long Range Planning Comm Suffolk Univ; renway consortium Retention Comt; pres, Human Resources Cons; pres, Alpha Kappa Alpha Sorority, Boston chap; exec brd, ACE & NIP, 1985; exec brd, Freedom House, 1985; Leadership Memphis, 1989-90; brd, phis Urban League; Family Serv phis; phis Symphony Orchestra; Porter Leath C's Ctr, phis; Young Women Christian Asn; natl pres, Soc Inc, 1997-2001; sr fel, Am Coun Educ, 1999; phis Symphony League, 2002-. **Home Addr:** 2826 Cent Ave, Memphis, TN 38111, **Home Phone:** (901)323-9963. **Business Addr:** President, Educational Leadership Consultant, Lamar-Jordan Associates Inc, 2826 Cent Ave, Memphis, TN 38111, **Business Phone:** (901)229-1832.

### JORDAN, CHARLES WESLEY

Clergy. **Personal:** Born May 28, 1933, Dayton, OH; son of David Morris and Naomi Azelia Harper; married Margaret Crawford; children: Diana Elizabeth & Charlie Jordan Brookins. **Educ:** Roosevelt Univ, BA, 1956; Garrett-Evangel Theol Sem, Mdiv, 1960. **Career:** Clergy (retired); United Methodist Church, minister, 1960; Woodlawn United Methodist Church, pastor, 1960-66; Rockford Ill Urban Ministries, dir, 1966-71; Northern Ill Conf Cou, prog staff, 1971-82; Chicago Southern Dist, supt, 1982-87; St Mark United Methodist Church, Chicago, IL, sr pastor, 1987-92, bishop, 1992; Iowa Area United Methodist Church, bishop, 1992-2000; Claremont Sch Theol, Bishop Residence, 2001-. **Orgs:** Comnr, Rockford Housing Authority, 1967-71; fel Northern Ill Conf Coun, 1971-82; bd dir, United Methodist Bd Global Ministries, 1972-80; United Methodist Coun Ministries, 1980-88; bd trustee, Garrett-Evangel Theol Sem, 1982-97, elected life trustee, 2000; Proj Image, 1987-92; bd dir, Chicago Community Ment Health Coun, 1989-92; bd dir, Cent Iowa Health Syst, 1992-2000; bd mem, United Methodist Church & Soc, 1992-2000, pres, 1996-2000; bd dir, Mid-Iowa Coun Boy Scouts Am, 1995-2000; pres, Iowa Ecumencial Ministries, 1999-2000; life mem, Kappa Alpha Psi fraternity; Sigma Pi Phi fraternity; life mem, Nat Asn Advan Colored People; life mem, Black Methodists Church Renewal; City Human Rels; bd, County Community Action Agency; N Cent Jurisdiction Comn Relig Race; bd Progressive Christians Uniting, 2003-10. **Home Addr:** 1014 Deborah St, Upland, CA 91784, **Home Phone:** (909)946-6785.

### JORDAN, HON. CLAUDIA J.

Judge. **Personal:** Born Raleigh, NC. **Educ:** Univ NC, Charlotte, NC, BA, 1975; Univ Colo Sch Law, Boulder, CO, attended 1980. **Career:** Colo Pub Defenders Off, Denver Off, trial atty, 1982-87; sole practr, 1987-94; Denver County Ct, judge, 1994-; dep state pub defender. **Orgs:** Colo Bar Asn; Sam Cary Bar Asn; Denver Bar Asn; Colo Women's Bar Asn. **Business Addr:** Judge, Denver County Court, 1437 Bannock St Rm 256, Denver, CO 80202, **Business Phone:** (720)865-8301.

### JORDAN, DARIN GODFREY

Football player. **Personal:** Born Dec 4, 1964, Boston, MA; married Andrea Hayes; children: Jonah & Jenelle. **Educ:** Northeastern Univ, BA, speech commun, 1988. **Career:** Football player (retired); Pittsburgh Steelers, line backer, 1988; Los Angeles Raiders, 1990; San Francisco 49ers, line backer, 1991-94. **Special Achievements:** Elected to the Northeastern Univ Hall of Fame, 2002.

### JORDAN, DAVID LEE

Educator, city council member. **Personal:** Born Apr 3, 1934, Leflore County, MS; son of Cleveland and Elizabeth; married Christine Bell; children: David Jr, Joyce Jordan Dugar, Donald & Darryl. **Educ:** Miss Valley State Univ, BS, 1959; Univ Wyo, MS, 1969. **Career:** Teacher (retired), city councilman; Greenwood Voters League, pres, 1965-; Greenwood Pub Sch Syst, sci teacher, 1970-; Greenwood City Council, pres, 1985; Mississippi State Senate, Greenwood City, councilman, 1993-. **Orgs:** Leflore Co Br & Nat Asn Advan Colored People, 1960-; Leflore Co & Dem Exec Comt 1976-; Nat Dem Platform Civil Rights Adv Comt, 1978; chmn, Miss Valley State Univ Nat Alumni Asn, 1980; Miss Municlpal Asn; Miss Wayport Authority Adv Coun; chmn, Investigate State Off Comt; vice chmn, Elections Comt; vice chmn, Legislative Reapportionment; chmn, Agriculture Comt; chmn, Educ Comt; chmn, Finance Comt; chmn, County Affairs; chmn, Forestry Comt; chmn, Labor Comt; chmn, Municipalities Comt; chmn, Tourism Comt; chmn, Housing. **Home Addr:** PO Box 8173, Greenwood, MS 38930, **Home Phone:** (662)453-5361. **Business Addr:** Greenwood City Councilman, Democratic Member, Mississippi State Senate, Rm 405 A, Jackson, MS 39215-1018, **Business Phone:** (601)359-3244.

### JORDAN, DR. DEDRA R.

Manager, entrepreneur, educator. **Personal:** Born Aug 10, 1953, Portsmouth, VA; daughter of Paul Wilson and Delores Wilson; married Melvin C; children: Milton Ray Dixon II. **Educ:** Va State Univ, BS, educ; James Madison Univ, MA, educ; Kennedy-Western Univ, PhD, bus admin; cert strategic mgt human resources. **Career:** VA Beach Pub Schs, band teacher, 1976-77; Norfolk Pub Schs, teacher, 1978-81; Super Eng & Electronics Co, personnel mgr, indust security supvr, 1981-90; Casde Mfg, personnel mgr/ indust security supvr, 1990-93; Norfolk Airport Auth, dir employee & community rels, 1994-98; SE Pub Serv Auth, hr analyst, res trainer, 1999-2001; PEMCO, HR coord, 2001-02; FSS Alutiiq JV, hr mgr, 2002-03; New Horizons Reg Educ Ctr, hr dir, currently; BET Consult Serv, founder, currently; Lorman Educ Serv, prin consult, owner, currently. **Orgs:** Int Personnel Mgt Asn; Soc Human Resource Mgt; Employ Mgt Asn; C's Ctr, 2003; Am Soc Trng & Develop; Nat Asn Female Execs; Am Bus Women's Asn; Alpha Kappa Alpha; Va & Tidewater Asn Sch Personnel Adminr; Human Roads Chap Am Bus Women's Asn. **Honors/Awds:** Creative Application Award, Yoder-Heneman HR Mgt (small co), Soc HR Mgt, 1995; InterNat Who's Who of Professional, 1995; Sterling Who's Who Directory, Executive Edition; A Phillip Randolph Award, Outstanding EEO & Affirmative Action, Airport Authority, 1998; numerous other leadership awards. **Home Addr:** 3929 Spring Meadow Crescent, Chesapeake, VA 23321, **Home Phone:** (757)405-3783. **Business Addr:** Founder, BET Consulting Service, 3929 Spring Meadow Crescent, Chesapeake, VA 23321, **Business Phone:** (757)405-3783.

### JORDAN, DR. EDDIE J., JR.

Attorney general (U.S. federal government), government official. **Personal:** Born Oct 6, 1952, Ft. Campbell, KY; son of Eddie J Sr and Gladys McDaniel (deceased); married Charmaine E; children: Aisha Zakiya, Chad-Hassan Akil & Julian Khalid. **Educ:** Wesleyan Univ, Middletown, CT, BA, social studies, 1974; Rutgers Law Sch, Newark, NJ, JD, 1977. **Career:** Southern Univ Law Sch, prof, 1981-84; US Atty's Off, assist US atty, 1984-87; Sessions & Fishman, assoc, 1987-90, partner, 1990-92; Bryan, Jupiter & Lewis, coun, 1992-94; US Dept Justice, US atty, 1994-2001; Orleans Parish, La, dist atty, 2003-07; Pepper, Hamilton & Scheetz, assoc; Eddie J. Jordan, Jr. LLC, proprietor, 2009-. **Orgs:** Bd govs, LA State Bar Asn, 1984; bd dir, 1989-94, vpres, bd dir, 1991-93, Planned Parenthood LA; bd dir, Metrop Area Community, 1990-94; bd dir, St Thomas/Irish Channel Consortium, 1990-94; adv comm human rels, Human Rels Comn, City N Orleans, 1993; Nat Asn Advan Colored People, 1993-95; adv comt, Atty Gen's, 1998-2000; adv bd & bd dir, Reducing Alcohol Accessibility Youth; bd dir, New Orleans chap Fed Bar Asn; adv bd, Pediat AIDS Prog; adv bd, New Orleans Community, Teach Am; vice chair, Atty Gen's Adv Comm, Subcomt Controlled Substances/Drug Abuse Prev; subcomts Justice Progs & Organized Crime/Violent Crime. **Home Addr:** 7821 Windward Ct, New Orleans, LA 70128. **Business Addr:** LA.

### JORDAN, ATTY. EDDIE JACK, JR.

District attorney. **Personal:** Born Jan 1, 1952, New Orleans, LA; son of Eddie J Sr. **Educ:** Wesleyan Univ, Middletown, CT, attended 1974; Rutgers Univ Sch Law, NJ, attended 1977. **Career:** US attorney (retired), district attorney; Southern Univ, law prof, 1981-84; New Orleans, asst US atty, 1984-94; Eastern Dist La, US atty, 1994-2001; Orleans Parish, dist atty, 2003-07. **Orgs:** La bar Asn; La Polit Mus & Hall Fame, 2005. **Honors/Awds:** Louisiana Political Museum and Hall of Fame, 2005. **Special Achievements:** First African-American to be elected the District Attorney of New Orleans; First African-American U.S. Attorney in La. **Business Addr:** District Attorney, Orleans Parish, 619 S White St, New Orleans, LA 70019, **Business Phone:** (504)822-2414.

### JORDAN, EDWARD MONTGOMERY (EDDIE JORDAN)

Basketball coach, basketball player. **Personal:** Born Jan 29, 1955, Washington, DC; son of Edward Lee Jr and Marguerite; children: Justin, Eddie Jr & Paul; married Charrisse; children: Jackson & Skylar. **Educ:** Rutgers Univ, BS, health & phys educ, 1977. **Career:** Basketball player (retired), basketball coach; Cleveland Cavaliers, 1977-78; Nj Nets, 1977-81, asst coach, 1999-2003; Los Angeles Lakers, 1980-84, asst, 2012-13; Wyo Wildcatters, 1983; Portland Trail Blazers, 1983-84; Boston Col, asst coach, 1986-88; Rutgers Univ, asst coach, 1988-91; Sacramento Kings, asst coach, 1992-97, coach, 1997-98; Wash Wizards, head coach, 2003-08; Philadelphia 76ers, head coach, 2009-10; Rutgers, head coach, 2013-. **Orgs:** Vol asst, Rutgers Univ. **Home Addr:** 158 Monroe Ave, Belle Mead, NJ 08502-4632.

### JORDAN, PROF. EMMA COLEMAN

Educator, lawyer, civil rights activist. **Personal:** Born Nov 29, 1946, Berkeley, CA; daughter of Earl and Myrtle Coleman; children: Kristen Elena & Allison Elizabeth. **Educ:** San Francisco State Univ, BA, 1969; Howard Univ, JD, 1973. **Career:** Stanford Law Sch, teaching fel, 1973-74; Univ Santa Clara, asst prof, 1974-75; White House, fel, 1980-81; Atty Gen US, spec asst, 1981; Univ Calif, Davis, fac; Georgetown Univ Law Ctr, prof law, 1987-; Books: Beyond Rational Choice: Alternative Perspectives on Economics, 2006; A Woman Place is in the Marketplace: Gender and Economics, 2006; When Markets Fail: Race and Economics, 2006; Cultural Economics: Markets and Culture, 2006; The Short End of The Stick: The Role of Race in Law, Markets and Social Structures, 2009; Economic Justice: Race; Gender; Identity & Economics, 2011. **Orgs:** Am Law Inst, 1984; pres, Soc Am Law Teachers, 1986-88; exec comt, Asn Am Law Schs, 1988-91, pres, 1992-93; Nat Conf Black Lawyers; Nat Bar Asn; Am Soc Int Law; pub mem, Calif State Bd Dent & Exmnrs; Am Asn Law Schs Sects Com Law & Contracts, Minority Groups; Charles Houston Bar Asn; bd dir, Calif Asn Black Lawyers; chmn, Calif St Bar Financial Inst Comn; chmn, AALS Financial Inst & Consumer Financial Serv Sect; bd mem, Consumer Action; adv comm, Nat Consumer Union Northern Ca. **Business Addr:** Professor of Law, Georgetown University, McDonough 578 600 NJ Ave NW, Washington, DC 20001-2075, **Business Phone:** (202)661-6585.

**JORDAN, ERIC BENET.** See BENET, ERIC.

### JORDAN, FREDERICK E., SR.

Association executive, civil engineer, executive. **Personal:** Born Apr 27, 1937, Loveville, MD; son of Lewis E. **Educ:** Howard Univ, BS, civil engineering; Stanford Univ, MS, civil engineering. **Career:** Sandrestrom Afb Greenland, asst chief engr pvt pract, 1968; W Asn Minority Consult Engr, pres, 1974; Am Soc Civ Engr SF Sect, dir, 1974; Nat Coun Minority Consult Engr, pres, 1976-77; Bonelli, Young, Wong & Biggs, San & Fran, div civ-struct engr; Bechtel Corp San Fran & Charles T Main Consult Engrs, Boston, struct engr; Riverside Dept Pub Works Riverside CA, civ engr; LA Air Def Command, dir civ engr; US Environ Protect Agency, tech adv; FE Jordan Assocs Inc, prin, pres & chief exec officer, currently; San Francisco, comnr; Calif State, comnr. **Orgs:** Nat Soc Prof Engr; consult Engrs Asn US;

Struct Engrs Asn CA; Soc Am Mil Engrs; fed mem, pres, chmn bd, dir Engr Soc Com Manpower Training Inc; founding mem, first chmn, N Calif Coun Black Prof Engrs; vpres, San Fran Forum Am Soc Civ Engrs; mem engr adv & bd, Calif State Univ San Fran; San Fran Engr Coun; pres, bd dir Bay Area Urban League Inc, 1972-73; pres, San Francisco Black Chamber Com, 1989-94; pres, Calif Asn Better Govt, 1990-91; councilman, San Francisco Pvt Indust Coun; councilman Calif, Dept Transp Bus Coun; Comnr, San Francisco Parking & Traffic Comn; comnr, Calif State Comn Status African Male; pres, African Am Chamber; co-founder, Calif Black Chamber Com; Nat Black Chamber; Greenlining Inst. **Honors/Awds:** Bay Area & State Calif outstanding civil engr comn activity, Am Soc Civ Engr, 1967-68; Distinguished Alumni Award, Bay Area Howard Univ Alumni Club, 1972; Distinguished Black Sci & Eng, US Oakland Mus Asn, 1973; Governor's Award, Best Small Bus Contractor, State CA, 1993; Minority Serv Firm, Five Western States, 1993; One of Ten Outstanding Bus in the US, 1993; several Publs, 20 other awards. **Special Achievements:** Co-founder of the first African American Civil Engineering and Construction Management firm in the western part of the US; Published "The Lynching of the American Dream", 1996. **Business Addr:** President, Chief Executive Officer, FE Jordan Associates Inc, 90 New Montgomery St Suite 1320, San Francisco, CA 94105, **Business Phone:** (415)243-9080.

**JORDAN, DR. GEORGE LEE, JR. See Obituaries Section.**

### JORDAN, GEORGE WASHINGTON, JR.

Executive. **Personal:** Born Mar 11, 1938, Chattanooga, TN; son of George W Sr and Omega Davis; married Fredine Sims; children: George W III. **Educ:** Tuskegee Univ, BSEE, 1961; Emory Univ, mgt inst, 1976; GA Inst Tech, MSIM, 1978. **Career:** Boeing Co, engr, 1961-64, test engr. 1964-65; Gen Elec Co, design engr, 1965-66; Lockheed-Ga Co, engr & engineering dept mgr, 1966-. **Orgs:** Life mem, Alpha Phi Alpha Fraternity, 1957-; Nat Mgt Asn, 1966-; sr mem, Am Inst Aero Astro, 1973-; Merit Employees Asn, 1975-; Asn MBA Execs, 1978-; Inst Mgt Sci, 1978-; chmn, Atlanta Zoning Bd, 1978-84; nat mem, Flt Sim Tech Comm AIAA, 1984-; Nat Asn Advan Colored People, 1985-; Am Mgt Assoc, 1991; Smithsonian Nat Assoc, 1991; United Way; bd deacon, Christian Fel Baptist Church; coun Christian ed, youth leadership coun, Sunday sch teacher, royal ambassador counr, fin comm, asst treas, chmn march bd, bus mgr; bd trustee, Shorter Col; Asn Master Bus Admin Execs; Am Defense Preparedness Asn. **Honors/Awds:** Outstanding Business & Professional Award, Dollars & Sense, 1991. **Home Addr:** 120 Moss Creek Walk, Fayetteville, GA 30214-2692, **Home Phone:** (678)817-0457. **Business Addr:** Engineering Department Manager, Lockheed Georgia Co, 86 S Cobb Dr, Marietta, GA 30063-0001.

### JORDAN, DR. HAROLD WILLOUGHBY

Physician, educator, army officer. **Personal:** Born May 24, 1937, Newnan, GA; son of Edward P (deceased) and Dorothy W (deceased); married Geraldine Crawford; children: Harold II, Vincent, Karen & Kristie. **Educ:** Morehouse Col, BS, biology, 1958; Meharry Med Col, MD, 1962; G W Hubbard Hosp, rotating internship, 1963, med residency, 1964; Vanderbilt Univ Hosp, psychiat residency, 1967. **Career:** Meharry Med Col, Dept Psychiat clin instr, 1965-67, instr, actg dir outpatient dept, 1967-68, asst prof, dir psychiat outpatient clin, 1968-71, prof, chmn dept psychiat, 1979-97, Sch Med, actg dean; Florence Crittendon Home, psychiat consult, 1967; State Div Voc Rehab Intensive Treat Ctr, psychiat consult, 1967-71; Vanderbilt Univ Hosp, courtesy staff mem, 1967-, clin instr, 1968-72, clin asst prof, 1972-; Fisk Univ Stud Couns Ctr, psychiat consult, 1969-71; Tenn Dept Ment Health, Ment Retardation, asst comnr, 1971-75, comnr, 1975-79; Tenn State Univ, psychiat consult, 1984-; Cumberland Hall Hosp, attend physician, 1985-; pvt pract, currently. **Orgs:** Nat Asn Advan Colored People, 1957; Am Psychiat Asn, 1967; Am Asn Univ Profs, 1967; R F Boyd Med Soc, 1968; Nat Med Asn, 1970; Black Psychiatrists Am, 1973; Tenn Med Asn, 1975; Nashville Acad Med, 1975; Am Asn Chmn Psychiat, 1979; Alpha Omega Alpha Hon Med Soc, 1980; Sigma Pi Phi. **Honors/Awds:** Certificate of Recognition, Nashville Chap, Asn Black Psychologists, 1976; certificate of appreciation, Joseph P Kennedy Jr Found, 1976; certificate of recognition, Metro Atlanta Chap Nat Asn Human Rights Workers, 1976; Awarded Plaque, Nat Asn Black & Social Workers, 1977; plaque, Harriet Cohn Mental Health Ctr, 1979; plaque, Meharry Med Col Class, 1980; President's Award, Meharry Med Col, 1987; A state building, the Harold W. Jordan Habilitation Center, is named in his honor. **Special Achievements:** Harold W Jordan Habilitation Center, dedicated in Nashville, TN, 1987; First black medical resident on record at Vanderbilt University; First black Commissioner of Mental Health for the State of Tennessee. **Home Addr:** 4204 Kings Ct, Nashville, TN 37218, **Home Phone:** (615)342-1400. **Business Addr:** Psychiatry, 2400 Parmer Pl, Nashville, TN 37203, **Business Phone:** (615)342-1400.

### JORDAN, J. PAUL

Executive, chief executive officer, president (organization). **Personal:** Born Duquesne, PA; son of William and Rebecca. **Educ:** Univ Mich; Univ Detroit, BS. **Career:** Jordan & Assoc, chief exec officer; Meadow Village Partnership, chief exec officer; Ujama Develop Co, chief exec officer. **Orgs:** Adv bd, Fed Res Bank; adv bd, Fed Home Loan Bank; multicultural comt, Greater Milwaukee Conv & Visitors Bur; Nat Black Comt; dist dir, Am Defense Preparedness Asn; adv bd, US Small Bus Asn; pres & exec dir, Milwaukee Minority Chamber Com. **Home Addr:** 725 N 22, Milwaukee, WI 53233, **Home Phone:** (414)933-6000. **Business Addr:** President, Executive Director, Milwaukee Minority Chamber of Commerce, 509 W Wis Ave Suite 606, Milwaukee, WI 53203, **Business Phone:** (414)226-4105.

### JORDAN, DR. J. ST. GIRARD

Lawyer. **Personal:** Born Feb 29, 1944, Philadelphia, PA; son of Henderson and Emma Jane; married L Elaine Bullock; children: Daniel, Mark, Chonda & Kijsa. **Educ:** Temple Univ, ABS, 1969, BS, 1970; Univ Pa, Law Sch, JD, 1973. **Career:** SmithKline Corp, sr mkt res analyst, 1960-70, financial analyst, 1967-69, group gen coun, 1974-, asst gen coun, asst secy, 1986-87; Black Bk TV Prod, vpres & treas, 1969-72; Norden Labs Lincoln & VPO Inc, Omaha, corp officer; Goodis Greenfield Henry Shaiman & Levin, assoc, 1973-74; Municip Tax Bur Inc, coun, 1980-97; Consumer Prod Inc, gen coun, dir & secy, 1987; Expert Comt Drug Dependence, Geneva, Switz, consult; UN Coun Narcotic Drugs, Vienna, Austria, 1989-92; Menley James Inc, coun; WKW Inc, coun, 1990; St Assocs, currently. **Orgs:** Pres, Barristers Asn Philadelphia Inc, 1976-77; Nat Bar Asn; Am Bar Asn; Pa Bar Asn; Philadelphia Bar Asn; NJ Bar Asn; Camden County Bar Asn; legal comt, United Negro Col Fund Dr, 1977; vice chmn, AHI Law Comt, Washington, DC; pres, Philadelphia Fed Black Bus & Prof Orgs; Nat Asn Advan Colored People; Mt Zion Baptist Church; United Fund Way; Neighborhood Servs Comn; adv bd, Christian St Young Women's Christian Asn; bd dir, United Comn United Way Agency, 1982-84; chmn, AHI Law Comn, 1982; exec comt, Barristes Asn Philadelphia, 1986-87; Delta Epsilon, Southern NJ; Govt Affairs Comn Proprietry Asn; bd, Camden County Girl Scouts, NJ, 1991-92; Fed Judiciary Mediation Bd, 1992-; Municip Tax Bur, off coun, 1995-; secy bd, Philadan co. **Honors/Awds:** Outstanding Student Award, Temple Univ, 1968; Tribune Outstanding Citizen Centennel Award, 1984. **Home Addr:** 6 Rockledge Ct, Marlton, NJ 08053-9774, **Home Phone:** (856)767-3984. **Business Addr:** Principal, 6655 Mccallum St, Philadelphia, PA 19119, **Business Phone:** (215)438-5840.

### JORDAN, JACQUELYN D.

Educator, nurse. **Personal:** Born Mar 3, 1948, Waterbury, CT; children: Ayanna & Derek. **Educ:** Mattatuck Community Col, AA, nursing; Western Conn State Univ, BS, nursing, RN-BSN, 1979; Yale Univ, MS, neuroscience nursing, 1982; Adelphi Univ, PhD, nursing, 1994. **Career:** Mt Sinai Hosp, clin nurse supt, 1982-86; Univ Conn, asst prof nursing, 1985-86; Bristol Hosp, nurse mgr, 1986-88; Bridgeport Hosp, nurse mgr, neuro intensive care unit, 1988-89; Western Conn St Univ, assoc prof, nursing, 1989-98; Howard Univ, asst dean, undergrad nursing, 1998; Towson Univ, Dept Nursing, acad chair & prof, currently. **Orgs:** Asn Black Nursing Fac Higher Educ, 1990-; Sigma Theta Tau, 1982-; Nat Black Nurses Asn, 1991; Nat Polit Cong Black Women, 1989; bd dir, Nat Polit Cong Black Women, 1997; Am Nurses Asn; bd dir, Am Red Cross; Conn's Statewide Health Coord Coun. **Home Addr:** 7806 Regal Ct, Clinton, MD 20735, **Home Phone:** (301)877-3274. **Business Addr:** Chairperson, Professor, Towson university, Burdick Hall Rm 134 8000 York Rd, Towson, MD 21252-0001, **Business Phone:** (410)704-4212.

### JORDAN, REV. JOHN WESLEY

Educator, minister (clergy), clergy. **Personal:** Born Sep 10, 1941, Edenton, NC; son of Earl Holley and Annie Louise; children: Johann, Christian & Stanley. **Educ:** Elizabeth City State Univ, BS, Eng, 1963; Teachers Col, Columbia Univ, MA, eng, 1964; A Phillip Randolph Inst, attended 1973; Columbia Univ, adv study, 1974; NC State Univ, attended 1976. **Career:** Savannah State Col, instr humanities, 1964-66; Elizabeth City State Col, instr humanities, 1965; Claflin Col SC, instr humanities, 1966; Hampton Univ, instr humanities, 1966-67; New York Bd Educ, eng teacher, 1967-74; HQ USAG Ft Bragg, NC, personnel actions spec, 1975-77; Camp Casey, Korea, awards & decorations spec, 1977-78; Ft Bragg, NC, ID card sargent, NCOIC, 1978-81; Ft Shafter, HI, Non-Comn Officer Charge, personnel actions, 1982-84; Ft Drum NY, personnel actions sgt, SFC & E7, 1984-86; personnel admin ctr supvr, HHC First Bench Seventh Fa, 1986-88, supvr Transition Ctr, 1989-91; Watertown Correctional Facil, Watertown, NY, eng teacher, GED prog summer, 1988; Watertown Urban Mission, Watertown, NY, dir Oper Breakthrough, 1988-89; Faith Fel Christian Sch, vol eng teacher, 1990-91; City Refuge Christian Church, pastor, 1988-; Carthage Cent Schs, sub teacher, 1999-. **Orgs:** Ed, Refuge Flame City Refuge Christian Church, HI, 1982-84; Metro-Jefferson Pub Safety Bldg, 1984-; vol minister, Watertown Correctional Facil Watertown, NY, 1984-; vol lay relig leader, Ft Drum Prayer, Bible Study, fel 1984-88; Watertown, Jefferson County, Nat Asn Advan Colored People, 1988-; Cape Vincent Correctional Facil, 1988-; relig adv bd, Watertown & Cape Vincent Correctional Facil, 1988-; regist & cert foster father, 1989-2005; Gov Correctional Facil, 1991-92; vpres, Full Gospel Bus Men's Fel Int, Ft Drum, Charthage Chap, 1985, pres, 1986; chmn worship comn, Ft Drum Gospel Servs; bd mem, New Gate Prison Ministry; bd sch, Faith Fel Christian Sch, 1990-95, 1990-; bd mem, Barnabas Ministries, 1997-; Steering Comt, Communities That Care, Jefferson County, NY, 1998; bd mem, Alcohol & Substance Abuse Coun, 1998; Rotary Int Watertown, NY Noon Club, 2005-. **Honors/Awds:** Omega Psi Phi Fraternity Undergrad Scholarship, 1962; Grad Scholarship, 1963; American Spirit Honor Award, Ft Jackson, SC, 1975; Administration Ft Ben Harrison IN; Meritorious Service Medal, AUS, 1988; First Annual Freedom Fund Award, Watertown & Jefferson County Nat Asn Advan Colored People, 1989; USA Pastor of the Year, Day Spring Cards, 1998; Dewitt Clinton Masonic Award, 1999; Army Commendation Medal, AUS; First Oak Leaf Cluster, AUS; Army Achievement Medals, AUS; Certificates Appreciation, AUS. **Special Achievements:** Eight trips to Haiti as part of Barnabas Ministries pastor training in Haiti, 1997-. **Business Addr:** Pastor, City of Refuge Christian Church, 32500-32504 New York State Hwy Suite 3, Great Bend, NY 13643, **Business Phone:** (315)493-6463.

### JORDAN, JOSEPHINE E. C.

Transportation consultant. **Personal:** Born Dec 13, 1935, Philadelphia, PA; daughter of Clarence Connor and Josephine Connor; married Rev Harry A Sr. **Educ:** Allied Corp, bus cert, 1971. **Career:** Amtrak, res & info agt. **Orgs:** Daughter Isis, 1983-; Heroines Jericho, 1983-; Past Worthy Matron, Hadassah Chap No 91 OES, 1985-87; Ct Cyrenes, 1987-; Order Golden Circle; Past Royal Perfect Matron Faith & Fidelity, Ladies Circle Perfection; Past Dist Dep, Past Dist Lectr, 4th OES Dist. **Home Addr:** 2202 Airacobra St, Levittown, PA 19057, **Home Phone:** (215)943-3485.

### JORDAN, DR. JOY ANN

Dentist. **Personal:** daughter of Eugene. **Educ:** Howard Univ Sch Dentist, DDS. **Career:** Pvt pract, Cleveland, OH, currently. **Orgs:** Pres, Nat Dent Asn, 2004-; Adv Bd, Church & Dwight's Arm & Hammer Oral Care Div; rep, Greater Cleveland Dent Soc; pres, E Cleveland City Schs Bd Educ; Am Asn Women Dentists; Am Dent Asn; secy, Black Women's Polit Action Comt; coun woman, E Cleveland City Coun; Coalition 100 Black Women. **Honors/Awds:** Martin Luther King Jr Award, Nat Asn for the Advan of Colored People; Women of Achievement, YWCA, 2004. **Home Addr:** 13145 Euclid Ave, Cleveland, OH 44112-4740, **Home Phone:** (216)451-8500. **Business Addr:** Dentist, 4074 Lee Rd, Cleveland, OH 44128-2165, **Business Phone:** (216)491-8100.

### JORDAN, KENNETH ULYS

Educator. **Personal:** Born Apr 10, 1944, South Pittsburg, TN; children: Kenneth II & Michael. **Educ:** Univ Tenn, BS, pub admin, 1966; Vanderbilt Law Sch, JD, 1974. **Career:** Gen Foods Corp, employ specialist, 1970-71; Blue Heaven Farms, Dep Dir Oper, 1971; Nat Alliance Bus Men, loan ed exec, 1970-71; Sequatchi Valley Planning & Employ Agency, summer intern, 1972; Fair Employ Practices Clin, assoc dir, 1974; consult, 1975-2010; Vanderbilt Univ Law Sch, assoc dir, 1974-75, asst dean, 1975-76, opportunity develop officer & dir, 1977-81; Meharry Med Col, exec asst pres & interim vpres, 1981-82, vpres admin & gen coun, 1981-83; Air Univ, Air Command & Staff Col, resident stud, 1983-84; US Dept Justice, Justice Mgt Div, exec asst to asst atty gen, 1985-86, chief staff, 1986-87; Gov Task Force Housing, exec asst, 1987-88; Air, Mil Dept Ten, staff, 1988-95; Nat Comt Employer Support Guard & Res, dir, 1997-2000; City Atlanta, chief operating officer, 2001-. **Orgs:** Family & C Servs; Nashville Urban League; Univ Club Nashville; Nashville Bar Found; United Way Mid Tenn; Tenn State Mus Fund; Vanderbilt Univ Credit Union; Asn Vanderbilt Alumni; Napier-Looby Bar Asn; E Coast Chap; AMVETS; Am Legion; Air Force Assoc; VFW; Vanderbilt Bar Asn; pres, Law Stud Civil Rights Res Coun; Black Am Law Stud Asn; dir, Tenn Housing Develop Agency, 1987-90; Tenn Task Force Supply Minority Teachers, 1988-95; Napier-Looby Bar Asn; Vet Foreign Wars; bd, Nat transp Safety, 1995-97; Phi Kappa Phi; Reassessment Comt. **Honors/Awds:** US Law Week Award, Vanderbilt Univ Law Sch, 1974; Performance Award, Nat Transportation Safety Bd, 1995-97; Walter P Murray Distinguished Alumnus Award, Asn Vanderbilt Black Alumni, 1995; Martin Luther King Jr Fellowship Award, Woodrow Wilson Found, 1971. **Home Addr:** 224 M St SW, Washington, DC 20024-3602, **Home Phone:** (204)488-8825. **Business Addr:** Chief Operating Officer, City of Atlanta, 55 Trinity Ave SW, Atlanta, GA 30335-0300, **Business Phone:** (404)330-6100.

### JORDAN, KEVIN

Baseball player, executive. **Personal:** Born Oct 9, 1969, San Francisco, CA. **Educ:** Univ Nebr, Lincoln, Nebr. **Career:** Baseball player (retired), exec; Brisbane Bundits, 1993-97, mgr, 2011-; Philadelphia Phillies, player, 1995-2001, free agt, 2001-02; Cincinnati Reds, free agt, 2002; San Francisco Giants, free agt, 2002; Detroit Tigers, 2003. **Business Addr:** Manager, Brisbane Bandits, 29 Mkt St, Newmarket4051, **Business Phone:** (731)62-8316.

### JORDAN, LEROY A.

Administrator, association executive, educator. **Personal:** Born Dec 27, 1941, Murphysboro, IL; married Johnetta Williams; children: Laura, Loralean & Jennifer. **Educ:** So Ill Univ, BS, elem educ, 1964; Sangamon State Univ, MA, educ admin, 1972; Ill State Univ, ABD, 1997. **Career:** Hopkins Park Pembroke Twp Sch, teacher, 1964-65; Sch Dist 186 Springfield IL, teacher adult educ & prin, 1965-69; State Bd Educ Div Voc Tech Educ, consult res & develop, 1969-72; Sangamon State Univ, asst dir appl studies, 1972-75, dean innovative studies, 1972-90, dir appl studies & exp learning, 1975-81, dean innovative & exp studies, 1982-85, asst supvr, 1990-91, dir, res & develop, 1992-98; Inst Recovery Racisms, Racial Sobriety, facilitator, currently; Black Catholic Ministry for the Springfield Diocese, dir, 1991-; Rail Task Force, chair. **Orgs:** Ill Asn Sch; educ adv com, Springfield Jr League; corp bd dir, Meml Hosp Springfield Jr League; corp bd dir, Meml Hosp; pres bd educ, Springfield; Nat Sch Bd Asn, 1976-82; pres bd dir, Statesmen Drum & Bugle Corps, 1978-81; Nat Com Campaign Human develop Nat Cath Conf, 1979-82. **Honors/Awds:** Outstanding Leadership Award, Black Caucus Sangamon State Univ, 1979-80; Cert Appreciation, Bd Control Springfield Area Voc Ctr, 1979-80; Outstanding Citizen, Urban League, 1980; Nat Asn Advan Colored People; The Leroy Jordan Social Justice Scholarship, Univ of Illinois at Springfield. **Special Achievements:** Only academic African American Dean in Sangamon State Univ; First black male elementary school teacher in Springfield. **Home Addr:** 2051 Randall Ct, Springfield, IL 62703-3320, **Home Phone:** (217)753-0215. **Business Addr:** Coordinator, Diocese of Springfield, 1615 W Wash St, Springfield, IL 62702, **Business Phone:** (217)698-8500.

**JORDAN, MARJORIE W. See Obituaries Section.**

### JORDAN, MICHAEL B.

Actor. **Personal:** Born Feb 9, 1987, Santa Ana, CA; son of Michael A. Jordan and Donna David Jordan. **Career:** Actor: HBO series "The Wire," character Wallace, 2002; ABC soap opera "All My Children," character Reggie Montgomery, 2003-06; Canadian sitcom "The Assistants," as Nate Warren, 2009; NBC TV series "Friday Night Lights," as Vince Howard, 2009-11; NBC TV series "Parenthood," as Alex, 2010-11; feature film "Chronicle," as Steve Montgomery, 2012; lead role in feature film "Fruitvale Station," as Oscar Grant, 2013. **Honors/Awds:** "Nylon Magazine," 55 Faces of the Future, 2010; Hollywood Film Awards, Hollywood Spotlight Award, 2011; Gotham Awards, Breakthrough Actor, 2011; National Board Review of Motion Pictures, Breakthrough Actor, 2013; "Time" Magazine, 30 Under 30: World Changers (with director Ryan Coogler), 2013; Satellite Awards, Breakthrough Award Performance, 2013; Santa Barbara International Film Festival, Virtuoso Award, 2013; "Entertainment Weekly," New Hollywood: Entertainers on the Rise, 2013; "Variety," Top 10 Actors to Watch, 2013; "The Root" Magazine, The Root 100 Honorees, 2013; "People" Magazine, Sexiest Man Alive list, 2013; "GQ" Magazine, Breakout of the Year, 2013. **Special Achievements:** Youngest African American cast in the history of "All My Children".

### JORDAN, MICHAEL JEFFREY

Basketball player, entrepreneur, executive. **Personal:** Born Feb 17, 1963, Brooklyn, NY; son of James R Sr and Deloris Peoples; married Juanita Vanoy; children: Jeffrey Michael, Marcus James & Jasmine Mickael; married Yvette Prieto; children: Victoria & Ysabel. **Educ:** Univ NC, BA, geog, 1984. **Career:** Basketball player (retired), entrepreneur, executive; Chicago Bulls, guard, 1984-93, 1995-98; Chicago White Sox, minor league player, 1994-95; Birmingham Barons, 1994-

95; Scottsdale Scorpions, 1994; Launched own line athletic clothing, JORDAN Brand, a subdivision NIKE, 1997; Wash Wizards, part owner, 1999-2001, shooting guard, 2001-03; Michael Jordan Celebrity Golf Classic, founder; Charlotte Bobcats, prin owner & chmn, head basketball opers, currently. **Business Addr:** Chairman, Owner, Charlotte Bobcats, 333 E Trade St, Charlotte, NC 28202, **Business Phone:** (704)688-8600.

### JORDAN, MICHELLE DENISE
Lawyer. **Personal:** Born Oct 29, 1954, Chicago, IL; daughter of John A and Margaret (O'Dood) J. **Educ:** Loyola Univ, BA, 1974; Univ Mich Law Sch, JD, 1977. **Career:** States Atty Off Cook Co, asst state atty, 1977-82; pvt law pract, 1982-84; Ill Atty Gen Off, trial atty trial div & dep chief environ control div, 1984-90; Young Lawyers Intensive Trial Pract Prog, instr, 1986; Ill Atty Gen's Training Prog, instr, 1988-90; Hopkins & Sutter Law Firm, partner, 1991-93; US Environ Protection Agency Region Five, dep regional adminr, 1994-2001; US Dept Justice, spec asst US atty, 1998-2001; Rainbow & Push Coalition, nat dir fund develop, 2001-03; Ill Dept Pub Aid, asst dir, 2003; sole practr, 2003-; Circuit Ct, First Munic Dist, judge, 2004; State Ill, Circuit Ct Cook County, Dist 1, circuit judge, 2004-16. **Orgs:** Chicago Bar Asn, 1977-, Cook County Bar Asn, 1977-, Ill State Bar Asn, 1978-; Nat Bar Asn, 1980-; prof, Women's Auxiliary Provident Hosp, 1981-82; bd mem, Loyola Univ Alumni Asn, 1984-87; subcomt co-chmn, Chicago Bar Asn, Young Bar Asn, 1986-87; investr, invests, Chicago Bar Asn, Judicial Eval Comt, 1987-88; chmn, criminal law comt, 1987-88; Hearing Div, Chicago Bar Asn, Judicial Eval Comt, 1987-88; Child Witness Proj, Task Force, 1987-88; environ law comt mem, Chicago Bar Asn, 1989; Art Inst Chicago, 1990; Alpha Sigma Nu. **Honors/Awds:** Operation PUSH Womens Day Award, 1978; America's Top 100 Business & Professional Woman, Editorial Bd Dollars & Sense Mag, 1988; Susan E Olive National EEO Award, US EPA, 1996. **Home Addr:** 7750 S Hoyne, Chicago, IL 60620, **Home Phone:** (312)846-5343.

### JORDAN, MONTELL DUSEAN
Singer, clergy. **Personal:** Born Dec 3, 1968, Los Angeles, CA; son of Elijah and Deloris; married Kristin Hudson; children: 4. **Educ:** Pepperdine Univ, BS, commun. **Career:** Def Jam, vocalist; Songs: "This Is How We Do It", 1995; "Somethin' 4 da Honeyz", 1995; "Daddy's Home", 1995; "Falling", 1996; "I Like, What's On Tonight", 1996; "What's On Tonight", 1997; "Let's Ride", 1998; "I Can Do That", 1998; "When You Get Home", 1998; "Get It On Tonite", 1999; "Once Upon a Time", 2000; "You Must Have Been", 2001; "Supa Star", 2003; "Me and U", 2008; "Not No More", 2008; Albums: This is How We Do It, 1995; Let's Ride, 1998; Get It On. Tonite, 1999; Montell Jordan, 2002; Life after def, 2003; Freedom Writers, 2007; How She Move, 2007; Step Brothers, 2008; Let It Rain, 2008; Film: The Fighting Temptations, 2003, TV series: "Johnny Bravo", 1997; "Motown Live", 1998; "Touched by an Angel", 1999; "The Tonight Show with Jay Leno", 2000; Victory World Church, Norcross, Ga, worship pastor, 2010-. **Orgs:** Kappa Alpha Psi Fraternity. **Special Achievements:** First Def Jam R&B artist to hit Number 1 on pop chart, This Is How We DoIt, 1995; 1995 MTV Video Music Award nominations and 1995 Grammy Awardnomination. **Business Addr:** Worship Pastor, Victory World Church, 5905 Brook Hollow Pkwy, Norcross, GA 30071, **Business Phone:** (770)849-9400.

### JORDAN, PATRICIA
Educator. **Personal:** Born Sep 26, 1951, New York, NY; daughter of Clifford James and Juanita James (deceased); married Jack M; children: Alexa Juanita. **Educ:** Vassar Col, BA, 1972; City Col, MS, 1976; Hofstra Univ, PhD, 1991. **Career:** Cross High Sch, math instr, 1972; Bronx high sch, math instr; Lee High Sch, math instr, 1972-73; Pk E High Sch, math instr & advisor, 1973-74; Martin Luther King Jr High Sch, math instr & dean, 1974-76; Malverne High Sch, math instr, 1976-80; Roslyn High Sch, math instr, 1980-2001. **Orgs:** Asn Black Psychologist; Nat Asn Advan Colored People; Memorial Scholar Found; adv bd mem, New York Dept Juv Justice. **Home Addr:** 21 Stuyvesant Oval Apt 3E, New York, NY 10009-2036, **Home Phone:** (212)529-3208.

### JORDAN, PATRICIA CARTER
Government official. **Personal:** Born Jan 23, 1946, Washington, DC; daughter of Nelver Sherman and Olivette Glaude; married Richard O Jr; children: Orisha Katrina. **Educ:** Howard Univ, Wash, DC, BA, sociol; Top 40 Mgt Training Prog, City NY, grad; Columbia Univ Grad Sch Arts & Scis, grad. **Career:** City NY Bd Educ, asst to dep chancellor; City NY High Div, mgt consult; Communs Inst, NY, commun supvr; Found Chg Inter-Racial Bks C, consult & instr; Pub Educ Asn, consult; US Dept Justice, Community Rels Serv, community rels specialist & trainer; Hunter Col Dept Urban Affairs, res asst & adj lectr; HARYOU-ACT Assoc, res assoc; Columbia Univ Grad Sch Arts & Sci, res & teaching asst; City NY Housing Preserv & Develop & Off Housing Mgt & Sales, admin mgr. **Orgs:** Dir res & develop, Black Citizens Fair Media, 1971-; Chairperson Bd dir, Upper Manhattan Ment Health Inc; bd mem, Found Minority Interest Media; chair, prin, Emma L. Bowen Found. **Home Addr:** 50 W 97th St Apt 4R, New York, NY 10025, **Home Phone:** (212)866-1070.

**JORDAN, PAUL SCOTT.** **See JORDAN, RICKY.**

### JORDAN, RANDY LOMENT
Football player, football coach. **Personal:** Born Jun 6, 1970, Manson, NC; married Romonda Baxter; children: Raven, Jalen & Justin. **Educ:** Univ Nc, Chapel Hill, BS, speech commun, 1993. **Career:** Football player (retired), coach; Univ NC, Chapel Hill, running back, 1989-92, running backs coach, 2012-13; Los Angeles Raiders, running back, 1993; Jacksonville Jaguars, running back, 1995-97; Oakland Raiders, running back, 1998-2002, spec teams asst, 2003-04; Nebr Cornhuskers, running backs coach, 2004-07; Tex A&M Univ, running backs coach, 2008-12; Wash Redskins, running backs coach, 2014-. **Orgs:** Fel Christian Athletes. **Honors/Awds:** NFL Unsung Hero Award, 2001; Ed Block Courage Award, 2001. **Special Achievements:** Films: Celebrity, 1998. **Home Addr:** , Henderson, NC. **Business Addr:** Running Backs Coach, Washington Redskins, 21300 Redskin Pk Dr, Ashburn, TX 20147, **Business Phone:** (703)478-8900.

### JORDAN, REGINALD
Basketball coach, basketball player. **Personal:** Born Jan 26, 1969, Chicago, IL. **Educ:** Southwestern Univ, 1989; NMex State Univ, BA, jour, 1991. **Career:** Basketball player (retired), coach; Grand Rapids Hoops, Conn Basketball Asn, guard, 1991-93; Yakima Sun Kings, Conn Basketball Asn, 1993-94, 1994-95; Los Angeles Lakers, shooting guard, 1994; Sioux Falls Skyforce, CBA, 1995-96; Atlanta Hawks, point guard, 1996; Portland Trail Blazers, 1996; Minn Timber wolves, shooting guard, 1996-99; Wash Wizards, guard & point guard, 2000; Fuerza Regia, head coach, 2010-12. **Honors/Awds:** All-League first team, Conn Basketball Asn, 1996; All-Defensive team, Conn Basketball Asn, 1993, 1996.

### JORDAN, RICHARD LAMONT
Football coach, football player. **Personal:** Born Dec 1, 1974, Holdenville, OK; son of Ray and Jannie; children: 5. **Educ:** Mo Southern State Univ, BA, educ, 1996. **Career:** Football player (retired), coach; Detroit Lions, linebacker, 1997-99, 2002-03, Kans City Chiefs, 2001-02; Clear Channel Radio, on-air host, 2006-09; Lee M Thurston High Sch, teacher & varsity football & track coach, 2006-12; Jordan Compound, 2012-. **Orgs:** Active mem, Local Boys & Girls Club community; Alpha Phi Alpha Fraternity Inc. **Honors/Awds:** Hughes Award; Defensive Most Valuable Player, Mass Interscholastic Athletic Asn, 1996; Athletic Hall of Fame, Mo Southern State Univ, 2006. **Business Addr:** The Jordan Compound, 1008 Brady Ave NW, Atlanta, GA 30318, **Business Phone:** (404)898-1702.

### JORDAN, RICKY (PAUL SCOTT JORDAN)
Baseball player. **Personal:** Born May 26, 1965, Sacramento, CA. **Career:** Baseball player (retired), baseball coach; Philadelphia Phillies, infielder, 1base, left field, outfield, 1988-94; Calif Angels, 1995; Seattle Mariners, designated hitter, 1996; Ronald Reagan High Sch, coach, 2002. **Orgs:** Diabetes Help; Kids Basketball Camp; Baseball Camp; Homeless People. **Honors/Awds:** Player of the Year, Phillies Orgn, 1987. **Special Achievements:** Film appearance: High Hopes: The Anatomy of a Winner, 2003; Thirty first National League Player to hit Home run in First Major League At Bat. **Home Addr:** 5691-A Power Inn Rd, Sacramento, CA 95824, **Home Phone:** (830)226-5086.

### JORDAN, ROBERT
Educator, pianist. **Personal:** Born May 2, 1940, Chattanooga, TN; son of Ira and Mamie McCamey J. **Educ:** Eastman Sch Music, BM, 1962; Juilliard Sch Music, MS, 1965; Goethe Inst Ger Lang, dipl, 1965; Hochsch fur Musik, Ger, dipl, 1967; Sorbonne, Paris, dipl, 1969. **Career:** Triad Presentations Inc, bd dir, adv coun; Morgan State Univ, artist-in-residence, 1976-78; Paris Inst Music, New York, pres; Univ Del, artist-in-residence, 1979; State Univ New York, Fredonia, NY, Sch Music, prof piano, 1980-2004, asst to dir, 1988-89, prof emer, 2004-; Northern Mich Univ, vis Martin Luther King Prof, 1987; Univ Mich, Ann Arbor, Mich, vis prof, 1990. **Orgs:** Inaugurated Minority Scholar Fund, Univ Del, 1979; bd dir & adv coun, Triad Presentations Inc. **Home Addr:** 1101 St Paul St Suite 707, Baltimore, MD 21202-2626, **Home Phone:** (410)659-9581. **Business Addr:** Professor Emeritus, State University of New York, 280 Cent Ave, Fredonia, NY 14063, **Business Phone:** (716)673-3111.

### JORDAN, ROBERT A.
Social worker. **Personal:** Born Dec 4, 1932, Atlanta, GA; married Edna Fraley. **Educ:** Clark Col, AB, 1958; Atlanta Univ, MA, 1969; Univ GA, attended 1973. **Career:** Fulton County Sch Syst, teacher, 1961-66; Atlanta Pub Sch Syst, teacher, 1966-72, reading teacher, 1972-, social worker, 1972; Jazz Radio Prog, Stat WYZE, co-host. **Orgs:** Bd dir, Atlanta Asn Educ, pres; Ga Educ Asn; Nat Educ Asn; Prof Rights Comn Asn Am Educ; educ chmn, Forward Ga Assembly; pres, Jazz Disciples Club; State Dem Party; Phi Beta Sigma; bd trustee, Ebenezer Baptist Church. **Special Achievements:** Articles written "Parent Input In Publ Schs" & "Why SAT Scores Are Low"; Appeared on Radio WRNG & TV (ch 5, 2, 11, 30); Collector of Jazz Records five thousand albums; Interviewed for article "State of Jazz in Atlanta", Constitution Nwspaper; Author article "Profile of a VIP"; Article "What's Wrong with Education". **Home Addr:** 3236 Rabun Dr SW, Atlanta, GA 30311, **Home Phone:** (404)696-5905.

### JORDAN, DR. ROBERT HOWARD, JR.
Television journalist. **Personal:** Born Aug 31, 1943, Atlanta, GA; son of Robert H and Millicent Dobbs; married Sharon E Lundy; children: Karen Millicent. **Educ:** Roosevelt Univ, Chicago, Ill, BA, 1977; Northeastern Ill Univ, MA, speech, 1994; Loyola Univ, PhD, philos educ, 2000. **Career:** WSM TV, Nashville, Tenn, reporter & announcer, 1970-73; WGN TV, Chicago, Ill, reporter & anchor, 1973-78, 1980-, "News at Nine", weekend anchor, currently; CBS News Midwest Bur, Chicago, Ill, reporter, 1978-80; Jordan & Jordan Commun Inc, founder & owner, pres, 1998-. **Orgs:** Am Fedn Radio & TV Artists, 1972-; Chicago Asn Black Journalists, 1983-; bd dir, John G Shedd Aquarium, 1987-; bd dir, Evanston Hosp Corp, 1987-; Chicago Lung Asn; Chicago Sinfonietta Aquarium; Safer Found; Night Ministry. **Honors/Awds:** Black Achievers of Industry Award, YMCA Metrop Chicago, 1975; Appreciation Award, Chicago Dent Soc, 1976; Master of Ceremony, Black & Hispanic Achievers Indust, 1985-89. **Special Achievements:** Many writing credits including two screenplays, Anthony's Key & Multi-Man, written articles for the Chicago Tribune. **Home Addr:** 1704 Keeney St, Evanston, IL 60202, **Home Phone:** (312)864-4291. **Business Addr:** Anchor, Reporter, WGN-TV, 2501 Bradley Pl, Chicago, IL 60618-4718, **Business Phone:** (773)528-2311.

### JORDAN, PROF. SANDRA D.
Educator. **Personal:** Born Dec 3, 1951, Philadelphia, PA; married Byron N; children: Nedra Catherine & Byron Neal II. **Educ:** Wilberforce Univ, BS, 1973; Univ Pittsburgh Law Sch, JD, 1979. **Career:** US Dept Justice, asst US atty, 1979-88; US Dept Independent Coun, Iran Contra, assoc coun, 1988-91; Iran/Contra prosecution; Univ Pitt Law Sch, assoc prof law, prof law, assoc dean, acad affairs, currently; Western Dist Pa, Asst Us Atty, White Collar Crimes unit, dir; Charlotte Sch Law, prof, law, 2008-15, emer prof; Books: casebook, White Collar Crime: Cases Materials & Problems, second edition, author; Pennsylvania Law Encyclopedia: Evidence to Execution, editor; Pennsylvania Law Encyclopedia: Criminal Law, editor. **Orgs:** Homer S Brown Law Asn, 1979-; Nat Bar Asn, 1979-; disciplinary bd, Supreme Ct Pa, 1990-94; vice chair, Pa Judicial Conduct Bd, 1994-. **Special Achievements:** Professor Jordan has been a frequent commentator in many publications including Reuters News Service, N.Y. Times, USA Today, Los Angeles Times, Washington Post, Pittsburgh Tribune Review, Charlotte Observer, Jurist, and the Pittsburgh Post-Gazette. In addition, she has appeared on National Public Radio, WSOC, News 14 Charlotte, WBTV, and America Now. **Home Addr:** 100 Dewey St, Pittsburgh, PA 15218-1408, **Home Phone:** (412)241-4211. **Business Addr:** Professor of Law, Associate Dean, University of Pittsburgh School of Law, Rm 529 3900 Forbes Ave, Pittsburgh, PA 15260, **Business Phone:** (412)648-1988.

### JORDAN, STANLEY
Composer, jazz musician, guitarist. **Personal:** Born Jul 31, 1959, Chicago, IL; married Sandra kilpatrick; children: Julia. **Educ:** Princeton Univ, BA, music theory & compos, 1981; Ariz State Univ, music ther. **Career:** Jazz guitarist & composer; Sedona Bks & Music, owner, currently. Albums: Touch Sensitive, 1983; Magic Touch, 1985; One Night With Blue Note Preserved; Hideaway, 1986; Standards, Volume 1, 1987; Blind Date, 1987; Flying Home, 1988; Morning Desire; Artists Against ApartheiSunCity; RU Tuff Enough; Cornucopia, 1990; Stolen Moments, 1991; Stanley Jordan Live in New York, 1998; Relaxing Music for Difficult Situations I, 2003; Ragas, 2004; Dreams Of Peace, 2004; State of Nature, 2008; Friends, 2011; Duets, 2015. **Orgs:** Am Music Ther Asn. **Honors/Awds:** Award, Reno Jazz Festival; two Grammy nominations. **Special Achievements:** Has played with Dizzy Gillespie, Benny Carter, Quicy Jones, MichalUrbaniak, and Richie Cole. **Home Addr:** 5 Chrysona Lane, Sedona, AZ 86336-9510, **Home Phone:** (520)204-1327. **Business Addr:** Jazz Musician, c/o The Management Ark, 116 Village Blvd, Princeton, NJ 08540, **Business Phone:** (609)734-7403.

### JORDAN, STEVE RUSSELL
Football player, manager, executive. **Personal:** Born Jan 10, 1961, Phoenix, AZ; married Anita; children: Cameron Tyler. **Educ:** Brown Univ, BS, civil engineering, 1982. **Career:** Football player (retired), manager; Minn Vikings, tight end, 1982-94; Ryan Co Inc, sr proj mgr, dir construct, currently; civil engr, currently; term trustee emer, 1993-97; corp fel, 1998-. **Orgs:** Bd fel Brown Univ; adv bd mem, Nat Football Found; Col Hall Fame; Phx Thunder birds; bd dir, Brown Sports Found, 1996-; chmn, Leukemia Golf Classic; bd mem, Cystic Fibrosis Found; Nat Missing Children's Found; Multiple Sclerosis Soc; Steve R Jordan Endowed Scholar Minority Athletes, Brown Univ, 2000. **Honors/Awds:** NCAA Silver Anniversary Award, 2006. **Special Achievements:** Pro Bowl, 1986, 1987, 1988, 1989, 1990 & 1991. Film: 1987 NFC Championship Game, 1988. **Home Addr:** , Chandler, AZ. **Business Addr:** Director of Construction, Ryan Companies US Inc, 1 N Central Ave Suite 1300, Phoenix, AZ 85004-4418, **Business Phone:** (602)322-6100.

### JORDAN, REV. DR. TERNAE T., SR.
Clergy. **Personal:** Born Dec 3, 1955, Chattanooga, TN; son of Melvin and Maggie; married Angela Faye; children: Ternae Jr, Dejuan & JaMichael. **Educ:** Univ Tenn, BS, bus educ, 1977; Harvard Sch Divinity, Leadership Inst, dipl. **Career:** Johnson & Johnson, Territorial Sales mgr, 1978-79; Chattanooga Sch Syst, trainer/teacher/coordr; Natl Life & Mutual Omaha Ins Co, sales agt, 1981-83; KBL Enterprises, exec vpres, 1983-88; Greater Progressive Baptist Church, sr pastor; Unlimited Dimensions Mgt Corp, chief exec officer, 2002-; Bethlehem Baptist Church, Chattanooga, sr pastor; Mt Canaan Baptist Church, Chattanooga, Tenn, pastor, currently. **Orgs:** Paul Clarke Found, 1993-; founder & pres, Stop Madness Inc, 1993-2001; prog dir, Value-Based Initiative, 1999-2004; Pk & Recreation Comners; Community Outreach Adv Coun, Ivy Tech Col; Harvard Sch Divinity, partic, 2000; chmn, Midland Community Resource Centerl pres, Servant Leadership Coun; Front Porch Alliance; Alternative Sem; Hatch's House Hope; Weed & Seed; chmn, Day Serv, 2009 & 2010; Destiny Theater. **Honors/Awds:** Jefferson Award, Am Inst of Pub Serv, 1993; Citizen of the Year, J Gazette Newspaper, 1997; Elizabeth Dobynes Award, NAACP-Ft Wayne, 1998; Sagamore of the Wabash Award, 2004; DDiv, Huntington Col, Huntington, Ind, 2005. **Home Addr:** 1319 Ardsley Ct, Fort Wayne, IN 46815, **Home Phone:** (260)749-7289. **Business Addr:** Pastor, Mt Canaan Baptist Church, 2800 N Chamberlain Ave, Chattanooga, TN 37406, **Business Phone:** (423)624-4080.

### JORDAN, THURMAN
Accountant. **Personal:** Born Dec 2, 1938, Harrisburg, IL; son of Joseph and Lutishia; married Teiko Ann; children: Eric, Neal & Philip. **Educ:** Roosevelt Univ, BS & BA, 1966; Univ Chicago, MBA, 1982; Univ Ill, CPA, 1972. **Career:** Unisource Network Serv, pres & chief exec officer; Arthur Andersen & Co, audit mgr, 1966-76, partner; Signode Corp & Ill Tool Works Inc, vpres, controller & chief financial officer, 1976-88; Chicago Osteop Health Systs, exec vpres & chief financial officer, 1989-94; Financial consult, 1994-95; Meris Labs Inc, sr vpres & chief financial officer, 1995-97; Spectra LLC & Detroit Chassis LLC, vpres finance & chief financial officer; Magnys Innovative Solutions, chief financial officer, currently. **Orgs:** Ill Soc CPA's Am Inst CPA; Alumni Chicago Forum Chicago United; vice chmn, Oper & Effectiveness Comn; Agency Serv Com Comn Fund; bd mem, United Way Chicago, Evanston Art Ctr; bd mem, Bd trustee, Gould Acad; bd dir, Northlight Theater; Econ Club Chicago & MAPI; pres, Evanston Art Ctr. **Honors/Awds:** Black Achiever Award, YMCA, 1974. **Home Addr:** 2743 Ridge Ave, Evanston, IL 60201, **Home Phone:** (708)491-0393. **Business Addr:** Chief Financial Officer, Magnys Innovative Solutions, 42500 Suite B W 11 Mile Rd, Novi, MI 48375, **Business Phone:** (248)449-2600.

### JORDAN, VERNON EULION, JR.
Executive, lawyer. **Personal:** Born Aug 15, 1935, Atlanta, GA; son of Vernon and Mary; married Ann Dibble Cook; married Shirley M Yarbrough; children: Vickee J Adams. **Educ:** DePauw Univ, BA, 1957; Howard Univ Law Sch, JD, 1960. **Career:** Law clerk atty Donald Hollowell, 1960-64; Voter Educ Proj Southern Regional Coun, pvt pract lawyer & dir, 1964-70; Nat Urban League Inc, pres & chief exec officer, 1972-81; United Negro Col Fund, exec dir, 1970; Voter Educ Proj,

Southern Regional Coun, dir, 1964-68; US Off Econ Opportunity, atty, consult; Nat Asn Advan Colored People, field dir; GA & AK, pvt legal pract; Akin, Gump, Strauss, Hauer & Feld, LLP, sr exec partner, 1982-99, of-coun, 2000-; Am Express Co, dir; Dow Jones & Co Inc, dir; J C Penney Co Inc, dir; Sara Lee Corp, dir; Xerox Corp, dir; Lazard Freres & Co LLC, sr managing dir & bd dir, 2000-. **Orgs:** Ga field secy Nat Asn Advan Colored People, 1962-64; Dir, Voter Educ Proj Coun, 1965; exec dir, United Negro Col Fund, 1970; exec dir, Nat Urban League, 1972; Am Revolution Di-Centennial Comn, 1972; Presidential Clemency Bd, 1974; Adv Coun Social Security, 1974; Secy State's Adv Comt SafricA, 1985; Points Light Initiative Found, Pres's Adv Comt, 1989; trustee, DePauw Univ; trustee, Howard Univ; trustee, LBJ Found; trustee, Nat Acad Found; Int Adv Comt Daimler-Chrysler; Alfalfa Club; Am Asn Advan Sci; Metrop Club; Univ Club; bd gov, Joint Ctr Polit & Econ Studies, 1998-; sr adv, Shinsei Bank Ltd; Iraq Study Group; Omega Psi Phi; Sigma Pi Phi; life mem, Coun Foreign Rels. **Business Addr:** Senior Managing Director, Lazard Freres & Co LLC, 30 Rockefeller Plz, New York, NY 10020, **Business Phone:** (212)632-6000.

### JORDAN, DR. WILBERT CORNELIOUS

Physician. **Personal:** Born Sep 11, 1944, Wheatley, AR; son of William and Annie Mae. **Educ:** Harvard Col, AB, 1966; Case Western Res Univ, MD, 1971; Univ Calif, Los Angeles, MPH, 1978. **Career:** Beth Israel Deaconess Med Ctr, residency, 1971-73; Ctr Dis Control, epidemiologist, 1973-76; US Pub Health Svcs, lt comdr, 1973-78; Univ Calif, Los Angeles Med Ctr, fel, 1976-78; Los Angeles County, area pub health chief, 1979-83; Drew Med Sch, assoc prof, 1979-87; King-Drew Med Ctr, dir grad educ; Unic Calif Los Angeles, asst prof, pub health; St. Francis Med Ctr, physician; Promise Hosp E Los Angeles, physician; King-Drew Med Ctr, Oasis Clin, dir & founder, currently. **Orgs:** Life mem, Nat Asn Advan Colored People, 1978-; sec bd PSRO Area XXIII, 1980-84; chmn bd, Minority AIDS Proj LA City, 1984-87; bd mem, Nat Asn Minority Media Execs, 1984-87; Coalition Against Black Exploitation, 1985-87; chmn bd, Sallie Martin Found, 1986-87; dir, Nat Conv Gospel Choirs & Choruses Inc; Undersea Med Soc; Am Venereal Dis Asn, Assoc Am Med Col, Nat Med Asn; pres Ingle wood Physicians Assoc; liaison Nat Assoc Minority med Educrs; chmn, Black Los Angeles AIDS Comn; ed, S Cent AIDS Newsletter; bd dir, AIDS Res Alliance; Los Angeles County HIV Planning Coun. **Honors/Awds:** Outstanding Physician of Year, SNMA, 1973; Recognition Award, Nat Assoc Minority med Educrs, 1984; Recognition Award, Nat Assoc Minority med Educrs, 1988; Recognition for Service, Warwick Found, 1990; Recognition for Service, Brotherland Crusade, 1991; Physician of the Year, Charles R Drew Med Soc, 1992; Man of the Year, Los Angeles Sentinel Newspaper, 1992; Special Humanitarian Award, Tau Eta Psi Nursing Sorority, 1992. **Special Achievements:** He reported the first heterosexual case of HIV in Los Angeles County in 1983. **Home Addr:** 2380 Venus Dr, Los Angeles, CA 90046-1644, **Home Phone:** (323)876-1336. **Business Addr:** Medical Director, King Drew Medical Center, 12021 S Wilmington Oasis Clinic, Los Angeles, CA 90059, **Business Phone:** (310)668-4213.

### JORDAN, WILLIAM CHESTER

Educator. **Personal:** Born Apr 7, 1948, Chicago, IL; son of Johnnie Parker and Marguerite Jane; married Christine Kenyon Hershey; children: Victoria Marie, John Mark, Clare Kenyon & Lorna Janice. **Educ:** Ripon Col, AB, 1969, BA, hist, math & Russ studies, DHL, 2001; Princeton Univ, PhD, 1973. **Career:** Princeton Univ, instr, 1973-74, lectr, 1974-75, asst prof, assoc prof, 1975-86, prof hist, 1986-; Univ Pa, vis lectr, 1981-82; Swarthmore Col, vis assoc prof, 1985; Dickinson Col, morgan lectr, 1985; Behrman, sr fel humanities, 1989-94; Shelby Cullom Davis Ctr Hist Studies, dir, 1994-99, dept chair, 2008-; Dayton-Stockton, prof, 2005-. **Orgs:** Counr, Medieval Acad Am, 1998-2001; fel Am Philos Socs, 2000; assesseur, Int Comt Hist Sci, 2000-; pres, Am Cath Hist Asn, 2009; Am Coun Learned Soc; Soc Study Fr Hist; Soc Study Crusades & Latin E; Haskins Soc; fel AAAS, 2009; pres fel, Medieval Acad Am, 2011-12; pres, Medieval Acad Am, 2014-15; vice chmn, Bd trustee, Nat Humanities Ctr, 2014-. **Business Addr:** Professor, Princeton University, 232 Dickinson Hall, Princeton, NJ 08544, **Business Phone:** (609)258-4165.

### JOSEPH, ABRAHAM, JR.

Accountant. **Personal:** Born Mar 12, 1954, Kingsland, GA; son of Abraham Sr and Maude R; married Denese; children: Arika, Bianca & Andre. **Educ:** Morris Brown Col, BS, acct, 1976; Troy State Univ, MS, personnel mgmt, 1983. **Career:** Ga Dept Revenue, tax auditor, 1977-85; Army Audit Agency, auditor, 1985-87; AJ's Acct & Tax Serv, acct & consult, 1977-; Dept Navy, supvr auditor, 1988-, investr & internal auditor, 2012-; Dept Veterans Affairs, systs auditor, 2006-09; NAVAIR, staff acct, 2009-; Black Data Processing Assocs, nat vpres finance, currently. **Orgs:** Life mem, Alpha Phi Alpha, 1973-; Morris Brown Col Alumni, 1977-; treas, Camden Co Black Bus Asn, 1987-; Am Soc Mil Comptrollers, 1987-; acct/trustee, St Paul AME Church, 1988-; nat asst treas, Blacks Govt, 1988-01; bd mem, Camden Kings Bay Chamber, 1990-92; Asn Govt Accts, 2000-; Nat Asn Black Accts, 2004-; bd mem, Black Data Processing Assocs, Austin Chap, TX; life mem, Blacks Govt; secy, Sons Allen Grant AME. Worship Ctr, Austin, TX; treas, Kin law Community Ctr; Cent Fla Black MBA Chap, currently. **Honors/Awds:** Community Service Award, Morris Brown Col Alumni, 1990; Business Award, Camden County Black Bus Asn, 1992. **Home Addr:** 538 Joseph, PO Box 2787, Kingsland, GA 31548-2787, **Home Phone:** (912)729-5127. **Business Addr:** National Vice President of Finance, Black Data Processing Associates, 9500 Arena Dr Suite 350, Largo, MD 20774, **Business Phone:** (800)727-2372.

### JOSEPH, DAVID E.

Executive, chief executive officer, president (organization). **Career:** Specialized Servs Inc, pres, chmn & chief exec officer, currently. **Business Addr:** Chairman & President, Chief Executive Officer, Specialized Services Inc, 23077 Greenfield Rd Suite 470, Southfield, MI 48075-3736, **Business Phone:** (248)557-1030.

### JOSEPH, JAMES ALFRED

Executive director, chief executive officer, educator. **Personal:** Born Mar 12, 1935, Opelousas, LA; son of Julia and Adam; married Mary Braxton; children: Jeffrey & Denise. **Educ:** Southern Univ, BA, 1959; Yale Univ, BD, MA, 1963; Southeastern Univ, LLD, 1982; Univ Md, DPS, 1984. **Career:** Claremont Col, chaplain & prof, 1969-70; Irwin-Sweeney-Miller Found, exec dir, 1970-72; Cummins Engine Co, vpres, 1972-77; US Dept Interior, undersec, 1977-81; Yale Divinity Sch, vis prof, 1981-82; Coun Found, pres & chief exec officer, 1982-95; Duke Univ, Southern Africa Ctr Leadership & pub values, exec dir, Pract Pub Policy Studies, prof, currently, founder; Stillman Col, civil rights organizer. **Orgs:** Pitzer Col, 1972-77; chmn, US Comn Northern Marianas, 1980-86; bd dir, Cummins Engine Found, 1981-87; Colonial Williamsburg, 1981-87; Coun Foreign Rel, 1981-85; bd Visitors, Duke Univ 1981-83; adv Comt, US Dept State, 1982-84; bd dir, Africare, 1982-; adv comt, Nat Acad Sci, 1982-83; bd dir, C Defense Fund, 1983-; Hague Club, 1983-87; bd dir, Brooking Inst, 1985-; Salzbert sem, 1985-; Atlantic Coun, 1985-; UN Assoc, 1986-; Leader-in-Residence, Hart Leadership Prog; chmn emer, Childrens Defense Fund; dir, Mgt & Training Corp; bd mem, Advisors Kenan Inst Ethics, Duke Univ; Alpha Phi Alpha fraternity; US senate, U.S. Ambassador SafricA; pres, Baptist Club; ordained minister, Yale Divinity Sch & Claremont Cols. **Home Addr:** 7726 Crossover Dr, Mc Lean, VA 22102. **Business Addr:** Professor, Duke University, 110 Sanford Bldg, Durham, NC 27708-0545, **Business Phone:** (919)613-7321.

### JOSEPH, JENNIFER INEZ

School administrator, educator, vice president (organization). **Personal:** Born Mar 25, 1948, New Amsterdam; daughter of Vincent Percival Chung and Inez Gwendolyn Chung; married Richard A; children: Mark Vincent, R Anthony & Robert Lionel. **Educ:** British Open Univ, BA, 1975; Harvard Grad Sch Educ, MEd, 1984. **Career:** Univ Ibadan, Nigeria, publ, admin officer, 1976-79; Oxford Univ, Eng, clin trial coordr, 1979; Dartmouth Col, asst affirmative action officer, 1980-81, asst dir, career & employ servs, 1981, dir, intensive acad sup-port prog, asst dean freshmen, 1981-85, asst dir, admis & financial aid, 1985-86, sr assoc dir, admis & financial aid, 1986-89; Ctr Dis Control, Epidemiol Prog Off, assoc dir, 1989-90; Morehouse Col, exec asst pres, 1991-92, vpres, policy & planning, 1992-; Coun Freely Elected Heads Govt, Int Observer Team, Guyana Elections, 1992. **Orgs:** Co-chair, Asn Black Admin & Financial Aid Officers Ivy League & Sister Schs, 1985-89, 1987-88; consult, adv bd mem, Emory Univ & Pew Charitable Trusts Sci & Math Prog, 1989-90; co-founder, coord comt chair, Saturday Youth Enrichment Prog, Atlanta, GA, 1990-; adv bd mem, Atlanta Youth Enrichment Prog, 1991-. **Special Achievements:** First women to VP position for Morehouse College. **Business Addr:** Vice President for Policy & Planning, Morehouse College, 830 Westview Dr SW, Atlanta, GA 30314, **Business Phone:** (404)681-2800.

### JOSEPH, KERRY

Football coach, executive, football player. **Personal:** Born Oct 4, 1973, New Iberia, LA. **Educ:** McNeese State Univ, grad. **Career:** Football player (retired); Cincinnati Bengals, 1996; London Monarchs, quarterback, 1997; Wash Redskins, slot back, 1997; Rhein Fires, safety, 1998; Seattle Seahawks, strong safety, 1999-2000, 1998, 2001; Ottawa Renegades, quarter back, 2003-05; Sask Rough riders, 2006-07, 2014; Toronto Argonauts, 2008-09; Edmonton Eskimos, 2010-13; Cross Gates Athletic Club, personal trainer, 2011; Parisi Speed Sch, Slidell, LA, prog dir, currently. **Honors/Awds:** Most valuable player & Conf Player of the Year, McNeese State, 1995; James J Corbett Mem Award, 1995; State Offensive Football Player of the Year, La Sports Writers Asn, 1995; CFL's Most Outstanding Player Award, 2007; CFL All-Star, 2007; CFL West All-Star, 2007. **Business Addr:** Program Director, Parisi Speed School, 200 N Mil Rd, Slidell, LA 70461, **Business Phone:** (985)685-1466.

### JOSEPH, LLOYD LEROI

Engineer, manager. **Personal:** Born Sep 18, 1934, Los Angeles, CA; son of Al Lee and Blondine; married Jeannette S Jones; children: Darnetta. **Career:** KIIX Channel 22, chief brdcst audio eng, 1963; RPM Rec Studio, chief rec eng, 1965-66; Genisco Technol Corp, Compton, test eng, 1967-69; CB Sound, rec eng, 1969; KNXT/CBS News, newsreel soundman, 1969-77; Universal Studios, Universal City, transfer prod recordist, 1977-. Films: Melvin & Howard, Psycho III, Best Little Whore House in Tex, boom operator; Promise Kept: The Oksana Baiul Story, boom operator; Televison Ser: "Columbo", "Magnum PI", "Murder She Wrote", "Simon & Simon"; Documentaries: Blacks in the Media, Plight of the Jews in Russia. **Honors/Awds:** Emmy Award, TV, 1976. **Home Addr:** 1920 Lake Ave Suite 108, Altadena, CA 91001-3059, **Home Phone:** (818)564-1545. **Business Addr:** Sound Recordist, Universal City, 100 Universal Plz, Universal City, CA 91608, **Business Phone:** (818)777-1295.

### JOSEPH, HON. RAYMOND ALCIDE

Journalist. **Personal:** Born Aug 31, 1931, San Pedro de Macoris. **Educ:** Wheaton Col, BA, anthrop, 1960; Univ Chicago, MA, social anthrop, 1964. **Career:** Haiti-Observateur, founder, 1971, co-ed; Wall St J, Div Dow Jones, financial reporter; New York Sun, columnist; Haitian Govt, Charge de Affaires; Embassy Haiti, ambassador, 2005-10. **Orgs:** Founder, printshop Wis Mission Haiti, 1950; ed, Creole Mmthly Reyon & Lumie; transl, ed, publ, New Testament Creole Am Bible Soc, 1960; organizer, daily pol bd cast Haiti Fr; ed, Le Combattant Haitien Fr & Eng. **Home Addr:** 865 West End Ave, New York, NY 10025.

### JOSEPH, SHAWN

School administrator, teacher, school superintendent. **Personal:** married Ocheze; children: 2. **Educ:** Lincoln Univ, BS, 1996; Johns Hopkins Univ, MSEd, 2000; George Washington Univ, EdD, 2009. **Career:** Roberto Clemente Mid Sch, Montgomery County Pub Schs, Eng teacher, reading specialist, team leader, 1996-2002; Redland Mid Sch, Montgomery County Pub Schs, asst prin, 2002-05; Roberto Clemente Mid Sch, Montgomery County Pub Schs, 2005-09; McDaniel Col, adj prof, 2008-11; Montgomery County Pub Schs, dir sch performance, 2009-11; Hillel at George Washington Univ, adj prof, 2009-11; Seaford Sch Dist, supt, 2012-14; Prince George's County Pub Schs, dep supt, 2014-16; Metro Nashville Pub Schs, dir schs, 2016-. **Orgs:** AASA. **Honors/Awds:** Middle Level Principal of the Year, Md Asn Sec Sch Principals, 2009; Outstanding Dissertation Award, Am Educ Res Asn, 2010; Ambassador Andrew Young Certificate of Distinguished Services, 2016. **Special Achievements:** First African-American director of schools for Metro Nashville Public Schools. Author, The Principal's Guide to the First 100 Days of the School Year, 2012; contributor, educational journals. **Business Addr:** Metro Nashville Public Schools, 2601 Bransford Ave, Nashville, TN 37204, **Business Phone:** (615)259-INFO.

### JOSEPH, TAROME ALFORD

Educator. **Personal:** Born May 3, 1960, Milwaukee, WI; son of Joe and Joyce Alford; married Milva McGhee. **Educ:** Univ Wis-Oshkosh, BA, BS, 1982; Southern Ill Univ Carbondale, MA, 1985. **Career:** Univ Wis-Oshkosh, resident asst, 1980-82; Southern Ill Univ, Carbondale, grad asst, 1982-84; Cornell Col, residence hall dir, 1984-85; Univ Nebr, residence hall dir, 1985-88; SUNY, Col New Paltz, asst dir residence life, 1988-89; Eastern Conn State Univ, assoc dir housing & res life; Tex A&M Univ, Kingsville, dir housing; Prof Stand Inst, fac, 2002-; Cent Conn State Univ, dir residence life, 2005-. **Orgs:** NASPA Region I, Conf Planning Comm, 1989-92; chair, NTWK Edu Equity & Ethnic Diversity, 1989-92; chair, Elections & Nominations Comm, 1992-94, Regional Liaison Minority Undergrad Fel Prog, 2002-; ACPA, Comm Multical Affairs, 1990-92; ACUHO-I, Multical Affairs Comm, 1993-; Nat Chair, Mem Comm, 1994-96; Found Bd Trustee, 1996-99. **Home Addr:** PO Box 1191, Providence, RI 02901, **Home Phone:** (401)454-6713. **Business Addr:** Director of Residence Life, Springfield College, 263 Alden St, Springfield, MA 01109-3797, **Business Phone:** (413)748-3000.

### JOSEPH-MCINTYRE, MARY

Administrator, executive director. **Personal:** Born Jan 12, 1942, Shreveport, LA; children: Jarrett. **Educ:** Contra Costa Jr Col, attended 1962; Willis Col Bus, attended 1963; Univ Calif, attended 1966; Univ San Francisco, continuing educ, bus admin, 1983. **Career:** Univ Calif, Berkeley, secy, 1963-78, coordr sec pool, 1968-71, psychol dept, 1972-74; N Peralta Jr Col, secy pres, 1971-72; Oakland Met Enterprises, adv asst, 1975-76, exec dir, 1976-79; Dukes, Dukes & Assoc, proj adminr, 1979-83; "Sweet Touch", owner, 1984-; City Oakland Youth Adv Comn, staff liaision, 1989-91; City Oakland, Off Parks & Recreation, adv serv mgr, 1989-; Alameda County Youth Serv Forum Mem, 1989-; Third Ace Inc, bd secy, 1989-. **Orgs:** Nat Frat Stud & Teachers, 1958-60; Nat Asn Advan Colored People, 1961-65; League Women Voters, 1964-70; vol, Kilimanjaro House, 1968; Black Caucus, 1968-69; Nat Contract & Mgt Asn, 1977-; Negro Women Bus & Prof Inc, 1977-84. **Honors/Awds:** PRS, TAPS Prog; Albany Youth Coun, 1959-60; March of Dimes Award, Alameda County, 1960; Northern Calif Adoption Agency; Outstanding Merit Increase, Univ Calif, 1968. **Home Addr:** 3922 Turnley Ave, Oakland, CA 94605, **Home Phone:** (510)562-4394.

### JOSEY, LERONIA ARNETTA

Government official, commissioner. **Personal:** Born Norfolk, VA; children: Quenton C. **Educ:** Spelman Col, BA, 1965; Univ Md Sch Soik & Comm Plang, MSW, 1973; Syracuse Univ, Col Law, JD; Maxwell Sch Citizenship Pub Affairs, MPA, 1977. **Career:** US Dept Housing & Urban Develop, Wash, DC, atty, 1977-81; Md Parole Comn, comnr, 1981-; Leronia josey & Assc Llc Md, pres & chief exec officer, 2005-. **Orgs:** Dir, Echo House Found, 1978-82; Med Eye Black Bd, 1981-82; Luic Carroll Jackson Mus, 1982-; pres, Nat Asn Black Women Atty, 1983-; bd mem, Leadership Md. **Honors/Awds:** Maryland's Top 100 Women, 1966; Third honorable graduate, Spelman Col; Law School Senate Award, 1977; White House fel finalist, 1977. **Home Addr:** 3700 Locheam Dr, Baltimore, MD 21207, **Home Phone:** (410)298-5931. **Business Addr:** Commissioner, Maryland Parole Commission, Suite 601 1 Investment Pl, Towson, MD 21204.

### JOSEY-HERRING, ANITA MARIE

Judge. **Personal:** Born Sep 19, 1960, Portsmouth, VA; daughter of Edward and Katie; married Albert Herring Esq; children: 1. **Educ:** Va Commonwealth Univ, BA, 1982; Georgetown Univ Law Ctr, JD, 1987. **Career:** Occup Safety & Health Admin. Dept Labor, paralegal specialist, 1984-85; Us Dept Energy Solicitors Off, law clerk; KOH Systs Inc, law clerk, 1985-87; Judge Herbert B Dixon, Jr, judicial clerk, 1987-88; Pub Defender Serv, staff atty, 1988-94, dep dir, 1994-97; Super Ct, DC, assoc judge, dep presiding judge family div, 2000-. **Orgs:** Nat Bar Asn; Women Lawyer's Div, Greater Wash Area Chap, Community Outreach Comn; Wash Bar Asn; Fed Bar Asn; DC Super Ct Domestic Violence Coun, 1994-; co-chair, DC Super Ct Task Force Families & Violence, Domestic Violence Task Force Treat Subcomt, 1994-95; Greater Wash Urban League; Delta Sigma Theta Sorority; fac mem, Nat Legal Aid & Defender Training Conf. **Honors/Awds:** Superior Court Medal of Excellence, 2000; Powerful Voice for Children Award, 2005. **Special Achievements:** Georgetown Legal Ethics Law Journal, Georgetown Univ, 1980. **Home Addr:** 4801 Colo Ave NW, Washington, DC 20011, **Home Phone:** (202)291-0034. **Business Addr:** Deputy Presiding Judge, Superior Court of District of Columbia, 500 Ind Ave NW Rm 2500, Washington, DC 20001, **Business Phone:** (202)879-2700.

### JOSHUA, DR. ALEXA A.

Physician. **Educ:** Wayne State Univ, MD, 1986. **Career:** Henry Ford Hosp, internship; Henry Ford Hosp, resident; Doc Rxtor Patience Med, physician; Pvt practioner, internal med, currently. **Orgs:** Am Bd Internal Med. **Business Addr:** Physician, Internist, Doc Rxtor Patience Medical, 3741 McDougall St Suite 2, Detroit, MI 48207-2345, **Business Phone:** (313)921-8866.

### JOURNEY, LULA MAE

Government official, executive. **Personal:** Born May 8, 1934, Doddsville, MS; children: Larry, Callie Sanders, Linda, Ronnie, Marilyn Kirk & Blondina. **Educ:** Delta Indust Inst Bus Sch, MS, 1954; Mkt Training Inst, attended 1958; Purdue Univ, attended 1979. **Career:** Ctr Twp Trustees Off, investr; Marion County Home, asst supvr, supvr investr, asst chief supvr oper, 1965-. **Orgs:** Pres, Indianapolis Pre Sch, 1972; bd dir, Citizens Neighborhood Coaltion, 1976-; city-county counr, 10th Dist City-County Coun, 1976-; bd dir, Mapleton/Fall Creek Asn, 1977-; chmn, Mem Comt, Am Bus Women Asn, 1981; state coordr munic women govt, Nat League Cities, 1982-; minority leader dem caucus, City-County Coun, 1985; Health & Corp Mgt; bd trustee,

Health Hosp Corp. **Honors/Awds:** Key to the City, City-County Coun, 1976; Cert Coop, Beyond Call Duty Ctr Twp Trustees Off, 1978; Cert of Appreciation, Indianapolis Pre-Sch, 1978; Suprv of the Month, Ctr Twp Trustees Off, 1979; Cert, IN Asn Motorcycle Clubs, 1983. **Home Addr:** 2020 New Jersey St, Indianapolis, IN 46202, **Home Phone:** (317)925-1056. **Business Addr:** Assistant Chief Supervisor of Operations, Center Township Trustees Office, 863 Massachusetts Ave, Indianapolis, IN 46204, **Business Phone:** (317)633-3610.

### JOWERS, JOHNNIE EDWARD, SR.
Teacher, association executive. **Personal:** Born Jul 1, 1931, Lynchburg, SC; son of Loro (deceased) and Bernice (deceased); married Paltine Horton; children: Johnnie E Jr & Deborah J. **Educ:** Shaw Univ, BA, 1957; NCA Cent Univ, MS, 1958; Johns Hopkins Univ, cert, advan studies educ, 1964; NYK Univ, cert org & admin, 1965. **Career:** Edge combe Co Bd Educ, sec sch teacher, 1958-59; Salvation Army Boys & Girls Clubs, phys dir, 1959-60, prog dir, 1960-63, unit dir, 1963-68, exec dir, 1974-96; Baltimore City Schs, sec sch teacher, 1968-74; CARE Inc, spec educ teacher, 1997-. **Orgs:** Trustee, Progressive First Baptist Church, 1975-; corresp secy, Shaw Univ Alumni Asn, 1975-; United Way Cent MAR Speaker's Bur, 1978-94; Baltimore club pres, Frontiers INT Inc, 1979-80; chmn, Shaw Univ Nat Homecoming Banquet, 1990; area co-chmn, Shaw Univ Capital Campaign, 1991-; chaplin, Baltimore Frontiers Club, 1992-; Greensboro Shaw Univ Alumni Asn; Soc African Am Am Profs; Northeast Region Manpower Develop Comt; Nat Comn; Nat Adv Group. **Honors/Awds:** Student of the Year, Shaw Univ, 1953; Outstanding TCR Award, Baltimore City Schs, 1970; Man & Boy Award, Salvation Army Boys Club, 1973; Distinguished Serv Award, Salvation Army, 1984; Distinguished Alumni Award, NC Cent Univ, 1998; Distinguished Award, Shaw Univ, 1998. **Special Achievements:** History of Intercollegiate Athletics at Shaw Univ, 1958; "Boosting Your Speeches", 1989; "Publicity: Everybody's Job", 1989. **Home Addr:** 2800 E Coldspring Lane, Baltimore, MD 21214-2804, **Home Phone:** (410)254-1557. **Business Addr:** Trustee, Progressive First Baptist Church, 3220 Garrison Blvd, Baltimore, MD 21216, **Business Phone:** (410)664-6454.

### JOY, DANIEL WEBSTER
Judge. **Personal:** Born Apr 15, 1931, Middleton, NC; son of Andrew and Mattie Griffith; married Ruby M Collins; children: Darryl & Kathry. **Educ:** State Univ NY, Albany, BA, 1952; Brooklyn Law Sch, JD, 1957. **Career:** Judge (retired); Rent & Rehab Admin, chief coun, 1967-70, comnr, 1970-73; Housing Preserv & Develop Dept, comnr, 1973-83; Queens Co Civil Ct, judge, 1984-85; Supreme Ct, justice, 1985-2000; Ctr for Pub Theol, judge. **Orgs:** Spring Civic Asn, 1968-; vpres, chmn, New Hope Lutheran Church, Jamaica, NY, 1973-; Asn Bar City NY, 1976-83; Edwin Gould Found, 1980-; bd mem, Queens Co Bar Asn, 1981-; bd chmn, Macon B Allen, Black Bar Asn, 1982-; Nat Bar Asn, 1983-; nat treas, Lutheran Men in Mission, 2002; pres, AALA Chap; bd dir, Lutheran Social Serv New York, currently; Mayor's Comt City Marshals; chair, Stewardship Committee; bd mem, Jamaica Services for Older Adults; bd mem, Ctr for Pub Theol; Task force mem, Evangel Lutheran Church. **Home Addr:** 14438 168th St, Jamaica, NY 11434-4815, **Home Phone:** (718)723-0438. **Business Addr:** Board of Director, Lutheran Social Services of New York, 475 Riverside Dr Suite 1244, New York, NY 10115, **Business Phone:** (212)870-1100.

### JOYCE, ELLA (CHERRON HOYE)
Actor. **Personal:** Born Jun 12, 1954, Chicago, IL; daughter of Bunnie Hoye; married Dan Martin. **Educ:** Eastern Mich Univ; bus Col; Yale Repertory Theater, trained with Lloyd Richards. **Career:** Ford Motor Co, secretary; actress, theater experience includes: Don't Get God Started, Two Trains Running, Milestones in Drama, The First Breeze of Summer, Chapter, Ma Rainey's Black Bottom. Films: Stop or My Mom Will Shoot, 1992; Set It Off, 1996; Her Married Lover, 1999; Clockin' Green, 1999; Frozen Hot, 2000; Bubba Ho-tep, 2002; Salvation, 2002; Salvation, 2003; Who Made the Potatoe Salad, 2005; Forbidden Fruits, 2005; My Nappy Roots, 2005; Lost Signal, 2006; A Simple Promise, 2008; Busted, 2009; Preacher's Kid, 2009; Our Family Wedding, 2010; Hopelessly in June, 2011; Saybrook: The Tully Girls, 2011; California Solo, 2012; Temptation: Confessions of a Marriage Counselor, 2013. TV series: "Newlywed Game"; "Search for Tomorrow"; "One Life to Live"; "Roc", 1991-94; "Choices", 1992; "Selma, Lord, Selma", 1999; "Frozen Hot", producer, 1999; "Clockin Green", assoc producer, 2000; "Stranger Inside", 2001; "The Old Settler", 2001; "What About Your Friends: Weekend Getaway", 2002; "My Wife and Kids", 2003; "Belle", 2013. **Honors/Awds:** Audelco Best Dramatic Actress, for Black Theater Excellence; TOR Award for Best Dramatic Actress, in Off-Broadway category; Cass Tech Hall of Famer; Joseph Jefferson Award, Goodman Theatre Chicago, 2006. **Special Achievements:** Author, Kink Phobia: Journey Through A Black Woman's Hair, 2002. **Business Addr:** Actor, Landmark Artists Management, 4116 W Magnolia Blvd Suite 101, Burbank, CA 91505, **Business Phone:** (818)848-9800.

### JOYNER, CLAUDE C.
Government official, chief financial officer. **Personal:** Born Nov 8, 1950, New Haven, CT; son of Minnie (deceased) and Claude (deceased); married Dolores Brandow. **Educ:** Maple Springs Baptist Bible Col & Sem, MRE, 1997; Cent State Univ, BS,1974; Pepperdine Univ, MBA, 1983; Maple Springs Baptist Bible Col & Sem, MRE, 1997. **Career:** Lincoln Nat Life Ins Co, syst designer, 1974-76; First Interstate Bank, opers officer, 1977-79; Aerospace Corp, programmer, 1979-80; Trans Tech Inc, systs analyst, 1980-84; Electronic Data Systs, sr systs analyst, 1984-85; Booz Allen & Hamilton, assoc, 1985-86; Contel ASC, sr syst analyst, 1986-87; Mt Sinai Baptist Church, sunday sch teacher, 1986-94, lic minister, 1991-, asst supt, 1992-94; Comput Based Systs Inc, staff analyst, database adminr, 1987-91; Joyner Design Ltd, chief financial officer, 1990-; Crystal City, Va, sr database specialist, 1991-96; Kendall Baptist Church, disciple training dir, 1994-, sunday sch teacher, asst training union dir, 1995-, dir nenevolence Comn, 1997-; US Patent Trademark Off, comput Specialist, 1996-; Wash Grace Church, pastor, 2008-. **Orgs:** Deaf Pride Inc, 1980-86; stud outreach comn, Nat Black MBA Asn, 1984-87; educ chairperson, Black Data Processing Asn, DC Chap, 1985-87; staff vol, treas, Mt Sinai Outreach Ctr, 1987-94; treas, Right Way Ministries Inc, 1992-96, chmn trustee bd, 1997-. **Home Addr:** 4102 Buck Creek Rd, Temple Hills, MD 20748-4931, **Home Phone:** (301)894-7947. **Business Addr:** Computer Specialist, US Patent & Trademark Office, 2131 Crystal Dr Suite 1100A, Alexandria, VA 22202, **Business Phone:** (703)305-9352.

### JOYNER, DONNA RICHARDSON
Personal trainer, executive director. **Personal:** Born May 13, 1957; married Tom. **Educ:** Hollins Col, health educ. **Career:** Aerobics instructor, author, television sports commentator & producer; Aerobics instr, 1980; Donnaerobics, 1984; Stay Fit Plus, 1989; ESPN, co-host fitness Pro show, 1992, sports commentator, currently; StayFit Kids, founder; Donna Richardson LLC, owner, currently; President's Council Physical Fitness & Sports, mem, 2006; TV Series: "Donna Richardson: Mind, Body, & Spirit", producer; "Sweating In The Spirit", producer; Videos: Donna Richardson-Attitude Aerobics, 1993; Platinum Series: Thighs of Steel 2000, 1993; Perfect Balance Workout, 1994; Platinum Series: Buns of Steel 2000, 1994; Platinum Series: Arms & Abs of Steel 2000, 1994; 4-Day Rotation Workout, 1995; Donna-Mite Aerobic Workout, 1995; 30 Days to Firmer Abs & Arms, 1995; Donna Richardson - 30 Days To Thinner Thighs, 1995; Back to Basics, 1995; Step & Awesome Abs, 1995; Donna Richardson: 3-Day Rotation 2000, 1999; Sweating In The Spirit, 2003; Sweating In The Spirit 2, 2006; The Brazilian Workout, 2006; Old School Dance Party, 2006. **Orgs:** Spokesperson, Am Heart Asn; Women's Sports Found Bd trustees; adv bd mem, Boys & Girls Clubs Am. **Honors/Awds:** World's largest line dance, Guinness Book of World Records; One out of 25 most inspiring women in America, Essence Magazine, 2006; Fitness Magazine Fitness Hall of Fame; Top 10 Movers and Shakers, Fitness Magazine. **Special Achievements:** Presidential appointee of President George W. Bush's Council on Physical Fitness and Sports; The author of the best-selling book Let's Get Real: Exercise Your Right To A Healthy Body, 1998; selected by the "Oprah Winfrey Show" as one of the Top 5 Fitness Video Instructors; Also selected by Fitness Magazine as one of their Top 10 Movers And Shakers; has lectured in 40 countries and has been a featured motivational speaker with several national tours including God's Leading Ladies, Sisters In The Spirit and the Pantene Total You. Also entered the Guinness Book of World Records for creating the world's largest line dance, with over 50, 000 participants. Has done numerous TV shows. **Business Addr:** Owner, Donna Richardson LLC, 13760 Noel Rd Suite 750, Dallas, TX 75240, **Business Phone:** (800)475-6399.

### JOYNER, ESQ. GORDON L.
Lawyer, county commissioner. **Personal:** Born Feb 11, 1950, Fort Valley, GA; son of Henry W and Helen L; children: Ashley & Shannon. **Educ:** Morehouse Col, Atlanta, Ga, BA, bus admin, econs & polit sci, 1972; Harvard Law Sch, Cambridge, Mass, JD, corp, civil litigation, const law & civil rights, 1975. **Career:** Kilpatrick & Cody Law Offices, Atlanta, Ga, atty, 1975-78; Am Bar Asn, Wash, DC, asst dir, 1978-79; US Dept Housing & Urban Develop, Wash, DC, legal coun, dir fair housing enforcement, 1979-82; Atlanta Munic Ct, Atlanta, Ga, judge, 1985-87; Fulton County Bd Commissioners, comnr, 1987-2000; State Ga Civil Rights Dept, Ga Comn Equal Opportunity, exec dir & adminr, 2000-11; Law Offices Gordon L. Joyner, owner, currently; self-employed atty, currently. **Orgs:** Secy, Atlanta Harvard Club, 1983; chmn, Fulton County Bd Elections, 1985-87; life mem, Nat Asn Advan Colored People; Nat Urban League; exec bd mem, Atlanta Nat Asn Advan Colored People; Phi Beta Kappa; Alpha Phi Alpha Frat; Mayor's Task Force Pub Educ; Southern Christian Leadership Conf; trustee bd, usher bd, Friendship Baptist Church; family adv comt, Atlanta Hist Ctr; Sigma Pi Phi. **Honors/Awds:** Government Executive-In-Residence & Vis Prof, Morehouse Col, 1981-82; Official Guest of Israel & Germany Governments, 1989-90. **Home Addr:** 663 Cativo Dr SW, Atlanta, GA 30311. **Business Addr:** Attorney, Owner, The Law Offices of Gordon L Joyner, 945 Ashby Circle NW, Atlanta, GA 30314-0816, **Business Phone:** (404)524-2400.

### JOYNER, IRVING L.
Lawyer, educator. **Personal:** Born Dec 11, 1944, Brooklyn, NY; son of McLean Spaulding and Dorothy; children: Lauren, Kwame & Tuere. **Educ:** Long Island Univ, BS, 1970; Rutgers, State Univ NJ, JD. **Career:** United Church Christ Comt Racial Justice, dir criminal justice, 1968-78; Currie & Joyner, atty law, 1978-80; Nat Prison Proj ACLU, staff atty, 1980-81; Currie, Pugh & Joyner, atty law, 1981-85; NC Cent Univ Sch Law, prof law, 1982-, assoc dean, 1984-92. **Orgs:** Pres, NC Asn Black Lawyers, 1977-; NC State Bar, 1977-; Nat Bar Asn, 1977-; NC Acad Trial Lawyers, 1977-; Fed Bar Adv Coun, 1985-; Ebenezer Missionary Baptist Church. **Business Addr:** Professor of Law, North Carolina Central University Law School, 1512 S Alston Ave Off 132, Durham, NC 27707, **Business Phone:** (919)530-6293.

### JOYNER, LAUREN CELESTE (LAUREN JOYNER BOWERS)
Lawyer. **Personal:** Born Brooklyn, NY. **Educ:** Univ NC, BA, psychol, 1989; Georgetown Univ Law Ctr, JD, 1992. **Career:** Kings County Dist Attorneys Off, asst dist atty, 1992-95; MasterCard, franchise mgt, mgr, 1995-98; Am Express, mgr, 1998, dir, dir risk mgt, 2000-03; Am Bankers Asn, gen coun, sr vpres & sr coun, 2004-. **Orgs:** Team leader, New York Cares, 1995-; mentor, C's Aid Soc, Yes Prog, 1997-; Am Bankruptcy Inst, 1998-; Am Bankers Asn; Georgetown Univ Law Ctr Alumni. **Honors/Awds:** President's Award, MasterCard, 1998; Chairman's Award, Am Express, 2000. **Home Addr:** 213 Lafayette Ave, Brooklyn, NY 11238, **Home Phone:** (718)398-3311. **Business Addr:** Senior Vice President, Senior Counsel, American Bankers Association, 1120 Conn Ave NW, Washington, DC 20036-3971, **Business Phone:** (800)226-5377.

### JOYNER, LEMUEL MARTIN
Administrator, mental health counselor. **Personal:** Born Jun 20, 1928, Nashville, TN; married Barbara; children: Lemuel Jr, John M, Christopher A, Dennis L, Victor P & Lonnie. **Educ:** Univ Notre Dame, BFA, 1957, MFA, 1969. **Career:** St. Christophers Workshop, designer ch interiors; liturgical artist, 1958-65; St Mary's Col, Notre Dame, asst prof art, 1965-71; Off Inter-Cult Develop, spec asst pres, 1970; Day Treat Ctr, co-develop; Ctr Integrative Healing, art therapist, 1985; Memorial Hosp, S Bend, Ctr Integrative Healing, spiritual therapist, currently. **Orgs:** Am Art Therapists Asn; S Bend Art Asn; S Bend St Acad; Nat Coun Artist; Alpha Phi Alpha; Ctr Integrative Healing S Bend's Memorial Hosp. **Honors/Awds:** Model Upward Bound Prog, 1966; Excellence in Teaching Award, St Mary's Col, 1969; Outstanding Contribution to Standard Life Award; Black Dimensions In Am Art, 1969; Rev Anthony J Lauck CSC Award. **Home Addr:** PO Box 654, Notre Dame, IN 46556. **Business Addr:** Spiritual Therapist, Memorial Hospital of South Bend, 615 N Mich St, South Bend, IN 46601, **Business Phone:** (574)647-1000.

### JOYNER, OSCAR ALBERT
Executive. **Personal:** Born Jan 27, 1975, Dallas, TX; son of Tom Sr and Dora. **Educ:** Darden Univ; Fla Agr & Mech Univ, MBA, mkt & finance, 1998. **Career:** ABC Radio Networks, producer, 1997-99; Joyner & Assoc, chief exec officer, 1999-2003; Reach Media Inc, pres & chief operating officer & chief exec officer, 2003; Tom Joyner Morning Show, exec producer, sr vpres. **Orgs:** Omega Psi Phi Inc, 1995-; bd dir, sr vpres, Tom Joyner Found, 1998-; bd mem, bd dir, Nat Black MBA Asn; 100 Black Men Am; bd mem, Fla A&M Univ Found; bd mem, Nat Asn Broadcasters Educ Found; co founder, prin educ, Develop Corp Am. **Honors/Awds:** Benjamin L Hooks Award; Freedom Fighter Award, Nat Asn Advan Colored People; Civic Community Award, NV Mag, 2003; Nat Coalition of Black Civic Participation Award. **Business Addr:** Board of Director, Tom Joyner Foundation, PO Box 630495, Irving, TX 75063-0495, **Business Phone:** (972)789-1058.

### JOYNER, RUBIN E., JR.
School administrator. **Personal:** Born Dec 5, 1949, Trenton, NJ; married Phyllis A; children: Zanada & Ciarra. **Educ:** Rider Univ, BA, 1973; Trenton State Col, MEd, 1977; Temple Univ, EdD. **Career:** E Windsor sch syst, guid counr; Monmouth Univ, dir educ opport prog; Ocean County Col, dir educ opport, 1982-86; Rider Univ, dir educ opport prog, 1987-. **Orgs:** NJ Ed Opp Asn, 1978; Am Asn Coun Dept, 1979; Soc Spec & Ethnic Studies, 1979; dir black stud union, Monmouth Col, 1979-85; co-founder, Acceleration Comput Sci Prog, 1983-85; Orgn Black Unity, dir, 1985; founder, Access Prog, 1986; co-chairperson, Stud Leadership Educ Opport, 1986. **Home Addr:** 706 Berkeley Lane, Neptune, NJ 07753, **Home Phone:** (732)774-7339. **Business Addr:** Director Education Opportunity Program, Rider University, Acad Annex Rm 6 2083 Lawrenceville Rd, Lawrenceville, NJ 08648-3099, **Business Phone:** (609)896-5354.

### JOYNER, SETH
Sports promoter, football player. **Personal:** Born Nov 18, 1964, Spring Valley, NY; married Wanda; children: Jasmine. **Educ:** Univ Tex, El Paso, attended 1985. **Career:** Football player (retired), sports promoter; Philadelphia Eagles, linebacker & right linebacker, 1986, left linebacker, 1987-93; Ariz Cardinals, left linebacker, 1994, 1996, left linebacker & strong safety, 1995; Green Bay Packers, left linebacker, 1997-98; Denver Broncos, linebacker, 1998; All Am Speakers, sports speaker, currently; Joyner Coaching LLC, coach, 2009-. **Orgs:** Philadelphia Eagles; Broncos, 1999; 20/20 Club; pres & co-founder, Joyner-Walker Found Inc, 2007-. **Honors/Awds:** Pro Bowl, 1991, 1993, 1994; Defensive Player of the Year, Asniated Press, 1991; NFL Player of the Year, Sports Illustrated, 1991; Super Bowl XXXIII, 1999. **Special Achievements:** TV appearance: "Rome Is Burning, " 2005-07. **Home Addr:** 7755 N 71st St, Paradise Valley, AZ 85253. **Business Addr:** Sports Speaker, All American Speakers, 200 Alexander Dr, Durham, NC 27707, **Business Phone:** (919)403-7004.

### JOYNER, THOMAS
Radio host, business owner, disc jockey. **Personal:** Born Nov 23, 1949, Tuskegee, AL; son of Frances and Hercules L; married Dora Chatmon; children: Thomas Jr & Oscar; married Donna Richardson. **Educ:** Tuskegee Univ, BS, sociol, 1978. **Career:** WVON, staff; WBMX-FM, staff; WJPC, staff; Chicago Radio Sta, disc jockey; KDKA, Dallas, Tex, morning air personality, 1983-93; WGCI Chicago, afternoon host, 1985-93; ABC Radio, Tom Joyner Morning Show, host & producer, 1994-; BlackAmericaWeb.com, founder; REACH Media Inc, founder, chair, majority owner, 2003-. **Orgs:** Founder, Tom Joyner Found, 1998-. **Honors/Awds:** National Radio Hall of Fame, 1998; Trumpet Award, 2002; Cong Black Caucus, Mickey Leland Humanitarian/Relig Award; NAB Marconi Radio Award, 2004; International Civil Rights Walk of Fame, 2008; The Official R&B Music Hall of Fame, 2013; Humanitarian Award, 2015. **Special Achievements:** First African American to be inducted into The National Radio Hall of Fame, 1998; First African American to become a syndicated radio show host. **Business Addr:** Owner, REACH Media Inc, PO Box 801565, Dallas, TX 75380-1565, **Business Phone:** (972)789-1058.

### JOYNER-KERSEE, JACKIE (JACQUELINE JOYNER KERSEE)
Athlete. **Personal:** Born Mar 3, 1962, East St. Louis, IL; daughter of Alfred and Mary; married Bob Kersee. **Educ:** Univ Calif, LA, BA, 1985. **Career:** Track & field athlete (retired), asn exec; track & field athlete, 1987-98; Richmond Rage, prof basketball player, 1996-98; Bd USA Track & Field orgn, 2012; Jackie Joyner-Kersee Found, founder, chairperson & dir currently. **Orgs:** Jackie Joyner-Kersee Found; Univ Calif Alumni Asn; Athletic Cong Athletics Adv Bd; St Louis Sports Comn; Founding Athlete, Athletes Hope. **Home Addr:** 8319 Paul Jones Dr, Jacksonville, FL 32208-2822. **Business Addr:** Chairperson, Director, Jackie Joyner-Kersee Foundation, 101 Jackie Joyner-Kersee Cir, East St. Louis, IL 62204, **Business Phone:** (618)274-5437.

### JUDGE, DR. PAUL QANTAS
Executive. **Personal:** Born Mar 5, 1977, Baton Rouge, LA; son of Paul and Mary. **Educ:** Morehouse Col, BS, comput sci, 1998; Ga Inst Tech, MS, network security, 2000, PhD, comput sci, 2002. **Career:** Nat Aeronaut & Space Admin, res asst, 1995-98; Ga Tech, researcher, 1998-2003; Int Bus Mach, developer, 1998; Cipher Trust, chief tech officer, 2000-06; CipherTrust, chief technol officer, 2000-06; Secure Comput Corp, chief technol officer & sr vpres, 2006-07; Purewire, founder & chief technol officer, 2007-09, chief res officer, 2009-; Barracuda Networks, chief res officer & vpres, 2009-; Pindrop Security, co-founder, exec chmn, 2011-; Tech Sq Labs, founding partner; Monsieur, co-founder; Judge Ventures, head, currently. **Orgs:** Internet Res

Task Force; Anti Spam Res Group, founder; Inst Elec & Electronics Engrs; ACM. **Honors/Awds:** Innovators to Watch in 2006, InfoWorld, 2005; Black Engineer of the Year Special Recognition Award, 2006; 50 Most Powerful Players Under 40, Black Enterprise, 2005; 40 Under 40, Network Journal, 2005; "100 Top innovators under 35", MIT Technology Review Magazine, 2003; 30 under 30, Atlanta Power, 2007; Top 25 CTOs, InfoWorld, 2007; Top Forty Under 40, Baton Rouge Business Report, 2008; Georgia Corporate CIO Of The Year, 2009. **Special Achievements:** About 20 publications in academic journals & conferences; regularly speaks at leading industry events including Federal Trade Commission, RSA Conference & congressional panels; featured in hundreds of media outlets including CNN, Business Week, and The Wash Post; MIT's Technol Review Magazine, TR100-100 Top Young Innovators in the World, 2003; The Network Journal "40 Under 40"; Black Enterprise "50 Most Powerful Players Under 40". **Business Addr:** Chairman, Pindrop Security, 817 W Peachtree St NW Suite 770, Atlanta, GA 30308, **Business Phone:** (404)721-3767.

**JUDSON, DR. HORACE AUGUSTUS**
College administrator, college president, educator. **Personal:** Born Aug 7, 1941, Miami, FL; married Beatrice Gail; children: Tamara Renee, Sonya Anita, Sojourner Maria & Jessica Gail. **Educ:** Lincoln Univ, BA, 1963; Cornell Univ, PhD, phys org chem, 1970. **Career:** Cornel Univ, res fel, 1965-69; Bethune-Cookman Col, asst prof, 1969; Morgan State Col, assoc dean, 1973-74, from asst prof to assoc prof, 1969-72; Morgan State Univ, vpres acad affairs, 1974-79, prof, 1974-86, Col Sci, assoc dean & dean, Col Sci Improv Prog, assoc dir & dir, chair chem dept; Calif State Univ, provost & vpres acad affairs & dean col lett & sci, 1994; State Univ NY Col, Plattsburgh, pres & chancellor, 1994-2003; Grambling State Univ, pres, 2004-09; Knoxville Col, pres, 2010-13, interim pres, currently. **Orgs:** Am Chem Soc; Am Asn Higher Educ; Omega Psi Phi; Miner Inst Bd; Am Asn Univ Admin; pres, Int Asn Univ; Am Asn State Col & Univ; bd dir, Res Found State Univ NY; bd trustee, Trudeau Inst; bd dir, Clinton Cty Area Develop Corp; Boy Scouts Am, Adirondack Coun Adv Bd; Am Chem Soc; Sigma XI; Kappa Delta Pi; Phi Kappa Phi; Sigma Beta Delta. **Business Addr:** President, Knoxville College, 901 Knoxville Col Dr, Knoxville, TN 37921, **Business Phone:** (865)524-6525.

**JUNIOR, E. J. (ESTER JAMES JUNIOR, III)**
Executive, football player, football coach. **Personal:** Born Dec 8, 1959, Salisbury, NC; married Yolanda; children: Adam, Aja, E J IV, Kyle, Ashley, Shandon, Torren & Cameron. **Educ:** Univ Ala, BA, pub rel, 1997. **Career:** Football player (retired), coach; St Louis Cardinals, linebacker, 1981-88; Miami Dolphins, linebacker, 1989-91; Tampa Bay Buccaneers, linebacker, 1992; Seattle Seahawks, linebacker, 1992-93, coach, 1994; Nat Basketball Asn, Alonzo Mourning, exec dir; Miami Dolphins, dir player develop progs, 1996-98; Minn Vikings, coach, 2003; Miami-Dade County Pub Schs, distrit coordr, 1999-2003; Overtown Youth Ctr, exec dir, 2003-04; Rhein Fire NFLE, linebacker coach, 2005; Jacksonville Jaguars, coach, 2005; NFL Europe, coach, 2005-06; E-W Shrine Game, coach, 2005 & 2006; Southwest Baptist Univ, linebackers coach, 2006-07, defensive coordr, 2007-09; Cent State Univ, head coach, 2009-13; Middletown High Sch, asst football coach, 2014; Ohio Mid Western Col, asst football coach & defensive coordr, 2014; Del State Univ, dir player develop, defensive line coach, 2015-. **Orgs:** Asst youth pastor, Bethel Full-Gospel Baptist Church; Kappa Alpha Psi Fraternity Inc; NFL Player Progs, Steering Comt; motivational speaker. **Honors/Awds:** Alabamas Team of the Decade, 1970; Strength Coaches All-American team; All-SEC Defensive Player of the Year, 1980; Sr Bowl, Outstanding Defensive Performer, 1981; named to several All-Rookie teams, 1981; Pro Bowl, 1984, 1985; ordained, 1997; Nashville, TN, Public Schools Hall of Fame, 2006; Senior Bowl Hall of Fame, 2007; Lombardi Award finalist; Inducted Alabama Sports Hall of Fame, 2012. **Home Addr:** 1001 NW 78th Terr, Plantation, FL 33322-5122, **Home Phone:** (513)217-1274. **Business Addr:** Head Coach, Delaware State University, 1200 N Dupont Hwy, Dover, DE 19901, **Business Phone:** (302)857-6060.

**JUNIOR, MARVIN**
Singer. **Personal:** Born Jan 31, 1936, Harrell, AR. **Career:** The Dells, lead baritone & mem, 1952-; Albums (With the Dells): Oh What a Night, 1957; It's Not Unusual, 1965; There Is, 1968; Love Is Blue, 1969; The Dells' Musical Menu/Always Together, 1969; The Dells' Greatest Hits, 1970; Like It Is, Like It Was, 1971; Freedom Means, 1971; Sweet As Funk Can Be, 1972; The Dells Sing Dionne, 1972; Give Your Baby a Standing Ovation, 1976; The Dells, 1973; The Mighty Mighty Dells, 1974; The Dells vs. The Dramatics, 1975; The Dells' Greatest Hits Volume 2, 1975; We Got To Get Our Thing Together, 1975; No Way Back, 1976; They Said It Couldn't Be Done But We Did It, 1977; Love Connection, 1977; New Beginnings, 1978; Face to Face, 1979; I Touched a Dream, 1980; Whatever Turns You On, 1981; One Step Closer, 1984; The Second Time, 1988; On Their Corner, 1992; I Salute You, 1992; Dreams of Contentment, 1993; Bring Back the Love: Classic Dells, 1996; I Touch a Dream/Whatever Turns, 1998; Reminiscing, 2000; Open Up My Heart: The 9/11 Album, 2002; Hott, 2003; (With Michael Ross): We Finally Meet, 1995; Last Love Letter, 1996; The Wailers Band, guitarist, currently; Solo album: Wailin' For Love, 2007; Jah Roots, 2008. **Honors/Awds:** Rock and Roll Hall of Fame, The Dells, 2004. **Business Addr:** Lead Baritone, The Original Dells Inc, PO Box 1133, Harvey, IL 60426-7133, **Business Phone:** (708)474-1422.

**JUNIOR-SPENCE, REV. SAMELLA E.**
Educator, musician. **Personal:** Born Dec 15, 1931, Chattanooga, TN; married Ester James; children: Avis & E J. **Educ:** Spelman Col, AB, 1953; La State Univ, MA, music educ, 1957; George Peabody Col, PhD, 1977. **Career:** Educator (retired), musician; Leland Col, instr & dir, 1956-57; Jarvis Christian Col, 1957-59; Livingstone Col, prof, 1959-60; E Baker High Sch & Elem Sch, teacher, 1961-63; Carver Jr High Sch, teacher, dir & chmn, 1963-68; Highland Heights Jr High Sch, teacher, 1969-71; Isaac Litton Jr High Sch, 1971-74; Joelton High Sch, asst prin, 1974-75; Cumberland Jr High Sch, prin, 1975-78; Pearl High Sch, prin, 1975-78; Whites Creek Comprehensive High Sch, assoc prin; E Nashville High Sch, prin, 1978-86; Pleasant Green Baptist Church, minister music, currently. **Orgs:** Choir dir & minister, Mt Zion Bapt Ch; First Bapt Ch; Disciples Christ Ch; asst organist, First Bapt Ch; choir dir, minister music & pres, Spelman Club; pres, vpres, secy & comm chmn, Delta Sigma Theta Inc; treas, Nat Coun Negro Women; treas, Black Expo; secy, Albany State Col Wives; com chmn, Nat Educ Asn; comm chmn, Mo Nat Educ Asn; com chmn, Tex Educ Asn; com chmn, Nat Asn Sec Sch Principals; com chmn, Tex Asn Sec Sch Principals; com chmn, Asn Supv & Curric Develop; com chmn, Asn Teacher Educrs; com chmn, Phi Delta Kappa; com chmn, Am Asn Univ Women; com chmn, Nashville Pin; pres elect, Mid Region Tex Educ Asn; chmn, Metro Coun Teachers Educ; Nat Fel Ch Musicians; Nat Asn Advan Colored People; vice chmn bd, Oper PUSH; bd dir, Leadership Nashville Found, 2006-07. **Honors/Awds:** Molly Todd Cup, Nashville CABLE, 1998. **Home Addr:** 130 Bluegrass Dr, Hendersonville, TN 37075. **Business Addr:** Minister of Music, Pleasant Green Baptist Church, 1410 Jefferson St, Nashville, TN 37208, **Business Phone:** (615)329-1189.

**JUPITER, CLYDE PETER**
Educator, executive. **Personal:** Born Oct 31, 1928, New Orleans, LA; married Pat; children: Carol A Gariboldi, Lisa A Jupiter-Byles, Joan C, Jeannie Ritchie, Deanna, Matthews, Mike Schank, Steve Schank, Chris Schank & Erika Schank. **Educ:** Xavier Univ New Orleans, BS, physics, 1949; Univ Notre Dame, South Bend, MS, physics, 1951. **Career:** Teaching Fel, Univ Notre Dame S Bend IN, 1949-50; Douglas Aircraft Co, aerodynamicist, 1951; Lawrence Radiation Lab, Livermore CA, 1956-64; Gen Atomic Co San Diego, staff sci, 1964-69; Nuclear Calibration Lab, dir; EG&G Inc Santa Barbara, mgr radiation physics dept, 1969-70; EG&G Inc Albuquerque, dir appl sci, 1970-71; EG&G Inc Las Vegas, mgr radiation & environ sci dept, 1971-75; US Nuclear Reg Comn, tech asst dir res, 1975-78, prog mgr waste mgt res, 1978-82; Howard Univ Sch Eng, adj prof nuclear Eng prog, 1981-86; US Nuclear Regulatory Comm, sr policy analyst Off policy eval, 1982-86; Jupiter Corp, pres, 1986-2001, chmn & founder, chief operating officer, 2001-. **Orgs:** Alpha Phi Alpha Fraternity, 1947-; fel Am Nuclear Soc, 1980; bd dir, Am Nuclear Soc, 1976-79 & 1994-97; Nat Asn Advan Colored People; Health Physics Soc; AAAS; Fel Am Nuclear Soc, 1980. **Honors/Awds:** Frazier Thompson Pioneer Award; Black Alumni, Notre Dame Club. **Home Addr:** 265 Amberleigh Dr, Silver Spring, MD 20905-5992, **Home Phone:** (202)255-2002. **Business Addr:** Chairman, Founder, Jupiter Corp, 2730 Univ Blvd W Suite 900 Westfield N, Wheaton, MD 20902, **Business Phone:** (301)946-8088.

**JUSTICE, DAVID CHRISTOPHER**
Broadcaster, baseball player, television journalist. **Personal:** Born Apr 14, 1966, Cincinnati, OH; son of Robert and Nettie; married Halle Berry; children: Dionisio, Raquel & David Jr; married Rebecca Villalobos; children: Dionisio & Raquel. **Educ:** Thomas More Col, criminal justice, 1985. **Career:** Baseball player (retired), broadcaster, tv journalist; Atlanta Braves, outfielder & infielder, 1989-96; Cleveland Indians, 1997-2000; NY Yankees, 2000-01; Oakland Athletics, 2002; ESPN, baseball telecasts, commentator; YES Network, NY Yankees, game & studio analyst, contribr, currently. **Orgs:** Omega Psi Phi. **Home Addr:** 311 Glenwood Ave, Cincinnati, OH 45217. **Business Addr:** Contributor, YES Network, 405 Lexington Ave 36th Fl, New York, NY 10174-3699, **Business Phone:** (646)487-3600.

# K

**KAALUND, SEKOU H.**
Financial manager, executive director, association executive. **Personal:** Born Jun 29, 1975, Raleigh, NC; son of Jackie Mburu and Barry; married Jennifer. **Educ:** Univ Granada, Spain, 1995; Hampden-Sydney Col, BA, pub policy, classics & span, 1997; Duke Univ, MPP, public policy, 1999. **Career:** White House Off Gen Coun; SK Solutions, pres, 1998-99; Fed Res Bank NY, sr bank examr & sr relationship specialist, 1999-2004; Citigroup, dir strategic initiatives, 2004-06, head strategy, securities & funds serv, 2004-07; JP Morgan, Global Head Pvt Equity Fund Serv, managing dir, 2007-09, Americas Head Sales, Pub & Corp Pension & Tax Exempts, managing dir, 2009-13, Investor Client Mgt, managing dir, 2013-; Head Pension Coverage, 2016-. **Orgs:** Chair corp develop fund raising, Next Gen Network, 2000-03, vpres, 2003-; Banking our Future, 2002-; asst treas, Kappa Alpha psi, 2003-; Urban Financial Servs Coalition, 2003-; Woodrow Wilson fel; Donnelly Found fel; bd visitor, Duke Univs Sch Pub Policy. **Honors/Awds:** Nat Youth of the Year Finalist, Boys & Girls Club Am, 1992; Merit Scholar, Hampden-Sydney Col, 1993; Ford Foundation/AED, Woodrow Wilson Fel, Public Policy, 1996; President's Award for Excellence, Fed Reserve Bank, 2001; Nat Orator of the Year, Urban Financial Service Coalition, 2002; President's Award; Featured on 22 "Young Leaders of the Future", Ebony magazine. **Business Addr:** Managing Director, JPMorgan Chase Bank, 231 Grand St, New York, NY 10013, **Business Phone:** (212)552-4001.

**KADREE, DR. MARGARET ANTONIA**
Physician, educator, college teacher. **Personal:** Born Jun 25, 1952, Tunapuna; daughter of Fitzroy Vidale and Ella; married Adegboyega J; children: Temilade, Shijuade, Yewande & Hafsa. **Educ:** NY Univ, BA, 1979; State NY Buffalo Sch Med, MD, 1983. **Career:** Howard Univ Hosp, fel, 1986-88; Morehouse Sch Med, dir clin residence prog, 1984-, asst prof med, 1993-, chief infectious dis, 1993-, dir HIV prev youth, Sub proj MSM Zambian HIV Prev Proj, 1993-; Ctr Dis Control, guest researcher, 1994-, dir, clin res prog, 1994-, Ctr Devices, 1997; St Marys Hosp, Dean Clin E, 2011; pvt pract physician, currently. **Orgs:** Atlanta Metrop TB Task Force, 1993-; Food & Drug Admin, Microbiologic Devices Comt, 1994-; Ga State Task Force AIDS, 1994-; Am Lung Asn, Educ Comt, 1994-; vice chair, Our Lady Mercy High Sch, Ann Giving Comt. **Home Addr:** 202 Peters Rd, Fayetteville, GA 30214, **Home Phone:** (770)306-8373. **Business Addr:** Physician, Private Practice, Fairburn, GA 30213.

**KAFELE, BARUTI KWAME**
School principal, writer, public speaker. **Personal:** Born Oct 22, 1960, Orange, NJ; son of Norman G Hopkins and Delores C James; married Kimberley Broughton; children: Baruti, Jabari & Kibriya. **Educ:** Middlesex County Col, AS, 1985; Kean Univ, BS, mgt sci & mkt, 1986; NJ City Univ, MA, educ admin. **Career:** New York Bd Educ, teacher, 1988-89; Baruti Publ, owner, pres, publ, 1990-; E Orange Bd Educ, teacher, 1992-; Sojourner Truth Mid Sch, prin, 1998-2002; Hubbard Mid Sch, prin, 2002-03; Patrick F. Healy Mid Sch, prin, 2003-05; Newark Technol High Sch, prin, 2005-11; Prin Kafele Consult LLC, from consult & speaker to educ speaker & consult, 2011-. **Orgs:** Lambda Alpha Sigma; Phi Kappa Phi. **Honors/Awds:** Phi Kappa Phi Nat Hon Soc, 1986; Lambda Alpha Sigma Lib Arts & Sci Hon Soc, 1986; Black Stud Union Academic Achievement Award, 1986; UB & US Lit Achievement Awards, Best New Writer Male, 1991; E Orange School District & Essex County Public Schools Teacher of the Year, 1996-97; District & County Teacher of the Year. **Special Achievements:** Selected for Who's Who Among Americans Teachers six times; Author: Motivating Black Males to Achieve in School & in Life; A Black Parent's Hand book to Educating Your Children, 1991; Goal Setting: For Serious Minded Black Folks, 1991; A Black Student's Guide to Goal Setting, 1992; Goal Setting: A Black View, 1992; A Handbook For Teachers of African American Children, 2004. **Home Addr:** 12 Audubon Ave 404, Jersey City, NJ 07305, **Home Phone:** (201)433-9484. **Business Addr:** Consultant, Education Speaker, Principal Kafele Consulting LLC, 396 Stegman Pkwy, Jersey City, NJ 07305, **Business Phone:** (201)433-0622.

**KAIGLER, MARIE.** **See KAIGLER-REESE, MARIE MADELEINE.**

**KAIGLER-REESE, MARIE MADELEINE (MARIE KAIGLER)**
Broadcaster, counselor. **Personal:** Born Jan 25, 1945. **Educ:** Fisk Univ, BA, 1965; Wayne State Univ, attended 1969, 1983. **Career:** Wayne County Juvenile Ct, caseworker aide, 1965-66; Mich Employment Security Comn, employ counr, 1966-67; Northern Systs Co, behav counr, 1967-70; Wayne County Community Col, part-time instr, 1969-82; Detroit Bd Educ, sch community agent, 1970-78; WJLB, People Want to Know, co-host & producer, 1972-79; MORE, group individual instr & sem instr, 1975-85; Wayne State Univ, Col Educ, res asst dean's off, 1985-86; WXYT, radio journalist; Republican Nat Conv Mich, alt del, 1988. **Orgs:** Exec bd chair polit awareness, Mich Asn Coun & Develop, 1989-90; chair educ bd dir, Am Asn Univ Women, 1990; chair & exec bd, Republican Women's Forum, 1986-; chair polit awareness, Mich Employ Coun Asn, 1987-. **Honors/Awds:** Most Inspiring Counr, Oakland Community Col, 1982; Cert of Appreciation, Guest Lectr, Col of Nursing, Wayne State Univ, 1988; Mich Citizen Newspaper articles: "The Single Homemaker", 1989; "Aging Black Leadership", 1989; "Being Black Is Not Enough", 1989; "Why Republican?", 1989; "The Black Agenda 1900-2000: Get Real!", 1989; "Appreciation Serv" commendation, Pres of the U S, Wash, DC, 1981; cand, state rep, 1990; cand, Wayne County Comnr, 1990; various others. **Special Achievements:** Candidate for Michigan State House of Representatives, 5th Dist, 2000. **Business Addr:** Radio Journalist, WXYT, Southfield, MI 48037, **Business Phone:** (313)569-8000.

**KAISER, ERNEST DANIEL**
Editor, writer. **Personal:** Born Dec 5, 1915, Petersburg, VA; son of Ernest B and Elnora B Ellis; married Mary G Orford; children: Eric & Joan. **Educ:** City Col NY, attended 1938. **Career:** Erie Rr, redcap, 1938-42; Negro Quart, ed staff, 1943; Cong Indust Orgn, Polit Action Comt, shipping clerk, 1944-45; NY Pub Libr, Schomburg Ctr Res Black Cult, mem staff, 1945; Arno Press, ed, reviewer & consult; Crowell-Collier, ed, reviewer & consult; Beacon Press, ed, reviewer & consult; McGraw-Hill Bk Co, ed, reviewer & consult; RR Bowker Co, ed, reviewer & consult. **Honors/Awds:** Plaque, Kappa Sigma Chap Sigma Gamma Rho, 1982; Humanitarian Award, Harlem Sch Arts, 1985; Ernest D Kaiser Index to Black Resources, named in honor, Schomburg Ctr, 1985; African Heritage Award, 2006. **Special Achievements:** Books: Black Titan: W. E. B. DuBois, Beacon Press, co-ed, 1970; In Defense of the People's Black & White History & Culture, 1971; No Crystal Stair: A Bibliography of Black Literature, co-ed, 1971; The Correspondence of W. E. B. DuBois, Vol I: Selections, 1877-34, co-ed, 1973; The Correspondence of W. E. B. DuBois, Vol II: Selections, 1934-44, co-ed, 1976; The Correspondence of W. E. B. DuBois, Vol III: Selections, 1944-63, co-ed, 1978; Harlem: A History of Broken Dreams, co-author, 1974; A Freedomways Reader: Afro-America in the Seventies, ed & contibr, 1977; Paul Robeson: The Great Forerunner, ed & contibr, 1978. **Home Addr:** 3137 95th St, East Elmhurst, NY 11369-1745, **Home Phone:** (718)225-4520.

**KAISER, JAMES GORDON (JIM KAISER)**
Executive. **Personal:** Born Feb 28, 1943, St. Louis, MO; son of Samuel Arthur and Jane Aileen; married Kathryn Juanita Mounday; children: Lauren Elizabeth. **Educ:** Univ Calif, Los Angeles, BA, polit sci, 1966; Mass Inst Technol, MS, mgt, 1973. **Career:** Corning Glass Work Corning NY, sales rep, 1968-70, sales prom specialist, 1970-72, prod line mgr, 1973-75, bus planning mgr, 1975-76, gen mgr sales & mkt, 1976-79, mgr new bus develop, 1979-81, bus mgr, 1981-84, vpres & gen mgr, 1984-86, sr vpres, 1986-92; Intl Technol Corp, pres & chief exec officer, 1992; Enseco Inc, pres & chief exec officer, 1992-94; Quanterra Inc, pres & chief exec officer, 1994-96; Avenir Partners Inc, chmn & chief exec officer, 1998-2011; Kaiser Serv LLC, founder & pres, 1997-; Ridgeway Avenir LLC, 2001-13; Pelican Banners & Signs Inc, chmn & chief exec officer, 2001-03; Kaiser Ridgeway LLC, mgr, 2002-; Lexus Memphis, chmn & chief exec officer; Div Corning Inc, pres. **Orgs:** Bd mem, Stanley Works, 1992-2000; bd dir, Int Asn Environ Testing Labs, 1994; bd trustee, Keystone Ctr, 1993; bd dir, Sunoco Inc, 1993-98; bd mem, MeadWestvaco, 1995-2002; bd dir, Wharton Spencer Stuart Dirs Inst; founding mem, pres & bd mem, Exec Leadership Coun; bd mem, Toyota Lexus Minority Dealers Asn; bd mem, Kaiser Serv LLC; adv bd mem, Dartnell Corp; bd mem, AutoTradeCenter Inc; bd mem, Dartnell Enterprises Inc. **Honors/Awds:** Hon DHL, Fla A&M Univ, 1988; The Partner Development Award, Soc of Black Profs, 1991; Blue Ribbon Giver's Award, Corning Hosp & Founders Pavilion, 1991; Houghton Award, Total Quality Corning Inc, 1992. **Special Achievements:** First African American vice president at Enesco Inc. **Home Addr:** 111 Falcon Hills Dr, Highlands Ranch, CO 80126-2911, **Home Phone:** (303)470-1996. **Business**

Addr: Manager, Kaiser Ridgeway LLC, 111 Falcon Hills Dr, Littleton, CO 80126.

### KAISER-DARK, PHYLLIS E.
Government official. **Educ:** Univ DC; Prince George's Community Col. **Career:** White House, Off Mgmt & Budget, confidential asst, 1993-2001, confidential asst adminr, 2000; Off Mayor, Wash, DC, exec asst city adminr, 2001-, human resources advisor, currently. **Business Addr:** Administrative Officer, Government of the District of Columbia, 1 Judiciary Squ 441 4th St NW 330 S, Washington, DC 20001, **Business Phone:** (202)671-0543.

### KALU, NDUKWE DIKE
Radio broadcaster, football player. **Personal:** Born Aug 3, 1975, Baltimore, MD; son of Dike and Carolyn; married Dana; children: 5. **Educ:** Rice Univ, attended 1997; BA, 2002. **Career:** Football player (retired), broadcast; Philadelphia Eagles, defensive end, 1997, 2001-05; Wash Redskins, defensive end, 1998-2000; Houston Texans, defensive end & defensive tackle & left defensive tackle, 2006-08; NFL, free agt, 2009; Comcast Sports Southeast & Charter Sports Southeast, occas analyst; KBME, currently; CSN Houston, occas analyst, currently. **Honors/Awds:** NFC Defensive Player of the Week, 2002; Jack Edelstein Memorial Award, 2003; Mickey Herskowitz Award, 2006. **Business Addr:** Occasional Analyst, Comcast SportsNet Houston, 1201 San Jacinto St Suite 200, Houston, NY 77002, **Business Phone:** (713)457-6700.

### KAMAU, KWADWO AGYMAH
Writer. **Educ:** Bernard M Baruch Col, City Univ NY, BBA, 1981, MS, 1985; Va Commonwealth Univ, MFA, 1992. **Career:** NY Off Econ Develop, res asst, 1983-85; UN Secretariat, res asst int econ & social affairs, 1984; NY Dept Invest, statistician, 1985-86; NY State Dept Taxation & Finance, Off Tax Policy Anal, sr economist, 1986-89; Va Commonwealth Univ, adj prof, 1989-; New Va Rev, ed asst, 1991-92; Richmond Free Press, copy ed, 1992-93; freelance copy ed & proofreader, 1993-94; writer, 1994-; Centrum & Ucross Found, writer-in-residence, 1998; Univ Okla, fac creative writing; Books: Flickering Shadows: A Novel, 1996; Pictures of a Dying Man, 1999. **Orgs:** Fel, Va Comn Arts, 1992, 1997. **Business Addr:** Writer, Faith Childs Literary Agency, 915 Broadway Suite 1009, New York, NY 10010, **Business Phone:** (212)995-9600.

### KAMAU, MOSI (ANTHONY CHARLES GUNN WHITE)
Educator. **Personal:** Born May 5, 1955, Chicago, IL. **Educ:** Univ Minn, BFA, 1979; Fla State Univ, MFA, 1983; Temple Univ, PhD, African-Am Studies, 1989. **Career:** Tutle Contemp Elem Sch, pottery instr, 1977-78; Talbot Supply Co Inc, welder, 1979-80; Fla State Univ, asst prep, 1980-81; Williams Foundry, foundry man, 1981-82; St Pauls Col, asst prof art, 1984-89; Philadelphia Sch Arts; Johnson C Smith Univ; Chicago Pub Libr, Woodson Regional Libr, cyber navigator, currently. **Orgs:** Nat Coun Black Studies; African Am Asn Ghana; African Heritage Asn. **Home Addr:** 1639 W Grange Ave, Philadelphia, PA 19141, **Home Phone:** (215)924-7145. **Business Addr:** Cyber Navigator, Chicago Public Library, Commissioners Off 10N, Chicago, IL 60605, **Business Phone:** (312)747-4090.

### KANE, EUGENE A.
Columnist. **Personal:** Born May 15, 1956, Philadelphia, PA; son of Eugene and Hattie. **Educ:** Temple Univ, BA, jour, 1980; Stanford Univ, John S Knight Prof jour prog, 1993. **Career:** Philadelphia Bull, reporter, 1980; Milwaukee J, reporter, 1981-85, features writer, columnist, 1985; J Sentinel, columnist, currently; Marquette Univ, lectr, 1998; Wis Pub TV, host, 2002-06; Univ Milwaukee Wis, lectr, 2004-05; Milwaukee J Sentinel, columnist, 1981-; OnMilwaukee.com, sr writer & columnist, 2013-. **Orgs:** Wis Black Media Asn, 1984-; Nat Asn Black Journalist, 1994. **Home Addr:** 1732 N Prospect Ave, Milwaukee, WI 53212, **Home Phone:** (414)291-0131. **Business Addr:** Senior Writer, Columnist, OnMilwaukee.com, 735 N Water St, Milwaukee, WI 53202-4144, **Business Phone:** (414)272-0557.

### KANE, DR. JACQUELINE ANNE
Consultant, president (organization), educator. **Personal:** Born Aug 27, 1946, New York, NY; daughter of Jacqueline Jones and Philip Gough. **Educ:** Morgan State Univ, AB, sociol, 1968; State Univ NY Col, Oneonta, MS, counr educ, 1974; State Univ NY, Albany, PhD, sociol, 1997. **Career:** New York Dept Soc Serv, caseworker, 1968-70; State Univ New York Col, Oneonta, coordr coun & acad adv, 1970-75; Ny Educ Dept, assoc higher educ opportunity, 1975-99, dir resource ctr higher educ, 1976-80, Bur Higher Edu Opp Prog, 1976-99, Off Col & Univ Eval, 1999-2009; State Univ New York, Albany, adj fac, 1984-88, 1996-98; JAK Prod, pres & Higher Educ Mgt Specialist, owner, 1989-2006; Kane Consult & Coaching, Higher Educ Mgt consult & coach, 2009-. **Orgs:** Hon bd mem, Asn Black Women Higher Educ, 1978-, 1997-2009; NY State Plng Comn, Am Coun Educ Nat Ident Proj, 1980-92 & 1999-; Albany NY Alumnae Chap Delta Sigma Theta Sor, 1983-98; Albany Area Chap Am Red Cross, 1984-97; pres, Capital Chap Asn Black Women Higher Educ, 1989-92; chair, adv comn, MNY Women's issues, Ctr Women Govt, 1991-2001; bd mem, Ctr Women Govt & Civil Soc, 1991-2001. **Home Addr:** 30 Limerick Dr, Albany, NY 12204-1742, **Home Phone:** (518)465-2146. **Business Addr:** Higher Education Management Consultant, Coach, Kane Consulting & Coaching, 30 Limerick Dr, Albany, NY 12204-1742, **Business Phone:** (518)465-2146.

### KANI, KARL (CARL WILLIAMS)
Fashion designer, president (organization). **Personal:** Born Mar 22, 1968, Brooklyn, NY. **Career:** Threads for Life Corp, designer, 1990-93; Cross Colours, 1991-94; Karl Kani Infinity Inc, founder, pres & chief exec officer, 1989-; Kani Inc, dir. Films: Awakening World, 2012; Fresh Dressed, 2015; TV: "The 1999 Source Hip-Hop Music Awards", 1999. **Orgs:** Bd mem, Nat Asn Advan Colored People; bd mem, Urban League. **Special Achievements:** First African-American man to launch a Hip Hop Fashion brand. **Business Addr:** President, Chief Executive Officer, Karl Kani Infinity Inc, 500 S Molino St Suite 215, Los Angeles, CA 90013-2267, **Business Phone:** (213)626-6076.

### KAPPNER, DR. AUGUSTA SOUZA
School administrator, educator. **Personal:** Born Jun 25, 1944, New York, NY; daughter of Augusto Souza and Monica Fraser; married Thomas; children: Tania & Diana. **Educ:** Barnard Col, NY, AB, 1966; Hunter Col, NY, MSW, 1968; Columbia Univ, NY, DSW, PhD, 1984. **Career:** St Univ, NY Sch Social Welfare, asst prof, 1973-74; La Guardia Community Col Queens, assoc prof, 1974-78, dean continuing educ, 1978-84; City Univ NY, univ dean, acad affairs, 1984-86; Bor Manhattan Community Col, pres, 1986-92; City Col New York, actg pres; US dept Edn, asst sec voc & adult edn, 1993-95; Bank Str Col Ed, pres, 1995-2008, Bank Str Col Ed, pres emer, currently. **Orgs:** Bd dir, Nat Coun Black Am Affairs; NY State Child Care Comn; New York Temp Comn Early Childhood & Child Caring Progs; vice chair, bd trustee, Mary mt Manhattan Col; chmn, Mary mt Manhattan Col Pres Search Comt; pres, chair & bd dir, Women's Ctr Educ & Career Advan; New York Mayors Educ Policy Panel; Carnegie Fel; chair, Governance Comt; bd dir, Wallace Found, 2006-; New York Gov's Educ Transition Comt; chair, Improv Postsecondary Educ; bd dir, Nat Writing Proj & Res Alliance New York Schs, currently; Mid States Asn's Comn Higher Educ; Am Asn Community Cols; Am Coun Educ's Comns Women Higher Educ; Advan Racial & Ethnic Equity; Teaching Matters, After Sch Corp; States Nat Adv Bd Sch Governance; adv bd, Adult Literacy Media Alliance. **Home Addr:** 600 W 111 St, New York, NY 10025, **Home Phone:** (212)663-9235. **Business Addr:** President Emeritus, Bank Street College of Education, 285 Mercer St 3rd Fl, New York, NY 10003, **Business Phone:** (212)992-7697.

### KARANGU, DAVID M.
Automotive executive. **Personal:** Born Jan 1, 1967, Atlanta, GA; married Jane; children: 1. **Educ:** Morgan State Univ, BS, acct & mkt. **Career:** Fairway Ford Augusta, pres & chief operating officer, 1997-; Lincoln dealership, sales mgr; Ford Motor Co, qual care mgr; Mercedes Benz Augusta, pres, chief operating officer, 2005; Ivory Chevrolet, owner, currently. **Orgs:** Bd dir, MCG Health Syst, 2005-; Kenya Diaspora Adv Coun, chmn; bd mem, Augusta Prep Sch; bd mem, Boys & Girls Club, Augusta. **Honors/Awds:** President's Award, Ford Motor Co, 2005; Black Enterprise Top 50 Dealers in the US; Ebony Magazine 2001 Dealer of the Year. **Business Addr:** Owner, Ivory Chevrolet, 4200 Jonesboro Rd, Union City, GA 30291, **Business Phone:** (678)369-6497.

### KARPEH, ENID JUAH HILDEGARD
Lawyer, legal consultant. **Personal:** Born Apr 4, 1957, Mainz; daughter of Martin Sieh Jr and Marion Catherine White Cooper. **Educ:** Univ Pa, BA, int rels, 1979; NY Univ Sch Law, New York, NY, JD, 1983. **Career:** O'Donnell & Schwartz, assoc atty, 1983-85; WNET, channel 13, NY, assoc gen coun, 1986-88; MTV Networks Inc, NY, coun law & bus affairs, 1988-90; CBS Broadcasting Inc, NY, independent legal coun, 1990; URLjam Media, pres & cofounder, 1994-2006; Kidsites 3000 Inc, co-founder & pres, 1994-2000; ABC Inc, asst chief coun, 2001-; Arts & Entertainment Network, dir, legal & bus affairs. **Orgs:** Bar Asn City New York; Black Entertainment & Sports Lawyers Asn. **Home Addr:** 300 W 53rd St 5D, New York, NY 10019. **Business Addr:** Co-Founder, President, Kidsites 3000 Inc, 320 Riverside Dr Suite 5H, New York, NY 10025, **Business Phone:** (212)210-1333.

### KASHIF, GHAYTH NUR (LONNIE KASHIF)
Writer, clergy. **Personal:** Born Sep 9, 1933, Raeford, NC; son of Lonnie Smith (deceased) and Annie Mae Bethea Dale; married Hafeeza N A; children: Alif-Ahmed, Rul-Aref, Shazada Latifa & Sadara Barrow. **Educ:** Keesler Commun Chenute USAF, dipl, 1953; Univ Md Grant Tech, CA, 1953; NY Sch Writing, dipl, 1955. **Career:** Muhammad Speaks Bilalian News, Wash bur chief, 1968-78; Bilalian News AMJ, ed, 1978-81; Int Graphics Kashif News Serv, consult writer, 1981-85; Int Graphics/IQraa Mag, consult, 1981-87; Int Inst Islamic Thought, ed, 1987; Am J Muslim Social Scientists, consult, 1986-87; J Iqraa & Open Mag & Metrop Mag, exec ed, 1982-84, 1985; Warner Cable TV, VA, Islam Focus, TV dir & producer; Masjidush-Shora, Wash, DC, imam, 1990; Am Muslim Coun, Wash, DC, dir, founding mem; Black Cong Watch, ed, 1990; Int Inst Islamic Studies, VA, in-house ed; Muslim Am Mil Asn, counsellor, currently. Books: Sacred Journey, 1986; Questions, The Quranic Response. **Orgs:** Pres & chmn, Bilalian News, 1978-81; dir, secy & treas, Metro Mag, 1982-83; rep, Black Media, 1982-83; dir commun, Majdush Shura; Bilalian Econ Develop Corp, 1985-87; dir, Shaw Bus, 1985; Nat Red Cross, 1985; Capital Press Club, 1985; Org 3rd World J NNPA, 1987; dir, Roundtable Strategic Studies, 1989. **Honors/Awds:** Fred R Doug Award, HU (Muhammad Speaks), 1977; 1st Annual Freedom Journal Award, Univ DC, 1979; Excel in Journalism, CM Found, 1979. **Business Addr:** Imam, Masjid Ush Shura, 3109 Martin Luther King Jr Ave SE, Washington, DC 20032, **Business Phone:** (202)574-8417.

### KASLOFSKY, THOR
Government official. **Personal:** Born Feb 25, 1970, San Francisco, CA; son of Leslie Kaslof and Norma Krieger. **Educ:** John Jay Col Criminal Justice, BA, pub admin, 1997; City Univ NY, Baruch Col, MBA. **Career:** City NY, Mayor's Off, events capt, Off Opers, policy analyst, proj planner, Off Mgmt & Budget, budget analyst, 1993-98, Dept Homeless Serv, Div Facil Maintenance & Develop, dep dir budget & policy, 1998-2001; dir, regulatory & oversight compliance; San Francisco Redevelop Agency, asst proj mgr, proj mgr, currently. **Orgs:** Community Bd, Brooklyn NY; John Jay Alumni Asn; Police Res Asn; bd mem, Calif Redevelop Asn; bd mem, Bayview Opera House. **Home Addr:** 163 E Pkwy, Brooklyn, NY 11238, **Home Phone:** (718)399-1016. **Business Addr:** Project Manager, San Francisco Redevelopment Agency, 1 S Van Ness Ave 5th Fl, San Francisco, CA 94103, **Business Phone:** (415)749-2464.

### KAZADI, MUADIANVITA MACHEZ
Football player, football coach. **Personal:** Born Dec 20, 1973, Kinshasa; married Monique N; children: Ra-sun, Isis & Rohon. **Educ:** Tulsa Univ, BA, 1997; Univ Mo, ME, 2006. **Career:** Football player (retired), football coach; St Louis Rams, linebacker, 1997-2001; Kans City Chiefs, 2001, strength & conditioning asst coach, 2006-; Barcelona Dragons, 2001-02; Buffalo Bills, 2002; Baylor Univ, asst athletic dir athletic performance. **Honors/Awds:** Defensive Player of the Year. **Home Addr:** 206 Edinburgh, Woodway, TX 76712-4065, **Home Phone:** (254)845-1300. **Business Addr:** Strength Coach, Conditioning Assistant Coach, Kansas City Chiefs, 1 Arrowhead Dr, Kansas City, MO 64129, **Business Phone:** (816)920-9300.

### KAZI, ABDUL-KHALIQ KUUMBA
Editor, writer, consultant. **Personal:** Born Dec 15, 1951, New Orleans, LA; son of Wilbur F and Yvonne Gavion; married Sandra Pierre; children: Zijazo, Ambata, Mandela, Ahmad & Jathiya. **Educ:** Tulane Univ, attended 1971; Univ New Orleans, attended 1986; Stanford Univ, attended 1993. **Career:** Moret Press, printer, 1971-80; Figaro Newspaper, prod assoc, 1980-81; Black Col Serv Inc, copy ed, 1981-83, assoc ed, 1983-86, managing ed, 1986-, prod mgr, 1989-; Worldwide Concepts Inc, ed, writer, consult & prin, 1992-; Times-Picayune Publ Corp, ed, 1994-. **Orgs:** Founding mem, Black Runners Orgn, 1980-; Nat Asn Black Journalists, 1988-89; Am Muslim Coun, 1992; Coun Am-Islamic Rels, 1994; founder, Holy Land, 1994. **Home Addr:** 22 Chatham Dr, New Orleans, LA 70122, **Home Phone:** (504)288-6355. **Business Addr:** Writer, Consultant, Worldwide Concepts Inc, 6221 S Claiborne Ave Suite 310, New Orleans, LA 70125, **Business Phone:** (504)289-3507.

### KEA, ARLEAS UPTON
Lawyer, government official. **Personal:** Born Mar 31, 1957, Weimar, TX; daughter of Henry and Lillie Mae Upton; married Howard E; children: Chase & Arlyce Mallory. **Educ:** Univ Tex, BA, 1979; Univ Tex Sch Law, JD, 1982. **Career:** US Dept Labor, benefits rev bd atty, 1982-85; Fed Deposit Ins Corp, sr atty, Fidelity Bd Claims, 1985-89, sr coun, Criminal Restitution, 1989-91, asst gen coun, 1994-96, Corp Affairs & Admin Br, acting dep gen coun, 1995, ombudsman, dir div admin, currently; White House Adv Group, currently. **Orgs:** US Supreme Ct Bar; State Bar Tex; Nat Bar Asn; Fed Bar Asn, 1985-87; secy, Nat Conf Black Lawyers, 1982-88; Alpha Kappa Alpha Sorority; chmn bd stewards, Lomas African Methodist Episcopal Zion Church, 1988-90; vice chair, Tutor & Mentoring Prog. **Home Addr:** 8911 Ellsworth Ct, Silver Spring, MD 20910, **Home Phone:** (301)587-2177. **Business Addr:** Director, Federal Deposit Insurance Corp, 550 17th St NW, Washington, DC 20429, **Business Phone:** (202)942-3100.

### KEARNEY, ERIC HENDERSON
Lawyer, publisher. **Personal:** Born Oct 27, 1963, Cincinnati, OH; son of Jasper William and Rose Powell; married Jan Michele Lemon; children: Emerson Celeste Flora & Asher. **Educ:** Dartmouth Col, BA, eng, 1985; Univ Cincinnati, Col Law, JD, 1989. **Career:** Strauss & Troy, atty, 1989-94; Sesh Commun, pres, 1995-, chief exec officer, currently; Cohen, Todd, Kite & Stanford LLC, partner atty, 1995-; Gile, Hanover, Fr Presse Inc, pres, 1998; Cincinnati Herald, publ, pres & chmn; KGL Media, publ, pres & chmn; Ohio Dist 9, state sen, 2005-, minority leader, 2012-; Kearney LLC, owner. **Orgs:** Trustee, Amateur Athletic Comn, 1997, 2012; pac founder & treas, African Family Asn Small Bus Commun; steering comt mem, Nat Underground Rr Freedom Ctr; trustee, Greater Cincinnati African Family Asn C; trustee, Downtown Cincinnati; exec comn, Greater Cincinnati Conv & Visitors Bur; trustee, Independent Living Options; trustee, Cincinnati Zoo; ranking minority mem, Senate Judiciary Civil Justice Comt; treas, Ohio Legis Black Caucus. **Home Addr:** 3 Lenox Lane, Cincinnati, OH 45229-1907, **Home Phone:** (513)602-1154. **Business Addr:** Minority Leader, Ohio Senate, 1 Capitol Squ 3rd Fl, Columbus, OH 43215, **Business Phone:** (614)466-5980.

### KEARNEY, JESSE L.
Lawyer. **Personal:** Born Jan 14, 1950, Gould, AR; son of Thomas James and Ethel Virginia Curry; married Sheryl Rene Rogers; children: Phillip James & Jessica Leigh. **Educ:** Univ Ark, Fayetteville, AR, BA, polit sci, 1973; Univ Ark, Sch Law, JD, 1976; Nat Judicial Col, Reno, NV, cert, 1989. **Career:** Kearney Law Off, atty, Magnolia, AR, 1976-77, Pine Bluff, AR, 1981-82; State Ark, Off Atty Gen, Little Rock, AR, asst atty gen, 1977-79; State Ark, Off Gov, Little Rock, AR, admin asst gov, spec asst gov, 1979-81; Ark State Claims Comn, Little Rock, AR, comnr, 1981-82; Cross, Kearney & McKissic, Pine Bluff, AR, atty, partner, 1982-89, 1990-; State Ark Judicial Dept, Pine Bluff, AR, ciruit chancery ct judge, 1989-91; atty pvt pract, currently. **Orgs:** W Harold Flowers Law Soc, 1977-, Jefferson County Bar Asn, 1981-, Ark Bar Asn, 1977-, Ark Trial Lawyers Asn, 1987-, Am Bar Asn, 1977-, Am Trial Lawyers Asn, 1984-; Nat Bar Asn. **Home Addr:** 3620 S Olive St, Pine Bluff, AR 71603-6740, **Home Phone:** (870)535-8266. **Business Addr:** Attorney, Partner, Cross & Kearney PLLC, 1022 W 6th Ave, Pine Bluff, AR 71611-6606, **Business Phone:** (870)536-4056.

### KEARSE, AMALYA LYLE
Judge. **Personal:** Born Jun 11, 1937, Vauxhall, NJ; son of Robert Freeman and Myra Lyle Smith. **Educ:** Wellesley Col, BA, 1959; Univ Mich Law Sch, Ann Arbor, JD, cum laude, 1962. **Career:** Hughes Hubbard & Reed, assoc, 1962-69; NY Univ Law Sch Wash Sq, adj lectr, 1968-69; Ny, atty, 1969-72; US Ct Appeals, 2nd Circuit, judge, 1979-. **Orgs:** Exec comt, Lawyers Comt Civil Rights Under Law, 1970-79; Am Law Inst; fel Am Col Trial Lawyers; Pres's Comt Selection Judges, 1977-78; Nat Asn Advan Colored People LD&E Fund 1977-79; bd dir, Nat Urban League 1978-79; Mich Law Rev; Am Bar Asn. **Business Addr:** Circuit Judge, US Ct Appeals, 40 Foley Sq, New York, NY 10007, **Business Phone:** (212)857-8603.

### KEARSE, GREGORY SASHI
Publisher, association executive, editor. **Personal:** Born Feb 13, 1949, Brooklyn, NY; children: Nina Monique. **Educ:** Howard Univ, BA, Eng, 1974, Commun Res, PhD. **Career:** New York Times, internship, 1969; WABC-TV NY, news asst, writer, 1970-71; Etcetera Mag, assoc ed, 1971-72; Mutual Black Radio Network, news ed, writer, 1974-78; Howard Univ Press, ed, 1978-85, ed consult, 1985-88; Aplns Syst, tech writer, 1989; Kearse & Legall Inc, pres & chief exec officer; Bluelight Publ Co, pub, pres & chief exec officer, currently; Publ: Ebony Mag; Encore; Mod Black Men Mag; Essence Mag; Wash African-Am Newspaper Columnist; Chess Life; Karate Illus; Conti-

nenet Newspaper, writer, bk rev ed; African Faces Mag, ed-in-chief; Campus Lifestyle Mag; New Directions; Chronicle Higher Educ; Scottish Rite Jour, Phylaxsis Notes, Masonic Dig, managing ed. **Orgs:** St John's 12, Prince Hall Grand Lodge, Mt Vernon Chap 1 Royal Arch Masons; Nat Rifle Asn; Sigma Delta Chi Soc Prof Journalists; Auth League & Auth Guild Am; Am Asn Univ Presses; Wash Area Publ Asn; Big Bros Greater Wash; Am Fedn TV & Radio Artists; Johnathon Davis Consistory 1 Supreme Coun 33rd Degree; Scottish Rite Res Soc; Phylaxis Soc. **Honors/Awds:** Writer's Digest Creative Writing Award, 1970; Radio Commentary Award, 1976; Public Service Award, Sec Labor, 1977. **Special Achievements:** First African-American to Hold This Vaunted Position of New Editor and writer of the Scottish Rite Journal. **Home Addr:** 15147 Deer Valley Terr, Silver Spring, MD 20906-6224, **Home Phone:** (301)438-9718. **Business Addr:** President & Chief Executive Officer, Publisher, Bluelight Publishing Co, 15147 Deer Valley Terr, Silver Spring, MD 20906-6224, **Business Phone:** (301)438-9718.

## KEE, JOHN P. (JOHN PRINCE KEE)

Gospel singer, clergy. **Personal:** Born Jun 4, 1962, Durham, NC; married Felice Sampson; children: 9. **Educ:** NC Sch Arts; Yuba Col Conserv Sch Music. **Career:** Discography: "There is Hope", 1990; "Churchin Christmas", 1992; "Churchin", 1992; "Lilies of the Valley", 1993; "Color Blind", 1994; "Just Me This Time", 1990; "Never Shall Forget", 1991; "Wash Me", 1991; "We Walk By Faith", 1992; Lily in the Valley, 1993; "Yes Lord", 1987; "Wait on Him", 1989; "Show Up", 1995; "Stand", 1996; "Livin on the Ultimate High", 1995; "Christmas Album", 1996; A Special Christmas Gift, 1996; "Thursday Love", 1997; "Strength", 1997; "Any Day", 1998; Not Guilty, 2000; Mighty in the Spirit, 2001; Blessed By Association, 2002; Color of Music, 2004; Live at the Fellowship, 2005; The Reunion, 2005; New Life Community Chair, founder; Gospel vocalist; New Life Fel Ctr, founder & pastor, 1995-. **Orgs:** Founder & choral leader, New Life Community Choir, 1980-; musical ensemble mem, Miss Black Universe beauty pageant, 1980-; founder, New Life Fel Church, Charlotte, NC, 1990-. **Honors/Awds:** GMWA Excellence Award, Best New Urban Contemporary Female Group, 1991; GMWA Excellence Award Best Video Concert, 1992; Stellar Award best Music Video, 1992; GMWA Excellence Award for Contemporary Male Vocalist of the Year, 1992; GMWA Excellence Award for Contemporary Choir of the Year, 1992; GMWA Excellence Award Best Contemporary Album of the Year & Producer of the Year, 1992, 1994; 2 Billboard Music Award No1 Gospel Artist, 1992; Stellar Award Best Traditional Album, 1993; Inside Gospel Award Best Male Artist, 1994; Stellar Award for Best Solo Performance Male Contemporary, 1994; GMWA Excellence Award for Album of the Year, 1995; GMWA Excellence Award for Producer of the Year, 1995; Diamond Award for Excellence, Int Asn African-Am Music, 1995; 5 Stellar Awards, 1996; Soul Train Music Award Album of the Year; Grammy Nomination, 1996, 1999, 2001, 2004; Stellar Award, 2002; A Trailblazer Award, former President Bill Clinton; Nine Waljo Awards. **Special Achievements:** Dove Nomination for Traditional Album, 1993; Grammy Nomination for Best Gospel Album, 1996; 7 Stellar Award nominations, 1999; Grammy Nomination for Best Traditional Soul Gospel Album, 2001; Stellar Award Nomination, 2002; Grammy Nomination for Best Gospel Choir/Chorus Album, 2004; Stellar Nomination Traditional Male Vocalist of the Year, 2006; Grammy Nomination Best Gospel Choir Album Live at the Fellowship, 2006; Stellar Nomination Traditional Male Vocalist of the Year The Color of Music, 2006; Traditional CD of the year, Stellar award nominated, 2007. **Business Addr:** Pastor, New Life Fellowship Ceter, 1337 Samuel St, Charlotte, NC 28206, **Business Phone:** (704)377-4004.

## KEE, LINDA COOPER (LINDA G COOPER WALTON)

Management consultant. **Personal:** Born Jun 1, 1954, Jacksonville, FL; daughter of Freddie and Benjamin Groomes; married Steven. **Educ:** Fla State Univ, BS, 1974; Ind Univ, MBA, 1977; Nat Multicultural Inst, diversity training cert. **Career:** Hallmark Cards, budget analyst, 1977-80, mgr sales admin, 1980-85, dir minority affairs, 1985-92; LGC & Assocs, pres, 1992-. **Orgs:** Black MBA Asn; Alpha Kappa alpha Sorotity, 1972-; Soc Human Resource Mgt; treas, GKC Chap Links; Women's Employ Network; Urban League Greater Kans City; Full Employ Coun; Mo State Bd Mediation; Defense Adv Comn Women Armed Serv. **Honors/Awds:** Hundred Most Influential African Americans, KC Globe Newspaper, 1992, 1993-97; Up & Comers Award, Jr Achievement, 1995; Dollars & Sense. **Special Achievements:** Often cited in various national publications. **Home Addr:** 4010 NW Claymont Dr, Kansas City, MO 64116, **Home Phone:** (816)459-8694. **Business Addr:** President, LGC & Associates, 1601 E 18th St Suite 120, Kansas City, MO 64108, **Business Phone:** (816)842-0542.

## KEE, MARSHA GOODWIN

Government official. **Personal:** Born Oct 3, 1942, Durham, NC; daughter of Lewis Marshall Goodwin and Margaret Catherine Kennedy Goodwin (deceased). **Educ:** Spelman Col, Atlanta, GA, BA, 1964; Atlanta Univ, Atlanta, GA, MA, 1969. **Career:** NC Cent Univ, Durham, NC, instr sociol, 1966-72; NC State Univ, Raleigh, NC, instr sociol, 1973-74; Durham Col, Durham, NC, counr/dir, 1974-80; NC Off State Personnel, Raleigh, NC, personnel analyst, 1980-89; County Durham, NC, dir, equal opportunity/affirmative action, 1989. **Orgs:** Delta Sigma Theta Sorority Inc, 1967-; Int Personnel Mgt Asn, 1985-; Nat Asn Advan Colored People, 1987-; Nat Forum Black Pub Admin, 1989-; NC Minority Women's Bus Enterprise, 1989-; Fin Secy, NCCU Educ Advan Found, 1989-; chap mem, Durham Alummae Chap, currently; NCCU Eagle Club. **Home Addr:** 620 Dupree St, Durham, NC 27701, **Home Phone:** (919)682-3938. **Business Addr:** NC.

## KEELER, VERNES

Executive, business owner, construction engineer. **Personal:** son of John W; married Yolanda. **Career:** V Keeler & Assoc Inc, New Orleans, La, owner, pres & chief exec, 1971. **Home Addr:** 7431 W Renaissance Ct, New Orleans, LA 70128-2584, **Home Phone:** (504)245-3133. **Business Addr:** Chief Executive Officer, President, V Keeler & Associates, 3750 Alvar St, New Orleans, LA 70126, **Business Phone:** (504)947-0447.

## KEELS, JAMES DEWEY. See Obituaries Section.

## KEENE, SHARON C.

Executive. **Personal:** Born Feb 27, 1948, Philadelphia, PA. **Educ:** Morgan State Univ, BS, 1970; Univ PA, MLA, 1976. **Career:** Nat Pk Serv, chief planning & fed prog, 1980-, Div Resource Area Studies, chief. **Home Addr:** 1493 SW Willis Mill Rd, Atlanta, GA 30311, **Home Phone:** (404)758-5201. **Business Addr:** Division Chief, National Park Service, 75 Spring St, Atlanta, GA 30303-3109.

## KEENON, DR. UNA H. R.

Judge. **Personal:** Born Dec 30, 1933, Nashville, TN; daughter of Charles L and Mary L Gowins; children: Gregory M Rhodes & Patrick Washington. **Educ:** Tenn State Univ, BA, 1954; Cleveland State Univ, Col Law, JD, 1975; Ashland Theol Sem. **Career:** Judge (retired); Cuyahoga County Welfare Dept, social worker, 1957-60; Cleveland Pub Schs, teacher, 1960-74; Legal Aid Soc, atty, 1975-78; Cuyahoga County Pub Defender, Juv Div, atty-in-charge, 1978-80; Johnson, Keenon & Blackmon Law Firm, partner, 1980-83; UAW Legal Servs Plan, managing atty, 1983-86; E Cleveland Munic Ct, judge, 1986-05; E Cleveland City Sch Dist, Bd Educ, pres, currently. **Orgs:** AKA Sorority, 1952-; founding pres, 1982-86, bd mem, 1986-, Black Women Polit Action Comt; NCW, 1986-; bd mem, YWCA, Northern Br, 1989-; bd mem, Nat Asn Advan Colored People, 1992-; bd mem, Hitchcock House, 1992-; bd mem, COT Guid, 1992-; Cleveland Metrop Bar Asn. **Honors/Awds:** Meritorious Service Award, E Cleveland Black Police Officers Asn, 1988-89; Servant Award, St James Lutheran Church, 1990; Role Model for Women Award, Women Community Serv, 1992; E Ohio Gas Honor Award, 1992; Woman in Service Award, 1993; MLK Jr Altruism Award, E Cleveland Citizens Sound Gov, 1993; Hitchcock Center Award, 1993. **Special Achievements:** Chronical (Past Editor), Official Newsletter of the Association of Municipal County Judges Association. **Home Addr:** 16148 Cleviden Rd, East Cleveland, OH 44112, **Home Phone:** (216)932-5090. **Business Addr:** President, East Cleveland City Schools, 1843 Stanwood Rd, East Cleveland, OH 44112, **Business Phone:** (216)268-6676.

## KEFFERS, JAMIE L.

City commissioner. **Career:** US Parole Comn, comnr. **Business Addr:** Commissioner, US Parole Commission, 10th St Const Ave NW, Washington, DC 20530, **Business Phone:** (301)492-5990.

## KEGLAR, SHELVY HAYWOOD

Psychologist, executive. **Personal:** Born Dec 13, 1947, Charleston, MS; son of John H Ratliff and Minnie M Miller; married Robbia G Steward; children: Shelvy Jr, Robalon, Skyler H, Ronelle & Stanford. **Educ:** Kaskaskia Jr Col, Centralia, Ill, assoc degree, 1969; Ark State Univ, Jonesboro, Ark, BA, sociol, 1970, MA, rehab coun, 1974; Ind Univ, Bloomington, Ind, PhD, psychol, 1979; Campbell Univ, MBA. **Career:** Hamilton Ctr, Terre Haute, Ind, assoc dir, 1974-84; Atterbury Job Corps, Edinburgh, Ind, psychologist, 1979-; Midwest Psychol Ctr Inc, Indianapolis, Ind, clin psychologist, founder & pres, 1984-; Ind Consortium Ment Health Serv Res, fac, currently. **Orgs:** Vpres, mem chmn, 1988-89, pres, 1986-87, Nat Black Child Develop Inst, Indianapolis affil; pres, Terre Haute Minority Bus Assoc, 1983-84; pres, Ind Asn Black Psychologists, 1982-84; Am Psychol Asn; Asn Black Psychologists; bd dir, Sterling Sports Mgt; Soc Clin & Exp Hypn; MPC Corp; Joy Adult Day Care Inc; Indianapolis Black Chamber Com; Kappa Alpha Psi; chair, Ind Hypnotist Comt; Forensic Psychol; Int Who's Who med. **Honors/Awds:** Outstanding Service Award, Ind Asn Black Psychologists, 1984; Service Award, Strong-Turner Alumni Club, Ark State Univ, 1988; Outstanding Alumnus, Ark State Univ, 1991; Centralia Sports Hall of Fame, 1991; Distinguished Alumnus For The Department Of Counseling And Psychology, Ark State, 2015; America's Best & Brightest Business & Professional Men, Dollars & Sense Mag. **Special Achievements:** Author: "Workfare and the Black Family", Black Family, vol 6:2, 1986; "Alcohol & Drug Abusers in a Family Practice Resident's Ward", w/M Clarke, Alcohol & Research World, 4, 1980. **Home Addr:** 9208 Fordham St, Indianapolis, IN 46268-1222, **Home Phone:** (317)872-9727. **Business Addr:** President, Midwest Psychological Center Inc, 3676 N Wash Blvd, Indianapolis, IN 46205, **Business Phone:** (317)923-3930.

## KEITH, HON. DAMON JEROME

Judge, circuit court judge. **Personal:** Born Jul 4, 1922, Detroit, MI; son of Perry A and Annie L Williams; married Rachel Boone; children: Cecile, Debbie & Gilda. **Educ:** WVa State Col, AB, 1943; Howard Univ Law Sch, LLB, 1949; Wayne State Univ Law Sch, LLM, 1956. **Career:** Off Friend Ct, City Detroit, atty, 1951-55; Wayne County, bd supvr, 1958-63; Keith, Conyers, Anderson, Brown & Wahls, Detroit, Mich, sr partner, 1964-67; Eastern Dist Mich, chief US judge, 1967-77; US Ct Appeals, 6th Circuit Ct, Detroit, Mich, judge, 1977-95, sr judge, 1995-. **Orgs:** Co-chair, chmn, Mich Civil Rights Comn, 1964-67; trustee, Med Corp Detroit; trustee, Interlochen Arts Acad; trustee, Cranbrook Sch; Citizen's Adv Comn Equal Educ Opportunity Detroit Bd Educ; vpres, United Negro Col Fund Detroit; first vpres emer, Detroit Chap Nat Asn Advan Colored People; comn mgt, Detroit YMCA; Detroit Coun Boy Scouts Am; Detroit Arts Comn; Am Bar Asn; Nat Bar Asn; Mich Bar Asn; Detroit Bar Asn; Nat Lawyers Guild; Am Judicature Soc; Alpha Phi Alpha; Detroit Cotillion; Univ Notre Dame Law Sch, Adv Coun; bd trustees, Univ Detroit Mercy; vice chmn, Detroit Symphony Orchestra; Leukemia Soc Am Inc. **Honors/Awds:** Spingarn Medalist, Nat Asn Advan Colored People, 1974; received numerous honorary degrees from various universities including: Univ Mich; Howard Univ; Wayne State Univ; Mich St Univ; NY Law Sch; Detroit Col Law; W Va St Col; Univ Detroit; Atlanta Univ; Ohio St Univ; Cent Mich Univ; Eastern Mich Univ; Morehouse Col; NY Law Sch; Hofstra Univ; DePaul Univ; Yale Univ; Western Mich Univ; Tuskegee Univ; Lincoln Univ; Menorah Award, Afro-Asian Inst Histadrut Israel, 1988; Governor's Minuteman Award, The Rotary Club Lansing, 1991; Champion of Justice Award, State Bar Mich, 1991; Trumpet Award, Turner Broadcasting Syst, 1991, 2000; C Francis Stratford Award, Nat Bar Asn, 1992; Martin Luther King Jr Freedom Award, Progressive Nat Baptist Conv, 1992; Thurgood Marshall Award, Wolverine Bar Asn, 1993; Alumni Award for Distinguished Postgraduate Achievement, Howard Univ, 1994; Earl Burru Dickerson Award; Spirit of Excellence Award, Am Bar Asn, 2001; dr, Howard Univ, 2008; LD, Harvard Univ, 2011. **Special Achievements:** Named one of 100 Most Influential Black Americans, Ebony Magazine, 1971, 1977; Publications: "We the People Have Lots to Celebrate," Detroit Free Press, 1987; "Ashmore: Hearts and Minds: The Anatomy of Racism from Roosevelt to Reagan," University of Michigan Law Review, 1983; "A Responsibility to Serve Black Community," Detroit Free Press, 1988. **Home Addr:** 3130 W Outer Dr, Detroit, MI 48221. **Business Addr:** Senior Judge, US Court of Appeals, 100 E 5 St, Cincinnati, OH 45202, **Business Phone:** (513)564-7000.

## KEITH, FLOYD A.

Football coach, executive director. **Personal:** Born Aug 22, 1948, St. Marys, OH; married Nicole R; children: Kenyari, Imani, Mikia & Kailan. **Educ:** Ohio Northern Univ, BS, educ, 1970. **Career:** Miami Univ, asst coach, offensive backfield coach, 1970-73; Col, coach, 1970-99; Univ Colo, offensive backfield coach, asst coach, quarterback & receiver coach & passing game coordr, Colo Buffaloes, 1974-78; Howard Univ, head football coach, 1979-82; Univ Ariz, running back coach, 1983; Ind Univ, quarterback coach & passing game co-coordr, 1984-92; Univ RI, head football coach, 1993-99; Howard Bison, head coach; RI Rams, head coach. **Orgs:** Memorial High Sch Class, 1966; Guest & panelist, ESPN; Black Coaches Asn, Black Coaches & Adminrs Off, exec dir, 2001-; Hons Ct Nat Found; St Marys Memorial High Sch Alumni found; Hons Ct Nat Found & Col Football Hall Fame. **Business Addr:** Executive Director, Black Coaches Association, 201 S Capitol Ave Suite 495, Indianapolis, IN 46225, **Business Phone:** (317)829-5600.

## KEITH, KAREN C.

Athletic coach. **Personal:** Born Apr 16, 1957, Boston, MA; daughter of Albert and Margaret Stokes. **Educ:** Fla State Univ, BS, 1978; Boston Col, MA, MEd, admin & supv, 1989. **Career:** Beth Israel Hosp, Brookline MA, phlebotimist, 1978-83; US Youth GamesTeam, coach, 1980-81; Newton S High Sch, coach, 1981-83; Brown Jr HighSch, Newton MA sci & phy educ teacher, sports coach team leader, adminr, 1981-87; Boston Col, head coach track & field, 1987-93. **Honors/Awds:** Mem, New England Select Side Rugby Team, 1985-86; First Coach of the Year, Div first Region, 1987; Hall of Fame Sagamore Award, Brookline High Sch, 1988. **Home Addr:** 63 Roanoke Rd, Hyde Park, MA 02136, **Home Phone:** (617)361-1181.

## KEITH, DR. LEROY, JR.

Executive. **Personal:** Born Feb 14, 1939, Chattanooga, TN; son of Roy and Lula; married Anita Halsey; children: Lori, Susan, Kelli & Kimberly. **Educ:** Morehouse Col, BA, 1961; Ind Univ, MA, 1968, PhD, 1970; Bowdoin Col, LLD, 1990. **Career:** Chattanooga Pub Sch, sci teacher, 1961-66; Neighborhood Serv Prog, dir, 1966-68; Ind Univ, Human Rels Comt, exec secy, 1968-69, Bur Educ Placement, admin asst, 1969-70; Dartmouth Col, asst prof educ, William Jewett Tucker Found Internship Prog, dir, 1970-71, asst dean, asst prof educ, 1971-72, assoc dean & asst prof educ & urban studies, 1972-73; Univ Mass Syst, assoc vpres, 1973-75; Mass Bd Higher Ed, chancellor, 1975-78; Univ DC, exec vpres, 1978-82; Aspen Inst Humanistic Studies, Alvin & Peggy Brown fel, 1980; Univ Md, vpres policy & planning, 1983-87; Morehouse Col, pres, 1987-94; Carson Prod Co, chmn, 1998-2000; Keystone Group, bd dir; Phoenix Ser Fund, bd dir; dir, Obagi Med Prod Inc; Stonington Partners Inc, partner; Almanac Capital Mgt, managing dir; Diversapack Co, dir. **Orgs:** Trustee, Phoenix Funds Family, 1980-; One One Mentoring Partnership; bd, Savannah Bus Group; Found Mem Med Ctr; Telfair Mus Art; First City Club; Savannah Area Chamber Com; CEO Coun Savannah Area Chamber Com; dir, Value Am; Phi Beta Kappa; trustee, Virtus fund complex; trustee, Evergreen Invest, 1983-2010; trustee, St Andrews Episcopal Sch; treas, Capital Formation & Enterprise Develop; bd dir, Siskin Childrens Inst; chair, Bloc Global Serv; trustee, Wells Fargo Advantage Funds, 2010-. **Honors/Awds:** Resolution for Outstanding Achievement Award, Tenn House Reps, 1976; Distinguished Alumni Service Award, Ind Univ, 1977; Named 100 top Young Leaders in the American Academy; Change Mag & Am Coun Educ. **Special Achievements:** First African American to hold chancellor of the Massachusetts Board of Higher Education. **Business Addr:** Director, Diversapack Co, 1770 The Exchange SE Suite 220, Atlanta, GA 30399, **Business Phone:** (770)874-8003.

## KEITH, LUTHER

Executive director, editor. **Personal:** Born Oct 9, 1950, Detroit, MI; son of Luther Caesar and Mittie Savella Ashworth; married Jacqueline Hall; children: Erin. **Educ:** Univ Detroit, jour, 1972. **Career:** Journalist (retired), executive director, commissioner; Wayne State Univ, Journ Inst Minorities, founding dir, 1985-87; Detroit News, gen assignment reporter, 1972-73, sportswriter, 1973-79, bus ed, asst managing ed, sr ed, Asst City Ed, 1987, Night City Ed, 1988, writer, copy ed, bus ed, asst managing ed, pub ed, sr ed & columnist, 1988-2005; ARISE Detroit, exec dir, 2000-; Detroit Pub Libr, comnr, currently. **Orgs:** Founding dir, Wayne State Univs Journalism Inst Minorities, 1985-87; vpres, Nat Asn Black Journalists; bd mem, Rosa Parks Scholar Found; bd mem, Plowshares Theater Co. **Business Addr:** Executive Director, ARISE Detroit!, 5830 Field St Suite 103, Detroit, MI 48213, **Business Phone:** (313)921-1955.

## KEITT, LIZ ZIMMERMAN

Purchasing agent, president (organization). **Personal:** Born Nov 28, 1938, Cameron, SC; married Joseph L; children: Vincent Lewis & Marvin. **Educ:** Claflin Univ, BS, phys educ, 1970; SC State Col, MEd, 1974. **Career:** Orangeburg County, mayor pro team; Claflin Univ, purchasing agt; Mt Carmel Bapt Church, Cameron, SC, supt, 1971; Claflin Univ Gospel & Choir, adv, 1974-78; Proj Life: Positeen Prog, founder & exec dir, 1992-. **Orgs:** Chairperson, Lower Savannah Grassroots Adv Comt, 1976-; Claflin Col Nat Alumni Asn; Dem Women's Club, 1977-79; coordr, Ward III Voters, 1978; Miss Black Universe Pageant, reg dir, Orangeburg Co, 1979; Nat Asn Advan Colored People State; Stud Govt Asn; Alpha Kappa Sor; Beta Zeta Omega Chap Alpha Kappa Alpha Sorority Inc; pres, Claflin Univ Int Alumni Asn. **Honors/Awds:** Outstanding Community Leader, 1975; Outstanding Adviser, Nat Asn Advan Colored People, 1976-77; Outstanding Service, 1978. **Special Achievements:** First African American who served in the Orangeburg City Council; first woman ever to serve as Mayor Pro Tem and served the City of as Mayor for three months; first woman president of the Eastern Intercollegiate Athletic Conference. **Home Addr:** 505 Bayne St, Orangeburg, SC 29115, **Home Phone:** (803)534-8967. **Business Addr:** Founder, Executive Director, Project Life: Positeen, 349 Summers Ave, Orangeburg, SC 29115, **Business Phone:** (803)534-4263.

### KEIZS, MARCIA V.
President (organization), executive. **Personal:** Born Jamaica, NY. **Educ:** Univ Man, Winnipeg, Can, BA, 1967; Columbia Univ's Teachers Col, MA, 1971, EdD, 1984; Harvard Univ's Grad Sch Educ, cert duc mgt, 1995. **Career:** Queensborough Community Col/City Univ New York, Eng prof, vpres & dean stud serv, 1988-94; LaGuardia Community Col/City Univ New York, asst dean; Bronx Community Col, vpres acad affairs; City Univ New York, York Col, pres, 2005-; New York Carib News, founding ed. **Orgs:** Bd chair, Morris Heights Health Ctr; Greater Jamaica Develop Corp; Jamaica YMCA; Regional Plan Asn; Regional Econ Develop Coun; Nat Col Athletic Asn; Am Coun Educ. **Business Addr:** President, City University of New York, 94-20 Guy R Brewer Blvd, Jamaica, NY 11451, **Business Phone:** (718)262-2000.

### KELLER, C. RANDOLPH
Public prosecutor. **Educ:** Case Western Res Univ Sch Law, JD, 1987. **Career:** City Shaker heights, OH, chief prosecutor, currently; Pyramid Inst Inc, pres & chief exec officer, 2009-. **Orgs:** Past pres, Norman S. Minor Bar Asn. **Business Addr:** President, Chief Executive Officer, The Pyramid Institute Inc, 3417 Rumson Rd, Cleveland Heights, OH 44118, **Business Phone:** (216)402-6222.

### KELLER, DR. EDMOND JOSEPH
School administrator, educator. **Personal:** Born Aug 22, 1942, New Orleans, LA; married Genevieve Favorite; children: Vern A & Erika V. **Educ:** La State Univ, New Orleans, BA, govt, 1969; Univ WI, Madison, MA, polit sci, 1970, PhD, polit sci, 1974. **Career:** Univ Wis, Nat Defense Educ Act, title IV fel, 1969-71; Univ Nairobi, Inst Develop Studies, vis res fel, res assoc, 1972-73; Ind Univ Bloomington, from asst prof to assoc prof, 1974-83; Ford Found, fel, 1971-72, Mid E & Africa Field Res fel, 1972-73, fel, 1981-82; Nat Fel Fund, fel, 1981-82; Comm Inst Coop, dir cic minority fel prog, 1982-83; Univ Calif Santa Barbara, chmn black studies, 1983-84, from assoc prof to prof, 1983-90, Dept Black Studies, chair, 1983-84, assoc dean grad div, 1984-87, actg dean; Univ Calif, Los Angeles, Am Coun Educ fel, 1987-88, Acad Affairs, Off Pres, fac asst, 1988-90, African studies, prof & vpres, polit sci, 1990-; James S Coleman African Studies Ctr, dir, 1992-2001; Pres's Task Force Black Stud Eligibility, exec dir, 1988-90; Globalization Res Ctr, dir, 2001; consult; Afro-marxist Regimes: Ideology & Pub Policy with Donald Rothchild, 1987; SafricA Southern Africa: Domestic Chg & Int Conflict with Louis Picard, 1989; Africa New Int Order: Rethinking State Sovereignty & Regional Security with Donald Rothchild, 1996, co-ed. **Orgs:** Ed bd, Western Polit Sci Asn & Nat J Polit Sci; ed bd specialist, CP; ed bd, Nat J Polit Sci; ed J African Policy Studies; treas, N Am Chap African J Polit Sci; pres & vpres, African Studies Asn; Exec Comt Comparative Polit Sect APSA, 1996-98; Coun Am Polit Sci Asn, 2000-02. **Honors/Awds:** APSA, exec comt, 1996-98; Dissertation Research Fellowship, Ford Found, 1972-73; African-Am Scholars Council Post-Doctorate, 1976-77; Post Doctorate, Nat Fel Fund, 1980-82; Rodney Higgins Award of the National Conference of Black Political Scientists, 1981; Ford Found Post Doctorate Ford Found, 1981-82; Eminent Scholar, Norfolk State Univ, 1983; Distinguished Lecturer in Pan Africanist Studies, Ind State Univ, 1987; African Studies Association Distinguished Africanist Award, 2008. **Special Achievements:** Contributed numerous publications; Monographs: Education, Manpower & Development: The Impact of Educational Policy in Kenya, 1980 & Revolutionary Ethiopia: From Empire to People's Republic, 1988. **Home Addr:** 24150 Mariano St, Woodland Hills, CA 91367, **Home Phone:** (818)203-1539. **Business Addr:** Director of Political Science, Globalization Research Center-Africa, 10359 Bunche Hall 405 Hilgard Ave, Los Angeles, CA 90095, **Business Phone:** (310)267-4054.

### KELLER, MARY JEAN
Controller. **Personal:** Born Nov 6, 1938, Mt. Vernon, NY; daughter of Raymond Mizell and Grace McNair Mizell; children: Ericka. **Educ:** NY Univ, Sch Com, BS, 1960; Columbia Univ, MS, 1978. **Career:** Controller (retired); Hoffberg & Oberfest, Cert Pub Acct's; Bedford Stuyvesant Restoration Corp, asst treas & dir fin; nd Inc, treas; Lisc Inc, controller; Foreign Policy Study Found. **Orgs:** St. Paul Church Orchestra; Sisters Assisting SAfrica; Black Child Develop Inst, NY Affil. **Home Addr:** 198 E 91st St, Brooklyn, NY 11212, **Home Phone:** (718)774-7135.

### KELLEY, DR. DELORES G.
Educator, state government official. **Personal:** Born May 1, 1936, Norfolk, VA; daughter of Stephen and Helen Jefferson; married Russell Victor Jr; children: Norma, Russell III & Brian. **Educ:** Va State Col, BA, philos, 1956; NY Univ, MA, educ, 1958; Purdue Univ, MA, speech commun, 1972; Univ Md, PhD, Am studies, 1977. **Career:** NY City Protestant Coun, dir christian educ 1958-60; Plainview JHS, teacher eng, 1965-66; Morgan State Univ, instr eng, 1966-70; Purdue Univ, grad teaching fel speech, 1971-72; Coppin State Col, Lang Lit & Philos, dept chmn, 1973-79, dean lower div, 1979-89, prof communs, 1990-2004; Md State Deleg 42nd dist, 1991-94; Md Gen Assembly, state sen, 1991-; Md State Sen, 10th Dist, state senate, 1995-. **Orgs:** Life mem, Alpha Kappa Alpha Sorority, 1955-; Vol Host Family Baltimore Coun Int Visitors, 1976-; Roots Forum Proj Grant Md Com Humanities & Pub Policy 1977; eval team, Hood Col Md State Dept Educ 1978; reviewer & panelist, Nat Endowment Humanities, 1978-82; chairperson, Adv Coun Gifted & Talented Educ Baltimore City Sch, 1979-; Mayor's Ment Health Adv Coun, Baltimore City, 1980-88; Values Educ Comn, 1981-85; Dem State Cent Comt, 1982-86; fel Am Coun Educ, 1982-83; exec bd, Baltimore Urban League, 1986-89; sec, Md Dem Party 1986-90; vice-chair & bd dir, Harbor Bank Md, 1987-; bd, Inst Christian Jewish Studies, 1988-; pres, Black/Jewish Forum Baltimore, 1990-92; State Comn Hereditary & Congenital Dis, 1991-95; State Comn Hereditary & Congenital Dis, 1991-; Women Legislators Md, 1992 &1995-; chair, Baltimore Chap, Nat Polit Cong Black Women, 1993-95; pres-elect, Gov's Comn Adoption, 1995-; deleg, White House Conf Aging, 1995; Family Violence Coun, 1995-; Baltimore County Dem Cent Comt, 1995-; Md Legis Black Caucus, 1995-; Gov's Task Force Judicial Nominating Comns, 1995; Md Comner Criminal Sentencing Policy, 1996-98; Adoption Oversight Team, Dept Hr, 1997-; Women Legislators Md, 1997-98; Task Force to Study Anti-Asian Violence, 1997-99 pres, Women Legislators MD, 1998-99; Gov's CounAdolescent Pregnancy, 1998-; Md Medicaid Adv Comm, 1998-; Atty Gen's & Lt Gov's Family Violence Coun, 1998-; Md Comn Infant Mortality, 1999-; Baltimore County Schs Strategic Plng Task Force, 1999-; State Comn Criminal Sentencing Policy, 1999-; Task Force Study Licensing & Monitoring Community-Based Homes C, 2000-01; Task Force Study Col Readiness Disadvantaged & Capable Students, 2000-01; Task Force Study Repealing Disenfranchisement Convicted Felons Md, 2001; Md Educ Coun, 2003-; Oversight Comt Qual Care Nursing Homes, 2003-; Unemploy Ins Funding Task Force, 2003-04; Task Force Access Ment Health Serv, 2003-04, co chair, 2007; Task Force Common Ownership Communities, 2005-06; State Traumatic Brain Injury Adv Bd, 2005-; Comt Unemploy InsOversight, 2005-06; co-chair, Task Force Study Identity Theft, 2007; Work Grp Cult Competency & Workforce Develop Ment Health Prof, 2007-; Task Force Study Develop Disabilities Admin Rate-Payment Syst, 2007-; chair, Exec Nominations Comt, 2007; trustee bd chair, Union Baptist Church; Senate Finance Comt; vice chair, Joint Comt Health Care Delivery & Finance; senate rep, Md State Comn Criminal Sentencing Policy. **Special Achievements:** First African-American Senator elected in Baltimore County. **Home Addr:** 9437 Joleon Rd, Randallstown, MD 21133-2809, **Home Phone:** (410)922-5085. **Business Addr:** Senator, Senate of Maryland, Rm 302 James Sen Off Bldg 11 Bladen St, Annapolis, MD 21401, **Business Phone:** (410)841-3606.

### KELLEY, WILLIAM E.
Association executive, executive director. **Personal:** Born Feb 15, 1939, Los Angeles, CA; son of LeRoy Sr (deceased) and Laura Mae; married Joann Oliver; children: Darren LeRoy & Jason Wardell. **Educ:** Whittier Col, BA, sociol, 1960; US Naval War Col, attended 1972; George Washington Univ, MS, indust personnel mgt, 1972. **Career:** Association executive (retired); Int Comn Young Men's Christian Asn, fel, 1960-61; Young Men's Christian Asn Los Angeles, prog dir, 1961-62; Smith, Bucklin & Assoc, acct exec, 1990; Cong Award Found, chief exec officer & nat dir, 2001-04; Nat Asn Corp Treas, exec dir; CNL Bank, exec vpres. **Orgs:** Nat Naval Officers Asn, 1972-; Am Soc Asn Exec, 1989-; Naval Order US, 1990; Retired Officers Asn, 1990-; Disabled Am Veterans, 1990; Greater Wash Soc Asn Execs, chmn. **Honors/Awds:** Alumni Achievement, Lancer Soc Whittier Col, 1989. **Business Addr:** National Director, Chief Executive Officer, Congressional Award Foundation, PO Box 77440, Washington, DC 20013, **Business Phone:** (202)226-0130.

### KELLEY, WILLIAM MELVIN
Short story writer, educator, writer. **Personal:** Born Nov 1, 1937, New York, NY; son of William Sr and Narcissa Agatha; married Karen Isabelle Gibson; children: Jessica & Cira. **Educ:** Harvard Univ, attended 1961. **Career:** Free-lance writer & photographer; State Univ NY, Geneseo, writer in residence, 1965; New Sch Social Res, instr, 1965-67; Univ Paris, Nanterre, guest lectr am lit, 1968; Univ W Indies, Mona, guest instr, 1969-70, Sarah Lawrence Col, prof creative writing, 1989-; Articles: "If You're Woke You Dig It", New York Times Mag, 1962; "The Ivy League Negro", Esquire, 1963; "An Am in Rome", Mademoiselle, 1965; "On Racism, Exploitation & the White Liberal", Negro Digest, 1967; "On Africa in the United States", Negro Digest, 1968; Dancers on the Shore, Howard Univ Press, 1983; Taos Inst Art, guest lectr; State Univ New York, writer-in-residence. Author: A Different Drummer, 1962, Dancers on the Shore, 1964, A Drop of Patience, 1965, Dem, 1967, Dunfords Travels Everywhere, 1970. **Honors/Awds:** Dana Reed Literary Prize, Harvard Univ, 1960; Bread Loaf Scholar, 1962; John Jay Whitney Found Award, 1963; Rosenthal Foundation Award, Nat Inst Arts & Letters, 1963; Transatlantic Review Award, 1964; Black Academy of Arts & Letters Prize for Fiction, 1970; Wurlitzer Found; New York Found Arts; Rockefeller Found; Am Acad Arts and Lett; Anisfield-Wolf Book Award, 2008. **Business Addr:** Professor of Creative Writing, Sarah Lawrence College, 1 Mead Way, Bronxville, NY 10708, **Business Phone:** (914)337-0700.

**KELLMAN, DENIS ELLIOTT.** **See Obituaries Section.**

### KELLOGG, CLARK CLIFTON, JR.
Actor, basketball player, executive. **Personal:** Born Jul 2, 1961, Cleveland, OH; married Rosella Swayne; children: Talisa, Alex & Nicholas. **Educ:** Ohio State Univ, BA, mkt, 1996. **Career:** Basketball player (retired), executive, actor; Ohio State Univ, 1979-82; Ind Pacers, draft pick, 1982-86, tv analyst, color commentator, vpres player rels, currently; ESPN, basketball analyst, 1990; Big E Network; Prime Sports; CBS Sports, game analyst, 1993-94, studio & game analyst, 1997-2008, studio analyst, 2014; NCAA Tournament, studio co-host, 1994-97. TV Series: "NCAA Men of March", 2014. **Orgs:** Bd dir, Com Nat Bank. **Special Achievements:** Kellogg appeared in the popular NBA video game NBA 2K9 as the co commentator. **Business Addr:** Vice President, Indiana Pacers, 125 S Pennsylvania St, Indianapolis, IN 46204, **Business Phone:** (317)917-2500.

### KELLOGG, GEORGE
Executive. **Personal:** Born Brooklyn, NY. **Educ:** Univ NDak, BBA, human resources mgt; City Univ NY, Baruch Col, MBA, human resources mgt. **Career:** Chase Manhattan Bank, position eval analyst; Hoffmann-LaRoche Inc, assoc personnel mgr; Revlon Inc, mgr human resources; Cent Pk Conservancy, dir human resources; Bugle Boy Industs, dir human resources & admin; Joseph P Addabbo Family Health Ctr, dir human resources; Lee Hecht Harrison; Bedford Stuyvesant Famility Health Ctr, dir human resources. **Orgs:** Delta Sigma Pi Prof Bus Fraternity; WorldatWork; Nat Black MBA Asn; Soc Human Resources Mgt; Human Resources Asn New York; Mercy Col Adv Bd. **Home Addr:** , Pomona, NY 10970, **Home Phone:** (917)687-9415.

### KELLOGG-RAY, CARRIE WALLS
Accountant.

### KELLUM, ANTHONY O.
Executive, real estate executive. **Personal:** Born May 5, 1965, VA; married Doreen A; children: Bryann, Anthony, Nicole & Nathan. **Educ:** Lewis Col Bus, Hon, humane lett, 1990. **Career:** Kellum Mortgage, pres, 1995-2006, Power by Wells Fargo Home Mortgage, dir emerging markets, 2005-07, Kellum Capital Group Inc, pres & chief exec officer, 2006-; Kellum Mortgage Financial Serv Inc, pres, founder, owner. **Orgs:** Vpres, Mich Mortgage Brokers Asn, 1999-2000; comt mem, Detroit Sym Orchestra, 2000-01; bd mem, Boysville, 2000-01; comt chait, Mich Mortgage Brokers Asn, 2000-01; adv comt, Lewis Col Bus, 2000-01. **Business Addr:** Chief Executive Officer, President, Kellum Capital Group LLC, 1442 Brush St 4th Fl, Detroit, MI 48226, **Business Phone:** (646)483-5237.

### KELLY, BRIAN PATRICK
Football player. **Personal:** Born Jan 14, 1976, Las Vegas, NV; children: Brian, Kiaran & Kyu Blu. **Educ:** Univ Southern Calif, attended 1997. **Career:** Football player (retired); Tampa Bay Buccaneers, defensive back, 1998, 2007, cornerback, 1999-2000, right cornerback, 1999, 2007, left cornerback, 2001-06; Detroit Lions, left cornerback, 2008. **Honors/Awds:** Excellence Sports Performance Yearly Awards, 2003; MTV Video Music Awards, 2004; Champion, Super Bowl, XXXVIII. **Special Achievements:** TV Series: "The Tonight Show with Jay Leno", 1992. Film: Super Bowl XXXVII, 2003.

### KELLY, ERNECE BEVERLY
Journalist, educator. **Personal:** Born Jan 6, 1937, Chicago, IL; daughter of William and Lovette Nathalia. **Educ:** Univ Chicago, BA, 1958, MA, 1959; Northwestern Univ, PhD, 1972. **Career:** Univ of Wis, asst prof, 1978-81; Kingsborough Community Col, assoc prof eng, 1980-95; New York Beacon Newspaper. **Orgs:** Dir, Nat Coun Teachers Eng, task force racism & bias teaching Eng, 1970-80; exec comm, Conf Col Compos & Commun, 1971-74; Col Lang Asn, 1972-; Humanities Coun NY; Speakers Humanities, 1992-99; bd dir, Audience Develop Comt Inc. **Home Addr:** 286 10th St, Brooklyn, NY 11215, **Home Phone:** (718)832-3772. **Business Addr:** Associate Professor of English, Kingsborough Community College, 2001 Oriental Blvd, Brooklyn, NY 11235, **Business Phone:** (718)368-5000.

### KELLY, REV. DR. HERMAN OSBY, JR.
Clergy. **Personal:** Born Feb 28, 1954, Jacksonville, FL; son of Herman; married Linda M; children: H Osby III & Tiffany Marie. **Educ:** Morehouse Col, BA, 1975; Springfield Col, MEd, 1976; Boston Univ, MDiv, 1983; Memphis Theol Sem, DMin, 2000. **Career:** Mt Zion AMEC, pastor, 1986-89; RI Col, chaplain, 1987-89; St James AMEC, pastor, 1989-93; Meridian Community Col, instr, 1990-93; Friendship African Methodist Episcopal Church, pastor, 1993-98; La State Univ, instr, 2000-; Bethel African Methodist Episcopal Church, pastor, 2000-. **Orgs:** Nat Asn Advan Colored People, 1989-93; life mem, Kappa Alpha Psi; Black Fac & Staff Asn, La State Univ, 2000-; La Interfaith Conf, 2000-; mentor, fac friend, Football Team mentor, La State Univ. **Honors/Awds:** Man of the Year, Nat Asn Advan Colored Peop, 1992; Special Citation, City of Meridian, MS, 1993; Academic Bar Award, St Josephs Academy. **Special Achievements:** Published, "Spiritual Formation of Young Leity in Bethel AME Church", 2000. **Home Addr:** 1146 Arcedia Dr, Baton Rouge, LA 70810, **Home Phone:** (229)768-7535. **Business Addr:** Pastor, Bethel African Methodist Episcopal Church, 1358 S St, Baton Rouge, LA 70802, **Business Phone:** (225)344-6931.

### KELLY, IDA B.
Business owner. **Personal:** Born Jun 2, 1925, Yazoo City, MS; children: 7. **Career:** Pizza Queen Inc, owner, currently. **Orgs:** Nat Asn Advan Colored People. **Honors/Awds:** Businesswoman of the Year, Nat Asn Bus & Prof Women, 1988. **Home Addr:** 1956 Hyde Pk Dr, Detroit, MI 48207. **Business Addr:** Owner, Pizza Queen Inc, Cobo Hall Cor.f Ctr, Detroit, MI 48231, **Business Phone:** (313)259-1100.

### KELLY, REV. JAMES CLEMENT
Clergy. **Personal:** Born Sep 29, 1928, Bethlehem, PA; married Loretta; children: Lynne, James Jr & Susan. **Educ:** Va Union Univ, BA, 1964; Va Union Sch Rel, MDiv, 1967. **Career:** Calvary Baptist Church, clergyman, pastor & founder, 1977-2004, pastor emer, 2004-; New Jerusalem Baptist Church, 1988-2004. **Orgs:** At Large BSA; Queens Fed Churchs; Rotary Club Jamaica; Prog Nat Bapt NY; life mem, vpres, Nat AsnAdvan Colored People; NY Mission Soc; vpres, Home Mission Bd; PNBC; admin bd, Am Baptist Churchs Metro NY; pres, Calvary Baptist Fed Credit Union; Fedn Churches; pres, Nat Baptist Conv; pres emer, Southeast Queens Clergy Community Empowerment; treas, Am Baptist Churches Metrop. **Honors/Awds:** Combat Infantry Man's Badge, AUS; Honorary Doctor of Divinity, Virginia Union Univ, 1983. **Special Achievements:** Fellowship hall named in honor of Rev. James C. Kelly. **Home Addr:** 187 Pennsylvania Ave, Freeport, NY 11520. **Business Addr:** Pastor Emeritus, Calvary Baptist Church, 5201 Dayton Blvd, Chattanooga, TN 37415, **Business Phone:** (423)875-8154.

### KELLY, JAMES JOHNSON
Military leader. **Personal:** Born Mar 29, 1928, High Point, NC; son of Nathan (deceased) and Elsie Johnson (deceased); married Sallie Mae Williams; children: Eva Mae Kelly-Jones, Thomas Edward & Cheryl Yvonne Kelly-Oliver. **Educ:** Univ Md, 1957; Our Lady Lake Univ, BA, 1971, MEd, 1973. **Career:** Military leader (retired). USAF, opers officer, sqdrn comdr, remote air base comdr, sr pilot & expert weapons controller, int pilot, maj, 1971; City San Antonio, TX, planning comnr, 1988, vice chmn, 1990-93. **Orgs:** NCP, S Poverty Law Ctr; Retired Officers Asn; Disabled Am Vets, County Workers Coun San Antonio; San Antonio Club OLLU, San Antonio; Lackland AF Base Officers Club, Chap No 5 DAV; lifetime mem, Tex Cong PTA; Star W Masonic Lodge 24, New St Mark Missionary Bapt Church, San Antonio; former mem bd trustees, Our Lady Lake Univ; former pres, OLLU Alumni Asn; adv Brentwood Jr H PTA; chmn, Brentwood Athletic

Booster Club; St John Bosco PTC; treas, John F Kennedy H Athletic Booster Asn; pres, Bethel Neighborhood Coun, 1986-91; pres, County Workers Coun, San Antonio, TX, 1987-91; Tex Dem Party, 1992-; Nat Asn Advan Colored People, 1958-; Southern Christian Leadership Conf, 1962-; Am Asn Retired Persons, 1986-. **Honors/Awds:** UN Service Medal; National Defense Medal; Outstanding Unit Award, USAF; Good Conduct Medal w/3 OLC, USAF; ROKPUCE; WW II Occupation Medal Japan; Community Distinguished Service Award, 1994. **Special Achievements:** First black candidate for city council Dist 6, San Antonio, TX, 1977; First black budget officer, Edgewood Urban-Rural Coun, 1977. **Home Addr:** 5010 Enid St, San Antonio, TX 78237-1715, **Home Phone:** (210)434-3273.

### KELLY, JOHN PAUL, JR.
Banker, consultant. **Personal:** Born Mar 8, 1941, New Orleans, LA; son of John P Sr (deceased) and Dorothy M Jones; married Lethia A Robinson; children: John P III, Byron M Smith, Phillip L Smith, Kelli C Smith & Lauren E. **Educ:** Manhattan Col, Bronx, NY, BS, sec educ & teaching, 1963; City Univ NY, MS, social sci, 1965. **Career:** Citicorp, NY, asst vpres, 1970-74; Midwest Nat Bank, Indianapolis, IN, pres, 1974-83, chief exec officer; Unibind Wash, DC, managing partner, 1987; MMB & Assocs, Wash, DC, partner, 1988; Dryades Savings Bank, consult & organizer, 1993-94; World Corp Group, asst vpres; Founder's Nat Bank, Los Angeles, pres & chief exec officer, 1991-93, 1999-2001; Enterprise Fed Savings Bank, pres & chief exec officer, 1994-99; Brookstone Financial Group Inc, founder, chmn, pres & chief exec officer, 2001-08; Independence Fed Savings Bank, chief lending officer; Castine Managment Group, prin, 2009-; New York Life Ins Co, financial serv prof, 2011-13. **Orgs:** Kappa Alpha Psi, 1965-; bd mem, Indianapolis Chamber Com, 1979-85; statetreas, Air Force Asn, 1979-81; bd mem, Citizens Gas & Coke Utility, 1980-85; bd mem & secy, Indianapolis Airport Authority, 1981-85; Gov Ind Fiscal Policy Adv Coun, 1981-85; chmn, Capital Fund Dr, 1982; bd mem, Nat Bus League, 1987-; bd mem, Am Soc Asn Execs, 1988-; Nat Ctr Missing & Exploited C; pres & chief staff officer, Nat Bankers Asn, Wash, DC, 1984-91; bd dir, Bowie State Univ. **Honors/Awds:** Four-Year Academic Scholarship, Manhattan Col, 1959; Academic Scholarship, City Univ NY, 1964. **Home Addr:** 3905 Hudee Dr Suite 100, Mitchellville, MD 20721, **Home Phone:** (301)464-9438. **Business Addr:** Principal, Castine Management Group.

### KELLY, DR. JOHN RUSSELL
Government official, president (organization). **Personal:** Born Nov 18, 1947, Utica, MS; son of John H; married Bernell Topp; children: Jon Felice & Kristi Bernell. **Educ:** Alcorn State Univ, BS, music performance, 1970; Wayne State Univ, MEd, urban sociol, 1972; Univ Southern Miss, PhD, 1979. **Career:** AUS, educ specialist, 1971-72; MS Coop Ext Serv, youth develop specialist, 1973-79; Univ Southern MS, adj prof, 1974-2001; Sea Grant Adv Serv, marine specialist, 1979-83; Navy Region Southeast, regional dir, 2001-05; USN Family Serv Ctr, dir; City Gulfport, chief admin officer, 2007-; pres & chief vol officer, S Miss United Way. **Orgs:** Pres, Res Mgt Inc, 1981; dep dir, Navy Family Serv Ctr, 1983-90; pres, gov bd, Phillips Col, 1985-93; pres, MS div Am Cancer Soc, 1986-88; gen vpres, Alpha Phi Alpha Frat, 1987-91; pres, Harrison Co United Way, 1987-89; pres, J & B Printing Inc; DBA Print Shack, 1987-93; chmn, vice chair & Secy, Am Cancer Soc Nat Bd dir, 2005; chair, Gulf Coast Med Ctr Bd trustee, 2000-04; trustee Leadership Gulf Coast; chmn, Bd Deacons & churchs Rebuilding Comt; chmn bd, Miss State Bd Educ, 2011-. **Home Addr:** 11397 Palm Valley Cove, Gulfport, MS 39503. **Business Addr:** Chief Administrative Officer, City of Gulfport, PO Box 1780, Gulfport, MS 39502, **Business Phone:** (228)868-5700.

### KELLY, JOSEPH WINSTON, JR.
Football player, executive. **Personal:** Born Dec 11, 1964, Sun Valley, CA; son of Joe Sr. **Educ:** Univ Wash, BA, criminal justice, 1986. **Career:** Football player (retired); Cincinnati Bengals, right inside linebacker, 1986-89; New York Jets, right inside linebacker, 1990-92; Los Angeles Raiders, mid inside linebacker, 1993; Los Angeles Rams, left linebacker, 1994; Green Bay Packers, linebacker, 1995; Philadelphia Eagles, linebacker, 1996; KELLY Youth Serv Inc, exec dir, prin owner, currently. **Orgs:** NFL Alumni Asn. **Honors/Awds:** Am Football Club Championship Game; Nat Football League Championship Game. **Business Addr:** Executive Director, Principal Owner, KELLY Youth Services Inc, 800 Compton Rd Unit 11, Cincinnati, OH 45231, **Business Phone:** (513)761-0700.

### KELLY, MARION GREENUP
Manager, association executive, executive. **Personal:** Born Nov 28, 1947, Baton Rouge, LA; married Harlan H; children: Ingrid & Ian. **Educ:** H Sophie Newcomb Col Tulane Univ, BA, psychol, 1969; Tulane Univ, MEd, educ early childhood develop, 1970; Columbia Univ, Sch Pub Health, MS. **Career:** New York Univ Child Study Ctr, admin dir; Columbia Univ Health Sci, asst vpres admin; Columbia Univ, dept adminr pediat; Headstart, tchr, 1970-71; Neighborhood Coordr, asst exec dir, 1971-73; Mayors Off New Orleans, city partic coordr, 1975; City's Human Rels Comt, dep dir; Audubon Pk Comn, asst dir & bus mgr, 1981. **Orgs:** Nat Asn Planners, 1971-73; Am Soc & Planning Officials, 1971-74; sr vpres educ & health prom, March Dimes; Hons Educ Soc, 1970-73; Gr New Orleans Presch Asn, 1970-74; Childrens Bur New Orleans, 1973-74; secy, Foresight proj Inc, 2006; vpres admin, Simons Found. **Honors/Awds:** Civic Organization Awards, Pub Schs Baton Rouge, 1963-64. **Home Addr:** 2811 Audubon St, New Orleans, LA 70125. **Business Addr:** Secretary, The Foresight Project Inc, PO Box 341, Harvard, MA 01451, **Business Phone:** (978)621-8549.

### KELLY, MIKE (MICHAEL RAYMOND)
Baseball player. **Personal:** Born Jun 2, 1970, Los Angeles, CA. **Educ:** Ariz State Univ. **Career:** Baseball player (retired); Atlanta Braves, outfielder, 1994-95; Cincinnati Reds, outfielder, 1996-97; Tampa Bay Devil Rays, outfielder, 1998-99; Colo Rockies, outfielder, 1999.

### KELLY, ROBERT SYLVESTER
Singer, writer. **Personal:** Born Jan 8, 1967, Chicago, IL; son of Joann (deceased); married Andrea Lee; children: Jaya, Joann & Robert Jr; married Aaliyah. **Career:** Singer, songwriter, producer, dancer; USBL, Atlantic City Seagulls, basketball player, 1997.Albums: Born into the '90s, 1992; 12 Play, 1993; R Kelly, 1995; TP-2.com, 2000; The Best of Both Worlds, 2002; Chocolate Factory, 2003; The R in R&B Collection, Vol. 1, 2003; Happy People/U Saved Me, 2004; Unfinished Business, 2004; TP-3: Reloaded, 2005; Remix City Vol. 1, 2005; Double Up, 2007; Untitled, 2009. Hot singles include: Sex Me (Parts 1 +2); Bump N' Grind; Your Body's Callin; self-titled album, 1998; Shaft, 2000; Osmosis Jones, 2001; Drumline, 2002; Old Sch, 2003; Fun with Dick & Jane, 2004; Trapped in the Closet, 2005, 2007; Write Me Back, 2012. **Business Addr:** Vocalist, c/o Jive Records, 137-139 W 25th St, New York, NY 10001, **Business Phone:** (212)727-0016.

### KELLY, THOMAS, JR.
Financial manager, chief financial officer. **Personal:** Born Apr 2, 1951, Augusta, GA; married Geraldine; children: Thomas III & Tiffany Nicole. **Educ:** Augusta Col Sch Bus, BBA, Augusta Col, MBA, 1978. **Career:** Med Col Ga Talmadge Memorial Hosp, gen assountant, 1973-74, cost Acct, 1974-75, fiscal & affairs analyst, 1975-76, asst hosp adminstr, 1976-78, assoc hosp adminr; Community Med Ctr, interim chief financial officer, 2006-10; Moses Taylor Found, interim chief financial officer, 2013-15, chief financial officer, 2016-; MCG Health Inc, sr vpres & chief financial officer; Med Col Ga Health Syst, sr vpres, chief financial officer, currently. **Orgs:** Hosp Financial Mgt Asn; chmn, Internal Audit Com Health Ctr Credit, 1977-79; loan exec, United Way Agency, 1978-79; bd dir, First Bank Ga; Tabernacle Baptist Church; Augusta United Way; treas, Augusta Prep Day Sch; Ga Finance Comt; Savannah River Regional Diversification Initiative; Ga Dept Community Health Hosp Adv Bd. **Home Addr:** 3317 Greening Lane, Augusta, GA 30906. **Business Addr:** Chief Financial Officer, Moses Taylor Foundation, 150 N Washington Ave 6th Fl, Scranton, PA 18503, **Business Phone:** (570)207-3731.

### KELSEY, JOSEPHINE
School administrator, president (organization), executive director. **Career:** Ctr Creative Studies, pres, 1991-93; Mich Guild Artists & Artisans, exec dir; Humane Soc Huron Valley, exec dir. **Orgs:** Mayor's Comn State Art Fairs. **Special Achievements:** First chief executive officer of the corp formed by the merger of the Coll of Art & Design & the Inst of Music & Dance. **Business Addr:** Executive Director, Humane Society of Huron Valley, 3100 Cherry Hill Rd, Ann Arbor, MI 48105, **Business Phone:** (734)662-5585.

### KELSO-WATSON, ANGELA R.
Vice president (organization), college administrator. **Personal:** Born Mar 21, 1961, Guthrie, OK; daughter of JM and Ruth Harris; married Cleovis Watson II; children: Crystal Kelso & Jade Watson. **Educ:** BS, 1991; MBA, 1995. **Career:** Langston Univ, secy receptionist, pres off, 1980-82, secy pres off, 1982-84, exec asst to pres, 1984-95, exec asst pres assoc vpres admis, 1995-97, chief staff, pres off, 1997-2000, actg vpres admin & fiscal affairs, 2000-01, vpres admin & fiscal affairs, 2001-. **Orgs:** Nat Asn Col & Univ Bus Officers, NACUBO; Okla Asn Col & Univ Bus Officers; chmn, Langston Econ Develop Authority; Langston Univ Nat Alumni Asn; charter mem, Epsilon Epsilon Chap, Phi Beta Delta Hon Soc; Alpha Kappa Alpha; Women Higher Educ; Mt Zion Missionary Baptist Church. **Home Addr:** 1713 Kyle Dr, Guthrie, OK 73044-6424. **Business Addr:** Vice President, Administrative & Fiscal Affairs, Langston University, Page Hall Rm 218, Langston, OK 73050, **Business Phone:** (405)466-3299.

### KEMP, EMMERLYNE JANE
Musician, songwriter. **Personal:** Born May 6, 1935, Chicago, IL; daughter of Robert Louis (deceased) and Janie Lee Harris (deceased). **Educ:** Northwestern Univ, piano, 1954; Monterey CA, MPC, 1960; Berklee Sch Music, Boston, MA, jazz subjects, 1965; NY Univ, music educ, 1971. **Career:** Beth Eden Bapt Church 1st Concert, 1942; Berkeley Little Theater, class piano, 1950; theater show piano, 1958; Santa Clara Col, concert with jazz group, 1961; Radio & TV com voice overs, 1966; CBS-TV, staff, 1968; Ballad Box Brown, creator, 1974; Musicals: Bubbling Brown Sugar, 1975-76; Tomorrow's Woman; Someone To Sing To, 1992; First Awakening. **Orgs:** Harlem Arts Alliance. **Honors/Awds:** First place, National Talent Competition, Bapt Ushers, Washington, DC, 1953; Second place, Golden State Chap, Nat Asn Negro Musicians, 1954; National Endowment for the Arts Grant, San Francisco Choral Artists, 1977; ASCAP Awards; Audelco Pioneer Award. **Home Addr:** 626 Riverside Dr Apt 21j, New York, NY 10031-7233, **Home Phone:** (212)281-4363. **Business Addr:** Musician, c/o Dunlop Enterprises, 8 Lillian Dr, Spring Valley, NY 10977, **Business Phone:** (914)623-8418.

### KEMP, LEROY PERCY, JR. (DARNELL FREEMAN)
Automotive executive, wrestler, association executive. **Personal:** Born Dec 24, 1956, Cleveland, OH; son of Leroy Percy Sr and Jessie Bell; married Linda Diane Isabell; children: Brandon Elliott, Jordan Lee & Mercedes Christina. **Educ:** Univ Wis-Madison, BBA, mkt, 1979, MBA, mkt, 1983. **Career:** Wrestler (retired), entrepreneur, wrestling coach; Burrell Advert, acct exec, 1985-86; Lever Bros Co, Personal Prod Div, asst prod mgr, 1986-87; Clairol Inc, Consumer Prod Div, assoc prod mgr, 1987-89; Ford Motor Co Minority Dealer Training Prog, 1989-91; Forest Lake Ford Inc, pres & owner, 1991-. **Orgs:** Ford Lincoln Mercury Minority Dealer Asn; Nat Asn Minority Automobile Dealers; USA Wrestling Nat Gov Body; Raise His Praise Worship Ctr; FORZA Technologies, co-founder & pres. **Honors/Awds:** Two-time Ohio State High School Wrestling Champion, 1973-74; World Champion, 1978; World Champion, 1979; US Freestyle Champion, 1979-83; Two-time Gold Medalist, Pan America Games, 1979, 1983; FILA Wrestling World Cup, Gold, 1979-82; Bronze Medal, 1981; World Champion, 1982; National Wrestling Hall of Fame, 1990; George Martin Wisconsin Wrestling Hall of Fame, 1983; FILA International Wrestling Hall of Fame. **Special Achievements:** First American to become Three-time World Freestyle Wrestling Champion, 1978, 1979, 1982; At age 21, the youngest American to win world championships, 1978; Four-time World Cup Champion; Ghost & Goblins, film. **Home Addr:** 127 S Quentin Rd, Palatine, IL 60067, **Home Phone:** (228)200-6153. **Business Addr:** President, Owner, Forest Lake Ford Inc, 231 19th St SW, Forest Lake, MN 55025, **Business Phone:** (651)464-4600.

### KEMP, MATTHEW RYAN (MATT KEMP)
Baseball player. **Personal:** Born Sep 23, 1984, Midwest City, OK; son of Carl and Judy Henderson. **Career:** Maj League Baseball, Los Angeles Dodgers, outfielder, 2006-14; San Diego Padres, 2015-16; Atlanta Braves, 2016-. **Orgs:** Kemp's Kids, 2008, 2009. **Honors/Awds:** Gold Glove, 2009, 2011; Silver Slugger, 2009, 2011; Hank Aaron Award, 2011; Player of the Year, Baseball America Major League, 2011; Roy Campanella Award, 2011. **Special Achievements:** In 2011, became the first player to finish in the top two in both home runs and stolen bases since Hank Aaron in 1963. **Business Addr:** Professional Baseball Player, Los Angeles Dodgers, 1000 Elysian Park Ave, Los Angeles, CA 90012, **Business Phone:** (323)224-1507.

### KEMP, SHAWN T.
Basketball player, basketball executive. **Personal:** Born Nov 26, 1969, Elkhart, IN; married Marvena L Thomas; children: 11. **Educ:** Univ Ky, attended 1989; Trinity Valley Community Col, attended 1989. **Career:** Basketball player (retired), basketball executive; Seattle SuperSonics, forward, 1989-97; Cleveland Cavaliers, 1997-2000; Portland Trail Blazers, 2000-02; Orlando Magic, 2002-03; Premiata Montegranaro, forward, 2008; Shawn Kemp Basketball Clin, owner, currently.

### KENAN, RANDALL G.
Writer, educator. **Personal:** Born Mar 12, 1963, Brooklyn, NY. **Educ:** Univ NC, Chapel Hill, NC, BA, 1985. **Career:** Alfred A Knopf, New York, NY, ed, ed staff, 1985-89; Sarah Lawrence Col, Bronxville, NY, lectr, beginning 1989; Vassar Col, Poughkepsie, NY, lectr, 1989-; Columbia Univ, New York, NY, lectr, beginning 1990; Univ Miss, vis writer; Univ Nebr-Lincoln, vis writer; Duke Univ, vis prof creative writing, 1994; Univ Memphis, vis prof creative writing; Univ Nc Chapel Hill, assoc prof, currently; Author: A Visitation of Spirits, 1989; Let the Dead Bury Their Dead, Harcourt, Brace, 1992; A Time Not Here: The Mississippi Delta, 1997; Walking on Water: Black American Lives at the Turn of the Twenty-first Century, 1999; The Fire This Time, 2007; Only The Dead Know Chapel Hill; The Cross of Redemption: The Uncollected Writings of James Baldwin; Theres a Man Going Round Taking Names, forthcoming. **Business Addr:** Associate Professor, University of North Carolina at Chapel Hill, Chapel Hill, NC 27599-3520, **Business Phone:** (919)962-2211.

### KENDALL, ESQ. JOHN S.
Lawyer. **Personal:** Born Chicago, IL. **Educ:** Univ Dayton, BEEE, 1985; Ohio State Univ, JD, 1990. **Career:** Northrop Defense Systs Div, Commun Systs Engr; Sughrue, Mion, Zinn, McPeak & Seas, law clerk; Davis & Kendall PC, sr partner, atty, currently; Law Off John S Kendall PC, atty & owner, currently. **Orgs:** Chmn, Metrop Reclamation Dist Greater Chicago Civil Serv Bd; Vice Chair Develop, 100 Black Men Chicago; Am Bar Asn. **Business Addr:** Attorney, Owner, Law Office of John S Kendall PC, 225 W Wash Suite 2200, Chicago, IL 60606, **Business Phone:** (312)857-1997.

### KENDALL, LETTIE M.
Educator, government official. **Personal:** Born May 2, 1930, Magnolia, AR; married Robert B; children: Yvonne, Sharon, Donald & Ronald. **Educ:** Ariz Bapt Col, BS, 1951; Bishop Col, attended 1951; Tenn State Univ; Austin Peay State Univ, MA, 1974; Austin Peay State Univ, EdS, 1979. **Career:** Woodruff County Sch Syst, teacher, 1951-52; Clarksville & Mont City Sch, 1961; Byrns L Darden Sch, 1966; Moore Elem & Cohen Schs, prin, 1977-; Clarksville Sch; Ringgold Elem Teacher; Montgomery County, Dist 13 County Comnr, 2006-. **Orgs:** Clarksville Mont City Educ Asn; TEA, MTEA, NEA; Kappa Delta Pi; Dept Byrns L Darden Sch; Mid Tenn Coun IRA; attended numerous workshops; County Comnrs Asn Tenn; Adv Comt EEO bd, Ft Campbell, KY; Sch Com County Ct; Nat Asn Advan Colored People; Clarksville Community Develop Comn; vice chmn, Recreational & Hist bd County Comn; dir, St John Baptist Church Sunday Sch; John Missionary Baptist Church. **Honors/Awds:** Honored with a park named in her name, 2006; Robert M Wormsley Outstanding County Official of the Year, Tenn County Serv Asn, 2011; Bridge of Honor Award, NAACP, 2015. **Home Addr:** 388 A St, Clarksville, TN 37042, **Home Phone:** (931)648-5625. **Business Addr:** District 13 County Commissioner, Montgomery County, PO Box 368, Clarksville, TN 37041-0368, **Business Phone:** (937)648-5625.

### KENDALL, MICHELLE KATRINA
Pharmacist, executive. **Personal:** Born Aug 5, 1952, Detroit, MI; daughter of Louis A Cayce and Evelyn Cayce; married Jeffrey M; children: Christopher M. **Educ:** Wayne State Univ, BA, biol, 1983, BS, pharm, 1987. **Career:** Wayne State Univ, stud res asst, 1972-84; C Hosp, pharm intern, 1984-87; Perry Drug Store Inc, pharm supvr, 1987-. **Orgs:** Lambda Kappa Sigma, 1986-; adv bd, Crockett Voc Ctr, 1992-; Detroit Pharm Guild. **Home Addr:** 30235 Woodgate Dr, Southfield, MI 48076, **Home Phone:** (248)647-3523. **Business Addr:** Pharmacy Supervisor, Perry Drug Stores Inc, 5400 Perry Dr, Pontiac, MI 48340, **Business Phone:** (313)538-2780.

### KENDALL, ROBERT, JR.
Lawyer. **Personal:** Born Feb 11, 1947, Thomaston, GA; married Lolita Marie Toles; children: Yolanda Yvette & Robert III. **Educ:** Ft Valley State Col, BS, educ, 1969; Tex State Univ Sch Law, JD, 1973. **Career:** US Dept Justice, atty; Civil Div, Off Immigration Litigation, asst dir, currently. **Orgs:** Phi Beta Sigma Fraternity, 1968; Phi Alpha Delta Law Fraternity, 1969. **Honors/Awds:** Special Achievement Awards for Sustained Superior Performance of Duty, US Dept Justice, 1977, 1985, 1989, 1990 & 1992. **Home Addr:** 150 Little Falls St Suite 203, Falls Church, VA 22046, **Home Phone:** (703)533-7756. **Business Addr:** Assistant Director, Attorney, US Department of Justice, 950 Pa Ave NW, Washington, DC 20530-0001, **Business Phone:** (202)514-2217.

**KENDRICK, CAROL YVONNE**
Counselor. **Personal:** Born Jan 29, 1952, New York, NY; daughter of E Curtis and Marguerite Holloway; married John A DeMicco. **Educ:** New York Univ, BA, 1974; New York Univ Sch Law, JD, 1977. **Career:** Off Bronx Dist Atty, asst dist atty, 1977-81; New York Life Ins Co, assoc coun, 1981-97; AnnTaylor, asst gen coun, 1997-02; Hahn Hessen LLP, contract litigation atty, 2003-04; MetLife, sr coun; Song Noway, prodn mgr; Desert Song, stage mgr; Village Light Opera Grp; Opera Ensemble; Village Dinner Theatre NC; Stage Productions; Fate Productions. **Orgs:** Speaker, Minority Interchange, 1983-84; founding mem & treas, Riverside Opera Ensemble, 1984-. **Honors/Awds:** Best & Brightest Black Women in Corporate America, Ebony Mag, 1990. **Home Addr:** 92 Pinebrook Rd, New Rochelle, NY 10801-1307, **Home Phone:** (914)235-1976. **Business Addr:** Treasurer, Founding Member, The Riverside Opera Ensemble Inc, 488 Madison Ave 14th Fl, New York, NY 10022.

**KENDRICK, CURTIS L.**
Librarian. **Personal:** Born Jun 13, 1958, New York, NY; son of Ercell Curtis and Marguerite Sanford Holloway; married Mary Beth; children: James Mitchell & Caroline Lindsay. **Educ:** Brown Univ, Providence, RI, BA, 1980; Simmons Col, Boston, MA, MLS, 1984; Emory Univ, Atlanta, GA, MBA, 1992. **Career:** Brown Univ, Providence, RI, libr asn specialist, 1981-83; Oberlin Col, Oberlin, OH, asst to dir libs, 1984-86; State Univ New York, Stony Brook, NY, head, circulation & reserves dept, 1986-90; Harvard Univ, asst dir librs, 1992-98; Columbia Univ, dir access serv, 1998-2004; City Univ New York, univ librn, 2004-08, univ dean libr & info resources, 2010-. **Orgs:** Am Libr Asn, 1983-; Asn Col & Res Librs, 1985-; Asn Col & Res Librs Afro-Am Studies Sect, chair, Nomination Comt, 1990-92; Libr Admin & Mgmt Asn, 1990-2008; Libr Info Technol Asn, 1990-; Libr Admin & Mgmt Asn Prog Comt Chair, 1995-97; Libr Info Technol Asn Nat Conf Prog Cot, 1996; Libr Admin & Mgmt Asn Budget & Finance Comt, 1997-2001; Asn Col & Res Librs Univ Libr Sect Pub Serv Dirs, 1998-2003; Libr Admin & Mgmt Asn LOMS Exec Bd Secy, 1999-2001; Access Serv 21st Century Symp, Founder, 2001; Am Libr Asn Coun Comt Pay Equity, 2004-05; Am Libr Asn Comt Res & Statist, 2004-06; NY State Higher Educ Initiative Bd Mem, 2004-; bd dir, NY Higher Educ Initiative, 2004-; Am Nat Stand Inst/Nat Info Stand Orgn Stand, 2004 Maintenance Adv Comt, 2005-06; Asn Lib Coll & Tech Srvs, 2005-; Yonkers Pub Libr Bd Trustees, 2006-; NY Online Virtual Electronic Libr Steering Comt, 2007-; Urban Libr J Adv Bd, 2008-; bd dir, MOUSE, 2008-; Beta Phi Mu; Beta Gamma Sigma; bd dir, Yonkers Partners Educ, 2013; adv coun, Queens Col Grad Sch Libr & Info Studies. **Honors/Awds:** Beta Phi Mu, Nat Honor Soc, 1983; Fac Travel Res Grant, SUNY, Stony Brook, 1989; Title II-B Fel, US Dept Educ, 1983; Emory Scholar Fel, 1990-92; 'George Mew Organisation & Management Award', 1992; Frye Leadership Institute Fellow, 2002 (sponsored by Council on Library & Information Resources, EDUCAUSE, & Emory University); Archons of Colophon, 2005. **Special Achievements:** Author, To Perpetuity and Beyond, Urban Library Journal, 2007; Library Offsite Shelving: Guide for High-Density Facilities; 2001; The Paradox and Politics of Off-site Shelving, in Library Offsite Shelving: Guide for High-Density Facilities, 2001; High Density Storage Libraries : The Harvard Depository Model, in Solving Collection Problems Through Repository Strategies, 1999; A User-Centered View of Document Delivery & Interlibrary Loan, Library Admin and Mgmt, 1994; The Competitive Advantage of Librarians, Managing Resource Sharing in the Electronic Age, 1996; The Design & Operation Off-site Storage in Support of Preservation Programs, Erice 96 Conservation and Restoration of Archive & Library Materials Conference, 1996; Performance Measures of Shelving Accuracy, Journal of Academic Librarianship, 1991; Minority Internship/Scholarship in Library and Information Sciences, College & Research Libraries News, 1990; Cavalry to the Rescue, Col & Research Libraries News, 1989. **Home Addr:** 54 Sunnyside Dr, Yonkers, NY 10705-1731, **Home Phone:** (914)963-2851. **Business Addr:** University Dean for Libraries and Information Resources, City University of New York, 535 E 80th St, New York, NY 10075, **Business Phone:** (212)794-5481.

**KENDRICK, JOY ANTOINETTE**
Lawyer. **Personal:** Born Burlington, NC; daughter of Charles and Sarah L. **Educ:** Univ NC, Chapel Hill, BA, 1977; State Univ NY, Buffalo, JD, 1981; Ind Univ, MBA, 1985. **Career:** Alamance Tech Col, orientation librn, 1977-78; law clerk, 1979-81; Cora P Maloney Col, acad coordr, 1980-81; Neighborhood Legal Serv Inc, staff atty, 1981-83; NCR Corp, bus intern, 1984; JA Kendrick Bus Enterprises Inc, pres & lawyer, 1985-; Law Off Joy Kendrick, managing coun, 1985-; Joy A Kendrick Atty At Law, atty. **Orgs:** Bd mem, Chamber Com, 1987-90; Leadership Buffalo, 1988; bd mem, Buffalo Pvt Indust Coun, 1990-; contrib writer, Buffalo Bus; bd dir, Minority Bus Coun; bd dir, Housing Asst Ctr; Erie County Bar Asn; New York Bar Asn; Am Bar Asn. **Business Addr:** Attorney, Joy A Kendrick Attorney At Law, 534 Del Ave Suite 420, Buffalo, NY 14202-1340, **Business Phone:** (716)855-2251.

**KENDRICK, L. JOHN, SR.**
Executive, association executive. **Personal:** Born May 13, 1932, Monticello, KY; son of Wesley and Marie; children: L John Jr, Rozalind Denese Hopgood & Debra Jo Hopgood. **Career:** Kendrick Paper Stock Co, owner, chief exec officer, pres, 1954-. **Orgs:** Jefferson County Chamber Com, 1968-81; Jefferson County NCP, 1968-92; Just Mens Club, 1969-72; chmn, Jefferson County Housing Authority, 1972-74; Govs Club, 1990-; finance comt, Corinthian Baptist Church. **Honors/Awds:** Cert Recognition, Efforts Recycling, 1988; Governors Corp Recycling Award, State Ill, 1989. **Home Addr:** 5106 Richview Rd, Mount Vernon, IL 62864, **Home Phone:** (618)244-3962. **Business Addr:** Chief Executive Officer, Owner, Kendrick Paper Stock Co, 1000 Salem Rd, Mount Vernon, IL 62864-3429, **Business Phone:** (618)242-4527.

**KENDRICK, TOMMY L.**
School administrator. **Personal:** Born May 29, 1923, Sycamore, GA; son of George and Salbe; married Geneva Bhanton; children: Deborah Elane, Welchel, Diane H & Denise. **Educ:** Ft Valley State Col, BSA, 1948; Tuskegee Inst, MS, educ, 1958, MA, admin & Supv, 1969. **Career:** Ft Baptist Church, Sunday Sch, supt, 1955-85, clerk, 1961-85; Chatto Valley Bible Col, Sch Theol, Edison, Ga, dean, 1989-93; elem sch prin. **Orgs:** Worshipful master, Prince Hall Masons, 1950-85; Masonic Lodge, wishful master; GTA, 1970-85; Nat Asn Educr, 1970-85; Co Bd Comn, 1976-95; State Asn Co Community, 1976-95; Order Consery 32 Mason, 1979-95; Page Prof Org, 1983-; dep grand master, Prince Hall Masons, 1987-95. **Honors/Awds:** Man of the Year, 1988. **Special Achievements:** Citation from first Baptist Church of Georgetown, 1992. **Home Addr:** 214 Kaigler Rd, Georgetown, GA 39854, **Home Phone:** (229)334-2656.

**KENLAW, JESSIE**
Executive, basketball coach. **Personal:** Born Guyton, CA. **Educ:** Savannah State, BS, health & phys educ, 1977. **Career:** Basketball player (retired), basketball coach, executive; Houston Angels, 1979-82; Lamar Univ, asst coach, 1987-88; Univ Houston, women basketball head coach, 1990-98; Am Basketball League, Colorado Xplosion, asst coach, 1998-99; La Tech Univ, asst women basketball coach, 1999-2000; Women's Nat Basketball Asn, Portland Fire, asst coach, 2002; Women's Nat Basketball Asn, Seattle Storm, 2003-06; Women's Nat Basketball Asn, Houston Comets, 2007-08; Wash Mystics, asst coach, dir scouting, interim head coach, 2008-09; Sports Int Group, dir mkt, 2010-13; When I Nvest I AM, founder & chief exec officer, camp leader, motivational speaker, Ment Conditioning Coach, 2012-. **Orgs:** Women's Am Basketball Asn; Ladies Prof Basketball Asn. **Honors/Awds:** Coach of Year, baseball coaches asn, 1991. **Business Addr:** Founder, Chief Executive Officer, When I Nvest I AM.

**KENNARD, BILL.** See KENNARD, WILLIAM EARL.

**KENNARD, PATRICIA A.**
Television news anchorperson, radio journalist, government official. **Personal:** Born Canton, OH; children: Maya Khalilah. **Educ:** Cent State Univ, BS; Univ Akron Sch Grad Studies. **Career:** Hartford Jr High Sch, lang arts teacher; Canton Urban League; educ specialist (counr); WHBC, radio newscaster; tv reporter, TV-23, 1980-86; Rubber City Radio Group, mid-day news anchor; part-time fac, Univ Akron; WAKR-Radio, veteran news reporter & anchor; Ohio Dept Transp, Dist 4, spokeswoman & pub rels officer, 2007-. **Orgs:** Asn Black Prof Bus Women; Nat Asn Advan Colored People; Zeta Phi Beta Sorority; co-host, Nat Childrens Miracle Network; vol, Mentoring Mothers; House Lord. **Honors/Awds:** Black Women of Excellence Award, YWCA, 1998; Crystal Award for Community Service; Cleveland Press Club Award; National Broadcaster's Hall of Fame. **Business Addr:** Public Relations Officer, Spokeswoman, Ohio Department of Transportation, 2088 S Arlington Rd, Akron, OH 44306, **Business Phone:** (330)786-3100.

**KENNARD, WILLIAM EARL (BILL KENNARD)**
Government official. **Personal:** Born Jan 19, 1957, Los Angeles, CA; son of Robert A and Helen Z King; married Deborah Diane Kennedy; children: Robert. **Educ:** Stanford Univ, BA, communs, 1978; Yale Law Sch, JD, 1981. **Career:** Nat Asn Broadcasters, fel, 1981-82, asst gen coun, 1983-84; Nat Asn Broadcasters, asst gen coun, 1983-84; Verner, Liipfert, Bernhard, McPherson & Hand, assoc, 1982-83, partner, 1984-93; Fed Commun Comn, gen coun, 1993-97, comnr & chmn, 1997-2001; Carlyle Group, managing dir, 2001-; Global Telecommunications & Media, managing dir; Us Ambassador to Europ Union, 2009-. **Orgs:** Calif Bar Asn; Wash DC Bar; Fed Commun Bar Asn; Am Bar Asn; Nat Bar Asn; Phi Beta Kappa Soc; sr fel Aspen Inst, 2001-; Bd dir, mem finance comt, New York Times Co, 2001-; bd dir, Nextel Corp, 2001-05; dir, Handspring Inc, 2001-; bd dir, Dex Media, 2002-; Insight Commun Co Inc, dir & chmn, Compensation Comt, 2005-; dir, Media Access Proj; bd dir, eAccess Ltd; bd dir & chmn, Hawaiian Telcom, 2005-; bd dir, Sprint Nextel Corp, 2005-07; trustee, Gallaudet Univ; Joint Ctr Polit & Econ Studies; dir, One Econ Corp; dir, Common Sense Media Inc; dir, Yr up; Gore 2000; John Kerry Pres; Obama Am; bd dir, AT&T Inc, currently; fel & bd dir, Yale Univ Coun, currently; bd dir, Ford Motor Co, currently; bd dir, MetLife Inc, currently; bd dir, Duke Energy, currently; bd dir, Int African Am Mus, currently; bd dir, Ctr a New Am Security, currently; adv bd, Secy State John Kerry's Foreign Policy, currently. **Special Achievements:** First black Federal Communications Commission chairman. **Home Addr:** 5300 27th St NW, Washington, DC 20015. **Business Addr:** United States Ambassador, United States Mission, Zinnerstraat - 13 - Rue Zinner, BrusselsB-1000, **Business Phone:** (322)811-4100.

**KENNEDY, ADRIENNE LITA**
Lecturer, playwright, educator. **Personal:** Born Sep 13, 1931, Pittsburgh, PA; daughter of Cornell Wallace Hawkins and Etta Haugabook Hawkins; married Joseph; children: Joseph Jr & Adam. **Educ:** Ohio State Univ, BA, educ, 1953; Columbia Univ, grad study, 1956; New Sch Social Res, Am Theatre Wing, Circle Sq Theatre Sch & Edward Albee's workshop, playwright. **Career:** Mem playwriting unit, Actors Studio, New York, 1962-65; Yale Univ, lectr, 1972-74; Sch Drama, New York, CBS fel, 1973; Princeton Univ, lectr, 1977, prof, currently; Int Theatre Inst rep, Budapest, 1978; Brown Univ, vis assoc prof, 1979-80; Univ Calif, Berkeley, lectr, 1980, 1986; Harvard Univ, Cambridge, MA, vis lectr, 1981-91; Signature Theatre Co, New York, playwright-in-residence, 1996-97; Univ Calif, Davis, fac. Plays: A Movie Star Has to Star in Black & White, 1976; A Lancashire Lad, 1980; Black C's Day, 1980; Diary of Lights, 1987; She Talks to Beethoven, 1989; The Ohio State Murders, 1992; The Film Club, 1992; The Dramatic Circle, 1992; Motherhood 2000, 1994; June & Jean in Concert, 1995; Sleep Deprivation Chamber, 1996; Mom, How Did You Meet the Beatles, 2008. **Orgs:** Founding mem, Women's Theatre Coun, 1971; bd dir, PEN, 1976-77; fel Yakle Univ, 1974-75; Int Theatre Inst Rep Budapest, 1978. **Honors/Awds:** Obie Award, 1964; Guggenheim Award, 1967; Rockefeller Grants, 1967-69, 1974, 1976; CBS Fellow, 1973; Creative Artists Public Service grant, 1974; Manhattan Borough President Award, 1988; American Book Award, 1990; National Endowment for the Arts Award, 1993;The Lila Wallace Readers Digest Award, 1994; Academy Award in literature, Am Acad Arts & Letters, 1994; Literature Award, Am Acad Arts & Lett, 1994; Pierre Le comte du Novy Award, Lincoln Ctr, 1994; American Academy of Arts and Letters Award, 1994; Village Voice Obie Award, 1995; Lifetime Achievement Book Award, Anisfield-Wolf Book Awards, 2003; Pierre Lecomte du Novy Award, 2003; Hon doctorate Lit, Ohio State Univ, 2003; Lifetime Achievement Award, 2008; Theater Award, PEN/Laura Pels Int Found; Stanley Award. **Special Achievements:** First major play Funnyhouse of a Negro. **Home Addr:** 114-91 179th St, Jamaica, NY 11434. **Business Addr:** Professor, Princeton University, Princeton, NJ 08544, **Business Phone:** (609)258-3000.

**KENNEDY, BERNICE ROBERTS**
Educator, nurse. **Personal:** Born Sep 23, 1953, Eastover, SC; daughter of Samuel Roberts Sr and Irene Jacobs Roberts; children: Chrishonda M & Kenard J. **Educ:** Univ SC, BSN, 1975, MSN, ment health & admin, 1998; Walden Univ, PhD, health serv, 1998. **Career:** WBJD Veteran Med Ctr, advan pract nurse, 1993-99; SC State Univ, assoc prof, 1999-; Amy V Cock croft Leadership fel, Univ SC, 2003; psychiatnurse, pvt pract; BRK Healthcare Serv Inc, owner, sr consult, currently. **Orgs:** Sigma Theta Tau, Univ SC, 1998; Sister Care Inc, Women & C Domestic Violence Bur, 2000-03; Angel Nursing Inc, gov bd, 2001-03; Delta Sigma Theata, Columbia chap, 2002-03; Chi Eta Phi, Delta ETQ, SC State Univ, 2002-03; SC State Univ, Stud Affairs Comm, chair, 2002-03; post doctoral fel, Univ Sc, 2005. **Home Addr:** 1156 Old McGraw Rd, Eastover, SC 29044-9116, **Home Phone:** (803)353-2082. **Business Addr:** Owner, Senior Consultant, BRK Healthcare Services Inc, PO Box 90105, Columbia, SC 29209, **Business Phone:** (803)353-2082.

**KENNEDY, BRENDA PICOLA**
Judge. **Personal:** Born Sep 4, 1956, Mexia, TX; daughter of Jimmie Vernon and Lois Bertha Hobbs; married Derrell Caldwell; children: Mallore & Pilar Elise. **Educ:** Univ Tex, Austin, BA, jour, 1977; Univ Tex Sch Law, JD, 1981. **Career:** City Austin, asst city atty, 1981-82; Travis County, Dist Atty's Off, asst dist atty, 1982-87; Courty Court at Law #7, Judge, 1987-2002; 403rd Dist Ct, Travis County, Texas, dist judge, 2002-. **Orgs:** State Bar Tex, 1981-; Travis County Bar Asn; Autsin Black Lawyers Asn; Austin Chap Links Inc; Delta Sigma Theta Sorority Inc; Jack & Jill Am Inc; bd, Laguna Gloria Art Mus; bd, Leadership Tex Alumnae Asn, 1990-94; bd, Umlauf Sculpture Garden Mus, 1992-94; active bd mem, Austin Area Urban League; vice-president of membership, Austin Chapter of Links, Inc. **Honors/Awds:** Virgil C Lott Alumni Award, Thurgood Marshall Legal Soc, 1993. **Special Achievements:** First African-American to win a contested county-wide race in Travis County. **Home Addr:** 7300 Covered Bridge Dr, Austin, TX 78736-3345, **Home Phone:** (512)358-4107. **Business Addr:** District Judge, State of Texas District Court, Travis County Courthouse, Austin, TX 78701, **Business Phone:** (512)854-9808.

**KENNEDY, CALLAS FAYE**
Educator. **Personal:** Born Oct 13, 1954, Lisman, AL. **Educ:** Sacramento City Col, AA, 1975; Calif State Univ, Sacramento, BA, 1978. **Career:** Sacramento Co Head Start Progs, teacher/dir, 1978-83; C's Home Soc Calif, prog specialist, 1983-84; Pac Oaks Col, instr, 1984; Yuba Comm Col, instr, 1985; Child-Human Develop specialist; Ctr CP, Health educr, currently. **Orgs:** Chairperson, Nat Black Child Develop Inst, 1978-; chairperson, vice chair, Sacramento Area Black Caucus Inc, 1983-85; treas, Calif Child Passenger Safety Asn, 1983-; consult/speaker Child Develop Inc, 1985; Marriage & Family Counsr Inc, 1986; conf speaker Sacramento Valley Asn Educ Young C; Sacramento Black Women's Network & Sacramento Co C; Co-chair, Coalition Sacramento Women's Orgn; founding mem, Cong African Peoples; Black Group; SisterFriends; chair, Coalition Sacramento Womens Orgn. **Home Addr:** , Sacramento, CA 95822. **Business Addr:** Health Educator, Center for Collaborative Planning, 1401 21st St Suite 360, Sacramento, CA 95811, **Business Phone:** (916)498-6960.

**KENNEDY, CORTEZ C.**
Football player. **Personal:** Born Aug 23, 1968, Osceola, AR; son of Ruby; children: Courtney. **Educ:** Northwest Miss Community Col; Univ Miami, BA, criminal justice. **Career:** Football player (retired); Seattle Sea hawks, defensive tackle & right defensive tackle, 1990-2000. **Honors/Awds:** First-team All-America choice, Sporting News, 1989; Pro Bowl, 1991-98; Marcus Nalley Trophy, 1992; Defensive Lineman of the Year, NFL Players Asn, 1992; Defensive Player of the Year, Nat Football League, 1992; Defensive Player of the Year, Asniated Pres, 1993; Steve Largent Award, 1996; inducted, Seattle Seahawks Ring of Honor, 2006; Hurricanes Ring of Honor; Named the best athlete ever to wear the number 96, 2007; Awarded football scholarship, Univ Miami; Miami Sports Hall of Fame, 2004; Arkansania Sports Hall of Fame; Pro Football Hall of Fame, 2012. **Special Achievements:** Semi-Finalist for the Pro Football Hall of Fame, 2008 & finalist, 2009, 2011. **Home Addr:** 2121 George Halas Dr NW, Canton, OH 44708, **Home Phone:** (330)456-8207.

**KENNEDY, HENRY HAROLD, JR.**
Judge. **Personal:** Born Feb 22, 1948, Columbia, SC; son of Henry H and Rachel Spann; married Altomease Rucker; children: Morgan & Alexandra. **Educ:** Princeton Univ, AB, 1970; Harvard Law Sch, JD, 1973. **Career:** Law firm of Reavis, Pogue, Neal & Rose, 1973; US Atty Off, asst atty, 1973-76; US Dist Ct DC, US magistrate, 1976-79; Super Ct Dist Columbia, assoc judge, 1979-97; Us Dist Ct Dc, fed judge, 1997-2011. **Orgs:** Sigma Pi Phi; Am Bar Found; trustee, Princeton Univ; Am Law IST Barristers; bd dir, Wash Tennis Educ Found; bd dir, Jr Tennis Champions Ctr. **Home Addr:** 1733 Kalmia Rd NW, Washington, DC 20012, **Home Phone:** (202)829-1250. **Business Addr:** Judge, US District Court, 333 Const Ave NW, Washington, DC 20001, **Business Phone:** (202)354-3350.

**KENNEDY, HOWARD E.**
Fashion designer. **Personal:** Born Nov 30, 1941, Fernandina Beach, FL; son of Charles Emmanuel and Cecil D Watson Williams. **Educ:** Gibbs Col, AA, 1960; NY Inst Tech, New York, NY, biol/chem, 1979. **Career:** St Petersburg, Fla, assoc, 1962; Revlon, Bronx NY, apprentice perfumer, 1965-70; Pfizer Consumer Prod, chief perfumer, 1970-87; Royal Essence Ltd, New York, founder, pres, 1987-; H K Enterprises Inc, Union City, NJ, founder, pres, chief executive officer, 1990-. **Orgs:** Pres, Nat Advan Asn Colored People Youth Coun, 1961-62; Soc Cosmetics Chemists; Fragrance Found; Nat Bus Coun; bd dir, trustee, pres, United Methodist Home; pres, Am Soc Perfumers, 1997-98; pres, mem bd trustee, United Methodist Homes Found;

African Sci Inst fel Socs Cosmetic Chemists; Nat Minority Supplier Develop Coun; Am Red Cross; Rotary Club Parsippany Troy Hills; Black Retail Action Group; Black Child Develop Inst; Stanley M Isaacs Neighborhood Ctr; Broward County Schs; Elm St Little League Asn; Policemens Benevolent Asn; Nat Advan Asn Colored People Legal Defense Educ Fund; Riverland Elem Sch; Nassau County Vol Ctr. **Honors/Awds:** Black Achievers Industry, NY Chap Greater YMCA, 1985; Outstanding Entrepreneur of the Year, Nat Black MBA Assn, 1989; Business Achievement Award, Black Retail Action Group Inc, 1990; Ron Brown Award, Nat Black MBA Asn, 1998; Fragrance Found Award; Silver Torch Award, Asn Nat Black MBA; Award of Achievement, African Sci Inst Fellows; Past Presidents Award, Am Socs Perfumers; Academic Achievement, New York Inst Technol; Honorary Alumnus, Eckerd College, 2009; Doctor of Humanities, Eckerd Col, 2009. **Home Addr:** 380 Mountain Rd Apt 2106, Union City, NJ 07087, **Home Phone:** (201)865-5591. **Business Addr:** President & Chief Executive Officer, Founder, HK Enterprises Inc, 79 N Franklin Turnpike, Ramsey, NJ 07446, **Business Phone:** (201)995-1221.

### KENNEDY, INGA D.
Business owner, executive. **Educ:** Spelman Col, BA; GA inst technol, MA. **Career:** Planners Environ Qual Inc, pres & owner, 1992-. **Orgs:** Clayton County develop Authority; chair, Fulton Community Zoning Bd; pres, Old Nat Merchants Asn; bd dir, Atlanta Chap WTS; Am Planners Asn; COMTO; Water Envi Fed; S Fulton Chamber Com; Hisp Chamber Com; bd mem, Greater Atlanta Econ Alliance Inc; Conf Minority Transp Officials; Hisp Chamber Com; Women's Transp Sem. **Special Achievements:** First female Chair of the Fulton County Community Zoning Board. **Business Addr:** President, Owner, Planners for Environmental Quality Inc, 4405 Mall Blvd Suite 500, Union City, GA 30291-2068, **Business Phone:** (770)306-0100.

### KENNEDY, JAMES E.
Educator. **Personal:** Born Sep 30, 1933, Jackson, MS; son of Tim and Esther Shelwood; married Karen; children: Jia Lynette & Jason Edward. **Educ:** Ala State Univ, BS, 1954; Ind Univ, MAT, 1964. **Career:** Mobile Co Pub Sch, instr, 1958-67; admin, 1967-68; Univ S Ala, from instr to prof emer art & art hist, 1968-97. **Orgs:** Col Art Asn; Nat Conf Artist; Kappa Alpha Psi; Adv Eta Nu Chap Univ S Ala; Cult black & White mobile; bd mem, Mobile Mus Art; dir, cur Am Ethnic Art Slide Libr. **Honors/Awds:** Recipient of 19 awards. **Special Achievements:** Exhibitor in innumerable shows. **Home Addr:** 5408 Gaillard Dr, Mobile, AL 36608-2532, **Home Phone:** (251)343-1076. **Business Addr:** Professor Emeritus, University of South Alabama, 307 N Univ Blvd Suite 2100, Mobile, AL 36688-0002, **Business Phone:** (334)460-6101.

### KENNEDY, REV. JAMES E.
Manager, clergy. **Personal:** Born Jun 21, 1938, Weir, MS; son of Ethel (deceased) and Girtha (deceased); married Thelma Brown; children: Sandra, Sheri & Stephon. **Educ:** John Wesley Col, Owosso, Mich, BA, 1976; Southern Sem, Louisville, Ky. **Career:** Manager (retired), clergy; Gen Motors Corp, Flint, Mich, supvr, 1956-87; Baptist State Conv, Mich, family ministry consult; Mt Carmel Baptist Church, Flint, Mich, pastor, 1981-. **Orgs:** Bd dir, Genesee Baptist Asn; Genesee Baptist Asn; Sunday Sch; bd chmn, Genesee County Comn Substance Abuse; adv coun, Gulf Coast Community Serv Asn; Nat chmn, Pro-Minority Action Coalition; bd, Urban League Flint; bd, Urban Co Boy Scouts Am; chaplain, Flint Police & Fire Dept; pres, Interfaith Prev Group; Big Bro, Big Sisters. **Honors/Awds:** Frederick Douglas Award, Nat Asn Bus & Prof Women, 1989. **Home Addr:** 6530 Wreckenridge Rd, Flint, MI 48532, **Home Phone:** (810)230-7515. **Business Addr:** Pastor, Mount Carmel Baptist Church, 1610 W Pierson Rd, Flint, MI 48507, **Business Phone:** (810)785-4421.

### KENNEDY, DR. JOYCE S.
Educator. **Personal:** Born Jun 15, 1943, St. Louis, MO. **Educ:** Harris Teachers Col, BA, 1965; St Louis Univ, MEd, 1968; Mich State Univ, PhD, 1975. **Career:** Carver Elem Sch, teacher, 1966-68; St Louis Job Corps Ctr Women, counr, 1968-69; Forest Pk Jr Col, counr, 1969-71; Meramec Jr Col, counr, 1971-74; Mich State Univ, Nat Ment Health Inst, urban coun fel, 1972-74; Govs State Univ, Col Arts & Sci, occup educ coordr & univ prof commun, 1975-, distinguished prof, 1977, Div Lib Arts, chair, 1999-2001. **Orgs:** Keynote speaker, Roseland Community Sch Grad, 1978; facilitator, Career Awareness Workshop, 1978; speaker, Harvey Pub Libr, 1978; Am Personnel & Guid Asn; Ill Asn Non-White Concerns; Ill Guid & Personnel Asn. **Home Addr:** 500 Pk Ave Apt 2, Calumet City, IL 60409-5069. **Business Addr:** University Professor of Communication, Governors State University College of Arts & Sciences, F Bldg 1 Univ Pkwy, University Park, IL 60484-0975, **Business Phone:** (708)534-4085.

### KENNEDY, DR. KAREL RALPH
Educator, health services administrator. **Personal:** Born May 6, 1946, Greeleyville, SC; son of Ben and Susie. **Educ:** Howard Univ, BS, 1967, MD, 1971. **Career:** Greater Harlem Nursing Home, med dir; Mt Sinai Sch Med, asst clin prof; Karel Kennedy Med Ctr, currently. **Home Addr:** 4749 Hwy 17, Murrells Inlet, SC 29576. **Business Addr:** Physician, Karel Kennedy Medical Center, 137 Cedar Dr, St. Stephen, SC 29479, **Business Phone:** (843)567-6237.

### KENNEDY, LINCOLN (TAMERLANE FIZEL KENNEDY, JR.)
Football player, broadcaster, insurance executive. **Personal:** Born Feb 12, 1971, York, PA; son of Tamerlane F Sr and Carson Hope Brown; married Patricia; children: Zachary, Taylor, Thom, Tavon & Tye. **Educ:** Univ Wash, BA, commun & media studies, 1993. **Career:** Football player (retired), analyst, broadcaster; Atlanta Falcons, tackle, 1993-95; Oakland Raiders, offensive tackle, 1996-2003; NFLPA, team rep, 1998-2003; NFL Total Access, NFL Network, studio anal, 2004-05; Fox Sports Radio, broadcaster, 2006-; Premier Radio Networks, 2006-; Arena Football League, Tampa Bay Storm, 2007; Farmers Ins & Financial Serv, agency owner/operater, 2009-2013; Compass Media, broadcaster, 2013-. Film: The Marine, 2006; Super Bowl XXXVII, 2003; NFL Total Access, 2003. TV Series: "Two and a Half Men", 2005. **Orgs:** Am Red Cross; Reading Fundamental; AFT; SAG. Pres, NFL-RPA; Exec bd & vpres mkt, Boys & Girls Club E Valley. **Home Addr:** 3555 E Jasmine Clr, Mesa, AZ 85213. **Business Addr:** Owner, Chief Executive Officer, Kennedy & Associates Insurance Agency, 6677 W Thunderbird Rd Suite K-180, Glendale, AZ 85306, **Business Phone:** (480)707-7019.

### KENNEDY, NATHELYNE ARCHIE
Engineer, chief executive officer. **Personal:** Born Jun 1, 1938, Richards, TX; daughter of Nathaniel L Archie and Ernestine Linton Archie; married James D; children: Tracey A & David J. **Educ:** Prairie View A&M Univ, BS, archit engineering, 1959. **Career:** Alfred Benesch & Co, engr, 1960-72; Bernard Johnson Inc, engr, 1978-81; Nathelyne A Kennedy & Assocs, pres & chief exec officer, engr, 1981-. **Orgs:** Am Soc Civil Engrs; Nat Soc Prof Engrs; Tex Soc Prof Engrs; Am Coun Engineering Cos; bd trustee, Prairie View A&M Found; Women Transp Serv. **Home Addr:** 318 Teal Lane, Sugar Land, TX 77478, **Home Phone:** (281)242-2399. **Business Addr:** President, Chief Executive Officer, Nathelyne A Kennedy & Associates, LP, Regency Sq Twr 6200 Savoy Dr Suite 1250, Houston, TX 77036, **Business Phone:** (713)988-0145.

### KENNEDY, RANDALL L.
Educator, writer. **Personal:** Born Sep 10, 1954, Columbia, SC; son of Henry and Rachel; married Yvedt Matory; children: William Henry, Rachel & Thaddeus. **Educ:** Princeton Univ, BA, 1977; Oxford Univ, Balliol Col, grad studies, hist, 1979; Yale Law Sch, JD, 1982. **Career:** US Ct Appeals, Skelly Wright, law clerk, 1982-83; US Supreme Ct, Thurgood Marshall, law clerk, 1983-84; Harvard Univ, asst prof law, 1984-85, assoc prof, 1985-89, prof, 1989-, Michael R Klein prof law, 2005-; Auth: Race, Crim & Law, 1997; Nigger: Strange Career a Troublesome Word, 2002; Interracial Intimacies: Sex, Marriage, Identity & Adoption, 2003. **Orgs:** Wash DC Bar, 1983; Am Law Inst; Am Acad Arts & Sci; Am Philos Asn; trustee, Princeton Univ. **Business Addr:** Michael R Klein Professor of Law, Harvard University, Areeda 228, Cambridge, MA 02138, **Business Phone:** (617)495-0907.

### KENNEDY, RAY C.
President (organization), chief executive officer. **Educ:** La State Univ, grad sch banking; Univ NC; Univ Md Eastern Shore, BS; NC Cent Univ, MBA. **Career:** Am Product Distribr, founder, 1992, chief exec officer & pres, currently. **Orgs:** Bd dir, Carolinas Inc. **Business Addr:** Chief Executive Officer, President, American Product Distributors Inc, 8350 Arrowridge Blvd, Charlotte, NC 28273, **Business Phone:** (704)522-9411.

### KENNEDY, SANDRA DENISE
State government official, business owner, commissioner. **Personal:** Born Dec 25, 1957, Oklahoma City, OK; daughter of Leland W and Doll Baby Alford; children: Mahogany, Amber & Seth. **Educ:** Phoenix Col, attended 1975; Maricopa Community Col Dist, attended 1986; Ariz State Univ, acct & bus admin, 1986. **Career:** State Ariz, House Reps, rep, 1986-92, Dist 23, sen, 1992-98; Kennedy & Assocs, consult, 1984-; Ariz Legis, ariz state rep & sen, 1987-99; Kennedy Restaurants LLC, owner; Ariz Corp Comn, comnr, 2009-13; Sam s Hospitality Group, partner, 2012-. **Orgs:** Off aide, Nat Youth Corps, 1974-75; tutor, Valle del Sol City Phoenixper, Black Theatre Troupe, 1981; Nat Asn Exec Women, 1983-; vol, Valley Christian Ctr, 1983-84; bd mem, Ariz Cactus Pine Girls Scout Coun, 1987-; ex-officio mem, Phoenix Community Alliance, 1987; Phoenix Union High Sch Bd; City Phoenix, Surface Transp Adv Comt; Ariz Employ Training Coun; Nat Black Conf State Legislators; bd mem, Community Excellence Proj; Nat Asn Female Execs; Nat Conf State Legislators. **Home Addr:** 2333 E Wier Ave, Phoenix, AZ 85040. **Business Addr:** Commissioner, Arizona Corporation Commission, Commissioners Wing, Phoenix, AZ 85007, **Business Phone:** (602)542-3625.

### KENNEDY, TAMERLANE FIZEL, JR. See KENNEDY, LINCOLN.

### KENNEDY, TERESA KAY-ABA
President (organization), founder (originator). **Educ:** Wellesley Col, BA, sociol & studio art; Harvard Univ, MBA; PhD, world relig. **Career:** MTV Networks, media exec; Ta Life Inc, founder; Inst Integrative Nutrit, NY; Power Living Enterprises Inc, founder & pres, currently. **Orgs:** Bd dir, Yoga Alliance; nat spokesperson, Am Heart Asn. **Special Achievements:** Book: 40 Days to Power Living: Think, Eat & Live on Purpose, 2007. **Business Addr:** Founder, President, Power Living Enterprises Inc, 116 W 23rd St Suite 500, New York, NY 10011, **Business Phone:** (212)901-6913.

### KENNEDY, DR. THEODORE REGINALD
Educator. **Personal:** Born Jan 4, 1936, Winter Haven, FL. **Educ:** Univ Wash, Seattle, BA, 1970; Princeton Univ, NJ, MA, 1972, PhD, 1974. **Career:** Boeing Co Seattle, 1961-69; State Univ NY, Stony Brook, asst prof, anthrop, 1974-80, assoc prof, antrhop, 1980-. **Orgs:** Nat Asn Advan Colored People, 1967; Asn Am Anthropologists, 1970-; Nat Hist Soc, 1974-; Consult, Howard Univ Press, 1980; adv group, Nat Endowment Humanities, 1980. **Special Achievements:** Recipient numerous fellowships & grants Afro-Am, Study Prof Univ Washington; Princeton Univ; Univ Pa; Ford Found; HEW; Research Found of NY, 1969-75; numerous research experiences Seattle New York City Philadelphia NJ Spain So US W & E Coasts US Vigin Islands; "Relations in a So Comm "Oxford Press 1979; pub "Black Argot assoc languistic analysis of black life style through verbal & non-Verbal communication" oxford u press; dissertation "you gotta deal With It the relationship in the black domestic unit". **Home Addr:** 22 Brookhaven Blvd, Port Jefferson Station, NY 11776-3006, **Home Phone:** (631)331-4588. **Business Addr:** Assistant Professor, State University of New York, Circle Rd Social Behav Sci Bldg 5th Fl, Stony Brook, NY 11794, **Business Phone:** (631)632-7620.

### KENNEDY-OVERTON, JAYNE
Actor, fashion model, television show host. **Personal:** Born Oct 27, 1951, Washington, DC; married Bill Overton; children: Savannah Re, Kopper Joi & Zaire Ollyea; married Leon Issac Kennedy. **Career:** Show: "Speak Up, America", host, 1980; "Greatest Sports Legends", host, 1983; Happy 100th Birthday, Hollywood, host, 1987; Jackie Robinson: An American Journey, narrator, 1988; Films: Lady Sings the Blues, 1972; Group Marriage, 1973; Let's Do It Again, 1975; Big Time, 1977; Death Force, assoc producer, 1978; Body and Soul, 1981; Night Trap, 1993; TV Series: "Shaft", 1973; "Kojak", 1974; "The NFL Today", 1975; "That's My Mama", 1975; "The Rockford Files", 1976; "Police Story", 1977; "Trapper John, M.D.", 1979; "CHiPs", 1980-81; "The Love Boat", 1981-83; "Diff'rent Strokes", 1983; "Benson", 1984-86; "227", 1986; "Throb", 1988; Coca Cola, rep. **Orgs:** Great Am Talk Festival, 1982; pub serv, Nat Toll Free Numberfinding lost c; Health Hotline Nat Coun Negro Women; Black Women Portrait Dignity Black Hist Month, host; summer prog C Commun Bridge. **Honors/Awds:** Miss Ohio, 1970; Emmy Award, Image Award, Nat Asn Advan Colored People, 1982; Rose Bowl Parade; Belding Award, 1985. **Special Achievements:** First female host of CBS NFL.

### KENNEY, JAMES A.
Executive. **Career:** Fleet Boston Financial Corp, dir diversity recruiting. **Business Addr:** Director Diversity Recruiting, Fleet Boston Financial Corp, 100 Federal St Suite 10034F, Boston, MA 21100, **Business Phone:** (617)434-2200.

### KENNEY, WALTER T., SR.
Mayor, vice president (organization), government official. **Personal:** Born Dec 3, 1930, Richmond, VA; son of Jacob and Lois Virginia Moore; married Maime Mallory; children: Wilma Battle, Walter T & Marvette Denise. **Educ:** Old Dom Col; Fed City Col; WVa Univ. **Career:** US Postal Serv, clerk, 1954-85, postal worker, Nat Postal Union, vpres; City Richmond, VA, city coun mem, 1977-94, mayor, 1990-94, councilman, 2003-04. **Orgs:** Nat vpres, Am Postal Workers, AFL-CIO, 1970-80; life mem, Nat Am Advan Colored People; Big Bros Richmond. **Honors/Awds:** Outstanding Leadership, East view Civic League, 1970; Certificate of Appreciation, Richmond Crusade Voters, 1976; Outstanding Appreciation of Service, Black Awareness Asn, 1979. **Home Addr:** 1614 Bryan St, Richmond, VA 23223-3810, **Home Phone:** (804)644-9586.

### KENNISON, EDDIE JOSEPH, III
Football player, executive. **Personal:** Born Jan 20, 1973, Lake Charles, LA; married Shimika; children: Karrington & Jisiah. **Educ:** La State Univ, BS, phys ther, 1996. **Career:** Football player (retired); St Louis Rams, punt returner, wide receiver, 1996-98, wide receiver, 2008; New Orleans Saints, wide receiver, 1999; Chicago Bears, wide receiver, 2000; Denver Broncos, wide receiver, 2001; Kans City Chiefs, wide receiver, 2001-07; Barrel 87, owner, 2014-. **Orgs:** Founder, Quick Start; Eddie Kennison Found, 2003. **Honors/Awds:** Rams Rookie of the Year Award, 1995; St Louis Rams, Carroll Rosenbloom Memorial Award, 1996. **Special Achievements:** National Football League Draft, First round Pick, 18, 1996.

### KENNON, ROZMOND H., SR.
Physician, president (organization). **Personal:** Born Dec 12, 1935, Birmingham, AL; married Gloria Oliver; children: Shawn & Rozmond Jr. **Educ:** Talladega Col, BA, 1956; Univ Colo, cert, 1957. **Career:** St John's Hosp St Paul, asst chief phys therapist, 1957-58; Creighton Memorial St Joseph's Hosp Omaha, asst chief phys therapist, 1958-61; Sis Kenny Inst, asst chief & phys therapist, 1962, chief physther, 1962-64; Mt Sinai Hosp Minn, consult phys ther, 1963-70; Rozmond H Kennon RPT Inc, 1964; Physician's Phys Ther Serv, self-employed; Ebenezer Nurse Home Minn, chief phys therapist; Texa-tonka Nurse Home, consult physcther; Cedar Pines Nurse Home; Villa Maria Nurse Home; All Minn Midway Hosp, St. Paul; Daniel Kennon Jr & Verna Herron Kennon Found, pres, currently. **Orgs:** Am Phys Ther Asn; Am Reg Phys Therapist; Soc-econ Com; chmn, Prof Pract Com; bd mem & secy, Minn Chap Am Physchol Ther Asn; patner, Phys Therpartner RKR Asn; Minn Long-Term Care Physchol Ther Int & Grp Int Cong Physchol Ther; mem & bd dir, Southdale YMCA; Edina Human Rights; Southside Med Ctr; bd trustee, Talladega Col. **Special Achievements:** Author various articles on Phyical Therpay. **Home Addr:** 6108 Waterside Ct, Hoover, AL 35244-4158, **Home Phone:** (205)424-1588. **Business Addr:** President, Daniel Kennon Jr & Verna Herron Kennon Foundation, 420 10th Ct W, Birmingham, AL 35204-3027.

### KENNY, JAMES A.
Association executive. **Career:** FleetBoston Financial, dir exec search & diversity recruiting, currently. **Business Addr:** Director, Executing Search & Diversity Recruiting, FleetBoston Financial Corp, 100 Federal St, Boston, MA 02110, **Business Phone:** (617)434-2200.

### KENOLY, BINGO (RON KENOLY, JR.)
Singer, songwriter. **Personal:** Born Jan 18, 1977, Oakland, CA; son of Ronald and Tavita Kenoly; children: Deasia, Omari, Dezirae & Tre. **Career:** Next Generation Ministry Rec, owner & rec artist, 1999-; Who's There?God's There, Right hand Rec, 1998; All The Way, Next Generation Ministry Rec, 1999; No Distance, Next Generation Ministry Rec, 2002; No More Secrets; HOG Life. **Special Achievements:** Grand Avenue, movie with Robert Redford, HBO, 1995. **Business Addr:** Recording Artist, Owner, Next Generation Ministry Records, 4904 Keeneland Cir, Orlando, FL 32819, **Business Phone:** (407)295-4451.

### KENOLY, RON
Gospel singer. **Personal:** Born Dec 6, 1944, Coffeyville, KS; son of Edith; married Tavita; children: Ron Jr, Samuel & Tony. **Educ:** Alameda Col, attended 1982; Friends Int, BS, 1983, PhD, 1997; Faith Bible Col, MDiv, 1985. **Career:** Gospel singer; Alameda Col, instr, 1978-92; Jublee Christian Ctr, worship leader, 1985-87, minister music, 1987-99; Integrity Music, recording artist, 1991-; Faith World, minister music, 1999-; Praise Acad, founder, 1999-; Mellow Fellows, singer; Next Generation Ministry Rec, owner; Ron Kenoly Ministries Inc, founder, currently; Album: Jesus is Alive, 1991; Lift Him Up with Ron Kenoly, 1992; God Is Able, 1994; Sing Out with One Voice, 1995; Welcome Home, 1996; Majesty, 1998; We Offer Praises, 1999; Dwell

in the House, 2001; Ancient of Days. **Orgs:** RKM Worship Team. **Honors/Awds:** Doctorate in ministry, Sacred Music, 1966; Angel Awards, Lift Him Up, 1993; God Is Able, 1995; Dove Award, Gospel Music Asn, 1997; Psalmist of the Century, Missionary Charismatic Int Church Bogota, 2000; Doctorate of Ministry, Friends Int Christian Univ. **Special Achievements:** Auth: Charisma, Ministries Today. **Business Addr:** Owner, Ron Kenoly Ministries Inc, PO Box 2200, Windermere, FL 34786, **Business Phone:** (407)352-7800.

### KENOLY, SAMUEL

Singer, songwriter. **Personal:** Born Mar 14, 1979, Oakland, CA; son of Ronald and Tavita; married Vanessa Katzenberger. **Career:** NGMR LLC, recording artist, 1999-; Quick start Music Seminars, founder & chief exec officer, 2001-. Albums: Welcome Home, 1996; Who's There? God's There, 1998; All The Way, 1999; We Offer Praises, 1999; No Distance, 2002; HOG Life, 2005; Singles: "Eres Mi Gozo", 2000; "Forever You & I", 2000. **Honors/Awds:** Dove Award, 1996. **Business Addr:** Singer, c/o Capital Entertainment, 217 Seaton Pl NE, Washington, DC 20002, **Business Phone:** (202)636-7028.

### KENT, DEBORAH STEWART

Manager, automotive executive. **Personal:** Born Mar 10, 1953, St. Louis, MO; daughter of Leodas and Earline; children: Jessica, Jordon & Wendell L Coleman Jr. **Educ:** Southern Ill Univ, BA, psychol, 1975; Wash Univ, MA, psychol, 1977; Baker Col, MBA, int bus. **Career:** Gen Motors, staff, 1977-87; Ford Motor Co, area mgr, 1987-92, asst plant mgr, 1992-94, Chicago Assembly Plant, plant mgr, 1994-96, qual dir, vehicle opers, 1996-, mfg mgr, Wixom, MI, Dearborn Assembly Plant, mgr, OH Assembly Plant, head, 1996-. **Orgs:** Exec bd, Boy Scouts, 1992-94; bd dir, Gov's State Univ, 1992-94; exec dir, Fla Trls Asn. **Honors/Awds:** Outstanding Woman in the Automotive Industry, 1995. **Special Achievements:** First woman to head a vehicle assembly plant at the Ford Motor Company; First African-American woman to run an assembly operation for an auto makers plant manager of Avon Lake (Ohio) Assembly Plant. **Business Addr:** Head of Assembly Plant, Ford Motor Co, 650 Miller Rd, Avon Lake, OH 44012-2398, **Business Phone:** (440)933-1200.

### KENT, HERB

Radio broadcaster. **Personal:** Born Jan 1, 1929. **Career:** Radio host, 1949-; WVON, host; WJJD, host; WVAZ-FM 102.7, host; Chicago State Univ, fac radio broadcasting, lectr, currently, WCSU Radio, gen mgr, currently. **Honors/Awds:** Inducted into the Radio Hall of Fame in 1995. **Special Achievements:** Became the first black deejay inducted into the Radio Hall of Fame in 1995; Author: The Cool Gent: The Nine Lives of Radio Legend Herb Kent. **Business Addr:** Lecturer, General Manager, Chicago State University, 9501 S King Dr, Chicago, IL 60628-1598, **Business Phone:** (773)995-2832.

### KENT, MELVIN FLOYD

Manager, administrator. **Personal:** Born Oct 22, 1953, Panama City, FL; son of Floyd M Jr and Viletta McIntyre; married Donna Dunklin; children: Preston J, Shante D & Shanice L. **Educ:** Gulf Coast Community Col, AA, social serv, 1974; Univ S Fla, BA, sociol, BS, criminal justice, 1977. **Career:** Domestic Laundry & Cleaners, crew supvr, 1970-74; Int Paper Co, shopkeeper, 1975; Sears Roebuck & Co, credit interviewer, 1978; Bay County Juv Detention Ctr, detention supvr, 1978-94; Fla Dept HRS, Foster Care Unit, c& families counr, 1994-99; Fla Dept C & Families, family serv specialist, 1999-2000, oper prog adminr, ESS, 2000-; State Fla, pub assistance fraud investr, 2006-. **Orgs:** Vpres, secy, Xi Sigma Lambda Sphinx Club, 1985; secy, Xi Sigma Lambda Chap Alpha Phi Alpha, 1986. **Home Addr:** 909 Bay Ave, Panama City, FL 32401-4248, **Home Phone:** (850)257-5368.

### KENYATTA, MARY

Educator. **Personal:** Born Aug 14, 1944, Greenville, SC; children: Malcolm Joseph & Asante Luana. **Educ:** Temple Univ, Philadelphia, PA, BA, 1980; Harvard Grad Sch Educ, Cambridge, MA, EdM, 1986. **Career:** United Presby Church, USA, Wayne, co-dir, WIL Proj, 1971-75; Williams Col, Williamstown, assoc dean, 1981-88; NJ Dept Higher Educ, Trenton, exec asst vice chancellor, 1988-89; Millard Fillmore Col, Buffalo, assoc dean, 1989. **Orgs:** Vpres, Soc Organized Against Racism, 1985-88; chmn, nominations comt, Asn Continuing Higher Educ, 1990. **Home Addr:** 140 Linwood Ave C11, Buffalo, NY 14209, **Home Phone:** (716)883-3038. **Business Addr:** NY.

### KERN-FOXWORTH, DR. MARILYN L.

Educator. **Personal:** Born Mar 4, 1954, Kosciusko, MS; daughter of Manella LouBertha Dickens-Kern (deceased) and Jimmie Kern (deceased); married Gregory Lamar; children: Lamar II. **Educ:** Jackson State Univ, BS, speech, 1974; Fla State Univ, MS, mass commun, 1976; Univ Wis-Madison, PhD, mass commun, 1980; Harvard Univ, exec leadership prog, leadership, diversity, corp placement, 1998. **Career:** Fla State Univ, comm specialist, 1974-76; City Tallahassee, coordinato, 1975-76; Gen Tel, personnel rep, 1976-78; WWQM Radio, Madison, mgr, 1978-79; Mid-W Observer, columnist, 1979-80; Univ Tenn, asst prof, 1980-87; Aloca prof, pr fel, 1981; Tex A&M Univ, assoc prof, prof, 1987-2000; Poynter Inst fel, 1988; Am Press Inst fel, 1988; Agnes Harris AAUW Postdoctoral fel, 1991-92; Fla A&M Univ, Dept Jour, Media & Graphic Arts, garth c reeves endowed chair, 1994, fac, 1994, prof; Journalism & Educ Mass Commun, pres, 1999-2000; Kern-Foxworth Int LLC, pres, chief exec officer, 2003-; Michael Davis lectr. **Orgs:** Exec comt, Asn Educ Jour, 1980-; Nat Coun Negro Women, 1980-; Asn Black Communicators, 1980-; Nat Community Asn, 1982-; Int Platform Asn, 1982-; adv, Campus Practitioners, 1982; Pub Rels Soc Am, 1982-; pres, Asn Educ Journalism & Mass Commun; consult, assoc, Nashville Banner, 1983; Mt Calvary Baptist Church, 1983; staff mem, Grad Teaching Sem, 1983-; adv, Pub Rels Stud Soc Am, 1983-; Nat Fed Press Women, 1983-; Nat Asn Media Women, 1983-; Nat Fed Exec Women, 1983-; adv comt, YWCA, 1983-; Black Media Asn; newsletter ed, Black Fac & Staff Asn; Jackson State Univ Nat Alumni Asn; minister educ, Alpha Kappa Alpha Sorority; Nat Asn Advan Colored People. **Honors/Awds:** Readers Digest Travel Grant, 1979; First Prize, Alan Bussel Res Competition, 1980; Leadership Award, Asn Black Community, 1980; Kizzy Award, Black Women Hall of Fame Found, 1981; Amon Carter Evans Award Scholar, 1983; Women of Achievement, Univ Tenn, 1983; Unity Awards in Media, Lincoln Univ, 1984; Special Award Recognition of Excellence, PRSA Chap, Knoxville, TN, 1985; Pathfinder Award, Pub Rel Inst, 1988; Kreighbaum Under-40 Award, AEJMC. **Special Achievements:** One of 12 outstanding African-American women in America; First African-American female president of the Association for Education in Journalism and Mass Communications; First & only black in the nation to receive a PhD in Mass communications with a concentration in advertising & public relations; National Adviser of the Year, Pub Rels Stud Soc Am; Author of numerous publications; Author: Aunt Jemima, Uncle Ben and Rastus: Blacks in Advertising, Yesterday, Today and Tomorrow; Texas State Senate passed a proclamation in her honor and Public Relations Quarterly dubbed her "one of the most influential executives in public relations". **Home Addr:** 1514 Seminole Dr, Tallahassee, FL 32301-5736. **Business Addr:** President, Chief Executive Officer, Kern Foxworth International LLC, 1713 Woodwell Rd, Silver Spring, MD 20906, **Business Phone:** (301)460-6004.

### KERNER, MARLON LAVELLE

Football player. **Personal:** Born Mar 18, 1973, Columbus, OH; married Nicole. **Educ:** Ohio State Univ. **Career:** Football player (retired); Buffalo Bills, left corner back, 1995, 1996, defensive back, 1996, 1998.

### KERNISANT, DR. LESLY J.

Gynecologist, obstetrician, president (organization). **Personal:** Born Aug 15, 1949, Port-au-Prince; son of Claire Albert and Rene; married Danielle Duclos; children: Lesly Jr & Natalie. **Educ:** Howard Univ Liberal Arts, BS, 1971, Sch Med, MD, 1975. **Career:** Harlem Hosp, exec chief resident, Obstet & Gynec, 1978-79; Nat Health Serv Corps, physician 1979-81; Interfaith Hosp, clin instr, 1980-; Brookdale Hosp, assoc attend, 1981-; Mid-Brooklyn Health Asn, clin dir, 1981-86; Preferred Health Partners, chmn & chief exec officer; Cent Brooklyn Med Group, Obstet & Gynec partner, 1983-89, chief Obstet & Gynec dept, 1989-2003, vpres, med affairs, 2003-, chief med officer, chief exec officer, br mgr & pres, currently; Simact Inc, founder, chief exec officer, pres & chmn, currently; Jacmel, chmn & doctor. **Orgs:** Exec comt mem, Haitian Biomed Found, 1987, Cent Med Group, 1987; trustee, CBMG Retirement Funds Prog; bd dir, Rep Action Haiti; AMA; Am Bd Obstet & Gynec, Clini Provident Soc; fel Asn Haitian Physicians Abroad. **Home Addr:** 125 Ashland Pl Apt 4D, Brooklyn, NY 11201, **Home Phone:** (347)227-8342. **Business Addr:** President, Chief Executive Officer & Branch Manager, Central Brooklyn Medical Group PC, 71 Carroll St, Brooklyn, NY 11231, **Business Phone:** (718)858-1571.

### KERR, BROOK

Actor. **Personal:** Born Nov 21, 1973, Indianapolis, IN; married Christopher Oneal Warren; children: Chris Warren Jr. **Career:** TV series: "The Wayans Bros.", 1996; "Moesha", 1996; "City Guys", 1998; "Smart Guy", 1998; "Hang Time", 1998; "The Steve Harvey Show", 1998; "Talent", 1998; "Passions", 1999-2007; "Shoe Shine Boys", 2000; "The Brother", 2001; "Special Unit 2", 2001; "Soap Talk", 2003-04; "McBrided: Dogged", 2006; "Cane", 2007; McBride: Dogged, 2007; "CSI: Miami", 2008; True Blood", 2008; Flower Girl, 2009; NCIS: Los Angeles, 2010; "This Magic Moment", 2013. Films: Talent, 1998; Prank, 2000; Shoe Shine Boys, 2000. **Honors/Awds:** Nominee, Soap Opera Digest Award, 2005; Image Award, 2008. **Business Addr:** Actress, c/o William Morris Agency LLC, 151 El Camino Dr, Beverly Hills, CA 90212, **Business Phone:** (310)859-4000.

### KERR, STANLEY MUNGER

Lawyer, judge. **Personal:** Born Sep 30, 1949, Des Moines, IA; son of Richard Dixon and Arlene Munger; married Myrna Hill; children: Mila & Tamara Aldridge. **Educ:** Christian Col SW, 1969; Univ Tex, 1971; Huston-Tillotson Col, BA, 1975; Univ Tex Sch Law, JD, 1977. **Career:** Church Christ, preacher, 1966-71; Austin State Sch, relief supvr ment retarded, 1970-78; Austin Ind Sch Dist, bus driver & maintenance, 1972-78; pvt law pract, 1977-87; Huston-Tillotson Col, govt dept head, 1978-81; City Austin, Tex, sr civil rights investr, 1981-88; Travis County, Tex, Probate Ct, ment health atty; City Austin, Munic Ct Judge, substitute judge. **Orgs:** State Bar Tex, 1977-; Austin Black Lawyers Asn; precinct chair, state & county conv del, Dem Party; sr warden, stewardship chair, St James Episcopal Church; bd mem, Am Fed State, County & Munic Employ Local 1624, 1983-; del, Austin Metrop Ministries, 1978-; partner, Trinity Broadcasting Network. **Home Addr:** 11503 Hornsby St, Austin, TX 78753-2629. **Business Addr:** Lawyer, State Bar of Texas, 12920 James Madison St, Manor, TX 78653-3847.

### KERR, WALTER L.

Executive, manager, lawyer. **Personal:** Born Mar 26, 1928, Cleveland, OH; son of George H Sr; married Ruby Cowan; children: Diane. **Educ:** Kent St Univ, BBA, 1957; Cleveland Marshall Law Sch, JD, 1963. **Career:** Yellow Cab Co, taxicab driver, 1953-55; postal clerk, 1955-57; Internal Revenue Serv Cleveland, agt, 1957-83; atty law, currently. **Orgs:** Admitted Ohio Bar, 1963 Cleveland Bar Asn, 1963, Cuyahoga Co Bar Asn, 1963, Ohio Bar Asn, 1963; mem John Harlan Law Club, 1963; EEO counr Cleveland Dist Internal Revenue Serv, 1973-77; exec bd mem, Chap 37 NatlTreas Emp Union, 1974-83; Asn exec E 147 St Club, 1969-71; trustee, Shiloh Baptist Church, 1968-80; bus mgr, Shiloh Baptist Church Gospel Chor & Shiloh Male Church, 1968-76; Asn exec Shiloh Educ Bd, 1971-72; chmn, SupvAudit Comm Shiloh Credit Union, 1973-86; Asn execMetro Chorus, 1974-89; pres, Cleveland Chap Am Jr Bowling Cong, 1974-78; trustee, Forest City Hosp, 1974-76. **Honors/Awds:** Fed Community Service Award, Cleveland Program Exec Bd, 1976; Cleveland Dist Equal Opportunity Program Commendation IRS, 1976; Award Tax Inst Cleveland Public School System. **Home Addr:** 23305 Chagrin Blvd Apt 205, Beachwood, OH 44122-5523, **Home Phone:** (216)591-0773. **Business Addr:** Attorney, Rm 130 4500 Lee Rd, Cleveland, OH 44128-2959, **Business Phone:** (216)587-0785.

### KERRY, LEON G.

Chief executive officer, commissioner. **Personal:** Born Oct 14, 1948, Hampton, VA; married Angela J; children: Lisa & LeAnne. **Educ:** Norfolk State Univ, BS, bus admin, 1972; Am Inst Banking, AA, banking. **Career:** Executive (retired); Sovran Bank, Norfolk, VA, asst vpres, banking, 1976-84; Atlantic Nat Bank, Norfolk, VA, asst vpres, 1984-86; Syst Mgt Am, Norfolk, VA, asst vpres, 1986-88; Cent Intercollegiate Athletic Asn, Hampton, va, bus mgr, 1988-90, comnr & chief exec officer, 1990-2011; Am's oldest black col & univ conf, comnr. **Orgs:** NCAA Div II Comnrs Asn; NACDA John McLendon Minority Scholar Comt; Hampton Roads Comt 200+ Men; Bus Adv Coun, Nat Repub Cong Comt; Kappa Alpha Psi Fraternity; bus adv coun, Nat Republican Cong Comt; bd dir, Cent Intercollegiate Athletic Asn. **Home Addr:** , VA.

### KERSEE, JACQUELINE JOYNER. See JOYNER-KERSEE, JACKIE.

### KERSEY, ELIZABETH T.

Vice president (organization), secretary (organization), administrator. **Personal:** Born Oct 30, 1956, Wadesboro, NC; married Marion W; children: Mario, Kinyotta J & Fateana. **Educ:** Anson Tech Col, AAS, 1977. **Career:** Assistant, vice president (retired); Anson Tech Col, asst, assoc vpres, secy, dean instr, 1977; S Piedmont Community Col, Asst, VP Student Learning. **Orgs:** Prof Secy Intl, 1983-; chairperson, Anson Cty Soc Serv Adolescent Parenting Prog, 1984-; secy, Parent Teacher Org, 1984-; pres, Anson Tech Col Alumni Assoc; bd dir, Anson County. **Home Addr:** 5523 White Store Rd, Polkton, NC 28135-9401. **Business Addr:** Assistant to the Vice President of Student Learning, South Piedmont Community College, 4209 Old Charlotte Hwy, Monroe, NC 28110, **Business Phone:** (704)272-5436.

### KEYES, ALAN LEE

Talk show host, public speaker, writer. **Personal:** Born Aug 7, 1950, New York, NY; son of Allison and Gerthina; married Jocelyn Marcel; children: Francis, Maya & Andrew. **Educ:** Cornell Univ; Harvard Univ, BA, 1972, PhD, 1979. **Career:** US Dept State, foreign serv officer, 1978, consult officer, Bombay, India, 1979-80, desk officer, Zimbabwe, 1980-81, policy planning staff, 1981-83, US rep to UN Econ & Social Coun, 1983-85, asst secy int orgn affairs, Wash, DC, 1985-88; Am Enterprise Inst, resident scholar, 1987-89; US Sen Md, cand, 1988, 1992; Scripps Howard, syndicated columnist, 1991-92; Ala A&M Univ, interim pres, 1991; Republican Party, pres, currently; WCBM radio, Owings Mills, MD, "Am's Wake-Up Call", host; MSNBC, "AlanKeyes Making Sense", host, 2002; Books: Masters Dream: Strength & Betrayal Black Am, 1994; Our Character, Our Future: Reclaiming Am's Moral Destiny, 1996; Leadership Defined: In-Depth Interviews with Am's Top Leadership Experts, 2004; Judicial Tyranny, 2005. **Orgs:** Pres, Citizens Against Govt Waste, 1989-91; founder, Nat Tax payer Action Day, 1990; founder & chair, Declaration Found, 1996-; pres, Ronald Reagan Alumni Asn, 1998-; Cornell Univ Glee Club. **Special Achievements:** Republican candidate for presidential race, 1996; appeared in the 2006 comedy "Borat: Cultural Learnings of America for Make Benefit Glorious Nation of Kazakhstan". **Business Addr:** President, Republican Party, 310 First St SE, Washington, DC 20003, **Business Phone:** (202)863-8600.

### KEYMAH, CRYSTAL T. (CRYSTAL WALKER)

Actor, television producer, writer. **Personal:** Born Oct 13, 1962, Chicago, IL. **Educ:** Fla A&M Univ, BS, theater, 1984; Fla State Univ, theater, 1984; Univ Calif, Los Angeles, CA, screenwriting, 1993; Southern Univ, psychol, 2012. **Career:** Chicago Bd Educ, teacher, 1984-88; Christmas Carol, Goodman Theatre, actor, 1987-89; Call To Action Touring Co, member, 1989; Love Letters, stageplay, 1991; Some of My Best Friends, theatrical tour, writer, 1991-, Five Heartbeats Live, 1994; Quantum Leap, NBC-TV, guest artist, 1992; ROC-Live, HBO-TV, special guest, 1993; In Living Color, Fox-TV, cast member & writer 1990-94; The Commish, ABC-TV, guest star, 1994; John Larroquette Show, NBC-TV, guest star, 1994-95; On Our Own, ABC-TV, cast member, 1995; One Last Time, executive producer/actress & writer, 1995; Circle of Pain, producer & writer 1996; TV Series: "The Show", 1996; "Cosby", 1996-2000; "That's So Raven", 2001-; "Static Shock", 2003; "Wavelength", 2004; "Teen Titans", 2005; "American Dragon", 2005; "Crystal the Monkey", 2006; "Half Baked", 2006; "Hairy Christmas", 2006; "Am Dragon: Jake Long", 2006; Films: Tales from the Hood, 1995; Jackie Brown, 1997; The Gilded Six Bits, 2001; The Creature of the Sunny Side Up Trailer Park, 2004; Majique Movement Dance Theatre, vpres, 1980-84; In Black World, owner, 1991-; K W Properties, partner, 1998-2003; Stage Aurora Theatrical Co, artistic associate, currently; T'Keyah Keyman Inc, owner, 2001-. **Orgs:** Delta Sigma Theta Sorority Inc, 1983-; FAMU Alumni Asn, 1985-; vol, Ill Visually Handicapped Inst, 1986-87; vol, Citizens Comt Juv Ct, 1987-88; Nat Coun Negro Women, 1992-; Rainbow/Push Coalition; Nat Asn Advan Colored People, 1991-; active vol, Inst Black Parenting, 1991-; celebrity partner, My Good Friend, 1993-; Acad Tv Arts & Sci, 1995-12; Nat Asn Bros & Sisters In & Out, 1996; Chicago Urban League, 2002; Am Women Radio & TV, 2004; Greater Los Angeles African Am; Alliance Women Media, 2004-12; dir, dir Guild Am, 2005. **Home Addr:** , North Hollywood, CA 91605. **Business Addr:** Owner, T'Keyah Keyman Inc, 10061 Riverside Dr Suite 714, Toluca Lake, CA 91602, **Business Phone:** (818)569-5456.

### KEYS, ALICIA (ALICIA AUGELLO COOK)

Singer, songwriter, pianist. **Personal:** Born Jan 25, 1981, New York, NY; daughter of Craig Cook and Teresa Augello; married Swizz Beatz; children: Egypt Daoud Ibarr Dean & Genesis Ali Dean. **Educ:** Columbia Univ. **Career:** Albums: Songs in A Minor, 2001; Diary of Alicia Keys, 2004; Unplugged, 2005; As I Am, 2007; The Element of Freedom, 2007; Films: Smokin' Aces, 2006; The Nanny Diaries, 2007; The Secret Life of Bees, 2008; Jem and the Holograms, 2015. Songs: "Fallin'", 2001; "You Don't Know My Name", 2003; "Diary", 2004; "My Boo", 2004; "No One", 2007; "Like You'll Never See Me Again", 2007. TV Appearences: The Cosby Show, 1985; Charmed, 2001; American Dreams, 2003; The Proud Family, 2003; Sesame Street, 2005; The Backyardigans, 2006; Cane, 2007; Elmo's Christmas Countdown, 2007; Dive, Fresh Takes, 2008; Five, 2011; Firelight, 2012. **Orgs:** Hon mem, Alpha Kappa Alpha Sorority Inc, 2004-. **Business Addr:** Recording Artist, J Recs, 745 5th Ave, New York, NY 10151, **Business Phone:** (646)840-5672.

**KEYS, DORIS TURNER. See TURNER, DORIS.**

**KEYS, MADISON**
Athlete, tennis player. **Personal:** Born Feb 17, 1995, Rock Island, IL; daughter of Rick and Christine. **Career:** Professional tennis player, 2009-. **Orgs:** FearlesslyGIRL, ambassador. **Honors/Awds:** Tournament wins: WTA Aegon Classic, 2014, 2016. **Special Achievements:** Youngest player to be ranked in WTA the top ten for singles, 2016. **Business Addr:** WTA, 100 Second Ave S Suite 1100-S, St. Petersburg, FL 33701.

**KEYS, RANDOLPH**
Basketball player. **Personal:** Born Apr 19, 1966, Collins, MS. **Educ:** Univ Southern Miss, MS, 1988. **Career:** Basketball player (retired); Cleveland Cavaliers, 1988-90; Charlotte Hornets, 1990-91; Benetton Treviso, Italy, 1991; Paris Basket Racing, France, 1991-92; Taugres Vitoria, Spain, 1992-93; Quad City Thunder, 1993-95; Los Angeles Lakers, 1995; Milwaukee Bucks, forward, 1995-96; Verona, Italy, 1996-99; Scaligera Basket Verona, 1998; Panionios B.C., Greece, 1999.

**KHADAR, MOHAMED A.**
Engineer. **Personal:** Born Dec 17, 1946, Jimmi Bagbo; son of Haja Memunah and Achaj Yusuf; married Barbara R; children: Rasheeda J, Memunah M, Mounrah, Rajheed & Zahra. **Educ:** Cairo Polytecnical Inst, 1968; N Va County Col, AS, 1979; Univ Md, College Park, BA, bus & int affairs, 1982. **Career:** Columbia Plaza Apt, bldg engr, 1977-80; Holy Cross Hosp, power plant engr, 1980-2006; Metropol Condos Bldg, engr, 1990; Metrop Condominium, gen mgr, engr, 1991-2006; Selectproperties46 LLC, owner, 1995-; Summer Ridge Condominium, gen mgr, 2008-. **Orgs:** Dir & founder, Africa Cult Ctr, 1983. **Home Addr:** 7500 Elioak Terr, Gaithersburg, MD 20879-4504, **Home Phone:** (301)977-0042. **Business Addr:** General Manager, Summer Ridge Condominium, 18407 Guildberry Dr, Gaithersburg, MD 20879-5354, **Business Phone:** (301)926-8802.

**KHALFANI, NYESHA. See BUCHANAN, SHONDA T.**

**KHALFANI, SALIM KING**
Executive director, association executive. **Career:** Va State Conf, coord, interim exec dir, mem state exec comt, nat pres; Nat Asn Adv Colored People, Va, exec dir, pres, currently. **Orgs:** Dir, Nat Asn Advan Colored People; African Am Adv Coun; adv bd mem, Virginians Alternatives Death Penalty. **Business Addr:** Advisory Board Member, Virginians for Alternatives to the Death Penalty, PO Box 4804, Charlottesville, VA 22905, **Business Phone:** (434)960-7779.

**KHALI, SIMBI (SIMBI KALI WILLIAMS)**
Actor, screenwriter. **Personal:** Born Apr 28, 1971, Jackson, MS; married Cress Williams. **Educ:** Calif Inst Arts, BFA, actg. **Career:** TV series: "Martin", 1993-95; "The Sinbad Show", 1994; "Clifford the Big Red Dog"; "She TV", 1994; "3rd Rock from the Sun", 1996-2001; "Masquerade", 2000; "That '80s Show", 2002; "The Bernie Mac Show", 2004; "Sanctuary"; "Special Agent Oso", 2009; "Weeds", 2012; Films: Vampire in Brooklyn, 1995; A Thin Line Between Love and Hate, 1996; Plump Fiction, 1997; We Were Soldiers, 2002; Guild Wars Nightfall, 2006; The Incredible Hulk, 2008; Mississippi Damned, 2009. **Honors/Awds:** Nominee, Screen Actors Guild Award, 1998, 1999. **Business Addr:** Actress, CBS Studio Center, 4024 Redford Ave, Studio City, CA 91604, **Business Phone:** (818)760-5000.

**KHALID, ORA MCQUILLER LEWIS DELGADO. See LEWIS, ORA LEE.**

**KHAN, AKBAR. See ELLIS, ERNEST W.**

**KHAN, CHAKA (YVETTE MARIE STEVENS)**
Singer, music producer. **Personal:** Born Mar 23, 1953, Chicago, IL; daughter of Charles Stevens and Sandra Coleman; married Richard Holland, Aug 14, 1976?, (divorced 1980); children: Damien; married Hassan, Jan 1, 1970, (divorced 1971); children: Milini; married Doug Rasheed, Jan 1, 2001. **Career:** Singer, music producer; Lyfe, musical group mem; The Babysitters, musical group mem; Rufus, musical group mem, 1972-78; solo singer, 1978; Earth Song record label, co-founder, 1996; Raeven Productions, co-founder, 1996; Albums: (with Rufus) Rufus, 1973; Chaka, 1978; Naughty, 1980; What Cha Gonna Do for M, 1981; Echoes of an Era, 1982; Chaka Khan, 1982; I Feel for You, 1984; Destiny, 1986; CK, 1988; Life is a Dance: The Remix Project, 1989; The Woman I Am, 1992; Epiphany: The Best of Chaka Khan, Vol. 1, 1996; Come 2 My House, 1998; Dance Classics of Chaka Khan, 1999; I m Every Woman: The Best of Chaka Khan, 1999; Classi Khan, 2004; The Platinum Collection, 2006; Chaka Khan Greatest Hits Live, 2007; Funk This, 2007; Singles: "I'm Every Woman", 1978; "Life Is a Dance", 1979; "Clouds", 1980; "Papillon (Aka Hot Butterfly)", 1980; "Get Ready, Get Set", 1980; "What Cha' Gonna Do for Me", 1981; "We Can Work It Out", 1981; "Any Old Sunday", 1981; "Got To Be There", 1982; "Tearin It Up", 1983; "I Feel For You", 1984; "This Is My Night", 1985; "Eye To Eye", 1985; "Through the Fire", 1985; "(Krush Groove) Can't Stop the Street", 1985; "Own the Night", 1985; "The Other Side of the World", 1986; "Love of a Lifetime", 1986; "Tight Fit", 1986; "Higher Love", 1986; "Earth to Mickey", 1987; "It's My Party", 1988; "Soul Talkin'", 1988; "I'm Every Woman", 1989; "I Feel For You", 1989; "Baby Me", 1989; "I'll Be Good to You", 1990; "Love You All My Lifetime", 1992; "You Can Make the Story Right", 1992; "I Want", 1992; "Feels Like Heaven", 1993; "Don't Look At Me That Way", 1993; "Watch What You Say", 1995; "Missing You", 1996; "Never Miss The Water", 1996; "Spoon", 1998; "This Crazy Life of Mine", 1998; "I'll Never B Another Fool", 1998; "I Remember U", 1999; "All Good", 2000; "Disrespectful", 2007; "Angel", 2007; "You Belong To Me", 2007; "One For All Time", 2008; Films: The Blues Brothers, 1980; Globe hunters, 2000; TV series: "Hunter", 1987; "Malcolm & Eddie", 1999; "Friday Night with Jonathan Ross", 2008; "The 40 Year Old Virgin", performer, 2005; "Roll Bounce", writer, 2005; "Get Rich or Die Tryin", performer, 2005; "Madea's Family Reunion", 2006; "I Now Pronounce You Chuck & Larry", 2007; "27 Dresses", 2008; "Amongst Friends", 2009; "Vanity Fair: Decades", 2013. Raeven Productions, owner & singer, currently. **Orgs:** Chaka Khan Found; Afro-Arts Theater. **Honors/Awds:** Numerous honors & awards including 10 Grammy Awards, 1975-08; Lena HorneAward, 1998; Lifetime Achievement Award, Black Entertainment TV, 2006; Best R & B Award for "Funk This", 2008. **Special Achievements:** Ranked 17 on VH1's 100 Greatest Women of Rock N Roll; Co-author: Chaka!Through the Fire, 2003. **Home Addr:** 1516 Adeline, Oakland, CA 94607-2810. **Business Addr:** Singer, c/o Chaka Khan Enterprises, 9100 Wilshire Blvd ETwr Suite 515, Beverly Hills, CA 90212, **Business Phone:** (310)247-2400.

**KHAN, DR. RICARDO M.**
Artistic director. **Personal:** Born Nov 4, 2012, Washington, DC; son of Mustapha and Jacqueline; married Nita Khan. **Educ:** Rutgers Univ, Rutgers Col, BA, 1973; Mason Gross Sch Arts, MFA, 1977. **Career:** Crossroads Theatre Co, co founder & dir 1978-1999, creative advisor, 2003-2015, artistic dir emer, currently; Lincoln Ctr Performing Arts New York, NY, resident artist; World Theatre Lab, Johannesburg, London, NYC, founder; Univ Mo Prof Grad Training Prog, Kans City, Mo, vis prof, theatre; Lead Creative Consult to Opening Ceremonies Smithsonian's new Nat Mus African Am Hist & Cult, Wash DC. **Orgs:** Black Leadership Conf, 1993-99; pres Nat Bd, Theatre Commun Group, 1994-98; co-chmn, Nat Endowment Arts, Theater Adv Panel. **Home Addr:** 1125 Maxwell Lane, Hoboken, NJ 07030. **Business Addr:** Self Employed, Ricardo Khan, 1125 Maxwell Lane Suite 1111, Hoboken, NJ 07030.

**KID, CHRISTOPHER. See REID, CHRISTOPHER.**

**KIDD, HERBERT C., JR.**
President (organization), association executive. **Personal:** married Grace Erby; children: 5. **Career:** Asn exec. **Orgs:** Pres, Bessemer Br Nat Asn Advan Colored People; Bristol Steel Corp; New Zion No 2 Choir; vpres, Choir Union; Bessemer Voters League; Bessemer Civic League; Bessemer Progress Asn; Citizens Comt Bessemer; Cand Order Elks. **Home Addr:** 1321 8th Ave N, Bessemer, AL 35020-5632, **Home Phone:** (205)426-0273.

**KIDD, JASON FREDRICK**
Basketball player, basketball coach. **Personal:** Born Mar 23, 1973, San Francisco, CA; son of Steve and Anne; married Joumana Samaha; children: Trey Jason, Miah & Jazelle. **Educ:** Univ Calif, attended 1994. **Career:** Basketball player (retired), coach; Dallas Mavericks, pt guard, 1994-96, 2008-12; Phoenix Suns, pt guard, 1996-2001; NJ Nets, pt guard, 2001-08; New York Knicks, shooting guard, 2012-13; Brooklyn Nets, coach, 2013-14; Milwaukee Buck, head coach, 2014-. **Orgs:** Founder, Jason Kidd Found. **Honors/Awds:** Naismith Prep Player of the Year, 1992; National Freshman of the Year, Us Basketball League, 1993; Pac-10 Player of the Year, 1994; Co-Rookie of the Year, Nat Basketball Asn, 1995; All-Rookie First Team, 1995; Gold Medal, FIBA Championship, 1999, 2003, 2007; Gold Medal, sydney Olympic Games, 2000; NBA All-Star Skills Challenge champion, 2003; USA Basketball's Male Athlete of the Year, 2007; Gold Medal, Beijing Olympic Games, 2008; Nat Basketball Asn, Champion, 2011; Sportsmanship Award, Nat Basketball Asn, 2012-13. **Business Addr:** Head Coach, Milwaukee Bucks, 1001 N 4th St, Milwaukee, WI 53203, **Business Phone:** (414)227-0500.

**KIDD, WARREN LYNN**
Basketball player. **Personal:** Born Sep 9, 1970, Harpersville, AL. **Educ:** Mid Tenn State Univ, attended 1993. **Career:** Basketball player (retired); Philadelphia 76ers, power forward, 1993-94; Valencia, Spain, ctr, 1994-95; Caja San Fenando, Spain, ctr, 1995-96; Olimpia Milano, Italy, ctr, 1996-98, 2002-03; Virtus Roma, Italy, ctr, 1998-2000; Joventut Badalona, Spain, ctr, 2000-01; Canarias, Spain, ctr, 2001-02; Armani Jeans Milano, ctr, 2002-03. **Orgs:** Ohio Valley.

**KIDD, WILLIE MAE. See ROBINSON, DR. KITTY KIDD.**

**KILGORE, TWANNA DEBBIE**
Fashion model. **Personal:** Born Jan 1, 1954. **Career:** Immanuel Prod Inc, exec dir. **Honors/Awds:** Miss Black Washington DC, 1976; Miss Black America, 1976-77. **Special Achievements:** As title holder, traveled US & Europe, contracted with Avon as beauty consultant spokeswoman. **Home Addr:** 4170 Welcome All Terr, College Park, GA 30349.

**KILIMANJARO, JOHN MARSHALL**
Executive, association executive, educator. **Personal:** Born Jun 6, 1930, Little Rock, AR; married Culey Mae Vick. **Educ:** Ark AM&N Col, BA, 1952; Univ Ark, MA, PhD, 1965; NC Agr & Tech State Univ. **Career:** Educator (retired), exec; Carolina Newspapers Inc, publ pres, instr eng, 1955-58, 1962-69; State Univ IA, teaching fel, 1958-59; Ark AM & N Col, prof eng, 1959-61; NC Agr & Tech State Univ, dir drama, teacher theater arts & lang, prof speech & theatre, 1969; Carolina Peacemaker, founder, ed & publ, 1967-; Paul Robeson Theatre, founder, 1970, exec dir, 1970-81. **Orgs:** Exec dir, Richard B Harrison Players, 1970-81; pres, NC Black Pubs Asn; bd, Chome Soc Greensboro Arts Soc, past pres, NADSA ATA; former second vpres, NCP; consult, Civil Rights; Comn Action Progs NC Fund; Guilford Co Young Dem; bd, NC Autism Soc; Omega Psi Phi Fraternity Inc. **Honors/Awds:** O Henry Award, 1973. **Home Addr:** 4619 Charlottesville Rd, Greensboro, NC 27410, **Home Phone:** (336)299-2759. **Business Addr:** Founder, The Carolina Peacemaker, 400 Summit Ave, Greensboro, NC 27405, **Business Phone:** (336)274-6210.

**KILLENS, TERRY DELEON**
Football player. **Personal:** Born Mar 24, 1974, Cincinnati, OH; son of Terry Sr and Eleanor Carolyn; married Rhonda; children: Taylor Denise, Terry, Taryn Danielle & Tori. **Educ:** Pa State Univ. **Career:** Football player (retired); Houston Oilers, linebacker, 1996; Tenn Oilers, 1997, 2000, linebacker, 1998-99; San Francisco49ers, left outside linebacker, 2001-02; Seattle Seahawks, linebacker, 2002. **Home Addr:** 308 Jackson St Apt 401, Oakland, CA 94607-4356.

**KILPATRICK, CAROLYN JEAN CHEEKS**
Government official, politician. **Personal:** Born Jun 25, 1945, Detroit, MI; daughter of Marvel Cheeks Jr and Willa Mae Cheeks; married Bernard Nathaniel; children: Kwame & Ayanna. **Educ:** Ferris State Col, AS, 1970; Western Mich Univ, BS, 1972; Univ Mich, MS, educ, 1977. **Career:** REA Express, secy, 1962-63; Detroit Pub Schs, teacher, 1970-78; Mich House Reps, state rep, 1977-96; US House Reps, Mich 13th & 14th Dist, rep, 1997-2011. **Orgs:** bd trustees New Detroit, 1983; bd trustees Henry Ford Hosp, 1984; resource comt, Your C Our C, 1984; Nat Org 100 Black Women; Nat Order Women Legis; vice chair, Int Affairs Comt Nat Black Caucus State Legislators; chair, Mich Legis Black Caucus, 1983-84; Mich House Appropriations Comt, Dem chairpersonHouse Transp Budget Comt, 1993; co-chair, Cong Urban Caucus 107th Cong; House Appropriations Foreign Opers; USAF Acad Bd; chair, Cong Black Caucus, 2006-; Can-US Inter-Parliamentary Group; Detroit Substance Abuse Adv Coun; Delta Sigma Theta Sorority. **Honors/Awds:** Anthony Wayne Award for Leadership, Wayne State Univ; Distinguished Legislator Award, Univ Mich; Burton Abercrombie Award; appointed by Gov James Blanchard to represent MI in first African Trade Mission, 1984; Woman of the Year Award, Gentlemen Wall St Inc; Dr, Ferris State Univ. **Special Achievements:** First African American woman to serve on the Michigan House Appropriations Committee. **Home Addr:** 7445 LaSalle Blvd, Detroit, MI 48206-2537. **Business Addr:** Chairwoman, Congressional Black Caucus Foundation Inc, 1720 Massachusetts Ave NW, Washington, DC 20036, **Business Phone:** (202)263-2800.

**KILPATRICK, DR. GEORGE ROOSEVELT, JR.**
Physician. **Personal:** Born Dec 9, 1938, New Bern, NC; son of George Sr (deceased) and Priscilla Bryant; married Lillian Farrington; children: Michaux, Gregory & La Tonya. **Educ:** Meharry Med Col, Sch Med, MD, 1968. **Career:** G W Hubbard Hosp, internship, 1968-69; Harlem Hosp Ctr, resident, 1969-70; Fitzsimons Army Med Ctr, resident, 1971-75; NC Textile Occup Lung Dis Panel, physician; pvt pract; pulmonary dis & internal med, currently. **Orgs:** Am Thoracic Soc; Greensboro Med Soc; Nat Med Soc; AMA; Am Bd Internal Med, 1973. **Honors/Awds:** Appreciation Award, Triad Sickle Cell Anemia Found, 1991. **Business Addr:** Physician, 601 E Market St, Greensboro, NC 27401, **Business Phone:** (336)275-7658.

**KILPATRICK, RICHARDO IVAN**
Lawyer. **Personal:** Born Feb 14, 1952, Lakeworth, FL; son of George W and Winifred C; married Carole Camp, Aug 10, 1985. **Educ:** Harvard Univ, BA, econs, 1973; Univ Mich Law Sch, JD, 1982. **Career:** Shermeta, Chimko & Kilpatrick PC, partner, 1987-2000; Kilpatrick & Assoc, PC, pres & atty, 2000-; St Johns Univ, adj prof, currently. **Orgs:** Fed Bar Asn; Mich Bar Asn, 1983; US Dist Ct, Eastern & Western Dists Mich, 1984; US Ct Appeals, Sixth Circuit, 1988; US Supreme Ct, 1997; fel Am Col Bankruptcy, 1999; Nat Bankruptcy Arch Comt, 2001; pres, Am Bankruptcy Inst, 2001-02; Judicial Adv Comt Bankruptcy, 2011; fed ct comn, Oakland County Bar Asn; Asn Trial Lawyers Am; bd mem, Am Bankruptcy Inst, var comts; ethics comn, Nat Asn Bankruptcy Trustees; chair, creditor's auxiliary, Nat Asn Chap 13 Trustees; bd dir, ACB & Coun Cert Bankruptcy Specialists; Harvard Club Miami; Univ Mich Alumni Asn; co-founder & past pres, Consumer Bankruptcy Asn; Litigation comn, Am Bar Asn; bd dir, Bankruptcy Arbit & Mediation Serv. **Special Achievements:** Publisher: Toxins-Are-Us, Norton Bankruptcy Law and Practice. **Home Addr:** 4885 Gallagher, Rochester Hills, MI 48306, **Home Phone:** (313)652-8200. **Business Addr:** President, Attorney, Kilpatrick & Associates PC, 903 N Opdyke Rd Suite C, Auburn Hills, MI 48326, **Business Phone:** (248)377-0700.

**KILSON, MARTIN LUTHER, JR.**
Educator, consultant. **Personal:** Born Feb 14, 1931, East Rutherford, NJ; son of Martin Luther Sr and Louisa Laws; married Marion Dusser de Barenne; children: Jennifer Greene, Peter Dusser de Barenne & Hannah Laws. **Educ:** Lincoln Univ, BA, 1953; Harvard Univ, MA, polit sci, 1958, PhD, polit sci, 1968. **Career:** Educator (retired), Harvard Univ, Dept Govt, teaching fel, 1957-59, from tutor govt to prof, 1962-2003, frank g. thomson prof govt emer, 2003; Harvard Ctr Int Affairs, res fel, 1961-72; Univ Ghana, vis prof, 1964-65. **Orgs:** Res fel Ford Found Foreign Area Training Prog, 1959-61; Urban Polit, Int Polit, Afro-Am Polit, Ethnic Studies; Nat Asn Advan Colored People; fel Am Acad Arts & Sci; founding fel Black Acad Arts & Lett; bd dir, Am African Studies Asn, 1967-69; consult, Fulbright-Hayes Int Exchange Prog, 1972; vis scholar, Un Chpts Phi Beta Kappa, 1974-75; fel Guggenheim Found, 1975-76. **Special Achievements:** First African-American to be granted full tenure at Harvard University; Aprolific writer who has authored numerous social and political articles on Black life in scholarly journals; Publications: The Making of Black Intellectuals, 2007, The Transformation of Black American Intellectuals, 2008. **Home Addr:** 4 Eliot Rd, Lexington, MA 02421-5610, **Home Phone:** (781)862-0760. **Business Addr:** Professor Emeritus, Harvard University, 1737 Cambridge St, Cambridge, MA 02138, **Business Phone:** (617)495-2148.

**KIMBLE, BETTYE DORRIS**
School administrator, musician. **Personal:** Born Jun 21, 1936, Tulsa, OK; daughter of J C and Ethel; children: Jay Charles & Cheleste Kimble-Botts. **Educ:** Tulsa Univ, BME, 1959; Pepperdine Univ, MA, 1979, MS, 1980. **Career:** Police officer, music teacher (retired); Greenville Police Dept, sch adminr, musician; Sapulpa OK Bd Educ, music instr, 1959-61; Hamlin KS Sch Dist, coord music, 1961-62; Kansas City, Mo, Sch Dist, music instr, 1963-67; US Gypsum, Greenville, Miss, Finishing Dept, 1965-68; Willowbrook Jr High, choral dir & vocal music educr, 1967-79; MS, police officer, chief police, 1968-89; Compton Unified Sch Dist, chairperson, performing & visual arts, teacher, choral dir, 1967; Centennial High Sch, instr, 1979-90, supvr visual & performing arts, 1991-93; Broadcast Music Inc, composer; Play Production, music consult; Greenville Pub Schs, Greenville, Miss, student activities supvr; Music Publ; In the name of the Lord, 1998; kimble community choir, founder & dir. Album : Chancel Choir & Bettye D. Kimble, The-In Gospel Concert. songs: "I Surrender All"; "He's All

You Need To Get By"; "Keep Me In Touch With Thee"; "He'll See You Through"; "Walk Around Heaven All Day"; "Let Jesus Fix It For You"; "That's Enough"; "Up In Glory". **Orgs:** Phi Delta Kappa Pepperdine Chap, 1983-; dist missionary dir, Southern CA Conf, 1985-; Performing Arts Coun; Am Choral Dir Asn; Chairperson, Compton Nat Asn Advan Colored People Act-So Proj. **Home Addr:** 8013 Crenshaw Blvd, Inglewood, CA 90305-1217.

### KIMBLE, BO (GREGORY KEVIN KIMBLE)
Basketball player. **Personal:** Born Apr 9, 1966, Philadelphia, PA. **Educ:** Univ Southern Calif, Los Angeles, CA, attended 1986; Loyola Mary Mt Univ, Los Angeles, CA, attended 1990. **Career:** Basketball player (retired); Los Angeles Clippers, guard, 1990-92, New York Knicks, 1992-93; Nat Basketball Asn, player; CRO Lyon, France, 1993-94; Rapid City Thrillers, 1994-95; Hartford Hellcats, 1995; La Crosse Bobcats, 1996-97; Yakima Sun Kings, 1997-98. **Orgs:** Founder, Bo Kimble Found; owner, Forty Four Life Found, currently. **Business Addr:** Founder, Owner, Bo Kimble Foundation, 4001 Conshohocken Ave, Philadelphia, PA 19131, **Business Phone:** (215)473-8010.

### KIMBLE, GREGORY KEVIN. See KIMBLE, BO.

### KIMBRO, DENNIS PAUL
Educator, writer. **Personal:** Born Dec 29, 1950, Jersey City, NJ; son of Donald and Mary; married Patricia McCauley; children: Kelli, Kim & MacKenzie. **Educ:** Okla Univ, BA, 1972, MA; Northwestern Univ, PhD, polit sci, 1984. **Career:** Smithkline Beckman Corp, sales & mkt, 1978-87; ABC Mgt Consult Inc, consult, 1988-91; Ctr Entrepreneurship Clark Atlanta Univ Sch Bus & Admin, assoc prof & dir, 1992-96; P Kimbro Group, founder, currently. TV Shows: "Today" & "CNN's Larry King Live". Books: The Wall Street Journal; The New York Times And Usa Today; Think And Grow Rich : A Black Choice; What Makes The Great Great: Strategies For Extraordinary Achievement; The Wealth Choice: Success Secrets Of Black Millionaires: Featuring The Seven Laws Of Wealth; What Keeps Me Standing: A Black Grandmother's Guide To Peace, 2005; Hope & Inspiration; Daily Motivations For African-American Success; Think And Grow Rich A Black Choice. **Home Addr:** 3806 Brandeis Ct, Decatur, GA 30034-5520, **Home Phone:** (770)981-9610. **Business Addr:** Founder, The P Kimbro Group, 3806 Brandeis Ct, Decatur, GA 30034, **Business Phone:** (770)981-9610.

### KIMBROUGH, CHARLES EDWARD
Clergy, veterinarian. **Personal:** Born Jun 24, 1927, Prospect, TN; son of Sterling and Azie Smith; married Blondell M Strong; children: Adric L & Gwenell. **Educ:** Tenn State Univ, BS, 1956; Tuskegee Inst, DVM, 1960; Southern Ill Col Bible, cert, 1965. **Career:** Veterinarian (retired), business owner; Sparta, area vet, 1960-69; Meat & Poultry Inspection Prog, supvr vet med officer, 1969-75; New Hope Missionary Baptist Church, Sparta, Ill, pastor, 1964-69; Mt Zion Missionary Baptist Church, Watertown, Tenn, 1970-74; Bordeaux Realty Plus, broker, co-owner, currently. **Orgs:** Pres, Nat Asn Advan Colored People, Nashville Br, 1973-80; life mem, Phi Beta Sigma Fraternity; Eta Beta Chap; Nashville-Tuskegee Alumni Club. **Honors/Awds:** Sigma Man of the Year, Phi Beta Sigma, Eta Beta Chapter, 1974; Citizen of the Year, Omega Psi Phi Fraternity, 1977. **Special Achievements:** One of the first African Americans to hold a license to practice veterinary medicine in the state of Tennessee. **Home Addr:** 3852 Augusta Dr, Nashville, TN 37207-3502, **Home Phone:** (615)876-4863. **Business Addr:** Owner, Bordeaux Realty Plus, 3250 Dickerson Pike Suite 4, Nashville, TN 37207-2969, **Business Phone:** (615)227-3898.

### KIMBROUGH, DONNA L. (DONNA L KIMBROUGH-THOMPSON)
Manager. **Personal:** Born Aug 26, 1948, Oklahoma City, OK; daughter of Irvin Rodger and Irene Betty Jones; children: Dawn Marie & Jason Leigh. **Educ:** Univ WA, BA, 1977, MBA, Michael G. Foster Sch Bus, human resource systs, 1980; NFBPA-Exec Leadership Inst, 1993. **Career:** Dept Pub Welfare, Wash, DC, social serv caseworker, 1971-75; City Seattle Water Dept, personnel specialist, 1978-80; Seattle Pub Sch, classification admin, 1980-86; Pierce Transit, mgr personnel, 1986-89; City Seattle Water Dept, mgr human resources, 1989-94; Clover Pk Sch Dist, dir human resources, 1994-97; King Co Solid Waste, asst dir, 1999-2003; King County Housing Authority, asst dir solid waste, 2001-05, dir human resources, 2007-. **Orgs:** Delta Sigma Theta; pres, Urban League Metro Seattle Guild, 1995-98; NFBPA Seattle; King Co Womens Polit Caucus; Therapeut Health Serv Soc. **Honors/Awds:** Leadership Excellence Award, Seattle Water Dept, 1991; Advan Mgt, Prog Grad, City Seattle, 1991. **Home Addr:** 10233 66th Ave S, Seattle, WA 98178-2514, **Home Phone:** (206)723-1088. **Business Addr:** Director of Human Resources, King County Housing Authority, 12039 Roseberg Ave S, Seattle, WA 98168, **Business Phone:** (206)957-4501.

### KIMBROUGH, KENNETH RODGER
Government official. **Personal:** Born OK; son of Irvin and Irene; married Juneanne; married Cheryl; children: Karin. **Educ:** Okla State Univ, BA, indust engineering; Univ Rochester, MBA, finance, 1974. **Career:** Int Paper Co, 1980-87; Ameritech-IL Bell Tel, gen mgr real estate serv, 1987-93; Gen Serv Admin, comnr pub buildings, 1993; USAA Real Estate Co, asst vpres, Pub Sector Develop, managing dir, currently; Kimbrough & Assocs, prin; Carnegie Mellon Univ, asst vpres; Pub Bldg Serv, GSA, nat comnr. **Orgs:** NACORE; civil Res, Engineering Res Found; bd advisor, Govt Leasing News; dir, Off Property Mgt. **Home Addr:** 1535 Colonial Ct, Arlington, VA 22209, **Home Phone:** (703)351-0899. **Business Addr:** Director, USAA Real Estate Co, 9830 Colonnade Blvd Suite 600, San Antonio, TX 78230-2239, **Business Phone:** (210)641-8425.

### KIMBROUGH, MARJORIE L.
Educator, writer. **Personal:** Born Jul 11, 1937, Brookhaven, MS; daughter of William T Lindsay and Louise P; married Walter L; children: Walter M & Wayne M. **Educ:** Univ Calif, BA, math, 1959; Interdenominational Theol Ctr, MRE, 1965. **Career:** Lockheed Aircraft Corp, math engr, 1959-63; Burroughs Corp, programming lang consult, 1963-66, systs rep, 1966-70; Advan Systs Inc, video tech instr, 1970-72; Interdenominational Theol Ctr, instr, 1972-73; MGT Sci AME, sales training specialist, 1973-87; Clark Atlanta Univ, relig & philos instr, prof, 1987-98; Abingdon Press, writer. **Orgs:** Delta Sigma Theta, 1956-; Phi Beta Kappa, 1957-; lectr, Church Women United, 1987-; Grady Hosp, vol, 1987-2002; United Methodist Clergy Spouses; GEO Coun Arts, 1988-91; Cascade United Meth Church; Columbia Dr. United Methodist Church. **Special Achievements:** Writer of 11 books published by Abindon Press. **Home Addr:** 824 Dolly Ave SW, Atlanta, GA 30331-8733, **Home Phone:** (404)349-3074.

### KIMBROUGH, POLLYANNA CASANGA JOHNS. See JOHNS, POLLYANNA.

### KIMBROUGH, DR. ROBERT L.
Dentist. **Personal:** Born Aug 20, 1922, Birmingham, AL; married Luequster Murphy; children: Kernelia & Donna Lynn. **Educ:** Univ Ill, Chicago, BS, Col Dent, DDS, 1951. **Career:** Dentist (retired); Community Med Care Ctr, dentist; Pvt Pract, dentist, 1951-86. **Orgs:** Prog chmn, Chicago Dent Soc, 1975-76; pres, Chicago Dent Soc, 1984; pres, Kenwood Hyde Pk Dent Soc; vpres, Med Asn Chicago; fel Acad Gen Dent; treas, Legis Interest Comt Ill Dentist; chmn, Peer Rev Comt Ill State Dent Soc; dir, Highland Community Bk Chicago; Am Dent Asn; Nat Dent Asn; Lincoln Dent Soc; Ill State Dent Soc; Am Soc Pract Childrens Dent; pres, Southside Community Arts Ctr; past exec comt, Chicago Br; life mem, Nat Asn Advan Colored People; Urban League. **Special Achievements:** First African American President in the Chicago Dental Society 120 History. **Home Addr:** 5 Santa Maria Dr, Hilton Head Island, SC 29926-1970, **Home Phone:** (843)681-3614.

### KIMBROUGH, TED D.
Executive, school administrator, secretary general. **Personal:** Born Chicago, IL. **Educ:** Northern Ill State Univ, BS; Calif State Univ, MS; Pepperdine Univ; Univ Calif; Univ Southern Calif. **Career:** Compton Unified Sch Dist, supt, 1982-90; Chicago Pub Sch Syst, supt, 1990-93; Sacramento Unified Sch, interim supt, 1996, supt, 1996-97; Los Angeles Unified Sch Dist; Multi-Kim & Assocs Inc, pres, owner, dir; Quadratech, dir, chmn, secy, currently. **Orgs:** Coun Educ Facil Planners Int; Asn Calif Sch Adminr; Am Voc Asn; Calif Coun Adult Educ; pres, Pierce Community Col Found; bd dir, founding mem, Human Econs Liberation Poverty. **Home Addr:** 1933 Durango Ave Suite 1, Los Angeles, CA 90034, **Home Phone:** (916)453-1353. **Business Addr:** Secretary, Director, Quadratech Inc, 11401 Valley Blvd Suite 200A, El Monte, CA 91731, **Business Phone:** (626)401-2700.

### KIMBROUGH, THOMAS J.
Educator, teacher. **Personal:** Born Apr 24, 1934, Morristown, NJ; son of Gladys; married Eva Harden; children: Jerome Joseph. **Educ:** Wilberforce Univ, BS, 1956; Xavier Univ, MEd, 1969. **Career:** Educator (retired); Middletown, OH, educr, 1963-90, guid couns, 1969-70; Princeton Schs, adv staff race rel, 1970-72; Princeton City Schs, asst prin, 1972-73; Educ OH Youth Comn, asst supt, 1974-76; Stud Servs Laurel Oaks Career Devel Ctr, supvr, 1976-79; Sch Creative & Performing Arts, teacher, currently. **Orgs:** Consult, Nat Equal Educ Inst Hartford, CN; consult, Equal Educ Off Ind; treas, Interracial Interaction Inc; pres, Funds Legal Defense; chmn, Educ Com Middletown Coun Human Dignity; exec comm, Middletown Br Nat Asn Advan Colored People; chmn, Educ Comm Nat Asn Advan Colored People; co-founder, Anti-Klan Network; chmn, polit action comt, Nat Asn Advan Colored People, 1991. **Home Addr:** 6049 Todhunter Rd, Middletown, OH 45044-7926, **Home Phone:** (513)539-8961.

### KIMBROUGH, WALTER M.
College administrator, college president. **Personal:** Born Atlanta, GA; son of Walter L and Marjorie L; married Adria Nobles; children: Lydia Nicole & Benjamin Barack. **Educ:** Univ Ga, BSA, biol, 1989; Miami Univ, Oxford, OH, Col Stud Personnel Serv, MS, 1991; Ga State Univ, PhD, higher educ, 1996. **Career:** Ga State Univ, admin; Emory Univ, admin; Old Dom Univ, dir stud activ & leadership; Albany State Univ, vpres Stud Affairs, 2000-04; Philander Smith Col (Little Rock, AR), pres, 2004-12; Dillard Univ (New Orleans), pres, 2012-. Book: Black Greek 101: The Culture, Customs and Challenges of Black Fraternities and Sororities. **Orgs:** Asst vpres, Alpha Phi Alpha, Southern Region; Nat Asn Stud Personnel Adminr; Asn Fraternity Advisors; Bros Acad; bd dir, United Negro Col Fund, Chair Arch, Hist & Pub Info Comt; bd dir, Greater Little Rock Chamber Com; bd dir, Ark United Methodist Found.

### KIMBROUGH-THOMPSON, DONNA L. See KIMBROUGH, DONNA L.

### KIMMONS, CARL EUGENE
Educator. **Personal:** Born Apr 10, 1920, Hamilton, OH; son of Posey Meadows and Mary Vanduren Whitaker; married Thelma Jean Lewis; children: Karen Toni West, Larry Carlton & Kimberly Ann Kimmons-Gilbert. **Educ:** Conn Col, BA, hist, 1973; Univ Conn, MA, hist, 1976; S Conn State Univ, cert, 1986. **Career:** Military, Educator (retired); Brd Educ Waterford CT, teacher, 1973; Waterford HS, teacher, 1973-95; Top secret control officer, USN, mess attend third class & steward, 1940, master chief yeoman, 1960, lt, comn officer, 1963-70; navy liason officer, bi-racial com City New London CT, 1965-66; pvt airplane pilot, 1965-97; Bd Educ Waterford CT, teacher, 1973; Waterford HS, teacher, 1973-95. **Orgs:** Fitness leader, YMCA New London CT, 1978-99; comnr, Waterford Sr Citizens Comn, 2000-; vol, AARP's 55 Alive Mature Driving Course; vol, Lawrence & Memorial Hosp; vol, AARP; retired activ off, Submarine Base, Groton. **Special Achievements:** First man ever to have enlisted as a mess attendant and serve in every enlisted pay grade to become a commissioned officer. One of the very first black officers in the submarine service. **Home Addr:** 982 Hartford Tpke, Waterford, CT 06385, **Home Phone:** (860)443-5568.

### KIMMONS, DR. WILLIE JAMES
Educator, administrator, educational consultant. **Personal:** Born Apr 4, 1944, Hernando, MS; son of Annie F and Willie Greer; married Shirley A; children: 4. **Educ:** Lincoln Univ, BS, health educ & psychol, 1966; Northern Ill Univ, MS, curric & instr, 1970, PhD, educ admin & supv, 1974. **Career:** Sikeston HS, instr, 1966-67; Northern Ill Univ, instr, 1969-73; NC Cent Univ, asst vice chancellor, 1973-76; Nat Lab Higher Educ, consult, 1973-74; Shaw Univ, adj prof, 1974-76; Univ Dayton Grad Sch, lectr, 1976; Antioch Col, adj prof, 1976-; Cent State Univ, dir, 1976-77; St Francis Col, dean, 1977-79; Downtown Campus Wayne Community Col, dean, 1979; Lawson State Community Col, Birmingham, Ala, vpres; Trenholm State Tech Col, Montgomery, Ala, interim pres; Downtown Campus Wayne County Community Col, Detroit, Mich, pres; Ivy Tech State Col, Bloomington, Ind, chancellor; Pre-K-16 schs, educ consult, currently; Save C Save Schs Inc, Educ Servs, founder, pres & chief exec officer, 2005-. **Orgs:** Coun Black Am Affairs; Nat Alliance Black Educs; Kappa Alpha Psi Frat; Am Asn Higher Educ; Nat Univ Extensions Asn; Adult Educ Asn USA; Soc Ethnic & Spec Studies; Am Asn Jr & Comm Col; Phi Delta Kappa; Prof Educ Frat; Am Personnel Guide Asn; teaching fel 1969-70; post doc fel Am Mgt Asn, 1975-76; Cont Educ Elderly Ohio Dominican Col, 1976; Black Adminrs Pub Comm & Col Carlton Press Inc, 1977; bd dir, Volusia & Flagler Counties African Am Men's Prostate Cancer; African Am Men's Health Summit C & Family Serv Bd, Daytona Beach, Fla; vice chairperson, Daytona Beach Community Rels Coun; vice chairperson, Daytona Beach/Volusia County Asn Retarded Citizens; bd mem, Daytona Beach/ Volusia County Health Dept; vpres, Volusia County Fla Men Against Destruction-Defending Against Drugs & Social Disorder; bd mem, Daytona Beach/Volusia County Salvation Army; vpres, Volusia County Fla First Step Juv Residential Facil young males; bd mem, Volusia County Fla C & Family Serv. **Honors/Awds:** NEA Athletic scholarship, 1962-66; Educator of the Year, 1975-76; Distinguished Alumnus of his Alma Mater, Lincoln Univ, 2001; Distinguished Graduate Award; Furthering Rights, Investing in Equality & Nurturing Diversity Award, Fla Civil Rights & Human Rels Comn, 2003; Lifetime Achievement Award, Nat Alliance Black Sch Educr, 2006; honored & recognized for community service, civic & leadership contributions in the areas of race relations & community relations; inducted, Wall of Fame, Frederick Douglass High Sch, 2008; honored as an outstanding community leader, Daytona Deliverance Church of God, 2010; Honored as the Father of the Year, 16th Ann Int Fatherhood Conf, 2014. **Special Achievements:** Contributed more than 500 presentations & lectures; Awarded the key to 12 major cities in the United States by the mayors; Book: "A Parenting Guidebook". **Business Addr:** Founder, President/CEO, Save Children Save Schools Inc, 1653 Lawrence Cir, Daytona Beach, FL 32117, **Business Phone:** (386)253-4920.

### KINCAID, DR. BERNARD
Mayor. **Personal:** Born Jun 5, 1945, Birmingham, AL; married Alfreda Harris; children: Amy. **Educ:** Miles Col, BA, 1970; Miami Univ, MA, 1971; Univ Ala, PhD, 1980; Birmingham Sch Law, JD, 1994. **Career:** Social Security Admin, Prog Ctr, youth counr, 1970-71; Univ Ala, Birmingham, Cult Diversity & Minority Affairs, educ consult, Sch Health-Related Prof, asst prof & asst dean, 1971-95; Miles Col, contract dir develop, 1996-97; Birmingham City Coun, 1997; City Birmingham, mayor, 1999-2007. **Orgs:** Bd dir, Birmingham-Jefferson Co Conv Complex; Birmingham Racing Comn; Metrop Planning Orgn; vice chmn, Jefferson Co Mayors Asn; vice chair, Ala Conf Black Mayors; bd dir, Ala League Munic; US Conf Mayors; chair, Elections Comn; US Conf Black Mayor; Am Legion; Am & Ala Educ Asn; UAB Retired Employees Asn; Miles Col Alumni Asn; Miles Col Booster Club; Jefferson Co Progressive Dem Coun Inc; Omega Psi Phi Fraternity Inc; Sigma Pi Phi Fraternity Inc; vpres, pres, Ensley Highlands Neighborhood Asn; Metrop CME Church; Am Legion; Sigma Kappa Delta; Glenwood Ment Health Serv found; bd, Birmingham Jefferson Conv Complex. **Home Addr:** 1026 46th St Ensley, Birmingham, AL 35208, **Home Phone:** (205)786-6388. **Business Addr:** AL.

### KINCAID, PROF. JAMAICA (ELAINE CYNTHIA POTTER RICHARDSON)
Writer, educator. **Personal:** Born May 25, 1949, St. Johns; daughter of Annie Richardson; married Allen Shawn; children: Harold & Annie. **Educ:** NY Sch, photog; Franconia Col. **Career:** Bennington Col, educr; writer; New Yorker, New York, NY, staff writer, 1976-95; Harvard Univ, vis lectr, 2009; Claremont McKenna Col, Josephine Olp Weeks chair & prof lit, 2009-; Author: At the Bottom of the River (short stories), 1983; Annie John, 1985; Annie, Gwen, Lilly, Pam & Tulip, 1986; A Small Place, 1988; Lucy, 1990; At the bottom of the river, 1992; The Autobiography of My Mother, 1996; My brother, 1997; My garden, 1999; Talk stories, 2001; Mr. Potter, 2002; Among flowers: a walk in the Himalayas, 2005; Figures in the Distance; Fantabulosos vuelos, 2005; See Now Then, 2013. **Honors/Awds:** Frequent contributor to periodicals, including the New Yorker; PEN & Faulkner Award, 1984, 1997; Morton Darwen Zabel Award, Am Acad & First of Arts & Letters, 1985; Ritz Paris Hemingway Award, 1985; Guggenheim Award for Fiction, 1985; Honorary Degree, Williams Col, 1991, Long Island Col, 1991, Amherst Col, 1995, Bard Col, 1997, Middlebury Col, 1998; AnisfieldWolf Book Award, 1997; Lannan Literary Award for Fiction, 1999; DHL, Wesleyan Univ, 2008; Lila Wallace Readers Digest Award; Clifton Fadiman Medal, 2010; hon degree, Doctor Humane Lett, Tufts Univ, 2011; Anifield-Wolf Book Award; American Book Award, Before Columbus Found, 2014; hon degree, Doctor Humane Lett, Brandeis Univ; Lila Wallace-Readers Digest Award. **Special Achievements:** Write Story to the Film: Life and Debt, 2001. **Home Addr:** 284 Hudson St, New York, NY 10013. **Business Addr:** Professor of Literature, Josephine Olp Weeks Chair, Claremont McKenna College, Roberts S 220 500 E 9th St, Claremont, CA 91711, **Business Phone:** (909)607-3228.

### KINCHEN, ARIF S.
Actor, chief executive officer. **Personal:** Born Feb 7, 1973, Los Angeles, CA; children: 2. **Career:** Entertainment Partners, extra, 1990-96; Immortal Records, promoter, st mkt, 1993-94; Loud Records, Steven Rif kind Co, st mkt, video promotion, 1995-96; Ed Weinberger Co, MTM, actor, 1996-99; A.S.K. Inc, chief exec officer, dir promotions, 1996-; Films: Beverly Hood, 1999; Trippin', 1999; Clayton, 2000; The Wash, 2001; Nikita Blues, 2001; The Trailer, 2003; Runaways, com-

poser, 2004; One More Round, 2005; Holy Fit, 2006; Happy Feet, 2006; Video Game: Underground 2, 2004; Juiced, 2005; Ever Quest II: Desert of Flames, 2005; The Suffering: Ties That Bind, 2005; Saints Row, 2006; Downhill Jam, 2006; The Sopranos: Road to Respect, 2006; Juiced 2: Hot Import Nights, 2007; Mercenaries 2: World in Flames, 2008; Saints Row 2, 2008; Spider-Man: Web of Shadows, 2008; Prototype, 2009; Red Faction Guerrilla, 2009; MotorStorm: Apocalypse, 2011; TV series: "Hull High", 1990; "The Fresh Prince of Bel-Air", 1992; "Saved by the Bell: The New Class", 1994; "Sparks", 1996-97; "For Your Love", 2002; "Family Guy", 2003-05; "Method & Red", 2004; "Talk Show with Spike Feresten", 2006; "Holy Fit", 2006; "Talkshow with Spike Feresten", 2008; "INST MSGS (Instant Messages)", 2009; "Sym-Bionic Titan", 2010; "Mad", 2010; "Christmas in Compton", 2012; "Saints Row IV", 2013; TV Commercials: "Coca Cola"; 'At & T "; "Dominos Pizza"; Album: "What' You Call Dis An Album?", 2001; Voice: Crashbox, 1999; Tigerland, 2000; Remember the Titans, 2000; The Ladies Man, 2000; Save the Last Dance, 2001; Baby Boy, 2001; Hard Ball, 2001; Our America, 2002; Bad Company, 2002; Barbershop, 2002; 8 Mile, 2002; Conviction, 2002; Brown Sugar, 2002; The United States of Leland, 2003; Marci X, 2003; Honey, 2003; Love Don't Cost a Thing, 2003; Torque, 2004; Barbershop 2: Back in Business, 2004; Johnson Family Vacation, 2004; Soul Plane, 2004; Fat Albert, 2004; Curious George, 2006; Freedomland, 2006; Madea's Family Reunion, 2006. **Orgs:** Exec consult, Zera Found, 1997-; vol, Actors & Entertainers Kids, 1997-; Comics Kids, 1997-. **Honors/Awds:** Various city & state awards. **Home Addr:** 1425 N Detroit St Suite 304, Los Angeles, CA 90046. **Business Addr:** Actor, c/o Jazzmyne Public Relations, 3727 Magnolia Blvd Suite 167, Burbank, CA 91510, **Business Phone:** (818)848-6056.

### KINCHEN, DENNIS RAY

Law enforcement officer, executive. **Personal:** Born Oct 11, 1946, Shreveport, LA; son of M B and Heareace; married Ruthie Douglas; children: Darrick Ray. **Educ:** Bossier Community Col, AS, 1990; La Techol, BA, psychol, 1991, MA, psychol, 1993. **Career:** Police Captain (retired), executive; Shreveport Police Dept, patrolman, 1969-78, corporal, 1978-80, sgt, 1980-82, lt, 1982-87, capt, 1987; Casino Asn La, assoc exec, currently; Kinchen Consult Firm, currently. **Orgs:** Paradise Baptist Church; Nat Org Black Law Enforcement Execus; FBINA, La Chap; secy, Bros & Sisters Shield; Wood lawns Mentor Prog; La Tech Alumni Asn; Bossier Parish Community Col Alumni Asn; Leadership Coun. **Home Addr:** 108 Rambo Rd, Benton, LA 71006-8749, **Home Phone:** (318)965-5587. **Business Addr:** Member, LOUISIANA GAMING CONTROL BOARD, 9100 Bluebonnet Ctr Suite 500, Baton Rouge, LA 70809, **Business Phone:** (225)295-8450.

### KINCHLOW, BEN

Clergy, writer, television journalist. **Personal:** Born Dec 27, 1936, Uvalde, TX; son of Harvey and Jewel; married Vivian Carolyn Jordan; children: Nigel, Levi & Sean. **Educ:** SW Tex Jr Col, attended 1972; Univ Va, Darden Grad Sch Bus, MBA, 1984. **Career:** Minister, broadcaster, author & businessman; African Methodist Episcopal Church, ordained; 700 Club, co-host, 1975-88, 1992-96, host int ed; Christian Broadcasting Network, dir coun, 1975, vpres, 1982-85, pres; motivational speaker, currently; Christian Drug & Reha Ctr, exec dir; Front Page Jerusalem, co-host. **Orgs:** Founder & chief exec officer, African Am Polit Awareness Coalition; bd dir & vpres Kids Against Hunger; Front Page Jerusalem; founder, Amns for Israel; Phi Theta Kappa. **Honors/Awds:** Asniate Award, SW Texas Jr Col, 1972; American Legion award of Merit, 1972; Outstanding Alumni, Phi Theta Kappa, 1988. **Special Achievements:** Books: Plain Bread; You Don't Have To If You Don't Want To. **Business Addr:** Board of Director, Vice President, Kids Against Hunger, 5401 Boone Ave N, New Hope, MN 55428, **Business Phone:** (763)257-0202.

### KINDALL, DR. ALPHA S.

Business owner, consultant. **Personal:** Born Mar 5, 1944, Alamo, TN; daughter of B W Simmons; married Luther M; children: Kimberley & Katrina. **Educ:** Tenn State Univ, BA, 1964; George Peabody Col, MA, 1968; Univ Tenn, PhD, 1976. **Career:** Nashville Metro Sch BP, teacher, 1965-69; Knox Co Sch Bd, teacher, 1970-99; Kindall Assocs, chief exec officer, 1999-. **Orgs:** Alpha Kappa Alpha, 1962-; Phi Delta Kappa, 1975-; Gene Piaget Soc, 1975-99; Tenn Alliance Independent Voters, 1976-; Nat Edu Asn. **Home Addr:** 257 Newport Rd, Knoxville, TN 37934, **Home Phone:** (865)966-4177. **Business Addr:** Chief Executive Officer, Kindall Associates, 257 Newport Rd, Knoxville, TN 37934, **Business Phone:** (865)966-4177.

### KINDALL, DR. LUTHER MARTIN

Educator. **Personal:** Born Nov 1, 1942, Nashville, TN; son of Lucy Moore and Bruce; married Alpha J Simmons; children: Kimberly & Katrina. **Educ:** Tenn State Univ, BS, 1967, MS, 1968, EdD, 1973. **Career:** Tenn State Univ, asst prof psychol, 1968-70; Brushy Mountain State Prison, instr psychol, 1972; Roane State Community Col, asst prof psychol, 1972-73; Univ Tenn, prof educ psychol, 1973-2002, assoc prof, emer prof educ psychol, 2002-; Dem Primary Gov Tenn, cand, 1982; Kindall & ASC Consult Co, pres. **Orgs:** Founding mem, Nat Asn Black Psychologists, 1968; state coord, Proj Utilize Educ Talents, 1968; pres, TN Alliance Black Voters, 1979-; Omega Psi Phi Frat, 1973-; comnr, Tenn Human Rights Comn, 1985-92; pres, Community Rels CounKnoxville Job, 1986-95; pres, Elk Develop Co, 1988-2001; chmn, UT Commn Blacks; founding mem, UT Black Fac & Staff Asn; UT Comn Blacks; Ron McNair Summer Mentoring Prog. **Honors/Awds:** Alpha Kappa Mu Honor Soc, 1966-; Outstanding Teacher of the Year, UT Panhellenic & Greek Org, 1978-79; Received Several Awards. **Home Addr:** 257 Newport Rd, Farragut, TN 37922, **Home Phone:** (615)966-4177. **Business Addr:** Emeritus Professor, University of Tennessee, 535 Jane & David Bailey Educ Complex 1122 Vol Blvd, Knoxville, TN 37996-3452, **Business Phone:** (865)974-8145.

### KINDE, ISAAC

Biotechnologist. **Personal:** Born Jan 1, 1984?. **Educ:** University of Maryland Baltimore County, B.S. in Biological Sciences; Johns Hopkins School of Medicine, M.D.-Ph.D. Candidate. **Honors/Awds:** Invent Now, Collegiate Inventors Competition--3rd Place, 2013; "Forbes" 30 Under 30: Science and Healthcare, 2013; "The Root" Magazine, The Root 100 Honorees, 2013; The Baltimore Sun's "b" Magazine, 10 People to Watch Under 30, 2013. **Special Achievements:** Expert in DNA sequencing, researching how to fight cancer; published in many journals, including "Science Translational Medicine," "Journal of Molecular Biology," "Cancer Research," "Proceedings of the National Academy of Sciences," and "Nature".

### KINDLE, ARCHIE

Automotive executive. **Personal:** children: Travis & Lamont. **Educ:** Davidson County Community Col, attended. **Career:** Hull/Dobbs Ford, Winston-Salem, salesman; Cloverdale Ford, sales mgr; Pkwy Ford, sales mgr; Plaza Ford Lincoln-Mercury Inc, operator, owner & pres, 1987-2007; Plaza Auto Mart, owner, chief exec officer, currently. **Business Addr:** Owner & Operator, President, Plaza Ford Lincoln Mercury Inc, 1802 Cotton Grove Rd, Lexington, NC 27292-2552, **Business Phone:** (336)357-3505.

### KING, AJA NAOMI

Actor. **Personal:** Born Jan 11, 1985, Los Angeles, CA. **Educ:** Univ Calif, Santa Barbara; Yale Univ Sch Drama, MFA, 2010. **Career:** Professional actress, 2008-. TV series: "Blue Bloods", CBS, 2010; "Person of Interest", CBS, 2012; "Emily Owens, M.D.", The CW, 2012-13; "The Blacklist", NBC, 2013; "Deadbeat", 2014; "Black Box", ABC, 2014; "How to Get Away with Murder", ABC, 2014-; "BoJack Horseman", 2015. TV movies: "Onion News Empire", 2013. Films: "Damsels in Distress", 2011; "Four", 2012; "36 Saints", 2013; "The Rewriter", 2014; "Reversion", 2015. Theatre: "Edgewise", Walkerspace Theatre; "Good Goods", Eugene O'Neil Theatre Center. **Business Addr:** Talent Management Company, 115 W 29th St Suite 1102, New York, NY 10001.

### KING, ALBERT

Basketball player. **Personal:** Born Dec 17, 1959, Brooklyn, NY. **Educ:** Univ Md, MD, 1981. **Career:** Basketball player (retired); NJ Nets, forward, 1981-87; Philadelphia 76ers, forward, 1987-88; San Antonio Spurs, forward, 1988-89; Olimpia Milano, 1989; Philips Milano, 1989; Albany Patroons, 1990-91; Wash Bullets, forward, 1991-92.

### KING, ALONZO B.

Choreographer. **Personal:** Born Dec 31, 1957, Albany, GA; son of Slater Hunter and Valencia LaVerne Benham Nelson. **Educ:** Sch Am Ballet; Am Ballet Theatre; Harkness House Ballet Arts; Calif Inst Art, choreography. **Career:** NEA, Choreographers fel; Irvine Dance Fel; Dancer: Honolulu City Ballet, dancer; Santa Barbara Ballet, dancer; Dance Theatre Harlem, dancer; teacher, master classes: Ballet Rambert, London; Nat Ballet Can; Les Ballets de Monte Carlo; Ballet W; San Francisco Ballet; Alonzo Kings LINES Ballet, founder & artistic dir, 1982-; San Francisco Dance Ctr, founder, 1989-; art dance, writer & lectr; San Francisco county, comnr; city comnr; choreography: Aka Pygmies, 2001; The Moroccan Proj, 2005; Sky Clad, 2006; Long River High Sky, 2007; Writing Ground, 2010; Swed Royal Ballet; Frankfurt Ballet; Joffrey Ballet; Dance Theater of Harlem; Alvin Ailey Am Dance Theatre; Hong Kong Ballet; Nc Dance Theatre; Wash Ballet; Royal Swed Ballet; Ballett Frankfurt; Joffrey Ballet; Resin, 2011; Figures of Thought, 2011; Triangle of the Squinches, 2011; Film: One Last Dance, choreographer, 2003; Alonzo King Goes to Venice, choreographer, 2005. **Orgs:** Nat Endowment Arts; Calif Arts Coun; City Columbus Arts Coun; Lila Wallace-Readers Dig Arts Partners. **Honors/Awds:** Five Isadora Duncan Awards; Hero Award, Urban Bank; Excellence Award, KGO; Dominican Univ, hon Doctorate, 2005; prestigious Bessie Award, 2005; US Artists award, 2006; Community Leadership Award, San Francisco Found, 2007; Mayors Art Award, 2008; Princess Grace Award; hon degree, Dominican Univ Calif & Calif Inst Arts; Jacobs Pillow Creativity Award, 2008; Green Honors Chair Professorship, Tex Christian Univ; Lifetime Achievement Award, Corps de Ballet Int Teacher Conf, 2012; President Award; Los Angeles Lehman Award. **Special Achievements:** Master of African-Am choreography by the Kennedy Ctr, 2005; 50 outstanding living artists in America; First ever Barney Choreographic Prize from White Bird Dance, 2013. **Business Addr:** Founder & Artistic Director, Choreographer, Alonzo Kings LINES Contemporary Ballet, 26 7th St, San Francisco, CA 94103, **Business Phone:** (415)863-3040.

### KING, ANITA

Writer. **Personal:** Born Feb 3, 1931, Detroit, MI. **Educ:** Univ Detroit, BA, music, 1956. **Career:** Books: Quotations in Black, auth, 1981, 1997; An Introd to Candomble, 1987; Samba! & other Afro-Brazilian Dance Expressions, 1989; Dance Herald: A Descriptive Index, Compiler, ed, publ, 2002; Dragon Sings The Blues, 2011; The Last Applause for the Dragon, 2013. **Home Addr:** 10 E 138th St Apt 8E, New York, NY 10037, **Home Phone:** (212)862-9415.

### KING, DR. ARTHUR THOMAS

Educator, dean (education). **Personal:** Born Feb 10, 1938, Greensboro, AL; son of Harvey James and Elizabeth Williams; married Rosa Marie Bryant; children: Donald & Kevin. **Educ:** Tuskegee Univ, BS, biol, 1962; SDak State Univ, MS, econs, 1971; Univ Colo, PhD, econs, 1977. **Career:** Educator (retired); USAF Acad, asst prof econs, 1962-74; Air Force Inst Tech, assoc prof econs, dep head, 1979-82; Baylor Univ, prof econs, 1982-95, coordr minority affairs; Duke Univ, Am Coun Educ, fel, 1993-94; Winston-Salem State Univ, tenured prof econs & dean sch bus, 1995, prof, dir div bus & econs, 2004; Goodwill Indust Am Inc, bd dir; King Analytics LLC, owner, managing mem, 2005-. **Orgs:** Pres & bd dir, Heart Tex Goodwill, 1986-88; pres & bd dir, EOAC, 1987-89; pres, Nat Econ Asn; Am Econ Asn; Am Asn State Cols & Univs; bd dir, Tripath Imaging, 2003-. **Home Addr:** 212 Waite Hall Rd, Waco, TX 76712, **Home Phone:** (817)741-9959. **Business Addr:** Director, TriPath Imaging Inc, 780 Plantation Dr, Burlington, NC 27215, **Business Phone:** (336)222-9707.

**KING, B. B. See Obituaries Section.**

### KING, REV. DR. BARBARA LEWIS

Clergy. **Personal:** Born Aug 26, 1930, Houston, TX; children: Michael. **Educ:** Tex Southern Univ, BA, sociol, 1955; Atlanta Univ, MSW, 1957, course work EdD. **Career:** Henry Booth House, Chicago, IL, prog dir; 1957-59; Church Fedn Greater Chicago, prog consult, 1960-66; S Chicago Comm Serv Asn, exec dir, 1966-68; Chicago City Col, Malcolm X col, Chicago, dean, community rels, 1967-69; Atlanta Univ Sch Social Work, instr, 1970-71; S Cent comm Ment Health Ctr, dir, 1971-73; Barbara King Sch Ministry, founder & pres, 1971-; Hillside Chapel & Truth Ctr Inc, founder & minister, 1971-; Spelman Col, Atlanta, instr, dean stud, 1973-74; Nat & Int speaker, preacher & teacher; Emory Ment Health Ctr, Atlanta, adminr; Assin Nsuta, Ghana, W Africa, chief; Books: Piddlin for the Soul; Love Your Body Temple; What is a Miracle?. **Orgs:** Rules comt Dem Nat Comt, 1984; bd mem, Christian Coun Metro Atlanta; bd treas, Int New Thought Alliance; capt & chaplain Fulton County Sheriff's Dept, Atlanta Sheriffs Servs; Fulton County Develop Authority Bd; Atlanta Bus League Bd; Atlanta Bus League; Int New Thought Alliance; Nat Asn Social Workers; life mem, Nat Asn Advan Colored People; legendary Antioch Baptist Church; Nat Womens Law Ctr; Zeta Phi Beta Sorority Inc; Nat Womens Law Ctr; life mem, Apex Mus African Am Hist; Nat Rules Comt; Dem Nat Comt Elector; Ethics Bd Metro Atlanta. **Special Achievements:** She became the first female enstooled as a Chief at Assin Nsuta, Ghana, West Africa. **Home Addr:** 2660 Peachtree Rd NW, Atlanta, GA 30305. **Business Addr:** Minister, Founder, Hillside Chapel & Truth Center Inc, 2450 Cascade Rd SW, Atlanta, GA 30311, **Business Phone:** (404)472-1929.

### KING, BERNARD

Basketball player, sports manager. **Personal:** Born Dec 4, 1956, Brooklyn, NY; married Collette Caesar. **Educ:** Univ Tenn, attended 1977. **Career:** Basketball player (retired), speaker, broadcaster; player, 1964-; sports speaker; NJ Nets, 1977-79, 1992-93; Utah Jazz, 1979-80; Golden State Warriors, 1980-82; New York Knicks, 1982-85, 1987; Wash Bullets, 1987-91; Playing Field Promotions, sports speaker, currently; NBA TV, broadcaster, currently. TV Series: "Fast Break", actor, 1979; "NBA All-Star Game", 1982, 1984, 1985, 1991; "Miami Vice", actor, 1986; "Sons of the City: New York", 2011; "30 for 30", exec producer, 2013; "Mike & Mike", 2014. **Business Addr:** Sports Speaker, Playing Field Promotions, 277 S Forest St, Denver, CO 80246, **Business Phone:** (303)377-1109.

### KING, REV. DR. BERNICE ALBERTINE

Lawyer, minister (clergy). **Personal:** Born Mar 28, 1963, Atlanta, GA; daughter of Martin Luther Jr and Coretta Scott. **Educ:** Spelman Col, BA, psychol; Emory Univ, Theol & Law, 1990; Candler Sch Theol, Mdiv; Emory Univ Sch Law, JD. **Career:** City Atty Off, internship; Ga Retardation Ctr, stud chaplain; Ga Baptist Hosp; atty, currently; Voice Communs Network, minister; Juv Ct Judge, clerk, 1990-92; Greater Rising Star Baptist Church, asst pastor, cur; New Birth Missionary Baptist Church, minister, elder, 2002-11; Southern Christian Leadership Conf, chief exec officer, pres, 2009-. **Orgs:** Bd dir, King Ctr, Nat Black MBA; State Bar Ga; Alpha Kappa Alpha Sorority Inc. **Business Addr:** President, Southern Christian Leadership Conference, 320 Auburn Ave NE, Atlanta, GA 30312, **Business Phone:** (404)522-1420.

### KING, BILLY

Manager, president (organization). **Personal:** Born Jan 23, 1966; married Melanie Lynn Frantz; children: Natane Alexandra & Reggie. **Educ:** Duke Univ, polit sci. **Career:** Ill State Univ, asst coach; ESPN's basketball coverage, Ohio Valley Conf, color analyst; Ind Pacers, asst coach; USA Basketball, exec comn, athelete rep, 1997-2000, treas, 2001-04; Philadelphia 76ers, vpres basketball admin, 1997, gen mgr, 1998, pres, 2003-07; Brooklyn Nets, gen mgr, 2010-. **Orgs:** USA Basketball Mens Sr Nat Team Prog Adv Panel; bd dir, USA Basketballs; treas, USA Basketball Mens Sr Nat Team Comn, 1997-2000, 2001-04. **Business Addr:** General Manager, Brooklyn Nets, 15 MetroTech Ctr 11th Fl, Brooklyn, NY 11201, **Business Phone:** (718)933-3000.

### KING, BRETT

Executive. **Personal:** children: 2. **Educ:** Pa State Univ, BA, speech commun. **Career:** WNYC-TV, prod asst, 1981-86; TV show Saturday Night Live, prod coorr, 1986-87, unit producer, 1987-90; Lost Planet Prod, music video & promo producer, 1990-91; Quincy Jones Entertainment, dir tv develop, 1991; Vibe mag, exec consult; Twentieth Century Fox TV, dir current programming, 1993-96; Paramount TV Group, vpres current progs, 1996-2004; The WB Tv Network, SVP, Current Progs, 2004-06; Time Warner Inc, sr vpres; Black Entertainment Tv, head Original Programming, 2007-08; Non LP B-Side Media, independent producer, 2009-10; de Passe Jones Entertainment, exec vpres, 2010-12; Freelance, producer, develop consult, 2012-13; Creative Consult, 2014-15; Sony Pictures Entertainment, vpres, creative programming, diversity & inclusion, 2015-. **Business Addr:** Senior Vice President, Time Warner Inc, 1 Time Warner Ctr, New York, NY 10019-8016, **Business Phone:** (212)484-8000.

### KING, CEOLA

Government official. **Personal:** Born Jun 10, 1927, Macon, MS; children: Terasa. **Career:** Town Old Memphis, council mem. **Home Addr:** Rt 1 Box M 158C, Aliceville, AL 35442.

### KING, REV. CHARLES E.

Singer, clergy. **Personal:** Born Jul 6, 1920, Cleveland, OH; married Helen Grieb; children: Oolissa & Darla. **Educ:** Heidelberg Col, attended 1939; Juilliard Sch Music, attended 1948. **Career:** Singer, 1941-70; Wings Over Jordan Choir, dir & singer, 1941-48; CBS radio broadcasts, dir; Charles King Choir, dir & founder, 1948-50; Karamu Theater Cleveland, mgr, actor & voice teacher, 1950-53; CFO Int, song leader, speaker & leader, 1952-85; Albums: Porgy & Bess; Showboat; The Medium; Kiss Me Kate; Lost in the Stars; Mikado; Carmen Jones; The Maid in & Mistress; Baritone singer & minister; Musical Church, pastor, 1988-. **Orgs:** Minister & founder, Awareness Ctr, 1965-; song leader-retreat dir, Unity Sch Practical Christianity, 1968-; pres, Charles King Orgn, 1971-; pres & owner, King Worm Ranch, 1975-79; pres & owner, King Tree Nursery, 1979-81. **Honors/Awds:** Invited by the Pentagon to entertain servicemen in Vietnam & Korea, 1970-71. **Home Addr:** 3020 Issaquah Pine Lk Rd, PO Box 82, Sammamish, WA 98075, **Home Phone:** (425)557-9595. **Business Addr:** Pastor, Musical Church, 24015 SE 30th St, Issaquah, WA 98075-9412, **Business Phone:** (425)557-9595.

**KING, CLARENCE MAURICE, JR.**
Saxophonist, executive. **Personal:** Born Jul 25, 1934, Greenwood, MS; son of C Maurice and Eddie Mae; children: Mark, Michael, Jeffrey, Cierra & Lydia. **Educ:** Detroit Inst Com, acct cert, 1961; Wayne State Univ, BS, 1974; Cent Mich Univ, MS, 1981. **Career:** Internal Revenue Serv, tax auditor, 1961-65, group mgr, 1965-68, br & div chief, 1968-76, from asst dist dir to sidt dir, 1976-89; Langston Univ, Langston, Okla, asst prof acct, 1989-90; Wichita Minority Supplier Coun Wichita Area Chamber Com, Wichita, Kans, exec dir, 1990-92; Local 297 Wichita Musicians' Asn, secy & treas, 2000-; Wichita State Univ, lectr. **Orgs:** Alto saxophonist Clarence King Quartet; archon, Alpha Nu Boule Sigma Pi Phi, 1986-; life mem, Nat Asn Advan Colored People; bd dir, Nat Bus League; 32 degree Prince Hall Mason; IRS campus exec, Langston Univ & Wichita State Univ; Wichita Rotary; bd dir, Goodwill Industs. **Home Addr:** 6526 ONeil St, Wichita, KS 67212, **Home Phone:** (316)945-2588. **Business Addr:** Secretary, Treasurer, Wichita Musicians, 530 E Harry St Suite 105, Wichita, KS 67211, **Business Phone:** (316)265-6445.

**KING, COLBERT I.**
Vice president (organization), columnist, editor. **Personal:** Born Sep 20, 1939, Washington, DC; son of Isaiah and Amelia Colbert; married Gwendolyn Stewart; children: Robert, Stephen & Allison. **Educ:** Howard Univ, BA, 1961, grad studies. **Career:** Riggs Nat Bank; US Dept St Foreign Serv Attache, 1964-70; Us Dept State HEW, spec officer, 1964-80; spec asst under sec, 1970-71; VISTA, dir prog & policy dir, worker, 1971-72; Vols Serv Am, worker, 1971-72; Comn DC, US Senate, staff dir, 1972-76; re-election & campaign aid, 1974; Sen Mathias MD, legis dir, 1974-; Govt Rels, Potomac Elec Power Co, dir, 1975-77; Treas Dept, dep asst sec, legis affairs, 1976-79; World Bank, exec dir, 1979-81; Riggs Bank, exec vpres, 1980-90; lectr, Foreign Serv Inst, 1982-86; lectr, JFK Inst Polit, Harvard Univ, 1983; Wash Post, Posts ed page, dep ed & columnist, 1990-, dep ed & ed page, 2000-07; Wash, DC, opinion writer. **Orgs:** Nat Asn Advan Colored People, 1969; HEW Fel Prog, 1970-71; Dist Columbia Home Rule Act, 1972-76; bd dir, Africare, 1987-89; Kappa Alpha Psi; trustee, Arena Stage Theatre, 1986-88; mem ed bd, Wash Post, 1990-; supremacist, Racist Conservative Citizens. **Home Addr:** 1506 Hamilton St NW, Washington, DC 20011. **Business Addr:** Deputy Editor, Columnist, The Washington Post, 1150 15th St NW, Washington, DC 20071, **Business Phone:** (202)334-6000.

**KING, DR. DELUTHA PORTER HAROLD, JR.**
Physician. **Personal:** Born Jan 17, 1924, Weir City, KS; son of DeLutha Sr and Julia Banks; married Lois Weaver. **Educ:** Western Res Univ, BS, zool & eng, 1952; Howard Univ, Col Med, 1956. **Career:** Howard Univ Col Med, internship, 1957, residency surg urol, 1961; Veteran's Admin, chief urol serv, 1961-65 ; Freed men's Hosp, intern, 1957, resident, urol, 1961; VA Hosp, chf urol, 1961-65; Physician, pvt prac, 1965-; John A. Andrew VA Hosp, consult, 1966-72; pvt urol pract, 1966-70; Hughes Spalding Pavilion, staff & mem; GA Bapt Hosp; Crawford W Long Memorial Hosp; Physician & Surgeons Hosp; St Joseph's Infirmary; Atlanta W Hosp; Sickle Cell Found Ga Inc, founder, 1971-; Atlanta Health Care Found, founder, 1973; SW Comm Hosp, chief staff, 1979; Morehouse Sch Med, fac, 1980-86. **Orgs:** Found, Stud AM Medi Asn, 1956; founder, Southwest Atlanta Urol Assocs Inc, 1970; pres, Atlanta Hlth Care Found, 1973-; Am Urol Asn; Am Col Surgeons; Atlanta Urol Soc; Ga State Med Asn; Metro-Atlanta Med Asn; chmn bd, Metro Atlanta Hlth Plan; sec, co-founder, chmn bd, Sickle Cell Found, GA, 1971; pres, bd trustees, Atlanta Med Asn, 1974; Gov Task Force, HSA Devel, 1975; bd mem, Cancer Network, GA State Com; bd mem, Physicians Com, GA Partners, 1976, chmn; Kappa Alpha Psi; pres, N Ctr GA, Hlth Systs Agency; bd mem, Metro-Atlanta Coun Alcohol & Drug Abuse; 2nd vpres, Nat Asn Sickle Cell Disease; bd mem, Ga State Med Asn, pres; bd mem, Am Cancer Soc; nat pres, Howard Univ Alumni Asn, 1978-80; bd trustees, Nat Med Asn, 1979-; bd trustees, SW Comm Hosp, 1979-80; Health Maintenance Orgn, 1980; apptd Nat Coun Hlth Planning & Develop; p pres, Atlanta Club, Howard Univ Alumni Asn; Nat Asn Advan Colored People; Med Adv Bd, Morehouse Sch Med; Am Col Surgeons. **Honors/Awds:** Outstanding achievement as Chief Resident in Urology, Asn Former Interns & Residents, Freed men's Hosp, 1961; Spec Award for Service, Atlanta Med Asn; Alpha Omega Alpha; "Honorary Doctor of Humanities Degree", Morehouse Col, 2001; fifty years of medi practicing, 2006; Daniel Hale Williams Award, Association of Former Interns and Residents of the Freedmen's Hospital; Hon Doctor Humanities, Morehouse Col. **Special Achievements:** Published article "Hyperthyroidism" Journal of the Medical Assn of GA, 1966. **Business Addr:** Founder, The Sickle Cell Foundation of Georgia Incorporation, 2391 Benjamin E Mays Dr, Atlanta, GA 30311, **Business Phone:** (404)755-1641.

**KING, DEXTER SCOTT**
Association executive, chairperson, chief executive officer. **Personal:** Born Jan 30, 1961, Atlanta, GA; son of Martin Luther Jr and Coretta Scott. **Career:** Corrections officer, 1981-83; bus consult, music producer & music promoter, 1983-89; Martin Luther King Jr Ctr Nonviolent Social Chg Inc, entertainment coordr, 1988-89, pres, 1989, chmn & chief exec officer, 1995-; Series: "Living the Dream", producer, 1988; "King", actor, 1978; "The Rosa Parks Story", actor, 2002; "1-800-Missing", actor, 2004. **Business Addr:** Chairman, Chief Executive Officer, Martin Luther King Jr Center Nonviolent Social Change Inc, 449 Auburn Ave NE, Atlanta, GA 30312-1503, **Business Phone:** (404)526-8900.

**KING, DON (DONALD KING)**
Boxing promoter. **Personal:** Born Aug 20, 1931, Cleveland, OH; son of Clarence and Hattie; married Henrietta; children: Eric, Carl & Debbie. **Educ:** Kent State Univ; Case Western Res Univ. **Career:** Ernie Shavers, Larry Holmes, boxing mgr; George Foreman-Ken Norton, Ali-Foreman, Ali-Frazier, promoted prize fights; Don King Sports Entertainment Network, owner, pres; King Training Camp, owner; Don King Productions, pres, chmn & chief exec officer, 1974-; Film: Teenage Mutant Ninja Turtles III; Devil's Advocate; Scary Movie 4; TV Shows: "My Bro's Keeper"; "Boy Meets World". **Orgs:** United Negro Col Fund; Oper Push; Martin Luther King Ctr Social Chg; Trans-Africa; Anti-Apartheid Asn; bd mem, Pres's Phys Fitness Coun; bd trustee, Shaw Univ; Don King Found. **Home Addr:** 8089 Chubb Rd, Windsor, OH 44099. **Business Addr:** Chairman, Chief Executive Officer, Don King Productions, 501 Fairway Dr, Deerfield Beach, FL 33441, **Business Phone:** (954)418-5800.

**KING, DR. EARL B.**
Founder (originator). **Personal:** Born Jan 5, 1953, Chicago, IL; son of John Barksdale and Mildred R; married Darryl S; children: Earl B II. **Educ:** N Tex State Univ, BA, spec ed, 1976. **Career:** Basketball player (retired); Continental Basketball League, 1977-78; Kings Peaceful Solutions, chmn; San Diego Clippers, 1978-79, 1982-83; Cook County Night Basketball League, bd dir, chmn, currently; pres Off Employ & Training, dep dir opers, currently. **Orgs:** Western Basketball Asn, 1979-80; Europ Basketball League, 1980; pres, chief exec officer, No Dope Express Found, 1986-; Nat Asn Advan Colored People, 1994-. **Honors/Awds:** Outstanding Comm Serv & State, Secy of State, 1993; Man of the yr, Dollars & Sense, 1994; Bus & Prof, 1994; Nat Outstanding Comm Serv, Nat Asn Advan Colored People, 1994; Humanitarian of the Yr Black, Heritage Expo, 1994; Drug Enforcement Admin & Dept of Justice, Outstanding Contrib in Drug Law Enforcement. **Special Achievements:** First four year letterman in twenty two years at North Tex State Univ, 1976. **Home Addr:** 18416 Aberdeen St, Homewood, IL 60430-3526. **Business Addr:** Founder, No Dope Express Foundation, 901 E 104th St, Chicago, IL 60628, **Business Phone:** (773)568-5600.

**KING, EDGAR LEE**
Manager, accountant, health services administrator. **Personal:** Born Shellman, GA; son of J B and Bertha; married Georgia Roberta Chester; children: Laura Smith & Edgar Jr. **Educ:** Northwestern Univ; Ga State Col; Univ Ill, CPA, 1980. **Career:** Allied Radio Corp, sr acct, 1958-61; Schwab Rehab Hosp, bus mgr, 1961-63, controller, 1963-73, assoc adminr, 1980-88; Hosp Englewood, chief finance officer, 1973-79. **Orgs:** Am Inst CPAs; Ill Soc CPAs; Health Care Fin Mgt Asn; Am Hosp Asn; Ill Hosp Asn; serv exec, Nat Asn Hosp; Chicago Urban League. **Honors/Awds:** Delta Mu Delta, Beta Chap, Northwestern Univ. **Home Addr:** 9728 S Brennan Ave, Chicago, IL 60617, **Home Phone:** (773)721-9108.

**KING, EMERY C.**
Journalist. **Personal:** Born Mar 30, 1948, Gary, IN; son of Natalie Harridy and Emery H; married Jacqueline Casselberry. **Educ:** Ind Univ, Bloomington, IN, 1966; Purdue Univ, Hammond, IN, 1971. **Career:** WJOB-Radio, Hammond, Ind, reporter, 1970-72; WWCA-Radio, Gary, Ind, reporter, 1972-73; WBBM-Radio, Chicago, Ill, reporter, 1973-76; WBBM-TV, Chicago, Ill, reporter, 1976-80; NBC News, Wash, DC, white house corresp, 1980-86; WDIV-TV, Detroit, Mich, anchor & reporter; Detroit Med Ctr, dir commun, currently; Kingberry Productions, owner, 1995-. **Orgs:** Bd dir, Soc Yeager Scholars, Marshall Univ, 1986-91; bd dir, Detroit Symphony Orchestra; Nat Asn TV Arts & Sci; bd mem, Michigan Multiple Sclerosis Soc; chmn, Michigan Film Advisory Comn; bd visitors, Wayne State Univ Sch Fine, Performing & Commun Arts, 2006. **Honors/Awds:** Emmy Award, Nat Asn TV Arts & Sci, 1977, 1979; 1st Place, Monte Carlo International Film Festival Award for NBC White Paper Documentary, "America Black and White", 1982; Best Hard News Reporting & Best Documentary Award, Mich Asn Broadcasters. **Business Addr:** Director of Communications, Owner, Detroit Medical Center, 4707 St Antoine Suite W 514, Detroit, MI 48201.

**KING, FREDERICK L., JR.**
Government official. **Personal:** Born Nov 16, 1957, Washington, DC; married Teresa; children: Ryan & Erin. **Educ:** Cent State Univ, BS, 1980. **Career:** Pepsi Cola USA, regional sales mgr, 1987-90; Drackett Prod Co, bus develop mgr, 1990-92; Philip Morris USA, trade mkt dir, 1992-94, sales dir, 1994; M & M Mars Kal Kan, regional mgr, 1994-96; DC Lottery & Charitable Games Control Brd, exec dir, 1996-97, dir, 1998. **Orgs:** Bd mem, mem develop comt, Multi State Lottery; co-chair, Steering comt; mkt comt, Nat Asn State & Prov Lotteries; bd mem, CSU Bus Adv Coun; founder, FOCUS; pole march Cincinnati Alumni, Kappa Alpha Psi Fraternity, 1999. **Honors/Awds:** Volunteer Award, United Negro Col Fund, 1989.

**KING, GALE V.**
Executive, vice president (organization). **Educ:** Univ Fla, BJ, MPA. **Career:** Nationwide Life Ins N Am, Off Pres-Property & Casualty, admin officer, sr vpres property & casualty human resources, exec vpres & chief human resources officer, exec vpres & chief admin officer. **Orgs:** Bd mem, Franklin County C's Serv; bd mem, Nat Urban League; bd mem, Columbus Mus Art; Exec Leadership Coun. **Business Addr:** Executive Vice President, Nationwide, 1 Nationwide Plz, Columbus, OH 43215, **Business Phone:** (614)677-5805.

**KING, GAYLE**
Television news anchorperson, talk show host. **Personal:** Born Dec 28, 1954, Chevy Chase, MD; daughter of Scott and Peggy; married William G Bumpus; children: William & Kirby. **Educ:** Univ Md, BA, psychol & sociol. **Career:** WDAF-TV, reporter & weekend anchor; WFSB, news anchor, 1981-98; Cover to Cover, cohost, 1991; Gayle King Show, host, 1997-98; O, Oprah Magazine, ed, 1999, ed at large, currently; Oprah Winfrey Show, spec corresp; Good Morning America, spec corresp; Gayle King Show, 2011; CBS This Morning, co-anchor, currently. **Business Addr:** Editor at Large, Oprah Magazine, 1 S Wacker Dr, Chicago, IL 60607, **Business Phone:** (312)984-5166.

**KING, GERARD**
Basketball player. **Personal:** Born Nov 25, 1972, New Orleans, LA. **Educ:** Nicholls State Univ, attended 1995. **Career:** Basketball player (retired); Miami Tropics, 1995; Quad City Thunder, prof basketball player, 1995-96; Fontanafredda Siena, Italy, 1997-98; San Antonio Spurs, forward, beginning, 1999; Wash Wizards, forward, 1999-2001.

**KING, GREG (GREGORY KING)**
President (organization), chief executive officer. **Educ:** Howard Univ, BA, jour & commun, 1992; Vanderbilt Univ, Owen Grad Sch Mgt, MBA, 2009. **Career:** Fox Tv, exec assist, 1991-92; NBPC, mgr pub rels, 1992-94; Underworld Entertainment, dir, mkt & promotions, 1994-96; NBC Enterprises, bus develop exec, 1997-2000; Warner Bros, entrepreneur; Soundbreak.com, dir bus develop; Big Balloon Commun, founder, pres & chief exec officer, 2000-07; L'Oreal USA, brand mgr, 2008; Spin Master Ltd, brand mgr, 2010-11. **Orgs:** Nat Urban League Young Prof; Nat Asn Black Journalists; NABPR; VSED; EPPS. **Home Addr:** 4183 6th Ave, Los Angeles, CA 90008, **Home Phone:** (310)801-0441. **Business Addr:** Chief Executive Officer, The Big Balloon Communications, 1968 W Adams Blvd Suite 203, Los Angeles, CA 90018-3510, **Business Phone:** (323)730-0029.

**KING, GWENDOLYN STEWART**
Public utility executive. **Personal:** Born Jan 1, 1941, East Orange, NJ; married Colbert I; children: Robert, Stephen & Allison. **Educ:** Howard Univ, BA, 1962; George Washington Univ, attended 1974. **Career:** US Dept HEW, staff, 1971-76; US Dept HUD, dir div consumer complaints, 1976-78; US Sen John Heinz, sr legis asst, 1978-79; Common wealth PA, Dir, Wash Off, 1979-86; White House, dep asst to Pres & dir inter govt affairs, 1986-88; US Dept Health & Human Servs, Social Security Admin, comnr, 1989-92; Martin Marietta, dir, 1992-95; PECO Energy Co, sr vpres corp & pub affairs, 1992-98; Lockheed Martin Corp, bd dir, 1995-2016; Marsh & Mc Lennan Cos Inc, dir, 1998-2011; Podium Prose LLC, pres & founder, 2000-; Monsanto Co, dir, 2001-16; Pharmacia, dir; Countrywide Financial Corp, dir emer. **Orgs:** Founding partner, Dirs Coun,2003-05; dir, Nat Asn Corp Dirs, 2004-10; trustee, Coun Excellence Govt; trustee, Barnes Found; adv mem, Nat Adoption Ctr & George Wash Univ Grad Sch Polit Mgt. **Honors/Awds:** Drum Major for Justice Award, Southern Christian Leadership Conf, 1989; Annual Achievement Award, Xi Omega Chapter of Alpha Kappa Alpha, 1990; Ebony Black Achievement Award, 1992; Outstanding Director, Wash Bus J, 2012; honorary doctorates, Univ New Haven, Univ Maryland, Baltimore County; Howard University Alumni Award; American Black Achievement Award, Johnson Publ Co. **Business Addr:** President, Founder, Podium Prose LLC, 1025 Connecticut Ave NW Suite 1012, Washington, DC 20036, **Business Phone:** (202)857-9793.

**KING, HERMAN**
Entrepreneur. **Personal:** Born May 27, 1960. **Career:** VIP Exec Protection LLC, owner, currently. **Orgs:** Potter's House multiracial nondenominational church. **Home Addr:** PO Box 630604, Irving, TX 75063-0130. **Business Addr:** Co-Owner, VIP Executive Protection LLC, 9125 Oleanderway, Irving, TX 75063, **Business Phone:** (972)401-1172.

**KING, HOWARD O., SR.**
Executive, secretary general, association executive. **Personal:** Born Aug 24, 1925, Pensacola, FL; son of Lula and Willie; married Lillie Marie Pollard; children: Howard O, Joanne K Carr & William C. **Educ:** Fla A&M Univ, BS, 1956; Fed Exec Inst, 1979. **Career:** Naval Air Sta Pensacola, supvr storekeeper & personnel staffing specialist, 1941-65; Wash Adult Sch Pensacola, adult educ, 1957-65; HO King Sales & Serv Pensacola, proprietor, 1958-65; Dept Defense, Atlanta, contract compliance officer, 1965-67; US Forest Serv, Atlanta, regional intergroup rels specialist, 1967-70; FAA, regional civil rights officer, 1970-72, Off Civil Rights, dep dir, 1972-81; Madison County. **Orgs:** Bd dir, Md Transp Authority Pensacola, 1963-65; secy, Bi-Racial Comm Pensacola, 1963-65; officer, Ebenezer Baptist Church, 1985-, chmn church's bldg & grounds comt; Fla A&M Univ. **Honors/Awds:** Good Conduct Medal, USN, 1945; Business Award, SNEAD, 1956; Citizenship Award, NAACP, 1965; Citizenship Plaque, City Pensacola, 1965; Certificate of Achievement, Dept Transport, FAA, 1972; Outstanding Achievement Award, National Black Coalition FAA Employees, 1978; Key & Silver Beavers Awards, Scouters, 1992; The Livingston Ivy Award, for Making a Difference, Pensacola, FL, 1994; keys to cities, Tuskegee, AL, & Pensacola, FL; Distinguished Service Career Award, FAA. **Special Achievements:** Author of "You too can overcome". **Home Addr:** 3105 Duke of Gloucester, East Point, GA 30344, **Home Phone:** (404)763-2428.

**KING, HULAS H.**
Executive. **Personal:** Born Oct 9, 1946, East St. Louis, IL; son of Robert (deceased) and Willie Mae Patton; married Linda Bolton; children: Gail & LaTasha. **Educ:** Belleville Area Col, assoc degree, 1970; Southern Ill Univ, Edwardsville, BS, data processing, 1972, MBA, mkt, 1974, MS, int rel, 1975, MS, mgt sci & syst, 1978, health care mgt systs, 1979; Univ Mo-Columbia, MS, indust engineering, 1983. **Career:** USA, Collinsville, Ill, bagger, 1964-65; Dow Chem Co, scalper helper, 1965; Ford Motor Co, Hazelwood, body shop work, 1966; McDonnell Aircraft Co, St Louis, dir, knowledge based applications, 1966-91; McDonnell Douglas Syst Integration Co, St Louis, proj dir, Team Columbus mfg progs, 1989-91; EDS-Unigraphics, St Louis, dir, indust mkt team, 1992, dir, indust opers team, 1993-; Southern Ill Univ, lectr, engineering; UGS Corp, global community rels, dir, currently; Siemens, global opportunities in prod lifecycle mgt, dir, 2003-14; Siemens PLM Software, diversity, prof affilliations & community rels, dir, 2014-. **Orgs:** Bd mem, Soc Mfg Eng; bd mem, Worldwide Youth Sci & Eng; bd mem, Am Inst Industl Eng; bd, Greater St Louis HTH Syst Agency, 1977-81; prog evalutor, Accreditation Bd Eng & Technol, 1980-; reg coord, Numerical Control Soc, 1980-; adv bd, Child Assistance Prog, 1982-; bd mem, Prof Bus Leadership Coun, 1982-; bd, Jr Eng Technol Soc, 1985-; tech vpres, Asn Integrated Mfg-Tech, 1986-89; adv coun, Lewis & Clark Community Col, 1988-; chair, Bus Adv Coun, Southern Ill Univ, 1989; chair, Prof Bus Leadership Coun, 1992-; Int Fed Eng Educ Socs; Socs Automotive Engrs; Bd mem, Stone Soup Found; Nat Socs Black Engrs; Asn Advan Int Educ; Indust Engineering & Opers Mgt; Int Fedn Engineering Educ Soc. **Home Addr:** No 7 Lake Forest Ct E, Saint Charles, MO 63301, **Home Phone:** (314)946-4176. **Business Addr:** Director of Global Community Relations, UGS Corp, 13736 Riverport Dr, Maryland Heights, MO 63043, **Business Phone:** (314)334-8670.

**KING, DR. JAMES, JR.**
Educator, manager. **Personal:** Born Apr 23, 1933, Columbus, GA; son of James (deceased) and Lucille Jameson Williams (deceased); married Jean H; children: Jennifer Schlickbernd & Jeffrey. **Educ:** Morehouse Col, BS, chem, 1953; Calif Inst Technol, MS, chem, 1955, PhD, physics, 1958; Danforth Found, fel. **Career:** Manager (retired); Danforth Found, fel, 1953; Jet Propulsion Lab, mgr, 1969-74, prog mgr atmospheric sci, 1976-81, Space Sci & Appl, tech mgr, 1981-84, tech mgr, 1986-88, dep asst lab dir, Tech Div, 1988-93, asst lab dir, 1993-94; sr chemist, dir eng & sci, 1995; NASA, Wash, DC, space shuttle environ effects, 1974-75, dir upper atmosp res off, 1975-76; Morehouse Col, Atlanta, chem prof, 1984-86. **Orgs:** Sigma Xi, 1958-; Am Phys Soc, 1960-; Am Chem Soc, 1960-; bd dir, Pasadena Child Guid Clin, 1969-72, 1980-86; La Air Pollution Control, 1971-74; bd dir, Caltech YMCA, 1972-74; Phi Beta Kappa, 1975; AAAS, 1976-; dir, Caltech Alumni Asn, 1977-80; Am Geophys Union, 1977-80; chmn, Pasadena Community Develop Comt, 1982-83; Pasadena Planning Comn, 1989-93; City Pasadena Planning Comn. **Honors/Awds:** Scholarship, Gen Educ Bd, 1953; Certificate of Merit, Nat Coun Negro Women, 1968; US Jaycee's Distinguished Service Award, 1966; Equal Opportunity Medal, NASA, 1986; Technologist of the Year Award, Nat Tech Asn (NTA), 1993. **Special Achievements:** Author of 13 articles in professional journals. **Home Addr:** 1720 La Cresta Dr, Pasadena, CA 91103, **Home Phone:** (818)794-7932.

**KING, JAMES R.**
Episcopal clergy, bishop. **Personal:** Born Ashland, AL; married Margareta Rosetta Hayden; children: two sons and a daughter. **Educ:** Clark College (Atlanta, GA), B.A.; Interdenominational Theological Center (Atlanta, GA), M.Div., 1972. **Career:** Wesley Foundation at Tennessee State University, Director; Tennessee Conference Council on Ministries, Associate Director and Director; Mission team to Grenada, West Indies, Evangelist, 1984; Clark Memorial UMC in Nashville, Pastor, 1985-95; Murfreesboro District, Superintendent, 1996-99; Brentwood United Methodist Church (Brentwood, TN), Pastor, 1999-08; United Methodist Church--South Georgia area, Episcopal Leader, 2008-. **Orgs:** South Georgia Annual Conference, Episcopal Leader. **Special Achievements:** Central Alabama Conference, ordained as deacon in 1970, ordained as elder in 1972; elected as bishop in 2000, co-author of "366 Meditations for Men"; author of "CLU-Christlike Love Unit," 2013; first African American to serve as episcopal leader of South Georgia. **Business Addr:** Bishop, UMC, PO Box 7227, Macon, GA 31209-7227, **Business Phone:** ((47)8)475-92.

**KING, JEANNE FAITH**
Marriage counselor, manager, counselor. **Personal:** Born Sep 20, 1934, Philadelphia, PA; daughter of Julian Frederick and Minnie H Hines; children: Heather O Bond Bryant. **Educ:** Antioch Col LA, BA, 1977, MA, clin psychol, 1987. **Career:** Performing Arts Soc La, TV producer, 1969-70; Watts Media Ctr, pr instr, 1972-74; WTTW-Chicago Pub TV, TV prod, 1975; Self Employed, free lance comm & pr, 1976-78; Cent City Comm Ment Health Ctr, dir pub rel, 1978; Beginning Corp, pres, 1978; Jeanne King Enterprises, consult firm, 1984; Valley Cable LA, producer cable TV show Jazz n U, 1984; Local Jazz Clubs, free lance entertainment specialist, 1984; Julia Ann singer Ctr Family Stress Prog, intern, 1985-86, intern family ther prog, 1986-87; Rosa Pks Sexual Assault Crisis Ctr, LA, counr, 1987; Play It Safe SASA, consult & trainer focus consult teaching, 1987; MFCC pvt pract, 1988; Univ Calif Sch Med Doctoring Prog, instr; Marriage Family Child Counr, intern; New Horizons, consult; Day Drum Festival Bk, co-ed. **Orgs:** Exec dir, Performing Arts Soc, LA, 1973-74; cons, Contrib Black Art, An Int Quart, 1976-79; Black Womens Forum, 1978-80; bd dir, Ureaus Quart Mag, 1978-80; LA, Salvador Sister Cities Comt, 1978-80; Calif Asn Marriage, Family, Child Therapists, 1987; dirs, Centinela Child Guid Clin, 1988-89; IRB-Human Subjects Protection comt, Univ Calif, 1995-97; Womens Ment Health. **Honors/Awds:** Public Service Award; Watts Summer Festival Award, 1969; Commt Contribution Head Start Award, 1970; Outstanding Service Award, Compton Community Arts Acad, 1971; Outstanding Service Award, 1975; Nat Conf Artists Award, 1975; Day Drum Fest Mistress Ceremonies, 1984; Marla Gibbs Commt Award, 1987. **Home Addr:** 4614 Glenalbyn Dr, Los Angeles, CA 90065-5060, **Home Phone:** (323)747-1905. **Business Addr:** Mental Health Services, Marriage & Family Therapy, Jeanne King, 12520 Magnolia Blvd, Valley Village, CA 91607, **Business Phone:** (818)760-7676.

**KING, JIMMY HAL**
Basketball player. **Personal:** Born Aug 9, 1973, South Bend, IN. **Educ:** Univ Mich, attended 1995. **Career:** Basketball player (retired); Toronto Raptors, guard, 1995-96; Quad City Thunder, 1996-97, 1997-2000; Dallas Mavericks; Denver Nuggets, guard, 1997; Continental Basketball Asn, Europe, 1998; La Crosse Bobcats, 1999-2000; Sioux Falls Skyforce, 2000; Gary Steelheads (IBL), 2000-01; Trotamundos de Carabobo (Venezuela), 2001; Tulsa 66er; Asheville Altitude, 2001-02; Spojnia Stargard Szczecinski (Poland), 2002-03; Great Lakes Storm, guard, 2003-04; Tex Tycoons (ABA), 2004-05; Guaiqueries de Margarita (Venezuela), 2005; Merrill Lynch, financial advisor, currently.

**KING, JOHN L.**
Executive. **Personal:** Born Apr 29, 1952, Detroit, MI; son of Johnnie L and Lillie Mae Hannah. **Educ:** Oakland Univ, Rochester, MI, BA, human resources, 1975. **Career:** Oakland County, Pontiac, Mich, employ coordr, 1972-78; Vis Nurses Asn, Detroit, Mich, sr personnel rep, 1978-80; Rehab Inst, Detroit, Mich, dir human resources, 1980-88; Detroit Med Ctr, Detroit, Mich, compensation admin, 1988-89, mgr equal employ plan, 1989-92, dir equal employ planning, 1992; Diversified Systs Int Inc, Sr. Vice Pres Human Resources, 1999-2001; Detroit Workforce Develop Dept, proj mgr, currently, Long Term Care Regional Skills Alliance, proj dir, 2002-; JOHN L KING LLC, pres & sr. Consult, 2002-. **Orgs:** Nat Asn Advan Colored People; Mich Develop Disabilities Coun; Mayor's Handicapper Adv Coun; treas, SW Detroit Community Ment Health Servs Group, 1987-; Nat Asn Advan Blacks Health; prog develop chmn, Healthcare Personnel Admin Asn, SE Mich, 1988-90; spec proj chmn, 1989-90, pres, Healthcare Personnel Admin Asn SE Mich, 1990-92; chmn, Southeastern Mich Indust Liaison Group. **Home Addr:** 14287 Maiden, Detroit, MI 48213. **Business Addr:** Project Manager, Detroit Workforce Development Department, 707 W Milwaukee Ave, Detroit, MI 48202, **Business Phone:** (313)873-7321.

**KING, JOHN THOMAS**
Administrator. **Personal:** Born Dec 9, 1935, Detroit, MI; son of John and Frances Berry; married Joan Ardis; children: Victoria D, John K & Pamela A. **Educ:** Wayne State Univ, Detroit, Mich. **Career:** Administrator (retired); Detroit Police Dept, Detroit, Mich, police cadet, 1954-57; Detroit Fire Dept, Detroit, Mich, firefighter, 1957-72, Lt, 1972-77, fire marshal, 1977, from asst to fire commnr, 1978-87, chief adminr, 1987-93, dep chief. **Orgs:** Pres, Phoenix Black Firefighters, 1970-80; CYO, 1973-; comt mem, New Detroit, 1974-; pres, Toastmasters, 1976-78; alt, Detroit Police & Fire Pension, 1986-.

**KING, JOSEPHINE**
Insurance executive. **Career:** Chicago Metrop Assurance Co, sr vpres & chief exec officer. **Honors/Awds:** Company is ranked No 5 on the list of top Insurance Company, Black Enterprise, 1994.

**KING, KELLEY A.**
Executive director. **Educ:** Wharton Sch, Univ Pa, BS, econ. **Career:** Prof Womens Alliance, vpres; JB Polk Real Estate Develop Group, founding mem & partner; Am Express Co, dir strategic technol relationships, currently. **Orgs:** Co-chair, Career Develop Comm; Univ Penn Women's Track Alumni Asn; Black Employee Network's Career Comm. **Business Addr:** Director, American Express Co, 200 Vesey St, New York, NY 10285, **Business Phone:** (212)640-2000.

**KING, LAWRENCE C.**
Executive. **Personal:** Born Washington, DC; married Beulah; children: Larry & Craig. **Educ:** Howard Univ, BA, 1951. **Career:** Gen Foods Corp NY, regional sales mgr, assoc marketers mgr, dist sales mgr & sales develop mgr. **Orgs:** Urban League; Kappa Alpha Psi. **Business Addr:** Executive, 250 N St, White Plains, NY 10605.

**KING, LAWRENCE PATRICK**
Engineer, marketing executive. **Personal:** Born Feb 3, 1940, Detroit, MI; son of Samuel and Vivian; married Deborah Barrett; children: Dereck Jackson & Alexandria. **Educ:** Univ Detroit, 1962; Cleveland State Univ, BSME, mechanicl engineering, 1974; Univ Dayton, mechanicl engineering, 1979; Univ Mich, 1990. **Career:** Gen Elec, sr mkt develop engr, speciality mat dept, 1977-79, mgr, mkt serv, 1970-80; Babcock-Wilcox, sr mkt specialist, contract res div, 1980-81, sr mkt specialist, 1981-93; Edison Polymer Innovation Corp, dir mkt, 1997-99; Deblar & Assocs Inc, environ health scientist, 2006-11, vpres, 2000-; Stem Connector, consult, 2011-. **Orgs:** Kappa Alpha Psi Fraternity, 1985-; Pres, Nat Tech Asn, 1986-87; Am Asn Blacks Energy; trustee, Nat Invention Ctr; Pressure Sensitive Tape Coun; Nat Patent Law Asn; Atlanta Bus League, 2002-03; S Cobb Bus Asn, 2009-12; Nat Tech Asn. **Honors/Awds:** Samuel Cheevers Distinguished Service Award, Nat Tech Asn, 1985. **Special Achievements:** Challenges ASOd with Increased Coal Consumption, 1992; Incineration in the Mgt of Hazardous Wastes, 1986; Outreach Strategy for Equity in Environmental Issues, 1995. **Home Addr:** 320 Sunnyside St SW, Hartville, OH 44632-9648, **Home Phone:** (330)877-6718. **Business Addr:** Vice President, Deblar & Associates Inc, 3712 Auldyn Dr, Austell, GA 30106, **Business Phone:** (770)319-8189.

**KING, LEWIS HENRY**
Consultant. **Personal:** Born Birmingham, AL; son of Tony J and Lilly Bell Taylor; married Annie M Caster; children: Debra, Cynthia, Lewis Jr & Marlon. **Educ:** Samford Univ, Birmingham, AL, BS, 1978. **Career:** US Postal Serv, postman, 1951-81; United Mgt Enterprises Meeting Planning Agency, vice chmn, owner & pres, currently. **Orgs:** Bd mem emer, Nat Coalition Title I, Chap I Parents, Meeting Planners Int; Am Soc Asn Exec; Relig Conf Mgt Asn; Nat Coalition Black Meeting Planners; bd dir, Birmingham Jefferson Civic Ctr Authority. **Business Addr:** Owner, President, United Management Enterprises Meeting Planning Agency, 648 Ctr Way SW, Birmingham, AL 35211-2935, **Business Phone:** (205)322-3219.

**KING, LEWIS M.**
Scientist, college teacher. **Personal:** Born Oct 5, 1942; son of Henry and Gladys; children: Eric. **Educ:** Howard Univ, BS, 1967; Univ Calif, Los Angeles, MA, 1968, PhD, 1971. **Career:** Univ Calif Los Angeles, psychol lectr, 1967-71; Univ Calif Los Angeles Med Sch, assoc dean; Martin Luther King Jr Hosp, chief psychol, 1971-73; Drew Med Sch, dir res, 1972-74, dean, prof psychiat, 1972-74, Fanon Res & Devel Ctr, dir; Drew Univ, vpres; Charles R Drew Univ Med & Sci, Dept Psychiat, prof, currently. **Orgs:** Dir, Trinidad Drama Guild, 1960-63; bd dir, Behav Res & Develop, 1970-74; chmn, Community Res Rev Com, LA, 1972-74; sr fel Nat Ctr Health Behav Chg. **Honors/Awds:** Howard Univ Scholarship, 1964-67; Dean's honor role, 1964-67; UN Inst Int Educ Fel, 1965-67; Physics Honor Soc Howard Univ, 1965; Outstanding contribution to Student Life, Howard Univ, 1966; Distinguished Teaching Award, Univ Calif Los Angeles, 1969-70. **Special Achievements:** First African American PhD in Psychology from Univ Calif Los Angeles. **Business Addr:** Professor, Charles R Drew University of Medicine and Science, 1731 E 120 St, Los Angeles, CA 90059, **Business Phone:** (323)563-4800.

**KING, MARCELLUS, JR.**
Manager, marketing executive. **Personal:** Born Jun 14, 1943, Tampa, FL; married Romaine C Ruffin; children: Marcellus III. **Educ:** Hampton Inst, VA, BS (dean's list), 1965; Rutgers Univ, NJ, MBA, 1975; Am Col, CLU, 1978. **Career:** Prudential Investments LLC, assoc mgr grp pension, 1970-71, mgr grp pensions, 1971-74, dir grp pension serv, 1974-85, dir mkt, 1985-95, vpres mkt, 1995-. **Orgs:** pres, Omega Phi Epsilon, 1961; mem allocations com, United Way of Morris Co NJ, 1975-80; vpres, Urban League of Essex Co NJ, 1976-80; Guest speaker Minority Interchange, 1978-80. **Honors/Awds:** Designation CLU, Am Col, 1978; exec mgt prog Prudential Ins Co, 1980, registered representative, 1987. **Home Addr:** 15 Oakview Ave, Maplewood, NJ 07040-2213, **Home Phone:** (973)762-0687. **Business Addr:** Vice President Marketing, Prudential Investments LLC, 100 Mulberry St, Newark, NJ 07102.

**KING, MARTIN LUTHER, III**
Government official. **Personal:** Born Oct 23, 1957, Montgomery, AL; son of Martin Luther Jr (deceased) and Coretta Scott (deceased); married Arndrea Waters; children: Yolanda Renee. **Educ:** Morehouse Col, BA, polit sci & hist, 1979. **Career:** Fulton County Ga, comnr, 1987-93; Estate Martin Luther King Jr Inc, founder, 1993; Southern Christian Leadership Conf, pres, 1997-2004; King Ctr Nonviolent Social Chg, pres, chmn & chief exec officer, 2004-12; founder, Realizing Dream, 2006-. **Orgs:** Alpha Phi Alpha Fraternity; bd dir, Drum Maj Inst Pub Policy. **Special Achievements:** Acted in a film King, 1978. **Business Addr:** Founder, Realizing the Dream, PO Box 1684, Atlanta, GA 30301, **Business Phone:** (866)855-6286.

**KING, MARY BOOKER**
Educator. **Personal:** Born Jul 14, 1937, Quitman, GA; married Grady J; children: Felicia, Adriene & Karon. **Educ:** Morris Brown Col, BA, 1959; Atlanta Univ, MA, 1961; Nova Univ, MEd, 1975. **Career:** Miami Dade Comm Col, assoc prof eng, 1970-72, Dept Reading, chmn, 1973-75, prof lang & arts, 1975-, prof eng, 1979-97. **Orgs:** Commr, Dade Co Com Status Women, 1978-80; consult, Devel Col Progs Reading & Writing; Women Involved Comm Affairs, 1979-80; Educ Task Force Com, 1979-80. **Home Addr:** 8361 SW 142 St, Miami, FL 33158. **Business Addr:** Professor, Miami Dade Community College, 300 N E 2nd Ave, Miami, FL 33132, **Business Phone:** (305)237-8888.

**KING, NAOMI RUTH**
Activist. **Personal:** Born Nov 17, 1931, Dothan, AL; daughter of Bessie Barber; married A D Williams King; children: Alfred D W III, Alveda, Esther Darlene, Vernon & Derek B. **Educ:** Spelman Col, attended 1950; Univ Ala. **Career:** Department store fashion model, GA; civil rights activist, 1955-; speaker; A.D. King Foundation, co-founder, 2008. **Orgs:** NAACP; Southern Christian Leadership Conf; Southern Christian Leadership Conf Women; Am Bridge Asn. **Special Achievements:** Sister in law of Martin Luther King, Jr.; as activist, supported Rosa Parks, 1955, creation of the Southern Christian Leadership Conference, 1957, beginning of sit-ins in Greensboro, NC, 1960, Birmingham campaign, 1963, March on Washington, 1963, and vote in Selma, 1965; author, "A.D. King and M.L. King: Two Brothers Who Dared to Dream" (AuthorHouse LLC, 2014). **Business Addr:** A.D. King Foundation, 2505 Creel Rd, Atlanta, GA 30349, **Business Phone:** (678)736-4933.

**KING, PATRICIA ANN**
Educator. **Personal:** Born Jun 12, 1942, Norfolk, VA; daughter of Addison and Grayce; married Roger Wilkins; children: Elizabeth Wilkins. **Educ:** Wheaton Col, BA, 1963; Harvard Law Sch, JD, bioethics, 1969, Harvard Univ, LLD, 2014. **Career:** Dept State, budget analyst, 1964-66; Equal Employ Opportunity Comn, dep dir off civil rights, spec asst chmn, 1969-71; Off Civil Rights, Dept Health Educ & Welfare, dept dir, 1971-73; Hastings Inst, fel, 1977-; Civil Div Dept Justice, dept asst atty gen, 1980-81; Georgetown Univ, assoc prof law, 1974-88, prof law, 1988-, Carmack Waterhouse Prof law, med, ethics & pub policy, currently; John Hopkins Univ, adj prof, 1990-. **Orgs:** Fel John Hay Whitney Found, 1968; Nat Comn Protection Human Subjects, 1974-78; Harvard Law Sch Comt, 1975-81; chmn, Redevelop Land Agency, 1976-79; US Circuit Judge Nomination Comn, 1977-79; Recombinant DNA Adv Comn, 1979-82; pres, Comn Study Ethical Probs Med & Res, 1980-81; bd, Russell Sage Found, 1981-91; bd, Womens Legal Defense Fund, 1987-; Am Law Inst, 1988-; Nat Insts Health, 1990-94; Inst Med, 1998-2001; fel Hastings Ctr; bd trustee, Wheaton Col, 1989-, chair bd, 2000-05; Nat Acad Sci; fel Harvard Corp, 2005-13; bd trustee, Wheaton Col; vice chair, Henry J. Kaiser Family Found. **Honors/Awds:** The Juridicial Status of the Fetus, Mich Law Review, 1647, 1979; Distinguished Service Award, HEW, 1973; Secretary's Special Citation, HEW, 1973; Senior Research Scholar, Kennedy Inst Ethics, 1977; LLD, Wheaton Clearing, 1992. **Special Achievements:** The First African-American woman to became a permanent member of the faculty in Georgetown University; co-author "Cases and Materials on Law, Science and Medicine", 1984. **Home Addr:** 1253 4th St SW, Washington, DC 20024. **Business Addr:** Carmack Waterhouse Professor of Law, Medicine, Ethics, and Public Policy, Georgetown University, 600 New Jersey Ave NW 400 McDonough Hall, Washington, DC 20001, **Business Phone:** (202)662-9401.

**KING, PATRICIA E.**
Teacher, lawyer. **Personal:** Born Jan 16, 1943, Chester, SC. **Educ:** John C Smith Univ Charlotte, BS, 1965; NC Cent Univ, JD. **Career:** Chester, sch teacher, 1965-66; Pearson Malone Johnson & Dejermon, researcher, 1967-69; Bell & King, atty; Jenkin Perry Pride, researcher, 1969-70; funeral directress; NC State, pvt pract atty, 1971-. **Orgs:** NC Bar Asn; Black Lawyers Asn; Am Bar Asn; NC Bar Found; NC State Bar Asn. **Honors/Awds:** OIC Award, 1972. **Home Addr:** 129 Cemetery St, Chester, SC 29706. **Business Addr:** Attorney at Law, 4000 Beatties Ford Rd, Charlotte, NC 28216-3220, **Business Phone:** (704)398-0827.

**KING, PRESTON**
Educator, writer. **Personal:** Born Mar 3, 1936, Albany, GA; son of Clennon Washington and Margaret; married Raewyn; children: Akasi Peter; married Murreil Hazel Stern; children: Oona & Slater. **Educ:** Fisk Univ, BA, 1956, MSc, econ; London Sch Econ, PhD, 1966; Univ Vienna; Univ Strasbourg; Univ Paris. **Career:** Univ Lancaster, Dept Polit & Int Rel, chmn, prof emer, 1986-; Univ E Anglia, Dept Philos, vis prof, currently; Critical Rev Int Social & Polit Philos, found ed & co-ed; Emory Univ, Woodruff Prof Polit Philos, currently; Fisk Univ, distinguished vis prof polit sci, 2007; Macquarie Univ, distinguished vis prof polit sci, 2007; Morehouse Col, Distinguished Prof Polit Philos, currently; McGill Univ, vis prof; Australian Nat Univ Canberra, vis prof; London Sch Econs, vis prof; l'Institut des Rels Internationales, vis prof; Univ S Pac, vis prof; Emory Univ, vis prof; Auckland Univ, vis prof; Critical Rev Int Social & Polit Philos, founder, co-ed; Books: Fear of Power; The Ideology of Order, 1974; The study of politics: a collection of inaugural lectures. London, 1977; Socialism and

the common good: new fabian essays. London Portland, 1996; An African Winter; Toleration; Federalism and Federation and Thinking a Problem; Trusting in reason: Martin Hollis and the philosophy of social action; 2003; Editor: The Challenge to Friendship in Modernity; Trust in Reason and Black Leaders and Ideologies in the South; Friendship in Politics, 2007; Routledge, prof polit philos, 2000-. **Orgs:** Chair, Univ Nairobi, 1972-76; chair, Univ Nsw, 1976-86; chair, Lancaster Univ, 1986-2001; Ctr Civil & Human Rights; chair, nternational Polit Sci Asn. **Business Addr:** Department Of Political Science, Morehouse College, 830 Westview Dr SW, Atlanta, GA 30322, **Business Phone:** (404)614-8565.

### KING, RAY (RAYMOND KEITH KING)
Baseball player. **Personal:** Born Jan 15, 1974, Chicago, IL; married Cherie; children: Tyrell & Brookelynn. **Educ:** Lambuth Univ, Tenn. **Career:** Baseball player (retired); Chicago Cubs, pitcher, beginning, 1999; Milwaukee Brewers, 2000-02, 2007; Atlanta Braves, 2003; St Louis Cardinals, 2004-05; Colo Rockies, 2006; Wash Nationals, 2007, 2008; Chicago White Sox, 2008; Houston Astros, 2008; Free Agt, currently.

### KING, DR. REATHA CLARK
Administrator, philanthropist, scientist. **Personal:** Born Apr 11, 1938, Pavo, GA; daughter of Willie and Ola Watts Campbell; married N Judge King Jr; children: N Judge III & Scott Clark. **Educ:** Clark Col, BS, chem, 1958; Univ Chicago, MS, phys chem, 1960, PhD, phys chem, 1963; Columbia Univ, MBA, 1977. **Career:** Natural Bur Stand, res chemist, 1963-68; York Col, NY, asst prof chem, 1968-70, assoc prof chem & assoc dean natural sci & math div, 1970-74, chem prof & assoc dean acad affairs, 1974-77; Metrop State Univ, St Paul, MN, pres, 1977-88; Gen Mills Found, pres & exec dir, 1988-2002; Allina Health Systs, corp dir. **Orgs:** AAAS; Am Chem Soc; Nat Orgn Prof Advan Black Chemists & Chem Engrs; Sigma Xi; bd dir, Exxon/Mobil Corp; bd dir, H B Fuller Co Found; Hispanics Philanthropy; Cong Black Caucus Found; chair, Gen Mills Found Trustees; life trustee, trustee emer, Univ Chicago; Wells Fargo & Co; Minn Mutual Ins Co; Am Coun Educ; Coun Foundations; bd mem, Lenox Group Inc; bd mem, Int Trachoma Initiative; bd mem, Nat Asn Corp Dirs. **Honors/Awds:** Meritorious Publication Award, 1969; Educational Leadership Award, YMCA, St Paul, MN, 1984; Execeptional Black Scientist Award, CIBA-GEIGY Corp, 1984; Spurgeon Award for Community Work, Boy Scouts Am, Indian head Coun, 1985; Outstanding Publication Award, Nat Bur Standards; Honorary Doctorate, State Univ NY, Empire State Col, 1985; Civic Leader Award, League Women Voters, 2000; City Minneapolis Award, 2000; Director of the Year, Nat Asn Corp Dirs; Defender of Democracy Award; Exceptional Black Scientist Award, CIBA-GEIGY Corp; Received 14 honorary doctorate degrees. **Special Achievements:** First African American female chemist in National Bureau of Standards. **Home Addr:** 110 Bank St SE Suite 2403, Minneapolis, MN 55414-3906, **Home Phone:** (612)623-9810. **Business Addr:** Trustee Emeriti, The University of Chicago, 5801 S Ellis Ave, Chicago, IL 60637, **Business Phone:** (773)702-1234.

### KING, REGINA RENE
Actor, movie producer. **Personal:** Born Jan 15, 1971, Los Angeles, CA; daughter of Thomas and Gloria; married Ian Alexander Sr; children: Ian Jr. **Career:** Films: Boyz in the Hood, 1991; Poetic Justice, 1993; Higher Learning, 1994; Friday, 1995; A Thin Line Between Love & Hate, 1996; Jerry Maguire, 1996; How Stella Got Her Groove Back, 1998; Mighty Joe Young, 1998; Enemy of the State, 1998; Down to Earth, 2001; Final Breakdown, producer, 2002; Daddy Day Care, 2003; Legally Blond 2: Red, White & Blonde, 2003; A Cinderella Story, 2004; Miss Congeniality 2: Armed & Fabulous, 2005, Year of the Dog, 2007; This Christmas, 2007; Side by Side: The Story of the 50/50 Group of Sierra Leone, co exec producer, 2007; Living Proof, 2008; Our Family Wedding, 2010; Beastly, 2011; Planes: Fire & Rescue, 2014. TV: "Living Single"; "New York Undercover, Northern Exposure"; 227, 1985-90; "Silver Spoons"; "Frankly Female"; "Ira Joe Fisher"; "Leap of Faith", 2002; "Damaged Care", 2002; "The Boondocks", 2005-07; "Women in Law", 2006; "Framed", 2007; The S-Word, 2008; "Riley Wuz Here"; The Day of Change, 2009; Episode dated 9 April 2009, 2009; See the Woman, 2009; Sally in the Alley, 2009; Two Gangs, 2009; Westside, 2009; Derailed, 2009; "Southland", 2009-13; "The Big Bang Theory", 2013-14; "The Strain", 2014; "Shameless", 2014; "The Gabby Douglas Story", 2014; American Crime, 2015; The Leftovers, 2015. Theatre: Wicked Ways; Seymour & Shirley; 227; A Rainy Afternoon; This Family; The Weirdo; Southland. **Honors/Awds:** BET Award, Best Actress, 2005; Image Award, Outstanding Supporting Actress, Ray, 2005; Golden Satellite Award, 2005; Image Award, Nat Asn Advan Colored People, 2005, 2011, 2012, 2014 & 2016; BET Award, 2005; Primetime Emmy Awards, 2015; Satellite Awards, 2016. **Business Addr:** Actress, C/o Artists Investment Group, 1930 Century Pk W Suite 403, Los Angeles, CA 90067-4115, **Business Phone:** (310)552-1100.

### KING, REGINALD F.
Engineer. **Personal:** Born Mar 11, 1935, Powellton, WV; son of Isaiah and Marie Fairfax; married Grace V Tipper; children: Reginald T & Thaxton E. **Educ:** Youngstown State Univ, BE, 1961; San Jose State Univ. **Career:** Nat Aeronaut & Space Admin, res engr, 1961; Reynolds Electronics, co owner, dir engr, 1968-70. **Orgs:** Inst Elec & Electronics Engrs; Nat Asn Advan Colored people; KAY Frat; Int Studies Orgn. **Honors/Awds:** Technical Brief Award, Nat Aeronaut & Space Admin. **Special Achievements:** Patent in Field; Regis Prof Engr-Elec Engineering, State of Calif, 1975; Regis Prof Engr-Control Syst, State of Calif, 1978. **Home Addr:** 324 Gold Mine Dr, San Francisco, CA 94131-2526, **Home Phone:** (415)647-6536.

### KING, DR. RICHARD DEVOID
Psychiatrist. **Personal:** Born Nov 19, 1946, New Orleans, LA; children: Khent. **Educ:** Whittier Col, BA, 1968; Univ Calif, San Francisco Med Ctr, MD, 1972. **Career:** Univ Calif, Los Angeles, lab asst, 1964; Los Angeles, teacher aide, 1965; factory worker, 1967; lab tech, 1968; Neighbourhood Youth Cor, educ aide, 1969; Univ Calif, asst teacher, 1970; Univ Southern Calif Med Ctr, internship, 1972-73; Univ Calif Med Ctr, resident, 1973-76; San Francisco, psychother res, 1974; Goddard Col, fac adv, 1975-76; Fanon Ment Health Res & Develop Ctr, develop scholar, 1976; Aquman Spiritual Ctr, prin, 1976-77; Palm Springs, lectr, 1977; Martin Luther King Hosp, lectr, 1977; San Francisco State Univ, Sch Ethnic Studies, Dept Black Studies, lectr, 1978; pvt pract psychiatrist, currently. **Orgs:** Nat Islam, 1969-71; Nat Inst Ment Health Ctr Develop Prog, 1973-; Black Psychiatrist Am, 1975-; Am Psychiat Asn, 1975-; Nat Med Asn; Asn Black Psychologist, 1977; Pan-Am Conf, 1977; Black Health Leadership Conf, 1977; pres, Black Psychiatrists N Calif, 1978-80; pres, Black Psychiatrists Calif, 1980; Am Col Surg; Fanon Adv Coun; Atlanta Med Asn; US Pub Health Serv. **Honors/Awds:** Bibliography melannin, 1977; Pineal Gland Rev, 1977; Uracus, 1977-79. **Special Achievements:** Author: African Origin of Biological Psychiatry, 2001; Melanin: A Key To Freedom, 2001; iI African Origin of Biological Psychiatry, 2012; African Origin of Biological Psychiatry, 2012; Co-author, Why Darkness Matters, 2005. **Business Addr:** Psychiatrist, Private Practice, 3751 Stocker St, Los Angeles, CA 90008, **Business Phone:** (323)298-3647.

### KING, RICHARD L., JR.
Entrepreneur. **Personal:** Born Oct 17, 1942, Flint, MI; son of Richard and Johnnie E. **Educ:** Roosevelt Univ, BS, 1966; Harvard Bus Sch, MBE, 1972. **Career:** Richard King Sr Realtors, Property Mgt Dept, mgr, 1962-66; Chicago Bd Educ, admin asst to asst supt schs, 1966-70; City Flint, Econ Develop Div, adminr, 1972-94; Shape Future Habitats To Come Inc, pres, 1994-. **Orgs:** Nat Black MBA Asn; Nat Asn Homebuilders; Flint Community Develop Corp, 1982-94. **Honors/Awds:** Mich Municipal League First-Place, Annual Achievement Competition for the City of Flint, Genesee County Urban Investment Plan, 1994. **Home Addr:** PO Box 3283, Flint, MI 48502-0283. **Business Addr:** President, Shape of Future Things To Come Inc, 328 Cloverdale Pl, Flint, MI 48503-2345, **Business Phone:** (810)233-7483.

### KING, RONALD STACEY. See KING, STACEY.

### KING, DR. ROSALYN CAIN
Pharmacist, health services administrator. **Personal:** Born Sep 10, 1938, New York, NY; daughter of Samuel and Ethel Cain Davis; married Sterling Jr; children: Kristin & Aaron. **Educ:** Duquesne Univ, BS, 1962; Univ Calif Los Angeles, MPH, 1972; Univ Southern Calif, PharmD, 1976. **Career:** Howard Univ, guest lectr, 1977, Continuing Educ Instr, dir, currently; SECON Inc, vpres, 1977-80; Agency Int Develop, Charles R Drew, Univ Med & Sci, pub health adv to US AID, pharm & expert consult, 1980-85, assoc dir, off int health, 1985-86, dir, off int health, 1986-87; Dept Family Med, from instr to assoc prof, 1984-87; Fla A&M Univ, Col Pharm & Pharmaceut Scis, adj assoc prof, 1985; Int Health Inst, dir, 1987; Xavier Univ, Col Pharm, adj assoc prof, 1987; John Hopkins Univ Press, ed; Founding Dir, Howard Univ Pharmacists & Continuing Educ Ctr. **Orgs:** Chairperson, Ambulatory Care Comn, Am Pub Health Asn, 1979-; Am Pub Health Asn, Am Pharmaceut Asn, Nat Pharmaceut Found; deaconess, Mt Calvary Baptist Church, Rockville, MD; Nat Ed Bd; prog mgr, Off Int Progs.John Hopkins Univ Press, ed; Founding Dir, Howard Univ Pharmacists & Continuing Educ Ctr. **Special Achievements:** First Black Pharmacist to serve on professional team of American Pharmacists Association in 1969; Public Health Advisor on Pharmaceuticals to the Africa Bureau and Office of Science and Technology of US Agency for International Development, 1980-85. **Home Addr:** 915 S Belgrade Rd, Silver Spring, MD 20902, **Home Phone:** (301)649-6626.

### KING, RUBY DEAN
Educator. **Personal:** Born Jan 26, 1934, Oktaha, OK; married Clifford; children: Diane, Gerald & LaDonna. **Educ:** BS, 1957; MS, 1975; Okla State Univ, attended 1975; Tex Tech Univ; Univ Cent Okla. **Career:** Educator (retired); Okla Med Ctr, supvr, 1957-60; Morning side Hosp, Los Angeles, supvr, 1961-63; Langston Univ, Family Living Specialist Co op Extent Serv, 1972; Coop Exten Prog, asst dir, 1976; area prog agt, 1976. **Orgs:** Phi Upsilon Omicron; Langston Univ Alumni Asn; Upsilon Theta Omega Chap, Alpha Kappa Alpha Sor Inc; Order Eastern Star, Myra Chap 3; usher, Mt Olive Baptist Church. **Home Addr:** 10601 White Oak Canyon Rd, Oklahoma City, OK 73162-6631, **Home Phone:** (405)722-4459.

### KING, RUBY E.
Consultant. **Personal:** Born Mar 3, 1931; children: Cynthia, Paul, Gayle & Carol. **Educ:** Mich Univ, BA, 1963; Western Mich Univ, MA, 1968. **Career:** Elem sch educr, 1961-67; Mich Univ Campus Sch, supvr, 1967, educr, 1968-71. **Orgs:** Chmn educ comt, Grand Rapids Model Cities Prog, 1969-71; group leader, NEA Urban Educ Conf, 1969; bd dir, YWCA, 1970-71; Gov's Task Force Improving Educ, 1970; bd dir, Grand Rapids Legal Aid Soc, 1971; consult, Minority Affairs Div Mich Educ Asn, 1971-; chmn, Personnel Com Grand Rapids, YWCA, 1971; Mayor's Adv Bd Housing, 1971; state adv bd, Migrant Educ, 1971; bd dir, Asn Supv & Curric Develop, 1971-74; Mich Educ Asn Prof Staff Asn; Lansing Urban League; Gen Educ Adv Comt; Nat Educ Asn, asst exec dir pub affairs. **Honors/Awds:** Nominee Teacher of the Year, Grand Rapids, 1965. **Business Addr:** Assistant Executive Director of Public Affairs, National Education Association, 1201 16th St NW, Washington, DC 20036-3290, **Business Phone:** (202)833-4000.

### KING, SHAKA C.
Fashion designer, business owner. **Personal:** Born Mar 16, 1959, Miami, FL; son of Evelyn and Willie Jr. **Educ:** Pratt Inst, BFA, 1982. **Career:** Shaka King New York Mens Luxury Wear, owner, currently. **Orgs:** Black Alumni Pratt, 1992-; Founder, Black Fashion Collective, 1994-; Fashion Outreach, 1994-. **Honors/Awds:** TFA, Playboy New Talent Award, Absolut Subluxation Showcase. **Special Achievements:** First African to design a line of Hush Puppies, 1998; SKM customers include: Will Downing, Gregory Hines, Mayk Yoba; launched mail order catalog, 1997. **Business Addr:** Owner, Shaka King New York Fine Luxury Mens Wear, 7420 NE 6th Ct, Miami, FL 33138, **Business Phone:** (917)304-5895.

### KING, SHAUN EARL
Football player. **Personal:** Born May 29, 1977, St. Petersburg, FL; son of Sam and Carolyn; married Faith; children: 3. **Educ:** Tulane Univ, mkt, 1998. **Career:** Football player (retired), analyst, radio host; Tampa Bay Buccaneers, 2001, 2003, quarterback, 1999-2000, 2002; Ariz Cardinals, quarterback, 2004-05; Indianapolis Colts, quarterback, 2006; Arena Football League, Las Vegas Gladiators, quarterback, 2006; Detroit Lions, quarterback, 2006; Candian Football League, Hamilton Tiger-Cats, 2007; ESPN, analyst, 2007-10; King David Show, sports talk show host, 2010-12; Mid-day sports talk radio show, hosting, currently; Fox Sports, col football analyst, currently; South Florida Bulls, coaching staff, 2016. **Orgs:** Founder, Shaun King Found; Kappa Alpha Psi Fraternity. **Business Addr:** Founder, The Shaun King Foundation, 1270 Orange Ave Suite E, Winter Park, FL 32789, **Business Phone:** (407)644-1600.

### KING, SHAWN
Football player. **Personal:** Born Jun 24, 1972, West Monroe, LA; children: Charity. **Educ:** La State Univ; Northeast La Univ. **Career:** Football player (retired); Carolina Panthers, defensive end, 1995-97; Indianapolis Colts, defensive end, 1999; Tampa Bay Storm, 2004.

### KING, STACEY (RONALD STACEY KING)
Basketball player, basketball executive, basketball coach. **Personal:** Born Jan 29, 1967, Lawton, OK. **Educ:** Univ Okla, Norman, OK, attended 1989. **Career:** Basketball player (retired), basketball executive; Chicago Bulls, power forward, 1989-92, ctr, 1992-94; game analyst, 2006-07; coach, currently; Minn Timber wolves, ctr, 1994, power forward, 1994-95; Miami Heat, power forward, 1995-96; Boston Celtics, ctr, 1996-97; Dallas Mavericks, ctr, 1996-97; Atenas de Cordoba, 1998-99; Sioux Falls Skyforce, 1998, coach, 2002-03; CBA, Rockford Lightning, head coach & gen mgr, 2001-02; minor-league basketball, head coach; Comcast Sports Net, pre & post-game analyst & color commentator. **Honors/Awds:** NCAA All-American First Team, 1989; Big Eight Player of the Year, 1989; NBA All-Rookie Second Team, 1990; NBA champion, 1991-93.

### KING, STANLEY OSCAR
Sports agent, vice president (organization). **Personal:** Born Mar 21, 1958, Bronx, NY; son of Ellridge and Alberta; children: Stanley O II & Stephanie N. **Educ:** Oglethorpe Univ, BA, bus admin & polit sci, 1981; Rutgers Univ, Sch Law, JD, 1994. **Career:** CIGNA Corp, course designer, 1981-85; Xerox Corp, maj accounts sales mgr, 1985-89; Am Bus Alternatives, pres, 1989-92; First Round Sports Inc, exec vpres & chief operating officer, 1989-; King & King LLC, partner, currently. **Orgs:** Nat Black MBA Asn, Philadelphia Chap, 1988; chmn, Negro Baseball League Celebrations, 1994; youth mentor, Philadelphia Youth Entrepreneurs Inst, 1994; bd mem, Philadelphia Sports Cong, 1994. **Honors/Awds:** Sponsor's Award, Concerned Black Men, 1994. **Home Addr:** 11 Del Sol Pl, Sicklerville, NJ 08081, **Home Phone:** (609)228-8105. **Business Addr:** Executive Vice President, Chief Operating Officer, First Round Sports Inc, 109 E Laurel Rd, Stratford, NJ 08084, **Business Phone:** (856)782-1113.

### KING, DR. TALMADGE EVERETT, JR.
Physician, educator. **Personal:** Born Feb 24, 1948, Sumter, SC; son of Talmadge E Sr and Almetta; married Mozelle Davis; children: Consuelo & Malaika M. **Educ:** Gustavus Adolphus Col, BA, 1970; Harvard Med Sch, MD, 1974. **Career:** Emory Univ Affiliated Hosp, resident, 1974-77; Univ Colo Health Scis Ctr, pulmonary fel, 1977-79, prof med, 1991-97, vice chmn clin affairs, 1993-97; Nat Jewish Med & Res Ctr, sr fac mem, 1990-97, exec vpres clin affairs, 1992-96; San Francisco Gen Hosp, chief, med serv, currently; Univ Calif, San Francisco, Dept Med, Constance B Wofsy Distinguished prof & vice chair, Julius R Krevans distinguished professorship internal med, currently, Dept Med, chair, currently. **Orgs:** Fel Am Col Chest Physicians, Pulmonary PhysiciansFuture, 1983, 1984; fel Am Col Physicians, 1986; bd dir, Am Lung Asn Colo, 1986-97; Western Asn Physicians, 1993; ALA Nat Coun, 1993-98; Gustavus Adolphus Col, 1993-2002; adv bd, Glaxo-Welcome Pulmonary Fel 1994-99, sub specialty bd pulmonary dis, 1995-2000; pres, Am Thoracic Soc, 1997-98; Fleischner Soc, 1997; hon mem, Calif Thoracic Soc, 1998; Colo Thoracic Soc, 1998; Am Col Chest Physicians; Am Col Physicians; Am Lung Asn; Nat Med Asn; Nat Inst Health, Lung Biol & Pathol Study Sect, 1997-2000; Calif Inst Med; Asn Am Physicians, 1998; Am Clin & Climat Asn, 2002; San Francisco Regional Panel selection White House Fel, 2003-04; chmn, Univ Calif San Francisco, 2006-15; bd dir, NCQA, 2009-; fel Am Acad Arts & Sci, 2011; Adv Bd Clin Res Nat Inst Health; Bd Extramural Adv, Nat Heart Lung & Blood Inst, Nat Insts Health; Am Bd Internal Med; Nat Acad Sci, Inst Med. **Honors/Awds:** First Decade Award for Early Achievement, Gustavus Adolphus Col Alumni Asn, 1980; James J Waring Award Outstanding Leadership Treatment Lung Disease, Am Lung Asn Colo, 1992; Constance B Wofsy Distinguished Professor, Univ CA, San Francisco; inducted Colo Pulmonary Hall of Fame, 1998; San Francisco's Top Doctors, San Francisco Mag, 2001-05; PAR Excellence Award, Am Thoracic Soc, 2003; Trudeau Medal, Am Thoracic Soc, 2007; Trudeau Medal, Am Lung Asn, 2007; Breathing for Life Award, Found Am Thoracic Soc, 2012; Sesquicentennial Award, Gustavus Adolphus Col, 2012; Distinguished Chair of Medicine Award, Asn Professors Med, 2016. **Special Achievements:** Co-editor of eight medical textbooks; Author of over 200 articles; Publications, Prevailing and evolving hypotheses about its pathogenesis and implications for therapy, 2001; diopathic Pulmonary Fibrosis. Relation Between Histopathologic Features and Mortality, 2001; Interstitial Lung Disease, 2003; Pulmonary Medicine, 2004; A placebo-controlled trial of interferon gamma-1b in patients with idiopathic pulmonary fibrosis N Engl J Med, 2004; Analyses of Efficacy Endpoints in a Controlled Trial of Interferon gamma-1b for Idiopathic Pulmonary Fibrosis, Chest, 2005; Clinical Advances in the Diagnosis and Therapy of the Interstitial Lung Diseases, 2005; diopathic interstitial pneumonias, 2006; Co-authored Eight Books. **Home Addr:** 6411 Gwin Ct, Oakland, CA 94611, **Home Phone:** (415)206-8317. **Business Addr:** Julius R Krevans Distinguished Professorship in Internal Medicine, Chair, University of California, 400 Parnassus Ave 5th Fl, San Francisco, CA 94143, **Business Phone:** (415)353-2577.

### KING, THOMAS LAWRENCE
Librarian. **Personal:** Born Feb 21, 1953, Medina, OH; son of Thomas and Mozella; married Toni; children: Maria Louise. **Educ:** Univ Akron, Akron, Ohio, BA, geog, 1979; Univ Colo, Boulder, Colo, MA, geog, 1983; Univ Pittsburgh, Pittsburgh, Pa, MLS, 1986; Doctoral

cand, LIS; Simmons Col, Grad Sch Libr & Info Sci. **Career:** Libr Cong, Geog & Map Div, Wash, DC, ref librn, 1987-88; State Univ New York, Binghamton, NY, sci ref/maps librn, earth sci bibliogr, 1989-96; Marion Correctional Inst, librn, currently. **Orgs:** Asn Col & Res Lib; Bibliog Instr Sect, Black Caucus; Am Libr Asn, 1997. **Honors/Awds:** Grad Fel, Nat Sci Found, 1979. **Home Addr:** 608 Boulder Dr, Delaware, OH 43015. **Business Addr:** Librarian, Marion Correctional Institution, PO Box 57, Marion, OH 43302-0057, **Business Phone:** (740)382-5781.

## KING, VIRGIE M. DUNLAP

Educator. **Personal:** Born Oct 9, 1940, Fayette, MS; daughter of Edward Lee and Luetter Massie Hunt; children: Rufus Daniel Jr & Jessica Chase. **Educ:** Jackson State Univ, Jackson, MS, BS, lang arts, 1963; Univ Southern Calif, Los Angeles, CA, MA, educ, 1971; Univ Alaska, Fairbanks, AK, admin, 1982. **Career:** Educator (retired); Tanana Mid Sch, teacher; Fairbanks N Star Bor Sch Dist, Fairbanks, Alaska, teacher, 1973-97; Fairbanks Br Youth Summit, founder. **Orgs:** Alaska Juvenile Justice Adv Comt, N Star Youth Ct, 1997-; PGWM Prince Hall Grand Chap, OES; imperial dep, Desert D I; state loyal lady ruler, Heroines Jericho; chairperson, FEA Minority Caucus; chairperson, Alaska State Human Rights Comn; chair, NEAT Bd; life mem & pres, Nat Asn Advan Colored People; life mem, Jackson State Univ Alumni; Corinthian Baptist Church; coordr, African-Am Stud Leadership Conf. **Home Addr:** 4010 Dunlap Ave, Fairbanks, AK 99709, **Home Phone:** (907)479-3977.

## KING, W. JAMES

Executive. **Personal:** Born Aug 26, 1945, Evergreen, AL; son of John D and Vergie Smith; married Shirley; children: Monica & Sean. **Educ:** Univ Cincinnati, OH, attended 1966. **Career:** Mutual New York, Cincinnati, OH, sales rep, 1970-74; Jaytag Inc, Cincinnati, OH, vpres, opers, 1974-78; J King Contractors, Cincinnati, OH, owner & pres, 1974-80; Avondale Redevelop Corp, Cincinnati, OH, exec dir, 1980; King & Assocs, pres & chief exec officer; Walnut Hills Redevelop Found, pres & chief exec officer, currently; Avondale Redevelop Corp, exec dir; Calif Agr Labor Rels Bd, dir; Nat Farm Worker Serv Ctr, dir; Am Fedn Teachers, dir; Iniciativa Frontera, dir; Azteca Community Loan Fund, dir. **Orgs:** Exec bd, Hist Conserv Bd, 1980-; chmn, Nat Cong Community Econ Develop, 1983-; exec bd, Boys & Girls Club Am, 1989-; chairperson, Xavier Community Adv Comt. **Home Addr:** 756 S Fred Crescent, Cincinnati, OH 45229, **Home Phone:** (513)221-6382. **Business Addr:** Executive Director, Walnut Hills Redevelopment Foundation, 791 E Mcmillan St Suite 201, Cincinnati, OH 45206-1938, **Business Phone:** (513)281-7070.

## KING, WARREN EARL

Management consultant, chief executive officer, president (organization). **Personal:** Born Jul 9, 1947, Durham, NC; son of Leroy Lesley and Alice Mae Umstead; married Hiawatha Mechall Jackson; children: Justin Christopher. **Educ:** Naval Aviation Sch, radar, navig & commun systs, 1970; Univ Calif, Los Angeles, attended 1970; Purdue Univ, BSE, elec engineering, 1976; Ind Univ, Kelley Sch Bus, MBA, mgt, 1987. **Career:** Marine Air Group 33 3rd MAW MCAS El Toro, Calif, Staff Sgt Avionics Systs Specialist, 1966-70; US Postal Serv, distrib clerk, 1970-72; Gen Motors Corp, proj mgr, 1972-87; Delco Remy Div GMC, Anderson, eng proj mgr, 1976-87; Hewlett Packard Co, Sunnyvale, proj mgr, 1987-88; Crown Consult Group LLC, Indianapolis, managing prin, 1988-98, pres & owner, 1988-2001; Digital Equip Corp, global acct exec, 1998; King & Assocs LLC, pres & chief exec officer, 2001-. **Orgs:** Life mem, Nat Asn Advan Colored People, 1984; chmn rules & bylaws comn, CASA/SME, 1984, 1985; Nat Black MBA Asn, 1985; bd dir, Indianapolis Prof Asn, 1990-; life mem, Ind Univ Alumni Asn. **Business Addr:** President, King & Associates, 7934 N Richardt St, Indianapolis, IN 46256, **Business Phone:** (317)849-3019.

## KING, DR. WESLEY A.

Surgeon. **Personal:** Born Sep 25, 1923, Napoleonville, LA; son of Wesley Sr; married Barbara Johnson; children: Robin, Wesley, Jan & Erik. **Educ:** Dillard Univ, AB, 1943; Howard Univ, Md, 1951; Johns Hopkins Sch Med. **Career:** John Hopkins Sch Med, intern; Univ Calif, Los Angeles, Med Ctr, resident neurosurg; Meharry Med Col Inst Surg, surgeon, 1955-57; Los Angeles County Univ Southern Calif Med Ctr, attend surgeon, 1967-; Norstadt Hosp, fel; Univ Southern Calif Med Sch, assoc prof, clin surg, 1974; pvt pract, currently; Ctr Minimally Invasive Neurosurg, dir, currently. **Orgs:** LA County Med Asn; AMA; bd mgr, Crenshaw YMCA, 1972; jr warden ChristGood Shepherd Episcopal Church; founding bd mem, Good Shepherd Manor; Phi Beta Sigma; fel Am Col Surgeons; Cong Neurol Surgeons; N Am Skull Base Soc; Am Asn Neurol Surgeons; Neurosurg Soc Am; Western Neurosurg Soc. **Honors/Awds:** Certified by Am Bd Surg, 1958; Better Businessman's Award, 1962. **Business Addr:** Director, The Center for Minimally Invasive Neurosurgery, 120 S Spalding Dr suite 400, Beverly Hills, CA 90212, **Business Phone:** (310)385-1918.

## KING, DR. WILLIAM CARL

Dentist. **Personal:** Born Nov 29, 1930, Albany, GA; married Rosaria Thomas; children: Sarita Cofield & Sarmora E Chin. **Educ:** Paine Col, BA; Meharry Med Col, DT, DDS. **Career:** Val Community Col, adv dent hyg, 1977; pvt pract dentist, currently. **Orgs:** Cent Dist Dent Soc; Am Dent Asn; Nat Dent Asn; Fla Dent Asn; bd trustees, Valencia Community Col, 1971-75; treas, Goodwill Indust, Fla; Handicap Advs Bd, Fla; pres, Handicap Workshop. **Honors/Awds:** Acad Dentistry Award, Am Soc C, 1966; Excell scholarship, Alpha Omega Fraternity, 1966; Scholarship Award, Chi Delta Mu Fraternity, 1966; Certificate of Appreciation Award, Fla Dept Educ, 1977. **Home Addr:** 1137 Coretta Way, Orlando, FL 32805, **Home Phone:** (407)299-1908. **Business Addr:** Dentist, 809 S Goldwyn Ave, Orlando, FL 32805-4303, **Business Phone:** (407)295-1572.

## KING, ESQ. WILLIAM CHARLES

Lawyer. **Personal:** Born Sep 4, 1952, Pensacola, FL; son of Howard O Sr; married Gayle Surles; children: W Charles & Kristen Noel. **Educ:** Lincoln Univ, Pa, BS, 1973; N Va Sch Law, JD, 1984; Antioch Sch Law. **Career:** DC Govt, retirement examr, 1973-82, personnel mgt specist, 1982-89, gen coun, 1989-91, asst crp coun, 1991-95; US Dept Housing & Urban Develop, asst gen coun, 1995, Off Dept Equal Employ Opportunity, dir, 2005; Powell, Lewis & King Law Firm, partner. **Orgs:** Shiloh Baptist Church, 1983-; Nat Bar Asn, 1984-; Wash Bar Asn, 1984-; DC Bar Asn, 1984-; Am Bar Asn, 1984-; bd trustees, former vchair, chair, evaluations comt, Lincoln Univ, 1994-; Blacks Govt, 1995-. **Honors/Awds:** Employee of the Year, DC Govt, 1985. **Home Addr:** 10012 Tenbrook Dr, Silver Spring, MD 20901-2151, **Home Phone:** (301)681-6807. **Business Addr:** Director, US Department of Housing & Urban Development, 451 7th St SW Suite 10170, Washington, DC 20410-3087, **Business Phone:** (202)708-1112.

## KING, WILLIAM FRANK

Labor relations manager, chemist, educator. **Personal:** Born Dec 13, 1938, Bluffton, GA; son of Eulalia Bankston and Marcellus; married S V Edwards Debourg; children: William Jr & Kristina N; married Karen Aroyan; children: Julian, Isaac & Jason. **Educ:** Lincoln Univ, BA, chem, 1961; Fisk Univ, MA, org chem, 1963; Utah State Univ, PhD, org chem, 1972. **Career:** Atomic Energy Comn, Oak Ridge, Tenn, Nb NJ, tech intern, chemist, 1963-67; Univ Utah, Salt Lake City, fac, intern, fel, 1972-73; Univ N Fla, Chem Dept, asst prof, 1973-75; Chevron Chem Co, Richmond, Calif, sr res chemist, 1975-90; Chevron Res & Technol Co, Richmond, Calif, human resources rep, 1990; Chevron Corp, San Francisco, Calif, human resources rep, 1990-92; Chevron Chem Co, Oronite Technol Div, Additive Synthesis & Processing, sr res chemist, 1992-; Col Marin, chem instr, currently; Dominican Univ, fac. **Orgs:** Bd trustee, Novato Community Hosp, 1993-; Nat Org Prof Advan Black Chemists & Chem Engrs; Am Chem Soc; Nat Asn Advan Colored People; AABE; Am Asn Blacks Energy; ACLU, Marin County, Calif; Concerned Parents Novato; Whos Who Among African Am; bd N Bay Cs Ctr; Novato Pub Access Tv; Marin Educ Fund; Novato Nazarene Church. **Honors/Awds:** Thirty US & foreign Patents, Chevron Corp, 1980-88; Dr William King Scholar, Black Employee Network, named in hon, 2005; Newark Athletic Hall of Fame; Outstanding Work & Dedication, Novato Community Multicultural Comn. **Home Addr:** 1205 Lynwood Dr, Novato, CA 94947, **Home Phone:** (415)892-2162. **Business Addr:** Instructor, College of Marin, 835 College Ave, Kentfield, CA 94904, **Business Phone:** (415)457-8811.

## KING, REV. WILLIAM J.

Clergy, educator. **Personal:** Born Jul 21, 1921, Selma, AL; son of Joseph and Lillian; married Clarice Robinson; children: Judy Thornton, Eric & James. **Educ:** Talladega Col, BA, 1943; Howard Univ Sch Relig, 1946; Howard Univ, Eden Theol Sem, attended 1946; Chapman Col Family Ther Inst Marin. **Career:** Third Baptist Church, pastor, 1946-51; Shiloh Baptist Church, pastor, co-founder, lic counr, 1976-83; Antioch Progressive Church, interim pastor, 1985; Trinity Missionary Baptist Church, interim pastor; Solano Community Col, fac, currently. **Orgs:** Progressive Nat Baptist Conv; Am Asn Marriage & Family Counrs; Calif State Asn Marriage Counrs; Nat Alliance Family Life Inc; Alpha Phi Alpha Fraterity; Nat Asn Advan Colored People. **Home Addr:** 435 Reflections Cir Suite 27, San Ramon, CA 94583-5226.

## KING, WOODIE, JR.

Movie producer, administrator. **Personal:** Born Jul 27, 1937, Baldwin Springs, AL; son of Woodie and Ruby; married Willie Mae; children: Michelle, Woodie Geoffrey & Michael. **Educ:** Will-O-Way Sch Theater; Lehman Col, BA; Brooklyn Col, MFA. **Career:** Ford Motor Co, arc welder; Detroit Tribune, drama critic, 1959-62; Concept E Theatre, Detroit, founder, mgr & dir, 1960-63; Mobiliz Youth, dir, 1965-70; John Hay Whitney fel, 1965-66; Henry St New Fed Theatre NY, founder & dir, 1970-, pres, currently; Woodie King Asn, pres; Nat Black Touring Circuit, founder & producer; My One Good Nerve: A Visit With Ruby Dee, producer; Writer: Right on!, 1971; Hot L Baltimore, 1975; The Long Night, dir, 1976; Black Theatre: The Making of a Movement, producer & dir, 1978; Death of a Prophet, producer & dir, 1981; Segregating the Greatest Generation, producer & dir, 2006; The Torture of Mothers, dir, 1980; The Minority, associate producer, 2006; Men in Black 3, dir, 2012; Flims: Sweet Love, Bitter, 1967; Together for Days, 1972; Serpico, 1973; The Long Night, 1976; TV series: "Law & Order", 1994; "Law & Order: Special Victims Unit", 2009; "Treme", 2011. **Orgs:** Nat Theatre Conf; Soc Stage Dirs & Choreographers; Audelco; Theatre Commun Group; Asn Study Negro Life & Hist; Black Filmmakers Found; dir, Guild Am; Producer & dir, Black Beauties: 100 Years of African-American Women on Broadway, Broadway Cares Equity Fights AIDS, 2003. **Honors/Awds:** Ford Found Grant; Theatre Award, Nat Asn Advan Colored People; Audelco Award; NAACP Image Award, 1987-88; Obie Award, 1996-97; Honorary Doctorate, Wayne State Univ, 2000; Paul Robeson Award, 2003; Rosetta LeNoire Award, 2005; The Edwin Booth Award, 2013. **Special Achievements:** Author of Black Theatre: Present Condition, 1982; author of feature articles in magazines; editor of 5 books of plays, short stories & poems. **Home Addr:** 790 Riverside Dr Apt 3E, New York, NY 10032, **Home Phone:** (212)283-0974. **Business Addr:** President, Director, New Federal Theatre, 292 Henry St, New York, NY 10002-4804, **Business Phone:** (212)353-1176.

## KING-GAMBLE, MARCIA

Writer. **Personal:** Born St. Vincent. **Educ:** Elmira Col, BA, psychol & theater, 1979; MA, communs, currently. **Career:** Novels: Remembrance, 1998; Eden's Dream, 1998; East of Eden, 1998; Under Your Spell, 1999; Carnival Cruise Lines, dir guest relations, 1999-01; Royal Caribbean International, dir, 2001-03; Illusions of Love, 2000; A Reason to Love, 2001; Change of Heart, 2001; Jade, 2002; Come Fall, 2003; This Way Home, 2003; Come Back to Me, 2004; A Taste of Paradise, 2005; Designed for You, 2006; Flamingo Place, 2006; Shattered Images, 2006; All About Me, 2007; American Express. Leader, 2007-09; Down & Out In Flamingo Beach, 2007; Sex On Flamingo Beach, 2007; Hook, Line & Single, 2008; More Than a Woman, 2008; The Way He Moves, 2008; Tempting The Mogul, 2008; First Crush, 2008; Meet Phoenix, 2008; Jack; Island Bliss; Island Book; Harlequin Books, author, 1992-; ARE, mgr member services, 2009-. **Orgs:** Exec bd, Soc Consumer Affairs Prof Bus. **Home Addr:** 4905 N Travelers Palm Lane, Tamarac, FL 33319, **Home Phone:** (954)733-4036. **Business Addr:** Writer, Marcia King-Gamble, PO Box 25143, Tamarac, FL 33320.

## KING-HAMMOND, LESLIE

Dean (education), artist, educator. **Personal:** Born Aug 4, 1944, South Bronx, NY; daughter of Oliver King and Evelyne Alice Maxwell King; married O'Neill Troy; children: Rassaan Jamil King. **Educ:** Univ NY, Queens Col, BFA, 1969; La State Univ, Shreveport, MLA; Univ Md, MFA; Johns Hopkins Univ, MA, 1973, PhD, 1975. **Career:** Queens Col, Dept Performing Arts Workshops, chmn art, 1969-71; Harlem Youth Opportunities Unlimited, prog writer, 1971; Md Inst Col Art, lectr, 1973-76, dean grad studies, 1976-2008, dean emer, 2008-, Ctr Race & Cult, founding dir, 2008-; Kress Fel, 1974-45; Howard Univ, Dept African Studies, doctoral supvr, 1977-81; Nat Endowment Arts, panelist, 1980-82; Civic Design Comn, comnr, 1983-87; Phillip Morris Scholars Artists Color, proj dir, 1985-98; Afro-Am Hist & Cult Mus, art consult, 1990-96; Philip Morris Scholarships Artists Color, dir, 1990-98; Found Scholarships Humanities Visual Arts, coordr, 1985-90; Artscape, cur, 1992; Jacob Lawrence Catalog Raisonne Proj, vpres, 2000; Andy Warhol Curatorial Fel, 2008; Jacob Lawrence Catalog Riasonne Proj, vpres. **Orgs:** Advisor Mayors Comt Art & Cult, 1978; trustee, Baltimore Mus Art, 1981-1987; BLEWS, 1982; Greater Community Found, 1984-; adv bd, Edna Manley Sch Visual Arts, Kingston, 1988-; bd dir, Alvin Ailey Dance Theater Found, 1990-; fel, Cambridge Ctr Residency, GA, 1993 & 1994; pres, Col Art Asn, 1996-2000; bd overseer, Baltimore Sch Arts, 1996-99; fel Va Ctr Creative Arts Residency, 1999 & 2000; bd dir & exec dir, Int Asn Art Critics, 2000-03; fel Ragdale Found Artist Residency, 2000; Girls Baltimore; Ctr Emerging Artists, 2005-07; chmn, exhibs comt & bd dir, Reginald F Lewis Mus Md African Am Hist & Cult, 2007; Womens Art Caucus-Col Art Asn, 2008; James A Porter Colloquium, Howard Univ, 2008; Nat Conf Artists; Md Acad Sci; Creative Alliance. **Home Addr:** 2021 Madison Ave, Baltimore, MD 21217-3861, **Home Phone:** (410)383-0588. **Business Addr:** Dean Emeritus, Founding Director, Maryland Institute College of Art, 1300 W Mt Royal Ave, Baltimore, MD 21217-4134, **Business Phone:** (410)669-9200.

## KING-POYNTER, MARVA

Association executive, executive director. **Personal:** married Robert. **Career:** Ministry Caring Inc, prog dir. **Orgs:** Exec dir, Women & C's Ctr Milwaukee; prog dir, Mary Mother Hope House II & III; prog dir, Job Placement Ctr; prog dir, AmeriCorps prog; prog, Hope House I; prog dir, Samaritan Outreach. **Honors/Awds:** Wilmington Award. **Business Addr:** Program Director, Ministry of Caring Inc, 506 N Church St, Wilmington, DE 19801-4812, **Business Phone:** (302)652-5523.

## KINGDOM, ROGER NONA

Athlete, executive. **Personal:** Born Aug 26, 1962, Vienna, GA. **Educ:** Univ Pittsburgh, attended 2002. **Career:** Athlete (retired), exec; Pan Am Games, Caracas, Venezuela, 1983; Summer Olympics, Los Angeles, 1984, Seoul, S Korea, 1988; IAAF World Cup, Barcelona, Spain, 1989; IAAF World Indoor Championships, Budapest, Hungary, 1989; Goodwill Games, Seattle, USA, 1990; Calif Univ Pa, men & women's head track & field coach, 2004, interim coach, 2005-, dir track, field & cross country, currently. **Orgs:** New Image Track Club; Omega Psi Phi Fraternity Inc. **Home Addr:** 1209 Hawthorne Cir, Monroeville, PA 15071-1075. **Business Addr:** Director, Head Coach, California University of Pennsylvania, 250 Univ Ave, California, PA 15419, **Business Phone:** (724)938-4351.

## KINGI, HENRY MASAO, SR.

Stunt performer, actor. **Personal:** Born Dec 2, 1943, Los Angeles, CA; son of Masao D and Henriella Dunn Wilkins-Washington; married Lindsay Wagner; children: Henry Jr; children: Dorian & Alex. **Career:** Films as actor: Halls of Anger, 1970; Black Girl, 1972; Black Belt Jones, 1974; Truck Turner, 1974; Smoke in the Wind, 1975; The Ultimate Warrior, 1975; Car Wash, 1976; Swashbuckler, 1976; Mr. Billion, 1977; Zero to Sixty, 1978; Stir Crazy, 1980; Charlie Chan & the Curse of the Dragon Queen, 1981; Scarface, 1983; Predator, 1987; Road House, 1989; Secret Agt OO Soul, 1990; Far Out Man, 1990; Parker Kane, 1990; Predator 2, 1990; Grand Canyon, 1991; The Rapture, 1991; Batman Returns, 1992; Lethal Weapon 3, 1992; Conflict of Interest, 1993; Death Ring, 1993; Double Dragon, 1994; Out-of-Sync, 1995; Under Siege 2: Dark Territory, 1995; Barb Wire, 1996; Vampires, 1998; The Protector, 1998; Show time, 2002; The Sponge Bob Sq Pants Movie, 2004; From Mex with Love, 2008; Films asst stunt performer: Gun Shy, 2000; The Million Dollar Hotel, 2000; Here on Earth, 2000; Gone in Sixty Seconds, 2000; The Kid, 2000; Bless the Child, 2000; Get Carter, 2000; Double Take, 2001; The Fast & the Furious, 2001; Ghosts of Mars, 2001; Soul Survivors, 2001; The Salton Sea, 2002; The First $20 Million Is Always the Hardest, 2002; Like Mike, 2002; Austin Powers in Gold mem, 2002; xXx, 2002; Deliver Us from Eva, 2003; Daredevil, 2003; The Matrix Reloaded, 2003; The Ital Job, 2003; Bad Boys II, 2003; The Hard Easy, 2005; Constantine, 2005; The Island, 2005; The Fast & the Furious: Tokyo Drift, 2006; The Tex Chainsaw Massacre: The Beginning, 2006; deja vu, 2006; Mr. Brooks, 2007; Hell Ride, 2008; St Kings, 2008; TV series: Daniel Boone, 1970; "Kung Fu", 1975; "The Bionic Woman", 1978; "T.J. Hooker", 1983; "Matt Houston", 1983; "V", 1985; St of Justice, 1985; Destination Am, 1987; "Earth Star Voyager", 1988; "Disneyland", 1989; She Knows Too Much, 1989; "A Man Called Hawk", 1989; K-9000, 1991; In the Arms of a Killer?, 1992; Steel Justice, 1992; Sex, Love & Cold Hard Cash, 1993; "Walker, Tex Ranger", 1993-98; "Renegade", 1996; "Profiler", 1999; "Soldier of Fortune Inc", 1999; "Angel", 1999; "The Dist", 2002; Franken fish, stunt performer, 2004; "Sleeper Cell", stunt performer, 2005. **Orgs:** Bd dir, founder, Black Fashion Mag "Elegant", 1963; mgr, first maj, Black Pvt Key Club Maverick's Flat, Calif; organizer, Coalition Black Stuntman's Asn Hollywood; sec mem, Soc 10th Cavalry Buffalo Soldiers; Nat Asn Advan Colored People; chmn, Labor & Indust Com; co-chmn, Motion Picture Com; PUSH; CORE Worked with Image; co-founder, Black Stuntmen's Asn. **Honors/Awds:** Awards to get Blacks in motion pictures; Image Award; 10th Cavalry Cowboy Hall Fame; Image Award; Stunt Award, Black Stuntmen's Asn; Stunt Award, Most Spectacular Sequence, "To Live and Die in LA", Stuntmen Award Show, 1986; Taurus Award, 2004, 2005. **Business Addr:** Actor, Stunt Performer, c/o William Morris Agency Inc, 151 El Camino Dr, Beverly Hills, CA 90212, **Business Phone:** (310)859-4000.

**KINGTON, RAYNARD S.**
Educator, association executive. **Personal:** married Peter T Danilolos; children: Emerson & Basil. **Educ:** Univ Mich, BS, MD; Univ Pa, MBA, Wharton Sch, PhD, health policy & econs, Fontaine Fel; Michael Reese Med Ctr, resident, internal med. **Career:** Michael Reese Med Ctr Chicago, resident internal med; Univ Pa, Robert Wood Johnson Clin Scholar, Fontaine fel; Nat Inst Aging Explor Minority Aging Ctr; Charles R Drew Univ Drew/RAND Ctr Health & Aging, co-dir; RAND Corp, sr scientist; Nat Health & Nutrit Exam Surv, dir; Wharton Sch, Fontaine fel; Univ Calif-Los Angeles, asst prof med; Nat Ctr Health Statist, Div Health Exam Statist, dir; Nat Insts Health, Nat Inst Alcohol Abuse & Alcoholism, actg dir, 2002, Behav & Social Sci Res, assoc dir, 2000-03, prin dep dir, 2003-10, actg dir, 2008-09; Inst Med Nat Academies Sci, 2006, gov coun, currently; Grinnell Col, pres, 2010-. **Orgs:** Div dir, Centers DisControl & Prev; chiar, Sect Admin Health Serv, Educ, & Res, 2010; bd dir, Inst Int Educ Students. **Business Addr:** President, Grinnell College, 1115 8th Ave, Grinnell, IA 50112, **Business Phone:** (641)269-4000.

**KINNAIRD, MICHAEL LEON**
School administrator, educator. **Personal:** Born Jul 12, 1945, IN; son of David Renfroe and Thelma Renfroe; children: Eric Michael. **Educ:** Scottsbluff Col, AA, 1967; Chadron St Col, BA, Educ, 1969; Northern Ariz Univ, MA, 1973. **Career:** Educator (retired); Opportunity Sch Clark Co Sch Dist, prin, 1977-81; JimBridger Jr H Clark Co Sch Dist, teacher, 1970-71, dean, 1971-72, admin asst, 1972-73, asst prin, 1973-77; Clark County Sch Dist, Las Vegas, Nev, Sec Prin, 1981; Brinley Miss, fac, 1981-92; Area Tech Trade Ctr, staff, 1993-94; Advan Technol Acad, prin, 1994-2002. **Orgs:** Nat Asn Sec Prin, 1973; Phi Delta Kappa Chap 1113, 1974; treas, ClarkCounty Sec Prin Asn, 1976-77; pres, Clark Co Asn Sch Admin, 1977-78; treas, PDK Chap 1113, 1979-80; Chadron State Col Alumni Asn. **Honors/Awds:** Appreciation for Continued Support, Am Afro Unity Festival, Las Vegas, Nev, 1978; Nevada Secondary Principal of the Year, Nat Asn Sec Sch Principals, 1997; Distinguished Alumni Educator Award, Chadron State Col, 1998; Milken National Educator Award, 1998; Milken Family Foundation Award. **Home Addr:** 8000 Gothic Ave, Las Vegas, NV 89117, **Home Phone:** (702)258-9098.

**KINNEBREW, LAWRENCE D. (LARRY KINNEBREW)**
Football player. **Personal:** Born Jun 11, 1960, Rome, GA. **Educ:** Tenn State Univ. **Career:** Football player (retired); Cincinnati Bengals, fullback, 1983-87; Buffalo Bills, fullback, 1989-90. **Home Addr:** 3190 Patrisal Ct, Cincinnati, OH 45236-1332.

**KINNIEBREW, ROBERT LEE**
Real estate executive. **Personal:** Born Feb 13, 1942, Manhattan, NY; son of Covton and Daisy Crawford Cobb; married Raymona D Radford; children: Robertina & Rolanzo. **Educ:** Pace Univ, Lubin Sch Bus, BBA, int mgt, span, 1987; Acad Aeron NY; Commun Sch, AUS; Non Commiss Off Acad Bad Toelz W Ger; AUs Off Cand Sch Comn 2 Lt Artil Ft Sill, OK; Ins Underwriters Sch, PA; Nat Assoc Independent Fee Appraisers, NJ; MW Funk Sales Inst Real Estate NJ; S Jersey Realty Abstr Sales Sch NJ; Grad Realtors Inst NJ; Mgt Develop Course, Wash DC. **Career:** AUS W Ger, pole lineman, fixed sta transmitter repairman, 1963-65; Candid Realty Inc, pres, 1971, broker & owner, 1987-; Century 21 Candid Realty Inc, pres, 1972-87, broker, owner, 1987-2010; Century 21 Northeast, data entry clerk, 1983-85; Helstrom Int, info technologist, 1985-86; Stand Importing, comput operator, 1986; Veterans Admin, mgt broker; Fed Housing Admin, mgt broker; Vet Admin, appraiser; Lockheed Aircraft Co Idlewild Airport, flight line mech; Mutural NY Ins Co, dir sales underwriter; Protect A Life Burglar Alarm Co, dir sales; jewelry store chain, dir sales; Gen Sound Philadelphia, customer rel mgr; Westinghouse, mgr lighting dept; TREND, bd dir; Ft Dix NJ, post signal, oper & comndg officer; Ft Bliss TX & Viet-Nam, battalion commun officer. **Orgs:** Pres, Nj Asn Realtors, 1996; Edgewater Pk Jaycees, Burlington Cty Draft Bd, Burlington Cty Chamber Com, Masonic Lodge; Century 21 Brokers Coun SJ; Beverly Rotary Club; Boy Scouts Am; Make Am Better Comn; dir, Nat Asn Realtors; bd mem, chap chmn, exec comm, chmn, Burlington Cty Red Cross; rep, Century 21 Nat Brokers Commun Cong; pres, dir Burlington Cty Bd Realtors; dir NJ State Bd Realtors; Legal Action Comn; Nominating Comn; Equal Opportunity Comn; Libr Comn; Legal Action Comn, NJ Asn Realtors; dir, comnr, Nj Real Estate Comn; Burlington Camden County Asn Realtors; W Jersey Ski Club; Easter Pa Ski Coun. **Honors/Awds:** Community Service Award, Burlington City Bd Realtors, 1983; Realtor of the Year Award, NJ State Assoc Realtors, 1983; Century 21 Sales Achievement Award, 1994-2004; Award Appreciation, Dedicated Serv Beverly City Common Councilwoman, 2004-06. **Home Addr:** 106 Riverbank, Beverly, NJ 08010, **Home Phone:** (609)387-3648. **Business Addr:** Owner, President, Candid Realty Inc, 4259 B Rte 130 S, Beverly, NJ 08010-2801, **Business Phone:** (609)871-1444.

**KINSEY, BERNARD W.**
Executive, president (organization), founder (originator). **Personal:** Born Sep 20, 1943, West Palm Beach, FL; married Shirley; children: Khalil. **Educ:** Fla A&M Univ, attended 1967, Pepperdine Univ, MBA, 1973. **Career:** Humble Oil Co, sales rep, 1971; Xerox Corp, LA, field serv mgr, 1971, regional gen mgr, 1983, Voice Systs Div, vpres, 1991; Rebuild Los Angeles, chief operating officer & chmn; KBK Enterprise, pres & founder, currently. **Orgs:** Co-founder, Xerox Black Employees Asn; bd dir, Nat Underground Rr Freedom Ctr, 2009; bd mem, William H. Johnson Found, 2001; Omega Psi Phi. **Special Achievements:** First African American sales representative for Humble Oil Company. **Home Addr:** 301 Mt Holyoke Ave, Pacific Palisades, CA 90272-4602, **Home Phone:** (310)454-9304. **Business Addr:** President, Founder, KBK Enterprises Inc, 3018 W Kennedy Blvd, Tampa, FL 33609, **Business Phone:** (813)874-3302.

**KINSEY, JIM**
Basketball executive. **Personal:** married Darlene; children: Jackie Adonis. **Career:** Nat Basketball Asn, referee, 2001-02.

**KINSEY, SHIRLEY (SHIRLEY POOLER)**
Art collector, foundation executive, philanthropist. **Personal:** Born Feb 7, 1946, Lake City, FL; daughter of Eddie Pooler and Erma Pooler; married Bernard Kinsey; children: Khalil. **Educ:** Fla A&M Univ, BA, eng, 1967; Pepperdine Univ, MA, multi-cultural educ, 1976. **Career:** Art collector; Compton Unified Sch Dist, elem sch teacher, 1967-73; Xerox Corp, trainer & training mgr, 1973-82; KBK Enterprises Inc, proj mgr, 1985-95; Bernard & Shirley Kinsey Found Arts & Educ, co-founder, 2008, chmn emer. **Orgs:** Delta Sigma Theta. **Special Achievements:** Co-creator, national touring museum exhibit "The Kinsey Collection: Shared Treasures of Bernard and Shirley Kinsey-Where Art and History Intersect", 2006-; coauthor, "The Kinsey Collection: Shared Treasures of Bernard and Shirley Kinsey"; helped raise more than $22 million for charitable and educational institutions.

**KIRBY, ANTHONY T.**
Fashion designer, entrepreneur. **Educ:** Tobe-Coburn Sch Fashion, AOS, merchandising & mkt, 1984; Fashion Inst Technol, BS, merchandising & mgt, 2008. **Career:** Polo Ralph Lauren, menswear coordr, 1986-87, asst store mgr, 1987-91, Haberdashery Specialist, 2005-08; Barneys New York, dress furnishings mgr, 1994-96; David Glazer, merchandising & rep dress furnishings, 1997-98; Peter Elliot, asst menswear dir & menswear sales, 1999-2004; Anthony T. New York Dress Furnishings, owner & haberdasher, 1992-20 05; Polo Ralph Lauren, haberdashery specialist, 2005-08; Robert Talbott & Audrey Talbott, neckwear & MTM shirt sales, 2008-09; Ralph Lauren, mens clothing, dress furnishings, 2011-2012; CROCKETT & JONES, Men's & Women's Footwear Representative, 2013-.

**KIRBY, DR. JACQUELINE**
Physician. **Personal:** Born Dec 17, 1946, Atlanta, GA; married Edward G Helm; children: Lisa. **Educ:** Spelman Col, BA, 1968; Meharry Med Col, MD, 1973. **Career:** Grady Health Syst, resident, 1973-78; Harvard Univ, res & fel, 1971; Emory Univ Affiliated Hosp, externship, 1972, med intern, 1973-74, internal med, 1974-76, rheumatology, 1977-; Crawford W Long Hosp, emergency room physician, 1976-77; Tulane Univ, resident, 1984-85. **Orgs:** YWCA, 1973; assoc mem, Am Col Physicians. **Honors/Awds:** Res fel, Harvard Univ, 1971; honor, Dept Pharmcacol, 1971; fel Emory Univ, 1977. **Home Addr:** 2539 Shiloh Dr, Decatur, GA 30032.

**KIRBY, NANCY J.**
Consultant, college administrator. **Personal:** Born Apr 20, 1940, Haddonfield, NJ. **Educ:** Bennett Col, BA, psychol, 1960; Bryn Mawr Col, MSS, 1965. **Career:** Temple Univ Med Ctr, chief social worker outpatient med, 1966-69; Planned Parenthood SE Pa, dir social serv, 1969-71; Beaver Col, asst prof, 1971-79; Bryn Mawr Col Grad Sch Social Work & Social Res, lectr, asst dean & dir admis, 1979-2010, consult to dean, coordr alumni connections, 2010-. **Orgs:** Bd dir, Spectrum Health Serv, 1978-; Asn Blacks Philanthropy & new Safrica, Univ Nc Sch Social Work; Inglis Found, 1992-; bd dir, Inglis Innovative Serv, 1994-; trustee, Dowdy Found, 1995-; bd dir, Unitarian Universalist House, 1998-; trustee, staff, Valentine Found, 2007-13; Black Women Sport Found. **Business Addr:** Coordinator of Alumni Connections, Bryn Mawr College, 300 Airdale Rd, Bryn Mawr, PA 19010-1697, **Business Phone:** (610)520-2605.

**KIRBY-DAVIS, MONTANGES**
Executive, manager. **Personal:** Born Jan 6, 1953, Wadesboro, NC; daughter of Archie William (deceased) and Minnie Allen. **Educ:** Winston-Salem State Univ, Winston-Salem, BA, sociol, 1975; Cornell Univ, cert int human resources exec prog. **Career:** Sara Lee, Winston-Salem, personnel specialist, 1978-83, mgr, mgt employ, 1983-88; Am Soc Personnel Admin, cert trainer, accredited personnel specialist recruiting; Sara Lee Corp, Winston-Salem, NC, chief diversity strategist, mgr, training & develop, 1988-91, dir workforce diversity, 1991-97; Kirby Resource Group, founder & pres, 1997-. **Orgs:** Bd dir, Winston-Salem Personnel Asn, 1980-85; bd dir, Battered Women's Shelter, 1980-85; bd dir, YWCA, 1980-85; pres, Forsyth County YWCA, 1982-83; Am Soc Training & Develop; co-chair, First Piedmont Triad Prof Develop Conf Women, 1990-; chmn, United Way Training & Develop Comt, 1990-91; NC Gov's Comn Workforce Preparedness, 1994; Winston Salem State Univ, bd trustee, 1994; Olympics Employee Prog, 1997; assoc dir, Diversity Strategy Consortium. **Home Addr:** 21 Middlecreek Way, Greenville, SC 29607. **Business Addr:** President, Founder, The Kirby Resource Group, 535 N Pleasantburg Dr Suite 202, Greenville, SC 29616-0579, **Business Phone:** (864)292-7033.

**KIRCHHOFER, DR. WILMA ARDINE LYGHTNER**
Consultant, executive director, founder (originator). **Personal:** Born Sep 30, 1940, Mason City, IA; daughter of William and Tressie Traylor; married Guy Marbury; married Kirk; children: Gregory Luther & Douglas Bernard. **Educ:** Iowa State Univ, Col Home Econs, IA, BS, foods & nutrit, 1963; Emory Univ, Atlanta, GA, MPH, 1977; Univ Mo, Columbia, PhD, human nutrit & int community develop, 1986. **Career:** Ga State Univ, Atlanta, Ga, asst prof, 1976-80; Univ Mo, Columbia, Mo, asst prof, 1984-86; Lincoln Univ, Jefferson City, Mo, asst prof, 1982-86; Ross Labs, Columbus, Ohio, assoc dir med educ, 1986-87; Coca-Cola Co, Atlanta, Ga, mgr, health prom, 1987-2000; Youth Leadership Global Health Inc, co founder & dir, 2001-; WALK Assocs, health & productivity consult & prin, 2001-. **Orgs:** Bd mem, Ga Partners Americas, 1988-91; chair, Pub Rels Atlanta Dietetic Asn, 1989-91; ed, Newsletter Ga Nutrit Coun, 1989-91. **Home Addr:** 2000 Filbert Lane Suite A, Atlanta, GA 30349-5255, **Home Phone:** (404)559-9634. **Business Addr:** CoFounder, Director, Youth Leadership for Global Health Inc, 136 Cottsford Dr SW, Atlanta, GA 30331-8376, **Business Phone:** (404)559-9634.

**KIRK, ORVILLE, SR.** **See Obituaries Section.**

**KIRK, AMBASSADOR RONALD**
Lawyer, government official. **Personal:** Born Jun 27, 1954, Austin, TX; married Matrice Ellis; children: Elizabeth Alexandra & Catherine Victoria. **Educ:** Austin Col, BA, polit sci & sociol, 1976; Univ Tex Sch Law, JD, 1979. **Career:** US Sen Lloyd Bentsen, legis asst, 1981-93; City Dallas, asst city atty & chief lobbyist, 1983-89; Johnson & Gibbs PC, shareholder, 1989-94; State Tex, 98th secy state, 1994-95; Gardere & Wynne LLP, partner; City Dallas, mayor, 1995-2002; Gen Drew Days, US solicitor; Gen Eric Holder, dep atty; Chevron Corp, gen coun; Charles James & Gen Mills, gen coun; Roderick Palmore, gen coun; Vinson & Elkins LLP, partner, 2005-; Off Us Trade Rep, US trade rep, 2009-13; Energy Future Holdings, lobbyist; Merrill Lynch, lobbyist. **Orgs:** Leadership Dallas Alumni Asn, 1986-; Dallas Assembly, 1990-; bd trustee, Austin Col, 1991-; Mus African Am Life & Cult, 1991-; Cotton Bowl Athletic Asn, 1991-; Gen Serv Comn Tex, 1992-94; pres, Dallas Zool Soc, 1992-94; chmn, Gen Serv Comn Tex, 1993; State Fair Tex Bd, 1993-; State Bar Tex; Am Bar Asn; Nat Bar Asn; J L Turner Legal Asn; chmn bd, Dallas Educ Found; bd trustee, March Dimes; bd dir, Brinker Int; bd dir, Dean Foods Co; bd dir, PetSmart Inc; chmn, S Dallas/Fair Pk Trust Fund Adv Bd; chmn bd, Hart Global Leaders Forum, Southern Methodist Univ. **Business Addr:** Partner, Vinson & Elkins LLP, Trammell Crow Ctr 2001 Ross Ave Suite 3700, Dallas, TX 75201-2975, **Business Phone:** (214)220-7968.

**KIRK-DUGGAN, REV. DR. CHERYL ANN**
Clergy, musician, educator. **Personal:** Born Jul 24, 1951, Lake Charles, LA; daughter of Rudolph Valentino (deceased) and Naomi Ruth Mosely (deceased); married Michael Allan. **Educ:** Univ Southwestern La, BA, 1973; Univ Tex, Austin, MM, 1977; Austin Presby Theol Sem, MDiv, 1987; Baylor Univ, PhD, 1992. **Career:** Univ Tex, Austin, music Black Am coach accomp, 1974-77; Austin Community Col, music Black Ams, 1976-77; Prairie View A&M Univ, teacher, 1977-78; Williams Inst CME Church, organist, choir dir, 1979-83; The Actor's Inst, teacher, 1982-83; Self-employed, prof singer, voice teacher, vocal coach, 1980-85; Christian Methodist Church, ordained minister, deacons orders, 1984, elders orders, 1986; Baylor Univ, Inst Oral Hist, grad asst, 1987-89, Dept Relig, teaching asst, 1989-90; Meredith Col, asst prof, 1993-96; Ctr Women Relig, dir, grad theol union, asst prof, theol womanist studies, 1997-; Ed Bd, Contagion: Jour Violence, Mimesis Cult, 1994-; Asn Black Awareness, Meredith Col, adv, 1994-96. **Orgs:** Pi Kappa Lambda, 1976-; Omicron Delta Kappa, 1977-; assoc pastor, Trinity CME Church, 1985-86; pres, Racial Ethnic Faith Comm, Austin Sem, 1986-87; Golden Key Hon Soc, 1990; Colloquim On Violence Religion; Soc Biblical Lit; Am Acad Relig; Ctr Black Music Res; Soc Chritian Ethics; Am Soc Aesthetics; ed bd, Sigma Alpha Iota; Semeia, 1999-. **Honors/Awds:** Univ Southwestern LA, Magna Cum Laude; Univ Tex, Austin, Univ Fellowship, 1975-77; Fund for Theol Educ, Fellowship for Doctoral Studies, 1987-88, 1988-89. **Special Achievements:** Carnegie Hall debut, 1981; featured: "Life, Black Tress, Das Goldene Blatte, Bunte," 1981, 1982; recording: "Third Duke Ellington Sacred Concert," Virgil Thompson's Four Saints in Three Acts, EMI Records, 1981-82; "African Spirituals: Exorcising Evil Through Song," A Troubling in My Soul: Womanist Perspectives on Evil and Suffering, Orbis Press, 1991; "Gender, Violence and Transformation," Curing Violence: The Thought of Rene Girard, Polebridge Press, 1991; author: Lily Teaching Fellow, 1995, 1996; Collidge Scholar with Assoc for Religion & Intellectual Life, 1996; African Special Days: 15 Complete Worship Services, Abingdon Press, 1996; It's In the Blood: A Trildgy of Poetry Harvested from a Family Tree, River Vision, 1996; Exorcizing Evil: A Womanist Perspective on the Spirituals, Orbis, 1997; Refiner's Fire, A Religious Engagement with Violence, Augsburg- Fortress, 2000; The Undivided Soul: Helping Congregations Connect Body and Spirit, Abingdon, 2001; Misbegotten Anguish: Theology and Ethics of Violence, Chalice, 2001; Soul Pearls: Worship Resources for the Black Church, 2004; Sisters Bible Study Wising Up - Participant's Workbook: Applying the Wisdom of Proverbs to Daily Life, 2005; More African American Special Days: 15 Complete Worship Services, 2005; Violence and Theology, 2006; Wake Up: Hip-Hop, Christianity, and the Black Church, 2011; Wising Up: Applying the Wisdom of Proverbs to Daily Life: Participants Workbook. **Business Addr:** Assistant Professor, Director, Center for Women and Religion, 2400 Ridge Rd, Berkeley, CA 94705, **Business Phone:** (510)649-2400.

**KIRKLAND, REV. GWENDOLYN V.**
Executive. **Personal:** Born Apr 24, 1951, Chicago, IL; daughter of Warren and Smith. **Educ:** Bradley Univ, BS; DePaul Univ, MEd; Chicago Theol Sem, Mdiv. **Career:** Chicago Pub Schs, primary grades educr; AJ Nystrom Inc, sales rep; Dean Witter Reynolds, assoc vpres investments; Chapman Co, br mgr; Am Investment Serv Inc, CFP/Investment broker & br mgr; Kirkland, Turnbo & Assoc, managing prin, Covenant United Church Christ, assoc pastor Stewardship. **Orgs:** Delta Sigma Theta; bd mem, United Church Funds; Stewardship Comt Ill Conf UCC. **Special Achievements:** Executive Certificate in Religious Fundraising from Indiana University the Lilly Foundation of Philanthropy. **Home Addr:** 18531 Meadow Lane, Hazel Crest, IL 60429, **Home Phone:** (708)799-8235. **Business Addr:** Managing Principal, Kirkland Turnbo & Associates, 4747 Lincoln Mall Dr Suite 602, Matteson, IL 60443-3817, **Business Phone:** (708)481-8787.

**KIRKLAND, PROF. JACK A.**
Consultant, educator. **Personal:** Born Oct 28, 1931, Blythedale, PA; son of Aaron and Anna Mae; married Iris McWherter; children: Jack Jr, Adrianne & Kelly. **Educ:** Syracuse Univ, BA, 1959, MSW, 1961. **Career:** Peace Corps, Trng Community Develop, Honduras, dir, 1964-67; St Louis Univ, Social Grp Work Prog, chair, 1964-70, 1980; Wash Univ, assoc prof, social work, 1970-, chair, dir & co-founder, African-Am studies, 1974-76, Econ Develop Concentration, Sch Social Work, founder, 1980-89; State Mo, dir transp, 1976-80; Shatil, Nat Israeli Community Develop Corp, Int Inst Educ, consult; Jeff-Vander-Lou Develop Corp, dir. **Orgs:** Phi Delta Kappa End Hon Soc; Herbert Hoover Boy's Club; Mo State Dept Transp; consult, Int Inst Educ, S Africa; advisors, Native Ams Southwest Div Bur Indian Affairs. **Home Addr:** 10829 Chase Pk Lane Apt D, St. Louis, MO 63141. **Business Addr:** Associate Professor of Social Work, Washington University, 1 Brookings Dr, St. Louis, MO 63130-4899, **Business Phone:** (314)935-6600.

**KIRKLAND, LEVON (LORENZO LEVON KIRKLAND)**
Football coach, football player. **Personal:** Born Feb 17, 1969, Lamar, SC; married Keisha LeShun Tillman; children: Kennedy (deceased) &

Zach. **Educ:** Clemson Univ, BA, sociol, 2004. **Career:** Football player (retired), coach; Pittsburgh Steelers, left inside linebacker, 1992-2000, linebacker, 1999; Seattle Seahawks, mid linebacker, 2001; Philadelphia Eagles, mid linebacker, 2002; Nat Col Scouting Asn, educ speaker, currently; Wade Hampton High Sch, Greenville, SC, linebackers coach; Woodmont High Sch, linebacker coach, 2009-11; Shannon Forest Christian Sch, Greenville, SC, head coach, 2011-13; Fla A&M Univ, defensive coordr & linebackers coach, 2013-; Clemson Univ, coord minority recruitment. **Orgs:** Educ speaker, Nat Col Scouting Asn. **Honors/Awds:** All-American, 1991; All-Pro, 1996, 1997; Pro Bowl, 1996, 1997; Alumni Linebacker of the Year, Nat Football League, 1997; Most Valuable Player, Pittsburgh Steelers Team, 1998, 1999; Clemson Hall of Fame, 2001; South Carolina Athletic Hall of Fame, 2008. **Business Addr:** Defensive Coordinator, Linebackers Coach, Florida A&M University, Lee Hall Suite 400, Tallahassee, FL 32307, **Business Phone:** (850)599-3000.

### KIRKLAND, THEODORE

Writer, educator, association executive. **Personal:** Born Jan 1, 1934, Camden, SC; married Winona Washington; children: Sharon, Adrianne & Cynthia. **Educ:** State Univ NY, Buffalo, BA, sociol, 1976, MA, social sci, 1984. **Career:** Buffalo Police Dept, police officer, 1962-78; WKBW-TV, Buffalo, Kirkland & Co, tv host & producer, 1974-78; NY State Parole, bd comnr, 1978-85; State Univ New York, Buffalo, adj prof criminol & sociol; Hunter Col, Black & Puerto Rican Studies Dept, prof, currently. **Orgs:** Pres & founder, Afro-Am Police Asn Buffalo, 1969-71; Nat Black Police Asn, 1972; fel Buffalo State Col Comn, 1984; Sr ed, Buffalo Black Newspaper, 1985; bd mem, Harlem Restoration Proj, 1985; bd mem, NY State Civil Liberties Union, 1985; Nat Asn Blacks Criminal Justice, 1985; Nat Asn Advan Colored People. **Honors/Awds:** Presidential Citation for Exceptional Service, 1972; Received numerous community awards and citations from community groups, Youth groups and prison inmate organizations including the NAACP, Operation PUSH, ACLU, Black Prof Women's Org Black Firefighters, Afro-American Police Asn; President's Award, Empire State Fedn Women's Clubs. **Special Achievements:** Published an article "A Black Policeman's Perpective on Law Enforcement in "1979 " which is used in numerous colleges and police training academies. His writings appears periodically in the Black Community newspaper. Hosts "Kirkland's Korner" on WUFO Fridays at 10pm; Columnist with The Challenger & The Buffalo Criterion newspapers. Author: Spirit and Soul, Odyssey of a Black Man in America. **Home Addr:** 352 Pratt St, Buffalo, NY 14204, **Home Phone:** (716)856-9315. **Business Addr:** Professor, Hunter College, W Bldg 1711 695 Pk Ave, New York, NY 10021, **Business Phone:** (212)772-5035.

### KIRKLAND-BRISCOE, DR. GAIL ALICIA

Dentist. **Personal:** Born Apr 12, 1960, Tuskegee, AL; daughter of Levi S Sr and Mary L Pratt. **Educ:** Vanderbilt Univ, BS, 1982; Howard Univ Col Dent, DDS, 1986, Cert Orthod, 1988. **Career:** Gail Kirkland-Briscoe, DDS PC, owner, 1994-. **Orgs:** Alpha Kappa Alpha Sor; Alumni Asn Stud Clinicians Am Dent Asn; Omicron Kappa Upsilon; Nat Dent Asn; Am Asn Orthod; Nat Asn Female Exec. **Honors/Awds:** Deans Award, Alpha Omega Nat Soc, 1986; Int Col Dentists Award, 1986; Harold S Fleming Memorial Award, 1986; Orthodontic Award, Howard Univ, 1988. **Special Achievements:** Author of Forensic Dentistry- Solving the mysteries of identification, General Dentistry, 1987; Featured on Working Woman Television Show. **Home Addr:** 17006 Federal Hill Ct, Bowie, MD 20716-3512, **Home Phone:** (301)218-5914. **Business Addr:** Dentist, Orthodontist, Gail Kirkland-Briscoe DDS PC, 3012 18th St NE, Washington, DC 20018-2458, **Business Phone:** (202)526-4060.

### KIRKLAND-GORDON, DR. SHARON ELAINE

Psychologist. **Personal:** Born Oct 19, 1957, Buffalo, NY; daughter of Theodore and Winona. **Educ:** Spelman Col, BA, 1979; State Univ NY, Buffalo, NY, MS, 1983, PhD, coun psychol, 1991. **Career:** City Buffalo Common Coun, legis asst, 1979-80; State Univ New York, Buffalo, Upward Bound prog counr, 1984-85, Sch Med, prog coord & res spec, 1985-88; Univ Md Coun Ctr, pre-doctoral intern, 1988-89, staff counr & psychologist, 1990, internship training dir, 1998. **Orgs:** Minority fel Am Psychol Asn, 1986, Div 17 & 45, 1994-; Nat Asn Black Psychologists, 1991-94; bd dir, Am Psychol Asn, Asn Coun Ctr Training Agencies, 1998-, 2001-; Am Col Personnel Asn, 1998-. **Honors/Awds:** Outstanding Young Woman of the Year, 1977; Certificate of Appreciation, Govt Dominica, 1997; Certificate of Appreciation, Nat Weather Serv, 1998; Certificate of Appreciation, Am Psychologist Asn Minority Fel Prog, 2000; President's Distinguished Service Award, Univ Md, 2013. **Special Achievements:** Co-auth: "Univ Campus Consultation: Opportunities & Limitations", Jour Coun & Develop, 1993; "Organizational Racial Diversity Training", Racial Identity Theory: Applications to Individual, Group & Organizational Interventions, 1993. **Business Addr:** Training Director, Staff Counselor, University of Maryland, 1203 Shoemaker Bldg, College Park, MD 20742, **Business Phone:** (301)314-7651.

### KIRKLAND-HOLMES, DR. GLORIA

Educator. **Personal:** Born Aug 29, 1952, Charleston, SC. **Educ:** Fisk Univ, BA, elem educ, 1974; Ind State Univ, MS, elem educ, 1975, PhD, elem educ, 1978. **Career:** Margaret Ave Child Care Ctr, asst dir, parent coord, 1975-76; Maehling Terr Day Care Ctr, dir teacher, 1976; Ind State Univ, adj asst prof, 1976-78; Rose S side Child Care Ctr, dir, 1976-78; Ind State Lab Sch, nursery teacher, 1978; Malcolm Price Lab Sch, Univ Northern Iowa, nursery-kindergarten teacher, 1978-97, assoc prof, 1978-; coordr, African Am Read-in, 2006, coordr, Conf African Am C & Families, 2010, project coordinator, 2013-. **Orgs:** Nat Asn Educ Young C, 1975-; Iowa Asn Educ Young C, 1975-; Black Child Devel Inst, 1977; bd mem, Logandale Urban Housing Corp, 1979-; chairperson & secy, Iowa NE State Conf Nat Asn Advan Colored People, 1979-; youth adv, Black Hawk Co, Nat Asn Advan Colored People Youth Group, 1979-. **Special Achievements:** Book: Read Rap: Cognitive Learning with a Rhythmic Beat, 2000. **Business Addr:** Professor, University of Northern Iowa, Schindler Educ Ctr 624, Cedar Falls, IA 50614-0606, **Business Phone:** (319)273-2007.

### KIRKLIN, DR. PERRY WILLIAM (NANA KWAME BAFFOE, II)

President (organization), physical chemist, educator. **Personal:** Born Feb 28, 1935, Ellwood City, PA; son of Perry and Martha Peek; married Betty Jean Lampkins; children: Cheryl Merrell, Perry III & Pamela June. **Educ:** Westminster Col, New Wilmington, PA, BS, 1957; Univ Minn, Minneapolis, MN, PhD, 1964. **Career:** Phys chemist, educr (retired); Rohm & Haas Co, analyst grp leader, 1964-70; Mobil Res & Develop Corp, sr res chemist, 1970-78, assoc chemist, 1978-91; proj fuels res leader, 1978-91; assoc aviation fuels res; Bloomfield Col, assoc prof chem, 1991-95; St Mary's Hall-Doane Acad, sub teacher, 1995-2001; Montgomery County Col, Summer Bridge Prog, chem prof, 1995-2001; Cheyney Univ Pa, adj prof, 1996-97. **Orgs:** Dir, Bucks County Community Ctr, 1965-74; Salem Baptist Church Jenkingtown, Pa, 1968-2004; chmn, Bucks County Health Planning, 1968-72; dir, PHILA Reg Health Planning, 1968-74; pres, vpres & asst treas, Salem Fed Credit Union, 1968-2004; Pa State Health Planning Coun, 1970-74; chmn, ASTM Aviation Fuel Comn, 1977-91; Nat Org Black Chemists & Chem Engrs, 1979-; founder & pres, Kuntu Village (Ghana) Nkosohen Comt-USA, 2003-. **Home Addr:** 5534 Grey Hawk Lane, Lakeland, FL 33810, **Home Phone:** (863)816-8285. **Business Addr:** President, Kuntu Village Nkosohen Committee-USA, 5534 Grey Hawk Lane, Lakeland, FL 33810-4001, **Business Phone:** (863)816-8285.

### KIRKSEY, M. JANETTE

Administrator, writer. **Personal:** Born Apr 15, 1946, Brownsville, PA; daughter of George A Williamson (deceased) and Johnnie L (deceased); married Edward M Kirskey; children: Scott M (deceased) & Daniele B. **Educ:** Franklin Univ, ABA, BBA, bus admin, 1981. **Career:** Abbott Nutrit, contract mgr, 1973-2003; Ross Labs, from assoc buyer to sr buyer, contract mgr, 1996-; Ross Prod Div, packaging buyer, currently; J-Boo Bks, independent publ prof/auth/chief exec officer/pr mgr Nia, 2007-. **Orgs:** Delta Sigma Theta; Mt Herman Baptist Church; proj bus vol counr; Jr Achievement; Nia Performing Arts Theatre Co; Interdenominational Church Ushers Asn Columbus Inc; Sr Usher Bd. **Business Addr:** Chief Executive Officer, J-BOO BOOKS LTD, 8142 Bellow Pk Dr, Reynoldsburg, OH 43068.

### KIRVEN, MYTHE YUVETTE

Government official. **Personal:** Born Jun 12, 1956, Dallas, TX. **Educ:** Tex Tech Univ, BS, 1977; Atlanta Univ, MPA, 1980. **Career:** City Dallas, admin asst. **Orgs:** Nat Asn Advan Colored People; Conf Minority Pub Admin, 1978-; rec secy, Delta Sigma Theta Dallas Chap, 1980-84; Urban Mgt Assts N TX, 1983-; TX City Mgt Asn, 1983-; Int City Mgt Asn, 1983-; vpres, S Dallas Club Nat Asn Negro Bus & Prof Women's Clubs, 1985-; dir, S Dallas Health Access; Nat Forum Black Pub Adminr, currently. **Home Addr:** 2823 Tanner St, Dallas, TX 75215-3006, **Home Phone:** (214)565-1119. **Business Addr:** Member, National Forum for Black Public Administrators, PO Box 313, Cedar Hill, TX 75106-0313, **Business Phone:** (972)487-7304.

### KIRWAN, ROBERTA CLAIRE

Journalist. **Educ:** Manhattanville Col, Purchase, NY, BA, Russ; Fordham Univ Grad Sch Bus, NY, MBA, mkt, 1978. **Career:** Doyle Dane Bernbach, NY, personnel mgr, asst acct exec, 1978-80; freelance photogr & mkt res coordr, 1980-82; Merrill Lynch, NY, acct exec, 1982-83; freelance mkt res coordr, 1984-88; Time-Warner, Money Mag, New York, NY, assoc ed, 1989-. **Orgs:** Nat Asn Black Journ, 1990. **Home Addr:** 19 W 69 St, New York, NY 10023, **Home Phone:** (212)877-0104. **Business Addr:** Associate Editor, MONEY Magazine, 1271 6th Ave 32nd Fl, New York, NY 10020, **Business Phone:** (212)522-0670.

### KISPERT, DOROTHY LEE

Association executive, president (organization). **Personal:** Born Dec 10, 1928, Detroit, MI; daughter of Leo Priestley and Pearl Priestley; married Wilson G; children: Kimberly A & Cynthia L. **Educ:** Univ Mich, BA, 1950; Wayne State Univ, MA, 1971. **Career:** President, association executive (retired); Merrill-Palmer Inst, fac, 1975-80; Parent Child Develop Ctr, dir, 1975-80; Parent Child Ctr, dir, 1980-81; Parents & C Together, dir, 1981-91; Detroit Family Proj, dir servs, coordr, 1991-94. **Orgs:** Lay rep Children's Hosp, Mich, 1978-88; consult, Spelman Col, 1979; tech, rev panel CDA Bank St Col, 1981; pres, Metro Detroit Day Care Asn. **Home Addr:** 19310 Woodingham, Detroit, MI 48221, **Home Phone:** (313)341-0287.

### KITCHEN, WAYNE LEROY, JR.

School administrator. **Personal:** Born Sep 7, 1948, Sedalia, MO; son of Imogene Nurse and Edgar Roy Imogene Nurse. **Educ:** Lincoln Univ, BS, bus educ, 1970; Univ Mo, MEd, col admin, 1977. **Career:** Cogswell Col, Admis Dept, asst dir, 1978-80; St Mary's Col, Mkt Div, prog coord, 1980-82; Univ San Francisco, Mkt Div, assoc dir, 1982-84; Bay Area Urban League Training Ctr, dir, 1984-85; Peralta Comm Col Dist, educ consult; Mills Col, upward bound asst dir, 1986-90; Calif State Univ, Hayward, dir upward bound, 1990-. **Orgs:** Phi Delta Kappa, 1983-; bd dir, Nat Alumni Asn, Lincoln Univ, 1984-88, pres, Mo Alumni Asn, 1984-88, nat vpres, Nat Alumni Asn; vpres, Phi Beta Sigma, 1984-86; chmn, Community Elect Lloyd Vann Sch Bd, 1985; bd dir, Oakland Ensemble Theatre; United Negro Col Fund Inter-Alumni Coun; Western Asn Educ Opportunity Personnel. **Home Addr:** 44 Oak Hill Cir, Oakland, CA 94605-4548, **Home Phone:** (510)636-8644. **Business Addr:** Director Upward Bound, Calif State University, Rm LI-2158 25800 Carlos Bee Blvd, Hayward, CA 94542-3059, **Business Phone:** (510)885-2960.

### KITCHEN-NEAL, MARY KIM

College administrator. **Personal:** Born Apr 18, 1961, Ft. Riley, KS; daughter of John Morgan and Yuson Kim Williams; married Rickey Neal; children: Sandra, Raymond II, William, Michael, Sasha Neal, Tiffany Neal & Andrecia Wingfield. **Educ:** Kans State Univ, BA, eng lit, 1996; Yale Univ, contemp writing tech, 1997; Friends Univ, MS, marriage & family ther, 2010. **Career:** Delta Airlines Inc, sales agt, 1988-96; Int Aviation & Travel Acad instr, 1996-98; Univ Tex, Arlington, Upward Bound Prog, acad coordr, 1998-2005, educ consult, 2010-13, TRIO Pre-Col Progs, spec progs coordr, 2013-15; GrayMatter Consults, educ consult & acad life trainer, 2004-; SMSD, paraprofessional, 2008-10; Salvation Army, intern, 2009-10; Friends Univ, intern, 2009-10; Unique STEM Opportunities & New Solutions, chief training officer, currently. **Orgs:** Alpha Kappa Alpha Sorority, 1981; Work Advantage Youth Adv Coun, 1999-; adv, NACWC, 2003-; Kauffman Scholars Inc, educ consult, 2005-08, life coach staff, 2008-10; Child Abuse Prev Asn, intern, 2010; vpres, Univ Tex at Arlington Mediation Asn, 2014-15; Psi Chi Int Hon Soc Psychol; Delta Kappa Int Marriage & Family Ther Hon Soc. **Home Addr:** 2614 Fallcreek St, Arlington, TX 76014, **Home Phone:** (817)543-1642. **Business Addr:** Educational Consultant, Academic Life Trainer, GrayMatter Consultants, Arlington, TX.

### KITHCART, LARRY E., SR.

Legislator, executive director. **Personal:** Born Jul 25, 1939, Glasco, NY; married Audrey; children: Larry Jr. **Career:** Ulster Co, First Black legislator, Community Action Comt Inc, exec dir, 1975, currently; Co Legislator, elected 4th consecutive term. **Orgs:** Pres, Kingston City Recreation Com, 1968-77; comnr recreation, 1977; past pres, Kingston Dem Men's Club, Sheriff's comm; pub health- Indus develop; taxbase & study; bridge & hwy; prog aged; conser Vation com Chmn Mayor's policy making bd Kingston Rondout Neighborhood Ctr; ward chmn; YMCA; United Way; Cancer com; Jaycees; Nat Asn Advan Colored People; com pres, Ulster Cnty Community Action Adv Bd; Finance Com Co Legis; Audit & Ins Com, Legis, Finance Com Co Legis, Munic Power Study Commn Co Legis. **Home Addr:** 34 Brewster St, Kingston, NY 12401-5855, **Home Phone:** (845)338-5418. **Business Addr:** Executive Director, Ulster County Community Action Committee Inc, 70 Lindsley Ave, Kingston, NY 12401-3316, **Business Phone:** (845)338-8750.

### KITT, SANDRA ELAINE

Novelist. **Personal:** Born Jun 11, 1947, Bronx, NY; daughter of Archie and Ann. **Educ:** Bronx Community Col, AA, 1968; City Col City Univ NY, BA, fine arts, 1969, MA, fine arts, 1975. **Career:** Art asst, 1970-72; New York City Board Education, Cloisters Workshop Program, teacher, 1972-73; New York City, information specialist librarian, 1974-92; Am Museum Nat Hist, libr spec, Richard S Perkin Library, mgr library services, 1973-04; publ novelist, 1981-; graphic artist illusr; Novels: The Color of Love; Rites of Spring, 1984; All Good Things, 1984; Adam & Eva, 1984; Perfect Combination, 1985; Only With the Heart, 1985; With Open Arms, 1987; An Innocent Man, 1989; The Way Home, 1990; Someone's Baby, 1991; Love Everlasting, 1993; Serenade, 1994; Sincerely, 1995; The Colour of Love, 1995; Suddenly, 1996; Significant Others, 1996; Between Friends, 1998; Family Affairs, 1999; Homecoming, 1999; Close Encounters, 2000; She's the One, 2001; Southern Comfort, 2004; The Next Best Thing, 2005; Celluloid Memories, 2007; Omnibus: For the Love of Chocolate, 1996; Baby Beat, 1996; Sisters, 1996; Girlfriends, 1999; First Touch, 2004; Have a Little Faith, 2006; Back in Your Arms, 2006. **Orgs:** Int Astron Union Comn Astron Libr, 1986; New York chap pres, Spec Librs Asn, 1999-2000; chair, Affirmative Action Comm, 1993-96, Prof develop community, 1996-99; Am Libr asn, Black Caucus, 1995-2001; Romance Writers Am; Novelist Inc; Publ Authors Network; adv bd, First Step Job Training Prog through Coalition Homeless New York; adv bd, St Jude C Res Hosp, Memphis. **Honors/Awds:** NIA, Woman Excellence Award, 1993; Walden Books Award for "Sincerely", 1996; Romantic Times Lifetime Achievement Award, 2001; Romance Writers of America Service Award, 2002; Lifetime Achievement Award, New York Chap, Romance Writers Am, 2004. **Special Achievements:** First African American to publish with Harlequin Enterprises; Top 25 Romances for the 20th Century; Close Encounter is One of the Top 10 Contemporaries for 2000; Image Award, Nat Asn Advan Colored People, nominee for Girlfriends, 2000. **Home Addr:** 3215 Netherlands Ave Suite 5E, Bronx, NY 10463-3420, **Home Phone:** (212)818-0344. **Business Addr:** Writer, PO Box 403, New York, NY 10024-0403.

### KITTLES, KERRY

Basketball player, basketball coach. **Personal:** Born Jun 12, 1974, Dayton, OH. **Educ:** Villanova Univ, attended 1996; Villanova Univs Sch Bus, MBA. **Career:** Basketball player (retired), scout; NJ Nets, guard & shooting guard, 1996-2004, part-time scout, currently; Los Angeles Clippers, guard & shooting guard, 2004-05; IQ Sports Solutions, co-founder; Princeton Tigers, asst coach, 2016-. **Orgs:** Kappa Alpha Psi Fraternity Inc; merchant banking assoc, Ledgemont Capital Group LLC. **Honors/Awds:** Big East Conference Player of the Year, 1995; Gold Medal, World Univ Games, 1995; Consensus NCAA All-American Second Team, 1995; Robert V Geasey Trophy winner, 1995, 1996; One All-Rookie First Team, 1996; Consensus NCAA All-American First Team, 1996; NBA co-Rookie of the Month, 1996; NBA All-Rookie Second Team, 1997. **Special Achievements:** NBA Draft, First round pick, No 8, 1996; NBA co-rookie of the Month, 1996. **Business Addr:** Assistant Coach, Princeton Tigers Men's Basketball, Princeton, NJ 08544, **Business Phone:** (609)258-2388.

### KLAUSNER, WILLETTE MURPHY

Theatrical producer, business owner. **Personal:** Born Jun 21, 1939, Omaha, NE; daughter of William and Gertrude Jones; married Manuel S. **Educ:** Univ Calif, Los Angeles, BA, econs, 1961. **Career:** Carnation Co, res analyst, 1965; Audience Studies Inc, res analyst, 1965-66, proj dir, 1966-68, res unit dir, 1968-72, res, 1972-74; MCA Universal Studios, Calif, vpres mkt res & mkt, 1974-81; Theatrical: "Hurlyburly", Westwood Playhouse, 1988-89; "The Apprentice", The Richard Pryor Theatre, Hollywood, 1991; Edge work Prod, producer, "Twist", Walnut St Theater, 1992; "Twist", George St Playhouse, 1996; "The Man in Room 304", Watermark Theater, NY, 1997; "To Take Arms", Tamarind Theater, LA, 1997; "Three Mo' Tenors", "Kat & the Kings", Cort Theatre, Broadway, 1999-2000; "Fully Committed", Coronet Theater, Los Angeles, 2000; Edge work Productions, pres, owner; WMK Productions Inc, owner, currently; Three Mo'Tenors, producer, 2000-; co-producer "Twist, An American Musical" Atlanta, 2010, Pasadena, CA, 2011; co-producer "Porgy and Bess 75th Anniversary Tour". **Orgs:** Gold Shield, Univ Calif Los Angeles Alumni Asn, 1974-; founding mem, Am Inst Wine & Food, 1982-; mem bd dir, Const Rights Found, 1982; vpres, bd dir, Los Angeles Co Music Ctr Oper Co, 1987; mem bd dir, Audrey Skir Ball-Kenis Theatre, 1991-; mem bd dir, Individual Rights Found, 1994; bd dir, Am Cinema Found, 1995; bd dir, Los Angeles Music Ctr; bd trustee, Women Film Found; League Prof Theatre Women; Nat Women's Forum. **Honors/Awds:** Honorable Certificate, Tobe-Coburn Sch Fashion Careers NY, 1962; Mehitabel Award for

Outstanding Professional Achievement, Tobe-Coburn Sch Fashion Careers, 1978. **Special Achievements:** First African American model to appear in a major fashion magazine (Mademoiselle) & she modeled in Copenhagen, Denmark & other major European cities; First African American woman in fashion merchandising at Bloomingdale's in New York; First female corporate VP at MCA Universal Studios; First female Sr Class President at UCLA; First Female student body vice president at Santa Barbara High School. **Business Addr:** Owner, Producer, WMK Productions Inc, 675 3rd Ave 3rd Fl, New York, NY 10017, **Business Phone:** (646)415-8903.

**KLEVEN, PROF. THOMAS E.**
College teacher. **Personal:** Born Aug 30, 1942, Cambridge, MA; married Ella Faye Marsh; children: Deborah & Aaron. **Educ:** Yale Univ, New Haven, CT, BA, 1964; Yale Law Sch, LLB, 1967. **Career:** Goulston & Storrs, Boston, Mass, assoc, 1967-69; Boston Model Cities Prog, 1969-72; Univ Southern Calif, 1972-74; Univ San Diego, prof, 1975-79; Thurgood Marshall Sch Law, Houston, Tex, prof, 1980-. **Orgs:** Radical Philosophers Asn. **Home Addr:** 4914 N Braeswood Blvd, Houston, TX 77096-2708, **Home Phone:** (713)665-0067. **Business Addr:** Professor, Texas Southern University, 3100 Cleburne St, Houston, TX 77004, **Business Phone:** (713)313-7355.

**KLINE, JOSEPH N.**
Government official, county court judge. **Personal:** Born Oct 8, 1948, Dale, SC; son of Frances and Eddie; married Audrey Annette Wheelwright; children: Marwin, Mikima & Miesha. **Educ:** Hartford Data Inst, comput operator & programmer, 1968. **Career:** Savannah-Chatham County Pub Sch, sr analyst programmer, 1984; Beaufort County Magistrates Ct, SC, councilman, 1979-98, judge, 1998-02. **Orgs:** Bd mem, Black Elected Off Beaufort County, 1979-; bd dir, Burton-Dale-Beaufort Br Nat Asn Advan Colored People, 1979; deacon, Mt Carmel Baptist Church, 1984; bd dir, Dale-Lobeco Community Org, 1975; bd dir, Beaufort Marine Inst, 1987; bd dir, Beaufort Jasper EOC, 1984; bd dir, Low County Coun Govt, 1979-94; Beaufort County Coun, 1995-96; coordr, Beaufort County Local Organizing Comn; SC Legis House. **Honors/Awds:** Most Outstanding Young Man, Black Arise, 1973; One of a Million Man Marcher; Jaycee of the Year, Jaycees, 1973; Plaque of Appreciation, Beaufort County, 1977; Certificate of Appreciation, Beaufort Jasper Econ Opport Cmdr, 1991; Citizen of the Year, Omega Psi Phi Fraternity, 1992; Outstanding Contribution in Politics Award, Beaufort County Dr King Day Comn, 1993. **Home Addr:** 42 Kline Cir, Seabrook, SC 29940-3125, **Home Phone:** (803)846-4166. **Business Addr:** Judge, Beaufort County Magistrates Court, 539 William Hilton Pkwy, Hilton Head Island, SC 29926-3601, **Business Phone:** (843)842-4263.

**KLINE, WILLIAM M.**
School administrator. **Personal:** Born Feb 24, 1933, Paterson, NJ; married Lillian Thomas; children: Wayne, Michelle, William Jr & Wesley. **Educ:** William Paterson Col, BS, 1954, MS, 1959. **Career:** School administrator (retired); Paterson Bd Educ, teacher, 1957-65; Neighborhood Youth Corp, dir, 1965-68, vice prin, 1968-71; E side High Sch, prin, 1971-79, dir curric & spl educ proj, 1979, asst supt; Paterson, NJ, coun man-at large, 1998; City CNL, pres, 2000-01. **Orgs:** Bd Recreation, City Paterson, 1962-64; alderman, City Paterson, 1965-67; Nat Asn Advan Colored People; Omega Psi Phi; Phi Delta Kappa; IBPOE WIntegrity Lodge; 4th Ward Co Committeeman; Paterson Rotary Club; munic chmn, Dem Party; Bd Educ Paterson, NJ, 1996-97, chmn, 1997-98. **Home Addr:** 403 Main St, North Middletown, NJ 07748-5942, **Home Phone:** (732)495-3154.

**KLUGE, PAMELA HOLLIE (PAMELA GAIL HOLLIE)**
Administrator. **Personal:** Born Apr 17, 1948, Topeka, KS; daughter of Frances Hollie and Maurice Hollie; married P F. **Educ:** Washburn Univ, Topeka, KS, BA, eng, 1970; Columbia Univ, New York, NY, MS, jour, 1971; Univ Hawaii, Honolulu, HI, Asian studies, 1977; Columbia Univ, Am studies, 1987. **Career:** Wall St Jour, staff, 1969-75; Honolulu Advertiser, reporter, Pac corresp, Saipan, 1975-76; Trust Territory Pac Island, econs dept Micronesia, 1976; New York Times, nat corresp Los Angeles, foreign corresp Manilla, author, financial columnist New York, 1977-87; New York Stock Exchange, New York, NY, media consult, 1987-; Knight Bagenot Fel Econ & Bus Jour; Columbia Univ Grad sch Jour, dir, 1987-90; Poynter Inst, vis fac, 1989-; Kenyon Col, dir capital proj, 2005-, sr philanthropic advisor; Ohio State Univ, kiplinger prof. **Orgs:** Dir, Newspaper Found, 1973-75; contribr, Encyclopdeia Americana, 1985-; adv bd, Kans Ctr Bk, 1988-; consult, Paragon Group, 1989-; dir, Asia-Pac Region Nature Conservancy. **Home Addr:** 120 W 70th St 2A, New York, NY 10023. **Business Addr:** Director of Capital Projects, Senior Philanthropic Advisor, Kenyon College, 101 Scott Lane, Gambier, OH 43022-9623, **Business Phone:** (740)427-5153.

**KNABLE, BOBBIE MARGARET BROWN**
School administrator. **Personal:** Born May 20, 1936, Knoxville, TN; daughter of Jacqueline Jordan (deceased) and Isaac (deceased); married Norman; children: Jacob. **Educ:** Oberlin Conserv, Oberlin, OH, BA, music, 1958. **Career:** Tufts Univ, Medford, Mass, asst prof Eng, 1970-76, dir continuing educ, 1974-78, dean freshmen, 1978-79, dean stud, 1979-99, dean emerita, 1999-; City a Hill Pub Charter High Sch, sch head, 2003-04; educ consult, currently. **Orgs:** New Eng Deans, 1978-; steering comn, New Eng Col Alcohol Network, 1980-; trustee, Vt Acad, 1983-85; Mass Asn Women Deans, Adminr & Counrs, 1986-, rec secy, 1988-89; Deans Round Table, 1988-; Stud Affairs Think Tank, 1988-; trustee, Pine Manor Col, 1989-; comnr, New Eng Asn Sch & Col, 1989-95; gov bd mem, Mass Inst Psychoanalysis, 1990-96 & 2007-; trustee, Bennington Col, 1997-; bd mem, Tufts Univ, 1999-2008; vice chair, bd trustee, City Hill, 2004-; Mass Charter Pub Sch Asn, 2005-; Mass Ctr Pub Charter Sch Excellence, 2008-. **Honors/Awds:** Doctor of Humanities, Oberlin Col, 2009. **Special Achievements:** Town Meeting Member, Town of Brookline, MA; Member of Advisory Committee, Town of Brookline, MA. **Home Addr:** 243 Mason Terr, Brookline, MA 02446-2776, **Home Phone:** (617)852-6717. **Business Addr:** Vice Chair, City on a Hill Charter Public School, 58 Circuit St, Roxbury, MA 02119, **Business Phone:** (617)445-1515.

**KNIGHT, ATHELIA WILHELMENIA**
Educator, journalist. **Personal:** Born Oct 15, 1950, Portsmouth, VA; daughter of Daniel Dennis and Adell Virginia Savage. **Educ:** Norfolk State Univ, Norfolk, VA, BA, eng, 1973; Ohio State Univ, Columbus, OH, MA, jour, 1974; Fr Alliance, Paris, France, attended 1997. **Career:** DC Coop Exten Serv, Wash, DC, summer aide, 1969-72; Portsmouth Pub Schs, Portsmouth, Va, substitute teacher, 1973; Virginian-Pilot, Norfolk, Va, summer relief reporter, 1973; Chicago Tribune, Chicago, Ill, summer relief reporter, 1974; Wash Post, Wash, DC, metrop desk reporter, 1975-81, investigative reporter, 1981-94, sports reporter, 1994-2000, Young Journalists Develop Prog, asst dir, 2000-03, dir, 2003-08; Harvard Univ, Cambridge, Mass, Nieman Fel, 1986; Hampton Univ, Hampton, Va, Scripps Howard vis prof, 2001; Georgetown Univ, Wash, DC, Eng Dept, lectr, adj prof, 2008-; staff writer, currently; Hampton Univ, Sch Lib Arts & Educ, staff mass media arts, currently; Princeton Univ, Princeton, NJ, Ferris Prof Journalism, Coun Humanities, lectr, 2009-10. **Orgs:** Women in Communs; Nat Asn Black Journalists; Wash-Baltimore Newspaper Guild. **Business Addr:** Lecturer, Georgetown University, 3700 O St NW, Washington, DC 20057, **Business Phone:** (202)687-0100.

**KNIGHT, BREVIN ADON**
Executive, basketball player. **Personal:** Born Nov 8, 1975, Livingston, NJ; son of Melvin and Brenda; married Deena; children: Brenna, Kayla & Donevin. **Educ:** Stanford Univ, BA, sociol, 1997. **Career:** Basketball player (retired), executive; Cleveland Cavaliers, guard, 1997-2001; Atlanta Hawks, 2001; Memphis Grizzlies, guard, 2001-03, commentator, 2010-, analyst; Wash Wizards, 2003-04; Phoenix Suns, 2003; Milwaukee Bucks, 2004; Charlotte Bobcats, guard, 2004-07; Los Angeles Clippers, 2007-08; Utah Jazz, 2008-09. **Orgs:** Founder, Assist by Knight Found, 2002-. **Business Addr:** Commentator, Memphis Grizzlies, 191 Beale St, Memphis, TN 38103, **Business Phone:** (901)888-4667.

**KNIGHT, BUBBA (MERALD KNIGHT, JR.)**
Singer. **Personal:** Born Sep 4, 1942, Atlanta, GA; son of Merald Sr and Elizabeth Woods; married Kathleen C A. **Career:** Gladys Knight & the Pips, singer, 1952-; Shakeji Inc, mem; Albums: If I Were Your Woman, 1971; Neither One Of Us, 1973; Imagination, 1973; "I Feel a Song", 1974; 2nd Anniversary, 1975; The Best of Gladys Knight & the Pips, 1976; Visions, 1983; All Our Love, 1987. **Orgs:** Gladys Knight & Pips. **Honors/Awds:** Grammy Awards; American Music Awards; Georgia Music Hall of Fame, 1989; Rock and Roll Hall of Fame, 1996; Lifetime Achievement Award, Rhythm & Blues Found, 1998; Vocal Group Hall of Fame, 2001; Apollo Theater's Hall of Fame, 2006. **Business Addr:** Musician, c/o MCA Records, 70 Universal City Plz, Universal City, CA 91608.

**KNIGHT, REV. DR. CAROLYN ANN**
Educator, clergy. **Personal:** Born Denver, CO; daughter of Ed (deceased) and Dorothy (deceased). **Educ:** Bishop Col, Dallas, TX, BA, eng, philos & relig, 1977; Union Theol Sem, New York, NY, Mdiv, 1980, MA, sacred theol; United Theol Sem, Dayton, OH, DMin, 1995. **Career:** Benjamin E Mays, fel; Canaan Baptist Church, NYC, asst pastor, 1978-87; Philadelphia Baptist Church, NYC, pastor, 1988-93; Union Theol Sem, NY, asst prof, 1989-93; ITC, Atlanta, asst prof homiletics, 1995-, preacher; LaGuardia Community Col, adj prof; Carolyn Ann Knight/Can Do Ministries Inc, founder, pres, chief exec officer, pastor, currently; Interdenominational Theol Ctr, asst prof homiletics, preacher. **Orgs:** Nat Asn Advan Colored People, 1980-; Golden life mem, Delta Sigma Theta, 1982-; Harlem Congregations Community Improv; Breast Exam Ctr Harlem; Black Leadership Comn; adv bd, African Am Pulpit Judson Press. **Home Addr:** 868 Victoria Pl SW, Atlanta, GA 30310-2767, **Home Phone:** (404)758-9664. **Business Addr:** Founder, President, Carolyn Ann Knight/Can Do Ministries Inc, 904 Walton Way SE, Smyrna, GA 30314-4143, **Business Phone:** (770)433-8644.

**KNIGHT, DR. FRANKLIN W.**
Educator. **Personal:** Born Jan 10, 1942; son of Willis J and Irick M Sanderson; married Ingeborg Bauer; children: Michael, Brian & Nadine. **Educ:** Univ Col W Indies, BA, 1964; Univ Wis, MA, 1965, PhD, 1969. **Career:** State Univ New York Stony Brook, asst/assoc prof, 1968-73; Johns Hopkins Univ, assoc prof, 1973-77, prof, 1977-, Leonard & Helen R Stulman prof hist, 1991-, Undergrad Studies, dir, currently; Latin Am Studies Prog, dir, 1992-95; Howard Univ, vis prof, 1983, 1998-2000, 2002; Colgate Col, John D & Catherine T McArthur dist vis prof, 2000; Hist Soc, pres, 2004-06. **Orgs:** Bd dir, Social Sci Res Coun, 1976-79; fel Nat Endowment Humanities 1976-77; fel Ctr Adv Studyin Behav Sci 1977-78; consult, NEH, 1977-85; vis prof Univ Tex, Austin, 1980; exec comm, Asn Caribbean Hist, 1982-85; chmn, Int Scholarly Rels Comm Conf Latin Am Historians, 1983-86; comm mem, Inter-Am Found, 1984-86; res comm, Am Hist Asn, 1984-86; Am Coun learned Socs; adv comts, Nat Res Coun; pres, Latin Am Studies Asn, 1998-2000. **Home Addr:** 2902 W Strathmore Ave, Baltimore, MD 21209-3811, **Home Phone:** (410)358-8178. **Business Addr:** Leonard & Helen R Stulman Professor of History, Johns Hopkins University, 2850 N Charles St 322 Gilman Hall, Baltimore, MD 21218, **Business Phone:** (410)516-7591.

**KNIGHT, GLADYS L.**
Writer, scholar. **Career:** Freelance writer/scholar/researcher: "Icons of African American Protest: Trailblazing Activists of the Civil Rights Movement", Greenwood, 2008; "Female Action Heroes: A Guide to Women in Comics, Video Games, Film, and Television", Greenwood, 2010; "Pop Culture Places: An Encyclopedia of Places in American Popular Culture", Greenwood, 2014. **Special Achievements:** Has contributed to over 100 articles and essays in seven reference works and a trade magazine for the trucking industry. **Home Addr:** 1714 E 2nd St, Tacoma, WA 98404-4311.

**KNIGHT, GLADYS MARIA**
Lyricist, singer, actor. **Personal:** Born May 28, 1944, Atlanta, GA; daughter of Merald Woodlow Sr and Sarah Elizabeth Woods; married Barry Hankerson, Jan 1, 1974, (divorced 1981); children: Shanga; married Les Brown, Jan 1, 1994, (divorced 1997); married William McDowell, Apr 12, 2001. **Career:** Morris Brown Choir, singer, 1950-53; Gladys Knight & The Pips, singer, 1953-90, solo artist, 1990-; concert appearances in Eng, 1967, 1972, 1973, 1976, Australia, Japan, Hong Kong, Manila, 1976; Charlie & Co; Kenya's Cakes To The Stars, co-owner; Gladys & Ron's Chicken & Waffle Restaurant, co-owner, currently; Albums: Lett Full of Tears, 1961; Gladys Knight & the Pips, 1964; Everybody Needs Love, 1967; Feelin'Bluesy, 1968; Silk & Soul, 1968; Nitty Gritty, 1969; All in a Knight's Work, 1970; If I Were Your Woman, 1971; Standing Ovation, 1971; Imagination, 1973; Neither One of Us, 1973; All I Need Is Time, 1973; Help Me Make It Through the Night, 1973; Gladys Knight & the Pips Super-Pak, 1973; It Hurt Me So Bad, 1973; Gladys Knight & the Pips, 1974; Knight Time, 1974; Claudine, 1974; I Feel a Song, 1974; A Little Knight Music, 1975; 2nd Anniversary, 1975; Bless This House, 1976; Pipe Dreams, 1976; Still Together, 1977; Love Is Always on Your Mind, 1977; Miss Gladys Knight, 1978; The One & Only, 1978; Gladys Knight, 1979; Memories, 1979; That Spec Time of Yr, 1980; About Love, 1980; Midnight Train to Ga, 1980; Teen Anguish, Vol. 3, 1981; I Feel a Song, 1981; Touch, 1981; Visions, 1983; Life, 1985; All Our Love, 1988; Christmas Album, 1989; Good Woman, 1991; Just for You, 1994; Lost Live Album, 1996; Many Different Roads, 1998; At Last, 2000; Many Different Roads, 2000; Midnight Train, 2001; Christmas Celebrations, 2002; The Best Thing That Ever Happened to Me, 2003; Every Beat of My Heart, 2003; Before Me, 2006; Another Journey, 2013; Where My Heart Belongs, 2014. TV: Never Can Say Goodbye, 1997; Always & Forever, 2001; Hollywood Homicide, 2003; Unbeatable Harold, Centennial, 2005. Films: Pipe Dreams, 1976; Desperado, 1987; Twenty Bucks, 1993; Hollywood Homicide, 2003; Unbeatable Harold, 2006; Holidaze: The Christmas That Almost Didn't Happen, 2006; I Can Do Bad All by Myself, 2009; Seasons of Love, 2014-. **Orgs:** Alpha Kappa Alpha Sorority Inc. **Honors/Awds:** Grand Prize, Ted Mack Amateur Hour, 1952; 1 Gold Album; 1 Platinum Album; Grammy Award, 1972, 1987, 2001, 2004-05; Top Female Vocalist, Blues & Soul Mag, 1972; 6 Gold Buddah Records; NAACP Image, Ebony Music, Cash box, Billboard, Record World Awards, 1975; Spec Award for Inspiration to Youth, WA City Coun; Rolling Stone Award; American Music Award, 1984, 1988; Georgia Music Hall of Fame, 1989; DHL, Morris Brown Col, 1990; Essence Award, 1992; Ladies Home Journal Award; Star, Hollywood Walk of Fame, 1995; Rock & Roll Hall of Fame, 1996; Trumpet Awards Foundation Pinnacle Award, 1997; Heard It Through the Grapevine, Midnight Train to Georgia; Vocal Group Hall of Fame, 2001; Hon Doctorate, Shaw Univ; BET Lifetime Achievement Award, 2005; Las Vegas Music Awards Legendary Award, 2006; Image Award, Nat Asn Advan Colored People, 2007; Ella Award, Soc Singers, 2007; BET Inaugural Best Living Legend Award, 2008; Stardust Music Awards Lifetime Diva Award, 2008; National Black Arts Festival Honoree at Legends Celebration, 2008; Soul Train Music Awards Lifetime Achievement Award, 2011. **Special Achievements:** Appeared in "Sisters in the Name of Love", HBO, 1986; Author, Between Each Line of Pain and Glory, 1997. **Business Addr:** Singer, Sole Artist, Shakeji Inc, 3221 La Mirada Ave, Las Vegas, NV 89120-3011, **Business Phone:** (702)436-2913.

**KNIGHT, JOE. See KNIGHT, W. H, JR.**

**KNIGHT, JOHN F., JR.**
School administrator, president (organization). **Personal:** Born Jun 7, 1945, Montgomery, AL; son of Johnnie F Sr and Ruth Bateman; married Karen Neal; children: Tamara & Tehrik. **Educ:** Ala State Univ, BS, bus admin, 1974; Ala A&M Univ, hon doctor law. **Career:** Ala State Univ, dir pub rels, 1976, dir commun & pub affairs; Ala PSC, exec asst to pres; postal serv, clerk, 1969-74; Ala State Univ, spec asst to pres, exec vpres, chief operating officer, 1993; State Ala, rep, currently; WVAS-FM, gen mgr, currently; Ala State Univ, exec vpres & chief operating officer, currently. **Orgs:** Pres, adv coun Ala Dem Conf Young Dem, 1973; Studs Affairs Com, 1973; pres, Ala State Univ Stud Govt Asn, 1972-73; State Dem Exec Comn, 1975; chmn, Montgomery County Dem Conf, 1979-; Montgomery County Dem Exec Comt; comnr, Montgomery County Comn, 1980-; bd mem, Montgomery Housing Authority Bd, 1975-; bd dir, Kershaw YMCA; bd dir, Montgomery Improv Assoc, bd dir, Family Sunshine Ctr, bd dir, Southern Develop Coun Inc, bd dir, Retired Sr Vol Prog; bd dir, Cleveland Ave YMCA; Ways & Means Gen Fund; Montgomery County Legis. **Honors/Awds:** Highest ranking black in Ala State Govt, 1974; Presidential Citation, NAFEO, 1991; Man of the Year, Kappa Alpha Psi Fraternity, 1991; LLD, Ala A&M Univ, 2008. **Home Addr:** 875 John Brown Ave, PO Box 6148, Montgomery, AL 36106-1219, **Home Phone:** (334)834-7445. **Business Addr:** Representative, State Alabama, Rm 516 A 11 S Union St, Montgomery, AL 36106, **Business Phone:** (334)229-4286.

**KNIGHT, MERALD, JR. See KNIGHT, BUBBA.**

**KNIGHT, DR. MURIEL BERNICE**
Consultant, educator. **Personal:** Born Apr 21, 1922, Hartford, CT; daughter of Oscar Milton and Rosena Burnett Williams; children: Leo M (deceased), Philip A (deceased), Muriel Virginia, William & Sheila Eileen. **Educ:** Northeastern Univ, AS, 1970, BS, educ admin leadership & supv, 1972, EdD, 1988; Harvard Grad Sch Educ, EdM, sociol, 1973, PhD, educ mgt, leadership supv; Suffolk Univ, cert, consumer law, 1979. **Career:** Northeastern Univ, Grad Sch Educ, teaching asst, 1977-78; Boston State Col, lectr, 1979-81; Election dept Ward 5 Precinct 7, Warden, 1980-88; Mass Bay Comm Col, lectr, 1985; Beaver Co Day Sch, instr. **Orgs:** Northeastern Alumni, 1973-; Harvard Grad Alumni, 1974-; vpres, New Eng Woman's Press Asn, 1983-85; bd mem, Dimock St Health Ctr, 1983-85; warden, Election Dept City Boston, 1983-; Selective Serv Bd No 32; bd mem, S End Neighborhood Action Prog, 1985. **Honors/Awds:** Kennedy Federation Scholar; Martin Luther King Scholar, Northeastern Univ; Community Service Award; Professional Award, Educator's Award, Boston Chap, Negro Bus & Prof Women; Merit Media Award, Lambda Kappa Mu Sorority. **Special Achievements:** Audio Archeology Recordings: "Little Brown Jug", "Am the Beautiful", "Nearer My God to Thee", "Jesus in All the World to Me"; Harvard Chap, Phi Delta Kappa, historian-elected, 1985-86. **Home Addr:** 31-C Village Ct, PO Box 18366, Boston, MA 02118, **Home Phone:** (617)482-9018.

### KNIGHT, NEGELE OSCAR

Basketball player. **Personal:** Born Mar 6, 1967, Detroit, MI; son of Willie O and Alma. **Educ:** Univ Dayton, attended 1990. **Career:** Basketball player (retired); Phoenix Suns, guard, 1990-93; San Antonio Spurs, 1993-94; Portland Trail Blazers, 1994; Detroit Pistons, 1994-95; Europe Leagues, 1995-98; Toronto Raptors, 1998-99. **Home Addr:** 18624 N 4th Ave, Phoenix, AZ 85027-5665.

### KNIGHT, RICHARD, JR.

Executive. **Personal:** Born May 31, 1945, Ft. Valley, GA; son of Freddie and Richard; married Mavis Best; children: Richard L, Marcus E & Nolan C. **Educ:** Yale Univ, polit sci, 1967; Ft Valley State Col, BA, polit sci & econs, 1968; Univ NC, MPA, 1974. **Career:** Carrboro NC, town mgr, 1976-80; ICMA, vpres, 1980; Gainesville FL, dep city mgr, 1980-82; City Dallas, asst city mgr, 1982-86, city mgr, 1986-90; City Dallas, asst city mgr, 1982-86, city mgr, 1986; Caltex Petrol Corp, dir total qual & envir mgt, 1990, gen mgr admin, 1993, gen mgr mkt, dir, 1995; Vista Stores, chmn bd dir, 1998; Richard Knight Parking Co, owner, 1998-99; Knightco Oil Co, founder, pres, chmn, 1997-2004; Pegasus Tex Construct, owner & managing partner, currently; Knight Waste Serv, pres, currently. **Orgs:** Vpres, int City Mgt Asn, 1980; chmn, Dallas Regional Minority Purchasing Coun, 1984-85; chmn bd, D & FW Minority Bus Develop Coun, 1984-85; vchmn, Dallas Alliance, 1985; Salesmanship Club Dallas, 1989; bd dir, Comerica Bank, TX; bd dir, Dallas Int Sports Comn; bd dir, Dallas Zool Soc; bd dir, Comerica Bank; Bd Regents, Univ N Tex; bd trustee, Dallas Med Resource; bd dir, Arena Group; chmn, Goodwill Industs; C's Med Ctr; JP Morgan Chase Bank; exec bd mem, Circle Ten Coun Boy Scouts Am; Exec Comt State Fair Tex; Salesmanship Club Dallas & Dallas Citizens Coun; St Paul United Methodist Ch; Rotary Int; Salvation Army; Dallas Chamber Com; Ft Worth Black Chamber Com; comn, Cub Scout MAWAT Durham Dist Boy Scouts. **Honors/Awds:** Outstanding Alumnus Award, Univ NC, 1988; Horace Mann Bond Award, Fort Valley State Col, 1988; Whitney M Young Service Award. **Special Achievements:** First African-American city manager for the city of Dallas. **Home Addr:** PO Box 763337, Dallas, TX 75376-3337. **Business Addr:** President, Knight Waste Services, 4901 Parker Henderson Rd, Ft. Worth, TX 76119, **Business Phone:** (817)332-8333.

### KNIGHT, DR. ROBERT S.

Educator, dentist, dean (education). **Personal:** Born Aug 10, 1929, Montgomery, AL; married Patricia Tyler; children: Lynn, Robert, Joan & Stephen. **Educ:** Talladega Col, BA, 1949; Meharry Med Col, DDS, 1954. **Career:** Bridgeport, CT, pvt pract, 1964; Howard Univ, Col Dent, asst prof, 1965-74, assoc dean stud affairs, 1975-77, prof, 1978-90, dean, 1991-95. **Orgs:** Am Cancer Soc; fel oral path, NY Univ, 1963; Sigma Xi, 1971; Omicron Kappa Upsilon Hon Dent Soc, 1974; fel Am Col Dent, 1981; bd mem, Howard Univ, 2001-; Am Dent Asn; Nat Dent Asn; DC Dent Soc; Robert T Freeman Dent Asn; Am Acad Oral Path; Am Asn Dent Sch; Soc Teacher Oral Path; Capital Order Oral Path; Nat Urban League; com chmn, Explorer Scouts, BSA. **Home Addr:** 609 Elm Ave, Takoma Park, MD 20912-5431, **Home Phone:** (301)270-1480. **Business Addr:** Board Member, Howard University, 600 W St NW, Washington, DC 20059, **Business Phone:** (202)806-0400.

### KNIGHT, SAMMY D., JR.

Football coach, football player. **Personal:** Born Sep 10, 1975, Fontana, CA; son of Sam Sr; married Freda L; children: Shianne, Samone, Savannah & Aneka. **Educ:** Univ Southern Calif, commun, 1998, MS, commun mgt, currently. **Career:** Football player (retired), coach; New Orleans Saints, free safety & strong safety, 1997-2002, safety, 2008-09; Miami Dolphins, safty & strong safety, 2003-04; Kans City Chiefs, safety & strong safety, 2005-06; Jacksonville Jaguars, strong safety, 2007; Compass Media Networks, analyst, 2009; Univ Southern Calif, asst coach, 2010-11. **Orgs:** Founder, Sammy Knight Found, 2002. **Honors/Awds:** Pro Bowl selection, 2001; All-Pro selection, 2001; Hall of Fame, New Orleans Saints, 2011. **Special Achievements:** Serves as a spokesperson for Kansas Citys Hooked on Books campaign; Anavid player of the EA Sports Madden Football video game. **Home Addr:** 43 Hildene Way, Spring, TX 77382-6201.

### KNIGHT, THOMAS LORENZO

Executive, football player. **Personal:** Born Dec 29, 1974, Summitt, NJ. **Educ:** Univ Iowa, BA, hist, 1996. **Career:** Football player (retired), executive; Ariz Cardinals, right cornerback, 1997-2000, cornerback, 1999, left cornerback, 2000-01; Baltimore Ravens, defensive back, 2002-03; Tampa Bay Buccaneers, 2004; St Louis Rams, 2004; Sandbar Mex Bar & Grill, owner, investor, 2004-06; Univ Wis, asst football coach, 2006-07; KDUS 1060 AM Sports Radio, sales rep, 2007-09; Warner Chilcott, specialty sales rep, 2009-10; Stryker, sales rep, 2010-11; Smith & Nephew, Territory Mgr, 2011-13; Conmed Corp, sr territory mgr, 2013-15; Osiris Therapeut, regional sales specialist, 2015-. **Business Addr:** Regional Sales Specialist, Osiris Therapeutics Inc, 7015 Albert Einstein Dr, Columbia, MD 21046, **Business Phone:** (443)545-1800.

### KNIGHT, W. H., JR. (JOE KNIGHT)

Educator. **Personal:** Born Beckley, WV; son of W H and Frances; married Susan L Mask; children: Michael Joseph Mask & Lauren Louise Mask. **Educ:** Univ NC, Chapel Hill, BA, econs, speech & polit sci, 1976; Columbia Univ Sch Law, JD, 1979. **Career:** Colonial Bancorp, assoc coun & asst sec, 1979-83; Univ Bridgeport Sch Law, adj prof, 1981-83; Univ Iowa Col Law, assoc prof, 1983-88, vice provost, 1997-2000, prof, 1988-2001; Wake Forest Univ Law Sch, Winston-Salem, NC, guest prof, 1989, actg assoc dean, 1991-93; Duke Univ Law Sch, Durham, NC, vis prof, 1991; Wash Univ, Sch Law, St Louis, Mo, vis prof, 1992, dean & prof, 2001-08; WHK Consult, prin, 1993-; Univ Fla Law Sch, team chair, ABA AALS, site inspection team, 2003-; Seattle Univ Sch of Law, prof & distinguished acad, 2007-; Chapman Univ Sch of Law, vis prof, 2010. **Orgs:** Adv bd, Conn Econ Develop Authority, 1982-83; consult, Knight Financial Enterprises, 1982-; Lawyers Alliance Nuclear Arms Control, 1983-; Am & Iowa Civil Liberties Union, 1983-; pres, Iowa City, Nat Asn Advan Colored People, 1986-90; Nat Conf Black Lawyers; Soc Am Law Teachers, 1988-; Nat Bar Asn; Am Bar Asn; bd mem, Willow wind Sch, 1992-; bd mem, Mid-Eastern Coun Chem Abuse, 1992-; Am Law Inst, 1993-; bd mem, State Farm Fire &Casualty Co, 1995-; bd mem & chair, State Farm Mutual Automobile Co, 1996-; bd mem, State Farm Life Ins, Co, 1998-; bd trustee, Law Sch Admis Coun, 2001-03; Am & Iowa Civil Liberties Union; Columbia Human Rights Law Rev; Trinity Episcopal Church; trustee, Nat Univ Syst, currently. **Home Addr:** 3730 42nd Ave S, Seattle, WA 98144-7206. **Business Addr:** Dean, Professor, University of Washington Law School, William H Gates Hall, Seattle, WA 98195-3020, **Business Phone:** (206)685-3846.

### KNIGHT, WALTER R.

Government official, association executive. **Personal:** Born Aug 16, 1933, Camden, AR; married Sadie M Brown; children: Harriet, Vicki, Sabrena & Michelle. **Educ:** Univ Wis; Univ Minn. **Career:** City Councilman; USWA, vpres, 1969; UN Steelworkers Am Local 1533, pres, 1975-. **Orgs:** Bd dirs, Gr Beloit Asn Com; City Ambassadors Club; exec comn, Black Res Personnel; Beloit Improv Coalition; bd dirs, Wis Equal Employ Opportunity Asn; Rock Co Manpower Planning Coun, 1974. **Honors/Awds:** Service Award, Salvation Army, 1966. **Home Addr:** 2028 Masters St, Beloit, WI 53511-2724, **Home Phone:** (608)362-0285. **Business Addr:** President, Un Steelworkers Am Local 1533, 614 Broad St, Beloit, WI 53511.

### KNIGHT-PULLIAM, KESHIA

Actor. **Personal:** Born Apr 9, 1979, Newark, NJ; daughter of James Pulliam Sr and Denise. **Educ:** Spelman Col, BA, sociol, 2001. **Career:** TV series: "Sesame Street", 1969; "The Cosby Show", 1984-92; "A Different World", 1987-88; "The Little Match Girl", 1987; "Polly", 1989; "A Connecticut Yankee in King Aurthur's Court", 1989; "What About Your Friends: Weekend Getaway", 2002; "Christmas at Water's Edge", 2004; "House of Payne", 2007-12"; "The Last Supper", 2008; "Party Over Here!", 2008; "Your Wife's a Payne", 2008; "Payneful News", 2008; "Tyler Perry's House of Payne", 2008-; "Back Where We Belong", 2009; "Harlem Heights", 2009; "Psych", 2010; "Mr. Box Office", 2012; "Guys with Kids", 2013; "The Love Letter", 2013; Films: The Last Dragon, 1985; Polly: Comin' Home, 1990; Motive, 2004; Christmas at Water's Edge, 2004; Motives, 2004; Beauty Shop, 2005; The Gospel, 2005; Cuttin Da Mustard, 2008; Death Toll, 2008; Madea Goes to Jail, 2009; Atlanta based Production Company. **Orgs:** Delta Sigma Theta Sorority Inc. **Honors/Awds:** Emmy nomination for Outstanding Supporting Actress in a Comedy Series; Image Award, Nat Asn Advan Colored People, 1988, 2009, 2010 & 2010; People's Choice Award, 1988; Young Artist Award, 1989; Blimp Award, 1991; Golden Globe Awards, 2011; Impact Award, 2011. **Special Achievements:** Won a celebrity ed of the Weekest Link; Won a celebrity version of Fear Factor in September 2002; Won a celebrity ed of Fear Factor, 2003; Ranked No 19, VH1's list of the "100 Greatest Kid Stars"; Ranked #11on E! Television's "50 Cutest Child Stars All Grown Up" special, 2005. **Business Addr:** Actor, Carsey-Werner, 4024 Redford Ave Bldg 3, Studio City, CA 91604-2101, **Business Phone:** (818)655-5598.

### KNIGHTON, CHRISTINE B.

Business owner, army officer, founder (originator). **Personal:** Born Dec 23, 1957?, Cuthbert, GA; married Bennie Williams Jr; children: Tre. **Educ:** Tuskegee Inst, BA, sec educ-home econ, 1979; National War Col, MA, nat security & strategy; AUS Command & Gen Staff Col. **Career:** US Army officer, 1979-2008; Quartermaster Corps; Transportation Officer's Corps; US Department of Defense, 1980; Army V Corps in West Germany, flight section leader of 205th Transportation Battalion, platoon leader of 62nd Aviation Company and logistics officer of 11th Aviation Battalion; Delta Company, commander of 227th Aviation Regiment, 1988; 2nd Infantry Division, Aviation brigade logistics officer in Uijeongbu, South Korea; Combat Structure for the Army Study Group, Ft. Leavenworth, KS, aviation logistician, 1990; Center for Army Lessons Learned, Operation Desert Storm; Hotel Company, 159th Aviation Regiment, 1993; Blackhawk Helicopter Battalion, 1st Cavalry Division, commander, 1996-98; Army Officer Human Capital-Human Resources Command, Alexandria, VA, chief leader development officer. SHAPE (Self-esteem, Harmony, Awareness, Pride and Education), founder, 1990; Prince George's County (MD) Public School System, chief human resources officer, 2008-09; executive coach, 2009-; WINNERS!, owner and founder, 2010-. **Orgs:** Bd mem, Leave No Veteran Behind; vpres, Bessie Coleman Found; Delta Sigma Theta; Tuskegee Airman Asn. **Special Achievements:** Second African American woman in the U.S. State Department of Defense; first woman from Georgia to complete aviation training; first woman in the U.S. Army to command a tactical combat arms battalion, 1996. **Business Addr:** WINNERS!, LLC., 7481 Hunstman Blvd Suite 1005, Springfield, VA 22153, **Business Phone:** (202)577-5004.

### KNOTT, DR. ALBERT PAUL LOWE, JR.

Executive, educator. **Personal:** Born Mar 23, 1935, Pittsburgh, PA; son of Albert Paul Sr (deceased) and Fannie Merideth Scott (deceased); married Lynda Steenberg; children: Albert Paul III & Olivia Merideth. **Educ:** Yale Col, BA, human behav & cult anthrop, 1956; Seton Hall Col Med, MD, 1960; cert, advan trauma life support. **Career:** Georgetown Univ, internship, 1960; DC Gen Hosp, internship, 1961; Chicago's Michael Reese Hosp, cardiovasc res fel, 1961-63; Va Hosp Hines IL, sr med res, 1963-65; Us Naval Hosp, chief cardiol, 1965-67; Daniel Hale Williams Health Ctr, cardiol consults, 1966-81; Rush Presby St. Lukes Med Ctr; Mile Sq Community Health Ctr; Louise Burg Hosp; Provident Hosp; Bethany Hosp; Tabernacle Community Hosp, assoc med dir, 1972-77; Bethany/Garfield Pk Hosp, chief med & admin officer, 1977-81; Ill' Stateville Correctional Ctr, chief med officer & med adminr, 1981-83; Metrop Correctional Ctr, med dir, 1984-86; Luxury Yachts charaters, Miami, FL & Chicago, IL, pres, 1984-; CHA Ltd, Chicago Ill, pres, 1985-; Commun Equip Consults, pres, 1987-; Marine Cellular Specialists Chicago & Ft Lauderdale, vpres, 1988-; Knott Lock Corp, pres, 1988-; Loyola Univ, teaching med; Univ Ill, fac; Rush Med Col, fac. **Orgs:** Dir, Inner Cty Ind, 1967-; Am Col Phys, 1968-; dir, St Johns Entp, 1970-; dir, Kings Bay Ltd, 1972-; dir, Lux Yachts Ltd, 1980-; dir, Reg Ind, 1980-; fel Sigma Pi Phi. **Special Achievements:** Attended First World Black Festival of Arts and Culture in Dakar, 1966. **Home Addr:** 1501 N State Pkwy Apt 3a, Chicago, IL 60610-1665, **Home Phone:** (312)787-5532. **Business Addr:** President, Knott Lock Corp, 800 S Wells Suite 532, Chicago, IL 60607, **Business Phone:** (312)939-9200.

### KNOTT, MABLE M

Manager. **Personal:** Born Montgomery, AL; daughter of Joseph Paige (deceased) and Julia Kyle Alexander Mayberry (deceased); married Gerald Jordan; children: Deborah L & Gerald Jr; married Harold Wynne; married William Edgar. **Educ:** Sinclair Col; Univ Dayton. **Career:** Manager (retired); Wright Patterson AFB, reports control clerk, 1953-55; Gentile Air Force Depot, exec secy, 1959-72; Defense Electronic Supply Ctr, contract admin & negotiator, 1972-74, Columbus procurement analyst, 1974-77; Digital Equip Corp, buyer, 1977-80; Air Force Acquisition Ctr, Hanscom AFB, small bus specialist, 1982-91, Fed Womens Prog, mgr, 1989-93; Jazz Ensemble, May Knott, mgr. **Orgs:** Chmn, YWCA Swim-Ment Handicapped, 1980-82. **Honors/Awds:** Outstanding Performance, DLA, 1965, 1980; Letter of Commendation, DLA, 1974; Letter of Outstanding Fed Serv, AF; Nominated for Roy Wilkins Award, Nat Asn Advan Colored People, 1989. **Home Addr:** 52 Northwood Dr, Nashua, NH 03063.

### KNOWLES, BEYONCE GISELLE (BEYONCE GISELLE KNOWLES-CARTER)

Actor, singer, movie producer. **Personal:** Born Sep 4, 1981, Houston, TX; daughter of Mathew and Tina; married Jay Z; children: Blue Ivy. **Career:** R&B group, Destiny's Child, lead singer; Albums with Destiny's Child: Destiny's Child, 1998; The Writing's On the Wall, 1999; Survivor, 2001; Albums: Romeo Must Die, 2000; Charlie's Angels, 2000; Osmosis Jones, 2001; Head of State, 2003; Soul Plane, 2004; White Chicks, 2004; Dangerously In Love, 2003; Live at Wembley, 2004; B'Day, 2006; Dreamgirls, 2006; Good Luck Chuck, 2007; Bling: A Planet Rock, 2007; Karaoke Revolution Presents: American Idol Encore, 2008; TV series: "Smart Guy", 1998; "Carmen: A Hip Hopera", MTV, 2001; "Saturday Night Live", 2002-09; "The 79th Annual Academy Awards", 2007; "Premios Principales", 2008; "The X Factor", 2008; "Skins", 2009; "Fringe", 2009; "CSI: Miami", 2009; "20 to 1", 2009; Obsessed, 2009; "Dancing with the Stars", 2008-09; "Anima", 2009; "Loose Women", 2009; "So You Think You Can Dance", 2009-14; Dancing with the Stars", 2009-14; "Accidentally on Purpose", 2009; "Cougar Town", 2009; "Glee", 2009; "WWF Raw Is War", 2009; Films: Carmen: A Hip Hopera, 2001; Austin Powers in Goldmember, 2002; The Fighting Temptations, 2003; Bridget Jones: The Edge of Reason, 2004, Soul Plane, 2004; The Pink Panther, 2006; Dreamgirls, 2006; Lakeview Terrace, writer, 2008; Cadillac Records, writer, 2008; Wow! Wow! Wubbzy!: Wubb Idol, 2009; Obsessed, 2009; Epic, currently; A Star Is Born, currently. **Orgs:** Mem choir, St John's United Methodist Church. **Special Achievements:** First African-American woman to ever win the ASCAP Pop Songwriter of the Year Award, 2001. **Business Addr:** Recording Artist, Sony BMG Music Entertainment, 550 Madison Ave, New York, NY 10022-3211, **Business Phone:** (212)833-8000.

### KNOWLES, DR. EDDIE ADE

College teacher, percussionist, musician. **Personal:** Born May 3, 1946, New York, NY; son of Maggie and Ephraim; children: Alisa & Themba. **Educ:** Lincoln Univ, BA, 1970; Columbia Univ Teachers Col, MA, 1973; Univ Albany, PhD, 1998. **Career:** Bronx Community Col, from asst dir col discovery prog to dir col discovery prog, 1970-74; Hostos Community Col, asst prof, 1974-75; Rensselaer Polytech Inst, asst dean studs & foreign stud adv, 1977-79, dean minority affairs, 1979-82, dean studs, 1982-2000, interim vpres stud life, 2000-01, vpres stud life, 2001-, Arts Dept, Adjunct Faculty, 2000-11, Profesor of Practice in the Arts, 2011-. **Orgs:** Bd dir, Sponsors Educ Opportunity, 1970-; consult, Exxon Educ Found, 1984; consult, NY Educ Opportunity Ctrs, 1984; bd dir, Edwin Gould Found C; artistic dir, Ensemble Congeros, 2004-; bd dir, Hist Troy Savings Bank Music Hall. **Home Addr:** 95 Brunswick Rd, PO Box 1531, Troy, NY 12181-1531, **Home Phone:** (518)271-7919. **Business Addr:** Professor of Practice in the Arts, Rensselaer Polytech Institute, 110-8th St, Troy, NY 12180-3590, **Business Phone:** (518)276-8629.

### KNOWLES, DR. EM CLAIRE

School administrator. **Personal:** Born Jun 6, 1952, Sacramento, CA; daughter of Sidney S and Almeana Early. **Educ:** Univ Calif, Davis, BA, 1973; Univ Calif, Berkeley, MLS, 1974, cert mgt, 1975; Calif State Univ, Sacramento, MPA, 1986; Simmons Col, Boston, MA, doctor arts, libr admin, doctoral degree, 1988. **Career:** Univ Calif, Davis, ref librn, 1975-82, soc sci librn, 1982-85, coordr bib instr, 1985-88; Wentworth Inst Technol, fel, 1982; Wentworth Inst Tech, Boston, Mass, arch librn, 1982; Simmons Col, Boston, Mass, circulation librn, 1982, asst dean stud admin serv, 1988-, ALASC, fac adv, Libr Comnrs, chmn; freelance proof reader & reviewer, 1988-. **Orgs:** Calif Libr Asn, 1975-88, counr, 1978-90; Calif Gov's Conf Libr & Info Sci, 1979; Lambda Xi, 1980; Life mem, Am Libr Asn, 1984-; chmn, Librns Asn Univ Calif, Davis, CA, 1985-86; Mass Black Librns Network, 1988-; Nat Asn Waterfront Employers, 1990; Am Asn for Higher Educ, 1990; vpres, Greater Boston Inter-Univ Coun, 1998-99; comnr, Mass Bd Libr Comnrs, 2001-06; Delta Sigma Theta Sorority; Beta Phi Mu; bd trustee, Read Found. **Business Addr:** Assistant Dean of Student Administration Service, Simmons College, 300 The Fenway P-212L, Boston, MA 02115-5898, **Business Phone:** (617)521-2000.

### KNOWLES, MATHEW

Executive. **Personal:** Born Jan 9, 1952; married Tina; children: Beyonce & Solange; married Gena C Avery. **Educ:** Fisk Univ, BA, econs, BBA; Cornerstone Christian Bible Col, MBA, strategic leadership & orgn cult. **Career:** Tex Southern Univ, vis prof; Music World Entertainment & Global Entertainment Conglomerate, founder, pres & chief exec officer. **Orgs:** Grammy Awards Panel; voting mem, Nat Acad Rec Arts & Sci; Rec Indust Asn Am; Omega Psi Phi Fraternity; bd dir, Gospel Music Asn, 2011. **Business Addr:** Founder, Chief Executive Officer, Music World Entertainment, 1505 Hadley St, Houston, TX 77002-8927, **Business Phone:** (713)772-5175.

### KNOWLES, SOLANGE PIAGET

Singer, actor. **Personal:** Born Jun 24, 1986, Houston, TX; daughter of Matthew and Tina Beyonce; married Daniel Smith; children: Daniel Julez Smith Jr. **Career:** Albums: Solo Star, 2003; Sol-Angel and the Hadley St. Dreams, 2008. Films: Johnson Family Vacation, 2004; Bring It On: All or Nothing, 2006; Singles: "I Decided", 2008; "I Decided (Part2)", 2008; TV series: "Taina", 2002; "The Proud Family", 2002; "One on One", 2004; "Listen Up", 2005; "Ghost Whisperer", 2008. **Business Addr:** Recording Artist, c/o Columbia Records, 550 Madison Ave, New York, NY 10022-3211, **Business Phone:** (212)833-8000.

**KNOWLES, SUDANI**
Executive. **Career:** Detroit City Coun, Off Mayor, exec assist; Detroit Vacant Property Campaign, Americorps Vol. **Orgs:** Community Legal Resources. **Business Addr:** Executive Assistant, City of Detroit, Office of the Mayor, 2 Woodward Ave Suite 1126, Detroit, MI 48226, **Business Phone:** (313)224-3400.

**KNOWLES-CARTER, BEYONCE GISELLE. See KNOWLES, BEYONCE GISELLE.**

**KNOWLING, ROBERT E., JR.**
Executive. **Personal:** Born Jan 1, 1954?, Kokomo, IN; married Angela Denise; children: 4. **Educ:** Wabash Col, BA, theol, 1976; Northwestern Univ, Kellogg Sch Mgt, MBA. **Career:** Bell, operator, engr, mkt exec, 1977-92; Acordia, dir, 1987-91; Ameritech, lead architect re-eng corp transformation, 1992-94, vpres network opers, 1994-96; US W, exec vpres opers & tech, 1996-98; Covad Commun Group, chmn, pres & chief exec off, 1998-2001; Simdesk Technologies, chief exec officer, 2001-03; Internet Access Tech, chair, chief exec off, 2001-03; Vercuity Inc, chief exec off, 2002-05; New York Leadership Acad, chief exec off, 2002-05; Telwares, chief exec off, 2005-09; Bartech Group, dir, 2007-; Grupo Salinas, consult, 2009-; Eagles Landing Partners, chmn, dir, 2008-. **Orgs:** Bd dir, Ariba Inc, 1999-2012; speaker, Digital Divide; bd dir, Juv Diabetes Fndn Intl; adv bd, Northwestern Univ, Kellog Grad Sch Mgmt; vol, YMCA; chair, nat serv group; bd dir, Roper Industs, Sarasota, Fl; bd dir, Aprimo, Indianapolis, Ind; Broadmedia Inc; bd dir, Heidrick & Struggles Int Inc, 1998-; bd dir, Hewlett-Packard, 2000-05. **Business Addr:** Board of Director, Director, Heidrick & Struggles International Inc, 233 S Wacker Dr Sears Tower Suite 4200, Chicago, IL 60606-6303, **Business Phone:** (312)496-1200.

**KNOX, DOROTHY DEAN**
Law enforcement officer, police chief. **Personal:** Born Mar 10, 1940, Jayess, MS; daughter of Robert Earl Brent and Juanita Jones; married Stanley R. **Educ:** Wayne State Univ, BS, criminal justice admin, 1975. **Career:** Detroit Police Dept, policewoman, 1969-74, sgt, 1974-77, lt, 1977-80, inspector, 1980-86, comdr, 1986-93, dep chief, 1994, Community Serv Div, head, 2000; Wayne Co, prosecutor, chief investr, 1994-2004; Real Estate One, salesperson, 1979-11, sales assoc, 1979-. **Orgs:** Bd mem, Black Family Develop, 1984-91; bd mem, Detroit Police Athletic League, 1985-91; bd secy, Cs Aid Soc, 1985-96; bd mem, Child Care Coord Coun, 1986-92; bd mem, Old Newsboys Good Fel Detroit, 1992-94; trustee, Leadership Detroit, 1994-99; Int Soc Poetry. **Home Addr:** 18048 Marlowe St, Detroit, MI 48235. **Business Addr:** Sales Associate, Real Estate One Inc, 555 Briarwood Cir, Ann Arbor, MI 48108, **Business Phone:** (248)684-1065.

**KNOX, DR. GEORGE F.**
Lawyer. **Personal:** Born Oct 17, 1943, Cleveland, TN; son of George and Iris Long; married Odette Curry. **Educ:** Mich State Univ, BS, zool, 1966; Univ Miami Sch Law, JD, 1973. **Career:** Univ Miami Sch Bus Admin, lectr, 1973-74; City Miami, Fla, asst city atty, 1974-75; Univ Ark, Fayetteville, asst prof law, 1975-76; City Miami, Fla, city att & dir law dept, 1976-82; Univ Miami Sch Law, lectr, 1978-80; Nova Univ Ctr Study Law, lectr, 1980-82; Paul, Landy Bailey & Harper Pa, partner, 1982-84; Long & Knox, partner, 1984; Kubicki Draper Gallagher, Miami, Fla, atty, 1990; pvt pract lawyer, currently; Adorno & Zeder Pa, vice chmn, currently; Fla Int Univ Col Law, vis prof & dir, Non-Litigation Clin Progs, currently, atty & ethics prof; Y3K Holdings Inc Knox-Seaton LLC, sr prin, currently; dir, City Nat Bank, currently. **Orgs:** Fla Bar Asn; Nat Bar Asn; Am Bar Asn; DC Bar Asn; Nat Inst Munic Law Officers; Asn Am Law Sch; Black Lawyers Asn; Fla League Cities; Asn Am Trial Lawyers; Acad Fla Trial Lawyers; US Dist Ct Southern Dist Fla, US Ct Appeals Fifth Circuit, US Supreme Ct; Nat Asn Advan Colored People; bd dir, Miami-Dade Community Col Found Inc; bd trustee, Greater Miami Chamber Com; bd dir, Trust Pub Land, 2000-; bd trustee, Orange Bowl Comt; dir, Fla Wages Prog State Bd; Ctr Excellence; bd dir, YMCA Greater Miami; Dade Co Blue Ribbon Comt; bd trustee, Fla Mem Col; bd dir, United Way; Miami Coalition Drug-Free Community Iron Arrow Hon Socs Univ Miami; mem bd dir, Bapist Health Doctors Hosp; Fla Int Univ, bd mem; Baptist Health hosp, bd mem; Fla Bar Found, mem; bd mem; Jr League Miami Inc, bd mem, mem adv bd; Fla Memorial Univ, trustee, bd trustees; Miami Sports, original mem; Welfare, chmn. **Honors/Awds:** Jaycees Outstanding, Young Men Am, 1976; Miami-Dade Chamber Commerce Award of Outstanding Contribution to Social and Economic Development, 1977; Virgil Hawkins Achievement Award, Black Lawyers Asn, 1977; Alpha Phi Alpha Fraternity Achievement Award, 1977; Community Awareness Award, Fla Jr Col, Jacksonville; Community Service Award, Beta Beta Lambda Chap, Alpha Phi Alpha Fraternity, 1981; Appreciation Award, Nat Asn Advan Colored People, 1981; Jacksonville Achiever Award, Northwest Coun Jacksonville Chamber Comn, 1986; James W Mc Lamore Outstanding Volunteer of the Year Award, Miami Dade Community Foundation, 2001; Doctor of Law degree, Fla memorial Univ; History Miamis Legal Legends Award, 2010-11; Listed in 100 Most Powerful People In Miami, Miami Bus Mag; Silver Medallion Award, NCCJ. **Special Achievements:** The First Person of African Descent to Join the Faculty of the University of Arkansas School of Law. **Home Addr:** 2601 S Bayshore Dr, Miami, FL 33133, **Home Phone:** (305)858-5555. **Business Addr:** Senior Principal, KnoxSeaton LLC, 245 Pk Ave Fl 39, New York, NY 10167.

**KNOX, GEORGE L., III**
Executive, vice president (organization). **Personal:** Born Sep 6, 1943, Indianapolis, IN; son of George L II and Yvonne Nee Wright; married B Gail Reed; children: Reed & Gillian. **Educ:** Tuskegee Univ, Tuskegee, BA, polit sci, 1967; Harvard Bus Sch, Boston, MBA, 1975; Am Univ, Wash, DC. **Career:** Executive (retired); US Dept State, Wash, DC, Tokyo, foreign serv officer, 1968-73; McKinsey & Co, New York, assoc, 1975-77; Philip Morris, NY, mgr internal mgt consult, 1977-79, mgr financial rels, 1979-83, dir financial rels & admin, 1983-85, dir corp Communs, 1985-87, vpres, pub affairs, 1987-95, vpres corp affairs, 1995-2001. **Orgs:** Trustee, Studio Mus Harlem; Ford Found; chmn, Phil-Pac; dir, Franklin & Eleanor Roosevelt Inst; adv coun, Am Ballet Theatre; trustee, Afr Am Experience Fund; bd adv, Conn Can; chmn bd, Studio Mus, Harlem; bd mem, Am Ballet Theatre; bd mem, Southern Ctr Int Studies; advisor, Japan Found; vice chmn, Franklin & Eleanor Roosevelt Inst; mem emer, Pub Affairs Comt Us Mil Acad; trustee, African Am Experience Fund; bus adv coun, US Info Agency; dir, Harvard Bus Sch Club, New York, Independent Col Fund New York; Dea's Adv Coun Ala State Univ; gov, New Sch Univ. **Home Addr:** 1001 Genter St Suite 7H, Stamford, CT 92037, **Home Phone:** (858)456-2829.

**KNOX, MARK ALEXANDER. See ALEXANDER, FLEX.**

**KNOX, MARSHALL**
Executive. **Career:** Retired teachers Asn Chicago, dir, 2005-06. **Orgs:** Trustee, Pension Fund. **Business Addr:** Director, The Retired Teachers Association of Chicago, 20 E Jackson Blvd Suite 1500, Chicago, IL 60604-2235, **Business Phone:** (312)939-3327.

**KNOX, SIMMIE**
Portrait painter. **Personal:** Born Aug 18, 1935, Aliceville, AL; son of Simmie Sr and Amelia; married Roberta B; children: Zachary L & Amelia L; children: Sheri. **Educ:** Del State Col, attended 1960; Univ Del, BA, 1967; Temple Univ, Tyler Sch Art, BFA, 1970, MFA, 1972. **Career:** Mus African Art, artist, Wash, DC, 1971; Simmie Knox Portraits Inc, portrait artist & still life artist, 1971-; Portrait paintings: William Jefferson Clinton; Hillary Rodham Clinton; Bill Clinton's presidential portrait; Portrait of Joseph H. Rainey; Judith Ann Wilson Rogers; John Conyers; Donald Eugene Siegelman; Dr. Nathan Carter; Damon Bradley; Consuelo Marshall; John Wilson; Norman Minetta; Rodney Slater; Xernona Clayton; Clarence W. Blount; Joseph W. Hatchett; Dr. John Hope Franklin; Blanche Kelso Bruce; Quintin Primo; Damon Jerome Keith; Nathaniel R. Jones; Dr. Dorothy Height; Carol Reid Wallace; Rosemary McCarthy; Theodore R. Newman Jr; Ruth Bader Ginsburg; Spottswood William Robinson III; Alvin I. Krenzler; David Dinkins; H. Patrick Swygert; Frederick Douglas, 1975; Alex Haley, 1977; Justice Thurgood Marshall, 1989; Bill Cosby & family, 1983-91; Muhammad Ali, 1995; Bishop John T Walker, 1995; Henry Aaron, 1996. **Special Achievements:** First African American artist paint off presidential portrait; participant, Thirty Second Biennial Contemp Am Painting, The Corcoran Gallery Art, Wash, DC. **Business Addr:** Portrait Artist, Still Life Artist, Simmie Knox Portraits Inc, 13801 Ivywood Lane, Silver Spring, MD 20904-5471, **Business Phone:** (301)879-1655.

**KNOX, STANLEY**
Police chief. **Personal:** Born Jan 1, 1939, Summerville, GA; son of Doris; married Dorothy Brent. **Educ:** Wayne State Univ, BA, criminal justice, 1976. **Career:** Ppolice (retired); Detroit Police Dept, police officer, 1966, lt, 1977, inspector, 1978, head traffic sect, 1980, comdr, 1986, chief police, 1991-93. **Orgs:** Int Asn Chief Police; Mich Asn Chiefs Police.

**KNOX, WAYNE D. P.**
City planner, government official. **Personal:** Born Jun 19, 1947, West Reading, PA; son of John W and Mary V Peagram; children: Latina Marie. **Educ:** Cheyney State Col, BA, 1970; Pa State Univ, MA, 1984. **Career:** Bur Planning City Reading, urban planner, 1973-78; City Reading, dir orientation & training USAC proj, 1974-75; Neighborhood Housing Serv Reading, assoc dir, 1978-80, exec dir, 1980-82; Neighborhood Reinvestment Corp, field serv off, 1982-92; Martinsville Community Develop off, asst city mgr, currently. **Orgs:** Comt mem Reading Downtown Adv Comn, 1980-; dir, Old Bethel Cult Serv Ctr, 1985-91; CDC Martinsville/Henry County, 2013-. **Home Addr:** 332 Lakewood Trail, McKenney, VA 24112, **Home Phone:** (276)632-4280. **Business Addr:** Assistant City Manager, Director of Community Development, City of Martinsville, 55 W Church St Suite 217, Martinsville, VA 24114, **Business Phone:** (276)403-5169.

**KNOX, WAYNE HARRISON**
Executive, president (organization), chief executive officer. **Personal:** Born Apr 26, 1942, Atlanta, GA; son of Nazareth Sr (deceased) and Lessie Heard; married Isabel Houston; children: Michelle, Vanessa & Meredith. **Educ:** Clark-Atlanta Univ, BS, physics, 1965; Geo Inst Technol, MS, nuclear engineering, health physics. **Career:** Western Elec, elec engr, 1966-67; Clemson Univ, grad teaching asst, stud, 1971-72; Clark Col, instr, 1972-74; Westinghouse Hanford, oper health physics suv, 1974-77; Battelle Northwest, radiation safety auditor, res scientist, 1977-80; Inst Nuclear Power Opers, proj mgr, 1980-81; Advan Syst Technol Inc, pres, chief exec officer, 1981-; Cold War Soldiers, pres & chief exec officer, 2009-. **Orgs:** Health Physics Soc. **Home Addr:** 3931 Land O, Atlanta, GA 30342, **Home Phone:** (404)261-2194. **Business Addr:** President, Chief Executing Officer Chairman, Advanced Systems Technology Inc, 3490 Piedmont Rd NE Suite 1410, Atlanta, GA 30305-4810, **Business Phone:** (404)240-2930.

**KNOX, WILLIAM ROBERT, SR.**
Executive, football player. **Personal:** Born Jun 19, 1951, Elby, AL; son of Henry and Johnnie Finch; children: Jerett, Rashard & Rachelle. **Educ:** Purdue Univ, BS, 1974. **Career:** Chicago Bears, defensive back, kick return, punt return, 1974-77; Correct Piping Co Inc, estimator, 1978-83; W R Knox Corp, pres, 1980-. **Orgs:** Pres, Purdue Club Lake Co, 1983; E Chicago Sports Hall Fame. **Business Addr:** President, W R Knox Corp, 7836 Forest Ave, Gary, IN 46403-2139, **Business Phone:** (219)938-5422.

**KNOX-BENTON, DR. SHIRLEY**
School administrator, philanthropist. **Personal:** Born Aug 8, 1937, Carthage, TX; daughter of Napoleon and Rhoberdia Goodwin; married Sammy L; children: Reginald Jerome Knox. **Educ:** Huston-Tillotson Col, BA, music, 1959; Tex A&M Univ, summer study, 1965; Tex Women's Univ, MS, guid & coun, 1978, MA, admin mgt, 1982; Harvard Univ, educ spec, 1985. **Career:** Sch adminr, philanthropist (retired); Southwest High Sch, asst prin, counr, music teacher; Paul Laurence Dunbar High Sch, prin, 1992-2004. **Orgs:** Pres, Neighborhood Club, 1971-; deleg NEA, TSTA, FWCTA 1974-; consult, High Sch Workshops, 1982-; vpres & pres, Ft Worth Counselors Assoc, 1983-85; consult, B&B Assocs, 1984-; consult, Links Sororities 1984-85; Nat Asn Advan Colored People; Zeta Phi Beta; Tex Asn Sec Sch Prin, Ft Worth Admin Women, Phi Delta Kappa; bd dir, Camp Fire Girls; FWASSP; mus dir, Nat Cowboys Color Mus & Hall Fame. **Home Addr:** 5901 Eisenhower Dr, Ft. Worth, TX 76112-7710, **Home Phone:** (817)457-6542.

**KNUCKLES, KENNETH J.**
Vice president (organization), government official, association executive. **Educ:** Univ Mich, BS, archit; Howard Univ Sch Law, JD. **Career:** Dep Bronx Bor pres, 1987-90; New York Dept Gen Serv, asst housing comnr, 1990-93; S Bronx Overall Econ Develop Corp, sr vpres econ develop, 1990-93; Columbia Univ, chief procurement officer, 1994-95; Columbia Univ, vpres support servs, 1996-2003; New York Dept Gen Servs, comnr, 1990-93; New York Planning Comn, vice chair, 2002-; Upper Manhattan Empowerment Zone Develop Corp, pres & chief exec officer, 2003-. **Orgs:** Ny Bar Asn; New York Planning Comn, 2002-; bd dir, 2001-03, Upper Manhattan Empowerment Zone Develop Corp; trustee, Continuum Health Partners Inc; trustee, St Lukes-Roosevelt Hosp Ctr; bd trustee, NYC Big Bros & Big Sisters; bd trustee, Continuum Health Group; dir, pres, NYC2012 Inc; dir, NYC & Company Inc; dir, Carver Fed Savings bank, dir; Carver Bancorp Inc, 2013. **Special Achievements:** First African-American commissioner of New York City's Department of General Services. **Business Addr:** President, Chief Executive Officer, Upper Manhattan Empowerment Zone Development Corp, 55 W 125th St 11th Fl, New York, NY 10027, **Business Phone:** (212)410-0030.

**KOCH, FRANCENA JONES**
Counselor, educator, association executive. **Personal:** Born Dec 3, 1948, Bunnell, FL; daughter of Roosevelt Jones and Naomi Stafford; children: Ahmad Yussef Shaw. **Educ:** Fla Mem Col, BS, elem educ, 1972; Nova Southeastern Univ, MEd, 1984, specialist, early & mid childhood, 1994. **Career:** Miami Dade Co Pub Schs, intermediate instr, 1973-88, guid counr, 1988-; Fla Mem Col, adj prof, 1984-87; Dept Corrections, juv GED instr, 1994-97, Inmate to Inmate Tutoring, planner, 2000; Dorothy M Wallace Cope Ctr S, guid counr, currently. **Orgs:** Supt leadership cir, United Way, 1995-, ambassador, 1996-; Nat Asn Advan Colored People, Miami Br, 1997-; pres, Zeta Phi Beta, Beta Zeta Chap, 1997-99; Region 5 Steering Comt, Dade Co Schs, 1998-; Am Asn Univ Women, Miami Br, 2000-; pres-elect, Dade Co Coun Asn, 2001-02; chair, Herstory; adv bd, Beta Tau Zeta ROYAL Asn Inc. **Honors/Awds:** Southeastern Leadership Award, Zeta Phi Beta Sorority Inc, 2001. **Home Addr:** 10850 SW 164th St, Miami, FL 33157-2935, **Home Phone:** (305)232-9695. **Business Addr:** Guidance Counselor, Dorothy M Wallace COPE Center South, 10225 SW 147th Ter, Miami, FL 33176, **Business Phone:** (305)233-1044.

**KODJOE, BORIS (BORIS FREDERIC CECIL TAY-NATEY OFUATEY-KODJOE)**
Actor, fashion model. **Personal:** Born Mar 8, 1973, Vienna; son of Eric and Ursula; married Nicole Ari Parker; children: Sophie Tei Naaki Lee & Nicolas Neruda. **Educ:** Va Commonwealth Univ, Richmond, Va, mkt degree, 1996. **Career:** Films: Love & Basketball, 2000; Brown Sugar, 2002; The Gospel, 2005; America's Next Top Model, Cycle 4, 2005; What Ever She Wants, 2006; Madea's Family Reunion, 2006; Alice Upside Down, 2007; All About Us, 2007; Starship Troopers 3: Marauder, 2008; Surrogates, 2009; Resident Evil: Afterlife, 2010; The Confidant, 2010; clones, 2010; Take The Stand, 2011; Resident Evil: Retribution, 2012; Baggage Claim, 2013; Nurse 3D, 2013; Addicted, 2014. TV series: "Soul Food: The Series", 2000-04; "Street Time", 2003; Boston Public, 2003; Doing Hard Time, co-producer, 2004; "Second Time Around", 2004-05; If You Lived Here, You'd Be Home Now, 2006; "Crossing Jordan", 2007; "Women's Murder Club", 2007; "Nip Truck", 2007; "Tyler Perry's House of Payne", 2009; "Lopez Tonight", 2010; "Undercovers", 2010-12; "Scruples", 2012; "Franklin & Bash", 2012; "A Killer Among Us", 2012; "Unforgettable", 2014. **Orgs:** Eliminate Racism & Create Equality; Cascade United Methodist Church. **Honors/Awds:** Nominee, Image Award, 2002, 2003, 2004. **Special Achievements:** Named one of the "50 Most Beautiful People in the World 2002" by PeopleMagazine in 2002. **Business Addr:** Actor, Ujaama Talent Agency Inc, 501 Seventh Ave Suite 312, New York, NY 10018, **Business Phone:** (212)629-4454.

**KODJOE, NICOLE ARI PARKER (NIKKI KODJOE)**
Actor. **Personal:** Born Oct 7, 1970, Baltimore, MD; daughter of Donald and Susan; married Boris Kodjoe; children: Sophie Tei Naaki Lee & Nicolas Neruda Kodjoe; married Joseph Falasca. **Educ:** NY Univ, Tisch Sch Arts, drama, 1993. **Career:** Paramount Hotel, phone operator; Baltimore Actors Theatre, Washington Ballet Co, Signature Theatre Co, Metropolitan Playhouse, and the New Group, stage actor, 1990-; film actor, 1995-; television actor, 2000-; Films: The Incredibly True Adventure of Two Girls in Love, 1995; Stonewall, 1995; Boogie Nights, 1997; The End of Violence, 1997; Spark, 1998; The Adventures of Sebastian Cole, 1998; 200 Cigaretts, 1999; Mute Love, 1999; Mirar Mirror, 1999; Loving Jezebel, 1999; Blue Streak, 1999; A Map of the World, 1999; Harlem Aria, 1999; A Map of the World, 1999; Blue Streak, 1999; Dancing in September, 2000; Remember the Titans, 2000; Brown Sugar, 2002; King's Ransom, 2005; Welcome Home, Roscoe Jenkins, 2008; Never Better, 2008; Black Dynamite, 2009; Imagine That, 2009; Pastor Brown, 2009; 35 and Ticking, 2011; Big Mike, 2011; Repentance, 2013; TV series: "Divas", 1995; "Rebound: The Legend of Earl The Goat Manigault", 1996; "SUBWAY Stories: Cosby", 1996-2000; "SUBWAY Stories: Tales from the Underground", 1997; "Exiled", 1998; "Mind Prey", 1999; Cosby, 1999-2000; "The Loretta Claiborne Story", 2000; "Soul Food", 2000; "CSI: Crime Scene Investigation", 2000; "All of Us", 2003; "Second Time Around", consult, 2004-05; "The Deep End", 2010; "The Fran Drescher Show", 2010; "Let's Stay Together", 2011; "Secret Lives of Husbands and Wives", 2013; "Revolution", 2013; "Murder in the First", 2014. **Orgs:** Dem Party. **Honors/Awds:** FFCC Award, Fla Film Critics Circle, 1998; Special Award, Urban World Film Festival, 1999. **Special Achievements:** Appeared in shows with Naked Angels, Metropolitan Playhouse & Circle Rep

Lab. **Home Addr:** 6300 Power Ferrys Rd Suite 600-347, Atlanta, GA 30339. **Business Addr:** Actress, Showtime Networks Inc, 1633 E Broadway, New York, NY 10019, **Business Phone:** (212)708-1600.

## KOGER, DR. LINWOOD GRAVES, III

Physician. **Personal:** Born Feb 21, 1951, Baltimore, MD; son of Linwood G Jr Esq and Margaret Pigott; married Iantha Angela Hill; children: Brian Anthony & Kelsey Alexandria. **Educ:** Howard Univ Col Lib Arts, BS, chem, 1974, Col Med, MD, 1978. **Career:** Howard Univ, Dept Gen Surg, resident, 1983; pvt pract Baltimore, physician, 1983-85; Alvin C York Va Med Ctr, asst chief surg, 1985-; Morehouse Med Col, Atlanta, Ga, asst prof surg, 1985-89, prof surg, 1989-, course dir; Linwood G Koger III MD PC, pres, 1995-; pvt pract Baltimore, physician, currently. **Orgs:** Fel Am Col Surgeons; Asn Acad Surgeons; Soc Black Acad Surgeons. **Honors/Awds:** Diplomate, Am Bd Surg, 1984; Clinical Scis Fac Member of the Year, Meharry Med Col Pre-Alumni Coun, 1985-86; Mesenteric Ischemia; The York Va experience, presented Nat Med Asn Conv, 1989; Outstanding Surg Fac Mem, Morehouse Med Sch, Class 1994. **Home Addr:** 4474 Haverstraw Dr, Atlanta, GA 30338-6604. **Business Addr:** Physician, Linwood G Koger III MD PC, 4470 N Shallowford Rd Suite 104, Atlanta, GA 30338, **Business Phone:** (770)457-2228.

## KOGER, DR. MICHAEL PIGOTT, SR.

Physician. **Personal:** Born Jan 20, 1953, Baltimore, MD; son of Linwood and Margaret Pigott; children: Michael Pigott Jr. **Educ:** Fisk Univ; MIT; Meharry Med Col, MD, 1979; Univ Ala, MS, health educ & health prom, 2003. **Career:** Franklin Sq Hosp, resident physician, 1979-82; Provident Hosp, med staff, 1982-85; N Charles Gen Hosp, med staff, 1982-85; Jai Med Ctr, internist, 1982-84; Constant Care Med Ctr, internist, 1984; Basil Health Systs, internist, 1985; St Joseph Hosp, physician, 1985; Lutheran Hosp, house physician, 1985; Hancock Memorial Hosp, internist, 1985-86; Sparta Health Care Ctr, internist, 1986; Veterans Admin Med Ctr, internist, 1986-88; Cent St Hosp, med staff, 1988-92; Northwest Geog Regional Hosp, physician, 1992-96; S DeKalb Family Health Serv, 1997; Complete Wellness Med Ctr, 1997. **Orgs:** Baltimore City Med Soc, 1983-98, Med & Chirurgical Fac MD, 1983-07; chmn, Hancock Co Bd Health Sparta GA, 1985-86; Med Asn GA, 1985-86; chmn, Dept Utilization Hancock Memorial Hosp Rev & Qual Assurance, 1985-86; chmn physician's peer, Utilization Rev comt Hancock Memorial Hosp, 1985-86; vpres med staff, Hancock Memorial Hosp, 1986; Am Soc Internal Med, 1988-97. **Honors/Awds:** Physician's Recognition Award, Am Med Asn, 1985, 1988, 1991. **Special Achievements:** Publication "Your Health", a weekly column in The Sparta Ishmaelite newspaper, 1985-86. **Home Addr:** 2024 Binford St Apt 311, Laramie, WY 82072.

## KOMUNYAKAA, YUSEF (JAMES WILLIE BROWN, JR.)

Poet, educator. **Personal:** Born Apr 29, 1947, Bogalusa, LA; son of James William Brown Sr; married Reetika Vazirani; children: Jahan; married Mandy Sayer; children: 1. **Educ:** Univ Colo, BA, 1975; Colo State Univ, MA, writing, 1978; Univ Calif, Irvine, MFA, creative writing, 1980; Ind Univ, Afro-Am studies, 1997. **Career:** Writer, poet, essayist, educator; New Orleans Pub Schs, elem teacher; Southern Star Correspondent, ed; Univ New Orleans, Lakefront, instr Eng & poetry; Colo State Univ, assoc instr Eng compos, 1976-78; Univ Calif, Irvine, teaching asst poetry, writing instr remedial Eng compos, 1980; Univ New Orleans, instr Eng compos & Am lit, 1982-84; poet-in-the-schools, New Orleans, 1984-85; Ind Univ, Bloomington, vis asst prof Eng, 1985-86, assoc prof Eng & African Am Studies, 1986-93, Ruth Lilly Prof, 1989-90, prof Eng & African Am Studies, 1993-98; Univ Calif, Berkeley, vis prof Eng, 1991, Holloway lectr, 1992; Princeton Univ, Coun Univ Ctr Creative & Performing Arts, prof, 1997-; New York Univ, prof, creative writing, currently. Books: Dedications & Other Dark horses, 1977; Lost in the Bone wheel Factory, 1979; Copacetic, 1984; I Apologize for the Eyes in My Head, 1986; Toys in a Field, 1986; Dien Cai Dau, 1988; February in Sydney, 1989; Magic City, 1992; Neon Vernacular: New & Selected Poems, 1993; The Insomnia of Fire by Nguyen Quang Thieu, 1995; Thieves of Paradise, 1998; Talking Dirty to the Gods, 2000; Blue Notes: Essays, Interviews & Commentaries, 2000; Pleasure Dome: New & Collected Poems, 2001; Talking Dirty to the Gods, 2001; Pleasure Dome, 2001; Taboo: The Wishbone Trilogy, Part One, 2004; Gilgamesh: A Verse Play, 2006; Warhorses, 2008; The Chameleon Couch, 2011; The Emperor of Water Clocks, 2015. co-ed: The Second Set: The Jazz Poetry Anthology, Vol 2, 1996; Best American Poetry 2003, 2003. auth essay: Covenant: Scenes from an African American Church, 2007; Southern Cross, managing ed. **Orgs:** Phi Beta Kappa; Alpha Iota Chap; Fel Southern Writers; Fels from Fine Arts Work Ctr. **Business Addr:** Professor, New York University, 70 Washington Sq S, New York, NY 10012, **Business Phone:** (212)998-2415.

## KONDWANI, DR. KOFI ANUM

Consultant, educator. **Personal:** Born Mar 11, 1955, Dayton, OH. **Educ:** Maharishi Int Univ, Fairfield, IA, PhD, psychophysiol; Can Col Redwood City, CA, attended 1979; Univ Calif, Davis, attended 1980. **Career:** AUS, admin asst Korea, 1972-75; Can Col, Redwood City, Calif, recruitment consult, 1976-78; TMC Inc, San Francisco, transcendental meditation teacher, 1977-; Univ Calif, Davis, recruitment consult, 1979-80; James ETolleson, pub rel rep; Dayton & Calif, syndicated columnist; Univ Calif, affirmative action officer; Morehouse Sch Med, Atlanta, GA, Dept Community Health & Prev Med, prof, currently, Global Health Task Force, chair, 2007-; Nat Insts Health, meditation treat provider; Nat Ctr Primary Care, Morehouse Sch Med, consult, currently. **Orgs:** Nat Asn Advan Colored People, 1978-; vpres, Black Health Sci, 1979-80; chief exec officer, pres, Consciously Resting Meditation Progs; Cares Neway Forward. **Home Addr:** 861 St Agnes, Dayton, OH 45407. **Business Addr:** Assistant Professor, Global Health Task Force, Morehouse School of Medicine, 720 Westview Dr SW Suite 330, Atlanta, GA 30310-1495, **Business Phone:** (404)756-1478.

## KOONCE, GEORGE

Football player, executive. **Personal:** Born Oct 15, 1968, New Bern, NC; married Tunisia; children: George & Jayla. **Educ:** Chowan Univ, AA, lib arts & sci, 1989; NY Univ Regents, BA, lib arts & sci, 1999; E Carolina Univ, MA, sports mgt, 2006; Marquette Univ, PhD, interdisciplinary, 2012. **Career:** Football player (retired), executive; Ohio Glory, 1992; Green Bay Packers, left outside linebacker, 1992, 1999, left inside linebacker, 1993, right linebacker, 1994-95, mid linebacker, 1996, 1997, left linebacker, 1998, dir player develop, 2006-07; Seattle Seahawks, mid linebacker, 2000; E Carolina Univ, bd visitors bd mem, 2000-03, spec asst athletic dir, 2003-06; Marquette Univ, sr assoc athletic dir, 2007-09, dir develop, scholar progs, 2012-14; Univ Wis Milwaukee, dir athletics, 2009-10; Dampeer & Canady, partner, 2010-11; Marian Univ, sr vpres univ rels, 2014-. **Orgs:** Founder, George Koonce Sr Found, 1995-; bd mem, Athletic Dir Search Comt, 2003-04; bd mem, Wis Sports Develop Corp, 2007-; bd mem, Boule, 2009-; spokesperson, C's Serv Soc Family Finding Fatherhood Engagement Prog, 2012-; bd mem, Nat Football League Player Engagement Adv, 2012-. **Honors/Awds:** Hall of Fame, Nat Junior Col, 2000; Athletic Hall of Fame, E carolina Univ, 2002; Athletic Hall of Fame, Chowan Col, 2003; Hall of Fame, W Craven High Sch, 2005; American Hero Award, Holy Redeemer Acad, 2010; March of Champions Award, Boys & Girls Club, 2010. **Business Addr:** Senior Vice President for University Relations, Marian University, 45 S Nat Ave, Fond du Lac, WI 54935-4699, **Business Phone:** (920)923-7600.

## KOONCE, NORMAN L.

Executive. **Personal:** married Suzanne. **Educ:** La State Univ, architectural engineering, 1956. **Career:** Bogalusa City, city planning comn; Am Inst Architects, pres, 1988-89, exec vpres & chief exec officer, 1999-2005. chancellor, chair, currently. **Orgs:** Pres, secy, treas, La Architects Asn, 1978-82; Am Archit Found, 1998; Nat Campfire Girls & Boys; St. Paul's Cathedral Trust; Boyer Ctr Advan Studies; bd mem, Nat Ctr Preserv Technol & Training; chair, Fla Asn Ins Agents; dir, Treasures Truth Inc; Baton Rouge Chap; mem bd trustees, US Nat Comt Int Coun Monuments & Sites; bd dir, Acad Neuroscience Archit, currently. **Honors/Awds:** Edward C Kemper Award, Am Inst Architects, 1998; Doctor of Humanities, Northwestern State Univ, 2001; AIA La Medal of Hon, 2000. **Home Addr:** 7300 Old Dominion Dr, McLean, VA 22102-2644, **Home Phone:** (703)827-7383. **Business Addr:** Chancellor, The American Institute of Architects, 1735 New York Ave NW, Washington, DC 20006-5292, **Business Phone:** (202)626-7300.

## KORNEGAY, DR. WADE M.

Consultant, scientist. **Personal:** Born Jan 9, 1934, Mt. Olive, NC; son of Gilbert and Estelle Williams; married Bettie Joyce Hunter; children: Melvin, Cynthia & Laura. **Educ:** NC Cent Univ, BS, 1956; Bonn Univ Ger, attended 1957; Univ Calif, Berkeley, CA, PhD, phys chem, 1961; Mass Inst Technol Sloan Sch Mgt, attended 1979. **Career:** Scientist (retired); Univ Calif, postdoctoral fel, 1961-62, res assoc, 1962; Bonn Univ, Sloan Sch Mgt, fulbright fel; Mass Inst Technol, tech staff mem, 1962-71, Radar Signature Studies, tech group leader, 1970-86, assoc div head, 1986-93, Radar Measurements, div head, 1993-2000, Lincoln Lab, consult. **Orgs:** Am Phys Soc, 1959-; Sigma Xi Sci Res Soc, 1960-; vpres, Humphrey's Task Force Youth Motivation, 1964-68; exec coun, United Church Christ, 1971-77; bd dir, Nat Consortium Black Prof Develop, 1976-80; Boston City Mission Soc, 1977-; YMCA MA & RI Camp Community, 1977-99; NYAS, 1984-99; AMR IST Aeronaut & Astronauts, 1986-; div head, Radar Measurements; Alpha Phi Alpha; chmn, bd dir, Two State YMCA, 1990-94; AUS Sci Bd, 1991-98; bd trustee, Andover Newton Theol Sch, 2001-; fel, div fel, Air & Missile Defense Technol Div;Homeland Security/Homeland Defense Study, 2007; Innovative Army Orgn Study, 2008; Tactical Non-coop BiometSystems Study, 2010-11. **Home Addr:** 35 Hickory Rd, Sudbury, MA 01776, **Home Phone:** (978)443-8483. **Business Addr:** Division Fellow, Lincoln Laboratory, 244 Wood St, Lexington, MA 02420-9108, **Business Phone:** (781)981-5500.

## KORNEGAY, BR. WILLIAM F.

Labor relations manager, executive. **Personal:** Born Mar 9, 1933, Apalachicola, FL; married Dorothy L Little; children: Bill Jr. **Educ:** Edward Waters Col, AA; Bethune-Cookman Col, BS, sci edu, 1954; Fla A&M Univ, MEd, admin & supv, 1961; Univ Ill, PhD, mathedu, 1970. **Career:** Rosenwald HS FL, head sci dept, 1957-58; Univ High Sch, head sci dept, 1958-61; Hampton Jr Col, instr sci & math, 1961-66; Bethune-Cookman Col, asst prof math, 1966-67, acad dean instr, 1970-74; Ford fel, 1967; Univ Ill, coord math teachers, 1967-70; Gen Motors Inst, dean stud affairs, 1974-79; Fisher Body Div, dir qual work life, 1979-82; Gen Motors Corp, Detroit, dir res & devt, 1982-85; Gen Motors Corp, Flint, MI, dir, personnel, 1985-. **Orgs:** Phi Delta Kappa Educ Fraternity, 1965; bd trustee, Jr Achievement, 1975-80; bd trustee, Flint Urban Leag, 1977-79; bd trustee, United Way Chpn Allocations Com; 1978-80; life mem, Alpha Phi Alpha Fraternity. **Home Addr:** 1486 Kennebec Rd, Grand Blanc, MI 48439-4978, **Home Phone:** (810)694-3405. **Business Addr:** Director of Personnel, General Motors Corp, 6060 W Bristol Rd, Flint, MI 48554, **Business Phone:** (810)635-5612.

## KOTTO, YAPHET FREDERICK

Television producer, actor, administrator. **Personal:** Born Nov 15, 1939, New York, NY; son of Njoki Manga Bell Abraham and Gladys Maria; married Antoinette Pettyjohn, Jan 29, 1975?, (divorced 1988); children: Sarada, Mirabai & Salina; married Tessie Sinahon, Jul 12, 1998; married Rita Ingrid Dittman, Jan 1, 1962, (divorced 1975); children: Natascha, Fred & Robert. **Career:** Appeared in Off-Broadway & Broadway productions including: Great White Hope, Blood Knot, Black Monday, In White America, A Good Place to Raise a Boy; Films: 4 for Texas, 1963; Nothing But a Man, 1964; 5 Card Stud, 1964; Liberation of Lord Byron Jones, 1968; The Thomas Crown Affair, 1968; Man & Boy, 1972; Live & Let Die, 1973; Across 110th St, 1973; Report to the Commissioner, 1974; Truck Turner, 1974; Sharks Treasure, 1975; Friday Foster, 1975; Monkey Hustle, 1976; Drum, 1976; Roots, 1977; Blue Collar, 1978; Alien, 1979; Brubaker, 1980; Fighting Back, 1981; Hey Good Looking, 1982; Star Chamber, 1983; Terror in the Aisles, 1984; Warning Sign, 1985; Eye of the Tiger, 1986; The Park is Mine, 1986; Pretty kill, 1987; The Running Man, 1987; Prettykill, 1987; Midnight Run, 1988; Tripwire, 1990; After the Shock, 1990; Hangfire, 1991; Freddy's Dead: The Final Nightmare, 1991; Extreme Justice, 1993; Out of Sync, 1994; The Puppet masters, 1994; Two If by Sea, 1996; Witless Protection, 2008; TV appearances: "Losers Weepers", 1967; "The Big Valley", 1967; "High Chaparral", 1968; "Daniel Boone", 1968; "Hawaii Five-O", 1969; "Mannix", 1969; "The Name of the Game", 1970; "Gunsmoke", 1970; "Night Chase", 1970; "Doctors Hosp", 1975; "Raid on Entebee", 1977; "Death in A Minor Key", 1979; "Women on San Quentin", 1983; "For Love & Honor", 1983; "Rage", 1984; "Harem", 1986; "In Self Defense", 1987; "Badge of the Assassin"; "The Defenders: Payback", 1997; "Law & Order", 1997; "Homicide: The Movie", 2000; "The Ride", 2000; "Stiletto Dance", 2001, "Witless Protection", 2008; TV series: "Homicide", 1993-2000. **Orgs:** Actors Studio. **Business Addr:** Actor, NBC-TV, 30 Rockefeller Plz Fl 25, New York, NY 10012, **Business Phone:** (212)664-4444.

## KOTZIN, DR. DIANA

Psychologist, educator. **Personal:** Born Oct 28, 1941, Chicago, IL; daughter of John Ison and Gwendolyn Malva Armstead; married Joseph. **Educ:** Univ Chicago, BA, human develop, 1962, MA, human develop, 1964, PhD, human develop & clin psychol, 1968. **Career:** Univ Chicago, Grad Sch Educ, res assoc, 1966-67, asst prof behav sci human devel & dept educ, 1970-77; Howard Univ, Sch Med, instr psychiat, dept psychiat, 1967-68; Yale Univ, Sch Med, Child Study Ctr, asst prof psychiat, 1968-70; Northwestern Univ, Sch Educ, from asst prof to prof, 1977-97; Univ Pa, Grad Sch Educ, Constance E Clayton prof urban educ, 1998-. **Orgs:** Inst Int Educ New York & Inst African Studies, Univ Ghana, 1972; elected chairperson, Black Caucus Soc Res Child Devel, 1979-81; Nat Adv Bd Child Abuse & Neglect, 1979-81; elected mem, Gov Coun Soc Res Child Devel, 1981-87; Soc Res Child Devel Study Tour Peoples Repub China, 1984; Am Psych Asn; mem gov coun, Soc Res Child Devel; Am Educ Res Asn; Nat Asn Black Psych; Groves Conf Family; Delta Sigma Theta; Nat Assoc Educ Young C; bd ethnic & minority affairs, Am Psycholog Asn, 1986-88, bd sci affairs, 1995-97; Comt Child Develop Res & Pub Policy, Nat Res Coun, 1987-92; bd dir, Ancona Sch, Chicago Ill, 1989-91; adv panel, Head Sta Bur, ACF, 1988-; Appl Develop Psychol; Human Develop & NHSA; bd vistors, Learning, Res & Develop Ctr, Univ Pittsburgh, currently; Inst for Policy Res Studies & the dept African Am studies. **Honors/Awds:** Distinguished Research Award, Pi Lambda Theta, 1969; First Black Scholar Achievement Award, Black Caucus, Soc Res Child Develop, 1987; received many awards, 1987; Elected Fel, Am Psycholog Asn, 1993; Distinguished Contribution Research Public Policy, Am Psychol Asn, 1994; Distinguished Research Award, Pi Lambda Theta; Lifetime Professional Achievement Citation, Univ Chicago, 2007. **Special Achievements:** Published books: Visible Now: Blacks in Private Schools, Greenwood Press, 1988; Black Children & Poverty: A Developmental Perspective, Jossey-Bass Press, 1988; Black Educational Choice, 2012; Messages for Educational Leadership, 2012. **Home Addr:** 816 S Ogden Dr, Los Angeles, CA 90036, **Home Phone:** (323)964-9771. **Business Addr:** Constance E Clayton Professor Emeritus, University of Pennsylvania, 3700 Walnut St, Philadelphia, PA 19104.

## KOUNTZE, VALLERY J.

Executive. **Personal:** Born Cambridge, MA; daughter of Wallace H and Alberta M Yearwood Jackman. **Educ:** Chamberlain Sch Retailing, Boston, MA, 1975; Univ SC Grad Sch Bus, Los Angeles, CA, CME, 1986. **Career:** Executive, producer; RKO Gen, Boston, acct exec, 1976-78; Future Media, vpres, 1979-82; Mainstreet Commun, Los Angeles, Calif, vpres, 1981-83; RCA & Columbia Pictures Home Video, Los Angeles, Calif, vpres mkt, 1983-85, vpres, gen mgr mm & div, 1985-86; Repub Pictures Home Video, Los Angeles, Calif, vpres, mkt, 1986-87, sr vpres sales & mkt, 1987-89, pres, 1989-92; Main St Mkt, Los Angeles, Calif, pres, 1991-92; ITC Home Video, Los Angeles, Calif, exec vpres, gen mgr, 1992-94; Warner Music Group, vpres video mkt develop, 1994-97; Entertainment Mkt Solutions, managing partner, 1997-; Mi Casa Multimedia, bus develop, 2000-11; Insync Media, bus develop consult, 2003-08; Diversified Luxury Mkt, consult, 2007-09; James Beard Found, consult, 2008-09. Films: Mad Max: The Film Phenomenon, exec producer, 2002; Mel Gibson: The High Octane Birth of a Superstar, exec producer, 2002; Witnessed in Blood: A True Murder Invest, exec producer, 2007; The Man Behind Carlos Santana, exec producer, 2007; Mr Chili: Too Hot for TV, exec consult producer, 2007; All the Way to La, exec consult producer, 2007; Die Laughing, exec consult producer, 2008; How the Devil Was Made, exec producer, 2008; The Witless Protection Blooper Reel, exec consult producer, 2008; The Musicians of Witless Protection, exec consult producer, 2008; Making Witless: The Cast on the Cast, exec consult producer, 2008; Larry's Use of the Analogy, exec consult producer, 2008; A Cast of Critters, exec consult producer, 2008; The Kung Fu Dream Team, exec producer, 2008; Monkey King & the Eight Immortals: The Ancient Roots of Kung Fu, exec producer, 2008; Dangerous Beauty: The Women of 'The Forbidden Kingdom, exec producer, 2008; Making It in Beantown: Where It All Began, exec producer, 2009; The Prom: A Teen Rite of Passage, exec producer, 2009; The Cast's Guide to Dating, exec producer, 2009; A to Z: Prof Turner's Sexist Rating Syst, exec producer, 2009. TV Series: "Filming in Chinawood: Hengdian World Studios", exec producer, 2008; "Discovering China: The Extraordinary Locations of The Forbidden Kingdom", exec producer, 2008. **Orgs:** Pres & steering comt, 1989-, bd dir, co-pres, founder, Entertainment AIDS Alliance, 1989-; bd dir, AIDS Proj Los Angeles, 1990-96; Video Software Dealers Asn IAB, 1990-; founding mem, Video Indust AIDS Action Comt; chmn, bd dir, Break Cycle's. **Business Addr:** Board of Director, Founder, Entertainment AIDS Alliance, 7985 Santa Monica Blvd Suite 109-491, Los Angeles, CA 90046, **Business Phone:** (323)874-6497.

## KRAFT, DR. BENJAMIN F.

School administrator. **Personal:** Born Jan 15, 1948, Baton Rouge, LA; son of Benjamin F and Frances H Simons; married Yanick Douyon; children: Benjamin Robeson, Phillip Fouchard & Guileine Frances. **Educ:** Southern Univ & Agr & Mech Col, Baton Rouge, econs, 1966; Rutgers Col, BA, econs, 1970; Northeastern Univ, JD, 1973; Am Univ, MBA, employee rels, 1978. **Career:** Nat Labor Rels Bd, staff atty, 1973-77; Caribsun Export-Import Inc, pres, 1977-79; Big Ben Hardware Haiti, owner, gen mgr, 1979-86; Fla Mem Col, assoc dir, ctr community chg, 1986-87, chmnperson, Div Bus Admin, 1988-91, assoc dean fac, 1989-90, dir, Govt Rels & Sponsored Progs, 1992-94; Sc State Univ, asst to pres & vpres planning, eval & instnl advan, 1994-99; found exec dir, dir develop, Alcorn State Univ, asst to pres, 1999-2003; Windsor Village United Methodist Church, chief admin officer,

2003-07; US cong, interim dist dir, 2007; St Philip's Col, vpres col serv, 2008-11; Spirit Transp Serv, LLC, owner, 2011; Law Off Benjamin F. Kraft, prin, 2012-; DC Pub Employee Rels Bd, atty advisor, 2015-; Univ Vi, dir maj gifts, currently. **Orgs:** DC Bar Assoc, 1974-; credit community mem, NLRB Fed Credit Union, 1975-77; bd mem, treas, Haitian Am Chamber Com, 1984-86; Haitian Found Aid Women, 1985-86; bd mem Carib Am Enterprises Fla Inc, 1986-; bd mem, Ctr Family & Child Enrichment, 1988-90; Alpha Phi Alpha Frat Inc; Beta Beta Lambda, 1989-; 100 Black Men S Fla Inc, 1990-; Nat Asn Advan Colored People. **Honors/Awds:** ACE fel, Am Coun Educ, 1991-92; Performance Excellence Award, Univ Tex, 2009. **Home Addr:** 1430 Hawkins Mdw, San Antonio, TX 78248-1572. **Business Addr:** Director Major Gifts, University Virgin Islands, Fac W Bldg Suite 2 John Brewers Bay, Saint Thomas, VA 00802, **Business Phone:** (340)693-1046.

### KRAVITZ, LENNY (LEONARD ALBERT KRAVITZ)

Singer. **Personal:** Born May 26, 1964, New York, NY; son of Seymour (deceased) and Roxie Roker (deceased); married Lisa Bonet; children: Zoe Isabella. **Career:** Wrote "Justify My Love" for Madonna, 1990; Films: Coyote Ugly, performer, 2000; Blue Crush, writer, 2002; Bruce Almighty, writer, 2003; Peace One Day, writer, 2004; I'm Going to Tell You a Secret, writer, 2005; Precious: Based on the Novel Push by Sapphire, 2009; TV series: "The Simpsons", 2002; "Alias", 2003; "One Tree Hill", 2004; "My Super Sweet 16", 2005; "Ha-Shminiya", 2006; "60/90", 2008; Albums: Let Love Rule, 1989; Mama Said, 1991; Are You Gonna Go My Way, 1993; Circus, 1995; 5, 1998; Greatest Hits, 2000; Lenny, 2001; Baptism, 2004; It Is Time for a Love Revolution, 2008; Black and White America, 2011; Strut, 2014. Singles: "Spirit of the Forest", 1989; "Let Love Rule", 1989; "I Built This Garden for Us", 1990; "Mr. Cab Driver", 1990; "Always on the Run", 1991; "It Ain't Over 'Til It's Over", 1991; "Fields of Joy", 1990; "Stand by My Woman", 1990; "What the Fuck Are We Saying?", 1990; "Stop Draggin' Around", 1990; "What Goes Around Comes Around", 1990; "Believe", 1993; "Heaven Help", 1993; "Is There Any Love in Your Heart", 1993; "Heaven Help", 1994; "Spinning Around Over You", 1994; "Deuce", 1994; "Rock & Roll Is Dead", 1995; Can't Get You Off My Mind", 1996; "The Resurrection", 1996; "I Belong to You", 1998; "If You Can't Say No", 1998; "Thinking of You", 1998; "Fly Away", 1999; "Black Velveteen", 1999; "American Woman", 1999; "Again", 2000; "Dig In", 2001; "Stillness of Heart", 2002; "Believe in Me", 2002; "If I Could Fall inLove", 2002; "Show Me Your Soul", 2004; "Where Are We Runnin'?", 2004; "California", 2004; "Storm", 2004; "Calling All Angels", 2005; "Lady", 2005; "Breathe", 2005; "Bring It On", 2007; "I'll Be Waiting", 2007; "Love Love Love", 2008; Actor: The Rugrats Movie, 1998; Zoolander, 2001; Being Mick, 2001; Rebelde, 2004; The Diving Bell and the Butterfly, 2007; Precious, 2009; Selma, 2011; The Hunger Games, 2012; Lee Daniels' The Butler, 2013; The Hunger Games: Catching Fire, 2013. **Honors/Awds:** Received numerous awards including: MTV Video Music Awards, 1993; Brit Awards, 1994; VH1/Vogue Fashion Awards, 1998; Grammy Awards, 1999-2002; Radio Music Awards, 2001; My VH1 Awards, 2001; Blockbuster Entertainment Awards, 2001; American Music Awards, 2002; Microsoft Windows Media Innovation Award, 2002; BSFC Award, Boston Soc Film Critics Awards, 2009. **Business Addr:** Vocalist, Creative Artists Agency, 9830 Wilshire Blvd, Beverly Hills, CA 90212, **Business Phone:** (310)288-4545.

### KRIGGER, DR. MARILYN FRANCIS

Educator, teacher. **Personal:** Born Mar 27, 1940, St. Thomas; daughter of Charles Adolphus and Mary Augusta Skelton; married Rudolph E Sr; children: Rudolph E Jr. **Educ:** Spelman Col, BA, social sci, 1959; Columbia Univ, MA, hist, 1960; Univ Del, PhD, hist, 1983. **Career:** Charlotte Amalie High Sch, St Thomas, soc stud teacher, 1960-66; Univ VI, St Thomas, hist prof, hist prof emer, currently. **Orgs:** VI Hist Soc; Asn Caribbean Hist; Phi Alpha Theat; consult, VI; dept Ed, supporter, VI Hum Coun; VI Bd Ed, 1974-76; fel Nat Endowment Human, Summer, 1976-88; co-chair, VI Status Comm, 1988-93; VI State Rev Bd hist; VI, 2000; Alexander Hamilton Award Comt; adv bd, Univ Vi, Ctr Study Spirituality & Professionalism, currently. **Honors/Awds:** John Hay Whitney Found Fel, 1959-60; African Am Inst Ed-to-Africa Prog, 1972. **Home Addr:** Crown Mountain Rd, PO Box 4099, St Thomas00803, **Home Phone:** (809)776-8342. **Business Addr:** Professor Emeritus, University of the Virgin Islands, 2 John Brewer, St. Thomas00802-9990, **Business Phone:** (340)693-1057.

### KROLOFF, REED

Accountant. **Career:** Accountant. **Home Addr:** 2401 Calvert St NW Suite 910, Washington, DC 20008, **Home Phone:** (202)232-4750.

### KROON, MARC JASON

Baseball player. **Personal:** Born Apr 2, 1973, Bronx, NY; son of Raquel Altreche; married Tricia. **Career:** Baseball player (retired); New York Mets, 1991-93; San Diego Padres, pitcher, 1995, 1997-98; Memphis, 1996; Las Vegas, 1997; Indianapolis Indians, 1998; Seattle Mariners, free agt, 1998-2000; Cincinnati Reds, 1998; Azl Mariners, 1999; Tacoma Rainiers, 1999; Albuquerque Isotopes, 2000; Los Angeles Dodgers, free agt, 2000-01; Anaheim Angels, free agt, 2003; Ark Travelers, 2003; Salt Lake Stingers, 2003; Colo Springs Sky Sox, 2004; Colo Rockies, relief pitcher, 2004; Yokohama Bay Stars, 2005-07; Yomiuri Giants, closer, 2008-10; San Francisco Giants, free agt, 2011; Fresno Grizzlies, 2011. **Business Addr:** Professional Baseball Player, Yomiuri Giants.

### KUMANYIKA, DR. SHIRIKI K.

Nutritionist, educator. **Personal:** Born Mar 16, 1945, Baltimore, MD; daughter of Maurice Laphonso Adams and Catherine Victoria Williams; married Christiaan Morssink; children: Chenjerai. **Educ:** Syracuse Univ Col Arts & Sci, BA, psychol, 1965; Columbia Univ, MS, social work, 1969; Cornell Univ, PhD, human nutrit, 1978; Johns Hopkins Univ, Sch Hyg & Pub Health, MPH, epidemiol, 1984. **Career:** James Weldon Johnson Ment Health Clin; Bird S Coler Hosp; Windham Child Serv, caseworker, 1965-69; Nat Urban League, Family Planning Proj, dir, 1969-70; Addiction Res & Treat Corp, Dept Educ & Prevent, community organizer, 1970-71; Naomi Gray Assoc New York, proj dir, 1971-72; Cornel Univ, Ujamaa Residential Col, resident dir, 1973-74, Div Nutrit Sci, Gen Mills fel, 1974-76, Quaker Oats fel, 1976-77, asst prof, 1977-84; Johns Hopkins Univ Sch Hyg & Pub Health, asst prof, 1984-89, assoc prof, 1989; Pa State Univ, Univ Pk, Pa, assoc prof, sr scholar epidemiol, currently, prof epidemiol, currently, Health Prom & Dis Prev, assoc dean, currently, Grad Prog Pub Health Studies, dir, currently, C's Hosp Philadelphia Dept Pediat, Sect Nutrit, prof epidemiol, currently; Ctr Pub Health Initiatives, sr adv, currently, Penn Inst Urban Res, fac assoc, Dept Biostatistics & Epidemiol, Sch Med, prof epidemiol, currently, Ctr Clin Epidemiol & Biostatistics, Sch Med, sr scholar, currently, Penn-Cheyney Export Ctr Inner City Health, dir, currently; Robert Wood Johnson Health Soc Scholars Prog, from asst fac to fac; Penn's interdisciplinary, multi-sch Master Pub Health prog, founding dir; Ctr Africana Studies, affiliated fac. **Orgs:** Chair, Food & Nutrit Sect, Am Pub Health Asn, 1976-; Equal Health Opportunity Comt; Asn Black Cardiologists; Black Caucus Health Workers; Soc Nutrit Educ; Soc Epidemiol Res; fel Am Col Nutrit; Am Dietetic Asn, 1979-; Am Inst Nutrit, 1990-; Am Soc Clin Nutrit, 1990-; bd dir, Health Prom Coun Southeastern Pa; vice chair, Fed Adv Comt; sr fel Pa State Univ, Univ Pk, Pa, Inst Aging, currently; Leonard Davis Inst sr fel Health Econ, currently; founder, chair, African Am Collab Obesity Res Network, vice chair, Dept Health & Human Serv Secy's Adv Comt, 2008-11; co-chair, Inst Med;s Comt Childhood Obesity Prev; co-chair, Int Obesity Task Force; World Health Orgn's Expert Adv Panel Nutrit; Sect Pub Health, Col Physicians Philadelphia; bd dir, Food Trust. **Home Addr:** 324 S Barnard St, State College, PA 16801-4030, **Home Phone:** (814)238-2119. **Business Addr:** Professor of Epidemiology, Associate Dean for Health Promotion & Disease Prevention, University of Pennsylvania, Blockley Hall 8th Fl 423 Guardian Dr, Philadelphia, PA 19104-6021, **Business Phone:** (215)898-2629.

### KUMBULA, DR. TENDAYI SENGERWE

Journalist, educator. **Personal:** Born Nov 3, 1947, Harare; son of Isaac Sengerwe and Mandinema Edna Mungate; married Barbara Ann Jackson; children: Mandinema R, Runako T & Tendayi S Jr. **Educ:** Univ San Diego, BA, jour, 1968; Univ Calif, Los Angeles, CA, MA, jour, 1969, MA, polit sci, 1970; Univ SC, PhD, educ, 1976. **Career:** Los Angeles Times, Calif, CA, gen assignment reporter, 1968-82; Sunday Mail, Harare, Zimbabwe news, ed, 1982-86; Herald, Harare, Zimbabwe, asst ed, 1984-86; Calif State Univ, Long Beach, Calif, jour instr, 1987-89; Ball State Univ, Muncie, Ind, asst prof jour, news ed seq crd, asst prof emer jour, 1989-; Book: The Information Superhighway: Whither the Third World, 1995; The Role of the Media in Democratization: The Zimbabwe Case, 2001. **Orgs:** Soc Prof Journalists, 1989-; Nat Asn Black Journalists, 1990-; founder, fac adv, Nat Asn Black Journalists Study Chap, Ball State Univ, 1990-; Asn Educ Jour & Mass Comm, 1990-; fel African Studies Asn, 1991-; bd trustee, 1992, bd mem, 1996-, Motivate Our Minds; fel Poynter Inst Media Studies 1995 & 2002; fel Am Soc Newspaper Ed' Inst Journalism Excellence, 1997; Muncie Chap Ind Black Expo; Int Platform Asn; overseas dir, Mpisaunga, Mutandiro & Assocs, Harare, Zimbabwe; chair, Ball State Jour Dept, Multicult Affairs Adv Comt; chair & discussant, asn policy, Res & Develop Third world Countries; Ind Consortium Int Prog; Nat Alliance Black Sch Educrs Minorities & Media; fel Am Press Inst, 2003; fel Am Soc Newspaper Ed, 2003; ind holiday comn statewide adv comt, Day Serv Proj. **Home Addr:** 2807 W Wellington Dr, Muncie, IN 47304, **Home Phone:** (765)289-6930. **Business Addr:** Assistant Professor Emeritus of Journalism, Ball State University, Rm 300 Art & Jour Bldg 2000 W Univ Ave, Muncie, IN 47306, **Business Phone:** (765)285-1625.

### KUNES, KENNETH R.

Writer, insurance executive, association executive. **Personal:** Born Feb 7, 1932, Maywood, IL; son of Arthur F and Emily M; children: Ken, Leigh Ann & Jeff. **Educ:** Univ AZ, attended 1949; NE Univ, BS, 1955. **Career:** Phoenix-Am Inst Agency, fdr, 1965-85; Maricopa Co, assessor, 1968-81; Mid-City Glass & Mirror, owner, 1986; Security Reliable Inst, pres & chief exec officer. **Orgs:** Independent Ins Agents Asn; Phoenix Jaycees; vpres, Kiwanis; state rep, Int Asn Assessing Officers; past pres, Ariz Asn Assessing Officers; chmn, Maricopa Cty Sheriff's Relig Comn; lic res, N Phoenix Baptist Church; Alpha Tau Omega Fraternity; Moon Valley Country Club; Phoenix Chamber Comn. **Honors/Awds:** Boss of yr, Phoenix Midtowners Bus & Prof Women's Club, 1975; rec Cert Appraisal Evaluator prof design Int Asn Assessing Officers. **Special Achievements:** Book: "Introduction to Assessor's Salary Study". **Home Addr:** 6915 E Glenrosa Ave, Scottsdale, AZ 85251-2331, **Home Phone:** (602)870-8738.

### KUNJUFU, DR. JAWANZA

Writer, consultant. **Personal:** Born Jun 15, 1953, Chicago, IL; son of Eddie Brown and Mary Snyder Brown; married Rita Archer; children: Walker & Shikamana. **Educ:** Ill State Univ, Norm, IL, BS, econs, 1974; Union Grad Inst, Cincinnati, OH, PhD, bus admin, 1984. **Career:** Africentric Sch, teacher, 1974-80; African Am Images, Chicago, Ill, pres, 1980-; Films: "Up Against The Wall", exec producer; AUTHOR: Children Are the Reward of Life, 1978; Countering the conspiracy to destroy Black boys, 1982, 1986, 1990; Developing positive self-images & discipline in Black children, 1984; Motivating Black youth to work, 1986; Lessons from history, 1987; To be popular or smart, 1989; Talk with Jawanza: critical issues in educating African American youth, 1989; Black economics, 1991; Hip-hop vs. MAAT, 1993; Adam! where are you?, 1991; Restoring the village, values & commitment: solutions for the Black family, 1996; Good brothers looking for good sisters, 1997; Black college student's survival guide, 1998; Great negroes, & present, 1998; Satan, I'm taking back my health, 2000; State of emergency: we must save African American males, 2001; Black students-Middle class teachers, 2002; Solutions for Black America, 2004; Keeping black boys out of special education, 2005; African centered response to Ruby Payne's poverty theory, 2006. **Orgs:** Founder, Unity; Living Word Christian Ctr; ed adv bd, YSB mag. **Business Addr:** President, Founder, African American Images, 9204 Commercial Ave Suite 308, Sauk Village, IL 60612, **Business Phone:** (800)552-1991.

### KUYKENDALL, DR. CRYSTAL ARLENE

Educator, lawyer. **Personal:** Born Dec 11, 1949, Chicago, IL; daughter of Cleophus Avant and Ellen Campbell Logan; married Roosevelt Jr; children: Kahlil, Rasheki & Kashif. **Educ:** Southern Ill Univ, BA, govt, 1970; Montclair State Univ, MA, sociol, 1972; Atlanta Univ, EdD, educ admin, 1975; Georgetown Univ Law Ctr, JD, 1981. **Career:** Seton Hall US Orange NJ, Montclair State Univ, instr, 1971-73; DC Pub Sch, admin intern planning res & eval, 1974-75; Nat Comt Citizens Educr, dir, 1975-77; Nat Sch Boards Asn, Wash, DC, dir, urban & minority rel dept, 1978-79; PSI Assoc Inc, Wash, DC, dir ed devel, 1979-80; Nat Alliance Black Sch Ed, exec dir, 1980-81; Roy Little john Assoc Inc, sr assoc, 1982-; Kreative & Innovative Resources Kids, founder, pres & gen coun, 1989-; bd dir, Md Mentoring Partnerships; Author: Developing Leadership for Parent/Citizen Groups, 1976; Improving Black Student Achievement through Enhancing Self-Image, 1987; You and Yours: Making the Most of this School Year, 1989 & 1997; From Rage to Hope: Reclaiming Black and Hispanic Students, 1992; From Rage to Hope II, 2004. **Orgs:** Am Asn Sch Admin, 1974-; mem educ task force, Martin Luther King Jr Ctr Soc Chg, 1977-; consult, Nat Teachers Corp Proj, 1978-79; Black Am Law Students Asn, 1978-; chmn, Nat Adv Coun Continuing Educ, 1979-81; cons, mem, Nat Transition Team Off Elem Sec Ed, 1980; Am Bar Asn; Nat Bar Asn; DC Bar Asn, 1988, assoc supvr & curric developer, 1992-; bd dir, HealthPower Inc, 1994-02; bd dir, Cong Nat Youth Leadership Coun, 1995-; mentor, Help One Stud To Succeed, 1995; bd dir, Family Life Ctr, Shiloh Baptist Church, 1996-. **Business Addr:** President, Kreative & Innovative Resources for Kids Inc, 8925 Harvest Sq Ct, Potomac, MD 20854, **Business Phone:** (301)299-2057.

### KWAKU-DONGO, FRANCOIS

Chef. **Personal:** married Ruth Y Letson; children: Joseph-Paul & Christine-Elizabeth. **Educ:** Manhattan's Bor Col, lit. **Career:** Alo Alo Restaurant, part-time prep cook; Remi, NY, sous chef, 1984-89; line cook, 1989; Marc Meneau L'Esperance; Bernard Loiseau Cote D'Or; Baumaniere Provence; Trois Gros Roasanne; Spago W Hollywood, exec chef, 1991; Chinois Main; Postrio, San Francisco; Spago Chicago, exec chef & managing partner; L'Escale, exec chef, currently. **Orgs:** Meals On Wheels; Ronald McDonald Found; Rita Hayworth Alzheimer's Asn. **Home Addr:** 6 Idlewild Mnr, Greenwich, CT 06830-5219. **Business Addr:** Executive Chef, L'Escale, 500 Steamboat Rd, Greenwich, CT 06830, **Business Phone:** (203)661-4600.

### KWAME, PAUL T.

Music director, college teacher. **Educ:** Fisk Univ, 1985; Western Mich Univ, attended; Am Conserv Music, DM. **Career:** Fisk Jubilee Singers, part-time dir, fac mem, musical dir & Curb-Beam Chair; Fisk Univ, assoc prof, music dept chair, 1996-2003. **Orgs:** Bd mem, Nashville Adv Coun; bd mem, Gospel Music Asn Found; bd mem, Schermerhorn Symphony Comt (Nashville, TN); Nashville Music Coun; mem adv coun, W O Smith Community Music Sch (Nashville, TN). **Honors/Awds:** National Medal of Arts, Awarded by President George W. Bush and First Lady Laura Bush, 2008 (as Director of Fisk Jubilee Singers). **Special Achievements:** First African to direct the ensemble and hold the Curb-Beaman Chair position; under his directorship, the Fisk Jubilee Singers have performed at various locations including Apollo Theatre (NYC), Plymouth Congregational Church (NYC), Kennedy Center, Smithsonian Institute, Abraham Lincoln Presidential Museum, the White House, and to Ghana in 2007 to celebrate the country's 50th anniversary of its independence; led the group in performances with well-known singers including Faith Hill, Hank Williams Jr., Shania Twain, and Natalie Cole; featured in the documentary "The Fisk Jubilee Singers: Sacrifice and Glory" (1999).

### KWEKU, BABAKUBWA. See DAVIS, DR. WILLIE.

### KWELI, TALIB (TALIB KWELI GREENE)

Rap musician. **Personal:** Born Oct 3, 1975, Brooklyn, NY; son of Brenda Greene; married D J Eque; children: Amani Fela & Diani Eshe. **Educ:** NY Univ, exp theatre. **Career:** Albums: Black Star, 1998; Reflection Eternal, 2000; Quality, 2002; The Beautiful Struggle, 2004; Right About Now, 2005; Getting Up: Liberation, 2006; Eardrum, 2007; Liberation, 2007; Hold it Down, 2008; Revolutions Per Minute, 2010; Gutter Rainbows, 2011; Prisoner of Conscious, 2013; Gravitas, 2013. Films: Getting Up: Contents Under Pressure, actor, 2005; Blokhedz Mission G Animated Web Series, actor, 2009; MCA Rec, rec artist, currently. **Orgs:** Black August Benefit Concert. **Business Addr:** Recording Artist, c/o MCA Records Inc, 2220 Colorado Ave Suite 1, Santa Monica, CA 90404, **Business Phone:** (310)865-4500.

### KYLE, GENGHIS

Band musician, bandleader. **Personal:** Born Jun 7, 1923, Los Angeles, CA; married Dorothy F; children: Alfred Conrad & Marie J (Brooks). **Educ:** Los Angeles City Col; Univ SC, ext. **Career:** Vultee Aircraft Co, sub assembler, 1942; City Los Angeles, Calif Dept Water & Power, storekeeper, 1954-82; Genghis Kyle Enterprises, bandleader, personal mgr. **Orgs:** Broadcast Music Inc; Local 47 Musicians Union; shop co-dir, Signature Music Pub Co Imperial Youth Theater Work; Coaches & Mgr Assoc LA. **Home Addr:** 1645 W 108 St, Los Angeles, CA 90047. **Business Addr:** Bandleader, Genghis Kyle Enterprises, 1544 W 93 St, Los Angeles, CA 90047.

### KYLES, CEDRIC ANTONIO. See ENTERTAINER, CEDRIC THE.

### KYLES, DWAIN JOHANN

Lawyer, business owner. **Personal:** Born Aug 25, 1954, Chicago, IL; son of Samuel Billy and Gwendolyn Kyles Griffin; married Theresa Cropper; children: Chad Joseph. **Educ:** Lake Forest Col, BA, econ urban study, 1976; Georgetown Univ, Law Ctr, JD, 1979. **Career:** Congressman Harold Ford 9th Dist TN, staff aide, 1976-78; Off Civil Rights Dept Health Educ & Welfare, law clerk, 1978-79; Johnson Prods Co, staff atty, 1979-83; Off Mayor Harold Wash, spec coun minority bus develop, 1983-84; McCormick Pl Conv Ctr, house coun, mgt & inter govt liaison, 1984-88; Grill Inc, owner, 1987; Dept Econ Develop, spec coun comnr, 1989; Jackson's Rainbow/PUSH Coalition, atty, coun; Le Mirage Studio Ltd, pres, chief officer & owner; E2 club, owner; Mirage, owner; Le Mirage All-Night Studio Inc, pres, owner & prin officer; Dwain J. Kyles & Assocs PC, atty. **Orgs:** Am Bar Asn; Nat Bar Asn, 1979; Cook City Bar Asn, 1979; bd mem, Forum Evolution Progressive Arts, 1983-; founder & pres, New Chicago Comt; Oper

PUSH, Nat Asn Advan Colored People; admin asst, Black Am Law Students Asn. **Honors/Awds:** Mentor of the Year, Urban Focus, 1984. **Home Addr:** 5100 S Hyde Pk Blvd Suite 1C, Chicago, IL 60615-4258. **Business Addr:** Attorney, Dwain J Kyles & Associates PC, Chicago, IL 60615-4258, **Business Phone:** (312)907-4945.

# L

### LA SALLE, ERIK KI. See LASALLE, ERIQ.

### LABAT, ERIC MARTIN

Oceanographer, scientist. **Personal:** Born May 8, 1962, Bay St. Louis, MS; son of Rudolph H and Geraldine T; married Katrina R Lane; children: Arielle. **Educ:** Univ Southern Miss, BS, 1985; Naval Post Grad Sch, attended 1987; Faith Grant Col, Birmingham, AL, DLaw, 1994; Univ New Orleans. **Career:** Naval Oceanog Off, phys sci trainee, 1980-83, comput sci trainee, 1983-85; mathematician, 1986-91, oceanogr, 1991-. **Orgs:** Alpha Phi Alpha Fraternity; pres, Zeta Mu Lambda, 1991-94; vpres, St Rose de Lima Cath Church Pastoral Coun, 1991-93; chmn, Magic's AYSE Prog, 1992-95; black employ prog coord, Naval Oceanog Off EEOC, 1990-; Marine Technol Soc, 1992-; NCP, 1990-; co-chmn, GPS Enhancements VII, Joint Navig Conf, 2007; Blacks In Govt Stennis Chap. **Honors/Awds:** Walter "Duke" Williams Alumni Brother of the Year, Alpha Phi Alpha Fraternity, 1992; COT Service Award, N Gulfport Civic Club, 1991; Am Best & Brightest Bus & Prof Men, Dollars & Sense Mag, 1991. **Home Addr:** PO Box 2141, Chesapeake, VA 23327-2141. **Business Addr:** Oceanographer, Naval Oceanographic Office, 1002 Balch Blvd Code N333, Stennis Space Center, MS 39522-5001, **Business Phone:** (228)688-2211.

### LABEACH, NICOLE ANN

Consultant, chief executive officer, public speaker. **Personal:** married Calvin Thomas IV. **Educ:** Spelman Col, BA, psychol, 1993; St Louis Univ, MA, clin psychol, PhD, orgn psychol, 2001. **Career:** Provident Coun, prog mgr, developer, 1996-98; Vandaveer Group, od consult, 1997-98; Anheuser Busch Corp, od consult, intern, 1998-2000; Fortune 500 Co News Corp, dir training & orgn devlop, 2000-01; Millenium Consult, managing dir; Faithful Cent Bible Church, assoc dir; Volition Enterprises Inc, owner, chief exec officer, 2001-; Right Mgt, exec coach, 2008-. **Orgs:** Founder & bd mem, Liaison Prof Orgn Women; founder & vpres, Brightest Stars Found; bd mem, Training & Orgn Develop fortune 500 co News Corp; bd mem, Pace Ctr Girls; Int Coaching Fedn; mem soc, Human Resources Mgt; elta Sigma Theta Sorority Inc. **Business Addr:** Chief Executive Officer, Owner, Volitions Enterprises Inc, 1740 SW St Lucie W Blvd Suite 159, Port St. Lucie, FL 90036, **Business Phone:** (772)873-2753.

### LABELLE, PATTI (PATRICIA LOUISE HOLTE-EDWARDS)

Actor, singer. **Personal:** Born May 24, 1944, Philadelphia, PA; daughter of Henry Holt and Bertha Holt; married L Armstead Edwards; children: Stanley, Dodd & Zuri Kye. **Career:** Ordettes, singer, 1960; The Blue Belles, singer, 1961-65; Patti LaBelle & the Blue Belles, lead singer, 1965-70; LaBelle, lead singer, 1970-77; solo artist, 1977-; Live AID Benefit Rock Concert; TV specials: "PBS production", 1981; "Your Arm's Too Short to Box with God", gospel musical, 1981-82; "A Soldier's Story", 1985; "Unnatural Causes", 1986; "Sisters in the Name of Love", 1986, "Motown Returns to the Apollo"; "Out All Night", 1992-93; "Santa Baby!", 2001; "Living It Up with Patti LaBelle", exec producer, 2004; "All of Us", 2004; "Tommy & Quadrophenia Live: The Who", voice, 2005; "On the One", 2005; "Why I Wore Lipstick to My Mastectomy", 2006. Films: A Soldier's Story, 1984; Unnatural Causes, 1986; Sing, 1989; A Different World, 1990; Preaching to the Choir, 2005; Idle wild, 2006; Cover, 2007; Semi-Pro, 2008; Mama, I Want To Sing, 2011; TV Series: "A Different World", 1990; "Out All Night", 1992; "The Nanny", 1994; "Cosby", 1997; "Living It Up With Patti LaBelle", 2003; "The Dog Whisperer", 2007; "An Evening With The Stars: A Tribute to Patti Labelle", 2008; "American Horror Story", 2014. Video: Going Home to Gospel with Patti Labelle, 1991; Albums: When A Woman Loves, 2000; Timeless Journey, 2004; Classic Moments, 2005; The Gospel According to Patti LaBelle, 2006; Miss Patti's Christmas, 2007. **Orgs:** founding mem, Temptations. **Honors/Awds:** B'nai B'rith Creative Achievement Award; Congressional Black Caucus Medallion; Entertainer of the Year Award, Nat Asn Advan Colored People, 1986; Platinum album, "Winner in You", 1986; Favorite Soul/R&B Female Artist, Am Music Awards, 1986, 1992; Image Award, Nat Asn Advan Colored People, 1987, 1993, 1997, 1999; Grammy Award, 1992; Star on the Walk of Fame, 1993; Best Female R&B Vocal Performance, Grammy Award, 1994; Career Achievement Award, 1996; Essence Award, 1998; Best Traditional R&B Vocal Performance, Grammy Award, 1999; Hon Doctor Music Degree, Berklee Col Music, 1996; Lifetime Achievement Award, Songwriters Hall of Fame, 2003; Excellence in Media Award, GLAAD, 2007; Legend Award, World Music Awards, 2008; UNCF Award of Excellence, UNCF Evening Stars, 2009; Legends Hall of Fame, Apollo Theater, 2009; Lifetime Achievement Award, BET Awards, 2011. **Special Achievements:** Special Citation from President Ronald Reagan, 1986; Collaborated with Fiori Roberts Cosmetics to create a new line of lip and nail color products; Author: Recipes to Sing About; Don't Block the Blessings, 1995; Patti's Pearls: Lessons on Living Genuinely, Joyfully, Generously, 2001. **Home Addr:** 2041 Locust St, Philadelphia, PA 19103. **Business Addr:** Singer, Owner, PattisButterflies.com, 4 Brussels St, Worcester, MA 01610, **Business Phone:** (508)791-6710.

### LABODE, MODUPE GLORIA

Educator. **Educ:** Iowa State Univ, BS, hist, 1988, PhD, hist; Oxford Univ, DPhil, hist, 1992. **Career:** Iowa State Univ, Hist Dept, trainee, 1993-94, asst prof hist, 1994-2001; Rhodes Scholar; Colo Hist Soc, Colo Hist Mus, chief historian, dir, 2002-07; Harvard Univ, WEB Du Bois Inst Afro-Am Res; Berkshire Summer fel Mary Ingraham Bunting Inst, Radcliffe Col; Ind Univ-Purdue Univ Indianapolis, assoc prof, 2007-. **Orgs:** Am Asn State & Local Hist; Nat Coun Pub Hist; Orgn Am Historians; Western Hist Asn; Am Hist Asn; African Studies Asn; Coord Coun Women Hist; Rhodes Scholar Selection Comt; docent, Molly Brown House Mus, 2001-02. **Home Addr:** , CO. **Business Addr:** Assistant Professor, Indiana University-Purdue University Indianapolis, 420 Cavanaugh Hall, Indianapolis, IN 46202, **Business Phone:** (317)274-3829.

### LACEY, DR. BERNARDINE M.

Manager, educator, association executive. **Personal:** Born Jul 28, 1932, Vicksburg, MS; daughter of Leroy Jackson and Katie; married Wilbert; children: Amando Gomez, Elthon & Jacinta. **Educ:** Gilfoy Sch Nursing, Miss Bapt Hosp, Jackson, MS, nursing dipl, 1962; Georgetown Univ, Sch Nursing, BSN, 1968; Howard Univ, MA, sociol, 1985; Teachers Col, Columbia Univ, New York, NY, EdD, 1991. **Career:** Howard Univ, Nursing Grad Prog, admin supvr, Stud Health Ctr, dir nursing, 1980-85, Col Nursing, asst prof, 1985-94; W K Kellogg-Howard Univ, Col Nursing, Homeless Proj, proj dir, 1985-94; Univ Va, clin asst, 1991-95; Johns Hopkins Sch Nursing, lectr, 1991-93, adj asst prof, 1991-93; Howard Univ, Col Med, nurse dir, 1993-94; Western Mich Univ, dir sch nursing, prof & founding dean, 1994-99, spec asst, 1999; Prince George's Community Col, chair nursing dept, prof & chmn, 2001-02; C's Nat Med ctr, exec dir, 2002-04; Bowie State Univ, Dept Nursing, chmn, 2004-08; Coppin State Univ, Helene Fuld Sch Nursing, prof & asst dean, 2008-. **Orgs:** Am Acad Nursing; Am Nurses assn; DC Nurses assn; Nat Black Nurses assn; Sigma Theta Tau Int Nurses Hon Soc; Nat League Nursing; Soc Nursing Hist. **Honors/Awds:** Health Policy & Legislative Award, Univ Sch Educ, 1994; Pearl McIver Public Health Nurse Award, Am Nurses Assn, 1994; Community Serv Award, AKA Sorority Inc, Bowie State Univ, 1994; Distinguished Alumna Award, Sch Nursing, Goergetown Univ, 1993; Distinguished Scholar Lecturer, James Madison Univ, Dept Nursing, 1992; The Distinguished Scholars Award, W Mich Univ; Presidential Warrior Award, 2005-06. **Home Addr:** 247 Lake Forest Blvd, Kalamazoo, MI 49006-8309. **Business Addr:** Professor, Assistant to the Dean, Coppin State University, 2500 W N Ave, Baltimore, MD 21216-3698, **Business Phone:** (410)951-3000.

### LACEY, JACKIE

Lawyer, district attorney. **Personal:** Born Feb 27, 1957, Los Angeles, CA; daughter of Louis Phillips and Addie Phillips; married David; children: Kareem & April. **Educ:** Univ Calif, BA, psychol, 1979; Univ Southern Calif Law Sch, JD, 1982. **Career:** Los Angeles Dist Atty's Off, dep dist atty, 1986-2011, chief dep dist atty, 2011-12, 42nd Los Angeles, dist atty, 2012-. **Honors/Awds:** Los Angeles and San Francisco Daily Journal, Top 100 Women Litigators, 2009; TheGrio.com, 100 Making History Today, 2012. **Special Achievements:** First African American and first female district attorney in Los Angeles County. **Home Addr:** Granada Hills, Los Angeles, CA 91344. **Business Addr:** District Attorney, Los Angeles District Attorney's Office, 210 W Temple St, Los Angeles, CA 90012, **Business Phone:** (213)974-1484.

### LACEY, MARC STEVEN

Journalist. **Personal:** Born Nov 11, 1965, New York, NY; son of Earle Milton and Jean Lilian Moran; married Omaira Rivas. **Educ:** Cornell Univ, Ithaca, NY, BA, 1987; George Washington Univ, Wash, DC, MIPP, 2001. **Career:** Cornell Daily Sun, ed-in-chief; Wash Post, Wash, DC, intern, summer, 1987; Buffalo News, Buffalo, NY, journalist, 1987-89; Los Angeles Times, Los Angeles, Calif, suburban reporter, City Hall reporter & Wash corresp, 1989-99; NY Times, New York, NY, White House corresp, 1999-01, Nairobi Bur Chief, 2001-06, Mex Bur corresp, currently. **Orgs:** Nal Asn Black Journalists, 1988-; Cornell Univ Alumni Asn, 1989-; Freedom Forum Paul Miller Wash Reporting Fel. **Honors/Awds:** Nat Merit Achievement Scholarship, 1983-87; Quill & Dagger Senior Honor Society, Cornell University, 1987; Cornell Tradition Academic Scholarship Cornell, 1983-85; Summer Research Exchange Program, Univ California, Berkeley Summer, 1985; guest lectr, Univ Calif Los Angeles; guest lectr, Univ Md-Col Park; Times's in-house award. **Business Addr:** Foreign Correspondent, Mexico City Bureau, New York Times, 1627 I St NW Suite 700, Washington, DC 20006-4007, **Business Phone:** (212)556-7415.

### LACEY, DR. MARIAN GLOVER

School administrator. **Educ:** AM&N Col, BA, eng, 1960; Ind Univ, MEd, 1967; Univ Ark, EdD, 1985, EDAS, 1999. **Career:** Elizabeth Miller Sch, Helena, Eng Dept, chmn & teacher, 1967-69; Dunbar Jr High Sch, Eng Dept, chmn & teacher, 1974-81, prin; Little Rock Cent High Sch, asst prin, 1981-86; Horace Mann Arts & Sci Magnet Jr High Sch, prin, 1988-; Little Rock Sch Dist, Little Rock, AR, asst supt, currently. **Orgs:** Bd & Planning Comt, Univ Ark, Little Rock; bd trustee, Cent Ark Libr Syst. **Business Addr:** Board of Trustee, Central Arkansas Library System, 100 Rock St S, Little Rock, AR 72201, **Business Phone:** (501)918-3000.

### LACEY, WILBERT, JR.

Psychiatrist, educator. **Personal:** Born Dec 1, 1936, Washington, DC; married Bernardine M; children: 4. **Educ:** Howard Univ, BS, 1959, Col Med, MD, 1968; Am Bd Psychiat & Neurol, cert, 1977. **Career:** Howard Univ Col Med, Health Serv, univ psychiatrist, 1973, clin asst prof, 1975, internship prof staff. **Orgs:** Fox Ridge Civic Asn, 1977; DC Mem Soc; Nat Med Asn; Am Inst Hypertension; Am Col Health Asn; Metro WA Soc Adolescent Psychiat; Joint Coun WA Psychiat Soc; life mem, Kappa Alpha Psi Frat. **Home Addr:** 3601 Tyrol Dr, Glenarden, MD 20774, **Home Phone:** (229)244-8708. **Business Addr:** Psychiatrist, Internship Professional Staff, Howard University, 6th Bryant St NW, Washington, DC 20059, **Business Phone:** (202)806-6870.

### LACHMAN, DR. RALPH STEVEN

Physician, educator, radiologist. **Personal:** Born May 12, 1935; married Rose Katz; children: Nicole & Monette. **Educ:** Temple Univ, BA, 1957; Meharry Med Col, MD, 1961. **Career:** Bronx-Lebanon Med Cntr NYC, rotating intern, 1961-62; Mt Sinai Med Ctr, resident; AUS Hosp BadKreuznach, Ger, capt, 1964-66; Mt Sinai Hosp NYC, pres, 1962-64; radiol, 1966-68; C's Hosp, Boston, ped radiol, 1969-70; Univ Calif Los Angeles, from asst prof radiol to prof radiol, 1970-99, assoc chair radiol, 1980-99, prof emer, 1999-; Stanford Univ, Dept Pediat/Radiol, vis scholar, currently, Lucile Packard C's Hosp, clin prof radiol, currently; Int Skeletal Dysplasia Registry, Cedars-Sinai Med Ctr, co-founder, consult, currently. **Orgs:** Chmn, Equal Opportunity Acad Affirm Action Comn, Univ Calif Los Angeles, 1981-83; Soc Pediat Radiol; Am Col Radiol; Los Angeles Pediat Soc; AAAS; Western Soc Pediat Res Am Fedn Clin Respresident; Pac Coast Pediat Radiol Asn, 1985 Gold Medal Comt, SocsPediat Radiol; Am Bd Radiol; Am Bd Pediat. **Honors/Awds:** Fel Am Col Radiol, 1983. **Special Achievements:** Published 260 scientific articles, 4 books, 15 book chapters. **Home Addr:** 943 14th St, Santa Monica, CA 90403, **Home Phone:** (310)395-4703. **Business Addr:** Clinical Professor, Stanford School of Medicine, 725 Welch Rd MC5913, Stanford, CA 94305, **Business Phone:** (650)723-0705.

### LACOUR, NATHANIEL HAWTHORNE (NAT LACOUR)

Vice president (organization), school administrator, secretary general. **Personal:** Born Feb 11, 1938, New Orleans, LA; married Josie Brown; children: Carey Renee, Carla Cenee & Charlette Jene; married Connie Goodly. **Educ:** Southern Univ, BS & MS, biol. **Career:** Union exec vpres; exec, AFL-CIO; vpres, AFT exec coun; pres, AFT New Orleans affil, United Teachers New Orleans; secy-treas & pres AFT; secy-treas emer, Am Fedn Teachers; 2008. **Orgs:** Pres, United Teachers New Orleans, 1970; vpres, Am Fedn Teachers, 1987-94, exec vpres, 1998-2004; secy-treas, Labor Union Activist, 2004-08; secy-treas emer, 2008-; nat bd mem, A Philip Randolph Inst; founding mem, Nat Bd Prof Teaching Stand; chmn, New Orleans Manpower Adv Planning Coun; Am Inst Biologists; mem exec bd, Greater New Orleans AFL-CIO Exec Coun, 2004-; YMCA; Nat Asn Advan Colored People; exec bd, New Orleans Urban League; bd dir, New Orleans Pub Libr; comnr, WhiteHouse Comn Presidential Scholars, 1993; bd dir, Amalgamated Bank Chicago; bd dir, Albert Shanker Inst; bd dir, Nat Dem Inst; bd dir, Coalition Black Trade Unionists; bd, Learning First Alliance; bd, Educ Qual Inst; bd dir, Thurgood Marshall Scholar Fund. **Honors/Awds:** Prestigious Ellis Island Medal of Honor, 2006; first been elected as an AFT vice president, 1972. **Home Addr:** , Greenbelt, MD. **Business Addr:** Board Director, Albert Shanker Institute, 555 NJ Ave NW, Washington, DC 20001-2079, **Business Phone:** (202)879-4401.

### LACY, AUNDREA

Executive. **Personal:** Born San Francisco, CA. **Educ:** San Jose State Univ, BS, jour & pub rels; Golden Gate Univ, MBA. **Career:** Fortune 500 Comput Co; Hewlett Packard, field mkt & strategic events expert, sr events mkt mgr, 1990-2000; Black Enterprise, owner; Cloud Bakery, owner; AddShoppers, founder & chief exec officer; Luv's Brownies, founder, owner & chief exec officer, 1996-; high technol consult, 2000-. **Orgs:** Mentor, Big Sisters Santa Clara County. **Business Addr:** Owner, Chief Executive Officer, Luv Brownies, 2910 Stevens Creek Blvd Suite 109, San Jose, CA 95128, **Business Phone:** (408)881-0759.

### LACY, DONALD E., JR.

Administrator, actor, writer. **Personal:** Born Nov 26, 1958, Canton, OH; son of Donald and Mary; married Shaina; children: LoEshe (deceased), Donnie & Anwaar. **Educ:** San Francisco State Univ, BA, black studies, theater arts, 1984. **Career:** TV & Film: Metro; Bound By Honor; Jack; Blood In, Blood Out; Catherine Crier Live; Hangin' with Mr. Cooper, 1997; Wolf; Comic View; LA Heart, 1999; Def Comedy Jam; Bay Sunday; Bay TV; Stage Shows: The Shelter; Ballard of Pancho & Lucy; Fists of Roses; Hairy Ape; Good Person of Szechwan; Jitney; Soul of a Whore; Wheel of Fortune; Hotel Angulo; Color Struck; Loeshe, 1998; Boogie Woogie Land Scapes; Bloodlines to oblivion; Evolution of Soul Brother; Streamers; The Loudest Scream; Boseman & Lena; Death of Bessie Smith; Playwright: The Loudest Scream You'll Never Hear; Homebase; Evolution of Soul Brother; Loeshe, 1998; Director: The Dutchman; Streamers; Boseman & Lena; Homebase; The Loudest Scream You'll Never Hear; Short films: Four; Romeo & Juliet Gettin' Busy; Recreation Ctr Handicapped, staff, 1983-88; Writer: What Goes On When The Mike Goes Off; Love Life; KPFA Radio, host; KPOO Radio, pub affairs dir, show host, 1980-93, show host, 1997-; Harlem Globetrotters, announcer, 1995; actor, writer, comedian, 1984-2003; Kaleidovision Film works, exec dir, 1985-90; Explosion Comedy, host, currently; Martin & Glanz, conf organizer, 1999; Love life Found, founder & exec dir, 1997-; Silence The Violence, dir, currently. **Honors/Awds:** Black Filmmakers Hall Fame, 1999; Bay Area Cable Excellence Award, 1999; Fade to Gold, 1999; PSA Award, Nat Pub Programming, 1999; Excellence Award, City Oakland, 1999; The Angel Award, outstanding community service, Take Wings Foundation; Nominated, 10 Most Influential African Americans in The Bay Area, 2002; Nominee for 10 most influential African Americans in The Bay Area by City Flight magazine, 2002; Avanti Magic Award, 2003; Best Radio Talk Show Host, East Bay Express Newspaper, 2003; Healthy Oakland Father of the Year Award, 2003; Bay Area Blues society Hall of Fame, 2013. **Special Achievements:** Helped reduce the murder rate in Oakland to a 25-year low in 1998, and a32-year low in 1999. **Business Addr:** Executive Director, Lovelife Foundation, PO Box 70351, Oakland, CA 94612, **Business Phone:** (510)663-5683.

### LACY, HUGH GALE

Lawyer, educator. **Personal:** Born Mar 23, 1948, Huntsville, AL; son of Leo Marshuetz and Mary Crean Berry; married Paulette Nettles; children: Kenitra Irma & Hugh Shomari. **Educ:** Ala A&M Univ, BA, 1972, MEd, 1974; Miles Law Sch, JD, 1989. **Career:** Huntsville City Bd Educ, teacher corps intern, 1972-74; USY Ballistic Missle Defense Systs Command, supply mgt asst, 1974-75; USY Ord Missile & Munitions Ctr & Sch, educ spt, 1975-92; pvt pract, atty, 1990-; USY Corps Engrs, educ spt. **Orgs:** Bldg & educ comt, St Bartley Primitive Baptist Church; area dir, Assoc ed Sphinx, APA Fraternity; Ala Lawyers Asn; Ala Trial Lawyers Asn; Am Bar Asn, 1990-; Nat Bar Asn, 1990-; NCP, 1972-; counr, Spec Educ Action Com, 1989-; legis comn, Huntsville & Madison County BarAsn,

1990-. **Honors/Awds:** Club 4 H Leadership Award, 1974; Brother of the Year, APA Fraternity Inc, State Ala, 1990; Great American Family Award, 1990; Role Model of the Week, Speaking Out Newspaper, 1990; Brother of the Year, Delta Theta Lambda, 1991; Equal Employment Opportunity Counselor Appreciation Certificate, USY Missile Command, 1992. **Home Addr:** 146 Lauros Dr, Harvest, AL 35749-9468. **Business Addr:** Attorney, 300 E Clinton Ave Suite 2, Huntsville, AL 35804-8341, **Business Phone:** (256)652-6103.

### LACY, VENUS

Basketball player, college administrator. **Personal:** Born Feb 9, 1967, Chattanooga, TN; children: 1; children: 1. **Educ:** La Tech Univ, BA, sociol. **Career:** Basketball player (retired): Japan, Italy & Greece, 1990-96; Seattle Reign, ABL, ctr, 1996-97; Long Beach Stingrays, WNBA, 1997-98; Nashville Noise, 1998-99; WNBA, NY Liberty, 1999-2000; Univ Tenn Chatanooga, stud develop specialist, currently. **Business Addr:** Student Development Specialist, University of Tennessee Chatanooga, Dept 1951, Chattanooga, TN 37403, **Business Phone:** (423)425-4761.

### LACY, WALTER

Manager, educator. **Personal:** Born Nov 14, 1942, Huntsville, AL; son of Jessie Sr (deceased) and Lelia Acklin (deceased); married Julianne White; children: Lorraine Young, Walter Marcellus & Julian Crishon. **Educ:** Ala Agr & Mech Univ, BS, 1966, MS, 1972. **Career:** AUS Msl & Mun Cen & Sch, electronics instr, 1966-70; Gen Elec Co, equip specialist, 1970-71; Safeguard Logistics Command, equip specialist, 1971-73, equal opportunity specialist, 1973-74; AUS Missile Command, equip specialist, 1974-85, logistics mgt specialist, 1985-92, int prg mgt specialist, 1992-. **Orgs:** Free & Accepted Masons; tutor, bd dir, Seminole Serv Ctr, 1989-; Am Poetry Asn; parliamentarian, vpres, Blacks Govt, 1990-93; var comn, Alpha Phi Alpha Fraternity, 1991-. **Honors/Awds:** Exceptional Performance Awards, AUS Missile Command, 1990-97; Honorable Mention, poem, Am Poetry Soc, 1991. **Special Achievements:** Poetry published: American Poetry Anthology, 1989. **Home Addr:** 1322 Julia St NW, Huntsville, AL 35816-3760, **Home Phone:** (256)533-6192.

### LACY-PENDLETON, STEVIE A.

Journalist. **Personal:** Born Apr 19, 1956, Oklahoma City, OK; daughter of Robert and Bette J Lacy. **Educ:** John Jay Col Criminal Justice; Case Western Res Univ, BA, 1974. **Career:** Cleveland Urban Learning Ctr, teacher, 1973-75; Xenia Daily Gazette, reporter, 1975-78; Cent State Univ, coord stud recruitment, 1978-79; Dayton J Herald, reporter, 1979-80; Staten Island Advan, contribr, advan columnist news, 1980-, sunday prespective ed, 1995-2002, dep ed page ed & sr advan columnist, 2002-; NY 1 News & Staten Island Cable, Focus, co-anchor, 1997-98. **Orgs:** Bd trustees & sec vice chair, Soc C & Families; former bd mem, Polit Action Comt, former chair, Nat Coun Negro Women; gov bd mem, Friends Found; adv bd, Staten Island Univ Hosp, Univ Hospice; adv & former bd mem, Community Adv Bd, NY State Div Youth, Staten Island Community Residential Ctr; adv bd dir, Amethyst House Inc, Bayley Seton Hosp; adv, delivery vol, Meals Wheels, Staten Island Div; founder, pres, Ebony Elves; co-founder, Women's Health Initiative, Mary McLeod Bethune Ctr. **Honors/Awds:** Three Asniated Press Awards; Deadline Club Award; Front Page Award; Stevie Lacy-Pendleton Day, 1981; Leadership Award, United Negro Col Fund Inc, 1993; Front Page Award; Deadline Club Award, New York Deadline Club Soc Prof Journalists, 1996; Front Page Award, Newswomen's Club NY, 1997; Schools Chancellor Rudolph F Crew Caring Community Award Recognition of Excellence, Intergroup Relations Adv Coun, 1997; James Josey Memorial Community Harmony Award, 1997; Black American Achievement Award, State Island Borough Pres Guy V Molinari, 1997; Nat Asn of Black Journalists Award, 1998; Education Award, Port Richmond High Sch; Outstanding Young Women in America; First Place Columns, Nat Asn Black Journalist, 1999; Honorable Mention, Soc Silurians, 1999; 1st place, columns, NY State Asn Press, 2000; Community Service Award, Nat Coun Negro Women, Staten Island chap, 2001; Award of Excellence, NY Newspapers Eds & Publ, 2001; 1st place, columns, NY Asn Black Journalists, 2002; numerous community service awards. **Home Addr:** 10 Bay St Landing A2H, Staten Island, NY 10301, **Home Phone:** (718)981-7999. **Business Addr:** Deputy Editorial Page Editor, Advance Senior News Columnist, Staten Island Advance, 950 W Fingerboard Rd, Staten Island, NY 10305, **Business Phone:** (718)981-2214.

### LADAY, DR. KERNEY, SR. See Obituaries Section.

### LADD, FLORENCE CAWTHORNE

Association executive, educator, executive director. **Personal:** Born Jun 16, 1932, Washington, DC; daughter of William and Eleanor Louise Cawthorne; married John; children: Michael Cawthorne; married William Joseph Harris. **Educ:** Howard Univ, BS, psychol, 1953; Univ Rochester, PhD, social psychol, 1958. **Career:** Age Ctr New Eng, res assoc, 1958-60; Simmons Col, asst prof, 1960-61; Robert Col, Istanbul, assoc prof, 1962-63; Am Col Girls Istanbul, fac psychol; Harvard Grad Sch Educ, lectr & res assoc, 1965-70; Harvard Grad Sch Design, assoc prof, 1972-77; Sch Archit & Planning Mass Inst Techol, assoc dean, 1977-79; Wellesley Col, dean students, 1979-84; S African Educ Prog, consult, 1984-85; WEB DuBois Inst, vis scholar; Oxfam Am, dir educ & outreach, 1985-87, assoc exec dir, 1987; Harvard Univ, Mary Ingraham Bunting Inst Rad cliffe Col, dir, 1989-97, writer-in-residence, dir emer. **Orgs:** Fel Mary Ingraham Bunting Inst Rad cliffe Col, 1970-72; Bunting fel Radcliffe Inst, 1970-72; Black Women Policy Action; Trans Africa; bd mem, Overseas Develop Network, United Nat Int Res & Training Inst Advan Women; Nat Coun S African Progs; Asn Women Develop; trustee, Bentley Col; bd mem, Inst Contemp Art; bd mem, Overseer, WGBH; bd mem, Nat Coun Res Women; vice bd trustee, Hamshire Col; vice bd trustee, Amherst Univ; vice bd trustee, Mass Univ; Sigma Zi; Phi Betta Kappa. **Honors/Awds:** Hon mem, Am Inst Architects; Wellesley Alumnae Asn; Phi Beta Kappa; Sigma Xi; Best Fiction Award, Blk Caucus Am Libr Asn, 1997. **Special Achievements:** Author: Sarahs Psalm, Scribner, 1996; Paris Reunion, 2007; Cited by Mirabella magazine in 1994in their selection of 100 Fearless Women. **Home Addr:** 82 Larch Rd, Cambridge, MA 02138, **Home Phone:** (617)441-6782.

### LADNER, JOYCE ANN

School administrator, writer. **Personal:** Born Oct 12, 1943, Battles, MS; married Walter Carrington. **Educ:** Tougaloo Col, BA, 1964; Wash Univ, PhD, sociol, 1968. **Career:** S Ill Univ, asst prof & curric specist, 1968-69; Wesleyan Univ, 1969-70; Univ Dar es Salaam, Tanzania, res assoc, 1970-71; Hunter Col, CUNY, sociol fac, 1973-81; Brookings Inst, sr fel, govt studies, 1977-; Howard Univ, prof sociol, 1981-87; vp acad affairs, 1990-94, interim pres, 1994-95. Author: Tomorrow's Tomorrow: The Black Woman, 1971; Mixed Families: Adopting Across Racial Boundaries, 1977; The Ties That Bind:Timeless Values for Afr Amer Families, 1998; Co-Auth: Lives of Promise, Lives of Pain: Young Mothers After New Chance, 1994; Selected Papers from the Proceedings of the Conf on Ethics, Higher Educ & Social Responsibility, 1996; The Ties That Bind: Timeless Values for African American Families, 1997; The New Urban Leaders, 2001; Launching Our Black Children for Success: A Guide for Parents of Kids from Three to Eighteen, Johnson Publishing Co, 2003. **Orgs:** Bd dir, Am Sociol Asn; rev comm & mem Minority Ctr, Nat Inst Ment Health; fel Social Sci Res Coun; Soc for Study Social Probs; bd dir, Caucus Black Sociologists; Asn for Study Afro-Am Life & Hist; bd dir, 21st Century Found; Amn Sociol Asn. **Business Addr:** Senior Fellow, The Brookings Institution, 1775 Mass Ave NW, Washington, DC 20036, **Business Phone:** (202)797-6252.

### LADSON, GWINNETT

College teacher, college administrator, physician. **Personal:** Born Carrallton, GA; married James; children: Vincent James & Taylor Nicole. **Educ:** Tenn State Univ, BS; Meharry Med Col, MD, 1984. **Career:** Meharry/Hubbard Hosp, intern & resident, 1984-88; practicing OB/GYN, 1988-; Meharry Med Col, prof OB/GYN, chair OB/GYN & prog dir OB/GYN. **Orgs:** Nat Med Asn, Am Col Obstetricians & Gynecologists, Asn Professors Gynec & Obstet, R.F. Boyd Med Soc, Mid Tenn OB-GYN Soc; Cervical Cancer Coalition Bd; Nashville Gen Hosp Med Exec Comt; & Pharm & Therapeut Comt, Maternal, Child, & Adolescent Liaison Comt & Instnl Rev Bd Meharry Med Col. **Honors/Awds:** APGO-SOLVAY Educational Scholar; Women of Legend and Merit Award, Middle Tennessee State Univ. **Special Achievements:** Board certified in obstetrics and gynecology through the Specialty Board of the American Board of Obstetrics and Gynecology. **Business Addr:** Meharry Medical College, 1005 Dr DB Todd Jr Blvd, Nashville, TN 37208-3501, **Business Phone:** (615)327-6753.

### LADSON, LOUIS FITZGERALD

Pharmacist. **Personal:** Born Jan 3, 1951, Georgetown, SC; son of Henry and Susan Smith; married Sharon A; children: Eric & Tisha. **Educ:** St Olaf Col, BA, Hist, 1978; Creighton Univ, BS, Pharm, 1981; Cent Mich Univ, MA, Bus, 1982. **Career:** James A Haley Va Hosp, resident pharmacist, 1982-83; SuperX Univ, Sq Mall, pharm mgr, 1983-84; PCMC Pharm, consult, 1996; Lincourt Pharm Corp, owner & dir, 1984-. **Orgs:** Am Soc Hosp Pharm, 1979-, Kappa Psi Fraternity, 1980-, Nat Asn Retail Druggists, 1982-; Fla Pharm Asn, 1982-; pharm consult, Adult Care Living Facil, 1984-; Chamber Com Clearwater, 1985-; Nat Asn Advan Colored People, Clearwater Chap, 1985-; Alpha Phi Alpha Fraternity, 1988-; Prof Compounders Am; cub master, Boy Scouts, Pack #52, 1991; adv bd mem, careone, 1990; adv bd mem, Mt Zion AME Church, 1990; adv bd, Pharm Mag, Drug Topics; adv bd, CCH Home care. **Honors/Awds:** Outstanding Leadership Certificate, Creighton Univ, 1981; Outstanding Service Award, Creighton Univ, Black Fac, 1982. **Home Addr:** 1216 S Missouri Ave Apt 316, Clearwater, FL 33616, **Home Phone:** (727)724-4867. **Business Addr:** Owner, Director, Lincourt Pharmacy Corp, 501 S Lincoln Ave 10, Clearwater, FL 33756, **Business Phone:** (727)447-4248.

### LAFAYETTE, DR. BERNARD, JR.

Consultant, president (organization), school administrator. **Personal:** Born Jul 29, 1940, Tampa, FL; son of Bernard Sr and Verdell; married Kate Bulls. **Educ:** Am Baptist Theol Sem, BA, 1961; Harvard Univ, EdM, 1972, EdD, 1974. **Career:** SNCC AL Voters Regist Proj, dir, 1962-63; Chicago Open Housing Movement, 1966; Gustavus Adolphus Col, dir pr, 1974-76; SCLC, nat prog admin, 1976; Lindenwood Col Four, dir; Exce Inst, admin chief prog off, dep dir, PUSH, 1979-80; Ala State Univ Montgomery, fac, dean grad sch; Tuskegee Inst High Sch, Tuskegee, prin; Am Baptist Col, pres; distinguished-scholar-in-residence & consult, currently; Progressive Baptist Church, pastor, emer; Civil Rights Movement, civil rights activist & organizer; Gustavus Adolphus Col, dir; Emory Univ, distinguished scholar-in-residence; Am Baptist Theol Sem; Univ RI, dir ctr nonviolence & peace studies, currently. **Orgs:** Cong Racial Equality, 1961; nat coordr, Poor Peoples Campaign, 1968; chmn, Consortium Peace Res Educ & Develop, 1975; bd mem, Ministries Blacks Higher Educ, 1977; founder, chmn exec bd, Inst Human Rights & Res, 1979-; nat chmn, Founder Nat Black Christian Stud Leadership Consult, 1979-; treas, pres, Phi Delta Kappa; Am Friends Serv Comt; founder, Asn Kingian Nonviolence Educ & Training Works; Alpha Phi Alpha Fraternity; founder, God-Parents Clubs Inc; sr fel, Univ Ri; Selma Voting Rights Movement; Nashville Stud Movement; Stud Nonviolent Coord Comt; Southern Christian Leadership Conf; Am Friends Serv Comt; nonviolent rep, Fel Reconciliation. **Home Addr:** 873 Greenshire Ct, St. Louis, MO 63130. **Business Addr:** Distinguished-Scholar-in-Residence, Director, University of Rhode Island, 74 Lower Col Rd, Kingston, RI 02881, **Business Phone:** (401)874-2875.

### LAFAYETTE, EXCELL, JR.

Business owner, executive. **Educ:** McPherson Col, BA, broadcast jour, 1980; Langston Univ, BA, broadcast jour, 1982. **Career:** Executive, motivational speaker; KTUL-TV Channel 8, oper supvr, electronic field prod producer, photogr & news photojournalist, 1983-89; Conoco Phillips Petrol Co, video prod rep, 1989-93; Wal-Mart Stores Inc, TV Network, mgr, 1994-98, dir supplier develop, 1998-2012, dir, 2002-12, dir supplier admin, 1999-2012, admin & ins compliance, 2005; ABC; CBS; NBC; ESPN; FOX; La Fayette Enterprises LLC, chief exec officer & pres, 2012-. **Orgs:** Chmn, Ark Minority Bus Adv Coun; bd mem, Women's Bus Enterprise Nat Coun; bd mem, Nat Minority Supplier Develop Coun; bd trustee, Philander Smith Col; deacon, St James Missionary Baptist Church; bd mem, Rogers Community Support Ctr; Bd mem, Langston Univ Found; exec bd mem, Greater Ozarks-Ark Blood Serv Region Am Red Cross; chair & bd mem, Ark-Miss Minority Bus Develop Coun. **Honors/Awds:** Billion Dollar Round Table Award, Bus News USA, 2000-01; Outstanding Men of Minority Business Development Award, Minority Bus News USA, 2001; MBE Advocate of the Year, ARMSDC, 2001; Rising Star Award, African Am Bus Hall Fame & Mus, 2002; Corporate Partnership Award, ARMSDC, 2002; Commitment to Excellence Award, US Black Chamber Com, 2003; Global CEO Award, Ga Minority Bus Asn, 2004; Power Play Awards, 2005; Power Surge Award, 2005; Salute to Greatness Award, Ark M.L. King Comn, 2008. **Business Addr:** President, Chief Executive Officer, La Fayette Enterprises LLC, PO Box 1921, Bentonville, AR 72712-1921, **Business Phone:** (479)640-6800.

### LAGARDE, REV. FREDERICK H., JR.

Executive, clergy, president (organization). **Personal:** Born Apr 10, 1928, Teaneck, NJ; son of Floville Albert and Claudia; married Frances Frye; children: Frederica, Francine, Francella & Frederick Jr. **Educ:** Grand Music Acad, 1948; Va Union Univ & Sem, AB, MDiv, 1959. **Career:** First Baptist Church, pastor, 1956-58; Providence Baptist Church, pastor, 1958-66; Community Baptist Church Love, pastor, 1966-; Come-Unity & The Annual Greater Youth Crusade Paterson vicinity, pres & founder, 1980; La Garde Funeral Home Inc, vpres, currently. **Orgs:** Founder, United Neighborhood Indust Training & Econ Develop, 1967; Housing Opportunity Provided Everyone, 1969; House Action, 1970; Paterson Community Sch, 1983; co-writer & producer, Martin Luther King video & song, 1986; Nat Asn Advan Colored People reg rep, SCLC; ASCAP; Alpha Phi Alpha; Am Soc Composers Authors & Publishers; Nj State Bd Educ. **Honors/Awds:** Founder, United Neighborhood Indust Training & Econ Develop, 1967; Housing Opportunity Provided Everyone, 1969; House Action, 1970; Paterson Community Sch, 1983; co-writer & producer, Martin Luther King video & song, 1986; Nat Asn Advan Colored People reg rep, SCLC; ASCAP; Alpha Phi Alpha; Am Soc Composers Authors & Publishers; Nj State Bd Educ. **Special Achievements:** Co-writer Official Song Paterson, 1983. **Home Addr:** 255 17 Ave, Paterson, NJ 07504. **Business Addr:** Vice President, LaGarde Funeral Home Inc, 236 Union Ave, Paterson, NJ 07522, **Business Phone:** (973)720-9595.

### LAHR, DR. CHARLES DWIGHT

Educator, mathematician. **Personal:** Born Jan 1, 1944?, Philadelphia, PA; married Beatriz Pastor; children: Elena, Maria, Emilio, Sonia & Katerina. **Educ:** Temple Univ, AB (magna cum laude), math, 1966; Syracuse Univ, MA, math, 1968, PhD, 1972. **Career:** Willow Grove Naval Air Sta; Bell Labs, mathematician, 1971-73; Savannah State Col, vis prof mathematics, 1973-74; Amherst Col, vis prof mathematics, 1974-75; Dartmouth Col, from asst to assoc prof mathematics, 1975-84, assoc dean sci, dean grad studies, 1981-84, prof math & comput sci, 1984, dean fac, 1984-89, prof math & comput sci, permanent fac, currently. Book: Principles of Calculus Modeling An Interactive Approach. **Orgs:** Consult, Alfred P Sloan Found, 1982-90; reviewer, Math Reviews; Am Math Soc; Math Asn Am; AAAS; Phi Beta Kapa. **Home Addr:** 12 Rocky Hill Lane, Lyme, NH 03768. **Business Addr:** Professor of Mathematics & Computer Science, Dartmouth College, 6188 Kemeny Hall, Hanover, NH 03755-3551, **Business Phone:** (603)646-2415.

### LAINE, DAME CLEO (CLEMENTINA DINAH CAMPBELL)

Singer, actor. **Personal:** Born Oct 28, 1927, Middlesex; daughter of Alexander Campbell and Minnie Bullock; married John Philip William Dankworth; children: Alec & Jacqueline; married George Langridge; children: Stuart. **Educ:** Open Univ, MA, 1975; Berkee Col, MusD, 1982. **Career:** John Dank worth's Jazz Band, popularized Gimme a Pig foot & It's a Pity to Say Goodnight, singer, 1952; Recordings: A Beautiful Theme; Pierrot Lunaire All About Me; Born on a Friday; Day by Day; That Old Feeling; Cleo Sings Sondheim; Woman to Woman; Feel the Warm; I'm a Song; Live at Melbourne; Best Friends; Sometimes When We Touch; Actress: Seven Deadly Sins; Showboat; The Roman Spring of Mrs Stone, 1961; Colette, 1980; A Time to Laugh; Hedda Gabler; The Women of Troy; The Mystery of Edwin Drood, 1986; guest singer, One Man's Music; Marvelous Party; Talk of the Town; Not So Much a Programme; The Sammy Davis Show; Merv Griffin Show, 1974; Cotton Club, 1975; Dinah; Films: The Thief of Bagdad, 1940; The Third Alibi, actor, 1961; "Kraft Mystery Theater", 1961; The Last of the Blonde Bombshells, 2000; TV: I Love Muppets, 2002; Victoria Wood: A BAFTA Tribute, 2005; "Sunday AM", 2006; "The Paul O'Grady Show", 2007; "Legends", 2007. Discography: Get Happy Esquire ESQ317 Reissued, 1950-52; Cleo Sings British (10") Esquire, 1955. Albums: Meet Cleo Laine, 1957; In RetrospectMGM, 1957; She's the TopsMGM 2354026, 1957; Valmouth(original cast) Pye, 1959; Jazz Date (with Tubby Hayes)Wing, 1961; Spotlight on Cleo, 1961; All About MeFontana, 1962; Cleo Laine Jazz Master SeriesDRG Records MRS 502, 196?; CindyElla (orig cast of 1962 Xmas production)Decca, 1963; Beyond the Blues (American Negro Poetry) Argo, 1963; Shakespeare and All that JazzFontana, 1964; This is Cleo LaineShakespeare and All That JazzPhilips, 1964; Woman TalkFontana, 1966; Facade (with Annie Ross) British reissue: PhilipsFontana, 1967; If We Lived on Top of a MountainFontana, 1968; SoliloquyFontana, 1968; The Idol (Dankworth soundtrack w/ 2 Cleo vocals)Fontana, 1969; The Unbelievable Miss Cleo LaineFontana, 1969; Portrait-Philips, 1971; An Evening with Cleo Laine and the John Dankworth QuartetPhilips, Sepia, 1972; Feel the WarmPhilips, 1972; Showboat (single LP)EMIColumbia, 1972; Showboat (double LP)EMI/Stanyan, 1972; This is Cleo LaineEMI, 1972; I Am A SongRCA, 1973; Day by DayStanyan, 1973; Live at Carnegie HallRCA, 1974; CloseUpRCA, 1974; Pierrot Lunaire (Schoenberg) Ives SongsRCA, 1974; A Beautiful Thing (with James Galway)RCA, 1974; Easy Living (anthology of Fontana tracks)RCA, 1974; Spotlight on Cleo Laine (double LP) Philips, 1974; Cleo's ChoicePye, 1974; Cleo's Choice (abridged issue on Quintessence Jazz)Quintessence, 1975; The Unbelievable Miss Cleo LaineContour 6870675, 1975; Born on a FridayRCA, 1976; CloseUp (reissue?)Victor, 1976; Live at the Wavendon FestivalBBC (Black Lion), 1976; Porgy & Bess (with Ray Charles)London, 1976; Return to CarnegieRCA, 1976; Best Friends (with John Williams) RCA, 1976; Leonard Feather's Encyclopedia of Jazz in the '70'sRCA, 1976; 20 Famous Show HitsArcade, 1977; The Sly Cormorant (read by Cleo and Brian Patten)Argo (Decca), 1977; Romantic CleoRCA 42750, 19??; Showbiz Personalities of 19779279304, 1978; The Early YearsPye GH653, 1978; Gonna Get ThroughRCA, 1978; A Lover &

His LassEsquire Treasure, 1978; Wordsongs (double LP)RCA, 1978; One More DayDRG, 1979; The Cleo Laine Collection (double LP) RCA, 1979; Cleo's Choice (reissue?)Pickwick, 1980; Collette (original cast)Sepia, 1980; Sometimes When We Touch (with James Galway) RCA, 1980; One More Day, Sepia, 1981; Smilin' Through (with Dudley Moore), 1982, Platinum Collection (double LP), Off the Record, WEA Sierra GFE, 1983; Let the Music Take You (w/ John Williams), 1984, Cleo at Carnegie: The 10th Anniversary Concert, That Old Feeling, Johnny Dankworth and His Orchestra, The John Dankworth 7 featuring Cleo Laine, 1985; Wordsongs, Westminster, The Mystery of Edwin Drood, Philips, Unforgettable: 16 Golden Classics, Castle, Cleo Laine: The Essential Collection, Sierra, 1986; Unforgettable, PRT, Classic Gershwin (1 track, "Embraceable You"), CBS, 1987; Cleo Laine Sings Sondheim, RCA, Showboat (reissue of 1972 cast album), EMI & Stanyan, Cleo Laine & John Dankworth: Shakespeare and All That Jazz, Affinity, 1988; Woman to Woman, RCA, Jazz, RCA, Portrait of a Song Stylist, Harmony, 1989; Young at Heart Castle, Spotlight on Cleo Laine, Pachelbel's Greatest Hits (1 track), RCA, 1991; Nothing Without You (with Mel Torme), Concord, 1992; On the Town, 1993; I Am a Song, RCA, Blue and Sentimental, RCA, 1994; Solitude, RCA, 1995; The Very Best of Cleo Laine, RCA, Mad About the Boy, Abracadabra, 1997; Ridin' High (Early Sessions), Koch, Trav'lin' Light: The Johnny Mercer Songbook (1 track) Verve, Let's Be Frank (1 track) MCA, The Collection Spectrum Music, 1998; Sondheim Tonight Live From the Barbican (1 track) Jay, The Best of Cleo Laine Redial, The Silver Anniversary Concert (Carnegie Hall, Limited Edition), Sepia, Christmas at the Stables, That Old Feeling, Sony, 1999; Quintessential Cleo, Gold Label, Live in Manhattan, 2000; Quality Time, Universal/ Absolute, 2002; Loesser Genius, Qnote, 2003; Once Upon a Time, Qnote, 2005; London Pride, 2006; Jazz Matters, Qnote, 2010. **Honors/Awds:** Golden Feather Award, Los Angeles Times, 1973; Edison Award, 1974; Show Business Personality of the Year, Variety Club, 1977; Singer of the Year, TV Times, 1978; Grammy Award for Jazz Female Vocal, 1985; Grammy Award for Best Female Jazz Vocalist, 1985; Theatre World Award, 1986; Lifetime Achievement Award, 1991; Lifetime Achievement Award, Worshipful Co Musicians, 2002; BBC Jazz Award, 2008; Honorary doctorate, UnivLuton, Open Univ, Univ York, Univ Cambridge, Berklee Col Music, Boston; Made Honorary Fellow, Hughes Hall, Univ Cambridge. **Special Achievements:** Ambassador for SOS Children's Villages UK in recognition of her support for the Cambridge based charity. **Business Addr:** Singer, Actor, Gurtman & Murtha Artist Management, 450 7th Ave Suite 603, New York, NY 10123, **Business Phone:** (212)967-7350.

### LAIRD, REV. ALAN
Clergy, art museum director, artist. **Personal:** Born Dec 8, 1949, Oakland, CA; son of Levy and Sadie M; married Lorraine; children: Damon Alan, Aaron Jason, Mauryea, Chantalle & Rashaad. **Educ:** Laney Col, AA, 1976; Golden Gate Univ, attended 1980; Theol Union, Mdiv, 1997. **Career:** AMR PRS Lines, 1980-92; Bethel AME Church, 1993-; Expressions Art Gallery, owner & artist, 1996-; Oakland Unified Sch, teacher, 1998; Ameri Corp Vista, vol, 2005. **Orgs:** Working Artist Coalition Oakland; bd mem, Citizens United Rehab Errants, currently; bd mem, Fed Cure; bd mem, Expressions Art Gallery. **Business Addr:** Gallery Owner, Painter, Expression Art Gallery, 3463 San Pablo Ave, Oakland, CA 94607, **Business Phone:** (510)547-6646.

### LAIRET, DR. DOLORES PERSON
Educator, lecturer. **Personal:** Born Dec 27, 1935, Cleveland, OH; children: Christine & Evin. **Educ:** Wheaton Col, AB, 1957; Middlebury Col, AM, 1958; Case Western Res Univ, PhD, 1972; Univ Paris. **Career:** Educator (retired); Southern Univ Baton Rouge, instr, 1959; Fox Lane Sch Bedford NY, educr, 1960-62; John Marshall HS, Fr teacher, 1963-65; Western Res Univ, teaching fel lectr, 1965-67; City Cleveland, sr personnel asst, 1969-71; Cleveland State Univ, lectr, 1969-71, instr, 1971-72, assoc prof, 1972-77. **Orgs:** Secy & pres, Cleveland Chap Tots & Teens, 1963-73; Champs Inc, 1964-; Am Asn Teachers Fr, 1971-; Am Asn Univ Prof, 1971; Am Coun Teaching Foreign Lang, 1972-; NE Mod Lang Asn, 1974-; bd mem, Glenville Health Asn, 1974-; African Lit Asn; Music Critics Asn; Ohio Mod Lang Teachers Asn; Am Spec Lctr US Dept State Niger Mali Upper Volta Senegal & Togo; bd dir, bd mem & fac advisor, Nat Inst Restorative Justice. **Honors/Awds:** Published: The Francophone African Novel Perspectives for Critical Eval Presence Africaine; Various Art on Jazz Cleveland Press Showtime; Recipient of various Fellowships. **Home Addr:** 11012 Wade Park Ave, Cleveland, OH 44106, **Home Phone:** (216)421-4646.

### LAISURE, SHARON EMILY GOODE
Government official. **Personal:** Born Sep 3, 1954, Wiesbaden; daughter of Robert A Goode; married W Floyd. **Educ:** Univ NC, Chapel Hill, BA, polit sci, hist, 1976, MPA, pub admin, 1979. **Career:** Winston & Salem City, admin asst dep city mgr, 1977-78, admin asst city mgr, 1978-79, personnel analyst, 1979-80; Petersburg City, Va, personnel dir, 1980-85; Durham County, NC, personnel dir, 1985-86, asst mgr, currently; Richmond County, Va, dir, human resources & employee rels, 1986-89, dep city mgr, 1990; DigitalOwl.com, vpres, opers, 2000-02; Norfolk city, asst city mgr, 2005-09; Goode Laisure Tallent Performance Develop Partners, consult, 2009-; Nc Cent Univ, Sch of Bus, adj fac mem, 2011-. **Orgs:** Am Soc Pub Admin, 1979; bd dir, Southside Chap Am Red Cross, 1980; United Way Southside, VA, 1982, 1983; pres, Southern Region, Indian Paper Manufacturers Asn, 1984; Int City Mgt Asn; Nat Forum Black Pub Adminr; NC City & County Mgt Asn. **Home Addr:** 5231 Bemiss Rd, Richmond, VA 23234. **Business Addr:** Deputy City Manager, Durham County, 101 City Hall Pl, Durham, NC 27701-3328, **Business Phone:** (919)560-4222.

### LAKE, CARNELL AUGUSTINO
Football player, football coach. **Personal:** Born Jul 15, 1967, Salt Lake City, UT; married Monica; children: 3. **Educ:** Univ Calif, Los Angeles, BA, polit sci, 1993. **Career:** Football player (retired), coach; Pittsburgh Steelers, defensive back, strong safety, 1989-97, right cornerback, 1995, 1997, left cornerback, 1998, defensive backs coach, 2011-; Jacksonville Jaguars, defensive back, 1999-2000, free safety, 1999; Baltimore Ravens, defensive back, 2001-02, safety, 2001; Philadelphia Eagles, coaching intern, 2009; UCLA Bruins, cornerback coach, 2009; Marina High Sch, Boys Basketball team, asst coach, 2010. **Orgs:** Alpha Phi Alpha. **Honors/Awds:** Pro Bowl, 1994-96; Natl Football Foundation Hall of Fame Scholar Athlete Award, 1988-89; Joe Greene Great Performance Award, 1989; Defensive Player of the Year, Am Football Club, 1997; NFL 1990s All-Decade Team; Pittsburgh Pro Football Hall of Fame, 2014. **Home Addr:** , Irvine, CA. **Business Addr:** Coach Intern, UCLA Bruins, J D Morgan Ctr, Los Angeles, CA 90024, **Business Phone:** (310)825-8699.

### LAMAR, DR. HATTIE G.
College administrator. **Educ:** Paine Col, BA; Atlanta Univ, MA. **Career:** Chief fiscal officer, academic dean (retired); Miles Col, chief fiscal officer, dean acad affairs. **Home Addr:** 1414 Hendrix Dr, Birmingham, AL 35214.

### LAMAR, JAKE V., SR.
Educator, writer. **Personal:** Born Mar 27, 1961, Bronx, NY; son of Jacob V Sr and Jouce Marie Doucette; married Dorli. **Educ:** Harvard Univ, BA, Am hist & lit, 1983. **Career:** Time Mag, staff writer, assoc ed, 1983-89; Univ Mich, adj lectr, Commun Dept, 1993; Paris Writers Workshop, lectr, currently. **Home Addr:** 1115 Maiden Lane Ct Apt 104, Ann Arbor, MI 48105, **Home Phone:** (313)663-8544. **Business Addr:** Lecturer, Paris Writers Workshop, 7 City Falguiere, Paris75015, **Business Phone:** (014)566-7550.

### LAMAR, WILLIAM, JR.
Executive. **Personal:** Born Apr 25, 1952, Chicago, IL; son of William Sr and Jeanette Jarrett; married Kathy Amos; children: Brian & Andrew Marcus. **Educ:** Univ Ill, Chicago, IL, BS, 1973; Northwestern Univ, Kellogg Sch Mgt, Evanston, IL, MBA, 1976. **Career:** Executive (retired); Quaker Oats Co, Chicago, Ill, brand mgr, 1976-81; Burrell Advert Co, Chicago, Ill, vpres, acct supvr, 1981-82; United Airlines, Elk Grove Village, Ill, mkt mgr, 1982-84; McDonald's Corp, Oakbrook, Ill, staff dir mkt, Bloomfield NJ, dir opers, gen mgr, vpres nat mkt, 1984-2000, sr vpres mkt, chief mkt officer US, 2002-08; McDonald's Restaurants Ltd, chief mkt officer, 2002-08; McDonald's Atlanta Region, vice pres & gen mgr; Del Frisco's Restaurant Group Inc, dir, chmn nominating & corp governance comt, 2013-; Sionic Mobile Corp, dir, 2014-; 100 Black Men Atlanta Inc, chmn; Atlanta Football Classic, chmn; Univ Ill-Urbana-Champaign; J L Kellogg Sch Mgt, Northwestern Univ. **Orgs:** Dir, CS Memorial Med Ctr; Nat Caucus & Ctr Black Aged; Univ Ill Chicago Develop Comt; bd mem, Alliance Digital Equality; dir, Advert Coun Inc; Omega Psi Phi Fraternity Inc; 100 Black Men Atlanta; adv bd mem, Intellione Inc; bd dir, Sionic-mobile. **Home Addr:** 8325 Sentinae Chase Dr, Roswell, GA 30076, **Home Phone:** (312)946-1644.

### LAMARR, CATHERINE ELIZABETH
Lawyer. **Personal:** Born Chicago, IL; daughter of Carl Leonard and Sonya Frances Saxton. **Educ:** W Anchorage High Sch, 1978; Cornell Univ, Ithaca, NY, BA, 1982; Howard Univ, Sch Law, Wash, DC, JD, 1985. **Career:** Murtha, Cullina, Richter & Pinney, Hartford, CT, assoc, 1985-87; Levy & Droney LLP Farmington, CT, assoc, 1987-94; Bingham McCutchen LLP, off coun, 1994-98; Off Conn Treas, gen coun, 1999-. **Orgs:** Treass rep, Conn Lawyers Group; Nat Asn Pub Plan Attys; pres & bd mem, George W Crawford Law Asn; bd dir & mem, Legal Aid Soc Hartford, 1989-; treas, Conn Ctr Arts & Technol. **Business Addr:** General Counsel, Office of the Connecticut Treasurer, 55 Elm St, Hartford, CT 06106, **Business Phone:** (860)702-3018.

### LAMAUTE, DENISE
Government official, educator, lawyer. **Personal:** Born Mar 14, 1952, St. Louis, MO; daughter of Josephine Carroll and Frederick Washington; married Daniel. **Educ:** Brandeis Univ, Waltham, BA, 1973; Wash Univ, JD, 1977, LLM, tax, 1980. **Career:** Teachers Ins & Annuity Asn, sr tax atty, 1978-82; Ernst & Whinney, supvr, 1982-85; Lamaute Tax & Financial Servs, owner, 1985-; Howard Univ Sch Bus, adj prof; Fla A&M Univ, assoc prof; Lamaute Capital Inc, pres, founder, 1993-; Georgetown Univ Law Ctr, Social Security Admin, Off Policy, dir prog studies, currently; US Agency Int Develop, sr pension reform adv, Europe & Eurasia Bur Off Democracy Governance & Social Transition; Bur Europe & New Independent States; Bur Econ Growth, Agr & Trade, Mid E Bur, econ officer. **Orgs:** US Tax Ct, 1981-; Nzingha Soc, 1987-88; co-chmn, Nat Bar Asn, 1988-89; Nat Asn Securities Dealers, gen securities prin, investment advisor, munic finance prin & financial opers prin, life & health ins agt. **Home Addr:** 616 Hasselin Ave, Los Angeles, CA 90036, **Home Phone:** (213)965-0511. **Business Addr:** Director of Program Studies, Social Security Administration Office of Policy, 500 E St SW 8th Fl, Washington, DC 20254, **Business Phone:** (202)358-6225.

### LAMB, MONICA (MONICA LAMB-POWELL)
Basketball player. **Personal:** Born Oct 11, 1964, Houston, TX; married Felix; children: 2. **Educ:** Univ Southern Calif, BA, 1987. **Career:** Basketball player (retired); Palermo, Italy, basketball player, 1986-87; Milan, 1987-88; Madrid, Spain, 1988-89; Catanzaro, 1989-90; Bari, 1991-94; Clermont, France, 1995-96; Parma, 1996-97; Houston Comets, ctr, 1998-2000. **Orgs:** Founder & pres, Monica Lamb Wellness Found, 1998-. **Business Addr:** Founder, President, Monica Lamb Wellness Foundation, 5330 Griggs Rd Suite B106, Houston, TX 77099, **Business Phone:** (832)890-8790.

### LAMB, SABRINA
Radio host, writer, entrepreneur. **Educ:** Lincoln University, Graduate; St. John's University School of Law, Attended. **Career:** Radio 1600 WWRL (New York City), "The Morning Show" Co-host; Radio WRKS-FM, Co-host of "Open Line," "Week in Review," and "Wake-Up Club"; Radio WBAI-FM, Host and Producer of "Laughing, Lying and Signifying"; Film "UnBeweavable: Woman, What Did You Do to Your Hair?, Producer; WorldofMoney.org, CEO and Founder; Huffington Post, Contributor. **Honors/Awds:** "Black Noir" Magazine, 50 Top Black Women in Entertainment; BDPA Small Business Innovator Award; Rainbow Push/Wall Street Project Honors; New York State Z-Hope Award; "NV Magazine," Movers and Shakers Award, 2011; National Black MBA New York Metro Chapter, Entrepreneur of the Year Award; TheGrio.com, 100 Making History Today, 2012. **Special Achievements:** Author of "Have You Met Miss Jones? The Life and Loves of Radio's Most Controversial Diva," Random House, "Celebrity Elect: When Your Favorite Star Becomes President of the United States," CreateSpace Independent Publishing Platform (2008), "A Kettle of Vultures...Left Beak Marks on My Forehead," Simon & Schuster (2010), and "Do I Look Like an ATM? A Parent's Guide to Raising Financially Responsible Children," Chicago Press Review (2013); written many articles for a variety of publications including "Ebony," "Essence," and "Black Elegance; completed the New York City Marathon in 1995, 1996, and 2000.

### LAMB-POWELL, MONICA. See LAMB, MONICA.

### LAMBERT, BENJAMIN FRANKLIN. See Obituaries Section.

### LAMBERT, JOSEPH C.
Executive. **Personal:** Born Jul 4, 1936, Vauxhall, NJ; married Joan E Cross; children: Kim, George & Joseph Jr. **Educ:** Va State Col. **Career:** St Bank Plainfield, NJ, teller trainee, 1961-64; Security Nat Bank Newark, NJ, chief clerk, 1964-66; Nat State Bank Linden, NJ, admin asst, 1966-68; Nat State Bank Elizabeth NJ, asst br mgr, 1968-70; Nat State Bank, Plainfield, NJ, asst cashier, br mgr, 1970-72; E Orange Comt Bank, vpres, treas, 1972; Dreyfus Consumer Bank, sr vpres, treas. **Orgs:** Plainfield Area Urban Coalition; Plainfield Kiwanis; bd dir, S Second StYouth Ctr YMCA; finance chmn, S Plainfield Bd Educ. **Honors/Awds:** Apptd first Black Jury Comnr Union Co, 1974. **Home Addr:** 326 Muriel Ave, Piscataway, NJ 08854, **Home Phone:** (732)752-5383. **Business Addr:** Senior Vice President, Treasurer, Dreyfus Consumer Bank, 554 Central Ave, East Orange, NJ 07018.

### LAMBERT, LEONARD W.
Lawyer. **Personal:** Born Oct 27, 1938, Henrico County, VA; married Sylvia Jeter; children: Leonard Jr, Ralph, Linda, Brice & Mark. **Educ:** Va Union Univ, BA, 1960; Howard Univ Sch Law, JD, 1963. **Career:** Lambert & Assocs, atty, currently. **Orgs:** Vpres bd, Metrop YMCA; Jewish Comn Ctr; C Home Soc; Travelers Aid Soc; Richmond Chap Am Red Cross; Neighborhood Legal Aid Soc; Old Dom Bar Asn; Va Adv Coun Comn Youthful Offenders; Va State, Richmond Criminal Bar Asn; Va Trial Lawyers Asn; Nat Asn Defense Lawyers; Nat Bar Asn; Richmond Trial Lawyers Asn; Focus Club; Club 533; substitute Judge Juv & Domestic Rels Ct City Richmond Va; Omega Psi Phi Frat; selective appeal bd Eastern Dist Va; chmn trustee bd, Westwood Baptist Church; Nat Bd, YMCA; Nat Prog Chmn, YMCA; vpres, Va Ctr Performing Arts; vpres Federated Arts Coun. **Home Addr:** 815 Coleridge Lane, Richmond, VA 23229-6509, **Home Phone:** (804)282-7774. **Business Addr:** Attorney, Leonard W Lambert & Associates, 321 N 23rd St, Richmond, VA 23223-7140, **Business Phone:** (804)648-3325.

### LAMBERT, LILLIAN LINCOLN
Public speaker, founder (originator), president (organization). **Personal:** Born May 12, 1940, Ballsville, VA; daughter of Willie D and Arnetha B; married John Anthony Sr; children: Darnetha & Tasha. **Educ:** Howard Univ, BA, bus admin, 1966; Harvard Bus Sch, MBA, 1969. **Career:** Sterling Inst Wash; Ferris & Co, stockbroker, 1972; Bowie State Col, exec vpres Unified Serv, 1973-76; Centennial One Inc, founder & pres, 1976-01; Keller Williams Realty, agt, 2005-08; LilCo Enterprises, pres, 2002. **Orgs:** Bd Visitors, Va Commonwealth Univ; bd mem & bd dir, Harvard Bus Sch African Am Alumni Asn; mgr, Nat Bankers Asn; bd regents, Univ Syst Md; vice chmn, Manasota Chap Asn Study African Am Life & Hist. **Honors/Awds:** Small Business Person of the Year, State of Md, 1981; Alumni Achievement Award, Harvard Business School, 2003; inducted into "Enterprising Women" magazine's Hall of Fame, 2010; Honoree for Dominion Resources Strong Men Strong Women: Excellence in Leadership Series, 2011. **Special Achievements:** The first African-American woman to receive an M.B.A. from Harvard Business School; her memoir, "The Road to Someplace Better: From the Segregated South to Harvard Business School and Beyond", was released in 2010 by John Wiley & Sons. **Business Phone:** (804)353-5999.

### LAMBERT, LISA M.
Computer executive, vice president (organization). **Educ:** Pa State Univ, BS, mgt info systs, 1989; Harvard Bus Sch, MBA, bus admin & mgt, gen, 1997. **Career:** Owens Corning, software engr, 1989-92, sales & bus develop, 1992-97; Intel Corp, prod mkt, 1997-99; Intel Capital, Intel 64 Fund, investment dir, 1999-2001, Enterprise Software, sector dir, 2001-06, managing dir software & serv, 2006-10, vpres & managing dir software & serv, 2010-16, Diversity Fund, vpres & managing dir, 2015-16; Uniting Prof Women Accelerating Relationships & Develop, Founder, chief exec officer & chmn, 2013-; Westly Group, managing partner, 2016-. **Orgs:** Bd dir, VCE LLC; bd dir, Endeca; bd dir, CollabNet; bd dir, Acadia Enterprises; bd dir, iovation; bd dir, REvolution Comput; bd dir, SpikeSource; bd dir, Zend Technologies; dir, X+1 Inc. **Honors/Awds:** "Business Insider," 25 Most Influential Blacks in Technology, 2013. **Business Addr:** Managing Partner, The Westly Group, 2200 Sand Hill Rd, Menlo Park, CA 94025, **Business Phone:** (650)275-7420.

### LAMBERT, DR. VIOLET THERESA EARLY
School administrator. **Personal:** Born Sep 24, 1924, New Orleans, LA; daughter of William Sr (deceased) and Alphonsine Harris (deceased); married Joe R; married Joe R. **Educ:** YMCA, Sch Com, dipl, 1945; Agr Mech & Norm Col, BS, 1964; Henderson State Univ, MS, educ, 1977; Univ Ark, LLD, 1993. **Career:** School administrator (retired); Univ Ark, Pine Bluff, asst registr, 1961-85, foreign stud advisor, 1965-83, registr/dir admis, 1983-90. **Orgs:** Ark Am Asn Col Registrars & Admis Officers, 1960-; PB Social & Art Civic Club, 1960-; advisor, Alpha Rho Chap, Alpha Kappa Alpha Sorority, 1960-71; advisor, Alpha Kappa Mu Hon Soc, 1970-89; vice chmn, Econs Opport Comn, 1975-00; EOC, 1975-; Phi Delta Kappa Fraternity, 1977-; perpetuator Sylvester Early Endowment Scholar Fund, UAPB, 1980-; secy, Pine Bluff Boys Club, 1981-83; Kappa Delta Pi Educ Fraternity, 1983-; secy, Am Red Cross Chap, 1985-; secy, Phi Delta Kappa Educ Fraternity, 1985-; Phi Beta Lampda Bus Fraternity; lector, St Peter Cath Church; Golden

Lion Found; life mem, AMEN/UAPB Alumni Asn; UAPB Found; vol, Am Red Cross; ARR SVP, 1990-; financial sponsor, UAPB Cheerleaders, 1999-; 25 Yrs Am Red Cross, 2002. **Home Addr:** 706 W 14th St, Pine Bluff, AR 71601, **Home Phone:** (870)535-2321.

**LAMONT, JESSE. See MARTIN, JESSE LAMONT.**

### LAMOTTE, JEAN MOORE
Administrator, writer. **Personal:** Born Sep 2, 1938, Shreveport, LA. **Educ:** Calif State Univ, Sacramento; Am River Col, Sacramento; Central State Univ, Wilberforce, OH. **Career:** Campbell Soup Co, voc spec, 1966-70; Human Rights Comn, proj dir & Affirmative action prog, 1970-73; KXTV-10 Corinthian Broadcasting, host moderator daily pub serv talk show, 1973; Affirm Act Prog underutilizing employers, writer. **Honors/Awds:** Community Service Award, Golden Empire Chap Am Heart Asn, 1977-80; Woman of the Year, Sacramento Observer Newspaper, 1977; Sacramento's Most Influential Black Woman Sacramento Observer, 1978; Outstanding Community Service Award, Women's Civic Improvement Ctr, 1980. **Home Addr:** 6250 Gloria Dr, Sacramento, CA 95831-1751.

### LAMPLEY, DR. PAUL CLARENCE
Administrator, educator, vice president (organization). **Personal:** Born Dec 12, 1945, Louisville, MS; married Fannie Lumpkin; children: Samantha. **Educ:** Tougaloo Col, BS, biol, 1967; Atlanta Univ, MS, biol, 1971; Howard Univ; Memphis State Univ; Univ Miss, PhD, health care admin, 1981. **Career:** Atlanta Univ Ctr Health & Aging, post doctoral, geront; United Negro Col Fund, distinguished prof, 1985-86; Harris Jr Col, instr; NSF, grad trainee; Rust Col, asst develop dir, chair div social sci & acad dean, exec asst pres, SACS Reaffirmation Comt, chair, vpres assessment, 2004-, vpres acad affairs, currently. **Orgs:** Bd trustee & life mem, Nat Asn Advan Colored People; Yacona Area Coun; Omega Psi Phi; Nat Asn Fed Rel Officers; Phi Delta Kappa; Sigma Pi Phi Fraternity Anderson Chapel C.M.E. Church; vice chair, Holly Springs Sch Syst, chair. **Honors/Awds:** Outstanding Young Man in American, 1972. **Special Achievements:** Co-author: "A Ray of Hope". **Home Addr:** 601 Swaney Rd, Holly Springs, MS 38635, **Home Phone:** (662)252-5269. **Business Addr:** Vice President for Assessment, Vice President Academic Affairs, Rust College, 150 Rust Ave, Holly Springs, MS 38635, **Business Phone:** (601)252-8000.

### LANCASTER, HERMAN BURTRAM
Teacher, legal consultant, educator. **Personal:** Born Mar 6, 1942, Chicago, IL; son of Eddie and Louise; married Patricia L Malucci; children: Lauren E, Rachel J & Meredith E. **Educ:** Chicago State Univ, BS, 1965; Rosary Col, MA, 1968; De Paul Univ, JD, 1972. **Career:** Chicago Bd Ed, teacher, 1965-66; DePaul Univ Law Sch, asst dir law lib, 1966-70; Univ Chicago, psychiat dept dir info, 1970-72, legal coun, 1972-73; Glendale Univ Law Sch, prof law, dir res, 1973-, prof emer; Legal Inst Law Consult, dir, 1976-; US Cent Dist Bankruptcy Ct, mediator. **Orgs:** Nat Asn Advan Colored People, 1975-; Glendale Law Rev, 1976-; advisor, Subcontractors Inst, 1984-; arbitrator, AAA, 1986-; arbitrator, Am Arbit Asn. **Honors/Awds:** Omega Psi Phi Scholarship, 1963; Grad Fellowship, 1966; Man of the Year, Omega Psi Phi, 1966. De Paul Law School Scholarship, 1968; Blue Key Law Hon Soc, 1968; De Paul Law Review Scholarship, 1969-72. **Special Achievements:** Published numerous articles; First faculty member to be conferred with the title of Professor Emeritus. **Business Addr:** Professor Emeritus, Glendale University College of Law, 220 N Glendale Ave, Glendale, CA 91206, **Business Phone:** (818)247-0770.

### LANCASTER, RONNY B.
Executive. **Educ:** Cath Univ, BA, econs, 1973; Univ Pa, Wharton Sch, MBA, 1975; Georgetown Univ Law Ctr, JD, 1984. **Career:** US Off Personnel Mgt, Div Fee-For-Serv Plans, chief, 1984-86; Hamilton Enterprises Inc, gen coun, 1988; US Dept Health & Human Serv, exec asst secy & prin dep asst secy planning & eval, 1990-93; Morehouse Sch Med, vpres health & social policy, 1993-96, sr vpres, 1996-2005, chief operating officer, 2003-05; Assurant Inc, sr vpres fed govt rels, 2005-07, sr vpres pub affairs & govt rels, 2007-; US Off Personnel Mgt, Div Fee-For-Serv Plans, chief; Nat Inst Adv Studies, exec asst chmn. **Orgs:** Dir, chmn nominating & corp governance comt & mem compensation comt, OraSure Technologies, 2003-; bd mem fed govt rels, Assurant Inc, 2003-05; dir, Immucor Inc, 2008-; Pa Bar Asn; DC Bar; bd mem, Morehouse Col Res Inst; pres, Minority Health Professions Found; dir, Morehouse Sch Med Inc; sr Wash rep, Blue Cross & Blue Shield Asn; pres, Minority Health Profs Found; Bar Commonwealth Pa; Dist Columbia Ct Appeals; med adv bd, Henry Schein Inc; Wash DC Bar. **Business Addr:** Director, Chairman, OraSure Technologies Inc, 220 E 1st St, Bethlehem, PA 18015, **Business Phone:** (610)882-1820.

### LAND, DANIEL
Football player, football coach. **Personal:** Born Jul 3, 1965, Donaldsonville, GA; children: 2. **Educ:** Albany State, GA, grad. **Career:** Football player (retired) coach; Tampa Bay Buccaneers, defensive back, 1987; Los Angeles, defensive back, 1989-94; Oakland Raiders, defensive back, 1995-97; interim head coach.

### LAND-LATTA, THERESA E.
Police officer. **Career:** City New York, Dept Invest, dep inspector gen, currently. **Business Addr:** Deputy Inspector General, City of New York, 80 Maiden Lane 16th Fl, New York, NY 10038, **Business Phone:** (212)825-5900.

### LANDER, C. VICTOR
Lawyer, judge. **Personal:** Born Jun 29, 1954, Columbus, GA; son of Fred L III and Agnes Levy. **Educ:** Morehouse Col, BA, hon, polit sci & psychol, 1975; Univ Tex Sch Law, JD, 1978. **Career:** Tex Atty Gen Off, legal intern, law clerk, 1976-78; FDL Commun CMS, atty, 1978-86; Lander & Assocs, PC, atty, managing partner, 1986-; City Dallas Tex Munic Ct, assoc judge, 1991-96, munic judge, Ct 7, 1996-2008; City Balch Springs, Tex Munic Ct, munic judge, 1993-96; Paul Quinn Col, Dallas, adj prof, 2010-11; ITT Tech Inst, adj prof, 2011-12; Dallas Munic Ct, City Dallas, admin judge, 2008-12; City Dallas Munic Ct, munic judge, 2012-. **Orgs:** Bd gov, Nat Bar Asn, gov lawyers div chmn, 1977-89; chmn, Legal Redress Comt, Nat Asn Advan Colored People, Nominations Comt, Election Supv Comt, 1986-90, 1994-96; bd dir, YMCA, 1989-; bd mem, Dallas Urban League, 1996-; atty, JL Turner Legal Asn, currently. **Honors/Awds:** Certificate of Achievement, Nat Judicial Col, Reno, NV, 1997. **Special Achievements:** Periodic writer, Dallas Weekly Newspaper, 1990-94; Frequent speaker on employment, legal, judicial issues, 1986-; Participant & co-founder, CAW Clark Legal Clin, 1989-; AMR Inns Court; Col State Bar Tex. **Home Addr:** 6521 Putting Green Dr, Dallas, TX 75241, **Home Phone:** (214)374-7740. **Business Addr:** Municipal Judge, Dallas Municipal Court, Rm 210 2014 Main St, Dallas, TX 75201, **Business Phone:** (214)670-5573.

**LANDER, CRESSWORTH CALEB. See Obituaries Section.**

### LANDERS, NAAMAN GARNETT, JR.
Manager. **Personal:** Born Oct 23, 1938, Anderson, IN; son of Naaman Sr (deceased); married Stephanie E Cox; children: Naaman III. **Educ:** Purdue Univ, BS, CE, 1966; Univ Chicago, MBA, 1969. **Career:** Manager (retired); Amoco Oil Co, engr, 1966-69, mat mgr, 1972-76, proj dir, mgr, Bus & Financial Serv, 1980-91; Esso Chem Co, trans analyst, 1969-71; Stand Oil Co, coord inventory control, 1977-79. **Honors/Awds:** Presidential Citation Reconnaissance over Cuba. **Home Addr:** 1454 E Pk Pl, Chicago, IL 60637-1836, **Home Phone:** (773)955-0454.

### LANDREAUX, KENNETH FRANCIS (KEN LANDREAUX)
Baseball player. **Personal:** Born Dec 22, 1954, Los Angeles, CA; children: Antoine & Todd Xavier. **Educ:** Ariz State Univ; Ariz Sch Real Estate, attended 1992. **Career:** Baseball player (retired); Calif Angels, outfielder, 1977-78; Minn Twins, outfielder, 1979-80; Los Angeles Dodgers, outfielder, 1981-87; Sr ProfBaseball Asn, Orlando Juice, St. Petersburg Pelicans, 1989; Urban Youth Academy, coach, currently. **Orgs:** Community Affairs, Los Angeles Dodgers. **Home Addr:** 1211 N Chester Ave, Compton, CA 90221. **Business Addr:** Coach, Urban Youth Academy, 901 E Artesia Blvd, Compton, CA 90221, **Business Phone:** (310)763-3479.

### LANDRUM, TITO (TERRY LEE LANDRUM)
Baseball player. **Personal:** Born Oct 25, 1954, Joplin, MO; married Theresa; children: Melissa & Julie. **Educ:** Eastern Okla State. **Career:** Baseball player (retired), consultant; St Louis Cardinals, outfielder, 1980-83, 1984-87; Baltimore Orioles, outfielder, 1983, 1988; Los Angeles Dodgers, outfielder, 1987; Tex Rangers, free agt, 1988; Hydro-Tone Sports & Med Equip, dir res & develop, 1992-94; Play It Again Ltd, team consult, 1994. **Home Addr:** 1121 Ky SE, Albuquerque, NM 87108.

**LANDRY, BART. See LANDRY, L. BARTHOLOMEW.**

### LANDRY, DOLORES BRANCHE
Businessperson, executive. **Personal:** Born Oct 9, 1928, Philadelphia, PA; daughter of Merwin Edward (deceased) and Wilma Brown (deceased); married Lawrence A; children: Jennifer E & Michael H. **Educ:** Fisk Univ, BA, 1950; Denmark Int Hojskole Elsinore, Denmark, WI, dipl, 1951; Univ Chicago, MA, 1960. **Career:** Executive (retired); Sci Res Assocs, ed & guid dir, 1954-60, proj dir res & develop, 1960-61; Chicago Community Youth Welfare, actg dir city-wide youth serv, 1961-63; Joint Youth Develop Community, youth employ consult, 1963-64; Horizons Employ Counr Inc, founder & pres, 1964-66; Chicago Community Urban Oppor, chief planner, 1964-65; pvt consult, 1965-71; Assoc Consults Inc, co-founder & pres, 1971. **Orgs:** Chicago Guid & Personnel Asn, 1955-66; mem bd dir, Elliott Donnelly Youth Ctr, 1961-63; Asn Women Bus Owners, 1971-00; chmn, child guid comn vpres Murch Home & Sch Asn, 1973-78; vpres, Howard Univ Fac Wives Asn, 1974-75; vpres, mem bd dirs DC Asn C women & Learning Disabilities, 1974-87; Alpha Kappa Alpha; bd dir, Glenbrook Found Except C, Bethesda, MD, 1980-81; chair, budget & planning comt, DC Juv Justice Adv Group, 1987-90; Int Network Women Bus Owners, 1990-2000; adv bd, Nat Fed Teaching Entrepreneurship, DC, 1994-96. **Honors/Awds:** Woman of the Year Award, Sigma Gamma Rho Sorority, Chicago, 1960; Outstanding Volunteer Award, DC Pub Schs, Wash, DC, 1979; NE Regional Alumni Award, Outstanding Commitment Fisk Univ, 1990. **Home Addr:** 2936 Davenport St NW, Washington, DC 20008-2165, **Home Phone:** (202)244-8456.

### LANDRY, L. BARTHOLOMEW (BART LANDRY)
Educator, sociologist. **Personal:** Born Apr 28, 1936, Milton, LA. **Educ:** St Marys Sem & Univ, BA, 1961; Xavier Univ, BA, 1966; Columbia Univ, PhD, 1971. **Career:** Columbia Univ, fac fel, 1966-67; New Sch Social Res, Instr, 1969-70; Purdue Univ, Dept Sociol, asst prof, 1971-73; Univ Md, Dept Sociol, from asst prof to assoc prof, 1973-02, prof, 2002-, prof emer, currently. **Orgs:** African Studies Asn; Am Sociol Asn; Caucus Black Sociologists; Law Sociol Asn; Pop Asn Am Publ field; Asn Black Sociologists. **Home Addr:** 10744 Lester St, Silver Spring, MD 20902-3759, **Home Phone:** (301)649-1087. **Business Addr:** Professor Emeritus, University of Maryland, 2112 Art-Sociol Bldg, College Park, MD 20742-1315, **Business Phone:** (301)405-6390.

### LANE, ALLAN C.
City planner. **Personal:** Born Dec 21, 1948, Akron, OH; son of Sanford and Mable Farrior; married Nancy McClendon. **Educ:** Hiram Col, Hiram, OH, BA, social sci, 1971; Univ Cincinnati, MCP, community planning, 1973. **Career:** City Cin, city planner, 1972-73; Cin Comm Action Agency, asst proj dir, 1972; Model Cities Housing Corp, dep plng dir, 1973-75; City Dayton, sr city planner, 1975-89; City Atlanta, urban planner, 1989-92; GRASP Enterprises, dir cot develop, 1992-94, dir trng, 1999-; Atlanta Community Olympic Games, proj coordr, 1994-96; City Col Pk GA, econ develop specialist, 2002-07; City N Port, econ develop mgr, 2008-14. **Orgs:** Founder, artistic advisor Creekside Players, 1978-89; bd mem, Dayton Contemp Dance Co, 1984-86; bd mem, OH Theatre Alliance, 1984-87, touring panelist, 1984-86, theatre panel, 1989-91, Ohio Arts Coun; Fulton County Arts Coun, theatre panel, 1993-95; Ballethnic Dance CPN, bd mem, 1991-94; Proj Interconnections, bd mem, 1996-98; Old Ntl Merchants Asn, bd mem, 2001-; Atlanta Airport Area Com, 2003-04. **Honors/Awds:** Employee Year Dayton Dept Planning, 1981; Outstanding Service to Proj Alpha, Alpha Phi Alpha Frat, 1985-86; Service to Gifted C Dayton Pub Schs, 1986. **Home Addr:** 3150 Key Dr SW, Atlanta, GA 30311-3647, **Home Phone:** (404)696-2237. **Business Addr:** Economic Development Specialist, Georgia Department Community Affairs, 3667 Main St, College Park, GA 30337.

### LANE, AUSTIN A.
College teacher, college administrator, college president. **Personal:** Born NJ; married Loren; children: 3. **Educ:** Odessa Jr Col; Langston Univ, BA; Univ Okla, MA; Univ Ala, EdD. **Career:** Sam Houston State Univ, adj prof; Univ Tex at Arlington, adj prof, dean students; Tyler Jr Col, vpres stud affairs; Lone Star Col-Montgomery, pres, 2009-15, exec vice chancellor, 2015-16; Tex Southern Univ, pres, 2016-. **Orgs:** Amergy Bank Adv Bd; Montgomery County Women's Ctr; Rotary Club Woodlands; Tex Diversity Coun; Woodlands Area Chamber Com; Greater Conroe/Lake Conroe Area Chamber Com; Greater Conroe Econ Develop Coun; Educ Tomorrow Alliance. **Honors/Awds:** Pacesetter of the Year, National Council for Marketing and Public Relations, 2012; Drum Major Award, 2015. **Business Addr:** Texas Southern University, 3100 Cleburne St, Houston, TX 77004, **Business Phone:** (713)313-7011.

### LANE, CHARLES
Actor, movie director. **Personal:** Born Dec 26, 1953, New York, NY; son of Charles and Albertha; married Laura Lesser; children: Nicole Alysia & Julien Michael. **Educ:** State Univ NY, Purchase, BFA, 1980. **Career:** Filmmaker, 1976-; Films: A Place in Time, 1976; Sidewalk Stories, 1989; True Identity, 1991; Alma's Rainbow, 1994; Actor: Posse. **Orgs:** Nat Black Programming Consortium; Black Filmmakers Found; Acad Motion Pictures Arts & Sci; adv bd, Independent Film Prog; Actors Guild Am; Screen Actors Guild; Writers Guild; dir, Guild Am. **Honors/Awds:** Student Academy Award, 1976; Rockefeller Foundation grant, 1979; Prix du Publique award, Cannes Film Festival, 1989; Best Director & Best Film awards, Upsalla Film Festival, Sweden, 1989; Grand Prix & 2nd Prize, Journalise Jury, Chamrousse, France, 1989; Guggenheim Award, 1990; Best director award & public prize, Festival Comedy, Vevey, Switzerland, 1990; First prize for best film, Wurzburg Film Festival, Germany, 1990; International Festival of Humor, Chamrousse, France, 1990; Black Filmmakers Hall of Fame, 1990; CEBA Award, 1991; Nat Asn Advan Colored People, 1992; numerous other national & international awards. **Business Addr:** Filmmaker, 110 E 59th St 6th Fl, New York, NY 10022.

### LANE, CURTIS
Executive, government official. **Career:** Hillsborough County Police, chief investr; Tampa Police Dept, dep chief police; City Tampa, exec asst to mayor, 1995-, dir code enforcement, currently. **Orgs:** Nat Forum Black Pub Adminr; Nat Asn Human Rights Workers; bd dir, Int Asn Police-Community Rels Officers; Fed Bur Invest Nat Acad Assocs; Tampa Bay Area Police Chiefs Asn; Nat Asn Black Law Enforcement Execs. **Home Addr:** 8709 Tantallon Cir, Tampa, FL 33647-2238. **Business Addr:** Director, City of Tampa, 102 E 7th Ave, Tampa, FL 33602, **Business Phone:** (813)274-5545.

### LANE, DAPHENE CORBETT
Nurse, educator. **Personal:** Born Aug 24, 1964, Ivanhoe, NC; daughter of Billy and Laura; married Xavier; children: Brandon & Brandi. **Educ:** NC Cent Univ, BSN, 1986; E Carolina Univ, MSN, 1995. **Career:** Veterans Admin, staff nurse, 1986-87; Sampson Regional Med Ctr, staff nurse, 1987-90; Sampson Community Col, nursing instr, coordr pract nursing prog, 1990-. **Orgs:** NC Coun Practical Nurse Educr; Kenansville Eastern Missionary Baptist Youth Coun; NC Nurse's Asn; Community Outreach Mission; inductee, Sigma Theta Tau, 1994-95; co adv, Practical Nursing Stud Asn. **Home Addr:** 291 Cannady Rd, Harrells, NC 28444, **Home Phone:** (910)532-2252. **Business Addr:** Nursing Instructor, Sampson Community College, 1801 Sunset Ave Hwy 24 W, Clinton, NC 28328, **Business Phone:** (910)592-8081.

**LANE, DR. EDDIE BURGYONE, SR. See Obituaries Section.**

### LANE, ELEANOR TYSON
Educator. **Personal:** Born Feb 14, 1938, Hartford, CT; married James Perry Jr; children: Randall P & Hollye Cherise. **Educ:** Howard Univ, attended 1958; St Joseph Col, BA, 1960; Univ Hartford, MEd, 1975. **Career:** Educator (retired); Hartford Bd Educ, teacher, 1960-72; Amistad House, actg dir, 1973-75; Univ Conn, asst dir, 1976-90; Manchester Cot Col, Assoc Prof Edu, 1990-97. **Orgs:** New Eng Minority Women Adminr Ann Conf Wellesley Col, 1985; panelist Assoc Social & Behav Scientists Inc, 1985; partic Success full Enrollment, Mgt Sem sponsored by Consults Educ Resource & Res Inc, 1986; New Eng Minority Women Adminr, Assoc Social & BehavScientists, Urban League Greater Hartford, Nat League Bus & Prof Women, Delta Sigma Theta Sor Inc, Univ Conn, Prof Employees Asn, Conn Asn Co-lAdmis Officers; Nat Asn Women Deans Adminr & Counr, Nat Asn Col Admis Counr, New Eng Asn Col Registr & Admis Officers. **Home Addr:** 113 Vernwood Dr, Vernon Rockville, CT 06066-4920, **Home Phone:** (860)872-4230.

### LANE, ERIC, III
Actor. **Personal:** Born Chicago, IL. **Career:** Films: One Week, 2000; Novocaine, 2001; Love Relations, 2002; Barbershop, 2002; A Get2Gether, 2005; The Evil One, 2005; Trapped in the Closet, 2007; Subtle Seduction, 2008; Dance Fu, 2011; Ransum Games, 2014. TV series: "Soul Food", 2001; "The Parkers", 2004; "Prison Break", 2005; "The Beast", 2009; "Chicago Fire", 2013. **Home Addr:** 6948 S Harvard Ave, Chicago, IL 60621.

**LANE, JANIS OLENE**
Journalist. **Personal:** Born Kansas City, KS; daughter of Charles Thomas and Henrietta Perry. **Educ:** Univ Mo, Kans City. **Career:** KCPT-TV, Kans City, Mo, reporter/assoc producer, 1978-83; KB-MT-TV 12, Beaumont, Tex, anchor/producer, 1984; KCMO 81 AM, Kans City, Mo, anchor/reporter, 1984-86; KCTV 5, Kans City, Mo, talk show host/reporter, 1985-88; Power 95 FM, Kans City, Mo, news dir & anchor, 1986-88; WTOL-TV 11, Toledo, Ohio, weekend anchor & reporter.KCPT-TV, Kans City, Mo, reporter & assoc producer, 1978-83; KBMT-TV 12, Beaumont, Tex, anchor & producer, 1984; KCMO 81 AM, Kans City, Mo, anchor & reporter, 1984-86; KCTV 5, Kans City, Mo, talk show host & reporter, 1985-88; Power 95 FM, Kans City, Mo, news dir & anchor, 1986-88; WTOL-TV 11, Toledo, Ohio, weekend anchor & reporter. **Orgs:** Nat Asn Broadcast Journalists; Women Alive; prayer intecessor, Toledo Covenant Church. **Honors/Awds:** Crystal Award, News Reporting, 1989. **Home Addr:** 5101 Breezeway, Toledo, OH 43613, **Home Phone:** (419)472-0255. **Business Addr:** News Anchor, WTOL-TV - 11 News, 730 N Summit St, Toledo, OH 43604, **Business Phone:** (419)248-1107.

**LANE, JEFFREY D.**
Airplane pilot. **Personal:** Born Oct 7, 1955, Chicago, IL; married janine S McDonald. **Educ:** Wilberforce Univ, attended 1975; Marquette Univ, BS, bus admin, 1980. **Career:** Lockheed Support Syst, Black Hawk Helicopter Test Pilot, 1992-94; Pfizer Inc, Team Leader, 1995; Gulfstream Int Airlines, pilot, 1995-98; Northwest Airlines, pilot, 1998-, regional vpres midwest region, currently; Orgn Black Aerospace Professionals, Delta Airlines, nat dir, currently. **Orgs:** Alpha Phi Alpha Fraternity, 1974-; regional vpres, Orgn Black Airline Pilots, 2001-04; USAF; WVa Nat Guard. **Home Addr:** PO Box 511271, Livonia, MI 48151. **Business Addr:** Pilot, Regional Vice President, Northwest Airlines Corp, 2700 Lone Oak Pkwy, Eagan, MN 55121, **Business Phone:** (612)726-2111.

**LANE, JEROME**
Basketball player, manager. **Personal:** Born Dec 4, 1966, Akron, OH; children: 5. **Educ:** Univ Pittsburgh, attended 1988. **Career:** Basketball player (retired), supervisor; Denver Nuggets, forward, 1988-91; Ind Pacers, forward, 1992; Milwaukee Bucks, forward, 1992; Oximesa Granada, Spain, 1992; Cleveland Cavaliers, forward, 1992-93; La Crosse Catbirds, 1993-94; Rapid City Thrillers, 1994; Okla City Cavalry, 1994-96; Forum Filatelico, Spain, 1996-97; Caja Cantabria, Spain, 1997-98; Idaho Stampede, 1998-2000; Amateur Athletic Union, Team Akron, coach; Summit Lake Community Ctr, supvr, 2002-08; Firestone High Sch, asst basketball coach, currently. **Home Addr:** , Akron, OH 44304. **Business Addr:** Assistant Coach, Firestone High School, 333 Rampart Ave, Akron, OH 44313, **Business Phone:** (330)873-3315.

**LANE, PROF. JOHNNY LEE, JR.**
Percussionist, educator, founder (originator). **Personal:** Born Dec 19, 1949, Vero Beach, FL; son of Alfred A and Anna Lee; married Claudia Hickerson; children: Latoya T, Maxine A & Johnny A. **Educ:** Southern Univ, attended 1971; Southern Ill Univ, MM, 1972; Univ Ill, advan study; Bobby Christian Sch Percussion, advan study. **Career:** Johnny Lane Percussion Sextet Ensemble, conductor, 1971-72; Accent Music, percussion instr, 1971-72; Tenn State Univ, Univ Percussion Ensembles, dir, 1972-74, asst dir bands, 1972-74; Eastern Ill Univ, dir percussion studies, 1974; Ind Univ Sch Music; Univ Baptist Church, dir music, 1978-; Johnny Lane Percussion Enterprises, pres, 1980-83; MIDCO Int, percussion consult, 1983; US Percussion Camp, founder, host, 1987-99; percussion clinics & workshops; Univ Cent AK, 1996; Univ Mo, St Louis, fac, 1997; La State Univ, fac, 1999; Univ Tenn-Knoxville, fac, 1999; Clemson Univ, fac, 1999; Music Fest Can, 1999; Univ Miss, fac, 2000; Sam Houston State Univ, asst prof; Olathe N Productions, tech theatre dir, currently; VIC Firth, signature artist, currently; Remo Inc, dir educ mktg, currently; Author: Four Mallet Independence For Marimba; Rudimental Snare Drum Grooves. **Orgs:** Ed, Percussive Notes Mag Percussive Arts Soc, 1978-86; bd, Percussive Arts Soc, Ill State Chap, 1979-85, int bd, 1978-88, 1991-92, second vpres, 1981-83, mem comt chair, 1986-90; Nat Asn Rudimental Drummers; Kappa Kappa Psi, Nat Band Fraternity; Phi Mu Alpha, Nat Music Fraternity; Pi Kappa Lambda, Nat Music Hons Soc; fac adv, Sigma Alpha Iota. **Home Addr:** 1891 Zachary Lane, Indianapolis, IN 46231-1041, **Home Phone:** (317)839-3861. **Business Addr:** Director of Education, Remo Inc, 28101 Industry Dr, Valencia, CA 91355, **Business Phone:** (661)294-5600.

**LANE, NANCY L.**
Executive. **Personal:** Born Boston, MA; daughter of Samuel M and Gladys Pitkin. **Educ:** Boston Univ, BS, pub rels, 1962; Univ Pittsburgh Grad Sch Pub & Int Affairs, MPA, pub admin, 1967; Univ Oslo, Norway, undergrad studies; Harvard Univ Grad Sch Bus Admin, prog mgt devel, cert, 1975. **Career:** Vice president (retired); Chase Manhattan Bank, second vpres, 1972-73; Off-Track Betting Corp, New York, vpres, 1973-75; Johnson & Johnson Corp, corp personnel staff, 1975-76; Ortho Diag Systs Inc, Div Johnson & Johnson, dir personnel, 1976-78, vpres personnel & admin & mem bd dir, 1978-89, Worldwide Hq, Govt Affairs Div, vpres, 1989-2000. **Orgs:** Bd trustee, Studio Mus Harlem, 1973-, chmn; adv bd, prog founder, Black Exec Exchange Prog, 1970; bd dir, exec comt, 1972-80, Catalyst; bd dir, Nat Black MBA Asn, 1972-75; trustee, Benedict Col, 1974-84; trustee, Wilson Col, 1975-78; Nat Comn Working Women, 1980-84; bd dir, vice chmn, 1982-86, Better Chance; secy & treas, Harvard Bus Sch Alumni Asn, 1986-90; bd dir, Women's Forum, Woodrow Wilson Nat Fel 1987-; chair bd trustee, Bennett Col, 1989-90; bd gov, Rutgers Univ, 1990-98; pres, 1990-92, bd dir, 1992-, Harvard Bus Sch, Club Greater New York; bd dir, Ronald McDonald House New York, 1995-98; nat bd dir, Natl Asn Advan Colored People; Links Inc, 1998-; bd trustee, Freedom House Inc, currently; WARM2Kids Inc; Better Chance, CATALYST, Exp Int Living World Living; United Way Tri-State; bd mem, Int Ctr Photog; bd dir, SEED Found, bd dir, Nat Asn Advan Colored People; bd mem, Bloomfield Col, 2004-; co-chair, Stieglitz Soc at Metrop Mus Art. **Honors/Awds:** Living Legends in Black, JE Bailey III, 1976; Twin Award, YWCA Int, 1978; Graduation Speaker, Univ Col, Rutgers Univ, 1992; Chairman's Award for Distinguished Service, Studio Mus Harlem, 1996; Leadership Award, New York City Support Group, 1996; Distinguished Alumni Award, Boston Univ, 1997; Distinguished Award, Harvard Bus Sch African Am, 1998. **Special Achievements:** Published numerous articles; profiled in The New York Times, Fortune, Black Enterprise, BusinessWeek, O, The Oprah Magazine. **Home Addr:** 37 W 12th St Apt 10J, New York, NY 10011, **Home Phone:** (646)336-5994. **Business Addr:** Director, Board of Director, Harvard Business School Club of New York, 350 5th Ave Suite 4811, New York, NY 10118, **Business Phone:** (212)947-5544.

**LANE, TIFFANY. See BALTIMORE, CHARLI.**

**LANE, WILLIAM KEITH**
Clergy, bishop. **Personal:** Born Dec 26, 1923, Knoxville, TN; son of George Alexander and Bertha Irvin; married Marion Keene; children: Rhoda Darling, William Keith Jr, Marcia Elizabeth (deceased) & Brian Keith. **Educ:** Detroit Bible Col, attended 1952. **Career:** Eastside Church God, bishop; Church of God Sanctified Inc, sr bishop, currently. **Orgs:** Chmn, Nat Exec Bd Bishops & Elders. **Honors/Awds:** Hon Doctorate, Faith Evangelistic Christian Sch, 1990. **Home Addr:** 15483 Fairfield St, Detroit, MI 48238-1445, **Home Phone:** (313)341-7743. **Business Addr:** Senior Bishop, Pastor, Church of God Sanctified Inc, 1230 W Trinity Lane, Nashville, TN 37218, **Business Phone:** (615)255-5579.

**LANEUVILLE, ERIC GERARD**
Actor, administrator, television producer. **Personal:** Born Jul 14, 1952, New Orleans, LA; son of Alexander and Mildred; children: Sean. **Educ:** Santa Monica City Col, attended 1973; Univ Calif, Los Angeles, attended 1974. **Career:** MTM Prod, actor & dir; PBS, producer; Lorimar Prod, dir & producer; Universal City, dir; 20 Century Fox, dir; Citadel Prod, dir; Warner Bros, co exec producer & dir; Lan Ville Inc, pres; TV Series: "Head of the Class", 1988; "A Brand New Life", 1989; "Reasonable Doubts", 1991; "Going to Extremes", 1992; "McKenna", 1994; "Rescue 77", 1999; Films: The Omega Man, 1971; Black Belt Jones, 1974; Death Wish, 1974; A Piece of the Action, 1977; Love at First Bite, 1979; The Baltimore Bullet, 1980; Staying Afloat, 1993; Fear of a Black Hat, 1994; Someone She Knows, 1994; ER: Summer Run, 1995; If Someone Had Known, 1995; A Case for Life, 1996; Twisted Desire, 1996; Pandora's Clock, 1996; Born into Exile, 1997; Trapped in a Purple Haze, 2000; Scrubs, 2002; Critical Assembly, 2003; America's Prince: The John F. Kennedy Jr. Story, 2003; The Party's Over, 2004; Naughty or Nice, 2004; Monk: Mr Monk & the Other Detective, 2005. TV series: Rescue 77, The WB, 1999; A force of one; Dir; L.A. Law, 1986; Quantum Leap, 1989; Doogie Howser, managing dir, 1990; NYPD Blue, 1993; ER, 1995; 413 Hope St, Gilmore Girls, 2004; Invasion, Medium, Lost, 2005-08; Lie to Me, 2009; The Mentalist, 2009-12; Girlfriends, Everybody Hates Chris, Prison Break, Ghost Whisperer & Grimm, 2012-13; Producer; Midnight Caller, 1990-91; 413 Hope St, 1997; Executive producer: Bull, 2000, Supervising Producer; A Brand New Life. **Orgs:** Dirs Guild Am; Screen Actors Guild; Acad TV Arts & Sci; Dirs Guild Educ & Benevolent Found; Am Diabetes Asn. **Honors/Awds:** Outstanding Director, Dirs Guild Am, 1987, 1992; Christopher Award, The Christophers, 1987, 1996; Emmy Award, Acad TV Arts & Sci, 1992. **Special Achievements:** Nominated for Emmy for Drama and Comedy Series, 1993; On Ballot for Emmy, acting, 1968; Three nominations for Emmy for directing, 1989, 1992, 1993. **Home Addr:** 5140 W Slauson Ave, Los Angeles, CA 90056, **Home Phone:** (213)293-1277. **Business Addr:** President, Lan Ville Inc, 2566 Overland Ave Suite 700, Los Angeles, CA 90064-3367, **Business Phone:** (310)841-2626.

**LANG, ANDREW CHARLES, JR.**
Basketball player. **Personal:** Born Jun 28, 1966, Pine Bluff, AR; married Bronwyn; children: Trey & Chad. **Educ:** Univ Ark, attended 1988. **Career:** Basketball player (retired), chaplain; Phoenix Suns, ctr, 1988-92; Philadelphia 76ers, ctr, 1992-93; Atlanta Hawks, ctr, 1993-96, chaplain, currently; Minn Timberwolves, ctr, 1995-96; Milwaukee Bucks, ctr, 1996-98; Chicago Bulls, ctr, 1998-99; New York Knicks, ctr, 1999-2000. **Home Addr:** 1048 Woodruff Plantation Pkwy SE, Marietta, GA 30067-9106. **Business Addr:** Chaplain, Atlanta Hawks, 101 Marietta St NW Suite 1900, Atlanta, GA 30303, **Business Phone:** (404)827-3800.

**LANG, ANTONIO MAURICE**
Basketball player, basketball coach. **Personal:** Born May 15, 1972, Mobile, AL. **Educ:** Duke Univ, 1994. **Career:** Basketball player (retired), basketball coach; Phoenix Suns, small forward, 1994-95; Cleveland Cavaliers, small forward & guard, 1995-97, 1998-99; Miami Heat, small forward, 1997-98; Toronto Raptors, small forward & guard, 1999-2000; Philadelphia 76ers, forward & guard, 1999-2000; Mitsubishi Melco Dolphins, Japan, 2001-06, asst coach, 2006-10, head coach, 2010-14; Antonio Lang Sports Coun, owner, coach, currently; Utah Jazz, asst coach, 2014-. **Honors/Awds:** Philippine Basketball Association Best Import of the Conference Awardwee, 2001. **Business Addr:** Assistant Coach, Utah Jazz, 301 S Temple, Salt Lake City, UT 84101, **Business Phone:** (801)325-2500.

**LANG, KENARD DUSHUN**
Football player, football coach. **Personal:** Born Jan 31, 1975, Orlando, FL. **Educ:** Univ Miami, BS, lib arts, 1996. **Career:** Football player (retired), coach, free agent, teacher; Wash Redskins, left defensive end, 1997-98, defensive end, 1999-2002; Cleveland Browns, defensive end, 2002-04, 2006, linebacker, 2005; Denver Broncos, defensive end, 2006-07; NFL Denver Broncos, free agt, currently; Edgewater High Sch, asst football coach, 2007-08; Jones High Sch, head football coach, 2008-12; Nike NFTC, defensive line coach, 2012-; Wekiva High Sch, head football coach, 2013-15; Orange County Pub Sch, teacher, 2014. **Orgs:** Founder, Kenard Lang Found, 2002; Make-A-Wish Found. **Honors/Awds:** Big E Rookie of the Year; Defensive Player of the Week, Nat Football League, 1999; Defensive Player of the Week, AFC, 2004; Sportsman of the Year, Onyx. **Special Achievements:** First round pick, NFL Draft, No 17, 1997. **Home Addr:** . **Business Addr:** Head Football Coach, Wekiva High School, 2501 N Hiawassee Rd, Apopka, NY 32703, **Business Phone:** (407)297-4900.

**LANG, MARK**
Educator, teacher. **Educ:** Edith Cowan Univ, music; Wayne State Univ. **Career:** Snowden Elem Sch, music instr, teacher; Aurora High Sch, music instr, teacher; Pitt Community Col, music instr, teacher; Wayne County Community Col Dist, music instr, teacher, Downtown Campus, vice chancellor admin & finance, Eastern Campus, Entrepreneurial Inst & Resource Ctr provost, currently. **Orgs:** Prin Percussionist & Vocalist, abwe; exec dir, Southwest Detroit Immigrant & Refugee Ctr. **Business Addr:** Provost, Wayne County Community College District, 801 W Fort St, Detroit, MI 48226, **Business Phone:** (313)496-2600.

**LANG, DR. MARVEL**
Educator. **Personal:** Born Apr 2, 1949, Bay Springs, MS; son of Otha Sr and Hattie Denham; married Mozell Pentecost; children: Martin & Maya Susan Goree. **Educ:** Jackson State Univ, BA, 1970; Univ Pittsburgh, MA, 1975; Mich State Univ, PhD, 1979. **Career:** Lansing Community Col, 1976-78; Jackson State Univ, assoc prof, 1978-84; US Census Bur, res geogr, 1984-86; Contemp Urban Am, ed, 1986-91; US Census Bur Wash, DC, prof researcher; Walden Univ, fac, currently; Mich State Univ, Ctr Urban Affairs, dir & prof, currently. **Orgs:** Govs Coun Selective Serv, 1969-70; Nat Youth Adv Coun Selective Ser, 1969-70; steering comt mem, Southeastern Asn Am Geographers, 1980-81; consult, Miss Inst Small Towns, 1980-84; bd mem, Cath Social Servs St Vincents Cs Home, 1986-89; Boys & Girls Clubs Lansing, 1986-89; adv bd mem, Mich Legis Black Caucus Found, 1987-90; gov bd mem, Urban Affairs Asn; ed bd mem, Jour Urban Affairs, Urban Affairs Quart. **Home Addr:** 3700 Colchester Rd, Lansing, MI 48906, **Home Phone:** (517)323-8204. **Business Addr:** Faculty, Walden University, 155 5th Ave, Minneapolis, MN 55401, **Business Phone:** (612)925-3368.

**LANG-JETER, LULA L.**
Government official. **Personal:** Born Pickens County, AL. **Educ:** Cent State Univ, BS, 1951, attended 1970; Wright State Univ Grad Sch, attended 1969. **Career:** Internal Revenue Servs, auditor & supvr, 1963-71, br chief, 1971-78, sr exec, 1979-; Cent State Univ, supvr acct, 1968; Imp Ct Daughters Isis, imp internal auditor, currently; Arlington Va Chap, pres & corresp secy; Prince Hall Shriners Found, pres. **Orgs:** Co-chairperson, N VA Minority Task Force Am Cancer Soc; Am Inst Parliamentarians; partic, Nat Urban League's Black Exec Exchange Prog; Soc Women Accts; local pres & nat treas, Alpha Kappa Alpha Sor Inc; League Women Voters; life mem, Nat Coun Negro Women; bd dir, YM-YWCA, 1962-83; Nat Adv Bd Asn Improv Minorities, 1981-; nat treas, Alpha Kappa Alpha Educ Advan Found, 1982-; Nat Adv Bd Federally Employed Women, 1983-; pub rels, Arlington Chap Links, 1984-; nat treas, Links; bd dir, Va Hosp Ctr. **Home Addr:** 1001 S Queen St, Arlington, VA 22204-4732, **Home Phone:** (703)920-1268. **Business Addr:** Imperial Internal Auditor, Imperial Court Daughters of Isis, 3454 Oak Alley Ct, Toledo, OH 43606-9998, **Business Phone:** (419)720-9393.

**LANGE, LAJUNE THOMAS**
Judge, educator. **Personal:** Born Jan 29, 1946, Kansas City, MO; daughter of Thomas P. **Educ:** Augsburg Col, BA, psychol, 1975; Univ Minn Law Sch, JD, 1978; Minn Inst Criminal Justice, 1979; Harvard Law Sch, advan training prog, 1984, employ discrimination, 1985, Judicial Scholars Prog, 1987; Nat Judicial Col, advan gen jurisdiction, 1985, drugs & courts, 1989. **Career:** Judge (retired), educator; Twin Cities Opportunities Industrialization Ctr, counr, 1967; Univ Minn, Dept Civil Rights, field rep, 1968-70; Harry Davis Mayoral Campaign, media & pub rel staff vol, 1971; Dorsey, Marquart, Windhorst, W & Halladay, legal asst, 1971-73; self-employed, civillitigation matters, 1973-74; Oppenheimer, Wolff, Foster, Shepard & Donnelly, legal asst litigation, 1974-75; Hennepin County Pub Defender's Off, law clerk, 1976-78, asst pub defender, 1978-85; Nat Inst Trial Advocacy, fac, 1980; William Mitchell Col Law, civil rights clin, clin prof, adj prof, 1984-, trial advocacy, adj prof, 1983-; Hennepin County Munic Ct, judge, 1985-86; 4th Judicial Dist, judge; chmn, Independent Nat Electoral Comn. **Orgs:** Founding mem, Minn Minority Lawyers Asn, 1980-; bd dir, Minn Women Lawyers; co-chair, pub rel comt, Minn Women Lawyers, 1977-; comnr, Minn Civil Rights Comn, 1979-84, chair person, stand & procuedures comt; Nat Bar Asn; judicial coun, int law comt, criminal law & juv justice comt; impact drugs crime, educ & social welfare, Gov's Select Comt; chairperson, Nat Asn Women Judges; minority affairs comt, nominating comt, Nat Bar Asn judicial Coun; bd dir, Penumbra Theatre Co; adv bd mem, chancellor adv coun, Univ Minn; sr fel, Roy Wilkins Ctr Human Rel & Social Justice; chief exec, La June Thomas Lange Int Leadership Inst; bd mem, dir, Servant Leaders Support Inc; pres, founder, Int Leadership Institut; adv bd mem, Womens Forum Res & Training. **Business Addr:** Directors, Servant Leaders Support Inc, 2202 Storland Rd, Eagan, MN 55122, **Business Phone:** (651)402-6175.

**LANGE, TED W. (THEODORE WILLIAM LANGE)**
Actor. **Personal:** Born Jan 5, 1948, Oakland, CA; son of Ted and Geraldine L; married Sherryl Thompson; children: Ted IV & Turner Wallace; married Mary Ley. **Educ:** San Francisco City Col; Merritt Jr Col. **Career:** San Francisco City Col, fac; Univ Calif, fac; George Washington Univ, fac; "Othello", producer, dir & actor. Plays: Love Boat segment "Starmaker", 1981; "Driving Miss Daisy"; "Lemon Meringue Facade", 1998; "Family Matters". Films: Wattstax, 1973; Trick Baby, 1973; Blade, 1973; Larry; Passing Through, writer, 1977; The Redemption, 2000; Is This Your Mother, 2002; Banana Moon, co-producer, 2003; Gang of Roses, 2003; Monster Movie, 2006; Dorm Daze 2, 2006; Uncle Tom's Apartment, 2006; Last of the Romantics, 2007; Senior Skip Day, 2008; Who Shot Mamba?, 2008; The Adventures of Umbweki, 2008; Phil Cobb's Dinner for Four, 2008; For Love of Amy, dir, 2008. TV specials: "The Big Buttingin Episode", 2003; "Guitar", 2004; "Mindy's Back", 2005, "All of Us", dir, 2005; "Eve", dir, 2003; "Bottoms Up", 2006; "TV L &: Myths & Legends", 2007; Maxim Mag, writer; Psych, dir, 2008; "The First Family", dir, 2012; Movie: Steps of Faith, 2014; A Remarkable Life, 2016. **Orgs:** Am Film Inst, Musical Hair. **Honors/Awds:** Renaissance Man Theatre Award; The Heroes and Legends HAL Lifetime Achievement Award; The Dramalogue Award; James Cagney Directing Fellow Scholarship Award, Am Film Inst; Paul Robeson Awar, Oakland's Ensemble Theatre; Bartender of

the Year, 1983; Certificate of Achievement, Black Film makers Hall of Fame, 1989. **Special Achievements:** Book: "Ask Isaac", 2006. **Business Addr:** Actor, Artist Group, 1930 Sentry Pk W Suite 303, Los Angeles, CA 90067.

### LANGFORD, DARIA
Executive. **Educ:** Univ Ill, Chicago. **Career:** Jr High Sch, teacher; RCA, regional promotions mgr; Virgin Rec, promotions & sales; Mercury Rec, vpres, R& B promotions & sales, nat field dir; La Face Rec, sr vpres promotions & mkt, currently. **Business Addr:** Senior Vice President, LaFace Records, 1 Capital City Plz, Atlanta, GA 30326, **Business Phone:** (404)848-8050.

### LANGFORD, DEBRA LYNN
Executive. **Personal:** Born Mar 27, 1963, Los Angeles, CA; daughter of Roland and Barbara Jean Wilkins. **Educ:** Univ Southern Calif, Marshall Sch Bus, BS, bus admin, mkt & advert, 1984. **Career:** Golden Bird, dir mkt & advert, 1984-86; Hanna-Barbera Prod, dir develop, 1986-89; Warner Bros TV, dir current prog, 1988-92, vpres current programming, 1992-93; Quincy Jones Entertainment, vpres TV, 1992-97; Essence Mag, gen mgr & vpres, essence entertainment, 1998-2000; UrbanEntertainment.com, sr vpres, prod & develop, 2000-02; Warner Bros, sr vpres current programming, 2002; Time Warner Inc, dir strategic sourcing, 2003, exec dir strategic sourcing, corp vpres strategic sourcing, 2002-09; NBC Universal, corp vpres Inclusion & Bus Diversity, 2009-11; Langford Co, chief exec officer & Prin, 2012-; Univ Southern Calif Marshall Sch Bus, assoc dir, Diversity Progs, 2013-. **Orgs:** Nat Asn Female Exec, 1988-; Nat Asn Advan Colored People, 1989-; African Am Film & TV Asn, 1989-; Kwanza, 1989-; steering cot, Black Entertainment Alliance, 1990-. **Business Addr:** Associate Director, University of Southern California Marshall School of Business, 3670 Trousdale Pkwy, Los Angeles, CA 90089, **Business Phone:** (213)740-8674.

### LANGFORD, HON. DENISE MORRIS
Judge. **Personal:** Born Jan 1, 1953, Detroit, MI. **Educ:** Wayne State Univ, BA, guid & coun, 1975, MA, 1978; Univ Detroit, Sch Law, JD, 1982. **Career:** Child welfare worker; State Dept Social Serv, protective serv investr; Oakland Co, trial atty & asst prosecuting atty, 1984; Sixth Judicial Circuit Ct Mich, US Atty's Off, asst US atty, judge, 1992-. **Orgs:** Fed Bar Asn; Nat Bar Asn; Nat Asn Women Judges; Am Bar Asn; bd dir, Mich Judges Asn; Black Judges Asn; gov bd mem, Oakland-Livingston Human Servs Agency; bd mem, Salvation Army, William Booth Legal Aid Clin; bd mem, St Joseph Mercy Hosp; Wolverine Bar Asn; bd dir, D Augustus Straker Bar Asn; Oakland Co Bar Asn; Access Justice Group, Mich Supreme Ct; bd mem, child abuse & neglect coun; Univ Detroit Mercy; Women Officials Network & Women Lawyers Asn Mich. **Honors/Awds:** Cert of Recognition, Judicial Admini Div, Am Bar Asn; Us Dept of Agr Award, 1991; Cert of Recognition, Southeastern Mich Asn Chiefs Police; Wonder Woman Award, Women's Survival Ctr, 1993; Break the Glass Ceiling Award, Pontiac Urban League; Judicial Award, Nat Asn Advan Colored People, 1994; Sprit of Detroit Award, 1998; Professor Award, Oakland Co Bar Asn, 1998; Appreciation Award, Fed Bar Asn, 1998; Distinguished Alumni of the Year, Univ Detroit, 1998; Pontiac Urban League-Break the Glass Ceiling Award; Powerful Women of Purpose in the Legal Field, Rhonda Walker Foundation, 2008; Excellence in Law & Justice Award, 2009; Courage in Leadership Award, North Oakland NAACP William Waterman, 2009; One of Detroits Best Award, Native Detroiter Magazine. **Special Achievements:** First African American judge to serve at Oakland County Circuit Court; First African American elected to a county government position; Named one of Most Influention African-Am Women in Metro Detroit, 1998; Longest serving female judge on the Bench. **Business Addr:** Judge, 6th Judicial Circuit of Michigan, Bldg 12 E 1200 N Tel, Pontiac, MI 48341, **Business Phone:** (248)858-0363.

### LANGFORD, JEVON (JEVON DICORIOUS LANGFORD)
Boxer, football player. **Personal:** Born Feb 16, 1974, Washington, DC; son of Howard and Mary; married Jayna; children: 2. **Educ:** Okla State Univ. **Career:** Football player (retired), coach, boxer; football coach, 1984-94; Ohio State Univ, defensive end, 1993-95; Cincinnati Bengals, defensive end, 1996-2001; prof boxer, 2001-; Functional Conditioning, coach, currently. **Home Addr:** , Denver, CO. **Business Addr:** Coach, Functional Conditioning, 8120 Sheridan Blvd B 101, Westminster, CO 80003, **Business Phone:** (303)467-7954.

### LANGFORD, REV. VICTOR C., III
Clergy, army officer, president (organization). **Personal:** Born Aug 6, 1939, Detroit, MI; son of Victor Jr and Charlotte; married Luana Calvert; children: Tanya, Natalie, Kineta & Victor IV. **Educ:** Seattle Pac Col, BA, hist, 1970; Concordia Theol Sem, BDiv, 1970, MDiv, 1975. **Career:** National guard (retired), pastor; Nat Guard Bur, nat guard; Bethel Lutheran Church New Orleans, founder & pastor, 1962-64; Holy Cross Lutheran Church Houston, pastor, 1965-68; Lutheran Church Good Shepherd, Seattle, pastor, 1968-76; St Mark's Lutheran Church, minister, 1976-, pres, Parish pastor, currently; Seattle Pac Univ, instr, 1978; Seattle Univ, instr, 1978, 1980; Nu-Life Enterprises, pres, 1979-86; Army Nat Guard, asst chief chaplains, 1997-98; Lutheran Partners Mag, ed assoc; 3rd Battalion, battalion chaplain; 181st Support Battalion, battalion chaplain; 66th Aviation Brigade, battalion chaplain; Wash Army Nat Guard, state area command chaplain. **Orgs:** Treas, Black United Clergy Action, 1969-76; bd dir, Seattle Opportunities Indust Ctr, 1969-86; Nat Asn Advan Colored People, 1969-; chmn, Proj People Seattle, 1970-72; chmn exec com, Emerg Feeding Prog, Seattle, 1977-86; organizer & chmn, Filling Gap Conf March 26 & 27, 1982; exec bd, Asn Black Lutherans, 1983-87; exec comt bd dir, Church Coun Greater Seattle, 1983-86; pres, Aid Asn Lutherans, 1983-; ed assoc, Lutheran Partners Mag, 1985-; assoc educ, Lutheran Partners Mag, 1985-; exec bd, PNW Synod Lutheran Church Am, 1986-87; NW Wash Synod Coun, 1988-89; founding bd chmn, Emerald City Bank, Seattle, WA, 1988; pres, African Am Lutheran Asn, 1991-93; dean, Cluster 8, NW Wash Synod, ELCA, 1994; pres, Faith Ministries, 1996-; ELCA Lutheran/Orthodox Dialogue Comn; mem ministry teams, St Mark's Lutheran Church. **Honors/Awds:** Juneteenth Fathers Day Award, Future Prod Seattle, 1977. **Special Achievements:** First African-American general appointed in the Washington National Guard. **Home Addr:** 1200 NE 106th St, Seattle, WA 98125-7537, **Home Phone:** (206)365-2966. **Business Addr:** Parish Pastor, St Mark's Lutheran Church, 6020 Beacon Ave S, Seattle, WA 98108-3106, **Business Phone:** (206)722-5165.

### LANGHAM, COLLIE ANTONIO
Football player. **Personal:** Born Jul 31, 1972, Town Creek, AL; son of Willie and Deborah. **Educ:** Univ Ala, grad. **Career:** Football player (retired); Cleveland Browns, left defensive back, 1994-95, 1999; Baltimore Ravens, left defensive back, 1996-97; San Francisco 49ers, left defensive back, 1998; New Eng Patriots, cornerback, free safety, right cornerback, 2000. **Honors/Awds:** Consensus National Championship, 1992; Jim Thorpe Award, 1993; Jack Tatum Trophy, 1993; Defensive Player of the Year, Nat Football League Players Asn, 1994; Defensive Player of the Year, Football Digest, 1994. **Special Achievements:** Film: 1994 NFL Draft, 1994.

### LANGHAM, JOHN M.
Executive. **Personal:** Born Jan 1, 1927?; married Carvine; children: John Jr & Jimmy. **Educ:** Ala A & M, Ala State Col; Univ Southern Ala, phys sci. **Career:** Prichard Trading Post; self-employed. **Orgs:** Pres, PTA Mobile Co; pres, Toulminville Recreation Ctr; pres, Prichard City Coun; Ala & Am Teachers Asn; bd dir, Commonwealth Nat Bank; mem adv bd, Bishop State Jr Col; pres, Prichard Nat Asn Advan Colored People; supvry comn, Mobile Co Personnel Bd; Mobile United; Nat League Cities; Joint Ctr Polit Action; Southern Black Caucus Elected Officials; Nat Dem Party; Prichard Sr Citizen Org; ACT Educ Prog. **Honors/Awds:** Pichard C Of C week; Kappa Citizen of the Year.

### LANGSTON, DR. ESTHER J.
Educator. **Personal:** Born Jun 20, 1939, Shreveport, LA; daughter of Frank Jones and Daisy. **Educ:** Wiley Col, BA, bus educ, 1963; San Diego State Univ, MSW, 1970; Univ Southern Calif, cert, social work/geront, 1974; Univ Tex, PhD, human serv admin, 1982. **Career:** Nev State Welfare Dept, child specialist, 1965-70; Santee Sch Dist, social worke, 1969-70; Univ Nev Las Vegas, lectr, 1970-84, assoc prof, 1974-89, emer prof, 1980-, Baccalaureate prog coordr, 1989-93, interim dir, 1993-94, dir, 1998-2003, dir, Family Support Div, 2003-, prof, Social Work, 2003-08, Ctr Acad Advan & Enrichment, dir, currently; Univ Of Tex, Arlington, curric coordr specialist, 1979-81; Jet Away Travel, co-owner, 1982-84. **Orgs:** Social worker, San Diego C's Home, 1968-69; Child Welfare Worker, Dept Social Serv, 1969; bd mem, Oper Life Community Develop Corp, 1977-79, 2003-06; proj dir, Minorities Pub Policies & Laws & Their Effect Serv Delivery, 1977; pres, LV Chap Nat Asn Black Social Workers, 1983-85; fac senate, Univ Nev Las Vegas, 1984-85; pres, undergrad fac & assoc mem bd, Coun Social Work Educ, 1984-85; vice chairperson, Gov's Comn Ment Health M/R, 1985-89; vpres & bd dir, exec dir, Aids AIDS Nev, 1988-90; pres, Les Femes Douze, 1990-94, 1996-; pres, Nev Chap, Nat Asn Social Workers, 1996-98, Legal Defense Comn, 1997-2000; bd dir, BACC Prog dir, 1997-2000; Delta Sigma Theta Sorority. **Home Addr:** 1943 Hobson Dr, Henderson, NV 89014-1002, **Home Phone:** (702)458-3618. **Business Addr:** Director, University of Nevada, 4505 Md Pkwy CDC 10 Rm 1026, Las Vegas, NV 89154-5032, **Business Phone:** (702)895-4338.

### LANGSTON-JACKSON, WILMETTA ANN SMITH
Educator. **Personal:** Born Sep 16, 1935, Burlington, IA; daughter of William Amos Sr and Inez Jane Wallace; married Robert; children: Charles N III; married Robert; children: Robert Jackson Jr. **Educ:** Ft Valley State Col, Ft Valley, GA, BS, 1966; Atlanta Univ, Atlanta, GA, MLS, 1976. **Career:** Educator, administrator (retired); Fort Valley State Col, Div Vocational Home Econs, intermediate stenographer, 1960-64, Div Educ, secy, 1965-67; Houston County Bd Educ, Perry, Ga, media specialist, teacher, librn, 1967-88; Civil Serv, Warner Robins, Ga, comput programmer asst, 1988-94; Fort Valley State Col UNIV, adjunct Eng & instr, 1988-2000; libr, 2003-04. **Orgs:** Pres, Pink Ladies, Peach County Hosp; Sunday sch supt, youth dir, Trinity Baptist Church, 1954-; Middle GEO Girl Scouts, 1968-2003, bd, 1993-97; leadership team mem, Delta Sigma Theta Sorority, 1989-91; recording secy, GEO coun Auxiliaries, 1989-91, central district dir, 1996-98; Fort Valley State Col NAT Alumni ASN, bd, asst secy & secy, hist, life mem, 1990-93, 1994-2002; Peach County Pub Librs, bd trustee, 1992-2004; bd mem, Peach County Unit, Am Heart Asn; Atlanta Univ Nat Alumni Asn, Fort Valley Area Alumni Chap, charter mem, pres; life mem, NARFE; life mem, Nat Asn Advan Colored People; life mem, Georgia TCRs Asn; life mem, GSUSA; life mem, Nat Educ Asn; life mem, GaE; Ft Valley Area Alumni Chap, secy; secy, Peach County health Educ & Wellness Coalition, 1990-; charter mem, Women Military Serv Am. **Home Addr:** PO Box 1413, Ft Valley, GA 31030, **Home Phone:** (912)825-8675.

### LANIER, ANTHONY WAYNE
Editor. **Personal:** Born Aug 13, 1957, Louisville, KY; son of Austin and Ida Mae Smith; married Carlene Grace Foreman. **Educ:** Western KY Univ, BFA, 1980; Univ Louisville, MA, prog, 1982. **Career:** Reza Inc, graphic artist, 1981-82; US, cartogr asst, 1981-82; Courier-J, Louisville, Ky, news artist, 1984-90; Courier-J Newspaper, staff artist, 1984-90; USA Today, info graphics asst, 1988-89; Patriot Ledger, Quincy, Mass, graphics ed, 1990-98; freelance photogr. **Orgs:** Club, mentor, 1990-93; treas, Boston Asn Black Journalists, 1990-95; Soc Newspaper Design, 1990, bd, 1996; New Eng Soc Newspaper Eds, 1990; bd dir, New Eng Press Asn, 1993-96; Region One treas, Nat Asn Black Journalists, 1993-96; mid adult ministry coordr, Concord Baptist Church, 1994-95. **Honors/Awds:** Newspaper Design Sem participant, Am Press Inst, 1985; Black Achiever Volunteer Service Award, YMCA, Chestnut St Branch, 1987; The Club, Outstanding Service Award, Mentor, 1991-93; Nat Asn Black Journalists, Inst Journalism Educ Fel, 1992. **Special Achievements:** The JB Speed Museum, 10th Annual Black Artists Exhibition, 1990. **Home Addr:** 3 Douglass Pk Suite 319, Boston, MA 02118-1076, **Home Phone:** (617)445-8681.

### LANIER, GAYLE S.
Vice president (organization). **Personal:** daughter of Harmon Seawell Jrmarried Dwain K. **Educ:** NC State Univ, BS, indust engineering, 1982. **Career:** Nortel Networks, Nortel Knowledge Serv, vpres global corp opers & gen mgr time-div multiplexing; Progress Energy, vpres corp serv; Duke Energy Corp, sr vpres & chief customer officer, currently. **Orgs:** Bd trustee, NC State Univ, 2007-12. **Honors/Awds:** Distinguished Engineering Alumnus Award, NC State Univ, 2008; 25 Influential Black Women in Business, "The Network Journal: Black Professionals & Small Business Magazine", 2009. **Special Achievements:** Established Dwain K. & Gayle S. Lanier Endowment at North Carolina State University for minority engineering students in 2003. **Home Addr:** 2112 Oakton Dr, Raleigh, NC 27606-8908, **Home Phone:** (919)859-0659. **Business Addr:** Senior Vice President, Chief Customer Officer, Duke Energy Corp, 526 S Church St, Charlotte, NC 28202, **Business Phone:** (704)594-6200.

### LANIER, HORATIO AXEL (RAY LANIER)
Association executive, president (organization). **Personal:** Born Feb 7, 1955, Augusta, GA. **Educ:** Univ Ga, AB, jour, 1977; Georgetown Univ Law Ctr, JD, 1987; Columbia Col, MA, conflict resolution. **Career:** Southern Bell Tel Co, bus off mgr, 1977-79; Xerox Corp, mkt rep, 1980-82; Sears Bus Syst Ctr, mkt rep, 1982-84; US Justice Dept Off Legal Coun, legal edl asst, 1984-85; H Lanier Small Bus Develop Consult, pres, 1985-86; Nat Black Alumni Asn, nat pres, 1986-; Wash Metrop Area Transit Authority, Sr EEO & dispute resolution officer, currently. **Orgs:** Pres, Univ Ga Black Alumni Asn, 1980-82; Univ Ga Bicentennial Planning Comn, 1984-85; vice chmn, Black Law Stud Asn Georgetown Law Ctr, 1985-86; exec producer, UHURU Performing Arts Ensemble Georgetown Law Ctr, 1985-87; Am Bar Asn, 1986-; Nat Bar Asn, 1987-; pres & bd dir, Asn Conflict Resolution, 2006-; co chair, Mem & Develop Comts; Workplace Sect Leadership Coun; Diversity & Equity Comt; Governance Comt. **Business Addr:** President, Board of Directors, Association for Conflict Resolution, 1015 18th St NW Suite 1150, Washington, DC 20036, **Business Phone:** (202)464-9700.

### LANIER, JESSE M., SR.
Executive. **Personal:** Born May 2, 1941, Bath, NC; son of Daniel Sr and Beather O; married Barbara M; children: Audrey, Jesse Jr & Lucinda. **Educ:** NC A&T State Univ, BS, bus admin, 1968; Univ New Haven, MBA prog, 1973. **Career:** Lanier Trucking Co, partner & operator, 1959-69; C W Blakeslee & Sons Construct, acct, 1968-70; Southern New Eng Tel Co, staff acct, ade serv staff asst, cot rel mgr & purchasing mgr, 1970-83; Springfield Food Syst Inc, pres & chief exec officer, 1983-. **Orgs:** Life mem, NCP, 1972-; pres, NC A&T Alumni Asn, 1975-; Nat Asn Purchasing Mgr, 1980-; Asn Ky Fried Chicken Franchisee Inc, 1985-; officer, Urban League Springfield Inc, Mass, 1987-, bd chairperson, 1997-; bd mem, Greater Springfield Chamber Com, 1988-92; bd mem, KFC Minority Franchisee Asn, 1989-; bd mem, Jr Achievement Western Mas Inc, 1992-; New England Chamber Com. **Home Addr:** 310 Thompsonville Rd, Suffield, CT 06078-1312, **Home Phone:** (203)668-2523. **Business Addr:** President, Chief Executive Officer, Springfield Food System Inc, 644 State St, Springfield, MA 01109, **Business Phone:** (413)733-4300.

**LANIER, MARSHALL LEE. See Obituaries Section.**

**LANIER, RAY. See LANIER, HORATIO AXEL.**

### LANIER, ROB (ROBERT A LANIER)
Basketball player, basketball coach. **Personal:** Born Jul 24, 1968, Buffalo, NY; son of Bob; married Dayo; children: Emory & Kai. **Educ:** St Bonaventure Univ, psychol, 1990; Niagara Univ, MA, educ coun, 1993. **Career:** Basketball player (retired), basketball coach; Niagara Univ, grad asst & restricted earnings coach, 1990-92; St Bonaventure Univ, guard, 1986-90, asst coach, 1992-97; Rutgers Univ, asst coach, 1997-99; Univ Tex, recruiter, 1999-2001, asst mens head basketball coach, 2011-; Siena Col, head men's basketball coach, 2001-05; Univ Va, asst coach, 2005-07; Univ Fla, asst coach, 2007-10. **Business Addr:** Associate Head Men's Basketball Coach, University of Texas, 3102 Oak Lawn Ave Suite 350, Dallas, TX 75219, **Business Phone:** (214)526-2386.

### LANIER, SHELBY, JR.
Police officer. **Personal:** Born Apr 20, 1936, Louisville, KY; son of Shelby and Florine Bridgeman; children: Michael, Ricardo, Stephanie, Rasheedah & Ciara. **Educ:** Cent State Univ, Wilberforce, OH, 1956; Univ Louisville, Louisville, KY, BS, 1975. **Career:** Police officer (retired); Louisville Div Police, Louisville, Ky, detective, 1961-92. **Orgs:** Pres, Black Police Officers Orgn, 1971; Comnr, Metro Jr Football League, 1980-89; pres, Louisville Br Nat Asn Advan Colored People, 1988-92; chmn, Nat Black Police Asn, 1990-92; pres, Louisville Black Police Officers Org, 1990-92. **Honors/Awds:** Equality Award, Louisville Urban League, 1972; Citizen of the Year, Omega Psi Phi Fraternity, 1984; Outstanding Community Involvement, World Community Islam, 1986; Renault Robinson Award, Nat Black Police Asn, 1989; Community Service Award, Louisville Defender Newspaper, 1989. **Home Addr:** 3634 Breckenridge Lane, Louisville, KY 40218, **Home Phone:** (502)491-3429.

### LANIER, WILLIE EDWARD
Executive, football player. **Personal:** Born Aug 21, 1945, Clover, VA. **Educ:** Morgan State Univ, BS, bus admin. **Career:** Football player (retired), executive; Kans City Chiefs, Right linebacker, 1967, Middle linebacker, 1968-77; Baltimore Colts, 1978; Wheat First Butcher & Singer, sr vpres; First Union Securities, stock broker, dir bus develop & vice-chmn; Wachovia Securities, sr vpres, currently; Marriott Int, exec vpres & gen coun. **Orgs:** Bd visitor, Va State Univ; United Way Greater Richmond; YMCA; Garfield Childs Fund; WCVE Pub TV, Cent Va; Indust Develop Authority Chesterfield City; bd dirs, Huddle House Inc; bd dir, Venture Richmond; Pigskin Club Wash; Pro Football Hall Fame; adv bd mem, Crossflo Systs Inc. **Honors/Awds:** Man of the Year, Nat Football league, 1972; Linebacker of the Year, NFL Players Asn, 1970-75; Chiefs Super Bowl IV, Defensive Star; All AFL

& AFC, seven times; AFL All Star Games; six Pro Bowls; Hall of Fame, Kansas City Chiefs, 1985; Pro Football Hall of Fame, 1986; Virginia Sports Hall of Fame, 1986; Virginian of the Year, 1986; National Football League 75thAnniversary Team, 1995. **Special Achievements:** First African-American to play at middle linebacker position. **Home Addr:** 2911 W Brigstock Rd, Midlothian, VA 23113, **Home Phone:** (804)794-4328. **Business Addr:** Senior Vice President, Wachovia Securities, Riverfront Plz 901 E Byrd St, Richmond, VA 23219-4052, **Business Phone:** (804)649-2311.

### LANKFORD, RAYMOND LEWIS

Baseball player. **Personal:** Born Jun 5, 1967, Los Angeles, CA; married Yolanda M; children: Raquel & Danielle. **Educ:** Modesto Junior Col. **Career:** Baseball player (retired); St Louis Cardinals, outfielder, 1990-2001, 2004; San Diego Padres, 2001-02. **Honors/Awds:** Midwest League, 1988, Texas League Most Valuable Player, 1989; Texas League, 1989; American Association, 1990; National League Player-of-the-Week September 4-10, 1995; National League Outfield Fielding Champion, 1996; National League All-Star Team, 1997; Baseball Man of the Year, St Louis Chap Baseball Writers Asn Am, 1997. **Home Addr:** 15 Terry Hill Lane, Saint Louis, MO 63131-2422.

### LANSEY, YVONNE F.

Banker, executive. **Personal:** Born Sep 9, 1946, Baltimore, MD; daughter of E Gaines Sr and Priscilla. **Educ:** Morgan State Univ, Baltimore, MD, BS, 1969; Long Island Univ, Brooklyn, NY, MBA, 1974. **Career:** Fed Res Bank NY, credit analyst, 1969-74; Xerox Corp, Rochester, NY, financial analyst, 1974-76; Westinghouse Elec Corp, Hunt Valley, Md, financial analyst, 1976-79, proj dir, 1979-85; Ideal Fed Savings Bank, Baltimore, Md, vpres, 1985-88, pres & chief exec officer, 1988-; Real Estate Appraiser & Home Inspector Comn, Baltimore, Md, comnr, currently. **Orgs:** Trustee, Florence Crittenton Servs, 1986; trustee, Girl Scouts Cent Md, 1987; trustee, Combined Health Agencies Inc, 1987; financial secy, The Links Inc, Harbor City Chap, 1987-89; bd dir & secy, Am League Financial Insts, Wash, DC, 1988; trustee, Baltimore Mus Art, 1989; Alpha Kappa Alpha Sorority; secy, Baltimore Community Lending. **Honors/Awds:** Women on the Move, Sigma Gamma Rho, 1986; Booker T Washington Business League of Baltimore, 1989. **Home Addr:** 3303 Glen Ave, Baltimore, MD 21215, **Home Phone:** (410)542-4480. **Business Addr:** President, Chief Executive Officer, Ideal Federal Savings Bank, 1629 Druid Hill Ave Suite 6, Baltimore, MD 21217-0888, **Business Phone:** (410)669-1629.

### LAPOINT, DR. VELMA

College teacher. **Educ:** Hartford Univ, W Hartford, CT, BS, elem educ/sociol; Mich State Univ, E Lansing, MI, MA, coun, PhD, coun. **Career:** Howard Univ, Sch Educ, Sch Human Ecol, asst dean, 1987-92, Sch Educ, assoc dean, 1993-94, Dept Human Develop & Psychoeducational Studies, assoc prof, Sch Educ, Grad Sch, assoc prof, 1993-2005, assoc prof, Grad Sch, 1993-, Dept Human Develop & Psychoeducational Studies, from assoc prof to prof, 1993-. **Orgs:** Socs Res Child Develop; Educ Res Asn; Am Psychol Asn; Psychologists Social Responsibility; Socs Study Social Issues; Nat & Local Bd Mem; bd mem, Campaign Com Free Childhood; Healthy Community Stores Nat Network, Philadelphia, PA; Judge Baker Childrens Ctr, Harvard Univ, 2001-; Am Psychol Asn, 2002-03; mem, Adv Comt to Task Force Advert to C, Am Psychol Asn, 2002-03; mem, bd dir, Kids Can Make a Difference, Mystic, CT, 2004-; Johns Hopkins Bloomberg Sch Pub Health, 2004-; chair, SRCD Black Caucus, 2005-07; mem, trustee Coun, Wash Waldorf Sch, Bethesda, MD, 2005-. **Business Addr:** Professor of Human Development, Howard University School of Education, 2400 6th St NW, Washington, DC 20059, **Business Phone:** (202)806-6514.

### LARA, EDISON R., SR.

Executive. **Personal:** married Genevieve; children: Cecelia E, Valencia Ann, Edison Jr & Alysanne. **Career:** Co Club Malt Liquor, regional mgr; Westside Distributors, chief exec officer, pres, 1974-. **Orgs:** Black Bus Asn; YMCA; adv bd, Calif State Univ; UNCF Leadership Coun; Los Angeles Urban League; 100 Black Men; Tee Masters Golf Club; CBBD; NBWA. **Business Addr:** Chief Executive Officer, President, Westside Distributors, 2405 Southern Ave, South Gate, CA 90033-4219, **Business Phone:** (323)566-2304.

### LARGE, JERRY D.

Journalist. **Personal:** Born Jan 15, 1954, Clovis, NM; son of Viola Bailey; married Carey Gelernter. **Educ:** NMex State Univ, Las Cruces, NM, BA, jour & mass commun, 1976. **Career:** Farmington Daily Times, Farmington, NMex, reporter, 1976-77; El Paso Times, El Paso, Tex, reporter, 1977-80; Oakland Tribune, Oakland, Calif, copy ed, 1980-81; Seattle Times, Wash, asst city ed, 1981-92, columnist, 1993-; Knight fel, Stanford Univ, 2000-01. **Orgs:** Soc Prof Journalists, 1977-; Nat Asn Black Journalists, 1983-; treas, Black Journalists Asn Seattle, 1989-90. **Home Addr:** 4109 49th Ave S, Seattle, WA 98118-1229. **Business Addr:** Columnist, The Seattle Times, 1120 John St, Seattle, WA 98109, **Business Phone:** (206)464-3346.

### LARKE, CHARLES G.

School administrator. **Personal:** Born Kathwood, SC; son of Alvin and Staretha (deceased); children: Charles Derrick. **Educ:** Paine Col, BS, math, 1969; Univ SC, MEd, 1978; Univ Ga, cert, educ spec voc educ, 1983, DEd, 1987; Augusta Col, bus admin; Ga Tech, cert, environ sci; Ga State Univ, cert, voc curric supv. **Career:** Tutt High Sch, algebra teacher; Westside High Sch, algebra, acct & bus math teacher, 1970-84, cordor, Voc Acad Educ Prog, 1979-84, asst prin, 1984; Richmond County Pub Schs, dir sec voc educ, 1984-86, asst supt voc serv, 1986-95, interim supt, 1995-96, supt, 1996-. **Orgs:** Nat Educ Asn; Ga Sch Superintendents Asn; Ga Asn Educ Leaders; Richmond County Asn Educrs; Asn Career & Tech Educ; Educ Tech Consortium Adv Comt; Kappa Delta Pi Hon Soc Educ; Beta Kappa, Univ Ga; Sigma Pi Phi Fraternity Alpha Mu Boule; bd dir, Richmond/Burke Workforce Investment Bd; bd dir, Richmond/Burke Job Training Authority; bd dir, Am Red Cross; Boy Scouts Am; St. Catherine CME Church Tabernacle Baptist Church; Augusta-Richmond County Partnership Coun. **Business Addr:** Superintendent, Learning Consultant, Richmond County Public Schools, 864 Broad St, Augusta, GA 30901-1215, **Business Phone:** (706)826-1118.

### LARKIN, BARRY LOUIS

Baseball player, association executive, radio broadcaster. **Personal:** Born Apr 28, 1964, Cincinnati, OH; son of Bob and Shirley; married Lisa Davis; children: Brielle D'Shea, Cymber Nicole & DeShane Davis. **Educ:** Univ Mich, attended 1986. **Career:** Baseball player (retired), baseball coach, executive; Cincinnati Reds, infielder, 1986-2004; Wash Nationals, spec asst to gen mgr; Maj League Baseball Int, Europ Baseball Acad, lead infield instr & studio analyst, 2008-11; ESPN Baseball Tonight, analyst, 2011-. **Home Addr:** 5410 Osprey Isle Lane, Orlando, FL 32819-4015. **Business Addr:** Analyst, ESPN Baseball Tonight, ESPN Plz, Bristol, CT 06010.

### LARKIN, DR. BYRDIE A.

Educator, political scientist. **Personal:** Born Tuskegee, AL; daughter of Charles Haile and Lula Berry; children: Seve Mwangi Leonard. **Educ:** Ala State Univ, BS, 1973; Atlanta Univ, MA, 1975, PhD, 1983. **Career:** Ala State Univ, Dept Polit Sci, asst prof, 1977-82, actg chmn, 1982-85, coordr polit sci prog & assoc prof, currently, polit scientist, currently; Univ Miss, Ford Found fel, 1989. **Orgs:** Alpha Kappa Mu Nat Hon Soc; charter mem, Black Women Academicians; exec bd, Nat Conf Black Polit Scientists; Ala Asn Polit Scientists; chmn, Col Arts &Sci, Courtesy Comt; consult, bd dir, Local Govt Training Inst; Ala Comn Higher, exec bd, pres, Ala Polit Sci Asn; adv coun, Ctr Leadership & Nat Asn Advan Colored People, Ala State Univ; advisor, Pi Sigma Alpha Nat Polit Sci Hon Soc; trustee ministry, Mt Gillard Missionary Baptist Church. **Home Addr:** 114 Mountain Laurel Rd, Prattville, AL 36066-6753, **Home Phone:** (334)358-2463. **Business Addr:** Associate Professor of Political Science, Political Scientist, Alabama State University, GW Trenholm Hall 211, Prattville, AL 36066, **Business Phone:** (334)229-4373.

### LARKIN, MICHAEL TODD

Advertising executive. **Personal:** Born Mar 7, 1963, Cincinnati, OH; son of Robert L and Shirley J; married Sharon Denise Dean. **Educ:** Univ Notre Dame, BA, econ, 1985. **Career:** Cincinnati Reds Shortstop Barry Larkin, personal mgr; Hamer off, Milenthal Spence Inc, sports prom dir, currently. **Home Addr:** 1149 Vineyard Dr, Gurnee, IL 60031-3103. **Business Addr:** Director Sports Promotion, Hameroff Milenthal Spence Inc, 10 W Broad St 14th Fl, Columbus, OH 43215-3499, **Business Phone:** (614)221-7667.

### LARS, BYRON

Fashion designer. **Personal:** Born Jan 19, 1965, Oakland, CA. **Educ:** Brooks Col, AA, 1985; Fashion Inst Technol, attended 1987. **Career:** Freelance sketcher & pattern maker, Kevan Hall, Gary Gatyas, Ronaldus Shamask, Nancy Crystal Blouse Co, NY, 1986-91; showed first collection, 1991; Byron Lars Beauty Mark, fashion designer, 1991-; first full-scale New York show, 1992; En Vogue fashion collection, designer, 1993; Shirttails collection, 1995-97; Cinnabar Sensation Barbie, 1996; launched new collection, Green T, 1999. **Honors/Awds:** USA rep, Int Concours des Jeunes Creatures de Mode, 1986; Festival du Lin, 1989; Vogue Cecil Beaton award, 1990; Rookie of the Year, Women's Wear Daily, 1991. **Home Addr:** 202 W 40th St, New York, NY 10018. **Business Addr:** Fashion Designer, Byron Lars Beauty Mark, 241 W 37th St Suite 401A, New York, NY 10018, **Business Phone:** (212)764-7664.

### LARTIGUE, ROLAND E.

Engineer, executive. **Personal:** Born Mar 3, 1951, Beaumont, TX; son of Homer Sr and Emily; married Dell Malone; children: Jason. **Educ:** Mich State Univ, BS, mech engr, 1973; Xavier Univ, advan bus studies, 1984. **Career:** United Technol Automotive, vpres, pur & logistics, 1991-97, gen mgr, terminals & connectors, 1995-98; Valeo Raytheon, gen mgr, 2000-04, chief exec officer, 2004-08, Siemens Energy Inc, bus develop, 2009, mgr, elec vehicle infrastructure, 2009-; Eastman Kodak, res engr; Rockwell Int, res engr, sls engr, pur mgr & commodity mgr; Columbus Auto Parts, vpres, mat; Stahl Mfg, exec vpres, gen mgr; Saturn Electronics, vpres, gen mgr, currently. **Home Addr:** 29222 Lancaster Dr Apt 206, Southfield, MI 48034-1445, **Home Phone:** (248)352-7019. **Business Addr:** Vice President, Saturn Electronics, 255 Rex Blvd, Auburn Hills, MI 48326-2954, **Business Phone:** (248)299-8529.

### LARVADAIN, EDWARD, JR.

Lawyer. **Personal:** Born Aug 18, 1941, Belle Rose, LA; son of Edward Sr and Maxine; married Patricia Dorsett, Jan 1, 1965; children: Edward III (Cynthia Harvey) & Malcolm X. **Educ:** Southern Univ, BA, Eng, 1963, Law Sch, JD, 1966. **Career:** Ernest Morial, atty, 1966-67; Edward Larvadain Jr & Assoc, atty, currently. **Orgs:** Alexandria Br, NCP, 1968-; La State Bar Asn, 1968-; La Trial Lawyers Asn, 1970-; chair, State NCP Educ, 1985-; comt mem, YMCA Black Achiever, 1989-. **Honors/Awds:** Outstanding Contributions, Sickle Cell Anemia, 1984, 1992; Service Award, EDU, State NCP, 1984; Outstanding Service, 1988; Outstanding Service, Sickle Cell Anemia, 1990; Outstanding Contributions, Girl Scouts, 1992. **Home Addr:** 4207 Whitefield Blvd, Alexandria, LA 71303, **Home Phone:** (318)448-0469. **Business Addr:** Attorney, Edward Larvadain Jr & Associates, 626 8th St, Alexandria, LA 71301-7707, **Business Phone:** (318)445-6717.

### LASALLE, ERIQ (ERIK KI LA SALLE)

Actor, movie director, movie producer. **Personal:** Born Jul 23, 1962, Hartford, CT. **Educ:** NY Univ, BFA, 1984. **Career:** Films: Drop Squad, 1994; Coming to America, 1988; One Hour Photo, 2002; Crazy As Hell actor, producer & dir, 2002; Biker Boyz, 2003; Johnny Was, 2005; Inside Out, 2005; producer: The Salton Sea, 2002; TV series: "ER", 1994-2009; "The Twilight Zone", 2002-03; "Memphis", 2003; "Without a Trace", 2006; "Relative Stranger", 2009; "MegaFault", 2009; "Covert Affairs", 2010; "How to Make It in America", 2011; "A Gifted Man", 2012; TV Movies: Rebound: The Legend of Earl 'The Goat' Manigault, 1996; Mind Prey, 1999, Conviction, 2005; Inside Out, 2005; Johnny Was, 2006.Director: Lucifier; "Rosewood", 2015.Music: Rappin, 1985. Writer: Psalms From the Underground, 1994. **Business Addr:** Actor, c/o Allen Niprod, 232 N Cannon Dr, Beverly Hills, CA 90210-5302, **Business Phone:** (310)274-6611.

### LASANE, JOANNA EMMA

Theatrical director, consultant. **Personal:** Born Jul 24, 1935, Atlantic City, NJ; daughter of John Westley Foreman and Viona Marie Foreman; married Karlos Robert; children: Karlos Jr. **Educ:** Katherine Dunham Sch Dance, NY, attended 1955; Martha Graham Sch Mod Dance, NY, attended 1955; Am Sch Ballet & Int Sch Dance, attended 1957; Montclair St Col Theatre Arts & Speech, attended 1970; Negro EnsembleCo, NY, attended 1971; New Lafayette Theatre, NY, attended 1973. **Career:** Ebony Fashion Fair Johnson Publ, Chicago, high fashion model, 1965-66; Atlantic City Bd Educ, comm agt, 1972-75, drama consult, 1983-; Stockton Performing Arts Ctr, rep arts & lect ser, 1983-85; Atlantic City C's Theatre, dir, 1973-, bd mem; Atlantic Human Resources, Atlantic City, NJ, drama consult, 1973-; Ctr Early Childhood Educ, Atlantic City, NJ, drama consult, 1983-; Atlantic City Bd Educ, drama consult, currently; Dr Martin Luther King Jr Complex, dir & consult, currently. **Orgs:** Allied Arts; Nat Asn Advan Colored People; Urban League; NJ Educ Asn; bd dirs, Atlantic City Educ Found, 1987; Nat Educ Asn; Stockton St Col Friends Asn; adv coun, Dr Martin Luther King Jr Sch Complex; NJ St Coun Arts; NJ Speech & Theatre Asn; comt chmn, Boy Scouts Am, 1988-89; comnr, NJ-Atlantic City Coord Coun, 1990-; bd dirs, Police Athletic League; Altantic Co Cult & Heritage Adv Bd; Atlantic City Fine Arts Comn; bd trustees, South Jersey Stage Co; Children's Cult Arts Found; bd dirs, Atlantic Co Womans Hall Fame; Atlantic City Arts Comn Bd. **Honors/Awds:** Numerous honors & awards including Cultural Arts Award, Atlantic City Mag, 1981; Delta Sigma Theta Appreciation Award, 1983; Outstanding Citizen, Nat Asn Advan Colored People & Civic Betterment Asn, 1984; Theta Kappa Omega Arts Award, 1986; Community Service Award, Alpha Kappa Alpha, 1986; Omega Psi Phi Fraternity Upsilon Alpha Chapter Inspiration & Leadership Award, 1986; Role model Award, Sun Newspaper, 1989; People to Watch Award, Atlantic City Mag, 1989; Mary Church Terrell Award, 1992; NJ St Legislature Superlative Accomplishment in the Arts Award, 1994; Atlantic County Women's Hall of Fame, 1996; The Omega Psi Phi Award for Arts Excellence, 1996; Educ Fund Achievement Award, 1997; Kiwanis Club Key Award, Excellence in the Arts, 1997. **Special Achievements:** First African American model to do an international advertisement for Pepsi Cola, 1967; First African American woman appointed to the New Jersey St Council on the Arts. **Home Addr:** 1223 N Michigan Ave, Atlantic City, NJ 08401, **Home Phone:** (609)344-5457. **Business Addr:** Director, Drama Consultant, Atlantic City Public Schools, 3223 Arctic Ave, Atlantic City, NJ 08401, **Business Phone:** (609)343-1583.

### LASLEY, PHELBERT QUINCY, III (PHIL LASLEY)

Musician, music arranger or orchestrator, saxophonist. **Personal:** Born Mar 27, 1940, Detroit, MI; son of Phelbert and Josephine Wooldridge; married Trudy Diana Norresi; children: Felicia & Nagira. **Educ:** Inst Musical Arts, Detroit, Mich, attended 1958. **Career:** Saxophonist, 1958-; Detroit Jazz Orchestra, alto saxophonist, 1983-; Greenpeace, 1986; Guerilla Jam Bank, alto saxophonist, 1987; composition: Nkenge's Blues, Lady T Diana. **Orgs:** Jazz Heritage Soc, 1975-; Citizens Comt Save Jazz, 1975-. **Honors/Awds:** Best Alto Sax, Honorable Mention, Metro Times, Detroit, 1989-90; Jazz Hallof Fame, Graystone Jazz Mus, 1990. **Home Addr:** 4762 Second Ave, Detroit, MI 48201, **Home Phone:** (313)833-2064.

### LASSITER, PROF. CHAD DION

Activist, educator, social worker. **Personal:** Born Oct 5, 1972, Philadelphia, PA; son of Marilyn Adele; married Wanda Jamilah. **Educ:** Johnson C Smith Univ, BSW, 1995; Univ Pa Grad Sch Soc Work, MSW, 2001. **Career:** Gateway Group Homes, coun, 1994-95; Palumbo Elem Sch, sch based lead therapist, 1995-96; C's Hosp Philadelphia, soc worker, 1996-99; Univ PA, soc worker, 1998-2001, health educ, 1993-2003, Sch Social Policy & Pract, adj prof, 2003-, C's Hosp Pa, res, currently; Respecting All Cult Essential, co-founder, 2003-; W Chester Univ, adj lectr, currently. **Orgs:** Founder, Bright Outstanding Young Scholars, 2001-; res fel WEB Dubois Collective Res Inst, Univ Pa; Triumph Baptist Church, Gideon 300 Mens Ministry, 2001-; bd dir, Univ Pa Grad Sch Soc Work Alumni Asn, 2003-; bd mem, Leadership Learners Partners Charter Sch, 2003-; co-founder, pres, Black Men Penn Sch Soc Work, 2003-; co dir, Fostering Adopting & Mentoring to Improve Lives Youth. **Home Addr:** 6612 N 13th St, Philadelphia, PA 19126-3207, **Home Phone:** (215)927-2223. **Business Addr:** Behavioral Interventionist, Researcher, The Childrens Hospital Philadelphia, 34th St & Civic Ctr Blvd, Philadelphia, PA 19104, **Business Phone:** (267)426-5583.

### LASSITER, DR. JAMES EDWARD, JR.

Educator, dentist, association executive. **Personal:** Born Feb 12, 1934, Newport News, VA; children: Teri, Tina, James III & Judi. **Educ:** Howard Univ Col Dent, BMus Ed, 1957, DDS, 1963. **Career:** Overlook Hosp Summit NJ, assoc attend; Martland Hosp, assoc attend, 1972; Col Med & Dent, assoc prof, 1972-73; Col Dent Fairleigh Dickenson, asst prof, 1974-78; Col Med & Dent, asst prof, 1982-84; Patient First Dent Summit, pres, currently. **Orgs:** Morristown Dent Asn, 1973-78; Consul Union Co Voc Sch; adv comn, Col Med & Dent Sch, 1977-79; adv, comn Nat Health Prof Placement Network WK Kellogg Found, 1979; Consul Piedmont Res Ctr, 1979; Consul Dept Health Educ & Welfare, 1979; bd mem, Group Health Ins NY; Am Dent Asn; Nat Dent Asn; NJ Dent Asn; Commonwealth Dent Soc; Am Analgesia Soc; Acad Med NJ; NJ Dent Group PA; Paterson Dent Asn; Acad Gen Dent; Am Soc Dent C; fel Acad Dent Int; fel Am Col Dent; actg exec & sr consul, Nat Dent Asn; ADA's Spec Comn, "Future Dent", 1982; chmn & pres, Nat Dent Asn Found; life mem, Golden Heritage; Nat Advan Asn Colored People; Kappa Alpha Psi Frat; Wallace AME Chapel. **Honors/Awds:** Commission Service Award, Greater Newark Urban Coalition, 1975; Outstanding Service Award, Nat Dent Asn, 1976; President's Award, Nat Dent Asn, 1977; Citation Giant Excellence, Health Care Arena, 1979; Alumni Achievement Award, Howard Univ Col Dent, 1981; Bergen & Passaic Howard University Alumni Award, 1981; President's Award, Nat Dent Asn, 1982; Outstanding Achievement Award, Commonwealth Dental Soc NJ, 1983; Outstanding & Valuable Contribution for Scientific Session, Nat Dent Asn Baltimore, MD, 1983. **Home Addr:** 140 Hill HollowRd,

Watchung, NJ 07069-6442, **Home Phone:** (908)273-5656. **Business Addr:** President, Patient First Dentistry of Summit, 475 Springfield Ave Suite 210, Summit, NJ 07901-2600, **Business Phone:** (908)273-5656.

## LASSITER, KWAMIE

Football coach, football player. **Personal:** Born Dec 3, 1969, Hampton, VA. **Educ:** Univ Kans, BS, commun. **Career:** Football player (retired), coach, exec; Ariz Cardinals, free safety & defensive back & safety, 1995-2002, radio broadcaster, 2006-08; San Diego Chargers, free safety & strong safety, 2003; St Louis Rams, free safety, 2004; VoiceAmerica Sports, radio host, analyst, 2008-; Football Univ, defensive backs coach, 2008-; Mesa Community Col, coach, 2009-10; Nat Football League, Alumni Ariz Chap, pres, 2010-; Las Vegas Locos, defensive backs coach, 2012-13; NFL Alumni Ariz Chap, pres, 2010-14; ACN, independent bus owner, 2013-; NFL Legends Community, pac w coordr, 2015-. **Orgs:** Founder & pres, Kwamie Lassiter Found, 1988-. **Honors/Awds:** Aloha Bowl champion, 1992; Defensive Player of Week, Sports Illus; Defensive Player of Week, Nat Football League, 1998; Defensive Player of Month, Nat Football League, 2001; Defensive Player of Week, Pro Football Weekly, 2003. **Business Addr:** Independent Business Owner, ACN, 1000 Progress Pl, Concord, NC 28025-2449, **Business Phone:** (704)260-3000.

## LASSITER, REV. DR. WRIGHT LOWENSTEIN, JR.

College president, college administrator. **Personal:** Born Mar 24, 1934, Vicksburg, MS; son of Wright L Sr and Ethel F; married Bessie Loretta Ryan; children: Michele Denise & Wright Lowenstein III. **Educ:** Alcorn State Univ, BS, 1955; Tuskegee Inst, Inst Bus Mgmt, cert, 1956; Ind Univ, Bloomington, IN, MBA, 1962; Auburn Univ, EdD, 1975; Calif Western Univ, PhD, 1977. **Career:** Alcorn State Univ, instr; Hampton Inst, investments acct, 1956; Tuskegee Inst, sr acct, 1958-61, dir aux enterprises, 1962-76, asst prof mgmt, 1962, bus mgr; Ind Univ Bloomington, res assoc, 1961-62; Univ Ala, bus mgr; Morgan State Univ, vpres fin & admin, 1976-80; Schenectady County Community Col, pres, 1980-83; Bishop Col, pres, 1983-86; El Centro Col, pres, 1986-2006; Dallas County Community Col Dist, chancellor, 2006-, chief exec officer; Dallas Baptist Univ, distinguished adj prof mgt, currently. **Orgs:** Coun educ facil planner, Soc Advan Mgt; bd dir & sr dir, Dallas Urban League; State Fair Tex; bd dir, United Way Metro Dallas; Dallas Black Chamber Com; bd dir, Dallas Symphony Asn; Dallas County Youth Servs Comn; Dallas AIDS Educ Comn; bd dir, Young Men Christian Asn, Metrop Dallas; bd dir, Dallas Urban League; bd govs, Dallas Model UN; Downtown Dallas Rotary Club; bd dir & vpres, Dallas Black Chamber Comt; chmn bd trustee, African Am Mus; bd, Dallas Baptist Univ Found; bd mem, Univ Tex Southwestern Med Sch Found; Nat Adv Coun Nat Endowment Humanities; fel Ind Univ Acad Alumni, 1995; bd adv, Baylor Univ, Sch Bus; YMCA Found; trustee, Parker Univ, 2007-; dir, JP Morgan/Chase Manhattan Bank Tex; bd chair, African Am Mus; bd chair, Tex Coun Humanities. **Honors/Awds:** Martin Luther King Distinguished Leadership Award, State Univ New York, 1981; National Association Advanced Colored People Leadership Award, 1982; Outstanding Conributions in Education Award, Alpha Phi Alpha, 1983; Distinguished Service Award, Hamilton Hill Neighborhood Asn, 1983; Appreciation Award, State New York, 1983; Appreciation Award, Alpha Phi Alpha, 1984; Distinguished Achievement & Service Award, 1984; Meritorious Service Award, United Way Metro Dallas, 1984, 1985; Distinguished Service Award, Tex Baptist Conv, 1984; Distinguished Service Award, Inter First Bank, 1984; Distinguished Service Award, Interdenominational Nat Ministerial Alliance, 1984; Man of the Year Award, S Dallas Bus & Prof Women's Club Inc, 1984; Brotherhood Award, New Jersulaem Baptist Church, 1984; Certificate of Appreciation, Vet Admin Reg Med Ctr, 1985; Certificate of Special Congressional Recognition, US Congressman James Armey, 1985; Certificate of Appreciation, Dallas Reg Office US Agriculture, 1985; Appreciation Award in Education, Off Civil Rights Dallas Reg, 1985; Certificate of Recognition, Nat Republican Congressional Comn, 1985; Black Portfolio Excellence Award in Education, 1985; Distinguished Service Award, New Birth Baptist Church, 1985; Distinguished Service Award in Education, Arlington Asn Concerned Citizens, 1985; Outstanding Service Award in Education, Most Worshipful St Joseph Grand Lodge, 1985; DHL, Dallas Baptist Univ; African American Educators Hall of Fame; J. Erik Jonsson Award for Volunteer Service & Above, United Way Metrop Dallas; Beyond Award, United Way Metrop Dallas; George B. Allen Award, YMCA, Dallas; Pacesetter of the Year Award for marketing excellence, Nat Coun Mkt & Pub Rels; Johnnie Ruth Clark Award for excellence, Nat Coun Black Am Affairs Am Asn Community Cols; Russell H. Perry Free Enterprise Award, Dallas Baptist Univ, 2010. **Special Achievements:** First African American chairman of the board of the United Way of Dallas, 1989; In 2002, he was nominated by President George W. Bush & confirmed by the U.S. Senate to serve as a member of the National Advisory Council to the National Endowment for the Humanities; One of 47 international educators selected to participate in the Oxford Round Table at Oxford University in 2005. **Home Addr:** 7683 Pineville Cir, Castro Valley, CA 94552, **Home Phone:** (214)374-5009. **Business Addr:** Chancellor, Dallas County Community College District, 5001 N MacArthur Blvd, Irving, TX 75038, **Business Phone:** (972)273-3000.

## LATHAM, CHRISTOPHER JOSEPH (CHRIS LATHAM)

Athletic director, baseball player. **Personal:** Born May 26, 1973, Coeur d'Alene, ID; married Sarah Cunningham; children: Christopher. **Career:** Baseball player (retired); Minnesota Twins, outfielder, 1997-99; Colorado Rockies, 1999-2000; Toronto Blue Jays, outfielder, 2000-01; New York Yankees, outfielder, 2003; Yomiuri Giants, Japan, outfielder, 2003-04; Bridgeport Bluefish, Atlantic League, outfielder, 2005; World Cup Baseball, US, 2005; Top Recruit, dir player develop, 2007-. **Business Addr:** Director of Player Development, Top Recruit, 7437 S Eastern Suite 264, Las Vegas, NV 89123, **Business Phone:** (702)721-8671.

## LATHAM, ESQ. WELDON HURD

Lawyer, association executive, educator. **Personal:** Born Jan 2, 1947, Brooklyn, NY; son of Avril Hurd and Aubrey G; married Constantia Beecher; children: Nicole Marie & Brett Weldon. **Educ:** Howard Univ, BA, bus admin, 1968; Georgetown Univ Law Ctr, JD, 1971; George Washington Univ Nat Law Ctr, advan legal courses, 1976; Brookings Inst, exec educ prog, 1981; Dartmouth Col, Amos Tuck Sch, Exec Bus cert, 1997. **Career:** Checchi & Co, mgt consult, 1968-71; Covington & Burling, atty, 1971-73; Howard Univ Sch Law, adj prof, guest prof, 1972-82; Exec Off Pres, asst gen coun, 1973-76; White House Off Mgt & Budget, asst gen coun, 1974-76; Hogan & Hartson, atty, 1976-79; Univ Va Law Sch, guest prof, 1976-91; US Dept Housing & Urban Develop, gen dep asst secy, 1979-81; Sterling Systs Inc, vpres & gen coun, 1981-83; Planning Res Corp, exec asst & coun chair & chief exec officer, 1983-86; Reed Smith Shaw & McClay, managing partner, McLean Va off, 1986-92; Minority Bus Enterprise Mag, columnist, 1991-; Shaw, Pittman, Potts & Trowbridge, Nat Law Firm, sr partner, 1992-2000; Civilian Aide to Secy Army, 1994-99; TeleCommun Syst Inc, bd dir, 1999-; Holland & Knight, sr partner; Corp Diversity Coun Group, pract group leader, 2000-04, chmn, currently; Diversity Jour, columnist, 2002-; Davis Wright Tremaine LLP, sr partner, 2004-09; Jackson Lewis, sr partner, shareholder, 2009-; Georgetown Univ Law Ctr, adj prof. **Orgs:** Legal Defense & Educ Fund, 1976-96; bd dir, Prof Serv Coun, 1984-88; ed adv bd, Wash Bus J, 1985-88; bd dir, bd trustee, Va Commonwealth Univ, 1986-89; bd dir, Wash Urban League, 1986-90; founding mem & gen coun, Nat Coalition Minority Bus, 1993-; Small Bus Admin Nat Adv Coun, 1994-2003; managing trustee, maj sponsor, Dem Nat Comt, 1995-; Md Econ Develop Comn, 1996-98; Wash Hosp Ctr Found, 1996-97; Wash Hosp Ctr Found, 1996-97; Burger King Corp Diversity Action Coun, 1996-98; bd dir, chmn legal comt, Metrop Wash Airports Authority, 1997-; Joint Ctr Polit & Econ Studies, 1998-; bd trustee, Am Univ, 1999-2002; Coca-Cola Procurement Adv Coun, 2000-03; chair, Deloitte & Touche Diversity Adv Bd, 2002-; Georgetown Univ Law Bd Visitors, 2002-; trustee, Fed City Coun, 2003-; Capital Area Adv Bd, bd dir, Dem Nat Comn, DC; Nat Asn Advan Colored People; Nat Employ Law Coun, 2004-; Am Employ Law Coun, 2005-; Md Stadium Authority; capt, secy air force, Gen Coun's Hons Prog; Defense Dept Adv Comt Procurement & Tech Data Rights; adv comt, Omnicom Group Diversity; coun, PepsiCo Global Diversity; coun, Governance Coun; Econ Club Wash; adv bd & secy, Deloitte External Diversity; Greater Wash Bd Trade, adj prof; bd trustee, George Mason Univ. **Honors/Awds:** National Association of Equal Opportunity Higher Educational Achievement Award, 1987; Northern Virginia Min Bus & Prof Association Award, 1990; Private Industry Advocate of the Year, Small Bus Admin, 1992; Advocate of the Year, Minority Enterprise Development Week, US Dept Com, 1996; Washington Bar Association Hall of Fame, 2001; Ron Brown Legacy Award, Nat Black MBA Asn, 2002; Amtrak A. Philip Randolph Diversity Award; Outstanding Performance Award, US Dept HUD; Rev Al Sharpton National Action Network Excellence Award; Rev. Jesse L. Jackson Rainbow PUSH Coalition Martin Luther King Leadership Award. **Home Addr:** 7004 Natelli Woods Lane, Bethesda, MD 20817-3924, **Home Phone:** (301)469-7819. **Business Addr:** Partner, Shareholder, Jackson Lewis LLP, 10701 Parkridge Blvd Suite 300, Reston, VA 20191, **Business Phone:** (703)483-8333.

## LATHAN, SANAA MCCOY

Actor. **Personal:** Born Sep 19, 1971, New York, NY; daughter of Stan and Eleanor McCoy. **Educ:** Univ Calif-Berkeley, BA, Eng; Yale Sch Drama, MFA. **Career:** Films: Drive, 1996; Blade, 1998; Life, 1999; The Best Man, 1999; The Wood, 1999; Love & Basketball, 2000; Catfish in Black Bean Sauce, 2000; The Smoker, 2000; Brown Sugar, 2002; Out of Time, 2003; Nip & Tuck, 2006; A Raisin in the Sun, 2008; The Family That Preys, 2008; Powder Blue, 2009; Wonderful World, 2009; The Middle of Nowhere, 2009; Contagion, 2011; The Best Man Holiday, 2013; Repentance, 2014; The Perfect Guy, 2015-; The Best Man Wedding, 2016-; Now You See Me: The Second Act, 2016-. TV movies: "In the House", 1996; "Moesha", 1996; "Family Matters", 1997; "NYPD Blue", 1998; "LateLine", 1998-99"Disappearing Acts", 2000; "Brown Sugar", 2002; "Out of Time", 2003; "AVP: Alien Vs Predator", 2004; "The Golden Blaze", 2005; "Nip/Tuck", 2006 "Something New", 2006; "A Raisin in the Sun", 2008; "The Cleveland Show", 2009; "Family Guy", 2010-; "Tilda", 2011; "Boss", 2012; "Real Husbands of Hollywood", 2014; "Shots Fired", 2017. **Honors/Awds:** Rising Star Award, Acapulco Black Film Festival, 2001; Rising Star Award, 2001; Black Entertainment Award, Best Actress, 2001; Black Reel Award for Theatrical Best Actress, 2001, 2004; Image Award, 2001; Nominee for Teen Choice Award, 2000, 2003; Nominee for Image Award, 2000, 2003, 2004, 2007, 2009; Nominee for Independent Spirit Award, 2001; Black Reel Award, 2001, 2004; BET Award, 2001; Theatre World Award, 2004; Best Performance by an Actress, 2004; American Black Film Festival, 2004; Nominee for Black Movie Award, 2006; Hollywood Award, Acapulco Black Film Festival, 2014; NAACP Image Award, 2016. **Business Addr:** Actress, John Carrabino Management, 5900 Wilshire Blvd, Los Angeles, CA 90036, **Business Phone:** (323)857-4650.

## LATHAN, DR. WILLIAM EDWARD

Physician. **Personal:** Born Apr 14, 1937, Philadelphia, PA; son of Stanley Edward and Julia Elizabeth Dunston; married Melvina Smith; children: William Earl, Robert Edward, Edward, Honey Bea & John Calvin. **Educ:** Pa State Univ, BS, 1959; Drexel Univ Col Med, MD, 1963. **Career:** Hahnemann Univ Hosp, intern, 1963-64; Albert Einstein Med Ctr, resident Gen Surg, 1964-65; NY Athletic Comn, med dir, 1996-2000; Westchester Med Ctr, asst attend, currently; pvt pract, currently. **Orgs:** Am Bd Family Pract; Am Acad Family Physicians; fel NY Acad Med; fel Philadelphia Col Physicians; consult, NY State Off Prof Med Conduct. **Honors/Awds:** Obie Award for Distinguished Direction, NY Off Broadway, 1973; Rocky Marciano Sports Medicine Doctor Award, 1999; med advisor, World Boxing Orgn. **Special Achievements:** Contrib auth, "The Med Aspects of Boxing", CRC Press, 1993; contrib photogr, "The Family of Black America", Random House, 1996; "African Am Hist & Cult Catalog", Barnes & Noble, 1999; photographs exhibited in "A Hist of Black Photogr", St Martin Press, 1999; stage dir, The Confessions of Stepin' Fetch it, So Nice They Name it Twice, The Sirens, What If It Had Turned Up Heads, The Fabulous Miss Marie. **Business Addr:** Physician, 7 Dellwood Lane, Ardsley, NY 10502, **Business Phone:** (914)693-7795.

## LATHEN, DEBORAH ANN

Lawyer, executive director. **Personal:** Born Mar 28, 1953, St. Louis, MO; daughter of Olean and Levi. **Educ:** Cornell Univ, BA, 1975; Harvard Law Sch, JD, 1978. **Career:** Foley & Lardner, atty, 1978-81; Keck, Mahin & Cate, atty, 1978-82; Quaker Oats Co, litigation atty, 1982-88; TRW Inc, sr coun, 1988-90; Nissan Motor Corp USA, dir & nat consumer affairs & managing coun, 1990-98; Fed Commun Comn, chief cable serv bur, 1998-2001; Lathen Consult LLC, founder & pres, 2001-; US atty, currently; BT Group Plc, non-exec dir, 2007-10. **Orgs:** Bd dir, Nissan Found; bd dir, Leadership Calif; ABA; Black Women Lawyers Asn; Los Angeles Black Women Lawyers; bd mem, One Econ Corp; bd mem, Brit Telecommunications; bd mem, Dc Bd Ethics & Govt Accountability, 2011-. **Honors/Awds:** YWCA Women Leadership Award, 1987; Chairmans Award, Quaker Oats Co, 1988; Volunteer Award, Quaker Oats Co, 1992; Commendation from Mayor Thomas Bradley for Riot Relief Efforts, 1992; Americas Best & Brightest, Dollars & Sense Magazine, 1993. **Special Achievements:** first African-American woman to serve as a senior manager in nissan motor corporation. **Home Addr:** 1607 Allison St NW, Washington, DC 20011, **Home Phone:** (202)722-4356. **Business Addr:** Founder, President, Lathen Consulting LLC, 1607 Allison St NW, Washington, DC 20016, **Business Phone:** (202)722-4356.

## LATHON, LAMAR LAVANTHA

Football player, executive. **Personal:** Born Dec 23, 1967, Wharton, TX; children: Octavia & Madison. **Educ:** Univ Houston, educ. **Career:** Football player (retired), exec; Houston Oilers, linebacker & left linebacker & right defensive end, 1990-94; Carolina Panthers, left outside linebacker & linebacker & right defensive end, 1995-98; Sportscapers Inc, opers supvr, 2010-14; Fielder's Choice Inc, supvr, 2014-; Thuzio, prof serv, 2014-. **Honors/Awds:** Pre-season First Team All-Southwest Conference; Pro Bowl, 1996; All-Pro Selection, 1996. **Business Addr:** Professional Services, Fielder's Choice Inc, 15255 Gulf Freeway Suite 135 A, Houston, TX 77034, **Business Phone:** (281)484-6400.

## LATIF, NAIMAH

Newspaper publisher. **Personal:** Born Apr 15, 1960, Chicago, IL; married Sultan Abdul; children: Zakiyya Amirah. **Educ:** Univ Nebr Lincoln, BA, jour, 1982. **Career:** Chicago Black United Comn, youth chmn, 1982-84; Black United Front, secy, 1982-83; Task Force Black Polit Empowerment, secy, 1982-83; Intl Commun Corp, pres, 1986-89; Int Bus Network, Managing Ed; Latif Commun Group Inc, pres, 1989-; The Media Connection TV Show, Exec Producer, 1999-. **Orgs:** Oper Push, youth comt, 1982-84; PUSH Intl Trade Bur, 1984-; Int Black Writers, 1984-; Nat Asn Advan Colored People, 1985-; Urban League, 1985-; deleg, Nat Small Bus Conf, 1985-86; Chicago Asn Black Journalists; Nat Asn Black Journalists; fel Ahmadiyya Movement Islam; Chicago Asn African Am Photogr; Ahmadiyya Muslim Community. **Home Addr:** 7405 S Kimbark Ave Suite 2, Chicago, IL 60619-1431. **Business Addr:** President, Latif Communications Group Inc, 8 S Mich Ave Suite 1510, Chicago, IL 60603, **Business Phone:** (312)849-3456.

## LATIMER, ESQ. ALLIE B.

Lawyer. **Personal:** Born Jan 1, 1929?, Coraopolis, PA; daughter of Lawnye S and Bennie Comer. **Educ:** Howard Univ, Wash, DC, JD, 1953; Cath Univ Am Columbus Sch Law, LLM, 1958; Hampton Inst, Hampton, Calif, BS; Am Univ, Study Towards Doctorate; Howard Univ Sch Divinity, MDiv, DMin. **Career:** Lawyer (retired), general counsel; Fed Reformatory Women, correctional officer, 1949-51; Mitchel Afb, realty officer, 1955-56; atty, 1960-71; chief coun, 1966-71; Gen Serv Admin, Wash, DC, asst gen coun, 1971-76; NASA, asst gen coun, 1976-77, gen coun, 1977-87, spec coun, 1987-96. **Orgs:** Secy, Nat Bar Asn, 1966-76; co-chmn & bd dir, Presby Econ Develop Corp, 1974-80; pres, Nat Bar Found, 1974-75; pres, DC Ment Health Asn, 1977-79; founder & first pres, Federally Employed Women, 1968-69; vpres, Links Inc, 1976-80; bd gov, Nat Coun Church, USA, 1978-84; Supreme Ct US; US Ct Appeals DC; NC St Ct Appeals; Am Bar Asn; Fed Bar; Nat Bar; NC Bar; DC Bar; Wash Bar Asn; Nat Asn Advan Colored People & Nat Asn Advan Colored People Legal Def Fund, DC Steering Comt; vol work, Am Friends Serv Comn, Europe. **Honors/Awds:** Public Service Award & Gen Serv Admin, 1971; Exceptional Service Awards, Gen Serv Admin, 1976-79; Humanitarian Award, Sigma Delta Tau Legal Fraternity, 1978; Outstanding Achievement Award; Kiwanis Club Award DC, 1978; Presidential Rank Award, 1983, 1995; Distinguished Service Award, Gen Serv Admin, 1984; Ollie May Cooper Award, Wash Bar Asn, 1998; Hall of Fame Award, Nat Bar Asn, 1999; National Women's Hall of Fame, 2009. **Special Achievements:** First woman and the first African American to serve as General Counsel of a major United States federal agency. **Home Addr:** 3050 Mil Rd NW Suite 520, Washington, DC 20015-1364, **Home Phone:** (202)244-5078.

## LATIMER, CHRIS

Marketing executive, founder (originator). **Personal:** Born Dec 25, 1968, White Plains, NY; son of Benjamin and Sudie Hardy. **Educ:** Howard Univ, attended 1990. **Career:** Source Mag, tour coord, 1990-91, designer & co-owner, 1997; Am Col Alliance Inc, promos, 1990-91; NYA Area Entertainment Inc, pres & chief exec officer, currently; Ocean Christopher Group, owner, currently; Cancun All-Star Fiesta, founder, 1995, pres & chief exec officer, currently. **Honors/Awds:** Recognition Award, 1995; Mentor Award, Thomas H Slater Inc, 1997. **Business Addr:** President, Chief Executive Officer, NYA Area Entertainment Inc, 550 Broadway Suite 406, New York, NY 10012, **Business Phone:** (212)343-1700.

## LATIMER, INA PEARL

Educator. **Personal:** Born Oct 19, 1934, Okeechobee, FL; married Harold A; children: Cynthia L. **Educ:** Tuskegee Inst, BS, nursing, 1956; Northern Ill Univ, MS, educ, 1979. **Career:** Univ Ill, staff nurse charge, 1958-60; St Mary Nazareth, Sch Nursing, instr med-surg nursing, 1960-70; Triton Col, instr, 1970-73, chair person prac nursing prog, 1973-. **Orgs:** Home maker-Home Health Aide Comn; Ill Coun Home Health Servs; Nat League Nursing; Ill Voc Asn; accreditation site visr, Nat League Nursing, 1978-; bd rev, Nat League Nursing Coun Prac Nursing Progs, 1979-84; eval, Dept Voc & Tech Educ, 1981; Lakeside Community Church. **Honors/Awds:** Award, Delta Sigma Theta Sororoty; Alpha Kappa Mu, Nat Honor Soc. **Home Addr:** 520 Ryegrass Ct, Aurora, IL 60504, **Home Phone:** (630)585-

9006. **Business Addr:** Department Chairperson Practical Nursing, Triton College, 2000 5th Ave, River Grove, IL 60171, **Business Phone:** (708)456-0300.

### LATIMER, JENNIFER ANN
School administrator. **Personal:** Born Apr 29, 1953, Gastonia, NC; daughter of Robert E Grier and Susie M Kithcart; children: Faith G. **Educ:** Univ RI, BA, 1975; RI Col, MA, 1983; CAGS, 1990. **Career:** Atlanta Bd Educ, comt organizer, 1977-78; RI Educ Oppurtunity Ctr, follow-up counr, 1980; Community Col RI, counr access prog, 1981-83; RICol, coord minority prog, 1983-86, asst dir student life/minority affairs, 1986-01; Cornerstone Coun & Consult counr, 1989-93. **Orgs:** Vpres, URI Minority Alumni Coun, 1987-89; Providence Christian Outreach Ministries, 1988-90; Nat Asn Advan Colored People. **Home Addr:** 230 Summey Barker Dr, Dallas, NC 28034-7780, **Home Phone:** (704)922-6745. **Business Addr:** NC.

### LATIMORE, GAIL
Executive director. **Personal:** children: 3. **Educ:** Columbia Univ, BS, archit; Boston Univ, MS, urban affairs. **Career:** Codman Sq Neighborhood Develop Corp, exec dir, 1998-; Citi, dir community rels, 2008-10. **Orgs:** Founding bd mem, Dudley St Neighborhood Initiative; Metrop Boston Housing Partnership; bd mem, Mass Asn Community Develop Corps, 2005-; Four Corners Action Coalition; exec dir, Boston Found; Nat NeighborWorks Asn. **Business Addr:** Executive Director, Codman Square Neighborhood Development Corp Inc, 587 Wash St, Dorchester, MA 02124, **Business Phone:** (617)825-4224.

### LATNEY, HARVEY, JR.
Lawyer. **Personal:** Born May 26, 1944, Caroline County, VA; children: 2. **Educ:** Va Union Univ, BA, hist, 1966; Howard Univ, Sch Law, JD, 1969. **Career:** US Dept Transp, legal intern, 1969, 1971-72; Richmond Comn Sr Ctr, dir, 1972-73; Greene & Poindexter Inc, atty, 1973; Carolina County, Va, commonwealth atty, 1978-; State Va, atty; Villa's Housing Bd, chmn; St. Josephs villa, bd trustee; Circuit Ct, Va, substitute judge, currently. **Orgs:** Nat Bar Asn; Am Bar Asn; Va Bar & Asn; Va Trial Lawyer's Asn; Old Dominion Bar Asn; St James Baptist Church; bd trustee, St. Josephs Villa; Kappa Alpha Psi Fraternity Inc. **Home Addr:** 30415 Richmond Tpke, Hanover, MD 23069-2007. **Business Addr:** Substitute Judge, 15th Circuit Ct, 815 Princess Anne St, Fredericksburg, VA 22401-5819, **Business Phone:** (540)372-1066.

### LATTA, JUDI MOORE. See SMITH, DR. JUDITH MOORE.

### LATTIMER, DR. AGNES DOLORES
Physician, educator. **Personal:** Born May 13, 1928, Memphis, TN; daughter of Arthur O and Hortense M Lewis; married Bernard Goss; married Frank Bethel; children: Bernard C Goss Jr. **Educ:** Fisk Univ, BS (magna cum laude), biol, 1949; Chicago Med Sch, MD, 1954. **Career:** Physician (retired); Michael Reese Hosp, dir amb peds, 1966-71; Cook County Hosp, dir amb peds, 1971-84, dir Fantus Clin, 1984-85; Cook Co Hosp, med dir, 1986-95; Univ Health Sci & Chicago Med Sch, asst prof dept pediat; pvt pract physician; Agnes D Lattimer & Assoc, owner, mgr. **Orgs:** Fel Am Acad Pediat, 1960-; Ambulatory Ped Assoc, 1974-; pres, Ill Chap Am Acad Pediat, 1983-86; Physician's Task Force Hunger, 1984-86; Am Assoc Pub Health; bd trustee, Child serv; bd trustee, Family Inst; Chicago Pediat Soc. **Special Achievements:** First African American alumna of Chicago Medical School. **Home Addr:** 1700 E 56th St Apt 3709, Chicago, IL 60637-5801, **Home Phone:** (773)493-1670. **Business Addr:** Pediatrist, 333 W Wacker Dr Suite 1400, Chicago, IL 60606-1257, **Business Phone:** (312)782-4486.

### LATTIMER, ROBERT L.
Lawyer. **Personal:** Born Jul 16, 1945; son of James and Maryagnes; married Sarah; children: Ebony, Isoador, Hope & John. **Educ:** Rutgers Univ, BA, econs, polit sci, 1973; Columbia Univ, Grad Sch Bus, exec MBA mgt prog, Arden House, 1978. **Career:** J Walter Thompson Co, vpres, dir, 1976-81; CRE Operating Comn, 1976-81; Lattimer Group, chief exec officer, sr consult partner, 1981-90; Towers Perrin, global pract leader, 1981-95, managing partner; Andersen Consult, assoc partner, 1995-2008; City Atlanta, chief operating officer; Metrop Atlanta Rapid Transit Authority, dir corp bus, currently; Rutgers Univ, Diversity Studies, sr fel, 2008-; PRM Consult Inc, prin. **Orgs:** Vice chair, bd dir, Zoo Atlanta, 1993-; exec comn, chmn bd dir, Strategic Planning & Human Resources Comn, Atlanta Neighborhood Develop Partnership Inc, 1993; adv bd dir, Cong Black Caucus Found, 1996; sr fel Am Soc Competitiveness, dean; sr fel John J. Heldrich Ctr Workforce Develop. **Honors/Awds:** US Jaycees, One of the Ten Outstanding Young Men America, Honored with VPAlbert Gore Jr, 1987; Global Strategy Formulation & Execution, Am Soc Competitiveness, 1997. **Special Achievements:** Quoted in significant management books, journals, newspapers, & magazines such as: Fortune Magazine, Atlanta Journal Constitution, Atlanta Tribune; Completed book chapter, "Redefining Diversity", in book Beyond Affirmative Action, 1996. **Home Addr:** 1978 Sylvan Cir SW Apt A1, Atlanta, GA 30310-5096, **Home Phone:** (404)696-0837. **Business Addr:** Director of Corporate Business, Metropolitan Atlanta Rapid Transit Authority, 2622 Piedmont Rd NE, Atlanta, GA 30324-3311, **Business Phone:** (404)848-5000.

### LATTIMORE, DR. CAROLINE LOUISE
School administrator, college administrator. **Personal:** Born May 12, 1945, Winston-Salem, NC; daughter of Mary Rhodes and Earl R Sr. **Educ:** Hampton Inst, BS, 1967, MA, 1973; Duke Univ, PhD, 1978. **Career:** Richmond Pub Sch, VA, eng teacher, 1967-74; State Univ, coord sr citizens prog Winston-Salem, 1974; NTS Res Corp, Wash, coord, 1978; Duke Univ, psychol testing intern, 1974-75, educ consult & spec coun, 1978, dean minority affairs, asst provost, 1978-83, acad dean, 1987, asst dean, assoc acad dean & adj assoc prof, currently. **Orgs:** Pres, Coun Black Affairs, 1984-91; Reggie B Howard Scholar Selection Comn, 1985-01; Nat Asn Advan Colored People, 1985-; Defense Adv Comn Women Serv, 1999-2002; bd dir, AKA, 2002-06; WTVO-11 TV, 2003; bd dir, Duke Univ Fed Credit Union, 2003; NC Civil Rights Comn, 2003; Duke Resv Officer Training Corps, 2003; chair, memship comt, regional dir, Alpha Kappa Alpha, 2009. **Home Addr:** 234 Overlook Ave, Durham, NC 27712, **Home Phone:** (919)471-3764. **Business Addr:** Associate Academic Dean, Adjunct Associate Professor of the Practice, Duke University, 109 Acad Advising Ctr Allen Bldg, Durham, NC 27708, **Business Phone:** (919)684-2096.

### LATTIMORE, KENNY (KENNETH LEE LATTIMORE)
Singer. **Personal:** Born Apr 10, 1970, Washington, DC; married Chante Moore; children: Kenny Jr. **Educ:** Howard Univ, Wash, DC. **Career:** Albums: Kenny Lattimore, 1996; From the Soul of Man, 1998; Weekend, 2001; The Essential, Things That Lovers Do, 2003; Days Like This, 2004; Uncovered/Covered, For You, 2006; Timeless, 2008; TV: "Double Date", 1997; "Moesha", 1997; "An Evening of Stars: A Celebration of Educational Excellence", 2001; "To Love or Not to Love", 2002; "Abby", 2003; "The View", 2004; "The Tom Joyner Show", 2005; "Honors Reba", 2006; "In the Mix", 2006; "Black to the Future", 2009. TV series: "The Young and the Restless", 2003; "A Cross to Bear", 2012. Singles: "I Wanna Ride", 1989; "Funny Feeling" b/w "Why Do You Lie", 1989; "Never Too Busy", 1996; "Just What It Takes", 1997; "For You", 1997; "Days Like This", 1998; "If I Lose My Woman", 1999; "Heaven & Earth", 1999; "Love Will Find a Way", 1999; "Weekend", 2001; "Don't Deserve", 2001; "Loveable", 2003; "You Don't Have To Cry", 2003; "Tonight [2 Step]", 2005; "Figure It Out", 2006; "Make Me Like The Moon", 2006; "You Are My Starship", 2008; "Find a Way", 2012; "Back 2 Cool", 2012; "Heart Stops", 2013. **Honors/Awds:** Nat Asn Advan Colored People Image Award, Best New Artist, 1996. **Business Addr:** Singer, Arista Records, 6 W 57th St, New York, NY 10019, **Business Phone:** (212)489-7400.

### LAUDERBACK, BRENDA JOYCE
Executive. **Personal:** Born Apr 25, 1950, Pittsburgh, PA; daughter of Clayton (deceased) and Dorothy; married Boyd Wright; children: Phallon & Adam. **Educ:** Robert Morris Col, BA, mkt, 1972; Univ Pittsburgh, grad studies, voc educ, 1973. **Career:** Executive (retired); Gimbels, asst buyer, buyer; Dayton's Dept Store, asst buyer, 1975-76, buyer, 1976-79, mgr, 1979-82; Dayton-Hudson Corp, vpres, gen merchandise mgr, 1982-93; US Shoe Footwear, Wholesale Group, pres, 1993-95; Nine W Group Inc, Wholesale & Retail Group, pres, 1995-98; Target Corp, vpres & gen mgr; Irwin Financial Corp, dir, 1996-; Big Lots Inc, dir, 1997-; La-Pac Corp, dir, 1999-2005; Jostens Inc, dir, 1999-; La-Pac Corp, dir, currently; Wolverine World Wide Inc, dir; Dennys Corp, dir, currently; Select Comfort Corp, independent dir, 2004-. **Orgs:** NCP, 1975-; Urban League, 1989-; Comt 200, 1989-; Exec Leadership Coun, 1993; bd mem, Arthur Ashe Inst Urban Health, 1996-97; Irwin Fin, 1996; Consol Stores, 1997; Hord Found, bd trustee, 1997; All Kids Found Adv Comn, 1998; Minneapolis-St Paul Chap Links, pres; Rosie O'Donnell All Kids Found, adv bd; Wolverine World Wide Inc, chmn governance comt, audit comt, 2003-; Dennys Corp, chmn corp governance & nominating comt, audit comt, 2005-; Susan G Komen Cure, 2008; Select Comfort Corp, chmn corp governance & nominating comt, compensation comt. **Home Addr:** 58 Good Hill Rd, Weston, CT 06883. **Business Addr:** Director, Big Lots Inc, 300 Phillipi Rd, Columbus, OH 43228-5311, **Business Phone:** (614)278-6800.

### LAUDERDALE, PRIEST
Basketball player. **Personal:** Born Aug 31, 1973, Chicago, IL. **Educ:** Cent State Univ, OH, attended 1994; Kaskaskia Col, Centralia, Ill. **Career:** Football player (retired); Peristeri Nikas, Greece, 1995-96; Atlanta Hawks, ctr, 1996-97; Denver Nuggets, ctr, 1997-98; Grand Rapids Hoops, Continental Basketball Asn, 2000; Ft Wayne Fury, Continental Basketball Asn, 2000; Gaiteros del Zulia, Venezuela, 2001; Apollon Limassol, Cyprus, 2002; Lukoil Acad, Bulgaria, 2002-05; Al-Ittihad Jeddah, Saudi Arabia, 2005-07; Saba Mehr Kazvin, Iran, 2006; Al Nasr, United Arab Emirates, 2007; Al-Hilal, Saudi Arabia, 2008; Shandong Lions, China, 2008; Mahram Tehran, Iran, 2008-09; Saba Mehr Qazvin, Iran, 2010; Levski Sofia, Bulgaria, 2011; Chabeb-Zahle, Lebanon, 2011. **Honors/Awds:** Bulgarian Basket Center of the Year; Bulgarian Basket MVP of the Playoffs, 2004.

### LAUREN, GREEN
Television news anchorperson. **Personal:** Born Jun 30, 1958, Minneapolis, MN; daughter of Robert and Robert; married Ted Nikolis. **Educ:** Northwestern Univ, Medill Sch, jour; Univ Minn, BMus. **Career:** KSTP-TV, Minn, gen assignment reporter, 1988-93; WBBM-TV, news anchor, corresp, 1993-96; FOX News Channel, news anchor, 1996-, chief relig corresp, currently; TV Show: "FOX & Friends", news anchor, 1996. **Orgs:** African Methodist Episcopal Church. **Special Achievements:** Third runner-up, Miss America 1985 pageant; album, Classic Beauty, 2004. **Business Addr:** Chief Religion Correspondent, Fox News Channel, PO Box 900, Beverly Hills, CA 90213, **Business Phone:** (310)369-1000.

### LAVAILLE, MARTHA. See REEVES, MARTHA ROSE.

### LAVALAIS, LESTER JOSEPH
Executive, vice president (organization), manager. **Personal:** Born Dec 16, 1959, Houston, TX; son of Tommie and Lois E Jones; married Sherry Edine; children: Lael E & Raziel J. **Educ:** McMurry Univ, BS, appl sociol & social serv, 1984. **Career:** Woods Psychiat Inst, caseworker, 1983-85; Taylor County Detention Ctr, probation officer, 1985-88; Ment Health-Ment Retardation, Outpatient Servs, ment health prof, 1988-93; prog mgr, Goodwill Industs, Residential Youth Treat Ctr, 1993, Electronic Monitoring, prog mgr, 1994-97; JEMS, vpres, currently. **Home Addr:** 2316 Plain View Rd, Cheyenne, WY 82009, **Home Phone:** (307)638-1997. **Business Addr:** Vice President, JEMS, 117 W 9th St, Cheyenne, WY 82003, **Business Phone:** (307)635-8888.

### LAVAN, ALTON
**Personal:** Born Sep 13, 1946, Pierce, FL; married Bessie Lavonia Jewell; children: Travis Alton, Douglas Milo & Maeleeke. **Educ:** Colo State Univ, Ft Colins, BA, sociol, 1970. **Career:** Football player (retired), football coach; Philadelphia Eagles, defensive back, 1968; Atlanta Falcons, defensive back, 1969-70, asst coach, 1975-76; Colo St Univ, asst coach, 1972; Univ Louisville, asst coach, 1973; Iowa State Univ, asst coach, 1974; Ga Tech, asst coach, 1977-78; Stanford Univ, asst coach, 1979; Dallas Cowboys, offensive backfield coach, 1980-88; San Francisco 49ers, asst coach, 1989-90; Univ Wash, asst coach, 1992-95; Baltimore Ravens, asst coach, 1996-98; Kans City Chiefs, asst coach, 1999-2000; Eastern Mich Univ, asst coach, 2002-03, asst head coach, 2003; Del State Univ, head football coach, 2004-10. **Orgs:** Am Football Coaches Asn; Black Coaches Asn. **Special Achievements:** First African American Coach of Dallas Cowboys & Atlanta Falcons. **Business Addr:** DE.

### LAVAR, ELLIN
Founder (originator). **Educ:** Fordham Univ, BA, psychol. **Career:** LaVar Hair Designs, founder. **Honors/Awds:** Emmy Award, nominated; "The Network Journal: Black Professionals & Small Business Magazine", 25 Influential Black Women in Business, 2009. **Special Achievements:** Credited with creating the modern hairweave; First African-American stylist with a reality television program, "Hair Trauma", WE Channel, 2006-; Released product line "Ellin LaVar Textures". **Business Addr:** Founder, 134 W 72nd st, New York, NY 10023, **Business Phone:** (212)724-4492.

### LAVEIST, DR. THOMAS
Educator. **Educ:** Univ Md Eastern Shore, Princess Anne, MD, BA, sociol, 1984; Univ Mich, Ann Arbor, MI, MA, 1985, PhD, med sociol, 1988, PDF, 1990. **Career:** Johns Hopkins Univ, Baltimore, Md, prof, currently, Hopkins Ctr Health Disparities Solutions, dir, 1990-. **Orgs:** Pres, Acad Health Equity; bd dir, Bon Secour Health Syst; assoc regional dir, Phi Beta Sigma Fraternity, 1983-84; Paul B Cornely fel, Univ Mich, Sch Pub Health, 1988-90; Brookdale Nat fel, Brookdale Found, 1991; health sub-comt, Md Comn Status Black Males, 1991-; Asn Black Sociologists, 1985-; Am Pub Health Asn, 1988-; Am Sociol Asn, 1984-. **Business Addr:** Professor, Director, Johns Hopkins Bloomberg School of Public Health, 625 N Broadway, Baltimore, MD 21205-1996, **Business Phone:** (410)955-3774.

### LAVEIST, WILBERT FRANCISCO
Television producer. **Personal:** Born Brooklyn, NY; son of William and Eudora; married Rita Mildred Wilson; children: Daniel, Joshua & Coryn. **Educ:** Lincoln Univ, BA, jour, 1988; Univ Ariz, MS, 1992; Old Dom Univ, PhD, technol & media studies, 2011-. **Career:** Phoenix Gazette, copy ed, 1992-93; Ariz Repub, copy ed, 1992-93, reporter, 1993-95, online web ed, 1995-97; ArizonaCentral.com, online ed, 1995-97; Blackvoices.com, exec producer, proj mgr, 1997-2004; Daily Press, columnist; 2004-06; Hampton Univ, adj prof, 2004-; LELLC, pres, 2006-; Johnson Publ Co, dir, 2006-07; Medill Sch Journalism, Northwestern Univ, Adj, 2007; Target Publ, ed, 2007-09; Virginian Pilot Media Co, publ & ed, 2007-09; BWE Inc, Blog Contribr, 2008; Thomas Nelson Community Col, adj eng compos prof, 2009-10; Regent Univ, adj journalism prof, 2009-10; New J & Guide, columnist, 2009-11; Urban League Hampton Roads Inc, consult & pub rels, community outreach, 2010-11; UrbanFaith.com, cult columnist, 2010-; The Wil LaVeist Show, host, 2010-; Mennonite Mission Network, Managing Ed for Multimedia, 2011-. **Orgs:** Nat Asn Black Journalists; pres, Ariz Asn Black Journalists; Md Inst Journ Ed; exec, Nat Asn Minority Media. **Honors/Awds:** Arizona Press Club Creative Writing, 1995. **Home Addr:** 18514 Dundee Ave, Homewood, IL 60430, **Home Phone:** (708)647-7552. **Business Addr:** Managing Editor for Multimedia, Mennonite Mission Network, 3145 Benham Ave, Elkhart, IN 46517, **Business Phone:** (574)523-3000.

### LAVELLE, AVIS
President (organization), business owner, consultant. **Personal:** Born Mar 5, 1954, Chicago, IL; daughter of Adolph Eugene Sampson and Mai Evelyn Hicks. **Educ:** Univ Ill, BS, 1975; Keller Grad Sch Mgt, MBA. **Career:** WLTH Radio, news dir, 1978-79; WJJD/WJEZ, reporter, anchor, 1979-84; WGN-Radio/TV, chief polit reporter, 1984-88; Richard M Daley Mayor, campaign press secy, 1988-89; Off Mayor, Chicago, mayoral press secy, 1989-92; Clinton/Gore Campaign, nat press secy, 1992; Presidental Transition Team, spec asst chmn, 1992-93; US Dept Health & Human Serv, asst secy, pub affairs, 1993-95; Waste Mgt Inc, vpres commun & community rels; Chicago Bd Educ, vpres, 1997-2003; Foster Group, sr partner, 2003; A LaVelle Consult Serv LLC, founder & pres, currently; Univ Chicago Hosp, vpres govt & pub affairs. **Orgs:** Delta Sigma Theta Pub Serv, 1973; Nat Comn Working Women, 1980; Black Adoption Task Force Ill, Steering Comt, 1987; bd mem, Proj Image Inc, 1988-89; bd mem, Human Resources Develop Inst, 1988; Bd trustee, vpres, Chicago Schs Reform; bd dir, After Sch Matters Found. **Business Addr:** President, Founder, A LaVelle Consulting Services LLC, 101 W Grand Ave Suite 600, Chicago, IL 60654, **Business Phone:** (312)223-0581.

### LAVERGNE, HON. LUKE ALDON
Judge, lawyer. **Personal:** Born May 7, 1938, Lawtell, LA; son of Adam Jr and Ida Nero; married Catherine Ann Malveaux, Oct 15, 1960; children: Lance A & Cynthia A. **Educ:** Univ Nebr, Omaha, BS, bus & finance, 1969; Southern Ill Univ, Edwardsville, MS, guid & coun, 1974; La State Univ Law Ctr, JD, 1982. **Career:** Judge (retired); USAF, 2nd Lt; Travis Afb, Calif, officer, Avionics Squadron, 1970-73; Directorate Avionics, Hq Mil Airlift Command, officer, 1973-75; La State Univ, asst prof, aerospace studies, 1975-79; asst dist atty, 1982-84, asst parish atty, 1991-92; City Ct, Judge Pro Tempore, 1988; State La E Baton Rouge Parish Family Ct, judge, 1992-2008, chief judge, 2007; La Judicial Col, bd mem; Our Lady Lake Col, Bd Trustees, mem, currently; Southern Univ Law Ctr, adj prof, Child Support Comt, mem, Parenting Coordr Comt, mem, Visitation Comt, mem, currently; La State Civil Law Inst, coun mem, currently. **Orgs:** State dir, Phi Beta Sigma Fraternity, 1984-88, regional legal coun, 1987-92; pres, Lou-is A Martinet Legal Soc, 1989-92; bd dir, YMCA, 1989-96; La State Bar Asn; bd dir, Lions Club, 1989-96; bd dir, Baton Bar Asn, 1990-92; bd dir, Boy Scouts Am Istrouma Coun, 1990-96, scout show chmn, 1992-94; 100 Black Men BR Ltd; bd dir, Our Lady Lake Col; Kiwanis Club; life mem, Phi Beta Sigma; Phi Delta Phi; Baton Rouge Symphony; treas, Judicial Coun, Nat Bar Asn; pres, Black Lawyer group; La

Judicial Coun; chmn Finance Comt, chmn Capital Campaign, teacher Cath church hist, co-chair bldg comt, St Paul Apostle Cath Church. **Home Addr:** 5956 Valley Forge Ave, Baton Rouge, LA 70808, **Home Phone:** (504)924-0590. **Business Addr:** Adjunct Professor, Louisiana State Law Institute, Rm W-127 Paul M Hebert Law Ctr, Baton Rouge, LA 70803-1016.

## LAVERGNEAU, RENE L.

Administrator, educator, association executive. **Personal:** Born Nov 4, 1933, New York, NY; son of Armando and Myrtle. **Educ:** Community Col New york, BA, 1958; MS, 1963; MA, 1974. **Career:** Educator (retired); WNYE-TV, NY Ed TV, instr, 1965-67; Bur Audio-visual Instr NYC, writer & voice-over, 1966-68; NY City Bd Educ, bd examrs, 1968; Fair leigh Dickinson Univ PR, grad instr, 1969; Univ PR, Bayamon, instr, 1974; Hackensack Pub Schs, dir, bur foreign langs, bilingual ed & Eng second lang, 1986-96; coordr, foreign lang. **Orgs:** Consult, Princeton Conf Foreign Lang Curric Develop, 1967; chair, NE Conf Teaching Foreign Langs, 1974; chair, State wide Comt Bilingual &Teaching Eng Second Lang Ed Cert NJ, 1974; keynoter, Am Asn Teachers, 1974; chair, NJ Bilingual Minimum Stand, 1978; Bergen City Health & Welfare Coun, 1980; chmn, bd dirs Teatro Duo, 1986-87; bd dir, Hackensack Pub Sch Hist Soc, 1986; sel comt, Am Coun Teaching Foreign Langs & Nat Textbk Co Award Bldg Community Interest Foreign Lang Educ, 1987. **Honors/Awds:** Careers Community and Public Awareness Award, NE Conf Rept Pub, 1974; National Award, Bldg Community Interest Foreign Lang Educ Am Coun Teaching Foreign Langs & Nat Textbook Co, 1983. **Special Achievements:** Actor "The Wiz" 1977. **Home Addr:** 300 Winston Dr Suite 907, Cliffside Park, NJ 07010-3215, **Home Phone:** (201)886-2099.

## LAVIZZO-MOUREY, DR. RISA JUANITA

Physician, government official, chief executive officer. **Personal:** Born Sep 25, 1954, Seattle, WA; daughter of Philip V and Blanche Sellers; married Robert J; children: Rel & Max. **Educ:** Univ Wash, attended 1973; State Univ NY, Stony Brook, attended 1975; Harvard Med Sch, MD, 1979; Wharton Sch, Univ Pa, MBA, 1986. **Career:** Brigham & Women's Hosp, intership & med resident, 1979-82; Temple Univ Med Sch, clin instr, 1982-84; Univ Pa, Sch Med, dir Inst Aging, chief div geriat med, 1984-92, 1994-2001, asst prof, 1986-94, assoc prof, 1992-97, Sylvan Eisman prof med & health Care systs, 1997-2001; Philadelphia Veterans Admin Med Ctr, assoc chief staff geriat; US Dept Health & Human Servs, dep adminr agency health care policy & res; Robert Wood Johnson Found, pres, 2001-, chief exec officer, 2001-. **Orgs:** Asn Acad Minority Physicians, 1990-; adminr, Agency Health Care Policy & Res, 1992-94; fel Am Col Physicians, regent, 1993-94, master, 2002; Consumer Rights & Qual Healthcare Indust, 1997-98; fel Nat Med Asn; White House Task Force Health Care Reform; consultm, White House Health policy; trustee, Robert Wood Johnson Found, vpres, sr vpres & dir health care group, pres, 2002-; bd dir, Genworth Financial Inc, 2007; fel Am Geriat Soc; fel Am Soc Internal Med; co-vchair, Inst Med; fel NAS; fel Asn Acad Minority Physicians; servedseveral comts Task Force Aging Res, Off Technol Assessment Panel Prev Serv Medicare Beneficiaries. **Honors/Awds:** One of the 100 Most Powerful Women, Forbes; Robert Wood Johnson Foundation Clinical Scholar, Univ Pa, 1984. **Special Achievements:** Author: "Invasive Gynecologic Oncology", 1979; "Dehydration in the Elderly", 1987; "Amantad ine-related adverse reactions among African-American elderly nursing home residents", 1991; First woman and the First African-American to be president and chief executive officer of the Robert Wood Johnson Foundation; Numerous others. **Home Addr:** 711 Paper Mill Rd, Erdenheim, PA 19038-7832, **Home Phone:** (215)843-9875. **Business Addr:** President, Chief Executive Officer, The Robert Wood Johnson Foundation, Col Rd E Rte 1, Princeton, NJ 08543, **Business Phone:** (877)843-7953.

## LAW, BOB. See LAW, ROBERT LOUIS.

## LAW, ROBERT LOUIS (BOB LAW)

Executive, radio host. **Personal:** Born Apr 6, 1939, Brooklyn, NY; son of John and Lucille; married Munty Doggett; children: Patrice Aisha & Abina Napier. **Career:** WWRL Radio, prog dir; Midday Magic Music, radio personality, Nat Black Network, producer & host, vpres; Namaskar, Bob Law's Health & Wellness Shop, owner; Bob Law's Seafood Cafe, owner, currently. **Orgs:** Founder, Nat Respect Yourself, Youth Orgn; chair, NY Million Man March Orgn; founder & chair, Namaskar Community Assistance Prog; chair, Black Spectrum Theatre, currently. **Home Addr:** 14 Greentree Cir, Westbury, NY 11590, **Home Phone:** (516)334-6218. **Business Addr:** Owner, Bob Law's Seafood Cafe, 637 Vanderbilt Ave, Brooklyn, NY 11238, **Business Phone:** (718)789-4060.

## LAW, TY (TAJUAN E LAW)

Football player, executive. **Personal:** Born Feb 10, 1974, Aliquippa, PA. **Educ:** Univ Mich. **Career:** Football player (retired); New Eng Patriots, defensive back, 1995-2004, cornerback, 2003; New York Jets, corner back, defensive back, left corner back, right corner back, 2005, 2008; Kans City Chiefs, cornerback, 2006-07; Denver Broncos, 2009-10; Launch Trampoline Park, founder. **Honors/Awds:** Champion, Asian Football Conf, 1996, 2001, 2003, 2004; Alumni Defensive Back of the Year, Nat Football League, 1998, 2003; Pro Bowl, 1998, 2001, 2002, 2003, 2005; Champion, Super Bowl, XXXVI, XXXVIII, XXXIX; Co Most Valuable Player, Pro Bowl, 1998; Interceptions Leader, Nat Football League, 1998, 2005; Interceptions Yards Leader, Asian Football Conf, 2005; New England Patriots Hall of Fame, 2014. **Business Addr:** Founder, Launch Trampoline Park, 24 Walden Dr, Arden, NC 28704.

## LAWAL, KASE LUKMAN

Executive. **Personal:** Born Jun 30, 1954, Ibadan, OY; married Eileen. **Educ:** Tex Southern Univ, BS, chem, 1976; Prairie View A & M Univ, MBA, finance & mkt, 1978; Ft Valley State Univ, PhD; Tex Southern Univ, PhD. **Career:** Shell Oil Refining Co, process engr, 1975-77; Dresser Indust, res chemist, 1977-79; Suncrest Investment Corp, vpres, 1980-82; Baker Investments, pres, 1982-86; CAMAC Holdings, pres, chmn & chief exec officer, 1986-; CAMAC Int Corp, chmn & chief exec officer, 1986-2011; Allied Energy Corp, chmn, 1991-; Port Houston Authority Bd Comnrs, 1999-2000, comnr, 2000-, vice chmn; Port Houston Authority, vice chmn, 2000-13; Houston Airport Syst Develop Corp, vice chmn & bd dir, 2001; CAMAC Energy Inc, founder, exec chmn, 2010-, chief exec officer, 2011-16; CAMAC Energy Holdings Ltd, dir; Greater Houston Partnership, dir; Windy Hill Pet Food Co, dir; Us Bus Adv Coun, pres; Cullen Engineering Res Found, dir. **Orgs:** US Trade Adv Comt Africa; US Trade Rep Trade Policy Africa; dir, Cullen Eng Res Found; bd dir, Nat Urban League; mem bd dir, Unity Nat Bank; Nat Republican Cong Comt's Bus Adv Coun; bd dir, Cape Investment Holdings; chmn, Houston Mayoral Adv Bd, Int Affairs & Develop; bd dir, Houston Int Festival; bd trustee, Fisk Univ. **Honors/Awds:** US Entrepreneur of the Year Award, 1994; US Africa Business Person of the Year, US Africa Newspaper, 1997; Houston 100 Award; Business Leader Award, Prairie View Tex A & M Univ, 2003; Hon Dr Philos, Ft Valley State Univ; Hon DHL, Tex Southern Univ. **Special Achievements:** Listed in Black Enterprise 100s list, 2003; CAMAC International Corporation, has been named as the 2006 company of the year among African-American businesses. Second Richest African in the World. **Business Addr:** Executive Chairman, Chief Executive Officer, CAMAC Energy Inc, 1330 Post Oak Blvd Suite 2250, Houston, TX 77056, **Business Phone:** (713)797-2940.

## LAWES, VERNA

Executive. **Personal:** Born Philadelphia, PA; daughter of Thomas Jones and Jessie Lee Grier; married Sylvester; children: Anthony & David. **Educ:** Temple Univ, BS. **Career:** Cert Data Serv Inc, pres, 1970-; US Treas Dept, data coordr; IBM, libr; Sperry Univac Corp, res mgr; Nat Polit Cong Black Women, exec secy. **Orgs:** Howard Co Housing Alliance; Howard Co Drug & Alcohol Adv Bd; bd mem, Wilde Lake Village. **Home Addr:** 6200D Foreland Garth, Columbia, MD 21045, **Home Phone:** (410)997-5104.

## LAWHORN, ROBERT MARTIN

Military leader. **Personal:** Born Jan 8, 1943, Camden, SC; married Jacqueline Carter; children: Bridgett Tiffany & Brandon Tilman. **Educ:** NC A&T State Univ, BS, 1965; Nat Univ, MBA, 1985. **Career:** Aviation Officer Cand Sch, officer cand, 1966; Basic Naval Aviation Training, aviation trainee, 1966; Advan NFO Training, 1967; VF-101 NAS Oceana VA & Key W FL, 1967; VF-41 Oceana VA, power plants div off & asst admin off, 1967-70; Navy Recruiting Dist St Louis, exec officer minor recruiting officer, 1970-72; VF-124 Miramar CA, 1972-73; VF1 NAS Miramar, info training officer, admin officer, 1973-77; VF 124 Miramar, asst opers officer instr, 1977-79; VF 1 NAS Miramar CA, maintenance officer, safety off, 1980-81; USS Range CV 61 San Diego, weapons officer co-dept head, 1981-83; Comdr Naval Base San Diego, asst chief staff admin, 1983-. **Orgs:** Nat Naval Officers Asn, 1972-. **Home Addr:** 2106 Rancho Verde Dr, Escondido, CA 92025-7033, **Home Phone:** (760)741-0657. **Business Addr:** Assistant Chief of Staff for Admin, Commander Naval Base San Diego, Code N1, San Diego, CA 92132.

## LAWLAH, GLORIA GARY

State government official. **Personal:** Born Mar 12, 1939, Newberry, SC; married John Wesley III; children: John Wesley IV, Gloria Gene & Gary McCarrell. **Educ:** Hampton Univ, BS, social studies, 1960; Trinity Col, MA, eng & admin, 1970. **Career:** McCormick Co SC Pub Schs, teacher, 1961; Prince George County Pub Schs, teacher, 1961-62; Prince Georges County, state sen; Wash DC Pub Sch, teacher & adminr, 1965-95; Md Gen Assembly, deleg, 26th dist, 1986-90, sen, 26th dist, 1991-; Women Legislators Md, pres, currently; Women Govt Inc, secy & treas, currently; Dept Aging, off secy, 2007-, currently. **Orgs:** Nat Asn Advan Colored People; bd dir, Coalition Black Affairs, 1980-; Nat Coun Negro Women; Oxon Hill Dem; co-chair, PG Govt Rev Task Force Pub Safety, 1982; Dem State Cent Comn, 1982-86; bd dir, Hillcrest-Marlow Planning Bd, 1982-; bd dir, Family Crisis Ctr, 1982-84; Alpha Kappa Alpha Sorority, 1984-; del, Dem Nat Conv, 1984; founder, Nat Polit Cong BlackWomen, 1984-; Black Dem Coun, 1985-; John Hanson Women's Dem Club, 1985-; bd, Ctr Aging Greater SE Comn Hosp, 1985-; St Md legis Comn, Econ &Environ Affairs Comn, Senate-House Joint Comn Invest; Child Care Admin Adv Coun; Educ Block Grants Adv Comn; adv bd, Transp Planning Bd Wash; incorporator & treas, Prince George's Co Alliance Black Elected Off Inc, 1986-; Am Bus Women Asn, 1990-; Nat Conf St Legis, Nat Black CaucusSt Legislators, 1991-; vchmn, Prince Georgeocos Co Senators, 1998-; bd dir, Hospice Nat Capital Region, 1999-; treas, Nat Orgn Black Elected Legis Women Inc, 1999-; Regional Transp Comn Va & Md, 2000-; sen chair, Joint Comn Mgt Pub Funds, 2001-; Pierrians Inc, 2002-; vpres, Prince Georgeocos Chap, LINKS; bd, Prince Georgeocos Southern Christian Leadership Conf, 2002-03; co-chair, Sen Protocol Comn, 2002-; pres, Prince George's County Chap, Links Inc, 2006-; chair & bd dir, Women Govt, 2006-. **Honors/Awds:** Hall of Fame inductee, Prince George's Co Women's, 1991; J Richard CrouseLegislator of the Year Award, 1998; Edgemeade Hon, 1999; Citizen of theYear Award, Prince Georges Co Bd Trade, 2000; Maryland Leadership Award, Md Greater Wash Bd Trade, 2001; Champion Against Oral Cancer, Univ Md MedSyst, 2001; Outstanding Transp Leader of the Year, MWBT, 2002; Award ofExcellence, Mothers Against Drunk Driving, 2002; Nat Coalition of 100Black Women, 2002; hon, Md State Bd Educ, 2002; Humanitarian Award, UnivMd Dent Sch, 2003; Legislator of the Year, Health Facilities Asn of Md, 2006. **Home Addr:** 3801 24th Ave, Temple Hills, MD 20748, **Home Phone:** (301)894-3082. **Business Addr:** Senator, Secretary of Aging, Maryland Department of General Services, Rm 1007 301 W Preston St, Baltimore, MD 21201, **Business Phone:** (410)767-1102.

## LAWLESS, EARL

Administrator. **Personal:** Born Oct 10, 1947, Raceland, LA; married Otha M; children: Reneta & Sharmanice Bradley. **Educ:** Xavier Univ, attended 1967. **Career:** La Weekly Newspaper, asst ed, 1972-76; US Postal Serv, carrier, 1976-77, distrib clerk, 1984-86; Orleans Sheriffs Off criminal dept, dep sheriff, 1977-81; Verona Police Dept, sgt, 1982-84; Okolona Police Dept, sgt, 1987-89; Tupelo Police Dept, patrolman, 1989-90; Tupelo Pub Sch Dist, security chief, 1990-96; Jackson Advocate, news corresp. **Orgs:** Fed Commun Comn, 1974-02; Am Fedn Radio & TV Artists, 1976; chair, Adv Comt Legal Serv, 1982-90; Am Asn Retired Persons, 1997-2002; pres, Vietnam Veterans Am, 1998-2001; lay leader, NEMS Christian Methodist Episcopal Church, 1998-2001; pub policy advocate, Arthritis Found, 1999-2002; Int Soc Poets, 2001. **Home Addr:** 2723 Lawndale Dr, Tupelo, MS 38801-6722, **Home Phone:** (662)690-6568.

## LAWRENCE, ANNIE L.

Educator, nurse. **Personal:** Born Feb 14, 1926, VA. **Educ:** Freedman's Hosp Nursing; Loyola Univ, cert pub health nursing; DePaul Univ, BS, nursing, 1953, MS, nursing admin, 1973; Sarsota Univ, EdD; Ill Stat Univ, EdD. **Career:** Gov State Univ, prof nursing, nursing educ coord, nurse educr, Div Nursing & Hosp Sci, chair, 1997 (retired); St Ill Dept Regist & Educ, asst nursing educ coord; Evangel Sch Nursing, asst dir; Mt Sinai Hosp Sch Nursing, nursing educ; Provident Hosp Sch Nursing, sup instr & dir nursing educ. **Orgs:** Bd mem, Chicago State Univ, 2000; treas, Depaul Nursing Sch Alumni Asn; Northeastern League Nursing; chmn, Adv Stud Sect Am Nurses Asn; Nat League Nursing; parliamentarian, N Asn Lawyers Wives; aux vpres & immediate past pres, N Asn Lawyers Wives; N Ethical Guideline Community; United Church Christ; lay moderator, Pk Manor Ongregational UCC; pres, Women's Fel Pk Manor Cong Church; Am Inst Parliamentarians; corp mem bd, Homeland Ministries; nat pres, Sigma Gamma Rho Sorority; bd dir, Evangel Hosp Asn Pub; site visitor & panel reviewer, Nat League Nursing; vice chair & gov coun, Bethany Hosp; Ill Nurses Asn; Nat League Nurses; Am J Nursing. **Honors/Awds:** Service Award, Chicago State Univ, 2006-07; Successful Blacks Award. **Special Achievements:** Author of "Can an Evaluation Tool be Meaningful to Studies & Teachers?". **Home Addr:** 448 E 89th St, Chicago, IL 60619-6716, **Home Phone:** (773)846-1149.

## LAWRENCE, ARCHIE L.

Lawyer. **Personal:** Born Jun 21, 1947, East St. Louis, IL; son of Charlie and Addie; married Ernestine King; children: Chiestine, Crystal & Candace. **Educ:** Southern Ill Univ-Carbondale, BA, 1970; St Louis Univ, Sch Law, JD, 1975. **Career:** Legis Ref Bur, bill drafting agency, 1975-80; Internal Revenue Serv, estate tax atty, 1980-82; Ill Dept Revenue, staff atty, 1982-90; Sangamon County Bd, elected rep, 1986-92; Ill Atty Gen's Off, asst atty gen, 1991-, atty gen, currently. **Orgs:** Ill State Bar Asn, 1982-; rep, County Bd, 20th Dist, Sangamm County, Ill, 1986-; pres, Nat Asn Advan Colored People, Springfield Bd, 1984-88, bd, 1988-90, first vpres, 1990-92; bd dir, 1996-. **Honors/Awds:** Equal Opportunity Award, Sprinfield Ill Urban League, 1986; President's Award, Nat Asn Advan Colored People, Springfield Br, 1988, Political Action Award, 1989. **Home Addr:** 2420 Wimbledon Pl, Springfield, IL 62704-8708, **Home Phone:** (217)726-5698. **Business Addr:** Attorney General, State of Illinois, 500 S 2nd St, Springfield, IL 62701-1705, **Business Phone:** (217)782-1090.

## LAWRENCE, AZAR MALCOLM

Jazz musician, saxophonist. **Personal:** Born Nov 3, 1953, Los Angeles, CA; children: Daneka, Azar Malcolm III & Aisha. **Educ:** W La Jr Col; Calif State Univ; Univ Southern Calif. **Career:** McCoy Tyner's Quartet, jazz musician, 1973-77; Prestige Label Serv, leader, 1974-76; Azar Lawrence Quartet, saxist, currently; Albums: Bridge into the New Age, 1974; Summer Solstice, 1975; People Moving, 1976; Prayer For My Ancestors, 2009; Mystic Journey, 2010. **Orgs:** Sickle Cedd Fedn; Urban League Guild; Black Awareness Prog. **Special Achievements:** Featured in Downbeat Magazine, 1973 and Esq Magazine, 1975; Montreaux Jazz Festival, 1973. **Home Addr:** 4272 Don Jose Dr, Los Angeles, CA 90008.

## LAWRENCE, DR. BARBARA ANN

School administrator. **Personal:** Born Feb 4, 1938, Indianapolis, IN; daughter of Harold and Norma Price; married Leonard E; children: Courtney N, Leonard M & David W. **Educ:** Mich State Univ, BA, 1959; Butler Univ, MS, 1967; Tex Agr & Mech Univ, PhD, 1994. **Career:** Indianapolis Pub Sch, spec educ teacher, 1959-62; Sandia AFB, NMex, kindergarten teacher, 1964-65; Ind Univ Sch Med, psychometrist, 1967-69; N side ISD San Antonio, spec educ teacher, 1969-70, Northeast ISD, depthead, spec ed, 1976-84, lead teacher, pyschiatric hosp, 1984-91; Univ Tex, Inst Texan Cult, asst dir educ & technol initiative, 1994-. **Orgs:** Nat Med Asn, 1973-; pres, Links, San Antonio Chap, 1983-; vpres, bd mem, Community Guid Ctr, 1986-92; adv comn, Tex Cancer Coun, 1994-96; chair personnel comm, bd mem, San Antonio Child Advocates, 1994-99; Tex Agr & Mech Dev Bd, Col Educ, 1995-; chair dev comn, Merced Housing Tex, 1996-; dev bd mem, Univ Incarnate Word, 1998-. **Home Addr:** 3107 Sable Creek, San Antonio, TX 78259-2636, **Home Phone:** (210)481-7092. **Business Addr:** Director of the Educational & Technology Initiative, The University of Texas Institute of Texan Cultures, 801 S Bowie St, San Antonio, TX 78205, **Business Phone:** (210)458-2300.

## LAWRENCE, HON. BRENDA L.

Mayor, school administrator, government official. **Personal:** Born Oct 18, 1954, Southfield, MI; married McArthur; children: Michael & Michelle. **Educ:** Cent Mich Univ, BA, pub admin. **Career:** Community advocate; Southfield City Coun, pres, 1999; Southfield City, mayor, 2001-15; US House Representatives, Mich 14th dist, 2015-. **Orgs:** Parent Youth Guid Comn; adv comn, Oakland Co United Way; Oakland Co Aids Coun; Oakland Co Chap, Nat Asn Advan Colored People; adv bd, Mich Asn Mayor's; US Conf Mayors; Southfield-Lathrup Optimist Club; Women's Econ Club; bd dir, Women Off Network; adv bd, Birmingham YMCA; adv bd, Pepsi Community; bd gov, Renaissance & Skyline Club; Parent Teacher's Asn; pres, Southfield Pub Schs Bd Educ, vpres, & secy; Mich deleg, Dem Nat Conv, 2004; superdelegate, Dem Nat Conv, 2008; Go Red For Women, Am Heart Asn; Mich Suburbs Alliance Exec Bd; adv bd, MBN TV & Radio. **Honors/Awds:** Brotherhood Award, Jewish War Vet-State Mich; Challenging the Process Award, Leadership Detroit's; Woman of the Year Award, ABWA Millennium Chap; Enterprising Women Award, Detroit Historical Soc; Distinguished Leadership & Future Leaders Award, Leadership Oakland, 2004; 95 Most Influential Women in Michigan; Black Women Achiever Award; Wand Award, 2004; Enterprising Women, Detroit Historical Soc, 2004; 2007 Most Influential Women, Crain, 2007; Black Women Achiever Award. **Special Achievements:** First African American & first woman mayor of Southfield; Initiated the following community programs: The Mayor's Walk community health prog; Mayor's Roundtable-a citizen driven forum; Southfield Reads!; Ann Flower Day; City-wide Blood Dr; Today's Woman-a cable show; List of the Most Influential Black Women in Metropolitan Detroit,

Women's Informal Network; 95 Most Influential Women in Michigan, CORP Magazine. **Business Addr:** US House of Representatives, 5555 Conner Ave, Detroit, MI 48213, **Business Phone:** (313)423-6183.

### LAWRENCE, CHARLES, JR.

Lawyer, judge, association executive. **Personal:** Born Sep 27, 1955, Laurel, MS; son of Charels E and Mattie M; married Shirley Sutton; children: Charles E C J III & Chari E. **Educ:** Univ Southern Miss, BA, polit sci, 1976; Howard Univ Sch Law, JD, 1979. **Career:** Southeast Miss Legal Serv, staff atty, 1979-84; Pvt Pract, atty, 1984-; City Hattiesburg, councilman ward 5, 1985-97, munic ct judge, 1997-. **Orgs:** Omega Psi Phi Fraternity Inc, 1975-; Miss Bar & Magnolia Bar, 1979-; Hattiesburg Eve Optimist Club, 1987-; Nat Asn Advan Colored People; Hattiesburg Area Develop Partnership/Chamber Com, 1997-; Miss Munic Judges Asn, 1997-; Am Trial Lawyers Asn, 1997-; United Way Southeast Miss, 1997-. **Honors/Awds:** Outstanding Service Award, SEMLS, 1979-84; Outstanding Service Award, Miss Headstart, 1985; Juneteenth Community, Black Excellence Award City Gov, 1992; Man of the Year, Omega Psi Phi Fraternity, 1998; Pro Bono Volunteer Award. **Home Addr:** 606 John St, Hattiesburg, MS 39401, **Home Phone:** (601)583-4917. **Business Addr:** Attorney, 1105 Edwards St, Hattiesburg, MS 39401, **Business Phone:** (601)582-4157.

### LAWRENCE, EDWARD

Actor. **Personal:** Born Jan 8, 1935, Gadsden, AL; married Marion Winn; children: Rita, Edward Jr, Jill & Lawrence Jr. **Educ:** Empire State Col, BA, 1957; Studio Theatre Sch. **Career:** African-am Cult Ctr, prof actor, exec dir; Film: Everybody's All-American (When I Fall in Love), 1988. **Orgs:** Actors Equity; Studio Arena Theatre, 1966-68; Buffalo Urban League; Community Action Orgn; Buffalo & Build Orgn. **Honors/Awds:** Community Service Award Black Harmony. **Home Addr:** 129 Dartmouth, Buffalo, NY 14215.

### LAWRENCE, ELLIOTT

Association executive, executive. **Personal:** Born May 27, 1947, Mt. Vernon, NY; son of Muriel and Milford Brown. **Educ:** Albany State Univ, BA, Eng lit/dramatic arts, 1973. **Career:** Events Plus, vpres sales, 1989-91; Themes & Schemes, dir sales & mkt, 1991-92; San Diego Conv & Visitors Bur, nat sales mgr, 1994-99, scct dir, 1999-99, asst dir multicultural group sales, 2001; Am Property Mgt, dir sales, 2003-06; Coctail Jazz, owner, 2006-. **Orgs:** Nat Coalition Black Meeting Planners; Relig Conf Mgt Asn; Meeting Prof Int; bd mem, Jackie Robinson YMCA, San Diego; Nat Black MBA Asn; asst dir multicultural group sales, Int Asn Hisp Meeting Planners. **Honors/Awds:** Multicultural Award, Nat Univ, 1997; Apex Award, Black Meeting & Tanes in Mag, 1999. **Special Achievements:** BroadwaySinger/Dancer. **Home Addr:** 2810 31st St, San Diego, CA 92104. **Business Addr:** Owner, Coctail Jazz, San Diego, CA 92101.

### LAWRENCE, JAMES FRANKLIN

Journalist. **Personal:** Born Aug 19, 1949, Orlando, FL; son of James and Ethel L; married Betty A; children: Terrance, Jamil & Ebony. **Educ:** Howard Univ, Wash, DC, BA, 1971. **Career:** Cleveland Call & Post, Cleveland, OH, reporter, 1972-73; United Press Int, Denver, Colo, reporter & ed, 1973-85; Orlando Sentinel, Orlando, Fla, ed writer, 1985-87; Gannett Westchester Newspapers, White Plains, NY, assoc ed & ed; Rochester Dem & Chronicle, ed, currently. **Orgs:** Treas, Alpha Phi Alpha, 1989; Nat Asn Black Journalists; fel, McCormick Found, 1999. **Honors/Awds:** Second Place, Beat Commentary, The Orlando Sentinel, 1986; Mighty Pen, Gannett Westchester Newspapers, 1987-91. **Special Achievements:** One of 15 Gannett Supervisors of the Year, 2004. **Home Addr:** 23 Watergrant St 1K, Yonkers, NY 10701, **Home Phone:** (914)376-4680. **Business Addr:** Editor, The Rochester Democrat and Chronicle, 55 Exchange Blvd, Rochester, NY 14614, **Business Phone:** (585)232-7100.

### LAWRENCE, JAMES H.

Police officer. **Personal:** Born Apr 25, 1946, Harlem, NY; son of James and Alice; married Gail Brown; children: James III. **Educ:** Fordham Univ, BA, econs, 1978; CUNY Law Sch, JD, 1988; Columbia Univ, police mgt inst, 1993. **Career:** Police officer (retired); New York Police Dept, chief personnel, 1970-2002; Nassau County Police Dept, comnr police, 2002-07. **Orgs:** Sigma Pi Phi; Nat Org Black Law Enforcement Execs; Am Acad Pro Law Enforcement; Guardian's Asn; NY State Asn Chiefs Police; Int Asn Chiefs Police; mem chair, Law Enforcement Employer's Prog; Sigma Pi Phi; bd dir, Nassau County Munic Police Chief's Asn; bd dir, Old Westbury Col Found; Maj Cities Chiefs Asn; One Hundred Black Men Long Island Inc. **Honors/Awds:** Lloyd Sealy Award, NY Chap Nat Org Black Law Endorcement Execs, 2000; Man of the Year, NYPD Guardians Asn, 2001; Lifetime Achievement Award, Nubians Soc, 2001; Building Brick & Cornerstone Award, NY Chap, Urban League, 2002; Man of the Year, Police Self Support Group, 2002; 6th Criminal Justice Leadership Award, St. John's Univ, 2003; Man of the Year, Suffolk Minorities involved in Law Enforcement, 2004; Lifetime Achievement Award, Nassau County Guardians, 2005. **Special Achievements:** First African American police commissioner in Nassau County Police Dept. **Home Addr:** 329 Pkwy Dr, Westbury, NY 11590, **Home Phone:** (516)997-8954.

### LAWRENCE, DR. JAQUATOR HAMER

Executive, educator. **Personal:** Born May 16, 1968, Ashland, MS; daughter of Joseph Sr and Edith Mae. **Educ:** Miss State Univ, BBA, 1990, MS, 1995; Univ Ark, Fayetteville, EdD, 2000. **Career:** Univ AR-Fayetteville, asst dean, multicult stud serv, 1994-2000; Bradley Univ, dir multicult stud serv, 2000-02; Southern Univ & A&M Col, dir, retention & transition servs, 2002-08; La Dept of Educ, educ prog consult, 2008-10; River Parishes Community Col, dir, Stud Support Serv, 2010-. **Orgs:** Zeta Phi Beta Sorority, 1988-; Am Col Personnel Asn, 1995-; Asn Black Cult Ctrs, 1996-; Nat Asn Advan Colored People, 2001-. **Home Addr:** 8001 Jefferson Hwy, Baton Rouge, LA 70809, **Home Phone:** (225)928-8369. **Business Addr:** Director, Retention and Transition Services, Southern University and Agricultural and Mechanical College, Harris Hall Rm 122, Baton Rouge, LA 70813, **Business Phone:** (225)771-4312.

### LAWRENCE, JOHN EDWARD

Educator. **Personal:** Born May 11, 1941, Durham, NC; son of Harry and Lucille; married Virginia Landers; children: John II & Jason Earl. **Educ:** NC Cent Univ, BS, biol; Fla A&M Univ, MS, admin supv, adult educ; Fla State Univ, marine biol. **Career:** Lincoln High Sch, biol teacher, 1963-67; Godby High Sch, teacher, 1967-69, from asst prin to prin, 1969-78, prin, 1973; Fla Dept Educ, bur adult & community educ, chief, 1979-; JVL Educ Inc, chief exec officer, 1996-. **Orgs:** Community Educr; Nat Commmunity Educ Asn; NAPCAE; FAEA; Leon Dist Adv Comn; Kappa Delta Pi; Phi Delta Kappa; Frontiers Int; bd dir, Capital City Tiger Bay Club; Tallahassee Urban League; life mem, Nat Asn Advan Colored People; bd mem, Leon Co Housing Finance Authority; Fla Lemon Law Bd; bd mem, Thurgood Marshall Achievers; chair, Nat Dirs Adult Educ; bd mem, Coun Cult & Arts. **Honors/Awds:** Frontiersman of the Year Award, 1975, 1998. **Special Achievements:** First African-American principal in Godby High School. **Home Addr:** 1801 Quince Dr, Tallahassee, FL 32308-5237, **Home Phone:** (850)878-1502. **Business Addr:** Chief, Florida Department of Education, Rm 1244 FEC Bldg 325 W Gaines St, Tallahassee, FL 32399-0400, **Business Phone:** (850)487-4929.

### LAWRENCE, DR. LEONARD EUGENE

Educator, psychiatrist. **Personal:** Born Jun 27, 1937, Indianapolis, IN; son of Leonard A and Elizabeth M; married Barbara Ann Price; children: Courtney, L Michae & David. **Educ:** Ind Univ, BA, 1959, MD, 1962. **Career:** E. J. Meyer Memorial Hosp, internship, 1962-63; USAF, gen med officer, 1963-65, Child Psych Serv Wilford Hall USAF Med Ctr, chief, 1969-72; Ind Univ Sch Med, child psychol fel, 1962, psych resident, 1965-68, chief psychol res, 1967-69; San Antonio C Ctr, assoc med dir; Univ Tex Health Sci Ctr, asst prof, 1972, asst dean, assoc dean stud affairs, 1981-2005, prof psych pediats, fam pract, prof emer, 2010-. **Orgs:** Am Bd Psychol & Neurol, 1970-71; Tex Juv Corrections Master Plan Adv Coun, 1974-75; coun, C Adolesc & Their Families Am Psychol Asn, 1976, 1978-83, distinguished life fel; pres, Nat Med Asn, 1992-93, 1993-94; Tex Youth Comn, 1992-, chmn, 1995; Am Acad Child Psychol; Am Ortho Psychol Asn; Am Psychol Asn; Kappa Alpha Psi; ed bd, Jour Am Acad Child Psychol; chair, Group Stud Affairs; Minority Affairs Sect, Asn Am Med Cols; chair mem, Am Acad Child & Adolescent Psychiat, life fel; exec comt, United Way San Antonio, chair bd trustee; United Way Bexar, chair bd trustees; chair Mgt Bd, San Antonio Fighting Back; United Ways Partners Community Chg Coord Coun; Robert Wood Johnson Found; Alamo Area community Info Syst. **Honors/Awds:** Distinguished Service Award, Asn Am Med Cols Minority Affairs, 2004; Jeanne Spurlock Award, Am Acad of Child & Adolescent Psychiat, 2005. **Special Achievements:** Co-author with J Spurlock "The Black Child" Basic Handbook of Child Psychvol 1; JB Noshpitz Ed-in-Chief Basic Books Inc, NY, 1979. **Home Addr:** 3107 Sable Creek, San Antonio, TX 78259-2636, **Home Phone:** (210)481-7092. **Business Addr:** Professor Emeritus, University of Texas Health Science Centre School of Medicine, 7703 Floyd Curl Dr MC 7792, San Antonio, TX 78229-3900, **Business Phone:** (210)567-5403.

### LAWRENCE, LONNIE R.

Executive, manager. **Personal:** Born Jun 11, 1946, Miami, FL; married Carol Walker; children: Derek & Jonathan. **Educ:** Miami-Dade Community Col, attended 1972; St Thomas Univ, attended 1979; Northwestern Univ, Sch Police Staff & Command, attended 1989; Barry Univ, Miami, Fla, prof studies, 1989, BS, mgt, 1990; Harvard Univ, JFK Sch Gov, sr exec, 1990. **Career:** Manager (retired); Metro-Dade Police Dept, patrolman, 1968-80, sgt, 1980, comdr, 1981-83, maj & dist comdr, 1980-89; Metro-Dade HUD, asst dir, 1987-89; Metro-Dade Corrections, dir, 1989-93; Miami Dade Aviation Dept, dir opers, 1993-97; Off Congressman Kendrick Meek, dir spec opers, 2005-11; Independent Security & Law Enforcement Consult, freelance, 2011-. **Orgs:** Bd dir, Leadership Miami Alumni Asn, Big Bros & Big Sisters, Informed Families Dade; bd dir, treas, Miami-Dade Chamber Com; Fla Criminal Justice Exe Inst, 1990-; chmn, Youth Activ Dade County Asn Chiefs Police, 1984-; Am Correctional Asn, 1989-. **Honors/Awds:** Officer of the Year, Richmon-Porrine Jaycees, 1982; Public Serv US Dept Justice, 1984; Officer of the Year, MIK Develop Corp, 1985; Outstanding Participation Award, Hialeah-Miami Springs Co, 1991; Award of Honor, Alternatives Prog Inc, 1990; Cert Commendation, Bd County Comnr, 1991. **Home Addr:** 831 NW 207th St, Miami, FL 33169-2320, **Home Phone:** (305)652-1304.

### LAWRENCE, DR. MARGARET MORGAN

Physician. **Personal:** Born Aug 19, 1914, New York, NY; daughter of Sandy Alonzo and Mary Elizabeth Smith; married Charles R II; children: Charles R III, Sara Lawrence Lightfoot & Paula Wehmiller. **Educ:** Cornell Univ, AB, 1936; Columbia Univ, Col Physicians & Surgeons, MD & MS, pub health, 1943, cert, psychoanal med, 1951. **Career:** Physicians, surgeons (retired); Pediat Meharry Med Col, asso prof, 1943-47; Nat Coun Res fel, Babies Hosp, 1948; Pomona NY, practicing child psychiatrist & psychoanalyst, 1951; Northside Child Develop Ctr, City Col Educ Clin, NYC, psychiatrist, 1951-57; C's Ther, assoc dir, 1954-57; Sch Ment Health Unit, dir, 1957-63; Harlem Hosp Ctr, supv child psychiatrist & psychoanalyst, 1963-84; Col P& S Columbia, assoc clin prof psychiat, 1963-84; Child Develop Ctr, dir, 1969-74; Rockland Co Ctr Ment Health, Pomona, NY, co-founder. **Orgs:** Fel Rosenwald, 1942-43; Peace Fel Episcopal Church, 1943; fel Nat Res Coun, 1947-48; fel US Pub Health Serv, 1948-50; Licentiate Am Bd Pediat, 1948; Alpha Kappa Alpha Sorority, 1990; life fel Am Psychoanal Asn; life fel Am Psychiat Asn; Am Acad Psychoanalysis; Am Orthopsychiat Asn; Nat Med Asn; Black Psychiatrists Am; Med Soc Co Rockland. **Honors/Awds:** Publ "Mental Health Team in the Schools" Human Sci Press, 1971; publ "Young Inner City Families the Development of Ego Strength under Stress" Human Sci Press, 1975; Joseph R Bernstein Mental Health Award, Rockland Co, NY, 1975; EY Williams MD Clinical Scholars of Distinction Award, 1984; Outstanding Women Practioners in Medicine Award, Susan Smith McKinney Steward Med Soc, 1984; Cornell Black Alumni Award, 1992; Honorary Doctor of Civil Law, University of the South, 1987; Honorary Doctor of Science, Connecticut Col, 1989; Honorary Doctor of Divinity, General Theological Seminary, 1990; Honorary Doctor of Humane Letters, Marymount Col, 1990; Honorary Doctor of Education, Wheelock Col, 1991; Honorary Doctor ofHumane Letters, Berkeley Theological Seminary, 1998; Honorary Doctor of Science, Swarthmore Col, 2003; The 100 Most Notable Cornellians (Altschuler GC, Kramnick I, Moore RL, eds) Margaret Morgan Lawrence, 1936; Nevin Sayre Peace Award, Episcopal Peace Fellowship, 2003. **Special Achievements:** First African American trainee to be certified in psychoanalysis at Columbia University's Columbia Psycoanalytic Center; First African American to complete a residency at the New York Psychiatric Institute; First recipient of Rockland County New Yorks J R Bernstein Mental Health Award.; First African American psychoanalyst trained in the United States; First black female pediatrician certified by American Board of Pediatrics; Authored: The Mental Health Team in Schools, 1971; Young Inner City Families, 1975; First child psychiatrist in Rockland County. **Home Addr:** 34 Dogwood Lane, Pomona, NY 10970-3312, **Home Phone:** (845)354-1951.

### LAWRENCE, MARTIN FITZGERALD

Actor. **Personal:** Born Apr 16, 1965; son of John and Chlora; married Patricia Southall; children: Jasmine Page; married Shamika Gibbs; children: 2. **Career:** Actor, executive producer, writer & director; Films: Do the Right Thing, 1989; House Party, 1990; House Party II, 1991; Talkin' Dirty After Dark, 1991; Boomerang, 1992; You So Crazy!, actor & exec producer, 1994; Bad Boys, 1995; A Thin Line Between Love & Hate, exec producer & dir, 1996; Nothing to Lose, 1997; Life, 1999; Blue Streak, 1999; Big Mamma's House, exec producer, 2000; What's the Worst That Could Happen, actor & exec producer, 2001; Black Knight, exec producer, 2001; Martin Lawrence Live: Run teldat, exec producer, 2002; National Security, exec producer, 2003; Bad Boys II, 2003; Blue Streak II, 2003; Rebound, exec producer, 2005; Big Momma's House 2, exec producer, 2006; Wild Hogs, 2007; Welcome Home, Roscoe Jenkins, 2008; College Road Trip, 2008; Big Momma's House 3, 2009; Death at a Funeral, 2010; Big Mommas: Like Father, Like Son, 2011; Bad Boys 3, 2012; TV series: "What's Happening Now!", 1987-88; A Little Bit Strange, 1989; Private Times, 1991; Hammer, Slammer & Slade, 1990; "Martin", 1992-97; "Saturday Night Live", 1994; "The Soul Man", 2014; "Partners", 2014. **Honors/Awds:** ShoWest Award, ShoWest Convention, 1995; Image Award, Nat Asn Asvan Colored People, 1995 & 1996; Male Star of Tomorrow, 1995; NRJ Cine Award, 2004; BET Icon Comedy Award, 2005. **Home Addr:** c/o William Morris Agency, New York, NY 10019, **Home Phone:** (212)586-5100. **Business Addr:** Actor, William Morris Agency, 1 William Morris Pl, Beverly Hills, CA 90212, **Business Phone:** (310)859-4000.

### LAWRENCE, MERLISA EVELYN (MERLISA EVELYN LAWRENCE CORBETT)

Writer. **Personal:** Born Oct 14, 1965, Winter Haven, FL; daughter of Esther Mae Martin and Robinson Louis. **Educ:** Univ S Fla, Tampa, Fla, BA, jour, 1987. **Career:** Tampa Tribune, Tampa, Fla, sports writer, 1987-88; St Petersburg Times & Lakeland Ledger, reporter; Am Online, asst sports ed; Staten Island Advan, Staten Island, NY, sports writer, genl assignments, 1988-90; Pittsburgh Press, Pittsburgh, Pa, sports writer, 1990-92; Sports Illus, reporter, 1992-94; freelance writer, 1994-; Alexandria Coffee News, publ, 2005-09. **Orgs:** Nat Asn Black Journalists, 1988-; Pittsburgh Press sports staff; Garden State Asn Black Journalists, 1992; Am Soc Journalists & Authors; Nat Asn Black Journalists & Us Tennis Asn; ed, Nat Asn Black Journalists Sports Task Force Newsletter, 1990-. **Honors/Awds:** Outstanding Achievement on Brain Bowl Team, 1985; Public speaking to high school & college students, 1990-; Involved with local job fairs & workshops for minority high school & college students. **Home Addr:** 233 1/2 Summit Ave, Jersey City, NJ 07304, **Home Phone:** (201)451-1103. **Business Addr:** Publisher, Alexandria Coffee News, PO Box 22206, Alexandria, VA 22304, **Business Phone:** (703)966-7127.

### LAWRENCE, OLLIE, JR.

Airline executive, founder (originator), executive. **Personal:** Born Aug 3, 1951, Chicago, IL; son of Ollie and Minnie; married Robin Warr; children: Nicole. **Educ:** Univ Conn, BS, bus admin, 1973; Univ New Haven, attended 1978; George Washington Univ, attended 1990. **Career:** Cockerham & Assocs, LLC, pract leader, human resource officer; Pratt & Whitney Aircraft, compensation analyst, personnel counr, 1973-78; US Airways Inc, Human Resources, vpres, Employee Rels, vpres; Sodexho Inc, sr vpres, chief human resorces officer; Lawrence Consult, founder, 2003-. **Orgs:** Wash Personnel Asn; Am Compensation Asn; bd mem, Black Human Resource Network; US Air Mgt Club; pub arbitrator, Nat Asn Securities Dealers Inc; pub arbitrator, Am Stock Exchange; chap vpres, Soc Human Resources Mgt; Int Asn Bus Communicators; Capital Press Club; bd mem, Va Chamber Com; bd mem, Arlington Chamber Com. **Honors/Awds:** Mgt Achievement Award, US Air, 1990; Minority Human Resources Professor Award, Black Human Resources Network, 1992; Motivator of the Year Award, Elliot Groups, 2001; Pvt Sector Human Resources Prof Excellence Award, Black Human Resources Network, 2004. **Special Achievements:** Black Belt in Tae Kwon Do. **Home Addr:** 7714 Midday Lane, Alexandria, VA 22306, **Home Phone:** (703)765-6046. **Business Addr:** Founder, Lawrence Consulting Inc, 3506 W 37th Ave, Vancouver, BC V6N 2V8, **Business Phone:** (604)351-3606.

### LAWRENCE, PHILIP MARTIN

Executive, sales manager. **Personal:** Born Nov 12, 1950, Evansville, IN; son of William Henry and Pilar Elizabeth; married Sandra Authur Robinson; children: Kevin, M Demorrio & Rhonda; married Cheryl Darlene Moore; children: DeVonna M, Philip M II & Shane K. **Educ:** ISUE, Evansville, IN. **Career:** People's Voice, Black Newspaper, 1969-71; WUPS Radio, disc jockey, 1970-71; Family Rec Plan Heritage, from salesman to sales dir, 1977-77, 1981-82; ATSCO Inc, chief exec officer, owner, 1982-; WJPS, radio announcer; City Evansville, Evansville, Ind, contract compliance officer, bus develop supvr; Tomorrow's Treasures, Calif, regional mgr; Heritage, NJ, regional mgr; Community Action Evansville, Evansville, Ind, sr aide dir. **Orgs:** Bd dir, Nat Asn Advan Colored People, 1972-75, treas, 1980-82, 1983-86; Sr aides dir, Community Action Prog, 1977-78; Mich C chmn, IRMSDC, 1984-85; bd mem, Coun Aging, 1984-87; Steering Comt Head, 1986-89; State Chamber Com, 1986-89; treas, 1987-89, Evansville Area Minority Supplies Develop Coun; Rotary Int, 1987-89; bd dir, Pvt Indust Coun, 1987-89; pres, Grace Lutheran Church, 1990-; bd dir, ABCDE Corp. **Honors/Awds:** Master of Ceremonies for Black History Talent, 1978-88; Certificate for Outstanding Business Achievement, Black Enterprise Mag, 1990; Freedom Award, Nat Asn Advan Colored People, 1990; Leadership Award, Evansville Chamber Com, 1992; Nat Asn Advan Colored People, Minority Bus Leadership Award, 1992; Certificate of Appreciation, Downtown Master Plan Steering Comt, 1995. **Special Achievements:** Played the beast in "Beauty & the Beast" on local TV station, 1982. **Home Addr:** 907 E Gum St, Evansville, IN 47713-2350, **Home Phone:** (812)402-6027. **Business Addr:** Chief Executive Officer, ATSCO Inc, PO Box 3912, Evansville, IN 47737, **Business Phone:** (812)423-0054.

**LAWRENCE, RODELL**
Executive. **Personal:** Born Feb 19, 1946, Apopka, FL; son of Adell and Estella Richardson; married Cedar Lavern Evans; children: Christopher, Debora, Biram & Raegena. **Educ:** SC State Col, BSEE, 1970. **Career:** N Am Rockwell Missile Syst Div, mem tech staff, 1970-73; Xerox Corp, test engr, sr field engr, regional prod serv mgr midwest region hq, proj mgr I II III, multinat serv opers mgr, prod support mgr, prod serv mgr, mgr, multinat configuration mgt, 1973; Integrated Supply Chain, Off Doc Systs Div, mgr; Stillman Col, from exec asst to pres; Meharry Med Col; Ft Valley State Univ, dir develop, 2007-. **Orgs:** Bd dir, CARI, 1980-85; dean educ, Omega Psi Phi Frat, 1984, 1985, 1987; athletic dir, Irondequoit Football League, 1985-86; bd dir, Lewis St Settlement, 1986-87; bd visitor, Claflin Col; adv Coun, chmn engineering, SC State Col, 1991-94; vpres, Rochester Chap Nat Asn Advan Colored People, 1991-92; vpres, Dist Scholar Found, Omega Psi Phi, 1990-91; comt mem, Univ Syst Ga. **Honors/Awds:** Distinguished Corp, Alumni Citation NAFEO, 1983; Houston Engineers Society Award, SC State Col, 1986; SC State Col, Benjamin E Mays Most Distinguished Grauate Award, 1989; Outstanding Performance Award, Xerox, 1989; Leadership through Quality Award, Xerox, 1989; hon doctor law degree, SC State Univ, 1992; President Award, Claflin Col, 1992. **Business Addr:** Director of Development, Fort Valley State University, 1005 State Univ Dr, Ft. Valley, GA 31030-4313, **Business Phone:** (478)827-3878.

**LAWRENCE, THOMAS R, JR. See Obituaries Section.**

**LAWRENCE, DR. WILLIAM WESLEY**
Consultant, educator, counselor. **Personal:** Born Jan 27, 1939, Whiteville, NC; son of Horace and Mary; married Queen E Wooten; children: William Jr & Lori Elecia. **Educ:** NC Col, BS, chem, 1962; St Josephs Sch Med Tech, Tacoma, WA, cert med tech, 1967; NC Cent Univ, Durham, MA, coun, 1971; Univ NC, Chapel Hill, PhD, coun psychol, 1974. **Career:** Liggett & Myers Inc, res chem, 1969-71; Univ NC Chapel Hill, counr, 1972-73; NC Cent Univ Durham, assoc dir inst res & eval, 1973-74; NC A&T State Univ, Greensboro, chmn educ psychiat & guid, 1974-78; Nat Inst Environ Health Sci coun psychiat & dir human resource devel, 1978-87; Century21 NC Comm Col, real estate broker & instr, 1982-85; Fayetteville State Univ, prof educ, 1987-99; NC Cent Univ, Sch Educ, Dept Counr Educ, chmn, prof educ, currently, consult & prog evaluator educ & educ related progs, currently. **Orgs:** Pub notary, Durham City. **Home Addr:** 308 Wayne Cir, Durham, NC 27707, **Home Phone:** (919)682-6236. **Business Addr:** Professor, North Carolina Central University, Rm 2123 H M Michaux Jr Sch Educ Bldg 1801 Fayetteville St, Durham, NC 27707, **Business Phone:** (919)530-6212.

**LAWRIE-GOODRICH, MADELINE**
Vice president (organization). **Career:** ABC Radio Networks, sr dir affil rels, prod specialist ABC news programming; Reach Media, sr vpres affil rels, 2003-. **Business Addr:** Vice President of Affiliate Relations, Reach Media Inc, 13760 Noel Rd Suite 750, Dallas, TX 75240, **Business Phone:** (972)371-5844.

**LAWSON, ANTHONY EUGENE, SR.**
President (organization), manager, executive. **Personal:** Born Nov 15, 1954, Martinez, CA; son of Ardell Sr and Inez; married Gazelle Williams; children: Tony & Danielle. **Educ:** Univ Ariz, BS, pub admin, 1977; Univ LaVerne, MS, orgn mgt, 1985. **Career:** Rockwell Int Space, supvr, qual, reliable assurance, test qual engr, 1980-85; Rockwell Int NAAO, supvr qual assurance, 1985; Northrop Corp B-2 Div, qual assurance mgr, prod inspector mgr, maj, final inspection opers mgr, vpres prod, vpres site opers; Northrop Grumman Corp, vpres, dep prog mgr, 1985-97; Burke Industs, vpres & gen mgr, 1998-2001; Everett Charles Technologies, gen mgr, 2001-02; Hitco Carbon Composites Inc, exec vpres, vpres prog mgt, 2003-, pres, 2010-13; Hitco Carbon Components, pres. **Orgs:** Bd mem, S Bay Workforce Investment Bd. **Home Addr:** 7333 Dana Dr, Palmdale, CA 93551. **Business Addr:** President, Hitco Carbon Composites Inc, 1600 W 135th St, Gardena, CA 90249-2506, **Business Phone:** (310)527-0700.

**LAWSON, BRUCE BENJAMIN**
Executive. **Personal:** Born Mar 30, 1948, New Orleans, LA; son of Henry and Josephine Hirsch; married Ruth Evelyn Charles; children: Rachel Joyce & Roxanne Louise. **Educ:** Southern Univ, Baton Rouge, LA, BSEE, 1969; Univ Chicago, Chicago, IL, attended 1976. **Career:** AT&T, Morristown, NJ, int mkt dir, 1969; Hearst-Argyle TV Inc, gen sales mgr, 1998-2012; singer, songwriter, musician. **Orgs:** Chairperson, Comn Black Ministries, Diocese Paterson, NJ, 1988-91. **Home Addr:** 2 Thompson Way, Morris Plains, NJ 07950-2541, **Home Phone:** (973)898-0646. **Business Addr:** General Sales Manager, Hearst-Argyle Television Inc, 300 W 57th St, New York, NY 10106, **Business Phone:** (212)887-6800.

**LAWSON, DR. CASSELL AVON, SR.**
Educator, executive director, association executive. **Personal:** Born Mar 29, 1937, Little Rock, AR; married Amy Davison; children: 6. **Educ:** Langston Univ, BA, 1959; Ind Univ, MEd, 1970; Univ Notre Dame, PhD, 1974; Ind State Univ, postdoctoral, 1976. **Career:** Educator (retired); Grand Rapids Urban Leag, dir, 1956-68; S Bend Urban League, exec dir, 1968-70; Notre Dame Univ, dir Stud Outreach & Minority Stud Affairs, 1973-74; Univ Mass, asst prof & dir, 1974-75; Morgan State Univ, asst vpres dir, 1974-78; Coppin State Col, dean educ, 1978-79, vpres acad affairs, 1980-81, prof, 1981-83; Erie Community Col, vpres, 1983-86; Wayne County Community Col, exec dean, 1986-90; E Region Gateway Tech Col, vpres; Gateway Tech Col, vpres & provost, 2005. **Orgs:** Kappa Alpha Psi Fraternity; Phi Delta Kappa; Nat Educ Asn, 1965; chair, Ind Coun Urban Leag Exec, 1967-68; chair, Midwestern Rep Urban Leag Exec, 1968-69; chair, Black Stud Affairs, 1973-74; chair, S Bend Black Caucus, 1973-74; Am Personnel & Guid Asn, 1974-75; pres, Roxbury Community Col, 1974; Am Asn Higher Educ, 1975-76; Black Leadership Coun. **Honors/Awds:** Nat urban league scholarship, 1968; Community Service Award, Suburban Club, 1967; Community Service Award, Lamba Kappa Mu, 1968; Outstanding Man of the Year Award, 1968; Rockefeller fellow, Ind State Univ, 1975-76. **Home Addr:** 5942 Joanne Dr Apt 203, Mount Pleasant, WI 53406-4696, **Home Phone:** (262)633-2377.

**LAWSON, CHARLES J.**
Airline executive, association executive, manager. **Personal:** Born Jul 13, 1948, Jackson, GA; son of James and Eliza; married Jackie. **Educ:** Savannah State Col. **Career:** Delta Airlines, cargo serv agt, Atlanta, 1971-73, passenger serv agt, Philadelphia, 1973-77, zone mgr, New York, 1977-81, sales mgr, Cleveland, 1981-87, sales mgr, Detroit, 1987-90, regional mgr, Atlanta, 1990-93, dir sales, Atlanta, 1994-95, civic & promotional affairs, dir, 1996, vice chair, Civic & Promotional Affairs, currently. **Orgs:** Bd mem, 100 Black Men of Atlanta; bd mem, Atlanta Conv & Visitors Bur, 1994; bd mem, Atlanta Sports Coun, 1994-; bd mem, Fr Am Chamber, 1994-; bd mem, Brit Am Chamber, 1994-; bd mem, Dekalb County Chamber, 1995-; bd mem, Cobb County Conv & Visitors Bur, 1996-; bd mem, Atlanta Touchdown Club, 1996-; bd mem, Atlanta Tip-Off Club, 1996-. **Honors/Awds:** Crusade Award, American Cancer Society, 1983; Distinguished Leadership, United Negro Col Fund, 1983; Appreciation Award, UNCF Telethon, 1984; Corp Member of the Year, ACUB, 1997. **Home Addr:** 650 McCaskill Dr, Jackson, GA 30233, **Home Phone:** (770)775-1635. **Business Addr:** Director of Civic, Promotional Affairs, Delta Air Lines Inc, Dept 741, Atlanta, GA 30320-2544, **Business Phone:** (404)881-2541.

**LAWSON, DEBRA ANN (DEB PATTERSON)**
Media executive. **Personal:** Born Oct 25, 1953, Detroit, MI; daughter of Purvis Patterson and Lois Marie Patterson; children: Christina Marie. **Educ:** Wayne State Univ, BFA, 1975. **Career:** WJBK-TV, Fox Tv Stas Inc, part-time switchboard operator, 1972-76, typist clerk, acct, 1976-77, admin secy, acct & personnel, 1977-78, secy news dir, 1978-81, community affairs coordr, 1981-86, pub affairs dir, 1987-92; asst prog dir, 1993-96, pub rels dir, 1996-; WJBK-FOX 2 News, Staff, Educ & Viewer Rels, internship prog coordr, 1997-2013, mgr, currently, independent contractor, 2015-. **Orgs:** Nat Acad TV, Arts & Sci-Mich Chap, 1979-; Detroit Chap, Nat Asn Advan Colored People, 1987-; bus contrib comn mem, Greater Det Chamber Com, 1988-92; corp leadership group, Boys & Girls Clubs Southeastern Mich, 1989-92; community adv bd, Substance Abuse Prev Coalition Southeast Mich, 1990-92; adv bd, MADD, 1991-92; affil bd dir, Am Heart Asn Mich, 1991-94; bd dir, Gleaners Comn Food Bank, 1991-92. **Home Addr:** 18975 Hartwell, Detroit, MI 48235-1348, **Home Phone:** (313)864-6568. **Business Addr:** News Independent Contractor, WJBK-TV2, 16550 W 9 Mile Rd, Southfield, MI 48075, **Business Phone:** (248)557-2000.

**LAWSON, ELIZABETH HARRIS**
Educator, executive director. **Personal:** married Harris; children: Clyde H, Carol H Cuyjet & Leonard J. **Educ:** Ill Inst Technol, Chicago, BS; Chicago State Univ, MS, 1961; Univ Chicago, post grad, PhD, 1974. **Career:** City Chicago, hs & univ counr, teacher; Chicago St Univ, dir intensive educ prog, 1968-72, assoc prof, asst dir admis & foreign stud adv, 1974-. **Orgs:** NAFSA; Nat Asn Women Deans Couns & Admins; Nat Guid & Personnel Asn; Master Plan Com Chicago St Univ; chmn, CSU's 5th Div Univ Sen, 1968-74; Am Asn Sch Educr; Ill Guid & Personnel Asn; res ch, Delta Kappa Gamma Int Soc; Alpha Kappa Alpha Sorority; consult, SC Desegregation Ctr, 1968-69; N Cent Bd accreditation HS's, 1970-80; Ill del & co-chair White House Conf, Lib & Inf Serv Wash DC, 1979; vol coordr, Nat Conf Christians & Jews, 1980-84; bd, Gov's ICOLA, 1983-84. **Home Addr:** 371 E 89 Pl, Chicago, IL 60619.

**LAWSON, ERMA J.**
Educator. **Educ:** Howard Univ, RN, nursing, 1976; Atlanta Univ, MA, sociol, 1988; Univ Ky, PhD, med sociol, 1990. **Career:** Atlanta Univ, Phylon Fel, 1981; Nat Inst Aging, res assistan, 1985-89; Univ Ky, Dept Behav Sci, asst res profres assoc, 1986-90, proj dir, 1989-90, Lyman T. Johnson Fel, 1990-92, asst res prof, Dept Behav Sci, 1993-96; Univ Calif, vis scholar, 1990-91; Transylvania Univ, adj instr; Univ N Tex, assoc prof. **Orgs:** Univ Md, 1978; Am Sociol Asn; Asn Pub Health; Int Sociol Asn; Sociologists Women Soc; Southern Sociol Asn; Asn Black Social Behav Scientists; Int Res Prom Coun; Int Womens Cong Serv; Nat Women's Health Info Ctr; cong fel Univ N Tex, 2005-06. **Business Addr:** Associate Professor, University of North Texas, 2336 Northway Lane 390J Chilton Hall, Denton, TX 76203-1157, **Business Phone:** (940)369-7473.

**LAWSON, HERMAN ACE**
Consultant, state government official. **Personal:** Born Dec 25, 1920, Fowler, CA; son of Frances and Herman; married Pearl Lee Johnson; children: Betty, Patricia, Gloria, Yvonne, Thomas & Tracey. **Educ:** Fresno State Univ CA; Univ Pac, attended; Sacramento State Univ; Chapman Col, attended. **Career:** St Employ Develop Dept, minority employ rep & manpower consult, 1963-; Sacramento, councilman 2nd dist, 1973-75; State Manpower Planning Off, consult, currently. **Orgs:** Del Paso Heights Libr Comm; col awareness bd, Am River Col; adv, presidenton progs disadvantaged at Amer River Col; City Amendments Study Comm; adv coun, Sacramento Businessmans; 99th Fighter Squad Flight Leader Frt Pilot; bd dir, Tuskegee Airmen Inc, 1974-75, 1978-80; Nat Asn Advan Colored People; commodore Port Sacramento. **Home Addr:** 6851 Steamboat Way, Sacramento, CA 95831. **Business Addr:** Consultant, State Manpower Planning Office, 800 Capitol Mall, Sacramento, CA 95814.

**LAWSON, REV. JAMES MORRIS, JR.**
Clergy, activist, college teacher. **Personal:** Born Sep 22, 1928, Uniontown, PA; son of James Morris and Philane May; married Dorothy Wood; children: John, Morris & Seth. **Educ:** Baldwin-Wallace Col, BA, 1952; Boston Univ, STB, 1960; Vanderbilt Univ, Nashville, attended 1960. **Career:** Hislop Col, Hagpur, India, Dept Phys Educ, chmn, 1953-56; fel Reconciliation Southern Region, 1958-59; field secy, 1958-69; Stud Nonviolent Coord Comt, adv, 1960-64; Nonviolent Educ Southern Christian Leadership Conf, dir, 1960-67; Centenary United Methodist Church, Memphis, pastor, 1962-74; Holman United Methodist Church, pastor, 1974-99; Vanderbilt Univ, vis prof, 2006-07; Univ Calif Labor Ctr, vis prof, 2002. **Orgs:** Nat Coun, 1960-66; Stud Nonviolent Coord Comt, 1960-66; chmn educ comt, Nat Asn Adv Colored People, Memphis, 1963-65, 1974-, bd mem, 1964-74; World Coun Church, 1966-; chmn, Black Methodist Church Renewal, 1968-71; Theol Comt Nat Comn Black Churchmen, 1969-; W TN ACLU, 1969-74; Philadelphia Randolph Inst, 1971-; adv comt, Amnesty Prof, 1972-; bd mem, Southern Christian Leadership Conf, 1973-, Los angeles chap, pres, 1979-93; dir, Cong Racial Equality. **Honors/Awds:** Elk Award, 1960; National Association for Advanced Colored People Award, Memphis, 1965 & 1974; Special Award, AFSCME Int, 1968; Russwurm Award, 1969; Man of the Year, Cath Interracial Coun, Memphis, 1969; Citation of the Year, Prince Hall LodgeTenn, 1969; Distinguished Alumnus Award, Boston, 1970; Outstanding Witness Christ Award, AME Nat Laymen's Asn, 1971; Civic Award, Mallory Knights Memphis, 1974; Walter R. Murray Distinguished Alumnus Award, 2002; Ralph J. Bunche Trailblazer Award, 2003; Vanderbilt University's Distinguished Alumnus, 2006. **Home Addr:** 4521 Don Timoteo Dr, Los Angeles, CA 90008-4112, **Home Phone:** (323)291-9625.

**LAWSON, JASON L.**
Basketball player. **Personal:** Born Sep 2, 1974, Philadelphia, PA. **Educ:** Villanova Univ, attended 1997. **Career:** Basketball player (retired), free agent; Orlando Magic, ctr, 1997-98; Grand Rapids Hoops, 1999-2001; Wash Wizards, 1999-2000; Caja San Fernando, Spain, 2000; Pau-Orthez, France, 2001-02; Los Angeles Clippers, ctr, 2001-02; Panionios, Greece, 2002; Entente Orleanaise, France, 2002; Pa ValleyDawgs, 2003; Columbus Riverdragons, D-League, 2004; Halcones Rojos Veracruz, 2005-06; Barreteros de Zacatecas, Mex, 2005-06; Al-Wehdat, Jordan, 2008; free agt, currently.

**LAWSON, JENNIFER KAREN**
Television producer, manager. **Personal:** Born Jun 8, 1946, Fairfield, AL; daughter of William and Velma; married Anthony Gittens; children: Kai & Zac. **Educ:** Tuskegee Univ; Columbia Univ, MFA, film making, 1974. **Career:** Stud Nonviolent Coord Comm, spec educ proj dir & staff mem, 1964-67; Nat Coun Negro Women, 1968-69; Brooklyn Col, asst prof film, 1974-77; Quitman County, MS, dir adult educ prog; United Church Christ, publicity dir; William Greaves Prods Film Co, ed, 1975; Film Fund, exec dir, 1977-80; Corp Pub Broadcasting, TV fund dir, 1980-89; Pub Broadcasting Serv, fund coordr, 1980; exec vpres programming & promotional serv, 1989-95; Magic Box Mediaworks Inc, pres & exec producer, 1995-; Africa Ser, exec prod, 2001-; Howard Univ Tv, WHUT, gen mgr, 2004-; consult & producer, currently. **Orgs:** Bd mem, Am Pub TV, Boston, MA; community & friends bd, John F Kennedy Ctr Arts, Wash, DC; trustee, Sidwell Friends Sch, Wash, DC; hon bd mem, CINE; bd dir, Women Film & Video; bd dir, PBS. **Honors/Awds:** Dr, Teikyo Post Univ. & Med; Gold Camera Award; Woman of Vision Award, 2004. **Special Achievements:** Named one of 101 Most Influential People in Entertainment Today, Entertainment Weekly, Nov 2, 1990; appeared on the Hollywood Reporter's list of the "Power 50," the 50 most influential women in entertainment. **Home Addr:** . **Business Addr:** Producer, Consultant, Magic Box Mediaworks Inc, 1838 Ontario Pl NW, Washington, DC 20009, **Business Phone:** (202)232-7327.

**LAWSON, JOHN C., II**
Lawyer. **Personal:** Born Jul 17, 1961, Nashville, TN; son of James Jr and Dorothy. **Educ:** Oberlin Col, BS, 1983; Howard Univ Sch Law, JD, 1986. **Career:** Attorney (retired), commissioner, judge; Los Angeles County Pub Defenders Off, atty, 1988-2007; Los Angeles County Super Ct, comnr, 2007-; Long Beach Juv Ct Judge, Div 245, judge, 2009-. **Orgs:** Los Angeles Black Pub Defenders Asn; John M Langston Bar Asn; Am Bar Asn. **Home Addr:** 4227 Mt Vernon Dr, Los Angeles, CA 90008, **Home Phone:** (213)291-6064. **Business Addr:** Judge, Long Beach Juvenile Court, Long Beach Courthouse, Long Beach, CA 90802, **Business Phone:** (213)742-8809.

**LAWSON, LAWYER**
Mayor, government official, executive. **Personal:** Born Aug 29, 1941, Cincinnati, OH; son of Lawyer and Fannie M Grant (deceased); married Mary Bates; children: Mary Adale Hall, Kenneth L, George & Robert. **Educ:** Ohio Col Appl Sci; Pre-Med Xavier Univ; Univ Cincinnati. **Career:** Village Woodlawn, mayor. **Orgs:** Ohio Mayors Asn, 1980-; Nat League Cities, 1980-; bd dir, Nat Conf Black Mayors, 1984-; trustee, Hamilton County Develop Co, 1985-87; pres, Ohio Chap Black Mayors, 1985; second vpres, Nat Conf Black Mayors, 1990; pres, Hamilton County Munic League; Black Mayors Roster. **Home Addr:** 27 E Leslie Ave, Woodlawn, OH 45215, **Home Phone:** (513)772-5849. **Business Addr:** Mayor, Village of Woodlawn, 10141 Woodlawn Blvd, Woodlawn, OH 45215, **Business Phone:** (513)771-6130.

**LAWSON, QUENTIN ROOSEVELT. See Obituaries Section.**

**LAWSON, ROBERT L.**
School administrator. **Personal:** Born Feb 24, 1950, Gallipolis, OH; married Shannon Lynn Strom; children: Robert L Jr, James & Michael. **Educ:** Rio Grande Col, BA, eng, 1973; Marshall Univ, MA, eng, 1978; Nova Southeastern Univ, EdD, educ admin, 1988. **Career:** Gallia Acad HS, teacher, 1973-76; Marshall Univ, admin asst, 1977-83, dir continuing ed, 1984-; Georgetown Jr.-Sr. High Sch, teacher; Ohio Univ, Chillicothe, Ohio, adj fac; Ohio Univ, Zanesville Ohio, adj fac. **Orgs:** Consult, Continuing Ed & SUCCESS; speaker, SUCCESS; Community Col Coun; Comn Serv Round table; bd dir, Opportunity Indust Ctr; chmn, Affirmative Action Adv Comn. **Home Addr:** 1809 Hall Ave, Huntington, WV 25701-3936. **Business Addr:** Director of Continuing Education, Marshall University, Huntington, WV 25701.

### LAWSON, DR. WILLIAM DANIEL
Dean (education), educator. **Personal:** Born Nov 5, 1948, Alpine, AL; son of Sadie Brown (deceased); married Nora Davenport; children: Sonya Danette & Nicole Danielle. **Educ:** Knoxville Col, BA, 1968; Atlanta Univ, MA, 1970; Iowa State Univ, PhD, 1978. **Career:** Ala State Univ, instr sociol, 1971-74; NC A&T State Univ, asst prof rural sociol, 1978-79; Ala State Univ, assoc prof sociol, 1979-85, chmn dept sociol, dean col arts & sci; consult, Ala Ctr Higher Educ, 1982-83; XAP Corp; Tenn State Univ, dean col arts & sci, 2000, exec vpres, currently. **Orgs:** Fel Am Sociol Asn, 1977-78; licensure monitor, Am Sociol Asn, 1984-; polemarch, Montgomery Alumni Chap Kappa Alpha Psi, 1984-; pres, Tuskegee Area Knoxville Col Alumni Asn, 1984-; bd dir, Montgomery Area Coun Aging, 1985. **Home Addr:** 142 Elm Dr, Montgomery, AL 36117. **Business Addr:** Executive Vice President, Tennessee State University, 3500 John A Merritt Blvd, Nashville, TN 37209-1561, **Business Phone:** (615)963-2164.

### LAWSON, WILLIAM R.
Architect. **Personal:** Born Mar 8, 1943, Washington, DC; son of Charlotte Hughes and LaMont Harris; married Carol Cloud; children: Derrick Mark & Leslye Michelle. **Educ:** Howard Univ, Wash, DC, BA, archit, 1966. **Career:** HTB Inc, Wash, DC, vpres; Gen Serv Admin, Region 3, Wash, DC, architect & proj mgr, 1966-70; US Postal Serv, Wash Region, Wash, DC, chief, design sect, 1970-71, asst comnr design & construct, Hq, 1971-87; Jones Lang LaSalle, sr vpres, assoc; McDevitt St Bovis, vpres, 1987-93; PBS, asst comn planning; ARA PBS, NCR, GSA, 1993-; Nat Capital Planning comn, asst exec dir; Staubach Co, sr vpres, exec vpres; Fed Mkt Serv LLC, owner, pres; Trust Strategy Group, sr adv, currently. **Orgs:** Comt Pub Archit, Am Inst Architects, 1971-; Am Inst Architects, DC Chap, 1987-; Nat Trust Hist Preserv, 1987-; Am Consult Engrs Coun, 1988-; juror, Medals & Awards Comt, Air Force Design Awards Prog, Soc Am Mil Engrs, 1988-; past pres, Soc Mkt Prof Servs, DC Chap, 1988-89; Greater Wash Bd Trade, 1988-; Nat Asn Indust & Off Parks, 1988-; past mem, exec Comt, Leukemia Soc Am Nat Capitol Area Chap, 1988; Urban Land Inst, 1988-; Consultative Coun, Nat Inst Bldg Sci, 1990-; fel Am Inst Architects; Nat Trust Hist Preserv; Nat Bldg Mus. **Honors/Awds:** Outstanding Performance Certificates, Gen Serv Admin, 1971-87; Alpha R Chi Medal, 1966; Gold Medal for Design, Howard Univ, 1966; Architect of the Year, DC Council Engineers & Architects, 1972; Award for Exemplary Leadership, 1982. **Home Addr:** 11005 Saffold Way, Reston, VA 20190-3802, **Home Phone:** (703)437-5225. **Business Addr:** Senior Advisor, Trust Strategy Group, 6576 Timothy Lane, Warrenton, VA 20186-9658, **Business Phone:** (703)636-4879.

### LAWTON, MATTHEW, JR. (MATT LAWTON)
Baseball player. **Personal:** Born Nov 3, 1971, Gulfport, MS; married Cazesta; children: Chassity & Chaseton. **Educ:** Miss Gulf Coast Jr Col. **Career:** Baseball player (retired); Minn Twins, outfielder, 1995-2001; New York Mets, outfielder, 2001; Cleveland Indians, outfielder, 2002-04; Pittsburgh Pirates, outfielder, 2005; Chicago Cubs, outfielder, 2005; New York Yankees, outfielder, 2005; Seattle Mariners, outfielder, 2006.

### LAWYER, CYRUS JEFFERSON, III
Educator, executive director. **Personal:** Born Sep 21, 1943, Vicksburg, MS; married Vivian Moore; children: Lenaye Lynne & Sonya Denise. **Educ:** Tougaloo Col, BS, 1966; Bowling Green Univ, MS, 1969; Univ Toledo, PhD, 1974. **Career:** Bowling Green Univ, grad asst & teacher asst, 1967-69; Univ Toledo, 1969-71, admin intern, 1971-72, asst dean adj instr, 1972-73, asst dean & housing dir, 1973-75, sr prog assoc inst servs educ. **Orgs:** Am Chem Soc; Orgn Black Scientists; Am Asn Univ Professors; Phi Delta Kappa; Asn Col & Univ Housing Officers; Alpha Phi Alpha Frat; Nat Asn Advan Colored People. **Honors/Awds:** Outstanding Young Men of America, 1975. **Home Addr:** 3805 Ben Lomond Ctintern, Toledo, OH 43607. **Business Addr:** Educator, 2001 S St NW, Washington, DC 20009.

### LAWYER, VIVIAN MOORE
School administrator. **Personal:** Born Jan 6, 1946, Cleveland, OH; daughter of Walter Frank and Everine Moore; married Cyrus J III; children: Lenaye Lynne, Sonya Alyse, Cyrus Jefferson IV & Stanton Moore Bosley. **Educ:** Bowling Green State Univ, BS, educ, 1967, MA, educ, 1969; Cath Univ Am, JD, 1981. **Career:** Nat Coun Teachers Eng, coord human resources, 1967-68; Bowling Green Sate Univ, asst dean stud, 1967-72, dir, 1972-75; Ohio Asn Women Deans & Counrs, 1968-; Montgomery Col, dir affirmative action, 1975-99, dir employ & devel, 1989-99, chief human resources officer, 1999-2011; VML-Coaching LLC, owner, 2012-. **Orgs:** Ohio Affirmative Action Officers Asn; Nat Asn Womens Deans, Admin & Counrs; Nat Coun Negro Women; Lucas Ct Health Serv Comn NW Ohio Health Planning Asn, 1971-72; Delta Sigma Theta Sor Toledo Alumnae; bd trustee, Toledo YWCA, 1974-77. **Honors/Awds:** Distinguished Serv University Award, BGSU, 1967; Midwest Region's Advisory Award, Delta Sigma Theta, 1972. **Home Addr:** 11510 Homewood Rd, Ellicott, MD 21042-1506, **Home Phone:** (301)596-3822.

### LAY, CLORIUS L.
Lawyer. **Personal:** Born Sep 1, 1940, Mound Bayou, MS; son of Laddel and Arzzie; children: Rosmond M & Cloe R. **Educ:** Ind Univ, BS, 1966; Univ Chicago; Brunel Univ, Eng, 1973; Valparaiso Univ, JD, 1974; Ind Continuing Legal Educ Forum's Prog, 1995; Harvard Univ, John F Kennedy Sch Govt, 1996; John M Marshall Grad Sch Law. **Career:** New Careers, proj dir, 1968-69; E Chicago Hts Comn Ctr, exec dir, 1969; Black Ctr Strategy, vpres, 1969-71; Univ Nat Bank, vpres, 1971-72; Northwest Sickle Cell Found, exec dir, 1972-75; Clorius L Lay & Assocs, atty & owner, 1975-; Inland Steel Co, corp internal auditor & procedure designer. **Orgs:** Nat Fel Woodrow Wilson Fel Found, 1972-74; Ind Univ Northwest Med Sch Scholar Comt; councilman-at-large, Gary City Coun, 1996-; Nat Alliance Black Sch Educrs; recruiter, Valparaiso Univ, Sch Law; Northwest Ind Alliance Black Sch Educrs; bd mem, Lake County Med Ctr; liaison, Ind Sch Bd Asn; hon bd mem, Northwest Sickle Cell Found; sustaining mem, Urban League N w Ind Inc; Nat Asn Advan Colored People. **Honors/Awds:** Cleo Appointee, Coun Legal Educ Opport, 1973; US Top Master, Am Pool Checkers Asn; Service Award, Northwest Ind Sickle Cell Found Inc; Certificate of Appreciation, Kiwanis Int; Prog Sr Execs, State & Local Govt, Cambridge MA. **Home Addr:** 1164 Pyramid Dr, Gary, IN 46407, **Home Phone:** (219)883-8538. **Business Addr:** Attorney, Clorius L Lay & Associates, 1277 Broadway, Gary, IN 46407, **Business Phone:** (219)883-8539.

### LAYMON, HEATHER R.
Banker. **Personal:** Born Nov 10, 1948; daughter of Beryl O Harris Sealy and Ellis W Sealy; married John; children: Shawn M & Nasya H. **Educ:** Northeastern Univ, BA, polit sci, 1972; Nat Sch Savings Banking, banking dipl, gen studies & mgt 1978; Cambridge Col, MEd, 1980. **Career:** Suffolk Franklin Savings Bank, Boston, mgr, 1972-80; Mutual Bank Savings, Boston, asst treas, 1980-82; Bank Boston, asst vpres, 1982-87; Boston Bank Com, Boston, Mass, vpres, 1986-91; Citizens Bank, vpres, 1995-97; Philips Lifeline, human resource mgr & human resource bus partner, 1999-. **Orgs:** Boston Bankers Urban Forum, 1980-; trustee, Cambridge YWCA, 1983-87; pres, Boston & Vicinity Club Nat Asn Negro Bus & Prof Women, 1986-89; Plan Giving Comm, Andover Newton Theol Sem, 1988-; treas, Roxbury Multi Serv Ctr; ber, 1988-; Mass Mortgage Bankers Asn, 1990-; Mass Young Mortgage Bankers Asn, 1990-; pres, Beta Alpha Psi. **Honors/Awds:** Black Achiever's Award, YMCA, 1981; President Award, Nat Asn Negro Bus & Prof Women, 1988; Professional Award, Women Serv Club Boston, 1988. **Business Addr:** Human Resources Manager, Human Resources Business Partner, Philips Lifeline, 111 Lawrence St, Framingham, MA 01702, **Business Phone:** (508)988-1000.

### LAYMON, JOE W.
Vice president (organization). **Personal:** Born Jan 1, 1952?, MS; children: 3. **Educ:** Jackson State Univ, BA, econs, 1975; Univ Wis-Madison, MA, econs, 1977. **Career:** Eastman Kodak Co, dir human resources, 1996-2000; USAID; Ford Motor Co, group vpres corp human resources & labour affairs, 2000-08; Chevron Corp, corp vpres human resources, med & security, 2008-. **Orgs:** Dir, DTE Energy Co, 2005-06; dir & chmn compensation comt, Molex Inc, 2008-; bd trustee, Clark Atlanta Univ; nat trustee, Boys & Girls Clubs Am; bd dir, BoardRoomIQ.com; bd dir, United Way Bay Area; HR Policy Asn; dir, Nat Asn Corp. **Business Addr:** Corporate Vice President, Human Resources, Chevron Corp, 6001 Bollinger Canyon Rd, San Ramon, CA 94583, **Business Phone:** (925)842-1000.

### LAYNE, STEVEN
Clergy. **Career:** Reach Out & Touch Ministries Inc, pastor, currently. **Business Addr:** Pastor, Reach Out & Touch Ministers, 51 Cottage Pl, Staten Island, NY 10302, **Business Phone:** (718)442-5007.

### LAZARD, BETTY
Banker, chairperson. **Personal:** married Wardell R; children: 3. **Career:** Howard Univ, law prof; WR Lazard, vice chmn, currently. **Business Addr:** Vice Chairperson, WR Lazard, 300 Garden City Plz, Garden City, NY 11530-3302, **Business Phone:** (212)406-2700.

### LEACE, DONAL RICHARD
Educator. **Personal:** Born May 6, 1939, Huntington, WV; married Jakki Hazel Browner. **Educ:** Howard Univ, BFA, drama/theatre arts & stagecraft, 1966; George Washington Univ, MFA, directing & theatrical prod, 1978; Georgetown Univ, MA, lib arts & sci, 1984. **Career:** Carnegie Chap Hall, folk singing, 1959; Howard Univ Players, pres, 1965-66; Roanoke Va Total Action Against Poverty, dram & music consult, 1966-67; Duke Ellington Sch Arts, fac mem; Theatre Dept, chair, 1979-86, 1990, teacher; Georgetown Univ, adj fac, 1992; Wash Theater Awards Socs, judge. **Orgs:** Am Fed Music 161-710, 1960; Am Fed TV & Radio Artists, 1979; bd dir, Wa, DC, Tokama Theatre, 1983-85; fulbright memorial prog fel Govt Japan, 1998. **Home Addr:** 1883 Monroe St NW, Washington, DC 20010-1047, **Home Phone:** (202)462-9744. **Business Addr:** PO Box 4924, Washington, DC 20008, **Business Phone:** (202)462-9744.

### LEACOCK, DR. FERDINAND S., SR.
Physician, surgeon. **Personal:** Born Aug 8, 1934, New York, NY; children: 4. **Educ:** Columbia Col, BA, 1956; Howard Med Col, MD, 1960. **Career:** Surgeon (retired); San Joaquin Hosp, rotating internship, 1961; Ft Howard Va Hosp, residency, 1961-65; Univ Md Med Ctr, fel; Univ Md Hosp, thoracic surg residency, 1967-69; Johns Hopkins Hosp, resident gen surg; Univ Calif, Los Angeles, Sch Med, asst prof surg, 1972-76; Martin Luther King Jr Gen Hosp, chief div thoracic & cardiovasc surg, 1973-74; Charles R Drew Post grad Med Sch, asst prof surg, 1972-76, vchmn dept surg, 1974-75; CMA/CHA Educ Patient Care Audit Workshop Prog, 1974-76; pvt pract thoracic & cardiovasc surg, 1975-; Bon Secours Hosp, chief thoracic & cardiovasc surg, 1987-2004, chmn, dept surg, 1998-2004; Md Gen Hosp, chief thoracic surg, 1987-92; Liberty Med Ctr, vpres med affairs, 1990-92, Dept Surg, chmn, 1992-99. **Orgs:** Univ MD Surg Soc; Baltimore City Med Soc; Am Col Surgeons; Am Col Chest Physicians; Baltimore Acad Surg. **Honors/Awds:** Publications 3; 1 abstract; Healthgrades Honor Roll. **Home Addr:** 3442 Rockway Ave, Annapolis, MD 21403, **Home Phone:** (410)269-6841.

### LEACOCK, PROF. STEPHEN JEROME
College teacher, educator. **Personal:** Born Oct 28, 1943; married Phyllis Otway; children: Natasha, Talitha & Baron. **Educ:** City London Polytech, BA, 1970, MA; Garnett Col, grad cert educ, 1971; London Univ, LLM, 1971; Guildhall Univ, MA; Mid Temple, barrister, 1972. **Career:** Univ Wi, Barbados, fac law, 1972-75; Univ Cincinnati, Col Law, Ohio, fac, 1975-79; De Paul Univ, Col Law, Ill, fac, 1979-98; Univ Ind Sch Law, Bloomington, vis prof, 1992; Univ Ill Col Law, Chapaign-Urbana, vis adj prof, 1998; Barry Univ, prof law, currently. **Orgs:** Am Soc Int Law; hon mem, Brit Ins Securities Laws. **Special Achievements:** Publications: "Public Utility Regulation in a Developing Country"; "Lawyer of the Americas"; "Fundamental Breach of Contract & Exemption Clauses in the Commonwealth Caribbean"; "Anglo-American Law Review"; "Essentials of Investor Protection in Commonwealth Caribbean & US". Author of Several Articles. **Home Addr:** 7825 Del Ct, Darien, IL 60561, **Home Phone:** (630)971-0536. **Business Addr:** Professor of Law, Barry University, 6441 E Colonial Dr, Orlando, FL 32807-3650, **Business Phone:** (321)206-5656.

### LEAGUE, CHERYL PERRY
Manager. **Personal:** Born Nov 29, 1945, New York, NY; daughter of Robert and Alberta; children: Anthony, Robeson & Assata. **Educ:** Merritt Col, AS, 1977; Univ Calif, bus planning cert; San Francisco State Univ, BA, 1979; Univ San Francisco. **Career:** Legal Aid Soc, Alameda County, Calif, contract compliance officer, 1975; US Dept Com, Minority Bus Develop Agency, minority bus prog specialist, 1980; Mgt Prof Servs, Oakland, Calif, prin partner, 1982; Port Oakland, Calif, contract compliance officer, 1983-86, equal opport mgr, 1986-91, equal opportunity officer, 1991-, founding mem, Calif Affirmative Action Coun. **Orgs:** Nat Asn Adv Colored People; secy, treas, nat bd mem, dir equal opportunity, Nat Forum Black Pub Adminr, 1984-; Calif Asn Affirmative Action Officers; pres, Bay Area Contract Compliance Officers Asn; bd mem, Bay Area Black United Fund; women's adv comn mem, Oakland Police Dept; bd mem, Northern Calif Minority Bus Opportunity Comn; steering comt mem, Calif Bus Coun Orgn Equal Opport; adv & hon comt, Civic Pride; vpres, Calif Asn Equal Rights Professionals; chair, nat empowerment comt. **Honors/Awds:** Minority Advocate of the Year Award, US Dept Com, San Francisco, Calif, 1988; Special Recognition Award, Minority Bus Develop Agency, San Francisco, Calif, 1988; Outstanding Achievement Award, Minority Enterprise Develop Week Comt, Oakland, Calif, 1988; Community Service Award for outstanding service, Oakland/San Francisco Bay Area Chap Nat Forum Black Public Admin, 1989. **Home Addr:** 2636 Cole St, Oakland, CA 94601, **Home Phone:** (510)928-9912. **Business Addr:** Equal Opportunity Officer, Port of Oakland, 530 Water St, Oakland, CA 94607, **Business Phone:** (510)627-1417.

### LEAK, VIRGINIA NELL
School administrator, educator, administrator. **Personal:** Born Oct 18, 1950, Temple, TX; daughter of Frank and Doris Gregg; married William A Jr; children: Volney Willis III & Vance Antoin Willis. **Educ:** Temple Jr Col, AAS; Univ Mary Hardin-Baylor, BS, nursing, 1979; Tex Woman's Univ, MS, nursing, 1984; Tex A&M Univ; Univ Tex Health Sci Ctr, San Antonio, attended 1991. **Career:** Scott & White Hosp, lic voc nurse, 1973-75; Olin E Teague VA Med Ctr, licvoc nurse, 1975-79; Kings Daughters Hosp, staff nurse, 1979-80; Temple Col, voc nursing instr, 1980-88, nursing dir, 1988-07, emeriti, currently; chmn assoc deg prog & div dir nursing. **Orgs:** Secy, Tenoke Col, Fac Coun, 1980-; Temple Community Col Teachers Asn, 1980-; Pub Rels Comn, 1983-; bd mem, UMHB Consumer Adv Coun, 1993; Temple Educ Found Bd, 1993-; Stop Tobacco & Nicotine Damage Bell Co, 1994-; bd mem, King's Daughters Hosp Asn, 1994-; bd mem, Wilkerson Health Care Mgt, Prof Adv Comn, 1998-; Ebony Cult Soc, 1999-; chair, Nat Asn Advan Colored People, Mem Comn, 1999-; Univ Mary Hardin-Baylor, Alumni Bd, 1999; Am Nurses Asn; exec bd & sec, Tex Nurses Asn, Nominating Comn, chair; secy, Temple Br Nat Asn Advan Colored People; secy, Temple Col Found, currently; Temple Housing Authority Bd; 10th & Ave M Church Christ. **Home Addr:** 5120 Waterford, Temple, TX 76502, **Home Phone:** (254)778-2909. **Business Addr:** Secretary, National Association for the Advancement of Colored People, PO Box 157, Temple, TX 76503, **Business Phone:** (254)217-0298.

### LEAKS, EMANUEL, JR.
Basketball coach, basketball player, association executive. **Personal:** Born Nov 27, 1945, Cleveland, OH; son of Emanuel and Sadie; married Marna Hale; children: Richard W Leaks Hale Pace & DeAndre George. **Educ:** Niagara Univ, sociol, BA, 1968; Case Western Res Univ, Mandell Sch Appl Social Sci, MSSA, social admin & social work, 1994. **Career:** Basketball player (retired), basketball coach; Ky Colonels, 1968; New York Nets, ctr forward, 1968-72, 1972-74; Dallas/Tex Chaparrals, 1969-71; Utah Stars, 1971-72; Floridians, 1972; Philadelphia 76ers, 1972-73; Capital Bullets, 1973-74; E. L. United Horizons, property owner & landlord, 2002-05; City Cleveland, community rels rep; Hough Area Develop Corp, pub rels mgr; LegalShield, independent assoc; Somalian Nat Basketball Team, adv, coach; Ctr Families & C, dir, currently. **Orgs:** Am Basketball Asn. **Home Addr:** 13613 Vormere Ave, Cleveland, OH 44120, **Home Phone:** (216)371-3873. **Business Addr:** Director, Fathers & Families Together, Center for Families & Children, 1117 E 105th St, Cleveland, OH 44108, **Business Phone:** (216)451-9838.

### LEAKS, MARNA HALE. See HALE, MARNA AMORETTI.

### LEAL, SHARON ANN
Actor. **Personal:** Born Oct 17, 1972, Tucson, AZ; daughter of Jesse and Angelita; married Bev Land; children: Kai Mile. **Educ:** Diablo Valley Jr Col. **Career:** Films: Face the Music, 2000; What Are the Odds, 2004; Dreamgirls, 2006, Soul Men, 2008, Linewatch, 2008; Limelight, 2009; Why Did I Get Married Too?, 2010; Little Murder, 2011; Woman Thou Art Loosed: On the Seventh Day, 2012; 1982, 2013; The Last Letter, 2013; Freedom, 2014; Addicted, 2014. TV Series: "The Guiding Light", 1996-99; "Legacy", 1998-99; "Boston Public", 2000-04; "Chapter Forty-Five", 2002; "The Longest Morning", 2004; "Thanksgiving", 2004; LAX, 2004-05; "Las Vegas", 2005; "Senator's Daughter", 2005; "Sperm Whales & Spearmint Rhinos", 2005; "CSI: Miami", 2007; "Internal Affairs", 2007; "Private Practice", 2009; "Hellcats", 2010-11; "Suits", 2011-14; "Perception", 2014; "Grimm", 2014; "Recovery Road", 2016; "Supergirl", 2016. **Honors/Awds:** Golden Globe Award; Asian Excellence Award, 2008; Best Supporting Actress Award, New York Independent Film Festival. **Business Addr:** Actress, Boston Public, Bldg 4A 1600 Rosecrans Ave 3rd Fl, Manhattan Beach, CA 90266, **Business Phone:** (310)727-2700.

### LEATH, VERLYN FAYE
Educator, executive director. **Personal:** Born Jan 16, 1946, Burlington, NC; daughter of Ervin Isaiah Walker and Sallie Myrtle Phillips; children: Andrienne Lynnette Weeks. **Educ:** NC A&T State Univ, BS, 1975, MS, 1982. **Career:** Alamance Burlington Sch Syst, teacher, 1975-; Harvey R Newlin Elem Sch, dir at-risk serv, 2004-. **Orgs:** Comt chair, Jack O'Kelley La Sertoma Club; secy, comt chair, Alamance Co Chap AT&T Alumni; NC Asn Educr; hons comt, chair, First Baptist Church; bd dir, Sunday Sch; bd mem, community comput comt, long range planning comt mem, Christian Educ. **Home Addr:** 330 Doggett Dr, Graham, NC 27253-3114, **Home Phone:** (336)227-8256.

**Business Addr:** Director of At-Risk Services, Harvey R Newlin Elementary School, 316 Carden St, Burlington, NC 27215, **Business Phone:** (336)570-6125.

**LEATHERWOOD, LARRY LEE**
State government official. **Personal:** Born Sep 7, 1939, Peoria, IL; son of Larry and Helen Moody Brown; married Martha; children: Jeffrey & Stacy. **Educ:** Kellogg Community Col, AA, 1967; Western Mich Univ, BS, 1969, MPA, 1982. **Career:** Battle Creek Area Urban League, exec dir, 1970-73; Mich Dept Com, spec asst, 1973-77; Mich State Minority Bus Off, dir, 1977-83; Mich Dept Transp, liaison officer, 1983-85, dep dir admin, 1985-92; Harvard Univ, Boston, sr exec fel, 1985; self employed, currently; Univ Mich-Dearborn, adj lectr. **Orgs:** Vice chmn, Lansing Urban League, 1982-83; chmn, Minority Tech Coun Mich, 1983-; Midwest Rep, Howard Black Alumni Asn, 1989-; pres, Lansing YMCA, 1991-92; pres, YMCA, 1992-93; Mich Dept Civil Serv, State Officers Compensation Comn, 2004-08; exec dir, Citizens Coun Mich Pub Univ; vice chmn, State Adv Coun Voc Educ; Conf Minority Trans Officials, Am Pub Works Asn; founder & chairperson, Uplift Our Youth Found, 2002-; adj staff, Mich Asn Sch Bd. **Home Addr:** 812 Canton Dr, Lansing, MI 48917, **Home Phone:** (517)321-0132. **Business Addr:** Founder, Chairperson, Uplift Our Youth Foundation, PO Box 70099, Lansing, MI 48908, **Business Phone:** (517)321-0132.

**LEAVELL, ALLEN FRAZIER (CHUCK LEAVELL)**
Basketball player. **Personal:** Born May 27, 1957, Muncie, IN; married Gwethalyn; children: Alex & Amanda. **Educ:** Okla City Univ, attended 1979. **Career:** Basketball player (retired); Houston Rockets, 1979-89; Tulsa Fast Breakers, 1989-90; Rockford Lightning, 1991-92.

**LEAVELL, CHUCK. See LEAVELL, ALLEN FRAZIER.**

**LEAVELL, DOROTHY R.**
Administrator, editor, newspaper publisher. **Personal:** Born Oct 23, 1944, Pine Bluff, AR; daughter of Blane Gonder and Sallie Gonder; married John Smith; children: 2; married Balm L Jr; children: Antonio & Genice. **Educ:** Roosevelt Univ, Ill, psychiat social work, 1962. **Career:** Holy Name Mary Sch Bd, pres; Chicago Crusader, off mgr, 1961-64, bus mgr, 1964-68, publ, 1968-; Gary Crusader, publ, 1968; Nat Newspaper Publishers Asn, asst secy, 1976, treas, 1983-87, 1889-95, bd dir, pres, 1995-99, chmn, 2006; Amalgamated Publ Inc, chmn, 2002. **Orgs:** Pres, Nat Newspaper Publ Asn, 1995-97; bd dir, Wash Park YMCA, 1974; Nat Newspaper Publ Asn; secy, PUSH; bd mem, Directions Scholar Found. **Honors/Awds:** YMCA Award; PUSH Award; Holy Name of Mary Award; Fourth District Community Improvement Association Award; Publishing Award, Nat Asn Negro Bus & Prof Womens Club; Dollars and Sense Award; Mary McLeod Bethune Award; Publisher of the Year, Nat Newspaper Publishers Asn, 1989; Humanitarian Award, Coun African Affairs. **Special Achievements:** First female chief executive in the 40-year history of the nation's oldest African American placement firm; Second woman ever named to the position of President of National Newspaper Publishers Association. **Home Addr:** 10941 Lowe, Chicago, IL 60628. **Business Addr:** Editor, Publisher, Chicago Crusader, 6429 S King Dr, Chicago, IL 60637, **Business Phone:** (773)752-2500.

**LEAVELL, DR. WALTER F.**
Educator, executive director. **Personal:** Born May 19, 1934, Chicago, IL; son of Ernest and Grace Byrd; married Vivian G Gunnels; children: Pierce & Pierre. **Educ:** Univ Cincinnati Col Pharm, BS, 1957; Meharry Med Col, MD, 1964. **Career:** State Univ NY, Upstate Med Ctr Col Med, assoc dean, 1971-75, vice dean & tenured assoc prof med, 1975-82; Univ Cincinnati, Col Med, vice dean, 1975-85; Cincinnati Gen Hosp, assoc chief staff, 1977-79, prof affairs, assoc adminr, 1977-79; EDUCOM, consult, 1979-; Univ Cincinnati Col Law, scholar-in-residence, 1981; Meharry Med Col, dean sch med, 1982-87, dir med affairs, 1982-90; Hubbard Hosp, med dir, 1982-87, staff; Charles R Drew Univ Med & Sci, Los Angeles, CA, pres, 1990; Howard Univ, Wash, DC, interim vpres health affairs, consult & health advisor, currently; Acad Educ Develop, dir, currently. **Orgs:** Asn Am Med Cols/GSA Steering Comt, 1974-; nat chairperson, Asn Am Med Cols/GSA Minority Affairs Sect, 1976-; Coun Deans, 1982-; adv bd, Nat Fund Med Educ, 1983-; AAMC AdHoc MCAT Rev Comt, 1985; AAMC Spring Meeting Prog Comt, 1985-; LCME Accreditation Rev Team; Am Nat Cincinnati Med Asn; Nat Asn Med Minority Educr; Am Asn Med Cols; Acad Educ Develop; Alpha Omega Alpha Clubs: Boule; AMA; Nat Med Asn; past pres, Minority Health Professions Found; Univ Cincinnati med admis comt. **Honors/Awds:** Service Recognition Award, Asn Am Med Cols, 1979; NAMME Presidential Citation, 1985. **Home Addr:** 6445 Lewis Clark Trl, Cincinnati, OH 45241-6048, **Home Phone:** (513)469-0488. **Business Addr:** Advisor, Consultant, Howard University, 2400 6th St NW, Washington, DC 20059, **Business Phone:** (202)806-6100.

**LEAVY, WALTER**
Editor. **Educ:** Univ Memphis, BA, jour, 1975. **Career:** Memphis Press-Scimitar, reporter, 1976-80; Johnson Publ Co, managing ed EBONY mag, 1997-2009; Leavy Commun LLC, pres, 2009-; Celebrity Front Page Mag, ed, 2012-. **Orgs:** Am Foun Blind; Alpha Phi Alpha Fraternity; Nat Asn Black Journalists; Soc Prof Journalists; Writing & Editing Professionals; Freelance Writers Connection; Assoc Press Stylebook; Linked N Chicago. **Business Addr:** President, Leavy Communications LLC, 551 Roosevelt Rd 150, Glen Ellyn, IL 60137, **Business Phone:** (312)315-0837.

**LECESNE, ALVAREZ, JR.**
Executive director, lawyer. **Personal:** Born Aug 31, 1942, New Orleans, LA; son of Alvarez Louis Sr and Garnet Latisha Barra; married Brenda Irons; children: Craig & Ryane. **Educ:** E Los Angles Jr Col, AA; Calif State Univ, Los Angeles, BS; Loyola Marymount Univ, Sch Law, Los Angeles, JD, 1973; Stanford Univ, fed prog mgt cert, mgt develop, 1974. **Career:** Attorney (retired); US Dept Justice, Civil Tax Div, sr trial atty; US Internal Revenue Serv Income tax field agt, group mgr, regional & nat off, analyst. **Orgs:** Pres, Optimist Club Reston; chmn, Reston Community Coalition; Nat Asn Advan Colored People; Fairfax County, Va Exec Comt; Calif & DC Bar Asns; fel Fairfax County Nat Asn Advan Colored People; vpres, Alpha Phi Alpha Fraternitys charitable found; Martin Luther King Jr Found; Heritage Fel Church, Reston, Va, 1995-2012; bd dir, 2011, founding exec dir, 2012-, Emerging Scholars Prog. **Home Addr:** 10822 Hunt Club Rd, Reston, VA 22090, **Home Phone:** (703)471-6788. **Business Addr:** Founding Executive Director, Emerging Scholars Program, 4401 Ford Ave Suite 400, Alexandria, VA 22302, **Business Phone:** (571)312-0013.

**LECESNE, TERREL M.**
School administrator, government official, association executive. **Personal:** Born Apr 13, 1939, New Orleans, LA; married Gale H; children: Terrel Jr & Haydel. **Educ:** Xavier Univ, BA, 1961; Eastern Mich Univ, MA, 1967, EdS, 1973; Univ Mich, PhD, 1979. **Career:** City Inkster, Mich, mayor, 1975-78, coun mem, teacher, 1961-66; Jr high sch counr, 1966-68; Willow Run/Romulus Sch, elem prin, 1968-79; Romulus Sch, asst supt, 1979-95; Inkster Schs, supt, 1995-; Ypsilanti Pub Sch, exec dir opers & labor rels, currently; City Inkster, bd mem, Housing Comn, currently. **Orgs:** Pres Romulus Asn Sch Bldg Adminr; pres, Inkster Jaycees; Dearborn-Inkster Human Rel Coun bd Housing Comnr. **Honors/Awds:** Named Outstanding Young Man of the Year, Inkster Jaycees, 1970. **Home Addr:** 3723 Burns St, Inkster, MI 48141, **Home Phone:** (734)722-3426. **Business Addr:** Board Member, City Inkster, 2121 Inkster Rd, Inkster, MI 48141, **Business Phone:** (313)563-9770.

**LECOMPTE, PEGGY LEWIS**
School administrator, television show host, executive. **Personal:** Born Oct 7, 1938, St. Louis, MO; daughter of Obadiah Sr and Winnie Penguite; married Larry Ferdinand Sr; children: Larry F Jr. **Educ:** Lincoln Univ, BS, 1960; Sangamon State, MS, 1985; Nat Col Educ, Evanston, IL, MS, 1990. **Career:** E St Louis Sch Dist 189, educr, 1962; USAF, librn, 1968; E St Louis Sch Dist 189, educr, 1970; Channel 13 E St Louis, TV host, 1983; Lang Arts High Sch, dept head, Dist 189, 1998-; Time Network; Limelight Newspaper, columnist, 2000-; E St Louis News Jour; LeCompte Unlimited, owner, pres & chief exec officer, 2008-. **Orgs:** Bd pres, Boys Club E St Louis, 1978-86; cent regional dir, Alpha Kappa Alpha Sorority, 1978-82 & 1997-98; pres, E St Louis Fedn Teachers, Local 1220; vpres, Ill Fedn Teachers, 1985-90; pres, Area III dir & organizer, Top Ladies Distinction; nat workshop chmn & nat parliamentarian, 1987-91; secy bd dir, Girl Scouts Am, 1990-97; pres & bd dir, GEMM, 1990; nat vpres, Top Ladies Dist Inc, 10th Nat Pres, 2003-07; pres, Comp Ment Health Ctr; pres, St Clair County, SWAC; YMCA; Nat YWCA bd, Nat Policy Comm, Nat Const & Bylaws Comm; bd, Racial Harmony; int mem chmn & nat secy, Alpha Kappa Alpha Sorority. **Home Addr:** 212 Bunker Hill Rd, Belleville, IL 62221-5764, **Home Phone:** (618)277-9088.

**LEDAY, JOHN AUSTIN**
Executive, president (organization), business owner. **Personal:** Born Sep 11, 1931, Basile, LA; son of Alsay and Edna Papillian; married Christine Sandoval; children: Anna & Angela. **Career:** Warehouseman, 1948-52; People Chem Co, sales mgr, 1954-61; Southend Janitorial Supply Inc, owner & pres, 1962-. **Orgs:** Pres, Am Enterprises Inc; Govt Brown Adv Coun Econ Bus Develop State Calif, 1978; pres, MTM Corp; Nat Asn Black Manufacturers; Sanitary Supply Asn Southern Calif; Los Angeles C C; bd dir, Black Bus Men's Asn Los Angeles; exec comt, Los Angeles Off Urban Develop; dir, Equip Bank; bd dir, Pickett Enterprises; Nat Community Bus Develop; chmn, Community Pride. **Business Addr:** President, Owner, Southend Janitorial Supply Inc, 11422 S Broadway, Los Angeles, CA 90061-1833, **Business Phone:** (323)754-2842.

**LEDBETTER, CHARLES TED**
Educator. **Personal:** Born Dec 29, 1949, Muskogee, OK; son of Jerome and Dora; married Eva Blake; children: Vicki Ann. **Educ:** Lincoln Univ, BA, 1963; Golden Gate Univ, MPA, 1969; Univ Mo, Columbia, MO, 1975; Kent State Univ, PhD, 1991. **Career:** Educator (retired), executive; Univ Mo, assoc prof, 1972-75; WVa State Coll, chair, ROTC, 1979-83, vpres stud affairs, 1983-88, exec asst to pres & adj prof, 1988-97, dean prof studies & prof educ, 1997-2000, prof educ, 2000; vice chair, Archives and History Commission, currently. **Orgs:** Dunbar Torary Club, 1980-; pub ed comm, Am Cancer Soc, 1985-87; Charleston Job Corps, 1988-96; Charleston Regional Chamber Comm, 1989-92; Consortium WVa State Coll, 1992-95; bd dir, Family Servs Kanawua Valley, 1992-; bd dir, Red Cross, Cent Chp, 1992-; vice chmn, WVa Arch & Hist Comn.; Alpha Phi Alpha. **Home Addr:** 106 Leslie Pl, Scott Depot, WV 25560-8906, **Home Phone:** (304)775-7467. **Business Addr:** vice chair, Archives and History Commission.

**LEDE, DR. NAOMI W.**
School administrator, educator. **Personal:** Born Mar 22, 1934, Huntsville, TX; children: Susan & Paul. **Educ:** Univ Houston, Tex, EdD, multicultural studies, 1979; Mary Allen Col, Crockett, Tex, BA, social sci & eng; Tex S Univ, Houston, MA, sociol & polit sci; Univ Tex, Arlington, MA, urban affairs & transp. **Career:** Distinguished prof, exec dir emer (retired); Tex Southern Univ, prof transp & urban planning, dean & dir, Ctr Urban Progs, vpres instnl advan, distinguished prof, Dept Transp Studies, exec dir emer, Ctr Transp Training & Res, currently; Lifson Wilson & Ferguson Houston; Surv Res Ctr Ann Arbor; Juv Delinq Surv Univ, Houston; Fisk Univ, Race Rels Inst Surv, Nashville; Reg Transp Study, Arlington, Tex; Consumer Opinion Inst, NY; SRDS DATA Inc, NY; Batten Barton Drustine & Orborne, NY; Louis Harris & Asn; Univ SC, Inst Social Res; Nat Urban League, St Louis; St Louis Urban League, dir res; St Louis Univ, lectr; Wash Univ, urban intern; City St Louis, prog analyst & res cons; Bishop Coll Dallas Tex, asst prof & dir res; Samuel Walker Houston Mus & Cult Ctr, Huntsville, Tex, chmn bd; Tex Transp Inst, sr res scientist. **Orgs:** Am Asn Univ Profs; Nat Coun Univ Res Admins; Asn Study Negro Life & Hist; Tex Asn Col Teachers; Nat Asn Social Sci Teachrs; Am Sociol Soc; Res & Consult Dallas Urban League & Dallas Negro Chamber Com; Soc Study Negro Dent; Delta Sigma Theta Sor; Iota Phi Lambda Bus Sor; World Future Soc; Soc Res Admins; Counc Univ Inst Urban Affairs; bd mem, Urban Affairs Corp; Transportation Res Bd; Nat Acad Political & Social Sci; Smithsonian Inst; assoc mem, AIP; State Educ Comm AIP; Mayor's Manpower Adv Coun; Am Planning Asn; Univ Aviation Asn Conf Minority Transit Officials Iota Phi Lamba Bus Prof Orgn, Transp Res Bd; Iota Phi Lamba Bus & Prof Orgn. **Honors/Awds:** Received spec recognition for participation in prog 'Operation Champ from Vice Pres Hubert Humphrey'. **Special Achievements:** Author: "Mary Allen College: Its rich history, pioneering spirit, and continuing tradition", 1995. **Home Addr:** 187 Fm 1791 Rd, Huntsville, TX 77340-2006, **Home Phone:** (936)291-9781. **Business Addr:** Executive Director Emeritus, Texas Southern University Center for Transportation Training & Research, 3100 Cleburne Ave, Houston, TX 77004, **Business Phone:** (713)313-1841.

**LEDEE, ROBERT. See Obituaries Section.**

**LEDOUX, REV. JEROME G.**
Theologian. **Personal:** Born Feb 26, 1930, Lake Charles, LA. **Educ:** Divine Word Sem, Ordained, 1957; Ponitifical Gregorian Univ Rome, Italy, MST, 1961, JCD, 1961. **Career:** Divine Word Theol Bay, St Louis, MS, prof moral theol & canon law, 1961-67; Miss Hist Divine Word HS Sem, instr eng & civics, 1967-69; Xavier Univ, New Orleans, 1st black chaplain, 1969-71, assoc prof theol, 1971-80; St Martin de Porres Church, pastor, 1981-84; St. Paul Apostle Church, pastor, 1984-88; St Augustine Church, pastor, 1990-2006; Our Mother Mercy Cath Church, pastor, currently. **Special Achievements:** Author, Weekly Synd Column, 6 Cath Diocesan Papers & 3 Black Weeklies; author, Monthly Column, Nat Cath Paper. **Home Addr:** 1210 Governor Nicholls St, New Orleans, LA 70116. **Business Addr:** Pastor, Our Mother of Mercy Catholic Church, 1007 E Terrell St, Fort Worth, TX 76104, **Business Phone:** (817)335-1695.

**LEE, AARON**
Business owner, executive. **Personal:** Born Aug 29, 1948, Hinds County, MS; married Frances Jackson; children: Aaron Brennan. **Educ:** Utica Jr Col, AA, 1970; Jackson State Univ, BS, 1975, MS, 1976. **Career:** Maj Assoc Construct Co, estimator, 1975-77; Nat Bus League, construct mgr, 1977-80; Town Edwards, alderman, 1977-, fed prog coord, 1982; Jackson State Univ, super bldg serv, 1981-83; asst dir phys plant, 1983; Bestway Abatement & Construct Inc, pres, currently. **Orgs:** Phi Beta Sigma Frat, 1976; mem bd dir, Nat Asn Advan Colored People Bolton-Edwards Br, 1981-; Am Mgt Asn, 1984. **Home Addr:** 222 Vicksburg St, Edwards, MS 39066, **Home Phone:** (601)852-2408. **Business Addr:** President, Bestway Abatement & Construction Inc, 222 Vicksburg St, Edwards, MS 39066, **Business Phone:** (601)852-2408.

**LEE, DR. ALLEN FRANCIS, JR. (WILLIAM FRANCIS LEE)**
Educator, scientist. **Personal:** Born Apr 12, 1943, Notasulga, AL; married Lula M Wheat; children: Allen F III & Aryanna F. **Educ:** Tuskegee Inst, AL, DVM, 1967; Univ Ga, Athens, PhD, 1978. **Career:** Univ Ga, from res asst to res assoc, 1967-71; Emory Univ, NIH spec fel, 1971-72; Univ Ga, instr, 1972-73; La St Univ, assoc prof vet neurophysiology, 1973-. **Orgs:** Kappa Alpha Psi Fraternity, 1965-; Am Vet Med Asn, 1967-; Am Soc Vet Physiologists & Pharmacologists, 1969-; NIH Post Doctoral Fel Emory Univ, 1971; Am Radio Relay League, 1977-; bd dir, Campus Fed Credit Union, 1978-; bd dir, Kenilworth Civic Asn, 1980-; dir, Capital Area Omik Amateur Radio Club Inc, 1994, AAAS. **Honors/Awds:** Scholar in Veterinary Medicine, Tuskegee Inst, 1965; Outstanding Service, Vet Stud Womens Aux AVMA, 1967; res nerve/muscle physiol EMG. **Special Achievements:** Author, "Evaluation of Ulnar Nerve Conduction Velocity in the Dog", Univ Ga, 1978. **Home Addr:** 1572 Leycester Dr, Baton Rouge, LA 70808-5751, **Home Phone:** (225)937-3500. **Business Addr:** Associate Professor of Veterinary Neurophysiology, Louisiana State University, 114 David Boyd Hall, Baton Rouge, LA 70803, **Business Phone:** (225)578-2311.

**LEE, AMP (ANTHONEA WAYNE LEE)**
Football coach, football player. **Personal:** Born Oct 1, 1971, Chipley, FL; married Natalie; children: Saben. **Educ:** Fla State Univ, grad. **Career:** Football player (retired), football coach; San Francisco 49ers, running back, 1992-93; Minn Vikings, 1994, running back, 1995-96; St Louis Rams, running back, 1997-98, 1999; Philadelphia Eagles, 2000; Amsterdam Admirals, running backs coach, 2003; Berlin Thunder, running backs coach, 2004; Kans City Chiefs, area scout, 2004-05; Ariz Cardinals, qual control asst, 2006; Foothills Acceleration Sports Training, mgr & trainer; Scottsdale Prep Acad, actg head football & basketball coach; Las Vegas Locomotives, running backs coach, 2012-. **Honors/Awds:** Rookie of the Year, 1992; Daniel F Reeves Memorial Award, St Louis Rams, 1997; Most Valuable Player, St Louis Rams, 1997; Twelveth Man Award, 1998; Super Bowl Champion. **Business Addr:** Running Backs Coach, Las Vegas Locomotives, 750 Pilot Rd Suite A, Las Vegas, NV 89119, **Business Phone:** (702)877-5626.

**LEE, DR. ANDRE L.**
Health services administrator, school administrator. **Personal:** Born Aug 14, 1943, Detroit, MI; son of Clyde and Laura; married Katrina; children: Andre, Bryan, Tracey & Robin. **Educ:** Mich State Univ, BS, 1966; Cornell Univ, MPA, 1972; Nova Univ, DPA, 1978. **Career:** Hosp administrator (retired); Highland Park Gen Hosp, dir, 1972-76; Sidney Sumby Hosp, dir, 1976-78; St Joseph Hosp, asst dir, 1978-81; Hubbard Hosp, dir, 1981-88; Urban Health Assoc Inc, pres; Friendship Hospice Nashville Inc, founder, owner, pres, currently; United Community Hosp, pres & chief exec officer, currently; Cornell Univ, Johnson Sch, prof, currently; Heritage Hospice Care Inc, part owner; Extended Hospice CareSouthfield, part owner; Southern Christian Leadership Conf, chief exec officer; Leeway DME, owner; Leeway LLC, pres, 1999; Phyx Inc, chief exec officer; Natchez, owner; Meharry-Hubbard Hosp, chief exec officer; Sidney Sumby Hosp, chief exec officer; Highland Park Gen Hosp, chief exec officer; Meharry Med Col, fac; Eastern Mich Univ, fac; Shaw Col, fac; Tenn State Univ, fac; Northwood Univ, fac, currently; Cent Mich Univ, fac, currently. **Orgs:** Tech Sinai Hosp Detroit, 1966-67; state dir, Am Acad Med Admin Ind & Tenn, 1983-85; pres, Nat Asn Health Serv Execs, 1985-87; chmn, Mgt Housing Scholar Comt; Alpha Phi Alpha; Nat Asn Advan Colored People; proper Health Care Fin Syst; Am Prof Mgt Ltd;

Am Col Hosp Admin; Am Pub Health Asn; Am Acad Med Admin, Mich; Pub Health Asn; bd mem, Comprehensive Health Ctr; Model Neighborhood Health Ctr; Resident Manpower Ctr; Mich C C Ed Sub-Com; Reg Emergency Room Task Force; City Emergency Room Task Force; bd mem, Priority Hospice, Nashville; fel Am Col Health Care Execs; chmn, pres, Leeway Found Inc; bd mem, Detroit Med Soc. **Honors/Awds:** COGME Fellowship Award, 1970-72; Whitney Young Award, Boy Scouts Am, 1989; Silver Beaver Award, Boy Scouts Am, 1991. **Special Achievements:** He has published more than 75 articles in numerous professional journals and newspapers, & co-authored the book Loose Ends - Putting Your Personal Affairs in Order. In addition, he was the executive producer of a recent documentary "The Healers - the Legacy of African American Pioneers in Medicine". **Home Addr:** 317 E Crescent Lane, Detroit, MI 48207-5002, **Home Phone:** (313)393-2565. **Business Addr:** President, Leeway LLC, 24315 Northwestern Hwy, Southfield, MI 48075, **Business Phone:** (248)208-7400.

### LEE, ANDREA
Writer, novelist. **Personal:** Born Jan 1, 1953, Yeadon, PA; children: 2. **Educ:** Harvard Univ, BA, MA. **Career:** New Yorker mag, NY, contract writer; books: Russian Journal, 1981; Sarah Phillips, 1984; Anthropology, 2002; Interesting Women, 2002; Lost Hearts in Italy, 2006. **Honors/Awds:** American Book Award Nomination, Russian Journal, 1981; Jean Stein Award, Am Acad & Inst Arts & Letters, 1984. **Home Addr:** , Torino.

### LEE, AUBREY WALTER, JR.
Financial manager. **Personal:** Born Oct 14, 1956, Ashland, KY; son of Aubrey W Sr and Jeane F; married Janice D; children: Aubrey Bejamin, Lauren Nicole, Natalie Ann Booker & Nathan Alexander McGhee. **Educ:** Univ Mich Dearborn, attended 1976; Univ Mich Ann Arbor, attended 1978; Merrill Lynch Internal, cert, personal investment advisor, 2014. **Career:** Booth Am Co, radio announcer, 1978-81, 1987-90; Manufacturers Nat Bank Detroit, br asst mgr, 1980-87; Inner City Broadcasting, radio announcer, 1981-83; Amaturo Group Inc, radio announcer, 1983-85; Bank Am Corp, Merrill Lynch, Novi, Wealth Mgt Adv, 1st vpres, 1987-, Diversity Adv Coun Mgt, mem, 2005-06, sr resident dir, 2006-; Evergreen Media, radio announcer, 1990-; CBS Radio, WVMV-FM, radio announcer, 1997-2009; Aubrey Lee, Jr Group, vpres, currently; NorthRidge Church, small group leader, 2010, kingdom advisor, 2010-12. **Orgs:** Detroit Chap, Nat Asn Securities Prof, 1996; asst minister, Men Faith, Outer Dr Faith Lutheran Church, 1996; internship comt, Go lightly Voc Sch, 1996-97; Promise keepers, 1996; corp liaison, Mich Minority Bus Develop Coun, Merrill Lynch, 1996; Penn Ctr-Mich Support Group, 1996; Detroit Discovery Mus; bd trustee, Leadership Detroit; bd mem, Detroit Urban League. **Honors/Awds:** Father & Son Footsteps Award, YMCA, 1985; Guild Community Service Award, Detroit Urban League, 2003; Leadership in Diversity & Inclusion Award, Merrill Lynch 2007. **Home Addr:** 762 Natures Cove Ct, Wixom, MI 48393, **Home Phone:** (248)438-6876. **Business Addr:** Senior Resident Director, First Vice President, Merrill Lynch, 26200 Town Ctr Dr Suite 200, Novi, MI 48375, **Business Phone:** (248)348-3990.

**LEE, AUBREY WALTER, SR. See Obituaries Section.**

### LEE, BARBARA JEAN
Politician. **Personal:** Born Jul 16, 1946, El Paso, TX; daughter of Mildred Adaire and Garvin Alexander Tutt; children: Tony & Craig. **Educ:** Mills Col, BA, 1973; Univ Calif, Berkeley, MSW, 1975. **Career:** Congressman Ronald V Dellums, Cong aide advisor & sr advisor chief staff, 1975-87; bus owner, 1987-98; mem, Calif State Assembly, 1990-96; sen, Calif State Senate, 1996-98; 1987-98; US House Rep, congresswoman, 1998-. **Orgs:** Chair, CBC Task Force Global HIV/AIDS; co-chair, CBC Haiti Task Force; fel State Assembly, 1991; chair, Cong Out Poverty Caucus; founder, Calif Comn Status African-Am Males; co-chair, Cong Black Caucus Outreach Task Force; founder, Ronald V Dellums Dem Club; pres, Nat Conf State Legis, Women's Network; chair, Nat Conf State Legis, Women's Network; chair, Calif Rainbow Coalition. **Honors/Awds:** Received numerous awards including: Honorary doctorate Calif Sch Prof Psychiat; Mills Col, 1999; Certificate of CongratulationsCapital Bus & Prof Women, Award of AppreciationA Safe Place, National Legislator of the Year-Calif Pub Health Asn, Distinguished Public Health Legislator of the Year Award, Am Pub Health Asn San Francisco, National Peacemaker Award, Houston Peace & Justice Ctr, Physicians for Social Responsibility Award, 2003; Virtuous Woman Community Award, Muhsana Center for Health, 2006; 2006 Urban Education Leadership Award, Catapault Online, 2006; MLK Freedom Award, Progressive Nat Baptist Convention, 2006; Nat Achievement Award, Nat Asn Negro Bus & Professional Women's Clubs, 2006; Outstanding Woman Award, Black Expo, 2006; Peacemaker of the Year Award, Baptist Peace Fellowship of N Am Conv, 2006; Leadership In Advocacy Award, AIDS Alliance, 2006. **Special Achievements:** First woman to represent California's 9th congressional district. 13th district. **Business Addr:** Congresswoman, Oakland District Office, 1301 Clays St Suite 1000 N, Oakland, CA 94612, **Business Phone:** (510)763-0370.

**LEE, BILL. See LEE, WILLIAM JAMES EDWARDS, III.**

### LEE, CARL, III
Football player, football coach, executive. **Personal:** Born Feb 6, 1961, South Charleston, WV. **Educ:** Marshall Univ. **Career:** Football player (retired), football coach, executive; Minn Vikings, cornerback, defensive back, 1983, free safety, 1984, right cornerback, 1986-89, left cornerback, 1990-93; New Orleans Saints, right cornerback, 1994; W Va State Univ, yellow jacket, head coach, 1996-2005, dir develop athletics, 2005-13; City S Charleston, prog dir, 2013. **Honors/Awds:** Sporting News NFL All-Star Team, 1988; post-season play: NFC Championship Game, 1987, Pro Bowl, 1988, 1989.

### LEE, CHANDLER BANCROFT
Automotive executive. **Educ:** Western Mich Univ, BS, polit sci, 1974; Cent Mich Univ, MBA, finance, 1982; Gen Motors Univ, degree dealership mgt, 1985; Cent Mich Univ, MA, bus admin. **Career:** Gen Motors Corp, Fisher Body Div, sr proj engr; Classic Pontiac Buick-GMC Inc, pres, chmn & chief exec officer, 1984-2001; Chandler Lee Motors Inc, Southern Pines, NC, pres, 1986; Am Financial Automotive Serv Inc, mgr nat dealership develop, 2006-09; State Farm Ins, agency intern, 2009-10; Cornerstone Financial Partner MetLife, financial serv rep, 2010-. **Orgs:** Southern Pines Rotary Club; Southern Pines Chamber Com; civic & trade orgn; NC & Nat Automobile Dealers Asn; NC Real Estate Comn; Nat Automobile Dealers Asn; bus adv comt, Sandhills Community Col; Moore Count Sch; Nc Indust Comn, chmn, 2010-. **Business Addr:** Financial Services Representative, Cornerstone Financial Partner at MetLife, Baltimore, MD 21228.

### LEE, CHARLES GARY, SR.
Construction manager, business owner, president (organization). **Personal:** Born Sep 29, 1948, Jacksonville, FL; married Claudia Pittman; children: Charles, Marcus & Cedric. **Educ:** H Coun Trenholm Jr Col, A Masonry, 1969; Westfield State Col, cert occ educ, 1974; Univ Mass, BA, occup educ, 1984. **Career:** Springfield Sch Syst, adult educ instr, 1973-80; Lee-Hamilton Construct Co, pres, gen mgr, 1974-78; Neighborhood Housing Servs, asst dir, 1978-80; Charles Gary Lee Inc, owner & pres, 1980-; Lee-Brantley Inc, consult, 1986-. **Orgs:** Third Degree Master Mason FAM Ala Prince Hall, 1967-; dir, corp mem, Springfield Girl's Club Family Ctr Inc, 1979-; pres, Big Will Express Athletic Club, 1983-; cert mem, Minority Bus Enterprise, 1983-; affil mem, Western Mass Contractor's Asn, 1985-. **Honors/Awds:** Man of the Year Award, Big Will Express, 1984; Outstanding Citizen Award, Mass Black Caucus, 1986; Letter of Recognition, Mayor City of Boston, 1986. **Business Addr:** President, Owner, Charles Gary Lee Inc, 32 Briarwood Ave, Springfield, MA 01118-1312, **Business Phone:** (413)782-2920.

### LEE, CHARLIE
Football executive. **Educ:** Northern Ariz Univ, 1966. **Career:** Cent Sr High, coach; Univ Ariz, coach; Univ Tex, coach; Univ Purdue, coach; Northwest Mo State Univ, coach; Denver Broncos, dir player & community rels; Dir, pub rels, player & community rels, NFL franchise. **Honors/Awds:** Summit Award.

### LEE, DR. CHARLOTTE O.
Educator, chemist. **Personal:** Born Jul 13, 1930, Boligee, AL; married Ralph Hewitt; children: Krystal, Karla, Rachel & Rosalind. **Educ:** Knoxville Col, BS, 1953; Tuskegee Inst, MS, 1955; Univ Kans, PhD, 1959. **Career:** Am Asn Univ Women, res fel, 1958-59; Univ Kans, asst prof nutrit, 1963; Ala A&M Univ, prof chem, 1964-69; Nassau Community Col, asst prof chem, 1970-71; St Louis Univ, res assoc, 1971-72; Southern Ill Univ, Edwardsville, assoc prof, 1972-78; City Univ, parks comnr, 1976-78; Triton Col, instr, 1979-; Oak Pk River Forest Community Chest, dir, 1982. **Orgs:** Am Asn Univ Women, 1958-59; Women Sci Proj, NSF, 1977-78; proposal rev panelist, NSF, 1978 & 1979. **Home Addr:** 333 N Cuyler Ave, Oak Park, IL 60302-2302, **Home Phone:** (708)848-2847. **Business Addr:** Instructor, Triton College, 2000 Fifth Ave, River Grove, IL 60171, **Business Phone:** (708)456-0300.

### LEE, CHERYL TAYLORE
College teacher, college administrator, physician. **Personal:** Born Jan 1, 1966?, Babylon, NY; children: 2. **Educ:** Polytech Inst, BS, 1987; Albany Col, MD, 1991. **Career:** Univ Mich Hosps, urol resident, 1997; Univ Mich Comprehensive Cancer Ctr, physician; Univ Mich, Dr. Robert H. & Eva M. Moyad Res Prof Urol; Ohio State Univ, prof & chair dept urol, 2016-. **Orgs:** Educ Coun Am Urol Asn; chmn & pres sci adv bd, Bladder Cancer Advocacy Network; Am Cancer Soc, Lakeshore Div, Soc Urol Oncol; past pres, R. Frank Jones Urol Soc. **Honors/Awds:** Fellowship in urologic oncology, Memorial Sloan Kettering Cancer Center, NYC, 2000. **Special Achievements:** First woman to lead the department of urology at Ohio State University; served as the principal investigator, co-principal investigator, site principle investigator, or co-investigator for 50 clinical research trials. **Business Addr:** Ohio State University Wexner Medical Center, 410 W 10th Ave, Columbus, OH 43210.

### LEE, CLARA MARSHALL
Educator, administrator. **Personal:** Born Feb 14, 1946, Mobile, AL; daughter of Edward J Sr and Clara Mae; married Marion Sidney Lee Jr; children: LaToia Ejuan Marius Sidward. **Educ:** Ala State Univ, Montgomery Al, BS, 1967; Nat Col Educ, Chicago IL, MA, 1983. **Career:** Harvey Pk Dist, comnr, 1981; Delta Sigma Theta Sor Inc Joliet Area Alumni Chap, finance secy, 1984; Harvey Pub Schs Dist 152, hist teacher, asst prin, currently. **Orgs:** Bd mem, People Organized Secure Election Equalities, 1982; IEA, NEA, NPRA, IPRA, Nat Sor Phi Delta Kappa Inc. **Home Addr:** 14600 S Myrtle Ave, Harvey, IL 60426-1739, **Home Phone:** (708)370-4039. **Business Addr:** Assistant Principal, Harvey Public Schools District 152, 147th and Main, Harvey, IL 60426, **Business Phone:** (708)331-1390.

### LEE, CLIFTON VALJEAN
Physician, obstetrician, gynecologist. **Personal:** Born Jan 21, 1929, New York, NY; married Irene Warner; children: Marquetta, Michele & Jeanine. **Educ:** Howard Univ, Wash, DC, BS, 1951, MD, 1955; Am Bd Obstet & Gynec, dipl. **Career:** State Univ NY Health Sci Ctr Brooklyn, internship, 1955-56; Western Res Med Sch, Cleveland OH, MetroHealth, resident, Obstet & Gynec, 1959-63, demonstr obstet & gynec, 1962-63; Calif Col Med, Los Angeles, clin instr obstet & gynec; Cleveland metrop gen, resident training; Univ Southern Calif Med Sch, Los Angeles, physician & asst clin prof obstet & gynec. **Orgs:** Nat Med Fel, 1960-63; fel Am Col Obstetricians & Gynecologists; fel Am Col Surgeons. **Home Addr:** , CA 90062, **Home Phone:** (323)295-5446. **Business Addr:** Gynecologist, 4361 S Western Ave, Los Angeles, CA 90062, **Business Phone:** (323)295-5446.

### LEE, CONSELLA ALMETTER
Journalist. **Educ:** Wayne State Univ, Detroit, MI, jour, 1989. **Career:** Mich Chronicle, Detroit, Mich, staff writer, 1990; Dow Jones Newswires, currently. **Business Addr:** Staff Writer, Dow Jones Newswires, 1 World Financial Ctr 200 Liberty St, New York, NY 10281, **Business Phone:** (201)938-5400.

### LEE, DAMON
President (organization), movie producer. **Personal:** Born Jan 8, 1969, Washington, DC. **Educ:** Brandeis Univ, BA, Eng, 1991; Univ Southern Calif, MFA, 1994. **Career:** Flims: Higher Learning, prod asst; There Goes The Nation; My Babies Mamas; Hustlin' Hank; Undercover Bro; Disturbing Behav; Am Coffee, 2001; One Flight Stand, 2003; This Christmas, 2007; Who's Your Caddy?, 2007; Whisper, 2007; Silver Pictures, vpres prod; MGM, vpres prod; Urban Entertainment, pres; Univ Calif, Los Angeles, Adj Prof, 2010-11; Brandeis Univ, Adj Prof, 2012; Deacon Entertainment's, producer, founder & pres, currently; Our Stories Films, exec vpres prod, 2008-. **Orgs:** Teacher For Am; BDADS. **Business Addr:** President, Founder, Deacon Entertainment Inc, Rm 2 Bldg 9128 100 Universal City Plz, Universal City, CA 91608.

### LEE, ESQ. DEBRA L.
Chief executive officer, chairperson. **Personal:** Born Aug 8, 1955, Fort Jackson, SC; married Randall Coleman; children: Quinn & Ava. **Educ:** Brown Univ, BS, polit sci, 1976; Harvard Univ, John F Kennedy Sch Govt, MPP, 1980; Harvard Law Sch, MA & JD, 1980. **Career:** Steptoe & Johnson Assoc, atty, 1981-86; Black Entertainment Tv, BET Holdings Inc, vpres strategic bus develop & gen coun, 1986-92, exec vice pres legal affairs, 1992-95, pres & chief operating officer, 1995-2005, BET Networks, chief exec officer, 2005-. **Orgs:** Dir, WGL Holdings Inc, 2000-; bd mem, Girls Inc; trustee & bd dir, Nat Symphony Orchestra; bd dir, Alvin Ailey Am Dance Theater; bd dir, Nat Cable Tv Asn; bd mem, Nat Cable & Telecommunications Asn; bd dir, Ad Coun; bd dir, Eastman Kodak Co, 1999-2011; bd dir, Genuity Inc, 2000-; bd dir, Marriott Int Inc, 2004-; bd dir, Revlon, 2006-; chmn, bd dir Black Entertainment Tv, 2006-; trustee emeritus, Brown Univ; bd dir, Nat Womens Law Ctr. **Special Achievements:** First African American female executive to get the Distinguished Vanguard Award for Leadership from national Cable TV Association, 2003. **Business Addr:** Chief Executive Officer, Chairman, Black Entertainment Television LLC, 1235 W St NE, Washington, DC 20018-1211.

### LEE, DR. DEBRA LOUISE
Lawyer, executive director, businessperson. **Personal:** Born Aug 8, 1955, Ft. Jackson, SC; daughter of Richard M and Delma L; married Randall Spencer Coleman; children: Quinn Spencer & Ava. **Educ:** Brown Univ, AB, 1976; Harvard Law Sch, JD, 1980; Harvard Kennedy Sch Govt, MPP, pub policy, 1980. **Career:** US Dist Ct Judge Barrington Parker, law clerk, 1980-81; Steptoe & Johnson, atty, 1981-86; Black Entertainment TV, vpres & gen coun, 1986-92, exec vpres-Legal Affairs, 1992-95, chief oper officer, 1995-2005, pres, 1995-2006, chief exec officer, 2005-, chmn, 2006; Genuity Inc, bd dir, 2000-; Publ, Young Sisters & Bros Mag, pres; Eastman Kodak Corp, dir, 1999-2011; WGL Holdings Inc dir, 2000-; Marriott Int Inc dir, 2004-; Revlon Inc dir, 2006-. **Orgs:** Minority Recruitment Comn Fed Comn Bar Asn, 1982-; Pub Serv Activ Comn DC Bar, 1983-; bd dir, Legal Aid Soc DC, 1986-; nat bd dirNat Symphony Orchestra; nat bd dir, Nat Women's Law Ctr; nat bd dir, Alvin Ailey Dance Theater. **Honors/Awds:** Eva A Mooar Award, Brown Univ, 1976; Nat Achievement Award, Wash DC Area Chap Nat Alumnae Asn Spel Col, 1992; Woman of the Year Award, Women Cable & Telecommunications, 2001; Distinguished Vanguard Award, NCTA, 2003; C. J. Walker Award, Ebony magazine. **Special Achievements:** First firm owned and controlled by African-American to be listed on the New York Stock Exchange. **Business Addr:** President, Chief Operating Officer, Black Entertainment TV, 1900 W Pl NE, Washington, DC 20018-1211, **Business Phone:** (202)608-2000.

### LEE, DERREK LEON
Baseball player. **Personal:** Born Sep 6, 1975, Sacramento, CA; son of Leon and Pamela; married Christina; children: Jada. **Career:** Baseball player (retired); San Diego Padres, infielder, 1997; Fla Marlins, infielder, 1998-2003; Chicago Cubs, infielder, 2004-10; Atlanta Braves, 2010; Baltimore Orioles, 2011; Pittsburgh Pirates, 2011; Cincinnati Reds, advising batting coach. **Orgs:** Co owner, 1st Touch Found, 2005; Proj 3000. **Business Addr:** Professional Baseball Player, Chicago Cubs, Wrigley Field 1060 W Addison, Chicago, IL 60613-4397, **Business Phone:** (773)404-2827.

**LEE, DON LUTHER. See MADHUBUTI, DR. HAKI R.**

### LEE, DOROTHY A. H.
Educator. **Personal:** Born Jan 22, 1925, Columbia, MO; daughter of Victor Hicks and Helen; married George E; children: George V & Helen Elaine. **Educ:** Wayne State Univ, BA, 1945, MA, 1947; Radcliffe Col, MA, 1948; Radcliffe Col & Harvard Univ, PhD, 1955. **Career:** Wayne State Univ, asst prof, 1952-62; Henry Ford Community Col, instr, 1963-72; Univ Mich, Dearborn, Mich, prof, eng & comparative lit, 1972-93, prof emer, eng & comparative lit. **Home Addr:** 939 Green Hills Dr, Ann Arbor, MI 48105-2721, **Home Phone:** (734)213-6015. **Business Addr:** Professor Emeritus, University of Michigan-Dearborn, 4901 Evergreen Rd, Dearborn, MI 48128, **Business Phone:** (313)593-5000.

### LEE, E. JACQUES
Executive, manager, vice president (organization). **Personal:** Born Sep 5, 1953, Atlanta, GA. **Educ:** Simmons Col, BS, math & econ, 1975. **Career:** Fulton Fed Savings & Loan, mgt assoc, br mgr; First Union Nat Bank, br mgr; First Southern Bank Lithonia, regional br mgr; Citizens Trust Bank, div mgr retail banking, consumer banking div mgr & sr vpres retail banking, 2006-. **Orgs:** Ga Environ Facil Authority; United Way African Am Partnership. **Home Addr:** 1848 Farmer Rd, Conyers, GA 30012, **Home Phone:** (770)922-6804. **Business Addr:** Senior Vice President of Retail Banking, Consumer Banking Division Manager, Citizens Trust Bank, 75 Piedmont Ave NE, Atlanta, GA 30303, **Business Phone:** (404)575-8400.

**LEE, EDWARD S.**
Government official. **Personal:** Born May 12, 1935, Philadelphia, PA; married Fay E Jones; children: Michael & Eric. **Educ:** Cheyney State Col, BA, polit sci, 1968. **Career:** US Post Off; HELP Inc, exec dir, 1967-69; Philadelphia Urban Coalition, exec staff mem, task force coordr & chmn, 1969-71; City Philadelphia, elected clerk quarter sessions, 1971-; Nat Asn Postal & Fed Employees, union rep; Regional & Community Treat Ctrs Women, app attys, 1967, ward leader, 1970; Black Polit Forum, exec dir, 1968-70; Cheyney State Col, adj prof, 1974; Pa Gov's Justice Comn; Cernitian Am Inc, producer; Hall Realty Inc, agt, 2006-. **Orgs:** Bd mem, Nat Asn Ct Adminrs; Ile-Fe Black Humanitarian Ctr; Greater Ger town Youth Corps; bd trustee, Canaan Baptist Church; Ralph Bunche Club Philadelphia; Nat Asn Advan Colored People; Urban League Philadelphia; elected deleg, Democ Nat Mini Conv, 1974; exec asst chmn, Second World & Conf Arts & Cult; bd dir, Police Athletic League; bd dir, Community Servs & Develop Corp; chmn & bd trustee, Cheyney State Col, 1974; Snow Hill Chamber Com. **Home Addr:** 6146 Morton St, Philadelphia, PA 19144-1043. **Business Addr:** Agent, Hall Realty Inc, 269 S Gunnison Ave, Lake City, CO 81235, **Business Phone:** (970)944-8100.

**LEE, FELICIA R.**
Journalist. **Personal:** Born Nov 11, 1956, Chicago, IL; daughter of Felix and Sarah Crawford; married Adolfo Emanuele Profumo; children: 2. **Educ:** Northwestern Univ, Evanston, IL, BSJ, 1978. **Career:** Ft Worth Star-Telegram, Ft Worth, Tex, reporter, 1978-79; Cincinnati Enquirer, reporter, 1979-82; USA Today, Wash, DC, reporter, 1982-85; Cincinnati Enquirer, Cincinnati, OH, asst metro ed, 1985-86; Miami Herald, Miami, Fla, reporter, 1986-88; NY Times, New York, reporter, 1988-. **Orgs:** Nat Asn Black Journalists, 1982-; Meyer Berger Award, 1995; Nieman fel, Harvard Univ, 1996. **Home Addr:** 160 W 71st St Suite 6M, New York, NY 10023, **Home Phone:** (212)721-4931. **Business Addr:** Reporter, The New York Times, 229 W 43rd St 3rd Fl, New York, NY 10036, **Business Phone:** (212)556-1533.

**LEE, FORREST A., SR.**
Executive. **Personal:** Born Nov 19, 1937, Boley, OK; son of Maurice W Sr and Harriett Anderson; married Joyce A Kirksey; children: Forrest, Carole, Catherine, Brian, Gregory, Michael, Rachael, Reginald & Crystal Lee Otis. **Educ:** Okla City Univ, BA, 1961. **Career:** Liberty Tower Co, Ok City, draftsman, 1959; Cent State Hosp Norman, OK, psychiat aide, 1960-61; MW Lee Mfg Co, plant supvr, 1961-68; Leefac Inc, Boley, OK, pres, 1963-70; Farmers Home Adm Okemah, FHA loan committeeman, 1970-73, chmn, 1973; Smokaroma Inc, pres, 1975-90; Okla City Northeast Inc, pres, 1990-; Capitol Chamber Com, exec dir, 1999-2004; Privileged Info Inc, pres, owner, 1990-. **Orgs:** Councilman, Town Boley, 1961-73; pub Chap Boley Chamber Com, 1962; exec comm mem, Cent Okla Criminal Comm, 1970-73; bd mem, bd dir, Nat Asn Black Mfgrs, 1972-76; comm State Okla Human Rights Comm, 1973; bd trustee, treas, Ward Chapel AME Church Boley; Nat restaurant asn, 1977; Wewoka Alumni Chap Kappa Alpha Psi Fraternity; Nat Assoc Food Equip Mfgrs, 1980; Okla Human Rights Comn; chmn, Boley Sch Bd; dir fulfillment, Feed C, 1994-99; life mem, Nat Asn Advan Colored People. **Honors/Awds:** Communication Achievement Award, Lets Talk Toastmasters Club 4884, 2009. **Home Addr:** PO Box 7, Boley, OK 74829. **Business Addr:** President, Owner, Privileged Information Inc, 1512 Nw 125th St, Oklahoma City, OK 73120, **Business Phone:** (405)302-4826.

**LEE, FRED D., JR.**
Automotive executive. **Personal:** Born Apr 26, 1947, Tallahassee, FL; son of Fred Douglas Mosley Sr and Maude Sneed; married Patricia Mosley; children: Ronald, Adrienne Dionne & Fred Douglas III. **Educ:** Fla A&M Univ, Tallahassee, FL, BS, music, 1969, guid coun, 1971. **Career:** Ford Motor Co, Jacksonville, Fla, mkt analyst, 1971-74, Memphis, Tenn, dist sales rep, 1974-78, bus mgt mgr, 1978-79, truck merchandising, 1979, fleet leasing rental mgr, 1979-82, vehicle dist mgr, 1982-84; Shoals Ford Inc, Muscle Shoals, Ala, pres & owner, 1986-. **Orgs:** Black Ford Lincoln Mercury Dealer Asn, 1986-; vice chmn, Area New Car Dealers Asn, 1988-89; bd dir, Am Heart Asn, 1988-; Exec Comt, United WayShoals, 1988-; Sheffield, Ala, Rotary Club, 1988-; chair, Ala Comn Higher Educ, 1988-; Sheffield Rotary Club; vice chmn, Ala Comn Higher Educ, 1992-. **Home Addr:** 102 Moorsgate Dr, Florence, AL 35630, **Home Phone:** (205)764-6119. **Business Addr:** President, Shoals Ford Inc, PO Box 820399, Dallas, TX 75382-0399.

**LEE, GERALD BRUCE**
Chief executive officer. **Personal:** Born Jan 1, 1952?, Washington, DC. **Educ:** Am Univ, BA, 1973; Wash Col Law, JD, 1976. **Career:** Fairfax County, Va, pvt practice; Eastern Dist Va, judge, 1998-. **Orgs:** Active mem, Va Judges Judicial Conf; chmn, Circuit Ct Judicial Educ Comt; Circuit Ct Bench Bk Comt; legal community; Va St Bar; Va St Bar Coun; Pres, Northern Va Black Attorneys Asn; chmn, Judicial Selection Comt Alexandria Bar Asn; Bd dir, Metrop Wash Airports Authority; Am Bar Asn; chmn, Gen Pract Law Sect. **Business Addr:** Judge, Eastern District Virginia, US Courthouse, Alexandria, VA 22314-5798, **Business Phone:** (703)299-2100.

**LEE, DR. GERALD E.**
School administrator. **Personal:** Born Jan 11, 1958, Los Angeles, CA; son of Eugene and Erma Willis; married Tonya Marie Durley; children: Dawn Racquel, Gerald Eugene II, Darryl Eugene & Dennis Edward. **Educ:** Southwestern Christian Col, Terrell, TX, AS, theol & relig vocations, 1978; Okla Christian Col, Okla City, OK, BS, sociol & psychol, 1980; Amber Univ, Garland, TX, MA, prof develop, 1992, MA, coun psychol, 1997; Southwestern Christian Col, LLD, 2008. **Career:** First & Euclid Church Christ, minister, 1976-78; E side Church Christ, minister, 1978-81; Florence St Church Christ, minister, 1981-84; Metrop Church Christ, minister, 1984-87; Southwestern Christian Col, dir admis & recruitment, 1986-92, asst pres develop, assoc prof, 1992-2004; Lifestyle Mgt Coun Serv, Terrell, TX, pvt pract; G Lee & Assocs PC, Tex, founder, owner, sr practr & therapist, 2007-. **Orgs:** Am Coun Asn; Am Col Coun Asn; Asn Humanistic Educ & Develop; Asn Spiritual, Ethical & Relig Values & Coun; Int Asn Marriage & Family Counrs; Nat Career Develop Asn; Tex Coun Asn. **Home Addr:** 104 Lindell Dr, Terrell, TX 75160, **Home Phone:** (972)551-0504. **Business Addr:** Senior Practitioner, Owner, G Lee & Associates PC, 2825 Miller Ranch Rd Suite 225, Pearland, TX 77584, **Business Phone:** (713)340-3299.

**LEE, DR. GUY MILICON, JR.**
Educator, administrator, association executive. **Personal:** Born May 24, 1928, East Chicago, IN; married Trevor J; children: Kim Valerie, Rodney & L Smith. **Educ:** Roosevelt Univ, BA, 1954; Ind Univ, MS, 1959; Ball State Univ, EdD, 1969. **Career:** Educator (retired); Gary Community Schs, IN, pub sch teacher, 1956-64, adminr, 1964-70; Ball State Univ, Muncie, IN, doctoral fel, 1968-69; Saginaw Valley State Col, dir stud teaching, 1970-73, assoc dean sch educ prof, 1973-75, admin asst to pres, 1975-78, asst to pres, 1978-82, dean sch educ, 1982-86, prof educ, 1986-95, prof emer, col educ, 1995. **Orgs:** Asn Supv & Curric Develop; Nat Orgn Legal Prob Educ; Am Asn Sch Admin; rep, United Way Saginaw Co; Asn Teach Educ; Am Asn Higher Educ; bd dir, League United Latin Am Citizens, 1982-95; Metro Fayette Kiwanis Club, 1998-; Fayette County Sr Servs Bd, 1999-; Am Asn Col Teachers Educ; Phi Delta Kappa; Am Asn Affirmative Action; Col & Univ Personnel Asn. **Honors/Awds:** High Scholastic Achievement Award, Ind Univ, Bloomington, 1953; Citizen of the Age of Enlightenment Award, Am Found Sci Creative Intelligence, 1976; Keyman Award, United Way, Saginaw County, MI, 1979. **Home Addr:** 165 Hampstead Mnr, Fayetteville, GA 30214-3465, **Home Phone:** (770)460-1374.

**LEE, DR. GWENDOLYN B.**
Educator. **Personal:** Born Feb 3, 1950, Gary, IN; daughter of Willie and Emma Byrd; married Ronald Warren; children: Michelle Victoria. **Educ:** Ball State Univ, BS, 1971; Purdue Univ, MS, 1975, MS, 1984; Loyola Univ, PhD, 1998. **Career:** Thornridge High Sch, teacher, 1971-81, dean stud, 1981-85, asst prin, 1985-92, prin, 1994-99; Hillcrest High Sch, prin, 1992-94; assoc supt; Thornton Twp High Schs, assoc supt, 1971-2007; Newleaders New Schs, sch achievement coach, 2007. **Orgs:** Alpha Kappa Alpha Sorority, 1969-; pres, S Suburban Chap, 1978-82; Nat Mem-At-Large, 1986-90; Chairperson, Nat Nominating Comt, 1990-94; state dir, Ill Prins Asn, 1997-2000; Nat Trends & Serv, 1998; nat rec secy, 1998-2002, nat vpres, 2002-06; Nat Asn Sec Schs Prins, 1985-; Asn Supvn & Curric Develop, 1985-; bd dir, S Suburban Family Shelter, 1994-; Dir, Nat Coun Negro Women; Links Inc. **Home Addr:** 3014 Elliot Lane, Homewood, IL 60430-2846, **Home Phone:** (708)957-7962. **Business Addr:** School Achievement Coach, New Leaders for New Schools, 850 W Jackson Blvd, Chicago, IL 60607, **Business Phone:** (312)829-6567.

**LEE, HELEN ELAINE**
Educator, novelist. **Personal:** Born Mar 13, 1959, Detroit, MI; daughter of George Ernest and Dorothy Ann Hicks. **Educ:** US Dept Educ, Howard Univ, 1995; Harvard Col, BA, 1981; Harvard Law Sch, JD, 1985. **Career:** Univ Mich, Dearborn, adj lectr, 1995; Pine Manor Col, writers-in-residence; Mass Inst Technol, asst prof writing, assoc prof fiction writing & humanistic studies, currently; novelist; Auth: Serpent's Gift, Atheneum Publishers, 1994, London Headline Press, 1994; Marriage Bones, African Diaspora Short Fiction, ed; Charles Rowell W view Press, 1995; Silences, Best Short Stories by Black Writers vol II, ed, Gloria Naylor, Little, Brown & Co, 1995; Novel Water Marked, Scribner, 1999; Life Without about lives inmates Am prisons; The Hard Loss; Best African American Fiction, 2009. **Orgs:** Phi Beta Kappa; bd mem, PEN New Eng. **Home Addr:** 18 Glovesta St, Arlington, MA 02474, **Home Phone:** (781)648-7770. **Business Addr:** Associate Professor of Fiction, Massachusetts Institute of Technology, Rm 14N-425 77 Mass Ave, Cambridge, MA 02139-4307, **Business Phone:** (617)253-7894.

**LEE, HELEN SHORES**
Lawyer, psychologist, judge. **Personal:** Born Birmingham, AL; daughter of Arthur D Shores; married Robert M Sr; children: 3. **Educ:** Fisk Univ, BA, psychol, 1962; Pepperdine Univ, MA, clin psychol; Samford Univ, Cumberland Sch Law, JD, 1987. **Career:** Clin psychologist, 1971-87; Univ Ala Birmingham, Dept Psychiat, instr clin psychol, 1972-77; Birmingham' s Jefferson County, consult & dduc, dir, 1977-80, Dept Heath, Western Ment Health Ctr, clin outreach serv dir, 1980-84; T. A. Lawson State Jr Col, counr; Calif Job Corps Ctr Women, resident advisor; Univ Ala Med Ctr, Chair Minority Health Res Ctr Adv Coun; Los Angeles Girl Scouts Coun, field dir; Inst Child Study, teacher & counr; Shores, Lee, Sparks, Atha & Choy, lawyer, 1987-95, Shores and Lee, lawyer, 1995-2003; Jefferson County (Ala), 10th Judicial Ct Ala, circuit judge, 2003-. **Orgs:** Chairwoman, Ala State Ethics Comn, 1996-2000; Am Bar Asn; Ala State Bar; Birmingham Bar Asn; Magic City Bar Asn; Phi Alpha Delta Int Law Fraternity; Nat Bar Asn; Bd trustees Leadership Birmingham; adv bd, Cumberland Sch Law; bd trustees, Leadership Birmingham; bd dir, Blue Cross Blue Shield; bd trustees, First Congregational Christian Church; bd dirs, Campfire Inc; chairperson ala ethics comn, Nat Bd Gov Am Red Cross; dir, Birmingham Airport Authority; bd dir, Birmingham Mus Art; bd dir, AmSouth Bank; bd dir, Civil Rights Inst; bd dir, Blue Cross Blue Shield; bd dir, United Way; bd dir, United Cerebral Palsy; bd dir, Young Women's Christian Asn; bd dir, Am Red Cross (Birmingham Chap); bd dir, A. G. Gaston Boys Club. **Honors/Awds:** Women Who Make a Difference, Birmingham News, 2013. **Special Achievements:** The first African-American woman to serve in the civil division of the Circuit Court of Jefferson County; she worked at her father Arthur D. Shores' law practice. **Business Addr:** Circuit Judge, Tenth Judicial Court of Alabama, Jefferson County Courthouse, Birmingham, AL 35203, **Business Phone:** (205)325-5635.

**LEE, HOWARD N.**
Executive, government official, mayor. **Personal:** Born Jul 28, 1934, Lithonia, GA; married Lillian Wesley; children: Angela, Ricky & Karin Alexis Lou Tempie. **Educ:** Clark Col, 1956; Ft Valley State Univ, BA, sociol, 1959; Univ NC, MSW, 1966; Acad Cert Social Workers, 1968; Shaw Univ, LLD, 1971. **Career:** Juv Comestic Rel Ct Savannah, prob off, 1961-64; Univ NC, pres; Duke Univ, dir Youth Prog, 1966-68; NC Cent Univ, vis asst prof, 1967-68; Employee Rel Duke Univ, dir, 1968-69; Chapel Hill, Mayor, 1969-75; Lark Cinemas Inc, pres; Lee Dist & Mfg Co; Lark Entertainment Enter, pres & chmn bd; Plastiwood Prod Inc, pres; Shaw Univ, adj prof; Duke Univ, off human develop dir; Chapel Hill, NC, mayor, 1969-75; NC Dept Natural Resources & Community Develop, secy, 1977-81; NC, senate, 1990-94, 1996-2002; State Bd Educ, chmn, 2003; Jim Hunt Inst, sr adv, currently; NC Utilities Comn, comnr, 2004-08; State NC, exec dir educ cabinet, 2008-11; NC Educ Cabinet, exec dir, 2009; Howard N Lee Inst, founder & pres, 2011-. **Orgs:** Numerous prof mem; NC State Bd Educ, 2008; pres, NC Asn Independent Cols & Univs. **Honors/Awds:** Recip Ga St Teachers Hon Student's Award; honor student's Award, St Col; hunt fel Award Ft Valley St Col; achievement Award, Atlanta Br Nat Asn Advan Colored People; Achievement Award Phi Beta Sigma Fraternity, 1969; Nat Urban Leag Equal Oppor Day Award, 1970; publs field; William Richardson Davie Award, UNC; Distinguished Service Medal, UNC Gen Alumni Asn. **Special Achievements:** After graduate school he made history by becoming the youngest and most-recent graduate to be elected President of the NC Chapter of The Professional Association of Social Work; First African American to hold the mayor position in a mainly white city; First African American to serve in a governors cabinet in the south. **Business Addr:** President, Founder, Howard N Lee Institute, PO Box 14570, Research Triangle Park, NC 27709, **Business Phone:** (919)991-5128.

**LEE, IRMA. See THOMAS, IRMA.**

**LEE, IVIN B.**
Police chief, executive, association executive. **Personal:** Born Beard, WV; daughter of Carl Jr and Lenora Harmon; children: Carlene, Carlett, Carla, Carl & Carlton. **Educ:** BS, criminal justice. **Career:** Police chief (retired), executive; Charleston WVa Police Dept, sgt; Dunbar Police Dept, police chief; WVa Human Rights Comn, exec dir; Juv div, detective, dep dir corrections; spokesperson. **Orgs:** Mt Zion Baptist Church; WV Human Rights Comn, exec dir Hate Crimes Taskforce; WV BLEU; KCNC; NOBLE; WV Chiefs Police Asn; Bus & Prof Women's Club USA; Fraternal Order Police-Capitol City Lodge; Dunbar, WV Women's Club; Nat Asn Advan Colored People, Charleston, adv coun Salvation Army, Boys' & Girls' Club; exec bd Job Corps; Task force to study perceived racial disparity juv justice syst; Int Asn Off Human Rights Agencies. **Honors/Awds:** Community Reflection Award, Nat Asn Advan Colored People, 1995; Lifetime Achievement Award, Optimist Club, 1995; Community Service Award, Charleston Black Ministerial Alliance, 1996; Woman of the Decade 1986-96, Nat Asn Advan Colored People, 1996; 100-year Anniversary Community Award, Charleston Women's Improvement League, Inc; Appalachian Women of WV, Smithsonian Inst, 1996; Outstanding Law Enforcement Award, WV Trial Lawyers, 1997; Women of Achievement in Government, YWCA, 1998; African American Women of Distinction, 2002. **Special Achievements:** First Female Police Chief for Dunbar; First woman and the only African American to be appointed chief of the Dunbar Police Dept. **Home Addr:** , Charleston, WV. **Business Addr:** Executive Director, West Virginia Human Rights Commission, Rm 108A 1321 Plz E, Charleston, WV 25301-1400, **Business Phone:** (304)558-2616.

**LEE, DR. JAMES EARL, SR.**
Dentist. **Personal:** Born Mar 5, 1940, Conway, SC; son of Richard Allen and Ophelia Buck; married Patricia Ponds; children: James E Jr, Allen Earlington & Arrington Patrick. **Educ:** SC State Col, attended 1963; Howard Univ, Col Dent, DDS, 1971. **Career:** Carraway Meth Hosp, intern; Univ Hosp, Birmingham, resident; pvt pract dentist, 1973-; Appalachian Reg Health Policy & Planning Coun Anderson, SC, staff dentist, 1971-72; Dent Serv, Howard Univ Upward Bound Prog, dir, 1971; Franklin C Fetter Comprehensive Health Care Clin Charleston, staff dentist, 1972-74. **Orgs:** Chmn, Salvation Army Adv Bd, 1980; chmn, Conway Housing Authority, 1980-81; chmn, 1992-93, past pres, coun pres, Palmetto Med Dent & Pharmaceut Asn, 1984-; vpres, State Bd Dent, 1994; Int Col Dent, 1993; Col Dents, 1993; Palmetto Med Dent & Pharm Asn; Pee Dee Dist Dent Soc; SC Dent Soc; Am Dent Asn; Nat Dent Asn; Conway Alumni Chap; Kappa Alpha Psi; Bethel African Methodist Episcopal Church Young Adult Choir; exec comt, Palmetto Med Dent & Pharm Asn; Grand Strand Dent Soc; pres, Pee Dee Med Dent & Pharmaceut Asn; health adv comn, Waccamaw Econ Opptunity Coun; Ment Health Asn Horry County; steward Bd, Bethel African Methodist Episcopal Church. **Honors/Awds:** Dental Award, Howard Univ, 1958; Doctor of the Year, Palmetto Med Dent & Pharmaceut Asn, 1989. **Business Addr:** Dentist, James E Lee, 611 Church St, Conway, SC 29527, **Business Phone:** (843)248-4115.

**LEE, JEFFERI KEITH**
Executive director, association executive, executive. **Personal:** Born Jan 24, 1957, South Boston, VA; son of Nannie; married Tina Mance; children: Brandon (deceased) & Jefferi. **Educ:** Univ Md, Mo Valley Col, radio, tv & film. **Career:** WDVM-TV, Wash DC, freelance producer, 1979-81; PM Mag, prod staff, assoc producer; Univ Tex, vis prof; Black Entertainment TV, Network Opers, exec vpres, pres, 1982-98; Bio-Defense Res Group Inc, exec dir, pres & chief exec officer, 2005-08; Brandon Carrington Lee Found, chief exec officer; BET Holdings Inc, exec vpres; WHUT-TV, gen mgr, 2011. **Orgs:** Mem adv bd, Safe & Secure TV Channel Inc; Big Bros Big Sisters; Easter Seals; Nat Asn Tv Prog Execs. **Honors/Awds:** Lect, Howard Univ. **Business Addr:** General Manager, WHUT, 2222 4th St NW, Washington, DC 20059, **Business Phone:** (202)806-3200.

**LEE, JOHN C., III**
Executive. **Career:** John C Lee Construction & Supply Co, chief exec officer, 1977-. **Business Addr:** President, John C Lee Construction & Supply Co Inc, 470 MD Dr, Ft. Washington, PA 19034, **Business Phone:** (800)523-2200.

**LEE, JOHN M.**
Banker, president (organization). **Career:** Stand Savings Bank, co-founder, dir, chmn & pres, 1980-; E W Bank, vice chmn, managing dir community banking div, gen mgr, currently; E W BanCorp Inc, dir, 2006-. **Business Addr:** Vice Chairman, Director, East West Bank, 135 N Los Robles Ave 7th Fl, Pasadena, CA 91101, **Business Phone:** (626)768-6000.

### LEE, DR. JOHN ROBERT E.

Executive, president (organization). **Personal:** Born Jul 11, 1935, Tallahassee, FL; children: John Robert E IV. **Educ:** Fla A&M Univ, BA, 1959; Boston Univ, MA, 1961; Univ KS, PhD, 1973. **Career:** Commun Transp Real Estate Develop, pres, owner & entrepreneur; Silver Star Commun LLC, mgr. **Orgs:** Dir, Athletics TN State Univ, 1985; Nat Assoc Broadcasters, 1985; pres, Nat Assoc Black Owned Broadcasters; chmn, fund raising YMCA, 1985; comt mem, Boy Scouts Am, 1985; Nat Col Athletic Assoc, 1985; Ford Mercury Lincoln Minority Auto Assoc, 1985. **Business Addr:** Manager, Silver Star Communications LLC, 1100 A E Tennessee St, Tallahassee, FL 32308.

### LEE, JOIE SUSANNAH

Actor, movie director, movie producer. **Personal:** Born Jun 22, 1962, Brooklyn, NY; daughter of William James Edwards III and Jacquelyn Shelton (deceased). **Educ:** St Ann's Sch, Brooklyn; Sarah Lawrence Col, music, writing, dance. **Career:** Films: She's Gotta Have It, 1986; School Daze, 1988; Do the Right Thing, 1989; Mo' Better Blues, 1990; Bail Jumper, 1990; A Kiss Before Dying, 1991; Fathers & Sons, 1992; Crooklyn, 1994; Losing Isaiah, 1995; Girl 6, 1996; Get on the Bus, 1996; Nowhere Fast, 1997; Personals, 1999; Summer of Sam, 1999; Coffee and Cigarettes, 2003; She Hate Me, 2004; Full Grown Men, 2006; Starting Out in the Evening, 2007; Window on Your Present, 2010; Da Sweet Blood of Jesus, 2014. Screenwriter & assoc producer: Crooklyn, 1994; Nowhere Fast, 1997; Snapped, dir, 2001; Jesus Children of America, 2005; All the Invisible Children, exec producer, 2005; TV series: "Making 'Do the Right Thing'", 1989; "The Cosby Show", 1989; "100 Centre St", 2002; "Zero Tolerance", 2002; "Rotten", 2003; "Law & Order: Special Victims Unit", 2003. **Home Addr:** 165 Washington Pk, Brooklyn, NY 11205, **Home Phone:** (718)522-5802. **Business Addr:** Actress, co 40 Acres and a Mule Filmworks, 124 DeKalb Ave 2, Brooklyn, NY 11217, **Business Phone:** (718)624-3703.

### LEE, KERMIT J., JR.

Architect, educator. **Personal:** Born Mar 27, 1934, Springfield, MA; son of Kermit James Sr and Lillian B Jackson; married Lore Leipelt; children: Karin Justine & Jason Anthony. **Educ:** Syracuse Univ, BArch, 1957; Technische Hochschule Braunschweig Ger, Fulbright, 1958, 1959. **Career:** Afex, Wiesbaden Ger, chief architect, 1960-63; P Zoelly Arch Zurich Switz, assoc architect, 1963-66, vpres arch, 1969; Syracuse Univ, prof architect 1973, prof emer, currently; SU Inst Energy Res, fac assoc, 1978; Chimaera Energy Tech Corp, prin & chief exec officer, 1979; Syracuse Univ Pre-Col Prog, app dir, 1986; Energenesis Develop Corp, vpres, 1983; Kermit J Lee Jr, AIA architect & prin, 1989-. **Orgs:** Medary fel, Am Inst Archit, 1959-60; consult, Urban Designer Model Cities, Springfield, MA, 1969-75; dir, Campus Plan Group Syracuse Univ, 1970; bldg code bd appeal, 1970-; Am Inst Architect; mayors comm Revise City Charter, 1972-74; adj assoc prof, urban design, Columbia Univ, 1974; NY Coalition Black Architect, 1977; graphic exhib Proj Energy Syracuse Univ Sch Architect, 1979; tech consult Onondaga County Citizens Energy Comm, 1979-; NY Bd Architect, 1979-, Gov Cult Adv Comm Time Sq, Nat Coun Architect Regional Bd ARE, 1985; Citizen's Cult Adv Comt, Times Sq Develop, 1985-; chmn, NY Bd Architect, 1986-87. **Home Addr:** 301 Houston Ave, Syracuse, NY 13224-1755, **Home Phone:** (315)445-1021. **Business Addr:** Professor Emeritus of Architecture, Syracuse University, 350 W Fayette St Suite 13202, Syracuse, NY 13244, **Business Phone:** (315)443-3518.

### LEE, KEVIN BRIAN

Executive. **Personal:** Born Aug 15, 1967, Philadelphia, PA; son of William Keith and Grenthian. **Educ:** Pa State Univ, BS, 1990, MEd, 1995. **Career:** Pa State Univ, admis asst, 1990-91, human resources asst, 1991-92, staff develop, training coordr, 1992-96; TRW Syst Integration Group, mgr human resources, 1997-. **Orgs:** Nat Asn Advan Colored Peopel, Educ Comt, 1988-90; pres, Groove Phi Groove Social Fel Inc, Penn State, 1990-91, adv, 1991-92; exec asst, Univ Libr Diversity Coun, 1991-96; Am Col Personnel Asn, 1994-; Pa Col Personnel Asn, 1994-95; Penn State Univ, Black Grad Stud Asn, 1994-96; Grad Stud Asn, 1994-96. **Honors/Awds:** Community Service Award, 1989; Homecoming King, 1989-90; Black Caucus, Penn State Univ. **Home Addr:** 4421 Fairstone Dr, Fairfax, VA 22033. **Business Addr:** Human Resources Manager, TRW Systems & Information Technology Group, 1 Fed Syst Pk Dr, Fairfax, VA 22033, **Business Phone:** (703)803-5759.

### LEE, LARRY DWAYNE

Sports manager, football player, musician. **Personal:** Born Sep 10, 1959, Dayton, OH; son of Charles V and Evolia; married Daphne Y; children: Dayna & Danielle. **Educ:** Univ Calif, Los Angeles, CA, BS, US hist, 1981. **Career:** Football player (retired), football staff, musician; Detroit Lions, player, right guard, left guard, 1981-85, football admin opers, vpres, 1993-2001; Miami Dolphins, right guard, 1985-86; Denver Broncos, center, 1987-88; Mel Farr Ford, mgr, 1987-91; While Allen Honda, gen mgr, 1991-93; Larry Lee & Back Day, founder, pres, chief exec officer, 2002-. **Orgs:** Kappa Alpha Psi; bd mem, Dayton Pro Stars Football Camp, 1981-; fel Broncos. **Honors/Awds:** Man of the Year, Kappa Alpha Psi, 1981; Urban/Funk Musician of the year, 2006. **Special Achievements:** Detroit Music Awards, nominated, 2005-08. **Home Addr:** 3397 Sawgrass Ct, Rochester Hills, MI 48309, **Home Phone:** (810)852-1984. **Business Addr:** Founder, President, Larry Lee And Back In The Day, 2826 Tall Oaks Ct Suite 12, Auburn Hills, MI 48326, **Business Phone:** (248)852-1984.

### LEE, LAVERNE C.

Educator. **Personal:** Born Dec 19, 1933, Bayonne, NJ; daughter of Charles H Churn and Violet M Grayson Churn; children: Juvia A. **Educ:** Morgan St Col, BS, 1955; Loyola Col, MEd, 1969; Johns Hopkins Univ. **Career:** Baltimore Co Bd Educ, instr reading spl; teacher physically handicapped; Battle Monumental Sch Eastwood Ctr, prin; Baltimore County Pub Schs, coord recruitment. **Orgs:** Treas, 1970-74, vpres, 1974-75, CEC; sec, Teacher Asn Baltimore Co, 1973-; pres, Baltimore Co Chap Coun Excep C, 1974-76; del, Nat Educ Asn Conv; del, CEC Conv; Orton Soc; PTA; exec bd, TABCO; Delta Kappa Gamma; Phi Delta Kappa, 1988-. **Home Addr:** 8415 Bellona Lane Suite 701, Towson, MD 21204. **Business Addr:** Coordinator of Recruitment Personnel, Baltimore County Public Schools, 6901 N Charles St, Towson, MD 21204, **Business Phone:** (410)887-4554.

### LEE, LERON

Executive, baseball player, president (organization). **Personal:** Born Mar 4, 1948, Bakersfield, CA; son of Leon and Jewel Williams; married Vicquie Tanaka; children: Juliet M & Vivian Y. **Career:** Baseball player (retired), baseball coach; St Louis Cardinals, St Louis, Mo, player, 1969-71; San Diego Padres, San Diego, Calif, player, 1971-73; Cleveland Indians, Cleveland, OH, player, 1974-75; Los Angeles Dodgers, Los Angeles, Calif, player, 1975-76, free agt; Lotte Orions Baseball Club, Tokyo, Japan, player, 1977-88; Oakland Athletics, Oakland, Calif, coach, 1989-90; Pro-Elite Sports Inc, pres; Bold Tech Corp, owner; Cincinnati Reds, advising batting coach, currently. **Home Addr:** 8150 Warren Ct, Granite Bay, CA 95746, **Home Phone:** (916)797-0411. **Business Addr:** Advising Batting Coach, Cincinnati Reds, Great Am Ball Pk 100 Main St, Cincinnati, OH 45202, **Business Phone:** (513)765-7000.

### LEE, M. DAVID, JR.

Educator, architect. **Personal:** Born Aug 31, 1943, Chicago, IL; son of M David Sr and Mae Thomas; married Celeste E Reid; children: M David III, Aron Ford & Raquel Yvette. **Educ:** Univ Ill, BA, 1967; Harvard Univ, MA, 1971. **Career:** Candeub Flessig & ASC, planning draftsman, 1962-64; Roy D Murphy Architect, draftsman, 1965-67; David A Crane Architects, urban design draftsman, 1967-69; Stull ASC Inc, architects, arch & urban designer, 1969-83; Stull & Lee Architects, partner, 1983-; Harvard Univ, adj prof, 1988-; Rhode Island Sch Design, fac; Mass Inst Technol, fac.; WHBQ-TV, sports dir; Film; My Law/ Your Order, dir, 1991. **Orgs:** Pres, Boston Soc Architects, 1992; fel, Inst Urban Design; mayor's inst fac, Nat Endowment Arts; Boston Coc; Boys & Girls Clubs; vis comt, Mass Inst Tech Sch Arch; trustee, Berklee Col Music; fel, John Hay Whitney Found, 1970; fel, Am Inst Architects, 1992. **Home Addr:** 50 Waverly St, Brookline, MA 02445, **Home Phone:** (617)232-6439. **Business Addr:** Partner, Stull & Lee Inc, 38 Chauncy St, Boston, MA 02111, **Business Phone:** (617)426-0406.

### LEE, MALCOLM D.

Movie director, writer, movie producer. **Personal:** Born Jan 11, 1970, Queens, NY; married Camille Melika Banks. **Educ:** Georgetown Univ, BA, eng & fine arts minor, 1992; Packer Col Inst, Brooklyn, NY. **Career:** Malcolm X, post-prod asst, 1992; Clockers, asst to Spike Lee, 1995; Girl 6, dir trainee, 1996; The Best Man, writer, dir, actor, 1999; Undercover Brother, dir, 2002; Roll Bounce, 2005; "Everybody Hates Chris", dir, 2006; "The Music Makers", actor, 2005; "Everybody Hates the Lottery", tv series, 2006; Welcome Home, Roscoe Jenkins, dir, exec producer, writer 2008; Soul Men, dir, 2008; Life's Poison, dir, 2011; Scary Movie 5, dir, 2013; The Best Man Holiday, dir, writer, producer, 2013; The Best Man Wedding, dir, writer, producer, forthcoming, 2016; Barbershop 3, dir, forthcoming, 2016. **Business Addr:** Writer, Director, William Morris Endeavor Entertainment LLC, 9601 Wilshire Blvd, Beverly Hills, CA 90210, **Business Phone:** (310)859-4000.

### LEE, DR. MARGARET CAROL

Educator. **Personal:** Born Oct 3, 1955; daughter of Charles Henry Sr and Carol Rae Carruthers. **Educ:** Spelman Col, Atlanta, BA, polit sci, 1976; Univ Pittsburgh, PA, MA, 1981, PhD, pub & int affairs, 1985. **Career:** Tenn Technol Univ, Dept Polit Sci, assoc prof, 1986-94; Spelman Col, Atlanta, Ga, Dept Polit Sci, assoc prof, 1996; Am Univ, Sch Int Serv, scholar residence, 2000; Georgetown Univ, Wash, DC, vis assoc prof, 2000; Univ NC, Chapel Hill, Dept African & Afro-Am Studies, assoc prof, 2006-. Books: The Political Economy of Development in Southern Africa, 1989; The State and Democracy in Africa, 1997; The Land Crisis in Southern Africa, 2003; The Political Economy of Regionalism in Southern Africa, 2003. **Orgs:** African Studies Asn, 1988-; Nordic Africa Inst; Inst Security Studies; US African Growth & Opportunity Act; Dag Hammarskjold Found; Nordic Africa Inst. **Business Addr:** Associate Professor of African Studies, University of North Carolina, CB 3395 106 Battle Hall, Chapel Hill, NC 27599-3395, **Business Phone:** (919)966-5496.

### LEE, MARGARET S.

Association executive. **Personal:** Born Mar 31, 1936, Ocean City, NJ; daughter of Theodore Scott and Mary Roberta Outen. **Educ:** Temple Univ, 1957; Taylor Bus Inst, 1970. **Career:** Association executive (retired); City Philadelphia, zoning clerk, 1954-60; Bankers Trust Co, credit clerk, 1964-68; Leitner & Goodman, Esqs, legal secy, 1969-74; Nat Bowling Asn, exec secy-treas, 1974-2006. **Orgs:** Nat Coalition Black Meeting Planners, 1989-; trustee, Nat Bowling Hall Fame & Mus, 1990-; Nat Asn Female Execs, 1991. **Honors/Awds:** Received the NBA Mary L Wilkes Award, Outstanding Service, 1974; received numerous local, regional and national NBA Awards and citations for outstanding service from 1974-; Inducted into Local Chapter Hall of Fame, 1990. **Special Achievements:** First all female Executive Cabinet of TNBA. **Home Addr:** 365 Clinton Ave Apt 4D, Brooklyn, NY 11238, **Home Phone:** (718)789-6965.

### LEE, MARK ANTHONY

Football player. **Personal:** Born Mar 20, 1958, Hanford, CA. **Educ:** Univ Wash, attended. **Career:** Football player (retired); Green Bay Packers, left cornerback, punt returner, kick returner, 1980-90; New Orleans Saints, defensive back, 1991; San Francisco 49ers, defensive back, 1991. **Home Addr:** 6411 20th Way Ave, Redmond, VA 53188.

### LEE, MILTON B.

Chief executive officer, founder (originator), president (organization). **Personal:** married Sarah. **Educ:** Univ Tex, Austin, BS, mech engineering, 1971. **Career:** Gen Elec Co, staff, 1976; Pub Utility Comn Tex; Austin Energy, chief operating officer, chief exec, officer & gen mgr, 1976; Lower Colo River Authority; City Pub Serv, gen mgr, chief exec officer; CPS Energy, San Antonio, Tex, sr vpres, 2000, interim gen mgr, 2001, chief exec officer, gen mgr, 2002-10; Lee Energy Partners LLC, founder, pres, 2010; Univ Idaho, faculty, Corp Strategy at Utility Exec Course. **Orgs:** Pres, TPPA; Elect Reliability Coun Tex; Tex Pub Power & Am Pub Power Asns; adv bd, Univ Tex Austin Engineering Found; Univ Tex San Antonio's Develop Bd; bd dir, Greater San Antonio Chamber Com; trustee, bd dir, Southwest Found Biomed Res; bd dir, tech adv comt, ERCOT; bd trustee, Huston Tillotson Univ; Nat Socs Black Engrs; Tex Socs Prof Engrs; Tex Alliance Minorities Engineering; bd dir, Big Bros Big Sisters; vice chair, Large Pub Power Coun; bd gov, Cancer Ther Res Ctr; San Antonios Econ Develop Found; bd dir, Southwest Res Inst; Tex Res & Technol Found; P16Plus Coun Greater Bexar County Found; bd dir, BioMed San Antonio; bd dir, Greater San Antonio Chamber Com; Tex Pub Power & Large Pub Power Asn; San Antonio Med Found; bd dir, Alamo Col Found; bd dir, Masters Leadership Prog; bd dir, Leadership Austin; bd dir, Greater San Antonio Chamber Com; vice chmn, Southwest Res Inst. **Business Addr:** Faculty, Utility Executive Course College of Business & Economics, 875 Perimeter Dr MS 3161, Moscow, ID 83844-3161, **Business Phone:** (208)885-6265.

### LEE, MINNIE JOYCELYN. See ELDERS, DR. M. JOYCELYN.

### LEE, NATHANIEL

Lawyer, chairperson. **Educ:** Morehead State Univ, BA, 1977, MA, 1978; Univ Ga, JD, 1982. **Career:** Wilson, Coleman Roberts, 1981-83; Nathaniel Lee & Assocs, 1983-86; Watkins & Lee, partner, 1986-91; Lee & Fairman LLP, sr partner, 1984-. **Orgs:** Vpres, NCP, Indianapolis Br, 1986-88; life mem, chair bd dir, Marion Co Bar Asn, 1987-2009; bd mem, Ronald McDonald House, 1987-2000; golf chmn, Indianapolis Urban League, 1992-94; bd mem, Police Athletic League, 1993-96; mem litigation sect, Indianapolis Bar Asn, 1993-02, grievance comt, 1999-; co-chair, Judicial Eval Comt, 2002-; adv bd mem, Ind Supreme Ct CLEO, 1999-2006; life mem, spec asst pres, Nat Bar Asn, 2001, legal educ dir & civil advocacy chmn, 2001-09; Am Inns Ct, 2002; Legal Educ Comt, 2002; chmn, Lee Found; Ind Super Lawyers, 2005-15; Am Trial Lawyers Asn; Ind Trial Lawyers Asn; co-chmn, Ind Supreme Ct; chmn, Lee Found. **Honors/Awds:** COT Service Award, Marion County Bar Asn, 1992; COT Service Award, Nat Bar Asn, 1992; Distinguished Fellow Award, Indianapolis Bar Asn, 2002; Presidential Award, Nat Bar Asn, 2004, 2006-08; Indiana Super Lawyer, 2006-09; Leadership in Law Barrister's Award, 2009; Special Contributor Award, Wheelers Boys Club; Service to Organization Award, In Ronald McDonald House. **Business Addr:** Attorney, Senior Partner, Lee & Fairman LLP, 127 E Mich St, Indianapolis, IN 46204, **Business Phone:** (317)631-5151.

### LEE, OLIVER B.

Educator, executive director. **Personal:** Born Sep 27, 1926, Cleveland, OH; married Isis Edna; children: Brenda, Linda, Jacquelyn & John. **Educ:** Springfield Col, Springfield, Mass, BS, 1953, MS, 1957. **Career:** YMCA, Cleveland, Ohio, dir, 1954-59; Voc Rehab Cleveland, Cleveland, Ohio, counr supr, 1959-64; Ohio Bur Voc Rehab, Cleveland, youth prog dir, 1964-66; Rehab Serv Cleveland Soc Blind, Cleveland, Ohio, dir, 1966-67; Coun & Placement Aim-Jobs, Cleveland, dir, 1967-69; Cleveland State Univ, Comn Exten Prog, dir, 1969-73, assoc dean, 1973-. **Honors/Awds:** United Area Citizens Agency Leadership Devel Award, 1972; Lincoln HS Football Hall of Fame Hinton, WV, 1972; Youth Award, Kiwanis Club Service, 1973. **Home Addr:** 15987 Ravine Dr, East Cleveland, OH 44112, **Home Phone:** (216)761-4518. **Business Addr:** Associate Dean, Cleveland State University, Division of Continuing Edition, Cleveland, OH 44115-2214, **Business Phone:** (216)687-2000.

### LEE, OTIS KNAPP

Restaurateur. **Personal:** Born Detroit, MI. **Career:** Mr FoFo's Deli & Restaurant, owner, 1973-. **Special Achievements:** Commissioned by Kentucky Fried Chicken to create a sweet potato pie for mass marketing, beginning 1993. **Business Addr:** Owner, Mr FoFo's Delicatessen, 8902 2nd Ave, Detroit, MI 48202, **Business Phone:** (313)873-4450.

### LEE, PATRICE J.

Spokesperson. **Educ:** Tufts Univ, BA, 2004; Boston Col, MA, 2006. **Career:** Prince Cedza Dlamini, consult, 2004-07; Charles G. Koch Charitable Found, assoc, 2008-09; Fund Am Studies, media rels mgr, 2008-09; Philanthropy Roundtable, proj mgr pub policy, 2009-13; Generation Opportunity, dir outreach, 2013-, nat spokeswoman, 2015-; Independent Women's Forum, sr fel, 2013-. **Orgs:** Tufts Alumni Asn; Phi Sigma Alpha. **Business Addr:** Independent Women's Forum, 1875 I St NW Suite 500, Washington, DC 20006, **Business Phone:** (202)587-5201.

### LEE, PAULINE W.

Librarian. **Personal:** Born Nov 6, 1933, Simsboro, LA; daughter of Clinton Willis and Mionia Williams Willis; married Melvin. **Educ:** Southern Univ, Baton Rouge, La, BA, social studies/libr sci, 1955; Univ Mich, Ann Arbor, Mich, MALS, 1961; Calif State Col, Los Angeles, Calif, 1966; La Tech Univ, Ruston, La, 1972. **Career:** Librarian (retired); St Tammy High Sch, La, sch librn, 1955-58; Grambling State Univ, Grambling, La, circulation librn, 1958-62, educ librn, 1962-76, coordr pub serv, 1975-77, actg dir, 1977-78, assoc prof, dir, libr AC Lewis Memorial Libr, 1978-99; Staff Develop Workshop, SUSBO, consult, 1980; J Int libr Loan & Info Supply, consult ed, 1989. **Orgs:** Acad Libr Adminrs La; Am Libr Asn; Libr Develop Comt La; Grambling State Univ Alumni Asn; La Libr Asn; Trail Blazer Libr Syst; Ruston-Grambling League Women Voters; Black Caucus Am Libr Asn. **Honors/Awds:** Certificate of Recognition, Lewis Temple CME Church, 1972; Certificate of Appreciation, Future Bus Leaders Am, 1973; Awards of Recognition, Alpha Kappa Alpha Sorority, 1976; Certificate of Merit, Gov Edwin Edwards, 1978; Task Force on Academic Libraries/Library Master Plan, 1980; Service Award, New Rocky Valley Baptist Church, 1981; author, Courage Through Love: A Story of a Family, Ruston Daily Leader, 1982. **Home Addr:** 1229 Martin Luther King Jr Ave, PO Box 456, Grambling, LA 71245-0456, **Home Phone:** (318)255-8156.

### LEE, RITTEN EDWARD, II

Executive. **Personal:** Born Jun 25, 1925, Brighton, AL; son of Mattie Hogue (deceased) and Ritten (deceased); married Betty Allen; children: Anthony & Juliana Catherine Hogue. **Educ:** Earlham Col, BA, 1950; Univ CT, Sch Social Work, MA, 1953. **Career:** Rutgers Univ,

Newark, NJ, adj prof, 1965-81; Hudson Guild NYC, exec dir, 1972-77; Hunter Col Sch Social Work, adj lectr, 1977-78; United Neighborhood House NYC, dir manpower, 1977-80; Nat Info Bur NYC, asst dir, 1980-81; WCVI, WENY, WHRC, disc jockey, 1981-84; NYC Dept Law, consult, 1981; Seneca Ctr, exec dir, 1982-93; BLACFAX Jour, publ, 1982-98; Col New Rochelle, adj prof, 1997-98. **Orgs:** Trustee, Comm Church NY, 1973-77; founder & bd mem, RENA-COA Multi-Serv Ctr; trustee, Earlham Col, 1970-79. **Honors/Awds:** Sarah Addington Award, Earlham Col, 1950; Hon Mention Poetry Mag, 1950-51; Comn NCNCR Appt Newark Comm for Neighborhood Conserv, 1968; Certificate of Appreciation, RENA-COA Multi Serv Ctr, 1979; Henry McNeal Turner Community Service Award, 1993. **Special Achievements:** Poetry Published in Span, Botteghe Oscure Crisis, Flame, Crucible, Pittsburgh Courier, Chicago Defender, Michigan Chronicle, Ebony Rhythm (an anthology) & others. **Home Addr:** 200 Calif Rd Apt 12, Bronxville, NY 10708-4426, **Home Phone:** (914)667-2749.

### LEE, ROBERT EMILE

Executive, manager. **Personal:** Born Aug 19, 1948, New Orleans, LA; son of Robert Emile Sr and Mae Louise; married Glendarene Beck; children: Joseph. **Educ:** Tulane Univ, BS, 1970; Univ Chicago, MBA, 1973. **Career:** Martin Marietta Aerospace, eng admin specialist, 1973-75; Tenneco Oil, planning analyst, 1976-78, supply coord, 1978-80, mgr prod distrib, 1980-84, mgr mkt & planning, 1984-86, sr crude oil rep, 1986-87. **Orgs:** NBMBA Asn Houston Chap, 1986-. **Home Addr:** 2318 Sugarline Dr, Sugar Land, TX 77479, **Home Phone:** (713)980-3049. **Business Addr:** Sr Crude Oil Rep, Tenneco Oil Co, Tenneco Blgd, Houston, TX 77001, **Business Phone:** (713)757-2131.

### LEE, ROBINNE

Actor. **Personal:** Born Jul 16, 1974, Mt. Vernon, NY. **Educ:** Columbia Law Sch, law degree; Yale Univ, BA, psychol. **Career:** Films: Hav Plenty, 1997; National Security, 2003; 13 Going On 30, 2004; Deliver Us from Eva, 2004; Shook, 2004; Hitch, 2005; This Is Not a Test, 2008; Seven Pounds, 2008; Hotel for Dogs, 2009; Miss Dial, 2013; Being Mary Jane, 2013-. TV series: "The Runaway", 2000; "Cupid & Cate", 2000; "Almost a Woman", 2001; "Numb3rs", 2005; "Tyler Perry's House of Payne", 2007. **Honors/Awds:** Best Acting Performance, Boston International Film Festival, 2008. **Business Addr:** Actress, c/o Paradigm, 10100 Santa Monica Blvd 25th Fl, Los Angeles, CA 90067, **Business Phone:** (310)277-4400.

### LEE, SHALON D.

Chief executive officer. **Educ:** Univ Mich Sch Social Work, MSW, 1998. **Career:** PATH; Soka Serv LLC, owner, pres & chief exec officer, currently. **Business Addr:** President, Owner, Soka Services L L C, 280 Bondale Ave, Pontiac, MI 48341, **Business Phone:** (248)481-8654.

### LEE, SHEILA JACKSON

Government official. **Personal:** Born Jan 12, 1950, Queens, NY; daughter of Ivalita (deceased); married Elwyn Cornelius; children: Erica Shelwyn & Jason Cornelius Bennett. **Educ:** Yale Univ, BA, polit sci, 1972; Univ Va, Sch Law, JD, 1975. **Career:** John Courtney Murray Traveling & Res fel, Mudge Rose Guthrie & Alexander assoc, summer, 1974; Wld Harkrader & Ross, atty, 1975-78; Munic Ct city Houston, assoc judge; US House Reps & Select Comm Assassinations, staff coun, 1977-78; Fulbright & Jaworski, atty, 1978-80; United Energy Resources, atty, 1980-87; Brodsky & Ketchand, partner, 1987-; City Houston, assoc judge, 1987-90; pvt pract, atty, 1988-; Homeland Security Subcomt Transp Security & Infrastructure Protection, chwmn; Houston City Coun, 4 Dist, cnm large, 1990-95; Human rels Commt, Chwmn; Airport & Cables commt; US House Reps, congresswoman, 1995-2014. **Orgs:** Bd dirs, John Courtney Murray Found, Yale Univ, New Haven, 1972-73; Episcopal Ctr C, 1976-78; Wash Coun Lawyers, 1976-78; Houston Area Urban League, 1979-; State Bar Tex, Bar Jour Comm, 1980; bd dir, Am Asn Blacks Energy, 1980; chairperson, Black Women Lawyers Asn, 1980; pres, Houston Lawyers Assc, 1983-84; pres, Houston Metro Ministries, 1984-85; dir, C's Mus, 1985-; dir, Tex Young Lawyers Assc, 1986; dir, Sam Houston Area Coun Boy Scouts Am, 1987-; Alpha Kappa Omega Chap, Houston, TX, 1988-; Cong C's Caucus, Afghan Caucus; founder & co-chairperson, Pakistan Caucus; founder & co chairperson, Algerian Caucus; Alpha Kappa Alpha Sorority Inc; Dem Party. **Honors/Awds:** Outstanding Young Lawyer, Pampered Lady Boutique Awards, Luncheon NY, 1977; Womens Day Speaker Award, Linden Blvd Seventh Day Adven Chap, NY, 1978; Rising Star of Texas Award, Tex Bus Mag, 1983; Outstanding Young Houstonian Award, 1984; Outstanding Service Award, Houston Lawyers Asn, 1984; Outstanding Young Lawyer of Houston, 1985; Outstanding History Maker (Legal), Riverside Gen Hosp Awards Prog, 1987; 2006 Award for Policy, 16th Annual Phillip Burton Immigration & Civil Rights Awards, 2006; Revelation Urban Dev Inst, drum Major Award; Legislator of the Year Award, Nat Mental Health Asn. **Special Achievements:** Named one of Houston's 20 Most Influential Black Women 1984; the only female to serve as a Ranking Member of a Judiciary Subcommittee, has been hailed by "Congressional Quarterly" as one of the 50 most effective members of Congress and by "U.S. News and World Report" as one of the 10 most influential legislators in the House of Representatives. Introduced legislation to enhance federal enforcement of hate crimes with H.R. 254, the David Ray Hate Crimes Prevention of 2007; played a significant role in the recent renewal and reauthorization of the Voting Rights Act; contributed an amendment to the NASA reauthorization bill. **Home Addr:** 4428 N Roseneath, Houston, TX 77021, **Home Phone:** (713)741-0887. **Business Addr:** Congresswoman, US House of Representatives, 1919 Smith St Suite 1180, Houston, TX 77002, **Business Phone:** (713)655-0050.

### LEE, DR. SILAS H., III

Educator. **Personal:** Born Jul 24, 1954, New Orleans, LA; son of Henrietta Johnson and Silas Jr. **Educ:** Loyola Univ, BA, polit sci, 1976; Univ New Orleans, MS, urban studies, 1979, PhD, urban studies, 1999. **Career:** Silas Lee & Assoc, pres, 1982-; Ed Found, consult, 1984-; Xavier Univ, New Orleans, LA, sociol instr, 1988, pub opinion pollster & analyst local & nat media, asst prof sociol, currently, Ernest N Morial prof pub policy, currently; Silas Lee & Assocs, owner, currently. **Orgs:** Vice chmn, Nat Black Tourism Asn, 1989; bd trustees, Greater New Orleans Found. **Honors/Awds:** Honorary Secy State, LA, 1984; Court Certified Expert, Social & Econ Status Blacks & Pub Opinion Res, Eastern Dist La Court & Fed District Court. **Special Achievements:** First African American Opinion Pollster in New Orleans; Published the Economic Profile Blacks & Whites New Orleans. **Home Addr:** 1750 St Charles Ave Suite 536, New Orleans, LA 70130, **Home Phone:** (504)523-2308. **Business Addr:** Assistant Professor, Ernest N Morial Professor, Xavier University of Louisiana, 1 Drexel Dr, New Orleans, LA 70125-1098, **Business Phone:** (504)520-7400.

### LEE, SPIKE (SHELTON JACKSON LEE)

Movie director, actor, executive. **Personal:** Born Mar 20, 1957, Atlanta, GA; son of William James Edwards III and Jacquelyn Shelton; married Tonya Lynette Lewis; children: Satchel Lewis & Jackson. **Educ:** Clark Atlanta Univ, Morehouse Col, BA, mass commun; NY Univ, Sch Arts, MFA, film & TV, 1979. **Career:** Forty Acres & A Mule Film works, owner, 1986-; Spikes Joint, owner, 1990-; Spike DDB, pres & chief exec owner, currently; Films: She's Gotta Have It, dir, producer & writer, 1986; Sch Daze, dir, producer & writer, 1988; Do the Right Thing, dir, writer & producer, 1989; Mo Better Blues, dir, writer & producer, 1990; Jungle Fever, dir, writer & producer, 1991; Malcolm X, dir & producer, 1992; Crooklyn, dir, writer & producer, 1994; Clockers, dir, writer & producer, 1995; Drop Squad, 1994; New Jersey Drive, 1995; Tales from the Hood, 1995; Girl 6, 1996; Get on the Bus, dir & producer, 1996; 4 Little Girls, dir & producer, 1997; He Got Game, 1998; The Original Kings of Comedy, dir & producer, 2000; Lisa Picard Is Famous, 2000; Bamboozled, dir, writer & producer, 2000; 3 AM, 2001; Come Rainor Come Shine, dir, 2001; Jim Brown: All American, dir & producer, 2002; The 25th Hour, dir & producer, 2002; She Hate Me, dir, writer & producer, 2004; Sucker Free City, dir & producer, 2004; Jesus Children of America, dir, 2005; All the Invisible Children, dir & producer, 2005; Inside Man, dir, 2006; Lovers & Haters, dir, 2007; Miracle at St. Anna, dir & producer, 2008; Passing Strange, dir, 2009; Saint John of Las Vegas, exec producer, 2009; Dream Street, exec producer, 2010; Red Hook Summer, actor, dir & producer, 2012; You're Nobody 'til Somebody Kills You, exec producer, 2012; The Girl Is in Trouble, exec producer, 2012; Oldboy, dir & producer, 2013; Da Sweet Blood of Jesus, dir & producer, 2014; TV series: "Pavarotti & Friends for the Children of Liberia", 1998; "A Huey P. Newton Story", 2001; "The Concert for New York City", 2001; "Jim Brown: All American", 2002; "Sucker Free City", 2004; "Miracles Boys", 2005; "When the Levees Broke", 2006; "Shark", 2006; "Chapelles Show", 2006; "M.O.N.Y.", 2008; "Da Brick", dir & exec producer, 2011; "Mike Tyson: Undisputed Truth", dir & producer, 2013; "Katt Williams: Priceless", dir & producer, 2014. Music Videos:"Sunless Saturday", 1991; "White Lines (Dont Do It)", 1993; "Breakfast at Dennys", 1994; "They Dont Care About Us", 1996. Harvard Univ, instr; New York Univ, Kanbar Inst of Film & Television, artistic dir, 2002-; Co-author childrens book, Please Baby Please, 2002. **Honors/Awds:** Student Academy Award, Acad Motion Picture Arts & Sci, 1982; Ernest Artaria Award, Locarno Int Film Festival, 1983; Merit Award, Student Academy Awards, 1983; New Generation Award, Los Angeles Film Critics Asn, 1986; Prix de Jeunesse, Cannes Film Festival, 1986, 1991; Independent Spirit Award, 1987; LAFCA Award, Los Angeles Film Critics Asn, 1989; Filmcritica Bastone Bianco Award, Venice Film Festival, 1990; CFCA Award, Chicago Film Critics Asn, 1992; Filmmaker Award, 1992; Special Mention, Berlin Int Film Festival, 1997; Golden Satellite Award, Satellite Awards, 1998; Inspiration Award, 1999; Black Reel, 2001, 2007, 2011 & 2014; Maverick Tribute Award, Cinequest San Jose Film Festival, 2001; Honorary French Academy of Cinema Award, 2002; Special Award, BAFTA Awards, 2002; Lifetime Achievement Award, Las Vegas Film Critics Soc, 2003; Filmmaker Trumpet Award, 2003; Innovator Award, Am Black Film Festival, 2004; Ossie Davis Award, Atlanta Film Festival, 2005; Black Movie Award, 2006; FIPRESCI Prize, Venice Film Festival, 2006; Human Rights Film Network Award, Venice Film Festival, 2006; Venice Horizons Documentary Award, Venice Film Festival, 2006; Silver Bucket of Excellence Award, MTV Movie Awards, 2006; Image Award, 2007; Emmy Award, 2007; Biografilm Award, Venice Film Festival, 2012; Future Film Festival Digital Award, Venice Film Festival, 2012; Jaeger-LeCoultre Glory to the Filmmaker Award, Venice Film Festival, 2012; New York Emmy Awards, 2015; Academy Awards, 2016. **Special Achievements:** Nominated Oscar, 1990, 1998; Nominated Emmy, 1998. **Business Addr:** President, Chief Executive Officer, Spike DDB, 437 Madison Ave, New York, NY 10022, **Business Phone:** (212)415-3100.

### LEE, TAMELA JEAN

Executive. **Personal:** Born Feb 9, 1959, Denver, CO; daughter of Gentry and Patsy Burks; married Kyle Robert; children: Taja & Blaine. **Educ:** Howard Univ, finance, 1982. **Career:** Wells Fargo, credit analyst, 1982-83; Bank One, corp loan officer, 1983-89; Fedn Deposit Ins Corp, bank examr, liquidation specialist, 1989-93; pvt consult bus, 1993-94; Denver Office Economic Development, Division Small Business Opportunity, dir, currently; City & County Denver, dir, 2003-11; Dallas Ft/Worth Int Airport, vpres bus diversity & develop dept, 2011-. **Orgs:** Circuit rider, Small Bus Develop Ctr, Denver Metro Chamber Com, 1993-95, dir, 1995-2003; Leadership Denver Alumni Asn, 1996-; bd mem, Human Servs Inc, 1997-; Colo Lending Source, 1997-; Am Coc Execs, 1998-; bd mem, Colo Enterprise Fund, 1998-; Denver Urban Econ Develop Corp, 2002-; Better Bus Bur, 2002-; bd dir, Rocky Mountain Minority Supplier Develop Coun, 2002-. **Home Addr:** 5117 N Enid Ct, Denver, CO 80289, **Home Phone:** (303)371-4361. **Business Addr:** Vice President Business Diversity & Development Department, DFW International Airport, 2400 Aviation Dr, DFW Airport, TX 75261-9428, **Business Phone:** (972)973-5500.

### LEE, VIVIAN BOOKER

Government official, health services administrator. **Personal:** Born Jan 28, 1938, Spring, TX; daughter of Alvirita Wells Little; children: Anthony. **Educ:** Registered Nurse Cert, 1958; Pub Health Cert, 1959; Univ Wash, BS, 1959, MS, 1961; Sch Nurse Cert, 1967; Univ Puget Sound, MPA, 1980. **Career:** Government official (retired); Va Hosp, psychiat nurse, 1959-60; 50th Gen Hosp Army Reserve Corp, nurse instr, 1960-64; Group Health Corp Puget Sound, outpatient clinic nurse, 1961-66; Seattle Pub Sch, sch nurse, 1966-68; Renton Sch, supvr group health hosp & title I health supvr, 1968-72; US PHS, Region X, PHS EEO Officer, prog mgt officer, 1972-75; Region X Family Planning & Maternal & Child Health Progs, pub health adv, 1975-80, Region X Adolescent Health Coordr, 1975-91, Title X Family Planning Prog, Region X, reg mgr, 1980-93, Regional Women's Health, coordr, 1984-93, first PHS Region X Minority Health, coordr, 1987-92, PHS EEO investr; US Pub Health Serv, Off Women's Health, Off Regional Health Admin, Regional Mgr Title X Family Planning Prog, 1980, Region X, founding dir, 1993-94; Va Mason & Univ Hosp, emer rm nursing; Vet Admin Hosp, Psychiat Nursing; Pub Health Nursing, Seattle/King Co DPH; Sch Nursing Seattle & Renton Sch Dists; Outpatient Clin Servs, relief supvr; Hosp Nursing Supvr Group Health Cooperative, Puget Sound. **Orgs:** Univ Wash Nurses Alumnae Asn; Found Int Understanding through Studs; Delta Sigma Theta; Girls Clubs Inc; participant, White House Conf Civil Rights, 1966; Food Nutrit Health & C, 1969-70; Nat Family Planning & Reproductive Health Asn, Wash State Family Planning Coun; Wash Alliance Concerned With Sch Age Pregnancy; Univ Wash Minority Community Advy Comn; Rainier Beach United Methodist Church, Univ Wash Alumni Asn, bd, Multicultural Alumni partnership Club, Univ Wash Alumni Asn; Univ Wash Diversity Coalition; Univ Wash Diversity coun; Mary Mahoney Prof Nurses Orgn, Nat Family Planning & Reproductive Health Asn; Wash State Asn Black Health Profs; Alan Guttmacher Inst; vol, MAP; vol, Health Care Consult & Community, 1994. **Honors/Awds:** Nurse of the Year, Wash Sch, 1972; Outstanding Performance Award for Promoting Women's Equality, Dept HEW, 1975; DHHS Sustained Superior Performance Awards, 1973-90; Outstanding Dedication Award, Wash State Coun Family Planning, 1978; HRSA Award for Excellence, 1982; Annual Award of Family Planning Advocates of Oregon State, 1983, 1987 & 1990; Region X Clinician Award is named "The Vivian O Lee Clinician of the Year Award", 1987; WACSAP Award, 1988; NFPRHA Award, 1991; Chief Nurse Officer's Award, US Pub Health Serv, 1993; Certificate of Appreciation, US PHS, Region X, African-American Women's Health Care, 1994; Exemplary Service Award, Surgeon Gen US, Dr Joycelyn Elders, 24 yrs pub serv, 1994; Distinguished Service Award, US PHS Dep Asst Secy, Population Affairs, Wash, DC, 1994; Special Honors, nationwide group RPC's for FPS; Dep Asst Secy, Women's Health & the Dir of the PHS Office on Women's Health, US PHS, DHHS, 1994; Certificate of Recognition, Mary Mahoney Prof Nurses Orgn, 1995; Irving Kushner Award, Nat Family Planning & Reproductive Health Asn, 1995; PHS Region X Office Women's Health Annual Award, 1996; UWAA Volunteer of the Year, 1996; University Washington Annual Charles E Ode Guard Award, 2000; Nordstrom Community Service Award, 2001; WWAA Distinguished Alumnus Award, 2003. **Special Achievements:** Co-author of eight publications; Family Planning Services for Southeast Asians, Chlamydia, 1990 Health Objectives for the Nation, Title X Family Planning Prog, Pap Smear quality assurance; Region X Women's Health. **Home Addr:** 6323 Sand Point Way NE, Seattle, WA 98115, **Home Phone:** (206)524-1312.

### LEE, W. RANDOLPH

Administrator, business owner. **Educ:** Univ NC, BS, microbiol; Univ N Fla, MS, health admin & bus admin. **Career:** Anheuser-Busch Co Inc, mgr; Raven Transp Co, chief exec officer, pres & owner, 1985-. **Orgs:** Jacksonville Minority Bus Develop Coun. **Business Addr:** President, Owner & Founder, Raven Transport Co, 6800 Broadway Ave, Jacksonville, FL 32254, **Business Phone:** (904)880-1515.

### LEE, WILLIAM FRANCIS. See LEE, DR. ALLEN FRANCIS, JR.

### LEE, DR. WILLIAM H.

Founder (originator), president (organization), publisher. **Personal:** Born May 29, 1936, Austin, TX; son of Charles R; married Kathryn Charles; children: Roderick Joseph (deceased), William Hanford Jr & Lawrence Charles. **Educ:** Sacramento State Col, attended 1955; Univ Calif, BA, jour, 1957. **Career:** Lee Sacramento Observer, founder, 1962, pres & publ, 1965; Lee Publ Co, pres. **Orgs:** Secy, bd dir, Nat Newspaper Publs Asn, 1970-73; founding pres, W Coast Black Publs Asn, 1974; Delta Sigma Chi Journalism Fraternity; comnr, Sacramento County Welfare Commn; founder, pres, Mens Civil League Sacramento; bd dir, Sacramento Nat Asn Advan Colored People Credit Union; United Christian Ctr; dir, Sacramento Cent YMCA; Sacramento Urban League; United Way; Sacramento County, Am Cancer Soc; bd chmn, Sacramento Bus Coord Coun; co-founder, Sacramento Area Black Caucus; vice-chmn, Cancer Fund Dr; Sacramento Comm Urban Renewal; Statewide Comm Voter Regist; Blue Cross Calif; Methodist Hosp Sacramento; adv bd, Wells Fargo Bank; Super Valley Small Bus Develop Corp; bd mem, W Coast Black Publishers Asn; life mem, Nat Asn Advan Colored People. **Home Addr:** 2330 Alhambra Blvd, Sacramento, CA 95817-1124. **Business Addr:** Founder, Publisher, The Sacramento Observer, 2330 Alhambra Blvd, Sacramento, CA 95817, **Business Phone:** (916)452-4781.

### LEE, WILLIAM JAMES EDWARDS, III (BILL LEE)

Musician, writer. **Personal:** Born Jul 23, 1928, Snow Hill, AL; son of Arnold Wadsworth III and Alberta Grace Edwards; married Jacquelyn Shelton; children: Shelton, Chris, David, Joie & Cinque; married Susan Kaplan; children: Arnold Tone Kaplan VI. **Educ:** Morehouse Col, BA, 1951. **Career:** Self-employed jazz musician, 1950-; Folk Jazz Opera, Village Vanguard, 1968; Theatre St, Youth Action, C's Folk Jazz Opera, Little Johnny, dir & writer, 1971; Folk Jazz Opera, Alice Tully Hall, 1972; Folk Jazz Opera, Hampton Univ, 1973; Folk Jazz Opera, var Col campuses, 1975; Essex County Community Col, bass violin & ARO lit teacher, 1979-80; 29-B-Folk Jazz Opera, 1981; Colored Col Folk Jazz Opera, 1986; She's Gotta Have It, 1991; W chester Community Col, Lectr, Movie Music, 1992; Opera: Depot, One Mile E, Baby Sweets, Quarter, Rabbi, Monica, Juan Valdez. Films: She's Gotta Have It, 1986; Mo' Better Blues, 1990; Rage of Vengeance, 1993. Composer: Joe's Bed-Stuy Barbershop: We Cut Heads, 1983; She's Gotta Have It, 1986; School Daze, 1988; Do the Right Thing, 1989; Mo' Better Blues, 1990; Never Met Picasso, 1996; Window on Your Present, 2010. **Orgs:** Founder, pres, musical dir, NYK Bass Violin Choir, 1968-; Co-founder, co-musical dir, Brass Co, 1970; founder, musical dir, Desendents Mike & Phoebe, 1971-77; founder, dir, Natural Spiritual Orchestra, 1982-; co-founder, musical dir, Noah's Ark, 1989-; Bill Lee & Mo' Betta' Quartet, 1990; founder, Jacobs Ladder, c's chorus, 1991; musical dir, His Wonders to Perform, umbrella group, 1991; Family Tree Singers; Tone Is. **Honors/Awds:** Composing Grant, The Natioanal Endowment Arts, 1979, 1982; The LA Critics Awards, Best Movie Picture

Score, Do the Right Thing, 1988; Columbia Records Citation, 300000 record sales, Mo' Better Blues, 1990; Borough of Brooklyn, Howard Golden Citation Service, 1991; has written numerous folk-jazz operas. **Business Addr:** President, New Version Music, 165 Washington Pk, Brooklyn, NY 11201, **Business Phone:** (718)522-5802.

### LEE, WILLIAM THOMAS

Labor activist, executive director. **Personal:** Born Mar 27, 1942, Philadelphia, PA; son of Walter and Thelma Harper; married Celestine Tolbert; children: Marie, Thomas & Melissa Cora. **Educ:** Temple Univ, Philadelphia, PA, BA, acct, 1966. **Career:** Budd Co, Philadelphia, Pa, cost acct, 1966-67; Philadelphia Dress Joint Bd St, Philadelphia, Pa, asst mgr, bus agt, organizer, 1967-85; Local 132-98-102, ILGWU, New York, NY, mgr & secy, 1985-96; New York-Nj Regional Joint Bd, mgr, 1996-2001; Unite Here CLC, exec vpres, 2001-. **Orgs:** Dir, Bd dir, Empire Blue Cross & Blue Shield, 1988-2001; Nat Asn Advan Colored People, 1988-; Jewish Labor Comt, 1978-; Temple Varsity Club, 1966-; bd mem, A Philip Randolph Inst, 1988-. **Honors/Awds:** Achievement Award, Nat Asn Advan Colored People, 1988; Achievement Award, Philadelphia S Jersey Dist Coun, 1985; "Spirit of Life Award", City Hope Med Ctr, 1991. **Home Addr:** 2 Royal Ct, Roosevelt, NY 11575-1318, **Home Phone:** (516)867-0427. **Business Addr:** Executive Director, Unite Here CLC, 275 7th Ave, New York, NY 10001-6708, **Business Phone:** (212)265-7000.

### LEE-EDDIE, DEBORAH

Executive. **Educ:** Univ Mich, Ann Arbor, BA, psychol, 1976, MA, health serv admin, 1979; Am Col Healthcare Execs. **Career:** Erlanger Med Ctr, vpres Patient Serv, 1986-91; Brackenridge Hosp, Tex, chief exec officer, chief operating officer, 1991-94; Univ Miami & Jackson Memorial Hosp, sr v pres, chief admin officer, 1995-98; Nat Assoc Health Serv execs, pres, 1997-99; Kaiser Permanente, sr vpres, 1998-2000; Cath Health Initiatives, sr vpres opers, 2000-08, interim chief operating officer, chief exec officer, 2013-14; BE Smith Inc, interim chief operating officer, 2011-13; Alegent Health, dir; DLE Group, Interim Leader, Consult, 2009-; St Luke's Health Syst Corp, interim chief operating officer, currently. **Orgs:** Past nat pres, bd mem, comt chair, Nat Asn Health Serv Execs, 1980-. **Business Addr:** Interim Chief Operating Officer, Catholic Health Initiatives, 198 Inverness Dr W, Englewood, CO 80112, **Business Phone:** (303)298-9100.

### LEEKE, JOHN F.

Educator, president (organization). **Personal:** Born May 19, 1939, Indianapolis, IN; married Theresa Gartin; children: Michael, Madelyn, Mark & Matthew. **Educ:** Ind State Univ, BS, 1961; Univ Mich, MS, 1966; Union Grad Sch, PhD, orgn develop, 1977. **Career:** Ind State & Penal Farm, counsr, 1962; DC Pub Sch, teacher, 1962-63; Flint Community Schs, teacher, 1963-68; Nat Educ Asn, instr, prof, develop spec, 1968-85; Elsie Y. Cross & Assocs, Sr Consult, 1981-2009; John F Leeke Assoc Inc, orgn develop consult, 1985-, pres, currently; Nat Training Lab App Behav Sci, consult; Johnson & Johnson Pharmaceut Core States, staff; US Dept Agr Grad Sch, staff; Corning Inc, staff; Kodak, staff; Nat Inst Drug Abuse, consult; Consumer Prod Safety Comn, consult; Bell Labs, consult; GS USA, consult; Ind State Dept Inst, fac. **Orgs:** St Joseph Church, Landover, MD; Neighborhood Civic Orgn; Pi Lambda Phi; Nat Schs Brd Asn. **Home Addr:** 11305 Indian Wells Lane, Mitchellville, MD 20721. **Business Addr:** President, Consultant, John F Leeke Associates Inc, 11305 Indian Wells Lane, Mitchellville, MD 20721, **Business Phone:** (301)350-0925.

### LEEKE, MADELYN CHERYL (ANANDA KIAMSHA MADELYN)

Artist, writer, consultant. **Personal:** Born Dec 18, 1964, Flint, MI; daughter of John and Therese. **Educ:** Morgan State Univ, BA, 1986; Howard Univ Sch Law, JD, 1989; Georgetown Univ Law Ctr, LLM, 1991. **Career:** Commodities Futures Trading Comn, legal adv, 1989-90; John F Leeke Assoc Inc, res policy analyst, 1990-93; DC Off Treas, debt mgr, 1993-95; Hamilton Securities Group Inc, mgr, 1996-97; Kiamsha.com, found, pres, artist, auth & bus consult, 1997-; Smith Farm Ctr, artist resident, currently; State Union Fr Arrival Ceremony, social media corresp. **Orgs:** A Salon Ltd; Womens Caucus Art; bus vol, Cult Alliance Greater WASH; Yoga Alliance; Soc Arts Health care; Cult Alliance Greater Washs Bus Vol Prog; Sigma Gamma Rho Sorority Inc; All Souls Unitarian Church; Mid Atlantic Yoga Asn; Wash Buddhist Peace Fel; Insight Meditation Community Wash's People Color Sangha. **Home Addr:** 2000 16th St NW Apt 202, Washington, DC 20009, **Home Phone:** (202)332-5767. **Business Addr:** Founder, President, Kiamsha.com, PO Box 4444, Washington, DC 20010, **Business Phone:** (202)444-4444.

### LEEPER, RONALD JAMES

Administrator, government official. **Personal:** Born Dec 14, 1944, Charlotte, NC; married Phyllis Mack; children: Rhonda & Atiba. **Career:** LRT & Assoc Consult Firm, pres; L&S Housing Corp, pres; Charlotte City Coun, coun mem; Charlotte, NC, gen contractor; RJ Leeper Construct LLC, pres & owner, 1993-. **Orgs:** Chmn city coun, Community Develop Comm, 1979-87; pres, NC Black Elected Munic Off Assoc, 1982; mem bd dir, Urban League, 1983; chmn, Charlotte-Meck Lenburg Black Elected Off, 1984-85; organizer, Westpark Youth Athletic Asn; organizer, Colony Acres Home Owners Asn; bd dir, Nat Conf Christians & Jews; bd mem, Visitors Boys Town NC; organizer, Vote Task Force; pres, St Mark's United Methodist Church; bd mem, HabitatHumanities; chmn, bd dir, C W Williams Health Ctr; bd mem, Z Smith Reynolds; organizer, SaveSeed; bd mem, Metrop YMCA. **Honors/Awds:** Certificate of Appreciation, St Mark's United Methodist Church, 1978, 1980; Selected as one of ten Outstanding Men in America, 1979-81; Sr Citizen United Serv Christian Social Concern, 1980; Outstanding Community Service Award, Alpha Kappa Alpha Sorority, 1980; Award of Appreciation for Service to Senior Citizens & the Handicapped, Sr Citizens United, 1981; Recognized as Chart Pres, NC-BEMCO, 1982; Certificate of Appreciation, Black Polit Awareness League, 1984; Meritorious Award, Nat Asn Advan Colored People, 1984; Outstanding Community Serv, 1984; YMCA Outstanding Service Award, Community Serv Prog, 1987; Hon Neighbor of the Year Award, Charlotte Organizing Prog, 1987; Award of Appreciation, Charlotte Civic League Leadership, 1987; Award of Appreciation, Nat Asn Negro Bus & Prof Women's Club, 1987; Martin Luther King Gold Medallion, Charlotte-Mecklenburg Community Rels Comn, 1991; Citizen of the Year, Community Pride Mazina, 1994; LLD, Livingston Col, 2004; Luminary-Lifetime Achievement Award, Charlotte Post Found, 2009. **Home Addr:** 5544 Piper Glen Dr, Charlotte, NC 28277, **Home Phone:** (704)525-4589. **Business Addr:** Owner, President, Ronald J Leeper Construction LLC, 601 Morris St, Charlotte, NC 28202-1317, **Business Phone:** (704)334-3223.

### LEFEBVRE, DALE

Executive. **Personal:** Born Jan 1, 1971, Beaumont, TX. **Educ:** Mass Inst Technol, BS, elec eng; Harvard Law Sch, JD; Harvard Bus Sch, MBA. **Career:** Bell Labs, researcher; Testa, Hurwitz, Thibeault & LLP, law consult; McKinsey & Co, mgt consult & founder; Morgan Stanley Capital Partners, consult; Morgan Stanley M&A; Blue Capital, consult; First Union Pvt Equity Group, consult; etang.com, US Oper, head, chief financial officer; AIC Ltd, managing partner; Converge Global Trading, chmn, pres; Pharos Capital Group LLC, chmn, chief exec officer & managing partner, partner, currently; 3.5.7.11, founder & chmn, currently; PCG Trading LLC, chmn, pres. **Orgs:** Bd mem, dir, Smart Direct Inc; bd mem, Atherotech Inc; Nat Urban League Inc; African Am Stud Union; bd mem, Nat Asn Investment Co; dir, Alereon Inc; SmartDm Holdings Inc; SmartDM Inc. **Special Achievements:** Named as 10th largest African Am-owned US bus by Black Enterprise mag in 2004. **Business Addr:** Founder, Chairman, 3.5.7.11, 2710 Foxhall Rd NW, Washington, DC 20007-1127, **Business Phone:** (202)683-6835.

### LEFFALL, DR. LASALLE D., III

Chief financial officer, administrator, president (organization). **Educ:** Harvard Univ, BA, JD, & MBA. **Career:** Fed Home Loan Bank Atlanta, dir, 2007-; Mutual Am Instnl Funds Inc, dir, 2011-; Endeavor Group Inc, sr consult; LDL Financial Inc, founder, pres; Lockhart Caribbean Corp, dir, currently. **Orgs:** Actg chief exec officer, Nat Health Policy Forum; Econs Club Wash DC; sr exec, pres, chief operating officer, actg chief exec officer, chief financial officer, NHP Found, 2002-06. **Business Addr:** Member of the Board of Directors, The Endeavor Group Inc, 2001 K St NW Suite 206, Washington, DC 20006, **Business Phone:** (202)715-0924.

### LEFFALL, DR. LASALLE DOHENY, JR.

Oncologist, educator, association executive. **Personal:** Born May 22, 1930, Tallahassee, FL; son of LaSalle D Sr and Martha; married Ruthie McWilliams; children: LaSalle III. **Educ:** Fla A&M Col, BS, summa cum laude, 1948; Howard Univ, MD, 1952. **Career:** Homer G. Phillips Hosp, St. Louis, med training, 1953-54; Freedmans Hosp, from asst resident surg to chief resident surg, 1955-57; DC Gen Hosp, asst resident surg, 1954-55; Memorial Sloan-Kettering Hosp, sr fel, cancer surg, 1957-59; AUS Hosp, Munich, Ger, 1960-61; Howard Univ, fac, 1962, asst prof, 1970, chmn, dept surg; Am Col Surgeons, fel, 1964; Howard Univ Col Med, asst dean, 1964-70, actg dean, 1970, prof chmn dept surg, 1970-95, prof, dept surg, 1995-; Nat Housing Partnership Found, vpres, chief operating officer. **Orgs:** Nat Med Asn, 1962; SE Surg Cong, 1970; Soc Surg Chmn, 1970; Alpha Omega Alpha, 1972; Inst Med Nat Acad Sci, 1973; dir, Tyco Toys Inc, 1973; Amer Surg Asn, 1976; pres, Soc Surg Oncol, 1978-79; pres, Am Cancer Soc, 1979; Nat Urban League; Nat Asn Advan Colored People; YMCA; Alpha Phi Alpha; Sigma Pi Phi; Nat Cancer Adv Bd, 1980; Am Bd Surg, 1981; fel Am Col Gastroenterol; Cosmos Club; Comm Calif; Am Col Surg, 1983; pres, Soc Surg Chairmen, 1988-90; exec comt chmn, United Way Am, 1989-92; LaSalle D. Leffall Jr Surg Soc, 1995; bd dir, Nat Dialogue Cancer; pres, Am Col Surgs, 1995-96; chmn, Susan G. Komen Breast Cancer Found, currently; dir, Mutual Am Life Ins Co; dir, Charles A. Dana Found; dir, Warner-Lambert Co LLC; dir, Celsion Corp; adv bd, Lance Armstrong Found. **Honors/Awds:** First prize, Charles R Drew Fundamental Forum, 1954; Outstanding Young Man of the Year, 1965; Outstanding Educator in Am, Fla A&M, 1971, 1974; William H Sinkler Memorial Award, 1972; Star Surgeon Newsletter NMA, 1973; St George Medal & Citation, Amer Cancer Soc, 1977; Distinguished Volunteer Service Award, Secy U.S. Dept Health Human Serv; Named in Honor LaSalle D. Leffall, Jr Award, M.D. Anderson Hospital, Tumor Institute, Intercultural Cancer Council. **Special Achievements:** First African American president of the American Cancer Society. First African American president of the American College of Surgeons. Heauthored or co-authored over 130 articles and chapters. To honor him in Quincy, Florida and a hospital surgical wing has been given his name in 1989; First black educator at Howard University; Occupying the First Endowed Chair In the History of Howard's Department of Surgery. **Home Addr:** 2900 Ellicott St NW, Washington, DC 20008. **Business Addr:** Professor, Howard University Hospital, 520 W St NW, Washington, DC 20059, **Business Phone:** (202)806-6270.

### LEFLORE, DR. LARRY

Government official, educator, counselor. **Personal:** Born Oct 1, 1949, Cuba, AL; married Amanda L Collins. **Educ:** William Carey Col, BA, sociol, 1971; Univ Southern Miss, MS, community coun, 1974, MS, family life studies & psychol, 1980; Fla State Univ, PhD, sociol, 1984. **Career:** Columbia Training Sch, inst social worker, 1971-72; Miss Dept Youth Serv Forrest City, Youth Ct, youth ct counr, 1972-74, intake counr, 1974-76, regional supvr, 1976-77; Univ Southern Miss, from instr to assoc prof, 1977-94, prof & vpres acad affairs, 1994-97, prof & exec asst, 1997-99, adj prof, 2001-; pvt pract, marriage & family therapist, 1982-; US Dept Health & Human Serv, Ctr Substance Abuse Prev, grant reviewer, 1989-; US Dept Justice, Off Juv Justice & Delinq, grant reviewer, 1990-; Miss C Justice Act Prog, adminr, 1991-; Forrest Gen Hosps, Pine Grove, Life Focus Ctr, marriage & family therapist, 1992-; W Va Univ, Dept Family & Consumer Sci, adj prof, 1999-, Ctr 4-H & Youth, Family & Adult Develop, exten prof & ctr dir, 1999-; WVa Univ, prof & ctr dir, 1999-2003, Families & Health Progs, prof & prog dir, 2003-05; Substance Abuse Ment Health Serv Admin, 2001-; Tex Women's Univ, Dept Family Sci, prof & chair, 2005-12, Dean Grad Sch, 2012-. **Orgs:** Nat Col Juv Ct Judges; comnr, Gov Comn Stand & Goals Criminal Justice; bd dir, Spel Serv Prog, William Carey Col; Opportunity House; curric comn mem, Miss Judicial Col, 1984-; adv comn, Gov's Miss Juv Justice, 1984-; consult, Jackson County Dept Pub Welfare, 1987-; bd dir, Hattiesburg Miss Main St Proj, 1987-88; adv bd mem, Grad Sch Social Work, Univ Southern Miss, 1987-89; bd dir Gulf Pines Boy Scouts Am; founding bd mem, PineBelt Boys & Girls Club; bd mem, WVa Head Start Policy Coun; chair, Youth Coun, Workforce Investment Bd, Region Six, WVa Univ, 2001-. **Home Addr:** 3288 Univ Ave Apt 403, Morgantown, WV 26505. **Business Addr:** Dean of the Graduate School, Texas Woman's University, 304 Administration Dr, Denton, TX 76204, **Business Phone:** (940)898-2000.

### LEFLORE, LYAH BETH

Writer, television producer, administrator. **Personal:** Born Jan 1, 1970, St. Louis, MO. **Educ:** Stephens Col, BA, commun media, 1991. **Career:** Writer, Media Exec: Nickelodeon, asst vpres programming, 1991-93; Uptown Entertainment & Universal Tv, dir develop, 1993; Dick Wolf & Wolf Films, assoc producer; Alan Haymon Productions Inc, vpres prod & develop; "Midnight Mac", HBO, consult; "New York Undercover", assoc producer; "Between Brothers", Fox, develop exec; "Lawless", Fox, "Grown-Ups", "Off Limits", UPN, producer; Books: Cosmopolitan Girls, co-auth, 2004; Last Night a DJ Saved My Life, auth, 2006, I GOT YOUR BACK: A Father & Son Keep It Real About Love, Fatherhood, Family & Friendship, 2006; Haymon Develop, vice pres; novel: New York Times, Essence, Ebony, Jet, Sister 2 Sister & New York Daily News & it was featured BET, UPN-New York & Today New Yorknovel. **Orgs:** Alpha Kappa Alpha Sorority Inc; bd trustee, Stephens Col, 2005-; fel Nat Asn Black Journalists. **Business Addr:** Board Member, Stephens College, 1200 E Broadway, Columbia, MO 65215, **Business Phone:** (573)876-7133.

### LEFTWICH, BYRON ANTRON

Football player, football coach. **Personal:** Born Jan 14, 1980, Washington, DC; son of Brenda. **Educ:** Marshall Univ, WVA, bus. **Career:** Daytona Int Speedway, Pepsi 400, grand marshal, 2004; Jacksonville Jaguars, quarterback, 2003-06; Atlanta Falcons, quarterback, 2007; Pittsburgh Steelers, quarterback, 2008, 2010-12; free agt, currently; Tampa Bay Buccaneers, quarterback, 2009; Ariz Cardinals Football Club, intern coach, currently. **Honors/Awds:** MAC's Vern Smith Leadership Award; Walter Camp Nat Offensive Player of the Year Award; Super Bowl Champion (XLIII); Most Valuable Player, Motor City Bowl, 2000; Champion, Am Football Conf, 2008, 2010. **Special Achievements:** First repeat winner of conf's Offensive Player of the Year in a decade; Frequent guest on the NFL Total Access; Featured on Hey Rookie, Welcome to the NFL, 2003; Ending clip montage of the film "We Are Marshall", 2006. **Business Addr:** Intern Coach, Arizona Cardinals Football Club, PO Box 888, Phoenix, AZ 85001-0888, **Business Phone:** (813)870-2700.

### LEFTWICH, ESQ. NORMA BOGUES

Lawyer, executive. **Personal:** Born Aug 8, 1948, New York, NY; married Willie L Jr; children: Curtis. **Educ:** Univ Pittsburgh, BA, 1969; Harvard-Kennedy Sch Govt, Sr Govt Mgrs Prog, 1982; Georgetown Univ, Law Ctr, JD, 1992. **Career:** Boone Young & Assoc, sr consult, 1977; Dept Com, spec asst, 1978-79; Dept Defense, dir; Howard Univ, gen coun, 1995-. **Orgs:** Delta Sigma Theta Sorority, 1968; Dc Bar; vice chair, small bus comt am bar asn. **Honors/Awds:** Outstanding Achievement, Black Bus Asn LA, 1982, 1986; SBA Award of Excellence, 1984; Special Achievement Award, Dept Defense, 1985; The RoyWilkins Meritorious Service Award, Nat Asn Advan Colored People, 1985; Governor's Award Commonwealth of Puerto Rico, 1985. **Special Achievements:** First Woman in the 140-year history of Howard University. **Home Addr:** 1732 Shepherd St NW, Washington, DC 20011, **Home Phone:** (202)829-1797. **Business Addr:** General Counsel, Howard University, 2400 6th St NW Suite 321, Washington, DC 20059, **Business Phone:** (202)806-2650.

### LEFTWICH, DR. WILLIE L.

Lawyer, engineer, executive. **Personal:** Born Jun 28, 1937, Washington, DC; son of Willie and Maude; married Norma; children: Curtis. **Educ:** Howard Univ, BSEE, 1960; George Washington Univ, Sch Law, JD, 1967, LLD, 1972. **Career:** NASA, res aeronaut instrumentation engr; Naval Air Systs Command, res electro-optical engr; Tech Media Sys Inc, vpres & gen coun; Fed Aviation Admin, patent atty, 1968; Univ Dist Columbia, assoc prof; Ga Wash Univ Sch Law, prof & vis prof; Dept Transp FAA, patent atty; Naval Air Systs Command, adv, res engr, res electro-optical engr, 1963-68; NASA, res aero instrumentation engr; dir, Pa Ave Develop Corp; DC Redevelop Land Agency, dir; Neighborhood Legal Servs Prog, dir; Nat Inst Trial Advocacy, dir; Hudson Leftwich & Davenport, founding partner, 1970-74; Leftwich Moore & Douglas, managing partner, 1985-96; Potomac Surety Ins Co Inc, pres, chief exec officer; Willie's Pots, owner, currently. **Orgs:** DC Bar Asn; DC Redevelop Land Agency; Com Tech Adv Bd DC Judicial Nomination Comn; life mem, Nat Asn Advan Colored People; life mem, Am Bar Asn; Asn Trial Lawyers Am; dir, Pa Ave Develop Corp; dir, Neighborhood Legal Serv Prog; dir, Nat Inst Trial Advocacy. **Home Addr:** 1732 Shepherd St NW, Washington, DC 20011-5355, **Home Phone:** (202)882-0807. **Business Addr:** President, Willie's Pots, 12380 Yeawood Dr, Boston, VA 22713, **Business Phone:** (703)330-1173.

### LEGEND, JOHN (JOHN ROGER STEPHENS)

Songwriter, philanthropist, singer. **Personal:** Born Dec 28, 1978, Springfield, OH; son of Ronald Stephens and Phyllis Stephens; married Christine Teigen, Sep 14, 2013. **Educ:** University of Pennsylvania, Attended, studied English with an emphasis on African American Literature. **Career:** Singer/songwriter, albums "Get Lifted" (2004), "Once Again" (2006), "Evolver" (2008), "Love in the Future" (2013). **Orgs:** The Education Equality Project, Board Member; Harlem Village Academies, Board Member; Stand for Children, Board Member; Millennium Campus Network, Board of Advisors, 2008-; Teach for America, National Board Member, 2010-; World Economic Forum's Forum of Young Global Leaders, Appointee, 2012-; "Duets" television program judge, 2012. **Honors/Awds:** Black Entertainment Television Awards (BET Awards), Best New Artist, 2005; MOBO Awards, Best R&B Act, 2005; Soul Train Music Awards, Best R&B Solo Album, Best R&B Solo Song, 2006; Grammy Awards, Best New Artist, Best Male R&B Vocal Performance, Best R&B Album, 2006, Best Male R&B Vocal Performance, Best R&B Performance by a Duo or Group, 2007, Best R&B Performance by a Duo or Group with Vocals, 2009, Best R&B Song, Best Traditional R&B Vocal Performance, Best

R&B Album, 2011; Songwriters Hall of Fame, Starlight Award, 2007; Soul Train Music Awards, Best R&B/Soul Single Male, 2007. **Special Achievements:** Performed at Super Bowl XL in Detroit, the NBA All-Star Game, MLB All-Star Game in Pittsburgh, all in 2006.

**LEGENDRE, HENRI A.**
Executive, vice president (organization). **Personal:** Born Jul 11, 1924, New York, NY; son of Laurette M; married Ruth E Mills; children: Renee, Laurette & Jacques. **Educ:** Howard Univ, ASTP, civil engineering, 1943; City Col NY, lib arts, 1949; Pratt Inst, dipl arch, 1952. **Career:** Designs for Bus, designer, 1962; Ifill & Johnson Arch, partner, 1963-67; LeGendre Johnson McNeil Arch & Planners, pvt arch pract, 1978; LeGendre Purse Architects, PC, vpres, currently. **Orgs:** US Gen Serv Admin Adv Panel A/E Selections, 1977; Am Inst Arch; NY State Asn Arch; NY Soc Arch; Nat Orgn Minority Arch; Am Arbit Asn; 100 Black Men Inc; Bd Educ Valhalla; Alpha Phi Alpha; Promeatheans Inc; Rotary Int; St George Asn B&P Chap DAV; Order St Vincent, Euclid Lodge 70 F&AM; Arch State NY; Nat Asn Advan Colored People; Westchester Coalition; 9th & 10th Cavalry Horse Asn; Buffalo Soldiers Greater Nc Chap. **Home Addr:** 7218 Bevington Woods Lane, Charlotte, NC 28277, **Home Phone:** (704)542-6977. **Business Addr:** Vice President, LeGendre Purse Architects PC, 7218 Bevington Woods Lane, Charlotte, NC 28277, **Business Phone:** (704)542-6977.

**LEGETTE, TYRONE CHRISTOPHER**
Football player. **Personal:** Born Feb 15, 1970, Columbia, SC; son of Earl and Annie; married Reginene. **Educ:** Univ Nebr, grad. **Career:** Football player (retired); New Orleans Saints, corner back, 1992, defensive back, 1993-95; Tampa Bay Buccaneers, corner back, 1996, defensive back, 1997; San Francisco 49ers, corner back, 1998; Carolina Panthers. 1998. **Honors/Awds:** Seven-Year National Football League Veteran; Nebraska Football Hall of Fame Inductee, 2007.

**LEGGETT, DR. CHRISTOPHER J. W. B.**
Entrepreneur, cardiologist. **Personal:** Born Nov 8, 1960, Cleveland, OH; son of Willie and Ethel; married Denise Cleveland; children: Alexandria Nichol & Christopher James II. **Educ:** Princeton Univ, BA, sociol, 1982; Univ Cincinnati Sch Med, Cincinnati, OH, attended 1982; Case Western Res Sch Med, MD, 1986. **Career:** John Hopkins Hosp, intern & resident, 1986-89; Emory Univ Sch Med, Atlanta, Ga, cardiol fel, 1989; Emory Univ Sch Med Decatur, Ga, Cardiovasc Lab Veterans Admin Hosp Dept Med & Cardiol, physician, 1992-93; US Secy Dept Health & Human Serv, Nat Practicing Physician Adv Coun, cardiologist, 2002-06; Med Assoc N GA, dir cardiol, currently; St Josephs Hosp, cardiologist, currently. **Orgs:** Chmn, Case Western Res Univ Sch Med, Stud Nat Med Asn; dir cardiol, Med Assocs N Ga. **Business Addr:** Cardiologist, Medical Associates Of North Georgia, 320 Hospital Rd, Canton, GA 30114, **Business Phone:** (770)479-5535.

**LEGGETT, RENEE**
Manager, executive. **Personal:** Born Oct 7, 1949, Cleveland, OH. **Educ:** Fisk Univ, BA, 1972; Northwestern Univ, MA econs, 1973; NY Univ, MBA, 1980. **Career:** Cleveland State Univ, instr, 1973; Lincoln First Bank, mkt analyst, 1973-76; Fortune Mag, reporter, 1976-79; Mobil Corp, mkt analyst, 1979-81; NY Times, mkt analyst, 1981-82, plng mgr, 1982-83, circulation mkt mgr, 1983-86, advert mkt & prom mgr. **Orgs:** NY Univ Black Alumni Asn; Nat Black MBA Asn; Black Reps Adv NY; tutor, First World Alliance C Ctr; vol fund raiser, Boy Choir Harlem; speaker, New Alliance Pub Schs. **Honors/Awds:** Wall St Journal Student Achievement Award, 1972. **Home Addr:** 2017 N El Molino Ave, Altadena, CA 91001-3009, **Home Phone:** (213)316-3123.

**LEGGETTE, VIOLET OLEVIA BROWN**
Educator, mayor, librarian. **Personal:** Born Tallula, MS; daughter of Alfred Rufus and Theresa Gary Bowman; married Clyde Lamar Sr; children: Clyde, Melanye, Eric & Terrell. **Educ:** Natchez Jr Col, AA, 1955; Tougaloo Col, BS, elem educ, 1957; Univ Ill, MLS, 1974; educ admin, 1996. **Career:** Bob Woods Elem Sch, teacher, 1957-74; W Bolivar Dist Mid Schol, Rosedale, Miss, librn, media specialist, 1957-78, 1989-96, curric staff develop coordr, 1996-2000; Bolivar Co Sit, elem libr supr, 1974-78; Town Gunnison, mayor, 1977-97; Delta Pace Presch, dir, 1978-79; Bolivar Co Head Start, educ dir, 1979-89; Miss Dept Educ, Writing Instrnl Intervention Suppl, Creative Arts Work Group, 2002. **Orgs:** Pres, Bolivar Co Sch Dist I Teacher Asn, 1977; vpres, Miss Conf Black Mayors, 1978-88; chmn, Legis Com MCBM, 1978-88; chmn, Miss Inst Small Towns Bd, 1980-2000; Miss Asn Educrs; NEA, Alpha Kappa Alpha Sor; Nat Asn Advan Colored People; vice chairperson, MS Dem Party; chairperson, Bolivar Co Dem Comn; Nat Coun Negro Women. **Honors/Awds:** Outstanding Achievement Award Alcorn Col Chap/Negro Bus & Prof Women Club, 1978; Community Service Award, MS Valley St Univ, 1978; Leadership Award Black Genesis Found, 1979; Mother of the Year, First Baptist Church, 1988. **Home Addr:** PO Box 191, Gunnison, MS 38746.

**LEGGON, HERMAN W.**
Systems analyst, mathematician, software developer. **Personal:** Born Sep 20, 1930, Cleveland, OH; married Zara S. **Educ:** Case Western Res Univ, BS, chem, 1953; MS, chem, 1966. **Career:** Union Carbide Corp, systs analyst & mathematician; Dyke Col, part-time instr, bus math, comput sci & appl quant tech; Systs & Comput Techol Corp, supvr tech support micro comput. **Orgs:** Life mem, Alpha Phi Alpha Frat; Juv Delinq ACLD; bd chmn, Am Sickle Cell Anemia Asn; chmn, Am Soc Testing & Mat Comt E31 01; scoutmaster, Troop 370; Nat Asn Advan Colored People; Urban League; former serv dir, coun man & pres, Coun Oakwood Village; Case Alumni Asn & Found, Scholar Comt. **Home Addr:** 3470 Belvoir Blvd, Beachwood, OH 44122-3876, **Home Phone:** (216)561-3167. **Business Addr:** Member, Case Alumni Association & Foundation, 10605 Chester Ave Suite 309, Cleveland, OH 44106-2240, **Business Phone:** (216)231-4567.

**LEGRAND, ROBERT C., JR.**
Business owner, educator, basketball coach. **Personal:** Born Aug 28, 1943, Nashville, TN; son of Sarah H Joyner; married Gloria Jean Young; children: Lisa, Robert III, Christopher, Brianna & Brian. **Educ:** St Mary's Univ, San Antonio, TX, BA, polit sci & govt, 1970; Southwest Tex State Univ, MA, counr educ & sch coun & guid serv, 1974; Professional cert, guid & coun, 1974. **Career:** Jefferson High Sch, San Antonio, TX, head coach, 1970-75; Univ Tex, Arlington, from asst coach to head coach, 1975-87, Irving High Sch, Irving, TX, head coach, 1988; Sport 'n' Goods 4 U, owner, 1988-; Nichols Jr High Sch, counr; Lamar High Sch, counr, 1999-2011. **Orgs:** Chmn, Dist 6 Ed Community, Nat Asn Basketball Coaches; chmn, Dist 6membership Community, Nat Asn Basketball Coaches; bd dir, Arlington Boys Club, 1978-82; chmn, United Way Campaign, Univ Tex, Arlington, 1980; Arlington Noon Optimist Club; Tex Asn Basketball Coaches. **Home Addr:** 3112 Westwood Dr, Arlington, TX 76012, **Home Phone:** (972)261-4455. **Business Addr:** Owner, Sport N Goods 4 U, 500 Throckmorton St Suite 1504, Ft. Worth, TX 76012, **Business Phone:** (817)919-0750.

**LEGRAND, YVETTE MARIE**
Management consultant, executive. **Personal:** Born Nov 8, 1950, Chicago, IL. **Educ:** Loyola Univ Chicago, BA, hist & educ, 1971; Univ Chicago, Booth Sch Bus, MBA, 1975. **Career:** First Nat Bank, first scholar mgt trainee, 1972-75, acct mgr, 1975-77, loan officer, 1977; Int Mgt Asst United Way Met Chicago, dir, 1977-; Community Investment Corp, resource develop dir & lending prog mgr, 1985-99; Kenwood Fund, vpres, 1999-2001; Nat Housing Trust, Enterprise Preserv Corp, Chicago Regional Off, dir, 2002-05; MetLife Home Loans, 1st Reverse Financial Serv, Wells Fargo, reverse mortgage consult, 2005-11; Community Preserv Strategies, consult, currently. **Orgs:** Lois R Lowe Women's Div, United Negro Col Fund, 1972-79; Nat Black MBA Asn, Chicago Chap, 1974-77; vpres pub rel, Chicago Jaycees, 1977-78; dir, Chicago Jazz Gallery, 1978-80; vpres, Chicago Jr Asn Com & Indust Found, 1979-80; first black pres, Chicago Jaycees, 1980-81; adv comt, Mid-S Planning & Develop Comn; bd mem, Landmarks Preserv Coun Ill; chair, United Way Chicago Priority Grants Comt; First Cong Dist Housing Task Force; Urban Land Inst; Housing Task Force. **Honors/Awds:** President Award, Honor Chicago Jaycees, 1975-76; Outstanding Chaper Officer, Chicago Jaycees, 1978; Outstanding Young Woman of America, 1979. **Home Addr:** 4934 S Vincennes Ave, Chicago, IL 60615-2418, **Home Phone:** (773)624-1743. **Business Addr:** Director, First National Bank, 1620 Dodge St, Omaha, NE 68197.

**LEHMAN, DR. CHRISTOPHER PAUL**
Educator. **Personal:** Born Oct 14, 1973, Philadelphia, PA; son of Paul and Marion. **Educ:** Okla State Univ, BA, 1995; Univ Mass-Amherst, MA, hist, 1997, PhD, Afro-Am studies, 2002. **Career:** Bay Path Col, adj prof, 2000-01; Western New Eng Col, adj prof, 2000-02; Eastern CT State Univ, adj prof, 2001-02; St Cloud State Univ, prof, ethnic studies, asst prof, 2002-07, assoc prof, 2007-10, full prof 2010-; Harvard Univ, W. E. B. Du Bois Inst, Nat Endowment, Humanities Summer Inst, African & African Am Res, fel, 2011. **Orgs:** Phi Eta Sigma; Phi Kappa Phi. **Home Addr:** PO Box 2354, St Cloud, MN 56302, **Home Phone:** (320)339-6638. **Business Addr:** Full Professor, Saint Cloud State University, 51 Bldg Rm 205, St Cloud, MN 56301-4498, **Business Phone:** (320)308-5127.

**LEHMAN, DR. PAUL ROBERT**
Educator. **Personal:** Born Apr 18, 1941, Mansura, LA; son of Frances Revare and Kermit; married Marion W White; children: Christopher Paul, Karlyn Elizabeth (deceased) & Jeffrey Robert. **Educ:** La City Col, AA, commun & Eng, 1966; Cent State Col, BA, commun & Eng, 1969; Cent State Univ, ME, African-Am & black studies, 1971; Lehigh Univ, PhD, 1976. **Career:** Western Elec Co, tester insptct, 1963-66; Stand Oil Calif, credit dept, 1966-67; KOFM radio, music newsman, 1968-69; KWTV, newsman, reporter, writer, ed, photogr, producer & weekend anchorman, 1968-70; CSU, lectr, 1969-71, instr, 1971-73; NCACC, adj prof, 1974-76; Blk Am Lit, vol lectr col pub pvt sch churches, Radio/TV News, 1974-75; Northampton Co Area Community Col, develop co-ordinated col orientation workshop minority stud, 1975; Univ Cent Okla, dean; Cent State Univ, from assoc prof dept eng to prof dept Eng, 1977-88, dean grad col, 1985-88; Univ Cent Okla, dean studies, Dept Eng, prof, 1988, prof emer, currently; Edmond Arts & Humanities, 1991-. **Orgs:** Vice chmn, Okla Found Humanities, 1988-89; treas, Okla Alliance Arts Educ, 1988-; Nat Jaycees; Nat Asn Advan Colored People; Urban League; Heart Asn Nat Asn Press Photogr; stud exec officer, LACC, 1966; NEA, OEA, CSEA, NCTE, CEA; bd trustee, Okla Folk Life Coun; Edmond Community Housing Resource Bd; Afro-Am Southern Asn; bd trustee, Edmond Arts & Humanities Coun; bd trustee, Okla Arthritis Found; bd trustee, Okla Folk life Coun; bd trustee, Okla Connections; bd trustee, Okla Found Humanities; bd trustee, Let's Talk About It Okla; Okla State Regents Higher Educ Coun. **Honors/Awds:** Best actor in minor role, CSC, 1968; deans honor roll, CSC, 1968; listed in Contemporary Authors, 1977-78; Lehigh Univ Fel, 1973-76; first dissertation John Oliver Killens, 1976; Award for Service to Urban League Greater Okla City, 1984; Award for Service to Boy Scouts of Am, 1985; Fulbright Senior Specialist, 2004; Hall of Fame, Univ Cent Okla, 2006; Lifetime Achievement Service Award, Urban League Greater Okla City, Boy Scouts Am. **Special Achievements:** First black American to teach at CSU, 1969; first black in Oklahoma to anchor weekend TV news, 1969; first black American to receive PhD in English from Lehigh, 1976; Author: The Making of the Negro in Early American Lit, 2003, The Development of A Black Psych in the Works of John Oliver Killens, 2003; America's Race Problem: A Practical Guide to Understanding Race in America; book reviewer, The Oklahoman, The Making of the Negro in Early American Lit, second edition, 2006. **Home Addr:** 1313 Briarwood Dr, Edmond, OK 73034, **Home Phone:** (405)341-8773. **Business Addr:** Professor Emeritus, University of Central Oklahoma, 100 Univ Dr, Edmond, OK 73034, **Business Phone:** (405)974-5608.

**LEIGH, MAJOR GEN. FREDRIC H.**
Military leader, association executive. **Personal:** Born Mar 29, 1940, Columbus, OH; son of William F Sr and Cathrine A; married Karyn; children: Tracey, William & Jade Moore. **Educ:** Cent State Univ, BA, hist & polit sci, 1963; Syracuse Univ, MS, commun, jour, & related progs, 1972; USY, Command & Staff Col, MMS, 1973; Nat War Col, grad, mil strategic studies, gen, 1983; Univ Chicago, Exec Develop Prog, cert, 1986; Ctr Creative Leadership, Eckerd Col, FL, cert, 1990; Harvard Univ, JFK Sch Govern Sr Exec governprog, cert, 1993. **Career:** Off secy USY, sr mil asst, 1982-83; Off Chief Staff, USY, dep dir army staff, 1983-85; 19th Support Command, 8th USY, Korea, chief staff, 1985-87; 1st Brigade, 101st Airborne Div (Air Assault), Ft Campbell, KY, comdr, 1987-89; Army War Col, Sr Leadership Res, dir, 1989-90; 7th Inf Div (Light), Ft Ord, Calif, asst div commr(support), 1990-91; Nat Mil Command Ctr, dep dir, 1991-93; Chief Staff, Army Off, dir mgt, 1993; Joint Ctr Polit & Econ Studies, exec vpres, 1994-98; Intl Trust Co, exec vpres & gen mgr, Monrovia, Liberia; Karyn Trader & Assoc Global Partners, prin, exec vpres & chief operating officer, 2000-. **Orgs:** Past pres, Rocks Inc; New Initiatives Comt Historically Black ColROTC Assistance, chr; Korean-Am Friendship Asn, bd mem, 1985-87; Big Bros Inc, Clarksville, TN, 1977-78; Boy Scouts, Syracuse, NY, leader, 1971-72; exec dir, Taia Peace Found, 2007-; Modeling & Simulation Adv Coun, 2008-. **Honors/Awds:** Central State Univ, Hall of Achievement, 1991; Korean-Am Friendship Society, Outstanding Friendship Award, 1987; Taegu Korea Labor Union, Labor Development Award, 1987; Command & Staff Col, Commandant's List Graduate, 1973; Northern New York Public Relations Society of Am, Outstanding Graduate in Public Relations, 1972; New house School of Communications, Syracuse Univ, Faculty Award to Most Outstanding Graduate Student, 1972. **Home Addr:** 7768 Glade Ct, Manassas, VA 20112, **Home Phone:** (703)489-1111. **Business Addr:** Executive Vice President & Principal, Chief Operating Officer, Karyn Trader & Associates Global Partners LLC, 7768 Glade Ct, Manassas, VA 20112, **Business Phone:** (703)794-8682.

**LEIGH, WILLIAM A.**
Contractor, entrepreneur. **Personal:** Born Sep 12, 1929, Douglasville, GA; son of William and Beatrice; children: William, Cornell & Bernard. **Educ:** Miami Jacobs Bus Col; Sinclair Community Col. **Career:** Fleetline Cab Co, owner, 1950-61; Main Auto Parts & Glass Co, sales rep, 1960-68; Madden Inc, founder & pres, 1968-. **Orgs:** Bd mem, Newfields Comn Authority; treas, bd mem, Am Bus Coun; chmn, Black Contractors & Bus Asn; adv bd, Dayton Housing; bd mem, Miami Valley Coun Boy Scouts; United Fund Agency; Miami Valley Child Develop; vpres, Dayton Fund Home Rehab; bd mem, Southern Christian Leadership Conf; pres, Ohio Real Estate Investors Asn; bd mem, Montgomery Co Child Develop Corp; bd mem, Unity State Bank; pres, Greater Dayton Real Estate Investor Asn; facilitator, Barbara Jordan Comt Race Unity; Dayton City Sch Adv Bd; Frontiers Club Am; Dayton Fund; YMCA League; Home Builders Asn; Dayton Urban League; Black Enterprise Top 100 Nat Black Businesses. **Home Addr:** 1421 Albritton Dr, Dayton, OH 45408. **Business Addr:** Founder, President, Madden Inc, 2305 Heartsoul Dr, Dayton, OH 45408, **Business Phone:** (937)268-1314.

**LEIGHTON, HON. GEORGE NEVES**
Judge, lawyer. **Personal:** Born Oct 22, 1912, New Bedford, MA; son of Antonio Neves Leitao and Annay Sylvia Garcia; married Virginia Berry Quivers; children: Virginia Anne & Barbara Elaine. **Educ:** Howard Univ, AB, 1940, Sch Law, LLB, 1946; Loyola Univ, LLD. **Career:** Judge (retired); pvt pract, 1946-64; Ill State, asst state atty gen, 1949-51; Moore, Ming & Leighton, Chicago, Ill, partner, 1951-59; McCoy, Ming & Leighton, Chicago, Ill, partner, 1959-64; Circuit Ct Cook County, master chancery, 1960-64, judge, 1964-69, First Dist Appellate Ct, judge, 1969-76; US Dist Ct, Northern Dist Ill, judge, dist judge, 1976-89, sr dist judge, 1986-87; Earl L Neal & Assocs, coun; Rand Corp, overseer. **Orgs:** Mass Bar Asn, 1946; Ill Bar Asn, 1947; pres, Howard Univ Alumni Asn, 1947-48; chmn, Legal Redress Comt, Nat Asn Advan Colored People, Chicago Chap, 1947-53; pres, 1952-53; Chicago Bar Asn; US Supreme Ct Bar, 1958; Am Bar Asn; comnr, 1955-63; chmn, 1959-63, Character & Fitness Comt, First Appellate Dist Supreme Ct Ill; Joint Comt Rev Ill Criminal Code, 1964; life mem, Nat Asn Advan Colored People, 1964; bd dir, United Church Bd Homeland Ministries; United Church Christ; Grant Hosp; fel Am Bar Found; Howard Univ Chicago Alumni Club; coun, Nat Harvard Law Sch Asn; Phi Beta Kappa; trustee, 1979-83; trustee emer, Univ Notre Dame, 1983; bd overseers, Harvard Col, 1983-89; Fel Am Col Trial Lawyers, 1994. **Home Addr:** 8400 S Prairie Ave, Chicago, IL 60619.

**LELAIND, DETRA LYNETTE**
Chief executive officer. **Personal:** Born Jul 26, 1967, San Francisco, CA; daughter of Richard and Dorthy Matthews; children: Ayron Joseph & Laron Walker. **Educ:** Laney Col, AA, bus admin, 1988; San Francisco State Univ, BA, bus admin, 1990. **Career:** Detra Fashion Mag, owner, 1990; Century 21 Realty, real estate agt; AF Evans Property Mgt, property mgr, 1992-95; Acorn Housing Corp; Contra Costa County Housing Authority, property mgr; Insignia Financial Corp, property mgr, 1995-97; Brick Housing Mgt Inc, chief exec officer, 1997-; J Br Developments, Oakland, Calif, proj mgr, 2002-; Clayton-Bisch Developments, founder, 2004-; World Financial Group, Transamerica Co, 2014. **Orgs:** Nat Ctr Housing Mgt, 1997; Womens Initiative Self Employ, 1998; Nat Apt Asn, 1999; Asn Housing Mgt Agents, 2001; incorporator, A Lelaind Community; mgr, Community Harbor Bay Isle Owners Asn. **Home Addr:** 21 Shetland Ct, Oakland, CA 94605, **Home Phone:** (510)638-7555. **Business Addr:** Principal, Clayton Bisch Development, 1321 Evans Ave, San Francisco, CA 94124, **Business Phone:** (510)276-1452.

**LELAND, JOYCE F.**
Government official, consultant, police chief. **Personal:** Born Sep 8, 1941, Washington, DC; married John Watkins. **Educ:** Howard Univ, BA, sociol, 1965; Univ DC, Union Inst, PhD, clin psychol, 1998. **Career:** Police officer (retired): Metrop Police Dept, Wash, DC lt & inspector, 1965-78, 7th Police Dist, comdr, capt, 1978-83, eeo inspr, 1983-85, dep chief, 1985-96. **Orgs:** Bd dir, MPDC Boys & Girls Club, Police Mgt Asn; consult, Police Found, Ctr Youth Serv. **Honors/Awds:** Crime Reduction Awards; Numerous awards from citizens, law enforcement agencies, churches, business establishments. **Special Achievements:** First female deputy chief of the District of Columbia's metropolitan police force; First Black women in US history to reach such a height in law enforcement work. First female patrol officers

in the United States. **Home Addr:** 2326 Br Ave SE, Washington, DC 20020-1461.

## LEMELLE, IVAN

Judge. **Personal:** Born Jun 29, 1950, Opelousas, LA; son of Clifford J and Cecilia Comeaux; married Patricia Waddell; children: Christopher, Marc & Tricia. **Educ:** Xavier Univ La, BS, 1971; Loyola Univ Sch Law, JD, 1974. **Career:** Orleans Parish Criminal Dist Ct, law clerk, 1972-74; New Orleans Legal Assistance Corp, law clerk, 1972; Judge Robert Collins, law clerk, 1973-74; Dist Atty Off, asst dist atty, 1974-77; pvt pract, 1977-81; City Atty Off, asst city atty, 1977-78; Douglas, Nabonne & Wilkerson, law partner, 1977-84; La Dept Justice, asst state atty gen, 1980-84; US Dist Ct, Eastern Dist La, US magistrate judge, 1984-98, Sect B, dist judge, 1998-. **Orgs:** Co chmn, Fed Bar Asn, 1992-; pres comm bench & bar rels, La Bar Asn, 1994-, comm community involvement, 1995-; pres, vis commitee, Loyola Univ Sch Law, 1994-; Tulane Univ Med Sch, chancellor's comm, 1988-; pres advsior comm, Martinet Legal Soc, 1978-; adv bd mem, DeLille Inn Sr Citizen Ctr, 1986-98; Fed Judge's Asn; treas, Amistad Res Ctr, 1990-95. **Honors/Awds:** Legal Defense Fund Scholar, Nat Asn Advan Colored People, 1971-74; William H Mitchell Award, Xavier Univ, 1971; AP Tureaud Award, 1991; Ernest Dutch Morial Judicial Pacesetters' Award, 1998; Service Award, Fed Bar Asn, 1995. **Special Achievements:** First African American appointed US Magistrate Judge in LA. **Business Addr:** District Judge, US District Court-, 500 Camp St, New Orleans, LA 70130, **Business Phone:** (504)589-7555.

## LEMELLE, TILDEN J.

School administrator. **Personal:** Born Feb 6, 1929, New Iberia, LA; son of Eloi Sabas and Therese Marie; married Margaret Guillion; children: Joyce Marie, Stephanie Marie & Therese Marie. **Educ:** Xavier Univ, New Orleans, BA, 1953, MA, 1958; Univ Colo, Denver, PhD, 1965. **Career:** Grambling Col, La, asst prof, 1957-63; Fordham Univ, NY, assoc prof, 1966-69; Ctr Int Race Rel Univ, Denver, prof, dir, 1969-71; Hunter Col, NY, prof & actg dean, from asst provost to provost, vpres, vicechancellor, Dept Black & Puerto Rican Studies, prof & chmn, Dept Acad Skills & SEEK Prog, chmn & dir; New York Tech Col, actg pres, 1988-90; Univ DC, pres, 1991-96; City Univ New York, comnmr, actg vice chancellor, currently. **Orgs:** John Hay Whitney Fel NY, 1963-65; trustee, Africa Today Asn Inc, 1967-; ed & pub, Africa Today, 1967-; bd office pres, Am Community Africa, 1973-; trustee, New Rochelle Bd Educ, 1976-; Coun Foreign Rel, 1978-; trustee, Social Sci Found, 1979-; trustee, Africa Found, 1979-; trustee, Int Leaguer Human Rights, 1980-; trustee, Nurses Educ Fund, 1984-; Coun Int Exchange Scholars, Fulbright, 1991-; bd trustee, City Univ NY, 1997-; Coun Foreign Rels; reviewer & consult, Nat Sci Found; African Heritage Studies Asn. **Honors/Awds:** The Black Col Praeger, NY, 1969; Hon Consul-Senegal, Denver, Colo, 1969-71; Race Among Nations Heath-Lexington, 1971; New York Urban League Building-Brick Award, 1991. **Home Addr:** 3520 Rittenhouse St NW, Washington, DC 20015-2412. **Business Addr:** Commissioner, City University New York, 365 5th Ave, New York, NY 10016-4309, **Business Phone:** (212)817-7000.

## LEMMIE, VALERIE

Government official, commissioner. **Personal:** married Olan Strozier. **Educ:** Univ Mo, BS, BA, polit sci & urban sociol; Wash Univ, MA, urban affairs & pub policy planning. **Career:** Howard Univ, adj prof; Univ of Dayton, adj prof; Mgr, City of Dayton (OH), 1996; Cincinnati city, city mgr; Pub Utilities Comn Ohio, comnr, 2006-; Kettering Found, scholar in residence, dir, 2014-. **Orgs:** Cincinnati Zoo; Cincinnati Fine Arts Coun; Nat Civic League Coun Adv; bd dir, Nat Regulatory Res Inst; Financial Res Inst Adv Bd Univ Mo; pres, Nat Acad Pub Admin; fel Ctr Excellence Munic Mgt George Wash Univ; Dayton Hist, Initiatives Chg; fel Nat Acad Pub Admin; House Speaker Dennis Hastert's Comt, Urban Redevelop; Pres, Clinton's Greenhouse Gas Adv Comt. **Business Addr:** Director, Kettering Foundation, 200 Commons Rd, Dayton, OH 45459, **Business Phone:** (937)434-7300.

## LEMMONS, HERBERT MICHAEL

Clergy, executive director. **Personal:** Born Sep 25, 1952, Little Rock, AR; son of Herbert G and Deliah A Herron; married Karenga Rashida Hill; children: H Michael II & Malcolm R. **Educ:** Univ Detroit, Mich, BA, sociol, 1973; Interdenominational Theol Ctr, Atlanta, Ga, MDiv, 1976; Howard Univ Sch Law, JD, Law, 1979. **Career:** Seaton Mem AME Church, Lanham, Md, pastor, 1977-84; US Small Bus Admin, Wash, DC, atty adv, 1979-81; Univ Md, Col Pk, chaplain, 1982-84; Cong Nat Black Churches, Wash, DC, dep dir, 1984-85, exec dir, currently; Mt Moriah AME Church, Annapolis, Md, pastor, 1984-89; Hist Ebenezer AME Church, pastor, 1997-08; AME Church, presiding elder, 2008-. **Orgs:** Human Relations Comn, Annapolis, Md, 1986-88; Mayors Task Force on Substance Abuse, 1987-89; bd comnr, Annapolis Housing Authority, 1988-. **Honors/Awds:** Walder G Muelder Student Lectureship in Social Ethics, Interdenominational Theol Ctr, 1976; Clergy Award, Annual Kunte Kinte Celebration, 1990. **Home Addr:** 17491 Mt Vernon St, Southfield, MI 48075-3446, **Home Phone:** (248)557-2788. **Business Addr:** Presiding Elder, AME Church, Detroit, MI 48207.

## LEMMONS, KASI (KAREN LEMMONS)

Movie director, writer, actor. **Personal:** Born Feb 24, 1961, St. Louis, MO; married Vondie Curtis Hall; children: Hunter & Zora. **Educ:** NY Univ; Univ Calif Los Angeles, New Sch Social Res. **Career:** Director, writer, actor; Films: School Daze, 1988; Vampire's Kiss, 1989; The Five Heartbeats, 1991; The Silence of the Lambs, 1991; Candyman, 1992; Hard Target, 1993; Fear of a Black Hat, 1994; Drop Squad, 1994; Gridlock'd, 1997; Til There Was You, 1997; Eve's Bayou, dir & writer, 1997; Dr. Hugo, dir & writer, 1998; Liars' Dice, 1998; The Caveman's Valentine, dir, 2001; Waist Deep, 2006; Talk to Me, dir, 2007; Disconnect, 2012; Black Nativity, dir & screenplay, 2013. TV series: "11th Victim", 1979; "A Man Called Hawk", 1989; "The Court-Martial of Jackie Robinson", 1990; "The Big One; The Great Los Angeles Earthquake", 1990; "Under Cover", 1991; "After burn", 1992; "Override", 1994; "Zooman", 1995; "Er", 2002. **Honors/Awds:** Best Debut Director Award, Nat Bd Rev, 1997; Independent Spirit Award, Best First Feature, 1998; Director's Achievement Award, Palm Springs Int Film Festival, 1998; Black Film Award, 1998; AAFCA Award, African-Am Film Critics Asn, 2007; Image Award, Nat Asn Advan Colored People, 2008; Black Reel Award, 2014. **Business Addr:** Director, Trimark Pictures, 2644 30th St, Santa Monica, CA 90405-3009, **Business Phone:** (310)314-2000.

## LEMON, ANN

Executive. **Educ:** Smith Col, BA, lib arts, 1972; NY Univ, MS, food mgt, 1975; Columbia Univ, Columbia Bus Sch, MBA, finance, money & financial mkts, 1984; City Univ NY, Baruch Col, real estate, 2008; Levin Grad Inst Int Rels & Com, green finance & carbon trading, 2010. **Career:** NYU Med Ctr, clin nutritionist, 1975-80; HJ Heinz, nutritionist new prod develop & res, 1980-82; Superius Securities, asst portfolio mgr, 1983-85; PaineWebber Inc, vpres investments, 1994-2000; Ann Lemon Group, chief exec officer, 2005-; Levin Inst, Neil D. Levin Grad Inst Int Rels & Com, mgt consult, 2010; DUCE Construct, dir sustainability, 2010; Columbia Univ, vpres venues & menus, alumni sustainability cert prog, 2010-11, Columbia Bus Sch Alumni Asn New York, vpres corp & community relationships, sustainable bus comt, 2011-. **Orgs:** Nat Black MBA Asn; Financial Women's Asn; treas, Smith Col Alumnae Asn; Nat Structured Settlement Trade Asn; Smith Col Club; Columbia Bus Sch Alumni Asn; Smith Col Club New York Events Comt. **Business Addr:** Vice President, Columbia University, 116th St & Broadway, New York, NY 10027, **Business Phone:** (212)854-1754.

## LEMON, DON

Television journalist. **Personal:** Born Mar 1, 1966, Baton Rouge, LA. **Educ:** Brooklyn College, Bachelor's in Broadcast Journalism; Louisiana State University, Attended. **Career:** WNYW (New York City), News Asst.; WCAU (Philadelphia), Weekend Anchor; KTVI (St. Louis), Anchor and Investigative Reporter; WBRC (Birmingham, AL), Anchor; NBC News, New York City Operations, Reporter; "Today" Show, Correspondent; "NBC Nightly News," Correspondent; Weekend "Today" Show, Anchor; MSNBC, Anchor; NBC5 News, WMAQ-TV, Reporter and Co-Anchor, 2003-06; CNN, Reporter and Anchor, 2006-; "CNN Newsroom," Weekend Host; Brooklyn College, Adjunct Professor. **Honors/Awds:** Edward R. Murrow Award, For Coverage of Capture of the Washington D.C. sniper; Emmy Award, News & Documentary for Outstanding Live Coverage of a Current News Story--Long Form, for Special Report on Chicagoland Real Estate; "Ebony" Magazine, 150 Most Influential African Americans, 2009. **Special Achievements:** Wrote memoir "Transparent" in 2011.

## LEMON, MEADOWLARK, III

Athlete, preacher, basketball player. **Personal:** Born Apr 25, 1932, Wilmington, NC; son of Meadow Jr; married Cynthia; children: Richard, George, Beverly, Donna, Robin, Jonathan, Jamison, Angela, Crystal & Caleb. **Educ:** Fla A&M Univ; Vision Int Univ, DDiv, 1988. **Career:** Basketball player (retired), speaker, preacher; Harlem Globetrotters, 1954-79, 1994; Bucketeers, basketball group, 1980-83; Shooting Stars, 1984-87; Sweepstakes; ordained minister, 1986-2005; Meadowlark Lemon's Harlem All Stars, owner, 1988-; Meadowlark Lemon Ministries, founder, 1994-; Smoky Mountain Jam, partial owner, 2009-; Smoky Mountain Jam, Am Basketball Asn, partial owner, 2009-; preacher, currently; Meadowlark Lemon Line Acad, founder, currently. Films: Crash Island; The Fish That Saved Pittsburgh, 1979; Meadowlark Lemon Presents the World, 1979; Modern Romance, 1981. TV Series: "Harlem Globe Trotters", voice, 1970; "Hello Larry", 1979. **Orgs:** Founder, Meadowlark Lemon Found. **Special Achievements:** Meadowlark was voted as one of Americas most recognizable faces following Alan Alda, John Wayne and Bob Hope. **Business Addr:** Founder, Meadowlark Lemon Foundation, Meadowlark Lemon Ministries, 6501 E Greenway Pkwy Suite 103, Scottsdale, AZ 85254-2066, **Business Phone:** (480)951-0030.

## LEMON, MICHAEL WAYNE, SR.

Police officer. **Personal:** Born Nov 2, 1953, Detroit, MI; son of Primus and Mary Strong; married Valerie Mennifee; children: Michael Wayne Jr & Ashlee Michelle. **Educ:** Wayne County Community Col, attended 1988; Wayne State Univ. **Career:** Police officer (retired); Mich Bell Tel, consult, 1987-; Detroit Police Dept, Narcotics Div, police officer, 2001, sergent. **Orgs:** Bd mem, Community Vol, 1986-; Task Force Drug Abuse, Detroit Strategic Plan, 1987-91. **Honors/Awds:** Appreciation Award, Mich Bell Tel, 1986; Community Serv Award, Detroit Chamber Com, 1988; Man of the Year Award, Minority Women Network, 1988; Spirit of Detroit, Detroit Common Coun, 1989, Heart of Gold Award, United Found, 1989. **Home Addr:** 15745 Auburn, Detroit, MI 48223, **Home Phone:** (313)592-4059.

## LEMUWA, IKE EMMANUEL

Executive. **Personal:** Born Oct 1, 1961, Mband; son of Ononiwu and Cyrina Adim; married Chioma N. **Educ:** Univ DC, BA, develop econs & int develop, 1992. **Career:** Dickinson & Co, stockbroker, 1995-96; RAF Financial Corp, investment exec; Nat Hubzone Incubator Mgmt, owner, currently; Wash Premier Financial Serv inc, pres, chief exec officer, 2000-08; Ike Lemuwa Group LLC, pres, chief exec officer, 2009-12, 198TILG chief exec officer Branding Marketplace, Alexandria, VA, proj developer, 2013-; TIL Co LLC, chief exec officer, pres, 2004-, speaker, coach, auth, angel investor, 2011-. **Orgs:** Pres, Int Asn Friends Africa Inc, IAFA, founder; founder, Am Partnership Rural Re-Investment Corp. **Business Addr:** Founder, American Partnership for Rural Re-Investment Corp, 1090 Vt Ave NW Suite 800, Washington, DC 20005.

## LENARD, VOSHON KELAN

Basketball player. **Personal:** Born May 14, 1973, Detroit, MI; children: Tayler, Tyler & Tae Shon. **Educ:** Univ Minn, pre-speech commun, 1995. **Career:** Basketball player (retired); Okla City Calvalry, Continental Basketball Asn, 1995-96; Miami Heat, shooting guard, 1995-2000; Denver Nuggets, shooting guard, 2000-02, 2003-06; Toronto Raptors, shooting guard, 2002-03; Portland Trail Blazers, shooting guard, 2006. **Orgs:** Continental Basketball Asn. **Honors/Awds:** NBA Three Point Shootout champion, 2004.

## LENIX-HOOKER, CATHERINE JEANETTE

Executive director, administrator. **Personal:** Born May 10, 1947, Camden, SC; daughter of Frank and Annie Lenix; children: Frank R Jr. **Educ:** Howard Univ, BA, 1968; Univ MLS, MD, 1970; Victorian Soc Am Summer Sch, attended 1999. **Career:** Wash, DC Pub Libr, chief, black studies div, 1970-77; Corp Pub Broadcasting, consult, 1975, 1986; Anaheim Calif Pub Libr, dir pub servs, 1977-81; Schomburg Ctr Res Black Cult, asst chief, 1981-90, dep dir, 1984-90; Krueger-Scott Mansion Cult Ctr, actg exec dir, dir, Mkt & Develop, Newark Performing Arts Corp, 2000-; Newark Symphony Hall, actg mgr, 2000-; dir mkt & develop. **Orgs:** Am Libr Asn, 1970-; Black Caucus, 1970-; Crippled C's Soc, freelance writer, 1979-81; chairperson, S Calif Chap Howard Univ Alumni Scholar, 1980-81; chmn, Harlem Hosp Ctr Comm Adv Bd, 1981-90; bd dir, N Gen Home Attend Corp, 1982-84; Nat Asn Advan Colored People; Newark Jazz Festival, 1991-97; Victorian Soc Northern NJ; vol, Habitat Humanity, Newark, NJ Chap; Harlem Tourism Asn; trustee, Newark Prev & Landmark Comt, 2009-. **Home Addr:** 54A James St, Newark, NJ 07102-2005, **Home Phone:** (973)623-4031. **Business Addr:** Acting Manager, Assistant Manager, Newark Symphony Hall, 1020 Broad St, Newark, NJ 07102, **Business Phone:** (973)643-8468.

## LENNON, PATRICK ORLANDO (PAT LENNON)

Baseball player. **Personal:** Born Apr 27, 1968, Whiteville, NC. **Career:** Baseball player (retired); baseball coach; Seattle Mariners, outfielder, 1991-92; Kans City Royals, outfielder, 1996; Oakland Athletics, outfielder, 1997; Toronto Blue Jays, outfielder, 1998-99; Long Island Ducks, 2002-05; Matt Guiliano's Play Like A Pro, coach, 2004-. **Business Addr:** Baseball Coach, Matt Guiliano's Play Like A Pro, 1745 Express Dr, North Hauppauge, NY 11788, **Business Phone:** (631)342-9033.

## LENNOX, BETTY BERNICE

Basketball player. **Personal:** Born Dec 4, 1976, Oklahoma City, OK; daughter of Bernice and Bernice Jefferies. **Educ:** Trinity Valley Community Col, KS; La Tech Univ, BA, psychol, 2000. **Career:** Minn Lynx, guard, 2000-02; Elitzur Cellcom Holon, Israel, 2000-01; Miami Sol, guard, 2002; Cleveland Rockers, guard, 2003; Seattle Storm, guard, 2004-07; Coconuda Maddaloni, Italy, 2004-05; Lotos Gdynia, Poland, 2006-07; K. V. Imp EKA AEL Limassol, Greece, 2007-08; Atlanta Dream, 2008; Los Angeles Sparks, guard, 2009-10; Tulsa Shock, 2011. **Orgs:** Founder, The Lennox Foundation 22, 2005. **Honors/Awds:** Conference Player of the Year, Sun Belt, 2000; Rookie of the Year, WNBA, 2000; Most Valuable Player, WNBA, 2004; WNBA Champion, 2004; WNBA's Community Assist Award, 2006. **Business Addr:** Professional Basketball Player, Los Angeles Sparks, 888 S Figueroa St Suite 2010, Los Angeles, CA 90017, **Business Phone:** (213)929-1300.

**LENOIR, JUAN KIP.** See LENOIR, ESQ. KIP.

## LENOIR, ESQ. KIP (JUAN KIP LENOIR)

Lawyer. **Personal:** Born Apr 27, 1943, Knoxville, TN; son of Henry and Teri Adkins; married Richelle Guilmenot. **Educ:** Howard Univ, Wash, BS, 1966, JD, 1969; NY Univ, Grad Sch Law, BA, criminal justice. **Career:** Legal Aid Soc Crim, 1971-73; Mayor's Off, NY, supv atty, 1973-75; NY State Atty Gen Off, asst atty gen in charge, 1974-76; Lenoir & Bogan, PC, partner, 1977-85; Malcolm King Col, law instr, 1980; Bronx Community Col, City Univ NY, adj prof crim law, 1987-88; Kip Lenoir Prof Corp, owner, 1976-2012, pres, 1985, atty & owner, currently. **Orgs:** Mayor's Graffiti Comt, NY, 1974-75; NY St Bar Asn, 1975-; NY Co Lawyers Asn, 1975-; Coun Harlem Interfaith Coun Serv Inc, 1980-; bd mem, Metrop Black Bar Asn, 1987-88. **Honors/Awds:** Outstanding Achievement, Harlem Interfaith Coun Serv Inc, 1984. **Home Addr:** 19 W 122nd St, New York, NY 10027. **Business Addr:** Owner, Attorney, Kip Lenoir PC, 100 W 92nd St, New York, NY 10025-7502, **Business Phone:** (212)333-2225.

## LENOIR, DR. MICHAEL A.

Pediatrician. **Personal:** Born Feb 22, 1942; married Denise Washington; children: 4. **Educ:** Univ TX, Austin, BA, sci, 1965; Univ TX, Galveston, MD, 1967; Am Bd Allergy & Immunol, cert, 1973. **Career:** Los Angeles County Hosp, Calif, rotating intern, 1968; William Beaumont Army Hosp, El Paso, Tex, residency pediat, 1970; Letterman Army Hosp San Francisco, chief pediat serv, 1972-75; KCBS Radio, med ed, 1981-93; KPFA Pacifica Radio, med ed, 1996-; Ethnic Health Am, chief exec officer, 1985-; Univ Calif, assoc clin prof pediat, currently; Bay Area Multicultural Clin Res & Prev Ctr, dir & chief operating officer; Ethnic Health Inst, Summit Med Ctr, pres; Comprehensive Allergy Servs, med dir; San Francisco General Hospital, dir allergy serv; Bay Area Pediats, med dir, currently; Alta Bates Med Group, allergist & pediatrician, currently; Dr Michael A LeNoir, owner, currently. **Orgs:** Am Bd Pediats, 1972; chair, Allergy & Asthma initiative; Nat Med Asn; fel Am Acad Pediat; fel Am Acad Allergy & Immunol; fel Am Acad Cert Allergist & Immunol; lifelong mem, fel Am Col Allergy; chair, Allergy & Asthma Sect, Nat Med Asn, 1998-2000; past pres, Nat Asn Physician Broadcasters; pres, Clin Fac Asn, Univ Calif; pres, Northern Calif Allergy Asn; pres, Region VI, Nat Med Asn; pres, Sinkler Miller Med Asn; bd, E Bay Regional Ctr; chmn bd, Bay Area Black United Fund; Bd Calif Spec Olympics; bd, Int Visitors Ctr; chmn bd, Bd Bay Area Black United Fund; Bd Int Visitors Ctr; lifetime mem, Nat Asn Advan Colored People; lifetime mem, Alpha Phi Alpha Fraternity; Sigma Pi Phi Fraternity. **Honors/Awds:** Citizen of the Year, Oakland, 1988; Burbridge Award Community Service, Univ Calif; Positive Profiles Award, Am Med Asn; Lyda Smiley Award, Calif Sch Nurses Asn; John B. Jackson Community Service Award, Ethnic Health Inst Alta Bates Summit Med Ctr; East Bay's Top Doctors, Oakland Magazine, 2007; Floyd Malveaux Award; Ken Alvord Distinguished Community Service Award; Pfizer Positive Physician Award, AMA. **Special Achievements:** Over 50 Publ and Presentations on Asthma & Allergy; distinguished honor, one of the 50 most positive physicians in Am; one of the Nations Top 100Black Physicians, 2001, ed of Black Enterprise mag. **Business Addr:** Allergist, Pediatrician, Alta Bates Medical Group, 401 29th St Suite 201, Oakland, CA 94609, **Business Phone:** (510)834-4897.

**LEON, JEAN G.**
Executive, nurse. **Personal:** Born Trinidad; daughter of Vida Barrington. **Educ:** San Fernando Gen Hosp, Sch Nursing, dipl; Sch Midwifery, dipl; St Joseph's Col, BS, health admin, MPA; NY Univ, MA, pub admin. **Career:** Executive (retired); San Fernando Gen Hosp, staff nurse, 1968-71; Cumberland Hosp, staff nurse, 1971-73; Brooklyn Jewish Hosp, staff nurse, 1973-80; Interfaith Med Ctr, Q A coordr, 1980-85; Harlem Hosp ctr, nurse, 1984, sr assoc exec dir, dep exec dir, qual mgt, chief operating officer, 1992-94; Woodhull Med Ctr, from asst dir to assoc dir, nursing, 1985-89; Metrop Med Ctr, assoc exec dir, dir, qual mgt, 1989-92; Kings County Hosp Ctr, interim exec dir, exec dir, 2009. **Orgs:** Nat Asn Health Care Qual, 1981-; bd mem, NY Asn, 1984-94; pres, Caribbean Am Nurses Asn, 1990-94; Am Col Healthcare Exec, 1993-; New York Health & Hosps Corp, bd mem; sr vpres, Cent Brooklyn Family Health Network.

**LEON, DR. TANIA JUSTINA**
Composer, conductor (music), educator. **Personal:** Born May 14, 1943, Havana; daughter of Oscar de and Dora Ferran; married Francisco Javier Perez. **Educ:** Carlos Alfredo Peyrellade Conserv, BA, attended 1963; Nat Conserv, La Habana, CU, MA, music educ, 1964; NY Univ, BS, music educ, 1971; NY Univ, MA, compos, 1973. **Career:** Dance Theatre Harlem, co founder & music dir, 1970-79; conductor, 1971-; Brooklyn Col, prof, 1985-, Claire & Leonard Tow prof, 2000, dist prof, currently; Kurt Masur, music adv, 1993-97; NY Philharmonic, revson composer, 1993-; Yale Univ, vis prof, 1993; Harvard Univ, vis lectr, 1994; Concorso Int di Composizione, pres, 2002; NY Philharmonic, 1969-; Alvin Ailey Am Dance Theatre, Madrid Symphony Orchestra, 2002; Symphony Orchestra Marseille, 2003; Orquesta de la Comunidad de Madrid, 2004; MOSAIC Chamber ensemble, 2004; NY Univ Symphony Orchestra, 2004; Symphony Orchestra Marseille, 2005; Shangri La", Opera by Susie Ibarra, The Kitchen, 2005; Fargo Moorhead Symphony, 2005; City Univ New York, distinguished prof, 2006; MacDowell Colony, Peterborough, NH, resident fel, 2016; Univ Mich, vis lectr; Univ of Kans, vis prof; Musik schule, Hamburg, vis lectr; Ithaca Col Sch Music, Karel Husa vis prof composition; Jazz Composer Orchestra Inst, vis prof; Arthur Mitchell's Dance Theater Harlem, founding mem & first musical dir; Conductor & Composer: Beethoven halle Orchestra; Gewandhaus orchester; Santa Cecilia Orchestra; Natl Symphony Orchestra South Africa; Netherlands Wind Ensemble. **Orgs:** Byrd Hoffman Found, 1981; Queens Coun Arts, 1983; Manhattan Arts, 1985; artistic dir, Composers Forum Inc, 1987-89; bd mem, Am Composers Orchestra, 1988, 2001; bd mem, Am Music Ctr, 2001-07; founder, Composers Now Festival, 2009-; Fromm Music Found, Harvard Univ, 2010; nat adv coun, Cornish Col Arts, 2012; bd mem, Symphony Space, 2012-; bd mem, Chamber Music Am, 2012; ASCAP; NY, Local 802, AFL CIO; bd mem, NY Found Arts; bd mem, Meet Composer; bd mem, Am Acad Poets; bd mem, Chamber Music Am. **Honors/Awds:** Natl Endowment Arts Comn, 1975; CINTAS Award, 1976, 1979; ASCAP Composer's Awards, 1978-89; Natl Coun Women US Achievement Award, 1980; Key to the City, Detroit, 1982; Dean Dixon Achievement Award, 1985; NY State Coun Arts, 1988; Acad Inst Award, Am Acad & Inst Arts & Letters, 1991; Ann Residency Artists, Yaddo, John D & Catherine T MacArthur Found, 1991; Meet Composer & Reader's Digest Comn Award, 1992; Natl Endowment Arts Rec Award, 1993; Distinguished Alumni Award, NY Univ, 1994; BMW Music Theater Prize, Munich Biennale, 1994; NY Gov's Lifetime Achievement Award, 1998;Nobel Prize-winner, 2005; ASCAP Victor Herbert Award, 2013; Hon Doctorate, Colgate Univ & Oberlin Col; received numerous awards from various organization including: Chamber Music Am; NYSCA; Lila Wallace & Reader's Digest Fund; ASCAP; Koussevitzky Found; Fromm Music Found; Received Numerous Awards & Honors. **Special Achievements:** Publications: "Ritual" for solo piano, Southern Music Publishing Co, 1991; "Parajota Delate" for mixed quintet, Southern Music Publ Co, 1992; recordings: "De Orishas The Western Wind" Newport Classic; piano solo, Leonarda Records, Momentum; Chamber works by Tania Leon, Composers Recordings Inc, Indigena; The Western Wind, Western Wind Records, Batey; Ana Maria Rosado, Albany Records, Paisanos Semos; Louisville Orchestra, First Edition Records, Bata, Carabali; TV appearances: Univision, "Orgullo Hispano"; Two of her piano works, Ritua & Mistica were featured in the Chicago Symphony's Music Now Pierre Boulez's 80th Birthday Celebration. Film: The Sensual Nature of Sound, composer, 1993. **Business Addr:** Professor, Brooklyn College, 408 Whitehead Hall, Brooklyn, NY 11210, **Business Phone:** (718)951-2596.

**LEON, WILMER J., JR.**
Criminologist. **Personal:** Born Mar 6, 1920, LA; married Edwina T Devore; children: Valerie Leon Brown & Wilmer III. **Educ:** S Univ, BS, 1949; Univ Calif Berkeley, MA, 1954. **Career:** Calif Adult Auth, admin officer; Calif Dept Educ, Bur Intergroup Rels, consult; Calif Dept Corrections, parole agt; asst dist parole supr; State Dir Corrections, consult; Calif State Univ Sacramento, lectr Criminal Justice. **Orgs:** Calif Probation & Parole Asn; Proj Safer Calif, Off Criminal Justice Planning; Sacramento Reg Area Planning Comn, Calif Coun Criminal Justice; Am Sociol Soc; bd dir, Cath Welfare Bur; exec bd, Cath Youth Orgn; Golden Gate Psychother Soc; Nat Asn Advan Colored People; Sacramento Comt Fair Housing; Sacramento Unified Sch Dist Adult Educ Group; Urban League Formation Comt, educ coordr. **Home Addr:** 6390 S Land Pk Dr, Sacramento, CA 95831, **Home Phone:** (916)421-7799.

**LEONARD, CAROLYN MARIE**
School administrator. **Personal:** Born Nov 20, 1943, Portland, OR; daughter of Kelly Miller Probasco (deceased) and Grace Ruth Searcie Probasco (deceased); children: Cherice M & Chandra M. **Educ:** Portland State Univ, BS, bus admin, 1976, MS, educ, 1979; Stand Admin cert, 1988. **Career:** Ore Assembly Black Affairs, vpres, 1979-86; Portland Pub Sch, Portland, Ore, evaluator, 1979-85, coordr multicult educ, 1985-, Acad Stands Reform Unit, admin, currently, Multicultural & Multiethnic Educ Off, coord, educ adminr, currently; re Comn Black Affairs, 1986-; Ore Coun Excellence Educ, sec, 1987-99; Jefferson Comm Cluster, Stud Achiev, dir, 2000-01; Compliance, Diversity & State Fed Progs, dir, 2003-; Univ Portland, adj prof. **Orgs:** Treas, Alpha Kappa Alpha, 1982-86; Nat Alliance Black Sch Educ; bd mem & chair, Ore Comn Black Affairs, 1984-94, bd mem & exec comt, Nat Coun Black Studies, 1984-; sec, Black United Fund Ore, 1987-90; Metro Human Rels Community, 1987-91, chmn, 1990-91; Joseph J. Malone fel 1995; bd mem, Portland State Univ Alum, 1997-; bd, McCoy Acad, 1997-2000; bd, Multicult Resource Ctr, 1997-2000; bd, Hyalite, 1997-2000; pres, Black Resource Ctr; bd, Moral Re-Armament, 2000-; bd mem, Initiatives Chg, 2000-. **Honors/Awds:** President's Award, Ore Assembly Black Affairs, 1984; Community Leadership Award, Skanner Newspaper, 1987; Merit Award, Skanner Newspaper, 1987; Cheik Anta Diop Award, Outstanding Scholarly Achievement Multicultural Educ, 1988; Education Award, Delta Sigma Theta Sorority, 1988; Ancient Free & Accepted Masons OR, Recognition Outstanding Service, 1989; Certificate of Appreciation, Commercial Club Portland, 1989; Woman of Excellence Award Education, Delta Sigma Theta Sorority, 1989; Outstanding Community Service Award, Ore Black Resource Ctr Found, 1990; Alma "Nomsa"John Inspiration Award, Int Black Women's Congress, 1991; NABRLE Community Service Award, Nat Asn Black Reading & Language Educrs, 1991; Mary McLeod Bethune-Carter G Woodson Award, Nat Coun Black Studies, 1992; Joseph J. Malone fellow, 1995; Community Service Award, Muslim Educ Trust, 1996; Community Harmony Award, Metro Human Rels Ctr, 1997; Outreach Award, Mrs. J.M. Gates, 1998; Mrs JM Gates "Coming Out" Award, 1999. **Special Achievements:** Editor, AFA Baseline Essays, 1987; Hispanic-Am Women, 1988; chair, Martin Luther King Jr Street Renaming Comn, 1989. **Home Addr:** 311 NE Jessup St, Portland, OR 97211-3113, **Home Phone:** (503)286-7332. **Business Addr:** Coordinator, Multicultural & Multiethnic Education, Portland Public Schools, 501 N Dixon St, Portland, OR 97227-1807, **Business Phone:** (503)916-3183.

**LEONARD, DONIS**
Administrator, educator. **Educ:** Prairie View A&M Univ, BA, theatre arts; Wayne State Univ, MFA, actg. **Career:** Calif State Univ, dir speech forensics prog & assoc prof theater arts, currently. **Special Achievements:** Founder & director "New African Grove", Black Theatre Prog Univ; directing credits include August Wilsons "The Piano Lesson", "The Shadow Box", "Miss Evers Boys", "The Heiress", Pearl Cleages "Flyin West" recognized as "Best Drama South Bay", 2000, "Jitney", "Blues For an Alabama Sky", "Zooman and the Sign", "A Raisin in the Sun". **Business Addr:** Associate Professor of Theater Arts, Director of the Speech & Forensics Program, California State University, Dominiguez Hills, Carson, CA 90747, **Business Phone:** (310)243-2847.

**LEONARD, GLORIA JEAN**
Library administrator. **Personal:** Born Jan 12, 1947, Seattle, WA; daughter of Charles Ratliff Jr and Katie Mae Stratman Ashford; children: Melanie Renee Smith; married James; children: James Oliver Jr. **Educ:** Fisk Univ, Nashville, TN, 1967; Univ Wash, Seattle, WA, BA, 1971, MLS, 1973; City Univ, Seattle, WA, MBA, 1985. **Career:** Univ Wash, Seattle, Wash, ref & outreach librn, 1973-79; Seattle Pub Libr, Seattle, Wash, s region servs develop librn, 1979, mobile servs & bookmobile dept head, 1981, Libr dir, br librn, 1981-83, 1984-89, spec asst city librn, 1989, s region mgr, 1990, advocate & dir, neighborhood libr serv, 1990-, actg dir, 2002-03, dir, 2003-08. **Orgs:** Pres, Seattle Chap, Jack & Jill Am, Inc, 1981-; Am Libr Asn, 1973-; exec bd, Black Caucus Am Libr Asn, 1975-; Wash Libr Asn, 1973; memship comt mem, Pub Libr Asn, 1990-. **Honors/Awds:** Reading Aloud: A Good Idea Getting Better by Tom Watson, Wilson Library Bulletin, volume 61, February, 1987, p 20-22; Articles: "Bias Busting: Valuing Diversity Work Place", Library Administration & Management, Vol 5, No 4, Fall, 1991; "Learning to Get Along with Each Other", Library Personnel News, Vol 5, No 2, March-April, 1991. **Home Addr:** 5716 S Hawthorn Rd, Seattle, WA 98118-3005, **Home Phone:** (206)725-9615. **Business Addr:** Advocate, Director of Library-Community Partnerships, Seattle Public Library, 800 Pke St, Seattle, WA 98101-3922, **Business Phone:** (206)386-4133.

**LEONARD, JEFFREY**
Baseball player, baseball manager. **Personal:** Born Sep 22, 1955, Philadelphia, PA; married Karen. **Career:** Baseball player (retired), baseball coach, executive; Los Angeles Dodgers, outfielder, 1977; Houston Astros, outfielder, 1978-81; San Francisco Giants, outfielder, 1981-88; Milwaukee Brewers, outfielder, 1988; Seattle Mariners, outfielder, 1989-90; Oakland Athletics farm syst, coach; Montreal Expos, hitting coach; Independent Western League, mgr; Golden Baseball League, Reno Silver Sox, mgr, 2008; Antelope Valley Col, Marauders baseball team, coach, 2002-05; One Flap Down Found Inc, vpres & co-founder, currently. **Orgs:** Golden Baseball League. **Home Addr:** 920 Rutherford Cir, Brentwood, CA 94513. **Business Addr:** Co-Founder, Vice President, One Flap Down Foundation Inc, 1198 Melody Lane Suite 103, Roseville, CA 95678, **Business Phone:** (916)677-1726.

**LEONARD, RAY CHARLES. See LEONARD, SUGAR RAY.**

**LEONARD, SUGAR RAY (RAY CHARLES LEONARD)**
Boxer, actor, administrator. **Personal:** Born May 17, 1956, Rocky Mount, NC; son of Cicero and Getha; married Juanita Wilkinson; children: Ray Jr & Jarrel; married Bernadette Robi; children: Camille & Daniel Ray. **Career:** Boxer (retired), actor, founder; Amateur Fights Olympics, team capt, boxer, 1976; prof boxer, 1988; HBO, boxing analyst & commentator; Sugar Ray Leonard Boxing Inc, chmn & founder, 2001-; Films: Riot, 1997; I Spy, 2002. Boxin Buddies: Knockout Juvenile Diabetes, 2006; The Fighter, 2010; Real Steel, consult, 2011; TV Series: "Tales from the Crypt", 1992; "Vault of Horrorl", 1994; "Half & Half", 2003; NBC, "The Contender", 2005; Miss USA, 2005, celebrity judge, 2005, broadcaster, host & mentor; ESPN, broadcaster, host & mentor; ABC, broadcaster; Sugar Ray Leonard Foundation, owner & founder, currently. **Orgs:** Owner & founder, Sugar Ray Leonard Found, currently. **Home Addr:** RR 4, PO Box 232, Mullins, SC 29574-9328. **Business Addr:** Founder, Sugar Ray Leonard Foundation, 21731 Ventura Blvd Suite 300, Woodland Hills, CA 91364.

**LEONARD, DR. WALTER J. See Obituaries Section.**

**LEONEY, ANTOINETTE E. MCLEAN**
Lawyer, judge. **Personal:** Born Jul 22, 1950, Boston, MA; daughter of Calvin and Marie E Cardoza; children: Dasan C. **Educ:** Lesley Col, Cambridge, Mass, BA, legal employ hist, 1980; New England Sch Law, Boston, MA, JD, 1984. **Career:** Commonwealth Mass, Dept Social Serv, Legal Coun, Boston, Mass, 1984-86; Dept Atty Gen, Boston, Ma, asst atty gen, 1986-87; Gov Michael S Dukakis, Boston, Mass, dep chief coun, 1987-90; Brandeis Univ, Waltham, Mass, dir off govt regulation & compliance, 1990-91; McKenzie & Edwards PC, sr litigation assoc, 1991; US Attys Off, asst US atty, 1994-; Mass Dept Social Serv, asst div coun; trustee & pres, bd trustee, Mass Continuing Legal Educ Inc; Mass Trial Ct, assoc justice; Mass Bar Found, judge. **Orgs:** Trustee, Lesley Col, 1989-; vpres, Mass Black Women Atty Asn, 1990-; dir, Mass Pension Res Investment Mgt Bd, 1990-92; dir, Mass Crime & Justice Found, 1990-92; exec bd mem, Mass Black Lawyers Asn, 1990-; Mass Bar Asn, 1991-; Boston Bar Asn, 1991-; deleg, MBA's House Deleg, 1998-01; active mem, Nat Black Prosecutors Asn; adv bd, Mass Trial Court's Gender Equality, 1999-2002; pres, Womens Bar Asn Mass, 1999-2000; Women's Bar Found, 2002-03; mem gender equality adv bd, Massachusetts Trial Ct; elected bd mem, New Eng Sch Law Alumni Asn; trustee, secy bd trustee & fel, Mass Bar Found; Mass Supreme Judicial Ct's Comn. **Honors/Awds:** Young Alumni Award, Lesley Col, 1990; Outstanding Achievement Award, New England Sch Law, Women's Law Caucus. **Home Addr:** 80 Hope Ave Apt 604, Waltham, MA 02453-2747. **Business Addr:** Judge, Massachusetts Bar Foundation, 20 W St, Boston, MA 02111-1204, **Business Phone:** (617)338-0500.

**LEROY, CHARLES**
Writer, executive, educator. **Personal:** Born Dec 16, 1933, Norristown, PA; son of Charles E and Annie Parker; married Elizabeth Parker; children: Noelle. **Educ:** Pa State Univ, BA, 1956. **Career:** Pa State Univ, Armed Servs, 1957-58; Norristown High Sch, human rels advisor, 1970; auth, 1975-; Afro-Am Hist & Cult Mus, Philadelphia, cofounder, 1976; Pa Black Hist Comt, dir, 1976-; Pa Afro-Am Hist Bd, dir, 1976-; Pa State Hist & Rec Adv Bd & Black Hist Adv Bd, dir, 1980-; Temple Univ Charles L Blockson Afro-Am Collection Rare Texts, founder & cur emer, 1982-; lectr, US Inf Agency, 1990-; moderator, Black Writer's Conf Paris, France, 1992; Valley Forge African-Am Revolutionary Soldier Monument, chmn, 1990-; Pa State Univ, fullback football player. **Orgs:** Nat Asn Advan Colored People, 1974-; bd mem, Hist Soc Pa, 1976-83; coun mem, Pa State Univ Alumni Coun, 1982-; Montgomery County Pa Bicentennial Comt, 1982-83; comt mem, Temple Univ Centennial Comt, 1983-; Urban League PA; Am Antiqn Soc, 1996; Grolier Club, 1996; Underground Rr Adv Comt; Pa Abolition Soc; chairperson, Nat Pk Serv; chair, Adv Coun community; dir, Pa Black Hist Comt. **Honors/Awds:** Honorary Doctorate Degree in Education, Villanova Univ, 1979; Alumni Fellow Award, Pa State Univ, 1979; Underground Railroad PA, 1980; Pa St Quarterback Award, PA State Quarterback Club, 1984; "The Underground Railroad", Cover Story Nat Geographic Mag, 1984; Lifetime Achievement Award, Before Columbus Found, 1987; Honorary Degree, Lincoln Univ, 1987; Honorary Degree, Holy Family Col, 1995; Storytellers First Life Time Achievement Award, Columbus Found, 1996; Founder's Award, Hist Soc Pa, 2002; First Inductee, Norristown sch dist's Hall of Fame & Hall of Champions. **Special Achievements:** Publications: Pa Black Hist Book, 1975; Black Genealogy Book, 1977; The Underground Railroad First Person Narratives Book, 1987; "People of the Sea Island", 1987; Philadelphia State Historical Marker Guide, 1992; Hippocrene Guide: The Underground Railroad, 1994; Underground Railroad Sites Study, 1990-95; Damn Rare: Memoirs of an African-American Bibliophile, 1998; Book, African-Americans in Pennsylvania: Above Ground & Underground - An Illustrated Guide, 2001; The Liberty Bell Era: The African American Story. Harrisburg, PA: RB Books, 2003; The Haitian Revolution: Celebrating the First Black Republic. Virginia Beach, VA: Donning Co. Publishers, 2004. **Home Addr:** 133 Hancock Rd, Gwynedd, PA 19436. **Business Addr:** Curator Emeritus, Founder, Temple University, Rm 7 1330 Polett Walk, Philadelphia, PA 19122, **Business Phone:** (215)204-6632.

**LEROY, DR. GARY LEWIS**
Physician, administrator, dean (education). **Personal:** Born Jun 30, 1956, Dayton, OH; son of Abraham and Flora; married Sherlynn; children: Julia & Ciara. **Educ:** Wright State Univ, Sch Med, BS, 1984, MD, 1988. **Career:** Dayton Newspapers Inc, Circulation Dept, customer serv clerk, 1972-81, off supvr, 1977; Miami Valley Hosp, Dayton, Ohio, phlebotomist, 1981-82, Med technologist, 1982-84, E Dayton Health Ctr, Med Doctor, 1992-2007, med dir, currently; Miami Valley Hosp, inpatient attend, currently; Wright State Univ, Sch Med, asst dean minority & stud affairs, 2004-07, Boonshoft Sch Med, asst dean minority & stud affairs, 2008-, Interim vpres multicultural affairs & community enhancement, 2010-12; Community Health Centers Greater Dayton, staff physician, 2008-. **Orgs:** First Aiders Response Comt, 1980-92; Alpha Phi Alpha Fraternity Inc, 1987-, vpres, 1994-96, pres, 19996-98; Ohio Acad Family Physicians, 1988; AMA, 1988-; Am Acad Family Physicians, 1988-; gov bd mem, 1992-; bd trustee, Miami Valley Hosp, 1997-2006; bd dir, Mary Scott Nursing Home, 1998-2001; bd dir, United Health Servs, 1998-2001; fel Am Acad Family Physicians, 1998; Sigma Pi Phi Fraternity, 1999-; bd dir, WSU Alumni Asn, 1999-; bd dir, Am Red Cross, Dayton Chap, 1999-2002; Community Adv Bd; pres, Ohio Acad Family Physicians; Golden Key Int Horror Soc; secy, WSU Alumni Asn, 2000-01;vpres, WSU Alumni Asn, 2001-02; pres, WSU Alumni Asn, 2003-06; Serv Delivery comt, Am Red Cross, 2004-; med dir, Premier Community Health, 2006-08; bd chair, HOSPICE Dayton Found, 2006-09; Family & C First Comt, 2008; bd trustee, Mound St Academies, 2009-; co-chair, Unintentional Prescription Drug Death Taskforce, 2010-12. **Home Addr:** 761 Kenilworth Ave, Dayton, OH 45405-4051, **Home Phone:** (937)278-6447. **Business Addr:** Associate Dean for Student Affairs & Admissions, Wright State University, 268 Univ Hall 3640 Col Glenn Hwy, Dayton, OH 45435, **Business Phone:** (937)775-2934.

**LESLIE, LISA. See LESLIE-LOCKWOOD, LISA DESHAUN.**

## LESLIE, MARSHA R.
Editor, journalist. **Personal:** Born Apr 16, 1948, Lexington, MS; children: Michaela L Leslie-Rule. **Educ:** Univ Mo, BJ, jour, 1970; Columbia Univ, MS, jour, 1974. **Career:** Journalist, 1970-; KMOX Radio; The Associated Press; The Houston Chronicle; The Seattle Times; KCTS-TV, assoc producer; The Rochester Democrat & Chronicle; The Single Woman's Companion, The Single Mother's Companion, Seal Press, ed, 1994. **Home Addr:** 1209 NE 98th St, Seattle, WA 98115, **Home Phone:** (206)527-5409. **Business Addr:** Editor, c/o Seal Press, 3131 Wern Ave Suite 410, Seattle, WA 98121, **Business Phone:** (206)283-7844.

## LESLIE-LOCKWOOD, LISA DESHAUN (LISA LESLIE)
Basketball player, fashion model, actor. **Personal:** Born Jul 7, 1972, Gardena, CA; daughter of Walter and Christine Lauren; married Michael; children: Lauren Jolie & Michael Joseph II. **Educ:** Univ Southern Calif, BCS, commun, 1994; Univ Phoenix, MBA. **Career:** Basketball player (retired), author, sports analyst, model, actress; Atlanta Glory, ctr, 1996-97; Wilhelmina Models, model, 1996; Lisa L. Enterprises Inc, pres & owner, 1997-; Los Angeles Sparks, 1997-2009, co-owner, 2011-; Fox Sports Net, sports commentator & analyst, 2010-; Disney ABC Tv Group, studio analyst & commentator, 2010-; Americas' SAP Users' Group, entrepreneur exec coach, 2011-; Lisa Leslie Basketball & Leadership Acad, co-owner, 2012-; Am Fedn C, spokesperson, 2013-; ESPN, commentator; ABC, sports analyst, currently; Turner, sports analyst, currently; Film: Think like a man. **Orgs:** Us Olympic Comt. **Business Addr:** Co-Owner, Los Angeles Sparks, 2151 E Grand Ave Suite 100, El Segundo, CA 90245, **Business Phone:** (310)341-1000.

## LESTER, BETTY J.
Judge. **Personal:** Born Oct 14, 1945, Bristol, PA; daughter of John and Ollie Kimbrough; married Althear; children: Alyse Renee. **Educ:** Howard Univ, BBA, 1968; Rutgers Univ, JD, 1971; Marymount Manhattan, LLD, 1983. **Career:** Pub Defenders Off, asst dep pub def, 1972-74; Pub Advocates Off, asst dep pub advocate, 1974-76; Supermkts Gen, staff atty, 1976-77; Newark Munic Ct, judge, 1977-80, presiding judge, 1980-85; Super Ct NJ, super ct judge, 1985-; Lions Club Frederick, woman pres; State NJ, Super Ct, 5th Vicinage, criminal div, 1996-99, presiding judge, currently. **Orgs:** EC Bar Asn, 1971-; Nat Bar Asn, 1971-; bd mem, Goodwill Industs; bd mem & secy, Ont Asn Agr Socs; bd mem, Lions Club Frederick; Nat Asn Negro Bus & Prof Women's Club, 1977; bd dir, Joint Connection, 1978; bd dir, gov NJ State Bar Asn, 1978-80; treas, EC Mun Ct Judges Asn, 1982-; Nat Asn Women Judges, 1982-; NJ Coalition 100 Black Women, 1983-. **Honors/Awds:** Outstanding Achievement, Asn Black Women Lawyers, 1980; Mary Philbrook Award, Rutgers Law Sch, 1986; Woman of the Year, Zonta Club Int, 1986. **Home Addr:** 506 Longview Rd, South Orange, NJ 07079. **Business Addr:** Presiding Judge, State of New Jersey Superior Court 5th Vicinage, 50 W Mkt St Rm 514 NCB, Newark, NJ 07102, **Business Phone:** (973)693-5872.

## LESTER, BILL (WILLIAM ALEXANDER LESTER, III)
Engineer, race car driver. **Personal:** Born Feb 6, 1961, Washington, DC; married Cheryl; children: William Alexander IV. **Educ:** Univ CA, Berkeley, BS, elec engineering & comput sci, 1984. **Career:** Hewlett-Packard, software engr & proj mgr, 1982-98; Infineon Raceway, racing instr, 1992; pro racecar driver, 1998; Bill Davis Racing Inc, driver, 2004; Grand-Am Rolex Ser, 2007-; Rolex Sports Car Ser, driver, 2008-10; NASCraftsman Truck Ser, driver. **Orgs:** NASCAR Diversity Coun; Int Motor Sports Asns (IMSA); Nat Motorsports Appeals Panel. **Honors/Awds:** Rookie of the Year, SCCA N CA Region, 1985; Regional Road Racing Championship, SCCA GT-3, 1986; Four-Hour Endurance Race Championship, RDC, 1989, 1991; 20th position in NASCAR Camping World Truck Series, 2006; 68th Position in NASCAR Sprint Cup Series, 2006. **Special Achievements:** Filming his first TV commercial to advertise the NASCAR Craftsman Truck Series; First African American to drive in NASCAR Nextel Cup debut in 20 years; First African-American to run a Busch Series race in 1991; First African-American driver to win in any Grand-Am division, 2011; First African-American to Win NASCAR's; The First African-american Driver To Compete In An XFINITY Series Event. **Home Addr:** 9738 English Pine Ct, Windermere, FL 34786. **Business Addr:** Professional Racecar Driver, Rolex Sports Car Series, 1801 W Int Speedway Blvd, Daytona Beach, FL 32114-1243, **Business Phone:** (386)947-6681.

## LESTER, DONALD
Educator, teacher. **Personal:** Born Sep 20, 1944, Detroit, MI; children: Tarik. **Educ:** Wayne State Univ, BS, 1967; Western Mich Univ, EdM, 1972. **Career:** Detroit Pub Sch Syst, teacher; Wayne County Community Col, instr; Univ Detroit, instr; Western Mich Univ, instr; Shaw Col, assoc prof. **Orgs:** Nat dir Basic Training, Black Christian Nationalist Church; vice chmn Reg 1; bd ed, Detroit Schs; southern reg bishop, Shrines Black Madonna Pan-African Orthodox Christian Church; chmn, Atlanta Housing Auth; Kappa Alpha Psi Fraternity. **Business Addr:** Associate Professor, Shaw College, 944 Gordon St SW, Atlanta, GA 30310.

## LESTER, DR. ELTON J.
Lawyer. **Personal:** Born Sep 28, 1944, Bronx, NY; married Sandra Hight; children: Eric & Shawne. **Educ:** Atlantic Union Col, BA, history, 1966; Howard Univ, JD, 1969. **Career:** Off Mgt & Budget, examr; US Dept Housing & Urban Develop, legal hons intern, atty & adv, assoc gen coun, Assisted Housing, Community & Urban Develop, 1969-. **Orgs:** Fed Bar Asn; DC Bar Asn; Nat Bar Asn; Omega Psi Phi; Urban League; Concerned Black Fathers. **Honors/Awds:** Recipient, Ford Found Scholar, 1966. **Home Addr:** 10792 Folkestone Way, Woodstock, MD 21163-1376, **Home Phone:** (301)596-5162. **Business Addr:** Associate General Counsel, US Department Housing & Urban Develop, 451 7th St SW, Washington, DC 20410, **Business Phone:** (202)708-1112.

## LESTER, GEORGE LAWRENCE
Writer, executive, historian. **Personal:** Born Dec 11, 1949, Charleston, AR; son of George and Casteline Williams; married Valcinia Marie Boyd; children: Tiffany R Lester, Marisa & Erica Joi. **Educ:** Columbia Col, BA, 1978. **Career:** Negro Leagues Base Ball Mus, co-founder & res dir, 1990-95; Negro Leagues Comt, co-chmn, currently. **Orgs:** Nat Asn Advan Colored People; Asn Study Afro Am Life & Hist; Soc Am Baseball Res; Am First Day Cover Soc; Am Topical Asn; Black Am Philatelic Soc; vpres, Midwest Afro Am Geneal Interest Coalition, 1995; African Am Mus Asn; Am Jazz Mus; Asn Prof Basketball Res; Ebony Soc Philatelic Events & Reflections; Nat Asn Black Sch Educr; Nat Baseball Hall Fame & Mus; Negro Leagues Baseball Mus; N Am Soc Sports Hist; Prof Football Res Asn. **Home Addr:** 8212 Ash Ave, Raytown, MO 64138-2156, **Home Phone:** (816)358-0475.

## LESTER, ISAAC, JR.
Association executive. **Personal:** son of Isaac Sr. **Educ:** Ky State Univ, attended 1980; Univ N Tex, BS, advert, 1984. **Career:** Amalgamated Publ Co, mid-w reginal sales mgr, 1991-97; Educ Hwy Found, pres & nat sales mgr, currently; Diversity Publ Co, owner, pres, 1996-2011; Orange Truck Billboards, owner, 2011-. **Business Addr:** Owner, Orange Truck Billboards, 96 Linwood Plz Suite 325, Fort Lee, NJ 07024, **Business Phone:** (201)862-0206.

## LESTER, JULIUS
Educator, writer. **Personal:** Born Jan 27, 1939, St. Louis, MO; son of Woodie Daniel and Julia B Smith; married Alida Carolyn Fechner; children: Elena Milad & David Julius; married Joan Steinau; children: Jody Simone & Malcolm Coltrane; married Milan Sabatini. **Educ:** Fisk Univ, Nashville, TN, BA, eng, 1960. **Career:** Professor (retired), professor emeritus; AUTHOR: Look Out, Whitey! Black Power's Gon' Get Your Mama, Dial Press, 1968; To Be A Slave, Dial Press, 1968; Auth Fiction: Black Folktales, Baron, 1969; Revolutionary Notes, 1969; Search for the new land, 1969; The Thought & Writings of W E B Dubois, Random House, 1971; Two Love Stories, 1972; The Knee High Man & Other Tales, 1972; The Seventh Son, All Is Well, An Autobiography, Morrow, 1976; Lovesong: Becoming A Jew, Holt, 1988; Long Journey Home: Stories from Black Hist, Dial Press, 1972; POEMS: Who I Am, Dial Press, 1974; This Strange New Feeling, Dial Press, 1982; The Tales of Uncle Remus: The Adventures of Brer Rabbit, Dial Press, 1987, More Tales of Uncle Remus:The Further Adventures of Brer Rabbit, Dial Press, 1988, Do Lord Remember Me, Dial Press, 1984; How Many Spots Does a Leopard Have, Dial Press, 1989; Falling Pieces of the Broken Sky, Arcade Publ, 1990; The Last Tales of Uncle Remus, 1994; All Our Wounds Forgiven, 1994; John Henry, 1994; The Man Who Knew Too Much, 1994; Othello: A Novel!, 1995; Caldecott Hon Bk, 1996; Sam & The Tigers, 1996; From Slaveship to Freedom Road, 1998; Black Cowboy, Wild Horses, 1998; What a Truly Cool World, 1999; When the Began, 1999. Pharaoh's Daughter, Harcourt & Silver Whistle, 2000; Albidaro & the Mischievous Dream, Phyllis Fogelman Bks, 2000; Ackamarackus: Julius Lester's Sumptuously Silly Fabulously Funny Fables, Scholastic, 2001; When Dad Killed Mom, 2001, The Blues Singers:Ten Who Shook the World, Hyperiod & Jump At The Sun, 2001; Why Heaven is Far Away, Scholastic, 2001; Shining, Harcourt & Silver Whistle, 2003; Let's Talk about Race, 2003, The Old African, 2003; Day of Tears, 2003; The Autobiography of God, 2004; New Sch Social Res, Afro-Am Hist, 1968-70; Newport Folk Festival, Newport, RI, dir, 1966-68; WBAI-FM, New York, NY, producer & host, 1968-75; New Sch Social Res, lectr, 1968-70; WNET-TV, New York, NY, host, 1971-73; Univ Mass, Amherst, Mass, prof Afro-Am studies, 1971-88, Near Eastern & Judaic Studies, prof, 1982-03, Inst Advan Studies Humanities, actg dir & assoc dir, 1982-84, adj prof Eng & hist dept, 1988-03, prof emer, 2004-. **Home Addr:** 600 Sta Rd, Amherst, MA 01002. **Business Addr:** Professor Emeritus, University of Massachusetts, 744 Herter Hall, Amherst, MA 01003-9312, **Business Phone:** (413)545-2550.

**LESTER, NINA MARIE. See Obituaries Section.**

## LESTER, TIM LEE
Football player, football coach, advocate. **Personal:** Born Jun 15, 1968, Miami, FL; son of Johnny and Robbie; married Kendra; children: Brandi & Breanna. **Educ:** Eastern Kent Univ, criminol & psychol. **Career:** Football player (retired), Football coach, partner; Los Angeles Rams, running back, 1992-94; Pittsburgh Steelers, running back, 1995-98; Dallas Cowboys, running back, 1999; Melbourne Cent Cath High Sch, asst head football coach & offensive cord; Chamimade Madonna High Sch, volunt coach team couns, recrut cord & run backs coach, 2001; Scottish Claymores, coaching asst, 2004, Lovells, leader capital mkt & securitization team, partner, 1995-2008; Allens Arthur Robinson, partner corp & fin, managing partner, 2008-. **Orgs:** Founder, Tim Lester Cares Inc, 2000-; mem Exec Comt, Australia Japan Bus Coop Comt; mem bd, Dept Foreign Affairs & Trade's Australia Japan Found; chmn, Univ Western Australia's Bus Sch's Ambassadorial Coun; gov, trustee, Western Australian Mus Found; Atty Gen's Int Legal Serv Adv Coun. **Home Addr:** 10991 SW 222 Ter, Miami, FL 33170. **Business Addr:** Partner, Allens Arthur Robinson, Level 37 QV 1 250 St Georges Ter, Perth, WA 6000, **Business Phone:** (618)9488-384.

## LESTER, PROF. WILLIAM ALEXANDER, JR.
Theoretical chemist. **Personal:** Born Apr 24, 1937, Chicago, IL; son of William Alexander and Elizabeth Frances Clark; married Rochelle Diane Reed; children: William Alexander III & Allison Kimberleigh. **Educ:** Univ Chicago, BS, 1958, MS, 1959; Cath Univ Am, PhD, 1964. **Career:** Nat Bur Stand, phys chemist, 1961-64; Univ Wis-Madison, Theoret Chem Inst, from res assoc to asst dir, 1964-68; Univ Wis-Madison, Dept Chem, lectr, 1966-68; Int Bus Mach, San Jose Res Lab, from res staff mem to mgr, 1968-78; Int Bus Mach Corp, TJ Watson Res Lab, technol planning staff, 1975-76; Lawrence Berkeley Lab, assoc dir, 1978-81; Nat Resource Comput Chem, dir, 1978-81; Univ Calif, Berkeley, Calif, prof chem, 1981-2010, Col Chem, assoc dean, 1991-95, Grad Sch, Dept Chem, prof, 2010-12, prof emer, currently; NSF, Human Resource Develop, sr fel sci & eng, asst dir, 1995-96. **Orgs:** Vol Instr Proj, Spec Elem Educ Disadvantaged, 1970-72; chmn, Black Liason Comn, San Jose Unified Sch Dist, 1971-72; Chem Eval Panel, Air Force Off Sci Res, 1974-78; US Nat Comt Int Union Pure & Appl Chem, 1976-79; coun mem, chmn, Div Phys Chem, Am Chem Soc, 1979, fel 2011; Nat Res Coun Panel Chem Physics, Nat Bur Stand, 1980-83; Chem Adv Panel, NSF, 1980-83; Community Surv Chem Sci, Nat Acad Sci, 1982-84; bd mem, Marcus Foster Educ Inst, 1982-86; fel APS, 1984; Nat Orgn Prof Advan Black Chemists & Chem Engrs, 1984-88; Comt Recommendations Army Basic Sci Res, 1984-87; chmn, Div Chem Physics, Am Phys Soc, 1986-87; adv bd, World Bk Inc, 1989-93; fel AAAS, 1991; Adv Bd, Model Inst Excellence, Spelman Col, 1991-2005; Fed Networking Coun Adv Comt, 1991-95; fel Calif Acad Sci, 1994; Army Res Lab Tech Assessment Bd, 1996-99; at-large mem, Gordon Res Conferences, Coun Gordon Res Conferences, 1997-2000; External Vis Comt, Nat Partnership Advan Computational Infrastructure, 1999-2002; Sigma XI, 1999-2000; pres's comt mem, Nat Medal Sci, 2000-02; Dept Energy Adv Comt, Advan Computational Comput, 2000-04; bd mem, Chem Sci & Technol, Nat Res Coun, 2003-; Int Acad Quantum Molecular Sci, 2006; Site & Selection Comt, 2000-06, bd trustee, 2007-12. **Honors/Awds:** Outstanding Contribution Award, Int Bus Mach Corp, 1974; Percy L Julian Award, Nat Orgn Prof Advan Black Chemist & Chem Engrs, 1979; Alumni Award in Science, Catholic Univ Am, 1983; Outstanding Teacher Award, Nat Orgn Prof Advan Black Chemist & Chem Engrs, 1986; Professional Achievement Award, Northern Calif Coun Black Prof Engrs, 1989; Outstanding Service Award, NSF, 1996; History Maker, 2004; Berkeley Chancellors Award, Univ Calif, 2006; Festschrift, 2008; Israel Regional Award, Am Chem Soc, 2008. **Home Addr:** 4433 Briar Cliff Rd, Oakland, CA 94605, **Home Phone:** (510)635-9782. **Business Addr:** Professor Emeritus, University of California Berkeley, Pitzer Ctr 212 Gilman Hall Rm 8 & 13, Berkeley, CA 94720-1460, **Business Phone:** (510)643-9590.

**LESTER, WILLIAM ALEXANDER, III. See LESTER, BILL.**

## LESURE, JAMES
Actor. **Personal:** Born Sep 21, 1970, Los Angeles, CA. **Educ:** Univ Southern Calif, BFA, theater; Univ Kent. **Career:** Films: Giving It Up, 1999; The Package, 2005; The Ring Two, 2005; Love less in Los Angeles, 2007; Our Family Wedding, 2010; Fire with Fire, 2012.TV Series: "Macbeth"; "Martin", 1992-96; "Space: Above & Beyond", 1995; "Mad About You", 1996; "Pacific Blue", 1996; "Diagnosis Murder", 1996; "Dangerous Minds", 1996; "Seinfeld", 1996; "Saved by the Bell: The New Class", 1997; "The Burning Zone", 1997; "The Drew Carey Show", 1997; "Getting Personal", 1998; "For Your Love", 1998-2003; "George Lopez"; "Alias"; "Suddenly Susan", 2000; "What Wouldn't Jesus Do?", 2002; "The Johnny Chronicles", 2002; "The Division", 2003; "Las Vegas", 2003-08; "Monk", 2008; "Lipstick Jungle", 2009; "The New Adventures of Old Christine", 2009; "Studio 60 On The Sunset Strip"; "Seinfeld"; "NYPD Blue"; "The Drew Carey Show"; "Lost"; "Mr. Sunshine", 2010-; "Harry's Law", 2011; "Men at Work", 2012-14; "CSI: Crime Scene Investigation", 2014. **Honors/Awds:** Most Valuable Player, NBA Entertainment League, 2006; Distinguished Support Award, Sickle Cell Disease Found; Multicultural Prism Award, Outstanding Male Actor, 2006; Distinguished Support Award, Sickle Cell DisFound Calif, 2006. **Home Addr:** PO Box 251499, Los Angeles, CA 90025, **Home Phone:** (310)234-1992. **Business Addr:** Actor, Kyle Avery Public Relations, 1107 Fair Oaks Ave Suite 321, South Pasadena, CA 91030.

## LETSON, ALFRED, JR. (AL LETSON)
Poet, playwright, actor. **Personal:** Born Aug 8, 1972, Plainfield, NJ; son of Alfred Sr and Ruth; children: Brooklyn, Greg & Syrus. **Career:** Freelance Writer & Performer, owner, 1997-; Poet, 1998-; PoetCD. com, founder & pres, 1998-2000; playwright, 2001-; Pub Radio, host, 2006-07; State Re: Union, host & exec producer, 2008-; Radio host; Poem: Slam Movement; Author: Stoplights, short film, 1999; Essential Personal, play, 2001; Theatre Proj, Griot: He who Speaks the Sweet Word, poetry slammer; Julius X; Summer in Sanctuary, 2006; Crumbs; Chalk, 2004. **Honors/Awds:** Atlanta Grand Slam, 2000; 3rd rank National Poetry Slam, 2000; Individual Artist Fellowship, State Fla, 2005. **Special Achievements:** Film: Sign Language, On the Lot; One of the three finalists out of more than 1, 500 applicants to win the Public Radio Talent Quest. **Business Addr:** Playwright, Poetry Slammer, Theatre Project, 45 W Preston St, Baltimore, MD 21201, **Business Phone:** (410)752-8558.

## LETT, GERALD WILLIAM
Entrepreneur. **Personal:** Born Sep 28, 1926, Lansing, MI; married Ruby Truitt; children: William, Gerald & Debra. **Career:** Lett's Bridal Inc, owner & pres, 1952-. **Orgs:** Mich Retailers Asn; YWCA; Lansing Econ Develop Corp; Lansing Sexton HS PTA; Nat Asn Advan Colored People; Urban League. **Home Addr:** 534 Mc Pherson, Lansing, MI 48915, **Home Phone:** (517)484-2104. **Business Addr:** President, Owner, Lett's Bridal & Formal, 2225 E Grand River Ave, Lansing, MI 48912-3292, **Business Phone:** (517)484-0944.

## LEVELL, COL. EDWARD, JR.
Executive, manager, military leader. **Personal:** Born Apr 2, 1931, Jacksonville, AL; son of Edward A Sr (deceased) and Gabrella Williams (deceased); married Rosa M Casellas; children: Edward A III (deceased), Ruben C, Kenneth W (deceased), Raymond C (deceased), Randy C, Cheryl D & Michael K. **Educ:** Tuskegee Inst, BS, phys educ, 1953; USAF, Bryan AFB, USAF Pilot Training, 1954; Univ Northern Co, Greeley, MA, urban sociol, 1972; Air War Col, Maxwell AFB, Ala, leadership, mgt, 1974; Indust Col Armed Forces, MA, mgt, 1973. **Career:** Military leader, manager (retired); USAF, col, 1953-83, Acad Comdr, Colo Springs, Cadet Group l, 1970-72, dep commandant Cadets, 1972-73, Hurlburt AFB, comdr 1st Spec Opers WG Wing, 1976-77, USAF, Luke, AFB, comdr 58th Tactical Training Wing, 1977-78, Langley AFB, 20th Air Div, comdr, 1978-83; Chicago, dir aviation, 1984-89; New Orleans Airport, dep dir aviation, 1989-92, dir aviation. **Orgs:** Life mem, Kappa Alpha Psi Fraternity; life mem, The Retired Officers Asn; life mem, The Daedalian Found; life mem, The Tuskegee Airman Inc. **Honors/Awds:** Top Gun Award, USAFE, 1961; Top Gun, Tactical Air Command, 1961, 1965, 1969; Vietnam Campaign Medals, 1965-69; Distinguished Flying Cross, 1969; Air Force Commendation Medal, 1966; Meritorious Service Medal, 1970; Won Eight Air Medal Awards, 1970; Distinguished Service Award, Jacksonville,

1974; Air Force Asn Special Citation of Merit, State Fla, 1977; State Fla Comn Human Relations Award Special Recognition, 1977; Legion of Merit Award, 1983; Hall of Fame, Tuskegee Univ, 1991. **Special Achievements:** First & only African-American commander of the First Special Operations Wing at Hurlburt Field; First Air Force pilot to log 3, 000 flying hours in the F-100 Super Sabre aircraft. **Home Addr:** 1500 W Esplanade Suite 46F, Kenner, LA 70065, **Home Phone:** (504)464-9915.

**LEVENS, DORSEY (HERBERT DORSEY LEVENS)**
Actor, founder (originator), football player. **Personal:** Born May 21, 1970, Syracuse, NY; son of Herbert and Patricia; children: Amaya. **Educ:** Ga Tech, mgt; Univ Notre Dame. **Career:** Football player (retired); Green Bay Packers, 1994-2001; Philadelphia Eagles, 2002, 2004; New York Giants, 2003; PlayerPress, NFL analyst, currently; Sprint Exclusive Entertainments, analyst; Films: We Are Marshall, 2006; Three Can Play That Game, 2007; Gridiron UK, forthcoming; TV: "Arli$$", 1998; "Retreads", forthcoming. **Orgs:** Founder & chief exec officer, Dorsey Levens Found. **Home Addr:** 4249 Olde Mill Lane NE, Atlanta, GA 30342-3400, **Home Phone:** (404)256-0932. **Business Addr:** NFL Analyst, Player Press LLC, 679 9th Ave Apt 4f, New York, NY 10036, **Business Phone:** (212)956-7280.

**LEVENS, HERBERT DORSEY. See LEVENS, DORSEY.**

**LEVER, FAT. See LEVER, LAFAYETTE.**

**LEVER, LAFAYETTE (FAT LEVER)**
Basketball player, basketball executive. **Personal:** Born Aug 18, 1960, Pine Bluff, AR; married Charlene Manager; children: Anthony. **Educ:** Ariz State Univ, BS, educ & commun, 1982. **Career:** Basketball player (retired), basketball executive; Portland Trail Blazers, 1982-84; Denver Nuggets, 1984-90; Dallas Mavericks, 1990-94; Kings Radio Broadcasts, color analyst, currently; Sacramento Kings, dir player develop, 2007-. **Orgs:** Nat Basketball Players Asn, vpres, 1987; Nat Basketball Asn. **Home Addr:** 50 Regency Pk Cir, Sacramento, CA 95835-1780, **Home Phone:** (916)692-5314. **Business Addr:** Director of Player Development, Sacramento Kings, Sleep Train Arena, Sacramento, CA 95834, **Business Phone:** (916)928-0000.

**LEVERETTE, DR. MICHELLE A.**
Administrator, health services administrator. **Personal:** Born Oct 27, 1962, Washington, DC; daughter of James and Gloria Abram; children: Kristin M & James A. **Educ:** Tougaloo Col, BS, chem, 1984, summa cum laude; Johns Hopkins Sch Med, MD, 1988. **Career:** Bienville Med Group, pediatrician, 1991-93; pvt pract pediatrician, 1991-93; Johns Hopkins Med Serv, pediatrician, 1993-95; Johns Hopkins Hosp, Dept Pediat, instr, 1995-99; Baltimore Co Dept Health, dir & health off, 1995; Baltimore County, dir bur substance abuse. **Orgs:** Friends C MS, Med Adv Bd, Baltimore Co Med Asn; Md Med & Chirurgical Asn; Md Asn Co Health Offrs; Nat Asn Co & City Health Offs; Am Pub Health Asn; adv comn, Johns Hopkins Community Health Workers; res & adv panel, Inst Racial & Ethnic Health Studies, Univ Md; Md Sch-Based Heatlh Ctr Policy Adv Coun; State Inter agency Coord Coun Infants & Toddlers; Md Partnership C & Families; Gov Task Force Emerging Med & Surg Treatments; US Cong man Ben Cardin's Health Adv Comn; chair, Baltimore Co Local Mgt Bd. **Home Addr:** 9 Nearock Ct, Owings Mills, MD 21117, **Home Phone:** (410)654-3138. **Business Addr:** Director, Health officer, Baltimore County Department of Health, 400 Washington Ave, Towson, MD 21204, **Business Phone:** (410)887-3196.

**LEVERMORE, CLAUDETTE MADGE (CLAUDETTE N LEVERMORE)**
Educator, teacher, school administrator. **Personal:** Born Feb 28, 1939, St. Andrew; daughter of Herbert Willacy; married Oswald Burchell; children: Monique Althea & Jacqueline Maureen. **Educ:** McGill Univ, cert, 1968; Univ Miami, BBA, 1978; Wharton Univ, cert, 1981; Nova Univ, MBA, 1984. **Career:** Govt Jamaica, civil servant, 1958-64; Geigy Pharmaceut, admin asst, 1964-68; McGill Univ, admin asst, 1968-71; Univ Miami, dir admin serv, 1971-; Miami Dade County Pub Schs, instr, 1984-, bus educ teacher, currently; STARBURST Southwood Mid Sch, advisor; Levermore Mgt Serv Inc, dir. **Orgs:** Woodson Williams Marshall Asn, 1978-; Nat Black MBA Asn; bd mem, Black Cult Art Ctr & Black S Fla Coalition Econ Develop; Nursing Sch Bus Officers Asn; bd mem & treas, Un Fla Chap. **Home Addr:** 14865 SW 166th St, Miami, FL 33187, **Home Phone:** (305)233-3964. **Business Addr:** Instructor, Business Education Teacher, Miami Dade County Public Schools, 1450 NE 2nd Ave, Miami, FL 33132, **Business Phone:** (305)995-1000.

**LEVERMORE, JACQUELINE MAUREEN**
Publisher. **Personal:** Born Oct 10, 1968, Montreal, QC; daughter of Oswald and Claudette. **Educ:** Univ Miami, BA, 1990; Univ Iowa, Col Law, JD, 1993. **Career:** Mustered Seed Publishing Worldwide Inc, chief exec officer, 1993-; Book: Cherub: The Human Race, author. **Honors/Awds:** Gold Drum Award, 1986; Iron Arrow Hon Soc, 1990; Bowman Ashe Scholar. **Business Addr:** Chief Executive Officer, Mustered Seed Publishing Worldwide Inc, PO Box 192011, Dallas, TX 75219, **Business Phone:** (214)252-9704.

**LEVERMORE, DR. MONIQUE A.**
Psychologist, educator. **Personal:** Born Oct 29, 1966, Montreal, QC; daughter of Claudette and Oswald; married Mark Bartolone; children: Nino & Kai. **Educ:** Univ Miami, BA, psychol, 1988, MSEd, psychol, 1990; Howard Univ, MS, clin psychol, 1990, PhD, clin psychol, 1995. **Career:** Johns Hopkins Med Inst, psychol extern, 1993-94; Harvard Med Sch, psychol intern, 1994-95; Eckerd Youth Develop Ctr, resident psychologist, 1995-96; Palm Beach Atlantic Col, asst prof, dir couns ctr, 1996-97; Levermore Psychol Servs, pres, psychologist, 1997-; Fla Inst Technol, asst prof, 1998-2004; Miami teaching fel, 2006-08; Carlos Albizu Univ, prof, dir clin training, 2008-12; Pvt Guid Consult Corp, guid consult, 2011, co-founder; Univ Cent FL, lectr, 2013-. **Orgs:** Am Psychol Asn, 1995-; founder & dir, GIRLS, 1998-2003; Links, 2003; independent consult, Nat Asn Col Coun, 2011-; Asn Black psychol, pres, S Fla Chap, 2012-13; fel Am Col forensic examiners Inst; adv bd mem, Salvation Army. **Business Addr:** President, Clinical Psychologist, Levermore Psychological Services PA, Rialto Pl, Palmetto Bay, FL 32901, **Business Phone:** (786)293-0922.

**LEVERT, EDDIE, SR. (EDWARD LEVERT)**
Actor, singer. **Personal:** Born Jun 16, 1942, Bessemer, AL; married Raquel Capelton; children: 1; married Martha; children: Gerald (deceased), Sean (deceased) & Eddie Jr. **Career:** The O'Jays, singer, currently; Albums: Comin' Through, 1965; Back on Top, 1968; Back Stabbers, 1972; Peace, 1975; So Full of Love, 1978; My Favorite Person, 1982; Love Fever, 1984; Serious, 1989; Heartbreaker, 1993; Love You to Tears, 1997; For the Love, 2001; Imagination, 2004; Christmas With The O'jays, 2010; Eddie Levert: I Still Have It, 2012; TV Series: "Tavis Smiley", 2004-07; "The Apprentice", 2004; "The View", 2005; "Jimmy Kimmel Live!", 2005; "VH1 Rock Doc"s, 2010; "Tavis Smiley", 2004-10; "Unsung", 2010; "The Mo'Nique Show", 2010; "The Hot 10", 2011; Films: Coming to America, 1988; The Fighting Temptations, 2003; An Evening of Stars: 25th Anniversary Tribute to Lou Rawls, 2004; TV Movies: "Rock & Roll Hall of Fame Induction Ceremony", 2005; "An Evening with Quincy Jones", 2008; "19th Annual Trumpet Awards", 2011. **Honors/Awds:** American Music Award, Best Duo, 1990; Outstanding Vocal Group Award, Nat Asn Advan Colored People, 1991; Quincy Jones Award, 2002; Vocal Group Hall of Fame, 2004; Rock and Roll Hall of Fame, 2005; Lifetime Achievement Award, Black Entertainment Television, 2009; Trumpet Lifetime Achievement Award, 2011; Heroes and Legends Pacesetter Award. **Special Achievements:** Book: I Got Your Back: A Father and Son Keep It Real about Love, Fatherhood, Family, and Friendship issued in 2007. Lifetime Commitment to the Community for service and beautiful sounds that continue to change the face of music" from 100 Black Men, October 20, 2001. **Home Addr:** 1000 N Green Valley Pkwy Suite 440-629, Henderson, NV 89074, **Home Phone:** (702)565-1489. **Business Addr:** Singer, CBS Records, 51 W 52nd St, New York, NY 10019.

**LEVERT, DR. FRANCIS E., II**
Engineer, president (organization). **Personal:** Born Mar 28, 1940, Tuscaloosa, AL; married Faye Burnett; children: Francis, Gerald C & Lisa A. **Educ:** Tuskegee Inst, BS, 1964; Univ Mich, MS, 1966; Pa State Univ, PhD, nuclear engineering, 1971. **Career:** Tuskegee Inst, Sch Engr, actg head mech engineering, 1972-73; Commonwealth Edison Co, prin engr, 1973-74; Argonne Nat Lab, nuclear engr appl physics div, 1974-79; Tech Energy Corp, chief scientist, 1979-85; Trans-Africa Gas & Elec, tech adv, 1999-; KEMP Corp, inventor, pres, currently. **Orgs:** Am Nuclear Soc; exec comt, Plant Maintenance Div; Am Soc Mech Engrs; Phi Kappa Phi; Pi Tau Sigma; Beta Kappa Chi; Nat Soc Prof Engrs; fel Atomic Energy Comn, Univ Mich; Am Soc Engineering Educ; fel Ford Found; fel Pa State Univ. **Special Achievements:** Inventor: 23 US Patents; author of two books & 63 technical journals, articles. **Business Addr:** President, Kemp Corp, 1725 E Magnolia Ave, Knoxville, TN 37917, **Business Phone:** (865)525-3372.

**LEVINGSTON, BASHIR A.**
Football player. **Personal:** Born Oct 2, 1976, Seaside, CA. **Educ:** Eastern Wash Univ, admin justice. **Career:** New York Giants, defensive back, 1999-2000; Amsterdam Admirals, defensive back, 2000; Toronto Argonauts, 2002-07; Montreal Alouettes, 2007; free agt, currently. **Honors/Awds:** All-NFL Europe honors; CFL All-Star, 2003; CFL East All-Star, 2003-04; Grey Cup, 2004. **Special Achievements:** CFL record when he returned a missed field goal by Paul Mc Callum for a 129 yard touchdown.

**LEVINGSTON, CLIFFORD EUGENE (CLIFF LEVINGSTON)**
Basketball player, basketball coach. **Personal:** Born Jan 4, 1961, San Diego, CA. **Educ:** Wichita State Univ, attended 1982. **Career:** Basketball player (retired), basketball coach; Detroit Pistons, 1982-84; Atlanta Hawks, 1984-90; Chicago Bulls, 1990-92; PAOK Thessaloniki, 1992-93; Buckler Bologna, 1993; Denver Nuggets, 1994-95; Ft Wayne Furhead coachy, asst coach, 2000; Dodge City Legend, asst coach, 2001, head coach, 2002; Harlem Globetrotters, asst coach, 2003-04; St. Louis Flight, coach, 2004; Gary Steel heads, asst coach, 2005, head coach, 2007; Kans Cagerz, asst coach, 2006; Okla Cavalry, 2007; Mich City Marquette High Sch, asst coach, 2011; Rochester Razorsharks, head coach, 2012; Halifax Rainmen, head coach.

**LEVISTER, DR. ERNEST CLAYTON, JR.**
Physician. **Personal:** Born Feb 4, 1946, New York, NY; son of Ernest Sr and Ruth Amos; married Christine; children: E Clay & Michelle Nicole. **Educ:** Lincoln Univ, AB, chem, 1958; Lafayette Col, BS, chem engr, 1958; HowardUniv Col Med, MD, 1964. **Career:** Jersey City Med Ctr, internship internal med, 1964-65; Hahnemann Univ Hosp, residency, radiol, 1965-65; VA Med Ctr, residency, internal med, 1966-69; Norfolk VA, internal med & cardiol pvt pract, 1974-78; Embassy USA Lagos Nigeria, med attache, 1978-79; George Wash Sch Med, asst prof, prof, 1973-74; Eastern Va Med Sch, asst prof, 1974-81; Tuskegee Inst, Sch Eng, instr; San Bernardino CA, pvt pract internal & occup med, 1979-; Med Talk Show Norfolk, radio host, 1980-81; Am Col Prev Med, fel, 1991; Univ Calif-Irvine, clin prof internal & occup med, 2002-. **Orgs:** Inst Sch Engr Tuskegee Inst, 1958-59; fel Am Col Physicians, 1977; asst clin prof internal & occup med, 1986-01; Los Angeles Coun Black Prof Engrs, 1982-; comnr, Environ Protection Comn, Riverside CA, 1989-91; mem bd trustees, Lincoln Univ; co-founder & pres, JW Vines Med Soc, 1994-01; nat adv bd, Sci Edu New Civic Engagements & Responsibilites; Calif Sco Indust med & Surg. **Honors/Awds:** Media Award, Asn Black Women Entrepreneurs, 1995; Dr Rosemary Schraer Humanitarian Award, 1999; Leadership Award, Calif Med Asn; Black Rose Award, San Bernardino Black Cult Found, 2000; Silver Scalpel Award, Calif Sco Indust med & Surgery, 2000; Outstanding Contribution to the Community Award, San Bernardino County Med Soc, 2003; Robert D. Sparks Leadership Achievement Award, 2004; Champions of Health Professions Diversity Award, Calif Wellness Found, 2008. **Special Achievements:** First African-American to graduate from Lafayette College. **Home Addr:** PO Box 161, Lake Arrowhead, CA 92352-0161. **Business Addr:** Owner, Medical Practice, 1738 N Waterman Ave St 1, San Bernardino, CA 92404, **Business Phone:** (909)883-8683.

**LEVY, VALERIE LOWE**
Executive, social worker, government official. **Personal:** Born New York, NY; married Edward J Levy Jr; children: Vanessa Lynn & Edward Joseph III. **Educ:** NY Univ, BA; City Col NY, grad studies; New Sch Social Res, masters cand. **Career:** New York Dept Aging, dir, Manhatten field off, 1969-79, dir minority affairs, 1990. **Orgs:** Geront Soc Am, 1973-; bd mem, Nat Caucus & Ctr Black Aged, Wash, DC, 1974-2005; Am Pub Health Asn, 1979-; Delta Sigma Theta Sorority. **Honors/Awds:** Has written and presented many papers on aging and the elderly in the US; Also a recognized authority on the minority elderly. **Special Achievements:** One of original organizers & coordinator of the Harlem Interagency Council on Aging. **Home Addr:** 70 W 95 St, New York, NY 10025. **Business Addr:** Director of Minority Affairs, New York City Department for the Aging, 2 Lafayette St, New York, NY 10007, **Business Phone:** (212)442-1000.

**LEVYCHIN, RICHARD**
Accountant. **Personal:** Born Feb 13, 1959, London; son of Cosmo and Mary; married Belinda C; children: Richard Jr. **Educ:** City Univ New York-Baruch Col, BBA, 1980. **Career:** Deloitte Touche, sr acct, 1982-85; Adler & Topal, supvr, 1985-87; Backer, Berson & Adler, supvr, 1987-88; Richard Levychin, CPA, pres, 1988-93; Kahn Boyd Levychin LLP, managing partner, 1994-, managing patner, currently, chief exec officer; RFM Broadcasting Inc, chief financial officer, currently. **Orgs:** Am Inst Cert Pub Accts, 1982-; NY State Soc Cert Pub Accts, 1982-; 100 Black Men, 1985-; treas, 100 Black Men Inc; Nat Asn Black Accts Inc; Nat Asn Tax Prof; Nat Asn Black Accts Inc; US Hisp Advocacy Asn; bd mem, Entrepreneurs' Orgn; treas & bd mem, New York chap One; co-chairperson, EO 2030; Asn Latin Professionals Finance & Acct. **Honors/Awds:** The 40 Under 40, Network Jour, 1998; Nat Bus Coun Fel, US Hisp Advocacy Asn, 2009; Best Accountant, New York Enterprise Report, 2013. **Home Addr:** 20 Plz St E, Brooklyn, NY 11238, **Home Phone:** (718)638-0276. **Business Addr:** Chief Executive Officer, Managing Partner, Kahn Boyd Levychin, LLP, 110 Wall St, New York, NY 10005-4322, **Business Phone:** (212)785-9700.

**LEWELLEN, MICHAEL ELLIOTT**
Public relations executive, administrator. **Personal:** Born Jan 16, 1960, Marianna, AR; son of Herman L and Mildred King; married Merle Williams; children: Elliott. **Educ:** Ark State Univ, Jonesboro, AR, BS, jour, 1983. **Career:** Pine Bluff Com, Pine Bluff, Ark, sports reporter, 1982-85; Bloom Tennis Ctr, Pine Bluff, Ark, tennis pro, 1983-85; Southwestern Bell Tel, St Louis, Mo, pub rel mgr, 1985-91; FOX Sports Net, vpres media rels; Nike Inc, urban & minority affairs dir; Universal Orlando Resort, vpres media rels; Cent Fla Urban League, pres & chief exec officer, chmn dirs; Portland Trail Blazers, vpres, cr vpres commun & pub engagement; Black Entertainment TV, vpres corp commun, sr vpres corp commun, currently. **Orgs:** Treas, St Louis Asn Black Journalists, 1987-88; bd dir, nat adv coun, Nat Asn Partners Educ, 1989-; bd dir, St Louis Jour Found, 1990; pres, Int Asn Bus Communicators, St Louis Chap, 1990; Nat Asn Black Journalists, Nat Black Pub Rels Soc; Int Asn Bus Communicators; Pub Rels Soc Am; Kappa Alpha Psi Fraternity; US Prof Tennis Asn; Urban League Portland; Ore Asn Minority Entrepreneurs. **Home Addr:** 17453 SW McKnight Lane, Beaverton, OR 97006, **Home Phone:** (503)531-0699. **Business Addr:** Senior Vice President for Corporate Communications, Black Entertainment TV, 1900 W Pl NE, Washington, DC 20018, **Business Phone:** (202)608-2003.

**LEWIS, ALBERT RAY**
Football player, football coach. **Personal:** Born Oct 6, 1960, Mansfield, LA; children: Julian, Dylan & Dakota Gonzalez. **Educ:** Grambling State Univ. **Career:** Football player (retired), football coach; Kans City Chiefs, corner back & defensive back, 1983, left cornerback, 1984-91, 1993, right cornerback, 1992; Los Angeles Raiders, right cornerback, 1994-98; Oakland Raiders, right cornerback, 1995-97, free safety, 1998; San Diego Chargers, asst sec coach, 2006. **Honors/Awds:** Pro Bowl, 1987-90; NFL All-Star Team, Sporting News, 1989, 1990; AFC Top Defensive Back, Nat Football League Players Asn, 1989; PFWA All-Pro, 1989, 1990; Kansas City Chiefs Hall of Fame, 2007.

**LEWIS, HON. ALEXIS OTIS**
Judge. **Educ:** Wash Univ Sch law, JD; Southern Ill Univ, Carbondale, BA, child develop; Southern Ill Univ, Edwardsville, MA, coun. **Career:** Judge (retired); St Clair County, asst atty; Ill fed ct, E St Louis, pro se law clerk; St Clair State atty Off, prosecutor; State Ill, Circuit Ct, 20th Judicial Circuit, assoc judge. **Orgs:** Ill Bar Asn, 1985-. **Special Achievements:** First Black female judge of St Clair County. **Business Addr:** Associate Judge, State of Illinois Circuit Court 20th Judicial Circuit, 10 Pub Sq, Belleville, IL 62220, **Business Phone:** (618)277-7325.

**LEWIS, ALMERA P.**
Educator, social worker, association executive. **Personal:** Born Oct 23, 1935, Chicago, IL; married Thomas P; children: Tracy & Todd. **Educ:** Univ Wis, BS, 1957; Loyola Univ, MSW, 1959. **Career:** Day Care Ctrs & Sch, counr; Ment Health Ctr, psychiat & social worker, 1959-65; Crittenton Comprehensive Care Ctr, supvr prof staff, 1966-68; Pk Forest Sch Syst, social worker, 1968-69; Chicago Circle-jane Adams Sch Social Work, work prest; Univ Ill, prof, dean studs, social work, actg dean, 1990-91, assoc prof emerita, currently. **Orgs:** Nat bd dir, Nat Asn Social Workers; Ill Asn Sch Social Workers; Acad Cert Social Workers; Am Asn Univ Prof Bd; Women's Community United Cerebral Palsy Greater Chicago; Chicago Urban League PUSH; Art Inst Chicago. **Home Addr:** 635 E Groveland Pk, Chicago, IL 60616-4104, **Home Phone:** (312)949-1311. **Business Addr:** Associate Professor Emerita, University of Illinois-Chicago, 1040 West Harrison St, Chicago, IL 60607-7134, **Business Phone:** (312)996-7096.

**LEWIS, ALONZO TODD**
Health services administrator. **Personal:** Born Jun 29, 1969, Detroit, MI; son of Alonzo and Vera. **Educ:** Univ Mich, BA, sociol, 1991,

MHSA, 1993. **Career:** Mercy Health Serv, mgt fel, 1993-94; Mercy Hosp, dir sr servs, 1994; Henry Ford Health Syst, adminr, 1997-99; Root Learning, managing dir healthcare pract; William Beaumont Hosps, vpres pediat & cardiovasc med serv lines, 2008-. **Orgs:** Alpha Phi Alpha Fraternity, 1989-; assoc, Am Col Health Care Exec, 1991-; Nat Asn Health Serv Exec, 1991-; bd mem, Adult Well-Being Serv; Kaiser Permanente; GlaxoSmithKline; Kelli Gilpin. **Home Addr:** 742 Lothrop, Detroit, MI 48202, **Home Phone:** (313)875-7602. **Business Addr:** vice president for Pediatrics Service Line, Beaumont Hospital, 131 Kercheval Ave, Detroit, MI 48213, **Business Phone:** (313)579-4000.

## LEWIS, REV. DR. ALVIN, JR.

Clergy, executive, consultant, consultant. **Personal:** Born Oct 1, 1935, Chicago, IL; married Juanita L; children: Alvin Vaughn, Lydia Janese & Lystrelle Daneen. **Educ:** Northern Bapt Sem, theol studies, 1962; KS State Univ, BS, hist & sci, MS, family & child develop, 1970, PhD, adult develop & aging, 1974; Garrett Evangelicol Theol Sem, MDiv, christian educ & pastoral coun, 1992. **Career:** Consultant (retired); Minorities Res Ctr, family consult, 1966-74; Kans State Univ, from instr to asst prof, 1970-75; Minor Res & Res Ctr, dir, 1973-75; Bd Christian Educ Ch God, assoc secy, 1975-89; Nat Asn Church God, chief exec officer, 1989-92, exec dir; Vernon Pk Church God, minister admin & spec programmer, 1992-; Beverly Nat Bank, Adv Bd, mem, 1997-99; Christian Coun Ctr Madison County, vice chmn; Fourth Dist ChicagoYouthnet Chicago, Ill, chmn; Church God, Credentials Bd, secy; Church God, Miss, Ministerial Assembly, vice chmn; First Ch God, pastor, prof, dir; Emporia State Univ; Anderson Univ, Sch Theol; Mid-Am Bible Col; Chicago State Univ; Bay Ridge Christian Col; Wesley Bible Col; Wesley Bibl Theol Sem; Bay Ridge Christian Col, dir & pastor, currently; Mid-Am Christian Univ, instr, currently. **Orgs:** Pres, Jct Manhattan Nat Asn Advan Colored People, 1967-71; chmn, Madison County Urban League, 1987-89; Phi Alpha Theta, 1969-71; nat dir adult & family life educ, Nat Bd Christian Educ, Church God, 1974-89; Nat Coun Family Rel; dir, Nat Met Black Family Conf; Am Asn Univ Prof; vice chmn & comnr, Family Life Nat Coun Church; supvr & clin mem, Nat Acad Counr & Family Therapists Inc; cert leader marriage enrichment, Asn Couples Marriage Enrichment; Beverly Nat Bank; served educ consult Africa Caribbean & Europe; pres, Mahattan-Jct City, Kans Nat Asn Advan Colored People; chmn, Chicago Area Ministers & Laymen Fel. **Honors/Awds:** Omicron Hon Soc, 1968. **Business Addr:** Pastor, Director, Bay Ridge Christian College, PO Box 726, Kendleton, TX 77451, **Business Phone:** (979)532-3982.

## LEWIS, ANANDA (SARASVATI ANANDA LEWIS)

Television show host. **Personal:** Born Mar 21, 1973, San Diego, CA; children: Son. **Educ:** Howard University, B.A. in History. **Career:** Black Entertainment Television Network (BET Network), "Teen Summit" show, 1994-97; "MTV Live," Host, 1997; MTV's "Total Request Live," 1999-01; Hollywood Squares (TV game show), 2000-01; "The Ananda Lewis Show," (Syndicated), Host, 2001-02; "The Insider," Host, 2004-. **Honors/Awds:** NAACP Image Award, Interview with First Lady Hillary Rodham Clinton for "Teen Summit," 1997; "People" Magazine, 50 Most Beautiful People, 2000.

## LEWIS, ANDRE

Banker, president (organization). **Personal:** Born May 4, 1960, Walterboro, SC; son of William and Clara Lee Martino; married Queen E Govan; children: Shana Nicole & William Andre. **Educ:** SC State Col, Orangeburg, BS, acct, 1982. **Career:** First Union Nat Bank, Columbia, SC, br mgt, 1983-87; SC Nat Bank, Columbia, SC, assoc vpres corp banking, 1987-88; Victory Savings Bank, Columbia, SC, pres, 1988-92; Richland Teachers Coun FCU, pres, chief exec officer, 1992-99; TLC Real Estate Holdings, pres, 1997-. **Orgs:** Comt mem, United Way Midlands, 1989-90; bd mem, Greater Columbia Chamber Com, 1989-90; bd mem, Comt 100, 1990-92. **Honors/Awds:** Business Person of the Year, Phi Beta Lambda, 1988; Outstanding Alumnus, Upper Dorchester Alumni SC State Col, 1989; Outstanding Bus Achievement, Black Enterprise Magazine, 1990. **Home Addr:** PO Box 7432, Columbia, SC 29202-7432. **Business Addr:** President, TLC Real Estate Holdings, PO Box 7432, Columbia, SC 29202-7432, **Business Phone:** (803)799-6045.

## LEWIS, DR. ANGELA K.

Educator. **Personal:** Born Birmingham, AL. **Educ:** Univ Ala, BA, polit sci regional & urban planning, 1994; Univ Tenn, MPA, 1996, PhD, polit sci & regional & urban planning, 2000. **Career:** Univ Tenn, black grad fel recipient; Univ Ala, Birmingham, African Am Studies Prog, actg asst dir, dept govt, undergrad prog dir, from asst prof to assoc prof; Univ Ala, Tuscaloosa, asst prof, dept polit sci; High Pt Univ, High Pt, Nc, dept hist & polit sci, asst prof. **Orgs:** McNair fel Univ Tenn; Delta Sigma Theta Sorority Inc fel; Black Grad Opportunity Prog fel Univ Tenn; Am Polit Sci Asn; Am Asn Univ Professors; Nat Conf Black Polit Scientists; Midwest Polit Sci Asn; Southern Polit Sci Asn; Nat Coun Black Studies; Southern Polit Sci Asn; Emerging Scholars Interdisciplinary Network; Jack & Jill Am, Birmingham Chap; Ala State Social Action Comt, Delta Sigma Theta Sorority Inc; Jefferson County Alumnae Chap, Delta Sigma Theta Sorority Inc; Faith Chapel Christian Ctr, Life Group Host, iConnect Team; Nat Asn Advan Colored People; bd dir, pres, Love Temple Church Inc; Ala Citizens Const Reform, Deleg, Mock Const Conv; Whos Who Black Birmingham, 2008 & 2006; Ala Black Fac Asn; Delta Sigma Theta Sorority Inc; Univ Tenn, Pi Sigma Alpha, Polit Sci Hon Soc & Pub Admin Hon Soc. **Special Achievements:** Nominated for the UAB School of Social and Behavioral Sciences Alumni Teaching Award. **Business Addr:** Professor, University of Alabama at Birmingham, 1720 2nd Ave S, Birmingham, AL 35294-1152, **Business Phone:** (205)934-8416.

## LEWIS, ARTHUR A., JR.

Accountant, auditor. **Personal:** Born Nov 4, 1925, Los Angeles, CA; son of Arthur and Verna Deckard Williams; married Elizabeth; children: Ivy, Derek, Cornell, Arthur III, Jeffrey & Jason. **Educ:** Univ Calif, Los Angeles, BA, acct & finance, 1947. **Career:** Auditor (retired); acct; Dept Energy, audit investr; Defense Contract Audit Agency, auditor, 1952-82; Golden State Mutual Life Ins Co, 1947-52; Vending Mach Bus La, owner, 1954-; Lewis Tax Serv, La, owner, 1962-. **Orgs:** Bd dir, Southeast Symphony Asn; Fed Govt Accountants Asn; Nat Asn Advan Colored People; Urban League; Alpha Phi Alpha Frat; trustee, Lincoln Memorial Cong Church, Los Angeles. **Honors/Awds:** Cert, Cert Internal Auditor. **Home Addr:** 1749 Va Rd, Los Angeles, CA 90019, **Home Phone:** (323)737-2559. **Business Addr:** Owner, Lewis Tax Service, 2415 W Martin Luther King Blvd, Los Angeles, CA 90008, **Business Phone:** (323)295-2258.

## LEWIS, ARTHUR W.

Consultant. **Personal:** Born Jul 1, 1926, New York, NY; son of Arthur and Marlon; married Frances. **Educ:** Dartmouth Col, BA, 1966, MA, 1969; Foreign Serv Inst, postgrad, 1970. **Career:** US Info Agency, foreign serv, 1951-; US Embassy, cult affairs officer, Bucharest, 1970-72, counr pub affairs, Lusaka, 1972-74, Addis Ababa, 1974-77, Lagos, 1977-79, dir african affairs, 1979-; Repub Sierre Leone, US ambassador, 1983-86; Fletcher Sch Law & Diplomacy, edward r murrow fel, 1986-87; US Embassy Freetown, retired; Naval Res Officers Training Corps, fac; Nord Resources Corp, sr consult, currently. **Orgs:** Commmissioning crew USS Saratoga; bd mem, Whitfield Found. **Home Addr:** 1446 Jonquil St NW, Washington, DC 20012-1414, **Home Phone:** (202)882-0597. **Business Addr:** Senior Consultant, Nord Resources Corp, 1 W Wetmore Rd Suite 203, Tucson, AZ 85705, **Business Phone:** (520)292-0266.

## LEWIS, AYLWIN B.

Executive. **Personal:** Born May 28, 1954, Houston, TX; son of Albert and Rowena; married Novaline. **Educ:** Univ Houston, BBA, bus mgt, BA, eng lit, 1976, MBA, 1990; Houston Baptist Univ, MA, human resource mgt. **Career:** Jack Box, dist mgr opers; KFC, sr vpres, mkt & opers develop, 1995-96; Pizza Hut, sr vice pres opers, 1996-97, chief operating officer, 1997-99; YUM! Brands, chief operating officer, 1991-2003, pres, chief multibranding & operating officer, 2003-04; Tricon Global Restaurants, exec vice pres opers & new bus develop, 2000, chief operating officer, 2000-02; Halliburton, bd mem, 2001; Walt Disney Co, bd dirs, 2004; Starwood Hotels & Resorts, bd dirs; Kmart Holding Corp, pres & chief exec officer, 2004-05; Sears Holdings corp, bd mem, 2004-, pres & chief exec officer, 2005-08; Potbelly Corp, pres & chief exec officer, 2008-. **Orgs:** Trustee, Rush Univ Med Ctr; dir, World Bus Chicago; dir, Halliburton Co; chmn governance & dir, Walt Disney Co, 2004-. **Business Addr:** President, Chief Executive Officer, Potbelly Corp, 222 Merchandise Mart Plz 23rd Fl, Chicago, IL 60654, **Business Phone:** (312)951-0600.

## LEWIS, DR. BETTYE DAVIS

Association executive, president (organization). **Educ:** Univ Houston, psychol; Prairie View A&M Univ Col Nursing, BS, nursing, 1959; Univ Houston, BA, 1972; Tex Southern Univ, MA, EdD, PhD, 1982. **Career:** Allen Health Care Inc, dir nurses; Diversified Health Care Syst Inc, adminr & supv nurse, chief exec officer; Tex Southern Univ, adj prof; Nat Black Nurses Asn, pres, 2005; Nat Black Nurses Asn Inc, Diversified Health Care Systs, chief exec officer; Allen HealthCare Inc, Dir Nurses, Currently. **Orgs:** Bd mem, Ethnic Coalition Minority Nurse Asn; Black Nurses Asn Greater Houston; Jessie Jackson Acad; Negro Coun Black Women; Nat Cong Black Women; United Negro Col Fund; Am Cancer Soc; Alzheimer's & Related Diseases, St TX; St Bar Grievance Comt; bd mem, Nat Heartburn Alliance; sr fel & Bd mem, Am Leadership Forum; fel, Int Soc Hypertension Blacks; bd mem, Nat Black Nurses Asn Inc; trustee, NLN Foundation for Nursing Education. **Business Addr:** Director of Nurses, Allen Healthcare Inc, 111 Colchester Ave, Burlington, VT 05401-1473.

## LEWIS, BILL. See LEWIS, DR. WILLIAM A.

## LEWIS, BILLIE JEAN

Librarian. **Personal:** Born Dec 6, 1947, Eden, MI; daughter of William Manns and Darnella Blackstock Worthington; married Jerome M Jr; children: Jerome V & Jill Renee. **Educ:** Corning Community Col, AAS, bus Admin, 1983; Cornell Univ, cert, indust rels & human serv, 1984; Fla A&M Univ, BS, 1988; Univ Mich, MS, 1989. **Career:** Corning Glass Works, qual, ade aide, 1984-85; Fla State Univ, ade aide, 1985-88; Mich State Univ, GEAC operator, 1988; Wayne State Univ, res asst, 1989; Detroit Pub Libr, C librn, 1989-92, asst mgr, C librn, 1992-. **Orgs:** Am Libr Asn, 1989-90; chap, AFA C Bk C chap, Fund-Raising Community, C Bk Community, 1990-; Asn AFA Librns, 1992-; Detroit Pub Libr C Servs. **Home Addr:** 12751 W 10 Mile Rd, Oak Park, MI 48237, **Home Phone:** (313)541-0492. **Business Addr:** Librarian, Detroit Public Library, 3648 W Vernor Hwy, Detroit, MI 48216-1441, **Business Phone:** (313)297-9381.

## LEWIS, DR. BRENDA NEUMON

Educator, college administrator. **Personal:** Born NJ; daughter of Jacob and Mari Neumon; married Woodrow Jr; children: Kayin, Kimani & Killian. **Educ:** Univ Copenhagen, attended 1969; Doane Col, BA, 1970; Clark Atlanta Univ, MA, eng educ, 1974; Ohio State Univ, PhD, educ admin, 1985. **Career:** Educator (retired), college administrator (retired); Ohio State Univ, coordr, 1975-79; Univ Md, assoc dir coop educ, 1981-84; Old Dom Univ, dir interdisciplinary studs, 1985-99, actg assoc dean, 1995-96, asst vpres grad studies, assoc vpres grad studies, asst dean grad studies; Norfolk State Univ, spec asst to vpres, 1999-2000, assoc vpres acad affairs, 2000-04. **Orgs:** Bd mem, YWCA, 1993-99, bd pres, 1995-97; bd mem, Places C, 1994-97; bd mem, Old Dom Univ Credit Union, 1994-2000, chair, nominating comt, 1996, 1998; Va Symphony Edu Comm, 1997-98; personnel comt, UWCA S Hampton Roads, 1999-. **Home Addr:** 4325 Wishart Rd, Virginia Beach, VA 23455-5632, **Home Phone:** (757)318-7567. **Business Addr:** Associate Vice President for Graduate Studies, Old Dominion University, 212A Koch Hall Admin Bldg, Norfolk, VA 23529-0082, **Business Phone:** (757)683-4885.

## LEWIS, BYRON E., SR.

Executive, television producer. **Personal:** Born Dec 25, 1931, Newark, NJ; son of Thomas Eugene and Myrtle Evelyn Allen; children: Byron Eugene Jr; married Sylvia Wong. **Educ:** Long Island Univ, BA, 1953; NY Univ, grad study; City Col NY; Adelphi Univ, PhD. **Career:** Urbanite Mag, co-founder, 1961; Amalgamated Publs, asst advert mgr, 1963-64; Tuesday Mag, vpres & advert dir, 1963-68; Uniworld Group Inc, founder, chmn & chief exec officer, chmn emer, 1968-; Afro Mkt Co, pres, 1968-69; Kenneth Gibson's Mayoral Campaign, 1971; Black Polit Summit, 1972; Sounds City, exec producer, 1974-75; UniWorld Entertainment, 1977; This Far by Faith, creator, 1977; UniWorld Hispanic, 1980; Reverend Jesse Jackson's First Presidential Campaign, 1984; Black Forum, exec producer, 1989; Acapulco Black Film Festival, creator. Producer: Ann Black Filmmakers Hall Fame; UniWorld Healthcare, 2002; Black radio serial; America's Black Forum; This Far By Faith. **Orgs:** Lectr, Black Col; Black Exec Exch Prog Nat Urban League; Am Inst Pub Serv; Phoenix House Found; New York Sports Comn; metro bd gov, U.S. Olympic Comt; bd, Apollo Theater Found, Jackie Robinson Educ Found, NYC Mission Soc, Long Island Univ. **Home Addr:** 67 Pk Terr E, New York, NY 10034. **Business Addr:** Founder, Chairman & Chief Executive Officer, UniWorld Group Inc, Fl 16 100 Ave of the Americas 16th Fl, New York, NY 10013, **Business Phone:** (212)219-7110.

## LEWIS, CARL (FREDERICK CARLTON LEWIS)

Track and field athlete, actor. **Personal:** Born Jul 1, 1961, Birmingham, AL; son of William McKinley Jr (deceased) and Evelyn Lawler. **Educ:** Univ Houston, communs, 1979. **Career:** Track & field athlete (retired), actor, executive; track & field athlete, 1984-96; Films: Atomic Twister, 2002; Alien Hunter, 2003; The Last Adam, 2005; Tournament of Dreams, 2006; Material Girls, 2006; Fck You Pay Me!, 2007; Tournament of Dreams, 2007; Speed Zone!; The Weakest Link; Rift, exec producer, 2011; Christmas in Compton, 2012; Carl Lewis Found, founder, currently. **Honors/Awds:** World Championships: Pan American Games, San Juan, Bronze Medal, 1979; Helsinki, gold medal, 100m, 4x100 m, Long Jump, 1983; Rome, gold medal, 100 m, 4x100 m, Long Jump, 1987; Indianapolis, gold medal, 1987; Tokyo, gold medal, 100m, 4x100 m, Silver, Long Jump, 1991; Stuttgart, gold medal, 200 m, 1993; Olympic Games: Los Angeles, gold medal, 100m, 200m, 4x100m, long jump, 1984; Seoul, gold medal, 100 m, Long Jump, 1988, silver medal, 1998; Barcelona, gold medal, 4x100 m, Long Jump, 1992; Atlanta, gold medal, Long Jump; Sportsman of the Century, Int Olympic Comt; Olympian of the Century, Am sports mag; Received Numerous Awards. **Special Achievements:** World athlete of the year, 1982-86; Olympic Athlete of the Century. **Business Addr:** Actor, Cleve Lewis Management, 10940 S Parker Rd Suite 526, Parker, CO 80134, **Business Phone:** (303)531-4469.

## LEWIS, CARMEN CORTEZ

Educator. **Personal:** Born Detroit, MI; daughter of John E Farris and Maggie M Farris; married Thomas J. **Educ:** Univ Detroit, BA, 1973; Wayne State Univ, MEd, 1987. **Career:** Detroit bd Educ, Ruddiman Mid Sch, teacher, 1974-2001; Univ Pub Sch, teacher, 2001-. **Orgs:** Vpres, Zeta Phi Beta; treas, State Mich; NCP, Women's Community, Detroit Br; March Dimes Orgn; Retirement Community, Detroit Br; pres, Greater Ebenezer Baptist Church, Usher bd 2; comt mem, Ladies Distinction; comt mem, Nat Asn Bus Women; Greeters Ministry Greater Ebenezer Church. **Home Addr:** 9190 Dale Ave, Redford, MI 48239, **Home Phone:** (313)532-0462. **Business Addr:** Teacher, University Public School, 2001 Martin Luther King Jr Blvd, Detroit, MI 48208, **Business Phone:** (313)596-3780.

## LEWIS, CAROL J.

Association executive. **Orgs:** Bd dir, Women Color Found & Health Ministries. **Business Addr:** Member, Board of Directors, Women of Color Foundation & Health Ministries, PO Box 3835, Southfield, MI 48037, **Business Phone:** (248)569-3532.

## LEWIS, CHARLES HENRY

Consultant, business owner. **Personal:** Born Nov 22, 1930, Bessemer, AL; son of Charles M (deceased) and Erline Mills Carter; married Joyce Jean Hale; children: Joyce Rene Rich, Donna Kay (deceased) & Charles Michael. **Educ:** Langston Univ, BS, 1953; Wayne State Univ, MA, recreation & pk serv, 1967; Mich State Univ, MBA, 1974. **Career:** Consult (retired); City Detroit Recreation Dept, recreation instr, ctr supvr, 1956-64; Detroit Pub Sch, sch-community agt, 1964-66; City Detroit Comn C & Youth, proj dir, 1966-69; City Detroit Recreation Dept, recreation instr, 1969-71; Blvd Gen Hosp, dir, personnel serv, 1971-74; Wayne State Univ, assoc prof, chair, rec parks serv, 1974-83; Mich Coun Humanities grant, Urban Recreation Conf, 1975; City Detroit Recreation Dept, supt recreation div, 1983-93; Creative Holistic Leisure Serv, leisure consult, owner; host; writer; speaker. **Orgs:** Mich Recreation & Pk Asn, 1974-; Nat Recreation & Pk Asn, 1974-; pres, Nat Recreation & Pk Ethnic Minority Soc, 1981-83; fel Am Acad Pk & Recreation Admin, 1991-; chmn, Detroit Recreation Adv Comt, 2002-03; World Future Soc; pres, treas, Prof Recreation Employees, Detroit Local 836AFSCME; Alpha Phi Alpha Fraternity; Langston Univ Alumni Asn. **Honors/Awds:** Citation Award, 1978, 1984; Fel Award, Mich Recreation & Park Asn, 1985; State Mich 84th Legis, Spec Tribute, 1988; Ernest T Atwell Award, Nat Recreation & Park Ethnic Minority Soc, 1991; Various Awards from local community groups and organization. **Special Achievements:** First African Am Chmn, Wayne State Univ Recreation & Park Services Dept; First African Am Superintendant, Rec Div, Detroit Rec Dept; Established Leisure Resource Center & Charles H Lewis Collection, Detroit Gray Branch Library, 1992; Co-Chair, Community Analysis Committee UCS Report, "Looking At Leisure: A Study of the Negative Aspects"; Numerous articles, Papers and Proposals written; Hall of Fame, Mich Recreation & Pk Asn. **Home Addr:** 3202 Waverly St, Detroit, MI 48238-3346, **Home Phone:** (313)868-1592. **Business Addr:** Leisure Consultant, Owner, Creative Holistic Leisure Services, 3202 Waverly, Detroit, MI 48238, **Business Phone:** (313)868-1592.

## LEWIS, CHARLES MCARTHUR

Manager, librarian. **Personal:** Born May 29, 1949, Fitzgerald, GA; married Katrinda McQueen. **Educ:** Ft Valley State Col, BS, math, 1971; Univ Ga, MA, math, 1973; Ga State Univ, MBA, 1984. **Career:** Southern Bell Tel & Tel, engr, 1973-78, mgt skills assessor, 1978-80, staff engr, 1980-86; BellSouth Serv Inc, info systs planner, 1986-, staff mgr. **Orgs:** Alpha Kappa Mu Hon, Soc Ft Valley State Col, 1970; Church Affiliated Orgns, 1983-87; Nat Black MBA Asn, 1986-87. **Honors/Awds:** Speakers Award, 1986. **Home Addr:** 3424 Boring Rd,

Decatur, GA 30034-4401, **Home Phone:** (404)243-3407. **Business Addr:** Staff Manager, BellSouth Service Inc, 675 W Peachtree St NE, Atlanta, GA 30375, **Business Phone:** (404)927-2047.

## LEWIS, CHARLES MICHAEL

Manager, educator. **Personal:** Born Jul 17, 1949, Columbus, OH; son of Charles W and Irene V Fisher (deceased); married Anita Graham; children: Michael Jr, Christopher Morgan & Anicca. **Educ:** Cent State Univ, Wilberforce, OH, BS, bus, 1971. **Career:** Wilmington Col, Wilmington, OH, admis counr, 1972-74; Bliss Bus Col, Columbus, OH, instr, 1974-78; Huntington Bank, Columbus, OH, Br Load Serv, 1978-79; Anheuser Busch Cos, Columbus, OH, area mgr, 1979-82, dist mgr, 1982-87, Houston, Tex, Southwest regional mgr corp affairs, 1987-. **Orgs:** Bd mem, Houston Area Urban League, 1988-; bd mem, Houston Sun Literacy Acad, 1988-; Alpha Phi Alpha Fraternity Inc; Nat Asn Advan Colored People; New Orleans Urban League, Oakland, Calif. **Honors/Awds:** Black Achievers in Business & Industry, Harlem Branch YMCA, 1983; Second Degree Black Belt Karate, 1971-. **Home Addr:** 3 Tall Sky Pl, The Woodlands, TX 77381, **Home Phone:** (713)363-2154. **Business Addr:** Regional Manager, Corporate Affairs, Anheuser-Busch Co Inc, 1 Busch Pl, St Louis, MO 63118, **Business Phone:** (800)3425-283.

## LEWIS, CLARENCE K.

Automotive executive, business owner. **Career:** Pryor Ford Lincoln-Mercury Inc, owner, 1989-; Cloverleaf Chevrolet Oldsmobile, pres, owner & chief exec officer, 1995-. **Business Addr:** Owner, President, Cloverleaf Chevrolet Geo & Oldsmobile Inc, 150 Turnpike Rd, Westborough, MA 01581, **Business Phone:** (508)366-9996.

## LEWIS, CLEVELAND ARTHUR

Engineer, clergy. **Personal:** Born Apr 21, 1942, Selma, AL; son of Elsie and Levi; married Betty Faye Harris; children: Aisha & Jahmilla. **Educ:** Purdue Univ, AAS, 1972, BEng, indust engineering technol, 1976; Ind Wesleyan Univ, Marion, IN, MBA, 1991. **Career:** Chrysler Corp, indust engr, 1972-76; Clevetech Work Systs Inc, pres & chief exec officer, 1975-; Allison Transmission Div, sr prod engr, sr indust engr, currently; Ind Univ; Purdue Univ Indianapolis, mech engineering dept, instr & prof; US Food Serv; First Timothy Lutheran Church, deacon, currently. **Orgs:** Inst Indust Eng, 1970-; bd regents Concordia Col, 1986-; bd dir, Purdue Univ, Bd Alumni. **Home Addr:** 5085 Knollton Rd, Indianapolis, IN 46228-2929, **Home Phone:** (317)257-6383. **Business Addr:** Deacon, First Timothy Lutheran Church, 2190 Lafayette Rd, Indianapolis, IN 46222-3142, **Business Phone:** (317)257-6383.

## LEWIS, CLINTON A., JR.

President (organization). **Personal:** married Teresa; children: 1. **Educ:** Fairfield Univ, BS, biol; Fairleigh Dickinson Univ, MBA, mkt, 1993. **Career:** Pfizer Animal Health (PAH), sales rep, 1988-, Pratt Pharmaceut, regional mgr New Eng region, gen mgr, Pfizer Caribbean, vpres sales, pres US opers, 2007-2013; Zoetis, US Opers, pres & exec vpres, 2013-15, Int Opers, pres & exec vpres, 2015-. **Orgs:** Bd mem, Animal Health Inst (AHI), 2007-, vice chmn bd, 2009-10, chmn, 2011-12; Cornell Vet Col Adv Coun; bd trustee, Fairfield Univ; nat bd mem, INROADS Inc. **Home Addr:** , Baldwin, NY. **Business Addr:** President, Executive Vice President, Zoetis, 100 Campus Dr, Florham Park, NJ 07932, **Business Phone:** (973)822-7000.

## LEWIS, HON. DANIEL

Judge. **Personal:** Born Apr 22, 1946, New York, NY; son of Matthew Gray and Anna Copeland; married Vernice Jackson; children: Sharon Elaine & Morgan Nicole. **Educ:** New Lincoln Sch, acad degree, 1963; Brown Univ, BA, 1967; Pa Law Sch, JD, 1970. **Career:** State Dept Bur African Affairs, Wash, DC, intern, 1966; Am Emb Rome, intern 1967; Nat CORE, researcher 1968; Harlem Commonwealth Coun New York, writer, 1969; Dist Atty Off, asst dist atty, 1970-75; NY State, Appellate Div, First Dept, 1971; NY State Dept Law, Harlem Off, asst atty-gen--charge, 1975; NY State, Div Criminal Justice Servs, civil rights comp officer, 1975-77; NY K State Supreme Ct, prin law clerk, Justice Browne, 1977-91; New York Criminal Ct, judge, 1992-95; NY Supreme Ct, Queens County judge, 1996-. **Orgs:** Vol SCLC SCOPE Proj, AL, 1966; parliamentarian, Epsilon Sigma Chap, Phi Beta Sigma, 1982-; One Hundred Black Men; Am Civil Lib Union; trustee, Prof C's Sch arbitrator, Small Claims Ct, 1986-91; pres, Asn Law Secretaries, 1988-91; Nat Cong Racial Equality; Jamaica Nat Asn Advan Colored People; Dept State, Am Embassy, Rome; Brown Youth Guid. **Business Addr:** Judge, Supreme Court Queens County, 125-01 Queens Blvd, Kew Gardens, NY 11415, **Business Phone:** (718)298-1359.

## LEWIS, DARREN JOEL

Baseball player, athletic coach. **Personal:** Born Aug 28, 1967, Berkeley, CA. **Educ:** Univ Calif, Berkeley, BA, social sci, 2009. **Career:** Baseball player (retired), athletic coach; Oakland Athletics, 1990; San Francisco Giants, outfielder, 1991-95; Cincinnati Reds, 1995; Chicago White Sox, 1996-97; Los Angeles Dodgers, 1997; Boston Red Sox, 1998-2001; Chicago Cubs, 2002; Cal State Univ E Bay, asst baseball coach & recruiter, 2015-16, assoc head baseball coach, currently; Tastes Fly, pres & co-founder; Dougherty Valley High Sch, coach. **Orgs:** Chabot Col's Hall Fame. **Honors/Awds:** NL Gold Glove Award, 1994. **Business Addr:** Associate Head Baseball Coach, California State University East Bay, 25800 Carlos Bee Blvd, Hayward, CA 94542, **Business Phone:** (510)885-4381.

## LEWIS, DAVID BAKER

Lawyer, educator, administrator. **Personal:** Born Jun 9, 1944, Detroit, MI; son of Walton Adams and Dorothy Florence Baker; married Kathleen McCree; children: Aaron McCree & Sarah Susan; married Lisa Charles; children: Dallas Charles. **Educ:** Oakland Univ, BA, bus admin, 1965; Univ Chicago Grad Sch Bus, MBA, 1967; Univ Mich, JD, 1970. **Career:** Northern Trust Co, admin dept, 1966; Morgan Guaranty Trust Co, corp res analyst, 1967; Lewis & Thompson Agency Inc, 1968; Miller Canfield Paddock & Stone, law clerk, 1969; Univ Mich, Afro-Am & African Studies Dept, lectr, 1970; Hon Theodore Levin US Dist Ct, law clerk, 1970-71; Patmon Young & Kirk, assoc atty, 1971-72; Detroit Col Law, assoc prof, 1972-78; Lewis & Munday PC, pres, 1972-82, bd chmn, 1982-; Atty Law, sole practr, 1972; Lewis & Munday's Chmn, Pres & chief exec officer; Sr Shareholder, 1972-2014. **Orgs:** Life mem, Nat Bar Asn, Northern Trust Co, admin dept, 1966; Morgan Guaranty Trust Co, corp res analyst, 1967; Lewis & Thompson Agency Inc, 1968; Miller Canfield Paddock & Stone, law clerk, 1969; Univ Mich, Afro-Am & African Studies Dept, lectr, 1970; Hon Theodore Levin US Dist Ct, law clerk, 1970-71; State Bar Mich, 1970-; Wolverine Bar Asn, 1970-; Detroit Bar Asn, 1970-; fel Am Bar Asn, 1970-; Patmon Young & Kirk, assoc atty, 1971-72; Detroit Col Law, assoc prof, 1972-78; Lewis & Munday PC, pres, 1972-82, bd chmn, 1982-; Atty Law, sole practr, 1972; Lewis & Munday, 1972-2014; Nat Asn Bond Lawyers, 1979-; bd trustee, Mich Opera Theatre, 1982-99; bd dir, Music Hall Ctr Performing Arts, 1983-94; bd dir, Ctr Creative Studies, 1983-96; bd dir, Detroit Symphony Orchestra Inc, 1983-; bd dir, Metrop Affairs Corp, 1984-90; exec comt, bd dir, Inst Am Bus, 1985-; Nat Asn Securities Prof, 1985-; bd trustee, Am Bar Found, 1987-; Client Security Fund, 1988-89; bd dir, Booker T Bus Assoc, 1988-91; bd dir, Nat Conf Community & Justice, 1990-99; SEMCOG-Regional Develop Initiative Oversight Comt, 1990-92; bd dir, Greater Detroit & WindsorJapan-Am Soc, 1990-93; bd dir, Arts Comn City Detroit, 1992-99; bd dir, TRW Inc, 1995-99; bd dir, Comerical Inc, 1995-2004; chmn, LG & E Energy Corp, 1996-2000; bd dir, MA Hanna Co, 1997-2000; bd Mgrs, Fife Elec LLC, 1998-2000; chmn, Oakland Univ Found, 1998-2000; bd dir, Lakefront Capital Adv Inc, 1999-2010; bd dir, Consol Rail Corp, 2000-08; bd dir, chmn, Paradies Metro-Ventures, 2001-10; bd mgrs, Detroit Edison Securitization Funding, 2001-; life mem, Judicial Conf US Ct Appeals Sixth Circuit; mem comt visitors, Univ Mich Law Sch; life mem, Nat Asn Advan Colored People. **Home Addr:** 736 Step Beach St, Detroit, MI 89138, **Home Phone:** (702)778-6461. **Business Addr:** Of Counsel, Lewis & Munday PC, 535 Griswold St Suite 2300, Detroit, MI 48226, **Business Phone:** (313)961-2550.

## LEWIS, DAVID LEVERING

Historian, writer. **Personal:** Born May 25, 1936, Little Rock, AR; son of John Henry Sr and Urnestine A Bell; married Sharon Lynn Siskind; children: Eric Levering, Allison Lillian & Jason Bradwell; married Ruth Ann Stewart; children: Allegra Stewart. **Educ:** Fisk Univ, BA, 1956; Columbia Univ, MA, hist, 1958; London Sch Econs & Polit Sci, PhD, 1962. **Career:** AUS, Landstuhl, Ger, psychiat technician, 1961-62; Univ Md, lectr, 1961-62; Univ Ghana, lectr, 1963-64; Howard Univ, lectr, 1964-65; Univ Notre Dame, asst prof, 1965-66; Morgan State Univ, from asst prof to assoc prof, 1966-70; Univ DC, from assoc prof to prof, 1970-80; Univ Calif, San Diego, Calif, prof, 1981-85; Rutgers State Univ NJ, Martin Luther King Jr Prof, 1985-94, Martin Luther King Jr Univ Prof, 1994-; Univ New York, Grad Ctr, vis prof, 1995-96; MacArthur Found, fel; Ctr Advan Study Behav Sci, fel; Nat Humanities Ctr, fel; Am Philos Socs, fel; Woodrow Wilson Int Ctr Scholars, fel; John Simon Guggenheim Found, fel; New York Univ, Julius Silver Univ Prof & prof hist, 2003-; Writer: Dc: A Bicentennial Hist States & Nation, 1976; W E B Du Bois: Fight Equality & Am Century, 1919-63, 2001, UCSD, 1980-82; Rutgers, 1985-2001; NYU, 2003-2013; Harvard, 2001-02; Emer, 2013. **Orgs:** Fel Am Acad Arts & Sci; fel Am Philos Socs; Am Hist Asn; pres, Soc Am Historians, 2002-; trustee, Nat Humanities Ctr; sen, Phi Beta Kappa. **Special Achievements:** 12 honorary degrees: Emory, Northwestern, Columbia, Bard, Fisk, Bates, Lafayette, Wheaton, New School University, Marymount Manhattan, University of Pittsburgh, John Jay College. **Home Addr:** Hill House 195 S Rd, Stanfordville, NY 12581, **Home Phone:** (845)758-0208. **Business Addr:** Professor of History, Julius Silver University Professor and professor of history, New York University, King Juan Carlos I Ctr, New York, NY 10012-1098, **Business Phone:** (212)998-8619.

## LEWIS, DAWNN

Musician, actor. **Personal:** Born Aug 13, 1961, Brooklyn, NY; daughter of Carl and Joyce; married Johnny Newman. **Educ:** Univ Miami, BA, jour, 1982. **Career:** Television appearances: "Stompin' at the Savoy", 1992; "Kid-N-Play Cartoon"; "voice of Lela"; "A Different World"; "series regular"; "Hangin with Mr.Cooper", 1992-93; feature films: I'm Gonna Get U Sucka, 1988; Your Love, Woman in cleaners, 1999; Nicolas, 2001; Paula, 2002; co-writer; A Different World, theme song, singer; HBO's Dream On; Other works: The Cherokee Kid; Bad Day on the Block, 1997; How to Succeed in Business Without Really Trying; voices for several animated TV series: C Bear & Jamal; Mortal Kombat; Bruno the Kid, 1996; Wayne's Head; Spider Man, 1996; Black Jaq, 1998; The Poof Point, 2001; "A Leela of Her Own", "The Route of All Evil", 2002; "Bend Her", The Sting", 2003; "Medical Investigation"Little Girl True Crime: New York City, "The Boondocks", 2005; The Adventures of Brer Rabbit, 2006; Marvel: Ultimate Alliance, 2006; Holly Hobbie & Friends: Christmas Wishes, 2006; Dream girls, 2006; "Hell on Earth", 2006; "Grim & Evil", 2007; "Handy Manny", 2007; "One Tree Hill", 2008-09; Spider-Man 3, 2007; The Last Sentinel, 2007; Futurama: Bender's Big Score, 2007; Morning Jewel Inc, pres, 1984-; Hell on Earth, 2007; The Rise of the Argonauts, 2008; Futurama: Into the Wild Green Yonder, 2009; The Secret Life of the American Teenager, 2010; Billion Dollar Freshmen, 2011; CSI: Miami, 2012; Strange Frame: Love & Sax , 2012; Let It Shine, 2012; Second Chances, 2013; Monsters University , 2013; Regular Show, 2013; Toy Story of Terror, 2013. **Orgs:** Bd dirs & spokesperson, Campfire Boys & Girls; spokesperson, Nat 4H Club; spokesperson, Planned Parenthood; spokesperson, UNICEF; spokesperson, Inst Black Parenting; dir speakers bur, Arnold Schwarzenegger's Inner City Games. **Honors/Awds:** Illustrious Alumni Award, Univ Miami, 1991; Outstanding Service, Am Lung Asn, 1991; Act-So Award, NAACP; Smile of the Year, Am Dent Asn; Fred Award; Cebe Award; Outstanding Service Award, 1988, 1990, 1991, UNCF; Excellence in Achievement, Howard University, 1992; ASCAP Award & four BMI Honors for Best Song; Grammy, Handel's Messiah: A Soulful Celebration; Gold Record, on the Take 6 Album, So Much To Say; BMI TV Music Award, 1990, 1991, 1992; Integrity Award, Los Angeles Women's Theatre Festival. **Special Achievements:** First graduate to receive musical theatre degree in the University of Miami. **Business Addr:** President, Morning Jewel Inc, PO Box 56718, Sherman Oaks, CA 91413, **Business Phone:** (310)315-4150.

## LEWIS, DR. DELANO EUGENE

Government official, executive, businessperson. **Personal:** Born Nov 12, 1938, Arkansas City, KS; son of Raymond Ernest and Enna W; married Gayle Carolyn Jones; children: Delano Jr, Geoffrey, Brian & Phillip. **Educ:** Univ Kans, BA, 1960; Washburn Sch Law, Topeka, KS, JD, 1963. **Career:** US Dept Justice, gen atty, 1963-65; US Equal Employ Opportunity Comn, staff anal & advice, 1965-66; US Peace Corps, Nigeria & Uganda, assoc dir & country dir, 1966-69; Off Sen Edward W Brooke, legis asst, 1969-71; Off Rep Walter E Fauntroy, admin asst, 1971-73; Chesapeake & Potomac Tel Co, pub affairs mgr, 1973, vpres, 1973-88, pres, 1988-93, chief exec officer, 1990-93; Nat Pub Radio, pres & chief exec officer, 1993-98; Repub S Africa, US ambassador, 1999-2001; Lewis & Assocs, consult pract, 2001; Colgate-Palmolive Co, bd dir, 1991-99, 2001-; NMex State Univ, sr fel, 2006-; Hallburton Co, dir; Guest Serv, dir; Apple Comput, dir; BET, dir; Eastman Kodak Co, dir, currently; Univ Kans, pres. **Orgs:** Bd dir, Comt Found Greater Wash, 1978-; pres, Greater Wash Bd Trade, 1987; Mil Order Knights Malta, 1987-; chmn, Pro Clef Culinary Concepts Alpha Phi Alpha Fraternity; pres, City Nat Bank Wash; Black Entertainment Tv; sr fel Nmex State Univ, 2006, founding dir, 2007; Alpha Phi Alpha. **Honors/Awds:** Washingtonian of the Year, Wash Mag, 1978; President Medal, Catholic Univ Am, 1978; Honorary Degree, Marymount Univ, 1988; Distinguished Community Service Award, Washburn Univ, 1989; Distinguished Alumnae Award, Washburn Univ, 1990; Citizenship Award, Nat Coun Christians & Jews, 1989; Cultural Alliance of Washington Community Service Award, 1991; Honorary Degree, Loyola Col; Honorary Degree, Barry Univ Miami; Kansan of the Year, 2009. **Special Achievements:** First African-American president of National Public Radio, 1993. **Home Addr:** PO Box 1389, Mesilla, NM 88046-1389. **Business Addr:** Director, Colgate-Palmolive Co, 300 Pk Ave, New York, NY 10022-7499, **Business Phone:** (212)310-2000.

## LEWIS, DEREK

Manager, vice president (organization). **Educ:** Hampton Univ, Hampton, VA, BS, bus mgt; Xavier Univ, Cincinnati, OH, MBA. **Career:** Pepsi Beverages Co (PBC), acct rep, 1988-95, mkt mgr Taco Bell Cincinnati, 1995-98, regional sales mgr Phoenix, Ariz, 1998-2001, vpres & gen mgr Portland, Ore, 2001-08, vpres consumer & category insights Pepsi Bottling Group Inc, 2006-08; sr vpres & gen mgr Pepsi Beverages S Region Bus Unit, 2008-12, sr vpres & gen mgr Pepsi N Am, 2012-. **Orgs:** Bd dir, Fla Citrus Sports; bd dir, Cent Fla's Boy Scouts Am; bd dir, YMCA Cent Fla; Exec Leadership Coun; Nat Black MBA Asn; Kappa Alpha Psi Fraternity Inc; bd dir, Am Beverage Asn; Orlando Magic Youth Fund. **Home Addr:** , Orlando, FL. **Business Addr:** Senior Vice President, General Manager, PepsiCo, 700 Anderson Hill Rd, Purchase, NY 10577, **Business Phone:** (800)433-2652.

## LEWIS, DIANE Y.

Administrator, lawyer. **Personal:** Born New York, NY; daughter of George A and Alyce Morris. **Educ:** Beaver Col, Glenside, PA, BA, 1969; Columbia Univ, New York, NY, MS, 1977; Hastings Col Law, JD, 1995. **Career:** Nat Urban League, New York NY, proj dir, 1970-73; Ctr Urban Educ, New York NY, liaison, 1970-71; Trans Urban E, New York NY, consult, 1972-73; Jamaica Urban Develop Corp, Kingston, Jamaica, Wi, social planner, 1974-76; City Oakland, Oakland Calif, sr urban econ analyst, 1977-82, div mgr, 1982-92; Oakland city, dep city atty, 1999-2010; Lewis Law Group, prin, 2010-. **Orgs:** Consult, Trans Urban E Orgn, 1972-73; vpres, Progressive Black Bus &Prof Women, 1983-86; assoc mem, Urban Land Inst, 1984-; chmn, Econ Develop Comn, BAPAC, 1984-86; vpres & secy, chmn, nominations comn, Citi centre Dance Theatre, 1985-89; Niagara Movement Dem Club; Nat Asn Planners; Black Women Organized Polit Action; Nat Forum Black Pub Admin, 1985-; Am Soc Pub Admin, 1988-; mem chmn, Asn Black Families, 1989-92; loan comt mem, Womens Initiative Self Employ, 1990-93; Asn Symp ed, W Northwest Environ Law J; staff, Hastings Law News; Charles Houston Bar Asn; Am Bar Asn; Am Inns Ct; 2nd yr Hastings BLSA; Phi Alpha Delta; Calif Redevelop Asn. **Home Addr:** 1106 Trestle Glen Rd, Oakland, CA 94610-2519. **Business Addr:** Principal, Lewis Law Group, Oakland, CA.

## LEWIS, DUANE

Executive. **Educ:** Southern Univ, BA, mass commun, 1995. **Career:** Southern Dig, sports writer & sports ed, 1993-95; Advocate, newsroom aide/sports corresp, 1993-97, freelance writer, 2010-11; Times-Picayune, sports corresp, 1995-96; New Orleans Times-Picayune, sports corres; St. Louis Rams, pub rels asst, 1997-98, asst dir pub rels, 1998-2003, dir football media, 2003-06, dir new media, 2006-07; Allstate Sugar Bowl, dir commun, 2007-08; Baton Rouge Advocate, sports corres; Rams, St. Louis, staff, 1997-2003, pub rels dir, 2003-05, dir news media, 2006-07; Southwestern Athletic Conf, asst comnr, 2008-10; Dynomite Commun, dir, 2010-; Ala State Univ, dir sports info, 2011-. **Orgs:** Football Writers Asn Am. **Business Addr:** Director of Sports Information, Alabama State University.

## LEWIS, EARL

College administrator, educator. **Educ:** Concordia Col, BA, hist & psychol, 1978; Univ Minn, MA, am hist, 1981, PhD, hist, 1984. **Career:** Univ Calif, Afro-Am Studies Dept, asst prof, 1985-89; Univ Mich, Dept Hist & Ctr Afro-Am & African Studies, assoc prof, 1989-95, interim dir, 1990-91, dir, 1991-93, prof, 1995-, Horace H Rackham Sch Grad Studies, from interim dean to dean, 1997-2004, vice provost acad affairs & grad studies, 1998-2004; Elsa Barkley Brown & Robin DG Kelley Col Prof Hist & African Am & African Studies designate, 2003; Emory Univ, provost & exec vpres acad affairs, 2004-, Asa Griggs Candler prof hist, 2004-. **Orgs:** Am Antiqn Soc; prin investr, Nat Sci Found; Grad Rec Exam; Southern Spaces; Nat Acad Sci Bd Higher Educ & Workforce; Am Coun Learned Socs; fel Am Acad Arts & Sci, 2008-; Andrew W Mellon Found, 2013. **Business Addr:** Provost, Executive Vice President for Academic Affairs, Asa Griggs Candler Professor of History and African American Studies, Emory University, 201 Dowman Dr 404 Admin Bldg, Atlanta, GA 30322, **Business Phone:** (404)727-6055.

## LEWIS, EDWARD T.

Executive, association executive, publisher. **Personal:** Born May 15, 1940, Bronx, NY; married Carolyn Wright. **Educ:** Univ NMex, BA, polit sci, 1964, MA, polit sci & int rels, 1966, PhD, 2003; NY Univ, attended 1969; Harvard Bus Sch, small bus mgt prog. **Career:** Peace Corps Univ NM, lectr, 1963; City Mgr's Off Albuquerque, NM, admin analyst, 1964-65; First Nat City Bank, financial analyst, 1966-69, loan officer; Essence Mag, publ & founder; Essence Commun Inc, founder, chief exec officer & chmn, 1968-; Great Atlantic & Pac Tea Co, bd dir, 2000-; Cent Pk Conservancy Girls Inc; Latina Media Ventures LLC, chief exec officer, chmn bd, 2008-; Lower Manhattan Develop Corp, dir. **Orgs:** Bd dir, Vol Urban Consult Group; bd dir, Black Coun Africa; Fund New Horizons Retarded Inc; 21st Century Found; bd dir, Rheeland Found; bd dir, Negro Ensemble New York; Sch Vol Prog; trustee, Coty; 100 Black Men Inc; Uptown C C; New York Com & Indust; chmn, Mag Publ Am, 1997-99; chmn, Trans Africa Forum; trustee, Columbia Univ; dir, Partnership New York Inc; Cent Pk Conversancy; Times Sq Bus Improv Dist; Lincoln Ctr Performing Arts; Jazz Comt; Int Peace Comt; Greater Harlem Chamber Com; bd mem, Howard Univ Sch Publ; Time Inc; trustee, Teachers Col Columbia Univ; Spelman Col; trustee, Tuskegee Univ; Harlem Village Acad; bd advisor, Historically Black Cols & Univs; trustee, Leadership Coun Tanenbaum Ctr Inter relig Understanding; dir, Apollo Theater Found Inc; trustee, Cent Pk Conservancy Inc. **Honors/Awds:** Decision Maker Award, Nat Asn Media Women, 1974; Businessman of the Year, Black Africa Promotions Inc, 1974; Nat IGBO Award, 1979; Ellis Island Medal of Honor; Good Scout Award, Boy Scouts Am; Lifetime Achievement Award, United Negro Col Fund; Our World News Award, Dow Jones; Good Guy Award, Dem Womens' Polit Caucus; FL Yates Ruffin Ridley Award, NY's Asn Black Charities; The Men Who Dare Award, Black Women's Forum; Entrepreneur of the Year Award, Ernst & Young, 1994; Award Honor, Nat Asn Black Journalists, 1995; President's Award, One Hundred Black Men Am Inc, 1995; Frederick Douglass Award, New York Urban League, 1995; AG Gaston Lifetime Achievement Award, Black Enterprise Mag, 1997; Diversity Achievement Role Model Award, Am Advert Fedn, 1997; Media-Bridge-Builder Award, Tanen baum Ctr Inter Relig Understanding, 1998; Henry Johnson Fisher Award, Mag Publ Am, 2002; Minority Bus Round Table Joint Ctr Polit & Econ Studies; hon DHL, Univ Nmex, 2003; Robert C Maynard Legend Award, 2003; Henry Johnson Fisher Lifetime Achievement Award; Henry Luce Lifetime Achievement Award; Lifetime Achievement Award, Mag Publ Am; inducted, Advertising Hall of Fame, 2014. **Special Achievements:** Featured with other prominent businessmen on the cover of Black Enterprise Magazine as one of the "Marathon Men" for 25 yrs of Entrepreneurial Excellence, June 1997; first African American to chair Magazine Publishers of America; ESSENCE ranked seventh on Advertising Age's 2003 "A-List", which is the first time that an African-American targeted publication has received this honor; First African American to receive the Media-Bridge-Builder Award from the Tannenbaum Center for Inter religious Understanding. **Home Addr:** , New York, NY. **Business Addr:** Chairman, Founder, Essence Communications Inc, 135 W 50th St Fl 4, New York, NY 10020-1201, **Business Phone:** (212)642-0600.

## LEWIS, EMMANUEL

Actor. **Personal:** Born Mar 9, 1971, Brooklyn, NY; son of Margaret. **Educ:** Clark Atlanta Univ, BA, theatre arts, 1997. **Career:** TV Series: A Midsummer Night's Dream, 1982; Webster, 1983-89; The Love Boat, 1984; A Celebration of Life: A Tribute to Martin Luther King, Jr, 1984; Circus of the Stars #9, 1984; Night of 100 Stars II, 1985; The ABC All-Star Spectacular, 1985; "Lost in London", 1985; "The Tonight Show"; "The Phil Donahue Show"; "The World's Funniest Commercial Goofs, host", 1983-85; "Salute to Lady Liberty", 1984; "Mr T & Emmanuel Lewis in a Christmas Dream", 1984; "Secret World of the Very Young", 1984; "Life's Most Embarassing Moments", 1986; "Candid Camera: The First Forty Years", 1987; "Emmanuel Lewis: My Own Show", 1987; "The New Adventures of Mother Goose", 1995; "Family Matters", 1997; "Moesha", 1998; "Malcolm & Eddie", 1999; "GvsE", 1999; "The Surreal Life: Fame Games", 2003, 2007; "Tripping the Rift", 2004; "I Love the 80's 3-D", 2005; "One on One", 2005; "My Super Sweet Sixteen", 2005; "100 Greatest Kid Stars", 2005; "Child Star Confidential", 2006; The Lil Flex Show, 2008. Films: Frank McKlusky, CI, 2002; Dickie Roberts: Former Child Star, 2003; Kickin It Old Skool, 2007. Emmanuel Lewis Entertainment, owner & founder, 2000. **Orgs:** Am Fedn TV & Radio Artists; Screen Actors Guild; Actors Equity Asn. **Honors/Awds:** People Choice Awards, 1984, 1985, 1986 & 1987. **Special Achievements:** Ranked 6 in VH1's list of the "100 Greatest Kid Stars", 2005. **Business Addr:** Actor, c/o Schuller Talent Agency, 276 5th Ave Suite 207, New York, NY 10001, **Business Phone:** (212)532-6005.

## LEWIS, EPHRON H.

Executive, business owner, president (organization). **Personal:** Born Jul 1, 1935?; son of Jasper (deceased) and Adline Mathis (deceased); married Doris; children: Ephron Jr. **Educ:** Ark AM&N Col. **Career:** Lewis & Son Rice Processing Co, owner, pres, currently. **Orgs:** Pres, Ark Land & Farm Develop Corp, 1980-92; mem, Nat Rice Adv Comm. **Home Addr:** 1858 Edward Ave, Memphis, TN 38107, **Home Phone:** (901)278-7735. **Business Addr:** President, Owner, Lewis & Son Rice Processing Corp, 1127 County Rd 1005, Earle, AR 72331-8911, **Business Phone:** (870)755-2727.

## LEWIS, DR. FELTON EDWIN

School administrator. **Personal:** Born Oct 2, 1923, New Orleans, LA; son of Felton B (deceased) and Ethel Martin (deceased); children: Ronald, Anthony, Felton III, Marita & Karen. **Educ:** Xavier Univ, BA, cum laude, 1955; Univ Wis, Madison, MA, 1956; Univ Aix-Marseille France, dipl, 1958; Univ Interamericana Mex, PhD, 1970. **Career:** New York Bd Educ, intern educ admin & super prin intern, 1938-69, teacher, 1958-66, Dist 12, dep dist supt, 1969-71, Dist 12, actg comm supt, 1971-72, Dist 12, comm supt, 1972-78; Dist 16, community supt, 1978-82, asst comnr educ, 1985-86; Foreign Lang Dept JHS, actg chmn, 1963-66; Jr High Spec Serv Sch, actg asst prin, 1966-67; Title I New York Bd Educ, ESEA coordr, 1967-68; Urban House Corp. **Orgs:** Phi Delta Kappa; Am Asn Sch Adminr; New York Asn Supt; Doctoral Asn New York Educr; Int Reading Asn; Asn Supv & Curric Develop, Nat Asn Advan Colored People; Nat Urban League, Bronx Boys Clubs. **Home Addr:** 1705 Purdy St, Bronx, NY 10462.

## LEWIS, FLOYD EDWARD

Manager, association executive. **Personal:** Born Nov 23, 1938; married Ruth M. **Educ:** S Ill Univ, BS, 1961; M Urban Affairs Bus St Univ, attended 1972. **Career:** Monsanto Co, mgr equal oppor, 1974-75; Anheuser-Busch Co Inc, dir equal oppor affairs, 1975, dir corp affairs, consult, 2003-; AOL Time Warner Inc, dir corp affairs, 2003. **Orgs:** Agency rel asn, United Way St Louis, 1970-72; dir personnel, Urban League St Louis, 1972-74; bd mem, Carver House Asn, 1977; bd mem, Asn Black Psychologist, 1977; bd mem, Annie Malone C Home, 1978; St Louis Minority Coun. **Home Addr:** 10455 Litzsinger Rd, Frontenac, MO 63131-3500, **Home Phone:** (314)567-7098. **Business Addr:** Consultant, Anheuser Busch Inc, 1 Busch Pl, St. Louis, MO 63118, **Business Phone:** (314)577-2000.

## LEWIS, FREDERICK CARLTON. See LEWIS, CARL.

## LEWIS, GEORGE E.

Educator. **Personal:** Born Jul 14, 1952, Chicago, IL; married Miya Masaoka; children: 1. **Educ:** Yale Univ, BA, philos, 1974. **Career:** Univ Calif, San Diego, asst to prof music, 1991-2004; McArthur fel, 2002; Columbia Univ, Edwin H Case prof music, 2004-, vchair dept music, dir, Ctr Jazz Studies, dir grad studies, 2008-09; Sch Art Inst Chicago, prof music; Simon Fraser Univ's Contemp Arts Summer Inst, prof music; Nat Endowment Arts, fel. **Orgs:** Asn Advan Creative Musicians, 1971-; fel, MacArthur Found, 2002-; fel, Us Artists Walker. **Business Addr:** Edwin H Case Professor of Music, Columbia University, 615 Dodge Hall MC 1814, New York, NY 10027, **Business Phone:** (212)854-5837.

## LEWIS, GEORGE RALPH

Executive. **Personal:** Born Mar 7, 1941, Burgess, VA; son of Spencer and Edith Pauline Toulson; married Lillian Glenn; children: Tonya & Tracey. **Educ:** Hampton Univ, BS, 1963; Iona Col, New Rochelle, NY, MBA, 1968. **Career:** Executive (retired); Gen Foods Corp, sales analyst, 1963-64, profit planning analyst, 1964-65, prod analyst, 1965-66; WR Grace Co, financial analyst, 1966-67; Philip Morris Inc, corp analyst, 1967-68, sr planning analyst, 1968-70, mgr investor rels, 1970-72, mgr financial serv, 1972-73, asst treas, 1973-74, vpres financial & planning, treas, 1975-82; Seven Up Co, vpres finance, 1982-84; Philip Morris Cos Inc, vpres, treas, 1984-97; Cent Fidelity Banks, dir, 1985; Wachovia Corp, dir, 1997; Philips Morris Capital Corp, pres, chief exec officer, 1997-2001; Ceridian Corp, dir, 2001-07. **Orgs:** Nat Urban League, 1986; trustee, Hampton Univ, 1985; Kemper Nat Ins Co, 1993; Ceridian Corp, 1994; Prof Golfers Asn Am, 1995. **Honors/Awds:** Arthur A Loftus Achievement Award, Iona Col, 1980; Outstanding Twenty Year Alumnus Award, Hampton Inst, 1982; CNN Trumpet Tower of Power Award, 2000; Lifetime Achievement Award, Jackie Robinson Found, 2006. **Special Achievements:** First black member of Professional Golfers' Association of America, 1995. **Home Addr:** 236 S Lake Dr, Stamford, CT 06903-1028, **Home Phone:** (203)329-9812.

## LEWIS, GREEN PRYOR, JR.

Teacher, executive, labor activist. **Personal:** Born Apr 27, 1945, Columbus, GA; son of Green Pryor Sr and Minnie Jones; married Christine McGhee; children: Raquel, Green III & LeKeisha; married Christine McGhee; children: Raquel, Green III & LeKeisha. **Educ:** Ft Valley State Col, Ft Valley, Ga, BS, 1967; Am Univ Ft Benning, advan studies, 1969; Fla Int Univs Inst, labor res & studies. **Career:** Buckner Construct Co, Columbus, Ga, bricklayer apprentice, stud, 1963-64; Am Toy Co, Columbus, Ga, asst dept mgr, 1965-67; Muscogee County Sch Syst, Columbus, Ga, teacher, coach, 1967-69; Am Fedn Labor & Cong Indust Orgns, asst dir, 1969-, dir, currently; Field Rep Fedn AFL-CIO, vpres, 1979-84, Region V, dir, Field Serv Dept, asst nat dir, Community Serv, dir; Off & Prof Employees Int Union, Region III, int rep, 2001-, vpres, 2004-. **Orgs:** Keeper rec, Columbus Alumni Chap, Kappa Alpha Psi, 1968-69; pres, Proud Neighbors S De Kalb, 1973-75; vice chmn, fourth dist, Dem Party De Kalb County Ga, 1982-84; exec comt, A Philip Randolph Inst, 1985-; United Way Am Bd Gov, 1997. **Honors/Awds:** High Achievement Award, Kappa Alpha Psi, 1963; Distinguished Serv, Houston Organizing Proj, 1984; Distinguished Serv, Field Rep Fedn, 1985; Labor Award Outstanding Serv, Serv Employees Local 579, 1987; High Achievement Award, Lewis Family Reunion, 1988; Histadrut Menorah Award, 1989; A Philip Randolph Achievement Award, 1992; Keeper Flame Award, Nat Asn Advan Colored People, 1992. **Home Addr:** PO Box 12493, Columbus, GA 31917-2493. **Business Addr:** Vice President, Office & Professional Employees International Union, 80 8th Ave 20th Fl, New York, NY 10011, **Business Phone:** (800)346-7348.

## LEWIS, HANK. See LEWIS, WILLIAM HENRY.

## LEWIS, HAROLD

Restaurateur, business owner. **Personal:** married Tina; children: Jeremy, Jonathan & Jennifer. **Career:** United Airlines, sales & human resource mgt; Sir Speedy Printing (Los Angeles), franchise owner, 1982-86; HRL Group LLC, co-founder (with wife Tina Lewis), 1987-. **Orgs:** Founder, African Am Visionary & Inspirational Leaders (AVAIL) Scholar Prog; Trumpet Found (Atlanta, GA). **Honors/Awds:** McDonald's Corporation, "Ronald Award", Recipient, "Outstanding Store Award", Recipient; McDonald's 365Black Award, 2013. **Special Achievements:** Managed 20 McDonald's restaurant franchises from 1987-2011.

## LEWIS, HAROLD THOMAS

Educator, clergy. **Personal:** Born Feb 21, 1947, Brooklyn, NY; son of Frank Walston and Muriel Kathleen Worrell; married Claudette Richards; children: Justin Craig. **Educ:** McGill Univ, BA, 1967; Yale Divinity Sch, Mdiv, 1971; Univ Birmingham, Eng, PhD, 1994. **Career:** NY City Dept Social Serv, social worker, 1967-68; Overseas Missionary, Honduras, staff, 1971-72; St Monica's Church, rector, 1973-82; Episcopal Church Foundation, res fel, 1978; St Luke's Episcopal Church, assoc priest, 1983-96; Presiding Bishop of the Episcopal Church, Off of Black Ministries, dir, 1983-94; Episcopal Church Cent, staff officer, 1983-94; Mercer Sch Theol, prof homiletics, 1988-96; Yale Univ, res fel, 1990; NY Theol Sem, prof homiletics, 1995-96; Calvary Episcopal Church, Pittsburgh, Pa, rector, 1996-; Pittsburgh Theol Sem, adj prof, 1996-. **Orgs:** Racial Justice Working Group, Nat Coun Churches, 1986-96; exec comt, Prophetic Justice Unit, Nat Coun Churches, 1988-96; Sigma Pi Phi, 1991-. **Home Addr:** 138 Penham Lane, Pittsburgh, PA 15208-2637, **Home Phone:** (412)362-1830. **Business Addr:** Rector, Calvary Episcopal Church, 315 Shady Ave, Pittsburgh, PA 15206-4388, **Business Phone:** (412)661-0120.

## LEWIS, DR. HENRY L., III

Educator, school administrator. **Personal:** Born Jan 22, 1950, Tallahassee, FL; son of Henry Sr and Evelyn P; married Marisa Ann Smith. **Educ:** Fla A&M Univ, BS, pharm, 1972; Mercer Univ, PhD, clin pharm, 1978; Harvard Univ, Inst Educ Mgt. **Career:** Fla A&M Univ, asst dean, 1974-90, dean, 1994-2010, bd trustee, Col Pharm Pharmaceut Sci, dean, 1994-2001, prof, 1994-, interim pres, 2002-02, dir, dean, pres, currently; Tex Southern Univ, dean & prof, 1990-94; Am Univ Health Sci, provost & vpres acad affairs, 2013-. **Orgs:** Am Asn Col Pharm, 1974-; Rho Chi Hon Soc, 1975-; ASHP, 1978-; Am Pub Health Asn, 1980-; Alpha Phi Alpha, 1985-; Bd County Comnr, Leon County, 1986-90; pres, NPHA, 1988-90; Tex Pharm Asn, 1990-; bd adv, Nat Inst Gen Med Sci, 1992-96; pres, AMHPS, 1992-95; pres, MHPF, 1994-; bd dir, Fla Educ Fund Chair, 1999-; United Way; Habitat Humanity; Nat Urban League; Big Bend Hospice; Am Cancer Socs, 2007-2009; pres, Minority Health Professions Found; pres, Found's sister agency; Asn Minority Health Professions Schs; pres, Nat Pharmaceut Asn; Nat Ctr Res Resources Nat Adv Bd; bd dir, Capital City Bank Group; bd regents, Nat Libr Med, 2011-; bd dir, Miami-Dade Chamber Com, 2011-13. **Special Achievements:** First African American elected to the Leon County Board of County Commissioners, Tallahassee. **Home Addr:** 531 Tuskegee St, Tallahassee, FL 32305. **Business Addr:** Professor, Dean, Florida A&M University, 1415 S Martin Luther King Blvd, Tallahassee, FL 32307, **Business Phone:** (850)599-3301.

## LEWIS, IDA ELIZABETH

Educator, college teacher, publisher. **Personal:** Born Sep 22, 1935, Malvern, PA. **Educ:** Boston Univ Sch Pub Commun, BS, jour, 1956. **Career:** NY Amsterdam News, financial & bus writer, 1957-60; NY Age, financial ed, 1959-61; Life Mag, writer, 1964-65; BBC, writer & broadcaster, 1967; Jeune Afrique Mag, corresp, 1968-71; Essence Mag, ed-in-chief, 1970-71; Tanner Publ Co, pres, 1972; Encore: Am & Worldwide News, founder, publ & ed-in-chief; Nat Asn Advan Colored People, Crisis, ed-in-chief, 1998; Boston Univ Sch Pub Commun, Dept Jour, adj prof, lectr jour, currently. **Orgs:** Trustee Tougaloo Col; bd dir, Am Com Africa; Comn Inquiry Into High Sch Journ; Nat Coun Negro Women; Alpha Kappa Alpha Soc; Am Mgt Asn; founder, Ida E Lewis Scholar Fund; Boston Univ Alumni Coun; Boston Univ Commun, Deans Exec Adv Bd. **Honors/Awds:** Scarlet Key, Boston Univ, 1956; Journalism Award, Asn Study Afro-Am Life & Hist, 1974; Citizen of the Year, Omega Psi Phi, 1975; Bicentennial Award, 1975; Int Benih Award, 1975; Media Executive Award, Nat Youth Movement, 1975; Distinguished Alumni Award, Boston Univ, 1999; Woman of Distinction Award, Kingsborough Col, City Univ NY. **Special Achievements:** Lewis became the first editor in chief of "Essence" magazine and later founded " Encore: American & worldwide News", 1971; First African American woman in the US to publish a magazine; first woman editor-in-chief of Crisis, the magazine of the Nat Asn Advan Colored People, 1998. **Home Addr:** 165 W 66th St, New York, NY 10023. **Business Addr:** Lecturer in Journalism, Boston University, 1 Sherborn St, Boston, MA 02215, **Business Phone:** (617)353-2000.

## LEWIS, J. B., JR.

Funeral director. **Personal:** Born Oct 22, 1929, Clifton Forge, VA; son of J B Sr (deceased) and Mattie E Douglas (deceased); married Mary Louise Colbert; children: Aaron. **Educ:** Eckels Col Mortuary Sci, grad, 1957. **Career:** Ins underwriterm, 1958-63; Greyhound Lines, optr, 1964-65; Mt View Terr Apts, mgr & agt, 1970-; JB Lewis Funeral Serv, owner. **Orgs:** Va Mortic Asn, 1959; pres, Lylburn Downing PTA, 1962-63; treas, Sec Cub Scouts, 1963; vpres, Rockbridge Area Housing Corp, 1967-70; vpres, Human Rel Coun, 1968; councilman City Lexington, 1969; adv bd, Coreast Savings Bank, 1972; VA Funeral Dir Asn, 1976; Nat Funeral Dir Asn, 1976; Nat Asn Advan Colored People; Am Legion Post 291. **Honors/Awds:** Eye Enucleat Cert, 1976. **Home Addr:** 420 Wills Rd, Lexington, VA 24450-2827, **Home Phone:** (540)463-5101. **Business Addr:** Owner, JB Lewis Funeral Service, 112 N Randolph St, Lexington, VA 24450, **Business Phone:** (540)463-5101.

## LEWIS, JAMES B.

Government official, commissioner, administrator. **Personal:** Born Nov 30, 1947, Roswell, NM; son of William Reagor and Dorris; married Armandie Lillie Johnson; children: Teri Seaton, James Jr, Shedra & LaRon. **Educ:** Bishop Col, BS, educ, 1970; Univ NMex, MPA, 1977; Nat Col Bus, AS, bus admin, 1980, BS, bus, 1980, BS, bus admin, 1981; Duke Univ, chief staff cert; Univ Va, minority leadership cert. **Career:** Chief admin officer (retired); Univ Albuquerque, Afro-Studies Admin/instr, 1974-77; Dist Atty Off, investr/purchasing dir, 1977-83; Bernalillo Co, treas, 1983-85; NMex State Govt, state treas, 1985-90, 2006-14; Chief Staff Gov Bruce King, 1991-94; NM State Land Off, Oil Gas & Minerals Div, dir, 1995-99; US Dept Energy, Off Econ Impact & Diversity, dir, 1999-2001; City Albuquerque, chief opers officer, 2001-04, chief admin officer, 2004-05. **Orgs:** State housing chair, Nat Asn Advan Colored People, 1980-; bd mem finance comn, Victims Domestic Violence, 1983-; treas, Am Soc Pub Admin, 1983-; Nat State Treas, 1985-; bd mem, State Investment Coun, NM, 1985, Pub Employee Retirement Bd, 1985, Educ Retirement Bd, 1985; Am Legion PO 99, 1985; pres, NMex Chap, Am Soc Pub Admin, 1989; commencement speaker, Zuni High Sch, Zuni, NM 1989; Ad-Hoc Comt, State Investment Coun, 1989; hon mem, Beta Alpha Psi, CPA Hon Soc, 1989; PRS Bill Clinton Transition Team, 1992-; commencement speaker, Univ N Mex, Dept Pub Admin, 1992; Kiwanis Club Albuquerque; Am GI Forum; Int Alumni Asn, Bishop Col; Taylor Ranch Neighborhood Asn; Omega Psi Phi Fraternity; N Mex State Bd Finance; Educ Found Assistance Bd; Mid Rio Grande Coun Govts, Metrop Transp & Exec Bd; Albuquerque Armed Forces Adv Asn; Univ NMex Sch Eng, Diversity Coun; Metrop Criminal Justice Coord

Coun; bd dir, United Way; bd dir, Albuquerque Hall Fame; bd dir, St Joseph Community Health Serv; First State Bank, Metro Community Adv Bd; bd trustee, W Mesa Med Ctr; bd dir, Albuquerque Conv & Visitors Bur; Nat Asn Black Accountants; pres, Western State Treasurers Asn, 2007; pres, Nat Asn Auditors, Comptrollers & State Treasurers, 2014. **Home Addr:** 6117 Carousal Ave NW, Albuquerque, NM 87120-2152, **Home Phone:** (505)792-8771.

### LEWIS, JAMES D.
Publisher, president (organization). **Career:** Minority Bus J Inc, pres & publ, currently; James D Lewis Enterprises, currently. **Business Addr:** President, Publisher, Minority Business Journal Inc, 511 Junilla St, Pittsburgh, PA 15219-4837, **Business Phone:** (412)682-4386.

### LEWIS, DR. JAMES R.
Dentist. **Personal:** Born Aug 3, 1938, Asheboro, NC; married Barbara Walker; children: Krista & Erica. **Educ:** NC Cent Univ, BS, 1963; Howard Univ, DDS, 1968. **Career:** McGill Univ, Montreal, Can, rotating dent internship; VA Hosp, Albany, 1968-69; Univ NC Sch Dent, asst prof, 1969-71; Lincoln Health Ctr, Durham, NC, dent dir, 1971-75; Univ NC Dent, adj assoc prof dent ecol, 2002. **Orgs:** Am Dent Asn; Acad Cent Dent; NC Dent Soc; Am Endodontic Soc; Chi Delta MuMed & Dent Frat Bd NC Health Plan Agency; Highest Order Mystic Shrine 32nddeg Mason; health prof Coun Black Students Int Dent; admin comt, Sch Dent Univ NC, 1969-71. **Special Achievements:** First African American as mem Adm Comm for Sch of Dent UNC 1969-71. **Home Addr:** 5111 Shady Bluff St, Durham, NC 27704-1130, **Home Phone:** (919)477-3925. **Business Addr:** Associate Professor, University North Carolina, CB 7450, Chapel Hill, NC 27599-7450, **Business Phone:** (919)966-1161.

### LEWIS, JAMES R.
President (organization), chief executive officer, administrator. **Personal:** Born Jan 1, 1950, Somerset, KY; married Ernestine. **Educ:** Berea Col, Berea, KY, BA, math. **Career:** USF&G Corp, 1992-2001; Aetna Life & Casualty; CIGNA; St Paul Cos, sr vpres US field opers, reg pres northeast reg; sr vpres, personal lines; pres small com; CNA Ins Co, exec vpres, 2001-02, pres & ceo, 2002-08, chmn & dir, 2003-08. **Orgs:** Bd mem, Metrop Family Servs; bd mem, Young Mens Christian Asn Metrop Chicago; bd mem, Cs Home & Aid Soc; trustee, Berea Col; ChicagoLand Chamber Com; Goodman Theater. **Business Addr:** Trustee, Berea College, 101 Chestnut St, Berea, KY 40403, **Business Phone:** (859)985-3000.

### LEWIS, JANICE LYNN
Executive. **Personal:** Born Dec 11, 1958, Magnolia, MS; daughter of Joe and Ruth Robertson; children: Kerrington Lavern Howard. **Educ:** Southern Univ, BS, journ & advert, 1980; Barry Univ, MS, theol, 2001. **Career:** Wash Post, journalist, off mgr, circulation, 1981; Miami Herald, circulation mgr, 1989; WPLG, TV-10, sales asst, 1990; John S & James L Knight Found, jour prog asst, 1990-; Proj Hope Global Outreach Inc, reverend, 2006-. **Orgs:** Sherman Baptist Church, 1962; bd dir, exec forum, James K Batten Black, 1995; bd dir, Miami Mega City Spec Olympics, 1995-; New Mt.Olive Baptist Church, 2000-; Nat Asn Black Journalists. **Honors/Awds:** James K Batten Black Executive; Miami Black Executive, 1995. **Home Addr:** 709 NE 205 Terr, Miami, FL 33179, **Home Phone:** (305)653-4842. **Business Addr:** Reverend, Project Hope Global Outreach Inc, 2801 Somerset Dr 401, Fort Lauderdale, FL 33311, **Business Phone:** (954)663-3094.

### LEWIS, HON. JANNIE M.
Judge. **Personal:** Born Oct 4, 1958, MS; married Earl Blackmon. **Educ:** Jackson State Univ, BA, 1980; Univ Iowa Col, JD, 1983. **Career:** Legal Servs Corp, N MS rural legal serv, 1984-87, atty; pvt pract atty, 1987-94; Town Tchula, munic judge, 1992-94; State Mo Circuit Ct, 21st Circuit Ct Dist, judge, 1995-; Pub Defender Country, munic judge; City Lexington, prosecuting atty; Town Goodman, city atty; City Durant, munic judge. **Orgs:** Miss State Bar, 1984; Sunday Sch teacher; trustee, New Gordon Chapel Missionary Baptist Church; fel, Miss Bar Found. **Business Addr:** Judge, State of Mississippi Circuit Court, 101 1/2 Dr Martin Luther King Jr Dr, Lexington, MS 39095-0718, **Business Phone:** (662)834-1452.

### LEWIS, ESQ. JEFFREY MARK
Executive. **Personal:** children: 2. **Educ:** Rutgers Univ, BS, econs & BA, bus admin, 1980; Northwestern Univ, JL Kellogg Grad Sch Mgt, master, mgt, 1981. **Career:** Sands Hotel & Casino, acct, 1980; Anheuser-Busch, Spec Proj & Corp Investments, mgr, 1985; SmithKline Beckman, Financial Planning & Anal, mgr, 1981-85; Bus Improv Forum, exec dir, 1986; Mars Inc, 1986-91; Northwest Airlines Inc, int treas, dir, 1991-93; World Trade Inst Int Finance Prog, chmn, lectr; Ark State Univ; Lewis & Co Inc, pres, 1993-. **Orgs:** Rotary Int; fel Chase Manhattan Bank, 1981. **Home Addr:** 2195 Marilyn Ave, St. Paul, MN 55122. **Business Addr:** President, Lewis & Co Inc, 3432 Denmark Ave Suite 236, St Paul, MN 55123-1088, **Business Phone:** (612)707-8571.

### LEWIS, JENIFER JEANETTE
Actor, singer. **Personal:** Born Jan 25, 1957, Kinloch, MO. **Educ:** Webster Univ. **Career:** Films: Beaches, 1988; Sister Act, 1992; Frozen Assets, 1992; Poetic Justice, 1993; What's Love Got to Do With It, 1993; Undercover Blues, 1993; Sister Act 2: Back in the Habit, 1993; Renaissance Man, Corrina, Corrina, 1994; Panther, 1995; Dead Presidents, 1995; The Preacher's Wife, 1996; Girl 6, 1996; The Temptations, 1998; The Mighty, 1998; Mystery Men, 1999; Get Bruce, 1999; Blast From the Past, 1999; Jackie's Back, 1999; Partners, Dancing in September, Cast Away, 2000; The Brothers, 2001; Juwanna Man, 2002; The Cookout, 2004; Dirty Laundry, 2006; Cars, 2006; Madea's Family Reunion, 2006; Redrum, Who's Your Caddy?, Redrum, 2007; Meet the Browns, Prop 8: The Musical, 2008; Not Easily Broken, 2009; Voice: Princess and Frog, 2009; Hereafter, 2010; Cars 2, 2011; Think Like A Man, 2012; Baggage Claim, 2013; Think Like A Man Too, 2014. TV movies: Deconstructing Sarah, 1994; Temptaions, 1998; Little Richard, 2000; The Ponder Heart, 2001; TV Series: "Murphy Brown", 1988; "Fresh Prince of Bel-Air", 1990; "Cosby", 1996; "For Your Love", 1998; "Grown Ups", 1999; "The PJs", 1999-2008; "Time of Your Life", 1999; "Strong Medicine", 2000-06; "Girlfriends", 2002-06; "Family Affair", 2002; "The Proud Family", 2003; "The Proud Family", 2003; "That's So Raven ", 2004; "Day Break", 2007; "Shark", 2007; "Boston Legal", 2007-08; "The Cleveland Show", 2011; "State of Georgia", 2011; "The Playboy Club", 2011; "The Boondocks", 2014. **Honors/Awds:** Two National Association Advanced Colored People Theater Awards; Nominated, Image Award, 1997. **Business Addr:** Actress, William Morris Agency, 1325 Avenue of the Americas, New York, NY 10019, **Business Phone:** (212)586-5100.

### LEWIS, JERMAINE EDWARD
Football player. **Personal:** Born Oct 16, 1974, Lanham, MD; married Imara; children: J J, Ali & Geronimo. **Educ:** Univ Md, grad. **Career:** Football player (retired); Baltimore Ravens, kick returner, punt returner, 1996, 2001, kick returner, punt returner, wide receiver, 1997, punt returner, wide receiver, 1998-99, punt returner, 2000; Houston Texans, kick returner, punt returner, 2002; Jacksonville Jaguars, 2003, kick returner, punt returner, 2004. **Orgs:** Geronimo Lewis Found. **Honors/Awds:** Two time Pro Bowl selection, 1998, 2001; NFL Punt Return Yards Leader, 2001; Super Bowl champion (XXXV). **Special Achievements:** TV Series: Mike & Mike, 2016.

### LEWIS, JESSE CORNELIUS
School administrator. **Personal:** Born Jun 26, 1929, Vaughan, MS; son of Jefferson; married Emma Goldman; children: Peggy & Valerie. **Educ:** Tougaloo Col, BS, 1949; Univ Ill, MS, 1955, MA, 1959; Syracuse Univ, PhD, 1966. **Career:** Southern Univ, Baton Rouge, instr math, 1955-57; Prairie View Col, 1957-58; Syracuse Univ, res asst comput ctr, 1963-66; Jackson State Col, prof math, dir, comput ctr, 1966-84; Norfolk State Univ, Norfolk, Va, vpres, acad affairs, 1984-; NSF, sr scientist emer, MGE coordr, currently. **Orgs:** Fel Nat Sci Found Sci Fac, 1958, 1961; chmn, fac Senate, Jackson State Col, 1970-73; lectr, Am Math Asn, 1971; proj dir, Nat Sci Found Comput Network, 1973-; Am Asn Comput Mach; Math Soc; Alpha Phi Alpha. **Honors/Awds:** Administrators of the Year, 1990. **Home Addr:** 1041 Fairlawn Ave, Virginia Beach, VA 23455, **Home Phone:** (757)461-6191. **Business Addr:** Senior Scientist Emeritus, National Science Foundation, 4201 Wilson Blvd, Arlington, VA 22230, **Business Phone:** (703)306-1634.

### LEWIS, DR. JESSE J.
Businessperson, executive, association executive. **Personal:** Born Jan 3, 1925, Tuscaloosa, AL; married Helen Merriweather; children: James & Jesse Jr. **Educ:** Miles Col, Birmingham, Ala, BA, acct & bus admin, 1955; Troy State Univ, Montgomery, Ala, MS, 1977, MA, EdS; Atlanta Univ, EdD. **Career:** Jesse J Lewis & Assocs, founder, 1954; Birmingham Times Newspaper, founder, pres & chief exec officer, 1963-74; Off Hwy Traffic Safety Montgomery, dir, 1974-78; Lawson State Community Col, pres, 1978-87; Lewis Group, pres, chief exec officer & owner, 1995-; Birmingham Jefferson Conv Complex, consult, currently. **Orgs:** Law Enforcement Planning Agency; Birmingham Urban League; life mem, Alpha Phi Alpha; bd trustee, Birmingham Bus Alliance. **Honors/Awds:** Citation for Outstanding Service, Gov Ala, 1975; Outstanding Acadamy Excellence Award, Miles Col, 1975. **Special Achievements:** First black-owned advertising agency, Jesse J. Lewis and Associates was opened by him in 1954. **Home Addr:** 300 10th Ct W, Birmingham, AL 35204. **Business Addr:** Consultant, Birmingham Jefferson Convention Complex, 2100 Richard Arrington Jr Blvd N, Birmingham, AL 35203, **Business Phone:** (205)458-8400.

### LEWIS, JIM (JAMES LEWIS)
Administrator, president (organization), certified public accountant. **Personal:** Born Jan 1, 1961?, Hammond, IN; married LaFaye Floyd; children: Jalen & Jaren. **Educ:** Ind State Univ, BS, acct, 1984; Krannert Sch Bus, Purdue Univ, MBA, int finance, 1992. **Career:** PricewaterhouseCoopers, sr acct, 1984-86; Tokheim Corp, mgr internal audit, 1986-88; Pepsi-Cola Co, mgr internal audit, 1988-89, sr mgr planning & anal, 1989-92, controller, 1992-93, dir investor rels, 1993-94; vpres & gen mgr, 1994-96; Walt Disney Attractions, dir planning & finance, 1996-98; Walt Disney World, vpres finance, 1998-99, vpres bus develop, 1999-2001; sr vpres bus develop & pub affairs, 2001-03; Disney Vacation Club, sr vpres & gen mgr, 2003-06, pres, 2006-11; Wal-Mart, corp officer, vpres, regional gen mgr opers, currently. **Orgs:** Chmn, Orlando Regional Chamber Com; chmn, Am Resort Develop Assoc, 2009-11; Fla CPA Soc; Am Inst Cert Pub Accountants; Nat Black MBA Asn. **Business Addr:** Vice President, Regional General Manager of Operations, Wal-Mart, 13300 Cortez Blvd, Brooksville, FL 34613, **Business Phone:** (352)597-3807.

### LEWIS, JIMMY
Manager, executive director. **Personal:** Born Sep 3, 1952, Elizabethtown, NC; son of Gaston and Martha; married Hsieh Y; children: Sandra, Dexter S & Tiffany. **Educ:** Univ NY, BS, 1990; Cent Mich Univ, MSA, 1992. **Career:** USN, tele commun opers mgr, 1987-90, tele commun mgr, 1990-93, dir Commun, 1993-96, Communs network mgr, 1996-99; Ai Metrix Inc, opers mgr, dir opers, currently. **Orgs:** Arm Forces Commun Asn, 1990-93; mentor, Hawaii Youth Challenge, 1996-99; pres, Makakilo Housing Asn, 1998-99; supporter, advisor, Fishing Sch, 1990-. **Home Addr:** 43173 Cardston Pl, Leesburg, VA 20176-6453, **Home Phone:** (703)771-9073. **Business Addr:** Director of Operations, Ai Metrix Inc, 1821 Michael Faraday Dr Suite 400, Reston, VA 20190, **Business Phone:** (703)668-1000.

### LEWIS, JOHN ROBERT
Government official. **Personal:** Born Feb 21, 1940, Troy, AL; son of Eddie and Willie Mae Carter; married Lillian Miles (Deceased); children: John. **Educ:** Am Baptist Theol Sem, BA, 1961; Fisk Univ, BA, relig & philos, 1967. **Career:** Southern Regional Coun, comm orgn proj dir, 1967-70; Voter Educ Proj Inc, exec dir, 1970-77; Atlanta City Councilman-At-Large, 1981, Congressman, 1986-; US Gov, dir, 1977-, house representatives Ga's 5th cong dist, 1987-, sr chief dep whip, 1991-, leader; Nat Consumer Co-op Bank, community affairs dir. **Orgs:** Nonviolent Coord Comm, chmn stud, 1963-66; Field Found, assoc dir, 1966-67; Leadership Atlanta, 1974-75; Am Civil Liberties Union; Afro-Am Inst; adv comm, Biracial Com Atlanta Bd Educ; adv bd, Black Enterprises; Martin Luther King Jr Ctr Social Chg; life mem, Nat Asn Advan Colored People; SCLC; leading speaker, organizer & worker, Civil Rights Movement; Speaker's Bur during Sen Robert Kennedy's campaign; secy, Southern Christian Leadership Conf; Atlanta City Coun, 1981; Cong Black Caucus; Cong Caucus Global Rd Safety; Bipartisan Taskforce Nonproliferation; Dem Party; co-chair, Chronic Obstructive Pulmonary Disease (COPD) Caucus. **Honors/Awds:** Martin Luther King Jr Peace Prize, 1975; Wallenberg Medal, Univ Mi, 1999; Dole Leadership Prize, Univ Kans, Robert J. Dole Inst Polit, 2007; Presidential Medal of Freedom, 2011. Got numerous Honorary degrees from Spelman Col, Princeton Univ, Univ of Nh, Johnson C. Smith Univ, Del State Univ Duke Univ, Morehouse Col, Clark-Atlanta Univ, Howard Univ, Brandeis Univ, Columbia Univ, Fisk Univ, Williams Col, Georgetown Univ, Troy State Univ, Univ Vt, 2007; Brown Univ, Harvard Univ, & Univ Conn Law, 2012; Cleveland State Univ, 2013; Emory Univ, 2014. Numerous awards includes: Lincoln Medal, Ford's Theatre; Golden Plate Award, Acad Excellence; Preservation Hero Award, National Trust for Historic Preservation. **Special Achievements:** Appointed by President Johnson to White House Conference "To Fulfill These Rights" 1966, named "One of Nation's Most Influential Black" Ebony Magazine, 1971-72, "One of America's 200 Rising Leaders" by Time Mag, 1974, author of Walking with the Wind, 1998. **Home Addr:** 1520 Pinehurst Dr SW, Atlanta, GA 30311. **Business Addr:** Congressman, U.S. House of Representatives, 343 Cannon House Office Bldg, Washington, DC 20515, **Business Phone:** (202)225-3801.

### LEWIS, KAREN A.
Marketing executive, association executive. **Personal:** Born Mar 9, 1962, Philadelphia, PA; daughter of Wallace and Anita. **Educ:** La Salle Univ, BS, bus, 1985, media rels, cert prog, 1999; Univ Pa, fund raising, cert prog, 1996. **Career:** USN Int Logistics Control Off, mgt analyst, 1985-91; Greater Philadelphia Chamber Com, prog develop specialist, 1990-91; Mayor's Off, asst dep mayor, 1992-94; City Philadelphia, dep city rep, 1994-96; Greater Philadelphia Tourism Mkt Corp, vpres, 1996-99; Greater Philadelphia Cult Alliance, vpres; Ave Arts Inc, exec dir, currently. **Orgs:** Travel Indust Am, 1996-99; Nat Asn Female Execs, 1997-99; bd mem, Optum Inc, 1999-2001; bd mem, Cult Fund, Nominating Comm chair, 1999-2003; bd mem, Welcome Am, 1999-2001; bd mem, Multucultural Affairs Cong, 1999-2001. **Special Achievements:** Appointed by Mayor Rendell to President Clinton's Summit, 1997; Appointed by Governor Ridge to Quebec/Pennsylvania Task Force, 1998. **Home Addr:** 6811 Ardleigh St, Philadelphia, PA 19119-1425, **Home Phone:** (215)842-1697. **Business Addr:** Executive Director, Avenue of the Arts Inc, 123 S Broad St Suite 1240, Philadelphia, PA 19109, **Business Phone:** (215)731-9668.

### LEWIS, KEIRSTON
Singer. **Personal:** married Toni Braxton; children: Denham Cole & Diezel Ky. **Career:** Mint Condition, mem, 1991-99; Writer: Mo' Money, 1992; Albums: Meant to Be Mint, 1991; From the Mint Factory, 1993; Definition of a Band, 1996; The Collection, 1998; Life's Aquarium, 1999; Snowflakes, producer & composer, 2001; TV appearances: "New York Undercover", 1997; "Intimate Portrait", 2002; "Soul Train", 2005. Innovative International Group Inc, chief exec officer. **Business Addr:** Singer, c/o Atlantic Records Incorporation, 1290 Ave of the Americas, New York, NY 10104, **Business Phone:** (212)707-2000.

### LEWIS, KENNETH DWIGHT
Engineer, clergy, college administrator. **Personal:** Born Aug 11, 1949, Newark, NJ; son of Joseph Sr and Carrie Attles; married Pamela Josephine Masingale; children: Caleb & Sarah. **Educ:** Rutgers Univ, AB, physics, 1971; Lehigh Univ, MS, physics, 1972; Stanford Univ, MS, nuclear engineering, 1974; Univ Ill, Urbana-Champaign, MA, appl math, 1979, PhD, nuclear engineering, 1982; Trinity Theol Sem, Newburgh Ind, ThD, 1986; Moody Bible Inst Chicago, cert bibl studies, 1992; Anderson Baptist Sem, Camilla, GA, Ministry degree prog. **Career:** Lockheed Martin Energy Systs, sr engr, 1982-88, dev staff mem I, 1988-90, engr specialist, 1990-95, sect mgr, nuclear calculations sect, 1994-98, sr staff engr, 1995-, cre nuclear criticality safety mgr, 1995-97; Knoxville Col, adj prof physics, 2000-; Master Ministry, Andersonville Baptist Sem, Camilla, Ga, 2001-; BWXT Y-12, LLC Oak Ridge, Tenn, sr staff engr II; SC State Univ, B&W Y-12 Prof Nuclear Engineering, Col Sci, Math & Engineering Technol, dean, currently. **Orgs:** Sigma Xi Hon Soc; Pi Mu Epsilon Math Hon Soc; Lic Prof Engr; assoc pastor & youth dir, Little Leaf Baptist Church, TN, 1993-; assoc pastor, Second Baptist Church, Stockton CA, 1988-90; asst pastor, trustee, First Baptist Church, Chillicothe, OH, 1983-87; deacon, Salem Baptist Church, Champaign Ill, 1979-82; Dept Adv Bd, Univ Ill, NUCE, 2000-; fel Am Nuclear Soc; Network Sr Scientists & Engrs; speaker, NPRE Hons Banquet, 2007-. **Honors/Awds:** Certificate of Merit, Ohio Soc Prof Engr, 1983; Outstanding Achievement Award, Univ Ill, Black Alumni Asn, 1992; Lockheed Martin Cash Awards, Tech Achievement, 1992, 1994, 1998, 2000, 2003; Certificate of Recognition, Ohio House Reps, 1983; Grad Col Fel, Univ Ill, 1977-78; Letter of Appreciation, Pres Clinton, 1995; Black Engineer of the Year President's Award, 1998; Engineer of the Year, Lockheed Martin Energy Systs, 1998; Lockheed Martin Corp NOVA Award; DOE Award of Excellence, 2000, 2001. **Special Achievements:** Delegate to People's Republic of China Radiation Protection Conference, 1987; Session Chair, Am Nuclear Soc Annual Meeting, PA, 1995; Over 20 Technical Publications; Visiting Prof Math, Univ the Pacific, 1989-90; Authored over two dozen journal articles and technical reports, including works presented in Germany and in Shanghai, China, before China's largest nuclear science association. **Home Addr:** 128 Capital Cir, Oak Ridge, TN 37830, **Home Phone:** (423)481-8319. **Business Addr:** Dean, South Carolina State University, 300 Col Ave NE, Orangeburg, SC 29117, **Business Phone:** (803)536-7000.

### LEWIS, KIRK J.
Administrator, president (organization). **Educ:** Mich State Univ, BS, acct, 1984; Wayne State Univ, MBA, finance, 1993. **Career:** Price Waterhouse, staff acct, 1983-85; Ford Motor Credit Co, debt analyst, 1988-94; Bing Group, pres, 1994-2009; Integrated Supply Chain Solutions LLC, pres, 2008-10; City Detroit, chief govt & corp affairs officer, 2010-11, dep mayor, 2011-13; Blue Springs Metals LLC, chmn & pres, 2013-. **Orgs:** Habitat Humanity; Health Alliance Plan Mich; bd dir, Integrated Supply Chain Solutions LLC; Detroit Econ Growth Corp; Urban Policy Adv Group; Harvard Kennedy Sch Detroit Zool

Soc; Parade Co; Mich Econ Develop Corp; Nat Asn Black Automotive Suppliers; New Detroit; Downtown Detroit Partnership; Bus Leaders Mich; Cs Hosp; Vanguard CDC; bd dir, Blue Springs Metals LLC; bd dir, Am Promise Schs; Rainbow/PUSH Coalition. **Business Addr:** President, Chairman, Blue Springs Metals LLC, 1036 Corolla Lane, Blue Springs, MS 38828, **Business Phone:** (662)539-2700.

## LEWIS, LAURETTA FIELDS

Educator. **Personal:** Born Chattanooga, TN; daughter of Mark Sr and Lula Ballard Hogue; children: Jeffrey L & Mark F. **Educ:** Univ Tenn, Chattanooga, BSW, 1971, MSW, 1974; Univ Mich Inst Geron, cert, 1982; NC A&T State Univ, Summer Inst Aging, 1986. **Career:** Educator (retired); Family Serv Agency, social worker aide, 1966-68; Community Action Prog, out reach soc worker, 1968-70; Neighborhood Youth Corp, youth counsr, 1972; Clover Bottom Dev Ctr Nashville TN, social worker, 1973; Florence Crittenton Home TN, social worker aide, 1973-74; E Carolina Univ, assoc prof, social work, instr, Univ Geroutol Ctr. **Orgs:** Consult Long Term Care, 1976-; vice chmn, treas, 1980-82, chmn, 1983 NC Coun Social Work Ed; pres, exec bd, Pitt Coounty Ment Health Asn, 1983-92; chmn bd, Pitt County Coun Aging, 1983-85; exec comm & chap rep state bd Pitt County Ment Health Asn, 1987; exec bd, Creative Living Ctr Day Prog Geriatric Patients; grants & res comt mem, Southern Gerontol Soc, 1990-92; chair, personnel action, Pitt County Coun Aging, 1989-92; scholarshipliaison, Sch Social Work & Pitt County Ment Health Asn, 1985-93; Greenville/Pitt County Habitat Humanity, PORT Adolescent Substance AbuseProg, MH/Pitt County, bd mem; Pitt County Coalition Adolescent Pregnancy Prevention Inc, comt mem; East Carolina Organization Black Fac & Staff, prog comt mem; Hospice Volunteer, Home Health & Hospice Care Inc; Certified Clin Practitioner, recertified CCSW, 1994; Chi Zeta-Phi Alpha ECU-Sch Social Work Chapter Phi Alpha Nat Social Work Hon Soc, fac adv. **Home Addr:** PO Box 21061, Greenville, NC 27858.

## LEWIS, LEMUEL E.

Manager, chief financial officer. **Personal:** son of Minnie and Charles (deceased); married Sandra; children: Tanya. **Educ:** Darden Grad Sch; Univ Va, BA, econs; Univ Va, MBA, 1972. **Career:** Chief financial officer (retired); Landmark Commun Inc, exec vpres & chief financial officer, 2000-06, vpres; Fed Res Bank Richmond, dir, 2004, dep chmn, 2007-08, chmn, 2009-, Fed Res Bank Atlanta, 2008-10, chmn; Class C, Dir Richmond Bd, 2005-; Q Interactive Inc, staff, 2005, dir, 2013-; Markel Corp, dir, 2007-, bd mem; LocalWeather.com, pres, 2008-; KLAS-TV, pres & gen mgr; NewsChannel5, pres, gen mgr; Owens & Minor Inc, dir, 2011-. **Orgs:** Bd mem, Fed Res Bank Richmond, 2004, Chmn audit comt, 2005-08; bd mem, Class C; bd mem & bd trust mem, Vi Found Independant Col; bd mem, Landmark Commun Inc, 2006-08, dir; bd mem & mem audit comt, Dollar Tree Stores Inc, dir, 2007-; chmn bd dir, LocalWeather.com, 2009. **Business Addr:** Chairman, Federal Reserve Bank of Richmond, 502 S Sharp St, Baltimore, MD 21203, **Business Phone:** (410)951-4655.

## LEWIS, LEO E., III

Athletic director, football player, consultant. **Personal:** Born Sep 17, 1956, Columbia, MO; son of Leo (deceased) and Doris (deceased); married Benita; children: Lauren & Lindsay. **Educ:** Univ Mo, BS, educ, 1980; Univ Tenn; Univ Minn, PhD, kinesiol & sports psychol, 1997. **Career:** Football player (retired), consultant; Calgary Stampeders, wide receiver, 1980; Hamilton Tiger-Cats, wide receiver, 1980; Minn vikings, wide receiver, 1981-89, 1990-91, dir player develop, 1992-2005; Univ Minn, Dept Kinesiology & Leisure Studies, instr, 1986-94, assoc athletic dir, currently; Athletic Serv LLC, cert consult & pres, 1993-; St Cloud State Univ, Dept Health Phys Educ, adj instr, 1999-2000. **Orgs:** Sigma Pi Phi; AAASP; NASSS; Mizzou Alumni Asn; Capital Campaign Steering Comt; founder & pres, Lewis Sports Found, 1999-. **Home Addr:** PO Box 46451, Eden Prairie, MN 55344, **Home Phone:** (612)382-7160. **Business Addr:** Founder, President, Lewis Sports Foundation, PO Box 46451, Eden Prairie, MN 55344, **Business Phone:** (952)886-3399.

## LEWIS, LILLIAN J.

Social worker. **Personal:** Born Apr 20, 1926, Chicago, IL; children: Robert, Gloria, Benjamin & Vivian. **Career:** US Naval Hosp, 1955-63; DeWitt Army Hosp, nurs div, 1963-65; Group Health Assoc, clin asst, 1966-70; Manpower Admin, chief support serv, 1971-. **Orgs:** Comn elect, Marvin Mandel; chmn, Community Affairs, 1970-72; Prince George County Pub Sch Emergency Sch Assistance Prog, 1971; Nat Org Women, Nat Polit Womens Caucus, Mass State Dem Steering Comt, 1976, Nat Women's Polit Caucus Affirm Action Task Force; vpres, Nat Asn Advan Colored People; c; adv bd, Model Cities Fel League Women Voters; Prince Georges Pol Womens Caucus & Affirm Action Coord; Prince George Ment Health Asn; bd dir, SChristian Leadership Conf Md Chap, Prince Georges County Md Black Dem Coun. **Honors/Awds:** Certificate of Appreciation for Meritiroius Assistance, US Dept Com, 1970; Certificate of Merit, Nat Asn Advan Colored People, 1973; Delegation At Large, Dem Conv State Md, 1976. **Home Addr:** 7311 Sheriff Rd, Landover, MD 20785. **Business Addr:** Chief Support Service, Manpower Administration.

## LEWIS, DR. LLOYD ALEXANDER

Educator, clergy. **Personal:** Born Nov 12, 1947, Washington, DC; son of Lloyd Alexander and Alice Christine Bell. **Educ:** Trinity Col, AB, 1969; Va Theol Sem, Mdiv, 1972, PhD, 1992; Yale Univ, MA, 1975, MPhil, 1981, PhD, 1985. **Career:** World Coun Churches, comnr; Union Black Episcopalians; Gen Theol Sem, New York, tutor; St Monicas Church, Hartford, asst; St Georges Church, Brooklyn, curate; consult, Standing Liturgical Comn, Episcopal Church, deacon & priest; Gen Theol Sem, New York, adj new testament; Episcopal Bishop Long Island, Canons Theologian; Church St James Jerusalem, Long Beach, New York, hon asst; Episcopal Diocese Long Island, bishops dep educ; George Mercer Jr Memorial Sch Theol, dean; Va Theol Sem, fac, 1978-91, Molly Laird Downs Prof New Testament Lang & Lit at Protestant Episcopal Theol Sem Alexandria Va, 2000-. **Orgs:** Soc Study Black Relig; Soc Bibl Lit; Prog Theol Educ; Comn, Standing Liturgical; Gen Bd Exam Chaplains Episcopal Church. **Home Addr:** 200-16 Hilton Ave, Hempstead, NY 11550, **Home Phone:** (703)461-0977. **Business Addr:** Professor, Virginia Theological Seminary, 3737 Sem Rd, Alexandria, VA 22304, **Business Phone:** (703)461-1713.

## LEWIS, LOIDA NICOLAS

Civil rights activist, executive, lawyer. **Personal:** Born Dec 7, 1942, Sorsogon; married Reginald F; children: Leslie & Christina. **Educ:** St Theresas Col, Manila; Univ Philippines Col Law, law, 1960. **Career:** Law Students Civil Right Res Coun, 1969; Manhattan Legal Serv, 1970-73; Immigration atty, 1979-90; TLC Beatrice Int Holdings Inc, chmn, founder & chief exec officer, 1994-2000; TLC Beatrice, China, chmn & chief exec officer, currently; TLC Beatrice Foods, Philippines, chmn & chief exec officer; Lewis Col, founder & pres, 1999-. **Orgs:** Nat chair, Nat Fedn Filipino Am Asn, 2002-06. **Honors/Awds:** No 1 in Top 50 Women Business Owners in America number, Working Woman Mag, 1994. **Special Achievements:** Book written: "How to Get a Green Card; First Asian American to pass the American Bar without having been educated in the United States". **Home Addr:** 116 Springy Banks Rd, East Hampton, NY 11937-1171, **Home Phone:** (631)324-3770. **Business Addr:** President, Founder, The Lewis College, 479 Magsaysay St Cogon, Sorsogon City4700, **Business Phone:** (635)6-211-34.

## LEWIS, DR. LONZY JAMES

Educator, scientist. **Personal:** Born Aug 29, 1949, Sharon, GA; son of Joseph and Lillian (Seals); married Cynthia Patterson; children: Lillianne Marie, Brianna Nicole & Adrianne Zanetta. **Educ:** Morehouse Col, BS, 1971; Ga Inst Technol, MS, physics, 1973; State Univ NY, Albany, PhD, 1980. **Career:** Deutsches Elektronen-Synchrotron, work study fel, 1970; Ga Inst Technol, EPA trainee, physics dept, Chem dept, 1972-73, Sch Geophys Sci, res sciII, 1980-83; Atmos Sci Res Ctr, res asst, 1974-80; Col St Rose, HCOP prog, math instr, 1979-80; State Univ NY, Albany, res fel; State Miss, Dept Environ, Air Qual Control Off, consult, 1983-93; Jackson State Univ, Dept Physics & Atmos Sci, chmn, 1983-87, assoc prof, 1983-93; Clark Atlanta Univ, Dept Physics, chmn, 1993-98, assoc prof, 1993-; Clark-Atlanta Res Ctr Sci & Technol, fac. **Orgs:** Mem bd, meteor & ocean ed univ, 1983-87, mem 1978-, Am Meteorol Soc; treas, finance comt chmn, 1990-95; conf chmn, 1991-92, 1994-95, 1998-99; Proj Kalleidoscope, 1994-; fac assoc, curric supv, mentor, sci res agt, 1994-00, Ronald E McNair Found; vice chmn, 1995-96; pres, sci ambassador, Nat Soc Black Physicists (NSBP), 1996-98. **Home Addr:** 970 Forest Overlook Dr SW, East Point, GA 30331-8352, **Home Phone:** (404)696-3408. **Business Addr:** Associate Professor, Clark Atlanta University, McPheeters Dennis Hall Rm 102, Atlanta, GA 30314, **Business Phone:** (404)880-8798.

## LEWIS, DR. LYN ETTA

School administrator, educator, chief executive officer. **Personal:** Born Oct 1, 1947, Monroe, LA; daughter of Rufus and Onita. **Educ:** Grambling State Univ, BA, 1968; Univ Tenn, MA, 1970; Wayne State Univ, PhD, 1978. **Career:** Spelman Col, inst sociol, 1969-72; Univ Detroit, assoc prof, sociol, 1973-90; Univ Detroit-Mercy, chair & assoc prof, 1990-2007; Lyn Lewis & Assocs Inc, chief exec officer & pres, 2000-; Detroit Pub Schs, consult, 2001-02; Wayne County Community Col Dist, adj prof, 2009-14. **Orgs:** Boysville Mich; pres, Detroit Adv Coun, 1993-. **Special Achievements:** Book: Don't Hate the Player Learn the Game. **Home Addr:** 14368 Warwick, Detroit, MI 48223, **Home Phone:** (313)836-1877. **Business Addr:** MI.

## LEWIS, DR. MARGARET W.

Educator, administrator. **Personal:** Born Aug 12, 1932, Oviedo, FL; daughter of Morris T Williams and Margaret Ellis Williams; married Howard E; children: Morris T. **Educ:** Fla A&M Univ, Tallahassee, FL, BSN, 1958, PhD, 1977; Ohio State Univ, Columbus, OH, MSN, 1968. **Career:** Fla A&M Univ Hosp, Tallahassee, Fla, staff nurse, 1958-59; Fla A&M Univ, Tallahassee, Fla, instr, 1959-61, asst prof, 1966-78, dean, sch nursing, dean emer, currently; Ctr County Hosp, Belafonte, Pa, supvr, 1961-66; Albany State Col, Albany, Ga, assoc prof, 1978-79; Winston-Salem State Univ, Winston-Salem, NC, dir, div nursing, 1979-82; Brevard Pub Sch, Off Career & Tech Educ, dir, currently. **Orgs:** Bd mem, Fla League Nursing, 1983-84, 1991; bd mem, Big Bend Deaf Ctr, 1989-; Am Nurses Asn, 1958-; Nat League Nursing, 1975-; Fla League Nursing, pres, 1992-. **Home Addr:** 1805 Skyland Dr, Tallahassee, FL 32303, **Home Phone:** (850)386-9270. **Business Addr:** Director of Career & Technical Education, Brevard Public Schools, Office Of Career & Technical Education, Viera, FL 32940, **Business Phone:** (321)633-1000.

## LEWIS, MARTIN

Basketball player. **Personal:** Born Apr 28, 1975, Liberal, KS. **Educ:** Butler Co Comm Col, attended 1994; Seward Co Comm Col, attended 1995. **Career:** Basketball player (retired); Toronto Raptors, small forward, 1995-97; Mobile Revelers, Nat Basketball Asn, D-League, 2001; Roanoke Dazzle, Nat Basketball Asn, D-League, 2002; Kans Cagerz, US Basketball League, 2002.

## LEWIS, MARVIN RONALD

Basketball coach. **Personal:** Born Sep 23, 1958, McDonald, PA; son of Marvin Sr and Venetta; married Peggy; children: Whitney & Marcus. **Educ:** Idaho State Univ, BA, phys educ, 1981, MA, athletic admin, 1982. **Career:** Id State Univ, linebackers coach, 1981-84; Long Beach State Univ, linebackers coach, 1985-86; Univ New Mex, linebackers coach, 1987-89; Univ Pittsburgh, linebackers coach, 1990-91; Kans City Chiefs, coaching internship; San Francisco 49ers, coaching internship; Pittsburgh Steelers, linebackers coach, 1992-95; Baltimore Ravens, defensive coordr, 1996-2001; Wash Redskins, defensive coordr & asst head coach, 2002; Tampa Bay Buccaneers, head coach, 2002; Cincinnati Bengals, head coach, 2003-; Minnesota Vikings, head coach, 2010-; Oakland Raiders, head coach, 2011-. **Orgs:** Marvin Lewis Community Fund, 2003. **Business Addr:** Head Coach, Cincinnati Bengals, 1 Paul Brown Stadium, Cincinnati, OH 45202, **Business Phone:** (513)621-3550.

## LEWIS, MATTHEW MARVIN

Photographer, editor. **Personal:** Born Mar 8, 1930, McDonald, PA; son of Alzenia Heath and Matthew; married Jeannine Wells; children: Charlene, Matthew & Kevin. **Educ:** Howard Univ; Univ Pittsburgh. **Career:** Photographer & editor (retired); Baltimore Afro-Am Newspaper, freelance photogr; Wash Post, asst mgr, ed & photogr; Morgan State Col, instr, 1957-65; Thomasville Times, photogr, 1994-2001; High Pt Enterprise; Our State Mag. **Orgs:** White House New Photograph Asn; Nat Press Photograph Asn; Nat Asn Black Journalists. **Home Addr:** 2 Clark St, Thomasville, NC 27360, **Home Phone:** (910)472-6683.

## LEWIS, MAURICE

Journalist, television news anchorperson. **Personal:** Born Aug 23, 1943, Chicago, IL; married Terry Sloat; children: Stephanie & Kevin. **Career:** Bell Tel; AF Radio, reporter & commentator; Boston TV, reporter; CNL Radio, mgr, 1965-67; WBZ Radio News, reporter, 1969-74; WHDH TV, anchor, 1972-79; WNAC-TV, anchorman & reporter, 1974-76, co-anchorman, 1975-76, news anchorman & reporter, 1976; WHYY, guest journalist, 1976-77; Marlborough Pub Libr, host prog, 2007; Massachusetts Dept Employ & Training Resources, bus serv rep. **Orgs:** Chmn & co-founder, Afro Am Media Asn, 1975-; bd dir, Elma Lewis Sch Fine Art, 1977; bd dir, Family Serv Ctr, 1976; Nat Asn Advan Colored People; bd dir, Urban League, 1976; bd trustee, Graham Jr Col, 1977; Marlborough Regional Chamber Com; dir event planning, Mass Exec Off Transp & Construct. **Home Addr:** 11 First Rd, Marlborough, MA 01752, **Home Phone:** (508)303-8311. **Business Addr:** Reporter, WBZ NewsRadio, 1170 Soldiers Field Rd, Boston, MA 02134, **Business Phone:** (617)787-7000.

## LEWIS, DR. MEHARRY HUBBARD

Educator, president (organization). **Personal:** Born Aug 2, 1936, Nashville, TN; son of Felix E and Helen M; children: Karen Anita & Arlan David. **Educ:** Tenn State Univ, BS, 1959, MS, 1961; Ind Univ, PhD, 1971. **Career:** Educator (retired), executive; Ind Univ, NDEA fel, 1966-67; Sch City Gary, bio teacher, 1966-91; Stud Activ Off, Ind Univ, frat affairs adv, 1967-69, lectr, 1970, vis asst prof, 1970-72; Bullock County Bd Ed, coordr res & eval, 1972-73; Nat Alliance Black Sch Educrs, dir res proj, 1973-74; Tuskegee Inst, Sch Educ, prof educ, asst dean, dir inst res & planning, 1974-84; MGMT Inc, pres, dir, 1984-91; Bullock County, Bd Educ, sr counr, 1992-2000; Tuskegee Inst Relig & Sacred Music, pres & founder, 2000-01; Church Living God, Pillar & Groundthe Truth Inc, pres, chief overseer, 2001-. **Orgs:** Nat Alliance Black Sch Ed; Kappa Delta Pi; Phi Delta Kappa Int; Alpha Kappa Mu Nat Hon Soc; Am Personnel & Guid Asn; ACES Div & AsnNon-White Concerns; gen sec, trustee, ChurchLiving God, Pillar &GroundTruth Inc; youth community, YMCA, 1963-66; Beta Kappa Chi; Chi Sigma Iota Hon Coun & personal servs; Nat & Ala Educ Asn. **Honors/Awds:** President Award, Nat Alliance Black Sch Educrs, 1974. **Special Achievements:** Published numerous poems & articles; published seven in a series of Books: Mary Lena Lewis Tate: vision, The New and Living Way Publishing Company, Nashville, TN, 2005. **Home Addr:** 2301 Tenita Ave, Tuskegee, AL 36083-0384. **Business Addr:** Chief Overseer, Church of the Living God, PO Box 830384, Tuskegee, AL 36083, **Business Phone:** (334)727-5372.

## LEWIS, MELANIE

Journalist. **Personal:** Born Dec 19, 1964, Wilmington, DE; daughter of Leurhman Saulsberry and Pearle Saulsberry. **Educ:** Univ Del, Newark, DE, BA, eng, 1986. **Career:** Univ Del, Newark, Del, resident asst, 1983-84, hall dir, 1984-86; WXDR; WILM-AM, Wilmington, Del, pub affairs reporter, 1984, 1985, traffic reporter, 1986; Des Moines Regist, Des Moines, IA, zone reporter, gen assignment reporter, educ reporter & staff writer, 1986-90; Dallas Morning News, Dallas, Tex, staff writer, 1990-94, bur reporter, 1990; educ reporter, 1991-. **Orgs:** Nat Asn Black Journalists, 1990-; Delta Sigma Theta Sorority, 1990-; Dallas-Ft Worth Asn Black Communicators, 1990-; Educ Writers Asn; Phi Sigma Sigma. **Honors/Awds:** Omicron Delta Kappa, 1985-; Mortar Bd, 1985; Pulitzer Prize, 1986; Media Award, Tex Coun Family Violence; School Bell award, Tex State Teachers Asn; National reporting award, Educ Writers Asn; Two School Bell awards, Tex State Teachers Asn. **Home Addr:** 2506 Wedglea Dr Apt 904, Dallas, TX 75211, **Home Phone:** (214)559-0559.

## LEWIS, MICHAEL WARD

Executive. **Personal:** Born Sep 15, 1949, Detroit, MI; married Jacqueline; children: Kamilah & Neamen. **Educ:** Western Mich Univ, BBA, mgt, 1971; Ind Univ, MBA, finance, 1976. **Career:** Detroit Bank & Trust, opers analyst, 1976-74; Harris Bank, com banking trainee, 1976, com banking officer, 1979, asst vpres, 1981, vpres, 1983, team leader, 1987, svp & mkt exec, 1994, exec vpres com banking, 1998, city region, pres, 2003-13. **Orgs:** Prin & bd chair, bd mem, Chicago United, currently; bd adv, Local Initiatives Support Corp; adv bd, Western Mich Univ's Haworth Col; Exec Club Chicago; Union League Club; Ill Govt Finance Officers Asn; Black MBA Asn; zoning bd, Village Olympia Fields; adv bd, Urban Fin Serv Forum; Kappa Alpha Psi Fraternity; Alumni Asn Ind Univ; Alumni Asn Western Mich Univ. **Home Addr:** 2551 Glen Eagles Dr, Olympia Fields, IL 60461, **Home Phone:** (708)481-7410. **Business Addr:** Board Member, Chicago United, 300 E Randolph St Suite CL920, Chicago, IL 60601-5075, **Business Phone:** (312)977-3060.

## LEWIS, MICHELE

Business owner. **Educ:** Southern Univ, New Orleans, bus admin. **Career:** Afro Am Bk Stop, owner, 1992-. **Business Addr:** Owner, Afro-American Book Stop, 3951 Mag St, New Orleans, LA 70115, **Business Phone:** (504)896-9190.

## LEWIS, MO (MORRIS CLYDE LEWIS)

Football player. **Personal:** Born Oct 21, 1969, Atlanta, GA; married Christy; children: Mo IV & Chirs. **Educ:** Univ Ga. **Career:** Football player (retired); New York Jets, linebacker & right linebacker & left linebacker & mid linebacker & left outside linebacker, 1991-2003, 2005. **Honors/Awds:** Miller Lite Player of the Year, 1994, Three Pro Bowls, 1998-2000; AFC s defensive player of the week, 2000; All-Pro, 1998-2000.

## LEWIS, NATHAN L.
Investment banker. **Personal:** Born GA. **Educ:** Univ Ga, BBA, risk mgt; Clark Atlanta Univ, MBA, finance. **Career:** Security Capital Brokerage, owner, pres & chief exec officer; Nestle USA, Strategy & Treas Dept; Jackson Securities Inc, equity res analyst, 2001, investment banker, vpres, 2006-. **Orgs:** Bd mem, Community Found Financial Literacy; bd mem, Cool Girls. **Business Addr:** Vice President, Jackson Securities Inc, 233 S Wacker Dr, Chicago, IL 60606, **Business Phone:** (312)283-8650.

## LEWIS, NICOLE M.
Executive, vice president (organization). **Educ:** Wayne State Univ, BS, bus admin, 1985, MBA, mkt, 1989. **Career:** Chrysler Corp, dealer representation planner, 1985-89; Adia Personnel Serv, br mgr, 1989-90; United Parcel Serv, area sales mgr, 1990-92, sr mkt mgr, 1992-95; Kelly Serv, sls mgr bus solutions, 1995-98, sls dir, mid markets div, 1998-2000, sr dir corp accts, vpres corp accts nat sales, 2000-04, vpres, supplier diversity develop global sales, 2004-08 & vice pres indust mgt global mkt, 2008-10, vice pres client mkt global mkt, 2010-11, vice pres prod develop global mkt, 2011-. **Orgs:** Bd dir, co-chair & mentor, Exec Leadership Coun, 2006; bd dir, Youth Law Ctr; Delta Sigma Pi, Asn Black Bus Students; bd visitor, Wayne State Univ Irvin D Reid Hons Col, 2012; Prod Develop Mgt Asn, 2012; charter mem, Prod & Serv Develop Coun-Conf Bd, 2013; co-chair, Black Women's Leadership Summit. **Business Addr:** Vice President of Supplier Diversity Development, Kelly Services, 999 W Big Beaver Rd, Troy, MI 48084, **Business Phone:** (248)362-4444.

## LEWIS, ORA LEE (ORA MCQUILLER LEWIS DELGADO KHALID)
Association executive, executive, executive director. **Personal:** Born Apr 27, 1930, Port Huron, MI; daughter of William and Essie Hogan; married Cornelius W; children: Vincent Cornel (deceased), Andrea (Keith King), Craig (Marietta), Lawrence (deceased), Dawn (Bryant Perkins), T Daynean & Caroline Allahna; married Tony Delgado; children: Maria, Madelaine Delgado-Massey & Anthony Jr (deceased). **Educ:** Erie Comn Col, AA, 1973; Univ Buffalo, attended 1994. **Career:** Executive (retired); United Mutual Life Ins Co, sec, 1947-51; Hope Lodge, part-time mgr; Buffalo Criterion, pres, rptr clmnst, 1947-65; Frienship House, prog asst, 1947-49; Mrs Sims, sec atty, 1951-54; Ora-Lee's Sec Serv, owner; YWCA, chaperone, 1956-67; Westminster Comn House, adminr asst, 1967-71; Comn Youths Boys Town, coun; Arts, exec dir; NY State Div Youth, supvr coun; Langston Hughes Inst, admin asst, exec dir, 1975-96. Bk: Memories Time. **Orgs:** Human Serv Asn; E Side Coalition; bd, Rev & Referral, 1972-74; vpres, Embassy Educ Cult Com Model Cities, 1972-74; Consortium Human Serv, 1975-77; Westminster Comn House, 1972-74; Buffalo Sister City Ghana, 1974-77; rep, City Buffalo, 1975; Am Asn Retired Persons; treas, Int League Muslim Women; vol, Am Cancer Soc. **Honors/Awds:** Honor Member Award, vol serv Friendship House, 1949; Community Service Award, Westminster Comn House, 1975; Certificate of Completion, Erie Comn Col, 1976; Outstanding Achivement, Arts Comn Univ, 1976; Certificate of Award, Victoria Sch Reporting, 1976; exhib, Buffalo Savings Bank, 1976; Honorary Doctor of Laws Degree, Faith Grant Col, 1994; Citizenship Award, Empire State Fedn Womens Clubs; Meritorious Service Award, Nat Asn Negro Bus & Prof Womens Clubs Inc; Community Service Award, Minority Mgt Asn; Institute s most sacred African Ancestor s Award, Int Adv Bd. **Home Addr:** 1003 Northland Ave, Buffalo, NY 14215.

## LEWIS, PATRICIA
Administrator, educator. **Career:** La Southwest Col Bookstore, arts, dept chair, dir, commun studies, adj instr, currently. **Orgs:** Chair, Arts Patricia McCollum. **Business Addr:** Director, La Southwest College Bookstore, 1600 W Imperial Hwy, Los Angeles, CA 90047-4899, **Business Phone:** (323)241-5225.

## LEWIS, PEGGY
Government official. **Educ:** Trinity Col, BA, eng, 1977; Howard Univ, MA, hist, 2015. **Career:** WPLG-TV reporter/anchor, 1983-95; White House, spec asst pres, asst chief staff, media affairs, 1995-96; US Dept Labor, dep asst secy pub affairs, 1997-99; Childrens Defense Fund, commun dir, 1999-2002; Alliance Retired Am, dir Commun; Howard Univ, teacher journ, asst prof, broadcast sequence coordr, 2003-13; Trinity Wash Univ, dir media studies, 2013-. **Orgs:** Pres, S Fla Asn Black Journalists, 1991-93; vpres, Alumnae Asn Bd dir, Trinity Col; pres, Big Bros/Big Sisters Greater Miami; Nat Asn Black Journalists; Broadcast Educrs Asn; Delta Sigma Theta Sorority; Links Inc. **Business Addr:** Director of Media Studies, Trinity Washington University, 125 Michigan Ave NE, Washington, DC 20017, **Business Phone:** (202)884-9000.

## LEWIS, RAMSEY EMANUEL, JR.
Musician. **Personal:** Born May 27, 1935, Chicago, IL; son of Ramsey Emanuel and Pauline Richards; married Geraldine Taylor; married Janet Tamillow; children: Vita Denise, Ramsey Emanuel III, Marcus Kevin, Dawn, Kendall, Frayne & Robert. **Educ:** Chicago Music Col, attended 1954; Univ Ill, attended 1954; De Paul Univ, attended 1955; pvt music study. **Career:** Hudson-Ross Inc Chicago, mgr rec dept, 1954-56; Ramsey Lewis Trio, organizer & mem, 1956-; prof appearance, 1957; Randalls Island Jazz Fest, New York, 1959; Saugatuck, Mich Jazz Fest, 1960; Newport Jazz Fest, 1961, 1963; Argo-Cadet recs, rec artist; CBS Recs, 1971-90; Black Entertainment TV, BET Jazz, co-host, 1990-; WNUA-FM Jazz, Ramsey & Yvonne, co-host, 1990-97, Ramsey Lewis Morning show, host, 1997-; lectr music, 1990-; Legends Jazz, co-host, 1990-; Ravinia Festival "Jazz at Ravinia", ser, Chicago, IL, artistic dir, 1992-; Albums: Gentlemen Swing, 1956; Gentlemen Jazz, 1958; Down to Earth, 1959; An Hour With Ramsey Lewis Trio, 1959; Stretching Out, 1960; Ramsey Lewis Trio Chicago, 1960; More Music From Soil, 1961; Never Sunday, 1961; Sound Christmas, 1961; Bossa Nova, 1962; Sound Spring, 1962; Crowd Live at Bohemian Cavern, 1962; Pot Luck, 1963; Barefoot Sunday Blues, 1963; Bach to Blues, 1964; More Sounds Christmas, 1964; At Bohemian Caverns, 1964; Country Meets Blues, 1964; Greatest Sides Vol 1, 1964-67; Crowd, 1965; Choice! Best Ramsey Lewis Trio, 1962-64; Hang Ramsey, 1965; Wade Water, 1966; Movie Album, 1966; Groover, 1966; Hang Sloopy, 1966; Goin' Latin, 1967; Dancing St, 1967; Up Pops Ramsey Lewis, 1967; Maiden Voyage, 1968; Mother Nature's Son, 1968; Live Toyko, 1968; Solid Ivory, 1963-68; Another Voyage, 1969; Piano Player, 1969; Best Ramsey Lewis, 1970; Them Chas, 1970; Back to Roots, 1971; Upendo Ni Pamoja, 1972; Funky Serenity, 1973; Golden Hits, 1973; Solar Wind, 1974; Sun Goddess, 1974; Don't It Feel Good, 1975; Salongo, 1976; Love Notes, 1977; Tequila Mockingbird, 1977; Legacy, 1978; Ramsey, 1979; Routes, 1980; Best Ramsey Lewis, 1981; Blues Night Owl, 1981; Three Piece Suite, 1981; Live At Savoy, 1982; Chance Encounter, 1982; Les Fleurs, 1983; Reunion, 1983; Two Us, 1984; Fantasy, 1985; Keys to City, 1987; A Classic Encounter, 1988; Urban Renewal, 1989; We Meet Again, 1989; Elec Collection, 1991; This Jazz 27, 1991; Ivory Pyramid, 1992; Sky Island, 1993; Urban Knights, 1995; Between Keys, 1996; Urban Knights II, 1997; Dance Soul, 1998; Appassionata, 1999; Urban Knights III, 2000; Ramsey Lewis's Finest Hour, 2000; Urban Knights IV, 2001; Meant To Be, 2002; Collection: Best Ramsey Lewis, 2002; Urban Knights V, 2003; 20th Century Masters-Millennium, 2002; Simple Pleasures, 2003; Time Flies, 2004; Urban Knights VI, 2005; With One Voice, 2005; Best Urban Knights, 2005; Very Best Ramsey Lewis, 2006; Mother Nature's Son, 2007; Songs from Heart: Ramsey Plays Ramsey, 2009; Taking Another Look, 2011. **Orgs:** Bd dir, Merit, 1986-; bd dir, CYCLE, 1987-; bd dir, Gateway Found, 1990-; bd dir, Ravinia Mentor Prog, 1995-; bd dir, Cares Kids Found, 1997-. **Business Addr:** Composer, Pianist & Jazz Legend, Ted Kurland Agency, 173 Brighten Ave Suite 2, Allston, MA 01234, **Business Phone:** (617)254-0007.

## LEWIS, RASHARD QUOVON
Basketball player. **Personal:** Born Aug 8, 1979, Pineville, LA; son of Juanita Brown; married Giovanni Fortes; children: 3. **Career:** Seattle Supersonics, forward, 1998-2007; Orlando Magic, 2007-11; Wash Wizards, 2010-12; Miami Heat, 2012-14. **Home Addr:** 351 Elliott Ave W Suite 500, Seattle, WA 98119.

## LEWIS, RAYMOND ANTHONY, JR. (RAY LEWIS)
Football player. **Personal:** Born May 15, 1975, Bartow, FL; son of Elbert Ray Anthony Sr and Sunseria Keith; children: Ray Anthony III & Rayshad. **Educ:** Univ Miami; Univ Md Univ Col, BA, arts & sci, 2004. **Career:** Football player (retired); Baltimore Ravens, linebacker, 1996-2012. **Orgs:** Founder, Ray Lewis Found; Vietnam Veterans Am Found; Miami Hurricanes football. **Business Addr:** Professional Football Player, Baltimore Ravens, 11001 Owings Mills Blvd, Owings Mills, MD 21117, **Business Phone:** (410)654-6200.

## LEWIS, RETA JO
U.S. attorney. **Personal:** Born Sep 22, 1953, Statesboro, GA; daughter of Charlie and Aleathia; married Carlton. **Educ:** Univ Ga, BA, polit sci, 1975; Am Univ, MA, admin justice, 1978; Emory Univ, JD, 1989. **Career:** Democracy S Africa, Nelson Mandela USA Tour, trip dir, 1991; Verner Liipfert Bernhard McPherson & Hand, atty, 1989-91; DC Govt, DC Dept Pub Works, chief staff, 1992-93; Exec Off Pres, White House, spec asst pres, polit affairs, 1993-95, sr domestic polit advisor & prin staff coordr; Arter & Hadden, coun, 1996-97; Greenberg Traurig, partner, 2000-07; Edwards Wildman Palmer LLP, coun, 2007-10; US Chamber Com, vpres & counr to pres, 1998-2000; Vanderbilt Consult LLC, founding partner, managing prin; US govt Denver, prin liaison; Edwards Angell Palmer & Dodge LLP, coun; Obama-Biden Transition Comt, bus liaison to pvt sector, 2010; US Dept State, spec rep global intergovernmental affairs, 2010-13. **Orgs:** Delta Sigma Theta, 1997; chair, DC Comn Women; nat tour dir, Nelson Mandela eight city USA tour; Broader Image Inc, 1997; adv coun, Women's Info Network, 1997; Emory Law Sch Coun, 1998; Outreach Prog head, US Chamber Com, 2002-, vpres & counr, US Chamber Com, 2002-; State Bar Ga. **Home Addr:** 2030 16th St NW, Washington, DC 20009, **Home Phone:** (202)328-9355. **Business Addr:** Managing Principal, Founder, Vanderbilt Consulting LLC, 888 16th St NW Suite 800/814, Washington, DC 20001, **Business Phone:** (202)349-0880.

## LEWIS, DR. RICHARD ALLEN, SR.
Administrator, chief financial officer. **Career:** African Methodist Episcopal Church, treas & chief financial officer, 1996-, Connectional Lay Econ Develop Corp (CLEDC), advisor, consult. **Home Addr:** 512 8th Ave S, Nashville, TN 37203, **Home Phone:** (615)259-3771. **Business Addr:** Treasurer, Chief Financial Officer, African Methodist Episcopal Church, 1134 11th St NW, Washington, DC 20001, **Business Phone:** (202)371-8700.

## LEWIS, RICHARD JOHN, SR.
Government official. **Personal:** Born Jun 7, 1936, Manheim, WV; son of Thomas Ellington (deceased) and Ida McLane Carroll; children: Richard Jr & Thomas. **Educ:** Numerous Govt, Com Insts & Comput Manufacture Sponsored Training, 1983; Liberty Univ, Lynchburg, VA, 1991. **Career:** Government official (retired); Dept Health & Human Servs, Washington, DC, from clerk/typist to comput programmer, 1964-70, sr comput systs programmer, 1970-80, chief, software mgt div, 1980-84; Adv Mgt Inc, McLean, Va, comput security consult, 1984-91. **Orgs:** Past chmn, Audit Comt, Pitts burghers Wash, DC Inc, 1985-90; Am Legion, 1972-; Marine Corps Asn. **Home Addr:** 3214 SE Quay St, Port St Lucie, FL 34984, **Home Phone:** (772)336-7751.

## LEWIS, ROBERT ALVIN, JR.
Airline executive, executive. **Personal:** Born Jul 10, 1945, Henderson, NC; son of Robert A Sr and Dorothy A; married Joanne Mangum; children: Derek Robert. **Educ:** NCA State Univ, BS, aero space engineering, 1966; Univ Conn, MS, aerospace engineering, 1969, MBA, 1975. **Career:** Pratt & Whitney, dir, int sales & serv, 1995-. **Orgs:** Am Inst Aeronaut & Astronaut, 1966. **Honors/Awds:** Outstanding Contributor to Corporation, UTC, 1992. **Special Achievements:** Propfan Power, Asn Singapore Licensed Aircraft Engrs, 1988; "Choosing Propulsion Technology," Alfred Wegener Inst, Germany, 1988; "Advances in Commercial Aviation," Indian Aeronautical Soc", 1990; "High Thrust Engines for Middle East," Abu Dhabi, 1994. **Home Addr:** 197 Fairview Dr, South Windsor, CT 06074-2200, **Home Phone:** (860)644-8780. **Business Addr:** Director of International Sales & Services, Pratt & Whitney, 400 Main St, East Hartford, CT 06108, **Business Phone:** (860)565-4321.

## LEWIS, RODERICK ALBERT
Football player. **Personal:** Born Jun 9, 1971, Washington, DC; married Becky. **Educ:** Univ Ariz, grad. **Career:** Football player (retired); Houston Oilers, tight end, 1994-96; Tenn Oilers, tight end, 1997. **Business Addr:** Tight End, Tennessee Titans, 460 Great Circle Rd, Nashville, TN 37228, **Business Phone:** (615)565-4000.

## LEWIS, RONALD ALEXANDER
Football player. **Personal:** Born Mar 25, 1968, Jacksonville, FL. **Educ:** Fla State Univ, commun, 1989. **Career:** Football player (retired); San Francisco 49ers, wide receiver, 1990, 1992; Green Bay Packers, wide receiver, 1992-94. **Home Addr:** 5812 Geranium Rd, Jacksonville, FL 32209.

## LEWIS, RONALD C.
Government official, firefighter. **Personal:** Born Jun 15, 1934, Philadelphia, PA; married Leslie Annette Williams; children: Terri Anne, Anita Marie & Audrey Yvonne. **Career:** Government Official (retired); Philadelphia Fire Dept, fire fighter, fire lt & fire capt, 1956-78, fire battalion chief, 1974-78; Int Asn Black Prof Firefighters, regional vpres, 1974-77, affirm action officer, 1978-82; City Richmond, dir dept fire & emergency serv, fire chief, 1978-95. **Orgs:** Life mem, Nat Asn Advan Colored People, 1960-; Int Asn Black Prof Fire Fighters, 1970-; pres, Valiants IncI ABPFF Local, 1970-74; Int Asn Fire Chiefs, 1978-; bd dir, Offenders Aid & Restoration, 1979-81; Muscular Dystrophy Asn, 1979-81; Bldg Officials &Code Admin, 1979-; Alcohol & Drug Abuse Prev & Treat Serv, 1984-90; bd, Rich Chap Am Red Cross, 1989-. **Honors/Awds:** S Singleton Award of Excellence, Valiants IA BPFF Philadelphia, 1977; Outstanding Service Award, NE Reg IABPFF, 1978; Outstanding Achievement Award, Nat Asn Advan Colored People Richmond Chap, 1978; Outstanding Firefighter, Phoenix Soc, 1979; Person of the Year, State Va EEO, 1991; Freedom Award, Nat Asn Advan Colored People, 1994. **Special Achievements:** Was Richmond's first African-American fire chief, from 1978-95. **Home Addr:** 3709 Birdwood Rd, Richmond, VA 23234-2917, **Home Phone:** (804)275-7700.

## LEWIS, RONALD N.
Executive. **Career:** Trans World Airlines; Greater Orlando Aviation Authority, staff, 1992-, dir airport oper & interim dep exec dir opers, 1994-2010, dep exec dir opers, 2010-. **Orgs:** Chmn, Ground Transp Comt, Greater Orlando Aviation Authority. **Business Addr:** Deputy Executive Director - Operations, Greater Orlando Aviation Authority, 1 Jeff Fuqua Blvd, Orlando, FL 32827-4399, **Business Phone:** (407)825-2001.

## LEWIS, RONALD STEPHEN (RON LEWIS)
Counselor, television producer. **Personal:** Born Sep 3, 1950, Raleigh, NC; son of Thomas J and Beatrice H; married Veronica Nichols; children: N'Zinga Monique & Preston Stanford-Hashim. **Educ:** NC Cent Univ, BA, sociol, 1973. **Career:** Wake County Opportunities Inc, social servs coordr, 1973-78; Rhodes Furniture, collection Officer, credit counr, 1978-81; K-Mart, mgt, 1981-82; Va CARES, pre/post release counr, 1982-83; Small Bus Broadcasting Serv, studio supvr, 1983-89; St Augustine's Col, WAUG-TV, producer, host, 1990-; Drug Action Inc, Awareness Ctr, coordr, substance abuse counr, 1990-; Shaw Univ, NC Cent Univ, radio progr, 1990-; Chapel Hill & Carrboro Sch Syst, dir fam resource ctr, 1994-. **Special Achievements:** Produced a four-part television series on substance abuse recovery, 1992; co-produced additional programing for local base origination such as: Black Male, Are we an Endangered Species?. **Home Addr:** 2600 Talbot Ct, Raleigh, NC 27610, **Home Phone:** (919)255-1486.

## LEWIS, DR. SAMELLA SANDERS
Educator, artist, writer. **Personal:** Born Feb 27, 1924, New Orleans, LA; daughter of Rachel Taylor and Samuel; married Paul G; children: Alan & Claude. **Educ:** Hampton Univ, BA, 1945; Hampton Inst, MA, 1947; Ohio State Univ, MA, art hist, 1948; PhD, art hist, cult anthrop, 1951. **Career:** Author, artist, art educator; writer; film maker; Hampton Inst, instr, 1946-47; Morgan State Univ, assoc prof, 1948-53; Fla A&M Univ, prof & chair Fine Arts Dept, 1953-58; State Univ NY, Plattsburgh, prof, 1958-68, Fulbright fel, 1962; Nat Defense Act fel, 1964-65; Ford Found fel, 1965, 1981; Calif State Univ, assoc prof, 1966-67; Los Angeles Co Mus Art, coordr educ, 1968-69; Scripps Col, prof art hist, 1969-84, prof emer, 1984-; Nat Conf Artists, nat co-chairperson, 1972-74; Clark Humanities Mus, dir, 1976-84; Int Rev African Am Art, founder, 1975-; Nat Endowment Arts, proj dir, 1980-; Nat Res Coun, 1981; Col Art Asn Am, adminr, 1990-94; Bks: Black Artists Art, 2 vols, 1976; Art: African Am, 1978; Art Elizabeth Catlett, 1984; Mus African Am Art, Los Angeles, founder, 1986-; African Am Art & Artists, 1990; African Am Art Young People, 1991. **Orgs:** Abbr Arts Panel, NEA, 1975-78; dir & founder, Mus African Am Art, 1976-80; pres, Contemp Crafts Inc, co-founder, 1970; bd mem, Mus African Am Art; Art Educ Black Art Int Quart Nat Conf Artists; Col Art Asn Am; pres, Oxum Int; Nat Asn Advan Colored People. **Honors/Awds:** Hon doctorate, Chapman Col, 1976; Who's Who in Black Am Award, 1982; Senate of Calif Spec Award, 1983; Vesta Award, 1984; Scripps Col Fac Recognition Award, 1985; Los Angeles Achievement in the Visual Arts Award, 1985; Citation for Distinguished Alumnae, Ohio State Univ, 1986; Nat Conf of Artists Achievement Award, 1988; Legendin Our Time Tribute, Essence, 1990; Hon doctorate, Hampton Univ, 1990; Lifetime Achievement Award, Brandywine Workshop, 1992; Charles White Lifetime Achievement Award, 1993; Hon doctorate, Univ Cincinnati, 1993; UNICEF Award, 1995; Hon doctorate, Bennett Col, 1996; Distinguished Scholar Award, Getty Ctr Hist Art & Humanities, 1996; Alumni Association Award, Ohio State Univ, 2005. **Special Achievements:** Written five books and five scholarly articles; First African American woman to receive her doctorate in fine arts and art history; First African American-owned art publishing house, Contemporary Crafts. **Home Addr:** 1237 S Masselin Ave, Los Angeles, CA 90019-2544, **Home Phone:** (323)935-2693. **Business Addr:** Professor Emeritus, Scripps College, 1030 Columbia Ave, Claremont, CA 91711-3948, **Business Phone:** (909)621-8000.

## LEWIS, DR. SAMUEL L., JR.
Transport worker. **Personal:** Born Jul 19, 1953, Philadelphia, PA; son of Samuel Sr and Georgianna Johnson. **Educ:** Penn State Univ, BA, 1976; Community Col Philadelphia, AS, Mgt, 1986; MS, Admin Info Resource Mgt, 1998. **Career:** Transport worker (retired); WPHL-TV Philadelphia, broadcast dir, 1976-77; Consolidated Rail Corp, opers mgr, 1977-83; New Jersey Transit Rail Opers, revenue analyst, 1983-85, sr opers planner, 1985. **Orgs:** Conf Minority Transp Officials, Am Pub Transit Asn Minority Affairs Comn, Omega Psi Phi Frat, F&AM, Brain Trust, Penn State Alumni Asn, Concerned Black Men Philadelphia, Nat Asn Watch & Clock Collectors, Black Music Asn; Historically black cols & univs Transp Consortium; transp res bd, Nat Acad Scis; Columbia Univ Master Bus Admin Conf; Wharton Sch Black Master Bus Admin Conf. **Honors/Awds:** Outstanding Young Men of America, 1984, 1986, 1987; Honorary Doctorate of Humane Letters, Faith Grant Col, 1995. **Home Addr:** 1643 Cobbs Creek Pky, Philadelphia, PA 19143-5212, **Home Phone:** (215)726-8890.

## LEWIS, SARASVATI ANANDA
Television show host, executive. **Personal:** Born Mar 21, 1973, San Diego, CA; daughter of Stanley and Yvonne; children: 1. **Educ:** Howard Univ, BA, hist, 1995. **Career:** Black Entertainment TV, "Teen Summit", host, "1st Annual BET Awards", host, "Politically Incorrect", host, "The View", host, "The Chris Rock Show", host, "The Late Late Show with Craig Kilborn", host; MTV, video jockey, 1997, "Total Request Live", host; "Wanna Be a VJ Too", host; "Hot Zone", host; "The Ananda Lewis Show", 2001; A&E, "America's Top Dog", co-host; ABC, "Celebrity Mole: Yucatan", contestant, 2004; Radio Show, "The John Salley Block Party", co-host; TV Series: "The Ultimate Survival", 2000; "Whitney T.V", 2000; "Method & Red", 2004; "Pilot", 2004; "America's Top Dog", 2004; "High School Reunion", 2004; The Insider, chief corresp, 2004-; L.A. Radio Station 100.3, "The Beats Morning Show", co-host, 2005. **Orgs:** Nat spokesperson, Nat Reading Fundamental; Am People Native Am Descent; Blackfoot People; Journalists Mont. **Honors/Awds:** Image Award, Nat Asn Advan Colored People, 1996; 14th Annual Inner City Destiny Awards, 2006. **Special Achievements:** Featured in People magazines as 50 Most Beautiful People in 2000; Nominated for Cable Ace Award; Nominee, Teen Choice Award, 2000, 2002. **Home Addr:** , San Fernando, CA. **Business Addr:** Chief Correspondent, The Insider, 5555 Melrose Ave, Hollywood, CA 90038.

## LEWIS, SHARMA
Bishop, clergy. **Personal:** Born Jan 1, 1964, Statesboro, GA. **Educ:** Mercer Univ, BS, 1985; Univ W Ga, MS, 1988; Gammon Theol Sem, MDiv, 1999. **Career:** Res biologist acad & corp sectors, 1988-96; Ben Hill United Methodist Church, Atlanta, assoc pastor, sr assoc pastor, 1999; Powers Ferry United Methodist Church, Marietta, GA, sr pastor; Wesley Chapel, sr pastor, 2007-10; Atlanta-Decatur-Oxford Dist, United Methodist Church, 2010; Southeastern Jurisdiction United Methodist Church, elected bishop & resident bishop Richmond episcopal area, 2016-. **Orgs:** Atlanta Alumnae Chap Delta Sigma Theta, Black Clergywomen & Black Methodists Church Renewal United Methodist Church, Southeastern Jurisdiction Comt Coord & Accountability, SEJ Intentional Growth Ctr; Wesley Woods Found, SEJ Comt Episcopacy; Standing Comt Evangelism World Methodist Coun United Methodist Church; Wesley Theol Sem bd gov; ex-officio six United Methodist cols Va Conf. **Honors/Awds:** G. Ross Freeman Leadership Award, 2010; Harry Denman Evangelism Award, 2010; Gammon Theological Seminary Distinguished Alumna Award, 2014; Delta Sigma Theta Pinnacle Award; Torch Award. **Special Achievements:** First African-American woman elected to lead the delegation of the North Georgia Conference to the General and Jurisdictional Conferences, 2012; first African-American woman to be elected bishop in the Southeastern Jurisdiction of the United Methodist Church; first female senior pastor and first African-American pastor of Powers Ferry United Methodist Church; first woman to serve as senior minister of Wesley Chapel UMC; first woman to serve as district superintendent in the Atlanta-Decatur-Oxford District. **Business Addr:** PO Box 5606, Glen Allen, VA 23060, **Business Phone:** (804)521-1102.

## LEWIS, SHERMAN PAUL
Football coach. **Personal:** Born Jun 29, 1942, Louisville, KY; married Toni; children: Kip & Eric. **Educ:** Mich State Univ, educ admin, 1974. **Career:** Football player, coach (retired); Toronto Argonauts, 1964-65; New York Jets, 1966-67; Mich State Univ, asst head coach & defensive coord, 1969-82; San Francisco 49ers, running back coach, 1983-88, receiver coach, 1989-91; Green Bay Packers, offensive coordr, 1992-99; Minn Vikings, offensive coordr, 2000-01; Detroit Lions, offensive coordr, 2002-04; Redskins mid-way, head coach, 2009, offensive consult. **Honors/Awds:** College Player of the Year, 1963. Super Bowl champion, XIX, XIII, XXIV, XXXI. **Home Addr:** PO Box 10628, Green Bay, WI 54307.

## LEWIS, DR. SHIRLEY ANN REDD
Executive, school administrator. **Personal:** Born Jun 11, 1937, Winding Gulf, WV; daughter of Robert F and Thelma Danese Biggers; married Ronald; children: Mendi. **Educ:** Univ Calif Berkeley, BA, span & speech, 1960, MSW, 1970; Stanford Univ, PhD, 1979; Ghana & Univ, London, cert, African studies. **Career:** Educational administrator (retired); Numerous teaching positions, 1962; Meharry Med Col, educ specialist, from asst to vpres, 1981-84, assoc dean, acad affairs, 1984-86; Gen Bd Higher Educ & Ministry United Methodist Church, educ exec, 1986-91, asst gen secy, 1992-94; Paine Col, pres, 1994-2007. **Orgs:** Bd dir, United Negro Col Fund; Augusta United Way; GA Bank & Trust; Assoc Gov Bds; Zeta Phi Beta Sorority Inc; bd mem, Augusta Metro Chamber Com. **Home Addr:** 1238 Beman St, Augusta, GA 30904, **Home Phone:** (706)737-6063.

## LEWIS, STEPHEN CHRISTOPHER
Chief executive officer, executive. **Personal:** Born Aug 19, 1950, Chicago, IL; son of Robert and Elizabeth Stewart; married Stefanie Woolridge. **Educ:** Bradley Univ, BSIE, 1972; Marquette Univ, MBA, 1975, EMBA, 1995; Duke Univ, Exec MBA. **Career:** Jos Schlitz Brewing Co, supt prod scheduling, 1974-78; Ford Motor Co, Escort/Lynx, planning analyst, 1978-82, Taurus/Sable, planning analyst, 1982-83, small car import mgr, 1983-86, Dearborn, MI, advan prod mgr, 1988-91, assoc dir, dir, strategic planning & mfg exec off; New Mkt Develop, dir mfg, 2000-; Auto Alliance Inc, gen mgr, 1998-; Success Guide, Cleveland, OH, regional dir, 1990-; Nat Black MBA Asn, vpres, 1986-89, pres, 1994-97, actg pres, 2010-11, interim chief exec officer. **Orgs:** Omega Psi Phi, baselius, 1971-72; Nat Asn Advan Colored People, 1978-; Nat Tech Asn, 1983-85; pres, Nat Black MBA, detroit chap, 1984, life mem, 1988-, nat pres, 1994-98; chairperson, Nat Scholar, 1984-, nat vpres, 1985-; Detroit Econ Club, 1989-; Engineering Soc Detroit, 1989-; Black Achievers Indust, YMCA-Detroit, 1996; chair, Ford Employees African Ancestry Network, 2001-, dir mfg strategy; Am Bar Asn; Asn MBA Exec. **Honors/Awds:** Omega Man of the Year, Omega Psi Phi, 1971; Black Achievers Industry, YMCA Greater New York, 1976; President's Award, 1984; Outstanding MBA of the Year, 1990; Best in Business, Success Guides, 2000. **Home Addr:** 5944 Naneva Ct, West Bloomfield, MI 48322, **Home Phone:** (248)737-1620. **Business Addr:** Board of Director, National Black MBA Association Inc, 400 W Peachtree St NW Suite 203, Atlanta, GA 30308, **Business Phone:** (312)236-2622.

## LEWIS, STEVE EARL
Track and field athlete. **Personal:** Born May 16, 1969, Los Angeles, CA; son of Stella. **Educ:** Univ Calif, Los Angeles, BA (with hons), hist, 1992. **Career:** Track & field athlete (retired). **Orgs:** Santa Monica Track Club, 1987-93; Int Asn Athletics Federations. **Honors/Awds:** Gold medal, Olympic Games, Seoul, 400 meters, 1988, 4*400 metres relay, 1988; National Collegiate Athletic Association Championships 400 m, Winner, 1990; US Track and Field Championships; Gold medal, Olympic Games, Barcelona, 400 meters relay, 1992; Silver medal, Olympic Game Barcelona, 1992; Hall of Fame, Univ Calif, Los Angeles, 2004.

## LEWIS, TERRY STEVEN
Songwriter, music producer, business owner. **Personal:** Born Nov 24, 1956, Omaha, NE; married Indira Singh; children: Talin & Tierra; married Karyn White; children: Ashley Nicole. **Career:** Producer, business owner; Flyte Tyme Prod, owner, 1982-; Flyte Tyme Tunes, 1984-; Perspective Records, owner, 1991-; Albums: "On the Rise", 1983; "Just the Way You Like It", 1984; "Fragile", 1984; "High Priority", 1985; "Cherrelle & Alexander O'Neil", 1985; "Alexander O'Neal"; "Tender Love", 1985; "Force MD's"; "Control", 1986; "Rythm Nation", 1989; "janet", 1993; "The Velvet Rope", 1997; "Rainbow", 1999; "Mountain High", "Valley Low", 1999; "When A Women Loves", 2000; Own Label Artists: Sounds of Blackness, Mint Condition, Lo-Key, Raja-Nee, Ann Nesby. **Home Addr:** PO Box 36038, Minneapolis, MN 55435. **Business Addr:** Owner, Flyte Tyme Productions Inc, PO Box 398045, Edina, MN 55435-5106, **Business Phone:** (952)897-3901.

## LEWIS, REV. THEODORE RADFORD, JR.
Clergy. **Personal:** Born Jul 23, 1946, Galveston, TX; son of Theodore Radford Sr and Carrie Ann Eaton; married Martha Fox; children: Geoffrey Bernard & Carrie Elizabeth. **Educ:** Univ Houston, BA, 1970; Sam Houston State Univ Grad Sch, attended 1974; Univ Houston Continuing Educ Ctr, attended 1977; Episcopal Theol Sem, MDiv, 1982. **Career:** Fed Pre-Release Ctr, asst counr, 1970-71; Harris County Adult Probation Dept, probation officer, 1971-75; US Probation & Parole Off, probation & parole officer, 1975-79; St James Episcopal Church, asst rector, 1982-83; St Luke Episcopal Church, rector, 1983-91; Tex Southern Univ, Episcopal chaplain, 1983-91; Calvary Episcopal Church, rector & pastor, 1992-; Charleston Youth Leadership League, elder, 1997-. **Orgs:** Union Black Episcopalians, 1982-; chaplain, dean educ, rec & seal keeper, mem comt chair, Nu Phi Chap, Omega Psi Phi Fraternity, 1987-91; Bd Edu Redirection, 1995-98; chaplain, Mu Alpha Chap, Omega Psi Phi Fraternity, 1992-; Bd Crisis Ministries, Inc, 1997-2003; chaplain, vol, Homeless Shelter Crisis Ministries, 1997-; gov bd, Charlestown Acad, 1997-98; Charleston County Sch Bd, 1998-2003. **Honors/Awds:** Omega Man of the Year, Nu Phi Chapter, Omega Psi Phi Fraternity, 1990; Scroll of Honor, Mu Alpha Chapter, Omega Psi Phi Fraternity, 1992; Omega Man of the Year, Mu Alpha Chapter, Omega Psi Phi, 1999; Delta Sigma Theta, Merit Award for Service, N Charleston Alumnae Chapter, 1999; Scroll of Honor, NCP, Mu Alpha Chapter, 2002; honoree in the field of religion, MOJA Arts Festival, Charleston, SC, 2003. **Home Addr:** 2945 Limestone Blvd, Charleston, SC 29414-7044, **Home Phone:** (843)769-6106. **Business Addr:** Rector, Calvary Episcopal Church, 106 Line St, Charleston, SC 29403-5305, **Business Phone:** (843)723-3878.

## LEWIS, THERTHENIA WILLIAMS
Educator. **Personal:** Born Mar 1, 1947, Dayton, OH; daughter of Alexander Williams and Mattie Williams; married Jerry J. **Educ:** Univ Dayton, BS, 1975; Ohio State Univ, MS, 1978; Atlanta Univ, MSW, 1986; Univ Pittsburgh, MPH, 1992. **Career:** Ohio State Univ, grad admin asst, 1976-78; Wernle Residential Ctr, adolescent therapist, 1978-81; Ga State Univ, Col Arts & Sci, asst dir, 1982-84; Bur Planning City Atlanta, HUD fel intern, 1984-85; Univ Pittsburgh, grad stud asst, 1986-87; C Hosp, Family Intervention Ctr, Pittsburgh, Pa, 1988-92; Clark Atlanta Univ, Sch Social Work, Kellogg Proj, 1992-94, asst prof, 1994-, dir stud affairs, instr social work, currently; Southeast Ark Behav Healthcare Syst, DASEP proj dir, currently. **Orgs:** Adv community mem, Big Sisters/Big Bros Adv Bd, 1977-78; Am Soc Pub Admin, 1984-; Nat Asn Black Social Workers, 1987; Am Home Econs Asn, 1987; Black Child Develop Inst, 1987; Coun Social Work Educ, 1988; Am Pub Health Asn, 1988; Am Asn Univ Prof, 1994; Am Asn Ment Retardation, 1994; Community Health Promotions & Educ Network. **Home Addr:** 1515 Snapfinger Rd, Decatur, GA 30032-5170, **Home Phone:** (404)284-0470. **Business Addr:** Project Director, Southeast Arkansas Behavioral Healthcare System Inc, 2500 Rike Dr, Pine Bluff, AR 71613, **Business Phone:** (870)534-2206.

## LEWIS, THOMAS A.
Football player, athletic director. **Personal:** Born Jan 10, 1972, Akron, OH. **Educ:** Ind Univ, BS, commun, 1994. **Career:** Football player (retired), athletic dir; New York Giants, wide receiver, 1994-97; Club Beauty, owner, 1994-2010; Chicago Bears, wide receiver, 1998; MONY sports, exec; Syndicated Capital Inc, dir athletic mgt div, 2002-; Thomas Lewis, owner, 2006-08; Farmers Ins, RDM, 2008-10; Cambridge Financial, partner, 2010-; PepsiCo-Gatorade, mkt develop mgr, 2012-. **Orgs:** Pres, GladMan Foudation. **Business Addr:** Market Development Manager, PepsiCo - Gatorade, 700 Anderson Hill Rd, Purchase, NY 10577, **Business Phone:** (914)253-2000.

## LEWIS, TINA
Restaurateur, business owner. **Personal:** married Harold; children: Jeremy, Jonathan & Jennifer. **Career:** United Airlines & Continental Airlines, flight attend & in-flight serv, Sir Speedy Printing (Los Angeles), franchise owner, 1982-86; HRL Group LLC, co-founder (with husband Harold Lewis), 1987-. **Orgs:** Founder, African Am Visionary & Inspirational Leaders (AVAIL) Scholar Prog; Trumpet Found (Atlanta, GA), Scholar Providers; Susan G Komen Cancer Found Nat Speaker's Bur; Links Inc, San Diego Chap; former bd dirs, Susan G Komen Advocacy Alliance; former bd dirs, Scripps Polster Breast Ctr. **Honors/Awds:** California Legislature Assembly Entrepreneurial Spirit Award; United Negro College Fund Frederick D. Patterson Award; Urban League Equal Opportunity Award; National Coalition of 100 Black Women Economic Development Award; McDonald's Corporation "Ronald Award" for Community Service; McDonald's Corporation NBMOA Lifetime Achievement Award; 2010 Women of Distinction Award; McDonald's 365Black Award. **Special Achievements:** Managed 20 McDonald's restaurant franchises from 1987-2011.

## LEWIS, TOM
Activist, president (organization), school administrator. **Personal:** Born Aug 7, 1939, Chadbourn, NC; son of Gaston and Martha; married Lucille; children: Jason, Patrick & Tisha. **Educ:** Am Univ, BS, admin justice, law enforcement, 1975. **Career:** Metrop Police Dept, DC, police officer, 1965-86; Hope Village Community Treat Ctr, voc counr, 1986; Lutheran Social Serv, counr, 1987-89; ForLove C, coordr, child & family serv, 1989-93; Fishing Sch, founder, exec dir & chief exec officer, 1990-2005, pres emer, 2005-. **Orgs:** Coun mem, Lifers Lorton, 1970; pres, chair safety comn, PTA, 1974-86; chief steward, Fraternal Order Police, 1978-86; Leadership Wash; chairperson, Juv Justice Adv Group, 1988-97; steering comm governance, Mid NE Collab, 1996-97; Hands Across DC. **Home Addr:** 7017 16th St NW, Washington, DC 20012, **Home Phone:** (202)723-1522. **Business Addr:** President Emeritus, Founder, The Fishing School, 4737 Meade St NE, Washington, DC 20019, **Business Phone:** (202)399-3618.

## LEWIS, VICKIE J.
Chief executive officer, executive. **Personal:** married David L Sr; children: David L Jr. **Educ:** Davenport Col; Walsh Col Accountancy & Bus Admin. **Career:** Acct mgr; independent contractor; VMX Int LLC, owner, pres & chief exec officer, 2001-. **Orgs:** Bd mem, Environ Mgt Asn, pres; bd mem, Detroit Black Chamber Com; Detroit Regional Chamber Com; Nat Asn Woman Bus Owners; Booker T Wash Bus Asn; Nat Minority Waste Asn; Mich Minority Supplier Develop Coun; Wayne County Small Bus Enterprise. **Business Addr:** Chief Executive Officer, President, VMX International LLC, Fisher Bldg 3011 W Grand Blvd Suite 2401, Detroit, MI 48202-3099, **Business Phone:** (313)875-9450.

## LEWIS, VINCENT V.
Executive, consultant, president (organization). **Personal:** Born Oct 1, 1938, Wilmington, DE; son of Vincent and Matilda Janet; married Babirette Babineaux; children: Dawn C & Duane A. **Educ:** Upper Iowa Univ, Fayette, IA, BA, 1980; Loyola Col, Baltimore, MD, MBA, 1983. **Career:** Wilmington Housing Authority, Wilmington, DE, vpres & exec dir, 1972-77; Nat Ctr Community Develop, Wash, DC, 1978-79; HUD Hq, Wash, DC, housing mgt officer, 1979-85; Coopers & Lybrand, Wash, DC, mgr, 1982-85; Vinelle Assocs Inc, Wash, DC, pres, 1985-. **Orgs:** Am Soc Pub Admin; Am Mgt Asn; Asn MBA Execs; Nat Asn Housing & Redevelop officials. **Home Addr:** 732 6th St SW Suite 205, Washington, DC 20024, **Home Phone:** (202)484-0391. **Business Addr:** President, Vinelle Associates Inc, 717 D St NW Suite 309, Washington, DC 20004, **Business Phone:** (202)659-4466.

## LEWIS, VIRGINIA HILL
Manager, quality control inspector, chemist. **Personal:** Born Feb 13, 1948, Berria County, GA; daughter of H B and Mary; married Robert; children: Michael & Roslyn. **Educ:** Albany State Col GA, BS, chem, 1970; Univ Pac, Stockton CA, MS, 1972. **Career:** Grad Sch Univ Pac, lab asst, 1972; Albany State Col, advan chemist; 3M Co, Vis Tech Women Prog, Indust Chem Prod Div, process control specialist, qual mgr, 1973, Dyneon, qual mgr, 1998. **Orgs:** Summer training prog Argonne Nat Lab Argonne Ill, 1969; Sunday Sch Teacher, Mt Olivet Bapt Ch St Paul Minn, 1973, 1975-76; social affairs, 3M & community; Step Prog, 3M; Vis Tech Women, 3M; Delta Sigma Theta Sor, 1969. **Honors/Awds:** Alpha Kappa Mu Honor Soc Albany State Col GA, 1967-70; Affiliate ACS, 1968-70; "This Is Your Life" Award. **Home Addr:** 2220 Snowshoe Lane E, St Paul, MN 55119, **Home Phone:** (651)739-3587. **Business Addr:** Quality Manager, Dyneon, 6744 33rd St N, Oakdale, MN 55128, **Business Phone:** (651)733-5353.

## LEWIS, DR. VIVIAN M.
Physician. **Personal:** Born Pensacola, FL; daughter of Edward C and Vivian L Crawley (deceased); married Billie; children: Vivian V Sanford, William P & Beverly Gooden. **Educ:** Fisk Univ, BS, 1952; Univ Okla, Sch Med, MD, 1959. **Career:** Hurley Hosp, rotating intern, 1959-60, pediat residency, 1961-63; Mott Childrens Health Ctr, pediat staff, 1963-69; Lewis Med Servs, pediat pract, 1964-; Dept Maternal & Infant Health Mott Childrens Health Ctr, chairperson, 1967-69; St Joseph Hosp, mem teaching staff; McLaren Hosp, courtesy staff; Mich State Univ, Dept Human Med, asst prof clin pediat; Univ Mich, Med Sch, preceptor interflex prog. **Orgs:** Life mem, Alpha Kappa Alpha Sor Inc; Family Serv Bd; bd dir, Girl Scouts Am; bd dir, Flint Inst Arts; Flint Women Bus Owners' Coun; Mich State Med Soc; Am Med Asn; Nat Med Asn; Am Acad Pediat; Genesee Valley March Dimes Med Adv Comn; Genesee County Med Soc, 1963-; med adv, Flint Easter Seal Soc; Whaley C's Ctr Community Bd; bd mem, Genesee Valley Chap Am Lung Asn, 1969-78; chairperson, Genesee Co March Dimes Campaign, 1971; Flint Acad Med; co-chair, Flint United Negro Col Fund Dr, 1975; adv bd, Mich Nat Bank, Flint, 1976-; adv comn, Univ Mich-Flint; pres, Flint Chap Links Inc, 1983-; citizens adv comn, Univ

Mich-Flint; adv bd, Mich Nat Bank Flint; pres, Greater Flint Pediat Asn; adv bd, Univ Mich Corp, 1986-; pres, Prof Med Corp Hurley Med Ctr; pres, Zonta Club Flint I; Family Servs Bd, 1990-; Whaley C's Community Bd, 1993-; founding mem, bd treas, Hurley Found, 1993-; vpres, Flint Inst Arts Bd; trustee, Community Found Greater Flint; bd & med advisor, Collins Home Nursing Serv. **Honors/Awds:** Community Serv Award, Flint Chap Negro Bus & Prof Women's Club, 1973; Liberty Bell Award Genesee Co Bar Asn, 1975; Pan Hellenic Woman of the Year, 1978; Woman of the Year, Zeta Beta Omega Chap Alpha Kappa Alpha SorInc, 1978; Nana Mills Award, YWCA, 1985; Outstanding Citizen Award, Gamma Delta Boule, Sigma Pi Phi Fraternity, 1985; Behold the Woman Award, Top Ladies Distinction, 1987; Urban Coalition Service Award, 1989; Paul Harris Award, Rotary Club of Flint, 1994. **Special Achievements:** Recognized as an Outstanding African American Woman Physician in publication, Alpha Kappa Alpha Sorority, Heritage Series, 1993; First black woman graduate from University of Oklahoma Medical School; First woman president, Genesee County Medical. **Home Addr:** 1618 Kensington, Flint, MI 48503, **Home Phone:** (313)233-0539. **Business Addr:** Physician, Lewis Medical Services PC, 1910 Robert T Longway Blvd, Flint, MI 48503, **Business Phone:** (810)239-0011.

## LEWIS, W. ARTHUR

Housing developer, clergy. **Personal:** Born Dec 13, 1930, Princeton, NJ; son of George Peter Sr and Blanche E Taylor Chase; married Rose Marie Dais; children: Adrienne Richardson & Andrea. **Educ:** Trenton Jr Col, AA, 1957; Rider Col, Lawrenceville, NJ, BS, 1959, MA, 1977; Harvard Univ, John F Kennedy Sch Govt, cert, 1982; Lutheran Theol Sem, MAR, 1985; Luthern Sch Theol, DMin, 1992. **Career:** United Progress Inc, personnel dir, 1966-68; OIL Int, prog adv, 1968-69; consult, Econ & Manpower Corp, proj mgr 1969-71; NJ Dept Comm Affairs, div dir & asst comnr, 1972-82; Philadelphia OIC, exec dir, 1982-85; Lutheran C & Family Svcs, clergy/adminr, 1986-88; dir, community develop; Evangel Lutheran Church Am, Social Ministry, 1988-90; NJ Dept Comm Affairs, housing adminr, 1990-94; Calvary Lutheran Church, Philadelphia, PA, pastor, 1990-; Lutheran Coun Tidewater, exec dir, 1995-97; Lutheran Church Atonement, Atlanta; Off Gov, dir, currently. **Orgs:** Consult, Nat Urban Coalition, 1974; chmn, Nat State Econ Opportunity Off Dir Asn, 1976-77; bd trustee, Glassboro State Col, 1979-; vpres, NJ Chap ASPA, 1980-82; bd mem, Evesham Twp Sch Dist, 1981-; Alpha Phi Alpha, 1983-; Philadelphia Liberty Bell City Philadelphia 1984; consult, NJ Synod Lutheran Church Am, 1985; bd trustee, NJ Prison Complex, 1991-; Lilly Found; Evangel Lutheran Church Am. **Home Addr:** 41 Country Club Lane, Marlton, NJ 08053, **Home Phone:** (609)983-4596. **Business Addr:** Director Office of African-American Affairs, Office of the Governor, CN 001, Trenton, NJ 08625, **Business Phone:** (609)777-0991.

## LEWIS, W. HOWARD

Automotive executive. **Career:** Automotive Mgt Inst, accredited automotive mgr, 1994; L&B Auto Repair, owner; Esprit, vpres; Daimler Chrysler, Advan Qual Planning, sr mgr, currently. **Orgs:** Longtime mem, Automotive Serv Asn, 1990, gen dir, 1996, chmn, 2000-01, 2006-; Licensing Task Force Comt, 1993; chmn, Cong Automotive Repair & Serv, 2006. **Honors/Awds:** Chairman's Club Award, 1992-94; Outstanding Member of the Year, 1992; Top Shop Award, 2000. **Special Achievements:** Outstanding Member of the Year, 1992. **Home Addr:** 3388 Summit Ridge Dr, Rochester Hills, MI 48306. **Business Addr:** Senior Manager, Daimler Chrysler, 1000 Chrysler Dr, Auburn Hills, MI 48326-2751, **Business Phone:** (248)576-5741.

## LEWIS, WENDY

Manager, vice president (government). **Personal:** daughter of Emcee Williams and Alma Williams. **Educ:** Univ Wis-Oshkosh, BS, psychol; Northwestern Univ, J.L. Kellogg Grad Sch Mgt, MBA. **Career:** Chicago Cubs, dir human resources, 1989-95; Maj League Baseball, exec dir human resources, 1995, vpres strategic planning recruitment & diversity, currently, sr vpres diversity & strategic alliances, currently. **Honors/Awds:** Wise Woman of the Year Award, 2011. **Business Addr:** Senior Vice President Diversity & Strategic Alliances, Major League Baseball, 245 Pk Ave, New York, NY 10167, **Business Phone:** (212)931-7554.

## LEWIS, WILLARD C. (WILLARD CHUCK LEWIS)

Banker. **Personal:** Born Apr 9, 1961, LaGrange, GA; son of Willard (deceased) and Dora; married Patricia; children: Charles & Camille. **Educ:** Morehouse Col, BA, banking & fin, 1983. **Career:** Citizens Trust Bank, controller, 1983-91, sr exec vpres & chief operating officer, 1991-2005; First Southern Bank, exec vpres & COO, 1991-; One Ga Bank, pres, bd mem, chief exec officer & co-founder, 2005-10; WM Lewis Group, chmn & chief exec officer, 2010-; Community Reinvestment Fund, independent advisor, 2012-. **Orgs:** Chmn bd, Eastlake YMCA, 1992-94, 2000-; AUBA, 1995; Dekalb Med Ctr Found Bd, 1997-; exec bd mem, Berry Col Campbell Sch Bus; bd chmn, Sweet Auburn Bus & Improv Asn, 1998; Leadership, Atlanta Grad, 1999; treas bd, Nat Bankers Asn, 2000-; treas, co-founder, New Century Forum Bd, 2001-; bd dir, Ga Coun Econ Edu, 2002; bd, Com Club Operating, 2002; Morehouse Col Nat Alumni Asn; vice chmn, Dekalb Med Ctr Found; bd trustee, Communities in Schs, Ga; bd trustee, Ga Chamber of Com; bd visitors, Emory Univ; bd visitors, Berry Col; bd dir, Metrop YMCA; bd dir, Midtown Alliance. **Honors/Awds:** Spec Recognition, Nat Bankers Asn, 2000; Richard Wright Founders Award, Nat Bankers Asn, 2002; Man of the Year, Atlanta Tribune Mag, 2008. **Special Achievements:** Guest ed columnist, Atlanta Bus J & Columbus Times; Top 40 Exec Under 40 Ga, Ga Trend Mag, 1997. **Home Addr:** 5183 McCarter Ct, Stone Mountain, GA 30088-2517. **Business Addr:** Co-Founder & Board Member, President and Chief Executive Officer, One Georgia Bank, 1180 Peachtree St NE, Atlanta, GA 30309, **Business Phone:** (678)553-7020.

## LEWIS, DR. WILLIAM A. (BILL LEWIS)

Lawyer. **Personal:** Born Aug 15, 1946, Philadelphia, PA; son of William A and Constance Merritt; married Deborah Cover; children: Ryan. **Educ:** Am Univ, attended 1968; Susquehanna Univ, BA, 1968; Boston Univ Law Sch, JD, 1972. **Career:** City Philadelphia, Pa, asst dist atty, 1972-75; US Civil Rights Comn, atty, 1975-80, dir cong lia div, 1980-86, dir cong & community rels div, 1985-86, actg asst staff dir, cong & pub affairs, 1987, coun senate judiciary comt, 1987-; Senate Judiciary Comt, Wash, DC, coun, 1987-89; Equal Employ Opportunity Comn, Wash, DC, supvry atty, 1989-92; US Dept Energy, off admin & mgt, exec asst dir, 1992-94, sr exec, 1944, Off Sci Educ Progs, dir, 1994-96, Off Employee Concerns, nat ombudsman, dir, 1996-2005, Off Civil Rights Diversity, dep dir, 2005-. **Orgs:** Del, Legal Rights & Justice Task Force White House Conf Youth Estes Park County, 1970; Pa Bar Asn, 1972-; Eastern Dist Ct Pa, 1974-; pres, Blacks Govt US Civil Rights Comn, 1977-80; exec comt, 1980-83, sec vpres, 1987, pres, 1988-91, Susquehanna Univ Alumni Asn; bd dir, Susquehanna Univ, 1988-; Dept's Performance Rev Bd, 1997-2001; Secy Exec resources Bd, Dept Energy, 1998-2001; treas, african am fed execs asn. **Honors/Awds:** Legal Defense Fund Scholarship, NAACP, 1971-72; publ: "Black Lawyer in Private Practice", Harvard Law Sch Bulletin, 1971; Outstanding Young Men in America. **Home Addr:** 7224 Selkirk Dr, Bethesda, MD 20817-4648, **Home Phone:** (301)320-3164. **Business Addr:** Deputy Director, United States Department of Energy, Rm 5B 140 1000 Independence Ave SW, Washington, DC 20585, **Business Phone:** (202)586-6530.

## LEWIS, WILLIAM HENRY (HANK LEWIS)

Educator, writer, football coach. **Personal:** Born Denver, CO; married Sarah. **Educ:** Trinity Col, BA, 1989; Univ Va, MFA, 1994. **Career:** McCallie Sch, Eng teacher, 1989-92; Univ Va Fall, Instr Creative Writing, 1993; Denison Univ, asst prof, Eng, 1994-95; Mary Wash Col, asst prof, Eng, 1995-97; Trinity Col, asst prof creative writing 1997-2000; Col Bahamas, lectr creative writing, 2000-03; Centre Col, vis prof, 2004-05; Colgate Univ, assoc prof, Eng, currently; Author: Billy Bathgate, 1990; In the Arms of Our Elders, Carolina Wren Press, 1995; I Got Somebody in Staunton, 2005; outfield players, coach, 2001-02; Nat Team goalkeeping coach, 2000-03; Bears FC to league championship & league cup, co-coached, 2003-04; Goalkeeper Opers, dir, 2000-03; Bahamas Football Asn, tech staff coach, 2000-04; NCAA Div II Mo S&T, asst coach, 2007-08, 2012; Goalkeeping Develop & U13 boys coach with FC Boulder, dir, 2013-14; Men's Soccer, Colo Sch Mines, asst coach, 2014-. **Business Addr:** Associate Professor, Colgate University, 13 Oak Dr, Hamilton, NY 13346, **Business Phone:** (315)228-7100.

## LEWIS, WILLIAM M., JR.

Executive, chairperson. **Personal:** Born Apr 30, 1956, Richmond, VA; son of William M Sr and Essie Mae; married Carol Sutton; children: 3. **Educ:** Harvard Univ, BA, econs, 1978; Harvard Bus Sch Mgt, MBA, 1982. **Career:** Morgan Stanley Group Inc, Mergers & Acquisitions Dept, financial analyst, head real estate banking & pvt equity businesses, 1978-80, Midwest M&A Dept, Chicago, head, 1988, managing dir, 1989-91, NY City, managing dir, 1992-; Morgan Stanley Estate Funds, Worldwide Real Estate Dept, head, 1993-97, pres & chief oper officer; Red Roof Inn, dir, 1995-; Worldwide Mergers, Acquisitions & Restructuring Dept, head, 1999, Global Banking, co-managing dir, 2001-04; Freddie Mac, dir, 2004-; Lazard Ltd, managing dir & co-chmn investment banking, 2004-; Darden Restaurants Inc, dir, 2005-14; New York Investment Fund Mgr Inc, dir; Philharmonic-Symphony Soc New York Inc, dir. **Orgs:** Bd mem, Red Roof Inns, 1995-; Fed Home Loan Mortgage Corp, dir, 2004-08; dir, Darden Restaurants, 2005-; bd mem & trustee, Ariel Capital Mgt; trustee & bd mem, Phillips Acad Andover; chair, Better Chance Inc; co-chair, Nat Asn Advan Colored People Legal Defense & Educ Found; Task force mem, Exam Recruiting Tech Better Retaining African Am Talent, Morgan Stanley Group Inc; treas, Nat Urban League; bd mem, Am Mus Natural Hist; Carnegie Endowment Int Peace; bd mem, Northwestern Memorial Hosp; Urban Land Inst; trustee, Cancer Res Inst; vice chmn, Cent Pk Conservancy; Nat Asn Real Estate Investment Trust; Int Coun Shopping Centers. **Honors/Awds:** Ranked among Most Powerful Black Execs, Fortune, 2002; Named one of Top 50 African Americans Wall St, Black Enterprise, 2002; 75 Most Powerful Blacks on Wall Street, Black Enterprise, 2011. **Special Achievements:** First African American and the youngest individual to hold that title of managing director for Morgan Stanley. **Home Addr:** 7017 Long View Rd, Columbia, MD 21044-4230, **Home Phone:** (609)522-7482. **Business Addr:** Co-Chairman, Managing Director, Lazard Ltd, 30 Rockefeller Plz, New York, NY 10012, **Business Phone:** (212)632-6000.

## LEWIS, WILLIAM SYLVESTER, SR.

Educator, writer. **Personal:** Born Aug 31, 1952, Manhattan, NY. **Educ:** Columbia Univ Col, BA, sociol, 1974; Columbia Grad Sch Jour, MS, jour, 1976. **Career:** Columbia Univ Grad Sch Jour, CBS fel, 1976; Black Sports Mag, contrib ed, 1977-78; Encore Mag, sports ed, 1979-80; Good Living Mag, sr ed, 1979-80; Black Agenda Reports, producer, writer, 1979-81; Touro Col, adj prof, 1981, instr lang & lit, dep chair, currently. **Orgs:** Legacy Int Inc; Morrisania Educ Coun; Columbia Univ Club NY; Am Athletic Union Distance Running Div. **Honors/Awds:** Bennett Cert Award Writing, Columbia Univ, 1974; Loyal & Outstanding Service Award, Morrisania Educ coun, Bronx NY, 1978; Presidential Citation for Excellence Dist nine Comm School Bd, 1983, 1984. **Special Achievements:** Fiction Writer & published numerous articles. **Home Addr:** 348 W 123rd St, New York, NY 10027-5123, **Home Phone:** (212)666-5975. **Business Addr:** Instructor, Deputy Chair, Touro College, 27-33 W 23 St, New York, NY 10010, **Business Phone:** (212)463-0400.

## LEWIS, WILMA A.

Educator, business owner, lawyer. **Personal:** Born Jan 1, 1956. **Educ:** Swarthmore Col, BA, 1978; Harvard Law Sch, JD, 1981. **Career:** Steptoe & Johnson, Gen Litigation Group, assoc, 1981-86; DC, asst US atty, 1986-93; lectr & instr employ discrimination law, 1987-98; US Dept Interior, Civil Div, dep chief; US Dept Interior, Div Gen Law, assoc solicitor, 1993-95; George Washington Univ, Nat Law Ctr, adj fac mem, 1993, prof lectr law, currently; DC, US atty; US Dept Interior, inspector gen, 1995-98; US Dist Ct, DC, practr, 1998-2001; US Ct Appeals, DC, practr; Supreme Ct US, practr; Crowell & Moring Llp, partner, 2001-; Land & Mineral Mgmt, asst secy, 2009-; Fed Home Loan Mortgage Corp, managing assoc gen coun, 2007-08. **Orgs:** DC Bar Asn; US Dist Ct, Civil Justice Reform Act Adv Group, DC, 1992-93; fel, Am Bar Found; chmn, DC Bd Elections & Ethics; DC Judicial Nomination Comn; adv comm, US Dist Ct, DC; bd dir, Wash Lawyers Comn Civil Rights & Urban Affairs; bd mgr, Swarthmore Coll; bd visitors, Howard Univ Sch Law; bd trustee, Moravian Theol Sem; bd adv, Nat Youth Leadership Forum Law; Phi Beta Kappa; bd dir, Am Arbitration Asn, 2007-; adj fac mem, George Wash Univ Nat Law Ctr. **Home Addr:** 3911 Highwood Ct NW, Washington, DC 20007. **Business Addr:** Partner, Crowell & Moring LLP, 1001 Pa Ave NW, Washington, DC 20004-2595, **Business Phone:** (202)624-2500.

## LEWIS-HALL, FREDA

Vice president (organization). **Educ:** John Hopkins Univ, BA & BS, natural sci, 1976; Howard Univ Col Med, Md, 1980. **Career:** Howard Univ Col Med's, Dept Psychiat, vice chairperson & assoc prof, 1988-94; Eli Lilly & Co, prod team leader, 1994-02; Pharmacia Corp., vpres res & develop; Bristol-Myers Squibb Co, sr vpres, 2003-08; Vertex Pharmaceut, chief med officer & exec vpres, 2008-09; Pfizer Inc, exec vpres & chief med officer, 2009-. **Orgs:** Fel, Am Acad Psychiat; dir, Found Nat Insts Health Inc; trustee, Save C Fedn, 2012-. **Honors/Awds:** "Black Enterprise", 75 Most Powerful Women in Business, 2010. **Special Achievements:** Co-edited "Psychiatric Illness in Women: Emerging Trends in Research", 2002. **Business Addr:** Executive Vice President, Chief Medical Officer, Pfizer Inc, 235 E 42nd St, New York, NY 10017-5755, **Business Phone:** (212)733-2323.

## LEWIS-KEMP, JACQUELINE

Manager, president (organization), writer. **Personal:** daughter of James O Lewis. **Educ:** Univ Mich, BA, polit sci & commun, 1984, MPP, 1985. **Career:** Lewis Metal Stamping & Mfg Co, prod control mgr, 1985-93, pres & chief exec officer, 1993-2001; US Gen Acct Off, auditor, 1987-88; Segunda Vida LLC, auth, prin, 2004-. **Orgs:** Bd visitors, Sch Bus Admin, Oakland Univ; Nat Asn Black Automotive Suppliers. **Business Addr:** Author, Segunda Vida, LLC, 1758 Brandywine Dr, Bloomfield Hills, MI 48304, **Business Phone:** (248)844-9613.

## LEWIS-LANGSTON, HON. DEBORAH

Judge. **Personal:** Born Detroit, MI. **Educ:** Univ Mich, BA, 1978; Univ Mich Law Sch, JD, 1982. **Career:** Macomb Co, asst prosecutor; Detroit City, asst corp coun; Mich State Senate, assoc senate gen coun; 36th Dist Ct, judge, 1988-. **Special Achievements:** First African American individual to be hired as Assistant Prosecutor for Macomb County. **Business Addr:** Judge, 36th District Court, 421 Madison Ave, Detroit, MI 48226, **Business Phone:** (313)965-8717.

## LEWIS-SCOTT, AISHA

Engineer. **Personal:** Born Oct 30, 1971, Indianapolis, IN; daughter of Cleveland A and Betty F. **Educ:** Purdue Univ, AS, electronics engineering technol 1995, BS, electronics engineering technol, 1997, MS, microsoft off, 2016. **Career:** IBM Corp, electronic assembly mfg engr, 1997-99, mfg test engr, 1999-2003, mfg engineering proj mgr, 2003-06; Sony Ericsson, indus proj mgr, 2007-08; His Alto Ministries, prin, 2008-. **Orgs:** R4 adv bd & secy, Nat Soc Black Engrs, 1999-2010, exec bd, 1994-97; Ctr Leadership Develop Alumni, 1998. **Honors/Awds:** Engineering Technology Student Service Award, Purdue Univ, Indianapolis, 1993; IBM Women in Technology Award, 2002; US Women of Color in Science & Technology Award, 2002; Multicultural Women in Leadership Institute Alumni, 2003; IBM Bravo Award, 2004. **Special Achievements:** Independent gospel artist 2008-. "Aisha J. Lewis - A Spiritual Journey: Through The Past And Present" debut gospel CD release 2009; "FTL Series" Accompaniment CD Sampler Disc release April 2011; "Nightmare" (poem) published in Tomorrow's Dream, Natl Library of Poetry, 1996; Proficient in the Japanese and Mandarin; singer/songwriter/musician (piano, organ, cello, taiko drum, tenor guitar, tenor mandola, handbells). **Home Phone:** (919)875-9667. **Business Addr:** Principal, Lead Vocalist, His Alto Ministries, 5116 Dice Dr, Raleigh, NC 27616, **Business Phone:** (919)332-5213.

## LEWIS-THORNTON, RAE

Clergy, aids activist. **Personal:** Born May 22, 1962; daughter of Alfred Henry Lewis Jr and Judith; married Kenneth. **Educ:** Southern Ill Univ; Northeastern Ill Univ, Chicago, IL, BA, polit sci, 1991; McCormick Theol Sem, Mdiv, theol studies, 2003; Luthern Sch Theol, PhD, church hist, 2010. **Career:** Jesse Jackson Presidential Campaign, dep nat youth dir, 1984, nat youthdir, 1988; AIDS advocate & motivational speaker, 1993-; Barbara Mikulski & Carol Mosley Braun, staff. **Orgs:** Delta Sigma Theta Sorority; Leadership Bd Core Ctr; advocate & motivational speaker, AIDS, 1993-; founder & pres, Rae Lewis-Thornton Inc, 2009-; staff, Barbara Mikulski & Carol Mosley Braun. **Business Addr:** Founder, President, Rae Lewis-Thornton Inc, 1507 E 53rd St Suite 315, Chicago, IL 60615, **Business Phone:** (773)643-4316.

## LEWTER, REV. ANDY C., SR.

Clergy, president (organization), minister (clergy). **Personal:** Born Oct 6, 1929, Sebring, FL; son of Rufus Cleveland Sr (deceased) and Mary Lee; married Ruth Fuller; children: Rita Olivia Davis, Cleo Yvette, Veda Ann Pennyman, Andy C Jr, RosalynAaron & Tonya Marie. **Educ:** Morris Brown Col, BA, 1954; Atlanta Univ; Bible Sem, New York; James Teamer's Sch Relig, BD, 1964; T Sch Religion, LLD, 1975; NY Theol Sem, MDiv, 1985. **Career:** St John Baptist Church, Ft Myers, asst minister, 1951-52; Morris Brown Col, asst col pastor, 1953-54; Zion Grove Baptist Church, Atlanta, asst minister, 1953-54; Stitt Jr HS, teacher, 1954-60; First Baptist Church, Rockaway, asst minister, 1954-59; Hollywood Baptist Church Christ Amityville, pastor, 1959, pastor emer, currently; AC Lewter Interdenom Sch Relig, founder pres, 1975; Pilgrim State Psychiat Hosp, chaplain, pastor. **Orgs:** Pres, N Amityville Ministerial Alliance & Vicinity, 1989-; vice moderator, Eastern Baptist Asn, 1990-; Past vpres, Nat Asn Advan Colored People; past chmn mem, Interfaith Health Asn; Bd Gov Interfaith Hosp Queens; pres, Inter-denominational Ministerial fel Amityville; trustee, Long Island Health & Hosp Planning Coun; vpres, Lewter-Scott Travel Asn; supvr, Ushers Nat Baptist Conv, USA; adv bd, Suffolk County Off Aging; Amityville Taxpayers Asn; adv bd, Suffolk Co Off Aging; pres, New Millennium Develop Servs. **Honors/Awds:** Friendship Col, Hon DD, 1962. **Home Addr:** 796 Clocks Blvd, East Massapequa, NY 11758, **Home Phone:** (516)795-5570. **Business Addr:** President, New Millennium Development Services Incorporation, 1840 Wisteria Circle, Bellport, NY 11713, **Business Phone:** (516)223-3855.

**LIAUTAUD, JAMES**
Educator, chairperson. **Personal:** children: 2. **Educ:** Univ Ill, BS, mech engineering, 1963. **Career:** Univ Ill, Chicago, clin res prof; Gabriel Inc, Elgin, Ill, founder, chmn bd, 1968-; Entrepreneurship Inst, dir & trustee; Univ Ill Family Bus Coun, dir & trustee, clin prof, currently; Nat Interstate & Raffles Inc, dir; Blue Rhino Corp, dir; Capsonic Group Inc, chief exec officer, 1960-. **Orgs:** PdEI Group; founder, YPO's Chicago Windy City Chap; founder, UIC Family Bus Coun; founder, UIC Liautaud Grad Sch Bus; founder, UIC PdEI Leadership Adv Bd. **Business Addr:** Chief Executive Officer, Capsonic Group Inc, 460 2nd St, Elgin, IL 60123, **Business Phone:** (847)888-7300.

**LIDE, DR. WILLIAM ERNEST**
School administrator. **Personal:** Born Feb 14, 1950, Darlington, SC; married Cheryl Anita Leverett; children: Desiree Danielle, Amber Nicole, Lindsey Koren & Kristin Regina. **Educ:** Johnson C Smith Univ, Charlotte, NC, BS, health & phys educ, 1973; Univ NC, Charlotte, NC, MEd, educ leadership & admin, 1977; Ohio Univ, Columbus, OH, PhD, admin, phys educ, 1980. **Career:** Johnson C Smith Univ, Charlotte, NC, phys educ, 1975-78, 1980-84; Winston-Salem State Univ, Winston-Salem, NC, chair, phys educ, 1984-87; NC Cent Univ, dir athletics, 2000-; Univ Cent Ark, dir athletics, 2000-03; Southern Intercollegiate Athletic Conf, 2005-07; Benedict Col, assoc prof, 2010-12; Salisbury State Univ, Salisbury, Md, dir athletics, chair phys educ & recreation; Am Bk Publishers, writer, 2012-. **Orgs:** Nat secy, Nat Round table Parks, Conserv & Recreation, 1982-; bd dir, Nat Col Athletic Asn Coun, 1989-; Nat Asn Col dir Athletics Postgrad Scholar Comt, 1993-; pres, Easterm State Athletic Conf, 1989; Div III Steering Comt, NCAA, 1990; pres, Round table Asn, 1994; chair, Nat Col Athletic AsnCou Post grad Scholar Comt; Ark Literacy Coun; NCAA Gov Boards Coun. **Home Addr:** 207 W Philadelphia Ave, Salisbury, MD 21801, **Home Phone:** (410)543-8041. **Business Addr:** Director of Athletics, Chairman, North Carolina Central University, 1801 Fayetteville St, Durham, NC 27707, **Business Phone:** (919)530-6100.

**LIGGINS, ALFRED C., III**
Chief executive officer, president (organization). **Personal:** Born Jan 30, 1965, Omaha, NE; son of Alfred Jr and Cathy Hughes. **Educ:** Univ Calif, Los Angeles; Univ DC; Univ Pa, MBA, 1995; Wharton Sch Bus/Exec, MBA. **Career:** Light Rec, sales exec, 1984; CBS Rec, prod asst, 1984-85; Radio One Inc, acct mgr, 1985-87, gen sales mgr, 1987, gen mgr opers, 1988, pres, treas & dir, 1989-, chief exec officer, 1997-, chief operating officer, 2006; WOL, sales mgr, 1986-94. **Orgs:** Bd dir, Apollo Theater Found; bd dir, Reach Media; bd dir, Boys & Girls Clubs Am; bd dir, Ibiquity Corp; bd dir, Nat Asn Black Owned Broadcasters; bd dir, Nat Asn Broadcasters; dir, TV One Capital Corp. **Business Addr:** Chief Executive Officer, President, Radio One Inc, 5900 Princess Garden Pkwy 7th Fl, Lanham, MD 20706, **Business Phone:** (301)306-1111.

**LIGGINS, W. ANTHONY**
Fashion designer. **Personal:** Born Jul 4, 1965, Hampton, VA; son of Wilbert A; married Kym. **Educ:** Del State Univ, Am Col Appl Arts, AA, fashion design, 1989; Am Intercontinental Univ, Atlanta, London, AA, fashion merchandising, 1991. **Career:** Future Mode LLC dba Anthony Liggins, pres & fashion dir, currently; Anthony Liggins Studios, artist, 2000-. **Honors/Awds:** Alumni Hall of Fame, Am Inter-Continental Univ, 1998. **Special Achievements:** Annual 10 Best Man List, guest ed, Jezebel Mag, 50 Best Dressed Women In Atlanta, guest ed, Today's Atlanta Woman Mag, been featured on VH-1, E Entertainment, F-TV, Frankfurt, Ger, 1996, featured in Atlanta Bus Chronicle, 1995, Atlanta Mag, 1995, 1998, 1996, Atlanta J Const, 1995, 1996, 1997, 1998, 1999, Essence, 1997, Black Enterprise Mag, 1997, Swissotel OCo Spellbound, Atlanta, GA, 2000, Gallery Sklo, Red & Loaded, 2001, Sacred Ground, 2002, Shanghai Dreams, 2003, Sacred Language, 1000 Kisses from Shanghai, 2004. **Business Addr:** President, Creative Director, Anthony Liggins Studios, 254 E Paces Ferry Rd Suite 207/208, Atlanta, GA 30305, **Business Phone:** (404)842-0621.

**LIGHT, ALAN**
Executive. **Personal:** Born Jan 1, 1966?; married Suzanne. **Educ:** Yale Univ, BA, Am studies, 1988. **Career:** Rolling Stone Mag, fact checker, 1989, sr writer, 1990-93; VIBE Mag, ed in chief, 1994-97; SPIN Mag, ed in chief, 1999-2002; Tracks Mag, ed in chief, currently; Rock & Roll Hall Fame, consult; WFUV Radio sta, music reviewer; Nat Pub Radio, Weekend Am, music corresp, currently. **Business Addr:** Editor In Chief, Co Founder, Tracks Magazine, 304 Pk Ave S, New York, NY 10010, **Business Phone:** (212)219-7447.

**LIGHTFOOT, JEAN DREW**
Executive, government official. **Personal:** Born Hartford, CT. **Educ:** Howard Univ, BA, 1947; Univ Mich, MPA, 1950. **Career:** Government official (retired); Coca Cola, pub rels, 1954-55, asst dir, 1959-61; Dept State, foreign serv res officer, 1962-69; Consumer Protection & Environ Health Serv HEW, chief consumer spec sect, 1969-70, asst dir pub affairs, 1970-71; EPA, int affairs officer, 1971, Spec Asst Training & Upward Mobility, dep dir, 1978. **Orgs:** Actg dir, Community Rel Conf S Calif, dir, 1961-62; Women's Auxiliary Bd NW Settlement House; former bd mem, W Coast Reg Nat Negro Col Fund; Nat Asn Advan Colored People; Urban Laeague; Fred Douglass Mus African Art; Legal Def Fund; Int Club Wash Inc; Indian Spring Country Club; Univ Mich Club; Circle-Lets Inc; Neighbors Inc. **Honors/Awds:** Good Citizenship Award, Daughters of the Am Revolution, 1940; Ideal Girl Award, Hartford Pub High Sch, 1940; Nat Council Negro Women Mary McLeod Bethune Award, 1962; Community Service Award, Community Rels Conf S Calif, 1962; Community Service Award, Nat Asn Advan Colored People, 1975. **Home Addr:** 2000 Trumbull Terr NW, Washington, DC 20011.

**LIGHTFOOT, JEAN HARVEY**
Educator. **Personal:** Born Nov 29, 1935, Chicago, IL; married Ernest Brinkmann; children: Jaronda. **Educ:** Fisk Univ, BA, 1957; Univ Chicago, MA, 1969; Northwestern Univ, Evanston, PhD, 1974. **Career:** Chicago Pub Schs, eng teacher, 1957-69; Kennedy King Campus, Chicago City Col, prof eng, 1969-; Citizens Comn Pub Educ, exec dir, 1975-76; Comn Urban Affair Spec Proj, AME Church, exec dir, 1978-80; Neighborhood Inst, educ coordr, 1979; Univ Chicago, dir Educ Assistance Prog, 2002-. **Orgs:** Counr, Hillcrest Ctr C, NY, 1958-61; featured soloist, Pk Manor Cong Church, 1958-; John W Work Chorale, 1959-; asst prof educ, Northeastern Univ, Chicago, 1974-76; consult, Prescription Learning Inc, 1977-; staff dir, convener, S Shore Schs Alliance, 1979-80; Nat Asn Col Admis Coun. **Home Addr:** 195 M Harbor Dr, Chicago, IL 60601-7514. **Business Addr:** Director for the Educational Assistance Program, University of Chicago, 5801 S Ellis Ave, Chicago, IL 60637, **Business Phone:** (773)702-1234.

**LIGHTFOOT, DR. SARA LAWRENCE**
Socialist, educator, writer. **Personal:** Born Aug 2, 1944; daughter of Charles Radford and Margaret. **Educ:** Swarthmore Col, BA, psychol, 1966; Bank St Col Educ, 1967; Harvard Univ, EdD, sociol, 1972. **Career:** Educr, sociologist, writer; Albert Einstein Sch Med Dept Psychiat, res asst, 1967-68; Harvard Grad Sch Educ, supvr, 1970-71, asst prof, 1972-76, Fac Arts & Sci, fac fel, 1976-78, assoc prof, 1976-80, prof, 1980-98, Emily Hargroves Fisher prof educ, 1998-, Emily Hargroves Fisher endowed chair, 1998; Educ Develop Ctr, res & eval consult, 1970-71; writer, currently; Swarthmore Col, endowed prof; Sara Lawrence-Lightfoot endowed chair, 1993. **Orgs:** Fel Metrop Appl Res Ctr, 1970-72; fel Bunting Inst, Radcliffe Col, 1976-78; fel Ctr Advan Study Behav Sci, 1983-84; chair bd, MacArthur Found; Nat Acad Educ; Bright Horizons Family Solutions; Boston Globe; Berklee Col Music; spencer sr scholar, Spencer Found, 1995-2002. **Honors/Awds:** Outstanding Book Award, Am Educ Res Asn, 1984; Christopher Award, 1988; MacArthur Fellows Award, John D. & Catherine T. MacArthur Found, 1989; Candace Award, Nat Coalition 100 Black Women, 1990; Radcliffe College Graduate Society Medal, Harvard Univ, 1991; George Ledlie Prize, Harvard Univ, 1993; Meridian Award, Indianapolis C's Mus, 1995; Literary Award, Black Caucus Am Libr Asn, 1995; Medal for Distinguished Service, Columbia Univ, 1996; Sojourner Truth Award, Cambridge YWCA, 1998; Academy of Women Achievers, Boston YWCA, 2001; Crossing the River Jordan Award, 2003; Ferguson Award, Nat Louis Univ, 2004; Margaret Mead Award, Am Acad Polit & Social Sci, 2008; Marion Langer Award, Am Orthopsychiatric Asn, 2012; Received many honorary degree. **Special Achievements:** Featured on the 2006 Documentary on PBS, African American Lives; First African-American woman in Harvard's history to have an endowed professorship named in her honor; Books: Worlds Apart: Relationships Between Families and Schools, 1978; Beyond Bias: Perspectives on Classrooms, 1978; The Good High School: Portraits of Character and Courage, 1983; Balm in Gilead:-Journey of a Healer, 1988; The Good High Sch: Portraits of Character &Culture; "Portraits of Exemplary Secondary Schs: Highland Park," Daedalus, Fall 1981, p. 59; "Portraits of Exemplary Secondary Schs: George Washington Carver Comprehensive High Sch," Daedalus, Fall 1981, p. 17; "Portraits of Exemplary Secondary Schs: St Paul's Sch," Daedalus, Fall 1981, p. 97; I've Known Rivers: Lives of Loss & Liberation, 1994; The Essential Conversation: What Parents & Teachers Can Learn From Each Other, 2003; The Third Chapter: Passion, Risk, and Adventure in the 25 Years After 50, 2009. **Business Addr:** Emily Hargroves Fisher Professor of Education, Harvard University, Appian Way, Cambridge, MA 02138, **Business Phone:** (617)496-4837.

**LIGHTFOOT, SIMONE DANIELLE**
Government official, association executive. **Personal:** Born Oct 22, 1967, Detroit, MI; daughter of Henry and Mary Ann Patterson; married Phillip; children: Jaydaka & Jaydan. **Educ:** Eastern Mich Univ, BS, 2003. **Career:** USAF, air transp specialist, 1986-90; US EPA, mech engineering tech, 1990-91; Mich House Rep, legis asst, 1996-98, dep chief staff, 1998-; African Am Health Inst, state health conf dir, 1999; Green Couture Supply, founder & owner; Am Red Cross, regional rep; Mallory Campaign Cincinnati, campaign mgr, currently. **Orgs:** Nat Asn Advan Colored People, Detroit Br, 1987-; Tuskegee Airman, 1992-; Nat Coun Negro Women, 1998-; dir, Nat Asn Advan Colored People, Mich State, 2001-; dir, Wayne County off; trustee, Ann Arbor Pub Schs, 2009; nat dir, Nat Wildlife Fedn. **Honors/Awds:** Dr Martin Luther King Humanitarian Award, Huron High Sch, 1985; Distinguished Citizen Award, Cent Delaware Chamber Com, 1989; Minority Business Owner of the Year, Minority Bus Owner Washtenaw County, 1995; Best of Award, Craine Bus Mag, 1995; Annette Rainwater Political Award, Mich State Dem Party, 2001. **Special Achievements:** First Directly Elected African American Mayor Of Cincinnati. **Home Addr:** 2356 Arrowwood Trl, Ann Arbor, MI 48105-1215, **Home Phone:** (734)996-8230. **Business Addr:** Campaign Manager, NAACP Voter Empowerment, 5846 Hamilton Ave Col Hill, Cincinnati, OH 45224, **Business Phone:** (513)591-1100.

**LIGON, DORIS HILLIAN**
Museum director. **Personal:** Born Apr 28, 1936, Baltimore, MD; married Claude M; children: Claude M Jr & Carole Ann. **Educ:** Morgan State Univ, BA, social, 1978, MA, art hist, museol, 1979; Howard Univ, PhD, courses African hist. **Career:** Nat Mus African Art Smithsonian Inst, docent, 1976-88; Morgan State Univ, art gallery res asst, 1978-79, Goldseeker fel, 1978-79; Grade Studies MSU, 1978-79. **Orgs:** Asn Black Women Hist; African-Am Mus Asn; founder & exec dir, Md Mus African Art, 1980-; charter Columbia Chap Pierians Inc, 1983; charter Eubie Blake Cult Ctr 1984; Morgan State Univ Alumni; Nat Asn Advan Colored People; Urban League; Arts Coun African Studies Asn; Phi Alpha Theta; Alpha Kappa Mu. **Home Addr:** 6302 Raritan Ct, Columbia, MD 21045, **Home Phone:** (410)381-0528. **Business Addr:** Founder, Executive Director, African Art Museum of Maryland, 5430 Vantage Pt Rd Suite B, Columbia, MD 21044-0105, **Business Phone:** (410)730-7106.

**LILES, KEVIN**
Executive. **Personal:** Born Feb 27, 1968, Baltimore, MD; married Erika; children: Genevieve, Valentina, Khristian, Kevin & Kayla. **Educ:** Morgan State Univ, engineering. **Career:** Numarx, founder & contrib, 1989-90; Marx Bros Rec, founder & pres, 1991-92; Def Jam Recs, internship, pres, 1992-94, Mid-Atlantic Region, mgr, 1994, W Coast, gen mgr prom, 1994-96, gen mgr & vpres prom, 1996-98, pres, 1998-2002; Island Def Jam, exec vpres, 1994-2004; Warner Music Group, exec vpres, 2004-09; KWL Enterprises, chief exec officer & founder 2009-. **Orgs:** Bd mem, Hip-Hop Summit Action Network; DJ crew. **Home Addr:** Rockefeller Plz Fl 32, New York, NY 10019. **Business Addr:** Founder, Chief Executive Officer, KWL Enterprises, 304 Pk Ave S 9 th Fl, New York, NY 10010.

**LILLARD, KWAME LEO (LEO LILLARD, II)**
Activist, industrial engineer. **Personal:** Born Sep 16, 1939, Tampa, FL; son of Leo I and Louise Taylor; married Evelyn Downing; children: Leo III, Jessica, Joshua, Nyleve, Troy, Chiffonda & Edward. **Educ:** Tenn State A&I Univ, Nashville, TN, BS, mech engineering, 1961; City Col NY, MS, mech engineering, 1965; Hunter Col, NY, MS, urban planning, 1971. **Career:** Malcolm X Univ, Greensboro, NC, engineering instr, 1972; Weyer haeuser, Plymouth, NC, indust engr, 1972-76; Nashville City Planning Dept, Nashville, TN, sr planner, 1976-80; Textron, Nashville, TN, indust engr, 1981-91; C21 Architect Engrs, planning analyst, Tenn Dept environ & conserv, environ specialist, currently. **Orgs:** Pres, chief exec officer, African Am Cult Alliance, 1984-2004; co-founder, Men Distinction Youth Develop, 1989-; prog coordr, Nashville Peace Coalition, 1990-; exec bd, Nashville NCP Chap; exec bd, Coun COT Serv. **Honors/Awds:** Black Expo Education Innovator, Black Expo Inc, 1980; Martin Luther King Award, Nashville Martin Luther King Celebration, 1989. **Home Addr:** 2814 Buena Vista Pke, Nashville, TN 37218, **Home Phone:** (615)828-4325. **Business Addr:** Chief Executive Officer, African American Cultural Alliance, 1215 9th Ave N Suite 210, Nashville, TN 37202, **Business Phone:** (615)329-3540.

**LILLARD, LEO, II. See LILLARD, KWAME LEO.**

**LILLIE, DR. VERNELL AUDREY WATSON**
Educator, theatrical producer, artistic director. **Personal:** Born May 11, 1931, Hempstead, TX; daughter of Walter J Watson and Lillie Mae Watson; married Richard L Jr; children: Attorney Charisse Lillie McGill & Hisani Lillie Blanton. **Educ:** Dillard Univ, BA, speech and drama, 1952; Carnegie-Mellon Univ, MA, Eng, 1971, DA, Eng, 1972. **Career:** Julius C Hester House Settlement Asn, group work spec, 1952-56; Houston Indep Sch Dist Phillis Wheatley & Worthing HS, chair & teacher speech, drama & debate, 1956-59; Tex So Univ, Proj Upward Bound, instr eng, curric developer & drama specialist, 1965-69; Carnegie-Mellon Univ, Proj Upward Bound, dir stud affairs, 1969-71; Hester House Exper Theatre, dir & founder, 1972-2009; Kuntu Repertory Theatre, founder & dir, 1974-; Univ Pittsburgh, Dept Africana Studies, Feasibility Study Develop Independent Black Sch, assoc prof, chair, prof emer, (retired); Plays: The Buffalo Soldiers Plus One, She'll Find Her Way Home, dir; Difficult Days Ahead in a Blaze, dir; Ashes to Africa, dir; Whispers Want to Holler, dir; Mahalia Jackson: Standing On Holy Ground, dir; The Crawford Grill Presents Billie Holiday, dir; Zora: The Dark Town Strutter, dir; Papa's Blues, dir; Over Forty, dir; Little Willie Armstrong Jones, dir; Two Can Play, dir; Blues for an Ala Sky, dir; Pittsburgh Craw fords & the Homestead Grays, dir. **Orgs:** Am Soc Group Psych other & Psychodrama; Nat & Pa Counc Teachers Eng; Speech Asn Am; Nat Adult Day Servs Asn; Asn Theatre Higher Educ; Black Theatre Network; founding mem, Afro-Am Educrs; bd dir, Julius C Hester House Houston, 1965-69; Earnest T. Williams Mem Ctr, Pittsburgh Ctr Alterntive Ed, 1972-78; Women Urban Crisis, 1973-80; coord curric & staff devel mem, Hope Devel Houston; founding mem, Black Theatre Network; Pierian Asn. **Honors/Awds:** Award for Outstanding Contrib to Arts, Delta Sigma Theta, 1969; Award for Ed Achievements, Carnegie-Mellon Univ Proj Upward Bound, 1972; Pittsburgh Outstanding Ed Black Cath Ministries, 1973; Distinguish Teacher Award, Univ Pittsburgh, 1986; Arts & Lett Award, Alpha Kappa Alpha Sorority, 1987; Women of Color Caucus, 1985; Performances, Fringe Festival, Edinburgh Univ, Scotland, 1989, 1994; Career Achievement in Education Award, Career Award for Excellence, Black Theatre Network, 2003; Demonstrating the Faith Award, Eta Creative Arts foundation, 2004; hon doc, Seton Hill Univ, 2005; Lifetime Achievement Award, Nat Black Theatre Festival, 2005; Chancellor's Distinguished Teaching Award, Univ Pittsburgh; Outstanding Award for Women in the Arts, Alpha Kappa Alpha Sorority Inc; Career Achievement in Education Award, Asn Theatre Higher Educ. **Home Addr:** 7126 Wiltsie St, Pittsburgh, PA 15206, **Home Phone:** (412)363-8172. **Business Addr:** Professor Emeritus, University of Pittsburgh, 4140 Wesley W Posvar Hall, Pittsburgh, PA 15260, **Business Phone:** (412)648-7547.

**LINCOLN, JEREMY ARLO**
Football player, executive. **Personal:** Born Apr 7, 1969, Toledo, OH; married Lisa. **Educ:** Univ Tenn, attended 1991. **Career:** Football player (retired), executive; Chicago Bears, right cornerback, 1993-95; St Louis Rams, defensive back, 1996; Seattle Seahawks, defensive back, 1997; New York Giants, defensive back, 1998, right cornerback, left cornerback, cornerback, 1999; Detroit Lions, 2000-01; Ikon Partners LLC, partner, 2008-, player develop, 2011-; CB Richard Ellis, assoc, currently; Legacy Growth Partners, consult & owner, currently. **Orgs:** Founder, Jeremy Lincoln Found; CB Richard Ellis African-Am Network Group. **Honors/Awds:** Living Legend, Univ of Tenn, 1992. **Business Addr:** Consultant, Owner, Legacy Growth Partners, 130 5th Ave, New York, NY 10011, **Business Phone:** (212)463-5974.

**LINDO, DELROY GEORGE**
Actor. **Personal:** Born Nov 18, 1952, London; married Neshormeh; children: 1; married Kathi Coaston. **Career:** Films: Find the Lady, 1976; Malcolm X, 1992; Crooklyn, 1994; Congo, 1995; Clockers, 1995; Get Shorty, 1995; Broken Arrow, 1996; Ramsom, 1996; The Devil's Advocate, 1997; A Life Less Ordinary, 1997; Cider House Rules, 1999; Romeo Must Die, 2000; Gone in 60 Seconds, 2000; The Book of Stars, 2001; Heist, 2001; The Last Castle, 2001; The One, 2001; The Core, 2003; Wondrous Oblivion, 2003; This Christmas, actor & exec producer, 2007; The Big Bang, 2011; Cymbeline, 2014. TV series: "Soul Of The Game", 1996; "Glory & Honor", 1998; "Strange Justice", 1999; "Profoundly Normal", 2003; "The Core", 2003; "Wondrous Oblivion", 2003; "Lackawanna Blues", 2005; "The Exonerated", 2005; "Sahara", 2005; "Domino", 2005; "Kidnapped", 2006-07; "Law & Order: Special Victims Unit", 2009; "Mercy", 2009; "The Chicago Code", 2011; "Robot Chicken", 2013; "Believe", 2014. **Honors/Awds:** Golden Satellite Award, 1999; Image Award, Nat Asn Advan Colored People, 2010. **Special Achievements:** Was nominated for Broadway's 1988 Tony Award as Best Actor. **Business Addr:** Actor, William Morris Agency,

151 S El Camino Dr, Beverly Hills, CA 90212-2775, **Business Phone:** (310)274-7451.

### LINDSAY, DR. ARTURO
Educator, artist. **Personal:** Born Sep 29, 1946, Colon; son of Arthur and Louise; married Melanie Pavich; children: Urraca, Joaquin & Javier. **Educ:** Cent Conn State Univ, BA, span & theater, 1970; Univ Mass, MFA, painting, 1975; NY Univ, DA, 1990. **Career:** Nh Col, Conn Campus, Hamden, CT, fac adminr, 1979-82; Midtown Art Ctr, dir, 1983; Royal Athena Galleries, asst dir, 1984-89; Franklin & Marshall Col, scholar-in-residence, 1989-90; NY Univ, scholar-in-residence, 1993; Spelman Col, asst prof, 1990-96, assoc prof, 1996-2003, prof, 2003-13, Dept Art & Art Hist, prof & chair, 2013-; Univ Panama, Sch Art, fulbright vis prof, 1999; Rockefeller Found, Bellagio fel, 2003; Davidson Col, Kemp distinguished vis prof, 2005; Colgate Univ, Hamilton, NY, distinguished batza family chair, 2006. **Orgs:** Founding mem, Taller Portobelo, 1995-; bd dir, Col Art Asn, 1996-2000. **Special Achievements:** One of 15 elite artists selected by the U.S. Department of States Bureau of Educational and Cultural Affairs, to promote diplomacy as part of the new smart power initiative. **Home Addr:** 4026 Birchwood Cove, Decatur, GA 30034, **Home Phone:** (770)808-8497. **Business Addr:** Professor of Art & Art History, Spelman College, 350 Spelman Lane SW, Atlanta, GA 30314-4399, **Business Phone:** (404)223-7653.

### LINDSAY, EDDIE H. S.
Executive. **Personal:** Born Oct 23, 1931; married Joyce McCrae; children: Paul & Lisa. **Educ:** London Polytech Col, London; Queens Col, NY; Am Inst Banking NY, Hofstra Univ. **Career:** Ins Salesman, 1968; Mfrs Hanover Trust Co, credit officer; Broadway Bank & Trust Co, dir urban affairs, loan officer com minority econ develop, br mgr main off, asst vpres; Priority Chem Co, pres, currently. **Orgs:** Nat Bankers Asn; NJ Bankers Urban Affairs Comn; EDGES NY Prof Asn; dir, Cath Diocese Comm Human Develop; dir, Planned Parenthood Passaic Co; finance chmn mem, Boys Club Paterson-Passaic; Legal Aid Soc; YMCA; United Way. **Home Addr:** 3384 Misty View Dr, Spring Hill, FL 34609-6717, **Home Phone:** (352)686-3284. **Business Addr:** President, Priority Chemical Co, 725 River Rd Suite 56, Edgewater, NJ 07020, **Business Phone:** (201)945-7010.

### LINDSAY, GWENDOLYN ANN BURNS
Federal government official. **Personal:** Born Nov 13, 1947, Baltimore, MD; daughter of Lucinda Bowman Burns (deceased) and Robert Burns (deceased); children: Brock A. **Educ:** Coppin State Col, BA, social sci, polit sci & eng, 1975; Univ Baltimore, MPA, 1977. **Career:** Bur Prog Oper Prospective Reimbursement Br, social sci res analyst, 1975-77; Bur Prog Oper Prog Iniatives Br, prog analyst, 1977-79; Off Exec Oper Prog Liaison Br, prog liaison specialist, 1979-82; Dept Health & Human Serv Health Care Financing Admin, Off Regulations, health ins specialist, 1993-97, Off Commun & Opers Support, 1997-2002, Ctr Med & Medicaid Serv, sr tech health ins specialist, 2002. **Orgs:** Baltimore Alumnae Chap, 1995, first vpres, second vpres, third vpres, fin secy, Ebony, budget & finance, 1977-91; Nat Coun Negro Women, 1980-; bd mem & personnel comt, YWCA Greater Baltimore, 1986-92; bd mem, Md State Bd Dietetic Practices, 1988-92; bd mem, Towson Cath Adv Bd, 1989-94; pres, Delta Sigma Theta Sorority, 1991-93; Baltimore Metrop Chap Nat Black Women's Health Proj, workshop facilatator, 1993-2000, regional journalist, 1997-; corresp secy, 1994-99, vpres, 1999-, Baltimore Chap Continental Socs; regional journalist, Delta Sigma Theta Sorority Inc, 1997-2001; Alpha Kappa Mu Nat Hon Soc; Courier Newspaper Yearbk Staff; Pan Hellenic Coun; Womens League. **Home Addr:** 12 Garobe Ct, Baltimore, MD 21207-6411, **Home Phone:** (410)486-0420.

### LINDSAY, HORACE AUGUSTIN
Executive, executive director. **Personal:** Born Mar 1, 1938, New York, NY; son of Horace A Sr and Cecelia T Mitchell; married Donna McDade; children: Gloria & Horace. **Educ:** Prairie View A&M Univ, BS, 1959; Calif State Univ, MS, 1969. **Career:** Executive (retired); Boeing Co, res engr, 1961-63; Martin Co, sr engr, 1963-64; Bunker Ramo, prog mgr, 1964-68, mkt dir, 1969-73, prog dir, 1973-77, mkt vpres, 1977-84; Eaton Corp, plans & bus develop vpres, 1984-89; Contel Corp, vpres & gen mgr, 1989-91; GTE Govt Systs, IIPO, vpres & gen mgr, 1991-93; GTE Airfone, pres, 1993-96; GTE Corp, vpres technol mkt, 1996-2000, pres; pvt investor. **Orgs:** Armed Forces Commun & Electronics Asn; sec, Hibiscus C's Ctr. **Home Addr:** 5620 N Harbor Village Dr Apt 402, Vero Beach, FL 32967-7076, **Home Phone:** (772)569-9865.

### LINDSAY, SAM A.
Judge. **Personal:** Born Oct 16, 1951, San Antonio, TX. **Educ:** St Marys Univ, San Antonio, BA, 1974; Univ Tex Sch Law, JD, 1977. **Career:** Tex Aeronaut Comn, Staff Atty, 1977-79; Fed Litigation Sect, Head, 1979-86; Dallas City Attorneys Off, 1979-92; Dallas City, atty, 1992-98; Northern Dist Tex, fed judge, 1998-. **Orgs:** State Bar Tex; Dallas Legal Asn; Dallas Inn Ct; JL Turner Legal Asn; City Dallas Judicial Nominating Comn; Int Munic Lawyers Asn; Southwestern Legal Found; Leadership Dallas Class; fed Judiciary adv comt, Northern Dist Tex; adv comt, Dallas Bus Jour; trustee, Ctr Am & Int Law. **Honors/Awds:** Trailblazers Award, 1993; CB Bunkley Award, JL Turner Legal Asn, 1996. **Special Achievements:** First African American to serve on the District Court in Dallas. **Business Addr:** Federal District Judge, Northern District of Texas, Rm 1544 1100 Com St, Dallas, TX 75242-1003, **Business Phone:** (214)753-2365.

### LINDSEY, JEROME W., JR.
Educator, planner, architect. **Personal:** Born Apr 7, 1932, Phoenix City, AL; son of Jerome W II and Willie Mae Harper Swinton. **Educ:** Howard Univ, BArch, 1956; Mass Inst Technol, MA, archit & city planning, 1961. **Career:** Harold M Lewis, planner, 1955-56; John Hans Graham, planner, 1956-58; Samuel Glaser, planner, 1958-59; Jose Luis Sert, planner, 1959-61; Providence Redevelop Agency, sr planner, 1961-62; Howard Univ, assoc prof archit, 1962-68, chmn, 1969-70, from assoc dean to dean, 1970-79, prof, 1971-; Wash DC, dir planning, 1964-68; Yale Univ, vis prof, 1967-68; Jerome W Lindsey Assocs, owner, currently. **Orgs:** Regional architect; Am Inst Architects; Bd Educ; consult, World Bank Urban Devel Proj. **Honors/Awds:** NCARB Certificate. **Home Addr:** 501 Aspen St NW, Washington, DC 20012, **Home Phone:** (202)726-8645. **Business Addr:** Professor, Howard University School of Architecture & Planning, 2400 6th St NW, Washington, DC 20059, **Business Phone:** (202)806-6100.

### LINDSEY, PASTOR PATRICK O.
Executive. **Personal:** married Kathy; children: Kendall & Kaylyn. **Educ:** Univ Mich, BA, polit sci, 1981; Harvard Univ Kennedy Sch Govt, cert, sr execs state & local govt prog, 2003, leadership 21st century, 2006. **Career:** Chrysler LLC, exec security supvr, 1991-94, state & local govt rels exec, govt rels mgr, sr mgr state rels, 2002-08; Greater Bibleway Baptist Church, pastor, 1992-; DaimlerChrysler Group, mgr community rels, 1994-2002, sr mgr state rels, external affairs & pub policy, currently; Focus HOPE, dir, external rels & develop, 2009-11; Wayne State Univ, vpres govt & community affairs, 2012-. **Orgs:** Focus, dir govt affairs & external commun, 2009-; bd chair, Community Schs Metrop Detroit, 2014; bd mem, Urban League Detroit & Southeast Mich, 2014; bd mem, Detroit Community Health Connection Inc, 2016; bd mem, Warren/Conner Develop Coalition; FutureGen Ill Task Force; speaker, Growth Dimensions; bus mem, Eight Mile Blvd Asn; bd dir, Black Family Develop Inc; bd mem, Detroit Entrepreneurship Inst Inc; Alpha Phi Alpha Fraternity Inc; Viewpoint Lect Comt; Bursley Hall Minority Stud Pres; City Detroit Workforce Develop Bd; Warren Conner Develop Coalition; Detroit Entrepreneurship Inst Inc; Black Family Develop Inc; Pleasant Grove Baptist Dist Asn; Mich Alumni Asn; JFK Sch Govt Alumni Group; Wayne State Univ/DMC Instnl Rev Bd. **Honors/Awds:** Outstanding Young Men of America, 1994; Spirit of Detroit Award, 1996; Award of Excellence, Dale Carnegie, 2008; Men of Excellence Award, Mich Chronicle, 2013. **Business Addr:** Vice President for Government & Community Affairs, Wayne State University, 4145 Fac Admin Bldg 656 W Kirby, Detroit, MI 48202, **Business Phone:** (313)577-4228.

### LINK, JOYCE BATTLE
Lawyer. **Personal:** Born Dec 24, 1956, Columbus, OH; daughter of William R and Dorothy L; married Michael D. **Educ:** Wash Univ, St Louis, BA, educ & psychol, 1978; Ohio State Univ, Col Law, JD, 1983. **Career:** Asst city prosecutor, 1983-85; asst atty gen, 1985-89; Bricker & Eckler LLP, assoc, 1989-95, Litigation Dept, partner, 1995; Cent State Univ, Ohio Atty Gen, spec coun, 1996-2004; Ohio Supreme Ct Chief Justice Mayor, Ohio Supreme Ct's, civil rules comt, 2002-04; Montgomery, McCracken, Walker & Rhoads LLP, atty, 2006-. **Orgs:** Columbus Bar Asn, former chair judiciary comt, 1998; Ohio State Bar Asn; Am Bar Asn; Nat Bar Asn; Nat Asn Col & Univ Atty; Nat Coun Ohio State Univ Col Law Alumni Asn; vchmn, Community Shelter Bd, 2001-04; chair, Life Ins Law Comt Tort Trial & Ins Pract Sect, 2004. **Honors/Awds:** Panelist, Oxygen Media & Time Warner prod, 2002; Women of Achievement Award, Young Women Christian Asn, 2003; Columbus Community Black Women of Courage Award. **Home Addr:** 105 Woodland Ave, Columbus, OH 43203-1768, **Home Phone:** (614)262-5996. **Business Addr:** Attorney, Montgomery, McCracken, Walker & Rhoads LLP, 123 S Broad St 28th Fl Ave of the Arts, Philadelphia, PA 19109-1099, **Business Phone:** (215)772-7692.

### LINTON, GORDON J.
State government official, executive. **Personal:** Born Mar 26, 1948, Philadelphia, PA; son of James and Alberta James; married Jacqueline Flynn; children: Sharifah & Sabriya. **Educ:** Peirce Jr Col, AS, bus admin, mgt & opers, 1967; Lincoln Univ, PA, BA, econs, 1970; Antioch Univ, MEd, coun psycol, 1977. **Career:** Sch Dist Philadelphia, comn consult, 1971-74; Baptist C's House, educ dir, 1974-78; Philadelphia Child Guid Ctr, psych-ed spec, 1978-80; Dept Auditor Gen, reg dir, 1980-82; Pa House Rep, state rep, 1982-93; Southeastern Pa Transp Authority, dir, 1991-93; Us Dept Transp, Fed Transit Admin, adminr, 1993-99; Siebert Brandford Shank Co LLC, sr vpres transp group, 2000-02; Hagler Bailly Inc, sr adv, 2000-04; Wage Works Inc, sr adv & vpres, 2001-09; WMATA, dir, 2004-10; 200consult, sr advisor & prin, 2009-. **Orgs:** Nat Black Caucus State Legislators, 1982-, Minority Bus Enterprise Coun, 1982-; trustee, Lincoln Univ, 1982-; Philadelphia Econ Round table, 1983-; pres, Conf Minority Transp Officials, 1984; SEPTA, 1991-93, bd dir, 1993-99; Wash Metrop Area Transit Authority, alt dir, bd dir; chmn, Linton 200 Charitable Fund, 2011-; Alzheimer's Asn, New York Chap; Mem Bd Dirs, Brandywine Workshop & Arch, 2016-. **Honors/Awds:** Community Service Award, Hill Youth Asn, 1982; Community Service Award, Leeds Middle Sch, 1982; Community Service Award, Crisis Intervention Network, 1984; Appreciation Award, New Pa Del Minority Purchasing Coun, 1985; Appreciation Award, Independent Minority Businessmen Cent Pa, 1985; Outstanding Civic Leadership Award, Entrepreneurial Club-Bus & Technol Ctr, 1985; Dedicated Service to Higher Education Award, Lincoln Univ, 1986; Pride Peirce, Peirce Jr Col, 1989; Adviser of the Year Award, Nat Asn Women Bus Owners, 1989. **Home Addr:** 913 E McPherson St, Philadelphia, PA 19150. **Business Addr:** Alternate Director, Washington Metropolitan Area Transit Authority, 600 Fifth St NW, Washington, DC 20001, **Business Phone:** (202)962-1234.

### LINTON, JONATHAN C.
Football player. **Personal:** Born Nov 7, 1974, Allentown, PA; children: 2. **Educ:** NC State Univ, grad. **Career:** Football player (retired); Buffalo Bills, 1998, running back, 1999-2000, fullback, 1999; US Dept State. **Honors/Awds:** Rookie of the Year, 1998. **Business Addr:** Washington, DC.

### LINTON, SHEILA LORRAINE
Educator, association executive. **Personal:** Born Dec 19, 1950, Philadelphia, PA; daughter of Harold Louis (deceased) and Elvera Linton Boyd (deceased). **Educ:** Pa State Univ, BS, educ, 1972; Drexel Univ, MS, 1976. **Career:** Educator (retired); Sch Dist Philadelphia, teacher, 1972-78, 1988-2003, new teacher coach, 2003-10, consult teacher, 2010-13; Pew Charitable Trusts, prog officer, 1979-87. **Orgs:** Alpha Kappa Alpha Sorority Inc, 1970-; Nat Sec Bullock Family Reunions, 1978-85; adv comt, bd dir, Jack & Jill Am Found, 1981-87, 1989-2001; vol, United Negro Col Fund, 1982-87; Women Philanthropy, 1983-87; bd dir, Asn Black Found Exec, 1984-87; Friends Free Libr Philadelphia, 1989-96; bd dir, Family Reunion Inst, Temple Univ, 1990; bd, Kearsley Retirement, 1992-2003; Nat Coalition 100 Black Women. **Honors/Awds:** Presidential Award for Distinguished Service, Jack & Jill Am Found, 1984; Teacher of the Year, Audenried Cluster, Sch Dist Philadelphia, 2000; National Board Certified Teacher, 2002. **Home Addr:** 1030 Harbour Dr, Palmyra, NJ 08065-1216, **Home Phone:** (856)303-2286. **Business Addr:** Teacher, School District of Philadelphia, 4909 Chestnut St 1st Fl, Philadelphia, PA 19139, **Business Phone:** (215)400-4000.

### LINTZ, FRANK D. E.
Landscape architect. **Personal:** Born Feb 5, 1951, Ottumwa, IA; son of Franklyn and Margaret; married Lisa M Campos. **Career:** Mid-Continent Meats, union leader, 1972-79; Circle C Beef Co, union leader, 1979-83; Swift & Co, lead butcher, 1983-86; Nebr Turf Co, co-owner, 1994-98; Farmland Foods Co, Warehouse & Transp, coordr, 1998-. **Orgs:** Amalgamated Meat Cutters & Butcher Workmen, 1972-79, chief steward, 1979-83; United Food & Com Workers, 1983-86. **Special Achievements:** Des Moines Register, farming article in 1968; BET News Network, Drought in Midwest, television Interview in 1989. **Home Addr:** 4915 N 61st St, Omaha, NE 68104, **Home Phone:** (402)571-3251. **Business Addr:** 4736 S 131st St, Omaha, NE 68137-1822.

### LINYARD, RICHARD
Chief executive officer, manager, banker. **Personal:** Born Nov 16, 1930, Maywood, IL; married Maggie; children: Linda, Lance & Timothy. **Educ:** Northwestern Univ; Am Inst Banking, standard & advan cert; Univ Wis, Grad Sch Banking, dipl. **Career:** Oak Pk Trust & Savs Bank, janitor, elevator oper, savs bookkeeper, teller, gen bookkeeper, savs dept, asst mgr, asst cashier, 1950-64; Seaway Nat Bank Chicago, exec vpres, bd dir cashier, 1964-72, pres & chief exec officer. **Orgs:** Pres, dir, Chicago chap, Am Inst Banking.

### LIPPETT, RONNIE LEON
Football player. **Personal:** Born Dec 10, 1960, Melbourne, FL. **Educ:** Univ Miami. **Career:** Football player (retired); New Eng Patriots, corner back & left corner back, 1983-88, 1990-91. **Orgs:** Patriot, Nat Alliance Dedicated Patriots, 2003-; founder, Found Stud Educ. **Honors/Awds:** Post-season play, 1985: Am Football Club Championship Game, Nat Football League Championship Game.

### LIPPS, LOUIS ADAM, JR.
Football player, executive, radio host. **Personal:** Born Aug 9, 1962, New Orleans, LA. **Educ:** Univ Southern Miss. **Career:** Football player (retired), executive, host; Pittsburgh Steelers, wide receiver, 1984-91; New Orleans Saints, wide receiver, 1992; Steel City Mortgage Serv, mortgage banking officer, currently; ESPN radio, co-host, currently. **Orgs:** Hon chmn, Big Bros & Sisters Bowl Kids; chmn, MS Readathon; chmn, Variety Club Golf Tournament, Ronald McDonald House; owner, Halls Mortuary; Drug & Alcohol Educ Prog, Blue Cross Western Pa, 1986-. **Honors/Awds:** Offensive Rookie of the Year, Nat Football League, 1984; Pro Bowl, 1984, 1985; Professional Athlete of the Year; Joe Greene Great Performance Award, 1984; Steelers Most Valuable Player, 1985; Pittsburgh's Man of the Year in Sports; Louisiana Prof Athlete of the Year, Sugar Bowl's Sports Awards Community, 1985. **Special Achievements:** First Steeler rookie since Franco Harris to be named to AFC Pro Bowl. **Business Addr:** Mortgage Banking Officer, Steel City Mortgage Services, 17 Brilliant Ave, Pittsburgh, PA 15215, **Business Phone:** (412)784-8808.

### LIPSCOMB, CURTIS ALEXANDER
Publishing executive. **Personal:** Born Mar 23, 1965, Detroit, MI; son of Lester Lewis and Mary Salley. **Educ:** Parsons Sch Design, BFA, 1987; Wayne State Univ, attended 2015. **Career:** Dagger Grp, knitwear designer, 1987-89; Bonaventure, knitwear designer, 1989-90; Chelsea Young, knitwear designer, 1990; Ruff Hewn, knitwear designer, 1990-91; Banana Repub, knitwear designer, 1991-92; Kick Publ Co, pres & chief exec officer, exec dir, 1994-. **Orgs:** Men Color Motivational Grp, Detroit, 1992-; co-chair, Mich Clinton & Gore Lesbian Gay Leadership Counre-elect Pres Clinton, 1996; ed bd, Between The Lines; ed bd, Mich Community News Lesbians, Gays, Bisexuals & Friends. **Honors/Awds:** Adolf Klein Scholarship Award, 1986; Roz & Sherm Fashion Award, 1983; Brother of the Year Award, Community Service, SBC Magazine, 1996. **Special Achievements:** Traveled to Europe/UK, 1990; Traveled to Far East, 1990; Publications: Kick! Magazine, The Motivator, Detroit Pride Guide, The Official Resource Guide to Hotter Than July 1996 & 1997. **Home Addr:** 2208 John R, Detroit, MI 48201. **Business Addr:** Executive Director, Kick Publishing Co, 41 Burroughs St Suite 109, Detroit, MI 48202, **Business Phone:** (313)285-9733.

### LIPSCOMB, DARRYL L.
Government official. **Personal:** Born Jan 18, 1953, Chicago, IL. **Educ:** Univ Wis-La Crosse, BS, mass commun & media studies, 1977, MS, educ, 1982. **Career:** Univ Wis, admis counr, 1979-82; COE Col, asst dir admis, 1982-83, assoc dean admis, 1983-86; Cedar Ridge Publ, dir mkt, 1986-89; Civil Rights Comn, City Cedar Rapids, compliance mgr, 1989-2013; HUD, syst admin; Kirkwood Community Col, Stud Develop, adj counr, dir admis, part time counr, ICCSSA, web master, 1994-2011; Lipscomb & Assocs, pres & chief exec officer, 1995-2003, mediatiaton serv & EEO consult, 2003-; Iowa Comn Status African-Am, comnr, 1996-2000. **Orgs:** Equal Opportunity Prog Personnel, 1985-89; adv comt, Kirkwood Community Col, 1991-; bd dir, Friends Unity Inc, 1996-; life mem, Kappa Alpha Psi Frat; IC/CR Alumni Chap Kappa Alpha Psi; life mem, Nat Asn Advan Colored People; bd mem, Equal Employ Opportunity Affirmative Action. Nat Assoc Human Rights Workers; Nat Assoc Black Pub Officals; bd dir, Iowa Am Civil Liberties Union. **Home Addr:** 2035 Knollshire Rd NE, Cedar Rapids, IA 52402, **Home Phone:** (319)265-1927. **Business Addr:** EEO Consulting, Lipscomb & Associates, PO Box 102, Cedar Rapids, IA 52406, **Business Phone:** (319)431-4788.

### LIPSCOMB, DR. WANDA DEAN
Administrator. **Personal:** Born Jan 29, 1953, Richmond, VA; married Keith N; children: Nicholas K & Victoria N. **Educ:** Lincoln Univ, BA, 1974; Wash Univ, MA, 1975; Mich State Univ, PhD, 1978. **Career:**

Mich State Univ, Col Human Med, assoc chairperson educ prog, 1994, dir ctr excellence, currently, assoc prof psychol, currently, sr assoc dean diversity & inclusion, asst dean stud affairs, currently; Health Carrers Opportunity Prog, dir, 1984-2012; Centers Excellence Prog, 2012-. **Orgs:** Bd dir, nat pres, Asn Multicult Coun & Develop, 1980-88; bd dir, Am Asn Coun & Develop, 1982-85; Asn Black Psychologists, 1984-; bd dir, pres & chair, Nat Bd Cert Counselors, 1985-90; pres, Lansing Alumnae Chap Delta Sigma Theta Sorority Inc; Nat Prog Planning Comn Delta Sigma Theta Sorority Inc; bd dir, Mich State Univ Black Alumni Asn; Asn Am Med Cols; pres, Nat Coun Diversity Health Professions; nat pres, Nat Asn Med Minority Educr. **Home Addr:** 3422 Penrose Dr, Lansing, MI 48911, **Home Phone:** (517)977-0509. **Business Addr:** Assistant Dean for Student Affairs, Diversity & Outreach, Director & Associate Professor, Michigan State University, A-234 Life Sci Bldg, East Lansing, MI 48824, **Business Phone:** (517)355-2404.

## LIPSCOMBE, MARGARET ANN

Dancer, educator, executive director. **Personal:** Born Dec 12, 1939, AL. **Educ:** Univ Minn, BS, 1957; NY Univ, MA, 1960; Columbia Univ, attended 1968; Conn Col, attended 1967; Juilliard Sch, attended 1970; NY Studios, attended 1975. **Career:** Valmar Dance Co, performer, 1958-59; Spelman Col, instr, 1959-64; Hunter Col HS, instr, 1959-60; Women's Dance Proj Henry St Play house NY, performer, 1960; City Col NY, instr, 1964-67; Vassar NY, choreography performance under Mary Jean Corvele, 1965-68; Dance W Conn State Col, profdance workshops, instr, 1967-; Creative Daycare LLC, dir; Dancers Faith, performer, 1971-72. **Orgs:** Asn Ment Health; Am Asn Health Phys Educ & Recreation; Nat Teachers Asn; Univ Prof Women; Music Fedn Inc. **Home Addr:** PO Box 462, Georgetown, CT 06829-0462. **Business Addr:** Director, Creative Daycare LLC, 76 Merry Lane, Weston, CT 06883-1220, **Business Phone:** (203)227-9273.

## LISTER, ALTON LAVELLE

Basketball coach, basketball player. **Personal:** Born Oct 1, 1958, Dallas, TX; married Elaine; children: Avery, J Ross, Alton Jr, Alexa & Amari. **Educ:** Ariz State Univ, attended 1981. **Career:** Basketball player (retired), basketball coach; USA Olympic Basketball team, 1980; Milwaukee Bucks, ctr-forward, power forward, 1981-86, 1994-95; Seattle Super Sonics, ctr, 1986-89; Golden State Warriors, ctr, 1989-93; Boston Celtics, ctr, 1995-97; Portland Trailblazers, ctr, 1997-98; Mesa Community Col, head coach, ABCD Reebok camp, coach, 2006; Mike Woodson, asst coach, 2007; San Miguel Beermen, skills coach, 2008-15; Tropang TNT, asst coach, 2016-. **Honors/Awds:** Inducted into Woodrow's Hall of Fame in 1990. **Special Achievements:** First round pick, 21, NBA Draft, 1981. **Home Addr:** 626 E Kilbourn Ave Suite 1606, Milwaukee, WI 53202. **Business Addr:** Skills Coach, San Miguel Beermen, 40 San Miguel Ave, Mandaluyong City1475, **Business Phone:** (026)32-3000.

## LISTER, DAVID ALFRED

School administrator, educator. **Personal:** Born Oct 19, 1939, Somerset, NJ; son of James and Etoile Johnson; married Anita Louise Browne; children: Mimi & Gigi. **Educ:** Cent State Univ, BA, 1962; Stetson Univ Col Law, JD, 1977. **Career:** Johns Hopkins Med Inst, dir affirmative action, 1978-79; Univ Mass Med Ctr, assoc vice chancellor, 1979-82; Inst Int Educ, dir personnel, 1982-86; Fairleigh Dickinson Univ, univ dir & human resources, 1986-87, asst vpres admin, 1987-88; Univ Med & Dent NJ, vpres, human resources, 1988-94; Jersey City Med Ctr, vpres human resources, 1994-99; St Peter's Univ Hosp, vpres human resources, 1999-2001; Detroit Pub Schs, dep ceo human resources, 2001-. **Orgs:** Pres's adv Comn, Morgan State Univ, 1978; Nat Asn Advan Colored People; Soc Human Resources Adminr; Col & Univ Personnel Asn; Alpha Phi Alpha Fraternity Inc; bd mem, Chmn Prog Comm, Community Newark Pvt Indust Coun, mem exec comm; Am Asn Affirmative Action; Int Personnel Mgt Asn; Am Mgt Asn; Am Hosp Asn; Am Compensation Asn; Asn Hosp Personnel Adminr; NJ Col & Univ Personnel Asn; NJ Asn Hosp Personnel Adminr; Greater Newark Chamber Com; Urban League; Cent State Univ Alumni Asn. **Home Addr:** 21 Mountain View Dr, Chester, NJ 07930, **Home Phone:** (908)879-5174. **Business Addr:** Deputy Chief Executive Officer for Human Resources, Detroit Public Schools, 5057 Woodward Ave Rm 404, Detroit, MI 48202, **Business Phone:** (313)494-1810.

## LISTER, VALERIE LYNN

Writer. **Personal:** Born Jun 21, 1961, Niagara Falls, NY; daughter of Espinetta Griffin and Valentine Jonathan. **Educ:** Univ Tex, El Paso, Tex, BA, 1983. **Career:** Athens Daily News, Athens, Ga, sports writer, 1984; Pensacola News J, Pensacola, Fla, sports writer, 1984-88; USA Today, Arlington, Va, sports writer, 1988-. **Orgs:** Delta Sigma Theta Sorority Inc, 1982-; Natl Assn Black Journalists, 1987-; steering comt, NABJ Sports Task Force, 1989-; reg dir, Assn Women Sports Media, 1990-; co-dir, Reston Runners Youth Motion, 2006-09; bd mem, Reston Youth Cheerleading, 2009, 2010; liturgy coordr & eucharistic minister trainer, St John Neumann Cath Church. **Home Addr:** 2358 Tumbletree Way, Reston, VA 20191-4408. **Business Addr:** Sports Writer, USA Today, 1000 Wilson Blvd, Arlington, VA 22229, **Business Phone:** (703)276-3701.

## LISTER, WILLA MAE. See Obituaries Section.

## LITTLE, BENILDE ELEASE

Writer. **Personal:** Born Jan 1, 1959, Newark, NJ; daughter of Matthew and Clara; married Clifford Virgin III; children: Baldwin & Ford. **Educ:** Howard Univ, BA, Jour, 1981; Northwestern Univ, Grad Sch, 1982. **Career:** Cleveland Plain Dealer, reporter; Newark Star Ledger, reporter, 1982-85; People Magazine, reporter, 1985-89; Essence Magazine, sr editor, 1989-91; Heart & Soul, contrib ed; Author: Book Good Hair, National Bestseller, 75, 000 copies; Los Angeles Times, One of 10 Best Books, Good Hair, 1996; The Itch, Simon & Schuster, 1998, Acting Out, 2003; Who Does She Think She Is?, 2005; novel writing; Ramapo Col, writing prof, currently. **Honors/Awds:** Go On Girl Book Club, National Best New Author, 1996; Image Award, Nat Asn Advan Colored People, Finalist, 1996. **Home Addr:** 124 Bellevue Ave, Montclair, NJ 07043, **Home Phone:** (973)509-3596. **Business Addr:** Author, Journalist & Editor, Writing Professor, c/o Little-Virgin Inc, PO Box 588, South Orange, NJ 07079-0588.

## LITTLE, BRYAN

Physician, orthopedic surgeon. **Educ:** Univ Mich, BS, 1994; Northwest Univ Med Sch, residency, orthopaedics; Wayne State Univ Sch Med, MD, 1998; Adult Reconstruction, Ind Univs Hosps, fel. **Career:** Northwest Univ Med Sch, resident; fel, Ind Univs Hosps; Henry Ford Hosp, Dept Orthop, sr attend staff surgeon, 2004-09; DMC Detroit Receiving Hosp, orthopaedic surgeon, 2009-. **Special Achievements:** Minority Peer Advisor to 1500 students at the Univ of MI; won full tuition scholarships for both his undergraduate and medical school education; made presentations to the Am Assoc of Hip and Knee Surgeons; published research. **Business Addr:** Orthopaedic Surgeon, 4201 St Antoine Suite 6B2, Detroit, MI 48201, **Business Phone:** (313)745-1315.

## LITTLE, GENERAL T.

Physician. **Personal:** Born Sep 10, 1946, Wadesboro, NC; married Barbara McConnell; children: Christopher, Adrienne & Kimberly. **Educ:** NC A&T State Univ, BS, 1967; Meharry Med Col, MD, 1971; Walter Reed Gen Hosp, attended 1975. **Career:** Walter Reed Army Med Ctr, resident, internal med, 1971-76; Cardio-Pulmonary Assoc Charleston, Md; Kimbrough AUS Hosp, chief internal med, 1975-76; Am Bd Internal Med, dipl; pvt pract, currently; Roper Hosp; internist, currently. **Orgs:** Nat Med Asn; consult, internal med Sea Island Health Care Corp, 1976-77; Am Soc Internal Med; bd trustee, Charleston Co Hosp; bd trustee, Charleston Area Ment Health Bd; Omega Psi Phi Frat Inc. **Business Addr:** Physician, 280 Rutledge Ave, Charleston, SC 29403, **Business Phone:** (843)722-6336.

## LITTLE, HANNAH. See BERRY, HALLE MARIA.

## LITTLE, HERMAN KERNEL

School administrator, county government official. **Personal:** Born Jan 25, 1951, Wadesboro, NC; son of Bryant and Margie; married H Patricia; children: Kentrell & Karlton. **Educ:** Anson Tech Col, AAS, acct, 1980, AAS, retailing & mkt, 1980; Wingate Col, BA, bus admin mgt, 1984. **Career:** Anson Tech Col, asst proj dir, 1977-83, proj dir, 1983-, ed admin; Anson County Govt, Bd Commissioners, chmn. **Orgs:** Bd dir, Morven Area Med Ctr, 1978-, Anson City Red Cross, 1978-; NC Community Col Adult Ed Assoc, 1978-; bd dir, Anson County, Bd Adjust, 1980; Anson County Waste Mgt Bd, 1981-; Savannah AME Zion Church, 1982-; Am Soc Personnel Admin, 1982-; pres, Polit Action Community Concerned Citizens, 1982-; Anson County Young Dem Party, 1982-83; Phi Beta Lambda Wingate Col, 1982-; Grace Sr Ctr Adv Coun, 1983-; Anson County Personnel Asn, 1983-; bd dir, Anson County Art's Coun, 1984-; PDCOG Emergency Med Serv Adv, 1984-; Anson County Comnr, 1986; Anson County Health Bd, 1987; bd mem, NC United Way, 1991; bd mem, Sandhills Ctr Area, 2003-. **Home Addr:** PO Box 625 Rte 4, Wadesboro, NC 28170, **Home Phone:** (704)848-8165. **Business Addr:** NC 28170.

## LITTLE, IRENE PRUITT

Government official. **Personal:** Born Feb 9, 1946, Aliceville, AL; daughter of Bill and Ruth Wade; children: Christopher Sean & Shana Nicole Dawson. **Educ:** Wellesley Col, attended 1965; Stillman Col, BA, educ, 1967; Univ Md, MS, pub admin, 2000. **Career:** Government official (retired); Social Security Admin, personnel mgt specialist, 1972-77; US Customs, sr labor rels specialist, 1977-80; Environ Protection Agency, Off Civil Rights, dir, 1980-82, asst toregional admin, 1982-87; US Nuclear Regulatory Comn (NRC), regional personnel dir, 1987-89, dir resource mgt & admin, 1989-96, Off Small Bus & Civil Rights, dir, 1997-03. **Orgs:** Chicago Fed Recruitment Coun, 1972-90; vpres, 1986-89; Blacks Govt; Nat Asn Advan Colored People; pres, 1998-99, treas, 2000-, DC Metro Chap, Stillman Col Alumni; trustee, 1999-2000, pastoral search comm, 2000-, Resurrection Baptist Church; Nat Alumni Asn; Stillman Col, Souther Region vpres; Initial Steering Comt. **Honors/Awds:** Meritorious Service Award for Equal Employment Opportunity, NRC, 1989; Outstanding Contribution to Higher Education, NAFEO, 1990; Outstanding Client Award, GSA, 1994; Outstanding Alumnus, Stillman Col, 2000; Presidential Meritorious Executive Rank Award, 2003. **Home Addr:** 1053 Greystone Cove Dr, Silver Spring, MD 20905.

## LITTLE, LEONARD ANTONIO

Football player. **Personal:** Born Oct 19, 1974, Asheville, NC. **Educ:** Univ Tenn, psy chol. **Career:** Football player (retired); St Louis Rams, 1998, defensive end, 1999, 2001, 2002-09, linebacker, 2000, left defensive end, 2003. **Honors/Awds:** First-team All-SEC, 1997; First-team All-American, 1997; Champion, Nat Football Conf, 1999, 2001; All-Pro, 2003; Pro Bowl, 2003; Ed Block Courage Award, 2005; Super Bowl champion, XXXIV; St. Louis Rams 10th Anniversary Team; Super Bowl champion, XXXIV. **Special Achievements:** Film: Super Bowl XXXIV, 2000. TV Special: "Super Bowl XXXVI", 2002.

## LITTLE, DR. MONROE HENRY, JR.

Educator. **Personal:** Born Jun 30, 1950, St. Louis, MO; married Shelia Maria Josephine Parks; children: Alexander. **Educ:** Denison Univ, BA, hist, 1971; Princeton Univ, MA, 1973, PhD, Africana studies/hist, 1977. **Career:** Mass Inst Technol, instr, 1976-77, asst prof, 1977-80; Ind Univ-Purdue Univ, Indianapolis, Sch Lib Arts, from asst prof, 1980-81, African Am Studies Prog, dir, 1981-, dept chair, currently, assoc prof hist, currently; US Dept Labor, CSR Inc, consult, 1981. **Orgs:** Fel Rockefeller Fel Afro-Am Studies, 1972-75; Am Hist Asn; Orgn Am Historians; Nat Urban League; Study Afro-Am Life & Hist; consult, Educ Develop Ctr, 1980; consult, Black Women Mid-W Proj, Purdue Univ, 1983. **Honors/Awds:** Elected Omicron Delta Kappa Men's Leadership Hon, 1971. **Special Achievements:** Author of "Black Leaders of the Twentieth Century", 1983. **Home Addr:** 4629 Sunset Ave, Indianapolis, IN 46208. **Business Addr:** Associate Professor, Indiana University, CA 503C Cavanaugh Hall 504M, Indianapolis, IN 46202, **Business Phone:** (317)274-0098.

## LITTLE, REUBEN R., SR.

Manager, teacher. **Personal:** Born Sep 1, 1933; married Margaret Jean Davis; children: Reuben R Little II. **Educ:** Ala A&M Univ, BS, 1957; Univ Texas, grad study, 1963; Kans State Univ, attended 1964; Western Ill Univ, attended 1965; Ind Univ, MSS, 1966. **Career:** Teacher (retired); Dept Health & Human Serv & Social Security Admin, Meridian MS, oper supvr, cur; DHEW & Social Security Admin, Tuscaloosa AL, mgt trainee, 1974-75; tchr admin, jr high sch level; Neighborhood Youth Corp Prog, dir; Bonita Educ Ctr, tchr, social studies, 1995. **Orgs:** Kappa Alpha Psi, 1954; Rescue Lodge 439 3rd Deg Mason, 1958; IBPO Elk W, 1960; Nat Coun Geog Tchrs, 1964; Choctaw Area Coun BSA, 1965; charter mem, Cloverleaf Toastmaster Club, 1967; Nat Asn Advan Colored People, 1968; div chmn, Lauderdale Co March Dimes 1968-70; Nat Bus League 1970; Nat Assoc New York dir, 1970; EEO Assoc, 1970; vol Youth Ct Coun, 1972; lay minister trustee, chmn Bd, Elders Good Shepherd Luthern Ch Meridan MS; pres & area gov, Toastmasters Intl, 1973-74; Zoning Bd, City Meridian, 1978-92; life mem, Nat Asn Advan Colored People; pres, Sandwedge Golfers Asn, Meridian, 1982-92-; Cent Meridian Optimist Club, pres, charter mem, 1984, pres, 1990-91; pres, bod, retired sr vol prog, 1990-; pres, Area VI Gov, 1985-86-; pres, Meridian Area Toastmasters, 1989-93; chmn, Lauderdale Coun Planning & Airport Zoning CMS, 1992-; finance com Meridale Girl Scouts; AL & MS Dist, lt gov; Pub Off, Election Comn, Dist 4, 1994-. **Home Addr:** 3203 13th St, Meridian, MS 39301, **Home Phone:** (601)482-3407. **Business Addr:** Election Commissioner, Pub Off, 500 Constitution Ave 1st Fl, Meridian, MS 39301, **Business Phone:** (601)482-9809.

## LITTLE, DR. ROBERT BENJAMIN

Physician, surgeon. **Personal:** Born Apr 25, 1955, Dublin, GA; son of William Albert and Druzy Perry. **Educ:** Morehouse Col, BS, 1977; Meharry Med Col, MD, 1982. **Career:** Harlem Hosp, internship & residency, gen surg, 1983-85; USn, gen med officer, 1986-89; More house Med Sch, Atlanta, Ga, family med intern, resident, 1989-92, chief resident, 1991-92; Family Med & Emergency Med, independent contractor, 1992-; Little Assocs Inc, physician, currently. **Orgs:** Am Acad Family Physicians; Am Med Asn; Am Col Emergency Physicians; Asn Emergency Physicians; Am Med Stud Asn; Atlanta Med Asn; Ga State Med Asn; Am Asn Physician Specialists. **Honors/Awds:** Bd Certification, Family Med, 1992. **Home Addr:** 821 N Cobb St, Milledgeville, GA 31061, **Home Phone:** (478)454-3795. **Business Addr:** Physician, Little Associates Inc, 225 Canaan Glen Way SW, Atlanta, GA 30331, **Business Phone:** (404)346-0032.

## LITTLE, ROBERT E.

President (organization), public speaker. **Educ:** MA, educ psychol; PhD, educ psychol. **Career:** Relde Publ LLC, founder; Solutions Training & Develop LLC, pres, currently; books: What CAN I Be?, auth; Jamaal's LUCKY Day, auth; Grandma's Biscuits, auth; SPOKEN SUCCESS, auth. **Orgs:** Bd dir, Toastmasters Intl; Am Soc Training & Develop; Nat Speakers Asn. **Business Addr:** President, Chief Executive Officer, Solutions Training & Development LLC, 931 Hwy 80 W Suite 218-C, Jackson, MS 39289, **Business Phone:** (601)968-9052.

## LITTLEJOHN, HON. BILL C.

Judge, business owner. **Personal:** Born Jan 25, 1944, Gaffney, SC; son of Elviry Geter; married Gail Hodge; children: Erica A, Shai A & Eric. **Educ:** Cent State Univ, BS, acct, 1969; Ohio Northern Law Univ, JD, 1972; Payne Theol Sem. **Career:** Montgomery County Pub Defender, criminal defense atty, 1974-75; City Dayton, prosecutor, 1975-76, pvt pract, 1976-91, traffic ct referee, 1979-80, actg judge, 1978-91; Austin, Jones, Little john & Owens, trial atty, 1980-85; Littlejohn & Littlejohn, pres, 1985-91; State Ohio Munic Ct Dayton Municipality, judge, 1991-2009; N River Coffee House & Eatery LLC, owner, currently; WorldVentures, owner. **Orgs:** Nat Bus League, bd mem, 1985-, regional vpres, 1986, treas, 1990-93; bd mem, Pvt Indust Coun, 1985; chmn bd, Cent State Univ, Gleksto Inc, 1986; pres, Neighborhoods USA, 1986; 32 Degree Prince Hall Mason; distinguished pres, Optimist Int; bd mem, United Cerebral Palsy Found; bd trustee, Wesley Community Ctr Inc; bd trustee & pres, Mary Scott Nursing Ctr; Christian Educ Dir, Church; Habitat Humanity, 1993-; bd mem, Dayton African Am Legacy Inst. **Home Addr:** 301 W 3rd St, Dayton, OH 45402, **Home Phone:** (937)333-4369. **Business Addr:** Owner, North River Coffee House & Eatery LLC, 323 Salem Ave, Dayton, OH 45406, **Business Phone:** (937)226-1532.

## LITTLEJOHN, DONNA M.

Association executive. **Career:** Women Color Found & Health Ministries Inc, founder, 2001-. **Business Addr:** Founder, Women of Color Foundation & Health Ministries Inc, PO Box 3835, Southfield, MI 48037, **Business Phone:** (248)569-3532.

## LITTLEJOHN, DR. EDWARD J.

Educator, lawyer. **Personal:** Born Pittsburgh, PA. **Educ:** Wayne State Univ, BA, 1965; Detroit Col Law, JD, 1970; Columbia Univ Law Sch, LLM, 1974, JSD, 1982. **Career:** City Detroit, varied govt serv, 1959-70; Detroit Col Law, asst prof, 1970-72; Wayne State Law Sch, assoc prof & asst dean, 1972-76, prof law 1972-96, assoc dean& prof law, 1976-78, prof emer law, 1996-; Univ UtrechtNeth, vis prof, 1974; Wayne State Ctr Black Studies, fac res assoc; DamonJ Keith Law Collection & Archive, founder. **Orgs:** Charles Evans Hughes Fel Columbia Univ Law Sch, 1973-74; chmn, Bd Police Comners Detroit, 1977-78; Mich Bar Asn; NBA; ABA; Wolverine Bar Asn; Alpha Phi Alpha; ed bd, Urban Educr & Compleat Lawyer; hearing officer, Mich Dept Civil Rights; consult, Police Civil Liability & Citizen Complaints; reporter, Am Bar Assoc; Mich Comt Juv Justice, 1987-90; Task force Minorities Legal Prof; Mich Correctional Officers, training coun, 1990-93; trustee, Kurdish Mus & Libr NY, 1990-96; chmn, City Detroit Bd Ethics, 1994-97; Arts Comn, City Detroit, 2000-01. **Home Addr:** 7122 St Andrews Lane, Sarasota, FL 34243. **Business Addr:** Professor Emeritus of Law, Wayne State University, 471 W Palmer St, Detroit, MI 48202, **Business Phone:** (941)355-7844.

## LITTLEJOHN, JOSEPH PHILLIP

School administrator. **Personal:** Born Aug 31, 1937, Hackensack, NJ; children: Mavis & Marc. **Educ:** Rutgers Univ, BS, sociol, 1960;

NY Univ, MPA, 1972; Lancaster Ctr Mediation, Lancaster, PA, cert. **Career:** School administrator (retired); Steward AFB, NY, equal employ off, officer & fed women prog coord, 1968-70; Nat Asn Advan Colored People, New York, asst dir housing prog, 1970; Inter-relig Found Comm Organ Amilcar Cabral Inst, asst dir admins, 1972-73; Nat Coun Churches, coord, 1973; New York City Human Resources Admin, prog mgr, 1973-75; Jersey City State Col, dir affirmative action, 1975-78; Fairleigh Dickinson Univ, dir affirmative action, 1978-87; NJ Dept Trasp, Trenton, dir civil rights compliance, 1987-88; Shawnee Develop Corp, Pa, sales, owner rep, 1988-92; Pa Legal Servs, Harrisburg, dir, human resources & cult div, 1992-96; Hudson Valley Community Col, Troy, NY, asst pres affirmative action & human resources develop, 2005. **Orgs:** Bd dir, Orange County United Fund, 1968-71; bd dir, Jersey City Br Nat Asn Advan Colored People, 1977-83; bd dir, Hudson Co Opportunities Indust Ctr, 1978-82; regional dir, vpres, Am Asn Affirmative Action, 1984-; consult, Nat Urban League, NY; consult, Newburgh Community Action Agency; consult, United Church Christ, NY; consult, Nat Asn advan Colored People, NY; consult, Seton Hall Univ, Orange, NJ; consult, AT & T Bell Lab, Whippany, NJ; consult, Southern Col Technol, Marietta, GA; consult, Ron Jackson Assoc, Harrisburg, PA; One Hundred Black Men Albany; adv comt, Greater Harrisburg United Negro Col Fund; Unity Coalition Poconos. **Home Addr:** 66 Madison Ave, Jersey City, NJ 07304.

### LITTLEPAGE, CRAIG

Administrator, basketball coach. **Personal:** Born Aug 5, 1951, La Mott, PA; son of Quentin W and Erma S; married Margaret Murray; children: Erica, Murray & Erin. **Educ:** Univ Pa, Wharton Bus Sch, BA, econs, 1973. **Career:** Villanova Univ, asst coach, 1973-75; Yale Univ, asst coach, 1975-76; Univ Va, asst basketball coach, 1976-82, 1988-90, asst athletic dir, 1990-91, assoc athletic dir progs, 1991-95, sr assoc dir athletics, 1995-2001, athletic dir, 2001-; Univ Pa, head basketball coach, 1982-85; Rutgers Univ, head basketball coach, 1985-88. **Orgs:** Univ Va Athletics Admin, 1990-; NCAA Div I Infractions Comn; Re instatement Sub comt, 1999-2000; head, NCAA Men's Div I Basketball Comm, 2002-07. **Business Addr:** Athletic Director, University of Virginia, McCue Ctr, Charlottesville, VA 22904-4835, **Business Phone:** (434)982-5106.

**LITTLES, EUGENE SCAPES. See LITTLES, GENE.**

### LITTLES, GENE (EUGENE SCAPES LITTLES)

Basketball coach, basketball player. **Personal:** Born Jun 29, 1943, Washington, DC; married Loredana; children: Darren, Travis & Gino. **Educ:** High Point Col, attended 1969. **Career:** Basketball player (retired), basketball coach; Am Basketball Asn, Carolina Cougars, point guard, 1969-74; Am Basketball Asn, Ky Colonels, point guard, 1974-75; Appalachian State, asst player, 1975-77; Cleveland Cavaliers, asst coach, 1976-77, 1985-86; NC Agr & Tech State Univ, head coach, 1977-79; Utah Jazz, asst coach, 1979-82; Chicago Bulls, asst coach, 1986-87; Charlotte Hornets, asst coach, 1988-90, head coach, 1990-91; Denver Nuggets, asst head coach, interim coach, 1994-95; coach, currently. **Orgs:** Bd trustee, High Point Univ. **Honors/Awds:** Champion, Am Basketball Asn, 1975. **Business Addr:** Assistant Coach, Denver Nuggets, 1000 Chopper Cir, Denver, CO 80204, **Business Phone:** (303)405-1100.

### LITTLES, DR. JAMES FREDERICK, JR.

Physician. **Personal:** Born Nov 7, 1960, Florence, SC; son of James and Ella; married Barbara Moultrie; children: Jessica & Elena. **Educ:** SC State Univ, BS, 1982; Howard Univ Col Med, MD, 1986. **Career:** William Beaumont Hosps, internship, resident; Univ Mich, Med Sch, clin instr, 1990-; Veterans Affairs Med Ctr, chief, radiation oncol serv, 1991; Midland Bay Radiation Oncol Assocs, chief, radiation oncol dept, currently; Bay Regional Med Ctr, med dir, currently. **Orgs:** One Hundred Black Men Greater Detroit; Dipl Am Bd Radiol; Nat Asn Advan Colored People; S Carolina State Univ Alumni Asn; MI Soc Therapeut Radiol; Straight Gate Church, deacon. **Special Achievements:** The First African-American Faculty Member, Dept Radiation Oncol, Univ Mich, Med Sch; The First African-American Clinical Service Chief, Veterans Affairs Med Ctr, Ann Arbor, MI. **Home Addr:** 5391 Oakbrook Dr, Saginaw, MI 48603-6426, **Home Phone:** (989)799-6559. **Business Addr:** Medical Director, Radiation Oncologist, Bay Regional Medical Center, 3180 E Midland Rd, Bay City, MI 48706, **Business Phone:** (989)667-6670.

### LIVERPOOL, CHARLES ERIC

Financial manager, executive director. **Personal:** Born Mar 14, 1946, Ann's Grove Village; son of Ivy Thomas (deceased) and Eric C (deceased); married Joan Ann Paddy; children: Charles Jr, Dionne, Euisi & Jamal. **Educ:** Bronx Community Col, AA, 1978; Bernard M Baruch Col, BBA, 1982; Long Island Univ, attended 1988; Cent Mich Univ, MSA, 1995. **Career:** Navy Resale Serv Support Off, acct/liab ins asst, 1974-83, prog analyst, 1980-86; HQ 77th AUs Res Command, budget analyst, 1986-89; Fulton County Govt, Atlanta, GA, financial budget eval specialist, 1990-; Deskan Inst & Training Inc, asst dir, currently. **Orgs:** Educ vpres & secy, Navresso Toastmasters #2285, 1978-82; vice chmn & supv comn, 1980-85, mem bd dir, 1985-89, CGA Fed Credit Union Brooklyn, NY; literacy vol tutor, Queens Boro Pub Lib, 1984-89; new York Urban League, 1985-89; Nat Black MBA Asn, 1986-; prog comt mem/tutor support coordr, Literacy Vol Am, 1990-; Am Asn Budget & Prog Anal, 1994-; Med outreach Team; Voices Light-Black Poets Asn. **Special Achievements:** Author/Publisher: A Brother's Soul: Writings of a Country Boy-Poetry, 1992; Another Days Journey-Poetry, 1996. **Business Addr:** Associate Director, Deskan Institute & Training Inc, 424 Orchards Walk, Stone Mountain, GA 30087, **Business Phone:** (770)498-2152.

### LIVERPOOL, REV. HERMAN OSWALD

Clergy. **Personal:** Born Feb 12, 1925, Georgetown; son of Joseph Nathaniel and Hilda Beatrice Hinds; married Lucille Joycelyn Cleaver; children: Lorraine Janet, James Nathaniel & Lynda Alethea. **Educ:** Univ London, Avery Hill Col, teacher's cert, educ, 1971; Univ W Indies, BA, theol, 1977; Intl Sem, ThM, 1985, DMin, 1990. **Career:** Clergy (retired); The Inner London Educ Authority, teacher, 1971-73; The Bishop, Anglican Diocese Guyana, clergyman, 1977-80; The Bishop, The Episcopal Diocese FLA, vicar, 1983; St Cyprian's & St Mary's Episcopal Church, vicar, 1983-96. **Orgs:** Vestry mem, St Hilda's Anglican Church, Brockley Rise, England, 1971; exec mem, COT Rels Coun, London, England, 1971-73; founder, Holy Redeemer Boy Scouts, Guyana, 1977-80; initiator, East Coast Musical Church Festival, Diocese Guyana, 1980; founder, St Cyprian's Annual Church Festival, 1984-; founder, Friends St Cyprian's, 1984; St Augustine Ministerial Alliance, 1983, pres, 1987-88; bd mem, Vicar's Landing, Life Pastoral Care Servs, 1988-91; Brotherhood St Andrews, 2000. **Honors/Awds:** Awarded symbolic gavel, St Augustine Ministerial Alliance, 1986; Plaque & letter appreciation, Vicar's Landing, 1991. **Special Achievements:** A Brief History of the Anglican Church in Guyana, unpublished, 1826-70; Collection Poems, unpublished; Contributed to "Theatre of the Mind", Noble House Publishers-Poetry Division, 2003. **Home Addr:** 3988 Inverrary Dr, Lauderhill, FL 33319-4514, **Home Phone:** (954)485-9686.

### LIVINGSTON, RANDY ANTHONY

Basketball player, basketball coach. **Personal:** Born Apr 2, 1975, New Orleans, LA; married Tameka. **Educ:** La State Univ. **Career:** Basketball player (retired), basketball coach; Houston Rockets, guard & pt guard, 1996-97; Atlanta Hawks, free agt & pt guard, 1997-98; Sioux Falls Skyforce, 1998, 2004-05; Phoenix Suns, pt guard, 1998-2000; Golden StateWarriors, pt guard, 2001; Idaho Stampede, 2000-01, 2003-04, 2006-07, head coach, 2010-12; Gary Steelheads, pt guard, 2001; Seattle Supersonics, pt guard, 2002, 2007; New Orleans Hornets, 2003; Los Angeles Clippers, pt guard, 2004; Utah Jazz, pt guard, 2005-06; Turkish League, Galatasaray, pt guard, 2005-06; Chicago Bulls, pt guard, 2006; Maine Red Claws, asst coach, 2008-09; LivOn, chief scout & pres, 2012-; La State Univ, asst, 2016-. **Honors/Awds:** Naismith Prep Player of the Year, 1993; Champion, Continental Basketball Asn, 2005; NBA Development League Most Valuable Player, 2007. **Business Addr:** Chief Scout, President, LivOn, 6221 S Claiborne Ave, New Orleans, IA 70125, **Business Phone:** (504)343-5075.

### LIVINGSTON-WHITE, DR. DEBORAH J. H. (DEBI STARR-WHITE)

Educator, fashion model, consultant. **Personal:** Born Nov 21, 1947, DuQuoin, IL; daughter of Jetson Edgar and Tressie May Gaston; married William Tyrone; children: William Gaston White IV. **Educ:** Southern Ill Univ, BS, educ, 1968, MS, educ, 1971; Northern Ill Univ, EdD, admin, 1975; Mich State Univ, post doctoral studies, 1982; Univ Mich, post doctoral studies, 1984. **Career:** Dansville Ag Schs, teacher & consult, 1976-78; Mgt Recruiters, acct exec, 1976-78; Mich Dept Educ, spec educ consult, 1978-; Mich State Univ, asst prof; Yale Univ, guest lectr, 1984-2001; Affiliated Models & Talent Agency, Full-Figure, model & actress, 1987-; Talent Shop, Oak Park Sch Dist, dir spec educ, 1987-96; E Detroit Pub Schs, dir spec educ, 1996-2000; Int Consults, People's Network's "Success Channel", pub rels, personal develop & mkt consult, motivational keynote speaker, travel agent; Inkster-Edison Pub Schs, asst supt, chief acad officer, 2000-01; Int Consults Am LLC, pres, 1998-; PAX-Prog Acad Exchange, community coordr, 2008-; AMI kids, ese staffing specialist & consult, 2009-. **Orgs:** Consult & evaluator, US Dept Educ, 1979-; adv comm mem, Black Notes MSU Media Prod, 1980-83; Mich EPFP Alumni, 1980-84; pres & exec dir, Int Consult, 1981-; voc chairperson, Altrusa Int, 1982-83; regional coordr, Vols Spec Educ, 1982-; trainer, Proj Outreach MDE, 1984; founder & pres, Tressie Found; Mich Asn Artists & Songwriters, 1989-; Int Photographers Asn, 1990-; Nat Asn Black Journalists, 1990-; secy, vpres, Self-Esteem Inst, 1990-, Musicians', Entertainers', Composers' Creative ASN, 1992-; Ment Health Educ Exhibit Treas; pers, Alternative Living Positive Handicapped Adults, 1992-; Habitat Humanity fund raising comm, Detroit; chair, Archer, McNamara, Pub & Media Rels, 1995. **Business Addr:** Community Co-Ordinator, PAX - Program of Academic Exchange, 14 Willett Ave, Port Chester, NY 10573, **Business Phone:** (914)690-1340.

### LIVINGSTON-WILSON, KAREN E.

Insurance executive, lawyer, association executive. **Personal:** married Mark. **Educ:** Univ Mich, BA, polit sci, 1979; Wayne State Univ, JD, 1983. **Career:** Citizens Ins Co Am, gen coun, vpres & secy, 1996-98; Butler Snow O'Mara Stevens & Cannada PLLC, atty, currently. **Orgs:** Am Bar Asn; Am Health Lawyers Asn; Nat Bar Asn; Nat Asn Women Lawyers; Women Lawyers Asn; Mich Bar Asn; Ohio Bar Asn; Miss Bar; Magnolia Bar Asn; Hinds County Bar Asn; mem bd dirs & exec comt, YMCA Metrop Jackson; bd trustee, Miss Mus Art; bd dir, Bethany Christian Serv. **Special Achievements:** First woman & First African American to hold the posts of vice president, general counsel and secretary of Citizens Insurance Company of America in Howell, MI; One of 50 Leading Business Women, Mississippi Business Journal, 2007. **Home Addr:** PO Box 1831, Madison, MS 39130, **Home Phone:** (601)898-9933. **Business Addr:** Attorney, Butler Snow O'Mara Stevens & Canada PLLC, AmSouth Plz 17th Fl 210 E Capitol St Suite 1700, Jackson, MS 39225-2567, **Business Phone:** (601)985-4593.

### LL COOL J (JAMES TODD SMITH)

Rap musician, actor. **Personal:** Born Jan 14, 1968, Bay Shore, NY; married Simone; children: Najee, Italia, Samaria & Nina. **Career:** Discography: Radio, 1985; Bigger and Deffer, 1987; Walking with a Panther, 1989; Mama Said Knock You Out, 1990; 14 Shots to the Dome, 1993; Mr. Smith, 1995; Phenomenon, 1997; G.O.A.T, 2000; 10, 2002; The DEFinition, 2004; Todd Smith, 2006; Exit 13, 2008. Films: Krush Groove, 1985; Wildcats, 1986, The Hard Way, 1991; Toys, 1992; Out-of-Sync, 1995; B*A*P*S, 1997; Caught Up, 1998; Woo, 1998; Halloween H20: 20 Years Later, 1998; Deep Blue Sea, 1999; In Too Deep, 1999; Any Given Sunday, 1999; Charlie's Angels, 2000; Kingdom Come, 2001; Rollerball, 2002; Deliver Us from Eva, 2003; S.W.A.T., 2003; Mindhunters, 2004; Edison, 2005; Slow Burn, 2005; Last Holiday, 2006; The Deal, 2008; Grudge Match, 2013. TV series: "In The House", 1995-99; "All That", "Oz", 1998; "House", 2005; "The Man", 2007; "30 Rock", 2007; "WWII in HD[18]", 2009; "NCIS", 2009; "NCIS: Los Angeles", 2009-14; "Sesame Street", 2011; "2013 Do Something Awards", 2013; "CBS Cares", 2014. **Honors/Awds:** MTV Video Music Award for Best Rap Video, 1991; Grammy Award for Best Rap Solo performance, 1992; Mama Said Knock You Out, 1992; Hey Lover, 1997; Best Rap Artist, 1996, 1997; MTV Video Music Vanguard Award, 1997; Blockbuster Entertainment Award, 2000; NAACP Image Award, Nat Asn Advan Colored People, 2001, 2003 & 2011-14; Billboard Award; Source Foundation Image Award, 2003; ShoWest Award, 2003; 10 Soul Train Awards; 15 New York Music Awards; BET Comedy Award, 2004; Teen Choice Award, 2013. **Special Achievements:** Author of I Make My Own Rules, 1997; Was named the 10th greatest hip hop MC of all time by MTV. **Business Addr:** Rap Artist, c/o Def Jam Records, 160 Varick St 12th Fl, New York, NY 10013, **Business Phone:** (212)229-5200.

### LLEWELLYN-TRAVIS, CHANDRA

Association executive, executive director, educator. **Personal:** Born Jun 11, 1960, New York, NY; daughter of Gilbert Metcalfe Llewellyn Sr and Jenny Cody; married Jack; children: Sojourner Joy. **Educ:** City Univ NY-Lehman Col, BA, 1986; Norwich Univ-Vermont Col, MA, 1992; City Univ NYk-Grad Ctr, PhD cand. **Career:** New York Dept Health, health resource coord, 1984-86; Canaan Baptish Church, proj dir, living consortium, 1986-89; Colonial Pk Community Servs, family counr, 1986-89; Malcolm King Col, adj prof, 1989; New York Urban League, assoc & dir educ, 1989-91; Nat Urban League, dir youth serv, 1991-95; Intercultural Outreach Korea Soc, exec dir, 1994-97; Col New Rochelle, adj, 1997; Child Care Inc, credential trainer, currently. **Orgs:** Com chair, New York Bd Educ Multicultural Task Force, 1989-91; downstate adv mem, NY State Bd Regents, 1989-91; Educ Priorities Panel, 1989-91; Tri-State Parent Adv Coun, 1992-94; bd mem, White Wave Rising, 1995-; comt mem, Intercultural Alliance, 1995-; Meml Baptist Church-AIDS Ministry, prcom chair, 1996-; Walks Life, prof vol, 1996-; bd mem, NY Med Col, Westchester County Med Ctr. **Honors/Awds:** Awardee, Outstanding Young Women Am, 1987; Community Serv Award, Countee Cullen Sch Parent Asn, 1988; NY Bd Educ, Partner in Educ, 1990; Miss Black Am, Judge, 1994; Mentorship Recognition, Walks of Life, 1998. **Special Achievements:** The AFA Male: A Second Emancipation, co-editor, 1992; "AFA Male Immersion School: Segregation? Separation? or Innovation", proj dir, 1992;"Rap: Good? Bad? or Both?",exec producer, 1994. **Home Addr:** 100 St Nicholas Ave Suite 4D, New York, NY 10026. **Business Addr:** Credential Trainer, Child Care Inc, 322 8th Ave 4th Fl, New York, NY 10001.

### LLOYD, DR. BARBARA ANN

Educator. **Personal:** Born Sep 21, 1943, Fairfield, AL; daughter of Arthur Lee (deceased) and Alberta Salley (deceased). **Educ:** Tuskegee Inst AL, BS, nursing, 1965; Univ Ala, Birmingham AL, MS, community health nursing, 1975, Tuscaloosa, AL, EdD, admin higher educ, 1986. **Career:** Educator, president (retired); Univ Ala Hosp, Birmingham, AL, staff nurse, 1965; Veterans Admin Hosp, Birmingham, AL, staff nurse, 1966-68; Tuskegee Inst, Tuskegee, AL, instr, 1968-70; Jefferson St Jr Col, Birmingham, AL, instr, 1970-72, Lawson State Jr Col, instr, 1972-74; Univ Ala, Birmingham, AL, instr/asst prof/assoc prof, 1975-95, Western Ment Health Ctr, Birmingham, AL, 1984-88; Fairfield City Sch, Fairfield Bd Educ, pres bd, 2004-. **Orgs:** Pres, Tuskegee Univ; Nat Nursing Alumni Asn; Kappa Delta Pi Hon Soc Educ, 1982; Sigma Theta Tau Int; Hon Soc Nursing; Chi Eta Phi Sorority Inc; Order Eastern Stars, 1983-; bd educ, Fairfield City Sch Syst, AL, 1992-97; life mem, Chi Eta Phi Sorority Inc. **Home Addr:** 204 Westmoreland Cir, Fairfield, AL 35064, **Home Phone:** (205)923-3848.

### LLOYD, GREGORY LENARD, SR.

Football player. **Personal:** Born May 26, 1965, Miami, FL; married Rhonda; children: Greg Jr, Gregory Lenard II, Tiana Cassandra & Jhames Isaac. **Educ:** Fort Valley State Univ, grad. **Career:** Football player (retired); Pittsburgh Steelers, linebacker & right outside linebacker, 1988-97; Carolina Panthers, right outside linebacker, 1998; Tae Kwon Do, teacher, currently. **Orgs:** Kappa Alpha Psi Fraternity Inc. **Honors/Awds:** Pittsburgh Steelers, Ed Block Courage Award, 1988; Five Times Pro Bowler, 1991-95; Man of the Year Award, Pittsburgh YMCA, 1994; Defensive Player of the Year, UPI, 1994; Defensive Player of the Year, Kans City 101 Club, 1994; SIAC Player of the Year.

### LLOYD, REV. DR. J. ANTHONY

Clergy, college teacher. **Personal:** Born Aug 22, 1955, Philadelphia, PA; son of James (deceased) and Ruth. **Educ:** Houghton Col, BS, ministry, 1979; Gordon Conwill Theol Sem, Hamilton, MA, MDiv, 1982; United Theol Sem, DMin, 1996. **Career:** Camp Ladorol, staff prog coordr, 1980; Gordon Conwill Theol Sem, assoc dean students, 1982-2002, adj prof, 1990-; 12th Baptist Church, ministerial staff, 1985-92; Hillar Sch, consult, 1989-90; Greater Framingham Community Church, pastor, 1992-. **Orgs:** Benjamin E Mays fel Benjamin E Mays Found, 1980-82; Alumni chap pres, 1986-89, trustee, 1993-, Houghton Col; bd trustee, Bittnaz Hill Sch, 1995-98; bd dir, United Way, 1996-; MA NH RI chair comn ministry, United Baptist Conv, 1996-; conf comt, Vision NE, 1997; life time mem, Nat Asn Advan Colored People, 1997; mgr search comt, Framingham Town, 1998-99; Urban Ministerial Educ. **Honors/Awds:** Martin Luther King Award Award, Gordon Conwill Theol, 1982; License to Preach, 12th Baptist Church, 1992; Community Award, PFI, ALPA, PSY, 1996. **Special Achievements:** Gordon Conwill, certified supervisor of ministry, 1979; Evangelical Teaching Training Research, teaching diploma, 1979; Govt of Zaire, fact finding teacher, 1989; Seminar on Evangelism, CO, instructor of Evangelism, 1981; St Thomas, Virgin Islands, missionary, 1981. **Home Addr:** 40 Rr Ave, Beverly, MA 01915, **Home Phone:** (978)927-3472. **Business Addr:** Pastor, Greater Framingham Community Church, 44 Franklin St, Framingham, MA 01702, **Business Phone:** (508)626-2118.

### LLOYD, HON. LEONIA JANNETTA

Lawyer, judge. **Personal:** Born Aug 6, 1949, Detroit, MI; daughter of Leon and Naomi. **Educ:** Wayne State Univ, BS, educ, 1971, JD, 1979. **Career:** Lloyd & Lloyd, sr law partner; Double L Mgt, partner; Mich State 36th Dist Ct, 1992-2002; Mich State 36th Dist Ct, drug ct judge, 2002-. **Orgs:** Nat Conf Black Lawyers, 1975-79; Friends Afro-Am Mus, 1983-; Am Bar Asn; Wolverine Bar Asn; Mary McLeod Bethune Asn; Nat Asn Negro Bus & Prof Women; Asn Black Judges Mich; Nat Judicial Coun; 36th Dist Ct's Handgun Intervention Prog. **Home Addr:** 531 S Pk, Detroit, MI 48215. **Business Addr:** Judge, State of

Michigan District Court 36th District, 421 Madison Ave Suite 3066, Detroit, MI 48226-2358, **Business Phone:** (313)965-8741.

### LLOYD, LEWIS KEVIN
Basketball player. **Personal:** Born Feb 22, 1959, Philadelphia, PA; son of Lewis and Joanne; married Cassandra. **Educ:** NMex Mil Inst, attended 1979; Drake Univ, attended 1981. **Career:** Basketball player (retired); Golden State Warriors, guard, 1981-83; Houston Rockets, 1983-87, 1989-90; Philadelphia Aces, 1988, 1990; Cedar Rapids Silver Bullets, 1988-89; Philadelphia 76ers, 1990.

### LLOYD, MARCEA BLAND
Lawyer. **Personal:** Born Oct 12, 1948, Chicago, IL; daughter of Ralph and Beatriz; children: Randy Jr, Shomari & Malaika. **Educ:** Knox Col, BS & BA, 1968; Northwestern Univ, JD, 1971. **Career:** Pillsbury Co, atty, 1972-74; Montgomery Wards Co, sr antitrust coun, 1974-77; Pillsbury Co, coun; Univ Minn Bus Law, asst atty, 1977-78; Medtronic Inc, int coun, 1978-83, sr legal coun, 1983-91, asst gen coun, 1991-99, vpres, 1993-99; VHA Inc, gen coun & secy, 1999-2004, group vpres, chief admin officer, gen coun, 2004-07; Amylin Pharmaceut Inc, sr vpres govt & corp affairs, chief admin officer & gen coun, 2007-12; Medtronics Inc, asst gen coun; Health Partners Inc, vice chair. **Orgs:** Jack & Jill Am Inc; Links Inc; dir, NBA, 1971-; Turning Pt Inc Found; dir, chairperson, Exec Leadership Found; assoc, Women Bus Leaders, US Health Care Indust Found; bd dir, Calif Healthcare Inst; bd advisor, Bente Hansen & Assocs, currently. **Honors/Awds:** Pinnacle Award, Athena San Diego, 2012. **Home Addr:** 14319 Hughes Lane, Dallas, TX 75240-8501, **Home Phone:** (972)991-2508. **Business Addr:** Board of Advisor, Bente Hansen & Associates, 12707 High Bluff Dr Suite 200, San Diego, CA 92130, **Business Phone:** (858)350-4330.

### LLOYD, PHIL ANDREW
Automotive executive. **Personal:** Born Jun 24, 1952, Buffalo, NY; son of Otis and Mable Spivey; children: Phil A Jr. **Educ:** Erie Community, Buffalo, NY, AAS, 1972; Buffalo State, Buffalo, NY, BS, 1975. **Career:** Mfr Trader Trusts, Buffalo, NY, collector, 1975; Wicks Lumber, Orchard Pk, New York, sales mgr, 1976-80; Ed Mullinax Ford, Amherst, Ohio, salesman, 1981-86; Western Ford-Mercury, Clyde, Ohio, pres, 1987-. **Orgs:** Phi Beta-Lamba, 1971-73; Environ Pollution Control, 1972-73; pres, Twin City Kiwanis, 1980-81; Clyde Bus Asn, 1987-; trustee, Clyde Kiwanis, 1988-89. **Home Addr:** 118 Liberty St, Clyde, OH 43410, **Home Phone:** (419)547-0567. **Business Addr:** President, Western Ford-Mercury Inc, 1036 W Mcpherson Hwy, Clyde, OH 43410.

### LLOYD, DR. RAYMOND ANTHONY
Physician, educator, association executive. **Personal:** Born Nov 25, 1941; married Eveline Moore; children: Raymond II, Rhea & Ryan. **Educ:** Jamaica Col, attended 1958; Howard Univ, BS, 1962, Col Med, MD, 1966. **Career:** Vet Affairs Med Ctr, fel, 1968-71; Freedmen's Hosp, resident, 1967-68; Va Hosp, C's Hosp & Nat Inst Health, fel, 1971; Howard Univ Col Med, asst prof med, 1971-; Comm Group Health Found, consult, 1971-76; Narcotics Treat Admin, assoc admin treat, 1972-73; Div Prev, Nat Inst Alcoholism & Alcohol Abuse, initial rev comn, 1972; pvt pract, physician, currently. **Orgs:** DC Med Soc; Caribbean Am Intercultural Org; Nat Asn Intern & Residents; AMA; Nat Capital Med Found Inc; Am Heart Asn; Am Fedn Clin Res; Am Prof Pract Asn; fel Int Col Angiol; Wash Heart Asn; sub-comt, Cardiopulmonary Resuscitation; Nat Capital Med Found; sub-comt, Cardiovasc Dis; pres, L&L Health Care Asn; adv bd, Hemisphere Nat Bank; Bata Kappa Chi, 1962; Phi Beta Kappa, 1962; Cent Tex Med Found. **Honors/Awds:** BKX Award in Chemistry, 1961; Honors in Chemistry, 1962; Honors in Pediatrics, 1966; Daniel Hale & Williams Award. **Home Addr:** 9415 Turnbery Dr, Potomac, MD 20854-5446, **Home Phone:** (301)767-0963. **Business Addr:** Physician, Private Practice, 1160 Varnum St NE Suite 117, Washington, DC 20017-2107, **Business Phone:** (202)529-0771.

### LLOYD, WANDA
Educator, executive director, editor. **Personal:** Born Jul 12, 1949, Columbus, OH; married Willie Burk; children: Shelby Renee. **Educ:** Spelman Col, BA, eng, 1971. **Career:** Providence Eve Bull, copy ed, 1971-73; Columbia Univ, instr, 1972; Miami Herald, copy ed, 1973-74; Atlanta Jour, copy ed, 1974-75; Wash Post, copy ed, 1975-76; Univ Md, instr, 1978; Los Angeles Times-WA Post News Serv, dep ed; USA Today, dep managing ed, cover stories, managing ed, Admin, sr ed & admin, sr ed days & admin, 1986-96; Northwestern Univ's Kellogg Grad Sch Bus Mgt, fel, 1987; Greenville News, managing ed, 1996-2000; Vanderbilt Univ, Freedom Forum Diversity Inst, founding exec dir, 2001-04; Montgomery Advertiser, exec ed, 2004-13; Savannah State Univ, Dept Mass Commun, chair & assoc prof, 2013-; Editor: The Edge of Change: Women in the 21st Century Press, 2009. **Orgs:** Nat Asn Black Journalists, 1980-2015; Am Soc News Ed, 1989-2009; life mem, Delta Sigma Theta Sorority; bd trustee, Spelman Col, 1989-2008; bd mem, Ala Press Asn; bd mem, Ala Assoc Press Media Ed; Links Inc; life mem, Nat Alumnae Asn Spelman Col; MLK Observance Day Asn; founder, chair, Nat Asn Minority Media Execs; Dow Jones Newspaper Fund; Leadership Savannah, currently. **Home Addr:** 2615 Winchester Rd, Montgomery, AL 36106. **Business Addr:** Associate Professor, Chairperson, Savannah State University, 3219 College St, Savannah, GA 31404, **Business Phone:** (912)358-3376.

### LOC, TONE (ANTHONY TERRELL SMITH)
Actor, rap musician. **Personal:** Born Mar 3, 1966, Los Angeles, CA; son of James Smith and Margaret; married Anthony; children: Bijan, Anthony James, Tony, Sean, Stephen James & Tawny. **Career:** Albums: Loc-ed After Dark, 1989; Cool Hand Loc, 1991; Wild Thing & Other Hits, 2003. Singles: "Wild Thing", 1988; "Funky Cold Medina", 1989; "I Got It Goin' On", 1990; "We're All in the Same Gang", 1990; "All Through the Night", 1991. Films: The Adventures of Ford Fairlane, 1990; Fern Fully: The Last Rainforest, animated, 1992; Bebe's Kids, animated, 1992; Posse, 1993; Poetic Justice, 1993; Surf Ninjas, 1993; Car 54, Where Are You?, 1994; Ace Ventura Pet Detective, 1994; Blank Check, 1994; Heat, 1995; Spy Hard, 1996; Fakin' Da Funk, 1997; Freedom Strike, 1998; Titan AE, animated, 2000; Whispers: An Elephant's Tale, 2000; Deadly Rhapsody, 2001; They Crawl, 2001; Storm Watch, 2002; White T, 2011. TV Series: "C-Bear & Jamal", 1996-97, producer & composer; "Thieves", 2001; "Static Shock", 2002; "The District", 2002; "Storm Watch", 2002; "The Night B4 Christmas", 2003; "The WB's Superstar USA", 2004; "Yes, Dear", 2005; "King of the Hill", 2005; "Totally Awesome", 2006; Dreamweaver", 2006; "Celebrity Rap Superstar", 2007; Chowder, 2008; "White T ", 2013; "Uncle Grandpa", 2014. **Business Addr:** Actor, William Morris Agency, 1 William Morris Pl, Beverly Hills, CA 90212, **Business Phone:** (310)859-4000.

### LOCKARD, PROF. JON ONYE. See Obituaries Section.

### LOCKE, DR. DON C.
Educator. **Personal:** Born Apr 30, 1943, Macon, MS; son of Willie and Carlene; married Marjorie P Myles; children: Tonya E & Regina C. **Educ:** Tenn A&I State Univ, BS, 1963, MEd, 1964; Ball State Univ, EdD, 1974. **Career:** S Side High Sch, social studies teacher, 1964-70; Wayne High Sch, sch counsr, 1971-73; Ball State Univ, Europ Prog, asst prof, 1974-75; NC State Univ, asst & assoc prof, 1975-87, prof & dept head 1987-93, alumni distinguished grad prof, 2003-05, distinguished prof counr educ emer, 2005-, doctoral prog, dir; Univ NC, Asheville Grad Ctr, prof counr educ, 1993-2005, dir diversity & multicult affairs, 2005-07. **Orgs:** Alpha Phi Alpha Fraternity Inc; New Bern Ave Day Care Ctr Bd, 1978-86; summer fel Ctr Advan Study, Behav Sci, 1979, 1992; pres, NC Coun Asn, 1980-81, parliamentarian, 1989-91, 1992-95; Ed bd, ACES J, 1981-93, assoc ed, J Ment Health Coun, 1993-96; chmn, S Region Br ACA, 1983-84, parliamentarian, 1989-90; chmn, NC Bd Regist Practicing Counsrs, 1984-87; Gov Coun, Am Coun Asn, 1985-87 & 1991-92, parliamentarian, 1990-91; sec, Asn Counsr Educ & Supv, 1985-86; pres, Southern Asn counsr Educ & Supv, 1988-89; pres, Southern Asn Counr Educ & Supv, 1988-89; chair, Strategic Planning Comt, 1992-94; trustee, Coun & Develop Found, 1993-96; chair, Ed Bd, Asheville Citizen-Times, 1994-96, 1998-2000; parliamentarian, Am Sch Counr Asn, 1994-95; bd dir, Asheville Buncombe United Way, 1997-; pres, Chi Sigma Iota Int Hon Soc, 1999-2000; pres, Asn Counsr Edu & Supv, 2000-01; Phi Delta Kappa; life mem, Am Coun Asn; Am Ment Health Counors Asn; Asn Multicultural Coun & Develop; chair, Coun & Human Develop Found. **Home Addr:** 23 Scenic View Dr, Weaverville, NC 28787. **Business Addr:** Distinguished Professor Emeritus of Counselor Education, North Carolina State University, Raleigh, NC 27695.

### LOCKE, HENRY DANIEL, JR.
Government official, journalist. **Personal:** Born Nov 16, 1936, Greenville, SC; son of Henry Sr and Josephine; married Audrey Marie Harris; children: Daniel Leroy, Tara Yvonne & Henry III. **Educ:** Univ Md, attended 1958; Univ Buffalo, NY, attended 1961; Am Press Inst, Reston, VA, attended 1979. **Career:** MI Ave YMCA Buffalo, weekend exec, 1959-63; Buffalo Courier-Express, dist mgr, 1960-72; Buffalo, youth counr, 1964-78; Black Enterprise Mag NYC, contrib, 1979-; Buffalo Courier-Express, columnist & reporter, 1972-82; Nat Leader Phila, columnist & reporter, 1982-83; Chicago Defender, nat reporter, 1983-89, managing ed, 1988-92; Mayor's Off, City Chicago, Dept Human Serv, dir pub affairs, freedom info officer, 1992-2000; Chicago Dept Human Serv, Comm Rels Div, coordr Spec Proj; Chicago Dept Family & Support Serv, spec proj coordr; United Negro Col Fund; DFSS, coordr, photogr DFSS, Dir Veterans Affairs City Chicago, currently. **Orgs:** Comm Asn Black Journalists; bd dir, Mich Ave YMCA, 1960-64; bd trustees, Lloyd's Memorial United Church Christ, 1962-63; state pr dir, Nat Asn Advan Colored People Conf Br, 1976-77; Alpha Phi Alpha Frat, Nat Asn Advan Colored People, Buffalo Urban League, Oper PUSH; Black Commun Asn; Black Social Workers/ No Region Black Polit Caucus; NY State Affirmative Action Com; BUILD; vice chmn, Local 26 Am Newspaper Guild, 1975-; CABJ; Headlines Club; Marycrest Homeowners Asn. **Honors/Awds:** Nominee Pulitzer Prize, 1977; 6 awards, page-one competition, newspaper articles; first place On the Spot Newspaper Reporting, AP Wire Serv, 1977; 61 Awards Outstanding Comm Serv various orgns; Pulitzer Prize nominee, 1978, 1986, 1987; Man of the Year Award, Chicago, IL, 1988. **Special Achievements:** As a journalist, covered (investigative) stories in five continents--Africa, Asia, Europe, North America, and South America. Also interviewed five sitting U.S. presidents and most national political and elected leaders across the U.S. **Home Addr:** 7953 S Dobson Condo 3, Chicago, IL 60619-4409, **Home Phone:** (773)846-3063. **Business Addr:** Coordinator of Special Projects, Director of Veterans Affairs, City of Chicago, Chicago Department of Family & Support Services, 1615 W Chicago Ave Suite 3 East 5th Fl, Chicago, IL 60622-5127, **Business Phone:** (312)743-0300.

### LOCKE, DR. HUBERT G.
Educator, school administrator. **Personal:** Born Apr 30, 1934, Detroit, MI; son of Hubert H and Willa; children: Gayle & Lauren. **Educ:** Wayne Univ, BA, 1955; Univ Chicago, BD, 1959; Univ Mich, MA, 1961. **Career:** Wayne State Univ, dir relig affairs, 1959-62, fel & asst prof urban ed, 1967-72; City Detroit, Citizens Comt Equal Opportunity, exec dir, 1962-65; Detroit Police Dept, admin asst to comnr, 1966-67; Univ Nebr, Omaha, fac, assoc prof urban studies & dean pub affairs, 1972-76; Univ Wash, Daniel J Evans Sch Pub Affairs, assoc dean arts & sci, fac, 1976-77, vice provost acad affairs, 1977-82, dean, 1982-87, prof pub affairs, 1982-88, John & Marguerite Corbally prof emer pub affairs, dean emer, 1988-, Marguerite Corbally prof pub serv emer, currently; Richard Stockton Col, NJ, vis prof, 2001; Pac Sch Relig, actg pres, 2003; Whitman Col, vis prof relig, 2004; Antioch Univ, Seattle, distinguished vis fel, 2005-06; Journal: Criminology and Police Science; Journal of Urban Law; Univ Wash, sociol dept & comparative relig & jewish studies, adj fac; Book: Learning From History: A Black Christian's Perspective on the Holocaust; The Care and Feeding of White Liberals; The Church Confronts the Fatherland, Exile in the Fatherland: The Prison Letters of Martin Niemoller. **Orgs:** Exec dir, Citizens Community Equal Opportunity, 1962-65; DDiv, Payne Theol Sem, 1968; bd dir, Police Found, 1970-71; dir, Wm O Douglas Inst, 1972-; exec vpres, Inst Study Contemp Soc Probs, 1972-; DHL, Univ Nebr, Omaha, 1982; bd mem, Bullitt Found, Seattle; Disciples Divinity House, Chicago; Disciples Sem Found, Claremont; Comt Educ & Church Rels; US Holocaust Mem Mus, Wash, DC; Nat Coun Crime & Delinq, Oakland; Seattle Police Found; Seattle Symphony Orchestra; Inst Int Educ, Chicago; Lakeside Sch, Seattle; chmn, Ethics Bd, King Co; co-chmn, Wash State Comn Ethics & Polit Accountability; chmn, Wash State Sentencing Guidelines Comn; Wash State Comn Judicial Conduct; DHL, Univ Akron; DHL, Univ Bridgeport; DHL, Richard Stockton Col; bd, Common Cause; bd, Group Health Found; bd, Univ Wash Edward Carlson Leadership & Pub Serv Off & Lakeside Sch; vice chair, US Holocaust Memorial Mus Educ Comt; vice chair, Church Rels Comt; bd mem, Inst Europ Studies; bd mem, Pac Sch Relig; co founder, Ann Scholars Conf Holocaust & Churches. **Home Addr:** 2801 1st Ave Suite 609, Seattle, WA 98121, **Home Phone:** (206)374-0863. **Business Addr:** Professor Emeritus of Public Affairs, Dean Emeritus, University of Washington, PO Box 353055, Seattle, WA 98195-3055, **Business Phone:** (206)543-4900.

### LOCKE, DR. MAMIE EVELYN
Politician, school administrator, government official. **Personal:** Born Mar 19, 1954, Brandon, MS; daughter of Ennis and Amanda McMahon. **Educ:** Tougaloo Col, Tougaloo, BA, hist & polit sci, 1976; Atlanta Univ, Atlanta, MA, advan polit sci studies, 1978, PhD, 1984; Am Univ, Cairo, prog mid eastern studies, 1986; Harvard Univ, cert, mgt develop; Emory Univ, Ga Dept Arch & Hist, cert, arch admin. **Career:** Dept Arch & Hist, Jackson, archivist, 1977-79; Atlanta Hist Soc, Atlanta, archivist, 1979-81; Hampton Univ, assoc prof, 1981-97, asst dean, 1991-96, dean, sch lib arts, 1996-, prof, polit sci, 1997-; Nat Endowment Humanities, NEH fel, 1985; City Hampton, coun mem, 1996-2004, vice mayor, 1998, mayor, 2000-04; Legis Va, 2nd Dist, state sen, 2004-. **Orgs:** Alpha Kappa Alpha Sorority Inc, 1973-; Nat Conf Black Polit Scientists, 1976-, exec coun, 1989-92, pres, 1993-94; Am Polit Sci Asn, 1981-97, 1990-; Alpha Kappa Alpha Sorority Inc; Southeastern Women's Studies Asn, 1987-; adv, Alpha Kappa Mu Nat Hon Soc, 1990-; ed bd, PS: Polit & Polit Sci, 1992-95; ed bd, Nat Polit Sci Rev, 1994-; Hampton Dem Comm, 1994-; pres, Nat Conf Black Polit Scientists, 1997; Hampton City Coun; comnr, Hampton Planning CMS; Hampton Redevelop & Housing Authority; VA Munic League, Gov Affairs Comn; Nat Black Caucus Local Elected Officials; hampton chap, Links Inc, 1997-; bd mem, Women Munic Gov, 1998-99; United Way Va Pa, 2000-02; Downtown Hampton Child Develop Ctr, 2001-; Towne Bank, 2003-; Transitions Family Violence Ctr, 2006-; Start Strong Coun, 2006-07; Nat Asn Advan Colored People; Roman Cath Church. **Home Addr:** 37 Wills Way, Hampton, VA 23666-5002, **Home Phone:** (757)846-1085. **Business Addr:** Dean, Professor of Political Science, Hampton University, 119 Armstrong Hall, Hampton, VA 23668, **Business Phone:** (757)727-5400.

### LOCKE-MATTOX, BERNADETTE
Basketball coach. **Personal:** Born Dec 31, 1958, Rockwood, TN; daughter of Alfred M Locke; married Vince; children: Vincent. **Educ:** Roane State Community Col, Harriman, TN, 1979; Univ Ga, Athens, GA, BS, 1982. **Career:** Univ Ga, Athens, Ga, acad adv, 1982-83; Xerox Corp, Atlanta, Ga, customerserv rep, 1984-85; Univ Ga, Athens, Ga, asst coach, 1985-90; Univ Ky, Lexington, Ky, asst coach, 1990-94, asst athletics dir, 1994-95, head women's basketball coach, 1995-2003; Conn Sun, asst coach, 2004-2014. **Home Addr:** 3244 Malone Dr, Lexington, KY 40513-1236, **Home Phone:** (859)296-9669. **Business Addr:** Assistant Coach, Connecticut Sun, 1 Mohegan Sun Blvd, Uncasville, CT 06382, **Business Phone:** (860)862-4000.

### LOCKETT, ALICE FAYE
Nutritionist. **Personal:** Born Sep 6, 1944, Linden, TX; daughter of Bernice Fisher and Eddie. **Educ:** Prairie View A&M Univ, BS, 1968; Univ Iowa, cert, 1972; Col State Univ, MS, 1974; Montreal Diet Dispensary, cert, 1975. **Career:** Denver Dept Health & Hosps, pub health nutritionist, 1969-73; L&L Healthcare Asn, community nutritionist, 1974-76; Community Col Denver, nutrit instr, 1973; Dept Human Serv, pub health nutritionist, 1976-81; DC Gen Hosp, Maternal & Child Nutrit, chief, 1981-94; US Dept Agr, Food & Nutrit Serv, nutritionist. **Orgs:** Am Dietetic Asn, 1969-; DC Metrop Dietetic Asn, 1974-; health adv bd, March Dimes, 1978-; Soc Nutrit Educ, 1990-. **Honors/Awds:** Outstanding Performance Award, 1983-94, Outstanding Woman of Division, 1984; Employee of the Month, 1985; Certificate of Merit, 1997-02; Outstanding performance Awards, Food & Nutrition Serv, 1999-02; SCY's Honor Award, 2002. **Special Achievements:** Presentation, "The Impact of Drug Abusers on Prenatal & the Unborn,"1991, author of Preliminary Results from a Study to Examine the Effects of Breast feeding on Neonatal Intensive Care Cost, 1991, Prenatal Nutrition for Substance Abusing Women: Reaching the Unreachable, 1991, Perspectives on Breastfeeding for the High Risk Neonate, 1992, Nutrition Offset Drugs, 1993, coordinated USDA's WIC Nat Breastfeeding Promotion Loving Support Campaign, represented USDA'S under secretary for Food and Nutrition Service (FNS) in "People to People Ambassador Program", Breastfeeding & Human Lactation delegation to Israel and Egypt; nominee, Outstanding Woman of Col, DC Gen Hosps, 1972. **Home Addr:** 4914B Barbour Dr, Alexandria, VA 22304-7706, **Home Phone:** (703)567-3430. **Business Addr:** Senior Nutritionist, United States Department of Agriculture, 3101 Pk Ctr Dr, Alexandria, VA 22302, **Business Phone:** (703)305-2478.

### LOCKETT, BRADFORD R.
Designer, tailor. **Personal:** Born Sep 26, 1945, Norfolk, VA; married Brendale Joyce; children: Belinda Joyce. **Educ:** Nat Sch Dress Design, 1966; Tex Southern Univ, BS, clothing & textiles, 1968; EW Kyles Sch Voc Tailoring, Houston, TX, master cert, tailoring. **Career:** JC Penney Co Tucson, AZ, head tailor, 1970-71; Brotherhood Asn Mil Airmen Tucson, vpres, 1971-72; Tucson, master mason, 1971-72; Res & Anal DMAFB Tucson, AZ, clothing counr USAF, 1970-72; Joe Frank Houston, asst fashion designer, 1973; JCPenny Bullock Wilshire, head tailor; Neiman Marcus Beverly Hills, head tailor; Mr Creations Inc & Battlesteins, fashion designer & master tailor; Lockett Oshins Collection, pres, currently; BradLockett Forum Tailoring, owner, currently. **Orgs:** Gulf Coast Fashion Asn; Small Bus Admin; Basilus Omega Psi Phi Frat, 1966-67; Master mason 11th Degree Pima Lodge No 10 Tucson. **Honors/Awds:** Italian Designer Emilio Pucci, 1966; Man of Year Award, Omega Psi Phi, 1967; Outstanding Clothing Design Award, Yardley Co, 1969; Spec Air Force Doc Film Fashion Entertainment Brad Lockett, 1972; Creative Garment Design award, 1991; Grammy Awards, 1991; American Designers & Tailors Guild Award, 1997 & 1999; Special Support Award, 1997 & 1999; Yardley Fashion Award. **Home Addr:** 1811 Pleasantville, Houston, TX 77029. **Business**

**Addr:** Owner, BradLockett Forum Tailoring, 3711 S Valley View Blvd Ste G, Las Vegas, NV 89103, **Business Phone:** (702)338-4210.

### LOCKETT, DR. JAMES D.
Educator. **Personal:** son of Elvie Thomas and J D. **Educ:** Morehouse Col, BA, polit sci; Atlanta Univ, MS, lib serv, PhD, hist, humanities; Case Western Res Univ, MA, int rels, polit sci; Vanderbilt Univ, Nashville, state & local govt. **Career:** Allen Univ, nat teaching fel, 1966-67; Tenn State Univ, asst prof, polit sci & hist, 1967-69; Tuskegee Inst, asst prof, 1969-70; St Augustine Col, actg chmn, Dept Hist, polit sci, black studies, social sci, 1970-72; Miss Valley State Univ, asst prof TCCP, 1972-74; Opportunities Industrialization Ctr, staff; Stillman Col, assoc prof, hist, polit sci & geog, 1977-91, prof, 1991-. **Orgs:** Pres, W AL Chap, Asn Study Afro-Am Life & Hist, 1983; app mem, Econ Adv Coun, Ala Conf Black Mayors Inc, 1984; chmn bd, Ala Afro-Am Black Hall Fame, 1985; app mem, Econ Devt Comn, Ala Conf Black Mayors Inc, 1985; appmem, adv bd, Ala Hist Comn, 1985; NEA; Am Libr Asn; Asn Higher Educ; AmHisl Asn; Southern Hist Asn; Orgn Am Historians; Asn Study Afro-Am Life &Hist; Birmingham Astron Soc; adv bd, Ala Hist Comn; assoc comnr, AlaElection Comn; Exec Comn, W Ala Oral Hist Asn; campus coordr Kettering Pub Leadership; coordr, SREB; ed adv bd, Col Press, 1993-94; fnd bd, Murphy African Am Mus; campus coordr, Exxon Kettering Pub Leadership; adv comn, Govs Salute Great Black Alabamians. **Special Achievements:** First chairman of the board of the Alabama Afro-American Hall of Fame. **Home Addr:** 2745 Suite 11 Elm St, Tuscaloosa, AL 35401. **Business Addr:** Professor, Stillman College, 3601 Stillman Blvd, Tuscaloosa, AL 35401, **Business Phone:** (205)349-4240.

### LOCKETT, KEVIN EUGENE
Football player. **Personal:** Born Sep 8, 1974, Tulsa, OK; married Cheryl; children: Tyler, Sterling, Jacob & Jordan. **Educ:** Kans State Univ, BA, acct & finance, 1997. **Career:** Football player (retired); Kans City Chiefs, 1997, 2000, wide receiver, 1998, split end, 1999; Wash Redskins, wide receiver, 2001-02; Jacksonville Jaguars, wide receiver, 2002; New York Jets, 2003; Kauffman Found, consult-entrepreneur residence, 2004-05, mgr res & policy & minority entrepreneurship, 2005-10, chief operating officer, 2010-13; Kans Bioscience Authority, pres & chief exec officer, 2013-; Kauffman Fellows, 2016-. **Orgs:** Exec Comt Bd Trustees, Kans State Univ. **Honors/Awds:** Academic All-American, 1995, 1996; Rookie of the Year, 1997. **Business Addr:** President & Chief Executive Officer, Kansas Bioscience Authority, 10900 S Clay Blair Blvd, Olathe, KS 66061, **Business Phone:** (913)397-8300.

### LOCKETT, SANDRA BOKAMBA
Librarian. **Personal:** Born Nov 18, 1946, Hutchinson, KS; daughter of Herbert Wales Johnson and Dorothy Bernice Harrison; married Eyamba G Bokamba; children: Eyenga M Bokamba; married James C; children: Madeline B. **Educ:** Univ Kans, Lawrence, BS, educ, 1968; Ind Univ, Bloomington, Ind, MLS, 1973. **Career:** Hutchinson Community Jr Col, Hutchinson, Kans, assoc arts, 1966; Gary Pub Libr, Gary, Ind, Alcott Br, librn, 1973-76, asst dir pub rels & programming, 1976-78, head exten serv, Gary, 1978-79; Univ Iowa Law Libr, Iowa City, IA, head gov docs dept, 1979-84; Milwaukee Pub Libr Syst, Milwaukee, Ctr St Libr, Wis, br mgr, 1984-88, exten serv coordr, 1988-91, asst city librn & Mgr Neighborhood & Exten Serv, 1991-95, dep city librn, 2006-; MPLs 12 neighborhood libr, mgr. **Orgs:** Alpha Kappa Alpha Sorority, 1967-; Am Libr Asn, 1974-79 & 1988-; Wis Libr Asn, 1984-; Wis Black Librarians' Network, 1985-; Greater Milwaukee Literacy Coalition, 1986-; comt mem, Pub Libr Asn, 1987-; bd mem, Links Inc, 1996-; Phi Theta Kappa; Outstanding Young Woman Grad-Hutchinson Community Jr Col. **Honors/Awds:** Librarian of the Year, Bookfellows, Milwaukee Pub Libr, 1987; Management Merit Award, Milwaukee Pub Libr, City Milwaukee, 1988. **Special Achievements:** Author, "Adult Programming.", The Bottom Line, 1989; Who's Who of American Women, 1983-; Outstanding Young Woman Nominee, 1986. **Home Addr:** 6019 W Calumet Rd, Milwaukee, WI 53223. **Business Addr:** Deputy City Librarian, Milwaukee Public Library System, 814 W Wis Ave, Milwaukee, WI 53233, **Business Phone:** (414)286-3023.

### LOCKHART, BARBARA H.
Executive, consultant. **Personal:** Born Apr 1, 1948, Cleveland, OH; daughter of Willie and Estelle. **Educ:** Cleveland State Univ, BS, 1972; Cent Mich State Univ, MSA, 1987. **Career:** Aetna Casualty & Surety Ins, sr underwriter, 1972-77; Blue Cross NE Ohio, underwriting specialist, mkt res analyst, 1977-80; Mead Corp, health maintenance orgn & cost control coordr, 1980-83; Ohio Dept Health, health care cost analyst, 1983-84; Physicians Health Plan Ohio, vpres, gov progs, 1984-94; Medimetrix Group Inc, sr consult, currently. **Orgs:** Past chair, 1986-89, bd trustee, 1991-, State Legislators Medicaid Oversight Comt, 1986; Ohio Med Care Adv Comt, 1990-; Nat Acad State Health Policy, 1992-; Am Managed Care Asn Medicaid Adv Comt, 1992-; HCFA Medicaid Coordication Care Indust Group, 1992-; Asn Black Ins Professionals, 1992-; Ohio health maintenance orgn, Asn Human Servs Comt. **Honors/Awds:** Ohio House Representatives, Community Service Proclamation, 1992. **Home Addr:** 1694 Norma Rd, Columbus, OH 43229, **Home Phone:** (614)621-6097. **Business Addr:** Senior Consultant, Medimetrix Group Inc, 25 W Prospect Ave Suite 1100, Cleveland, OH 44115-1073, **Business Phone:** (216)523-1300.

### LOCKHART, EUGENE, JR.
Football player, restaurateur. **Personal:** Born Mar 8, 1961, Crockett, TX; married Sharon; children: Bryan, Brandon & Eugene III. **Educ:** Univ Houston, BA, mkt, 1983. **Career:** Football player (retired), restaurant owner; Dallas Cowboys, mid linebacker, 1984-90; New Eng Patriots, left inside linebacker, 1991, right inside linebacker, 1992; Lockhart One-Hour Photo, Dallas, TX, partner; Cowboys Sports Cafe, Irving, TX, partner; Lockhart Custom Pools, partner. **Honors/Awds:** NFL All-Star Team, Sporting News, 1989; Nat Cancer Soc Golf Tournament. **Business Addr:** Partner, Lockhart One Hour Photo Inc, 515 W Campbell Rd, Richardson, TX 75080.

### LOCKHART, JAMES ALEXANDER BLAKELY
Army officer, lawyer. **Personal:** Born May 27, 1936, New York, NY; son of Edgar and Margaret; married Ruth Yvonne Douglas; children: Marc & Diallo Henry. **Educ:** Palmer Mem Inst, attended 1954; Boston Univ Col, BS, bus admin, 1957; Boston Univ Sch Law, JD, 1959. **Career:** Lawyer (retired); Off Chief Coun US Treas Dept, atty adv, 1963-65; City Chicago, asst corp coun, 1965-67; Rivers Lockhart Clayter & Lawrence Attys Law Chicago, partner, 1967-71; Budget Rent A Car Corp, Sr vpres legal affairs & secy & dir1972-79; Chicago Community Ventures Inc, chmn bd, 1975-79; Transamerica Corp, vpres pub affairs, 1979-98. **Orgs:** Bd dir, Pub Affairs Coun; dep, Calif Bus Roundtable; Ill & SC Bar Asns; Sigma Pi Phi Boule Fraternity Inc; Kappa Alpha Psi Fraternity Inc; Episcopalian; bd dir & vice chmn, Legal Legis Comt, Int Franchise Asn; Car & Truck Rental & Leasing Asn; bd trustee & exec comn, Episcopal Charities Diocese Chicago; Standing Comt Episcopal Diocese Chicago; Comn Legis Conv Episcopal Diocese Chicago; life trustee, vpres & exec comt, Lawrence HallSch Boys; pres, Downtown Asn San Francisco; chair, Bay Area Urban League; dir & vice chairperson, Pub Broadcasting Serv; dir, Oakland Pvt Indust Coun; Bohemian Club; dir, founding chairperson, City Club San Francisco; Sequoyah Co Club; pres, bd port comnrs, Port Oakland; trustee emer, Fine Arts Mus San Francisco, 1986-; bd gov, San Francisco Tennis Club, 1988-91; bd trustee, Alta Bates Med Ctr & Hosp San Francisco; chmn, social action comt, Sigma Pi Phi Fraternity Inc; vice chair, Boule Found; chair, City Club San Francisco; Lockhart Family Found. **Honors/Awds:** WBEE (Radio) Community Service Citation, 1973; San Francisco Planning & Urban Research Associates Award, 1988; Good Scouts Award, San Francisco Bay Area Boy Scouts, 1997; Champion for Equality, Nat Asn Advan Colored People Legal Defense Fund, 1998. **Home Addr:** 6037 Ridgemont Dr, Oakland, CA 94619.

### LOCKHART, DR. ROBERT W., III
Dentist. **Personal:** Born Jul 19, 1941, Houston, TX; married Betty J Moore; children: Robert III, Chris & Lisa. **Educ:** Univ Tex, BA, 1962, DDS, 1966, MPH, 1973. **Career:** Harris Co Hosp Sunnyside Clin, dir dept serv, 1973-74; Calif George Dent Soc, vpres, 1974-76; pvt pract dentist, 1968-. **Orgs:** Am & Nat Dent Asn; Acad Gen Dent; Am Asn Pub Health Dent; Alpha Phi Alpha; Nat Asn Advan Colored People; Urban League. **Business Addr:** Dentist, South Main Dental Services, 9285 S Main St (Near Loop 610), Houston, TX 77205, **Business Phone:** (713)666-1116.

### LOCKHART, DR. VERDREE, SR.
Educator, association executive, army officer. **Personal:** Born Oct 19, 1923, Louisville, GA; son of Fred D and Minnie B Roberson; married Louise Howard; children: Verdree II, Vera Louise, Fernandez & Abigail. **Educ:** Tuskegee Univ, BS, 1949; Atlanta Univ, MA, 1957, PhD, 1975; George Peabody Col, attended 1960. **Career:** Educator (retired); Jefferson County High Sch, teacher, 1949-58, counr, 1958-63; GA Dept Educ, educ consult, 1963-80; Atlanta Univ, vpres, 1981-82; Phillips Col, dean educ, 1984-85, regional asbestos inspector, 1985-86; N Fulton High Sch, counr, 1986-92; W Fulton Mid Sch, counr, 1992-2000. **Orgs:** Alpha Phi Alpha Fraternity, 1949-; Parliamentarian, Eta Lambda Chap; Am Coun Asn, 1960-; Former state pres, Asn Coun & Devel, 1963-65; mem exec bd, Atlanta Area Coun, Boy Scouts Am, 1965-; treas, Atlanta Br Nat Asn Advan Colored People, 1972-90; trustee, Atlanta Univ, 1975-81; Tuskegee Univ Forest Resource Coun, 1978-88, 1995-; Tuskegee Univ Nat Alumni Asn, 1980-84; Phi Delta Kappa, 1981-; mem bd dir, Econ Opportunity Atlanta Inc, 1985-88; Am Voc Asn; Ga Adult Educ Asn; Ga Educ Artic Com; Nat Educ Asn; former mem, Youth Employ & Planning Coun, Atlanta CETA Off; Mayor'sTask Force Pub Educ, 1986-92; pres, Atlanta Univ Consortion Chap, Phi Delta Kappa, 1988-89; asst parlimentarian, Tuskegee Univ Nat Alumn Asn, 1990-92; bd mem, Atlanta Asn Eucators, 1990-95; Zion Hill Baptist, 1996-; exec bd mem, Clark Atlanta Univ Nat Alumni Asn; Am Sch Counr Asn; treas, exec bd mem, Fulton Atlanta Community Action Authority Inc, 1995-2001; pres, Tuskegee Univ, Col Agr, Environ & Nat Scis Alumni Asn, 1997-; chmn, Eminent Assoc Prog, Tuskegee Univ, 1998-, chmn exec bd, Fulton-Atlanta Community Action Authority, 2002-; Eminent Presidential Assocs chmn, Tuskegee Nat Alumni Asn Exec Bd. **Honors/Awds:** Ga Gov Medallions, Gov State GA, 1967-68; Silver Beaver Award, Atlanta Area Coun, Boy Scouts Am, 1968; Alumni Merit Award, Atlanta Univ Alumni Asn, 1972; Alumni Brother of the Year, Alpha Phi Alpha Fraternity, 1980; Presidential Award, Atlanta Univ Consortium Chapter of Phi Delta Kappa, 1989; George Washington Carver Outstanding Alumni Award, Tuskegee Univ Agr, Environ & Nat Scis Alumni Asn; A Heritage of Leadership Plaque, Atlanta Area Coun, Boy Scouts Am; Presidential Citation, Nat Asn Equal Opportunity Higher Educ; Alumni Merit Award, Tuskegee Univ. **Home Addr:** 2964 Peek Rd NW, Atlanta, GA 30318-6181, **Home Phone:** (404)794-5208.

### LOCKLEY, CLYDE WILLIAM
Law enforcement officer, police officer. **Personal:** Born Jul 14, 1938, Jacksonville, FL; married Barbara Elaine; children: Rhonda M, Karen P, Larry K, Brian K, Darrell W & Rodney A; married Mary Frances Jordan. **Educ:** Calif Hwy Patrol Acad, attended 1965; Lib Arts Los Angeles SW Col, AA, 1971; Univ Southern Calif, AA, 1971, BA, polit sci, 1974, MS, pub adminr, 1976; Calif Specialized Inst, cert, 1976; Univ Va, cert Criminal Justice, 1978; FBI Acad Quantico, VA, attended 1978. **Career:** Law enforcement officer (retired); Calif State Dept Correction, Inst Men, chino, 1961; Calif Hwy Patrol, 1965,W Los Angeles, patrol officer, training officer, 1969-71, actg field supvr, 1971, W Los Angeles sgt field supvr, lt in-chg, 1976, exec officer, field operating officer, capt, 1989, Los Angeles Commun Ctr & Traffic Opers Ctr, comdr; Compton Community Col, part-time instr criminal justice; Los Angeles Commun & Traffic Opers Ctr, capt-comdr, currently. **Orgs:** Vice chmn, Environ Commn City Cars Calif; FBI Nat Acad Asn; Calif Asn Hwy Patrolman; Los Angeles County Peace Officers Asn; life mem, Univ Southern Calif Alumni Asn; Calif State Employees Asn. **Honors/Awds:** Outstanding Airman-Special Honor Guard VIP Guard March AFB, CA, 1959. **Home Addr:** 19326 Tajauta Ave, Carson, CA 90746.

### LOCKLEY-MYLES, BARBARA J.
Librarian. **Educ:** Fla A&M Univ, Col Educ, BS, 1996; Fla State Univ, MSLS, 1999. **Career:** Fla A&M Univ, Sci Res Ctr Libr, Col Pharm & Pharmaceut Sci, fac, 1974, instr & digital librn, currently. **Business Addr:** Instructor, Digital Librarian, FAMU Library, 1500 S Martin Luther King Blvd 525 Orr Dr, Tallahassee, FL 32307, **Business Phone:** (850)599-3330.

### LOCKLIN, JAMES R.
Marketing executive, executive, chief executive officer. **Personal:** Born Jan 20, 1958, Monroe, GA; son of Orell and Geneva Malcolm; married Sherry Jackson; children: Jacques & Kimberly. **Educ:** Albany State Univ, attended 1977; Clark Atlanta Univ, BA, mass commun, 1980. **Career:** WCLK-FM, announcer, reporter, prog mgr, 1978-80; WAOK-AM, admin asst, 1979-80; WORL-AM, news, pub affairs dir, 1980; Clarke City, Ga, probation officer, 1980-82; WXAG-AM, gen mgr, 1982-83; Leon Farmer & Co, vpres mkt, 1983-94; First Class Mkt Ltd, pres, 19; Premier Mgt Group, pres, 1994-98; Charter Commun, mkt mgr, 1998-2002; Elements Commun Solutions, Dir Acct Serv, 2004; WATV-AM, gen mgr, 2004-07; E's Lawn Care Inc, sales mgr, 2008-09; Ferst Found Childhood Literacy, Opers Dir, 2010-11; Locklin Mkt Group, chief exec officer, 2011-; Nalley Toyota Stonecrest, e sls mgr, 2014-15. **Orgs:** Athens Ad Club, 1983-; bd mem, Morton Theatre Corp, 1984; bd mem, Hope Haven Sch, 1985; bd mem, Athens Tutorial Prog, 1985; exec comt, Athens Area Human Rel Coun; Zeta Beta Beta Chap Omega Psi Phi Frat Inc; Athens Bus Coun; Huntington Pk Homeowners Asn; Ga Plng Asn; Am Plng Asn; Greater Athens Jazz Asn; Nat Asn Advan Colored People; Northeast Ga Bus League; Athens Area Chamber Com; comn mem, Athens Clarke County Plng Comn; comn mem, Athens Clarke County Clean & Beautiful Comn. **Honors/Awds:** Leadership Athens Participant, 1985; Man of the Year, Omega Psi Phi Fraternity, 1989; Local Business Person of the Year, Nat Asn Advan Colored People, 1990. **Home Addr:** 910 James Huff Rd, Monroe, GA 30656-4842, **Home Phone:** (770)267-2100. **Business Addr:** Vice President Marketing, Leon Farmer & Co, PO Box 249, Athens, GA 30603, **Business Phone:** (404)353-1166.

### LOCKWOOD, JAMES CLINTON
Executive, educator, association executive. **Personal:** Born May 22, 1946, Philadelphia, PA; son of William and Signora; married Carolyn Francina McGowan; children: Jason Perry & James Andrew. **Educ:** West Chester Univ, BS, 1968; Salisbury State Univ, attended 1976; Univ Md, College Park, MA, sociol, 1990. **Career:** Oxford Area Sch Dist PA, fifth grade teacher, 1968-70; Lincoln Univ, PA, asst financial aid, 1970-71; Salisbury State, MD, dir financial aid, 1971-77; Coppin State Col, dir financial aid, 1977-78; Univ MD, Eastern Shore, dir financial aid, 1979-89; Sociol Univ, MD Eastern Shore, instr, 1983, 1985-89; Montgomery Col, dir financial aid, 1989-97. **Orgs:** Nat Appeals Panel, US Dept Educ, 1981; stud fin aid trainer, Nat Asn Stud Fin Aid ADM & US Dept Educ, 1981, 1983, 1989, 1993; chairperson, FED Rels Com, 1981-82; Middles States Sociol, Univ MD Eastern Shore, 1983, 1985-89; Asn Stud Fin Aid ADM Inc; Moton Consortium Admis & Fin Aid, instr, 1986; Nat Regional Assembly, 1994-96; trainer, exec coun, Eastern Asn Stud Fin Aid ADM, 1996; life mem, US Chess Fedn. **Home Addr:** 1404 Timberwolf Dr, Frederick, MD 21703-2221, **Home Phone:** (301)696-1893.

### LOFTERS, ESQ. CECILIA O'BRIEN
Lawyer. **Educ:** Mass Inst Technol, BS, mech engineering, 1983; Univ Calif, Berkeley, MS, mech engineering, 1984; Harvard Univ, JD, cum laude, 1987. **Career:** Gen Elec Co, sr corp intellectual property coun, 2000-; White & Case LLP, partner. **Orgs:** Chairperson, Am Intellection Property Law Educ Found Sydney B. Williams Scholar; bd trustees mem, Woods Serv; Minority Corp Coun Asn Inc. **Honors/Awds:** The Network Journal: 25 Influential Black Women in Business, Black Professionals & Small Bus Mag, 2007. **Special Achievements:** First African American partner at White & Case LLP. **Business Addr:** Senior Corporate Intellectual Property Counsel, Junior Lawyer, General Electric Co, 3135 Easton Turnpike, Fairfield, CT 06828-0001, **Business Phone:** (203)373-2211.

### LOFTON, ANDREW JAMES
Government official. **Personal:** Born Oct 16, 1950, Longstreet, LA; son of Junius E and Ethel M Peyton; married Verda J Minnix; children: Junius & Lamar. **Educ:** Univ Puget Sound, Tacoma, WA, BA, urban studies, 1972; Univ Wash, Seattle, WA, MUP, 1974. **Career:** City Seattle, WA, Off Policy Planning, human resource planner, 1974-76, capital improv planner, 1976-78, Dept Community Develop, block grant adv, 1978-80, dep dir, 1980-87, Dept Lic & Consumer Affairs, dir, 1987-89, Off Mgt & Budget, dir, 1990-92, dep chief staff, mayor's off, 1992-94, dep dir, Dept Community Trade & Econ Develop, 1994-95; Seattle City Light, Customer Serv, dep supt, 1995-; Seattle Housing Authority, dep exec dir finance & admin, 2004-12, exec dir, 2012-; City Seattle, budget dir; Wash State Dept Community Trade & Econ Develop, dep dir. **Orgs:** Nat Forum Black Pub Admin, 1983-90; Region X Coun Mem, Blacks Govt, 1983-87; pres, Seattle Chap, Blacks Govt, 1983-86; bd mem, Seattle Mgt Asn, 1986-87; bd mem, Rainier High Boys & Girls Club, 1987-; region IX rep, Conf Minority Pub Adminr, 1989-91. **Home Addr:** 5157 S Graham, Seattle, WA 98118, **Home Phone:** (206)722-2673. **Business Addr:** Executive Director, Seattle Housing Authority, 120 6th Ave N, Seattle, WA 98109-5003, **Business Phone:** (206)615-3500.

### LOFTON, DR. BARBARA
Administrator. **Personal:** Born May 2, 1954, Jackson, MS; daughter of Fred Alexander Jr and Alberta Alexander; married Jon C; children: Torri A Irving, Norman W Irving & Anastasia A. **Educ:** Jackson State Univ, BS, health, phys educ & recreation, 1975; Univ Iowa, MA, recreation educ, 1977; Grambling State Univ, EdD, 1993. **Career:** Chicago Asn Retarded Citizens, activ coordr & supvr, 1980-82; Cs Haven Inc, recreation specialist & supvr, 1982-83; Grambling State Univ, Dept Health, asst prof, 1983-93; Univ Ark, Pine Bluff, Dept Health, asst prof, 1993-95, dir diversity progs, 1996-, Sam M Walton Col Bus, dir minority affairs, currently. **Orgs:** Nat Asn Academics; Am Asn Univ Women; Am Asn Black Higher Educ. **Home Addr:** 2217 Sweetbriar, Fayetteville, AR 72701, **Home Phone:** (479)575-4557. **Business Addr:** Director of Minority Affairs, Director of Diversity Programs, University of Arkansas, 301 Bus Bldg 220 McIlroy Ave, Fayetteville, AR 72701, **Business Phone:** (479)575-5949.

**LOFTON, DOROTHY W.**
Executive, educator. **Personal:** Born Jun 22, 1925, Marlin, TX; married Donald D; children: Ronald & Deanne Michelle. **Educ:** Baylor Univ, BA, 1971. **Career:** Marlin Independent Sch Dist, teacher; Lofton Cement Contractor, owner, currently. **Orgs:** Tex Classroom Teachers Asn; Falls County Teachers Asn; Tex St Teacher Asn; pres, City Fedn Women's Clubs; vpres, Strivette Club; secy, Falconerstamps Comn Ctr; secy & treas, Marlin Parents Orgn; treas, Carrie Adams Dist Tex Women & Girls' Clubs. **Honors/Awds:** Adult leader certificate, 4H Coun, 1974. **Business Addr:** Owner, Lofton Cement Contractor, 302 Grimes St, Marlin, TX 76661-3378, **Business Phone:** (254)883-5233.

**LOFTON, ERNEST**
Labor activist, vice president (organization). **Personal:** Born Feb 25, 1932, Detroit, MI; children: Terry & Penny Holloway. **Career:** Labor activist (retired); Dearborn Iron Foundry, water tester, 1950; Ford Motor Co, Specty Foundry Unit, bargaining comt man, pres, 1967-76; United Auto Workers Local 600, second vpres, 1976-81, first vpres, 1981-82; United Auto Workers Int Exec Bd, region 1A dir, 1983-89, int vpres, 1989; United Auto Workers Mich Community Action Prog Dept, dir, 1989-99. **Orgs:** Bd dir, Blue Cross & Blue Shield Mich; bd dir, United Found; New DetroitInc; bd dir, Detroit Police Athletic League; Transafrica; bd, Save Our Sons & Daughters; United Auto Workers Int Exec Bd, 1983-; dir, United Auto Workers Mich Community Action Prog Dept, 1989-; bd dir, dir, Metropolitan Realty Corp, 1991-; bd mem, Detroit Econ Growth Corp; adv bd, Detroit Repertory Theatre; Econ Policy Coun United Nations Asn USA; nat secy, Coalition Black Trade Unionists; vpres, Nat Asn Advan Colored People, Detroit chap; vpres, UAW Int Union; dir, United Auto Workers Nat Ford Dept; dir, UAW Region 1A; Nat Asn Advan Colored People; Blue Cross & Blue Shield Mich; New Detroit Inc; Detroit Econ Growth Corp; Econ Alliance Mich; Nat Secy Coalition Black Trade Unionists; Econ Policy Coun UNA. **Home Addr:** 535 Griswold, Detroit, MI 48226, **Home Phone:** (313)961-5552.

**LOFTON, JAMES**
Football player, football coach. **Personal:** Born Jul 5, 1956, Fort Ord, CA; married Beverly Fanning, Jan 1, 1980; children: David, Daniel & Rachel. **Educ:** Stanford Univ, BA, 1978. **Career:** Football player (retired), coach; Green Bay Packers, wide receiver, 1978-86; Los Angeles Raiders, wide receiver, 1987-88; Buffalo Bills, wide receiver, 1989-92; sports commentator, 1990; Los Angeles Rams, 1993; Philadelphia Eagles, wide receiver, 1993; Westwood One Radio, color analyst & sideline reporter, 1999-2001, Sunday Night Football broadcasts, analyst, 2009; San Diego Chargers, wide receiver coach, 2002-07; Oakland Raiders, wide receiver coach, 2008-09, asst coach, 2009-. **Orgs:** Theta Delta Chi Fraternity; Pro Football Hall Fame. **Honors/Awds:** All-Pro, Assoc Press, 1980-83; Pro Football Hall of Fame, 2003; Green Bay Packers Hall of Fame. **Special Achievements:** TV Series: "The NFL on CBS", 1978-93; "NFL Monday Night Football", 1979-94; "The NFL on NBC", 1984-87; "ESPN's Sunday Night Football", 1987-92; "TNT Sunday Night Football" 1990; "Requiem for a Running Back". Films: 1990 AFC Championship Game, 1991; Super Bowl XXV, 1991; Super Bowl XXVI, 1992; 1991 AFC Championship Game, 1992; Super Bowl XXVII, 1993; 1992 AFC Championship Game, 1993. **Business Addr:** Wide Receiver Assistant Coach, Oakland Raiders, 1220 Harbor Bay Pkwy, Alameda, CA 94502, **Business Phone:** (510)864-5000.

**LOFTON, KENNY**
Baseball player, executive. **Personal:** Born May 31, 1967, East Chicago, IN. **Educ:** Univ Ariz, studio prod. **Career:** Baseball palyer (retired), executive; Houston Astros, outfielder, center fielder, 1991; Cleveland Indians, 1992-96, 1998-2001, 2007; Atlanta Braves, 1997; Chicago White Sox, 2002; San Francisco Giants, 2002; Pittsburgh Pirates, 2003; Chicago Cubs, 2003; New York Yankees, 2004; Philadelphia Phillies, 2005; post-game color commentator, Los Angeles Dodgers, 2006; Tex Rangers, 2007; Am Century Celebrity Golf Classic, 2008; Post-prod Co, Hollywood, co-owner, currently; FilmPool Inc, co-founder, chief exec officer, currently. **Honors/Awds:** Fastest player, 1990; Best Bunter, 1990; AL Gold Glove-CF, 1993-96; Indians Gordon Cobbledick Golden Tomahawk Award, 1994; AL All Star Team, 1994, 1995, 1996; Major League Baseball stolen base champions, 1992-96; NL All Star Team, 1997; Cleveland Indians Hall of Fame, 2010. **Special Achievements:** co writer: "What If", Ruben Studdards, 2006. **Business Addr:** Co-founder, Chief Executive Officer, FilmPool Inc, 1112 W Magnolia Blvd, Burbank, CA 91506, **Business Phone:** (818)729-9970.

**LOFTON, MELLANESE S. (MELLANESE SLAUGHTER LOFTON)**
Lawyer, association executive. **Personal:** Born Aug 24, 1941, Houston, TX; children: Frederick Douglas & Robin Mellanese. **Educ:** Univ Tex, BA, 1962; Univ Calif, Boalt Hall Sch Law, JD, 1974. **Career:** Univ Tex, photog teacher, 1961-62; Alameda & Co, soc worker employ counslt, 1963-69; Contra Costa Co, social worker, 1969-73; Jacobs Sills & Coblentz, law clerk, 1973-74; US Steel Corp, atty, 1974-82; Siemens Corp, Tel Plus Commun, 1984-92; Lofton & Lofton, owner, managing partner & atty, 1999-, Exeter 1031 Exchange Serv, LLC, Kona Hawaii, br mgr, 2008-; My Corp Coach, chief exec officer, co-founder, 2014-; Lofton Law Search, pres, 2015-. **Orgs:** Pa Bar; Calif State Bar; Alpha Kappa Alpha Sorority; Pub Proj Future chair, Rotary Club N Hawaii; Kona Bd Realtors. **Special Achievements:** Author: The Medi-Cal Advantage: How to Save the Family Home from the Cost of Nursing Home Care; "Corporate Chess How to Outplay Management", 2008. **Home Addr:** 7122 McCormack Rd, Rio Vista, CA 94571-1006. **Business Addr:** Branch Manager, Partner, Exeter 1031 Exchange Services LLC, 68 1773 Auhili Loop, Waikoloa, HI 96738, **Business Phone:** (808)883-3595.

**LOFTON, MICHAEL (MIKA'IL SANKOFA)**
Athlete, public relations executive. **Personal:** Born Dec 10, 1963, Montgomery, AL; son of Inez. **Educ:** NY Univ, BA, econ, 1988; Semmelweis Univ, Budapest, Hungary, attended 2006. **Career:** Shearson Lehman Hutton, broker, 1988-90; Ernst & Young, pub rels assoc, 1990-; Grey Advert; Kirshenbaum; Bond & Partners & Shandwick Int; Peter Westbrook Found, dir athletics & fencing coach, 1990-2009; Un Int Sch, head fencing coach; National Broadcasting Company Sports, analyst; Stevens Inst Technol Men's fencing team, head coach, 2005-09; Ross Schs summer prog, E Hampton, NY, head sabre coach, Thrust Fencing Acad Nyack, coach, currently. **Orgs:** Dir bus affairs, Peter Westbrook Found, 1990-. **Business Addr:** Head Coach, Thrust Fencing Acad, 35 S Broadway, Nyack, NY 10960, **Business Phone:** (917)371-5603.

**LOFTON, STEVEN LYNN**
Football player. **Personal:** Born Nov 26, 1968, Jacksonville, FL; married Tarita; children: Christian & Courtney. **Educ:** Tex A&M Univ. **Career:** Football player (retired); Montreal Mach, 1991; Phoenix Cardinals, defensive back, 1991, 1992-93; Carolina Panthers, defensive back, 1995-96, right cornerback, 1998-99; New Eng Patriots, 1997-98.

**LOGAN, DR. BARBARA N.**
Educator, executive. **Educ:** Bronx Community Col, AA; Loyola Univ, BSN, 1970; Univ Ill, MS, 1972; Northwestern Univ, MA, 1978, PhD, sociol, 1980; RN, FAAN. **Career:** Clemson Univ, Sch Nursing, dir, 1993-2003, prof emer, currently, EXPORT Ctr, prin investr, 2003-07, res core dir, 2007-, Ctr Res Health Disparities, assoc dir, currently. **Orgs:** Fel Am Nurses Asn Minority Fel Prog, 1976; fel Am Acad Nurses, 1994; Nat & int res conferences; NIH, Dept Health & Human Serv, Clemson Univ; Univ Ill, Chicago; Nat Black Nurses Asn. **Home Addr:** 1520 W Little River Dr, Seneca, SC 29672-6861, **Home Phone:** (864)888-0709. **Business Addr:** Associate Director, The EXPORT Center, 407 Edwards Hall, Clemson, SC 29634-0743, **Business Phone:** (864)656-0779.

**LOGAN, JUDGE BENJAMIN HENRY, II**
Lawyer, judge. **Personal:** Born Jun 25, 1943, Dayton, OH; son of Ben H Sr and Jeanne Ross; married Creola; children: Fonda, Benjamin M & Barry; married Denice M; children: Bradford & Benjamin W. **Educ:** Ohio Northern Univ, Ada, OH, BA, acct & hist, 1968; Ohio Northern Law Sch, Ada, OH, JD, 1972. **Career:** Ben's Enterprise, Dayton, Oh, mgr, 1960-68; Dayton Tire & Rubber, Dayton, OH, cost acct, 1968-69; Dayton Bd Educ, Dayton, OH, sub teacher, 1969-70; G R Legal Aid, Grand Rapids, Mich, staff atty, 1972-74; Davenport Col, instr, 1973-75; Logan & Beason, Grand Rapids, MI, partner, 1974-88; Grand Valley State Univ, instr, 1975-77; Mich Civil Rights, referee, 1984-88; 61st Dist Ct, Grand Rapids, Mich, judge, 1988-94, chief judge, 1994-2014. **Orgs:** Bd mem, 1972, life mem, 1985, Nat Asn Advan Colored People, Grand Rapids Chap; bd mem, Grand Rapids Bar Asn, 1973-, 1990-, 1991-94; Grand Rapids Urban League, 1973-; Am Bar Asn, 1974-, judicial admin div, 1992-; Task force opportunities minorities & ABA Standing Comt Judicial Selection, Tenure Compensation, 1995-96 & Comn Minorities, 1997-; co-chair, 1974-, bd dir, 1989-92, 1991-94, judicial coun chair, 1994-95, Nat Bar Asn; Press Club, 1975-; bd dir, mem, A Philip Randolph, 1978-; Wolverine Bar Asn, 1980-; gen coun, 1980-88, bd dir, 1993-, YMCA; charter mem, 1982-, pres, 1986-87, 1993-95, Sigma Pi Phi Fraternity; founder & pres, Floyd Skinner Bar Asn, 1982-88; vpres, 1983-, bd mem, 1986, Boy Scouts Western Shores; Grand Rapids Jr Col Pres's Comt, 1984-; founding mem, exec bd, vice chmn, Citizens Rep Govt, 1985-88; bd mem, 1986-, 1991-94, Lions Club; Mich Supreme Ct Hist Soc, 1989-; Asn Black Judges, Mich, 1989-; Dispute Resolution, 1990-; bd mem, 1990-, trustee, 1992-, Law Alumni Asn Ohio Northern Univ-Ada; US Supreme Ct Hist Soc, 1992-; Fair Housing Bd, 1992-; Leadership Grand Rapids, 1993-; YWCA Tribute Comn, 1993-; Arkon City Club, 1994-; Fel State Bar Mich, 1995; nat bd mem, Pan Hellenic Coun, 1996-; nat bd mem & gen coun, Kappa Alpha Psi Found, 1996-; chair, United Negro Col Fund Chair, 2000-03; advisor & consult, Men's Ministry, Messiah Missionary Baptist Church, currently. **Home Addr:** 2243 Breton Rd SE, Grand Rapids, MI 49546-5559, **Home Phone:** (616)942-9519. **Business Addr:** Men's Ministry, Messiah Missionary Baptist Church, 513 Henry Ave SE, Grand Rapids, MI 49503, **Business Phone:** (616)458-2651.

**LOGAN, CAROLYN GREEN**
Law enforcement officer. **Personal:** Born Jul 5, 1957, Asheville, NC; daughter of Mack and Gladys; married Karl; children: Christopher Green, Morgan & Taelor. **Career:** Master trooper (retired); Asheville Police Dept, police officer, 1977-84; NC State Hwy Patrol, master trooper, state dir, 1984-07. **Orgs:** Friendship chmn, Onyx Optimist Club, 1995-96; infant & toddler counr, First Mayfield Mem Baptist Church, 1995-96; AAST, 2004-. **Business Addr:** NC.

**LOGAN, ERNEST EDWARD, II**
Football player, football coach, executive. **Personal:** Born May 18, 1968, Ft. Bragg, NC; married Diana; children: Ernest III. **Educ:** East Carolina Univ. **Career:** Football player (retired), football coach, exec; Cleveland Browns, right defensive end, 1991, 1992; Atlanta Falcons, nose tackle, 1993-94; Jacksonville Jaguars, nose tackle, 1995-96; New York Jets, nose tackle, 1997, 1999-2000, right defensive tackle, 1998; Jacksonville Univ, defensive coach, 2004-15; Independent Assoc Pre-Paid Legal Serv Inc & Identity Theft Shield, sales assoc, 2014-; IMG Acad, line coach, currently. **Business Addr:** Line Coach, IMG Academy, 5650 Bollettieri Blvd, Bradenton, FL 34210.

**LOGAN, HON. GEORGE, III**
Lawyer, judge. **Personal:** Born Dec 23, 1942, Elizabeth City, NC; married Sheila Jacqueline Miller; children: Natalie, Camille & George Spencer. **Educ:** Rutgers Col, BA, 1964; Rutgers Sch Law-Newark, JD, 1967. **Career:** Judge (retired); Ctr Const Rights, staff atty, 1967-68; USAF, asst staff judge advoc, 1968-72; Deprima Aranda & de Leon, 1972-73; Karl & N Stewart, 1973-74; Lindauer & Goldberg, assoc atty, 1975; Lindauer & Logan, 1975-76; atty, self-emp, 1976-78; Logan Marton Halladay & Hall, partner, 1978-99; Ariz Dept Econ Security, chief admin law judge & asst dir, 1980-91; Ariz Supreme Ct, proj mgr & ct specialist, 1992-97; Phoenix Munic Ct, ltd jurisdiction judge, 1999-2006; Surprise City Coun, Ariz, presiding judge, 2006-13. **Orgs:** Pres, Ariz Black Lawyers Asn; Phoenix Urban League; Nat Bar Asn; Am CivilLiberties Union; bd dir, Casa Linda Lodge; pres, Community LegalServ; City Phoenix, Comn Aging; Joint Legis Comn Conflict Interest; mem bd dirs & secy, Gamma Mu Educ Serv Corp. **Home Addr:** 12640 N 17th Pl, Phoenix, AZ 85022-5713, **Home Phone:** (602)997-4333. **Business Addr:** Presiding Judge, Surprise City Council of Arizona, 16000 N Civic Ctr Plz Suite 105, Surprise, AZ 85374, **Business Phone:** (623)222-1000.

**LOGAN, HAROLD JAMES**
Publishing executive, executive director, association executive. **Personal:** Born Feb 27, 1951, Washington, DC; son of Jean Rhodes and Harold Green; married Etienne Gabrielle Randall; children: Justin & Gabrielle Randall. **Educ:** Harvard Univ, Cambridge, BA, econ, 1973; Stanford Univ, Grad Sch Bus, MBA, 1980. **Career:** Wash Post, Wash, reporter, 1973-78, mgr, electronic publ, 1980-84; Dow Jones & Co, Princeton, dep dir bus dev, 1984-88; Pac Bell diry, San Francisco, dir bus dev, 1988; Vicinity Corp, chief exec officer; Third Set Partners, mgr; Manheim Interactive Inc, pres & chief exec officer; Manheim, sr vpres mkt & sr vpres strategic plng; BuyBook Technologies Inc, chief exec officer, currently. **Orgs:** Nat Black MBA Asn, 1980-; founding mem, Black Harvard Alumni, Wash, 1982-84; bd dir, Crossroads Theatre, 1986-88; bd dir, Princeton Nursery Sch, 1986-88; Minority caucus, New Oakland Comn, 1991-; dir, WEB Du Bois Soc. **Home Addr:** 1325 Peachtree St NEApt 201, Atlanta, GA 30309-3249. **Business Addr:** Chief Executive Officer, BuyBook Technologies Inc, 1373 Lancaster Rd, Manheim, PA 17545, **Business Phone:** (866)552-8948.

**LOGAN, JAMES EDDIE**
Football player. **Personal:** Born Dec 6, 1972, Opp, AL. **Educ:** Univ Memphis, grad. **Career:** Football player (retired); Houston Oilers, linebacker, 1995; Cincinnati Bengals, linebacker, 1995; Seattle Seahawks, 1996, 2000, linebacker, 1997-99; Scottish Claymores, 1997.

**LOGAN, DR. JOHN C., JR.**
Executive, educator. **Personal:** Born Nov 23, 1948, Dayton, OH; son of John and Harleen; married Tracy; children: Tina & Marquetta Walker. **Educ:** Union Inst, Cincinnati, PhD, mass commun, 1997. **Career:** WDAO-FM, prog dir & announcer, 1970-83; Acad Broadcasting, owner, pres, 1983-86; Cent St Univ, WCSU-FM, gen mgr, 1986-2009; Cosby Mass Commun Ctr, dir, 1989-; Logan Commun, pres & chief exec officer, 1991-; Historically black cols & univs, Wilberforce Univ, prof commun, 1993-2010; Presidential Leadership Inst. **Orgs:** Unity Lodge 115, 1983; nat chair, Logan Family Reunion, 1984; St JamesCath Church; chair, United Negro Col Fund; chair, Sickle Cell Anemia Drive; local host, Jerry Lewis Muscular Dystrophy Telethon. **Business Addr:** General Manager, WCSM FM, Central State University, 1400 Brush Row Rd, Wilberforce, OH 45384, **Business Phone:** (937)376-6011.

**LOGAN, JUAN LEON**
Artist. **Personal:** Born Aug 16, 1946, Nashville, TN; married Geraldine Johnson; children: Sidney & Jonathan; married Lorna Hosein; children: Kim. **Educ:** Howard Univ, attended 1965; Clark Col, attended 1967; Md Inst Col Art, MFA, painting & mixed media, 1998. **Career:** Univ NC, Chapell Hill, assoc prof, prof studio art, 1999-2012; artist, 1974-. Exhibitions: Jefferson Gallery, 1969; Charlotte Arts & Cult Soc, 1970; Davidson Col Art Gallery, 1973; Winthrop Gallery Winthrop Col, 1974; SC State Col, 1976; Winston-Salem Univ Art Gallery, 1979; Nat Mus African Art Washington, DC, 1980; Rowe Gallery, Univ NC, Charlotte, 1983; Six NC Artists Pfeiffer Col Gallery, Afro-Am Artists NC Ctr/Gallery, La Watercolor Soc 14th Annual Int Exhibit, 1984 Invitational/Black & White Spirit Square Arts Ctr, 1984; Spirit Sq Ctr Art & Educ, Deborah Peverall Gallery, 1985; Portsmouth Mus, Mus Sci & Indust, Hickory Mus Art, Gaston City Mus Art & Hist, Afro-Am Cultural Ctr, 1986; NC Cent Univ, Green Hill Ctr NC Art, 1987; Waterworks Visual Arts Ctr, Johnson C Smith Univ, 1988; Hodges Taylor Gallery, 1989; Lawton Gallery Univ Wis Green Bay, NC State Univ, Marita Gilliam Gallery, 1990; NC Arts Coun Artists fellowship, Greenville Mus Art, VA Polytechnic Inst & State Univ, 1991; Arts Coun Artistfel, 1991-92; Tubman Mus, Lincoln Cultural Ctr, Gainesville Col, Univ Ill, Chicago, 1992; Asheville Art Mus, Ga Southern Mus, Southeast Ark Arts & Sci Ctr, Wilmer Jennings Gallery, Kenkeleba, Isobel Neal Gallery, McIntosh Gallery, Potsdam Col State Univ, NY, 1993; St John's Mus Art, Mint Mus Art, Jerald Melberg Gallery, Montgomery Mus Art, 1994; Diggs Gallery Winston-Salem State Univ, 1994; Southeastern Ctr Contemporary Art, Cleveland Ctr Contemporary Art, 1995; June Kelly Gallery, Anderson Gallery, Va Commonwealth Univ, 1996; Phillips Morris fel, 1996-98; Howard Univ Art Gallery, Asheville Art Mus, Budapest Galeria, Corcoran Gallery, 1997; Litografiska Akademien, Waterloo Mus Art, Landmark Gallery, Tex Tech Univ, 1998; Gomez Gallery, John Hopkins Univ, Md Art Place, 1999; Carolina Minority fel, 1999-2001; Print Ctr Sande Webster Gallery, James E Lewis Mus, Philadelphia Mus Art, San Francisco Craft & Folk Art Mus, World Bank, Tryon Ctr Visual Arts, artist-in-residence, 2000; Art Fusion MIA, 2013; Hoi Polloi-Kaplan Gallery, 2014. Collections: Afro-Am Cultural Ctr; Asheville Art Mus, 1995; Atlanta Fulton Pub Libr; BellSouth; Blue Cross Greater Philadelphia; Glaxo Inc; Hammonds House Galleries, 1995; Lincoln Nat Ins; Mint Mus Craft & Design; Mus African Am Art; NC A&T State Univ; NC Mus Art; Northwestern Univ; Philadelphia Mus Art, 2000-01; Mint Mus Art, 2003; Sch Law, Univ NC, Chapel Hill; SE Ark Arts & Sci Ctr; Davidson Col, Smith Gallery, 2011; St John's Mus Art; Tubman African Am Mus; Winston-Salem State Univ. **Orgs:** Bd trustees, Gaston County Public Library, 1995. **Honors/Awds:** The Romare Bearden Award for Creativity/Innovation, Medium Carnegie Inst, 1972; Honorable Mention-PIC Award/Nonprocess Educ, Posters Assoc Printing Co, Charlotte, NC, 1974; First Place Award, La Watercolor Soc 14 Annual Int Exhib, New Orleans, 1984; Artist as Catalyst, Mid Atlantic Arts Found, 2000. **Home Addr:** 14 Brandon Rd, Chapel Hill, NC 27514-5601. **Business Addr:** Artist, c/o June Kelly, 591 Broadway Suite 3C, New York, NY 10012, **Business Phone:** (212)226-1660.

**LOGAN, LEWIS E.**
Executive, executive director. **Career:** Md State Treas Off, dir, chair. **Business Addr:** Deputy Treasurer, Maryland State Treasurer Office, Rm 108 Treas Bldg 80 Calvert St, Annapolis, MD 21401-1991, **Business Phone:** (410)260-7920.

**LOGAN, LLOYD**
Executive, pharmacist, association executive. **Personal:** Born Dec 27, 1932, Columbia, MO; married Lottie A Pecot; children: Terri, Connie, Gerald, Michael & Kevin. **Educ:** Purdue Univ, attended 1952; Belleville Jr Col, attended 1954; St Louis Col Pharm, BS, 1958. **Career:** Pharmacist (retired); Mound City Pharm, owner; Dome Pharm, owner; St Louis Univ Hosp, staff pharmacist, 1958-59, chief pharmacist, 1959-67, dir pharm, purchasing, 1966-69; Rhodes Med Supply Inc, 1968-72; Daughter Charity Nat Health Syst, asst vp contracts, 1970-95, consult. **Orgs:** Am Hosp Asn; pres, People Inc; Chi Delta Mu Med Frat; YMCA; Help Inc; treas, Page Community Develop Corp; Lindell Hosp; Am Pharmaceut Asn; Nat Pharmaceut Asn; Mound City Pharmaceut Asn; Nat Asn Retail Druggists; St Engelbert Sch Bd; St Louis Archdiocesan Sch Bd; St Louis Urban League. **Home Addr:** 6055 Lindell Blvd, St. Louis, MO 63112, **Home Phone:** (314)726-0427.

**LOGAN, WARREN E., JR.**
President (government). **Personal:** married Linda; children: 2. **Educ:** Tenn State Univ, BS. **Career:** Off Minority Bus Enterprise, Statewide Bus Develop Ctr, Chattanooga, Memphis & Nashville, exec dir; Tenn Valley Authority, Div Power; Tenn Urban League Affil, Knoxville, Memphis & Nashville, chmn & chief operating officer, 1998; Urban League Greater Chattanooga, pres & chief exec officer, currently. **Orgs:** Pres, Nat Urban League; bd trustee, Mem Health Care Syst, 2008-; pres, Asn Execs; vice chmn, Elec Power Bd; Brightbridge Inc. **Business Addr:** President, Chief Executive Officer, Urban League of Greater Chattanooga, 730 ML King Blvd, Chattanooga, TN 37403, **Business Phone:** (423)756-1762.

**LOGAN, WILLIE FRANK**
Mayor, state government official. **Personal:** Born Feb 16, 1957, Miami, FL; son of Willie and Ruth Sr; married Lyra Blizzard. **Educ:** Miami Dade Community Col, AA, 1976; Univ Miami, BS, acct, 1977. **Career:** Opa-locka Mayor, comnr, 1980-82; Opa Locka Community Develop CRP, consult; Fla House Rep, state rep, 2000; Performing Arts Ctr Trust Inc. **Orgs:** Nat Asn Advan Colored People; Urban League; Nat CNF State Legislators; pres, Phi Beta Sigma; Alpha Kappa Psi; Alpha Phi Omega; vpres, UBS; chair, Black State Legislators, 1990-92; comn chair, Alternative Educ Inst; comt chair, Cent Voter File Study; chair, Finance & Taxation Comt; Cs Serv Coun; Performing Arts Ctr Trust Inc; Greater Miami Nat Asn for Advan Colored People; Dem Nat Comt; Nat Conf State Legislatures. **Home Addr:** 18870 NW 53rd Pl, Opa Locka, FL 33055-2399, **Home Phone:** (305)623-4072. **Business Addr:** FL.

**LOGAN, WILLIS HUBERT**
Social worker. **Personal:** Born Nov 23, 1943, Springfield, IL; married Joyce A Day; children: Gennea & Andre. **Educ:** Western Ill Univ, attended 1943; Sangamon State Univ, BA, 1972. **Career:** Springfield Recreation Commn, youth supvr, 1962; Allis Chalmers, mach operator, 1963; Ill Nat Bank, bank teller, 1967; Dept Conser, employ coordr, 1979; Dept Community Develop & Progs, Springfield, Ill, exec dir, 1979; Springfield Housing Authority, exec dir, 1984-89; dir Housing Progs, Dept Com & Community Affairs, 1991-97, exec dir, 1997-2005; Springfield Pk Dist, Comnr, currently; Ill Asn Pk Districts, treas, vice chair, currently; Citizens Club of Springfield, vpres. **Orgs:** Frontiers Int, 1976; vice chmn, Springfield Planning Comn, 1979; bd mem, United Fund, 1976; pres, Springfield E Asn, 1977; secy, Alpha Phi Alpha Mu Delta Lambda, 1980; chmn, Springfield Sangamon Co Reg Planning Comn, 1980; Capital City Rr Relocation Authority; assoc dir, Springfield Progressive Movement Youth; presidential adv comt, Univ Ill; Springfield Golf Club. **Honors/Awds:** Community Service Award, NAACP, 1977; Community Service Award, United Way, 1978. **Home Addr:** 2704 Johnathan Pl, Springfield, IL 62711-6385, **Home Phone:** (217)546-9124. **Business Addr:** Vice Chair, Illinois Association of Park Districts, 211 E Monroe St, Springfield, IL 62701-1186, **Business Phone:** (217)523-4554.

**LOGAN-TOOSON, LINDA ANN**
Executive. **Personal:** Born Aug 7, 1950, Cincinnati, OH; daughter of Harold John and Amelia Edna. **Educ:** Fisk Univ, BA, bus admin & econs, 1972; Xavier Univ, MBA, 1975. **Career:** Frigidaire Gen Motors, mkt analyst, 1972-75; IBM, mkt trainee, 1975-76; Drackett Co Bristol Myers, proj dir, 1977-82, mgr consumer res, 1982-84, sr mgr consumer res, 1984-92; Tucson Limousine Serv Inc, vpres, 1991; W Shell Coldwell Banker, realtor, 1993-. **Orgs:** Life mem, chap vpres, 1996-97, pres, 1998-2000, Alpha Kappa Alpha Sorority Inc; Nat Urban League Black Exec Exchange Prog, 1978-; Nat Asn Female Execs, 1982-; youth prog chairperson, YMCA Black Achievers Prog, 1983-84; bd mem, Gross Br YMCA, 1984-85; vpres, Am Mkt Asn, mem bd dir, 1985-86, exec adv bd, 1986-89; Nat Black MBA Asn, 1986-; acct mgr, United Way Campaign, 1987, 1989, 1990; exec secy, bd dir, 1986-88, pres, 1990-91, Cincinnati Scholar Found; bd realtors, Nat Asn Realtors, 1993-; vpres, Greater Cincinnati Limousine Asn, 1994-96. **Home Addr:** 1230 Springfield Pke, Cincinnati, OH 45215-2142, **Home Phone:** (513)821-3800. **Business Addr:** Realtor, Coldwell Banker West Shell, 6700 Ruwes Oak Dr, Cincinnati, OH 45248, **Business Phone:** (513)922-9400.

**LOGANS, ANDREA RENEE**
Consultant, chief executive officer. **Educ:** Univ Fla, BA. **Career:** Smith Inc, financial consult; Fenner, financial consult; Pierce, financial consult; Merrill Lynch, financial consult; Xerox/Control Data Inc, acct mgr, sales exec; Control Data, sales & mkt, acct rep; Access Data Supply Inc, pres & chief exec officer, 1990-; Access Data Support Serv, pres & chief exec officer, 2000-. **Orgs:** Houston Minority Bus Coun; bd Houston Area Women's Ctr; Da Camera Houston; trustee bd mem, Ensemble Theatre; bd mem, dir, Greater Houston Partnership; bd dir, Ctr Houston's Future; fel Am Leadership Forum; bd mem, Boy Scouts Am; mentor, Houston Independent Sch Dist; mentor, Shell Youth Acad; mentor, Wheeler Ave Baptist Church; chaired fundraising, W. L. Davis Dist Boy Scouts Am; bd mem, Ctr Houston's Future, currently. **Honors/Awds:** Who's Who US Execs, 1991; Woman Entrepreneur of the Year, Asn Urban Women Entrepreneurs, 1992; Individual Technical Achiever Award, Nat & Greater Houston Area Tech Achievers Acad, 1992; Administrator's Award for Excellence, US Small Bus Admin, 1993; Woman on the Move, 2000; Ensemble Theatre Presidents Award, 2013; Pinnacle Award, Great Hills Baptist Church, 2013. **Special Achievements:** Was the Texas Executive Women (TEW) Women On The Move 2000 recipient and is named by the Steed Society as one of 2011 Top 25 Women of Houston. **Business Addr:** President, Chief Executive Officer, Access Data Supply Inc, 2425 W Loop S Suite 855, Houston, TX 77027, **Business Phone:** (713)439-0370.

**LOGUE-KINDER, JOAN**
Vice president (organization), executive. **Personal:** Born Oct 26, 1943, Richmond, VA; daughter of John Thomas and Helen Harvey; married Lowell A Henry Jr; children: Lowell A Henry III, Catherine Dionne Henry & Christopher Logue Henry; married Randolph S. **Educ:** Wheaton Col, attended 1962; Adelphi Univ, BA, sociol, 1964; NY Univ, Mercy Col, cert educ, 1971. **Career:** TWA NYC, ticket agt, 1964-65; US Census Bur, from admin asst to dist mgr, 1970; Bd Educ Yonkers, social studies teacher & admin, 1971-75; Nat Black Network, dir pub rels, 1976-83; World Inst Black Commun Inc, co-dir, co-founder, 1978-90; NBN Broadcasting Inc, vpres, 1984-90; Mingo Group Plus Inc, sr vpres, 1990-91; Edelman Pub Rels Worldwide, vpres, 1991-93; US Dept Treas, Wash, dep asst sec pub affairs, 1994-95; Joseph E Seagram Co, NY, dir corp comn prog, 1995-96; Save C, Westport, Conn, vpres, 1997-98; Lynch Jones & Ryan Inc, sr vpres, dir mkt & communs, 1998-99; Govt DC, commun dir; Overseas Pvt Investment Corp, Wash, vpres investment devel, 1999-2001; Greater Jamaica Devel Corp, consult, 2001-; Sari Katz Mayor, consult, 2001-; Philadelphia Acad Fine Arts, consult, 2001-; Off Mayor DC, dir comn, 2001. **Orgs:** Asst coord, Howard Samuels Gov NY, 1974; adv pers rep, Morris Udall, 1976; consult, KLM Royal Dutch Airlines, 1976; consult, Ky Fried Chicken, 1976; consult, ATESTA Span Nat Tourist Bd, 1977; coord, Nat Asn Black Owned Broadcasters, 1977-; bd dir, NY Chap PUSH, 1983; bd dir, Girl Scout Coun Greater NY, 1985-; bd dir, Nat PUSH, 1985; bd dir, Nigerian-Am Friendship Soc; 100 Black Women; del, White House Conf Small Bus; consult, Sony Corp; sr black media advisor, Dukakis-Bentsen; consult, Who; consult, Lincoln Univ; consult, Save C Fedn; consult, Kraft Foods. **Home Addr:** 1800 7th Ave 9B, New York, NY 10026, **Home Phone:** (212)864-7152. **Business Addr:** Consultant, Greater Jamaica Development Corp, 90-04 161st St, Jamaica, NY 11432, **Business Phone:** (718)291-0282.

**LOKEMAN, JOSEPH R.**
Accountant. **Personal:** Born Jul 24, 1935, Baltimore, MD; son of Joseph Miles and Beulah V; married Shirley M; children: Pamela C, Kimberly S, Sherre & Shereen J. **Educ:** AS, 1967; BS, 1969. **Career:** Pub acct, enrolled agt, pvt pract, 1967-; Bur Pub Debt Treas, auditor, 1968-70; Bur Acct Treas, staff acct, 1971-73; Bur Govt Fin Opers Treas, syst acct, 1973-84, chief gen ledger br, treas, 1984-90. **Orgs:** Fed Govt Accts Asn; Nat Soc Pub Accts; Nat Soc Black Accts; Nat Soc Enrolled Agents; Md Soc Accts, Notary Pub; White Oak Civic Asn Silver Spring. **Honors/Awds:** Gallatin Award, 1990. **Home Addr:** 12 David Ct, Silver Spring, MD 20904, **Home Phone:** (301)622-2695. **Business Addr:** Public Accountant, 4022 Edmondson Ave, Baltimore, MD 21229, **Business Phone:** (410)362-6500.

**LOMAS, DR. RONALD LEROY**
Educator. **Personal:** Born May 21, 1942, Rock Island, IL. **Educ:** Western IIll Univ, BA, speech commun, 1965, MA, speech commun, 1967; Bowling Green State Univ, PhD, speech commun, 1976. **Career:** Western Ill Univ, grad asst dept speech, 1965-66; Lorain City Comm Col, adj prof, speech & dir forensics, reg adv, 1969-76; Bowling Green State Univ, grad asst dept speech, 1969-70, instr speech & ethnic studies, asst prof, 1969-75, asst dir ethnic studies, 1970-75; Univ Cincinnati Med Sch, coord supportive serv, 1975-76, Med Sch Libr, adminr; Tex Southern Univ, Houston, assoc prof, speech comm, 1976-2009; San Jacinto Col, adj prof, 1987-98; Houston Community Col, adj prof, 1999-, prof speech. **Orgs:** Chmn fac eval comt, Lorain County Community Col, 1968-69; chmn, Minority Affairs Comt, 1968-69; adv, Black Progressives, 1968-69; producer, "Black Perspectives", WBGU Channel 70, 1971; consult & lectr, Black Cult St Pauls Episcopal Church Maumee, Ohio, 1972-73; leadership consult B'naiB'rith Youth Org, S Euclid, OH, 1972-73; Lorain Coun, 1970-71; Mich Coun, 1973; Int Commun Asn; Speech Commun Asn; producer, host & writer prog WBGU Channel 57, 1973; commun consult, Title I Grant Toledo Minority Businessmen, 1974-75. **Honors/Awds:** Foreign Serv Scholar, 1964; Omicron Delta Kappa, 1973; Distinguish Faculty Award, 1974; Outstanding Instructor, Texas Souther University, 1980; student organization named in honor, Texas Southern University; Teacher of the Year, Bowling Green State Univ, Tex Southern Univ. **Home Addr:** 22618 Meadowgate Dr, Spring, TX 77373. **Business Addr:** Adjunct Professor, Houston Community College, 3100 Main St, Houston, TX 77002, **Business Phone:** (713)718-6360.

**LOMAX, JANET E.**
Television journalist. **Personal:** Born Jan 18, 1955, Louisville, KY; daughter of James A and Sedalia M; married Charles V Smith; children: Erica Claire Smith & Charles Smith. **Educ:** Murray State Univ, BS, jour & radio/TV prod, 1976. **Career:** WAVE-TV3, Louisville, Ky, photogr, host, producer, journalist & reporter, 1976-80; WHEC-TV, anchor, 1980; NEWS 10NBC, Rochester, NY, reporter, co-anchor, currently, broadcast journalist. **Orgs:** Nat Asn Black Journalists, 1978-; founding pres, Rochester Asn Black Communicators, 1982; Delta Sigma Theta, 1975-; pres, Rochester Chap; bd dir, Community Heating Fund; RABJ; Jack & Jill Am Inc; Links Inc. **Honors/Awds:** Numerous awards, Louisville, KY, 1976-80; Communications Award, Delta Sigma Theta, 1987; Communicator of the Year, Rochester Advert Asn, 1989; Award winning News Anchor, News10NBC. **Business Addr:** Co-Anchor, NEWS 10NBC, 191 E Ave, Rochester, NY 14604, **Business Phone:** (585)546-5670.

**LOMAX, MICHAEL WILKINS**
Educator, executive. **Personal:** Born Philadelphia, PA; married Dr A Faye Rogers; children: Lauren. **Educ:** St Josephs Univ, BS, soc, 1973; Am Col Ins, cert; Pa State Univ, Sch Grad Prof Studies, Great Valley, MS, leadership develop, 2009. **Career:** Colonial Penn Ins, asst vpres claims, 1984-87; Allstate Ins, claims mgt, 1973-84, field sales leader, 1984-2010; Strategic Leadership Systs, Sr Managing Mem, 2010-; Force 5 Group LLC, chief bus develop officer, 2013-16; Jones Col, adj prof & Assoc Dean, 2016-; Va Col Jacksonville Fla, adj prof, 2014-15; Keiser Univ, Adv Bd Mem, 2014-. **Orgs:** Ins Ed Dir Soc, 1982; Black Exec Exchange Prog Urban League, 1982; bd dir, Brockport Found, 1983-84; mem Wayne PA chaptet, Bus Network Int, 2011-13. **Home Addr:** 2041 Stoneridge Lane, Villanova, PA 19085-1735, **Home Phone:** (610)525-6009. **Business Addr:** Managing Member, Strategic Leadership Systems LLC, 600 W Germantown Pke Suite 400, Plymouth Meeting, PA 19462-1046, **Business Phone:** (570)337-3497.

**LOMBARD, GEORGE PAUL**
Baseball player, baseball executive. **Personal:** Born Sep 14, 1975, Atlanta, GA; son of Posy. **Educ:** Univ Phoenix, attended 2013. **Career:** Baseball player (retired), baseball coach; Atlanta Braves, 1994, 1998-2000; Eugene Emeralds, 1995; Macon Braves, 1995-96; Durham Bulls, 1997, 2003; Greenville Braves, 1998, 2002; Richmond Braves, 1999-2002; Detroit Tigers, 2002; Tampa Bay Devil Rays, 2003; Boston Red Sox, outfielder, 2004; Portland Sea Dogs, 2004; Pawtucket Red Sox, 2004-05; Wash Nationals, 2006, 2007; New Orleans Zephyrs, 2006; Columbus Clippers, 2007, 2009; Las Vegas 51s, 2008; Albuquerque Isotopes, 2008; Marlins, 2008; Cleveland Indians, 2009; Lowell Spinners, hitting coach, 2010; Boston Red Sox, Gulf Coast League mgr, 2011-12, outfield & baserunning coordr, 2012-. **Special Achievements:** First American baseball player to hit a home run, MLB China Series, 2008. **Business Addr:** Base Running Coordinator, Boston Red Sox, Fenway Pk, Boston, MA 02215, **Business Phone:** (617)267-9440.

**LOMBARD, KEN**
Executive. **Personal:** Born Jan 1, 1954?, Seattle, WA. **Educ:** Univ Wash, BA, commun advert. **Career:** IBM, sales assoc; Johnson Develop Co, pres, cochmn, 1992-2004; Starbucks Coffee Co, pres, Starbucks Entertainment, 2004-08; Econ Resource Corp, exec vpres; investment Banking Div Grubb & Ellis, regional dir; Capri Capital Partners LLC, pres, partner, 2009-. **Orgs:** Bd dir, Timberland Co, 2006-11. **Business Addr:** Partner, Capri Capital Partners, 875 N Mich Ave Suite 3430, Chicago, IL 60611, **Business Phone:** (312)573-5300.

**LONDON, DR. CLEMENT B. G.**
Educator. **Personal:** Born Sep 12, 1928, Trinidad, CO; son of John and Henrietta Myrtle Simmons; married Pearl Cynthia Knight; children: Al Mu. **Educ:** City Univ NY, City Col, BA, 1967, MA, 1969; Columbia Univ, Teachers Col, NY, EdM, 1972, EdD, 1974. **Career:** Toco & Morvant EC Elem Schs, Trinidad-Tobago Sch Syst, Trinidad, WIndies, asst prin, 1953-60; St Augustine Parochial Sch, Brooklyn, NY, teacher, 1960-61; Harlem Hosp Sch Nursing, New York, sec & registr, 1963-66; Develop & Training Ctr, Dist rb tv Trades Inc, NYC, instr math & eng, 1967-70; Crossroads Alternative HS, asst prin & dean, 1970-71; Columbia Univ, Teachers Col, New York, grad asst & instr, 1971-73; Intermediate Sch, substitute teacher math, 1974; Fordham Univ, Lincoln Ctr, Grad Sch Educ, from asst prof educ to assoc prof educ, 1974-91, prof educ, prof emer educ, currently. **Orgs:** Nat Alliance Black Sch Educr, 1975; ed Curric Career, Ed & Dev Demonstration Proj Youth, 1978; ed consult, Nat Coun Negro Women, 1978; Asn Teacher Educr, 1979; summer chmn, Div Curric & Teaching, 1979; bd elders, Coun Mwamko Wa Siasa Educ Inst, 1980; Nat Sch Bd Asn, 1980-; Org Am Historians, 1980; Asn Caribbean Studies, 1980-; Am Asn Advan Humanities, 1980; Am Acad Polit & Social Sci, 1980-; reporter & bd dir, Kappa Alpha Psi, 1980-; fac & sec, Sch Educ, Fordham Univ, 1981; Salem Cot Serv Coun New York, 1981; Jour Curic Theorizing, 1982-; dir, Proj Real, 1984; bd dir Solidaridad Humana, 1984; bd mem, Schomburg Corp, Ctr Res Black Cult, 1992-; bd mem, ALL Bereavement Ctr Ltd, 1996-; fac adv, exec comt, Phi Delta Kappa; Kappa Delta Pi; adv bd, curric consult, La Nueva Raza Half House prog; bd mem, African Heritage Studies Asn; Am Mus Natural Hist; Libr Cong; Acad Am Poets; Asn Supv Curric Develop; Ed Bd, Col Stud Jour; advisor, Ndak State Univ. **Honors/Awds:** Clement London Day, Celebrant, Toco Anglican Elem Sch, 1977; Spec Recognition Award, Outstanding Quality, Proj Real, 1983. **Special Achievements:** Author, numerous research publications & professional activities including: "Black Women of Valor," African Heritage Studies Association Newsletter, p 9, 1976; History and Other Disciplines, 1977; 2 video-taped TV appearances: Natl TV Trinidad, WIndies, featuring emotionally oriented issues, 1976-77; "Conf Call, The Caribbean & Latin America", WABC Radio, 3 hour broadcast, 1979-80; "Career & Employment, Critical Factors in Ed Plng," African American Journal for Research & Education, 1981; "Crucibles of Caribbean Conditions, Factors of Understanding for Teaching & Learning Caribbean Students American Editorial Settings" Journal of Caribbean Studies, 2&3, p 182-188, Autumn/Winter 1982; Through Caribbean Eyes, 1989; Test-taking Skills:Guidelines for Curricular & Instructional Practices, 1989; A Piagetian Construct vist Perspective on Curriculum, 1989; On Wings of Changes, 1991; "Multicultural Curriculum Thought: A Perspective," 1992; "Multicultural Education and Curriculum Thought: One Perspective," 1992; "Curriculum as Transformation: A Case for the Inclusion of Multi culturality", 1992; "ARO Catholic School NYC", Black Educator in the Univ Role as Moral Authority Clg Stdnt Jrnl Monograph 18(1 Pt 2), Career Ed for Educational Ldrs, A Focus on Decision Making 1983, Parents and Schools, 1993: A sourcebook, Garland Publishings, Inc, 1993; A critical perspective of multi culturality as a philosophy for educational change, Education, 114(3), p 368-383, 1994; Three Turtle Stories, 1993; New Mind Productions, Inc, 1994; Linking cultures through literacy. A perspective for the future, In NJ Ellsworth, CN Hedleyand AN Baratta (Eds), Literacy: A redefinition, Lawrence Erlbaum Associates, 1994; Queens Public Access Television, discussing Fordham University Graduate School of Education and its leadership role in Language, Literacy, and Learning, 1994; Enchanted Village & Other Stories, Crossing Boundaries, Spring Poems for Children Everywhere, Beyond the Beaches, 2000; On an Archipelago of Words, 2000; Caribbean Visions in Folktales, 2002. **Home Addr:** 352 Greenwich St Apt B, New York, NY 10013-2332, **Home Phone:** (212)962-0682. **Business Addr:** Professor Emeritus of Education, Fordham University, Lincoln Ctr Campus, New York, NY 10023-7478, **Business Phone:** (212)636-6453.

**LONDON, DENISE**
Marketing executive. **Educ:** Glassboro State Col; Tex A&M Univ, bus admin; Univ Cambridge, Eng; Rowan Univ, BA, law. **Career:** Tex State Aquarium, dir mkt, 1989-91; Nat Aquarium Baltimore, vpres mkt, sr mkt dir, 1995-99; London Group Ltd, chief exec officer, 1998-2008; NJ Performing Arts Ctr, asst vpres corp, 2007-08; Denijon

Enterprises LLC, mkt & commun exec, pres, 2008-; Bariatric Beauty Queen, owner, 2011-; Patrol officer; Ford Motor Co, zone mgr; Brdcst sta, acct exec. **Orgs:** Assoc vpres commun, Am Bible Soc, 2001-06; Am Mkt Asn; Am Zool Aquarium Asn; Am Asn Mus; Pub Rels Soc Am. **Honors/Awds:** Best of Tex & Silver Spur Award, Tex Pub Rels Soc; Award of Excellence, YWCA Am; Gold Key Award, Ford Motor Co; Comm Serv, Mayor's Baltimore Citation; Torchbearers Award, 100 Black Women; Marketing Excellence, American Marketing Assn; Award of Excellence for Magazine, EPA. **Special Achievements:** First African-American to be named senior director of marketing, The Nat Aquarium, Baltimore; First female patrol officer, Camden co, NJ. **Home Addr:** 12039 White Cord Way, Columbia, MD 21044. **Business Addr:** President, Denijon Enterprises LLC, 15 Masters Blvd, Piscataway, NJ 08759, **Business Phone:** (917)509-6664.

## LONDON, EDDIE

Educator, executive. **Personal:** Born Nov 25, 1934, Morgan City, LA; married Karolyn L; children: Lori B. **Educ:** Pepperdine Univ, AA, BA, electronics, econs, MBA. **Career:** Design technician, 1965-70; Navy, mgt analyst, 1970-71, oper res analyst, 1971-73; Pac Missile Ctr Div Head, analyst, 1974-90; London Enterprise Info Syst, pres, 1990-; Oxnard Col, Instr; Lifestyles Recovery Ctr, chmn & chief financial officer, currently. **Orgs:** Nat Asn Advan Colored People, 1992-; pres, Oxnard-Ventura Nat Asn Advan Colored People; bd, Prof Employees; chmn, Grass Roots Poverty Prog; pres, San Luis Obispo Co. **Honors/Awds:** Fed Exe Bd Outstanding Mgt, 1983. **Special Achievements:** Certified by the American Red Cross as a HIV/AIDS instructor. **Home Addr:** 2655 Campo Rd, Atascadero, CA 93422, **Home Phone:** (805)461-3841. **Business Addr:** Chairman, Chief Financial Officer, Lifestyles Recovery Center Inc, 715 24th St Suite P, Paso Robles, CA 93446, **Business Phone:** (805)238-2290.

## LONDON, DR. EDWARD CHARLES

Real estate executive. **Personal:** Born Aug 18, 1944, Memphis, TN; son of James Sr and Juanita S; married Nell R; children: Edwin C & Torrick. **Educ:** LeMoyne-Owen Col, BA, econ, 1967; Atlanta Univ, MBA, 1972; John Marshall Law Sch, JD, 1975. **Career:** Metrop Atlanta Rapid Transit Authority, fed grants, sr acct, 1973-75, sr contracts admin, 1975-79, mgr contracts, 1979-81; Edward C London & Assocs, Real Estate & Mgt Consult, pres, 1981-, chmn, prin, chief exec officer, deacon & vpres, 2005-; Cornelius King & Son Inc, Atlanta, GA, chief exec officer, managing broker, 1988-94; Empire Bd Realtists Inc, pres & chief exec officer, 1989-90, 1993-95; Harold A Dawson Co Inc, exec vpres. **Orgs:** Chmn bd dir, Reach-Out Inc, 1979-84; comt mem, Ga Real Estate Comn Educ Adv Comt, 1983-87; coordr, Pastor's Higher Ground Task Force Antioch Baptist Church, 1984-86; bd mem, GA Chap Nat Soc Real Estate Appraisers, 1986-87; Real Estate Educr Asn, 1987; mem bd dir, 1st vpres Empire Real Estate Bd Inc, 1987; sr mem & cert real estate appraiser, Nat Asn Real Estate Appraisers, 1987; cert sr mem, Nat Soc Real Estate Appraisers, 1989-; Bd Zoning Appeals, Fulton County GA, 1987-; bd dir, Community Housing Resources Bd Atlanta, 1987-; US Dept HUD, Reg Adv Bd, 1991-95; bd dir, Atlanta Urban Residential Finance Authority/Atlanta Develop Authority, 1993-; vpres, pres & CEO, Nat Asn Real Estate Brokers, 2001-03, 2011; Fannie Mae Nat Adv Coun Nat Housing Impact Coun, 2001-03; Chase Home Finance Corp Adv Bd, 2003-04; Bd Comnrs, Ga Equal Employ Opp Comm; Atlanta Com Club; Metro Atlanta Lions Club; Ga Real Estate Comn's Brokerage Task Force; Fulton county Bd zoning Appeals; bd dir, Atlanta Urban Residential Finance Authority; Atlanta Develop Authority; Com Club Atlanta; Alpha Phi Alpha Fraternity, Nat Asn Advan Colored People Atlanta Bus League, Atlanta Exchange, Progressive Alliance, Minority Purchasing Coun, Atlanta Chamber Com; comnr, Ga Comn Equal Opportunity; Geo Real Estate Comn Task Force Brokerage Indust; chmn, bd trustee, Antioch Baptist Church N. **Honors/Awds:** Outstanding Leadership Award, Reach-Out Inc, 1981; Century Club Award, Butler St YMCA, 1986; Outstanding & Dedicated Service Award, Empire Real Estate Bd Inc, 1986; Basic Budgeting & Accounting for Property Management, 1986; Real Estate Broker of the Year, Empire Real Estate Board Inc, 1988; Local Board President of the Year, Nat Asn Real Estate Brokers, 1989; Realtist of the Year, Nat Asn Real Estate Brokers Inc, 1992; Realtist of the Year, Empire Real Estate Bd Inc, 1994; Outstanding Alumnus Award, United Negro Col Fund (UNCF), 1995; Presidential Citation, Nat Asn Equal Opportunity His Her Educ, 1997; Association Partner Award; Ga Real Estate Comn Task Force on Brokerage Indus; National Alumni Councils Outstanding Alumnus Award. **Special Achievements:** Publications Principles of Apartment Management, 1983. **Home Addr:** 3144 Valleydale Dr SW, Atlanta, GA 30311-3064, **Home Phone:** (404)505-7470. **Business Addr:** Principal & Chairman, Chief Executive Officer, EC London & Associates, 101 Marietta St NW Suite 3310, Atlanta, GA 30303-2720, **Business Phone:** (404)688-6607.

## LONDON, GLORIA D.

Banker, executive director. **Personal:** Born Jul 24, 1949, Clinton, LA; daughter of Hampton and Georgia Lee; children: Kena Elizabeth. **Educ:** Southern Univ, A&M Col, BS, bus mgt, 1971, MPA, 1993. **Career:** Premier Bank NA, staff, 1971-91; Life Savings Bank, chief opers officer, 1991-92, chief admin officer, 1992; Southern Univ A&M Col, bus develop specialist, 1994-97; Los Angeles County Develop Capital Fund, exec dir, 1997-; Southern Univ Agr Res & Exten Ctr, Ctr Rural & Small Bus Develop, dir, currently. **Orgs:** Philacter, Alpha Kappa Alpha Sorority; Pi Gamma Mu Hon Soc; Phi Beta Lambda Hon Soc; Beech Grove Baptist Church; NCP; Community Develop Initiative Comt State LA. **Honors/Awds:** Outstanding Soror, Alpha Kappa Alpha Sorority Inc, 1985; Black Achievers Award, Young Men's Christian Asn, 1992. **Home Addr:** 6339 Cedar Grove Dr, Baton Rouge, LA 70812-1732, **Home Phone:** (225)356-3091. **Business Addr:** Director, Southern University Agricultural Research and Extension Center, Rm 191 Ashford O Williams Hall, Baton Rouge, LA 70813, **Business Phone:** (225)771-4107.

## LONDON, DR. HARLAN

Executive, educator. **Personal:** Born Syracuse, NY; married Arcenia Phillips; children: Doran Jarvis (deceased), Judy Karen & David. **Educ:** PhD. **Career:** Professor (retired); Syracuse Univ, Human Develop, dept child & family studies, assoc prof & chair, adv to vice chancellor & provost, 1997, emer prof, currently. **Business Addr:** Emeritus Professor, Syracuse University, 217 Edgemont Dr, Syracuse, NY 13214, **Business Phone:** (315)443-4291.

## LONDON, ROBERTA LEVY

Executive. **Personal:** Born New York, NY; daughter of Carrie Belle Calier Levy and Henry Edward Levy; married Lester Jr. **Educ:** Nassau Community Col, Garden City, NY, AA, 1972; Hunter Col, New York, NY, BA, 1977; Queens Col, Flushing, NY, educ credits, 1978; Adelphi Univ, Garden City, NY, grad cert, 1988. **Career:** Presby Church, New York NY, mgr human resources, Prog Agency, 1981-89; Turner/Santa Fe Construct Co, Brooklyn, NY, coordr Local Laws 49/50; Delta Minerva Life Develop Ctr Inc, chmn. **Orgs:** Lakeview Pub Libr; One Hundred Black Women Long Island, 1979-83; gov, NE Dist, Nat Asn Negro Bus & Prof Women's Clubs Inc, 1987-91; chair, Delta Sigma Life Develop Ctr; bd trustee & chmn, Union Baptist Church, Hempstead, NY. **Home Addr:** 425 Columbia Ave, Rockville Centre, NY 11570, **Home Phone:** (516)678-1894.

## LONEY, CAROLYN PATRICIA

Banker. **Personal:** Born Jun 16, 1944, New York, NY; daughter of Daniel and Edna. **Educ:** Morgan State Univ, BS, 1969; Columbia Univ, MBA, 1971. **Career:** Royal Globe Ins Co, rater, 1962-65; NY Nat Asn Advan Colored People, br mgr, 1965; Human Resources Admin, field auditor, 1967; NY State Senate, res worker, 1967; Citibank, corp lending officer, 1969-77, vpres; Fed Res Bank NY, spec asst, 1977. **Orgs:** Adv bd, Columbia Univ Alumni, 1971-; Nat Credit & Financial Women's Orgn, 1972-74; Urban Bankers Coalition, 1973-80; Nat Asn Accts, 1973; bd dir, New Harlem YWCA, 1975-76; 100 Black Women, 1977-; founder, Carolyn P Loney Scholarship Award, Morgan State Univ; Am Mgt Asn, 1977-; Uptown C C, 1977-. **Home Addr:** 363 Murray Ave, Englewood, NJ 07631, **Home Phone:** (201)569-7418.

## LONG, DR. CHARLES H.

Educator, writer. **Personal:** Born Aug 23, 1926, Little Rock, AR; son of Samuel Preston and Geneva Diamond Thompson; married Alice M Freeman; children: John, Carolyn, Christopher, & David. **Educ:** Dunbar Jr Col, dipl, 1946; Univ Chicago, BD, 1953, PhD, hist relig, 1962. **Career:** Univ Chicago, instr hist relig, 1956-59, asst prof, 1960-62, from assoc prof to prof, 1963-74; Princeton Univ, vis prof, 1961-62; St Xavier's Col, Chicago, Ill, vis prof, 1969; Carleton Col, Northfield, Minn, vis prof, 1970; Duke Univ, prof hist relig, 1974-87; Univ NC, Chapel Hill, NC, Wm Rand Kenan, jr prof hist relig, 1974-88; Univ Tenn, Dept Relig, vis prof, 1980; Univ Pittsburgh, vis prof, 1983-87; Univ Calif, Santa Barbara, Calif, Ctr Black Studies, Dept Relig Studies, prof & dir hist relig, 1992-96, prof emer, 1996-; Syracuse Univ, vis prof; Univ Queensland, Brisbane, Australia, vis prof; Tsukuba Univ, Tsukuba, Japan, Inst Philos, vis prof; Univ SC, vis prof, 2003; Univ Mich, vis prof, 2004; Univ Mo, vis prof, 2005; Univ Capetown, SafricA, vis prof; African Heritage Mus, Philadelphia, consult. **Orgs:** Pres, Am Acad Relig, 1973; Soc Relig Higher Edn; Int Asn Historians Relig; pres, co-founder, Soc Stud Black Relig, 1987-90; Am Soc Stud Relig; bd gov, Univ NC; Press Nat Humanities Fac; chair, Hist Religions Field, Univ Chicago; chair, Comt African Studies, Univ Chicago; dir, Humanities Doctoral Prog; dir, Res Ctr Black Studies; adv bd, Inst Signifying Scriptures at Claremont Grad Univ. **Home Addr:** 405 Wesley Dr, Chapel Hill, NC 27516. **Business Addr:** Emeritus Professor of Religious Studies, University of California, 4001 HSSB, Santa Barbara, CA 93106-3130, **Business Phone:** (805)893-5681.

## LONG, EDDIE L.

Clergy, bishop. **Personal:** Born May 12, 1953, Charlotte, NC; son of Floyd and Hattie; married Vanessa Griffin; children: Eric, Jared & Taylor; married Dabara S Houston; children: Edward. **Educ:** Charlotte Pub Sch Syst; NC Cent Univ, BS, bus admin, 1977; Atlanta Interdenominational Theol Ctr, divinity, 1986; Int Col Excellence, PhD pastoral ministry. **Career:** Ford Motor Corp, sales rep; Atlanta's Morning Star Baptist Church, pastor, 1981; New Birth Missionary Baptist Church, sr pastor, 1987-; Full Gospel Baptist Conv, bishop; Ford Co; Faith Acad, founder & chief exec officer. **Orgs:** Co-chair, Hosea Feed Hungry Proj, 2001; bd trustee, NC Cent Univ, 2002; vice chair, Morehouse Sch Relig; Kappa Alpha Psi Inc; founder & chief exec officer, New Birth Christian Acad; bd visitor, Emory Univ; bd trustee, Young Life; bd trustee, Ft Valley State Univ; bd dir, Safehouse Outreach Ministries. **Honors/Awds:** Hon doctorate, NC Cent Univ; Mdiv, Interdenominational Theol Ctr; Received hon doctorates from NC Cent Univ, Beulah Heights Bible Col Atlanta & Morehouse Sch Relig; Legacy Award, Big Bros & Big Sisters Metro Atlanta, 1999; Faith/Community Leadership Award, 100 Black Men Am, 2003; Trumpet Awards, 2005; Relig Contemp Award, IRC; Champion Award; New York Festival's Silver World Medal; World Media Festival's Intermedia Golden Globe. **Special Achievements:** America's 125 most influential leaders; One of the Most Influential Leaders in Black America, Savoy Magazine; One of first among Baptist clergy appointed to office of Bishop in the newly formed Full Gospel Baptist Convention; Nation's best-known and most influential black clergy to craft a new role for US; Publications: I Don't Want Delilah, I Need You; Power of a Wise Woman; What a Man Wants, What a Woman Needs; Called to Conquer; Taking Over; It's Your Time!; Gladiator: The Strength of a Man; The Blessing in Giving; Deliver Me From Adam; New Birth Missionary Church; Our Mission; The mission of New Birth Missionary Baptist Church is to lead the world to worship God through serving, loving, evangelizing, and making disciples; Attracting.Relating.Transforming; Taking Over. **Business Addr:** Bishop, Senior Pastor, New Birth Missionary Baptist Church, 6400 Woodrow Rd, Lithonia, GA 30038, **Business Phone:** (770)696-9600.

## LONG, GERALD BERNARD

Accountant. **Personal:** Born Oct 19, 1956, Bessemer, AL; son of Edward Beckon Sr and Ruby Stein; married Darlene Gillon; children: Claudia Miranda Horn. **Educ:** Univ Ala, Birmingham, BS, acct, 1983; Mich State Univ, Grad Sch Bus Admin, attended 1989. **Career:** KPMG US, auditor, 1983-87; Peat Marwick Main, asst acct, 1983-84, staff acct, 1984-85, sr acct, 1985-86, level 1 suv, 1986-87, level 2 suv, 1987-88; Booker T Wash Ins Co, dir internal audit, 1988; State Ala Pub Serv Cms, adv staff cpa, 1988-93, dir telecommunications div, 1993-96; Gerald B Long & Co, owner, 1995-; Fresh Anointing House Worship, chief financial officer, 2005-; Premier Financial Serv PC, chief exec officer, 2014-. **Orgs:** Ala Soc CPA's, 1985-; Am Inst CPA's, 1988-; chief financial officer, Fresh Anointing House Worship, 2005-; chief financial officer, Utilities Bd City Tuskegee, 2008; Am Inst CPA's; Govt Finance Officers Asn. **Honors/Awds:** Scholastic Achievement Award, Ala State Univ, 1978; Goldstein Scholar, Goldstein Fund, 1982. **Home Addr:** 7312 Rolling Hills Blvd, Montgomery, AL 36116, **Home Phone:** (334)284-5241. **Business Addr:** Chief Financial Officer, Fresh Anointing House of Worship, 150 E Fleming Rd, Montgomery, AL 36105, **Business Phone:** (334)613-3363.

## LONG, GRANT ANDREW

Baseball executive, basketball player. **Personal:** Born Mar 12, 1966, Wayne, MI; married Nikki; children: Garvis, Gavar, Abagayl & Amiala. **Educ:** Eastern Mich Univ, Ypsilanti, MI, attended 1988. **Career:** Basketball player (retired), broadcast analyst, reporter; Miami Heat, forward, 1988-94; Atlanta Hawks, 1994-96, 1998-99; Detroit Pistons, 1996-98; Vancouver Grizzlies, 1999-2001; Memphis Grizzlies, 2001-02; Boston Celtics, 2002-03; Nat Basketball Asn, 2003; Oklahoma City Thunder Telecasts, broadcast analyst, 2008-14; Fox Sports Detroit, detroit pistons analyst, sideline reporter, 2014-. **Orgs:** Lorenzo Benz Youth Detention Ctr. **Home Addr:** 8501 Morton Taylor Rd, Belleville, MI 48111-5313. **Business Addr:** Detroit Pistons Analyst, Sideline Reporter, Fox Sports Detroit, 26555 Evergreen Meadows Rd Suite 90, Southfield, MI 48076, **Business Phone:** (248)226-9700.

## LONG, DR. IRENE DUHART

Physician. **Personal:** Born Nov 16, 1951, Cleveland, OH; daughter of Andrew Duhart and Heloweise Davis Duhart. **Educ:** Northwestern Univ Evanston Ill, BS, biol, 1973; St Louis Univ Sch Med, MD, 1977; Wright State Univ Sch Med, MS, aerospace med. **Career:** Physician (retired): Cleveland Clin, internship gen surg; Mt Sinai Hosp, resident gen surg; Wright State Univ, Dayton, Ohio, resident aerospace med; Ames Res Ctr, resident, 1981-82; Nat Aeronaut & Space Admin, physician, 1982, Kennedy Space Ctr, Biomed Opers, dir, 1994-2000, chief med officer, assoc dir, 2000. **Orgs:** Aerospace Med Asn; pres, Soc NASA Flight Surgeons, 1999. **Honors/Awds:** Kennedy Space Center Federal Woman of the Year Award, 1986; Women in Aerospace Outstanding Achievement Award, 1998; Soc NASA Flight Surgeons President's Award, 1995; Equal Opportunity Action Committee Group Achievement Award; NASA Outstanding Leadership Medal, 1997; NASA Exceptional Serv Medal, 2000; Ohio Women' Hall of Fame, 2001; Women of Color Technology Awards Conference Lifetime Achievement Award, 2005; Strughold Award, Space Med Asn, 2010. **Special Achievements:** First black woman chief of med at Kennedy Space Ctr. **Business Addr:** Chief of Medical Operations, Associate Director Support Services, NASA, MD-MED, Orlando, FL 32899, **Business Phone:** (321)867-5000.

## LONG, JAMES, JR.

Executive. **Personal:** Born Apr 26, 1931, St. Francis County, AR; son of James Sr and Almamie Gray; married Patricia Hardiman; children: Karen R, Kathryn C, Kaye Patrice H Allen & James III. **Educ:** Lincoln Univ Mo, BS, educ & commun rotc corp engrs, 1954; Northeastern Univ, Boston, MA, Grad Sch, MBA, 1976. **Career:** US Govt Army, Ft Belvoir, officer & AUS, 1954-57, Ft Riley, Kans, officer & AUS Corp Engr, 1954-57; Lincoln Univ Jefferson City, Mo, asst instr & dir stud union, 1957-61; Lincoln Sr High Sch, Kans City, Mo, teacher & coach, 1961-64; Western Elec Co, Lee's Summit, Mo, supvr mfg & safety dir, 1964-69; Gen Elec Co, Lynn, Mass, mgr mfg manpower develop, mgr personnel practices, 1970-74, mgr employee rels LUO, 1974-81, mgr equal opportunity & compliance, 1982-. **Orgs:** Chmn, Lynn Corp Adv Bd Salvation Army, 1982-86; dir, Pvt Indust Coun, 1983-; dir, Action Boston Community Develop, 1984-; dir, vpres, Indust Rels Mass Pre-Engineering Prog, 1985-; dir, Lynn, Mass Hist Soc, 1986-. **Home Addr:** 149 Adams St, Lexington, MA 02420-1840, **Home Phone:** (781)861-9311. **Business Addr:** Manager Equal Opportunity, Compliance, Gen Electric Co, 1000 Wern Ave Suite 14512, Lynn, MA 01910, **Business Phone:** (617)594-2687.

## LONG, JAMES ALEXANDER

Executive. **Personal:** Born Dec 26, 1926, Jacksonville, FL; son of Willie James and Ruby Hawkins; married Ruth Beatrice Mitchell; children: John Alexander. **Educ:** NC Agr & Tech State Univ, BS, 1950; Univ Mich, MA, 1962; Wayne State Univ, post grad study. **Career:** Executive (retired); NC Agr & Tech State Univ, instr Eng & jour, 1950-52; St Paul's Col, instr Eng & jour, 1952-57; Foch Jr High Sch, teacher eng & soc studies, 1957-62, eng dept head, 1962-65; Cooley High Sch, guid counr, 1965-67, asst prin, 1967-70; Northwestern High Sch, prin, 1970-72; Storer Broadcasting Co, gen exec & coordr trng progs, 1972-74, mgr personnel develop, 1974-80, recruiter; Storer Communs Inc, corp vpres personnel develop, 1980-87; Am Civil Liberties Union Fla, exec dir, 1987-88; Am Civil Liberties Union Fla, exec dir, 1987-88; Dade County Pub Schs, educ specialist, 1988-99. **Orgs:** Am Mgmt Asn, 1973-; Am Soc Personnel Admin, 1975-; admin mgmt soc, Phi Delta Kappa Educ Frat; Ind Labor Coun Hr Ctr Albertson NY; Dade's Employ Handicapped Community; exec bd, Goodwill Ind Miami; Lafayette Pk Kiwanis Club; Church Open Door United Church Christ; Alpha Phi Alpha Frat Inc; Alpha Rho Boule Sigma Pi Phi Frat Inc; bd dir, Family Coun Serv Miami; chairperson employ comn, Pvt Ind Coun, Miami. **Honors/Awds:** NC A&T State Univ Gate City Alumni Chap Award; Achiever's Award Family Christian Asn Am Inc, Miami, 1986; Presidential Citation Nat Asn for Equal Opportunity in Higher Educ, Wash, DC, 1986. **Home Addr:** 20 NW 89th St, El Portal, FL 33150-2432.

## LONG, HON. JAMES L.

Judge, lawyer, executive. **Personal:** Born Dec 7, 1937, Winter Garden, FL; son of James J and Susie L. **Educ:** San Jose State Col, BA, 1960; Howard Univ Law Sch, JD, 1967. **Career:** Legis Coun Bur Calif State Legis, grad legal asst; Legal Aid Soc Sacramento Co, grad legal asst; pvt pract atty; Super Ct Bar Asn Liaison Comt, mem; Supreme Ct, judge; Calif State Univ, Sacremento, Calif, asst prof criminal justice; Sacramento Co Super Ct, judge, currently. **Orgs:** Hon mem, Wiley W Manual Bar Asn, Sacramento, Calif; Appellate Dept Super Ct Sacramento Co, 1987; Sacramento City/Co Comn Bicentennial US Const; spec coun, Nat Asn Advan Colored People Western Region. **Honors/Awds:** Law & Justice Award, Sacramento Br, Nat Asn Advan Colored People; Outstanding Contribution Award, Riverside Br, Nat Asn Advan Colored People; Pro Tem Justice Supreme Ct, 1985; Justice Pro Tem, Ct Appeal Third Appellate Dist, 1987; Judge of the Year Award, Sacramento Co Bar Asn, 1998. **Special Achievements:** Co-author "Amer Minorities, The Justice Issue", Prentice Hall Inc, 1975. **Business Addr:** Judge, Sacramento County Superior Court, 720 9th St, Sacramento, CA 95814, **Business Phone:** (916)874-7001.

**LONG, JERRY WAYNE**
Computer executive, president (organization). **Personal:** Born Jun 6, 1951, Murfreesboro, TN; son of Delois and Ernest; married Marjorie E Russell; children: Julian, Jamaal & Khalilah. **Educ:** Mid Tenn State Univ, BS, bus admin, 1972; Univ Tenn, MBA, 1980. **Career:** Gen Elec, prog mgr; Conn Gen Co; CG Aetna, proj mgr; Hartford Ins Group, mgr data archit planning; PC Consult, founder & owner, 1988-94; PCC Technol Group LLC, founder, pres & chief exec officer, 1994-; Simsbury Bank, bd dir, dir, 2010-; SBT Bancorp Inc, bd dir; Charter Oak State Col, vice chmn, bd trustee, currently. **Orgs:** Pres, Black Data Processing Asn, Bloomfield Chamber Com; Bus Leadership Circle, 1998; bd dir, Conn Bus & Indust Asn; Kappa Alpha Psi Fraternity; chmn, Metro Hartford Chamber Com, currently; treas, Hartford Chap, Black Data Processing Assocs; chmn, Bloomfield Econ Develop Comn; dir, Hartford Educ Found; Rotary Club Bloomfield; dir, Hartford Youth Scholars Found; pres, Conn Chamber Com. **Honors/Awds:** Metro Hartford Bus Leader Year Technol, 2000. **Home Addr:** 17 Avery Rd, Bloomfield, CT 06002-4318. **Business Addr:** President, Chief Executive Officer, PCC Technology Group, 2 Barnard Lane, Bloomfield, CT 06002, **Business Phone:** (860)242-3299.

**LONG, JOHN EDDIE**
Radio host, basketball player. **Personal:** Born Aug 28, 1956, Romulus, MI. **Educ:** Univ Detroit Mercy, attended 1978. **Career:** Basketball player (retired), radio analyst; Detroit Pistons, shooting guard, 1978-86, 1988-89, 1990-91, radio analyst, currently; Ind Pacers, shooting guard, 1986-89; Atlanta Hawks, shooting guard, 1989-90; Tours Joue Basket, France, 1990-91; Sioux Falls Skyforce, 1994; Toronto Raptors, shooting guard, 1996-97. **Honors/Awds:** NBA Champion, Nat Basketball Asn, 1989. **Business Addr:** Radio Analyst, Detroit Pistons, 4 Championship Dr, Auburn Hills, MI 48326, **Business Phone:** (248)377-0100.

**LONG, JOHN EDWARD**
Educator. **Personal:** Born Mar 16, 1941, Philadelphia, PA; son of William (deceased) and Lena R Bowman (deceased); married Carolyn Yvonne Wakefield. **Educ:** Temple Univ, BA, psychol, 1963; Theol Sem Reformed Episcopal Ch, BD, 1966; Westminister Theol Sem, MA, mediter studies, 1970; Brandeis Univ, MA, PhD, class & orient studies, 1978. **Career:** Western Ky Univ, dept head, assoc prof relig studies, currently. **Orgs:** Fulbright-Hays Res Fel, Algeria, 1974-75; Mid E & Studies Asn, 1975; Mid E Inst, 1975; Am Asn Teachers Arabic, 1979. **Home Addr:** 5 Proctor Ct, Bowling Green, KY 42101-3410, **Home Phone:** (270)781-4571. **Business Addr:** Associate Professor, Western Kentucky University, 1906 College Hts Blvd, Bowling Green, KY 42101, **Business Phone:** (270)745-3136.

**LONG, LEONARD C.**
Executive. **Educ:** Univ Tex, MSSW. **Career:** W Dallas Community Ctr, chief exec officer, exec dir, currently. **Business Addr:** Chief Executive Officer, Executive Director, West Dallas Community Center, 8200 Brookriver Dr Suite N704, Dallas, TX 75247-4069, **Business Phone:** (214)630-6281.

**LONG, MONTI M.**
Automotive executive. **Personal:** Born Sep 24, 1957, Chicago, IL; son of Curtis and Edna Phillips Carlson; married Dana L Lucas; children: Tiffany Nicole & Tonya Renee. **Educ:** Glen Oaks Community Col, attended 1977; Ford Dealer Training, 1988; Chrysler Dealer Sem, attended 1989; Chrysler Financial Sem, 1990. **Career:** Clark Equip, qual control, 1979-82; Monti Long's Automobile Referral Serv, pres & owner, 1980-81; M & M Dodge-Honda Inc, salesman, 1982-85; Dick Loehr's Auto Mart, bus mgr, 1985-87; Brighton Ford-Mercury Inc, vpres & gen mgr, 1987-89; Vicksburg Chrysler-Plymouth-Dodge Inc, pres, gen mgr & dealer prin, 1989-; Albion Ford Mercury, pres, 1995-96; Premier Motor Cars Bonita Springs, Owner, 2013-. **Orgs:** Vpres, Jeep Eagle Div, Chrysler Minority Dealers Asn; pvt capitol dealers chmn, 1982-; Chamber Com, 1988-; Nat Asn Minority Auto Dealers, 1988-; Better Bus Bur, 1988-; Mich Automobile Dealers Asn, 1988-; Ford Black Dealers Asn, 1988-; Chrysler Advert Asn, 1989-; Chrysler Dealer Adv Coun, 1992-. **Home Addr:** 5727 Briarhill Dr, Kalamazoo, MI 49009-9536. **Business Addr:** President, Dealer Principal, Vicksburg Chrysler-Plymouth-Dodge Inc, 13475 Portage Rd, Vicksburg, MI 49097-9497, **Business Phone:** (269)649-2000.

**LONG, NIA (NITARA CARLYNN LONG)**
Actor. **Personal:** Born Oct 30, 1970, Brooklyn, NY; daughter of Doc and Talita Long; married Massai Dorsey; children: Massai Zhivago Dorsey II & Kez Sunday Udoka. **Career:** Films: Buried Alive, 1990; Boyz N The Hood, 1991; Made in America, 1993; Friday, 1995; Love Jones, 1997; Soul Food, 1997; Hav Plenty, 1997; The Best Man, 1999; Stigmata, 1999; Held Up, 1999; The Secret Laughter of Women, 1999; In Too Deep, 1999; The Broken Hearts Club, 2000; Boiler Room, 2000; Big Momma's House, 2000; How to Get the Man's Foot Outta Your Ass, 2003; BAADASSSSS!, 2003; Alfie, 2004; Are We There Yet, 2005; Big Momma's House 2, 2006; Premonition, 2007; Are We Done Yet?, 2007; Gospel Hill, 2008; Mooz-lum, 2010; The Best Man Holiday, 2013; The Single Moms Club, 2014. TV Series: "227", 1986; "The BRAT Patrol", 1986; "Fresh Prince of Bel-Air", 1991-95; "The Guiding Light", 1991-93; "Living Single", 1993; "Live Shot", 1995-96; "Moesha", 1996; "ER", 1996; "Black Jaq", 1998; "Butter", 1998; "If These Walls Could Talk 2", 2000; "Judging Amy", 2001-02; "Sightings: Heartland Ghost", 2002; "Third Watch", 2003-05; "Everwood", 2006; "Big Shots", 2007; "Boston Legal", 2007; Big Shots, 2007-08; "The Cleveland Show", 2009-10; "Boston's Finest", 2010; "Chase", 2011; "House of Lies", 2013; "The Divide", 2014. Documentary: The N-Word, 2004; Good Hair, 2009. **Honors/Awds:** Black Star Award, Acapulco Black Film Festival, 2000; Black Reel Award, 2000; Image Award, Nat Asn Advan Colored People, 2000, 2004 & 2005; BET Comedy Award, 2005; Nominated for Blockbuster Entertainment Award, 2001; Hollywood Award, Acapulco Black Film Festival, 2014. **Special Achievements:** Image Award Nomination, Guiding Light, 1993. **Home Addr:** 5851 Bowcroft St Suite 2, Los Angeles, CA 90016. **Business Addr:** Actor, Paradigm Talent & Literary Agency, 10100 Santa Monica Blvd Suite 2500, Los Angeles, CA 90067, **Business Phone:** (310)277-4400.

**LONG, STEFFAN**
Executive, banker. **Personal:** Born Oct 6, 1929, Philadelphia, PA. **Educ:** Howard Univ; Univ Mex; Univ Bridgeport; Am Inst Banking. **Career:** Conn Nat Bank, vpres & mgr. **Orgs:** Treas, Family Serv SE Fairfield Co; Greater Bridgeport Heart Asn; bd mgr, YMCA; exec bd mem, Greater Bridgeport-Stratford Nat Asn Advan Colored People; treas, Hall Neighborhood House; bd mem, St Marks Day Care Ctr; UNA; Nat Negro Col Fund; 2nd pres, UNA Fairfield Co; pres, Japanese Scholar Comt, Univ Bridgeport; treas, Greater Bridgeport Opera Co; treas, Greater Bridgeport Vis Nurses Asn; bd mem, Ital Community Ctr Guild. **Home Addr:** 1087 Broad St, Bridgeport, CT 06604.

**LONG, TERRENCE DEON**
Baseball player. **Personal:** Born Feb 29, 1976, Montgomery, AL; son of Diane. **Career:** Baseball player (retired); New York Mets, 1999; Oakland Athletics, 2000-03; San Diego Padres, 2004; Kans City Royals, outfielder, 2005; New York Yankees, 2006.

**LONG, WILLIAM H., JR.**
Judge. **Personal:** Born Jun 7, 1947, Daytona Beach, FL; children: William III & Cherylen. **Educ:** Univ Miami, BA, 1968; Univ Miami Law Sch, JD, 1971. **Career:** Univ Miami Law Sch, instr, 1970; Opa Locka Mun Ct, assoc judge, 1972; Long & Smith Pa, partner; Long Knox Mays, Pa; Coun Legal Educ Oppor. **Orgs:** Founder, United Black Students Univ Miami, 1968; pres, Black Am Law Students Asn, 1971; chmn, adv comn, Dade Co Comprehensive Offender Rehab Prog Inc; Phi Alpha Delta; Colo Bar Asn. **Honors/Awds:** James E Scott Community Service Award, 1973. **Home Addr:** 8850 N Miami Ave, El Portal, FL 33150.

**LOPES, DAVID EARL (DAVEY LOPES)**
Athletic coach, baseball player. **Personal:** Born May 3, 1945, East Providence, RI; married Linda Lee Van Dover; children: Vanessa. **Educ:** Washburn Univ, BS, educ, 1969. **Career:** Baseball player (retired), baseball coach; Los Angeles Dodgers, infielder & outfielder, 1972-81; Oakland Athletics, infielder, outfielder & designated hitter, 1982-84; Chicago Cubs, infielder & outfielder, 1984-86; Houston Astros, outfielder & infielder, 1986-87; Rangers, first base coach, 1988-91; Tex Rangers, coach; Baltimore Orioles, first base coach, 1992-94; Orioles, first base coach, 1992-94; Padres, first base coach, 1995-99; Brewers, mgr, 2000-02; San Diego Padres, first base coach, 1995-99, 2003-05; Wash Nationals, first base coach, 2006; Philadelphia Phillies, first base coach, 2007-10; Los Angeles Dodgers, first base coach, 2011-.15; Washington Nationals, first base coach, 2016. **Honors/Awds:** All-Star team;NL Gold Glove winner 1978; Nat League All-Star Team, 1978-81; World Series Champion, 1981 & 2008. **Home Addr:** 16984 Ave De Danta Ynez, Poway, CA 90272. **Business Addr:** Los Angeles Dodgers, 1000 Elysian Pk Ave, Los Angeles, CA 90012-1199, **Business Phone:** (215)463-6000.

**LORD, DR. CLYDE ORMOND, SR.**
Physician. **Personal:** Born Aug 10, 1937, Brooklyn, NY; son of F Levi and Mildred Agatha; married Barbara; children: Sharon, Clyde Jr & David. **Educ:** Univ Vt, BA, 1959; Meharry Med Col, MD, 1963. **Career:** Kings County Hosp, internship, 1963-64; Columbia Presby Med Ctr, resident, 1964-66, fel pharmacol, 1966-67; AUS Hosp, chief anesthesia, 1967-69, asst prof dept anesthesia, 1969-70; SW Community Hosp, staff physician, 1970-; Westside Anesthesia Asn, anesthesiologist; pvt pract physican, currently; Atlanta, GA, pvt prac anesthesiol. **Orgs:** Elder Westend Presby Church, 1973-; AMA; Nat Med Asn; Am Soc Anesthesiologist; Alpha Omega Alpha Hon Med Soc; Am Bd Anesthesiol; fel Am Col Anesthesiol; dipl, Am Acad Pain Mgt. **Honors/Awds:** AUS, maj, 1967-69. **Home Addr:** 1251 Shanter Trl SW, PO Box 42985, Atlanta, GA 30311, **Home Phone:** (404)699-0775. **Business Addr:** Anesthesiologist, Westside Anesthesia Association, PO Box 311135, Atlanta, GA 30311, **Business Phone:** (770)850-1887.

**LORENZO, IRVING DOMINGO, JR.** **See GOTTI, IRV.**

**LORTHRIDGE, DR. JAMES E.**
School administrator, school superintendent, executive director. **Educ:** Prairie View A&M Univ, BS, 1964; Calif State Univ, Long Beach, MA, 1970; Claremont Grad Sch, PhD, 1974. **Career:** School superintendent (retired), school administrator; Mt Pleasant Sch Dist, asst supt, 1978, supt, 1978-79; Rockefeller Found, post doctoral, 1978; W Valley Community Col, dir personnel, 1979-83; Stockton Unified Sch Dist, supt, 1983-86; Ithaca City Sch Dist, supt. **Orgs:** Bd mem, Mt Pleasant Sch Bd; Calif Asn Sec Sch Admin, Am Asn Sec Sch Admin, Asn Calif Sch Admin; Phi Delta Kappa, Nat Asn Advan Colored People; hon life mem, PTA; panel mem, Am Arbit Asn. **Honors/Awds:** Hon Serv PTA. **Home Addr:** 5609 Pintail Ct, Stockton, CA 95207.

**LOTT, RONNIE (RONALD MANDEL LOTT)**
Football player. **Personal:** Born May 8, 1959, Albuquerque, NM; son of Roy; children: Ryan Nece; married Karen Collmer; children: Hailey, Isaiah, Anthony Jose Leon & Chloe. **Educ:** Univ Southern Calif, BA, public admin, 1981. **Career:** Football player (retired), executive; San Francisco 49ers, corner back, 1981-84, free safety, 1985-90, 1995; All Stars Helping Kids, owner & pres, 1989-; Los Angeles Raiders, strong safety, 1991-92; New York Jets, 1993-94; Kans City Chiefs, 1995; Fox NFL Sunday, analyst, 1996-97; Tracy Toyota, owner, 2000-; HRJ Capital, managing partner & founder; PAC-12 tv network, currently. **Orgs:** Founder & chmn, All Stars Helping Kids, 1989-; bd dir, GSV Capital Corp, 2015; bd dir, Positive Coaching Alliance; bd selector, Jefferson Awards Pub Serv. **Honors/Awds:** Pro Bowl, 1981-91; Defensive Back of the Year, NFL Alumni Asn, 1983; Pro Football Hall of Fame, 2000; Pro Hall of Fame, 2001; Inducted, Col Hall of Fame, 2002; Defensive IMPACT Player of the Year, 2006; runner-up, NFL Rookie of the Year; All-Pac 10 performer. **Special Achievements:** Films: Fight to Win, 1987; Hawkeye , 1988. **Business Addr:** Owner, President, All Stars Helping Kids, 2901 Tasman Dr Suite 218, Santa Clara, CA 95054, **Business Phone:** (408)934-6980.

**LOTTIER, PATRICIA ANN**
Publisher. **Personal:** Born Feb 18, 1948, Ashland, KY; daughter of Ruth and Melvin; married George; children: Christopher & Shawn. **Educ:** Western Conn State Univ, BS, nursing, 1980; Emory Univ, MS, pub health admin, 1984. **Career:** Baxter Int, southeastern opers mgr, 1982-86; Atlanta Tribune, founder & publ, 1986-. **Orgs:** Jack & Jill, 1984-97; Coalition 100 Black Women, 1990; Links, 1995-; Ga Asn Minority Entrepreneurs; Atlanta Chamber Com; Atlanta Bus League; adv bd, Clark All Bus SCh; Nat Newspaper Asn; Ga Minority Supplier Develop Coun; Atlanta Asn Black Journalist; Atlanta Asn Media Women; Nat Asn Mkt Developers; Nat Asn Advan Colored People; bd visitor, CDC Found; bd mem, Atlanta AD Club; bd mem, Atlanta Women Network; bd mem, Atlanta Press Club; adv bd, Emory Univ Pub Health. **Honors/Awds:** Hundred Atlanta Women of Power, 1992, Diamond Award, 1993, Trailblazer Award, 1993; Atlanta Bus League Nontraditional Bus Owner, 1998; Female Eentrepreneur of the Year, US Dept Com Minority Develop Agency; Founders Award, GMSDC; Women of Achievement, YWCA. **Special Achievements:** Selected as attache for the 1996 Olympic games by Cayman Island. **Home Addr:** 10005 Fairway Village Dr, Roswell, GA 30076-3718, **Home Phone:** (770)475-2530. **Business Addr:** Publisher, Founder, Atlanta Tribune: The Magazine, 875 Old Roswell Rd Suite C100, Roswell, GA 30076, **Business Phone:** (770)587-0501.

**LOU, DAPPER.** **See DELCY, LUDGET.**

**LOUARD, AGNES ANTHONY**
Educator. **Personal:** Born Mar 10, 1922, Savannah, GA; daughter of Joseph and Agnes; married V Benjamin; children: Rita, Diane & Kenneth. **Educ:** Univ Pa, BA, 1944; Fisk Univ, MA, 1945; Columbia Univ, MS, 1948; NY Univ, add studies, 1972. **Career:** Educator (retired); Manhattanville Neighborhood Ctr, C Div, supvr, 1950-52; Union Settlement Asn, dir rec & educ, 1952-57; E Harlem Proj, dir, 1958-59; Speedwell Serv C NYC, sr caseworker, 1959-61; Leake & Watts C's Home, sr caseworker, 1962-63; Patterson Home Aged, supvr, 1964-65; Columbia Univ, from asst prof to assoc prof, 1965-92, prof, 1992. **Orgs:** Bd mem, Harriet Tubman Comt Ctr, 1965-; James Weldon Johnson Ctr, 1964-69; City Col New York Psychol Ctr, 1969-70; vpres, Pleasant Ave Day Care Ctr, 1971-; Harlem Hosp, 1971-73; bd mem, Peninsula Couning Ctr, 1972-, pres, 1985-88; consult, Spence Chapin Serv Families & C, 1974-; exec comt, State Manpower Servcs Coun, 1977; NY State Employ & Training Coun, 1977-82; consult, Harlem Teams, 1979-82; Alumni Asn Columbia Univ; adv bd, JW Jr Comm Ment Health Bd, 1982-84; panel chmn, staff mediation comm Columbia Univ, 1984-89; consult, Brooklyn Bur Community Servs, 1988-; bd mem, Schomburg Corp, 1988-; NY Coalition hundred Black Women, 1988-; ACLU, Nat Asn Advan Colored People, Common Cause, Urban League, Cottagers; trustee, Union Chapel Marthas Vineyard; NASW; hon comm, Schs centennial, Columbia Univ; founder, V Benjamin & Agnes Louard Scholar; Co-chair, 50th Class Reunion, Alumni Asn Bd conf planning & Int comt, Columbia Univ; Ivy stone Soc. **Honors/Awds:** Class of 1968; Award for dedicated Serv, Peninsula Coun Ctr & Town of Hempstead, NY, 1988; Outstanding Teacher Award, Columbia Univ Sch of Social Work, 1993; Alumini Medal, Columbia Univ, 1998. **Home Addr:** 560 Riverside Dr Apt 6l, New York, NY 10027-3211, **Home Phone:** (212)749-2092.

**LOUCHIEY, COREY**
Football player, executive. **Personal:** Born Oct 10, 1971, Greenville, SC; married Nicole. **Educ:** Univ SC-Columbia, BA, bus, mgmt & retail, 1993. **Career:** Football player (retired), exec; Buffalo Bills, tackle & right tackle, 1993-98; Atlanta Falcons, tackle, 1998-99; Laser Expedited Transp, vpres sales & bus develop, 2006-07; Sterling Interiors Group, bus develop, 2007-10; Axiom Sports & Entertainment, vpres bus develop, 2010-11.

**LOUD, KAMIL KASSAM**
Football player. **Personal:** Born Jun 25, 1976, Richmond, CA. **Educ:** Calif Polytech, San Luis Obispo. **Career:** Football player (retired); Buffalo Bills, wide receiver, 1998-99; Pittsburgh Steelers, 2000. **Honors/Awds:** Rookie of the Year, 1998.

**LOUIS, CONAN N.**
Executive. **Educ:** Georgetown Univ, BS, appl ling, 1973; MS, sociol, 1978; Georgetown Univ Law Ctr, JD, 1986. **Career:** Pvt Law Pract, Wash Off; Wash, social sci res; Georgetown Univ, asst to dean, 1973-75; assoc vpres alumni rel & assoc vpres ext rels; Smithsonian Inst, asst prog dir, 1973-75, 1976-77; DC PRE-TRIAL AGENCY, STAFF INTERVIEWER, 1976-77; Am Correctional Asn, asst prog dir, 1977-79; Univ City Sci Ctr, sr res assoc; dir ling & educ res, 1979-83; WASH & CHRISTIAN, SR ASSOC, 1986-92; GEORGETOWN UNIV, ASSOC VICE PRES EXTERNAL RELS, 1997-98; Howard Univ, vpres adv, 1998-2001; CNL Consult, founder, 2001-; Bentz Whaley Flessner, sr assoc, 2001-05; Nat Asn Adv Colored People, Legal Defense & Educ Fund, dir develop, 2005-06; SEED FOUND, CHIEF DEVELOP OFFICER, 2006-07; Coun Adv & Support Educ, Int J Educ Adv, ed bd; Lassiter & Assocs LLC, vpres & gen coun, 2008-11; JCMCS, COUN & DIR BUS RELS, 2009-11; Nat Soc Black Engrs, chief develop officer, 2010-11. **Orgs:** Nat Asn Adv Colored People; Coun Adv & Support Educ; Nat Col Athletic Asn.SEED Found, chief develop officer, 2006-07. **Business Addr:** Founder, President, CNL Consulting.

**LOUIS, JOSEPH**
Manager. **Personal:** Born Apr 4, 1948, Vacherie, LA; son of Albertha Davis and Marshal; children: Crystal Michelle, Jeremy Allen, Jennifer Ann, Pernell Joseph & David Wayne. **Educ:** Southern Univ, attended 1970; Lamar Univ, environ mgt. **Career:** Manager (retired); BMC Holdings, shift prod mgr; Terminal technician. **Orgs:** Nat Asn Advan Colored People, 1964-; Southern Univ Alumni Fedn, 1970-; Hiram Lodge No 12 Free & Accepted Masons, 1974-. **Special Achievements:** Stratford Business School Achieved an "A" in Business Management, 2008. **Home Addr:** 3046 29th St, Port Arthur, TX 77642-5326, **Home Phone:** (409)982-1569.

**LOUIS, DR. SUCHET LESPERANCE**
School administrator. **Personal:** Born Dec 23, 1935, Port-au-Prince; son of Joseph and Anaida; married Mathilde Clerge. **Educ:** Fac Agron & Vet Med, Damien, Haiti, BS, 1963; Inter Am Inst Agr Fural Scis, Turrialba, Costa Rica, MS, 1967; Univ Calif, Davis, CA, PhD, 1973; Univ Calif, Berkeley, CA, post doctoral studies, 1975. **Career:** Univ Calif, Berkeley, Calif, res assoc, 1974-75; Tuskegee Univ, Tuskegee, AL, asst prof & assoc prof, 1975-83, prof & assoc dir int progs, 1986-89, assoc provost & dir int progs, 1989-, Centennial Planning Comt, OIP, currently, assoc vpres & dir; Tufts Univ, N Grafton, Mass, vis assoc prof, 1983-86. **Orgs:** Am Asn Animal Sci, 1970-; liaison officer, Nat Asn Equal Opportunity, 1986-; trustee, SE Consortium Int Develop, 1989-; Int Adv Coun & Int, 1986-89; chairperson, Interdisciplinary Working Comt & Int, 1989-. **Home Addr:** 612 Green St, Auburn, AL 36830, **Home Phone:** (334)887-6549. **Business Addr:** Associate Vice Provost, Tuskegee University, 1200 W Montgomery Rd, Tuskegee Institute, AL 36088, **Business Phone:** (334)727-8953.

**LOURY, DR. GLENN CARTMAN**
Educator. **Personal:** Born Sep 3, 1948, Chicago, IL; son of Everett and Gloria Roosley; married Charlene; children: Lisa & Tamara; married Linda Datcher; children: Glenn II & Nehemiah. **Educ:** Northwestern Univ, BA, math, 1972; Mass Inst Technol, PhD, econ, 1976. **Career:** Northwestern Univ, asst prof econ, 1976-79; Univ Mich, assoc prof econs, 1979-80, prof econs, 1980-82; Harvard Univ, John F Kennedy Sch Govt, prof econ & afro-am studies, 1982-84, prof polit econ, 1984-91; Boston Univ, prof econ, 1991-2005, univ prof, 1994-2005, Inst Race & Social Div, founder & dir, 1997-2003; Am Enterprise Inst Pub Policy Res, lectr, 1992, 1994; Oxford Univ, vis prof; Tel Aviv Univ, vis prof; Univ Stockholm, vis prof; Delhi Sch Econs, vis prof; Univ de los Andes, Bogota, vis prof; New Repub, ed; Brown Univ, Merton P Stoltz prof social sci & prof econ, 2005-. Books: One by One; From the Inside Out: Essays and Reviews on Race and Responsibility in America, Free Press, 1995; The Anatomy of Racial Inequality, Harvard University, 2002; Ethnicity, Social Mobility and Public Policy: Comparing the US and the UK, Cambridge University, 2005. **Orgs:** John Simon Guggenheim fel, 1985-86; Econ Soc fel, 1994-; Coun Foreign Rels, 1999-; fel AAAS, 2000-; Pub Interest; Ed Adv Bd, First Things; vpres, Am Econ Asn, 1997; Templeton Hon Roll Educ Free Soc, 1997-98; ed bd, Boston Rev; fel Am Econ Asn; fel Economet Socs; fel Am Philos Soc, 2011-; fel Am Acad Arts & Sci; Nat Res Coun; ed adv bd, Am Interest, currently. **Special Achievements:** First black tenured professor of economics in the history of Harvard University. **Home Addr:** 11 Copley St, Brookline, MA 02446. **Business Addr:** Merton P Stoltz Professor of the Social Sciences, Professor of Economics, Brown University, 64 Waterman St, Providence, RI 02912, **Business Phone:** (401)863-2606.

**LOVE, DR. BARBARA J.**
Executive director, consultant, educator. **Personal:** Born Apr 13, 1946, Dumas, AR. **Educ:** Ark State AM & N, BA, 1965; Univ Ark, MA, 1967; Univ Mass, PhD, EdD, 1972. **Career:** Speaker, presenter, consult & writer; Univ Mass, Am herst Campus, assoc prof, assoc prof emer, currently; Fel House, exec dir; Kans City, teacher, 1969-70; Ctr Urban Educ, grad asst, 1970-71, instr, 1971-72; NGO Forums, speaker; U.S Europe Caribbean & Africa, consult. **Orgs:** Panel Am Women, 1968-70; Urban Coalition Task Force Educ, 1968-70; comm rep, Nat Teachers Corps, 1969-70; task force, Nat Alternative Schs Prog, 1971-73; Nat Alliance Black Sch Educr, 1973; Phi Delta Kappa, 1974; Am Educ Studies Asn, 1974; chair, local sch comt; Diversity & Social Justice; United End Racism; Multicultural orgn develop. **Home Addr:** 23 Arbor Way, Amherst, MA 01002-1694. **Business Addr:** Associate Professor Emeritus, University of Massachusetts, 813 N Pleasant St, Amherst, MA 01003, **Business Phone:** (413)545-6984.

**LOVE, BOB. See LOVE, ROBERT EARL.**

**LOVE, CAROLYN DIANE**
Manager, executive director. **Personal:** Born Dec 30, 1950, Gary, IN; daughter of James and Catherine Ross; married David R; children: Leslie N Holloway. **Educ:** Ind State Univ, BA, social work, 1971; Regis Univ Denver, MA, nonprofit mgt; Antioch Univ, PhD, leadership & chg; Col Inst Leadership Training, cert, 1998; Naropa Univ, cert, authentic leadership; Amos Tuck Sch Bus, advan minority bus exec prog; Univ Wis, cert, minority bus mgt prog cert, minority bus mgt prog. **Career:** JC Penney, retail mgt, 1978-81; Conn Nat Bank, prod mgr, 1981-91; Minority Enterprises Inc, exec dir; Kebaya Coaching Consult Inc, prin, currently. **Orgs:** Exec dir, Denver Metro COC, Small Bus Develop Ctr, 1991-95, vpres county develop; exec dir, Denver Metro Chamber Found, 1994-97; Denver County Leadership Forum, 1992; Leadership Denver Alumni Asn; founding mem, Epsilon Xi Chap Alpha Kappa Alpha Sorority; Assoc Consults Int; Colo Black Women Polit Action; Bd Pres Asian Pac Ctr Human Develop, 1993-95; Shorter AME Church Scholar Comt, 1993-; Leadership Denver, 1994; bd mem, Platte River Industs, 1995-; Jr League Denver Citizen's Adv Comt, 1995-; Conn Housing & Fin Authority, bd mem, 1997-; exec dir, Rocky Mountain Minority Supplier Develop Coun, 1998-2003; bd mem, Mile High United Way; chair, Diversity Giving Campain, 1999; bd mem, Key Bank Conn Adv Bd, 1999; Conn Small Bus Develop Ctr, Adv Bd, 1999; bd dir, Colo Nonprofit Asn, 2011-. **Business Addr:** Principal, Kebaya Coaching Consulting Inco, 3166 W 11th Ave Ct, Broomfield, CO 80020, **Business Phone:** (303)438-0953.

**LOVE, DARLENE (DARLENE WRIGHT)**
Entertainer. **Personal:** Born Jul 26, 1941, Los Angeles, CA; daughter of Joseph Wright and Ellen Wright; married Alton A Allison; children: Marcus Peete, Chawn Peete & Jason Mitchell. **Career:** Songs: "White Christmas", "Winter Wonderland", "Marshmallow World", Back To Mono 1958-69, 1991; "(Today I Met) The Boy I'm Going to Marry, " 1963; "Wait Til My Bobby Comes Home, " 1963; "Christmas (Baby Please Come Home), " 1986; Albums: A Christmas Gift F; Producer of "a celebrated Christmas album", 1963; "Late Night with David Letterman", 1986-92; "Late Show with David Letterman", 1993-; "Rock and Roll Forever", 1978; "Leader of the Pack Original Broadway Cast ", 1985; "Darlene Love Live", 1985; "Paint Another Picture", 1988; "Dick Tracy: Music from and inspired by the film", 1990, "Back to Mono", 1991, "A Very Special Christmas 2", 1992; "The Best of Darlene Love", 1992; "Bringing It Home", 1992; "Grease Is the Word", 1998; "Unconditional Love", 1998; "It's Christmas of Course", 2007; ""So Much Love: A Darlene Love Anthology", 2008; "The Sound Of Love: The Very Best Of Darlene Love", 2011; "The Sound Of Love: The Very Best Of Darlene Love", 2011. **Orgs:** Make a Wish. **Honors/Awds:** Image Award, NCP, 1972; Honorary Citizen, City of Atlanta, 1985; Darlene Love Day delcared, Tocca, Ga, Aug 3, 1991; Rythm & Blues Pioneer Award, 1995; One of the 12 finalists for 2010 induction into the Rock and Roll Hall of Fame, 2009. **Special Achievements:** Published: My Name is Love: The Darlene Love Story, 1998; Film Appearance: 20 Feet From Stardom, 2013. **Home Addr:** PO Box 762, Nanuet, NY 10954, **Home Phone:** (212)242-9551. **Business Addr:** Actor, Talent Consultants International, 1560 Broadway Suite 1308, New York, NY 10036, **Business Phone:** (212)730-2701.

**LOVE, EDWARD TYRONE**
Dean (education), educator. **Personal:** Born Dec 8, 1954, Philadelphia, PA; children: Danielle J Floyd & Keith T Morris. **Career:** Sch Dist Philadelphia, prog dir, 1997-, dean, currently; Elec Factory Concerts, security dir, 1998. **Orgs:** Omega Psi Phi Fraternity, 1975-; Prince Hall Masons, 1977-. **Home Addr:** 5801 Rodman St, Philadelphia, PA 19143, **Home Phone:** (215)748-1134. **Business Addr:** Program Director, Dean, The School District of Philadelphia, 1400 Stitesbury Ave, Wynnmoor, PA 19038, **Business Phone:** (215)581-5647.

**LOVE, DR. ERIC TYRONE LOWERY**
Manager, educator. **Educ:** Brown Univ, BA, hist; Idaho State Univ; Univ Vt, MA; Univ Princeton, MA, PhD. **Career:** Univ Colo, undergrad dir, Dept Hist, assoc prof, hist; Ind Univ, proj cord. **Orgs:** Am Hist Asn. **Special Achievements:** Author: 'Race Over Empire: Racism and U.S. Imperialism", 1865-1900, 2004; "The Way of All Flesh". **Business Addr:** Associate Professor, University of Colorado, Rm 204 234 UCB Hellems, Boulder, CO 80309-0234, **Business Phone:** (303)492-6683.

**LOVE, FAIZON (LANGSTON FAIZON SANTISIMA)**
Actor. **Personal:** Born Jun 14, 1968, Santiago de Cuba. **Career:** Films: Bebe's Kids, 1992; The Meteor Man, 1993; Fear of a Black Hat, 1994; Friday, 1995; Don't Be A Menice, 1996; A Thin Line Between Love & Hate, 1996; BAPS, 1997; The Players Club, 1998; The Replacements, 2000; Made, 2001; Mr Bones, 2001; Blue Crush, 2002; Wonderland, 2003; Elf, 2003; TheFighting Temptations, 2003; Torque, 2004; Rumble, 2006; Who's Your Caddy?, 2007; Tao of the Golden Mask, writer & dir, 2007; A Day In my life, 2009; Couples Retreat, 2009; Life as We Know It, 2010; Big Mommas: Like Father, Like Son, 2011; Zookeeper, 2011; Shredd, 2011; King of the Underground, thanks, 2011; Budz House, 2011; Co2, 2011; White T, 2013; Q, 2014; Matthew 18, 2014; Tell, 2014. TV series: "Comic Justice", writer, 1993; "The Parent Hood", 1995-98; "Play'd: A Hip Hop Story", 2002; "Just My Luck", 2005; "Animal", 2005; "It's Always Sunny in Philadelphia", 2007; "My Name Is Earl", 2009; "Mr. Box Office", 2013. **Honors/Awds:** Action on the Film Award, Action Film Int Film Festival, 2007. **Business Addr:** Comedian, Actor, The Artists Group, 10100 Santa Monica Blvd Suite 2490, Los Angeles, CA 90067-4144, **Business Phone:** (310)552-1100.

**LOVE, DR. HELEN ALTHIA MENDES**
President (organization), social worker, consultant. **Personal:** Born May 20, 1935, New York, NY; daughter of Arthur Davenport and Louise Davenport; married Gregory R; children: Sheila & Leon. **Educ:** Queens Col, BA, music, 1957; Columbia Univ, MSW, 1964; Univ Calif, Los Angeles, CA, DSW, 1975; Fuller Theol Sem, 1989; Univ Calif, Los Angeles, PhD. **Career:** Jewish Family Serv, social worker, 1964-67; Big Bros Res Treat Ctr, actg dir, 1967-69; Albert Einstein Col Med, ment health consult, 1969; Hunter Col Sch Soc Work, lectr, 1970-72; Univ Calif, Los Angeles, assoc, 1972-75; Univ Southern Calif, assoc prof, 1975-86; Mendes Consult Serv, founder & pres, 1976-; Pepperdine Univ, social work minor prog, dir, 2001-05. **Orgs:** Chmn, Pastor Parish Rels Comt Wilshire UM Church, 1981-87; Alt Pvt Indus Coun LA, 1984-86; Distrib Success Motivation Inst, 1985-89; bd dir, Jenesse Ctr Inc, 1985-86; Nat Asn Black Soc Workers; Black Womens Network; mem bd dir, House Ruth, 1985-89; vpres, Prof Develop NASW, CA, 1986-88; vpres NASW, CA, 1988-90; bd dir, SISCA; Hollygrove C'sHome, 1987-2004, vpres, 2000-04; bd dir, W Angeles Church God Christ; Acad Cert Soc Workers; Nat Asn Soc Workers. **Home Addr:** 833 5th St Suite 2, Hermosa Beach, CA 90254, **Home Phone:** (310)798-4164. **Business Addr:** President, Mendes Consultation Services, PO Box 62111, Houston, TX 77205, **Business Phone:** (281)540-2124.

**LOVE, CH. J. GREGORY**
Firefighter, commissioner. **Educ:** Wayne County Community Col, AS, fire protection technol; Univ Detroit Mercy, BA, pub admin; Wayne State Univ, ME. **Career:** City Detroit, Detroit Fire Acad, firefighter, capt & instr, 1971-95; Royal Oak Twp Pub Safety Dept, fire chief, 1995-96; Jackson Fire Dept, fire chief, 1996-; Buffalo Fire Dept, dep comnr, 2004-06; Buffalo Niagara Int Airport, Niagara Frontier Transp Authority (NFTA), 2006-09; Int City/County Managers Asn (ICMA), sr assoc ctr pub safety mgt, 2012-. **Honors/Awds:** Numerous citations for bravery & rescue. **Special Achievements:** First African American fire chief in Jackson, MI; Certified by the Michigan State Police Firefighter Training Council as a Fire Officer III. **Business Addr:** Deputy Commissioner, Buffalo Fire Department, Detroit, MI 48226.

**LOVE, JAMES O., SR.**
Law enforcement officer. **Personal:** Born Jan 12, 1957, Chicago, IL; son of Jerry L and Henrietta; children: James O Jr & Jerry L II. **Career:** Chicago Police Dept, police officer, 1985-. **Orgs:** Fraternal Order Police; Carter Harrison/Lambert Tree Soc; Ill Police Asn; Ill Drug Enforcement Officers Asn. **Business Addr:** Officer, Chicago Police Department, 121 N La Salle St Suite 107, Chicago, IL 60602, **Business Phone:** (312)744-4000.

**LOVE, JAMES RALPH**
Executive, president (organization), chief executive officer. **Personal:** Born Apr 2, 1937, Hahira, GA; married Bernice Grant; children: Rhita V, James R II, Gerald K & Reginald. **Educ:** Ky State Col, BS, 1958; Tuskegee Inst, MS, 1968. **Career:** Proj MARK Jackson MS, job developer, 1968; Nat Alliance Bus Denver C of C, mgr, 1968-71; Mt Bell, pub rels, 1971-74; Mutual Benefit Life, thsagt, 1974-79; James R Love & Assocs Inc, pres, 1980-86; Pyramid Fin & Ins Serv Inc, pres & ceo, 1986-. **Orgs:** Pres, Delta Psi Lambda, 1971-74; treas, Denver Bd Ment Retarded & Physically Handicapped, 1972-78; vpres, Park Hill Br Nat Asn Advan Colored People, 1979-80; adv Gov Love Govt, 1969-71; dir, UNCF Co, 1971-72; ethics comm, Denver Area Life Under writers, 1978-79. **Home Addr:** 1532 Galena St Suite 200, Aurora, CO 80010-2236. **Business Addr:** President, Chief Executive Officer, Pyramid Financial & Insurance Services Inc, 1532 Galena St Suite 200, Aurora, CO 80010-2236, **Business Phone:** (303)367-5577.

**LOVE, JON**
Executive. **Personal:** Born Jul 3, 1961, Washington, DC; son of Charles James and Anne Lucinda; married Jeanette Victoria Dorsey; children: Ryan Michael & Jonee Denise. **Educ:** Knoxville Col, attended 1981; Bowie State Univ, BS, 1983; Rutgers Univ, advan mgt prog, 1989; Columbia Univ Exec Educ Prog, mkt mgt, 1995; Mich State Univ, attended 1998. **Career:** AT&T Inc, mgr, 1983-93, gen mgr, sales, 1983-96; Alcatel-Lucent, vpres sales, 1996-2000; Fed Govt Markets, gen mgr bus commun systs, 1993-96; Lucent Technologies, vpres, sales, 1996-2000; Avaya Inc, nat vpres, serv opers, 2000-03; HCI Technologies Inc, chief operating officer, 2003-04; Robbins Gioia LLC, exec vp sales & mkt, 2004-05; Pitney Bowes Govt Solutions Inc, pres, 2005-11; CSC, vpres, bus develop & strategy, 2012-14; ISS Facil Serv, exec vice pres bus develop, 2014-. **Orgs:** Steering comt mem, Mayors Scholar Ball; bd mem, United Way Nat Capital Area, currently; Lau Rawls Telethon; Habitat Humanity; United Negro Col Fund; bd dir, United Serv Orgn; bd dir, Fishing Sch; bd advisor, Us Postal Serv Supplier Mgt; Exec Leadership Coun, 2009-; bd dir, CSC Found, 2013-; bd mem, Hampton Univ Sch Bus, currently; bd mem, United Way Worldwide; bd mem, Detroit Regional Chamber. **Home Addr:** 24068 Windridge Lane, Novi, MI 48374-3652. **Business Addr:** Executive Vice President, Business Development, ISS Facility Services Inc, 1019 Cent Pkwy N Suite 100, San Antonio, TX 78232, **Business Phone:** (210)495-6021.

**LOVE, KAREN ALLYCE (KAREN A WISE-LOVE)**
Newspaper executive, chief executive officer. **Personal:** Born May 22, 1946, River Rouge, MI; daughter of Ruth Lee McIlwain and Joseph William Wise; married John L; children: Schari Alana Dixon & Lloryn Ruth. **Educ:** Ferris State Col, attended 1965; Col DuPage, attended 1975; Los Angeles City Col, attended 1978; Wayne Co Community Col, 1991; Eastern NC Theol Inst, BS, christian studies, 2004; Eastern Mich Univ, sociol, psychol & geront, 2011; Univ Southern Calif, MS, geront, 2013. **Career:** Commonwealth Edison Co, Syst Security Div, 1972-76; Los Angeles Times Co, acct exec, 1976-78; Western States Asn Los Angeles, regional acct exec, 1978-79; Chicago Tribune Media Group, acct exec, regional rep, 1979-86; Security Bank & Trust, acct dept, 1986; Asod Newspapers, retail mgr, 1986-89; Mich Chronicle Newspaper, exec admin asst, 1989, chief operating officer, 2009; KarYzma Media Consult, pres & chief exec officer, 2010-; Presby Village Mich, community connections coordr, Greater Midtown, 2013-; Miss Dept Employ Security, admin law judge iii; Detroit Rescue Mission Ministries, community & media rels; Project LoveSHARE, founder. **Orgs:** Grand officer, Order Eastern Star, 1975-, officer, Heroines Jericho, 1984-; life mem, Publicity Comn, Nat Asn Advan Colored People, 1990-; Ladies Cir Perfection, 1990-; life directions, publicity comn, 1992-; Urban League, publicity comn, 1992-; Nat Newspaper Publ Asn; bd mem, Detroit Symphony Orchestra Inc. **Honors/Awds:** Black Achievement Award, City Chicago, 1981; Benjamin Hooks Outstanding Black Leader, 1991; Woman of the Year, Nat Polit Congr Black Women, 1992. **Home Addr:** 541 Frazier St, River Rouge, MI 48218, **Home Phone:** (313)213-0800. **Business Addr:** President, Chief Executive Officer, KarYzma Media Consulting, 541 Frazier St, River Rouge, MI 48218.

**LOVE, LAMAR VINCENT**
Executive, business owner. **Personal:** Born Oct 20, 1964, Columbus, OH; son of Lamar E and Marie C. **Educ:** Ohio State Univ, BA & BS, 1989. **Career:** Banc Ohio, crt operator, 1981-83, group leader, 1983-86; Lamar Love Co, owner, 1988-2002; Foster & Assoc, sales rep, 1989-90, sales & opers mgr, 1991-92, vpres, 1993-95; Action Int, founder, 1993, owner, currently; CML Group, founder, pres & chief exec officer, 2002-10; ActionCOACH, pres & chief exec officer, 2005-09; Synergy Nat, mem, spec proj, 2006-; Wealth Systs LLC, pres & chief exec officer, 2009-13; HealthLinx, mgr client solutions, 2011-. **Orgs:** Vpres, Ohio State Entrepreneur Network, 1988-89. **Home Addr:** 1423 Cottingham Ct W, Columbus, OH 43209-3143, **Home Phone:** (614)235-6158. **Business Addr:** Owner, Action International, 2459 Dorset Rd, Columbus, OH 43221, **Business Phone:** (614)486-4970.

**LOVE, LONI**
Actor, electrical engineer, comedian. **Personal:** Born Jul 12, 1971, Detroit, MI. **Educ:** Prairie View A&M Univ, Tex, BS, elec engineering. **Career:** Xerox, engr; Laugh Factory, performer; IBM, engr; Actress--movie: "Soul Plane", 2004. TV series: "I Love the 70s", 2003; "Hollywood Squares", 2003-04; "I Love the '90s", 2004; "Ned's Declassified School Survival Guide", 2004-07; "TV Land's Top Ten", 2005; "Comics Unleashed", 2006-14; "Chelsea Lately", 2007-14; "Master of Dance", 2008; "The Smoking Gun Presents: World's Dumbest", 2008-13; "Comedy.TV", 2009-12; "The Gossip Queens", 2010-11; "Loni Love: America's Sister", 2010; "Whitney", 2011-13; "Kickin' It", 2011-13. Co-host, TV series "The Real", 2013-14; "Ellen: The Ellen DeGeneres Show", 2013-14; "Bethenny", 2013-14. Movie: "Gunshot Straight", 2014; "Bad Ass 3", 2015; "Paul Blart: Mall Cop 2", 2015; "Mother's Day", 2016. **Orgs:** mem, Delta Sigma Theta. **Honors/Awds:** U.S. Comedy Arts Festival, Jury Prize for Best Stand-up, 2003; "Campus Activity" magazine, Hot Comic, 2009; "Variety" magazine, Top 10 Comics to Watch; Comedy Central, Top 10 Comics to Watch. **Special Achievements:** Author of "Love Him or Leave Him But Don't Get Stuck with the Tab" (Simon & Schuster, 2013).

**LOVE, LYNNETTE ALICIA**
Athletic coach, educator. **Personal:** Born Sep 21, 1957, Chicago, IL; daughter of Dolores Merritt. **Educ:** Wayne State Univ, BFA, 1983. **Career:** Maryland Federal Savings, asst mgr, 1986-89; City Alexandria, recreation supvr, 1993-94; National Team, coach, 1995-2000; Love's Taekwondo Acad, pres, 1994-. **Orgs:** Women's Sports Found, 1988-; vice chairperson, United States Taekwondo Union, 1988-96, vpres, 2001-. **Honors/Awds:** Gold Medalist, Pan American Championship, 1980, 1982, 1984, 1986, 1988, 1990; World Silver Medalist, 1983; Outstanding Female Player, United States Taekwondo Union, 1984, 1988; World Champion, 1985, 1987, 1991; Alumni Award, Cass Technical High Sch, 1988; Sullivan Award Outstanding Sports Performance, Nominated AAU, 1988; Bronze Medalist, Olympic, Barcelona, Spain, 1992; World Cup Silver Medalist, 1983; Gold Medalist, Olympics, Seoul, Korea, 1988; American Female Winner Of The Most National And World Records, Guinness Book Of Records, 1989; World Cup Champion, Madrid, Spain, 1990; Bronze Medalist, Olympic, Barcelona, Spain, 1992. **Special Achievements:** Female Coach, World Championships, 1993; Female Coach, Pan American Games, 1995; Ten-Time National Champion, 1979-87, 1990; Five-Time Pan American Champion, 1982, 1984, 1986, 1988 & 1990; Two-Time Olympic Medalist, Gold, 1988, Bronze, 1992; WMAC Masters, 1995-96; Team Captain, 1989-92; Three-Time World Champion, 1985, 1987 & 1991. **Home Addr:** 6125 Sea Lion Pl, Waldorf, MD 20603-4448. **Business Addr:** President, Owner, Loves Takewondo Academy, 7605 Barbara Lane C, Clinton, MD 20735-1429, **Business Phone:** (301)645-9125.

**LOVE, MIA (LUDMYA BOURDEAU)**
Congressional representative (U.S. federal government). **Personal:** Born Dec 6, 1975, Brooklyn, NY; daughter of Jean Maxine Bordeau and Mary Bordeau; married Jason Love; children: 3. **Educ:** Univ Harford, BFA. **Career:** Continental Airlines, flight attendant; call center manager; fitness instructor; city council of Saratoga Springs, UT, member, 2004-10; mayor of Saratoga Springs, UT, 2010-14; US House of Representatives, member representing the Fourth District UT, 2015-. **Orgs:** House Financial Serv Comt, 2015-. **Special Achievements:** First Republican African American woman elected to Congress; first African American elected to Congress from Utah; first Haitian American elected to Congress. **Business Addr:** U.S. House of Representatives, 217 Cannon House Office Bldg, Washington, DC 20515, **Business Phone:** (801)890-4355.

**LOVE, PRISCILLA MARIE WINANS.** **See WINANS, CECE.**

**LOVE, ROBERT EARL (BOB LOVE)**
Basketball player, basketball executive. **Personal:** Born Dec 8, 1942, Bastrop, LA; married Rachel Dixon. **Educ:** Southern Univ, attended 1965. **Career:** Basketball player (retired), director; Trenton Colonials (EPBL), 1965-66; Cincinnati Royals, 1966-68; Milwaukee Bucks, 1968; Chicago Bulls, 1968-76; New York Nets, 1976-77; Seattle SuperSonics, 1977; Chicago Bulls, dir community rels, 1993. **Business Addr:** Director of Community Affairs, Chicago Bulls, United Ctr 1901 W Madison St, Chicago, IL 60612-2459, **Business Phone:** (312)455-4000.

**LOVE, ROOSEVELT SAM**
Executive. **Personal:** Born Jun 11, 1933, Bulloch County, GA; children: Katheleen, Patricia, Bonnie, Julia & Sandra. **Career:** Love's Fina Serv St, operator; JP Stevens, cement mixer; Gulf Inc, serv sta attend. **Orgs:** Rep, JP Stevens Employ Twisting Dept, 1971; Negotiations Com Textiles Workers Union, 1974; Comn Rels Counc, 1975-77; DUSO develop Unique Serv Ourselves; Comn Action Club; SCWC; pres, Bulloch Co Br Nat Asn Advan Colored People; Bethel Primitive Bapt Ch. **Honors/Awds:** Outstanding Service Award, NAACP, 1977. **Business Addr:** Operator, Loves Auto Shop, 116 E Parrish St, Statesboro, GA 30458-4338.

**LOVE, DR. RUTH BURNETT**
Founder (originator), school administrator, newspaper publisher. **Personal:** Born Apr 22, 1932, Lawton, OK; daughter of Alvin E and Burnett C; married James A Holloway. **Educ:** San Jose State Univ, BA, 1954; San Francisco State Univ, MA, guid & coun, 1959; US Int Univ, Cal Western, PhD, 1970. **Career:** Oakland Unified Sch Dist, teacher, 1954-59, ford found, consult & supt, 1960-62, adult educ teacher, supt, 1975-84; cheshire, Eng, exchange teacher, 1960; oper crossroad, Ghana, proj dir, 1962; Calif State Dept Educ, bur chief & consults, 1963-65, dir, 1965-71; US Off Educ, Wash, DC, dir, Right to Read, 1971; Chicago Bd Educ, gen supt; Calif Voice, publ, currently; San Francisco State Univ, distintuished prof; Ex-publ 9 weekly Black Newspapers; RBL Enterprises LTD, founder, chief exec officer & pres, currently. **Orgs:** Am Asn Sch ADR, 1974-; bd trustee, Morehouse Med Sch, 1976-; vice chair, Pres Ment Health Comn, 1976-79; bd dir, Cities Schs, 1977-; bd dir, NUL, 1977-82; Asn Suv & Counr Develop, 1979-; chair, scholar comt, Links Inc; bd dir, Nat Newspaper Publishers Asn, 1988-; PRSial Con HBUC, 1989-92; bd dir, Pac Grad Sch Psychol; Downs Community Develop Corp; Nat Urban League, Am Asn Sch Adminr; Coun Great City schs; Women Adminr Inc. **Special Achievements:** First African-American and woman to serve as superintendent for the Chicago Public School district. **Business Addr:** Founder, President, RBL Enterprises LTD, 1300 Clay St Suite 600, Oakland, CA 94612, **Business Phone:** (510)622-7707.

**LOVE, THOMAS CLIFFORD**
Editor, college teacher. **Personal:** Born Jul 23, 1947, New Rochelle, NY. **Educ:** Howard Univ, BA, 1969. **Career:** WRC-TV AM-FM, Wash, employ spec, pub serv dir, 1969-71; WABC-AM Radio, New York, pub serv dir, 1971-72, dir comm affairs, 1972-73; WABC AM-Radio NY, ed, community affairs dir, 1973-79; St Johns Univ, adj prof, 1976-78; Montclair St Col, vis prof, 1978-; WABC-TV, ed dir, 1979. **Orgs:** Nat & Int Radio & TV Soc; Nat Broadcast Ed Asn; Alpha Phi Alpha. **Honors/Awds:** NY State Broadcasters Award, 1979, 84; Black Achievers Industry Award, YMCA, 1974; UPI & AP Award, 1974; Andy Award, Merit Ad Club NY, 1978; NY Emmy Award, 1980. **Home Addr:** 65 W 96 St, New York, NY 10025.

**LOVELACE, DEAN ALAN**
Consultant, vice president (organization), government official. **Personal:** Born Jan 31, 1946, Ford City, PA; married Phyllis Jean Rutland; children: Leslie Denise, Laeina Deandra & Dean Nyerere. **Educ:** Sinclair Community Col, AS, bus, 1971; Univ Dayton, BSBA, 1972; Wright State Univ, MS, appl & social econs, 1981. **Career:** Nat Cash Regist, lathe operator, 1965-71; Community Leadership Consult, 1970-; City Dayton, Dept Planning, neighborhood planner, 1973-79, NW Off Neighborhood Affairs, community serv adv, 1977-79, coordr & dir, 1979-80; Univ Dayton, dir neighborhood develop, Strategies Responsible Develop Off, 1983, dir, Dayton Civic Scholars Prog, currently; City Dayton, OH, comnr, 1993-. **Orgs:** Citizens adv coun, Model Neighborhood Community Ctr, 1977-; Econs Resources Comt, Miami Valley Regional Planning Coun, 1977-; chmn, Dayton, Ohio Black Polit Assembly, 1977-; trustee, Housing Justice Fund Inc, 1978-; pres, Edgemont Neighborhood Coalition Inc, 1980-; vpres, Dayton Urban League, 1982-; adv bd, Dayton Found Neighbor Neighbor, 1983-; coun mem, Montgomery County Human Serv Levy, 1984-; chmn, Dayton-Montgomery County Rainbow Coaltion, 1984-; Dayton Anti-Apartheid Comn, 1985-; chair, Dayton Poverty Reduction Forum, Workforce Develop Task Force & Earned Income Tax Credit Initiative; chair, Dayton Community Reinvestment Inst; bd mem, Nat Community Reinvestment Coalition; bd mem, CityFolk; bd mem, Community Action Partnership Dayton; bd mem, Ombudsman's Off; bd mem, Parity Inc; bd mem, St Mary Develop Corp; bd mem, ISUS; Montgomery County Solid Waste Adv Comt & Mgt Police Comt; co-founder, Dayton Dialogue Race Rels; co-founder, Black Leadership Develop Prog, Dayton Urban League; comnr, Social Justice. **Home Addr:** 2532 Madden Hills Dr, Dayton, OH 45417-4448, **Home Phone:** (937)268-4160. **Business Addr:** Commissioner, City Commissioner Office, City Hall 2nd Fl 101 W 3rd St, Dayton, OH 45401-0022, **Business Phone:** (937)333-3636.

**LOVELACE, JOHN C.**
Executive. **Personal:** Born Mar 4, 1926, West Point, GA; married Mary Jean Roebuck; children: Juan Carlos & Carlita Joy (Thomas). **Career:** Pittsburgh Plate Glass Indust Inc; Allegheny-Kiski Valley, pres, 1985-2008. **Orgs:** Drug & Alcoholic Comn; Nat Asn Advan Colored People; mgr, Valley Choraliers Leechburg, 1960-75; Youth Comn, 1968; planning comn Gilpin Twp, 1973-75; bd dirs, Kiski Valley Med Facil Inc, 1974-75; pres, Nat Asn Advan Colored People. **Honors/Awds:** Thalheimer Award, Nat Asn Advan Colored People, 1970. **Home Addr:** PO Box 215, Leechburg, PA 15656.

**LOVELESS, THERESA E.**
Association executive, executive director. **Career:** Executive (retired); Girl Scout Coun, Greater St Louis, assoc exec dir, 1996, chief exec officer. **Orgs:** Missouri Bot Garden Subs Dist Comn; Regional Arts Comn. **Honors/Awds:** Woman of Achievement, 1992. **Special Achievements:** First African American to take helm of Girl Scout Council in St Louis. **Home Addr:** 12773 Pky Estates Dr, St. Louis, MO 63146-3769, **Home Phone:** (314)434-9394.

**LOVETT, DR. REV. LEONARD**
Clergy, consultant, executive director. **Personal:** Born Dec 5, 1939, Pompano Beach, FL; son of Charles and Cassie; married Phyllis Marie Bush; children: Laion, Lamont, Lamar & Mandon. **Educ:** Saints Jr Col, AA, 1959; Morehouse Col, BA, hist/relig & social sci, 1962; Crozer Theol Sem, MDiv, theol, 1965; St Jr Col, DLaw, 1972; Emory Univ, PhD, ethics & soc, 1978; Univ Ghana, cert African studies, 1994. **Career:** Memorial Church God Christ, pastor, 1962-70, ecumenical officer urban affairs; Health & Welfare Coun, Philadelphia, NY City Proj, coordr, 1965-67; Bryn Mawr Grad Sch Social Res, res fel, 1969-70; Stephen Smith Towers 202 Sr Citizens, proj mgr, 1967-70; Church Mason Theol Sem, pioneer pres, 1970-74; Grad Theol Union, Berkeley, visit prof, 1975; Fuller Theol Sem, Black Ministries, assoc dir, 1977-81; Ecumenical Ctr Black Church Studies, prof ethics & theol, 1978-; Am Baptist Sem W, prof ethics & theol, 1984; Black Perspective, Ministries Today Mag, columnist, 1988-; Seminex Ministries, founding chief exec officer, 1994-, consult; Church God Christ Inc, Off Ecumenical & Urban Affairs, exec dir, 2004-14; Ministries Today, columnist; Oral Roberts Univ Sch Theol; C H Mason Sem, dean emer. **Orgs:** Res fel, Community Orgn Res Fel 1969-70; Soc Study Black Relig, 1972-; reactor, Vatican-Pentecostal Dialogue W Ger, 1974; pres, Soc Pentecostal Studies, 1975; vis fel Human Behav Am Inst Family Rels, 1982-85; bd mem, Watts Health Found, United Health Plan, 1985-; bd dir, Interfaith Worker Justice; bd mem, Bread; Order Comn; Nat Coun Churches Faith. **Honors/Awds:** Martin Luther King, Jr. celebrant speaker at scores colleges, universities, churches & military bases throughout North America. **Special Achievements:** Conditional Liberation Spirit Journal, 1977; What Charismatics Can Learn from Black Pentecostals Logos Journal 1980; Tribute to Martin Luther King in Outstanding Black Sermons Vol 2 Judson Press 1982; contrib Aspects of the Spiritual Legacy of the Church of God in Christ in Mid-Stream an Ecumenical Journal Vol XXIV No 4 1985, Black Witness to the Apostolic Faith Eardmans 1988; Black Holiness-Pentecostalism, Black Theology, Positive Confession Theology, Dictionary of the Pentecostal Charismatic Movement, Zondervan 1988; Author: Close Your Back Door, 2002; Kingdom Beyond Color, 2009. **Home Addr:** PO Box 762, Inglewood, CA 90307, **Home Phone:** (213)257-4411. **Business Addr:** Founding Chief Executive Officer, Consultant, Seminex Ministries, 107 SW St Suite 422, Alexandria, VA 22314, **Business Phone:** (800)619-9394.

**LOVETT, MACK, JR.**
Educator. **Personal:** Born Aug 31, 1931, Shreveport, LA; married Marlene; children: Alice, Pamela, Michelle & Albert. **Educ:** Oakland City Col, AA, 1959; Calif State Univ, BA, 1965, MPA, 1970. **Career:** Munic Ct, ct clerk, 1956-65; Litton Indus, instr, 1965-66, admin, 1966-68; Calif State Univ, asst pres, 1968-72, dir instr serv, 1972, asst vpres instr serv, 1978-2000. **Orgs:** Chmn, Polit Actn Com Nat Advan Asn Colored People So Alameda Co Chap, 1958-64; pres, Nat Advan Asn Colored People, 1964-68; bd dir, So Alameda Co Econ Opportunity Orgn, 1965-67; consult, Hayward Univ Sch Dist, 1966-73; dir, Plnd & Appl Res Inc, 1967-68; consult, Calif Employ Serv, 1968; consult, Chabot Comm Col, 1969; dir & treas, Ebony Constr Co, 1972-73; Gr Hayward Kiwanis Serv Club; bd dir, New Lady mag, 1965-70; reg adult, Voca Educ Advis Com; bd mgrs, YMCA Eden area. **Special Achievements:** Published "How to File Your Income Tax", Litton Industrial Education Systems Division. **Home Addr:** 2642 Aspen Valley Lane, Sacramento, CA 95835-2137, **Home Phone:** (916)419-8941. **Business Addr:** Assistant Vice President, Instructional Service, California State University, 25800 Carlos Bee Blvd, Hayward, CA 94542, **Business Phone:** (510)885-3000.

**LOVICK, CALVIN L.**
Publisher, chief executive officer, president (organization). **Personal:** Born Aug 6, 1950, Belhaven, NC; son of Nathan; children: Scott, Christian & Jeannie. **Educ:** Kean Col, BS, 1974. **Career:** CL Lovick & Assocs Inc, chief exec officer, pres, publ, 1979-. **Business Addr:** President, Publisher, CL Lovick & Associates Inc, 8825 Penridge Pl, Inglewood, CA 90305, **Business Phone:** (310)686-8881.

**LOVILLE, DEREK KEVIN**
Football player. **Personal:** Born Jul 4, 1968, San Francisco, CA; married Nina; children: Derek II. **Educ:** Univ Ore, Am studies. **Career:** Football player (retired); Seattle Seahawks, running back, 1990-91; San Francisco 49ers, running back, 1993-96; Denver Broncos, 1997-99; St Louis Rams, runningback, 1999-2000. **Honors/Awds:** Super Bowl Championship, 1994, 1997-98.

**LOVING, JAMES LESLIE, JR.**
Executive. **Personal:** Born Aug 14, 1944, Boston, MA; son of James Leslie and Wauneta Barbour; married Leebertha Beauford; children: Robyn Leslie. **Educ:** Boston Bus Sch, dipl, 1964; Harvard Univ, EdM, 1974, CAS, 1975; Aenon Bible Col, DD. **Career:** City Boston, spec asst mayor, 1972-77; US Dept HHS, spec asst, 1977-80, prin regional off Denver, 1980, actg dep, 1980-81; Stud Nat Med Asn, exec admin, 1981-83; Data Processing Inst, vpres, 1983-86; Career Bus Acad, pres, 1986-90; Long & Foster Real Estate Inc, real estate agt, currently; Global Mortgage Bankers Corp, pres. **Orgs:** Treas, Boston Br Nat Asn Advan Colored People, 1972; dir, Boston Legal Asst Proj, 1972; Norfolk Prison Fel 1972-76; chmn, Roxbury Cancer Crusade, 1974; bd dir, Montessori Sch, 1974-76; hew fel US Dept Health Ed & Welfare, 1977; trustee, Emmanuel Temple Church, 1977; nat coord, Dr King 51st Celebration, 1980; treas, Nat Young Peoples Union, 1982. **Honors/Awds:** United Student Oakwood Coll Huntsville, 1975; Outstanding Young Men of America, 1976; 100 Black Influentials, 1976; Finalist White House Fellows Prog, 1977; Outstanding Leader, JCs Boston Chap, 1978. **Home Addr:** 8717 Baskerville Pl, Upper Marlboro, MD 20772-5101, **Home Phone:** (301)627-5267. **Business Addr:** Real Estate Agent, Long & Foster Real Estate Inc, Ellipse at Westfield's 14501 George Carter Way, Chantilly, VA 20151, **Business Phone:** (301)843-3600.

**LOWE, EUGENE YERBY, JR.**
Clergy, school administrator. **Personal:** Born Aug 18, 1949, Staten Island, NY; son of Eugene Y Sr and Miriam V; married Jane Pataky Henderson; children: Benjamin & Sarah. **Educ:** Princeton Univ, BA, relig, 1971; Union Theol Sem, MDiv, Divinity, 1978, PhD, 1987. **Career:** Princeton Univ, dean studs, 1983-93; Union Theol Sem, tutor, 1979-82; Gen Theol Sem, tutor, 1978-80; Parish Calvary & St George's, asst minister, 1978-82; Chase Manhattan Bank, vpres, 1973-76; St Agatha Home C, soc work asst, 1971-73; Northwestern Univ, assoc provost fac affairs, sr lectr relig, 1995; Northwestern Univ, asst to pres, 1999-, Mellon postdoctoral prog humanities, prin investr, 1996, coordr, Mellon Mays Undergrad Fel Prog, 2008-09; Weinberg Col Arts & Sci, sr lectr. **Orgs:** Trustee, Princeton Univ, 1971-83; trustee, Elizabeth Seton Col, 1972-83; Comn Soc Responsibility & Investments, Exec Coun Episcopal Church, 1976-81; dir, Forum Corp Responsibility, 1976-80; Coun Foreign Rels, 1977-81; Northwestern Fac Adv Coun Ill Bd Higher Educ; Sr Diversity Officers Group Comt Instnl Coop; trustee, Berea Col, 1995-; Relig dept, Princeton Univ; pres bd, Episcopal Charities & Community Serv Chicago; trustee, Seabury-Western Sem, 1996-; Teagle Found, Am Acad Relig relig studies maj & lib educ; consult-evaluator, US Dept Educ & Pew Charitable Trusts; mem external adv bd, Stanford Univ Ctr Comparative Study Race & Ethnicity; trustee, Berea Col, Berea, Ky, & Seabury Western Theol Sem Evanston; Phi Beta Kappa; fel FundTheol Educ, 1976-77; fel Episcopal Ch Found, 1978-80. **Honors/Awds:** The Harold Willis Dodds Prize, Princeton Univ, 1971. **Special Achievements:** Promise and Dilemma, Perspectives on Racial Diversity and Higher Education, Princeton University Press, 1999; Charles H; Williams, Peter, Encyclopedia of Religion in America, SAGE Publications, 2010. **Home Addr:** 624 Colfax St, Evanston, IL 60201-2808, **Home Phone:** (847)866-9211. **Business Addr:** Assistant to the President, Senior Lecturer, Northwestern University, Rm 2-145 Rebecca Crown Ctr, Evanston, IL 60208-1100, **Business Phone:** (847)491-5255.

**LOWE, JACK, JR.**
Law enforcement officer. **Personal:** Born Sep 5, 1936, Gadsden, AL; son of Jack Sr. **Career:** Law enforcement officer (retired); Baptist Hosp, staff; Calhoun County, dir nursing; Etowah County Sheriff's Dept, capt, Internal Affairs Comt, chief investr. **Orgs:** Ala New S Coalition.

**LOWE, JACKIE**
Actor. **Personal:** Born Bamberg, SC. **Educ:** Rider Col, attended 1973. **Career:** TV series: "The Guiding Light"; "Edge of Night"; "Ryan's Hope"; "The Merv Griffin Show"; "Easter Seals Telethon"; Films: The Wiz; Daddy Daddy; The First; Eubie; Best Little Whorehouse in TX; Story ville, Selma; West Side Story; Sweet Charity; The Tap Dance Kid; Pippin; J Walter Thompson Advertising, prod asst, 1973-76; Wind in the Willows, 1985; Ain't Misbehavin, 1988-89; performer, currently. **Orgs:** Cord Mothers March March Dimes, 1972; Am Fedn Tv & Radio Artists; Screen Actors Guild; Am Guild Variety Artists; Equity Unions. **Honors/Awds:** Nominated Best Supporting Actress Santa Monica Theatre Guild, 1977; First recipient of Capitol City Dance Award in Recognition for accomplishments in dance fine arts Trenton NJ, 1985. **Home Addr:** 539 Atlantic Ave Apt 2, Brooklyn, NY 11217. **Business Addr:** Actor, Minskoff Theater, 200 W 45th St, New York, NY 10036, **Business Phone:** (212)869-0550.

**LOWE, DR. JAMES EDWARD, JR.**
Physician. **Personal:** Born Dec 5, 1950, Warsaw, NC; son of James Edward and Alice Mae Gavins; married Philamina Lucy Lozado; children: James Edward III, Joseph Alexander & Jesse J Carattini. **Educ:** Harvard Univ, Health Careers Prog, 1970; Livingstone Col, BS, 1971; Univ NC, Chapel Hill, Health Careers Prog, 1971; Meharry Medical Col, MD, 1975. **Career:** State Univ NY Health Sci Ctr, internship, resident; Lutheran Med Ctr, resident; Lenox Hill Hosp,

resident; Downstate Med Ctr, resident surg, 1975-78; Lutheran Med Ctr, resident & chief resident, 1978-81, teaching fel, gen surg, 1981-82, assoc attending plastic & reconstructive surg; Lenox Hill Hosp, plastic surg residency, 1982-84, asst attending plastic & reconstructive surg, 1985-; Beautiful Body Plastic Surg Ctr, surgeon; Roseboro, surgeon. **Orgs:** Phi Beta Sigma Fraternity, 1968-, Nat Asn Advan Colored People, 1985-; CORE, 1985-; NY County Med Soc, 1985-; Nat Med Asn, 1986-; Am Soc Plastic & Reconstructive Surgeons, 1986-; fel Am Col Cardio. **Honors/Awds:** Physician Recognition Award, Am Med Asn, 1998-01; spec lectr, Non-Caucasian Rhinoplasty, Keloid & Hypertrophic Scans; spec lectr, Breast reconstruction with Auto Genous Tissue Lenox Hill Hosp. **Special Achievements:** Publications: "Adriamycin Extravasation Ulcers", Ame Soc Plastic & Reconstructive Surg Meeting, 1983; "Non-Caucasian Rhinoplasty","Common Pressure Ulcers and Treatment", "History of the Carter-Morestin Society", presented at Nat Med Assoc Convention, New Orleans, LA, 1987; "Autologous Secondary Breast Augmentation with Pedicled Transverse Rectus Abdominus Musculocutaneous Flaps", Annals Plastic Surg, 1995. **Home Addr:** No 3 Charlotte Ct Rosecliff, Briarcliff Manor, NY 10510. **Business Addr:** Physician, A Beautiful Body Plastic Surgery Center, 4155 Ferncreek Dr Suite 102, Fayetteville, NC 28314, **Business Phone:** (910)323-4823.

### LOWE, MARTHA P.

Business owner. **Personal:** Born Mar 17, 1945, Pocahontas, VA; daughter of Nathaniel Fitzgerald and Josephine Fitzgerald; married Arthur F; children: Patrice White, Cherri Latta, Timothy & Arthur Jr. **Educ:** Ohio State Univ; Wilberforce Univ, attended 1995; Cent Mich Univ, MSA, 1998. **Career:** Ohio State Univ, develop assoc, 1978-97; Accountants Assoc, vpres, 1997-98; ADT/US Alert Inc, dist mgr, 1998-99; Shekinah Grande Salon & Day Spa, 1999-. **Orgs:** Pres & bd mem, Nat Asn Working Women Inc, 1987-97; event planning & fund raising comt, Alpha Kappa Alpha Sorority, 1996-; Victory Matrons ClubInc, 1996-; steering comt, Nat Black Women's Health Proj, 1997-99; scholarcomt, N easterners Inc, 1997-; bd mem, Hannah Neil Ctr C, 1997-; fund raising comt, Jack & Jill Am Inc, 1997-; vol, Am Cancer Found, 2004-. **Honors/Awds:** Outstanding Teacher, Bible Way Church of Our Lord Jesus Christ Inc, 1997; Outstanding Mentor, Bible Way Church of Our Lord Jesus Christ Inc, 1998; #1 sales nationally, ADR/US Alert Inc, 1998. **Home Addr:** 2706 Mitzi Dr, Columbus, OH 43209, **Home Phone:** (614)231-0554. **Business Addr:** Chief Executive Officer, Shekinah Grande Salon & Day Spa, 3435 E Livingston Ave, Columbus, OH 43227, **Business Phone:** (614)239-8119.

### LOWE, SIDNEY ROCHELL

Basketball player, basketball coach. **Personal:** Born Jan 21, 1960, Washington, DC; children: Sidney II. **Educ:** NC State Univ, 1983. **Career:** Basketball player (retired), basketball coach; Ind Pacers, prof basketball player, 1983-84; Detroit Pistons, 1984, asst coach, 2005-06; Atlanta Hawks, prof basketball player, 1984-85; Continental Basketball Asn, Tampa Bay Thrillers, 1986-88; Continental Basketball Asn, Albany Patroons, 1988-89; Charlotte Hornets, prof basketball player, 1988-89; Continental Basketball Asn, Rapid City Thrillers, 1989; Minn Timberwolves, prof basketball player, 1989-90, asst coach, 1990-93, interim & head coach, 1993-94, asst coach, 1999-2000, asst coach, 2003-05, asst coach, 2014-16; Cleveland Cavaliers, asst coach, 1994-99; Memphis Grizzlies, head coach, 2000-02; Minn Timberwolves, asst coach, 2003-05; NC State Univ, head coach, 2006-11; Utah Jazz, asst coach, 2011-14; Wash Wizards, asst coach, 2016-. **Special Achievements:** Nat Basketball Asn's youngest Head Coach, 1993. **Business Addr:** Assistant Coach, Washington Wizards, 601 F St NW, Washington, DC 20004, **Business Phone:** (202)661-5050.

### LOWE, VICTORIA

Chief executive officer, president (organization). **Personal:** Born St. Louis, MO. **Educ:** Univ Mo, BA, psychol, 1984. **Career:** Pac Coast Regional Corp; Remedy Intelligent Staffing, regional dir, 1988-95; Alert Staffing, founder, pres & chief exec officer, 1995-2005; I Am Whole Inc, pres, 2005-; Victoria Lowe Enterprises / Kaptivate Inc, pres & chief exec officer, 2014-. Publications: 10 Spiritual Principles of Successful Women, 2004. **Orgs:** Bd mem, Destiny Outreach Inc; bd mem, Nat Assoc Women Bus Owners; bd mem, Black bus Assoc; exec dir, Kindom@Work, 2012-. **Business Addr:** President, Chief Executive Officer, Victoria Lowe Enterprises, 300 Corp Pt Suite 300, Culver City, CA 90230, **Business Phone:** (310)665-9380.

### LOWE, WALTER EDWARD, JR.

Chairperson, executive. **Personal:** Born Aug 20, 1951, Milford, VA; son of Walter E Sr and Fraulein C; married Sheryl Ferguson; children: Ashley Patrice & Walter Edward III. **Educ:** Univ Va, BA, psychol, 1976. **Career:** Gen Dynamics, buyer spt, 1983, chief procurement, 1983-85, Land Systs Div, mgr procurement, 1985-90, Land Systs Div, dir procurement, 1990-93, dir mat mgt, 1983-98; Ford Motor Co, buyer, 1976-83, N Am Vehicle Logistics, mgr, 2006-. **Orgs:** Am Mgt Asn, 1983-; Cert mgr, Inst Cert Prof Mgr, 1985-; NCP, 1988-; chmn, United Way Allocation Panel, 1990-; bd trustee, Henry Ford HTH Syst, 1992-; mat steering comt, Electronic Indust Asn, 1995-; bd dir, Automotive Indust Action Group, 2006-; chmn, Automotive Indust Logistics Steering Comt, 2008-. **Home Addr:** 4899 Peggy St, West Bloomfield, MI 48322, **Home Phone:** (810)737-6942. **Business Addr:** Manager, North America Vehicle Logistics, Ford Motor Co, PO Box 6248, Dearborn, MI 48126, **Business Phone:** (800)367-5690.

### LOWERY, DR. BIRL

Educator. **Personal:** Born Dec 24, 1952, Starkville, MS; son of Clem and Katie Collins; married Ester Hamblin; children: Ramona C & Tyson B. **Educ:** Alcorn Univ, Lorman, BS, agr educ, 1975; Miss State Univ, Starkville, MA, agr engineering technol, 1975; Ore State Univ, Corvallis, PhD, soil physics, 1980. **Career:** Univ Wis, Madison, Dept Soil Sci, asst prof, 1980-86, assoc prof, 1986-92, prof emer, 1992-2015, Dept Soil Sci, chair, 1999-2004; Jour Soil & Water Conserv, assoc. **Orgs:** Soil Sci Soc Am; Int Soil Tillage Res Org; Soil & Water Conserv Soc; Am Socs Agron, 1977-; Sci Res Socs, Sigma Xi, 1980-96; Soil Water Conserv Socs, 1981-; Am Soc Agr Engrs, 1984-94; Gamma Sigma Delta, 1984-; InterNatSoil Sci Socs, 1986-98; InterNatSoil Tillage Res Orgn, 1987-; Vilas Res Assoc, 1998-2000; Int Union Soil Sci, 1998-. **Business Addr:** Professor, University of Wisconsin-Madison, 55A Soils Bldg, Madison, WI 53706-1299, **Business Phone:** (608)262-2752.

### LOWERY, BOBBY G.

Executive. **Personal:** Born Nov 26, 1932, Blacksburg, SC; son of Eliza Morgan and Garance Lee; married Betty Mason; children: Regina Jones, Reginald, Revonsia Dozier & Robert. **Educ:** Carver Col, lib arts, 1957. **Career:** US Post Off, lett carrier, 1957-70; Better Cleaning Janitor Serv Inc, pres; Better Cleaning Maintenance Supply Inc, pres, 1970-. **Orgs:** Vice chmn, Nat Minority Supplier Develop Counl, Minority Input Comt, 1978-79; pres, Charlotte Bus League, 1981-82; chmn, bd deacons, St Paul Baptist Church, 1982-; dir, Bldg Serv Contractors Asn Int, 1985-88; exec comt, Charlotte Chamber Com, 1985-86; trustee, Univ NCA Charlotte, 1987-95. **Honors/Awds:** Outstanding Citizen Award, Sigma Gamma Rho Sorority, 1978; Minority Business Enterpriser of the Year, Charlotte Chamber Com, 1985. **Home Addr:** 5930 Sierra Dr, Charlotte, NC 28216-2240, **Home Phone:** (704)392-2377. **Business Addr:** President, Better Cleaning Janitor Service Inc, 1801 N Tryon St Suite 125, Charlotte, NC 28206-2215, **Business Phone:** (704)372-9242.

### LOWERY, CAROLYN T.

Social worker, executive director, association executive. **Personal:** Born Jul 7, 1940, New Iberia, LA; daughter of Genivie Thomas Davis and Eldridge Thomas; children: Donald Jr, Valencia, Michael, Peter & Donald Wayne. **Educ:** Maricopa Tech Col, AA, 1978; Ariz State Univ, Sch Social Work. **Career:** Palmade Sch, teacher's aide; Motorola Plant, assembly worker; Ebony House rehab prog men, 1977-81; Wesley United Methodist Church, black community developer, 1981-85; Kid's Pl, founder & dir, 1989; Ariz Black United Fund Inc, exec dir, dir, 1985-. **Orgs:** Co-chairwoman, Ariz New Alliance Party, 1985-; co-chairwoman, Westside Neighborhood Community Ctr, 1988-; bd mem, Ariz Future Forum Prog; bd mem, Ariz Regional Pub Transp Authority; co-founder, Ariz Black Cult Mus, 1981-; co-founder, Ariz Stop Police Brutality Orgn, 1981-; co-founder, Ariz New Alliance Party, 1986; founder, Moms Moms Orgn, 1998; founder, Pennies Heaven Found, 1999; Ariz Repub Champion C. **Honors/Awds:** Outstanding Community Service Citations, Masons, 1982, Nation Islam, 1983, City Phoenix, 1984, Black Engineers & Scientists, 1986 & Black Community, 1988; Leadership Award, Black Women Task Force, 1995; As They Grow Awards, Parents Mag, Ceremony White House, 1997; Foot Soldier Award, Ariz Nat Asn Blacks Criminal Justice, 1997; Nat Freedoms Foundation at Valley Forge Award, 2005; Hon Kachina Volunteer Award, 2006. **Home Addr:** 5602 S 20th St, Phoenix, AZ 85040-3311, **Home Phone:** (602)268-0666. **Business Addr:** Executive Director, Arizona Black United Fund Inc, PO Box 24457, Phoenix, AZ 85074, **Business Phone:** (602)268-0666.

### LOWERY, DONALD ELLIOTT

Investment banker. **Personal:** Born Jan 6, 1956, Chicago, IL; son of R D and Annie. **Educ:** Wesleyan Univ, Middletown, CT, BA, econ, 1977. **Career:** Landmark Newspapers, reporter, 1977-79; Ariz Rep, Phoenix, reporter, 1979-80; Boston Globe, Mass, reporter, 1980-82; WHDH-TV, Boston, Mass, dir, pub affairs & ed, 1982-91; Lazard Freres & Co, investment banker, 1992; New Eng Patriots, vpres, commun & pub affairs, 1994-2002; Viacom Boston, exec vpres commun & pub affairs, 2002-04; Nielsen Media Res, sr vpres govt & pub affaris, 2004-; Nielsen Co, sr vpres govt & pub affairs, 2004-. **Orgs:** Nat Asn Black Journalist, 1980-; pres, Nat Broadcast Ed Asn, 1982-; Bus Assocs Club, 1984-; bd dir, Bay State Games, 1990-. **Honors/Awds:** Emmy, Nat Acad TV Arts & Scis, 1985, 1986; UPS Tom Phillips Award, 1985; Lincoln University Unity Award, 1988, 1989, 1991. **Home Addr:** 70 W Rutland, Boston, MA 02118. **Business Addr:** Senior Vice President of Government & Public Affairs, The Nielsen Co, 85 Broad St, New York, NY 10004, **Business Phone:** (800)864-1224.

### LOWERY, REV. DR. JOSEPH E.

Association executive, president (organization), chief executive officer. **Personal:** Born Oct 6, 1921, Huntsville, AL; son of LeRoy and Dora Fackler; married Evelyn Gibson; children: Leroy, Joseph Jr, Yvonne, Karen & Cheryl. **Educ:** Chicago Ecumenical Inst, DD, 1950; Payne Theol Sem, BA, BD; Knoxville Col; Ala A&M Col; Payne Col; Wayne Univ; Morehouse Univ, DD; Atlanta Univ, LLD; Dillard Univ, LittD. **Career:** Pastor (retired); Warren St United Methodist Church, pastor, 1952-61; Bishop Golden, admin asst, 1961-64; St Paul Church, pastor, 1964-68; Southern Christian Leadership Conf, founder, vpres, 1967, nat chmn, bd dir, 1967-77, pres, 1977-98, chief exec officer, pres emer, 1997-; Cent United Methodist Church, minister, 1968-86; Emory Univ, Candler Sch Theol & Nursery Sch, instr, 1970-71; Cascade United Methodist Church, minister, pastor, 1986-92; Enterprises Now Inc, pres. **Orgs:** Gen Bd Pub Housing, 1960-72; Comt Race Rels, United Methodist Church, 1968-76; bd dir, MARTA, 1975-78; bd dir, Comt Relief, Global Ministry, 1976; Mayors Comt Human Rels; chmn, Civil Rights Coord Comt; pres, InterdenomiNat Ministry All, Nashville, Tenn; pres, OEO Comt Act Agency; bd dir, United Way; Martin Luther King Jr Ctr Social Change; bd dir, Urban Act Inc; Nat Leadership Coun Civil Rights; bd trustee, Paine Col; founder& pres, Cascade First Comt Asn; Ga Coalition Peoples Agenda; co-founder & pres, Black Leadership Forum; vice chmn, Atlanta Community Rels Comt; Ala Civic Affairs Asn. **Home Addr:** 3121 Cascade Rd SW, Atlanta, GA 30311-3631, **Home Phone:** (404)699-0261. **Business Addr:** President Emeritus, Southern Christian Leadership Conference, 334 Auburn Ave NE, Atlanta, GA 30303-2604, **Business Phone:** (404)522-1420.

### LOWERY, MICHAEL DOUGLAS

Educator. **Personal:** Born Feb 21, 1950, Madisonville, KY; son of Hendrix and Lila. **Educ:** BORE, 1980; BS, hist polit sci, 1992; MA, 1993. **Career:** City Recreation, dir; Elliott Mortuary, gen asst; State Hwy Dept, libr, spec worker; Paralegal, gifted educr, teacher, gifted dir, 1999-2000. **Orgs:** Pres, Nat Asn Advan Colored People; HCEA, Vic II; KEA; NEA; Nat Funeral dir; founder, OPP, Murray State Univ Chap; Nat Baptist, Progressive Baptist, Ky Bapt. **Home Addr:** 343 N Church St, Madisonville, KY 42431-1501, **Home Phone:** (270)821-7803. **Business Addr:** Teacher, Browning Springs Middle School, 357 W Arch St, Madisonville, KY 42431, **Business Phone:** (502)825-6006.

### LOWERY, MICHAEL ZANTEL

Football player. **Personal:** Born Feb 14, 1974, McComb, MS. **Educ:** Univ Miss. **Career:** Chicago Bears, linebacker, 1996-97.

### LOWERY, QUENTON TERRELL

Baseball player. **Personal:** Born Oct 25, 1970, Oakland, CA; married Denise Nicole Burch; children: 3. **Educ:** Loyola Marymount Univ. **Career:** Baseball player (retired); Texas Rangers, 1991-96; Chicago Cubs, outfielder, 1997-98; Tampa Bay Devil Rays, outfielder, 1999; San Francisco Giants, outfielder, 2000.

### LOWERY-JETER, DR. RENECIA YVONNE

Association executive. **Personal:** Born Jul 2, 1954, Detroit, MI; daughter of Harold and Sarah; married Darrell. **Educ:** Wayne State Univ, BA, mass commun, 1976; Marygrove Col, MA, human resource mgt, 1991, MEd, eng, 2005; Capella Univ, PhD, orgn develop, 2011. **Career:** United Way Servs, dir human resources, 1990-97; Detroit Inst Arts, dir human resources, 1998-99; Genesis Training & Develop, 2000-03; Detroit Pub Sch, dir benefits, 2004-07; Pretty Prod LLC, vpres human resources, 2007-; Isaac Group, vpres human resources, 2007-08; N Gen Hosp, vpres, 2009-11; Detroit Symphony Orchestra, dir human resources, 2012-13; Genesis Training, Develop & Human Resources, founder, prin, 2000-. **Orgs:** Bd mem, Spaulding C, 1993-96; pres, Am Soc Training & Develop, 1997-98; vol, Jr Achievement; Soc Human Resource Mgt; Am Soc Training & Develop; Nat Asn Women Bus Owners. **Home Addr:** 16146 Kentfield, Detroit, MI 48219-3372, **Home Phone:** (313)531-2509. **Business Addr:** Vice President, Pretty Products LLC, 1513 Redding Dr, LaGrange, GA 30240, **Business Phone:** (706)884-1711.

### LOWMAN, CARL D.

Executive, vice president (organization). **Personal:** Born Dec 1, 1962, Philadelphia, PA; son of Carl N and Delores Guy. **Educ:** Univ Mass, Amherst, BBA, 1984; Colo State Univ, MBA. **Career:** The Gillette Co, budget analyst asst, 1984-85, ade & controls analyst, 1985-86, budget analyst, 1986-87; Continental Airlines Inc, financial analyst, 1987-89, sr financial analyst, 1989-91, mgr budget & forecasting, 1991-95; Western Pac Airlines Inc, dir financial serv, 1995-96, treas, 1995-97; MWH Global Inc, vpres & dir global financial planning & analysis, currently. **Home Addr:** 9574-D Brentwood Way, Westminster, CO 80021, **Home Phone:** (303)940-6193. **Business Addr:** Director, Vice President, MWH Global Inc, 380 Interlocken Cres Suite 200, Broomfield, CO 80021, **Business Phone:** (303)533-1900.

### LOWMAN, DR. ISOM D.

Physician, commander. **Personal:** Born Jun 3, 1946, Hopkins, SC; married Irma Jean Smith; children: Joye Katrese, Isom Batrone & Robin Patrese. **Educ:** SC State Col, BS, chem, 1968; Meharry Med Col, MD, 1972. **Career:** Ft Benning, chief med, 1975-78; Wm Beaumont Army Med Ctr, nuclear fel, 1978-80; Moncrief Army Hosp, Ft Jackson, SC, chief nuclear med, 1980-82, dep comdr, chief nuclear med & med, 1983-. **Orgs:** Alpha Phi Alpha Fraternity, 1965-; Palmetto Med Soc; pres, Cong Med Soc; fel Am Col Physicians; Soc Nuclear Med; Am Med Asn; Nat Asn Advan Colored People. **Honors/Awds:** Outstanding Alpha Alpha Phi Alpha Fraternity; Distinguished Grad Hopkins High Sch, 1984. **Home Addr:** 51 Running Fox Rd, Columbia, SC 29223, **Home Phone:** (803)736-0585. **Business Addr:** Chief Nuclear Medicine, Deputy Commander, Moncrief Army Hospital, 1 Medical Parks Dr, Chester, SC 29706, **Business Phone:** (803)581-3151.

### LOWNES-JACKSON, DR. MILLICENT GRAY

School administrator, entrepreneur, writer. **Personal:** Born Dec 24, 1951, Philadelphia, PA; daughter of James Gray and Mildred Gray; married Arthur; children: Robert Jr & Monique. **Educ:** Fisk Univ, BA, bus, admin, 1972; Vanderbilt Univ, MBA, bus, mgt, 1975, PhD, admin/bus, 1981; cert bus coach. **Career:** Tenn State Univ, Col Bus, Dept Bus Admin, prof, 1976-2011, assoc dean & prof, 1995-2011, interim provost & exec vpres, 2011-13, dean, 2013-; pvt pract gen & fam pract, currently. **Orgs:** Founder, Inter denomi Nat Serv Orgn Am, 1990-; 100 Black Women, 1994-; Links Inc, 1994-; Jack & Jill Am; Phi Kappa Phi Hon Soc, 1995-; Beta Gamma Sigma Hon Bus Frat, 1995-; founder, Bus Exchange Entrepreneurially Minded, 1995-; founder, Women's Inst Success Entrp, 1995-; co-founder, World Inst Sustainable Educ & Res Group; dir, Tenn Small Bus Develop Ctr; dir, Tenn State Univ Small Bus Inst Prog; dir, TSU Kauffman Entrepreneurial Internship Prog. **Special Achievements:** Books: Savvy Leadership: A Woman's Guide to 21st Century Entrepreneurial Leadership; Starting A Child Care Center; Starting A Flower and Gift Shop; Starting A Craft Business. **Home Addr:** 205 Augusta Nat Ct, Franklin, TN 37069, **Home Phone:** (615)646-8881. **Business Addr:** Professor, Associate Dean, Tennessee State University, 330 10th Ave N, Nashville, TN 37203-3401, **Business Phone:** (615)963-7127.

### LOWRY, DONNA SHIRLYNN

Television journalist. **Personal:** Born May 19, 1957, Pittsburgh, PA; daughter of Walter J S and Alma M; married Bennet W Reid Jr; children: Nicole Fuller, Lakisha & Sparkle. **Educ:** Chatham Univ, BA, commun & admin & mgt, 1979; Northwestern Univ, MSJ, 1981. **Career:** WEEK-TV, news anchor, reporter, 1981-83; WESH-TV, news anchor, reporter, 1983-86; WXIA-TV, educ ed, 1986-. **Orgs:** Adv bd, Save The C, 1991-; Bd, W End Boys & Girls Clubs, 1992-; bd dir, Old Nat Christian Acad, 1994-; hon chaplian, S Fulton PTA, 1991; Atlanta Asn Black Journalists, 1987-; Alpha Kappa Alpha Sorority Inc; Magnolia Chaplian, Links Inc, 1994-; Statewide Safety Belt Task Force, 1994-; adv bd, Ga Asn Family Daycare, 1994; bd dir, Ga Asn Sch Age Care, 1996-; The Sheltering Arms Child Care Ctrs; Beulah Baptist Church Dollars Scholars; Black Women Film Preserv Proj; Educ Writers Asn; Nat Acad Tv Arts & Scis; Magnolia Chap LINKS Inc; Atlanta Asn Black Journalists. **Honors/Awds:** Outstanding Bus & Prof Award, Dollars & Sense Mag, 1992; Positive Image Award, The Minority Recruiter Newspapers, 1993; Media Award, GEO Psychol Asn, 1992; var Child Care Media Awards, 1991; Salute to Women of Achievement, YWCA, 1987, 1990. **Business Addr:** Education Editor, WXIA-TV, 1611 W Peachtree St NE, Atlanta, GA 30309, **Business Phone:** (404)892-1611.

### LOWRY, JAMES E.
Executive. **Personal:** Born Jul 8, 1942, Wyoming, OH; son of Henry and Mamie. **Educ:** Xavier Univ Cincinnati, BS, bus admin, 1975. **Career:** Gen Elect Co, equal opportunity minority rels, adminr, 1970-71, mgt trainee, 1975-78, buyer machined parts, 1978-79, mgr specialty parts, 1979-84, mat adminr, 1984-89, mgr sourcing advan tech, 1989-93, mgr purchasing; Lincoln Heights, OH, mayor, 1972-74; Indirect Mat & Serv, mgr, 1993-95; Bus Practices, mgr, 1995. **Orgs:** Bd dir, Community Action Comn Cincinnati, 1972-74; bd dir, Lincoln Heights Health Clin, 1972-74; consult, Community Chest Cincinnati, 1972-74; bd dir, People United Save Humanity, 1972-74; bd dir, Freedom Farm Ruleville MS, 1972-74; bd dir, Ohio Black Polit Assembly, 1972-74; bd dir, Gen Elec Credit Union, 1984; Union Experimenting Col & Univ, 1986; City Forest Pk Civil Serv Comn, 1989-94; chmn, AECU Credit Union, 1993; chmn, Forest Pk Civil Serv Community, 1994; Friendship Community Develop Inc. **Honors/Awds:** Key to City Cincinnati, 1972; Award of Appreciation, City Fayette, 1973; Outstanding Polit Serv to the Community, Ohio Black Polit Assembly, 1973; Extra Step Award, Gen Elec Co, 1980; Extra Step Award, Gen Elec Corp, 1980; GE Purchasing Gold Cup Award, 1982. **Home Addr:** 2420 Larkfield Dr, PO Box 37194, Cincinnati, OH 45237-1504.

### LOWRY, JAMES HAMILTON
Executive. **Personal:** Born May 28, 1939, Chicago, IL; son of Wlliam E and Camille; married Doris Davenport; children: Aisha. **Educ:** Grinnell Col, BA, 1961, DHL; Univ Pittsburgh, MPIA, 1968; Harvard Univ, prog mgt develop (PMD), 1973. **Career:** Pepsi-Cola, helper, 1957-60; Grinnell Col, Travel fel, 1961-62; Kivokoni Col, teacher, 1961; Peace Corps Lima, Peru, training officer, 1961-62, assoc dir, 1964-66; Univ Pittsburgh, John Hay-Whitney fel, 1963-65; Bedford-Stuyvesant Restoration Corp Brooklyn, from spec asst to pres proj mgr, 1966-68; McKinsey & Co Chicago, sr assoc, 1968-75; James H Lowry & Assoc, pres, chief exec officer, 1975-; Northwestern Univ, adj instr mgt, 1987-92; Kellogg Sch Bus, acad advisor to advan mgt educ prog, 1996-; Boston Consult Group, vpres, 2000-05, sr vpres, global diversity dir, sr advisor, currently. **Orgs:** Inst Mgt Consult, 1980-85; Nat Black MBA Asn, 1981-85; prin, Chicago United, 1982-85; Harvard Alumni Asn, 1980-85; pres, chmn, Chicago Publ Libr Bd, 1981-85; bd trustee, Northwestern Mem Hosp, 1980-85; bd trustee, Grinnell Col, 1971-85; bd dir, Independence Bank, Chicago, 1983-85; Kellogg's Adv Bd, 1998-; bd dir, Howard Univ Sch Bus, 1995-; diversity adv bd mem, Toyota Motor Corp, 2002-; Kraft Multicultural Coun; Chicago Coun Foreign Rels; chair, Durban SafricA/Chicago Sister Cities Comt; bd mem, Africa Am Inst; bd dir, Johnson Prod; chair, Chicago-Durban Sister City Prog; adj fac mem, Northwestern Univ's Kellogg Sch Mgt; Exec Leadership Coun; chmn, Howard Univ's Inst Entrepreneurship, Leadership, & Innovation; Toyota Diversity Adv Bd; chair, RLJ Equity Fund Exec Network; chmn, Chicago Pub Libr Bd; Kraft Multicultural Coun; Harvard Bus Sch Vis Comt; chair, Durban S Africa/Chicago Sister Cities Comt. **Honors/Awds:** President of class, Harvard Bus Sch, 1973; Minority Business Enterprise Hall of Fame, 2005; Lifetime Achievement Award, Nat Minority Supplier Develop Coun, 2009. **Special Achievements:** Co-author of "The New Agenda for Minority Business Development", Kauffman Found, 2005. First African American recruit; first African-American to join McKinsey & Company in 1968. **Home Addr:** 3100 N Sheridan Rd, Chicago, IL 60657-4954, **Home Phone:** (773)296-6844. **Business Addr:** Senior Advisor, Boston Consulting Group, 200 S Wacker Blvd 27th Fl, Chicago, IL 60606, **Business Phone:** (312)993-3300.

### LOWRY, WILLIAM ELBERT, JR.
Executive, president (organization), broadcaster. **Personal:** Born Feb 16, 1935, Chicago, IL; son of Camille and William; married Teri; children: Kim Maria & William Andre. **Educ:** Kenyon Col, AB, 1956; Loyola Univ, Chicago, MS, indust rels, 1969. **Career:** Francis W Parker Sch, athletic dir, coach, 1960-62; Inland Steel Co, supvr, 1962-65; Inland Steel Container Co, personnel mgr, 1965, 1968-76; Opportunity Line WBBM TV, host TV ser, 1967-82; Objective Jobs WBBM TV, host TV ser, 1982-; Jos T Ryerson & Son Inc, mgr human resource, 1976-86; Personnel Admin dir, 1986-88; Inland Steel Indust, dir personnel & recruitment, 1988-93; John D & Catherine T MacArthur Found, vpres hr, 1994-2005, sr advisor pres; James H Lowry & Assoc, chief operating officer. **Orgs:** Hr Asn, Chicago, 1965-; secy, Midwest Col Placement Asn, 1967-68; bd dir, Childrens Home & Aid Soc Ill; vpres, bd dir, Chicago Boys & Girls Clubs, 1967-92; bd dir trustee, Kenyon Col; Chicago United, 1975-93; bd dir trustee, Lake Forest Col, 1984-88; bd dir, Rehab Inst Chicago, 1988-; chmn, Chicago Pvt Indust Coun, 1990-; bd dir, United Way Crusade Mercy, 1996-; bd dir, Donors Forum Chicago, 1996; chair, City Co Task Force Welfare Reform, 1996-2000; bd dir, Ill Issues, 1998-; Chicago Workforce Bd; bd, Cath Theol Union; vpres, MacArthur Found. **Honors/Awds:** George Foster Peabody Award, 1968; Emmy Award, Nat Acad TV Arts & Sci, 1968-69; Human Rel Mass Media Award, Am Jewish Comn, 1968; 10 Outstanding Men of Chicago, 1969; Blackbook's Black Business Man of the Year, 1981; Distinguished Jour Award, AICS, 1984; Peabody Award; KAA Don May Award; Gregg Cup, the Colleges Highest Alumni Award. **Special Achievements:** First black student initiated into Beta Theta Pi; Inducted into the Kenyon Athletic Associations Hall of Fame, 1994. **Home Addr:** 1023 W Vernon Pk Pl Apt A, Chicago, IL 60607-3447, **Home Phone:** (312)929-2689. **Business Addr:** Senior Advisor to the President, John D & Catherine T MacArthur Foundation, 140 S Dearborn St, Chicago, IL 60603-5285, **Business Phone:** (312)726-8000.

### LOYD, WALTER, JR.
Executive, manager. **Personal:** Born Dec 23, 1951, Tampa, FL; children: Stacey, Tracey, Symon & Samuel. **Educ:** Univ Ariz-Pine Bluff, BS, 1974. **Career:** Ark Power & Light, sales rep, 1974-77, adm rate analyst, 1977-78, procedures analyst, 1974-78, contracts adminr, 1979-84, Minority Bus Develop, mgr, 1984-; Entergy Servs Inc, mgr, 1991-97, dir, supplier diversity, 1997-. **Orgs:** Treas, Am Asn Blacks Energy; century club & leadership mem, Quapaw Area Boy Scouts Am; chair bd dir, Ark Regional Minority Supplier Develop Coun; bd dir, Ouachita Girl Scout Coun; chair, Little Rock Bd Housing & Appeals; bd mem, Ariz Regional Minority Purchasing Coun; bd dir, Nat Minority Supplier Develop Coun; Greater Little Rock COC, Small Bus Coun; NCP, Econo Develop Coun; SBA; chair emer, Edison Elec Inst; leadership mem, Boy Scouts Am, 1984; century mem, Boy Scouts Am, 1987-90. **Honors/Awds:** Exceptional Leadership & Dedication EEI Minority Bus Develop Comt, Edison Electric Inst, 1996. **Special Achievements:** Publication: Enlightened Interest, Minority Business Enterprise, 1993. **Home Addr:** 14205 Clairborne Ct, Little Rock, AR 72211. **Business Addr:** Director of Supplier Diversity, Entergy Services Inc, 639 Loyola Ave, New Orleans, LA 70113, **Business Phone:** (504)576-6116.

### LOZADA, DE JUANA
Business owner. **Personal:** Born May 20, 1970, Raleigh, NC; daughter of Clarence Boone Jr and Dorothy Jeffries; married Victor; children: Deryian & Jhaylen. **Educ:** Univ NC, FSU campus, BA, commun, 1991; Univ Md, Europ campus, MA, commun, 1996; Defense Info Sch, advan pub affairs officer course, 1998. **Career:** Tex Higher Educ Coord Bd, asst dir commun; Dept Defense, AUs Europe, pub affairs officer, 1991-99; Copydesk, pub rels firm, founder & chief exec officer, 1999-. **Orgs:** Am Women Radio & TV; Pub Rels Soc Am; Nat Asn Advan Colored People; Am Civil Liberties Union; Urban League. **Honors/Awds:** Keith L Ware Military Awards Journal; Civilian Journalist of the Year, 1997. **Home Addr:** , CO. **Business Addr:** Chief Executive Officer, Founder, The CopyDesk, 627 N Weber St, Colorado Springs, CO 80903, **Business Phone:** (719)633-6765.

### LUCAS, DR. C. PAYNE, SR.
Association executive. **Personal:** Born Sep 14, 1933, Spring Hope, NC; son of James Russel and Minnie Hendricks; married Freddie Emily Myra Hill; children: Therese Raymonde, C Payne Jr (Deceased) & Hillary Hendricks. **Educ:** Md State Col, Princess Anne, MD, hist, 1953, BA, 1959; Am Univ, Wash, DC, MA, govt, 1961. **Career:** Peace Corps, Wash, DC, Togo, asst dir, 1962, Niger, dir, 1964-66, Africa Region, dir, 1967-69, dir, off/returned vol, 1969-71; Afri care, Wash, DC, exec dir & pres, 1971-2002; Lodestar LLC, chief exec officer, currently. **Orgs:** Bd dir, Overseas Develop Coun, 1977-; Int Develop Conf; bd mem, Environ Energy Inst, 1986-; bd dirs, Interaction; adv bd, Nat Peace Corps Asn; adv bd, Discovery Channel Global Educ Fund; Coun Foreign Rels, 1983-; bd mem, Pop Action Int, 1990-; Nat Asn Advan Colored People; Africa Soc; Mod Africa Fund Mgrs; Constituency Africa; Kennedy Ctr Community & Friends Bd; Univ Md Found; chmn & founding mem, US Comt Un Develop Programme; Comn Post-Conflict Reconstruction; founding mem, Corp Coun Africa; &Andrew Young Ctr Int Affairs, Morehouse Col; US Africa Trade & Aid Link Corp; DC Campaign Prevent Teenage Pregnancy; bd dir, US Comt Un Develop Prog; Helping Enhance Livelihood People Comn. **Honors/Awds:** President's Award for Distinguished Federal Civilian Service, 1967; Distinguished Federal Service Award Peace Corps, 1967; Honorary Doctorate of Law, Univ Md, 1975; Capitol Press Club's Humanitarian of the Year, 1980; Presidential Hunger Award Outstanding Achievement, 1984; Phelps-Stokes Fund Aggrey Medal, 1986; Officers of the Order of Distinguished Service Award, 1986; Recognition from the National Order of the Republics of Niger, Zambia & Ivory Coast, 1988; Land Grant Colleges Distinguished Bicentennial Award, 1990; Nation Order of Merit Award, Govt Senegal, 1990; Hubert H Humphrey Public Service Award, Am Polit Sci Asn. **Special Achievements:** First African American Recipient of the American Political Science Association's Hubert H Humphrey Public Service Award. **Home Addr:** 4241 Mathewson Dr NW, Washington, DC 20011, **Home Phone:** (202)722-0061. **Business Addr:** Chief Executive Officer, Lodestar LLC, 780 Newtown Yardley Rd Suite 325, Newtown, PA 18940, **Business Phone:** (215)860-1223.

### LUCAS, DAVID EUGENE, SR.
State government official. **Personal:** Born Apr 23, 1950, Peach County, GA; son of David and Beatrice; married Elaine Huckabee; children: David Jr, Leonard, Aris & Albert. **Educ:** Tuskegee Inst, BS, polit sci, 1972; Mercer Univ Med Sch, JD; Atlanta Law Sch. **Career:** Lucas Supply Co, owner; Northeast High Sch, Macon GA, social studies teacher & coach, 1972-73; Bibb Tech High Sch, Macon, GA, social studies teacher & varsity girls basketball, 1973-74; Barney A Smith Motors, Macon, GA, car salesman, 1974-75; Ga House Representatives, 1974-2011; Ga State House, dist 124, 1996, 1998, 2000, dist 105, 2002, dist 139, 2004, 2006, 2008, 2010, dist 26, 2011, 2012; independent ins agt, 1980-86; Horace Mann Co, ins agt, 1986-88; TBL Inc, pres, 1988-; Ga State Senate elections, 2012, 2014. **Orgs:** Vpres, Macon Chfs Amtr football team; Black Eagles Motorcycle Club; C CMacon; fel, Christian Athletes; GA Asn Black Elected Offs; Nat Conf Black State Elected Offs; bd mem, Boys Club Macon; Coalition Polit Awareness; bd mem, Small & Minority Bus Coun, City Macon; bd gov, app Mercer Univ Sch Med, 1994; Steward Chapel AME Church, currently; 100 Black Men Macon-Mid Ga, currently; mem, Ga State Senate 26th Dist, 2012-; mem, Dem party; Ga Comt Assignments, 2013. **Home Addr:** 2594 Saratoga Dr, Macon, GA 31211, **Home Phone:** (478)742-2387. **Business Addr:** Representative, Georgia House Representatives, 509A Coverdell Legislative Office Bldg, Atlanta, GA 30334, **Business Phone:** (404)656-0220.

### LUCAS, DR. REV. DOROTHY J.
Physician, educator, consultant. **Personal:** Born Nov 27, 1949, Lambert, MS; daughter of Garvie Sr (deceased) and Elizabeth Killebrew Sr (deceased). **Educ:** Kennedy-King Col, AA, 1971; Roosevelt Univ, BS, biol & chem, 1973; UHS Chicago Med Sch, MD, 1977; Univ Ill, MPH, 1993; FACOG; Colo Theol Sem, Dmin; Univ Ill, Chicago, postgrad, pub health. **Career:** Columbus Cuneo Cabrini, resident, 1977-81, assoc attend physician, 1981-; Mercy Hosp Med Ctr, asst attend physician, 1986-87; Cath Health Partners, sr attend physician, 1986-; Roosevelt Univ, instr; Am Col Obstetricians & Gynecologists, fel; Greater Bethesda Baptist Church, health ed; pvt pract physician, currently; Cook Co Dept Pub Health, med dir, currently; Chicago Med Soc, Health Care Econs Comt, consult, currently. **Orgs:** Alpha Kappa Alpha, 1986-; CMC; ISMA; dipl, Am Bd Ob-Gyn; fel Am Col Ob-Gyn; AMA; Am Soc Addiction Med; Adv Bd Mem, Univ Chicago Cancer Res Ctr; Adv Bd Mem, GIRLS LINK Cook County; Adv Bd Mem, Ill Maternal & Child Health Coalition; chair, Work Force Comt, Chicago Med Soc; chair, Ill State Med Soc; Nat Consortium Black Women Ministry; Chair, Southside Chicago Br, vpres & pres; mem chair, exec comt mem, 1st vice-pres & pres, Nat Asn Advan Colored People. **Honors/Awds:** ACOG, Am Col Ob-Gyn, 1985; AMA Physician recognition, Am Med Asn, 1985; Chicago Jaycees Ten Outstanding Young Citizens, 1987; Distinguished Alumni City Colleges Trustee Award, 1987; Push-Andrew Thomas Health Award, 1987; Urban League Women in Health Award, 1999. **Special Achievements:** Author of "A History Of Women In Religion", 2010. **Home Addr:** 65 E 75th St, Chicago, IL 60619-1651, **Home Phone:** (773)874-1776. **Business Addr:** Medical Director, Cook County Department of Public Health, 1010 Lake St Suite 104, Oak Park, IL 60301-1133, **Business Phone:** (708)492-2000.

### LUCAS, HON. EARL S.
Government official, executive director, mayor. **Personal:** Born Jan 1, 1938, Renova, MS; married Marilee Lewis; children: Eric, Vicki, Carla, Tina, Mark & Kendric. **Educ:** Dillard Univ, BA, 1957; De Pauw Univ; Beloit Col. **Career:** Bolivar County Sch Syst, teacher, 1958-65; Star Inc, exec dir, 1965-73; City Mound Bayou, mayor, 1969, Syst Training & Redevelop Prog, dir; Nat Conf Black Mayors, founder, currently. **Orgs:** Treas, So Conf Black Mayors; dir, Mound Bayou Develop Corp; dir, Fund Educ & Community Develop; Com Delta Ministry Nat Coun Church; dir, Delta Found; Alpha Phi Alpha Fraternity; Conf Black Mayors. **Home Addr:** PO Box 476, Mound Bayou, MS 38762. **Business Addr:** Founder, National Conference of Black Mayors, 1151 Cleveland Ave Bldg D, East Point, GA 30344, **Business Phone:** (404)765-6444.

### LUCAS, GERALD ROBERT
Educator, government official, social worker. **Personal:** Born Sep 18, 1942, Washington, DC; son of Mack and Sylvia Coats Jiles; married Patricia Selena Jones; children: Gerald R Jr, Kenya & Kimberlee. **Educ:** Brandeis Univ, attended 1971; State Univ, NY Stoney Brook, MSW, 1973; Univ Minnesota, PhD, 1976. **Career:** US Dept Health, Educ & Wealth, personnel mgt specialist, 1969-71; Wash Urban League, prog dir, 1967-69; Minneapolis Urban League, proj dir, 1974-76; Univ Cincinnati, assoc prof, 1976-78; US Dept Comn, spec asst secy admin, 1978-; US Dept Com, dir off civil rights, 1982-; US Dept Com, Eastern Admin Support Ctr, dir; Econ Develop Admin, dep chief financial officer, 2002; Dir Civil Rights, Dept Com, sr adv, currently. **Orgs:** Bd dir, Minneapolis Zion Group Home, 1975-76; Nat Asn Black Social Workers Minneapolis Chap, 1973-76; Am Soc Pub Adminr, Nat Capital Area Chap, 1979-80; Cincinnati Title XX Adv Comn, 1975-76; Barnaby Manor Civic Asn, 1978-80; Conf Minority Pub Admin, 1979-80. **Honors/Awds:** Commendation Award, AUS. **Home Addr:** 12006 Hazem Ct, Ft Washington, MD 20744-6069, **Home Phone:** (301)972-3388. **Business Addr:** Senior Advisor, US Department of Commerce, 1401 Const Ave NW, Washington, DC 20230, **Business Phone:** (202)482-2000.

### LUCAS, JOHN HARDING, II
Baseball player, basketball coach, president (organization). **Personal:** Born Oct 31, 1953, Durham, NC; son of John and Blondola; married Debbie; children: Tarvia, John Jr & Jai. **Educ:** Univ Md, BS, bus admin, 1976; Univ San Francisco, MA, educ. **Career:** Basketball player, tennis player (retired), actor, coach; Houston Rockets, 1976-78, 1984-86, 1989-90; Golden Gaters World Tennis Team, 1977; New Orleans Nets World Tennis Team, 1978; Golden State Warriors, 1978-81; Wash Bullets; 1981-83; Lancaster Lightning, 1983; San Antonio Spurs, 1983-84, coach, 1992-93; Milwaukee Bucks, 1986-88, Seattle Super Sonics, 1988-89; John Lucas Enterprises, founder & pres, 1990-; Miami Tropics, coach, 1993; Philadelphia 76er's, coach & gen mgr, 1994-96; Denver Nuggets, asst coach, 1998-2001; Cleveland Cavaliers, head coach, 2001-04; Houston Wranglers, head coach, 2004; Lori McNeil, coach, 2006; Nigeria nat team, coach, 2009-; Shaw Univ, pres; Los Angeles Clippers, asst coach, 2009-10; JaMarcus Russell, life coach, 2010-11. Tv series: "ESPN SportsCentury", 1999. Films: Inside Moves, 1980; Tragedy to Triumph:The Maryland Terrapin Odyssey, 2003. **Orgs:** Bd dir, Nat Coun Alcoholism & Drug Dependence Inc; pres, Nc Educ Asn; bd dir, Nat Educ Asn. **Home Addr:** 1502 Wash St, Durham, NC 27701, **Home Phone:** (919)682-0660. **Business Addr:** Assistant Coach, Los Angeles Clippers, 714 W Olympic Blvd Suite 622, Los Angeles, CA 90015-1438, **Business Phone:** (213)765-0740.

### LUCAS, DR. JOHN HARDING, SR.
Educator, founder (originator). **Personal:** Born Nov 7, 1920, Rocky Mount, NC; son of John William and Rebecca Bowles; married Blondola O Powell; children: Cheryl & John Harding Jr. **Educ:** Shaw Univ NC, BS, 1940; NC Cent Univ, MA, 1951; NY Univ, cert advan study educ; NY Univ, Univ NC, Duke Univ; Appalachian State Univ; Durham Tech Community Col. **Career:** Educator (retired); Adkin HS NC, asst prin, sci teacher, 1940-44, guid dir coordr diversified occupations, basketball & football coach admin asst, 1946-52; Orange St Elem Sch Oxford NC, prin, 1952-57; Mary Potter HS Oxford NC, prin, 1957-62; Hillside Sr HS Durham NC, prin, 1962-86; Shaw Univ, pres, 1986-87; Durham City Bd Educ, prin emer, 1986-; Durham Pub Schs, Bd Educ, 1992-96; Durham Pub Educ Network, founder, 1997. **Orgs:** Pres, Kinston Teacher Asn, 1942-44; dir, NC Nat Educ Asn, 1961-72; US Deleg to World Assembly World Confederation Orgn Tchr ProfessionAfrica, Asia Brit Columbia & Ireland, 1965-73; adv com, Gov Commn Study Pub Sch NC, 1967-68; bd dir, NC Asn Educrs, 1970-72; Task Force NC Ment Health Ctr, 1970; Nat CommnTX Educ Asn Eval, 1970; adv com, White House Conf C & Youth, 1970; bd dir, Nat FoundImprov Educ, 1970-; bir, Learning Inst NC, 1971-; Durham Civic Conv Cntr Comn, 1972-; hon mem bd dir, NEA, 1973; chmn, Durham Human Rels Comn, 1973-75; White House Brief Conf Educ, 1975; pres, NC Asn Educs, 1974-75; chmn, bd trustee, Shaw Univ, 1978-; pres, Clean Community Syst Durham City Durham CountyInc, 1984-85; Gov Adv CNL Aging; chair, bd deacons, White Rock Baptist Church, 1990-; deacon trustee, White Rock Bapt Ch Durham NC; NC Cit Com Sch; consult, Race Rels; contr, Educ & Prof Jours; chmn, NC Delegationsto Ann Conv NC Asn Educrs at Nat Educ Asn Nat Rep Assemblies; ed, Beta Phi Chap Omega Psi Phi Frat Inc; bd dir, Durham Pub Sch Fund; Boy's Adv Coun Salvat; bd dir, NC Pub Sch Forum; Liaison Com NC Tchr Asn NC Edn Asn; life mem, Nat Asn Advan Colored People; Omega Psi Phi Fraternity Beta Phi Chapter; Durham Comt Affairs Black People. **Honors/Awds:** Man of the Year Award, Citizen's Welfare League NC, 1951; Distinguished Service Award, NC Teachers Asn, 1968; Meritorious Award, NC Resource Use Educ, 1969; Honor Award, NC State Fair, 1969; Distinguished Service Award, Durham City Asn Educrs, 1971-72; Durham's Father of the Year, 1972; Honorary Citizen, Durham NC, 1974; DHL, Shaw Univ, 1982; Wachovia Principal of the Year, 1984; Above & Beyond Award, NCAE, 1986; Honored for human and civil rights efforts, Nc Asn Educr, 1986; Martin Luther King, Jr Meritorious Award, General Baptist Convention of North Carolina, 1987; Citizen of the Year, Omega Phi Psi Fraternity, 1988; Hall of Distinction, Shaw Univ, 1990; NCAE Lobby named Lucas-Radar Lobby,

NCAE Equity Award, 1995; DHL, Shaw Univ; Benjamin Elijah Mays Lifetime Achievement Award, The Nat Sch Boards Associations Coun Urban Boards Educ, 2009. **Special Achievements:** Father of the Decade City of Durham, NC, 2011. **Home Addr:** 1502 Washington St, Durham, NC 27701-1220, **Home Phone:** (919)682-0660. **Business Addr:** Founder, Durham Public Schools, PO Box 30002, Durham, NC 27702, **Business Phone:** (919)560-2000.

## LUCAS, L. LOUISE

Government official. **Personal:** Born Jan 22, 1944, Portsmouth, VA; daughter of Joseph Boone and Lillie Boone; married Charlie C Trotter; children: Jeffrey (deceased), Lisa Burke & Theresa. **Educ:** Norfolk State Univ, BS, voc-indust educ, 1976, MA, urban affairs, human resources planning & admin, 1982. **Career:** Norfolk Naval Shipyard, from apprentice ship fitter to ship fitter, 1967-71, Engineering draftsman, 1975-76, naval archit technician, 1976-79; SE Tidewater Opportunity Proj, interim exec dir, 1985-86, exec dir, 1986-92; Old Dominion Univ, congional liaison sponsored progs, 1992-94; Virginia State Senate, senator, 1992-; Norfolk State Univ, asst prof, 1994-98, spec asst, vpres univ advan, 1998-; Southside Direct Care Provider, pres & admin, 1998-; Lucas Lodge, pres, chief exec officer & exec dir, 1998-; Lucas Transp, pres & chief exec officer; Portsmouth Day Support Prog, pres & chief exec officer; Outreach with Dem Party Va, vice chair; US Atlantic Fleet (CINCLANTFLT), command fed womens prog mgr; Supvr Shipbuilding Conversion & Repair (SUPSHIP), equal employ mgr; Comn Elec Utility Regulation, 2010; Fed Action Contingency Trust Fund, 2012; Medicaid Innovation & Reform Comn, 2013. **Orgs:** Golden life mem, Delta Sigma Theta Sorority Inc; Portsmouth Naval Civilian Adminr's Asn; bd mem large, Portsmouth Torch Club; Order Eastern Star, Brighton Light Chap, No 118; African Methodist Episcopal Church; golden heritage mem & pres, Nat Asn Advan Colored People; Nat Coun Christians & Jews; Hon Deputy Sheriff; steering comt, charter mem, Martin Luther King Leadership; bd mem, Torch Club Portsmouth; active mem, Va Legis Black Caucus; deaconess, New Mt Olivet Baptist Church; Norfolk State Univ Alumni Asn; Portsmouth Chap Links Inc; chmn, Brown v. Bd Educ Scholar Comt Va; chmn, Senate Local Govt; Comts Agr, Conserv & Natural Resources; Rehab & Social Serv; Transp; chmn, Educ & Health Spec Sub-comt Pub Smoking Legis; Govs Comn Info Technol, currently; Portsmouth City Coun, 1984; Nat Womans Polit Caucus, currently. **Business Addr:** State Senator, Virginia State, 1819 Elm Ave, Portsmouth, VA 23705-0700, **Business Phone:** (757)397-8209.

## LUCAS, LINDA GAIL

Counselor, president (organization). **Personal:** Born Jul 18, 1947, Charleston, SC; married Henry Jr; children: Ayoka L. **Educ:** Herbert Lehman Col, BA, 1969; Citadel, MEd, 1984. **Career:** Rockland C Psych Ctr, sr speech pathologist, 1972-80; Dorchester Co Schs III, speech correctionist, 1980; Chas Co Sch Dist, speech correctionist, 1980-84; Hunley Pk Elem, guid counr 1984-85; Buist Acad, guid counr 1985; Wands High Sch, guid counr, 1988-90; Septima P Clark, guidance dir, 1990; Charleston Southern Univ, adjunct cour, 1992-99; Charleston County Sch Dist, Neighborhood Planning Team, guid/parent educr, 2012; Malcolm C Hursey Elem Sch, sch counr, currently. **Orgs:** Sec Tri-County Foster Parents Assoc, 1982; adjunct staff mem Dorchester Ment Health Ctr 1984; guardian ad litem GAL Prog, 1985; delegate Alice Birney Sch Bd, 1986-87; Womens Aglow Int, 1988; pres, Tri-County Counr Develop Asn, 1991-92; adv coun, Youth Empowerment Serv, currently. **Home Addr:** 5315 Eileen St, Charleston, SC 29418, **Home Phone:** (803)767-0947. **Business Addr:** School Counselor, Malcolm C Hursey Elementary School, 4542 Simms St, North Charleston, SC 29406-5256, **Business Phone:** (843)745-7105.

## LUCAS, MAURICE F., SR.

Government official, mayor. **Personal:** Born Oct 10, 1944, Mound Bayou, MS; son of Julius and Glady Collins; married Carolyn Cousin; children: Maurice F Jr. **Educ:** Delta State Univ, Cleveland, MS, BBA, 1971. **Career:** Mayor (retired); Cleveland Sch Dist, secy & trustee, 1987-; Town Renova, Renova, Miss, mayor, 1978-09. **Orgs:** Dep grand master, PH Masons Miss, 1984-; dir, Indust Develop Found, 1985-; dir, Chamber Com, 1985-; dir, United Way, 1985-; active mem, United Supreme Coun; trustee, Bolivar County Hosp Med Found; bd mem & treas, Bolivar County Community Action Agency; adv bd mem, Miss Pub Serv Comn; lifetime mem, Nat Asn Advan Colored People; trustee, Calvary Baptist Church. **Special Achievements:** First African American to serve as president of the agency. **Home Addr:** 25 Popular St, Cleveland, MS 38732. **Business Addr:** MS.

## LUCAS, RAYMOND J.

Executive, football player, broadcaster. **Personal:** Born Aug 6, 1972, Harrison, NJ; son of Tom. **Educ:** Rutgers Univ, criminal justice, 1996. **Career:** Football player (retired); Tv game show host; New Eng Patriots, quarterback, 1996; New York Jets, quarterback, 1997-2000; Miami Dolphins, quarterback, 2001-02; Baltimore Ravens, quaterback, 2003; Platinum Maintence Serv Corp, acct exec, 2005-08; SportsNet, Jets Nation, NY, studio analyst, 2006-; Rutgers Football Radio Network, color analyst, 2009; Ocean Pac Interiors Inc, acct exec, currently; SportsNet New York, analyst, currently. **Orgs:** Rutgers Campaign Nat Steering Comt, 2001. **Honors/Awds:** Hudson County Sports Hall of Fame, 2008. **Special Achievements:** Film: Super Bowl XXXI, 1997. TV Series: "Late Show with David Letterman", 2000; "The Jersey", 2000; "Jets Nation", 2006; "Jets Extra Point", 2006; "Jets Game Plan", 2007; "Jets Post Game Live", 2008; "Casualties of the Gridiron", 2013. **Business Addr:** Account Executive, Ocean Pacific Interiors Inc, 7 Hanover Sq 8th Fl, New York, NY 10004, **Business Phone:** (212)239-1557.

## LUCAS, DR. RENDELLA (RENDELLA LUCAS GAYTON)

Social worker. **Personal:** Born Oct 30, 1910, Cheriton, VA. **Educ:** Va Union Univ, BA, 1932; Hampton Inst, MA, 1943. **Career:** Fauquier High Sch, teacher, 1932-36; Pa Dept Pub Welfare, case worker supvr admin asst, 1945-73. **Orgs:** Youth leader, Salem Baptist Church, 1937-55; supvr, Youth Dept Northern Baptist Missionary Union, 1940-55; pres, Bapt Ministers' Wives Union, 1943-45; corrs sec, Nat Asn Ministers Wives Inc, 1943-55; vpres, Woman's Aux Eastern Baptist Keystone Asn, 1945-48; vpres, Woman's Aux Sub Baptist Church Asn, 1951-53; pres, Nat Asn Ministers' Wives Inc, 1957-78; 2nd pres, Int Asn Ministers' Wives & Ministers' Widows, 1957-78; fed first ed Newsletter, 1965; Philadelpha Nat Asn Advan Colored People; exec secy, Nat Asn Ministers' Wives Inc, 1970-74; Salem Baptist Church; Church Women United; life mem, Nat Asn Ministers' Wives Inc; exec bd, Northern Baptist Missionary Union & Woman's Aux Suburban Baptist Church Asn; scholar secy, Northern Baptist Missionary Union; rec sec Inter denom Ministers Wives Fel Philadelphia; vpres, Pa Baptist Bus & Prof Women; vpres Baptist& Women's Ctr Philadelphia; communist Ministers' Wives Herald; ML Chepard Chap Va Union Univ Alumni; Comn Disadvantaged Students Eastern Sem & Col; vol, Leukemia Soc Am; adv coun, Rose Butler Brown Fund, RI Col Educ. **Honors/Awds:** Testimonial & Distinguished Achievement Award, Philadelphia Chap Comn, 1957; cert merit, Va Union Univ, 1958; Distinguished Service Award, Philadelphia Nat Asn Advan Colored People, 1961; Distinguished Service Award, Bapt Ministers' Wives Philadelphia, 1961; Elizabeth Coles Beueymem Leadership Trophy, Nat Asn Ministers' Wives, 1962; National Achievement Award, Salem Baptist Church, 1965; Certificate of Achievement, Baptist Ministers' Wives Union, 1967; Certificate of Award, Pa Baptist Asn, 1968; Community Service Award, Chapel 4 Chaplains, 1968; Outstanding Award, Plaque Baptist Ministers' Philadelphia Conf, 1967; Outstanding Service Award, Plaques New York & Rose City Portland Ministers' Wives. 1969; Shriner's Woman of the Year Award, 1970; Outstanding Service Citation, Pa Dept Welfare, 1973; DHL, Va Sem, 1982. **Home Addr:** 938 E Roumfort Rd, Philadelphia, PA 19150.

## LUCAS, RUBYE

Executive, vice president (organization). **Personal:** Born Sep 26, 1935, Ft. Myers, FL; daughter of Viola Hendley and Booker T Mims; married William; children: William Jr, Wonya & Andrea. **Educ:** Fla A&M Univ, social sci degree; Atlanta Univ, MEd. **Career:** Atlanta Pub Sch Syst, teacher, 1965-90; Turner Broadcasting Syst Inc, human resources admin/mgmt training, 1990-91, mem bd, vpres community rels, 1999; The Atlanta Proj, dir community rels, 1991-96; Fla Pub Sch Syst, teacher. **Orgs:** Bd dir, Atlanta Braves Nat Leagues Baseball Club; bd dir, Bill Lucas Scholar Found; bd dir, Bill Lucas Br Butler St YMCA; bd dir, Alliance Theatre; co-founder, Hank Aaron Rookie League; sect, Ga World Cong Ctr Authority; Fulton County Comn C & Youth; bd dir, Turner Broadcasting Syst Inc, dir, 1981-. **Home Addr:** 3154 Topaz Lane, Atlanta, GA 30331. **Business Addr:** Director, Turner Broadcasting System, 100 International Blvd, Atlanta, GA 30303, **Business Phone:** (404)827-1700.

## LUCAS, VICTORIA

Public relations executive. **Personal:** Born Chicago, IL; daughter of John Meredyth. **Educ:** Malcolm King Col; Chicago Ill, lib arts; Univ NY, bus admin. **Career:** Am Mus Immigration, pub rels asst, 1955-57; Nat Coun Alcoholism, mgr publ dept, 1957-63; Norman Craig & Kummel, copywriter & acct exec, 1964-66; Cannon Advert, pub rels dir & copywriter, 1966-67; Victoria Lucas Assoc, pres & owner. **Orgs:** Bd dir, Publicity NY; Nat Assoc Media Women; pub rel, New Sch Social Res NY, 1977-; Pub Rel Soc Am, NY Chap Comt Minorities, 1985; Acad Motion Picture Arts & Sci. **Honors/Awds:** Woman of the Year Award, Nat Asn Media Women Media; Outstanding Mentor Award, D Parke Gibson. **Special Achievements:** scripts Writer: The Body; Extreme Ops; The I Inside; The Mark of Zorro; Adventures of Don Juan. **Business Addr:** President, Victoria Lucas Associates, 888 7th Ave Suite 400, New York, NY 10019, **Business Phone:** (212)489-8008.

## LUCAS, DR. WILLIAM

Judge. **Personal:** Born Jan 15, 1928, New York, NY; son of George and Charlette Hazel; married Evelyn Daniel. **Educ:** Wayne State Univ; Manhattan Col, BS, 1952; Fordham Univ, law, 1962. **Career:** New York Police Dept, patrol officer & undercover vice squad officer, 1953; teacher, social worker, policeman, civil rights investr & FBI agt, 1966; lawyer; Wayne County Mich, 1st wayne county chief exec officer, dep wayne county sheriff, 1968, sheriff, 1969-82, county exec, 1982-87; US Govt, Wash, DC, dir off liaison servs, 1989-93; Recorder's Ct, judge, 1993-94; US Justice Dept, legal asst, dir community rel servs; Circuit Ct Three, Wayne Co, judge, 1997-2001; Fed Bur Invest, spec agt. **Orgs:** Nat Asn Advan Colored People; bd dir, Hutzel Hosp; bd gov, Manhattan Col; fel Harvard Univ. **Honors/Awds:** Michigan Man of the Year, 1986; Honorary doctorate, Manhattan Col; Sports Hall Fame; Jr Achievement Vol Am. **Special Achievements:** Wayne County's (Michigan) first Chief Executive Officer. **Home Addr:** 749 Pallister, PO Box 02733, Detroit, MI 48202.

## LUCAS, WONYA

Vice president (organization). **Educ:** Ga Inst Technol, BS, indust engineering; Univ Pa, Wharton Sch Bus, MBA, finance & kkt; Betsy Magness Leadership Inst. **Career:** Clorox, brand asst, 1990-91; Coca Cola, brand mgr, 1991- 94; Turner Broadcasting Syst, sr vpres strategic mkt, vpres bus opers & network develop, 1997-99; Cable News Network, sr vpres strategic mkt, 1999-2002; Weather Channel Networks, gen mgr & exec vpres, 2002-08; Discover Commun, chief mkt officer, 2008-10; Discovery Channel & Sci Channel, exec vpres & chief operating officer, 2010-11; TV One, pres, chief exec officer, 2011-12. **Orgs:** Bd mem, WICT Inc; bd mem, Cable & Tv Asn Mkt; bd mem, Girl Scouts USA, 2011-. **Honors/Awds:** Cablefax Daily, "Leading Women in Business" & "Leading Minorities in Business", 2009; Women in Cable Telecommunications, "Woman To Watch"; Promax & BDA Conference, Brand Builders Award, 2006; "Women To Watch", Wonder Women of Cable TV Awards, 2005; WICT-Atlanta's Red Letter Awards Inspiration Award, "Woman of the Year", 2007; "Black Enterprise", 75 Most Powerful Women in Business, 2010.

## LUCK, DR. CLYDE ALEXANDER, JR.

Surgeon. **Personal:** Born Mar 3, 1929, Danville, VA; son of Clyde Sr (deceased); children: Kelli. **Educ:** Howard Univ, BS, 1950; New York Univ, MA, 1952; Howard Univ, Md, 1959. **Career:** Samaritan Hlth Ctr-Mercy Hsp, resident gen surg; St Joseph Mercy Hosp & Detroit Receiving Hosp, resident gen surg, 1960-64; Kaiser Found Hosp, La, fel, 1964-65; Crenshaw Hosp, chmn dept surg, 1974-78; Clyde A Luck Inc, owner & surgeon, currently. **Orgs:** Omega Psi Phi; Nat AsnAdvan Colored People; Urban League; Los Angeles City Med Soc; fel Am Col Surgeons; Int Col Surgeons. **Home Addr:** . **Business Addr:** Surgeon, Owner, Clyde A Luck Inc, 6200 Wilshire Blvd Suite 1012, Los Angeles, CA 90048, **Business Phone:** (323)937-6182.

## LUCKEY, DR. EVELYN F.

Educator. **Personal:** Born Apr 30, 1926, Bellefonte, PA; daughter of Arthur R Foreman and Agnes A Haywood Foreman; children: Jennifer & Carolyn. **Educ:** Wilberforce Univ, attended 1945; Ohio State Univ, BA, BsEd, eng, psychol, 1947, MA, Eng, 1950, PhD, educ, 1970. **Career:** Educator (retired); Columbus Pub Sch, Fair Ave, Title I teacher, spec educ, 1957-59; exec dir, 1972-77, asst supt elem schs, 1977-90; Beatty Pk teacher, 1959-62; Ohio State Univ, asst prof, 1971-72; Otterbein Col, Westerville, Ohio, asst prof, 1990-98, researcher. **Orgs:** Curric Develop, 1972-93; Am Assoc Sch Admin; Assoc Suprv, trustee, pres, Bd Pub, Libr Columbus & Franklin City, 1973-89; Links Inc; trustee, pres, bd, Columbus Metrop Libr, 1973-89; Nat Alliance Black Sch Ed; Cent Ohio Mkt Coun, 1984-89; trustee, Cent Ohio Mkt Coun, 1984-89; Bd, Planned Parenthood Cent Ohio, 1984-87; Adv Bd, Urban Network Northern Cent Reg Ed Lab, 1985-90. **Honors/Awds:** Outstanding Educator Award, Alpha Kappa Alpha, 1978; Woman of the Year, Omega Psi Phi, 1980; Distinguished Kappan Award, Phi Delta Kappa, 1981; Distinguished Alumnae Award, Ohio State Univ, 1982; Cert Honor City Columbus, 1984; Woman of Achievement Award, YWCA, 1987, 1991; United Negro Col Fund Eminent Scholar, 1990. **Special Achievements:** First African American woman trustee; First African American woman board president, 1985. **Home Addr:** 404 Brookside Dr, Columbus, OH 43209-2005, **Home Phone:** (614)231-9186.

## LUCKEY, DR. IRENE

Administrator, educator. **Personal:** Born May 29, 1949, New York, NY. **Educ:** NC Agr & Tech State Univ, BA, 1971; Univ Chicago, Sch Soc Serv Admin, MA, 1973; City Univ NY, Grad Sch, PhD, 1982. **Career:** Metrop Hosp, New York, med social worker, 1973-76; NC Agri & Tech St Univ, asst prof social work, 1976-78; Brookdale Ctr Aging-Hunter Col, dir educ prg, 1979-81; LeMoyne Owen Col, vis prof, 1981-82; Clark Col, asst prof, 1982-84; Univ W Fla, asst prof soc work, assoc dir ctr aging, 1985-89; Univ Mich, Ann Arbor, res fel, 1987-89; St Univ New York, Albany, asst prof, 1989-90; Rutgers Univ; St Univ Nj, asst prof, 1990; Univ SC, Inst Family & Soc, proj evaluator, consult, res assoc prof soc work & dir, res eval & prog integration, currently. **Orgs:** Consult, Admin Aging, 1981; Atlanta Reg Comn Aging, 1984; Clark Col SocWork Prog, 1985-86; chair educ prog, Nat Asn Black Soc Workers, 1985-; adv mem, Ment Health Asn, Escambia County, 1985-; State Fla Long Term Care Coun, 1986-; bd dir, Northwest Fl Area Agen Aging, 1986; Geriat Residential & Treat Northwest Fl, 1986-; Phi Alpha; Kappa Alpha Kappa; Alpha Kappa; adv bd, Rutgers Univ, Undergrad Soc Work Prog; Gerontological Task Force, Geront Soc Res, Planning & Pract; Task Force Minority Issues, Sub comt Policy & Serv Pract; referee & reviewer, Nat Soc Sci J Geront Soc; Sisters Charity Foun. **Business Addr:** Research Associate Professor, Institute for Families in Society, 1600 Hampton St Suite 507, Columbia, SC 29208, **Business Phone:** (803)777-9124.

## LUCKIE, MARK S.

Journalist. **Educ:** Bethune-Cookman College, B.A. in Broadcast Journalism, 2005; University of California, Berkley, Master's of Journalism and Digital Journalism, 2007. **Career:** "The Daytona Beach News-Journal," Crime and Legal Reporter, 2003-05; "Los Angeles Times," Intern/Online Producer, 2007; "Entertainment Weekly," Associate Producer, 2007-08; Center for Investigative Reporting, Multimedia Producer, 2009-10; "The Washington Post," National Innovations Editor, 2010-12; Twitter, Manager of Journalism and Media, 2012-. **Orgs:** National Association of Black Journalists, Member. **Honors/Awds:** NLGJA, Excellence in Student Journalism Award, 2007; GLAAD Media Award Nominee in Digital Journalism, 2008; Sunlight Labs, Winner of Design for America Challenge, 2010; Poynter Institute, 35 Influencers in Social Media, 2010; TheGrio.com, 100 History Makers in the Making, 2011; Pulitzer Prize Finalist Team, Local News Reporting, 2012; "The Root" Magazine, The Root 100 Honorees, 2013. **Special Achievements:** Author of "The Digital Journalist's Handbook" and founder of the digital journalism blog "10,000 Words".

## LUCY, WILLIAM

Engineer. **Personal:** Born Nov 26, 1933, Memphis, TN; son of Joseph and Susie B Gibbs; married Dorotheria; children: Benita Ann & Phyllis Kay. **Educ:** Univ Calif, Berkeley, CA, civil engineering, 1950; Contra Costa Jr Col, Richmond, VA. **Career:** Contra Costa Co, CA, asst mat & res eng, 1950-66; Am Fedn State, County & Munic Employees, Local 1675 union Contra Costa employs, staff, 1956, pres, 1965, Dept Legis & Community Affairs, assoc dir, 1966-72, secy, treas, 1972-, exec asst; Coalition Black Trade Unionists, pres, 1972-; Pub Serv Int, pres, 1994-. **Orgs:** pres, co founder, Coalition Black Trade Unionists, 1972-; founder, Free SafricA Movement, 1984; Employs Asn Contra Costa Co, Calif; pres, Pub Serv Int, 1994-; bd trustee, African Am Inst; bd trustee, Transafrica; vpres, exec coun mem, Indust Union Dept Am Fedn Labor & Cong Indust Orgn; vpres, Maritime Trades Dept Am Fedn Labor & Cong Indust Orgn; bd dir, Am Dem Action; bd dir, Nat Laws Black Aged; Judicial Nomination Comn, Wash, DC; bd trustee, Martin Luther King Ctr Social Chg; pres, Local 1675; Black Leadership Forum; Africa Am Inst; bd mem, African Am Labor Ctr; bd mem, Ctr Policy Alternatives; Coun Instnl Investors. **Honors/Awds:** DHL, Bowie State Col. **Special Achievements:** One of the founders of the Free South Africa Movement; highest-ranking African American in the Labor movement; Ebony, named one of "The 100 Most Influential Black Americans"; First African American elected as president of Public Services International. **Home Addr:** 1831 Sudbury Lane NW, Washington, DC 20012, **Home Phone:** (202)429-1054. **Business Addr:** Founder, President, Coalition of Black Trade Unionists, 1150 17th St NW Suite 300, Washington, DC 20036, **Business Phone:** (202)778-3318.

## LUDACRIS (CHRISTOPHER BRIAN BRIDGES)

Rap musician. **Personal:** Born Sep 11, 1977, Champaign, IL; son of Wayne and Roberta Shields; children: Karma. **Educ:** Ga State Univ. **Career:** Hot 107.9 FM, disc jockey; Disturbing Tha Peace Rec, chief exec officer; Albums: Incognegro, 2000; Back for the First Time, 2000; Word of Mouf, 2001; Chicken-N-Beer, 2003; The Red Light Dist, 2004; Release Therapy, 2006; Theater of the Mind, 2007, 2008; Battle of the Sexes, 2010. Films: The Wash, 2001; The Bros, 2002; 2 Fast 2 Furious, 2003; Crash, 2005; The Heart of the Game, 2005;

Hustle & Flow, 2005; The Bros, 2006; American Hustle, 2007; Fred Claus, 2007; RocknRolla, 2008; Max Payne, 2008; Ball Don't Lie, 2009; Gamer, 2009; Fast Five, 2011; No Strings Attached, 2011; New Year's Eve, 2011; Breakaway, 2011; Ludaversal, 2012; Fast & Furious 6, 2013; Parking Lot Pimpin, producer, 2013. TV series: Eve, 2005; Law & Order: Special Victims Unit, The Simpsons, 2006-07; The Simpsons, 2007; Being Mary Jane, 2014. **Honors/Awds:** Hollywood Film Award, 2005; Black Reel Award, 2006; Screen Actors Guild Award, 2006; Critics Choice Award, Broadcast Film Critics Asn, 2006; Grammy Award, 2007. **Special Achievements:** Nominated for numerous awards. **Business Addr:** Recording Artist, Def Jam Records, 825 8th Ave, New York, NY 10019, **Business Phone:** (212)333-8000.

### LUE, TYRONN JAMAR

Basketball player. **Personal:** Born May 3, 1977, Mexico, MO; son of Kim Miller and Kim Jones. **Educ:** Univ Nebr, BA, sociol, 1998. **Career:** Basketball player (retired), coach; Los Angeles Lakers, pt guard, 1998-2001; Wash Wizards, pt guard, 2001-03; Orlando Magic, pt guard, 2003-04, 2009; Houston Rockets, pt guard, 2004-05; Atlanta Hawks, pt guard, 2004-08; Dallas Mavericks, pt guard, 2008; Milwaukee Bucks, pt guard, 2008-09; Orlando Magic, pt guard, 2009; Boston Celtics, asst coach, 2009-13, dir basketball develop, 2009-11; Los Angeles Clippers, asst coach, 2013-14; Cleveland Cavaliers, assoc head coach, 2014-16, head coach, 2016-. **Honors/Awds:** Rookie Year, Nat Basketball Asn, 1998; Champion, Nat Basketball Asn, 2000-01; ESPY Award, 2016. **Business Addr:** Head Coach, Cleveland Cavaliers, 1 Ctr Ct, Cleveland, OH 44115-4001, **Business Phone:** (216)420-2000.

### LUE-HING, DR. CECIL

Association executive, engineer. **Personal:** Born Nov 3, 1930; children: Cecil Barrington & Robert James. **Educ:** Marquette Univ, BS, civil engineering, 1961; Case Western Res Univ, MS, sanit engineering, 1963; Wash Univ, St Louis, PhD, environ & sanit engineering, 1966. **Career:** Univ Wis, Col Med, chief technician, 1950-55; Mt Sinai Hosp, sch med tech, Wis, instr histol & cytol chem & lab suv, 1955-61; Huron Rd Hosp, Wis, res assoc clin biochem, 1961-63; Wash Univ, res assoc, environ engr, 1963-65, asst prof, 1965-66; Ryckman, Edgerley, Tomlinson & Assoc, 1966-68, sr assoc, 1968-77; Metrop Water Reclamation Dist Greater Chicago, dir res & develop, 1977; Ill Inst Technol, invited lectr, adj prof; Gov bd Environ & Water Resources Inst Am Soc Civil Engrs, pres; Nat Asn Clean Water Agencies, pres; Cecil Lue-Hing & Assocs Inc, pres & chief exec officer, currently; Environ Engineering & Sci Found, pres, currently. **Orgs:** Bd trustee & pres, Am Acad Environ Engrs & Scientists, 2010; AAAS; Nat Acad Scis Task Force; Water Pollution Control Fed; Am Water Works Asn; Am Pub Works Asn; Sigma Si, hon mem, Nat Eng Soc; Hon Mem, Am Soc Civil Engrs; vice chmn, Ill Environ Regulatory Rev Comn; Asn Metrop Sewerage Agencies; chmn, Bd Ed Rev Water Environ Res; fel Wash Univ. **Honors/Awds:** Professional Achievement Award, Marquette Univ Alumni Asn, Col Engineering, 2006; Sustained Achievement Award, Renewable Natural Resources Found, 2007; National Government Civil Engineer Award; Simon W Freese Environ Engineering Award; Gordon Maskew Fair Award, Am Acad Environ Engrs' Kappe; Presidental Award; Environmental Award, Asn Metrop Sewerage Agencies AMSA; Charles Alvin Emerson Medal, Water Environ Fed; App by the mayor Atlanta nine-mem independent coun citys Clean Water Plan. **Special Achievements:** Published numerous industry-recognized books and reference materials, and has contributed more than 30 chapters to various other publications; Metrop Water Reclamation Dist Greater Chicago's res facility renamed the Dr. Cecil Lue-Hing Research and Development Complex, 2005. **Home Addr:** 6101 N Sheridan St 40B E, Chicago, IL 60660. **Business Addr:** President, Chief Executive Officer, Cecil Lue-Hing & Associates Inc, 6815 County Line Lane, Burr Ridge, IL 60527-5724, **Business Phone:** (630)986-5751.

### LUIS, DR. WILLIAM

Educator. **Personal:** Born Jul 12, 1948, New York, NY; son of Petra Diluvina Santos and Domingo; married Linda Garceau; children: Gabriel, Diego, Tammie & Stephanie. **Educ:** State Univ NY, Binghamton, BA, 1971; Univ Wis, Madison, MA, 1973; Cornell Univ, MA, 1979, PhD, 1980. **Career:** Bd Educ, NY City, teacher, 1971-72 & 1973-74; Cornell Univ, teaching asst, 1976-78; Dartmouth Col, instr, 1979-80, asst prof Latin Am & Caribbean, 1980-85, assoc prof, 1985-88, fac fel, 1983; Handbk Latin Am Studies, contrib ed & consult, 1981-91; Latin Am Lit Rev, mem ed bd, 1985-; Nat Endowment Humanities, reader, 1985; Nat Res Coun, Ford Found Fel Panel, staff, 1986; Wash Univ, vis assoc prof, 1988, Latin Am & Caribbean Area Studies Prog, assoc prof & dir, 1988-91; Binghamton Univ, vis assoc prof, 1988-89, Latin Am & Caribbean Area Studies Prog, actg dir, 1988-89, dir, 1989-90, assoc prof, 1989-91; Vanderbilt Univ, Dept Span & Port, assoc prof Span, 1991-96, Robert Penn Warren Ctr Humanities, fel, 1991-94, mem, 1991-2004, African & African Am Studies Steering Comt, mem, 1995-2004, prof Span & Port, 1996, prof Eng, 2001, Afro-Hisp Rev, ed, 2004-, chancellor's Prof Span, 2006-11, Gertrude Conaway Vanderbilt Prof Span, 2011-, Latino & Latina Studies Prog, dir, 2013-; Am Coun Learned Soc, fel, 1993-94; Yale Univ, vis prof, 1998. **Orgs:** Vpres, Asn Caribbean Studies, 1985-86; ed bd, Afro-Hisp Rev, 1987-; Latin Am & Iberian Studies Prog, 1991-; speakers bur, Tenn Coun Humanities, 1992-93; African Afro-Am Studies Steering Comt, 1995-; ed bd, J Afro-Latin, Am Res Asn, 1996; Exec comt, Afro-Latin Am Res Asn, 2000-; Mod Lang Asn; Asn Caribbean Studies; Am Asn Teachers Span & Port; adv bd, Comt Spec Educ Proj; Ad Hoc Comt Study Hisp Admis & Recruitment; Minority Educ Coun; Black Caucus; Lit Criticism Sem; co-dir, Latin Am Lit Sem; fac adv, Phi Sigma Psi; African & Afro-Am Studies Sem; exec comt mem, Asn Caribbean Studies; dir, Screening Comt; adj cur, Film DC; Native Am Studies Steering Comt; Exec Comt Fac DC; dir grad studies, Dept Sp & port, Fall, 2002; Agenda Subcomt Exec Comt Fac DC; Libr Search Comt Humanities Bibliogr. **Honors/Awds:** Editorial Board Award, State Univ NY, Off Spec Prog, 1989 & 1994; Distinguished Alumnus Award, State Univ New York, 1989; Certificates of Recognition & 13th Annual Affirmative Action & Diversity Initiatives Award, 1999. **Special Achievements:** Published: Literary Bondage: Slavery in Cuban Narrative, 1990; Dance Between Two Cultures: Latino-Caribbean Literature Written in the United States, 1997; Culture and Customs of Cuba, 2001; Lunes de Revolucion: Literatura y cultura enlos Primeros Anos de la Revolucion Cubana, 2003; Autobiografia del esclavo Juan Francisco Manzano y Otros Escritos, Iberoamericana-Vervuert Verlag, 2005; Edited with Edmundo Desnoes, Losdispositivos en la flor, Ediciones del Norte, 1981; Edited Voices from Under: Black Narrative in Latin America and the Caribbean, 1984; edited with Julio Rodriguez-Luis, Translating Latin America: Culture as Text and Translation Perspectives VI, 1991; edited Modern Latin American Fiction Writers, 1992; edited with Ann Gonzalez, Modern Latin American Fiction Writers, Second Series, 1994; edited "Antologia: Poesia hispano-caribena escrita en los Estados Unidos,"Boletin de la Fundacion Federico Garcia Lorca, 1995; Bibliografia yantologia critica de las vanguardias literarias: El Caribe, Iberoamericana, 2005. **Home Addr:** 2112 Piccadilly Pl, Nashville, TN 37215, **Home Phone:** (615)481-2112. **Business Addr:** Gertrude Conaway Vanderbilt Professor of Spanish, Vanderbilt University, Furman 323 2301 Vanderbilt Pl, Nashville, TN 37240-1617, **Business Phone:** (615)322-6862.

### LUKE, DR. LEARIE B.

Educator, vice president (organization). **Personal:** married Sharon; children: Sharlene. **Educ:** Caribbean Union Col; Andrews Univ; Morgan State Univ; Howard Univ. **Career:** SC State Univ, chairperson, 2002, Dept Social Sci, asst prof hist & interim chair, 2011-, interim assoc vpres acad affairs, 2011-13, Off int & Nat Stud Exchange Progs, dir, 2011-, assoc provost acad affairs, actg provost, currently; Sc Dept Arch & Hist, Comnr. Book: Identity and Secession in the Caribbean: Tobago Versus Trinidad 1889-1980, Univ Wi Press, 2007. **Orgs:** Fel, Sasakawa Young Leaders Fel Fund, Howard Univ, 1998-2001; Adv ComtAcad Progs, SC Comn Higher Educ; life mem, Asn Caribbean Historians;Asn Study African Am Life & Hist; prin investr, Montford Pt Marines; departmental & univ-wide comt; Black Hist Month Coord Comt, Fac Handbk Comt; bd mem, Educ S Atlantic Conf; chmn bd, Vanard J. Mendinghall Jr. Acad; vpres, Univ Southern Caribbean Alumni Asn. **Home Addr:** 703 Kings Rd, Orangeburg, SC 29115-3061, **Home Phone:** (803)536-1670. **Business Addr:** Assistant Professor, Chairperson, South Carolina State University, 300 Col St NE, Orangeburg, SC 29117, **Business Phone:** (803)536-8969.

### LUKE, SHERRILL DAVID

Actor, judge, air force officer. **Personal:** Born Sep 19, 1928, Los Angeles, CA; son of Mordecai and Venye Luke Corporal; children: David & Melana. **Educ:** Univ Calif, Los Angeles, BA, 1950; Univ Calif, Berkeley, MA, 1954; Golden Gate Univ, JD, 1960. **Career:** Judge (retired), mediator; Films: Sunny, 1941; Syncopation, 1942; South of Dixie, 1944. Dist Columbia Govt, dir prog dev, 1967-69; Aetna Life & Casualty, dirurban affairs, 1969-71; Conn Val Dev Corp, pres & dir, 1971-73, Pacht Ross Coun, 1973-76; Jacobs Kane Luke, partner, 1976-78; Los Angeles County, chief dep assessor, 1978-81; Loyola Law Sch, adj prof, 1979-81; Los Angeles Munic Ct, judge, 1981-88; super ct judge, 1989; Am Arbit Asn, arbit & mediator, currently. **Orgs:** Cabinet Sec Calif Gov's Off, 1964-65; consult, Ford Found, 1966-67; pres, Los Angeles City Planning Comn, 1975-76; bd gov, Univ Calif Los Angeles Found, 1976-; pres, Univ Calif Los Angeles Alumni Assoc, 1988-90; regent, Univ Calif, 1988-90; bd visitor, Univ Calif Los Angeles, 1991-94; Calif Judges Asn; Judicial Div Langston Bar Asn; Judicial Coun Calif Asn; bd dir, Univ Calif Los Angeles Stephens House Scholar Asn; adv bd, Southeast Symphony Asn; adv bd, Univ Calif Los Angeles Chancellor's Community Adv Comn. **Honors/Awds:** Outstanding Senior Award, Univ Calif Los Angeles Alumni Asn, 1950; Outstanding Achievement Award, Kappa Alpha Psi, 1963-; Justice Pro Tem CA Ct Appeal, 1985-86, 1995; University Service Award, Univ Calif Los Angeles Alumni Asn, 1994; Hall of Fame Award, John M. Langston Bar Asn, 1999. **Special Achievements:** First African-American to be elected president of undergraduate student government at UCLA. **Home Addr:** 725 S Lorraine Blvd Suite C, Los Angeles, CA 90005, **Home Phone:** (323)933-3845. **Business Addr:** Arbitrator, Mediator, American Arbitration Association, 335 Madison Ave Fl 10, New York, NY 10017-4605, **Business Phone:** (212)716-5800.

### LUMBLY, CARL

Actor. **Personal:** Born Aug 14, 1951, Minneapolis, MN; married Vonetta McGee; children: Brandon. **Educ:** Macalester Col, St. Paul, eng. **Career:** Undercover with the KKK, 1979; Assoc Press, journalist; Films: Caveman, 1981; The Adventures of Buckaroo Banzai, 1984; The Bedroom Window, 1987; Everybody's All-American, 1988; To Sleep With Anger, 1990; Pacific Heights, 1990; Brother Future, 1991; South Central, 1992; Back to the Streets of San Francisco, 1992; "Going to Extremes", 1992-93; How Stella Got Her Groove Back, Out of Darkness, 1994; M.A.N.T.I.S., 1994; SeaQuest 2032, 1994, 1998; Men of Honor, 2000; Just A Dream, 2002; Nat Turner: A Troublesome Property, 2003; Namibia: The Struggle for Liberation, 2007; The Alphabet Killer, 2008; Nominated, 2010; America Is Still the Place, 2014. TV Series: "Emergency! ", 1978; "Escape from Alcatraz", 1979; "Taxi", 1980; "Caveman ", 1981; "Nurse", 1981; "Lifepod", 1981; "The Jeffersons", 1981; "B.J. and the Bear", 1981; "Cagney & Lacey", 1981-88; "Judgment in Berlin", 1988; "Cagney and Lacey", 1982-88; "L.A. Law", 1989-90; "To Sleep with Anger", 1990; "Moe's World", 1990; "Conspiracy: "The Adventures of Buckaroo Banzai Across the 8th Dimension ", 1984; "Great Performances", 1985; Conspiracy: The Trial of the Chicago 8, 1987; The Trial of the Chicago 8", 1987; "M.A.N.T.I.S", 1994; "On Promised Land", 1994; "Night john", 1996; "The Ditch digger's Daughters", 1997; "Buffalo Soldiers", 1997; SubZero, 1998; The Real Adventures of Jonny Quest", 1997; "The Ditchdigger's Daughters", 1997; "EZ Streets", 1996-97; "The Wedding", 1998; How Stella Got Her Groove Back, 1998; "Any Day Now", 1998; "Strange World", 1999; "Superman", 1997-99; "Border Line", 1999; "ER", 1999; "The Wild Thornberrys", 1999-2000; "Family Law", 2000; "The American Experience", 1991-2000; "Batman Beyond", 1999-2000; "The Magnificent Seven", 2000; Men of Honor ", "9mm of Love", 2000; "The Color of Friendship", 2000; "The West Wing", 2000; "Little Richard", 2000; "Night Visions", 2001; "Kate Brasher ", 2001; "Justice League", 2001-04; "Alias", 2001-06; "Just a Dream", 2002; "Static Shock", 2003; "Sounder", 2003; "Independent Lens", 2004; "Alias", 2004; "Slavery and the Making of America", 2005; "Justice League", 2001-06; "Justice League Unlimited", 2004-06; "Battlestar Galactica", 2006; "Chuck", 2008; "Cold Case", 2008; "Grey's Anatomy", 2008; "Black Panther", 2009-10; "Batman: The Brave and the Bold, "Batman: The Brave and the Bold", 2009; "Trauma", 2010; "Criminal Minds", 2010; "NCIS", 2011; "Southland", 2012; "Hope: The Last Paladin", 2014; "Family Guy", 2014. **Special Achievements:** Nominated for Image Awards, Cable ACE Awards and Black Reel Awards. **Business Addr:** Actor, 1033 Miller Ave, Berkeley, CA 94708.

### LUMPKIN, ADRIENNE KELLY (ADRIENNE LORRAINE KELLY)

Business owner. **Personal:** Born Apr 12, 1957, Bronx, NY; daughter of James and Lorraine; married Kelly M; children: 4. **Educ:** Wesleyan Univ, BA, psychol sociol, 1979; Harvard Univ, MBA, mkt, 1983. **Career:** IBM, systs engr, 1979-81; Hewlett-Packard, mkt mgr, 1983-92; Wake County Pub Sch Bus Alliance, chair, Engaged Parent & Citizen, 1992-; Alt Access, fonder & pres, 1993-; NAWBO, pres-greater raleigh chap, 2004-05; Jack & Jill Am Inc, chair, by laws comt, 2006-09, chair educ comt, 2009-11. **Orgs:** Vpres, Raleigh/Durham Chap, 1994-96, bd dir, 1997-2002, Nat Black MBA Asn; Nat Asn Women Bus Owners, 1995-; Coun Entrepreneurial Develop, 1993-; bus adv bd, Meredith Col, 1999-; bd adv rep, Wiley Int Elem, 2010-; bd mem, NAWBO Nat Nominating Comm, Greater Raleigh Chamber Com & Raleigh Little Theatre, 2011-; chair acad women, YWCA the Greater Triangle, 2011; exec comt, bd mem, United Arts Coun Raleigh & Wake County, 2011-; bd adv chair, Wake County Pub Sch Syst, 2012-. **Honors/Awds:** MBA of the Year Award, Raleigh/Durham Chap, Nat Black MBA Asn, 1993, 1997; Outstanding MBA Award, 1997; Future 30 Award, 1997, Pinnacle Award, 1998, 1999, Greater Raleigh Chamber Com, 1997; Super Gazelle, southeast region, Entrepreneurial Educ Found, 1997; North Carolina Tech 50 Award, 1998-2000; Triangle Women in Business Award, 1998; Forbes ASAP Fast 500 Award, 1999; H Naylor Fitzhugh Award of Relevance, 1999; 2005 Entrepreneur inductee, YWCA Acad Women; Women Extraordinaire Award & Women in Business Award, Triangle Bus Jour. **Business Addr:** President, Director of Marketing, Alternate Access Inc, Glenwood Ctr, Raleigh, NC 27612-2700, **Business Phone:** (919)831-1860.

### LUMPKIN, ELGIN BAYLOR. See GINUWINE.

### LUNDIN-HUGHES, DONNA

Public relations executive. **Personal:** Born Nov 25, 1949, Chicago, IL; daughter of Donald and Estella Walker Madden; married Michael Dean; children: Lyn, Natalie & Melissa. **Educ:** Iowa Wesleyan Col, BA, 1971. **Career:** S Cook County Girl Scout Coun, field exec, 1971-72, currently. **Orgs:** Girl Scouts-Seal Ohio Coun Inc, field exec, 1972-76, dir commun, 1976-84, field supvr, 1984-86, pub rels dir, 1986-90, asst dir, resource develop & serv, pub rels dir, mem dir, currently; Alpha Kappa Alpha; Pub Rels Soc Am, 1990-; Jack & Jill Am; Nat Coalition 100 Black Women, 1991-92. **Home Addr:** 5649 Dorsey Dr, Columbus, OH 43235, **Home Phone:** (614)459-0333. **Business Addr:** Membership Director, Girl Scouts-Seal of Ohio Council Inc, 1700 WaterMark Dr, Columbus, OH 43215-1097, **Business Phone:** (614)487-8101.

### LUNDY, DR. HAROLD W., SR.

President (organization), school administrator, founder (originator). **Educ:** Dillard Univ, attended 1971. **Career:** Grambling State Univ, vpres admin & strategic planning, 1991, pres, 1991-2001; Lundy Enterprises LLC, founder, chief exec officer & pres, 1994-. **Business Addr:** Chief Executive Officer, President, Lundy Enterprises LLC, 4505 N Sherwood Forest Dr, Baton Rouge, LA 70814, **Business Phone:** (225)275-1773.

### LUNDY, LARRY

Executive, executive director. **Personal:** Born New Orleans, LA; married Marilyn; children: 3. **Educ:** Dillard Univ, BA, acct; Pepperdine Univ, MBA. **Career:** Peat, Marc & Mitchell, staff; Alexander Grant & Co, staff; Pizza Hut, controller, 1980, vpres/controller, vpres, restaurant develop, 1988; Lundy Enterprises Inc, prin, pres & chief exec officer, currently. **Honors/Awds:** New Orleanian of the Year, Gambit Newspaper, 1993; Company is ranked 69 on the list of Top 100 businesses, Black Enterprise, 1994. **Special Achievements:** Controller of the largest minority owned fast food franchise in America. **Business Addr:** President, Chief Executive Officer, Lundy Enterprises Inc, 10555 Lake Forest Blvd Suite 1J, New Orleans, LA 70127-5206, **Business Phone:** (504)241-6658.

### LUNEY, PERCY R., JR.

Educator, vice president (organization). **Personal:** Born Jan 13, 1949, Hopkinsville, KY; son of Percy R; married Beverly Marshall; children: Jamille & Robyn. **Educ:** Hamilton Col, BA, geol, 1970; Harvard Law Sch, JD, law, 1974. **Career:** US Dept Interior, Off Solicitor, atty, adv, 1975-77; Fisk Univ, univ legal coun spec asst to pres, 1977-79; Birch, Horton, Brittner, Monroe, Pestinger & Anderson, assoc, 1979-80; NC Cent Univ Sch Law, asst dean, prof, dean, 1980-98; Duke Univ, adj prof law, 1985-98; Cornell Univ, adj prof; Nat Judicial Col, pres, 1998-2001; Fla A&M Univ Sch Law, dean & prof law, 2001-05; Space Fla, vpres, educ res & develop & workforce, 2008-; Fulbright Lectr & Scholar; sr Fulbright Specialist. **Orgs:** Fel Thomas J Watson Found, 1970; Hamilton Col, Alumni Asn, 1970-; Harvard Law Sch, Alumni Asn, 1974-; Dist Columbia Bar, 1975-; Am Bar Asn, 1983-; fel NC Japan Ctr Fac, 1983; NC Bar Asn, 1983-; Nat Bar Asn, 1994-; fel Am Bar Found, 1996-; Univ NC Chapel Hill, Parents Coun, 1999-. **Home Addr:** PO Box 162642, Altamonte Springs, FL 32716. **Business Addr:** Vice President, Director, Space Florida, Bldg M6-306 Rm 9030 State Rd 405, Cape Canaveral, FL 32920, **Business Phone:** (321)730-5301.

### LUSTER, JORY

Executive, president (organization). **Personal:** son of Fred Sr. **Educ:** Bradley Univ, BS, bus admin; Kellogg Grad Sch Mgt, Northwestern Univ, MBA; Harvard Univ Grad Sch Bus Admin, cert. **Career:** Luster Prod Inc, pres, currently. **Business Addr:** President, Luster Products Inc, 1104 W 43rd St, Chicago, IL 60609, **Business Phone:** (773)579-1800.

### LUSTER, ROBERT

Executive, president (organization), chief executive officer. **Educ:** US Mil Acad, BS, gen engineering; Long Island Univ, MBA, finance. **Career:** Luster Nat Inc, owner, pres & chief exec officer, 1990-; Century 22 Communities LLC, managing gen partner; Can Do Kid Inc, pres, co-founder & financial opers, 2004. **Orgs:** Bd dir, Bay Planning Coalition, San Francisco, CA; bd dir, W Pt Soc San Francisco; bd dir, Golden Gate Bank; founding trustee, Univ Calif; Construct Mgt Asn Am; Soc Am Mil Engrs. **Business Addr:** President, Chief Executive Officer, Luster National Inc, 1701 Westwind Dr Suite 116, Bakersfield, CA 93301, **Business Phone:** (661)869-0157.

### LUTEN, THOMAS DEE

Educator, administrator. **Personal:** Born Mar 12, 1950, Youngstown, OH; son of Ernest D and Christine Motley; married Nedra Farrar; children: Thomas David & Christian Douglas. **Educ:** Kenyon Col, Gambier, attended 1969; Ohio State Univ, BS, coun & personnel serv,

MA, 1974; Mich State Univ, PhD, coursework, higher educ admin, 1982; Univ NC, orgn behav, econs & mkt, attended 1984. **Career:** Cornell Univ, asst dir, 1973-76; Mich Dept Com, admin analyst, 1977-78; Mich Dept Ment Health, personnel specialist, 1978-80, dir, staff develop & EEO, 1978-80; Univ NC, Chapel Hill, assoc dir, univ career planning & placement, 1980-83, Sch Dent, dir stud serv & asst prof dente col, 2000-07; GTE S, orgn effectiveness spec, 1984; NC Cent Univ, dir, career coun, placement & coop educ, 1984-88; Mich State Univ, dir, career devt & placement, 1988-91; Wayne County Community Col, vpres stud develop, 1993-95; Hampton Univ, Career Ctr, dir, 1998-2000; Henry Schein, diversity consult, 2007-08; First Tee, Vol, 2007-11; self-employed, edu & human resource consult, 2008-11; pvt diversity consult, currently; Meharry Sch Dent, admis sch dent, dir, asst prof, co chair, 2011-13; Premiere Dent Staffing, recrutiment consult, 2013-14; MakeATransition Consult Serv, sr partner, 2015-. **Orgs:** Am Acad Cosmetic Dent, 1972-81; Am Col Personnel Asn, 1984-92; Sch Community & Pub Affairs, 1984-91; Minn Col Personnel Asn, 1988-91; ASCUS, 1985-86, 1988-91; IMPA, 1978-81, 1985-88; Nat Coun Stud Dev, 1993-; Southeastern Asn Stud Personnel Admin, 1993-96; bd mem, Better Health 4Kids, 2012-15. **Home Addr:** 1511 Edgeside Ct, Raleigh, NC 27609. **Business Addr:** NC.

### LYDE, JEANETTE S.

Educator. **Personal:** Born Apr 23, 1946, Paterson, NJ; daughter of William Smith and Delphine Williams; married Ray; children: Ray Jr & Jalyn Elizabeth. **Educ:** William Paterson Col, BA, 1969; Montclair State Col, MA, 1982; Seton Hall Univ, doctoral cand, cur. **Career:** Paterson Pub Sch, high sch guid dir, 1986-92, high sch vice prin, 1988-89, elem sch vice prin, 1992-93, elem sch prin, 1993-94, high sch prin, 1994-98, high sch coordr, 1998-. **Orgs:** Delta Sigma Theta Sorority, Paterson Alumnae Chap, 1974-; NJ Prin & Supvr Asn, 1993-; Asn Supvr & Curric Devel, 1993-; Nat Asn Soc Sch Prin, 1994-; pres, Paterson Prin Asn, 1994-98; Kappa Delta Pi, 1997-; life mem, local exec bd mem, Nat Asn Advan Colored People. **Home Addr:** 268 E 31st St, Paterson, NJ 07504, **Home Phone:** (973)278-1760. **Business Addr:** District High School Coordinator, Paterson Public School, 90 Delaware Ave, Paterson, NJ 07503, **Business Phone:** (973)321-1000.

### LYGHT, TODD WILLIAM

Football coach, football player. **Personal:** Born Feb 9, 1969, Kwajalein; son of William; married Stefanie; children: Logan & Luca. **Educ:** Univ Notre Dame, psychol, 1991. **Career:** Football player (retired); Los Angeles Rams, left cornerback, 1991-93, right cornerback, 1994; St Louis Rams, left cornerback, 1995-2000, strong safety, 1999; Detroit Lions, right cornerback & left cornerback, 2001-02; Bishop Gorman High Sch, defensive backs asst coach, 2009-10; Univ Ore, defensive intern, 2011-12; Philadelphia Eagles, asst defensive backs coach, 2013-14; Univ Notre Dame, defensive backs coach, 2015-. **Honors/Awds:** All American, 1988-89; Jim Thorpe Award, 1989; Kris Samons Trophy; Rams Rookie of the Year, 1991; Pro Bowl, 1999; All-Pro, 1999; Super Bowl Champion (XXIV). **Special Achievements:** Film: Super Bowl XXXIV, 2000. TV Series: "NFL Monday Night Football", 1991; "ESPN's Sunday Night Football", 1992-98; "NFL on FOX", 1994-95; "The NFL on CBS", 1998-99; "The Daily Show with Jon Stewart", 2000. **Business Addr:** Defensive Backs Coach, University of Notre Dame, 116 Joyce Ctr, Notre Dame, IN 46556, **Business Phone:** (574)631-5450.

### LYLE, DR. FREDDRENNA MARGARET

Judge, lawyer. **Personal:** Born Jun 1, 1951, Chicago, IL; daughter of Delores Murphy Harris and Fred. **Educ:** Univ Ill-Chicago, BA, 1973; John Marshall Law Sch, JD, 1980. **Career:** Cornelius E Toole & Assocs, Chicago, Ill, assoc, 1980-83; F Lyle & Assocs, Chicago, Ill, partner, 1983-85; Smith & Lyle, Chicago, Ill, partner, 1985; 6th Ward City Chicago, alderman, 1998-2011, Dem Committeeman, 2004-12; Black Elected Officials State Ill, chmn, currently; State Ill' Circuit Ct Cook County, First Munic Dist, judge, 2011-; Cook County Dem Party, vice chair, currently. **Orgs:** Pres, Cook County Bar asn, 1980-; bd mem, Nat Bar asn, 1981-; bd mem; Const Rights Found, 1985-; Nat Black Child Devt Inst, 1989-; Ill Supreme Ct Comt; Chatham Avalon Park Community Coun, currently; Park Manor Neighbors Community Org; Nat Asn Advan Colored People; Rainbow PUSH; co-chair, Lawyer's Comt Harold Wash. **Honors/Awds:** William Ming Award, Cook County Bar Asn, 1987. **Home Addr:** 7241 S Rhodes, Chicago, IL 60619, **Home Phone:** (312)224-9402. **Business Addr:** Judge, State of Illinois' Circuit Court of Cook County, Rm 2505 50 W Wash St, Chicago, IL 60602, **Business Phone:** (312)603-4347.

### LYLE, KEITH ALLEN

Football player. **Personal:** Born Apr 17, 1972, Washington, DC; son of Garry. **Educ:** Univ Va, BS, psychol. **Career:** Football player (retired); Los Angeles Rams, 1994; St Louis Rams, free safety, 1995-2000, safety, 1999; Wash Redskins, defensive back, 2001; San Diego Chargers, free safety, 2002. **Honors/Awds:** Interceptions leader, Nat Football League, 1996; Super Bowl champion (XXXIV); Interception return yards leader, Nat Football Conf, 1996. **Home Addr:** 9615 Maypan Pl, Largo, FL 33777, **Home Phone:** (727)391-4197.

### LYLE, PERCY H., JR.

Salesperson. **Personal:** Born Oct 15, 1947, Detroit, MI; married Glenda Wilhelma; children: Kipp E, Jennifer B & Anthony S. **Educ:** Commun Univ Colo, BA, 1970; Webster Univ, MA, 1972; Univ Denver, PhD, 1997. **Career:** Int Bus Mach, systs mkt rep; Community Col Aurora, instr, dir diversity, adv, Black Stud Allicance; Red Rocks Community Col, instr; Community Col Denver, instr; Radio Talk Show, host. **Orgs:** Pk Hill Bus Asn; Optimist Club; Mt Gilead Baptist Ch; comnr, Elect George Brown Lt Gov; exec bd, Malcolm X Ment Health Ctr; YMCA; Pk Hill Improv Asn. **Home Addr:** 911 Locust St, Denver, CO 80220, **Home Phone:** (303)388-7245.

### LYLE, ROBERTA BRANCHE BLACKE

Teacher. **Personal:** Born Jul 20, 1929, Glasgow, VA; children: Valerie, Robert Jr & Carl. **Educ:** Va State Col, BS, 1966; Univ Va, MEd, 1972. **Career:** Teacher (retired); Rockbridge City Sch Bd, teacher. **Orgs:** Past mem, bd dir Stonewall Jackson Hosp, 1972-78; towncoun, Town Glasgow, Budget & Finance Parks & Recreation Comt, 1974; scholar comt Burlington Indust Glasgow, 1976-77; Grand Worthy Matron Grand Chap OES VA, 1998-2000; REA, VEA, NEA, 1958, Order Eastern Star, 1952, secy, Nat Asn Advan Colored People, PTA, Ann Ellen Early 209 OEA; usher bd, sr choir, teacher Sunday Sch, chair, Union Bapt Church; secy, Mt Olivet Cemetary Comn; secy, Concerned Citizens Inc, Glasgow; chaor, Parks & Recreation Comn; Lylburn Downing Asn; Concern Citizens Glasgow. **Home Addr:** 1306 2nd St, Glasgow, VA 24555, **Home Phone:** (540)258-2993. **Business Addr:** Town Council, Town of Glasgow, 1100 BlueRidge Rd, Glasgow, VA 24555, **Business Phone:** (540)258-2246.

### LYLES, DEWAYNE

School administrator. **Personal:** Born Mar 8, 1947, Clanton, AL; married Michelle Billups; children: Raquel Lynn, Ryan Milton & Roderic. **Educ:** Miles Col, sociol & educ, 1969; Univ Ala, Birmingham, AL, coun & guid, 1975; Marshall Univ, mgt, 1981. **Career:** Miles Col Spec Prog, counr, 1971-75, instr, 1975; Miles Col, Emergency Sch Aide Act Prog, asst dir, 1975-76; Miles Col, dir admiss, 1976-77; Marshall Univ, dir minority stud affairs; Denison Univ, asst dean educ serv, 1985-, asst dir admis, 1985-. **Orgs:** Nat Assessment Stud; consult, WV Sch Osteop Med, 1983; Fairfield W Community Ctr Jobs, 1983-84; Progressive Black Men's Asn, 1983-; treas, Omega Psi Phi; vpres, Men's Asn Church. **Home Addr:** 2842 E 6th St, Columbus, OH 43217-7851. **Business Addr:** Assistant Dean for Educational Services, Denison University, 100 W Col St, Granville, OH 43023, **Business Phone:** (614)587-6666.

### LYLES, JAMES V. (JAMES VERNON LYLES)

Clergy. **Educ:** Philander Smith Col, BA, 1952; Perkins Sch Theol, ThM, 1955; Grad Theol Found, DMin, 1994; Univ Calif, Los Angeles. **Career:** United Methodist pastor, 1955-98; hospital chaplain, 1998-2004. **Orgs:** Gen Bd Evangelism, Educ, & Cultivation; World Div, Gen Bd Global Ministries. **Honors/Awds:** Distinguished Alumnus Award, Perkins School of Theology, 2015. **Special Achievements:** In first group of African-American graduates of Perkins School of Theology. Contributor, The Christian Century, 1972. Author, Hard Trials, Great Tribulations: A Black Preacher's Pilgrimage from Poverty and Segregation to the 21st Century, 2014. **Business Phone:** (626)319-8094.

### LYLES, LESTER EVERETT

Football player, executive. **Personal:** Born Dec 27, 1962, Washington, DC. **Educ:** Univ Va, attended 1986. **Career:** Football player (retired); New York Jets, defensive back, 1985, strong safety, 1986, defensive back, 1987; Phoenix Cardinals, cornerback & defensive back, 1988-89; San Diego Chargers, defensive back, 1989-90; Ariz State Univ, facil mgr; Mutual Investment Groups Inc, mkt & bus develop mgr, mkt dir, currently.

### LYLES, MARIE CLARK

Government official, educator. **Personal:** Born Oct 12, 1952, Sledge, MS; daughter of Dave Clark and Mary McCoy Clark; married Eugene D; children: Jamaal Ventral, Justin Eugene & Jessica Marie. **Educ:** Coahoma Jr Col, AA, 1972; Miss Valley State Univ, BS, 1974. **Career:** Quitman Caenties Sch, Marks, Miss, teacher, 1970-89; Town Crenshaw, Crenshaw, Miss, mayor, 1987-; South side Jr High Sch, teacher. **Orgs:** Nat Teacher Org, 1970-89; treas, Crenshaw Community Builders, 1985; troop leader, Brownie Troop (Girl Scouts, ) 1986; vpres, Ebonette, 1988. **Honors/Awds:** Outstanding Religion Leader, Quitman Co, 1978; Outstanding Young Women, 1988. **Home Addr:** PO Box 560, Crenshaw, MS 38621, **Home Phone:** (662)382-5810. **Business Addr:** Teacher, Southside Junior High School, 26535 La Hwy 16, Denham Springs, LA 70726, **Business Phone:** (225)664-4221.

### LYNCH, ERIC D.

Football player. **Personal:** Born May 16, 1970, Woodhaven, MI. **Educ:** Grand Valley State Univ, grad. **Career:** Football player (retired); Detroit Lions, running back, 1992-96; Scottish Claymores, running back, 1998.

### LYNCH, GEORGE DEWITT, III

Basketball player, basketball coach, executive. **Personal:** Born Sep 3, 1970, Roanoke, VA; married Julie; children: Jalen, Mia & Santana. **Educ:** Univ NC, Chapel Hill, NC, BA, arts & sci, 1993. **Career:** Basketball player (retired), basketball coach; Los Angeles Lakers, small forward & shooting guard, 1993-96; Vancouver Grizzlies, small forward & shooting guard, 1996-98; Philadelphia 76ers, small forward & shooting guard, 1998-2001; Charlotte Hornets, small forward & shooting guard, 2001-02; New Orleans Hornets, small forward & shooting guard, 2002-05; personal trainer, 2005-09; Southern Methodist Univ, admin asst & grad mgr, 2006-07, asst coach, 2012-13, strength & conditioning coach, 2013-14, dir player develop, 2014-; Flight Nine Basketball, founder & dir, 2006-10; Univ Calif, Irvine, asst athletics dir community rels, strength & conditioning coach, 2010-12. **Orgs:** Nat Basketball Asn. **Honors/Awds:** Gold Medal, Summer Universiade, 1991; Citizen of the Year, Police Athletic League; Champion, Nat Col Athletic Asn, 1993; Community Hero of the Month, Nat Basketball Asn, 2001. **Business Addr:** Director of Player Development, Southern Methodist University, 6425 Boaz Lane, Dallas, TX 75205, **Business Phone:** (214)768-2000.

### LYNCH, HOLLIS RALPH

Educator. **Personal:** Born Apr 21, 1935, Port-of-Spain; married Sharon A; children: Shola Ayn (Vincent Scott Morgan), Nnenna Jean, Ashale Herman & John Benjamin. **Educ:** Univ BC, BA, 1960; MA, 1961; Univ London, PhD, 1964. **Career:** Educator (retired); Univ IFE Nigeria, lect, 1964-66; Roosevelt Univ Chicago, asst prof to assoc prof, 1966-68; State Univ NY, assoc prof, 1968-69; Columbia Univ, prof, 1969-, Inst African Studies, dir, 1971-74, 1985-90, vis prof, prof emer, currently; Am Coun Learned Soc, fel, 1978-79, 1964-66. **Orgs:** Am Hist Asn, 1971-73; African Studies Asn; Asn Study Afro-Am Life & History; Caribbean Studies Asn. **Honors/Awds:** Recipient Commonwealth Fellow, London Univ, 1961-64; Hoover National Fellow, Stanford Univ, 1973-74; Fellow, Woodrow Wilson Int Ctr Scholars, 1976. **Special Achievements:** Author of Edward Wilmot Blyden Pan Negro Patriot 1967 & The Black Urban Condition 1973; Author of many books and articles; The Foundation of American-Nigerian Ties: Nigerian Students in the United States, 1939-48, Black Ivory, The Pan-African Magazine, 1989. **Home Addr:** 100 La Salle St Suite 6G, New York, NY 10027, **Home Phone:** (212)316-0667.

### LYNCH, REV. LORENZO A., SR.

Clergy, preacher. **Personal:** Born Oakland City, NC; married Lorine Harris; children: Lorenzo A Jr, Loretta E & Leonzo D. **Educ:** Shaw Univ, BA, 1955, Divinity Sch, BD, 1957; Univ NC, Chapel Hill, 1957; Boston Univ, grad stud, 1958; Southeastern Theological Seminary, 1959; Duke Univ, Divinity Sch, attended 1965. **Career:** White Rock Baptist Church Durham, pastor, 1965-; Davis Chapel Wash; End street Baptist Church, Scotland Neck; Mt Zion, Arapahoe; St Delight, Nashville; Reid's Chapel, Fountain; Mt Olive, Ayden; Bazzel Creek, Fuquay Springs; Providence Baptist Church, Greensboro, pastor; Lynch Chapel, Oak City; Jones Chapel, Palmyra; Peoples Baptist Church, Boston, asst pastor; Religious Educ Prog, sponsored Boston Coun Week-day Religious Educ, teacher; Baptist Student Union, A&T Col, adv; Palmer Memorial Inst, Sedalia, preacher. **Orgs:** Pres, Durham Minister's Asn, 1967-68; bd dir, Edgemont Community Ctr, 1968-71; adv bd, Durham Co Mental Health Ctr, 1968-74; unsuccessful candidate, Durham's Mayor, 1973; critic Interdenominational Minister's Alliance, 1975; bd dir, Triangle Kidney Found, 1975-; Gen Baptist Conv NC Inc; exec bd, Durham Nat Asn Advan Colored People; chmn, Comn Econ Develop; Durham's Com Affairs Black People; Durham's Clergy Hosp Chaplain's Asn; Greensboro Br Nat Asn Advan Colored People; bd dir, United Southern A&T Col; bd dir, Cumberland Ct Inc. **Honors/Awds:** Hon DD, Shaw Divinity Sch, 1982. **Home Addr:** 1219 Fayetteville St, Durham, NC 27707. **Business Addr:** Pastor, White Rock Baptist Church, 3400 Fayetteville St, Durham, NC 27707, **Business Phone:** (919)688-8136.

### LYNCH, LORETTA E.

**Personal:** Born May 21, 1959, Greensboro, NC; married Stephen Hargrove. **Educ:** Harvard Col, AB, cum laude, 1981; Harvard Law Sch, JD, 1984. **Career:** Cahill Gordon & Reindel, 1984-90; US Dept Justice, Criminal Trial Advocacy Prog, frequent instr; NY firm, litigation assoc; St John's Univ Sch Law, adj prof; Long Island Off, dep chief, chief, 1994-98; asst US atty, 1990-99; US Atty Eastern Dist New York, June, 1999-2001; Dist, dep chief gen crimes, chief asst; St John Univ Sch Law, adj prof, 2000; Eastern Dist NY, chief asst US atty, 1999-2001, 2010-; Hogan & Hartson LLP, partner, 2002-10. **Orgs:** Bd dir, Fed Res Bank New York, 2003-05; bd dir, Legal Aid Soc; bd adv, Brennan Ctr Justice, New York Univ Sch Law; Eastern Dist Comt Civil Litigation; Fed Bar Coun; Judicial Screening Panel, Sen Charles Schumer; Magistrate Judge Selection Panel, Eastern Dist, NY; bd dir, Nat Inst Trial Advocacy; bd dir, Off Appellate Defender; bd dir, Nat Inst Law & Equity; chmn, Fed Bar Found; vpres, New York Bar Asn; Atty Generals Adv Comt; cochair, White Collar Crime Subcomt; New York Bar; Litigation Group. **Special Achievements:** First African-American woman to U.S. Attorney General. **Business Addr:** US Attorney General, Eastern District of New York, 271 Cadman Plz E, Brooklyn, NY 10601, **Business Phone:** (718)254-7000.

### LYNCH, MARSHAWN

Football player. **Personal:** Born Apr 22, 1986, Oakland, CA; son of Delisa. **Educ:** Univ Calif, Berkeley, 2007. **Career:** Football player; University of California, Berkeley, 2004-07; Buffalo Bills, running back, 2007-10; Seattle Seahawks, running back, 2011-. **Orgs:** Fam First Foundation, founder. **Special Achievements:** Second player in Cal history to gain more than 1000 yards in consecutive seasons, 2005, 2006; Superbowl Champion XLVIII, 2014; Seattle Seahawks post-season rushing record, NFC Championship game, 2015. **Business Addr:** Seattle Seahawks, 12 Seahawks Way, Renton, WA 98056.

### LYNCH, DR. RUFUS SYLVESTER

Social worker, educator. **Personal:** Born Nov 30, 1946, Baltimore, MD; son of Rufus and Marie; married VeRita Amelia Barnette; children: Marie Rachel & Kirkland Alexander. **Educ:** Morgan State Univ, BA, sociol, 1968; Univ Pittsburgh, Grad Sch Social Work, MSW, 1970; Univ Pa Sch Social Work, PhD, advan cert, social work admin, 1971, DSW, social work admin & policy, 1973. **Career:** Westing house Defense & Space Ctr, urban soc scientist, 1967-68; Cath Diocese Pittsburgh, prog dir & consult, 1969; Ford Motor Co, staff coordr, 1969; Philadelphia Health Mgt Corp, res develop & outreach specialist, 1973-74; Community Col Philadelphia, dir serv aging, 1975-76; Off Lt Gov PA, sr human serv policy adv, 1975-76; Off Majority Leader PA H R, exec asst chief staff, 1976-77; Off Speaker Pa H R, exec asst chief staff, 1977-78; MLB Inc, pres, 1978-84; Nat Geront Soc, res fel, 1978; Temple Univ, sr exec mgt, cons, spec asst exec vpres univ admin, 1984-85; Pa State Supreme Ct, dep ct adminr; Admin Off Supreme Ct Pa, asst ct admin, 1986-87, dir ct mgt, 1987-94; Nat Ctr State Courts, Inst Ct Mgt, grad fel, 1990; Univ Pen Sch Social Work, adj fac; Cheyney Univ Pa, prof, 1994-97; Ctr Studying Social Welfare & Community Develop, Philadelphia, Pa, pres, 1994-; Ctr Studying Social Welfare & Community Develop, pres, 1994-; Lincoln Univ Multidisciplinary Ctr Aging, assoc prof, 1995-2000; Chestnut Hill Col, adj criminal justice fac; Chestnut Hill Col Accelerated Prog, lectr, 1996-2001; Fresh Start Community Develop Corp, founder, pres, 1997-99; Pvt Indust Coun Philadelphia, Transitional Workforce Dept, vpres, 1999-2000; Philadelphia Workforce Develop Corp, sr vpres, 2000-; Inst Advan Working Families, founder, pres & prin investr, 2001-13; Clark Atlanta Univ, Whitney M Young Jr, Sch Social Work, Clark, prof & dean, 2004-07; Bryn Mawr Col, Grad Sch Social Work & Social Res, Stoneleigh Found Fel Social Chg, res assoc. **Orgs:** Justice Syst Jour ed bd; Nat Asn Ct Mgt; Am Bar Asn, Judicial Admin Div; Asn Black Social Workers; Am Bar Asn, Criminal Justice Div; Coun Social Work Educ; Nat Ctr State Courts; Ctr Studying Social Welfare & Community Develop, 1979; cong deleg, White House Conf Aging, 1981; Bicentennial Comn US Const, 1985; Nat Ctr Social Policy & Pract, founding mem, 1986; Black Caucus/African Am Network, NASW, convenor, 1990; Nat Community Inquiry, NASW; 1991-94; Pa Rep Nat Deleg Assembly, 1992-95; Continuing Ed Comn, Pa Chap NASW, 1992-94; Adjudication Prog Issues Advy Group, 1993-95; pres, Pa Chap Nat Asn Social Workers (NASW), 1994-98; proj dir, Philadelphia Juv Ctr Inc, 1995-; pres, Fresh Start Community Develop Corp, 1995-; bd dir, Blacks Educating Blacks Sexual Health Issues, 1996-; Asn Addiction Professionals; bd dir, W Philadelphia YMCA & Family Ctr, 1996-; chair, Morehouse Sch Med Adv Comt, 2009; nat consult, Whitney Young Film & Leadership Develop Proj; nat consult, PRWT Serv Inc; nat consult, Ill One Family One Child; nat consult, Nat Asn Former Foster Care C Am; nat consult; Carol Ann Campbell Found; Bread &

Roses Community Fund; founding mem, Ctr Working Families Inc. **Honors/Awds:** Pennsylvania Social Worker of the Year Award, 1978; Social Worker of the Year, NASW PA, 1978; Certificate of Appreciation, City Philadelphia Personnel Dept, 1980; Alumni of the Year Award, Univ Pittsburgh Sch Social Work, 1981; Pa Asn Spec Courts Spec Award, 1988; President's Friendship Award, Pa State Constable's Asn, 1988; Distinguished Service Award, Nat Constable's Asn, 1989; Distinguished Minority Scholars in Residents Prog, Pa State Univ, 1991; Man of the Year Award, Pa State Constables Asn, 1991; President's Award, Nat Asn Ct Mgt, 1991; Summit Award, City Charleston, SC, 1994; Distinguished Alumni Award,Univ Pittsburgh's Sch Social Work; Outstanding Young Man of America, U.S. Jaycee. **Special Achievements:** First African American elected President of Pennsylvania Chapter of National Assoc of Social Workers, 1995. **Home Addr:** 1730 N 71st St, Philadelphia, PA 19151-2304, **Home Phone:** (215)879-1775. **Business Addr:** Dean, Professor, Clark Atlanta University, 223 James P Brawley Dr SW, Atlanta, GA 30314, **Business Phone:** (404)880-8863.

### LYNN, ANTHONY RAY
Football player, football coach. **Personal:** Born Dec 21, 1968, McKinney, TX; children: D'Anton & Danielle. **Educ:** Tex Tech Univ, BS, exercise sport sci, 1992. **Career:** Football player (retired), football coach; Denver Broncos, running back, 1993, 1997-99, coaching staff, offensive asst & spec teams asst, 2000-02; San Francisco 49ers, 1995, running back, 1996; Jacksonville Jaguars, running backs coach, 2003-04; Dallas Cowboys, running backs coach, 2005-06; Cleveland Browns, running backs coach, 2007-08; New York Jets, running backs coach, asst coach, 2009-14; Buffalo Bills, running backs coach & asst head coach, 2015-. **Orgs:** Life Athletes. **Honors/Awds:** Super Bowl Champion, XXXII, XXXIII. **Business Addr:** Assistant Head Coach, Running Backs Coach, The Buffalo Bills, 1 Bills Dr, Orchard Park, NY 14127, **Business Phone:** (716)648-1800.

### LYNN, BARBARA (BARBARA LYNN OPEN)
Singer, songwriter, musician. **Personal:** Born Jan 16, 1942, Beaumont, TX; children: 3. **Career:** Bobbie Lynn and the Idols, founder, 1954; solo artist, 1956-; recorded for Jamie, 1962-66, Tribe, 1966-67, Atlantic, 1967-72. **Honors/Awds:** Rhythm and Blues Foundation Pioneer Award, 1999. **Special Achievements:** Albums: You'll Lose a Good Thing, 1962; Sister of Soul, 1964; Here is Barbaray Lynn, 1968; You Don't Have to Go, 1984; So Good, 1993; Until Then I Suffer, 1996; Live in Japan, 2000; Hot Night Tonight, 2000. Singles: "You'll Lose a Good Thing," 1962: "You're Gonna Need Me," 1965, and "You Left the Water Running, 1966." "(Until Then) I'll Suffer," 1972. Had number one hit with "You'll Lose a Good Thing". **Business Addr:** c/o Light in the Attic Records, PO Box 31970, Seattle, WA 98103.

### LYNN, LONNIE RASHID, JR. (COMMON SENSE)
Rap musician, actor. **Personal:** Born Mar 13, 1972, Chicago, IL; son of Lonnie and Mahalia Ann Hines; children: Omoye Assata. **Educ:** Fla A&M Univ. **Career:** Albums: Can I Borrow A Dollar?, 1992; Resurrection, 1994; One Day It'll All Make Sense, 1997; Like Water for Chocolate, 2000; Electric Circus, 2003; Be, 2005; Finding Forever, 2007; Universal Mind Control, 2008; The Dreamer/The Believer, 2011; Films: Brown Sugar, 2002; Girlfriends, 2003; Chappelle's Show, 2004; One on One, 2004; Smokin' Aces, 2006; This is me Then, 2007; The Believer, 2008; Actor: Dave Chapelle's Block Party, 2006; Smokin' Aces, 2007; American Gangster, 2007; Street Kings, 2008; Wanted, 2008; Wanted:Weapons of Fate, 2009; Terminator Salvation, 2009; Date Night, 2010; Just Wright, 2010; Bouncing Cats, 2010; Happy Feet Two, 2011;TV series: "Hell on Wheels", 2011-2014; New Year's Eve, 2011; The Odd Life of Timothy Green, 2012; L.U.V., 2012; Now You See Me, currently. **Business Addr:** Artist, MCA Records, 2220 Colorado Ave, Santa Monica, CA 90404, **Business Phone:** (310)865-4500.

### LYNN, DR. LOUIS B.
Research scientist, president (organization), horticulturist. **Personal:** Born Mar 8, 1949, Bishopville, SC; son of Lawton and Dorothy Evans; married Audrey Johnson; children: Adrienne N, Krystal & Bryan B. **Educ:** Clemson Univ, BS, hort (hons), 1970, MS, hort, 1973; Univ Md, PhD, hort, 1975. **Career:** Elanco Prod Co, field res scientist, 1976-80; Monsanto Agr Co, prod mgr, 1980-83, sr scientist, 1983-88; Environ Affairs, mgr, 1988-90; Environ Ag Sci Inc, pres & chief hort, 1985-; Univ SC, adj prof pub health; Benedict Col, adj prof biol; SC Dept Agr, crop prod consult; Atlanta Parks Dept, hort consult; Laidlaw Environ Serv, agrichem waste consult; US Dept Energy, conserv tillage consult; Agr Ministry Bahamas, crop consult; Trinidad & Tabago Govts, crop consult; Clemson Univ, adj prof hort, currently. **Orgs:** Clemson Black Alumni Coun, 1986-88; Clemson Univ Alumni Asn; SC Hort Soc, 1987-88; bd dir, SC Chamber Com; Am Soc Hort Sci; SC Agr Study Comt; bd trustee, Clemson Univ, 1988-; bd dir, BB&T Bank, 2013-; Pres's Club; Maj Gifts Club; Sc Hort Soc; bd mem, Nat Asn Minority Contractors. **Home Addr:** 85 Olde Springs Rd, Columbia, SC 29223-6002, **Home Phone:** (803)788-7612. **Business Addr:** President, Chief Horticulturist, ENVIRO AgScience Inc, 1190 Buckner Rd, Columbia, SC 29224, **Business Phone:** (803)714-7290.

### LYONS, A. BATES
State government official, consultant. **Personal:** Born Nov 20, 1944, Philadelphia, PA; son of Archie and Irma; children: Joanna, Daniel & Ashley. **Educ:** Cent State Univ, Wilberforce, OH, BS, bus admin, 1966; Columbia Univ, New York, NY, MBA, orgn behav, 1972; Mass Inst Technol, cert, exec mgt. **Career:** Atlantic Richfield, Philadelphia, Pa, mgr, 1969-72; Philip Morris, NewYork, NY, mgr, 1972-79; Heublein, Farmington, CT, mgr, 1977-78; Off Policy Mgt, Hartford, CT, under secy, 1978-87; State Tech Col, Hartford, CT, dep exec dir, 1987-92; consult, 1992-; Torrington Pub Sch, staff, 1999-, elected vice chair, 2007-; Univ Conn Sch Bus, adj prof, currently; Capital Community Tech Col, adj prof; A Bates Lyons & Assocs, staff develop consult, currently. **Orgs:** Pres, Fedn Black Dem, 1982-84; polemarch, Kappa Alpha Psi Fraternity, 1982-84; State Retirement Comn, 1985-; Conn Asn Bd Educ; chair, vice chair & comt chairs, Budget Comt & Negotiations-Adminr Comt; prov coordinators, Episcopal Church Ctr. **Home Addr:** 212 Carriage Lane, Torrington, CT 06790-4181, **Home Phone:** (860)489-5524. **Business Addr:** Vice Chair, Torrington Public Schools, 355 Migeon Ave, Torrington, CT 06790, **Business Phone:** (860)489-2327.

### LYONS, CHARLOTTE
Editor, educator, food writer. **Educ:** Morris Brown Col, BS, home econ & educ, 1972. **Career:** Gen Mills, prod group supvr, 1979-84; Johnson Publ Co, food ed, 1985-2010; Ebony Mag, food ed, auth, currently; Charlotte Lyons Consult, consult, 2011-; Betty Crocker Test Kitchen; Campbell Soup Co. Book: New Ebony Cookbook. **Business Addr:** Food Editor, Author, Ebony Magazine, 820 S Michigan Ave, Chicago, IL 60605-2190, **Business Phone:** (312)322-9200.

### LYONS, DONALD WALLACE, SR.
Athletic director, educator. **Personal:** Born Dec 11, 1945, Lexington, KY; son of Joseph Bailey and Sam Ella; married Myra Briggs; children: Donald Wallace & Reginald. **Educ:** Ky State Univ, AB, hist & polit sci, 1968; Univ Ky, MSLS, 1971. **Career:** Athletic director (retired); Detroit Mich, teacher, 1968; KY State Univ, teacher, 1969, supvr adult educ, asst librn, lib, 1971, dir libr, 1976-89, athletic dir, 1999, retired, Blazer Libr, assoc prof, 1971-95; Am Libr Asn, teacher; Am Asn Univ, prof; Ky State Univ Found, exec secy, currently; prof emer, currently. **Orgs:** Great Lakes Valley Conf; Nat Col Athletic Asn; past pres, Gamma Beta Lambda Chap Alpha Phi Alpha; Grammateus Delta Tau Boule Sigma Pi Phi Fraternity. **Honors/Awds:** Pub African & African Am History & Cult a bibliography; Follow-up of on the job training placements; Blazer bugle; Honorary Doctorate, Faith Grant Col, 1994. **Home Addr:** 517 Collier Ct, Lexington, KY 40505, **Home Phone:** (859)299-6420. **Business Addr:** Executive, Kentucky State University, 400 E Main St, Frankfort, KY 40601, **Business Phone:** (502)875-0187.

### LYONS, ELLIOTT J.
Chief executive officer, automotive executive, vice president (organization). **Educ:** Southern Univ, BS, mech engineering, 1988; Stanford Univ, MS, 1990; Univ Phoenix, MBA, 1998. **Career:** Gen Motors Corp, design & release engr, 1986-97; United Technologies Automotive, div engineering mgr, 1997-99; Navistar Int Transp Corp, dir severe serv prod ctr & global defense & export, 1999-2006; Leggett & Platt, corp vpres, group pres com vehicle prod group, 2006-13; EJL Group & Costello Elec Co, managing mem, chief exec officer, 2014-. **Orgs:** Bd mem & dir, Operating Coun Sci & Engineering Fair Metrop Detroit (SEFMD), 1994-95; Nat Soc Black Engrs; Am Soc Mech Engrs (ASME); Alpha Phi Alpha Fraternity Inc. **Business Addr:** Managing Member, Chief Executive Officer, EJL Group LLC, 3580 Cantrell Industrial Ct NW, Acworth, GA 30101, **Business Phone:** (770)966-1946.

### LYONS, GEORGE, JR.
Executive, vice president (organization). **Educ:** Univ NC, Chapel Hill, BA, econ, MBA, JD. **Career:** Parke-Davis, state govt regional mgr; Peco Energy Co, exec, vpres, community & external affairs, regulatory commun & external affairs; Exelon Corp, vpres, govt & pub affairs; Pepco, DC region vpres, govt affairs & pub policy issues, 2006-; Pfizer Inc, govt rels; Am Gas Asn, govt rels; PetroAlgae Inc, vice pres, govt rels. **Orgs:** DC Bar; Fed Energy Bar; Nat Health Lawyers Asn; Nat Bar Asn; bd, World Affairs Coun; bd, Greater Philadelphia Urban Affairs Coalition; bd, Philadelphia Urban League; bd, WYBE Pub TV Arts & Bus Coun. **Business Addr:** PetroAlgae Inc., 1901 S Harbor City Blvd Suite 300, Melbourne, FL 32901, **Business Phone:** (321)409-7970.

### LYONS, DR. JAMES E.
College president. **Personal:** married Jocelyn; children: Jack, Jamal & James Jr. **Educ:** Univ Conn, BA, Span, 1965, MA, stud personnel, 1971, PhD, prof higher educ admin, 1973; Harvard Univ Inst Educ Mgt, attended 1976. **Career:** Ky State Univ, assoc prof educ, 1973-74; Fayetteville State Univ, prof educ, 1974-75; Barber Scotia Col, vpres acad affairs, 1975-78; Del State Col, vpres & dean acad affairs, 1978-83, prof educ, 1978-83; Bowie State Univ, pres, 1983-92, prof educ, 1983-92; Jackson State Univ, pres, 1992-99; Calif State Univ, Dominguez Hills pres, 1999-2007; Md Higher Educ Comn, secy higher educ, 2007-11; Univ DC, interim pres, 2013-. **Orgs:** Comt Diversity & Social Chg, Am Asn State Cols & Univs, 1996-99; USaF Bd Advisors Hist Black Cols & Univs & Minority Inst, 1997; bd dir, Nat Asn Equal Opportunity Higher Educ, 1997-99; bd trustee, Citizens Scholar Found Am, 1998; bd dir, Golden Eagle Educ & Training, Int Youth Inst, 1998; evaluator, Vis Comt, Southern Asn Cols & Schs, Comn Cols, 1998; Coun Educ & Human Resources, Miss Econ Coun, 1998-99; Alcohol Abuse & Misuse Col Campuses Comt, Nat Inst Alcohol Abuse & Alcoholism, Dept Health & Human Servs, 1998; Comt Standing Rules, Miss Conf, United Methodist Church, 1998; Nominating Comt, Comn Cols, 1998-2000; Coun Exec Bd, Andrew Jackson Coun Boy Scouts Am, 1998; pres, Calif Coliate Athletic Asn, 2001-02; comnr, Am Coun Educ, Comn Minorities Higher Educ, 2001-04; Nat Coliate Athletic Asn, Div II, Pres Coun, 2003-07; Md K-16 Partnership Leadership Coun, 2007; Educ Coord Coun Correctional Insts, 2007-08; Statewide Comn Shortage Health Care Workforce, 2007-08; Comn Develop Md Model Funding Higher Educ, 2007-08; Task Force Implement Holocaust, Genocide, Human Rights Tolerance Educ, 2007-08; Instrnl Mat Access Guidelines Comt, 2007-10; Gov's Exec Coun, 2007-11; Base Realignment Closure Subcabinet, 2007-11; Gov's Subcabinet Int Affairs, 2007-11; Smart Growth Subcabinet, 2007-11; chair, Segmental Adv Coun, 2007-11; Comn Civic Literacy, 2007-11; Col Savings Plans Md Bd, 2007-11; Coord Coun Juv Serv Educ Progs, 2007-11; Educ Coord Comt, 2007-11; Md Educ Coun, 2007-11; Md Heritage Areas Authority, 2007-11; Gov's Comn Hisp Affairs, 2007-11; Md Adv Coun Libr, 2007-11; Md Adv Comn Mfg Competitiveness, 2007-11; Interdepartmental Adv Comt Minority Affairs, 2007-11; P-20 Leadership Coun Md, 2007-11; Southern Regional Educ Bd, 2007-11; Gov's Workforce Investment Bd, 2007-11; Workforce Creation Adult Educ Transition Coun, 2008; Task Force Preserv Heritage Lang Skills, 2008-09; Task Force Rev Physician Shortages Rural Areas, 2008-09; Educ Workforce Training Coord Coun Correctional Insts, 2008-11; Educ Curric Adv Comt Md War 1812 Bicentennial Comn, 2009-11; bd dir, Md Workforce Corp, 2009-11; Md Longitudinal Data Syst Ctr Gov Bd, 2010-11; Gov's Warrior Worker Coun, 2010-11; Am Asn Cols Teacher Educ; Am Asn State Cols & Univs; Am Coun Educ; Hisp Asn Cols & Univs; CSU Comt Alcohol Policies & Progs; CSU Comn Extended Univ; CSU Arch; chair, Accreditation Team, Mid States Comn Higher Educ; S Bay Econ & Develop Partnership; S Bay Work force Investment Bd; S Bay Bus Round table; Citizens Scholar Found Americas Scholar Mgt Servs Sub comt & Dollars Scholars Sub comt; Nat Asn State Col & Univs; US Dream Acad. **Honors/Awds:** Distinguished Alumni Award, Neag Sch Educ, Univ Conn, 2000; Named Regional Citizen Year, Omega Psi Phi Fraternity, 2001; Franklin H Williams Award, Peace Corps, 2001; Heritage Award, 100 Black Men of Maryland, 2008; Richard Allen Man of the Year Award, Bethel African Methodist Episcopal Church, Baltimore, 2009. **Special Achievements:** Published numerous articles. **Business Addr:** Interim President, University of the District of Columbia, 4200 Conn Ave NW, Washington, DC 20008, **Business Phone:** (202)274-5000.

### LYONS, DR. LAMAR ANDREW, SR.
Chief executive officer, banker. **Educ:** Univ Calif, Los Angeles, CA, BS, philos & math, 1975; Howard Univ, Sch Law, JD. **Career:** Morgan Stanley Inc, staff; L F Rothschild & Co Inc, staff; Rideau Lyons & Co Inc, chief exec officer & exec managing dir, currently. **Orgs:** Bd mem, Univ Calif Black Alumni Asn. **Business Addr:** Chief Executive Officer, Executive Managing Director, Rideau Lyons & Co Inc, 5455 Wilshire Blvd Suite 2131, Los Angeles, CA 90036, **Business Phone:** (323)965-1710.

### LYONS, DR. LAURA BROWN
Consultant, public speaker. **Personal:** Born Jul 15, 1942, Birmingham, AL; daughter of Jesse and Annie M; married Edward; children: Kobie. **Educ:** Dillard Univ, New Orleans, LA, BA, 1963; NY Univ, MSW. **Career:** Kaiser Corp, asst personnel mgr, 1975-80; BVI Govt, Rd Town, Tortola, BVI, asst cot develop off, 1980-81; Career Dynamics Int, Tortola, BVI, pres, chief exec officer, currently; motivational speaker & consult; WBNB-TV, CBS Affil, TV talk show hostess; Ann Wigmore Health Inst, mkt & promotions; Lyons Property Mgt, owner, cheif exec officer; Berkeley City Col Berkeley, CA, job developer extraordinaire, speaker, 2012, currently. **Orgs:** Caribbean Exec Woman's Network, 1985-; Am Soc Training & Develop, 1985-; Int Prof Pract Asn, 1989-; Cities by Bay Chap Am Bus Women's Asn, 2009. **Honors/Awds:** Multi-Cultural Trainer Year Award, ASTD, 1990; Outstanding Bus Person, Virgin Islands Bus Journal, 1988 Outstanding Female Exec, CEWN, 1990, 1997; Educator Year, US Virgin Islands Bus Jour, 1988; Am Express Recognition Award, Excellence Motivational Training, 1989; Business Person Year, nominee, British Virgin Islands Hotel & Com Asn, 1990; Black Career Women's Asn, "Legacy Messenger", Cincinnati, OH, 1997; Nominee, Avon/US Small Bus Women Year Award; USVI Woman of the Year, CEWN, 1997; CBB-ABWA Woman of the Year; Who's Who's Among Black Americans, 2008. **Special Achievements:** Author: Lyon's Guide to the Career Jungle, Odenwald Connection Publishing, 1989. **Business Addr:** Chief Executive Officer, President, Career Dynamics International, 6363 Curistis Ave Suite 1412, Emeryville, CA 94605, **Business Phone:** (510)658-8133.

### LYONS, PATRICK ALAN
Financial manager, consultant, business owner. **Personal:** Born Feb 18, 1972, Ft. Belvoir, VA; son of Gwendolyn A and Charlie J; married Kelly. **Educ:** Fla A&M Univ, BS, math, 1994; NC State Univ, MSM, finance, 2001. **Career:** Wake Tech Community Col; NCM Capital Mgt Group, sr res analyst, 1995-2001, assoc portfolio mgr, portfolio mgr, 2001-08; Lyons Den Press, owner, currently; Lyons Den Capital LLC, pres, owner, 2004-. **Orgs:** Prince Hall Masons; Nat Black MBA Asn; Alpha Phi Alpha Frat Inc, 1993-; Mkt Technician Asn; 100 Black Men Am. **Honors/Awds:** Featured in Black Enterprise magazine and on Bloomberg Radio. **Special Achievements:** Author: Map Your Financial Future: Starting on the Right Path in Your Teens and Twenties; numerous publications and shows including in Black Enterprise magazine, WHUR 96.3, Washington, DC, Bev Smith Show, WJZ, CBS Affiliate, WNCN, NBC Affiliate & Bloomberg Radio. **Home Addr:** 5404 Granada Hills Dr, Raleigh, NC 27613-1441. **Business Addr:** President, Owner, Lyons Den Capital LLC, PO Box 1341, Durham, NC 27675, **Business Phone:** (919)727-9529.

### LYONS, VINCENT S.
President (organization), vice president (organization). **Educ:** Southern Univ, Baton Rouge, LA, BS, mech engineering, 1988; Stanford Univ, MS, mech engineering, 1990; Univ Phoenix, MBA, mgt, 1999. **Career:** Gen Motors, Truck & Bus Group, Flint, Mich, gm scholar intern, sr engr, 1986-96; United Technologies Automotive, platform mgr, 1996-98; Lear Corp, Gen Motors Switch Progs, platform mgr, 1996-2000; Visteon Corp, engineering dir & dept mgr, 2000-01; Maytag Corp, vpres r&d & engineering refrig div, 2001-03; Leggett & Platt, vpres engineering & prod develop & pres mach & technol group, 2006-. **Orgs:** Bd mem, Sci Engineering Fair Metrop Detroit (SEFMD), 2003; Am Soc Mech Engrs; Alpha Phi Alpha Fraternity Inc. **Business Addr:** Vice President-Engineering, LEGGETT & PLATT INC, No 1 Leggett Rd, Carthage, MO 64836.

### LYTHCOTT, JANICE LOGUE (JANICE LYTHCOTT HILL)
Executive. **Personal:** Born Jun 19, 1950, St. Albans, NY; daughter of John Thomas and Helen Harvey; married Michael; children: Omi & Shade. **Educ:** Simmons Col, Boston, MA, 1969; Lehman Col, Bronx, NY, 1971; Howard Univ, Wash, DC, BA, commun, 1975. **Career:** WHUR, Wash, DC, spec asst to gen mgr, 1976; Gil Scott Heron, New York, NY, mgr, 1977-78; CBS Rec, New York, NY, mgr, admin, 1978-80, assoc dir progs & proj develop, 1980-88; Sony Music CBS Rec, New York, NY, dir, prog & proj develop, 1978-96; Cong Black Caucus Found, dir, mkt & event mgt, 2003-06; Lincoln Theatre, exec dir, 2006-. **Orgs:** Comt chair, Jackie Robinson Found, 1982-89; bd mem, Alvin Ailey Am Found, 1987-; bd mem, Jamison Proj, 1988-89; dir proj, Int Jazz Acad. **Business Addr:** Executive Director, The Lincoln Theatre, 1215 U St NW, Washington, DC 20009, **Business Phone:** (202)328-6000.

### LYTLE, JUDGE ALICE A.
Judge. **Personal:** Born Jersey City, NJ. **Educ:** Hunter Col, New York, NY, AB, physiol & pub health; Hastings Col Law, JD, 1973. **Career:** Judge (retired); New Col Law, instr criminal law; Albert Einstein Col Med, med res tech, 1961-70; Univ Calif, San Francisco Cardiovasc Res Inst; Gov Edmund G Brown Jr, dep legal affairs sec, 1975-77; Dept Indust Rels Div Fair Employee Pract, chief, 1977-79; State & Consumer Serv Agency, Cabinet Off Admin Gov Brown, secy, 1979-82; Sacramento Munic Sup Ct, judge, 1983-88, presiding judge, 1988-89; Juv Div Super Ct, judge. **Orgs:** Pres, Black Law Students Asn; Legal Defense Fund, Nat Asn Advan Colored People. **Honors/Awds:** Hall of

Fame, Hunter Col, New York City; Rose Bird Memorial Award, 2005. **Special Achievements:** First African-American woman to serve on the Sacramento branch; First female African American Superior Court judge in California.

## LYTLE, MARILYN MERCEDES

Association executive, educator. **Personal:** Born May 10, 1948, Mound Bayou, MS; daughter of C Preston Holmes and Pauline J Thompson; married Erskine Lytle III; children: Brandon Kyle & Kiera Danine. **Educ:** Fisk Univ, Nashville, TN, BS, 1969; Stanford Univ, Palo Alto, CA, MAT, 1970. **Career:** Wash High Sch, San Francisco, CA, music teacher, 1970-71; Jordan High Sch, Durham, NC, choral music teacher, 1972-78; INROADS Inc, Nashville, TN, coordr, asst dir, 1979-83, dir, 1983-86, regional dir, 1986-88, regional vpres, 1988-93, vpres, 1994-95, exec vp, 1995-99, pres affil org, chief operating officer, 1998-2006; Univ Tenn, Knoxville, exec-in-residence, 1997; State Tenn, asst comnr human resources, 2007-12. **Orgs:** Bd mem, United Way, 1987-94; head, Allocations Comt, United Way, 1984-86; bd mem, St Mary's Villa, 1984-87; Selection Comt, Bootstraps Scholars, 1988; Leadership Nashville, 1986-; Alpha Kappa Alpha Sorority Inc; bd mem, exec comt mem, Nashville CARES, 1994-2001; exec comt mem, YWCA, 1995-97; bd mem, Community Found Mid Tenn, 1999-. **Honors/Awds:** Community Role Model Award, St Peters AME Church, 1994; Outstanding Community Leadership and Service Award, Alpha Delta Omega Chap, Alpha Kappa Alpha Sorority; Project Cherish Honoree, Delta Sigma Theta Sorority Inc, 1995; President's Citation for Excellence, INROADS Inc, 1995; Inductee, Acad Women Achievement, YWCA, 2002. **Special Achievements:** Selected to 100 Top African-American Business & Professional Women, Dollars and Sense Magazine, 1989; selected, Phelps Stokes West Africa Heritage Tour, Phelps Stokes Fund, 1978. **Home Addr:** 4704 Aaron Dr, Antioch, TN 37013, **Home Phone:** (615)834-4523.

# M

## MABIN, JOSEPH E.

Executive. **Career:** Mabin Construct Co Inc, Kans City, Mo, exec dir, 1980-, owner & chief exec officer. **Orgs:** Pres, Black Chamber Com Greater Kans City; exec dir, pres, Minority Contractors Asn Greater Kans City, currently; pres, exec dir, Nat Asn Minority Contractors. **Business Addr:** Executive Director, President, Minority Contractors Association of Greater Kansas City, 3200 Wayne Ave Suite 202, Kansas City, MO 64109, **Business Phone:** (816)924-4441.

## MABREY, HAROLD LEON

Executive, government official, military leader. **Personal:** Born May 24, 1933, Pittsburg, TX; son of Horace L and Ethelyn E Brown; married Barbara J Johnson; children: Vicki Lynn, Lesley Harold & Kevin Frank. **Educ:** Lincoln Univ, BS, bus admin, 1956; George Washington Univ, MBA, 1971; Indus Col, Armed Forces, attended 1978; Harvard Univ, dipl, Nat & int security affairs, 1987. **Career:** Military leader (retired); USY Avn Res & Develop Cmdr, GM-15 suprv contract specialist & chief proc div, 1977-83, GS-14 supv contr spec, 1973-77, GS-13 supv contr spec, 1969-73, GS-12 supv contr spec, 1966-69, GS-11 supv contr spec, 1964-66, aviation systs command, 1983-86, GM-15 supv cont sp; AUS, troop sup comd, sr exec serv-04, SES-04, 1986-91, Avn Sys Cmd, GM-15, supr cont sp & div chief, 1983-86, dir proc & prod, 1985-91, Acquisition Ctr, exec dir; Mabrey & Asn. **Orgs:** Vchmn, EEO Working Group AUS, 1980; Nat Black MBA Asn Inc; Nat Contract Mgt Asn; Minority Bus Oppor Comn; Omega Psi Phi Frat; Lincoln Univ Alumni Asn; Berea Presby Church. **Honors/Awds:** Good Conduct Medal, Marksman, USY, 1955-57; Stained Sperior Prformance Award, USY Transp Cmd, 1962; Meritorous Civilian Serv Award, USY, 1970, 1976-77, 1980, 1991; Outstanding Performance Award, USY, 1971, 1977 & 1980; honor grad def adv proc mgt, USY, 1973; Cert Achievement, USY, 1977; Distinguished Alumni Award, 1986; Secy Defense Superior Mgt Award, 1989; Prsial Rank Meritorious Service Award, 1989; Exceptional Civilian Service Award, US Army, 1990. **Home Addr:** 4363 Keevenshore Dr, Florissant, MO 63034-3452, **Home Phone:** (314)921-4006.

## MABREY, PROF. MARSHA EVE

Educator, conductor (music), teacher. **Personal:** Born Nov 7, 1949, Pittsburgh, PA; daughter of Theodore R and Ella Jones. **Educ:** Univ Mich Sch Music, BM, music educ, 1971, MM, music educ, 1972; Univ Cincinnati Col Conserv Music. **Career:** Sch Music & Cincinnati Conserv Music, asst conductor, 1973-76; Winona State Univ, Symphony Orch, MN, instr music, 1978-80; Grand Rapids Symphony Orch, asst conductor, 1980-81; Grand Valley State Col, Symphony Orch, MI, asst prof music, 1980-82; Interlochen All State Music Prog, conductor, All State Orchestra Concer Prog, 1982; Univ Ore Symphony Orch, asst prof music, 1982-89; Eugene Chamber Orch, music dir, conductor comn orchestra, 1984-91; Univ Ore Sch Music, asst dean, 1989-91; Detroit Symphony Orchestra Hall, vpres educ affairs; Philadelphia Orchestra, interim dir educ; Interlochen Nat Music Camp Mich & Encore Music Camp Pa; Detroit Symphonys African-Am Composer Forum & Symp; Seattle Philharmonic Orchestra, music dir & conductor, 1996-2002. **Orgs:** Guest conducting Mich Youth Symphony Orch, 1977; coordr dir, W Coast Women Conductor & Composer Symp, 1984-85; orchestra chmn, Ore Music Ed Assoc, 1984-86; Sinfonietta Frankfort, Ger, 1988; keynote speaker, Ore String Teacher Assoc, 1984; guest conducting, Music Ed Assoc All-Star Orchestras; Nat Sch Band & Orchestra Assoc, Col Music Soc; Am Symphony Orchestra League; Conductors Guild; MENC; OMEA; guest conductor, Ore Symphony, 1988; Allendale Symphony, Mich; guest conductor, Utah All-State Orchestra, 1990; Savannah Symphony Orchestra, GA, 1991; Allen Pk Symphony, 1992; Women's Philharmonic, CA; Vancouver Symphony, WA; presenter, guest lectr, educ consult, San Jose Symphony, CA, Wash; New World Symphony, Fla; Duke Univ; Ore Symphony, OR. **Special Achievements:** Program: "Thistle Theatre Puppets"; "Tours de Force!"; "The American Horn Quartet"; "The Esoterics and Seattles Arts West"; "Janice Giteck", composer; "Bern Herbalsheimer", composer; "Regina Harris Bioacchi", composer; "Joseph Curiale", composer; "June Kirlin", composer; "sopranos Rebecca Hilgraves"; "Anne Tedards"; "Thomasa Eckert"; "tenor John Duykers"; "Jay Clayton"; "Jazz vocalist"; "Warren Chang"; "Er-Hu"; "soloist"; "Craig Sheppard"; "pianist William Wilde Zeitler"; "Glass Armonica soloist"; "Rubin Alvarez"; "percussionist"; "conductors Don Thulean and Salvador Brotons". **Home Addr:** 80 35th Ave, Eugene, OR 97405, **Home Phone:** (425)453-7455.

## MABREY, VICKI L.

Journalist, writer. **Personal:** Born Apr 3, 1956, St. Louis, MO; daughter of Harold and Barbara. **Educ:** Howard Univ, BA, polit sci, 1977. **Career:** WUSA-TV, Wash, DC, reporter trainee, 1982-83; WBAL-TV, Baltimore, MD, reporter, 1984-92; CBS News, corresp, 1992-95, foreign corresp, 1995-98, 60 Minutes II, corresp, 1998-2005; ABC News, corresp, 2005-. TV Series: "ABC News Nightline", 2006-07. **Orgs:** Am Fedn TV & Radio Artists, 1984-. **Business Addr:** News Correspondent, ABC news, 7 W 66th St, New York, NY 10023, **Business Phone:** (212)456-4060.

## MABRIE, DR. HERMAN JAMES, III

Physician. **Personal:** Born Jul 10, 1948, Houston, TX; married Linda; children: David, Herman IV & Brent. **Educ:** Howard Univ, BS, 1969; Meharry Med Col, MD, 1973. **Career:** Baylor Affiliated Hosp, gen surg res, 1973-75, otolaryngol, res, 1975-78; Conroe Regional Med Ctr, physician; St Lukes Episcopal Hosp, physician; Pk Plaza Hosp, physician; Plaza Specialty Hosp, physician; Doctor's Hosp-Tidwell, physician; pvt pract otolaryngologist, currently. **Orgs:** Houston Med Forum; Alpha Phi Omega Serv Frat; Deafness Res Found; AMA; Nat Med Asn; Harris Co Med Asn; Tex Med Asn; Am Coun Otolaryngol; Houston Otolaryngol Asn. **Special Achievements:** First black otolaryngol res, Baylor Affiliated Hosp, 1975-78; One of the first 10 Nat Achievement Scholarship, 1965. **Home Addr:** 8810 Delilah St, Houston, TX 77033. **Business Addr:** Physician, 509 W Tidwell Rd Suite 303, Houston, TX 77091, **Business Phone:** (713)697-8382.

## MABRY, EDWARD L. (EDDIE MABRY)

Educator. **Personal:** Born Nov 21, 1936, Brownsville, TN; son of Charlie and Mary Palmer. **Educ:** Millikin Univ, BA, 1966; Princeton Theol Sem, MDiv, 1969; Princeton Theol Sem, PhD, 1982. **Career:** Princeton Theol Sem, Rockerfeller fel, 1967-69; Millikin Univ, dir relig activ, 1969-70, vis prof, 1988; Princeton Theol Sem, master residence, 1970-73; NJ State Home Girls, chaplain, 1971-72; Talladega Col, dir relig action & asst prof relig, 1973-75; Morning Star Baptist Church Tulsa, minister educ, 1975-, organist, 1975; Okla Sch Relig, dean; Richard Community Col, instr & eve coordr, 1988-90; Augustana Col, assoc prof, 1990, chmn relig dept, 1995-, prof church hist, profesor emer relig, 1990-2002. **Orgs:** Am Asn Univ Prof, 1973-; dir, Christian Educ Okla Baptist State Conv, 1975-; lifetime mem Nat Asn Advan Colored People; assoc minister, Second Baptist Church, Rock Island, IL. **Honors/Awds:** Student Senate Appreciation Award, Talladega Col, 1974; Swank Prize in Homiletics, Princeton Theol Sem. **Home Addr:** 2202 Main St, Decatur, IL 62526, **Home Phone:** (309)755-3776. **Business Addr:** Professor Emeritus, Augustana College, 639 38th St, Rock Island, IL 61201, **Business Phone:** (309)794-7000.

## MABRY, MATTIE

Association executive. **Career:** Tupelo Neighborhood Asn Coun, past pres, vpres; Haven Acres Neighborhood Asn, Boys & Girls Club, dir clubhouse, vpres, pres, currently. **Home Addr:** 3138 Moore Ave, Tupelo, MS 38801-9066, **Home Phone:** (662)566-4720. **Business Addr:** Vice President, Tupelo Neighborhood Association Council, 71 E Troy St, Tupelo, MS 38804, **Business Phone:** (662)841-6513.

## MABSON, GLENN T.

Manager. **Personal:** Born Feb 23, 1940, Tulsa, OK; son of Lowell and Ozella; children: Athena, Darvell, Kimberly & Daniel. **Educ:** Calif Inst Technol, BEE, 1966; Nat Tech Sch, MS, 1968; PhD. **Career:** MGM/Sony Studios, prod sound mixer, 1968-75; Burbank Studios, prod sound mixer; 20th Cent Fox, W La, prod sound mixer; Paramount Studios, prod sound mixer; NBC News, prod sound mixer; CBS News, prod sound mixer; ABC News, prod sound mixer; Universal Studios, prod sound mixer; Mabson Audio Eng, Hawaii, prod sound mixer, currently. **Orgs:** Co founder, Pres & exec dir, Epileptic Found Maui. **Honors/Awds:** Community Leader of Achievement of Volunteers. **Special Achievements:** First African American to be in charge of production sound for a motion picture TV series; First African American to be hired as a Production Audio Engineer in the TV industry; First African American to produce a perfect sound track for a TV series; Emmy Winner "Reflections," 1981; First person to produce a perfect sound track for a motion picture "Car Wash," 1981; "The Greatest, Muhammed Ali Story," 1982. **Home Addr:** 2777 S Kihei Rd Apt I205, Kihei, HI 96753-9647, **Home Phone:** (808)879-8999.

## MACK, ALLY FAYE

School administrator, college administrator. **Personal:** Born Apr 6, 1943, Marthaville, LA; married Robert; children: Robert III, Ryan, Renfred & Jessica. **Educ:** Grambling State Univ, BA, 1963; Atlanta Univ, MA, 1964; Tex A&M Univ, further study, 1971; Univ So, MS, PhD, 1979. **Career:** Prairie View A&M Univ, asst prof, 1968-69; Tex A&M Univ, instr, 1969-71; Langston Univ, asst prof, 1971-74; Jackson State Univ, assoc prof, actg chmn, dir int progs, 1993-, Dept Polit Sci, prof, currently, Int Prog, dean, currently; Boren Fel Advisor. **Orgs:** Hinds Co Dem Exec Domm, 1975-; MS Health Systs Agency State Brd, 1978-79; consult, Tenn Valley Authority, 1979-; trainer, Nat Womens Educ Fund, 1980-; dist chmn, Dem Women, 1982-. **Home Addr:** 5927 Waverly Dr, Jackson, MS 39206. **Business Addr:** Professor, Director of International Programs, Jackson State University, 1400 J R Lynch St, Jackson, MS 39217-0103, **Business Phone:** (601)979-3792.

## MACK, DR. ASTRID KARONA

Educator, colonial administrator. **Personal:** Born Aug 21, 1935, Daytona Beach, FL; son of Meta Marietta; children: Astrid Kyle & Kristen Nichole. **Educ:** Bethune-Cookman Univ, BS, biol & chem, magna cum laude, 1960; Univ Minn, MS, zool, 1965; Mich State Univ, PhD, human & med genetics, 1974. **Career:** Dade Co Fla Pub Schs, teacher, biol & chem, 1960-66; Miami-Dade Community Col, instr & asst prof, assoc prof, 1966-73; Univ Miami Sch Med, Miller Sch Med, asst assoc prof, res assoc prof, Sickle Cell Clin Ctr, assoc dean minority affairs, 1988, assoc dean minority affairs, 2008. **Orgs:** Am Soc Human Genetics, 1969-; AAAS, 1974-; Am Genetics Asn, 1978-; exec dir, Dade Co Sickle Cell Found, 1978-; first five dist rep, Omega Psi Phi Fraternity Inc, 1982-85; dist rep, Omega Psi Phi Fraternity Inc, 1985-89; King Clubs Greater Miami Inc; Sickle Cell DisAsn Am, Miami-Dade County Chap Inc; Dr. Astrid Mack Diversity Endowment Fund. **Home Addr:** 5020 NW First Ave, Miami, FL 33127, **Home Phone:** (305)757-2525.

## MACK, C.

Banker, vice president (organization), manager. **Personal:** Born Mar 8, 1959, Canton, OH; son of Henry; married Tenetia; children: Lauren, Sean & Ryan. **Educ:** Univ Cincinnati, BFA, broadcasting, 1982; Ind Univ, MBA, mkt, 1984. **Career:** Consortium Grad Study Mgt fel, 1983; Procter & Gamble, brand mgr, 1984-91; Ryder Syst Inc, dir consumer trade rental mkt, 1991-92, group dir consumer truck mkt & mkt serv, 1992-93, vpres consumer track rental mkt, 1994, vpres, mkt serv, worldwide, 1994-96; Citibank FSB, sr vpres br sales & opers, 1986-97, Citibank FSB, pres & chief exec officer, 1996-2002; Citibank's Cent & Mid-Atlantic Regions, pres & chief exec officer; JP Morgan Chase & Co, exec vpres & retail banking exec, 2003-05; PNC Bancorp Inc, PNC Financial Serv Group, exec vpres & dep mgr, currently; Ankole Sporting Goods LLC, managing mem, 2006-. **Orgs:** Bd dir, Nat Black MBA Asn, 1987-95; co-chair, Super Bowl Mkt Comt, 1995; prin & co-chair, Chicago United, Econ Develop Comt, 1997-; bus adv coun, Chicago Urban League, 1997-; Lincoln Found Bus Excellence, bd trustee, 1997-; Neighborhood Housing Serv Chicago, Leadership Comt, 1997-; bd mem, Steppenwolf Theatre, 1997-; adv coun, DePaul Univ, Col Com, 1997-; fel Ind Univ, Kelley Sch Bus, 1998. **Honors/Awds:** Keepers of the Flame, Black Enterprise Mag, 1997. **Special Achievements:** Speaks fluent German & Portuguese. **Home Addr:** 1747 N Mohawk St, Chicago, IL 60614, **Home Phone:** (312)944-9528. **Business Addr:** Managing Member, Ankole Sporting Goods LLC, 3315 E Russell Rd A-4 Suite 278, Las Vegas, NV 89120, **Business Phone:** (855)462-5862.

## MACK, CHARLES RICHARD

Educator. **Personal:** Born Oct 2, 1942, Clarke County, NV; married Joan Jacqueline Thomas; children: 6. **Educ:** Univ Ga, BS, MEd. **Career:** Clarke Co Sch Syst, teacher, asst prin; Macedonia Baptist Church, Athens, GA, Baptist minister; City Athens, ward alderman, 1974-75. **Orgs:** Vpres, Clarke Chap Nat Asn Advan Colored People; CCAE; GEA; Nat Educ Asn; secy, NE Ga Baptist Ministerial Union; vpres, 8 Dist Gen Missionary Baptist Conv Ga; secy, 8th Dist Layman Group; pres elect, Clarke County Asn Educr; Phi Beta Kappa. **Home Addr:** 123 Pearl St, Athens, GA 30601.

## MACK, CLEVELAND J., SR.

Chief executive officer. **Personal:** Born Dec 5, 1912, AL; married Mary Holly; children: Cleveland Jr, Mary & Clarence. **Career:** Detroit, Mich, contractor; C J Mack Improv Co, owner, 1956-. **Orgs:** Asn Gen Contractors Am; Met Contract Asn; BTWBA; Urban League; Prince Hall Masons. **Business Addr:** Owner, C J Mack Improvement Co, 14555 Wyo St, Detroit, MI 48238, **Business Phone:** (313)931-0624.

## MACK, DANIEL J.

Insurance executive, executive. **Career:** Mutual Benefit Life Ins Co Inc, Richmond, Va, chief exec. **Business Addr:** Chief Executive, Virginia Mutual Benefit Life Insurance Co Inc, Richmond, VA.

## MACK, DR. DEBORAH L.

Consultant, administrator. **Educ:** Univ Chicago, BS, geog; Northwestern Univ, MA, PhD, anthrop. **Career:** Schomburg Ctr Res Black Cult, New York, consult; Nat Mus African Am Hist & cult, consult, selection comt, Community & Constituent Serv, assoc dir; Smithsonian Inst, Wash, consult; Chicago Hist Soc, consult; Ill State Bd Educ, consult; Mus Int Folk Art, Santa Fe, NM, consult; UNESCO, Paris, consult; His Mus, Senegal, consult; Palace Mus, Cameroon, consult; Orgn Mundo Afro, Uruguay; Nat Underground RR Freedom Ctr, Cincinnati, Ohio, mgr, exhibs & educ progs, 2003; Sch Art Inst, teacher; Northwestern Univ, res assoc & cur; Terranova Pictures, chief sci consult, currently; Chicago Field Mus Africa exhib, proj dir, currently. **Orgs:** Scholarly adv comt, Asn African Am Mus; McIntosh Sustainable Environ & Econ Develop; Smithsonian Coun; AFRICOM. **Home Addr:** 704 E 39th St, PO Box 1987, Savannah, GA 31401-1987, **Home Phone:** (912)443-3032. **Business Addr:** Chief Scientific Consultant, Terranova Pictures, 22430 Turkey Lane, Morrison, CO 80465.

## MACK, DR. DEBORAH LYNN

Consultant, curator, educator. **Educ:** Univ Chicago, BA, geog, 1976; Northwestrn Univ, MA, anthrop, 1977, PhD, anthrop, 1986. **Career:** Sociol & Anthrop, Lake Forest Col, asst prof, 1986-88; Northwestern Univ, vis scholar, 1988-89; Sch Art Inst Chicago, vis asst prof, 1989-90; Field Mus Natural Hist, proj dir, sr exhib developer, 1990-95; Field Mus, resassoc, dept anthrop; Northwestern Univ, res assoc & cur, 1996-; Mus Acad Consult, consult & advisor, 2002-; Terranova Pictures, chief sci consult, currently; Nat Underground Rr Freedom Ctr, mgr exhibs & educ progs, dir Pub Progs; Inst Mus & Libr Serv, field reviewer; Mus Group, consult, currently. **Orgs:** AFA Mus Asn; African Studies Asn; Am Anthrop Asn; Asn Am Mus; US Comt, Int Comt Mus; Mus Grp; adv coun, McIntosh Sustainable Environ & Econ Develop, Ga; adv bd, Smithsonian Coun; adv bd, McIntosh SEED; consult, Presidential Comn, 2002-03; scholarly adv, Smithsonian Inst, Nat African Am Mus Hist & Cult, 1999-2005, scholarly adv comt, 2005-11, assoc dir community & constituent serv; fulbright sr specialist, Musee Theodore Monod, Dakar, 2010; Nat Mus African Am Hist & Cult; vpres, Asn African Am Mus; Int Coun African Mus; ed bd, J Pub Hist. **Honors/Awds:** Illinois State Scholarship, 1970-74; Fellowship, Univ Chicago, 1970-74; Ralph Bunche Fellow, United Nations Asn,

1974-75; Fellowship, North westernUniv, 1976-77; Fulbright-Hays, US Dept Educ, Group Proj Abroad, 1988; Nat Endowment for the Humanities, Field Mus Africa Exhibit, 1992. **Special Achievements:** The Beni Amer, "Greenwood Press, 1984; Film Review of "The South-East Nuba," Am Anthropologist, 1986. **Home Addr:** 209 W Bolton St, Savannah, GA 31401, **Home Phone:** (912)443-3032. **Business Addr:** Consultant, The Museum Group, 704 E 39th St, Savannah, GA 31401, **Business Phone:** (912)443-3032.

## MACK, DONALD J.

Publisher. **Personal:** Born Jun 1, 1937, Port Arthur, TX; son of Howard (deceased) and DorothVack; married Gussie Lee Vinson; children: Todd. **Educ:** Lamar State Col, BS, 1963. **Career:** Tex Univ, teacher, 1964-66; Galveston Co, Calif, asst dir, 1966-67; Neighborhood Action Inc, dir, 1967-72; Community Action Agency, dir, 1972-74; Ft Worth Ctr Ex-offenders Inc, exec dir; Ebony Mart, publ. **Orgs:** Chmn, Neighborhood Action Apts, 1973; bd mem, Conf Christians & Jews, 1974; Leadership Ft Worth, 1974. **Home Addr:** 3304 Lawndale, Ft. Worth, TX 76133.

**MACK, FRED CLARENCE. See Obituaries Section.**

## MACK, GLADYS WALKER

President (organization), government official. **Personal:** Born Feb 26, 1934, Rock Hill, SC; daughter of Zenith Walker and Henrietta Alexander; married Julius L; children: Geofrey, Kenneth W & Johnathan. **Educ:** Morgan State Univ, Baltimore MD, BS, 1955; Cath Univ Am, Wash, DC, 1958. **Career:** Urban Renewal Admin Housing & Home Finance Agency, Wash, DC, budget analyst, 1955-65; Off Econ Opportunity, VISTA Prog, Wash, DC, budget analyst, 1965-67, prog anal officer, 1967-69; Exec Off Mayor, Wash, DC, sr budget analyst, 1969-72; Wash Tech Inst, Wash, DC, dir budget & finance, 1972-75; Exec Off Mayor, Wash, DC, dep budget dir, 1975-78, actg dir, 1978-79, asst city admin, 1979-82, dir Off Policy & Prog Eval, 1983-85, gen asst mayor, 1985-86; DC Bd Parole, Wash, DC, chairperson, 1986-91; Financial Planning and Mgt, Policy Develop & Career Coun, consult; United Planning Orgn, chief operating officer; Asn Paroling Authorities, Int, pres; Wash Metrop Area Transit Authority, chmn bd, currently. **Orgs:** Pres, Asn Paroling Authorities Int; dep exec dir, United Planning Orgn; Am Pub Transp Asn; Am Correctional Asn; Mid Atlantic States Correctional Asn; Delta Sigma Theta; dep exec dir, United Planning Orgn; secy/treas, bd dir DC Agenda; bd dir, vice chair, Wash Metrop Area Transit Authority; vol, community serv orgn; cabinet mem, Dist govt; Links Inc. **Home Addr:** 7030 Oregon Ave NW, Washington, DC 20015-1422, **Home Phone:** (202)244-8151. **Business Addr:** Chairman, Washington Metropolitan Area Transit Authority, 600 5th St NW, Washington, DC 20001, **Business Phone:** (202)962-1234.

**MACK, JAMES KEVIN. See MACK, KEVIN.**

## MACK, JOAN GLADDEN

Journalist, association executive. **Personal:** Born Nov 23, 1943, Charleston, SC; daughter of Harriet Robinson Gladden and Alonzo Gladden; married Charles Henry; children: Dandria Williams-Clark, Charles Austin & Kashauna Simmons. **Educ:** SC State Univ, BS, biol, 1964; City Col NY, cert, 1965. **Career:** Manpower Training & Devel Ctr, teacher, 1970-72; WCSC TV Channel 5 Charleston SC, pub serv dir/TV hostess, 1972-78; WCBD-TV Channel 2, Charleston SC, news reporter & news anchor, 1977-84; Col Charleston, media resources coord, adj prof, asst dir col rel & media commun, pub rels dir, dir admin, 5-Minute Linguist Talkin' About Talk, host, prin consult & producer, 1985-2009; New York Youth Bd, prog dir; Young Mens Christian Asn, prog dir. **Orgs:** Am Women Radio & TV, 1972-80; bd mem, Mayor's Comm Handicapped, 1976-80; March Dimes, 1976-80; Charles Webb Ctr Crippled C, 1977-80; Gov Comm Phys Fitness, 1980; Nat Fed Press Women, 1983-85; ITVA, 1986-87; Charleston County Heart Asn, 1986-87; Charleston County Substance Abuse Comn, 1987-; pub rels comn, Young Mens Christian Asn Auxiliary, 1988-; speakers bur, Young Mens Christian Asn. **Honors/Awds:** Communications Award, Omega Psi Phi Fraternity, 1974; Voluntary Service Award, United Negro Col Fund, 1974; Sch Bell Awards, SC Educ Asn, 1975-76, 1979; Outstanding Young Woman of America, 1977-78; YWCA Tribute to Women in Industry Award, 1981; Women Broadcast Award, SC Comn, 1981; Nat Federation of Press Women Award, 1983; Silver Reel Awards, Int TV Asn, 1986, Merit Award, 1988; Communicators Award, Carolina Asn Bus, 1987; Papal Award, "Pro Eccelesia Pontifice", 1999; Southern Regional EMMY Award, 2001; Listed, Who's Who Among Outstanding Black Americans. **Special Achievements:** First women of color to work at Channel 5. **Home Addr:** 1345 Pinnacle Lane, Charleston, SC 29412. **Business Addr:** Principal Consultant, Producer, College of Charleston, 66 George St, Charleston, SC 29424, **Business Phone:** (843)805-5507.

## MACK, JOHN L.

Executive, government official. **Personal:** Born Jul 25, 1942, Philadelphia, PA; son of Norman and Catherine; married Bettie Taylor; children: Monica, Michael, Mark & Gwendolyn. **Educ:** Mass Inst Technol, BS, 1973; Suffolk Univ, Sawyer Sch Mgt, MBA, 1979; Univ Tex, postgrad, int finance, 1980. **Career:** Personel staff rec, 1974-75; Mass Inst Technol, assoc dir admin, 1975-78; Univ Providence RI, assoc dir admin, 1978-79; Sonicraft, Chicago, dept prog mgr control, 1980-82; US State Dept Wash DC, admin officer, 1982-83; US Embassy Abidjan Ivory Coast, admin officer, 1983-85; US Embassy Paris France, mgt officer, 1985-87; US State Dept, Wash DC, Regional Admin Mgt Ctrs, coordr, 1987-; Mass Inst Technol, fel; House Foreign Affairs Comt, staff consult; Bandwidth Consortium, exec dir; Nsf, co-prin investr; WorldSpace Africa, managing dir; African Internet Forum, founder; Partnership Info & Commun Technologies Africa, founder; USAID, Leland Initiative, founder; Africa & Mid E Telecommunications Trade & Develop Policy, dir; John L Mack & Assocs, chief exec officer, currently. **Orgs:** Election consult, Fed Dearborn Proj; bd dir & pres, Cambridge Community Ctr; Mass Inst Technol Community Serv Fund; chmn, Mass Inst Technol Urban Act Comn; Mass Inst Technol Res Training Adv Comn; bd dir, Hope Housing; co-chmn, Mass Inst Technol Black Stud Union; Mass Inst Technol Task Force Educ Opportunity; Int Asn Fin Planners; Int Asn Black Prof Foreign Affairs; Inst Elec & Electronics Engrs, MENSA; bd mem, Suffolk Univ. **Honors/Awds:** American Spirit Medal of Honor. **Special Achievements:** Selected as Outstanding Young American, Jaycees, 1977. **Home Addr:** 12206 Kinloch Ct, Upper Marlboro, MD 20772, **Home Phone:** (301)627-2188. **Business Addr:** Staff Consultant, House Foreign Affairs Committee, 709 O'Neill HOB, Washington, DC 20515-6136.

## MACK, JOHN W.

Executive, association executive, civil rights activist. **Personal:** Born Jan 6, 1937, Kingstree, SC; married Harriett Johnson; children: Anthony, Deborah & Andria. **Educ:** NC Agr & Tech State Univ, BS, appl sociol, 1958; Clark Atlanta Univ, MA, 1960. **Career:** Camarillo St Hosp, P SW, 1960-64; Urban League Flint, Mich, exec dir, 1964-69; Los Angeles Urban League, pres, 1969-2005; Mayor Antonio R. Villaraigosa, Bd Police Commissioners, vpres, 2005-07, pres, 2007-09. **Orgs:** Leader, Atlanta Stud Civil Rights Protest, 1960; co-founder & vice chmn, Comt Appeal Human Rights, 1960; bd mem, KCET-TV-CHANNEL 28, 1975-; co-founder & Co-chair, La Black Leadership Coalt educ, 1977; bd mem, La County & County Pvt Ind Coun, 1983; vpres, United Way Corp Coun Execs, 1984; La Basin Equal Opport League, 1984; La Basin Equal Opport League, 1984; La Bd Zoning Applications, 1984; Calif's Atty Gen John Van DeCamp's Racila, Ethnic, Rel & Minority Violence Comt; teaching fel residence Prestigious Harvard Univ John F. Kennedy Sch Govt's Inst, 1998; bd mem, Cedars Sinai Med Ctr; bd mem, Calif Inst Technol Bd Trustees; Wells Fargo Bank Community Bd; State Farm Bank Adv Comt, bd govs, City Club Bunker Hill; Alpha Phi Alpha Fraternity; Xi Boule Sigma Psi Pi Fraternity; head, NAACP stud chap col. **Honors/Awds:** Mary McCleod Bethune, Nat Coun Negro Women, 1984; Outstanding Public Service Award, Asn Black Law Enforcement Exec, 1984; Thurgood Marshall Civil Rights Award, Alpha Phi Alpha Fraternity, 1992; Whitney M. Young, Jr. Award, Los Angeles Urban League, 1993; Hollzer Memorial Award, Jewish Fedn Coun Community Rels Comt, 1993; Black Women of Achievement's Special, NAACP Legal Defense & Educ Fund, 1997; Legend of the Century, Nat Urban League, 2000; Lifetime Achievement Award, NAACP, 2000; Lifetime of Giving Achievement Award, 2001; First C.I. Newman Lifetime Achievement Award, American Jewish Comt, 2003; Martin Luther King, Jr. President's Award, Southern Christian Leadership Conf, 2004; NCCJ Lifetime Achievement Award, 2004; The Magic Johnson Foundation Humanitarian Spirit Award, 2004; Honored "John W. Mack Day", City Los Angeles, 2005; Honorary Doctorate of Management Degree, Claremont Grad Univ Sch Educ, 2006; Inducted into the National Black Alumni Association Hall of Fame, 2006; Lifetime Achievement Award, Calif Afro Am Mus, 2007. **Home Addr:** 1838 Victoria Ave, Los Angeles, CA 90019. **Business Addr:** President, Los Angeles Urban League, 3450 Mount Vernon Dr, Los Angeles, CA 90008, **Business Phone:** (323)299-9660.

## MACK, KEVIN (JAMES KEVIN MACK)

Football player, actor, executive. **Personal:** Born Aug 9, 1962, Kings Mountain, NC; son of Calvin and Mary Francis; married Ava Bassett. **Educ:** Clemson Univ. **Career:** Football player (retired), executive; USFL, Los Angeles Express, running back, 1984; Cleveland Browns, running back, 1985-93, Nat Football League, player developement, 2007-10, alumni rels, 2010-. Film: "1986 AFC Championship Game", 1987; "1987 AFC Championship Game", 1988; "1982 Orange Bowl", 1982. **Honors/Awds:** National Championship, Clemson Tigers, 1981; Co-Most Valuable Player of the Year, Akron Browns' Backers; Kevin Mack Day, Hometown Kings Mountain, named in honor; Offensive Rookie of the Year, Nat Football League, Football Digest; AFC Rookie of the Year, UPI; Most Valuable Player, Cleveland TD Club; Pro Bowl, 1985, 1987. **Special Achievements:** Drafted by the Cleveland Browns in the first round (11th overall) of the 1984 Supplemental Draft. **Home Addr:** , TX. **Business Addr:** Alumni Relations, Cleveland Browns, 76 Lou Groza Blvd, Berea, OH 44017, **Business Phone:** (440)891-5000.

## MACK, LEVORN (VON MACK)

Government official. **Personal:** Born McBee, SC. **Career:** Town McBee, SC, town councilman, mayor. **Orgs:** Nat Conf Black Mayors; bd dir, Herman Martin Jr Found. **Business Addr:** Board Director, Herman Martin Jr Foundation, PO Box 658, McBee, SC 29101, **Business Phone:** (843)917-4850.

## MACK, LURENE KIRKLAND

School administrator. **Personal:** Born May 20, 1948, Graceville, FL; married Robert Eastmon; children: Uhura Jamal & Niesha Rochet. **Educ:** Miami Dade Community Col, AA, 1970; Barry Col, BS, 1982. **Career:** Dade Co, consumer protection agt, 1970-74; Dade Co Schs, investr, 1974-79, area supvr, 1980-; Early Advantage Kinder garden Inc, Miami, Fla, pres, 1980-; Scholar Fund Inc, officer, currently. **Orgs:** Nat Asn Advan Colored People, 1979-; Youth Crime Watch Adv Bd, 1982-; Black Pub Admin Asn, 1983-; exec bd, YEW, 1984-; vpres, NOBLE-FL Chap Sect6, 1984-. **Home Addr:** 18635 NW 38th Ave, Opa Locka, FL 33055. **Business Addr:** Officer, Scholarship Fund Inc, 6100 NW 2nd Ave, Miami, FL 33127.

## MACK, LUTHER W., JR.

Restaurateur. **Personal:** Born May 7, 1939, Sunflower, MS; son of Luther and Frances Mack; married Eugeni; children: Janelle. **Educ:** Univ Nev, Reno; LaSalle Univ. **Career:** State Nev, dept employ security, 1968, job coordr, 1969, dept hwy, equal opportunity coordr, 1970; US Small Bus Admin, dep contract compliance officer, 1971; McDonald's, owner, operator 11 franchises, 1974-; Boyd Gaming corp, dir, 2003-; Washoe Med Hosp Health Plan, bd dir, currently; Wells Fargo Bank Nev, Community Bd, currently. **Orgs:** Bd trustee, chmn affirmative action comn, chmn archit rev comn, Airport Authority Washoe County; comnr, chmn, 2001-03, Nev State Athletic Comn; bd dir, budget comn, found comn, chmn, 1997-98, Univ Nev, Reno; bd mem, freestockmarketreport.com; bd mem, bd dir, Nev Cancer Inst; bd mem, Boyd Gaming Corp; bd mem, Washoe Med Hosps Health Plan; bd mem, Wells Fargo Bank Nev; chair, Univ Nev Reno; northern nev bus owner, owner, chmn, Nev Athletic Comn; chmn, Nev State Athletic Comn; Mack Assocs Inc, owner, operator, founder, pres & chief exec officer. **Honors/Awds:** Hon doctorate, Univ Nev; Civic Leader of the Year, Raymond I Smith, 1990; Appreciation Award, Reno Police Dept; Ronald McDonald Awards, San Francisco Region McDonald's; Humanitarian Award, Nat Conf Christians & Jews, 1984; Distinguished Nevadan Award, Univ Nev, Reno; Honorary Doctorate Degree, Univ Nev, Reno, 1998. **Home Addr:** 35 Cassas Ct, Reno, NV 89502. **Business Addr:** Director, Boyd Gaming Corp, 3883 Howard Hughes Pkwy Ninth Fl, Las Vegas, NV 89169, **Business Phone:** (702)792-7200.

## MACK, MELVIN

Government official, mayor. **Personal:** Born May 28, 1949, Laurel, MS; son of Roger and Lennie; married Doneater; children: Trina. **Educ:** Meridian County Col, AA, 1970; Miss Valley State Univ, BS, 1972; Jackson State Univ, MS, 1979. **Career:** Cent State Univ, Univ Ctr, dir; MS Valley State Univ, asst basketball coach; Ellisville State Sch, staff develop dir; Jones County, supvr; City Laurel, coun, mayor, currently. **Orgs:** Omega Psi Phi Fraternity; MS Asn Supervisors; pres, Laurel High Sch Booster Club. **Home Addr:** 1307 Wheaton St, Laurel, MS 39440, **Home Phone:** (601)428-4844. **Business Addr:** Mayor, City of Laurel, City Hall, Laurel, MS 39441, **Business Phone:** (601)428-6405.

## MACK, NATHAN WESLEY

Salesperson, association executive, president (organization). **Personal:** Born Oct 15, 1956, Detroit, MI; son of Uler and Dorothy; married Jamie Baker; children: Ramone. **Educ:** Wayne St Univ, BS, mgt, mkt, real estate syndication, 1978. **Career:** Syntex Labs, Palo Alto, Calif, sales rep, 1979-84; Glaxo Inc, Res Triangle Pk, NC, sales, pres, 1984-89; Coalesce, co-founder, vpres, mkt & investor rels, 1991-95; Rayfred Group, pres, 1993-97; Adv Bd Co Mfg, pres, 1995-97; Man-mach interface, managing dir, 1995-; Centrifuge Mgt, pres, managing partner, 1999-2004; PinPointe Properties, pres, 2002-. **Honors/Awds:** Man of the Year, Coan Tennis Asn. **Home Addr:** 2361 Beecher, Atlanta, GA 30311, **Home Phone:** (404)758-4635. **Business Addr:** President, PinPointe Properties, 2155 Martin Luther King Jr Dr, Atlanta, GA 30310, **Business Phone:** (404)753-0031.

## MACK, PEARL WILLIE

Educator, chairperson, association executive. **Personal:** Born Aug 16, 1941, Laurel, MS; daughter of Sammie Lee Gilmer and Delia Ann Jones Moncrief; married Tommie Lee; children: Dwayne. **Educ:** Ill State Univ, BA, 1962; Roosevelt Univ; Gov's State Univ, MA, 1975. **Career:** Teacher (retired); Harvey Educ Asn, teacher, 1962-71, treas, 1971-75, chair grievance comn; Ill Educ Asn, resolutions comn, 1972-74, teacher; Women's Caucus, planning comn; Minority Caucus, chairperson, 1974-75; Nat Educ Asn, exec comn, 1987-87, chair elections comn, 1987-89, chairperson spec community black concerns, teacher. **Orgs:** Pol Action Comn Ill Educ Asn, 1975-; bd mem, Nat Educ Asn, 1975-; Pol Action Comn, Nat Educ Asn, 1976-; bd dir, World Confederation Org Teaching Prof, 1976, 1978, 1984, 1986; Grievance Com Harvey Educ Asn, 1977-; PUSH, Nat Asn Advan Colored People, Gov State Univ Alumni Asn, 1977; deleg, Dem Nat Conv, 1980; Coalition Labor Union Women, 1980-; Women Arts, 1984-; Citizens Utility Bd, 1984-; del rep, Nat Educ Asn. **Special Achievements:** Top 100 Outstanding Women in Educ, Nat Educ Asn, 1975; co-writer, Mini-grant Proposal for Cult Studies Prog, 1974-75; Intl Bus & Prof Women, Dollars & Sense Mag, 1987. **Home Addr:** 10324 S Peoria Ave, Chicago, IL 60643-3008, **Home Phone:** (773)233-1764.

## MACK, PHYLLIS GREEN

Librarian. **Personal:** Born Jul 1, 1941, Charleston, WV; daughter of Leroy Stanley Green and Gladys Webster Green; married Arnold Rudolph; children: Stephanie Michele & Nicole Renee. **Educ:** WVa State Col, BS, educ, 1963; Pratt Inst Grad Sch Libr Sci, MLS, 1967; Columbia Univ Sch Libr Serv, cert, advan librarianship, 1985; New York Univ, cert, New York real estate salesperson, 2003. **Career:** Librarian (retired); New York Pub Libr, clerk, 1963-65, librn trainee & librn, 1966-68, sr br librn & sr first asst, 1968-73, supv br librn, 1973-83, Cent Harlem Region, regional librn, 1984-02; Hunter Col Libr, jr libr asst, 1965-66; Columbia Univ, fel, 1983-84. **Orgs:** St Marks United Methodist Church; Black Caucus-Am Libr Asn; Upper Manhattan Rotary Club Int; pres, New York Black Librn Caucus, 1981-83; first vpres, Delta Sigma Theta Inc, N Manhattan Alumnae Chap, 1989-93; chmn, Community Bd 10 Manhattan, 1989-90; trustee, Sch Bd, Dist 5, NY, 1997-98. **Honors/Awds:** Special Performance Award, New York Pub Lib, 1988; Citation for Community Service, New York City Coun, 1990; Dr Charles A Wahlburg Service Award, Cent Harlem Meals Wheels, 2001; 5 elected officials' citations upon retirement, New York Public Library, 2002. **Home Addr:** 1901 Madison Ave, New York, NY 10035, **Home Phone:** (212)426-6961.

## MACK, RODERICK O.

Business owner, manager. **Personal:** Born Jul 30, 1955, Birmingham, AL; son of Edward and Irene; married Votura E Hendeson; children: Amrette, Shanta, Roderick Jr & Tamarka. **Educ:** Miles Col, Birmingham, Ala, BS, acct, 1977; Jefferson St Jr Col, Birmingham, Ala, AAS, fin, 1981; Samford Univ, Birmingham, Ala, MBA, 1981. **Career:** Liberty Nat Life Ins Co, acct intern, 1975-76; Emergency Sch Aid Act, tutor, 1976-77; Am S Bank NA Birmingham, corp acct officer, 1977-85; Am Inst, instr, 1982-83; Mack & Assoc, sr managing owner, 1982-; Southern Jr Col Bus, instr, 1986; Miles Col, Birmingham, Ala, instr, 1991. **Orgs:** Treas, pres, 1988-89, Nat Black MBA Asn, Birmingham Chap, 1985-87; treas, Family & Child Servs A United Way Agency, 1985-87; pres, Birmingham Minority Bus Adv Community, 1986-88; co-chair, Youth Leadership Forum Birmingham, 1987; Edward Lee Norton, Bd Adv Mgt & Prof Educ, Birmingham-Southern Col, 1990-93; adv comt, Birmingham Pub Schs Bus Educ, 1992-95; assoc dir, Nat Asn Accts Birmingham Vulcan Chap; Inst Mgt Accts, Birmingham Inter Prof Asn; Nat Soc Tax Prof; Birmingham Asn Urban Planners. **Honors/Awds:** Outstanding Member Award, Nat Asn Accts, 1983, 1985; Member of the Year, Nat Black MBA Asn Birmingham Chap, 1987; Presidents Award, Birmingham Assn Urban Bankers, 1993. **Home Addr:** 809 6th Ave W, Birmingham, AL 35204-3401, **Home Phone:** (205)781-2872. **Business Addr:** Senior Managing Owner, Mack & Associates, 801 Graymont Ave W, Birmingham, AL 35204-3923, **Business Phone:** (205)787-2870.

### MACK, RUDY EUGENE, SR.
Airplane pilot. **Personal:** Born Feb 9, 1941, Miami, FL; son of Flossie M; married Denise; children: Rudy Jr, Derek, Maurice & Jason; children: Angie & Brandon. **Educ:** Tenn A&I State Univ, BS, 1967. **Career:** Airplane Pilot (retired); Prudential, inst agt, 1967-71; Burnside OTT, flight instr, 1968-71; Northwest Airlines, capt; TAB Express Airline Inc, Turbine & Sim Instr. **Orgs:** Airline Pilot Asn; co-chmn com rel com, Airline Pilot Union; aeromed chmn, Orgn Black Airline Pilot. **Honors/Awds:** Orgn Black Airline Pilot ACE Camps Dirs Award, 1999-01; Parent Appreciation Award, 1999-01. **Home Addr:** 4803 Tangerine Cir, Oakwood, GA 30566-2423, **Home Phone:** (770)718-9428.

### MACK, SHANE LEE
Baseball player. **Personal:** Born Dec 7, 1963, Los Angeles, CA. **Educ:** Univ Calif, Los Angeles. **Career:** Baseball player (retired); San Diego Padres, outfielder, 1987-88; Minn Twins, outfielder, 1990-94; Yomiuri Giants, outfielder, 1995-96; Boston Red Sox, outfielder, 1997; Oakland Athletics, outfielder, 1998; Kans City Royals, outfielder, 1998. **Honors/Awds:** Most Valuable Player, Pac-10 Conf, 1983; Silver Medal, Olympic Games, 1984; American League Pennant, 1991; World Series Champion, 1991; Univ Calif, Los Angeles Athletic Hall of Fame, 2002.

### MACK, SYLVIA JENKINS
School administrator, cosmologist, association executive. **Personal:** Born Dec 22, 1931, Deal Island, MD; daughter of William E and Violet Armstrong; children: Alphonso L, Michael L, Don Frederick, Thomas Everett & Anthony Charles. **Educ:** Newman Col, BS, prof educ; Cert Trade & Indust Inst, Del State Bd Educ; St Joseph Univ, Philadelphia, Pa, MS, prof educ. **Career:** Cosmetologist (retired); Del State Bd Cosmetology, licensed cosmetologist, licensed cosmetol instr; New Castle Co Sch Dist, voc instr, 1970-93; Mas Aivlis Acad Cosmetol & Barbering, owner & curator. **Orgs:** Brandywine Prof Asn; bd mem, Brandywine Sch Dist Del, 1981-89; bd mem, Nat Asn Black Sch; vpres, Brandywine Sch Dist Bd Educ; Nat Asn Univ Women; life mem, Nat Asn Advan Colored People; Pilot Cong Black Women; pres, Moss-Robertson Auxiliary; vol, Del Veterans Nursing Ctr. **Home Addr:** 2121 Jessup St, Wilmington, DE 19802, **Home Phone:** (302)652-7370. **Business Addr:** Owner, Mas Aivlis Academy of Cosmetology & Barbering, 216 E 22nd St, Wilmington, DE 19802, **Business Phone:** (302)652-7370.

### MACK, TREMAIN FERRELL
Football player, special education teacher. **Personal:** Born Nov 21, 1974, Tyler, TX. **Educ:** Univ Miami, attended 1996. **Career:** Football player (retired); Cincinnati Bengals, defensive back & Kick Returner, 1997-2000; Louisville Fire, 2004; San Jose SaberCats, 2005-06; Mt Rainier High Sch, head coach, Currently. **Honors/Awds:** Pro Bowls, 1999. **Business Addr:** Head Coach, Mount Rainier High School, 22450 19th Ave S, Des Moines, WA 98198, **Business Phone:** (206)631-7000.

**MACK, VON. See MACK, LEVORN.**

### MACK, DR. WILHELMENA
Hospital administrator, chief executive officer, president (organization). **Personal:** Born Oct 1, 1951, Kendall, FL; daughter of Eugene and Gladys Terry; children: Shannon Lynnette. **Educ:** Univ Miami, BA, 1972, MEd, 1973; Fla Atlantic Univ, EdS, 1983, EdD, educ leadership, 1988. **Career:** Dade County, personnel officer, 1973-74; Jackson Memorial Health care Syst, personnel officer, 1974-75, educ coordr, 1975-78; Memorial Healthcare Syst, asst dir mgmt training, 1978-79, training & develop dir, 1979; Right Mgmt Consults, vpres consult Servs; N Broward Hosp Dist, vpres, chief human resource officer, 2002-04; W Mack & Assocs Inc, chief exec officer & pres, 2004-. **Orgs:** Am Asn Univ Women, 1991-; Am Soc Health Educrs & Trainers, 1989-; Broward Econ Develop Counc; Exec comt, 1993-; Educ Comt, 1994-; Dania Chamber Com; bd, 1988-91, exec comt, 1989-91; Hollywood Chamber Com, Phi Delta Kappa, 1991-; Greater Ft Lauderdale Chamber Com; bd, 1994-, Exec Comt, 1995-97; Leadership Hollywood, 1994; BAND (Bus Against Narcotics & Drugs)bd, 1994-; Browards County Sch Bds Blu Ribbon Comt, Bus Coalition Educ Excellence; World Class Schs; co-chair, Community Outreach Comt, 1998 & 2007. **Honors/Awds:** Woman of the Year, Ft Lauderdale Chap, Nat Asn Negro Bus & Prof Women, 1986; Bronze Leadership Award, National Junior Achievement, 1987; Up & Comers Award, Price Waterhouse, 1989; Outstanding Service Award, 1990; Dania Chamber Com, President's Award for Outstanding Service, 1990; Appreciation Award, Council for Black Economic Develop, 1990; America's Up Coming Business and Professional Women Award, Dollars & Sense Magazine, 1991; Greater Ft Lauderdale Chamber Com, Abraham S Fischler Award, 1992; Woman of the Year, Am Cancer Soc; President Award, American Lung Asn; Community Service Award, TJ Reddick Bar Asn. **Special Achievements:** Appointed, Council for Black Econo Develop. **Business Addr:** Chief Executive Officer, President, W Mack & Associates Inc, 8301 NW 48th St, Ft. Lauderdale, FL 33351, **Business Phone:** (954)741-8138.

### MACKAY, DR. LEO S., JR.
Chief executive officer. **Personal:** Born Jan 1, 1961?; married Heather; children: Sarah & Josiah. **Educ:** US Naval Acad, BS, hist, 1983; Harvard Kennedy Sch Govt, MPP, int security, 1991; Harvard Univ, PhD, int security & polit econ, 1993; Stanford Univ Grad Sch Bus, finance & acct non-financial exec, 1998; Univ Chicago Booth Sch Bus, finance execs, 1999; Concordia Sem, Doctor Laws honoris causa, 2005. **Career:** State Ga, Medicaid adminr; Lt Comdr, USN, 1983-95; Fighter Pilot, USN, 1983-89; Bell Helicopter, vice pres & gen mgr-aircraft serv bus unit, 1997-2001; Veterans Affairs, dep secy, 2001-03; US Govt, dep secy, 2001-03; Affiliated Comput Serv State Healthcare Solutions, Atlanta, Ga, chief operating officer & sr vpres, 2003-05; Lockheed Martin Corp, ICGS LLC, pres, 2005-07, corp vpres, domestic bus develop, 2007-11; vpres & corp officer 2011-; Ethics & Bus Conduct, chmn & chief excecutive officer; Cognizant Technol Solutions, independent dir, 2012-; Pegasus Capital Advisors, strategic advisor, 2014-. **Orgs:** Bd dir, Ethics & Corp Responsibility Comt; bd mem, Cook's C's Hosp, Ft Worth, Tex, 1998-2001; bd mem, Ctr a New Am Security, Wash, DC; Secy Health & Human Serv Adv Comt Minority Health, chmn, 2004-05; fel Grad Prize Harvard Univ; Aspen Strategy Group, 2005; chmn, bd visitors, Grad Sch Pub Affairs, Univ Md Sch Pub Policy, 2006-14; Coun Foreign Rels, 2007-15; vice chmn, bd regents, Concordia Theol Sem Ft. Wayne, 2010. **Business Addr:** Vice President, Corporate Officer, Lockheed Martin Corp, 6801 Rockledge Dr, Bethesda, MD 20817, **Business Phone:** (301)897-6000.

### MACKEL, DR. AUDLEY MAURICE, III
Surgeon. **Personal:** Born Dec 3, 1955, Natchez, MS; son of Audley M Jr and Nannie Love Blassingame; married Sharon White; children: Ashley Monique & Audley Maurice. **Educ:** Morehouse Col, BS, 1977; Meharry Med Col, MD, 1981. **Career:** Northwestern Univ Med Ctr, intern, 1981-82, orthop resident, 1982-86; Centinela Hosp Med Ctr, orthop resident, 1986-87; Kerlan Jobe Orthop Clin, orthop surgeon, arthritis, joint implant fel, 1986-87; Charles Drew Med Sch, Los Angeles, CA, Calif orthop surgeon, 1987-88; Assocs Orthop, Cleveland, Ohio, orthop surgeon, 1988-. **Orgs:** Nat Med Asn, 1982-; Cleveland Orthop Club, 1989-; fel Am Acad Orthop Surgeons, 1991-; Am Asn Hip & Knee Surgeons; Knee Socs, 2006-07; Am Orthopaedic Asn, 2007-; treas, J. Robert Gladden Orthopaedic Socs, 2007-. **Honors/Awds:** Alpha Omega Alpha Med Hon Soc, 1981; Outstanding Young Men of America, 1983; Anatomy Award, Dept Orthop Surgery, 1984; Physician Recognition Award, Am Med Asn. **Home Addr:** 23200 Lyman Blvd, Shaker Heights, OH 44122-2150, **Home Phone:** (216)360-9543. **Business Addr:** Orthopaedic Surgeon, Associates in Orthopaedics Inc, 5 Severance Cir Suite 609, Cleveland, OH 44118, **Business Phone:** (216)691-9000.

### MACKEY, MALCOLM
Basketball player, executive. **Personal:** Born Jul 11, 1970, Chattanooga, TN. **Educ:** Ga Inst Technol, bus mgt & bus, 1993. **Career:** Basketball player (retired), executive; Phoenix Suns, ctr, 1993-94; Continental Basketball Asn, Omaha Racers, 1994-95; Jeanne d'Arc Dijon, France, 1995-96, 2001-02; Konya Kombassan, Turkey, 1996; CB Murcia Arte, Spain, 1996-97; Dallas Mavericks, 1997; Continental Basketball Asn, Rockford Lightning, 1997; Tiburones de Aguadilla, Pr, 1997; Caceres CB, Spain, 1997-98; Leon Caja Espana, Spain, 1998; Sporting Athens, Greece, 1999; Sacramento Kings, 1999; Quad City Thunder, 1999-2000; Continental Basketball Asn, Quad City Thunder, 2000; Leones de Ponce, Pr, 2000; Giallorosso Basket Messina, 2000-01; Media Broker Messina, Italy, 2000-01; Atleticos de San Ger, Pr, 2001; FIBA Europe, Saos Jda Dijon Bourgogne, 2002; Jilin Northeast Tigers, China, 2002-03; Besancon, France, 2003-04; SIG Strasbourg, 2003-04; Anwil Wloclawek, Poland, 2004-05; Chattanooga Steamers, 2005-06; Mercedes-Benz Buckhead, 2010-13; Mercedes Benz Sales, team leader, 2012-15; Mercedes Buckhead, accomplished cert mercedes benz sales consult, 2012-; 92.9fm Game, sports anal, 2013-; ABA, Z Chattanooga, power forward; E Pt Jaguars, head coach, consult & advisor, currently. **Honors/Awds:** Georgia Tech Hall of Fame, Nat Basketball Asn & Europe Prof Basketball, 2005. **Business Addr:** Sports Analysis, 92.9 FM The Game, 1201 Peachtree St Suite 800, Atlanta, GA 30361, **Business Phone:** (404)898-8900.

### MACKIE, DR. CALVIN
College teacher, business owner, consultant. **Personal:** Born Jan 1, 1969?, New Orleans, LA; married Tracy; children: Myles Ahmad & Mason Amir. **Educ:** Morehouse Col, BS, math, 1990; Ga Inst Technol, BME, 1990, MS, mech engineering, 1992, PhD, mech engineering, 1996. **Career:** Morehouse Col, instr mathematics; Channel ZerO, co-founder & pres, 1992-; Tulane Univ, Dept Mech Engineering, fac, 1996-2002, tenured assoc prof mech engineering, 2002-06; Univ Mich, Dept Chem Engineering, vis prof, 2004-05; Prof, Speaker, Auth, Inventor & Entrepreneur; La Recovery Authority, ambassador; Golden Leaf Energy, partner. **Orgs:** Phi Beta Kappa; Pi Tau Sigma; Tau Beta Pi; bd mem, La Recovery Authority; Nat Speaker Asn; 100 Black Men Metro New Orleans; life mem, Nat Socs Black Engrs; fel, Effective Leadership Prog, 2008; chair, La Coun Social Status Black Boys & Men, 2009. **Business Addr:** President, Channel Zero, PO Box 312, Harvey, LA 70059-0312, **Business Phone:** (504)391-0730.

### MACKIE, TIMOTHY
Vice president (organization). **Personal:** Born New Orleans, LA; married Karen; children: Kwency, Wynston & Timme. **Educ:** Univ Alaska, AA; Southern Univ, BA; Community Col Air Force, AA, appl sci; Am Col, CLU/CHFC, prof designations. **Career:** UsaF, capt, 1979-99; AXA Advisors LLC, br mgr, div exec vpres, 1987-. **Orgs:** Booker T Wash Bus Asn; Nat Asn Black Accountants; Double Oo Riders Asn; Double OO Ranch, A Day Ranch Prog; 102nd US Colored Troops Civil War Re-enactment Group; Tuskegee Airmen. **Business Addr:** Executive Vice President, Branch Manager, AXA Advisors LLC, 201 W Big Beaver Suite 300, Troy, MI 48084, **Business Phone:** (504)218-1146.

### MACKLIN, DR. JOHN W.
Chemist, educator. **Personal:** Born Dec 11, 1939, Ft. Worth, TX; son of Vera L; married Toni L Stockton; children: Marcus E. **Educ:** Linfield Col McMinnville, BA, 1962; Cornell Univ, PhD, inorg, 1968. **Career:** Univ Wash, dept chem, from asst prof to assoc prof, prof emer, currently. **Orgs:** Am Chem Soc, 1966-; AAAS, 1978-; Int Soc Study Origin Life, 1984-; Nat Orgn Prof Advan Black Chemists & Chem Engrs, 1986-. **Home Addr:** 4307 1st NE, Seattle, WA 98105, **Home Phone:** (206)633-4917. **Business Addr:** Professor Emeritus, University of Washington, Bagley Hall 36 PO Box 351700, Seattle, WA 98195, **Business Phone:** (206)543-7199.

### MACON, MARK L.
Basketball player, basketball coach. **Personal:** Born Apr 19, 1969, Saginaw, MI. **Educ:** Temple Univ, BS, 1991. **Career:** Basketball player (retired), basketball coach; Temple, 1987-91; Denver Nuggets, guard, 1991-93; Detroit Pistons, guard, 1993-96, 1999; Fla Beach Dogs, 1996-97; Mabo Pistoia, 1997; Oyak Bursa Spor Kulubu, 1999-2000; Toros de Aragua, 2000-01; Atlantic City Seagulls, 2001; Temple Owls, Temple Univ, asst coach, 2003-06; Ga State Univ, asst coach, 2006-07; Binghamton Univ, asst coach, 2007-09, interim head coach, 2009-12. **Orgs:** Founder, Mark Macon Found, 1991. **Honors/Awds:** Mr. Basketball of Michigan, 1987; USBWA National Freshman of the Year, 1988; Atlantic 10 Player of the Year, 1989; Robert V. Geasey Trophy, 1991; NBA All-Rookie second team, 1992; Athletics Hall of Fame, Temple Univ, 2004; Silver Anniversary Team, ESPN, 2006.

### MACON-RUE, PAMELA A.
Executive. **Educ:** Wayne State Univ, BA, bus admin, mkt, 1988; Walsh Col Accountancy & Bus Admin, MBA, finance, 1996. **Career:** Comerica Bank, vpres, portfolio mgr, 1997-2008; Colo State Bank & Trust, sr portfolio mgr, 2008-; Bosc Inc, 2013-. **Business Addr:** Senior Portfolio Manager, Colorado State Bank & Trust, 1600 Broadway, Denver, CO 80202, **Business Phone:** (303)861-2111.

**MADDOX, DR. ELTON PRESTON, JR. See Obituaries Section.**

### MADDOX, GARRY LEE
Baseball player. **Personal:** Born Sep 1, 1949, Cincinnati, OH; married Sondra; children: Garry & Derrick. **Educ:** Harbor Col. **Career:** Baseball player (retired); San Francisco Giants, outfielder, 1972-75; Philadelphia Phillies, outfielder, 1975-86; Phillies, spring training instr; Philadelphia's now-defunct cable-sports network PRISM, broadcaster; A Pomerantz & Co, chief exec officer, 1995-; pres, World Wide Concessions Inc. **Orgs:** Philadelphia Child Guidance Clinic, bd dir; Federal Reserve Bank, bd dir, currently; investor, Washington Philadelphia, Foxwoods; Youth Golf & Academics Program, founder & pres. **Special Achievements:** Film: High Hopes. **Business Addr:** Chief Executive Officer, A Pomerantz & Co, 701 Mkt St Suite 7000, Philadelphia, PA 19106, **Business Phone:** (215)408-2100.

### MADDOX, JACK H.
Real estate agent. **Personal:** Born Jul 17, 1927, Detroit, MI; son of John (deceased) and Wylma (deceased); children: 1. **Educ:** Wayne State Univ, BS; Univ MI, cert; MI State Univ, cert. **Career:** Real estate & rel subj, teacher; Assoc Ins Agency, pres & gen agt; Past Brokers Invest Co, past vpres; J H Maddox & Co, proprietor & real estate broker, currently. **Orgs:** Secy, dir, Ebony Dist County; Real Estate Alumni, Mich; chmn fund raising comt local state, Nat Police Candidates; chmn, Alpha Phi alpha; guardsman, Jaycees; Nat Asn Advan Colored People, 1975-88, dir, Freedom Fund Dinner Comt; chmn, Housing Comn; Detroit Real Estate Brokers Asn; Police Action Comt; Million Dollar Club; dir, Housing Owners US Exchange; original chmn, 1300 Lafayette E Co-op Bd Dir; Detroit Bd Realtors; chmn, Govt Affairs Comt, 1988-95. **Special Achievements:** Named as representative of City of Acapulco, Mexico to the City of Detroit by El Pres Municipal De Acapulco, 1994. **Business Addr:** Real Estate Broker, Proprietor, J H Maddox & Co, 1300 Lafayette E St Apt 1602, Detroit, MI 48207, **Business Phone:** (313)393-9430.

### MADDOX, JULIUS ARNELL
Association executive, educator. **Personal:** Born Oct 9, 1942, Philadelphia, PA; son of Fannie; children: Marcus & Christopher. **Educ:** Wayne State Univ, BS; Oakland Univ, MA. **Career:** Highland Pk Schs, educr, 1974-76; Pontiac Schs, educr, 1976-91. **Orgs:** Prof Stand Comn Teachers; Mich Dept, Educ Periodic Rev Coun; life mem, Nat Asn Advan Colored People; bd dir, Delta Dent Mich; Phi Delta Kappa; pres, Mich Educ Asn, 1991. **Honors/Awds:** Man of the Year, MEA Women's Caucus, 1980; Apple Award, Jefferson Co Ky Teachers Asn; One Detroit's Fifteen Top Educrs, Success Guide. **Home Addr:** 1429 Somerset Close, East Lansing, MI 48823, **Home Phone:** (517)351-7863. **Business Addr:** MI.

### MADDOX, MARK ANTHONY
Football player. **Personal:** Born Mar 23, 1968, Milwaukee, WI. **Educ:** Northern Mich Univ. **Career:** Football player (retired); Buffalo Bills, 1991, linebacker, 1992, 1995, 1997, right inside linebacker, 1993-94, 1996; Ariz Cardinals, 2000, linebacker, 1998-99. **Honors/Awds:** Rookie of the Year, 1992.

### MADDOX-SIMMS, DR. MARGARET JOHNNETTA
Educator, executive. **Personal:** Born Aug 31, 1952, Clio, SC; married Odinga Lawrence Maddox. **Educ:** Livingstone Col, BA, 1973; Ohio State Univ, MA, 1975, PhD, 1991. **Career:** TRW Marlin-Rockwell Div, syst analyst, 1977-78; Fla A&M Univ, fac, 1978-80; Sen Wm F Bowen OH, admin asst, 1980-83; MJ Simms & Assocs Inc, chief exec officer, pres, 1983-; Wilberforce Univ, Wilberforce prof, polit sci, 1991-; Livingstone Col, assoc prof polit sci, 2005-. **Orgs:** Columbus Area C C 1983-; Am Mkt Assoc Cent OH, 1984-; Pub Rel Soc Am, 1986-; Livingston Col Alumni Asn, vpres local chap, pres. **Home Addr:** 1295 E Gates St, Columbus, OH 43206-3229, **Home Phone:** (614)443-4010. **Business Addr:** Associate Professor of Political Science, Livingstone College, 701 W Monroe St, Salisbury, NC 28144-5298, **Business Phone:** (704)216-6174.

**MADELYN, ANANDA KIAMSHA. See LEEKE, MADELYN CHERYL.**

### MADGETT, DR. NAOMI LONG (NAOMI WITHERSPOON)
Publisher, college teacher, editor. **Personal:** Born Jul 5, 1923, Norfolk, VA; daughter of Maude Selena Hilton Long and Clarence Marcellus Long Sr; married Julian F Witherspoon, Mar 31, 1946, (divorced 1949); married William Harold Sr, Jan 1, 1954, (divorced 1960); children: Jill Witherspoon Boyer; married Leonard P Andrews, Mar 3, 1972. **Educ:** Va State Col, BA, 1945; Wayne State Univ, MEd, 1955; Int Inst Advan Studies, Greenwich Univ, PhD, 1980; Michigan State Univ, DFA. **Career:** Poet & auth: 1941-; MI Chronicle, staff writer, 1946-47; MI Bell Tel Co, serv rep, 1948-54; Detroit Pub Sch, teacher, 1955-65, 1966-68; pub speaker, poetry readings only, 1956-; Oakland Univ, res assoc, 1965-66; Eastern MI Univ, assoc prof eng, 1968-73; Univ MI, lectr, vis prof, 1970; Eastern Mich Univ, prof, 1973-84, prof emer, 1984-; Lotus Press, publ & ed, 1972-; poetry ed, Mich State Univ Press, 1993-98; Adam of Ife: Black Women in Praise

of Black Men, 1992; Star by Star, 1965, 1970; Pink Ladies in the Afternoon, 1972, 1990; Exits & Entrances, 1978; Phantom Nightingale, 1981; Octavia and Other Poems, 1988; Remembrances of Spring: Collected Early Poems, 1993; Octavia: Guthrie and Beyond, 2003; Pilgrim Journey, 2006; poems widely anthologized & translated; poem: One and the many, 1956; Octavia: Guthrie and Beyond, 2002; Connected Islands: New and Selected Poems, 2004. **Orgs:** Col Lang Asn; Alpha Kappa Alpha Soc; Nat Asn Advan Colored People; Detroit Women Writers; Southern Poverty Law Ctr; Langston Hughes Soc; Charles H Wright Mus African Am Hist; Detroit Inst Arts; Fred Hart Williams Geneological Soc; Plymouth United Church Christ. **Honors/Awds:** Distinguished English Teacher of the Year, Met Detroit; first recipient Mott Fel eng, 1965; Disting Soror Award, Alpha Rho Omega Chap, Alpha Kappa Alpha Sor, 1969; Key to the City of Detroit, 1980; Resolutions from Detroit City Coun, 1982 & MI State Legis, 1982 & 1984; Recognition by Black Caucus Nat Coun Teachers Eng, 1984; Nat Coalition 100 Black Women, 1984; Induction into Stylus Soc Howard Univ, 1984; Distinguished Artist Award, Wayne State Univ, 1985; Robert Hayden Runagate Award, 1985; Creative Artist Award, MI Coun arts, 1987; Creative Achievement Award, Col Lang Asn, 1988; "In Her Lifetime" Award, Afrikan Poets Theatre Inc, 1989; Literature Award, Arts Found Mich, 1990; Honorary Degrees: Siena Hgts Col, 1991; Recognition by Black Caucus of American Library Asn, 1992; Loyola University, Chicago, 1993; MI Artist Award, 1993; Am Book Award, 1993; Honorary Degree: MI State Univ, 1994; Sumner HS Hall of Fame, 1997; Nat Literary Hall of Fame for Writers of African Descent, 1999; City of Detroit, poet laureate, 2001-; MI Women's Hall of Fame, 2002; Alain Locke Award, DIA Friends of African Am Art, 2003; life size bronze bust created by sculptor Artis Lane part of the permanent collection of the Charles H Wright Mus of African Am Hist, 2005; Naomi Long Madgett & Lotus Press Papersin the Special Collection Library, Univ Mich, Ann Arbor; Kresge Eminent Artist Award, 2012; name in honor Naomi Long Madgett Poetry Award; American Book Award; Michigan Artist Award; DHL, Siena Heights Univ; Lifetime Achievement Award. **Home Addr:** 18080 Santa Barbara Dr, Detroit, MI 48221-2531, **Home Phone:** (313)342-9174. **Business Addr:** Publisher, Editor, Lotus Press Inc, PO Box 21607, Detroit, MI 48221, **Business Phone:** (313)861-1280.

### MADHUBUTI, DR. HAKI R. (DON LUTHER LEE)

Educator, association executive, editor. **Personal:** Born Feb 23, 1942, Little Rock, AR; son of Jimmy L Lee and Maxine Graves Lee (deceased); married Johari Amini; children: 2. **Educ:** Wilson Jr Col, Roosevelt Univ, Univ Ill, Chicago Circle; Univ Iowa, MFA, 1984. **Career:** DuSable Mus African Am Hist, Chicago Ill, apprentice cur, 1963-67; Montgomery Ward, Chicago Ill, stock dept clerk, 1963-64; US Post Off, Chicago Ill, clerk, 1964-65; Spiegels, Chicago Ill, jr exec, 1965-66; Third World Press, Chicago Ill, found, pres, publ & ed, 1967-, chmn bd; Cornel Univ, Ithaca NY, writer-in-residence, 1968-69; Inst Positive Educ, Chicago, Ill, founder, dir, 1969-; Northeastern Ill State Col, Chicago Ill, poet-in-residence, 1969-70; Univ Ill, Chicago Ill, lectr, 1969-71; Howard Univ, Wash, DC, writer-in-residence, 1970-78; Morgan State Col, Baltimore Md, 1972-73; Chicago State Univ, Chicago Ill, assoc prof Eng, 1984-; Betty Shabazz Int Charter Sch, co-founder, 1998; Chicago State Univ, Master Fine Arts Creative Writing prog, dir, Gwendolyn Brooks Ctr Black Lit & Creative Writing, distinguished univ prof, co-founder & dir emer. **Orgs:** Apprentice cur, DuSable Mus African Am Hist, 1963-67; founding mem, Orgn Black Am Cult, Writers Workshop, 1967-75; fels Nat Endowment Arts, 1969-82; vice-chmn, African Liberation Day Support Comn, 1972-73; pres, African-Am Publ, Booksellers & Writers Asn, 1990-; founder & dir, Nat Black Writers Retreat; past exec coun, Cong African People; founder & bd mem, Nat Asn Black Bk Publishers; founder & chmn bd, Int Lit Hall Fame Writers African Descent. **Honors/Awds:** American Book Award; Kuumba Workshop Black Liberation Award; Broadside Press Outstanding Poet's Award; National Endowment for the Humanities. **Special Achievements:** Published works include Think Black, Broadside Press, 1967; Black Pride, Broadside Press, 1967; For Black People (and Negroes Too), Third World Press, 1968; Don't Cry, Scream, Broadside Press, 1969; We Walk the Way of the New World, Broadside Press, 1970; Dynamite Voices I: Black Poets of the 1960s, Broadside Press, 1971; Direction score: Selected and New Poems, Broadside Press, 1971; From Plan to Planet-Life Studies: The Need for Afrikan Minds & Institutions, Broadside Press, 1973; Book of Life, Broadside Press, 1973; Earthquakes and Sunrise Missions: Poetry and Essays of Black Renewal, 1793-1983, Third World Press, 1984; Say That the River Turns: The Impact of Gwendolyn Brooks, Third World Press, 1987; Black Men: Obsolete, Single, Dangerous'; Claiming Earth: Race, Rage, Rape, Redemption, 1994; Blacks Seeking A Culture of Enlightened Empowerment, 1994; GroundWork: New and Selected Poems, 1966-96; HeartLove: Wedding and Love Poems, 1998; Yellow Black. **Home Addr:** 7647 Bennett, Chicago, IL 60619. **Business Addr:** Founder, President, Third World Press, 7822 S Dobson Ave, Chicago, IL 60619, **Business Phone:** (773)651-0700.

### MADISON, EDDIE L., JR.

Writer, publicist, editor. **Personal:** Born Sep 8, 1930, Tulsa, OK; son of Laverta Mae Pyle and Eddie L Sr; married Davetta Jayn Cooksey; children: Eddie III, Karyn Devette & David. **Educ:** Lincoln Univ Mo, Jefferson City, BJ, 1952; Univ Tulsa, MA, mass commun, 1959. **Career:** Chicago Tribune, sect ed, 1963-65; Info Div US Dept Com, info spec, 1965; Off Publ & Info Domestic & Intl Bus, dept dir, publ div, 1965-69; WMAL-TV & Radio, community serv dir; Wash Star Sta Grp, mgr comm serv, 1969-77; Wash Star Comm Inc Brdcst Div, mgr admin serv, 1977-78; US Indsl Outlook, 1979, chief ed, 1978-79; US Dept Com Bus Am Mag, asst ed, 1979-81; Congressman Gus Savage Ill, chief press asst, 1981-82; US Dept Health & Human Serv radio, writer, ed & pub affairs coord, 1982-92, mgr, 1991-92; Lincoln Univ, asst prof & dept chmn, 1992-99; Three Elms & Assoc Inc, founder, pres & chief exec officer, 2001-; Eve Star Broadcasting sta group, dir. **Orgs:** Commn Human Rights, DC, 1970-75; dir, DC United Way, 1970-78; Industrialization Ctr, 1971-78; Nat Brdcst Asn Community Affairs, 1974-76; pub rel dir, Alpha Phi Alpha Fraternity; Int Bus Serv; US Dept Com; bd trustee, C's Hosp Nat Med Ctr, 1975-78; Nat Asn Educ Broadcasters, 1978-79; mem & officer, numerous orgn & comts. **Home Addr:** 1120 Netherlands Ct, Silver Spring, MD 20905, **Home Phone:** (301)236-9511. **Business Addr:** President, Chief Executive Officer, Three Elms & Associates, PO Box 90603, Washington, DC 20090, **Business Phone:** (202)436-8586.

### MADISON, JACQUELINE EDWINA

Manager, librarian, entrepreneur. **Personal:** Born Jul 16, 1951, Darlington, SC; daughter of John Brown and Lula Mack McLeod; married Calvin Lee; children: Jaquenette & Calexandria. **Educ:** Fayetteville State Univ, BS, 1972; Baylor Univ, Waco, cert, 1974; Kans State Univ, attended 1986; Emporia State Univ, MLS, 1991. **Career:** Principal information scientist (retired); FDA, Orlando, FL, food & drug inspector, 1972-73; AUS, Nurnberg, Ger, sanit engr, 1974-77, sup appt clerk, 1977-79; Cent Tex Col, Ft Lewis, WA, substitute teacher, 1980-82; Ft Riley Libr, Ft Riley, KS, libr tech, 1987-90; Youth Serv, Ft Riley, KS, secy & personal admin asst, 1990-; Jaqcal's Info phone, parent, teacher, stud commun line; Wyeth Ayerst Res Lab, prin info scientist. **Orgs:** Delta Sigma Theta, 1971-; Parent Teacher Asn, 1988-; Kan Libr Asn, 1989-; Black Caucus Ala, 1989-; SLA, 1989-; N Country Girls Scouts; Phi Beta Kappa; Phi Kapa Phi; advocacy, Northern New York Libr Network, 2010-, trustee. **Honors/Awds:** Science Awards, Phi Beta Kappa, 1971-72; Scholarship, E Stroudsburg Univ, 1989; Golden Poet Awards, World Poetry, 1990-91; Gold Poet Awards, World of Poetry, 1992, Phi Kapa Phi, 1991; Woman of the Year, Nominee & Finalist, 1996. **Home Addr:** 6571 State Rte 22, Plattsburgh, NY 12901, **Home Phone:** (518)562-5686.

### MADISON, KRISTEN DOROTHY

Lawyer. **Personal:** Born Jun 13, 1972, Rochester, NY; daughter of William and Barbara. **Educ:** Univ Va, BA, 1994; Univ Conn Sch Law, JD, 1997. **Career:** US Dept Labor-OECCP, jr officer, 1998-2000; Jackson Lewis LLP, assoc atty. **Honors/Awds:** Sr Compliance Off, OFCCP, 1998-00. **Home Addr:** 3 Spring Ct, Huntington, NY 11743-3619, **Home Phone:** (631)424-9392. **Business Addr:** Associate Attorney, Jackson Lewis LLP, 1 N Broadway 15th Fl, White Plains, NY 10601-2305, **Business Phone:** (914)328-0404.

### MADISON, PAULA WILLIAMS

Journalist, executive, president (organization). **Personal:** Born Jan 1, 1952, Harlem, NY; married Roosevelt; children: Imani. **Educ:** Vassar Col, BA, 1974; Syracuse Univ, Newhouse Sch Communs. **Career:** Executive (retired); Syracuse Herald Jour, reporter, 1974-80; Ft Worth Star-Telegram, reporter, 1980-82; Dallas Times Herald, asst city ed, 1982; WFAA-TV, community affairs dir, 1982-84, news mgr, 1984-86; KOTV-TV, news dir, 1986; KHOU-TV, exec news dir, 1987-89; WNBC, asst news dir, 1989-96, news dir, 1996-99; NBC, vpres, sr vpres diversity, 2000-02; KNBC, pres & gen mgr, 2000-; KNBC, KVEA, KWHY, regional gen mgr, 2002-07; NBC Universal, lead diversity, exec vpres diversity, 2007-11; Gen Elec Co, vpres, co officer, 2007-11; Nations second largest pub libr syst, libr commissioners, 2010; Maynard Inst Journalism Educ, fels; Los Angeles Pub Libr Comn, fels; Cardinal Spellman High Sch, fels; Chair Nell Williams Family Found, fels; fel Police Commissioners, vpres, currently; Williams Group Holdings LLC, partner, currently, Madison Media Mgt LLC, Chmn & chief exec officer, currently; Los Angeles Sparks, chmn & chief exec officer; Judge Nathaniel Jones, judicial clerk, 1995-96; O'Melveny & Myers LLP, assoc, 1996-97; US Dept Justice, sr coun policy, dep asst Atty Gen, 1997-2000; Fannie Mae, vpres & dep gen coun, 2000-02, sr vpres, dep gen coun & chief compliance officer, 2002, sr lawyer & bus exec, 2002-06; Housing & Community Develop, sr vpres & chief compliance officer; Latham & Watkins LLP, partner; Nat Col Athletic Asn, gen coun & vpres legal affairs, currently. **Orgs:** Nat Asn Black Journalists; Chinatown Serv Ctr; bd mem, Nat Med Fel; bd mem, Ctr Pub Integrity; bd mem, Poynter Inst; bd mem, Maynard Inst; NY Vassar Club; NY Press Club; bd mem, Greater Los Angeles United Way; chmn, Calif Sci Ctr Found; vice chair, Nat Med; Bd Police Commissioners, 2013-; Womens Nat Basketball Asn Bd Gov. **Business Addr:** Partner, Chairman & CEO, Williams Group Holdings LLC, 444 N Mich Ave Suite 3530, Chicago, IL 60611, **Business Phone:** (312)281-5570.

### MADISON, ROBERT P.

Architect. **Personal:** Born Jul 28, 1923, Cleveland, OH; son of Robert James and Nettie Josephine Brown; married Leatrice Lucille Branch; children: Jeanne M Anderson & Juliette M Little. **Educ:** Western Res Univ, BA 1948; Harvard Univ, MA 1952; Ecole Des Beaux Arts Paris, 1953. **Career:** Robert A Little Architects, designer, 1948-51; Howard Univ, asst prof, 1952-54; Robert P Madison Int, pres, chmn & chief exec officer, 1954-; Case Western Res Univ, 1969-81; trustee, Univ Circle, Inc, 1974-; dir, Indust Bank WA, 1975-81; engineering & nuclear teaching facil at Tuskegee Univ; trustee, Cuyahoga Metrop Gen Hosp, 1982-; trustee, Midtown Corridor Inc, 1982-; OH Bd Bldg Stand State OH, 1984-; City Planning Commn, Cleveland Heights OH, 1987-. **Orgs:** Fel Am Inst Architects, 1974; chmn, Jury Fel Nat AIA, 1985; trustee, Cleveland Chap Am Red Cross, 1986-; trustee, OH Motorists Asn, 1986-; Cleveland Downtown Plan Steering Comm, 1986; Alpha Phi Alpha, Sigma Pi Phi; trustee, Cleveland Opera, 1990-. **Honors/Awds:** Architect US Embassy Dakar Senegal, 1965-77; Architect's delegation Peoples Republic of China, 1974; Distinguished Service Award BEDO State of Ohio; President's Award Cleveland Chap AIA; Distinguished Firm Award, Howard Univ, 1989; Distinguished Serv Award, Case Western Reserve Univ, 1989; Honorary DHL, Howard Univ, 1987, AIA Ohio, Gold Medal Firm Award, 1994, Gold Medal Architect Award, 1997; Cleveland Opera honors, Robert P Madison & Leatrice Madison, 1999. **Special Achievements:** First black student to graduate from the Western Reserve University School of Architecture; First black registered architect in Ohio; First architectural firm established by an African-American in the State of Ohio. **Home Addr:** 18975 Van Aken Apt 410, Shaker Heights, OH 44122, **Home Phone:** (216)991-4347. **Business Addr:** President, Chairman, Robert P Madison International, 2930 Euclid Ave, Cleveland, OH 44115, **Business Phone:** (440)523-9889.

### MADISON, DR. ROMELL J.

Dentist. **Personal:** Born May 25, 1952, Nagoya; son of James and Fuki Tanaka; married Grace Perkins; children: Romell Jarrod & Leslie. **Educ:** Univ New Orleans, attended 1973; Xavier Univ, BS, pharm, 1976; Meharry Med Col, DDS, 1984. **Career:** Pharmacist, 1975-80; Dr Romell J Madison & Assoc, dentist, 1984-. **Orgs:** Life mem, Kappa, 1986; pres, New Orleans Dent Soc, 2001, 2002; pres, Pelican State Dent Asn, 2001, 2002; past pres, Nat Dent Asn, 2003; Am Dent Asn; Am Asn Dent Boards; CITA; polemarch, Kappa Alpha Psi Fraternity Alumni Chap, 2003; La State Bd Dent, 2004. **Honors/Awds:** Student National Dental Association Scholarship, 1981; Oral Medicine and Oral Diagnosis Award, Meharry Medical College, 1983, Dean's Award, 1984; American Academy of Dental Radiology Award, 1984. **Home Addr:** 3700 Orleans Ave Apt 5233, New Orleans, LA 70119-4861, **Home Phone:** (504)301-9097. **Business Addr:** Dentist, Dr. Romell J Madison & Assoc, 743 Terry Pkwy, Gretna, LA 70056, **Business Phone:** (504)394-9907.

### MADISON, SAMUEL ADOLFUS, JR.

Football player, executive, radio host. **Personal:** Born Apr 23, 1974, Thomasville, GA; married Saskia; children: Kellen, Kaden & Kennedy. **Educ:** Univ Louisville, BA, justice admin, 1996. **Career:** Football player (retired), exec; Miami Dolphins, defensive back & right corner back & corner back, 1997-2006, co-host, 2010-; New York Giants, corner back & right corner back & left corner back, 2006-09; Madison Ave Ventures, chief exec officer, 2007-; Nat Scouting Report, area scout s fla, 2012-13. **Orgs:** Founder, Madison Ave Kids, 2000-. **Honors/Awds:** Pro Bowl, 1999-02; NFL Interceptions Co-Leader, 1999; Nat Moore Community Service Award, 2004; Super Bowl Champion XLII. **Home Addr:** 13153 SW 25th Pl, Davie, FL 33325-5140. **Business Addr:** Chief Executive Officer, Madison Avenue Ventures, 1112 Weston Rd, Weston, FL 33326, **Business Phone:** (954)655-3595.

**MADISON, SHANNON L. See Obituaries Section.**

### MADISON, WILLIAM EDWARD

Executive. **Personal:** Born Jan 31, 1947, Rochester, NY; son of Williams E White and Addie D Adkins; married Barbara D; children: Kristen D & William E Jr. **Educ:** City Col NY, BS, 1970; Harvard Bus Sch, exec develop prog, 1991; Duke Univ, Fuqua Sch Bus, Exec Develop, human resource strategy; City Univ, criminal justice. **Career:** Xerox Corp, vpres, human resourses & qual, 1973-97, region personnel mgr, 1981-84, div hr mgr, 1984-87, employee resources, dir, 1989-91, hr Americas vpres, 1991-94, vpres, hr & qual, 1973-97; E I DuPont de Nemours & Co, hr, US ops, vpres, US Region, pres, 1997-2000; Talents Alliance Inc, dir, 1998-2000, pres, US Region; AVIS Grp Holdings Inc, sr vpres & chief hr officer, 2000-01; Entergy Inc, hr & admin, sr vpres, 2001-07; Gatestone Grp, chief exec officer, 2007-. **Orgs:** Omega Psi Phi Fraternity; dir, Boy Scouts Am, 1992-; dir, Urban Park Housing, 1984-97; dir, Boys & Girls Club Rochester, 1984-87; Nat Action comt minority Engrs, 1998-2000. **Business Addr:** Chief Executive Officer, Gatestone Group, 6230 Busch Blvd Suite 410, Columbus, OH 43229, **Business Phone:** (614)895-9027.

### MADISON, YVONNE REED (YVONNE REED MATHEWS)

Educator, association executive. **Personal:** Born Feb 22, 1954, Mobile, AL; daughter of Fred and Leila Roberts; children: Henry Clay Scott, Lucy Yvette Hillery & Sonya Williams. **Educ:** Univ S Ala, BM, 1976, ME, music, Eng & admin, 1982. **Career:** St Joseph Baptist Church, minister music, 1972-; Mobile County Bd SchComnr, teacher, 1982-, adminr, 2004-, clin dir; LeFlore Magnet Sch, chorus & piano instr, currently. **Orgs:** Music coordr, Alpha Kappa Alpha Sorority, Undergrad Chap, 1974-76; music dir, asst rep, Port City United Voices, 1981-; Ala Vocal Asn, 1982-; Nat Educ Asn; Mobile County Educ Asn; Music Educrs Nat Conf; Ala Music Educrs Asn; founder, pres, Nu Image, 1990-2013; music coordr, Nazaree Full Gospel Church. **Honors/Awds:** Career Women of the Year, Gayfers, 1996; Coalition of 100 Black Women Coral Award nominee, 1998; Outstanding Citizen Award, Alpha Alpha Fraternity, Beta Lambda Omicron Chapter, 1999. **Special Achievements:** Black Nativity/Blues City Cultural Center of Memphis, TN, 1994; Nat Governors Conference, performance, 1994; Nat Baptist Convention, Inc, Mid Winter Board Meeting Musical, 1996; Church Music Workshop, Jackson State Univ, AME Churches, 1998; Youth on the Winning Side, Summer Youth Program, 1998. **Home Addr:** PO Box 40042, Mobile, AL 36640-0042, **Home Phone:** (251)433-7553. **Business Addr:** Administrator, Mobile County Public School System, 1 Magnum Pass, Mobile, AL 36618, **Business Phone:** (251)221-4500.

### MADISON POLK, SHARON L.

Architect, business owner. **Personal:** Born Aug 17, 1953, Cleveland, OH; daughter of Julian C and Mildred R Madison; married Robert G. **Educ:** Univ Mich, BA, 1975, MA, Natural Resources, Urban Planning, 1994. **Career:** Madison Madison Int, owner, 1978-; M2 Int, chmn, 1987-. **Orgs:** Bd, Nat Women's Bus Coun, 1998-99; founder & pres, Bus Women's Alliance, 1999-; trustee, Detroit Inst Art, 1999-; chair, Friends African & African Am Art, 1999-; trustee, Detroit Downtown Develop Authority, 2000-; Am Planning Asn. **Honors/Awds:** Lifetime Achievement Award, NAACP; Small Business Female Entrepreneur Award, Detroit Chamber Com; Economic Achievement Award, SCLC; Alain Locke Award, FAAAA. **Business Addr:** Chairperson, Chief Executive Officer, Madison Madison International, Julian C Madison Bldg 1420 Wash Blvd Suite 200, Detroit, MI 48226-1718, **Business Phone:** (313)963-6110.

### MADLOCK, BILL, JR.

Baseball player, baseball manager. **Personal:** Born Jan 12, 1951, Memphis, TN; married Cynthia Johnson; children: Sarah, Stephen, William Douglas & Jeremy Joseph. **Educ:** Southwestern Community Col, Keokuk, IA. **Career:** Baseball player (retired), baseball coach; Tex Rangers, infielder, 1973; Chicago Cubs, infielder, 1974-76; San Francisco Giants, infielder, 1977-79; PittsburghPirates, infielder, 1979-85; Los Angeles Dodgers, infielder, 1985-87; Detroit Tigers, infielder, 1987; Lotte Orions, 1988; Tiffin Saints, mgr Independent League, 2013-. **Orgs:** Cystic Fibrosis "65 Roses" Campaign. **Home Addr:** 104 Prairie Ave Apt 1, Highwood, IL 60040-1714, **Home Phone:** (847)748-8341.

### MADU, DR. ANTHONY CHISARAOKWU

Educator, research scientist. **Personal:** Born Jun 10, 1956, Ulakwo; son of John and Pricilla Madu; married Mary Ellis; children: Geoffrey & Theandra. **Educ:** Benedict Col, BS, 1979; Meharry Med Col, PhD, microbial genetics, 1985. **Career:** Univ Mich, Molecular Biol, post-doctoral training, 1985-90; Univ MI, lect, 1989, Dept Biol, res fel, 1985-89, sr assoc, 1989-90; Emory Univ, Dept Biol, sr assoc, 1990-91; Univ MI, Post Doctoral fel molecular biol, 1990; VA Union Univ, Dept Biol, assoc prof, 1991-; Med Col VA, Dept Surg, fac assoc, 1992-; Va Union Univ, Dept Natural Scis, MARC, prog dir, 1992-. **Orgs:** Co-chair, Am Soc Microbiol, 1983-; Am Asn Advan Sci, 1985-; Alpha Kappa Mu Honor Soc, Kappa Pi Chapter, 1988-; Coun Undergrad Res, 1994-. **Home Addr:** 2302 Lockwood Rd, Richmond, VA 23294, **Home Phone:** (804)672-7341. **Business Addr:** Associate Professor, Program Director, Virginia Union University, 1500 N Lombardy St, Richmond, VA 23220, **Business Phone:** (804)257-5600.

## MADYUN, NASHID

Museum director, administrator. **Educ:** Miss Valley State Univ, BA, hist; Delta State Univ, MA, hist educ, 2000; Univ Phoenix, PhD, orgn leadership, 2012. **Career:** Gibson Musical Instruments, pres/gen mgr-retail group, 2005-08; Bob Bullock Tex State Hist Mus, Austin, TX, mus dir, 2008-09; Mid-S Planning & Mgt, COO, 2009-11; City Memphis, TN, adminr-mayor's off youth serv, 2009-11; Hampton Univ, dir mus & arch, 2011-15; Fla A&M Univ, dir Carrie Meek-James M. Eaton, Sr. Southeastern Regional Black Arch & Res Ctr, 2015-. **Orgs:** Asn Art Mus Dirs. **Special Achievements:** Former publisher of the "International Review of African-American Arts". **Business Addr:** Carrie Meek-James M. Eaton, Sr. Southeastern Regional Black Archives and Research Center, 445 Gamble St, Tallahassee, FL 32307.

## MAGEE, DR. ROBERT WALTER

Physician. **Personal:** Born Apr 23, 1951, New Orleans, LA; married Deborah Ketcheus. **Educ:** Southern Univ, BS, 1973; Meharry Med Col, Nashville, Tenn, MD, 1977. **Career:** Plasma Alliance, staff physician, 1979-82; Mathew Walker Health Ctr, staff physician, 1980-82; G W Hubbard Hosp & Meharry Col, resident family med; Meharry FP Prog, asst prof, 1980-82; New Orleans Health Corp, med dir, 1982-85; HMO, staff physician; Midsouth Health Care, pvt pract, currently. **Orgs:** Staff Physician Health Am, 1985-. **Home Addr:** 1523 Adams St, New Orleans, LA 70118-4001, **Home Phone:** (504)866-7373. **Business Addr:** Physician, Midsouth Health Care04-866-7373, 1700 Woodlawn Ave, Dyersburg, TN 38025, **Business Phone:** (731)287-4500.

## MAGEE, WENDELL ERROL, JR.

Baseball player. **Personal:** Born Aug 3, 1972, Hattiesburg, MS; married Vanedra; children: Joshua. **Educ:** Pearl River Jr Col; Samford Univ. **Career:** Baseball player (retired); Philadelphia Phillies, outfielder, 1996-98; Detroit Tigers, outfielder, 2000-02; Colo Rockies, outfielder, 2002; Long Island Ducks, outfielder, 2004-05.

## MAHAL, TAJ (HENRY SAINT CLAIRE FREDERICKS, JR.)

Musician. **Personal:** Born May 17, 1942, Harlem, NY; son of Henry Sr and Mildred Shields; married Inshirah Geter; children: Aya, Taj, Gahmelah, Ahmen, Deva & Nani. **Educ:** Univ Mass, BA, agr & animal Husb, 1964. **Career:** Performing & recording artist, 1964-; Taj Mahal & Elektras, group mem; Albums: Taj Mahal, 1968; The Natch'l Blues, 1968; Giant Step, 1969; The Real Thing, 1971; Happy Just to Be Like I Am, 1971; Recycling The Blues & Other Related Stuff, 1972; Big Sur Festival - One Hand Clapping, 1972; Oooh So Good 'n Blues, 1973; Mo' Roots, 1974; Music Keeps Me Together, 1975; Satisfied 'N Tickled Too, 1976; Music Fa'Ya, 1976; Brothers, 1977; Evolution, 1977; Live & Direct, 1979; Take A Giant Step, 1983; Taj, 1987; Shake Sugaree, 1988; Live at Ronnie Scott's, 1990; Mule Bone, 1991; Like Never Before, 1991; VolPour Sidney, 1991; Taj's Blues, 1992; Dancing The Blues, 1993; An Evening of Acoustic Music, 1993; The Source by Ali Farka Toure, 1993; MumtazMahal, 1995; Phantom Blues, 1996; Senor Blues, 1997; Sacred Island, 1998; In Progress & in Motion: 1965-98, 1998; Kulanjan, 1999; houtin' In Key, 2000; Hanapepe Dream, 2003; Blue Light Boogie, 1999; Shoutin' In Key, 2000; Hanapepe Dream, 2003; Martin Scorsese Presents The Blues - Taj Mahal, 2003; Blues with Feeling, 2003; Musicmakers with Taj Mahal, 2004; Live Catch, 2004; Etta Baker with Taj Mahal (Music Maker 50), 2004; Mkutano Meets The Culture Musical Club Of Zanzibar, 2005; The Essential Taj Mahal, 2005; Maestro, 2008; Compilations: Going Home, 1980; The Best of Taj Mahal, 1981, 2000; World Music, 1993; Sing a Happy Song, 2001; Martin Scorsese Presents the Blues - Taj Mahal, 2003; Blues with a Feeling: The Very Best of Taj Mahal, 2005. Films: Sounder, 1972; Bill & Ted's Bogus Journey, 1991; The Rolling Stones Rock and Roll Circus, 1996; Outside Ozona, 1998; Six Days Seven Nights, 1998; Blues Brothers 2000, 1998; Scrapple, 1998; Songcatcher, 2000; Divine Secrets of the Ya-Ya Sisterhood, 2002. TV series: "New WKRP in Cincinatti", 1992; "Arthur", 2003; "Theme song Peep and the Big Wide World", 2004. **Honors/Awds:** Grammy Award, 1997 & 2000; Grammy Award, Shoutin In Key, 2000; Blues Music Award, 2006; Honorary Doctorate, Fine Arts, Univ Mass, 2006.

## MAHOMES, PATRICK LAVON (PAT MAHOMES)

Baseball player. **Personal:** Born Aug 9, 1970, Bryan, TX; married Randi; children: Patrick Jr & Jackson. **Career:** Baseball player (retired); Minn Twins, pitcher, 1992-96; Boston Red Sox, 1996-97; Yokohama BayStars, 1997-98; New York Mets, 1999-2000, 2005; Tex Rangers, 2001; Chicago Cubs, 2002; Pittsburgh Pirates, 2003-04; Montreal Expos, 2004; Fla Marlins, 2004; Los Angeles Dodgers, 2005; Long Island Ducks, 2006; Kans City Royals, 2006; Toronto Blue Jays, 2007; Sioux Falls Canaries, 2007; Southern Md Blue Crabs, 2008; Grand Prairie AirHogs, 2009.

## MAHONE, BARBARA J.

Automotive executive. **Personal:** Born Notasulga, AL; daughter of Freddie Sr and Sarah L Simpson. **Educ:** Ohio State Univ, Columbus, OH, BS, bus admin, 1968; Univ Mich, Ann Arbor, MI, MBA, 1972; Harvard Bus Sch, Boston, MA, Mgt Develop, cert, 1981. **Career:** Executive director (retired); Gen Motors Corp Hq, Detroit, Mich, 1968-79; Gen Motors Rochester Prod, Rochester, NY, dir personnel admin, 1979-82; Gen Motors Packard Elec, Warren, OH, mgr labor rels & safety, 1982-83; Fed Govt, Wash, DC, chmn, fed labor rels auth, 1983-84; Gen Motors C-P-C Group, Warren, Mich, dir, HRM, 1984-86; Gen Motors Corp, Warren, Mich, gen dir, employee benefits, personnel, 1986-93; GM Truck Group, group dir, human resources; William Beaumont Hosp, dir; Charter One Financial Inc, dir, 2002-; Gen Motors Prod Develop, exec dir, 2008; Gen Motors Corp, Human Resources Global Prod Develop, exec dir, 2008; Talmer Bancorp Inc, dir, non-exec dir, 2013-. **Orgs:** Ad bd mem, Univ Mich Bus Sch, 1986-; bd dir, Urban League Detroit, 1990-; bd dir, Merrill-Palmer Inst, 1990-; adv bd mem, Nat Black MBA Asn, 1985-; adv bd mem, Cong Assistance Prog, 1989-; bd mem, Charter One Financial Inc, 2002; Am Soc Employers; treas, bd dir, William Beaumont Hosp; life mem, Nat Asn Advan Colored People; bd trustee, Walsh Col Accountancy & Bus Admin, 2008-; Shiloh Community Restoration Found; United Negro Col Fund; non-exec dir, bd dir, Talmer Bank & Trust, 2013-; bd dir, Beaumont Health Syst; bd dir, Shiloh Community Restoration Found Bd; bd dir, Bizdom Bd; adv coun, City Detroit Cult Affairs Dept; adv coun, Henry Ford Mus & Greenfield Village Pres Adv Bd. **Business Addr:** Executive Director, Shiloh Community Restoration Foundation, 7 Shiloh Rd, Notasulga, AL 36866, **Business Phone:** (334)257-4765.

## MAHONE, DR. CHARLIE EDWARD, JR.

Educator, school administrator. **Personal:** Born Aug 26, 1945, Washington, DC. **Educ:** Wayne State Univ, BS, bus admin, 1976; Univ Mich, MBA, 1978, PhD, 1981. **Career:** US Depts Educ & Com, prin investr; Prof Trng Prog, 1979-; Univ Mich, lectr, 1979-81; Ga State Univ, asst prof int bus, 1981-83, dir res, 1981-83; Fla A&M Univ, assoc prof int bus, 1985-89; Howard Univ, Sch Bus, assoc prof, 1989, dept chmn, 1994-98, assoc dean, 1998-2000, dir grad progs, 2000-03, prof int bus, 2000, dept fin int bus & ins, prof, 1989-2007; Univ DC, Sch Bus & Pub Admin, dean, 2007-. **Orgs:** Chmn social action comt, 1990-94, asst keeper rec, 1991-92; Wash DC Alumni Chap, Kappa Alpha Psi; bd dir, Japan-Am Stud Conf, 1996; Kappa Scholar Endowment Fund Inc, pres, 1984, chmn bd, 1996-98, bd dir, 1991-95, 1999-, vpres, 1991-95, 1999-; Acad Int Bus Studies; Bk Reviewer Southwestern Publ Co; ed comt, Competitiveness Rev; Int Acad Bus Disciplines; Int Jour Com & Mgt, reviewer; Fel Nat Econ Asn; Soc Int Bus; Fel DC Mayor's Task Force; Fel DC Local Bus Opportunity Comn. **Home Addr:** 1318 Emerson St NW, Washington, DC 20011-6906, **Home Phone:** (202)723-7356. **Business Addr:** Dean, University of the District of Columbia, 4200 Conn Ave NW Bldg 39 Rm A-08, Washington, DC 20008, **Business Phone:** (202)274-7000.

## MAHONEY, DWAYNE

Executive. **Career:** Boys & Girls Club Rochester, exec dir & chief prof officer. **Orgs:** Bd mem, E3 Rochester. **Business Addr:** Chief Professional Officer, Executive Director, Boys & Girls Club of Rochester, 500 Genesse St, Rochester, NY 14611-3696, **Business Phone:** (585)328-3077.

## MAHONEY, KEITH WESTON

Counselor, executive, association executive. **Personal:** Born Jan 12, 1939, Montego Bay. **Educ:** Brooklyn Col, BA, sociol, 1968, MA, polit sci, 1975, MSc, educ, 1982. **Career:** Counselor (retired); Dept Welfare, caseworker, 1968-72; Sch Dist 22 Drug Prev Prog, specialist, 1972-99; Caribbean Action Lobby, health coordr, 1983-. **Orgs:** Comt organiser, Vanderveer Pk Actions Coun, 1973-79; bd dir, Amersfort Flatlands Dev elop Corp, 1980-; mediator, C Aid Soc, 1982-; mediator, Brooklyn Col Dispute Resolution Ctr, 1982-; comt organiser, Amersfort Jct Anti Drug Task Force, 1983-; comn bd mem, Community Bd 14, 1985-; Nat Asn Black Counr, 1985-; vpres, E Region; co-founder, vpres, Howard Educ & Cult Inst; pres, Jamaica Nat Guild. **Honors/Awds:** Outstanding Effort to Prevent Drug Abuse, Sch Dist 22 Drug Prev Prog, 1972-; Serv to Community, Amersfort Flatlands Develop Corp, 1980-83; Excellence & Serv to Community, Brooklyn Col Grad Guid & Coun Stud Orgns, 1982-83. **Business Addr:** President, Jamaica National Guild N A Inc, 1655 Flatbush Ave Suite Apt B-208, Brooklyn, NY 11210, **Business Phone:** (718)692-0768.

## MAHORN, DERRICK ALLEN. See MAHORN, RICK.

## MAHORN, RICK (DERRICK ALLEN MAHORN)

Basketball player, basketball coach, radio broadcaster. **Personal:** Born Sep 21, 1958, Hartford, CT; married Donyale; children: 6. **Educ:** Hampton Univ, BS, bus admin, 1980. **Career:** Basketball player (retired), basketball coach; Wash Bullets, forward, 1980-85; Detroit Pistons, forward, 1985-89, 1996-98; radio analyst, currently; Philadelphia 76ers, forward, 1989-91, 1999; Il Messaggero, forward, 1991-92; Ital Serie A league, forward, 1991-92; Virtus Roma, 1991-92; Nj Nets, forward, 1992-96; Rockford Lightning, Detroit Shock, asst coach, 2005-, head coach, 2009; NBA TV, Tuesday Night with Ahmad, co-host. **Business Addr:** Radio Analyst, Detroit Piston, 5 Championship Dr, Auburn Hills, MI 48326, **Business Phone:** (248)377-0100.

## MAITH, SHEILA FRANCINE

Lawyer. **Personal:** Born Sep 9, 1961, Baltimore, MD; daughter of Warren Edward and Georgia Vinau Haddon; married David Lloyd Douglass. **Educ:** Duke Univ, Durham, NC, AB, pub policy, 1983; Harvard Law Sch, Cambridge MA, pub policy, JD, 1987; Kennedy Sch Govt, Cambridge, MA, pub policy, 1987. **Career:** Hill & Barlow, Boston, Mass, assoc, 1987-89; Boston Redevelop Authority, spec asst, 1989; Fannie Mae Found, Policy & Leadership Develop, managing dir, 2002; Fed Res Syst, Div Consumer & Community Affairs, community affairs officer, 2005-08, advisor, 2007-08, asst dir; Local Initiatives Support Corp, dir pub policy; Sen Edward M Kennedy, Senate Labor Comt, sr coun; Fed Res Bd Gov, sr advisor & community affairs officer; Enterprise Community Partners, prog dir; Enterprise Found, prog dir; Maith Consult, Achieving Excellence prog, coach & consult, currently; Kela Assocs, consult, currently. **Orgs:** Bd dir, Tent City, 1987-; dir, United S End Settlements, 1987-; Boston Bar Asn & Young Lawyers Div, 1987-89; alumni adv admis comt, Duke Univ, 1989-. **Home Addr:** 1905 Elkhart St, Silver Spring, MD 20910-2154, **Home Phone:** (301)589-7805. **Business Addr:** Coach, Consultant, Maith Consulting, Washington, DC 20551, **Business Phone:** (301)821-5689.

## MAITLAND, DR. CONRAD CUTHBERT

Physician. **Personal:** Born Jan 17, 1947, St. Georges; son of Denis and Mavis; children: Nicholas. **Educ:** Univ Detroit, BS, 1973; Wayne State Univ, Sch Med, MD, 1978. **Career:** Sinai Hosp, Wayne St Univ Affil Hosp, resident urol; Sinai-Grace Hosp/Sinai Hosp, internship, resident gen surg; self-employed, med dr, pvt pract, 1984-; Detrit Med Ctr, med doctor, currently. **Orgs:** Am Med Asn; Mich State Med Soc; Wayne County Med Soc Legislation/Community Affairs; Southeastern Med Soc; Wayne State Univ, Med Alumni; Wayne County Med Soc Project HOW Volunteer Physician; Black Med Alumni Asn. **Honors/Awds:** WCMS-Project HOW, Certificate of Appreciation, 1991; US member of Congress, Certificate of Appreciation, 1991. **Home Addr:** 2106 Hyde Pk Dr, Detroit, MI 48207, **Home Phone:** (313)393-0086. **Business Addr:** Medical Doctor, Detrit Medical Center, 7441 W 7 Mile Rd Suite 323, Detroit, MI 48221, **Business Phone:** (313)864-4452.

## MAITLAND, TRACY V. (TRACY VINCENT MAITLAND)

Founder (originator), president (organization), executive. **Personal:** Born New York, NY. **Educ:** Columbia Univ, BA, econ, 1982. **Career:** Merrill Lynch & Co Inc, corp intern, NY, corp finance, securities res, Wash, DC, equities sales, Detroit, vpres, sales, dir, convertible bond sales, New York, dir, 1982-96; Advent Capital Mgt L.L.C., founder, pres, chief investment officer, 1996-, chief exec officer. **Orgs:** Bd dir, Apollo Theater. **Honors/Awds:** Listed as one of 25 "Hottest Blacks on Wall Street", Black Enterprise, 1992; "Black Enterprise", 75 Most Powerful Blacks on Wall Street, 2011. **Business Addr:** President, Advent Capital Management LLC, 1271 Avenue of the Americas 45th Fl, New York, NY 10020, **Business Phone:** (212)482-1600.

## MAJETE, DR. CLAYTON AARON

Educator. **Personal:** Born Apr 19, 1941, Woodland, NC; son of Doreather Jefferson (deceased) and Barnabas (deceased); children: Lisa & Kim. **Career:** City Univ New York, Baruch Col, lectr, researcher, sociol & anthrop, currently. **Home Addr:** 1104 Pk Pl, Brooklyn, NY 11213-2602, **Home Phone:** (718)774-1000. **Business Addr:** Lecturer, Researcher, City University of New York, Baruch College, Rm 260 4th Fl Vertical Campus, New York, NY 10010, **Business Phone:** (646)312-4260.

## MAJETTE, DENISE L.

Politician, lawyer. **Personal:** Born May 18, 1955, Brooklyn, NY; daughter of Voyd Lee and Olivia Foster; married Rogers J Mitchell Jr; children: 2. **Educ:** Yale Univ, BA, 1976; Duke Univ, JD, 1979. **Career:** Legal Aid Soc Winston-Salem, NC, atty, 1981-83; GA Ct Appeals, law asst, 1984-89; Jenkins, Nelson & Welch, partner, 1989-92; GA Atty Gen's off, spec asst, 1991-92; GA State Bd Worker's Comp, admin law judge, 1992-93; State Ct DeKalb County, judge, 1993-2002; Wake Forest Law Sch, Winston-Salem, NC, prof; US House Reps, rep, 2003-05; Pvt pract, atty; Ga State, Politician. **Orgs:** State Bar Ga; Budget, Educ & Workforce Comt; Small Bus Comt. **Special Achievements:** First woman to be nominated for a U.S. Senate seat in Georgia. **Business Addr:** Congresswoman, US House Representatives, 1517 Longworth House Off Bldg, Washington, DC 20515-1004, **Business Phone:** (202)225-1605.

## MAJOR, DR. CLARENCE

Poet, educator, novelist. **Personal:** Born Dec 31, 1936, Atlanta, GA; son of Inez Huff and Clarence; married Pamela Jane Ritter. **Educ:** Art Inst, Chicago, IL, attended 1954; Armed Forces Inst, 1956; New Sch Social Res, attended 1971; Norwalk Community Col, CT, 1972; Howard Univ, attended 1975; State Univ NY, BS, 1976; Union Inst & Univ, Yellow Springs & Cincinnati, OH, PhD, 1978. **Career:** Coercion Rev, Chicago, Ed, 1958-66; Proof & Anagogic & Paideumic Rev, Chicago, staff writer, 1960-61; Simulmatics, New York, res analyst, 1966-67; New Lincoln Sch, New York, dir creative writing prog & Harlem Educ Prog, 1967-68; Ctr Urban Educ, writer-in-residence, 1967-68; Columbia Univ Teachers Col, Teachers & Writers Collab, 1967-71; Caw, New York, assoc ed, 1967-70; San Francisco, J Black Poetry, 1967-70; Brooklyn Col, City Univ New York, lectr, 1968-69; Essence mag, reviewer, 1970-73; Sarah Lawrence Col, Bronxville, New York, 1972-75; Am Poetry Rev, columnist 1973-76 & contrib ed, 1976-86; Aurora Col, Ill, writer-in-residence, 1974; Howard Univ, Wash, DC, lectr & asst prof, 1974-76; Univ Wash, Seattle, asst prof, 1976-77; Univ Md, Col Pk, vis asst prof, 1976; State Univ New York, Buffalo, vis asst prof, 1976; Univ Colo, Boulder, from assoc prof to prof, 1977-89; Am Bk Rev, New York, ed, 1977-78 & assoc ed, 1978-; Bopp, Providence, Ri, assoc ed, 1977-78; Univ Nice, France, Vis prof, 1981-82; Albany State Col, Ga, writer-in-residence, 1984; Wesleyan Univ Press, Middletown, Conn, ed consult, 1984; Univ Ga Press, Athens, 1987; Clayton Col, Denver, Colo, writer-in-residence, 1986-87; High Plains Lit Rev, Denver, fiction ed, 1986; Temple Univ, Philadelphia, distinguished vis writer, 1988; Warren Wilson Col, guest writer, 1988; Univ Calif, Davis, dir creative writing, 1991-93, prof eng, 1989-; Novels: All-Night Visitors, 1969, 1998; No, 1973; Reflex & Bone Structure, 1975, 1996; Emergency Exit, 1979; My Amputations: A Novel, 1986, 2008; Such Was Season, 1987, 2003; Painted Turtle: Woman with Guitar, 1988; Dirty Bird Blues, 1996, 1997; One Flesh, 2003; Poems: Fires That Burn Heaven, 1954; Configurations: New & Selected Poems: 1958-98; Love Poems a Black Man, 1965; Human Juices, 1965; Swallow Lake, 1970; Symptoms & Madness, 1971; Pvt Line, 1971; Cotton Club: New Poems, 1972; Syncopated Cakewalk, 1974; Inside Diameter: France Poems, 1985; Surfaces & Masks, 1988; Some Observations a Stranger at Zuni Latter Part Century, 1989; Parking Lots, 1992; Port Townsend, 1998; Dict Afro-Am Slang, 1970; Dark & Feeling: Black Am Writers & Their Work (essays), 1974; Such Was Season: A Novel, 1987; Juba to Jive: A Dict African-Am Slang, Penguin, 1994; Ed: Writers Workshop Anthology, ed, 1967; Man Like a Child: An Anthology Creative Writing by Students, 1968; New Black Poetry, 1969; Calling Wind, Anthology, 1993; Garden Thrives, Anthology, 1996; short stories: Church Girl, 1967; An Area Cerebral Hemisphere, 1975; Dossy O, 1978; Tattoo, 1987; Fun & Games, 1990; Necessary Distance: Essays & Criticism, 2001; Come by Here: My Mother's Life; Waiting Sweet Betty, 2002; auth numerous articles, reviews & anthologies; ed; Publ: Waiting Sweet Betty, 2002; Come by Here: My Mother's Life, 2002; Such Was Season, 2003; Myself Painting, 2008. **Orgs:** Ed bd mem,

Umojo, 1979-80. **Business Addr:** Professor, University of California, Voorhies Hall 1 Shields Ave, Davis, CA 95616, **Business Phone:** (530)752-2257.

### MAJOR, HENRYMAE M.

Counselor. **Personal:** Born Mar 9, 1935, Earle, AR; daughter of Andrew and Clara Sims; married Isadore; children: Kelly Dianne. **Educ:** Lincoln Univ, BS, 1956; Wayne State Univ, MA, guid & coun, 1963. **Career:** St Ill, recreational therapist, 1957; Cent High Sch Detroit, health, phys educ teacher, bd & educ teacher, 1958-65; guid counr, 1965-70, guid dept head, 1970-. **Orgs:** Nat Bd Cert Counr, 1979-; Am Asn Coun Develop, 1980-; Mich Asn Coun Develop, 1980-; Phi Delta Kappa, 1988-; Detroit Counrs Asn; Guild Asn Metro Detroit; Orgn Sch Admin & Supvr; Asn Black Admin; Future Teachers Am Sponsor; Lincoln Univ Alumni Asn; Delta Sigma Theta Alum Chap; Women Wayne St Univ Alumni Chap; Estab Coord Health Clin, Spain Mid Sch health coun socio-econ areas; Nat Asn Advan Colored People; Hartford Mem Baptist Church; Mich Asn Col Admis Counr. **Special Achievements:** Co-author, Role of the Counselor. **Home Addr:** 8120 E Jefferson Ave Apt 5M, Detroit, MI 48214-2672, **Home Phone:** (313)822-2843. **Business Addr:** Department Head Guidance, Counseling, 2425 Tuxedo, Detroit, MI 48206, **Business Phone:** (313)252-3017.

### MAJORS, ANTHONY Y. (TONY MAJORS)

Business owner, automotive executive. **Career:** Varsity Ford Lincoln Mercury Inc, owner & pres, currently; Tm Management LLC, dir. **Special Achievements:** Co is ranked No 29, Black Enterprise mag's list of top 100 auto dealers, 1992. **Business Addr:** Owner, President, Varsity Ford Lincoln Mercury Inc, 1351 Earl Rudder Fwy S, College Station, TX 77845-6034, **Business Phone:** (979)694-2022.

### MAJORS, JEFF

Musician, media executive. **Personal:** Born Nov 3, 1955, Washington, DC; son of Major Graham and Annie Pauline Fitzgerald. **Career:** Radio One, Magic 102.3, announcer, 1991-92; WWIN-AM, announcer, 1992-93, asst prog dir & music dir, 1993-95, host, 1994, prog dir, 1995-98; WXCB-AM, prog dir, 1997-98, vpres gospel programming, 1998-; rec artist, 1998-; WMAL-TV, "Grace & Glory show", host; Tv One, host, 2004-. Albums: Sacred, Universal Music, 1998; Sacred Holidays, 2000; Sacred 2000, 2001; Sacred 4 You, 2002; Sacred Chapter 6, 2005; Sacred Major 7th, 2008; Sacred Eight, 2009; Sacred Duets, 2010. **Orgs:** Network Doves. **Business Addr:** Host, TV One, 5900 Princess Garden Pkwy Suite 400, Lanham, MD 20706, **Business Phone:** (301)429-3270.

### MAJORS, MATTIE CAROLYN

Public relations executive, journalist. **Personal:** Born Jan 16, 1945, Waynesboro, GA; daughter of Carrie L Skinner and Willis Van; children: Brandon Matthew Quentin Van. **Educ:** Cent State Univ, BA, chem, 1970. **Career:** CWRU Cleveland, rsch lab tech, 1970-72; WABQ Radio Cleveland, newsreporter, 1970; WJMO Radio Cleveland, news reporter, actg news dir, 1970-72; WKBN Radio-TV, minority affairs coord, 1972-77; WJKW-TV, reporter, 1977-82; WJBK-TV Channel 2, news reporter, 1982-88; PM Mag, 1982-88; Simons Michelson Zieve Advert, 1991; Detroit Pub Schs, media rels & radio producer; Ambrose Assocs Inc, dir pub rels, currently. **Orgs:** Pres mem, Youngstown Sickle Cell Anemia Found, 1973-76; MENSA, Cleveland Press Club, 1980; Negro Bus & Prof Women's Club, 1980; Young Black Businessmen, 1979; Youngstown Fedn Women's Clubs; Freedom Inc; United Negro Improv Asn; Omega Psi Phi Frat; hon co-chmn, 1986, hon chair, 1987; Black United Fund Campaign, 1986; local AFTRA Chap. **Honors/Awds:** Volunteer Award, State of Mich, 1987; American Cancer Society, 1990. **Home Addr:** 18301 Manor St, Detroit, MI 48221-1940, **Home Phone:** (313)864-7758. **Business Addr:** Director of Public Relations, Ambrose Associates Inc, 429 Livernois, Ferndale, MI 48220, **Business Phone:** (313)547-4100.

### MAJORS, RICHARD G.

Psychologist, educator. **Personal:** Born Ithaca, NY; son of Richard II and Fannie Sue. **Educ:** Auburn Community Col, AA, humanities, 1974; Plattsburgh State Col, BA, hist, 1977; Univ Ill, Urbana, PhD, educ psychol, 1987. **Career:** Univ Kans, fel, 1987-89; Harvard Med Sch, clin fel psychiat, 1989-90; Univ Wis, asst prof, 1990-93; Urban Inst, Wash, DC, sr res assoc, 1993-95; Mich State Univ, David Walker Res Inst, fel, 1996-; Georgetown Univ, Social Policy Prog, hon vis scholar, 1996-97; Univ Manchester, Eng, Leverhulme fel & hon sr scholar, 1996-; Glasgow Univ, Ctr Learning & Support, head, currently; Univ Col, adj assoc prof, currently; J African Am Men, founder, dep ed; J African Studies, founder & dep ed, currently; Appl Centre Emotional Literacy Leadership & Res, dir, currently; Wolverhampton Col, dir innovation; Univ Colo, educ psychologist & vis & adj prof. **Orgs:** Greenpeace, 1988; Nat Coun African Am Men, chmn, 1990-92, bd dir; Am Psychol Asn, 1987; Soc Psychol Study Ethnic Minority Issues, 1989; Am Ortho Psychiat Asn, 1990; Initiative African Am Males, co-chmn, 1996. **Home Addr:** N44023 Lee Rd, Strum, WI 54770, **Home Phone:** (715)695-3476. **Business Addr:** Associate Professor, University Colorado, 140 Austin Bluffs Pkwy, Silver Springs, CO 80918, **Business Phone:** (719)255-3121.

### MAJORS, SHEENA L.

Lawyer. **Career:** Wayne County Neighborhood Legal Serv AIDS Law Ctr, managing atty; Majors Law Firm PLLC, owner, 2002-; Majors Law Ctr PLLC, atty, currently. **Business Addr:** Owner, The Majors Law Firm PLLC, 17380 Livernois Ave, Detroit, MI 48221.

### MAJORS, TONY. See MAJORS, ANTHONY Y.

### MAJOZO, ESTELLA CONWILL

Executive, educator, poet. **Personal:** Born Jan 1, 1949?, Louisville, KY. **Educ:** Univ Louisville, BA, 1975, MA, 1976; Univ Iowa, PhD, 1984. **Career:** Blackaliedoscope Cult Ctr Inc, founder & dir, 1975-77; Ky State Univ, asst prof, 1986-88; City Univ NY, Hunter Col, prof, 1988-2000; Univ Louisville, Dept Eng, prof creative writing, 2000-, internship coordr, currently. **Business Addr:** Professor of Creative Writing, Internship Coordinator, University of Louisville, Bingham Humanities 315, Louisville, KY 40292, **Business Phone:** (502)852-6801.

### MAKAU, ESQ. ELENA K.

Lawyer. **Personal:** Born Jun 20, 1966, New York, NY; daughter of Marjorie Ann Mathias and Peter M. **Educ:** Hamilton Col, BA, 1988; Albany Law Sch, JD, 1991. **Career:** King's County Dist Atty's Off, asst dist atty, 1991-95; Dienst & Serrins LLP, atty, litigation assoc, 1995-98; Law Off Elena K. Makau, atty, 1998-. **Orgs:** AKA Sorority Inc, 1987-; Metrop Black Bar Asn, 1991-; Nat Bar Asn, 1991-; New York County Lawyers Asn, 1991-; Brooklyn Bar Asn, 1991-; Kings County Criminal Bar Asn. **Business Addr:** Attorney, Law Offices of Elena K. Makau, 26 Ct St Suite 603, Brooklyn, NY 11242-1106, **Business Phone:** (718)643-1922.

### MAKOKHA, JAMES A. N.

Educator, government official. **Personal:** Born Jun 20, 1951, Kakamega; son of Ali N and Anjema Mitungu; married Patricia Brown; children: Audrey, Jarrett & Justin. **Educ:** Albany State Col, Albany, GA, BBA, bus admin, 1978; Auburn Univ, Auburn, AL, MS, econs, 1979; Century Univ, Los Angeles, CA, PhD, 1987. **Career:** Genesee County, Flint, Mich, dir elections, 1979-83, dep county clerk, 1984-87; Baker Col, Flint, Mich, Adj Instr, Econs, 1981-99; State Mich, Lansing, Mich, economist, 1987-88; City Flint, Flint, Mich, dir parks & recreation, 1988-90, dir policy & inter Govt rels, 1991-; Detroit Col Bus, Flint, Mich, exec dir community rels, 1990-91; Vincennes Univ, Indianapolis, Ind, Adj Instr, Econs, 2001-02; N Lake Col, Irving, Tex, Prof Econs, 2009-; N Cent Tex Col, adj fac; Collin County Community Col, Frisco, Tex, Prof Econs, 2004-. **Home Addr:** 713 Brendon Hills Pl, Louisville, LA 40245-5718, **Home Phone:** (214)491-6055. **Business Addr:** Professor, Collin County Community College, 3452 Spur 399, McKinney, TX 75070, **Business Phone:** (972)548-6790.

### MAKUPSON, AMYRE ANN PORTER

Television news anchorperson. **Personal:** Born Sep 30, 1947, River Rouge, MI; daughter of Rudolph Hannibal and Amyre Ann Porche Porter; married Walter H; children: Rudolph Porter & Amyre Nisi. **Educ:** Fisk Univ, BA, dramatics & speech, 1970; Am Univ, MA, speech arts commun theory, 1972. **Career:** WSM-TV, Mich Health Maintenance Orgn Plans, pub rels dir, 1973-75; WRC-TV; WGPR-TV, anchor; UPN 50, news anchor & pub affairs mgr, 1975-02; CBS Eyewitness News, news anchor; WSM-TV, anchor; WKBD-TV, news anchor & dir pub affairs, 1977-. **Orgs:** Bd mem, March Dimes, 1983-; bd mem, Alzheimers Asn, 1985-; bd mem, Merrill Palmer Inst, 1985-; bd mem, Sickle Cell Asn, 1990-; bd mem, Providence Hosp Found, 1995-; bd mem, Skillman Found, 2001; bd mem, Covenant House Mich; bd mem, AAA Mich; bd mem, Home Fed Savings Bank. **Honors/Awds:** Oakland County Bar Association Media Award, 1992, 1995; Media Person of the Year, Southern Christian Leadership Conf, 1995; Humanitarian of the Year, March Dimes, 1996; Bishop Harrington Award, Providence Hosp, 1999; Hon Nat Hon Soc, Howard Univ, 2001; Emmy Awards: Best Anchor, Best Interview Prog, Best Commentary; Michean Year, 2002; Distinguished Woman of the-Year, GM Womens Club; Exemplary Volunteer Service Award, Mich Govt, 2007. **Special Achievements:** March of Dimes, telethon host, 1980-85; C Miracle Network, telethon host, 1986-; UNCF, telethon host, 2001-02; Author of So What s Next, Author House, Book about death; Honored by City Detroit, City Pontiac, Nat Acad TV Arts & Sci, March Dimes, Oakland Co Bar Asn, Allstate Ins, Ment Illness Res Asn; Women In Communs; Nominated for an Exemplary Volunteer Service Award. **Home Addr:** 23475 Coventry Woods, Southfield, MI 48034, **Home Phone:** (248)357-4544.

### MALBROUE, JOSEPH, JR.

Executive, manager. **Personal:** Born Aug 24, 1949, Grand Coteau, LA; son of Joseph Sr and Earline Key; married Joretta Leauntine Tyson. **Educ:** Univ Southwestern La, BS, chem, 1970. **Career:** Executive (retired); Union Carbide Corp, prod engr, 1970-73, tech sales rep, 1973-76, asst customer serv mgr, 1976-78, dist planner, 1978-84, LPG supply mgr, 1984-2001; SAP Proj Implementation Team, 1997-98. **Orgs:** Dir & coun, Union Carbide Corp, 1975; Gas Processors Asn. **Honors/Awds:** Chairman's Award Union Carbide, 1993; E I Dupont scholarship, Univ Southwestern LA, 1968. **Home Addr:** 17114 Canyon Stream Ct, Houston, TX 77095-4300, **Home Phone:** (281)550-0520.

### MALCOLM, CATHERINE (CATHERINE J MALCOLM)

Restaurateur. **Personal:** married Desmond A. **Educ:** Broward Community Col. **Career:** Jerk Mach Inc, pres & co-owner, 1989-. **Orgs:** Founder, It Takes a Village. **Honors/Awds:** Caribbean Business Women of the Year 2000 Award, Nat Asn Carribean Women, S Fla; Excalibur Awards, Sun Sentinel Excalibursmall business award, 2005, USA Chamber of Commerce business award, 2006. **Home Addr:** 2280 SW 139th Ave, Davie, FL 33325-5047, **Home Phone:** (954)370-1005. **Business Addr:** Co-Owner, Jerk Machine Inc, 111 NW 2nd St, Ft. Lauderdale, FL 33301, **Business Phone:** (954)467-8332.

### MALCOLM, DESMOND (DESMOND A MALCOLM)

Restaurateur. **Personal:** married Catherine J. **Career:** Jerk Mach Inc, co-owner, 1989-. **Orgs:** Founder, It Takes a Village, 1988. **Honors/Awds:** Caribbean Business Women of the Year, Nat Asn Caribbean Bus Women S Fla, 2000; Sun-Sentinel Business Award, 2005. **Home Addr:** 2280 SW 139th Ave, Davie, FL 33325-5047, **Home Phone:** (954)370-5096. **Business Addr:** Co Owner, Jerk Machine Inc, 111 NW 2nd St, Ft. Lauderdale, FL 33302, **Business Phone:** (954)467-8882.

### MALCOM, DR. SHIRLEY MAHALEY

Association executive. **Personal:** Born Sep 6, 1946, Birmingham, AL; daughter of Ben Lee Mahaley and Lillie Mae Funderburg; married Horace; children: Kelly Alicia & Lindsey Ellen. **Educ:** Univ Wash, Seattle, Wash, BS, zool, 1967; Univ Calif, Los Angeles, Calif, MA, zool, 1968; Pa State Univ, Univ Pk, Pa, PhD, ecol, 1974; NJ Inst Technol, ScD, 1991; Knox Col, attended 1993; Bennett Col, attended 1993; Hood Col, attended 1994. **Career:** Univ NC, Wilmington, NC, asst prof, 1974-75; AAAS, Wash, DC, res assoc, staff assoc, proj dir, 1975-77, head, off opportunities sci, 1979-89, head educ & human resources prog, 1989-; Nat Sci Found, Wash, DC, Minority Insts Sci Improv Prog, prog officer, 1977-79. **Orgs:** Am Mus Nat Hist; Nat Sci Bd, 1994-; bd mem, Nat Ctr Educ & Econ; bd mem, Sci Serv; trustee, Carnegie Corp New York; Pres Comt Adv Sci & Technol; bd dir, Howard Heinz Endowment; Sigma Xi; fel AAAS; trustee, Caltech; State Univ New York Syst Res Coun; Pub Agenda; Nat Math-Sci Initiative; Digital Promise; co-chair, Gender Adv Bd, S&T Develop & Gender InSITE. **Honors/Awds:** Black Women Who Make It Happen, Nat Coun Negro Women, 1987; Humanitarian of Year Award, Nat Coalition Title I/Chap I Parents, 1989; Scroll of Honor, Nat Med Asn, 1989; DHL, Col St Catherine, 1990; DHL, St Joseph Col, 1992; hon doctorate, Uppsala Univ, Sweden, 2000; Public Welfare Medal, Nat Acad Sci, 2003; Holds 16 honorary degrees. **Special Achievements:** Publications: The Double Bind: The Price of Being a Minority Woman in Science, 1976; Our Ground: A Guidebook for STEM Educators in the Post-Michigan Era, 2004. **Home Addr:** 12901 Wexford Pk, Clarksville, MD 21029-1401, **Home Phone:** (410)531-3104. **Business Addr:** Head of Education and Human Resources Programs, American Association for the Advancement of Science, 1200 New York Ave NW, Washington, DC 20005, **Business Phone:** (202)326-6400.

### MALDON, HON. ALPHONSO, JR.

Executive. **Educ:** Fla A&M Univ; Univ Okla, MA; Command & Gen Staff Col; Armed Forces Staff Col. **Career:** Pres Legis Affairs, spec asst, 1993; Force Mgt Policy, asst secy defense, 1999; Wash Nationals, sr vpres, external affairs, pres, 2006-; Maj Leagues Wash Nat Baseball Club, founding partner, 2006-; Partnership Strategies Consult, founder, pres & chief exec officer, 2009-; Fleet Boston Financial Corp, Wash, DC, exec vpres; Fed Govt Banking, vpres, sr relationship mgt officer; PNC Bank, Corp Banking, sr vpres; dep asst to pres legis affairs; Pub Sector, vpres; US Senate & House Reps, White House Mil Off, dep asst to pres, dir; Dream Found, nat sr vpres, external affairs, pres; Lerner Group, partner, currently. **Orgs:** Am Legion Veterans Asn; Boston Col Club; Boston Partnership; Nat Minority Supplier Develop Coun Inc; Nat Retired Mil Officers Asn; Nat Urban League Inc; Prince Hall Masons Asn; bd dir, D.C. Chamber Com; bd dir, CM2; Greater Wash Bd Trade; Wash Nat Baseball Team Steering & Policy Comt; bd dir, Indust Bank. **Honors/Awds:** Distinguished Civilian Public Service Medal; United States Congressional Award; Legion of Merit; Defense Meritorious Service Medal. **Special Achievements:** In 1999 he held the highest ranking African-American in the Department of Defense. **Business Addr:** Senior Vice President External Affairs, President, Washington Nationals, Nationals Pk 1500 S Capitol St SE, Washington, DC 20003-1507, **Business Phone:** (202)675-6287.

### MALLEBAY-VACQUEUR DEM, JEAN PASCAL

Automotive executive. **Personal:** Born Apr 3, 1953, Paris; son of Raymonde and Oumar; married Mada Dao; children: Alain Moussa, Nelhai Adama, Sara Macora & Alexandre Sega Oumar. **Educ:** Ivory Coast Univ, BA, 1969; ESME, Sch Mech & Electronical Eng, BSME & MSME, 1974; INSEAD, Europ Sch Bus Admis, MBA, 1978; Pantheon Sorbonne, Paris Univ, postgrad, 1978; Ctr Creative Leadership, 2000. **Career:** Mauritania Sch Syst, tech asst, 1974-76; Regie Renault, mfg eng, 1978, asst to exec vpres, 1979-81; mfg plant mgr, mgr, body mfg, 1981-84, gen mgr, vehicle engineering opers, 1985-87, gen mgr, opers new int indust proj, 1988-89; RUSA, asst to exec vpres, 1979-80; Chrysler Corp, spec proj eng gen mgr, 1989-93; Environ Testing Labs, exec eng, environ & emissions testing, exec eng, dir; DaimlerChrysler AG, Sci Labs, 1994-2008; Re-Source Group, prin, 2008-; Heritage, anticorruption advocate, 2009-14; Environ Labs Chrysler, dir. **Orgs:** INSEAD Alumni, 1978-; Eng Soc Detroit, 1990-; Chrysler African Am Network, 1995. **Home Addr:** 1830 E Valley Rd, Bloomfield Hills, MI 48304-2153, **Home Phone:** (248)540-4174. **Business Addr:** Environmental & Emissions Testing Executive Engine, Chrysler Corp, 800 Chrysler Dr, Auburn Hills, MI 48326-2757, **Business Phone:** (248)576-5741.

### MALLETT, DR. CONRAD L., JR.

Judge, executive. **Personal:** Born Oct 12, 1953, Detroit, MI; son of Conrad L Sr and Claudia Gwendolyn; married Barbara Straughn; children: Mio, Alex Conrad & Kristan Claudia. **Educ:** Univ Calif, Los Angeles, BA, 1975; Univ Southern Calif, MBA, 1979, JD, 1979. **Career:** Judge (retired), executive; Miller, Canfield, Paddock & Stone, assoc, 1981-82, partner, 1999; State Mich, Lansing, Mich, gov, legal adv, dir legis affairs, 1983-84; dir, exec asst to Detroit Mayor, 1985-86; Jaffe, Raitt, Heuer & Weiss PC, Detroit, Mich, atty, 1986-90; Mich Supreme Ct, Detroit, Mich, assoc judge, 1990, 1992-94, chief judge, 1997-98; Detroit Med Ctr, gen coun & chief admin afficer, 1999-2002, chief legal & admin officer, 2003, chief admin officer, 2012-; City Detroit, chief operating officer, 2002; Lear Corp, bd dir, 2002-; La-Van Hawkins Food Group LLC, pres & gen coun, 2002-03; Detroit Med Ctr's, Sinai-Grace Hosp, pres & chief exec officer, 2003-11; Mich Pioneer ACO, LLC, dir. **Orgs:** Am Bar Asn; Mich State Bar Asn; Detroit Bar Asn; Wolverine Bar Asn; Genesee County Bar Asn; Nat Asn Advan Colored People; Nat Asn Bond Lawyers; Mich Supreme Ct Hist Soc; YMCA. **Special Achievements:** First African American to serve as Chief Justice on the Michigan Supreme Court; one of only five African American chief justices in the country. **Home Addr:** 6597 Torybrooke Cir, West Bloomfield, MI 48323. **Business Addr:** Chief Administration Officer, Detroit Medical Center, 4201 St Antoine St, Detroit, MI 48201, **Business Phone:** (313)745-3000.

### MALLETTE, CAROL L.

Executive, educator. **Personal:** Born Philadelphia, PA; daughter of Lewis Moore and Florence Evans Moore; married Kenneth; children: Tashia & Sydney. **Educ:** Morgan State Univ, Baltimore, MD, BS, psychol, 1963; Kean Col NJ, Union, NJ, MA, 1973. **Career:** Bd Educ, Pleasantville, NJ, teacher, 1963-65; DC Pub Schs, Wash, DC, teacher, 1966-70; Kean Col Nj, Union, NJ, coordr colprojs, 1971-79; Harris town Develop Corp, Harrisburg, Pa, coor dr community events, 1981-85; Penn State Univ, Middletown, Pa, asst provost/dean, spec events coor dr; Southern Jersey Family Med Ctrs, dir diabetes outreach & educ syst, 2000-12, dir prenatal access to care prog, 2010-. **Orgs:** Jack

& Jill Inc; Delta Sigma Theta Sorority; Pa Legis Black Caucus Found; Atlantic County Human Servs Adv Coun; pres, Atlantic City Chap Links Inc; Pleasantville Planning Bd; bd dir, Mainland Chamber Com; Atlantic County Women's Hall Fame. **Home Addr:** 4926 Lancer St, Harrisburg, PA 17109, **Home Phone:** (717)652-7535. **Business Addr:** Director of the Prenatal Access to Care Program, Southern Jersey Family Medical Centers Inc, 1 White Horse Centre, Hammonton, NJ 08037, **Business Phone:** (609)567-0200.

## MALLIET, SCHONE

Executive, president (organization), chief executive officer. **Personal:** Born South Bronx, NY. **Educ:** Holy Cross, MA, BA, econ, 1974; Pepperdine Univ, MBA, 1983. **Career:** Appl Data; Comput Assoc; Unisys, dir new prod; Western Region Sales Info Resources, vpres; Max Madison Group, managing partner; Info Resources Inc, vpres, 1988-91; Ziff Davis Mkt Intelligence, vpres, 1995-98; Nat Brotherhood Skiers Inc, exec vpres, competition dir & corp develop dir, 1996-2006; ViaNovus, pres, chief exec officer & founder, 1998-2000; Citadon Inc, sr vpres, 2000-01; AlyxSys, chmn & chief exec officer, 2001-05; Merrill Lynch, financial advisor, 2005-08; Bank at Wachovia, A Wells Fargo Co, vpres, 2009-2013. **Orgs:** Bd dir, Valley; nat youth competition dir, Nat Brotherhood Skiers; Coaches Educ Comn, US Skiing & Snowboard Asn; bd mgr, YMCA Harlem; bd mem J3 chairperson, NJ Ski Racing Assoc; bd mem, Noel Pointer Found, 2008-10; chief exec officer, Nat Winter Sports Educ Found, 2010-; chief exec officer, Nat Winter Activ Ctr, 2014-; bd dir, Col Holy Cross Alumni Asn, 2014-. **Business Addr:** Chief Executive Officer, National Winter Activity Center, 44 Breakneck Rd, Vernon, NJ 07462, **Business Phone:** (973)846-8250.

## MALLORY, GEORGE L., JR.

Lawyer. **Personal:** Born Apr 13, 1952, Washington, DC; son of George L and Anna P. **Educ:** Occidental Col, BA, polit sci, 1974; Western State Univ Law Sch, JD, 1977. **Career:** Los Angeles City Atty, dep city atty, 1979-86; State Bar Calif, pres; George L Mallory & Assoc APLC, atty, princ, 1986-. **Orgs:** Langston Bar Asn, 1982-; Ncp Los Angeles Br, 1982-; Ctr Early Educ, 1988-; pres, John M Langston Bar Asn, 1991. **Honors/Awds:** Recognition of Service, USS Congressinal Records, 1991; Recognition of Service, Calif State Legis, 1991; Recognition of Service, Los Angeles District Atty, 1990-91; Hall of Fame, Western State Univ Law Sch; Recognition of Service, City of Inglewood, 1991. **Special Achievements:** Roy Wilkins Dinner; 1986, 1987, 1991. **Business Addr:** Principal, George L Mallory & Associates, 1925 Century Pk E Suite 2000, Los Angeles, CA 90067-2701, **Business Phone:** (310)788-5555.

## MALLORY, GLENN OLIVER, JR.

Executive. **Personal:** Born May 2, 1927, Colorado Springs, CO; son of Ruth B and Glenn; children: Stephen V & Kim F. **Educ:** Univ Calif, Los Angeles, BS, 1951; Calif State Univ, MS, 1975. **Career:** Witco, Allied-Kelite Div, vpres res & develop, 1966-85; Electroless Technologies Corp, founder, 1986-, pres & owner. **Orgs:** Am Electroplaters Soc, 1953; Electrochem Soc, 1970; Am Socs Testing & Mat, 1974; fel Inst Metal Finishing, UK, 1974; Nat Asn Corrosion Engrs, 1979. **Business Addr:** President, Founder, Electroless Technologies Corp, 3860 S Cloverdale Ave, Los Angeles, CA 90008-1104, **Business Phone:** (323)292-4100.

## MALLORY, JAMES A.

Journalist. **Personal:** Born Aug 1, 1955, Detroit, MI; son of Gertrude P; married Frances; children: Allison & Allen. **Educ:** Western Mich Univ, BBA, 1977; Mich State Univ, MA, 1982. **Career:** Lansing State J, reporter, 1981-83; Grand Rapids Press, bus reporter, 1983-84; Detroit News, bus reporter, 1984-86, asst bus ed, 1986-88; Atlanta J & Const, bus reporter, 1988-90, asst bus ed, 1990-93, news personnel mgr, 1993-96, asst managing ed nights, 1996-99, asst managing ed bus, 1999-01, dep managing ed, 2001-02, managing ed, Initiatives & Opers, 2002-07, sr managing ed & vpres news, 2007-12; Commun Consult, Self-employed, 2012-; Kennesaw State Univ, Part-time instr, 2012-. **Orgs:** Atlanta Asn Black Journalists, 1988-97; Nat Asn Minority Media Execs, 1993-; Nat Asn Black Journalists, 1993-; bd visitors, Sch Journ, Mass Media & Graphic Arts, Fla A&M Univ, 1994-; Western Mich Univ, Alumni Asn, 1994-; Am Socs News Ed; Nat Asn Multicultural Media Execs. **Honors/Awds:** First Place Bus Reporting, Ga Asoc Press, 1992; First Place Bus Reporting, Nat Asn Black Journalists, 1992. **Home Addr:** 2626 Twin Lakes Way, Marietta, GA 30062, **Home Phone:** (770)579-9645. **Business Addr:** Senior Managing Editor, Vice President News, The Atlanta Journal & Constitution, 72 Marietta St NW, Atlanta, GA 30302, **Business Phone:** (404)526-5325.

## MALONE, AMANDA ELLA

Government official. **Personal:** Born May 30, 1929, Lafayette County, MS; daughter of Jerry Ingrom and Leona; married James; children: Lawrence (deceased), Malcolm L, Kenneth Leon, Kelsey Lee, Sheila Elaine (deceased), Cheryl Leona, Travis & James Roland (deceased). **Educ:** Rust Coll Holly Springs MS, AS. **Career:** Marshall County Bd Educ, vice chmn; Elem Sch, sub teacher; Head Start, teacher, parent involvement coord, social serv dir; Marshall & Lafayette County, Social Serv Orgn, pres. **Orgs:** Counr, Sunrise Chap Order Eastern Star, 1989-91; Nat Asn Advan Colored People; sunday sch teacher, New Hope MB Church; Marshall City Bd Educ; Marshall County Hosp Adv Bd; Holly Springs Baptist Asn Banking Comt. **Honors/Awds:** Outstanding Community Service Award, Galena Elem Sch, 1980; Citation, Inst Community Serv Head Start Agency, 1980; Cert Recognition for Outstanding African Am Elected Official Chulahoma MB Church. **Business Addr:** Vice Chairman, Marshall County Board of Education, 2217 Lawshill Rd, Holly Springs, MS 38635.

## MALONE, DR. CHARLES A.

Lawyer. **Personal:** children: Charles, Vicki, Keith, Kevin, Julian & Tony (deceased). **Educ:** McKendree Col, BS, 1957; Mich State Univ Col Law, JD, 1970. **Career:** Mobil Oil Corp, anal chemist, 1966-72; Sura & Malone, Inkster, Mich, atty law. **Orgs:** Mich Bar Asn; Detroit Bar Asn; charter mem, Mich State Bar Crim Law Sect, Nat Asn Advan Colored People; chmn, Inkster & Elected Officers Compensation Bd; co-chmn, Westwood Community Sch Dist Ad Hoc Comn; Elks; Golden Gate Lodge; IBPOE W; Lions. **Home Addr:** 26162 Penn, Inkster, MI 48141.

## MALONE, CLAUDINE BERKELEY

Executive. **Personal:** Born Louisville, KY. **Educ:** Wellesley Col, AB, philos; Harvard Bus Sch, MBA, high distinction. **Career:** IBM Corp, systs engr, 1963-65; Raleigh Stores, controller, mgr dp, 1966-70; Crane Co, sr systs engr, 1966; Harvard Bus Sch Bus Admin, asst prof to assoc prof, 1972-81; Fin & Mgt Consult Inc, pres, 1982-, chief exec officer, 1984-; Sch Bus Admin, Georgetown Univ, adj prof, 1982-84; Colgate-Darden Bus Sch, Univ Va, vis prof, 1984-87; Hannaford Bros Co, dir, 1991-; Hasbro Inc, independent dir, 1992-2008; Sci Applications Int Corp, dir, 1993-2006; Saic Inc, dir, 1993-; Leidos Holdings Inc, dir, 1993-Mallinckrodt Inc dir, 1994-; Lafarge Can Inc, dir, 1994-; Lowe's Co Inc, dir, 1995-2005; Anadarko Holding Co, dir, 1995-; Union Pac Corp, dir, 1995-; Fed Res Bank, Richmond, VA, chmn bd, 1996-99, dir, 1994-; Aviva Life Ins Co, dir, 2001-10; Novell Inc, dir, 2003-10; Apollo Investment Corp, dir, 2007-11; Dell, dir; Union Pac Resources, dir; MTV, dir; Cardinal Health Inc, sr exec, chief info officer; Horizon Inst, pres, founder; CGNU Life Ins Co; Univ Kathy Brittain White, prof; Ltd Stores Inc, dir, currently. **Orgs:** Trustee, Dana Hall Sch, 1974-77; treas, Wellesley Col Alumni Asn. 1977-80; trustee, Wellesley Col, 1982-; dir, Houghton Mifflin Harcourt Publ Co, 1982-; dir, Scott Paper Co; Campbell Soup Co; MTV Networks Ltd; Dart Drug, Supermarkets Gen Corp; Penn Mutual Life, Boston Co; trustee, Massachusetts Inst Technol; trustee, Asia Soc; trustee, Mass Inst Technol. **Honors/Awds:** Candace Award, Nat Coalition Black Women, 1982. **Home Addr:** 7570 Potomoc Fall Rd, McLean, VA 22102, **Home Phone:** (703)821-3879. **Business Addr:** President, Chief Executive Officer, Financial Management Consulting Inc, 7570 Potomoc Fall Rd, McLean, VA 22102, **Business Phone:** (703)821-8861.

## MALONE, EUGENE WILLIAM

Educator. **Personal:** Born Aug 8, 1930, Washington, DC; son of Austin; married Roberta Joanne Miller; children: Gina Dawn. **Educ:** Cent State Univ, BA, sociol, 1957, BS, educ, 1958; Ky State Univ, MEd, guid & couns, 1962; Nova Univ, EdD, 1976. **Career:** Canton Pub Schs, teacher, 1958-59; Cleveland Pub Schs, teacher, 1959-64, guid counr, 1965-67, group discussion leader, 1966-67; Community Action Youth, guid counr, 1964-65; Cent State Univ, dean men, 1967-68; Curber Assoc, consult, 1968-71; Shaker Heights Pub Schs, consult, 1969-70; Cleveland State Univ, coordr stud develop proj, 1968-70, dir stud develop prog, 1970-72; Cuyahoga Community Col, dir coun admin & recs, 1972-75, dean stud servs, 1975-. **Orgs:** Voc Educ Adv Bd, 1979; Ohio Asn Staff Prog & Orgn Develop, 1979; Nat & Asn Stud Pers Adminr; Am Pers & Guid Asn; Ohio Pers & Guid Asn. **Home Addr:** 2292 Coventry Rd, Cleveland Heights, OH 44118-3547, **Home Phone:** (216)932-5155. **Business Addr:** Dean, Cuyahoga Community College, 25444 Harvard Rd, Cleveland, OH 44122, **Business Phone:** (216)987-2202.

## MALONE, DR. GLORIA S.

Educator, administrator, association executive. **Personal:** Born May 12, 1928, Pittsburgh, PA; daughter of John H Snodgrass and Doris Harris Snodgrass; married Arthur A; children: Merrick, Deanna & Myrna. **Educ:** Cent State Col, Ohio, BS, 1949; Kent State Univ, MEd, 1956, MA, 1969, PhD, 1979. **Career:** Alliance OH Pub Schs, elem teacher, 1949-53, high sch teacher, 1953-69; Mt Union Col, prof eng, 1969-90, prof emer, 1991-; Ohio Northern Univ, vis prof, 1990-91; Stark Co Head Start Prog, educ coordr, 1991-93; SCCPA, employ develop officer, currently. **Orgs:** Nat Asn Advan Colored People; Second Baptist Church; Nat Educ Asn; Am Asn Univ Prof; Delta Kappa Gamma Soc; grand worthy matron, Amaranth Grand Chap OES PHA, 1972-74; bd dir, Alliance United Way; bd dir, Alliance Salvation Army; Alpha Kappa Alpha Sorority; bd dir, Alliance YWCA; bd dir, Church Women United. **Honors/Awds:** State Scholarship Awards, Delta Kappa Gamma, 1967, 1974; Teacher of the Year, Alliance High Sch, 1969; Outstanding Member, Al Kaf Ct Dts Isis Akron, 1970; Citizen of the Year, 1986; Martin Luther King Award, 1996. **Home Addr:** 11754 Webb Ave NE, Alliance, OH 44601, **Home Phone:** (330)821-8396. **Business Addr:** Professor Emeritus, Mount Union College, 1972 Clark Ave, Alliance, OH 44601, **Business Phone:** (800)992-6682.

**MALONE, DR. J. DEOTHA.** **See Obituaries Section.**

## MALONE, JEFFREY NIGEL

Actor, basketball coach, basketball player. **Personal:** Born Jun 28, 1961, Mobile, AL; married Alicia Hill; children: Jay, Joshua, Justin & Jasmine. **Educ:** Miss State Univ, BS, polit sci, 1983. **Career:** Basketball player (retired), basketball coach; Wash Bullets, 1983-90; Utah Jazz, 1990-94; Philadelphia 76ers, 1993-96; Miami Heat, 1995-96; Vyzantinos Athlitikos Omilos, 1997; Yakima Sun Kings, asst coach, 1998; San Diego Stingrays, head coach, 2000; Columbus River dragons, head coach, 2001-05; Fla Flame, head coach, 2005-06.TV series: "Space Jam", 1996. **Home Addr:** , Chandler, AZ.

## MALONE, KARL ANTHONY

Basketball executive, basketball player, basketball coach. **Personal:** Born Jul 24, 1963, Summerfield, LA; son of J P and Shirley Turner; married Kay Kinsey; children: Kadee Lynn, Kylee Ann, Karl Jr & Karlee. **Educ:** La Tech Univ, Ruston, LA, attended 1985. **Career:** Basketball player (retired); Utah Jazz, forward, 1985-2003; Los Angeles Lakers, forward, 2003-04; La Tech Univ, dir basketball promotions & asst strength & conditioning coach, 2007-11. **Business Addr:** Director, La Tech University, 305 Wisteria St, Ruston, LA 71272, **Business Phone:** (318)257-2000.

## MALONE, MAURICE

Fashion designer, business owner. **Personal:** Born Jan 1, 1965, Detroit, MI. **Career:** Hardware Maurice Malone, founder, 1984; Label X, founder, 1988; Maurice Malone Designs Blue Jeans Your A-, founder, 1990; Hip Hop Shop, owner, 1991-97; Hostile Takeover Rec, founder, 1995; Maurice Malone Designs, pres & chief exec officer, currently; MM Licensing Group LLC, owner, mgr, designer & founder, 2000-; Williamsburg NY Blog, Publ & Ed, 2011-; Williamsburg Garment Co, owner, 2011-. **Orgs:** Coun Fashion Designers Am. **Honors/Awds:** Perry Ellis Menswear Designer of the Year award, CFDA, 1998. **Business Addr:** Owner, Designer, MM Licensing Group LLC, 89 Grand St, Brooklyn, NY 11211, **Business Phone:** (718)486-0088.

## MALONE, MICHAEL GREGORY

Administrator, manager. **Personal:** Born Oct 27, 1942, Evansville, IN; son of Eugene Jr and Norma Louise; children: Malik LeRoi & Stephanie Nicole. **Educ:** Butler Univ, attended 1961; Ind State Univ, Evansville, 1971; Univ Evansville, BS, polit sci, 1974. **Career:** Iglehart Opers, qual control tech, 1966-68; CAPE, dir youth prog, 1968-71, dir commun serv, 1971-72, exec dir; Malone Assoc Inc, pres, mgr, chief operating officer, 1979-. **Orgs:** Nat Asn Social Workers; charter mem, bd dir, Nat Council Transp Disadvantaged; bd mem, Govs Coun Addictions; Downtown Civitans; Lakeview Optimist; exec bd mem, Boy Scouts Am Buffalo Trace Coun; SouthernSoccer Officials Asn. **Honors/Awds:** Community Service Award, Gov Ind, 1976; Outstanding Man Award, Commun Affairs Evansville Black Expo, 1978. **Home Addr:** 2607 Belize Dr, Evansville, IN 47725-6789, **Home Phone:** (812)626-2231. **Business Addr:** 1315 Read St Suite H, Evansville, IN 47710, **Business Phone:** (800)264-0624.

## MALONE, ROSEMARY C.

Law enforcement officer. **Personal:** Born Jun 23, 1954, Detroit, MI; daughter of Jesse James (deceased) and Rosetta M Cook; children: LaNetha P. **Educ:** Univ Detroit, MA, 1990; Univ Detroit-Mercy, doctoral cand, clin psychol. **Career:** Detroit Police Dept, police officer, 1974; Family Investment Admin, chief, currently. **Orgs:** Co-dir, Adopt-A-Cop, 1992-; Nat Asn Advan Colored People; World Prophetic Outreach Ministries. **Home Addr:** 3478 Yorkshire Rd, Detroit, MI 48224-2324, **Home Phone:** (313)640-9917. **Business Addr:** Chief, Policy & Training, Family Investment Administration, Saratoga State Ctr 311 W Saratoga St, Baltimore, MD 21201, **Business Phone:** (410)767-7949.

## MALONE, SANDRA DORSEY

Educator, executive. **Personal:** Born Mexia, TX; married Joseph L; children: Terence Dorsey. **Educ:** Prairie View A & M Univ, BS; MEd, 1972. **Career:** Team Teaching Sch Chattanooga, team leader, 1961-65; Guaranteed Performance Proj Dallas, educ analyst, 1970-71; Accountability, asst dir, 1972-74; Dallas Independent Sch Dist, teacher, adminr, asst dir, 1974-75, dir syst-wide testing; US Dist Ct, Northern Dist Tex, desegregation ct auditor, 1993-2003; The Links Inc, western area dir, 2003-07. **Orgs:** Dallas Sch Adminr & Asn; Am Asn Sch Adminr; Am Educ Res Asn State; organizer, Nat Coun Negro Women, 1973-75; pres, Dallas Alumnae Chap Delta Sigma Theta, 1973-75; pres, RL Thornton PTA, 1973-74; vpres, Hulcy Mid Sch PTA, 1975-76; leadership dallas class, 1979; Dallas County Appraisal Rev Bd; Prairie View A&M Alumni Asn; Uganda C's Charity Found; Nat Asn Advan Colored People; Urban League; Oak Cliff & Dallas Black Chambers Com; African Am Mus Dallas; Dallas Black Dance Theatre; Dallas Women's Found; Dallas Arboretum; Westview Dist; Boy Scouts Am; Women's Coun Dallas County; Cedar Crest CME Cathedral, Dallas, TX. **Honors/Awds:** Pres Award, Pan Hellenic Coun, 1973; Pres Award, RL Thornton PTA, 1974; Community Serv Award, United Action Dallas Negro Chamber Com, 1975; Serv Award, Delta Omega Chap Delta Sigma Theta, 1975; African Am Educr Hall Fame; Distinguished Alumna-Waco Independent Sch Dist; Kutokeza Kazi Award; Dallas Pub Schs Sponsor Yr Award; A. Maceo Smith Community Serv Award; Maura Award; Silver Beaver Award, Boy Scouts Am. **Home Addr:** 1907 Matagorda Dr, Dallas, TX 75232-2723, **Home Phone:** (214)333-3328. **Business Addr:** Western Area Director, The Links Inc, 1200 Mass Ave NW, Washington, DC 20005, **Business Phone:** (202)842-8686.

## MALONEY, CHARLES CALVIN

Physician. **Personal:** Born May 24, 1930, West Palm Beach, FL; married Ethel Pearl Covington; children: Charda Corrie & Charles Calvin III. **Educ:** Fla A&M Univ, BS, 1951; Franklin Sch, Med Tec, 1956. **Career:** N Dist Hosp Inc, chief med tech; Christian Hosp Miami, chief tech, 1956-58; Provident Hosp, 1958-62; Broward Gen Med Ctr, 1962-75; Gen Diagnostics Sci Prod, clin specialist. **Orgs:** Am Med Tech; Omega Psi Phi; Boys Club; Jacs Inc; vpres, secy, Broward Med Ctr Credit Univ, 1971; Jack & Jill Am Inc; secy, Omega Psi Phi, 1962-65; Connecting Link; All Am Tackle FL Agr & Mech Univ, 1950-55; Basilus, 1970-71. **Honors/Awds:** Man of Year, Omega Psi Phi, 1960-62. **Home Addr:** 2601 N W 16th St, Ft. Lauderdale, FL 33311-4418, **Home Phone:** (954)735-1650.

## MALRY, DR. LENTON, SR.

Educator, government official. **Personal:** Born Sep 30, 1931, Shreveport, LA; married Joy; children: Lenton Jr. **Educ:** Grambling State Univ, BS, elem educ, 1952; Tex Col, MEd, 1957; Univ NMex, PhD, admin, 1968. **Career:** John Marshall Elem Sch, prin, 1964-67; Albuquerque Pub Sch, teacher, human resources eeo dir, dir cult awarness, coun & guid advisor, 1967-68; NMex House Representatives, rep, 1968-78; La Mesa Elem Sch, prin, 1968-72, equal opportunity officer, 1975; Univ NMex, adj prof, 1975-89; NMex Legis, Bernalillo County Bd County Comnrs, comnr, 1980-83, chmn, 1983-84, 1987-88; Malry & Assocs, pres, 1987-97; Albuquerque Sch Syst, jr high sch teacher & prin, 1987; Bernalillo County govt, neighborhood prog coordr, county mgr, county treas, 2000-12; Albuquerque, co-comnr. **Orgs:** USAF Stationed Eng, 1952-56; pres, Western Interstate Comn Higher Educ, 1976-1984; bd regents, Nmex Inst Mining & Technol, 1985-91; Univ NMex African Am Studies Prog; bd dir, United Way, UNM Cancer Ctr, Heights Psychiat Hosp. **Honors/Awds:** Hall of Fame, Grambling State Univ, 2007; Trailblazers Award, Univ Nmex Black Alumni Chap, 2012. **Special Achievements:** Albuquerque's First Africa American Negro School Principal, 1964; The first black elected to the New Mexico House Representatives, 1968; The first African American to be elected as Bernalillo County Commissioner, 1980. **Home Addr:** 3000 Santa Clara Ave SE, Albuquerque, NM 87106-2350, **Home Phone:** (505)268-6344. **Business Addr:** Neighborhood Program Coordinator, Bernalillo County Government, Rm 5012 1 Civic Plz NW, Albuquerque, NM 87102, **Business Phone:** (505)768-2500.

**MALVEAUX, ANTOINETTE MARIE**
Association executive. **Personal:** Born Mar 19, 1958, San Francisco, CA; daughter of Warren and Proteone. **Educ:** Univ San Francisco, BA, econ, 1981; Univ Pa, Wharton Sch Bus, MBA, 1985. **Career:** Bank Am, remittance clerk, collections clerk, stud loan officer, res asst, asst & financial analyst, 1977-80; Am Express Bank, planner, 1985-86, sr planner, 1986-88, dir, strategic planning, 1988-90, dir, strategic planning & global mkt, 1990-91; Nat Black MBA Asn, dir opers, 1991-93, exec dir, 1993-2000, pres & chief exec officer, 2000-02; Casey Family Prog, dir strategic alliances, 2004-07, managing dir, strategic alliances, 2007-09, managing dir strategic engagements & initiatives, 2009-. **Orgs:** Alumni Admis rep, Wharton Sch, Univ Pa, 1985-; Alumni Adv Comt, Delta Sigma Theta Sororities Inc, 1986; bd mem, chap pres, Nat Black MBA Asn, 1987; Nat Urban League, Black Exchange Prog, 1989; chair, Mamott Customer Diversity Leadership Forum, 1993-; bd mem, Behav Res & Action Social Sci Found, 1993-97; bd mem, Mgt Asn Ill, 1996-99; bd mem, Girl Scouts Am, 1998-99; bd mem, Better Bus Bur, 1998-; bd trustee, Univ San Francisco, 2003-12; bd dir, pres, chair, Seattle Cent Community Col Found, 2004-15; Philanthropy Northwest, 2005; bd mem, Philanthropy Southwest, 2010; Seattle Art Mus, 2011; bd trustee, Asn Black Found Execs, 2015-; Southeastern Coun Foundations, 2016-. **Honors/Awds:** Outstanding Young Women of America, 1987; Black Achievers Award, Harlem Young Mens Christian Asn, 1989; Today's Chicago Women, 100 Women Making a Difference, 1995, 1999; Rainbow/PUSH Reginald Lewis Trailblazer Award. **Special Achievements:** People to People Ambassador Programs, Delegation Leader to South Africa, 1998. **Business Addr:** Managing Director, Casey Family Programs, 2001 8th Ave Suite 2700, Seattle, WA 98121, **Business Phone:** (206)282-7300.

**MALVEAUX, DR. FLOYD JOSEPH**
Immunologist, executive director. **Personal:** Born Jan 11, 1940, Opelousas, LA; son of Delton and Inez Lemelle; married Myrna Ruiz; children: Suzette, Suzanne, Courtney & Gregory. **Educ:** Creighton Univ, Omaha, NE, BS, 1961; Loyola Univ, New Orleans, MS, 1964; Mich State Univ, E Lansing, PhD, microbiol & pub health, 1968; Howard Univ Col Med, MD, 1974. **Career:** Howard Univ Col Med, asst prof microbial, 1968-70, assoc prof med, 1978-84, assoc prof microbiol & med & chair, Dept Microbiol, chmn, 1989-94, prof microbiol & med & dean, 1995-05, interim vpres Health Affairs, 1996, vice provost health affairs, 2000-03; Johns Hopkins Univ, assoc prof med, 1984-89; Urban Asthma & Allergy Ctr, Baltimore, founder & pres, 1986-89; Merck Childhood Asthma Network Inc, exec dir, 2005-. **Orgs:** Fel Am Col Physicians; Am Acad Allergy Asthma & Immunol; bd dir, Am Lung Asn; bd dir, Nat Allergy & Infectious Dis Adv Coun; comt chmn, Underrepresented Minorities, Am Acad Allergy Asthma & Immunol; bd trustee, Asthma & Allergy Found Am; Nat Asthma Educ & Prev Prog, Nat Heart Lung Blood Inst, NIH; founder & pres, Urban Asthma & Allegory Ctr, Baltimore, MD, 1986-89; bd trustee, Nat med Asn, 1988-84; Alpha Omega Alpha Hon Med Soc; elected mem, Inst Med, Nat Acad Scis; Nat Asn Advan Colored People; Sigma Xi Sci Res Soc; Sci Adv Bd, 2009. **Honors/Awds:** Medical Service Award, Nat Med Asn, 1986; National Research Service Award, NIH; Clemens von Pirquet Research Award, Georgetown Sch Med; Outstanding Faculty Research Award, Howard Univ; Legacy of Leadership Award, Howard Univ Hosp. **Home Addr:** 11910 Farside Rd, Laurel, MD 20707, **Home Phone:** (301)596-5006. **Business Addr:** Executive Director, Merck Childhood Asthma Network Inc, 1400 K St NW Suite 750, Washington, DC 20005, **Business Phone:** (202)326-5200.

**MALVEAUX, JULIANNE**
Economist, writer, columnist. **Personal:** Born Sep 22, 1953, San Francisco, CA; daughter of Paul Warren and Proteone Alexandria. **Educ:** Boston Col, BA, econs, 1974, MA, econs, 1975; Mass Inst Technol, PhD, econs, 1977. **Career:** Economist, author & commentator; Books: Slipping Through the Crack: The Status of Black Women, contribr, 1989; Sex, Lies & Sterotypes: Perspectives of a Mad Economist, 1994; What is Robeson's Legacy?; Paul Robeson: Artist & Citizen, contribr, 1998; Minister Farrakhan's Econ Rhet & Reality; The Farrakhan Factor, 1998; Wall St, Main St & the Side St: A Mad Economist Takes a Stroll, Pines One Publ, 1999; Unfinished Bus: A Dem and A Republican Take On the 10 Most Important Issues Women Face, 2002; San Francisco State Univ, asst prof, 1981-85; Univ Calif-Berkeley, vis scholar, vis fac, 1985-92; Pacifica Radio Network, The Julianne Malveaux Show, host, exec producer, 1994-96; Nat Coun Negro Women, Voice of Vision: African-Am Women on the Issues, ed-in-chief, 1996; WLIB, Julianne Malveaux's Capitol Report, radio host, 1997-98; Black Issues in Higher Educ, columnist, 1993-; Last Word Productions, pres & chief exec officer, 1995-; USA Today, guest columnist, currently; Bennett Col, pres, 2007-2012; Last Word Productions Inc, founder & thought Leader, 2012-. **Orgs:** Pres, Nat Asn Negro Bus & Prof Women's Club Inc, 1995-99; chair, bd dir, Nat Child Labor Comm, 1996-; hon co-chair, Delta Sigma Theta Sorority Inc, 2004-; Econ Policy Inst; Liberian Educ Trust; Recreation Wish List Comt Wash; Am Econ Asn; Nat Econ Asn; Bay Area Asn Black Journalists; mem numerous Bds & comts; EmergeAmerica; Push/EXCEL. **Honors/Awds:** Hon Doctorate, Sojourner Douglas Col; Hon Doctorate, Benedict Col; Hon Doctorate, Univ DC. **Special Achievements:** Became the 15th President of Bennett College for Women in Greensboro, NC, 2007. **Business Addr:** President Emerita, Chief Executive Officer, Last Word Productions Inc, 1318 Corcoran St NW, Washington, DC 20009, **Business Phone:** (202)298-9490.

**MANAGER, VADA O.**
Government official, executive, chief executive officer. **Personal:** Born Nov 26, 1961, East St. Louis, IL; son of Ethel; married Charlene; children: 5. **Educ:** Ariz State Univ, BS, polit sci, 1983; London Sch Econ, grad work, 1989. **Career:** Ariz Dept Com, spec asst, 1984-86; Off Gov, spec asst, 1986-87, pres secy, spec asst, 1988-91; Babbit PRS, polit adv, spec asst pres, 1987-88; Young Smith Res, vpres pub finance, 1988; Off Mayor, pres secy, 1991; Dem Nat Conv, network liaison, 1992-2004, sr commun prof team administering, 1992, 1996, 2004; Comn Presidential Debates, staff, 1992-96; Wash, DC based pub affairs firm, vpres; Levi Strauss & Co, sr mgr global commun, 1995-97; Nike Inc, dir global issues mgt, 1997-2009; Ashland's bd dirs, finance & personnel & compensation comm, 2008-; Mgr Global Consult Group, founder & chief exec officer, 2009-; APCO Worldwide's Wash, DC, sr counr, 2010-; Powell Tate, vpres; Young Smith & Peacock, vpres pub finance; New York Stock Exchange, regist broker. **Orgs:** Ariz Bd Regents, 1982-83; Am Coun Ger, leader, 1988-; NCP; Am Coun Ger, 1990; pres, CMS Presial Debates, 1992; Coun USS & Italy, 1992; task force mem, Rainbow Push Task Force Sports, 1999-2009; chairperson, Civilian Pub Affairs Coun, US Mil Acad W Pt, 2003-; chair, bd dirs, Issue Mgt Coun, 2005-10; exec bd mem, Ariz Centennial Comn, 2010-12; nat alumni coun, Ariz State Univ; bd dr, Helios Educ Found, 2015-. **Honors/Awds:** Young Alumni Achievement, Ariz State Univ Alumni Asn, 1989; Inductee Hall Fame, Col Lib Arts, 2000. **Home Addr:** 1304 R St NW, Washington, DC 20009, **Home Phone:** (202)387-6513. **Business Addr:** Senior Counselor, APCO Worldwide, 1299 Pennsylvania Ave NW #300, Washington, DC 20004, **Business Phone:** (202)778-1000.

**MANDLE, PAULA R.**
President (organization), chief executive officer. **Educ:** Susquehanna Univ, BS, physics, Chartered Property Casualty Underwriter. **Career:** The Swarthmore Group, chief compliance officer & chief exec officer, 1995-; Gov of PA, Twenty Sixth Senate Dist, Pub Employees Retirement Comn, comnr, 2002-08. **Orgs:** Bd dir, Thomas Jefferson Univ. **Business Addr:** President, Chief Executive Officer, The Swarthmore Group Inc, 1650 Arch St Suite 2100, Philadelphia, PA 19103, **Business Phone:** (215)557-9300.

**MANDLEY-TURNER, M ANNETTE. See TURNER, M. ANNETTE.**

**MANDULO, RHEA**
Editor, writer, educator. **Personal:** Born Jun 6, 1950, Brooklyn, NY; daughter of William H Wilkins Sr and Martha Benson; children: AmTchaas Nera Adea, Tais Seshua, Sihmen & Kaitu Maat. **Educ:** Marymount Manhattan Col, BA, 1973; Teachers Col, Columbia Univ, attended 1975; Brooklyn Col, MA, engineering & teaching, 1996. **Career:** USVI, Dept Educ, chair, reading teacher, 1977-80, Title I prog, St Thomas USVI, 1979-80; United Press Int, city desk ed, reporter, 1982-90; New York Law J, feature writer, 1992-93; City Sun Newspaper, exec ed, 1993; NYC Bd Educ, eng teacher, elem teacher, 2005-13; Daily Challenge, freelance writer, 1999-2001; A&B Bks, freelance ed, 2000-01; Bks: Princess Queen Mother, 2011; Senemeh-t SaSen Aat, founder, writer, ed, 2014-. **Orgs:** Ausar Auset Soc, 1980-. **Honors/Awds:** Outstanding Contribution Col Community, Marymount Manhattan Col, 1973. **Special Achievements:** Published in worldwide newspapers, 1987-92; Published in Black Enterprise, Essence & NY Newsday; Touring the World of New York's First Africans, 1995. **Home Addr:** 301 Jefferson Ave, Brooklyn, NY 11216, **Home Phone:** (718)623-6042. **Business Addr:** Founder, Senemeh-t SaSen Aat, 2409 Clarendon Rd, Brooklyn, NY 11226, **Business Phone:** (347)513-9907.

**MANGUM, ELMIRA**
College president, college administrator. **Educ:** NC Cent Univ, BA, geog; Univ Wis-Madison, MA, pub policy & pub admin & urban & regional planning; Univ Buffalo, PhD; Millennium Leadership Inst, cert; Harvard Grad Sch Educ Mgt Develop Prog, attended; Cornell's Admin Mgt Inst, cert. **Career:** Univ Wis-Madison, opers specialist; Univ Buffalo, vice provost; Univ NC-Chapel Hill, exec; Cornell Univ, vpres planning & budget, 2010-14; Fla A&M Univ, pres, 2014-. **Orgs:** Bd dirs, Higher Educ Resource Serv (HERS); bd dirs, NC Cent Univ (NCCU)-Creating Vision; bd dirs, Network Chg & Continuous Improv (NCCI); former univ chair, Am Asn Univ Women; bd mem, Nat Action Coun Minorities Engineering Inc; life mem, Nat Coun Negro Women; life mem, Zeta Phi Beta Sorority Inc. **Special Achievements:** First woman in FAMU's history to be named as a permanent president.

**MANGUM, ERNESTINE BREWER (ERNESTINE T BREWER)**
Educator, librarian. **Personal:** Born Aug 7, 1936, Durham, NC; daughter of Patti Brewer (deceased) and Robert Brewer (deceased); married Billy Lee; children: Bill Jr. **Educ:** NC Cent Univ, BA, span, libr sci, 1957; Rutgers Univ, MLS, 1965; Fairleigh Dickinson Univ, MA, human develop, 1982. **Career:** Educator (retired); Civil Rights & Human Rights Comn, officer, 1963; sch teacher & librn. **Orgs:** NJ Educ Asn, 1957; Nat Educ Asn, 1957; NJ Hist Soc, 1960; NJ Media Asn, NC Cent Univ Alumni Asn, 1960-; Rutherford Educ Asn, 1962-; Elmwood Presby Church, 1964-74; mem & officer, Mt Ararat Women's Club, 1974-; Mt Ararat Baptist Church, 1975; vol counr, var self-help groups, 1980; vol, Rutherford Child Care Ctr, 1999-; deaconess, Mt Ararat Baptist Church; outreach vol, Civil Rights Comn. **Honors/Awds:** Publ article NJEA Rev, 1970, 1994; interviewed three editors during Black History Month, 1984; Gov's Teachers Recognition Prog, 1986; Lifetime Achievement Award, Stud Aide & Coun Comt Rutherford & E Rutherford NJ, 1996; Civil Rights Commission Recognition Award, Keri Bennett Multicultural Festival Comt. **Home Addr:** 80 W Erie Ave, Rutherford, NJ 07070-1219.

**MANIGO, REV. GEORGE F., JR.**
Clergy. **Personal:** Born Nov 10, 1934, Bamberg, SC; son of George F Sr and Ertha M Ramsey; married Rosa L Lewis; children: Marcia B & George F III. **Educ:** Claflin Col, BS, edu, 1959; Gammon Theol Sem, BD, 1962. **Career:** Hurst Memorial United Methodist Church, 1960-62; Mkt St United Methodist Church, 1962-65; Wesley Church St James, 1965-70; St Mark & St Matthew Chs Taylors SC, minister, 1970-; Camden First United Methodist Church, pastor, 1977-86; United Methodist Church, dist supt, 1986; Trinity United Methodist Church, pastor. **Orgs:** SC Conf Merger Comt, 1973-; trustee, Columbia Col, Columbia, SC, 1978-; chmn, bd dir, Greenville CAP Ageny; Nat Asn Advan Colored People; secy, Greenville Urban Ministry; trustee, methodist oaks, Phi Beta Sigma; Claflin Univ. **Home Addr:** 3013 Char Augusta Rd, Bamberg, SC 29003-8203.

**MANLEY, DR. AUDREY FORBES**
Physician, college administrator. **Personal:** Born Mar 25, 1934, Jackson, MS; daughter of Ora Buckhalter and Jesse Lee; married Albert E. **Educ:** Spelman Col, AB, 1955; Meharry Med Col, MD, 1959; Johns Hopkins Univ Sch Hyg & Pub Health, MPH, 1987. **Career:** Educator (retired); Spelman Col, med dir, family plan prog, chmn healthcareers adv comn, 1972-76, orgn prog consult family plan prog & inst, 1972-76; Emory Univ, Family Planning Prog Grady Memorial Hosp, chief medserv, 1972-76; Us Pub Health Serv, comn officer, med dir, chief family health & prevserv, 1976-78, comn officer, chief sickle cell dis, 1978-83; Howard Univ Dept Pediat, clin asst prof, 1981; Nat Naval Med Ctr, Dept Peds, CourtClin attend, 1981; NIH Inter-Inst Genetics Clin, guest attend, 1981; Us Pub Health Serv, capt 06, med dir, assoc admin clin affairs, 1983-85; Nat HealthServ Corps, dir, 1987-89; US Pub Health Serv, asst surgeon gen, 1988-97; Us Pub Health Serv, Dept Health & Human Serv, dep asst secy health, 1989-93; Dep Surgeon Gen& Actg Dep Asst Ser minority health, 1993-95; Actg Surgeon Gen, 1995-97; Spelman Col, alumna pres, 1997-2002. **Orgs:** Bd trustee, Spelman col, 1966-70; Fel Am Acad Pediat; Nat Med Asn; Am Pub Health Asn; Am Asn Univ Women; Inst Med, Nat Acad Sci; AAAS; Comned Officers Asn; Am Soc Human Genetics; Nat Soc Genetic Counr; NY Acad Sci; Nat Coun Negro Women; Asn Mil Surgeons US; UNICEF, WHO, comt health policy, 1990-92; bd dir, March Dimes, COC Found, Am Cancer Soc Found, FDA adv ctm Vaccines & Biologies; Quelcty Educ Minorities; Spelman Col Alumni Asn; Meharry Med Col Alumni Asn. **Special Achievements:** First African American woman to be appointed chief resident at Cook County Children's Hospital, Chicago, 1962; First African American woman appointed Principal Deputy Assistant Secretary for Health in the United States Public Health Service, 1987; First African American woman to achieve the rank of Assistant Surgeon General (Rear Admiral), 1988. **Home Addr:** 2807 18th St NW, Washington, DC 20009, **Home Phone:** (202)462-5214.

**MANLEY, REV. JOHN RUFFIN**
Clergy. **Personal:** Born Oct 15, 1925, Murfreesboro, NC; married Gloria Roysler; children: JR Manley Jr. **Educ:** Shaw Univ, AB, BD, 1949, DA, 1955; Duke Univ, ThM, 1967. **Career:** First Bapt Ch, Chapel Hill, NC, founder, pastor, 1946, pastor emer, currently; Manley Estate, founder; Hickory Bapt Ch; New Hope Asn, moderator; Nat Baptist Conv, vpres; Interdenominational Ministerial Alliance Chapel Hill-Carrboro, pres. **Orgs:** Vpres, pres & chmn Polit Action Comn Gen Baptist Conv & NC Inc; Chapel Hill-caraboro Sch Bd; Chapel Hill Planning Bd; pres, Nat AsnAdvan Colored People; 2nd Masonic Lodge; vice chmn, Gov's Coun Sickle Cell Syndrone; chmn, Proj Area Comn Redevelop Comt; Task Force Community Develop Act Chapel Hill; Manley john ruffin trustee; chmn, Chapel Hill Carrboro Anti Poverty Prog; pres, Nat Asn Advan Colored People; founder, S Orange Black Caucus. **Honors/Awds:** Man of the Year, Shaws Theol Alumni; deleg to World, Baptist Alliance; Named honor Rev. John R. Manley Day. **Special Achievements:** First African American elected to Chapel Hill-Carrboro city school board; Declared Dec 9, 2006 as Rev John R Manley day. **Home Addr:** 101 Apple St, Chapel Hill, NC 27516. **Business Addr:** Pastor, First Baptist Church of Chapel Hill, 106 N Roberson St, Chapel Hill, NC 27516, **Business Phone:** (919)942-2552.

**MANLOVE, BENSON**
President (organization), executive. **Personal:** Born Jan 1, 1943. **Educ:** Wayne State Univ, BBA, 1969. **Career:** Wayne State Univ, asst to pres, 1968-70; Amtask Inc, dir mktg, 1970-71; L&M Off Prod, co-owner, 1970-79; Mich Consol Gas Co, exec asst to pres, 1979-81, exec dir, int support serv, 1981-83, vpres admin, 1983, co-dir, vpres econ develop; Detroit Econ Growth Corp, actg pres, 1995-. **Orgs:** Chmn & bd dir, Detroit Urban League, 1989-. **Business Addr:** Chairman, Detroit Urban League, 208 Mack Ave, Detroit, MI 48201, **Business Phone:** (313)832-4600.

**MANN, CHARLES ANDRE**
Business owner, television show host, football player. **Personal:** Born Apr 12, 1961, Sacramento, CA; married Tyrena; children: 3. **Educ:** Univ Nev, attended. **Career:** Football player (retired), TV Host, business owner; Wash Redskins, defensive end, 1983, left defensive end, 1984-93; San Francisco 49ers, defensive line, 1994; Black Entertainment TV, football Analyst; WJFK-FM, host, currently; WUSA-TV Channel 9, host, currently; NFL CBS, color analyst, currently; Mann All Pro Grill, owner, currently. **Orgs:** Co-founder, Good Samaritan Found; Nat Serv Initiative Comt; Nat Kidney Found; United Way; Ronald McDonald C Charities; Border Babies Found; Lever Bros; Why Sch Cool prog; Metrop Police Boys & Girls Clubs; C Hosp; C's Cancer Found; bd mem, Inova Health Systs; chmn, Inova Alexandria Hosp Qual Comt; bd, McLean Sch Deacon with Grace Covenant Church Chantilly; Read Achieve Prog. **Honors/Awds:** Most Valuable Defensive Lineman, Big Sky Conf, 1981-82; Washingtonian of the Year Award, 1994; Nevada Athletics Hall Of Fame, 1995; Super Bowl Champion, (XXII, XXVI, XXIX). **Special Achievements:** TV series: "A Man Called Hawk", "Just in Time", 1993. **Home Addr:** , WA. **Business Addr:** Host, WUSA-TV, 4100 Wisconsin Ave NW, Washington, DC 20016, **Business Phone:** (202)895-5999.

**MANN, DR. MARION**
Pathologist, educator, army officer. **Personal:** Born Mar 29, 1920, Atlanta, GA; son of Levi J and Cora Casey (deceased); married Ruth Maureen Reagin; children: M Nicholas & Judith R. **Educ:** Tuskegee Inst, BS, 1940; Howard Univ Col Med, MD, 1954; Georgetown Univ Med Ctr, PhD, 1961; Nat Bd Med Examiners, Am Bd Path, dipl. **Career:** Educator (retired); Howard Univ col med, asst prof path, 1961, Med Sch, dean, 1970-79, assoc vpres & res, 1988-91; Univ's Off Res & Admin, founder. **Orgs:** Sigma Pi Phi Fraternity, 1997; Nat Med Asn; Inst Med; Nat Acad Sci; Am Bd Path; Sigma Pi Phi. **Honors/Awds:** DSc, Georgetown Univ, 1979; DSc, Univ Mass, 1984; DSC, Tuskegee Univ, 1998. **Home Addr:** 1453 Whittier Pl NW, Washington, DC 20012-2845, **Home Phone:** (202)291-4409. **Business Addr:** Physician, Pathologist.

**MANN, RICHARD**
Football coach. **Personal:** Born Apr 20, 1947, Aliquippa, PA; son of Broadies Hughes; married Karen; children: Deven, Richard II, Mario & Brittany. **Educ:** Ariz State Univ, BS, elem educ. **Career:** Aliquippa High Sch, teacher & wide receiver coach, 1970-73; Ariz State Univ, asst wide receivers & tight end coach, 1974-79; Univ Louisville, asst wide receivers coach, 1980-81; Indianapolis Colts, wide receivers

coach, 1982-84; Cleveland Browns, wide receivers coach & tight end, 1985, wide receivers, 1986-93; New York Jets, wide receivers coach, 1994-96, tight end coach, 1995; Baltimore Ravens, wide receivers coach, 1997-98; Kans City Chiefs, wide receivers coach, 1999-2000; Wash Redskins, wide receivers coach, 2001; Tampa Bay Buccaneers, wide receivers coach, 2002-09, asst head coach, 2009; Pittsburgh Steelers, wide receivers coach, 2013-15. **Orgs:** Chmn, Charlotte Housing Authority Scholar Fund, 1990. **Honors/Awds:** Aliquippa Sports Hall of Fame, 1982; Black Image Achievement Award, 1989; Beaver County Hall of Fame in 1999; Joe Greene Great Performance Award.

## MANN, THOMAS J., JR.

Lawyer, state government official. **Personal:** Born Dec 15, 1949, Brownsville, TN; son of Thomas and Flossie; married Leala Ann Salter; children: Nari & Kari. **Educ:** Tenn State Univ, BS, polit sci, 1971; Univ Iowa Law Sch, JD, 1974. **Career:** St IA, asst atty gen, 1974-76 & 1980-82, st sen, 1983-91; IA CivilRights Comn, exec dir, 1978-79; Mann & Mann Law Off, partner, 1983-92 & 1995; Tex Comn Alcohol & Drug Abuse, gen coun, 1993-95. **Orgs:** IA St Bar Asn; Polk Co Bar Asn; bd mem, Des Moines Br Nat Asn Advan Colored People; Omega Psi Phi; Tex Bar Asn; Am Red Cross. **Home Addr:** 12606 Deer Falls Dr, Austin, TX 78729-7228, **Home Phone:** (512)219-0242. **Business Addr:** Attorney, 101 E 15th St, Austin, TX 78778, **Business Phone:** (512)463-8253.

## MANNEY, WILLIAM A.

Executive, radio host. **Personal:** Born Jul 12, 1931, Little Rock, AR; married Alice Leonard; children: Pamela Denise. **Educ:** Philander Smith Col, BA. **Career:** WBEE 92.5 Radio, sales mgr, 1966, gen mgr, 1970, acct exec, 1966-70, mgr to gen mgr, 1970-; WENN Radio, gen mgr; WAAF, Chicago Sta, acct exec; Rollins Inc, sales mgr; WJBC, gen mgr & pres. **Orgs:** Past pres, Nat Asn Mkt Developers; black media rep, bd dir, Cosmopolitan C C; second vpres, Jane Dent Home Aged; vice chmn, Leslie Rosenblum Boy's Club. **Honors/Awds:** Media Man of the Year, Chicago Chap. **Business Addr:** General Manager, WBEE 92.5, 70 Commercial St, Rochester, NY 14614, **Business Phone:** (585)423-2900.

## MANNING, BLANCHE MARIE

Educator, judge. **Personal:** Born Dec 12, 1934, Chicago, IL; daughter of Julius L Porter and Marguerite Anderson Porter; married William; children: 6. **Educ:** DePaul Univ, BS, educ; Chicago Teachers Col, BE, 1961; John Marshall Law Sch, JD, 1967; Roosevelt Univ, MA, 1972; Univ Nev, gen jurisdiction cert, 1982; Univ Va Sch Law, LLM, 1992. **Career:** Chicago Bd Educ, sch teacher, 1961-67; Cook Co State Attys Off, asst states atty, 1968-73; Malcolm X Community Col, lect, 1970-71; Equal Employ Opportunity Comn, supvry trialatty, 1973-77; United Airlines, gen atty, 1977-78; US Attys Off, asst US atty, 1978-79; NCBL Community Col Law, adj prof, 1978-79; Circuit Ct Cook Co, from assoc judge to judge, 1979-86; Dept Justice, Atty Gen Adv Inst, adj fac mem, 1979; IL Judicial Conf New Judges Sem, Prof Develop Prog New Asn Judges, IL Judicial Conf Asn Judges Sem, lectr, 1982-86; First Munic Dist Circuit Ct Cook Co, supv judge, 1984-86, supv circuit judge, 1986-87; Justice Ill Appellate Ct, First Dist, 1987-94; Harvard Law Sch, Univ Chicago Law Sch, Trial Advocacy Workshops, teaching team mem, 1991-; De Paul Univ Col Law, adj prof, 1992-94; US Dist Ct, Northern Dist Ilinois, judge, 1994-, dist ct jurist, 1994. **Orgs:** Nat Asn Women Judges; Cook County Bar Asn; Ill Judicial Coun; New Judges Sem; Chicago Bar Asn; Symphony Orchestra; Chicago State Univ Community Concert Band & Jazz Band; fel Am Bar Asn. **Honors/Awds:** Edith Sampson Memorial Award, 1985; Award of Appreciation, Int Asn Pupil Personnel Workers, 1985; IL Judicial Coun; Kenneth E Wilson Judge of the Year Award, Cook County Bar Asn; Distinguished Alumna Award, Chicago State Univ, 1986; Award of Excellence in Judicial Admin, Women Bar Asn, 1986; Black Rose Award, League Black Women, 1987; We Care Role Model Award, Chicago Police Dept, 1987-94; Thurgood Marshall Award, IIT Kent Law Sch BALSA, 1988; Professional Achievement Award, Roosevelt Univ, 1988; Distinguished Service Award, John Marshall Law Sch, 1989; Distinguished Service Award, Guardians Police Orgn, 1991; Citizen's Award, The Guardians Police Orgn, 1991; We Care Outstanding Role Model Award, Chicago Pub Schs & Chicago Police Dept, 1992-94; Honorary Doctor of Humane Letters Degree, Chicago State Univ, 1998. **Special Achievements:** First African-American female member of that court. **Home Addr:** 10346 S Martin Luther King Dr, Chicago, IL 60628. **Business Addr:** Judge, United States District Court, Everett McKinley Dirksen Bldg, Chicago, IL 60604, **Business Phone:** (312)435-7608.

## MANNING, BRIAN

Counselor, research scientist. **Personal:** Born Apr 22, 1975; son of Ray and Marvelyn; married Roxanne M; children: Micah & Caleb. **Educ:** Stanford Univ, BS, sociol; Univ KS Med Ctr, MPH. **Career:** Miami Dolphins, wide receiver, 1997-98; Green Bay Packers, wide receiver, 1998-99; Univ KS Med Ctr, researcher & counr, 1999-. **Orgs:** Stanford Alumni Asn; Nat Football League Players Asn; Lenexa Christian Ctr; Am Pub Health Asn. **Honors/Awds:** Overall Best Student Entry, Univ Kans Med Ctr, 2000. **Home Addr:** 616 SE Cumberland Dr, Lees Summit, MO 64063-1005, **Home Phone:** (816)524-7367. **Business Addr:** Counselor, KU Med Center, 3901 Rainbow Blvd Suite 3001S, Kansas City, KS 66160-7313, **Business Phone:** (913)588-1227.

## MANNING, DANIEL RICARDO (DANNY MANNING)

Basketball coach, basketball player. **Personal:** Born May 17, 1966, Hattiesburg, MS; son of Edward and Darnelle; married Julie; children: Taylor & Evan. **Educ:** Univ Kans, communs, 1988. **Career:** Basketball player (retired), basketball coach, director; Los Angeles Clippers, forward-ctr, 1988-94; Atlanta Hawks, forward-ctr, 1994; Phoenix Suns, forward-ctr, 1994-99; Milwaukee Bucks, forward-ctr, 1999-2000; Utah Jazz, forward-ctr, 2000-01; Dallas Mavericks, forward-ctr, 2001-02; Detroit Pistons, forward-ctr, 2003; Univ Kans, dir stud-athlete develop & team mgr, 2003-07, asst coach, 2006-12; Tulsa, asst coach, 2012-. **Orgs:** Kappa Alpha Psi Fraternity Inc; ambassador, Kans Gov's Coun Fitness; Lawrence (Kan.) High Sch Hall Fame. **Business Addr:** Assistant Coach, University of Tulsa, Westby Hall 800 S Tucker Dr, Tulsa, OK 74104, **Business Phone:** (918)631-2342.

## MANNING, DR. EDDIE JAMES

Administrator, dean (education), executive director. **Personal:** Born Mar 19, 1952, Philadelphia, PA; married Carolyn; children: Eddie Jr & C Jamal. **Educ:** Cheyney Univ, BS, 1974; Temple Univ, MEd, 1976, EdD, 1984. **Career:** Chester Upland Sch Dist, teacher & guid counsr; Ashbourne Sch, teacher; Act 101 Prog Temple Univ, dir 1975-86, coord, 1979-80, actg assoc dean, 1998; Temple Univ Spec Recruitment & Admis Prog, counr & acad adv, 1977-79; Rutgers Univ, Acad Support Progs, actg dir, 1999, Stud Access & Educ Equity, inaugural dir, Educ Opportunity Fund Prog, interim exec dir, assoc dean & exec dir, currently. **Orgs:** Am Asn Couns & Develop; Pa Coun Asn; Pa Asn Multi-Cult Coun & Develop; treas, Pa Chap Am Asn Non-White Concerns Personnel & Guid, 1982-; chmn, Act 101 Eastern Reg Exec Comt, 1982-83; chmn, State Chapts Div Am Asn Multi-Cult Couns & Develop, 1983-85; Temple Univ Sub-Comm Acad Excellence Athletics, 1985-; Temple Univ Resident Review Bd, 1985-. **Home Addr:** 7834 Williams Ave, Philadelphia, PA 19150. **Business Addr:** Associate Dean, Executive Director, Rutgers The State University of New Jersey, 611 George St Lucy Stone Hall- Rm A324, New Brunswick, NJ 08901-8533, **Business Phone:** (848)445-3090.

## MANNING, DR. JEAN BELL

Educator. **Personal:** Born Aug 14, 1937, LaMarque, TX; married Reuben D. **Educ:** Bishop Col, BA, 1958; N Tex State Univ, MEd, 1964, EDd, 1970. **Career:** Douglas High Sch, Ardmore, OK, instr, 1958-60, 1964-65; Reading Lab, Jarvis Col, Hawkins, TX, instr & dir, 1961-64; Southern Tex Univ, Houston, TX, vis prof, 1964-65; Paul Quinn Col, Waco, TX; chmn dept educ, 1970-73, 1974-78; Univ Liberia, Liberia, W Africa, prof eng, 1973-74, pres; Okla City Chap, prog coordr & facet dirs; Langston Univ, OK, assoc prof & dir resources, 1978-86; vpres, acad affairs, 1987-2007; vpres, emer acad affairs, 2007-. **Orgs:** Alpha Kappa Alpha Sor, 1956-; Phi Delta Kappa Sor, 1956-; Links Inc, 1974-; Educ Leadership Black Ch Lilly Found Sponsored Houston TX, 1975-77; curric devel Wiley Col Marshall TX, 1978; competency based educ Dallas Independent S Dist, 1979. **Honors/Awds:** Doctoral Grant, Ford Found, 1969; Outstanding Sorority, SW Phi Delta Kappa Sorority, 1978; Hall of Fame, Okla Higher Educ Heritage Soc, 2007; Waco, Texas as Woman of the Year, Phi Delta Kappa Nat Sorority. **Special Achievements:** First female Vice-President Emeritus, Langston Univ, 2007. **Home Addr:** PO Box 1203, Langston, OK 73050-1203, **Home Phone:** (405)282-4089. **Business Addr:** Vice President Emeritus, Langston University, 201 Univ Women, Langston, OK 73050, **Business Phone:** (405)466-3207.

## MANNING, DR. RANDOLPH H., SR.

Educator, school administrator. **Personal:** Born Dec 18, 1947, New York, NY; son of Ruthfoy and Gertrude Webber; married Monica S McEvilley; children: Randolph, Craig C & Corey A. **Educ:** Suffolk Co Community Col, AA, 1969; State Univ NY, Stony Brook, BA, 1971, MA, 1975, PhD, 1998. **Career:** R H Manning Enterprises, consult, 1972, owner & operator, 1973-; Suffolk Co Community Col, counr, 1971-80, prof psycol & sociol, 1980-85, dean instr, provost, 1985-97, assoc dean acad affairs, div bus & technol, 2008-11; CleanTech Rocks, chief operating officer, 2011-. **Orgs:** Educ consult, BOCES; adv bd mem, Re-Rout Dept Labor, BOCES, SOCC, SC Correction; bd dir, LI Sickle Cell; bd dir, Gordon Heights Fed Credit Union; Pres, NY State Spec Prog Personnel Asn; Suffolk City Youth Bd; adv community, Brookhaven Social Serv; Long Island Asn Black Counr; Long Island Minority Educrs; E End Guid Asn; pres emer, chmn, Supvry & Publicity Community; Gordon Hgts Fed Credit Union; treas, Long Island Sickle Cell Proj; co-dir, Coun Int Prog; Am Sociol Asn; State Univ NY Asn; steering comm, Suffolk City Probation Dept, Day Reporting Ctr; nat pres, Community Col Gen Educ Asn; NY State bd Prof Med Conduct; United Way steering comm, Proj Blueprint; restoration adv bd, USn; Alpha Beta Gamma Nat Bus Hon Soc, 1986. **Home Addr:** 3 Indian Valley Rd, Setauket, NY 11733-4037, **Home Phone:** (631)689-6277. **Business Addr:** Consultant, R H Manning Enterprises, New YorK, NY.

## MANNING, SHARON (SHARON MANNING BEVERLY)

Basketball player, basketball coach. **Personal:** Born Mar 20, 1969; married Randy. **Educ:** NC State Univ, BA, sociol, 1991; Queens Col, BA, MA; Capella Univ, PhD. **Career:** Basketball player (retired), basketball coach; NC State Univ, 1988-91; US Olympic Festival N Team, asst coach, 1994; Charollete Swing, 1997-99; Women's Basketball Open Div, state chmn; Charlotte Sting, ctr-forward, 1997-99; Miami Sol, 2000; St Joseph's Univ, asst coach, 2000-01; Wake Forest Univ, asst coach, 2001-; Nj Inst Technol, 2001-02; Vassar Col Athletics, assoc dir athletics & sr woman adminr, 2002-04, interim dir athletics, 2004, dir athletics & phys educ, 2005-; Queens Col, head women's basketball coach; Fairleigh Dickinson Univ, head women's basketball coach; Nj Inst Technol, head women's basketball coach. **Orgs:** NCAA Div III Nominating Comm; NCAA Div III Conv Planning Subcomt; pres, Nj State Coaches Asn; New York Metrop Coaches Asn. **Business Addr:** Director of Athletics, Physical Education, Vassar College Athletics, 124 Raymond Ave, Poughkeepsie, NY 12604-0750, **Business Phone:** (845)437-7450.

## MANSFIELD, DR. CARL MAJOR

Physician, educator, association executive. **Personal:** Born Dec 24, 1928, Philadelphia, PA; married Sarah Lynne; children: Joel & Kara. **Educ:** Lincoln Univ, AB, 1951; Temple Univ, attended 1952; Howard Univ, MD, 1956; Lincoln Univ, PhD, 1991. **Career:** Physician, educator (retired); Episcopal Hosp, resident intern, 1956-58, resident, 1960; USAF, radiologist, 1958-60; Jefferson Med Col Hosp, assoc radiologist, chief div, chernicoff fel, instr radiologist, NIH post doct fel, resident, 1960-67; Jefferson Med Col, adv clin fel, 1965-68, asst prof, 1967-69; Univ Pa Sch Med, lectr, 1967-73; Thomas Jefferson Univ Hosp, from assoc prof to prof, 1970-76, prof emer, currently, chmn dept radiation thermo & nuclear med, 1983-94; Hahnemann Med Col Hosp, vis prof, 1971; Univ Kans Med Ctr, prof chmn dept radiation, 1976-83; Univ Md Sch Med, chmn dept radiation oncol, 1998. **Orgs:** Am Bd Radiol, 1962; Mt Carmel Baptist Church, 1965-73; adv bd, Boys Scout Am, 1965-66; Pharm Com, 1965-66; Admis Com, 1968-72; Stud Affairs Com, 1968-71; Alt Judiciary Com, 1971-72; Am Bd Nuclear Med, 1972; AMA; Am Soc Therapeut Radiologists; Asn Univ Radiologists; Brit Inst Radiol; Am Col Nuclear Physicians; Nat Med Asn; Radiol Soc N Am; Royal Soc Med; Soc Nuc Med Gardens Bd; Hall-Mercer Comm Ment Health & Ment Retardation Ctr Pa Hosp, 1973-74; Philadelphia Redevelop Authority, 1973-75; Stud Prom Com, 1973-75; Pharma & Therapeut Comn, 1974-76; Radiation Safety Comn, 1974-76; Comput Comn, 1974-76; bd trustee, Peter's Sch, 1975-76; fel Am Col Radiol, 1976; nat bd, Am Cancer Soc; fel Philadelphia Col Physicians, 1984; pres, Am Radium Soc, 1988-89; fel Am Col Nuclear Med, 1989; pres, Philadelpia Am Cancer Soc, 1989-90. **Honors/Awds:** Over 150 publications, exhibits, presentations; Natl & Intl meetings; Bronze Medal, Am Cancer Soc, 1990. **Home Addr:** 336 S Front St, Philadelphia, PA 19106-4336, **Home Phone:** (215)592-8063. **Business Addr:** Professor Emeritus, Thomas Jefferson University Hospital, 1020 Walnut St, Philadelphia, PA 19107, **Business Phone:** (215)955-6000.

## MANSFIELD, W. ED

Administrator, government official, executive. **Personal:** Born May 7, 1937, Clifton Forge, VA; married Maxine L; children: Amy & Yolanda. **Educ:** Univ Denver, attended 1970. **Career:** Radio Sta KTLN, moderator, commentator, newscaster, 1966-67; Lincoln Nat Life Ins Co, spec agt, 1966-69; Pub Rels, dir, 1967-68; Univ Denver, asst to chancellor, 1969-71; Nat Urban Coalition, asst dir field opers, 1971; mkt & enrollment, dir, 1971-72; Gen Mills Inc, from consult to chmn bd & pres, 1972; Affirmative Action Progs Dept, leader, 1972-75; Alternative Mgt, consult, 1975-76; Minority Affairs Corp Pub Broadcasting, dir, 1976; US Equal Employ Opportunity Comn, St Louis Dist Off, dist dir. **Orgs:** Exec dir, Colo Asn Indust Cols & Univs, 1969-71; consult, EEO Laws Affirmative Action; Gen Mills Inc; Nat Asn Cos; Nat Civil Serv League; Int Personnel Mgt Asn; Minn League Cities; N Dak League Cities; Am Compliance Soc & Inc; Int Asn Off Human Rights Orgn; City & County Denver; Affirmative Action Asn; chmn Hennep Co Bicentennial Planning Comn; Affirmative Action Adv Comt; 1st vice chmn, Minneapolis Urban Coalition; Minn State Bd Nursing; Abbot-Northwestern Hosp; Minneapolis Citizens Concered Pub Educ; Am Soc Personnel Admin; Nat Orgn Women; Nat Asn Adv Colored People; Nat Urban League. **Home Addr:** 2416 Harmon Rd, Silver Spring, MD 20902.

## MANSON, RICHARD

Lawyer, association executive, executive director. **Educ:** Fisk Univ, Nashville, TN, BA, 1971; Vanderbilt Univ Sch Law, Nashville, TN, JD, 1975. **Career:** Dudley Cosmetology Sch, fac; Criminal Justice Dept, Tenn State Univ Nashville, assoc prof; Belmont Univ, Nashville, TN, adj prof; Citizens Savings Bank & Trust Co, dir bd & Legal Coun; Manson Jones & Whitted, pvt pract atty, currently; Manson Johnson Stewart & Assocs, founding partner, currently; SourceMark LLC, chief exec officer, owner, 2010-. **Orgs:** Tenn Bar Asn; Nashville Bar Asn; Am Bar Asn; Napier Looby Bar Asn; Tenn Trial Lawyers Asn; Nat Acad Rec Arts & Sci; Black Entertainment & Sports Attys; Jefferson St Com Revitalization Dist Citizens Adv Comt. **Business Addr:** Founding Partner, Attorney, SourceMark LLC, 100 Winners Circle, Brentwood, TN 37027, **Business Phone:** (615)269-6010.

## MANUEL, JERRY

Baseball manager, baseball player. **Personal:** Born Dec 23, 1953, Hahira, GA; married Renette Caldwell; children: 4. **Career:** Baseball player (retired), baseball coach, mgr & exec; Detroit Tigers, second baseman & shortstop, 1975-76; Montreal Expos, second baseman & shortstop, 1980-81, instr, 1987, field coordr, 1988-89, third base coach, 1991-96; SanDiego Padres, second baseman & third baseman & shortstop, 1982; Fla Marlins, bench coach, 1997; Chicago White Sox, scout, 1985, mgr, 1998-2003; New York Mets, base coach, 2005, outfield coach, bench coach, 2006-08, mgr, 2008-10; MLB Network, analyst, currently; William Jessup Univ, dir, 2014-. **Orgs:** Founder, Jerry Manuel Foundation. **Honors/Awds:** Southern League Co-Manager of the Year, 1990; World Series champion, 1997; California Black Sports Hall of Fame, 2000; C.I. Taylor Award; Manager of the Year, Am League, 2000. **Special Achievements:** First permanent African American manager in Chicago White Sox history. **Business Addr:** Analyst, MLB Network, 1 MLB Network Plz, Secaucus, NJ 07094.

## MANUEL, LIONEL, JR.

Football player, football coach. **Personal:** Born Apr 13, 1962, Rancho Cucamonga, CA; married Paulina; children: Lionel M III, Brittany M, Mikala M, Leo & Celysia. **Educ:** Citrus Col; Univ Pac. **Career:** Football Player (retired), football coach, professional chef; New York Giants, wide receiver, 1984-90; Fontana High Sch, coach; Univ La Verne, coach; Citrus Col, coach; NJ High Sch, coach; Riverside Community Col, wide receiver coach, currently; prof chef & restaurateur. **Honors/Awds:** Nat Football League Championship Game, 1986; Hall of Fame, Univ Pac, 2012. **Home Addr:** 827 E Cedar Dr, PO Box 12091, Chandler, AZ 85249-3319. **Business Addr:** Wide Receiver Coach, Riverside Community College, 3845 Market St, Riverside, CA 92501.

## MANUEL, DR. LOUIS CALVIN

Physician. **Personal:** Born Jun 13, 1937, Cleveland, OH; married Idabelle Todd; children: Donna L, April D, Erika L & Louis C. **Educ:** Bowling Green St Univ, BA, 1960; Meharry Med Col, MD, 1965. **Career:** Homer G Phillip Hosp, resident, internship; Wash Univ Med Ctr; Louis C Manuel MD Eye Serv Inc, ophthal; St. Luke's Hosp, physician. **Orgs:** Secy, Kans City Med Soc; pres, secy, Mo Pan Med; House Delegates; Nat Med Soc; AMA; Mo St Med; Jackson Co Med; SW Med Asn; APPA KC Oph & Otol; Roman Barnes Soc; Castroviejo Soc; Am Soc Con Oph; life mem, Nat Advan Asn Colored People; consult, Ophthal Model Cities Health Orgn KC Mo, 1971-80; fel Royal Soc Med, 1973; deacon Covenant Presby Ch KC Mo; youth coun, career develop United Presby Ch; bd dir, Civic Plaza Nat Bk KC Mo; Alpha Phi Alpha; YMCA; Univ Mo Asn; Midwesterners Greater KC Med Serv. **Honors/Awds:** Commendation Medal; Vietnamese serv ribbon AUS. **Business Addr:** Opthalmologist, Eye Services Inc, 1734 E 63rd St Suite 501, Kansas City, MO 64110, **Business Phone:** (816)363-4700.

### MAPLE, DENNIS
President (organization). **Educ:** Univ Tenn, BS, acct, 1982. **Career:** Quaker Oats Co, key acct mgr, 1982-85, sales planning mgr, 1985-86, dist mgr, 1986-87, broker territory mgr, 1987-88, zone develop mgr, 1981-89; Pepsi-Cola, regional sales mgr, 1989-91; Kraft-Gen Foods, dist mgr, 1991-93; Coors Brewing Co, dir sales, 1994-96, regional mkt dir, 1997-98, dir mkt develop, 1999, area vpres, 2004-05; ARAMARK Inc, sr vice pres higher educ, 2004-05, exec vpres, educ-facil serv, 2004-06, pres, 2006-14; First Stud, pres, 2014-. **Orgs:** Bd mem, Urban League Philadelphia; bd mem, Philadelphia Academies; La State Univ, EJ Ourso Col Bus, Dean's Adv Coun; bd trustee, Paoli Hosp Found; New York Univ, Metrop Ctr Urban Educ, Exec Coun. **Business Addr:** President, First Student, 600 Vine St Suite 1400, Cincinnati, OH 45202, **Business Phone:** (513)241-2200.

### MAPP, BERNELL
Chief executive officer. **Personal:** married Amy; children: 3. **Career:** Co-Principal Investr, Health Resource Servr; Admin Health Serv Inc, chief exec officer. **Orgs:** Co-founder, Acts Peace Ministries; bd mem, Amazing Facts Worldwide television ministry. **Business Addr:** Chief Executive Officer, Health Services Inc, 1000 Adams Ave, Montgomery, AL 36104, **Business Phone:** (334)832-4338.

### MAPP, DAVID KENNETH, JR.
Law enforcement officer. **Personal:** Born Nov 15, 1951, Norfolk, VA; married Cynthia Gaines; children: Shomarr & Patrice. **Educ:** Norfolk State Univ, BA, sociol, 1973. **Career:** Norfolk Sheriff's Dept, recreation dir, 1973-75, classification officer, 1975-78, dir classification & rehabilitative progs, 1978-80, sheriff, 1981-93; Eureka Lodge, officer, 1973. **Orgs:** Officer, Norfolk State Univ Alumni Asn, 1973; officer, Norfolk Jaycees; Nat Sheriff's Asn, 1981; VA State Sheriff's Asn, 1981; VA Asn Law Enforce Const Officers, 1981; JJDP State Adv Coun, 1982; chmn, Norfolk United Way, 1983. **Honors/Awds:** Citizen of the Year, Alpha Phi Omega Frat, 1983; Cardiac Arrest Award, Norfolk Heart Asn, 1984. **Home Addr:** 6825 Silverwood Ct, Norfolk, VA 23513-1118.

### MAPP, DR. EDWARD C.
School administrator, writer. **Personal:** Born Aug 17, 1929, New York, NY; son of Edward Cameron and Estelle Sampson; children: Andrew, Elmer & Everett. **Educ:** City Col NY, BA, 1953; Columbia Univ, MS, 1956; NY Univ, PhD, mass commun, 1970. **Career:** School administrator (retired), writer; Books: Blacks in American Films, 1972; Puerto Rican Perspectives, 1974; Blacks in Performing Arts, 1978, 2nd edition, 1990; A Separate Cinema, 1992; African Americans & the Oscar, 2003; New York City Bd Educ, teacher, 1957-64; New York City Tech Col, dir Libr Learning Resources Ctr, 1964-77; Borough Manhattan Community Col, dean fac, 1977-82, prof, 1983-92; Movie & TV Mkt, feature columnist, 1979-91; City Col Chicago, vchancellor, 1982-83; New York City Comn Human Rights, Comnr, 1987-94; prof emer, 1994; Univ New York, prof speech & commun, 1998. **Orgs:** Treas, City Univ New York Fac Senate, 1972-77; bd dir, United Nat Assoc New York, 1975-78; 100 Black Men Inc, 1975-85; bd mem, Brooklyn Region, Nat Conf Christians & Jews, 1972-81; adv comt, Nat Proj Ctr Film & Humanities, 1974-75; bd dir, Un Asn New York, 1975-78; bd trustee, New York Metro Ref & Res Agency, 1980-81; Brooklyn Bor Pres, Ed Adv Panel, 1981; dir, Nat ServCorp, 1984-87; comnr, vchair, New York Human Rights Comn, 1988-94; chmn, bdmem, Friends Thirteen, 2000-, 2005; co-chmn, Thirteens Legacy Soc, currently. **Honors/Awds:** Founders Day Award for Outstanding Scholarship, New York Univ, 1970; Distinguished Service Award, Borough Manhattan Community Col, The City Univ New York, 1982; Black Collectors Hall of Fame, 1992; Community Service Award, Knoxville Col Alumni Asn, 1993. **Special Achievements:** Curator: Edward Mapp African American Film Poster Collection, presented to Center for Motion Picture Study of the Academy of Motion Picture Arts and Sciences, 1996; "Close Up in Black": A Smithsonian Touring Exhibition from the Mapp Collection, 2003-05. **Home Addr:** 155 W 68th St, New York, NY 10023.

### MAPP, DR. JOHN ROBERT
Physician. **Personal:** Born Jan 26, 1950, Springfield, MA; son of Alexander B and Edna Royster; married Maria Mejia; children: Alexandra & Lorean. **Educ:** Hillsdale Col, Hillsdale, MI, BA, 1971; Meharry Med Col, MD, 1975; Calif St Univ, San Diego, MPH, 1987. **Career:** Med Col, Pa, residence Pediat, 1975-77; Univ Southern Calif Med Sch, clin instr pediat, 1977-79; Pediat Los Angeles, Calif, symp reneonatol, 1978; Univ Southern Calif, Los Angeles County Med Sch, neonatal pathologist, 1979-80; Hosp Italiano Rosario S Am, guest lectr neonatol, consult neonatol, 1979; Glendale Adventist Med Ctr, co chief neonatol dept, 1979-. **Orgs:** Co-founder & Pres, Blacks United Hillsdale Col, 1969-71; Am Asn Pediat, 1976-. **Special Achievements:** Appeared in TV Series, Nat TV Prog "Lifeline", 1978; Geronimo, 1993, Dr Quinn, Medicine Woman, 1993; Rides in Rose Bowl Parade, 1995; The District, 2003. **Home Addr:** 135 Thompson St, Springfield, MA 01109, **Home Phone:** (413)734-8868. **Business Addr:** Physician, Glendale Adventist Medical Center, 1509 Wilson Terr St, Glendale, CA 91206, **Business Phone:** (818)409-8247.

### MAPP, RHONDA (TOYJA RHONDA MAPP)
Basketball player. **Personal:** Born Oct 13, 1969; daughter of Kenneth. **Educ:** NC State Univ, commun & pub rels, 1992. **Career:** Basketball player (retired); Trogylos Priolo, 1996-97; Charlotte Sting, ctr-forward, 1997-2000; Galatasaray SKB, 2000-01; Los Angeles Sparks, 2001-03; Pool Comense, 2003; Sache.Exclusive, ceo & pres, 2004-; Kool Kutz Barbershop, ceo & pres, 2012-. **Orgs:** Founder, Follow Your Dreams Inc, 1998. **Business Addr:** Founder, Follow Your Dreams Inc, 636 Plank Rd Suite 205, Clifton Park, NY 12065, **Business Phone:** (518)631-6227.

### MAPP, TOYJA RHONDA. See MAPP, RHONDA.

### MARABLE, HERMAN, JR.
Judge. **Personal:** Born Oct 4, 1962, Flint, MI; son of Herman Sr and Iris Butler. **Educ:** Mich State Univ, James Madison Col, BA, am pub policy, 1984; Ohio State Univ, Col Law, JD, 1987. **Career:** Dist 68th Judge Lee Vera Loyd, law clerk, 1983-84; UAW-GM Legal Serv, law clerk, 1985; Garan Lucow Miller Seward Cooper & Becker, summer assoc, 1986; Riegle Senate Comt, regional coord, 1987-88; Atty Kathie Dones-Carson, dir res & spec proj, 1988-91; County Allegheny, asst dist atty, 1991-93; County Genesee, asst prosecuting atty, 1993-2000; 68th Dist Ct, judge, 2000-. **Orgs:** Intern, Nat Asn Advan Colored People, Wash Bur, 1983; Nat Bar Asn, 1985-; Mallory-Scott-Van Dyne Bar Asn, 1987-; sec nominating comt chair, Urban Coalition Greater Flint, 1987-91; bd dir, MSU James Madison Col Alumni Asn, 1987-89, 1990-94; adv bd chair, United Way Genesee & Lapeer Counties, 1988-91; vpres, Flint Br, Nat Asn Advan Colored People, 1988-94; state cent comt mem, Mich Dem Party, 1989-93, 1995-98; treas, Genesee County Black Caucus, 1989-91; Urban League Flint, 1991-; vice chmn admin, Boy Scouts Am, 1989-91; 9th Cong Dist Dem Exec Comt, 1995-97; vice chair, Genesee County Black Caucus, 1997-98; Homer S Brown Law Asn, 1990-93; Allegheny County Bar Asn, 1990-93; Pa Dist Atty's Asn, 1991-93; Nat Black Prosecutor's Asn, 1993-00; Pa Bar Asn; vpres, Mich Chap Nat Black Prosecutors Asn, 1993-00; 1994-95; Prosecuting Atty's Asn Mich, 1993-00; Genesee County Bar Asn, 1993-; Flint City Wide Hate Crimes Task Force, Human Rels Comn, 1993-98; Int F & A M Masons, 1994-; co-chmn, Legal Redress, Mich NAACP, 1994-00; exec bd mem, Genesee County Black Caucus, 1995-00; Cent Flint Optimist Club, 1996-; bd dir, Flint Neighborhood Coalition, 1997-; Prosecution Diversity Comt, 1997-00; vpres, Flint Neighborhood Coalition, 1998-00; Genesee County Dem Party, officer-at-large, 1988-91, 1994-00; Evergreen Valley Block Club; Southeast Crime Watch; State Bar Mich; Nat Bar Asn; Am Bar Asn; Judges Asn; Mallory-Scott Van Dyne Bar Asn; Mich Dist Judges Asn, 2001-; Asn Black Judges Mich, 2000-; Am Judges Asn, 2001-; Nat Bar Asn Judicial Coun, 2001-. **Honors/Awds:** Stud Leadership Award, Housing Programs Office, MSU, 1983; Outstanding Black Student Scholarship, Kappa Alpha Psi, MSU, 1983; Olive R Beasley Volunteer Award, Urban League Flint, 1989; Flint NAACP Service Award, 1992; Outstanding Service Award, Nat NAACP Radiothon, 1994; Honorary Page, State Senate of Tenn, 1980; Best Petitioner's Brief Award, Frederick Douglass-Midwest Regional Moot Court Competition, Black Law Students Asn, 1986; Outstanding Young Men of America, 1986, 1988, 1989, 1996, 1998; Who's Who in American Law; Who's Who Among African-Americans. **Special Achievements:** First challenger to defeat an incumbent judge in Genesee County, Michigan. **Home Addr:** 2031 Eckley Ave, Flint, MI 48503, **Home Phone:** (810)743-7626. **Business Addr:** Judge, 68th District Court, 630 S Saginaw St, Flint, MI 48502, **Business Phone:** (810)766-8985.

### MARBURY, REV. DONALD LEE
Broadcaster. **Personal:** Born Nov 26, 1949, Pittsburgh, PA; son of Sherrill and Susie Burroughs; married Sheila JoAnn King; children: Cara Jean & Evan Lee. **Educ:** Univ Pittsburgh, BA, Eng, 1971; Wesley Theol Sem, MDiv, exeg, syst theol, 2002. **Career:** Pittsburgh Post Gazette, gen assignment reporter, 1969-71; WQED-TV, air reporter & anchor, 1971-74, exec prod, 1973-80, prod, 1977-80, co-producer, 1977, prod & broadcast host, 1973-77, prod, 1976-77, instr, 1978-79, exec prod & coordr local programming, 1978-80; Chatham Col, Commun Dept, instr, 1976-80; KQED-TV, Scriptwriter, 1979; Tv Prog Fund, Cult & C's Progs, assoc dir, 1980-89, dir, 1989-95; Corp Pub Broadcasting, Dept Educ & Programming, vpres programming, 1980-97; Univ DC, Black Film Inst, instr screenplay writing, 1988-85; Under One Sky Media, Pres, 1997-; Montgomery Col, adj prof reading & Eng, 2000; Howard Univ, Sch Commun, Dept Radio, Tv, Film, lectr, 2002-10; St John African Methodist Episcopal Church, pastor; Ebenezer African Methodist Episcopal Church, sr pastor, 2006-, ordained African Methodist Episcopal Church elder, currenlty. **Orgs:** Bd dir, Intercultural House, 1971-; bd dir, Pittsburgh Black Media Coalition, 1971-74; bd dir, WYEP-FM, 1974-75; steering comm, Producers Coun, 1976-80; bd dir, Nat Black Prog Consortium, 1978-80; exec steering comm, Producers Coun Nat Asn Educ Broadcasters, 1978-80; Task Force Pub Participation, 1978; bd dir, Louise Child Care Ctr; bd dir, C's Advocacy Newspaper, 1989. **Honors/Awds:** Golden Quill Western Pa Journalism Honorary, 1973; Pittsburgh Goodwill Ambassador, Pittsburgh Goodwill, 1975; Black Achiever of the Year, Talk Mag, 1975; Founders Award, Nat Black Programming Consortium, 1983; Certificate of Appreciation, Nat Black Programming Consortium, l988; Leokoeberlein Distinguished Alumnus Award in Journalism, Univ Pittsburgh, 1990. **Home Addr:** Ste 1 Tupelo Ct, Rockville, MD 20855, **Home Phone:** (301)963-9380. **Business Addr:** Senior Pastor, Ebenezer African Methodist Episcopal Church, 720 N Maple Ave, Brunswick, MD 21716, **Business Phone:** (301)834-8767.

### MARBURY, MARTHA G.
Administrator. **Personal:** Born Nov 22, 1946, Morgantown, WV; daughter of John Dobbs Jr (deceased) and Georgia Johnson Dobbs (deceased); children: Anthony Vaughn. **Educ:** Univ Md, College Park, MD, BS, 1980. **Career:** USDA Soil Conserv Serv, Morgantown, WV, clerk steno, 1967-73; USDA Soil Conserv, Ser Col Pk, Md, personnel clerk, 1973-75, personnel asst, 1975-76, personnel mgt specialist, 1976-78, personnel officer, 1978-83; USDA Soil Conserv Serv, Wash, DC, classification specialist, 1983-85, chief, employ br, 1985-88, chief, EEO br, 1988-92; Human Resources Mgmt Serv, assoc dir, 1992-94; USDA, Natural Resources Conserv Serv, admin off, SE Region, 1994-. **Orgs:** Nat Orgn Prof NRCS Employees; Int Personnel Mgt Asn. **Home Addr:** 62 Winward Way SE, Smyrna, GA 30082, **Home Phone:** (770)435-2502. **Business Addr:** Administrative Officer Southeast Region, USDA Natural Resources Conservation Services, 1720 Peachtree Rd NW Suite 446N, Atlanta, GA 30309.

### MARBURY, STEPHON XAVIER
Basketball player. **Personal:** Born Feb 20, 1977, Brooklyn, NY; son of Don (deceased) and Mabel; married La Tasha; children: Stephanie, Xaviera & Stephon Jr. **Educ:** Ga Inst Technol, attended 1996. **Career:** Minn Timberwolves, pt guard, 1996-99; NJ Nets, pt guard, 1999-2001; Phoenix Suns, pt guard, 2001-04; New York Knicks, pt guard, 2004-09; Boston Celtics, pt guard, 2009; Shanxi Zhongyu Brave Dragons, 2010; Foshan Dralions, 2010-11; Beijing Ducks, Chinese Basketball Asn, 2011-. **Honors/Awds:** Gold Medal, FIBA Americas U18 Championship, 1994; All Rookie team, Nat Basketball Asn, 1997; All Nat Basketball Asn Third Team, 2000, 2003; Hometown Hero Award, 2001; NBA's most underrated player, 2003-04; NBA Community Assist of the Month Award, 2004; Bronze Medal, Olympic, 2004; All-Star Game MVP, Chinese Basketball Asn, 2010; Champion, Chinese Basketball Asn, 2012; All-Star, Chinese Basketball Asn, 2012; Most Valuable Player Award, 2014; Nat High School Player of the Year, Parade Mag. **Special Achievements:** First round pick, No 4, NBA Draft, 1996; listed in "Good Guys in Sports," Sporting News, 2005. Co-Author: The Adventures of Young Starbury: Practice Makes Perfect, 2007. 5th American basketball player to receive a Chinese green card. **Home Addr:** 4 Sycamore Ct, Purchase, NY 10577-1102. **Business Addr:** Professional Basketball Player, Beijing Ducks.

### MARCHAND, INGA FUNG (FOXY BROWN)
Rap musician. **Personal:** Born Sep 6, 1978, Brooklyn, NY; daughter of Judith. **Career:** Solo Albums: Ill Na Na, 1996; Chyna Doll, 1998; Broken Silence, 2001; Black Roses, 2005; Group Albums: The Firm, 1997; Songs: "Get Me Home", 1996; "I'll Be", 1997; "Hot Spot", 1999; "B.K. Anthem", 2001; "Ill Na Na 2: The Fever", 2002; "Too Much For Me", 2003; "I Need a Man", 2003; "Come Fly With Me", 2005; "Brooklyn's Don Diva", 2007; Films: Rush Hour 2, 2001; Marci X, 2003; Cradle 2 the Grave, 2003; The 40 Year Old Virgin, 2005; The Firm, group mem; Universal Music Group, currently; Def Jam Rec, currently. **Special Achievements:** Rapped on "I Shot Ya", with LL Cool J; "Touch Me, Tease Me", with Case; "No One Else", with Total, lil' Kim, and Da Brat; "You're Makin' Me High", with Toni Braxton. **Business Addr:** Rapper, Universal Music Group, 1755 Broadway Lobby, New York, NY 10019-3743, **Business Phone:** (212)841-8000.

### MARCHAND, MELANIE ANNETTE
Chemical engineer, chief executive officer. **Personal:** Born Mar 12, 1962, New Orleans, LA; daughter of Edward Janvier and Sandra Baker. **Educ:** Tulane Univ, New Orleans, La, BS, chem engineering, l984; Wharton Sch Bus Univ Pa, MBA, 1991. **Career:** Union Carbide Corp, Taft, La, prod, efficiency eng, l984-86; Air Prods & Chem Inc, New Orleans, La, process eng, l986-87; Air Prods & Chem Inc, Allentown, PA, process eng; corp planning, prod mgt, tech sales & mkt mgt; Sisters Shape Fitness Consult, founder, pres & chief exec officer, currently. **Orgs:** La Engineering Soc; Soc Women Engrs, l988-90; Asn Integrated Mgt; Minority Community Adv Bd Muhlenberg Col, l989; fitness consult, Philadelphia Black Women's Health Proj Black Men; Founder, SIS Fitness. **Honors/Awds:** Appreciation Award for Leadership & Dedication, Union Carbide Corp Family Safety & Health Comm, l985; Quality Recognition Variable Compensation Award, Air Products & Chem Inc, 1989. **Home Addr:** 7416 Scottsdale Dr, New Orleans, LA 70127, **Home Phone:** (504)241-4146. **Business Addr:** President, Chief Executive Officer, Sisters In Shape Inc, 1320 Somerville Ave, Philadelphia, PA 19141, **Business Phone:** (215)457-8663.

### MARCHANT, ANN WALKER
Government official, chief executive officer. **Personal:** children: 1. **Educ:** Sarah Lawrence Col. **Career:** Burson Marsteller, staff commun; ImagiNations SA, Paris, partner & sr pub rels dir; White House, spec asst pres, dir res & spec proj commun pres; Weber Shandwick Int, exec vpres & dir global bus develop; Walker Marchant Group, founder & ceo, currently. **Orgs:** Bd dir, Washington Ballet; bd dir, Decatur House Nat Hist Trust & Preservation; bd visitors, Howard Univ; trustee, George Wash Univ; exec comt, Knock Out Abuse. **Home Addr:** , Washington, DC. **Business Addr:** Founder, Chief Executive Officer, Walker Marchant Group, 1050 17th St NW Suite 1200, Washington, DC 20036, **Business Phone:** (202)466-6040.

### MARDENBOROUGH, LESLIE A.
Consultant, executive, executive director. **Personal:** Born Mar 25, 1948, Bronx, NY; daughter of Victor E and Dorothy Richards; children: Adina N, Keith A Clark & Kevin A Clark. **Educ:** Albright Col, AB, 1968, PhD, 1990; Simmons Col Grad Sch Mgt, prog develop execs, 1989. **Career:** Brooklyn Col, career counr, 1969-73; Wildcat Serv Corp, vpres opers, 1978; firms mag group, group personnel dir; New Life Group Inc, consult, Career Ctr, exec dir, 1979-81; NY Times Co, proj mgr, human resources, 1981-84, dir employee rels, 1984-86, dir personnel, 1986-87, dir corp personnel, 1987-90, vpres human resources, 1990; The Times Co, career press; Mardenborough Assoc, mgt consult & prin, currently. **Orgs:** Bd mem, Human Resource Planners Asn, 1982-, 1991; bd mem & mem officer, NY Human Resource Planners, 1986-88; NAA Employee Rels Comn, 1988-; Newspape rPersonnel Rels Assn, 1988-; bd dir, NY Brd Trade, 1989-92; bd dir, Westchester Residential Opportunities, 1989-; bd dir, Westchester Housing Fund, 1991-94; bd dir, United Neighborhood Houses, 1991-; pres, Bd Dirs Sch Alumnae Assn, 1996-; Gen Mgt Adv Brd, Am Press Inst; New Rochelle Pub Libr Found; bd mem, bd trustee, Albright Col. **Honors/Awds:** Black Achievers in Industries, YMCA, Harlem, 1986; Hon Doctorate, Albright Col, 1990; Rappaport Alumni Achievement Award, Simmons Col GSM, 1992. **Special Achievements:** Hundred of the Best and Brightest Black Women in Corporate America, Ebony Mag, 1990. **Business Addr:** Principal, Management Consultant, Mardenborough Associates, 256 Hamilton Ave, New Rochelle, NY 10802, **Business Phone:** (914)632-0589.

### MARIEL, SERAFIN U (SERAFIN UWALDO MARIEL)
Banker, chief executive officer, president (organization). **Personal:** Born Nov 14, 1943, Spanish Harlem, NY; married Milagros Lora; children: Laura Marie. **Educ:** Rutgers Univ, Stonier Grad Sch Banking. **Career:** Bankers Trust, teller, 1965, br mgr, regional dir; New York Nat Bank, pres & chief exec officer, 1982-05, Bus Develop & Community Responsibility. **Orgs:** Chmn, New York Yankees Stadium Community Benefits Fund Inc; chmn, Bronx Overall Econ Develop Corp; treas, Nat Minority Supplier Develop Coun; founder, chmn, bd mem emer, Nat Hisp Bus Group, currently; bd mem, Cent Pk Conservancy; bd mem, Ad Hoc Comt Historically Underutilized Businesses; bd mem, Early Steps; bd mem, Promesa Found; bd mem, United Way New York; bd mem, Upper Manhattan Empowerment Zone; vpres, Latin Am group Bankers Trust Int Dept; Triad Capital Corp, pres & chief operating officer. **Honors/Awds:** Honorary Doctorate, Univ New York; Community Banking Award; Paul Harris, Bronx econ; The Spirit of the Bronx, S Bronx Overall Econ Develop Corp, 2010. **Busi-**

ness Addr: Founder, New York National Bank, 960 Southern Blvd, Bronx, NY 10458, **Business Phone:** (212)589-5000.

### MARINER, JONATHAN D.

Executive. **Personal:** Born Jan 1, 1954; married Mildred; children: Brian, Matthew & Phillip. **Educ:** Univ Va, BS, acct; Harvard Bus Sch, MBA; CPA. **Career:** MCI Communs, Wash, DC, sr financial analyst; Fla Marlins Baseball Club, Miami, exec vpres & chief financial officer, 1992-2000; Tribune CNLBC LLC, chief financial officer & exec vpres finance; Marlins Ballpark Develop Corp, pres; Chicago Nat League Ball Club LLC, chief financial officer & exec vpres finance; The New York Metrop Baseball Club Inc, chief financial officer; Houston Astros LLC, exec vpres finance; Charter Schs USA, exec vpres & chief operating officer, 2000-02; Maj League Baseball & MLB Advan Media LP, New York, NY, chief operating officer, sr vpres & chief financial officer, 2002-, exec vpres finance, currently; Baseball Assistance Team Inc, treas; BankAtlantic Bancorp, dir; Ryan, Beck & Co, bd dir. **Orgs:** Chmn, Broward Community Col Found Bd; adv bd, Univ Va McIntire Sch Com; adv bd, Stanford Parents' Adv Bd; adv bd, Pine Crest Sch Ft Lauderdale; mem exec comt, Exec Comt Greater Miami Chamber Com; bd dir, United Way Greater Miami; Beacon Coun; dir, BBX Capital Corp, 2001-; dir, Factory Mutual Ins Co; dir, Harvard Bus Sch Club Greater New York Inc. **Business Addr:** Senior Vice President and Chief Financial Officer, Executive Vice President Finance, Major League Baseball, 75 9th Ave 5th Fl, New York, NY 10011, **Business Phone:** (212)485-3444.

### MARION, BROCK ELLIOT

Football player, football coach. **Personal:** Born Jun 11, 1970, Bakersfield, CA; son of Jerry; married Keri; children: Brianna, Olivia & Brock Jr. **Educ:** Univ Nev, Reno, grad. **Career:** Football player (retired) football coach; Dallas Cowboys, 1993, defensive back, 1994, free safety, 1995-97; Miami Dolphins, free safety, 1998, 2001-03, safety, 1999; Detroit Lions, free safety, 2004; St. John Lutheran High Sch, head coach, 2013. **Orgs:** Founder, Brock Marion Found; Cystic Fibrosis Found. **Honors/Awds:** Super Bowl champion, XXVIII, XXX; All-Pro, 2000; Pro Bowl selection, 2000, 2002, 2003; Interception Return Yards Leader, Nat Football League, 2001; Nevada Athletics Hall of Fame, 2006. **Special Achievements:** TV Series: "ESPN SportsCentury ", 2004; Ranked fourth on Dolphins with 100 tackles and had three interceptions, eight passes defensed and two forced fumbles in 2003; Participated in Var Social Service Program.

### MARION, FRED DONALD

Football player, restaurateur. **Personal:** Born Jan 2, 1959, Gainesville, FL; married Anne; children: Monica Nicole, Natasha Monigue, Alycia Dinita & Fred Donald. **Educ:** Univ Miami, Fl, Bus Mgt. **Career:** Football player (retired), restaurant owner; Miami Hurricanes football team, 1978-81; Am col, defensive back; Nat Football League, defensive back, 1980-90; Pro Bowler; New Eng Patriots, safety, 1982-83, free safety, 1984-91; Damons franchise restaurants, owner, currently. **Honors/Awds:** Post-season play, 1985: AFC Championship Game, NFL Championship Game, Pro Bowl; Ed Block Courage Award. **Business Addr:** Owner, Damon's Franchise Restaurants, Gainesville, FL 32608.

### MARION, DR. PHILLIP JORDAN

Physician. **Personal:** Born May 14, 1958, Albany, NY; son of G W and Marie; married Tanya C Lumpkins. **Educ:** State Univ NY Purchase, BA, 1981; NY Univ Sch Med, MD, 1985; NY Univ, MS, 1989; George Wash Univ, MPH, 1993. **Career:** NY Univ, resident, 1985-86, resident, 1986-89; Rusk Ist Rehab Med, chief resident, 1989; Howard Univ Sch Med, asst prof; Nat Rehab Hospl, asst med dir, 1990-95, Ambulatory Serv, med dir, 1990-95; Health Policy Fel, Off Sen Orrin G Hatch; Senate Judiciary Comt, Health Policy Fel; Capital Med Serv, pres, chief exec officer; George Wash Univ Sch Med & Health Sci, asst prof; George Wash Med Fac Assocs, assoc clin prof phys med & rehab dir phys med & rehab, currently. **Orgs:** Exec, Am Col Physician; fel Am Acad Phys Med & Rehab, 1990; Concerned blk Men, 1992-95; Nat Mentorship Prog; Am ment asn; Asn Acad Physiatrists; Health Policy Fel Robert Wood Johnson, 1994-95; Am Acad Electrodiagnostic Med. **Home Addr:** 3620 Cumberland St NW, Washington, DC 20008, **Home Phone:** (202)966-1606. **Business Addr:** President, Director, George Washington Medical Faculty Associates, 2021 K St NW, Washington, DC 20006, **Business Phone:** (202)741-3250.

### MARIUS, DR. KENNETH ANTHONY

Physician. **Personal:** Born Feb 22, 1937, New York, NY; son of Edwin and Aldith; married Esther Bailey; children: Kenneth Jr & Robert. **Educ:** Howard Univ, BSEE, 1960; NJ Inst Technol, MS, 1965; Howard Univ Col Med, MD, 1970. **Career:** Community Coop Corp, pres, 1972; Tricities Progress Women, consult, 1972; NJ Col Med & Dent, clin prof, 1976-; pvt practr. **Orgs:** Essex Co Med Soc; Consult City Newark; Orange Bd Educ; med dir, team physician, Weeguanic HS; speaker, Essex Co Heart Asn; Alpha Omega Alpha Med Hon Soc; Tau Beta Pi Eng Hon Soc; deleg, Nat Med Asn, 1981-; adv bd, Sickle Cell Found, 1983-; pres, N Jersey Med Soc, NJ Med Soc, 1984. **Honors/Awds:** Distinguished Service Award, Sports Physician, Weequahic, 1983-86; Distinguished Service Award, Tricities Chamber Com, 1985; Board Of Concerned Citizens Award, 1986; Award, Col Med & Dent NJ, 1992. **Home Addr:** 1326 Marcella Dr, Union, NJ 07083, **Home Phone:** (908)964-8164. **Business Addr:** 202 Clinton Ave, Newark, NJ 07108, **Business Phone:** (973)824-8201.

### MARK, RICHARD J.

Chief executive officer. **Educ:** Iowa State Univ, BS, 1977; Nat Louis Univ, MS, bus mgt. **Career:** Collinsville, high sch football coach & spec educ teacher; State Ill, asst to Mayor, customer serv Ill Power; St Clair Co Inter govt Grants Dept, exec dir; St Mary's Hosp, sr vpres & chief oper officer, pres & chief exec officer, 1994-2002; Ancilla Syst, sr vpres; Ameren Serv, vpres customer serv, 2002-03, vpres govt policy, econ develop & community rels, 2003-05; Ameren UE, sr vpres, 2002-. **Orgs:** Chmn Financial Oversight Panel, E St. Louis Sch Dist 189, 1994; bd dir, E St Louis Nat Asn Advan Colored People; bd dir, Maj Case Squad; bd dir, Belleville Dioceses Cath Community Found; bd dir, St Louis, 2004; St Clair Co Sheriffs Dept Merit Comn. **Business Addr:** President, Chief Executive Officer, Ameren Services, PO Box 66884, St. Louis, MO 63166-6884.

### MARKHAM, HOUSTON, JR.

Educator, football coach. **Personal:** Born Dec 20, 1942, Brookhaven, MS; son of Houston Sr and Ethel Tanner; married Annie Davis; children: Yolanda & Houston III. **Educ:** Alcorn State Univ, Lorman, BS, phys educ, 1965; Tenn State Univ, Nashville, TN, MS, 1971. **Career:** Educator, football coach (retired); Vicksburg High Sch, Vicksburg, Miss, head football coach, 1967-75; Jackson State Univ, Jackson, Miss, asst football coach, 1975-87; Ala State Univ, Montgomery, Ala, head football coach, 1987. **Home Addr:** 3102 Bankhead Ave, Montgomery, AL 36106-2446, **Home Phone:** (205)262-6177.

### MARKS, DR. JOHN

Mayor, educator, government official. **Personal:** married Jane Awkard; children: John IV. **Educ:** Fla State Univ Sch Bus, BS, 1969; Fla State Univ Col Law, JD, 1972. **Career:** Katz, Kutter PA; Knowles, Marks & Randolph, Pa; Tallahassee Off Adorno & Yoss, managing partner; chmn, Fla Pub Serv Comn, 1979-81; Fla State Univ Col Law, adj prof; charter pres, Fla League Mayors, 2005-07; City Tallahassee, mayor, 2003-. **Orgs:** Chmn, admin Law Judge, Fla Pub Serv Comn, 1979; trustee, Collins Ctr Bd, Fla State Univ; fac mem, Nat Asn Regulatory Utility Comnrs; Am, Nat, Fla &Tallahassee Bar; Tallahassee Barristers Asn; Am Law Inst; Fla Bars Local Gov & Admin Law Sect; bd dir, Fringe Benefits Mgt Co; bd dir, Fla League Cities; bd dir, Tallahassee Econ Develop Coun; bd dir, Tallahassee & Leon County Civic Ctr Authority; bd dir, Sunshine State Gov Financing Comn; bd dir, Econ Club Fla; Energy & Arts & Cult Comt; life mem, Nat Asn Advan Colored People; admin law judge, Fed Pub Utility Regulatory Policies Act; Omega Psi Phi Fraternity; bd dir, Tallahassee Urban League; Nat Bar Asn; pres, Fla League Cities, 2009-10. **Home Addr:** 3713 Bobbin Brk E, Tallahassee, FL 32312, **Home Phone:** (850)893-1700. **Business Addr:** Mayor, City of Tallahassee, 300 S Adams St, Tallahassee, FL 32301, **Business Phone:** (850)891-0000.

### MARKS, KENNETH HICKS, JR.

Lawyer. **Personal:** Born Sep 15, 1951, Lawrenceville, VA; son of Kenneth H Sr and Nethel H; married Fe Morales; children: Kenisha Maria Morales. **Educ:** Columbia Col, BA, psychol, 1974; Columbia Univ Sch Law, JD, 1977. **Career:** Shearman & Sterling, assoc, 1977-80; Webster & Sheffield, assoc, 1980-84; Wickwire, Gavin & Gibbs PC, partner, 1984-89; Ginsburg, Feldman & Bress, partner, 1989-91; Alexander, Bearden, Hairstonetal, 1991-97; Reid & Priest LLP, coun, 1997-98; Columbia Energy Group, asst gen coun, 1998-2000; Exostar LLC, secy & gen coun, 2001-.. **Orgs:** Chair pub rels comt, Hisp Bar Asn DC, 1983-85, bd dir, 1984-85; bd dir, Ayuda Inc, 1984-89; pub arbitrator, Munic Securities Rulemaking Bd, 1986-89; planning & zoning comt, Reston Community Asn, 1986-91; bd dir, Turnbridge Cluster Asn, 1987-90, pres, 1989-90; DC Bar Asn Elections Comt, 1988-91; co-vice chair, Pub Fin Comt Sect Urban, State & Local Govt Law, 1993-96; fel Am Bar Found, 1993-; Nat Bar Asn; Hisp Nat Bar Asn; NY Bar Asn; Nat Asn Bond Lawyers; Japan Soc; Am Bar Asn; bd dir, Hisp Bar Asn Dc; Minority Partners Majority-Owned Law Firms. **Home Addr:** 11515 Turnbridge Lane, Reston, VA 20194-1220, **Home Phone:** (703)478-0336. **Business Addr:** General Counsel, Exostar LLC, 13241 Woodland Pk Rd Suite 400, Herndon, VA 20171, **Business Phone:** (703)561-0500.

### MARKS, LEE OTIS

Football player, football coach, educator. **Personal:** Born Nov 17, 1944, Carthage, AR; married Karen Vaughn; children: Cynthia Lynne, Valerie Jeanne & Allison Marie. **Educ:** Sioux Falls Col, BA, 1966; Univ Ill, Urbana-Champaign, MS, 1974. **Career:** Player (retired) coach, co-capt; MVP football Sioux Falls Col, 1965; Lincoln Pk Elem Sch, teacher, 1966-67; Madison Mustang, football player, 1966-67; Rockford Guilford High Sch, Phys Educ teacher, head track coach, asst football coach, 1967-; Rockford Rams, football player, 1969-70. **Orgs:** SFC Letterman Club Sioux Falls Col Alumni Asn, 1966; prog dir, BT Wash Comm Cent, 1966-70; exec bd dir, Rockford Educ Asn, 1971-73; Ill Human Rels Commn, 1971-73; bd dir, Rockford Black Educrs Asn, 1971-73; deleg, Nat Educ Asn Conv, 1971; bd dir, Cent Terr Coop, 1972; Rockford Educ Asn; Ill Educ Asn; Nat Educ Asn; Ill Health Phys Educ & Recreation Asn; Ill Coaches Asn; Nat Letterman Asn; Rockford Coaches Asn; Nat Educ Asn Black Caucus; Allen Chapel AME Church. **Honors/Awds:** Teacher of the Year, Guilford High Sch Stud Body, 1971; Coach Inductee, Sports Hall of Fame, Annual Service Award, Rockford Guilford High Sch. **Home Addr:** 5961 Twin Orchard Dr, Rockford, IL 61114-5540, **Home Phone:** (815)654-8720.

### MARKS, ROSE M.

Librarian. **Personal:** Born Mar 17, 1938, Chicago, IL; children: Deborah & Charles. **Educ:** Sacramento City Col, attended 1958; Sacramento State Univ. **Career:** Sacramento City Co Libr, libr clerk, 1961-77; Martin Luther King Jr Libr; Oak Pk Br Libr, br supvr. **Orgs:** Bd dir, KVIE Educ TV; bd dir, Sacramento Reg Arts Coun; secy, Oak Pk Comn Theatre; mgr band, co-mgr singing group, Sacramento Black Women's United Front; vpres, Sacramento City Employ Asn; pres, Sacramento City Libr Asn. **Home Addr:** 7513 Schreiner St, Sacramento, CA 95822.

### MARQUEZ, DR. CAMILO RAOUL

Physician. **Personal:** Born Feb 25, 1942, New York, NY; son of Cecil and Gloria. **Educ:** Colby Col, AB, 1963; Howard Univ Sch Med, MD, 1976. **Career:** St Vincent's Hosp, resident psychiat, internship, 1977-79, chief resident, 1978-79; Manhattan Psychiat Ctr, res psychiatrist, 1979-80; Harlem Hosp, staff psychiatrist, 1980-82, attend physician div child & adolescent psychiat, 1988-92; N Gen Hosp, dir inpatient psychiat, 1982-84; St Univ NY, Health Sci Ctr, Brooklyn, asst instr; Columbia Univ, Col Physicians & Surgeons, asst clin prof psychiat, 1988-92. **Orgs:** Am Psychiat Asn, 1978-; Black Psychiatrists Am, 1979-; bd trustee, Wooster Sch, 1986-92; Am Acad Child & Adolescent Psychiat, 1986-; co-chmn, Black Health Professionals Sch Based Health & Sex Educ Progs, 1986-88; bd trustee, C's Annex, 1998-. **Honors/Awds:** Falk Fel, Am Psychiat Asn, 1978-79. **Special Achievements:** Diagnosis of Manic Depressive Illness in Blacks, Comprehensive Psychiatry, Vol 26, No 4 1985. **Home Addr:** 139 Fawn Hill Rd, Phoenicia, NY 12464-0361, **Home Phone:** (845)688-2151.

**MARR, CARMEL CARRINGTON.** **See Obituaries Section.**

### MARRETT, DR. CORA BAGLEY

Educator. **Personal:** Born Jun 15, 1942, Kenbridge, VA; daughter of Horace S Bagley and Clorann Boswell Bagley; married Louis E. **Educ:** Va Union Univ, BA, sociol, 1963; Univ Wis, MA, sociol, 1965, PhD, sociol, 1968. **Career:** Univ NC, Chapel Hill, asst prof, 1968-69; Western Mich Univ, asst prof, assoc prof, 1969-74; Ctr Advan Study, fel, 1976-77; Univ Mass, provost, 1997-2001; Univ Wis, assoc prof, prof, sr vpres acad affairs, 2001-. **Orgs:** Nat Acad Sci, 1973-74; bd govs, Argonne Nat Lab, 1982-89, 1996-; bdtrustee, Ctr Adv Study Behav Sci, 1983-89; asst dir, Social, Behav, and Econ Sci, 1992-96; fel Am Acad Arts & Sci, 1998; fel AAAS; asst dir, Nat Sci Found, Educ & Human Resources, 2007-2009, sr advisor, actg dep dir, dep dir, 2009-10, actg dir, 2010-. **Home Addr:** 7517 Farmington Way, Madison, WI 53717, **Home Phone:** (608)827-5388. **Business Addr:** Acting Director, National Science Foundation, 4201 Wilson Blvd, Arlington, VA 22230, **Business Phone:** (703)292-5111.

### MARRIOTT, MICHEL

Writer. **Personal:** Born Mar 8, 1954. **Educ:** Morehead State Univ, BA, 1976; Northwestern Univ, Medill Sch Jour, MA, 1978; Harvard Univ, attended 2002. **Career:** Columbia Univ Grad Sch Jour, adj prof; City Col, New York, prof jour; Marion Chronicle-Tribune, reporter; The New York Times, reporter, 1987-94; Newsweek Mag, New York, gen ed, 1994; Film: Nj Dr, co-writer, 1995; The Skull Cage Key, Agate Bolden, Auth, 2008; Frederick Douglass Creative Arts Ctr, head workshop; Baruch Col, Prof, 2007-09; New York Times, staff writer, currently. **Honors/Awds:** Nieman fel, 2002. **Business Addr:** Staff Writer, New York Times, 229 W 43rd St, New York, NY 10036, **Business Phone:** (212)556-1234.

### MARRIOTT, DR. SALIMA SILER

Legislator. **Personal:** Born Dec 5, 1940, Baltimore, MD; daughter of Cordie Ayers Siler and Jesse James Siler; married David Small; children: Terrez Siler Marriott Thompson & Patrice Kenyatta Siler. **Educ:** Morgan State Univ, BS, 1964; Univ Md, MSW, 1972; Howard Univ, DSW, 1988. **Career:** Baltimore City Pub Schs, teacher, 1964-65; Woman Power, co-ed; Dept Social Serv, NY, social worker, 1965-68; Dept Social Serv, Baltimore, social worker, 1968-72; Morgan State Univ, Baltimore, MD, instr, 1972-90, asst prof, 1972-96, chairperson, 1981-87; Md Gen Assembly, deleg, 1991-2007; Fleming Fel, 1995; Cantonsville Community Col, adj fac, 1998-99; Hood Col, 1999-2000; Foreign Policy Inst, fel, 2001; Bowie State Col, vis lectr, 2001-03; Community & Econ Develop, Baltimore City, dep mayor, 2006-10. **Orgs:** Dem State Cent Comt, 1987-90; chair, Pk Heights Develop Corp, 1988-92; founding mem & vpres, African-Am Women Caucus, 1982-85; vice chmn, Md Chap Nat Rainbow Coalition, 1988-89; Delta Sigma Theta Sorority Inc, 1989-, chair, 1993-95; Women Legislators Md, 1991-2007; Nat Black Caucus State Legislators, 1991-2007, regional chair, 1994-98; Legis Black Caucus Md, 1991-07; Ways & Means Comt, 1991-2007; chair, Nat Black Women's Health Proj, 1993; Joint Comt Mgt Pub Funds, 1993-2007; Joint Legis Workgroup Community Col Financing, 1994-95; secy, Nat Rainbow Coalition, 1994-96; Nat Am Advan Colored People; vice chair, Md Legis Black Caucus, 1994-95; Women Legislators; regional chair, Nat Black Caucus State Legislators, 1994-; Task Force Educ Assts & Paraprofessionals Pub Schs Md, 1996; trustee, Bethel AME Church, 1997-; trustee, African Methodist Episcopal Church, 1997-2004; vice chair, Baltimore Substance Abuse Systs Bd, 1998-; Task Force Pub Charter Schs, 1998; Effectiveness Comt Task Force to Study Increasing Availability Substance Abuse Progs, 1998-2001; vice-chair, Baltimore City Drug & Alcohol Abuse Coun, 1998-2007; human serv & welfare comt, Nat Conf State Legislatures, 1998-2007; chair, Baltimore City Deleg, 1999-2007; Spec Comt Higher Educ Affordability & Accessibility, 2003-04; chair, Joint Comt C, Youth & Families, 2003-07; chair, Citywide Re-entry & Re-integration Steering Comt, Baltimore City, 2004-07; Adv Coun C, 2005-07; Drug & Alcohol Abuse Coun, Baltimore City, 2006-08; House Delegates, 1991-2007. **Honors/Awds:** Workshop Convener, United Nation's Decade Women Conf, 1985; Outstanding Teacher Award, Dept Social Work & Ment Health, Morgan State Univ, 1988; Baltimore's Black Women of Courage Exhibit, 1988; Outstanding Teacher Award, Dept Social Work & Ment Health, Morgan State Univ, 1990; African American Humanitarian Award, 1991; Senator Verda Welcome Political Award, 1992; Perseverance Award, Consortium of Doctors, 1992; Delegate of the Year, Mid Atlantic Div Am Asn Marriage & Family Therapist, 1993; Sarah's Circle Award, Col Notre Dame, MD, 1994; National Legacy Award, Delta Sigma Theta Sorority, 1994; Labor Roundtable Award, Nat Black Caucus of State Legislators, 1999; Chairman Meritorious Award, Md Legislative Black Caucus, 2000; Cor Women Policy Studies Foreign Policy Inst, 2001; Bold Dreamer Award, Quixote Ctr Justice USA, 2002; Pacesetters Award, Women Legislators Lobby, 2003; Nat Coalition Abolish Death Penalty's Abolition Year, 2003; Abolitionist of the Year Award, Nat Coalition to Abolish the Death Penalty, 2003. Woman of the Year, Zonta Int, 2005. **Special Achievements:** Editor of US Policy Toward Southern Africa, 1984. **Home Addr:** 4515 Homer Ave, Baltimore, MD 21215, **Home Phone:** (410)664-4241.

### MARROW, TARA CENTEIO

Administrator, editor. **Personal:** daughter of John Centeio and Marlene; married Gino L; children: Ilyse April. **Educ:** Spellman Col, GA, attended 1996. **Career:** Mahogany card line, writer, currently; Hallmark Cards Inc, writer, ed dir, vpres creative, writing & ed, currently. **Business Addr:** Vice President of Creative, Hallmark Cards Inc, 2501 McGee St, Kansas City, MO 64108, **Business Phone:** (816)274-5111.

### MARROW, TRACY LAUREN

Actor, rap musician. **Personal:** Born Feb 16, 1958, Newark, NJ; son of Alice and Solomon; married Darlene Ortiz; married Coco Austin; children: Tracy Jr & Letesha. **Career:** Rapper, Actor, currently; Rapper, recs include: "The Coldest Rap", 1982; Rhyme Pays, 1987; Power,

1988; Colors, motion picture soundtrack, 1988; The Iceberg & Freedom of Speech Jack Hustler, 1991; O G-OriginalGangster, 1991; Body Count, 1992; Home Invasion, 1993; Films: Breakin', 1984; New Jack City, 1991, Ricochet, 1992; Trespass, 1993; Surviving The Game, 1994; Johnny Mnemonic, 1995; Judgement Day, 1999; The Heist, 1999; Leprechaun in the Hood, 2000; 3000 Miles to Gracel &, 2001; Lexie, 2004; Tracks, 2005, Copy That, 2006; Apartment 309, 2007; BelzerVizion, 2007; Tommy and the Cool Mule, 2009; The Other Guys, 2010; The Passions of Jesus Christ, 2012; Santorini Blue, 2013; Assaulted: Civil Rights Under Fire, 2013; Crossed the Line, exec producer, 2014; The Ghetto, 2015. TV Series: New York Undercover, 1994-98; "Players", 1997-98, writer; "Law & Order: Special Victims Unit", 2000-; "Beyond Tough", co-exec producer & host, 2004; "Smoke Out Festival", 2003 & 2005; "Law & Order", 2005; "The Magic 7", 2006 & 2009, composer, 2009; "Law & Order: Special Victims Unit", 2006 & 2008; "Outside", 2007; "Burned", 2007; Good Hair, 2009; Tommy & the Cool Mule, 2009; The Other Guys, 2010; Goat, 2011; "30 Rock", 2011-13; Something from Nothing, 2012. Music Albums: Gangsta Rap, 2006; Coco's 2007 Exotics Calendar DVD, cinematographer, 2007; Murder 4 Hire, 2006; Urban Legends, 2008; Manslaughter, 2014; "Chicago P.D.", 2015-15. Producer: Ice-T presents: 25 to life, exec producer, 2008; CoCo SSX Tribute Issue DVD, exec producer, 2008; 25 to Life: Ice T Presents, exec producer, 2008; Coco California Girl DVD Nicole Austin, exec producer, 2008; "The Peacemaker", exec producer, 2010; Ice Loves Coco, exec producer, 2011-13; Planet Rock: The Story of Hip-Hop and the Crack Generation, doc, exec producer, 2011; Something From Nothing: The Art Of Rap, doc, exec producer, dir, 2012; Iceberg Slim: Portrait of a Pimp, exec producer, doc, 2012; "Ice & Coco", exec producer, 2015. **Home Addr:** Priority Records, 6430 W Sunset Blvd, Hollywood, CA 90028. **Business Addr:** Rapper, Actor, c/o Susan Blond Inc, 250 W 57th St Suite 622, New York, NY 16107.

## MARROW-MOORING, BARBARA A.

Government official, executive director. **Personal:** Born May 4, 1945, Trenton, NJ; married Kelly Daniel; children: Carla, Paula, Connie, Venessa Culbreth, Kelly D Mooring Jr, Anthony Mooring & Shawn Mooring. **Educ:** Mercer County Community Col, AA, social sci & humanities, 1973; Trenton State Col, BS, elem educ, 1975. **Career:** Government official, executive director (retired); Educ Testing Serv, Princeton, NJ, div mgr, 1982-83, asst vpres, 1983-86, field serv rep, 1982-89; Trenton Bd Educ, teacher, 1983-88; NJ Gen Assembly, Trenton, NJ, clerk, 1986-87; NJ Lottery, Trenton, NJ, exec dir, 1987. **Orgs:** Pres, Nat Asn Univ Women, 1977-79; vpres, Lawrence Township Sch Bd, 1978-87; founder, past pres, Coalition 100 Black Republicans; treas, Mercer County Improv Authority, 1983-88; trustee, Rider Col, 1987-; Capital City Redevelopment Corp, 1987-; NJ Job Training Coord Coun, 1987-89; trustee, Urban League Metrop Trenton Inc, 1988-. **Honors/Awds:** Outstanding Achievement Award, NJ State Fedn Colored Women's Clubs Inc, 1986; Community Service Award, BAC Publ Co, 1988; Women of Achievement Award, NJ Fedn Bus & Prof Women Inc, 1989. **Home Addr:** 571 Bellevue Ave, Trenton, NJ 08625, **Home Phone:** (609)396-6301.

## MARRS, DR. STELLA

Writer, activist, singer. **Personal:** Born Mar 22, 1932; daughter of Theodore and Mary; children: Lynda, Joseph, Walter, Maria-Tita, Jude & Nellie. **Educ:** Hunter Col; St Thomas Aquinas Col, PhD, humanities. **Career:** Lional Hampton Orchestra, vocalist, 1969-73; TV spec Toots Thielmans, 1977; recorded album Belg Dicovers Stella Marrs, 1977; toured US, Australia, Europe, jazz artist; Stella Marrs Cable TV Show, hosted; WRVR Radio, jazz DJ; WNJR, bright moments jazz; Jazz Festivals Belg, France, Amsterdam, Holland; Martin Luther King Multi-Purpose Ctr Inc, exec dir & chief exec officer; Rockland County's Human Rights Comn, community liaison specialist, 2006-12. **Orgs:** Int Jazz Fed; contrib ed, African Am Class Music/Jazz Publ; Jazzat Home Club, 1972, Westchester Jazz Soc, 1975, Bi-Centennial Jazz Citation Manhattan Boro Pres, 1976; Rockland County Womens Issues, 1986; adv comn, Coop Exten 4H Club, 1986; Crystal Run Environ Ctr Adv Bd, 1986; Spring Valley Nat Asn Advan Colored People Educ Comn, 1987; adv coun, Village Spring Valley Community Develop Adv Coun, 1987; Rotary Int, 1989; bd mem, Ramapo Housing Authority, 1988; Jazz Fed Am Coalition Jazz Musicians Health &Welfare; Jazz Interactions Audience Develop; treas, People to People; bd dir, Leadership Rockland Inc; adv bd, Jamaican civic & cult asn rockland, 2007-08; bd mem, Legal Aid Soc Rockland County Inc; adv bd mem, Rockland Community Found; bd mem, Martin Luther King Multi Purpose Ctr. **Honors/Awds:** Woman of the Year, Kennedy Ctr, Harlem, 1976; Consortium of Jazz Artists Award of Excellence, 1981; Certificate of Excellence, A proud Heritage; St Paul Honorary Black Belt; Certificate of Appreciation, 1989; Certificate of Appreciation, Rockland County Dept Soc Serv, 1989; Distinguished Service Award, County Rockland, 1992; Distinguished Service Award, Senator Joseph R Holland, 1993; Citation, NY State Assembly, 1994; Positive Image Award, Delta Sigma Theta, Rockland County Alumni chap, 1997; Al Dykstra Memorial Award, 1998; Jan 19, 1999 declared Dr Stella Marrs Day, Rockland County; Outstanding Female Advocate Activist, Spring Valley NAACP, 2000; Joseph R Bernstein Memorial Award, Mental Health Asn Rockland County, 2000; Humanitarian Award, Rockland Co Ladies & Mens Club, 2000; Dr Stella Mars scholar prog established, 2000; Certificate of Recognition, Town Orangetown, 2000; Certificate of Merit, NY State Assembly, 2000; Cert Spec Congressional Recognition, 2000; Image Award, NAACP, Nyack chap, 2003; DHum, St Thomas Aquinas Col. **Home Addr:** 15 Bird Pl, Hillcrest-Spring Valley, NY 10977-2912, **Home Phone:** (845)352-9865. **Business Addr:** Board Director, Leadership Rockland Inc, 2 New Hempstead Rd Suite 208, New City, NY 10956, **Business Phone:** (845)708-7258.

## MARSALIS, BRANFORD

Composer, jazz musician, saxophonist. **Personal:** Born Aug 26, 1960, Breaux Bridge, LA; son of Ellis Louis Jr and Dolores Ferdinand; married Nicole; children: Peyton; married Teresa Reese; children: Reese Ellis. **Educ:** Southern Univ, attended 1979; Berkeley Col Music, attended 1981. **Career:** Lionel Hampton Orchestra, musician, 1980; Clark Terry Band, musician, 1981, Art Blakey & the Jazz Messengers, musician, 1981, Herbie Hancock Quartet, musician, 1981 & 1986; Wynton Marsalis Quintet, musician, 1982-85; Sting, musician, 1985-89; The Police, 1985; English Chamber Orchestra, musician, 1986; Buckshot LeFonque, musician, 1995-97; The Tonight Show, music dir, 1992-95; Films: Bring on the Night, recording artist, 1985, Sch Daze, recording artist, 1987, Throw Momma from the Train, recording artist, 1987; Columbia Rec, creative consult & producer jazz recordings, 1997-2001; Mich State Univ & San Francisco State Univ, music prof, 2000-; Marsalis Music, head & owner, 2002-; Cincinnati Symphony's Ascent ser, creative dir, 2012-13; Nat Pub Radio, host; Albums: Scenesin the City, 1983; Royal Garden Blues, 1986; Renaissance, 1986; Romancesfor Saxophone, 1986; Random Abstract, 1987; Trio Jeepy, 1988; Crazy People Music, 1990; The Beautiful Ones Are Not Yet Born, 1991; Bloomington, 1991; I Heard You Twice the First Time, 1992; Dark Keys, 1996; Requiem, 1999; Contemporary Jazz, 2000; Creation, 2001; Footsteps of Our Fathers, 2002; Romare Bearden Revealed, 2003; Steep Anthology, 2004; Eternal, 2004; A Love Supreme Live, 2004; Braggtown, 2006; Metamorphosen, 2009; Songs of Mirth and Melancholy, 2011; Four MFs Playin Tunes, 2012; In My Solitude: Live at Grace Cathedral, 2014; Branford Marsalis Quartet Performs Coltrane's a Love Supreme Live in Amsterdam, 2015; Upward Spiral, 2016. TV appearences Wait Wait... Don't Tell Me!; Shanice's, 1992; Space Ghost Coast to Coast, 1994; The Fresh Prince of Bel-Air, 1994; Top Chef (Season 5). **Honors/Awds:** Grammy Award, 1993; Grammy Award Best Pop Instrumental Performance, 1994; Grammy Award Best Jazz Instrumental Album, 2001; Am Soc Composers, Authors & Publ Film & Tv Music Awards, 2001-06; Drama Desk Award, 2010; NEA Jazz Masters Award, 2011. **Special Achievements:** Grammy Award nominations, 1987. **Home Addr:** 9056 Santa Monica Blvd Suite 538, West Hollywood, CA 90069. **Business Addr:** Jazz Musician, Wilkins Management, 323 Broadway St, Cambridge, MA 02139, **Business Phone:** (617)354-2736.

## MARSALIS, DELFEAYO

Musician, composer, trombonist. **Personal:** Born Jul 28, 1965, New Orleans, LA; son of Ellis Jr and Dolores. **Educ:** Tanglewood Inst; Berklee Col Music, BA, performance & audio prod, 1989; Univ New Orleans, grad studies, eng; Univ Louisville, MA, jazz performance, 2005. **Career:** La Div Arts, artistic fel, 1998; Three Fifths Prod, founder & producer, currently; Uptown Music Theatre, founder, 2000; Minnesota Orchestra, concerts, currently; Blues in C, producer, 1994; Albums: The List, 1986; Crystal Stair, 1987; Truth is Spoken Here, 1988; Vision's Tale, 1989; Jazzy Wonderland, 1990; Mo' Better Blues, 1990; The Beautiful Ones Are Not Yet Born, 1991; As Serenity Approaches, 1991; Citi Movement, 1992; I Heard You Twice the First Time, 1992; It Don't Mean a Thing, 1993; Series, 1993; Joe Cool's Blues, 1994; Loved Ones, 1995; Musashi, 1996; Dark Keys, 1996; Jazz Machine, 1997; Irvin Mayfield, 1998; Citizen Tain, 1999; Blessed, 2000; Late Night at the Blue Note, 2000; How Passion Falls, 2001; Half Past Autumn Suite, 2003; Steep Anthology, 2004; Grey Mayfield, 2005; Minions Dominion, 2006; King Bolden, 2007; Sweet Thunder: Duke and Shak, 2011; The Last Southern Gentlemen, 2014. **Orgs:** Dir summer prog, Found Artistic & Musical Excellence, 1998-. **Honors/Awds:** Outstanding Performance Award, Jefferson Performing Arts Soc, 1983; 3 MVisionary Award, 1996; hon doctorate, New England Col, Henniker. **Special Achievements:** Earned a cover article for the industry source, Mix magazine in 1997. **Home Addr:** 150 Massachusetts Ave, Boston, MA 02115. **Business Addr:** Musician, Braithwaite & Katz Communications, 248 S Great Rd, Lincoln, MA 01773, **Business Phone:** (781)259-9600.

## MARSALIS, ELLIS LOUIS, JR.

Pianist, composer, educator. **Personal:** Born Nov 14, 1934, New Orleans, LA; son of Ellis L Sr (deceased) and Florence Robertson (deceased); married Dolores Ferdinand; children: Branford, Wynton, Ellis III, Delfeayo, Miboya & Jason. **Educ:** Dillard Univ, BA, 1955; Loyola Univ, MM, music educ, 1986; Dillard Univ, 1989. **Career:** Musician, educr, host, tenor saxophonist; Am Jazz Quartet, pianist, mid-1950; Dillard Univ, freshman music maj, 1951; Marine Corps TV, "Dress Blues", pianist, 1956-58; US Marine Corps, 1957; New Orleans High Sch, music teacher, 1960; Carver High Sch, band & choral dir, 1964; Playboy Club, 1966; "Leatherneck Song bk", radio show, pianist; played with Al Hirt's band, 1967-70; Fr bros' Storyville Jazz Band, 1971; ELM Rec, founder, owner, 1972-; New Orleans Ctr Creative Arts, head, 1974-86; Al Hirt's Dixieland group, piano chair; New Orleans Ctr for Creative Arts High Sch, staff, 1974; Va Commonwealth Univ, Jazz Studies Prog, head, 1986-89; Univ New Orleans, Jazz Studies Prog, head, 1990; Xavier Univ, adj prof; Va Commonwealth Univ, commonwealth prof; Univ New Orleans, Coca Cola endowed chair, Jazz studies, dir; Albums: The Monkey Puzzle, 1963; Gumbo, 1976; Fathers & Sons, 1982; Syndrome, 1984; Homecoming, 1986; The New New Orleans Music: Vocal Jazz, 1989; The Vision's Tale, 1989; Univ of New Orleans, fac, 1989; The Resolution Of Romance, 1990; Piano in E, 1991; Ellis Marsalis Trio, 1991; The Classic, 1991; Heart of Gold, 1992; Whistle Stop, 1994; Joe Cool's Blue, 1995; A night At Snug Harbour, 1995; Duke In Blue, 1999; Jazz Studies, dir, 2001;Jazz At Christmas in New Orleans, 2002; Marsalis Family-A Jazz Celebration, 2002; Afternoon Session August 17th 1968 Sparks Nev, 2003; On The First Occasion, 2004; An Eve With The Ellis Marsalis Quartet, 2005; Ruminations in New York, 2005. Songs: "Zee Blues", 2005; "Blame It on the Sun", "Mo Betta Blues", "My One and Only Love", "Like a Star & Don't Know Why", 2008; "Mo Better Blues", 2011; "So In Love", 2013. TV Series: "Gimme a Break", 1984; "Treme", 2010; "The Mark of Beauty", 2013. **Orgs:** Panelist, grant evaluator & bd mem, Nat Endowment Arts & Southern Arts Fedn.

## MARSALIS, JASON

Musician. **Personal:** Born Mar 4, 1977, New Orleans, LA; son of Ellis Jr and Dolores Ferdinand. **Educ:** Loyola Univ, class percussion. **Career:** Los Hombres Calientes, co-founder; Basin St Rec, jazz drumer; Album: Yr Drummer; Music Motion; You Don't Have To See It To Believe It; Roots, Br & Leaves; A Jazz Celebration; Twelves It; Live At Blue Note; Los Hombres Calientes; Hon Duke; Music Update. **Honors/Awds:** NEA Jazz Masters Award, 2011. **Business Addr:** Jazz Drumer, Basin Street Rec, 4130 Canal St, New Orleans, LA 70119, **Business Phone:** (504)483-0002.

## MARSALIS, WYNTON LEARSON

Composer, teacher, jazz musician. **Personal:** Born Oct 18, 1961, New Orleans, LA; son of Ellis Jr and Dolores; married Candace Stanley; children: 2; married Victoria Rowell; children: Jasper Armstrong. **Educ:** New Orleans Ctr Performing Arts; Tanglewoods Berkshire Music Ctr, Juilliard Sch Music, attended 1981. **Career:** Trumpet soloist, New Orleans Philharmonic Orchestra, 1975; recitalist, New Orleans Orchestra; Art Blakey's Jazz Messengers, mem, 1980; Herbie-Hancock's VSOP quartet; formed own group, 1981; Albums include: Father & Sons, 1982; Wynton Marsalis; Think of One, 1983; Trumpet Concertos, 1983; Hot House Flowers, 1984; Black Codes from the Underground, 1985; Joe Cool's Blues, 1994; CITI Movement; Blood on the Fields, jazz oratorio, 1997; The Marciac Suite, 1999; Big Train, 1999; Immortal Concerts: Jody, 2000; Listen to the Storyteller, 2000; All Rise, 2002; Angel Eyes-PRISM, 2002; Angel Eyes-SWEDEN IMPORT, 2003; Unforgivable Blackness: The Rise & Fall of Jack Johnson, 2004; The Magic Hour, 2004; Live at the House of Tribes, 2005; From the Plantation to the Penitentiary, 2007; Jazz at Lincoln Ctr, artistic dir; Colorblind, composer, 2006. **Honors/Awds:** Named Jazz Musician of the Year, Downbeat readers' poll, 1982, 1984, 1985; Wynton Marsalis album named best jazz recorded, Downbeat readers poll, 1982; best trumpet player Downbeat critics' poll, 1984; Acoustic Jazz Group of the Year Award, 1984; Grammy Awards for solo jazz instrumental, 1983-85, classical soloist orchestra, 1984, best trumpet player, 1985, Group Award, 1986-88, Best Spoken Word Album for Children, 2000; Hon Degrees: Manhattan Col, Yale Univ, Princeton Univ, Hunter Col; inducted into Big Band & Jazz Hall of Fame, 1996; Pulitzer Prize, 1997; Young STAR Award, 1998; Marsalis has also written five books namely: Sweet Swing Blues on the Road; Jazz in the Bittersweet Blues of Life; To a Young Musician: Letters from the Road; Jazz ABZ; Moving to Higher Ground: How Jazz Can Change Your Life; Harvey Shapiro Award, Tanglewoods Berkshire Music Ctr; Netherlands Edison Award; NEA Jazz Masters Award, 2011. **Special Achievements:** First jazz musician to win the Pulitzer Prize in music, 1997; UN, named cult ambassador, 2001; Book: A Young Jazz Musician, 2004. **Business Addr:** Trumpeter, Sony Music Entertainment Inc, 550 Madison Ave, New York, NY 10022, **Business Phone:** (212)833-8000.

## MARSH, BEN FRANKLIN

Government official, manager. **Personal:** Born Feb 17, 1940, Holly Springs, MS; son of Willie (deceased) and Lizzie Dawkins; married Jessie Floyd; children: Kimberly; married Gloria. **Educ:** Ohio State Univ, Columbus, OH, BS, 1963; Boston Univ, Heidelberg, Germany, MET, 1980. **Career:** Clayton County Bd Educ; Third Army, Ft McPherson, Ga, progs/plans officer; Parking Co Am, shift mgr, 1995-. **Orgs:** Pres, Clayton County Br, Nat Asn Advan Colored People, 1990-92; co-chair, Clayton United Negro Col Fund, 1985-; div lt gov, Ga Toastmasters Int; bd mem, Clayton County Water Authority; communs comn, Clayton United Way, 1991; adv comt, Clayton County Rainbow House; Ga Agr Exposition Authority, 1992. **Home Addr:** 1250 Kay Terr SE, Conyers, GA 30013-2928, **Home Phone:** (770)679-0165. **Business Addr:** Shift Manager, Atlanta Airport Parking, PO Box 20786, Atlanta, GA 30320.

## MARSH, DOUG WALTER

Football player. **Personal:** Born Jun 18, 1958, Akron, OH. **Educ:** Univ Mich. **Career:** Football player (retired); St Louis Cardinals, tight end, 1980-86. **Special Achievements:** Listed in Top 10 Mich Football Players, 1969-2000. **Home Addr:** 8 Beaujolais Dr, Florissant, MO 63031.

## MARSH, SEN. HENRY LEANDER, III

Politician, lawyer, government official. **Personal:** Born Dec 10, 1933, Richmond, VA; married Diane Harris; children: Nadine, Sonya & Dwayne. **Educ:** Va Union Univ, BA, sociol, 1956; Howard Univ Sch Law, LLB, 1959; Howard Univ, JD, 1959. **Career:** Hill Tucker & Marsh, partner, atty, 1961; City Richmond Va, councilman; 1966-77, 1982-92, mayor, 1977-82; Metrop Econ Develop Coun, partner, 1978; Richmond Renaissance, partner, 1981; Senate Va, sen, 1991-; Va Dept Alcoholic Beverage Control, comnr, 2014. **Orgs:** US Conf Mayors Spec Comn Decennial Census; chmn, subcom urban hwy syst US Conf Mayors; past pres, Nat Black Caucus Local Elected Officials; youth task force, bd dirs, chmn, income security comn & adv bd, Nat League Cities; Human Resources Steering Policy Comn; chmn, Effective Govt Policy Comn; Judicial Coun Nat Dem Party; mem adv, State Dem party; Judicial Selection Comn US Ct Appeals 4th Circuit, Alpha Phi Alpha; bd dir, Voter Ed Proj; Lawyers Comn Civil Rights Under Law; Local Govt, Finance, Rules & Transp; chair comt, Courts Justice, chmn, Martin Luther King, Jr. Memorial Comn Va; chmn, Capital Outlay Subcomt Senate Finance; bd trustees & chmn, Va Alcohol Safety Action Prog. **Honors/Awds:** Numerous public service awards including: Legislator of the Year Award, Va Sheriff's Asn; Humanitarian Award, Nat Conf Christians & Jews, 1994. Outstanding Man of the Year Kappa Alpha Psi; Outstanding Mason of the Year Va; Man of the Year Alpha Phi Alpha. **Special Achievements:** First African American Mayor of Richmond, 1977; First African American Chairman of The Senate Courts of Justice Committee, 2008. **Home Addr:** 3211 Q St, Richmond, VA 23223-6753, **Home Phone:** (804)226-9637. **Business Addr:** Senator, Senate of Virginia, 600 E Broad St Suite 201, Richmond, VA 23218, **Business Phone:** (804)698-7516.

## MARSH, MCAFEE A.

Executive, businessperson, executive director. **Personal:** Born Aug 29, 1939, Meridian, MS; married Ruby Putmon; children: Marcellus G. **Educ:** Wilson Col; LIAMA Mgrs Sch. **Career:** Chicago Metrop Mutual Assurance Co, 1960-72; Supreme Life Ins Co, assoc agency dir, vpres, 1972-79; Cosmopolitan Chamber Com Sch Bus Mgt, instr; Al Johnson Cadillac, 1979-80; United Ins Co, 1980-82; McAfee Marsh Ins Agency & Mutual Funds, pres, owner, 1982-. **Orgs:** Pres, grad class LUTC, 1969; secy, Chicago Ins Asn, 1975; vpres, Nat Ins Asn; Oper Push; Christ Universal Temple; pres, Men Cuc Christ Universal Temple, Chicago Ill, 1987-89. **Honors/Awds:** President Award, Hong Kong & Tokyo, 1987, Hawaii, 1990; Excellence Award, Time Ins Co, 1989; Leaders Circle, Time Ins Co, 1991; Fortes Investors Excellence Award, 1999; Certificate of Merit, Chicago Asn Com. **Business Addr:** President, Owner, McAfee Marsh Insurance & Mutual Funds, 2952 Polly Lane, Flossmoor, IL 60422, **Business Phone:** (708)798-5746.

## MARSH, MICHAEL L.

Manager, vice president (organization), president (organization). **Educ:** Queens Col, BA, 1979; Cornell Law Sch, JD, 1982; Columbia

Univ, Columbia Bus Sch, cert, transition gen mgt, 2001. **Career:** Monroe County Dist Atty's Off, Rochester, NY, spec asst. dist atty, 1982-89; Nixon, Hargrave, Devans & Doyle, assoc atty, 1989-93; Eastman Kodak Co, atty legal dept, 1993-98, asst to chmn, pres & chief exec officer, 1998-2001, gen mgr, Digital Capture, Com Imaging Group & vpres, 2001-03, Digital Output, gen mgr health group, 2003-05, Digital Capture Solutions Bus, pres & vpres health group, 2005-07; Carestream Health, mgt, 2007-08; Eastman Kodak Co, gen mgr inkjet printing solutions, digital & functional printing, 2008-12, corp vpres, 2009-; IDEX Corp, gen mgr, Optical Systs Bus Unit, 2014-. **Orgs:** Bd dir, State Ohio Chamber Com; bd trustee, Goodwill/Easter Seals Miami Valley. **Home Addr:** 10710 Lakeview Rd, Richmond, IL 60071-9653, **Home Phone:** (815)678-4980. **Business Addr:** General manager, IDEX Corporation, 1925 W Field Ct Suite 200, Lake Forest, IL 60045-4824, **Business Phone:** (847)498-7070.

## MARSH, MICHAEL LAWRENCE

Track and field athlete. **Personal:** Born Aug 4, 1967, Los Angeles, CA; son of Jonnie Brown and Thamas Brown. **Educ:** Univ Calif, Los Angeles, hist & bus, 1989. **Career:** Track & field athlete (retired); US Summer Olympic Team, track & field team, athlete. **Honors/Awds:** Gold medal, World Championships, Tokyo, 1991; Gold Medal Track & Field, Olympic Games, Barcelona, 200 metres, 1992, 4*100 metres relay, 1992; Silver Medal, Olympic Games, Atlanta, 1996. **Home Addr:** 2425 Holly Hall St Suite 153, Houston, TX 77054-3968, **Home Phone:** (713)835-9821.

## MARSH, DR. PEARL-ALICE

Political scientist. **Personal:** Born Sep 6, 1946, La Grande, OR; daughter of Amos Sr and Mary Patterson. **Educ:** Sacramento State Col, Sacramento, CA, BA, 1968; Univ Calif, Berkeley, CA, MPH, 1970, PhD, 1984. **Career:** Neighborhood Health Ctr Sem Prog, Berkeley, CA, coordr, 1970-73; Alameda County Ment Health Servs, Oakland, CA, assoc dir planning, 1973-76; Asn Bay Area Govt, Oakland, CA, researcher, 1984-85; Univ Calif, Berkeley, CA, prog dir African studies, 1986-93; Joint Ctr Polit & Econ Studies, Wash, DC, sr res fel, 1993-96; Africa Policy Info Ctr, exec dir, 1996-99; Africa Policy Info Ctr, actg exec dir, 1997; Rep Juanita Millender-McDonald, sr policy adv, 1999-2000; US House Representatives, sr prof staff mem, 2000-, House Foreign Affairs Comt, sr prof staff mem, 2002-. **Orgs:** Comnr, Berkeley Rent Stabilization Prog, 1989-92; elected officer, bd mem, Asn Concerned African Scholars, 1989-; African Studies Asn, 1984-; Polit Sci Asn, 1989-; Afro-Am Gen & Hist Soc; Afri Geneas; African-Am Geneal Asn; Northern La Geneal Soc. **Home Addr:** 1801 16th St NW Suite 405, Washington, DC 20009, **Home Phone:** (202)328-6607. **Business Addr:** Senior Professional Staff Member, US House of Representatives, 110th Cong 2nd Session, Washington, DC 20515, **Business Phone:** (202)224-3121.

## MARSH, ESQ. SANDRA M.

Lawyer, police officer. **Personal:** Born Jan 14, 1943, Charleston, SC; daughter of William Baker and Ethel Baker; children: David. **Educ:** Brooklyn Col, City Univ NY, BA, 1977; NY Univ Sch Law, JD, 1981; NY Univ Wagner Grad Sch, MS, 1995. **Career:** Pub Educ Asn, staff atty, 1981-82; NY Educ Dept, Off Prof Discipline, prosecuting atty, 1982-85; New York Police Dept, asst trial commnr, 1985-88, dep police commnr, exec dir, 1988-93; US Equal Employ Opportunity, asst dep comnr, dep commnr, 1998-99; Admin Law Judge Environ Control Bd, 1999-2001; Family Ctr Inc, sr atty, 2001-. **Orgs:** Asn Black Women Attys, 1981-; mentor, Black Law Stud Asn, 1981-; Nat Asn Black Law Enforcement Execs, 1986-; vpres, New York Univ Law Sch Alumni Asn, 1993-; Metrop Black Bar Asn, 1993-; bd mem, NY Univ Alumni Asn; Asn Bd City NY. **Honors/Awds:** Alumna Award for Excellence, NY Univ Law Sch, 1996; Honorary Director, NY Univ Law Sch. **Special Achievements:** First African-Am female appointed trial commnr, NYPD, 1985; First African-Am female to head NYPD Civilian Complaint Review Bd, 1988; first African-Am to head NYPD OEEO, 1993. **Home Addr:** 315 8th Ave, New York, NY 10001, **Home Phone:** (212)255-8010. **Business Addr:** Attorney, The Family Center Inc, 315 W 36th St 4th Fl, New York, NY 10007, **Business Phone:** (212)766-4522.

## MARSH, WILLIAM A., JR.

Lawyer, executive. **Personal:** Born Jan 31, 1927, Durham, NC; married Bernice Sawyer; children: William Andrew & Jewel Lynn. **Educ:** NC Cent Univ, BS, 1949; NC Cent Univ, LLB, 1953; NC Cent Univ, JD, 1970. **Career:** Self-employed, atty; Mech & Farmers Bank, gen coun; Mutual Community Savings Bank, gen coun; UDI-CDC Garrett Sullivan Davenport Bowie & Grant CPA's, atty; Marsh & Marsh Attorneys, managing partner, currently. **Orgs:** Urban Develop Inst Comn Develop Corp; Found, Community Develop; Durham Opportunities Found; chmn, Legal Redress Comn; Am Bar Asn; Nat Bar Asn; Durham Comn Negro Affairs; Durham Chap, Nat Advan Asn Colored People; Beta Phi Chap; Ont Prov Police; Durham C C; NC Cent Alumni Asn; Masonic Lodge; Shriners; histrorian, NC Asn Black Lawyers; chmn, NC State Bd Elections. **Home Addr:** 1003 Cana St, Durham, NC 27707-4905, **Home Phone:** (919)688-5390. **Business Addr:** Managing Partner, Marsh & Marsh, 120 E Parrish St, Durham, NC 27701-3346, **Business Phone:** (919)688-2374.

## MARSH, HON. WILLIAM ANDREW, III

Lawyer. **Personal:** Born Mar 6, 1958, Durham, NC; son of William A Jr and Bernice S; married Sonja Denalli; children: William Andrew IV, Kylie Alexandra & Nicholas Emerson. **Educ:** Hampton Inst, Hampton Univ, BA, polit sci & govt, 1979; Univ NC Sch Law, Chapel Hill, JD, 1982. **Career:** Marsh & Banks, 1982-83, assoc, 1985-86; Judge James B. Hunt, asst legal coun, 1983-85; State NC, asst legal coun to gov, 1983-84, dist ct judge, 2007-; Pvt Pract, 1985-87; Dist Off Corp Coun, Juv Div, asst corp coun, prosecuting atty, 1987-92; Marsh & Marsh, atty & gen partner, 1993-2007. **Orgs:** Kappa Alpha Psi Fraternity, 1978-; Am Bar Asn, 1983-; Dist Bar Asn, 1983-; NC State Bar, 1984-; NCA Asn Black Lawyers, 1984-; pres, Durham County Bar Asn, 1998-99; pres, 14th Judicial Dist Bar NC, 1998-99; trustee, St Joseph's Am Church; Ancient & Accepted Scottish Rite Free Masons Prince Hall Affil; African Methodist Episcopal Church; George H. White Bar Asn; Dc Bar; Nc Bar. **Honors/Awds:** General Counsel AME Church. **Business Addr:** District Court Judge, State of North Carolina, PO Box 7001, Raleigh, NC 27695, **Business Phone:** (919)515-2011.

## MARSHALL, AMEILA

Fashion model, actor. **Personal:** Born Apr 2, 1958, Albany, GA; married Kent Schaffer; children: Dylan; married Daryl Waters. **Educ:** Univ Tex, Austin, BA, bus admin. **Career:** Films: Cul-de-Sac, 1995; According to Spenser, 2001; Stuart Little, 2002; Actress: Big Deal; Harrigan & Hart; Porgy & Bess; TV series: "Robert Klein on Broadway", 1986; "One Life to Live", 1988; "Guiding Light", 1990-93; "All My Children", 1996-99; "Lizzie McGuire", 2001; "The District", 2001; "Strong Medicine", 2001; Houston Jazz Ballet Co, mem; NBC soap opera Passions, actress, currently. **Honors/Awds:** Nominee, Image Award, 1998, 1999, 2000; Nominee, Soap Opera Digest Award, 2005. **Business Addr:** Actress, Passions NBC, GE Bldg, New York, NY 10112, **Business Phone:** (212)664-7174.

## MARSHALL, ANITA

Librarian. **Personal:** Born May 30, 1938, Newark, NJ; daughter of Noah Willis and Estelle Mitchell; children: Harry Vaughn Bims. **Educ:** Newark State Col, Newark, NJ, BS, educ, 1959; Chicago State Univ, Chicago, IL, MS, christian educ, 1974; Univ Chicago, attended 1986; Mich State Univ, E Lansing, attended 1989; Garrett Evangel Theol Sem, MCE, 1999. **Career:** Newark Bd Educ, Newark, NJ, teacher, 1959-62; Peace Corps, Philippine Islands, TESL, Sci & ESL, teacher, 1969-82; Chicago Bd Educ, Chicago, media specialist, ESEA, coordr, workshop facilitator, 1964-82, 1995-04; Chicago State Univ, Chicago, lectr libr sci, HEW proj dir, 1976-77; Mich State Univ, head, gift unit, ethnic studies & sociol bibliogr, 1982-95; Chicago Conf Am Church, S Dist, consult, 1999-02; Christian Educ Workshop, presenter; Am Church, Sunday Sch, curric writer; Chicago Bd Educ, librn; Bethel African Methodist Episcopal Church, ministerial team mem, currently; African Methodist Episcopal Church, Dept Christian Educ, Writers Guild coordr, 1992-. **Orgs:** Pres, Gamma Zeta Chap, Alpha Kappa Alpha Sorority, 1957-59; Am Libr Asn, 1968-95; Phi Delta Kappa, 1981-; chair, Tech Servs Caucus, Mich Libr Asn, 1988-92; Women's Adv Comt to Provost, Mich State Univ, 1988-91; Planning comt, Black Caucus Am Libr Asn, First Nat Conf, 1990-92; Mission & Ethics Comt, St Lawrence Hosp Exec Bd, 1991-95; Mich State Univ Mus Assocs Bd, 1992-96, co-chair, 1995-95; Kresge Art Mus Docent, Lansing Pub Libr Adv Bd, 1995-96; Womens Missionary Soc, Am Church, 1999-2004; secy & vpres, Mich State Univ, Black Fac & Adminrs Asn; Women's Missionary Soc, Chicago Conf Committe Chair & Fourth Dist Worship Leader & Comt Chair; Comt Uniform Ser, Nat Coun Churches; Stewardship & Finance Comn. **Honors/Awds:** State Acad Scholar, New Jersey, 1955-59; Archibald Carey Scholar, 1997-98; Outstanding Christian Educator, Chicago Cult Found, 1999; Am Bible Soc Award for Christian Educ, Garrett Theol Sem, 1999; Dedicated Teacher Award, Dusable High Sch, Chicago, Ill. **Special Achievements:** Contributor, Liberation & Unity Lenten Meditation Guide, 1993-98, 2000; Quilting Bibliography in "African-Am Quilting in Mich," 1998. **Home Addr:** 4358 S Ind Ave, Chicago, IL 60653-3216, **Home Phone:** (773)924-3159. **Business Addr:** Writers Guild Coordinator, African Methodist Episcopal Church, 500 8th Ave S, Nashville, TN 37203, **Business Phone:** (800)525-7282.

## MARSHALL, ANTHONY DEWAYNE

Football player. **Personal:** Born Sep 16, 1970, Mobile, AL. **Educ:** La State Univ. **Career:** Football player (retired); Chicago Bears, 1994, defensive back, 1995-97; New York Jets, 1997; Philadelphia Eagles, 1998; Memphis Maniax, Xclusive Football League, 2001.

## MARSHALL, BETTY J.

Executive, vice president (organization), manager. **Personal:** Born Oct 15, 1950, Youngstown, OH; daughter of L V Sharpe Mitchell and Grant Mitchell; married Richard H Young; children: Melanie D. **Educ:** Youngstown State Univ, Youngstown, OH. **Career:** Arbys Inc, Atlanta, Ga, dir purchasing, 1975-89; Rax Restaurants Inc, Columbus, Ohio, dir purchasing & distrib, 1989-90; Shoney's Inc, Nashville, Tenn, dir purchasing, 1990, dir corp & community affairs, 1990, vpres corp & community affairs, 1991-96, sr vpres, corp communs; Phoenix Restaurant Group Inc, sr vpres, chief admin officer, asst secy, sr exec, 2001; Sams Club, vpres & div merchandise mgr, regional gen mgr & vpres purchasing, 2006-. **Orgs:** Treas & steering comt mem, Nat Restaurant Asn, 1987-; hospitality mgt adv bd mem, Eastern Mich Univ, 1990-; tourism task force mem, Nashville Area Chamber Com, 1990-; vice chair, Health & Rehabilitative Servs Community Initiatives Steering Comt, United Way, 1990-; bd dir, Tenn Minority Purchasing Coun, 1991; Union Planters Community Bank Bd; Tenn Minority Supplier Develop Coun; Nashville Airport Authority; adv bd, Meharry Med Col Ctr Womens Res; bd mem, YWCA USA; Tenn Minority Supplier Develop Coun. **Business Addr:** Regional Vice President, Sam's Club, 12920 Foothill Blvd, San Fernando, CA 91340, **Business Phone:** (818)365-7710.

## MARSHALL, BRANDON TYRONE

Football player, business owner, broadcaster. **Personal:** Born Mar 23, 1984, Pittsburgh, PA; married Michi Nogami. **Educ:** Univ Cent Fla, BA, lib studies, 2006; Harvard Univ, exec educ cert, bus entertainment, media, & sports, 2014. **Career:** Football player, University of Central Florida, 2002-06, Denver Broncos, wide receiver, 2006-09, Miami Dolphins, 2010-11, Chicago Bears, 2012-14, New York Jets, 2015-; FitSpeed Athletic Performance, co-founder & partner, 2010-; Showtime Networks, broadcaster, 2014-. **Orgs:** Founder & bd mem, Project375, Chicago, IL, 2011-. **Business Addr:** The Atlantic Health Jets Training Center, 1 Jets Dr, Florham Park, NJ 07932.

## MARSHALL, REV. CALVIN BROMLEY, III

Clergy. **Personal:** Born Jun 13, 1932, Brooklyn, NY; son of Evans B and Edith Best; married Delma Mann; children: Sharon Wallinger, Smitn, Edythe L & Chad. **Educ:** Anderson Col, Anderson, IN, BA, 1955; Anderson Theol Sem, BD, 1958; Grasslands Hosp, Valhalla, NY, CPC, 1965; Teamer Sch Relig, NC, DD, 1972, LHD, 1973. **Career:** Pk St AME Zion Church, Peekskill, NY, pastor, 1960-68; Cumberland Hosp, dir pastoral care, 1972-83; Varick Memorial AME Zion Church, pastor; Woodhull Med & Ment Health Ctr, dir pastoral care. **Orgs:** Chief Protocol, AME Zion Church; vice chair, Nat Action Network; Am Asn Christian Counrs US Chaplains Asn; Am Asn Pastoral Counrs; Asn Clin Pastoral Educ. **Special Achievements:** Articles: "Living on the Left Hand of God, " Theol Today, 1968; "The Black Church-Its Mission Is Liberation," Black Scholar, 1970. **Home Addr:** 125 Fairway Dr, Hempstead, NY 11550-4700, **Home Phone:** (516)485-2399. **Business Addr:** Pastor, Varick Memorial AME Zion Church, 120 Atlantic St, Hackensack, NJ 07601, **Business Phone:** (201)343-8240.

## MARSHALL, CHARLENE JENNINGS

State government official. **Personal:** Born Sep 17, 1933, Osage, WV; daughter of Charles Jennings and Christine J Cranford; married Rogers Leon; children: Gwendolyn, Roger Jr & Larry R. **Career:** Rockwell Intl, mach operator & stores attend, 1963-78; United Steel workers Am Local 6214, rec secy, 1976; Mon Preston Labor & Coun, 1968-78; W Va Dept Labor, state insp; W Va mayor, 1991-98; W Va House Del, vice chmn Monongalia County mn polit sub-div; St House, currently; W Va State House Delegates, deleg, 1998-2004 & 2004-14, Dist 44, house chaplain, 2004-, Const Rev, mem, currently, Dist 51, cand, 2004-2014, Finance Comt, mem, currently, Health & Human Resources Comt, mem, currently, House Rules, Comt, mem, currently, Energy, Indust & Labor & Econ Develop & Small Bus, Comt, mem, currently, Sr Citizen Issues Comt, mem, currently, Joint Finance, 2013-14, Health, 2013-14, Minority Issues, 2013-14. **Orgs:** Dir, W Va Women's Bowling Asn; chmn, Morgantown Human Rights Comn, 1974-79; pres & vpres, Nat Advan Asn Colored People, Morgantown Bd, 1973-76; St. Paul African Methodist Episcopal; pres, Vis Comt Stud Affairs & Social Justice, W Va Univ; Boys & Girls Club Am; Leadership Monongalians First Class; rec secy, Monongalia Preston Labor Coun; bd mem, Morgantown Theater Co; exec bd mem, Red Cross; Steelworks Local 6214; Valley Health Care; W Va Bar Asn; W Va Univ Local 814; W Va Univ Pres Vis Commt Stud Affairs; W Va Univ Sch Nursing Adv Bd; Energy, Indust & Labor & Econ Develop & Small Bus; Sr Citizen Issues; W Va Univ Presidents Vis Comt Stud Affairs. **Home Addr:** 1010 Ashton Dr, Morgantown, WV 26508, **Home Phone:** (304)292-7757. **Business Addr:** House Chaplain of District 44, West Virginia State House of Delegates, Rm 214 E Bldg 1 St Capitol Complex 1900 Kanawha Blvd E, Charleston, WV 25305, **Business Phone:** (304)558-2000.

## MARSHALL, HON. CONSUELO B.

Judge. **Personal:** Born Sep 28, 1936, Knoxville, TN; married George E Jr; children: Michael & Laurie. **Educ:** Los Angeles City Col, AA, 1956; Pepperdine Univ, attended 1957; Howard Univ, BA, 1958; Howard Univ Sch Law, LLB, 1961; Univ Southern Calif Law Ctr, attended 1971. **Career:** City Los Angeles, dep city atty, 1962-67, super ct comnr, 1971-76; Cochran & Atkins, pvt pract, 1968-70; Juv Ct, Los Angeles Super Ct, comnr, 1971-76; Inglewood Munic Ct, Civil & Criminal Div, judge, 1976-77; Los Angeles Super Ct, Criminal Div, judge, 1977-80; US Dist Ct, Cent Dist CA, fed judge, 1980, chief judge, 2001-05, sr dist judge, 2005-. **Orgs:** Black Women Laywers Asn; Calif Women Lawyers Asn; Calif Judges Asn; State Bar Calif; Los Angeles City Bar Asn; Nat Asn Advan Colored People; Urban League; Beta Phi Sigma; Los Angeles Women Lawyers' Asn; Asn Black Lawyers; Nat Asn Women Judges; bd mem, Legal Aid Found; YMCA; Beverly Hills WestLinks Inc; mem bd dir, Antioch Sch Law Wash, DC; 9th Circuit Ct Appeals Educ Comn, 1984-86; fac mem, Trial Advocacy Workshop Harvard Law Sch, 1984-85; 9th Circuit Ct Appeals Libr Comn, 1985-86. **Business Addr:** Judge, United States District Court for the Central District of California, 312 N Spring St Rm G 8, Los Angeles, CA 90012, **Business Phone:** (213)894-5288.

## MARSHALL, DAVID

Manager, president (organization), accountant. **Personal:** Born Aug 27, 1960, Orange, NJ; son of Ruth; married Shirley Ann. **Educ:** Upsala Col, BA, bus admin, 1982. **Career:** Macy's Corp, sales mgr, 1982-84; Pk Tower Assoc, acct exec, 1985-90; Super Personnel, sr acct exec, 1990-92; Krow Assoc, exec recruiter, 1992-93; Solvay Pharmaceut, sales prof, 1993-94; Target Pros Inc, founder, pres, 1994-. **Orgs:** Nat Sales Network, 1992-. **Business Addr:** President, Founder, Target Pros Inc, 80 Main St Suite 340, West Orange, NJ 07052-3034, **Business Phone:** (973)324-0900.

## MARSHALL, DONALD JAMES

Actor. **Personal:** Born May 2, 1936, San Diego, CA; son of Ernest and Alma; married Diane. **Educ:** San Diego City Col, eng, 1957; Los Angeles City Col, theater arts, 1960. **Career:** Bob Gist Group, Frank Silvera Theater Being, Theater E Workshop, Richard Boone Repertory Co, 1960-67; Land Giants ABC-TV, co-star, 1967-71; DJM Productions Inc, past actor, 1970-73; Jo Co Int Enterprises Inc, dist ribr, licensing agt, 1984; Stage Work: Of Mice & Men, A Cat Called Jesus; Films: The Interns, 1962; Shock Treatment, 1964; Sergeant Ryker, 1968; The Thing with Two Heads, 1972; Terminal Island, 1973; Uptown Saturday Night, 1974; Hugo, a vizilo, 1975. TV series: "Kraft Suspense Theatre", 1963; "The Alfred Hitchcock Hour", 1963-65; "Great Gettin' Up Mornin'", 1964; "Rawhide", 1964; "The Lieutenant", 1964; "Bob Hope Presents the Chrysler Theatre", 1964-65; "The Rogues", 1965; "Ben Casey", 1965; "Daktari", 1966; "Mission: Impossible", 1966; "12 O'Clock High", 1966; "Mr. Terrific", 1967; "Tarzan", 1967; "Star Trek", 1967; "Ironside", 1967; "Dragnet 1967", 1967-68; "Braddock", 1968; Julia, 1968; "Land of the Giants", 1968-70; "Bewitched", 1970; "The Reluctant Heroes", 1971; "Police Story", 1974-75; "Good Times", 1976; "The Bionic Woman", 1976; "The Hardy Boys/Nancy Drew Mysteries", 1977; "Benny & Barney: Las Vegas Undercover", 1977; "The Incredible Hulk", 1978-80; "Rescue from Gilligan's Island", 1978; "Buck "Rogers in the 25th Century", 1979; "The Suicide's Wife", 1979; "Capitol", 1984; "Finder of Lost Loves", 1984; "Highway Heartbreaker", 1992. **Orgs:** Mem equity, Am Fedn TV & Radio Artists; Screen Actors Guild; Nat Acad TV Arts & Sci; nat mem, Am Film Inst; charter mem, Fedn Negro Actors Action; vpres & nat mem, Nat Asn Advan Colored People. **Honors/Awds:** Actor's Achievement Award, African Meth Epis Church, 1970; Black Achiever Award, 1976. **Special Achievements:** first African American male to have such a prominent role in a science fiction television series. **Business Addr:** Actor, c/o Abrams-Rubaloff & Lawrence, 8075 W Third St Suite 303, Los Angeles, CA 90048, **Business Phone:** (323)935-1700.

**MARSHALL, DONYELL LAMAR**
Basketball player, basketball coach. **Personal:** Born May 18, 1973, Reading, PA; son of Alonzo Cook Jr and Stephanie; children: Marquis Lamar, Paryss, Donyell Jr & Devynn. **Educ:** Univ Conn, attended 1994. **Career:** Basketball player (retired), coach, analyst; Minn Timberwolves, small forward, 1994-95; Golden State Warriors, small forward, 1995-99, power forward, 1999-2000; Utah Jazz, small forward, 2000-02; Chicago Bulls, power forward, 2002-03; Toronto Raptors, power forward, 2003-05; Cleveland Cavaliers, power forward, 2005-08; Seattle Supersonics, power forward, 2008; Philadelphia 76ers, power forward, 2008-09; Comcast SportsNet, game analyist, 2009-10; George Washington Colonials, asst coach, 2010-11; Maine Red Claws, asst coach, 2011-13; Rider Univ men's basketball, asst coach, 2013-15; Univ Buffalo, 2015-16; Cent Conn men's basketball team, head coach, 2016-. **Honors/Awds:** NCAA All-American First Team, 1994; Big East Conference Player of the Year, 1994; NBA All-Rookie Second Team, 1995; Good Guys, Sporting News, 2003. **Special Achievements:** First round, fourth pick, NBA Draft, 1994; TV Series: Arli$$, 1998. **Business Addr:** Head Coach, Central Connecticut Men's Basketball, 1615 Stanley St, New Britain, CT 06050, **Business Phone:** (860)832-3732.

**MARSHALL, DR. EDWIN COCHRAN (ED MARSHALL)**
School administrator, optometrist. **Personal:** Born Mar 31, 1946, Albany, GA; children: Erin C & Erika H. **Educ:** Ind Univ, BA, zool, 1968, BS, optom, 1970, OD, 1971, MS, 1979; Univ NC, MPH, 1982. **Career:** Professor (retired); Ind Univ Sch Optom, assoc prof, 1977-92, chmn dept clin sci, 1983-92, assoc dean acad affairs, 1992-, prof, 1992, emer prof, currently; Cebu Drs Col Optom Philippines, consult, 1980-87; Nat Optom Asn, exec dir, 1981-89, 1993-; Inter Am Univ PR, consult, 1982; Nat HBP Educ Prog, coord comn, 1984-; Nat Univ Malaysia, consult, 1992; 1995-; Ind Univ Sch Med, adj prof pub health, 1998-; Ind Univ Sch Optom, assoc dean acad affairs & stud admin, vpres. **Orgs:** Life mem, Kappa Alpha Psi Fraternity; pres, Ind Optom Asn; chair, Minority Health Care Data & Qual Subcomt Ind Comn Excellence Health Care; pres, Ind Pub Health Asn; pres, Nat Optom Asn, 1979-81; pub health exam comn, Nat Bd Examrs Optom, 1983-94; coun acad affairs, Asn Schs & Cols Optom, 1983-84; secy, Black Cong Health Law & Econ, 1985-87; pres, Eye Ski Inc, 1986-94; Nat Adv Coun Health Prof Educ, 1987-91; dipl pub health, Am Acad Optom, 1987; vice chmn, Black Cong Health, Law & Econ, 1987-92; chmn, Vision Care Sect, Am Pub Health Asn, 1988-90; chair dipl prog, Pub Health Am Acad Optom, 1990-93; chair, Task Force Health Policy, Asn Schs & Cols Optom, 1991-92; Ind Health Care & Develop Comt, 1995-; exec bd, Am Pub Health Asn, 2000-; vice chair, Exec Bd Am Pub Health Asn, currently. **Home Addr:** 4426 Cambridge Ct, Bloomington, IN 47408. **Business Addr:** Professor Emeritus, Indiana University, IN.

**MARSHALL, ERIC A.**
Executive, founder (originator). **Personal:** Born Oct 16, 1963, Marion, IN; son of Frank and Alice. **Educ:** Ind Univ Bloomington, BA, jour & psychol, 1987. **Career:** Clique Creative Serv, founder, creative dir, owner & pres, 1987-. **Orgs:** Ind pres, Am Soc Media Photogr; Ind Univ Sch Jour Alumni Bd; bd dir, Marion Gen Hosp; bd dir, Main St Marion. **Business Addr:** Owner, President, Clique Creative Services, 422 E 4th St, Marion, IN 46952, **Business Phone:** (765)664-2300.

**MARSHALL, GLORIA A. See SUDARKASA, NIARA.**

**MARSHALL, H. JEAN (H JEAN MARSHALL-MCENTIRE)**
Executive. **Personal:** Born Jun 7, 1945, Lake Providence, LA; daughter of William L and Thelma Jones Harden; children: Lyndon E & Tangie F. **Educ:** Univ Cincinnati, BS, psychol, 1972. **Career:** St Leo Sch, teacher, 1976-78; Cincinnati Pub Schs, work training coor, 1978-82; Ohio Lottery Comn, regional mgr & field coodr, 1983-87, dep dir sales, 1990-92; Brit Am Bank Note Co, acct mgr, 1987-89; Ohio Dept Rehab, consult, 1989-90; Interlott, dir retailer rels, 1992-93, dir, 1992-93, vpres mkt, 1993-97, consult, 1997-98; Ohio Civil Rights Comn, regional dir, currently. **Orgs:** Harriett Beecher Stowe Hist Cult Asn, 1981-; vpres, bd trustee, Arts Consortium Cincinnati, 1993-; United Way, commun chest-field serv, 1993-; secy, bd dir, Cincinnati Minority Bus Develop Ctr, 1994-; vice chair, C & Youth Field Serv; adv bd, WCPO TV; Boys Scout Am. **Home Addr:** 6731 Grange Ct, Cincinnati, OH 45239, **Home Phone:** (513)729-2935. **Business Addr:** Cincinnati Regional Director, Ohio Human Rights Commission, 7162 Reading Rd Suite 1001, Cincinnati, OH 45237, **Business Phone:** (513)852-3344.

**MARSHALL, HENRY HOWARD**
Football player. **Personal:** Born Aug 9, 1954, Broxton, GA. **Educ:** Univ Mo, grad. **Career:** Football player (retired); Kans City Chiefs, wide receiver, 1976-87. **Honors/Awds:** Chiefs 25 Year All-time Team, 1987.

**MARSHALL, JOHN W.**
Government official, speaker of the house of representatives (U.S. federal government), police officer. **Personal:** Born Jul 6, 1958, Manhattan, NY; son of Thurgood (deceased) and Cecilia Suyat; married Jean Marie. **Educ:** Georgetown Univ, BA, govt, 1988; Va Commonwealth Univ, post-baccalaureate cert, admin justice, 1998. **Career:** Va Secy Pub Safety, va state police, state trooper, narcotics div spec agt, training acad instr & field opers sergeant, 1980-94; Eastern Dist Va, marshal, 1994-99; US Marshals Serv, dir, 1999-2001; Cabinet Va, secy pub safety, 2002-10; Thurgood Marshall Col Fund, consult & sr advisor, 2011. **Orgs:** Chmn, Leadership Coun; Va Gov's Cabinet.

**MARSHALL, JONNIE CLANTON**
Executive, social worker, association executive. **Personal:** Born Jul 24, 1932, Memphis, TN; married Kenneth Evans; children: James Kwame & Evan Keith. **Educ:** Morgan State Col, BA, 1956; Columbia Univ Sch Social Work, MSW, 1963; Fashion Inst Tech, attended 1986. **Career:** Social worker (retired); Retreat Living Hartford, psych aide, 1958-59; Grant Houses Community Ctr, supvr & dir, 1964-67; Designer Fine Millinery, 1980; Bd Educ Community Spec Educ, NY, sch social worker, 1967-91. **Orgs:** Alpha Kappa Alpha Sor Inc, Tau Omega Chap, 1954-; grp leader, YWCA NY, 1959-61; bd, Friend C's Art Carnival, 1968-; bd dirs, Harlem Community Coun Inc, 1971-; chair, Commonwealth Holding Co Inc, 1971-, pres, dir; vpres, Nat Asn Milliners Dressmakers, 1983-; Harlem Fashion Inst New York, 1983-; mem fashion show coord, pres, Cottagers Martha's Vineyard MA, 1985-86; life mem, Morgan State Univ Alumni Asn. **Honors/Awds:** Fashions have appeared in numerous fashion shows at the Black Fashion Museum, Howard Univ Alumni Fashion Show, Cottagers, Salem United Methodist Church Affairs. **Home Addr:** 470 Malcolm X Blvd Apt 17P, New York, NY 10037-3003, **Home Phone:** (212)281-6583.

**MARSHALL, DR. JOSEPH EARL, JR. (JOE MARSHALL)**
Association executive, teacher. **Personal:** Born May 12, 1947, St. Louis, MO; son of Joseph E Sr and Odessa; children: Malcolm, Sydney-Nicole & Cassie. **Educ:** Univ San Francisco, BA, polit sci & sociol, 1968; San Francisco State Univ, MA, educ, 1974; Wright Inst, Berkeley, CA, PhD, psychol, 1997. **Career:** Woodrow Wilson High Sch San Francisco, teacher, 1969; Omega Boys Club (Alive & Free), co-founder & exec dir, 1987-; KMEL, host syndicated radio show "St Soldiers", 1991; San Francisco Unified Sch Dist, teacher, adminr. **Orgs:** Ashoka Fel, 2004; Adv bd, Harvard Univ, Community Violence Prev Prog; founder, Alive & Free Movement; founder & pres, St Soldiers Nat Consortium; trustee emer, Univ San Francisco; planning bd mem, Surgeon Gen's Report Youth Violence; pres, San Francisco Police Comn. **Honors/Awds:** Received numerous awards including: Fel MacArthur Found, 1994; Genius Award, MacArthur Found, 1994; Childrens Defense Fund Leadership Award, 1994; Essence Award, Essence Mag, 1994; Martin Luther King Jr Memorial Award, Nat Educ Asn, 1996; Congressional Freedom Works Award, 1997; Candle in Community Serv Award, Morehouse Col, 1998; National Trust Award, African Am Men, 1999; Service to Youth Award, Links Inc, 2000; Use Your Life Award, Oprah Winfrey, 2001; Alumni Educators Award, UnivSan Francisco, 2003; Human Rights Leadership Award, Harvard Univ Alumni San Francisco, 2003; Living History Makers Award, Turning point Mag, 2004; Angel Award, Take Wing Found, 2006; Community Leadership Award, San Francisco Found, 2006; Jefferson Award, 2006; San Francisco Foundation Community Leadership Award, 2006; Jefferson Award, American Institute for Public Service, 2006; African American Excellence in Business Award, 2007; Local hero Award, Bank Ams Neighborhood Excellence Initiative, 2008; Best Community-Oriented Radio Program Award, St Soldiers, 2012; Spotlight on Crime Award, Nat Crime Prevention Coun; Certificate of Recognition, Calif State Assembly; DHL, Morehouse Col; DHL, Univ San Francisco. **Special Achievements:** Author of Street Soldier: One Man's Struggle to Save a Generation, One Life at a Time, 1996. **Home Addr:** 1060 Tennessee St Suite 4, San Francisco, CA 94107. **Business Addr:** Executive Director, Co-Founder, Omega Boys Club, 1060 Tennessee St, San Francisco, CA 94107, **Business Phone:** (415)826-8664.

**MARSHALL, JULYETTE MATTHEWS. See Obituaries Section.**

**MARSHALL, LEONARD ALLEN, JR.**
Executive, football player, capitalist or financier. **Personal:** Born Oct 22, 1961, Franklin, LA; son of Leonard Sr; married Maryann; children: Erika Christina & Arianna Nicole. **Educ:** La State Univ, BA, bus finance, bus admin; Fairleigh Dickerson Univ, Teaneck, NJ, BS; Seton Hall Univ, MA, bus finance, 2007. **Career:** Football player (retired), executive & football coach: mortage lender, exec residence; New York Giants, 1983-92; New York Jets, 1993; Wash Redskins, 1994; Pro Star Athletic, chmn & chief exec officer, 1999; Promise Healthcare, dir corp diversity, 2004; Pro Star Athletic, co-founder, chmn & chief exec officer; Capital Source Mortgage, lic corresp mortgage lender, owner & chief exec officer, currently; Seton Hall Univ, Sports Mgt, prof & exec residence, 2004-09; Athena Financial Group, pres, chief exec officer & consult; Philanthropic Develop Seeman Holtz Financial Group, vpres, 2007; Hudson Cath, head football coach, 2010; Leonard Marshall Football Acad Camp, host; Cannabis World Cong & Bus Expo, speaker. **Orgs:** Nat sports chmn, Leukemia Soc, Westchester & Putnam Valley, NY; New York Bd; March Dimes; Nat Asn Advan Colored People. **Honors/Awds:** Most Valuable Person, La State Univ, 1983; All-NFL, 1985 & 1986; United Way Lifetime Achievement Award, 1986; NFC Defensive Lineman of the Year, NFLPA, 1986; Pro Bowl, 1986 & 1987; Byron Whizzer White Award, 1990. **Home Addr:** , Paramus, NJ. **Business Addr:** Executive in Residence, Seton Hall University, 400 S Orange Ave, South Orange, NJ 07079, **Business Phone:** (973)761-9000.

**MARSHALL, MARVIN ALI**
Football player, football coach. **Personal:** Born Jun 21, 1972, Aschaffenburg; married Lascotia; children: Marvin Jr & Matlin. **Educ:** SC State Univ, grad. **Career:** Football player (retired), football coach; Barcelona Dragons, wide receiver, 1996; Tampa Bay Buccaneers, wide receiver, 1996-97; Carolina Cobras, arena football league, 2000; Hephzibah High Sch, defensive backs coach, 2001; Josey High Sch, offensive coordr, 2002-04; NFL Europe, coach, 2005; San Diego Chargers, offensive asst; Augusta Spartans, coach, 2006; San Diego Chargers, coach, 2007; Miami Dolphins, coach, 2008; Detroit Lions, coach, 2008. **Home Addr:** 854 Rollo Domino Cir, Evans, GA 30809-3482. **Business Addr:** Coach, Miami Dolphins, 347 Don Shula Dr, Miami Gardens, FL 33056, **Business Phone:** (305)943-8000.

**MARSHALL, PATRICIA PRESCOTT**
Educator, school administrator. **Personal:** Born Apr 4, 1933, Houston, TX; daughter of Willie Mae and St Elmo Leonidas; married Cornelius. **Educ:** Calif State Univ, BA, 1955, MA, 1960; Univ Southern Calif, EdD, 1980. **Career:** Educator, school administrator (retired); Los Angeles Unified Sch Dist, teacher, 1955-60; Berkeley Unified Sch Dist, teacher, 1960-63; Los Angeles Unified Sch Dist, training teacher, 1963-66, prin, 1966-79; Mount St Mary's Col, instr, part-time, 1972-76; Los Angeles Unified Sch Dist, prog dir acad, 1979-86; King County Libr Syst, sta mgr, asst supt, 1986. **Orgs:** Bd, Nat Mus Women Arts; bd, Educ Adv Los Angeles Co Mus Art; bd, YWCA Greater Los Angeles; UNICEF; Acad TV Arts & Sci; Am Women Radio & TV; Women Target; Pub Broadcasting Serv Adv Comn; Elem & Sec Educ Act. **Home Addr:** 4919 Shenandoah Ave # 1704, Los Angeles, CA 90056-1063, **Home Phone:** (310)649-2833.

**MARSHALL, PAULE BURKE**
Writer, college teacher. **Personal:** Born Apr 9, 1929, Brooklyn, NY; daughter of Samuel and Ada Clement; married Kenneth E; children: Evan; married Nourry Menard. **Educ:** Brooklyn Col, BA, 1953; Hunter Col, attended 1955; Bates Col, LHD, 1993. **Career:** Our World Mag, staff writer, 1953-56; Yale Univ, lectr creative writing, 1970; Oxford Univ, lectr black lit; Columbia Univ, lectr black lit; Mich Univ, lectr; Lake Forest Univ, Lectr; Cornell Univ, lectr; Va Common wealth Univ, prof Eng; New York Pub Libr, 1994; New York Univ, Helen Gould Sheppard prof, currently; Novel: Brown Girl, Brownstones, Random House, 1959; Brown Girl, Brownstones, 1960; Soul Clap Hands & Sing, Atheneum, 1961; Chosen Pl, Timeless People, Harcourt, 1969; Praisesong Wid, Putnam, 1983; Reena & Other Stories, Feminist Press, 1983; Fisher King, Scribner, 2000. **Orgs:** Phi Beta Kappa, Asn Artists Freedom; MacArthur Fel. **Home Addr:** 503 S Davis Ave Apt 6, Richmond, VA 23220-5757. **Business Addr:** Helen Gould Sheppard Professor, New York University, 19 Univ Pl 214, New York, NY 10003, **Business Phone:** (212)998-8845.

**MARSHALL, PLURIA W., SR.**
Executive director, civil rights activist, photographer. **Personal:** Born Oct 19, 1937, Houston, TX; married Corbin Carmen; children: Pluria Jr, Mishka, Jason, Natalie & Christopher. **Educ:** Tex Southern Univ, BA, photog. **Career:** Nat Black Media Coalition, nat organizer, treas, chmn, 1975, sr chmn & chief exec officer; prof photogr; Oper Breadbasket TX, exec dir; Los Angeles Wave, publ, currently. **Orgs:** Tex State Adv Comn, US Comn Civil Rights; co-founder, off photogr & freelancer, Nat Asn Black Journalists, 1975-; nat organizer, treas & chmn, Nano-Bio Mfg Consortium; Nat Asn Radio & Tv Announcers. **Honors/Awds:** Community Service Award, Nat Asn Mkt Developers, 1973; Community Service Award, Omega Psi Phi, Houston Chap, 1973; Outstanding Ex-Student Award, Tex Southern Univ, 1974; Marketeer of the Year Award, Houston Chap, NAMD, 1974. **Home Addr:** 12912 Bluet Lane, Silver Spring, MD 20906-3303. **Business Addr:** Co-Founder, Freelancer, National Association of Black Journalists, 8701-A Adelphi Rd, Adelphi, MD 20783-1716, **Business Phone:** (301)445-7100.

**MARSHALL, PLURIA WILLIAM, JR.**
Executive, radio broadcaster. **Personal:** Born Jan 17, 1962; son of Pluria W Sr and Olivia F; married Paula; children: Kaelin & Pluria III. **Educ:** Clark Col, Atlanta, GA, BS, 1984. **Career:** KTRE-TV, Lufkin, Tex, sales & mkt, 1982, sales & acct exec, 1983; WTBS/Turner Broadcasting, Atlanta, Ga, res, 1982-83; WLBT-TV, Jackson, Miss, mgt develop sales, 1983-84; WLBM-TV30, Meridan, Miss, sta mgr & sales mgr, 1985-86, vpres/gen mgr, 1986; KHRN-FM, genl mgr, owner; Marshall Media Group, pres; WLTH Radio, gen mgr, 1993-; Los Angeles Wave Publ Group, group publ, currently. **Orgs:** Nat Black Media Coalition; Nat Asn Broadcaster; Nat Asn TV Programming Execs; chmn bd, pres, Watts Willowbrook Boys & Girls Club. **Home Addr:** 3803 Alta St, Houston, TX 77021-2519. **Business Addr:** Group Publisher, Los Angeles Wave Publications Group, 3731 Wilshire Blvd Suite 840, Los Angeles, CA 90010, **Business Phone:** (323)556-5720.

**MARSHALL, REESE**
Lawyer. **Personal:** Born Sep 3, 1942, Ft. Lauderdale, FL; married Leonora Griffin; children: Dara Isabelle, Kemba Lee & Reese Evans. **Educ:** Morgan State Col, BA, 1963; Howard Univ, LLB, 1966. **Career:** Fla Comn Human Rels, chmn; Fla Chap NBA, pres; Johnson & Marshall, partner, 1971-79; Reese Marshall Law Off, atty, 1979-. **Orgs:** Kappa Alpha Psi Frat; chmn, Jacksonville Urban League; Past pres, Nat Bar Asn, Fla Chap; Downtown Develop Authority. **Home Addr:** 9100 Westlake Cir, Jacksonville, FL 32208, **Home Phone:** (904)764-8803. **Business Addr:** Attorney, Reese Marshall Law Office, 214 E Ashley St, Jacksonville, FL 32202-3120, **Business Phone:** (904)354-8429.

**MARSHALL, THURGOOD, JR.**
Government official, lawyer. **Personal:** Born Aug 12, 1956, New York, NY; son of Thurgood and Cecilia S; married Colleen P Mahoney; children: Thurgood William III & Edward Patrick. **Educ:** Univ Va, BA, 1978, Sch Law, JD, 1981. **Career:** Judge Barrington D Parker, law clerk, 1981-83; Kaye Scholer Fierman Hays & Handler, atty, 1983-85; Sen Albert Gore Jr, coun & staff dir, 1985-87, Us Senate Govt Affairs Comt, subcomt staff dir & chief coun to sen gore, 1985-87; Us Senate Com Comt, consumer subcomt coun, 1987; Gore Pres, dep campaign mgr, 1987-88; Sen Judiciary Comt, Sen Edward M Kennedy, coun, 1988-92; Clinton-Gore Campaign, Sen Al Gore Traveling Staff, sr policy adv, 1992; Off vpres, dep coun, dir legis affairs, 1993-97; White House, asst to pres Clinton, Cabinet secy, 1997-2001; Swidler Berlin Shereff Friedman, partner, 2001-06; Bingham McCutchen LLP, partner, 2001-; Salt Lake Winter Olympic & Paralympic Games, Involvement Fed Govt Preparations, coord, 2002; Bingham Consult Group, prin, currently; Swidler Berlin's Harbor Group, dir, 2005-06; Bingham Consult, prin; Morgan Lewis & Bockius LLP, Partner, 2014-; Morgan Lewis Consult LLC, prin, 2014-. **Orgs:** Am Bar Asn; DC Bar Asn; Bars US Dist Ct DC Second Circuit Ct Appeals; Comn Advan Policy Affecting Disadvantage ed, 1978-80; bd mem, Fed Bar Asn, DC Chap, 1984-86; bd mem, Am Coun Young Polit Leaders, 1993; bd trustee, Supreme Ct Hist Soc; co chair, White House Olympic Task Force; bd mem, Nat Women's Law Ctr, 2004; Interagency Task Force US. Coast Guard Roles & Missions; mem bd gov, US Postal Serv; bd dir, Ford Found 2007-; bd dir, Ethics Resource Ctr, 2011-; Corrections Corp Am; Nat Bar Asn; Dem Conv deleg, 1996; bd dir, Nat Fish & Wildlife Found, 2001-07; bd trustee, Third Way, 2005-; Rules Comt, Dem Conv, 2004; chmn & bd gov, US Postal Serv, 2012. **Home Addr:** , Falls Church, VA 22040. **Business Addr:** Partner, Bingham McCutchen LLP, 2020 K St NW, Washington, DC 20006-1806, **Business Phone:** (202)373-6598.

**MARSHALL, TIMOTHY H.**
Consultant, musicologist. **Personal:** Born Dec 8, 1949, Aiken, SC. **Educ:** Lone Mtn Col San Francisco, BA, 1974. **Career:** Nat United Comn free Angela Davis & all Pol Prisoners Commun Fund, nat staff mem, 1971-72; Black Scholar Speakers Bur, nat dir; Comn Lieson Cinema Lone Mountain; Col San Francisco, promotional coord; Jamaica Bus Resource Ctr, pres, chief exec officer, currently. **Orgs:** Founding mem pres & min affairs, Progressive Black Orgn, 1967-70; Founder & pres, Black Stud Union, Agusta Col, 1968-69; Jr League Follies, musical dir Extravaganza, 1970; prof, musician Episcopal Diocese Augusta, Ga, 1970-71; Creator & dir, Concert Angela, 1972; Black Expo Concert Prod Staff, 1972; promotional dir, Black World Found, 1973-74; Afro-Am Music Opportunites Asn; Nat Alliance Against Racist & Pol Repression; Inst BlackWorld; African-Am Hist & Cult Soc; Nat Coordr Elayne Jones Defense Com; Wake Forest Baptist Med Ctr. **Honors/Awds:** Silver Ring, Loatian Delegation; Fraternal pin deleg Guinea Bissau Africa, 1973; outstanding service trophy Laney HS Agusta, Ga, 1968; Omega Psi Phi Scholarship, 1967; Augusta Chronical Newspaper Gold Plaque, 1966-67. **Home Addr:** 1331 20th Ave, San Francisco, CA 94122. **Business Addr:** President, Chief Executive Officer, Jamaica Business Resource Center, 9033 160th St, Jamaica, NY 11432, **Business Phone:** (718)206-2255.

**MARSHALL, WILBER BUDDYHIA**
Football player. **Personal:** Born Apr 18, 1962, Titusville, FL. **Educ:** Univ Fla, grad. **Career:** Football player (retired); Chicago Bears, linebacker, 1984-87; Wash Redskins, linebacker, 1988-92; Houston Oilers, linebacker, 1993; Ariz Cardinals, linebacker, 1994; New York Jets, linebacker, 1995. **Honors/Awds:** Lombardi Award Finalist, Nat Defensive Player of the Year, ABC Sports, 1983; University of Florida Athletic Hall of Fame, Col Football Hall of Fame, Pro Bowl, 1986; 1987; 1992; NFC Defensive Player of the Year, 1992; NFL Alumni Linebacker of the Year, 1993; NFLPA NFC Linebacker of the Year, 1992; 1993; 70 Greatest Redskins, All Southern Player of the Year & Acad All Am sr; Col Football Hall of Fame, 2008. **Special Achievements:** Films: 1985 NFC Championship Game, 1986; Super Bowl XX, 1986; Super Bowl XXVI, 1992. TV Series: 1984 NFL Draft, 1984.

**MARSHALL-MCENTIRE, H JEAN. See MARSHALL, H. JEAN.**

**MARSHBURN, EVERETT LEE**
Executive, television broadcaster. **Personal:** Born Jan 4, 1948, Baltimore, MD; son of William A Hall and Theresa G. **Educ:** Morgan State Univ, Baltimore, MD, BA, 1976. **Career:** Producer: Md Pub TV, Owings Mills, Md, dir regional prod, 1993, vpres broadcast prod, exec producer, vpres, currently. TV Series: Black Nouveav, producer; Black Men: Uncertain Futures, exec producer; Other Faces Aids, exec producer; Morgan Choir: A Silver Celebration, exec producer. **Orgs:** Charter mem, Beta Omega Epsilon Frat Inc, 1965-; Md Humanities Coun, 1987-92; Black Ment Health Alliance, 1990-92; Nat Asn Black Journalists; bd mem, Fund Educ Excellence. **Business Addr:** Vice President, Maryland Public Television, 11767 Owings Mills Blvd, Owings Mills, MD 21117, **Business Phone:** (410)356-5600.

**MARTIN, ALBERT LEE (AL MARTIN)**
Baseball player. **Personal:** Born Nov 24, 1967, West Covina, CA; married Cathy; children: Brandon. **Career:** Baseball player (retired); Pittsburgh Pirates, outfielder, 1992-99; San Diego Padres, outfielder, 2000; Seattle Mariners, outfielder, 2001; Tampa Bay Devil Rays, outfielder, 2003; LG Twins, outfielder, 2004.

**MARTIN, DR. AMON ACHILLES, JR.**
Dentist. **Personal:** Born May 21, 1940, Anderson, SC; married Brenda Watts; children: Jocelyn, Amon III & Theodore. **Educ:** Fisk Univ, BA; Howard Univ, Col Dent, DDS, 1966. **Career:** St Bd Dent, Labor licensing & regulation, pres, 1999-2005; pvt pract dentist, currently. **Orgs:** Am Dent Asn; Nat Dent Asn; Palmetto Med Dent & Pharmaceut Asn; fel Int Col Dentists; Omega Psi Phi; past pres, Anderson Dent Soc; Seneca Adv Bd; mem bd visitors, Clemson Univ, 1984-86; Sigma Pi Phi Frat; SC St Bd Dent; mem comn, pres comn, Clemson Univ. **Home Addr:** 1031 Shiloh Rd, Seneca, SC 29678, **Home Phone:** (864)882-7408. **Business Addr:** Dentist, 208 N Walnut St, Seneca, SC 29678, **Business Phone:** (864)882-2372.

**MARTIN, AREVA**
Activist, lawyer, television broadcaster. **Personal:** children: 3. **Educ:** Univ Chicago, BA, econs, 1984; Harvard Law Sch, JD, 1987. **Career:** Martin & Martin LLP, founding & managing partner, 2005-; Spec Needs Network Inc, founder & pres, 2007-15; tv talk show host, civil rights atty & legal, social issues & pop cult commentator, 2010-. **Orgs:** United Healthcare C's Found, bd dirs; Women Leadership at Ebell Los Angeles, chair; S Los Angeles Regional Task Force Senate Select Comt Autism, chair; Calif Blue Ribbon Comn Autism, Educ & Professions Comt, chair; Los Angeles County Bar; Black Women Lawyers; Langston Bar Asn. **Honors/Awds:** Los Angeles County, Woman of the Year Award, Recipient; L'Oreal Paris, Women of Worth, Recipient; KCET, Local Hero Award, Recipient; Farmers Insurance, Living Legends Award, Recipient; California Legislative Black Caucus, Civil Rights Leadership Award, Recipient; New Frontier Democratic Party, Leadership Award, Recipient; National Association of University Woman, Community Service Award, Recipient; Bank of America, "Local Hero Award", Recipient; California Association of Black Attorneys Community Service Award and the California Black Caucus, "Trailblazer Award", Recipient; "LA Focus Newspaper", Top Lawyers, 2007 and 2011; Southern California's Super Lawyers List, Listee, 2014. **Special Achievements:** Regular appearances on TV shows "The Dr. Phil Show," "Anderson Cooper 360," "Nancy Grace," "The Doctors," "The CBS Early News," "Fox News," and "Dr. Drew On Call"; author of "Journey to the Top: 12 Steps to Take Control of Your Career and Your Life" and "The Everyday Advocate: Standing Up for Your Child with Autism and Other Special Needs" (Penguin, 2010); blog writer for Huffington Post; featured in magazines such as "Redbook," "The Los Angeles Times," and "Ebony". **Home Addr:** , Los Angeles, CA.

**MARTIN, ARNOLD LEE, JR.**
Health services administrator. **Personal:** Born Jan 10, 1939, Hartford, CT; married Mary Remona Garner; children: Zena Monique & Arnold Lee III. **Educ:** FBI Nat Acad, attended 1981; NH Col, BS, 1983. **Career:** Hartford Police Dept, chief's adv, 1962-83; WTIC 1080 Corp, chmn adv comn, 1974-82; Am Red Cross Hartford, bd dirs, 1975-84, exec dir 1986-. **Orgs:** Chmn, Proj 90 USN Recruiting Team, 1974-75; bd dir, Nat Asn Advan Colored People, 1975; first vpres, Conn Asn Police Community Rel Off, 1979-81; Hartford Hosp Pub Rels Bd, 1981-83; first vpres, W Hartford Lions Club, 1982; Urban League, 1982; rhetoricos, Sigma Pi Phi Fraternity, 1985-; pres, Alpha Phi Alpha Fraternity, 1986-87. **Home Addr:** 626 Pk Rd, West Hartford, CT 06107. **Business Addr:** Executive Director, American Red Cross Blood Donor Center, 75 Pearl St, Hartford, CT 06103, **Business Phone:** (860)524-7800.

**MARTIN, B. HERBERT, SR.**
Religious leader, civil rights activist. **Personal:** Born Dec 28, 1942, Mound Bayou, MS; children: 3. **Educ:** Philander Smith Col, BS, 1967; Payne Theol Sem; Garrett Theol Sem, Mdiv, 1970. **Career:** Sherman, Clair Christian, Gresham & St. Mark United Methodist churches, pastor, 1968-79; Black United Methodist Church Renewal, exec dir Chicago chap, 1979-81; Progressive People's Community Ctr-People's Church, pastor, 1981-; Chicago Housing Authority, mem bd dirs, 1986-87, chmn, 1987-88; Chicago Comn Human Rels, exec dir, 1988-89. **Orgs:** Nat Asn Advan Colored People; Chicago S Side-Nat Asn Advan Colored People, pres, 1985-87, exec dir, 1980-82; bd mem Christian Laity Chicago, One Church One Child, Million Man March-Chicago Organizing Comt, & Oper PUSH. **Special Achievements:** Served as the pastor to former Chicago mayor Harold Washington. **Business Addr:** Progressive Community Church, 56 E 48th St, Chicago, IL 60615, **Business Phone:** (773)538-2677.

**MARTIN, BARBARA ANITA. See BLACKMON, BARBARA MARTIN.**

**MARTIN, BARON H.**
Judge. **Personal:** Born Sep 14, 1926, Boston, MA. **Educ:** Suffolk Univ, AA, BA, 1951, JD, 1957, LLB; Univ Chicago, exec mgt training, 1972; Boston Univ; Howard Univ. **Career:** Judge (retired), executive, educator; MA Bay Transit Authority, clerk, 1951, atty, 1958, sr atty, 1970, Comn MA, spl asst atty gen, 1972, asst gen coun, 1976, dir, 2001; Roxbury Dist Ct, Spec Justice, 1972-80; Wareham Dist Ct, presiding justice, 1981-85; Appellate Div Dist Cts, Southern Dist, presiding justice, 1985-95; Southern New Eng Sch Law, sr adj prof law, bd trustee, currently. **Orgs:** Metrop Transit Authority, 1952; MA Bar Asn; Am Bar Asn; MA Trial Lawyers; chmn, Dem Ward Comt, 1950-64; Am Judges Asn; US Dist Ct, 1959; US Supreme Ct, 1966; Am Jud Soc; Int Acad Law & Sci; Urban League; Nat Asn Advan Colored People; alt deleg, Dem Nat Conv, 1968; dir, Southern ME Law sch; gen coun & chmn, Exec Bd Unity Bank & Trust, 1990-. **Business Addr:** Board of Trustee, Southern New England School of Law, 333 Faunce Cor Rd, North Dartmouth, MA 02571-2112, **Business Phone:** (508)998-9600.

**MARTIN, BLANCHE W.**
Dentist, football player. **Personal:** Born Jan 16, 1937, Millhaven, GA; children: Gary, Steven, Michael, Gunnar, Skye, Koffar, Rane & Hantar. **Educ:** Mich State Univ, BS, 1959; Univ Detroit, DDS, 1963. **Career:** Football player (retired), dentist; New York Titans, fullback, 1960; Los Angeles Chargers, fullback, 1960; pvt pract dentist, currently; E Lansing Dent Assocs, owner. **Orgs:** Cent Dist Dent Asn, 1967-; Omicron Kappa Upsilon Nat Den Hon, 1967; African Am mem bd trustee, Mich State Univ, 1969-76, 1977-84; chmn bd, 1975-76; Am Dent Asn; Mich Dent Asn; SPP; A & A Fraternities; Golden Heritage; NCP. **Honors/Awds:** Academic All American Football player, 1957-58; Recipient Award for excel in General Dental. **Special Achievements:** First African American member of the Michigan State University Board of Trustees. **Home Addr:** 816 Ravenwood Ct, Mason, MI 48854, **Home Phone:** (517)749-0906. **Business Addr:** Dentist, Blanche Martin, 201 1/2 E Grand River, East Lansing, MI 48823, **Business Phone:** (517)351-9070.

**MARTIN, CARL E.**
Government official. **Personal:** Born Feb 14, 1931, Birmingham, AL; married Patricia; children: Ennis, Joel, Carla & Dana. **Educ:** Miles Col, BA, 1953; Pepperdine Univ, MPA, 1973; La Col Law, JD, 1978. **Career:** La County Human Rel Comn, exec dir; Calif Youth Auth, group supvr, parole agt; La County Probation Dept, sr dep prof officer; La Inglewood Culver City Duarte Sch Dist, coun; Univ S Calif & Univ Calif, Los Angeles, Calif State Univ Sys, coun. **Orgs:** Bd dir, Econ & Youth Opport Agency; pres, Fedn Black Hist & Arts Inc; bd dir, HELM Scholar Found; bd dir, RAKESTRAW Educ & Community Ctr; Wesley United Methodist Church; Employ Develop Comn, La Urban League; bd dir, Westminster Neighborhood Asn. **Home Addr:** 409 Golf Dr, Hoover, AL 35226-2316, **Home Phone:** (205)823-5861. **Business Addr:** 320 W Temple St 1184 Hall Rec, Los Angeles, CA 90012, **Business Phone:** (213)974-7611.

**MARTIN, CAROL (FRANCES MARTIN)**
Executive, journalist, vice president (organization). **Personal:** Born Jul 15, 1948, Detroit, MI; daughter of Daniel (deceased) and Idessa; married Joe Terry. **Educ:** Wayne State Univ, BA, 1970. **Career:** Journalist, executive; WWJ-TV, Detroit, dept asst pub affairs, 1970-71; Detroit Free Press, ed features dept, feature writer, 1971-73; WMAL-TV, Wash, DC, gen assignment reporter, 1973-75; WCBS-TV, NY, gen assignment news corresp, 1975-95; WJLA-TV, Wash, DC, reporter & producer; Syndicated TV, 1996-; Bayer, Intel & Johnson & Johnson, voice over artist; Making Hist Ltd, sr vpres & founder, 2001-. **Orgs:** Am Fed TV & Radio Artists; US Sen & House Representatives Radio TV Gallery; adv bd, Nat Child Day Care Asn, 1974-75. **Business Addr:** Founder, Senior Vice President, Making History Ltd, 954 W Wash Blvd, Chicago, IL 60607, **Business Phone:** (312)492-9160.

**MARTIN, PROF. CAROLYN ANN**
Educator. **Personal:** Born Aug 14, 1943, Versailles, MO. **Educ:** Lincoln Univ, BS, phys educ & psychol, 1968; Univ Calif, Riverside, grad courses, 1972; Calif State Poly Univ Pomona, MS, 1974; Pepperdine Univ, Los Angeles, CA, attended 1984. **Career:** Lincoln Univ Miss, Dept Phys Educ, teaching asst, 1964-68; Perris High Sch Dist, instr phys ed, 1968-78, phys educ teacher, nursing women's athletic dir, 1968-74; Perris Jr High Sch, chmn phys educ, 1970-74; Calif State Univ, assoc prof phys educ, 1974, prof phys educ, prof emer, currently, Stanislaus, coordr; Calif St Univ Summer Upward Bound, recreation cord, 1976; San Bernardino High Sch, head coach womens varsity softball, 1981-84. **Orgs:** Calif Asn Health Phys Educ Recreation & Dance, 1973-74, 1979-80; St Sch Supt Wilson Riles, St Task Force Athletic Injuries, 1976-77; bd mem, 3 Sports Inc, 1977; Am Alliance Health Phys Educ Recreation & Dance, 1979; Natl Girls & Womens Speed ball Guide Comt, 1980-84; San Bernardino Sexual Assault Serv Ctr, 1983-84; Joint Comn Am Asn Leisure & Recreation, Am Alliance Health Phys Educ, Recreation & Dance, Natl Assessment Elem Sch Playgrounds, 1985; Am Alliance Health; Calif Teachers Asn; Calif Fac Asn; Natl Bowling Coun; Natl Asn Sport & Phys Educ; Natl Asn Girls & Womens Sports; Calif Asn Black Fac & Staff; Delta Kappa Gamma. **Home Addr:** 1123 Montrose Ave, San Bernardino, CA 92404. **Business Addr:** Professor Emeritus, Lecturer, California State University San Bernardino, 5500 Univ Pkwy, San Bernardino, CA 92407-2318, **Business Phone:** (909)537-5353.

**MARTIN, CECIL. See MARTIN, DANYEL CECIL.**

**MARTIN, PROF. CHARLES HOWARD**
Lawyer. **Personal:** Born Nov 13, 1952, Washington, DC; son of John and Hestlene. **Educ:** Harvard Univ, BA, econs, 1974; Univ Calif, Berkeley, Boalt Hall Sch Law, JD, 1977; Columbia Bus Sch, MBA, bus, 2001. **Career:** State Fla, asst atty gen, 1982-84; Fla State Univ, asst prof law, 1984-85; Villanova Univ, asst prof law, 1985-87; Sallie Mae, asst gen coun, 1987-2000; UDC David A Clarke Sch Law, vis assoc prof, 2005-06; Open Soc Inst, vis fac fel, 2003-05, lectr, 2005; Fla Coastal Sch Law, asst prof law, 2006-10; Harriet Fulbright Col, instr, 2010-13; Every1's Guide Press, auth, 2016-; Hogan & Hartson, law pract; Civic Educ Proj, vis facfel; US Dep Navy, law pract; DC Off, Corp Coun, law pract; Off Legal Affairs Fla, law pract; U.S. Dept Navy, asst to gen coun. **Orgs:** Fla Bar; DC Bar. **Special Achievements:** Author: Every1's Guide to Electronic Contracts, 2013-. Publications: Comparative Human Rights Jurisprudence in Azerbaijan: Theory, Practice and Prospects, Journal of Transnational Law & Policy, 2005; Electronic Contracts: Emerging Dimensions, Amicus Books/ICFAI University Press, 2008; International Sale of Goods - Application and Implication, Amicus Books/ICFAI University Press, 2010; Every1's Guide to Electronic Contracts - Contract Law on How to Create Electronic Signatures and Contracts, Every1's Guide Press, 2013; Lawyerball - The Courtroom Battle of the Orioles Against the Nationals and MLB for the Future of Baseball, Every1's Guide Press, 2016. **Home Addr:** 1613 Otis St NE, Washington, DC 20018-2321, **Home Phone:** (202)635-3729. **Business Addr:** Assistant Professor of Law, Florida Coastal School of Law, 8787 Baypine Rd, Jacksonville, FL 32256, **Business Phone:** (904)680-7668.

**MARTIN, CHARLES WESLEY**
Insurance executive. **Personal:** Born Apr 23, 1937, Middlesboro, KY; son of Allen and Cora; married Ella K; children: Tracy M Cargo, Charla M Sturdivant, Katheryn & Angela. **Educ:** Ky State Univ, attended 1960. **Career:** Proctor & Gamble Co, sales rep, 1970-71; Eastern Life Zone, vpres, 1981-82; Allstate Ins Co, sales agt, 1971-72, sales mgt, 1972-80, reg vpres, Denver, Colo, 1982-86, reg vpres southern calif, 1986-94, vpres sales corp off, 1995-. **Orgs:** First vpres, Nat Asn Advan Colored People, Waukegan, Ill chap, 1967; bd trustee, Shaker Heights Community Church Christ, Shaker Heights, OH, 1980-81; bd trustee, Second Baptist Church, Santa Ana, Calif, 1988-91; bd trustee, bd deacons, Zion Baptist, Denver, Co, 1984-86; bd mem, Urban League, Orange County, Ca, 1991-94; Prison Fel Ministry, Inland Empire, Orange City, Ca, 1992-94; Calif Ins Commissioners, anti discrimination task force, 1993-94; Kappa Alpha Psi Fraternity. **Honors/Awds:** Black Achievers of Industry, YMCA Metrop Chicago, 1976. **Home Addr:** 2115 Royal Ridge Dr, Northbrook, IL 60062-8610.

**MARTIN, CHERYL**
Television news anchorperson. **Educ:** Northwestern Univ, BS, radio-tv, MS, brdcst jour. **Career:** WJLA-TV, reporter & producer; WRC-TV, reporter & producer; Black Entertainment TV, anchor, 2002-; Excellent Living, host; Book: 1st Class Single; Be the Dreaming You, 2009; "Moms, Kids & Crack", "The Legacy: Dreaming and Living Success", "Mission in the Hood". **Orgs:** Kappa Alpha Pi Jr Socs; Mortar Bd Sr Socs; US bd World Vision. **Honors/Awds:** First alumni, Hall of Achievement for excellence in journalism, Sch Journalism; Silver Award, 1991. **Home Addr:** 5301 Westbard Circle Suite 134, Bethesda, MD 20816-1425. **Business Addr:** Anchor, Owner, Cheryl Martin LLC, PO Box 15285, Chevy Chase, MD 20825, **Business Phone:** (301)907-8215.

**MARTIN, CHRISTOPHER**
Singer, actor, business owner. **Personal:** Born Jul 10, 1962, New York, NY; married Shari Headley; children: Skyler & Vannessa. **Career:** Actor, singer, producer, director, business owner; Film: The Cosby Show; 2 Hype, 1988; House Party, 1990; Kid 'N Play, 1990; House Party 2, 1991; Face the Nation, 1991; Class Act, 1992; House Party 3, 1994; Rising to the Top, 1999; Welcome to Durham, USA, 2007; The Return, 2010; Singer: Traveling Companion, 1998; TV Show: "Sealab 2021", 2002; Kid n Play; Amen Films, exec dir, currently; BrandNewz.com, chief exec officer; HP4 Digital Works & Solutions, founder & chief exec officer, currently; Nc Cent Univ, hip hop teacher, currently . **Home Addr:** , Durham, NC 27701. **Business Addr:** Chief Executive Officer, Founder, HP4 Digitalworks & Solutions, PO Box 606, Durham, NC 27702, **Business Phone:** (205)781-4411.

**MARTIN, CLARENCE L.**
Air force officer, lawyer. **Personal:** Born Baxley, GA; married Annie D; children: Anthony L & Bernard E. **Educ:** Savannah St Col, BS,

1970; Emory Univ, Notre Dame Law Sch, 1973. **Career:** City Savannah, asst city atty, judge pro temporo recorders ct; C & S Bank; SS Kresge Co; Hill, Jones & Farrington; Whitcomb & Keller Mortgage Co; Martin, Thomas & Bass PC, atty; Clarence L Martin PC, chief exec officer, currently. **Orgs:** Savannah Bar Asn; Ga Bar Asn; Am Bar Asn; Nat Asn Advan Colored People; Oper Push; Martin Luther King Fel Woodrow Wilson Found. **Special Achievements:** First African American to become the assistant attorney in the city of Savannah. **Home Addr:** 15 Anchorage Ct, Savannah, GA 31410-2124. **Business Addr:** Chief Executive Officer, Clarence L Martin PC, 109 W Liberty St, Savannah, GA 31412, **Business Phone:** (912)233-6685.

### MARTIN, CURTIS JAMES, JR.

Football player. **Personal:** Born May 1, 1973, Pittsburgh, PA; son of Curtis Sr (deceased) and Rochella Dixon; married Carolina Williams; children: Ava. **Educ:** Univ Pittsburgh, pub admin. **Career:** Football player (retired); New Eng Patriots, running back, 1995-97; New York Jets, running back, 1998-2006; AFC Championship, hon capt, 2010. **Orgs:** Founder, Curtis Martin Job Found. **Honors/Awds:** City League Player of the Year, Pittsburgh Post-Gazette & Pittsburgh Press, 1990; Pro Bowl, 1995, 1996, 1998, 2001, 2004; Rookie of the Year, Nat Football League, 1995; Rookie of the Year, Asian Football Conf, 1995; Offensive Rookie of the Year, Nat Football League, 1995; Dennis Byrd Award, 2001, 2002; Most Valuable Player Award, 2004; Bart Starr Man of the Year Award, 2005; Pro Football Hall of Fame, 2012. **Home Addr:** 2017 Karen Dr, Pittsburgh, PA 15237-1437.

### MARTIN, HON. DANIEL E., SR.

Judge. **Personal:** Born Apr 14, 1932, Bluffton, SC; son of John Henry and Rena Johnson; married Ruby Mae Nesbitt; children: Daniel E Jr & Max Maurice. **Educ:** Allen Univ, Columbia, SC, BS, health & phys educ, 1954; Howard Univ Sch Law, attended 1955; SC State Col, JD, 1966; Univ Nev, National Judicial Col, gen jurisdiction course. **Career:** Judge (retired); Wallace HS, phys educ dept, 1959-62; Gresham Meggett HS, math teacher, 1962-63; Neighborhood Legal Asst Prog, founder & dir, 1968-72; 9th Jud Circuit, asst solicitor first black, 1974-84; SC House Rep, vchair, judicial comt, 1984-92; Ninth Judicial Circuit SC, presiding judge, 1992-2001. **Orgs:** Am Bar Asn; SC Bar Asn; Charleston Co Bar Asn; Judges Selection Comt State SC Black Lawyer; Gov Energy Comn; State Bd Voc Rehab; US Tax Ct; US Ct Customs & Patent Appeals; Fed Dist Ct, Dist SC; US Supreme Ct; trustee, Emanuel AME Church; trust bd, Allen Univ; charter mem, Choraliers Music Club; life mem, treas, Alpha Phi Alpha Fraternity; Downtown Charleston Rotary Int Club; Charleston Bus & Prof Asn; Us Ct Claims; Fourth Circuit Ct Appeals; life mem, Gamma Lambda Boule Sigma Pi Phi Fraternity; bd dir, Pub Defender Corp; finance chmn, Palmetto Dist Coastal Carolina Boy Scouts Am; Charleston Trident Chamber Com, 1971-75; vicepresident Dem Party Charleston County, 1968-76; bd mem, Legal Advisor, Proj Pride Inc, 1970-; vice chmn, Charleston County Bicentennial Comt, 1975-77; First Cong Dist State Comt Judicial Reform, 1976; Pub Defender Corp Charleston County; Greater Charleston YMCA; Carolina Low Country Chap Am Nat Red Cross; S Carolina State Agency Voc Rehab, 1970-84; Trident United Way; selective serv advisor, Local Bd #10, 1972-; Gov's Comt Energy Coun; founder, dir, Neighborhood Legal Assistance Prog Inc, 1967-72; asst solicitor, Ninth Judicial Circuit; spec homicide prosecutor, 1974-84. **Home Addr:** 117 Gordon St, Charleston, SC 29403, **Home Phone:** (843)723-3046. **Business Addr:** 61 Morris St, Charleston, SC 29413.

### MARTIN, JUDGE DANIEL EZEKIEL, JR.

Lawyer, judge. **Personal:** Born Jan 21, 1963, Charleston, SC; son of Daniel E Jr and Ruby N; married Reba Hough. **Educ:** Howard Univ, BA, 1985; Univ SC Sch Law, JD, 1988. **Career:** House Rep, law clerk, 1986-88; Martin, Gailliard & Martin, atty & partner, 1988-; Charleston part-time magistrate, 1989-93; Martin & Martin, atty, 1989-2011; Town Lincolnville, legal coun, 1991-98; Martin Law Off, atty & partner, currently; Ninth Judicial Circuit, family ct judge, 2011-. **Orgs:** Pres, Network Charleston, 1989-; treas, SC Black Lawyer Asn, 1990-; corresp secy, Beta Kappa Lambda Chap, Alpha Phi Alpha, 1990-; bd trustee, Emmanuel AME Church, 1990-; exec bd, Charleston, Nat Asn Advan Colored People, 1991-; exec bd, Cannon St YMCA; Mayor's Comt 12; Charleston Comm C; Masonic Lodge No 51; George Wash Carver Consistory No 162; Arabian Temple No 139; Owl's Whist Club; 100 Black Men Charleston. **Honors/Awds:** Community Service, Charleston Chap, 1990; Celebrity Reader, Charleston Co Lib Asn, 1990. **Home Addr:** 1902 Capri Dr, Charleston, SC 29407-7606, **Home Phone:** (843)766-9280. **Business Addr:** Attorney, Partner, Martin Law Offices, 61 Morris St, Charleston, SC 29403-6038, **Business Phone:** (843)723-1686.

### MARTIN, DANYEL CECIL (CECIL MARTIN)

Executive, football player, broadcaster. **Personal:** Born Jul 8, 1975, Chicago, IL; son of Diana. **Educ:** Univ Wis, BA, commun arts & bus, 1999. **Career:** Football player (retired), exec, analyst; Philadelphia Eagles, running back, 1999-2003; Tampa Bay Buccaneers, running back, 2003-04; Oakland Raiders, running back, 2003; BSkyB, sports broadcaster, 2003-; Ocean Tomo, consult, 2004-; Guggenheim Partners, vpres, 2006-07; Athletic Recruiting Network, sr nat speaker, 2007-; Nat Col Scouting Assoc, educ speaker, currently; Sky Sports, studio analyst, currently. **Orgs:** Bd dir, Nat Wis Alumni Asn, 2006. **Honors/Awds:** Eagles Ed Block Courage Award, 2000; NFL Unsung Hero Award for community services, 2001, 2002; NFL Ed Block Courage Award for community, 2002. **Business Addr:** Educational Speaker, National Collegiate Scouting Association, 1415 N Dayton St 4th Flr, Chicago, IL 60642, **Business Phone:** (888)333-6846.

### MARTIN, DARNELL

Movie director. **Personal:** Born Jan 7, 1964, Bronx, NY; daughter of Marilyn; married Giuseppe Ducret. **Educ:** Sarah Lawrence Col, BA; New York Univ Film Sch, MA. **Career:** Deadly Obsession, actress, 1989; Nowhere Fast, actress, 1997; Prison Song, exec producer, 2001; Circulo vicioso, El, assoc producer, 2003; Filmmaker, currently; Film: suspect, 1992; I Like It Like That, writer & dir, 1994; Their Eyes Were Watching God, writer & dir, 2005; Cadillac Records, writer & dir, 2008; tv series: Law & Order; Grey's Anatomy; Homicide Life on the Street, 1993; ER, 1994; Oz, 1997; Special Victims Unit, 1997; Criminal Intent, 2001; Dragnet, 2003. **Orgs:** Writers Guild Am. **Honors/Awds:** Directing fellowship, Sundance Inst, Utah. **Special Achievements:** First African-American woman to make a movie with the sponsorship of a major Hollywood studio. **Business Addr:** Filmmaker, Columbia Pictures, 10202 W Wash Blvd, Culver City, CA 90232-3195, **Business Phone:** (310)244-4000.

### MARTIN, DARRICK DAVID

Basketball player, basketball executive, basketball coach. **Personal:** Born Mar 6, 1971, Denver, CO; son of Pam and Jesse. **Educ:** Univ Calif-Los Angeles, attended 1992. **Career:** Basketball player (retired), basketball exec; Sioux Falls Skyforce, guard, 1994-95, 2003-04; Minn Timberwolves, pt guard, 1995, 2003-04, asst dir Player develop, 2009-; Vancouver Grizzlies, 1995-96; Los Angeles Clippers, pt guard, 1996-99, 2004-05; Sacramento Kings, pt guard, 1999-2001; Dallas Mavericks, pt guard, 2001-02; Yakima Sun Kings, 2002-03; Harlem Globetrotters, 2003; Avtodor Saratov, 2002; Toronto Raptors, guard & pt guard, 2005-08; Los Angeles Lightning, 2009; Minn Timberwolves, asst dir, 2009; St John's Red Storm men's, asst coach, 2012; UCLA Bruins IMG Sports network, host, 2015; Reno Bighorns, head coach, 2016-. **Honors/Awds:** Newcomer of the Year, Continental Basketball Asn, 1995; Most Valuable Player, Continental Basketball Asn, 2003. **Business Addr:** Assistant Coach, Reno Bighorns, 50 W Liberty St, Reno, NV 89501, **Business Phone:** (775)853-8220.

### MARTIN, DEWAYNE NATHANIEL, JR.

Government official. **Personal:** Born Oct 18, 1967, Chicago, IL; son of DeWitt N Jr and Anne. **Educ:** Morehouse Col, BA, 1989; Ga State Univ Col Law, JD, 1994. **Career:** US Census Bur, mgr field opers, 1989-90; City Atlanta, legis aide, 1991-94, dep chief staff, 1994-97, chief staff, 1997. **Orgs:** Butler St YMCA, 1975-; bd mem, Greater Atlanta Community Corps, 1996-; State Bar Asn, 1996-; bd mem, Nat Black Arts Festival, 1997-; bd adv, Metro Atlanta Super Bowl XXXIV, 1998-. **Home Addr:** 1238 Spring Crk SW, Atlanta, GA 30311, **Home Phone:** (404)254-0832. **Business Addr:** GA.

### MARTIN, DUANE

Actor. **Personal:** Born Aug 11, 1965, Brooklyn, NY; married Tisha Campbell; children: Xen & Ezekiel Czar. **Educ:** NY Univ. **Career:** Impact Sports, owner, currently; Writer: Ride or Die, 2003; The Seat Filler, 2004; Producer: Getting Personal, producer, 1998; Ride or die, 2003; The Seat Filler, 2004; TV series: "Moe's World ", 1990; "Against the Law", 1991; "Different Worlds: A Story of Interracial Love", 1992; "Roc", 1992; "Out All Night", 1992-93; "CBS Schoolbreak Special", 1992; "The Fresh Prince of Bel-Air", 1993-95; "Happily Ever After: Fairy Tales for Every Child", 1995; "Living Single", 1997; "Between Brothers", 1997; "Getting Personal", 1998; "Mr. Headmistress", 1998; "Mutiny", 1999; "Sugar Hill", 1999; "Girlfriends", 2000; "One on One", 2001; "Blind Men", 2001; "I Got You", 2002; "Yes, Dear", 2002; "All of Us", 2003; "Abby", 2003-07; "Ghost Whisperer", 2006; "Rita Rocks", 2009; "The Paul Reiser Show", 2011; "LA Live the Show", 2013. Films: White Men Can't Jump, 1992; Above the Rim, 1994; The Ink well, 1994; Down Periscope, 1996; Scream 2, 1997; Fakin' Da Funk, 1997; Woo, 1998; The Faculty, 1998; Any Given Sunday, 1999; The Groomsmen, 2001; Ride or Die, 2003; Al Of Us, 2003; Deliver Us from Eva, 2003; What Boys Like, 2003; The Seat Filler, actor, writer & producer, 2004; Killer Movie, 2007. **Honors/Awds:** Nominated for Image Award, 2007; Nominated for BET Comedy Award, 2004; Nominated for Day Time Emmy Award, 1993. **Special Achievements:** Nominee, BET Comedy Award, 2004, 2005, 2007. **Business Addr:** Owner, Impact Sports, Phoenixville, PA 19460, **Business Phone:** (610)679-9139.

### MARTIN, REV. EDWARD, JR.

Clergy. **Personal:** Born Jun 30, 1936, Grove Hill, AL. **Educ:** Ala State Univ, BS, 1969; Carver Bible Inst, BTh; Interdenom Theol Ctr & Horehouse Sch Rel Atlanta, Mdiv, 1973. **Career:** Bethel Baptist Church, pastor, 1967-; Union Acad Baptist Church; Selma Univ Sch Rel, instr. **Orgs:** Nat Asn Advan Colored People, 1958-; YMCA, 1966-; Montgomery Improv Asn Inc, 1967-; Phi Beta Sigma, 1969-; Pres Montgomery-Antioch Dist SS & Bapt Training Union Cong, 1970; Nat Bapt Conv USA Inc; Am Beatury Lodge 858; Charlie Garrett Chap Royal Arch No 78a; United Supreme Coun 32; Prince Hall Affil Grand Orient Wash. **Honors/Awds:** Nat Found March of Dimes Award, 1971. **Business Addr:** Pastor, Bethel Baptist Church Montgomery, 1110 Mobile Rd, Montgomery, AL 36108.

### MARTIN, EDWARD ANTHONY

Podiatrist. **Personal:** Born Dec 25, 1935, Mason City, IA; married Barbara C Payne; children: Gail Ingrid, Edward Brian & Stephen Vincent. **Educ:** Mason City Jr Col, attended 1954; Ill Col Podiatric Med, DPM, 1958. **Career:** Podiatrist, 1958-; Ill Dept Regist & Educ, podiatry examr, 1978. **Orgs:** Pres, Acad Ambulatory Foot Surg, 1973-74; Nat Podiatry Asn; Am Podiatry Asn. **Honors/Awds:** Henri L Du Vries Award, Proficiency Clin Surg, 1958. **Special Achievements:** First National President of Academy of Ambulatory Foot Surgery, 1973-74; Private pilot Single Engine-land, 1974; "Podiatry A Step Toward Healthy Happy Feet", Ebony Article, 1978; Instructor in surgery-instructional movie on ambulatory surgery, 1979. **Home Addr:** 2106 Mill St, Montgomery, AL 36108. **Business Addr:** Podiatrist, Private Practice, 637 E Homestead Rd, San Jose, CA 94087, **Business Phone:** (408)269-6030.

### MARTIN, DR. EDWARD WILLIFORD

Dean (education), administrator, educator. **Personal:** Born Nov 29, 1929, Sumter, SC; son of Eddie and Frances; married Pearl Evelyn Sewell; children: Andrea Michelle, Debra Yvette & Christopher Edward. **Educ:** Fisk Univ, BA, 1950; Univ Ind, MA, zool, 1952; Univ Iowa, PhD, zool, 1962. **Career:** Prairie View A&M Univ, instr biol, 1952-55, asst prof biol, 1955-59, assoc prof, 1962-66, prof, 1966-, chmn, div nat sci, 1968-81, prof & head dept biol, 1973-81, Coll Arts & Sci, interim dean, 2003-04, Biol Dept, Chair, dean, 1981-2000, dean emer, 2000-, prof, 2002-, currently. **Orgs:** Am Soc Zoologists; Am Men Sci; adv bd, Baylor Col Med; Omega Psi Phi Fraternity; Sigma Pi Phi Fraternity Nu Boule; Beta Kappa Chi Scientific Honor Soc; Beta Beta Beta Biol Honor Soc; Alpha Kappa Mu Nat Honor Soc; Tx Higher Educ Coord Bdl; Am Asn Advan Sci; Tex Acad Sci; Socs Cell Develop Biologists; former mem, Adv Comt, Baylor Col Med; exec comt, Tex Asn Advisors Health Professions; Nat Naval ROTC Scholar Selection Comt; Nsf Rev Panel; Rev Panel Nat Insts Health; chmn, Premedical Adv Comt; treas, Socs Sigma Xi Sci Res Socs; Core Curric Adv Comt Tex Higher Educ Coord Bd; Coord Bd Comt Civil Rights Issues; Syst Employee Benefits Adv Comt (SEBAC), Tex A&M Univ Syst. **Honors/Awds:** Nat Sci Fac Fel, Nat Sci Found, 1961-62; Beta Kappa Chi Distinguished Award, Beta Kappa Chi Sci Hon Soc, 1965; Minnie Stevens Piper Professor Award, 1979; Who's Who in the South & Southwest; American Men & Women of Science; Beta Beta Beta Biology Honor Society (Charter Member, Sigma Chi Chapter); Alpha Kappa Mu National Honor Society (Sponsored the Alpha Pi Mu Chapter for undergraduates for 16 years); Theta Chi Chapter of the Omega Psi Phi Fraternity Achievement Award; Omega Psi Phi Fraternity Distinguished Service Award; Prairie View A&M University National Alumni Association Faculty Recognition Award; Prairie View A&M University Top Achievement Award for the College of Arts & Sciences; Johnson-Phillip All Faiths Chapel Distinguished Service Award; University Distinguished Professor Award. **Home Addr:** 315 Elm St, PO Box 878, Prairie View, TX 77446-0878, **Home Phone:** (409)857-3258. **Business Addr:** Dean Emeritus, Professor & Chair, Prairie View A&M University, PO Box 277, Prairie View, TX 77446-0519, **Business Phone:** (936)261-3171.

### MARTIN, EMANUEL C. (MANNY MARTIN)

Football coach, football player. **Personal:** Born Jul 31, 1969, Miami, FL; married Kimarya; children: Emanuel, Tyree & Kimar. **Educ:** Ala State Univ. **Career:** Football player (retired), coach; Houston Oilers, 1993; Can Football League, Ottawa Rough Riders, 1994-95; Buffalo Bills, defensive back, 1996-99; Cent High Sch, head football coach, 2007; Dillard High Sch, head football coach, 2009-; All-American safety Wayne Lyons, coach, Currently. **Business Addr:** Head Football Coach, Dillard High School, 2501 NW 11th St, Ft. Lauderdale, FL 33311-5796, **Business Phone:** (754)322-0800.

MARTIN, FRANCES. See MARTIN, CAROL.

### MARTIN, FRANK C., II

Curator, educator. **Personal:** Born Aug 17, 1954, Sumter, SC; son of Frank C and Leola Glisson; married Shirley Fields. **Educ:** Yale Univ, BA, art hist, 1976; City Univ NY, Hunter Col, MA, art hist, 1990; NY Univ, Inst Fine Arts. **Career:** Metorp Mus Art, curatorial asst, educ assoc, 1979-87, Off Educ Servs, asst mgr, 1988-89, assoc mgr, 1989-91; IP Stanback Mus & Planetarium, SC State Univ, instr, Hist Art, lectr, 1991-, Cur Exhibs & Collections, 1991-2004; Claflin Univ, consult, 1991-2013, Univ SC, Salkehatchie, instr; Univ S Carolina, Carolina Diversity Professors' Prog Doctoral Scholar, 2008-. **Orgs:** Artists Color, SC; Renaissance Soc Am, 1988-91; Col Art Asn, 1988-91; exe bd, Eboni Dance Theatre; Orangeburg Arts Coun; Grants in Aid Panel, SC Arts Comn, visual arts chair, 1992; Orangeburg Arts League; Int Asn Art Critics, Paris, France. **Honors/Awds:** Honorable Mention, Scholastic Arts Awards Comt, 1970; Nat Achievement Commended Scholar, Educ Testing Service, 1972; Kiwanis of America, Key Club Scholar Award, 1972; lect & gallery talk, 701 Ctr Contemp Art; Yale Nat Scholar, Yale Univ, 1976; City Univ New York; William Graf Grant Travel & Study Abroad, Hunter Col, 1986. **Special Achievements:** Author: "The Museum as an Artists' Resource, Am Artist Mag", 1991; "Cultural Pluralism: A Challenge for the Arts in SC, Triennial Exhibition Catalogue", 1992; "The Acacia Historical Collection, Am Visions Mag", 1992; "Art, Race, and Culture: Context & Interpretive Bias in Contemporary Africa Art in Transcendence and Conflict: Africa Art in SC 1700-Present", 1992. **Home Addr:** 145 Lovell St SE, Orangeburg, SC 29115-5537, **Home Phone:** (803)531-2190. **Business Addr:** Instructor, South Carolina State University, 300 Col St NE, Orangeburg, SC 29117, **Business Phone:** (803)536-8406.

### MARTIN, FRANK T.

Executive. **Personal:** Born Jul 24, 1950, Nashville, TN; son of William Henry and Maureen Kimbrough; married Pamela Johnson; children: Jessica Maureen. **Educ:** Tenn State Univ, BS, bus admin, 1973; Fisk Univ, MURP, 1974. **Career:** N Cent Fla Region Planning Coun, local assistance & mass transit planner, 1974-77; Greater Richmond Transit Co, oper planning dir, 1978-80; Birmingham Jefferson County Transit Authority, from asst gen mgr to gen mgr, 1980-84; ATE, Ryder Systs Inc, Transit Mgt SE La, vpres, gen mgr, 1984-87; Miami-Dade County Transit Agency, dep dir, 1987-89, rail opers asst dir, 1987-99; Santa Clara Valley Transp Authority, chief operating officer, 1999-2004; Atkins, sr vpres, 2004-13; Frank T. Martin Consult LLC, pres, 2014-; PBS&J transit serv div, sr vpres, nat bus sector mgr, currently. **Orgs:** Nat Forum Black Pub Admin, 1987-; pres, Tenn State Univ, Alumni Asn, Miami Chap, 1990-93, 1997-; bd mem, Am Pub Transit Found, 1991-97; bd mem, New Miami Group, 1991-97; bd mem, Conf Many Transp Officials, 1992-; dir, Am Pub Transp Asn; chair, Transp Res Found. **Home Addr:** 8538 Glencairn Lane, Miami Lakes, FL 33016-1466, **Home Phone:** (305)884-7520. **Business Addr:** Senior Vice President, Manager of National Business Sector, PBS&J Transit Services Division, 1666 K St NW, Washington, DC 20006, **Business Phone:** (202)496-4800.

### MARTIN, GEORGE DWIGHT

Football player, executive. **Personal:** Born Feb 16, 1953, Greenville, SC; married Diane; children: Teresa Michelle, George Dwight II, Benjmain Dean & Aaron. **Educ:** Univ Ore, grad. **Career:** Football player (retired), executive; New York Giants, defensive end, 1975; left defensive end, 1976-81&1986-87; defensive end, 1982-84; Nat Football League Alumni, exec dir & pres, currently. **Orgs:** Former rep, United Way Pub Serv TV Community. **Honors/Awds:** Byron Whizzer White Award; Sports Hall of Fame of New Jersey, 2004; New York Giants Ring of Honor, 1986.

### MARTIN, GERALD WAYNE

Football player, real estate executive. **Personal:** Born Oct 26, 1965, Forrest City, AR; married Gladys; children: Wayne Jr, Whitley & Wishawn. **Educ:** Univ Ark, criminal justice, 1990. **Career:** Football player (retired), real estate agent; New Orleans Saints, 1989, left defensive end, 1990-94, right defensive tackle, 1995, left defensive tackle, 1996-99, defensive end & defensive tackle, 1999; real estate bus, currently. **Honors/Awds:** Ed Block Courage Award, 1991; New Orleans Saints Hall of Fame, 2003. **Special Achievements:** Film: 1989 NFL Draft, 1989.

## MARTIN, GERTRUDE S.

Public relations executive, association executive. **Personal:** Born Savannah, GA; daughter of Walter S (deceased) and Laura McDowell (deceased); married Louis Emanuel; children: Trudy Hatter, Anita, Toni, Linda Purkiss & Lisa. **Educ:** Ohio State Univ, Columbus, BA, 1934, MA, 1936. **Career:** United Planning Orgn, Wash, educ coord, 1963-66; Willmart Serv, Wash, coordr, 1966-68; Univ Chicago, Dept Educ, ed, 1970-74; Integrated Educ Assoc, Evanston, ed, 1974-78; Calmar Commun, Chicago, vpres, 1978-88; free-lance ed, 1988-. **Orgs:** Bd mem, Ill Child Care Soc, 1955-58; bd gov, Am Red Cross, 1966-72; comt, A Better Chance, Wash, 1983-85; bd mem, Black Women's Agenda, Wash, 1989-92; life mem, Nat Coun Negro Women. **Honors/Awds:** Nat Coun Negro Women; New Horizons, George Washington Univ. **Home Addr:** 3675 Gracey Field Lane, Diamond Bar, CA 91765, **Home Phone:** (714)861-1432.

## MARTIN, HAROLD B.

Dentist, college teacher. **Personal:** Born Oct 26, 1928, Petersburg, VA; married Dolores A; children: Harold, Lisa & Gregory. **Educ:** Lincoln Univ, AB, 1950; Howard Univ, DDS, 1957; John Hopkins Univ, MPH, 1971. **Career:** College teacher (retired), dentist; Howard Univ Col Dent, Dept Comm Dent, prof, 1959-87, assoc dean advan educ & res, 1987-96; Dept Corrections, DC, 1960-70; founder, Century Ltd Inc; Pvt Pract, dentist, currently; Martin Harold B DDS PC, owner, currently. **Orgs:** Vpres, Nat Dent Asn; bd dir, E River Health Asn; Am Dent Asn; Nat Dent Asn; DC Med Care Adv Comt; Nat Rev Comn Guidelines Expanded Function Training Prog; Midway Civic Asn; US Youth Games Community; Nat Asn Advan Colored People; Urban League; Omega Psi Phi; pres, Huntsmen; bd dir, Ionia Whipper Home Unwed Mothers; bd dir, Pigskin Club, Wash; Am Pub Health Asn; Sigma Xi, 1975; Omicron Kappa Upsilon, 1976; fel Am Col Dentist; pres, Howard Univ Chap, 1984-85; fel Int Col Dent, 1985. **Home Phone:** (202)667-5815. **Business Addr:** Private Practice Dentist, Martin Harold B DDS PC, 1804 Nh Ave NW, Washington, DC 20001, **Business Phone:** (202)265-5825.

## MARTIN, HAROLD L., SR.

Chancellor (education), vice president (organization), college teacher. **Personal:** Born Oct 22, 1951, Winston-Salem, NC; married Davida Wagner; children: Harold L Jr & Walter. **Educ:** NC A&T State Univ, Greensboro, BS, elec engineering, 1974, MS, elec engineering, 1976; Va Polytech Inst & State Univ, PhD, elec engineering, 1980. **Career:** NC A&T State Univ, asst prof elec engineering, 1980-82, assoc prof elec engineering, 1982-84, Dept Elec Engineering, actg chair, 1984-85, chair, 1985-87, Col Engineering, dean, 1989-94, acad affairs vice chancellor, 1994-99; Winston-Salem State Univ, 2000-06; NC A&T State Univ (Greensboro), sr vpres, 2006-09, chancellor, 2009-. **Orgs:** Winston-Salem Chamber Com, bd mem; Piedmont Club, bd dirs; Forsyth County United Way, bd mem; Winston-Salem State Univ Found, bd mem; Ctr Intercollegiate Athletics Conf, bd mem; SACS Comn Cols & Schs, bd mem; Winston-Salem Found, bd mem; Res Triangle Inst, bd mem. **Honors/Awds:** Winston-Salem Chronicle, Man of the Year, 2001; "Triad Business Journal", 10 to Watch, 2001; Virginia Tech's Distinguished Graduate Alumni Award, 2004; McDonald's 5th Annual African American Achievement Award for Education, 2005; Thurgood Marshall College Foundation, Award for Excellence, 2008; Virginia Tech College of Engineering, Distinguished Alumnus, 2010. **Special Achievements:** First alumnus in North Carolina A&T's history to hold the chancellor position; Winston-Salem University named a new residence hall in honor of Martin and his predecessor Alvin J. Schexnider in 2012; writer and co-author of numerous engineering-related articles.

## MARTIN, HAROLD L., SR.

College teacher, college administrator. **Personal:** Born Jan 1, 1952?; married Davida; children: Walter Harold Jr. **Educ:** NC Agr & Tech State Univ, BS, MS; Va Polytech Inst & State Univ, PhD. **Career:** N Carolina Agr & Tech State Univ, fac mem, 1980-94, actg chmn dept elec engineering, 1984-85 chmn dept elec engineering, 1985-89, dean Col Engineering, 1989-94, vice chancellor acad affairs, 1994-2000; Winston-Salem State Univ, chief adminr & chancellor, 2000-06; Univ N Carolina syst, sr vice syst acad affairs, 2006-09; N Carolina Agr & Tech State Univ, chancellor, 2009-. **Orgs:** Tau Beta Pi-Engineering Hon Soc; Eta Kappa Nu; Hon Soc Phi Kappa Phi; Beta Gamma Sigma; Alpha Fi Alpha Fraternity Inc; Southern Asn Cols & Schs Rev Adv Bd; Res Triangle Inst; Piedmont Triad Regional Develop Coun; Nat Col Athletic Asn Historically Black Cols & Univs Comt Acad Performance & Ltd-Resource Insts Adv Group; Bd Int Food & Agr Develop; MCNC; Blue Cross & Blue Shield NC; Res Triangle Inst; chair, Winston-Salem Found Space Admin, 2009. **Honors/Awds:** Alumnus of the Year, North Carolina Agricultural and Technical State University, 1976; Distinguished Graduate Alumni Award, Virginia Tech, 2004; Duke Power's Citizen and Service Award, 2005; McDonald's African American Achievement Award for Education, 2005; honorary degree, Wake Forest University, 2007; Academy of Engineering Excellence, Virginia Tech, inductee, 2008; Thurgood Marshall College Foundation Award for Excellence, 2008. Ebony Power 100 list, 2015; Triad's Most Influential People, Triad Business Journal, 2015; Most Admired CEOs, Triad Business Journal, 2016. **Business Addr:** North Carolina Agricultural and Technical State University, Dowdy Bldg Suite 418, Greensboro, NC 27411, **Business Phone:** (336)334-7940.

## MARTIN, HOSEA L.

Marketing executive, association executive, army officer. **Personal:** Born Aug 10, 1937, Montezuma, GA; son of Marion Cannon and H L. **Educ:** Univ Chicago, BA, 1960; Univ Chicago, Grad Sch Bus, attended 1966. **Career:** Public relations, market executive (retired); Prudential Ins Co, advert specialist, 1966-67; Coca-Cola Co, nat prom mgr, 1967-75; Safeway Stores Inc, mkt progs mgr, 1975-86; Paragraphs Unlimited, pres, founder, 1984-89; Univ Calif, ed specialist, 1986-89; United Way San Francisco, assoc vpres, vpres, 1989-2000; Int Asn Bus Communicators, media rels dir, 2000-01. **Orgs:** San Francisco Media Alliance, 1986-. **Honors/Awds:** First Place, Am Advert Fedn, Direct Mail Develop, 1968. **Special Achievements:** Articles: Wall Street Journal, 1991; Essence, 1992; Author: The Wrong Place to Die, 2002; Down by the Deadly Riverside, 2010. **Home Addr:** 6 Greenbank Ave, Piedmont, CA 94611, **Home Phone:** (510)652-4233.

## MARTIN, HOYLE HENRY

Government official, college teacher. **Personal:** Born Oct 21, 1927, Brooklyn, CA; son of Mattie Garrett and Jesse T (deceased); married Mary Campbell; children: Hoyle Jr, Michael C, David E & Cheryl L. **Educ:** Benedict Col, BA, 1957; Syracuse Univ, MA, 1961; New Life Theol Sem, DCSM, 1999. **Career:** NC & SC, col educr, teaching, 1958-66; Charlotte Concentrated Employ Prog, chief exec officer, exec dir, 1967-71; Univ NC, Urban Inst, Charlotte, assoc dir, 1972-76; Charlotte Post, NC, chief ed writer, 1974-89; City Charlotte, NC, housing develop admin, 1977-88, city coun mem, 1989-95; Mecklenburg County, comnr, 1996-98; New Life Theol Sem, prof, dept head, currently. **Orgs:** Adv mem, WBTV Black Adv Comt, 1983-89; adv bd mem, Habitat Humanity, 1987-94; bd mem, Charlotte Civilian Club, 1989-98; bd mem, Reachline Inc, 1989-92; bd mem, W Charlotte Bus Incubator, 1990-. **Home Addr:** 3012 Burbank Dr, Charlotte, NC 28216-4406, **Home Phone:** (704)392-4623. **Business Addr:** Department Head, Professor, New Life Theological Seminary, PO Box 790106, Charlotte, NC 28206-7901, **Business Phone:** (704)334-6882.

## MARTIN, I. MAXIMILLIAN

Executive. **Career:** Berean Savings Asn, Philadelphia, PA, chmn, pres, currently; Eden Cemetery Co, treas. **Orgs:** Life heritage mem, Nat Asn Advan Colored People. **Business Addr:** Chief Executive Officer, President, Berean Savings Association, 5228 Chestnut St, Philadelphia, PA 19139, **Business Phone:** (215)472-4545.

## MARTIN, IONIS BRACY

Artist, educator, painter (artist). **Personal:** Born Aug 27, 1936, Chicago, IL; daughter of Francis Wright Bracy and Hattie O Robinson Bracy; married Allyn A; children: Allyn B. **Educ:** Fisk Univ, BA, lib arts, 1957; Univ Hartford, MEd, art educ, 1968; Pratt Inst, MFA, art educ, 1987; Art Inst Chicago, Chicago Pub Schs, continuing studies, sculpture & ceramics, 2010. **Career:** YWCA Y-Teen Assoc, dir, 1957-59; Hartford Bloomfield Pub Schs, sec art teacher, 1961-2001; Weaver High Sch, Hartford, art educr, 1961-67; Artist's Collective Inc, artist & educr, 1970-73; Bloomfield Pub Schs, art educr, 1971-2001; WFSB TV/Wadsworth Atheneum, produced art segments c's prog, 1972-75; Northwestern Conn Community Col, lectr, 1985-90; Cent Conn State Univ, instr & lectr, 1985-2003; Hartford Courant, illusr, 1986-90; SkidmoreCol, art fel, 1987; Getty Ctr Educ Arts, Los Angeles, Calif, consult, 1990-93; Gale Res, consult, 1992; Harvard's WEB Dubois Inst, fel, 1994; Ionis Life Art, 2009-; Univ Hartford, Hartford Art Sch, co-founder, currently. **Orgs:** chmn, Ella Burr Mc Manus Trust, 1958-2006; Comnr, Hartford Fine Arts Comn; dir, Greater Hartford Arts Coun, Charter Oak Temple Cult Ctr & Hartford Stage Co; co-founder, vpres & dir, Artists Collective, 1970-; trustee, Wadsworth Atheneum, 1977-85, 1986-96; Links Inc, 1985-; pres, Greater Hartford Chap, 1998-2002, secy, 1994-98; mem adv comn, Conn Bd Educ, 1986-87; NAEA; CAEA; Delta Sigma Theta; pres, Artworks Gallery, 1986-87; Romare Bearden/Jackie McLean "Sound Collages & Visual Improvizations", 1986; cur/producer, Cotra Gallery "Five CT", 1987; JP Getty Trust Curric Devel Inst, 1988-; co-trustee, Burr McManus Trust, 1990-2001; Capital Comn Col, 2000; Anchor Club, 2008; Huntington House Mus, 2001-05. **Honors/Awds:** Outstanding Community Service Award, Univ Hartford, 1974; 200 Years of Achievement Against the Odds Black Women of CT; One Woman Show, Christ Church Cathedral, Hartford, 1990; Best in Show, Pump House Gallery, 1990; One Woman Show, Lindgren Gallery, Manchester, 1990; One Woman Show Northampton Arts Center, Northampton, MA, 1990; One Woman Show, Wethersfield Hist Soc, 1991; Jubilee, One Woman Show, Fisk Univ, 1992; Solo exhibit, Univ Vt, 1993; Group shows: Artworks Gallery, The CRT Gallery and Pump House Galley, 1993-94; Secondary Art Educator of the Year, Conn Art Ed Asn, 1993-94; One Woman Show, First Church of Christ Art Gallery, New Britain, CT, 2003. **Home Addr:** 1234 Prospect Ave, Hartford, CT 06105-1123, **Home Phone:** (860)232-4283. **Business Addr:** Co-Founder, University of Hartford, 200 Bloomfield Ave, West Hartford, CT 06117-1599, **Business Phone:** (860)768-4100.

## MARTIN, DR. JAMES LARENCE

Dentist. **Personal:** Born Sep 3, 1940, Dubuque, IA; son of James and Ada; married Willie Mae; children: Linda, James Larence III & John Lance. **Educ:** Loras Col, BS MicroBiol, 1959; Tenn State Univ, MS, 1960; Meharry Med Col Sch Dent, DDS, 1966; Univ Mich, MPH, 1975. **Career:** Meharry Med Col, instr, 1960-62, instr, 1967-69, dent dir, 1967-72, assoc prof, 1969-72, asst prof dept pediat, 1972-, dir, 1973-75, asst prof dept oper, 1974-75, coord, 1975-77, assoc prof, 1977-, prof, 1981-, pres, 1989-93, Dept Dent Pub Health, chmn & dir, 1999-; Comprehensive Health Care Prog C & Youth Prom, proj dir, 1972-73. **Orgs:** Am Dent Asn; Nat Dent Asn; Am Pub Health Asn; Int Asn Dent Res; Am Asn Dent Res; Am Acad Oral Med; Am Acad Gold Foil Operators; AAAS; Am Asn Dent Schs; Am Asn Med Schs; Tenn Pub Health Asn; Capitol City Dent Soc; Human Rights Comn; Alpha Phi Alpha; St Vincent DePaul Men's Club; Boy Scouts Am; Meharry Century Club; Nashville Area Chamber Com; 50 Critics Orgn; Civitan Int St Vincent DePaul Church Coun; exec adv, Am Bd Forensic Dent. **Honors/Awds:** Dlitt, Loras Col, 1982. **Special Achievements:** First African American admitted to Loras Academy; First black hired to teach in the Waterloo, Iowa, parochial school system. **Home Addr:** 3515 Geneva Cir, Nashville, TN 37209, **Home Phone:** (615)320-7237. **Business Addr:** Professor, Chair, Meharry Medical College, 1005 Dr 18th Ave N, Nashville, TN 37208.

## MARTIN, DR. JAMES TYRONE

Physician, clergy, pediatrician. **Personal:** Born Aug 17, 1942, Elkhorn, WV; son of Henry. **Educ:** Bluefield St Col, Bluefield, WV, BS, 1966; Meharry Med Col, MD, 1973. **Career:** Tri-Dist Community Health Serv, med dir; McDowell Col, teacher, 1966-69; Community Health Serv, Raleigh County, Beckley, WV, med dir, 1988-95; Emmanuel Tabernacle Baptist Church, asst pastor, 1965-88, pastor, 1992-; AccessHealth Inc, Stanaford Health Ctr, physician, 2010-. **Orgs:** Beta Kappa Chi Hon Sci Fraternity; F&AAY; Royal Arch Masons; Am Acad Family Physicians; WVa Acad Family Physicians. **Home Addr:** 211 Leon Sullivan Way, Charleston, WV 25301, **Home Phone:** (304)252-8551. **Business Addr:** Physician, AccessHealth, 201 Woodcrest Dr, Beckley, WV 25801, **Business Phone:** (304)250-0272.

## MARTIN, HON. JANICE R.

Judge. **Personal:** Born Jan 1, 1956, Morganfield, KY; daughter of Herschel and Carrie E; married Paul Porter. **Educ:** Univ Louisville, BA, polit sci, 1977; Univ Louisville Law Sch, JD, 1980. **Career:** Judge(retired); Univ Louisville, instr; pvt pract, atty; Jefferson County Attys Off, Juv Div, Jefferson Dist Ct, Louisville, KY, judge, 1993-2009. **Orgs:** Womens Lawyers Asn; bd mem, Lousiville Bar Asn; bd mem, Jewish Hosp; bd mem, NAWJ; bd mem, Ky Bar Asn; adv bd, Ctr Elders & Courts. **Special Achievements:** First elected African American woman judge in Kentucky, 1991; First African American woman to serve as bar counsel for the Kentucky Bar Association. **Home Addr:** 1302 Oxmoor Woods Pkwy, Louisville, KY 40222, **Home Phone:** (502)425-4754.

## MARTIN, JESSE LAMONT (JESSE LAMONT)

Actor, singer. **Personal:** Born Jan 18, 1969, Rocky Mount, VA; son of Jesse Reed Watkins (deceased) and Virginia Price. **Educ:** NY Univ, Tisch Sch Arts, theatre prog; Lee Strasberg Theatre & Film Inst. **Career:** Actor, singer; Stage: The Government Inspector, 1994; Rent, original cast, 1996; The Merchant of Venice, 2010; The Winter's Tale, 2010; TV series: "New York Undercover", 1995, 1998; "413 Hope St", 1997; "Ally McBeal", 1997; "The X-Files", 1999; "Law & Order", 1999-2008; "Deep in My Heart", 1999; "A Christmas Carol", 2004; "The Philanthropist", 2009 "Smash", 2013; "The Flash", 2014. Films: Restaurant, 1998; Burning House of Love, 2002; Season of Youth, 2003; Rent, 2005; The CORPS, 2007; The Cake Eaters, 2007; A Muppet Christmas: Letters to Santa, 2008; Sexual Healing, 2008; Buffalo Bushido, 2009; Peter and Vandy, 2009; Puncture, 2011; Joyful Noise, 2012; Long Live TOY, 2013. **Orgs:** John Houseman's Actg Co; Robinhood Found; bd trustee, Jonathan Larson Performing Arts Found. **Honors/Awds:** Obie Award; Best Ensemble for Rent; Entitled "Real men know how to listen, & real men know how to be honest", People Magazine, 2000; SunDeis Entertainer of the Year Award, 2006; Critics Choice Award, 2008; Attended the prestigious Lee Strasberg Theatre & Film Institute. **Home Addr:** , Manhattan, NY. **Business Addr:** Actor, Law & Order Production Office, W 23rd St & Hudson River Pier 62, New York, NY 10011.

## MARTIN, DR. JOANNE MITCHELL

President (organization), chief executive officer, educator. **Personal:** Born Jun 12, 1947, Yulee, FL; daughter of Jeremiah Mitchell and Bessie Russell Mitchell; married Elmer P. **Educ:** Fla Agr & Mech, Tallahassee, FL, BA, fr, 1969; Atlanta Univ, Atlanta, GA, MA, fr, 1971; Case Western Res Univ, Cleveland OH, MA, reading, 1976; Howard Univ, Wash DC, PhD, educ psych, 1985. **Career:** Nassau County Bd Educ, Fernandina Beach, FL, teacher, 1969-70; Coppin State Col, Baltimore MD, dir & coordr, learning skills ctr, 1977-92; Nat Great Blacks Wax Mus, co-founder, pres & chief exec officer, 1983-; Author: The Black Extended Family, 1978; The Helping Tradition in the Black Family and Community, 1985; Social Work and the Black Experience, 1998; Spirituality and the Black Helping Tradition in Social Work, 2003. **Orgs:** Bd dir, Great Blacks Wax Mus, 1985-; African Am Heritage Tour Asn, 1987-. **Home Addr:** 7018 Queen Anne Rd, Baltimore, MD 21207, **Home Phone:** (410)653-8874. **Business Addr:** Co-Founder & President, Chief Executive Officer, The National Great Blacks In Wax Museum, 1601-03 E N Ave, Baltimore, MD 21213, **Business Phone:** (410)563-7809.

## MARTIN, HON. JOSHUA WESLEY, III

Judge, president (organization), executive. **Personal:** Born Sep 14, 1944, Columbia, SC; son of Joshua W Jr and Bernice Baxter; married Lloyd E Overton; children: Victoria & Alexis. **Educ:** Case Inst Tech, BS, 1966; Drexel Univ, attended 1973; Rutgers Univ Sch Law, JD, 1974. **Career:** EI DuPont De Nemours & Co, sr physicist, 1966-71; Hercules Inc, sr patent atty, 1974-82; DE Pub Serv Comm, chmn, 1978-82; Goldey Beacom Col, life trustee, 1982-; Wilmington Col, adj prof, 1984-89; Del Law Sch, adj prof, 1988-89; Del Super Ct, judge; Bell Atlantic, DE, vpres, gen coun & secy, 1990-96; PNC Bank, DE, dir, 1990-2007; Verizon, DE, pres & chief exec officer, 1996-2005; Nuclear Elec Ins Ltd, dir, chmn, 2000-09; Potter Anderson & Corroon LLP, partner & diversity comt chmn, 2005-; SCANA Corp, dir; Case Western Res Univ, trustee emer; Southwest Power Pool Inc, dir, currently; Christiana Care Corp, trustee & dir, currently. **Orgs:** Del Bar Asn, 1975-, pres; Nat Bar Asn, 1975-; Philadelphia Patent Law Asn, 1976-82; Better Bus Bur Del, 1978-82; adv comn, Univ Del Legal Asst Prog, 1982; chmn, Wilmington Renaissance Corp; chmn, United Way Del; trustee, Del Community Found; trustee, Wilmington Friends Sch; New Castle County Vo-Tech Sch Bd; chmn, YMCA Black Achievers Prog; trustee, Del Community Found, 1988-; fel Am Bar Found; pres, Del State Bar Asn; chmn, Del Econ & Financial Adv Coun; Am Arbit Asn; Int Inst Conflict Prev & Resolution; Episcopal Diocese Del; Saints Andrew & Matthew; trustee, Winterthur Mus. **Home Addr:** 3433 Midvale Ave, Philadelphia, PA 19129-1405. **Business Addr:** Partner, Potter Anderson & Corroon LLP, Hercules Plz, Wilmington, DE 19801, **Business Phone:** (302)984-6010.

## MARTIN, DR. JUANITA K.

Psychologist, educator. **Personal:** Born Mar 22, 1955, Mt. Vernon, NY; daughter of Willie C and Irene G. **Educ:** Brown Univ, AB, psychol, 1977; Univ Hartford, MEd, 1979; Kent State Univ, PhD, clin psychol, 1990. **Career:** Univ Akron, Coun Testing & Career Ctr, exec dir, 1988-; Massilon State Hosp, psychol assist, 1989-88; Minority Behav Health. **Orgs:** Western Res Girl Scouts, 1997-; African Am Bd YWCA Rape & Sexual Assault Servs, 1997-; Univ Akron Acad Leadership Forum. **Home Addr:** 530 Mineola Ave, Akron, OH 44320, **Home Phone:** (330)869-9523. **Business Addr:** Executive Director for Counseling Center, Psychologist, University of Akron, Simmons Hall 306, Akron, OH 44325-4303, **Business Phone:** (330)972-7082.

**MARTIN, KEVIN**
Aeronautical engineer. **Personal:** Born Sylmar, CA; son of Juanita Roberson Acker; children: Kameron. **Career:** JMR Electronics, qual control supvr, currently. **Business Addr:** Quality Control Supervisor, JMR Electronics, 20400 Plummer St, Chatsworth, CA 91311-5372, **Business Phone:** (818)993-4801.

**MARTIN, DR. KIMBERLY LYNETTE**
College administrator, activist, dean (education). **Personal:** Born Sep 5, 1963, Detroit, MI; daughter of Eldon and Linda. **Educ:** Univ Mich, BA, orgn behav, 1985; Clark Atlanta Univ, MBA, mkt/info systs, 1988; Wayne State Univ, PhD, higher educ. **Career:** Highland Park Bd Educ, adult educ instr, 1990-; Wayne State Univ, stud orgn adv, commserv dir, 1992-2003; Purdue Univ, asst dean stud community engagement & involvement, 2003-. **Orgs:** Grad adv, Alpha Kappa Alpha Sorority, 1982-84; Univ Mich Alumni Asn, 1985-; Nat Black MBA Asn, 1986-; Atlanta Univ Alumni Asn, 1988-; Am Asn Univ Prof, 1992-; Nat Asn Stud Personnel Adminr. **Home Addr:** 8102 E Jefferson Suite 204-B, Detroit, MI 48214. **Business Addr:** Assistant dean, Purdue University, Stewart Ctr Rm G4, West Lafayette, IN 47906, **Business Phone:** (765)496-2453.

**MARTIN, REV. DR. LAWRENCE RAYMOND**
Clergy, president (organization), teacher. **Personal:** Born Sep 4, 1935, Archie, LA; married Barbara Thompson; children: Lawrence II, Perry & Chantel. **Educ:** Grambling State Univ, BS, social studies, 1959; United Theol Sem, BTh, 1973; Interdenom Theol Ctr & Morehouse Sch Relig, MDiv, 1974; UTS & Bible Col, DD, 1993; Inter Baptist Theologicial Sem Shreveport, La, DD, 2001. **Career:** Tenth Dist Asn, bible instr, 1970-; Monroe City Edu Asn, pres, 1971-; Nat Asn Adv Colored People, Monroe, La, pres, 1973-74; Trenton Baptist Church, pastor, currently; Union Theol Sem, instr, currently; Am Baptist Exten Classes, teacher. **Orgs:** Monroe City Educ Asn; La Educ Asn; Nat Educ Asn; Los Angeles Baptist Conv; Nat Baptist Conv Inc; Los Angeles Bicentennial Comn; bd mem, Drug Abuse & Alcoholism Co, Gov Edwin Edwards. **Home Addr:** 2000 Evans St, Monroe, LA 71201, **Home Phone:** (318)388-4436. **Business Addr:** Pastor, Trenton Baptist Church, 2117 Cypress St, West Monroe, LA 71291, **Business Phone:** (318)325-8840.

**MARTIN, LEE**
Educator. **Personal:** Born Aug 4, 1938, Birmingham, AL; married Nora White; children: Lee Jr, Kristi & Dia. **Educ:** Eastern Mich Univ, BS, 1963, MA, 1965; Univ Mich, PhD. **Career:** Univ Detroit, instr, 1973-74; Romulus Sch, dir, 1974-; Metro Learning & Ment Health Clin, co-dir, 1974-; Detroit Pub Schs, Stud Support Serv, exec dir, 2000. **Orgs:** Pres, Annapolis Park Home owner's Asn, 1965-67; trustee, Inkster Sch Bd, 1973-; Coun Except C, 1975-; bd dir, NW Guid Clin, 1975-; trustee, Peoples Comt, 1975; MI Dept Ment Health, 1976; MI Soc Ment Health, 1976-; Task Force, 1977; mgt bd, Western Wayne County, YMCA; aiding fel-minorities, Mich Asn Retarded Citizens. **Home Addr:** 30049 Matthew Dr, Westland, MI 48185. **Business Addr:** Director, Romulus School, 36540 Grant Rd, Romulus, MI 48174, **Business Phone:** (313)494-1405.

**MARTIN, MANNY.** **See MARTIN, EMANUEL C.**

**MARTIN, MAXINE SMITH**
School administrator. **Personal:** Born Aug 9, 1944, Charleston, SC; daughter of Henry Wilmot and Emily Simmons; married Montez C Jr; children: Emily Elise & Montez C III. **Educ:** Hampton Inst, Hampton, Calif, BS, Eng, Educ, 1966; Atlanta Univ, MA, 1973; State Univ Orangeburg, Ed.D. **Career:** Suppl Educ Ctr, pub specialist, 1970-71; Atlanta Univ, pub rels asst, 1971-72; Morehouse Col, fedn rels coord, 1972-73; Col Charleston, pub info specialist, 1973-79, dir col rels, 1979-80; Charleston Co Sch Dist & Trident Tech Col, eng instr, 1980-85; Col Charleston, stud prog coord & advisor, Ctr Continuing Educ, 1985-; Charleston Co Sch Dist, reading consult, 1988-89; Trident Urban League Inc, dir, pres & chief exec officer, 1998; Trident Urban League Inc, pres & chief exec officer, 2000-. **Orgs:** Charleston Chap Hampton, Univ Alumni Asn, 1966-; Delta Sigma Theta Sorority, 1969-; YWCA, 1971-; Coun Advan & Support Educ, 1973-80; Col News Asn, 1973-80; comn chmn, SC Chap Links Inc, 1974-; bd mem, Charleston Area Ment Health Asn, 1976-80; Univ & Col Designers, 1977-80; bd mem, Charleston Civic Ballet, 1983-85; Florence Crittenton Home, 1983-85, SC Asn Higher Continuing Educ, 1985-; bd dir, Young Charleston Theatre Co, 1988-; exec dir, Mayors Comn C Youth & Families. **Honors/Awds:** Certificate for Public Relations Service, Delta Sigma Theta, 1975; Certificate for Public Relations Service, YWCA, 1975; Certificate for Public Relations Service, Am Freedom Train Found, 1977; Public Relations Award, YWCA, 1984; Twin Women Award, YWCA, 1985; Radio Community Service Award, WPAL, 1986. **Home Addr:** 21 Devereaux Ave, Charleston, SC 29403-3340, **Home Phone:** (843)722-1590. **Business Addr:** Chief Executive Officer, President, Charleston Trident Urban League, 1064 Gardner Rd Suite 216, Charleston, SC 29407, **Business Phone:** (843)769-8173.

**MARTIN, DR. MCKINLEY C.**
School administrator, association executive, army officer. **Personal:** Born Dec 2, 1936, Clarksdale, MS; married Willie Beatrice Burns; children: McKinley C II, Myron Craig & Marcia Corteze. **Educ:** Coahoma Jr Col, AA; Jackson State Univ, BS, 1961; Delta State Univ, ME, 1967; Fla State Univ, PhD, 1972. **Career:** Sandy Bayou Elem Sch, prin, 1962-65; Coahoma Jr Col, registr, 1965-66; FlaState Univ, instr, admin asst, 1970-72; Coahoma Jr Col, dir continuing educ, 1973-80, pres, 1980-92; Northside High Sch, counsr; LeMoyne-OwenColl, Memphis, Tenn, prof, Grad Div, asst to the pres & dean. **Orgs:** Exec bd mem, Coahoma City Chamber Com; planning com, Gov's Office Job Develop & Training; spec steering comg, US Dept Interior Historically Black Col & Univ; state chmn, Child Develop Asn, Delta Agency Progress; Coahoma County Port Community; Prince Hall Mason; Alpha Phi Alpha Fraternity; planning comn, US Dept Educ, Off Student Fin Assistance; US Dept Interior's Nat Parks Servs; Coahoma Co Comt Lower MS Delta Develop Act; bd dir, Leadership Clarksdale; MS Jr & Community Col Econ Coun; vpres, Miss Asn Community & Jr Col; vice chmn, Miss Asn Community & Junior Col Legis Comm; M Univ MS Minority Adv Bd; Black Bus Asn Memphis; pres, Miss Asn Community & Jr Col; pres, guidance div, Tenn Vocational Asn. **Honors/Awds:** Citizen of the Year, Clarksdale Coahoma Co, 1990. **Home Addr:** PO Box 1013, Clarksdale, MS 38614-1013, **Home Phone:** (662)624-2021.

**MARTIN, MONTEZ CORNELIUS, JR.**
Government official, construction engineer. **Personal:** Born Jun 11, 1940, Columbia, SC; married E Maxine Smith; children: Tanya Elayne, Terrie Lanita, Emily Elise & Montez Cornelius III. **Educ:** Hampton Univ, BS, archit engineering, 1963; Polytech Inst Brooklyn, grad studies, 1967. **Career:** WSB-TV, acct exec, 1970; WSOK Radio, dir opers, 1973-74; Col Charleston, dir construct, 1974-80; Montez Real Estate, broker-in-charge 1976-92; Charleston County Housing & Redevelop Authority, vpres, chief exec officer, 1992-2012, exec dir, currently. **Orgs:** SC Chap Nat Asn Real Estate Brokers, 1977-; Greater Charleston Bd Realtors, 1979-; pres, Charleston Citywide Local Develop Corp; Nat Asn Community Col trustee, 1996-97; pres, SC Asn Tech Col Comnr; chmn, Trident Tech Col, Area Comn; dir, SC Coun Econ Ed; bus ed sub-comt, SC Comt Excellence Ed; City Charleston Hqs Comt; Trident Urban League Formation Comt; Leadership SC Alumni Asn; pres, Lowcountry Housing & Econ Develop Found, 1994-; SC State Bd Tech & Comprehensive Educ, 2000-; vpres, Nat Asn Housing & Redevelop Officials, 2007-2009; Rotary; Nat Asn Housing & Redevelop Officials; Nat Asn Housing & Redevelop Officials fel, 2008. **Home Addr:** 21 Devereaux Ave, Charleston, SC 29403-3340, **Home Phone:** (843)577-2546. **Business Addr:** President, Lowcountry Housing and Economic Development Foundation, 2106 Mt Pleasant St, Charleston, SC 29403-6188, **Business Phone:** (843)722-0596.

**MARTIN, MYRON C.**
Consultant. **Personal:** Born Oct 4, 1969, Clarksdale, MS; son of McKinley C Sr and Willie B. **Educ:** Coahoma Community Col, AA, 1989; Univ Va, BS, 1991. **Career:** Coopers & Lybrand LLC, assoc, 1991-95; Price Waterhouse LLP, sr consult, 1995-97; Perot Systs Corp, sr consult, 1997-. **Orgs:** Victory Apostolic Church, Chicago Heights, IL; Country Club Hills Youth Baseball, Country Club Hills, IL. **Home Addr:** 22382 Karlov Ave, Richton Park, IL 60471, **Home Phone:** (708)748-2403. **Business Addr:** Senior Consultant, Perot Systems Corp, 2300 W Plano Pkwy, Plano, TX 75075, **Business Phone:** (972)577-0000.

**MARTIN, PATRICIA ELIZABETH**
Law enforcement officer. **Personal:** Born May 29, 1951, Brooklyn, NY; daughter of Malverse Sr and Helen Elizabeth Smith; children: Linese Antoinette. **Educ:** NY Community Col, Brooklyn, AAS, nursing, 1972; City Col, NY, BS, nursing, 1990; NY City Tech Col, AAS, hospitality, 1995, BTech, hospitality mgt, 2000. **Career:** St Vincent's Hosp, NY, regist nurse, 1973-81; NY City Police Dept, NY, sgt, 1981-91; lt, 1991-. **Orgs:** Guardians Asn, 1982-; Nat Org Black Law Enforcement Exec, 1989-; Police Women Endowment, 1984-; NOBLWE, 1985-; Int Asn Women Police, 1986-; St George Asn, 1987; church usher, Bentel Tabernacle Am Church; Northeast Asn Women Police, 1988; usher, Bridge St AWME Church. **Honors/Awds:** Centurion Found Award, 2000. **Home Addr:** 204-04 45th Rd, Bayside, NY 11361-3119, **Home Phone:** (718)281-1634. **Business Addr:** Lieutenant, Employee Relation Section, 127 Utica Ave, Brooklyn, NY 11213, **Business Phone:** (718)735-0616.

**MARTIN, DR. PATRICK M.**
Research scientist. **Personal:** married Sharla M. **Educ:** Univ Va, PhD, cell biol. **Career:** Univ Va, Dept Path, res scientist, postdoctoral fel, currently. **Business Addr:** Research Scientist, University of Virginia, 415 Lane Rd, Charlottesville, VA 22908-0214, **Business Phone:** (434)924-1946.

**MARTIN, DR. PAUL W.**
Dentist. **Personal:** Born Dec 4, 1940, Columbus, OH; son of Emmeal and Pauline Locke; married Barbara Burts; children: Todd Christopher Emmeal. **Educ:** Ind Univ Sch Dent, BS, DDS, 1962. **Career:** Ind State Teachers Col, 1955-58; Ind Univ Sch Dent, instr, 1965-69; Harlem Hosp, oral surg residency, 1969-72; Prison Health Serv, dir, 1973-75; Hostos Community Col, asst prof, 1975-76; pvt pract oral surg, 1976; NY Univ Col Dent, 1978; Govt Hosp, staff oral surg; N Gen Hosp, actg chief oral surg, 1985; Harlem Hosp Ctr, attend surg, 1986-; Mt Sinai Sch Med, clin instr, 1986-; attend oral surg, dir clins, 1998-. **Orgs:** Royal Soc Health, 1962; Am Dent Asn, 1962-; Frontiers Int, 1963-; Nat Dent Asn, 1963-; co-founder & mem exec comt, Nat Dent Acupuncture Soc, 1984-; Am Col Oral & Maxillo facial Surgeons, 1989-; Nat Soc Oral & Maxillo facial Surgeons, 1990-; Int Soc Plastic Aesthet & Reconstructive Surg, 1990-; Am Acad Pediat Dent. **Home Addr:** 10 Pryer Pl, New Rochelle, NY 10804-4504, **Home Phone:** (914)654-9646. **Business Addr:** Dentist, Harlem Hospital Center, 506 Malcolm X Blvd, New York, NY 10037, **Business Phone:** (212)939-2878.

**MARTIN, DR. RALPH C., II**
Government official, lawyer. **Educ:** Brandeis Univ, BA, 1974; Northeastern Univ Sch Law, JD, 1978. **Career:** Dist Atty Middlesex, prosecutor, 1983; Northeastern Univ, lectr, 1987-92, sr vpres & gen coun; chief law enforcement officer, 1992-2002; Suffolk County, dist atty, 1992-2002; Brandeis Univ, adj assoc prof, 2000-01; Bingham Consult Group, managing prin, currently; Bingham McCutchen LLP, co-chair, currently; Northeastern Univ, chief legal officer, 2011. **Orgs:** Ny Bar Asn; Nat Bar Asn; life mem, Mass Black Lawyers Asn; Boston Bar Asn; Mass Bar Asn; trustee, Boston C's Hosp, 1994-04, 2009-; chmn, Judicial Nominating Comt, 2003-05; dir & vice chair, Greater Boston Chamber Com, 2002-06; chmn, Greater Boston Chamber Com, 2006-; dir, Blue Cross & Blue Shield Mass Inc, 2002; vice chair, Human Resources Comt, 2009-; Audit Comt, 2009-; Fin & Bus Performance Comt, 2007-2009; chmn, Partnership Inc, 2013; trustee, Brandeis Univ; dir exec comt, Greater Boston YMCA. **Special Achievements:** First Republican and African-American District Attorney in Suffolk County's History. **Business Addr:** Co-Chair, Bingham McCutchen LLP, 150 Federal St, Boston, MA 02110-1726, **Business Phone:** (617)951-8844.

**MARTIN, RAYFUS**
Educator, politician, teacher. **Personal:** Born Jan 12, 1930, Franklinton, LA; married Elnora Lowe; children: Mechelle Denise. **Educ:** Leland Col, BA, 1956; Southern Univ, attended 1973; S Eastern La Univ, MEd, 1974. **Career:** Educator, politician (retired); St Tammary High Sch, Eng teacher, 1957; Wash Parish High Sch, hist teacher, 1962-90; Franklinton High Sch, Eng teacher, 1969-90; Franklinton County, city coun man, 1975-96. **Orgs:** Bd dir, Good Samaritan Living Ctr. **Honors/Awds:** Received a Plaque, Mayor of Franklinton for having served on the Council for 20 Years, 1996. **Special Achievements:** First African American council member Town of Franklinton in 1975; Poems: A Readers Creed, 1995; Twenty Frogs, 1995. **Home Addr:** 2020 Williams St Suite 93, Franklinton, LA 70438-1338, **Home Phone:** (985)839-3604. **Business Addr:** Board of Director, Good Samaritan Living Center, 605 Hilltop Ave, Franklinton, LA 70438, **Business Phone:** (985)839-6706.

**MARTIN, REDDRICK LINWOOD**
Real estate agent. **Personal:** Born Jul 20, 1934, Anderson, SC; son of Reddrick B and Mamie Lee; married Ernestine Heath. **Educ:** Allen Univ, BS, 1962. **Career:** Winnsboro SC Pub Schs, teacher, 1962-63; Lancaster SC Pub Schs, teacher, 1963; Columbia Coca-Cola Bottling Co, Columbia SC, sales & Mkt rep, 1963-73; Miami Coca-Cola Bottling Co, reg mkt mgr, 1973-76; Coca Cola USA, area mkt mgr, 1976-82, mkt develop mgr, 1982-83; Martin Real Estate Invest Co, pres, currently; real estate agt, 1989-. **Orgs:** Palmetta Bus Asn, 1970-73; OIC Columbia, SC, 1972-73; adv, Bus Dept Ft Valley State Col, 1980; Indust Cluster A&T State Univ, 1980; Nat Asn Advan Colored People; Urban League; Nat Asn Mkt. **Honors/Awds:** Outstanding Service Award Community Affairs, Save Our Community Club Columbia, SC, 1970; Meritorious Service Award, S Reg Press Inst Savannah State Col, 1980; Community Service Award, Richmond Perrine Optimist Club, 1974; Service Award, MEAC Conf, 1981; Service Award, Business Department, Ft Valley State Col, 1987. **Home Addr:** 1123 Braemar Ave SW, Atlanta, GA 30311, **Home Phone:** (404)696-0069. **Business Addr:** President, Martin Real Estate Investment Co, 1123 Braemar Ave SW, Atlanta, GA 30311, **Business Phone:** (404)696-0069.

**MARTIN, DR. RICHARD CORNISH**
Clergy. **Personal:** Born Oct 15, 1936, Philadelphia, PA; son of Leon Freeman and Virginia Lorette Bullock. **Educ:** Pa State Univ, BA, sci, 1958; Episcopal Theol Sem VA, MDiv, 1961; St Augustine's Col, Canterbury; Howard Univ, Wash DC, DMin, marian studies & soc mary hist, 1988; Nashotah House, DD, 2012. **Career:** Penn State Univ, chaplain, 1961-64; St Andrew's Church State Col, Pa, assoc rector, 1961-64; George Wash Univ, Wash, DC, chaplain, 1964-66; St Paul's Parish, Wash, DC, assoc rector, 1966-73, rector, 1989-96; St George's Parish, Wash, DC, rector, 1973-89; Church Advent, interim rector, 1996-99; St. Mark's Church, interim rector, 2000-01; Grace Church, interim rector, 2001. **Orgs:** Super Soc Mary Am Region, 1966-; pres, Prev Blindness Soc, 1982-84; Studia Liturgica; dir, Community Outreach Ministry; Inter-Church Club; bd, Hospice DC; chair, Ams Friends Anglican Ctr Rome; Anglican Int Liturgical Consult; bd trustees, Nashotah House Sem; founder, Anglo-Cath Rectors, coordr; Soc Holy Cross; bd, Guild All Souls. **Special Achievements:** Editor Studies & Commentaries I & IV; editor The Dragon; Composer Liturgical Music; Venerable Order of St John. **Home Addr:** 2926 Saint Paul St, Baltimore, MD 21218.

**MARTIN, ROBERT E.**
Television journalist, television producer, educator. **Personal:** Born Dec 17, 1948, Bronx, NY; son of Robert and Mary; children: LeRonne. **Educ:** Royal Col Art Inst, attended 1973. **Career:** WABC-TV, assoc producer, 1971-72; Capital Formation Inc, dir commun, 1972-75; WNEW-TV, producer, 1976-83; WNBC-TV, producer, 1983-88; Fox-TV, reporter & producer, "A Current Affair", 1988-93; MSNBC, currently; Unified Force Zujitsu-Ryu Martial Arts, founder & chief instr, currently. **Orgs:** Writers Guild Am E; Coun Concerned Black Exec; YMCA; dir, Male Echoes 1stUnion Bapt Church; Am Fedn TV & Radio Artists; NYAJB; Nat Asn Black Journalists; bd mem, Am Chi Kung Int Asn; founding mem, Zujitsu Fedn. **Honors/Awds:** Emmy Award, 1972; Special Award, NY Jaycees, 1973; Service Award, Salvation Army, 1977; CEBA Award, 1988; Inducted, World Head of Family Sokeship Council Hall of Fame, 2000; World Karate Union Hall of Fame Master Instructor Zujitsu-Ryu, 2003; Outstanding Contributions to the Martial Arts, Action Martial Arts Mag, 2004; Legends Champion Martial Arts Hall of Fame Master of the Year, 2004; WKU Hall of Fame Golden Lifetime Achievement, 2005; International Federation of Ju Jutsuans Shogan Award, 2007; WKU Grand Master of the Year, 2008; Great Grand Master Aaron Banks World Professional Martial Arts Org, 2009. **Special Achievements:** Has conducted Women's Self Defense/Self Protection Seminars for major corporations including NBC, Pain Webber, CNBC, MSNBC and Reed Travel Group; inducted by the World Head of Family Sokeship Council Hall of Fame Millennium Master Instructor, 2000. **Home Addr:** 1 Pegasus Pl, Hackettstown, NJ 07840-0000, **Home Phone:** (908)451-4776. **Business Addr:** Founder, Chief Instructor, Unified Force Martial Arts, 77 Kim Lane, Long Valley, NJ 07853, **Business Phone:** (908)850-9289.

**MARTIN, ROLAND S.**
Television broadcaster, journalist, radio host. **Personal:** Born Nov 11, 1968, Houston, TX; married Jacquie Hood Martin. **Educ:** Texas A&M Univ, BS, jour, 1991; La Baptist Univ, master's degree, Christian commun, 2008. **Career:** Bryan-College State Eagle, employee; KBTX-TV, employee; Austin-American Statesman, journalist, 1991; Fort Worth Star Telegram, city hall reporter; KRLD, sports reporter, 1995; KKDA-AM, news editor and morning anchor; Dallas Weekly, editor; Dallas-Fort Worth Heritage, owner & publisher; Houston Defender, managing editor; freelance producer, 2000; BlackAmericaWeb.com, editor, 2001; American Urban Radio Network, news correspondent; Fifth Quarter, WOL, Washington, D.C., sports commentator; ROMAR Media Group Dallas, founder; Savoy magazine, news editor; Chicago Defender newspaper, consultant, executive editor and gen-

eral manager; WVON-AM, mid-day host then morning drive host, 2005-08; syndicated newspaper columnist, 2007-; CNN, contributor, 2007-13; Washington Watch with Roland Martin, host and managing editor; Roland: A Fresh Perspective for the 21st Century, RolandMartin.com; The Tom Joyner Morning Show, senior analyst; NewsOne Now, Radio One and TV One, host and managing editor, 2013-. **Orgs:** Alpha Phi Alpha. **Special Achievements:** Author, "Listening to the Spirit Within: 50 Perspectives on Faith" (2007); "Speak, Brother! A Black Man's View of America" (2003); "The First: President Barack Obama's Road to the White House" (2010); contributor, "Paradox of Loyalty: An African-American Response to the War on Terrorism", "Black Women Redefined: Dispelling Myths and Discovering Fulfillment in the Age of Michelle Obama", and "Faivish Pewzner New York and Fatherhood: Rising to the Ultimate Challenge"; contributor to periodicals, Ebony, Essence.

### MARTIN, DR. ROSALEE RUTH
Educator. **Personal:** Born Mar 10, 1944, New York, NY; daughter of Lucille; children: Deshon, Tishana & Yvette. **Educ:** Univ Tex El Paso, BA, 1967; Univ Tex Austin, MSW, 1970, PhD, sociol, 1979. **Career:** Meridell Achievement Ctr, social worker & adminr, 1969-73; Ment Health-Ment Retardation, caseworker, 1981-88; Huston-Tillotson Univ, Sociol Dept, prof social, 1973-, head social sci div; outreach dir proj reach, 1988-95; pvt therapist, 1987-; Licensed Chem Dependency, counr, 1993-. **Orgs:** Social work cert State TX, 1983-; licensed prof counr, TX Bd Examiner, 1983-; vpres, Black Arts Alliance, 1985-94; teacher, Vocation Bible Sch Belize, Cent Am, 1985, 1986, 1988-95. **Home Addr:** 2105 Teakwood Dr, Austin, TX 78757. **Business Addr:** Professor of Sociology, Huston-Tillotson University, J-M 213 900 Chicon St, Austin, TX 78702-2753, **Business Phone:** (512)505-3098.

### MARTIN, ROSETTA P.
Librarian, teacher. **Personal:** Born Jun 20, 1930, Charleston, SC; daughter of Phoenix Poaches Sr and Della Scott Poaches; married George E. **Educ:** Morgan State Col, BA, hist, 1953; Simmon Col, MS, 1962. **Career:** Manning HS, teacher, 1954-55; Boston Pub Lib, C librn, 1958-63; Tufts Univ, ref libr, 1970-78, supr curric lab, 1965-, asst ref librn, 1963-70, Wessell Lib, 1976-77; Trident Tech Col, Main Campus, Charleston, librn, 1978-95; Avery Res Ctr Study African Am Hist, bd dir. **Orgs:** Am Libr Asn; Spec Libr Asn; New Eng Libr Asn; Am Asn Univ Prs; Librns Educ & Res NE; Nat Asn Advan Colored People; Civic Asn; Black Bibliogr; Asn Study Negro Life & Hist; S Carolina Libr Asn; Charleston Libr Consortium; Bibliog Instr Sect. **Home Addr:** 851 Bent Hickory Rd, Charleston, SC 29414-9071, **Home Phone:** (843)766-5475.

### MARTIN, SHEDRICK M., JR.
Government official, real estate developer. **Personal:** Born Jan 5, 1927, Savannah, GA; son of Shedrick and Hattie Mew; married Laura B Randolph; children: Beverly Anne & Brenda Annette. **Educ:** Savannah State Col, BS, biol, 1951; FBI Nat Acad, 1970. **Career:** US Postal Serv, Atlanta, GA, rwy postal clerk, 1951-52; Chatham Co Bd Educ Savannah, teacher, 1952-57; Savannah GA, Police Dept, detective, 1957-70; Savannah, personnel asst training, 1971-72; City Savannah, Savannah, GA, dept pub, serv adminr, 1972, dir code enforcement, 1988-94; US Marshall, Spec Dept, city security officer, 1994-. **Orgs:** Am Pub Works Asn; Fraternal Order Police; Nat Asn Advan Colored People; Cath Holy Name Soc; Wolves Social Club; vpres, Chatham S Lions Club, 1988-. **Home Addr:** PO Box 60626, Savannah, GA 31420-0626. **Business Addr:** Director of Code Enforcement, City Savannah, 2 East Bay St, Savannah, GA 31402, **Business Phone:** (912)651-6579.

### MARTIN, SHIRLEY
Administrator. **Personal:** Born Nov 21, 1948, Kosciusko, MS; daughter of Henry and Leora Beamon; married Wisdom; children: Wisdom T & Timothy D. **Educ:** Jackson State Univ, BS, 1973; Miss State Univ, MA, 1993. **Career:** Leake County Schs, eng teacher, 1974-91; Attala County Sch, guid counr, 1991-92; Miss dept educ, prog supvr, 1992-96, prog specialist, 1996-98, div dir, 1998-. **Orgs:** Awards chmn, Miss Teacher asn, 1980-82; adv, Miss Asn Needy Students, 1998-. **Home Addr:** 2685 Beamon Rd, Kosciusko, MS 39090, **Home Phone:** (662)289-9734. **Business Addr:** Division Director, Mississippi Department of Education, 500 Greymont Bldg Suite H, Jackson, MS 39205-0771, **Business Phone:** (601)576-5010.

### MARTIN, STEVEN ALBERT
Football player. **Personal:** Born May 31, 1974, St. Paul, MN; married Catherine; children: Evan & Emanuel. **Educ:** Univ Mo. **Career:** Football player (retired); Indianapolis Colts, defensive tackle & right defensive tackle, 1996-98; Philadelphia Eagles, defensive tackle & right defensive tackle, 1998-99; Kans City Chiefs, 2000; New York Jets, nose tackle, 2001; New Eng Patriots, defensive tackle & left defensive tackle, 2002; Houston Texans, left defensive tackle & nose tackle, 2003; Minn Vikings, 2004. **Orgs:** Anna Mae Martin Foundation, 2000.

### MARTIN, SYLVIA COOKE (CLARA SYLVIA COOKE)
Government official, manager. **Personal:** Born May 2, 1938, Baltimore, MD; daughter of Emanuel Levi and Clara M Evans; children: Donald E K & Marcia Lauren. **Educ:** Univ Md, College Park, MD, attended 1957, BS, econs, 1972, MPS, 1978; Univ Va, Charlottesville, VA, cert, 1975; Bowie State Univ, cert, 1987. **Career:** Soc Security Admin, Baltimore, Md, file clerk, 1963-66, health ins analyst, 1966, mgt intern, 1968-70; Soc Security Admin & Health Care Financing Admin, Baltimore, Md, manpower develop specialist, 1967-68, career develop specialist, 1970-78; Social Security Upward Mobility, mgt intern, 1968-70; Antioch Col, fac, 1975-79; Libr Cong, Washington, DC, chief staff training & develop, 1978-93; Self-employed Mgt Consult, 1979-; Bowie State Col, Bowie, Md, instr, 1986-89, lectr; Univ Md Baltimore County, mcnair scholars prog coordr, 1994-99; Ellicott City Colored Sch Restoration Proj, proj mgr to chief exec officer, 1997-2002; Friends Ellicott City Sch dist, pres & chief exec officer, 2000-02; Pres Lyndon B Johnson's Conf Medicare & Medicaid. **Orgs:** Historian, Nat Asn Negro Bus & Prof Women's Clubs, 1978-89; Md Hist Soc, 1980-89; Oral Hist Asn, 1984-89; pres, Daniel Murray AFA Cult Asn, 1984-85, 1987-88; historian, Afro Am Hist & Geneal Socs, 1984-85; parliamentarian, 1985-88, pres, 1988-90; parlimentarian, Nat Pierians, 1985-89; rec secy, 1989-91, 1999-2001, pres, 2001-03; Nat Coun Negro Women; life mem, Nat Am Advan Colored People; life mem, Delta Sigma Theta Sorority; Omicron Delta Kappa, 1997; Md Geneal Soc, 1980-91; Coalition 100 Black Women, 1999; pres, Am Soc Freedmen's Descendants; Nat Asn Advan Colored People. **Home Addr:** 6375 Shadowshape Pl, Columbia, MD 21045, **Home Phone:** (410)381-1292. **Business Addr:** MD.

### MARTIN, TONY DERRICK
Football player. **Personal:** Born Sep 5, 1965, Miami, FL; married LisaRaye McCoy. **Educ:** Bishop Col; Mesa State Col, MBA. **Career:** Football player (retired); New York Jets, 1989; Miami Dolphins, punt returner, wide receiver, 1990-93, 1999-2000; San Diego Chargers, wide receiver, 1994-97; Atlanta Falcons, wide receiver, 1998, 2001. **Honors/Awds:** Champion, Asian Football Confederation, 1994; Pro Bowl, 1996; Super bowl; Champion, Nat Football Conf, 1998.

### MARTIN, WALTER L.
Educator, manager. **Personal:** Born Apr 15, 1951, New York, NY; son of Robert and Elizabeth Monterio Brito; married Regina Marvel Montgomery; children: Shalya Mekeela Kelly & Merissa Tarla Mekeshia. **Educ:** Northeastern Univ, BS, finance & small bus mgt, 1975; Clark Atlanta Univ, MA, MBA, 1977. **Career:** Pyramid w Develop Corp, financial analyst & acct, 1979-82; Deloitte & Touch, staff; Pyramidwest Develop Corp, staff; Mobil Chem Co, financial analyst, 1982-83; Fed Express Corp, sr financial analyst, 1983-86, sta oper mgt, 1986-; Walt Disney World Resort, Area & Finance Mgt, 1997-2002, food & beverage finance mgr, 1999; Dekalb County Community Col, fac; Valencia Col, adj prof, 1999-, prof bus & acct, 2001-; Valencia Community Col, prof bus, 2002-. **Orgs:** Dir, Changes Full Arts Prod Co, 1977-82; chmn allocation comt, Youth Servs United Way Atlanta, 1985-; dir, Nat Black MBA Asn Atlanta, 1985-86; dirstud affairs, Nat Black MBA Asn Atlanta, 1987; partner, E Coast mgt Group. **Home Addr:** 5959 Pattillo Lane, Lithonia, GA 30058. **Business Addr:** Professor, Valencia College, Off 7-145, Orlando, FL 32802, **Business Phone:** (407)582-2849.

### MARTIN, WANDA C.
Manager, business owner. **Personal:** Born Mar 10, 1953, Gratham, NC; daughter of Nathaniel Cogdell (deceased); married Louis D; children: David Durand & Louis Demar. **Educ:** NC Agr & Tech State Univ, BS, 1975; Univ NC, Chapel Hill, MPH, pub admin, 1992. **Career:** Manager (retired), instructor; Martin Janitorial Serv Corp, owner; Guilford Co, Dept Pub Health, staff nurse, 1975, team leader, 1976, nursing supvr, 1980, health prom & dis prev mgr, 1994-2006; NC Agr & Tech State Univ, adj clin instr, currently. **Orgs:** Community assignments prog, Sigma Theta Tau, Mu-Tau, 1992; exec bd, Nat Asn Advan Colored People, 1999; treas, Guilford County AIDS Partnership Bd. **Honors/Awds:** Service Award, Guilford County, 1981; Volunteer Award, Project Head Start, 1991; Dr Joseph Holiday Scholarship Award, NAPHA, 1992; Outstanding Service, HIV/STD Prev & Care Sect, 1997. **Home Addr:** 4809 Olde Forest Dr, Greensboro, NC 27406-8748, **Home Phone:** (336)674-3397. **Business Addr:** Adjunct Clinical Instructor, North Carolina Agricultural and Technical State University, 1601 E Market St, Greensboro, NC 27401, **Business Phone:** (336)334-7500.

### MARTIN, WILLIAM R.
Chemist. **Personal:** Born Dec 19, 1926, Washington, DC; married Mildred Dixon; children: William R Jr & Janice Y. **Educ:** Morgan St Col, BS, 1951; Southeastern Pa Univ, MBA, 1976. **Career:** Nat Insts Health, biologist, 1952-55; Walter Reed Ins, res biochem, 1955-60; NIMH res, neurochemist, 1960-62, chief; Howard Univ, res proj, 1962-63; Food & Drug Admin, chemist drug mfg controls, 1963-. **Orgs:** Am Soc Qual Control, 1972-; Plymouth Cong United Church Christ; Bowie St Col; Prince George Co; Nat Asn Advan Colored People, 1979; Chillum-ray Citizens Asn; Morgan St Univ Nat Alumni Asn; DC Metro Chap, Nat Conf Community & Justice; Org Black Sci; Omega Psi Phi Frat. **Home Addr:** 1204 Raydale Ct, Hyattsville, MD 20783-3062, **Home Phone:** (301)559-0552. **Business Addr:** Research director, National Institute on Drug Abuse, 5600 Fishers Lane, Rockville, MD 20852.

### MARTIN, WISDOM T.
Television journalist, television news anchorperson. **Personal:** Born Sep 25, 1970, Kosciusko, MS; son of Wisdom D Sr and Shirley; married Monifa Alexander; children: Anaya & Wisdom. **Educ:** Jackson State Univ, BA, broadcast jour, 1993. **Career:** WAPT TV News, Jackson, photographer & reporter, 1991-95; KNDO TV News, reporter & sports anchor, 1995-97; KSEE TV News, reporter, 1996-97; WRAL TV News, reporter, 1998-99; CNN, anchor & reporter, 1999; WKRN News, anchor & reporter, 1999-2003; WTTG TV News, gen assignment reporter, 2003-, tv news anchor & reporter, currently. **Orgs:** Lake Providence Baptist Ch. **Honors/Awds:** Two awards as news photographer, Miss Broadcasters Asn, 1992; Kenya Hale Communication Award, Nat Broadcasting Soc, 2001; Outstanding Reporting, Tenn State Univ Nat Asn Broadcasters, 2001; School Bell award, Tenn Sch Bd Asn, 2002; guest panelist, Black Enterprise Conf, 2002; honors for excellence in journalism. **Home Addr:** 13211 Keverton Dr, Upper Marlboro, MD 20774-1821, **Home Phone:** (615)369-7206. **Business Addr:** TV News Reporter, Anchor, WTTG Fox 5 News, 5151 Wis Ave NW, Washington, DC 20016, **Business Phone:** (202)895-3000.

### MARTIN-OGUNSOLA, DELLITA LILLIAN
Educator. **Personal:** Born Oct 27, 1946, New Orleans, LA; daughter of Ret Sgt Wellie Martin (deceased) and Wilma M Martin (deceased); married David Olajire; children: Oludare Ajayi-Martin & Oladimeji Ade-Olu. **Educ:** La State Univ, New Orleans, BA, 1968; Ohio State Univ, MA, 1971, PhD, 1975. **Career:** St Mathias High Sch, instr Span & Fr, 1975-76; Univ Ala-Birmingham, from asst prof span to assoc prof Span, 1976-99, chair dept foreign lang, 1993-, prof span, 1999-, prof emer, currently, African-Am Studies, interim dir. **Orgs:** Mod Lang Asn, 1976-, secy, 1977-78, chair Afro-Am Exec Comt, 1979; Ala Asn Teachers Span, 1977-; Col Lang Asn, 1977-, foreign lang rep, 1996-98, from vpres to pres, 1998-2002; S Atlantic Mod Lang Asn, 1979-; secy exec sub comt, Ala Humanities Found, 1978-80, chair nominations subcomt, 1979; liaison secy, Asn Caribbean Studies, 1979, 1982-84; Hisp Conf Greater Birmingham, 1984-89; dir, Am Scholars Listings, 1978, 1982. **Home Addr:** 5017 Fulmar Dr, Birmingham, AL 35210, **Home Phone:** (205)956-8655. **Business Addr:** Professor Emeritus, Chair of Department Foreign Language, University of Alabama at Birmingham, HB 407 1720 2nd Ave S, Birmingham, AL 35294-1260, **Business Phone:** (205)934-4652.

### MARTINEZ, RALPH
Executive, chief executive officer. **Personal:** Born New York, NY. **Educ:** Queens Col, BA, polit sci, 1976. **Career:** Martinez Motors, pres, 1982-85; Town & Country Chrysler-Plymouth Inc, Milwaukie, Ore, founder, chief exec officer; Town & country Ford Body Shop, chief exec officer, 1985-; Town & Country dealerships, chief exec officer; Zenitram Inc, 1985-. **Orgs:** Bd dir, SAIF Corp, 2006-13, brand ore adv; vpres, Chrysler Minority Dealership Asn. **Business Addr:** Chief Executive Officer, Town & Country Dealerships, 16800 McLoughlin Blvd SE, Milwaukie, OR 97267-4956, **Business Phone:** (866)270-9655.

### MARTINEZ, RAMON JAIME
Consultant, baseball player. **Personal:** Born Mar 22, 1968, Santo Domingo. **Career:** Baseball player (retired); Los Angeles Dodgers, pitcher, 1988-98; Boston Red Sox, 1999-2000; Pittsburgh Pirates, 2001; Baltimore Orioles, sr advisor, currently. **Home Addr:** Bo San Miguel Sute 9 Managuayaba, Santo Domingo10700. **Business Addr:** Senior Advisor, Baltimore Orioles, Oriole Pk Camden Yards 333 W Camden St, Baltimore, MD 21201, **Business Phone:** (410)685-9800.

### MARTS, LONNIE, JR.
Football player, athletic coach, executive. **Personal:** Born Nov 10, 1968, New Orleans, LA; married Gionne Taylor; children: 5. **Educ:** Tulane Univ, BA, sociol, 1990. **Career:** Football player (retired), athletic coach, exec; Kans City Chiefs, linebacker, 1991-93; Tampa Bay Buccaneers, 1994-96; Tenn Oilers, 1997-98; Jacksonville Jaguars, 1999-2000; Godspeed Elite Sports Performance, owner, founder, coach, dir, currently; Harvest Community Sch, head football coach, currently. **Orgs:** Life Athletes; bd mem, Mayors Sports & Entertainment, Jacksonville Econ Develop Coun. **Home Addr:** 13650 Bromley Pt Dr, Jacksonville, FL 32225-2635. **Business Addr:** Director, Trainer, Godspeed Sports Performance, 11202 St John's Indust Pkwy N, Jacksonville, FL 32246, **Business Phone:** (904)379-9480.

### MARVE, EUGENE RAYMOND
Football player. **Personal:** Born Aug 14, 1960, Flint, MI; son of Robert (deceased) and Dorothy; married Erin; children: Robert & Rebecca. **Educ:** Saginaw Valley State Univ, grad. **Career:** Football player (retired); Buffalo Bills, linebacker, left linebacker, 1982, 1985-86, right linebacker, 1983-84, linebacker, 1987; Tampa Bay Buccaneers, left linebacker, 1988-90, linebacker, 91; San Diego Chargers, linebacker, 1992. **Honors/Awds:** All-Rookie teams; AP Defensive Rookie-of-the-Year; Most Valuable Player; Man of the Year, Nat Football League, 1984-85. **Special Achievements:** Inducted into the Saginaw Valley State University Athletic Hall of Fame, 2010; Greater Flint Afro-American Hall of Fame Inductee, 2011; First Saginaw Valley State University player for NFL. **Home Addr:** 4510 S Cameron Ave, Tampa, FL 33611.

### MARYLAND, MARY ANGELA
Nurse, educator. **Personal:** Born Sep 27, 1953, Cincinnati, OH; daughter of James Pearl and Christine Nero. **Educ:** Elmhurst Col, Elmhurst, IL, BA, psychol, 1975; Malcolm X Col, Chicago, IL, AAS, nursing, 1977; Chicago State Univ, Chicago, IL, BSN, 1980; Govs State Univ, Univ Park, IL, MSN, nursing admin, 1983. **Career:** Mt Sinai Hosp Med Ctr, Chicago, Ill, staff nurse II, 1977-83; Evangel Health Systs, Oak Brook, Ill, mgt Engr, 1983-85; City Cols Chicago, Chicago, Ill, nursing fac, 1985-87; Univ Ill Chicago Col Nursing, Chicago, Ill, coord, urban health prog recruiter, admis counr, 1987-90, res asst, 1990; Jackson Pk Hosp & Med Ctr, nurses practr. **Orgs:** Am Asn Critical Care Nurses, 1980-; Asn Black Nursing Fac, 1988-; People People Int, 1988-; Nominating Comt, Med Surg Nursing, 1989-92, bd dir, Am Nurses Asn; steering comt, Ill Nurses Asn, 1989-91. **Home Addr:** 420 Home Ave Apt 102, Oak Park, IL 60302-3713, **Home Phone:** (708)383-8161. **Business Addr:** 1900 W Taylor St Suite 172, Chicago, IL 60612-3742, **Business Phone:** (312)413-2042.

### MASERU, DR. NOBLE A. W.
Government official. **Educ:** Wayne State Univ, BS; Emory Univ Sch Med, MPH; Atlanta Univ, PhD. **Career:** Accrediting Comn Health Educ, fel; Clark Atlanta Univ Sch Social Work, fac; Ga Dept Human Resources, state dir, 1986-88; Ga Dept Human Resources, Family Health Sect, asst dir; Women Infants & C Suppl Food & Nutrit Prog, dir; Atlanta Pub Schs, coordr, 1990-94; Pub Health Sci Inst, Morehouse Col, acad & pub health policy scientist; Morehouse Sch Med, Master Pub Health Prog, founding dir, 1994; USAID Africa Div, consult; City Detroit Dept Health & Wellness Prom, dir & health officer, 2003-06; City Cincinnati Health Dept, health comnr, 2006-. **Orgs:** Cong Black Caucus Found; African Am Acads Pub Health Progs; vpres, Health Coun, Div Community Health, Greater Detroit Area, 1998-2000; bd trustee, Wayne State Univ; bd mem, St George's Univ; Grenada Wi; Detroit Receiving Hosp & Detroit Brownfield Redevelop; Nat Asn County; City Health Officials Strategic Direction Comt Social Justice & Health Equity; bd dir, Walter Rodney Found, currently. **Business Addr:** Health Commissioner, City of Cincinnati, 801 Plum St, Cincinnati, OH 45202, **Business Phone:** (513)352-2400.

### MASHBURN, JAMAL
Basketball player, television show host. **Personal:** Born Nov 29, 1972, New York, NY; son of Bobby; married Michelle; children: Taylor & Jamal. **Educ:** Univ Ky, attended 1993. **Career:** Basketball player (retired), TV show host; Dallas Mavericks, forward, 1993-97; Miami Heat, 1997-2000; Charlotte Hornets, 2000-03; New Orleans Hornets, forward, 2002-04; Philadelphia 76ers, forward, 2005-06; ESPN, studio

analyst, NBA Fastbreak, host, 2006-. **Orgs:** Spokesperson, Boys & Girls Club; partner, Ol Memorial Stable; owner, Outback Steakhouse Franchises; 37 Papa Johns. **Home Addr:** , FL. **Business Addr:** Host, ESPN, ESPN Plz 935 Middle St, Bristol, CT 06010, **Business Phone:** (860)766-2000.

## MASK, DR. SUSAN L.

Executive. **Personal:** Born New York, NY; daughter of Joseph C and Eleanor G; married W H Knight; children: Michael Joseph Knight & Lauren Louise Knight. **Educ:** City Univ NY, BA, polit sci, 1975; NY Univ, JD, law, 1978. **Career:** Univ Iowa, Off Affirmative Action, asst pres, dir, 1989-2001; Wash Mutual, first vpres, asst gen coun, 2001-09; Trillium360 Consult LLC, co-pres, managing dir, 2009-. **Orgs:** Nat Bar Asn; bd dir, Salvation Army. **Honors/Awds:** Vanderbilt Medal, NY Univ, 1978; State Board of Regents Staff Excellence Awards, Univ Iowa, 2001. **Home Addr:** 10 Brickwood Knoll, Iowa City, IA 52240, **Home Phone:** (319)337-8312. **Business Addr:** Co-President, Managing Director, Trillium360 Consulting LLC, 600 1st Ave Suite 221, Seattle, WA 98104, **Business Phone:** (206)682-1142.

**MASON, ANTHONY.** **See Obituaries Section.**

## MASON, DR. CHERYL ANNETTE

Physician. **Personal:** Born Jul 2, 1954, McAlester, OK; daughter of Lucious C III and Helen M Stuart; married Mack Henderson; children: Alisha Dixon & Samuel Dixon. **Educ:** Univ CA, San Diego, BA, human biology, 1977; Howard Univ Col Med, MD, med, 1981; Georgetown Univ Hosp, MD, obstet-gynec, 1987; Inner Vision, grad, spiritual develop, 2006-08; Johns Hopkins Univ, MPH, pub health, 2011. **Career:** San Pedro & Peninsula Hosp, family pract intern, 1983; Georgetown Univ Hosp, resident Ob-Gyn, 1983-87; Memorial Hosp Danville, Va, staff physician, chief med officer, 1987-90; Teen Ctr, health educr, 1990-93; DeWitt Army Hosp, 1994-96; Howard Univ med students, mentor, 1995-98; pvt pract physician, 1987-98; Since You Asked, pres, 1998-; Alexandria Youth Detention Home, health educr, 2000-06; Kingdom Vision Ministry, health educr, 2007-; McDougall Int Inc, health educr, 2007-; Johns Hopkins Bloomberg Sch Pub Health, physician, 2009-11. **Orgs:** Am Bus Women's Asn, 1988-90; Pittsylvania County Med Soc, 1988-; bd mem, Am Cancer Soc. **Home Addr:** PO Box 2034, Merrifield, VA 22116-2034.

## MASON, CLIFFORD L.

Playwright, writer. **Personal:** Born Mar 5, 1932, Brooklyn, NY. **Educ:** City Univ NY, Queens Col, BA, eng lit, 1958. **Career:** New Dramatists, writer, 1966; Manhattanville Col, teacher; Rutgers Univ, NEH Grant Theatre, resident, 1978; Playwright: Captain At Cricket, 1982; Boxing Day Parade, 1983; Gabriel, The Story Of A Slave Rebellion; Half Way Tree Brown; O T Fairclough & Roger Mais; Othello In The Night; Pilgrim Fathers; Return To Guys Hill; Royal Oak; Sister Sadie; Time Out Of Time; Trial of Denmark Vesey; Two Bourgeois Blacks; Verandah; Books: When Love Was Not Enough, 1980; Murder mysteries: When Love Was Not Enough, Street Martins Press, 1981; Case of the Ashanti Gold, Street Martins Press, 1985; Jamaica run, Street Martins Press, 1987; The African-American Bookshelf, 2004. Acted in: PBS; Anspacher Public Theatre; New Federal Theatre; Theater Row. **Business Addr:** Playwright, c/o Bertha Klausner, 71 Pk Ave, New York, NY 10016.

## MASON, DEREK

Football coach. **Personal:** Born Phoenix, AZ; married Leighanne; children: Makenzie & Sydney. **Educ:** Northern Ariz Univ, attended. **Career:** Northern Ariz Univ Football Team, corner back, 1989-92; Mesa Community Col Football Team, wide receiver coach, 1994; Weber State Univ, wide receiver coach, 1995-96; Idaho State Univ, running back coach, 1997-98; Bucknell Univ Football Team, defensive backs coach, 1999-2001; Utah Col, wide receiver coach, 2002; St. Mary's Col Football Team, asst head coach, 2003; New Mex State Univ Football Team, wide receiver coach, 2004; Ohio State Univ Football Team, wide receiver coach, 2005-06; Minn Vikings NFL team, defensive backs coach, 2007-09; Stanford Univ Football Team, defensive back coach, 2010, assoc head coach & defensive coordr, 2011-13; Vanderbilt Univ Football Team, head coach, 2014-. **Business Addr:** Head Coach, Vanderbilt University, 2301 Vanderbilt Pl, Nashville, TN 37235, **Business Phone:** (615)322-7311.

## MASON, DR. DONNA S.

Educator. **Personal:** Born Jan 15, 1947, Mt. Vernon, NY; daughter of Alexander and Olga Spence; married Charles L Sr; children: Charles L Jr. **Educ:** Howard Univ, BA, 1969, MEd, 1972; Univ Md, College Park, AGS, 1975, PhD, 1987. **Career:** Dist Columbia Pub Schs, classroom teacher, bldg resource teacher, comput camp teacher, comput curric writer, comput teacher trainer, comput educ instr/lab cord, 1969-; US Off Educ, Christa McAuliffe fel, 1988, 1994; Cafritz Found, teacher fel, 1988; Alice Deal Jr High Sch, comp instr & comp lab cord, currently. **Orgs:** Md Instrnl Comp Cordr Asn; Univ Md Alumni Asn; Int Soc Tech Educ; Spec Interest Group Comp Cords; NCSSM Found. **Home Addr:** 5724 Nevada St, Berwyn Heights, MD 20740-2655, **Home Phone:** (301)474-1718. **Business Addr:** Computer Instructor/Lab Coordinator, Alice Deal Junior High School, 3815 Ft Dr NW, Washington, DC 20016, **Business Phone:** (202)282-0100.

## MASON, EDDIE LEE

Football player, athlete, executive. **Personal:** Born Jan 9, 1972, Siler City, NC. **Educ:** Univ NC, Chapel Hill, BS, social psychol, 1994. **Career:** Football player (retired), exec; New York Jets, linebacker, 1995; Jacksonville Jaguars, 1998; Wash Redskins, 1999-2002; NC Tar Heels football; MASE Training LLC, pres, 2003-, owner, 2004-; NIKE Leadership Challenge, head trainer, 2011-; ARMOUR Xtreme Precision Analytics Div, owner, exec dir. **Business Addr:** President, Owner, MASE Training LLC, 21580 Atlantic Blvd Suite 110, Sterling, VA 20166, **Business Phone:** (571)434-6273.

## MASON, FELICIA LENDONIA

Journalist, writer. **Personal:** Born May 8, 1962, Pittsburgh, PA; daughter of Rev William L Sr and G Bernice. **Educ:** Hampton Inst, BA, 1984; Thomas Nelson Community Col, paralegal course work; Ohio State Univ, MA, 1986; Poynter Inst Media Studies, media mgt fel, 1988. **Career:** Pittsburgh Post Gazette, reporter, 1984-85; Hampton Univ, asst prof, 1986-90; Daily Press, copy ed, 1989-90, assoc ed, 1990-92, asst metro ed, 1992-94, columnist, metro ed, 1994-; United Way, loaned exec, 1991; Novels: Body & Soul, 1995; For the Love of You, 1995; Seduction, 1996; Rhapsody, 1997; Foolish Heart, 1998; Forbidden Heart, 2000; Testimony, 2002; Sweet Accord, 2003; Enchanted Heart, 2004; Sweet Devotion, 2004; Sweet Harmony, 2004; Gabriel's Discovery, 2004; Seductive Hearts, 2005; What Ana Mae Left Behind, 2005. **Orgs:** Nat Asn Black Journalists; Romance Writers Am; Chesapeake Romance Writers; Va Romance Writers. **Honors/Awds:** Print Alumni Award, Hampton Univ, 1991; Leadership Award, WICI, 1983; Emma Award; Best Multicultural Romance of the Year, Romantic Times, 1998; Reviewer's Choice Award, Career Achievement Award, Romantic Times, 1999. **Special Achievements:** Top 10 Romance Writer, Affaire de Coeur, 2002; two best of 2002 listings from Black Issues Book Review; a two-time winner of the Best-Selling Multicultural Title Award from Waldenbooks for Body and Soul and Seduction; First black romance to make the Top Ten on Ingram's Most Requested Romances list. **Home Addr:** PO Box 1438, Yorktown, VA 23692. **Business Addr:** Metro Editor, Daily Press Inc, 7505 Warwick Blvd, Newport News, VA 23607, **Business Phone:** (757)247-7860.

## MASON, REV. HERMAN SKIP, JR.

School administrator, writer. **Personal:** Born Jul 14, 1962, Atlanta, GA; son of Herman Sr and Deloris Harris Hughes; married Harmel Codi; children: Jewel & Jodari. **Educ:** Morris Brown Col, Atlanta, GA, BA, mass commun & hist, 1984; Clark Atlanta Univ, MS, libr & info sci, 1989; Jimmy Carter Presidential Libr, Atlanta, GA, archival mgt, 1989; Atlanta Univ, Atlanta, GA, MS, libr sci, 1989; Jimmy Carter Presidential Libr, cert, archival studies. **Career:** Herndon Home Mus, Atlanta, Ga, historian, interpreter, 1983-86; US Dept, Interior Interpreting Hist Significance, Martin Luther King Nat Hist Site, Atlanta, Ga, historian, 1986; Atlanta-Fulton Pub Lib, Atlanta, Ga, black studies archivist & historian, 1987-92; Morris Brown Col, dean, 2003; Morehouse Col Arch, interim vpres stud serv, dean, archivist; Digging It Up Inc, founder & pres; Apex Mus, consult, Music Masters, currently. **Orgs:** Pres, African-Am Family Hist Asn, 1988-91; chmn, Southern Region Hist Comn; historian, Eta Lambda Chap Alpha Phi Alpha Fraternity, 1985-90, pres 2009, nat archivist; bd mem, Ga Asn Mus & Galleries, 1988-91; Outstanding Atlanta; founder, corr secy, African-Am Male Study Group; pres, W Side Community CME Church Sr Usher Bd, 1988-91; Nat Asn Advan Colored People; Asn Study Afro Am Life & Hist; Sigma Pi Phi; Socs Am Archivists. **Honors/Awds:** National Alumni Brother of the Year, Alpha Phi Alpha Fraternity Inc, 1989; Volunteer Service Award, United Negro Col Fund, 1988-91; Distinguished Alumni Citation, Nat Coun Negro Women, 1987-89; Distinguished Alumni Citation, NAEFEO, 1989; Iota Chapter Brother of the Year; Georgia Alumni Brother of the Year; Southern Region Brother of the Year; Georgia Governors Award, 2006. **Special Achievements:** Books: "Hidden Treasures: African-American Photographers in Atlanta, 1870-70"; "African-American Life in Jacksonville", 1997; "Black Atlanta in the Roaring Twenties", 1997; "Alpha In Atlanta: A Legacy Remembered, 1920-87". Editor: "Going Against the Wind: A Pictorial History of African-Americans in Atlanta", 1993. **Home Addr:** 4233 Ivy Run, Ellenwood, GA 30294-6520, **Home Phone:** (404)241-1561. **Business Addr:** Archivist, Morris Brown College, 643 Martin Luther King Jr Dr, Atlanta, GA 30314, **Business Phone:** (404)681-2800.

## MASON, JOHN (EARNEST WOOTEN)

Radio host. **Career:** WJLB-FM, disc jockey; WDMK-FM, air personality, 2001-06; Detroit Pistons, pub add announcer, currently; Mason Radio Inc, WGPR, morning host. **Honors/Awds:** Emmy Award. **Special Achievements:** Consistently ranked the number one African-American morning show in Detroit; was honored for his community service or cheering the Detroit Pistons to victory; Served as the announcer for the international ALL-STAR game in Cyprus & Turkey, 2005; Chosen to serve as the PA announcer at the 2007 NBA All-Star Game in Las Vegas. **Business Addr:** Public Address Announcer, Detroit Pistons, 5 Championship Dr, Auburn Hills, MI 48326, **Business Phone:** (248)377-0100.

## MASON, LUTHER ROSCOE

Administrator, executive director. **Personal:** Born Feb 21, 1927, Georgetown, KY; married Anne Nutter; children: Gregory K & Kurt D. **Career:** Am Red Cross, dir, 1975-; Ky Sch Bds, dir, 1979-; Scott Co Sch, chmn, 1983-84, bd mem, 1976-. **Orgs:** Council mem, Scott City Agr Exten Serv, 1981-; Burley Tobacco Adv Comn. **Honors/Awds:** Treas Scott City, Nat Asn Advan Colored People, 1984-85. **Special Achievements:** First African American selected to Scott County Board of Education in 1976. **Home Addr:** 1290 Delaplain Rd, Georgetown, KY 40324-9582, **Home Phone:** (502)863-1857. **Business Addr:** Board Member, Scott County Schools, 2168 Frankfort Pk, Georgetown, KY 40324, **Business Phone:** (502)863-3663.

## MASON, MAJOR ALBERT, III

Consultant, musician, association executive. **Personal:** Born Jul 15, 1940, McKeesport, PA; married Ann Mathilde Floberg; children: Major Albert IV & Arianna Melany. **Educ:** Univ Pittsburgh, MEd, 1976, PhD, 1984. **Career:** NOW Enterprises Inc, exec dir, founder, 1968-73; Comm Col Allegheny Co, res plng consult, 1974-75, res assoc, 1974-96; Informason & Assocs Inc, founder & pres, 1995-. **Orgs:** Bd mem, Allegheny OIC, 1972-76; bd mem, United Ment Health Inc, 1973-75; radio show host, WEDO Radio, 1973-75; Community Col African-Am Caucus, 1990-97; Convener, 1995-97; Prog to Aid Citizen Enterprise (PACE), bd mem, secy, 1990-96; Comm Media, pres, bd dir, 1998-; Black Men Solidarity Day Mobilization Endorsements; facilitator, Racial Inequity Child Welfare Syst. **Honors/Awds:** Outstanding Young Men of America, 1971. **Special Achievements:** Co-ed, The State of Black Youth in Pittsburgh, 1999. **Business Addr:** President, Informason and Associates Inc, 1409 Bailey Ave, McKeesport, PA 15132-4606, **Business Phone:** (412)672-1519.

## MASON, MARK

Executive, association executive. **Educ:** Howard Univ, BA, bus & admin finance, 1991; Harvard Bus Sch, MBA, 1995. **Career:** Marakon Assocs, strategy consult; Lucent Technologies, dir strategy & bus develop; Citi Holdings, chief financial officer, 2001-, chief exec officer, 2012-; Citigroup Inc, vpres corp develop, 2001, Global Wealth Mgt, chief financial officer, 2006-; CITI Pvt Bank, chief exec officer, 2013-14; Citi's Instnl Clients Group, chief financial officer, 2014-; Citigroup Real Estate Investments, chief financial officer & chief operating off. **Orgs:** Independent bd dirs, Primerica Inc, 2010-. **Honors/Awds:** "Crain's New York Business," 40 Under Forty, 2008; "Black Enterprise," 75 Most Powerful Blacks on Wall Street, 2011. **Business Addr:** Chief Financial Officer, Citigroup Inc, 388 Greenwich St, New York, NY 10013, **Business Phone:** (212)559-1000.

## MASON, RONALD EDWARD (RON MASON)

Executive, vice president (organization), dean (education). **Personal:** Born Aug 22, 1948, New York, NY; son of Thurman and Eleanor Pierce; married Louise Orazio; children: Brian & Jonathan. **Educ:** Utica Col, BA, psychol, 1974; Long Island Inst Ment Health, cert, 1976; City Col NY, MEd, guid & coun, 1978; Baruch Col, NY, cert, 1979. **Career:** State Univ NY, Brooklyn, placement dir, 1974-76, dean stud, 1979-80; Fordham Univ, NY, HEOP, dir, 1976-79; La Guardia Community Col, bd mem, 1978-; SCM Corp, NY, asst mgr, AA & EEO, 1980-81; NBC, NY, dir, personnel, 1981-89; Reader's Dig, Pleasantville, human resources dir, 1989-92; BBDO Worldwide, NY, human resources exec vpres, bd dir, 1992-2000; New York Tech Col Found, bd mem, 1993-; Rockland Community Col Found, bd mem, 1995-; State Univ New York; Fordham Univ; Utica Col; Ny Educ Dept; Empire Blue Cross Blue Shield, human resources sr vpres; Platform Learning, Human Resources, human resources sr vpres, exec vpres human resources, 2004-. **Orgs:** Nat Urban Affairs Coun, 1974-; Am Asn Personnel Admin, 1979-; bd mem, NY, Metro Asn Develop Educ, 1989-; coun mem, Westchester Acad, 1990-; NY Urban League, bd mem, 1993-; exec bd mem, Edges Group, 1993-; bd mem, Am Red Cross, Rockland Cty Chap, 1993-; bd mem, Am Advert Found, EEO & AA Community, 1994-; Am Asn Affirmative Action Prof; Soc Human Resources Mgt; Black Human Resources Network; Nat Urban Affairs Coun Human Resources Forum. **Home Addr:** 303 Bliss Lane, Valley Cottage, NY 10989, **Home Phone:** (845)268-2704. **Business Addr:** Executive Vice President-Human Resources, Platform Learning, 55 Broad St 25th Fl, New York, NY 10004, **Business Phone:** (646)442-2500.

## MASON, DR. TERRY

Physician, surgeon. **Personal:** Born Sep 13, 1951, Washington, DC; children: Terry Jr & Shaakira. **Educ:** Loyola Univ, BS, biol sci, 1974; Univ Ill, MD, 1978. **Career:** Univ Ill, Abraham Lincoln Sch Med, Gen Surg, residency, 1978-80, asst prof, currently; Michael Reese Hosp & Med Ctr, urol residency, 1980-83; Comprehensive Urol SC, pres, 1983-2005; WVON 1690 AM, radio host, 1991-; Prairie Med Asn, pres, 1994; Mercy Hosp-Chicago, Dept Urol, chmn, chief urologist, currently; Rush Presby Chicago; Pub Health Comnr, Chicago, currently; pvt pract, currently; Prairie Med Asn, urologist, partner, pres, med doctor, currently; Chicago Dept Pub Health, comnr; Ctr New Life, owner, 2002-07; City Chicago, Dept Pub Health, comnr, 2005-09; Urolpartners, partner, 2005-10; Cook County Health & Hosp Syst, syst chief med officer, 2009-11, 2011-, interim chief exec officer, 2011, Dept Pub Health, chief operating officer, 2013-. **Orgs:** Am Col Surgeons, fel; Am Urol Asn; Chicago Urol Asn, exec comt mem; Chicago Med Soc; Am Med Asn; Nat Med Asn; R Frank Jones Urol Soc Nat Med Asn; Ill State Med Asn; N Cent Sect Am Urol Asn; Cook County Physicians Asn; regional dir, Impotence Inst Am; life mem, Nat Asn Advan Colored People; bd mem, Saltpond Redevelop Inst Ghana; founder, Proj Cooperates; founder, Health Solutions Inc; bd mem, Hosp Syst; adv bd mem, Thapelo Inst Inc. **Honors/Awds:** Human Resources Develop Inst, On the Move In Med, 1988; Chicago Health & Med Careers Prog, Ill Inst Technol Award, 1981; City of Chicago, Teen Opportunity Award; Dollars & Sense, Men In Med; Monarch Awards Foundation, Men in Med, 1988; Outstanding Young Doctor Award, Dollars & Sense; Nigerian American Forums Distinguished Persons award. **Special Achievements:** Surveillance Study of Diltiazem Use in Black & Non-Black Patients, Journal of Natl Med Assn, 1988; Making Love Again, Renewing Intimacy & Helping Your Man Overcome Impotence, Valarie Contemporary Books, 1988. **Home Addr:** , Chicago, IL. **Business Addr:** Physician, Prairie Medical Assoc, 2850 S Wabash Ave Suite 106, Chicago, IL 60616, **Business Phone:** (312)842-4400.

## MASON, WILLIAM E., SR.

Government official. **Personal:** Born Mar 12, 1934, Shuqualak, MS; married Catheryn; children: Terry & William Jr. **Educ:** Tenn State Univ, BS, 1952; Southern Ill Univ, MS; Univ St Louis, PhD, 1975. **Career:** Instnl Res & Assoc, pres; Dist 189, teacher, prin, personnel dir, dist supt; E St Louis, IL, mayor, 1975-79, precinct comt man; State Ill, human rights specialist; E St Louis pub sch, teacher. **Orgs:** E St Louis Chamber Com; first pres, exec bd Comprehensive Educ Comn; Model Cities Plng Comn; mem bd dir Madison, St Clair Urban League; Phi Delta Kappa; Alpha Phi Alpha; Friendship Baptist Church; Beta Omicron Alumni Asn. **Home Addr:** 1800 Tudor Ave, East St. Louis, IL 62207-2128, **Home Phone:** (616)482-5052. **Business Addr:** President, Institutional Research & Associate, 1800 Tudor Ave, East St. Louis, IL 62207.

## MASON, WILLIAM THOMAS, JR.

Lawyer. **Personal:** Born Jul 27, 1926, Norfolk, VA; son of William T Sr (deceased) and Vivian Carter M. **Educ:** Colby Col, BA, 1947; Howard Univ, LLB, 1950. **Career:** William T Mason, jr atty, pvt pract, 1951-63; Justice Dept, ED, asst US atty, 1963-72; Mason & Robinson Atty, partner, 1972-79, 1976-79; Mason, Moore & Robinson, partner, 1973-76; Norfolk Community Hosp, vice chmn, bd dir, 1975; Robinson Eichler Zaleski & Mason, partner, 1980-87; Overseer Colby Col, bd dir; Robinson, Zaleski & Lindsey, coun, 1987-92; Robinson, Madison, Fulton & Anderson, coun, 1992-95; Robinson, Banks & Anderson, coun, 1995-97; Robinson, Shelton & Anderson, coun, 1997-98; Robinson & Anderson, coun, 1998-2000; Robinson, Neeley & Anderson, coun, 2000-. **Orgs:** Secy bd, Visitors Norfolk State Univ, 1969-73; secy, Old Dom Bar Asn, secy, vpres, pres, 1969-90, exec comt, newsletter ed; vice chmn, Norfolk Community Hosp, 1975-98, chmn bd dir; bd mem, Planning Coun, 1976-; secy, Norfolk State Univ Found, vpres & pres bd dir, 1980-; overseer, Colby Col, 1982-94;

bd dir, Cult Alliance Greater Hampton Roads, 1984; Va State Bar Asn; bd dir, Urban League Hampton Roads, 1985; Players Guild Norfolk Inc. **Honors/Awds:** Award for Devoted Service, Old Dominion Bar Asn, 1983. **Special Achievements:** First African American assistant US attorney for Virginia. **Home Addr:** 2113 Carriage Lane, Norfolk, VA 23518, **Home Phone:** (804)853-3005. **Business Addr:** Counsel, Robinson Neeley & Anderson, 256 W Freemason St, Norfolk, VA 23510, **Business Phone:** (757)622-4686.

### MASS, EDNA ELAINE
Executive. **Personal:** Born Mar 17, 1954, Escatawpa, MS; children: Edward Juwan. **Educ:** Tougaloo Col, BS, 1976; Jackson State Univ, MEd, 1978. **Career:** AT&T Network Systs, supvr software tools develop. **Home Addr:** 1251 Folkstone Ct, Wheaton, IL 60189-7648, **Home Phone:** (630)668-8194. **Business Addr:** Supervisor Software Tools Development, AT&T Network Systems, 2600 Warrenville Rd, Lisle, IL 60532, **Business Phone:** (312)510-6498.

### MASSENBURG, KEDAR
President (organization), executive, music director. **Personal:** Born Jan 1, 1963, CA. **Educ:** Cent State Univ, Ohio, grad, 1985; Univ NC, Chapel Hill, law degree. **Career:** Pepsico Corp, dist mgr; SmithKline Beecham Clin Labs Pharmaceut, sales work, 1980; Motown Records, pres, 1997-2004; Universal Records, sr vpres, 1999; Kedar Beverages, founder, 2005; Kedar Entertainment, founder, pres & chief exec officer, 1995-2012; Massenburg Media, 2012-. **Special Achievements:** Massenburg is best known for bringing Erykah Badu to fame; Album: Long Time No See, 1994. **Home Addr:** , Saddle River, NJ. **Business Addr:** President, Chief Executive Officer, Kedar Entertainment, 21 W 39th St 6th Fl, New York, NY 10018, **Business Phone:** (212)391-1111.

### MASSENBURG, TONY ARNEL
Entrepreneur, basketball player. **Personal:** Born Jul 13, 1967, Sussex, VA; children: Tony James. **Educ:** Univ Md, attended 1990. **Career:** Basketball player (retired), executive; San Antonio Spurs, forward, 1990-91, 2004-05;; Charlotte Hornets, 1991-92; Pallacanestro Reggiana, 1992; Boston Celtics, 1992; Golden State Warriors, 1992; Unicaja-Mayoral, Spain, 1992-93; FC Barcelona, Spain, 1993-94; Los Angeles Clippers, 1994-95; Toronto Raptors, 1995-96; Philadelphia 76ers, 1996; NJ Nets, 1996-97; Vancouver Grizzlies, 1997-99, 1999-2002; Houston Rockets, 1999-2000; Memphis Grizzlies, 2000-02; Utah Jazz, 2002-03; Sacramento Kings, 2003-04; Wash wizards, 2007-08; Arecibo Captains, Pr, 2008; 44 Sports Bar, owner, 2010-12. **Business Addr:** Basketball Player, Washington Wizards, Verizon Ctr 601 F St NW, Washington, DC 20004, **Business Phone:** (202)661-5100.

### MASSEY, ARDREY YVONNE
Administrator, manager. **Personal:** Born Feb 18, 1951, Charlotte, NC; daughter of LeRoy and VeElla. **Educ:** Nat Univ, BBA, mkt, comput & bus, 1988; Strayer Univ, MPA, 2006. **Career:** Royal Globe Ins Co, asst underwriter, 1975-78; Nat Univ, acad adv, 1984-86, asst educ coordr, 1986-88; CMSDC, field coordr, 1989-94; Roots & Wings Unlimited, owner, 1994-2006; Barber Scotia Col, Pub Rels & Alumni Affairs dir, 1999; Charlotte Mecklenburg Urban League, placement specialist, spec employ serv; Cent Piedmont Community Col, Northeast Campus, eve dir; Strayer Univ N Charlotte Campus, Learning Resources Ctr, LRC mgr, currently. **Orgs:** New Birth Charlotte Mem, Carolinas Minority Supplier Develop Coun Inc, 1991-94; chairperson, Bus Opportunity Conf, Educ & Regist Comn, 1991-94; chairperson, Rockwell AME Zion, Youth Develop Prog, 1992-94; vpres, Hemphill Heights Community Orgn; Diversity Coun Carolinas, 1995-; mgr, One Accord Charlotte Gospel Group, 1995; Boy Scouts Am Nominating Comn, 1996. **Home Addr:** PO Box 26666, Charlotte, NC 28221, **Home Phone:** (704)449-6169. **Business Addr:** Manager, Strayer University North Charlotte Campus, 1133 15th St NW Suite 300, Washington, DC 20005, **Business Phone:** (202)408-2400.

### MASSEY, BRANDON
Writer. **Personal:** Born Jun 9, 1973, Waukegan, IL. **Career:** Computer systs admin, 1990-; Author: Thunderland, 1999; Kensington Publ Corp, 2002; Dark Corner, 2004; contributed short stories: Tomorrow: Speculative Fiction mag; After Hours anthology, Dark Dreams, 2004, Within The Shadows, Kensington, 2005; Voices From The Other Side: Dark Dreams II, 2006; Thunderland; Twisted Tales, 2006; Vicious, 2006; Dark Dreams III: Whispers in the Night, 2006; The Other Brother, 2006; Don't Ever Tell, 2008; Ancestors, 2008; Cornered, 2009; Covenant, 2010, In the Dark, 2013. **Home Addr:** PO Box 1416, Fairburn, GA 30213, **Home Phone:** (770)855-7777.

### MASSEY, JACQUELENE SHARP
School administrator. **Personal:** Born Oct 8, 1947, Jackson, MS; married James P; children: Jermane Edward & Jamie Patrice. **Educ:** DC Teacher Col, WA, cert, 1970; Knoxville Col, TN, BA, sociol, 1979; Col Notre Dame, Baltimore, MS, gen mgt courses. **Career:** US Dept Housing & Urban Develop, Wash, DC, summer coordr, 1970; Delta Sigma Theta Inc/Pub Serv Sorority, mem off, 1970-71; Fed Educ Prog/Direct Search Talent, Md, admin prog coordr, 1973-77; Baltimore City Pub Sch, 1977-78; Univ Md, Baltimore, assoc dir, spec prog, 1978-; US Dept Labor, Job Corps, voc specialist, 1994-97; DC Pub Sch, teacher; Off Employ Develop, Sch-To-Work Educ Alternative Learning prog, mgr, 1997-; Career Acad, Baltimore City Mayors Off Employ Develop, prog mgr, currently. Community Partnership & Resource Develop, dir, currently; Acad Col & Career, dir & conf coordr. **Orgs:** Second vpres, Delta Sigma Theta Inc, Pub Serv Sorority, 1965-67; cons/decision making prog Col Entrance Exam Bd, New York, 1976; vpres, Girl Scouts Cent Md, 1977-; Speakers Bur, United Fund Cent, Md, 1977-78; cons/cosmetic Bus Fashion Two-Twenty Co, 1978-; chmn, Hebbville Elem Sch PTA, 1979-; Echo House Multi-Svc Ctr, 1995-; Svc Acad Rev Bd, 7th Cong Dist, 1996; Gov Comn Serv, 1996; bd mem, Elijah Cummings Youth Pro, 1997-; community adv bd, Johns Hopkins Univ, currently. **Home Addr:** 3419 Ripple Rd, Windsor Mill, MD 21244-3604, **Home Phone:** (410)922-2536. **Business Addr:** Director of Community Partnership & Resource Development, Program Manager, Baltimore City Office of Employment Development, 101 W 24th St, Baltimore, MD 21218, **Business Phone:** (410)396-6722.

### MASSEY, DR. JAMES EARL
Clergy, school administrator, educator. **Personal:** Born Jan 4, 1930, Ferndale, MI; married Gwendolyn Inez Kilpatrick. **Educ:** Detroit Bible Col, BRE, BTh, 1961; Oberlin Grad Sch Theol, AM, 1964; Asbury Theol Sem, DD, 1972; Pac Sch Relig, attended 1972; Univ Mich; Boston Col Grad Sch. **Career:** Ch God Detroit, assoc minister, 1949-51, 1953-54; Metro Ch God, sr pastor, 1954-76; Jamaica Sch Theol, prin, 1963; Anderson Col, Sch Theol, campus minister, prof relig studies, 1969-77; Gautschi Lect Fuller Theol Sem, lectr, 1975-86; Christian Brotherhood, speaker, 1977-82; Anderson Univ, Sch Theol, prof new testament, 1981-84; Tuskegee Univ Chapel & Univ Prof Relig, dean, 1984-90; Southwestern Bapt TheolSem, northcutt lectr, 1986; Anderson Univ, Sch Theol, dean, prof preaching & Bibl studies, 1989-95, dean emer & prof large, currently; Pk Pl Ch God, Anderson, Ind, Preacher Resident, 1994-95; Metrop Church God, Detroit, pastor emer; Tuskegee Univ, prof, dean emer, currently. **Orgs:** Bd dir, Detroit Coun Chs; theol study commiss, Detroit Coun Ch; corp mem, Inter-Varsity Christian Fel; matl comn Black Churchmen; Wesleyan Theol Soc; ed bd, Christian Scholars Rev; bd dir, Warner Press Inc; vchmn, Pub Bd Ch God; ed adv, Tyndale House Publ, 1968-69; comn chmn; Christian Unity; Nat Asn Col & Univ Chaplains; bd dir, Nat BlackEvangelical; Nat Advan Asn Colored People; Lausanne Continuation Comn; Underwood Fel Danforth Found, 1972-73; pres, Anderson Civil Serv Merit Com miss, 1975-81; ed bd, Leadership Mag; bd dir, Nat Relig Broadcasters; ed bd, Preaching Mag, 1987; resource scholar, Christianity Today Inst, 1985; sr ed, Christianity Today, 1993-95. **Honors/Awds:** Staley Distinguished Christian Scholar, Staley Found, 1977; Distinguished Service Award, Anderson Univ; Freitas Lectures Asbury Theol Sem, 1977; Rall Co-Lectr Garrett-Evangel Sem, 1980; Mullins Lect So Bapt Sem, 1981; Swartley Lect Eastern Baptist Sem, 1982; Jameson Jones Lectr Iliff Sch Theol, 1983; Rom Lect Trinity Evangelical Div Sch, 1984; Lifetime Achievement Award, Wesleyan Theological Socs, 1995. **Special Achievements:** Author: Designing the sermon, 1980; The burdensome joy of preaching, 1998; Sundays in the Tuskegee Chapel, 2000; Aspects of My Pilgrimage, 2002. **Home Addr:** 367 Beverly Rd, Greensboro, AL 36744-6034, **Home Phone:** (334)624-4297. **Business Addr:** Dean Emeritus, Tuskegee University Chapel, 1200 W Montgomery Rd, Tuskegee, AL 36088, **Business Phone:** (334)727-8702.

### MASSEY, DR. JANELLE RENEE
Lawyer, teacher. **Personal:** Born Dec 7, 1976, New Orleans, LA; daughter of Johnny (deceased) and June. **Educ:** Southern Univ A&M Col, BS, psychol, 1998; Southern Univ Law Ctr, JD, 2001. **Career:** Orleans Parish Sch Bd, teacher, 2001-02; Orleans Parish Criminal Ct, law clerk, 2003-. **Orgs:** Golden Key Nat Hon Soc, 1996-; Nat Psychol Hon Soc, 1996-; Delta Sigma Theta Sorority Inc, 1997-; Delta Theta Phi Legal Fraternity, 2000-; La State Bar Asn. **Special Achievements:** Trombonist, Pinettes Brass Band. **Home Addr:** 4010 Virgil Blvd, New Orleans, LA 70122-2426, **Home Phone:** (504)282-4864. **Business Addr:** Law Clerk, Criminal District Court of Orleans Parish, Rm 114 2700 Tulane Ave 7th Fl, New Orleans, LA 70119, **Business Phone:** (504)658-9100.

### MASSEY, REV. REGINALD HAROLD
Clergy. **Personal:** Born Jun 23, 1946, Rowan County, NC; married Arletta Bingham; children: Angela, Marc & Reginald Jr. **Educ:** Livingstone Col, BS, sociol; Hood Theol Sem, Livingstone Col, MDiv; Rowan Tech Col, Cert Crisis Counseling; Baptist Hosp, Winston Salem, CPE cert. **Career:** Town E Spencer Police Dept, police officer, 1971-73; Town E Spencer, mayor, 1973-81; Salisbury Rowan Community Serv Coun Inc, asst planner, 1976-78, asst dir, 1978; Herndon Chapel AME Zion Church, pastor, 1979-81; Ezekiel AME Zion Church, 1979-83; Ctr Grove AME Zion Church, 1983-89; VA Med Ctr Salisbury, chaplain, 1984-; Hood Memorial AME Zion Church, pastor, 1989-; Southern City AME Zion Ch, minister & pastor. **Orgs:** E Spencer Planning bd; Aux Police, 1971-73; water qual policy adv comn, Gov's Appointment, 1980; intergovt rels comn, NC League Munic, 1980; Southern Conf Black Mayors; comn chmn, NC League Munic Com; Boy Scout Troup 383; Am Legion Post 107; E Spencer Civic League; Salisbury-Rowan Civic League; Livingston Col Alumni Asn; bd trustees, Southern City AME Zion Ch; Nat League Cities; Nat Conf Black Mayors; exec comt, Durham Col; vpres, NC Conf Black Mayors; Masonic Lodge Western Star #9. **Honors/Awds:** Martin Luther King Jr Humanitarian Award, 2004; Chief of Chaplain Service, NC Civitan Club, 2004. **Special Achievements:** Southern City AME Zion Church Town's first black mayor. **Home Addr:** 3275 Jake Alexander Blvd, Salisbury, NC 28144, **Home Phone:** (704)638-3330. **Business Addr:** Pastor, Hood Memorial AME Zion Church, 215 Sacco St, Belmont, NC 28012, **Business Phone:** (704)825-6007.

### MASSEY, DR. REV. SELMA DIANE REDD
Chief executive officer, association executive. **Personal:** Born Sep 8, 1953, Ft. Campbell, KY; daughter of Redd and Gaynelle. **Educ:** Univ Detroit, BA, sociol, 1974, MA, coun, 1975; Western Mich Univ, EdD, orgn & leadership, 1993. **Career:** C's Aid Soc, social worker, 1974-75; State Mich, social worker, 1975-79; Wayne Co Community Col, instr, 1977-; Detroit's Most Wanted, producer/host, 1986, chief exec officer, 1995; Proj Start Inc, chief exec officer & exec dir, 1981-; Whosoever Ministry, pres, currently; Proj BAIT (Black Awareness Tv), host, 1994-; Hist Full Truth Fel Christ Church, Mi, asst pastor; My People, host, 1994; Between Lines Newspaper, Mich, writer. **Orgs:** Univ Detroit Alumni Asn, 1974; Am Correctional Asn, 1983-; WDTR Educ Broadcasting, 1986-; Urban League, Detroit, 1994-; Mich Asn Community Corrections Advan, 1987-; Western Mich Univ Alumni Asn, 1993; Faith Action Network. **Honors/Awds:** Leadership Commitment, IBM Leadership Develop, 1992; Excellence Recognition, Detroit Pub Schs, 1993, Certificate of Participation, 1994; Teen Violence Accomplishment, Urban League, 1994. **Special Achievements:** Continue the Fight Against Crime, Mich Chronicle, 1994; "We Cannot Afford Short-Sightedness", Mich Chronicle, 1994; "A Study Needed to Understand", Behavior, Mich Chronicle, 1994; "I Don't Care", 1994; "Hurry Up! Bring it Back Home", 1995; "Outside the City Gate", 2014. **Home Addr:** 3320 Spinnaker Lane Suite Ten C, Detroit, MI 48207-5005. **Business Addr:** President, Whosoever Ministry, PO Box 14242, Detroit, MI 48214-0242, **Business Phone:** (313)259-9922.

### MASSEY, WALTER EUGENE
Scientist, school administrator, educator. **Personal:** Born Apr 5, 1938, Hattiesburg, MS; son of Chester and Essie; married Shirley Anne; children: Keith & Eric. **Educ:** Morehouse Col, BS, math & physics, 1958; Wash Univ, MS, PhD, physics, 1966. **Career:** Scientist, school administrator, educator (retired); NDEA, fel, 1959-60; Nat Sci Found, fel, 1961; Argonne Nat Lab, post doctoral fel, 1966-68, staff physicist, 1966-68, dir, 1979-84; Univ Ill, asst prof, 1968-70; Brown Univ, assoc prof, 1970-75, prof, dean, 1975-79; Am Coun Educ, fel, 1974; Univ Chicago, prof, 1979-91; vpres res, 1984-91; Nat Sci Found, dir, 1991-93; Univ Calif-Syst wide, provost & sr vpres acad affairs, 1993-95; Bank Am, chmn; Morehouse Col, pres emer, 1995-2007; Sch Art Inst Chicago, pres, 2010-. **Orgs:** Rev comt, Nat Sci Found, 1971; rev comt, Nat Acad Sci, 1973; Nat Sci Bd, 1978-84; fel bd dir, 1981-85; pres elect, 1987; pres, 1988; Am Asn Advan Sci; Am Nuclear Soc; Am Phys Soc; NY Acad Sci; Ill Gov Comn Sci & Technol; Ill Gov Sci Adv Comt; Sigma Xi; bd dir, BP Amoco; bd dir, Argonne-Chicago Develop Corp; bd dir, Motorola; bd dir, Chicago Tribune Co; bd dir; Continental Mat Corp; bd dir, First Nat Bank Chicago; bd dir, Bank Amer, BP oil; bd dir; Hewlett Found Commonwealth Fund; bd fels, Brown Univ; bd trustee, Rand Corp; Mus Sci & Indust; Chicago Orchestral Asn; bd gov, JF Symphony; bd dir, Mellon Found; bd dir, McDonalds; bd, Atlanta Symphony Orchestra, Woodruff Arts Ctr; Am Asn Physics Teachers; pres, AAAS; chmn, Salzburg Global Sem; trustee, Andrew W Mellon Found; Am Acad Arts & Sci, Am Philos Socs, Am AsnAdvan Sci &Coun Foreign Rels; fel Am Phys Soc; Omega Psi Phi Fraternity. **Honors/Awds:** Distinguished Service Citation, Am Asn Phys Teachers, 1975; Archie Lacey Memorial Award, NY Acad Sci, 1992; Bennie Trailblazer Award, Morehouse Col, 1992; Morgan State Univ, Distinguished Achievement Award, 1992; Golden Plate Award, 1992. **Special Achievements:** Numerous science publications; Recipient of 25 honorary Doctor of Science degrees; first black vice president for research, 1984. **Home Addr:** 833 Fair St, Atlanta, GA 30314. **Business Addr:** President, The School of the Art Institute of Chicago, 37 S Wabash Ave, Chicago, IL 60603, **Business Phone:** (312)259-2968.

### MATCHETT, JOHNSON
Executive. **Personal:** Born Oct 17, 1942, Mobile, AL; son of Johnson Sr. **Educ:** Ala State Univ, BS, 1963; Univ Ala, MA, 1969; Univ Southern, MS, EdS, 1975. **Career:** Anniston Pub Schs, teacher, 1963-64; Mobile Pub Schs, teacher, 1964-69; Miles Col, dir teacher educ, 1969-73; Ala State Univ, part-time instr, 1972-75; Univ S Ala, curric consult, 1974; BellSouth Serv Inc, mgr training, 1974-. **Orgs:** Am Soc Training & Develop, 1975-, Phi Delta Kappa Hon Educ Fraternity, 1975-, Nat Soc Performance & Instr, 1982-; Nat Asn Advan Colored People, 1983-; exec bd, Ala State Univ Gen Alumni Asn, 1985-89; Nat Black MBA Asn, 1986-, Ala Initiative Black Col Recruitment & Retention Birmingham Chapt, 1987-89, Holy Family HS bd dir, 1987; Acad Affairs Com, Nat Soc perf & instr, 1992-; PRS Birmingham Chap Nat Black MBA Asn, 1992-. **Home Addr:** PO Box 752, Birmingham, AL 35201. **Business Addr:** Manager/Training, Bell South Telecommunications, 65 Bagby Dr Rm 315, Birmingham, AL 35209, **Business Phone:** (205)945-2165.

### MATEEN, MALIK ABDUL
Association executive, firefighter. **Personal:** Born Oct 19, 1949, Hialeah, FL; son of Rubbie L Laughlin and Zula M Jackson; married Fern K; children: Africa & Clifford. **Career:** Life Geo Ins Co, ins agt, 1973; Dade County Solid Waste Dept, truck driver, 1973-81; Metro Fire Rescue, firefighter, 1981-. **Orgs:** Pres, Progressive Firefighters Asn, 1989. **Home Addr:** 17031 NW 12th Ave, Miami, FL 33169-5204, **Home Phone:** (305)216-8841. **Business Addr:** FL.

**MATHABANE, JOHANNES. See MATHABANE, MARK.**

### MATHABANE, MARK (JOHANNES MATHABANE)
Writer, lecturer. **Personal:** Born Oct 18, 1960, Alexandra Township; son of Jackson and Geli Mabaso; married Gail Ernsberger; children: Bianca Ellen, Nathan Phillip & Stanley Arthur. **Educ:** Limestone Col, attended 1978; St Louis Univ, attended 1979; Quincy Col, attended 1981; Dowling Col, BA, econ, 1983; Columbia Univ, attended 1984. **Career:** Author, lecterur, 1985-; Books: Kaffir Boy: True Story a Black Youth's Coming Age Apartheid SafricA, 1986; Kaffir Boy Am, 1989; Love Black & White, co-auth with Gail Ernsberger, 1992; African Women: Three Generations, 1994; Ubuntu, 1999; Miriam's Song, 2000; Deadly Memory; Last Lib; Dowling Col, black ed; The Proud Liberal, 2010. **Orgs:** Authors Guild; PEN Am Ctr; Authors League Am; Magdalene Scholar Fund, 2000. **Honors/Awds:** Christopher Award, 1986; White House Fellow, Dept Educ, 1996-97; Robert Kennedy Memorial Award, finalist. **Special Achievements:** The First Black Editor of The School Magazine. **Home Addr:** 341 Barrington Pk Lane, Kernersville, NC 27284. **Business Addr:** Author, Lecturer, Mathabane Books & Lectures, 1320 NW Frazier Ct, Portland, OR 97229, **Business Phone:** (503)758-9024.

### MATHEWS, GARY C.
Chief executive officer. **Career:** Afro-Am Newspapers Group Inc & Nat Newspaper Pubs Asn, consult; Diversity Media, advocate; Educ Communicate, pres; ETC Info Inc, pres & nat chmn, currently. **Orgs:** Bd mem, Browns Community Outreach. **Business Addr:** Chief Executive Officer, President, ETC Information Inc, 1327 Lafayette Ave, Baltimore, MD 21207-4836, **Business Phone:** (410)788-6471.

### MATHEWS, GEORGE
Executive, chief executive officer. **Personal:** Born Montgomery, AL. **Career:** WGPR Inc, WGPR-FM, Detroit, Mich, chief exec officer & pres, gen mgr, currently. **Orgs:** Int Free Accepted Modern Masons Inc. **Business Addr:** President, Chief Executive Officer, WGPR Inc, 3146 E Jefferson Ave, Detroit, MI 48207, **Business Phone:** (313)259-8862.

### MATHEWS, MAJ. K. KENDALL (K KENDALL STEVENS)
Manager, army officer, social worker. **Personal:** Born Detroit, MI; married Katrina; children: 5. **Educ:** Greenville Col, BA, social work,

1985, MA, theol; Andersonville Theol Sem, Camilla, Ga, PhD, christian psychol, 1994. **Career:** US Salvation Army, Chicago Midwest Corps & Community Ctr, case mgr & community ctr dir, 1985-89, corps officer, 1991-2001, div secy, 2001-08, regional coordr, 2008-12, ARC adminr, 2012-; Pontiac Pub Sch Syst, mentor; Oakland Univ, supvr; Greenville Col, admin assoc; Nat Network Social Work Mgr, social work mgr, 1998-; Eastern Mich Div Headquarter, lt, corps officer, capt, secy, detroit city comdr, 2001-08, regional coordr, 2008-. **Orgs:** Founder, Booth Acad; Stud Asn; Social Life Comt; dipl, Am Psychotherapy Asn; adminr, St. Louis Salvation Army Adult Rehab Ctr. **Honors/Awds:** Honor, Former Mich Gov John Engler; Whos Who Among Outstanding Corporate Executives, Salvation Army; Finalist for the George Romney Lifetime Achievement Award. **Special Achievements:** One of the top 50 African American men in the Southeastern Michigan Region for his leadership and effective interpersonal skills. **Business Addr:** ARC Administrator, Salvation Army, 16130 Northland Dr, Southfield, MI 48075-5218, **Business Phone:** (248)200-3448.

### MATHEWS, KEITH E.
Judge. **Personal:** Born Mar 2, 1944, Steubenville, OH. **Educ:** Morgan State Univ, BS, chem, 1966; Univ Baltimore, JD, 1972. **Career:** Judge(retired); Police Dept, Baltimore City, police officer, 1968-69; Water Dept, Baltimore City, chemist, 1969; Community Col Baltimore, instr, 1971-72; Legal Aid Bur Inc, Baltimore, staff atty, 1972-73; Congressman Parren Mitchell, legis asst, 1973-74; US Dept Justice, Antitrust Div, atty, 1974-75; Foster Mathews & Hill, atty, partner, 1975-82; States Atty Off Baltimore, asst states atty, 1978-83; Dist Ct Md, assoc judge, 1983-10, admin judge 1999-2010. **Orgs:** Bd govs, Univ Baltimore Alumni Asn, 1973; vice chmn, Consumer Affairs Adb Bd Howard Co, 1978; Monumental Bar Asn; Nat Bar Asn; Chair, Comt Civil Procedures, Dist Ct Md, 1998-99; founding mem, Univ Baltimore Law Rev; Admin Judges Comt, Dist Ct Md, 1999-10; Criminal Law & Procedure Comt, 2000-01; Judicial Coun, 2000-03; Monumental City Bar Asn; Drug & Alcohol Abuse Coun, Baltimore City, 2004-; Co-Chair, Access [to Ct Rec] Rules Implementation Comt, 2004-05; Md Judicial Conf. **Home Addr:** 1040 Deer Ridge Dr Suite 504, Baltimore, MD 21210. **Business Addr:** Administrative Judge, District Court of Maryland, Borgerding Dist Ct Bldg 5800 Wabash Ave, Baltimore, MD 21215-3330, **Business Phone:** (410)764-8714.

### MATHEWS, LAWRENCE TALBERT
Executive, financial manager, executive director. **Personal:** Born Oct 12, 1947, Michigan City, IN; married Beverly Ann Hoze; children: Gerald. **Educ:** Univ Mich, Flint, AB, 1969; Univ Detroit, MBA, 1975. **Career:** Arthur Young & Co, sr auditor, 1972-75; Comn Credit/Mc Cullagn Lsng, controller & treas, 1975-78; Mich Peninsula Airways, vpres finance, 1978-80; Clipper Int Mfg, vpres finance, 1980-82; Comprehensive Health Serv Detroit, dir finance oper; Wellness Plan, vpres, chief financial officer, currently; Mich Asn Ceritified Pub Acct, dir, currently. **Orgs:** Asst exec dir, Detroit Area Agency Aging, 1984; pres, Nat Asn Black Acct, 1992-94; Mich Asn Health Maintenance Org Finance Comn. **Honors/Awds:** Distinguished Service, Nat Asn Black Accts, 1985. **Home Addr:** 35376 Glengary Cir, Farmington, MI 48331-2622. **Business Addr:** Director, Michigan Association of Certified Public Accountants, PO Box 5068, Troy, MI 48007-5068, **Business Phone:** (248)267-3700.

**MATHEWS, YVONNE REED.** **See MADISON, YVONNE REED.**

**MATHEY, JORGE ANTONIO BELL.** **See BELL, GEORGE ANTONIO.**

### MATHIS, DAVID L.
Executive. **Personal:** Born Sep 16, 1947, Riverhead, NY; son of Freddie Mae Thompson; married Dorothy; children: David, Denise & Doreen. **Educ:** Mohawk Valley Community Col, AAS, 1970; Syracuse Univ, Uitca Col, BS, 1972. **Career:** Mohawk Valley Opportunity Indus Ctr, dir training, 1972-73, exec dir, 1973-74; Career Develop Ctr, dir manpower serv, 1974-79, dir job develop, 1979-80; Oneida Co Employ Training, dep dir, 1980-86, dir, Off Workforce Develop, 1986-. **Orgs:** Bd dir, Cosmopolitan Community Ctr; bd trustee, Hope Chapel AME Zion Church; adv bd, Oneida Co Youth Bur; bd trustee, Mohawk Valley Community Col, 1977; bd dir, Asn Gov Bds NY State Comm Cols; chmn, Utica Col Ed Bass Black Stud Scholar Fund; bd dir, Ferre Inst, l988; bd dir, Neighborhood Ctr Utica, l988; bd trustee, Munson-Williams-Proctor Inst, l988; Rotary Club Utica, 1989; bd dir, Utica Found, 1989; bd dir, Asn Community Col trustee, 1990; bd dir, Alumni Asn, 1990, vpres; Commit, 1991; bd dir, Utica Neighborhood Housing Serv; bd pres, Utica Head Start; bd dir, ARC Oneida Lewis Counties, 1993; adv bd, Fleet Bank New York, CRA, 1993; Am Red Cross, Northeast Reg Com, 1994; bd dir, State Univ NY Alumni Confederation, 1995; pres, Ny Affirmative Action Officers, 1995; bd dir, Ct St Family Health Ctr, 1996; bd dir, Am Lung Asn Mid NY, 2000-03; bd dir, House Good Shepard, 2000; pres, NY Asn TRG Employ Prof, 2002. **Home Addr:** 833 Symonds Pl, Utica, NY 13502-5619, **Home Phone:** (315)797-8069. **Business Addr:** Director, Oneida County Office of Employment & Training, 209 Elizabeth St Paul Bldg, Utica, NY 13501, **Business Phone:** (315)798-5908.

### MATHIS, DEBORAH F.
Journalist. **Personal:** Born Aug 24, 1953, Little Rock, AR; daughter of Rachel A and Lloyd H; children: Meredith, Allison & Joseph. **Educ:** Univ Ark, Little Rock, attended 1972. **Career:** Ark Dem newspaper, reporter, Ark Gazette, ed columnist & assoc ed, 1988-91; KTHV-TV, gen assignment reporter, 1973-74; WTTG-TV, weekend anchor, 1974-76; KARK-TV, asst news dir, 1976-82; KATV-TV, "Live at Five", anchor, 1983-88; Clarion-Ledger, columnist, 1992-93; Tribune Media Serv, syndicated columnist, 1992-, Am's Black Forum, commentator; Gannett News Serv, White House corresp, 1993-; Northwestern Univ Medill Sch Jour Wash Prog, asst prof; Medill News Serv Wash Bur, Managing ed, currently; freelance writer, 2001-; Book: Yet a Stranger: Why Black Americans Still Don't Feel at Home, 2002. **Home Addr:** 6702 Kenwood Forest Lane, Chevy Chase, MD 20815, **Home Phone:** (301)913-9553. **Business Addr:** Managing Editor, Medill News Service Washington Bureau, 1325 G St NW Suite 730, Washington, DC 20005-3195, **Business Phone:** (202)347-8700.

### MATHIS, DEDRIC RONSHELL
Football player. **Personal:** Born Sep 26, 1973, Cuero, TX. **Educ:** Univ Houston. **Career:** Football player (retired); Indianapolis Colts, defensive back, 1996, right defensive back, 1997; Chicago Bears, 1997-98; Seattle Seahawks, 1999; Xtreme Football League, Chicago Enforcers, 2000; Orlando Predators, 2000; Hamilton Tiger Cats, 2001-05. **Home Addr:** 703 2nd St, Cuero, TX 77954-2006, **Home Phone:** (361)275-6699.

### MATHIS, GREGORY
Judge, writer, broadcaster. **Personal:** Born Apr 5, 1960, Detroit, MI; son of Charles and Alice (deceased); married Linda; children: Jade, Camara, Greg Jr & Amir. **Educ:** Eastern Mich Univ, BS, pub admin, 1984; Univ Detroit, JD, 1987. **Career:** Judge (retired), Broadcaster; Detroit City Coun, admin asst councilman Clyde Cleveland, 1984-88; Off Mayor, City Detroit, mgr, neighborhood city hall, 1989-93, lawyer pvt pract, 1993-95; State Mich, 36th Dist Ct, judge, 1995-98; TV courtroom show, Judge Mathis, host, 1999-. **Orgs:** Chmn, Reclaim our Youth Crusade, 1993-; founder & chmn, Young Adults Asserting Themselves, 1986-; spec asst Rev Jesse Jackson, Nat Rainbow Coalition, 1994-; life mem, NAACP; Alpha Phi Alpha Fraternity Inc. **Honors/Awds:** Has recieved more than 100 awards including Man of the Year, Southern Christian Leadership Conf, 1995; Detroit City Coun, Testimonial Resolution, 1995; Proclaimation from Mayor, Off Mayor, City Detroit, 1995; Spec Tribute Proclamation, Mich Legis, 1995. **Special Achievements:** Co-author, play, Inner City Miracle, 1995, Ebony, 2007; Books; Street Judge; Being a Judge to Criminals and Such; Author of Black men must fight back against obstacles, 2007. **Home Addr:** 14455 Stahelin, Detroit, MI 48223, **Home Phone:** (313)836-5682. **Business Addr:** Television Show Judge, Warner Brothers Domestic Television, 4000 Warner Blvd, Burbank, CA 91522.

### MATHIS, JOHNNY (JOHN ROYCE MATHIS)
Songwriter, singer, actor. **Personal:** Born Sep 30, 1935, Gilmer, TX; son of Clement and Mildred Boyd. **Educ:** San Francisco St Col. **Career:** San Francisco Night Clubs, singer; Albums include: Johnny Mathis, 1956; Chances Are, 1957; Warm, 1957; It's Notfor Me to Say, 1957; Twelfth of Never, 1957; Wonderful! Wonderful!, 1957; Wild Is the Wind, 1957; No Love (But Your Love), 1957; Come To Me, 1957; All the Time, 1957; Teacher, Teacher, 1957; Good Night, Dear Lord, 1958; Johnny's Greatest Hits, 1958; A Certain Smile, 1958; Call Me, 1958; Winter Wonderland, 1958; Let's Love, 1958; You Are Beautiful, 1958; Small World, 1958; Swing Softly, 1958; Someone, 1958; Merry Christmas, 1958; Winter Wonderland, 1958; Open Fire, Two Guitars, 1959; More Johnny's Greatest Hits, 1959; Heavenly, 1959; Faithfully, 1959; You Are Everything To Me, 1959; Misty, 1959; The Story of Our Love, 1959; The Best of Everything, 1959; Starbright, 1960; The Rhythms and Ballads of Broadway, 1960; Johnny's Mood, 1960; Maria, 1960; My Love For You, 1960; How To Handle a Woman, 1960; You Set My Heart To Music, 1960; Jenny, 1961; Wasn't the Summer Short, 1961; I'll Buy You A Star, 1961; Portrait of Johnny, 1961; Live It Up!, 1962; Rapture, 1962; Sweet Thursday, 1962; Marianna, 1962; Gina, 1962; Johnny's Newest Hits, 1963; Johnny, 1963; Romantically, 1963; Sounds of Christmas, 1963; What Will My Mary Say, 1963; Every Step of the Way, 1963; I'll Search My Heart and Other Great Hits; Sooner or Later, 1963; Come Back, 1963; Your Teenage Dreams, 1963; I'll Search My Heart, 1963; Bye Bye Barbara, 1964; Bye Bye Barbara, 1964; Taste of Tears, 1964; Listen Lonely Girl, 1964; Take the Time, 1965; Sweetheart Tree, 1965; On a Clear Day You Can See Forever, 1965; So Nice (Samba de Verao), 1966; Two Tickets and a Candy Heart, 1967; Don't Talk To Me, 1967; Misty Roses, 1967; Venus, 1968; You Make Me Think About You, 1968; The 59th Street Bridge Song, 1969; I'll Never Fall In Love Again, 1969; Love Theme from Romeo and Juliet, 1969; Midnight Cowboy, 1969; Odds and Ends, 1970; Wherefore and Why, 1970; Pieces of Dreams, 1970; Evil Ways, 1970; Ten Times Forever More, 1971; Long Ago and Far Away", 1971; Make It Easy On Yourself, 1972; Soul and Inspiration/For Once In My Life, 1972; Take Good Care of Her, 1973; Show and Tell, 1973; I'm Coming Home, 1973; Life Is a Song Worth Singing, 1973; Sweet Child, 1974; Sail On White Moon, 1975; I'm Stone In Love With You, 1975; Stardust, 1975; One Day In Your Life, 1976; Yellow Roses On Her Gown, 1976; Do Me Wrong, But Do Me, 1976; Loving You-Losing You, 1977; Arianne, 1977; Too Much, Too Little, Too Late, 1978; You're All I Need To Get By, 1978; The Last Time I Felt Like This, 1979; Begin the Beguine, 1979; Gone, Gone, Gone, 1979; Different Kinda Different, 1980; Friends In Love, 1982; Love Won't Let Me Wait, 1984; Simple, 1984; Right From the Heart, 1985; I'm On the Outside Looking In, 1988; Small World; In a Sentimental Mood: Tribute to Duke Ellington, 1990; In A Sentimental Mood-Mathis Sings Ellington, 1990; Better Together, 1992; How Do You Keep the Music Playing, 1993; The Christmas Music Of Johnny Mathis, 1993; How Do You Keep The Music Playing, 1993; This Heart of Mine, 1994; All About Love, 1996; Johnny Mathis-40th Anniversary Edition, 1996; The Global Masters, 1997; Because You Loved Me: Songs of Diane Warren, 1998; The Ultimate Hits Collection, 1998; Because You Loved Me, 1998; For Christmas, 1998; Christmas Is, 1999; Mathis on Broadway, 2000; Christmas Album, 2002; That's What Friends Are For, 2003; Frosty the Snowman, 2003; Merry Christmas, 2003; 20 Grandes Exitos, 2003; Over the Rainbow, 2004; The Essential Johnny Mathis, 2004; Isn't It Romantic: The Standards Album, 2005; Isn't It Romantic-The Standards Album, 2005; The Very Best of Johnny Mathis 6 UK Pop Albums, 2006; A Night to Remember 29 UK Pop Albums, 2008; Let It Be Me: Mathis in Nashville, 2010; The Ultimate Collection #17 UK Albums, 2011; Sending You a Little Christmas, 2013. **Orgs:** Founder, Shell & Johnny Mathis Golf Classic. **Honors/Awds:** Hollywood Walk of Fame, 1972; Lifetime Achievement Award, Acad Rec Arts & Sci, 2003; Grammy Hall of Fame, 1998; Great American Songbook Hall of Fame, 2014; Society of Singers Lifetime Achievement Award, 2006. **Special Achievements:** Nominated for a Grammy, 1961, 1992; one of only five recording artists to have Top 40 Hits spanning each of the four decades since 1955; listed in Guinness Book, 490 continuous weeks (almost ten years) on the BILLBOARD Top Albums Chart; author, Cooking for You Alone, 1982. **Business Addr:** Singer, Richard De La Font Agency Inc, 4845 S Sheridan Rd Suite 505, Tulsa, OK 74145, **Business Phone:** (918)665-6200.

### MATHIS, KEVIN BRYANT
Football player, president (organization). **Personal:** Born Apr 29, 1974, Gainesville, TX; married Kimberly; children: Kennedy & Kaleb. **Educ:** Tex A&M Univ, com. **Career:** Dallas Cowboys, defensive back, 1997-99; New Orleans Saints, 2000-01; Atlanta Falcons, defensive back, 2002-06; Prime Prep Acad, asst coach, 2012-; Another Chance Properties LLC, pres, currently. **Orgs:** Founder, Kevin Mathis Found; bd mem, Cowboys Prof Rodeo Asn. **Home Addr:** 2400 Taylor St Suite 202, Commerce, TX 75428-3459. **Business Addr:** Founder, Kevin Mathis Foundation, 7204 Stilton Ct, Colleyville, TX 76034-7326, **Business Phone:** (888)939-2323.

### MATHIS, ROBERT LEE, JR.
Health services administrator. **Personal:** Born Apr 21, 1934, Concord, NC; son of Minnie V; married Margaret Miller; children: Calven, Rodney, Jeffery & Kim West. **Educ:** USn, Cooks & Bakers Sch, 1956; Cent Piedmont Comm Col, polit sci, 1976; NC State Univ, personnel mgt dipl, 1978; St Louis Univ, Food Serv Dipl, 1978. **Career:** Health service administrator (retired); Cabarras Memorial Hosp, cook spec diets, 1958, cook & baker supvr, 1965, asst food serv dir, 1979-94; Concord, mayor pro-team, 1995. **Orgs:** Dir, Cabarrus City Boys Club, 1979-; Mt Zion Lodge 26 Concord NC, 1980-, NC Chap Am Soc Hosp; Food Serv, 1980; adv bd, Salvation Army, 1981-; leader Boy Scouts, 1983; dir, Cab County United Way, 1983; mem bd visitor, Barber-Scotia Col, Concord NC, 1984; delegcity NC Centralina Coun Gov; elder First Christian Church; bd dir, Life Ctr & Logan Day Care; Bd Corrections, 1994; chmn, Cabarrus Cty, offical assoc, 1994; bd dir, Acad Learning Ctr. **Honors/Awds:** Represented the largest ward in NC, 1980; Outstanding Citizen of the Year, Kannpolis Daily Independence, 1981; co-founder, Fourth Word Develop Corp, 1982; Citizen of the Year, Phi Chi, 1985. **Special Achievements:** First African American elected as Concord Bd of Alderman, 1980-. **Home Addr:** 2676 RocK Hill Church Rd NW, Concord, NC 28027-8050, **Home Phone:** (704)782-9757.

### MATHIS, SHARON BELL
Executive, writer, educator. **Personal:** Born Feb 26, 1937, Atlantic City, NJ; daughter of John Willie Bell and Alice Mary Frazier Bell; married Leroy Franklin; children: Sherie, Stacy & Stephanie. **Educ:** Morgan State Col, BA, 1958; Cath Univ Am, MLS, 1975. **Career:** C Hosp DC, interviewer, 1958-59; Holy Redeemer Elem Sch, teacher, 1959-65; Stuart Jr High Sch, spec educ teacher, 1974-75; Charles Hart Jr High Sch, fac, 1965-72; DC Black Writers Workshop, founder & writer-in-charge C lit div; Howard Univ, writer-in-residence, 1972-73; Benning Elem Sch, librn, 1975-76; Patricia Roberts Harris Educ Ctr, librn, 1976-95; Author: Brooklyn Story, 1969; Sidewalk Story, 1971; Teacup Full of Roses, 1972; Ray Charles, 1973; Listen for the Fig Tree, 1974; The Hundred Penny Box, 1975; Cartwheels, 1977; Red Dog & Blue Fly: Football Poems, 1991; Running Girl, 1997. **Orgs:** Bd adv lawyers comt, DC Comn Arts, 1972; Black Womens Community Develop Found, 1973; Am Libr Asn, 1995-. **Honors/Awds:** Award, Coun Interracial Books C, 1970; Author Award, 1974; Coretta Scott King Award, 1974; Newbery Honor, Book Am Libr Asn, 1976; Arts & Humanities Award, Archdiocese Wash, 1978; Wallace Johnson Memorial Award, 1984; Arts & Letters Award, Delta Sigma Theta Sorority, 1985; Outstanding Writer Award, Writing-to-Read Prog, 1986. **Home Addr:** PO Box 780714, Orlando, FL 32878-0714, **Home Phone:** (407)249-1386.

### MATHIS, DR. THADDEUS P.
Educator. **Personal:** Born Sep 8, 1942, Americus, GA; married Deborah Moore; children: Latanya, Evan & Talani; married Deborah Moore-Stewart. **Educ:** Bluefield State Col, BS, sec educ, 1965; Bryn Mawr Col, MSS, social serv, 1968; Temple Univ, MA, African Am studies, PhD, polit sci, 1985. **Career:** Dept Pub Welfare, group leader, 1965-66; Child Study Ctr Philadelphia Temple Univ Hosp, social work intern, 1966-68; Dept Pub Welfare, social worker, 1968; Philadelphia Model Cities Prog, planning coordr, 1968-70; Temple Univ, prof social admin, 1970, adj prof, African Am Studies Dept, assoc dean, 1999-, Col Pub Health, Sch Social Work, Ctr African Am Res & Pub Policy, co-dir, prof emer, currently. **Orgs:** Exec comt, Philadelphia Cong Racial Equality, 1971-75; chairperson, Philadelphia Black Polit Conv, 1971-80; presiding officer, Nat Black Independent Polit Party, 1981-83; chairperson, Sch Soc Admin Grad Dept, 1981-84; pres, Philadelphia Alliance Black Soc Workers; bd mem, Housing Asn Del Valley; Philadelphia Alliance Black Social Workers; bd Housing ASN DEL Valley; chairperson, IST AFA Develop; dir, IST African Social Work; Nat Asn Black Social Workers. **Honors/Awds:** Shapp Found Scholar Shapp Foundation Philadelphia, 1961-65; PEP Fellow State PA Off Children & Youth, 1966-68; Fellow, Urban Affairs Inst Am Univ, 1971; Bernard C Watson Award, 1985; Distinguished Teaching Award, Christian R & Mary F Lindback Found. **Home Addr:** 8100 Rodney St, Philadelphia, PA 19150-3012, **Home Phone:** (215)247-2441. **Business Addr:** Professor Emeritus, Temple University, Ritter Annex 5th Fl 1301 W Cecil B Moore Ave, Philadelphia, PA 19122-6091, **Business Phone:** (215)204-8623.

### MATHIS, WALTER LEE, SR.
Government official. **Personal:** Born Feb 2, 1940, Columbus, MI; son of Willie and Ludell; married Patricia E Grier; children: Walter, Tracy, Daryl & Melissa. **Educ:** Davenport Col, MI, cert, acct & real estate. **Career:** Meijer Inc, shipping clerk, mgr trainee; Mathis Tax Serv, owner; Party Store, owner; Take Pride, Community Mag, founder; real estate broker, 1975-; Afro-Am Gazette, publ & ed, 1990-2005; Oper Resources Inc, pres, chmn bd & chief exec officer, 1993-; ULC One race-Oneblood Ministry, pastor, 2005-. **Orgs:** Mem, Grand Rapids Housing Bd Appeals; bd mem, Freedom Homes Inc; Nat Asn Advan Colored People; Kent-CAP Gob Bd; Take Pride! Community. **Honors/Awds:** Named VIP of Grand Rapids Press, 1972. **Home Addr:** 1313 Spencer St NE, Grand Rapids, MI 49505-5527, **Home Phone:** (616)458-7773. **Business Addr:** Chairman, Chief Executive Officer, Operation Resources Inc, 1014 Franklin St SE, Grand Rapids, MI 49507-1327, **Business Phone:** (616)243-1919.

### MATTHEW, CLIFTON, JR.
Baseball player, educator. **Personal:** Born Sep 25, 1943, Brooklyn, NY; married Claraleata Cutler; children: Darryl & Adrian. **Educ:** NC

Agr & Tech State Univ, BS, 1966; Rutgers Univ, MEd, 1973. **Career:** Baseball player (retried); Bluefield Orioles, baseball player, 1965-66; Aberdeen Pheasants, baseball player, 1966; Stockton Ports, baseball player, 1966-67, 1969; Baltimore Orioles, prof baseball player, 1966-71; Camden Sch Syst, teacher, 1966-71; FIL Orioles, baseball player, 1967, 1969; Stockton Ports, baseball player, 1967; Miami Marlins, baseball player, 1968-69; Dallas-Ft Worth Spurs, baseball player, 1970; Educ Opportunity Fund Trenton St Col, asst dir, 1971-74; Trenton State Col, baseball coach, 1974; Upward Bound, dir; Camden City Bd Edn, supr recreation, 1974-79; Pleasantville Pub Sch, dir comm educ, 1979-83; Lower Camden County Bd Ed, asst prin, 1983; Edgewood Jr High Sch, prin, 1990; Winslow Twp Schs, prin. **Orgs:** Kappa Alpha Psi; Nat Assoc Sec Sch Prins; NJ Princs & Supvr's Assoc; Phi Delta Kappa Fraternity. **Home Addr:** 340 Farmdale Rd, Moorestown, NJ 08057, **Home Phone:** (856)608-6883.

## MATTHEWS, ALBERT D.

Judge. **Personal:** Born Feb 19, 1923, Oklahoma City, OK; son of Samuel and Della; married Mildred; children: Angela M. **Educ:** Howard Univ Sch Law, LLB, 1954; Howard Univ, attended 1951. **Career:** Judge (retired); pvt pract, 1955-58; Los Angeles Co, dep dist atty, 1958-60; Dept Employ, state referee hearing officer, 1960-62; Pro Tempr, super ct comnr, 1962-68; munic ct judge, 1968-73; State Calif, super ct judge, 1973-89; Los Angeles Co Super Ct, judge, 1989-204, adv bd mem. **Orgs:** Los Angeles Bar Asn; Langston Law Club; Nat Conf Trial Ct Judges; Am Bar Asn; bd dir, Henderson Community Ctr, S Los Angeles; bd mgrs, Am Baptist Pac SW; chmn, MATE; deacon, Church Sch Admin, second Baptist Church, Los Angeles; exec bd, Am Baptist Churches, USA Valley Forge, Pa; christian educr, Sunday Sch Teacher; adv bd mem, Charles Dolo Coker Jazz Scholar Found Inc. **Home Addr:** PO Box 3928, City of Industry, CA 91744.

## MATTHEWS, BOB. See MATTHEWS, ROBERT L.

## MATTHEWS, CANDACE SHEFFIELD

Businessperson. **Personal:** Born New Brighton, PA; married Bruce; children: Sydney & Simone. **Educ:** Carnegie-Mellon Univ, BS, metal eng, admin & mgt sci; Stanford Grad Sch Bus, MBA. **Career:** Gen Mills, asst prod mgr, 1985-88; Proctor & Gamble, mkt dir, cover girl cosmetics, 1988-93; Bausch & Lomb Oral Care Div, dir mkt, 1993-95; Cent Inst Brackishwater Aquacult Vision Corp, exec dir, advan res progs, 1995-98; Coca-Cola Co, vpres, new prod & packaging innovation, 1998-2000; L'Oreal, pres, 2001-07; Soft Sheen-Carson, pres, 2001-; Amways, chief mkt officer, 2007-. **Orgs:** Bd trustee, Carnegie Mellon Univ; Stanford Grad Sch Bus Adv Coun; bd trustee, Peggy Notebaert Nature Mus; bd trustee, Cosmetic Exec Women & Figure Skating Harlem; bd trustee, Carnegie-Mellon Univ, 2003-08, 2011-; exec leadership coun, Cosmetic Exec Women, 2004-07, 2010-; Fifth Third Midwest Regional Bd Dirs, 2011-; Spectrum Health Found, 2011-. **Honors/Awds:** Women of Color iBusiness Person Year Award; Alumni Merit Award, Carnegie Mellon, 2003; Technology Business Person of the Year Award, Oper Push, 2004; United Cerebral Palsy Women Who Care Award, 2005; HELP USA Leadership Award, 2005; Advertising Working Mother of the Year Award, 2005; Outstanding Women in Marketing & Communications Award, Ebony, 2006; Power Award, Essence, 2006; Cosmetic Executive Women Achiever Award, 2007; Corporate Executive of the Year, Black Enterprise, 2009. **Special Achievements:** Has been featured in major publications, such as Ebony, Essence, Black Enterprise, Glamour, Salon Sense, and the Wall Street Journal. **Business Addr:** President, Soft Sheen/Carson Inc, 575 5th Ave, New York, NY 10017, **Business Phone:** (212)818-1500.

## MATTHEWS, CHRISTY S.

Executive. **Personal:** Born May 1, 1964, Orlando, FL. **Educ:** Hampton Univ, BA, multidisciplinary studies, 1992, MA, mus studies, 1996. **Career:** Baltimore City Life Mus, asst educ & asst dir educ prog, 1986-89; Colonial Williamsburg, dir. **Orgs:** IMTAL; CDR; AAAM; AAM; Colonial Williamsburg Found, character interpreter, 1982-86, dir prog & interpretive prog develop, 1989-99, dir African Am prog. **Business Addr:** Director, African-American Program, The Colonial Williamsburg Foundation, PO Box 1776, Williamsburg, VA 23187-1776, **Business Phone:** (757)229-1000.

## MATTHEWS, CLAUDE LANKFORD, JR.

Television producer. **Personal:** Born Jun 18, 1941, High Point, NC; son of Claude and Georgianna; married Cynthia C Clark; children: Georgeanne N. **Educ:** Howard Univ, BA, 1963; Georgetown Univ Law Ctr, JD, 1978. **Career:** WTOP-TV, reporter, 1968-70, "Harambee", talk show host, 1970-74; NBC News, ed network radio, 1976-77, ed network TV, 1977-80, Wash producer weekend nightly news, 1980; Pvt Pract, atty, currently. **Orgs:** Pa Bar Asn; Am Bar Asn; DC Bar Asn. **Home Addr:** 2805 31st Pl NE, Washington, DC 20018-1603, **Home Phone:** (202)529-0727. **Business Addr:** Attorney, 2805 31st Pl NE, Washington, DC 20018-1603, **Business Phone:** (202)526-8150.

## MATTHEWS, CYNTHIA CLARK

Lawyer. **Personal:** Born Aug 27, 1941, Nashville, TN; married Claude Lankford; children: Georgeanne. **Educ:** Wellesley Col, attended 1961; Howard Univ, BA, 1965; George Washington Univ Nat Law Ctr, JD, 1973. **Career:** Lawyer (retired); Hon John Conyers US Cong, legis & press asst, 1965-69; United Planning Orgn, pub info officer, 1970-72; US Comm Civil Rights, equal opportunity specialist, 1973-75; Onyx Corp, vpres mkt & contract mgr, 1975-76; Housing Com Coun DC, exec asst to coun mem & atty, 1976-79; US Equal Employ Opportunity Comn, dir, off equal employ opportunity, 1979-99; Vanderbilt Univ, admis evaluator, 2009-. **Orgs:** DC Bar, 1975; Supreme Ct Bar, 1980; US Dist Ct DC Bar, 1980; Nat Asn Black Women Atty; Am Bar Asn; bd dir, Anacostia Mus. **Home Addr:** 1609 Wilson Pl, Silver Spring, MD 20910. **Business Addr:** Admissions Evaluator, Vanderbilt University, 2201 W End Ave, Nashville, TN 37235, **Business Phone:** (615)322-7311.

## MATTHEWS, REV. DAVID

Vice president (organization), clergy, president (organization). **Personal:** Born Jan 29, 1920, Indianola, MS; son of Albert and Bertha Henderson; married Lillian Pearl Banks; children: Denise D. **Educ:** Morehouse Col, BA, 1950; Atlanta Univ; Memphis Theol Sem; Delta State Univ; Reformed Sem. **Career:** Ordained Baptist minister, 1946-; Sunflower City & Ind Pub Schs, teacher, 1950-83; Strangers Home Baptist Church, pastor, 1958-; Mt Heroden Baptist Church, Vicksburg MS, pastor, 1951-53; St Paul Baptist Church, pastor, 1954-58; Bell Grove Baptist Church, pastor, currently. **Orgs:** Indianola Community Rels Comt; Phi Delta Kappa; Miss State Dept Educ Task Force; moderator, Sunflower County Baptist Asn; vpres, oratorical contest supvr, Nat Baptist Conv USA Inc, 1971-94; pres, Gen Missionary Baptist State Conv Miss, 1974-98; first Black Dem Election Comnr, first Black Dep Chancery Clerk, Sunflower County; Indianola's biracial comt; Gov's Comn. **Home Addr:** PO Box 627, Indianola, MS 38751. **Business Addr:** Pastor, Bell Grove Baptist Church, 512 Chandler St, Indianola, MO 38751, **Business Phone:** (662)887-4963.

## MATTHEWS, DENISE (DENISE KATRINA MATTHEWS)

Singer, actor, clergy. **Personal:** Born Jan 4, 1959, Niagara Falls, ON; married Anthony Smith. **Career:** Song writer & singer; Vanity 6, lead singer, 1982; Pure Heart Ministries, evangelist & head, currently; Songs: Nasty Girls, He's So Dull, Drive Me Wild, single, 1982; Pretty Mess, 1984; Wild Animal, Motown, 1984; Skin On Skin, Motown, 1986; Under The Influence, 1986; He Turned Me Out, 1988; Film: The Last Dragon, 1985; Never Too Young To Die, 1986; 52 Pickup, 1986; Love You To Death; Deadly Illusion, 1987; Action Jackson, 1988; Neon City, 1992; South Beach, 1992; Da Vinci's War, 1993; Kiss of Death, 1995; TV Series: "The Late Show", 1987; "The New Mike Hammer", 1987; "Miami Vice", 1987; "Ebony/Jet Showcase", 1988; "T. and T", 1988; "Friday the 13th: The Series", 1989; " Booker", 1989; "Memories of Murder", 1990; "Tales from the Crypt", 1991; "Tropical Heat", 1991; "Silk Stalkings", 1992; "Lady Boss", 1992; "Highlander", 1992; "Counterstrike", 1993. **Honors/Awds:** Gold Single, Nasty Girls. **Home Addr:** 38625 Paseo Padre Pkwy Apt 201, Fremont, CA 94536-6130. **Business Addr:** Evangelist, Head, Pure Heart Ministries, 39270 Paseo Padre Pkwy Suite 214, Fremont, CA 94538, **Business Phone:** (510)744-9822.

## MATTHEWS, DOLORES EVELYN

School administrator. **Personal:** Born Jul 23, 1938, DuBois, PA; daughter of George Daniel and Evelyn Goodrich. **Educ:** NY City Community Col, AA&S, assoc, 1961. **Career:** School administrator (retired); Columbia Univ, Col Physicians & Surgeons, Dept Psychiat, prog coordr, post grad educ officer, 1979-2001. **Orgs:** Nat pres, Continental Socs Inc, 1993-97; exec comt, Nat Coun Negro Women; moderator, Presbytery New York, 2000-02; chair, Gen coun, Presbytery New York, 2002-03; vice moderator, Presby women, 2005; trustee, N Presby Church; Harlem Hosp Ctr's. **Home Addr:** 790 Riverside Dr Apt 5N, New York, NY 10032-7435, **Home Phone:** (212)368-5144.

## MATTHEWS, DOROTHY

Advertising executive. **Personal:** Born Jan 21, 1962, St. Louis, MO. **Educ:** Maryville Col, BA, 1983. **Career:** NY Ins, salesperson, 1983; Channel 4 Newsroom, res person, 1984; Sch Bd Dist 188, secy. **Orgs:** Elks Purple Temple 126; Black Media Coalition; St Louis First Freewell Baptist Church; United Parcel Holiday Club. **Honors/Awds:** Best Essay, First Freewill Bapt Church, 1979. **Home Addr:** 412 Jefferson St, Lovejoy, IL 62059.

## MATTHEWS, GARY NATHANIEL, JR.

Baseball player, actor. **Personal:** Born Aug 25, 1974, San Francisco, CA; son of Gary Sr and Sandra Smith. **Educ:** Mission Community Col. **Career:** Baseball player (retired); San Diego Padres, outfielder, 1999, 2003; Chicago Cubs, 2000-01; Pittsburgh Pirates, 2001; New York Mets, 2002; Baltimore Orioles, 2002-03; San Diego Padres, 2003; Texas Rangers, 2004-06; Los Angeles Angels of Anaheim, 2007-09; New York Mets, 2010; free agt, currently. TV Series: "Sunday Night Baseball", 2001-10; "Rome Is Burning", 2007. Movie: 2006 MLB All-Star Game, actor, 2006.

## MATTHEWS, DR. GERALD EUGENE

Educator. **Personal:** Born Oct 25, 1943, Michigan City, IN; son of Andrew and Cassie; married Carolyn S; children: Gregory, Corwin & McKenzie Sproul. **Educ:** Univ Mich-Flint, BA, 1978; Univ Mich, MSW, 1980, EdS, 1983, PhD, 1985. **Career:** CS MOH Community Col, adj instr, 1985-; Hamilton Family Health Ctr, exec dir, 1986-92; Wayne State Univ, lectr, 1993-94; Eastern Mich Univ, lectr, 1995-97; Univ Mich, Flint, adj instr Africana studies, 1998-2006; Ferris State Univ, assoc prof social work, prof social work, 1997-. **Orgs:** Nat Asn Soc Workers, 1980 & 1992-; planning comnr, Genesee Co, 1984-91; bd dir, Mich Primary Care Asn, 1985-91; bd gov, Univ Mich, Flint, 1990-93; chair, Ferris State Univ, PAC Sub comt, 1998-; adv bd mem, Mich State Univ Kinship Care Prog, 2000-; Phi Alpha Kappa, 2000; Ferris State Univ Prof Develop Comt, currently; proj dir, Community Found Greater Flint. **Home Addr:** 1079 Dye Meadow Lane, Flint, MI 48532-2315, **Home Phone:** (810)733-7381. **Business Addr:** Professor of Social Work, Ferris State University, ASC 2106 820 Campus Dr, Big Rapids, MI 49307-2225, **Business Phone:** (231)591-2752.

## MATTHEWS, GREGORY J.

Administrator. **Personal:** Born Oct 25, 1947, Baltimore, MD; married Paula Allen. **Educ:** Morgan State Univ, BA, 1970; Coppin St Col, MA, 1973. **Career:** Adult Ed Econ Manpower develop, instr, 1970; Conciliation & Compliance-MD Comn on Human Rel, dir, 1970-75; Int Asn Offical Human Rights Agencies, EEO consult, 1975; Affirmative Action-Great Atlantic Pac Tea Co, dir, 1975-78; GJ Matthews & Assoc, managing partner; Staffing & Equal Opp Prog, dir, 1978-85; SMP Corp, corp mgr; Am Express Travel Related Serv Co Inc, dir employee rels, 1985-. **Orgs:** Chmn, Nat Urban Affairs Coun; chmn, Fed Corp Prof; bd mem, Assoc Black Charities; life mem, Nat Asn Advan Colored People; bd mem, Nat Assoc Mkt develop; Edges Group. **Honors/Awds:** Distinguished service citation, Nat Black MBA Assoc, 1984; Herbert H Weight Award, 1985. **Home Addr:** 200 Vesey St, New York, NY 10285-0001. **Business Addr:** Director Employee Relations, American Express Travel, World Financial Ctr, New York, NY 10285.

## MATTHEWS, HARRY BRADSHAW

College administrator. **Personal:** Born Mar 1, 1952, Denmark, SC; son of James Edgar and Lucretia Killingsworth Parler; married Pamela Davis. **Educ:** State Univ NY, Col Oneonta, BA, black-hisp studies & polit sci, 1974; Carnegie Mellon Univ, attended 1979; Northern Mich Univ, MA, coun educ, 1981. **Career:** NYS Minority Ways & Means Res Div, trainee, intern, 1973-74; SUNY Col Oneonta, asst dean res, 1974-78; Northern Mich Univ, dir black stud serv, 1978-81; Hobart & William Smith Col, asst dean, 1981-85; Gettysburg Col, dean intercultural advan, 1985-93; Hartwick Col, assoc dean, 1993-, US Pluralism Prog, dir & US Colored Troops Inst, Inst Local Hist & Family Res, pres, exec dir, currently. Books: African American Genealogical Research: How to Trace Your Family History, 1992; Whence they came: The families of United States Colored troops in Gettysburg, Pennsylvania, 1815-1871, 1992; Honoring New York's Forgotten Soldiers: African Americans of the Civil War, 1998; Voices from the Front Line: New York's African American Statesmen of the Underground Railroad Freedom Trail, United States Colored Troops Organized in the Empire State, 1863-1865. **Orgs:** Mich Gov & Bd Educ Task Force, 1980-82; Human Rights Comn, Geneva NY, 1983-85; Penn Hist & Mus Comns Black Hist Adv Comn, 1989; dir & founder, Minority Youth Educ Inst, 1988-; co-chmn, Ann Conf, Afro-Am Hist & Geneal Soc, 1991; New York Comnr Educs Adv Coun State & Local Hist; New York Sch Bds Asns Diversity Comt; Ordinary fel Col Preceptors, Eng; exec dir, pres, Us Colored Troops Inst; NY Comnr Educ's Adv Coun, 2006-07. **Home Addr:** 140 W Broadway, Gettysburg, PA 17325, **Home Phone:** (717)337-3836. **Business Addr:** Associate Dean, Director of US Pluralism Programs, Hartwick College, PO Box 4022, Oneonta, NY 13820, **Business Phone:** (607)431-4150.

## MATTHEWS, DR. HEWITT WILLIAM

Educator, school administrator, vice president (organization). **Personal:** Born Dec 1, 1944, Pensacola, FL; son of Hewitt and Jestine; married Marlene Mouzon; children: Derrick & David. **Educ:** Clark Atlanta Univ, BS, chem, 1966; Mercer Univ Sch Pharm, BS, pharm, 1968; Univ Wis Madison, MS, pharmaceut biochem, PhD, pharmaceut biochem, 1973. **Career:** Fac, Mercers Sch Pharm, 1973; Ctr Dis-Control, res chemist, 1976; TX Southern Univ, vis assoc prof, 1979; Mercer Univ Sch Pharm, asst dean, 1980-83, vis scientist, summer 1987, 1988; Mercer Univ Atlanta, prof & asst provost; Mercer Univ Sch Pharm, prof, assoc dean, 1985-89; Mercer Health Sci Ctr Atlanta, Sch Pharm, Hood-Meyer Alumni prof, dean, 1990, sr vpres health sci, currently. **Orgs:** AACP, NPhA; ASHP; AphA; Rho Chi; Sigma Xi; Phi Kappa Phi; bd dir, Geo Pharm Asn; chmn, Comn Pharmaceut Care; gov adv coun, Sci & Technol Dev; Nat Asn Chain Drug stores, educ comt; Nat Community Pharmacist Asn; Deans Award, Am Col Apothecaries. **Home Addr:** 120 Hanover Cir, Fayetteville, GA 30214-1233, **Home Phone:** (770)461-9712. **Business Addr:** Senior vice president for health sciences, Mercer Health Sciences Center, 3001 Mercer Univ Dr, Atlanta, GA 30341-4155, **Business Phone:** (678)547-6306.

## MATTHEWS, IRVING J.

Executive. **Educ:** Southern Univ, BS, Eng; A&M Col, MS, Eng. **Career:** Procter & Gamble, opers mgr, 1970-84; Frito Lay, plant mgr, 1984-90; Matthews Automotive Group, Eustis, FL, gen mgr, owner, pres & chief exec officer, 1991-; Bethune-Cookman Col, chmn trustee & presidential search comt; Daytona Lincoln Mercury, owner. **Orgs:** Daytona Beach Symphony Soc; chmn trustee, bd trustee, chmn presidential search comt, Bethune-Cookman Col; Beta Xi Boule; Advan Technol Ctr Williamson Blvd; bd mem, Ford Lincoln Mercury Dealer Develop Alumni Asn Inc; bd dir, Volusia County Advan Technol Ctr. **Business Addr:** Chief Executive Officer, Prestige Ford Inc, 17701 US Hwy 441, Mount Dora, FL 32757-6743, **Business Phone:** (352)357-5522.

## MATTHEWS, REV. JAMES VERNON, II

Clergy. **Personal:** Born Oct 25, 1948, Berkeley, CA; son of James Vernon and Yvonne Feast. **Educ:** St Patrick's Col, Mountain View, Calif, BA, Humanities, 1970; St Patrick's Sem, Menlo Pk Calif, MDiv, 1973; Jesuit Sch Theo, Berkeley, Calif, DMin, cand, 1979; Pontif Gregorian Univ, abbatical studies Church Hist. **Career:** St Louis Bertrand Church, Oakland, Calif, assoc pastor, 1974-78; All Saints Church, Hayward, Calif, admin, 1978-80; St Cyril Church, Oakland, Calif, admin, 1980-83; Oakland Diocese, Oakland, Calif, vicar Black Catholics, 1983-87; St Cornelius Church, Richmond, Calif, admin, 1987-89; St Benedict Church, Oakland Calif, pastor, 1989-; Anthony Church, Oakland, assoc; St Columba, Oakland, Deacon; Bishop O'Dowd High Sch Oakland & Serra High Sch, San Mateo, Calif, Teacher; Diocese, Oakland, Youth Minister. **Orgs:** Knights St Peter Claver Third & Fourth Degrees, 1971-; past bd mem, Nat Black Cath Clergy Caucus, 1973-; rev bd, Alameda Co Revenue Sharing, 1975-76; bd dir, Campaign Human Develop, 1979-84; comnr, Oakland Sch Dist, Comn Educ & Career Develop, 1982-83; Bay Area Black United Fund Relig Task Force, 1982-; bd dir, Cath Charities Parish Outreach Prog, 1983-87; adv bd, Oakland Mayor's Task Force Hunger, 1984-87; adv bd, Oakland Mayor's Task Force Black & Jewish Rels, 1984-87; diocesan coordr, Nat Conf Interracial Justice, 1984-; chaplain, African-Am Cath Pastoral Ctr, 1990-; Oakland Mayor's Adv Coun, 1991-; Oakland Strategic Planning, 1991-; bd mem, Alameda Co Health Care Found; NAACP, New Oakland Comt; Casa Vincentia; Martin Luther King, Jr Birthday Observance Comt; Nat Asn of Black Cath; Oakland Mayor's Adv Coun on Educ; Oakland think tank; City of Oakland Police & Fire departments, New Oakland Comt & United Negro E Bay. **Honors/Awds:** Outstanding Black Sermons, Judson Press, Publishers, 1975; Rose Casanave Service Award, Black Cath Vicariate, Oakland CA, 1982; Martin Luther King Jr Award, United E Oakland Clergy, 1984; Marcus Foster Distinguished Alumni Award, Marcus Foster Educ Inst, 1984; Religious Award, Alameda/Contra Costa Chap Links Inc, 1985; Service Award, Xavier Univ Alumni Asn, 1985; Community service awards, Knights & Ladies St Peter Claver. **Special Achievements:** Father James Vernon Matthews, II was ordained as the First Black Catholic Priest in northern California on May 3, 1974. **Home Addr:** 2245 82nd Ave, Oakland, CA 94605, **Home Phone:** (510)632-1847. **Business Addr:** Pastor, Saint Benedict Catholic Church, 2245 82nd Ave, Oakland, CA 94605, **Business Phone:** (510)632-1847.

**MATTHEWS, LEONARD LOUIS**
Educator. **Personal:** Born Dec 4, 1930, New Orleans, LA; son of Alex and Angie Bell; married Dolores B; children: Mallory Louis & Cassandra Duere. **Educ:** Southern Univ, BS, BA, 1959; Calif State Univ, credential psychol, 1965, MA, 1974; Univ Calif, Los Angeles, credential psychol, 1972; Pepperdine Univ, Los Angeles, credential educ, 1974. **Career:** Educator (retired), director; St John Sch Dist, elem prin, 1952-59; La Unified Sch Dist, drama spec, master teacher, 1959-70, counsr, 1970-74; Inglewood Unified Sch Dist, sec prin, 1974-91; Youth Positive Alternatives, organizer, educ dir; Atherton Christian Sch, prin, 2000-02. **Orgs:** Secy, Alpha Phi Alpha, 1963-64; chmn, Young Men's Christian Asn, 1981-85; Organizer Citizens Against Prostitution, 1982-84; Dr Martin L King Jr Mem, 1983-86; Citizens Against Crime & Drugs, 1984-86; vpres, Parents Teachers Asn, 1985-86; vpres, Inglewood Mgt Asn, 1986; Calif Continuation Educ Asn; City Inglewood, Leadership Coun, chmn, Educ Award Youth Comt; pres, Block Club; educ chmn, City Inglewood Leadership Coun. **Home Addr:** 9626 5th Ave, Inglewood, CA 90305, **Home Phone:** (213)777-0856.

**MATTHEWS, MARY JOAN HOLLOWAY**
Educator, mayor. **Personal:** Born Dec 19, 1945, Boley, OK; daughter of Lawrence C Holloway (deceased) and Qvetta Ashley Holloway (deceased). **Educ:** Langston Univ, BS, elem educ, 1967; Calif State Col, Dominguez Hills, MA, learning disabilities, 1976; Univ Okla, cert psychometry, 1980. **Career:** Paramount Unified Sch Dist, teacher, 1968-70; Sapulpa City Sch, teacher, 1971-74; Boley Pub Sch, teacher, 1976-79; Okla State Dept Educ, psychometrist, 1979; mayor, Boley, Okla, 1999-. **Orgs:** Secy, Greater Boley Area Nat Asn Advan Colored People Br, 1981; Okla Coun Voc Educ, 1982-97; secy, Boley Chamber Com, 1983-96; bd dir, CREOKS Ment Health, 1983-2000; Grammateus, Epsilon Rho Omega Chap Alpha Kappa Alpha Sorority, 1989; secy, Self Cult Club Okla Federated Colored Women's Club. **Home Addr:** PO Box 352, Boley, OK 74829. **Business Addr:** Mayor, Town of Boley, PO Box 158, Boley, OK 78429, **Business Phone:** (918)667-9790.

**MATTHEWS, DR. MERRITT STEWART**
Physician. **Personal:** Born Jul 8, 1939, Atlantic City, NJ; son of George and Bessie; married Patricia Anne Delgado; children: Shari, Luis, Merritt Jr, Michael & Marguerite. **Educ:** Howard Univ, Lib Arts, BS, 1961, Sch Med, MD, 1965. **Career:** St Joseph's Hosp, internship, 1965-66, resident, 1966-68, chief resident family pract, 1967-68; Sharp Gateway Med Group, group pract; USAF Med Corps, 1968-70; Otay Med Clin SD, Calif, 1971-74; Family Pract Community Paradise Valley Hosp, chairperson, 1983-86, 1993-96; Skilled Nursing Facil, San Diego Physicians & Surgeons Hosp, med dir, 1983-87; San Diego Acad Family Physicians, pres, 1984-85; Gateway Med Group, pvt pract physician, currently. **Orgs:** Physician, San Diego County Jails, 1976-92; bd dir, San Diego Acad Family Physicians, 1982-; co-dir, Western Med Group Lab, 1982-87; bd dir, Jackie Robinson YMCA San Diego, 1983-85; Task Force SD Police Dept, 1983; dir, Calif Acad Family Physicians, 1988-95; alt deleg, Calif Med Asn, 1987-93; chair, Comn Minority Health Affairs AAFP, 1992-95, 1995; bd, San Diego AIDS Found, 1992-94; Sharp Community Med Group. **Honors/Awds:** Certified, Am Bd Family Physicians, 1970, recertified, 1976, 1982, 1988, 1995, 2001; Delegate, Calif Med Asn, 1994-; fel, Am Acad Family Physicians, 1974; Spec Achievement Award, Jackie Robinson YMCA, 1985; Competitive Award for Practicing Phys, Family Pract, NMA, 1993-94. **Special Achievements:** Publ Article "Cholelithiasis: A Differential Diagnosis in Abdominal Crisis of Sickle Cell Anemia", Journal of NMA, 1981. **Home Addr:** 383 Winewood St, San Diego, CA 92114, **Home Phone:** (619)262-4741. **Business Addr:** Physician, Gateway Medical Group, 752 med Ctr Ct Suite 210, Chula Vista, CA 91911, **Business Phone:** (619)656-0206.

**MATTHEWS, ROBERT L. (BOB MATTHEWS)**
Teacher, school principal, consultant. **Personal:** Born Jun 2, 1930, Tonganoxie, KS; son of Suzie Jane Brown and Mark Hanna; married Ardelle Marie Dunlap; children: Mark Douglas, Brian Louis & Scott Wallace. **Educ:** Kans State Teachers Col, Emporia, Kans, BS, 1952; Columbia Univ, MA, 1955; US Int Univ, PhD, 1971. **Career:** San Diego City Sch, teacher, 1955-64, prin, 1965-72, dir elem educ, 1972-83, prin, 1983-84; US Govt, NDEA fel, 1965; Rockefeller Found fel, 1971-72; Humanities fel, Nat Endowment Humanities, 1976; Educ Cult Complex, pres, 1984-86; San Diego Community Col Dist, pres, San Diego Unified Sch Dist, teacher & prin; 1986-92; self-employed, educ consult; Mt Erie Christian Acad, prin. **Orgs:** Officer, San Diego Urban League, 1965-; Educ Comt, San Diego Zool Soc, 1973-; pres, Elem Inst Sci, 1983-84, bd dir; pres, Zeta Sigma Lambda Alpha Phi Alpha, 1984-85; bd dir, Mus Nat Hist, 1984-; Nat Asn Advan Colored People; Black Leadership Coun; Inst Black Child Develop; Jackie Robinson YMCA Bd; San Diego Human Rels Comn; RADY C's Hosp Auxiliary & Kids News Day; Encanto Planning Comn; Jacobs Ctr Comt Investments; Southeast Community Theater; Common Ground Theatre; Jack & Jill Women Inc; Tema Ghana Sister. **Home Addr:** 4931 Dassco Ct, San Diego, CA 92102-3717, **Home Phone:** (619)264-0542.

**MATTHEWS, ROBERT L.**
Law enforcement officer. **Personal:** Born Oct 8, 1947, Wilmington, DE; married Elsie Nichols; children: Miel & Amne. **Educ:** Fla A&M Univ, BS, (magna cum laude), sociol, 1972; Ind State Univ, MS, criminol, 1973. **Career:** Bur Prisons, US Penitentiary Leavenworth, assoc warden, 1980, warden, 1981; FCI Ashland, warden, 1981; US Marshals Serv, Dist Columbia, US marshal, 1983; FCI Lexington, warden, 1985; USP Atlanta, warden, 1990, regional dir, 1991-94, asst dir, Southeast Region, regional dir; Correctional Serv Corp, Adult Div, sr vpres, 2001-; Correctional Consult Firm, pres; Matthews Correctional Consult, pres. **Orgs:** Am Correctional Asn, 1981-; Nat Asn Blacks Criminal Justice, 1982-; FDL Exec Bd, Atlanta, 1990-91, San Francisco, 1991; Leavenworth Civil Serv Comn, 1990; exec mem, Correctional Employees Comt ACA, 1992. **Home Addr:** 705 Birkdale Dr, Fayetteville, GA 30215, **Home Phone:** (770)461-6361. **Business Addr:** Senior Vice President, Correctional Services Corp, 1819 Main St Suite 1000, Sarasota, FL 34236, **Business Phone:** (941)953-9199.

**MATTHEWS, VINCENT EDWARD (VINCE EDWARD MATTHEWS)**
Athlete. **Personal:** Born Dec 16, 1947, Queens, NY. **Educ:** Johnson C Smith Univ, attended 1970. **Career:** Athlete (retired); Olympic Track Runner. **Orgs:** Mem Olympic Teams, 1968, 1972.

**MATTHEWS, DR. VIRGIL E.**
Scientist, politician. **Personal:** Born Oct 5, 1928, Lafayette, AL; son of Virgil (deceased) and Izetta Roberta Ware (deceased); married Shirley McFatridge; children: Brian Keith, Michael Andre & Deborah Michelle. **Educ:** Univ Ill, BS, chem, 1951; Univ Chicago, SM, chem, 1952, PhD, chem, 1955. **Career:** Scientist (retired); Univ Chicago, teaching asst, 1951-52; Carbide & Carbon Chem Co, fel, 1952-53; Union Carbide Corp, res chemist, 1954-67, proj scientist, 1967-75, develop scientist chem & plastics div, 1975-86; W Va State Col, instr part time chem, 1955-63, prof part-time chem, 1964-70, Dept Chem, prof & chmn, 1986-94. **Orgs:** Vpres, Nat Asn Advan Colored Pres, Charleston Br, 1964-72; pres, Charleston Bus & Prof Men Club, 1965-66; councilman-at-Large Charleston, 1967-83; Alpha Phi Alpha Fraternity, 1967-; Dem Nat Conv W Va, 1968; Dem nominee state senate 8th Dist W Va, 1970; Munic Planning Comn, Charleston, 1971-83; chmn Planning Comn City Coun Charleston, 1971-83; Am Chem Soc; elected mem, W Va State Dem Exec Comn, 1978-82; Fel Am Inst Chemists; Fel AAAS; Sigma Xi; Phi Lambda Upsilon; Am Men Sci; alt deleg, Dem Nat Conv W Va, 1980; Dem Nominee City Treas, Charleston, WV 1983. **Home Addr:** 835 Carroll Rd, Charleston, WV 25314, **Home Phone:** (304)343-0724.

**MATTHIS, JAMES L., III**
Marketing executive, business owner, executive director. **Personal:** Born Mar 21, 1955, Chicago, IL; son of James L and Doris Buckley; married Michelle Englander; children: Jordan. **Educ:** Ala A&M Univ, Huntsville, BS, acct, 1977; Univ Chicago, MBA, 1994. **Career:** Miller Brewing Co, Chicago, IL, merchandiser, 1977-78, Miller Brewing Co, Bloominton, IN, area sales mgr, 1978-81, Miller Brewing Co, St Louis, MO, area sales mgr, 1981-85, Miller Brewing Co, Milwaukee, WI, talent & video mkt mgr, 1985-96; Educ Innovations, owner, 1995-2006; Proj Equality Wis, exec dir; Community Econ Develop Corp Inc, exec dir, 2007-09; Marquette Univ, adj prof; Rays Hope Parent Empowerment Serv, consult; Potter House T. D. Jakes Ministries, chief mktg officer, 2011-14; Educ Presenters Network, bus develop, 2013-. **Orgs:** Am Mkt Asn, 1984-; Nat Asn Advan Colored People, 1978-; World Tae Kwon Do Fedn, 1980-; exec dir, Proj Equality Wis, 2001-03. **Home Addr:** 2227 N First St, Milwaukee, WI 53212, **Home Phone:** (414)264-5356. **Business Addr:** Executive Director, Community Economic Development Corp Inc, 718 N Mem Dr, Racine, WI 53404, **Business Phone:** (262)635-8908.

**MAULDIN, JERMAINE DUPRI.** See DUPRI, JERMAINE.

**MAULTSBY, DR. PORTIA K.**
Educator. **Personal:** Born Jun 11, 1947, Orlando, FL; daughter of Valdee C and Maxie Clarence Sr. **Educ:** Mt St Scholastica Col, Atchison, KS, BM, piano & theory compos, 1968; Univ Wis, Madison, WI, MM, musicol, 1969, PhD, ethnomusicology, 1974; Mozarteum Salzburg, Univ Salzburg, Salzburg, Austria, piano, music hist & Ger. **Career:** Ind Univ, Bloomington, Ind, vis asst prof, 1971-74, asst prof, 1975, assoc prof, 1981, assoc chmn, afro-am studies, 1981-84, dept chmn, afro-amstudies, 1985-91, prof, 1992, dir, arch African Am music & cul, 1991-; Ind Comt Humanities Summer, Res Fel, 1984; Swarthmore Col, Music Dept, vis prof, 1982; Seattle Pac Univ, Music Dept, vis prof, 1983; Mus Am Hist Smithsonian Inst, Wash, DC, sr vis scholar, 1984-85; Ind Music Educr Asn, bd dir, 1993-95; Colo Col, Music Dept, vis prof, 1994; Nat Res Coun, Ford sr fel, 1984-85; Utrecht Univ, Neth, Musicol Dept, Belle van Zuylen prof African Am music, 1998; Ctr Advan Study Behav Sci, Stanford, Calif, vis prof, 1999-2000. **Orgs:** Exec bd, Int Asn Study Popular Music, Am Br, 1987-95, ed bd, 1989-; counmem, Soc ethnomusicology, 1973-76, 1977-80, 1988-91; Asn African Am Mus; Am Music Soc; fel, Ctr Advan study Behav Sci, Stanford, Calif, 1999-2000; res fel, Ind Comt Humanities; Ford Found & Nat Res Coun. **Home Addr:** 537 Plymouth Rd, Bloomington, IN 47408-3025, **Home Phone:** (812)333-2544. **Business Addr:** Professor, Indiana University, 506 N Fess 104, Bloomington, IN 47405, **Business Phone:** (812)855-2708.

**MAULTSBY, REV. DR. SYLVESTER**
Government official. **Personal:** Born Oct 24, 1935, Whiteville, NC; son of Reather; married Mildred Baldwin; children: Jerome, Hilda & Thimothy. **Educ:** Atlanta Col, Mortuary Sci, grad, 1959; Penn Univ, attended 1973; Hampton Inst, CT Sch Rel, cert, 1978; Liberty Univ, attended 1985; Wheaton Col, Sch Evangelism, attended 1992; Shaw Divinity Sch, Ddiv, 1990; Liberty Univ, PhD, 1995. **Career:** Edwards Co, expediter, 1960-62; Norwalk Police Dept, patrolman, 1962-68; Norwalk Area Ministry, youth dir, 1968-70; New York Life Ins Co, underwriter, 1970-75; Gen Motors, Finance Div, 1973-75; Conn State Police, chaplain, 1985-; Prudential Life Ins Co Am, dist agt, 1975-; State Conn, justice peace, 1993-. **Orgs:** Exec bd, Nat Asn Advan Colored People; 32 degree Prince Hall Masonic Order; William Moore Lodge 1533, Elks IBPOEW; patron, Eastern Star PHA; founding bd dir, PIVOT, alcoholic & drug rehab ctr; founder & dir, Norwalk Interdenomi Nat Youth Movement; Conn Baptist Missionary Conv; Assoc minister, Calvary Baptist Church, Norwalk, CT, 1976-; Nat Black Caucus Local Elected Officials, 1976; Hampton Univ Minister Conf, 1976; vpres, Greater Norwalk Black Dem Club, 1976-; city sheriff, Norwalk City, 1977-80; Counman, City Norwalk, 1981-; Baptist Ministers Conf, Greater New York & Vicinity, 1986-; chmn, Polit Affairs Conn Missionary Baptist Conv, 1987-; Am Asn Christian Counr, 1992-; Int Conf Police Chaplains, 1993; comnr, Second Taxing Dist Norwalk City, CT. **Honors/Awds:** Distinguished Achievement Greater Norwalk Black Dem Club; Outstanding Citizen Norwalk Area Improvement League; US Jaycees Spoke Award Junior Chamber Commerce; Service Award, United Way; Holy Order of Past High Priesthood Award, 1974; Man of the Year Award, The Norwalk Youth Comm Concert Choir, 1983; CT Gen Assembly Official Citation for Presidential Campaign of Jesse Jackson, 1984; Realities of Empowerment Award CT State Fed of Black Dems, 1985. **Special Achievements:** First African American Democrat for State Senator from Fairfield County, CT 1980. **Home Addr:** 4415 Foxberry Run, Loganville, GA 30052-5176, **Home Phone:** (203)853-3084. **Business Addr:** Commissioner, Second Taxing District of the City of Norwalk, 164 Water St, Norwalk, CT 06856-0468, **Business Phone:** (203)866-4446.

**MAUNEY, DONALD WALLACE, JR.**
Executive, president (organization). **Personal:** Born Oct 16, 1942, New Castle, PA; children: Michael A, Dawnya M & Donovan T. **Educ:** New Castle High Sch, attended 1960. **Career:** State Dept Fed Govt, budget analyst, 1962-69; Robert Hall Store, asst mgr, 1969-70; Gen Acct Br DC Land Agency, chief, 1970-75; Tenant Ledger Br DC Dept Housing & Comn, chief, 1988; Diversified Payments & Loan Servicing Br, chief, 1985; DM Prod Corp, chief exec officer; DWM Enterprises Inc, pres, currently; Awards & Things, pres, currently. **Orgs:** Pres, Tri-State Enterprises Inc; proprietor, Tri-State Engraving Co, 1969-70; state pres, DC Jaycees, 1975-76; vpres, US Jaycees, 1976-77; treas, Com Dept Toastmasters, 1976-77; AFA, USA Elected Jaycess Int World V Pres Johannesburg S Africa, 1977; AFA mem, US Jaycees Exec Com; NE & SE regional bd dir, Greater Wash Boys & Girls Clubs, 1994-95; chmn bd, DC Coun Clothing Kids Inc; exec com, DC Vol Clearing House; bd dir, DC Jacyee Youth develop Trust; trustee, Plymouth Congregational United Ch Christ; pres, Jaycee Int Senate, Wash DC; secy, Assoc Renewal Educ Inc. **Honors/Awds:** Jaycee of Year, 1973; Special DC City Council Community Award Resolution, 1976; Hon Citizen Baton Rouge LA. **Home Addr:** 1541 Brentwood Rd NE, Washington, DC 20018-3700, **Home Phone:** (202)832-1012. **Business Addr:** President, Awards & Things, 2811 12th St NE, Washington, DC 20017, **Business Phone:** (202)635-3555.

**MAUPIN, DR. JOHN E., JR.**
Dentist, school administrator, educator. **Personal:** Born Oct 28, 1946, Los Angeles, CA; married Eilene; children: Deanne, Henry & Virgil J (deceased); married Linda Mays. **Educ:** San Jose State Col, pre-dentistry & bus admin, 1968; Meharry Med Col, DDS, 1972; Loyola Col, MBA, 1979. **Career:** Military service (retired), educator, dentist; AUS Dent Corps, capt, 1972-81; W Baltimore Community Health Care Corp, dent dir, 1976-81; Baltimore City Health Dept, assist commnr health servs, 1981-84, dep commnr med servs, 1984-87; Southside Healthcare Inc, chief exec officer, 1987-89; Morehouse Sch Med, execu vpres & chief operating officer, 1989-94, pres, 2007-; Meharry Med Col, pres & chief exec officer, 1994; Monarch Dent Corp, dir, 1997-; LifePoint Health Inc, dir, 1999-; Health S Corp, dir, 2004-; Regions Financial Corp, dir, 2007-. **Orgs:** Pres, Nat Dent Asn, 1984; Am Asn Higher Educ; Asn Am Med Cols; Nat Asn Health Serv Execs; Nat Asn Community Health Centers; Am Dent Asn; N Ga Dent Asn; Nat Inst Health;Trustee, int opportunities, high yield bond fund, small cap growth fund, socially responsible fund, mid cap growth fund, small cap value fund, large cap value fund, 1998-; bd mem, Regions Financial, 2007-; chmn, Community Found Mid Tenn. **Home Addr:** 2 Morningside, Nashville, TN 37215-5831. **Business Addr:** President, Chief Operating Officer, Morehouse School of Medicine, 720 Westview Dr SW, Atlanta, GA 37208-3599, **Business Phone:** (404)752-1500.

**MAUSI, SHAHIDA ANDREA**
President (organization). **Personal:** Born Dec 27, 1954, Detroit, MI; daughter of Nathan T Garrett and Joyce Finley Garrett; children: Dorian, Sulaiman, Rashid & Malik. **Educ:** Univ Detroit, Detroit, MI, BA, 1976. **Career:** Arts Pub Places, Detroit, coordr & dir, 1976-78; Detroit Pub Libr, progspecialist, 1978-81; Capricorn Enterprises, producer, 1979-80; DetroitCoun Arts, Detroit, Mich, exec dir, 1982-93; Greater Detroit YWCA, exec dir, 1993-; Right Prods Inc, owner chief exec officer & pres, 1996-; Chene Pk, gen mgr, 1996-2012, chief exec officer, 1996-; Producer: "Amen Corner", 1980; "Nina Simone Concert", 1985; "Fela Concert", 1986; "Debut Jamison Proj", 1988. **Orgs:** New Detroit Art Comt, 1982-; bd mem, Mus African Am Hist, 1984-; Mich Dem Party, 1985-; panel mem, Nat Endowment Arts, 1985-; Detroit People Mover Art Comn, 1986-; bd mem, Jamison Proj, Repertory Dance Am Found, 1989-. **Home Addr:** 200 River Pl Dr, Detroit, MI 48207-4487, **Home Phone:** (313)869-8783. **Business Addr:** Owner, President, The Right Productions Inc, PO Box 32778, Detroit, MI 48232, **Business Phone:** (313)869-1367.

**MAXEY, MARLON LEE**
Basketball player. **Personal:** Born Feb 19, 1969, Chicago, IL. **Educ:** Univ Minn, attended 1988; Univ Tex-El Paso, attended 1992. **Career:** Basketball player (retired); Minn Gophers, 1987-88; Univ Tex-El Paso Miners, 1989-92; Minn Timberwolves, forward, 1992-94; Breogan Lugo, 1994-95; Gymnastikos S Larissas, 1995-96; Peristeri, 1996-97; Iraklis Thessalonique, 1997-98; Peristeri, 1998-99; ASVEL Villeurbanne, forward, 1999-2000; Lucentum Alicante, 2000-01; Galatasaray, 2001-03. **Home Addr:** 9013 S Blackstone Ave, Chicago, IL 60619-7909, **Home Phone:** (773)375-6013.

**MAXEY, DR. RANDALL W.**
Educator, physician. **Personal:** Born Dec 1, 1941, Cincinnati, OH; married Gem L; children: 5. **Educ:** Univ Cincinnati, Col Pharm, BS, 1966; Howard Univ Grad Sch, PhD; Howard Univ, Col Med, MD, 1972. **Career:** Howard Univ, chmn & founder, 1969-72, instr, 1969-72, dir, 1969-71, chair, 1970-71; Univ Hosp, Downstate Med Ctr, dir, 1976-78; State Univ Ny, clin asst prof, 1977-78, asst prof, 1977-78; Kings County Hosp, asst dir, 1977-78; Daniel Freeman Memorial Hosp, attend physician, 1978-, dir, 1983-88; Centinela Hosp Med Ctr, attend physician, 1978-; Robert F Kennedy Med Ctr, attend physician, 1978-04, dir, 1983-96; Brotman Med Ctr, attend physician, 1978-00; Cedars Sinai Med Ctr, attend physician, 1978-00; Charles R. Drew Univ, Dept Med & Sci, Los Angeles, Calif, clin asst prof, 1980-88; Pac Coast Dialysis Ctr, med dir, 1986-98; Church Health Network, Calif, founder & pres, 1990-; Guam Memorial Hosp, attend physician, 1992-2000; Los Angeles Dialysis Ctr, supv med dir, 1993-98; Pac Dialysis Ctr, supv med dir, 1993-98; Assoc Primary Care Physicians Med Group, Inglewood, pres, 1994; Charles R Drew Univ; Downstate Med Ctr; Kings County Hosp; Calif based hosps; Daniel Freeman Marina Hosp; Howard Univ; Los Angeles Metrop Hosp; Guam Renal Care, supv med dir, 1996-98; pvt pract, currently. **Orgs:** Am Soc Pharmacol & Exp Therapeut, 1960-75; Am Soc Nephrology, 1975-; Int Soc Artificial Internal Organs, 1975-80; Am Soc Artificial Internal Organs,

1975-80; founding pres & mem bd, Asn Minority Nephrologists, 1986-; pres, Charles R Drew Med Soc, 1992-94, exec db, 1992-95, bd dir, 1992-2000; pres, Golden State Med Asn, 1994-95; chmn, Integrated Health & Managed Care Task Force, 1996-99; pres, bd trustee, Nat Med Asn, 1996-, secy, 1999-2001, chmn, 2001-02, pres, 2002-04; pres, Alliance Minority Med Asn, 2004-; Res Found Ethnic-Related Dis; Nat Asn Patients Hemodialysis & Transplantation; Unity One-Anti-Gang Advocacy Prog Adv Bd; Opportunities Industrialization Centers Int; Nat Minority Qual Forum; founding pres, Alliance Minority Med Asn. **Home Addr:** 575 E Hardy St Suite 207, Inglewood, CA 90301, **Home Phone:** (310)680-1810. **Business Addr:** 575 E Hardy St Suite 207, Inglewood, CA 90301, **Business Phone:** (310)680-1810.

## MAXIE, PEGGY JOAN

Executive, consultant. **Personal:** Born Aug 18, 1936, Amarillo, TX; daughter of Cleveland and Reba Harris M Jackson. **Educ:** Seattle Univ, BA, psychol, 1970; Univ Wash, MSW, 1972. **Career:** Off Atty Gen; Seattle Univ; Seattle Urban League, housing counr; State Wash, state rep, 1971-82; Mental Health Therapist; Life Coach; House Higher Educ Comm, chair, 1972-76; Joint Comn Higher Educ, officer, 1972-76; Cent Area Coun Alcoholism, exec dir & consult; Peggy Maxie & Assoc, pres, 1978-; Permanent Prof Staff Employ Comn & Session Staff Employ Comn, 1979-84. **Orgs:** Nat Asn Social Workers; Employee Assistance Prof Asn; US Tennis Asn; Nat Rehab Coun Asn; League Women Voters; bd mem, Capital Hill Chamber Com; Alpha Kappa Alpha; Delta Epsilon Sorority; Ladies Auxiliary, Knights Peter Claver; Iota Phi Lambda Sorority Inc; Munic League; Madrona Community Coun; Seattle Chamber Com; Seattle Exec Asn; Self-Insured Org. **Honors/Awds:** Hon LLD, St Martin's Col, 1975; Elder of Distinction Award; Certificate, Seattle Univ. **Special Achievements:** First African American Woman Elected in Washington Legislature; Featured in The Washington Story' a History of Our State, published by the Board of Directors of Seattle Public Schools. **Business Addr:** President, Peggy Maxie & Associates, 1441 Madrona Dr, Seattle, WA 98122-3519, **Business Phone:** (206)325-6088.

## MAXWELL (GERALD MAXWELL RIVERA)

Singer. **Personal:** Born May 23, 1973, Brooklyn, NY. **Career:** Professional singer, 1991-; signed with Columbia Records, 1994. **Honors/Awds:** Grammy Award, 2009. **Special Achievements:** Albums: Maxwell's Urban Hang Suite, 1996; MTV Unplugged, 1997; Embrya, 1998; Now, 2001; BLACKsummers'night, 2009; blackSUMMERS'night, 2016. **Business Addr:** c/o Sony Music, 25 Madison Ave, New York, NY 10010.

## MAXWELL, ANITA

Basketball player, executive. **Personal:** Born Apr 7, 1974, Dallas, TX; daughter of Minnie Mitchell. **Educ:** NMex State Univ, BA, int bus, 1996; Univ Tex, Arlington, MA, urban affairs/nonprofit mgt. **Career:** Basketball player (retired), executive; Asa Jerusalem, Israeli Pro League, basketball player; Cleveland Rockers, forward, 1997; United Way Va Peninsula, vpres community initiatives, 2006-12; Consumers' Choice Health Plan, dir community rels, 2012-. **Business Addr:** Director of Community Relations, Consumers' Choice Health Plan, 101-A W Ct St, Greenville, SC 29601.

## MAXWELL, BERTHA LYONS

Educator. **Personal:** Born Seneca, SC. **Educ:** Johnson C Smith Univ, BA, 1954; Univ NC, Greensboro, MEd, 1966; Union Grad Sch, PhD, 1974; Cath Univ; Howard Univ; Univ SC. **Career:** Alexander State Sch, teacher, 1954-60, corrective reading teacher, 1960-67; Villa Heights Elem Sch, asst prin, 1967; Morgan Elem Sch, prin, 1967-68; Albemarle Rd Elem Sch, prin, 1968-70; Univ NC Charlotte, dir black studies prog, 1970-, chair black studies prog, 1975, pres, 1976-78, assoc prof educ, prof educ. **Orgs:** Cons head, Start Winthrop Col Rock Hill SC, 1965; vis comn, Southern Asn Accreditation Gastonia City Sch Syst, 1967; local consult, ACE Workshop UNCC, 1969; mem bd dir, Int Reading Asn, 1969-72; African Heritage Study Asn; Resolutions Comn, 1970; chmn, Resolutions Comn, 1971; consult, So Regional Educ Bd Regional Conf, 1971; So Asn Accreditation Cabarrus Co Sch, 1972; chmn, vis comn Greensboro City Sch, 1973; pres, Nat Coun Black Studies, 1976; NEA; Nat Asn Elem Sch Prin; Afro-Am Study Asn; secy, Charlotte-Mecklenburg Elem Pring Unit; Greater Charlotte Coun Int Reading Asn; Int Platform Asn; League Women Votes; chmn, Charlotte-Mecklenburg Human Resources Comn League Women Voters; bd dir, Johnston Memorial YMCA; Jack & Jill Inc; pres, Merry Makers Inc; Organizer & coordr, Charlotte's First Vol Teacher Corps; chmn, vis comn Harrisburg Sch. **Honors/Awds:** Outstanding Community Services Award, Las Amagis Inc, 1967; outstanding leadership, Sigma Gamma Rho Sorority, 1969; outstanding community leader, 1971; outstanding educator, Las Amagis Inc, 1973. **Special Achievements:** First Chair of African American Studies at the University of North Carolina-Charlotte. **Home Addr:** 3508 Colony Rd, Charlotte, NC 28211-3797. **Business Addr:** National First Vice President, Delta Sigma Theta Sorority Inc, Rte 1, Catawba, SC 29704.

## MAXWELL, DR. MARCELLA J.

Government official, educator, advocate. **Personal:** Born Nov 6, 1927, Asbury Park, NJ; daughter of William B Redwood and Ethel Click; married Edward C; children: Deborah Young. **Educ:** Long Island Univ, Brooklyn NY, BS, elem educ, 1956, MS, 1958; Fordham Univ, NY, EdD, 1972. **Career:** New York Comm Status Women, asst acad dean; Pub Sch Dist 20, elem sch teacher & teacher trainer, 1958-63; Pr Sch Dist, exchange teacher, 1963; Bank State Col, curric coordr; Bd Higher Educ Medgar Evers Col, 1971-84; Medgar Evers Col, City Univ, dean, 1972-; NY City Comn Human Rights, chairperson, 1984-88, comnr; advocate; Brooklyn Col, clin supvr teaching fel, currently. **Orgs:** Bd mem, Women's Forum; vpres, Nat Coun Women, 1989-; treas & pres, Nat Comn Status Women; chairperson, New York Commn Status Women, Comn Human Rights, 1978-84, 1988-; trustee. Brooklyn Hosp Ctr; Governance Coun Links Inc; secy, Carver Bank Scholar Fund; bd dir, Am Heart Asn; vice chairperson, Spec Contrib Fund, Nat Asn Advan Colored People; dir, New York Found Sr Citizens. **Honors/Awds:** Nat Achievement Award, Nat Asn Negro Bus & Prof Women's Clubs; Exxon Scholarship, Harvard Bus School; Keynote Speaker, Older Women's League; Human Relations Award, NCCJ; Doctor Law Pratt Inst Brooklyn NY, 1985; Doctor Humane Letters Marymount Manhattan Col, 1984; Frederick Douglass Award, May, 2006; 25 Influential Black Women, NetWork J, 2009; Good Citizens Award, Coun Sr Centers & Serv; Delta Dear of the Year Award, Eastern Region, 2009-2010. **Home Addr:** 35 Prospect Pk W, Brooklyn, NY 11215, **Home Phone:** (718)789-5379. **Business Addr:** Clinical Supervisor, Brooklyn College, 2900 Bedford Ave, New York, NY 11210, **Business Phone:** (718)951-5000.

## MAXWELL, ROGER ALLAN

Government official, composer. **Personal:** Born Jul 31, 1932, Marshalltown, IA; married Arenda Randolph; children: Jennifer, Courtney, David & Matthew. **Educ:** Univ N Iowa, BA, music educ, 1954. **Career:** Iowa State Bd Regents, field rep, 1968, affirmative action off, 1969-, equal opportunity compliance officer. **Orgs:** Nat pres, Nat Asn Affirmative Act Officers, 1979-80; Nat Asn Music Educ. **Special Achievements:** Composer, "Mass in Honor of the Uganda Martyrs", 1964; composer, "Fourteen Weeks to a Better Band", Books I & II publ, CL Barnhouse Co, 1973-74; composer, "Twelve Weeks to a Better Jazz Ensemble", publ, CL Barnhouse Co, 1978. **Home Addr:** 7803 College Dr, Windsor Heights, IA 50322-5742, **Home Phone:** (515)270-6549.

## MAXWELL, VERNON

Basketball player. **Personal:** Born Sep 12, 1965, Gainesville, FL; married Shell Wiley; children: Vernon Jr, Brandon & Ariel. **Educ:** Univ Fla, attended 1988. **Career:** Basketball player (retired); San Antonio Spurs, guard, 1988-90, 1996-97; Houston Rockets, 1990-95; Philadelphia 76ers, free agt, 1995-96, guard, 2000-01; Charlotte Hornets, 1997-98; Orlando Magic, 1998; Sacramento Kings, 1998-99; Seattle Supersonics, free agt, 1999-2000; Dallas Mavericks, free agt, 2000-01.

## MAY, DERRICK

Musician. **Personal:** Born Apr 6, 1963, Detroit, MI. **Career:** Deep Space Sound works, dj, 1980; Transmat Rec, founder, 1986-; Albums: Let's Go, 1986; Nude Photo, 1987; Strings Of Life, 1987; It Is What It Is, 1988; Beyond The Dance, 1989; The Beginning, 1990; Icon / Kaotic Harmony, 1993; Mayday Mix, 1997; Innovator, 1997; I Travel EP, 2009; Films: High Tech Soul, 2006; Mastercuts Life Style Summer House, 2007; Things To Be Frickled, 2008; Balance 014, 2009; Remix: Truck On Road, 2009. Documentary: Movement: Detroit Electronic Music Festival, producer & composer, 2004. **Business Addr:** Founder, Transmat Records, 1492 Gratiot Ave, Detroit, MI 48207, **Business Phone:** (313)567-0080.

## MAY, DERRICK BRANT

Athletic coach, baseball player. **Personal:** Born Jul 14, 1968, Rochester, NY; son of Dave; married Alicia; children: Derrick Jr, Donovan & Devon. **Educ:** Univ Del, attended 1987; Univ Phoenix, attended 2004. **Career:** Baseball player (retired), athletic coach; Chicago Cubs, outfielder & left fielder & right fielder, 1990-94; Milwaukee Brewers, left fielder & out fielder, 1995; Houston Astros, out fielder & first base & right fielder & left fielder, 1995-96; Philadelphia Phillies, out fielder & first base & right fielder & left fielder, 1997; Montreal Expos, Designated hitter & right fielder & left fielder, 1998; Baltimore Orioles, Designated hitter & outfielder & right fielder & left fielder, 1999-2000; Japan, Chiba Lotte, 2003; St Louis orgn, Palm Beach Cardinals, Fla State League, hitting coach, 2005-06; Springfield Cardinals AA, hitting coordr, 2005-16, asst hitting coach, 2016-. **Honors/Awds:** George Kissell Award for Excellence in Player Development, 2014. **Business Addr:** Assistant Hitting Coach, St Louis Cardinals, 700 Clark St, St Louis, MO 63102, **Business Phone:** (314)345-9600.

## MAY, DICKEY R.

Manager, controller, administrator. **Personal:** Born Dec 14, 1950, Dublin, GA; son of Clarence W Sr and Zelma Smith; married L Yvonne Fambrough; children: Andrea Lynette & Ronald Maurice. **Educ:** Ft Valley State Col, Ft Valley Ga, BBA, 1972. **Career:** Ch's Fried Chicken Inc, Atlanta Ga, exec mgr candid, 1972-73, mgr area mgr, 1973-75, San Antonio TX, auditor, 1975-80, regional liason, 1980-84, dircorp planning, 1986-89, dir oper acct, 1989-; Ron's Krispy Fried Chicken, Houston TX, regional controller, corp controller, 1984-86. **Orgs:** Inst Internal Auditors, 1975-; Long Range Planning Comn; Northminister Presby Ch, 1988-. **Home Addr:** 5210 Timber Trace St, San Antonio, TX 78250-4421, **Home Phone:** (210)520-4205. **Business Addr:** Director of Operational Accounting, Church's Fried Chicken Inc, 355 Spencer Lane, San Antonio, TX 78201, **Business Phone:** (512)737-5742.

## MAY, FLOYD O.

Government official. **Personal:** Born Dec 2, 1946, Kansas City, MO; married Connie S Brown; children: Cheriss Dachelle & Floyd O; married Connie S Brown; children: Cheriss Dachelle & Floyd O. **Educ:** Pittsburg State Univ, Pittsburg, KS, BS, 1970, MS, 1971. **Career:** Miss Dept Voc Rehab, counr 1971-75; US Dept HUD, investr, 1975-77, mgt liaison officer, 1977-85, dept dir & dir comp, 1985, regional dir off Fair Housing & Equal Opportunity, 1998-2006; Floyd O. May LLC, owner, 2006-. **Orgs:** Lees Summit Chamber Com; Urban League KC; pres, Channel, 19 Pub TV Comm; adv bd, Heart Am Pop Warner Football Asn; Urban League; bd mem, Nat Asn Advan Colored People, Kans City, MO, Chap; KC Civil Rights Consortium; managing dir, Nat Oceanic & Atmospheric Admin, 2006-12. **Business Addr:** owner, Floyd O May LLC, 12914 Bay Hill Dr, Beltsville, MD 20705, **Business Phone:** (202)409-8380.

## MAY, DR. GARY STEPHEN

Dean (education), president (organization), educator. **Personal:** Born May 17, 1964, St. Louis, MO; son of Warren and Gloria Hunter; married LeShelle; children: Simone & Jordan. **Educ:** Ga Inst Technol, BEE, elec engineering, 1985; Univ Calif, Berkeley, MS, elec engineering & comput sci, 1987, PhD, elec engineering & comput sci, 1991. **Career:** GA Inst Technol, res asst, 1985, prof, 1991-2000, Motoral Found, prof, assoc chair fac develop, 2001-02, exec chair, 2002, exec asst to pres, 2002-05, prof, Steve W Chaddick Sch, Chair, 2005-11, dean, 2011, founder & dir, FACES; AT&T Bell Lab, tech staff, 1985-86; Univ Calif, Berkeley, res asst, 1986-91, grad stud instr, 1988-90, workshop coord, 1990-91; ECE fac, 1991; IEEE Trans, ed-in-chief, 1997-2001; Leidos Inc, dir; Ga Tech's Summer Undergrad Res Engineering/Sci prog, founder; Fundamentals Semiconductor Mfg & Process Control, co-auth, 2006. **Orgs:** ANAK Socs, 1985-, fac advisor, 2007-; Microelectronics res group, 1991; nat young investr, Nsf, 1993-98; Amer Soc Engr Educ, 1995-; Int Microelectronics & Packaging Soc; Int Soc Optical Engr; fel, NSF; Nat Soc Black Engrs; Soc Mfg Engrs; fel, AT&T Bell Labs; NSBE; Motorola Found, chair, 2001; fel, Inst Elec & Electronics Engrs, 2005; fel, IEEE, 2006; fel, AAAS, 2008; nat adv bd, Nat Socs Black Engrs; fac advisor, ANAK Socs; dir, Ethics & Corp Responsibility Comt; Human Resources & Compensation Comt, Leidos Holdings Inc, 2015-. **Home Addr:** 1310 Regency Ctr Dr SW, Atlanta, GA 30331, **Home Phone:** (404)696-7444. **Business Addr:** Dean, Steve W Chaddick School Chair, Georgia Institute of Technology, 777 Atlantic Dr NW, Atlanta, GA 30332-0250, **Business Phone:** (404)894-2901.

## MAY, JAMES F.

Educator, mayor, consultant. **Personal:** Born Feb 10, 1938, Millry, AL; married Bessie Hill; children: Keita & Katrice. **Educ:** Ala A&M Univ, BS, 1962; Tuskegee Inst, MEd, 1968. **Career:** Bus planning consult, 2014-; May's Plumbing & Elec Serv, owner; Union town, Al, mayor; Perry County Bd Educ, teacher; city councilman. **Orgs:** Union town Civic League; keeper recs, Omega Chi Chap, Omego Psi Phi; AVATA Perry Co Teacher Asn; AEA; NEA; Pride AL Elks No 1170, Perry County Chamber Com; Perry County Indust Bd; M & M Consult. **Honors/Awds:** First Black Councilman Award, 1972. **Home Addr:** Hwy 80, PO Box 24, Uniontown, AL 36786-0024, **Home Phone:** (334)628-5501.

## MAY, LEE ANDREW

Baseball player, athletic coach. **Personal:** Born Mar 23, 1943, Birmingham, AL; married Terrye; children: Yelandra (Mike Daniels), Lisa & Lee Jr. **Educ:** Miles Col. **Career:** Baseball player (retired), baseball coach; Cincinnati Reds, infielder, outfielder, 1965-71, first base coach, 1988-89; Houston Astros, first baseman, 1972-74; Baltimore Orioles, infielder, 1975-80; Kans City Royals, infielder, 1981-82, hitting coach, 1984-86, 1992-94; Tampa Bay Rays, first base coach, 2001-02. **Home Addr:** 5533 Hill & Dale Dr, Cincinnati, OH 45213-2615, **Home Phone:** (513)531-0884.

## MAY, MARK ERIC

Football player, television sportscaster. **Personal:** Born Nov 2, 1959, Oneonta, NY; married Kathy; children: Abra & Bryce. **Educ:** Univ Pittsburgh, BA, hist & psychol, 1980. **Career:** Football player (retired), sportscaster; Wash Redskins, guard, offensive tackle, 1981-90; WJLA-TV, sports asst, 1981-84; San Diego Chargers, 1991; Phoenix Cardinals, 1992-93; Ariz Cardinals, 1992-93; TNT, "Sunday Night Football", studio analyst, 1995-96, game analyst, 1997; CBS Sports, game analyst, 1998-2000; ESPN, football analyst & commentator, 2001-, "Col Game Day", analyst, currently. **Orgs:** C's Hosp; chmn, Ams Helping Am Prog, Christian Relief Serv, 1989; hon chmn, Wash, DC chap Juv Diabetes Asn; charter mem, Hogs; Nat Col Football Hall Fame; Nancy Reagan's Team Up Against Drugs. **Home Addr:** 3010 Cottonwood Springs Lane, Jamul, CA 91935. **Business Addr:** Football Analyst, Commentator, ESPN, ESPN Plz, Bristol, CT 06010, **Business Phone:** (860)766-2000.

## MAY-PITTMAN, INEVA

Educator, association executive, teacher. **Personal:** Born Jul 6, 1934, Jayess, MS; married Joe; children: Albert Jefferson & Davion Jamaal. **Educ:** Jackson State Col, BS, elem educ, 1956; Jackson State Univ, MS, educ & supv, 1973; AA, 1974; Univ Ala; Southern Univ; Belhaven Col; Miss Baptist Sem. **Career:** Jackson Missionary Baptist Dist Asn, asst teacher; Jackson Sch Syst, first grade teacher. **Orgs:** Pleasant Hill Missionary Baptist Church; vpres, N Jackson Community Boy's Club; chmn, trustee bd, NCNW; bd mem, Jackson Golden Heritage; Nat Asn Advan Colored People, vpres, 1965; pres, Nat Coun Negro Women, 1974; life mem, Jackson State Univ Nat Alumni Asn; MS Teachers Asn; Nat Coun Negro Women; Bus & Prof Women's Club; life mem, Nat Educ Asn; pres, Nat Asn Advan Colored People Garden Club Coun New Hope Baptist Church; State Dem Exec Comt; Jackson State Univ Nat Alumni Asn; vpres, Bus & Prof Women's Club; CSA, bd mem, poverty prog; exec bd mem, Jackson Sch Syst. **Honors/Awds:** Teacher of the Year, 1959; President of the Year, Jackson Dist Missionary, 1970; Nat Asn Advan Colored People Fight for Freedom Cert of Merit, 1973; John W Dixon Outstanding Community Service Award, Nat Asn Advan Colored People, 1977; Finer Womanhood Award, Jackson Sect NCNW, 1978; Community Service Award for Leadership in Christian Service Award, VOC, 1982; Dedicated Service, Nat Coun Negro Women, 1984; Distinguished Service Award, Jackson Pub Schs, 1986; Dedicated Service Award, Jackson Asn Educr, 1987; Dedicated Service Award, City Usher Bd, 1989; Exceptional Achievement Award, Black Women's Polit Action, 1989; Hope Award, 2006; Golden Diploma Citation, 2006; Personality of the South. **Business Addr:** Executive Board Member, Jackson School System, 5110 Inwood Dr, Jackson, MS 39206, **Business Phone:** (601)497-4360.

## MAYBERRY, DR. CLAUDE A., JR.

Publisher, entrepreneur. **Personal:** Born Feb 17, 1933, Detroit, MI; son of Claude Sr and Anna Johnson Riley; children: Lawrence, Karen, Cheryl, Claude III & Eric. **Educ:** Purdue Univ, W Lafayette, IN, BS, 1965, MS, 1968; Columbia Univ, Teachers Col New York, NY, PhD, 1973. **Career:** Univ Pa, Philadelphia, dean stud, 1973-76; Colgate Univ, Hamilton, NY, provost, 1976-81; US Dept Educ, Wash, DC, spec asst secy math & sci, 1981-84; Sci Weekly Inc, Silver Spring, Md, pres & chief exec officer, 1984-; CAM Publ Group Inc, founder, currently; Teachers Col Columbia Univ, trustee, currently. **Orgs:** Alumni Asn, Purdue Univ, 1965-; Alumni Asn, Columbia Univ, 1973-; Nat Alliance Black Sch Educr, 1975-; chair, Black Entrepreneurs Educ Publishers, 1984-; chair, Minority Entrepreneurs Comt, 1987-; pres, alumni adv comt, Teachers Col, Columbia Univ, 1990-93; Nat chairperson, Nat Conf Educating Black Child, 1990-92; pres, Nat Citizens Comn African Am Educ, 1994-; bd mem, Reading Is Fundamental Inc; former advisor, Nat Comn Excellence Educ; fel RIF Bd Dirs; pres, Nat Coun Educating Black C; Col's Alumni Coun, pres. **Honors/Awds:** Teacher of the Year Award, Ind State Jr Chamber Com, 1968; Marcus Foster

Distinguished Black Educator Award, Nat Alliance Black Sch Educr, 1988; African American Businessman Award, Montgomery County, MD, 1990; School of Science Distinguished Alumni Award, Purdue Univ, 1991; Hammond Achievement Award, 1992; American Educational Publishers Hall of Fame. **Home Addr:** 4450 S Pk Ave, Chevy Chase, MD 20815, **Home Phone:** (301)656-3777. **Business Addr:** President, Science Weekly Inc, 2141 Indust Pkwy Suite 202, Silver Spring, MD 20904, **Business Phone:** (301)680-8804.

### MAYBERRY, EINO ANTHONY. See MAYBERRY, TONY.

### MAYBERRY, JERMANE TIMOTHY
Football player, executive. **Personal:** Born Aug 29, 1973, Floresville, TX; married Danielle; children: Jermane. **Educ:** Tex A&M Univ, grad. **Career:** Football player (retired); Philadelphia Eagles, guard, 1996, left tackle, 1997-98, right guard, right tackle, tackle, 1999-2004, left guard, 2004; New Orleans Saints, tackle, right guard, 2005-06; Jayberry's Water Ice Franchise, founder, 2003. **Honors/Awds:** Extra Effort Award, Nat Football League, 1996; Pro Bowl, 2002; Super Bowl XXXIX, 2005. **Special Achievements:** NFL Draft, First round pick, #25, 1996. Film: 1996 NFL Draft, 1996.

### MAYBERRY, PATRICIA MARIE
Social worker, judge. **Personal:** Born Aug 25, 1951, St. Louis, MO; daughter of Samuel and Shirley Hawkins. **Educ:** Univ Mo, BA, 1973; Univ Houston, MSW, 1976; Tex Southern Univ, Thurgood Marshall Sch Law, JD, 1979. **Career:** USAF, atty/asst staff judge advocate, 1980-84; Alvin Dillings, PC, atty, 1984-87; pvt pract, atty, 1987-89; Immigration & Naturalization Serv, trial atty, 1989-93; African Methodist Episcopal Judicial Coun, pres; Calif Unemploy Ins Appeals Bd, admin law judge, 1993-96; Judicial Coun, pres, atty; Lay Activ, dist dir; Dept Air Force, labor law atty, 1996-. **Orgs:** Delta Sigma Theta Sorority, 1973-; Phi Alpha Delta, 1977; State Bar Tex, 1979; Colo Bar, 1985; Top Ladies Distinction, 1990; exec bd, Nat Asn Advan Colored People, 1990; trustee, Calif Conf, 1991-; judicial coun mem, pres, African Methodist Episcopal Church, 1992-; bd dir, Fel Manor, 1992-97. **Special Achievements:** The 100 Outstanding African Americans, Dollars & Sense Mag, 1991. **Home Addr:** 3027 Arthur MacArthur Rd, San Pedro, CA 90731-6798, **Home Phone:** (310)764-2101. **Business Addr:** President, Judicial Council AMEC, 17887 Balsam Ct, Carson, CA 90746, **Business Phone:** (310)653-3168.

### MAYBERRY, TONY (EINO ANTHONY MAYBERRY)
Football player. **Personal:** Born Dec 8, 1967, Wurzburg; married Rachel; children: Joshua & Briana. **Educ:** Wake Forest Univ, BA, sociol. **Career:** Football player (retired); Tampa Bay Buccaneers, offensive lineman & corner, 1990-99. **Honors/Awds:** Rookie of the Year, 1990; Most Valuable Player, Tampa Sports Club, 1997; Pro Bowl, 1997-99; Athletics Hall of Fame, 2002; TJR Hall of Fame, 2005. **Home Addr:** 15704 Cochester Rd, Tampa, FL 33647-1100, **Home Phone:** (813)971-0536.

### MAYBERRY-STEWART, DR. MELODIE IRENE
Health services administrator. **Personal:** Born Sep 4, 1948, Cleveland, OH; daughter of Marie Hague; children: George & Jay. **Educ:** Union Col, BS, bus admin & sociol, 1970; Univ Nebr, MA, sociol res & statist; Pepperdine Univ, MBA, 1972; Claremont Grad Sch, MA, 1988; exec mgt, PhD, info systs. **Career:** IBM Corp, regional mkt & tech support mgr, 1976-88; community health corp, vpres & chief info officer, 1988-91; St Thomas Hosp, vpres & chief info officer, 1991-95; Beth Israel Hosp, vpres, chief info officer, 1995-97; BP Amoco Oil Corp, gen mgr & vpres, info technol corp & shared servs, 1997-99; Black Diamond IT Consult Group LLC, founder, pres & chief exec officer, 1999-2002; City Cleveland, chief technol officer, 2002-07; State NY, chief technol officer & dir off technol, 2007-. **Orgs:** Bd dir & treas, Tenn Sports fest; bd mem, Ltd Way Mid Tenn; exec comt mem, Nashville Nat Asn Advan Colored People; bd mem, Sun Trust Bank; finance comt chmn, Cumberland Valley Girl Scout Coun; Nat Asn Female Execs; Nat Black MBA Asn; Nat Coun Negro Women; Healthcare Info & Mgt Systs Soc; Am Hosp Asn; Col Healthcare Execs; Nat Asn Health care Execs; bd chair woman, Nat Black MBA Asn. **Business Addr:** Chief Technology Officer, Chief Information Officer, State of New York, State Capitol, Albany, NY 12220, **Business Phone:** (518)402-2537.

### MAYDEN, RUTH WYATT
Dean (education), executive, educator. **Personal:** Born Dec 20, 1946, Baltimore, MD; daughter of John Clifton Jr and Wilhelmenia Outerbridge. **Educ:** Morgan State Univ, Baltimore, MD, BA, 1968; Bryn Mawr Col, Bryn Mawr, PA, MSS, 1970. **Career:** Educator (retired), administrator; Day Care Asn Montgomery County, Blue Bell, Pa, social serv coordr, 1970-72, exec dir, 1972-79; Bryn Mawr Col Grad Sch Social Work & Social Res, Bryn Mawr, Pa, asst dean, 1979-81, assoc dean, 1981-86, dean, 1986-02; Mid States Comn Elem Educ, comnr, currently. **Orgs:** Chair, Child Welfare Adv Bd, 1985-91; bd exec comt, United Way Southeastern PA, 1986-91; Nat Asn Deans & dir Schs Social Work, 1987-; treas, PA Chap, Nat Asn Social Workers, 1989-91; Am Asn Black Women Higher Educ, 1989-91; bd mem, Nat Asn Social Workers; pres, Nat Asn Social Workers, 1999-2001; dir, Annie E. Casey Found, 2002-. bd dir, Coun Social Work Educ, 2006-; Nat Asn Black Social Workers; bd dir, Women's Christian Alliance; Philadelphia Citizens C & Youth; adv bd mem, Child Care Matters; nat adv bd mem, Whitney M Young Sch Social Work, Clark-Atlanta Univ; Morgan State Univ. **Home Addr:** 4942 Larchwood Ave, Philadelphia, PA 19143, **Home Phone:** (215)471-1090. **Business Addr:** Director, Annie E Casey Foundation, 701 St Paul St, Baltimore, MD 21202, **Business Phone:** (410)547-6600.

### MAYERS, JAMAL DAVID
Hockey player. **Personal:** Born Oct 24, 1974, Toronto, ON; son of Doreen; married Natalie; children: Langley & Harper. **Educ:** W Mich Univ, BBA, mkt, 1996. **Career:** Hockey player (retired), analyst; Thornhill MTJHL, 1990-92; Western Mich CCHA, 1992-96; WorcesterAHL, 1996-98, 1998-99; St Louis Blues, right wing, 1996-97, 1998-99, 1999-2000, 2000-04, 2005-08; Can WC-A, 1999-2000; Hammarby Sweden-2, 2004-05; Mo UHL, 2004-05; Toronto Maple Leafs, 2008-10; Calgary Flames, 2009-10; San Jose Sharks, 2010-11; Chicago Blackhawks, 2011-13, community liaison, 2015-; NHL Network, analyst, 2013-15; Comcast SportsNet Chicago, hockey analyst, 2014-; David Crew Clothing, owner, 2015-; Jam & Sal's Comm Stars, developer; Hockey Acad St Louis, designer & instr. **Orgs:** Ice Hockey Harlem. **Honors/Awds:** Russia World Championships, Gold Medal, 2007; Canada World Championships, Silver Medal, 2008. **Business Addr:** Hockey Analyst, Comcast SportsNet Chicago, 350 N Orleans St Suite S1-100, Chicago, IL 60654, **Business Phone:** (312)222-6000.

### MAYERS, ONIDA COWARD. See COWARD, ONIDA LAVONEIA.

### MAYES, ALONZO LEWIS, JR.
Football player. **Personal:** Born Jun 4, 1975, Oklahoma City, OK. **Educ:** Okla State Univ, grad. **Career:** Football player (retired); Chicago Bears, tight end, 1998-2000, wide receiver, 1999; Miami Dolphins, 2000-02. **Honors/Awds:** Rookie of the Year, 1998; Consensus All-American, 1998.

### MAYES, CLINTON, JR.
Executive. **Career:** State Mutual Fed Savings & Loan Asn, Jackson, Miss, chief exec officer, mgr, currently. **Business Addr:** State Mutual Federal Savings & Loan Association, 1072 Lynch St, Jackson, MS 39203.

### MAYES, DERRICK BINET
Football player, chief executive officer. **Personal:** Born Jan 28, 1974, Indianapolis, IN; married Gayle; children: Hudson. **Educ:** Univ Notre Dame, BS, film & tv, 1996. **Career:** Football player (retired); Green Bay Packers, wide receiver, 1996-98; Seattle Seahawks, wide receiver, 1999-2000; Action Sports & Entertainment, chief exec officer & dir exec, currently. **Home Addr:** 3335 N Keystone Ave, Indianapolis, IN 46218-2075. **Business Addr:** Chief Executive Officer & Director, ExecutiveAction LLC, 1300 Conn Ave NW Suite 501, Washington, DC 20036, **Business Phone:** (202)223-4888.

### MAYES, DORIS MIRIAM
Educator, musician, opera singer. **Personal:** Born Dec 10, 1928, Philadelphia, PA; daughter of James and Evelyn Bulter; married Jurgen Ploog; children: Flavia Miriam. **Educ:** Philadelphia Conserv Music, Philadelphia, PA, BM, teaching cert; HochshuleFur Musik, Munich, Ger; Juilliard Sch Music, New York, NY. **Career:** Fulbright fels; Syracuse Univ, Syracuse, NY, assoc prof, 1966-68; Oberlin Col, Oberlin, Ohio, asst prof, 1968-74; Western Res Univ, Hudson, Ohio, voice technician, 1974-80; Univ Arts, Philadelphia, Pa, teacher conserv div, 1982-; Lincoln Univ, Lincoln, Pa, artist residence & asst prof voice & opera, 1988-. **Orgs:** Scholar chairperson, Pro Arts Soc, 1983-. **Home Addr:** 201 S 18th St Apt 1402, Philadelphia, PA 19103. **Business Addr:** Assistant Professor of Music, Lincoln University, 1570 Old Baltimore Pke Ware Ctr Rm 122, Lincoln, PA 19352, **Business Phone:** (610)932-8300.

### MAYES, GEORGE S., JR.
Vice president (organization). **Educ:** US Mil Acad, W Pt, BS, engineering, 1980. **Career:** Delphi, dir, 1985-2000; Supply Chain Mgt, vpres, 2000-02; Stanley Works, vpres mfg, fastening systs, 2000-02; Tinnerman Palnut Engineered Prod LLC, chief operating officer; Diebold Inc, exec vpres global opers, 2005-2013; Diebold, exec vpres, chief operating officer, 2013-. **Orgs:** Bd dir, Mfg Advocacy & Growth Network (MAGNET); bd dir, Stoneridge Inc, 2012-. **Business Addr:** Executive Vice President, Chief Operating Officer, Diebold, 5995 Mayfair Rd, North Canton, OH 44720, **Business Phone:** (330)490-4000.

### MAYES, HELEN M.
College administrator. **Personal:** Born May 28, 1918, Waycross, GA; daughter of Oscar Moody Sr (deceased) and Mary Woodson Moody (deceased); married Nathaniel H Sr; children: Nathaniel H Jr. **Educ:** Savannah State Col, BS, 1938; NY Univ, MA, 1961. **Career:** College administrator (retired); Savannah State Col, clerk nat youth admin, 1938-40, sub-dir div gen exten, 1940-44; Albany State Col, asst regist, dir admis & rec, 1944-76, emer dir admis & rec, 1976-; Semper Fidelis Nursery Sch Inc, dir finance, 1979-, finance secy, 1982-. **Orgs:** First black pres, Ga Asn Col Registr & Admis Officers, 1971-72; exec secy, Nat Asn Col Deans Registr & Admis Officers, 1978-; Albany State Col, chmn adv comt, 1978-80, vice chmn social work adv comt, 1983, chmn social comt, 1983; dir finance, SemperFidelis Club, 1980-; bd dir, 1980-, mem venture grant comt, 1982-, United Way Dougherty County; HARAMBEE Women's Auxiliary, 1982-; bd dir, Albany Symphony Asn, 1983-; Ga Teachers & Educ Asn; Nat Educ Asn; Alpha Kappa Alpha; Am Asn Col Registr & Admis Officers; selection comt, Nat Merit Achievement Scholar Prog; Steward, Bethel AME Church. **Home Addr:** 917 Dorsett Ave, Albany, GA 31701, **Home Phone:** (229)435-4945. **Business Addr:** Albany, GA 31701, **Business Phone:** (912)435-4945.

### MAYES, DR. MCKINLEY
Government official. **Personal:** Born Oct 7, 1930, Oxford, NC; son of Henry and Julia; married Mattie Louise Dupree; children: Byron Christopher. **Educ:** NC A&T State Univ, BS, agr educ, 1953, MS, agr educ, 1956; Rutgers Univ, PhD, 1959. **Career:** Government official (retired); Southern Univ, Baton Rouge LA, prof, 1959-76; US Dept Agr, Coop State Res Serv, Wash, DC, 1976-2004. **Orgs:** Fel Am Soc Agron; Sigma Xi; Global ministries; VA Conf; vice chair, admin bd, Roberts United Methodist Church, 1987; USDA Task Force; bd trustee, Agron Sci Found, 2000. **Home Addr:** 9012 Lake Braddock Dr, Burke, VA 22015-2131, **Home Phone:** (703)978-2330. **Business Addr:** DC.

### MAYES, NATHANIEL H., JR.
Consultant, educator. **Personal:** Born Aug 22, 1941, Waycross, GA; married Constantina; children: Nathaniel III & Muriel. **Educ:** Howard Univ, BS, 1962, MS, 1966. **Career:** Clark Col, Atlanta, instr psychol, 1966-68; Orgn Develop, consult, 1968-70; Greater Boston Area Pub Schs; Soc Dynamics Inc, Boston, prog mgr, 1970-71; Univ Mass, Inst Learning & Teaching, consult trainer, 1971; MIT Sloan Sch Mgt, Off External Rels, dir spec proj, Int Prog & Resource Develop, dir, currently. **Orgs:** Co-founder, Inter-Cult Inc, Cambridge; Soc Inter cult Educ Training & Res. **Honors/Awds:** Outstanding Teaching Certificate, Clark Col, 1965. **Special Achievements:** Co-author booklet on Multi-Cultural Tchr Training 1974. **Home Addr:** 7 S Normandy Ave Suite 1, Cambridge, MA 02138-1094, **Home Phone:** (617)864-0504. **Business Addr:** Director, MIT Sloan School of Management, E60-200C 50 Memorial Dr 5 Fl, Cambridge, MA 02142-1347, **Business Phone:** (617)253-9650.

### MAYFIELD, JOANN M.
Government official. **Personal:** Born Jul 1, 1932, Jackson, AL; children: Joyce, Barbara & Theresa. **Educ:** Louise Beauty Col. **Career:** Cosmetology. **Orgs:** Dist pres, Am Legion Aux, 1963-64, unit pres, 1963-64, dist pres, 1965-66, unit pres, 1967-68, usher bd sec, 1972; chmn Cit Training Dist A B C, 1966-67; chmn ed & scholar 9th dists; Celebrity Club; Counwoman City Comn GA. **Home Addr:** 194 Pine Ave, Commerce, GA 30529, **Home Phone:** (706)335-4273. **Business Addr:** 324 S Elm St, Commerce, GA 30529.

### MAYHEW, RICHARD
Artist, educator. **Personal:** Born Apr 3, 1924, Amityville, NY; son of Alvin and Lillian. **Educ:** Art Stud League; Brooklyn Museum Art Sch, 1951; Columbia Univ, BA, art hist. **Career:** Educator (retired), professor emeritus; Freelance med, illusr & singer, 1945-50; MacDowell colony prof; John Hay Whitney Fel, 1959; Brooklyn Mus Art Sch, instr, 1963-68; Art Students League, instr, 1965-71; Smith Col, instr, 1971-75; Pratt Inst, fac; Hunter Col, fac; San Jose State Univ, fac; Sonoma State Univ, fac; Pa State Univ, prof art, 1977-91, prof emer art, 1991-. **Orgs:** Founder, Spiral Group, 1963-; academician, Nat Acad Design; founding dir, Creative Ctr Arts & Sci; Nat Acad Design; fel African Am artists formed Spiral Group. **Home Addr:** PO Box 7720, Santa Cruz, CA 95061, **Home Phone:** (831)476-3388. **Business Addr:** Professor Emeritus of Art, Penn State School of Visual Arts, 210 Patterson Bldg, University Park, PA 16802, **Business Phone:** (814)865-0444.

### MAYNARD, DR. EDWARD SAMUEL
Educator, psychologist. **Personal:** Born Jul 16, 1930, Brooklyn, NY; son of Robertine and Samuel; married Ernestine Gaskin; children: Jeanne & Charles. **Educ:** Brooklyn Col, BA (cum laude), 1958; Columbia Univ, MA, 1967; NY Univ, PhD, 1972; Grad Ctr, City Univ NY, PhD, 1984. **Career:** New York City Bd Educ, teacher, 1958-67; Brooklyn Col, lectr, 1967-69; Medgar Evers Col, dir pub rels, 1970-71; Hostos Community Col, prof, 1971-; psychologist, Pvt Practice, 1980-. **Orgs:** Nat Asn Advan Colored People, 1980-; Am Psychol Assoc, 1984-; minister couns, Howells Congregational Church. **Home Addr:** 52 Mine Rd, Monroe, LA 10950, **Home Phone:** (914)783-1552. **Business Addr:** Professor, Hostos Community College, 500 Grand Concourse, Bronx, NY 10451, **Business Phone:** (718)518-4444.

### MAYNARD, VALERIE J.
Educator, sculptor, curator. **Personal:** Born Aug 22, 1937, Harlem, NY; daughter of William Austin Sr and Willie-Fred Pratt. **Educ:** Mus Mod Art, New York, drawing & painting, 1955; New Sch, New York, printmaking, 1969; Goddard Col Plain field, VT, MA, sculpture, 1977. **Career:** Elaine Journet Art Sch, New Rochelle, NY, apprentice, 1955-60; Studio Mus, New York, instr printmaking, artist-in-residence, 1969-74; Langston Hughes Lib, NY, instr sculpture, 1971-72; Howard Univ, Wash, DC, instr sculpture, 1974-76; Jersey City State Col, NJ, instr sculpture, 1977-78; Commun Excellence to Black Audiences Award, statuette, 1978; Two person exhib, "Works Progress " Valerie Maynard & Carol Byard Gallery, 1978; Travelling xhibits "Impressions/Expressions", Black Am Graphics Studio Mus, New York, 1979-84; Harlem State Off Bldg NY, lectr; St Thomas, lectr, 1979-85; Col Vi, St Thomas, instr sculpture, 1984-85; "Tradition & Conflict, Images a Turbulent Decade", 1963-73, Studio Mus, NY, 1985-87; Baltimore Sch Arts, instr sculpture, 1980-81; Reichhold Ctr Arts, St Thomas, US Vi, 1983; First PA Bank, St Thomas, US Vi, 1984; "Orie's Potpourri", St Thomas Cable TV, "News ctr 10" WBNB-TV St Thomas, "AMVI", WBNB-TV St Thomas, "Sunday Morning", CBS-TV NY, films & videos, 1985-86; Caribbean Ctr, New York, 1989; New York COT Col, 1989; Northeastern Univ, Boston, Mass, lectr; Goddard Col, Plainfield, VT, lectr; Rutgers Univ, NJ, lectr; Univ Vi, St Thomas, sculpture instr & artist-in-residence, 1984-88; Women's Studio Workshop, 1986-87; Blue Mouin ctr, 1987-91; McDowell Colony, 1991; Mass Inst Tech, artist-in-residence, 1992; "No Apartheid Anywhere", Compton Gallery, MIT, 1992; Brandywine Workshop, 1992; Bob Blackburn Printing Workshop, 1992-93; Univ Rochester, Susan B Anthony Ctr Women's Studies, Rockefeller Humanities fel, currently; artist, currently. Works: One woman exhibs: creator/designer. **Honors/Awds:** CEBA Design Award, World Inst Black Commun, New York, 1978; Citation of Merit Seward Park Alumni, NY, 1979; Living Hist Award, New York Urban League Westchester, 1980; Bedford-Stuyvesant Arts Award, Brooklyn, NY, 1980; Finalist Nat Sculpture Competition, Columbus, OH, 1980; Finalist Independence Monument Antigua, Wi, 1981; Pub Sch 181, Brooklyn, New York; Womens Studio Workshops, residency, 1989-; Sculpture Award, Atlanta Life Ins CPN, 1990; New Eng Fund Artists Grant, 1992; randywine workshop, artist-in-residence grant, 1992; Life Am, Mac Dowell Colony, fel, 1991; Nat Endowment Arts; grant, for a stage set for play, "Nzinga", 1992. **Special Achievements:** Represented the United States at the Second World Black and African Festival of Arts and Culture in Lagos, Nigeria, 1977; Art of Justice: Articulating an Ethos and Aesthetic of the Movement conference, New York Univ, 2015. **Home Addr:** 2116 E Madison St, Baltimore, MD 21205-2337, **Home Phone:** (410)558-1475.

### MAYNOR, KEVIN ELLIOTT
Opera singer. **Personal:** Born Jul 24, 1954, Mt. Vernon, NY. **Educ:** Manhattan Sch Music, dipl, 1972; Bradley Univ, BME, 1976; Northwestern Univ, MM, 1977; Moscow Conserv, MMV, 1980; Ind Univ,

DM, 1983, DM, 1988. **Career:** Chicago Lyric Opera, soloist, 1978; Sante Fe Opera, soloist, 1979; Bolshoi Opera, soloist, 1980; VA Opera, soloist, 1984; New York Opera, soloist, 1986; Alice Tully Hall, soloist, 1985; Avery Fischer Hall, soloist, 1985; Carnegie Hall, 1986; Nashville Opera, soloist, 1986; Long Beach Opera, soloist, 1986; Mobile Opera, soloist, 1986; NYC Opera, 1985-98; Orlando Opera, soloist, 1986; Metrop Opera-Neth Dance Theatre, soloist, 1986-87; Triangle Music Theatre Asn, Durham, NC, soloist, 1987; Metrop Opera House, 1987; Opera Co Boston, soloist, 1988; Alice Tully Hall, New York, NY, soloist, 1988; Valparaiso Univ, soloist & recitalist, 1988; Ft Worth Symphony, soloist, 1988; Knoxville Symphony, soloist, 1988; Music Under The Stars Festival, soloist, 1988; Opera Music Theatre Int, soloist, 1989-90; Skylight Opera Theatre, 1990-91; Scottish Opera, 1991-92; Conn Opera, 1992-93; Cincinnati Opera, 1992-93; Chattanooga Symphony, 1993-94; Greensboro Opera, 1994-95; Opera Pac, 1996; Edmonton Opera, 1996; Mkt Theatre, Johannesburg S Africa, 1997; Lyric Opera Chicago, 1997-98; Sacramento Opera, 1998; Dallas Opera, 1998; Milwaukee Symphony, 1998; Lyric Opera Boston, 1999; Saraton Opera, Russia, 2000; Flint Symphony, 2000; Knoxville Opera, 2000; Friends of the Roanoke Symphony, 2000; Lyric Opera Austin, 2000-01; Pittsburgh Opera; Pac Opera Victoria, 2001; TAOC, artistic dir, 2004-; Trilogy An Opera Co, artistic dir, 2004-; Nat du Rhin Opera, Strasbourg, France, currently & Sacramento Opera, currently; Anchorage Opera; Opera Birmingham; New York Opera; San Antonio Symphony. **Orgs:** NCP, 1983-85; bd mem, Edler G Hawkins Fund Inc, 1989; bd, Univ Heights Sci Park; deacon bd, Bethany Baptist Church; bd, Greater Newark Conservacy; bd, Neward Comm Sch Arts. **Home Addr:** 32 Howard Ct, Newark, NJ 07103. **Business Addr:** Opera Singer, Sacramento Opera, PO Box 161027, Sacramento, CA 95816, **Business Phone:** (916)737-1000.

### MAYNOR, VERNON PERRY

Entrepreneur, accountant. **Personal:** Born Feb 8, 1966, Mt. Vernon, NJ; son of Godfrey and Josephine; married Shevella Brown. **Educ:** Hampton Univ, BS, finance, 1988. **Career:** Johnson & Johnson Consumer Products Inc, Cooperative Educ Prog, 1987-88; Johnson & Johnson Corporate, acct mgt trainee, 1988-90, financial acct, 1990-; Me 2 You Inc, pres, currently. **Orgs:** Ed, OPP Fraternity; acct, Nat Black Ans. **Home Addr:** 6002 Shadow Oaks Ct, Monmouth Junction, NJ 08852, **Home Phone:** (908)940-8813. **Business Addr:** President, Me 2 You Inc, 105 Willowbrook Dr, North Brunswick, NJ 08902, **Business Phone:** (732)940-3000.

### MAYO, BARRY ALAN

Radio director, executive, president (organization). **Personal:** Born Jun 30, 1952, Bronx, NY; son of Charles C and Anne Lewis; children: Barry A II, Alana Aisha & Alexander. **Educ:** Howard Univ, radiol, 1976. **Career:** WRAP, Norfolk, prog dir, 1978; WMAK, Nashville, prog dir, 1978; WGCI-FM, Chicago, prog dir, 1978-81; WJLB-FM, Detroit, prog consult, 1981-84; WDMT-Cleveland, prog consult, 1984; WRKS-FM, New York, NY, vpres, gen mgr, 1984-88; Broadcasting Partners Inc, presid, 1988-; WVAZ-FM, pres, gen mgr, 1988-95; Emmis Boradcasting, gen mgr, mkt mgr, sr vpres, 2003-06; Radio One Inc, consult, 2006, pres, 2007-12; WHBC, gen mgr. **Orgs:** Bd dir, secy, New York Mkt Broadcasters; bd, Providence St Mel High Sch, 1990-; bd dir, Black United Fund. **Business Addr:** President, Radio One Inc, 5900 Princess Garden Pkwy 7th Fl, Lanham, MD 20706, **Business Phone:** (301)306-1111.

### MAYO, BLANCHE IRENE

School administrator. **Personal:** Born Jan 24, 1946, Woodstock, OH; daughter of Gertrude E (deceased) and William E; married Terry; children: Terry Jr. **Educ:** Cent State Univ, BS, 1976, MBA, 1980, CMI dipl, 1989. **Career:** Cent State Univ, fed credit union treas & mgr, 1976-78, asst vpres acad affairs, asst title III, 1978-85, asst vpres acad affairs, title III coordr, 1980-85, exec asst pres, title III coordr, 1985-87, vpres admin support serv, adj fac, currently. **Orgs:** Comnr, Ohio Stud Loan Comn, 1987; steering comn, CACUBO Mgt Inst, 1990-93; chaplain & sr usher bd, Mid Run Baptist Church, 1991-92; bus officer, Exec Comm Cent Asn Col & Univ, 1991-93; consult & evaluator, N Cent Asn Col & Schs, 1992-93. **Business Addr:** Vice President, Central State University, 1400 Brush Row Rd Rm 211, Wilberforce, OH 45384-1004, **Business Phone:** (937)376-6603.

### MAYO, HARRY D., III

Financial manager, educator. **Personal:** Born Aug 28, 1939, Brooklyn, NY; son of Harry D Jr and Lillie Mae Clark; married Joan Etta Bradley. **Educ:** Pace Univ, BBA, finance, 1968, MBA, exec mgt, 1978; Harvard Univ, Harvard Bus Sch, Cert Exec Educ Prog, 1978. **Career:** Sperry & Hutchinson Co Inc, stand admin, Sr Syst Analyst, sr programmer, oper, 1957-67; pace Univ, 1957-68; Facts Inc, JP Morgan & Co, mgr fin serv, 1967-69, dir mkt, 1969-70; Borden's Inc, proj mgr, 1970-73; Arthur Young & Co, mgr, 1973-76; Int Paper Co, mgr syst develop, 1976-80; Merrill Lynch & Co Inc, dir MIS, 1980-82; Peters, Mayo & Co, pres & ceo, 1983-85; SRI Int, mgr info serv & syst div NY, 1985-86; HD Mayo & Assoc, founder & chmn, 1982-; Passaic Valley Sewerage Comnr, dir hr, 2000-; Fairleigh-Dickinson Univ, instr. **Orgs:** Asst vpres, Eastern Rgn, Chap pres, Pledge Line pres Alpha Phi Alpha Frat NC, 1963-66; Sem chmn, guest spkr Am Mgt Asn; prin mem, Am Nat Stand Inst, 1967-70; Asn Syst Mgt guest spkr, Data Process Mgt Asn, IBM Process Indust Users Grp NY Univ; MENSA; pres & dir, Parker Imp Asn Inc, 1975-; secy & mem Plng Bd Twp N Bergen, 1979-87, vice chmn, 1988-; chmn & guest spkr, Nat Inst Mgt Res, 1986-87; trustee & chmn, Investment Comn, St Lukes Found, 1994-; dir & mem, Develop, Strategic Plng & Search Comn, Youth Consult Serv, 1995-; chmn, Planned Giving Comn, St Luke's Episcopal Church, 1996-. **Home Addr:** 7855 Blvd E Apt 18K, North Bergen, NJ 07047. **Business Addr:** Chairman, HD Mayo & Associates, 7855 Blvd E, North Bergen, NJ 07047, **Business Phone:** (201)861-6173.

### MAYO, JAMES WELLINGTON

Administrator, educator. **Personal:** Born Mar 2, 1930, Atlanta, GA; married Sandra Bratton; children: Joanna, Janell & Jamila. **Educ:** Morehouse, BS, 1951; Howard Univ, SM, 1953; Mass Inst Technol, PhD, 1964, MS, 1961. **Career:** Morehouse clearing, prof chmn, 1964-72; Dept Sci Educ Res, NSF, dept dir, 1975-77, sec head, 1973-75, prg dir, 1971-73; Mass Inst Tech, tutor, 1961-63, res asst, 1957-63; Howard Univ, instr, 1955-57, res asst, 1951-52; Nat Bur Stand, physicist, 1952-53; Dept Energy, Energy Storage Syst, div dir, 1978-81, consult, 1981-82; AMAF, res group, mkt mgr, 1982-83; Sonicraft, mgr, 1983-88; Pailen-Johnson Assoc, dir, techserv, 1988-89; Comp Tech Group, vpres, mkt, 1989-90; Cath Univ Am, asst acad vpres res, 1990-2005, assoc provost; Byte Back Inc, chmn. **Orgs:** Nat Res Coun, CHR, 1975-; Sloan Found, 1975; Beep Nat Urban League, 1972-; pres, Brown Sta Sch, PTA, 1971; NSF, 1969-71; Ctr Res, 1969-71; consult, Atlanta Sci Cong, 1969-71; comr Comt Clearing Physics, 1968-71; Beta Kappa Chi; Sigma Pi Sigma; Sigma XI; Phi Beta Kappa; Am Phy Soc; Am Assc Physics Teachers; AAAS; Ga Acad Sci; Nat Inst Sci. **Home Addr:** 7505 Democracy Blvd Apt A314, Bethesda, MD 20817-1239, **Home Phone:** (301)365-3067.

### MAYO, DR. JULIA A. (JULIA MAYO JOHNSTON)

Sociologist, psychiatrist. **Personal:** Born Aug 16, 1926, Philadelphia, PA; daughter of Henry and Mamie Clark; married William E Johnston; children: Wilvena. **Educ:** Univ Pa, BA, 1947, PhD, 1958; Bryn Mawr Col, MS, 1949. **Career:** Ment Hyg Clin VA Hosp Wilmington, DE, asst chief, 1953-60; NIMH St Elizabeth Hosp Wash, DC, chief psychosocial stds, 1960-66; St Vincent Cath Med Ctr NY, chief clncl stds & eval, 1966-, prof emer, 1991-; Psychother, indiv/group part time pvt prac, 1966-; DHew Off Educ, consult, 1975-; S Beach Psycho Ctr NY, consult rsrch, 1978-; Med Col, New York, NY, assoc prof clin psychiat, 1989-91; New York Med Col, clin prof psychiat emer, 1991-. **Orgs:** Am Sociol Asn; APPA; Am Acad Pediat; Am Asn Marriage & Family Ther; Nat Asn Social Workers; dipl, Am Psychother Asn. **Special Achievements:** Numerous scientific publications. **Home Addr:** 205 W End Ave Suite 24 J, New York, NY 10023, **Home Phone:** (646)386-2227. **Business Addr:** Professor Emeritus, New York Medical College, Rm N324 Behavioral Health Center 3rd Fl, Valhalla, NY 10595, **Business Phone:** (914)594-4000.

### MAYS, DAVID W., III

Dentist, football player, educator. **Personal:** Born Jun 20, 1949, Pine Bluff, AR. **Educ:** Tex Sothern Univ, BA, 1971; Univ Sothern Calif, DDS, 1976. **Career:** Football player (retired), dentist; Houston Texans & Shreveport Streamer, 1974; Hawaiians, 1975; Cleveland Browns, quarterback, 1976-77; Buffalo Bills, quarterback, 1978; Los Angeles, pvt pract, dentist, 1978-; Univ Calif, Community Dent Dept & Pedodontic Dent Dept, clin prof, 1978. **Orgs:** Western Dent Soc; Angel City Dent Soc; Am Dent Asn; Alpha Phi Alpha Frat. **Home Addr:** 7427 S Figueroa St, Los Angeles, CA 90003, **Home Phone:** (323)751-2395.

### MAYS, DR. JAMES ARTHUR. See Obituaries Section.

### MAYS, KIVUUSAMA

Football player. **Personal:** Born Jan 7, 1975, Anniston, AL. **Educ:** Univ NC, grad. **Career:** Football player (retired); Minn Vikings, linebacker, 1998-99; Green Bay Packers, linebacker, 1999; Orlando Rage, 2001.

### MAYS, LESLIE A.

Executive, president (organization), vice president (organization). **Personal:** Born Houston, TX; daughter of Edward H and Donna L; married Antonio Martin. **Educ:** Tex Southern Univ, BA, commun. **Career:** Tex Air, flight attend, human resources mgr, 1970; Peoples Express Airline, personnel dir, city mgr; Am Works, recruitment officer; Jane C Edmonds & Assoc, consult; Kimberly Clark, lead D&I strategy advisor; Worldwide diversity, vpres; Reebok Int Ltd, human resources dir, 1989-94; Gen Mills, corp leadership roles, diversity dept, 1994-96; Shell Oil Co, exec dir diversity, 1996-99, vpres group global diversity, 1999-2005; Royal Dutch Shell PLC, vpres & head global diversity; Pfizer, vpres & head global diversity, 2005-08; Conf Bd, vpres diversity & inclusion, 2008-10; Avon, vpres & chief inclusion officer, 2011-. **Orgs:** Bd mem, pres, Nat Coalition 100 Black Women, 1997-2001, pres, 2001-; mem bd dir, Cornell Univ Chief Diversity Officers Roundtable; mem bd, Exec Leadership Found; mem bd, Evidence Dance Co; sr fel Am Leadership Forum. **Business Addr:** Vice President, Chief inclusion officer, Avon Products, Inc., New York, NY, **Business Phone:** (212)282-7000.

### MAYS, TRAVIS CORTEZ

Basketball coach, basketball player. **Personal:** Born Jun 19, 1968, Ocala, FL; married Mirella; children: Cherrell & Trevor. **Educ:** Univ Tex, BA, psychol, 1990. **Career:** Basketball player (retired), basketball coach; Assoc Press All-Am, 1989-90; Sacramento Kings, guard, 1990-91; Atlanta Hawks, guard, 1991-93; Rochester Renegade, 1993; Panionios, 1994-95; Ironi Ramat Gan, 1995-96; Tuborg Pilsener, 1996-97; Mabo Pistoia, 1998-99; Ducato Siena, 1999-2001; Montepaschi Siena, 2001-02; Panionios BC Athens, FIBA Europe, guard, 2001; WNBA San Antonio Silver Stars, asst coach, 2002-03, head scout, 2003-04; Univ Tex, asst basketball coach, 2004-07; La State Univ, asst coach, 2007-11, assoc head coach, 2012-. **Business Addr:** Associate Head Coach, Louisiana State University, Athletics Admin Bldg Nicholson Dr, Baton Rouge, LA 70894-5095, **Business Phone:** (225)578-8001.

### MAYS, DR. VICKIE M.

Educator. **Personal:** Born Jan 30, 1952, Chicago, IL; daughter of Leonard and Ruth. **Educ:** Loyola Univ Chicago, BA, psychol & philos, 1973, MA, clin psychol, 1979; Univ Mass, PhD, clin psychol, 1979; Univ Mich, MSPH, health servs, postdoctoral training psychiat epidemiol. **Career:** Loyola Univ, Dept Psychol, res asst, 1972; Univ Mass, teaching asst, 1973-74, instr & dorm counr, 1974, lectr, 1974, teaching asst & clin supvr, 1976-77, actg intake coordr & clin supvr, 1977, res asst, 1978; George Washington Univ, instr, 1975-76; Univ Calif Los Angeles, asst prof clin psychol, 1979-, Ctr Res, Educ, Training & Strategic Commun Minority Health Disparities, dir, Col Lett & Sci, Dept Health Sci, prof, currently, Dept Psychol, prof, currently; Univ Calif Los Angeles Acad Senate, vice chairperson, chairperson, 1997-99. **Orgs:** Am Psychol Asn, 1970-; Western Psychol Asn, 1981-; Am Pub Health Asn, 1986-, Black Caucus Health Workers Prog Comm, 1991-; chairperson, Am Col Epidemiol, Minority Affairs Comn, 1996-; Nat Comm Vital & Health Studies, 2000-; consult, adv govt & educ insts; ed bd mem, Clin Psychol Women, AIDS Educ & Prev & Jour Homosexuality; Jour Cult Diversity & Ment Health; chairperson, Subcomm Pop; chmn, Nat Comt Vital & Health Statist. **Honors/Awds:** Outstanding Woman of the Year, Bd Outstanding Young Women, 1984, 1986; Women & Psychotherapy Research Award, Div Psychol Women, Am Psychol Asn, 1985; Master Lecture, 1997; Received number of awards including: Lifetime Research on Women and HIV, AMFAR; Women and Leadership Award, Am Psychol Asn; Several Distinguished Contributions for Research awards. **Special Achievements:** Author: The Impact of Racial & Feminist Attitudes on the Educational Achievement & Occupational Aspirations of College Level Black Women, UCLA Center for Afro-American Studies Newsletter, May, 1980; Co-author of Educating Community Gatekeepers About Alcohol Abuse in Women: Changing Attitudes, Knowledge & Referral Practices, Journal of Drug Education, 15 (4), 1985, Introduction to the Special Issues: Psychology & AIDS, American Psychologist, 43 (11), 1988; Author of numerous other research reports, review articles, abstracts, book chapters, & articles on behavioral science & AIDS. **Business Addr:** Professor, University of California-Los Angeles, 405 Hilgard Ave 1189 Franz Hall, Los Angeles, CA 90095-1563, **Business Phone:** (310)206-5159.

### MAYS, WILLIAM, JR.

Executive director, president (organization). **Personal:** Born Oct 12, 1929, Detroit, MI; married Mary Louise Smith; children: Elisabeth & Adrienne. **Educ:** Eastern Mich Univ, BA, 1954; Univ Mich, MA, 1958. **Career:** Ann Arbor Pub Schs, speech therapist, 1958-66, elem prin, 1966-72, asst supt, 1972-74, dir elem educ, 1974-75; Mich Elem & Mid Sch Prin Asn, exec dir, 1975-97; E Mich Univ Alumni Asn, pres, currently. **Orgs:** Bd trustee, Washtenaw Community Col, 1974; E Mich Univ Alumni Asn; pres, Alumni Asn. **Business Addr:** President, Eastern Michigan University, 1349 S Huron St Suite 2, Ypsilanti, MI 48197, **Business Phone:** (734)487-0250.

### MAYS, DR. WILLIAM O.

Executive, physician. **Personal:** Born Dec 21, 1934, Little Rock, AR; married Deborah Easter; children: William III, Ryan Easter & Eric Easter. **Educ:** Howard Univ, BS, chem, 1956; Univ Ariz, MD, 1960. **Career:** Wayne County Gen Hosp, internshp, 1960, residency, 1965; Southwest Med Plaza, physician, currently; self employed independent peoplesoft consult, 1965-2003; physician, 1972-2003. **Orgs:** Pres & chmn bd, Mich Health Maint Org Plans Inc; pres chmn bd, Detroit Med Found; vpres, Harris Mays & Assocs PC; NMA; AMA; Detroit Med Soc; Wayne Co Med Soc; Mich State Med Soc; Wolverine Med Soc; bd dir, exec com, tres CHPC, SEM; bd dir, Blue Shield Mich; pres, Detroit Med Soc, 1972-74; Am Col Physician Execs. **Business Addr:** Physician, Southwest Medical Plaza, 2401 20th St, Detroit, MI 48216, **Business Phone:** (313)961-8450.

### MAYS, WILLIE HOWARD, JR.

Baseball executive, baseball player. **Personal:** Born May 6, 1931, Westfield, AL; son of William Howard Sr and Annie Sattlewhite; married Margherite Wendell Chapman; married Mae Louise Allen. **Career:** Baseball player (retired), baseball executive; Birmingham Black Barons Baseball Team, 1948-50; Trenton Team, 1950-51; Minneapolis Millers, 1951; New York Giants, 1951-57; San Francisco Girants, 1958-72; New York Mets, 1972-73; Bally Pk Pl Atlantic City, asst to pres; Ogden Corp & Gruntal & Co, pub rels; Health Spring, spokesperson, currently; spec asst to pres, currently. **Orgs:** Pres, Say Hey Found; Giants Community Fund; San Francisco Food Bank; Whitney Young Child Develop Ctr. **Special Achievements:** Film: When Nature Calls, 1985; Book: Say Hey: The Autobiography of Willie Mays, 1988. **Business Addr:** Baseball Player, San Francisco Giants, 24 Willie Mays Plz, San Francisco, CA 94107, **Business Phone:** (415)972-1800.

### MAYWEATHER, FLOYD, JR. (FLOYD JOY SINCLAIR)

Athlete, boxer. **Personal:** Born Feb 24, 1977, Grand Rapids, MI; son of Floyd Sr and Deborah; children: 4. **Career:** Boxer. **Orgs:** Founder, Floyd May weather Found. **Home Addr:** , Las Vegas, NV. **Business Addr:** Boxer, Mayweather Promotions LLC, 4616 W Sahara Ave Suite 290, Las Vegas, NV 89102, **Business Phone:** (702)778-8622.

### MAZON, LARRI WAYNE

Educator, college administrator. **Personal:** Born Dec 6, 1945, Roanoke, AL; son of Dewey and Fannie; married Dorothy Antrum; children: Jeffrey & Nikki. **Educ:** Univ New Haven, West Haven, CT, BS, criminal justice admin, 1976; State Univ NY, Stony Brook, MSW, 1983; Nova-Southeastern Univ, doctoral grad. **Career:** Dir Instnl Diversity Initiatives (retired); Fairfield Hills Hosp, rehab counr, 1968-72; Regional Network Progs, Bridgeport, Conn, dir, rehabilition servs, 1972-78; Conntac-Wesleyan, Middletown, Conn, counr & coordr, 1978-84; Inst Diversity Initiatives, dir, 1983-2010; Fairfield Univ, dir, Multicultural Rels & Stud Acad Support Serv, dir, 1984-07. **Orgs:** Inst Afro-Am Scholar, 1984-91; steering com mem, African-Am in Higher Educn Conn, 1988-90; chmn, Minority Adv Coun, Hamden Bd Educ & Suptd Schs, 1989-90, 1990-91; chmn, Asn Jesuit Cols & Univs, Conf on Minority Affairs, 1990-91; bd dir, Greater Bridgeport Coun Churches Inc; Kappa Alpha Psi Fraternity. **Special Achievements:** Awarded as the Reverend John LaFarge, S.J Award, named in honor of a leader and a spokesperson for the human rights of African Americans. **Home Addr:** 3 Valley View Ct, Hamden, CT 06518-2751, **Home Phone:** (203)230-2920.

### MC LYTE (LANA MICHELE MOORER)

Rap musician. **Personal:** Born Oct 11, 1970, Queens, NY. **Career:** Rap singer, currently; began rapping at age 12; released first single, "I Cram to Understand U (Sam)", 1987; single: "Cha Cha Cha", reached number one on rap charts; signed to Electra, 1996; Albums: The Lion & The Cobra, 1988; Lyte as a Rock, 1988; Eyes on This, 1989; The First Priority Music Family: Basement Flavor, 1989; Act Like You Know; 1991; Mo' Money, 2002; Ain't No Other, 1993; Panther, soundtrack, 1994; Sunset Park, soundtrack, 1996; Bad as I Wanna B, 1997; Badder Than B-Fore, 1998; Seven & Seven, 1998; TV: I Cram to Understand You, 1988; Cha Cha Cha, 1989; Ruffneck, 1993; janet, 1994; Brandy, 1994; Lyte of a Decade, 1996; Keep on Keeping On, 1997; I Can't Make

A Mistake, 1998; 1993, 1999; Everyday, 1999; Da Undaground Heat Vol One, 2003; Shit I Never Dropped, 2003; "Half & Half", 2004-06; Girlfriend's Story, 2004; Da Jammies, 2006; "The Big Hide & Sneak Episode", 2006; "The Big Diva Down Episode", 2006; Films: Fly by Night, 1993; Train Ride, 2000. **Business Addr:** Rap Singer, Elektra Records, 75 Rockefeller Plz, New York, NY 10019, **Business Phone:** (212)275-4000.

### MCADOO, BOB, JR. (ROBERT ALLEN MCADOO, JR.)

Basketball player, athletic coach. **Personal:** Born Sep 25, 1951, Greensboro, NC; married Patrizia; children: Rita, Robert III, Ross, Russell, Ryan & Rasheeda. **Educ:** NC Univ, attended 1972. **Career:** Basketball player (retired), basketball coach; Buffalo Braves, 1972-76; New York Knicks, 1976-79; Boston Celtics, 1979; Detroit Pistons, 1979-81; NJ Nets, 1981; Los Angeles Lakers, 1981-85; Philadelphia 76ers, 1985-86; Olimpia Milano, 1986-90; Forli, Milan, Italy, 1990-92; Teamsystem Fabriano, 1992-93; Miami Heat, asst coach, 1995-2014. **Orgs:** Nat Basketball Asn. **Home Addr:** 16710 SW 82nd Ave, Miami, FL 33157. **Business Addr:** Assistant Coach, Miami Heat, 1 SE 3rd Ave Suite 2300, Coconut Grove, FL 33133, **Business Phone:** (305)577-4328.

### MCADOO, HENRY ALLEN, SR.

Government official, commissioner, programmer analyst. **Personal:** Born Feb 9, 1951, Murfreesboro, TN; son of John Allen and Doris Ann Wade; married Gayle Elizabeth Howse; children: Carol N, Allen Jr & Lauren M. **Educ:** Mid Tenn State Univ, Murfreesboro, TN, BS, 1975; Univ Tenn Space Inst, Tullahoma, TN, attended 1977; Mid Tenn State Univ, attended 1979. **Career:** Scales & Son Funeral Home Inc; Sedrulp Technologies, appln programmer, 1972-82; NISSAN, sr analyst, 1982-86, sr systs analyst; Rutherford Co Comn, comnr 18th Dist, 1978-. **Orgs:** Chmn, Law Enforcement Rutherford County, 1978-79; chmn, Econ Comt Rutherford County, 1983-84; Mason Murfreesboro Lodge No 12; Elks EA DavisLodge No 1138; Kappa Alpha Psi Fraternity, Murfreesboro Alumni Chap; chmn pro term, Rutherford County Comn, 1998-2002. **Honors/Awds:** Nominated & appointed Rutherford County Bd Gov Mid-Cumberland, 1978-79, Bd Zoning Appeals, 1979-. **Home Addr:** 1223 Toddington Dr, Murfreesboro, TN 37130-5629. **Business Addr:** Commissioner, Rutherford County 18th District, PO Box 3132, Murfreesboro, TN 37130, **Business Phone:** (615)293-3384.

### MCADOO, ROBERT ALLEN, JR. See MCADOO, BOB, JR.

### MCAFEE, CHARLES FRANCIS

Architect. **Personal:** Born Dec 25, 1932, Los Angeles, CA; son of Arthur James Sr and Willie Anna; married Gloria Myrth Winston; children: Cheryl Lynn, Pamela Anita & Charyl Frena Duncan. **Educ:** Univ Nebr Col Archit, BS, 1958. **Career:** Educr & community leader; Charles F McAfee FAIA NOMA PA, managing prin, pres & chief exec officer, currently; McAfee3 Architects, founder, 1963-. **Orgs:** Fel AMR Inst Architects, 1963; sr vpres, Nat Bus League; Wichita Urban League; Wichita Chamber Com; Phyllis Wheatley C Home; Excelsior Club; Kappa Alpha Psi Fraternity; Sigma Pi Phi Fraternity; fed pres, Nat Asn Minority Architects; Cath Social Serv; fel Am Inst Architects; Nat Orgn Minority Architects. **Honors/Awds:** Numerous Design Awards, Am Inst Architects, 1964-96; Design Awards, Fed Housing Admin, 1964; Design Awards, Nat Orgn Minority Architects, 1983; Alumni Achievement Award, Univ Nebr; Distinguished Alumni Award, Col Archit; First Honor Award; Whitney M. Young Jr. Award, Am Inst Architects. **Special Achievements:** Joint Venture selected for program, construction and design Management, Olympic Games facilities, Atlanta, 1996; developer, architect: Richmond Health Dept; McAfee Manufacturing Modular Housing Systems, pres. **Home Addr:** 16 Crestview Lakes Estates, Wichita, KS 67220-2914, **Home Phone:** (316)684-5231. **Business Addr:** Founder, McAfee3 Architects, 2251 E 21st Suite 125, Wichita, KS 67214, **Business Phone:** (316)263-7001.

### MCAFEE, FLO

Government official. **Career:** Caraway Group Inc, sr vpres; White House, Off Pub Liaison, spec asst pres, 1993-97; Wisdom Works Inc, develop & mkt adv, currently; Summerland Studio LLC, pres, 2000-. **Orgs:** Bd mem, InsideOUT Writers; bd mem, Alethos Found; bd mem, int Episcopal Relief & Develop; Univ Ill Pres Circle. **Business Addr:** Board Member, InsideOUT Writers, 1680 N Vine St Suite 614, Hollywood, CA 90028, **Business Phone:** (323)871-1866.

### MCAFEE, FRED LEE

Football player, football executive. **Personal:** Born Jun 20, 1968, Philadelphia, MS; children: Jaela & Frederick. **Educ:** Miss Col, BS, mass commun; Stanford Univ, Exec Educ Grad Sch Bus, NFL mgrs prog. **Career:** Football player (retired), football executive; New Orleans Saints, 1991, kick returner, 1992, running back, 1993, 2000-06, dir player progs, 2007-; Ariz Cardinals, 1994; Pittsburgh Steelers, 1994-98; Kans City Chiefs, 1999; Tampa Bay Buccaneers, 1999. **Honors/Awds:** American Football Conference Champion, 1994; Pro Bowl, 2002. **Business Addr:** Director of Player Development, New Orleans Saints, 5800 Airline Dr, Metairie, LA 70003, **Business Phone:** (504)733-0255.

### MCAFEE, DR. LEO C., JR.

Educator. **Personal:** Born Dec 15, 1945, Marshall, TX; son of Leo Sr (deceased) and Doretha Lester (deceased); children: Leo III, LaRuth & Lawrence. **Educ:** Prairie View A&M Univ, BS, elec engineering, 1966; Univ Mich, MSE, elec engineering, 1967, PhD, elec engineering, 1970. **Career:** Bell Tel Res Labs NJ, tech staff, 1968; Univ Mich, instr, 1970, prof, 1971-2010, from asst prof to assoc prof, elect & comput engr, assoc prof emer, 2011-, Ctr Wireless Integrated MicroSystems, assoc dir educ & outreach; IBM Thomas J Watson Res Labs NY, summer fac, 1971 & 1978; Gen Motors Res Labs Mich, Semiconductor Electronics Dept, assoc sr res engr, 1973-74; Telecom Anal Systs NJ, sum fac, 1995. **Orgs:** Inst Elect & Electronics Engr Inc; Eta Kappa Nu; Tau Beta Pi; Sigma Xi; Phi Kappa Phi; Alpha Kappa Mu. **Honors/Awds:** Outstanding Engineering Student, Prairie View A&M Univ, 1965-66; Nat Sci Found Trainee Univ Mich, 1966-68; EECS Faculty Service Award, Univ Mich, 1992. **Special Achievements:** First African American professor hired by college of engineering in University of Michigan, 1971; Published and co-author for books like: Data Knowl. Eng. 6: 421-443, 1991. **Business Addr:** Associate Professor Emeritus, University of Michigan, 2231 EECS, Ann Arbor, MI 48109-2122, **Business Phone:** (734)764-0218.

### MCALLISTER, SINGLETON BERYL

Lawyer. **Personal:** Born Mar 25, 1952, Baltimore, MD; daughter of James Winfred and Ann Hughes. **Educ:** Univ Md, BA, govt & polit, 1975; Howard Univ, Sch Law, JD, 1984. **Career:** Parren J Mitchell, legis assist, 1975-78; Trans Africa Inc, asst dir, 1978-79; Congressman William H Gray, III, legis dir, 1979-81; Congressman Mickey Leland, spec asst, 1981-83; US Fed Dist Ct, law clerk, 1984-85; US House Reps, budget comt coun, 1986-88; Reed, Smith, Shaw & McClay, partner, 1988-92; Shaw, Pittman, Potts & Trowbridge, coun, 1992-96; US Agency Int Develop, gen coun, 1996-2001; Patton Boggs LLP, partner, 2001-; Howard Univ, teaching asst; Sonnenschein Nath & Rosenthal LLP, partner; Mintz, Levin, Cohn, Ferris, Glovsky & Popeo PC, partner, 2005-07; LeClair & Ryan LLP, partner, 2007-; Alliant Energy & United Rentals Inc, dir, currently. **Orgs:** Bd mem adv bd, AFR Develop Found, 1987; bd mem, Capitol Ballet Guild, 1988; bd mem, Vir Local Anti-Trust Fund Drug Authority, 1990; VIR Small Bus Financing Authority, 1990; gen coun & bd mem, Women Govt Rels, 1991; adv bd mem, Cong Black Caucus Found, 1991; Northern VIR Minority Bus & Prof Asn, gen coun, 1992; pres, Women Govt Rels, 1994; Dem Nat Comt Women Leadership Forum, 1994; Health Policy Adv Comt, Joint Ctr Polit Studies, 1994; Fed Affairs Comt, Greater Wa Bd Trade, 1994; bd dir, Int Human Rights Law Group; bd dir, Howard Univ Hosp; fel Nat Acad Pub Admin. **Honors/Awds:** AMR Federation Government Employees Award, Local 1733, 1978; Recognition Award, Am Lung Asn Dist Columbia, 1992; Minority Business Award; Notable American Women Award, the Most Distinguished Member Award from Women in Government Relations; 25 Influential Black Women, Network J's, 2006. **Special Achievements:** Nat Med Asn News, Articles, 1991; Asn Black Cardiol News, Articles, 1992. **Home Addr:** 750 17th St NW Suite 900, Washington, DC 20006, **Home Phone:** (703)759-4462. **Business Addr:** Partner, Patton Boggs LLP, 2550 M St NW, Washington, DC 20037-1350, **Business Phone:** (202)457-6000.

### MCALPINE, ROBERT

Teacher, association executive. **Personal:** Born Jul 13, 1937, New Haven, CT; son of Rachel Thomas Simpson; married Carole J Robinson; children: Monique & Angie. **Educ:** Southern Conn State Col, BS, 1960, MS, 1969; Yale Univ, cert urban studies, 1969; Occidental Col, MA, 1970. **Career:** Guilford Pub Sch, teacher, 1960-67; New Haven Pub Sch, admin, 1967-69; US Conf Mayors, prog analyst, 1970-74; Nat Urban League, cong liaison, 1974-89, dir policy & govt rels, 1989-, dir govt rels, 1997-. **Orgs:** dir, Nat Asn Advan Colored People; Wash Urban League; bd dir, Coalition Against Ins Fraud. **Honors/Awds:** National Urban Fellows, 1969-70; New Haven Jaycees Key Man of the Year, 1969-. **Home Addr:** 13 Ashmont Ct, Silver Spring, MD 20906-5719, **Home Phone:** (301)597-5178. **Business Addr:** Director of Policy and Government Relations, National Urban League, 120 Wall St 8th Fl, New York, NY 10005, **Business Phone:** (212)558-5300.

### MCANDREW, ANNE E. BATTLE

Educator. **Personal:** Born May 28, 1951, Philadelphia, PA; daughter of Turner Charles Battle III and Marian Louise Chester Battle; married John; children: Allison & Christina. **Educ:** Moore Col Art & Design, Philadelphia, PA, BFA, BS, 1972; Visual Studies Workshop, Rochester, NY, photog, 1974; Rochester Inst Technol, Rochester, NY, MFA, graphic design, 1983. **Career:** Nat Coalition Bldg Inst, prin; Panther Publ House, New York, NY, researcher, 1971; Rochester City Sch Dist, teacher & adminr, 1973-, art teacher, 1973-, lead teacher, 1988; Univ Rochester, Rochester, NY, mus video asst, 1974-75; Rochester Inst Technol, Rochester, NY, grad asst, 1982-83; Wedge Newspaper, Rochester, NY, managing ed, 1985-86; Theodore Roosevelt Sch No 43, prin, currently. **Orgs:** Curric comn dir, Prof Pract Sch Design Team, Am Fed Teachers, 1990-; Sch Based Planning Team, 1990-. **Home Addr:** 72 Penn Lane, Rochester, NY 14625-2218. **Business Addr:** Principal, Theodore Roosevelt School No 43, 1305 Lyell Ave, Rochester, NY 14606, **Business Phone:** (585)458-4200.

### MCBEAN, GEN. CLEAVE A.

Military leader. **Educ:** Col VI, BA, bus admin, 1976. **Career:** Command & Control HQS, VIARNG, St Thomas, VI, oper & training officer, 1979-81; 666th MP BN, VIARNG, St Thomas, C-E officer, 1981-83, BN S-3, 1983-84; HQ TARC-VI, Det 1 Trp Cmd, VIARNG, St Thomas, BN S-1, 1984-85; HQS TARC-VI, Det 2 VIMA, VIARNG, St Thomas, asst commandant sr instr, 1985-88; 666th MP BN & 786th S&S BN, VIARNG, St Thomas, exec off, 1988-90; 786th S&S BN VIARNG, St Thomas, battalion comdr, 1990-92; HQS TARC-VI, VIARNG, St Croix, VI, training officer, 1992-94, POMSO, 1994-95, dep TERARC comdr, 1995-96, POTO, 1996-97, dep TERARC comdr, 1997; res, 1997-2000; HQS TARC-VI, VI Nat Guard, adj gen, 2000-. **Business Addr:** The Adjutant General, Virgin Islands National Guard, 4031 La Grande Princesse Lot IB, Christiansted00820-4353, **Business Phone:** (340)712-7710.

### MCBEE, VINCENT CLERMONT

Criminologist. **Personal:** Born Nov 4, 1946, Greenville, SC; son of Bozie C and Scotia Marion Henderson; married Virginia Daniels; children: Vanessa Latasha & Victoria Simone. **Educ:** Johnson C Smith Univ, BS, 1971; Fla Int Univ, attended 1971; Univ Miami, attended 1976. **Career:** Nat Brewing Co, Southern Div, qual control chem dir, 1971-75; Southland Corp Velda Farms, qual control supvr, 1975-76; Metro-Dade Police Dept, Miami, FL, criminalist II, 1976-. **Orgs:** Southern Asn Forensic Sci, Prince Hall Masons, Omega Psi Phi Frat Inc, Ordained Elder New Covenant Presby Church; Nat Asn Fire Investrs; Am Acad Forensic Scis; Int Asn Arson Investrs. **Home Addr:** 8625 Claridge Dr, Miramar, FL 33025-2720, **Home Phone:** (954)704-2293. **Business Addr:** Criminalist II, Metro-Dade Police Department, 9105 NW 25th St Rm 2149, Miami, FL 33172-1505, **Business Phone:** (305)471-1780.

### MCBETH, HON. VERONICA SIMMONS

Judge. **Personal:** Born Feb 23, 1947, San Diego, CA; daughter of Lemuel Jackson and Judith LaBrie Jackson; married Jim; children: Ashley & Alison. **Educ:** Calif State Univ, BS, 1972; Univ Calif, JD, 1975. **Career:** Judge (retired); Off Los Angeles City Atty, trial dep, 1975-76, Van Nuys Br, Asst supv atty, 1976-77, Spec coun to city atty, 1977-78, Dir domestic violence prog, 1978-79, coordr-domestic violence prog, 1976-78, Dep city atty, 1975-81, supvatty, 1979-81; Los Angeles Muni Ct, asst presiding judge, 1996-98, presiding judge, 1999; Los Angeles Super Ct, judge, 1981-2004, Assigned judge, 2004-. **Orgs:** Pres, Black Women Lawyers Asn CA, 1979-80; Nat Bar Asn, 1975-; bd mem, LA-Nat Asn Advan Colored People, 1979-80; Nat Asn Women Judges, 1981-; dir, UCLA Law Sch Exec Comt, 1981-; exec comt, LA Muni Ct, 1982-, chair, comt, 1985, 1987; sec, Judicial Div Calif Asn Black Lawyers, 1984-85, vpres, 1986-; dir, Harriet Buhai Ctr Family Law; bd dir, judicial coun, Nat Bar Asn, 1985-; bd dir, Coalition 100 Black Women, 1985-; lectr, Nat Judges Col, Pa Trial Judges Conf, ABA Appelate Judges Sem; pres, judicial div CABL, 1988-89; Pres Munic Ct Judges Asn, 1988-89; chair elect, 1989-90, chair, 1990-91, judicial coun, Nat Bar Asn; bd dirs, Jack & Jill Am, 1987-91; pres, Nat Consortium Racial & Ethnic Fairness Ct, 1999-2003, bd emer. **Honors/Awds:** UCLA Law Review, 1973-74; Ed, Chief Black Law Jour, 1974-75; Bernard Jefferson Jurist of the Year Award, John Langston Bar Asn, 1991; Raymond Pace Alexander Award, Judicial Coun, Nat Bar Asn, 1989; Presidential Award, Nat Bar Asn, 1987; NAACP Thomas Griffith Award, 1991; Cal Asn Black Lawyers, Judge of the Year, 1991; Calif State Bar Pub Law Sec, Pub Law Award, 1992; Nat Ctr State Ct, Distinguished Service Award, 1996; Century City Bar Asn, Munic Ct Judge of the Year, 1996; Nat Ctr State Ct, WmRehnquist Award for Judicial Excellence, 1998; Margaret Bahai Ctr Family Law, Community Service Award, 1998; Am Bar Asn Judge R Flashner Award for Judicial Excellence, 1999; Gertrude Rush Award, Nat Bar Asn, 1999. **Special Achievements:** Became the first woman & the first African Am to receive the William H Rehnquist Award for Judicial Excellence.

### MCBETH-REYNOLDS, SANDRA KAY

Banker, president (organization). **Personal:** Born May 7, 1950, Loma Linda, CA; daughter of Timothy L Woods and Velma A Woods; married James L; children: Brandon Lincoln (deceased). **Educ:** Ind Univ, Bloomington, IN, BA, psychol, 1970; Pepperdine Univ, Malibu, CA, MS, urban planning & develop, 1972, MA, sci, pub admin, 1973; Univ W Los Angeles, Sch Law, JD, 1981. **Career:** Loyola Marymount Univ, Westchester, CA, dean stud serv, 1976-79; United Int Mortgage, pres, 1980-; Tobin & Assocs Inc, staff. **Orgs:** Alpha Kappa Alpha Sorority, 1969-; Jack & Jill Am, 1986-; Nat Asn Female Execs, 1987-; Coalition 100 Black Women, 1988-. **Honors/Awds:** Top 50 Bus Executives, La Chamber Com, 1985; Black Women of Achievement, Legal Defense Fund, 1988; Top 100 Black & Professional Women, Dollars & Sense Mag, 1989. **Home Addr:** 2049 Century Pk Suite 2550, Los Angeles, CA 90067, **Home Phone:** (310)645-9024. **Business Addr:** President, United International Mortgage, 5 Wilshire Blvd 21st Fl, Los Angeles, CA 90302, **Business Phone:** (310)207-5060.

### MCBRIDE, BRYANT

Executive, hockey coach. **Personal:** Born May 30, 1965, Chicago, IL; son of William and Julia; married Tina; children: Taylor Jake. **Educ:** Trinity Col, Hartford, CT, attended 1988; Harvard Univ, MA, pub admin, 1990. **Career:** Aldrich Eastman & Waltch, analyst, 1990-91; Taubman Co, analyst, 1991-92, chief staff, 1993; Pioneer Inst, 1992-93; Nat Hockey League, Bus Develop, dir, 1993-99; Diversity Task Force, vpres bus develop; myteam.com, sr vpres, 2002-02; Vision Sports & Entertainment Partners, pres & chief exec officer, 2002-09; Active Network, vpres & group dir; hockey coach; Rte 2 Digital Team, partner, chief exec officer, 2010-; Burst, co-founder & chief exec officer, 2011-. **Orgs:** Nat Sports Mkt Networking; NY Rd Runners Club; All Hallows High Sch; vice chmn, Tech Effective Alcohol Mgt; Citizens Sports Alliance; bd dir, New York Track & Field Armory; chmn, USA Fitness Corps; youth hockey coach. **Business Addr:** Vice President, Group Director, The Active Network, 300 5th Ave 6th Fl, Waltham, MA 02451.

### MCBRIDE, CHI (KENNETH MCBRIDE)

Actor, singer, songwriter. **Personal:** Born Sep 23, 1961, Chicago, IL. **Career:** AT&T, billing clerk, 1986; MCI, tel oper; Films: Revenge of the Nerds III: The Next Generation, 1992; The Distinguished Gentleman, 1992; What's Love Got to Do With It?, 1993; The Frighteners, 1996; Hoodlum, 1997; Mercury Rising, 1998; Dancing in Sept, 2000; Gone in 60 Seconds, 2000; The Kid, 2000; Undercover Brother, 2002; Paid in Full, 2002; Narc, 2003; The N-Word, 2004; Roll Bounce, 2005; Annapolis, 2006; Let's Go to Prison, 2006; Brothers Solomon, 2007; Pushing Daisies, 2007; The Family Tree, 2010; TV movies: King of the World, 2000, Squarepants, 2004; Inside 'The Terminal', 2004; Killer Instinct, 2005; Annapolis, 2006; Let's Go to Prison, 2006; Brothers Solomon, 2007; American Son, 2008; First Sunday, 2008; Who Do You Love, 2008; Still Waiting, 2009; Fruit of Labor, 2011; The Family Tree, 2011; Pawn Shop Chronicles, 2013; Draft Day, 2014. TV series: "Max Steel", 2000; "God, the Devil and Bob", 2000; "Boston Public", 2000; "Jimmy Kimmel Live", 2005; "Ellen: The Ellen DeGeneres Show", 2005; "The Late Late Show with Craig Ferguson", 2005; "Psych", 2010; "Human Target", 2010; "How I Met Your Mother", 2011; "Hawthorne", 2011; "Suits", 2011; "Fruit of Labor", 2011; "Ultimate Spider-Man", 2011-12; "Golden Boy", 2013; "Hawaii Five-0", 2013-; "Avengers Assemble", 2013-; "Phineas and Ferb: Mission Marvel", 2013; "Lego Marvel Super Heroes: Maximum Overload", 2013; "Murder Police", 2014. **Business Addr:** Actor, c/o Fox Broadcasting Co, 10201 W Pico Blvd, Los Angeles, CA 90035, **Business Phone:** (310)369-3553.

### MCBRIDE, FRANCES E.

Educator. **Personal:** Born Athens, GA; married Willie; children: Reginald. **Educ:** Savannah State Col, BS, 1945; Atlanta Univ, MA, 1953. **Career:** Jones Co, 1945-46; Lagrange, GA, 1946-47; Polk Co, 1949-53; Alps Rd Elem Sch Clarke Co, teacher, 1954-83; Univ Ga, supporter, currently. **Orgs:** Resolution Comm NEA, 1973-74; Ebenezer Bapt Ch; Am Asn Univ Women Athens Br; Nat Asn Advan Colored

People; Delta Sigma Theta Sor; Savannah St Col Alumni Asn, 1976-77; Atlanta Univ Alumni Asn, 1976-77; Eval Team Southern Asn Schs Habersham Co Sch, 1977; pres, Silhouette Club Athens; chmn, Kappa Alpha Psi Frat Clarke Co; state pres, GEO CRs, ASN, 1988-89; Clarke Co Asn Educr; Ga Asn Edn; Nat Asn Educs. **Home Addr:** 284 Plz St, Athens, GA 30606-2988, **Home Phone:** (706)549-6978. **Business Addr:** Supporter, University of Georgia, 225 Herty Dr, Athens, GA 30602-6012, **Business Phone:** (706)542-3000.

## MCBRIDE, JAMES

Writer. **Personal:** Born Sep 11, 1957, New York, NY; son of Andrew D and Ruth Jordan; children: 3. **Educ:** Oberlin Col, Ohio, music, 1979; Columbia Univ, Ma, jour, NY. **Career:** Jazz saxophonist, composer, producer; Wash Post, journalist; Boston Globe, journalist; People Mag, journalist; freelance writer; Author: The Color of Water: A Black Man's Tribute to His White Mother, memoir, 1996; Miracle of St Anna, 2002; Song Yet Sung, 2008; Red Hook Summer, 2012; Hard Listening, The Good Lord Bird, 2013; NY Univ, distinguished writer-in-residence, currently. **Honors/Awds:** Stephen Sondheim Award, Am Music Fest, 1993; Am Arts & Letters Richard Rogers Award, for work in musical theater, 1996; Anisfield-Wolf Book Award; ASCAP Richard Rodgers Horizons Award, 1996. **Special Achievements:** Featured in People, Newsweek, Savoy & USA Today; Appeared on several national radio and television shows including The Rosie O'Donnell Show, NPR's All Things Considered, Fresh Air, Morning Edition, and in major news outlets in Australia, New Zealand, and across Europe. **Home Addr:** PO Box 829, New York, NY 10108. **Business Addr:** Musician, Writer, c/o Samantha Grabler, New York, NY 10036.

## MCBRIDE, JONATHAN

Media executive, consultant, presidential aide. **Personal:** Born Jan 1, 1970?. **Educ:** Conn Col, BA, econs & US hist, 1992; Univ Pa, Wharton Sch, MBA, finance, 1997. **Career:** Off U.S. Sen Herb Kohl, legis corresp, 1992-95; Goldman Sachs, assoc, 1997-2000; Jungle Media Group, co-founder, 2000-07; Universum, chief strategy officer, 2007-09; White House, spec asst, 2009-12, dep asst to pres, 2012-13, asst to pres & dir presidential personnel, 2013-14; BlackRock, managing dir, 2014-. **Orgs:** Connecticut College, former Trustee; National Urban League, former Trustee. **Honors/Awds:** "The Root" Magazine, The Root 100 Honorees, 2013. **Business Addr:** Managing Director, BlackRock, 40 E 52nd St, New York, NY 10022, **Business Phone:** (212)810-5300.

## MCBRIDE, KENNETH. See MCBRIDE, CHI.

## MCBRIDE, SHELIA ANN

Registered nurse. **Personal:** Born Aug 27, 1947, Albany, GA; married Mathis; children: William Alexander Corbett & Erica Monique Corbett. **Educ:** Albany St Col, BS, 1971. **Career:** Orthop & Newborn Nursery, Pheobe Putney Mem Hosp, 1971-74, Intensive Care Unit, charge nurse, 1975-76; Albany Urban League Fam Planning Prgm, proj dir, nurse, 1974-75; Coatesville Vet Adminstrn Hosp, Intensive Care Unit, staff nurse, 1976-77. **Home Addr:** 79 Gilbert Ave, New Haven, CT 06511.

## MCBRIDE, TOD ANTHONY

Football player. **Personal:** Born Jan 26, 1976, Los Angeles, CA. **Educ:** Univ Calif, Los Angeles, grad. **Career:** Football player (retired); Green Bay Packers, defensive back, 1999-2002, left cornerback, 2000, 2002, right cornerback, 2002; Atlanta Falcons, right cornerback, 2003; St Louis Rams, cornerback, 2004; Seattle Seahawks, 2004.

## MCBRIDE, DR. ULYSSES

Educator. **Personal:** Born Nov 27, 1938, Atmore, AL; son of George and Mamie; married Mabel Copridge; children: Valeri. **Educ:** Knoxville Col, BA, 1959; Ind Univ, MA; Auburn Univ, PhD, 1974; Ala State Univ, Montgomery, doctoral degree, law, 1990; Univ NY, Stony Brook, Coe fel; Troy State Univ, post doctoral studies. **Career:** James H Faulkner Col, prof, sec social sci, dean, 1988-; Escambia Cty Training Sch, Atmore AL, teacher, coach; No Norman HS Brewton AL, dir; Ala State Univ, dept chair, prof & adj prof; Faulkner State Community Col, dean; Reid State Tech Col, pres. **Orgs:** Past grand polemarch, Kappa Alpha Psi Fraternity, 1988-91, pres, 1989-; pres, Escambia City Teachers Asn; pres, Faulkner State Col Educ Asn; dist dir, Ala Coun Social Studies; Polemarch S Prov KAY; Kappa Delta Pi; Alpha Kappa Mu; dir, United Fund; bd mem, Ala Libr; mem grand bd dir, Kappa Alpha Psi; Pensions & Security Bd Escambia County; chmn bd dir, Ala Dem Conf; reader, Fed Grants Wash DC; dir, Self Study Southern Asn Col & Schs Faulkner State Col.; interim pres, Bishop State Community Col. **Honors/Awds:** Teacher of the Year, Faulkner State Col, 1974; Atmore Area Hall of Fame, 2010; Achievement Awards. **Special Achievements:** The 100 Most Influential Black Americans, Johnson Publishers 1989. **Home Addr:** 173 M L King Ave, PO Box 1026, Atmore, AL 36502-1527, **Home Phone:** (251)368-3030. **Business Addr:** Grand Polemarch, Kappa Alpha Psi Fraternity Inc, 2322-24 N Broad St, Philadelphia, PA 19132, **Business Phone:** (215)228-7184.

## MCBURROWS, GERALD

Football player. **Personal:** Born Oct 7, 1973, Detroit, MI. **Educ:** Univ Kans, BA, mgt, 1994. **Career:** St Louis Rams, defensive back, 1995, strong safety, 1996, defensive back, 1997, 1998; Atlanta Falcons, strong safety, 1999-2003, free safety, 2000, 2002; free agt, currently.

## MCCAA, JOHN K.

Television journalist, naval officer. **Personal:** Born Feb 24, 1954, Rantoul, IL; son of Johnnie and Margaret Britt; married Michele Moore; children: Collin. **Educ:** Creighton Univ, Omaha, NE, BA, jour & mass commun, 1976; Univ Dallas, MS, polit, 2002; Univ Tex, Dallas, PhD, hist ideas, 2008-. **Career:** WOWT-TV, Omaha, Nebr, reporter & photogr, 1976-84, reporter, 1984-2009; WFAA-TV, Fortworth, reporter, Dallas, TX, chief newsroom, anchor & mgr, 1984-2011; WFAA TV/Channel 8, news anchor/reporter, 1984-; Belo Corp, news anchor, 1984-. **Orgs:** Pres, Dallas-Ft Worth Asn Black Communicators, 1984-; Nat Asn Black Journalists, 1987-; pres, Press Club Dallas. **Business Addr:** News Manager, Anchor, WFAA-TV, 606 Young St, Dallas, TX 75202, **Business Phone:** (214)977-6213.

## MCCABE, JEWELL JACKSON

Association executive, consultant. **Personal:** Born Aug 2, 1945, Washington, DC; daughter of Harold Hal and Julia O Hawkins; married Frederick Ward; married Eugene L Jr. **Educ:** Bard Col, lib arts, 1966. **Career:** Receptionist, 1969; NY Urban Coalition, dir pub affairs, 1970-73; Spec Serv C, pub rel officer, 1973-75; Women's Div Off Gov, NY, assoc dir pub info, 1975-77; WNET-TV/Thirteen, dir gov comt affairs, 1977-82; NCBW/Community Serv Fund, pres; Nat Coalition 100 Black Women, pres, 1976, founder & chair, 1978-; Jewell Jackson McCabe Assoc Inc, pres, currently. **Orgs:** bd dir, Bus Mkt Corp; NY Urban League; New York Planned Parenthood; Lenox Hill Hosp; Settlement Housing Fund Inc; Community Planning Bd four; Exec Comt, Asn Better NY; bd dir, Women's Forum; co-chair, Women United NY, Planned Parenthood New York Pub Issues & Answers; Edges; bd dir, Harlem Interfaith Coun Serv, Comt Coun Gr NY; David Rockefeller chmn, Policy Planning Comt, NY Partnership, founding mem, 1981-2000; New York Comn Status Women, 1982-2002; Reliance Group Holdings Inc; Alight.Com; New York Investment Fund LIC, founding mem, 1996-2001; Wharton Sch Bus; Bard Col; Nat Alliance Bus; Res Am; Nat Assoc Advan Colored People; Ny Coun; chair, New York States Job Training Partnership Coun. **Honors/Awds:** E Region Urban League Guild Award, 1979; Seagrams Civic Award, 1980; Links Civic Award, 1980; Dep Grand Marshal, Annual Martin Luther King Jr Parade, New York City, 1980; Outstanding Community Leadership Award, Malcolm King Col, 1980; The Jewell Jackson McCabe Emerging Leaders Institute Inc, named in honor, 2003; Hon Doctorate, Tougaloo Col & Iona Col; Citation, YWCA; Eastern Region Urban League Guild Award; Seagram's Civic Award. **Special Achievements:** Publications: Give A Damn, 1970-73; Women New York, 1975-77. **Business Addr:** Founder, President, National Coalition of 100 Black Women Inc, Capitol Hill Bus Ctr, Washington, DC 20001, **Business Phone:** (212)222-5660.

## MCCAIN, ELLA BYRD

Librarian, educator. **Personal:** Born Mar 8, 1925, Dothan, AL; daughter of Olivia Claudia Woods and Erskine; married John. **Educ:** Ala A&M Univ, Normal, BS, 1945; Univ Mich, Ann Arbor, MLS. **Career:** Educator, librarian (retired); Opelika Bd Educ, AL, teacher, 1945-47; Jefferson County Bd Educ, teacher, 1947-52, librn, 1952-72; SC State Col, vis instr, 1953; Atlanta Univ Sch Libr & Scis, Atlanta, Ga, asst prof, 1956-82; Rogers Area Voc Ctr, librn, 1972-87; John & Ella Byrd McCain Health & Coun Serv. **Orgs:** Ala State Dept Educ Accreditation Comt, 1954-67; pres, Ala Asn Sch Librarians, 1956-58; bd dir, Birmingham Int Educ Film Festival, 1985-; vol, Am Red Cross, 1986-; 2nd vpres, Birmingham Urban League Guild, 1989-; parliamentarian, Ala Instrnl Media Asn, 1989; vpres, Progressive Action Club Birmingham, AL; Jefferson County Retired Teachers Asn; Ala Retired Teachers Asn; pres, Ala Instrnl Media Asn; Am Asn Retired Persons; Am Voc Asn; Am Asn Sch Librarians; Asn Educ Commun & Technol; Phi Delta Kappa Fraternity; Friends Ala Libr; Univ Mich Alumni Asn; Ala A&M Univ Alumni Asn; Seasoned Performers; vol, Mc Wane Ctr. **Home Addr:** 1 Green Springs Ave SW, Birmingham, AL 35211.

## MCCALL, BARBARA COLLINS

Educator. **Personal:** Born Nov 17, 1942, Norfolk, VA; daughter of Gladys George Collins and Joseph Collins Sr; children: Monsita, Monique Lavitia & Clifton III. **Educ:** Norfolk State Univ, BS, 1965, MA, 1982. **Career:** Norfolk State Univ, confidential secy & pres, 1966-75, instr eve Col, 1970, asst dir couns upward bound, 1975-76, dir asst instr irc, 1976-81, instr, Engl Lang skills Ctr, 1981-91, asst dir writing ctr & Eng instr, 1991-, Dept Eng, asst prof, currently. **Orgs:** Secy, Lambda Chap, Nat Sorority Phi Delta Kappa Alpha, 1985-87, treas; Nat Coun Negro Women, Nat Asn Negro Bus & Prof Womens Club Norfolk; charter mem, Metrop Club; fac advisor, Sigma Tau Delta Nat Eng Hon Soc, 1987-; Delta Sigma Theta Sorority, Chesapeake-VA Beach Alumnae Chap, 1990-; Citizens Drug Adv Comn, app Chesepeake, VA mayor Dr William Ward, 1991-; Col Lang Asn; Nat Coun Teacher Eng. **Home Addr:** 3032 Sunrise Ave, Chesapeake, VA 23324, **Home Phone:** (757)545-6695. **Business Addr:** Assistant Professor, Norfolk State University, 700 Pk Ave, Norfolk, VA 23504, **Business Phone:** (757)823-2371.

## MCCALL, REV. DR. EMMANUEL LEMUEL, SR.

Clergy. **Personal:** Born Feb 4, 1936, Sharon, PA; son of George and Myra Mae Preston; married Emma Marie Johnson; children: Emmanuel Jr & Evalya Lynette. **Educ:** Univ Louisville, BA, 1958; Southern Baptist Theol Sem, BD, 1962, MRE, 1963, MDiv, 1967; Emory Univ, Dmin, 1976. **Career:** Simmons Bible Col, Louisville, prof, 1958-68; Twenty-eighth St Baptist Church, Louisville, pastor, 1960-68; Coop Ministries Nat Baptist, Southern Baptist Conv, assoc dir, 1968-74, dir dept black church rels home missions bd, 1974-88; Southern Baptist Theol Sem Louisville, vis fac, 1970-96; Black Church Exten Div, Home Mission Bd, SBC, dir, 1989-91; Christian Fel Baptist Church, pastor, 1991-2004; Mercer Univ Sch Theol, adj prof, 1996-; Emory Univ, vis prof baptist studies; Mercer Univ, McAfee Sch Theol, adj prof, currently; Fel Group, founding pastor; Nat Coop Baptist Fel, moderator, 2006-07; Fel Group Baptist Church, pastor, currently. **Orgs:** Bd dir, Morehouse Sch Relig, 1972-85; Am Soc Missionology, 1975-80; bd trustee, Interdenominational Theol Ctr, 1978-2002, from co-chmn to chmn, 1990-96; pres, Nat Alumni Asn; pres, Southern Baptist Sem Alumni Asn, 1991-92; bd trustee, Atlanta Univ Ctr, 1993-96; trustee, Truett McConnell Col, 1994-98; vpres, chair, Ethics Baptist World Alliance, 1995-2000; vice chair, Ga Asn Pastoral Care, 1997-99, chair, 1999-2001. **Honors/Awds:** Hon DD, Simmons Bible Col, 1965; Ambassador of Goodwill, City of Louisville, 1967; Hon DD United Theol Sem, 1977; Victor T Glass Award Home Mission Bd So Bapt Conv, 1979; E Y Mullins Denominational Service Award, Southern Bapt Theol Sem, 1990, E Y Mullins Humanitarian Award; American Baptist College, 1990; James H Costen Award, Interdenominational Theol Ctr; Inducted, M.L. King Board of Preachers, Morehouse Col, 1999. **Home Addr:** 3280 Hazelwood Dr SW, Atlanta, GA 30311. **Business Addr:** Adjunct Professor, Mercer University, 3001 Mercer Univ Dr, Atlanta, GA 30341-4155, **Business Phone:** (888)471-9922.

## MCCALL, H. CARL

Executive, government official, chairperson. **Personal:** Born Oct 17, 1935, Boston, MA; son of Herman (deceased) and Caroleasa Ray (deceased); married Cecilia; children: Marci; married Joyce S Brown. **Educ:** Dartmouth Col, BA, 1958; Univ Edinburgh; Andover-Newton Theol Sch, Mdiv. **Career:** Comptroller (retired), teacher; bank manager, politics, ambassador; UN under Pres Jimmy Carter; NY State Div Human Right, comnr; State NY, sen, 1974-79; WNET-TV, sr vpres, 1981; NY State, cand lt gov, 1982; state; s comnr, 1983-84; Citicorp, vpres, 1985-93; Human Rights, NY City Bd Educ, pres, 1991-93; State NY, comptroller, 1994-2003; NYSE, chmn bd Audit & Finance comt, 1999-2003; Bd Comt Corp Accountability, co-chair, 1999-2003; bd mem, Tyco Intl, 2003-; HealthPoint, vice chmn, currently. **Orgs:** Dir, Blue Hill Protestant Ctr, 1961-63; dir, church comt serv NY City Missionary Soc, 1964-; proj dir, Taconic Found Inc, 1964-66; Founder, pres, Inner City Broadcasting Corp; chmn, ed bd NY Amsterdam news; dep admin, NY City Human Resources Admin; chmn, NY City Coun Against Poverty, 1966-69; ordained minister, United Church Christ; preaching minister, Met Comt Methodist Church Harlem; trustee, NY Med Col; vice chmn, bd Ctr NY Affairs New Sch; Gamma Delta Chi; Alpha Phi Alpha; bd dir, NYSE, 1999-2003; bd mem, Apollo Theater Found; bd mem, Fiscal Control Bd, bd mem, SUNY, currently; bd mem, TYCO Int; bd mem, TAG Entertainment Corp; bd mem, Ariel Mutual Fund; chmn, Ny Pub Higher Educ Conf Bd. **Business Addr:** Board Director, State University of New York, State Univ Plz 353 Broadway, Albany, NY 12246, **Business Phone:** (518)320-1100.

## MCCALL, NATHAN

Journalist, writer. **Personal:** Born Jan 1, 1955, Portsmouth, VA; children: Monroe, Ian & Maya. **Educ:** Norfolk State Univ, BA, jour, 1981. **Career:** Va Pilot & Ledger Star, reporter; Atlanta Const, reporter; Wash Post, reporter, 1989, writer; Atlanta J-Const, reporter; Virginian Pilot-Ledger Star; Emory Univ, Dept African Am Studies, Jour Prog, sr lectr, currently; Novel: Them, 2007; Author: "Makes Me Wanna Holler: A Young Black Man in America", 1994; "What's Going On", 1997, "Them". **Orgs:** Fac mem, African Am Studies dept; Nat Action Network; an orgn dedicated to social activism. **Honors/Awds:** Blackboard Book of the Year, 1955; Hon DHL, Martin University; Townsend Prize for Fiction, 2008. **Special Achievements:** Has written numerous articles and essays; award-winning author; Ernest J. Gaines Award for Literary Excellence, nominee; Hurston/ Wright Legacy Award for Debut Fiction, nominee, 2008 outstanding novel, nominee. **Business Addr:** Senior Lecturer, Emory University, 201 Dowman Dr, Atlanta, GA 30322, **Business Phone:** (404)727-6123.

## MCCALL, PATRICIA

State government official. **Personal:** Born Jul 29, 1948, Columbus, OH; daughter of Theodore Hollingsworth Sr (deceased) and Mildred L (deceased); children: Stacie R. **Educ:** Franklin Univ, attended 1981. **Career:** State Ohio Civil Rights Comn, secy, typist, 1973-74, admin asst, clerk staff supvr, 1974-80, civil rights compliance coordr, compliance Officer, 1980-99; Mary Kay Cosmetics, beauty consult, 1996-; spec enforcement Officer, 1999-; MCS Properties, owner. **Orgs:** Nat Asn Human Rights Workers, 1989-, Hosp chap; spec communion minister, Christ King Cath Church, 1986-, women's club, 1980-; tutor, math, reading, Eastgate Elem Sch, 1991-; steward secy, treas, OCSEA-AFSCMECHA 2540, 1986-, lead educ advocate, 1997-; secy, Christ King Cath Sch Bd, 1983-86, combined charitable co-coord, 1992-98; secy, Bishop Hartley Athletic Bd, 1986-89; Nat Nominating Com, Outstanding Young Ams, 1996-; Christ King Church Coun, 2000-03. **Honors/Awds:** San Kuy Ninjabudo Martial Arts, Third Degree Brown Belt, 1972; Model of the Year, D&W Alinatha Estello Modeling Agency, 1977; Outstanding Young Woman of America, 1984. **Home Addr:** 3469 Liv-Moor Dr, Columbus, OH 43227, **Home Phone:** (614)235-0099. **Business Addr:** Special Enforcement Officer, State of Ohio Civil Rights Commission, 1111 E Broad St Suite 301, Columbus, OH 43215, **Business Phone:** (614)466-7384.

## MCCALLUM, LEO. See SALAAM, DR. ABDUL.

## MCCAMMON, MARQUES

Association executive, executive. **Personal:** children: 3. **Educ:** NC Agr & Tech State Univ, BS, mech engineering, 1998; Univ Mich, MS, mech engineering, 2002. **Career:** DaimlerChrysler's Chrysler Group, Prod Strategy Team, sr analyst, 2001-03; ASC Inc, dir prod & bus planning, 2003-06; Am Specialty Cars Inc, gen mgr w coast design & develop opers, 2006-07; Saleen, gen mgr, 2007-08; Aptera Motors, chief mkt officer, 2008-11. NSTIG8, founder, managing dir, 2012-14; NimbleSott, co-founder, 2012-; Wind River, Sr Dir Auto Prod, 2014-16, gen mgr, 2016-. **Orgs:** X Prize Found; bd dir, Boys & Girls Club Vista; bd mem, Pac Southwest Sport Asn, 2010-. **Honors/Awds:** Boys & Girls Club of Vista Helping Hands Award; National Association of Black Automotive Suppliers Young Leader, 2003; Inaugural Chrysler Group "Everyday Hero", 2003; Automobile Hall of Fame, Young Leaders Nominee, 2005, 2006. **Special Achievements:** Young Leaders Nominee for the Automobile Hall of Fame in 2005 and 2006; one of Detroits top 40 execs under the age of 40. **Business Addr:** General Manager, Wind River, 500 Wind River Way, Alameda, CA 94501, **Business Phone:** (510)748-4100.

## MCCAMPBELL, RAY IRVIN

Songwriter, singer. **Personal:** Born Jun 22, 1959, Flint, MI; son of Victoria and Ellsworth. **Educ:** Olivet Col, Olivet MI, Music, 1979; Tex Southern Univ, Houston TX, BA, commn, 1982. **Career:** Self Employed, saxophonist, 1975-77, singer, 1977-82, singer/songwriter, 1983-87; MCA Records, Los Angeles, Calif, singer/songwriter, 1987; Lorimar Productions, Los Angeles CA, actor, 1988; Albums: The Mac Band, 1988; Love U 2 the Limit, 1990; The Real Deal, 1991; Singles: "Jealous", 1989; "Roses are Red", 1989; "Stalemate", 1989; "That's the Way I Look at Love", 1989; "Love U 2 the Limit", 1990; "Someone to Love", 1990; "Everything", 1992. **Orgs:** Kappa Alpha Psi Fraternity, 1980-; Oak Cliff Bible Fel, 1983-. **Honors/Awds:** Symphonic Award, Flint Northwestern High Sch, 1977; NBA Pre Game Song, Dallas Mavericks, 1988; Appearance, Lorimar Productions, 1988; NBA Legend's All star Pre Game Song, NBA, 1989; Soul Train Performance, 1988; McDonald's Commercial, 1989; Dallas City Proclamation, 1989;

Houston City Proclamation, 1989; Arsenio Hall Show Performance, 1989. **Home Addr:** 921 Mockingbird Ln, Glenn Heights, TX 75154-8415.

## MCCANE, CHARLOTTE ANTOINETTE

Educator. **Personal:** Born Oct 1, 1937, Washington, DC; daughter of Charles A (deceased) and Margaret Perea (deceased). **Educ:** Albright Col, BA, hist; Univ Mysore, India, Fullbright Grant, 1964; N Western Univ, NDEA Grant, 1968; Fairleigh-Dickinson Univ, MA, hist. **Career:** Educator (retired); New London CT Bd Ed, educr, 1957; Red Bank NJ Bd Ed, educr, 1957-69; Ridgewood NJ Bd Ed, educr, 1969-94. **Orgs:** Group leader World Youth Forum Tour Europe, 1965; Oper Cross roads Africa Liberia, 1966; mem eval comt, Mid State Asn Sec Sch; mem eval comt, Yorkers & Hempstead Sch; NASDTEC Eval Comn, Princeton Univ, Glassboro State; assoc inst, adv comm Racism & Social Justice Nat Coun Social Studies; sec & treas, Multicultural Ed SIG Life Assoc Study Afro-Am Life & Hist Am Asn Univ Women; Nat Asn Advan Colored People; life mem, Nat Coun Negro Women; Falmouth Woman's Club; AARP; Falmouth Sr Ctr; Anti-Racism Task Force; sec, Falmouth Women's Club; secy, Cape CodHollyberry Quilter's Guild, 2000-02. **Honors/Awds:** Falmouth Year of the Reader Comn, 2002. **Home Addr:** 493 Old Meeting House Rd, East Falmouth, MA 02536-4826, **Home Phone:** (508)457-1250.

## MCCANN, RENETTA

College teacher, advertising executive, media executive. **Personal:** Born Dec 8, 1958, Chicago, IL; married Kevin Williams; children: Ella & Alexander. **Educ:** Northwestern Univ, BS, 1978, MS, 2011. **Career:** Leo Burnett, client serv trainee, 1978-79, media supvry, 1979-82, asst media dir, 1982-86, vpres, 1986-88, media dir, 1989-95, sr vpres, 1995-99; Starcom MediaVest Group, chief exec officer, 1999-2008; Vivaki, chief talent officer, 2008-09; BPI Group, coach, 2012; Renetta McCann LLC, prin, 2012-; Leo Burnett U.S., chief talent officer, 2012-; Northwestern Univ, adj fac mem, 2016-. **Orgs:** Genius Motion, 2011-; Ctr Excellence Advert, 2011-; Chicago Shakespeare Theater, 2011-; Ancona Sch, 2011-. **Honors/Awds:** Pantheon Award, 4A's; Diversity Achievement Award, American Advertising Federation; Corporate Executive of the Year, Black Enterprise Magazine; named one of Essence's 50 Women Who Are Changing the World, Ebony's 57 Most Intriguing Blacks, Wall Street Journal's Top 50 Women to Watch, and Forbes' 100 Most Powerful Women. **Business Addr:** Walter Annenberg Hall, Evanston, IL 60208.

## MCCANNON, DINDGA FATIMA

Writer, educator, artist. **Personal:** Born Jul 31, 1947?, Harlem, NY; daughter of Ralph Miller and Lottie Porter Miller; married Percival E; children: Afrodesia (Zumhagen) & Harmarkhis. **Educ:** Bob Blackburn Workshop, Nyumba Ya Sanaa Galleries, NY. **Career:** Artist, auth, illusrator, painter, printmaker fashion designer, quiltmaker, teacher, fiber artist, currently; Books: Peaches, Dell, 1977; Wilhemina Jones, Future Star, Delacorte, 1980. **Orgs:** Where We At, Black Women Artists; New York Found Arts; Black Artist Am; African Americans Visual Arts. **Home Addr:** 800 Riverside Dr Apt 1B, New York, NY 10032-7403, **Home Phone:** (212)781-4585. **Business Addr:** Artist, 800 Riverside Dr, New York, NY 10032, **Business Phone:** (212)781-4585.

## MCCANTS, ALVIN KEITH. See MCCANTS, KEITH.

## MCCANTS, PROF. JENNIFER BARNES

Educator. **Educ:** Tenn State Univ, BS; Ind Univ, MDS; Meharry Med Col, DDS. **Career:** Univ Louisville Sch Dent, Diag Sci Prosthodontics & Restorative Dent, asst prof. **Business Addr:** Assistant Professor, General Practitioner, University of Louisville School of Dentistry, 501 S Preston St Suite 334, Louisville, KY 40202, **Business Phone:** (502)852-1233.

## MCCANTS, KEITH (ALVIN KEITH MCCANTS)

Football player. **Personal:** Born Apr 19, 1968, Mobile, AL. **Educ:** Univ Ala, gen studies. **Career:** Football player (retired), diver; Tampa Bay Buccaneers, linebacker & defensive end, 1990, right defensive end, 1991-92; Houston Oilers, 1993-94; Ariz Cardinals, linebacker & defensive end, 1994-95. **Honors/Awds:** Defensive Player of the Year, CBS-TV, 1989; Butkus Award Runner Up, 1989; Iron Bowl Most Valuable Player, 1989. **Special Achievements:** First black marine police officer in the state of Alabama.

## MCCANTS, DR. ODELL

Physician. **Personal:** Born Sep 5, 1942, Winnsboro, SC; married Laura; children: Odell Jr. **Educ:** Howard Univ, BS, 1965, MD, 1970. **Career:** Howard Univ Hosp, internship, 1970-71, resident, 1972-75; Automobiles Int, chief exec officer; Greater SE Comm Hosp, pres & designate; Automobiles Int, broker & founder; pvt pract, 1975-. **Orgs:** Fel Am Col Obstetricians & Gynecologists; Int Col Surgeons; mayor's task force, Adolescent Health City Alexandria, VA; instr, Howard Univ Col Med; bd dir, Northern VA, 1978-79; house specialist, Alexandria Hosp & Dept Health Commonwealth, VA, 1982; dir, United Black Fund, WA; mem & bd dir, Am Cancer Soc. **Honors/Awds:** Daniel Hale Williams Award, Asn Former Residents & Interns Freedmen's Hosp. **Business Addr:** Physician, Private Practice, 4717 Marshall Ave, Newport News, VA 23607, **Business Phone:** (757)380-8709.

## MCCARRELL, CLARK GABRIEL, JR.

Mechanical engineer. **Personal:** Born Apr 13, 1958, Chicago, IL; son of Clark G Sr and Melva Lee Washington; married Errika; children: Clayton Gabriel. **Educ:** Wright Col, Chicago Ill, AA, 1984; Wash Col, Chicago Ill, dipl, comput sci, 1986; Univ Nev, Las Vegas NV, BS, mech engineering, 1991, MS, engineering mgt, 1999. **Career:** Donohue & Assocs, Milwaukee, Wis, engineering aide, 1978-80; Consult Consortium, Chicago, Ill, engineering apprentice, 1980-82; Dunham & Assocs, Las Vegas, NV, mech designer, 1986-87; Sci Appln Inter Corp, Santa Barbara, Calif, CAE designer, 1987-88; Clark County Sch Dist, Las Vegas, NV, CAD designer, 1989-90; Southwest Gas Corp, Las Vegas, NV, 1990-2002; Univ Phoenix, Las Vegas, instr, area chair, 2001-; NV Energy Inc, sr engr, 2004-; Nev Power Co, Las Vegas, NV, sr proj mgr & sr engr, 2005-; Univ Nev, Las Vegas, NV, Dept Mech Engineering, Adv Bd, mem, currently. **Orgs:** Am Soc Mech Engineering, 1977-, vpres leadership & diversity, 2001-09; Nat Soc Black Engrs, 1979-; asst prog coordr, Ray Col Design, 1983-86; Diaconate Bd, Congional Church Pk Manor United Church Christ, 1984-86; Nat Fire Protection Asn; Procurement consult, Nev Econ Develop Co, 1986; Am Nuclear Soc, 1987-88, Am Soc Plumbing Engineering, 1987, Nat Soc Prof Engineering; pres, Am Soc Heating, Vent & Air Conditioning Engrs, 1989; Stud Adv Comt, Univ Nev Las Vegas, 1990; pres, TNBA Mixed Bowling League, Las Vegas, 1994-; deacon, 1994-96, ecclesiastical dir, 2001-, Mountain Top Faith Ministries, Las Vegas; Opers & Maintenance Aux, Toastmasters Int, 1993; dir, treas, Daybreak Christian Fel 1998-2000; bd chmn, Howard R Hughes Col Engineering; bd dir alumni, Univ Nev Las Vegas; sr vpres, Am Soc Mech Engrs. **Honors/Awds:** Outstanding Alumni Award, Hales Franciscan High Sch, Chicago Ill, 1994; Outstanding Alumnus Award, Univ Nev, Las Vegas, 1997; Faculty Member of the Year Award, Univ Phoenix, 2007. **Home Addr:** PO Box 95351, Las Vegas, NV 89193, **Home Phone:** (702)287-3306. **Business Addr:** Senior Project Manager, Generation Planning & Engineering, Nevada Power Co, 6226 W Sahara Ave, Las Vegas, NV 89146, **Business Phone:** (702)367-5381.

## MCCARTHY, GREGORY O'NEIL (GREG MCCARTHY)

Baseball player. **Personal:** Born Oct 30, 1968, Norwalk, CT. **Career:** Baseball player (retired), baseball coach; Cleveland Indians, free agt; Chicago White Sox, free agt, 1994; Seattle Mariners, pitcher, 1996-98; Macon Peaches, pitcher, 2003; Atlantic City Surf, pitcher, 2004; Mosquito Athletics Attnang-Puchheim, head coach, 2009; AVG Draci Brno, coach, 2010.

## MCCARTY, WALTER LEE

Basketball player, basketball coach. **Personal:** Born Feb 1, 1974, Evansville, IN; married Erin; children: Gabrielle & Sasha. **Educ:** Univ Ky, BA, commun, 1996. **Career:** Basketball player (retired), basketball coach; New York Knicks, forward & power forward, 1996-97; Boston Celtics, Small forward, 1997, power forward, 1998-2005, asst coach, 2013-14; Phoenix Suns, forward, 2005; Los Angeles clippers, forward & power forward, 2005-06; Univ Louisville, asst coach, 2007-10; Ind Pacers, asst coach, 2010-11. **Orgs:** Founder, I Love Music Found, 2002. **Honors/Awds:** Championship, Nat Col Athletic Asn, 1996. **Special Achievements:** Film Appeared: He Got Game, 1998; Solo album: "Moment for Love", 2003. **Home Addr:** , Lincoln, MA. **Business Addr:** Assistant Coach, Boston Celtics, 226 Causeway St 4th Fl, Boston, MA 02114, **Business Phone:** (617)854-8000.

## MCCASKILL, CAROLYN

Writer, counselor, educator. **Personal:** children: Jamel & Deron. **Educ:** Gallaudet (Col) Univ, BA, psychol & minor social work, 1977, MA, coun deaf, 1979, PhD, spec educ admin & supv, 2005; Ala Sch Deaf (Talladega). **Career:** Gallaudet Univ, assoc prof, deaf studies dept, 1996-, Cult & Lang Colloquium, assoc prof, 1999, coordr deaf studies prog, 2005-; Diversity Felsgallaudet Univ Representing Acad Affairs, 2006-07; Model Sec Sch Deaf, several positions incl residence & high sch counr; Houston Community Col Syst, Counr. **Orgs:** Nat Asn Deaf; Nat Black Deaf Advocates; Gallaudet Univ Alumni Asn; Dc's Chap Black Deaf Advocates. **Honors/Awds:** Thomas & Julia Mayes Award, 2005; Gallaudet University, Provost office, Diversity Fellow, 2006, and Office of Diversity & Inclusion, Diversity Fellow, 2011-12; TheGrio.com, 100 Making History Today, 2012, 2013; National Action Network, Deaf Humanitarian Award, 2013. **Special Achievements:** Second deaf African American female to complete the Ph.D. program at Gallaudet; has given numerous presentations on topics related to deafness and diversity issues; co-authored the 1992 publication "A Minority Within a Minority: Being Black, Deaf and a Female" with sister Angela McCaskill; co-author of the groundbreaking book/DVD on the evolution of ASL within the African American community, "The Hidden Treasures of Black ASL: Its History and Structure," May 2011. **Business Addr:** Associate Professor, Gallaudet University, Sorenson Lang & Commun Ctr (SLCC) 1203, Washington, DC 20002, **Business Phone:** (202)250-2337.

## MCCAULEY, JAMES R.

Government official. **Personal:** Born Nov 6, 1952, Rochester, NY; son of James and Virginia; married Carolyn; children: James, John & Kelli. **Educ:** St John Fisher Col, BA, 1975. **Career:** Monroe County, Off Employ & Training, mgr emp serv, Child Support Enforcement, asst admin, Child Support, ct liaison, investr, regional dir, Div Affirmative Action, Employ Serv & Affirmative Action, mgr. **Orgs:** Vpres, bd dir, Monroe County, Fed Credit Union; bd dir, Camp Good Days & Spec Times; adv bd, Boces I; adv bd, United Way, human resources; usherbd, Mt Oliver Bapt Church, men's chorus; adv bd, Baden St Settlement. **Honors/Awds:** Coordinator of the Year, United Way, 1998; Outstanding Service, Urban League, 1998. **Special Achievements:** Renegotiated all county contracts for a cost savings to County approximately $5300/month, 1992. **Home Addr:** 449 Fernwood Ave, Rochester, NY 14609, **Home Phone:** (716)467-6953.

## MCCLAIN, ANDRE

Circus performer, singer. **Personal:** Born Kansas City, MO; son of Lu; married Daniele. **Educ:** Univ Mo, Kans, MO, BA, bus mgt, 2000. **Career:** Three Ring Adventure 133rd Eds, host; Ringling Bros & Barnum & Bailey, singer, songwriter, trick roper, rodeo cowboy, ringmaster, horse & camel trainer, currently. **Orgs:** Int Prof Rodeo Asn. **Business Addr:** Cowboy, Animal Trainer, Ringling Bros & Barnum & Bailey, 8607 Westwood Ct, Vienna, VA 22182, **Business Phone:** (703)790-2500.

## MCCLAIN, ANDREW BRADLEY

School administrator, lawyer. **Personal:** Born Nov 12, 1948, Akron, OH; son of Andrew H and Margaret L Greene; children: Andrew & Peter. **Educ:** Univ Akron Sch Law, Akron, OH, BA, 1970, JD, 1988; Kent State Univ, Kent, OH, attended 1978. **Career:** Akron Bd Educ, eng teacher, 1970-73; Western Reserve Acad, Upward Bound, dir, 1973-87; Univ Akron, Upward Bound, dir, 1987, Pre Col Progs, dir, 1988, Acad Achievement Progs, dir, currently; pvt pract atty, currently. **Orgs:** Consult A Better Chance, 1975-86; dir, Sch Scholar Serv, 1979-84; consult, Mid-South Assoc Independent Schs, 1981-83, Marquette Univ, 1984; African Am Male Community, 1989-; dir & pres state chap, Mid-Am Asn Educ Opportunity Prog Personnel, treas, 1992-95; Nat Asn Advan Colored People; consult, Nat Coun Educ OpportunityAsn; parlamentarian, Nat Coun Educ Opportunity Asns, 1993-94; Akron Bar Asn; Ohio State Bar Asn, currently. **Home Addr:** 1004 Amelia Ave, Akron, OH 44302, **Home Phone:** (330)864-6558. **Business Addr:** Attorney, A Bradley Mcclain Law Office, 209 S Main St Suite 800 8th Fl, Akron, OH 44308-1307, **Business Phone:** (330)535-4450.

## MCCLAIN, DR. PAULA DENICE

Educator. **Personal:** Born Jan 3, 1950, Louisville, KY; daughter of Robert Landis and Mabel T Molock; married Paul Crane Jacobson; children: Kristina L McClain-Jacobson Ragland & Jessica A McClain-Jacobson. **Educ:** Howard Univ, Wash, DC, BA, 1972, MA, polit sci, 1974, PhD, 1977. **Career:** Adaptive Systs Annapolis, consult, 1976; Howard Univ, Social Sci Res Ctr, consult, 1976; Univ Wis-Milwaukee, Milwaukee, Wis, asst prof polit sci studies & African Am studies, 1977-81; Univ Pa, Wharton Sch, Anal Ctr, res assoc, 1981-82; Ariz State Univ, Tempe, Ariz, assoc prof, prof, 1982-90, Doctorate Pub Admin Prog, actg dir, 1990, prof, 1990-91; Univ Va, prof govt & foreign affairs, 1991-2000, dept chair, 1994-97, Shannon Ctr Advan Studies, 1997-98; Duke Univ, Dept Polit Sci, prof, 2000-; Duke Univ, prof law, pub policy & African Am studies, currently; Duke Univ, Ctr Study Race, Ethnic & Gender, co-dir, 2004-; Duke Univ, Grad Sch & Vice Provost Grad Educ, dean 2013-. Books: Alienation and Resistance: The Political Behavior of Afro-Canadians, auth, 1979; Urban Minority Administrators: Politics, Policy and Style, co-ed, 1988; Race, Place and Risk: Black Homicide in Urban America, co-auth, 1990; Minority Group Influence: Agenda Setting, Formulation and Public Policy, co-ed, 1993; Can We All Get Along? Racial and Ethnic Minorities in American Politics, auth, 2006, 2009, 2014; American Government in Black and White, co-auth, 2010; The Encyclopedia of Political Science, co-auth, 2010; American Government in Black and White, co-auth, 2014. **Orgs:** Phoenix Urban League, 1982-87; Midwest Polit Sci Asn, 1984; bd dir, Phoenix Black Theatre Troupe, 1986-87; Policy Studies Orgn, 1987-91; Am Polit Quart, ed bd, 1987-; pres, Nat Conf Black Polit Scientists, 1989-90; vpres, Am Polit Sci Asn; Womens Caucus Polit Sci, 1988-90; exec coun, Western Polit Sci Asn, 1989-92; pres, Southern Polit Sci Asn. **Special Achievements:** Became the third woman and the first African American elected to serve as Chair of Academic Council at Duke University, 2007-09. **Home Addr:** 9 Skipwith Ct, Durham, NC 27707. **Business Addr:** Professor of Political Science & Public Policy, Dean, Duke University, 2127 Campus Dr, Durham, NC 27708-0067, **Business Phone:** (919)681-1560.

## MCCLAIN, WILLIAM ANDREW. See Obituaries Section.

## MCCLAIN, WILLIAM L.

Automotive executive. **Personal:** Born Apr 25, 1958, Bronx, NY; son of Willie Lee and Jacqueline Francis Jackson Winters; married Pamela Kay Johnson. **Educ:** Ore State Univ, Corvallis, OR, BS, bus admin, 1981. **Career:** Westside Timber Inc, vpres, 1985-; Stayton Motors Inc, dealer, owner, 1985-; Jackies Ribs Inc, vpres, 1985-; Reedsport Motors Inc, dealer & owner, 1988-; Stayton Motorsports, pres, 1996-; Zale Corp, Salem, Ore, mgr. **Home Addr:** 3301 Wiltsey St, Salem, OR 97301, **Home Phone:** (503)769-6666. **Business Addr:** President, Stayton Motors Inc, 11361 Mill Creek Rd, Aumsville, OR 97325, **Business Phone:** (503)769-6666.

## MCCLAIN-THOMAS, DOROTHY MAE

Government official. **Personal:** Born Jun 17, 1931, Hartsville, SC; daughter of Eloise Eltridge and Chester; married Thurman McClain; children: Thurman Jr, Roxcella McClain Brown & Vaness McClain Smith; married Donald. **Educ:** Wash Tech Inst, cert, 1972; Howard Univ, attended 1980; Morgan State Univ. **Career:** Government Official (retired); DC Govt, clerk-typist, 1962-79; DC Govt Environ Serv, off supvr, 1975-79; DC Govt Newspaper Recycling, prog coordr, 1979-81; DC Govt Pub Works Mayor's Beautification Community, exec dir, 1984-89; McClain & Assocs. **Orgs:** Coun woman, Town Cheverly, Md, 1974-86; bd dir, Combine Communities Action, 1975-; bd dir, Md Munic League, 1977-78; pres, Iota Phi Lambda Sor Epsilon Delta Chap, 1979-81; dir, Ander-Mac Video Prod, 1983-84; Prince George's County Vol Action Ctr, S County rep, 1989-91; Prince George's County Pub Schs, Group Activ Leader Gladys Noon Spellman Elem Sch, 1991-; bd mem, Prince George's County Housing Develop Corp. **Honors/Awds:** Outstanding Job Performance, Dept Environ Serv, 1974, 1975, 1979, 1980; Outstanding Community Service, Los Amigos Serv Club, 1976; Plaque, 25th Legis Distinguished Alliance Club, 1976; Sorority of the Year, Iota Phi Lambda Sorority, 1984; Certificate of Appreciation, Dept Environ Serv Women's Prog, Adams-Morgan Comm, 1984. **Business Addr:** Staff, D T Enterprises, 6547 Bock Rd, Oxon Hill, MD 20745-3002.

## MCCLAMMY, DR. THAD C.

College president, state government official, real estate agent. **Personal:** Born Oct 22, 1942, Beatrice, AL; son of Ukla Maye and T C; married Patricia Larkins; children: Christopher & Patrice. **Educ:** Ala State Univ, Montgomery, AL, BA, 1966; Auburn Univ, Montgomery AL, MS, voc & adult educ, 1975; Selma Univ, LLD, 1982. **Career:** City Montgomery, AL, real estate officer & broker, 1968-68, developer, 1968-74; Lomax-Hannon Jr Col, Greenville, AL, develop officer, 1974; Trenholm State Tech Col, Montgomery AL, instr, 1974-77, dean, 1974-81, coordr community serv, 1977-81, pres, 1981-95; State Ala, House Rep, 76th Dist, Montgomery County, rep, 1994-; Capitol Realty, owner, 1995-; Nat Financial Secy Tots & Teens Inc, real estate broker & developer, currently. **Orgs:** Omega Psi Phi Frat, 1963-; Phi Delta Kappa Prof Coun; Press Club, Nat Dem Party, 1976-80; bd dirs, Montgomery Area United Way, 1982; Montgomery Lion's Club, 1987-; Ala & Montgomery Dem Confs; Adeen Oversight, 1998; Ment Health Adv, 1998; State Parks Oversight, 1998; chair, Black Belt Infrastructure Comt, 2000; St Matthews Baptist Church; Cosmospolital Civic Club; Kershaw YMCA; Phi Bolue; Ala & Nat Educ Asns; Southern Placement Coun; Iota Lambda Sigma Frat; chmn, House Pub Safety Comt; Montgomery Dem Club; Ala Educ Asn. **Honors/**

**Awds:** Honorary Doctor of Laws, Selma Univ. **Home Addr:** 3035 Rosa Pks Ave, Montgomery, AL 36105, **Home Phone:** (334)264-6767. **Business Addr:** Representative, State of Alabama, Rm 534-A 11 S Union St, Montgomery, AL 36130, **Business Phone:** (334)284-1769.

### MCCLANE, PROF. KENNETH ANDERSON, JR.
Educator, poet. **Personal:** Born Feb 19, 1951, New York, NY; son of Kenneth A and Genevieve Dora Greene; married Rochelle Evette Woods. **Educ:** Cornell Univ, AB, 1973, MA, 1974, MFA, 1976. **Career:** Colby Col, instr Eng, 1974-75; City Univ New York, asst dir SEEK, 1977-78; Williams Col, Luce, vis prof Eng, 1983-84; Cornell Univ, asst prof, lit, 1976-83, assoc prof, lit, 1983-89, prof, lit, 1989-206; prof emer, currently, WEB DuBois, prof Eng; Poems: "Out Beyond Bay", 1975; "Moons & Low Times", 1978; "At Winter's End", 1982; "A Tree Beyond Telling"; Take Five, 1987; Essays: "A Death Family", 1985; "Sch", 1985; Walls, 1991. **Orgs:** Dir, Cornell Univ, Creative Writing Prog, 1983-86; bd dir, Salton Stall Found; Epoch Mag, ed, 1984-86; script consult, "Bluest Eye", 1984; col scholar adv bd mem, Cornell Univ, 1984-; bd dir, Human Affairs Training Prog, 1986-; Mod Lang Asn, 1989-; bd trustee, Adelphi Univ, 2002; Stephen H Weiss Presidential Fel, 2004; Tompkins Co Libr Found. **Special Achievements:** In 1978 he was nominated for the Lamont Poetry Prize. **Home Addr:** 114 Glenside Rd, Ithaca, NY 14850, **Home Phone:** (607)277-3497. **Business Addr:** WEB Du Bois Professor of Literature, Cornell University, 278 Goldwin Smith Hall, Ithaca, NY 14853-3201, **Business Phone:** (607)255-9314.

### MCCLEARN, BILLIE MARIE
Activist, clergy. **Personal:** Born Aug 6, 1937, Cushing, TX; daughter of Charlie Smith and Ida G Smith; married Sylvester; children: Richard Kyle, Michael Anthony, Sylvester Darnell, Billy Cathel (deceased) & Alex Bernard. **Career:** Black Community Develop Inc, exec dir; First United Methodist Church, Newburgh, NY, community developer, currently. **Orgs:** Dir, Community Outreach. **Home Addr:** 101 Patton Rd, Newburgh, NY 12550-2481, **Home Phone:** (845)566-6585. **Business Addr:** Community Developer, First United Methodist Church, 241 Liberty St, Newburgh, NY 12550, **Business Phone:** (845)565-4267.

### MCCLELLAN, FRANK MADISON
Lawyer, educator. **Personal:** Born Feb 5, 1945, Marion, SC; married Linda J Hughey; children: Malik & Toussaint. **Educ:** Rutgers Univ, AB, 1967; Duquesne Univ, JD, 1970; Yale Univ, LLM, 1974. **Career:** Chief Judge William H Hastie, US Ct Appeals, law clerk, 1970-71; Wilmer Cutler & Pickering, assoc atty, 1971-72; Duquesne Univ, asst prof law, 1972-74, assoc prof law, 1974-76, prof law, 1981; Temple Univ, I Herman Stern prof law, prof law, prof law emer, Ctr Health Law, Policy & Pract, co-dir, currently, Sch Med, lectr, 1981-; Southern Ill Univ Sch Law, garwin distinguished visitor, law clerk, Chief Judge William H Hastie, US Ct Appeals; Wash DC law firm, assoc atty; Temple Univ Res & Creative Achievements Awards Comt, chair. **Orgs:** Pa Bar Asn; DC Bar Asn; bd dir, House Crossroads; law rev ed, United Way Rev Comn; Aids Law Proj; Philadelphia Fight; To Our C's Future With Health; Adv Coun Nat Heart; lead trial coun, Whittington v Episcopal Hosp; lead trial coun, Taylor v Einstein Med Ctr; pres, Pa Legal Serv Ctr; Nat Steering Comt Health Disparities Orthop Health; Heart, Lung & Blood Inst Nat Insts Health. **Honors/Awds:** Lindback Award for Distinguished Teaching, Temple Univ, 1986; Friel-Scanlon Prize for Outstanding scholarship, Temple Univ, 1995; Philadelphia Book Clinic Certificate of Award, 1995; George D Harris Memorial Award, 1999; Shusterman Alumni Faculty Award, Temple Law Alumni Asn, 2009; Phyllis S. Beck Chair Award; Herman Stern Chair Award for excellence in teaching; advisor, Inst Med; Am Law Inst; Soc Am Law Teachers; Merit Award; Felix S Cohen Prize in Jurisprudence. **Special Achievements:** First recipient of the Dr. George D. Harris Memorial Award, in recognition of his service as a founder and the first president of the Black Students Union at the university; Author: "Medical Malpractice: Law, Tactics & Ethics", 1995; Co author: "Torts: Cases, Problems & Materials", LexisNexis, 2007. **Home Addr:** 2361 Tilbury Ave, Pittsburgh, PA 15217. **Business Addr:** Professor of Law Emeritus, Co-Director, Temple University, 1719 N Broad St, Philadelphia, PA 19122, **Business Phone:** (215)204-1609.

### MCCLELLAND, MARGUERITE MARIE
Educator. **Personal:** Born Dec 6, 1919, St. Louis, MO; daughter of Brooks Manuel Sr and Minnie Mae Marshall; married John Clyde. **Educ:** Sch Art Inst Chicago, IL, BA, 1943; Wayne State Univ, Detroit, MI, MA, 1949; Temple Univ, Philadelphia, PA, attended 1963; Univ Mich, Ann Arbor, MI, attended 1975. **Career:** Educator (retired); Chicago Pub Schs, Chicago, Ill, art teacher, 1943-47; Detroit Pub Schs, Detroit, stud teacher & supvr; Wayne State Univ, teacher art educ, 1948-78, guid counr, 1963-78, guid dept head, 1978-83. **Orgs:** Alpha Kappa Alpha Sorority Inc, 1949; Am Guid Asn; Nat Coun Negro Women; Nat Assault Literacy; life mem, Nat Asn Advan Colored People; Nat Asn Univ Women; Org Sch Admins; Mich Personnel & Guid Asn; Mich Asn Career Educ; Detroit Sch Womens Asn; United Methodist Women; Top Ladies Distinction; Supreme basileus, Nat Sorority Phi Delta Kappa Inc, 1989-. **Home Addr:** 19211 Pennington Dr, Detroit, MI 48221, **Home Phone:** (313)861-4451. **Business Addr:** Supreme Basileus, Phi Delta Kappa Inc, 8233 S Martin Luther King Dr, Chicago, IL 60619, **Business Phone:** (812)339-1156.

### MCCLENDON, BISHOP CLARENCE E.
Clergy, educator, executive. **Personal:** Born Jun 7, 1965, Decatur, IL; son of Miriah and Rev Howell Levi; married Tammera; children: 4; married Priscilla Delgado. **Educ:** Friends Intl Christian Univ, PhD, 2001. **Career:** Harvest Fire Media Inc, chief exec officer; Clarence E McClendon Ministries, founder; Umbrella Corp, founder & pres; Siloam Bible Col, founder & pres; Clarence E McClendon Leadership Inst, founder & pres; Church Full Harvest Intl, sr pastor, currently. **Orgs:** Bishop's Coun, Full Gospel Baptist Church Fel Overseer Fel Rels; Intl Communion Charismatic Churches, Col Bishops; bd mem, Do Something Found; Calif Regent, Pres Bush's Faith Based Initiative Nat Ctr. **Honors/Awds:** Nominated, Stellar Award; Dove Award, Best New Gospel Artist Nominee, 2000. **Special Achievements:** Author: The X Blessing and When You Pray: The Key to Accessing the Presence of God; TV appearance: "Evening News", CBS; Nightline, ABC & Black Entertainment TV. **Home Addr:** 11736 Wetherby Lane, Los Angeles, CA 90077-1348. **Business Addr:** Founder, President, Clarence E McClendon Ministries, 1830 South La Cienega Blvd, Los Angeles, CA 90035, **Business Phone:** (310)323-2600.

### MCCLENDON, KELLEN
Lawyer, educator. **Personal:** Born May 7, 1944, New Castle, PA; son of Leroy and Sylest Butler; married Michele. **Educ:** Westminster Col, BA, 1966; Duquesne Univ Sch Law, 1974. **Career:** Pa Dept Justice, asst atty gen, 1974-79; pvt pract atty, 1979-82; City Pittsburgh, asst city solicitor, 1982-89; Robert Morris Col Legal Asst Prog, instr, 1985-89; Duquesne Univ Sch Law, adj prof, 1987-89, vis prof, 1989-90, asst prof, 1990-96, assoc prof, prof law, currently. **Orgs:** Allegheny County Bar Asn, 1974-; minority bus enterprise rev comn, City Pittsburgh, 1982-; bd dir, Housing Authority City Pittsburgh, 1990-. **Special Achievements:** Author: Do Hospitals Relieve the Government of Some of Its Burden?, 67 Temple Law Review 517, 1994; What the National Health Care Debate Tells Us About Whether Hospitals are Entitled to Exemption from Real Estate Taxes, 6 Widener Journal of Public Law 41, 1996; The Convergence of Thinking, Talking and Writing: A Theory for Improving Writing, 38 Duquesne Law Review 21, 1999; Fundamental Principles of Tort Law, Chapter 9 in Forensic Science and Law: Investigative Applications in Criminal, Civil & Family Justice 165-229, 2006. **Business Addr:** Professor of Law, Duquesne University, 600 Forbes Ave, Pittsburgh, PA 15282, **Business Phone:** (412)396-6300.

### MCCLENDON, LLOYD GLENN
Baseball manager, baseball player, baseball executive. **Personal:** Born Jan 11, 1959, Gary, IN; son of Grant and Hattie; married Ingrid Scott; children: Schenell & Beaudillio. **Educ:** Valparaiso Univ, attended 1981. **Career:** Baseball player (retired), athletic coach, baseball executive; Appalachian League, baseball player; New York Mets, 1980-82; Cincinnati Reds, 1987-88; Chicago Cubs, 1989-90; Pittsburgh Pirates, 1990-94, hitting coordr, 1996, hitting coach, 1997-2000, mgr, 2001-05; Detroit Tigers, bullpen coach, 2006-13; Seattle Mariners, mgr, currently. **Orgs:** Kappa Alpha Psi Fraternity; Four Div-Winning Clubs with Cubs, 1989. **Home Addr:** 2055 W 64th Pl, Merrillville, IN 46410. **Business Addr:** Manager, Seattle Mariners, Safeco Field, Seattle, WA 98194-0100, **Business Phone:** (206)346-4000.

### MCCLENDON, RAYMOND
Investment banker, chief executive officer, chairperson. **Personal:** married Ryland Needom; children: 4. **Educ:** Morehouse Col, BA, bus admin, 1972; Ga State Univ, MBA, finance, 1978. **Career:** City Atlanta, dir financial anal & auditing; Fed Nat Mortgage Asn, Mutli-Family Activ, vpres, 1984-88; R L McClendon Capital Corp, founder; Pryor, McClendon Counts & Co, vice chmn & chief exec officer, chief operating officer, 1990-97; iiQuest Consult, managing dir, 2006-; Gourmet Serv Inc, pres, 2007-. **Orgs:** Chmn, Nat Asn Securities Professionals, 1992-93; chmn & pres, 100 Black Men Atlanta, 1997-99; Atlanta Community; bd dir, Atlanta Interfaith Broadcasters, 2009-.

### MCCLENDON, REP. RUTH JONES
Government official. **Personal:** Born Oct 5, 1943, Houston, TX; married Denver; children: 4. **Educ:** Tex Southern Univ, BA, polit sci & hist; Webster Univ, MA, mgt; Guadalupe Col. **Career:** Worked with dysfunctional youth juv justice syst, 17 yrs; San Antonio city councilwoman & mayor pro tempore, 1993-96; Community Crime Prev Network Inc, founder; Nat Ctr Policy Alternatives, Fleming fel; RJMc Clendon & Co, pres & chief exec officer, currently; Tex House Representatives, rep, 1996-. **Orgs:** Sunset Adv Comn (SAC), 2006-10. **Home Addr:** 3811 Willowwood Blvd, San Antonio, TX 78219-2537, **Home Phone:** (210)281-9141. **Business Addr:** State Representative, Texas House of Representatives, 403 S WW White Rd Suite 210, San Antonio, TX 78219, **Business Phone:** (210)225-2107.

### MCCLENIC, PATRICIA L.
Administrator. **Personal:** Born Nov 13, 1947, Akron, OH; children: Richard L Jr, Dennis K & Nicole M. **Educ:** Akron Univ, BA, 1978. **Career:** WSLR Radio, dir pub affairs, 1970-75; United Way Summit City, dir comn, 1975-79; United Way S Hampton, dir comn, 1979-83; Am Cancer Soc, state pub info dir, 1983-84; United Way Am, Pub Rels, assoc dir, 1984-. **Orgs:** Pub Rels Soc Am; Int Asn Bus Comn; Nat Press Club, 1985. **Home Addr:** 6050 Haverhill Ct, Springfield, VA 22152. **Business Addr:** Associate Director, United Way of America, **Business Phone:** (703)836-7112.

### MCCLEON, DEXTER KEITH
Football coach, football player. **Personal:** Born Oct 9, 1973, Meridian, MS; children: Dexter Jr. **Educ:** Clemson Univ, attended 1996. **Career:** St Louis Rams, defensive back, 1997, right cornerback, 1998-2001, free safety, 1999, 2001, left cornerback, 2000-02, cornerback, 2000, 2002, strong safety, 2002; Kans City Chiefs, right cornerback, 2003-05; Houston Texans, cornerback, 2006; Meridian High Sch, asst football coach; Miles Col, Div II, cornerbacks coach, currently; Nat Football League, free agt, currently. **Home Addr:** , Hoover, AL. **Business Addr:** Cornerbacks Coach, Miles College, 5500 Myron Massey Blvd, Fairfield, AL 35064, **Business Phone:** (205)929-1100.

### MCCLESKEY, J. J. (THOMAS JOSEPH MCCLESKEY, JR.)
Football player. **Personal:** Born Apr 10, 1970, Knoxville, TN; married Susan R; children: Jalen Austin. **Educ:** Univ Tenn, BA, polit sci. **Career:** Football player (retired); New Orleans Saints, 1993-94, 1996, defensive back, 1995; Ariz Cardinals, defensive back, 1996-98, 2000, right cornerback, 1999. **Home Addr:** 156 Indian Trce, Madisonville, LA 70447-3006.

### MCCLESKEY, THOMAS JOSEPH, JR. See MCCLESKEY, J. J.

### MCCLINTON, CURTIS R., JR.
Investment banker. **Personal:** Born Jun 25, 1939, Muskogee, OK; married Devonne French; children: Tobi & Margot. **Educ:** Univ Kans, BS, 1962; Univ Nebr, sch banking; Cent Mich Univ, MPA; Univ Mo, Real Est Law; Am Inst Banking; Weaver Sch Real Est Pract Franklin Fin Serv Inst; Real Est Bd Inst; Wharton Sch, Univ Pa; Miles Col, PhD. **Career:** Football teams: Dallas Texans, halfback, 1962; Kans City Chiefs, halfback, 1963-69; Univ Kans, asst football coach & recruiter, 1962-63; Franklin Life Ins Co, ins salesman, 1963-; Interstate Securities, loan officer & collector, 1964-65; KPRS, tv, radio broadcaster, 1965-66; Douglass St Bank, community loan officer & asst cashier, 1965-67; Swope Pky Nat Bank, founder & exec vpres, 1969-; Tech Fab Inc, gen mgr & pres, 1972-; Midwest Prog Serv, lectr, 1974-; Franklin Fin Servs, reg securities broker & dealer, 1974-; Black Econ Union Gr KC, pres, founder & exec dir, 1985; McClinton Develop Co, owner, currently; Dept Com, Wash, nat exec dir; Black Econ Union, nat exec dir; Valdes & Moreno Inc, invest banker; Real Estate Partnerships, developer & gen partner; Govt Leased Facil Dep Mayor Econ Develop, Wash, DC; Amtraks Real Estate Mgt & Mkt, nat dir, currently. **Orgs:** Am Mgt Asn; Black Econ Union Gr KC; C C KC; Nat Asn Mkt Develop; Nat Brokers Asn; Nat Security Dealers Asn; past pres, Comm Econ Develop Cong; Counr, Urban Econ Develop; Mid-Am Reg Coun; Planned Ind Abbr Comn City; Univ Mo Ext Prog Adv Coun; Fel Christian Athlets; Kappa Alpha Psi Frat; Nat Asn Advan Colored People; Urban League; YMCA; bd dir, Who's Who Outstanding Young Men Am; St Mary's Hosp; United Negro Col Fund; Selec Counl Sch Med Univ Mo; Prof Football Club, 1962-70; Inst Brokers & Invest Bankers; comr & vice chmn, Jackson County Tax Increment Finance Comn; pres, Black Econ Union, Kans; Mo Kan Minority Contractors Asn; Prof Athletes Fed Credit Union; comr, Kans Keys Inner City Football League. **Honors/Awds:** American Football League Rookie of the Year, 1962; Outstanding player, 1962; AFL All-Star Game, 1962; DHL, Miles Col; Leader of the Month, C C, 1970; Outstanding Young American, 1971; Boss of the Year, C C, 1975; Outstanding Cit Award, Interracial Coun. **Special Achievements:** Professional Concert Singer; Runner-up to MrKS Cit Annual C of C Hon 1970; A Writer and lecturer of economic and sports development, and international singer of the songs of the renowned Paul Robeson, Esq. **Home Addr:** 11714 Jefferson St, Kansas City, MO 64114-5580, **Home Phone:** (816)942-3078. **Business Addr:** Owner, McClinton Development Co, 11714 Jefferson St, Kansas City, MO 64114, **Business Phone:** (816)942-8287.

### MCCLOMB, GEORGE E.
College administrator, educator. **Personal:** Born Apr 24, 1940, Long Island, NY; married Audrey Hamilton; children: George Jr. **Educ:** Colgate Univ, BA, 1962; Univ Pittsburgh, MSW, 1964, MA, polit sci, 1974, PhD, polit sci, 1984. **Career:** Homewood Brushton Health Ctr, asst proj dir, 1967-68, proj dir, 1968-71, Community Orgn & Soc Admin; Univ Pittsburgh, adj asst prof, 1969, guest lectr, 1970, health care consult, 1971-72, assoc prof, 1973-, chair social admin; Health Syst, asst dir, 1971-73; UCLID Ctr, C's Hosp Pittsburgh, dir, Community Strand. **Orgs:** Pres & bd dir, Lemington Home Aged, 1971-83; bd dir, W Pa Comprehensive Health Planning Ageny; W Pa Reg Med Prog; Vis Nurses Asn; Pittsburgh Model Cities Health Task Force; Urban League Health Comn; Comprehensive Care Task Force, Sickle Cell Anemia; comnr, Pub Parking Auth City Pittsburgh; comnr, Prog Aid Citizen Enterprise; deleg, White House Conf Aging, 1981; Pa State Conf Aging, 1984; Nat Asn Social Workers; Asn Community Orgn & Social Admin; Am Polit Sci Asn; Hill House Asn, Pittsburgh, PA. **Home Addr:** 1160 Stanton Ter, Pittsburgh, PA 15201. **Business Addr:** Director, Children's Hospital of Pittsburgh, 3705 5th Ave, Pittsburgh, PA 15213, **Business Phone:** (412)692-6300.

### MCCLOUD, AARON CURTIS
Educator. **Personal:** Born Oct 28, 1933, Saginaw, MI; married Doris Jean Godbee; children: Sylvia Lynn & Monica Delis. **Educ:** AA, 1954; BA, pub admin, 1957; MA, 1967; EdD, 1973. **Career:** Eng & soc studies teacher, 1960-68; eve adult ed, 1967-69; counr, 1968. **Orgs:** Exec bd, Winter halter PTA, 1966-67; Concerned Cit Action, 1966-70; pres, Mumford Constel Cit Group, 1968-71; pres, Mich Asn Supv Curr Develop, 1969; pres exec bd, Hampton PTA, 1971-72; Phi Delta Kappa, 1972; Messiah Baptist Church. **Honors/Awds:** Outstanding Community Contribution, WJR Radio, 1970; Recipient Whitney Young, Outstanding Contribution Black Culture, 1971. **Home Addr:** 3557 Sherbourne, Detroit, MI 48221-1818, **Home Phone:** (313)863-7138. **Business Addr:** 2470 Collingwood, Detroit, MI 48206.

### MCCLOUD, ANECE FAISON
School administrator, association executive, writer. **Personal:** Born May 29, 1937, Dudley, NC; daughter of J D Faison and Nancy Simmons Cole; married Verable L; children: Aja Siobhan & Carla D. **Educ:** Bennett Col, BS, 1959; Univ Nebr, MA, 1989. **Career:** Lincoln Jr High Sch, teacher, 1959-60; Univ NE Med Ctr, asst registr, 1972-76, dir minority affairs, 1976-85, asst instr med juris prudence & humanities, 1980-85; Wash & Lee Univ, assoc dean stud, int Stud Affairs, 1985-99. **Orgs:** Peer reviewer, Health Career Opportunity Prog Grant, 1982-84; Div Disadvantaged Assist Bur Health Prof HHS; consult, Life & Career Planning Workshop Urban League, NE, 1985; bd dir, Rockbridge Comm Unit Am Cancer Soc, Va Div, 1986; Nat Asn Women Deans Admins & Counr; Am Asn Coun & Develop; Asn Multicult Coun & Develop; Nat Asn Foreign Stud Adv; Asn Am Med Col. **Honors/Awds:** Certificate Black Hist Month Prog Speaker Veterans Admin Med Ctr, 1984; Certificate Acknowledgement of Contrib, Educ Omaha Pub Sch, 1984; Plaquein Appreciation, Minority Health Career Opportunity, 1984; Plaque in Appreciation, Stud Nat Med Asn, UNMC Chap, 1985; Excellence in Diversity Award, named in hon. **Special Achievements:** Black students in private white colleges, author, 1989. **Home Addr:** 1002 Shenandoah Rd, Lexington, VA 24450, **Home Phone:** (540)463-9779. **Business Addr:** Associate Dean, Washington and Lee University, Lexington, VA 24450, **Business Phone:** (540)458-8400.

### MCCLOUD, GEORGE AARON, III
Basketball player. **Personal:** Born May 27, 1967, Daytona Beach, FL; son of George; children: Travis. **Educ:** Fla State Univ, criminol, 1989. **Career:** Basketball player (retired); Ind Pacers, forward, 1989-93;

Scavolini Pesaro, Italy, 1993-94; Rapid City Thrillers, CBA, 1994-95; Dallas Mavericks, 1995-97; Los Angeles Lakers, 1996-97; Phoenix Suns, 1997-99; Denver Nuggets, 1999-2002; Tampa Bay Windjammers, 1999; Golden State Warriors, forward, 2000.

**MCCLOUD, REV. DR. J. OSCAR**
Executive, clergy, association executive. **Personal:** Born Apr 10, 1936, Waynesboro, GA; married Robbie J Foster; children: Ann Michelle, Cassandra Anita & Tony Delancy. **Educ:** Berea Col, Berea, KY, BA, sociol & psychol, 1958; Union Theol Sem NY, MDiv, 1961; Mary Holmes Col, West Point, MS, 1974; Whitworth Col, Spokane, WA, DHL. **Career:** Clergy (retired); Davis St United Presby Ch, Raleigh NC, pastor, 1961-64; United Presby Ch, Atlanta, Ga, field rep, bd christian educ, 1964-67; Div Church & Race Bd Nat Missions, 1968-69; United Pres Church New York, 1969-71; Gen Sec Comm Ecumcl Mission & Rel, assoc gen secy, 1971-72; Prog Agency United Presby Church, gen dir, 1972-86; The Fund Theol Educ, New York, exec dir, 1986-95; Fifth Ave Presby Church, assoc pastor, assoc pastor emer, 1995-2005. **Orgs:** Proj coordr, Am Forum Int Study Tour W Africa, 1971; bd trustee, Berea Col, 1990-; bd dir, Southern Christian Leadership Conf, Ga Coun Churches; black pres united, Nat Conf Black; vice-chairperson, Div Overseas Ministries, Nat Coun Churches, mem exec comn, gov bd; Comn World Mission & Evangelism; World Coun Churches; NE Community Org C, Teaneck; Proj Equality Inc Nat; mem exec comt, cent comm World Coun Churches; bd dir, Independent Sector; chair, adv bd, Comun Rels, Teaneck, NJ; pres, Pres by Ctr Holmes Camp & Conf Ctr; bd Advisor, Covenant Network; actg exec Presbyter, NYC Presby YouthAction Fifth Ave Presby Church. **Honors/Awds:** Community Service Award, Black Cong Caucus, 1978; hon doctorate, Mary Holmes Col. **Special Achievements:** First alumnus to receive Berea Col Community Serv Award in 1981. **Home Addr:** 1101 Dartmouth St, Teaneck, NJ 07666. **Business Addr:** Associate Pastor Emeritus, Fifth Avenue Presbyterian Church, 7 W 55th St, New York, NY 10019, **Business Phone:** (212)247-0490.

**MCCLOUD, THOMAS HENRY**
Educator, association executive, manager. **Personal:** Born Jul 29, 1948, Jersey City, NJ; son of Robert Sr and Pearline; married Georgia. **Educ:** Rutgers Univ, BA, 1974, MPA, 1977; Georgetown Univ Law Ctr, JD, 1989. **Career:** Rutgers Univ, counr spec progs, 1974-76; City Newark, dep dir, PSE, 1977, actg dir, 1977-78; Nat League Cities Wash, DC, dir, employ & training proj, 1978-81, dir, Urban Noise Progs, 1981-82; Wash Conv Ctr, dir, human resources & bus servs, 1982-86, asst gen mgr, 1986-87; Nat League Cities, dir mem serv, 1987-91, dir, pub affairs, 1991-; Network Fighting Back Partnership, exec dir, 1993-96; 18th Cong Dist, chief staff, 1996; Pub Technol Inst, vp, dept & interim exec dir, chief operating officer, dep exec dir, 1996-2005; Prince Georges Community Col, adj prof, 2010-; Key Bridge Found, mgr, 2011-. **Orgs:** Chmn, EOF Comt Adv Bd, 1972; treas, Rutgers Univ Alumni Asn, Nazareth Col Arts & Sci, 1976; pres, MPA Alumni Asn, 1976-77; trustee, Leaguers Inc, 1977-78; Am Soc Pub Admin, 1978-; Nat Bar Asn; bd mem, Nat Forum Black Pub Adminrs; Nat Bd Mem; pres, DC Chap Nat Forum Black Pub Adminr; chair, Educ Opportunity Community Adv Bd; comnr, Essex County Youth Comn; sr consult & lead instr, Mattocks Bus Advisors; Nat Bar Asn; Asn Conflict Resolution; Md Coun Dispute Resolution; MD Prog Mediator Excellence; Community Emergency Response Team; Md Notary Pub; bd dir, Community Mediation Prince Georges. **Honors/Awds:** Strauss Human Relations Scholar, 1972; Robert A Wynn Member Award, Rutgers Univ, 1974; Public Service Education fellow, Dept HEW Wash, DC, 1974; Manager of the Year, Wash Convention Ctr, 1984. **Home Addr:** 1310 Merganser Ct, Upper Marlboro, MD 20774-7020, **Home Phone:** (301)249-7706. **Business Addr:** Adjunct Professor, Prince Georges Community College, 301 Largo Rd, Largo, MD 20774-2199, **Business Phone:** (301)322-0900.

**MCCLOUD, TYRUS KAMALL**
Football player, executive. **Personal:** Born Nov 12, 1974, Ft. Lauderdale, FL; son of Armie. **Educ:** Univ Louisville, BA, justice admin, 1997; Kaplan Univ, MA, pub admin, 2011. **Career:** Football player (retired), exec; Baltimore Ravens, linebacker, 1997-98; Wash Redskins, linebacker, 2000; Miami Dolphins, linebacker, 2001; Ga Force, Arena Football League, linebacker, 2002-03; Kaplan Univ, acad advisor, 2005-10; Prison Fel, field dir, 2010-. **Orgs:** Prison Fel. **Honors/Awds:** Defensive Player of the Year, Conference USA, 1995, 1996. **Business Addr:** Field Director, Prison Fellowship, 6916 NW 34th Ave, Ft. Lauderdale, FL 33309, **Business Phone:** (954)978-9012.

**MCCLUNG, REV. WILLIE DAVID, II**
Clergy. **Personal:** Born Apr 3, 1939, Aliceville, AL; married Maria Antoinette Larkin; children: 5. **Educ:** Miles Col, BS; Samford Univ; Capella Univ, PhD. **Career:** Detroit Counc Baptist Pastors, secy, 1966-67; Comm Human Rel, Highland Pk, 1969-73; New Grace & Univ Detroit, minister; New Grace Baptist Church, assoc minister, 1978-79; Mt Seir Baptist Church, asst pastor, 1980-83; Sardis Baptist Church, youth minister, 1985-91; Holt St Baptist Church, assoc minister, 1993-; Beulah Baptist Church, assoc minister, 1998-99; Rising Sun First Baptist Church, asst, pastor, 2000-03; Emmaus Missionary Baptist Church, founder, 2003-, pastor, currently. **Home Addr:** 18015 Fairfield, Detroit, MI 48221. **Business Addr:** Pastor, Founder, Emmaus Missionary Baptist Church, 9928 Lyons Mill Rd, Owings Mills, MD 21117, **Business Phone:** (410)655-2095.

**MCCLURE, BRYTON ERIC**
Actor, singer. **Personal:** Born Aug 17, 1986, Lakewood, CA; son of Eric and Bette; married Ashley Leisinger. **Career:** TV series: "Family Matters", 1990-97, "Thirty Something"; "The Kids From Room 402", 1999; "The Young & the Restless", 2004-14; "Hero Factory", 2010-13; "Vampire Diaries", 2010-11; "Winx Club: Beyond Believix", 2012-13; "Miles Across the Sea", 2013; "Young Justice", 2013; "Star Wars Rebels", 2014. Films: The Jungle Book: Rhythm 'n Groove, 2001; The Intruders, 2009. **Orgs:** Screen Actors Guild AME; AFTRA Union. **Honors/Awds:** Youth in Films Award, 1992; Michael Landon Award, 1998; Daytime Emmy Award, 2007; Image Award, Nat Asn Advan Colored People, 2009. **Business Addr:** Actor, Barbara Cameron & Associates, 8369 Squsalito Ave Suite A, Canoga Park, CA 91304, **Business Phone:** (818)888-6107.

**MCCLURE, FREDERICK DONALD**
Investment banker. **Personal:** Born Feb 2, 1954, Ft. Worth, TX; son of Foster and Mayme Barnett; married Harriet Jackson; children: Lauren Elizabeth & Frederick Donald Jr. **Educ:** Tex A&M Univ, Col Sta, TX, BS, agr econ, 1976; Baylor Univ, Waco, TX, JD, 1981. **Career:** Reynolds, Allen & Cook, Houston, TX, trial atty, 1981-83; Sen John Tower, Wash, DC, legis dir, legal coun, 1983-84; Dept Justice, Wash, DC, assoc dep atty gen, 1984-85; White House, Wash, DC, spec asst legis affairs to pres Ronald Reagan, 1985-86, asst legis affairs to pres George H W Bush, 1989-92; Automatic Data Processing Inc, pres; Pub Strategies Inc, managing dir; Tex Air Corp, Wash, DC, staff vpres, 1986-89; First Southwest Co, Dallas, TX, managing dir, 1992-; Sonnenschein Nath & Rosenthal LLP, partner, 2001-07, managing patner, 2007-; Dentons US LLP, sr coun, currently. **Orgs:** Int vpres, Tex A&M Univ Asn Former Studs, 1984-88; bd dir, Nat Fraternity Alpha Zeta, 1985-; bd dir, Tex Lyceum, 1986-; Am Coun Ger, 1988-; pres, Nat Capital A&M Club, Tex A&M Univ Asn Former Studs, 1990-92; bd, Childrens Med Ctr Dallas, 1992-; bd, US Naval Acad, 1992-; chmn, Cotton Bowl Athletic Asn, 2000; Bush-Cheney Transition Comt, 2001; bd dir, Alex Lee, Inc; bd mem, exec dir, George Bush Presidential Libr Found, 2012-; chmn, pres, NC Asn Coucnty Commissioners. **Honors/Awds:** Nat FFA Hall of Achievers, Nat FFA Org, 1990; Distinguished Alumnus, Texas A&M Univ, 1991; Outstanding Young Alumnus, Baylor Univ, 1991; Jon Ben Sheppard Outstanding Texas Leader, 1992. **Special Achievements:** First Black ever to head a presidential congressional liaison team. **Home Addr:** 6722 Lakehurst Ave, Dallas, TX 75230, **Home Phone:** (214)369-8566. **Business Addr:** Managing Partner, Sonnenschein Nath & Cotton Bowl LLP, 1301 K St NW Suite 600 E Tower, Washington, DC 20005-3364, **Business Phone:** (202)408-3235.

**MCCLURE, FREDRICK H. L.**
Lawyer. **Personal:** Born Oct 21, 1962, Chattanooga, TN; son of Howard Jr and Carrie M Green. **Educ:** Earlham Col, BA, 1984; Univ Cincinnati, Col Law, JD, 1987. **Career:** Univ Cincinnati, instr, 1986-87; Grant, Konvalinka & Grubbs PC, assoc & partner, 1987-98; Holland & Knight, LLP, partner, 1998-2002; Piper Rudnick LLP, partner, 2002-. **Orgs:** Pres, Chattanooga Bar Asn, Young Lawyers Div, 1987-; Tenn Bar Asn, Young Lawyers Div, 1987-; Am Bar Asn, career issues comt, minorities profession commt nat conf team, 1991-; Alpha Phi Alpha, 1988-; justice, Phi Alpha Delta Legal Fraternity, 1986; Hillsborough County Bar Asn; life fel Am Bar Found; George Edgecomb Bar Asn; Fla Bar Asn; Alpha Phi Alpha Fraternity Inc. **Honors/Awds:** Man of the Year, Alpha Phi Alpha, 1990; Service Award, Tenn Young Lawyers Conference, 1989; Young Leader of the Future, Ebony Magazine, 1991. **Home Addr:** 1020 Talley Rd, Chattanooga, TN 37411, **Home Phone:** (615)629-9980. **Business Addr:** Attorney, Partner, Piper Rudnick LLP, 100 N Tampa Suite 2200, Tampa, FL 33602-5809, **Business Phone:** (813)222-5908.

**MCCLURKIN, DONNIE**
Minister (clergy), gospel singer. **Personal:** Born Nov 9, 1959, Copiague, NY. **Career:** Marvin Winans Perfecting Faith Church, associate minister, Detroit, 1989, ordained, 2001, sr pastor; Perfecting Faith Church, Freeport, New York, senior pastor, currently; Albums: Donnie McClurkin, 1996; Tis So Sweet, 2000; Live in London & More, 2000; Donnie McClurkin. Again, 2003; Psalms, Hymns & Spiritual Songs, 2005; The Essential Donnie McClurkin, 2007; Valley Of God, 2008; We All Are One: Live in Detroit, 2009; Attachments, 2009; Films: 25 Strong: The BET Silver Anniversary Spec; The Prince of Egypt, 1998; The Fighting Temptations, 2003; Apollo at 70: A Hot Night in Harlem, 2004; The Donnie McClurkin Story: From Darkness to Light, 2004; Diary of a Mad Black Woman, 2005; The Gospel, 2005; Valley Of God, 2008; Hopeville, 2007; Tv Ser: Girlfriends, 2001; An Eve of Stars: A Celebration of Educ Excellence, 2001; The Parkers, 2002; An Eve of Stars: Tribute to Stevie Wonder, 2006; Perfecting Your Faith, broadcaster, 2009. **Orgs:** Founder, New York Restoration Choir. **Honors/Awds:** Ten Stellar Gospel Awards, 2002-05; Grammy Award, Best Contemporary Soul Gospel Album for Again, 2004; NAACP Image Award; Two BET Award; Two Soul Train Award; Dove & Steller Awards. **Special Achievements:** Author of "Eternal victim/ Eternal victor", has appeared in numerous television shows Television Appearances: Good Morning America, CBS Saturday's Early Show, the View, Girlfriends and The Parkers. **Business Addr:** Senior Pastor, Perfecting Faith Church, 311 N Main St, Freeport, NY 11520, **Business Phone:** (516)223-8300.

**MCCLURKIN, JOHNSON THOMAS**
Executive. **Personal:** Born Sep 25, 1929, Chester, SC; married Evelyn Rudd; children: Gary. **Educ:** Morgan State Univ, BS, 1958. **Career:** Nat Asn Real Estate Brokers Inc, exec dir; Nat Corp Housing, asst dir; Rouse Co, asst to dir property mgt, 1970-72; Wash, DC, partner, 1972-73; City Balto Mayor's off, asst opers, 1987-96. **Orgs:** Bd dir, Nat Asn Real Estate Brokers Inc; life mem, Nat Asn Advan Colored People; Leadership Conf Civil Rights; Nat Bus League; St John Bapt Ch Columbia Interfaith Ctr; Columbia Asn; Exec, Am Soc Asn. **Home Addr:** 10968 Eight Bells Lane, Columbia, MD 21044-2704, **Home Phone:** (410)730-9350.

**MCCLUSKEY, AUDREY THOMAS**
Educator. **Personal:** Born Aug 30, 1947, Valdosta, GA; daughter of Paul and Eva; married John Jr; children: Malik, Jerome & Toure. **Educ:** Clark Col, BA, 1967; Howard Univ, MA, 1969; Ind Univ, PhD, 1991. **Career:** Ford Found, post grad fel, 1994; Ind Unit, Univ Div, asst to dean; Cleveland State Univ, asst prof womens studies & African Am studies, assoc dir womens studies, assoc dir, Black Film Ctr Archive, prof African Am studies, currently; dir, Neal Marshall Black Cult Ctr, 2007-; Ind Univ Bloomington, prof; Books: A Forgotten Sisterhood: Black Women A Educators and Activists in the Jim Crow South; Mary McLeod Bethune and the Education of Black Girls; Mary McLeod Bethune: Building a Better. World; Imaging Blackness: Race and Racial Representin in Film Poster Art; The Devil You Dance With: Film Culture in Post Apartheid South Africa; Richard Pryor: The Life and Legend of a 'Crazy' Black Man. **Orgs:** Asn Study African Am Life & Hist; Life mem, Nat Asn Advan Colored People; chmn, Monroe Co Chap Educ Comn; pres, Alpha Kappa Alpha; grad chap, Kappa Tau Omega; Asn Study African Am Life; Nat Womens Studies Asn; Orgn Am Historians; Nat Coun Black Studies; Asn Black Women Historians; Am Studies Asn; Asn Black Cult Centers; dir, Black Film Ctr; dir, Neal-Marshall Black Cult Ctr; dir, Grad Studies Dept AAADS. **Home Addr:** 3300 Moores Pke, Bloomington, IN 47401. **Business Addr:** Professor, Director, Indiana University, Memorial Hall E Rm M18, Bloomington, IN 47405, **Business Phone:** (812)855-3875.

**MCCLUSKEY, JOHN A., JR.**
Educator, novelist, scholar. **Personal:** Born Oct 25, 1944, Middletown, OH; son of John A and Helen Harris; married Audrey Thomas; children: Malik Douglass, Jerome Patrice & John Toure. **Educ:** Harvard Univ, BA, 1966; Stanford Univ, MA, 1972. **Career:** Miles Col, Birmingham, AL, instr Eng, 1967-68; Valparaiso Univ, Ind, lectr humanities, 1968-69; Case Western Res Univ, from coordr to lectr, Afro-Am Studies, 1969-72, asst prof am studies, 1972-74, asst prof Eng, 1974-77; Ind Univ, assoc prof, Afro-Am Studies, 1977-85, adj prof Eng, 1983-, dir, CIC Minorities Fels Prog, 1983-88, fac am studies, 1983-, assoc dean grad sch, 1984-88, assoc dean, Grad Sch, 1984-88, founding co-ed, Blacks Diaspora Ser, 1985-2000, prof, Afro-Am Studies, 1985-, prof emer, chair, Afro-Am Studies, 1994-2000; dir, Black Atlantic Seminars, 1996-98.Novel: Mr. America's Last Season Blues, 1983. **Orgs:** Am Studies Asn; Mod Lang Asn; Am Asn Univ Prof; Asn African-Am Life & Hist; Nat Coun Black Studies; Midwest Mod Lang Asn; Nat Soc Arts & Lett; Yaddo Fel, Yaddo Corp, 1984, 1986; Authors Guild Inc; life mem, Sapelo Island Ga Cult & Revitalization Socs Inc; life mem, Nat Asn Advan Colored People, Monroe County Chap; Bloomington Bd Pub Safety, 1983-1988; Harvard Club Ind Schs Comt; Harvard Black Alumni Socs; Nat Socs Arts & Lett Bloomington Chap. **Business Addr:** Professor, Professor Emeritus, Indiana University, Mem Hall E M-28, Bloomington, IN 47405, **Business Phone:** (812)855-0143.

**MCCOLLUM, JUDGE ALICE ODESSA**
Judge. **Personal:** Born Feb 15, 1947, Oklahoma City, OK; daughter of Irving A and Maryland G. **Educ:** Univ NC Greensboro, BA, math, 1969; Univ Cincinnati Sch Law, JD, 1972. **Career:** Reginald Heber Smith Community Lawyer, fel, 1972-74; Legal Aid Soc Dayton, co-dir, 1974-75; Wilberforce Univ, dir, pre-law, 1975-76; Univ Dayton Sch Law, asst prof, asst dir clin legal, 1976-79; Dayton Munic Ct, judge, 1979-2003; Montgomery County Ohio, Common Pleas Probate Div, judge, 2002-; Childrens' Med Ctr. **Orgs:** Bd mem, United Theol Sem, 1980-95; United Way, 1980-84; Dayton Contemp Dance Co, 1980-84; Am Judges Asn; Nat Bar Asn; Ohio State Bar Asn; Am Bar Asn; Thurgood Marshall Law Soc; bd trustee, Victoria Theatre Asn, 1987-93; Ohio Criminal Sentencing Comn, 1991-2002; bd trustee, C's Med Ctr, 1993-99; pres, Dayton Bar Asn, 2006-07; Nat Asn Women Judges. **Honors/Awds:** Marks of Excellence Award, Nat Forum Black Pub Admin Dayton Chap, 2000; Woman of Influence, YWCA, 2002; Community Service Award, Dayton Chap Nat Asn Advan Colored People, 2002. **Special Achievements:** First Woman Dayton Municipal Court Judge; First Woman & African American Probate Judge in Montgomery County; Ten Top African-Am Women, African-Ame CEO, 2002. **Business Addr:** Judge, Montgomery County Court, 41 N Perry St, Dayton, OH 45422, **Business Phone:** (937)225-4512.

**MCCOLLUM, ANITA LAVERNE (SILHOUETTE ANITA LAVERNE MCCOLLUM SHELTON)**
Executive, association executive. **Personal:** Born Aug 20, 1960, Cleveland, OH; married Fred D; children: 5. **Educ:** Ky State Univ, BS, mgt, 1983; Atlanta Univ, MBA, 1985. **Career:** Veterans Admin, accounts mgr; IBM, admin asst, 1981, sales asst, 1984; NASA Lewis Res Ctr, procurement coordr summers, 1981-83; Atlanta Exchange, asst to exec vpres, 1984-; AT&T Communs, supvr residence mkt. **Orgs:** Undergrad mem, Nat Bd Dirs Alpha Kappa Alpha, 1982-84; Toastmaster's Intl, 1983-85; stud mem, Nat Black MBA Asn, 1985; NAACP; First Baptist Church, Chesterfield; Int Directorate; silver star life mem, Alpha Kappa Alpha Sorority Inc; Jack & Jill Am Inc; Mocha Moms; Mother of Twins Club; Morehouse Col; Howard Univ. **Honors/Awds:** Soror of the Year, Alpha Kappa Alpha, 1982; Nat Dean's List, KY State Univ, 1981-83; Executive Management Scholarship, AUGSBA, 1983. **Home Addr:** 16512 Invermere Ave, Cleveland, OH 44128. **Business Addr:** Staff Supervisor Residence Marketing, AT&T Communications, 295 N Maple Ave, Basking Ridge, NJ 07920.

**MCCOMBS, ANTONIAS ORLANDO.** **See MCCOMBS, TONY.**

**MCCOMBS, TONY (ANTONIAS ORLANDO MCCOMBS)**
Football player. **Personal:** Born Aug 24, 1974, Hopkinsville, KY. **Educ:** Eastern Ky Univ. **Career:** Football player (retired); Ariz Cardinals, 1997, right linebacker, 1998. **Honors/Awds:** OVC Defensive Player of the Year; I-AA National Defensive Player of the Year.

**MCCONNELL, CONRAD**
Editor. **Personal:** Born Sep 2, 1952, Denver, CO; son of Geraldine Blanche Christian and Conrad N. **Educ:** Univ Ore, Eugene, BS, jour, 1974. **Career:** Ore Jour, Portland, reporter, 1975-82; Portland Ore, Portland, reporter, 1982-83; Seattle Post-Intelligencer, Seattle, ed, reporter, 1983-. **Orgs:** Nat Asn Black Journalists, 1983-; Seattle Asn Black Journalists, 1983-; Seattle Youth-at-Risk, 1989-; Amnesty Int, 1989-.Nat Asn Black Journalists, 1983-; Seattle Asn Black Journalists, 1983-; Seattle Youth-at-Risk, 1989-; Amnesty Int, 1989-. **Honors/Awds:** C B Blethen Memorial Award, Blethen, 1985; Pacific Northwest Excellence Journalism, Soc Prof Journalists, 1986; St Matthew Award, Northwest Harvest, 1986; Fair Housing Award, Seattle Bd Realtist, 1987; Challenge of Excellence, Wash Press Asn, 1987. **Home Addr:** 5644 36th Ave SW, Seattle, WA 98126, **Home Phone:** (206)938-2037. **Business Addr:** Night Assistant City Editor, Seattle Post-Intelligencer, 101 Elliott Ave W, Seattle, WA 98119, **Business Phone:** (206)448-8048.

### MCCONNELL, DOROTHY HUGHES

Educator. **Personal:** Born Cleveland, OH; daughter of Harry and Genevieve Harris; children: Jan Yvette Evans. **Educ:** Ohio State Univ, BS, 1946; Western Reserve Univ, MA, 1956. **Career:** Specialist (retired), consult; Los Angeles Unified Sch Dist, training teacher, 1960-79, sch improvement coordr, 1979-80, integration coordr, 1980-81, lang arts specialist, 1982-90; Black Studies, specialist, consult, 1990. **Orgs:** Los Angeles Alumnae; Delta Sigma Theta Sor; life mem, Nat Asn Advan Colored People, Los Angeles Br, 1995; pres, Nat Asn Univ Women, Los Angeles Br, 1996-98; deacon, Park Hills Reformed Church, 1998-2001. **Home Addr:** 5547 Secrest Dr, Los Angeles, CA 90043, **Home Phone:** (323)295-0133.

### MCCOO, MARILYN

Singer, actor. **Personal:** Born Sep 30, 1943, Jersey City, NJ; daughter of Wayman Glenn and Mary Ellen Holloway; married Billy Davis Jr. **Educ:** Univ Calif, BS, bus admin; Talladega Col, doctorate. **Career:** Art Link letters Talent Scout, singer; The Hi-Fi's, singer; The Fifth Dimension formerly the Versatiles, mem, 1965-75; It Takes a Thief, 1970; The Love Boat, 1978; The Fantastic World of D.C. Collins, 1984; New Love, American Style, 1986; Days of our Lives, 1986-87; Punky Brewster, 1988; My Mom's a Werewolf, 1989; Night Court, 1990; The Kingdom Chums Original Top Ten, 1990; Broadway Performedas "Julie" in "Showboat", 1995; Chicago, Role of "Julie" in "Showboat", 1996; Solid Gold, host, 1981-84, 1986-88; Road Tour with Billy Davis Jr, Duke Ellington Review, 1999; Los Angeles Role of "Aldonza" in "Man of LA Mancha", Miami, Role of "Reno Sweeny" in "Anything Goes"; Grizzly Adams & the Legend of Dark Mountain, 1999; "The Jamie Foxx Show", 1999-2001; Miss Rising, 2005; Albums: The Me Nobody Knows, 1991; White Christmas, 1996. **Orgs:** Bd gov, C Miracle Network; chair, Los Angeles Mission Bd; Meharry Med Col Bd; Cancer Res Found Bd; Sigma Gamma Rho Sorority. **Honors/Awds:** Miss Bronze California, 1962; Grammy Award for "You Don't Have to be a Star", 1977; 4 Grammy Awards for Up, Up & Away 1968; 2 Grammy Awards for Aquaris & Let The Sun Shine, 1969; Prestigious Grand Prize, Tokyo Music Fest; 14 Gold Recs & Albums with the 5th Dimension; One Gold Rec & Albums with husband Billy Davis Jr; Grammy nominee for The Me Nobody Knows, 1992; Harvard Found Award, Harvard Univ; 14 Gold Recs & Albums with the fifth Dimension; 3 Platinum Recs with the Fifth Dimension; star on the Hollywood Walk of Fame, 1991; Children's Miracle Network, Achievement Award, 2002. **Special Achievements:** First to record Whitney Houston's "Saving All My Love For You", 1978. **Home Addr:** PO Box 7905, Beverly Hills, CA 90212. **Business Addr:** Singer, Actress, The Sterling Winters Co, 10900 Wilshire Blvd, Los Angeles, CA 90024, **Business Phone:** (310)557-2700.

### MCCORD, LANISSA RENEE

Executive. **Personal:** Born May 4, 1969, Kansas City, MO; daughter of Ingrid and Derrick. **Educ:** Rutgers Univ, Mason Cross Sch Arts, attended 1990; Univ Mo, Kans City Conserv, attended 1992. **Career:** DANCE, choreographer, 1991-2000; Le Ballet Ivoire Spectacle, mgt, 1997-2000; Orlando Sch Cult Dance, 1998-99; Cent Fla YMCA Syst, 1998-2000; Nu Look Performers, 1999-2000. **Orgs:** Arts Complete Educ; United Arts Cent Fla; Orlando Sch Cult Dance, counelders, 1998. **Home Addr:** 4328 Lake Lawne Ave, Orlando, FL 32808, **Home Phone:** (407)298-7688.

### MCCORMACK, HURVIN

Football player. **Personal:** Born Apr 6, 1972, Brooklyn, NY. **Educ:** Ind Univ, grad. **Career:** Football player (retired); Dallas Cowboys, defensive tackle, 1994-98; Cleveland Browns, defensive end, 1999; Nat Football League Players Asn, Secy, currently. **Honors/Awds:** Honorable-mention All-American, 1993. **Business Addr:** Secretary, National Football League Players Association, 1133 20th St NW Suite 600, Washington, DC 20036, **Business Phone:** (800)372-2000.

### MCCORVEY, ANTOINETTE P.

Chief financial officer, vice president (organization). **Educ:** Univ W Fla, Pensacola, FL, BS, finance & acct, MBA, finance & acct. **Career:** Monsauto/Solutia, vpres, gen mgr; Eastman Kodak Co, dir finance-imaging mat mfg, 1999, dir finance-global mfg & logistics, dir finance-corp financial planning & anal, dir finance & vpres, consumer digital imaging group, dir & vpres investor rels, 2007-10, corp vpres, 2007, chief financial officer, 2010-12, sr vpres, 2010-12. **Orgs:** Bd dir, Info Technol Indust Coun, 2009-10; chmn, Asn Blind & Visually Impaired--Goodwill Industs Greater Rochester Inc; bd dir, ESL Fed Credit Union; Rochester Inst Technol (RIT), 2010-11.

### MCCORVEY, DR. EVERETT D.

Educator. **Personal:** Born Dec 3, 1957, Montgomery, AL; son of David and Olga; married Alicia Helm; children: Elizabeth, Julia & David. **Educ:** Univ Ala, BM, 1979, MM, 1981, DMA, 1989. **Career:** Newtown High Sch, Queens, NY, music instr, 1983-84; Knoxville Col, prof voice, 1984-85; Univ Ky, prof voice, dir opera theatre, 1991-; Am Spiritual Ensemble, artistic dir, founder, 1995-; Ky Arts Coun, vice chmn, 1999-; Lexington Opera Soc Endowed Chair, currently. **Orgs:** Opera Cent Ky, 1992-; Lexington Ballet, 1994-97; UK Athletics Asn, 1996-; chair, Univ Ky, visit by Archbishop Desmond Tutu, Convocation Comn, 1999; Ky Advocates Higher Educ, 1999; chair, Lexington Opera Soc; bd dir, Nat Assembly State Arts Agencies; bd trustee, Univ Ky, 2008-; Alltech World Equestrian Games Fedn Bd. **Home Addr:** 214 Bell Ct E, Lexington, KY 40508, **Home Phone:** (606)233-0789. **Business Addr:** Professor of Music, University of Kentucky, College of Fine Arts, 105 Fine Arts Bldg, Lexington, KY 40506-0022, **Business Phone:** (859)257-4900.

### MCCORVEY, KEZ (KEZARRICK MONTINES MCCORVEY)

Football coach, executive, football player. **Personal:** Born Jan 23, 1972, Gautier, MS; married Loris; children: Imoni, Kez Jr, Micah & Cristian. **Educ:** Fla State Univ, BA, sociol, 1994. **Career:** Football player (retired), coach, executive; Detroit Lions, wide receiver, 1995-97; Carolina Panthers, wide receiver; Rhein Fire, Europe, 1999; Edmonton Eskimos, wide receiver, 2000-01, wide receivers coach, 2014-15; Titus Sports Acad, owner/operator, 2001-09; Maclay Sch, head coach, 2009-10; Bethel Univ Tenn, receivers coach, passing game coordr/strength conditioning coach, 2011-12; Toronto Argonauts Football Club, asst coach over receivers, 2012-13; N E High Sch, head coach, 2013-14; Mid Tenn State Univ, receivers coach, 2016-. **Honors/Awds:** Florida State's Hall of Fame, 2005. **Special Achievements:** Named to a pair of All-America teams as a senior. **Business Addr:** Receivers Coach, Middle Tennessee State University, 1301 E Main St, Murfreesboro, TN 37132, **Business Phone:** (615)898-2300.

### MCCOULLUM, DR. VALARIE ENA SWAIN-CADE

Vice president (organization). **Personal:** Born Sep 16, 1952, Philadelphia, PA; daughter of William Arch Swain Sr and Ena Lindner Swain; married Henry W Jr; children: Ena Marietta Cade & David Lloyd. **Educ:** Pa State Univ, BA, 1973; Temple Univ, MEd, 1977, EdD, 1978; Univ Pa, Philadelphia Child Guid Clin, post-doctoral family ther, 1981; Wharton Sch Exec Educ Finance & Org Develop Prog, 1987; Harvard Univ, IEM, 1988. **Career:** Pa State Univ, tutor, 1971-72, peer counr, 1971-73; Sch Dist Philadelphia, teacher lang arts, 1972-74; Camden Schs, lang arts & reading teacher, 1974-76; Camden County Community Col Learning Skills Ctr, adminr & study skills specialist, 1976-77, counr, 1976-77; Dept Educ, field reader & curric consult, 1976-; Rutgers Univ, asst prof eng, 1976-78; Camden County Community Col, Learning & Study Skills specialist, 1976-77; Univ Pa, psychol educ specialist, 1978-80, asst prof/lectr 1978-82, fac master, WEB Du Bois Col House, 1978-80, asst vice provost undergrad studies, dir commonwealth prog, 1978-83, Grad Sch Educ, Sch Social Work, Sch Arts & Sci, adj fac, 1978-, asst assoc provost, 1983-85, exec asst provost, 1985-86, asst provost, 1986-88; Mellon Minority Undergrad fel Prog, prog coordr, 1989-, asst provost & asst pres, 1989-91, actg pres, 1991-92, 1994, chmn, Commonwealth Ct Pa Sch Dist Phil Equity Team, assoc vpres, 1992-95, vice provost div univ life, 1995-. **Orgs:** Pa coord Tri-State Coun Equal Educ Opportunity, 1978-81; eastern regional rep ACT-101 Adv Comn, 1979-81; pres, Pa Asn Educ Opportunity, 1981-83; pres, Mid-Eastern Asn Educ Opportunity, 1983; bd mem & Mid-Atlantic Regional pres emer, Nat Coun Educ Opportunity; exec bd mem, Mid-Eastern Asn Educ Opportunity; League United Latin Am Citizens Adv Bd; Am Found Negro Affairs Med Steering Comt; Nat Asn Educ Opportunity, 1988; IEM fel Harvard Univ, 1988; Cornell Univ Vis Comt, 1990; Philadelphia Urban League; chair, Commonwealth Ct Pa Educ Team Restructure Sch Dist Philadelphia, 1994-95; Philadelphia Open Studio Tours Planning Comm, 2006-; Ctr Emerging Visual Artists, 2007-; Pennylvania State Univ Col Lib Arts Centennial fel 2009. **Home Addr:** 3611 Locust Walk, Philadelphia, PA 19104. **Business Addr:** Vice Provost, University of Pennsylvania, 3611 Locust Walk Suite 201, Philadelphia, PA 19104-6222, **Business Phone:** (215)898-5337.

### MCCOVEY, WILLIE LEE

Businessperson, baseball player. **Personal:** Born Jan 10, 1938, Mobile, AL. **Career:** Baseball player (retired); restaurateur; Pacific Coast League; Phoenix Giants; San Francisco Giants, sr advisor, gen mgr, spec asst to pres, 1959-73 & 1977-80; San Diego Padres, 1974-76; Oakland Athletics, 1976; Mc Covey's Restaurant, partner, 2003-. **Orgs:** Chmn, Willie McCovey March Dimes Ann Charity Golf Tournament. **Home Addr:** PO Box 620342, Woooside, CA 54062. **Business Addr:** Partner, McCovey's Restaurant, 1444 N Calif Blvd, Walnut Creek, CA 94596, **Business Phone:** (925)944-9444.

### MCCOY, ANTHONY BERNARD

Clergy, football player. **Personal:** Born Jun 10, 1969, Orlando, FL; married Jodie; children: Khrystyna, T J & Isaiah. **Educ:** Univ Fla, BS, 2001. **Career:** Football player (retired), pastor; Indianapolis Colts, 1993, 1999, defensive tackle, 1992, left defensive tackle, 1994-98; Arizona Cardinals, left defensive tackle, 2000; Hope International Church, sr pastor, currently. **Honors/Awds:** SEC championship, 1991; Honorable mention All-American, 1991; Noble Max Award, 1994; Ed Block Courage Award, 1994. **Special Achievements:** Films: 1992 NFL Draft, 1992; 1995 AFC Championship Game, 1996. **Business Addr:** Senior Pastor, Hope International Church, 7432 Hwy 50 Suite 109, Groveland, FL 34736-9322, **Business Phone:** (352)429-4722.

### MCCOY, JAMES F.

Librarian. **Personal:** Born Aug 1, 1925, Clarkton, NC; son of Frank and Gertrude Smith. **Educ:** Lincoln Univ, AB, 1952; Rutgers Univ, MLS, 1956; Univ Denver, advan cert, 1973; Appalachian State Univ, HEW Inst. **Career:** NJ State Libr, ref librn, 1956; Elizabeth Pub Libr, ref librn, 1956; Mercer County Community Col, Libr Dept, chmn, 1956-74; Hudson Valley Community Col, dir learn resources, 1974-84, dir emer, currently; Community & Jr Col libr sect, Asn Vollege & Resource Libr, vice chair & chair. **Orgs:** Pres, Alumni Asn GSLS Rutgers, 1958 & 1975; Adv Comt, Grad Sch Libr Serv Rutgers, 1958-59; secy, NJ Jr Col Asn, 1960 & 1965; Bks Jr Col Libr, 1963; pres, Col & Univ Sect, 1964-65; Trenton Hist Soc, 1965-74; chmn, Scholar Comt, 1966-67; Adv Comt Trenton Urban Renewal, 1966-68; contrib Biblio Negro NJ, 1967; Mayor's Adv Comt, Trenton Model Cities, 1968-73; NJ Libr Asn Exec Bd, 1968-70; vpres, 1969-70; secy, NJ Exec Bd, 1970-72; Nominating Comt, ALA-ACRL, 1971-72; pres, Trenton Neighborhood Health Ctr, 1971-72; Ad Hoc Comt Interns, 1972-77; Ed Bd, CHOICE, 1974; AV Comt, 1975; pres, Am Asn Univ Prof Mercer Co Col; Am Asn Univ Prof; Adv Comt, Grad Sch Libr Serv Rutgers, 1975-76; secy, Coun Head Librn, State Univ New York, 1977; chmn, Adv Asn, GLIS Rutgers Univ, 1979; pres, Alumni Asn, Sch Libr & Info Mgt, Univ Denver, 1979; chmn, Intellectual Freedom & Due Process, New York Libr Asn, 1979; Basic Kappa Alphsi Frat; ALA; New York Libr Asn; NJ Libr Asn; NAACP; chair, State Univ New York Coun Head Librn, 1984; chair, Mem Comt, Am Libr Asn, 1985; chair, Comt & Jr Col Lib Sect, 1986; trustee, Elder Pres Scholar Comt, Berean Presby Church. **Honors/Awds:** Colleges & Universities Section Award Distinguished Service, NJ Librn Asn; Distinguished Alumni Award, Lincoln Univ; Certificate of Achievement Trenton Model Cities; Founders Award, Black & Hispanic Fac & Admin Asn, 1984; Sire Archon Beta Psi Boule Sigma Pi Phi Frat, 1984; 50th Anniversary Award of Appreciation, 1985; Appreciation Award, Beta Psi Boule, Sigma Beta Psi Fraternity, 1986; Outstanding Contribution, Comt Org, 1986. **Home Addr:** 317 N Broad St Apt 604, Philadelphia, PA 19107, **Home Phone:** (215)281-7933. **Business Addr:** Director Emeritus, Hudson Valley Community College, 80 Vandenburgh Ave, Troy, NY 12180, **Business Phone:** (518)629-7358.

### MCCOY, JELANI MARWAN (J-MAC MCCOY)

Basketball player. **Personal:** Born Dec 6, 1977, Oakland, CA; son of Frederick and Bettie. **Educ:** Univ Calif, attended 1998. **Career:** Seattle Supersonics, ctr, 1998-2001; Los Angeles Lakers, 2001-02; Toronto Raptors, 2002-03; Cleveland Cavaliers, 2003-04; Atlanta Hawks, ctr & forward, 2004; Long Beach Jam, 2004-05; Jiangsu Nangang Dragons, 2004-05; Reggio Calabria, Azovmash Mariupol, 2005-06; Viola Reggio Calabria, Ital Club, 2006; Menorca Basquet, 2007; Menorca Basquet, Santa Barbara Breakers, Span Club, 2007; Denver Nuggets, 2007-08; Los Angeles D-Fenders, 2007-08; Los Angeles Clippers, 2008; Zhejiang Guangsha, 2009; Fujian Xunxing, 2009-10; Caceres, 2016, 2010-11; Mets de Guaynabo, 2011; Marinos de Anzoategui, Osos de Guadalajara, 2012.

### MCCOY, JESSIE HAYNES

School administrator. **Personal:** Born Nov 17, 1955, Mound Bayou, MS; children: Raven & Tameka. **Educ:** Coahoma Jr Col, AA, eng, 1975; Univ S MS, BA, jour, 1976; MS State Univ, 1984; Bloomsburg Univ, attended 1985. **Career:** Delta Dem-Times Newspaper, Greenville, news reporter, 1976-79; Miss Valley State Univ, Itta Bena, dir univ rels, 1979-84; exec coun, MS Valley State Univ, 1982-84; freelancer var print media; Bloomsburg Univ Pa, Bloomsburg, univ rels dir, 1984-86; City Chesapeake, asst city mgr, pub info officer, 1986-; J & R Enterprises, co-owner, 1987-; City Norfolk, dir info & mkt; Inside City Hall, host; J Haynes & Assocs, Va Beach, founder. **Orgs:** Pres, PTA, Fulwiler & LS Roger Elem Schs, 1978-82; ford fel Ford Found Wash, journalism, 1979; case fel Coun Adv & Support Educ, 1981; dist chairwoman, MS Press Women, 1981-83; pres, Col Pub Rels Asn MS, 1982-83; pub rels officer, Am Asn Univ Women, 1983; mgt intern comn, Bloomsburg Univ, 1984-85, telecommun coun & pres coun; Columbia-Montour Tourist Prom Agency, 1984-85, Black Coun Higher Educ, 1984-85; mayorstask force, War Drugs; mayors bicentennial const comn, Jubilee Comn, C C PR Comn, city hall grand opening comn, rd bond referendumcomn, mayors youth day comn; curricullum adv bd comn, Tidewater Community Col; Nat Asn Advan Colored People, Chesapeake, VA; Nat Forum Black Pub Admin; Int City Mgrs Asn, Pub Rels Soc Am; Am soc Pub Admin; Am Mkt Asn; Va Munic League; Conf Minority Pub Admin. **Special Achievements:** Regional Finalist in President's Commission on White House Fellows. **Home Addr:** , TX. **Business Addr:** Founder, J Haynes and Associates, PO Box 64939, Virginia Beach, VA 23464, **Business Phone:** (757)490-4410.

### MCCRACKEN, QUINTON ANTOINE

Baseball player, executive. **Personal:** Born Aug 16, 1970, Wilmington, NC; son of Saundra; married Maggie Moskal; children: Isaiah Cicero. **Educ:** Duke Univ, BA, polit sci & hist, 1992. **Career:** Baseball player (retired), executive, owner; Colo Rockies, outfielder, 1995-97; Tampa Bay Devil Rays, 1998-2000; Minn Twins, 2001; Ariz Diamondbacks, outfielder, 2002-05, asst dir, player develop, 2010-; Seattle Mariners, 2004; Cincinnati Reds, 2006; Rochester Red Wings, 2006; Bridgeport Bluefish, 2007; Leones del Escogido, currently; Classic Car Spa, owner; Upper Deck Sports Grill, owner; Houston Astros, dir, player develop, 2012-. **Business Addr:** Assistant Director of Player Development, Arizona Diamondbacks, Chase Field 401 E Jefferson St, Phoenix, AZ 85004, **Business Phone:** (602)462-6500.

### MCCRACKIN, OLYMPIA H.

**Personal:** Born Jun 8, 1950, Tuscaloosa, AL; daughter of Oliver G Hines Sr and Susie Seltz Hines. **Educ:** Stillman Col, BA, 1972; Univ Ala, MLS, 1990. **Career:** Social Security Admin, Tuscaloosa, AL, claims rep, 1973-85; FBI, Birmingham, AL, rotor clerk, 1985-88; Tuscaloosa Pub Libr, librn, 1988-90; Bryce Hosp, librn, 1991-2001; Tuscaloosa City Schs, teacher, 2001-09. **Orgs:** Bd dir, Hospice W Ala, 1985-87; Ment Health Asn Tuscaloosa County, 1988-99; vpres, Eta Xi Omega Chap, Alpha Kappa Alpha Sorority, Inc, 1989-90; Am Libr Asn, 1989-2001; Ala Pub Libr Asn, 1989-2001; dep registr, Tuscaloosa County Bd Registrars; co-moderator, Presby Women, Brown Memorial Presby Church, 1990-91, moderator, Presby Women, 1991-95; pres, Eta Xi Omega Chap, Alpha Kappa Alpha Sorority, Inc, 1993-94; bd mem, bd chmn, ALA Adv CNL Libr, 1995; mentor, Big Bros Big Sisters, 1997-99; pres, Lucy Sheppard Art Federated Club, 1997-98; Tuscaloosa Asn Women's Clubs; Challenge 21 Vision Coun, area rep, 1998-2001; bd mem, Westside Community Develop Corp, 2011-13; financial secy, Presby Women Sheppards & Lapsley Presbytery, 2007-09; Tuscaloosa Cluster Leader, Presby Women Sheppards & Lapsley Presbytery, 2010-12; Tuscaloosa City Sch BRD EDU, 1999-2001; Nat Mid Sch Asn, 2001-04; AEA & NEA, 2001-; Nat Coun Teachers Eng, 2003-09; Delta Kappa Gamma Soc Int, 2003-06; Asn Supv & Curric Develop, 2004-09; asst Sunday sch supt, Brown Memorial Presby Church, 2008-; Clerk Session, Brown Memorial Presby Church, 2010-12; mem search comt, Synod Living Waters PCUSA, 2013-; Ala Educ Asn Legis Comn, 2008-10; Tuscaloosa Riverfront Pub-Pvt Partnership Steering Comt, 2009-11. **Honors/Awds:** Alabama Public Library Asn Scholarship, Ala Pub Libr Asn, Montgomery, Ala, 1989; Louise Giles Minority Scholar, Am Libr Asn, Chicago, Ill, 1989; AEA Emerging Leader, 2003; grad, Tuscaloosa City Schs, Sch Leadership Prog, 2003. **Home Addr:** 3 Greenbriar, Tuscaloosa, AL 35405, **Home Phone:** (205)343-7456. **Business Addr:** Retired Educator, Westlawn Middle School, 1715 ML King Jr Blvd, Tuscaloosa, AL 35401, **Business Phone:** (205)759-3673.

### MCCRAE, LARRY C.

Chief executive officer. **Career:** Larry C McCrae Inc, pres & chief exec officer, currently. **Orgs:** Greater Philadelphia Chamber Com. **Business Addr:** President, Chief Executive Officer, Larry C McCrae Inc, 3333 W Hunting Pk Ave, Philadelphia, PA 19132, **Business Phone:** (215)227-5060.

### MCCRARY, FRED DEMETRIUS

Football player. **Personal:** Born Sep 19, 1972, Naples, FL; married Sanquenette; children: 3. **Educ:** Miss State Univ, BS, criminol. **Career:** Football player (retired); Philadelphia Eagles, fullback, 1995;

New Orleans Saints, 1997; San Diego Chargers, fullback, 1999-2002; New Eng Patriots, fullback, 2003; Atlanta Falcons, fullback, 2004, 2005-06; Seattle Seahawks, 2007. **Honors/Awds:** Super Bowl XXXVIII Champions, 2003. **Special Achievements:** TV apeearance: Larry King Now, 2013.

### MCCRARY, MICHAEL
Singer, actor. **Personal:** Born Dec 16, 1971, Philadelphia, PA; son of Robert McCary Sr and Omarnetta Thomas. **Career:** R & B singer; Boys II Men, 1988-2003; Albums with Boys II Men: Cooley high harmony, 1991; Christmas Interpretations, 1993; II, 1994; Evolution, 1997; Nathan Michael Shawn Wanya, 2000; Full Circle, 2002; Throwback, Vol. 1, 2004; The Remedy, 2006; Motown: A Journey Through Hitsville USA, 2007; The Mannsfield 12, 2007; Beyond the Pretty Door, 2007; TBA, 2009. **Business Addr:** Recording Artist, Arista Records, 6 W 57th St, New York, NY 10019.

### MCCRARY-SIMMONS, SHIRLEY DENISE
Lawyer. **Personal:** Born Nov 7, 1956, Boston, MA; daughter of Eupha McCrary and Earlie McCrary; married Nathaniel O; children: Charity Denise. **Educ:** Brown Univ, AB, 1978; Boston Univ Sch Law, JD, 1982. **Career:** Ga Legal Serv, law intern, 1982; Internal Revenue Serv, tax rep/revenue officer, 1983-84, atty estate tax, 1984-90; atty, 1990-93; Arrington & Hollowell, PC, atty, 1993; pvt pract, attroney, currently. **Orgs:** Pres, Black Am Law Stud Asn, 1980-81; JD Curric Comn, 1981-82; Nat Bar Asn, 1983; dep registr, Fulton Co, Ga, 1983; St Bar Ga, 1983-; Gate City Bar Asn, 1985 & 1987; union steward, Nat Treas Employees Union, 1985-88; legal adv, Africare Atlanta Inc, 1985-89; Ga Asn Black Women Attorneys; Metrop Atlanta Chap 100 Black Woman; bd dir, Joseph E Mertz Memorial Educ Found; Antioch Urban Ministries Inc; Walton Mgt Inc. **Honors/Awds:** Superior Performance Award, IRS, 1988, 1989. **Special Achievements:** First African American female to be hired as an estate tax attorney in the Atlanta District. **Home Addr:** 191 Peachtree St, Atlanta, GA 30301. **Business Addr:** Attorney, Private Practice, PO Box 335, Fort Monmouth, NJ 07703, **Business Phone:** (732)380-9489.

### MCCRAVEN, MARCUS R.
Executive. **Personal:** Born Dec 27, 1923, Des Moines, IA; son of Marcus H and Buena Rollins; married Marguerite Mills; children: Carol J, Stephen A & Paul A. **Educ:** Howard Univ, BS, elec engineering; Univ Md; Univ Calif. **Career:** Executive (retired); Naval Res Lab, engr, elec engr, proj leader; Calif Lawrence Radiation Lab, res staff, engr group leader nuclear test; Phelps Dodge Community Co, chief engr; Bridgeport Elec Co, vpres; United Illum Co, dir environ engineering, vpres, 1970. **Orgs:** Dir, First Const Financial Corp; pres, Middletown Ave Asn Real Est; dir, Metrodata Inc Okla City; bd trustee, Conn State Cols; chmn bd, So Cent CT Am Red Cross; Sigma Pi Phi Fraternity; exec comn, EPA Sci Adv Bd; bd trustee, Quinnipiac Univ, Graduates Club, Jr Achievement; chmn bd, So Cent Ct Health Planning; pres, Yale Univ Peabody Mus Assoc; Quinnipiack Club; Golden Heritage Life Mem, Nat Asn Advan Colored People; State Conn Statewide Grievance co; aso fel, Yale univ; pres, N Haven CT Rotary; Urban League; United Way. **Home Addr:** 5 Rayzoe Terr, Hamden, CT 06514, **Home Phone:** (203)248-3008.

### MCCRAW, TOM (TOMMY LEE MCCRAW)
Baseball player, athletic coach. **Personal:** Born Nov 21, 1940, Malvern, AR; children: Bryan & Marla. **Career:** Baseball player (retired), athletic coach; Chicago White Sox, first baseman, 1963-70; Wash Senators, 1971; Cleveland Indians, 1972, infielder, 1974-75; Calif Angels, 1973-74; Cleveland Indians, coach, 1975, minor league hitting instr, 1976-79, first-base coach, 1980-82; San Francisco Giants, hitting instr, 1983; New York Mets, first-base coach, 1992-96; Montreal Expos, hitting coach, 2002; Wash Nat, hitting coach; Wash Senators, hitting coach, 2005; Gulf Coast Mets, hitting instr & mgr, 2006-. **Home Addr:** 2225 Clyde Suite 1, Los Angeles, CA 90016. **Business Addr:** Hitting Coach and Instructor, Manager, Gulf Coast League Mets, Tradition Field 525 NW Peacock Blvd, Port St Lucie, FL 34986, **Business Phone:** (772)871-2132.

### MCCRAY, ALMATOR FELECIA
Art museum director. **Personal:** Born Sep 16, 1956, Charlotte, NC; daughter of Robert Lee and Alma O; children: Ryan Lamar. **Educ:** Queens Col, BA, hist, 1992. **Career:** Belk Stores Serv, cre buyer, 1975-88; Ubiquitous Art Space Inc, dir, currently. **Orgs:** Nat Asn Negro Bus & Prof Women's Asn; adv bd, NC Mus Art, Am Fed Arts; art adv bd, UNCC, Nat Black Child Dev Inst; Nat Asn Female Execs. **Home Addr:** 2120 Aberdeen St, Charlotte, NC 28208-4624, **Home Phone:** (704)393-8514. **Business Addr:** Director, Ubiquitous Art Space Inc, 200 S Tryon St Suite 110, Charlotte, NC 28202.

### MCCRAY, CHRISTOPHER COLUMBUS
Government official. **Personal:** Born Sep 16, 1925, Waycross, GA; son of Pompey (deceased) and Rosa Lee (deceased); married Jewel Hollis; children: Cynthia, Linda Bacon & Christi. **Career:** Government official (retired); CSX Rr Co, equip operator, 1943-92; Waycross/Ware Co, co-chmn bi-racial comm, 1966-71; Waycross, Ga, sch bdmem, 1967-71; City Waycross, mayor pro-tem. **Orgs:** Waycross Community Concert Asn; John Sutton Am Legion Post No 517; Keystone Voters League; Nat Asn Advan Colored People, Waycross Chap; hon life mem, Future Bus Leaders Am; Supreme Grand Lodge Ancient & Accepted Scottish Rites Free Masons. **Honors/Awds:** Kiwanis Club Miller Medal Award, 1976; Martin Luther King Jr Commission Award, 1994; Citizen of the Year, Woodmen of the World, Way cross Chap, 1994; Gaines Chapel Merit Award of Civics; Silver Bowl Award, Waycross City Sch Bd; Waycross College Appreciation Award; Certificate of Appreciation, Keystone Voters & Civic League; Certificate of Appreciation, Nat Law Enforcement Community; Certificate of Appreciation, Jacksonville Fla Urban League; Certificate of Appreciation, CSX Transp; Merit Award of Civics, Greater Mt Zion AME Church; Delta Zeta Chapter Public School Award, Phi Delta Kappa Sorority; Public Service Award of Achievement in Community Service, Groveland Park Community Club; Sunday School Award for Civic & Christian Leadership, Mt Zion AME Church; Morris Jacobson Award; Certificate of Merit for Outstanding Service, SE Ga Area Planning & Develop Comn; E E Moore Membership Award for Outstanding Solicitation of Members, Nat Asn Advan Colored People; Distinguished Service Award for Service Rendered, Nat Guard Ga; Honorary Life Member, Future Bus Leaders Am; Award for Outstanding Service to the Community, Northside Community Club. **Special Achievements:** First African American mayor of the city of Waycross. **Home Addr:** 105 Santander Ct, Royal Palm Beach, FL 33411, **Home Phone:** (561)207-6010.

### MCCRAY, DARRYL K.
Fashion designer. **Personal:** Born Oct 3, 1963, Bronx, NY; children: Akira, D'Andra, Darryl II & D'Yon. **Educ:** Univ Phoenix, MBA, bus. **Career:** IBEW LU no 3, purchasing agt, 1985-90; Midtown Elec Supply, purchasing agt, 1987-90; House Nubian Inc, pres & chief exec officer, 1989-. **Business Addr:** Chief Executive Officer, President, House of Nubian Inc, PO Box 3510, Jersey City, NJ 07303, **Business Phone:** (201)547-3553.

### MCCRAY, MELVIN M.
Executive, manager. **Personal:** Born Aug 9, 1946, Ft. Benning, GA; married Rosie M Thompson; children: Kimya Nicole, Keisha Michelle, Cora Danielle & Diedra Marie. **Educ:** Ga State Univ, BS, 1972. **Career:** Atlanta City Aviation, admin asst II, 1975-76, admin asst III, 1976-77, proj coordr, 1977-80, Atlanta Hartsfield Int Airport, dir maintenance, 1980-. **Orgs:** Fin field City Atlanta City Hall, 1972-; collector dep marshal, 1975; Am Assoc Airport Exec, Southeastern Airport Mgrs Assoc, Conf Minority Pub Admin, Nat Forum Black Pub Admin; bd dir, Cty Atlanta Credit Union. **Honors/Awds:** Cert of Appreciation, ASPA, 1982; Cert of Recognition, GA Engg Found, 1982; Pres City of Atlanta Employees Club, 1982; Cert of Merit, Cty Atlanta & Andrew Young, 1983; Cert of Appreciation, COMPA, 1983; Christmas Fundraiser, 1983. **Home Addr:** 3070 June Apple Dr, Decatur, GA 30034-4535, **Home Phone:** (404)289-5691. **Business Addr:** Director of Maintenance, Hartsfield Atlanta International Airport, Commissioners Office, Atlanta, GA 30320.

### MCCRAY, NIKKI
Basketball coach, basketball player. **Personal:** Born Dec 17, 1971, Collierville, TN; married Thomas Penson; children: Thomas Nikson Penson. **Educ:** Univ Tenn, BA, sports mkt, 1995. **Career:** Basketball player (retired), basketball coach; Am Basketball League, Columbus Quest, 1996-98; Wash Mystics, 1998-2001; Pres's Coun Phys Fitness & Sports, mem, 2000; USA Olympic basketball team, 2000; Ind Fever, 2002-03; Launched Cubby Bear Daycare Ctr, Knoxville, Tenn, 2003; Phoenix Mercury, guard, 2004-06; San Antonio Silver Stars, 2005; Western Ky, asst coach, 2006-08; Chicago Sky, 2006; Univ SC, asst coach, 2008-, head coach; Women's Nat Basketball Asn. **Business Addr:** Assistant Coach, University of South Carolina, 1600 Hampton St, Columbia, SC 29208, **Business Phone:** (803)777-4227.

### MCCRAY, DR. ROY HOWARD
Dentist. **Personal:** Born Mar 14, 1946, Birmingham, AL; son of Maceo Cleggett and Annie Cleggett; children: Kenja, Kendyl & Kennethia. **Educ:** Ala A&M Univ, BS, 1972; Meharry Med Col, DDS, 1978. **Career:** Pvt practr, dentist, 1978-; Meharry Med Col, instr oper dent, 1978-81; Ala Dent Soc, parliamentarian, 1985-86. **Orgs:** Huntsville Madison Co Dent Soc, 1980-86; vpres, No Ala Med Asn, 1985-; Nat Asn Equal Opportunity, 1985; pres, Roy H Mccray Dds. **Honors/Awds:** CV Mosby III Award, Dr Martin Luther King Award, Meharry Dent Sch, 1977; Int Col Dentists, 1978; Am Asn Endodontists & Orthodontists, 1978. **Home Addr:** 180 Bentley Dr, Toney, AL 35773-9704. **Business Addr:** President, Roy H Mccray Dds, 2510 Pulaski Pike NW, Huntsville, AL 35810, **Business Phone:** (205)852-6954.

### MCCREARY, BILL
Journalist. **Personal:** Born Aug 18, 1933, Manhattan, NY. **Educ:** Baruch Col, City Col NYC; NY Univ Sch Commun. **Career:** Radio Sta WWRL Woodside Queens, staff anchor eng, 1960, co-producer, 1961; Night Prog, mgr, 1962; Radio Sta WLIB, newscaster, 1963; News Dir, 1965; Metro Media Broadcasting Inc, TV newscaster, 1967; WNEW & TV'S 10 O'Clock News, co-anchorman; 1 Hour TV Newscast, anchorman; Black News, anchorman, 1970, managing ed & exec dir, 1971; Gen Assignment reporter; Fox Broadcasting Co, exec producer "McCreary Report" & vpres, 1987-2000; Quest Media Entertainment, Spec Ed, co-producer & co-host, vpres, journalist, media consult & host, currently; Fox Tv sta WNYW - TV, former vpres, pres; Fox Tv, vpres, pres. **Orgs:** Cambria Hghts Civic Asn Queens; vpres, Royal Crusdrs Bowling Club; bd mem, New York Urban League; lifetime mem, National Association for the Advancement of Colored People; bd mem, Rich Inc, 2013-. **Honors/Awds:** Emmy Award, New York Chap Nat Acad TV Arts & Sci, 1969-70; Citation of Merit, 1971-72; Achievement Award, Berkeley Chap Nat Assoc Negro Bus & Prof Women's Club Inc; Cambria Heights Service Award, 1975; Achievement Award, NAACP LI Chap, 1975; Emmy Award for co-anchoring 10 o'clock news, 1980-81; Public Service Award, FDA; Black Heritage Award, NAACP, 1987; Floyd Flake Image Award, Mackee Williams Memorial Award, 1990; Distinguished Service Award, Fedn of Negro Civil Serv orgn. **Special Achievements:** Special Citation from the Commissioner, voted Most Watched and Believed Black Correspondent in Metro Area. **Home Addr:** 120-35 219 St, Cambria Heights, NY 11411. **Business Addr:** Vice President, Media Consultant & Host, Quest Media Entertainment Inc, 1000 Richmond Ter, Staten Island, NY 10301, **Business Phone:** (718)727-3777.

### MCCRIMMON, NICOLE (NICKY MCCRIMMON)
Basketball player. **Personal:** Born Mar 22, 1972, Harlem, NY. **Educ:** Univ Southern Calif, BS, commun & sociol, 1994. **Career:** Flims: Space Jam, 1996; TV Series: "Sports Theater with Shaquille O'Neal", 1997; "Smart Guy"; "Before & After'noon Movies". Seattle Reign, guard, 1997; Long Beach Stingrays, 1997; Atlanta Glory, 1997-98; Los Angeles Sparks, 2000-03; Women's Nat Basketball Asn, 2000; Houston Comets, guard, 2005; Lubbock Hawks, guard, 2005; LA County, probation officer. **Orgs:** Founder, Play Mode Inc.

### MCCRIMON, AUDREY L.
Government official, secretary (government). **Personal:** Born Oct 21, 1954, Covington, KY; daughter of Arthur and Letha Lewis Patrick. **Educ:** Northern Ill Univ, BS, educ, 1974, MS, educ, 1975; Harvard Univ, Boston, MA, 1993. **Career:** Jewish Voc Serv, Chicago, Ill, counr, 1975-77; City Cols Chicago, coordr, 1977-84; Chicago Dept Aging & Disability, dep comnr, 1984-90; Ill Dept Rehab Serv, Chicago, Ill, assoc dir, 1990-91, dir, 1991-97; Ill Dept Human Serv, asst secy, 1997-, asst compliance access & workplace safety, asst secy, currently. **Orgs:** Ill Asn Deaf, 1978-; Coalition Citizens Disabilities, 1985; Renaissance Women, 1990-; Nat Coun Disability, 1994-97; bd men, United Way Chicago Coun, 1994-; bd trustee, Comn Accreditation Rehab Facil, 1995-; Res Agenda Steering Comt, Nat Inst Disability & Rehab Res, 1995-. **Business Addr:** Assistant to the Secretary, Illinois Department of Human Services, 535 W Jefferson St, Springfield, IL 62702, **Business Phone:** (312)793-4605.

### MCCROOM, EDDIE WINTHER
Lawyer, naval officer. **Personal:** Born Sep 11, 1932, Memphis, TN; married Shirley Kathryn Lewis; children: Darren Winther, Audrey Jay & Sandra Marguerite. **Educ:** Univ Ark, BS, 1955; Case Western Res Univ, LLB, 1961. **Career:** OH Civil Rights Comn, field rep, 1961-63; US Dept Justice, asst US atty, 1964-69; Univ Cincinnati, lectr bus law, 1971-72; State OH Dept Admin Serv, state EEO coordr, 1972-74; E Winther McCroom & Assoc, pvt law pract, 1976-, pres. **Orgs:** Exec vpres, Indust Fed S & L Asns, 1969-70; legal coun Jaycee, 1970-; Ohio Legal Adv; NCP, 1970-; IBPOE W Elks, 1980. **Home Addr:** 724 Colonial Dr, Youngstown, OH 44505. **Business Addr:** Attorney, E Winther McCroom & Associates, 402 Legal Arts Ctr 101 Mkt St, Youngstown, OH 44503-1795, **Business Phone:** (330)747-1163.

### MCCUISTON, DR. STONEWALL, JR.
Physician. **Personal:** Born Feb 23, 1959, Chicago, IL; son of Stonewall and Annie M. **Educ:** Grinnell Col, BA, 1981; Meharry Med Col, MD, 1985. **Career:** John H Stroger Jr Hosp, intern, 1985-86, resident, 1986-89; Cook County Hosp, resident physician; pvt med pract, internal med & pediat, currently; Riverside Med Ctr, physician, currently. **Orgs:** Pres, Cook County Hosp House Staff Asn, 1988; pres, Cook County Hosp Black Physicians Asn, 1987-88; Cook County Hosp Union Coalition, 1988; Cook County Hosp Exec Med Staff, 1988; Chicago Med Soc; Ill State Med Soc; AMA. **Honors/Awds:** Research grant March of Dimes, 1982-83; First place Research Day, Med Div Meharry Med Col, 1983. **Home Addr:** 7810 S Ridgeland, Chicago, IL 60649, **Home Phone:** (312)731-3717. **Business Addr:** Physician, 3400 S Main St, Hopkins Pk, IL 60944, **Business Phone:** (815)944-5545.

### MCCULLERS, EUGENE
Executive. **Personal:** Born Jan 30, 1941, Garner, NC. **Educ:** Shaw Univ, BA, 1962; Univ Wis; Univ PR. **Career:** Executive (retired); US Peace Corps, vol, 1963-65; Capitol Coca-Cola Bottling Co, Raleigh, NC, spec markets rep, 1965-67; Coca-Cola Bottling Co, Thomas, Tenn, acct exec, 1968-76; Coca-Cola USA, Atlanta, Ga, mkt mgr, 1976-81, mgr community affairs, 1981-96; Almirante Consult, prin. **Orgs:** Bd dir, trustee, Shaw Univ; bd dir, Grambling State Univ Athletic Found; bd dir, Nat Black Col Hall Fame Found; bd dir, Jacquelyn McClure Lupus Ctr; bd dir, Nat Asn Mkt Develop; life mem, Nat Asn Advan Colored People; Elks; Kappa Alpha Psi. **Home Addr:** 3210 Hazelwood Dr SW, Atlanta, GA 30311-3036, **Home Phone:** (404)696-1858.

### MCCULLOUGH, GARY
President (organization), chief executive officer. **Educ:** Wright State Univ, BS, mgt, 1981; Northwestern Univ, Kellogg Grad Sch Mgt, MBA, mgt policy, mkt, finance, 1987. **Career:** Procter & Gamble, exec, N Am Homecare Prod, gen mgr, 1987-2000; Wm. Wrigley Jr Co, Americas sr vpres, 2000-03; Sherwin-Williams Co, dir & audit comt chmn, 2002-11; Abbott Labs, Ross Prod Div, pres, 2003-07; Career Educ Corp, pres & chief exec officer, 2007-11; Willow Partners LLC, pvt investor, 2012-; Abundant Venture Partners, investor & advisor, 2012-; Advert Resources Inc/ARI Packaging, chief exec officer & bd mem, 2014-. **Orgs:** Bd dir, Acad Urban Sch Leadership, 2011; bd trustee, Rush Univ Med Ctr, 2011. **Honors/Awds:** "Black Enterprise," 75 Most Powerful African Americans in Business, 2005; The 100 Most Powerful Executives in Corporate America, 2010; Meritorious Service Medal. **Business Addr:** Chief Executive Officer, ARI Packaging, 11601 S Cent Ave, Alsip, IL 60803, **Business Phone:** (888)311-3246.

### MCCULLOUGH, REV. DR. JACQUELINE E.
Preacher. **Personal:** Born Kingston. **Educ:** Drew Theol Sem, DMin; NY Univ, MA, philos; Jewish Theol Sem. **Career:** Harlem Hosp, regist nurse pediat, nurse practr; Gospel vocalist; reverend; Beth Rapha Bible Inst, founder & pres, currently; Int Gathering at Beth Rapha, sr pastor & founder, currently; Beth Rapha Christian Col & Theol Sem, pres & chief exec officer, currently. **Orgs:** Pres & chief exec officer, Daughters Rizpah; pres & chief exec officer, JEM Ministries. **Special Achievements:** The "Most Influential African-American Ministers In The Nation", 1996; Discography: This Is For You Lord, 1999; Author: Daily Moments With God: In Quietness and Confidence, 2001; 105 Days of Prayer, 2005. **Business Addr:** President, Founder, The International Gathering at Beth Rapha, 1540 Rte 202 Suite 3 & 4, Pomona, NY 10970, **Business Phone:** (845)362-8900.

### MCCUMMINGS, DR. LEVERNE
Executive, school administrator. **Personal:** Born Oct 28, 1932, Marion, SC; son of Henry and Mamie; married Betty L Hall; children: Gregory, Gary & Ahada. **Educ:** St Augustine's, BA, 1960; Univ Pa, MSW, 1966; Ohio State Univ, PhD, 1975. **Career:** Assoc Prof, 1977; GSSW Dean, 1978-85; Competency Cert Bd, Bd Health & Human Servs, Futures Think Tank, chmn, 1981-82; Denver Univ, dean & prof graduate sch social work; Natl Conf Grad Deans/Dirs & Off Soc Work Progs, pres, 1982-85; Cheyney Univ Pa, pres, 1985-91. **Orgs:** Pres, Alliance Black Social Workers; pres, Coun Deans & dir, 1982-85. **Special Achievements:** First African American to serve as a graduate dean; First person of color to serve as director or dean. **Home Addr:** 160 William Penn Blvd, West Chester, PA 19382. **Business Addr:** Presi-

dent, Philadelphia Alliance of Black Social Workers Inc, 1924 W Diamond St, Philadelphia, PA 19121, **Business Phone:** (215)235-1626.

### MCCURDY, DR. BRENDA L. (WRIGHT MCCURDY)

Microbiologist. **Educ:** Va Union Univ, BS, 1968; Va Commonwealth Univ, Sch Med, MS, 1970; Wayne State Univ, Sch Med, PhD, 1980. **Career:** Henry Ford Hosp Detroit, microbiologist III, 1970-72; Wayne State Univ, res asst, 1972-75; Wayne State Univ, adj asst prof immunol & microbiol, 1980-; Veterans Admin Med Ctr, sect chief microbiol, 1979; US Food & Drug Admin, Lab Br, dir, currently. **Honors/Awds:** Graduate Professional Scholarship, Wayne State Univ, 1976-77; 'National Fellowship Award', 1977-78; Augusta T Calloway Fellowship Award, 1979. **Home Addr:** 4646 John R St, Detroit, MI 48201-1932. **Business Addr:** Director, US Food & Drug Administration, Detroit Dist Off, Detroit, MI 48207, **Business Phone:** (313)393-8203.

### MCCURDY, WRIGHT. See MCCURDY, DR. BRENDA L.

### MCCUTCHEN, ANDREW STEFAN

Baseball player. **Personal:** Born Oct 10, 1986, Fort Meade, FL. **Career:** Maj League Baseball, Pittsburgh Pirates, ctr fielder, 2009-. **Honors/Awds:** Baseball America Rookie of the Year, 2009; All-Star Game, 2011, 2012; Gold Glove Award, 2012; Silver Slugger Award, 2012, 2013; Players Choice National League Outstanding Player Award, 2012; National League's Most Valuable Player, 2012; Dapper Dan Sportsman of the Year, 2012; Roberto Clemente Award, 2015. **Special Achievements:** TV Series: "Ellen: The Ellen DeGeneres Show", 2013; "Mike & Mik", 2013-14. **Business Addr:** Professional Baseball Player, Pittsburgh Pirates, 115 Fed St, Pittsburgh, PA 15212, **Business Phone:** (412)323-5000.

### MCCUTCHEON, LAWRENCE P.

Scout, executive director, football player. **Personal:** Born Jun 2, 1950, Plainview, TX; son of Roland and Leanna Bell; married Myra Emerson; children: Adrian Campbell & Daylon. **Educ:** Colo State Univ, attended 1972. **Career:** Football player (retired), scout; Los Angeles Rams, running back, 1972-79; Seattle Seahawks, running back, 1980; Denver Broncos, running back, 1980; Buffalo Bills, running back, 1981; Los Angeles Rams, dir player personnel, 2003-06; St Louis Rams, dir player personnel, 2006-. **Orgs:** Mem, Colo state hall flame. **Honors/Awds:** Outstanding Offensive Back, 1973-77; NEA'S Third Down Award, 1974 & 1977; Second team ALL-NFC, UPI; Pro Bowl for 4th Staight Time; Daniel F Reeves Mem Award, 1974 & 1977; Most Valuable Player; All-Rookie Team, UPI; All-Western Athletic Conf; Colo State Univ; NFC All Star Team, Sporting News, 1974; Inducted into the Tex Panhandle Hall of Fame, 2005. **Home Addr:** 19981 Weems Lane, Huntington Beach, CA 92646. **Business Addr:** Director Player Personnel, Saint Louis Rams, 1 Rams Way, St Louis, MO 63045, **Business Phone:** (314)982-7267.

### MCDADE, JOE BILLY

Judge. **Personal:** Born Jan 1, 1937, Billville, TX; married Mary Evelyn. **Educ:** Bradley Univ, BS, 1959, MS, 1960; Mich Univ, JD, 1963. **Career:** US Dept Justice, staff atty antitrust div, 1963-65; First Fed Savs & Loan Asn, exec trainee, 1965; Hafele & McDade, Peoria, Ill, partner, 1968-77; pvt pract, Peoria, 1977-82; Peoria COC Leadership Sch, guest lectr, 1977; Ill State, Peoria, assoc circuit judge, 1982-98, ciruit judge, 1988-91; US Dist Ct, Cent Dist Ill, chief justice, 1998-2004; judge, currently. **Orgs:** Exec dir, Greater Peoria Ill Legal Aid Soc, 1965-69; bd dir, Ill Judges Asn; chmn, Legal Action Comn, Peoria Chap, Nat Asn Advan Colored People, 1966-67; bd dir, Ct Counors Prog Inc, 1968-75 & 1983-86; bd dir, Tri-Co Peoria Urban League, 1970-72; panel mem, Heart Ill United Fund, 1974-77; bd dir, Peoria YMCA, 1975-77 & 1985-92, prog comn, 1989-92; bd dir, Ill Cent Health Systs Agency, 1975-82, pres, 1978-80; adv bd, Comprehensive Work & Training Prog, 1975-83; Creve Coeur Club, 1978-82; bd dir, Greater Peoria Sports Hall Fame Inc, 1980-82; trustee, St Peter's Catholic Church, 1980-85; bd dir, Cent Ill Bradley Alumni Club, 1982-83; bd dir, Upgrade Non-Profit Housing Corp, 1983-89; exec bd, Boy Scouts Am, WD Boyce, 1984-86; chmn, House Prayer Comn, 1987-89; bd dir, SHARE Foods Inc, 1987-92; Ill Eagle Scouts, Citizenship Prom Comn, 1988-94; bd dir, Amateur Musical Club Peoria, 1988-92; bd dir, Peoria Tri-Centennial, 1990-92; bd dir, Am Red Cross Central Ill Chap, 1991-94; Ill State Bar Asn; Peoria Co Bar Asn. **Honors/Awds:** NIT Championship Team, Bradley Univ, 1957; All NIT Team, Bradley University, 1959; Shriner's East/West All-Star Basketball Team, Bradley Univ, 1959; Outstanding Academic Athlete, Bradley Univ, 1959; Watonga Award, Bradley Univ, 1959; Highest Student Award, Bradley Univ, 1959; Bradley University Hall of Fame, Bradley Univ, 1961; Leadership Award, First Presbyterian Church Youth Retreat, 1966; Bradley Honorary Coach Award, Bradley Univ, 1980; Citizen of the Year Award, Omega Psi Phi Fraternity, 1983; IBPO Elms of the World Achievement Award, Bethel United Meth Men's Club, 1989; Distinguished Alumnus Award, 1990; Bradley Univ, 1990; Bradley University Centurion, Bradley Univ, 1990; Certificate of Appreciation, Ill Dept C & Family Serv, 1991; Recognition Award, African Hall Fame Mus, 1991; Award of Appreciation, Share Food Prog Cent Ill, 1992; Certificate of Recognition, Peoria Christian Leadership Coun, 1992; Certificate of Recognition, Peoria Christian Leadership Coun, 1992; Award of Appreciation, Share Food Prog Cent Ill Inc, 1992; Award of Recognition, Houston Area Urban League, 1994. **Business Addr:** US District Judge, US District Court, Fed Bldg 100 NE Monroe St Suite 122, Peoria, IL 61602, **Business Phone:** (309)671-7821.

### MCDANIEL, DR. ADAM THEODORE

Dentist. **Personal:** Born Jun 8, 1925, Rock Hill, SC; son of Therlo and Maggie Falls; married Lois Butler; children: Jenita A & Frederic. **Educ:** NC Cent Univ, BS, 1946; Howard Univ, DDS, 1951; Friendship Jr Col. **Career:** Jersey City Med Ctr, internship, 1951-52; pvt pract dentist, currently; Rahway Geriat Ctr, dent consult. **Orgs:** Rahway Rotary Club; state rep, Rahway Housing Auth, 1959-70; pres, Rahway Mun Coun Caucus Elected Black Officials, 1960-72; Union Co & NJ Dent Soc; 100 Black Men NJ; Omega Psi Phi Fraternity; NJ Chap Nat Guardsmen Inc; Correctional Health Serv Invest Comn NJ State Prisons; Lay Comm Pub Sch Systs; Urban League. **Honors/Awds:** Honoree, Beta Kappa Chi Hon SJI Soc; Testimonial Dinner, 1961, 1973. **Business Addr:** Dentist, Private Practice, 97 E Milton Ave, Rahway, NJ 07065-4031, **Business Phone:** (732)381-9005.

### MCDANIEL, EDWARD

Business owner, football player. **Personal:** Born Feb 23, 1969, Batesburg, SC. **Educ:** Clemson Univ, BA, human resources & develop. **Career:** Football player (retired), bus owner; Minn Vikings, 1992, linebacker, 1993, 1999-2001, right linebacker, 1994-95, left linebacker, 1996-97, middle linebacker, 1998-99; D1 Sports Training, Greenville, SC, co-owner, currently. **Honors/Awds:** Pro Bowl, 1998. **Special Achievements:** Film: 1998 NFC Championship Game, 1999. TV Series: "TNT Sunday Night Football", 1994; "ESPN's Sunday Night Football", 1994-99; "NFL Monday Night Football", 1994-2001; "NFL on FOX", 1998-2000. **Business Addr:** Co-owner, D1 Sports Training, 1334 Miller Rd, Greenville, SC 29607, **Business Phone:** (864)288-3868.

### MCDANIEL, ELIZABETH B.

Health services administrator. **Personal:** Born May 3, 1952, St. Louis, MO; children: Paul R. **Educ:** Forest Park, BA, arts, 1981. **Career:** Forest Pk Admin Bldg, work study, 1978; Forest Pk Community Col, workstudy, 1981, stud asst, 1982; Coalition Sch Desegration, secy, 1982; St Louis Comp N Health Ctr, secy & clerk 1982; Vis Nurse Asn, billing clerk, 1984; St Louis Univ Hosp, lead clerk, 1986; St Louis Regional Physician's Billing, treas, 1987. **Orgs:** Vpres, Wellston Sch Bd. **Home Addr:** 6562 Jesse Jackson Ave, St. Louis, MO 63121-5707, **Home Phone:** (314)382-0051. **Business Addr:** Treasurer, St Louis Regional Medical Center, St. Louis, MO 63112, **Business Phone:** (314)367-0513.

### MCDANIEL, EMMANUEL

Football player, football coach. **Personal:** Born Jul 27, 1972, Griffin, GA; married Lynn A Viehmeyer; children: Jaylen. **Educ:** E Carolina Univ, BA, criminal justice, 1995. **Career:** Football player (retired), football coach; Carolina Panthers, 1996, defensive back & right corner back, 2002; Indianapolis Colts, 1997; New York Giants, right cornerback, 1999-2000, 2001; Ariz Cardinals, 2003; Univ Akron, asst coach, 2007-09; E Carolina Univ, asst coach. **Honors/Awds:** East Carolina Rookie Year, 1996. **Business Addr:** Assistant Coach, University of Akron, 373 Carroll St, Akron, OH 44325, **Business Phone:** (330)972-6245.

### MCDANIEL, DR. JAMES BERKLEY, JR.

Physician. **Personal:** Born Aug 8, 1925, Pittsburgh, PA; son of James Sr; children: James B III & Nancy Alben Lloyd. **Educ:** Howard Univ, BS, 1950, Col Med, MD, 1957. **Career:** Freedmens Hosp, intern, resident; Physician Obest & Gynec, prv pract, 1962; State Univ NY, Buffalo, asst clin prof, 1974; Geneva B Scruggs Community Health Care Ctr Inc, head, Obest & Gynec Dept; pvt pract, physician, currently. **Honors/Awds:** First Achiever Award, Stud Nat Med Asn & Buffalo, 1972; Achiever Award, Buffalo Youth Bd; Chief Executive Officer's Lifetime Achievement Award, Geneva B Scruggs Ctr, 1989. **Home Addr:** 800 W Ferry St Apt 5bb, Buffalo, NY 14222-1688. **Business Addr:** Physician, Private Practice, 945 Wash St, Buffalo, NY 14203, **Business Phone:** (716)885-1885.

### MCDANIEL, KAREN COTTON

Librarian, college administrator. **Personal:** Born Nov 16, 1950, Newark, NJ; daughter of Alphonso C Jr and Maude Smoot Bledsoe; married Rodney Sr; children: Rodney Jr, Kimberly Renee & Jason Bradley. **Educ:** Berea Col, BS, bus admin, 1973; Univ Ky, MS, libr sci, women's studies cert, 1975, PhD, 2013. **Career:** KY State Univ, asst librn, 1975-83, dir libr, 1989-2005, prof emer, currently; KY Dept Pub Advocacy, law librn, 1983-85; KY Dept Librs & Arch, prog coord, 1985-89; Eastern Ky Univ, vis scholar, 2007-10; Berea Col, asst prof, 2010-11. **Orgs:** Delta Sigma Theta Sorority, 1976-; KY Coun Arch, 1987-; Am Libr Asn, 1989-; Asn Col & Res Librs, 1989-; secy, 1989-, 1991-92, chair, 1992-93, State Assisted Acad Libr Coun KY; sect secy, KY Libr Asn, 1990-91, 1975-; Black Caucus Am Libr Asn, 1991-; chair, 1994-98, vice chair, 1992-94, 1989-, Land Grant Lib dir Asn; bd dir & treas, 1995-96, secy, 1996-97, 1994-97, SOLINET; chair, Asn Agr Admin, 1996-98, 1989-; chair, Womens Hist Coalition KY, 1997-98, 1993-2004; HBCU Libr Alliance, 2002-, treas, 2004-; Asn Black Women Historians; bd mem, Ky Heritage Coun; Am Hist Soc; Asn Study African Am Life & Hist; Ky Hist Soc; Nat Women's Studies Asn. **Home Addr:** 147 Northwood Rd, Frankfort, KY 40601, **Home Phone:** (502)695-7437. **Business Addr:** Professor Emeritus, Kentucky State University, 400 E Main St, Frankfort, KY 40601, **Business Phone:** (502)597-6029.

### MCDANIEL, REV. PAUL ANDERSON

Clergy. **Personal:** Born Jul 5, 1930, Rock Hill, SC; son of Adam T and Maggie; married Edna Carolyn Phillips; children: Paul Jr, Pamela Anita (deceased), Patricia Ann & Peter Adam; married Linda Isadora; children: Paul Jr, Patricia, Peter & Pamela (deceased). **Educ:** Morehouse Col, Atlanta, BA, hist polit sci, 1951; Colgate Rochester Div Sch, MDiv, 1955; Univ Rochester, MA, 1959. **Career:** Second Baptist Church Mumford, pastor, 1952-56; Second Baptist Church, pastor, 1956-66; Second Missionary Baptist Church, Chattanooga, pastor, 1966-; Nat Baptist Cong Christian Educ, instr; Nat Baptist Sunday Sch, instr; BTU Cong, instr; Baptist Bible Ctr Chattanooga; Omega Psi Phi Fraternity Inc, bro. **Orgs:** Tenn Const Conv, 29th Dist Nashville, 1977; chmn, Ga-Tenn Regional Health Comn, 1978-80; chmn & past vice chmn, Hamilton Co Comn, Chattanooga, 1979; Chattanooga African Am Black Chamber Com; pres, Clergy Asn Greater Chattanooga; chmn, Unity Group; Nat Asn Advan Colored People; People United to Save Humanity; pres, Tenn Leadership Educ Cong; bd chmn, Westside Community Develop Corp, currently; chmn, Unity Group; chmn, Clergy Koinonia Fed Credit Union; Nat Asn Advan Colored People; People United Save Humanity; chmn, Clergy Koinonia Fed Credit Union; Hamilton County Comn, chmn. **Honors/Awds:** DD Friendship Jr Coll Rock Hill SC, 1975; Legacy Award, univ of tenn Chattanooga, 2004; June Hero of the Month. Received numerous awards. **Special Achievements:** First African American minister to serve as President of the Clergy Association of Greater Chattanooga. **Home Addr:** 722 Belle Vista Ave, Chattanooga, TN 37411, **Home Phone:** (432)622-8842. **Business Addr:** Member, Chattanooga African American Chamber of Commerce, 535 Chestnut St Suite 200, Chattanooga, TN 37402, **Business Phone:** (423)265-0021.

### MCDANIEL, RANDALL CORNELL

Football player. **Personal:** Born Dec 19, 1964, Phoenix, AZ; married Marianne. **Educ:** Ariz State Univ, BS, phys educ. **Career:** Football player (retired); Minn Vikings, guard & left guard, 1988-99; Tampa Bay Buccaneers, guard & left guard, 2000-01; McDaniel's high sch, athletic dir & asst prin, currently. **Honors/Awds:** Pro Bowl, 1989-2000; Most Inspirational Man of the Year, Nat Football League, 1990; Midwest Sports Channel, 1996; Unsung Hero Award, Nat Football League Players Asn, 1997; Minnesota Vikings "Ring of Honor", 2006; College Hall of Fame, Nat Football Found, 2008; Pro Football Hall of Fame, 2009; Randall McDaniel Sports Complex, Avondale, named in honor, 2010. **Special Achievements:** TV appearance: Rome Is Burning, 2009. **Home Addr:** 20405 Manor Rd, Excelsior, MN 55331-9470.

### MCDANIEL, PROF. REUBEN R, JR. See Obituaries Section.

### MCDANIEL, ROBERT ANTHONY (ROBERT PETE MCDANIEL)

Writer, journalist. **Personal:** Born Aug 2, 1952, Arden, NC; son of Theodore Roosevelt and Mary Alice Spain; married Angela L Tribue; children: 4. **Educ:** Univ NC, Asheville, NC, BA, eng, 1974. **Career:** Asheville Citizen-Times, Asheville, NC, sports writer, 1974-75; Life Ga Ins Co, Asheville, NC, ins agt, 1975-78; Piedmont Airlines, Asheville, NC, ticket agt trainee, 1978-79; Times-News, Hendersonville, NC, sports writer, 1979-82, sports ed, 1982-93; Golf World Mag, Trumbull, Conn, sr writer, 1993-97; Golf Dig, sr writer, 1997-. **Orgs:** Assoc Press Sports Ed, 1982-93; Nat Asn Black Journalists, 1989-; Golf Writers Am Assn, 1993-. **Honors/Awds:** Spot Sports News, 3rd Pl, NC Press Assn, 1981; Sports Feature, 2nd Pl, NC Press Assn, 1984; Sports Feature, 2nd Pl, NC Press Assn, 1985; 1st Place, Sports Reporting, NC Press Association, 1992; Denzel Washington Youth Service Award, Westchester Hills Country Club, 2009; Black Achiever in Bus/Industry Award, 1997; Harlem YMCAs Black Achiever. **Special Achievements:** Co-Author of best-selling book "Training A Tiger", How I Play Golf; Author; Uneven Lies: The Heroic Story of African Americans in Golf; Co-wrote and co-produced the documentary "Uneven Fairways". **Home Addr:** 1245 Azalea Cir, Conyers, GA 30013, **Home Phone:** (407)903-1367.

### MCDANIEL, SHARON A.

Arts administrator, music critic. **Personal:** Born Jan 3, 1950, Hampton, VA; daughter of James Cornelius and Mae Hallie Payne. **Educ:** Paris Am Acad Music, Paris, France, cert piano & cert fr, 1967; Col-Conserv Music, Cincinnati, OH, BA, music theory, 1971; Eastman Sch Music, Rochester, NY, 1974, 1988. **Career:** Gen Tel & Electronics, Los Angeles, Calif, regional sales mgr, 1974-78; Oakland Symphony Orchestra, Oakland, Calif, orchestra mgr, 1978-79; Dayton Contemp Dance Co, Dayton, Ohio, gen mgr, 1982-83; Springfield Symphony, Springfield, Ohio, gen mgr, 1984-86; Hochstein Music Sch, Rochester, NY, dir commun, 1988-; About Time Mag, Rochester, NY, ed asst, 1991. **Orgs:** Class music announcer/host WRUR-FM, Rochester, NY, 1986-; singer, Rochester Bach Festival Choir, Rochester, NY, 1972-74 & 1987-; Rochester Asn Black Communicators, Rochester, NY, 1987-; bd dir, publicity, Madrigalia Ltd, Rochester, NY, 1987-; fund raising comts, IBM-PC Club Rochester, NY, 1988; Music Critics Asn, 1984, 1991. **Home Addr:** 357 Hammocks Trl, Greenacres, FL 33413-2133, **Home Phone:** (561)649-3932. **Business Addr:** Critic, Democrat & Chronicle, 55 Exchange Blvd, Rochester, NY 14614, **Business Phone:** (585)232-7100.

### MCDANIEL, TERRENCE LEE (TERRY MCDANIEL)

Football player. **Personal:** Born Feb 8, 1965, Saginaw, MI; children: Isaiah. **Educ:** Univ Tenn. **Career:** Football player (retired); Los Angeles Raiders, defensive back, 1988, left cornerback, 1989-94; Oakland Raiders, left cornerback, 1995-97; Seattle Seahawks, defensive back, 1998. **Honors/Awds:** Pro Bowl, 1992- 96; All-Pro, 1992-94; Hall of Fame, Saginaw County, 2002. **Special Achievements:** Film: 1988 NFL Draft , 1988; 1990 AFC Championship Game, 1991. **Home Addr:** 1343 Norman St, Saginaw, MI 48601-1132.

### MCDANIEL, WILLIAM T., JR.

Educator, jazz musician. **Personal:** Born Sep 24, 1945, Memphis, TN; married Bernice Dowdy; children: William Theodore III. **Educ:** Morehouse Col, BA, 1967; Univ IA, MA, 1968, PhD, music educ, 1974. **Career:** NC Agr & Tech State Univ, prof, chmn dept music; Morehouse Col, dir bands, 1968-72, chmn dept Music, dir bands, 1974-77; Univ IA, instr black music, 1973-74; OSU Marching Band, music arranger, 1981-; Sch Music, Ohio St Univ, prof african am music, 1981-, dir Jazz studies, dir award winning OSU Jazz Ensemble, dept chair, 1989-96. **Orgs:** Mus Ed, Nat Conf; Am Musicol Soc; Col Mus Soc; Col Band Dir Nat Asn; Nat Asn Col Wind & Percsn Instrs; Nat Band Asn; Alpha Phi Alpha; Ctr Black Music Res; Nat Asn Negro Musicians; Nat Asn Music Educ; Nat Coun Black Studies; Asn Study Afro Am Life & Hist; Int Asn Jazz Educ; pres, founder, Nat Asn Study & Performance African Am Music. **Honors/Awds:** Distinguished Teaching Award, 1987; Distinguished Scholar Award, Sch Music Ohio State, 1994; Distinguished Diversity Enhancement Award, The Ohio State Univ, 2000. **Business Addr:** Professor, Ohio State University, 314 Hughes Hall, Columbus, OH 43210, **Business Phone:** (614)292-4657.

### MCDANIEL, XAVIER MAURICE

Basketball player, executive, basketball coach. **Personal:** Born Jun 4, 1963, Columbia, SC; married Pesters; children: Xylina. **Educ:** Wichita State Univ, attended 1985. **Career:** Basketball player (retired), basketball coach, executive; Seattle Super Sonics, forward, 1985-90; Phoenix Suns, forward, 1990-91; NY Knicks, forward, 1991-92; Boston Celtics, forward, 1992-95; Iraklis BC, 1995-96; NJ Nets, forward, 1996-98;

Riders Slamball, head coach; 34 X-man, owner, currently. **Business Addr:** Owner, 34 X-man, Blythewood, SC 29016, **Business Phone:** (803)600-5980.

### MCDANIELS, ALFRED F.
Athletic coach, educator. **Personal:** Born Sep 21, 1940, Muskogee, OK; son of Alvin; married Cheryl Kieser; children: Alfred Jr & Debbie. **Educ:** Bakersfield Jr Col, AA, 1961; Univ Nev, Reno, BS, 1965, Univ Nev, Las Vegas, MED, 1971; Univ Nev, BS, 1965, MEd, 1972. **Career:** PE Health Educ, teacher, 1965-70; Varsity Football, asst varsity head jr varsity asst track coach, 1965-67; Merced HS, head track coach, 1968-80; Univ NV, asst football coach, 1970-72, asst track coach, 1971-74, asst prof phys educ head track coach, 1975-92, Dept Kinesiology, teacher, PE Activ, teacher, vol coach, sprints, mid distance, currently. **Orgs:** Designed & develop, USA Youth Track & Field Prog Nev, 1980-93; trained & organized, Southern Nev Track & Field Off Asn, 1975-92; Nat Educ Asn; NSEA; NAHPER; AAHPER; United Teaching Prof; US Track & Field Coaches Asn; Women's Track & Field Coaches Asn. **Honors/Awds:** Outstanding Athlete, Bakersfield Col, 1959, Bakersfield HS, 1960, Univ NV, 1965; Most Outstanding in Track, 1963; Most Outstanding in Football, 1964; Most Outstanding Senior Athlete, Univ NV Reno, 1965; Women's PCAA Team Champion Track & Field, 1984-86 & 1989; Womens PCAA Coach of the Year Track & Field, 1984-86 & 1989; Big west coach of year, PCAA, 1989; District Eight Coach of the Year, Nat Col Athletic Asn, 1989 & 1991; Las Vegas Black Sports Hall of Fame, 1991; Bakersfield Col Track & Field Hall of Fame, 1993; USA Track & Field President's Award, 1993; Big West Coach of the Year, 1984-86 & 1989; publication in athletic journal, speaker at numerous clinics. **Special Achievements:** Wrote a chapter on track and field in "Sports & Recreational Activities for Men and Women", January 1994. **Home Addr:** 10599 Angelo Tenero Ave, Las Vegas, NV 89135, **Home Phone:** (702)240-7346. **Business Addr:** Teacher, University of Nevada, 4505 S Md Pkwy, Las Vegas, NV 89154, **Business Phone:** (702)895-4179.

### MCDANIELS, DARRYL
Publisher, rap musician. **Personal:** Born May 31, 1964, New York, NY; son of Byford and Banna; married Zuri L Alston, Sep 1, 1992?; children: Darryl M Jr. **Educ:** St. John's Univ. **Career:** Run-DMC, rapper, 1981-2002; solo rapper, 2004; DMC: My Adoption Journey, contributor, 2006; Darryl Makes Comics, LLC, publisher, 2014-. **Orgs:** Felix Organization, co-founder. **Honors/Awds:** Rock and Roll Hall of Fame, inductee, 2009. Grammy Lifetime Achievement Award, 2016. **Special Achievements:** Albums Run-DMC: Run-D.M.C., 1984; King of Rock, 1985; Raising Hell, 1986; Tougher Than Leather, 1988; Back from Hell, 1990; Down with the King, 1993; Crown Royal, 2000. Solo albums: Checks, Thugs, Rock-N-Roll, Elektra, 2006. Author: King of Rock: Respect, Responsibility and My Life with Run-DMC, 2001, Ten Ways Not to Commit Suicide, Amistad, 2016. **Business Addr:** c/o Universal Attractions Agency Inc, 15 West 36th St 8th Fl, New York, NY 10018.

### MCDANIELS, JEANEEN J.
Lawyer. **Personal:** Born Mar 29, 1960, Canton, OH; daughter of Albert H (deceased) and Nadine McIlwain Williams. **Educ:** Cent State Univ, Wilberforce, OH, attended 1981; Univ Akron, Akron, OH, JD, 1984. **Career:** Co Prosecutor's Off, Canton, Ohio, asst prosecuting atty, 1985-86; City Prosecutor's Off, Canton, Ohio, asst prosecuting atty, 1986-90; Timken Co, Canton, Ohio, sr personnel & logistics analyst, 1990-91, indust rels rep, 1992-, Gam Roller Plant, mgr hr, 1992-; We'll Do It You Inc, owner; pvt pract atty, currently; TimkenSteel Corp, mgr, Employee Rels & Compliance, 2011-14, sr mgr med serv, employee rels & regulatory compliance, 2014-. **Orgs:** Legal adv, Indian River Sch, 1987-92; vpres, 1988-90, pres, 1990-92; Stark Co Delta Sigma Theta Inc; pres, Mahogany Asn, 1988-90, treas, 1990-92; secy, Canton City Sch Found, 1990-92; secy, Canton Urban League, 1990-92. **Home Addr:** 2328 Raintree St NE, Canton, OH 44705, **Home Phone:** (330)492-4733. **Business Addr:** Industrial Relations Representative, Manager of Human Resources, Timken Co, 1835 Dueber Ave SW, Canton, OH 44706, **Business Phone:** (330)471-4131.

### MCDEMMOND, DR. MARIE VALENTINE
School administrator, president (government). **Educ:** Xavier Univ, BS; Univ New Orleans, MA; State Univ NY, grad studies, pub finance & mgt; Univ Mass, Amherst, EdD. **Career:** Emory Univ, asst vpres; Atlanta Univ, vpres, budget & fin; Univ Mass, assoc vice chancellor, finance & budget dir; Fla Atlantic Univ, vpres, finance & chief operating officer, chief finance officer; Norfolk State Univ, pres emer, 1997-2006; Fla Int Univ, interim dean, 2009-10. **Orgs:** Pres, bd mem, Southern Asn Col & Univ Bus Officers; bd mem, United Way & Urban League Hampton Rd; AAAS; adv bd, Historically Black Col & Univ; Nat bd dir Leukemia; pres, Coun Minority Educr, Mass Pub Cols & Univs; pres, Fla Asn Women Educ; bd dir Am Coun Educ's Comn; Nat Asn Equal Opportunity Higher Educ; United Way Greater Hampton Roads; Urban League Hampton Roads. **Business Addr:** President, Norfolk State University, 555 Pk Ave, Norfolk, VA 23504, **Business Phone:** (757)823-2916.

### MCDONALD, ALDEN J., JR.
Banker. **Personal:** Born Sep 16, 1943, New Orleans, LA; married Rhesa Ortique; children: 3. **Educ:** La State Univ Sch Banking, grad; Columbia Univ, com banking mgt prog. **Career:** Int City Bank, New Orleans; Liberty Bank & Trust Co, New Orleans, LA, pres & chief exec officer, 1972-; Port New Orleans, dir; Entergy New Orleans, adv bd, mem; Southern Univ New Orleans, Adv Coun, mem; Tulane Univ, Sch Med, bd mem; Access Capital Strategies LLC, dir, currently; Access Capital Strategies Community Investment Fund Inc, mgr, currently; Stewart Enterprises Inc, dir, 2001-. **Orgs:** Chmn, New Orleans Chamber Com; FannieMae Found; Am Bankers Asn; Nat Bankers Asn; La Bankers Asn; bd mem, Stewart Enterprises; chmn, Lindy Boggs Med Ctr; Minority Alliance Capital; Ernest N Morial Conv Ctr; Port Authority New Orleans; co-chair, New Orleans Educ Found; Fed Deposit Ins Corp; chmn, Greater New Orleans, 2004. **Honors/Awds:** R R Wright Presidential Award, Nat Banker's Asn; Whitney Young Award, Urban League Greater New Orleans; Civil Rights Award, Nat Dent Asn; Minority Suppliers Award, JC Penney; Business Hall of Fame, J Achievement; Loving Cup, Times Picayune, 2001; A G Gaston Lifetime Achievement Award, Black Enterprise, 2005. **Home Addr:** 10 Pk Island Dr, New Orleans, LA 70122-1229, **Home Phone:** (225)216-7311. **Business Addr:** President, Chief Executive Officer, Liberty Bank & Trust Co, 4101 Pauger St, New Orleans, LA 70122, **Business Phone:** (504)240-5115.

### MCDONALD, ANITA DUNLOP
Social worker. **Personal:** Born May 11, 1929, Morgantown, WV; daughter of William J (deceased) and LaFronia Chloe (deceased); married James J; children: Janice-Marie. **Educ:** WVa State Col, BA, 1951; WV Univ, MSW, 1953. **Career:** Social worker (retired); Syracuse Memorial Hosp, med soc worker, 1954-56; Family Serv Jamestown, social worker, 1975-79; Chautauqua Co Ment Health-Jamestown, psychiat social worker, 1980-94. **Orgs:** Am Asn Univ Women Jamestown Br, 1968-; sec bd trustee, Jamestown Comm Col, 1969-78; pres bd dir, YWCA, 1973-75; chmn pub affairs bd dir, YWCA, 1984-85; Ebony Task Force, 1986-; Sch Community Rels Coun, 1989-91; adult leader, Emmanuel Baptist Church Youth Group, 1990-; pres, Chaut Co Am Baptist Women, 1990-; nominating comt, Girl Scouts, Jamestown, 1991-94; Jamestown Chap, Links, 1993-, pres, 1998-; bd mgr, Am Baptist NY State, 1994-; NY State Am Baptist Church, 1994-2000; pres, Ebony Task Force, 1995-02; vpres, Girl Scouts, 1996-01; treas, Emmanuel Baptist Church, 1996-; pres, Int Chap Links, 1998-2000; adv bd, Jamestown Community Learning Coun, 1998-2003; adv bd, Safe House Chautauqua County, 2000-02; fin secy & chmn trustee bd, Emmanuel Bapt Church. **Honors/Awds:** Lifetime Achievement Award, Western Division New York State Chapter NASW, 1994; 3rd VP, Girl Scouts, Jamestown, 1996; Jamestown Woman of the Year, 1997. **Home Addr:** 40 W 22nd St, Jamestown, NY 14701, **Home Phone:** (716)484-7027.

### MCDONALD, AUDRA
Actor, singer. **Personal:** Born Jul 3, 1970, Berlin; daughter of Stanley Jr and Anna; married Peter Donovan, Jan 1, 2000?, (divorced 2009); married Will Swenson, Jan 1, 2012?; children: Zoe Madeline & Sally James. **Educ:** Juilliard Sch. **Career:** Singer and actress, 1993-. Theater: The Secret Garden, 1993; Carousel, 1994; Master Class, 1995, 1996; Ragtime, 1998; Marie Christine, 1999; Henry IV, 2004; A Raisin in the Sun, 2004; La voix humaine/Send, 2006; Rise and Fall of the City of Mahagonny, 2007; 110 in the Shade, 2007; Twelfth Night, 2009; The Gershwins' Porgy and Bess, 2012; Lady Day at Emerson's Bar & Grill, 2014; Shuffle Along, Or, The Making of the Musical Sensation of 1921 and All That Followed, 2016. Film: Seven Servants, 1996; The Object of My Affection, 1998; Cradle Will Rock, 1999; It Runs in the Family, 2003; The Best Thief in the World, 2004; She Got Problems, 2009; Rampart, 2012; Ricki and the Flash, 2015. Television: Having Our Say: The Delany Sisters' First 100 Years, 1999: Annie, 1999; Law & Order: Special Victims Unit, 2000; Wit, 2001; Mister Sterling, 2003; The Bedford Diaries, 2006; Kidnapped, 2006-07; Private Practice, 2007-11; A Raisin in the Sun, 2008; Live from Lincoln Center, 2012-; The Sound of Music, 2013; It Could Be Worse, 2013. **Orgs:** Covenant House Int. **Honors/Awds:** Tony Awards, 1993, 1996, 1998, 2004, 2012, 2104; Grammy Awards, 2007; Musician of the Year Award, 2013; National Medal of Arts, 2015; Emmy Award, 2015; Rockefeller Award for Creativity, 2015; Jason Robards Award for Excellence in Theatre, 2016; honorary doctorate, Yale University, 2016. **Special Achievements:** Albums: Way Back to Paradise, 1998; How Glory Goes, 2000; Audra McDonald-Live at Donmar London, 2000; Happy Songs, 2002; Build a Bridge, 2006; Go Back Home, 2013. **Business Addr:** c/o William Morris Endeavor Entertainment, 9601 Wilshire Blvd 3rd Fl, Beverly Hills, CA 90210-5213.

### MCDONALD, AUDRA ANN
Actor. **Personal:** Born Jul 3, 1970, Berlin; daughter of Stanley Jr (deceased) and Anna; married Will Swenson; married Peter Donovan; children: Zoe Madeline Donovan. **Educ:** Juilliard Sch, BM, 1993. **Career:** Films: Seven Servants, 1996; The Object of My Affection, 1998; Cradle Will Rock, 1999; It Runs in the Family, 2003; Tea Time with Roy & Sylvia, 2003; The Best Thief in the World, 2004; Rampart, 2011; TV series: "Great Performances", PBS, 1998; "Homicide: Life on the Street", 1999; "Having Our Say: The Delany Sisters' First 100 Years", 1999; "Annie", 1999; "Law & Order: Special Victims Unit", 2000; "Wit", 2001; "The Last Debate", 2000; "Mister Sterling", 2003; Partners & Crime, 2003; "Live from Lincoln Center", 2005; "The Bedford Diaries", 2006; "Kidnapped", 2006-07; A Raisin in the Sun, 2008; "Grey's Anatomy", 2009; "Private Practice", 2007-13; "Sesame Street", 2012-13; "The Good Wife", 2013; "The Sound of Music Live!", 2013. Narration: The Music Instinct: Science and Song, 2009. **Honors/Awds:** American Theater Wing, Tony Antoinette Perry, Best Featured Actress, 1994; Theatre World Award, 1994; Outer Critics Circle, Outer Critics Circle Award, Best Actress, 1994; Drama Desk, Best Supporting Actress, 1994; Theater World, Outstanding New Talent in a Musical; Tony Award for Best Supporting Actress in a Play, 1996; La Ovation Award, 1996; Ragtime, Tony Award, 1998; Tony Award for Portrayal of Ruth Younger in "A Raisin in the Sun", 2004; Nominated for Tony Award for playing Lizzie Curry in 110 in the Shade, 2007; Drama Desk Award for Outstanding Actress in a Musical, 2007; Nominated for Emmy Award, 2008; Grammys Award, 2009; Nominated for Image Award, 2008, 2009; Grammy Award for Best Opera Recording, 2009. **Home Addr:** 220 W 98th Suite 4, New York, NY 10025. **Business Addr:** Actress, c/o William Morris Agency LLC, 151 El Camino Dr, Beverly Hills, CA 90212, **Business Phone:** (310)859-4000.

### MCDONALD, DR. CHARLES J.
Physician, educator. **Personal:** Born Dec 6, 1931, Tampa, FL; son of George B and Bertha C (Harbin); married Maureen; children: Marc S, Norman D & Eric S. **Educ:** NC Agr & Tech State Univ, BS, 1951; Univ Mich, MS, 1952; Howard Univ, MD, 1960; Am Bd Dermat, dipl. **Career:** Hosp St Raphael New Haven, intern, 1960-61, asst resident, 1961-63; Yale Univ, Sch Med, asst resident dermat, 1963-65; US Pub Health Serv, Spec Res Fel, Yale Univ Sch Med, chief resident dermat, 1965-66; Yale Univ Sch Med, Yale-New Haven Med Ctr, instr, assoc physician, 1966-67, asst prof, asst attend physician med & pharm, 1967-68; Brown Univ Providence, RI, asst prof med sci, 1968-69, assoc prof, 1969-74; Roger William Hosp, head dermat, assoc chief med, 1968-97; Brown Univ, dermat prog dir, 1970, prof med sci, head subsect dermat, 1974-96, chmn, dept dermat, founding chmn, 1996, prof emer dermat, currently; RI Hosp, Dept Dermat, physician chief, 1997-. **Orgs:** Bd dir, vpres, pres, RI Div Am Cancer Soc, 1969-80; FDA Dermat Adv Comt, 1970-75; chmn, AAAS, secy dermat, 1973-75; Nat Inst Gen Med Scis, Pharmaeological Scis Rev Comt, 1978-82; bd, Nat Am Cancer Soc, 1983-; vpres, pres, New Eng Dermat Soc, 1983-85; bd dir, Noah Worcester Dermat Soc, 1983-86; bd dir, Am Acad Dermat, 1986-90; bd dir, Providence Pub Libr, 1987-; secy, 1990-96, chair nominating comt, 1990-96; Ri Commodores, 1990-; residency rev comn, Accreditation Coun Grad Med Educ, 1991-97, vice chair, 1995-97; nat adv bd, Nat Inst Arthrites, Musculoskeletal & Skin Disease, 1992-95; bd trustee, Howard Univ, 1993-2012, chair, Med Affairs, 1994-98; vpres, pres elect, Nat ACS, 1997-98, pres, 1998-99; chair, bd advisor, 1997-; pres elect, Am Dermat Asn, 2002-03; New Eng Dermat Soc; Soc Investigative Dermat; Am Fed Clin Res, Am Acad Dermat; Nat Med Asn; RI Dermat Soc; Noah Worcester Dermat Soc; Am Soc Clin Oncol; Dermat Found; Assoc Profs Dermatol; consult, Nat Inst Arthritis Metab & Digestive Dis; consult, RI State Dept Health; consult, Providence Health Ctrs Inc; former chmn, Health Task Force, RI Urban Coalition; former mem, Govs Conf Health Care Cost; mem bd trustee, Citizens Bank Providence, RI; Alpha Omega Alpha, Med Soc; Sigma Xi; Dermat Soc, New Eng; Ri Hall Fame, 2013. **Honors/Awds:** Certified Am bd Dermat, 1966; Honorary MS, Brown Univ, 1970; Distinguished Alumni Award, Col Med, Howard Univ, 1983; Eric Zwerling Memorial Lecturer & Outstanding Dermatology Professor, Nat Med Asn, 1987; St. George Medal, Am Cancer Soc, 1992; The Best Doctors in America, 1992, 1994, 1997, 2001, 2002; WW Keen Award, Brown Sch Med, 2002; RI Black Heritage Soc Award, Med & Community Affairs, 2005; Highest Academic Achievement Award, Col Med, Howard Univ; First Annual Distinguished Service Award, Hosp Assoc RI; National Division Award, Am Cancer Soc; DHS, Ri Col, 2014. **Special Achievements:** Published more than 100 articles on Dermitology. **Business Addr:** Professor Emeritus of Dermatology, Rhode Island Hospital, 593 Eddy St APC-10, Providence, RI 02903-4971, **Business Phone:** (401)444-7137.

### MCDONALD, DARNELL ALI
Football player. **Personal:** Born May 26, 1976, Fairfax, VA. **Educ:** Kans State Univ. **Career:** Football player (retired); Tampa Bay Buccaneers, wide receiver, 1999; Xtreme Football League, Los Angeles Xtreme, 2001; BC Lions, 2001-02; Miami Dolphins, wide receiver, 2002; Calgary Stampeders, 2003-04, 2006; Winnipeg Blue Bombers, 2005. **Honors/Awds:** Rookie of the Year, 1999.

### MCDONALD, DONZELL
Baseball player, athletic coach. **Personal:** Born Feb 20, 1975, Long Beach, CA; son of Donzell Sr; married Kamaria; children: 2. **Educ:** Trinidad Community Col; Yavapai Community Col. **Career:** Baseball outfielder (retired); coach; NY Yankees, 2001; Kans City Royals, 2002-04; Mex League; Acereros de Monclova, ctrfield; Ariz League Rangers, coach, 2011-13. **Business Addr:** Baseball Player, Arizona League Rangers.

### MCDONALD, ELLA SEABROOK
Administrator. **Personal:** Born Adel, GA. **Career:** Nurse; Health & human serv specialist, currently; Richard Allen Ctr Life, exec dir, currently. **Orgs:** Black Agency Execs; Nat Asn Univ Women; Schomung Corp; Black Adminr Child Welfare. **Business Addr:** Executive Director, Richard Allen Center on Life, 1872 Amsterdam Ave, New York, NY 10031, **Business Phone:** (212)862-7160.

### MCDONALD, FARNESE HAYNES. See HAYNES, FARNESE N.

### MCDONALD, GABRIELLE KIRK (GABRIELLE ANNE KIRK MCDONALD)
Judge. **Personal:** Born Apr 12, 1942, St. Paul, MN; daughter of James G. Kirk Jr (deceased) and Frances Retta English (deceased); married Mark T; children: Michael & Stacy. **Educ:** Boston Univ, attended 1961; Manhattan's Hunter Col, attended 1963; Howard Univ Law Sch, LLB, 1966; Georgetown Univ Law Ctr, LLD; Univ Notre Dame, LLD; Howard Univ, LLD; Stetson Col Law, LLD; Amherst Col, LLD. **Career:** Nat Asn Advan Colored People Legal Defense & Educ Fund, NY, staff atty, 1966-69; McDonald & McDonald, Houston, partner, 1969-79; Tex Southern Univ, Houston, asst prof, 1970, adj prof, 1975-77; Univ Tex, Houston, lectr, 1977-78; US Dist Ct, Houston, judge, 1979; Mathews Branscomb, atty; Int Criminal Tribunal former Yugoslavia, judge, pres, 1997-99; Iran-US Claims Tribunal, Hague, judge & arbitrator, 2001-; UN Gen Assembly, Int War Crimes, Trial Chamber II, fed judge, chief judge, currently. **Orgs:** Bd dir, Commun Serv Option Prog, Alley Theatre Houston; Nat Coalition 100 Black Women, ARC; trustee, trustee emerita, Howard Univ, 1983-; bd visitor, Thurgood Marshall Sch Law Houston; Am Bar Asn; Nat Bar Asn; Houston Bar Asn; Houston Lawyers Asn; Black Women Lawyers Asn; Nat Asn Advan Colored People; pres, Int Criminal Tribunal, 1993; Am Bar Asn Human Rights Ctr & Genocide Prev Task Force; bd dir, Am Arbit Asn. **Honors/Awds:** Equal Justice & Ronald Brown International Law Award, Nat Bar Asn; Goler Teal Butcher Award, Am Soc Int Law; Profession Margaret Brent Women Lawyers of Achievement Award, Am Bar Asn Comn Women; Leadership Award, Cent Eastern Europ Law Initiative, 1999; Horatio Alger Award, Horatio Alger Asn Distinguished Americans, 2004; First Women Groundbreakers in International Justice Award, Open Soc Inst, 2007; Dorothy I Height Lifetime Achievement Award, 2008. **Special Achievements:** First African American appointed to a federal court in Texas; First Female President of the International Criminal Tribunal for the Former Yugoslavia. **Business Addr:** Chief Judge, Iran-United States Claims Tribunal, Parkweg 13, The Hague2585 JH, **Business Phone:** (317)0352-006.

### MCDONALD, HERBERT G.
Architect. **Personal:** Born Feb 11, 1929, Jamaica, NY; son of Priscilla A Young and Herbert C; married Debra H; children: Gail Louise & Cathy Allison. **Educ:** Howard Univ, BArch, 1953. **Career:** Gitlin & Cantor Architects, Wash, DC, assoc, 1959-60; Edwin Weihe, architect, 1960-62; Herbert G McDonald & Assoc, architect, 1962-65; McDonald & Williams AIA, architect, partner, 1965-90; McDonald Williams Banks Architects, architect, 1990-. **Orgs:** Dir, Lawrence Johnson As-

socs, Washington, DC; vpres, dir, Barkingside Develop Inc, Bahamas; dir, secy, Davis Construct Co; adv, Independence Fed Savings & Loan, Washington, DC; Am Inst Archit; DC Coun Black Archit; Aircraft Owners & Pilots Asn; Omega Psi Phi Archit Clifton Ter Apts, 1969; DC Correctional Detention Facil, 1974; Archit NECIP, 1977; Lincoln Westmoreland Apts, 1972; DC Legis Comn Housing; dir, Nat Housing Rehab Assoc; vpres, dir, chief exec officer, H Bear Enterprises Inc. **Home Addr:** 4243 Blagden Ave NW, Washington, DC 20011, **Home Phone:** (202)829-2343. **Business Addr:** Architect, McDonald Williams Banks Architects, 7705 Ga Ave NW, Washington, DC 20012, **Business Phone:** (202)291-5103.

## MCDONALD, JASON ADAM

Baseball player. **Personal:** Born Mar 20, 1972, Modesto, CA. **Educ:** Univ Houston; Sacramento City Col. **Career:** Baseball player (retired); Oakland Athletics, outfielder, 1997-99; Texas Rangers, outfielder, 2000.

## MCDONALD, JEFFREY BERNARD

Executive. **Personal:** Born Oct 12, 1952, Benham, KY; son of Nathan and Orya Jr; children: R Malik. **Educ:** Ky State Univ, BS, bus admin, 1976; Boston Univ, MBA, 1978. **Career:** Monsanto, supvr, internal audit, 1977-87; Ralston Purina Co, mgr, financial serv, dir, financial serv, 1987. **Orgs:** Nat Asn Black Accountants; MBA Asn; Internal Audit Asn; Cash Mgt. **Special Achievements:** Fluent in Spanish. **Home Addr:** 14526 Greencastle Dr, Chesterfield, MO 63017-8110, **Home Phone:** (636)256-0987.

## MCDONALD, JON FRANKLIN

Educator, painter (artist). **Personal:** Born Jun 28, 1946, Jackson, MS; son of Ruby Tripplet and Charles; married Mary Ann Davies; children: Gabriel Charles & Beau Richards. **Educ:** Kendall Sch Design, cert, 1969; San Francisco Art Inst, MFA, 1972. **Career:** Painter; Spung buggy Works, asst animator, 1974-75; Every woman's Village, teacher, 1977-79; Kendall Col Art & Design, Grand Rapids, MI, prof, prog chair, 1980-. **Orgs:** Visual arts adv Frauenthal Ctr Performing Arts, Muskegon, Mich, 1986-89; comm mem, Mayor's Adv Comm Art/Grand Rapids, 1989-90; artist-in-residence, Grand Haven Pub Sch, 1989-90. **Honors/Awds:** Ellen Hart Bransten Scholarship, San Francisco Art Inst, 1970-72; One Man Show in Congressional Offices, Washington, DC, 1986; Best of Show in the Festival of the Arts, Grand Rapids, 1997; Docents Award, W Mich Reg, Muskegon Mus Art, 2002. **Special Achievements:** Moscow/Manhattan Connection, 48 paintings travelled in USSR & USA, 1989-91. **Home Addr:** 1602 Robinson Rd SE, Grand Rapids, MI 49506-1758, **Home Phone:** (616)458-2934. **Business Addr:** Professor of Visual Communication, Chair of Illustration Program, Kendall School of Design, 17 Fountain St NW, Grand Rapids, MI 49503-3102, **Business Phone:** (616)451-2787.

## MCDONALD, KATRINA BELL

Educator. **Personal:** Born Nov 5, 1961, Denison, TX; daughter of Gladys Murrel Bell (deceased); married Arnold Ray; children: Jordan Ray Bell. **Educ:** Mills Col, Oakland, CA, BA, written commun, 1983; Stanford Univ, MA, appl commun res, 1984; Univ Calif, MA, 1990, PhD, sociol, 1995. **Career:** San Francisco Newspaper Agency, mkt res analyst, 1984-85; Calif State Univ, res analyst, 1985-88; Univ Calif, res asst, 1988-90, 1992, teaching asst, 1991-93, assoc instr, 1990-94, 1996, 1998, 2000; Johns Hopkins Univ, from instr to asst prof, 1994-2000, assoc prof sociol, 2000-; Johns Hopkins Pop Ctr, fac, 1994, new prog develop grant, 2000-01, assoc dean multicultural affairs, 2008-10; assoc prof, currently. **Orgs:** Minority fel Am Sociol Asn, 1989-92, dissertation fel, 1992-93; Pop Asn Am; Asn Black Sociologists; Nat Asn Advan Colored People; Hopkins Black Fac & Staff Asn. **Special Achievements:** Book: Embracing Sisterhood; Three years as International Scholar to the AUIA and ONPS summer programs in Asia. **Home Addr:** 220 E University Pkwy, Baltimore, MD 21218, **Home Phone:** (410)467-9353. **Business Addr:** Associate Professor, Johns Hopkins University, 540 Mergenthaler Hall 3400 N Charles St, Baltimore, MD 21218, **Business Phone:** (410)516-7624.

## MCDONALD, LARRY MARVIN

Executive, association executive. **Personal:** Born Mar 12, 1952, Louisville, KY; son of Charles S and Angie V; married Denise Harker; children: 5; married Terry. **Educ:** Univ Ky Col Bus & Econs, Lexington, Ky, BBA, 1974; Univ Louisville, Louisville, Ky, MBA, 1992. **Career:** Ford Motor Co, prod supvr; Humana Inc, Louisville, Ky, equip specifier & buyer, 1982-85, mgt develop intern, 1985-87, personnel mgr, 1987-89, dir equal employ opportunity, affirmative action, 1989, corp dir assoc rels & serv; Lincoln Found Inc, pres, 2001-. **Orgs:** Vice chmn, trustee bd, First Congregational Methodist Church, 1981-; Steering Comt, Black Achievers Orgn, 1983-89, 1992-; pres, Steering Comt, Proj BUILD, 1985-; bus consult, Proj Bus, Jr Achievement, 1986-88; bd mem, BETA Adv Bd, Univ Louisville Speed Sci Sch, 1986-; bd mem, Class Roots, 1990; bd mem, Louisville Urban League, 1990-; bd mem, Louisville Orchestra, 1992-; fel Bingham, 2007; Ctr Nonprofit Excellence; Lincoln Found; Univ Louisville Bd Overseers; African Am Heritage Found; Canaan Community Develop Corp; 100 Black Men Louisville; Ky Statewide Adv Coun Voc Rehab; Sigma Pi Phi Fraternity; Community Found Louisville; Home Innocents; Norton Healthcare; Metro United Way Personnel Comt. **Honors/Awds:** Black Achiever, Chestnut St YMCA, 1983; Outstanding Volunteer of the Year, YMCA Greater Louisville, 1986; honoree, Leadership Louisville, 1987; Golden Apple Award, Jefferson County Pub Sch, 1988; Hon Vol, Spirit Louisville Found Inc, 1989; Citizen of the Month, Louisville Jaycees, 1989; Honored Volunteer Award, WLKY Spirit of Louisville Foundation, 1989, 1996; Night of 1, 000 Stars, Cathedral Heritage Found, 1995; Whitney MYoung, Jr. Equal Employment Opportunities Award, 1997; Diversity Role Model, Humana Inc, 1999; Appreciation Award, Whitney M Young Job Corp Ctr, 2002; Honorary Award, Lincoln Inst Kentucky Alumni Asn Inc, 2003; Presbyterian Community Center Hall of Fame, 2004; Leadership Network, 2005; Bingham Fel, 2007. **Business Addr:** President, The Lincoln Foundation Inc, 200 W Broadway Suite 500, Louisville, KY 40202-2125, **Business Phone:** (502)585-4733.

## MCDONALD, LYNETTE MARIA BOGGS

Government official. **Personal:** Born Jul 28, 1963, Washington, DC; daughter of Nathaniel Boggs Jr and Janice Costello Anderson; married Steve; children: Adam. **Educ:** Univ Notre Dame, BBA, mkt, 1985; Univ Ore, Grad Sch Jour, attended 1990; Univ Nev, MPA, 1998; St Mary's Univ Sch Law, doctor jurisp, 2012. **Career:** City Las Vegas, asst city mgr, 1994-97; Univ Nev Sch Med, dir mktg; Univ Nev, Las Vegas, dir mktg & community rels, 1997-2000; City Las Vegas, councilwoman, 1999-2004; Las Vegas Valley Water Dist, gov bd mem; Univ Med Ctr, gov bd mem; McCarran Int Airport, gov bd mem; Clark County Govt Ctr, Bd County Comnrs, Comnr dist F, 2004-07; Chief Judge Piper Griffin Orleans Parish Civil Dist Ct New Orleans, judicial extern, 2010; Justice Rebecca Simmons Tex Fourth Ct Appeals, judicial intern, 2011; Trial Div Pub Defender Serv Dc, law clerk, 2011; St. Mary's Law J, assoc ed; FaithWorks Inc, pres & co-founder, currently. **Orgs:** Bd mem, Nat Conf Community & Justice, 1999; bd mem, S Nev Health Dist; Alpha Kappa Alpha Sorority, 2000; vpres, Nev League Cities & Munic, 2001; trustee, Cath Charities Southern Nev, 2000; bd mem, Summerlin C's Forum, 2000; Nat Black Caucus Local Elected Officials, 2000; pres, Keep Memory Alive, found Lou Ruvo Alzheimer's Inst; Nat Comn Abraham Lincoln Study Abroad Fel Prog; bd mem, Miss Am Org; Liturgical Choir, Fighting Irish cheerleading squad. **Home Addr:** , NV.

## MCDONALD, MARK T.

Lawyer. **Personal:** Born Jun 20, 1935, Henderson, TX; married Gabrielle Kirk; children: Mark T Jr, Micheal K & Stacy Frances. **Educ:** Prairie View A&M Col, BA, hon, 1956; Tex Southern Univ, LLB, 1962. **Career:** McDonald & McDonald Atty Law, atty, 1962; Legal Serv Div OEO, consult, 1965; Tex Southern Univ, asst prof law, 1964-70; Prarie View A&M Col, assoc prof polit sci, 1963-64. **Orgs:** State Bar Tex; Am Bar Asn; Asn Trial Lawyers Am; pres, Nat Bar Asn; Am Judicature Soc; Nat Asn Criminal Def Attys; Tex Trial Lawyers Asn; Houston Bar Asn; Houston Trial Lawyers Asn; Nat Advan Asn Colored People; Houston Bus & Prof Men's Club; Am Civil Liberties Union, Houston; YMCA Century Club. **Home Addr:** 2316 Truxillo St, Houston, TX 77004-4366, **Home Phone:** (713)665-3410.

## MCDONALD, MICHAEL, JR.

Football coach, football player. **Personal:** Born Jun 22, 1958, North Hollywood, CA. **Educ:** Univ Southern Calif. **Career:** Football player (retired); Univ Southern Calif, grad asst coach, 1980, 1981; Burroughs CA High Sch, asst coach, 1982, 1983, 1985; Los Angeles Rams, linebacker, 1983-91; Detroit Lions, linebacker, 1992. **Honors/Awds:** NFC Championship Game, 1989. **Business Addr:** Linebacker, Detroit Lions, 222 Republic Dr, Allen Park, MI 48101, **Business Phone:** (313)335-4131.

## MCDONALD, DR. R. TIMOTHY

Administrator, association executive. **Personal:** Born Sep 29, 1940, Pittsburgh, PA; son of Ralph and Harriett; married Beverly Clark; children: Lawana, Monica, Lanita & Patrick. **Educ:** Oakwood Col, BS, elem educ, 1963; Atlanta Univ, MS, educ admin, 1968; Univ Miami, EdD, admin, 1972. **Career:** School administrator (retired); AL A&M Univ, prof educ, 1972-78; Oakwood Univ, Adult & Continuing Educ Prog, dir, vpres, vpres info technol & vpres advan & develop, vpres develop, 1975-78, provost & sr vpres, 2011-; Barber Scotia Col, vpres acad affairs, 1978-79; OH State Univ, develop officer, 1979-83, dir develop; Seventh-day Adventist Church, dir educ; Morehouse Sch Med, dir develop; Baltimore County Community Col, dir develop; Greater Atlanta Adventist Acad, teacher; DuPont Pk Sch, teacher; Larchwood SDA Sch, teacher; Univ Africa, pres, currently; Univ Eastern Africa, vice chancellor, 2003-07. **Orgs:** Consult, Higher Educ Asns, 1975-; proposal writer-reader Fed Govt, 1975-; bd mem, Columbus Ment Health Asn, 1980-83; bd mem, Columbia Union Col, 1983-; dir, SDA, Columbia Union Conf. **Honors/Awds:** Higher Education Fellowship, Fed Govt, 1969-72; Title III Grant, Fed Govt, 1972-78; Special Service Award, OH State Univ, 1981. **Home Addr:** 10516 E Wind Way, Columbia, MD 21044. **Business Addr:** Provost, Senior Vice President, Oakwood University, 7000 Adventist Blvd NW, Huntsville, AL 35896, **Business Phone:** (256)726-7000.

## MCDONALD, RAMOS

Football player. **Personal:** Born Apr 30, 1976, Dallas, TX. **Educ:** Univ NMex, Phys educ. **Career:** Football player (retired); Minn Vikings, cornerback, defensive back, 1998, left corner back, 1999; San Francisco 49ers, cornerback, right corner back, 1999; NY Giants, 2000; Oakland Raiders, corner back, 2001; Seattle Seahawks, corner back, 2002.

## MCDONALD, RICARDO MILTON

Football player. **Personal:** Born Nov 8, 1969, Kingston. **Educ:** Univ Pittsburgh. **Career:** Football player (retired); Cincinnati Bengals, left inside linebacker, 1992, right inside linebacker, 1993, 1997, right linebacker, 1994-96; Chicago Bears, left linebacker, 1998, linebacker, 1999; Denver Broncos, 2000-01. **Honors/Awds:** Ed Block Courage Award, 1995. **Business Addr:** Football Player, Denver Broncos, 13655 Broncos Pkwy, Englewood, CO 80112, **Business Phone:** (303)649-9000.

## MCDONALD, TIMOTHY (TIM MCDONALD)

Football player, football coach, executive. **Personal:** Born Jan 6, 1965, Fresno, CA; married Alycia; children: Timothy Jr, Tevin & Taryn. **Educ:** Univ SC, bus admin. **Career:** Football player (retired), football coach, owner; St Louis Cardinals, defensive back, 1987-92; Phoenix Cardinals, 1987-92; San Francisco 49ers, 1993-99; World Sports Cafe, owner, 1999-2014; Malloch Elem Sch, 2001-03; alma mater Edison High Sch, fresno, coach, 2012; New York Jets, defensive backs coach, 2013-14; Buffalo Bills, defensive backs coach, 2015-. **Business Addr:** Defensive backs coach, Buffalo Bills, 1 Bills Dr, Orchard Park, NY 14127, **Business Phone:** (716)648-1800.

## MCDONALD, WILLIAM EMORY, SR.

Engineer, air force officer, executive director. **Personal:** Born Mar 9, 1924, Detroit, MI; son of Emory S and Willie Mae Burrill; children: Varnell M, William & Jeannette. **Educ:** Univ Mich, BS, 1950. **Career:** Air force officer, engineer (retired); Pub Lighting Comn, jr engr, 1950-54; Detroit Arsenal, electronic scientist, 1954-57; Farrara Inc, chief proj engr, 1957-58; Chrysler Missile, design engr, 1958-59; Rockwell Int, sr proj engr, 1959-72; NC Cent Univ, phys plant dir, 1972-91. **Orgs:** Pres bd, Urban Ministries, 1970-71; Alpha Phi Alpha Fraternity; secy & treas, S Eastern Reg Asn Phys Plant Admin, 1980-89; mem bd adjust, City Durham, NC, 1981-91; NC Synod Coun, Evangel Lutheran Church Am, 1988-; secy, treas, Asn Phys Plant Admin, 1989-91; Cong Gold Medal, US Cong, 2007. **Honors/Awds:** Meritorious Service Award, SE Reg Asn Phys Plant Admin, 1987. **Special Achievements:** First African American officer Southeastern Regional Association of Physical Plant Administration. **Home Addr:** 902 Cana St, Durham, NC 27707-4941, **Home Phone:** (919)688-7577.

## MCDOUGALL, DR. GAY J.

Lawyer. **Personal:** Born Aug 13, 1947, Atlanta, GA. **Educ:** Bennington Col, BA, 1969; Yale Univ Law Sch, JD, 1972; London Sch Econs & Polit Sci, LLM, pub int law, 1978. **Career:** Debevoise, Plimpton, Lyons & Gates Law Firm, New York, assoc, 1972-74; Bd Corrections, Minimum Stand Unit, New York, staff atty, 1976-77; Off Dep Mayor Criminal Justice, New York, assoc coun, 1979-80; Southern Africa Proj Lawyer's Comt Civil Rights Under Law, dir, 1980-94; Comn Independence Namibia, 1989; UN Human Rights Bodies, independent expert, 1997-2001; Int Human Rights Law Group, Global Rights Hq, DC, exec dir, 1994-2006; Wash Col Law, Am Univ, Washington, DC, fac, distinguished scholar residence, 2006-08, law acad human rights & humanitarian law, vis scholar; Georgetown Univ Law Ctr, Father Robert F. Drinan vis prof, 2011-12; Howard Univ Sch Law, guest lectr, currently; Fordham Univ Sch Law, Mulligan distinguished vis prof int law, currently. **Orgs:** Gen coun, Nat Conf Black Lawyers, 1975-76; UN Comn Human Rights, 1996-00; DC Bar Asn; SafricA's 16-mem Independent Electoral Comn; CARE Int, 1994-03; Robert F Kennedy Memorial Found, 1994-04; fel Mac Arthur Found, 1999; chair, UN Comt Elimination Racial Discrimination; Am Soc Int Law, 2003-; UN Independent Expert Minority Issues, 2005-11; Un Forum Minority Issues, convener, 2007-11 Global Fund Women, 2005-; Afri Care, 2005-; Equal Rights Trust, 2006-; Open Soc Inst Sub-Bd Women's Rights, 2006-; Jimmy Carter Presidential Ctr, Int Human Rights Coun. **Honors/Awds:** MacArthur Fellows Award, 1999; Hon Degree, City Univ NY Law Sch, 2000; Lamplighter Award Human Rights, 2003; Hon Degree, Univ Georgetown Law Ctr, 2006; Butcher Medal, Am Soc Int Law; Thurgood Marshall Award, Dc Bar Asn. **Special Achievements:** First black student to integrate Agnes Scott College in Decatur, Georgia; first United Nations Independent Expert on Minority Issues, 2005; first American to be elected to the body of 18 international experts who oversee compliance by governments. **Business Addr:** Mulligan Distinguished Visiting Professor, Fordham University School of Law, Rm 7-166 150 W 62nd St, New York, NY 10023, **Business Phone:** (212)636-7348.

## MCDUFFIE, DEBORAH JEANNE

Composer, music producer. **Personal:** Born Aug 8, 1950, New York, NY; daughter of Thomas and Nan Wood; children: Kijana Saunders & Kemal Gasper. **Educ:** Western Col Women, Oxford, OH, BA, music, 1971. **Career:** McCann-Erickson Advert, New York, NY, music producer & composer, 1971-81; Mingo Group, New York, NY, music dir, 1981-90; Strachan McDuffie CommunsInc, New York, NY, exec vpres & creative dir, 1990-92; Jana Prods Inc, NewYork, NY, pres & chief exec officer, 1981-; Ritz Theatre & Lavilla Mus, ritz voices, prod mgr, artistic dir, currently, Ritz Voices, founder; Jacksonville Mass Choir, Art dir, currently. **Orgs:** Bd dir, NY Urban League, 1990-; Am Soc Composers, Authors & Publ, 1980; AmFedn Musicians, 1978; Screen Actors Guild, 1982; Am Fedn TV-Radio Artists, 1977-; chairperson, Fine Arts Dept Paxon Sch Adv Studies, 2001-; exec dir, NE Fla Found Arts Inc, Jacksonville, Fla, 2004-; Jacksonville Sch Music. **Honors/Awds:** Clio Award, 1981; Ceba Awards, Advertising Black Consumer Mkt, 1982-90; Telly Awards, 1986; Award Music & Entertainment, Onyx Mag, 2004. **Business Addr:** Owner, Miz McDuffie Music, 634 Lomax St Unity Church-Grenson Hall, Jacksonville, FL 32204, **Business Phone:** (904)504-2763.

## MCDYESS, ANTONIO KEITHFLEN

Basketball player. **Personal:** Born Sep 7, 1974, Quitman, MS; son of Gloria; married Liara Williams. **Educ:** Univ Ala, attended 1995. **Career:** Basketball player (retired); Los Angeles Clippers, 1995; Denver Nuggets, forward-center, 1995-97, 1999-2002; Phoenix Suns, 1997-98, 2004; New York Knicks, forward, 2003-04; Detroit Pistons, forward, 2004-09; San Antonio Spurs, 2009-11.

## MCEACHERN, D. HECTOR

Banker. **Personal:** Born Fayetteville, NC; married Brenda Britt; children: Todd, Natashia, Dorian & Brandon. **Educ:** Fayetteville State Univ, BS, eng, 1969; NC State Univ, grad study psychol, 1971; Am Mgt Asn, mgt study, supvry mgt, 1977; Interaction Mgt Instr cert; Univ Va, darden partnership prog; Duke Univ, Fuqua Sch Bus, Wachovia Sr Mgt Develop prog. **Career:** Fayetteville Observer Newspaper, news reporter, 1968-70; Cumberland County Ment Health Ctr, social worker, 1970-72; Mt Vernon Psychiat Clin, psychiat social worker, 1972-74; Texfi Indust Inc, plant personnel mgr, 1974-78, group personnel dir, 1978-90; Wachovia Bank & Trust Co, sr vpres, mgr personnel serv, 1980-87; Wachovia Bank NC, dir personnel, sr vpres, group exec, chief diversity officer, 2001-09; Hr Group Inc, consult, currently; McEachern Group, pres, 2009-. **Orgs:** Bd mem, United Way NC, 1992; bd mem, Work Family Resource Ctr, 1992; bd mem, Leadership Winston-Salem; former chmn, Bank Admin Inst, Human Resources Comn; bd trustee, Fayetteville State Univ; bd dir, Winston-Salem Urban League; Leadership Winston-Salem, Bi-Racial Comt; found bd mem, Fayetteville State Univ Alumni Asn; former chmn, C Home Soc; Am Bankers Asn's Human Resources Exec Comt; LeMoyne-Owen Col; Guilford Col; Wells Fargo Greensboro adv bd. **Home Addr:** 3601 Stonebrook Farms Ct, Greensboro, NC 27406-9675, **Home Phone:** (336)674-3889. **Business Addr:** President, The McEachern Group, Greensboro, NC, **Business Phone:** (336)287-1988.

### MCEACHIN, JAMES
Novelist, actor, playwright. **Personal:** Born May 20, 1930, Rennert, NC; married Lois Davis; children: Felecia, Alainia & Lyle. **Career:** Actor, author, director & producer; Films: Uptight!, 1968; If He Hollers, Let Him Go!, 1968; True Grit, 1969; Hello Dolly!, 1969; The Undefeated, 1969; Play Misty for Me, 1971; Buck & the Preacher, 1972; The Ground star Conspiracy, 1972; Short Walk to Daylight, 1972; Fuzz, 1972; Every Which Way But Loose, 1978; Sudden Impact, 1983; 2010, 1984; Double Exposure, 1993; Reveille, 2004; TV Series: "Cowboy in Africa", 1967; "Mannix", 1968; "The Good Guys", 1968; "Hawaii Five-O", 1968; "The Name of the Game", 1968-69; "It Takes a Thief", 1968-70; "Adam-12", 1968-72; "Then Came Bronson", 1969; "The Bold Ones: The Protectors", 1969; "The Wild Wild West", 1969; "The Outsider", 1969; "Dragnet 1967", 1969-70; "Ironside", 1969-71; "The F.B.I.", 1970; "The Bold Ones: The Senator", 1970; "Men at Law", 1970; "The D.A.", 1971; "McCloud", 1971; "O'Hara, U.S. Treasury", 1971; "That Certain Summer", 1972; "Jigsaw", 1972; "The Sixth Sense", 1972; "Escape", 1972-73; "Insight", 1972-75; "All in the Family", 1972-77; "Columbo", 1972-78; "The Tonight Show Starring Johnny Carson", 1973; "Tenafly", 1973-74; "Emergency!", 1973-77; "The Rockford Files", 1974; "Chase", 1974; "Griff", 1974; "Petrocelli", 1974; "Harry O", 1974-75; "The Six Million Dollar Man", 1974-77; "McMillan & Wife", 1975; "The Invisible Man", 1975; "Police Story", 1975-76; "The Bionic Woman", 1976; "Westside Medical", 1977; "The Feather & Father Gang", 1977; "Kingston: Confidential", 1977; "Grandpa Goes to Washington", 1978; "The Eddie Capra Mysteries", 1978; "Buck Rogers in the 25th Century", 1979; "Quincy M.E.", 1979; "Lobo", 1979; "The White Shadow", 1980; "McClain's Law", 1981; "Hill Street Blues", 1982-86; "T.J. Hooker", 1983; "Murder, She Wrote", 1984-85; "Trapper John, M.D.", 1986; "Crazy Like a Fox", 1986; "Matlock", 1986-95; "Hunter", 1988; "Perry Mason: The Case of the Poisoned Pen", 1990; "Perry Mason: The Case of the Silenced Singer", 1990; "Father Dowling Mysteries", 1990; "Perry Mason: The Case of the Glass Coffin", 1991; "Perry Mason: The Case of the Maligned Mobster", 1991; "Perry Mason: The Case of the Ruthless Reporter", 1991; "I'll Fly Away", 1991-92; "Perry Mason: The Case of the Fatal Framing", 1992; "Perry Mason: The Case of the Heartbroken Bride", 1992; "Perry Mason: The Case of the Reckless Romeo", 1992; "I'll Fly Away", 1992; "Perry Mason: The Case of the Wicked Wives", 1993; "Perry Mason: The Case of the Killer Kiss", 1993; "Perry Mason: The Case of the Skin-Deep Scandal", 1993; "Perry Mason: The Case of the Telltale Talk Show Host", 1993; "Willie, Sworn To Vengeance", 1993; "Diagnosis Murder", 1993-94; "Perry Mason: The Case of the Lethal Lifestyle", 1994; "Perry Mason: The Case of the Jealous Jokester", 1995; "City of Angels", 2000; "First Monday", 2002; Novels: Tell Me a Tale: A Novel of the Old South, 1996 & 2003; Farewell to the Mockingbirds, 1997; The Heroin Factor, 1999; Say Goodnight to the Boys in Blue, 2000; The Heroin Factor; The Great Canis Lupus, 2001; Pebbles in the Roadway: Tales & Essays, Bits & Pieces, 2003; USAR, army res ambassador, 2005-08; ambassador emer, currently; VOICES: A Tribute to the American Veteran, 2005; Old Glory DVD, producer, 2007; Above the Call; Beyond the Duty, A one-man, two-act play, 2008. **Orgs:** Mil Order Purple Heart, Am Legion. **Honors/Awds:** Benjamin Franklin Award, Publishers Mkt Asn, 1998; Best Fiction Award, Farewell to the Mockingbirds; Distinguished Achievement Award, Morgan State Univ, 2001; honored by the Maryland House Delegates, 2001; Benjamin Franklin Award, 2005; Best Audio for VOICES: A Tribute to the American Veteran, 2003; Audio Book of the Year for Pebbles in the Roadway: Essays and Tales, Bits and Pieces, Foreword Magazine, 2007; Best Film Short for Old Glory, GI Film Festival; American Airlines Honorary Captain of the Flagship Liberty; Military Order of the Purple Heart; George Washington Medal of Merit, 2007; Veterans Brain Trust Award, 2008. **Special Achievements:** Silver Star, multiple-wound Purple Heart Veteran of the Korean War. AUS, Ambassador Emeritus; First African-American man to have his own show on NBC, Tenafly. **Home Addr:** PO Box 5166, Sherman Oaks, CA 91403. **Business Addr:** Actor, C/o Rharl Publishing Group, 16161 Ventura Blvd PMB Suite 550, Los Angeles, CA 91436, **Business Phone:** (818)519-5453.

### MCELRATH-FRAZIER, WANDA FAITH
Security guard, musician, artist. **Personal:** Born Jan 11, 1959, Sylacauga, AL; daughter of Danfort (deceased) and Josephine L; married James. **Educ:** Troy State Univ, BME, 1983. **Career:** Anchor Club, sr dir, 1976; Avondale Mills, winder operator, 1977-82; Troy State Univ, stud secretarial asst dean fine arts & arts & sci, 1977-82; self-employed, pvt trumpet instr & performer, 1983-, karate instr, cert, 1988-, air brusher, 1988-, security officer, 1994-; Ala Sports Festival, co-tournament dir, currently; Sylacauga Parks & Recreation, instr, currently; Coosa Valley Fraternal Order of Police, assoc mem. **Orgs:** Prin's Adv Comt, 1971-72; Sr Scholastic Soc, 1976, 1977; US Yoshukai Karate Asn, 1976; founding pres, Troy State Karate Club-Dojo, 1978-82; Women Band Dir's Nat Asn, 1979; pres, Music Educrs Nat Conf, 1980-81; regional secy, Tau Beta Sigma Nat Hon Band Sorority, 1981-83; pledge class pres & social chair, Alpha Phi Omega Nat Serv Fraternity, 1981; Alpha Phi Omega, 1983-; secy, Nat Asn Advan Colored People, 1991-; secy, S Talladega County Amateur Radio Soc, 2002-04; vol examr, Am Radio Relay League; Talladega Radio Amateur Club; bd mem, Troy State Alumni Band Asn; bd mem, Sylacauga Alliance for Family Enhancement Inc. **Home Addr:** PO Box 462, Sylacauga, AL 35150, **Home Phone:** (205)249-0508. **Business Addr:** Instructor, Sylacauga Parks & Recreation, 2 W 8th St, Sylacauga, AL 35150, **Business Phone:** (256)249-8561.

### MCELROY, CHARLES DWAYNE, SR. (CHUCK MCELROY)
Baseball player. **Personal:** Born Oct 1, 1967, Port Arthur, TX; son of Herman C and Elizabeth Simmons Mayfield; married Shari Lannette Cooper; children: C J. **Career:** Baseball player (retired); Philadelphia Phillies, pitcher, 1989-90; Chicago Cubs, pitcher, 1991-93; Cincinnati Reds, pitcher, 1994-96; Calif/Anaheim Angels, pitcher, 1996-97; Chicago White Sox, pitcher, 1997; Colo Rockies, pitcher, 1998-99; New York Mets, pitcher, 1999; Baltimore Orioles, pitcher, 2000-01; San Diego Padres, pitcher, 2001. **Orgs:** Professional Baseball Players Asn, 1986-. **Home Addr:** 6230 17th St, Port Arthur, TX 77642-0411, **Home Phone:** (409)982-6769.

### MCELROY, DR. COLLEEN J.
Educator, writer. **Personal:** Born Oct 30, 1935, St. Louis, MO; daughter of Ruth Celeste (deceased) and Purcia Purcell Rawls; children: Kevin D & Vanessa C. **Educ:** Kans State Univ, Manhattan KS, BS, 1958, MS, 1963; Univ Wash, Seattle WA, PhD, 1973. **Career:** Professor (retired), poet, writer, editor, memoirist, professor emeritus; Rehab Inst, Kans City MO, chief, speech & hearing serv, 1963-66; Western Wash Univ, Bellingham WA, asst prof speech, 1966-74; Univ Wash, Seattle, WA, supvr, EOP Compos, 1972-83, creative writing, dir, 1984-87, prof Eng, 1983, prof emer, currently; Seattle Rev, Ed-in-chief, 1995-2006. Books: Speech and Language Development of the Preschool Child, 1972; The Mules Done Long Since Gone, 1973; Music from Home: Selected Poems, 1976; Winters without Snow, 1979; Lie and Say You Love Me, 1981; Looking for a Country under Its Original Name, 1984; Queen of the Ebony Isles, 1984; Jesus and Fat Tuesday and Other Short Stories, 1987; Bone Flames, 1987; Driving Under the Cardboard Pines, 1990; What Madness Brought Me Here: New and Selected Poems, 1968-88, 1990; A Long Way from St. Louie, 1997; Travelling Music, 1998; Over the Lip of the World: Among the Storytellers of Madagascar, 2001; Sleeping with the Moon, 2007; Here I Throw Down My Heart, 2012. **Orgs:** Writers Guild Am E, 1978-, Dramatists Guild, 1986-, PEN Writers, 1989-; Auth's Guild, 1989-; Writer's Union, 1989-. **Special Achievements:** First African American professor of University of Washington, 1984. **Home Addr:** 2616 4th Ave N, Seattle, WA 98109, **Home Phone:** (206)284-2829. **Business Addr:** Professor Emeritus, University of Washington, A101 Padelford Hall, Seattle, WA 98195-4330, **Business Phone:** (206)543-2690.

### MCELROY, DR. LEE A., JR.
Executive, educator. **Personal:** Born Mar 19, 1948, Beaumont, TX; son of Lee A Sr and Ada Mae Ford; married Karen A. **Educ:** Univ Calif, Los Angeles, BS, polit sci & hist, 1970; Univ Southern Calif, MEd, 1974; Univ Houston, EdD, 1984. **Career:** Santa Monica Schs, Santa Monica, Calif, coach & teacher, 1971-76; S Parks High Sch, Beaumont, Tex, vice prin, 1976-81; Univ Houston, Tex, assoc athletic dir, 1981-88; Univ Dist Columbia, athletic dir, vpres & stud affairs, 1988-89; Calif State Univ, Sacramento, dir inter athletics, 1989-; Univ Albany, Dept Athletics & Recreation, vpres athletic admin & dir intercollegiate athletics, 2000-; Nat Asn Col Dirs Athletics, pres, 2006-07; Eagle Club, founder. **Orgs:** Pres, Nat Asn Acad Advs, 1986; consult, Am Inst Res, 1987; bd dir, Doug Williams Found, 1988-; bd dir, Sacramento Sports Med, 1989-; Pub Rels, Rotary, 1989-; bd dir, Com stock Mag, 1990; pres, Am E Conf Exec Comt, 2003-04; vpres & pres, Nat Asn Col Dirs Athletics, 2006-07;pres, Am E Bd Dirs, 2007, 2011; bd dir, Minority Opportunities Athletic Asn, 2010; interim dir athletics, Rensselaer Polytech Inst, 2015; bd dir, Nat Consortium Academics & Sports; fel Univ RI; Nat Minority Golf Asn; Colonial Athletic Asn; chair, Sears Dirs Cup Comt, Sears Dirs Cup; bd dir, US Sports Acad. **Honors/Awds:** Outstanding Athletic Director Award, Gen Robert R. Neyland, 2004; John McLendon Minority Athletics Administrators Hall of Fame, 2010; America East Conference Commissioner's Cup, Great Danes Awarded, 2012-13; NACDA Hall of Fame, 2012. **Home Addr:** 74 Gullane Dr, Slingerlands, NY 12159-9798. **Business Addr:** Vice President for Athletic Administration, Director of Intercollegiate Athletics, University at Albany, 1400 Washington Ave, Albany, NY 12222, **Business Phone:** (518)442-2562.

### MCELROY, LEELAND ANTHONY
Football player. **Personal:** Born Jun 25, 1974, Beaumont, TX; married Vinita. **Educ:** Tex A&M Univ. **Career:** Football player (retired); Ariz Cardinals, running back, 1996-97, kick returner, 1996; Tampa Bay Buccaneers, 1998; Denver Broncos, 1999; Indianapolis Colts, running back, 1999; V.L. Mcelroy Enterprise Llc, pres, 2000. **Business Addr:** President, V L Mcelroy Enterprise LLC, 216 Hawthorne Dr, Murphy, TX 75094.

### MCELROY, DR. NJOKI
Executive, educator, writer. **Personal:** Born Sherman, TX; daughter of J D Hampton and Marion Hampton; married Clenan C; children: Ronald, Phillip, David, Marian, Harry & Larry. **Educ:** Xavier Univ, BS, 1945; Northwestern Univ, MA, 1969, PhD, 1973. **Career:** Northwestern Univ, adj prof, 1970-; Black Fox Enterprises Ltd, founder, 1972-, pres, 1978-; storyteller, performer, 1980-; Southern Methodist Univ, adj lit, 1987-, prof master Lib arts, currently; DFW Int Community Alliance, storyteller, currently; Back Home Folk Festival, founder & dir. Author: "Black Journey", play on African-Am hist, 1975; "The Gods Were Watching Them", play, Northwestern Univ, 1991; Common Bond, 1991; "La Bakaire", play, Northwestern Univ, 1992; Spiritual Walks, 1993. **Orgs:** Northwestern Univ. **Home Addr:** 1700 20th St, North Chicago, IL 60064, **Home Phone:** (214)823-3897. **Business Addr:** Adjunct in Literature, Professor of the Master of Liberal Arts, Southern Methodist University, 3101 University Blvd Suite 163, Dallas, TX 75205, **Business Phone:** (214)768-4273.

### MCELROY, RAYMOND EDWARD
Football player. **Personal:** Born Jul 31, 1972, Bellwood, IL; married Michelle; children: Miray, Ramiah, Jamaria & Janae. **Educ:** Eastern Ill Univ, BS, econs; MS, theol, 1995. **Career:** Football player (retired); Indianapolis Colts, defensive back & strong safety, 1995-98; Chicago Bears, 2000; Detroit Lions, 2001-02; Sportsworld Inc, Professional Speaker, 2003-10; Chicago Bears, team chaplain, currently; motivational speaker, currently. **Orgs:** Founder, A Ray of Hope on Earth. **Special Achievements:** Appeared on the MTV show "Made" as a personal football coach. **Home Addr:** 1410 June Lane, Lombard, IL 60148-4433, **Home Phone:** (630)261-0771. **Business Addr:** Team Chaplain, Chicago Bears, 1920 Football Dr, Lake Forest, IL 60045, **Business Phone:** (866)805-8555.

### MCELVANE, PAMELA ANNE
Insurance executive, publisher, chief executive officer. **Personal:** Born Sep 4, 1958, Stockton, CA; daughter of Charlene Penny; children: Joshua & Cameron. **Educ:** Univ Calif, Berkeley, BA, social welfare & sociol, 1980, MBA, finance & int mkt, 1984, MA, pub policy. **Career:** US Dept Labor, contract mgr, 1980-82; Gelco-Cti Leasing Co, lease admin & sys supvr, 1982-84; Allstate Ins Co, mkt mgr, 1984-88; Chubb Groupof Ins Cos, dept mgr & off, 1988-92; Hanover Ins Co, dir personal lines, 1992-; Diversity MBA, founder, publ, chief exec officer mag, 1997-; P & L Publ Group, chief exec officer & publ, 1997-; Legacy Bancorp Holding Co Bd, dir, 2006; StreetWise Inc, bd chair, 2006; Diversified Recruitment Inc, chief exec officer, strategic partner; DRi Consult, chief exec officer, currently. **Orgs:** Newsletter ed, 1984-86, exec bd mem, 1984-87, co-chair std affrs, 1987, mgr ed, SFMBA, 1987; coordr, Bay Blk Profiles, 1984-; bd mem, newsletter ed, vpres, UCB Alumni Assoc, 1985-; recruiter Big Bros, 1985-86; organizer March Dimes, 1986; pres, UCB Alumni Asn, 1988-89; Cinti MBA, 1989-90; chap commun dir, Mentor, 1989-91; Ins Professionals, 1990-95; MBA, Boston Chap, vpres opers, 1995; NBMBAA, conf pub rels dir, 1995; dir, Gamaliel Found, 2006; bd develop chair, Am Cancer Soc, 2011; independent bd mem, Howard Univ Exec MBA Adv Bd, 2012; ministry dir, apostolic strategy team, Triedstone Baptist Church, 2012; bd dir, DePaul Univ Mkt Adv Bd, 2013. **Honors/Awds:** Coach of the Year, Madeliene Sch, 1984-86; Merit Award, Big Brothers, 1984; Rosalie Stern Outstanding Comm Achiev UC Berkeley, 1986; Community Service Award, March of Dimes, 1986; Mentor Award, Cincinnati Public Schools, 1989-90; Outstanding MBA, Unti Chapter, 1992; Woman of the Year Award, Whos Who, 2005; Minority Business Enterprise Media Cornerstone Award, 2005; Media Ambassador Award, Boardroom bound, 2005; Named in Chicagos Whos Who Most Influential for 2006-08; Entrepreneurship of the Year Award, Triedstone Full Gospel Baptist Church, 2007; Board Service Award, 2007; Woman of the Year Award, 2009; Phenomenal Woman Award, Triedstone Full Gospel Baptist Church, 2009; Black Women's Expo, 2009; Rosalee Stern Award, UC Berkeley. **Home Addr:** 1416 N Cleveland Ave Suite 2, Chicago, IL 60610. **Business Addr:** Chief Executive Officer, P & L Publishing Inc, 9730 S Western Ave, Evergreen Park, IL 60805, **Business Phone:** (708)422-1506.

### MCEWEN, MARK
Television show host. **Personal:** Born Sep 16, 1954, San Antonio, TX; son of Alfred and Dolores; married Judith Lonsdale; children: Maya Alexis. **Educ:** Univ Md, College Park, attended 1975. **Career:** WKTK-FM, sports dir and disc jockey, 1977-78; WWWW-FM Radio, Detroit, MI, music dir & disc jockey, 1978-80; WLUP-FM Radio, Chicago, IL, res dir & disc jockey, 1980-82; WAPP-FM Radio, New York, NY, disc jockey, 1982-83; WNEW-FM Radio, New York, NY, disc jockey, 1983-86; CBS, Morning Prog, weatherman, 1987, CBS This Morning, weatherman, music ed, 1987-92, entertainment ed, 1992-96, co-anchor, 1996, Early Show, weather & entertainment reporter, 2000-02, 2010-; WKMG Local 6, morning news co-anchor & First News, News at Noon, anchor, 2005-; Writer & host: Live by Request: Kenny Loggins, 1997; "Live by Request: Michael Bolton", 1998; Live by Request: Johnny Mathis, 1998; Live by Request: Phil Collins, 1998; Live by Request: Gloria Estefan, 1998; "Tony Bennett Live by Request: An All-Star Tribute", 1998; "Live by Request: Vince Gill", 1999; Live by Request: Kenny Rogers, 1999; Live by Request: Reba McEntire, 1999; Live by Request: Eurythmics, 2000; Live by Request: Trisha Yearwood, 2000; "Live by Request: Willie Nelson", 2000; Live by Request: Neil Diamond, 2001; "Live by Request: Elton John ", 2001; Live by Request: Chicago, 2002; "Live by Request: Santana", 2002; Actor: Tickits, 1992; "Celebrity Dish", 2000; Producer: An Am Tragedy, 2007; Host: "The Morning Prog", 1987; "The New Hollywood Squares", 1988; Happy New Yr, Am, 1988; "Guiding Light", 1994; 1996 Tony Bennett Live by Request: A Valentine's Spec, 1996; "Murphy Brown", 1991-96; Tony Bennett Live by Request: A Valentine's Day Spec, 1997; "CBS This Morning", 1996-99; "Space Ghost Coast to Coast ", 1996-98; "Hollywood Squares", 1998; "The Early Show", 1999-02; "The Rosie O'Donnell Show ", 2002; "The 127th Westminster Kennel Club Dog Show", 2003; "The 128th Westminster Kennel Club Dog Show", 2004; An American Tragedy, co-producer, 2007. **Orgs:** Nat Asn Black Journalists. **Honors/Awds:** Electronic Media Journalist of the Year, Country Music Asn, 1992. **Special Achievements:** Listed as one of the 10 Most Trusted News people in TV Guide, Feb 1995, has covered almost every imaginable television event including the Oscars, the Cannes Film Festival, the Golden Globe awards, the Grammy awards, and the Country Music Association awards. **Business Addr:** Anchor, WKMG-TV, 4466 N John Young Pkwy, Orlando, FL 32804, **Business Phone:** (407)521-1200.

### MCEWING, MITCHELL DALTON
School administrator. **Personal:** Born May 16, 1935, Jacksonville, TX; married Verta Lee Ellis; children: Andre R & Veronica Lee. **Educ:** Wiley Col Marshall, Tex, BS, 1958; Tex Southern Univ, degree credits summers, 1964; N Tex State Univ, MEd, 1973, degree credits, 1975; Tex State Bd Examiners Prof Counrs, Licensure Prof Counr, 1982. **Career:** School administrator (retired); Bethlehem United Comn Ctr, athletic dir, 1958-63; IM Terrell Jr & Sr High Sch, teacher & asst coach, 1963-67, teacher & head coach, 1968-69; Tarrant Cty Jr Col, counr & instr, 1971-75, dean stud develop serv. **Orgs:** Soc worker Bethlehem United Comt Ctr, 1971; vpres, United Com Ctrs, Ft Worth, 1971-73; bd mem, Adv Coun Coun Stud N Tex State Univ, 1981-82; Phi Delta Kappa; Coun Black Am Affairs; secy & treas, E St Paul Bapt Church. **Honors/Awds:** Coach of the Year, IM Terrell High Sch, 1959-69; Dedicated Serv, The Dukes, 1975-76; Serv Awd Phi Theta Kappa, 1984. **Home Addr:** 3445 Denbury Dr, Ft Worth, TX 76133-3138, **Home Phone:** (817)292-0941.

### MCFADDEN, BERNICE L.
Writer. **Personal:** Born Sep 26, 1965, Brooklyn, NY; daughter of Robert Lewis and Vivian Hawkins; children: R'yane Azsa. **Educ:** NYC Fashion Col, Lab Inst Mdsg, NY; Fordham Univ; Marymount Col, travel & tourism course. **Career:** Books: Glorious; Sugar, 1998; The Warmest December, 2001; This Bitter Earth, 2002; Loving Donovan, 2003; Camilla's Roses 2004; Nowhere Is A Place, 2006; As Geneva Holliday:Groove 2005; Fever 2006; Heat 2007; Seduction 2008. **Honors/Awds:** Honor Award, Black Caucus, Ala, 2000; Best New Author of the Year, Go On Girl Book Club, 2000; Best Mainstream Fiction Award, Golden Pen Award, 2001; Best New Author Award, Golden Pen Award, 2001; Zora Neale Hurston Award, 2002; Black Caucus, Ala, 2004; MacDowell Colony Fel, 2005. **Special Achievements:** Pulitzer Prize nominations & Hurston Wright Award Nominations: The Warmest, 2001; Nowhere is a Place, 2006. **Business Addr:** Writer, Plume Books, 375 Hudson St 3rd Fl, New York, NY 10014.

### MCFADDEN, CORA (CORA COLE-MCFADDEN)

Government official, city council member. **Personal:** Born Oct 3, 1945, Durham, NC; children: Lori Yvette & Larry Everette. **Educ:** NC Cent Univ, BA, bus educ, MA, coun & sociol, 1972; Univ NC, Chapel Hill, post grad. **Career:** Government official (retired), coun member; Durham Co Dept Social Serv, social worker, 1969-76, foster care supvr, 1976-78; City Durham, community serv, supvr, 1978-81, affirmative action dir, 1981-; NC Dem Party, secy, vice chmn to chmn; Durham City Coun, coun mem, 2001-, Coun Procedures Comt, chmn, currently, Legis Comt, vice chmn. **Orgs:** NC Asn Black Social Workers, 1972; bd mem, Vol Servs Bur, 1980-83; bd mem, YWCA, 1983-84; state coordr, Am Asn Affirmative Action, 1985; Durham County Coun Women, 1985; pres, Ebonettes Serv Club, 1985; bd dir, Durham Chap, NC Symphony; bd dir, Vol Serv Bur; chmn, Durham Community Martin Luther King Steering Comt; Zeta, Eastern Star, Golden Circle; vice chmn, Durham Br, Nat Asn Advan Colored People; human develop comt, Nat League Cities; youth comt, NC League Cities; People's Alliance; Old Farm Neighborhood Asn; Durham Community Martin Luther King Steering Comt; polit comt, Durham Comt Affairs Black People; Upper Neuse River Asn; Durham-Chapel Hill-Orange County Work Group; Weed & Seed Comt; Durham Cult Master Plan Adv Bd; Cult Arts Master Plan Adv Comt; Homeless Serv Adv Comt. **Home Addr:** 5613 Old Well St, Durham, NC 27701, **Home Phone:** (919)560-4396. **Business Addr:** City Council Member, City Durham, 101 City Hall Plz, Durham, NC 27701, **Business Phone:** (919)560-1200.

### MCFADDEN, ERNEST

Philanthropist. **Personal:** married Patricia; children: 2. **Educ:** Marist Col, BS, bus admin, 1988. **Career:** Yonkers Pvt Indust Coun, dep dir, 1989-97; Purchase Col, SUNY, dir, 1997-99; Heineken USA Inc, dir pub affairs, 1999-2005; New York Dept Labor; Pepsi Cola, mgr global corp citizenship, 2005-08, dir, global corp citizenship, 2005-09; Westchester Community Oppportunity Prog Inc, 2009-; Alcoa, dir workforce inclusion, 2010-. **Orgs:** Nat Blacks Govt; Nat Asn Advan Colored People; Cong Black Caucus Found; Nat Urban League; Lighthouse Int; Int Amateur Athletic Asn; Nat Coun La Raza; bd trustee, Village Bd, 1996; Ossining Community Action Prog; African Am Chamber Com; Ossining Recreation Adv Coun; African Am Men Westchester; Westchester Community Opportunity Prog; Westchester Corp Vol Coun; Nat Blacks Govt; Westchester County Chamber Coms Govt Action Coun; Bus Coun Ny; fel Bethlehem Baptist Church. **Business Addr:** Director, Alcoa, 390 Pk Ave, New York, NY 10022, **Business Phone:** (412)553-4545.

### MCFADDEN, DR. GREGORY L.

Physician. **Personal:** Born Jun 18, 1958, Tallahassee, FL; son of Robert L and Alma L Johnson; married Cynthia A Williams; children: Desiree Y. **Educ:** Florida A&M Univ, BS, biology, 1980; Howard Univ Col Med, MD, 1984. **Career:** Orlando Regional Med Ctr, resident physician, 1984-87; Cigna Health Plan, staff physician, 1988-. **Orgs:** Am Col Physicians; Am Med Asn; Alpha Phi Alpha Fraternity Inc; diplomate, Nat Bd Med Examiners; Am Bd Internal Med; Am Soc Bariatric Physicians. **Honors/Awds:** Nat Dean's List, 1980; Physicians Recognition Award, Am Medical Asn, 1987. **Home Addr:** 4308 Ellenville Pl, Valrico, FL 33594. **Business Addr:** Staff Physician, Cigna Health Plan, 303 W Platt St, Tampa, FL 33606, **Business Phone:** (813)254-1020.

### MCFADDEN, JAMES L.

Educator, art consultant. **Personal:** Born Nov 9, 1929, Darlington, SC; married Gertha Moore; children: Dionne Jametta. **Educ:** Claflin Col, AB, 1954; NY Univ, MA. **Career:** Morris Col, Art instr, 1954-56; Orangeburg City Sch chair person Jr High Sch, art teacher, 1954-70; Art & Music Texts, 1969; SC State Col, Orangeburg, prof art, 1970-; Claflin Col, first art teacher. **Orgs:** Am Legion Post No 210, 1954; Edisto Masonic Lodge No 39 AF & M, 1966; Shriner Jeddah Temple No 160, 1966; treas, SC Art Educ Asn, 1971-75; Orbg Alumni Chap KAY; adv, Alpha Lambda Chap KAY; Attend William Chapel AME Church; Nat Asn Advan Colored People; SC Educ Asn; Nat Educ Asn; Nat Art Educ Asn; NY Univ Alumni Asn. **Honors/Awds:** South eastern Province Achievement Award, Kappa Alpha Psi Fraternity, 1950; Outstanding Leadership & Dedication Award, Alpha Lambda Chap Kappa Alpha Psi Fraternity, 1976. **Home Addr:** 2696 Old Cameron Rd, Orangeburg, SC 29115-3931, **Home Phone:** (803)536-1960. **Business Addr:** Professor, South Carolina State College, PO Box 1962, Orangeburg, SC 29115.

### MCFADDEN, NATHANIEL JAMES

School administrator, government official. **Personal:** Born Aug 3, 1946, Philadelphia, PA; married Rachel Tift; children: Nathaniel Jr, Byron & Devon Dodson. **Educ:** Morgan State Col, BA, geog & hist educ, 1968, Urban Educ Admin Degree Prog; Morgan State Univ, MS, hist & social sci, 1972. **Career:** Baltimore City Pub Schs, teacher, 1968-75, dept head, 1975-82, 1987-88, prin, 1979-82, coordr, 1988-94, work-based learning mgr, 1997-98; Dunbar High Sch, teacher, 1968-75; Lombard Jr High Sch, head social sci dept, 1975-82; Dunbar Adult Eve Sch, prin, 1979-82; City CounBaltimore, coun mem, 1982-87; Sojourner-Douglass Col, coordr community affairs, 1985-88; Southwestern Sr High Sch, head social sci dept, 1987-88; Lake Clifton & Eastern Sr High Sch, coordr educ opportunity prog, 1988-94, facilitator, 1998-; State Md, sen, 1995-, Majority Leader, 2003-07; Pro Tem, pres, 2007-; Spec Joint Comt Pensions, Senate chmn, 2008-. **Orgs:** Gamma Theta Upsilon, 1963-; Urban League; Phi Alpha Theta, 1967-; Nat Asn Advan Colored People; Alpha Kappa Mu, 1968-; Kappa Delta Pi, 1968-; E Baltimore Women's League, 1974-; bd mem, Eastside Dem Org, 1975-; Asn Study Negro Life & Hist Baltimore City Chap, 1980-82; Lakewood Chase Improv Asn, 1982-; Eastern Dist Police Community Rel Coun, 1982-; Eastside Neighborhood Asn, 1983-; Eastern Dist Police Community Rels Coun Baltimore, 1982-87; adv bd, Johns Hopkins Med Plan, 1985-; Optimist Club E Baltimore, 1985-; asst rec keeper, Baltimore Alumni Chap, Kappa Alpha Psi Fraternity, 1989-; Alpha Phi Omega, Nat Serv Fraternity, Baltimore Area Alumni; Youth Fair Chance, adv bd, 1994-; Juv Justice, adv bd, Baltimore City, 1994-; Comt 100 Asn Black Charities, 1994-; RAIDE-EOP Inc, bd dirs; Gov's Task Force Afr Am Entrepreneurship Baltimore City, 1996-99; Task Force Charitable Giving, 1996-; Small Bus Develop Ctr Netwok, adv bd, 1997; Privatization Adv Panel, Mass Transit Admin, 1997-98; 100 Black Men Md Inc; bd dir, 1 to 1 Baltimore Mentoring Partnership, 1997-; Chair, Baltimore City Senate Deleg, 1997; Partnership Policy Coun Block Grants, 1998; Task force End Smoking MD, vchair, 1999; Joseph Fund Bd, 1999-2001; Coun Mgmt & Productivity, 2000-04; State Coun Cancer Control, 2001-; Task Force to Study Pub Sch Facil, 2002-04; Oversight Comt Qual CareNursing Homes, 2002-05; Md State Drug & Alcohol Abuse Coun, 2004-08; Adv Comt Naming State Facil, Roads, & Bridges, 2005-06; Pres Pro Tem, 2007-; Task Force to Study Raising Compulsory Pub Sch Attendance Age to 18, 2006-07; Task Force Minority ParticipationEnviron Community, 2006-07; Blue Ribbon Comn Md Transp Funding, 2010-; vice-chair, Budget & Taxation Comt, 2011-. **Honors/Awds:** Legislator Recognition Award, Maryland Asn Counties, 2002; First Citizen Award, Maryland Senate, 2009; Lifetime Achievement Award, Md Nat Guard Freestate Challenge Acad, 2009; Alumni of the Year Award, Morgan State Univ, 2009. **Special Achievements:** First Black President Pro Tem in history of Maryland State Senate. **Home Addr:** 3301 Belair Rd Suite 2A, Baltimore, MD 21213-1228, **Home Phone:** (410)563-4500. **Business Addr:** Senator, Miller Senate Office, Rm 422 Miller Senate Off Bldg 11 Bladen St, Annapolis, MD 21401-1991, **Business Phone:** (410)841-3165.

### MCFADDIN, THERESA GARRISON (TERRI MC-FADDN-SOLOMON)

Teacher, counselor. **Personal:** Born Jul 23, 1943, Philadelphia, PA; daughter of Alvin Prunty and Barbara Campbell Prunty; married Charles Solomon; children: Roslyn Ballard & Theresa. **Educ:** Fuller Theol Sem, MA, theol; Am Jewish Univ, LA, Hebrew Studies. **Career:** Educator, author & minister; Motown Rec, Los Angeles, CA, writer, producer; Christian Broadcasting Network, Va Beach VA, writer, producer; Terri McFaddin & Friends, Pasadena, CA, teacher & counr; Books: God Made Me Beauty-full; Only a Woman; Sapphires & Other Precious Jewels. **Orgs:** Women Discipleship Group, 1999-. **Honors/Awds:** Grammy Award, Nat Acad Rec Arts & Sci US, 1986; Citizen of the Yr, Zeta Phi Beta Sorority, 1989; Grammy Award, Nat Acad Rec Arts & Sci US, 1998. **Home Addr:** 65 W Figueroa Dr, Altadena, CA 91001, **Home Phone:** (818)791-3640. **Business Addr:** Teacher, Counselor, Terri McFaddin & Friends, 686 Arroyo Pkwy Suite 174, Pasadena, CA 91101, **Business Phone:** (626)794-5402.

### MCFALL, MARY

School administrator, president (organization), lawyer. **Personal:** Born Aug 30, 1938, San Angelo, TX; children: Brick & Jamila Agbon. **Educ:** San Angelo Jr Col, dipl, 1955; Univ Tex, BA, 1957; Univ Tex, JD, 1978. **Career:** Soc Security Adm, serv rep, 1965-66; Comm Action Agy, asst nghbr hd servs dir, 1967-69; Intercultural Devel S Meth Univ, dir, 1971-; Tarrant Co YWCA, br exec, 1969-71; Tex Asn Black Personnel Higher Educ, co-founder, 1st vpres conf coord, 1973-79; Soc of Ethnic & Spec Studies, sec, 1975-; Tex Asn Black Personnel Higher Educ, pres, 1979-81. **Orgs:** Co-founder Students Direct Action Univ Tex; del Nat Students Asn, 1961; chmn, Am Civil Liberties Union Ft Worth Chap, 1968-70; vpres, Minority Cultural Arts Asn, 1970-71; Citizen's Planning Com Ft Worth, 1971; Univ Stu Personnel Adm Goals Black Dallas Com, 1976-77; bd dir, Family Guidance Asn, 1979-; Coalition Educ Black C; Tex Asn Col; Alpha Kappa Alpha Sor. **Honors/Awds:** First Black Student Admitted to San Angelo Col; 1st Black Student to Receive BA from Univ of TX; Listed Golden Profiles of Dallas Ft Worth, 1980; Golden Ex of the Year. **Special Achievements:** First black women accepted to the University of Texas School of Law. **Home Addr:** 322 Ave F, Dallas, TX 75203.

### MCFARLAND, ANTHONY DARELLE

Football player. **Personal:** Born Dec 18, 1977, Winnsboro, LA. **Educ:** La State, BS, bus mgt, 1999. **Career:** Football player (retired), analyst, free agent; Tampa Bay Buccaneers, 1999, left defensive tackle, 2000-01, 2004, nose tackle, 2000, 2002, defensive tackle, 2000, 2003-06, right defensive tackle, 2002; Indianapolis Colts, left defensive tackle, 2006, 2007; SEC Network, football analyst, 2014-; free agt, currently. **Orgs:** Kappa Alpha Psi Fraternity. **Honors/Awds:** Super Bowl champion XXXVII, XLI. **Business Addr:** Football Analyst, SEC Network, 11001 Rushmore Dr, Charlotte, NC 28277, **Business Phone:** (704)973-5000.

### MCFARLAND, ARTHUR C.

Lawyer, legal consultant. **Personal:** Born Feb 5, 1947, Charleston, SC; married E Elise Davis; children: Kira Jihan & William Joseph. **Educ:** Univ Notre Dame, BA, govt, 1970; Univ Va, JD, 1973. **Career:** Pvt pract atty, 1974-; City Charleston SC, munic ct judge, 1976-78, chief munic judge, 1978-; McFarland & Assoc, atty & mgr, currently; Knights Peter Claver Inc, supreme knight, chief exec officer, 2000-06; KPC, legal coun; consult, Us Conf Cath Bishops. **Orgs:** Nat Bar Asn; Am Bar Asn, 1974-; Nat Conf Black Lawyers, 1974-; Am Judges Asn; NBA Judiciary Coun, 1976-; bd dir, Trident United Way, 1977-; pres, Robert Gould Shaw Boys Club, 1978-; Chas SC Nat Asn Advan Colored People Exec Com, 1978-; pres, Charleston Bus & Prof Asn, 1983-85; Charleston Waterfront Pk Comt, 1983-; bd dir, Charleston Neighborhood Legal Assistance Prog, 1984-86; Nat advocate, Knights Peter Claver, 1994-; SC Bar; Am Bar Asn; St Peter Coun No 110; bd dir, Med Univ Found; bd dir, Daniel Joseph Jenkins Inst C; bd dir, Choraliers Music Club; bd dir, 100 Black Men Am; pres, Charleston County Human Serv Comn; Gamma Lambda Boule; Col Charleston Found; Charleston Waterfront Pk Comn; St. Patrick Cath Church; Cath Educ Found; Phillip Simmons Found; Med Univ Sc Found; Domestic Policy Comt; trustee, Nat Black Cath Cong; natl pres, Gadsden Family Reunion. **Honors/Awds:** Earl Warren Fel NAACP Legal Defense Fund, 1973-74; Earl Warren Fel Nat Asn Advan Colored People Legal Defense & Educ Fund, 1973-77; He received many awards & honors for his community service; African American Male Image Award; Humanitarian of the Year Award. **Special Achievements:** Listed in Who's Who in Black America. **Home Addr:** 204 Grove St, Charleston, SC 29403, **Home Phone:** (843)577-4889. **Business Addr:** Chief Executive Officer, Supreme Knight, Knights of Peter Claver Inc, 2815 Forbes Ave, Montgomery, AL 36110, **Business Phone:** (334)265-3214.

### MCFARLAND, ROLAND C.

Executive, television producer. **Personal:** Born Aug 13, 1940, Devern, TX; son of Booker and Ada; married Paulette; children: Curtis & Roselyn Daniels. **Educ:** San Diego State Univ, BA, speech arts, 1961. **Career:** Old Globe Theater, Repertory actor & dir, San Diego & Los Angeles, Calif, 1961-70; ABC TV, sr ed, mgr broadcast stand, 1970-73; FOX Broadcasting Co, dir broadcast stand, 1993-, vpres broadcast stand & pract, sr vpres, 1993-2007; MyNetworkTV, vpres broadcast stand & pract, 2007-; Hollywood & Beverly Hills Nat Asn Advan Colored People, vpres, currently. **Orgs:** Chair, Image Award, Nat Asn Advan Colored People, 1988-90; vpres & advisor, Nat Comt Youth Opportunity; adv, C Now; adv, Media Scope; adv, Ctr Commun Police, UCLA; adv, SAG, media awareness comt; Chrysalis Found Homeless; Calif Dance Ctr; Boys & Girls Club Am; San Diego Nat & Int Film Fest; dir coun pub rep, Nat Insts Health; bd dir, Hollywood & Beverly Hills Nat Asn Advan Colored People, currently; bd mem, Chrysalis Found; bd dir, EIC. **Home Addr:** 10901 Sunnybrae Ave, Chatsworth, CA 91311-1625, **Home Phone:** (818)882-5105. **Business Addr:** Senior Vice President, FOX Broadcasting Co, 10201 W Pico Blvd 1003220, Los Angeles, CA 90035, **Business Phone:** (310)369-1000.

### MCFARLIN, EMMA DANIELS

Teacher, consultant, government official. **Personal:** Born Nov 14, 1921, Camden, AR. **Educ:** Philander-Smith Col, BA, 1950; Univ Wis, MS, 1961; US Int Univ San Diego, PhD, 1976. **Career:** Low Rent Housing Proj Little Rock Redevelop & Housing Authority, mgr, 1952-64; San Francisco Unified Sch Dist, teacher, 1964-65; US Dept HUD, spec rep, 1965-70; US Dept HEW, regional rep, 1970-73; Menlo Pk, asst city mgr, 1973-74; Off Mayor Los Angeles, spec asst mayor, 1974-75; Univ Calif, asso prof urban planning, 1975-77; US Dept HUD, regional adminr, 1977; HUD, consult, currently. **Orgs:** Omicron Nu Nat Honor Soc, 1961. **Honors/Awds:** Emma McFarlin Day Award, City of Menlo Park, 1974; Newsmaker Award, Nat Asn Media Women, 1975; Outstanding Serv & Achievement City Council Los Angeles, 1975. **Special Achievements:** First African-American female to head the western region of the US Department of Housing and Urban Development. **Home Addr:** 2629/2 6th Ave, Birmingham, AL 35234. **Business Addr:** Consultant, HUD, 4207 Enoro Dr, Los Angeles, CA 90008.

### MCFERRIN, BOBBY (ROBERT KEITH MCFERRIN, JR.)

Singer, actor, songwriter. **Personal:** Born Mar 11, 1950, New York, NY; son of Robert K Sr and Sara; married Debbie Lynn Green; children: Taylor John, Jevon Chase & Madison. **Educ:** Sacramento State Univ, attended; Cerritos Col, attended. **Career:** Singer, 1977-. Solo: Bobby Mc Ferrin, 1982; The Voice, 1984; Spontaneous Inventions, 1985; Elephant's Child, 1987; Simple Pleasures, 1988; How the Rhino Got His Skin/How the Camel Got His Hump, 1990; Medicine Music, 1990; Many Faces of Bird, 1991; Hush, 1992; Sorrow Is Not Forever, 1994; Paper Music, 1995; Bang! Zoom, 1997; Circle songs, 1997; Mouth Music, 2001; Beyond Words, 2002; Konzert fur Europa, 2004; VOCAbuLarieS, 2010. Collaborations: The Just So Stories, 1987; Play, 1990; Hush, 1991; The Mozart Sessions, 1996; Circlesongs, 1997; Beyond Words, 2002; Konzert fur Europa, 2004; Live in Montreal, 2005; VOCAbuLarieS, 2010; Spirit you all, 2013. TV series: "For Our Children: The Concert ", 1993; "Sessions at West 54th", 1997; "In My Life", 1998; "VH-1 Where Are They Now?", 2000; "Great Performances", 2003. St Paul Chamber Orchestra, artistic leadership, creative chair, 1994. **Honors/Awds:** Grammy Award, 1985-88 & 1992. **Business Addr:** Singer, EMI-Manhatten, 1750 N Vine St, Hollywood, CA 90028, **Business Phone:** (323)462-6252.

### MCFERRIN, ROBERT KEITH, JR. See MCFERRIN, BOBBY.

### MCFERRIN, SARA ELIZABETH COPPER

School administrator, musician, educator. **Personal:** Born Sep 10, 1924, Washington, DC; daughter of Charles and Elizabeth; married Robert; children: Robert Jr Bobby & Brenda. **Educ:** Howard Univ, attended 1942; Univ Southern Calif; Calif State Univ, Los Angeles. **Career:** CBS-TV, Christmas specials; solo recitalist & oratorio soloist throughout USA; symphony soloist; New York Ctr, Opera Chorus, soloist; Hollywood Greek Theatre Opera Chorus, soloist; Calif State Univ, Long Beach/Nelson Sch Fine Arts, Can, Pasadena City Col, Cerritos Col, teacher; Fullerton Col Music Dept, chmn voice dept, 1973-90; chmn, 1990-93; Pac Chorale Bd dir & Personnel, dir; Guest speaker; prof emer, Univ Okla, Norman, Okla, vis prof voice, 1986, currently. **Orgs:** Nat Asn Teachers Singing; Adjudicator Met Opera Western Region Auditions Calif, Ariz, Nev; Adjudicating Panels Vocal comp Southern Calif; San Francisco Opera, S Calif Opera Guild; bd assoc, Los Angeles Master Chorale Assoc; bd dir, Pac Chorale, Costa Mesa Co-educ comm; A Cappella Soc, laureate. **Honors/Awds:** Staff of Distinction Award, Fullerton Col, 1993. **Special Achievements:** Appeared in films: Porgy & Bess, Elmer Gantry; Appeared in Television shows, "Lost in the Stars", "Troubled Island". **Home Addr:** 630 Brookline Pl, Fullerton, CA 92835, **Home Phone:** (714)441-1153. **Business Addr:** Professor Emeritus, Fullerton College, 321 E Chapman Ave, Fullerton, CA 92832-2095, **Business Phone:** (714)992-7000.

### MCGARITY, WANE KEITH

Football coach, football player, executive. **Personal:** Born Sep 30, 1976, San Antonio, TX. **Educ:** Univ Tex, Austin, BS, educ, 1999. **Career:** Football player (retired), exec, coach; Dallas Cowboys, wide receiver, 1999-2001; New Orleans Saints, 2001; Calgary Stampeders, 2002-04; Winnipeg Blue Bombers, 2005; H-E-B, health & wellness prog mgr; Cent Cath High Sch, wide receiver coach, currently. **Business Addr:** Wide Receiver Coach, Central Catholic High School, 1403 N St Mary's St, San Antonio, TX 78215, **Business Phone:** (210)225-6794.

### MCGATHON, CARRIE M.

Nurse. **Personal:** Born Feb 3, 1936, Mendenhall, MS; daughter of Lena Hays (deceased) and James Sr; married John A; children: Berlinda, Brenda & John Reginald. **Educ:** Dillard Univ, BSN, 1964; Col Holy Names, PHN, 1970; Jackson State Univ, MEd, 1978. **Career:** Naval Regional Med Ctr, Oakland, Calif, clin supvr Ob/Gyn, 1975-80; Health Care Serv Inc, dir/adminr; Alameda Community Hosp, Alameda, Calif, RN, labor & delivery, 1980-; COGIOC, lic, evangelist, 1980-; Healthforce, case mgr, nursing dept; Corp Regist Nurses, staff ltd; pvt pract, nursing, currently. **Orgs:** Calif Nurses Asn, 1964-; Dillard Alumnus, 1964-; NAACOG, 1970-; Biblesway CIGOGC, 1975-; Black Nurses Asn Greater E Bay; Coun Black Women Female Execs; Order Eastern Star 49A; Heroines Jericho. **Honors/Awds:** Commendation, Juris Doctoral Bishop EE, Cleveland, COGIOC; JD Bishop Larry J McEathon, Woman of Boldness Award. **Special Achievements:** Certified herbalist, nutritional consultant, iridologist, 1994. **Business Addr:** Nurse, 2653 76th Ave, Oakland, CA 94605-2807, **Business Phone:** (510)569-8790.

### MCGEE, ADOLPHUS STEWART
Football coach, association executive. **Personal:** Born Jan 29, 1941, Dos Palos, CA. **Educ:** Coalinga Col, BA, 1960; Calif State Univ, BA, 1963, MA, 1970, MA, 1972. **Career:** Union High Sch Dist Sacramento, teacher math, head track football coach, 1963-66; Grant Joint Union High Sch Dist, head track coach, 1963-65; Luther Burbank High Sch Sacramento, teacher math sci, track coach & asst football coach, 1966-68; Sacramento City Unified Sch Dist, asst, supt, 1968-70; inter-group rels adv, 1969-70; All-conf & All-Am, footballer; Sacramento Sr High Sch, prin, 1970; Potato Bowl Team, capt. **Orgs:** Asn Calif Sch Adminr; chmn, Minority News Media Joint Task Force Urban Coalition, 1969-71; Joint Legis Comn Educ Goals & Eval; pres, Sacramento Sr High Sch Mem Scholar Fund, 1970-; Joint Task Force Goals & Eval State Calif, 1972-; community bd, YMCA; Nat Asn Advan Colored People; Blue Key; Phi Delta Kappa; Omega Chi Delta; chair investment comt, State Teachers Retirement Syst; community bd, Camellia Symphony. **Honors/Awds:** Hall of Fame; CSUS Hall of Fame; California Legislature Black Hall of Fame; Men for Outstanding Leadership Campus-Wide, Blue Key Hon Soc. **Home Addr:** 7476 Franklin Blvd, Sacramento, CA 95823-0000. **Business Addr:** 2315 34 St, Sacramento, CA 95817, **Business Phone:** (916)549-5662.

### MCGEE, BENJAMIN LELON
Executive. **Personal:** Born Feb 18, 1943, Booneville, MS; married Rose M Jackson; children: Ivy, Ben II, Brian & Holly. **Educ:** Ark AM&N Col Pine, Buffalo, AR, agron sci, 1967; Memphis State Univ, attended 1975. **Career:** Dept Agr ASCS, compliance supr, 1967-75; GMAC, credit rep, 1976-77; Liquor Ctr, owner, 1977-. **Orgs:** Bd mem, Marion Sch Dist, 1975; vice chmn, bd trustee, AR State Univ, 1977-; state comt man, Dem Party, 1979; bd trustee, Ark State Univ Jonesboro, 1980; bd trustee, AME Ch. **Special Achievements:** First black chairperson of the Arkansas State University. **Home Addr:** PO Box 240, Marion, AR 72364-0240, **Home Phone:** (501)739-4171. **Business Addr:** Owner, The Liquor Center, 3107 E Broadway, West Memphis, AR 72301.

### MCGEE, BUFORD LAMAR
Football player. **Personal:** Born Aug 16, 1960, Durant, MS. **Educ:** Univ Miss, BS, bus, 1984. **Career:** Football player (retired); San Diego Chargers, 1984-86; Los Angeles Rams, running back, 1987-91; Green Bay Packers, fullback & running back, 1992. **Honors/Awds:** Daniel F. Reeves Memorial Award, 1990. **Special Achievements:** Film: 1989 NFC Championship Game, 1990.

### MCGEE, COL. CHARLES EDWARD
Military pilot, executive. **Personal:** Born Dec 7, 1919, Cleveland, OH; son of Lewis Allen (deceased) and Ruth Elizabeth Lewis (deceased); married Frances E Nelson; children: Charlene McGee Smith, Ronald A & Yvonne G. **Educ:** Columbia Col, MO, BA, 1978. **Career:** Military pilot, executive (retired); Army Air Corps & USaF, col, 1942-73, 44th Fighter Bomber Squadron, Philippines, comdr, 1951-53, 7230th Support Squadron, Italy, 1961-63, 16th TRS, 1967-68, Richard-Gebaur ARB, Mo, 1972; ISC Financial Corp, dir real estate & purchasing, 1973-78, vpres real estate, 1974-78; City Prairie Village, asst dir admin, 1979; City Kans, Downtown Airport, mgr, 1980-82; George Lucas film, consult; Red Tails; consult. **Orgs:** Life mem, Tuskegee Airmen Inc, 1972-; pres, Nat Pres Asn, 1983-85; life mem, Mil Order World Wars; life mem, Air Force Asn; life mem, Alpha Phi Alpha; life mem, Nat Asn Advan Colored People; Boy Scouts Am; Boy's & Girls Clubs Greater Kans; Christian Church; Aviation Adv Comn, Kans City; dir, Munic Assistance Corp, Kans City; life mem, S African Korean War Veteran's Asn. **Honors/Awds:** Eagle Scout Award, 1940; Elder Statesman of Aviation, Nat Aeronaut Asn, 1998; Brig Gen Noel F Parrish Award, Tuskegee Airmen Inc, 1988; Distinguished Eagle Scout Award, Nat Scout Jamboree, 2010; National Aviation Hall of Fame, 2011; Boy Scouts of America, Silver Beaver Award; Nations Highest Civilian Award. **Special Achievements:** First black airman in American history to obtained his flying certificate. **Home Addr:** 5002 Elsmere Pl, Bethesda, MD 20814-2826, **Home Phone:** (301)530-1960.

### MCGEE, EVA M.
Educator, association executive. **Personal:** Born Jun 13, 1942, Nashville, AR. **Educ:** AM & N Col, BS, 1963; Univ Ark, Fayetteville, MEd, 1971. **Career:** Educator, executive (retired); AM & N Col Pine Bluff, educ secy, 1963-69; Univ Ark, instr, dir instnl advan, 1969-86; Broadcast Media, dir; Univ Ark Pine Bluff, assoc vice chancellor, secy, asst prof, dir instnl advan, dir develop, dir planning & dir mgt & eval; Links Inc. **Orgs:** Treas, Nat Bus Educ Asn, 1970-72, pres, 1972-74, st coordr, 1974-; secy, Ark Bus Ed Asn, 1972-73; pres, Ark Bus Ed Asn, 1973-74; Ark Col Teachers Educ & Bus; Southern Bus Educ Asn; Pine Bluff Alum Chap Delta Sigma Theta Sorority; bd dir, Pine Bluff OIC, 1973-74; Nat Coun Negro Woman; Jeff County Adv Comn, Blk Adaptation, 1973-74. **Honors/Awds:** Listed Leaders Black American, 1973-74; named Outstanding Educator of America, 1974-75; Leadership Award, Pine Bluff Alum Chap Delta Sigma Theta, 1973; Delta of the Year, 1974; Distinguished Alumni Award, High Sch; Leadership Award, Delta Sigma Theta Sorority. **Home Addr:** 3 Buckshot, Pine Bluff, AR 71603, **Home Phone:** (870)535-5237.

### MCGEE, GLORIA KESSELLE
Nurse, psychotherapist. **Personal:** Born Jul 12, 1954, Monrovia; daughter of Andrew Belton and Izola Lewis; married Waddell. **Educ:** Wayne State Univ, BS, 1977; Univ Mich, MS, 1981. **Career:** Lafayette Clin, clin nurse specialist, 1981-87; Va Med Ctr, Okla City, head nurse, 1987-90; Va Med Ctr, Lincoln, NE, assoc chief nurse, 1990-; Inner Visions Coun Ctr Inc, bd pres, 1990-. **Orgs:** Sigma Theta Tau Int, 1980-; bd, Nat Asn Advan Colored People, 1980-; Am Nurses Asn, 1980-; Univ Mich Alumni Asn, 1981-; Lincoln Human Rights Comn, comnr, 1991-; bd, Am Red Cross, 1991-; Altrusa Int, 1992-; secy & treas, Am Veterans Alliance Auxiliary Inc. **Honors/Awds:** Special Advancement for Achievement, Va Med Ctr, 1988, Special Advancement for Performance, 1991; Woman of the Year, Inner Visions Counseling CTR Inc, 1991. **Special Achievements:** Reducing and Controling Absenteeism in Nursing, 1991. **Home Addr:** 2861 E 84th St, Tulsa, OK 74137-1402. **Business Addr:** Associate Chief Nurse, Veterans Affairs Medical Center, 600 S 70th St Suite 597, Lincoln, NE 68510, **Business Phone:** (402)489-3802.

### MCGEE, PROF. HENRY W., JR.
Educator. **Personal:** Born Dec 31, 1932, Chicago, IL; son of Henry W and Attye Belle Truesdale; married Victoria; children: Henry III, Kevin, Byron, Gregory & Erik; married Alice. **Educ:** Wilson Col, AA, 1952; Northwestern Univ, BS, jour, 1954; DePaul Univ, JD, 1957; Columbia Univ, LLM, 1970. **Career:** Negro Press Int, news ed, 1954-56; Gottlieb & Schwartz, law clerk, 1955-56; Ming & Leighton Moore, law clerk, 1957-58; Cook County, asst state atty, 1958-62; Jesmer & Harris, Chicago, Ill, atty, 1962-66; US Off Econ Opportunity, coord, Great Lakes Region, Regional Legal Serv dir, 1966-67; Univ Chicago, Law Sch Ctr, Studies Criminal Justice Legal Serv, Youth Action Res Proj, legal dir, admin, 1967-68; Univ Calif, Los Angeles Sch Law, from asst prof to prof, 1969-94, Grad Prog, dir, prof emer law, 1994-; Fordham Univ Sch Law, vis prof law, 1992, 1993 & 1994, 1995-98; Seattle Univ Sch Law, prof law, 1994-, Mex & Latin Am Initiatives, dir, currently. **Orgs:** Nat Bar Asn; Nat Hisp Bar Asn; consult, City Poverty Comn, London, Eng, 1973; draftsman, Nat Conf Bar Examiners, 1974-95; consult & lectr, Urban Planning USIS Italy, 1976; US Equal Employ Opportunity Comn; Am Arbit Asn; Asn Am Law Sch Teaching Clin; fel Mex Acad Pvt Int & Comparative Law Breakfast Group. **Honors/Awds:** Blue Key Nat Honor Frat, 1957; Distinguished Service Award, Black Law Journal of UCLA, 1979, 1980; Fulbright professor, Univ Madrid, 1982; Pub numerous articles; Arthur Sutherland Public Service Award, 1990; Frederic P. Sutherland Public Interest Award, Univ Calif, Los Angeles, Law Sch, 1990; Hall of Fame Award, Langston Law Club, 2003; Black Law Student Legal Legacy Award, Seattle University, 2007; Dean's Award, University Law School, 2008; Clyde Ferguson Award, Association of American Law Schools, 2011. **Business Addr:** Professor of Law, Mexico/Latin American Initiatives Director, Seattle University School of Law, Rm 437 901 Broadway 12th Ave, Seattle, WA 98122, **Business Phone:** (206)398-4026.

### MCGEE, HENRY WADSWORTH
Lecturer, executive, president (organization). **Personal:** Born Jan 22, 1953, Chicago, IL; married Celia; children: 1. **Educ:** Harvard Univ, Cambridge, MA, BA, social studies, 1974; Harvard Bus Sch, Cambridge, MA, MBA, 1979. **Career:** News week Mag, NY & Wash, reporter, 1974-77; HBO, mgr film acquisition, 1979-80, Family Programming Dept, mgr, 1982-83, Enterprises, dir, 1983-85, Home Video, vpres, 1985-88, sr vpres programming, 1988-95, pres, 1995-2013; Time-Life TV, 1979, dir prog acquisitions, 1980-81; Cine max, dir budgeting & planning, 1981-82; Amerisourcebergen Corp, dir, 2004-; Harvard Bus Sch, sr lect, 2013-; Film Soc Lincoln Ctr. **Orgs:** Bd dir, New 42nd St Inc, 1990-; pres, Film Soc Lincoln Ctr; dir, Black Filmmaker Found; pres, Alvin Ailey Dance Theater Found; Sundance Inst. **Honors/Awds:** Professional Achievement Award, Harvard Business School African-American Alumni Asn, 2004. **Special Achievements:** One of New Yorks Top 100 minority executives by Crains New York Business, 1998; Black Enterprise Magazine named him one of the 50 most powerful African-Americans in the entertainment business, 2002, 2007. **Business Addr:** Senior Lecturer, Harvard Business School, Soldiers Field, Boston, MA 02163, **Business Phone:** (617)496-9700.

### MCGEE, JAMES MADISON
Association executive, president (organization). **Personal:** Born Dec 22, 1940, Nashville, TN; married Mary Francis Wilkins; children: Andrea, LaSandra & James Jr. **Educ:** Fisk Univ, attended 1960; Mid-S Sch Electronics, dipl, 1970; Masons Sch Bus, dipl, acct. **Career:** US Postal Serv, clerk, 1965, LSM operator, 1967, LSM instr trainer, 1973-76; Nat Alliance Postal & Fed Employees, treas, 1968-72, vpres, 1976-89, nat vpres, 1982-89, nat pres, 1989-; Credit Union, chmn, currently; World Confederation Labor, vpres, 1989-. **Orgs:** Nat Black Leadership Roundtable; Tenn Voters Coun, 1967-80; Nat Asn Advan Colored People, 1968-80; Benevolent Protective Order Elks Tenn, 1970-80. **Business Addr:** National President, National Alliance of Postal & Federal Employees, 1628 11th St NW, Washington, DC 20001-5086, **Business Phone:** (202)939-6325.

### MCGEE, DR. JOANN
Counselor, executive director, educator. **Personal:** Born Buffalo, NY; daughter of Rev Cephus Jr and Verlene Freeman. **Educ:** Elmira Col, NY, BA, MS, reading educ, 1992; Univ Scranton, MS, couns, 1987; Columbia Univ, Teachers Col, MA, EdD, adult & continuing educ, 1992; Bank St Col Edu, MEd, spec educ, 1992. **Career:** State Univ NY, Binghamton, NY, instr, 1980-81; Arnot Art Mus, traveling artist, instr, 1982-85; Southern Tier fice Social Ministry, community residence counsr, 1985-86; Elmira Correctional Facility, suv vol tutors, 1984-94; Elmira City Sch Dist & Corning City Sch Dist, home teacher, 1994-; MG Ed Serv, exec dir, currently; Art/Reading Educ, instr, Mansfield Univ, 1998-2000; Johnson City Sch Dist, specl ed teacher, currently. **Orgs:** Reading Reform Found, NY, 1999-00. **Honors/Awds:** MNY Group Scholarship, Teachers Col, 1989-92. **Home Addr:** 811 W Water St, Elmira, NY 14905, **Home Phone:** (607)737-6777. **Business Addr:** Teacher, Elmira City School District, 951 Hoffman St, Elmira, NY 14905, **Business Phone:** (607)735-3000.

### MCGEE, PAMELA
Basketball coach, basketball coach. **Personal:** Born Dec 1, 1962, Flint, MI; married Kevin Stafford; children: Javale & Imani. **Educ:** Univ SC, econ & commun, 1984. **Career:** Basketball player, basketball coach (retired); Chicago State Univ women's basketball team, asst coach; Sacramento Monarchs, ctr, 1997-98; Los Angeles Sparks, 1998; Detroit Shock, asst coach.

### MCGEE, PATRICIA J. HORNE (PAT HORNE MCGEE)
School administrator, executive director. **Personal:** Born Dec 23, 1946, Ypsilanti, MI; daughter of Louise Hardwick Horne and Lacy Horne Sr; married Columbus J. **Educ:** Mich State Univ, BA, 1968; Univ Mich, MSW, 1971, cert, infant ment health; Eastern Mich Univ, MA, 1973. **Career:** Mich State Dept Social Serv, caseworker, 1968-69; Ann Arbor Model Cities, social coordr, 1970-72; Washtenaw Co Community Coord Child Care, exec dir, 1971-74; Eastern Mich Univ, adj prof; Univ Mich, adj prof; Ferris State Univ, asst prof, 1974-79; Mercy Col Detroit, assoc prof & prog dir social work dept, 1979-88; Wayne Co Intermediate Sch Dist, assoc dir, 1987-94; Wayne State Univ, adj prof, 1988-; Washtenaw Community Col, Ann Arbor, MI, adj prof, 1989-; Univ Calif, Los Angeles, mgt fel, 1993; Wayne County Regional Educ Serv Agency, dir, 1994-99; Washtenaw Co Head Start, exec dir, 1999-. **Orgs:** Sec Huron Valley Asn Black Social Workers, 1971-; head start consult, Wayne Co, Washtenaw Co, Region V, Emprise Design, CSR, 1980; plng comnr, City Ypsilanti, 1982-96; bd mem, Huron Valley Girl Scouts, 1983-, second vpres, 1988-94; pres, Ann Arbor Delta Sigma Theta Sorority, 1985-87; Nat Asn Social Workers; Zoning Bd Appeals City Ypsilanti; vpres, Mich Coun, Delta Sigma Theta Sorority; Ypsilanti Area Community Found; Literacy Coalition Washtenaw County; Success by Six. **Home Addr:** 925 Frederick St, Ypsilanti, MI 48197-5290, **Home Phone:** (734)482-0951. **Business Addr:** Director, Washtenaw County Head Start, 1661 Leforge Rd, Ypsilanti, MI 48197, **Business Phone:** (734)484-7119.

### MCGEE, REV. PAULA L.
Basketball player, preacher, president (organization). **Personal:** Born Jan 1, 1963, Flint, MI. **Educ:** Univ Southern Calif; Inter denominational Theol Ctr, Atlanta, GA, Mdiv; Vanderbilt Univ, MA, relig; Claremont Grad Univ, Claremont, CA, PhD, women's studies relig. **Career:** Basketball player (retired), preacher, motivational speaker; WNBA, Harlem Globetrotters, basketball player; WNBA, Dallas Diamonds, basketball player; Europe League, Italy, basketball player; Europe League, Spain, basketball player; Fisk Univ, dean chapel, ordained minister, currently. **Orgs:** Pres & minister, Paula McGee Ministries, currently; co-founder, Christian Bus Success Network. **Business Addr:** President, Minister, Paula McGee Ministries, 1325 N Col Ave D-225, Claremont, CA 91711, **Business Phone:** (909)244-9559.

### MCGEE, SHERRY
Business owner, educator. **Personal:** Born Nov 16, 1957, Honolulu, HI; daughter of Winnie R Johnson; children: Michael L. **Educ:** Wayne State Univ, BS, bus admin, 1987, MBA, 1991, PhD, health psychol. **Career:** CDI Corp, div sales mgr, 1978-89; McGee & Co, sales training consult, 1990-92; Bartech Inc, dir mkt, 1992-97; Apple Bk Ctr, founder & pres; Apple Kids LLC, founding pres & consult, owner, currently. **Orgs:** Vol, Jr Achievement, lifetime mem, Nat Black MBA Asn; consult, proj dir, workforce solution, City Connect Detroit. **Home Addr:** 18843 Gainsborough Rd, Detroit, MI 48223-1341, **Home Phone:** (313)836-1640. **Business Addr:** Founding President, Consultant, AppleKids LLC, PO Box 23574, Detroit, MI 48223, **Business Phone:** (313)268-7156.

### MCGEE, SYLVIA WILLIAMS
School administrator. **Personal:** Born Aug 5, 1952, Macon, GA; daughter of John Paul and Nora Cunningham; married Terry D Sr; children: Terese Lynette & T Dwight Jr. **Educ:** Tift Col, BA, 1974; Univ Ga, MSW, 1976. **Career:** Mercer Univ, Proj Upward Bound, counr, 1976-77; Bibb County Pub Schs, sch social worker, dir, admin, prin, dep supt, currently. **Orgs:** Reg dir, Jack & Jill Am, 1991-93, nat vpres & bd trustee, 1996-00; exec comm, Ga Indust Home C, 1994-97; corresp secy, Jr League Macon, 1996; chmn progs, Youth Leadership Bibb County, 1996-97; chmn eval comm, United Way Cent GEO, 1997-; bd dir, Family Coun Ctr, 1998-; comm chmn resource serv, Macon 2000; fin secy, New Hope Missionary Bapt Church; trustee, Mid Ga State Univ Found. **Home Addr:** 1542 Westminister Dr, Macon, GA 31204-4830, **Home Phone:** (478)477-9464. **Business Addr:** Deputy Superintendent, Bibb County Public Schools, 484 Mulberry St Suite 390, Macon, GA 31201, **Business Phone:** (478)765-8711.

### MCGEE, TIMOTHY DWAYNE HATCHETT
Football coach, executive, football player. **Personal:** Born Aug 7, 1964, Cleveland, OH. **Educ:** Univ Tenn, BA, lib arts, family & community serv, 1986. **Career:** Football player (retired), coach, executive; Cincinnati Bengals, wide receiver, 1986-93, 1994-95; Wash Redskins, wide receiver, 1993; Nat Basketball Asn, sports agt, currently; Luxury Motor Sales, owner & operator, 2010-; Courts 4 Sports, founder; Advan Football Learning, founder & coach, 2014-; Ursuline Acad, head basketball coach, currently. **Honors/Awds:** Post-season play, 1988: AFC Championship Game, NFL Championship Game; Greater Cleveland Sports Hall of Fame, 2008. **Home Addr:** , Cincinnati, OH. **Business Addr:** Head Basketball Coach, Ursuline Academy, 5535 Pfeiffer Rd, Cincinnati, OH 45242.

### MCGEE, TONY L.
Football player, executive. **Personal:** Born Apr 21, 1971, Terre Haute, IN. **Educ:** Univ Mich, BA, lang, sci & arts commun, 1993. **Career:** Football player (retired), analyst, executive; Cincinnati Bengals, tight end, 1993-2001; Dallas Cowboys, tight end, 2002-03; New York Giants, tight end, 2003; Big Ten Network, sports analyst, 2008-10; HNM Enterprises, pres & chief exec officer, 2004-. **Business Addr:** President, Chief Executive Officer, HNM Global Logistics Inc, 9901 Satellite Blvd, Orlando, FL 32837, **Business Phone:** (407)472-7575.

## MCGEE, WADDELL
Consultant, manager. **Personal:** Born Dec 13, 1946, Hattiesburg, MS; son of Ovell and Corine; married Gloria Kesselle. **Educ:** Alcorn State Univ, BS, 1968; Southern Univ, LLB, 1976; Am Univ, Sch Environ Studies, MS, 1980, PhD, 1985. **Career:** US, nuclear & environ engr, 1968-73; Oil Field Environ Safety, consult, dir opers, 1977-86; asst mayor, law dir, 1986-87; Calif Environ Waste Mgt, consult, vpres opers, 1987-88; Mid-Am Environ Consults Engrs, chief exec officer, 1988-; Mid-Am Archit Design & Engrs, owner, mgr, 1999. **Orgs:** Soc Am Mil Engrs; Am Bar Asn, 1975-; chair, Clean Am, 1989-; chair, NEB Energy CMS, 1991-; bd dir, Goodwill Industs, 1991-; pres, Int Soc Environ Professionals, 1991-; pres, Nat Asn Advan Colored People, 1992-; bd dir, Am Red Cross, 1992-; NEB Environ CMS, 1992-; bd dir, Ky Pollution Prev Ctr. **Honors/Awds:** Senatorial Citation, 1989; Man of the Year, Clean Am Inc, 1990; Professional Award, Int Soc Environ Professionals, 1991. **Special Achievements:** Author, Blacks & the Environment, 1992. **Home Addr:** 13618 9th, Miami, FL 33182, **Home Phone:** (305)228-7201. **Business Addr:** Owner, Manager, Mid-America Architectural Design & Engineers, 1613 Farnam St Suite 625, Omaha, NE 68102, **Business Phone:** (402)345-8797.

## MCGEE, WILLIAM TORRE
Journalist, editor. **Personal:** Born Sep 3, 1966, Miami, FL; son of William (deceased) and Betty Jean. **Educ:** Northwestern Univ, BS, jour, 1988. **Career:** Miami Herald Media Co, reporter, 1995-99; copy ed, 1999-2011; Miami Times, copy ed, reporter, 1988-90; Miami Herald, copy ed, 1990-92, reporter action line, 1992-94, reporter, 1994-99, staff writer, news copy ed, 1999; Chicago Tribune, copy ed, designer, 2011-. **Orgs:** S Fla, Black Journalists Asn, 1988-; National Association for the Advancement of Colored People; Am Copy Ed Soc. **Home Addr:** 2423 NW 179th St, Opa Locka, FL 33056-3623, **Home Phone:** (305)626-8837. **Business Addr:** Copy Editor, Designer, The Chicago Tribune, 435 N Mich Ave, Chicago, IL 60611.

## MCGEE, WILLIE DEAN
Baseball executive, baseball player. **Personal:** Born Nov 2, 1958, San Francisco, CA; son of Hurdice and Maddie; married Vivian Manyweather; children: 5. **Educ:** Diablo Valley Community Col. **Career:** Baseball player, baseball coach (retired); St Louis Cardinals, outfielder, 1982-90, 1996-99; Oakland Athletics, outfielder, 1990; San Francisco Giants, outfielder, 1991-94; Boston Red Sox, outfielder, 1995; Contra Costa Col, asst baseball coach, 1999, St. Louis Cardinals, spec asst gen mgr, 2013. **Orgs:** Founder, coach & co-chairperson, Willie McGee Found; Police Activ League, Greater Richmond Souper Kitchen, ACORN Track Club; E Bay Consortium; Terrance Kelly Youth Found. **Home Addr:** 3008 Autumn Lakes Ct, St. Louis, MO 63144. **Business Addr:** Founder, Coach, Willie McGee Foundation, 1160 Brickyard Cove Rd Suite 200, Richmond, CA 94801, **Business Phone:** (510)439-4114.

## MCGHEE, DAEDRA A VON MIKE. See MIKE, DAEDRA ANITA VON.

## MCGHEE, JACQUELINE EASLEY. See EASLEY, JACQUELINE RUTH.

## MCGHEE, JAMES LEON
Executive. **Personal:** Born Mar 3, 1948, Wayne, IN. **Educ:** Univ Puget Sound, Tacoma, WA, BA, pub admin, 1974. **Career:** City Planning Comn Tacoma WA, asst planner, 1972-73; US Treas Dept, asst bank examr, 1973-76; Housing & Devel Seattle, DC, dir, 1977-78; Northwest Tech Inc, pres, chmn, 1983-; Medsco Inc Med Supply Corp, pres, chmn, 1983-85; Greater Telecommunication Syst Inc, pres & chief exec officer, 1985-88; McGhee & Assocs, pres & chief exec officer, 1989-93; Am Automotive, distribr, 1989-96; Global Automotive distribr, pres & chief exec officer, 1996-99; JLM Mgt Group, pres & chief exec officer, 1990-; Serbin Assocs, consult. **Orgs:** Pres, Alpha Phi Alpha & Sphinx OH State, 1968; Fin treas NW Black Elected Off Assoc, 1973-85; founder, United Trade Worker Assoc, 1975; co-founder, Seattle Cent Comn Col Found, 1978; pres, chmn bd, Wash State Bus League, 1980-85; bd dir, NW Tech Inc, 1981-85; planning comn, City Seattle, 1981-85; asst reg vpres, Nat Bus League, 1983-85; bd dir, Medsco Inc, 1983-85; bd dir, United Negro Col Fund, 1985; nat chair, Minority Enterprise Develop; vice chair, Civil Rights Comn; chair, Calif Asn Local Ment Health Boards; pub mem, bd psychol, 2003; Wash State Lottery Comn; vice chair, King County Civil Rights Comn; pvt consult, Calif Energy Comn; Field Res Corp; treas, San Francisco African Am Chamber Com. **Honors/Awds:** Honors for Serv, EFP Rhomania, 1979; Community Black Leader, 1980; NW Conf Black Public Official, 1980. **Home Addr:** 5110 1 2 Othello St, Seattle, WA 98118. **Business Addr:** President, Chief Executive Officer, J L M Management Group, 200 Warren Dr, San Francisco, CA 94131-1032, **Business Phone:** (415)665-5940.

## MCGHEE, MALESA OWENS
Executive. **Educ:** Howard Univ, BA, broadcast jour & pub rels, MFA, cinematography & film/video prod; Spring Arbor Univ, MA, coun psychol. **Career:** Wayne Co Community Col Dist, pub rels consult; Detroit Acad Arts & Sci, dir commun, 2002-11, community rels & commun coordr, Pub Rels Mgr, 2011-; Eye To Eye Inc, owner, 1998-; Team Ment Health Serv, counr & life coach, 2012-; Super Bus Girl Asia Newson, publicist, 2013-; Detroit Nation Radio, exec producer, 2015-; Pashon Murray Detroit Dirt, brand & pr mgr, 2015-; Celebrity Bridal Stylist Keasha Rigsby, publicist, 2016-. **Business Addr:** Director of Communications, Community Relations & Communications Coordinator, Detroit Academy of Arts & Sciences, 2985 Jefferson Ave, Detroit, MI 48207, **Business Phone:** (313)259-1744.

## MCGHEE, ODELL G., II
Judge, educator. **Personal:** Born Jul 11, 1952, Liberty, MS; son of Odell and Eunice; married Jacqueline Easley; children: Carey & Ty. **Educ:** Cornell Col, BS, 1974; Drake Law Sch, JD, 1977. **Career:** Dist 5C, dist assoc judge, 2002-; Iowa Supreme Ct, Continuing Legal Educ Comn, comnr, currently; Iowa Comn Aging, prog planner; Iowa Dept Environ Qual, admin hearing officer; Polk Co Atty's Off, supvr, drug & vice docket; Des Moines Area Community Col, adj fac mem. **Orgs:** Nat Bar Asn; Iowa Nat Bar Asn; Nat Prosecutor Asn; Exec Bd Polk Co Bar Asn; Nat Asn Dist Attys; officer, Nat Asn Prosecutors; Iowa Judges Asn; Iowa State Bar Asn. **Home Addr:** 3113 Southern Hills Dr, Des Moines, IA 50321-1430, **Home Phone:** (515)243-3803. **Business Addr:** District Associate Judge, District 5C, 500 Mulberry St Ct Rm 101, Des Moines, IA 50309-4238, **Business Phone:** (515)285-3854.

## MCGHEE, SAMUEL T.
Executive director, mayor. **Personal:** Born May 29, 1940, Jersey City, NJ; son of Samuel T and Lucile Bitten; children: Darren, Elissa, Samuel III & Jeffrey. **Educ:** Jersey City State Col, BA, social sci, 1962; Seton Hall Univ, MA, admin & supv, 1965. **Career:** Educator (retired), executive; Jersey City State Col, from asst dir admis to dir admis, 1971-98, asst dean stud affairs, 1998-2001; Hillside, NJ, finance comnr, 1987; Hillside Twp, mayor, 1988, 1991, 1997-98; police comnr, 1989-90, 1993-94, pub works comnr, 1992, 1996, fire comnr, 1995-96, coun mem, 1999; Nj City Univ, dir admis & dean; Joint Meeting Essex & Union Counties, exec dir, 2004-. **Orgs:** Omega Psi Phi Fraternity, 1988-; Nat Conf Black Mayors, 1988-; Local Adv Comm Alcoholism & Drug Abuse, 2001-03; Nat Asn Clean Water Agencies; Union County Improv Authority; Libr Bd; Hillside Develop Corp; Newark Pub Radio; bd trustee, WBGO-Pub Radio. **Honors/Awds:** Black Merit Acad E St Louis, 1973; Distinguished Alumni Award, Jersey City State Col, 1981; Phi Delta Kappa, 1990; Omega Psi Phi Superior Service Award, 1991, 1995; Omega Man of the Year, 2010. **Special Achievements:** First African American mayor of Hillside. **Home Addr:** 1548 Maple Ave, Hillside, NJ 07205-1437, **Home Phone:** (973)923-8485. **Business Addr:** Executive Director, Joint Meeting of Essex & Union Counties, 500 S 1st St, Elizabeth, NJ 07202, **Business Phone:** (908)353-1313.

## MCGILL, CHARLES LEONARD, III. See MCGILL, LENNY.

## MCGILL, LENNY (CHARLES LEONARD MCGILL, III)
Football player, scout. **Personal:** Born May 31, 1971, Long Beach, CA. **Educ:** Ariz State Univ, BS, criminal justice, 1993. **Career:** Football player (retired), scout; Green Bay Packers, 1994, Defensive Back, 1995, col scout, 2000-09; Atlanta Falcons, 1997, left cornerback, 1996; Carolina Panthers, cornerback, 1998; Seattle Seahawks, defensive back, 1999; Denver Broncos, asst dir coll scouting, 2009-14, southwest regional scout, 2014-15; Miami Dolphins, w regional scout, 2015-. **Honors/Awds:** Hall of Fame, San Diego High Sch Sports, 2002; Most Improved Defensive Player, Sun Devils. **Business Addr:** West Regional Scout, Miami Dolphins, 347 Don Shula Dr, Miami Gardens, FL 33056, **Business Phone:** (305)943-8000.

## MCGILL, MICHAEL
Singer. **Personal:** Born Feb 17, 1937. **Career:** Albums; There Is, 1968; On Their Corner, 1992; I Salute You, 1992; Dreams of Contentment, 1993; Bring Back the Love; Classic Dells, 1996; I Touch a Dream/Whatever Turns, 1998; (With Michael Ross); We Finally Meet, 1995; Last Love Letter, 1996; The Dells, mem, currently. **Honors/Awds:** Rock and Roll Hall of Fame, Original Dells, 2004; Vocal Group Hall of Fame, Original Dells, 2004. **Business Addr:** Singer, The Original Dells Inc, PO Box 1133, Harvey, IL 60426-7133, **Business Phone:** (708)474-1422.

## MCGILL, MICHELE NICOLE JOHNSON
Writer, artist, librarian. **Personal:** Born Jul 14, 1966, San Diego, CA; daughter of Leonard and Dianne Campbell. **Educ:** Univ Fla, Gainesville, FL, BS, journ, 1988; Valdosta State Univ, Master Libr & Info Sci, community bldg, 2012. **Career:** Independent Fla Alligator, Gainesville, FL, layout ed, 1987-88; Fla Times-Union, Jacksonville, FL, copy ed, 1988-90, columnist, 1990-2002, staff writer, asst reader advocate; Greenville News, asst features ed, 2002-03; Charlotte Observer, arts ed, 2003-05; Sapelo Island Cult & Revitalization Soc Inc, prog officer, 2005-06; Hog Hammock Pub Libr, librn, 2005-; Gould Memorial Libr/Col Costal Ga, info specialist, 2013-. **Orgs:** Nat Asn Black Journalists, 1987-90; past pres, Univ Fla Asn Black Communicators, 1987-88; pres, Jacksonville Asn Black Communicators, 1991-93; pres, Soul Autonomy Inc, 1991-; newsletter dir, Jacksonville Urban League Auxiliary, 1991-92; First Baptist Church Mandarin Youth Group. **Home Addr:** 8996 Adams Walk Dr, Jacksonville, FL 32257, **Home Phone:** (904)777-5363. **Business Addr:** Assistant Reader Advocate, Florida Times-Union, 1 Riverside Ave, Jacksonville, FL 32231, **Business Phone:** (904)359-4427.

## MCGILL, THOMAS L., JR.
Lawyer. **Personal:** Born Aug 13, 1946, Martinsburg, WV; son of Thomas L Sr and Dorthy Kathryn Baylor (deceased); married Charisse R Lillie; children: Leslie Janelle, Thomas L III & Alison Charisse. **Educ:** Lincoln Univ, BA, 1968; Occidental Col, MA, 1972; Notre Dame Law Sch, JD, 1975. **Career:** Olney HS, teacher, 1968-71; Hon Kenneth Gibson Mayor, mayor's aide, 1971-72; Hon Paul Dandridge Judge, law clerk, 1975-82; Pa Human Rels Comn, comnr, 1981-90, chairperson, 1986-90; McGill & Seay, atty, 1975-90; Clark, McGill, Newkirk & Seary, 1990; Clark & McGill PC, managing partner, currently. **Orgs:** Philadelphia Bar Asn, 1975-; Am Bar Asn, 1975-; Nat Bar Asn, 1977-; Rec Sec Barristers Asn, 1977-78; pres, Barristers Asn, 1980-81; bd mem, Veritas Inc, 1980-83, Germantown Boys Club, 1982-84; bd dir, W Mt Airy Neighbors, 1986-87; bd dir, Friends Neighborhood Guild, 1995; Pa Asn Criminal Defense lawyers. **Honors/Awds:** Sr Class Award for Creative Writing, Lincoln Univ, 1968; Nat Urban Fellow, Nat Conf Mayors, Yale Univ, 1971-72. **Home Addr:** 7000 Emlen St, Philadelphia, PA 19119-2556. **Business Addr:** Attorney, Managing Partner, Clark & McGill PC, 2 Penn Ctr Plz Suite 200, Philadelphia, PA 19102, **Business Phone:** (215)735-5300.

## MCGINEST, WILLIE
Football player, broadcaster, business owner. **Personal:** Born Dec 11, 1971, Long Beach, CA; son of Willie and Joyce; children: Riley & Halie. **Educ:** Univ Southern Calif, pub admin, 1994. **Career:** Football player (retired), bus owner, actor; New Eng Patriots, defensive end, 1994-2005; Cleveland Browns, linebacker, 2006-08; NFL Network, football analyst; Fox Sports, analyst; ESPN, analyst; 55 Entertainment, owner, 2006-. Films: Super Bowl XXXVI, 2002; Super Bowl XXXVIII, 2004; Super Bowl XXXIX, 2005, I Tried, 2007. TV Series: "The Gentlemen's League", 2010. **Orgs:** Founder, Willie Mc Ginest Freedom Sch. **Honors/Awds:** Rookie of the Year, 1776; Quarterback Club New Eng, 1994; Player of the Game, Staples Star, 1995; Pro Bowl, 1995, 2003; Defensive Player of the Month, Asian Football Confederation, 1996; Defensive Player of the Week, Asian Football Confederation, 1996, 1999, 2003; Am Football Conf champion, 1996, 2001, 2003 & 2004; Miller Lite Player of the Game, 2001; Levitra Play of the Week, Nat Football League, 2003; Super Bowl XXXVI; All-Conf hons; All-Pac-10 conf hons; Defensive Player of the Year, Southern Calif; Willie was voted as one of the twenty hottest influencers by Urban Influence Magazine, 2009; New England Patriots Hall of Fame, 2015. **Special Achievements:** Lombardi Award finalist; appeared in various TV shows; City Council of Long Beach declared May 3rd of every year will be recognized as Willie McGinest Day. **Business Addr:** Owner, 55 Entertainment, Los Angeles, CA.

## MCGINNIS, JAMES W.
Educator, lawyer. **Personal:** Born Jul 8, 1940, Fairfield, AL; son of James and Reatha Saunders Felton; married Debra Hughes; children: Ayana Marie. **Educ:** Wayne State Univ, BS, 1963; San Francisco State Univ, MA, 1965; Yeshiva Univ, PhD, 1976; Wayne State Univ Law Sch, JD, 1977. **Career:** Col Entrance Exam Bd, asst dir, 1967-69; Univ Calif, Berkeley, instr, 1970-72; Far W Lab Educ Res, res assoc, 1972-73; Oakland Univ, asst prof, 1976-81; pvt pract, lawyer, 1978-. **Orgs:** Pres, Kappa Alpha Psi Frat; Wayne State Univ, 1961-62; Asn Black Psychologists, 1963-73; researcher, Black Studies Inst Wayne St Univ, 1975-76; off coun, Hall & Andary Law Firm, 1982-84; chmn, PAC, 1982-; Nat Conf Black Lawyers; Nat Bar Asn, 1989-. **Home Addr:** 1979 Hyde Pk, Detroit, MI 48207, **Home Phone:** (313)259-6336. **Business Addr:** Attorney, 985 E Jefferson Ave Suite 100, Detroit, MI 48207-3127, **Business Phone:** (313)446-9582.

## MCGINNIS, ROBERT LAWRENCE
Insurance executive, chief executive officer, vice president (organization). **Personal:** Born Oct 1, 1966, Minneapolis, MN; son of Ronald and Judy; married Jennifer Latwesen; children: Lauren M & Nathan. **Educ:** Univ Wis - Madison, BA, polit sci, 1990. **Career:** Prudential Ins, group mgr, 1990-95; United Healthcare Small Bus Group, chief operating officer, regional vpres Tex & Western region, 1995-2001; AmeriChoice Corp, dir, 2001-; CNA Ins Co, group oper, exec vpres, pres & chief exec officer, 2003-; CNA Financial Corp, CNA Life & Group Opers, chief exec officer & pres, 2003-; Marsh Inc, head consumer bus, 2007-; Marsh Global US Consumer, Affinity & Pvt Client Solutions, pres & chief exec officer, 2007-. **Orgs:** Dir, AAHP/HIAA, 2001-04; dir, ACLI, 2004-; adv bd mem, Univ Wis, 2005-06. **Honors/Awds:** Crain's Chicago Business, 40 Under 40, 2002. **Home Addr:** 2340 Woodpath Lane, Highland Park, IL 60035-2046, **Home Phone:** (847)372-7957. **Business Addr:** President, Chief Executive Officer, Marsh Global Consumer, Affinity & Private Client Solutions, 12421 Meredith Dr, Urbandale, IA 50398, **Business Phone:** (515)243-1776.

## MCGLOTHAN, ERNEST
Executive. **Personal:** Born Oct 25, 1937, Tuscaloosa, AL; married Willa Rean May; children: Wilma, Kecia & Corey. **Educ:** Tuskegee Inst Sch Arch, BS, 1961. **Career:** Mac-Pon Co Gen Contractors, pres & owner; Gaillard Construct Co, Birmingham; A H Smith Construct Co, Birmingham; Steel City Serv, Birmingham, Ala, pres & owner, currently. **Orgs:** Alpha Phi Alpha Frat; Mayor's Adv Com; Nat Asn Minority Contractors; Birmingham Zoning Bd Adjustments; bd dir, BSA, Omicron Lambda; chmn, Cooper Green Golf Course Comt. **Home Addr:** 1403 Miami Dr, Birmingham, AL 35214, **Home Phone:** (205)798-1211. **Business Addr:** President, Owner, Steel City Services LLC, Two 20th St N Suite 1050, Birmingham, AL 35203, **Business Phone:** (205)324-3249.

## MCGLOTTEN, ROBERT
Lobbyist. **Personal:** married Cheryl Good. **Educ:** Univ Pa; St Josephs Col Indust & Labor Mgt. **Career:** AFL-CIO, Fedns Dept Civil Rights, 1967-70; Human Resources Dept Inst, exec dir, 1970-72, legis rep, 1974-80, Legis Dept, asst dir, 1980-86; legis dir, 1986-95; US Dept Labor, spec asst secy, 1973; McGlotten & Jarvis, partner, currently. **Orgs:** Transp Workers Union; consult, Off & Prof Employees Int Union, lobbyist; Cong Black Caucus Found Inc; George Wash Univ, Grad Sch Polit Mgt, Coun Am Polit; mem bd trustee, Benedict Col, Columbia, Sc. **Business Addr:** Partner, McGlotten & Jarvis, 1901 L St NW, Washington, DC 20036, **Business Phone:** (202)452-9515.

## MCGLOVER, STEPHEN LEDELL
Executive, president (organization). **Personal:** Born Nov 8, 1950, Los Angeles, CA; son of Theo and Octavia Bell. **Educ:** Woodbury Col, BS, int bus mgt, 1978; Univ Md, int bus mgt, 1980; Black Businessmen Asn, BS, bus, 1981; Ohio State Univ, NOPA Dealer Mgt Inst, 1984; Nat Off Prod Asn, IBM sales course, 1984; Southern Methodist Univ, Edwin Cox Sch Bus, 1984; Minister Training Inst, CCC, 1995; Golden Gate Baptist Sem, attended 1996; Amos Tuck exec, met course, 1996. **Career:** Occidental Ins, salesman, 1974-76; Inventory Data Supplies, shipping mgr, 1975, dir & collections, 1976, gen mgr, 1977-78; McGlover Enterprises, salesman, 1977-79; Oasis Off Supplies, pres & partner, 1979-83; Oasis Off Prods Inc, pres & chief exec officer, 1983-. **Orgs:** Black Bus Asn, 1980-; Mayors Small Bus Adv Bd, 1988-; Nat Off Prods Asn; LAMBOC Comt, GSA Small bus Coun; chair, BBA, Church & Comt Rels; minister asst, pastor. **Home Addr:** 1940 1/2 S Harcourt, Los Angeles, CA 90016. **Business Addr:** President, Chief Executive Officer, Oasis Office Products Inc, 4600 W Washington Blvd, Los Angeles, CA 90016-1728, **Business Phone:** (323)938-6211.

## MCGOODWIN, DR. ROLAND CARYLE
Dentist. **Personal:** Born Jul 15, 1933, Evansville, IN; married Lillian Pollard; children: Nina Marie & Roland Jr. **Educ:** Cent State Col, BS, 1955; Meharry Med Col Sch Dent, DDS, 1963. **Career:** Hubbard

Hosp, intern, 1964; Albert Einstein Med Ctr, resident, 1965; Lincoln Heights Health Ctr, staff; Bethesda Hosp; Cincinnati OH, pvt pract, currently. **Orgs:** Dentist Crippled C; bd educ, Am Dent Asn; Nat Dent Asn; Ohio State Dent Asn; Ohio Valley Dent Soc; Cincinnati Dent Soc; Acad Gen Dentists Bd Mt Auburn Health Ctr; adv coun, Walnut Hill Area; Health Manpower Linkage Sys; Ohio Dept Health; bd mem, Dent Care Plus Ins Co; pres, Union Found. **Honors/Awds:** Dr Martin L King Jr Award, St Mark Catholic Church, 2007. **Home Addr:** 1715 Bella Vista, Cincinnati, OH 45237. **Business Addr:** Dentist, Roland C McGoodwin, 645 E Mc Millan St, Cincinnati, OH 45206, **Business Phone:** (513)861-1900.

## MCGOUGH, ROBYN LATRESE

Health services administrator, manager. **Personal:** Born Sep 15, 1961, Spokane, WA; daughter of Harold (deceased) and Eva. **Educ:** Univ Nev, Las Vegas, BSW, 1985, MSW, 1993. **Career:** Sunrise Hosp, food serv worker, 1978-79, diet clerk, 1979-86, med social worker, 1987-93; THC Las Vegas, social serv dir, 1993-97; Vencor Hosp, Las Vegas, soc serv dir; Kindred Health care Inc, social work/case mgr, 1993-. **Orgs:** Nat Asn Social Workers, 1986-98; asst youth dir, Progressive Nat Baptist Conv, Southwest Region; 1989-91; financial secy, Delta Sigma Theta Sorority Inc, 1986-, 1988-90; debutante adv, 1994-, Les Femmes Douze, 1996-. **Home Addr:** 1342 Alvo Ct, Las Vegas, NV 89104-5102, **Home Phone:** (702)438-9987. **Business Addr:** Case Manager, Kindred Healthcare Inc, 680 S 4th St, Louisville, KY 40202, **Business Phone:** (502)596-7300.

## MCGOWAN, DR. ANNA-MARIA

Scientist. **Educ:** Purdue Univ, BS, aeronaut & astronaut engineering, 1992; Old Dom Univ, MS, aerospace engineering, 1999. **Career:** Independent Res Activ, 1992-99; NASA, Langley Res Ctr, VA, aerospace technologist, 1992-, NSF vis scientist, DARPA/AFRL/NASA Smart Wing Prog, agency lead, tech consult, 1995-, Aerospace Vehicle Systs Technol Prog Off, proj mgr morphing proj, actg dep dir, 2000-, Subsonic Fixed Wing Proj, technol integration mgr, Complex Systs Design, sr engr, flight test leader, wind-tunnel test engr, sr researcher, NASA spokesperson, Convergent Aeronaut Solutions, proj mgr; Piezoelectric Aeroelastic Response Tailoring Invest, co lead, 1994-96, lead, 1996-97; Smart Struct Aeroelastic Focus Area, Aeroelasticity Br, chmn, 1996-2000; NATO-Sponsored Short Courses Smart Struct & Aeroelasticity, Instr, 1998-99. **Orgs:** Air Force Asn; chmn, Indust & Com Applications Conf, Int Soc Optical Engineering, 2000; Am Soc Mech Engrs Tech Comt; sr mem, Am Inst Aeronaut & Astronaut; stud judge & co chmn, Pre-Col Comt; Soc Women Engrs. **Business Addr:** Senior Engineer for Complex Systems Design, NASA, 100 NASA Rd, Hampton, VA 23681-2199, **Business Phone:** (757)864-5800.

## MCGOWAN, ATTY. CLARENCE ROY

Lawyer. **Personal:** Born Oct 20, 1921, Bryan, TX; son of Elihu and Ollie Mae; married Gloria Helen, Nov 19, 1958; children: Valorie. **Educ:** Prairie View Univ, BS, 1943; Iowa State Col, MS, 1950; St Mary Univ, JD, 1963. **Career:** Attorney (retired); San Antonio Sch Dist, math & sci teacher, 1945-60, sch prin, 1960-63; pvt pract, atty, 1963-99; City San Antonio, City Water Utility Syst, vpres. **Orgs:** Bd dir, United Way, 1950-55; Phi Delta Kappa Scholar Fraternity, 1965-99; coun, Nat Asn Advan Colored People, 1965-99; basileus, Omega Psi Phi Fraternity, 1973-75; Nat Bar Asn, 1990-99; founder, San Antonio Black Lawyers Asn; Blockbusters. **Honors/Awds:** Achievement, Nat Asn Advan Colored People, 1965; MLK Distinguished Achievement Award, Martin Luther King Comn, 2004. **Special Achievements:** First African American black man to graduate from St Mary's Univ, Law Sch, 1963; first African Am Judge San Antonio, Bexan County, TX, 1974. **Home Addr:** 311 N New Braunfels Ave, San Antonio, TX 78202-3031, **Home Phone:** (210)226-0337.

## MCGOWAN, ELSIE HENDERSON

Executive director. **Personal:** Born Jul 3, 1947, Pell City, AL; daughter of Rannie Collins and Franklin; married James Oliver; children: Kenneth Eugene & LaCindra DeNae. **Educ:** Knoxville Col, Knoxville, TN, BS, bus educ, 1969; Univ Ala Birmingham, AL, MA, educ admin, 1982, educ spec, edu admin, 1989. **Career:** Executive (retired); St Clair County Bd Edu, Ashville, Ala, bus edu teacher, 1969-83, asst prin elem, 1983-94, dir migrant edu prog, 1986-94; Moody Elem Sch, asst prin, 1983-89; John Pope Eden Career Tech Ctr, part-time instr adult educ prog; Migrant Educ Prog, Chandler Mountain, 1972; St. Clair County Head Start Prog, exec dir, 1994-2010. **Orgs:** Nat State & Local Prof Educ Asns, 1969-; pres, St Clair County Educ asn, 1979; Fel Johnson & Johnson, Univ Calif; Kappa Delta Pi Hon Socs, Univ Ala, 1980; Nat Alumni Soc, Univ Alab, 1981; coordr, Substitute Teachers' Workshop, 1987; United Way; Red Cross Auxiliary; Pell City Schs Educ Found; Habitat Humanity; Community Resource Develop, St Clair County Exten Syst; John Pope Eden Adv Coun; Pell City Chamber Com; golden life mem, Delta Sigma Theta Sorority; prog chair, Womens Socs Orgn; mem choir, First Missionary Baptist Church. **Home Addr:** 4306 Stemley Bridge Rd, PO Box 268, Pell City, AL 35125-0268, **Home Phone:** (205)884-2648.

## MCGOWAN, THOMAS RANDOLPH

Manager. **Personal:** Born Apr 19, 1926, Baltimore, MD; son of Robert and Mary; married Roedean Olivia Oden; children: James, Karen White, Terry V Stevens, Kevin & Kurt; married Bernice A Bernard. **Educ:** Oakland City Col, AA, 1964; San Francisco State Col, attended 1966; Univ Calif, Berkeley, CA, attended 1967; Univ Md, BS, 1978. **Career:** Army Base, lt security police Oakland, 1955-60; San Francisco Procurement Agency, chief motor pool, 1960-64, contract specialist, 1964-68; AUS Harry Diamond Labs, 1968-79, br chief, 1972-79; AUS Yuma Proving Ground, dir proc dirate, 1979-82; Roman Cath Diocese, Oakland, dir ecumenism, 1983-96; Graymoor, div bd consult, 1990-; African Am Cath Pastoral Ctr, dir, 1991; St John Baptist Church, deacon, currently. **Orgs:** Bd dir, Columbia Found, 1972-74, chmn bd, 1978-79; dir, Youth Serv, 1985-; convenor, Interreligious Coun Oakland, 1988-; trustee, Greater Oakland Interfaith Network, 1989-92; bd dir, Thea Bowman Manor, 1989-; E Oakland Renewal Task Force, 1990-; deacon, Diocese Oakland, 1995-; bd dir, St Mary's Ctr; Knights Peter Claver. **Honors/Awds:** James Fitzgerald Award for Ecumenism, 1999. **Home Addr:** 139 Pinto Dr, Vallejo, CA 94591-8451, **Home Phone:** (707)557-4039. **Business Addr:** Deacon, St John Baptist Church, 11150 San Pablo Ave, El Cerrito, CA 94530, **Business Phone:** (510)232-5659.

## MCGRADY, TRACY LAMAR, JR.

Basketball player. **Personal:** Born May 24, 1979, Bartow, FL; married CleRenda Harris; children: Layla Clarice, Laycee Aloe, Laymen & Layden. **Educ:** Ferris State Univ, BS, physics, 1998. **Career:** Basketball player (retired); Toronto Raptors, forward-guard, 1997-2000; Orlando Magic, 2000-04; Houston Rockets, guard, 2004-10; New York Knicks, 2010; Detroit Pistons, 2010-11; Atlanta Hawks, 2011-12; Qingdao Eagles, china, 2012-13; San Antonio Spurs, 2013. **Orgs:** Founder, Tracy McGrady Found; Us men's nat basketball team, 2003. **Business Addr:** Professional Basketball Player, Houston Rockets, 2 E Greenway Plz Suite 400, Houston, TX 77046, **Business Phone:** (713)627-3865.

## MCGREGOR, REV. MIGUEL D.

Clergy. **Career:** Team Zion Ministries Inc, chief exec officer & founder; Rock Int Church, staff. **Business Addr:** Chief Executive Officer, Founder, Team Zion Ministries Inc, PO Box 51048, Ft. Worth, TX 76105-8048, **Business Phone:** (817)658-7465.

## MCGREW, REGGIE (REGINALD GERARD MCGREW)

Football player. **Personal:** Born Dec 16, 1976, Mayo, FL; son of Taylor; married Nina Foster. **Educ:** Univ Fla, BS, sociol, 2010. **Career:** Football player (retired); San Francisco 49ers, defensive tackle, 1999-2001; Atlanta Falcons, 2002; St. Louis Rams, 2008. **Honors/Awds:** Bowl Alliance National Championship, 1996; SEC Championship, 1996; First-team All-SEC, 1998.

## MCGRIER, HON. JERRY, SR.

District attorney. **Personal:** Born Apr 4, 1955, Dallas, TX; son of Joseph and Irve Leen Bass Looney; married Diane Jones; children: Jerry Jr. **Educ:** Col Wooster, Wooster, OH, BA, polit sci, 1977; State Univ NY, Buffalo, NY, JD, 1980. **Career:** Neighborhood Legal Serv, Buffalo, NY, staff atty, 1980-82; Erie County Dist Atty, Buffalo, NY, asst dist atty, 1982; State NY, Law Dept, asst atty gen, currently. **Orgs:** Erie County Bar Asn, 1980-; Nat Dist Atty's Asn, 1982-; Nat Bar Asn, 1984-; NY State Bar Asn, 1984-; chmn, Minority Bar Asn Western NY, 1986-88; bd dir, Grace Manor Nursing Home, 1987-; bd dirs secy, Buffalo Fedn Neighborhood Ctrs Inc; NY State Defenders Asn; chair, Young Men's Christian Asn Bd Mgr; Grace Manor; Bd, Community Action Info Ctr. **Honors/Awds:** Lawyer's Service Award, Minority Bar Asn Western NY, 1988; Special Faculty Award, State Univ NY, Buffalo Law Sch, 1989. **Home Addr:** 42 Gerald Ave, Buffalo, NY 14215, **Home Phone:** (716)893-4880. **Business Addr:** Assistant Attorney General, State of New York Law Department, Statler Towers 107 Del Ave, Buffalo, NY 14202-3473, **Business Phone:** (716)855-2424.

## MCGRIFF, DR. DEBORAH M.

School administrator. **Personal:** Born Jun 6, 1949, Portsmouth, VA; daughter of Everlena Madkins and Ernest Boyd Madkins; married Howard Fuller; children: Jacqueline Denise. **Educ:** Norfolk State Col, BS, 1970; Queens Col, MEd, pedag, 1975; Fordham Univ, PhD, admin, policy & urban educ, 1985. **Career:** NY Pub Sch, exec asst supt, 1983-85, teacher & adminr; Ctr Educ Leadership, NY, proj mgr, 1985-86; Cambridge Pub Sch, Mass, asst supt, 1986-88; Teachers Col, pres; Milwaukee Pub Sch, exec asst supt, 1988-89, dep supt, 1989-91; Detroit Pub Sch, gen supt, 1991-93, Exec vpres; Edison Proj, sr exec, exec vpres & pres, 1993; Edison Sch, chief commun officer, exec vpres & chief Relationship officer, currently; Charter Schs Div, sr vpres; Edison Teachers Col, exec vpres, 1998-2000, pres, 2000-. **Orgs:** Adv Panel, Harvard Urban Supt Prog; Nat Urban Alliance; Bd trustee, Educ Testing Serv; C Defense Fund Educ Task Force; bd trustee, United Am Health care Found; pres, bd dir, Edison Sch Inc; ED Ventures plng comn; pres, Educ Indust Asn, currently; bd mem, Prog Educ Policy; adv bd, Nat Coun Teacher Qual, currently; MD, NewSchools Venture Fund; bd, Nat Alliance Pub Charter Schs; founder & nat bd mem, Black Alliance Educ Options; adv bd, Nat Coun Teacher Qual; Governance, Harvard Univ John F. Kennedy Sch Govt; bd mem, Educ Indust Asn; bd mem, Friendship Pub Charter Sch; Adv Bd, Games & Learning Publ Coun; Hechinger Report; bd dir, DC Prep; bd dir, Policy Innovators Educ Network; bd dir, Leadership Pub Schs; bd mem, Matchbook Learning. **Business Addr:** Executive Vice President, Chief Relationship Officer, Edison Schools Inc, 521 5th Ave 11th Fl, New York, NY 10175, **Business Phone:** (212)419-1612.

## MCGRIFF, FREDERICK STANLEY (FRED MCGRIFF)

Baseball player, athletic coach, broadcaster. **Personal:** Born Oct 31, 1963, Tampa, FL; married Veronica Watts; children: Erick & Ericka. **Career:** Baseball player (retired), athletic coach, broadcaster, advisor; Toronto Blue Jays, infielder, 1986-90; San Diego Padres, 1991-93; Atlanta Braves, 1993-97; Tampa Bay Devil Rays, 1998-2001, 2004; Chicago Cubs, 2001-02; Los Angeles Dodgers, 2003; Tampa Bay Rays, front office adv, currently; Catch 47, co-host, currently; radio show, co-host, currently; Jesuit High Sch Tampa, asst baseball coach, currently; The Baysball Show, co-host, currently. **Home Addr:** 16314 Millan De Avila, Tampa, FL 33613-1089. **Business Addr:** Assistant Baseball Coach, Jesuit High School of Tampa, 4701 N Himes Ave, Tampa, FL 33614, **Business Phone:** (813)877-5344.

## MCGRIGGS-JAMISON, IMOGENE

Lawyer, judge. **Personal:** Born Jan 1, 1965, Frankfurt. **Educ:** Alcorn State Univ, BA, 1986; Bowling Green State Univ, MA, Am lit, 1987; Univ Miss Col Law, JD, 1991. **Career:** AUS, Judge Advocate Gen Corps, capt, prosecutor, defense atty, 1993-. **Orgs:** Miss Bar Asn, 1991; DC Bar Asn, 1991; Delta Sigma Theta Sorority Inc. **Honors/Awds:** Outstanding Young Military Service Lawyer Award, nominee, Am Bar Asn, 1996. **Home Addr:** 7042 Old Brentford Rd, Alexandria, VA 22310-4332. **Business Addr:** Trial Defense Attorney, US Army, Usa Armor Ctr & Fort Knox, Ft. Knox, KY 40121-5000, **Business Phone:** (502)626-0547.

## MCGRUDER, AARON VINCENT

Cartoonist or animator, writer. **Personal:** Born May 29, 1974, Chicago, IL; son of Bill and Elaine. **Educ:** Univ Md, BA, Afro-Am studies, 1997. **Career:** Writer, cartoonist, pub speaker; Creator of "The Boondocks", Universal Press Syndicate comic strip, 1996-; Books: The Boondocks: Because I Know You Don't Read the Newspapers, 2000; Fresh for '01 You Suckas!: A Boondocks Collection, 2001; A Right to Be Hostile: The Boondocks Treasury, 2003; Birth of a Nation: A Comic Novel, 2004; Public Enemy Number 2: An All-New Boondocks Collection, 2005. Writer: Ballin, 2007. TV Series: "Charlie Rose", 1999; "Real Time with Bill Maher", 2003-04; "The Boondocks", actor, 2005-07, producer, 2005-10; "The Super Rumble Mixshow", exec producer, 2008; The S-Word, 2008; The Story of Catcher Freeman, 2008; The Hunger Strike, 2008; "Black Jesus", producer, 2014, writer, 2015. Film: Red Tails, screenwriter, 2012. **Business Addr:** Cartoonist, c/o Universal Press Syndicate, 4520 Main St Suite 500, Kansas City, MO 64111, **Business Phone:** (816)932-6600.

## MCGRUDER, DR. CHARLES E. See Obituaries Section.

## MCGUFFIN, DOROTHY BROWN

Consultant, counselor, educator. **Personal:** Born Jul 27, 1944, Metropolis, IL; daughter of Lester Brown and Mary Brown; married Robert R; children: Denise & Toni Greathouse. **Educ:** Southern Ill Univ, Carbondale, IL, BS, home econ educ, 1965, MS, educ, 1968; Drake Univ, MS, coun & stud personnel serv, 1985. **Career:** Lawrence Adult Ctr, adult educr, 1977-81; Des Moines Area Community Col, adult educr, 1981-84; Young Women's Resource Ctr, community outreach counr, 1984-86; St Louis Community Col Forest Pk, assessment specialist, 1986-87; St Louis Community Col Florissant Valley, NSBE advisor, coun, assoc prof, prof coun, scholar coordr, career counr, currently. **Orgs:** Prog chmn, secy, treas, Black Women's Coalition, 1976-80; bd mem, Continuing Educ Comn, St Louis Asn Coun & Develop; lic teacher & counr 4 states; Am Couns Asn; troop leader, consult, bd rep, Girl Scouts Coun; pres, St Louis Coun Asn; pres, MO Multicultural Coun Asn; bd mem, Licensing PRO Counr Mo; adv, Florissant Valley Chap Nat Soc Black Engr; co-chmn, Dist Diversity Comt; co-chmn, Florissant Valley Martin Luther King Celebration; bd mem, Span Lake Community Asn; coun mem, bd dir & chairperson, Diversity St. Louis Community Col; cosponsor, Nat Socs Black Engrs. **Home Addr:** 1821 Lakemont Lane, St. Louis, MO 63138-1224, **Home Phone:** (314)438-0610. **Business Addr:** Career Counselor, St Louis Community College at Florissant Valley, 300 S Broadway, St. Louis, MO 63102-2800, **Business Phone:** (314)513-4269.

## MCGUIRE, ALFRED D., JR.

Educator. **Personal:** Born Dec 7, 1981, Decatur, GA; son of Al and Dorothy G. **Educ:** Savannah State Univ, BA, hist, 2003; Armstrong Atlantic State Univ, MA, educ, 2007; Mercer Univ, Specialist Degree, educ leadership & admin, gen, 2011. **Career:** Coastal Heritage Soc, intern & interpreter, 2001-; Savannah Chatham County Pub Schs, Woodville-Tompkins High Sch, substitute teacher, 2003, prin, 2011-. **Orgs:** Pres, Stud Govt Asn, 2001-03; Alpha Phi Alpha, Delta Eta Chaplain, 2001-; adv bd mem, St Joseph's Candler Afr Am Health Ctr, 2001; pub rels chair, Nat Asn Advan Colored People, 2001-; tutor, May St Young Men Christian Asn, 2001; stud activ coordr, Savannah Black Heritage Festival, 2001-; basketball coach, May St Young Men Christian Asn, 2002-; bd dir, Achievers Today & Tomorrow Inc, 2002-; Ga Bd Regents, Task Force Enhancing Access Afr Am Males, 2003-. **Home Addr:** 3388 Hunters Chase Way, Lithonia, GA 30038-1643, **Home Phone:** (770)987-3180. **Business Addr:** Principal, Savannah-Chatham County Public School System, 208 Bull St, Savannah, GA 31401, **Business Phone:** (912)395-6750.

## MCGUIRE, DR. CHESTER C., JR.

Consultant, educator. **Personal:** Born Oct 29, 1936, Gary, IN; married Julieivory; children: Michael, Angela & Gail. **Educ:** Dartmouth Col, BA, 1958; Univ Chicago, MBA, 1964; Grad Sch Bus, PhD, 1974. **Career:** Inland Steel Co, financial analyst, 1962-64; Real Estate Res Corp, economist, 1965-68; Winston A Burnett Const Co, vpres & gen mgr, 1968-70; Univ Calif, Berkeley, Dept City & Regional Planning, fac, 1970, asst prof, prof, currently; HUD, consult; City San Francisco, consult; Metrop Transp Comn, consult; Berkeley Neighborhood Traffic Study, consult; E Palo Alto 701 Planning Progs, consult; AUS Corps Engrs, consult; Asn Bay Area Governments, consult. **Orgs:** Chairperson, Master Plan Rev Com, Berkely, 1973-75; bd dir, Alameda-Contra Costa Co Transit Dist, 1974; vpres, secy, Berkeley Planning Assocs, 1972-; pres, McGuire Assocs, 1972-; BCDC Adv Comt; Am Inst Planner; Am Econ Asn; asst secy, Housing & Urban Develop. **Special Achievements:** Author: "Operational Problems of New Communities", The Journal of Sociology & Social Welfare: Vol. 3: Iss. 2, Article 5, 2014; published numerous article on housing, transport & urban subjects. **Home Addr:** 140 Fairlawn Dr, Berkeley, CA 94708-2108, **Home Phone:** (510)848-8941. **Business Addr:** Professor, University of California, 228 Wurster Hall, Berkeley, CA 94720-1850, **Business Phone:** (510)642-3256.

## MCGUIRE, JEAN MITCHELL

Association executive. **Personal:** Born Apr 11, 1931, Canton, MA; married Clinton; children: Johanna, David & Clinton Jr. **Educ:** Howard Univ, attended 1951; Boston State Col, BS, 1961; Tufts Univ, MA, educ, 1963. **Career:** Boston Pub Schs, pupil adjust counr, 1963-73; Simmons Col, instr, 1971-74; Metrop Coun Educ Opportunity, exec dir, 1973-; Boston Sch Comn, staff, 1982-. **Orgs:** Boston Teachers Union, 1962; bd mem, Black Educ Alliance Mass; Negro Air Masns Int; Nat All Black Sch Educ; adv bd & bd mem, Mass Womens Polit Caucus; corporator, Homes Savings Bank; mem bd, Mass Conf United Church Christ; trustee, Boston C Mus; Negro Airmen's Int New Eng Chap; Delta Sigma Theta Sorority, Boston Alumnae Chap; Mass Black Polit Task Force; life mem, Nat Asn Advan Colored People; Eta Phi Chap; Omega Psi Phi Fraternity Inc; bd mem, Community Chg Inc; bd mem, Encampment Citizenship; chmn, Metrop Coun Educ Opportunity Inc; bd mem, C's Mus. **Honors/Awds:** Alice K Politzer Award, Encampment Citizenship, 1978; Zeta Phi Beta Sorority Award, 1980; Black Achievers Award, Boston, 1982; Fred Douglass Publication Service, YMCA, 1982; DHL, Salem State Col, 1983; Humanitarian Award Of The Year, 2004; Lifetime Achievement Award,

Community Change's, 2012; WGBH Community Achievement Award; Bristol Co Juvenile Court Award; Big Brothers Asn Award; Founders Award, Omega Psi Phi Fraternity Inc; Mass Teachers Asn Award. **Special Achievements:** Second African American female to be elected to the Boston School Committee, 1981. **Home Addr:** 35 Dennison St, Roxbury, MA 02119-1329, **Home Phone:** (617)442-6454. **Business Addr:** Executive Director, Metropolitan Council for Educational Opportunity Inc, 40 Dimock St, Roxbury, MA 02119, **Business Phone:** (617)427-1545.

## MCGUIRE, RAYMOND J.

Banker. **Personal:** Born Jan 1, 1957, Dayton, OH. **Educ:** Hotchkiss Sch, Harvard Col, AB, 1979; Harvard Bus Sch, MBA, 1984; Harvard Law Sch, JD, 1984; Univ Nice, rotary fel, France, 1980. **Career:** First Boston Corp, Mergers & Acquisitions Group, assoc, 1984-88; Wasserstein Perella & Co, partner, managing dir, 1988-94; Wasserstein Perella & Co Inc, managing partner, 1991-; Merrill Lynch, Mergers & Acquistions, managing dir; Patterson, Belknap, Webb & Tyler, assoc; Skadden, Arps, assoc; Morgan Stanley, global co-head mergers & acquisitions; Citigroup, head global invest banking & instnl clients group, currently. **Orgs:** Chmn bd, De La Salle Acad; pres bd, Int Ctr Photog; trustee, Lincoln Ctr; trustee, NY Presby Hosp; trustee, mem exec comt, NY Pub Libr; pres bd, San Remo Tenants Corp; chmn bd, Studio Mus, Harlem; trustee, Alex Hillman Family Found; vice chmn, chmn nominating comt Whitney Mus Am Art; trustee, New Mus Contemp Art; dir nominating & governance comt, Wyeth Corp, 2006-; bd mem, Joseph & Claire Flom Found; bd mem, Howard Gilman Found; bd mem, Hotchkiss Sch; bd mem, Found Art & Preserv Embassies; several vis comts, Harvard Univ; Overseers/Dirs Nominating Comt; Citi's Bus Develop Comt; Instnl Clients Group Exec Comt; Instnl Clients Group Bus Practices Comt; mem exec comt, trustee, New York Pub Libr; inaugural mem, Martin Luther King, Jr. Int Bd Renaissance Leaders, Morehouse Col. **Honors/Awds:** Rotary Fel, 1980; Black Enterprise, One of the 25 Hottest Blacks on Wall Street, 1992-97; Make-A-Wish Found & Art for Life Found; Distinguished Alumni Award & Distinguished Alumni Speaker Series, Harvard Bus Sch; Patron of the Arts, Pratt Inst; African-American Student Union's Professional Achievement Award, Harvard Business Sch; Frederick Douglas Award, New York Urban League, 2008; Humanitarian Leadership Award, Coun Urban Professionals, 2009; Recognitions: One of New York's 50 Smartest, Avenue Mag; One of the 100 Most Powerful Executives in Corporate America, Black Enterprise Mag, 2009. **Special Achievements:** First African managing dir at Wasserstein Perella; specialist in mergers & acquisitions; Distinguished Alumni Speaker Series. **Business Addr:** Head of Global Banking Institutional Clients Group, Citi Markets & Banking, 399 Pk Ave, New York, NY 10043, **Business Phone:** (212)559-1000.

## MCGUIRE, RAYMOND J.

Executive. **Personal:** Born Jan 23, 1957, Dayton, OH. **Educ:** Harvard Col, AB, 1979; Univ Nice, France, attended 1980; Harvard Bus Sch & Harvard Law Sch, MBA & JD, 1984. **Career:** First Boston Corp, Mergers & Acquisitions, 1984-88; Merrill Lynch & Co Inc, Mergers & Acquisitions Group, managing dir, 1993-2000; Wasserstein Perella & Co, partner & managing dir, 1991-94; Morgan Stanley, global co-head mergers & acquisitions, 2000-05; Citigroup Inc, Global Investment Banking, co-head, managing dir, 2005-11, Global Banking Instnl Clients Group, head, Global Technol Media & Telecommunications Group, co-head, 2011-; Lincoln Ctr Performing Arts Inc, dir; Wyeth LLC, dir, 2006. **Orgs:** chmn bd, De La Salle Acad; former pres bd, Int Ctr Photog; trustee, Lincoln Ctr; pres, New York-Presby Hosp; trustee, New York Pub Libr; chmn bd, Studio Mus Harlem; chmn bd, Alex Hillman Family Found; vice chmn, trustee, Whitney Mus Am Art; dir, Wyeth Corp; pres bd, San Remo Tenants' Corp; mem adv bd, MutualArt Serv Inc; bd mem, Enterprise Found; bd mem, Joseph & Claire Flom Found; Howard Gilman Found; bd mem, Mayor's Cult Affairs Adv Comt. **Honors/Awds:** "Avenue," New York's 50 Smartest; Frederick Douglas Award by the New York Urban League, Recipient, 2008; Morehouse College's Martin Luther King, Jr. International Board of Renaissance Leaders, 2008; "Black Enterprise," 75 Most Powerful Blacks on Wall Street, 2011. **Business Addr:** Director, Lincoln Center for the Performing Arts, 10 Lincoln Ctr Plz, New York, NY 10023, **Business Phone:** (212)875-5456.

## MCGUIRT, MILFORD W.

Certified public accountant. **Personal:** Born Aug 15, 1956, Niles, MI; son of Milton and Vhuaness; married Carolyn J Sconiers; children: Shavonne L, Andrea M & Brittany N. **Educ:** Western Mich Univ, BBA, cum laude, 1978. **Career:** Coopers & Lybrand, audit mgr, 1978-85; Peat Marwick Mitchell & Co, sr audit mgr, 1985-90; KPMG Peat Marwick, partner, 1990-; KPMG LLP, sr partner & audit sector leader, audit partner, 1986-. **Orgs:** Bd mem, S Bend Ind Chap Urban League, 1981-82; Am Inst CPA's, 1980; Mich Asn CPA's, 1980; Ga Soc CPA's, 1986; Nat Asn Black Acct, 1986; Fin Mgrs Soc, 1986; Atlanta Chamber Com Pres Comn, 1986; bd mem, Atlanta W End Rotary Club, 1986; bd mem, W End Boys & Girls Club, 1995; bd mem, UNICEF Atlanta, 1997; Atlanta Steering Comt, 2005-06; bd advisor, Ga Found Independent Col Inc; trustee, KPMG Found. **Honors/Awds:** Outstanding Alumni Award, Beta Alpha Psi, Western Mich Univ, 1995; Best Mentor, KPMG Peat Marwick, 1997. **Home Addr:** 4234 Nobleman Pt, Duluth, GA 30097-2360, **Home Phone:** (770)446-6314. **Business Addr:** Senior Partner, Audit Sector Leader, KPMG LLP, 303 Peachtree St NE Suite 2000, Atlanta, GA 30303, **Business Phone:** (404)222-3000.

## MCHENRY, DONALD F.

Executive, ambassador, educator. **Personal:** Born Oct 13, 1936, St. Louis, IL; children: Michael Stephen, Christina Ann & Elizabeth Ann. **Educ:** Ill State Univ, BS, 1957; Southern Ill Univ, MS, 1959; Georgetown Univ, post grad studies, 1962; Bates Col, LHD, 1986. **Career:** Southern Ill Univ, prof, 1957-59; Howard Univ Wash, instr, 1959-62; US State Dept, var positions, 1963-73; Brookings Inst, guest scholar, 1971-73; Coun Foreign Rels, intl affairs fel, 1971-73; Sch Foreign Serv Georgetown Univ, lect, 1971-72; Carnegie Endowment INTL Peace, humanitarin policy studies, proj dir, 1973; Am Univ Wash, lect, 1975; US State Dept, Pres Jimmy Carter's transition staff, 1976; UN Security CNL, app US dep rep, 1977-79; Un, US permanent rep, ambassador, 1979-81; Georgetown Univ, Distinguished Prof Diplomacy Int Affairs, 1981-; Coca-Cola Co, dir, 1981-; Fleet Nat Bank, dir; Am Tel Tel Co, dir; Intl Paper Co, dir, 1981-2008; SmithKline Beecham Corp; dir, AT&T Corp, dir; Fleet Boston Financial Corp, dir; UN Security Coun, dep rep; IRC Group, pres, 1981-2007. Author: Micronesia: Trust Betrayed. **Orgs:** UN Western Five Contact Group; gov, Am Stock Exchange; dir, Coun Foreign Rels; ed bd mem, Foreign Policy Mag; Am Acad Diplomacy; Ctr Transitional Justice; Alpha Phi Alpha; Am Ditchley Found; US Comt UN Pop Fund; fel Am Acad Arts Sci; Partnership a Secure Am, bd dir; Global Leadership Found; Trustee Emer Columbia Univ; Trustee Emer Mayo Found; Sr Advisor to Nat Dem Inst; Advisor to Women's Foreign Policy Group; Advisor to Wash Centre; dir, Am Assembly; dir, Coca Cola Africa Found; chmn emer, Africare. **Business Addr:** Professor, Georgetown University, 37th & O St NW, Washington, DC 20057, **Business Phone:** (202)687-6083.

## MCHENRY, DOUG

Administrator, movie producer, movie director. **Personal:** Born Jan 6, 1958, New York, NY. **Educ:** Stanford Univ, BA, econs, 1973; Harvard Bus Sch, MBA, 1977; Harvard Law Sch, JD, 1977. **Career:** Producer, director, actor, business owner; Krush Groove, 1985; Disorder lies, 1987; House Party 2, producer & dir, 1991; New Jack City, 1991; Private Times, 1991; Jason's Lyric, dir, 1994; House Party 3, producer, 1994; The Walking Dead, producer, 1995; Scenes for the Soul, producer, 1995; A Thin Line Between Love & Hate, producer, 1996; "Malcolm & Eddie", 1996-2000; Body Count, producer, 1998; Two Can Play That Game, 2001; How to Make Your Man Behave in 10 Days... Or Less, 2001; The Brothers, producer, 2001; Double Tap, 2006; Boogie Town, 2012; House Party: Tonight's the Night, 2013. Direcor: House Party 2, 1991; Jason's Lyric, 1994; Kingdom Come, dir, 2001; "Keep the Faith, Baby", 2002; Borrowed Moments, dir, 2014. Actor: Fear of a Black Hat, 1994; Road to' New Jack City', 2005. Casablanca Rec & Film works, dir bus affairs; Avco Embassy Pictures, dir legal & bus affairs, TV exec; Solar Rec, vpres film entertainment; Quincy Jones Entertainment, prod exec; Jackson/McHenryEntertainment, pres & partner; Elephant Walk Entertainment, partner, chief exec officer & pres, currently. **Orgs:** Adv bd, eWorld Entertainment Inc; Calif Bar; adv bd, NAFTC Studios, currently; dir Guild Am; Producers Guild Am; Acad Motion Picture Arts & Sci; adv bd, Gold Coast Productions, currently; adv bd, eWorld Co Inc, currently. **Business Addr:** President, Chief Executive Officer, Elephant Walk Entertainment, 9200 Sunset Blvd Suite 430, Los Angeles, CA 90069, **Business Phone:** (310)887-3977.

## MCHENRY, EMMIT J.

Executive, founder (originator), consultant. **Personal:** Born Jul 12, 1943, Forrest City, AR. **Educ:** Univ Denver, BS, commun, 1966; Northwestern Univ, MS, commun studies & indust engineering, 1979, qual exam PhD; Shaw Univ, hon PhD. **Career:** Network Solutions Inc, co founder, chmn & chief exec officer, 1979-95; Allstate Ins, regional vpres, 1983-86; Enterprise Mags, NetCom Solutions Int Inc, founder, chmn & chief exec officer, 1995-; Archura LLC, founding prin, chair & chief exec officer, 1995-; Int Bus Mach; Conn Gen, mgr; Union Mutual; VisuTel, chmn. **Orgs:** dir, Stratesec Inc, 2000-; Exec comt, bd dir, NetCom Solutions Int Ltd, UK; chair, Governance Comt, Phelps Stokes Fund; adv bd, DECIS Technol; chmn bd, Learn City Inc; Fairfax Co Econ Develop Authority; State Va Econ Develop Authority; bd dir, James Martin Govt Intelligence; chair bd dir, NetCom Solutions S Africa; founding mem, Am Productivity Mgt Asn; exec comt, Coun Competitiveness; Fairfax County Econ Develop Authority; Nat Minority Supplier Develop Coun; bd mem, NetCom Solutions Int Ltd; bd dir, Global Technol LLC; chaired bd dir, NeCom Solutions Safrica. **Honors/Awds:** Vendor Award for Quality Service Provider, IBM; Subcontractor Quality Service Provider Award, NASA; Highest Vendor Quality Award, AT&T; Partner in Excellence Award, Lucent Technologies. **Business Addr:** Chairman, Chief Executive Officer, Archura LLC, 673 Potomac Sta Dr Suite 808, Leesburg, VA 20176, **Business Phone:** (561)424-9122.

## MCHENRY, DR. JAMES O.

Administrator, army officer, association executive. **Personal:** Born Nov 9, 1940, Sterlington, LA; son of S O and Rebecca; married Esther C Johnson; children: Stephanie Diane & Ali Kenyatta. **Educ:** Grambling State Univ, BS, sociol, 1963; Wayne State Univ, MEd, 1970, EdD, sociol, 1979. **Career:** Educator, government official (retired); Monroe Los Angels Bd Educ, music teacher, 1962-63; AUS Educ Ctr, Europe, GED teacher, 1965; Mich Bd Educ, res teacher, 1966-67; Wayne City Recorders Ct, probation officer, 1967-73; Recorders Ct Probation Dept, asst supvr, 1973-78; Mich Dept Licensing & Reg, cert marriage counr, 1975-80; Recorders Ct Drug Prog, dir, 1978-80; Recorders Ct Pretrial Serv, dir, 1980-82; Oakland Univ, lectr, 1984-; US Pretrial Serv Agency, Detroit, Mich, chief pretrial serv officer; Dr.ofLetters.com, owner. **Orgs:** Omega Psi Phi Frat, 1960-; Restoration Comt; Formal Dance Comt; Assault Illiteracy Comt; block chmn, San Juan Pennington Block Club; vpres-rec Partner, Fifteen Investors Group. **Honors/Awds:** Special Award, NARCO, 1983; Leadership Award, Recorders Ct Probation Dept, 1983; President's Award, Grambling State Univ, 1983. **Home Addr:** 17191 Pennington Dr, Detroit, MI 48221, **Home Phone:** (313)345-7316. **Business Addr:** MI.

## MCHENRY, MARY WILLIAMSON

Educator. **Personal:** Born Jan 23, 1933, Washington, DC; married Hillary Rodham Clinton; children: Michael S, Christina A & Elizabeth A; married Harry Saunders Murphy Jr; married Donald F; children: Donald & Mary. **Educ:** Mt Holyoke Col, AB, 1954; Columbia Univ, MA, 1960; George Washington Univ, 1964. **Career:** Howard Univ, instr eng, 1960-63; George Washington Univ, asst prof eng, 1964-69; DC Teachers Col, guest lectr eng, 1967-68; Fed City Col, asst prof eng, 1969-74; Mt Holyoke Col, assoc prof eng, assoc dean studies, prof eng, 1974-99, prof emer eng, 1998-; Am lit scholar. **Orgs:** Phi Beta Kappa MHC Chap, 1954; fel John Jay Whitney Opportunity, 1954-55, 1957-58; Danforth Found fel 1961-62; instr, Am Studies Peace Corps Training Prog, 1962-63; consult ed, Univ Mass Press, 1978-79; adv bd, Radcliffe Seminars Forum Continuing Ed, 1980; Am Studies & Black Studies. **Honors/Awds:** Nat Endowment for the Humanities, 1972-73. **Home Addr:** 3001 Veazey Terr NW Apt 1401, Washington, DC 20008-5408, **Home Phone:** (202)362-2962. **Business Addr:** Professor Emeritus of English, Mount Holyoke College, 111 Shattuck Hall 50 Col St, South Hadley, MA 01075, **Business Phone:** (413)538-2146.

## MCILWAIN, NADINE WILLIAMS (NADINE MCILWAIN-MASSEY)

President (organization), school administrator. **Personal:** Born Jul 29, 1943, Canton, OH; daughter of Willie J and Mabel W; married Albert H; children: Jeaneen & Floyd; married William P Massey. **Educ:** Malone Col, BA, 1970; Univ Akron, MA, 1978; Ashland Univ, MA, educ, 1990. **Career:** Canton City Health Dept, lab asst, 1962-65; Ohio Bell Tel Co, opr, 1965-71, consult, 1970-71; Timken Sr High Sch, teacher, 1971-90; Canton City Sch, teacher, teacher, 1971-90, curric specialist, 1985-90, bd & pres, currently; Nefertiti Nuptials, owner, operator, 1984-; Canton City Coun, ward coun person, 1985-86; Alliance City Sch, prin, 1990-2002; Allen Elem Sch, prin; Sisters Charity Found, prog officer, 2001-05; Coming Together Stark County, exec dir. **Orgs:** Pres, Frontiers Int Aux, 1971; educ mem, dir, bd pres, Canton City Sch, 1975-82; pres, LeilaGreen Educrs Coun, 1978; sec, Am Bus Womens Assoc, 1980; st parliamentarian, Nat Black Womens Leadership Caucus, 1983-84; owner & operator, Nadine's Nuptials, 1984-; vpres, Alliance Symphony Asn, 1991-; chair stark, Metrop Housing Authority, 1992; elected mem, Canton City Bd Educ, 2002-06, pres, 2003-05; bd dir, Canton Players Guild; Nat Asn Advan Colored People; Canton Urban League; Alliance Area Farmworkers Housing Asn; Alliance Proj Hope; Nat Alliance Black Sch Educr; Nat Educ Asn; Nat Sociol Hon Soc; Ohio Mid Sch Asn; Ohio Coun Social Studies; Ohio Educ Asn; Canton Prof Educr Asn; Leila Green Alliance Black Sch Educr; tark County African-Am Fedn; Delta Sigma Theta. **Honors/Awds:** Woman of the Year, Canton Negro Oldtimers Athletic Asn, 1979; Political Award, Black Womens Leadership Caucus, 1981; Woman of the Year, Greater Canton Am Bus Womens Assoc, 1982; Nat Educ Award, Milken Family Found; Ohio Humanitarian Award, Educ Martin L King Jr Holiday Comn, State Ohio Recipient of numerous awards including Teacher of the Year, National Educator & as Woman of the Year for various organizations. **Special Achievements:** Author: From Ghetto to God, 2002; My Father's Child, 2006. Contributing Author: My Soul to His Spirit; Chicken Soup for the African American Woman's Soul. **Home Addr:** 3409 Tradewinds Cove NW, Canton, OH 44708, **Home Phone:** (330)456-5778. **Business Addr:** President, Canton City Schools, 617 McKinley Ave SW, Canton, OH 44707, **Business Phone:** (330)438-2500.

## MCILWAIN, TONI

Executive. **Personal:** Born Jan 26, 1948, Akron, OH; daughter of Julius and Dorothy; married Roger; children: Luther, Lance, Lashon & Lanette. **Career:** Wayne State Univ, Harmony Proj, dir; Metro E, coun; Twin Sisters, Same Spirit, co-founder; Ravendale Community Inc, cheif exec officer, founder & pres, currently; US Census Bur, recruiter, leader, 2009-10. **Orgs:** Secy, Detroit Revitilization Inc; co-chair, Metro E; Lakewood Manor; bd dir, Activating Resources & Inspiring Serv & Empowerment, currently; bd mem, Arise Detroit Inc. **Home Addr:** 9136 E Outer Dr, Detroit, MI 48213-4006, **Home Phone:** (313)527-4783. **Business Addr:** Chief Executive Officer, President, Ravendale Community Inc, 13903 Harper Ave, Detroit, MI 48213, **Business Phone:** (313)527-1603.

## MCILWAIN-MASSEY, NADINE. See MCILWAIN, NADINE WILLIAMS.

## MCINNIS, JEFF LEMANS (JEFFREY MCINNIS)

Basketball player. **Personal:** Born Oct 22, 1974, Charlotte, NC; son of Frank and Cynthia. **Educ:** Univ NC, Chapel Hill, psychol, 1996. **Career:** Basketball player (retired); Denver Nuggets, 1996; Panionios, Greece, 1996-97; Quad City Thunder, 1997-99, 1999-2000; Wash Wizards, guard, 1999; Los Angeles Clippers, 2000-02; Portland Trailblazers, free agt, 2002-04; Cleveland Cavaliers, guard, 2004-05; Nj Nets, guard, 2005-07; Charlotte Bobcats, guard, 2007-08. **Home Addr:** 34e4 Lazy Day Lane, Charlotte, NC 28269-e144.

## MCINTOSH, DR. FRANKIE L.

Educator. **Personal:** Born Dec 15, 1949, Quitman, GA; daughter of Frank and Ida Hardy. **Educ:** NC Cent Univ, Durham, NC, BA, 1972; Atlanta Univ, Atlanta, GA, 1973; Univ Ga, Athens, GA, MPA, 1981; Ga State Univ, Atlanta, GA, PhD, 2000. **Career:** Professor (retired); Social Security Admin, Atlanta, GA, claims rep, 1974-78; Social Security Admin, Atlanta, GA, supvr, 1978-80; Social Security Admin, Atlanta, GA, mgr, 1974-86; Ga Perimeter Col, Clarkston, GA, prof polit sci, 1986-2010, dept chair, 1988-2002, Acad Adv Comt Polit Sci, mem, currently. **Orgs:** Alpha Kappa Alpha Sorority, 1970-; NC Cent Univ Alumni Asn, Atlanta Chap, 1972-; Am Bus Women's Asn, 1980-86; SSA Southern Regional Mgt Asn, 1980-87; Ga Polit Sci Asn, 1986-; Nat Conf Black Polit Scientists, 1986-; Nat Educ Asn/GAE/DCFA, 1987-; Ga Asn Women Deans, Administrators, & Counsr, 1988-91; Southern Polit Sci Asn, 1989-; Am Bus Women's Asn, 1999-. **Honors/Awds:** Superior Performance Award, Social Security Admin, 1976 & 1980; Woman of the Year, Am Bus Women's Asn, Mableton Chap, 1983; Outstanding Public Service Award, Social Security Admin, 1986-; Teaching Excellence Award, Dekalb Col, 1995; Outstanding Faculty Award, 1996; NISOD Teaching Excellence Award, 1996. **Home Addr:** 99 Tyler Ridge, Jonesboro, GA 30238, **Home Phone:** (770)472-7791.

## MCINTOSH, HELEN YOUNG

Chief executive officer. **Personal:** married William E Jr; children: Blair & Brian. **Career:** Kirkland Chrysler Jeep, chief exec officer. **Orgs:** Premier mem, Nat Asn Minority Automobile Dealers. **Business Addr:** Chief Executive Officer, Kirkland Chrysler Jeep, 12828 NE 124th St, Kirkland, WA 98034, **Business Phone:** (866)435-2999.

## MCINTOSH, DR. LEVI H., JR.

Educational consultant. **Educ:** NMex State Univ, BS; San Francisco State Univ, MS, educ admin; Nova Southeastern Univ, PhD. **Career:** McIntosh & Assocs LLC Consult Group, pres & chief exec officer. **Orgs:** Exec Comt Mem, 100 Black Men Am; Asn Supvr & Curric Develop; Fla Asn Sch Adminr; Nat Alliance Black Sch Educr; Duval County Asn Sch Adminr; Am Asn Sch Administrations; Nat Asn Multi-Cult Educ; Riverside Fine Arts Bd; Bethel Baptist Instnl

Church. **Business Addr:** President and CEO, McIntosh & Associates LLC, 6061 Alderfer Springs Dr, Jacksonville, FL 32258.

### MCINTOSH, MARC

Executive, vice president (organization). **Personal:** Born Chicago, IL. **Educ:** De Paul Univ, BS; Harvard Univ, MBA; Argosy Univ, DBA. **Career:** Goldman, Sachs & Co, finance, vpres, 1989; PaineWebber Group Inc, managing dir, Telecommunications Group, head, 1989-, Latin Am group, head, 1991-; MCM Financial Advisors LLC, founder & pres; Asian Develop Bank, consult; Walden Univ, fac. **Orgs:** Bd dir, Greater New York, Coun Boys Scouts Am.

### MCINTOSH, RHODINA COVINGTON

Lawyer, educator, executive. **Personal:** Born May 26, 1947, Chicago Heights, IL; daughter of William George and Cora Jean Cain; married Gerald Alfred; children: Gary Allen, Garvey Anthony & Ayana Kai. **Educ:** Mich St Univ, BA, indust & orgn psychol, 1969; Univ Detroit, JD, corp law & bus admin, 1977. **Career:** Mich St Univ Off Equal Opportunity, asst dir, 1969-70; Bell & Hudson PC Detroit, law clerk, 1977-79; Covington McIntosh & Assocs Int, pres, Detroit MI, Wash, DC & Mbabane, Swaziland, 1980-83; Univ Swaziland & Botswana Kwaluseni Swaziland, lectr, 1981-83; US AID Off Pvt & Vol Coop, chief info & tech assistance, 1983-87, chief info & prog support, 1987-88; Automation Res Systs Ltd, corp coun, 1988-93; Konsider It Done Mgt Corp, 1993-, pres, 2000-, owner, currently. **Orgs:** NCP, 1960-70; founding bd mem, Women's Justice Ctr Detroit, 1975-77; PhiAlpha Delta Law Fraternity, 1977-; coord, Women's Leadership Conf Wayne St Univ Detroit, 1979; bd mem & counr, Awareness Inc Detroit, 1979-80; consult, Polit Educ Workshops Detroit, Flint, Lansing, Saginaw, Grand Rapids MI, 1979-80; bd mem, Detroit Urban League, 1980-; founding bd mem, Wayne Co Chap MI Republican Women's Task Force Detroit, 1980; Detroit Urban League, 1980; main rapporteur, First All Africa Law Conf Univ, Swaziland & Botswana Kwaluseni Swaziland, 1981; charter mem, Nat Asn Female Execs, 1983-; chairperson foreign rels subcom, Nat Black Women's Polit Caucus Wash, 1984; bd mem, Am Opportunity Found Wash, 1984-87; Mich St Univ Alumni Asn, 1985-; GOP Women's Network, 1986-87; Teacher Asn Springbrook High Sch, 1986-90; Naval Acad Athletic Asn, 1987-90; St Teresa Avila Roman Cath Church, 1987-89; Nat Bar Asn, 1989-; Am Bar Asn, 1989-; Univ Calif, Berkeley Booster Club Track, 1990-93; vice chair, SmallBus Community ABA, 1991-92; chair bd, Christian Vision Ctr Homeless Shelter, 1995-, Far S Suburban Cook Co; prog chair, Goodwill Charity Club, 1995-; adv bd mem, Suburban Recovery Ctr Inc, 1996-00; ed, UnionBanner, Union Evangelistic Baptist Church, 1996-99; City Chicago Heights Beautification Comn, 1998; City Chicago Heights Cable Comn, 2000; DeltaSigma Theta. **Honors/Awds:** National Achievement Scholar Finalist National Merit, 1965; Scholar, Martin Luther King Jr Ctr Social Change Atlanta, 1976; Award, Detroit Women's Justice Ctr, 1978; Award, Goodwill Charity Club, Chicago Heights, IL, 1978; Award Outstanding Volunteer Service Reagan/Bush Campaign, 1980; Award Detroit Edison, 1980; Award, Wayne Co Chap Republican Women's Task Force, 1980; Distinguished Leadership Award, ABI, 1987; Activist of the Year Award, Far So Sub Cook Co, Nat Asn Advan Colored People, 1999; Certificate of Achievement, Welfare Work Initiative, Chicago Heights Ministerial Alliance, 1999; Pioneer Award, Frederick Douglas Soc, Detroit, MI, 1994; Woman of the Decade Award, Bloom Township High Sch Centennial Celebration, 2000. **Business Addr:** President, Owner, Konsider It Done Management, 1508 Hanover St, Chicago Heights, IL 60441, **Business Phone:** (708)753-6408.

### MCINTYRE, DIANNE RUTH

Choreographer. **Personal:** Born Jul 18, 1946, Cleveland, OH; daughter of Francis Benjamin and Dorothy Layne. **Educ:** Ohio State Univ, Columbus, OH, BFA, dance. **Career:** Choreographer, 1972-; Sounds in Motion, New York, NY, choreorapher & founder, 1972-88; tv progs, choreographer; Nat Endowment Arts, choreographers fels, 1990-93; Choreography: Melting Song, 1971; A Free Thing I, 1972; Dead Center, 1974; The Great MacDaddy, 1974, 1977; Union, 1974; Shadows, 1975; Memories, 1975; Deep South Suite, 1976; The Voyage, 1976; Spell #7, 1979; Life's Force, 1979; Be-Bop, 1979; Triptych, 1980; Boogie Woogie Landscapes, 1980; Paul Robeson, 1981; How Long Brethren, 1981; Love Poems to God, 1982; Eye of the Crocodile, 1982; Mississippi Talks, Ohio Walks, 1984; Take-Off From a Forced Landing, 1984; Harlems legendary studio, mentor; Their Eyes Were Watching God, 1986; Shout Up a Morning, 1986; Black Girl, 1986; Gratitude, 1987; The Coming of Eagles, 1988; 80 Days, 1988; A Brand New People on the Planet, 1987; Miss Evers' Boys, 1989; Invincible Flower, 1989; In Living Color: A Gullah Story, 1993, 1994; I Could Stop on a Dime & Get Ten Cents Change, 1995-99; The Darker Face of the Earth, 1996; King, The Musical, 1999; Death and the King's Horseman, 1999; Mule Bone, 1991; King Hedley II, 2000-01; Polk County, 2002, 04; Crowns, 2003-05; Lyric Fire, 2006; Club, 2008; If you don't know, 2009; Joe Turner's Come and Gone, 2009. **Orgs:** Soc Stage Dirs & Choreographers; Am Fedn TV & Radio Artists; founder, Harlem Popular Dance Studio; Nat Endowment Arts & Ny Coun Arts; Soc Stage Dir Choreographers. **Honors/Awds:** AUDELCO Black Theatre Awards, United Black Artists Cornell Univ, choreography, 1979; Bessie Award, 1989; Performance Award, 1989; Helen Hayes Award; Thelma Hill Award; Woodie Award; AUDELCO Pioneer Award; hon doctorate, State Univ New York, 2009. **Home Addr:** 3703 E 140th St, Cleveland, OH 44120, **Home Phone:** (216)337-1376. **Business Addr:** Choreographer, 3703 E 140th S, Cleveland, OH 44120, **Business Phone:** (216)337-1376.

### MCINTYRE, NATALIE RENEE. See GRAY, MACY.

### MCIVER, EVERETT ALLEN

Football player. **Personal:** Born Aug 5, 1970, Cumberland, NC; children: Everett, Eric & Briallen Dutches Lynn. **Educ:** Elizabeth City State Univ. **Career:** Football player (retired); San Diego Chargers, 1993; Dallas Cowboys, 1993, right guard, 1998-99, right tackle, 1999; New York Jets, guard, 1994-95; London Monarchs, 1996; Miami Dolphins, right guard, 1996-97; Atlanta Falcons, guard, 2000. **Honors/Awds:** All-CIAA, 1990-92; CIAA Defensive player of the year 1991-92; Pigskin Club of Washington Player of the Year, 1992.

### MCIVER, JOHN DOUGLAS

Mayor, paper industry worker, executive. **Personal:** Born Nov 7, 1941, Savannah, GA; son of James and Hagar Norman; married Gloria Grant; children: 6. **Educ:** Liberty County High Sch. **Career:** Interstate Paper Corp, paper maker first asst, 1968-99; City Riceboro, mayor, 2001; Co Comn, chmn, 2003-. **Orgs:** Liberty County Ind Authority, 1980; vice chmn, Riceboro Community Found, 1982; chmn, New Zion Baptist Church, 1977, vice-chmn, 1989; vice-pres, pres, Ga Conf Black Mayors, 1989; bd mem, Coastal Ga Community Action Agency Inc, 1988-91, vpres, 1991-92, br dir; vice-chmn, chmn, Liberty County Joint Planning Comn; bd dirs, Ga Regional Develop Ctr. **Honors/Awds:** First Black Dorchester Credit Union, 1978; community leader, Riceboro Community Found, 1983; Outstanding Achievement Award, Omega Psi Phi Fraternity Inc, 1992. **Special Achievements:** First African American mayor of the City of Riceboro. **Home Addr:** PO Box 341, Riceboro, GA 31323-0341, **Home Phone:** (912)884-2034. **Business Addr:** Chairman, Liberty County of Georgia, PO Box 829, Hinesville, GA 31310, **Business Phone:** (912)876-2164.

### MCKANDERS, JULIUS A, II. See Obituaries Section.

### MCKANDERS, KENNETH ANDRE

Lawyer. **Personal:** Born Nov 18, 1950, Inkster, MI; son of Julius Aaron and Addye N Norwood Smith; married Carolyn M Welch; children: Kimberly, Karla, Kristal & Kenneth. **Educ:** Mich State Univ, East Lansing, BA, polit sci, 1972; Wayne State Univ, Detroit, MI, JD, 1977. **Career:** Recorders Ct, Detroit, Mich, probation officer, 1973-78; Wayne State Univ, Detroit, Mich, asst gen coun, 1978-86; Wayne County Community Col, Detroit, Mich, exec dir legal affairs, asst gen coun, 1986-87; Eastern Mich Univ, Ypsilanti, Mich, gen coun, 1987; Tex Southern Univ, gen coun, assoc gen coun, dep gen coun, 2011-. **Orgs:** Mich State Bar Asn, 1978-; Am Bar Asn, 1980-; bd mem, pres, Wayne State Univ Campus Ministry, 1984-; bd mem & vchair, Hartford Agape Inc, 1984-90; bd mem & pres, Renaissance Optimist Club, 1986-; Tex Bar, 2011-; chair, NACUA, Bd Adv Coun Diversity & Inclusivity; bd dir, Nat Asn Col & Univ Atty. **Honors/Awds:** Distinguished Service Award, Nat Asn Col & Univ Atty, 2009. **Home Addr:** 11512 Wilson, Belleville, MI 48111, **Home Phone:** (734)697-6847. **Business Addr:** Deputy General Counsel, Texas Southern University, Hannah Hall Off 310B 3100 Cleburne St, Houston, TX 77004, **Business Phone:** (713)313-1818.

### MCKANDES, DARNELL DAMON

Educator. **Personal:** Born Aug 26, 1966, Honolulu, HI; son of Robert Henry Sr and Dorothy Clark. **Educ:** SC State Col, attended 1988. **Career:** Gen Motors Corp, Saginaw Div, security officer, 1986; Maple Hill Golf Club, asst prof, 1991; Jackson State Univ, golf coach, girls golf team, 1992; PGA Am, prof golf player, currently. **Orgs:** Kappa Youth Leadership League; Frontiers Ann Christmas Shopping Spree Under priviledged C, 1982-84; Saginaw Alumnae Chap Kappa Alpha Psi Fraternity Inc, 1983-84; vol, Bethel AME Church. **Home Addr:** 1016 Spatz Ct, Saginaw, MI 48602, **Home Phone:** (517)752-9961. **Business Addr:** Professional Golf Player, The PGA of America, 100 Ave of the Champions, Palm Beach Gardens, FL 33418, **Business Phone:** (561)624-8400.

### MCKANDES, DOROTHY DELL

Executive, educator. **Personal:** Born Jul 5, 1937, Saginaw, MI; daughter of William Henry Clark and Katherine Halliday Clark (deceased); married Robert Henry; children: Robert Henry Jr & Darnell Damon. **Educ:** Leeward Community Col, Pearl City, Hawaii, AA, 1974; Cent Mich Univ, Mt Pleasant, Mich, BA, community develop educ, 1975, MA, educ admin, 1977; Delta Col, cert, adult lit, 1986; State Mich Works, cert, employ skills. **Career:** Educator (retired), executive; Leeward Community Col, Pearl City, Hawaii, asst instr, 1975; Pub Schs Saginaw, Saginaw, Mich, elem teacher, 1977-84; Stud Task Force Prog, jobshadow coordr, 1982; Mich Child Care Ctr, asst dir, 1986-89; Kiddie Kingdom Pre-Sch Ctr, Saginaw, Mich, dir, 1990; State Mich Works, classroom instr, 1994-2003; Delta col, residential advisor, 1994. **Orgs:** Co-owner, Cosmopolitan Roller Arena, 1978-83; founding organizer, charter mem, Tri-City Chap, Links Inc, 1980-; Alpha Kappa Alpha Sorority Inc; bd mem, Saginaw County Foster Care, 1988-89; bd mem, Bethel African Methodist Episcopal Church, Courtesy Ministry, secy; United Way Saginaw County; fund distrib comt, Lit Task Force, 1991; life mem, Cent MI Univ; bd dir, READ Asn Saginaw County, 1997; bd dir, Mitten Bay Girl Scout Coun, 1997-98; life mem, Saginaw County Sports Hall Fame. **Honors/Awds:** State Scholarship, Hawaii Fedn Bus & Prof Women's Club, 1977; Dedicated Service & Distinguished Service Awards, Tri-City Links Inc, 1990; Kool Achiever Awards, Brown & Williamson Tobacco Corp, Ky, Certificateof Recognition; Community Service Award, Nestle USA Inc, 1992; Certificate of Appreciation, Int Revenue Serv, 1992; J. C. Penney Golden Rule Nominee, 1995; Woman of Distinction, Mitten Bay Girl Scout Coun, 1997; Lifetime Achievement Award, 2013; Outstanding Community Service, 2013. **Special Achievements:** Co-Founder of First African-american Family-owned and Operated Roller Skating Business In Saginaw. **Home Addr:** 4862 W Michigan Ave, Saginaw, MI 48638-6312, **Home Phone:** (989)799-2841.

### MCKAY-DAVIS, MONIQUE DIONNE

Educator, state government official, politician. **Personal:** Born Aug 19, 1936, Chicago, IL; daughter of James McKay and Constance McKay; married Robert; children: Robert Jr & Monique C Conway. **Educ:** Chicago State Univ, BS, elem educ, 1966, MS, guid & supv, 1975; Univ Ill; DePaul Univ. **Career:** Chicago Bd Educ, teacher, 1967-86; City Cols Chicago, teacher, 1976-84; Chicago Bd Educ, coordr & adminr, 1986-; Ill Gen Assembly, Dist 27, state rep, 1987-. **Orgs:** Chmn, Southside Chap IVI-IPO, 1980-84; chmn, Legis Comt Chicago Area Alliance Black Sch Educr, 1981-83; coordr, Chicago Bd Educ, 1986-; bd mem, Christian Bd Trinity United Church Christ; Chicago State Univ, Alumni Bd, 1992-94; Nat Asn Advan Colored People; Phi Delta Kappa; Beverly Area Planning Asn; Alpha Kappa Alpha Sorority Inc. **Honors/Awds:** Teacher of the Year Award, Gresham Sch, 1978; Teacher Who Makes a Difference Center for New Schools; Excellent Legislator, Dept Aging, 1988; Excellent Legislator, Oper PUSH, 1989; Presidential Award, Nat Asn Equal Opportunity Higher Educ; Legislative Award, Ill Bd Regents Comt; Best & Brightest Award, Dollars & Sense Mag; Women for Work & Dedication to Education Award, Second Congressional Dist. **Business Addr:** State Representative, Illinois General Assembly, 1234 W 95th St, Chicago, IL 60643, **Business Phone:** (773)445-9700.

### MCKAYLE, DONALD COHEN

Educator, writer, choreographer. **Personal:** Born Jul 6, 1930, New York, NY; son of Philip Augustus and Eva Wilhelmina Cohen; married Leah Levin; married Lea Vivante; children: Gabrielle, Liane & Guy. **Educ:** Col City NY, attended 1949. **Career:** Mod dancer, choreographer, teacher, dir & writer; Dance instr: Juilliard Sch Music, Sarah Lawrence Col, Bennington Col, Neighborhood Playhouse, New Dance Group, Martha Graham Sch; Cult Prog Tunisia, adv, 1964; choreographer: Donald McKayle Dance Co, Alvin Ailey Am Dance Theater, Batsheva Dance Co, Israel; Repertory Dance Theater; Dayton Contemp Dance Co; Cleo Parker Robinson Dance Ensemble; Los Angeles Contemp Dance Theatre, artistic mentor & resident choregrapher; Limon Dance Co; Choreographer; Cindy, 1978; Private Debts, 1989; Films: Saturday's Child, 1948; Creole Afternoon, 1950; Games, 1951; Her Name was Harriet, 1952; Nocturne, 1953; St, 1954; Prelude to Action, 1954; Four Excursions, 1956; Rainbow 'Round My Shoulder, 1959; Dist Storyville, 1962; Blood Lamb, 1963; Reflections Pk, 1964; Incantation, 1968; Bedknobs & Broomsticks, 1970; Great White Hope, 1972; Minstrel Man, 1975-76; Jazz Singer, 1980; Broadway plays: GoldenBoy, 1964; I'm Solomon, 1969; Last Minstrel Show, 1974, Raisin, 1974; Dr Jazz, 1975; Sophisticated Ladies, 1981; It Ain't Nothin' But Blues, 1999; dir/choreographer: Hollywood Palace, 1969; Good Times, 1974; Free to Be You & Me, 1974; Komedy Tonite, 1977; The 49th Annual Academy Awards, 1977; Richard Pryor Spec, 1977, 1978; choreographer & creator: Regional Theatre, Denver Ctr Theatre Co, Mark Taper Forum, dir, choreographer & fac: Inner City Cult Ctr; Univ Wash; Portland State Univ; Fla State Univ; Alvin Ailey Dance Ctr; Calif Inst, Sch Dance, dean; Univ Calif, Irvine, prof finearts, dance, artistic dir, currently. **Orgs:** Bd dir, Am Dance Festival, Durham, NC, New Dance Group, New York; Clarke Ctr Performance Arts, NYC; Soc Stage Dir & Choreographers, NYC; Mod Dance Found; Dance Circle Boston, MA; Nat Ctr Afro-Am Artists Rox bury, MA; Irvine Barclay Theatre, St Joseph Ballet; Nat Endowment Arts Dance Panel; bd trustee, Nat Found Advan Arts; Asn Am Dance Co; ASCAP; AEA; AGMA; AFTRA; AGVA; fel, Black Acad Arts & Lett; fel, Dir Guild Am. **Home Addr:** 20 La Costa Ct, Laguna Beach, CA 92651-4401. **Business Addr:** Professor of Dance, Emeritus, University of California, 300 Mesa Arts Bldg, Irvine, CA 92697-2775, **Business Phone:** (949)824-6798.

### MCKEE, DR. ADAM E., II

Veterinarian. **Personal:** Born Apr 12, 1932, Fairfield, AL; married Barbara Nance; children: Adam III, Eric & Brett. **Educ:** Dillar Univ New Orleans, AB, 1954; Tuskegee Inst, DVM, 1958. **Career:** Istanbul, Turkey, vet, 1958-60; Lackland AFB, Tex, sentry dog clinian, 1960-63, chief altitude chamber unit aerospace path, 1966-67; Vet Path Armed Forces Inst Path, res, 1963-66; Biol & Med Scis Div Naval Radiol Defense Lab, San Francisco, chief vet & path, 1967-69; Naval Med Res Inst Nat, Naval Med Ctr, Bethesda, Md, chmn Qqqexptl path dept, 1969-. **Orgs:** USAF Distinguished Unit, 1960-64; chmn, Naval Med Res Inst Policy Adv Coun sci & Managerial bd, 1975-; pres, Tuskegee Vet Med Alumni Asn, 1975, mem; Am Vet Med Asn; Int Acad Path; Wash So Scanning Electron Micros; Am Soc Micro Biol; Post Doctoral Res Asso Prog Com; 76; Am Asn Lab Animal Sci; Omega Psi Phi; exec comt mem, deans adv bd, Tuskegee Univ Sch Vet Med, 2009-. **Honors/Awds:** Keynote speaker 6th Annual Intl Scanning Electron Microscopy Symposium Chicago, 1973; Special Merit Award, Naval Med Res Inst, 1976; chmn, Scanning Electron Ciroscopy Application in Med Microbiology 10th Annual Interna Scanning Electron Microsocpy Symposium Chicago, 1977. **Home Addr:** 3912 Fox Valley Dr, Rockville, MD 20853-3211, **Home Phone:** (301)260-9484. **Business Addr:** Member, Tuskegee Veterinary Medical Alumni Association, PO Box 1303, Bethesda, MD 20814, **Business Phone:** (301)319-7487.

### MCKEE, ESQ. CLARENCE VANZANT

Executive, lawyer, association executive. **Personal:** Born Nov 16, 1942, Buffalo, NY. **Educ:** Hobart Col, BA, sociol, 1965; Howard Univ Sch Law, JD, 1972. **Career:** New York Cent RR, waiter; bartender; disc jockey; Dept HEW, civil rights compliance officer, 1966-67; Pres's Coun Youth Opportunity, w coast coordr, 1968-69; Sen Jacob Javits, legal asst, 1969-71; Sen Charles MacMathias, legal asst, 1971-72; Off Cong Rel US Civil & Aeronaut Bd, actg dir, 1972; Fed Commun Comn, dep chief, 1973-75, legal asst, 1975-77; Indust EEO Unit Off Gen Coun FCC, dep chief, 1973-76; FDL Commun CMS, legal asst; Comnr Ben Hooks FCC, legal asst, 1976-77; Law, Murphy & McKee, atty, 1977-79; Reagan Pres, surrogate speaker-advan team, DC state finance chmn, 1979-80; Pepper & Corazzini, coun, 1979-87; Off Pres-Elect, Fed Home Loan Bank Bd Transition Team, team leader, 1980-81; Legal Serv Corp, dir, vice chmn, chmn spec comt grants-contracts, 1982; DC Republican Exec Comt, vice chmn, 1982-84; DC Reagan-Bush, chmn, 1984; DC Reagan-Bush '84 Comt, chmn, 1984; Campaign DC Deleg Republican Nat Comt, Critical Issues Task Force, Nat Black Republican Coun, vice chmn, 1983-84; Nat Union Total Independence Angola, regist foreign agt, coun & pub/media rels adv, 1985-87; WTVT, Channel 13, co-own, chief exec officer, chmn, pres, 1987-92; McKee Holdings, McKee Acquistion Corp, chmn, chief exec officer, pres, 1992-2005; Ruden McClosky Consult, prin, 2004-08; McKee Commun, founder, pres, 2008-. **Orgs:** Bd mem, DC United Way; Am Bar Asn; Nat Conf Black Lawyers; Fed Bar Asn; Unified Bar DC; NY, PA, DC Bars; Wash commentator, FOX Broadcasting Co; Fla Progress Corp; Fla Power Corp; Am Heritage Life Ins Co; Checkers Dr Restaurants Inc; Fla Asn Broadcasters; sr fel Broward Chamber Com; chmn, Broward Republican Party; co chmn, Hillsborough Co Mid Schs Task Force; Barnett Banks; chmn & mem, Univ Tampa, bd dir, Gulf Ridge Coun Boy Scouts Am; chmn, Fla Asn Broadcasters; comnr, Destination Fla Comn, 2002-03; fel Fla Coun 100; bd dir, Assoc Industs Fla; comnr, 17th Circuit Judicial Nominating Comn, 2007-11; comnr, N Broward Hosp Dist Bd, 2010-12; commun chmn, Broward County Republican Exec Comt; Hillsborough County Jail Comn; Broward County Sheriff's Found; bd dir, Lee & Renaissance Charter Sch; bd trustee, Collins Ctr Pub Policy; Exec Adv Bd Assoc Industs Fla. **Honors/Awds:** Outstanding Alumni Public Service Award, Hobart Col; John Mercer Langston Award, Outstanding

Achievement Law & Pub Serv, Howard Univ Sch Law; inductee, Hall of Fame, Tampa Bay Bus, 1998. **Special Achievements:** Appearances on national media and his articles have been published in The Washington Post, The Washington Times, Human Events Magazine, The Tampa Tribune, Electronic Media and on ProfileAfrica.com. **Home Addr:** 2525 Bayshore Blvd, Tampa, FL 33629. **Business Addr:** President, McKee Communications Inc, 1155 Heron Bay Blvd, Coral Springs, FL 33065, **Business Phone:** (954)509-7080.

### MCKEE, EVELYN PALFREY

Judge. **Personal:** Born Jun 24, 1950, Texarkana, AR; daughter of John and Lois; married Darwin; children: 2. **Educ:** Southern Methodist Univ, BA, 1971; Univ Tex, Law Sch, JD, 1981. **Career:** State Tex, City Austin Munic Ct, presiding judge, 1989-; novelist, 1995-; Austin Pub Libr Found, bd dir; Travis County Lawyer Referral Serv, bd dir; Travis County Women Lawyers, govt serv, 2002. **Orgs:** State Bar Tex, 1982-, bd mem, 1994; Austin Community Radio, 1987-; Travis County Bar Asn, 1989-; Writers League Tex, 1996-; Austin Romance Writers Am, 1998-; bd mem, Austin Black Lawyers Asn. **Honors/Awds:** Distinguished Judge of the Year, Tex Munic Cts Asn, 2000. **Special Achievements:** Author: Three Perfect Men, 1996; The Price of Passion, 1997; Dangerous Dilemmas, 1999; Everything In Its Place, 2002; Nominated for Career Achievement Award, Romantic Times Magazine. **Home Addr:** PO Box 142495, Austin, TX 78701, **Home Phone:** (512)773-8776. **Business Addr:** Judge, State of Texas Municipal Court Austin Municipality, 700 E 7th St, Austin, TX 78768-2135, **Business Phone:** (512)974-4800.

### MCKEE, LONETTE

Writer, singer, television producer. **Personal:** Born Jul 22, 1954, Detroit, MI; daughter of Lonnie and Dorothy; married Leo Compton. **Career:** Actress, singer, songwriter, director, screen writer, producer, self; Actress: Sparkle, 1976; Which Way Is Up, 1977; Cuba, 1979; Illusions, 1982; The Cotton Club, 1984; Brewster's Millions, 1985; Round Midnight, 1986; Gardens of Stone, 1987; The Women of Brewster Place, 1989; Jungle Fever, 1991; Malcolm X, 1992; To Dance with Olivia, 1997; Blind Faith, 1998; He Got Game, 1998; A Day in Black & White, 1999; Fast Food Fast Women, 2000; Men of Honor, 2000; Lift, 2001; The Paper Mache Chase, 2003; Honey, 2003; She Hate Me, 2004; ATL, 2006; Dream Street, 2010; This Narrow Place, 2010, 2011; Deauville, 2010, 2012; Honey 2, 2011; LUV, 2012; TV Series: "Spenser: For Hire", 1985; "The Equalizer", 1985; "Miami Vice", 1986; "Amen", 1989; "Dangerous Passion", 1990; "Queen", 1993; "Some Enchanted Evening: Celebrating Oscar Hammerstein II", 1995; "Having Our Say: The Delany Sisters' First 100 Years", 1999; "Third Watch", 1999-2003; "The Tys That Bind", 2000; "32 Bullets & a Broken Heart", 2000; "This Band of Brothers", 2000; "For Love of Olivia", 2001; "Chameleon", 2002; "Law & Order: Special Victims Unit", 1 Episode, 1991; "My Opening Farewell", 2003; "Superheroes: Part 2", 2002; "The Big Thanks for Nothing Episode ", 2004; "Tonya, Spencer's Mother", 1 Episode, 2004; "Half & Half", 2006; "1-800-Missing", 2006; "Exposure", 2006, "It's Hard Being Kelly Pitts", 2007; "The Game", 2007; Director, producer, Writer & Composer: The First, composer; Dream Street, writer, dir, producer, composer, 2010; Lonette Productions Ltd, owner, currently; Centenary Col Nj, master actg workshop, teacher, adj prof, theater arts dept. **Orgs:** Actors Equity Asn; Am Fedn Tv & Radio Artists. **Special Achievements:** First black actress to play Julie in a major American stage production of "Show Boat".

### MCKEE, HON. THEODORE A.

Judge. **Personal:** Born Jun 5, 1947, Rochester, NY; son of Clarence V and Etta V Payne; married Ana Luisa Pujols; children: Emilia & Marisol. **Educ:** State Univ NY, Cortland, BA, 1969; Syracuse Univ, Col Law, JD, 1975. **Career:** State Univ NY, Binghamton, dir minority recruitment & admis; Wolf Block Schorr & Solis-Cohen, assoc, 1975-77; Eastern Dist PA, asst US atty, 1977-80; Philadelphia Parking Authority, gen coun; Law Dept, City Philadelphia, dep city solicitor, 1980-83; Rutgers Univ Sch Law, Camden, trial advocacy, 1980-91; Ct Common Pleas Commonwealth PA, judge, 1984-94; US Ct Appeals, circuit judge, 1994-2010, chief judge, 2010-; Am Law Inst Proj, advisor. **Orgs:** Bd dir, Crises Intervention Network; Crime Prev Asn; Concerned Black Men; New Directions Women; World Affairs Coun; Urban League Philadelphia; bd dir, Fox Chase Cancer Ctr, Temple Univ; bd dir, City Yr Greater Philadelphia; Crime Prev Asn; trustee, Edna McConnell Clark Found; bd trustee, Temple Univ, 2002, vice chmn, Stud Affairs Comt; dir, State Univ New York Cortland; chair, Afro-Am studies prog; Diag Rehab Ctr; Fox Chase Cancer Ctr; Adv Comt City Yr Philadelphia; Pa Sentencing Comn; co-chaired Comn Racial Ethnic Bias Task Force. **Honors/Awds:** Order of the Coif, Syracuse Univ, 1975. **Special Achievements:** Fourth African American to serve on the 3rd Circuit bench. **Home Addr:** 636 St Georges Rd, Philadelphia, PA 19119-3340, **Home Phone:** (215)247-2064. **Business Addr:** Circuit Judge, US Court of Appeals, 20614 US Courthouse 601 Mkt St Suite 21400, Philadelphia, PA 19106, **Business Phone:** (215)597-9601.

**MCKEEVER, SARA. See PRIOLEAU, DR. SARA NELLIENE.**

### MCKELPIN, JOSEPH P.

Educator. **Personal:** Born May 6, 1914, Leflore County, MS; married Peggy A Jones; children: Joseph P Jr & Emmett O. **Educ:** AB, 1943; Univ Wis, MS, 1948, PhD, 1952. **Career:** Educator (retired); Southern Univ, prof ed, 1952-62; S Asn Cols & Schs, dir res & eval, 1967-73; Morris Brown Col, dean, 1973-74; Fed City Col, prof ed, 1974. **Orgs:** Phi Delta Kappa; Kappa Delta Pi; Kappa Phi Kappa; Omega Psi Phi. **Special Achievements:** Author: Some factors associated with school district reorganization in Wisconsin, 1952. **Home Addr:** 4106 Edgevale Ct, Chevy Chase, MD 20815.

**MCKELVEY, FELDER. See FELDER, DR. LORETTA KAY.**

### MCKENNA, DR. GEORGE J., III

School administrator. **Personal:** Born Sep 6, 1940, New Orleans, LA; son of George Jr and Leah. **Educ:** Xavier Univ, New Orleans, La, BS, math, 1961, EdD, 1989; Loyola Univ, Chicago, Ill, MA, math, 1964; Calif State Univ, Los Angeles; Loyola Univ Law Sch. **Career:** Jordan High Sch, teacher, 1960; Los Angeles Unified Sch Dist, Los Angeles, Calif, math teacher, 1962-70, prin, admin, 1970-88, local dist 7 supt, 2009-; N Am Aviation, engr; Wash Prep High Sch, prin; George Washington Prep High Sch, prin; Inglewood Unified Sch Dist, Inglewood, Calif, supt, 1986-92; McKenna & Assocs Educ Consults, chief exec officer, 1986-2009; Compton Unified Sch Dist, dep supt, 1992-2001; Los Angeles Unified Sch Distric, dist I supt, 2000-01; Pasadena Unified Sch Dist, asst supt sch opers & support, 2001-08; educ consult. **Orgs:** Bd mem, Los Angeles Southern Christian Leadership Conf, 1978-; pres, Los Angeles Unified Schs, Coun Black Adminrs, 1981-82, 1986-87; comn mem, Nat Drug Free Schs Comn, 1989-90; Nat Alliance Black Sch Educr. **Honors/Awds:** UNCF Achievement Award, 1988; Congressional Black Caucus CHR's Award, 1989; Inducted into the National Alliance of Black School Educators Hall of Fame, 1997. **Special Achievements:** Subject CBS television movie, "The George McKenna Story," starring Denzel Wash; Great Black Educs Calendar, 1988. **Business Addr:** Assistant Superintendent of School Operations & Su, Pasadena Unified School District, 351 S Hudson Ave, Pasadena, CA 91109, **Business Phone:** (626)568-4517.

### MCKENZIE, KEITH DERRICK

Football player, football coach. **Personal:** Born Oct 17, 1973, Detroit, MI; married Tamiko; children: Keith Jr, Kalen & Karson. **Educ:** Ball State Univ, BS, hist. **Career:** Football player (retired), football coach; Green Bay Packers, 1996-98, 2002, defensive end, 1999; Miami Dolphins, 1999; Cleveland Browns, 2000-01; Chicago Bears, defensive end, 2002; Buffalo Bills, 2003; Wayne State Univ, Dept Athletics, defensive line coach & assist linebackers, 2008, linebackers coach, 2009-. **Honors/Awds:** Super Bowl, 1996; NFC Champion, 1997; BSU Athletic Hall of Fame, 2006. **Home Addr:** , Farmington Hills, MI. **Business Addr:** Linebackers Coach, Defensive Line Coach, Wayne State University, 5101 John C Lodge 101 Matthaei, Detroit, MI 48202, **Business Phone:** (313)577-4280.

### MCKENZIE, MICHAEL TERRANCE

Football player, executive. **Personal:** Born Apr 26, 1976, Miami, FL; married Rachel McNeil; children: Reigni & Michael. **Educ:** Univ Memphis, bus mgt, 1998. **Career:** Football player (retired); Green Bay Packers, defensive back, 1999-2004; New Orleans Saints, cornerback, 2004-09. **Orgs:** 34 Ways Found, owner, currently. **Business Addr:** Cornerback, New Orleans Saints, 5800 Airline Dr, Metairie, LA 70003, **Business Phone:** (504)733-0255.

### MCKENZIE, MIRANDA MACK

Executive. **Personal:** Born Jun 21, 1955, Atlanta, GA; daughter of Dennis and Jewel Hillman; married Therman; children: Terrence Denard. **Educ:** Morris Brown Col, BA, Eng, lang & lit, gen, 1977; Univ Ga, masters prog, mass commun/media studies, 1978. **Career:** WAOK Radio, copy writer, 1977-79, acct exec, 1979-80; City Beverage Co, dir mkt develop, 1980-84; Coors Brewing Co, asst mgr spec mkt, 1984-85, asst nat prog mgr, comm rel field mgr, 1985-86, comm rel regional mgr, 1986-93; Atlanta Comt, Olympic Games, dir commun, 1993; Anheuser-Busch Co, corp affairs, dir, regional mgr, dir community affairs, consumer outreach & supplier diversity, 1994-2011; United Negro Col Fund, ambassador, area develop dir, 2011-14; TechBridge, dir develop. **Orgs:** Bd mem, Atlanta Nat Asn Advan Colored People, 1977-95; bd mem, Nat Asn Advan Colored People, 1983-; bd mem, Atlanta Urban League, secy, 1987-; bd mem, Ga Asn Minority Entrepreneurs, 1988-; founding bd mem, Coalition 100 Black Women, 1988; bd mem, Atlanta Bus League, 1989-91; Morris Brown Col Athletic Found, 1989-95; nat pres, Nat Asn Mkt Developers, 1991-92; Albany State Univ Found Bd, 1998-; found bd, Atlanta Area Tech Sch, 1999-; bd trustee, Morris Brown Col, 2003-04; Atlanta Tech Col Found, interim dir, develop & community engagement exec, 2015-16; founding mem, Coalition 100 Black Women Atlanta; Miss Morris Brown Col; Nat Hon Soc; Zeta Phi Beta Sorority; bd mem, Nat Black Col Alumni Hall Fame; Stud Govt Asn; bd mem, Decide Dekalb. **Honors/Awds:** Media Woman of the Year, Nat Asn Media Women, 1986; Leadership Atlanta, 1986; Leadership Award, Coun Nat Alumni, 1986; C L Harper Award, Nat Asn Advan Colored People, 1986; Marketer of the Year, NAMD, 1987; Athletic Hall of Fame, Morris Brown Col, 1987; Top African Am Bus & Prof Women, Dollars & Sense Mag, 1987, 1992; Leadership Am, 1989, 1992; Bronze Woman of the Year, Iota Phi Lambda, 1989; Leadership Ga, 1992.WAOK Radio, copy writer, 1977-79, acct exec, 1979-80; City Beverage Co, dir mkt develop, 1980-84; Coors Brewing Co, asst mgr spec mkt, 1984-85, asst nat prog mgr, comm rel field mgr, 1985-86, comm rel regional mgr, 1986-93; Atlanta Comt, Olympic Games, dir commun, 1993; Anheuser-Busch Co, corp affairs, dir, 1994, regional mgr, currently; United Negro Col Fund, ambassador, area develop dir, currently. **Special Achievements:** Named 1 of 10 Outstanding Atlantans, Outstanding Young People Atlanta, 1986; 100 of the Best & Brightest Black Women Corp Am, Ebony Mag, 1990. **Home Addr:** 1257 Weston Dr, Decatur, GA 30032. **Business Addr:** Area Development Director, United Negro College Fund, 229 Peachtree St NE Suite 2350, Atlanta, GA 30303, **Business Phone:** (404)302-8623.

### MCKENZIE, OBIE L.

Executive. **Educ:** Tenn State Univ, attended 1967; Harvard Bus Sch, MBA, finance, 1972. **Career:** Morgan Stanley, corp finance assoc, 1972; McKenzie & Co, founder, 1984-87; New York Times Co, mgr banking & pensions, 1975; UBS Asset Mgt, exec dir, 1987-90; Merrill Lynch Investment Managers, managing dir, 1990-2006; BlackRock Inc, managing dir, global client group, 2005-; Chase Investors, managing dir; Citibank, com banker; Chem Bank, com banker; Freedom Nat Bank, com banker. **Orgs:** Former pres, Asn Investment Mgt Sales Execs; founding bd mem, ToigoFound; founding bd mem, Tex Asn Pub Employees Retirement Systs; founding bd mem, Nat Asn Securities Professionals; chair, WorldofMoney.org; bd dir, Cocoon Resources Inc. **Honors/Awds:** Wall Street Hall of Fame Award, 2001; "Black Enterprise," 75 Most Powerful Blacks on Wall Street, 2011; Lifetime Achievement Award., Youth Found Gala, 2014.

### MCKENZIE, REGINALD (REGGIE MCKENZIE)

Football player, executive. **Personal:** Born Jul 27, 1950, Detroit, MI; son of Hazel and Henry; married Ethellean Hicks. **Educ:** Univ Mich, BS, 1972. **Career:** Football player (retired), executive; Buffalo Bills, offensive guard, left guard, 1972-82; Reggie McKenzie Football Clin, 1974; Seattle Seahawks, offensive guard, left guard, 1983-84; Seattle Seahawks, dir mkt & sales, offensive line coach; Reggie McKenzie Indust Mat Inc, pres, currently. **Orgs:** Comm Proj, Spec Olympics, United Way, Boys Clubs Am; Cent Area Youth Asn Seattle; bd dir, King County Boys & Girls Club; founder & pres, Reggie McKenzie Found. **Honors/Awds:** All-NFL player, 1973-74; Unsung Hero Award, Detroit Sports Media, 1986; Sportsman of the Year, Detroit March Dimes, 1986; Brotherhood Award, BTWBA, 1988; Outstanding Young Citizen, Wash State Jaycees, 1989; Michigan Sports Hall of Fame, 1994; College Football Hall of Fame, 2002. **Home Addr:** 11220 53rd NE, Kirkland, WA 98033. **Business Addr:** Founder, President, Reggie McKenzie Foundation, 13853 Trumbull, Highland Park, MI 48203, **Business Phone:** (313)869-8081.

### MCKENZIE, BISHOP VASHTI MURPHY

Clergy. **Personal:** Born May 28, 1947; daughter of Ida Murphy Smith Peters and Samuel Edward Smith; married Stan; children: Jon-Mikael, Vashti-Jasmine & Joi-Marie. **Educ:** Univ Md, College Park, BA, jour; Howard Univ, Mdiv; United Theol Sem, DMin. **Career:** African Methodist Episcopal Church, ordained, 1984; Payne Memorial African Methodist Episcopal Church, pastor; 18th Episcopal Dist, SE Africa, chief pastor, 2000-04; African Methodist Episcopal Church, titular head, 2005, bishop, 13th Episcopal Dist, presiding prelate, currently; Cong Black Caucus Prayer Breakfast, preacher, 2006; Hampton Minister's Conf, preacher, 2007; WJZ-TV, corp vpres. Books: Not Without Struggle, 1996; Strength in the Struggle, 2000. **Orgs:** African Methodist Episcopal Sch Ann Conf, Lesotho & Swaziland; pres, Coun Bishops; chairperson, Gen Conf Comn; chairperson, Bd Ministers Retirement Prog; chair, Quadrennial Theme Comt; nat chaplain, Delta Sigma Theta Sorority; life mem, Nat Asn Advan Colored People; chmnn, Bd trustee Paul Quinn Col; Bd trustee Int Theol Ctr. **Business Addr:** Presiding Prelate, African Methodist Episcopal Church, 500 8th Ave S, Nashville, TN 37203, **Business Phone:** (615)254-0911.

**MCKERSON, MAZOLA. See Obituaries Section.**

### MCKEY, DERRICK WAYNE

Basketball player. **Personal:** Born Oct 10, 1966, Meridian, MS; children: Mackenzie & Austin. **Educ:** Univ Ala, attended 1987. **Career:** Basketball player (retired); Seattle Supersonics, forward, 1987-93; Ind Pacers, 1993-2001; Philadelphia 76ers, forward, 2002. **Home Addr:** 4243 Creekside Pass, Zionsville, IN 46077-9290.

### MCKIE, AARON FITZGERALD

Basketball player, basketball coach. **Personal:** Born Oct 2, 1972, Philadelphia, PA; married Kianna Williams; married Lisa. **Educ:** Temple Univ, attended 1994. **Career:** Basketball player (retired), basketball coach; Portland Trail Blazers, shooting guard, 1994-97; Detroit Pistons, shooting guard, 1996-97, small forward, 1997-98; Philadelphia 76ers, small forward, 1997-98, 2002-04, shooting guard, 1999-2002, 2004-05, asst coach, 2007-13; Los Angeles Lakers, pt guard, 2005-06, small forward, 2006-07; Temple, asst coach, 2014-. **Honors/Awds:** Robert V. Geasey Trophy, 1993; Player of the Year, Atlantic 10 Conf, 1993; Sixth Man of the Year, Nat Basketball Asn, 2001; Community Assist Award, Nat Basketball Asn, 2003. **Special Achievements:** TV appearance: ESPN SportsCentury, 2003. **Business Addr:** Assistant Basketball Coach, Temple University, 1801 N Broad St, Philadelphia, PA 19122, **Business Phone:** (215)204-7000.

### MCKINES, CHARLOTTE O.

Marketing executive, executive director. **Educ:** Kent State Univ, BS, med technol; Boston Univ, MBA, health mgt. **Career:** Merck & Co Inc, mkt dir, global brand promos, integrated mkt commun, exec dir, global mkt commun, vpres, currently; Asn Nat Advertisers Inc, dir, 2009-. **Orgs:** Nat exec bd mem, Delta Sigma Theta Sorority Inc; bd trustee, Gwynedd Mercy Col; corp adv bd, Healthcare Businesswomen's Asn; Exec Leadership Conf. **Business Addr:** Vice President of Global Marketing Communications, Merck & Co, 1 Merck Dr, Whitehouse Station, NJ 08889-0100, **Business Phone:** (908)423-1000.

### MCKINNEY, ALMA SWILLEY (ALMA MCKINNEY WYNN)

Educator. **Personal:** Born Mar 4, 1930, Lamont, FL; children: Matthew M. **Educ:** Fla A&M Univ, Tallahassee, BA, 1951; Fla State Univ, MS, math, 1966; Univ Minn. **Career:** Madison City Sch Bd, Madison, Fla, teacher, 1951-60; Greenville Training Sch, Greenville, Fla, math instr, 1960-63; Suwannee River Jr Col, Madison, Fla, head math dept, 1963-67; N Fla Jr Col, assoc prof math, 1967-73, cordr learning lab, 1976-80; Univ Minn, teaching asst, 1973-76; Dept Corrections, chmn regional adv coun, 1977-79; ACTT Inc, Madison, corp dir, 1978-80; State Dept Educ, Tallahassee, consult. **Orgs:** Bd dir, Madison City Mem Hosp, 1981-84; pol action comt, Nat Asn Advan Colored People; Zeta Phi Beta Sor; voters League, RECS Serv Club. **Honors/Awds:** Teacher of the Year, Suwannee River Jr Col, 1964; Citizen of the Year, Iota Alpha Zeta Chap Zeta Phi Beta, 1979. **Home Addr:** 2668 US Hwy 90, Madison, FL 32340, **Home Phone:** (850)973-2567.

### MCKINNEY, BILLY

Sports manager, radio broadcaster. **Personal:** Born Jun 5, 1955, Waukegan, IL. **Educ:** Northwestern Univ, BS, educ, 1977. **Career:** Basketball player (retired); Kans City Kings, Utah Jazz, Denver Nuggets, San Diego Clippers, Chicago Bulls, Pt guard; W.F. Hall Printing Co, sales mgt trainee; Chicago Bulls, asst vpres basketball opers, 1985-87; dir player personnel, 1988-90, radio analyst, currently; Detroit Pistons, vpres basketball opers, 1992-95; Billy McKinney Enterprises Inc, pres; Seattle Sonics & Storm, vpres basketball opers, exec vpres, 1995-2004; Minn Timberwolves, broadcast analyst, 2004-08; gen mgr; Milwaukee Bucks, dir scouting, 2008-; City Zion, comnr, 2015-. **Orgs:** Harlem Globetrotters; Wash Boys & Girls Club; Big Bros & Big Sisters; Jr Achievement; dir, scouting Milwaukee Bucks; Seattle-King County Sports & Events Coun; Zion Benton Twp High Sch, 2014-. **Honors/Awds:** Northwestern Hall of Fame; Hall of Fame, Ill Basketball Coaches. **Home Addr:** , MN, **Home Phone:** (612)280-3165. **Business Addr:** Radio Analyst, Minnesota Timberwolves, 600 1st Ave N, Minneapolis, MN 55403, **Business Phone:** (612)673-1600.

### MCKINNEY, DR. CYNTHIA ANN

**Personal:** Born Mar 17, 1955, Atlanta, GA; daughter of Leola and Billy; children: Coy Grandison Jr. **Educ:** Univ Southern Calif, BA, int rels, 1978; Tufts Univ, Fletcher Sch Law & Diplomacy, MA, law & diplomacy, PhD, cand, 1993. **Career:** Spelman Col, diplomatic fel, 1984; Clark Atlanta Univ, instr polit sci; Agnes State Col, educr; State Ga, House Reps, rep, 1988-92; US House Reps, congresswoman, 1992-2003, 2005-07; One Hundred Third & to four succeeding Congresses, dem 1993-2003; One Hundred Ninth Cong, dem, 2005-07; Green Party presidential cand, US, 2008. **Orgs:** Bd mem, Metro Atlanta, HIV Health Serv Planning Coun; Nat Coun Negro Women; Nat Asn Advan Colored People; Sierra Club; Agr Comt; Cong Black Caucus; Women's Caucus; Progressive Caucus; secy, 103rd Cong Freshman Class; Intl Rels Comt. **Special Achievements:** First African American woman to represent Georgia in the House of Representatives. **Business Addr:** DC.

### MCKINNEY, GENE C.

Military leader. **Personal:** Born Nov 3, 1950, Monticello, FL; married Wilhemina Hall; children: Zuberi. **Educ:** El Paso Community Col, assoc sci degree gen mg; Park Col, BS, mgt human resources. **Career:** Sergeant major (retired); AUS Europe, infantryman, 2d Battalion, 503d Inf, 173d Airborne Brigade, Vietnam, 1969-70, Rigger, 612th Qm Battalion, Ft. Bragg, Nc, 1970-71, Scout Team Leader, 1st Battalion 58th Inf, 197th Inf Brigade, Ft. Benning, Ga, 1971-73, Squad Leader, Light Armored Vehicle Sect Leader, 3d Squadron, 12th Cavalry, 3d Armored Div, Budingen, Ger, 1973-77, Scout Sect Leader, Commun Sgt, Platoon Sgt 3d Squadron & 4th Squadron, 3d Armored Cavalry Regt, Ft. Bliss, Tex, 1977-83, First Sgt, Fox Troop, 2d Squadron, 2d Armored Cavalry Regt, Bamberg, Ger, 1983-84, First Sgt, Sgt Maj, Air Cavalry Troop & 4th Squadron (Provisional), 3d Armored Cavalry Regt, Ft. Bliss, Tex, 1984-87, Command Sgt Maj, 2d Squadron, 2d Armored Cavalry Regt, Bamberg, Ger, 1988-90, Command Sgt Maj, 1st Brigade, 1st Armored Div, Vilseck, Ger, 1990, Command Sgt Maj, 8th Inf Div, Bad Kreuznach, Ger, 1990-92, Command Sgt Maj, Aus, Europe & 7th Army Training Ctr, Heidelberg, Ger, 1992-95, Sgt Maj Army, 1995-97, Mil Dist Wash, 1997-98; AUS, sergeant major, 1995-97. **Honors/Awds:** Bronze Star Medal with 1 Oak Leaf Cluster; Meritorious Service Medal with 3 Oak Leaf Clusters; Republic of Vietnam Campaign Medal; Vietnam Service Medal; Army Service Ribbon; Overseas Service Ribbon; Combat Infantryman Badge; The Parachutist Badge; Legion of Merit; Army Commendation Medal; Army Achievement Medal; Good Conduct Medal; National Defense Service Medal; Vietnam Gallantry Cross Unit Citation. **Special Achievements:** First African American sergeant major. **Home Addr:** 11881 Coloriver Rd, Manassas, VA 20112.

### MCKINNEY, BISHOP GEORGE DALLAS

Clergy, founder (originator). **Personal:** Born Aug 9, 1932, Jonesboro, AR; married Jean C; children: George, Grant, Gregory, Gordon & Glenn. **Educ:** Ark State AM & N Col, Pine Bluff, BA, 1954; Oberlin Col, MA, 1956; Univ Mich, attended 1958; Calif Grad Sch Theol, PhD, 1974; Geneva Col, DD. **Career:** Chargin Falls Pk Comm Ctr, dir, 1955-56; Toledo State Ment Hosp, protchaplain, 1956-57; Family Ct Toledo, counr, 1957-59; San Diego Co Probation Dept, sr probation officer, 1959-65; St Stephen's Cathedral Church God Christ, pastor, 1962, founder & chief exec officer, sr pastor, currently; Econ Opportunity Comn, asst dir, 1965-71; Community Welfare Coun, consult, 1968-71; pvt pract marriage family & child counr, 1971-; St Stephan's Day Care Ctr, founder; Southeast Coun & Consult Serv, founder; St Stephan's Christian Sch, founder; St Stephen's Retirement Ctr, founder; Am Urban Univ, founder; San Diego Monitor Newspaper, publ, currently; Southern Calif Second Ecclesiastical Jurisdiction, Church God Christ, jurisdictional prelate. **Orgs:** Calif Probation Parole & Correctional Asn; founder & chmn bd dir, St Stephen's Group Home; Sandiego Co Coun Churches; bd trustee, Interdenomi Nat Theol Ctr Atlanta; bd dir, C H Mason Theol Sem, Atlanta; bd dir, Bob Harrison Ministries; bd elder, Morris Cerillo, World Evangelism; Sigma Rho Sigma Social Sci Frat; San Diego Rotary Club; Alpha Kappa Mu Nat Hon Soc; Oper Push; vol chaplain, summer camp BSA; San Diego Ment Health Asn; Nat Asn Advan Colored People; Young Men Christian Asn; San Diego Urban League; bd adv, Black Comun Ctr San Diego State Univ; Calif Ment Health Asn; sr ed, African Am Devotional Bible; gen bd, Church GodChrist Inc, 2001. **Honors/Awds:** JF Kennedy Award; Outstanding Pastor Award, San Diego State Univ Black Stud; Award For Services To Youth, Black Bus & Prof Women San Diego; listed in Contemporary Authors; Social Worker of the Year Award, San Diego County, 1963; Outstanding Man of the Year Award, Int Asn Aerospace Workers Dist 50, 1969; Outstanding contributions to the San Diego Community in Field of Religious Activities, Nat Asn Advan Colored People, 1975; Achievement Award, So CA Church God Christ; honorary DD, Geneva Col, Beaver Falls; Racial Reconciliation Man of the Year Award; "Mr. San Diego.", San Diego Rotary Club, 2001; Racial Reconciliation Man of the Year Award, Nat Asn Evangelicals; Author of eight books and has contributed to many more; Peace Maker Award. **Special Achievements:** African American Devotional Bible, sr editor, 1997; author of numerous books. **Home Addr:** 5848 Arboles St, San Diego, CA 92120-3722. **Business Addr:** Founder, Senior Pastor, St Stephen's Cathedral Church of God in Christ, 5825 Imperial Ave, San Diego, CA 92114, **Business Phone:** (619)262-2671.

### MCKINNEY, REV. JESSE DOYLE

Clergy. **Personal:** Born Oct 9, 1934, Jonesboro, AR; son of George D Sr (deceased) and Osie L (deceased); married Mary Francis Keys; children: Antoinette, Patrick, Bruce, Gloria & Carla. **Educ:** Univ Ariz, BA, 1957; San Diego State Univ, MSW, 1972. **Career:** San Diego State Univ, Grossmont Community Col, teacher & lectr, 1972-74; Southeast Coun & Consult Servs, counr & dir, 1974-76; San Bernardino Co Ment Health Dept, ment health clinician II, 1977-79; Pleasant Pl Group Home, dir, 1979-82; lic clin social worker; St Stephen's Church God Christ, pastor, social serv dir, currently; Samaritan Coun Ctr, founder. **Orgs:** Bd mem, Home Neighborly Serv, 1985-; adv bd, Grad Sch Social Work, 1989-; Nat Asn Social Workers; founder, pastor, St Stephen's Church Samaritan Shelter; psychiat social worker, Ment Health Dept, San Bernardino City; San Diego Co Health Adv Bd; Calif Personnel & Guid Asn; Asn Black Social Workers; bd dir, San Diego Oper PUSH. **Special Achievements:** Author of the popular cookbook Soul to Soul. **Home Addr:** 1883 Myrtlewood Ave, Colton, CA 92324-4837, **Home Phone:** (909)825-6210. **Business Addr:** Pastor & Counselor, Director, St Stephen Church of God in Christ, 12219 W 3rd Ave, San Bernardino, CA 92407, **Business Phone:** (909)881-1693.

### MCKINNEY, LEWIS L., JR.

Basketball player, legislator. **Educ:** St Louis Univ, BA; Univ St Etienne, France, fr. **Career:** Basketball player (retired), legislator; Anheuser-Busch Inc, Indust & Govt Affairs div, vpres & group dir govt strategies; World Conf Mayors Corp Roundtable, chmn; Corp Affairs Group, founder; Ashcroft Group LLC, chief bus develop, currently. **Orgs:** Vice Chmn Bd Commissioners, treas, Metro, 2005; Cong Black Caucus Found; bd Mem, St Louis Univ Sch Arts & Sci Adv Bd; bd mem, Southside Health Ctr; bd mem, Butler St YMCA; bd mem, Cong Black Caucus Corp Adv Coun; Cong Black Caucus Polit Educ & Leadership Inst; La Legis Black Caucus Found; Mo Legis Black Caucus Found; African Am Golf Found Inc; Leadership Mo Alumni Asn, Jefferson City, Mo; Queen Peace Ctr, St Louis; Monsanto Family YMCA, St Louis; bd mem, St Louis Airport Comn; bd mem, Metro Bi-State Comn. **Business Addr:** Chief of Business Development, The Ashcroft Group LLC, Arlington, VA 22203, **Business Phone:** (703)247-5454.

### MCKINNEY, NORMA J.

Banker. **Personal:** Born Dec 30, 1941, Banks, AR; daughter of Jesse Marks and Lorene Fry Bizzell; married Herman; children: Kristal, Kevin & Kent. **Educ:** Northwest Intermediate Banking Sch, attended 1986; Babson Col, Human Resource Sch, attended 1989; Univ Wash Sch Bus Admin Mgt Sch, attended 1990. **Career:** Security Pac Bank, Seattle, Wash, 1968-78, vpres & human resource specialist, 1978-89, vpres & human resource mgr, 1987-89, first vpres & human resource mgr, 1989-. **Orgs:** Bd dir, United Negro Col Fund; bd dir, First AME Headstart Prog; Nat Urban Bankers Assocs; facilitator, Diversity Training, Security Pac Bank; Seattle Human Rights Comn, 1990. **Honors/Awds:** National Urban Bank Award, 1988. **Home Addr:** 1711 36th Ave, Seattle, WA 98122, **Home Phone:** (206)325-6997. **Business Addr:** First Vice President, Manager Human Resources, Security Pacific Bank, Security Pac Bank Bldg T18 4, Seattle, WA 98126, **Business Phone:** (206)585-5088.

### MCKINNEY, RUFUS WILLIAM

Executive. **Personal:** Born Aug 6, 1930, Jonesboro, AR; son of GD Sr; married Glendonia Smith; children: Rufus Jr, Frederick Warren, Ann Marie & Paula Elaine. **Educ:** AM&N Col, AK, BS, 1953; Ind Univ Sch Law, JD, 1956. **Career:** Executive (retired); US Dept Labour, atty, 1956-69; Pac Lighting Corp, from atty to sr atty, 1969-72, asst vpres, spec coun, 1972; nat pub affairs Southern CA Gas Co, from asst vpres to vpres, 1975-92; Wash DC, vpres & spec coun. **Orgs:** Vpres, bd dir, Wash ChapNat Asn Advan Colored People, 1963-69; Nat Urban League; pres, Gas Men's Roundtable, 1975; chmn, Amer Assn Blacks Energy, 1980-82; CA & Bar Asn; Kappa Alpha Psi; Sigma Pi Phi Frat; MD Comn Human Rel, 1996-2003; Epsilon Boule. **Home Addr:** 5832 Tanglewood Dr, Bethesda, MD 20817, **Home Phone:** (301)320-5227.

### MCKINNEY, SAMUEL BERRY

Clergy, banker. **Personal:** Born Dec 28, 1926, Flint, MI; son of Wade Hampton and Ruth Berry; married Louise Jones; children: Lora Ellen & Rhoda Eileen. **Educ:** Morehouse Col, BA, 1949; Colgate-Rochester Div Sch, MDiv, 1952, Doctor Ministry, 1975. **Career:** Clergy (retired); Aenon Bapt Church, stud asst, 1950-52, asst to pastor, 1952-54; Olney St Bapt Church, pastor, 1954-58; Mt Zion Baptist Church, pastor, 1958-98; Liberty Bank, founder. **Orgs:** Life mem, Nat Asn Advan Colored People; Alpha Phi Alpha; Sigma Pi Phi Alpha Omicron Boule; Princehall Mason 33rd deg; Wash State Voc Educ Comn; pres, N Pac Bapt State Conv; pres, Black Am Bapts; pres, Seattle Coun Churchs; bd exec comt mem, Am Bapt Bd Natl Ministries; bd exec com mem, Am Bapt Gen Bd; fedr Seattle OIC; 2nd nat vpres, OIC Am; fdr & bd mem, Liberty Bank of Seattle; former mem bd trustee, Wash Mutual Savings Bank; Meredith Mathews E Madison YMCA, Fred Hutchinson Cancer Res Ctr; Sigma Pi Phi Grad Fraternity; Seattle Rotary. **Special Achievements:** Co Author: "Church Administration in the Black Perspective"; The first black-owned bank in Seattle and was the first black president of the Church Council of Greater Seattle. **Home Addr:** 1916 E Madison St, Seattle, WA 98122-2891, **Home Phone:** (206)568-8334.

### MCKINNEY, VENORA WARE

Library administrator. **Personal:** Born Jun 16, 1937, Meridian, OK; daughter of Odess and Hazel Parrish; married Lafayette; children: Carole Louise & James Christopher. **Educ:** Langston Univ, Langston, OK, BS, 1959; Univ Ill, Urbana, IL, libr sci, 1965; Univ Wis-Milwaukee, Milwaukee, WI, attended 1974; Marquette Univ, Milwaukee, WI, attended 1980, 1982. **Career:** Library administrator (retired); Milwaukee Pub Libr, Milwaukee, Wis, librn, 1963-69; Peoria Pub Schs, Peoria, Ill, librn, 1970-71; Milwaukee Pub Schs, Milwaukee, Wis, librn, 1972-79, br mgr, 1979-83, dep city librn, 1983-97. **Orgs:** Delta Sigma Theta Sorority; Links Inc, NCP; 1990-97; pres, Wis Libr Asn, 1995; co-founder & coordr, High Pt Fund, 1997; secy, Langston Univ Nat Alumni Asn, currently; Am Libr Asn. **Home Addr:** 1717 W Green Tree Rd Suite 207, Glendalee, WI 53209-2960, **Home Phone:** (414)352-7259.

### MCKINNEY, WADE HAMPTON, III

Administrator. **Personal:** Born Sep 6, 1925, Flint, MI; married Sylvia Lawrence; children: Wade Hampton IV. **Educ:** Western Res Univ, BA, 1948. **Career:** Administrator (retired); Cleveland Press, copy ed & reporter, 1949-53; Urban League, Ft Wayne, indust rels secy, 1953-56; Denver, indust rels secy, 1956-59; Milwaukee, indust rels dir, 1959-61; Chicago, youth guid proj dir, 1961-63, employ & guid dir, 1963-68, prog dir, 1968-71; Nat Urban League Skills Bank, midwest rep, 1963-66; Econ Develop Corp, vpres, 1965-68; Northwestern Univ Bus Sch, Mgt Assistance Class, dir, 1971-72; US Postal Serv Hq, Washington, DC, staff, 1972-92. **Home Addr:** 11215 Oak Leaf Dr Apt 1919, Silver Spring, MD 20901-1383, **Home Phone:** (301)593-8345.

### MCKINNEY-JOHNSON, ELOISE

Writer, lecturer. **Personal:** Born Dec 7, 1926, Greensboro, NC; children: Myron H Johnson Jr. **Educ:** Spelman Col, AB, 1947; Boston Univ, Col Lib Arts, AM, 1948; Univ Wis, 1951; Univ Colo, 1953; Univ Calif, 1967, 1970; San Francisco State Univ, 1976, 1998; Stanford Univ, cert publ course, 1986. **Career:** Winston Salem St Col, instr, 1948-52; Morehouse Col, instr, asst prof, 1953-61; NC Agr Tech St Univ, assoc prof, 1961-65; SF Unified Sch Dist, eng reader, 1965-67; San Fran Comm Col, teacher, 1966-71; N Peralta Col, instr, chairperson, 1971-73; Laney Col, Oakland, CA, instr eng, 1973-89; Praisesinger, ed, currently; freelance writer & lectr, currently. **Orgs:** San Francisco Chap, Un Asn; bd dir, San Francisco Acad World Studies; Nat Asn Advan Colored People; essay contest judge, San Francisco Chap Eng-Speaking Union; Asn Study Afro-Am Life & Hist; Col Lang Asn; Am Asn Univ Women; Friends Johnson C Smith Univ; Spelman Col Nat Alumnae Asn; Sanderson Trustee bd, San Francisco African-Am Hist & Cult Soc; San Francisco Bay Area Chap, Asn Study Class African Civilizations; adv bd, Langston Hughes Soc; AAAS; adv bd, Charlotte Hawkins Brown Mem State Hist Site; Alpha Kappa Alpha Sorority; Junos & Junos W; ed, Praise singer, San Francisco African Am Hist & Cult Soc, 1998-2000. **Home Addr:** 1280 Ellis St Suite 10, San Francisco, CA 94109, **Home Phone:** (415)346-9296.

### MCKINNEY-WHETSTONE, DIANE

Educator, writer. **Personal:** Born Aug 14, 1953, Philadelphia, PA; daughter of Paul McKinney and Bessie; married Gregory; children: Taiwo & Kehinde. **Educ:** Univ Pa, BA, eng, 1975. **Career:** USDA Forest Serv, pub affairs officer; writer, currently; Univ Pa, writing instr, currently; Novel: Tumbling, 1996; Tempest Rising, 1998; Blues Dancing, 1999; Leaving Cecil Street, 2004; Trading Dreams at Midnight, 2008; Lazaretto, 2016. **Business Addr:** Faculty, University of Pennsylvania, Fisher-Bennett Hall Rm 127 3340 Walnut St, Philadelphia, PA 19104-6273, **Business Phone:** (215)898-7341.

### MCKINNON, DARLENE LORRAINE

Government official. **Personal:** Born Jul 28, 1943, Baltimore, MD; daughter of Percy Otto McClaine Jr and Ruth Estelle Thurston McClaine. **Educ:** Morgan State Univ; Univ Redlands, BA, bus mgt, 1985. **Career:** Rouse Co, new projs, spec asst to Develop dir, 1974-79; Baltimore Coun Equal Bus Opportunity, Procurement Servs, dir, 1977-79; US Small Bus Admin, asst dir bus develop, dist dir develop, dir, 1979, Score Prog, women's rep, 1983-92, dep dist dir, San Francisco Dist Off, 1992-, actg dir, currently; TheaterGoers Int, owner; San Diego State Univ, instr, bus courses. **Orgs:** Bd mem, YWCA, 1990; Scripps Hosp Women's Health Source, 1990-; adv bd, San Diego Community Col Dist, 1992-; adv bd, San Diego Housing Comn, 1992-; co-founder, San Diego Chap Nat Asn Women Bus Owners, 1990; bd mem, Northern Calif Supplier Develop Coun; Pres's Bd C's Hosp Oakland. **Honors/Awds:** Women's Bus Representative Year, 1988; Wonder Woman in Bus, Women's Times, 1990; Regional & District Employee Year, Small Bus Admin, 1991, 1986; Soroptomist Inter Nat, Woman Distinction, 1992; Woman of Achievement Award; Fifty Most Influential Women in Silicon Valley, 2003. **Special Achievements:** One San Diego 100 Bus & Community Leaders, San Diego Bus Jour, 1992. **Home Addr:** 201 Harrison Suite 919, San Francisco, CA 94105, **Home Phone:** (415)546-0460. **Business Addr:** Deputy District Director, US Small Business Administration, 455 Mkt St 6th Fl, San Francisco, CA 94105-2420, **Business Phone:** (415)744-8475.

### MCKINNON, DR. ISAIAH

Police chief, educator, public speaker. **Personal:** Born Jun 21, 1943, Montgomery, AL; son of Cota and Lula; married Patrice; children: Jeffrey & Jason. **Educ:** Mercy Col Detroit, BA, hist & law enforcement, 1975; Univ Detroit, MA, criminal justice, 1978; Mich State Univ, PhD, admin higher educ, 1981; Fed Bur Invest Nat Acad, police mgt & procedures, 1987. **Career:** Detroit Police Dept, 1965-71, sgt, 1971-74, lt, 1974-77, inspector, 1977-84; Mercy Col Detroit, asst prof, 1978-86; Univ Detroit, dir pub safety, 1984-89; Univ Detroit, adj prof, 1984; Wayne State Univ, adj prof, 1985-86; Wayne County Community Col, adj prof, 1988; Renaissance Ctr, dir security, 1989-93; Detroit Police Dept, chief police, 1994-98; Univ Detroit Mercy, assoc prof, 1998-; speaker; WDIV-TV Detroit, safety consult; Author: Police and the Nurse, 1984, Police and Child Abuse, 1992; City Detroit, dep mayor. **Orgs:** Mgt Adv Bd; FBI Nat Acad Grads Orgn; Int Asn Chiefs Police; Am Soc Indust Security; pres, Citizens Crime Watch; Detroit Police Officers Asn; Lt & Sergeants Asn; Mich Trial Lawyers Asn; dom violence, Ala State Univ; dom violence, Nat Orgn Black Law Enforcement Officers; trustee, Grosse Pt Acad; bd dir, Ronald McDonald House; bd dir, Cs Ctr Wayne County; bd dir, Univ Detroit, 1974; bd dir, Wayne County Community Col, 1975; Fed Bur Invest Nat Acad; Youth develop comt Detroit Urban League; Dads Club Univ Detroit Jesuit High Sch; bd mem, Cath Charities Southeast Mich. **Business Addr:** Associate Professor, University of Detroit Mercy, 4001 W McNichols Rd Rm 205, Detroit, MI 48219-0900, **Business Phone:** (313)578-0451.

### MCKINNON, PATRICE BAUER

Government official. **Personal:** Born Jan 1, 1948?; married Isaiah; children: Jeffrey & Jason. **Career:** Wayne County GIS, dir budget. **Home Addr:** 1324 Nicolet Pl, Detroit, MI 48207-2838, **Home Phone:** (313)259-0809.

### MCKINNON, RONALD

Football coach, football player. **Personal:** Born Sep 20, 1973, Ft. Rucker, AL; married LaShana White; children: Guiliana, Raven, Rya & Rocky. **Educ:** Univ N Ala, BA, gen studies, 1995. **Career:** Football player (retired), coach; National Football League, linebacker; Univ N Ala, tackler; New Orleans Saints, linebacker, 1994-96, 2005; Ariz Cardinals, linebacker, mid linebacker, right linebacker, 1996-2004; Southern Intercollegiate Athletic Conf, staff; Miles Col, Golden Bears, linebackers coach, currently. **Honors/Awds:** Harlon Hill Trophy,

1995; State Professional Athlete of the Year, Ala Sports Writers Asn, 1998; College Football Hall of Fame, 2008; Alabama Sports Hall of Fame, 2010; Hall of Fame, Gulf S Conf, 2014. **Home Addr:** 1063 Grand Oaks Dr, Bessemer, AL 35022-7237, **Home Phone:** (205)426-2693. **Business Addr:** Linebackers Coach, Golden Bears, 5500 Myron Massey Blvd, Fairfield, CT 35064, **Business Phone:** (205)929-1615.

### MCKINZIE, BARBARA ANNE

Auditor, association executive, certified public accountant. **Personal:** Born Jan 2, 1954, Ada, OK; daughter of Leonard T and Johnnie M Moses Watson. **Educ:** E Cent OK Univ, BS, 1976; Northwestern Univ, MBA, 1997; Stillman Col, LHD. **Career:** Touche Ross & Co, supvr & health care coordr, 1976-83; DeLoitte Haskins & Sells, mgr, 1983-85; Coopers & Lybrand, mgr, 1987-94; Whitman Corp, Internal Audit & dir, 1994-96; Ill Toll Authority, chief internal audit, 1996; Hollywood Casino, chief financial officer, 2000-02; Emerging Bus Solutions LLC, shareholder, 2000-12; Cook Co Forest Preserve, chief financial officer, 2002-05; Alpha Kappa Alpha Sorority Inc, int pres, 2006-; MSL LLC, managing partner, 2010-; BMC Assocs, chief exec officer; Chicagos Neighborhood Housing Serv, dep dir finance & admin; Chicago Housing Authority, comptroller; BMC Consult, pres, currently. **Orgs:** Am Inst Cert Pub Accts, 1978; Nat Asn Black Accountants, 1980, pres, 1990-92; minority recruitment subcomm, IL Soc CPA's, 1983; exec dir, Alpha Kappa Alpha Sorority Inc, 1985-87, pres, 2006-10; Am Womens Soc CPAs, 1986; pres, Educ Advan Found, 1998-2006; chmn & bd dir, Alpha Kappa Alpha Inc, 1998-2010; treas, bd dir, Africare, 2005-14; nat adv bd, JP Morgan Chase, 2006-08; chmn, coun presidents, Nat Pan Hellenic Coun, 2007-10; bd dir, United Negro Col Fund, 2007-11. **Honors/Awds:** Outstanding Alumnae, E Cent Okla Univ, 1976; Valuable Contribution Award, Okla City, 1983; Outstanding Young Woman of America, 1980 & 1985; hon DHL, Stillman Col, 2007; Keys & Proclamations from over 50 cities; Stalwart Award, New York's Law & Policy Group; Carey B. Preston Leadership Award, Alpha Kappa Alpha Sorority; Outstanding Service Award, Ill CPA Soc; "2001 Woman of the Year" Am Biog Inst; Public & International Service Award, Onyx Mag; "Top 25 Outstanding Bus Women of 2002", New York Network Jour; Outstanding Graduate Award. **Home Addr:** 301 Wysteria Dr, Olympia Fields, IL 60461-1229, **Home Phone:** (708)679-1048. **Business Addr:** International President, Alpha Kappa Alpha Sorority Inc, 5656 S Stony Island Ave, Chicago, IL 60637, **Business Phone:** (773)684-1282.

### MCKISSACK, CHERYL MAYBERRY

Business owner, educator. **Personal:** Born Jun 24, 1955, Seattle, WA; daughter of Donald Mayberry and Thelma; married Eric. **Educ:** Seattle Univ, BS, polit sci, 1976; Northwestern Univ, Kellogg Sch Mgt, MBA, 1989. **Career:** IBM Corp, sales & mkt exec, area br mgr; 3Com, Network Systs Div, vpres, founding mem; Open Port Technol, sr vpres & gen mgr; Nia Enterprises LLC, founder, pres & chief exec officer, 2000-; Kellogg Sch Mgt, adj asst prof entrepreneurship, 2005-; Johnson Publ Co, chief operating officer, 2013-14. **Orgs:** Info Technol Resource Ctr; bd mem, LINK Unlimited, Chicago, IL; bd dir, PrivateBanCorp; dir, Deluxe Corp; bd mem, Univ Chicago Med Ctr; bd mem, Gaylord & Dorothy Donnelley Found; bd mem, Chicago Pub Libr Found; bd mem, Shedd Aquarium; adv mem, Corp Bd Diversity Coun; Outstanding dir Adv Bd; Econ Club Chicago. **Special Achievements:** Co-editor, Nia Guide Black Women: Balancing Work & Life, Nia Guide Black Women: Achieving Career Success Your Terms. **Business Addr:** Chair & Chief Executive Officer, Founder, Nia Enterprises LLC, 23 W Hubbard Suite 200, Chicago, IL 60610, **Business Phone:** (312)222-0943.

### MCKISSACK, LEATRICE BUCHANAN

Executive, executive director. **Personal:** Born Jul 27, 1930, Keytesville, MO; daughter of Archie Buchanan and Catherine Brummell; married William DeBerry; children: Andrea McKissack Krupski, Cheryl & Deryl. **Educ:** Fisk Univ, BS, math, 1951; Tenn State Univ, MS, psychol, 1957. **Career:** Executive (retired); Metrop Bd educ, teacher, 1952-69; McKissack & McKissack, chief exec officer, 1979-83. **Orgs:** Nashville Symphony Guild, 1975; Nashville Chamber Com, 1983-; United Way, 1983; comnr, Metro Planning Comn, 1989-95; Fed Res Bank Bd, 1990-95; adv bd mem, State Tenn Employ Sec, 1991-; Cheekwood Fine Arts ctr, 1991-; YMCA adv bd, 1994-; Nat Conf Christians & Jews, 1995-; Tenn Bd Econ Growth, gov's appointee, 1995-; bd trustee, Fisk Univ, 1995-; bd gov, 1995-; Nashville Symphony Bd, 1997-. **Honors/Awds:** Nat Female Entrepreneur, Dept Comm, PRS Bush, 1990; Business Woman of the Year, State Tenn, 1990, Women Owned Business of the Year, 1990; Distinguished Alumni Award, NAFEO, 1991; Business Award, Howard Univ, 1993; Human Relations Award, Nashville chap Nat Conf Christians & Jews, 1996. **Home Addr:** 6666 Brookmont Terr Suite 610, Nashville, TN 37205-4625, **Home Phone:** (615)353-0482.

### MCKISSACK, PATRICIA CARWELL (L'ANN CARWELL)

Writer. **Personal:** Born Aug 9, 1944, Smyrna, TN; daughter of Robert and Erma Carwell; married Fredrick L Sr; children: Fredrick L II, Robert & John. **Educ:** Tenn State Univ, BS, eng, 1964; Webster Univ, MA, early childhood lit & media programming, 1975. **Career:** Inst C's Lit, 1884-; educ consult, currently; Nipher Jr High Sch, teacher, 1969-75; Concordia Publ Co, ed, 1975-81; Forest Park Col, instr, 1977-84; Univ Mo, instr, Eng, 1979-84; Lindenwood Col, instr, Eng, 1977-80; All-Writing Servs, co-owner, 1978-; Auth: A Long Hard Journey: The Story of the Pullman Porter; Sojourner Truth: Ain't I a Woman?; A Long Hard Journey: The Story of the Pullman Porter; Black Diamond; Black Hands, White Sails; Christmas in the Big House, Christmas in the Quarters; The Diary of Clotee, a Slave Girl, Color Me Dark: The Diary of Nellie Lee Love, The Great Migration North, Chicago, Illinois, 1919; Look to the Hills: The Diary of Lozette Moreau, a French Slave Girl; Days of Jubilee: The End of Slavery in the United States; Dear America: Look to the Hills; The Honest-to-Goodness Truth; Tippy Lemmey; To Establish Justice: Citizenship & the Constitution; Where Crocodiles Have Wings; Loved Best; Abby Takes a Stand; Precious & the Boo Hag; Amistad: Station Stop 3; Away West; A Song for Harlem: 1928. books: Paul Laurence Dunbar: A Poet to Remember, 1984; Aztec Indians, 1985; Messy Bessey, 1987; Flossie and the Fox, 1986; Run Away Home, 1997; novel: Royal Diaries series: Nzingha: Warrior Queen of Matamba; Color Me Dark: The Diary of Nellie Lee Love, the Great Migration North, 2000; Carter G Woodson: The Father of Black History, 2002; Satchel Paige: The Best Arm in Baseball, 2002; Sojourner Truth: A Voice for Freedom, 2002; Zora Neale Hurston: Writer and Storyteller, 2002; A Friendship for Today, 2006. **Orgs:** Ark Sorority; AME Church Olive Chapel; MO Arts & Educ Coun; bd mem Nat C's Bk & Literacy Alliance. **Honors/Awds:** Hon doctorate; Univ Mo, C S Lewis Silver Medals 2, 1985; A Long Hard Journey--The Story of Pullman Porter won the Coretta Scott King Award, Jane Addams Peace Award; Ain't I A Woman won the Coretta Scott King Honor book, an ALA Notable title, a NCSS Notable title & winner of the Boston Globe--Horn Book Award for Nonfiction; NAACP, Image Award, for work in children's literature, 1994; Newberry Honor, ALA, for The Dirty Thirty: Southern Tales of the Supernatural, 1994; Regina Medal, Catholic Library Assn, 1998; NAACP Image Award, for Let My People Go: Old Testament Bible Stories; numerous others; Orbis Pictus Award. **Home Addr:** 14629 Timberlake Manor Ct, PO Box 967, Chesterfield, MO 63017, **Home Phone:** (636)519-0726. **Business Addr:** Co-Owner, All-Writing Services, 5900 Pershing Ave, Saint Louis, MO 63112, **Business Phone:** (314)725-6218.

### MCKISSACK, PERRI ALETTE

Executive, singer, social worker. **Personal:** Born Aug 29, 1964, Oakland, CA; married Antonio Reid, Jan 1, 1989?, (divorced 1996); children: Aaron; married Otis Nixon, Jan 1, 2000, (divorced 2004); married George Smith, Nov 29, 1982; children: Ashley. **Career:** Social worker, singer, entertainment industry (retired); Albums: Pebbles, 1987; Always, 1990; Straight from the Heart, 1995; Greatest Hits, 2000. Savvy Records, pres, 1993-97; Women of God Changing Lives Through Christ, founder & owner, 1997-; R&B Singer & Savvy, founder. **Business Addr:** Founder, Women of God Changing Lives Through Christ, PO Box 93523, Atlanta, GA 30377-0523, **Business Phone:** (404)355-9163.

### MCKISSICK, FLOYD B., JR.

Lawyer. **Personal:** Born Nov 21, 1952, Durham, NC; son of Floyd B Sr and Evelyn Williams; married Cynthia Heath; children: Alicia Michelle, Floyd B III & Graison Heath. **Educ:** Clark Univ, BA, 1974; Univ NC Chapel Hill, Sch City & Regional Planning, MRP, 1975; Harvard Univ, Kennedy Sch Gov, MPA, 1979; Duke Univ Sch Law, JD, 1983. **Career:** Floyd B McKissick Enterprises, asst planner, 1972-74; Soul City Com, dir planning, 1974-79; Peat, Marwick & Mitchell, mgt consult, 1980-81; Dickstein, Shapiro & Morin, atty, 1984-87; Faison & Brown, atty, 1987-88; Spaulding & Williams, atty, 1988-89; McKissick & McKissick, atty, 1989-; NC Gen Assembly, NC Senate, sen, 2007-, dep minority leader, 2011-; Durham County Dem Party, chmn. **Orgs:** Durham City Coun, 1994-; pres, NC Ctr Study Black Hist; past chmn, Land Loss Prev Proj; Durham City-Coun Planning Comn; St Joseph's Hist Soc; Mus Life & Sci; Durham City Adjustments; Rural Advan Found Int; chmn, NC Legis Black Caucus. **Special Achievements:** Co-author of Guidebook on Attracting Foreign Investment to the US, 1981; Author of books like: When an Owner can Terminate a Contract Due to Delay, 1984; Mighty Warrior, Floyd B McKissick, Sr, 1995. **Home Addr:** 6903 Herndon Rd, Durham, NC 27713-9726, **Home Phone:** (919)544-1994. **Business Addr:** Senator, North Carolina General Assembly, 628 Legis Off Bldg, Raleigh, NC 27603-5925, **Business Phone:** (919)733-4599.

### MCKNIGHT, FR. ALBERT J. See Obituaries Section.

### MCKNIGHT, BRIAN

Singer, songwriter, musician. **Personal:** Born Jun 5, 1969, Buffalo, NY; children: Brian Jr, Clyde, Niko & Briana. **Career:** Albums: Brian McKnight, 1991; I Remember You, 1995; Anytime, 1997; Bethlehem, 1998; Back at One, 1999; Superhero, 2001; From There to Here: 1989-2002, 2002; U-Turn, 2003; Gemini, 2005; Ten, 2006; Evolution of a Man, 2009; Just Me, 2011; More Than Words, 2013. Songs: "The Way Love Goes", 1992; "Goodbye My Love", 1992; "One Last Cry", 1993; "After the Love", 1993; "Love Is", 1993; "Crazy Love", 1995; "On the Down Low", 1995; "Still in Love", 1995; "You Should Be Mine (Don't Waste Your Time)", 1997; "Anytime", 1998; "Hold Me", 1998; "The Only One for Me", 1998; "Back at One", 1999; "6, 8, 12", 2000; "Stay or Let It Go", 2000; "Win", 2000; "Love of My Life", 2001; "Still", 2001; "What's It Gonna Be", 2002; "All Night Long (With Nelly)", 2003; "Shoulda, Woulda, Coulda", 2003; "What We Do Here", 2005; "Everytime You Go Away", 2005; "Find Myself In You", 2006; "Used To Be My Girl", 2006; "I ll be Home for Christmas", 2008; Brian McKnight Live from Fifteen", 2009; TV series: "Sister, Sister", 1998-99; "Platinum", 2003; "American Dreams", 2005; "The Mumblesteens", 2012; "A Country Christmas Story", 2013; "Minute Motivations", 2013; "CoffeeHouse", 2014. Films: The Beat, 2003; Leverage, 2005; Black Dynamite, 2009; Note to Self, 2012. Where house Music, singer, currently. **Honors/Awds:** Soul Train Award, Best R&B/Soul Male Album, 1999; American Music Award, Favorite Soul/R&B Male Artist, 2000; Image Award, Nat Asn Advan Colored People, 2000; Blockbuster Awards; BillBoard Songwriter of the Year. **Special Achievements:** A few Grammy nominations; worked with Sean "P Diddy" Combs, Justin Timberlake of NSync, Mary J Blige, Boyz II Men & Take 6. **Business Addr:** Singer, Wherehouse Music, 100 N La Cienega, Los Angeles, CA 90048.

### MCKNIGHT, CLAUDE V., III

Singer. **Personal:** Born Oct 2, 1962, Brooklyn, NY; son of Claude Jr and Elaine; children: Jessica. **Educ:** Oakwood Col. **Career:** The Gentlemen's Estate Quartet, founder & mem, 1985-87; Take 6, founder & mem, 1987-; Do the Right Thing, music, lyrics, performer, 1989; Albums: Take 6, 1988; So Much 2 Say, 1990; He Is Christmas, 1991; Join the Band, 1994; Brothers, 1996; So Cool, 1996; The Greatest Hits, 1999; We Wish You a Merry Christmas, 1999; Tonight: Live, 2000; Live, 2000; Beautiful World, 2002; Feels Good, 2006; The Standard, 2008; The Most Wonderful Time of the Year, 2009; Smooth Jazz, 2011; ICM, singer, currently. **Business Addr:** Singer, International Creative Management, 825 Eighth Ave, New York, NY 10019, **Business Phone:** (212)556-5600.

### MCKNIGHT, JAMES EDWARD

Executive, football player, football coach. **Personal:** Born Jun 17, 1972, Orlando, FL; married Mikki; children: David. **Educ:** Liberty Univ, criminal justice. **Career:** Football player (retired), coach; Seattle Seahawks, wide receiver, 1994-98; Dallas Cowboys, wide receiver, 1999-2000; Miami Dolphins, wide receiver, 2001-03; New York Giants, 2004; financial serv advisor; Cypress Bay High Sch, wide receiver & track team coach, currently. **Home Addr:** 16705 Berkshire Ct, Southwest Ranches, FL 33331-1331, **Home Phone:** (954)434-7368. **Business Addr:** Wide Receivers & Track Team Coach, Cypress Bay High School, 18600 Vista Pk Blvd, Weston, FL 33332, **Business Phone:** (754)323-0350.

### MCKNIGHT, REGINALD

Educator, writer. **Personal:** Born Feb 26, 1956, Furstenfeldbruck; son of Frank and Pearl M Anderson; married Julie Scott Buchness; children: Eve; married Michele Davis; children: Rachae. **Educ:** Pikes Peak Community Col, Colo Springs, CO, AA, gen studies, 1978; Colo Col, Colo Springs, CO, BA, African studies, 1981; Am Cult Ctr Dakar, Senegal, Eng, 1982; Univ Denver, Denver, CO, MA, creative writing, 1987. **Career:** USMC, corporal E-4, 1973-76; Univ Pittsburgh, Pittsburgh, Pa, asst prof, Eng, 1988-91; Carnegie Mellon Univ, Pittsburgh, Pa, assoc prof, Eng, 1991; Univ Md, prof, Eng creative writing prog, 1994-2000; Univ Mich, prof, Eng, 2000-02; Univ Ga, Hamilton Holmes prof Eng, 2002-; Novel: Moustapha's Eclipse, 1998; I Get on the Bus, 1990; The Kind of Light That Shines on Tex, 1992; African Am Wisdom, 1994; Wisdom of the African World, 1996; White Boys & Other Stories, 1998; He Sleeps, 2001. **Orgs:** Thomas J Watson Found Fel, 1981; Phi Beta Kappa, 1981; PEN Am, 1989-; African Lit Asn, 1989-. **Business Addr:** Hamilton Holmes Professor, University of Georgia, 111 Pk Hall, Athens, GA 30602-6205, **Business Phone:** (706)542-2233.

### MCLAREN, DOUGLAS EARL

Management consultant, lawyer. **Personal:** Born Nov 3, 1948, Wilmington, NC; son of Huldah E and Austen E; married Rosemarie P Pagon; children: Damion Earl & Kaili Elizabeth. **Educ:** Univ W Indies, BSc, civil engineering, 1970; McGill Univ, MBA, 1974; Harvard Law Sch, JD, 1984. **Career:** Hue Lyew Chin, construct engr, 1970-72; Peat Marwick Mitchell, mgt consult, 1974-76; Jamaica Nat Investment Co, proj officer, 1976-78; Exxon Int Co, financial & planning analyst, 1979-84; ICF Kaiser Engrs, proj mgr, 1984; Law Off Douglas Earl McLaren, prin, 1985-; TRW, sr pub policy analyst; KPMG, mgt consult; Bechtel SAIC Co LLC, sr govt affairs rep, legal educ coordr, currently. **Orgs:** Admitted to NY & DC Bars, 1985; Am Bar Asn, 1985; Panel Com Arbitrators Am Arbit Asn; chair, coordr, DC Bar Int Law Sect; bd dir, Wash Foreign Law Soc; Nat Asn Securities Dealers; Int Centre Dispute Resolution; com mediator, Am Arbit Asn; London Ct Int Arbit; chair, Steering Comt DC Bar Int Law Sect; bd gov, Wash Foreign Law Socs; Financial Indust Regulatory Authority; founding co-chair int mediation comt, ABA Sect Int Law; Am Corp Coun Asn. **Special Achievements:** Publisher & Co-author of numerous articles. **Business Addr:** Principal, Law Office of Douglas Earl McLaren, 1825 Tulip St Nw, Washington, DC 20012, **Business Phone:** (202)291-5383.

### MCLAUGHLIN, DR. ANDREE NICOLA

Poet, educator. **Personal:** Born Feb 12, 1948, White Plains, NY; daughter of Willie Mae Newman and Joseph Lee. **Educ:** Cornell Univ, BS, 1970; Univ Mass Amherst, MEd, 1971, EdD, 1974. **Career:** Medgar Evers Col, City Univ NY, asst prof & proj dir, 1974-77, chairperson, 1977-79, dean admin & assoc prof, 1979-82, planning coord Women's Studies Res & Devel, 1984-89, prof lang, lit & philos prof interdisciplinary studies, 1992-, Off Int Women's Affairs, dir, 1996-, Dr Betty Shabazz Distinguished Chair Social Justice, 2001-, chairperson, currently; Nat Endowment Humanities fel, 1976, 1979, 1984, 1989, 1993; Univ London Inst Educ, distinguished vis scholar, 1986; Hamilton Col, Jane Watson Irwin, vis prof Women's Studies, 1989-91. **Orgs:** Bd mem, Where We At, Black Women Artists, 1979-87; Nat Womens Studies Asn, 1980-84; Am Asn Univ Profs, 1982-; founding int coord, Int Resource Network Women African Descent, 1982-85, founding mem, Sisterhood Support Sisters SAfrica 1984-; adv bd mem, Sisterhood Black Single Mothers, 1984-86; founding int coord, Cross-Cult Black Womens Studies Inst, 1987-; chair, Ed Bd, Network: Pan African Women's Forum, 1987-91; Policy & Publ Comn, Feminist Press, City Univ NY, 1988-99; Am Coun Educ. **Home Addr:** PO Box 2010, White Plains, NY 10602. **Business Addr:** Chairperson, Professor, Medgar Evers College, 1650 Bedford Ave, Brooklyn, NY 11225, **Business Phone:** (718)270-5051.

### MCLAUGHLIN, BENJAMIN WAYNE

Manager, executive. **Personal:** Born Feb 24, 1947, Danville, VA; son of Lucy S and Daniel S; married Gwen Stafford; children: LaShandra & Sonya. **Educ:** Johnson C Smith Univ, Charlotte NC, BA, econ, 1969. **Career:** Lockheed Martin, buyer, 1969-70, maintenance engineering tech asst, 1970-76, ORGDP, affirmative action coordr, 1975-79, wage & salary assoc, 1979, employ dept supvr, 1979-81, barrier mfg div supt, 1981-82, maintenance engrg dept supt, 1982-83, wage & salary dept head, 1983-84, energy syst dir minority prog develop, 1984-86, personnel mgr; Portsmouth OH gaseous diffusion plant, 1986-95, admin support mgr, 1995-. **Orgs:** Mem pres circle, United Way Ross County; comnr, Chillicothe, Ohio, Civil Serv Comn; Omega Psi Phi; Ionic Lodge no 6, F & AM. **Honors/Awds:** Distinguished Service Award, State Tenn, 1980; Martin Marietta Energy Syst Community Service Award, 1985; Omega Man of the Year Award, Zeta Gamma Gamma Chap Omega Psi Phi Frat, 1985; Light From the Hill Award, Knoxville Col, 1985; Jefferson Award for Community Service, 1986. **Home Addr:** 1055 Edgewood Dr, Chillicothe, OH 45601-2155, **Home Phone:** (740)772-1272. **Business Addr:** Member of President, United Way of Ross County, 53 E 2nd St, Chillicothe, OH 45601, **Business Phone:** (740)773-3280.

### MCLAUGHLIN, BRIAN P.

Government official. **Personal:** Born Jan 1, 1974. **Educ:** Duke Univ, BA, pub policy studies, 1995; Mass Inst Technol, MCP, 1997; Am Univ, MA, econs, emphasis banking & finance, 2005. **Career:** Crispus Attucks Community Develop Corp, dir, 1997-2000; Fannie Mae, Am Communities Fund, sr asset mgr; Cyber Corps, co-founder, currently; Md Dept Housing & Community Develop, Div Neighborhood Revitalization, Community Revitalization Subcomt, vice chair, asst secy, 2003-06; Fannie Mae, sr asset mgr, dir, 2000-11; Com Develop Inc, vpres, 2011-14; Lantian Develop, chief exec officer, 2014-. **Orgs:** Rural Md Coun. **Home Addr:** 10602 Lake Arbor Way, Bowie, MD 20721-3135. **Business Addr:** Assistant Secretary, Vice Chair, Maryland Department of Housing & Community Development, 100 Community Pl, Crownsville, MD 21032-2023, **Business Phone:** (410)514-7015.

**MCLAUGHLIN, DR. GEORGE W.** **See Obituaries Section.**

**MCLAUGHLIN, REV. DR. JACQUELYN SNOW.** **See Obituaries Section.**

## MCLAUGHLIN, DR. LAVERNE LANEY

Educator, library administrator. **Personal:** Born Jul 29, 1952, Ft. Valley, GA; daughter of John and Gladys Slappy; married Frederick; children: Frederick Laney. **Educ:** Spelman Col, BA, polit sci, 1974; Altanta Univ, MSLS, libr & info sci, 1975; Ft Valley State Univ, MEd, 1975; Kennedy Western Univ Thousand Oaks, PhD, pub admin, 2003. **Career:** Atlanta Univ, Andrew Mellon fel, 1974-75; Byron Elem Sch, Bryon, Ga, teacher, 1975-76; Ga Southwestern State Univ, Americus, Ga, James EarlCarter Libr, Instr, assoc prof & librn & head tech serv, 1975-98; Albany State Univ, James Pendergrast Memorial Libr, libr dir, assoc prof, 1998-; HBCU Leadership Inst Proj, mentor, currently; Wayne State Univ, proj mentor; HBCU Libr Alliance, mentor. **Orgs:** Pianist, St John Baptist Church, 1968-; Organist Allen Chapel AME Church, 1977-81; bd dir, Am Cancer Soc; Am Libr Asn; vice chair, chair, Ga Libr Asn; Southeastern Libr Asn; Ga Pub TV Adv Bd, 1980-85; Data Base Qual Control Comt Southeastern Libr Network, 1981-87; Sumter Co Chamber Com & Educ Comt, 1989; Martin Luther King Jr State Holiday Comn Ga, 1991-; organist, Bethesda Baptist Church, 1992-; commencement comt, Albany State Univ, 1998-99, acad leadership comt, 1998-2004; DLG Civil Rights Digital Libr steering comt, 1999-2000, vpres acad affairs search comt, 2000-01, aaron brown acad, 2005-06; bd mem, HBCU Libr Allianc; Beta Phi Mu; Phi Delta Kappa; Spelman Col Nat Alumnae Asn; Clark Atlanta Univ Nat Alumni Asn; Alpha Kappa Alpha Sorority Inc; Galileo Steering Comt; Grassroots Re-granting Comt Ga; Ga Dept Natural Resources & Minority Preserv Network; chair, Mass Commun Search Comt; recorder, Curric & New Progs Comt; recorder, Mass Commun Comt; chair, Blue Ribbon Centennial Hist Sub-Comt; Chair, 2002 GIL User Group Conf Planning Comt; bd dirs, Americus-Sumter County Unit; bd dirs, Southwest Civic Chorus; Pres, Americus High Sch PTO; pres, Eastview Elem Sch PTO; Adv Comt Americus City Bd Educ; Boy Scouts Am Coun Rep; Human Rels Coun, Americus City Schs; asst coordr, Tiger Cubs Am; vpres, Sarah Cobb Elem Sch PTO; vpres, Staley Mid Sch PTO; treas, Cherokee Elem Sch. **Honors/Awds:** Cum laude, Spelman Col, 1974; Beta Phi Mu, Atlanta Univ, 1975; Outstanding Young Women America, 1983; Recipient of the Grant for the HBCU Archives I, II, III; Recipient of the Grant: Looking At Jazz: An American Art Form; Title III Grant: Enhancing Library Collections, 2000-05; Title III Grant: Revitalizing Library Collections & Library Technology, 2005-07; Strengthening Library Collections, 2007-12; Building A Digital Infrastructure of Library Resources, 2012-17; Recipient of Service Award for Outstanding Support of Student Organizations; Award of Appreciation for Planning and Hosting, 13th Ann MAP/MRO Conf Univ Syst Ga. **Special Achievements:** ML King State Holiday Commission, HBCU Library Alliance Board, Chair, Regents Committee on Academic Libraries (RACL), Civil Rights Digital Library Steering Committee, IMLS Grant participant for Galileo Knowledge Repository. **Home Addr:** 536 E Jefferson St, Americus, GA 31709-3726, **Home Phone:** (229)924-9456. **Business Addr:** Associate Professor, Director of Library & Archives, Albany State University, 536 E Jefferson St, Albany, GA 31705, **Business Phone:** (229)924-9426.

## MCLAUGHLIN, DR. MEGAN E.

Social worker. **Personal:** children: Afiya McLaughlin-White. **Educ:** Howard Univ, BA, 1966, MSW, 1968; City Univ NY Grad Ctr, Doctoral work Cult Anthrop, 1972; Columbia Univ Sch Social Work, Cert Advan Social Welfare, 1976, PhD, social work, 1981. **Career:** Executive, social worker (retired); Columbia Univ Sch Social Work, lectr, 1975-78; New York Community Trust, prog officer, 1978-83, sr prog officer, 1983-86; Fed Protestant Welfare Agencies Inc, exec dir & chief exec officer, 1986-2003. **Orgs:** Adv coun Columbia Univ Sch Social Work; Caribbean Women's Health Asn; Dept Social Serv Adv Comt, Health Syst Agency; Neighborhood Family Serv Continuing Crisis Implementation, Task Force Human Servs; Agenda C Tomorrow; Black Leadership Comn AIDS; Interagency Task Force Food & Hunger Policy; chmn, Ny Assembly Braintrust C & Families; adv comt, Human Resources Admin; adv comt, New York Dept Aging; New York Partnership; co-chmn, Human Servs Coun; New York Chap, Nat Asn Social Workers; Nat Black Leadership Comn Aids; New York Admin C's Serv Adv Bd; Human Serv Coun NY; adv bd, Bor Manhattan Community Col; Partnership New York; Int Youth Leadership Inst; bd dir, Abyssinian Develop Corp, currently; bd dir, Ny Aids Adv Coun, currently. **Special Achievements:** Authored 8 publications including "West Indian Immigrants, Their Social Network & Ethnic Identification" Distribution Columbia Univ, 1981. **Home Addr:** 404 W 149th St, New York, NY 10031-2801, **Home Phone:** (212)491-9342. **Business Addr:** Council Member, New York State Department of Health, Corning Twr Empire State Plz, Albany, NY 12237.

## MCLAURIN, DANIEL WASHINGTON

Executive, real estate executive. **Personal:** Born Nov 24, 1940, Philadelphia, PA; son of Abraham and Dorothy E Foster; married Delores E White; children: Craig Blair & Brian Keith. **Educ:** LaSalle Col, BS, mkt, 1981. **Career:** Gulf Oil Corp, retail marketer, 1970-73, coordr, 1973-76, dir admin serv, 1976-83; Chevron Gulf Oil Corp, dir security & safety, 1983-85, supv buildings mgt, 1985-; Chevron Real Estate Mgt Co, rep, bldg proj, 1994-. **Orgs:** Am Soc Indust Security; Soc Real Prop Admin; Bldg Owners & Mgr Inst Int. **Home Addr:** 1301 McKinney, Houston, TX 77010, **Home Phone:** (713)530-1892.

## MCLAWHORN, JAMES THOMAS, JR.

Executive, association executive, chief executive officer. **Personal:** Born Apr 27, 1947, Greenville, NC; son of James T Sr; married Barbara Campbell; children: Karla (Eric) Hawkins, James III & Mark. **Educ:** NC Agr & Tech State Univ, BS, polit sci, 1969; Univ NC Chapel Hill, MA, city & regional planning, 1971; Univ Miami, MBA, 1977. **Career:** Model Cities, prog planning coord, 1971-74; City Charlotte, prog mgt coord, 1974-76; First Union Bank, loan develop analyst, 1977-78; Dem Nat Community Cong Black Caucus, admin asst, 1978-79; Columbia Urban League Inc, pres, chief exec officer, chair, 1979-. **Orgs:** City Columbia Community Minority & Small Bus; Seven Thirty Breakfast Club; Govs Vol Awards Selection Comt; Crime Stoppers; Indian Waters Boy Scouts Am Exec Coun; chmn, Govs Primary Health Care Task Force Richland Co; founder, Nat Black Family Summit; MNY Prof Develop Prog; Black Male Workshop, Midland; Sanders Mid Sch Improv Coun; bd visitors, Columbia Col; Richland Co Pvt Indust Coun; CHOICE, Study Community; Alliance Carolina's C; SC Equal Policy Coun; chief planner, King Day at Dome. **Honors/Awds:** Mayor of Columbia, JT McLawhorn Day Honoree, Nov 28, 1989; Governor of South Carolina, Order Palmetto, 1992; Whitney M. Young Jr. Race Relations Award, Nat Urbans League; Inducted, SC Black Hall of Fame; Directors Community Leadership Award, 2010. **Special Achievements:** Publication: The State of Black SC: An Agenda for the Future; Ten for the Future Columbia Record; one of 60 civilian leaders in the nation invited to participate in the Joint Civilian Orientation Conf Sec of Defense 1985; assisted in bringing national attention to the plight of the rural poor and small farmers who were devastated by Hurrican Hugo, 1989. **Home Addr:** 204 Elmont Dr, Columbia, SC 29203-2808, **Home Phone:** (803)754-4569. **Business Addr:** President, Chief Executive Officer, Columbia Urban League Inc, 1400 Barnwell St, Columbia, SC 29250, **Business Phone:** (803)799-8150.

## MCLEAN, DENNIS RAY

Executive. **Personal:** Born Dec 8, 1951, Fuquay, NC; son of Mathew Jr and Minnie Mae; married Hyesuk McLean Ohm; children: Louis, Enoch & Tiffany. **Educ:** Midlands Tech Col, AA, 1978; Benedict Col, BS, 1980. **Career:** SC Youth Serv, family counr, 1975-82; SKM3 Transax Inc, founder & pres, 1982-. **Orgs:** Greater Columbia Chamber Com, 1982-; co-founder & pub rels officer, Greater Columbia Tennis Asn, 1983-86. **Honors/Awds:** Private Pilot Certificate, Midlands Aviation, 1984; Dr King Living the Dream, Prof Black Women Asn, 1986; Academic Small Business Man of the Year, Gen Dynamics, 1989; Top Supplier of the Year, Gen Dynamics, 1992. **Home Addr:** 1800 Broadview Ct, Columbia, SC 29212, **Home Phone:** (803)781-1611. **Business Addr:** President, Founder, SKM3 Transax Inc, 108 F White Oak Lane, Lexington, SC 29072, **Business Phone:** (803)754-1531.

## MCLEAN, DOLLIE CLARICE H.

Executive, executive director. **Personal:** Born New York, NY; daughter of Cleveland Robert and Gladys T Hamilton; married Jackie; children: Rene, Vernone & Melonae. **Educ:** Fashion Inst, fashion design, 1958; Univ Hartford, tv prod & creative writing, 1985. **Career:** Negro Ensemble Co, dancer & actress; Arnold Originals, showroom & design asst; NY Eye & Ear Infirmary, ENO Lab, secy, 1960-71; Wadsworth Antheneum Mus, community liaison; Artists Collective Inc, founder & exec dir, currently. **Home Addr:** 261 Ridgefield St, Hartford, CT 06112-1537, **Home Phone:** (860)247-7308. **Business Addr:** Founding Executive Director, The Artists Collective, 1200 Albany Ave, Hartford, CT 06112, **Business Phone:** (860)527-3205.

## MCLEAN, DR. HELEN VIRGINIA

School administrator, educator. **Personal:** Born Jul 23, 1933, Southern Pines, NC; daughter of Nora Jackson and Mitchell. **Educ:** NC Cent Univ, BA, 1954; Univ Pa, MA, 1956; Univ Fla, EdD, 1974. **Career:** Educator (retired); Wilberforce Univ, assoc prof lang, 1956-58; Gibbs Jr Col, chair person commun dept, 1958-64; St Petersburg Jr Col, chairperson directed studies dept, 1964-75, dir div commun, 1975; Tangley Oaks Educ, fel, 1972-73; Univ Fla, EDDA-E, grad fel, 1972-74. **Orgs:** Am Asn Univ Women; Mod Lang Asn; Col Eng Asn; Fla Eng Asn; Coun Black Am Affairs Southern Region; YWCA; secy exec comt mem, Pinellas Co Dist Ment Health Bd; Nat Asn Advan Colored People; bd, United Negro Col Fund St Petersburg Fla; Greater St Petersburg Coun Human Rel. **Special Achievements:** Published "Reading-A Total Faculty Commitment," "Career Educ and Gen Edn, ""Every Tchr a Reading Tchr," "Teaching Strategies for a Developmental Studies Curriculum"; various other publications. **Home Addr:** 1583 McAuliffe Lane, Palm Harbor, FL 34683-7209, **Home Phone:** (727)736-5143.

## MCLEAN, DR. JOHN ALFRED, JR.

Educator. **Personal:** Born Nov 8, 1926, Chapel Hill, TN; son of John Alfred Sr and Anna Belle Sheffield; married Esther Ann Bush; children: Jeffery, David & Linda. **Educ:** Tenn A&I State Univ, BS, chem, 1948; Univ Ill, MS, 1956, PhD, inorg chem, 1959. **Career:** Educator, professor emeritus (retired); Univ Detroit Mercy, asst prof chem, chmn dept chem & chem engineering, 1983-93, prof chem, 1994, prof emer, 1995; State Bd Pub Community & Jr Col, chmn, 1965-81. **Orgs:** Phi Delta Kappa; Phi Lambda Upsilon; Sigma Xi; bd dir, Am Heart Asn, 1988-; Optical Soc Am; Am Chem Soc. **Home Addr:** 9260 W Outer Dr, Detroit, MI 48219-4060, **Home Phone:** (313)534-4616. **Business Addr:** Professor Emeritus, University of Detroit Mercy, 4001 W McNichols Rd, Detroit, MI 48221-3038, **Business Phone:** (313)993-1245.

## MCLEAN, RENE (RENE PROFIT-MCLEAN)

Educator, musician, composer. **Personal:** Born Dec 16, 1946, New York, NY; son of Jackie and Dollie; married Thandine January; children: Rene Jr, Sharif, Thandine-Naima & Nozipho-Jamila. **Educ:** NY Col Music; Univ Mass. **Career:** EDR, band leader, 1965-; NY Narcotic Control Comm, Melrose Community Ctr, band master, 1970-73; Univ Hartford, Dept African Am Music, artist residence, 1984-85, sr artist teacher, currently, Jackie McLean Inst, prof african-am music, currently; MMABANA Cult Ctr, Safrica, consult, music dept head, 1987-90; Triloka Rec, rec artist, producer, 1988-; New Sch Jazz, New York, vis mem, 1991-92; Univ Capetown, lectr Jazz studies, 1994-98; McLean Entertainment Group, founder & chief exec officer, 1997-; Artists Collective, Hartford, Conn, master artist/dir-in-residence music, currently; Broadcast Music Inc, writer, publ; Harry Fox Agency, publ; Nordisk Copyright, publ. **Orgs:** AFM 802. **Honors/Awds:** Scholar, Outward Bound Mountaineering Sch, 1963; Cultural Medallion, presented by Mayor Karlstad, Sweden, 1977; Survival Black Artist Award, Howard Univ Fine Arts Festival, 1983; Creative Artist Fel Award, Japan-US Friendship Comn, Nat Endowment Arts, 1986-87. **Special Achievements:** Alubum: Watch Out, 1975, In African Eyes, 1993, Generations to Come, 2002. **Home Addr:** 330 W 38th St Rm 210, New York, NY 10018-2999, **Home Phone:** (212)947-4858. **Business Addr:** Professor, Senior Artist Teacher, University of Hartford, 200 Bloomfield Ave, West Hartford, CT 06117-1599, **Business Phone:** (860)768-4454.

## MCLEAN, RHONDA JOY

Law enforcement officer. **Personal:** Born Chicago, IL; married William Craig. **Educ:** Aurora Univ, BA, criminol & social work, 1972; NC A&T State Univ, MS, adult educ & leadership develop, 1979; Yale Law Sch, JD, 1983. **Career:** Fed Trade Comn, asst regional dir; Time Inc, asst gen coun, 1999-2005, assoc gen coun, 2005-. **Orgs:** Greater New York Chap Links, mem; Yale Law Sch Alumni Asn, chair, 2004-06; bd dir, Better Bus Bur Metrop New York.

## MCLEAN, DR. ZARAH GEAN

Physician, pediatrician. **Personal:** Born Aug 28, 1942, Tallulah, LA; married Russell; children: Paul, Crystal & Grant. **Educ:** Fisk Univ, BA, 1964; Howard Univ Col Med, MD, 1968. **Career:** Pediat C's Hosp Wis, internship; Med Col Wis, resident, assoc prof pediat, 1972-86; pvt pract pediatrician, currently. **Orgs:** Pbd dir, Emma Murry Child Care Ctr, 1982-86. **Honors/Awds:** Physician of Yr, Cream City Med Soc, 1989; Outstanding Community Serv, St Mary's Col Women of Color Alliance, 1990. **Home Addr:** 4016 W Good Hope Rd Apt C, Milwaukee, WI 53209-2282, **Home Phone:** (414)352-5114. **Business Addr:** Physician, 5310 W Capitol Dr Suite 218, Milwaukee, WI 53233, **Business Phone:** (414)342-5262.

## MCLEMORE, ANDREW G., SR.

Executive, founder (originator), president (organization). **Personal:** Born Dec 13, 1931, Memphis, TN; son of Benjamine and Belle; married Dorothy Ellison; children: Andrew Jr & Raymond S. **Educ:** WVa State Col, BS, 1953. **Career:** A-MAC Sales & Builders Co, pres, defendants. **Orgs:** Asn Black Gen Contractors. **Home Addr:** 892 W Boston Blvd, Detroit, MI 48202-1408, **Home Phone:** (313)869-4725. **Business Addr:** President, A-MAC Sales & Builders Co, 15780 Schaefer Hwy, Detroit, MI 48227, **Business Phone:** (313)659-9999.

## MCLEMORE, LESLIE BURL

Government official, educator. **Personal:** Born Aug 17, 1940, Walls, MS; son of Christine Williams and Burl; married Betty Mallett; children: Leslie Burl II. **Educ:** Rust Col, BA, social sci & econs, 1964; Atlanta Univ, MA, polit sci, 1965; Univ Mass, Amherst, PhD, govt, 1970. **Career:** Educator (retired); Atlanta Univ, res asst, 1960-65; Freedom Vote campaign, northern regional coordr, 1963; Southern Univ, 1965-66; Univ Mass Amherst, teaching asst, 1966-69; Johns Hopkins Univ, post-doctoral fel, 1970, Dept Polit Sci, prof, 1976-; Miss State Univ, Dept polit sci, vis prof, 1979-80; Harvard Univ, res assoc, 1982-83; Rockefeller Found, resfel, 1982-83, dean grad sch, dir res & admin, 1984-90, actg dir, 1990-; Jackson, Miss, interim mayor, 2009; Miss Freedom Dem Party, vice chmn; Jackson State Univ, prof polit sci; Jackson City Coun, coun pres; Univ Ctr Jackson, actg dir; Hammer Inst, dir, fac, currently. **Orgs:** Am Asn Higher Studies, 1992; pres, Rust Col Nat Alumni Asn; past vpres, S Polit Sci Asn; former pres, Nat Conf Black Polit Scientist; Jackson League Task Force Local Gov; exec comt, Black Miss Coun Higher Educ; chair, Liaison Community NCEA; chair, Task Force Minorities Grad Educ; Pi Sigma Alpha Polit Sci; pres, City Coun Jackson; chair, Miss Humanities Coun; pres, Nat Asn Advan Colored People; vice chair, Bd Fedn State Humanities Coun; pres, Coun Historically Black Grad Sch; Veterans Miss Civil Rights Movement; founding pres, Rust Col's Chap Nat Asn Advan Colored People. **Honors/Awds:** Spotlight Scholars Award, Jackson State Univ, 1980-81; Chancellor's Medal, Univ Mass, Amherst, 1986; Cert Commendation Outstanding Serv, US Secy Energy, 1990; Cert Appreciation, Miss Ctr Technol, 1992; Award Appreciation, Sci & Eng Alliance, 1992; Hon Woodrow Wilson Fel, Rust Col; Travel Grant Awards, Jackson State Univ, 2005. **Special Achievements:** Hundred Black Men of Jackson, 1991; Appointed to the Commission on the Status of Black Americans. **Home Addr:** 746 Windward Rd, Jackson, MS 39206, **Home Phone:** (601)366-4207.

## MCLEMORE, MARK TREMELL

Baseball player, baseball executive. **Personal:** Born Oct 4, 1964, San Diego, CA. **Career:** Baseball player (retired), baseball executive; Calif Angels, second baseman, outfielder & third baseman, 1986-90; Cleveland Indians, second baseman, outfielder & third baseman, 1990; Houston Astros, second baseman, outfielder & third baseman, 1991; Baltimore Orioles, second baseman, outfielder & third baseman, 1992-94; Tex Rangers, second baseman, outfielder & third baseman, 1995-99; Seattle Mariners, second baseman, outfielder & third baseman, 2000-03, free agt, 2003; Oakland Athletics, second baseman, outfielder & third baseman, 2004; Entertainment & Sports Programming Network baseball, color commentator; Fox Sports Southwest, mlb analyst, 2005-; TXA 21, baseball analyst, 2009-; Mark McLemore Sports Complex, pres, owner, currently. **Special Achievements:** Robbin' in da Hood, assoc producer, 2009. **Business Addr:** Owner, President, Mark McLemore Sports Complex, 2020 Industrial Blvd, Rockwall, TX 76087, **Business Phone:** (972)772-0556.

## MCLEMORE, NELSON, JR.

Government official. **Personal:** Born Jan 29, 1934, Chicago, IL; married Ollie Stokes; children: Nelson III. **Educ:** Tenn A&M State Univ, BS, 1955; Gov State Univ, MA, cult studies, 1978; Chicago Teachers Col & John Marshall Law Sch. **Career:** Government official (retired); Chicago Pub Elem & Sec Sch, teacher, 1955-65; Chicago Comn Youth Welfare, community unit dir, 1965-69; Chicago Dept Human Resources, asst comnr, coordr community serv, 1972-74; Planning-Human Serv, asst dir, 1978-79, chief-of-staff; Human Serv, dir personnel

& training, 1979-80; Human Serv, dep comnr, 1980; Kennedy King Col, coordr, 1990. **Orgs:** Nat Asn Comm Develop; pres, 2nd Ard Reg Dem Orgn Boosters Club; Kappa Alpha Psi; cert, social worker; dir, Dept Pub Works, 1985-90. **Home Addr:** 401 E 32nd St Apt 415, Chicago, IL 60616-4096, **Home Phone:** (312)225-7668.

## MCLEOD, DR. GEORGIANNA R.

Social worker. **Personal:** Born Oct 6, 1937, New York, NY; daughter of George and Annie Coles. **Educ:** NY Univ, BS, 1959; Inst Appl Res, London, eng, PhD, humanities. **Career:** Social worker (retired); Morningside Community Ctr Camp 41, group work & recreation, 1952; Rusk Inst, recreation therap, 1957-58; Neighborhood House, 1959; New York Dept Soc Serv Emer Asst Unit & Bronx, dir & social worker, 1984-89; Willow Star II, Womens Shelter for Substance Abusers, dir, social serv; Social Servs 68 Lex Womens Shelter, dir, 1996. **Orgs:** Am Pub Works Asn; Nat Charter Sch Watch; Nat Asn Black Social Workers; Am Chama Soc; Am Soc Prof Exec Women; trustee & grand secy, Eureka Grand Chap, PhOES; matron, Alpha Chap; pres, exec bd mem & life mem, founder & dir, New York; Nat Asn Advan Colored People, 1960-; vpres, Nat Black Presby Caucus, Ny Col; founder & dir, Proj THRESH, Nat Asn Advan Colored People, 1967-; chap, Consumer Educ Econ Develop, New York; Nat Asn Advan Colored People, 1966-; Migrant Workers Comm; dir, Westchester County; voter rep dir, St Compt Carl McCall; vpres, Black Dems Westchester, 1968-. **Honors/Awds:** Woman of the Year, Interboro Civic 5, 1980; Community Service Award, Nat Asn Advancement Colored People, 1983; Outstanding Service, Church Master, 1983; Employee of the Year, Willow Star II, 1993; Certificate of Appreciation, Nat Park Trust. **Home Addr:** 28 Univ Ave, Yonkers, NY 10704-1126.

## MCLEOD, DR. GUSTAVUS A. (GUS MCLEOD)

Business owner, airplane pilot. **Personal:** Born Jan 1, 1954?, Corinth, MS; married Mary Alice Lockmuller; children: 3. **Educ:** Cath Univ Am, BA, chem, 1976; Univ Md, MS, chem engineering, 1977; Fla Atlantic Univ, Hon Doctorate, 2002. **Career:** CIA, chemist; Raytheon Corp, chemist; surg supply co, owner; Beerdistrib co, owner; 3 Roads Commun Inc, aviator, currently. **Honors/Awds:** Distinguished Achievement Award, Air Force Asn; Distinguished Flying Cross, Distinguished Flying Cross Soc, 2004; Hon Researcher, Korea Aerospace Res Inst, 2005. **Special Achievements:** First person to fly the first open cockpit aircraft over the magnetic North Pole, 1999; First person to fly an open cockpit aircraft over the Geographic North Pole, 2000; first person to cross the treacherous Drake Passage at night in an experimental aircraft; Author: Solo to the Top ofthe World: Gus McLeod's Daring Record Flight. TV series: Inside Base Camp, 2002; The Amazing Race 6, 2004. **Business Addr:** Aviator, 3 Roads Communications Inc, 1 W 2nd St, Frederick, MD 21701, **Business Phone:** (301)662-4121.

## MCLEOD, KEVIN

Football player, football coach. **Personal:** Born Oct 17, 1974, Montego Bay; married Sharon. **Educ:** Auburn Univ. **Career:** Football player (retired), football coach, exec; Jacksonville Jaguars, 1998; Tampa Bay Buccaneers, fullback, 1999; ResCare Workforce Serv, 2000-03; Excel Alternatives, proj mgr, 2002-07; Clear Options Inc, pres, 2003-08; Cleveland Browns, fullback, 2003; Inlet Grove High Sch, coach, 2007; Silver Oak Acad, head coach & headmaster, prog dir, 2009-. **Honors/Awds:** Rookie of the Year, 1999. **Business Addr:** Program Director, Silver Oak Academy, 999 Crouse Mill Rd, Keymar, PA 21757, **Business Phone:** (410)775-1745.

## MCLEOD, DR. MICHAEL PRESTON

Dentist. **Personal:** Born Aug 16, 1954, Tulsa, OK; son of Jeanne and Wallace B; married Corlis Clay; children: Lauren Micah & Kathleen Blake. **Educ:** Howard Univ, BS, cum laude, 1976; Univ Okla, DDS, 1980; Martin Luther King Genl Hosp, GPR, 1981. **Career:** Pvt pract, dentist; Univ Okla, Col Dent, Okla City, OK, part-time fac, 1984-. **Orgs:** Kappa Alpha Psi, 1975-; Okla City Med Dent-Phar, 1982-; Citizen's Adv Comm, Capital-Med Ctr Improv & Zoning Commn, 1984-. **Honors/Awds:** Amer Acad of Periodontology Award, 1980; Amer Soc Dentistry for Children Award, 1980; Div Comm Dent Award, 1980; Univ Okla Assoc Black Personnel Award, 1980. **Business Addr:** Physician, Dentist, 2216 Martin Luther King Ave Suite B, Oklahoma City, OK 73111, **Business Phone:** (405)427-0237.

## MCLEOD, ROSHOWN

Basketball player, basketball coach, social worker. **Personal:** Born Nov 17, 1975, Jersey City, NJ; married Tiffani; children: Anthony & Anisa. **Educ:** St John's Univ, BA, sociol, 1995; Duke Univ, BA, sociol, 1998. **Career:** Basketball player (retired), basketball coach; Atlanta Hawks, small forward, 1998-2001; Philadelphia 76ers, 2000-01; Boston Celtics, 2001-02; Fairfield Univ, asst basketball coach, 2002-03; Ind Univ, coaching staff, asst coach, 2008-10; St. Benedict's Prep Sch, head, 2010-11; Cobb County Community Serv Bd, community & social serv technician, 2014-16; Johnson's Ferry Christian Acad, head basketball coach, 2014-. **Orgs:** Exec dir, Roshown McLeod Found, 2014-; bd mem, Nat Asn Parents, 2016-. **Honors/Awds:** Swett Memorial Trophy, Duke MVP, 1998. **Home Addr:** 4906 Vinings Ridge Trl SE, Mableton, NJ 30126-5905, **Home Phone:** (770)432-7957. **Business Addr:** Head Basketball Coach, Community and Social Service Technician, Johnson Ferry Christian Academy, 955 Johnson Ferry Rd, Marietta, IN 30068, **Business Phone:** (678)784-5231.

## MCLIN, REV. LENA JOHNSON (LENA MAE JOHNSON)

Educator, composer. **Personal:** Born Sep 5, 1928, Atlanta, GA; daughter of Benjamin J and Bernice Dorsey; married Nathaniel; children: Nathaniel Jr & Beverly. **Educ:** Spelman Col, BMus, 1951, BM, piano & violin, Spelman Col, Atlanta, Ga; Am Conserv, Mm, 1954; Roosevelt Univ, Chicago State Col, electronic music & voice; Am Conserv Music, grad degree, music. **Career:** Julius H Hess Upper Grade Ctr, teacher, 1959; Hubbard High Sch, teacher, 1960; John Marshall Harlan High Sch, teacher, 1963-70; Singer; composer numerous works; clinician; Kenwood High Sch, Chicago, teacher, dir, head music dept; small opera co "Mclin Ensemble", founder, dir; Trinity Congregational Church, founder; Ill House Representatives, 1981-2008. **Orgs:** Founding pastor, Holy Vessel Baptist Church, 1982; Chicago Bd Educ; TCI Educ Film Co MENC; Nat Asn Negro Musicians; NJE; Inst Black Am Music; founder & pastor, Holy Vessel Christian Ctr, Chicago. **Honors/Awds:** Critics Association Outstanding Composer, 1971; Outstanding composer Award, Va Union Univ, 1973; Best Teacher of the Year, 1983; outstanding musician, Nat Advan Asn Colored People; hon degree HHD, VA Union Univ, 1975; Outstanding Teacher Award, 1983; Lifetime Achievement Award, Chicago Music Awards, 2003; Hon Degree, Spelman Col. **Special Achievements:** Publisher: Pulse: A History of Music, 1977.

## MCLURKIN, JAMES DWIGHT, IV

Consultant, scientist. **Personal:** Born Jan 1, 1972. **Educ:** Mass Inst Technol, SB, elec engineering minor mech engineering, 1995; Univ Calif, Berkeley, MS, elec engineering, 1999; Mass Inst Technol, SM, comput sci, 2003, PhD, comput sci, 2008. **Career:** Gen Motors Advan Technol Group, intern, 1994; Sensible Technologies, consult, 1995; Mass Inst Technol, Artificial Intelligence Lab, res scientist, 1995-97; MicroDisplay Corp, consult, 1998; Walt Disney Imagineering, consult, 1998; Sensable Technologies, consult, 1998; iRobot, lead res scientist & mgr swarm proj, currently, tech lead & proj mgr, 1999-2003; Mass Inst Technol, CSAIL, res asst, 2000-08; St Paul's Sch Conroy, vis lectr, 2007; Univ Wash CSE, res assoc, 2008-09; Rice Univ, asst prof, dept comput sci, 2009-, grad admis comt, 2010, grad recruiting comt, 2011-; McMurtry Col, fac assoc, 2010-; Publications: From Theory to Practice: Dynamic Task Assignment in Robot Swarms, 2005; Distributed Coverage Control with Sensory Feedback for Networked Robots, 2006; Distributed Coverage Control Experiments with Groups of Robots, 2008; Measuring the Accuracy of Distributed Algorithms on Multi-Robot Systems with Dynamic Network Topologies, 2008; A Distributed Boundary Detection Algorithm for Multi-Robot Systems, 2009; A Low-Cost Multi-Robot System for Research, Teaching and Outreach, 2010; Agreement on Stochastic Multi-Robot Systems with Communication Failures, 2010; Design of a Low-Cost Series Elastic Actuator for Multi-Robot Manipulation, 2011; Hexagonal Lattice Formation in Multi-Robot System, 2012. **Orgs:** Inst Elec & Electronics Engrs; PC mem, Distrib Autonomous Robotic Systs, 2010; assoc ed, IEEE Robotics & Automation, 2011. **Business Addr:** Assistant Professor, Rice University, 6100 Main St MS132, Houston, TX 77005, **Business Phone:** (713)348-3049.

## MCMICHAEL, EARLENE CLARISSE

Journalist. **Personal:** Born Sep 29, 1963, New York, NY; daughter of Norma Krieger and Earl. **Educ:** Cornell Univ, Ithaca, NY, BS, 1984; Columbia Univ Grad Sch Jour, New York, MS, 1987. **Career:** The Oakland Press, Pontiac, Mich, reporter, 1987; Kans City Times, Kans City, Mo, reporter, 1987; Shoreline Newspapers, Guilford, Conn, reporter, 1988; Jersey J, Jersey City, NJ, reporter, 1988-; Kalamazoo Gazette, ed, 2011; WMUK, local host NPR's Morning Ed, 2012-. **Orgs:** Vpres, Brooklyn chap, Zeta Phi Beta Sorority, 1986-87; sec, Nj chap, Nat Asn Black Journalists, 1988-90. **Honors/Awds:** WNBC-TV Minority Fellow Scholarship, 1986-87; participant in the Capital Cities/ABC Inc Minority Training Program, 1987-88. **Home Addr:** 163 Eastern Pkwy Suite D4, Brooklyn, NY 11238, **Home Phone:** (718)857-7290. **Business Addr:** Reporter, The Jersey Journal, 30 J Sq, Jersey City, NJ 07306, **Business Phone:** (201)795-6147.

## MCMILLAN, FRIAR DOUGLAS JAMES (FRIAR DOUGLAS MCMILLAN)

Educator. **Personal:** Born Feb 8, 1947, New York, NY; son of James and Irene Wilson. **Educ:** Community Col, Allegeny Co, AA, Eng, 1975; Univ Pittsburgh, BA, lang commun, 1977; Xavier Univ La, New Orleans, LA, ThM, 1990. **Career:** Canevin High Sch, Pittsburgh, Pa, teacher, 1973-80; Assum Acad NY, teacher, 1980-81; Bishop Grimes High Sch, NY, Eng Dept, teacher, 1981-89, 1997-, asst prin, 1989-90, chair, 1999-; Diocese Syracuse, Syracuse, NY, dir, off Black Cath Ministry, 1990-97; Archbishop Curley High Sch, Eng Dept, instr & chair, 2005-; St. Frances Acad, Eng Dept, instr & chair, 2014-16. **Orgs:** Order Friars Minor Conventuals, 1968-; Nat Black Cath Clergy Caucus, 1984-; bd mem, Off Black Cath Ministry Diocese Syracuse; Nat Asn Black Cath Adminr, 1990-; Conventual Franciscan Prov Immaculate Conception; moderator, Speech & Debate Club, Archbishop Curley High Sch; moderator, Forensics Club; bd mem, Nat Black Cath Clergy Caucus; bd mem, Nat Black Cath Cong. **Honors/Awds:** Teacher of the Year, St. Frances Academy, 2015. **Home Addr:** 12290 Folly Quarter Rd, Ellicott City, MD 21042, **Home Phone:** (410)531-2800.

**MCMILLAN, FRIAR DOUGLAS. See MCMILLAN, FRIAR DOUGLAS JAMES.**

## MCMILLAN, JACQUELINE MARIE

Educator, management consultant. **Personal:** Born Dec 15, 1966, Jamaica, NY; daughter of Vincent Savage and Margaret; married LeMorris Neil; children: De Morris Jourdan Baity. **Educ:** Col Holy Cross, BA, 1989; Kent State Univ, MPA, 1993, PhD, 1998. **Career:** Stud Progs Urban Develop, co-dir, 1986-89; Col Holy Cross, resident asst, 1987-89; NY City Child Welfare Admin, case mgr, 1990-92; Kent State Univ, acad adv, 1992-95, res asst, 1995-. **Orgs:** Nat Forum Pub Adminrs, 1992-; Womens Network, 1993-; mentor, Cs Serv Bd, 1994-; prog adv, Black Grad Stud Asn, 1994-; Am Asn Higher Educ, 1994-95; bd mem, Phi Delta Kappa, 1995-; fel, World Bible Way, 1995; Kappa DeltaPi, 1996-; Nat Asn Women Educ, 1996-. **Home Addr:** 325 Beechwood Dr, Akron, OH 44320. **Business Addr:** Research Assistant, Kent State University, 404 White Hall, Kent, OH 44242, **Business Phone:** (330)672-2580.

## MCMILLAN, JAMES C.

Educator. **Personal:** Born Dec 23, 1925, Sanford, NC; son of James Ernest and Sadie; children: Eric Wesley & Frances Lynne. **Educ:** Howard Univ, BA, art, 1947; Fresco Mural Skowhegan Sch Art ME, fel, 1947; Acad Julian, cert, 1951; Cath Univ Am, Wash DC, MFA, sculpture, 1952; Syracuse Univ NY, attended 1961. **Career:** US Naval Air Sta, art instr & illusr, 1945-46; Bennett Col, Greensboro NC, prof & chmn art dept, 1947-50, 1952-53, 1956-69, prof emer, currently; Syracuse Univ, Bennett Col, NY, Danforth teacher fel, 1960-61; Guilford Col, prof art, chmn, 1966-88, dir London/Europ arts sem, 1968-72, painter, sculptor, prof art emer, 1988; Va State Univ, Petersburg, eminent scholar fine arts, 1990. **Orgs:** Dir cult enrichment, EPDA Bennett Col, 1969-70; dir, NY Art Sem, Guilford Col, 1971-75; Col Art Asn, 1984-85; Nat Conf Artists, 1984-85; DC Art Asn, 1985; co-founder, pres, Afro-Am Atelier Inc Gallery, Greensboro, NC, 1990-91. **Honors/Awds:** Mural Providence Baptist Church Greensboro, NC, 1977. **Special Achievements:** Became the first African-American to receive a fellowship at the Skowhegan School of Painting and Sculpture in Maine in 1947; first African-American chair of the Art Department, Guilford College; First president of the African American Atelier, 1991. **Home Addr:** 1915 Drexmore Ave, Greensboro, NC 27406-3212, **Home Phone:** (336)379-9376. **Business Addr:** Professor Emeritus, Guilford College, 5800 W Friendly Ave, Greensboro, NC 27410, **Business Phone:** (336)316-2000.

## MCMILLAN, DR. JOSEPH TURNER, JR.

College administrator. **Personal:** Born Jul 19, 1944, Valdosta, GA; son of J T Sr and Olivia Cooper. **Educ:** Howard Univ, BS, psychol, 1965, MA, stud personnel admin, 1970; Teachers Col, Columbia Univ, doctorate, higher educ admin, 1986; Harvard Univ, cert, educ mgt, 1990. **Career:** United Church Bd Homeland Ministries, secy higher educ relationships, exec secy coun higher educ, 1970-88; Huston-Tillotson Col, Austin, Tex, pres, 1988-2000, pres emer, 2000-; Tex Col Traditional Chinese Med, acad dean & chief acad officer, 2005-08, vpres acad affairs, assessment & pres, Tex Health and Sci Univ, currently. **Orgs:** Bd trustee, Pension Bds United Church Christ; bd dir, Amistad Res Ctr; bd dir, United Negro Col Fund, 1990-99; Austin Regional Adv Bd, JP Morgan Chase Bank Tex, 1990-2000; chmn & bd trustee, Tex Asn Develop Cols, 1993-97; chmn bd deacons, Congregational Church Austin, currently; chair, Coun Higher Educ United Church Christ, 1996-99; chair, site teams Tex Higher Educ Coord Bd & Accreditation Comn Acupuncture & Orient Med, 2000-; life mem, Alpha Phi Alpha Fraternity Inc. **Home Addr:** 115 Heritage Dr, Austin, TX 78737-2602, **Home Phone:** (512)301-1466. **Business Addr:** Vice President for Academic Affairs, Assessment & Research, Texas College of Traditional Chinese Medicine, 4005 Manchaca Rd, Austin, TX 78704, **Business Phone:** (512)444-8082.

## MCMILLAN, DR. MAE F.

Physician, psychiatrist. **Personal:** Born May 12, 1936, Austin, TX; daughter of Ben S Sr and Annie M Walker. **Educ:** Wiley Col Marshall, TX, BS, BA, 1955; Meharry Med Col, MD, 1959. **Career:** Wayne Co Gen Hosp Mich, intern, 1960; Baylor Univ Col Med Houston, affiliated hosp residency, 1963, 1965, Dept Psychiat & Child Psychiat, asst prof, 1966, clin assoc prof; Hampstead Child Ther Course & Clin, London, fel, 1967; pvt pract part time child psychiat specialty pre-schoolers; Tex Res Inst Ment Sci, asst dir div child psychiat, 1968-72, dir div child Psychiat, 1972-74, dir early childhood ther course & clin; Univ Tex Med Sch Houston, clin assoc prof; Fac Advan Studies Univ Tex Sch Biomed Sci, asst prof, 1975; Univ Tex Health Sci Ctr Houston, clin assoc prof, 1976; Tex Woman's Univ Child Develop & Family Living, adj prof. **Orgs:** Bd mem, Can Do It, 1973-80; chair, Am Psychiat Asns Comt Black Psychiatrists, 1978; bd dir, Girls Clubs Houston Sect; Nat Coun Negro Women; Delta Sigma Theta; Ment Health Asn; coord, Child Care Coun Houston Harris Co; United Methodist Women; treas, Tex Community Corp; chmn, Child Advocacy com, Houston Psychiat soc, 1992; Tex Soc Psych Physicians; bd trust, vchmn, Harris county Ment Health & Ment Retardation Authority, bd mem, 1998-, chair, prog Comt; Med Planning Adv Coun; Ment Retardation Authority Harris County, vchmn, bd ment health, 1999; distinguished life fel Am Psychiat Asn, 2002. **Honors/Awds:** Criminal Justice Award, Delta Sigma Theta; One Amer Proj, 1973; Distinction of Merit; Nat Coun Negro Women, 1977; YWCAs Outstanding Womens Luncheon, 1979; Woman of Distinction Award, YWCA Houston Sect, 1980; Notable Women of Texas Award, Govs Comn, 1983; Psychiatric Excellence Award, Tex Soc Psychiat Physicians, 2004. **Special Achievements:** Only African-American child psychiatrist to have completed part of her training at the Hempstead Clinic in London; Published Numerous Articles. **Home Addr:** 4114 Cornell St, Houston, TX 77022, **Home Phone:** (713)692-6851. **Business Addr:** Vice Chairman, Mental Health Mental Retardation Authority of Harris County, 7011 Southwest Freeway, Houston, TX 77074, **Business Phone:** (713)970-7000.

## MCMILLAN, NATE (NATHANIEL MCMILLAN)

Basketball player, basketball coach. **Personal:** Born Aug 3, 1964, Raleigh, NC; married Michelle; children: Jamelle & Brittany. **Educ:** Chowan Col, attended 1984; NC State Univ, attended 1986. **Career:** Basketball player (retired), basketball coach; Seattle Supersonics, guard-forward, 1986-98, asst coach, 1998-2000, interim head coach, 2000-01, head coach, 2000-05; Portland Trailblazers, head coach, 2005-12; US nat team, asst coach, FIBA World Championship, 2006; US nat team, asst coach, Beijing Olympics, 2008; Indiana Pacers, asst coach, 2013-. **Business Addr:** Assistant Coach, Indiana Pacers, 1 Conseco Ct 125 S Pa St, Indianapolis, IN 46204, **Business Phone:** (317)917-2500.

## MCMILLAN, REGINA ELLIS

Lawyer, executive. **Personal:** Born Mar 27, 1964, Louisville, CO; daughter of Geoffrey S and Mary A; married Antonio B. **Educ:** Fisk Univ, BA, polit sci & econs, 1985; Georgetown Univ Law Ctr, JD, 1988. **Career:** Brown-Forman Distillers Corp, summer intern, 1984-85; Georgetown Univ Law Ctr, res asst, 1987; Perpetual Savings Bank, law clerk, 1987; Wyatt, Tarrant & Combs, assoc atty, 1988-89; Thomas, Kennedy, Sampson & Patterson, assoc atty, 1989-95; Danley & Assoc, assoc atty, 1995-96; Regina Ellis McMillan PC, solo pract, 1995-97, atty, 2001-03; Atlanta Tech Col, paralegal studies instr, 1998-2000, interim coord staff support, grievance facilitator, 2000-01; Fulton County Dist Atty's Off, chief asst dist atty, 2003-11, sr asst dist atty, 2011-14; Mincey Law Pract, owner atty, 2014-. **Orgs:** Pres, Mortar Bd, 1984-85; Phi Beta Kappa, 1985; Nat Bar Asn, 1987; Geo Asn Black Women Attys, 1990-; State Bar Ga, 1992-; Nat Asn Female Execs, 1993-; truancy proj, Atlanta Vol Lawyers Found, 1993-; coach & evaluator, GA High Sch MockTrial Competition, 1995-; Nat Asn Advan Colored People. **Honors/Awds:** Youth Achiever of the Year, YMCA, 1981; National Dean's List, Fisk Univ, 1982-85; Rhodes Scholar State Finalist, 1984-85; Adult Black Achievers Award, YMCA, 1989; TRIO Achiever

Award, Nat Coun Educ Opportunity Asn, 1991. **Home Addr:** 11235 Chelsea Lane, Hampton, GA 30228, **Home Phone:** (770)472-5988. **Business Addr:** Owner, The Mincey Law Practice, 1 Hartsfield Bldg, Atlanta, GA 30354, **Business Phone:** (678)575-3501.

## MCMILLAN, ROBERT FRANK, JR.

Executive. **Personal:** Born Jul 8, 1946, Glassboro, NJ; son of Robert F Sr and Kurt Yvonne (deceased); children: Ayisha Nell & Marcia Akillah. **Educ:** Temple Univ, BS, civil engineering, 1972; Northwestern Univ, MBA. **Career:** Turner Construct, field engr, supt, 1972-76; Hudson Corp, proj mgr, 1976-80; Urban Investment & Develop Co, sr real estste mgr, 1978-90; Fox Valley Mall-Developer, sr real estate mgr, 1980-88; Joseph J Freed & Assocs Inc, dir develop, 1985-87; Wil-Freds Develop Inc, develop officer, 1988; McMillan Garbe Struct Inc, owner & pres; Shurgard Self Storage, real estate mgr, 2000-04; Fifth Third Bank, sr real estate mgr, 2005-06; Freeman Funding Solutions, pres, 2006-; McMillan Group Inc, owner, 2006-. **Orgs:** Charter mem, Rotary Int, 1984-; African Am Chamber Com, 1998-2000; bd chmn, Greater Aurora Chamber Com, 2000-01; bd mem, Aurora Crime Stoppers; bd mem, Merchants Bank; Ely Chap-Lambda Alpha; Land EconomicsSociety. **Home Addr:** 39W636 Prairie St, Aurora, IL 60506-5123, **Home Phone:** (630)897-3674. **Business Addr:** Owner, Mc Millan Group Inc, 25 Otter Trail, Westport, CT 06880, **Business Phone:** (203)227-8696.

## MCMILLAN, ROSALYN A.

Writer. **Personal:** Born Oct 14, 1953, Port Huron, MI; daughter of Edward (deceased) and Madeline Washington; married John D Smith; children: Vester Jr, Shannon, Ashley & Jasmine. **Career:** Ford Motor Co, seamstress; Books: Knowing, 1996-; Once Better, 1997; Blue Collar Blues, 1998; The Flip Side of Sin: A Novel, 2000; This Side of Eternity, 2001. **Orgs:** Toastmasters; 100 Black Women; exec adv bd, Memphis Black Writers Conf; ed bd, VIP Memphis Mag. **Honors/Awds:** Rosalyn McMillan Day, Southfield, Mich, named in honor, 1996; Black Board Fiction Novel of the Year, 1998; Blackboard Book of the Year award, 1999. **Business Addr:** Author, Warner Books, 1271 Avenue of the Americas, New York, NY 10020, **Business Phone:** (212)522-7200.

## MCMILLAN, TERRY L.

Educator, novelist, editor. **Personal:** Born Oct 18, 1951, Port Huron, MI; daughter of Edward (deceased) and Madeline Washington Tillman; married Jonathan Plummer; children: Solomon Welch. **Educ:** Columbia Univ, MFA, 1979; Univ Calif, Berkeley, BA, jour, 1978. **Career:** NY Times, HERS Column, guest columnist, Bk Rev, Atlanta Const, Philadelphia Inquirer, bk reviewer; NY Found Arts, fel, 1986; Univ Wyo, Laramie, WY, vis prof, 1987-90; Univ Ariz, Tucson, AZ, assoc prof, 1990-92; Stanford Univ, vis prof; Doubleday Columbia Univ, lit fel; Los Angeles City Col, lectr; Ed: Breaking Ice, Viking Penguin, 1990; Novels: Getting To Happy, The Sequel To Waiting to Exhale; Mama, Houghton Mifflin, 1987; Disappearing Acts, Viking Penguin, 1989; Waiting to Exhale, Viking Penguin, 1992; How Stella Got Her Groove Back, 1996; A Day Late & A Dollar Short, 2001; Interruption Everything, 2005; The Black Nation's Cry, 2007; Its Ok If You re Clueless; Short stories: The End, 1976. **Orgs:** PEN; Authors League; Harlem Writer's Guild. **Home Addr:** PO Box 2408, Danville, CA 94526-7408, **Home Phone:** (510)736-9364. **Business Addr:** Author, c/o Viking Penguin, 375 Hudson St, New York, NY 10014.

## MCMILLAN, WILTON VERNON

Educator. **Personal:** Born Jun 5, 1943, Hope Mills, NC; son of Eunice E; married Lenora W; children: Valerie Kay. **Educ:** St Paul's Col, BS, 1973; George Mason Univ, MEd, 1979. **Career:** Fairfax Co Pub Schs, teacher, 1972-; Woodlawn Elem Sch, teacher. **Orgs:** Founder & chair, Phi Delta Kappa, 1995-; baseluis, Omega Psi Phi Fraternity, 1995-; master, Prince Hall Mason, 1980-; Fairfax Educ Asn; Va Educ Asn; Nat Educ Asn; pres, Alumni Chapters & Chap, St Paul's Col. **Home Addr:** 3208 Norwich Ter, Alexandria, VA 22309, **Home Phone:** (703)780-1679. **Business Addr:** Teacher, Woodlawn Elementary School, 8505 Highland Lane, Alexandria, VA 22309, **Business Phone:** (703)780-5310.

## MCMILLIAN, DR. FRANK L.

Chemist. **Personal:** Born Jun 9, 1934, Mobile, AL; son of Walter J and Roberta E; married Ruby A Curry; children: Franetta L & Kecia L. **Educ:** Dillard Univ, BA 1954; Tuskegee Univ, MS 1956; Univ KS, PhD, 1965. **Career:** Chemist (retired); Ft Valley State Col, instr, 1956-58; NC Cent Univ, instr chem, 1959-60; Norfolk State Col, asst prof chem, 1960-62; E I du Pont de Nemours & Co, res chemist sr tech specialist, 1965-99; Dillard Univ, vis assoc prof chem, 1968-69. **Orgs:** Omega Psi Phi Frat, 1954-; Phi Lambda Upsilon Chem Soc, 1964-; Sigma Xi, 1967-. **Honors/Awds:** Fellow NSF, 1963. **Home Addr:** 66 Bay Rd, Rehoboth Beach, DE 19971, **Home Phone:** (302)226-9985.

## MCMILLIAN, JOSIE ANDERSON

Executive. **Personal:** Born Oct 21, 1940, Childersburg, AL; children: 3. **Educ:** Cornell Univ, trade union study & george meany labor & women studies, 1977; Fla Int Univ, ctr labor res & studies, 1991. **Career:** NY Metro Area Postal Union, sector aide, chief, chief steward, shop steward, 1969, ex dir clerk, 1975, orgl vpres, 1976, exec vpres, 1979, pres. **Orgs:** Labor adv coun, NY Nat Urban League; Coalition Labor Union Women; Nat Org Women; NY Cty Black Trade Leadership Comt; adv bd mem, Cornells Sch Indust & Labor Rels; bd dir, United Way NY Cty; bd mem, NY City & NJ combined Fed Campaign; life mem, Nat Asn Advan Colored People; clerk craft rep NYS Am Postal Workers Union; adv mem, NY Cty Cent Labor Coun; bd dir, NYC Arthritis Found Inc; Am Postal Workers Union Comt Safety & Violence; founder, organizer, Am Postal Workers Union Mechanization Comt; Am Postal Workers Union NY; Post Off Women Equal Rights; dir, Human Rels; Postal Press Asn; bd mem, Ny Am Fedn Labor & Cong Indust Orgn; Women Against Domestic Violence; adv coun mem, Nat Urban League; Nat Coun Negro Women; bd mem, Am Red Cross; Asn a Better New York; Nat Orgn Women; Women Racial & Econ Equality; chairwoman, NY Metro Area Postal Union Comt. **Honors/Awds:** Hispanic Labor Committee Award, NY Cty Central Labor Coun, 1978; Outstanding Achievement Award, New York City Chap Coalition Labor Union Women, 1981; Mary McLeod Bethune Award, Nat Coun Negro Women, 1981; Achievement Award, NY Cty Br NAACP, 1981; Distinguished Service Award, NY Cty Central Labor Coun, 1981; Sojourner Truth Loyalty Award, NY Chap Blk Trade Unionist, 1982; Hoey Ecumenical Award, NY Catholic Interracial Coun, 1982; Appted Admiral, Great Navy NE, 1982; Award of Appreciation, NY Chap Arthritis Found, 1983; Pacific Group Home Award, Little Flower Children's Serv, 1983; Outstanding Labor Leader Award, Nat Asn Negro Bus & Prof Women's Clubs, 1984; Citan of Appreciation, Brooklyn Borough Pres H Golden, 1984; Appreciation Award, Women Racial & Econ Equality, 1985; Women's Achievement Award, YWCA, 1985; Labor Leaders' Award, NY Cty Arthritis Found, 1988; Leadership Award, Borough Manhattan Community Col, 1989; Ellis Island Medal of Honor Award, Nat Ethnic Coalition Orgn, 1998; Citation of Appreciation, Am Legion Dan Tallon Post 678. **Home Addr:** 111 Childersburg Fayette Hwy, Childersburg, AL 35044-3108, **Home Phone:** (256)404-0921.

## MCMILLIAN, MARK D.

Football player. **Personal:** Born Apr 29, 1970, Los Angeles, CA. **Educ:** Glendale JC, Ala, grad. **Career:** Football player (retired); Philadelphia Eagles, defensive back & left defensive back, 1992-95; New Orleans Saints, left defensive back, 1996; Kans City Chiefs, defensive back & left corner back, 1997-98; San Francisco 49ers, 1999; Wash Redskins, defensive back, 1999. **Honors/Awds:** Led NFL in interception yards, 1997. **Special Achievements:** Film: 1992 NFL Draft, 1992.

## MCMILLON, BILLY (WILLIAM EDWARD MCMILLON)

Baseball player, sports manager. **Personal:** Born Nov 17, 1971, Alamagordo, NM; married Krista; children: Kennedy & Jackson. **Educ:** Clemson Univ, attended 1993. **Career:** Baseball player (retired), executive; Fla Marlins, outfielder, 1996-97; Philadelphia Phillies, outfielder, 1997; Detroit Tigers, outfielder, 2000-01; Columbus Clippers, outfielder, 2001; Oakland Athletics, outfielder, 2001, 2003-04; Triple-A Sacramento, outfielder, 2004; Oakland Raiders, outfielder, 2004; Boston Red Sox, outfielder, 2005, mgr, 2014-; Single A Greenville Dr, batting coach, 2008-10, mgr, 2010-11; Salem Red Sox, mgr, 2012-13; Portland Sea Dogs, mgr, 2013; Double-A Eastern League, mgr, 2014; Boston Red Sox, mgr, 2014. **Business Addr:** Manager, Greenville Drive, 945 S Main St, Greenville, SC 29601, **Business Phone:** (864)240-4500.

## MCMILLON, WILLIAM EDWARD. See MCMILLON, BILLY.

## MCMORRIS, DR. JACQUELINE WILLIAMS

Physician. **Personal:** Born Mar 18, 1936, Washington, DC; daughter of John D; married James Oliver. **Educ:** Temple Univ, AB, 1958; Howard Univ Col Med, MD, 1962. **Career:** Dc Gen Hosp, intership; Kings County Hosp Ctr, resident; Off Econ Opportunities, med consult, 1965; DC Pub Health Dept, med officer child health & sch health servs, 1965-69; Health Servs C Spec Needs, clin dir, 1969-95, supvr med officer, chief med officer; pvt pract pediat consult, currently. **Orgs:** Church choir dir, 1962-82; Howard Univ Med Alumni, 1962-87; bd dir, DC Spec Olympics, 1978-79; chairperson, Mamie D Lee Neighborhood Sch Coun, 1982-86; Mayor's Develop Disabilities Coun, 1984-87, secy, St Anthonys Grade Sch PTA, 1984-86; Mayors Develop Disabilities & Planning Coun, 1980-; Med Adv Rehab Serv, 1985-87, Mayors Community Handicapped, 1985-87, Am Med Women's Asn, 1985-86; Howard Univ Trans generational Proj C Learning Disabilities, 1986-87; Mayors Comt Early Child Develop, 1990-; DC Early Intervention Consortium Providers, 1990-98; Missies Diabetes adv, 1998-; chairperson, DC C with Spec Health Care Needs Adv Bd; chair, fel Am Acad Pediat; Alliance Healthy Homes. **Honors/Awds:** Appreciation Award, Inst Integration Handicapped Children Early Educ Progs, 1974; Award for Outstanding Service to Mentally Retarded Citizens, DC Spec Olympics, 1978; Silver Lily Membership Club Award, Easter Seals Soc, 1986; The Second Roland J Queene Sr Memorial Award, Information, Protection & Advocacy Ctr Handicapped Individuals, 1987; Angels with Tears Award, 1998; Champions of Children Award, HSC Found, 2002. **Business Addr:** Chief Medical Officer, Health Services for Children with Special Needs Clinic, 19th Massachusetts Ave SE, Washington, DC 20003, **Business Phone:** (202)675-5214.

## MCMORRIS, LAMELL

Political consultant, chief executive officer. **Educ:** Morehouse Col, BA, relig & soc, 1995; Princeton Theol Seminary, Mdiv, social ethics & pub policy, 1998. **Career:** Fulton County Comnr, Ga, asst Tom Lowe, 1996; Democratic Nat Convention, Chicago, Ill, press asst, 1996; New Jersey Mayor Sharpe James, Aide, Newark; Youth Develop Initiative, Chicago Urban League, dir; Southern Christian Leadership Conf, exec dir; Perennial Strategy Group & Perennial Law Group, founder & chief exec officer, prin, currently. **Orgs:** Wash Govt Rels Group; Wash Bd Trade; US Chamber Com; Rainbow PUSH Trade Bureau Chicago & Wash; DC Urban Leagues; Nat Advan Asn Colored People; Morehouse Col Nat Alumni Asn; Young Democratic Candidates Network; Unity Parenting & Coun; bd mem, Democratic Nat Comt Bus Coun; dir, chief exec officer, Southern Christian Leadership Conf; nat coordr, Redeem Dream; chmn, Am Red Cross; Alpha Phi Alpha Fraternity Inc; Chicago 2016 Olympic Bid Comt; bd trustee, Elmhurst Col; trustee, Miles Col; Nat Bd dir; trustee, spec contrib fund bd; Diamond Life; Legal Comt; Image Awards Comt; Econ Develop Comt; bd dir, Nat Action Network; bd dir, Crisis Publ Co; Nat Urban League; trustee, Life Pieces to Masterpieces. **Business Addr:** Principal, Chief Executing Officer, Perennial Strategy Group, 1455 Pennsylvania Ave NW Suite 225, Washington, DC 20004, **Business Phone:** (202)638-5090.

## MCMORRIS, DR. MICHAEL ANTHONY

Educator, writer. **Personal:** Born Highland Park, MI; children: Montina L. **Educ:** Saginaw Valley State Univ, BA, criminal justice, 1985, MA, polit sci & criminal justice, 1988; Capella Univ, PhD, educ, 2001. **Career:** Saginaw Police Dept, police officer, 1985-89; Saginaw Sch Dist, criminal justice coordr, 1989-93; US Treas Dept, spec agt, 1993-95; Ocean County Col, instr criminal justice, 1995-96; Beijing Polytech Univ, vis scholar; Capital Univ Econs & Bus, China, vis scholar; Ferris State Univ, assoc prof, 1996; State Univ Mich, assoc prof criminal justice; NC Cent Univ, dept criminal justice, assoc prof, currently; Auth: Perceptions Criminality, 2003; Hostile Corridors, 2003; Criminal Justice Scenarios, 2004; Am Law Enforcement Trainers LLC, founder & exec dir. **Orgs:** Horizons Upward Bound Alumni Asn, 1981-; Acad Criminal Justice Scis, 1996-; Midwestern Criminal Justice Asn, 1996-; Nat Educ Asn, 1996-; Nat Asn African Am Studies, 1999-. **Home Addr:** 7099 Reflection Dr NE, Comstock Park, MI 49321-9639, **Home Phone:** (616)784-2688. **Business Addr:** Associate Professor, North Carolina Central University, 309 Whiting 1801 Fayetteville St, Durham, NC 27707, **Business Phone:** (919)530-5206.

## MCMULLINS, TOMMY

Executive. **Personal:** Born Sep 15, 1942, Macon, GA; son of Ulysses Anderson and Alummer; married Gwendolyn Williams; children: Tommy, Tyrone & Timothy. **Educ:** Ft Valley State Col, BS, social sci, 1964; Am Inst Banking, bank courses, 1975; Pepperdine Univ, 1972; Pac Coast Banking Sch, grad cert, 1980. **Career:** Bank Executive (retired); Ylwstn Nat Pk, seasonal pk rgr, 1963-64; First Int Bank, mgr reg sales mgr vpres, 1965-82; US MarinesCorps, 1966-68; Crocker Nat Bank, vpres, 1982-85; Wells Fargo Bank, 1985-94; Citibank, N Hollywood Br, mgr, vpres, 1994-2001; Pasadena Unified Sch Dist Bd Educ, pres, 2001-02; Bank Whittier, NA, pres, chief exec officer, 2002; Pasadena Schs Bd, pres. **Orgs:** Pres, Pasadena Chap Alpha Phi Alpha, 1961; co-chairperson, Emerg Hispanic Mjty, 1978-80; bd mem, Pasadena Nat Asn Advan Colored People, 1979-82; bd mem, Comm Bell Gdns Rotary, 1981-85; bd mem, Monrovia Kiwanis; chmn, Int Visitors Coun Los Angeles. **Home Addr:** 1245 Rubio Vista Rd, Altadena, CA 91001, **Home Phone:** (626)797-7410.

## MCMURRY, DR. KERMIT ROOSEVELT, JR.

School administrator. **Personal:** Born Jul 31, 1945, Kansas City, KS; married Valerie M; children: James Patrick, Chris, Nikii, Kermetria & Justin. **Educ:** Univ Colo, BS, 1968, MS, 1970; Univ Nebr, PhD, 1975; Harvard Univ, attended 1979; Univ Nebr-Lincoln, PhD; Cowley Community Col, assocs degree. **Career:** Dept Admin Serv Exec Br State Govt State Nebr, asst dir, 1974-75; Nebr Coord Comt Post Sec Educ, exec dir, 1975-77; Grambling State Univ, exec vpres, 1977; Nebr Dept Social Serv, dir, 1986-90; Okla State Regents Higher Educ, assoc vice chancellor acad affairs, 1990-95, Stud Serv, vice chancellor, 1995-; Okla State Regents Higher Educ, vice chancellor, stud affairs, 1996-; Gov's Transformation, adv bd; guest speaker; Fairfield Univ, Grad Sch Educ & Allied Professions, vis prof. **Orgs:** Asst dir, Leisure Serv, Univ Nebr, 1970-74; vice chmn, United Campus Ministers; Lincoln Total Com Action Prog; chief exec officer, Nebr Dept Social Serv. **Honors/Awds:** Outstanding Young Man, Nebr Jaycees, 1971; Pioneering Coord Award, Nebr Coord Comn Post Sec Educ, 1977; Outstanding Tiger Alumini, 1995; Hall of Fame, Cowley Community Col's, 2004, 2007; Hall of Fame, Okla Stud Govt Asn's. **Special Achievements:** Author of numerous articles, books & journals. **Home Addr:** 23391 Hunters Spring Dr, Edmond, OK 73003, **Home Phone:** (405)359-6647. **Business Addr:** Vice Chancellor for Student Services, Oklahoma State Regents for Higher Education, 655 Res Pkwy Suite 200, Oklahoma City, OK 73104, **Business Phone:** (405)225-9100.

## MCMURRY, MERLEY LEE

Government official. **Personal:** Born Aug 20, 1949, Kansas City, MO; daughter of Andrew Jackson Owens III; married Murvell; children: Steven Andrew & Courtney Michelle. **Educ:** Univ Mo, Columbia, MO, BA, 1971; Cent Mich Univ, Mt Pleasant, MI, MA, 1974. **Career:** Mi Employ Security, Kansas City, Mo, employ counr, 1972-74; Metro Community Cols, Kans City, Mo, counr, 1974-78, proj coordr, 1978-83, tutorial coordr, 1983-85; Am Nurses' Asn, Kans City, Mo, educ consult & dod coordr, 1985-86; Greater Kans City Chamber Com, Kansas City, Mo, vpres & mem serv, 1986-2001; Kansas City Power & Light, community bus mgr, currently, govt & community affairs bus mgr, 2001-. **Orgs:** Small & Minority Bus Networking Comt, vice chair, 1986-; Univ Mi Jackson County Extension Bd, 1988-; Teenage Parent Ctr Adv Bd, secy, 1989-; Pres's Adv Univ Mi Extension Bd, 1989-; Univ Mi Small Bus Develop Adv Bd, 1990-; chairperson, S Kans City Chamber Com; Santa Fe Neighborhood Asn; Northland Regional Chamber Com; Urban League; Guadalupe Ctr; ReDiscover. **Home Addr:** 2627 Victor St, Kansas City, MO 64128, **Home Phone:** (816)923-6452. **Business Addr:** Community Business Manager, Kansas City Power & Light, 1201 Walnut, Kansas City, MO 64106, **Business Phone:** (816)556-2493.

## MCNABB, DONOVAN JAMAL

Football player, founder (originator). **Personal:** Born Nov 25, 1976, Chicago, IL; son of Samuel and Wilma; married Raquel Ann Nurse; children: Alexis, Sariah, Donovan Jr & Devin James. **Educ:** Syracuse Univ, BA, speech commun, 1998. **Career:** Football player & basketball player (retired); Syracuse Univ, res guard; Philadelphia Eagles, quarterback, 1999-2009; Wash Redskins, quarterback, 2010; Minn Vikings, quarterback, 2011; NFL Network, analyst, 2012; Fox Sports Live, analyst, 2013; Syracuse Univ, mem bd trustee; Super Five, owner, currently; McNabb Unlimited, founder, currently; beIN Sports, lead analyst, currently. **Orgs:** Founder, Donovan McNabb Golden Arm Scholar, 2000; Nat spokesperson, Am Diabetes asn; Pinnacy Soc Am Diabetes asn; exec dir, Donovan McNabb Found. **Honors/Awds:** NFL Player of the Year, CBS Radio, 2000; Terry Bradshaw Awards, Fox Sports, 2000; All-Madden team, 2000; NFC Pro Bowl squad, 2001-05 & 2010; NFC Offensive Player of the Month, September 2002, November 2003, September 2004, September 2005; Wanamaker Award, 2002; Horse Trailer Player of the Game hons, Monday Night Football, 2002; Big East Rookie of the Year; Most Caring Athlete, USA WEEKEND Mag, 2003; NFL Man of the Year finalist, 2003, 2005; NFC Offensive Player of the Year, Kans City Touchdown Club, 2004; Three time NFL Offensive Player of the Week; Five time NFC Offensive Player of the Week; NFC Offensive Player of the Year, CBS Radio, 2004; Pudding Pie Award winner, 2008; FedEx Air Player of the Week, 2008; Father of the Year, Am Diabetes Asn, 2009. **Special Achievements:** Youngest person to be named to the Syracuse University Board of Trustees; First NFL player with his own line of clothing. **Business Addr:** Lead Analyst, Minnesota Vikings, 7291 NW 74th St, Miami, FL 33166, **Business Phone:** (305)777-1900.

### MCNAIR, CHRIS

Government official, chief executive officer, photographer. **Personal:** Born Nov 13, 1926, Fordyce, AR; son of Jewel and Lilliebelle; married Maxine; children: Denise (deceased), Lisa & Kim. **Educ:** Tuskegee Univ, BSc, agr, 1942. **Career:** Comnr (retired), photogr, chief exec officer; Chris Mc Nair Health Ctr; Fed Med Ctr; Jefferson County Courthouse, county comnr, 1994-95, judge; Chris McNair Studio & Art Gallery, founder, owner, chief exec officer, currently. **Orgs:** Ala House Representatives, 1973; County Comn, 1986. **Home Addr:** . **Business Addr:** Chief Executive Officer, Chris McNair Studio & Art Gallery, 45 6th Ave S, Birmingham, AL 35205, **Business Phone:** (205)322-2685.

### MCNAIRY, DR. FRANCINE G.

School administrator, president (organization), association executive. **Personal:** Born Nov 13, 1946, Pittsburgh, PA; daughter of F E and Gladys. **Educ:** Univ Pittsburgh, BA, sociol, 1968, MSW, 1970, PhD, com, 1978; Harvard Univ Inst Educ Mgt. **Career:** President (retired); Allegheny Co Child Welfare Servs, supvr & soc worker, 1970-72; Comm Action Regional training, tech asst specialist, 1972; Clarion Univ, assoc prof & coun, 1973-82, coord acad devel & retention, 1983, dean acad support serv & asst to acad vpres, 1983-88; W Chester Univ, assoc provost, 1988-94; Millersville Univ, pres, 2003-13. **Orgs:** Adv, Clarion Univ Black Stud Union, 1973; Sunday News, guest columnist; Presenter, Nat Conf Freshmen Yr Experience Univ SC, 1982-86; Wesleyan Col, 1983; St Lawrence Col, 1984; vchmn, Clarion Co Human Resources Devel Comm, 1983-86; presenter, Int Conf First Yr Exp Eng, 1986; Creative Mgt Higher Educ, Boston, 1986; consult, Univ NE, Briar Cliff Col, Marshall Univ, 1986; Pa Adv Bd to ACT; AAHE; Nat Asn Black Women Higher Educ; Lancaster County Comm; speaker, Asn Baccalaureate Social Work Prog Dirs; Lancaster Chamber Com & Indust; Lancaster Gen Med Group; YWCA; Pa State Bd Educ. **Honors/Awds:** Publs "Clarion Univ Increases Black Student Retention"; co-author, "Taking the Library to Freshman Students via Freshman Seminar Concept", 1986; "The Minority Student on Campus" 1985; Named Outstanding First-Year Advocate by the National Resource Center; The President's Martin Luther King Jr Award, Edinboro Univ Pa; Heritage Award, Urban Connection the Capital Region; University of Pittsburgh's Distinguished Alumni Fellows Award, 2005. **Special Achievements:** First Female African American university president in the state system of higher education; She is the first black woman to lead a Pennsylvania state university. **Home Addr:** 46 W Cottage Ave, Millersville, PA 17551-1402. **Business Addr:** President, Millersville University, 1 S George St, Millersville, PA 17551, **Business Phone:** (717)872-3011.

### MCNARY, OSCAR LEE

Executive, artist, educator. **Personal:** Born Mar 23, 1944, San Antonio, TX; married Maudene J; children: Omar. **Educ:** Tex Southern Univ; Southern Methodist Univ; Hunters Sch Art, attended 1974. **Career:** Internet Art Resources, dir, currently; pvt art consult, currently. **Orgs:** Dallas Mus Fine Arts; Nat Conf Artists, 1975-80; adv bd mem, Phoenix Cult Arts Ctr, 1975-81; Tex Arts Alliance; state & local mem, Tex Fine Arts Asn, 1975-81; assoc mem, Am Watercolor Soc, 1976-81; nat mem, Artists Equity Asn, 1977-81; Int Platform Asn, 1978-81; vpres & bd mem, Artists Coalition Tex, 1979; bd trustee & pres, Richardson Civic Art Soc, 1979-81; Schomberg Soc; Af Am Mus; Studio Mus Harlem; Irving Black Arts Coun; guest cur, Artist & Elaine Thornton Found Arts Dallas Mus Art, 2000; vpres, Dallas art revenue. **Honors/Awds:** Man Exhib, Phoenix Cult Arts Ctr, 1979. **Special Achievements:** First Black vpres & first Black board mem of Artists Coalition of Tex, 1979; first Black pres of Richardson Civic Art Socs, 1979-81; An Inventory her Rec at African Am Libr at Gregory Sch. **Business Addr:** Director, PO Box 832627, Richardson, TX 75083-2627, **Business Phone:** (214)250-0548.

### MCNEAL, PASTOR DON (DONALD M MCNEAL)

Religious leader, public speaker, football player. **Personal:** Born May 6, 1958, Atmore, AL; married Rhonda; children: Jessica Morgan. **Educ:** Univ Ala, BS, social welfare. **Career:** Football player (retired), public speaker, pastor; Miami Dolphins, corner back, 1980-89; New Testament Baptist Church, coun pastor, c's pastor, currently; Sports World Inc, spokesman; Power Talent, speaker. **Orgs:** Univ Ala, All-Centennial Team. **Honors/Awds:** Captain of the Team for the 1979 Crimson Tide; NFL all rookie; Tommy Fitzgerald Member Award Outstanding Rookie, 1980; Dolphins' Player of the Year, 1982, 1984; Dolphins' Silver Anniversary team, 1982; Super Bowl XVII, 1983; Super Bowl XIX, 1985; Alabama Sports Hall of Fame, 2008; South Florida Bible College & Theological Seminary, DDiv. **Business Addr:** Pastor, New Testament Baptist Church, 6601 NW 167th Ave, Hialeah, FL 33015, **Business Phone:** (305)558-4930.

### MCNEAL, GLENDA G.

Vice president (organization), manager, financial manager. **Personal:** Born Jan 1, 1961?; married Philip. **Educ:** Dillard Univ, BA, acct, 1982; Univ Pa - Wharton Sch, MBA, finance & entrepreneurial mgt, 1986. **Career:** Arthur Andersen, auditor, 1982-84; Salomon Bros, mortgage specialist, 1986-89; Am Express, asst mgr, 1989-2000, GM New Indust Develop, vpres, 2000-03, Global Partnerships, sr vpres, 2003-05; GM Retail & Emerging Industs, sr vpres, 2005-09, GM Global Client Group, sr vpres, 2009-. **Orgs:** Pepsico Ethnic Adv Bd; trustee, Dillard Univ; bd, Ralph Lauren Ctr Cancer Care & Prev; United Negro Col Fund; PepsiCo, 1999-2011; Nat Retail Fedn Found, 2006-09; Bd dir, US Steel Corp, 2007-; RLJ Lodging Trust, 2011-; Newark Acad, 2014-15; Am Hotel & Lodging Asn, 2015-. **Honors/Awds:** "Black Enterprise", 100 Most Powerful Executives in Corporate America, 2009 "Black Enterprise", 75 Most Powerful Women in Business, 2010. **Business Addr:** Senior Vice President, American Express Co, Brookfield Pl 200 Vesey St, New York, NY 10285, **Business Phone:** (212)640-2000.

### MCNEAL, REV. JOHN ALEX, JR.

School administrator. **Personal:** Born Jun 18, 1932, Metter, GA; married Earlene Hazel; children: Lydia Tryphenia & Kezia Ruth. **Educ:** Ft Valley State Col, BS, 1961; Grace Theol Sem, BRE, 1964; Ga State Univ, MEd, 1975; Carver Bible Col, DD, 1986. **Career:** Atlanta Bible Baptist Church, sr pastor & founder, 1964-; Carver Bible Inst & Col, prof, rev & dean students, 1964-87; Fundamentalist Baptist Asn, publicity chmn, 1964, pres, 1975-77, vpres, 1977-80, pres, 1996-2000; Evangel Baptist Mission N Am, ethnic rep, 1985. **Orgs:** Evangel Baptist Mission; Fundamental Baptist; Asn Regular Baptist Churches; Baptist Bible Col; Baptist Bible Sem. **Honors/Awds:** Outstanding Educators of America, 1972; Award for Dedicated Serv, Carver Alumni Asn, 1972; Carver Bible Inst & Col Founder's Award, 1999; Pastor of the Year Award, Moody Bible Inst & Col, 1999. **Home Addr:** 2679 Rainbow Ct, Decatur, GA 30034-2212, **Home Phone:** (404)288-7444. **Business Addr:** Founder, Senior Pastor, Atlanta Bible Baptist Church, 1419 Peachcrest Rd, Decatur, GA 30032, **Business Phone:** (404)241-1176.

### MCNEAL, TIMOTHY KYLE (TIM MCNEAL)

Executive. **Personal:** Born Jun 27, 1960, Sacramento, CA; son of Carol and Homer. **Educ:** Univ Calif, CA, BA, polit sci, 1983. **Career:** AFS-USA, SP 77, returnee, 1977; Hughes Entertainment, Prod Assoc, 1985-88; Int Creative Mgt, agt, 1992-94; WB TV Network, vpres drama develop, 1994-99; Disney ABC TV Group, vpres talent develop & diversity, 2006-. **Orgs:** Bd dir, Univ Calif Los Angeles Alumni Asn; Nat Asn Mutual Ins Co. **Home Addr:** 800 S Shanandoah St, Los Angeles, CA 90035. **Business Addr:** Vice President, Disney ABC Television Group, 500 S Buena Vista St, Burbank, CA 91521-4016, **Business Phone:** (818)560-1000.

### MCNEAL, WILLIAM R., JR.

School superintendent, executive director. **Personal:** Born Jan 1, 1948. **Educ:** NC Cent Univ, BA, 1971, MA, 1976. **Career:** Teacher, school superintendent (retired), executive director; Danbury, CT, teacher, 1971-74; Wake County Schs Syst, Carroll Jr High Sch, teacher social studies, 1974-76, asst prin, 1976-78, E Garner Mid Sch, prin, 1978, from asst supt to assoc supt, 1979-2000, nat supt, 2000-06; from asst supt to assoc supt auxiliary serv, 1985, assoc supt instrnl serv, 1992; Martin Mid Sch, prin; NC State Bd Educ, supt advisor, 2005-06; NC Asn Sch Adminrs, exec dir, 2006-. **Orgs:** Bd mem, Wake Med Found; Everybody's Bus Coalition; Lightner Found; bd mem, Peace Col; bd mem, Golden Corral; bd mem, Triangle New Sch; bd mem, NC Pub Sch Forum. **Honors/Awds:** National Superintendent of the Year, Am Asn Sch Adminr, 2004; Bill McNeal Day named in honor, Wake County Schs, June 9, 2006. **Special Achievements:** Book: A School District's Journey to Excellence. **Business Addr:** Executive Director, North Carolina Association of School Administrators, 333 Fayetteville St Suite 1410, Raleigh, NC 27601, **Business Phone:** (919)828-1426.

### MCNEELY, DR. CAROL JEAN

Dentist, consultant. **Personal:** Born Jul 17, 1954, Chicago, IL; daughter of Lewis W and Jessie O Woodfin; children: Matthew Allan Ivy. **Educ:** Univ Ill Col Dent, DDS, 1979; Kellogg Sch Mgt Northwestern Univ, MM, 1995. **Career:** Tyrone Holiday DDS, assoc dentist, 1979-80; Dr Carol McNeely & Assocs, owner, 1979-; Provident Dent Assocs, owner, 1984-; Soulful Expressions, owner, 1987; Dent Network Am, consult, 1988-. **Orgs:** Speaker, Am Asn Women Dentists, 1982; treas, Lincoln Dent Soc Nat Dent Soc, 1982-83; assoc bd mem, Chicago Child Care Soc, 1982-85; Am Acad Cosmetic Dent, 1988; Am Dent Asn; Nat Dent Asn; co-chairperson, Chicago Urban League Sholarship Comt, 1989; Task force Women & Minorities, Am Dent Asn, 1992; pres, Chicago Metro Asn Black Women Dentists, 1992; Am Asn Health care Execs. **Honors/Awds:** Partners, Comt Nat Bar Asn Chicago Chap, 1985. **Business Addr:** Dentist, 4800 S Lake Pk Ave Suite 1707, Chicago, IL 60615-2190, **Business Phone:** (773)285-5880.

### MCNEELY, CHARLES E.

Government official. **Personal:** Born Jun 24, 1951; son of Louise Johnson and Aubrey; married Rosalind Gulley; children: Leslie, Brian & Brandon. **Educ:** Univ Kans, Lawrence, BA, polit sci, 1973, MPA, pub admin, 1975. **Career:** City San Diego, int rels intern, 1971; City Palo Alto, admin analyst, budget & staff servs, 1974-75, personnel adminr, 1975-76, mgt asst, 1976-78, asst city mgr, 1978-83; City Seaside, city mgr, 1983-93; E Bay Utility Dist, asst gen mgr; Golden Gate Univ, instr, 1991; Reno City, NV, mgr, 1996; San Bernardino City, CA, mgr. **Orgs:** Bd mem, CRA, 1990; chairperson, Coalition African Am Men, 1990-91; comt mem, League Calif Cities Advan Minorities & Women, 1990-91; comt mem, League Calif Cities Housing & Community & Econ Develop, 1991. **Home Addr:** 7481 Celeste Dr, Reno, NV 89511. **Business Addr:** NV.

### MCNEIL, DEEDEE

Poet, singer, playwright. **Personal:** Born Detroit, MI; daughter of Frank Lawton and Mary Virginia; children: Maricea Lynn , Harry Lawrence III & William A Chappell Jr. **Educ:** Pasadena City Col; Los Angeles City Col, music & jour. **Career:** Jobete Publ Co, Motown Rec Co, Detroit, contract songwriter, 1968-71; Ala Rec Co, Los Angeles, rec artist, 1971; Watts Prophets, col campus lectr & traveling poet, 1971-77; songwriter, singer, freelance jour & publ, 1971-; A&M Rec Co, Hollywood, publicist, 1972-73; United Artist Recs, Hollywood, Nat Press & Media Coord, 1973-74; contrib writer: var newspapers & mag in US & Can, 1974-75; Soul & Jazz Rec Mag, contrib ed, assoc ed & co-publ, 1975-77; Great Legends & Great Music Co, pres, currently; Double Dee Prod & Publ Co, founder; Novel: Jooziefruit. **Orgs:** Asst, David Gest & Assoc PR Firm, Hollywood; col speaker, sem promotional publ & publicity & co-establisher, Al-Bait Haram Publ Co, Calif, 1971; co-publ & operator, House Haram Publ Found; co-producer, Ar-Tee/Double Dee Prod Co; consult & pub rels specialist, KWANZA Orgn; Eddie Beal Scholar Fund Creative Youth; bd dir & lifetime mem, prog coordr, free prog C, Jazz & You, Jazz Heritage Found; Clifford Brown Found; founder, Great Legends & Great Music Co, Detroit; pres, Great Legends & Great Music Co; Nat Asn Advan Colored People. **Honors/Awds:** The Outreach Award, Pasadena, 1976; Shreveport Regional Bicentennial Comm Award, KWANZA Org, 1976; Named Director of Publicity, NATRA, 1976-77; Dean's honor list, Pasadena City Col Music Dept, Los Angeles City Col; Certificate of Merit, Am Song Festival, 1977; Nominee, Best Spoken Word Image Award, Nat Asn Advan Colored People, 1972; Winner, BET Jazz Nationwide Jazz Discovery Contest, 2001; Vocal Coach & Artist Develop Coach, Pasadena Int Music Acad, 2002-04. **Special Achievements:** Numerous articles published in Black Stars Magazine, Essence, Soul & Jazz Record Mag, numerous poems, wrote numerous songs; The Four Tops; Edwin Starr; Supremes; Kiki Dee; Gladys Knight; Diana Ross Nancy Wilson; Performed various col concerts with Watts Prophets, various TV appearances, featured vocalist, recordings & concerts, listed as west coast rap originator in "The Black Music History Los Angeles, It's Roots," 1992, wrote jazz column, Michigan Chronicle, 2000-04, was the first female, African-American Publicist for a major record label in Hollywood to establish a premiere comprehensive press list to service African-American newspapers and magazines across the country; Poem: Haiku In My Neighborhood, 2009; First female African-American Publicist for a major record label in Hollywood to establish a premiere comprehensive press list to service African-American newspapers and magazines across the country. **Business Addr:** Founder, President, Double Dee Productions & Publishing Co, 132 N El Camino Real Suite 154, Encinitas, CA 92024, **Business Phone:** (248)262-6877.

### MCNEIL, FRANK, SR.

Mayor, executive, government official. **Personal:** Born Jan 6, 1937, St. Louis, MO; married Annetta Cropp; children: Frank, Anita Louise, Patricia Ann, Betty Marie & Scott Kevin. **Career:** Wellston Mayor, city treasurer; Block Mothers, dir, 1973-. **Orgs:** Treas, Wellston Youth League Boys; Nat Roster Black Elected Officials, 1974. **Home Addr:** 6424 Myrtle, St Louis, MO 63133. **Business Addr:** 1804 Keinlin, St. Louis, MO 63133.

### MCNEIL, FRANK WILLIAM

Lobbyist. **Personal:** Born Dec 12, 1948, High Point, NC; son of Walter H and Madge Holmes; married Barbara Jean Curtain; children: Kwahme & Kofi. **Educ:** NC Cent Univ, Durham, NC, BA, polit sci, 1971; NC Cent Univ Sch Law, JD, 1974. **Career:** Ill Law Enforcement Comm, Springfield, Ill, legis specialist, 1974-76; State Bd Ethnics, Springfield, Ill, admin asst, 1976-77; Secy State Corp Div, Springfield, Ill, corp specialist, 1978-79, admin asst, 1979-81; Senate Dem Staff Parliamentarian, Springfield, Ill, 1981-86; Chicago Urban League, govt rel coordr, 1986-87; Springfield, Ill, consult & lobbyist, 1987-; Ill Dept Transp, dir, Off Bus & Workforce Diversity, 2003-; Ill Dept C & Family Serv, assoc dep dir, off monitoring & qual assurance, 2005-. **Orgs:** Springfield Urban League Guild; Springfield Pub Sch Found Springfield Br Nat Asn Advan Colored People; bd dir, Family Serv Ctr Sangamon County Bd, 1987; bd dir, Boy's Club; City Coun, City Springfield; exec dir, Ill Asn Minorities Govt; Kappa Alpha Psi Fraternity; Govs Task Force Human Serv Reform; chmn, African Am Family Comn; Springfield Community Fedn. **Honors/Awds:** Political Action Award, Nat Asn Advan Colored People, 1986; Man of the Year, Omega Psi Phi, 1986, 1987; Webster Plaque, Nat Asn Advan Colored People, 1987; Plaintiff in successful voting rights suit, McNeil vs City Springfield; Elected Alderman Ward 2 City of Springfield, 1987. **Special Achievements:** First African American Parliamentarian for the Illinois Senate. **Home Addr:** 2010 E Brown St, PO Box 20543, Springfield, IL 62703-2722, **Home Phone:** (217)753-2842. **Business Addr:** Deputy Director, Office of Business and Workforce Diversity, 2300 S Dirksen Pkwy, Springfield, IL 62764, **Business Phone:** (217)785-5394.

### MCNEIL, FREEMAN, III

Football player, manager. **Personal:** Born Apr 22, 1959, Jackson, MS; son of Freeman (deceased) and Gladys. **Educ:** Univ Calif, Los Angeles. **Career:** Football player (retired), computer executive; New York Jets, runningback, 1981-92; Advan Digital Data & Technol Inc, mgr, currently. **Honors/Awds:** Most Valuable Player, New York Jets, 1981-84; Mackiey Award, 1981; Rushing leader, National Football League, 1982; Three Pro Bowl, 1982, 1984, 1985; Three All-Pro, 1982, 1984, 1985; UCLA Athletic Hall of Fame, 1984; AFC Offensive Player of the Month, 1986; Ed Block Courage Award, 1990; Sidewalks of Newyork Award, Big Bros Big Sisters Newyork City, 1991; United Way Spokesman, 1994; Lougehrig Sports Award, ALS Asn, 1998; Certificate of Appreciation, Are Bergen & Passaic Counties Inc, 1999; President's Award, 1999; Heart of Gold Award, 2000; Arc, 2000; Nassau County Sports Hall of Fame, 2005; New York Jets Ring of Honor. **Home Addr:** 52 Dunlop Rd, Huntington, NY 11743-3934. **Business Addr:** Manager, Advance Digital Data & Technology Inc, 1490 N Clinton Ave, Bay Shore, NY 11706, **Business Phone:** (631)969-2600.

### MCNEIL, LORI MICHELLE

Association executive, tennis player. **Personal:** Born Dec 18, 1963, San Diego, CA; daughter of Charlie and Doris. **Educ:** Okla State Univ, attended 1983. **Career:** Prof tennis player (retired); tennis coach; tennis player, 1984-2002; US Tennis Champions Ctr, sr tennis prof, Col Park, Md; Coached AmandaCoetzer, 2001-04; US Olympic Women's Team, asst coach, 2004-08; US Tennis Asn, highperformance coach, nat high performance coach, 2004-12; Houstons Zina Garrison Acad, dir tennis; Asst Coach, US Olympic Womens Tennis Team, 2004; US Womens Tennis Coach, 2005. **Orgs:** Women Tennis Asn, 1983-; Wightman Cup Team, 1989; founder & chmn, LoriMcNeil Tennis Found. **Business Addr:** National High Performance Coach, United States Tennis Association, 7310 Crandon Blvd, Key Biscayne, FL 33149, **Business Phone:** (305)365-8782.

### MCNEIL, DR. OGRETTA V.

Educator, physiologist. **Personal:** Born Sep 2, 1932, Washington, DC; married Kingsley R; children: John & Robert Vaughn. **Educ:** Howard Univ, BS, 1954; Clark Univ, MA, 1959; PhD, 1967. **Career:** Educator (retired), psychologist; Worcester Youth Guid Ctr, psychologist, 1967-68; Worcester Pub Schs, clin psychologist, 1968-70, mentor; Assumption Col, asst prof, 1968-71; Anna Maria Col, consult clin psychologist, 1968-78; Holy Cross Col, assoc prof psychol, 1971-97, adv, dean; Clark Univ, visit lectr, 1972; Xavier Univ, founding mem. **Orgs:** Danforth assoc, 1971-77; NSF, 1971; Am Psychol Asn; AAUW corp laison; bd trustees, Univ Mass, 1976-81, 1992-97; Sigma Xi; bd trustees, LeMoyne Col, 1977-82; exec com, Asn Soc & Behav Sci, 1978-; AAUP Phi Beta Kappa; Worcester Sch Comt; pres, New Eng Psychol Asn, 1988-89. **Home Addr:** 14 Tahanto Rd, Worcester, MA 01602, **Home Phone:** (508)595-0219.

**MCNEIL, RANDY C.**
Association executive. **Career:** Youth Sports & Recreation Comn, founder, exec dir & pres, 2004-. **Orgs:** Founder, Youth Develop Comn; chmn, bd mem, Arise Detroit Inc; bd mem, Youth Sports & Recreation Comn; Detroit Workforce Develop Bd. **Business Addr:** President, Executive Director, Youth Sports & Recreation Commission, 1274 Library St Suite 201, Detroit, MI 48226-2291, **Business Phone:** (313)963-8916.

**MCNEIL, ROBERT LAWRENCE**
Business owner, consultant, association executive. **Personal:** Born Oct 3, 1969, Atlanta, GA; son of Robert L and Yvonne Sr; married Stacey R. **Educ:** Ga State Univ, exec, MBA; Nat Minority Supplier Develop Coun, grad; Kellogg Grad Sch Mgt, Advan Mgt Educ Prog; Tuck Sch Bus, advan MBE. **Career:** Images USA, pres & chief exec officer, founder, 1989-. **Orgs:** Am Mkt Asn; Atlanta Ad Club; Ga Minority Supplier Develop, Coun, AID Atlanta; Alpha Phi Alpha; Big Bros Big Sisters; bd mem, Nat Conf Community & Justice; bd mem, Am Inst Mng Diversity; bd mem, Nat Black Arts Festival; bd dir, Nat Underground Rr Freedom Ctr. **Business Addr:** President, Chief Executive Officer, Founder, Images USA, 1320 Ellsworth Indust Blvd, Atlanta, GA 30318, **Business Phone:** (404)892-2931.

**MCNEIL, RYAN DARRELL, II**
Executive, football player. **Personal:** Born Oct 4, 1970, Ft. Pierce, FL. **Educ:** Univ Miami. **Career:** Football player (retired), exec; Detroit Lions, defensive back & left corner back, 1993-96; St Louis Rams, defensive back & right defensive back, 1997-98; Cleveland Browns, defensive back & corner back & left corner back, 1999; Dallas Cowboys, right defensive back & defensive back, 2000; San Diego Chargers, defensive back & right defensive back & corner back, 2001-02; Denver Broncos, defensive back, 2003; Prof Bus & Financial Network, founder, currently. **Honors/Awds:** Consensus All-American, 1992; Interceptions Leader, Nat Football League, 1997; Pro Bowl, 2001. **Special Achievements:** TV appearance: 30 for 30, 2009; Bell Rung, 2012; Publisher of OT Magazine. **Business Addr:** Founder, Professional Business & Financial Network, 315 14th St NW Suite 2550, Atlanta, GA 30318, **Business Phone:** (866)536-4600.

**MCNEILL, CERVES TODD**
Artist, advertising executive. **Personal:** Born Jun 20, 1950, Jamaica, NY; son of Todd Cerves and Ella Mae; married Elizabeth Straka; children: Nigel Isaiah. **Educ:** NY Univ, Inst Film & Tv, BA, mkt & music, 1971; Univ Calif, LA, screenwriting, 1981, film prod, 1985; pvt study with Bess Bonnier, Jazz Piano Improvisation, 1990; Continental Cable Pub Access, prod cert, 1993. **Career:** Bassist, composer & actor; Freelance bassist, guitarist, vocalist, composer, actor, 1965-; Broadcast Music Inc, writer & publ affil, 1972-; Young & Rubicam Inc, NY copywriter, 1976-79; Benton & Bowles Inc, NY, sr copywriter, 1980; SSC&B Inc, Los Angeles, sr copywriter, 1980-81; Dancer Fitzgerald Sample Inc, Los Angeles, sr copywriter, 1982-84; self-employed, freelance copywriter & screenwriter, 1984-; Campbell-Ewald Advert, sr vip, assoc creative dir, 1986-98; O'Neal McClure, Detroit, exec, creative dir, 1998-99; Asher & Gal & Partners, Los Angeles, African Am Smoking Cessesion Proj, freelance copywriter, composer & producer, 1999-; Freelancealot Productions, owner, writer, dir, prod, composer, 2000-; Veriad, Brea, Calif, copywriter, web content writer, 2000-; Integrated MarketingWorks, Creative Consult, 2003-06; Songs: "Chaffed Elbows", bass player, 1965; Putney Swope, actor, 1969; "The White Whore & the 2 Bit Player", bass player, 1970; "My Heart & I Don't Believe, ", co-writer, bass player, 1972; "Plantation", writer, co-producer, actor, 1979; "The Great Steal", co-writer, co-producer, co-dir, music dir, 1991; Play: "Zodiocracy", 2002. **Orgs:** Am Fed Musicians, 1965-93; Christians In Advert, 1985-86; evangelist, Raulerson Evangelistic Asn, 1987-90; First & Second Ann Am Adv Fed, Top 25 Minority Adv Students Roundtables, 1997-98; music minister, Arise Christian Ctr, 1999-. **Honors/Awds:** CEBA Award, World Inst Black Commun Inc, United Negro Col Fund, 1979; CEBA Award, UNCF & Poster, 1980; ANDY Merit Award, Interagency Coun Child Abuse & Neglect, 1983; Merit Award, Art Dirs Club NY, Chevrolet, 1987; NY Festival Bronze Award, Int Film & TV Festival, 1990; Caddy Award of Merit, Detroit Creative Dirs Coun, GMAC Financing/TV, United Way & TV, 1990; Caddy Silver Award, Delta Faucet & TV, 1991; ADDY Award, Delta Faucet & TV, 1992; Continental Cable Access Award, 1993; O'Toole Award, Chevrolet Diversity & African Am, 1998. **Business Addr:** Freelance Bassist, Freelancealot Productions, 4900 Overland Ave Apt 329, Culver City, CA 90230-4289, **Business Phone:** (310)836-8271.

**MCNEILL, SUSAN PATRICIA**
Military leader. **Personal:** Born Oct 3, 1947, Washington, DC; daughter of Robert H and Lula M. **Educ:** Wilson Col, BA, 1969; Creighton Univ, JD, 1978; Pepperdine Univ, MBA, 1980. **Career:** Military leader (retired); USF, Edwards AFB, asst staff judge advocate, contract atty, 1978-81; Norton AFB, Ballistic Missile Off, asst staff judge advocate, staff atty, 1981-84; Lindsey Air Sta, Ger, Staff Judge Advocate, chief legal officer, 1984-87; Dept Justice, Defense Procurement Fraud Unit, trial atty, 1987-89; Pentagon, Air Force Contract Law Div, trial atty, 1989-91, Air Force Gen Coun Off, staff atty, 1991-92; Defense Systs Mgt Col, Acquisition Law Task Force, assoc dir, sr atty, 1992-93; AF Gen Couns Off, civilian staff atty, 1993-95. **Orgs:** Big Sisters Omaha, 1977-78; Nebr Bar Asn, 1978-; chap pres, Nat Contract Mgt Asn, Wiesbaden, Ger, 1985-87; exec bd mem, Air Force Cadet Off Mentor Prog, 1991-; Am Bar Asn, Gov Contracts Sect, 1991-; pres, Md Citizen Planners Asn, 2002-03; vice chair, sec, St Mary's County Bd Zoning Appeals. **Honors/Awds:** Big Sister of the Year, Judge Advocate, Big Sisters Omaha, 1978; Serv Award, Nat Coalition, 100 Black Women, VA Commonwealth Chapter, 1993. **Special Achievements:** Highest ranking AFA female Judge Advocate in all branches of the Armed Forces, 1993. **Home Addr:** PO Box 297, Leonardtown, MD 20650, **Home Phone:** (301)475-1745.

**MCNEILL-HUNTLEY, ESTHER MAE**
Government official, educator. **Personal:** Born May 7, 1921, Fayetteville, NC; daughter of Margaret; children: Micheline E, Karen D & Frances M. **Educ:** NC Agr & Tech State Univ, BS, home econ, 1944; Bank St Col NYC, teachers cert; NY Univ, admin, attended 1953; Fayetteville State Univ, small bus mgt, attended 1977. **Career:** Educator (retired); NY, postal clerk; day care teacher; Headstart teacher; Wash Ave Day Care Ctr, first dir; Rainbow Nursery Sch, proprietor & dir, currently. **Orgs:** Girl Scout Leader, NY, 1970-72; third dist chairwoman, Women Munic Govt, 1982-85; found bd, Bladen Tech Col; NC Black Leadership Caucus; Nat Black Caucus Local Elected Officials; vpres, NC Minority Pub Officials; Bladen Co Improv Asn; charter & former mem, Bladen Co Arts Coun; Mt Zion AME Zion Church; Rainbow Nursery Parent Club, Sch Parent Teach Asn. **Honors/Awds:** County Chmn, LINC Children's 100, 1974; Lobbyist in Wash DC for Newtown Comn Block Grant awarded, 1983; Outstanding Community Serv, Zeta Phi Beta, 1983; Appointed by Gov James G Martin, serve Local Govt Advocacy Coun, 1985 (2 yr term); State of NC Human Relations Comn, Gov Jim B Hunt, Certificate of Appreciation, 1994; Outstanding Service to Family & Community, Rainbow Nursery Sch, 1994; Nat Asn Advan Colored People, W Bladen Br, 50 Years Service to Children, 1945-95, Humanitarian Award, 1996; Represented, City of Elizabethtown Nat League of Cities; First woman to be elected to City Coun; Cert of Appreciation, Holshouser Jr; Treas, Rainbow Nursery Parents Club Inc. **Special Achievements:** First Black elected to Elizabethtown's City Council in 1979. **Home Addr:** 303 S Morehead St, PO Box 2391, Elizabethtown, NC 28337-2391, **Home Phone:** (919)862-3393. **Business Addr:** Director, Rainbow Nursery School, 303 S Morehead St, Elizabethtown, NC 28337, **Business Phone:** (910)862-3393.

**MCNORRIELL, MOZELL M.**
Executive. **Personal:** Born Oct 20, 1922, Marshall, TX; children: Robert Jr. **Educ:** Wayne State Univ, Labor Sch, attended 1971. **Career:** AFL-CIO, int vpres, 1974; Wayne Co Local 409 AFSCME, int vpres, pres; Metro Cist Coun 23, secy. **Orgs:** Life mem, Nat Asn Advan Colored People; Elliottorian Bus Women's Club; Plymouth United Ch Christ; nat co-ordinating com mem, Coalition Labor Union Women; dir, Civil Rights Trade Union Leadership Coun; Coalition Black Trade Unionists. **Honors/Awds:** Harriet Tubman Award. **Home Addr:** 4103 Kendall, Detroit, MI 48238.

**MCNORTON, BRUCE EDWARD**
Football player, football executive. **Personal:** Born Feb 28, 1959, Daytona Beach, FL; children: Brittney. **Educ:** Georgetown Col, KY, BA, social work, 1982. **Career:** Football player (retired), football exec; Spruce Creek, corner back, safety & wide receiver; Detroit Lions, corner back & safety & right corner back, left corner back, 1982-90; Miami Dolphins, 1991; Pittsburgh Steelers, Football Opers, col scout, 2007-. **Honors/Awds:** Georgetown Col Athletic Hall of Fame, 2000; Col fotball hall of fame. **Special Achievements:** One of the first players ever drafted from Georgetown. **Business Addr:** College Scout, Pittsburgh Steelers, 100 Art Rooney Ave, Pittsburgh, PA 15212-5721, **Business Phone:** (412)697-7700.

**MCPHAIL, DR. CHRISTINE JOHNSON**
Administrator, educator, manager. **Personal:** Born Feb 1, 1946, Tyler, TX; children: Ralph Bessard & Roderic Bessard. **Educ:** Fresno City Col, BA, 1967, MEd, educ, 1976; Calif State Univ, MA, 1972; Univ Southern Calif, Berkeley, EdD, higher educ/higher educ admin, 1987, PhD. **Career:** Fresno County Econ Opportunities Comn, counr job develop, 1968-69; Fresno State Univ, Live & Learn Ctr, coordr, 1969-70; Fresno State Univ, asst prof, 1971-74; Contra Costa Col, chair person coun-instrs, 1974-76; Col Alameda, asst dean, 1976-78; Cypress Col, pres & chief instrnl officer, 1995-98; Morgan State Univ, prof & prog dir, 1998-2009, emerita prof, Community Col Leadership Doctoral Prog, founder; McPhail Group, managing partner, 2001-; Achieving Dream Inc, leadership coach, 2004-; Col Alameda, dean stud serv; Kings River Community Col, Reedley, Calif, dean stud; Editor: AACC publ, Community Col Leadership Doctoral Prog, Baltimore, Md, prof & coordr; Am Assoc Community Cols & Coun Study Community Cols, bd dir, adv coun. **Orgs:** Consult Regional Off Health & Welfare Head Start San Francisco; CalifState Univ Law Enforcement Training Prog; com on status women Univ Calif Berkeley; mem Am Personnel & Guid Asn; mem Am Asn Univ Women; mem Coun on Black Am Affaris; CounStudy Community Cols & Am Educ Res Asn; bd dir, Am Asn Community Cols; ed bd, Community Col J Res & Pract. **Honors/Awds:** White house fellows finalist Commn on White House Fellows, 1972; Golden Educator's Award, Fresno state Col, 1973; Outstanding young women of America, 1976; Summer institute fellow, Bryn Mawr Summer Inst, 1979; Research Award, Am Asn Univ; Outstanding Alumini of the Year, Fresno City Community Col, 1990; Outstanding Alumini of the Year, Calif State Univ, Fresno, 1998; Terry O'Banion Leadership Award, League for Innovation in the Community Col, 2008; National Leadership Award, Am Assoc of Community Col, 2010. **Special Achievements:** Co-author of "Transforming Classroom Practice for African American Learners: Implications for the Learning Paradigm", Books such as "Walk the Rainbow: When You Get Tired of Waiting to Exhale" and "A Pocket Book of Mother Wit: Leadership Principles for the New Millennium". Guest columnist and featured writer for newspapers in California and Texas; State Center Community College Educator's Hall of Fame. **Home Addr:** 4338 Walnut St, Oakland, CA 94619. **Business Addr:** Managing Principal, The McPhail Group, PO Box 713, Amawalk, NY 10501, **Business Phone:** (410)245-9955.

**MCPHAIL, DR. IRVING P.**
School administrator, chancellor (education), association executive. **Personal:** Born Mar 27, 1949, New York, NY; married Carolyn Jean Carver; children: Kamilah Carole. **Educ:** Cornell Univ, BS, develop sociol, 1970; Harvard Univ, MAT, 1971; Univ Pa, EdD, 1976. **Career:** Univ Pa, Nat Fels Fund Fel; Morgan State Univ Baltimore, coord freshman reading prog, 1971-73, assocprof ed, chmn dept curr & instr, 1977-80; The Johns Hopkins UnivBaltimroe, spec asst to pres & provost, 1978-79; Univ MD Col Park, asstprovost div human & comm res, assoc prof curric & instr; BaltimoreCity Pub Sch, chief operating officer, 1984-85; Kamilah Educ EnterprisesInc, pres, prin cons; Del State Col, vpres, dean acad affairs, prof educ, 1985; Lemoyne-Owen Col, pres, 1993-95; St. Louis Community Col Florissant Valley, pres, 1995-98; Community Col Baltimore Co, chancellor, 1998-2005; Morgan State Univ, sr tenured fac; Del State Univ, sr tenured fac; LeMoyne-Owen Col, sr tenured fac; Pace Univ, sr tenured fac; Am Educ Res Asn Comn, comnr; Nat Asn Black Reading & Lang Educr, co-founder, pres; Am Coun Educ, secy bd dir; Teaching African Am Learners to Read, Co-ed, currently; Nat Action Coun Minorities Engineering, pres, Chief exec officer, currently; Transforming Classroom Pract African Am Learners, Co-auth, currently. **Orgs:** Antioch Univ, 1975-76, 82-; co-found & pres, Nat Asn Black Reading & LangEd; Nat Alliance Black Sch Educrs; Int Reading Asn; Am Asn Higher Ed; Nat Coun Teachers Eng; Phi Delta Kappa; Col Reading Asn; consult, AID Prog Staff Devel Sch Dist Philadelphia, 1976; consult off Right to Read Baltimore City Publ Sch, 1977; auth over 25 articles chaps & meno graphs inprof lit; Alpha Phi Alpha, ZetaRho Lambda; vchmn Del Coalition Literacy. **Honors/Awds:** Am Counc Ed Fel Acad Admin, 1978-79; Nat Fel Fund Doctoral Fel Phi Delta Kappa Univ of Pa; Certs Outstanding Contribs & Servs, Morgan State Univ, 1973; Md Reading Inst, 1977, 81, 85; Baltimore City Pub Sch, 1977, 85; IRA, 1978, 81, 82, 85; Teacher Corps, 1979; DC Public Schs, 1983; Copping State Col, 1984; Md State Dept of Educ, 1985; Concord Black Parents Hartford City, 1986; Listed in Men of Achievement, 1977; Selected as Eminent Scholar Norfolk State Univ, 1981; Exemplary Leader and Pioneer Award, Nat Coun Black Am Affairs; Learning Facilitator and Distinguished Service Award, Community Col Leadership Doctoral Prog, Morgan State Univ; Emerging Scholars Award, St. Louis Community Col. **Special Achievements:** One of Americas Ten Outstanding Young Men, US Jaycees, 1982. **Home Addr:** 3 Shadow Ct, Owings Mills, MD 21117, **Home Phone:** (410)560-1577. **Business Addr:** Chancellor, Community College Baltimore Co, Col Syst Off, Baltimore, MD 21228, **Business Phone:** (410)869-1220.

**MCPHAIL, JERRIS CORNELIUS**
Football player. **Personal:** Born Jun 26, 1972, Clinton, NC; married Mahogany; children: Jizzel & Jene. **Educ:** E Carolina Univ. **Career:** Football player (retired); Miami Dolphins, running back, 1996-97; Detroit Lions, running back, 1998; Cleveland Browns, 1999.

**MCPHAIL, SHARON M.**
Government official, lawyer. **Personal:** Born Nov 6, 1948, Cambridge, MA; daughter of Robson Bacchus and Natalie Fowler; married David Snead; children: Angela & Erika. **Educ:** Coe Col, attended 1968; Northeastern Univ, BA, sociol & eng, MA, 1972; Univ Mich Law Sch, attended 1976; Northeastern Univ Law Sch, JD, 1976. **Career:** Ford Motor Co, staff atty, 1976-80; US asst atty, 1980-82; US spec asst atty, 1982-83; Dickinson, Wright, Moon, Van Dusen & Freeman, assoc, 1982-84; Bushnell, Gage, Doctoroff & Reizen, assoc, 1984-86; Wayne Co Corp Coun, prin atty, 1986-87; Wayne Co Prosecutors Off, chief screening & dists, 1987-94; Feikens, Stevens, Hurley & PC, partner, 1995-; City Detroit, gen coun; Detroit City Coun, councilwoman, 2002-06; pvt pract atty, currently. **Orgs:** Mich Bar, 1976; chairperson, pres, Detroit Bd Police Comnrs, 1985-90; secy, treas & bd dir, Detroit Br, Nat Asn Advan Colored People; pres, Wolverine Bar Asn, 1985-86; vpres, 1986-89, pres, 1992, Nat Bar Asn; vice chair, Wayne County Neighborhood Legal Servs, 1987-; dir, Nat Coun Northeastern Univ, 1988-; vice chair, State Officers Compensation Comn, 1988; Sixth Circuit Judicial Conf, US Ct Appeals; bd dir, Fed Bar Asn, 1988; bd dir, Music Hall Ctr Performing Arts, 1988; fel Mich State Bar Found, 1988; dir, Kirwood Ment Health Ctr, 1990; Women Lawyers Asn, Mich; Asn Defense Trial Coun; vpres, Nat Asn Adv Colored People, Detroit. **Special Achievements:** First female attorney to be elected to Detroit's City Council. **Home Addr:** 1220 W McNichols, Detroit, MI 48203.

**MCPHERSON, DAVID**
Executive. **Personal:** Born Jan 1, 1968, St. Louis, MO; married Virginia. **Educ:** William Patterson Univ, Wayne, NJ. **Career:** Elecktra Rec, intern; Mercury Rec, intern, Mkt Dept, A&R mgr; Jive Rec, A&R dir; Epic Rec, Urban Music, sr vpres, 1998-2000, A&R, exec vpres, 2000-, urban music, exec vpres, 2000-; Mcphersongs, pres & chief exec officer; Sony Corp, exec vpres. **Business Addr:** Exec Vice President, Epic Records Group, 550 Madison Ave, New York, NY 10022, **Business Phone:** (212)833-8000.

**MCPHERSON, JAMES ALAN.** See Obituaries Section.

**MCPHERSON, JAMES R.**
Lawyer, manager. **Personal:** Born Mar 26, 1953, Fayetteville, NC; son of Willie D Wright and Annie R Wright; married Michelle Bagley. **Educ:** Fayetteville State Univ, BS, bus admin, 1975; Univ Wis, Madison, WI, MBA, 1980; Georgetown Univ Law Ctr, JD, 1985. **Career:** Univ Wis, advan opportunity fel, 1982; Scott Paper CPN, personnel asst, 1981-82; SUU DPT Lab, prog analyst, 1983-84; US Claims Ct, legal intern, 1983-84; Int Brotherhood Teamsters, law clerk, 1984-85; Clark, Klein & Beaumont, assoc, 1985-88; Carolina Power & Light CPN, assoc gen coun, 1988-92, human resource projs mgr, asst vpres, employee rels dept, area employee servs mgr, 1992-94; Area Human Resources, mgr, 1994, Northern Region asst vpres, 1994-95; Sanford, dist mgr, 1995-96; Progress Energy, mgr, 1988-2000; Sanford, Southern Pines, dist mgr, 1996; IBM, exec resources prog mgr, orgn leadership consult, hr bus partner, 2000-05; Vision & Destiny Group, founder, chief exec officer, 2002-; Tekelec, dir global resource & learning, 2005-07; Duke Univ & Health Syst, Learning & Org Develop, dir, 2007-13; Tilt Inc, exec coach, 2010-13; Carolinas Healthcare Syst, vpres & chief learning officer, 2013-15. **Orgs:** Charter mem, Fayetteville State Univ, Delta Mu Delta Nat Hon Soc Bus Admin, 1976; fel Consortium Grad Study Mgt, 1979-80; NCA Bar Asn, Labor & Employ Sec, 1989-91; Am Asn Blacks Energy, 1989-; Am Creative Coun Asn, 1989-92; Wake County Bar Asn, 1989-92; chair, Bar Exam Stipend Sub Community, Minorities Prof Community, 1989-92; Nat Bar Asn, 1989-92; NC Asn Black Lawyers, 1989-92; Soc Human Resource Mgt, 1992-95; bd dir, Triangle Orgn Develop Network; bd dir, Bibl Wellness Ministries; bd dir, Sanford & Lee County Chamber Com; bd dir, Duke Univ; bd dir, Wachovia Bank. **Honors/Awds:** Earl Warren Legal Scholar, 1982. **Home Addr:** 2122 Jasony, Sanford, NC 27330, **Home Phone:** (919)708-7202. **Business Addr:** Executive Coach, Tilt Inc, PO Box 31743, Raleigh, NC 27622, **Business Phone:** (919)789-0737.

**MCPHERSON, ROOSEVELT**
Educator, clergy, writer. **Personal:** Born Nov 27, 1948, Fayetteville, NC; son of Clara Mae Hill and Arthur; married Carrie Lee Ratliff; children: Ratliff, Kenyatta Troy & Tameka McGilvary. **Educ:** Fayette-

ville State Univ, Fayetteville, NC, BA, 1974, MA, educ admin & supv, 1997; Nova Southeastern Univ, Ft Lauderdale, FL, EdD, educ leadership & admin, 2007. **Career:** Burlington Industs, Raeford, NC, prod supvr, 1974-76; Kane-Miller, Fayetteville, NC, admin asst, 1976-78; Sears Roebuck, Fayetteville, NC, credit corresp, 1978-81; Gen Productions Inc, Raeford, NC, publ & ed, 1981-; Sandhills Community Col, Raeford, NC; Renaissance Bks, chief exec officer & pres, 1997-. **Orgs:** Bd dir, Sanctuary Deliverance Churches Inc, 1986-89; assoc minister, Mt Sinai Sanctuary Deliverance Church, 1985-88; minister/deacon, Mt Carmel Holy Church God, 1978-83; Hoke County Black Caucus, 1985; Hoke County Br, Nat Asn Advan Colored People, 1981; Hoke County Civic League, 1981; Nat Newspaper Publishers Assn, 1985-; Nc Black Publishers, 1985-.Faith Christian Temple, pastor, 1999-; Innovative Church Community; NorthCarolina Asn Educr; Asn Supv & Curric Develop; Nat Educ Asn; bd mem, Northwest Water Supply Inc. **Home Addr:** 190 Maj Evans Rd, Raeford, NC 28376-6250, **Home Phone:** (919)875-5845. **Business Addr:** Chief Executive Officer, President, Renaissance Books, 100 Hay St Suite 801, Fayetteville, NC 28311, **Business Phone:** (910)551-2913.

## MCPHERSON, ROSALYN J.

Publishing executive, writer. **Personal:** Born Mar 27, 1953, New Orleans, LA; daughter of James and Lillie; children: Jackie Robert Kelley II, Monique Cheri Kelley & Jasmin Renee Andrews. **Educ:** Southern Univ, A&M Col, BS, sec ed, 1973; Fairleigh Dickinson Univ, MBA, mkt, 1982. **Career:** Roosevelt Pub Schs, teacher, 1975-76; CBS Inc, ed, 1976-79; McGraw-Hill, ed, 1979-80; Time Warner Educ Task Force, NY, chmn; Scholastic Inc, prod mgr, 1980-83; Time Inc, source mgr, circulation, 1983-85; McPherson Andrews Mkt Inc, pres & founder, 1985-92; Rutgers Univ, adj prof, 1986-92; Time Life Inc, sr vpres & publ, 1993-2000; Franklin Inst, sr vpres, mkt & sci ctr, 2000-04; RJM Consult Group Inc, pres, currently; ROZ Group, pres & founder, 2005-; Forum Exec Women, Bd dir, currently; Auth: Milestones Sci & Mathematics, Facts-on-File, 1996; African Americans: Voices Triumph; Urban League Philadelphia, pres & chief exec officier, 2014-16. **Orgs:** Nat Asn Black Sch Educ; Int Reading Asn; Nat Coun Social Studies; bd mem, Northern Va Urban League; bd mem, Models Excellence, NASA, NSF; bd mem, Women's Proj & Prod; Col Bd, Task Force mem; bd trustee mem, Nat Philanthropic Trust Inc; bd gov mem, Philly Ad Club; bd mem, First Person Arts; Community Col Philadelphia; Philadelphia Educ Fund; Greater Philadelphia Chamber Com; Girl Scouts Eastern Pa; Ment Health Asn Southeastern Pa. **Home Addr:** 2808 Holland Ct, Alexandria, VA 22306, **Home Phone:** (703)360-5921. **Business Addr:** President, The ROZ Group Inc, 1700 Sansom St Suite 501, Philadelphia, PA 19103, **Business Phone:** (215)564-6151.

## MCPHERSON, VANZETTA PENN

Judge. **Personal:** Born May 26, 1947, Montgomery, AL; daughter of Luther L and Sadie G; married Thomas Jr; children: 4. **Educ:** Howard Univ, BA, speech path & audiol, 1969; Columbia Univ, MA, speech path, 1971; Columbia Law Sch, JD, 1974. **Career:** Judge (retired); NMSC, nat achievement scholar, 1965-69; Legal Serv Elderly Poor, summer assoc, 1972; Thatcher, Proffit & Wood, summer assoc, 1973; Hughes, Hubbard & Reed, assoc, 1974-75; State Ala, asst atty gen, 1975-78; pvt pract, atty, 1978-92; US Govt, US Dist Ct, Mid Dist Ala, judge, 1992-06; co-owner, Roots & Wings, 1989. **Orgs:** Fel Am Asn Univ Women, 1974-85; pres & vpres, Ala Lawyers Asn, 1980-81, vpres; life mem, Am Bar Asn, 1981-; bd mem, Ala Shakespeare Festival, 1987-; Leadership Montgomery; master bencher, Montgomery County Inn Ct, 1990-; Nat Coun Negro Women; pres, Fed Bar Asn, 1997-99; Montgomery Symphony Orchestra; life mem, Nat Bar Asn; Alas Fed Judicial Nominating Comn; Eleventh Circuit Adv Coun; adv comts, Ala Supreme Ct; pres, Montgomery Chap Fed Bar Asn; chmn, Family Law Sect Ala State Bar. **Honors/Awds:** Legacy of the Dreamer Award, SCLC, 1981; Law Off Design Award, Am Bar Asn, 1985; Women of Achievement, Montgomery Advertiser, 1989; Awards from Southern Christian Leadership Conference, the Women of Distinction, South Central Alabama Girl Scout Council, & Delta Sigma Theta Sorority, Inc. **Special Achievements:** Introduction of Blood Tests in Paternity Litigation, ABA, 1986.

## MCPHERSON, WILLIAM H.

Editor, technical writer. **Personal:** Born May 18, 1927, Ft. Worth, TX; married Olivia T Denmon; children: Valencia D & Olivette R. **Educ:** Morehouse Col, BS, 1948. **Career:** Editor (retired); N Am Aviation Space & Info Systs Div, tech writer, 1963-67; N Am Rockwell Corp Autonetics Div, tech writer, 1967-68; The Aerospace Corp El Segundo, Calif, publ ed, supvr. **Home Addr:** 3723 Monteith Dr, Los Angeles, CA 90043, **Home Phone:** (323)296-6272. **Business Addr:** El Segundo, CA 90245.

## MCQUARN, TRACEY ELAINE. See EDMONDS, TRACEY E.

## MCQUARTERS, ROBERT WILLIAM, II

Football player, television sportscaster. **Personal:** Born Dec 21, 1976, Tulsa, OK; married Monique; children: Robert III, Rylan, Reagan & Ricki Wrene. **Educ:** Okla State Univ. **Career:** Football player (retired), free agt; San Francisco 49ers, defensive back & right corner back & punt returner & left corner back, 1998-99; Chicago Bears, corner back & right corner back & left corner back & free safety, 2000-04; Detroit Lions, defensive back & right corner back & left corner back, 2005; New York Giants, corner back & right corner back & left corner back & defensive back, 2006-08; Free agt; TV ser: ESPN's Sunday Night Football, 2001-05; NBC Sunday Night Football, 2007-08; Rachael Ray, 2009. **Orgs:** Founder, RW McQuarters Found. **Honors/Awds:** Super Bowl XLII, New York Giants, 2007; First-team All-Pro, Sports Illus. **Home Addr:** 20th St N, Tulsa, OK 74126.

## MCQUATER, PATRICIA A.

Executive director, lawyer. **Personal:** Born Sep 25, 1951, Washington, DC; daughter of Matthew and Margaret Jackson. **Educ:** Boston Univ, Col Bus Admin, BS, 1973; Univ San Diego Sch Law, JD, 1978. **Career:** San Diego City Coun, admin intern, 1976-78; US Supreme Ct, intern, 1977; Country San Diego, admin asst, 1979-82; Foodmaker Inc, corp coun, 1982-84; Solar Turbines Inc, atty, sr corp atty, 1984-2010; San Diego Balbo Park Celebration 2015 Inc, dir, chmn, Risk Mgt Comt. **Orgs:** Nat Bar Asn, 1981-; bd govs, Earl B Gellium Bar Asn, 1982-; Am Bar Asn; Calif Asn Bulk Lawyers; San Diego Country Bar Asn; Am Arbitration Asn; secy & bd dir, San Diego Urban League, 1982-, chairperson, bd chair, 1988-89, nat delegate, 1986-89, chair, budget & finance comn, 1986-88; EO-Chr Country San Diego Affirm Action Comn, 1983-; Girl Scouts, San Diego-Imperial Coun Inc, 1985-90, nat deleg, 1986-89, exec dir search comm, coun nominating comt, 1990-92; San Diego Conv Ctr Corp, pres, 1989-95, chair, 1992-93; vpres, San Diego Convention Ctr, corp bd dir, 1990-; bd dir, Univ San Diego Sch Law Admin, 1990-; Calif Bar Asn; Am Immigration Lawyers Asn; Am Corp Coun Asn; USD Sch Law Alumni Asn, 1991-, pres, 1995-96; exec comn, Children's Hosp & Health Ctr, 1992-94; port/airport comnr, San Diego Unified Port Dist, 1994-, vice chair, 1998, chair; Port San Diego, bb port Commissioners, chair; trustee, Conserv's Bd; trustee, San Diego Youth Symphony. **Honors/Awds:** California Women Governor Award, 1992; TWIN Award, Solar Honoree, 1992; San Diego Mus Art, Songs My People: 100 Role Models, 1994; San Diego Hotel-Motel Asn, Gold Key Award, 1994; Outstanding Alumni Award, USDWomen's Law Caucus, 1997; Tribute to a Living History, Palavra Tree Inc, 1998; Distinguished Alumni Award, Univ San Diego Sch Law, 1999; Career Achievement Award, 2000. **Business Addr:** Attorney, Solar Turbines Inc, 3676 Keating St, San Diego, CA 92110.

## MCQUAY, JAMES PHILLIP (FURRIER JAMES MCQUAY)

Business owner. **Personal:** Born Nov 15, 1924, Baltimore, MD; married Doris; children: James Jr, Kevin & Jamal. **Educ:** NY Fashion Sch Design; Yonkers High Sch, attended 1943. **Career:** Fur Bus, owner; James McQuay Furnitures Inc, owner, currently. **Honors/Awds:** Fur Design Award, 1972, 1975, 1976; Spec furniture showing for congressional black caucus Wash, 1977; First Place Award for Design Century Furniture Trade Show, 1980; Madame C J Walker Award, 2008; Featured in Alpha Kappa Alpha Sorority. **Special Achievements:** First African American furrier in the US; Featured in Essence, Ebony, Jet and The New York Times and has appeared on David Letterman and Today. **Home Addr:** 600 W Harvey St Apt B1205, Philadelphia, PA 19144-4388. **Business Addr:** President, James McQuay Furnitures Inc, 151 W 30th St, New York, NY 10001.

## MCQUEEN, KEVIN PAIGE

Banker, president (organization), manager. **Personal:** Born Jul 8, 1958, Brooklyn, NY; son of Robert Paige and Constance Marie Jackson; married Ruthanna Graves. **Educ:** Brown Univ, Providence, RI, AB, ethics & polit philos, 1980. **Career:** Nat Westminster Bank, USA, New York, NY, banking officer, 1980-82; Citibank, NA, New York, NY, relationship mgr, 1982-85; Nat Cong Community Econ Develop, Wash, DC, prog dir, 1985-88; Nat Coop Bank Develop Corp, Wash, DC, vpres, 1988; NCB Capital Impact, vpres, 1988-94; New Columbia Capital Advisors, prin, 1994-2001; Nat Bank USA; Brody Weiser Burns, partner, 2001-. **Orgs:** Metrop Delta Adult Literacy Coun; bd mem, Nat Neighborhood Coalition, 1987-88; pres, Brown Univ Club, Wash, DC, 1988-90; steering comt coordr, Third World Alumni Network Brown Univ, 1990-; Pres, Wash Area Community Investment Fund, 1998-2002; chair bd dir, Dance Pl, 2000-04; partner, Common Good, 2003; adv bd mem, Consortium Am CDE, 2005; Community Adv Bd Mem, CityFirst Bank CDE, 2005; dir, Social Enterprise Alliance, 2006-10; bd mem, treas, Community Health Accreditation Prog Inc, 2011-14; dir, SeaChange Capital Partners, 2012-15; treas, Enterprising Staffing Servs; bd, Wash DC Local Develop Corp; Nat Neighborhood Coalition; Community Adv Bd; community adv bd mem, City First Bank CDE. **Home Addr:** 6711 Conway Ave, Takoma Park, MD 20912. **Business Addr:** Partner, Brody Weiser Burns, 250 W Main St Suite 110, Branford, CT 06405, **Business Phone:** (203)481-4199.

## MCRAE, EMMETT N.

Restaurateur, government official. **Personal:** Born Feb 12, 1943, Rennert, NC; son of Donnie and Katie Smith; married Helen McLean; children: David, Linda F & Lori A Strickland. **Career:** CS&X Transp Rr, Florence, cook, 1968-90; E & H BBQ Hut, Rennert, owner, operator, 1984-; City Rennert, mayor, currently. **Orgs:** Deacon, 2nd St Matthew Baptist Church, 1970-; Carpenters Consistory No164, 1975-; worship master, St Pauls Masonic Lodge, No 354, 1979-87; pres, Sunday Sch Conv, 1986; master, St Pauls Masonic Lodge No 354, 1987-; bd mem, Lumber River Coun Govt, currently. **Home Addr:** Rt 1 Box 42, Shannon, NC 28386, **Home Phone:** (919)843-5755. **Business Addr:** Mayor, Town of Rennert, 62 Pk St Rte 1, Shannon, NC 28386, **Business Phone:** (910)843-2162.

## MCRAE, HAROLD ABRAHAM (HAL MCRAE)

Baseball manager, baseball player. **Personal:** Born Jul 10, 1945, Avon Park, FL; son of Willie James and Virginia Foster; married Johncyna Williams; children: Brian, Cullen & Leah. **Educ:** Fla A & M Univ, attended 1966. **Career:** Baseball player (retired), baseball coach; Minor Leagues, baseball player, 1965-68; Cincinnati Reds, baseball player, 1968, 1970-72; World Series, 1970, 1972, 1985; League Championship Series, 1970, 1972, 1976-78, 1985; Kans City Royals, baseball player, 1973-87, hitting instr, 1987, mgr, 1991-94; Pittsburgh Pirates, minor league hitting instr, 1987-89; Montreal Expos, Montreal, Canada, hitting instr, 1990-91; Cincinnati Reds, hitting instr, 1995-96; Philadelphia Phillies, hitting instr, 1997-2000; Tampa Bay Devil Rays, mgr, 2001-02, asst to gen mgr, 2002; St Louis Cardinals, hitting coach, 2005-09. **Home Addr:** 2431 Landing Cir, Bradenton, FL 34209. **Business Addr:** Hitting Coach, St Louis Cardinals, Busch Stadium, St. Louis, MO 63102, **Business Phone:** (314)421-3060.

## MCRAE, LAWRENCE D. (LARRY MCRAE)

Executive, vice president (organization). **Educ:** Morgan State Univ, BS, acct, 1980; Harvard Bus Sch, MBA. **Career:** Financial, sales & mkt, 1985; Price Waterhouse, sr acct; Corning Inc, 1985-, mgr int sales sci prod, 1990-93; Revere Ware Corp (Corning Consumer Prod Co), bus dir, pres, 1995-96, div vpres global develop telecommunications prod div, 1996-2000, vpres corp develop, 2000-03, sr vpres corp develop, 2003-05, sr vpres strategy & corp develop, 2005-10, exec vpres strategy & corp develop, 2010-. **Orgs:** Bd dir, Dow Corning Corp, 2005; bd dir, Samsung Corning Precision Mat Co; Corning Mgt Comt, 2007-.

## MCRAE, RONALD EDWARD

Salesperson. **Personal:** Born Feb 7, 1955, Dillon, SC; son of Dudley and Betty. **Educ:** Macalester Col, BA, 1976; Northwestern Univ Sch Mgt, MBA, 1978; DePaul Univ Sch Law, JD, 1986. **Career:** Toro Co, mkt internship, 1976; Fed Savings & Loan Ins Corp, res asst, 1977; Searle Pharmaceut Inc, asst prod mgr, 1978-79, prod mgr, 1979-84, key acct hosp consult, 1984-88; Westwood Pharmaceut Inc, mgr, new bus develop, 1988-93; Bristol-Myers Squibb, sr dir Lic, 1993-. **Orgs:** Am Mgt Asn; Am Bar Asn; Nat Black MBA Asn; Midwest pharmaceut Advert Club; Asn MBA Execs; Chicago Vol Legal Servs; Lic Exec Soc. **Home Addr:** 101 Whisper Wood Ct, Wrightstown, PA 18940. **Business Addr:** Senior Director of Licensing, Bristol Myers Squibb Co, 100 Nassau Pk Blvd, Princeton, NJ 08540, **Business Phone:** (609)419-5000.

## MCREYNOLDS, ELAINE A.

Government official, executive, consultant. **Personal:** Born Feb 5, 1948, Louisville, KY; married George R; children: Jennifer, Jason & Julie. **Educ:** Univ Montpellier, France, attended 1965; Ctr Col, Ky, 1968; Univ Tenn, BS, psychol, 1975. **Career:** Nat Life & Accident Ins Co, comput programmer, 1970-73, programmer analyst, 1974-75, expense mgt analyst, 1975-76, admin asst, 1976-78, asst sec & mgr, 1978-83; Dir Crisis Intervention, bd dir, 1977-78; Cumberland Mus, bd dir, 1978-81; bd dir, Citizens Bank; Am Gen Life & Accident Ins Co, asst vpres, 1970-85; real estate, 1985-87; Tenn Dept Com & Ins, 1987-94; FEMA, fed ins admin, 1994-96; Am Gen Life & Accident Ins Co, corp sr vpres, ins servs, 1996-2000; Elaine A McReynolds Consult Serv, consult & expert witness, 2000-10; Elaine A McReynolds, independent ins agt, 2010-. **Orgs:** Trustee, Univ Tenn Bd Trustees, 1974-83; alumni bd mem, Leadership Nashville, 1977-92; bd dir, St Bernard Acad, 1982-84; bd dir, Harpeth Hall Mid Sch, 1987-89; bd mem & Officer, 1996-2000; bd mem, YMCA, 1990-2000; comt chair & mem, Links Inc, 1990-2000; trustee, Centre Col Ky, 2000-09; parish coun mem, St Vincent de Paul Cath Church, 2001-03; Diocese Nashville, Cath Church, adv bd mem, 2003-12. **Honors/Awds:** Woman of Achievement Award, 1993; Person of the Year, March Dimes, 1994; Insurance Person of the Year, Md Asn Independent Insurors, 1996. **Special Achievements:** Top Ten Outstanding Grads Nashville Mag, 1976. **Home Addr:** 1517 Naples Ave, Nashville, TN 37207, **Home Phone:** (615)868-1291.

## MCRIPLEY, DR. GIL WHITNEY

Government official, lawyer, attorney general (U.S. federal government). **Personal:** Born Nov 29, 1957, Detroit, MI; married Sandie Cameron; children: Marlena L & Gil Whitney Jr. **Educ:** Univ Detroit, BA, 1979; Univ Mich, MA, 1983; Thomas M Cooley Law Sch, JD, 1984. **Career:** Detroit Pub Schs, teacher, 1980-81; Waverly Pub Sch, teacher, 1981-83; City Lansing, dir div dept, 1983-84; Charter Twp Royal Oak, supvr; pvt pract, currently. **Orgs:** Pi Sigma Alpha; Dem Party; pres, Royal Oak Twp Bus Asn, Royal Oak Twp Mainstream; secy, MI Conf Black Mayors; State Bar Mich, currently. **Home Addr:** 10640 Oak Pk Blvd, Oak Park, MI 48237, **Home Phone:** (248)398-4060. **Business Addr:** Member, State Bar of Michigan, 306 Townsend St, Lansing, MI 48933, **Business Phone:** (517)346-6300.

## MCROY, DR. RUTH GAIL

Educator. **Personal:** Born Oct 6, 1947, Vicksburg, MS; daughter of Lucille A McKinney Murdock and Horace David Murdock; married Dwight D Brooks; children: Myra Louise & Melissa Lynn. **Educ:** Univ Kans, BA, psychol & sociol, 1968, MSW, 1970; Univ Tex, PhD, social work, 1981. **Career:** Family Consult Serv, social worker, 1970-71; KS C's Serv League, adoption worker, 1971-73; Univ Kans, Sch Social Welfare, grad asst, 1972-73, asst prof, 1973-77, coordr minority affairs, 1973-74, dir admis, 1974-75; Prairie View A&M Univ, Dept Sociol & Social Work, asst prof, 1977-78; Danforth fel, 1978; Black Anal fel, 1978; Univ Tex, Sch Social Work, from asst prof to assoc prof, 1981-90, Serv C & Families, Ruby Lee Piester fel, 1985, prof, 1990, Ruby Lee Piester Centennial Prof Serv C & Families, 1990-2005, Ctr African & African Am Studies & Sci Social Work, prof, 1990-2005, Ctr Social Work Res, dir, 1994-2005, dir diversity inst, 1997-2005, distinguished teaching prof, 1999-2005, assoc dean res, 2001-05, res prof & Ruby Lee Piester Centennial prof emer, 2005-; Boston Col Grad Sch Social Work, vis prof, 2001, vis res prof, 2005-08, consult, 2008-09, Donahue & DiFelice endowed prof, 2009-; Univ Southern Calif Sch Social Welfare, consult, 2009-11. **Orgs:** Bd pres, Black Adoption Prog & Serv, 1975-77; Coun Social Work Educ, 1977-; Nat Asn Social Workers, 1977-; Phi Kappa Phi, 1979; bd pres, Carver Mus, 1983-86; Nat Asn Social Workers Steering Comn, Austin, 1986-90; bd mem, Carver Mus, 1987-90; Casey Family Adv Comn, 1989-; Adoptive Families Am Adv Comn, 1989-92; bd dir, Marywood, 1991-94; bd mem & pres, N Am Coun Adoptable C; Bd Cath Charities; Archdiocese Boston; Rudd Adoption Adv Bd; chair, Comn Diversity & Social & Econ Justice; Donaldson Adoption Inst Bd mem; fel Am Acad Social Work & Social Welfare, 2010. **Honors/Awds:** Outstanding Dissertation Award, Univ Tex, 1981; Lora Lee Pederson Teaching Excellence Award, 1984; Phi Kappa Phi Scholar Award, 1985; Rishon Lodge Wilhemina Delco Award for Excellence in Educ, 1987; Texas Excellence Teaching Award, 1990, Leadership Tex, 1995; Flynn Prize, Univ Southern Calif; George Silcott Lifetime Achievement Award, Black Adminr Child Welfare; Society of Social Work and Research National Distinguished Achievement Award, 2006; Outstanding Alumna, Univ Tex, 2007; St. Johns Outstanding Scholar in Adoption Award, 2010; U.S. Childrens Bureau Adoption Excellence Award, 2013; Child Advocate of the Year Award, 2014; Charles I. Wright Distinguished Alumna Award, Univ Tex at Austin Sch Social Work, 2014. **Special Achievements:** Author: Transracial and Inracial Adoptees: The Adolescent Years, 1983; Emotional Disturbance in Adopted Adolescents, 1988; Openness in Adoption, 1988; Social Practice with Black Families, 1990; Openness in Adoption Exploring Family Connections; First holder of the prestigious Ruby Lee Piester Centennial Professorship in Services to Families and Children; Challenging Racial Disproportionality in Child Welfare; Building Research Culture and Infrastructure. **Home Addr:** 5705 Sam Houston Cir, Austin, TX 78731. **Business Addr:** Research Professor, Ruby Lee Piester Centennial Professor Emerita, University of Texas at Austin, 1925 San Jacinto Blvd D3510, Austin, TX 78712-0358, **Business Phone:** (512)471-0551.

### MCSWAIN, MICHAEL CRITTENDEN
Military leader. **Personal:** Born Jun 11, 1956, Detroit, MI; son of Louis and Theda; married Sherelyn; children: Michael Jr. **Educ:** Columbia Col, AA, 1977, BS, 1997. **Career:** Advisor (retired); AUS, first line supr, 1986, sr personnel supr, 1990-95, sr opers adv, 1996-97, chief sr adv, 1997-99, chief sr adv, 1999-2002. **Orgs:** Secy, Sergeants Maj Asn, Redstone Arsenal, Ala. **Honors/Awds:** Army Commendation Medal, 1986, 1992, 1995; Meritorious Service Medal, 1997, 1999; Humanitarian Service Award, 1998; Legion of Merit, 2002. **Home Addr:** 5705 Montrose Dr, Killeen, TX 76542, **Home Phone:** (254)699-9707.

### MCSWAIN, RODNEY
Football player. **Personal:** Born Jan 28, 1962, Caroleen, NC. **Educ:** Clemson Univ. **Career:** Football player (retired); Atlanta Falcons, defensive back, 1984; New Eng Patriots, defensive back. 1984-89, strong safety, 1990; Detroit Dr, 1992-93. **Honors/Awds:** NFL draft, 1984; ArenaBowl VI Champion, 1992.

### MCTEER, DR. GEORGE CALVIN, SR.
Dentist. **Personal:** Born Mar 9, 1938, Barnwell, SC; son of Henry A (deceased) and Janie Elizabeth Williams (deceased); married Norma Jean Eaddy; children: Sonja Nichelle, Arlene Veronica & George Calvin Jr. **Educ:** SC State Univ, BS, 1960, MEd, 1968; Med Univ SC Col Dent Med, DMD, 1974. **Career:** Fairfield Co Schs, math & sci teacher, 1960-63; Charleston Co Schs, math teacher & adult sch teacher, 1963-69; Franklin C Fetter Family Health Ctr Inc, chief dent serv, 1974-76; pvt pract, 1976-; Sea Island Health Care Nursing Home, former dent consult. **Orgs:** Alpha Phi Alpha Frat, 1958-; Psi Omega Dent frat, 1974-; chmn adhoc comt health, Charleston Bus & Prof Asn, 1981-; pres, Charleston Co Med Asn, 1982-86; bd dirs, Sea Island Health Care Corp, 1984-90; mem bd chmn, Personnel Comn Cannon St YMCA, 1986-87; state pres, Palmetto Med Dent & Pharmaceut Asn; SC Dent Asn; Coastal Dist Dent Soc, Am Dent Asn; bd deacons, Cent Baptist Church; Charleston Dent Soc; Acad Gen Dent; Charleston Mules; Nat Asn Advan Colored People; Jack & Jill Am; Owl's Whist Club; secy & pres, CBC Men Club, 1991-. **Honors/Awds:** Management Development Award, Franklin C Fetter Family Health Ctr, 1976; Certificate of Achievement, Alpha Phi Alpha Frat, 1982; Appreciation for Outstanding Leadership, Charleston County Med Asn, 1984; Volunteer Award, Coming St YWCA, 1985; Volunteer Award, Stono Park Elem Sch, Parent Teachers Asn, 1986; Merit Award, Nat Dental Asn, 1987; Recognition of Service in Dentistry, Sigma Gamma Rho Sorority, 1987; Distinguished & Exemplary Service, Delta Sigma Theta Sorority, 1988. **Special Achievements:** First black graduate College of dental Medicine, Medical University of South Carolina in 1974. **Home Addr:** 1405 Rainbow Rd, Charleston, SC 29412-8154. **Business Addr:** Dentist, 967 King St, Charleston, SC 29413, **Business Phone:** (843)577-6097.

### MCTYRE, ROBERT EARL, SR.
Journalist. **Personal:** Born Aug 2, 1955, Detroit, MI; son of Earl Melvin and Barbara Jean; married Dianne Denise Ball, Nov 1, 1978, (divorced 1982); married Earn Diane Fortune, Mar 1, 1975, (divorced 1977); married Carmela, Sep 22, 1990; children: Tamika Baldwin, DuJuan Robinson, Cornelius Fortune & Rob Jr. **Educ:** Wayne County Commun, cert, training emergency med tech, 1976; Highland Pk Commun, lib arts; Wayne State Univ, jour scholar, 1989; Capella Univ, PhD, orgn mgt & leadership. **Career:** Ambro Ambulance, Detroit, Mich, attend/driver, 1973-75; Detroit Gen Hosp, Detroit, Mich, emergency room attend, 1975-77; Detroit Fire, EMS, Detroit, Mich, EMT, 1977-85; Metro Times, Detroit, Mich, classified salesman, freelance writer, 1984-86; Citizen News, Detroit, Mich, managing ed, gen mgr, 1985-87; Mich Chronicle, Detroit, Mich, reporter, assoc exec ed, 1987-93, exec ed, 1993-.Mich Legis, chief legis asst; Pvt Univ, Mich, dir writing, currently. **Orgs:** Detroit Chap, Nat Asn Black Journalists, 1985; Investigative Reporters & Ed Inc, 1990; Soc Environ Journalist, 1991. **Honors/Awds:** Licensed Baptist Minister, New Resurrection MB Church. **Home Addr:** 93 Elmhurst, Highland Park, MI 48203, **Home Phone:** (313)869-0305. **Business Addr:** Associate Executive Editor, Michigan Chronicle, 479 Ledyard, Detroit, MI 48201, **Business Phone:** (313)963-5522.

### MCWHORTER, DR. GRACE AGEE
Educator, association executive, executive. **Personal:** Born Jan 15, 1948, Mobile, AL; married George R MD; children: Kenya & Lia. **Educ:** Tuskegee Inst, BS, hort/plant & soil sci, 1970, MS, hort/plant & soil sci, 1972; Univ Fla, PhD, plant path/ bot, 1978; Besson Divinity Sch, Samford Univ, MDiv, 1992. **Career:** Univ Fla, res assoc, 1973-75; Univ Mo, vis prof biol, 1976-77; Talladega Col, asst prof biol, 1980; Jacksonville State Univ, asst prof biol, 1980-81; Univ Tex, San Antonio, lectr biol, 1981-82; Fla Agr & Mech Univ, assoc prof agr, 1982-86; La Fontain Floral Design, owner, 1984-; Farmers Home Admin USOA, vis prof, 1984-85; State Univ Syst Fla Bd Regents, prog rev assoc, 1986; Lawson State Community Col, chairperson, Natural Sci Dept, 1993, Biomed Bridge to Baccalaureate Degree Prog, proj site dir. **Orgs:** Delta Sigma Theta Sor; Jack & Jill; Am Assoc Higher Educ Black Caucus; United Fac Fla Polit Action Chmn; bd vols, Tallahassee Memorial Hosp; Toastmasters Int; Tuskegee Alumni Club; chair, State Ala's Master Teacher Plan; chair, State Articulation Comt; Am Asn Univ Women; bd mem, George Wash Carver Soc; Ala Acad Sci; Nat Asn Biol Teachers; chair, State Ala's Master Teacher Plan; chair chem, State Articulation Comt. **Honors/Awds:** BOR Res Fel, 1977; Distinguished Service Award, Fla A&M Univ; Outstanding Alumnus Award, Tuskegee Univ; Chancellor's Award, Ala Col Syst. **Special Achievements:** Published numerous articles on small farm issues & concerns 1977. **Home Addr:** 2421 Tempest Dr, Birmingham, AL 35211.

### MCWHORTER, ROSALYND D.
Manager. **Personal:** Born Dec 19, 1960, Chicago, IL; daughter of Edward H and Earnestine Pollard; married Anthony Michael. **Educ:** Univ Ill, BA, Eng, 1982; Concordia Univ, MA, admin & leadership; Chicago State Univ, MAT, elem educ. **Career:** R J Dale Advert, acct exec, 1984-88; Burrell Pub Rels, acct group supvr, 1988-93; Summit Consult Group, acct group supvr, 1993; Quincy Univ, adj fac, 2010-; Flossmoor Sch Dist 161, educr, 2013-. **Orgs:** Black Pub Rels Soc, 1988; Publicity Club Chicago, 1990-; Nat Coalition 100Black Women, Chicago Chap, 1991; Delta Sigma Theta Sorority Inc; Girl Scouts Greater Chicago & Northwest Ind; Habitat Humanity Chicago S Suburbs. **Honors/Awds:** Certificate, McDonald's Corp Media Rels Training Prog; Certificate, Publicity Club Chicago. **Home Addr:** 2950 Bonnie Brae Cres, Flossmoor, IL 60422, **Home Phone:** (708)799-7455. **Business Addr:** Adjunct Faculty, Quincy University, 1800 Col Ave, Quincy, IL 62301, **Business Phone:** (217)222-8020.

### MCWHORTER, SHARON LOUISE
Executive, president (organization), chief executive officer. **Personal:** Born Feb 22, 1951, Detroit, MI; daughter of Leroy B Harris Jr and Josie Azeez; children: Abner III. **Educ:** Wayne State Univ, BA, 1988. **Career:** Galactic Concepts & Designs Inc, pres, 1976-81; Wayne County Community Col, acct tech, 1977-93; Am Resource Training Syst, pres & chief exec officer, 1983-; Idea Corp, facilitator, 1988-89; McWhorter Devel Co, pres & partner, 1999-. **Orgs:** Bd dir, Inventor's Coun Mich, 1979-80; MADD, pres, Wayne County Chap, 1985-87; Citizen's Rev Comt, appointee, 1990-94; bd chair, Neighborhood Family Initiative, 1991-93; bd dir & chair, Detroit Empowerment Zone Develop Corp, 1994-, bd sec, 1996-99, bd chair, 2000-; Detroit Grand Prix Asn; Citizen Band Patrol; S Cass Bus Asn; Nat Asn Advan Colored People. **Business Addr:** Board of Director, Chair, American Resource Training System Inc, Cadillac Towers 65 Cadillac Squ Rm 2401, Detroit, MI 48226, **Business Phone:** (313)224-1336.

### MCWILLIAMS, DR. ALFRED E., JR.
Educator. **Personal:** Born Feb 3, 1938, Wewoka, OK; son of Alfred E Sr and Elvira M Bowles; married Wilmer Jean Bible; children: Kimberly Beatrice, Esther Gabriel Moten, Cassandra Gabriel, Kenneth-Gabriel, Fredericka Gabriel Rice & Keith Gabriel. **Educ:** Colo State Col, BA, 1959, MA, 1960; Univ Northern Colo, PhD, 1970. **Career:** Denver Pub Sch Colo, teacher, counsr & admin asst, 1960-68; Proj Upward Bound Univ Northern Colo, dir, 1968-70; Univ Northern Colo, asst dean-spec educ & rehab, 1970-72; Univ Northern Colo, asst prof, 1970-72, assoc prof educ, 1976-82; Fed Rocky Mt States Inc, consult & career educ content coord, 1972-76; Univ Northern Colo, dir personnel AA/EEO, 1976-79, asst vpres, admin serv personnel, 1979-82; Univ Colo, vpres admin, 1982-84; Atlanta Univ, vpres admin, 1984-85; Atlanta Univ, dean, sch educ, 1985-87; Ga State Univ, prof, educ policy studies, 1987-09, coord, educa leadership prog, 1995-, Prof Educ Coun, chair, emer prof, currently, Col Educ, prof emer educ policy studies, currently. **Orgs:** Chmn, co-founder, Black Educrs United, 1967-68; bd mem, Colo Christian Home Denver, 1977-; sec, Aurora Colo Career Serv Comn, 1977-, chmn, 1980-84; bd mem, Nat Brotherhood Skiers, 1978-79, 1980-85, coun mem, 1978-; Am Asn Univ Admin; Colo Merit Syst Coun; Col & Univ Personnel Asn; Am Soc Personnel Admin, 1979-; consult & trainer, Nat Ctr Leadership Develop Atlanta Univ, 1979-80; consult & trainer, Leadership Develop Training Prog, Howard Univ, 1981-82; chmn elect, EEO, 1981-82; Rotary Club W End Atlanta, 1984-87, 1989-; army committeeman, Greater Atlanta Chap Res Officers Asn US, 1985-; chmn bd dir, APPLE Corps, 1986; Prof Jour Comt, Asn Teacher Educrs, 1987-; Am Asn Higher Educ, 1989-; Asn Supv & Curric Develop, 1989-; Am Asn Univ Profs, 1995-. **Home Addr:** 1221 Ashley Lake Dr, Marietta, GA 30062, **Home Phone:** (770)565-1953. **Business Addr:** Emeriti Professor, Georgia State University, 30 Pryor St Suite 300, Atlanta, GA 30303-3083, **Business Phone:** (404)651-2540.

### MCWILLIAMS, ESQ. JAMES D.
Lawyer. **Personal:** Born Dec 25, 1932, Fairfield, AL; son of James and Minnie; married Anne; children: Laura, Susan & Diana. **Educ:** Talladega Col, Talladega, Ala, BA, 1954; Univ Wis Law Sch, Madison, Wis, JD, 1962. **Career:** US Dept Interior, att adv, 1962-66; United Planning Organ, Wash, DC CAP, asst gen coun, 1966-67; US VI, asst att gen, 1967-72; US VI Port Authority, gen coun, 1969-72; Opp Funding Corp, gen coun sec, 1973-77; DC Govt Dept Transp, asst dir, 1979-90; Coop Assistance Fund, asst sec; pvt pract atty, currently. **Orgs:** State Bar Wis, 1962-; DC Bar Asn, 1972; Nat Bar Asn; Am Bar Asn. **Honors/Awds:** Drafted legislation which established US Virgin Islands Port Authority. **Home Addr:** 145 Monte Cristo Ave Suite 404, Oakland, CA 94611, **Home Phone:** (510)595-8486. **Business Addr:** Attorney, 5604 MacArthur Blvd NW, Washington, DC 20016-5301, **Business Phone:** (202)537-0544.

### MCWILLIAMS, JOHNNY E.
Football player. **Personal:** Born Dec 14, 1972, Pomona, CA; married Elizabeth; children: Johnny Jr. **Educ:** Univ Southern Calif, pub admin. **Career:** Football player (retired); Ariz Cardinals, tight end & wide receiver, 1996-99; Minn Vikings, tight end, 2000-01; New Eng Patriots, tight end, 2001.

### MCWILLIAMS-FRANKLIN, TAJ
Basketball coach, basketball player. **Personal:** Born Oct 20, 1970, El Paso, TX; daughter of Marvin and Stephanie Wiggins; married Reggie; children: Michele, Schera & Maia. **Educ:** Ga State Univ, attended 1989; St Edwards Univ, rhet. **Career:** Basketball player (retired), basketball coach; Wolfenbuettel, Ger, 1993-94; Contern, Luxembourg, 1994-95; Galilee, Israel, 1995-96; Philadelphia Rage, ctr, 1996-97; Orlando Miracle, 1999-2002; Famila Schio, 1999-2002; Shinhan Bank S-Birds, Korea; Conn Sun, 2003-06; Lavezzini Parma, 2003-04; Gambrinus Brno, 2004-05; Dandenong Rangers, 2005; CB Halcon Viajes, 2005-06; Ansan Shinhan Bank S-Birds, 2006, 2007; Spartak Moscow Region, 2006-07; Los Angeles Sparks, 2007; Wash Mystics, 2008; Galatasaray, 2008-09; Detroit Shock, 2008-09; Frisco Sika Brno, 2009-10; New York Liberty, 2010, asst coach, 2013-; Ros Casares, 2011; Spartak Moscow Region, 2011; Minn Lynx, 2011-12; Wisla Can-Pack Krakow, 2012; New York Liberty, asst coach, 2013; The Madison Sq Garden Co, asst coach, 2013; Boston Univ, asst coach, 2014; Post Univ, head coach, 2015-. **Business Addr:** Assistant Coach, New York Liberty, 4 Pa Plz, New York, NY 10121, **Business Phone:** (212)564-9622.

### MCWRIGHT, CARTER C.
Executive. **Personal:** Born Feb 7, 1950; son of John; children: Carter II. **Educ:** Southern Univ, BA, 1972. **Career:** Music Planet, owner, currently. **Orgs:** Vpres, Saginaw Black Bus Asn, 1982-84; vpres, Saginaw E Side Lions Club, 1983-84; bd mem, E Cent Mich Planners, 1984-87; Nat Asn Advan Colored People; Joy Baptist Church. **Home Addr:** 1072 Tahoe Trail, Flint, MI 48532-3565. **Business Addr:** Owner, Music Planet, 517 W Carpenter Rd, Flint, MI 48505-2034, **Business Phone:** (810)787-0099.

### MCZEAL, ALFRED, SR.
Executive, chief executive officer. **Personal:** Born Mar 6, 1931, Ridge, LA; son of Alzfall and Olivia; married Virgis Mary Sampay; children: Olivia Figaro, Myra Holmes, Alfred Jr & Janet Lynn. **Career:** Morgan & Lindsey, janitor, 1948-64; Southern Consumers Coop Inc, vol, 1962-64, gen mgr & ceo, 1964-; Arcadian Delight Bakery, mgr; World Wide Walkie Talkie Inc, regist agt. **Orgs:** Nat Asn Advan Colored People, 1955; supvr, St Pauls Credit Union, 1961; Better Bus Bur, 1986; MLK Holiday Comt, 1991; Inst Karamu Guid, Holy Family African Tour, 1992; secy, Black Alliance Prog; La Black Assembly; Nat Black Assembly. **Home Addr:** 315 Jackson St, Lafayette, LA 70501-8115, **Home Phone:** (318)232-2668. **Business Addr:** Chief Executive Officer, General Manager, Southern Consumers Coop Inc, 1006 Surrey St, Lafayette, LA 70501, **Business Phone:** (318)232-1126.

### MCZIER, ARTHUR
Management consultant, founder (originator). **Personal:** Born May 4, 1935, Atlanta, GA; married Ruby Burrows; children: Sandra & Jennifer Rose. **Educ:** Loyola Univ, BS, com, 1959; Harvard Bus Sch. **Career:** Seeburg Corp, intl sls & mktg rep, 1962-66; Ford Motor Co, mktg analyst, 1966-67; US Dept Com Off Foreign Direct Investments, 1968; US Small Bus Admin, assoc adminr minority enterprise, 1969-73; Gen Bahamian Co, bus exec, 1973-74; Resources Inc, mgt consult, 1974-. **Orgs:** Adv Bd, Inst Minority Bus Educ Howard Univ; Wash Bd Coun Fed City Col; bd mem, United Negro Col Fund Inc; employer trustee, bd trustees mem, Indust Tech Prof Employees Union; founder, Nat Bus Serv Enterprise, 1998. **Honors/Awds:** Special Achievement Award, US Small Bus Admin, 1969; Gold medal for Distinguished Service, US Small Bus Admin, 1969; Who's Who in Am Adv Bd; Robert Russo Moton Leadership Award, Nat Bus League, 1971; Honorary Doctor of Laws Degree, Daniel Payne Col, 1971; Award of Merit, Nat Econ Develop Admin, 1971; Recognition Award, outstanding contrib minority econ develop Black Businessmen's Prof Asn, 1971; Recognition Award, outstanding serv minority bus TX & USA Pylon Salesmanship Club, 1971; Hall of Fame, Loyola Univ, 1972; Certified Outstanding Perform, Small Bus Admin, 1972; City Economical Developement Center Award, Miami, 1972; Public Service Award, Houston Citizens C C, 1973; Arthur S Fleming Award, nominee Small Bus Admin, 1972; Key Award, Natl Asn Black Manufacturer's, 1974. **Home Addr:** 2200 N Atlantic Ave Apt 2102, Daytona Beach, FL 32118.

### MEACHAM, ROBERT B.
Educator, administrator. **Personal:** Born Mar 21, 1933, Tuscaloosa, AL; son of Manarah and Armond; married Grace A; children: Anthony & Alexander. **Educ:** AB, EdM, 1973. **Career:** Educator (retired); Univ Cincinnati, lectr psychol, counr, 1970-73, Col Appl Sci, asst dir, 1973-74, dir stud life & coun, 1974-, assoc vice provost minority prog & serv & int serv, assoc vice provost, stud serv, 1978-89, assoc athletic dir, 1989-, transfer coordr, currently. **Orgs:** Paddock Hills Assembly Inc, 1970-; United Black Fac Asn, 1973; Am Personnel & Guid Asn; Asn Non-White Concerns; treas, Asn Coun Educ & Supv Comn Develop Adv Coun, Cincinnati; bd mem, Talbert House. **Home Addr:** 1228 Westminster Dr, Cincinnati, OH 45229-1234, **Home Phone:** (513)242-2890.

### MEADE, DR. ALSTON B., SR.
Research scientist, biologist. **Personal:** Born Jun 28, 1930, Jamaica; son of Frank I R and Hepsy Condell; children: Alston B Jr, Allison D, Jule Anne, Brandon D & Fred A. **Educ:** Fisk Univ, BA, zool, 1956; Univ Minn, MS, entom, 1959, PhD, entom, 1962. **Career:** Research scientist & biologist (retired); EI du Pont de Nemours Co, res biologist, 1964, sr res biologist, 1971, res assoc, 1992; Govt Jamaica, Philadelphia, PA, hon consul, 2002-. **Orgs:** Pres, Nat Asn Advan Colored People, Southern Chester County Br, 1965-75; Bd Educ W Chester Area Sch Dist, 1970-80; chmn, Joint Community Spec Educ Chester County, Pa, 1974-80; Inter Unit Chester County, Pa, 1974-80; vpres, Bd Educ W Chester Area Sch Dist, 1975-77; fel African Sci Inst; pres, Int Soc African Scientists, 1988-90; pres, Nat Asn Jamaican & Supportive Orgn, 1993-98; pres, Nat Coalition Caribbean Affairs, 1998-. **Home Addr:** 2014 Valley Dr, West Chester, PA 19382, **Home Phone:** (610)436-0795. **Business Addr:** Honorary Consul, Consulate of Jamaica, PO Box 13117, Philadelphia, PA 19101, **Business Phone:** (215)313-9508.

### MEADE-TOLLIN, DR. LINDA C.
Consultant, business owner, cancer researcher. **Personal:** Born Aug 16, 1944, London, WV; daughter of Robert A and Virginia; married Gordon Tollin; children: Amina Rebecca. **Educ:** WVa State Col, BS, 1964; Hunter Col, MA, 1969; City Univ NY, PhD, 1972. **Career:** Professor (retired); Col Old Westbury, asst prof, 1972-75; Rockefeller Univ, vis asst prof, 1973-74; Univ Ariz, NIH postdoctoral fel, 1975-77, res assoc, 1978-80; Coord Women Sci & Engrg Off, staff, 1980-82, vis asst prof, 1982-85; Morehouse Sch Med, fac develop fel, 1985-86; Univ Ariz, sr lect & asst res sci, 1987-91, NIH, minority spec investigator, 1987-89, 1990-93, Ariz Health Sci Ctr, Dept Surg, res asst prof surg, 1987-2008; CCW Corporation, director, Anti-Metastasis Research, 2010-; Reiki, practitioner, 2011-; doTERRA Wellness, advocate, 2014-; 4Healing LLC, owner, 2014-. **Orgs:** Fel African Sci Inst; Alpha Kappa Alpha Sorority, 1962-; Nat Orgn Prof Advan Black Chemists & Chem Engrs, 1973-85, 1987-2005, chair exec bd, 1981; consult, Am Med Womens Asn, 1977-85; bd dir, Ododo Theatre Found, 1977-85; Am Med Womens Asn, 1979; Jack & Jill Inc, 1987-89; Univ Ariz Cancer Ctr. **Special Achievements:** Profiled in "African American Women Chemists" by Jeanette Brown, published 2012. **Home Addr:** , Tucson, AZ 85704, **Home Phone:** (520)742-2364. **Business Addr:**

Owner, director, CCW Corporation 4 Healing LLC, Tucson, AZ 85704, **Business Phone:** (520)742-2364.

### MEADOWS, CHERYL R.

Government official, executive director. **Personal:** Born Sep 7, 1948, Cincinnati, OH; daughter of Jack Pulliam and Ruth Pulliam; children: Jerry L Wilkerson Jr. **Educ:** Tenn State Univ, BA, 1970; Univ Cincinnati, MS, 1975. **Career:** City Cincinnati, planner, 1971-76, prog mgr, 1976-82, asst city mgr, dir; Human Serv Div, dir, 1981-95; Dept Neighborhood Serv, employ & training dir, exec dir, 1995-2000; Cincinnati Employ & Training Div, dir, 2000-05; Lincoln Heights, Ohio, village mgr, 2003-05; Cincinnati Human Rels Comn, exec dir, currently; Cincinnati Human Rels Comn, dir, 2006-12. **Orgs:** AS Conf Mayor/City Human Serv, 1976-; consumer serv; Human Serv Adv Comt; contract health centers; pub vehicle inspections; Nat Forum Black Pub Admin, 1986-; leader, vpes, Col Hill Community; Am Soc Pub Admin, 1989; Int Asn Off Human Rights Agencies. **Honors/Awds:** Fel, Aspo Ford Found, 1975; Univ Scholar, 1975; Outstanding Young Women of America, 1982; Community Chest's President Award, 1983; Community Action Commission Award, 1986; Outstanding Young Women of America, Talbert House Victim Services; Career Woman of Achievement Award, YWCA; Local Sch Decision-Making Comt; City of Cincinnati through the Outstanding Managers Award; Community Service Award, 1987; Career Women of Achievement, 1992; Outstanding Manager Award, City Cincinnati Managers Asn, 1992. **Home Addr:** 1215 Brushwood Ave, PO Box 24260, Cincinnati, OH 45224, **Home Phone:** (513)521-6209. **Business Addr:** Executive Director, Cincinnati Human Relations Commission, 801 Plum St City Hall Rm 158, Cincinnati, OH 45202-5407, **Business Phone:** (513)352-3237.

### MEADOWS, DR. RICHARD H.

Dentist. **Personal:** Born Dec 7, 1928, Roanoke, VA; married Dorothy M Magee; children: William C. **Educ:** Va Union Univ, BS, 1951; Howard Univ Sch Dent, DDS, 1955. **Career:** Freedman Hosp, intern, 1956; pvt pract dentist, currently; Richard H Meadows DDS, owner & dentist, 2008-. **Orgs:** Pres, PBR Dent Soc, 1961-68; pres, Old Dom Dent Soc, 1968-71; Nat Dent Soc; Int Endodontic Soc; Aircraft Owners & Pilots Asn; Omega Psi Frat; Nat Advan Asn Colored People. **Honors/Awds:** Award Oral Surgeon, Beta Kappa Chi Nat Sci Soc Howard Univ, 1955. **Home Addr:** 3338 Greenland Ave NW, Roanoke, VA 24012-3947. **Business Addr:** Dentist, Owner, Richard H Meadows DDS, 1720 Staunton Ave NW, Roanoke, VA 24017, **Business Phone:** (540)343-4354.

### MEADOWS, TIM

Actor, comedian. **Personal:** Born Feb 5, 1961, Highland Park, MI; son of Lathon (deceased) and Mardell; married Michelle Taylor; children: Isaiah Crosby & Julian. **Educ:** Wayne State Univ, tv & radio broadcasting. **Career:** Actor, currently; Second City, improv comedy troupe. TV series: "Saturday Night Live", 1991-2000; "The Michael Richards Show", 2000; "Leap of Faith", NBC, 2001; "Leap of Faith", 2002; 'You Don't Have to Go Home", 2004; 'The Ex Factor", 2005; "Perserverance", 2006; "Pink Freud", 2006; "Everybody Hates Corleone", 2006; "Everybody Hates Chris", 2006; "The Sperminator", 2006; "Lovespring International", 2006; "The Colbert Report", 2006; "Help Me Help You", 2006; "According to Jim", 2007; "Shredderman Rules", 2007; "Have You Seen My Muffins, Man?", 2007; "The Bill Engvall Show", 2007; "Curb Your Enthusiasm", 2007; "Walk Hard: The Dewey Cox Story", 2007; "Lil' Bush: Resident of the United States", 2007-08; "The Bill Engvall Show", 2007-09; "Carpet Bros", 2008-09; "Glory Daze", 2010-11; "Mean Girls 2", 2011; "The Gabriels", 2013; "Mr. Box Office", 2012-13; "Suburgatory", 2012-14; "Bob's Burgers", 2012-14; "30 Rock", 2013; "The Venture Bros", 2013; "Comedy Bang! Bang!", 2013; "Marry Me", 2014-15. Other: Aliens in the Attic, 2009; I Like It That Way, 2009; The Coffee Maker, 2009; Car Trouble, 2009; United Front, 2009; The Team Building Event, 2009; Easy to Assemble, 2009; Grown Ups, 2010; Mean Girls 2, 2011; Jack & Jill, 2011. Films: Cone heads, 1993; Wayne's World 2, 1993; It's Pat, 1994; The Ladies Man, 2000; Olive the Other Reindeer, 2000; 3 Days, 2001; The Stevens Get Even, Disney, 2002; Wasabi Tuna, 2003; The Cookout, 2004; The Bench warmers, 2006; Walk Hard: The Dewey Cox Story, 2007; Semi-Pro, 2008; Aliens in the Attic, 2009; Grown Ups, 2010; Mean Girls 2, 2011; Jack & Jill, 2011; Grown Ups 2, 2013; Chasing Ghosts, 2015; Trainwreck, 2015; Popstar: Never Stop Never Stopping, 2016. **Business Addr:** Actor, Brillstein-Grey, 9150 Wilshire Blvd Suite 350, Beverly Hills, CA 90212, **Business Phone:** (310)275-6135.

### MEANS, HON. BERTHA ELIZABETH

Educator, government official. **Personal:** Born May 1, 1920, Valley Mills, TX; married James H; children: Joan, Janet, James Jr, Patricia & Ronald. **Educ:** Huston-Tillotson Col, AB, Eng & educ, 1965; Univ Tex, MEd, educ psychol, 1955; Univ Tex. **Career:** Prairie View A&M Univ, vis instr, 1959-69, fac; Austin Independent Sch Dist, dir head start & coordr, 1969-70; Univ Tex, Dept Curric & Instr, instr, 1972-73; Austin-Maseru Comt, chair, currently; Austin Independent Sch Dist, instr coord sec reading, currently; Tillotson Univ, fac. **Orgs:** Pres, Austin Chap Jack & Jill Am Inc, 1956-58; Int Hospitality Coun Austin, 1958-; chmn, United Fund Austin & Travis County, 1965-72; Women Ed Area Church, United Fund, Austin & Travis Ctr, 1965-67; pres, Episcopal Women St James, 1966-67; City Coun appointee, Pk & Recreation Adv Bd, 1967-74; chmn, vpres, Austin Nat Asn Advan Colored People, 1970-74; Citizens Comt A More Beautiful Town Lake, 1972-75; Local Citizens Adv Comt & Tex Const Adv Comt, 1973; St Stephens Bd Trustees, 1980; Int Reading Asn; past pres, Capitol Area Coun; Tex State Teachers Asn; charter mem, Ad Hoc Com Enactment Human Rels Comt City Austin; bd mem, YWCA; Epsilon Kappa Chap Delta Kappa Gamma Soc; life mem, Alpha Kappa Alpha Sorority, St James Episcopal Chap; founding mem, St James Episcopal Church; Austin Chap Links Inc; adv bd, Channel 36, KTVV/KXAN; adv bd mem, Meals Wheels; Rock Springs Cumberland Presby Church. **Honors/Awds:** Woman of the Year Award, Zeta Phi Beta Sorority, 1965; Arthur B. DeWitty Human Relations Award, Austin Nat Asn Advan Colored People, 1966; DeWitty Civil Rights Award, Austin Br Nat Asn Advan Colored People, 1966; Committee Leadership Certificate of Appreciation, Capital City Lions & Optimist Clubs, 1972; one of Austins Outstanding Women, 1975; Austin Amer Statesman; Special Award for Service to Parks & Recreation Dept, Nat Asn Advan Colored People, 1975; Committee Service Award, Zeta Phi Beta, 1976; Woman of the Year Award, YWCA, 2004; delegate for Democratic Convention, 2008; Whitney M Young, Jr Lifetime Achievement Award, urban League, 2008; Heroes Award, Texas Nat Asn Advan Colored People, 2010; Received Numerous Awards & Honors. **Business Addr:** Chair, Austin-Maseru Committee, 7400 Valburn Dr, Austin, TX 78731, **Business Phone:** (512)345-0747.

### MEANS, DONALD FITZGERALD

Government official. **Personal:** Born Dec 29, 1966, Tuscaloosa, AL; son of Harry L and Mary Turner. **Educ:** Univ Ala, Tuscaloosa, AL, mkt mgt, 1989. **Career:** Greene County Racing Comn, Eutaw, AL, chmn comn, 1989-, financial mgt, analyst, 1989-90, dir; Dist 4, Ala, comnr, currently. **Orgs:** Chmn, Greene County Water Authority, 1990-; pres, Community Fire Dept, 1990; Extension Serv Adv Bd, 1990-; chmn, Agr Adv Bd, 1991-. **Home Addr:** 6208 US Hwy 43, PO Box 68, Eutaw, AL 35462-4046, **Home Phone:** (205)372-2745. **Business Addr:** Commissioner, Greene County, 400 Morrow Ave, Eutaw, AL 35462, **Business Phone:** (205)372-3349.

### MEANS, ELBERT LEE

Government official, executive. **Personal:** Born Feb 3, 1945, Sandy Ridge, AL; married Harriet Ivory; children: Madelene, Jennifer & Kristen. **Educ:** Selma Univ, attended 1964; AL State Univ, attended 1966 & 1969. **Career:** Sta Help Inc, supvr, 1969-73; Gen Motors, shipping clerk, 1973-75; Brockway Glass, laborer, 1975-79; Lowndes County, tax assessor; Ft Deposit, Ala, coun mem, currently. **Orgs:** State exec mem, Ala Dem Conf; county coord, Lowndes County Dem Party; mem adv bd, Lowndes County Community Org; vpres, Selma Univ Alumni-Chap. **Business Addr:** Council Member, Lowndes County, 205 E Tuskeena St, Hayneville, AL 36040-0065, **Business Phone:** (334)548-5375.

### MEANS, DR. FRED E.

School administrator, association executive. **Personal:** Born Jan 1, 1932?, Pacolet, SC; son of Fred Sr and Lemor E (Tucker) M; married Helen Pryor; children: Chad, Marc & Vincent. **Educ:** NY Univ, BS, 1959; Trenton State Col, MA, 1963; Rutgers Univ, EdM, 1973, EdD, 1975. **Career:** Livingston Sch, teacher, 1959-60; Dayton Elem Sch, teacher, 1960-64; S Side High Sch, band dir, 1964-67, proj coordr, 1967-70; Cleveland Elem Sch, prin, 1968-70; Rutgers Univ, lectr & dir, 1970-75; NJ City Univ, dir, 1975-78, asst dean & dean, 1978-94, adj prof, 1994, prof emer, 2000-. **Orgs:** Trustee, UCC Newark Anti Poverty Agency, 1965-66; Orgn Newark Educr, Newark, 1967-70; Newark Bd Educ, 1973-76; trustee, Action Sickle Cell Anemia Hudson County, 1982-88; bd dir, Res Better Schs, 1983-94; pres, AACTE; Am Educ Res Asn; Nat Alliance Black Sch; Phi Delta Kappa; Am Asn Col Teacher Educ. **Special Achievements:** Proj PRIME; paper presented, Norfolk State Univ, 1988; "The Process and Product of Restructuring an Urban Teacher Education Program," paper presented, Asn Teacher Educr Conf, New Orleans, 1991. **Home Addr:** 522 Abbot Ct, Monroe Township, NJ 08831-3779, **Home Phone:** (609)409-7373. **Business Addr:** Professor Emeritus, New Jersey City University, 2039 John F Kennedy Blvd, Jersey City, NJ 07305-1597, **Business Phone:** (201)200-2000.

### MEANS, NATRONE JERMAINE

Football player, football coach. **Personal:** Born Apr 26, 1972, Harrisburg, NC; married Shonda; children: 4. **Educ:** Univ NC. **Career:** Football player (retired), football coach; San Diego Chargers, running back, 1993-95, 1998-99; Jacksonville Jaguars, 1996-97; Carolina Panthers, running back, 2000; Livingston Col, asst coach, running backs coach, 2005, offensive coordr, 2006; W Charlotte High Sch, offensive coordr, 2007-; Winston-Salem State Univ, running backs coach, 2014. **Honors/Awds:** Pro Bowl, 1994; San Diego Chargers Hall of Fame, 2012. **Special Achievements:** Films: 1994 AFC Championship Game, 1995; Super Bowl XXIX, 1995. **Home Addr:** 14602 Greenpoint Lane, Huntersville, NC 28078-2624, **Home Phone:** (704)274-9995. **Business Addr:** Offensive Coordinator, West Charlotte High School, 2219 Senior Dr, Charlotte, NC 28216, **Business Phone:** (980)343-6060.

### MEANS, PAT

Founder (originator), business owner, management consultant. **Educ:** Univ Southern Calif, BS, bus admin; Univ Southern Calif, Marshall Sch Bus, MBA, int bus. **Career:** Turning Pt Commun, prin& co-founder, 1992-, sponsorship consult, 2014-; Los Angeles Fire & Police Pension Fund, comnr, 2005-08; Harris & Assocs/Skanska-Rados Joint Venture-Expo II Light Rail LIne, dir, 2011-12; Tall Ships Festival Los Angeles/San Diego Festival Sail/Dana Pt Tall Ship Festival, consult, 2014-; AltaSea, Port Los Angeles, dir commun & community, 2014-; Purex Corp, exec mgt; FCB (now Draftfcb), exec mgt; Motown Rec, exec mgt; ProServ Inc, exec mgt; KACE Radio, exec mgt; Expo 2 Light Rail Line, consult. **Orgs:** Los Angeles Fire & Police Pension Fund, former bd mem; Black Enterprise/Greenwich St Partners Pvt Equity Fund, former adv bd mem; W Angeles Community Develop Corp, former bd mem; Los Angeles African Am Women's Polit Inst Inc (LAAAWPPI), former bd mem; Greater Los Angeles African Am Chamber Com, former bd mem; Wells Fargo (Los Angeles Metro Region), community adv bd; TPC Found, bd mem. **Honors/Awds:** Professional Women in Business, Woman of the Year, 2000; "Los Angeles Business Journal," Women Who Make A Difference Awardee, 2000; USC Black Alumni Association, Outstanding Alumni of the Year, 2001; More than Shelter, Century Award, 2008; Los Angeles African American Women Political Action, Recognition; National Congressional Small Business Task Force, Recognition; The National Association of Women Business Owners (NAWBO-LA), Recognized; Los Angeles Commission on Women Business, Woman of the Year; California Black Chamber of Commerce, Female Entrepreneur of the Year. **Business Addr:** Director of Communications & Community, AltaSea, 222 W 6th St Suite 1010, San Pedro, CA 90731, **Business Phone:** (424)210-4320.

### MEAUX, RONALD

Artist, educator. **Personal:** Born Feb 15, 1942, Louisville, KY. **Educ:** Univ Ky, BA, art, 1965. **Career:** Cleveland Pub Schs, art instr. **Orgs:** Nat Conf Artists; Nat Asn Advan Colored People; Metro Opera Guild. **Special Achievements:** One man art show, Karamu, 1974. **Home Addr:** PO Box 14748, Cleveland, OH 44114-0748. **Business Addr:** Art Instructor, East Technical High School, 2439 E 55th St, Cleveland, OH 44104, **Business Phone:** (216)361-3116.

### MEDEARIS, VICTOR L.

Clergy. **Personal:** Born Apr 3, 1921, Austin, TX; son of James Ever and Pearl B Edgar; married Gladys Lonell Alexander; children: Victor L, Pamela Faye & Charlotte Briana. **Educ:** San Francisco Baptist Bible Col, attended 1953; City Col San Fran, AA, 1958; San Francisco Univ, attended 1961. **Career:** Double Rock Baptist Church, San Francisco, pastor, 1948-2003; Fed Employ, mech helper, warehouse foreman, heavy duty driver trainer, driver examr, mech inspector, equal employ spec, 1949; Christian radio prog, broadcasted. **Orgs:** Chmn, San Francisco Humn Rights Comn, 1971; secy bd, Fel Bible Inst, 1953; chmn, Civic Comn Bay view Baptist Min Fel; Bay Area Dist Asn; bd mem, San Francisco Chap, Nat Asn Advan Colored People; bd mem, Sickle Cell Anemia; W Bay Clergy Rep Northern CA; adv bd, United Negro Col Fund Bay Area Int Alumni Com; Org Calif State Baptist Conv; pres, instr & chmn, Fel's Bd Dirs; community leader, Urban Outreach Inc. **Honors/Awds:** Highest Award of Merit, City San Francisco, 1971; Honorary Award, Quartett Singers Asn Am, 1972; Honorary Award, Pelton Jr High Sch, 1973; Outstanding Community Achievement Award, San Francisco Bayview Hunters Point Multi-purpose Senior Service, 1989; 40th Pastoral Anniversary Commemoration, Senator Quentin Kopp, 1989. **Special Achievements:** Longest running Afro-american in San Francisco. **Home Addr:** 5185 Coach Dr, Richmond, CA 94803, **Home Phone:** (510)458-2719.

### MEDFORD, ISABEL

Lawyer. **Personal:** Born LA; children: Richard Kevin. **Educ:** Univ Calif, Berkley, BA, psych & polit sci, 1972; Univ Calif, Boalt Hall Sch Law, JD, 1975; Univ Calif, MCrim, 1976. **Career:** Robert T Cresswell Inc, atty, 1974-78; Nat Asn Advan Colored People Legal Def Fund, law clerk, 1974-75; Isabel Medford Law Firm, atty, 1978. **Orgs:** Chmn, Mem Com Niagra Movement Dem Club, 1974-; bd dir, A Safe Pl, 1979-; vpres, Univ Calif Black Alumni Asn, 1979-; legal adv, Oakland E Bay Chap, Delta Sigma Theta, 1979-; State Bar Calif. **Business Addr:** Attorney, 750 N Royal Crest Circle Suite 136, Las Vegas, NV 89109, **Business Phone:** (702)452-8104.

### MEDINA, BENNY

Television producer, executive, writer. **Personal:** Born Jan 24, 1958; son of Ahmad. **Career:** Apollo, vocalist, 1979; Warner Brothers Records, artists & repertoire, vpres; Handprint Entertainment, talent agent & partner, currently; Producer: "The Fresh Prince of Bel-Air", co producer, 1990-94, co exec producer, 1993-94; "Above the Rim", co producer, 1994; "You've Got to Be a Footbal"; "Maid in Manhattan", co producer, 2002; "Booty Call", co producer; Acts: "The Temptations", auth & produce; "Smokey Robinson", auth & producer; "Billy Preston", auth & producer; "Rick James", auth & producer; "Teena Marie", auth & producer; Warner Bros Rec; Medina Pollack Entertainment, co founder; Medina Co, chief exec officer, 2009-. **Honors/Awds:** Daytime Emmy Award, 2008. **Business Addr:** Talent Agent, Partner, Handprint Entertainment, 1100 Glendon Ave Suite 1000, Los Angeles, CA 90024, **Business Phone:** (310)481-4400.

### MEE, LAFARRELL DARNELL

Basketball player. **Personal:** Born Feb 11, 1971, Cleveland, TN. **Educ:** Western Ky Univ, attended 1993. **Career:** Basketball player (retired); Denver Nuggets, shooting guard, 1994-95; Continental Basketball Asn, Tri-City Chinook, 1995; Continental Basketball Asn, Yakima Sun Kings, 1995; NBL: Canberra Cannons, Australia, 1995-96; Gravelines, France, 1996-97; Adelaide 36ers, Australia, 1997-2001; Kinder Bologna, Italy, 2000; Bayer Giants Leverkusen, Ger, 2001-02; Cairns Taipans, Australia, 2002-03; Wollongong Hawks, Australia, 2004-05; Cairns Taipans, Australia, guard, 2005-09. **Orgs:** Nat Basketball Asn. **Honors/Awds:** Best Defensive Player, Nat Basketball League, 1999, 2000, 2001, 2005, 2006; Championships, Nat Basketball League, 1998, 1999.

### MEEK, CARRIE P.

Administrator, government official. **Personal:** Born Apr 29, 1926, Tallahassee, FL; daughter of William and Carrie; married Harold H Meek; children: Lucia Raiford, Sheila Davis Kinui & Kendrick. **Educ:** Fla A&M Univ, Tallahassee, FL, BS, biol & phys educ, 1946; Univ Mich, MS, pub health, phys educ, 1948. **Career:** Governement official (retired); Miami-Dade Community Col, spec asst, 1961; Fla Legis, seat, house reps, 1979-83; Fla State Senate, sen, 1983-93; US House Reps, congresswoman, 1993-2003; Bethune Cook man Col, phys educ, health instr; Fla A&M Univ, asst prof, health-phys educ. **Orgs:** Am-Israeli Coop Enterprise; bd advisor, Close Up Found; hon bd advisor, Nat Stud Leadership Conf; Delta Sigma Theta Sorority; bd mem, Health Syst-Health Planning Coun, 1972-75; bd mem, Pk People Prog, 1973-74; bd mem, Minority Bus Enterprise Comt Transp, 1978-79; Fla state house rep, 1979-83. **Business Addr:** Board of Advisor, Close Up Foundation, 1330 Braddock Pl Suite 400, Alexandria, VA 22314, **Business Phone:** (703)706-3300.

### MEEK, KENDRICK B.

Government official. **Personal:** Born Sep 6, 1966, Miami, FL; son of Carrie; married Leslie Dixon; children: Lauren & Kendrick B Jr. **Educ:** Fla A&M Univ, BS, criminol, 1989. **Career:** Fla Hwy Patrol, capt; Wacken hut Corp, develop rep; Dem Cong Campaign Comn, vice chair; Fla House Representatives, state rep, 1994-98; Fla State Senate, senator, 1998-2002; US House Representatives, Fla 17th Cong dist, congressman, 2003-11; K & L Security Serv Co, owner. **Orgs:** Numerous mem incl life mem, Nat Asn Advan Colored People; 100 Black Men; powerful House Armed Serv Comn; chair, bd dir, Cong Black Caucus Found; bd dir, Dem Nat Community Comn; hon co-chair, Col Dem Am; co-founder, Fla A&M Univ Col Dem; 100 Black Men S Fla; Biscayne Gardens Homeowners Asn; founding mem, Defending Against Drugs & Social Disorder; Nat Orgn Black Law Enforcement Execs; Omega Psi Phi Fraternity; mem, Fla Senate, 2002. **Business Addr:** Congressman, 17th Congressional District of Florida, 111 NW 183rd St Suite 325, Miami, FL 33169, **Business Phone:** (305)655-3213.

**MEEK, DR. RUSSELL CHARLES**
Educator, broadcaster, movie director. **Personal:** Born Sep 9, 1937, Springfield, IL; son of Albert Jackson and Josephine Snowden; children: 4. **Educ:** Milliken Univ, attended 1960; Nat Col, attended 1960; LaSalle Univ, attended 1960; Hwa Rang Do Martial Arts Acad, attended 1970; Universal Life Ch, DD, 1975. **Career:** Cook Co Dept Corrections, 1966-; Search for Truth Inc, pres, 1966-; Westside Art & Karate Ctr Inc, dir, 1968-; Univ Ill, instr radio TV prod psycholinguistics & philol; CETA V, Devel Educ & Employ Prog, proj dir; Malcolm X Col, instr, 1970-72; Radio Sta WVON, prod host, 1970-; Natl Black Writer's Workshop, lectr, 1973-75; Northeastern Ill Univ, rehab educ specialist, 1974-75; Study Commn Residential Schs Ill, hearing cord, 1974; Investigative Jour & Hist Rsch, writer; Malcolm X Col, bd dir; Parents Without Partners, comm adv commn; WBEZ, host. **Orgs:** Instr Martial Arts; pres, Black Karate Fed; Black United Front, Black Enpowerment Comm; SearchTruth Inc; radio commentator, talk show host, WBEE Radio; Dr Russ Meek's Jazz AllSTARS; bd dir, African Am ClergyAction, 1988-. **Honors/Awds:** Produced and directed TV & radioshows, 1966-; songs: "My Love", "You", "Shadows of the Night", 1969; produced and directed TV & radioshows, 1966-; received 10 humanitarian, community, integrity, merit & special awards, 1972-75; Westside Citizen of the Year, 1972-76; starred in 2 documentary films, "Crisis in the Cities" (Emmy Award winner), "A Letter to Martin"; Search for Truth News, editor; Comm Integrity Award, 1973; doctoral candidate, Univ the Pacific; publicist, co-sponsor, African-Amer Culture Center Imo State; The Can Do It Award, 1973; The Get It Done Award, 1973; Champion of Imprisoned Award, 1974; Special Commendation Award for Community Interest & Support, El Centro de La Causa, 1975; Nat Community Leaders; Gentlemen Distinction; Master of the MartialArts; Outstanding Serv to the Martial Arts & Community; playwright: "TheMessage", 1976; co-author: "Our Songs"; Image Makers Award, 1977; co-producer, actor, The Sinister Reign, Anna Lucasta, and Blues for MrCharlie; author, Poems for Peace, Justice and Freedom, 1966; co-director: "Mfundishi", Pan African Martial Ars Federation Inc. **Special Achievements:** First African American to produce & direct TV, radio shows since 1966 in the country. **Home Addr:** 10937 S Lowe Ave, Chicago, IL 60628-3129, **Home Phone:** (773)995-9727. **Business Addr:** President, Search for Truth Inc, 10937 S Lowe Ave, Chicago, IL 60628, **Business Phone:** (773)264-1691.

**MEEKS, GREGORY WELDON**
Government official, legislator. **Personal:** Born Sep 25, 1953, New York, NY; son of James and Mary; married Simone Marie; children: Ebony, Aja & Nia-Aiyana. **Educ:** Adelphi Univ, BA, 1975; Howard Univ, JD, 1978. **Career:** Queens Dist Atty Off, asst DA; Off Spec Narcotics Prosecutor, asst prosecutor; State Invest Comn, counr; NJS Workers Compensation Bd, supv judge; NY Assembly, 31st Dist, rep, 1992-98; US Cong, New York Sixth Cong Dist, rep, 1998-. **Orgs:** Alpha Phi Alpha; Nat Asn Advan Colored People; 100 Black Men; Nat Bar Asn; Meacon B Allen Black Bar Asn; New Dem Caucus; Dem Leadership Coun; Co-chair, Dialogue Caucus; Co-chair, Malaysia Caucus; Mid E Econ Partnership Caucus; Co-chair, Servs Caucus; bd mem, Nat Endowment Democracy; bd Advisors, Close Up Found; Nat Asn Advan Colored People; hon bd advisors, Nat Stud Leadership Conf; mem, House Comt Financial Serv; mem, Comt Foreign Affairs; Cong Black Caucus. **Home Addr:** 19424 109th Rd, St. Albans, NY 11412, **Home Phone:** (718)468-5106. **Business Addr:** US Congressman, US House of Representatives, 2234 Rayburn House Off Bldg, Washington, DC 20515, **Business Phone:** (202)225-3461.

**MEEKS, LARRY GILLETTE**
Writer. **Personal:** Born Apr 11, 1944, Bakersfield, CA; son of Henrietta and Reuben; married Dinnie Jean Williams; children: Kimerley & Corey. **Educ:** Bakersfield Jr Col, AA, 1963; Univ Calif, Davis, BS, 1970; Golden Gate Univ, MPA, 1973; Nat Univ, MA, 1995. **Career:** State Calif Off Health Planning & Develop, dir, 1983-92; Syndicated Columnist Ethnically Speaking, 1991-; Radio, talk show host, 1991-93; Los Rios Community Col Dist, col prof, 1995-. **Orgs:** Bd mem, Univ Southern Calif, 1983-92; gov bd mem, Natomas Sch Bd, 1985-2000; bd mem, Golden Gate Univ, 1989-; bd mem, Mercy Hosp Bd, 1992-94; Women Escaping a Violent Environ; Japanese Am Civil Liberties; League Women Voters; prof, Golden Gate Univ; Am Health Planers; chmn, Williams Memorial Church God Christ; life mem, Nat Urban League; Nat Asn Advan Colored People. **Honors/Awds:** Hons Docorate Humanity, Angeles Univ, 1989; Certificate of Appreciation, Los Angeles County, 1990. **Home Addr:** 26 Casa Vatoni Pl, Sacramento, CA 95834-7522, **Home Phone:** (916)920-8203. **Business Addr:** College Professor, Los Rios Community College District, 1919 Spanos Ct, Sacramento, CA 95825, **Business Phone:** (916)568-3041.

**MEEKS, HON. PERKER L., JR.**
Judge, lawyer, educator. **Personal:** Born Aug 6, 1943, Tallahassee, FL; married Patricia E Evans; children: Perker III & Alicia Nicole. **Educ:** Fla A&M Univ, BS, 1965; Fla State Univ Col, JD, 1968. **Career:** Judge (retired); Gov State Fla, admin aide, 1968-69; San Francisco Sch Dist, teacher, 1970-72; San Francisco Pub Defender's Off, trial lawyer, 1972-80; San Francisco Munic Ct, judge, 2004-07. **Orgs:** Pres & bd mem, OMI Comn Asn, 1970-80; secy & bd mem, Charles Houston Bar Asn, 1977-80; bd mem, San Francisco Chap Nat Advan Asn Colored People, 1978-79. **Honors/Awds:** CHBA Judicial Excellence Awards, 2004. **Home Addr:** 601 Miramar Ave, San Francisco, CA 94112-1231, **Home Phone:** (415)584-8145.

**MEEKS, REGINALD KLINE**
Legislator. **Personal:** Born Mar 21, 1954, Louisville, KY; son of Florian and Eloise M; children: Nilaja Nura-jehan. **Educ:** Wabash Col, BA, hist, 1976; Univ Iowa Col Law, JD, 1979; Univ Louisville, PhD. **Career:** Legal Aid Soc, community devel unit, 1981-82; Christian & Bynum Atty, law clerk, 1982-83; Bleidt, Barnett & Shanks Atty, law clerk, 1983-88; City Louisville, 11th ward alderman, 1982-2000; Jefferson County Pub Schs, career developer, 1988-91; Univ Louisville, assoc dir admis, 1991-; Ky House Representatives, 42nd Dis, state rep, 2000-; Univ La, Col Arts & Sci, dir external prog; McKendree Col, adj prof. **Orgs:** Nat Black Caucus Local Elected Officials, 1982-; secy bd dir, Seven Counties Servs, 1983-88; bd dir, Stage One, Louisville C's Theater, 1983-87; chmn, Shawnee Dist Old KY Home Coun Boy Scouts, 1984-87; Nat Asn Advan Colored People; Nat League Cities; KY Munic League; Nat Bar Asn; chmn, Mus Develop Comt KY African Am Mus, 1987-; bd dir, Farm & Wilderness Camps Plymouth, VT, 1987-90; adv coun, Salvation Army Boy's & Girl's Clubs, 1987-; bd dir, Neighborhood Housing Servs, 1991-; KY Polar Bear Club; founding mem, Ky Native Am Heritage Comn; Nat Asn Black Scuba Divers; founding mem, Ky Asn Black Scuba Divers; KY Native Am Arts & Cult Ctr; Lewis & Clark Bicentennial Comn. **Honors/Awds:** Dean's List Wabash Col; Black Achievers Award, YMCA, 1983; one of the 50 Young Leaders of the Future, Ebony Magazine, 1983; Outstanding Young Men of America. **Special Achievements:** Listed in Who's Who Among Black Americans; Who's Who in the South; Who's Who Among Emerging Leaders in America. **Home Addr:** 2301 Osage Ave, Louisville, KY 40210-1113, **Home Phone:** (502)772-1095. **Business Addr:** State Representative, Kentucky Legislation, PO Box 757, Louisville, KY 40201, **Business Phone:** (502)564-8100.

**MEEKS, STEPHEN ABAYOMI OBADELE**
Educator, physician. **Personal:** Born Aug 31, 1958, Philadelphia, PA; son of Clyde R and Pearl A Moore; children: Oji K, Kumasi D O & Adeyemi O. **Educ:** Howard Univ, BS, pre med, 1982; Inst TCM New York, dipl acupuncture, 1986; Inst Int D'Acupuncture et Medecine Chinois, Doctor Acupuncture, 1988. **Career:** Pro Martial Arts, 1968-; Family Planning Coun, health educr, 1983-84; Maternity, Infant Care Family Planning Coun New York, Health Educ, asst dir, 1984-89; prof musician, percussionist, vocalist, 1983-; prof speaker, health & cult confs, 1984-; Moyo Healing & Cult Arts Ctr Inc, owner, 1989-; Moyo Nguvu Cult Arts Ctr Inc, founder & fed dir, 1990-97; Moyo Health Assoc Inc, pres, doctor Asian Med, 1990-. **Orgs:** Qamata Int Martial Arts Asn, 1989-; Acupuncture Asn Colo, 1990-; Nat Black Child Develop, 1994-97; Denver Black United Fund, 1994-96; Nat Comn Cert Acupuncturist. **Home Addr:** 2512 High St, Denver, CO 80205. **Business Addr:** Founder, President, Moyo Nguvu Cultural Arts Center Inc, 5126 E Colfax Ave, Denver, CO 80220, **Business Phone:** (303)327-2511.

**MEEKS, WILLIS GENE**
Executive, vice president (organization). **Personal:** Born Jan 19, 1938, Harlan, KY; son of Maceo and Thelma; married Magalene Powell; children: Larry, Pamela Moore, Eric & Shauna. **Educ:** Allan Hancock Col, AA, electronics, 1964; Calif State Univ, BS, 1975, MBA, 1977. **Career:** Jet Propulsion Lab, Helios Proj engr, 1972-96, seasat chief, mission opers, 1975-78, mission opers mgr, 1978-83, mgr ulysess proj, 1983; OAO Corp, Corp Strategic Planning, sr vpres; NASA's Ulysses Solar Explor Proj, flight proj mgr & head, 1990. **Orgs:** Am Geophys Union, 1990-; Urban League; La Sickle Cell Found; Nat Asn Advan Colored People; La Coun Black Prof Engrs; Calif Tech Mgt Asn. **Special Achievements:** First flight project manager at JPL/NASA. **Home Addr:** 1159 Bradbourne Ave, Duarte, CA 91010, **Home Phone:** (818)303-5516.

**MEGGETT, DAVID LEE**
Football coach, football player, executive. **Personal:** Born Apr 30, 1966, Charleston, SC; children: Davin. **Educ:** Morgan State Univ; Towson Univ. **Career:** Football player (retired), football coach, executive; New York Giants, running back, 1989-94; New Eng Patriots, 1995-97; NY Jets, running back, 1998; Am Int Col, asst coach; Robersonville, NC, parks & recreation dir. **Honors/Awds:** Walter Payton Award, 1988; Pro Bowl, 1989, 1996; Super Bowl champion xxv.

**MEHRETEAB, GHEBRE-SELASSIE (GHEBRE SELASSIE MEHRETEAB)**
Management consultant. **Personal:** Born Jun 29, 1949, West Chester, PA; son of Ato Mehreteab Ogbou (deceased) and Weizero Leteyesus Woldeghabir (deceased). **Educ:** Haverford Col, BA, 1972, LLD, 2007. **Career:** Health & Welfare Coun, staff assoc, 1972-73; E Mt Airy Neighbors, dir, 1974-76; YMCA Germantown, assoc dir, 1976-78; New World Found, assoc dir, 1978-81; Ford Found, prog officer, 1981-87; Nat Corp Housing Partnerships, vpres, pres, chief exec officer; NHP Found, founder, chief exec officer, exec vpres, 1987-2007. **Orgs:** JP Morgan Chase Community Adv Bd; Comsos Club; City Club; Sigma Pi Phi; Coun Foreign Rels; bd dir, Na Housing Conf; dir, Douglas Emmett Inc, 2006-12; bd dir, Lockhart Co Inc; bd mem, Nat Housing Conf. **Honors/Awds:** Citation Senate of Pennsylvania, 1979; Key to the City Savannah GA, 1987. **Home Addr:** 600 Franklin Way, West Chester, PA 19380-5718.

**MEHU, GERALDINE**
Executive, executive director, association executive. **Personal:** children: 1. **Educ:** Seton Hall Univ, BA, criminal justice & sociol, MA, pub admin; Cornell Sch Indust Rels, cert, 2003; Securities Indust & Financial Markets Asn, Wharton Sch, Securities Indust Inst, cert, 2007. **Career:** NJ Gov's Off (Christine Todd Whitman), dep press secy, 1996-2002; NJ Dept State, dep chief staff; Barclays Capital, assoc dir global diversity & employee rels, 2002-04; UBS Wealth Mgt, dir pvt wealth mgt desk-client serv, 2005-07, dir piper jaffrey acquisition & integration, 2006-07, head prod strategy wealth mgt solutions, 2007-11, exec dir strategic initiatives, 2011-12, asst complex dir, 2012-14; Merrill Lynch, Assoc Mkt Exec, Currently. **Orgs:** Bd mem, Financial Women's Asn, 2005-; trustee, Marylawn High Sch, S Orange, NJ; Exec Leadership Coun, 2009-; Nat Asn Securities Professionals. **Honors/Awds:** 40 Under Forty, Network J, 2005; Women of Achievement Award, Marylawn High Sch, 2009; Top 100 Most Influential Blacks in Corporate America, Savoy, 2012. **Business Addr:** Merrill Lynch Wealth Management, 1 Crossroads Dr, Bedminster Township, NJ 07921, **Business Phone:** (800)526-0674.

**MELANCON, NORMAN, SR.**
Educator. **Personal:** Born Nov 6, 1939, Paincourtville, LA; son of Alphage Sr and Alice; married Joyce Carr; children: Norman E Jr, LaTisha & Marlon (deceased). **Educ:** Dillard Univ, BA, 1962; Nicholls State Univ, MEd, 1969; Loyola Univ, MS, 1972. **Career:** Assumption Parish, asst prin, 1964-85; Ward 6, police juror, 1976-85; Belle Rose Primary & Middle Schs, asst prin. **Orgs:** Sponsor 4-H Club; coordr, Boy Scout; supt, St Charles Baptist Church Sunday Sch. **Home Addr:** PO Box 91, Paincourtville, LA 70391. **Business Addr:** Assistant Principal, Belle Rose Middle School, 7177 Hwy 1, Belle Rose, LA 70341, **Business Phone:** (225)473-8917.

**MELENDEZ-RHINEHART, CARMEN M.**
Real estate agent, teacher, chief executive officer. **Personal:** Born Chicago, IL; daughter of Stanis S and Mae Hodge; married Vernon. **Educ:** Southern Ill Univ, BA, hist, 1968; Nat Louis Univ, MEd, 1977. **Career:** Teacher (retired), real estate agent, chief executive officer; Chicago PubSchs, hist dept, chair; Oscar C. Brown Real Estate, real estate assoc, broker, 1974-85; State Ill, real estate lic, assoc, 1974, broker, 1983; Melendez Realty Group Ltd, pres & chief exec officer, 1986-; White, Melendez & Hodge Inc, exec vpres. **Orgs:** Phi Delta Kappa Fraternity, 1979; Dearborn Real Estate Bd, 1983; formersecy, Links Inc, Windy City Chap, 1986; Delta Sigma Theta Sorority, Chicago Alumnae Chap, 1986; Nat Smart Set Inc, Chicago Chap, 1987; ArtInst Chicago, 1993; pres, Nat Sorority Phi Delta Kappa, Mu Chap, Krinonclub, 1999; Harris Young Women Christian Asn; Mikva Challenge. **Honors/Awds:** Citizens Award, Mayor Harold Wash, City Chicago, 1984; Achievement Award, Delta Sigma Theta Sorority, 1991; Quality Teacher of the Year, TeslaAlternative Sch, 1997; Armonk Institute Scholar, 1999; Citizen Award, Young Women Christian Asn. **Special Achievements:** Japan Project, participant, Chicago Public Sch, 1995; Univ Mass, Five College Center for Asian Studies, 1997; Rocky Mountain Project, Japan, Univ CO-Boulder, 1997. **Business Addr:** President, Chief Executive Officer, The Melendez Realty Group Inc, 9400 S Forest Ave, Chicago, IL 60619-7312, **Business Phone:** (773)821-7166.

**MELL, PATRICIA**
Dean (education), educator. **Personal:** Born Dec 15, 1953, Cleveland, OH; daughter of Julian Cooper and Thelma Webb; married Michael Steven Ragland; children: Lauren, Steven & Camille. **Educ:** Wellesley Col, BA, 1975; Case Western Res Univ Law Sch, JD, 1978. **Career:** Ohio Atty Gen Off, asst atty, 1978-82; Ohio Secy State Off, corp coun, 1982-84; Capital Univ Law Sch, Columbus, Oh, vis asst prof, 1984-85; Toledo Univ, Law Col, vis asst prof, 1985-86; Widener Univ Sch Law, DE, 1986-88; Lewis White & Clay; Mich State Univ, Detroit Law Col, prof, 1996-98, assoc dean acad affaris, 1998-2001; Univ Memphis, Cecil C Humphreys Sch Law, vis prof, 2002; John Marshall Law Sch, dean & prof, 2003-07; Mell Strategic Solutions & Consult, prin, 2009-. **Orgs:** Alliance Black Women, 1983-85; Black Am Law Stud Asn, Univ Toledo Law Sch, scholar screening comt, 1985-86; Case Western Res Univ Law Sch, Cleveland, gov body, 1985-88; Am Bar Asn; Nat Bar Asn; Nat Conf Black Lawyers; Am Arbit Asn; Nat Black MBAs, 1986-91. **Special Achievements:** First woman and first African American dean in the schools 104-year history. **Business Addr:** Principal, Mell Strategic Solutions & Consulting, 710 Crestview Dr, Bolingbrook, IL 60440, **Business Phone:** (630)456-0513.

**MELTON, BRYANT**
State government official, manager. **Personal:** Born May 9, 1940, Marion, AL; son of Bryant Sr and Bertha Dobyne; married Emma Jean Holmes; children: Tony, Delisa & Emily. **Educ:** Ala A&M Univ, attended 1958; Stillman Col, BS, 1965; Univ Ala, hon doctorate, 1968. **Career:** US Post Off, postman, 1965-69; Hale Co Bd Educ, teacher, 1969-72; Protective Ins Co, mgr, 1972-75; BF Goodrich, qual control mgr, 1976; Ala State House Reps, state rep dist 70, 2006; Shelton State Community Col, adminr, dean, dir human resources. **Orgs:** Nat Asn Advan Colored People, Tuscaloosa Co Chap; Boy Scouts; Stillman Col Alumni Asn; Alpha Phi Alpha; Masons; First African Baptist Church; Ala New S Coalition; Nat Asn Advan Colored People Sickle Cell Comn. **Honors/Awds:** Man of the Year & Charlie Green Award, Alpha Phi Alpha, 1977; Man of the Year, Nat Asn Advan Colored People, 1978.

**MELVIN, DR. ALEXANDER A.**
Dermatologist. **Personal:** Born Feb 4, 1943, Cleveland, OH; son of Alvin and Grace; married Leslie Gaillard; children: Hollie C & Allison L. **Educ:** Hillsdale Col, BS, 1965; Howard Univ Col Med, MD, 1968. **Career:** VA Med Ctr, internship; Howard Univ, resident; AUS Med Ctr Okinawa, chief dermat serv, 1972-74; Howard Univ, asst prof, 1975-80; Shaw Health Ctr, dermat consult, 1977-78; Alexander Dermat Ctr, PC, sr res assoc, dir, 1978-. **Orgs:** Consult, Am Safety Razor Co, 1980-82; chmn dermat sect, Nat Medial Assoc, 1985-87; consult, United Parcel Serv, 1992-; Gillette Res Inst, 1993-; Black Entertainment TV, 1993-; Am Bd Dermat. **Honors/Awds:** Upjohn Award for Excellence in Research, Howard Univ; contributor "Conn's Current Therapy," 1983 & 1984. **Special Achievements:** Author of several Published Professional Articles. **Home Addr:** 5601 Loch Raven Blvd Off Bldg Suite 203, Baltimore, MD 21239-2905, **Home Phone:** (410)464-5671. **Business Addr:** Physician, Dermatologist, Alexander Dermatology Center, 11085 Little Patuxent Pkwy, Columbia, MD 21044-2983, **Business Phone:** (301)596-4187.

**MENCER, DR. ERNEST JAMES**
Surgeon. **Personal:** Born Apr 24, 1945, Baton Rouge, LA; son of George E Jr and Maudra E; married Thomasine Haskins; children: Melanie Lynn & Marcus Kinnard. **Educ:** Morehouse Col, BS, 1967; Meharry Med Col, MD, 1972; Am Bd Surg, dipl, 1983. **Career:** Our Lady Lake Regional Med Ctr, chief surg, 1983; Earl K Long Hosp LSU Med Sch, asst prof surg; Baton Rouge Gen Med Ctr, vice chief surg; pvt pract gen surgeon, currently. **Orgs:** Bd dir, Baton Rouge Gen Med Ctr; fel Am Col Surgeons, 1985; bd dir, E Baton Rouge Parish Am Cancer Soc; LA Chap Am Col Surgeon. **Home Addr:** 5820 Stratford Ave, Baton Rouge, LA 70808-3526, **Home Phone:** (225)925-8941. **Business Addr:** Physician, 3401 North Blvd Suite 200-B, Baton Rouge, LA 70806, **Business Phone:** (225)341-7193.

**MENDENHALL, JOHN RUFUS**
Football player. **Personal:** Born Dec 3, 1948, Cullen, LA. **Educ:** Grambling State Univ. **Career:** Football player (retired); Green Bay Packers; New York Giants, right defensive tackle, left defensive back, nose tackle, 1972-79; Detroit Lions, right defensive tackle, 1980. **Orgs:** Nat Football League. **Business Addr:** WI.

**MENDES, DR. DONNA M.**
Surgeon. **Personal:** Born Oct 25, 1951, Oceanside, NY; daughter of Benjamin and Bernice Smith; married Ronald E LaMotte. **Educ:** Hofstra Univ, Hempstead, NY, BA, biol, 1973; Columbia Univ, Col Physicians & Surgeons, NY, MD, med, 1977. **Career:** Columbia Univ Col Physicians & Surgeons, Instr Clin Surg, assoc clin prof surg, 1984-; Self-employed surgeon, 1984-; Columbia Univ, clin asst prof, 1990-93; St Luke's Hosp, former chief vascular surg, 1992-98; N Gen Hosp, chief vascular surg, 2004-07; St Luke's-Roosevelt Hosp Ctr, fac, 1984-, sr vascular surgeon, 2003-; Mendes Vein Care, physician owner, 2009-. **Orgs:** Peripheral Vascular Surg Soc, 1984-; Manhattan Chap NMA, 1986-; Peripheral Surg Soc, 1986-; NY County Med Soc, 1986-2004; Soc Clin Vascular Surg, 1986-; Am Col Surgeons, 1987-; adv bd mem, Urban League, 1988-91; Am Med Women's Asn, 1988-; NY Cardiovasc Soc, 1989-; Susan Smith McKinney, 1989-91; sr mem, Socs Vascular Surgeons, 1992-12; adv panel, Vascular Surg, Am Bd Surg; Am Asn Vascular Surgeons, 1992-2003; Soc Clin Vascular Surgeons, 1992-2012; Int Soc Endovascular Surg, 1993-; Exec Mem Independent Physician Asn-St.Luke's-Roosevelt Hosp Ctr, 1996-97; Gala Steering Comt, 1997-98; Asn Black Cardiologists, 1998-2005; Soc Black Acad Surgeons, 1999-; Am Bd Vascular Surg; Leukemia & Lymphoma Soc, 2002-; chair minority comt, Soc Vascular Surgeons; Soc Vascular Surgeons, 2003-; Bergen County Urban League, 2005-. **Honors/Awds:** Outstanding Women of the Year, 1990; Teacher of the Year Award, StLuke's-Roosevelt Hosp Ctr Dept of Surgery, 1992; Student Nat Med Asn Award, 1995; Phenomenal Woman, KISS/FM, 2005; Hofstra University Alumnus of the Year, 2005. **Special Achievements:** First African-American female vascular surgeon certified by the American Board of Surgery. **Home Addr:** 311 Speer Ave, Englewood, NJ 07631. **Business Addr:** Senior Vascular Surgeon, St Luke's Roosevelt Hospital Center, 1000 Tenth Ave Suite 2B, New York, NY 10019, **Business Phone:** (212)636-4990.

**MENDOZA, GRACE. See JONES, GRACE.**

**MENEFEE, JUAN F.**
Executive, consultant. **Personal:** Born Jan 24, 1961, Chillicothe, OH. **Educ:** Univ Cincinnati, BBA, 1984. **Career:** Procter & Gamble, sales mgt; Johnson & Johnson, mgr; Frito Lay, regional sales mgr; Juan Menefee & Assocs, founder & pres, 1988-. **Orgs:** Omega Psi Phi Frat; Nat Black MBA Asn; pres, Nat Asn Black Sales Prof. **Business Addr:** President, Founder, Juan Menefee & Associates, 503 S Oak Pk Ave Suite 206, Oak Park, IL 60304, **Business Phone:** (708)848-7722.

**MENOGAN, ANNITA M.**
Secretary (office), executive, educator. **Educ:** Acad Art Col, San Francisco, CA, BFA, graphic design & lllustration, 1975; Univ Denver, Sturm Col Law, JD, corp, finance, & securities law, 1983. **Career:** Pvt pract law, Gen bus, corp, securities & telecommunications, 1983-97; Dorsey & Whitney LLP, partner, 1997-99; Molson Coors Brewing Co, asst gen coun, vpres, secy & dep gen coun, 1999-2005; Red Robin Intl Inc, vpres, 2006-07, chief legal officer & secy, 2006-, sr vpres, 2006-13; Inst Advan Am Legal Syst, educr, 2012-; Univ Denver, educr, 2012-; Sturm Col Law, educr, 2012-; Legal Exec Training & Adv Serv LLC, founder & prin, 2014-; Fortis Law Partners LLC, coun, 2014-15; Atkins Nutritionals Inc, Vpres & Gen Coun, 2015-. **Orgs:** Colo Lawyer Trust Acct Found; Colo Bar Asn; officer, Colo Supreme Ct comts; Atty Regulation Hearing Bd, 1999-2005; Comt Unauthorized Pract Law, 1999-2002; Bd Law Examiners, 2000-10; adv bd mem, Inst Advan Am Legal Syst, 2012-; adv bd mem, Univ Denver, 2012-; adv bd mem, Sturm Col Law, 2012-; mem bd dir, C's Hosp Colo, 2014-; mem bd dir, Denver Kids Inc, 2014-. **Honors/Awds:** Lawyer of the year, Law Week Colo, 2010. **Business Addr:** Vice President, General Counsel, Atkins Nutritionals Inc, 1050 17th St Suite1000, Denver, CO 80265, **Business Phone:** (303)633-2840.

**MENSAH, BERNARD**
Executive. **Educ:** Univ Bristol, BA, social sci, joint sch philos & econs, 1989. **Career:** Goldman Sachs, Global Head Bank Loans & Distressed Trading, african partner, global head bank loan, managing dir, 2001, partner, 2006; Bank Am Merrill Lynch, managing dir, global head emerging markets sales & trading, 2010-, exec dir, 2015-; Bank Am Corp, managing dir global head emerging markets. **Honors/Awds:** "Black Enterprise," 75 Most Powerful Blacks on Wall Street, 2011. **Business Addr:** Executive Director, Bank of America Merrill Lynch, 1 Bryant Pk 9th Fl, New York, NY 10036, **Business Phone:** (646)855-5000.

**MENSAH, E. KWAKU**
Executive, president (organization). **Personal:** Born Nov 1, 1945, Accra; son of Amuzu and Bertha Amuzu; married Linda May; children: Sidney, Sylvester, Tonyo, Asanvi & Delali. **Educ:** St Joseph's Univ, Philadelphia, PA, BS, bus admin, 1976; Univ Ghana, UN cert, statist. **Career:** Hilton Hotels Corp, Philadelphia Hilton Hotel, comptroller, area dir finance, 1974-84, Baltimore, Dir Finance/Comptroller, 1984, Parsipany, Nj, dir finance, 1984-86, Los Angeles Airport, dir finance, 1986-89; Wash, dir finance, 1989-; Gold Coast Financial Corp, pres, currently; Fortune 500 co, mid-Atlantic region, area dir finance. **Business Addr:** President, Gold Coast Financial Corp, 14919 Carry Back Dr, North Potomac, MD 20878-3712, **Business Phone:** (301)990-2600.

**MENZIES-WILLIAMS, DR. BARBARA ANN**
Physician. **Personal:** Born Oct 24, 1950, Memphis, TN; daughter of Simon Ledbetter; children: Simone Benai Williams. **Educ:** Mich State Univ, BS, 1972; Wayne State Univ, MS, 1974, Med Sch, MD, int med, 1978; Univ Wis-Madison, MS, prev med, 1996; Hutzel Hosp, internal med. **Career:** Harper Hosp, chief int med, 1995-97; Blue Cross Blue Shield Mich, exec med dir, 1997-2008; Henry Ford W Bloomfield Hosp; Self-employed, physician, currently. **Orgs:** Henry Ford Med Group. **Special Achievements:** Took part in the American College of Physicians Executive Delegation Visit to China; Representative of the People to People International Ambassador program. **Home Addr:** PO Box 04390, Detroit, MI 48204, **Home Phone:** (313)896-0935. **Business Addr:** Physician, Private Practice, 3011 W Grand Blvd Suite 568, Detroit, MI 48202, **Business Phone:** (313)875-1323.

**MERCADO-VALDES, FRANK MARCELINO**
Executive, president (organization), founder (originator). **Personal:** Born May 18, 1962, New York, NY; son of Frank Mercado and Lidia. **Educ:** Miami-Dade Col, AA, 1983; Univ Miami, BA, 1985. **Career:** Alto-Marc Commun, African Heritage Movie Network, pres & founder, 1985; Bush Quayle, media asst, 1988; Movie Marketing & Distributer: Cosby; Moesha; The Steve Harvey Show; Its Showtime at The Apollo. **Orgs:** Kappa Alpha Psi Fraternity, 1983-; Golden Gloves Fla Benefit Comn, 1987; Kappa Alpha Psi Scholar Found, 1989-92; Dancer's Alliance; African-Am Anti-Defamation Asn, 1991-; African-Am Film & Tv Asn; Nat Asn TV Prog Exec. **Home Addr:** 10 W 135 St Suite 6T, New York, NY 10037, **Home Phone:** (212)281-1141.

**MERCER, ARTHUR, II**
Manager. **Educ:** Univ Wyo, psychol, 1983. **Career:** Target Corp, Target Distrib Ctr, oper supvr, 1996-99, dist assets protection team leader, 1999-2002, group team lead invests e, 2002-04; Target Stores, sr group assets protection team leader, 2004-12; Sears Holdings Mgt Corp, regional loss prev mgr, 2012-13, nat mgr loss prev, 2013-14, Assoc Mil Support Network, chmn, 2014-, Assets Protection Learning & Develop, nat mgr, 2014-. **Business Addr:** National Manager, Sears Holdings Management Corp, 3333 Beverly Rd, Hoffman Estates, IL 60179, **Business Phone:** (847)286-2500.

**MERCER, LILLIAN ANN**
Teacher, educator, administrator. **Career:** Educator (retired); Laramie County Sch Dist, spec educ teacher. **Home Addr:** , Cheyenne, WY. **Business Addr:** WY.

**MERCER, RONALD EUGENE (RON MERCER)**
Basketball player. **Personal:** Born May 18, 1976, Nashville, TN. **Educ:** Univ Ky, attended 1997. **Career:** Basketball player (retired); Boston Celtics, 1997-99; Denver Nuggets, guard, 1999-2000; Orlando Magic, 2000; chicago bulls, 2001-02; Indiana Pacers, guard, 2002-03; San Antonio Spurs, guard, 2003-04; New Jersey Nets, guard, 2004-05.

**MERCER, VALERIE JUNE**
Curator. **Personal:** Born Jun 5, 1947, Philadelphia, PA; daughter of William J and Helen Kono. **Educ:** Sch Visual Arts, New York, NY, attended 1974; NY Univ, NY, BA, art hist, 1979; Harvard Univ, Cambridge, MA, art hist, 1982. **Career:** Harvard Univ Fel, 1982-86; Studio Mus, Harlem, sr cur, 1992-99; NY Times, New York, NY, freelance art writer, 1988-91; The Brooklyn Paper, Brooklyn, NY, freelance art writer, 1990-91; Am Visions, New York, NY, Wash, DC, 1991; Detroit Inst Art, cur african am art & head Gen Motors Ctr African Am Art, 2001-. **Orgs:** Nat Asn Black Journalists, 1989-; Col Art Asn, 1985-. **Honors/Awds:** Woman of the Year Award, NY Asn Prof Black Women, 1996. **Special Achievements:** First curator of the African American art. **Home Addr:** 74 Rutland Rd, Brooklyn, NY 11225, **Home Phone:** (718)282-6765. **Business Addr:** Curator of African American Art, The Detroit Institute of Arts, 5200 Woodward Ave, Detroit, MI 48202, **Business Phone:** (313)833-7900.

**MERCER-PRYOR, DIANA**
Executive director. **Personal:** Born Dec 4, 1950, Detroit, MI; daughter of Elisha and Dessie Hogan; married Donald Pryor; children: Eleasha De Ann Mercer & Jason Thomas Mercer. **Educ:** Univ Mich, Ann Arbor, BBA, bus/com, gen, 1973; Univ Detroit, Detroit, MI, MBA, finance, gen, 1975. **Career:** Executive director (retired); Chrysler Corp, Highland Pk, Mich, gen pur agt, procurement exec 1972-2006; Procurement & Supply orgn, 1989; DaimlerChrysler African Am Network, bd mem, NAO Non-Prod Procurement, dir, 1991-2006; Independent Automotive Prof, currently. **Orgs:** Bd mem, Univ Detroit Alumni Bd, 1989; assoc bd mem, Franklin Wright Settlement Bd, 1989; mem, Detroit Urban League; Faith Christian Ctr; vpres, Diversity Info Resources; bd mem, DaimlerChrysler African Am Network; Alpha Kappa Alpha Sorority Inc, currently; Girls Group, Communities United C, Oakland Woods-Presby Villages. **Home Addr:** 4261 Woodlands Lane, Orchard Lake, MI 48323-1622, **Home Phone:** (248)681-7707.

**MERCHANT, JAMES S., JR.**
Hotel executive, executive. **Personal:** Born Apr 28, 1954, Clarksburg, WV; son of James S and Millie A; married Joyce A Walton; children: Linel, Shelita & Ebony. **Educ:** WVa Univ, BS, bus admin, 1976. **Career:** Bob Evans Farms Inc, mgr trainee, 1977-78, from second asst mgr to first asst mgr, 1978-79, gen mgr, 1979-83, area dir, 1983-94, vpres & regional dir, restaurant opers, 1994-2005, sr vpres restaurant opers, 2005-. **Orgs:** Omega Psi Phi, 1974-; adv bd, Touchston Cafe, 1988-; trustee, Cent Ohio Restaurant Asn; Del County. **Honors/Awds:** Cent Zone Mgr of the Yr, Bob Evans Farms Inc, 1982; King Yr, WVa Black Heritage Festival, 2006. **Special Achievements:** Blue Chip Award, nominated, 1991. **Home Addr:** 1040 Melinda Dr, Westerville, OH 43081, **Home Phone:** (614)895-9764. **Business Addr:** Senior Vice President, Bob Evans Farms Inc, 3776 S High St, Columbus, OH 43207-4012, **Business Phone:** (614)491-2225.

**MERCHANT, ESQ. JOHN CRUSE**
Lawyer. **Personal:** Born Apr 1, 1957, Lexington, KY; son of John and Thelma; married Debra Spotts; children: Leah Cruse. **Educ:** Morehead State Univ, BA, 1979; Univ Ky, JD, 1982. **Career:** Shirley A Cunningham, law assoc, 1982-83; Off Lt Gov, admin asst, 1983-87; Wilkinson Govr Campaign, staff worker, 1987; Off Legal Serv, finance cabinet, staff atty, 1988-91; Peck Shaffer & Williams, assoc, 1991-94, partner, 1994-2014; Dinsmore & Shohl LLP, partner, currently. **Orgs:** Ky Bar Asn, 1982-; Nat Bar Asn, 1985-; Nat Asn Securities Prof, 1991-; Cincinnati Bar Asn, 1991-; Nat Forum Black Pub Adminrs, 1985-; Black Male Coalition, 1992-; exec bd, Jr Achievement Cincinnati, 1992-; mentor, Cincinnati Youth Collaborative, 1992-; Ohio Bar Asn, 1992-; fel Am Col Bond Coun; mem bd regents, Morehouse State Univ; bd mem, Ky League Cities; bd mem, Ohio State Bar Found; bd mem, Ky Sci & Technol Corp; Nat Asn Bond Lawyers; Asn Govt Leasing & Fin; Black Lawyers Asn Cincinnati; chair, bd regents, Morehead State Univ; bd mem, Cincinnati Ctr City Develop Corp; nd mem, Cincinnati Art Mus; Asn Govt Leasing & Finance. **Honors/Awds:** Alumni Award, Morehead State Univ, 1989; Black Business Award, Quinn Chapel AME Church, 1995. **Home Addr:** 4156 Allenhurst Close, Cincinnati, OH 45241, **Home Phone:** (513)769-5088. **Business Addr:** Partner, Dinsmore & Shohl LLP, 255 E 5th St Suite 1900, Cincinnati, OH 45202, **Business Phone:** (513)639-9224.

**MERCHANT, ESQ. JOHN F.**
Lawyer. **Personal:** Born Feb 2, 1933, Greenwich, CT; son of Essie L Nowlin and Garrett M; children: Susan Beth. **Educ:** Va Union Univ, BA, 1955; Univ Va, JD, 1958. **Career:** St Conn, atty, 1962-; ABCD Inc, dep dir, 1965-67; St Dept Community Affairs, dep comnr, 1967-71; Peoples Bank, dir, mem loan, 1969-; Fairfield Univ, vis lectr, 1970-75; Consumer Coun, St Conn, 1991-96; Nat Minority Golf Found Inc, pres, chief exec officer, 1996; Jomer & Asn, partner, 1998; JFM & Assocs, partner; Gen Elec Corp & Candeub Fleissig Asn, consult. **Orgs:** Chmn, Conn Coun Human Rights, 1964-65; pres, Brideport Area Ment Health Asn, 1968; dir, Bridgeport Hosp, 1968-79; dir, Child Welfare League Am, chmn, Pub Policy Comt, 1986-92, pres, 1993-96; trustee, St Vincent's Col Nursing; trustee, Fairfield Univ; founder, Walter N. Ridley Scholar Fund; trustee, Univ Bridgeport; partner, Merchant & Rosenblum Attorneys Law; Nat Asn Advan Colored People; pres, Child Guid Clin; dir, Regional Plan Asn; pres, Hartcom Inc. **Honors/Awds:** Community Service Award, Sacred Heart Univ, 1982; Citizen of the Year, Omega Psi Phi, 1983; Firstblack member, US Golf Asn Exec Comt; Tree of Life Award, Jewish Nat Fund; First Black President, Child Welfare League Am Inc. **Special Achievements:** First African American graduate, Univ Va Law Sch, 1958; First African American member of US Golf Asn Exec Committee. **Home Addr:** 289 A Agawam Dr, Stratford, CT 06614-8154, **Home Phone:** (203)386-1480. **Business Addr:** Attorney General, State of Connecticut, 490 Riders Lane, Fairfield, CT 06430, **Business Phone:** (860)808-5318.

**MEREDAY, RICHARD F.**
Government official, executive director. **Personal:** Born Dec 18, 1929, Hempstead, NY; son of Charles and Melta; married Emma; children: Philip, Richard & Meta. **Educ:** Hofstra Univ, BA, 1951; Brooklyn Law Sch, LLB, 1958. **Career:** Government official (retired); Charles Mereday Trucking Corp, vpres; Tri County Truck Owners Asn, sec scribe, 1956-63; lic NY Ins Broker, 1961; Town Hemp stead, probation officer supvr, 1964-65; Dept Pub Works, admin, 1965-70; Nassau County, Bur Career Planning & Develop, Dep Gen Servs, former dir, 1971-75; Off Manpower Progs, cord educ serv, nassau county govt, 1975-2002; Nassau County Met Regional Coun TV classes, speaker; Nassau County, Off Affil Action, exec dir. **Orgs:** Rep exec, Town Leader; vpres, Uptopia Comm Civic Asn; chmn, Roosevelt United Fund; inst rep, Nat Boy Scouts Coun; pres, Lions Club; adv bd, Salvation Army. **Honors/Awds:** Plaque Unselfish Service to the Community of Roosevelt, 1969; Recipient Good Neighbor Award, Nassau County Press Asn, 1973; recognition cert, Dist 20 K 2 Lions Intl, 1973; Active Participant, Rep Leadership Conf, 1975. **Home Addr:** 264 Frederick Ave, Roosevelt, NY 11575-2340, **Home Phone:** (516)379-0042.

**MEREDITH, LA'KEISHA FRETT. See FRETT, LA KESHIA.**

**MERENIVITCH, JARROW**
Executive, association executive, army officer. **Personal:** Born Jun 1, 1942, Alexandria, LA; son of Audrey Sr and Georgia N; married Hazel R Wilmer; children: Jarrow Jr, Marion E & Jonathan R. **Educ:** Grambling State Univ, BA, polit sci, 1964; Inst Appl Mgt & Law, cert, 1985; Tex Southern Univ, MBA. **Career:** Grambling State Univ, stud govt pres, 1963, 1964, alumni pres; Procter & Gamble Co, Green Bay, WI, team mgr, 1969-72, Albany, GA, plant personnel rels mgr, 1972-75, Cincinnati corp personnel develop consult, 1975-78, employee/employer rels mgr, 1978-80, personnel mgr, Macon, GA Plant, 1980-83, mgr indust rels, 1983-85, food mfg div human resources mgr, 1985-90, assoc dir, food & beverage personnel sector, 1990-93; Human Resources Customer Serv, Global, assoc dir, 1993-2001; Creative Mkt Consult LLC, pres, chief exec officer, currently; Judy Smith, campaign finance dir, 2000; Procter & Gamble, procter & gamble med acct mgr, 2001-08; Trop Salt Corp, exec dir int & domestic mkt & sales, 2008-10; Kraft Foods Group, customer sales, 2010-13, key acct mgr, 2013-; Kraft Heinz Co, territory bus mgr, 2015-. **Orgs:** Vpres, Grambling Univ Alumni, 1990; Omega Psi Phi Fraternity; Nat Asn Advan Colored People; bd dir, Quinn Chapel AMG Church; bd mem, Visions Inc, currently. **Honors/Awds:** Outstanding Service, Eta Omicron Chap, Psi Phi Omega, 1975; Citation Outstanding Contribution to Procter & Gamble Beverage Div, 1984; John Feldmann Diversity Leadership Award, 1988; Outstanding Contribution to Food PSS in the Diversity Area, 1989; Rosa Parks Award, Leadership Diversity & Multiculturalism; Diversity Planning Initiative Award, 1996; Diversity Globe Award, 1996. **Special Achievements:** Publication: "Toward a Multicultural Organization, " 1979. **Home Addr:** 1817 Forester Dr, Cincinnati, OH 45240, **Home Phone:** (513)825-4454. **Business Addr:** Board Member, Visions Inc, 48 Juniper St, Roxbury, MA 02119, **Business Phone:** (617)541-4100.

**MERIDETH, CHARLES WAYMOND**
Educator, association executive. **Personal:** Born Nov 2, 1940, Atlanta, GA; son of Charlie and Ruth Wilson; married Rebecca Little; children: Kelli & Cheryl. **Educ:** Morehouse Col, BS, chem & math, 1961; Univ Calif, Berkeley, PhD, phys chem, 1965; Harvard, Educ Mgt. **Career:** Educator (retired); Univ Ill, post doctoral fel; Lockheed Ga Co, res scientist; Univ Ill, fel, 1956-66; Morehouse Col, prof, 1965; Atlanta Univ, dir eng, 1969, provost, 1976, chancellor, 1978-90; Harvard Univ Inst Educ Mgt; New York Tech Col, pres, 1990-96; sci consult, NSF; sci consult, Nat Insts Health; Jet Propulsion Lab, sci consult. **Orgs:** Phi Beta Kappa; Soc Sigma Xi; Beta Kappa Chi Sci Soc; Am Chem Soc; Am Phys Soc; AAAS; NY Acad Sci; bd dir, Blayton Bus Col, 1971; vpres, 100 Black Men Atlanta Inc, 1988-90; pres, Jimmy Carter's Sci Adv Comt Comt Minorities, Nat Acad Eng. **Honors/Awds:** Fresman Achievement Award Chem, 1957; Woodrow Wilson Nat fel, 1961; Charles E Merrill Early Admis Scholar, Magna Cum Laude, 1961; Danforth Fac Asn. **Special Achievements:** Noted as one of the top ten Outstanding Young People of Atlanta by TOYPAin 1956. **Home**

Addr: 340 E 64th St, New York, NY 10021, **Home Phone:** (212)486-2455.

### MERIDITH, DENISE PATRICIA

Consultant, executive. **Personal:** Born Apr 14, 1952, Brooklyn, NY; daughter of Glenarva and Dorothy Sawyer. **Educ:** Cornell Univ, Ithaca, NY, BS, natural resouces & wildlife biol, 1973; USC, Sacramento, Calif, MPA, orgn behav, 1993. **Career:** Bur Land Mgt, Las Vegas, Nev, wildlife bio & env spec, 1973-77, SilverSpring, Md, environ spec, 1977-79, Wash, DC, wild life biologist, 1979-80, Alexandria, Va, dep state dir, 1980-86, Santa Fe, NMex, dep state dir, 1986-89, Sacramento, Calif, assoc state dir, 1989-91, Alexandria, Va, state dir, 1991-93, dep dir, Wash, DC, 1993-95, Ariz state dir, 1995-2002; Denise Meridith Consults Inc, pres & chief exec officer, 2001-; Colonial Life Phoenix, agency develop mgr, 2013-; Leo A Daly, subcontractor, 2002-03; Linking Sports & Communities, founder, 2004-; Putman Rovia Travel, travel agt, 2008-; US Dept Com, Census Bur, enumerator & clerk, 2010; Examr.com, Phoenix Bus Insight Examr, 2010-; Start Up Now Homes LLC, chief exec officier, 2009-11; Healthcare Success Strategies, bus develop exec, 2012; HealthNation, cert health advocate, 2013; NTCBDA/Trin & Assocs, assc, 2012-; Opportunities Youth Maricopa County, commun dir, 2015-16; VM&RC Enterprises LLC, dir pub & media rels, 2016. **Orgs:** Co founded, Ariz Tourism Asn, 1996; Bd dir, Ariz Cactus-Pine Coun Girl Scouts, 1996-2002; bd dir, Ariz Black, 1996-; pres, Phoenix Fed Exec Assoc, 1996; Bd, Soc Air Foresters; pres, Greater Phoenix Black Chamber Com, 1998-99; Forest Sci & Technol, 1998-2001; bd trustee, Cornell Univ, 2000-04; ceo, Leadership Consortium, 1999-2009; Girl Scouts AZ Cactus Pine Coun Bd; Socs Am Foresters, Partners Outdoors; Ariz Tourism & Sports Authority Bd; Phoenix Bond initiatives; Phoenix Conv & Visitors Bur; co chair, Nat Asn Black Journalists 25th anniversary conf, 2000; former mem, Phoenix Judicial Selection Comt; leader, 2001, 2006, chair parks, recreation & libr, co-chair human serv; Maricopa Community Col MultiCultural Adv Comt, 2007-. **Honors/Awds:** Meritorious Award, Dept Interior, 1987; Senior Executive Service Cert, 1990; BLM Legend Award, 2002; SBA Vision Award; BLM Legend Award; National Forum of Black Public Administrators Award. **Special Achievements:** First professional woman hired by the US Bureau of Land. **Home Addr:** PO Box 7305, Phoenix, AZ 85011. **Business Addr:** President, Chief Executive Officer, Denise Meridith Consults Inc, 5025 N Cent Ave Suite 259, Phoenix, AZ 85012, **Business Phone:** (602)763-9900.

### MERIWEATHER, MELVIN, JR.

Government official, executive. **Personal:** Born Oct 22, 1937, Hernando, MS; son of Melvin and Virgie; married Juliet Ilene Thomas; children: Kristel, Douglas & Dana. **Educ:** Isaac E Elston, grad 12th, 1957. **Career:** Riley Sch PTA, pres, 1968-79; Eastport Improv Asn, pres, 1971-73; Mich City PTA Coun, pres, 1974-75; N Cent Comn Action Agencies, pres, 1979-84, pvt rep; Mich City Sch Bd, pres; Mich City Area Sch, bd pres, 1987-88; secy, 1988-89; Midwest Steel, crew coordr, 1989. **Orgs:** Treas & deacon New Hope Baptist Church, 1963-85; parents adv bd, Rogers HS, 1978-79; health & safety chmn, 1980-82, 2nd vpres, 1982-84; Ind Cong Parents & Teachers; Daniel C Slocum Mem Found, 1982-85; vol fireman, Fire Brigade Midwest Steel, 1970-85; Ind Dept Educ "Parent/Community Involvement" task force. **Honors/Awds:** Mr Ind, Ind AAU Amateur Body building, 1966; Mr Most Muscular, AAU Mid States Competition, 1966; state life mem, Ind Cong PTA, 1974; vpres, Mich City Area Sch Bd, 1982-86; Sch Bd Pres, 1986-87; cert merit, Ind Dept Educ; Mr Am contest. **Home Addr:** 616 Monroe St, Michigan City, IN 46360-5042, **Home Phone:** (219)872-7109.

### MERIWETHER, LOUISE JENKINS

Writer, educator. **Personal:** Born May 8, 1923, Haverstraw, NY; daughter of Marion Lloyd and Julia Golphin; married Angelo; married Earl Howe. **Educ:** NY Univ, BA, Eng, 1950; Univ Calif, MA, jour, 1965. **Career:** Los Angeles Sentinel, newspaperwoman, 1961-64; Universal Studios, story analyst, 1965-67; City Col, Black studies teacher, 1979; Sarah Lawrence Col, creative writing teacher undergrad & grad, 1979-88; Univ Houston, instr creative writing teacher undergrads & grads, 1985; Author: Daddy Was A Number Runner, 1970; Civil War Hero Robert Smalls, 1971; The Freedom Ship of Robert Small, 1971; The Heart Man: The Story of Daniel Hale Williams, 1972; Don't Ride the Bus on Monday: The Rosa Parks Story, 1973; Fragments of the Ark, 1994; Daddy Was a Number Runner, 2002; Shadow Dancing, 2000; Incidents in the Life of a Slave Girl: The Givens Collection Classics, 2003; Contributor in: Black Review No 2, Morrow, 1972; Black-Eyed Susans, Anchor Press, 1975, confirmation: An Anthology of African-American Women, Morrow, 1983; Daughters of Africa, Pantheon, 1992; Shadow Dancing, 2000; Incidents in the Life of a Slave Girl, 2003; Watts Writers Workshop, staff mem; Sarah Lawrence Col, instr creative writing; freelance writer, currently. **Orgs:** PEN; Harlem Writers Guild. **Honors/Awds:** Fiction Grant, Rabinowitz Found, 1968; Fiction Grant, NY State Found Arts, 1973, 1977, 1992, 1996; Fiction Grant, Nat Endowment Arts, 1973; Mellon Research Grant, Sarah Lawrence Col, 1983. **Special Achievements:** First African-American story analyst in Hollywood's history. **Home Addr:** 392 Cent Pk W Apt 1C, New York, NY 10025, **Home Phone:** (212)749-3953. **Business Addr:** Author, Ellen Levine Literary Agency, 15 E 26th St Suite 1801, New York, NY 10010, **Business Phone:** (212)725-4501.

### MERIWETHER, ROY DENNIS

Pianist, composer, music arranger or orchestrator. **Personal:** Born Feb 24, 1943, Dayton, OH; children: Tammi & Cyd. **Career:** Columbia-Capitol-Gambit-Stinger-Faharenheit Rec Co, pianist, composer & rec artist, 1966; Howard Roberts Chorale & Dayton Contemp Dance Co, Composer & arranger, 1976; Dayton Philharmonic Orchestra, guest artist, 1980; Thomas A Edison St Col, composer lyricist col alma mater, 1984; Gemini Rec, producer, arranger, composer & rec artist, 1985; Albums: Soup & onion, 1965; Popcorn and soul, 1966; The stone truth, 1966; Soul knight, 1968; Preachin', 1970; Jesus Christ goes jazz, 1972; Nubian lady, 1973; Live, 1973; Black snow, 1975; Live at Gordy's, 1975; Journeys with Roy Meriwether, 1985; Opening night, 1986; Opening night II, 1989; Xtensions, 1995; This one's on me, 1999; Live at Gilly's, 2004; Twilight blues, 2005; The Art of the groove, 2007. **Orgs:** Am Fedn Musicians Local 802, 1966-; Am Soc Composers, Authors & Publishers, 1966-. **Honors/Awds:** Jazz Composition Fellowship Grant, Nat Endowment Arts, 1973; proclamation to honor Black Snow, Mayor, City Dayton, OH, 1976; Significant Achievement Award, Black Snow Powell & Assocs, 1976; Outstanding Jazz Instrumentalist, Manhattan Asn Cabarets, 1987; Lifetime Achievement honoree, Dayton Ohio Music Award, 1999; Man of the Year Award, Thessolonian Missionary Baptist Church, 1999; Jazz Community Award, Jamaica Queens, NY; Lifetime Achievement to Music Award. **Special Achievements:** Nominated for a Grammy Award. **Home Addr:** 7 W 87th St Suite 4D, New York, NY 10024, **Home Phone:** (212)874-7402. **Business Phone:** (212)874-7402.

### MERKERSON, SHARON EPATHA

Actor. **Personal:** Born Nov 28, 1952, Detroit, MI; daughter of Ann; married Toussaint Louverture Jones Jr. **Educ:** Wayne State Univ, BFA. **Career:** Broadway plays: The Piano Lesson; I'm Not Stupid; Three Ways Home; films: She's Gotta Have It, 1986; Navy Seals, 1990; Loose Cannons, 1990; Jacob'sLadder, 1990; Terminator 2, 1991; Random Hearts, 1999; Law & Order: Deadon the Money, voice, 2002; The Rising Place, 2003; Law & Order II: Double or Nothing, voice, 2003; Radio, 2003; Jersey Girl, 2004; Black Snake Moan, 2006; Slipstream, 2007; The Six Wives of Henry Lefay, 2009; Mother and Child, 2009; Lincoln, 2012; The Contradictions of Fair Hope, exec producer & dir, 2012; Peeples, 2013. TV movies: Christmas Special, 1988; Moe's World, 1990; Equal Justice, 1990; It's Nothing Personal, 1993; A Place for Annie, 1994; A Mother's Prayer, 1995; Breaking Through, 1996; An Unexpected Life, 1998; Exiled, 1998; A Girl Thing, 2001; The Rising Place, 2001; Inside TV Land: Cops on Camera, 2002; Lackawanna Blues, 2005; Girl, Positive, 2007; We the Peeples, 2011; Boomerang, 2013; The Gabby Douglas Story, 2014. TV series: "Peewee's Playhouse", 1987-89; "The Cosby Show", 1988; "The More You Know", 1989; "CBS Summer Playhouse", 1989; "The 44th Annual Tony Awards", 1990; "Law & Order", 1991-2010; "Mann and Machine", 1992; "Here and Now", 1992; "ABC Afterschool Specials", 1992; "South Beach", 1993; "Fifth Annual Screen Actors Guild Awards", 1999; "Late Night with Conan O'Brien", 1999; "Larry King Live", 2000; "Frasier", 2000; "Hollywood Squares", 2001; "Law & Order: Criminal Intent", 2002; "Life & Style", 2005; "The WIN Awards", 2005; "Ellen: The Ellen DeGeneres Show", 2005-06; "Tavis Smiley", 2005-07; "Law & Order: Trial by Jury", 2005; "The Sixty third Annual Golden Globe Awards", 2006; "Live with Regis and Kathie Lee", 2006; "2006 Independent Spirit Awards", 2006; "Inside the Actors Studio", 2006; "The Sixtyth Annual Tony Awards", 2006; "Comic Relief 2006", 2006; "The View", 2007; "The Late Late Show with Craig Ferguson", 2007; "The Closer", 2007; "Great Performances", 2009; "Drop Dead Diva", 2012; "The Good Wife", 2013; "Deception", 2013. **Honors/Awds:** Obie Award, 1992; Helen Hayes Award, 1999; Regulus Award, 2002; Emmy Award, 2005; Camie Award, Character & Morality Entertainment Awards, 2005; OFTA Television Award, Online Film & Tv Asn, 2005; Sun Deis Film Festival at Brandeis University Entertainer of the Year Award, 2006; Screen Actors Guild Award, 2006; PRISM Award, 2006; Obie Award, 2006; Image Award, Nat Asn Advan Colored People, 2006, 2010 & 2011; Gracie Allen Award, 2006; Golden Globe Award, 2006; Black Reel Award, 2006; Hon Doctor, Wayne State Univ, 2009. **Special Achievements:** Nominations for many awards including Tony Award Nomination, Drama Desk Award, Vision Award etc. **Business Addr:** Actress, NBC-TV, 30 Rockefeller Plz, New York, NY 10112, **Business Phone:** (212)664-4444.

### MERRITT, ELEANOR L. (LORI MERRITT)

Community activist, educator, artist. **Personal:** Born Aug 17, 1933, New York, NY; daughter of Wilbert and Lynette Lipsett; married WH Chris Darlington; children: Lori Ellen & Lisa Ann. **Educ:** Brooklyn Col, BA, 1955, MA, 1958; Hofstra Univ, attended 1972. **Career:** Educator (retired), artist; NYC Sch Syst, art teacher, 1955-58; Westbury Sch Dist, art teacher, 1959-70; chmn, art dept dist wide, 1970-82. **Orgs:** Charter mem, Womens Mus Art; bd mem, vpres, Womens Caucus Art, 1989-99; bd mem, Sarasota Visual Arts Ctr, 1992-98; Fla Artists Group, 1996-; vpres, Sarasota County Arts Coun, 1996-; chmn, Arts Pub Places, 1996-; pres, Venice Arts Ctr, 1999-2000; bd mem, Ringling Mus Art; charter mem, Nat Mus Women; practicing artist, Women Contemp Artist. **Home Addr:** 7632 Charleston St, Sarasota, FL 34201, **Home Phone:** (941)/358-718. **Business Addr:** Practicing Artist, Women Contemporary Artists, 8013 Waterview Blvd, Lakewood Ranch, FL 34202.

### MERRITT, JOSEPH, JR.

Executive. **Personal:** Born May 24, 1934, Tunica, MS; children: Joseph III. **Career:** Fillmore Taxi Svc, owner, 1968-. **Orgs:** YMCA, 1950; St John Bapt Ch, 1961; Black Men's Devel Found, 1963; Nat Asn Advan Colored People, 1963; Buffalo C C, 1973; Buffalo Metro Bus Asn, 1974; Better Bus Bur, 1974; Jefferson-Fillmore Revital Asn, 1975; vpres, Dem Party, 1976; apptd Civil Serv Commr Buffalo, 1977; Local Devel Corp. **Honors/Awds:** Black Achievement Award, 1976. **Business Addr:** Owner, Fillmore Taxi Service, 1000 E Ferry St, Buffalo, NY 14211-1410, **Business Phone:** (716)897-2300.

### MERRITT, LASHAWN

Businessperson, track and field athlete. **Personal:** Born Jun 27, 1986, Portsmouth, VA; son of Owen and Brenda. **Educ:** E Carolina Univ, BA, 2008. **Career:** Track and field athlete, 2004-; trucking business and day care center owner. **Honors/Awds:** USATF Junior Championships, gold medals 200m, 400m, 2004; World Junior Championships, gold medals 400m, 4x100m, and 4x400m, 2004; USATF Verizon Youth Athlete of the Year, 2004; World Outdoor Championships, gold medals 4x400m, 2005, 2007, 2008, 2011; World Outdoor Championships, gold medal 400m, 2007; Summer Olympics, gold medals 400m and 4x400m, 2008; USATF Outdoor Championships, gold medal 400m, 2008, 2009, 2012; World Outdoor Championships, gold medal 400m, 2009; World Outdoor Championships, gold medal 400m, 2011; World Outdoor Championships, gold medals 400m and 4x400m, 2013; World Championships, gold medal 4x400m, silver medal 400m, 2015; Summer Olympics, gold medal 4x400m, bronze medal 400m, 2016. **Special Achievements:** World Junior recordholder, 4x100m and 4x400m. **Business Addr:** c/o USA Track & Field, 132 East Washington St Suite 800, Indianapolis, IN 46204, **Business Phone:** (317)261-0500.

### MERRITT, LORI. See MERRITT, ELEANOR L.

### MERRITT, WENDY WARREN

Interior designer. **Personal:** Born Mar 4, 1953, Shelby, NC; daughter of Nevada and Lucy Buggs. **Educ:** N Calif Cent Univ, BS, 1974. **Career:** Montaldo's & Night Gallery, buyer, mgr couture retail, 1974-80; Games Prod, Inc, DC instant lottery sales exec, 1980-84; Condominium Rentals, Ltd, buyer & int design & sales, 1984-87; TBS Inc Turner Properties, interior serv coordr, 1990-; Speakers Forum & Lotus, PSS, chief exec officer, speakers bur & int design, 1980-. **Orgs:** S Phi S Inc; Sisters Interest Never Gone, proj mgr; Atlanta Grad Chap; United Negro Col Fund, spec events fundraiser, 1992-; Apex Mus, spec events coor dr, 1995; prog chmn, BLK Adults Action Sect Nat Coun Negro Women, 1985-88. **Honors/Awds:** Star Volunteer Award, Atlanta Chap, United Negro Col Fund, 1992-2000; Legacy Award, United Negro Col Fund, 2001. **Home Addr:** 827 Briarvista Way NE, Atlanta, GA 30329-3644, **Home Phone:** (404)315-0543.

### MERRITT, WILLIAM T.

Association executive, president (organization). **Educ:** NC Cent Univ; Rutgers Univ, Grad Sch Social Work. **Career:** Nat Black United Fund Inc, Newark, NJ, pres & chief exec officer, 1991-. **Orgs:** Dir, Girls Ctr Essex County; dir, Victory Home; dir, Janet Memorial Home; bd mem, Nat Black Leadership Round table; Model Child Abuse Reporting Law; Governor's Comt on Youth; pres, Nat Asn Black Social Workers, 1982-86; bd mem, Vol Consult Group; bd mem, Nat Ctr Black Philanthropy; pres, NJ Asn Children's Residential Facilities; active bd mem, Southern Rural Develop Initiative; active bd mem, Nat Comt Responsive Philanthropy. **Business Addr:** President, Chief Executive Officer, National Black United Fund Inc, 40 Clinton St 5th Fl, Newark, NJ 07102, **Business Phone:** (973)643-3402.

### MERRIWEATHER, BARBARA CHRISTINE

Educator. **Personal:** Born May 11, 1948, Philadelphia, PA; daughter of Robert C and Elizabeth Livingston; married Frank Washington; children: Frank Jr. **Educ:** Cheyney State Univ, BS, educ, 1969; Arcadia Univ, Beaver Col, MA, humanities, 1989; Cheyney Univ, cert prin, 1998. **Career:** Philadelphia Sch Dist, teacher, coach K-12, coordr, supvr, 1969-2002; Holy Family Univ, adj prof; Cheyney Univ, prof, 2000; Conscious Vigilance Educ Consult LLC, consult, currently. **Orgs:** Mem chair, Black Women's Ed Alliance, 1981-83; bd dir, Minority Asn Stud Support, 1981-; co-chair, pub rel, Salem Baptist Church 100 Anniversary, 1983-84; chair pub rel, 1984-87, pres, Philadelphia Fed Black Bus & Prof Orgn; recruiter, Am Fed Teachers, 1985; task force mem, Youth Serv Coord, Comn, 1986-; pres, Philadelphia Fed Black Bus & Prof Orgn, 1987-90; planning comm AFNA Educ & Res Fund, 1987; exec dir, Frank Wash Scholar Fund, 1990-; charter mem, Phi Beta Omega Chap Alpha Kappa Alpha Sorority, 1998; Second Anti-Basileus, 1998; fel Inst Learning Pittsburg; coordr, Nat Coun Accreditation Teacher Educ. **Home Addr:** 514 Greenhill Lane, Philadelphia, PA 19128, **Home Phone:** (215)508-9013.

### MERRIWEATHER, MICHAEL LAMAR (MIKE MERRIWEATHER)

Football player, football coach, business owner. **Personal:** Born Nov 26, 1960, Albany, NY; son of John (deceased); married Djuna Mitchell; married Sandra. **Educ:** Univ Pac, BA, hist, 1982. **Career:** Football player (retired), football coach, business owner; Pittsburgh Steelers, linebacker, 1982-87; Minn Vikings, linebacker, 1989-92; New York Jets, linebacker, 1993; Green Bay Packers, 1993; St Patrick-St Vincent, asst coach, 1990; Stanford Univ, E-W Shrine Game, defensive coach, 2005; Mike Merriweather, owner, currently; motivational speaker, currently; ins broker; Vacaville Christian High Sch, athletic dir, currently. **Orgs:** Alpha Phi Alpha Fraternity, 1980-; Big Bros Bowling Kids, 1986-87; founder, John Merriweather Athletic Scholar. **Business Addr:** Owner, Mike Merriweather, PO Box 8351, Stockton, CA 95208, **Business Phone:** (888)776-5728.

### MERRIWEATHER, ROBERT EUGENE

Consultant, manager. **Personal:** Born Sep 1, 1948, Cincinnati, OH; son of Andrew J and Ruth Hawkins; married Augustine Pryor; children: Tinia P, Andre & Tarani. **Educ:** Univ Cincinnati, BA, math, 1970. **Career:** Consultant (retired); Procter & Gamble Co, math consult, 1970-78, statist analyst, 1978-81, affirmative action mgr, 1981-83, sr syst analyst, 1983-89, personnel servs mgr, 1989. **Orgs:** Bd mem, Mt Zion Fed Credit Union, 1980-88; trustee, Mt Zion Baptist Church, 1986-; community adv bd, Univ Cincinnati, 1988-; Proj Alpha, chairperson, Alpha Phi Alpha Fraternity, 1989-91; Nat Asn Advan Colored People, Cincinnati Br. **Honors/Awds:** Black Achiever, YMCA, 1983; Black Networking Award, Procter & Gamble, 1986; Diversity Award, Procter & Gamble, 1988; Unsung Hero Award, Procter& Gamble, 1990. **Home Addr:** 9580 Heather Ct, Blue Ash, OH 45242-6059, **Home Phone:** (513)984-0738. **Business Addr:** Personnel Services Manager, Procter & Gamble Co, 1 Procter & Gamble Plz, Cincinnati, OH 45202, **Business Phone:** (513)983-1100.

### MESA, DR. MAYRA L.

Educator, dentist. **Personal:** Born Jul 20, 1949. **Educ:** Univ PR, BS, 1968; Univ PR Dent Sch, DMD, 1972; Boston Univ Sch Grad Dent, MSc, 1974. **Career:** Univ Med & Dent NJ, NJ Dent Sch, asst prof oral path, 1974-77, Dept Gen & Oral Path, assoc prof oral path, prof oral path, biol & diag sci, currently; Commonwealth Dent Soc, secy, 1977-79. **Orgs:** Bd dir, Act Boston Community Develop, 1973; bd dir, Act Boston Community Develop, 1973; Nat Dent Asn, 1975-; supvr, Black Coalition Health Law Fair, 1977-79; Table Clinics Nat Dent Asn, 1977-79. **Honors/Awds:** Outstanding Young Women of America, 1978. **Special Achievements:** Published numerous articles. **Business Addr:** Professor of Oral Pathology, Biology & Diagnostic Sciences, University of Medicine & Dentistry New Jersey, Rm C-829 110 Bergen St, Newark, NJ 07103-2400, **Business Phone:** (973)972-4506.

### MESIAH, RAYMOND N.

Manager, consultant. **Personal:** Born Sep 1, 1932, Buffalo, NY; son of Nicklos and Marie; children: 2. **Educ:** Canisius Col, BS, chem, 1954, MS, chem, 1960. **Career:** FMC Corp, Philadelphia, PA, res chemist, sr environ engr, 1977-90, eastern reg environ mgr, 1991-93, environ mgr, 1993-95, prod mgr, Specialty Chem Group, tech mgr; pvt environ consult, 1995. **Orgs:** Franklin Twp Jaycees, 1963-68; chmn, Franklin Twp Civil Rights Comn, 1967-68; treas, Franklin Twp Pub Libr, 1967-69; treas, Frederick Douglass Liberation Libr, 1969-70; Am Chem Soc; brd educ, Franklen town, 1969-75; Presenting team Worldwide Marriage Encounter, 1977-; Alpha Phi Alpha; cord, Camden diocese, 1985-87; cord, sect 3, 1992-95. **Honors/Awds:** One of Five Outstanding Men of the Year, NJ Jaycees, 1967. **Home Addr:** 12 Briarwood Dr, Voorhees, NJ 08043, **Home Phone:** (856)784-6889.

### MESSIAH-JILES, SONCERIA
Publisher. **Personal:** Born Baytown, TX; married Jodie Lee; children: Jodie & Clyde. **Educ:** Univ Houston, BA, polit sci & econs, 1974; Tex Southern Univ, MBA; Rice Univ, attended. **Career:** Houston Chronicle, radio news reporter, tv talk show host & advert acct exec; KYOK AM Radio, news reporter; KMJQ FM, adv acct exec; KHOU TV, talk show host; KRIV TV, talk show host; Defender Media Group, owner & publ, chief exec officer, 1981-; Grand Slam, vpres & dir, currently; Anderson Bd Visitors, managing dir, currently. **Orgs:** Secy, bd mem & adv bd, United Way Tex Gulf Coast; secy & bd mem, March Dimes Tex Gulf Coast Chap; chairperson, Nat Newspaper Publ Asn; nat alumni chair, Houston Alumni Orgn; bd mem, Greater Houston Partnership; adv bd, JP Morgan Chase-Houston; adv bd, Ctr Houston's Future; adv bd, Nat Asn Advan Colored People-Houston; adv bd, JobPlus; adv bd, Hester House; adv bd, Am Diabetes Asn; adv bd, Am Leadership Forum. **Home Addr:** 4720 Post Oak Timber Dr Unit 23, Houston, TX 77056-2225, **Home Phone:** (713)492-0245. **Business Addr:** Publisher, Chief Executive Officer, Houston Defender Newspaper, 12401 S Post Oak Suite 223, Houston, TX 77045, **Business Phone:** (713)663-6996.

### METCALF, ANDREW LEE, JR.
Executive, government official. **Personal:** Born Feb 21, 1944, Muskegon, MI; married Elizabeth Jane Lamb; children: Andrea & Andrew III. **Educ:** Muskegon Community Col, AA, police sci tech, 1971; Grand Valley State Univ, BS, pub serv, 1972; Thomas M Cooley Law Sch, JD, 1987. **Career:** Muskegon Heights Police Dept, patrolman & juv officer, 1967-71; Mc Croskey, Libner, Van Leuven, Cochcrane, Kortering & Brock Law Firm, legal investr, 1971-78; US Dept Justice, US marshal, 1978-81; Mich Dept Com, Liquor Control CMS, hearings comnr, 1982-83, Finance Sect, dirinternal audit, 1983-84; Mich Dept Licensing & Regulation, mich cemetery comnr, DLEG's, dir, Bur Com Serv, div dir enforcement, 1987-89, Bur Occup Prof Regulation, CIS Off Com Serv, dir, 1989-. **Orgs:** Asst regional dir, Nat Asn Legal Investigators, 1973-78; treas, Iota Phi Lambda Chap Alpha Phi Alpha Fraternity, 1973-; charter mem, Muskegon Heights Lions Club, 1975; W Mich Law Enforcement Officer Asn, 1978; exec bd mem, Nat Asn Advan Colored People, Grand Rapids Mich Chap, 1980; Citizens Responsible Govt, 1986; Freedom Fund Chair, 1987; pres, Grand Rapids Gentry Club, 1987-88. **Honors/Awds:** Academic scholarship (3.75 gpa), Ford Found, NY, 1971. **Home Addr:** PO Box 24002, Lansing, MI 48909, **Home Phone:** (517)675-2302. **Business Addr:** Director, State of Michigan Department of Commerce, 525 W Allegan St, Lansing, MI 48913, **Business Phone:** (888)767-6424.

### METCALF, DAVINCI CARVER
Librarian. **Personal:** Born Jul 1, 1955, Dayton, OH; son of Zubie West Jr and Maggie Lee Blake. **Educ:** Auburn Univ, BS, polit sci, 1977; E Carolina Univ, MS, community health, 1982; Univ NC, MLS, 1985; Fla State Univ, MLS, 1988; Nebr Fla Reg Libr Network, attended 1999; Fla State Univ, cert, 2000; Fla A&M Univ Media Ctr, NSLAD 2001. **Career:** Libr Cong, Wash, intern, 1984; W Va Univ, Main Libr, gen ref librn, col instr, 1985-86; Jacksonville Pub Libr, bus, sci, doc ref librn, 1989-2000; Jacksonville Jaguars Booster Club News, reporter, 1995-; Coleman Libr, Fla A&M Univ, asst univ librn, 2000-. **Orgs:** Am Libr Asn, 1985-; Fla Libr Asn, 1985-; Nat Asn Advan Colored People, 1988-; Black Caucus, Jacksonville Jaycees, 1992-94; Am Libr Asn; Panhandle Lib Access Network. **Honors/Awds:** Nat Catholic Scholarship Negroes, Nat Catholic Scholarship Found, 1973-82; Volunteer Service Award, Tuskegee Veteran's Admin Hosp, 1975-76; Pi Sigma Alpha Polit Sci Honor Soc, Pi Sigma Alpha Soc, 1981-83; McKnight Fellowship Scholar, McKnight Found, 1987-88; Certificate of Recognition, Outstanding Community Serv, Delta Sigma Theta, 1987. **Home Addr:** 1900 Ctr Pointe Blvd Paddock Club Apts Bldg 19 Suite 296, Tallahassee, FL 32308, **Home Phone:** (850)656-9510. **Business Addr:** Assistant University Librarian, FAMU Libraries, 1500 S Martin L King Jr Blvd 525 Orr Dr 214A, Tallahassee, FL 32307, **Business Phone:** (850)412-5163.

### METCALF, ERIC QUINN
Football coach, football player. **Personal:** Born Jan 23, 1968, Seattle, WA; son of Terry; married Lori; children: 3. **Educ:** Univ Tex, libr arts, 1990. **Career:** Football player (retired), football coach; Cleveland Browns, wide receiver, 1989-94, kick returner, 1989-91, punt returner, 1992-94; Atlanta Falcons, punt returner & wide receiver, 1995-96, kick returner, 1996; San Diego Chargers, punt returner, 1997; Ariz Cardinals, punt returner & kick returner, 1998; Carolina Panthers, wide receiver, 1999; Wash Redskins, 2001; Green Bay Packers, wide receiver, 2002; Pan Am Jr Team, coach, 2013; Rainier Beach Vikings, coach; Univ Wash, jump coach; Seatown Express, owner. **Honors/Awds:** AFC Championship Game, 1989; Pro Bowl, 1993, 1994 & 1997; Player of the Year, Wash DC Area Prep. **Special Achievements:** NFL All-Time Punt Return Touchdown Leader (10). **Home Addr:** , Seattle, WA.

### METCALF, DR. MICHAEL RICHARD, JR.
Physician. **Personal:** Born Jan 4, 1956, Detroit, MI; son of Adele C; married Ruth Chantell Holloman; children: Michael Jr, Leah, Jonathan & Christina. **Educ:** Dartmouth Col, BA, 1978; Howard Univ Col Med, MD, 1982. **Career:** DC Gen Hosp, internship, 1982-83, resident, 1983-85, chief resident, 1984; CW Williams Health Ctr, internist, 1985-94, health servs dir, 1991-94; Carolinas Med Ctr, assoc div, active staff, dept internal med, 1987-; Meridian Med Group, chief internal med, 1996-2003; pvt pract, currently. **Orgs:** Charlotte Med Soc, 1986-; Mecklenburg Med Soc, 1991. **Honors/Awds:** Dipl, Am Bd Internal Med, 1985. **Home Addr:** 6622 Harrison Rd, Charlotte, NC 28270, **Home Phone:** (704)321-9400. **Business Addr:** Physician, Metrolina Comprehensive Health Center, 3333 Wilkinson Blvd, Charlotte, NC 28208, **Business Phone:** (704)393-7720.

### METCALF, DR. ZUBIE WEST, JR.
School administrator, association executive. **Personal:** Born Jul 4, 1930, Ft. Deposit, AL; son of Zubie West Sr and Ella Louise Reasor; married Maggie L Blake; children: DaVinci C & Caroletta A. **Educ:** Univ Dayton, BS, 1957; Miami Univ, MAT, 1961; State Univ NY Buffalo, EdD, 1972. **Career:** School administrator (retired); Ball State Univ, dir acad opportunity prog, 1971-73; Tuskegee Inst, asst vpres acad affairs & dean grad prog, 1973-76; E Carolina Univ Sch Med, asst vice chancellor, assoc dean, dir med ctr stud opportunity & minority affairs, 1976-92. **Orgs:** Dir, Nat Sci Found Summer Inst, Fla A&M Univ, 1966-69; coordr, Teacher Educ Prog State Univ, NY, Buffalo, 1969-70; consult, US Dept Health & Human Serv Div Disadvantaged Asst, 1983-84; bd mem, Pitt-Greenville Cof C, 1983-87; chairperson, Southern Region Minority Affairs Sect Asn Am Med, 1984-86; bd Centura Nat Bank, 1986-92; vpres, Nat Asn Med Minority Educrs, 1987-89; bd dir, Am Lung Asn Fla, Big Bend Region, 2001-03. **Honors/Awds:** Hon Soc in Ed Univ of Dayton, OH, 1957; fel Nat Sci Found, Wash DC, 1960-61; fel Ford Found, NY, 1970-71; Distinguished Service Award, Nat Asn Med Minority Educrs, 1992; Merit Award, 16 Institutions Health Sci Consortium, 1993; Outstanding Leadership Award, 1992; Health & Human Serv Bd, Dist 2, State Fla, 1999. **Special Achievements:** Author, Career Planning Guide in the Allied Health Professions, 1997. **Home Addr:** 3518 Colonnade Dr, Tallahassee, FL 32309-3290, **Home Phone:** (850)668-1681.

### METOYER, ROSIA G.
Librarian. **Personal:** Born Mar 2, 1930, Boyce, LA; daughter of Eloise Pannell Washington and Horace Gilbert; married Granvel G; children: Renwick, Keith, Karlette & Toni Rosette. **Educ:** Grambling Col, BS, 1951; Webster Col, MA, bus mgt; Northwestern State Univ, BLS, 1964. **Career:** Acadian Elem Sch, libr; Lincoln Rd Elem Sch Rapides Parish Sch Bd, sch librn; Rapides Parish Libr, selections librn; Sickle Cell Anemia Res Found Inc, founder & exec dir, currently; Alexandria Human Rels Comn, pres. **Orgs:** Pres, La Classroom Teacher Asn, 1977-78; Exec Coun La Asn Educr, 1978-80; United Teaching Prof La Libr Asn; SW Libr Asn; Alexandria Zoning Bd Adjust & Appeals; Asn Classroom Teachers; La Libr Asn; YWCA; Nat Asn Advan Colored People; secy, La Asn Sickle Cell Disease, 1986-; secy, Rapides Parish Dem Exec Comt, 1988-92; chairperson, Nat Polit Cong Black Women, Alexandria Chap, 1990-92; Alapha Kappa Alpha Sorority, Zeta Lambda Omega Chapr, Basileus; dist coordr, La Fedn Dem Women, 1990-91; Alexandria Chap Jack & Jill Am, 1990-92; second vpres, La Fedn Dem Women, 1991-93; gov bd, Huey P Long Med Ctr; La Develop Disabilities Coun. **Home Addr:** 910 Papin St, Alexandria, LA 71302, **Home Phone:** (318)443-2439. **Business Addr:** Executive Director, Founder, Sickle Cell Anemia Research Foundation Inc, 2625 3rd St, Alexandria, LA 71301-6104, **Business Phone:** (318)487-8019.

### METTERS, DR. SAMUEL
Executive, chief executive officer, engineer. **Personal:** Born Jan 1, 1934. **Educ:** Prairie View A&M Univ, BS, archit eng; Univ Calif, Berkeley, BA, archit & urban planning; Univ Southern Calif, MS, systs mgt, MS, pub admin, PhD, pub admin; AUS Command & Gen Staff Col; Harvard Grad Sch Bus Admin, Cambridge, MA. **Career:** Hughes, Bendix & Holmes & Narver Eng, prog mgr & mgt info syst coordr; Metters Industs Inc, founder, chmn & chief exec officer, 1981-; NASA Career Explor Prog, co-founder; NASA Adv Coun; Nat Capital Area Coun Boy Scouts Am, pres & chief exec officer; Granville Acad, bd dir. **Orgs:** Dulles Corridor Metrorail Asn; bd trustee, Fairfax Bus Partnership; Northern Va Prof Serv Coun; Northern Va Urban League; Prairie View A&M Univ Found; Rosslyn Renaissance Urban Design Comt Arlington, Va; Shiloh Econ & Community Develop Corp; Shiloh Bd trustee; United Black Col Fund; US Black Enagr Yr Award Prog; S E Conf Minority Engrs; life mem, Kappa Alpha PSI Fraternity; pres & founder, Prairie View A&M Univ Nat Alumni Found; State Va, Vet Strategic Policy Bd; northeast region bd dir, Boy Scouts Am; co-founder, NASA Career Explor Prog; Armed Forces Commun & Electronics Asn; bd dir, US Black Engrs Publ Inc, 1987; Bd dir, Veteran's Corp Inc. **Business Addr:** President, Chief Executive Officer, Metters Industries Inc, 8200 Greensboro Dr, McLean, VA 22102, **Business Phone:** (703)821-3300.

### MEVORACH, KATYA GIBEL (KATYA GIBEL AZOULAY)
Educator. **Personal:** Born Jun 18, 1952; married Yorame Mevorach. **Educ:** Hebrew Univ Jerusalem, BA, African studies, 1982, MA, African studies, 1988; Duke Univ, cert, women's studies, 1992; Duke Univ, PhD, cult, 1995. **Career:** Duke Univ, Univy Writing Prog, instr, 1994, Inst Asian & African Lang, 1995; Grinnell Col, chmn, Africana Studies Concentration Minority Scholar-In-Residence, 1996-2006, chmn, Am Studies Concentration, 1996-2000, assoc prof, 1996-2010, Dept Anthrop & Am Studies Concentration, 1996-, prof, 2010-. Books: Katya Gibel Azoulay of Black, Jewish and Interracial: It's Not the Color of Your Skin but the Race of Your Kin, Other Myths of Identity. **Orgs:** Am Studies Asn; Am Anthrop Asn; Asn Black Anthropologists; consult & coordr, Safrica, Int Affairs Comt, Civil Rights & Peace Movement Party, Israel; ed bd, Iton Aher, Israel, 1989-91; ed bd, New Outlook, Israel, 1990-91; chair, Africana Studies Concentration, 1996-2000; Grinnell Col Diversity Steering Comm, 2002 & 2005; Presidential Diversity Comm Task Force. **Business Addr:** Associate Professor, Professor, Grinnell College, ARH 121, Grinnell, IA 50112, **Business Phone:** (641)269-4324.

### MEYER, ALTON J.
Automotive executive. **Career:** Meyer Acquisition Corp, pres, dir; Al Meyer Ford Inc, pres, dir, 1987-; Livingston Ford-Mercury Inc, pres. **Orgs:** Vice chmn, dir, Angelina County Chamber Com. **Business Addr:** President, Al Meyer Ford Inc, 800 N Medford Dr, Lufkin, TX 75901-5222, **Business Phone:** (936)632-6611.

### MEYERS, AUDREY WILLIAMS. See WILLIAMS, DR. AUDREY L.

### MEYERS, DR. CAROLYN W.
College president, college administrator, mechanical engineer. **Personal:** Born Newport News, VA; children: 3. **Educ:** Howard Univ, BA, mech engineering; Ga Inst Technol, MA, mech engineering, 1979, PhD, chem engineering, 1984; Harvard Univ, attended. **Career:** Gen Elec, systs analyst; Ga Inst Technol, fac & admin; Atlanta Univ Ctr Corp, fac & admin; Nat Sci Found, fac & admin; NC Agr & Tech State Univ, provost, vice chancellor acad affairs, Col Engineering, dean; Norfolk State Univ, pres, 2006-10; Jackson State Univ (Jackson, MS), pres, 2011-. **Orgs:** Am Soc Mech Engrs, fel; Am Coun Educ, bd mem; dir, Nauticus LLC; trustee, Moses Cone Health System Inc; bd chair, Nat Inst Aerospace Found. **Honors/Awds:** National Society of Black Engineers, Golden Torch Award; Career Achievement Award National Science Foundation, Presidential Young Investigator Award. **Special Achievements:** Published numerous articles and reports along with more than 200 presentations and technical papers on various topics including education, diversity, and research and technical. **Business Addr:** President, Jackson State University, 1400 Lynch St, Jackson, MS 39217, **Business Phone:** (601)979-2121.

### MEYERS, ISHMAEL ALEXANDER
Judge. **Personal:** Born Feb 3, 1939, St. Thomas; son of H Alexander and Elvera L; married Gwendolyn Lorraine Pate; children: Ishmael Jr, Micheline & Michael. **Educ:** Morgan State Univ, BS, 1962; Am Univ, MBA, 1964; George Washington Univ, JD, 1972. **Career:** Judge (retired); Interstate Com Comn, acct & auditor, 1963-64; VI Dept Housing & Comm Renewal, 1964-69; VI Dept Law, asst atty gen, 1973; US Dept Justice, asst US atty, 1973-78, US atty, 1978-82; Territorial Ct VI, from assoc judge to judge, 1982-2002; Super Ct Vi, sr sitting judge, 2004. **Orgs:** Charter mem, Nat Bar Asn, St Thomas Lions Club, 1968-; DC Bar Asn, 1973-; VI Bar Asn, 1973-; Am Bar Asn, 1973-; Bar Supreme Ct US, 1980-; vpres, historian, Theta Epsilon Lambda Chap, Alpha Phi Alpha Frat Inc. **Honors/Awds:** Alpha Kappa Mu Nat Honor Soc, Morgan State Univ, 1960-62; John Hay Whitney Found Fel, 1962-64; US Atty Gen Spec Achievement Award, US Dept Justice, 1976; Spec Achievement Award, Nat Alumni Asn Morgan State Univ, 1984. **Home Addr:** 15-31 Frenchman Bay, PO Box 7632, St Thomas00801. **Business Addr:** Senior Sitting Judge, Superior Court of the Virgin Islands, Alexander A Farrelly Justice Ctr 5400 Veteran's Dr, St. Thomas00802, **Business Phone:** (340)774-6680.

### MEYERS, LISA ANNE-MARIE
Publicist, executive. **Personal:** Born Feb 22, 1973, Atlanta, GA; daughter of Tim and Carolyn. **Educ:** Westminster, attended 1991; Univ Va, BA, communs, 1995; AmeriSpan/Valencia, Span, 2007. **Career:** Ketchum Pub Rels, assoc acct exec, 1995-97; BET Holdings, publicist, 1996-97; Black Entertainment Tv, mgr/publicist, 1997-98; Magic Johnson Enterprises, publicist, dir publicity, 1998-99, exec vpres commun & branding, 2007-09; Who Wants To Be A Millionaire Valleycrest Productions, assoc producer, 1999-2001; Johnson Family Corp, stay-at-home mom, 2008-13; Campbell Hall Episcopal, interim dir advan & dr commun, 2014-15; Love+Light Ventures, Co-Founder, 2014-. **Orgs:** Alpha Kappa Alpha Sorority, 1993-95; sr vpres commun & mkt, Am Cancer Soc, 2001-07; Nat Asn Multiethnicity Commun. **Honors/Awds:** Class Community Service Award, Univ Va Deans List, 1995; PRSA, Silver Anvil, 1996; Distinguished PR Professional, PRAME, 1998. **Business Addr:** Executive Vice President, Magic Johnson Enterprises Inc, 13701 Riverside Dr 8th Fl, Sherman Oaks, CA 91423.

### MEYERS, DR. ROSE M.
Association executive, research scientist, educator. **Personal:** Born Aug 18, 1945, Mt. Pleasant, SC. **Educ:** Bennett Col, Greensboro, BS, chem, 1966; NY Univ, MS, bio chem, 1972, PhD, biochem, 1976. **Career:** Howard High Sch, Georgetown, SC, math teacher, 1966-67; Yeshiva Univ NY, res teacher chem, 1967-68; NY Univ Med Sch, res teacher I cancer res, 1968-72, res teacher II cancer res, 1972-76; Univ Louisville Med Sch, resfel, 1976-78; Philip Morris Res Ctr, res scientist, 1978-81; Corning Life Sci, res scientist, 1981-85; Choate Rosemary Hall, chem teacher, 1988-90; Berlin Pub Schs, sci dept head, 1990-96; Univ Mass Amherst, Sci Enrichment Prog, dir, 1992-98; Bridgeport Pub Schs, sci supvr, 1996-99; New Brit Bd Educ, asst prin, 1999-2006; ROZIK Consult LLC, sci consult & educ mgt, 2009-. **Orgs:** Sister Cities Int, 1978-; Nat Asn Black Chem; Bennett Col; Bus & Prof Women's Club; Mus African Art. **Special Achievements:** Published article "Studies on Nucleoside Deaminase" J Biol Chem 24850901973; published "sialyltransferase in lympocytes" federation proceedings 351441 1976; Louis villecitz awd Mayor Harvey Sloane Louisville 1976-77; published "Immuno supprsn & Tobacco Smoke" federation proceedings 3612301977. **Home Addr:** 87 Columbia St 6K, New York, NY 10002.

### MFUME, KWEISI (FRIZZELL GERARD GRAY)
Association executive, government official. **Personal:** Born Oct 24, 1948, Baltimore, MD; son of Rufus Tate and Mary Elizabeth Willis; children: Ronald T Gray, Donald, Kevin, Keith & Michael. **Educ:** Morgan State Univ, BA, 1976; Johns Hopkins Univ, MLA, 1984. **Career:** Baltimore's, city coun, 1979-86; US House Rep, State Md, congressman, 1987-96; Cong Black Caucus, leader, 1992-94; Nat Asn Advan Colored People, pres & chief exec officer, 1996-2004; US Senate, cand, 2006; Nat Med Asn, exec dir, 2010-; Md's 7th Cong Dist, dem congressman; Community Col Baltimore County, head & ed; Radio Sta, prog dir. **Orgs:** Head, Cong Black Caucus, 1986; Baltimore City Coun, 1978; chmn, Morgan State Univ, 2013, bd Regents; Caucus Women's Issues; Cong Arts Caucus; Fed Govt Serv Task Force; bd trustees, Baltimore Mus Art; Sr Adv Comt, Harvard Univ John F Kennedy Sch Gov; Meyerhoff Nat Adv Bd, Univ Md; bd trustee, Enterprise Found; Big Bros & Big Sisters; hon chair, Ctr Stage, Theater New Generation Advocacy; Prince Hall Freemasons; Omega Psi Phi. **Honors/Awds:** Drum Major for Justice Award, SCLC, 1997; Inter generational Award, Sister 2 Sister Mag, 2000; Image Award, Nat Asn Advan Colored People, 2005; Honorary Doctorate, Brandeis Univ; Honorary Doctorate, Meharry Med Col. **Special Achievements:** Author: No Free Ride: From the Mean Streets to the Mainstream, 1996; Co-author: Harry Truman & Civil Rights: Moral Courage & Political

Risk, 2002. **Business Addr:** Executive Director, National Medical Association, 8403 Colesville Rd Suite 820, Silver Spring, MD 20910, **Business Phone:** (202)347-1895.

## MICHAEL, B.

Fashion designer. **Personal:** children: 2. **Educ:** Univ Conn, grad. **Career:** Oscar de la Renta, apprentice; Ab Apparel Group, Jazz Lincoln Ctr, fashion partner; DM Fashion Group Inc, fashion designer & partnership, 1999-; New York Fashion Inst Technol, guest lectr, currently. **Orgs:** Coun Fashion Designers Am, 1998; New Yorkers C; Styleworks; adv bd mem, Fashion Target Breast Cancer campaign; Autism Speaks; Dream Yard Proj; Cicely Tyson Sch Performing & Fine Arts. **Home Addr:** 453 W 143rd St Condo Suite 4, New York, NY 10031, **Home Phone:** (212)221-9400. **Business Addr:** Fashion Designer, DM Fashion Group Inc, 202 W 40th St 4th Fl, New York, NY 10018, **Business Phone:** (212)703-9494.

## MICHAEL, DR. CHARLENE BELTON

Consultant, manager, executive director. **Personal:** Born Heath Springs, SC; daughter of Charles Belton and Cherryane Powe; married Joseph Sr; children: Joseph M Jr & Charles B. **Educ:** Knoxville Col, BA, 1939; Teachers Col, Columbia Univ, MA, 1955; Univ Tenn, MS, 1958; Univ Tenn, PhD, 1976. **Career:** Knoxville City Schs, teacher, 1950-75; Knoxville City Sch & Univ Tenn, speech pathologist, 1958-75; Knoxville & Knox Co Proj Headstart, dep dir, 1965-66; Knoxville Col-Upward Bound, assoc dir, 1968-69; Educ & Training Adaption Serv Inc, ed dir, 1971-75; MAARDAC & Univ Tenn, assoc dir, 1974-; Univ Assoc, Johns Hopkins Univ, consult, 1979, 82-83; Mid Atlantic & Appalachian Race Desegregation Asst Ctr, actg dir, 1987. **Orgs:** Pres, Phi Delta Kappa Univ Tenn, 1979-80; bd trustee, Knoxville Col, 1984, pres, Nat Alumni Assoc Inc; pres, Knoxville Educ Assoc; Delta Sigma Theta Sor Alumnae Chapt; bd dir, Knoxville Womens Ctr, Matrix, C Ctr; Metrop Planning Commn. **Honors/Awds:** Certificate Record Knoxville Col SE Reg & Nat Alumni Assoc, 1977; Citizen of the Year Award, For Serv & Contrib Humanity, 1984; Selwyn Award, Knoxville Women's Ctr, 1985; YWCA Award Tribute Outstanding Women, 1986. **Special Achievements:** Publication: Why I Teach, The Effect of Parental Involment on the Learning Process, "Advantages of Lang-Experience Approach in the Teaching of Reading, Coping with Stresses in the Classroom, Student Team Learning, An Educational Equity Tool, Workshop Participants Perception Rankings Second General School Desegregation Issues; lic speech pathologist State Tenn. **Home Addr:** 1505 Pickett Ave, Knoxville, TN 37921-4862, **Home Phone:** (865)522-2204.

## MICHAUX, ERIC COATES

Lawyer, association executive, executive. **Personal:** Born Sep 23, 1941, Durham, NC; married Della Dafford. **Educ:** Univ NC, 1959; NC Cent Univ, Sch Law, 1965; Boston Univ, BS, bus admin, 1963; Duke Univ, Sch Law, 1966; Univ Denver, 1968. **Career:** Durham Col Durham, NC, teacher bus law, 1965; W G Pearson, atty, 1967; Pearson Malone Johnson & De Jormon, atty, 1971-73; NC Cent Univ, vis prof, 1971-73; Univ NC, Chapel Hill, Dept Health Educ, adj asst prof, 1972-73; 14th Solicitoral Dist, asst dist atty, 1973-75; Michaux & Michaux Pa, pres, partner, currently. **Orgs:** Vpres, Glenview Mem Pk Wash Terr Apts Inc; Am Bar Asn; Nat Asn Advan Colored People; Omega Psi Phi Fraternity; Phi Alpha Delta Legal Fraternity; Nat Soc Perishing Rifles; Durham Comt Affairs Black People; United Citizens Against Drug Abuse; steward trustee treas, St Joseph's African Methodist Episcopal Church; NC Bar Asn; bd dir, Durham Chap, Am Nat Red Cross; mem bd trustee, NC Cent Univ; gen coun, Nat Asn Real Estate Brokers; chmn, Nc Bd Law Examiners; bd dir, Nc Cent Univ Found; bd trustee, Louisburg Col, Triangle Transit Authority. **Honors/Awds:** Recipient of Nat Defence Service Medal; Vietnam Service Medal; Vietnam Campaign Medal. **Home Addr:** 5301 Fayetteville Rd, Durham, NC 27713, **Home Phone:** (919)544-7233. **Business Addr:** Attorney, Partner, Michaux & Michaux PA, 2515 Apex Hwy, Durham, NC 27713, **Business Phone:** (919)596-8181.

## MICHAUX, HENRY M., JR. (MICKEY MICHAUX)

State government official, real estate executive. **Personal:** Born Sep 4, 1930, Durham, NC; son of Henry M and Isadore C; married June; children: Jocelyn & Cicero. **Educ:** NC Cent Univ, BS, biology, 1952; Rutgers Univ, attended 1955; NC Cent Univ Law Sch, JD, 1952, attended 1964. **Career:** Union Ins & Realty Co, vpres, 1955-; Durham Co, chief asst dist atty, 1969-72; Michaux & Michaux, sr partner, 1970-; real estate broker; NC Gen Assembly & House Rep, 1972-76; Mid Judicial Dist NC, US atty, 1977-81; NC State House Reps, rep, 1973-77, Dist 31, 1983-. **Orgs:** Trustee, NC Cent Univ; exec comt mem, 14th Judicial Dist Bar; N State Bar; NC Bar Asn; George H White Bar Asn; Black Lawyers NC; Am Bar Asn; Judicature Soc; Criminal Code Comn State NC, 1973-77; Steering Comt Caucus Black Dem; NC Comn Human Skills & Resources; NC Com Law Focused Educ; NC Cent Alumni Asn; bd dir, NC Cent Univ Found Inc; Durham Bus & Prof Chain; Durham C C; Durham Merchants Asn; Nat Asn Advan Colored People; NC Med Soc; N Carolina Gen Assembly, 2014. **Honors/Awds:** Hon Doctorate, Durham Col & NC Cent Univ; Realist of the Year; Pub Affairs & Polit Achievement Award, 1973-74, 1976; Ann Award, Triad Sickle Cell Anemia Found, 1973; Citizen Com Sickle Cell Syndrome Award, 1976; Polit Achievement Award, Nat Asn Advan Colored People, 1975; Service Award, Phi Alpha Delta Law Fraternity; Achievement Award, Calif Real Estate Brokers, 1974; Service Award, 14th Judicial Dist Bar, 1972; Honored, Triangle "J" Coun Govt, 1973; Honored, NC Bar Asn, 1975; Public Service Award, NC Chiropractic Asn, 1977; Honored, NC Black Dem Leadership Caucus, 1977; North Carolina Central University was renamed the H. M. Michaux, Jr. School of Education in his honor in 2007; inducted, Black College Alumni Hall of Fame, 2011. **Special Achievements:** Longest-serving African American member of the North Carolina General Assembly; Durham's First African-American State Representative. **Home Addr:** PO Box 2152, Durham, NC 27702-2152, **Home Phone:** (919)596-8181. **Business Addr:** Representative, North Carolina State House of Representatives, Rm 1227 16 W Jones St, Raleigh, NC 27601-1096, **Business Phone:** (919)715-2528.

## MICHAUX, MICKEY. See MICHAUX, HENRY M, JR.

## MICHEL, HARRIET RICHARDSON

Executive director, mayor, association executive. **Personal:** Born Jul 5, 1942, Pittsburgh, PA; daughter of John Robert and Vida Harmony; married Yves; children: Christoper & Gregory. **Educ:** Juniata Col, Huntingdon, PA, BA, sociol & criminol, 1965. **Career:** Nat Scholar Serv & Fund Negro Students, prog officer, 1965-70; Off Mayor New York, asst, 1971-72; New York Found, exec dir, 1972-77; US Dept Labor, dir youth employ, 1977-79; John Jay Col, Criminal Justice, 1980-81; US Dept Housing & Urban Develop, consult, 1982-83; New York Urban League, pres, 1983-88; Harvard Univ, Kennedy Sch Gov, Inst Polit, resident fel, 1988; Nat Minority Supplier Develop Coun, pres & chief exec officer, 1988-; Women Against Crime Found, founder. **Orgs:** Citizens Comt, 1984; bd mem, African Am Inst, 1985; bd mem, NY Nat Bank; bd mem, TransAfrica Forum, 1988; bd mem, Juniata Col, 1989; founding mem, Asn Black Found Execs; vice chair, New York Charter Rev Comn, 1986-1991. **Honors/Awds:** First Nonprofit Leadership Award, New Sch, 1988; First Women on the Move Award, B Nai B rith, 1990; Ethnic New Yorker Award, 1985; Black Entrepreneurial Award, Wall St J, 1994; Building Bridges Award, Rainbow/PUSH Coalition, 2002; Legacy Award, Minority Bus Develop Agency, Ronald H. Brown Leadership Award, Dept Com, 2003; Champion Award, Black Enterprise Entrepreneurs Conf, 2003; Enterprising Woman of the Year Award, 2004; Executive Leadership Councils Achievement Award; Pioneer Award, Minority Business News USA. **Special Achievements:** first African American woman to head a major foundation. **Home Addr:** 616 W 147th St, New York, NY 10031. **Business Addr:** Founding Member, Association of Black Foundation Executives, 333 7th Ave 14th Fl, New York, NY 10001, **Business Phone:** (646)230-0306.

## MICHEL, SAMUEL PRAKAZREL (PRAKAZREL SAMUEL MICHEL)

Rap musician. **Personal:** Born Oct 19, 1972, South Orange, NJ. **Educ:** Rutgers Col; Yale Univ. **Career:** Solo albums: Ghetto Supastar, 1998; Win Lose Or Draw, 2005; Experience Magic, 2008; Solo singles: "Ghetto Supastar (That Is What You Are)", 1998; "Blue Angels", 1998; "Another One Bites the Dust" "What'cha Wanna Do", 1999; "Avenues", 1999; "Miss California", 2001; "Haven't Found", 2005; "Turn You On", 2007; Collaborations: "Pushin", 2007; "Le Blues de Toi", 2008; "Si je t'emmene/My Man", 2008; "Watch Out", 2010; "Untried", 2012. Films : Mystery Men, 1999; Turn It Up, actor & co-producer, 2000; Higher Ed, actor & exec producer, 2001; Go For Broke, actor & producer, 2002; Nora's Hair Salon, 2004; Careful What You Wish For (film)|-Careful What You Wish For, 2004; Feel The Noise, 2007; First Night, 2006; Skid Row, 2007; Go Go Tales, 2007; The Mutant Chronicles, actor & producer, 2008; TV series: "Fastlane", 2004. **Honors/Awds:** Best Rap Album, The Score, 1997. **Special Achievements:** Launching a line of urban sportswear called Refugee Camp; author of Ghetto Superstar; Winner, Grammy Award Winner.

## MICKELBURY, PENNY

Novelist, playwright. **Personal:** Born May 31, 1948, Atlanta, GA; daughter of Arthur Jennings and Mexico. **Educ:** Univ Ga, BA, 1971. **Career:** Novelist, print & tv journalist, writer, currently; Atlanta Voice, newspaper, 1968-69; Banner-Herald, reporter, 1970-71; Wash Post, reporter, 1971-72; Nat Caucus& Ctr on Black Aged, pub rels dir, 1972-75; WHUR-FM, news reporter, 1975-78; WJLA-TV, ABC, news reporter, 1978-84; asst news dir, 1984-87; City Kids Reperatory Co, teacher, 1988-89; Alchemy: Theatre Change, co-founder & managing dir, 1990-93; writing teacher, 1994-. Plays: Time Out, 1989; Waiting for Gabriel, 1991; Warm Robes of Remembrance, 1993; Hush Now, 2000. Author: Keeping Secrets, 1994; Nights Songs, 1995; Love Notes, 2002; Darkness Descending, 2005; One Must Wait, Simon & Schuster, 1998; A Carol Ann Gibson Mystery, 1999; Where To Choose, Simon & Schuster, 1999; The Step Between, Simon & Schuster, 2000; Paradise Interrupted, 2001; Two Graves Dug, 2005; A Murder Too Close, 2008; : The Mimi Patterson/Gianna Maglione Mysteries; Carole Ann Gibson Mysteries; Phil Rodriquez Mysteries; Belle City, 2014; That Part of My Face, 2016. print & tv journalist. **Honors/Awds:** Lambda Literary Award, Nightsongs; Golden Pen Award, 2001; Audre Lorde Estate Grant, 2003. **Home Addr:** , CA. **Business Addr:** Writer, c/o Lisa A Jones, 1200 G St NW Suite 370, Washington, DC 20005.

## MICKELL, DARREN

Football player. **Personal:** Born Aug 3, 1970, Miami, FL; children: Darren C, Delesha, Dereon & Anyae. **Educ:** Univ Fla. **Career:** Football player (retired); Kans City Chiefs, 1992, defensive end, 1993, right defensive end, 1994-95; New Orleans Saints, 1999, left defensive end, 1996-98; San Diego Chargers, defensive end, 2000; Oakland Raiders, defensive end, 2001. **Honors/Awds:** Rookie of the Year, 1992.

## MICKENS, MAXINE N.

Teacher, manager, executive. **Personal:** Born Dec 3, 1948, Clarksdale, MS; married Caesar Jr; children: Leonora. **Educ:** Univ Mich, AB, 1974; Comm Film Workshop Chicago, cert, 1976; ICBIF Small Bus mgmt Detroit, cert, 1978; Univ Phoenix, MBA, global mgt, 2001. **Career:** Detroit Bd Educ, voc & adult educ teacher, 1974-80; WJLB Radio Detroit, merchandising & prom dir, 1976-77; Max Belle & Assoc, co-owner & vpres, 1977-; Simpson's Wholesale Detroit, adv mgr, 1977; Detroit High Sch Fine & Performing Arts, govt & econ teacher. **Orgs:** Communs chairperson, Triedstone Baptist Church, 1972-73; communs chairperson, Jeffersn Chalmers Com Asn, 1974-75; WXYZ-TC Women's Adv Com Detroit Mich, 1974-76; Black Communicators Asn Detroit, 1979-; Nat Asn Media Women Detroit. **Home Addr:** 1425 W Grand Blvd, Detroit, MI 48208, **Home Phone:** (313)894-0204. **Business Addr:** Co Owner, Vice President, Max Belle & Associates, 1308 Broadway Suite 206, Detroit, MI 48226.

## MICKENS, DR. RONALD ELBERT

Research scientist, educator, mathematician. **Personal:** Born Feb 7, 1943, Petersburg, VA; son of Joseph and Daisy; married Maria Kelker; children: Leah & James. **Educ:** Fisk Univ, BA, math & physics, 1964; Vanderbilt Univ, PhD, theoret physics, 1968. **Career:** Woodrow Wilson fel; Dansworth fel; Nat Sci Found, postdoctoral fel, 1968-70; MIT Ctr Theoret Physics, post doctoral res, 1968-70; Fisk Univ, Dept Physics, asst prof, 1970-82; MIT Dept Physics, vis prof physics, 1973-74; Morehouse Col & Atlanta Univ, vis prof, physics, 1979-80; Vanderbilt Univ Dept Physics, vis scholar, 1980-81; Ford Found, postdoctoral fel, 1980-81; Joint Inst Lab astrophys Boulder, Colo, res fel, 1981-82; Clark Atlanta Univ, prof, 1982, chairperson, 1984-86, distinguished Fuller E Callaway prof physics, 1985-. **Orgs:** Consult, Nat Acad Sci; Los Alamos Sci Lab; Col Old Westburg; Nat Sci Found, Dept Energy; Nat Insts Health; Am Asn Physics Teachers; fel Am Phys Soc; AAAS; Sigma Xi; Beta Kappa Chi; Am Math Asn; London Math Soc; Soc Math Biologists; Soc Indust & Appl Math; Am Math Soc; Nat Soc Black Physicists; Soc Math Biol; Sigma Chi; Phi Beta Kappa; Nsf. **Honors/Awds:** Fisk University Chapter Elect, Phi Beta Kappa, 1964; Research Grants, Dept Energy, NASA, Nat Sci Found, GTE Found & Army Res Off; UNCF Distinguished Faculty Fellowship, 1984-85; Distinguished Lecturer for Sigma Xi, Res Soc, 2000-02. **Home Addr:** 2853 Chaucer Dr SW, Atlanta, GA 30311. **Business Addr:** Distinguished Fuller E Callaway Professor, Clark Atlanta University, Rm 102 McPheeters-Dennis Hall, Atlanta, GA 30314, **Business Phone:** (404)880-6923.

## MICKENS, WILLIAM RAY

Football player, executive. **Personal:** Born Jan 4, 1973, Frankfurt; married Nicole; children: Kamray, Ray Jr & Preston. **Educ:** Tex A&M Univ, BA, bus & acct, 1996. **Career:** Football player (retired), exec; New York Jets, corner back & right corner back & defensive back & left corner back, 1996-2005; Mickens Inc, pres, 2002-; Cleveland Browns, corner back, 2005-06; New Eng Patriots, corner back, 2006-07; M2 Concepts LLC, owner, 2010-. **Honors/Awds:** All-American, 1994 & 1995; All-Southwest, 1994 & 1995; Madden Bowl, 1999. **Business Addr:** President, Chief Executive Officer, Mickens Inc, 508 Villa Crossing, Southlake, TX 76092-9563, **Business Phone:** (214)562-2424.

## MICKLE, HON. ANDREA DENISE

President (organization). **Personal:** Born Jul 26, 1952, Kershaw, SC; daughter of John T and Mable Harris. **Educ:** Hampton Univ, BA, 1974; Adelphi Univ, cert, 1974; Howard Univ, MPA, 1985. **Career:** Howard Univ, financial aid officer; Minority Access Inc, pres & chief exec officer, currently. **Orgs:** Nat Asn Equal Opportunity Higher Educ, 1975-; Am Paralegal Asn, 1975-77; charter mem, Lawyer's Assts Inc, 1975; pres, Howard Univ Pi Alpha Alpha Hon Soc, 1984-85; DE-DC-MD Asn Stud Financial Aid Adminr; Am Soc Personnel Admin; Am Soc Pub Admin; Nat Asn Advan Colored People. **Home Addr:** 7201 Lena Way, Bowie, MD 20715. **Business Addr:** President, Chief Executive Officer, Minority Access Inc, 5214 Baltimore Ave Suite 200, Hyattsville, MD 20781, **Business Phone:** (301)779-5883.

## MICKS, DEITRA HANDY (DEITRA RAVERNE HANDY MICKS)

Lawyer. **Personal:** Born May 26, 1945, Bronx, NY; daughter of John and Mabel. **Educ:** Howard Univ, BA, 1967; Howard Univ, JD, 1971. **Career:** Lawyer (retired); Jacksonville, legal aid, 1971-73; pvt prac, atty; Jackson & Micks; Univ N Fla, teacher; Duval Co, Fla, city coun woman, 1987-91. **Orgs:** Bd dir, Legal Aid; life mem, Nat Advan Asn Colored People; Jackson villechap; stud articles Ed Howard Law J, 1970-71; Gamma Sigma Sigma Sorority; Bethel Bapt Inst Church. **Home Addr:** 6650 Kinlock Dr W, Jacksonville, FL 32219-3805, **Home Phone:** (904)764-9949.

## MIDDLEBROOKS, FELICIA

Television journalist, government official. **Personal:** Born May 29, 1957, Gary, IN; daughter of Raymond Jr and Geraldine Rembert. **Educ:** Purdue Univ, Hammond, IN, BA, mass commun, 1982, MBA, 2014. **Career:** Radio news broadcaster, anchor; WBAA, WJOB, WGVE, WLTH, 1976-77; WGVE Radio Handicapped, anchor, 1978-81; Jones& Laughlin Steel, laborer, 1978-82; WJOB Radio, reporter & anchor, 1979-82; WLTH Radio, reporter & anchor, 1982-84; Total Living Network's Chicago News makers, panelist; WBBM Radio 780, morning dr anchor & reporter, 1984-; Saltshaker Productions LLC, dir, producer, chief exec officer, currently; Purdue Univ Calumet. **Orgs:** Honorary chairperson, March Dimes Walk America, 1985-88; Chicago Asn Black Journalists, 1987-; bd mem, Cris Radio (Chicago land Reading Info ServHandicapped), 1987-; Sigma Delta Chi Prof Journalists, 1987-; Women Commun, 1989; bd dir, Chicagoland Radio Info Serv Blind; Ill News Broadcasters Asn; bd dir, New Regal Theater Found; Women Film; trustee; C's Home; trustee, Aid Soc; bd dir, Women Need Growing Stronger, Hands Hope, C's Home & Aid Soc; founder & pres, Hollywood Comes Chicago; consult, US Dept Homeland Security; Best Reporter Award; Edward R. Murrow Award, News. **Special Achievements:** First woman and African American, co-anchor mornings. **Home Addr:** 200 E Chestnut St Suite 1021, Chicago, IL 60611. **Business Addr:** Morning Drive Anchor, WBBM Newsradio 78, 630 N McClurg Ct, Chicago, IL 60611-4536, **Business Phone:** (312)202-3299.

## MIDDLETON, BENJAMIN AUGUSTUS. See VEREEN, BEN.

## MIDDLETON, DR. ERNEST J.

Educator. **Personal:** Born Dec 25, 1937, Franklin, LA; married Rosa Metz; children: Lance & Owen. **Educ:** Southern Univ, BA, 1962; Univ Colo, EdS, 1973, PhD, 1974. **Career:** Univ KY, asso prof; St Mary Par Pub Sch, prof, 1962-63, 1965-70; St Mary Human Rel Coun, vpres, 1966; Southern Univ, EPDA fel, 1971; Univ Colo, EPDA fel, 1972; Race & Sex Desegregation, Training Inst, dir, 1974-; State Univ New York, dean; Clark Univ, Sch Educ, dean, 2001-07, prof curric, currently. **Orgs:** Pres, St Mary Educ Asn, 1967-70; chmn, St Mary Comm Action Agency, 1969; La Educ Asn; Southern Univ, 1958-62; Kappa Alpha Psi Fraternity; Nat Asn Advan Colored People; Phi Delta Kappa Fraternity; Nat Alliance Black Sch Educ; Renaissance Group, Kremen Sch Educ & Human Develop; mem rep, Ga Asn Independent Col Teacher Educ, 2006; pres, Nat Coun Accreditation Teacher Educ. **Home Addr:** 3280 Bowie Dr, Lexington, KY 40502. **Business Addr:** Professor of Curriculum, Clark Atlanta University, 208 Clement Hall 223 James P Brawley Dr SW, Atlanta, GA 30314, **Business Phone:** (404)880-8000.

**MIDDLETON, FRANK, JR.**
Football player, football coach. **Personal:** Born Oct 25, 1974, Beaumont, TX; married Kristina; children: 3. **Educ:** Fort Scott Community Col, attended 1995; Ariz State Univ, criminal justice, 1995-. **Career:** Football player (retired), football coach; Tampa Bay Buccaneers, guard, 1997, right guard, 1998-2000; Oakland Raiders, right guard, 2001, left guard, right guard, 2002, left guard, 2003-04; Kountze High Sch, offensive coordr, 2012; Monsignor Kelly High Sch, asst football coach, 2007-, offensive coordr, 2013. **Honors/Awds:** Rookie of the Year, 1997. **Business Addr:** Offensive Coordinator, Kelly High School, 4136 S California Ave, Chicago, IL 60632, **Business Phone:** (773)535-4900.

**MIDDLETON, HERBERT, JR. See BLACQUE, TAUREAN.**

**MIDDLETON, JOHN ALLEN**
Educator. **Personal:** Born Nov 19, 1945, Hawthorne, FL; son of Theodore Agustus and Marguerite Ivey; children: Alicia, John II & LaTonya. **Educ:** Fla A&M Univ, BS, 1970; Univ Fla, MEd, 1974, EdD, 1984. **Career:** PCR Inc, chemist, 1970-72; Alachua County Sch Bd, teacher, 1972-78; Univ Fla, dir, 1978-79; Alachua County Sch Bd, prin, 1979-85; Volusia County Sch Bd, asst supt, 1985-90; Columbus City Sch, interim supt, supt, 1991-92; Ohio State Univ, assoc prof, dir sch rel, Col Educ, Off Dean, grad admin & res asst, teaching leadership consortium coordr, 1992-94; Univ Cent Fla, assoc dean, 1994-97, assoc prof, 1997-. **Orgs:** Am Asn Sch Admr; SPP Fraternity; life mem, APA Fraternity. **Special Achievements:** First African-American to hold the post superintendent in Columbus City School. **Home Addr:** 10960 Dearden Cir, Orlando, FL 32817. **Business Addr:** Associate Professor, University of Central Florida, 4000 Cent Fla Blvd Res Pavilion Suite 215, Orlando, FL 32816-8005, **Business Phone:** (407)823-2835.

**MIDDLETON, MICHAEL A.**
College teacher, college administrator, lawyer. **Personal:** married Julie N; children: 3. **Educ:** Univ Mo, BA, 1968, Univ Mo Sch Law, JD, 1971. **Career:** U.S. Dept Justice, Civil Rights Div, sr trial atty, 1971-75; Lawyers' Comt Civil Rights Under Law, sr atty, 1975-77; U.S. Dept Educ, dep asst secy, 1980-83; EEOC, assoc gen coun, 1983-85, dist dir, 1985; Univ Mo Sch Law, prof law, 1985-2015, interim vice provost minority affairs & fac develop, 1997-98, dep chancellor, 1998-2015, prof emer & interim pres, 2015-. **Orgs:** Am Bar Found, 1992-; Am Law Inst, 1999-. **Honors/Awds:** Distinguished Alumni Award, MU Black Alumni Organization, 1995; Harold Holliday Award, Missouri Legislative Black Caucus, 1998; Spurgeon Smithson Award, Missouri Bar Foundation, 1999; Citation of Merit, University of Missouri School of Law, 2001; Chief Justice's Award, Missouri Supreme Court, 2003; President's Award, Missouri Bar, 2003; MLK Dream Conference Trailblazer of the Year Award, 2006; MLK Jr. Distinguished Drum Major for Justice Award, 2016; Legislative Black Caucus Public Service Award, 2016; Trailblazer Award, Columbia NAACP, 2016. **Special Achievements:** Contributor, McGeorge Law Review, Southern Illinois Law Journal, Capital University Law, Saint Louis University Law Journal, and Oklahoma Law Review. **Business Addr:** c/o University of Missouri, Rm 101 Jesse, Columbia, MO 65211, **Business Phone:** (573)882-3394.

**MIDDLETON, PHILLIP B.**
Educator. **Personal:** Born Aug 10, 1947, Rocks, MD; married Theresa; children: Zoe Ross. **Educ:** Morris Brown Col, BA, 1969; Tenn State Univ, MA, 1974; Southern Ill Univ, PhD, 1979. **Career:** Al-Fetch Univ, Tripoli, Libya, asst prof Eng, 1978-80; Univ Niamey, Niger, W Afr, asst prof, 1980-83; Univ Khartoum, Sudan, Fulbright prof, 1984-87; Coun Int Exchange Scholars, Fulbright-Hays Fel, Sudan, 1984-87, Romania, 1995-97; Morris Brown Col, asst prof, 1987-89; Ferris State Univ, Col Arts & Sci, prof lang & lit, 1989-; Univ Cluj, Romania, Fulbright prof, 1995-97. **Orgs:** Nat Fulbright Asn; Sudan Studies Asn. **Home Addr:** 401 S Stewart Ave, Big Rapids, MI 49307-2025, **Home Phone:** (231)796-4518. **Business Addr:** Professor of Languages & Literature, Ferris State University, 820 Campus Dr, Big Rapids, MI 49307-2225, **Business Phone:** (231)591-5878.

**MIDDLETON, REV. DR. RICHARD TEMPLE, III**
Educator. **Personal:** Born Jan 17, 1942, Jackson, MS; son of Richard T II and Johnnie Beadle; married Brenda Marie Wolfe; children: Jeanna E & Richard T IV. **Educ:** Lincoln Univ, BS, 1963, MEd, 1965; Univ Southern Miss, EdD, 1972. **Career:** Tougaloo Col, instr educ, 1967-70; Woodrow-Wilson King, Doctoral Study, fel, 1969; Jackson State Univ, from asst prof to assoc prof, 1970-76, dir stud teaching, 1976-97; St Mark's Episcopal Church, priest, rector, 1995-. **Orgs:** Security Life Ins Co, 1985; pres, Beta Gamma Boule Sigma Pi Phi Fraternity, 1985-87; bd mem, Opera S Co, 1986-90; Cath Charities, 1986-90; Nat Exec Coun, Episcopal Church, 1987-88; vpres, Miss Relig Leadership Conf, 1988-89; vice chmn, Jackson, MS Planning Bd, 1990-94; bd examiners, Nat Coun Accreditation Teacher Educ; 100 Black Men Jackson; Union Black Episcopalians; Pi Lambda Theta. **Home Addr:** 944 Royal Oak Dr, Jackson, MS 39209-6737, **Home Phone:** (601)922-8047. **Business Addr:** Priest, St Mark's Episcopal Church, 903 Metro Pkwy, Jackson, MS 39203, **Business Phone:** (601)353-0246.

**MIDDLETON, ROSE NIXON**
Consultant, school administrator. **Personal:** Born Jun 3, 1932, Gum Tree, PA; daughter of Havard Downing Nixon and Margaret Black Nixon; married C T; children: Karen Ann Nixon & Tanya Hope Nixon. **Educ:** Univ Pa, Philadelphia, PA, AB, 1954; Bryn Mawr Col, Bryn Mawr, PA, MS, 1958. **Career:** Child Care Serv Chester County, W Chester, Pa, child welfare worker, 1960-62; Child Study Ctr Philadelphia, Philadelphia, Pa, psychiat social worker, 1962-66; Ment Health Ctr, W Chester, Pa, sr psychiat social worker, 1966-68; Chester County Intermediate Unit, Coatesville, Pa, admin asst dir spec educ pre-sch prog, 1968-89; Expertise & Assistance, Coatesville, Pa, pres, 1990-. **Orgs:** Commun Task Force mem, Downingtown Area Sch Dist, 1991-; treas & bd dir, United Cerebral Palsy Asn, 1989-; Chester County Head Start Inc, 1980-86; pres & bd dir, Chester County Head Start Inc 1985-86; bd dir, pres, Handi-Crafters Inc, 1971-73; secy & bd dir, Brandywine Red Cross, 1983-84; founder, Chester County Local Cs Team, 1979; handicapped serv comt chmn, Rotary Int, 1988-. **Home Addr:** Sky Vue Box 242A Rd Suite 1, Coatesville, PA 19320. **Business Addr:** President, Expertise & Assistance, 1263 Lone Eagle Rd, Coatesville, PA 19320, **Business Phone:** (215)383-4387.

**MIDDLETON, VERTELLE D. M.**
Educator, school administrator, counselor. **Personal:** Born Aug 10, 1942, Charleston, SC; daughter of Nazarene Baldwin Graham and Michael Graham; married James Jr; children: Jamela V, Gloria Holmes & Kylon Taylor. **Educ:** Johnson C Smith Univ, BS, psych & soc, 1964; NY Univ, adult educ cert, 1975; Bank Col, adult educ cert, 1975; Temple Univ, admin training cert, 1981; Webster Univ, Charleston, SC, MA, 1989. **Career:** Immaculate Conception High Sch, teacher, 1964-67; Charleston County OIC Inc, exec dir, 1968-82; Trident Tech, Col Fair Break Ctr, ctr dir, 1982-84, Col Manpower Skill Ctr, dir, 1984-86, Berkeley Campus, Moncks Corner SC, JTPA dir, 1987-90, minority affairs dir, 1991-97, counr, 1997-, prof, currently; Beaufort Tech Col, Walterboro, SC, dir Career Success, 1987. **Orgs:** Secy, Greater Bd Chapel Am Church, 1980-90; vice chmn, Steward Bd Greater Bd Chapel, 1980-90; Alpha Kappa Alpha Sorority, 1982-86; secy, Burke High Sch Adv Bd, 1983-; Pres, SC Prof Asn Access & Equity; SC Chap SETA, 1984-; SC Tech Educ Asn, 1984-; coordr, S Atlantic Region-Cluster, 1988-90; chmn, Burke High Sch Improv Coun, 1988-90; adv coun, Trident Tech Col Employee Assistance Prog, 1989; s atlantic regional dir, Alpha Kappa Alpha Sorority Inc, 1990-94; Am Jr Col Women Asn, 1990-; Charleston Speech & Hearing Adv Bd, 1993; nat mem, Comn S Atlantic region; pres, Sc Prof Asn Access & Equity; pres, Charleston Intercolgiate Consortium; bd mem, CIty Charleston, SC, Site & Design; bd dir, City Charleston Smoking Ban Community; Nat Asn Advan Colored People; Young Women Chrisitian Asn Greater Charleston. **Home Addr:** 1861 Taborwood Cir, Charleston, SC 29407, **Home Phone:** (843)556-3771. **Business Addr:** Professor, Counselor, Trident Technical College, 7000 Rivers Ave, North Charleston, SC 29406-4607, **Business Phone:** (843)574-6111.

**MIKE, DAEDRA ANITA VON (DAEDRA A VON MIKE MCGHEE)**
Government official, chief executive officer, manager. **Personal:** Born Aug 29, 1944, Urbana, OH; daughter of Clarence and Charlotta; married Curtis Thomas McGhee II; children: Curtis Thomas McGhee III. **Educ:** Wayne State Univ, BA, 1999; Brussels Belg, community psychol. **Career:** Detroit Med Ctr, admin personnel generalist & employ reveiwer, 1968-77; City Nat Bank, personnel reviewer, 1977-79; Crocker Nat Bank, corp admin personnel rep, 1979-81; First Pac Bank, corp exec asst chief exec officer, 1981-83; Carter Hawley Hale Stores Inc, exec admin asst to exec vpres & div pres, 1983-84; Nat Conf Community & Justice, vol, 1990-92, prog dir, 1992-99, assoc dir, 1989-2002; Sphinx Org, bd dir; Mich Gov's Off, dep dir govt & bus affairs, dir govt & bus affairs, 2003-10; US Dept of Justice, dir detroit field off, mediator, conciliation specialist, detroit field off mgr, 2011-; Fed Govt, mediator & conciliator, 2011-. **Orgs:** Wayne County Juv Ct Citizen's Adv Comt; Women Wayne Alumni Asn; life mem, Nat Asn Advan Colored People; youth leadership fel, WK Kellogg Found; develop comn, Goodwill Indust Detroit Found; serv learning adv bd, Detroit Pub Sch; fel Eureka Commun; fel Ctr Creative Leadership; Alliance a Safer Greater Detroit; Ctr Peace & Conflict Studies Alumni Asn, Wayne State Univ; advisor, Interdepartmental Task Force Serv At-Risk Youth Transitioning Adulthood. **Home Addr:** 2320 N LA Salle Gdns, Bloomfield Township, MI 48206-2579, **Home Phone:** (419)882-0933. **Business Addr:** Director Government & Business Affairs, State MI Gov Exec Off, 3022 W Grand Blvd Cadillac Pl Suite 14 150, Detroit, MI 48202, **Business Phone:** (313)456-0010.

**MIKELL, DR. CHARLES DONALD**
Health services administrator, president (organization). **Personal:** Born Jan 12, 1934, McKeesport, PA; son of Eugene and Sadie Bell Qualls; married Jacqueline Henry; children: Michelene Wofford & Charles D II. **Educ:** Lincoln Univ, AB, 1960; Univ Pittsburgh, PA, MPH, 1952, MPA, 1968. **Career:** Allegheny Co Health Dept, pub health san, 1960-64; Neighborhood develop worker, 1964-65; Hill Dist Community Action Prog, asst coord, 1965-66; Hill Emergency Lift Prog, supr, 1966-67; Hill Rehab Ctr, asst dir, 1967-68, acad & prof consult, 1968-69, dir, 1968-70; Alcoholic Couns & Recovery Prog CAP Inc, dir, 1970-74, exec dir, 1974-78; Univ Pittsburgh, field supr grad studs, 1971-; McKeesport Area Health Syst, asst adminr, 1978-89; Family Health Coun Inc, clin serv supvr, 1989-91; Women, Infants Develop Proj, prog dir, 1991-98; Primary Care Health Serv, consult, 1998-. **Orgs:** Pa HIV State Planning Com, Harrisburg, 1994-; Pa HIV Planning Coun, Harrisburg, 1997-; pres, City Coun, McKeesport; chair, McKeesport Redevelop Authority; chair, McKeesport Housing Authority; bd mem, Allegheny County Ment Health; Ment Retardation, Drug & Alcohol Bd, Pittsburgh; vpres bd, McKeesport YMCA; pres, McKeesport Nat Asn Advan Colored People; HIV Planning Coun. **Honors/Awds:** Bronze Key Award, Nat Coun Alcoholism Inc, 1975; Community Service Awards, Pittsburgh; Outstanding Achievements in the field of Alcoholism, Col Consults Inc; McKeesport High School Hall of Fame, 2007. **Special Achievements:** Author: "The Delivery of HTH Services to Low Income People, " dissertation; co-author: "Peer Networkers: One Key to HIV Prevention for Women in High Risk Communities," HIV Infection in Women Conference, 1995; "Teen Peers: HIV Prevention Through Teenage Peer Networkers," PA Pub Health Asn, 1996;"Peers in Public Housing: Case Studies in the Develop & Maintenance of Peer Networks for HIV & Unintended Pregnancy Prevention," Am Pub Health Asn meeting & exhibition, 1996. **Home Addr:** 1726 Eagle Ridge Dr, Monroeville, PA 15146-1769, **Home Phone:** (412)678-5053.

**MIKELL, JOHNNY**
Executive director. **Career:** Novartis Pharmaceut Corp, dir qual, vpres qual assurance, currently. **Business Addr:** Vice President of Quality Assurance, Novartis Pharmaceuticals Corp, 1 Health Plz, East Hanover, NJ 07936, **Business Phone:** (862)778-8300.

**MILBOURNE, LAWRENCE WILLIAM (LARRY MILBOURNE)**
Baseball player, baseball executive. **Personal:** Born Feb 14, 1951, Port Norris, NJ. **Educ:** Cumberland County Jr Col. **Career:** Baseball player (retired), baseball executive; Houston Astros, infielder, 1974-76; Seattle Mariners, infielder, 1977-80, 1984; New York Yankees, infielder, 1981-82, 1983; Minn Twins, infielder, 1982; Cleveland Indians, infielder, 1982; Philadelphia Phillies, infielder, 1983; New York Mets, instr. **Home Addr:** 7341 Tilden Way, Sacramento, CA 95822. **Business Addr:** Instructor, New York Mets, Shea Stadium, Flushing, NY 11368-1699.

**MILBURN, GLYN CURT**
Executive, football player. **Personal:** Born Feb 19, 1971, Los Angeles, CA; married Toya; children: Lauryn & Aaron. **Educ:** Univ Okla, attended 1988; Univ Stanford, BA, public policy, 1993. **Career:** Football player (retired), manager; Denver Broncos, punt returner, 1993-95, running back, 1994, kick returner, 1994-95; Detroit Lions, kick returner & punt returner, 1996-97; Chicago Bears, kick returner & punt returner, 1998, wide receiver, 1999, 2000-01; San Diego Chargers, 2001; Austin Wranglers, gen mgr & owner, 2003-07; Tex Af2 Holdings, vpres & owner, 2007-09; Hughes Develop Inc, chief operating officer, 2007-12; GW Real Estate Partners LLC, managing partner, 2010-12; City Los Angeles, spec asst, 2013; Jimmy Blackman & Assocs, partner, 2016-. **Orgs:** Bd dirs, Ronald McDonald House Charities, 2009-10. **Honors/Awds:** Pop Warner Trophy, 1992; Pro Bowl, 1995, 1999; All-Pro, 1995, 1999. **Special Achievements:** TV Series: "The NFL on NBC", 1993-94; "NFL Monday Night Football", 1993-96; "TNT Sunday Night Football", 1994; "NFL on FOX", 1995-2000; "ESPN's Sunday Night Football". 1995-2000; "The NFL on CBS", 1999. **Business Addr:** Partner, Jimmy Blackman & Associates, 11845 W Olympic Blvd Suite 645, Los Angeles, CA 90064, **Business Phone:** (213)220-6291.

**MILES, ALBERT BENJAMIN, JR.**
Executive. **Personal:** Born Jan 7, 1956, Brooklyn, NY; son of Albert Sr and Marguerite; married Susan J Burns; children: A Benjamin III & Claire. **Educ:** Wesleyan Univ, BA, 1978, MLS, 1990; Northwestern Univ, Kellogg exec prog, cert, 1987; Rensselaer Polytech Inst, MBA, 1992. **Career:** Southern New Eng Telecommunications, mgr, cre data ctr, 1988-94, dir cre data network, 1994-95; Citizens Utilities, dir pinnacle proj, 1995-96, dir cre strategic archit, 1997-, dir info technol; Starcast Inc, chief technol officer. **Orgs:** Bd mem, Dixwell Community Ctr, 1988-93, guide, 1988-90, share, 1988-90; bd mem, New Haven Boys Club, 1989-90; Meriden CT SNET Bus Partnership, founding mem, 1990-93; bd mem, Community Health Ctr, 1990-95; bd mem, Lenua S Williams, MD, 1991-; commun dir, Spec Olympics World Games, 1995. **Honors/Awds:** Service Award, Dixwell Community Ctr, 1993. **Home Addr:** 32 Greenleaf Farms Rd, Newtown, CT 06470-1866. **Business Addr:** Director, Citizens Utilities, High Ridge Pk Bldg 3, Stamford, CT 06905, **Business Phone:** (203)329-8800.

**MILES, DR. CARLOTTA G.**
Physician, administrator, educator. **Personal:** Born Sep 19, 1937, St. Augustine, FL; married Theodore A; children: Wendell Gordon, Cecily Allison & Lydia Carlotta. **Educ:** Wheaton Col, AB, 1959; Howard Univ Med Sch, MD, 1964. **Career:** Howard Univ Col Med, asst prof psychiat; Wash Sch Psychiat, fac; pvt pract physician, 1968-; Area B C's Prog, co-dir, 1969-71; Nat Cathedral Sch, consult psychiatrist. **Orgs:** Am Psychiat Asn; Am Acad Child Psychiat; affil mem, Am Psycho anal Inst; trustee, Wheaton Col; Black Stud Fund Wash; adv bd mem, Nat Urban Technol Ctr. **Honors/Awds:** Clerkship Prize, Howard Univ Med Sch, 1964. **Home Addr:** 2115 Yorktown Rd NW, Washington, DC 20012. **Business Addr:** Psychiatrist, 3000 Conn Ave NW Suite 206, Washington, DC 20008, **Business Phone:** (202)462-0770.

**MILES, DR. EDWARD LANCELOT**
Educator. **Personal:** Born Dec 21, 1939, Trinidad; son of Louise Dufont and Cecil B; married Wanda Elaine Merrick; children: Anthony Roger & Leila Yvonne. **Educ:** Howard Univ, BA, hist, 1962; Univ Denver Grad Sch Int Studies, PhD, int rels, 1965. **Career:** Univ Denver, instr, 1965-66, from asst prof to assoc prof, 1966-74; Univ Denver Grad Sch Int Studies, assoc prof, 1970-74; Univ Wash, prof, Marine Studies & Pub Affairs, 1974-, dir, Sch Marine Affairs, 1982-93, chmn Univ Comt Interdisciplinary Res & Grad Educ, 1991-92, Va & Prentice Bloedel prof, 1994-, chmn, Pres Task force Environ Educ, 1995-96; Nat Oceanic & Atmospheric Admin, Impacts Climate Variability, prin investr, 1995-; Joint Inst Study Atmosphere & Oceans, sr fel, 1995; Climate Impacts Group, Univ Wash, CSES co-dir; Univ Wash, Sch Fisheries, adj prof. **Orgs:** Bd ed, int org, 1969-77; Ocean Policy Comn; chmn, Nat Res Coun, 1970-79; exec bd, Univ Hawaii-Law Sea Inst, 1971-; assoc ed, Ocean Develop & Int Law J, 1973-; joint appointee, Micronesian Maritime Auth Fed States Micr, 1977-83; chief negotiator, Micronesian Maritime Authority, 1983-92; chmn, adv comt int prog, Nat Sci Found, 1990-93; US Nat Acad Sci, 2003; AAAS, 2005; fel am academt arts & sci; sr fel Joint Inst Study Atmosphere & Oceans. **Special Achievements:** One of the first four African Americans inducted into the National Academy of Sciences, 2003. **Home Addr:** 3136 Broadway E, Seattle, WA 98102. **Business Addr:** Virginia & Prentice Bloedel Professor, University of Washington, 3707 Brooklyn Ave NE, Seattle, WA 98105-6715, **Business Phone:** (206)543-7004.

**MILES, DR. ELIJAH WALTER**
Educator. **Personal:** Born May 4, 1934, Hearne, TX; married Frances Winfield; children: Tony W & Christopher W. **Educ:** Prairie View A&M Univ, BA, 1955; Ind Univ, AM, 1960, PhD, polit sci, 1962. **Career:** Prairie View A&M Univ, assoc prof, 1962-65, prof; Univ NC, vis fac scholar, 1965-66; Univ, vis summer prof, 1966; San Diego State Univ, prof polit sci, 1967, chmn, 1988; So Univ, 1967; Univ Tex, 1971. **Orgs:** San Diego Blue Ribbon Comn Charter Rev, 1968; assoc ed, W Pol Sci Quart; exec, Comn Calif State Assembly Fel Prog; State-Wide Anti-Discrimination Comn; Unit Prof CA; chmn, Comn Status Blacks Am Polit Sci Asn; past mem, exec coun, Western Polit Sci Asn; adv panel Calif Bd Educ, 1969-70; bd dirs, Law Am Soc Found; chmn bd, San Diego Urban League, 1983-; pres, deleg-at-large, Nat Bd, ACL, 1989-; San Diego & Imp Counties, 1990; trustee, Ctr Res & Develop Law Related Educ, 1991; Am Civil Liberties Union; chmn, San Diego Chap Am Civil Liberties Union. **Honors/Awds:** Distinguished

Teaching Award, San Diego State Univ, 1968. **Special Achievements:** Co-author of Vital Issues of the Constitution, 1975, author of various scholarly articles. **Home Addr:** 11474 Caminito Garcia, San Diego, CA 92131-2133, **Home Phone:** (858)695-9791.

### MILES, FRANK J. W., JR.
Executive. **Personal:** Born Dec 18, 1944, Orange, NJ; son of George L Sr (deceased) and Ula C (deceased); married Brenda B. **Educ:** Hampton Univ, BA; Columbia Univ, MBA. **Career:** State NJ, maj acct relationships; Citibank NA, vpres. **Orgs:** Vol Urban Consult Minority Bus; Mayor's Appointee Co Econ Develop Corp; Omega Psi Phi Fraternity; Urban Bankers Asn; NJ Real Estate Asn; Nat Black MBA Asn. **Home Addr:** 985 Glenwood Ave, Plainfield, NJ 07060, **Home Phone:** (908)753-4586.

### MILES, GEORGE L., JR.
Executive, chief executive officer, president (organization). **Personal:** Born Nov 13, 1941, Orange, NJ; son of George L Sr and Eula; married Janet; children: Tammy Brown. **Educ:** Seton Hall Univ, BA, acct, 1963; Fairleigh Dickinson Univ, MBA, 1970; LaRoche Univ, DHL, 2008. **Career:** Touche & Ross, mgr, 1969-78; KDKA-TV, Pittsburgh, bus mgr, controller, 1978-80; WPCQ-TV, Charlotte, NC, sta mgr, controller, 1980-81; Westinghouse TV Group, vpres, controller, 1981; WBZ-TV, Boston, sta mgr, 1981-84; Nat Pub Radio, chief admin officer, 1983; WNET-TV, NY, exec vpres/chief operating officer, 1984-94; WQED Multimedia, Pittsburgh, pres & chief exec officer, 1994-. **Orgs:** Bd mem, Sigma Pi Phi Frat; bd mem, Allegheny Conf Community Develop; bd mem, Black Broadcasters Asn; bd mem, Mentoring Partnership Southwestern Pa; bd mem, Pub Broadcasting Serv; bd mem, Urban League Pittsburgh; bd dir, Harley-Davidson; bd dir, Westwood One; bd dir, WESCO Int Inc; bd dir, Equitable Resources Inc; bd dir, Citizens Financial Group Inc; bd dir, Appl Technol Systs Inc; African Am Chamber Com Western Pa; Carnegie Mus Pittsburgh; WESCO Int Inc; chair, Urban League Pittsburgh; co-chair, Mentoring Partnership Southwestern Pa; bd dir, Am Int Group; bd dir, Chester Engrs Inc; bd dir, HFF Inc; bd dir, EQT Corp & Am Int Group;bd dir, Chester Engrs Inc, Univ Pittsburgh; Dir, Ararat Community Activ Ctr's Exec Bd. **Home Addr:** 611 Arthur St, Pittsburgh, PA 15219-4363. **Business Addr:** President, Chief Executive Officer, WQED Multimedia, 4802 5th Ave, Pittsburgh, PA 15213, **Business Phone:** (412)622-1370.

### MILES, DR. NORMAN KENNETH, SR.
Clergy, educator. **Personal:** Born Dec 5, 1946, Toledo, OH; son of Mervin and Sadie; married Doris Calandra Goree; children: Erica Lynette, Norman Jr, Candace Renee, Kira Danette & Neal Mervyn. **Educ:** Oakwood Col, BA, theol, 1968; Andrews Univ, Mdiv, 1973; Univ Mich, MA, 1974, PhD, 1978. **Career:** Econ Opportunity Planning Asn, work counr, 1968-69; S Cent Conf & Seventh Day Adventists, pastor, 1969-72; Lake Regional Conf Seventh Day Adventists, pres, 1974-77; Seventh Day Adventists, prof 1977-; Univ Mich, adj prof, relig, 1977-; Andrews Univ, Christian Ministry Dept, chmn, 1988-; Lake Region Conf, pres; Hyde Pk Seventh-Day Adventist Church, pastor & minister, 1989-; Andrews Univ, Urban Ministry, assoc prof, adj prof, prof, currently; Hattiesburg, MS, pastor; Detroit, MI, pastor; Chicago, IL, pastor; Trinity Temple Seventh-day Adventist Church, sr pastor, 2008. **Orgs:** Mp Ministerial Alliance, Hattiesburg, MS, 1969-72; bd dir, Southern Miss Chap, Am Red Cross; Nat Black Pastors Conf, 1980-; dir, Inst Human Rels Seventh Day Adventist Church, 1983; bd trustee, Andrews Univ. **Home Addr:** 8518 Hillcrest Dr, Berrien Springs, MI 49104. **Business Addr:** Senior Pastor, Trinity Temple Seventh-day Adventist Church, 14 S Bridge St, Poughkeepsie, NY 12601, **Business Phone:** (845)471-5815.

### MILES, RACHEL JEAN
Teacher. **Personal:** Born Sep 3, 1945, Memphis, TN; married Willie T; children: Lisa & Jason E. **Educ:** Lemoyne-Owen Col, BS, 1967; Memphis State Univ, EdM, guid & coun, 1970, post grad, 1971. **Career:** Memphis City Sch Syst, elem teacher, 1967-68; Memphis State Univ, counsr, 1969-70; Moorestown Twp Col Prep, guid counr, 1971; Fairview Jr High Sch, counr eng teacher, 1971-72; Shelby State Community Col, prof counr, 1972-75, coord coun adv, 1975; Tenn Indust Develop Coun, econ develop rep, currently. **Orgs:** JUGS Charitable Orgn, 1967-; Cherokee Community Civic Club, 1969-; Kappa Delta Pi Hon Soc, Memphis State Univ, 1970; Phi Delta Kappa, Memphis State Univ, 1971; secy, Westlawn-Galveston Block Club, 1972-; pres & bd dir, Human Employ Resources Inc, 1979-80; bd dir, Miss Black Memphis Pageant, 1979-80; workshop presenter, Am Personnel & Guid Asn, 1980; Chamber Staff. **Honors/Awds:** Col Aide De Camp, Gov Ray Blanton, 1977-78; Honorary Staff Member, Tenn House Rep, 1977-78. **Home Addr:** 3776 Deer Xing, Memphis, TN 38115-5244. **Business Addr:** Economic Development Representative, Tennessee Industrial Development Council, 100 Peabody Pl Suite 1400, Memphis, TN 38187, **Business Phone:** (901)543-3561.

### MILES, RUBY A. BRANCH
Librarian. **Personal:** Born Sep 6, 1941, Houston, TX; daughter of Richard Andrew and Ernestine Phelps; married Emerson Edward. **Educ:** Prairie View A&M Univ, BS, educ, 1963; Atlanta Univ, MLS, 1969. **Career:** Atlanta Fulton Pub Libr, child, young adult librn, 1969-71, br head, 1971-77; Houston Independent Sch Dist, Houston Tech Inst, librn, 1977-79, Gregory-Lincoln Educ Ctr, librn, 1979-85, Bellaire High Sch, librn, 1986-90, Michael DeBakey High Sch Health Prof, librn, 1990-; Houston Community Col Syst, part-time campus librn, 1985-; Houston Acad Med, Tex Med Ctr Libr, part-time librn, 1997-. **Orgs:** Am Asn Univ Women, 1971-; Am Libr Asn, 1984-, Young Adult Serv Asn Community, 1984-88 & 1992-96; Tex Libr Asn, 1991-92. **Honors/Awds:** Librarian of the Year, Houston Ind Sch Dist, 1993-94. **Home Addr:** 4514 Connies Ct Lane, Missouri City, TX 77459-2936, **Home Phone:** (281)499-7318. **Business Addr:** Librarian, Michael E DeBakey High School for Health Professions, 3100 Shenandoah St, Houston, TX 77021, **Business Phone:** (713)746-5215.

### MILES, STEEN
Television journalist, politician. **Personal:** Born Aug 20, 1946, South Bend, IN; daughter of Austin A Davis (deceased) and Rose E Wheeler Davis (deceased); children: Kellie J King Middleton & Heather Lynne King. **Educ:** Ball State Univ, bus educ, eng; Ind Univ, commun; Univ SC Daniel Sch Mgt; Univ Cincinnati; Ga State Univ. **Career:** Journalist, media relations consultant (retired), senator; WNDU-TV, reporter, anchor & talk show hostess, 1971-73; WMAQ, NBC Radio, reporter & anchor, 1973-78; WVON & WGCI, news dir, 1978-80; United Press Int, broadcast ed, 1980-84; WXIA-TV, assignment ed, 1984-86, managing ed, 1986-89, reporter & anchor, 1989-99; Metrop Rapid Transit Authority, chief media rels officer & spokesperson, 2001; Regional Leadership Inst, 2005; Software Mgt Consults Inc, pres & chief exec officer, currently; Ga State Senate, Dist 43, sen, 2005-, lt gov, 2006. **Orgs:** Ga Asn Broadcasters, 1982-84; bd mem, Salvation Army Adv Bd, 1988-92; pres, Jack & Jill Am Stone Mountain, 1988-92; bd mem, Dekalb Co Chamber Com, 1988-91; bd mem, Nat Acad TV Arts & Sci, 1988-91; Atlanta Asn Black Journalists, 1989-; Nat Asn Media Women, 1989-; bd mem, Victims Witness Assistance Adv Bd, 1992-; charter mem, Decatur-Dekalb Coalition 100 Black Women; Dekalb Acad Leaders; bd mem, Proj Impact, 1994-; mentor, SCLC, 1995-; trustee & assoc minister, Green forest Community Baptist Church; Banking and Financial Insts; Pub Safety and Homeland Security; Spec Judiciary; State Insts and Property. **Home Addr:** 2145 Tudor Castle Way, Decatur, GA 30035, **Home Phone:** (770)981-6769. **Business Addr:** Senator, Georgia State Senate, 325 B Coverdell Office, Atlanta, GA 30334, **Business Phone:** (404)463-2598.

### MILES-LAGRANGE, VICKI
Judge. **Personal:** Born Jan 1, 1953. **Educ:** Univ Ghana, cert, 1973; Vassar Col, attended 1974; Howard Univ Sch Law, JD, 1977. **Career:** TV news reporter; Speaker US House Reps, Carl Albert, cong aide; Fed Ct, Dist Judge Woodrow Seals, Southern Dist Tex, law clerk, 1977-79; US Dept Justice, criminal trial atty, 1979-80; African Develop Group, spec asst, 1980-81; Univ Md, Col Pk, lect, Womens Study Prog, 1981; US Dept Justice, Off Enforcement Opers, trial atty, 1982-83; Okla Co, asst dist atty, 1983-86; Okla Senate Judiciary Comt, chmn; Legis Black Caucus; pvt pratice, 1986-93; Okla Co, state sen, 1987-93; US Dist Fed, Western Dist Okla, judge, 1993-94, chief judge, 2008-. **Orgs:** Bd trustee, Vassar Col; bd dir, Kirkpatrick Mus & Planetarium; Alpha Kappa Alpha Sorority; Links Inc; Urban League; Nat Asn Advan Colored People; Okla Heritage Asn; Am Bar Asn; Okla Bar Asn; Okla Black Lawyers Asn; US Judicial Conf's Int Judicial Rels Comm, 1999-05; chair, Comn Africa Working Group, 1999-05; regional dir, Midwestern Region; Judicial Coun US Ct Appeals 10th Circuit & Am Bar Asn; Africa Law Initiative Adv Coun; Int Judicial Rels Comt Judicial Conf Us. **Honors/Awds:** Honarary Doctor of Laws, Oklahoma City Univ; Oklahoma Women's Hall of Fame, 2003. **Special Achievements:** First African American woman to be sworn in as US atty Western Dist Oklahoma; First African American female elected to the Oklahoma Senate. **Home Addr:** 6600 NE 63rd St, PO Box 796, Oklahoma City, OK 73101. **Business Addr:** Chief Judge, United States District Court, 200 NW 4th St Rm 1210, Oklahoma City, OK 73102, **Business Phone:** (405)609-5000.

### MILLEDGE, DR. LUETTA COLVIN UPSHUR
School administrator, educator. **Personal:** Born Savannah, GA; children: Marshall L Upshur. **Educ:** Ft Valley State Col, BA, Eng, 1948; Atlanta Univ, MA, Eng, 1949; Univ Ga, PhD, Eng, 1971. **Career:** Ford Found fel, 1969-71; Savannah State Col, asst instr, assoc prof, prof, chr div human, 1973-80, head, Dept Eng, 1972-80, head, Dept Humanities/Fine Arts, 1980-84, head, Dept Humanities, 1984-91, (retired), prof emer, 1991-. **Orgs:** Bd mem, Ga Endowment Humanities, 1980-83; Elder Butler Presbytery Church; pres, Community Future Savannah State Col; Phi Kappa Phi, Phi Beta Kappa; Ga Humanities Coun. **Honors/Awds:** George Washington Honor Medal; Freedoms Found Valley Forge Speech Vital Speech, 1973; Phi Kappa Phi, Phi Beta Kappa, Univ Ga; Co-Teacher of the Year, Sch Humanities, 1989. **Home Addr:** 918 Carver St, Savannah, GA 31415-5241. **Business Addr:** Professor Emeritus, Savannah State University, PO Box 20029, Savannah, GA 31404, **Business Phone:** (912)356-2368.

### MILLEGAN, MICHAEL H. (MIKE MILLEGAN)
President (organization). **Educ:** Angelo State Univ, San Angelo, TX, BS, bus mgt, 1980; MBA, 1982. **Career:** GTE Wireless, area pres & dir hr logistics, 1996-2000; Verizon Corp, sr vpres & pres logistics supply chain, 2000-04, sr vpres enterprise wholesale opers, 2004-05, sr vpres & area pres, verizon commun, 2005-07, pres global wholesale, 2007-13; Angelo State Univ, San Angelo, Tex, Wells Fargo Distinguished Lectr, 2003; Finsphere Corp, adv bd, 2015-. **Orgs:** Bd mem, Jr Achievement Bd, 1997-2000; bd mem, World Trade Ctr Seattle, 1998-2004; Springs Found; exec-in-residence, Univ N Tex; Schwab Found; Northeast Ind Corp Coun; bd appointee, Wash Comn Community Serv, 1998-2002; bus adv coun mem, Angelo State Univ, San Angelo, Tex; bd mem, Seattle Woodland Pk Zoo; Global 50, 2008-12; bd vice chmn, United Way Northern Nj, 2011-13. **Business Addr:** Advisory Board, Finsphere Corporation, 11747 NE 1st St Suite 330, Bellevue, WA 98005, **Business Phone:** (425)679-5700.

### MILLENDER, HON. B. PENNIE
Judge. **Personal:** Born Chicora, MS; son of Robert and Louise. **Educ:** Olivet Col, Southern Univ, BA, psychol, 1974; Wayne State Univ, MA, voc rehab coun, 1976; Detroit Col Law, JD, 1987. **Career:** Nat Labor Rels Bd, Region 7, atty, 1987-90; 36th Dist Ct, magistrate, 1997-2004; 36th Dist Ct, judge, 2004-. **Orgs:** Vpres, Wolverine Stud Bar Asn; chairperson, Mich Employ Security Bd, 1990-97; chairperson, Civil Liberties Comt, State Bar Mich, 1995-97; Asn Black Judges Mich; Robert L Millender Sr Mem Fund; life mem, Nat Asn Advan Colored People; bd mem, Black United Fund Mich Inc. **Business Addr:** Judge, Michigan's 36th District Court, Rm 2028 421 Madison Ave, Detroit, MI 48226, **Business Phone:** (313)965-8729.

### MILLENDER, DHARATHULA H. See Obituaries Section.

### MILLENDER, MALLORY KIMERLING, SR.
Publisher, editor, vice president (organization). **Personal:** Born Jul 11, 1942, Birmingham, AL; married Jacqueline Stripling; children: Mallory Jr & Marlon. **Educ:** Paine Col, BA, eng lit, 1964; Univ Toulouse, 1966; Clark Atlanta Univ, DA, 1996; Kans State Teachers Col, MS, foreign lang, 1969; Columbia Univ, MSJ, 1977; Emporia State Univ. **Career:** TW Josey High Sch, teacher, 1964-67; Augusta News Rev, ed & publ, 1974-; Paine Col, coord foreign lang, 1977, dean admis, 1971, assoc prof, 2005, asst prof, currently; prof fr & jour, currently, assoc prof mass commun, currently; Lucy Craft Laney Mus, exec dir, currently. **Orgs:** Pres, New Grow Inc, 1971-; vpres & bd trustee, Antioch Baptist Church, 1971-; bd trustee, Paine Col, 1980-82; bd dir, Paine Col Nat Alumni Asn; co-chmn, Blue Ribbon Comt. **Home Addr:** 523 Ellison Way, Augusta, GA 30907-2021, **Home Phone:** (706)863-2896. **Business Addr:** Professor, Paine College, 1235 15th St, Augusta, GA 30901, **Business Phone:** (706)821-8200.

### MILLER, ESQ. ALICE P.
Executive director. **Career:** Nat Asn State Election Dirs, pres, 2003; DC Bd Elections & Ethics, exec dir, 2008; US Election Assistance Comn, exec dir, chief operating officer, 2008-. **Orgs:** Bd dir, Election Ctr, currently. **Business Addr:** Executive Director, Chief Operating Officer, United States Election Assistance Commission, 1335 East West Hwy, Silver Spring, MD 20910.

### MILLER, DR. ANDREA LEWIS
Vice president (organization), dean (education), chancellor (education). **Personal:** Born Sep 10, 1954, Memphis, TN; married Robert A; children: Meredith Mechelle. **Educ:** Le Moyne Owen Col, BS, biol, 1976; Atlanta Univ, MS, cell & develop biol, 1978, PhD, cell & develop biol, 1980. **Career:** NIH, fel, 1977-80; Univ Cincinnati Col Med, fel, 1980-82; LeMoyne Owen Col, prof biol assoc investr, 1982-83, prof biol, prin investr, 1983, dept chmn, asst dean curric & instr, assoc prof biol, vpres acad affairs, dean fac; NIH, res grant, 1983-86; United Negro Col Fund, premed educ grant, 1984-; Doe res grant; Univ Nev, Col Human & Community Sci, asst dean; Shelby State Community Col, interim vpres acad & stud affairs; Southwest Tenn Community Col, exec vpres acad stud affairs, provost & exec vpres acad affairs admin & planning; Sowela Tech Community Col, chancellor, 2007-11; Baton Rouge Community Col, chancellor, 2011-; LeMoyne-Owen Col, pres, 2015. **Orgs:** Memphis Vol Placement Prog, 1973; Alpha Kappa, 1973; Am Soc Cell Biologist, 1981; pres, LeMoyne Owen Col Fac Orgn, 1984-86; Southeast Electron Micros Soc, 1985, Electron Micros Soc Am, 1985. **Home Addr:** 1119 Hayne Rd, Memphis, TN 38119-4946. **Business Addr:** President, LeMoyne-Owen College, 807 Walker Ave, Memphis, TN 38126, **Business Phone:** (901)435-1601.

### MILLER, ANTHONY. See MILLER, LAWRENCE ANTHONY.

### MILLER, ANTHONY
Basketball player. **Personal:** Born Oct 22, 1971, Benton Harbor, MI. **Educ:** Mich State Univ, BA, criminal justice, 1994. **Career:** Los Angeles Lakers, forward & power forward, 1994-96; Continental Basketball Asn, Fla Beachdogs, 1996-97; Atlanta Hawks, power forward, 1996-98, 2000, 2004-05; Houston Rockets, guard & power forward, 1999-2000, 2003; Philadelphia 76ers, power forward, 2001; Continental Basketball Asn, Yakama Sun Kings, 2006; Am Basketball Asn, Las Vegas Aces, 2008. **Orgs:** Continental Basketball Asn. **Special Achievements:** Actor: Space Jam, 1996; Eddie, 1996. **Business Addr:** Professional Basketball Player, Yakama Sun Kings, 1301 S Fair Ave Shattuck Bldg, Yakima, WA 98901, **Business Phone:** (509)248-1222.

### MILLER, REV. ANTHONY GLENN
Clergy. **Personal:** Born Sep 24, 1959, Los Angeles, CA; son of Isaac Nimrod and Lillian Lois Gray. **Educ:** Univ Southern Calif, BA, 1984; Gen Theol Sem, MDiv, 1988; Grad Inst Relig & Health, cert pastoral counr, 1993; Yale Univ, STM, 1994. **Career:** Parish Trinity Church, seminarian, 1985-86; St Philip's Episcopal Church, seminarian intern, 1986-87; Church Heavenly Rest, seminarian, 1987; Diocese Long Island, exec off bishop, 1988-92; Church Transfiguration, assoc rector, 1989-91; St Andrew's Episcopal Church, vicar, 1993; St Barnabas' Church, rector, currently. **Orgs:** Long Island rep Guatemala prog, Presiding Bishop's Fund World Relief, 1992; dean's search comt, 1992, jr tutorial prog, tutor, 1991, Gen Theol Sem; Diocese Long Island Comn Ministry, 1993; Diocesan Episcopal AIDS Comt, 1993; GOE reader, Gen Bd Examining Chaplains, 1993. **Special Achievements:** I Am Somebody, essay contest, 1973. **Home Addr:** 350 S Madison Ave Suite 207, Pasadena, CA 91101-4022. **Business Addr:** Rector, St Barnabas Church, 1062 N Fair Oaks Ave, Pasadena, CA 91103, **Business Phone:** (626)798-2996.

### MILLER, ARTHUR J. See Obituaries Section.

### MILLER, DR. BERNICE JOHNSON
School administrator, educational consultant. **Personal:** Born Chicago, IL; married George Benjamin; children: Benita & Michael. **Educ:** Chicago Teachers Col, MA, 1965; CAS Harvard Univ Grad Sch Educ, attended 1969, EdD, 1972; Roosevelt Univ Chicago, Ill, BA. **Career:** Chicago Bd Ed, teacher elem & hs, 1950-66; New Sch C Inc, headmistress, 1966-68; Jackson Col, assoc dean, 1968-70; Radcliffe, instr, 1970-73; Harvard Grad Sch Educ, assoc dir, 1971-75, High Tech Res Proj, dir, 1983-84; Boston Pub Sch Lucy Stone Sch, prin, 1977-78; Boston Pub Sch, sr officer, 1978-84; City Col Chicago, pres; City Col Chicago, pres emer, currently; Harold Wash Col, pres; Harold Wash Col, pres emer. **Orgs:** Bd mem, C's World Day Care Ctr Boston, 1972-84, Blue Cross & Blue Shield Boston, United Way; trustee, Brigham's & Women's Hosp Med Found; pres, United Commun Planning Corp, 1983-85; bd mem, Chicago Metro Hist Fair Bd; Mayor's Comn Women. **Honors/Awds:** Educator's Award, Boston 350th Anniversary, Boston MA, 1980; Educator of the Year, Urban Bankers Ed Award, Boston, 1982; Woman of the Year Award, Asn Mannequins, 1984; Woman in Education, Bus & Prof Women Boston & Vicinity, 1984; Freedom Award, Roosevelt Univ, 1985; Distinguished Alumni, Chicago State Univ, NABSE, 1985; Outstanding Achievement Award, Educ YWCA, 1986; Minority Networking Org Focus & Seana Mag Service Award, 1986. **Special Achievements:** Written journals like: Inner City Women in White Schools, The Journal of Negro Education. **Business Addr:** President Emeritus, Harold Washington College, 30 E Lake St, Chicago, IL 60601, **Business Phone:** (312)553-5600.

**MILLER, BUBBA (STEPHEN DEJUAN MILLER)**
Football player, television show host. **Personal:** Born Jan 24, 1973, Nashville, TN; married Gina; children: Stephen III. **Educ:** Tenn State Univ, grad. **Career:** Football player (retired), host; Philadelphia Eagles, corner, 1997-2000; New Orleans Saints, corner, 2002; B Miller Group, founder, 2005; TV & Radio appearnces: Philadelphia Eagles, TV analyst; "Mathews' show", guest host; co-host with Chris Low; "Trade winds", host; "ESPN's Sunday Night Football", 2000; ESPN 1180, "The Bubba Miller Show", host, currently. **Business Addr:** Host, ESPN 1180, 802 S Cent, Knoxville, TN 37902, **Business Phone:** (865)243-2877.

**MILLER, C. CONRAD, JR.**
Advertising executive. **Personal:** Born Jul 16, 1950, Little Rock, AR; son of Clarence Conrad Sr and Bernice Beatrice Jaudon; married Sherrin Ellen Johnson; children: Andrew & Lauren. **Educ:** Ft Hays Kans State Univ, BS, 1973; Univ Mich, MM, 1974, doctoral studies, 1976. **Career:** Ortho pharmaceut Corp, sales rep, 1977-78, sales training mgr, 1979-81, dist sales mgr, 1981-83, prod mgr, 1983-86, prod dir, 1986-88, sr dir, Gynec Therapeut, 1988-90; Ortho McNeil, sr prod dir, 1977-90; Dudnyk Co, acct group dir, 1990-91, dir client serv, vpres bus develop, 1990-97, dir healthcare commun group; Adis Int, dir acct servs & bus develop; MTI Info Technologies, sr vpre bus develop, 2001-11; Physicians Interactive, vpres, Bus Develop, 2011-. **Orgs:** Vol, Bus Coun Arts, 1983-84; Branchburg Environ Comn, 1985-86; Healthcare Mkt & Communs Coun, 1991-. **Home Addr:** 7036 Upper York Rd, New Hope, PA 18938-9516, **Home Phone:** (215)794-9975. **Business Addr:** Vice President Business Development, Physicians Interactive, 950 Technol Way Suite 202, Libertyville, IL 60048, **Business Phone:** (800)794-6757.

**MILLER, CAMILLE LOUISE STEARNS**
Lawyer. **Personal:** Born Apr 25, 1956, Guthrie, OK; daughter of Lila Hobson Stearns and Hollis D Stearns; married Daryl Lee; children: Kristen Danielle. **Educ:** Howard Univ, Wash, DC, BA, 1978; Case Western Res Sch Law, Cleveland, Ohio, JD, 1981. **Career:** Ohio Atty Gen Off, Columbus, Ohio, asst atty gen, 1981-83; Ohio Dept Natural Resources, Div Oil & Gas, gen coun, 1983-85; Lewis & Munday PC, Detroit, Mich, assoc atty, 1985-91, partner, 1991-2000; Holland & Knight LLP, partner & atty, 2001-06; Adorno Yoss White & Wiggins LLP, of coun, 2009-. **Orgs:** Alpha Kappa Alpha Sorority, 1981-; Nat Conf Black Lawyers, Columbus Chap, 1981-85; Am Bar Asn, 1981-; Detroit Bar Asn, 1985-; Detroit Pub Schs Role Model, 1985-91; Nat Coalition 100 Black Women, 1985-; bd mem & secy-treas, Wolverine Bar Asn, 1986-90, pres, 1991-92; asst secy, Nat Bar Asn, 1991; bd mem, Nat Bar Asn, 1995-; Detroit Renaissance Links, 1990-; Detroit Chap, Jack & Jill Am, 1996-; secy, San Antonio Chap, Jack & Jill Am Inc; bd mem, Alamo City Chamber Com; secy, San Antonio Youth Literacy Coun; vpres, San Antonio Chap Links Inc; Michael Kindred Community Singers; bd mem-at-Large, Nat Bar Asn; bd mem, Alamo City Chamber Com; exec bd, Alamo City Black Chamber Com; community adv bd, bd mem, Clear Channel Commun Inc; steering comt mem & former co-chair, State Tex Minority Coun Prog; Dallas Bar Asn; State Bar Mich Employ & Labor Coun; State Mich Atty Discipline Bd Panelist; treas, Metrop Detroit Bar Found; San Antonio Black Lawyers Asn. **Honors/Awds:** Outstanding Service Award, Black Law Students Asn, Case Western Res Sch Law, 1981; Outstanding Contributions to Legal Community, Black Law Students Asn, Columbus, Ohio, 1984; Certificate of Appreciation, Detroit Pub Schs, 1986-88; President's Award for Outstanding Service, Nat Bar Asn, 1991-92; Resolution for Outstanding Service to the Community, US Cong House Rep, 1992; Resolution for Outstanding Service to the Legal Community & Community-at-large, Mich State Legis Senate, 1992; Resolution for Outstanding Service to the County, Mayor Detroit Coleman A Young, 1992; Resolution for Outstanding Service to the Legal County, Wayne County Exec Ed McNamara; Resolution for Outstanding Service to the County, Detroit Bd Educ. **Home Addr:** 1900 Strathcora, Detroit, MI 48203, **Home Phone:** (313)368-2114. **Business Addr:** Partner, Attorney, Adorno Yoss White & Wiggins LLP, 1700 Pac Ave Suite 3740, Dallas, TX 75201, **Business Phone:** (214)665-4158.

**MILLER, CHARLES D., JR.**
Executive. **Personal:** Born Apr 13, 1952, Lexington, NC; son of Charles Sr; married Loretta W; children: Charles D III & Kellen A. **Educ:** NC Agr & Tech State Univ, BSME, 1974; Univ Ill, MBA, 1984. **Career:** John Deere, engr, 1974-77; Ford, sr engr, 1977; GE, dir eng, 1984-86, vpres mkt, 1986-91; Whirlpool Corp, from vpres mkt kitchenaid to pres kitchenaid, 1991-93, vpres mkt, 1993-. **Orgs:** Dir, Whirlpool Found, 1992-; Am Mgt Asn, 1992-; trustee, Mkt Sci Inst, 1994-. **Honors/Awds:** Nat YMCA, Achievers, 1993; Organization of the Year, Am Marketing Asn, 1993; Gold Award, Baldridge, 1994. **Home Addr:** 328 Cornatzer Rd, Mocksville, NC 27028-7127, **Home Phone:** (336)998-4158. **Business Addr:** Vice President of Marketing-North America, Whirlpool Corp, 2000 M-63 N, Benton Harbor, MI 49022-2692, **Business Phone:** (269)923-5000.

**MILLER, CHERYL DE ANN**
Athletic coach, television broadcaster, basketball player. **Personal:** Born Jan 3, 1964, Riverside, CA. **Educ:** Univ Southern Calif, BA, broadcast jour. **Career:** Outstanding Col & amateur basketball player, coach (retired); teams include: Junior National Team, 1981; US National Team, 1982; JC Penney All-American Five Team; World Championship Team, 1983; Univ SC, Women's Basketball Team, player; US Olympics, Women's Basketball Team, player, 1984; ABC Sports, commentator; Univ SC, head coach, women's basketball, 1993-95; Phoenix Mercury, head coach & gen mgr, 1997-2000; Turner Sports, TNT, TBS, NBA analyst; Nat Basketball Asn, NBA games, TNT, NBA TV, sideline reporter, Cal State Los Angeles, Coach, 2016. **Orgs:** US Olympic gold medal women's basketball team. **Honors/Awds:** Sports Illustrated Player of the Week, 1983; mem US Olympic Gold Medal Basketball Team, 1984; ABA & USA Female Athlete of the Year, 1986; Naismith Player of the Year, three consecutive yrs; Kodak All-Am, four consecutive yrs. **Special Achievements:** Recipient of more than 1, 140 trophies and 125 plaques; offered 250 scholarships to various college & Univ teams; participant in championship games including: CIF state championship, Nat Sports Festival, 1981, Pan Am Games, 1983; FIBA World Championships, Goodwill Games; player for US Olympic team winning first Gold Medal for women's basketball, 1984; First female analyst to call a nationally televised NBA game; US Olympic gold medal women's Basketball team; Women's Basketball Hall of Fame, 1999; FIBA Hall of Fame, 2010. **Business Addr:** Sideline Reporter, Turner Network Television - TNT, 1015 Techwood Dr 8th Fl, Atlanta, GA 30318, **Business Phone:** (404)827-1500.

**MILLER, CONSTANCE JOAN**
Consultant, manager. **Personal:** Born Sep 8, 1945, Frederick, OK; daughter of Arthur Lee and Esther Bell Herd; married Norman Engelsberg; children: Braswell & Michelle. **Educ:** Temple Univ, attended 1971; Univ Wash, attended 1974; Goddard-Cambridge Grad Sch, MA, attended 1976. **Career:** City Seattle, 1979-81; Phoenix Proj, 1982, managing dir, 1982-89; Med Legal Consult Wash, legal asst; Dalkon Shield, proj mgr, 1988-91; IUD Claim Info Serv, ICIS, managing dir, 1991-; Brain Injury Resource Ctr, founder & consult. **Orgs:** Founding bd mem, Int Dalkon Shield Victims Educ Asn, 1986-. **Special Achievements:** Co-author, From The Ashes, A Head Injury Self-Advocate Guide, The Phoenix Project Books, 1987-; Author, Dalkon Shield Claims Information Guide, ICIS Books, 1989-; Dalkon Shield Claims Legal Guide, ICIS Books, 1990-; Author, Dalkon Shield Claims Up-Date Service, ICIS Books; "Clap Your Hands el3", Essence, May, 1990, p 112; "Day of Reckoning", Ms. Magazine, June, 1989, p 50; "Are You a Victim of this Nasty-Looking Thing?" Woman's World Magazine, April 25, 1989, p 6. **Home Addr:** 2720 17th Ave S, Seattle, WA 98144-5112, **Home Phone:** (206)329-4355. **Business Addr:** Founder, International Dalkon Shield Victims Education Association, PO Box 84151, Seattle, WA 98104, **Business Phone:** (206)329-1371.

**MILLER, CYLENTHIA LATOYE**
Lawyer, judge. **Personal:** Born Dec 13, 1962, Pine Bluff, AR; daughter of George Boyer Jr and Sharon Elaine Bernard. **Educ:** Univ Mich, sociol, 1984; Wayne State Univ, BA, sociol, 1988; Mich State Univ, Col Law, JD, 1996. **Career:** Wayne Co Neighborhood Legal Servs, mediator, 1988-89; Mich Credit Union League, regulatory specialist, 1989-93; Neighborhood Servs Orgn, emergency phone counr, 1993-96; Dykema Gosset PLLC, assoc, 1996-98; Lewis & Munday PC, assoc; Detroit Police Dept, police cadet supvr & payroll asst; Detroit Workforce Develop Dept, dir; City Detroit, Employ & Training Dept, dir admin; Mich's 36th Judicial Dist Ct, judge, 2006-; Baker Col, adj prof, 2012-. **Orgs:** Golden Heritage life mem, Nat Asn Advan Colored People; Alpha Kappa Alpha Sorority Inc, 1984-; Am Bar Asn, 1993-; Nat Bar Asn, 1996-, Women Lawyers Div, bd mem, chmn; State Bar Mich, 1996-; Wolverine Bar Asn, 1996-; Women Lawyers Asn Mich, 1996-; Ark Bar Asn, 1997-; Nat Asn Female Exec, 1993-; Nat Coun Negro Women; Nat Cong Black Women; St. Cecilia Roman Cath Church; Gold Sustaining mem Trade Union Leadership Coun. **Honors/Awds:** Bk Award, Detroit Col Law, Probate Procedure; Bk Award, RWA II; Hons, RWA I & II, 1992-93; Scholar, Wolverine Bar Asn, 1994; Scholar, Wolverine Stud Bar Asn, 1993-94; Dent & Murphy Trailblazer Award, Wolverine Stud Bar Asn, 2000; President Award, Nat Bar Asn, 2000, 2006, 2009; Member of the Year, Wolverine Bar Asn, 2001; Nat Lawyers Guild; Top 5 Up & Coming Lawyer, Mich Lawyers Weekly, 2001; Distinguished Alumni Award, Wolverine Stud Bar Asn, 2003; Citizen Lawyer Award, State Bar Mich, 2005; Shining Star Award, Wolverine Bar Asn, 2005; Special Recognition Award, Wolverine Bar Asn, 2007; Sheroe Award, McKinney Elementary Sch, 2008; Distinguished Service Award, Detroit City Coun, 2008; Member of the Year, Asn Black Judges Michigan, 2009; Humanitarian of the Year Award, Mich Bus & Tech Inst, 2009; Alvin L. Storrs Outstanding Mentoring Award, 2011. **Special Achievements:** First African American female president of a graduating class, Detroit Col of Law at Mich State Univ, 1996. **Home Addr:** 620 Chrysler Dr Apt 202, Detroit, MI 48207-3054, **Home Phone:** (313)393-8736. **Business Addr:** Judge, Michigan's 36th Judicial District Court, 421 Madison Ave, Detroit, MI 48226, **Business Phone:** (313)965-2200.

**MILLER, DR. DENNIS WELDON**
Physician. **Personal:** Born Mar 12, 1949, Roanoke, VA; son of Henry and Rosa; married Carol; children: Damon & Jared. **Educ:** Fisk Univ, attended 1971; Meharry Med Col, attended 1975. **Career:** KC Gen Hosp & Med Ctr, resident obstet & gynec, 1975-76; Truman Med Ctr, resident obstet & gynec, 1976-79; Univ Kans, Med Ctr, Family Pract Dept, clin prof, 1983-; pvt pract physician, currently; St Margarets Health Ctr, chmn, 1987-89; Providence Med Ctr, physician; Overland Pk Regional Med Ctr, physician. **Orgs:** Gynec Soc, Southwest Clin Soc, Nat Med Asn, 1971-77; Am Med Asn, 1971-77; Nat Asn Advan Colored People; secy, treas, Kan Valley Med Soc, 1988-90; Am Asn Gynec Laparoscopists; Wyandotte Co Med Soc; KS Med Soc; KS Found Med Care; Gyn Laser Soc. **Business Addr:** Physician, 21 N 12th St Suite 350, Kansas City, KS 66102, **Business Phone:** (913)371-1667.

**MILLER, DONALD LESESSNE**
Vice president (organization), chief executive officer, executive. **Personal:** Born Jan 10, 1932, New York, NY; son of John H and Mamie Johnson; married Gail Aileen Wallace; children: Lynn Ann & Mark L. **Educ:** Univ Md, BA, 1967; Harvard Bus Sch, PMD, 1969. **Career:** Inmont Corp, New York, NY, asst pres, 1968-70; Seatrain Shipbuilding, New York, NY, vpres indust rels, 1970-71; US Dept Defense, Wash, DC, asst secy defense, 1971-73; Columbia Univ, New York, NY, vpres personnel & mgt, 1973-78; Int Paper, New York, NY, dir personnel, 1978-79; Con Edison, New York, NY, vpres employee rels, 1979-86; Community Banks, dir emer, 1983-; Dow Jones & Co, New York, NY, vpres, employee rels, 1986-95; Schering Plough Corp, pres, chief exec officer, 1995; Our World News, founder; Bank New York Inc, mem bd dir, currently; Schering-Plough Corp, mem bd dir, 1997-2004; Health Data Insights Inc, adv bd mem, chmn, currently. **Orgs:** Trustee, Pace Univ, 1979-; dir, United Way, Tri State, 1981-; dir, Jackie Robinson Found, 1981-; chmn bd, founder, Assoc Black Charities, 1982-. **Home Addr:** 1 Cove Ct, Secaucus, NJ 07094, **Home Phone:** (201)866-4452. **Business Addr:** Director, HealthDataInsights Inc, 2450 Fire Mesa St Suite 160, Las Vegas, NV 89128, **Business Phone:** (888)700-3282.

**MILLER, DORIS JEAN**
School administrator, president (organization). **Personal:** Born Oct 13, 1933, River Rouge, MI; married Olie; children: Carla A, Darryl S & Felicia C. **Educ:** Wayne State Univ, BA, 1957; Mich State Univ, cert, 1963; Wayne State Univ, MA, 1968. **Career:** School administrator (retired), retired; River Rouge Pub Schs, teacher, 1959-73, prin, 1973-74, teacher, 1974-79; Wayne County Community Col, trustee, 1978-88; Mich Fed Teachers & Sch Related Personnel, field rep, 1979-96, asst to pres, 1996-98; Doris Miller Educ Consult Servs, pres, 1998-2010. **Orgs:** Alpha Kappa Alpha Sor, 1952-; mem bd dir, Down river Guid Clin, 1970-88; chmn, Black Women's Task Force, 1982-85; Greater Metro Det Guid Assoc, 1982-88; Women's Conf Concerns, 1982-89; pres, Wayne County Community Col Found, 1982-84, treas, 1985; mem bd dir, Wayne County Pvt Indus Coun, 1983-89. **Honors/Awds:** Scholar, Ford Motor Co Fund, 1951-55; Golden Apple Award, Wayne County Regional & Educ Serv Agency, 1998. **Home Addr:** 431 Palmerston Dr, River Rouge, MI 48218, **Home Phone:** (313)294-0617.

**MILLER, DR. DORSEY COLUMBUS, JR.**
Educator. **Personal:** Born Jan 7, 1943, Ocala, FL; son of Dorsey C Sr and Eudora J; married Betty J Samuel; children: Kim Y, Eric T & Dorsey C III. **Educ:** Morehouse Col, BA, 1965; Univ Fla, masters, 1971; Fla Atlantic Univ, EdD, 1980. **Career:** Sch Bd Marion County, teacher, guid counr, 1965-68; Sch Bd Broward County, guid counr, 1972-73; Fla dept Educ, counsult, 1973-75, regional counr, 1975-79; Southern Bell Tel Co, mgr, 1979-80; Sch Bd Broward County, migrant educ, 1980-91, spec prog, dir, 1991-; DC Miller & Assoc, pres & chief exec officer, currently; secy, Com Carlos Gutierrez, currently. **Orgs:** Grand basileus, OPP Fraternity Inc; bd trustee chr, Broward County Col; bd trustee, Mt Olive Baptist Church; bd gov, Greater Fort Lauderdale; Nat CNF Christians &d Jews, bd; mem & pres, Kiwanis Club Cent Broward County; Am Cancer Soc. **Home Addr:** 6008 NW 62nd Ter, Parkland, FL 33064, **Home Phone:** (305)984-9777. **Business Addr:** President, Chief Executive Officer, DC Miller & Associates Inc, 545 N Andrews Ave, Ft. Lauderdale, FL 33301.

**MILLER, E. ETHELBERT**
School administrator, writer, college teacher. **Personal:** Born Nov 20, 1950, New York, NY; son of Enid Marshall and Egberto; married Denise King; children: Jasmine Simone & Nyere-Gibran. **Educ:** Howard Univ, BA, Afro-Am studies, 1972. **Career:** Howard Univ, African-Am Resource Ctr, dir, 1974-; Univ Nev, vis prof, 1993; African Am Rev, adv ed, currently; WDCU-FM, host; Art & Lett, contrib, currently; Bennington Col, fac, 2002; bd chmn, Inst Policy Studies, currently; Am Univ, adj prof; Poet Lore mag, ed. **Orgs:** Bd mem, Writer's Ctr & ed Poet Lore mag; former chair, Humanities Coun Wash; PEN Am Ctr; Faulkner Found; bd mem, Assoc Writing Progs; adv bd mem, J Contemp Cult; bd mem, Network Educr Americas; bd mem, Capitol Lett Writing Ctr; bd chmn, Provisions Learning Libr; bd mem, Split This Rock Writing. **Honors/Awds:** Mayor's Art Award for Literature, 1982; Tony Taylor Award, Cult Alliance Wash, DC, 1986; Public Humanities Award, DC Humanities Coun, 1988; Josephine Miles Award, Pen Oakland, 1994; Columbia Merit Award, 1994; O B Hardison Jr Poetry Prize, 1995; Honorary Doctorate of literature, Jessie Ball Du Pont Scholar, Emory & Henry Col, 1996; scholar in residence, George Mason Univ; Stephen Henderson Poetry Award, African-Am Lit & Cult Soc, 1997; Stephen E Henderson Poetry Award, African Am Lit & Cult Soc, 1997; Barnes & Noble/Writers for Writers Award, nat pub radio, 2007; Washington DC Hall of Fame, 2015; Mayors Arts Award, 31st Ann Mayors Arts Awards, 2016; George Garrett Award, AWP, 2016. **Special Achievements:** Published: Author: "Andromeda", 1974; "The Land of Smiles & The Land of No Smiles", 1974; "Migrant Worker", 1978; "Season of Hunger Cry of Rain", 1982; "Where Are the Love Poems for Dictators", 1986; "First Light, New & Selected Poems", 1994; "Whispers, Secrets & Promises", 1998; "Beyond the Frontier", 2002; "How we Sleep on the Nights We Dont Make Love", 2004; "The 5th Inning", 2009; Editor: "Synergy: An Anthology of Washington Do Co Poetry", 1975; "In Search of Color Everywhere", 1994; "Women Surviving Massacres & Men", 1997; "Fathering Words", 2000; "Buddha Weeping in Winter", 2001; "Beyond the Frontier", 2002; "Poem: Trouble the Water, 250 Years of African-American Poetry"; "The New Cavalcade; Erotique Noire Black Erotica"; "360 A Revolution of Black Poets; Spirit & Flame"; "I Am The Darker Brother"; "The Garden Thrives; I Feel A Little Jumpy Around You"; "Beyond Lament; Literature, The Evolving Canon"; "Catch the Fire; Furious Flower: African American Poetry from the Black Arts Movement to the Present"; "Poets of the World Bearing Witness to the Holocaust; New Bones; Tales from the Couch"; "Sept 28, 1979 proclaimed as E Ethelbert Miller Day"; "Made an honorary Citizen of Baltimore, MD, July 17", 1994; Hosted MaidenVoyage, WDCU-FM; Vertigo on the Air, WPFW-FM; Humanities Profiled, WDC-TV; Honored by Laura Bush & the White House, Nat Book Festival, 2001, 2003. **Home Addr:** 1411 Underwood St NW, Washington, DC 20012-2827, **Home Phone:** (202)494-5171. **Business Addr:** Director, Howard University, MSC 590 514, Washington, DC 20059, **Business Phone:** (202)806-7242.

**MILLER, ERENEST EUGENE**
High school principal, educator. **Personal:** Born Jun 13, 1948, Farmville, VA; son of William C and Maria G; married Alice Robinson. **Educ:** Va State Univ, BA, 1970, EdM, 1978. **Career:** Trophy & Plaque Luther P Jackson, fac, 1966; Gold Hill Elem Sch, teacher, 1970-71; Cumberland High Sch, educr, 1971-92; Cumberland Co Sch, adult educ teacher, 1973-; Longwood Col Summer Inst Talented & Gifted Students, facilitator, 1979; Prince Edward Co Mid Sch, teacher, 1992-, asst prin, 1993-. **Orgs:** Scout master, Robert E Lee Scout Troop 6280, 1971-74; pres, Cumberland Co Br, Nat Asn Advan Colored People 1976-80; bd mem, Va State Conf, 1978-; dir proj, Va Found Humanities & Pub Policy, 1979; vpres, 1988, pres, 1992-, Va State; sponsor, SCA Cumberland High Sch; dir, Summer Youth Employ & Trng Prog; coach, Battle Brains, 1988; coach, Social Studies AC Team, 1988; Plaque Central Piedmont Action Coun, 1989; vpres, Iota Tau Lambda Chap; pres, 1991, 1998, Alpha Phi Alpha; Tearwallet & Sharon Baptist Church; vpres, Inspirational Choir; dir, Voc Bible Sch; bd dir, Southside YMCA. **Home Addr:** 1135 Plank Rd, Farmville, VA 23901, **Home Phone:** (434)392-9929. **Business Addr:** Assistant Principal, Prince Edward County High School, 35 Eagle Dr, Farmville, VA 23901, **Business Phone:** (434)315-2130.

**MILLER, FAYNEESE**
College teacher, college administrator, college president. **Personal:** Born Danville, VA; married Bob Biral; children: David. **Educ:** Hampton Univ, BS, 1977; Tex Christian Univ MS, 1979, PhD, 1981;Yale Univ, postdoctoral studies. **Career:** Brown Univ, assoc prof & chmn ethnic studies, 1985-2005; Univ Vt, dean educ & social serv & prof, 2005-15; Hamline Univ, pres, 2015-. **Orgs:** Mem bd dir, United Way Chittenden County, Wheeler Sch; mem bd dir, RI Black Heritage Soc; mem bd dir, RI Hist Soc; mem bd dir, RI Youth Guid Ctr; mem bd dir, Big Sisters, Providence NAACP; mem bd dir, Community Prep Sch; mem bd dir, San Migel Sch; mem bd dir, Sojourner House; mem bd dir, Langston Hughes Ctr Arts; mem bd trustees, Hamline Univ; mem bd trustees, Vt State Bd Educ; mem bd trustees, Am Asn Cols Teacher Educ; mem bd trustees, Coun Deans from Res Extensive Insts; Outreach & Engagement Comt; Am Coun Educ. **Honors/Awds:** American Council of Education, fellow, 2004-05. **Special Achievements:** First African-American president of Hamline University, 2015; first African American to be granted at Ph.D at Texas Christian University; founding chairman and chief architect of ethnic studies concentration, Brown University; visiting scholar at the University of Cape Town, South Africa; special advisor to the chairman of the board at the University of Business and Technology, Jedda, Saudi Arabia. **Business Addr:** Hamline University, 1536 Hewitt Ave, Saint Paul, MN 55104-1284, **Business Phone:** (651)523-2800.

**MILLER, MAJOR GEN. FRANK LEE, JR.**
Military leader, vice president (organization). **Personal:** Born Jan 27, 1944, Atchinson, KS; son of Frank L and Evelyn A Wilson; married Paulette Duncan; children: Frank L III, Michael W & Toni K. **Educ:** Univ Wash, BA, 1973; AUS Command & Gen Staff Col, Ft Leavenworth, KS, attended 1977; Troy State Univ, attended 1979; Naval War Col, Newport, RI, attended 1984. **Career:** Major general (retired); AUS, pvt, 1965-97, Comndg Gen III Corps Artil, maj gen, currently; 101st Airborne Div, Rifle Co Comdr, rifle platoon leader, 1980-85; Spec Forces, spec forces officer, col, 1985; 1st Battalion; 1st Spec Forces Group; AUS War Col, Strategic Studies Inst, external researcher; Pub Opers Dell Comput Corp, vpres, vpres, pub supply chain & demand planning, currently. **Orgs:** Asn AUS, 1966-; Field Artil Asn, 1988-; Foreign Area Officer Prog. **Honors/Awds:** Meritorious Serv Medal; Distinguished Flying Cross; Joint Serv Commendation Medal, Legion of Merit with 3 OLC; Bronze Star Medal with "V" & 2 Oak Leaf Clusters; Air Medal with "V" and 19 Oak Leaf Clusters; Vietnamese Cross Gallantry with Silver Star. **Special Achievements:** First black chief of staff of the free world's ctr for fire support at Fort Sill, OK; First black commanding general of the Army's largest and most diverse Corps Artillery. **Home Addr:** 7 Scenic Ter, Round Rock, TX 78664-9635, **Home Phone:** (512)341-8057. **Business Addr:** Vice President of Public Supply Chain & Demand planning, Dell Computer Corp, 1 Dell Way, Round Rock, TX 78682, **Business Phone:** (512)338-4400.

**MILLER, FRED JUNIOR, JR.**
Football coach, football player. **Personal:** Born Feb 6, 1973, Houston, TX; married Kim; children: Grant & Evan. **Educ:** Baylor Univ, BA, sociol. **Career:** St Louis Rams, 1996, left tackle, 1997, left guard, 1998, right tackle & tight end, 1999; Tenn Titans, right tackle, 2000-04, tackle, 2000; Chicago Bears, right tackle, 2005-08; N Shore Country Day Sch, Varsity Football Team, asst coach, 2011-12, head coach, 2012-13; N Shore Titans youth football prog, coach. **Honors/Awds:** Super Bowl XXXIV, St Louis, 2000. **Special Achievements:** TV Series: "The NFL on CBS", 1999-2004; "NFL Monday Night Football", 2000-04; "ESPN's Sunday Night Football", 2000-04; "NBC Sunday Night Football", 2006-07.

**MILLER, FREDERICK A.**
Educator, manager, executive director. **Personal:** Born Nov 2, 1946, Philadelphia, PA; son of Frederick and Clarice Gaines; married Pauline Kamen; children: Kamen Kaleel & Shay Clarice. **Educ:** Lincoln Univ, PA, BA, 1968. **Career:** Conn Gen Life Ins Co, mgr, admin, 1968-72, officer & mgr, 1972, human develop consult, 1972-76, asst dir training, 1976-79; Kaleel Jamison Mgt Consult Group, partner, vpres, 1979-85, pres & chief exec officer, 1985-; Day & Zimmerman, dir; Seton Health Systs, dir; Sage Cols, dir; Promise Diversity, managing ed, 1994; Apple Comput, consult; Allstate, consult; Alyeska Pipeline Serv Co, consult; DuPont, consult; FedEx Kinkos; Eileen Fisher Inc, consult; Foxwoods Casino, consult; Merck & Co Inc, consult; Mobil, consult; Omega Inst, consult; Northeast Utilities, consult; Singapore Telecommunications, consult; Toyota, consult; United Airlines, consult; Am Univ, adj prof, 2008. **Orgs:** Bd dir, Living Sch, 1973-; Orgn Develop Network, 1974-; Am Soc Training & Develop, 1974-; Nat Training Labs, 1976-; bd dir, Nat Training Labs Inst, 1980-85; bd dirs, Orgn Develop Network, 1986-94; bd dir, Ben & Jerrys Homemade; Social Venture Network; co-founder, Inst Inclusion; co-convener, Community 2022, founder; Troy 100 Forum; bd mem, Hist Troy 2020, 1999-; bd mem, Ben & Jerrys Homemade Inc, 1992-00; bd mem, Seton Health Found Seton Health Systs, 1997-; bd mem, World Educ, 2000-01; bd mem, Day & Zimmermann, 2004-; bd mem, Sage Cols, 2005-; bd mem, One World Everybody Eats Found, 2008-; bd mem, Bainbridge Grad Inst, 2011-; bd mem, Pinchot Day & Zimmermann; One World Everybody Eats Found; Rensselaer Polytech Inst, 2011-. **Honors/Awds:** Outstanding Service Award, OD Network, 1999; Professional of the Year, Hudson-Mohawk ASTD's Independent Entrepreneurial Training & Develop, 2002; Small Business Person of the Year Award, The Bus Rev, 2006; Lifetime Achievement Award, Albany-Colonie Regional Chamber Com Small Bus Coun, 2006; OD Network Lifetime Achievement Award, 2007; Global HR Excellence Award, Accor Serv, 2008; HR Leadership Award, Asia-Pacific HRM Cong, 2008; Honored Legends Diversity Dinner, Int Soc Diversity & Inclusion Professionals, 2012. **Special Achievements:** Managing Editor of The Promise of Diversity, 1994; Co-author with J.H. Katz, "The Inclusion Breakthrough: Unleashing the Real Power of Diversity", 2002; Co-author with J.H. Katz, "Be BIG: Step Up, Step Out, Be Bold", 2008. **Home Addr:** 45 Meadows Dr, Melrose, NY 12121-2921, **Home Phone:** (518)663-9957. **Business Addr:** Chief Executive Officer, Kaleel Jamison Consulting Group Inc, 279 River St Suite 201, Troy, NY 12180-3270, **Business Phone:** (518)271-7000.

**MILLER, GEORGE CARROLL, JR.**
Executive, government official, management consultant. **Personal:** Born Mar 3, 1949, Atlanta, GA; son of George and Beatrice; married Nawanna Lewis; children: George III, John Elliott, Mikah Alexis & Victoria Melissa. **Educ:** Am Inst Banking, attended 1971 & 1975, cert, Basic & Stand; Ga State Univ, BBA, gen, 1971, MBA, finance, 1974; Univ Okla, com lending dipl, 1975. **Career:** Trust Co Ga, com lending officer, 1971-76; US Treas Dept, exec asst, 1977-79, asst secy econ policy; Cooper & Lybrand, state & local govt consult pract dir, 1980-89; Provident Capital Group LP, managing partner, 2013-; US Small Bus Admin, liaison; Minority Bus Develop Agency, liaison; Spectrum Consult Assocs Inc, pres, currently. **Orgs:** Fundraiser YMCA, 1972-74, United Negro Col Fund, 1973-74, United Way, 1973-74; vice chmn, treas, Atlanta Bus League, 1974-75; bd dir, Joint Action Community Serv, 1982-; pres, Ga State Univ Nat Capital Alumni Club, 1985-; bd dir, DC Lung Assoc, 1986-; Nat Asbestos Coun; bd dir, Metrop Towers Inc; bd trustee, Metrop Baptist Church; bd dir, Jobs Homeless People; bd dir, Capitol City Bank & Trust Co; chmn, Messiahs Temple Church; liaison, Nat Bankers Asn; founding mem, Omega Psi Phi. **Honors/Awds:** WSB Beaver Award, 1968; Herbert Leman Educ Grant, 1968-71; Alumni Appreciation Award, Ga State Univ, 1976. **Home Addr:** 1920 Sharpshooters Ct NW, Marietta, GA 30064, **Home Phone:** (770)499-9519. **Business Addr:** President, Spectrum Consulting Associates Inc, 1050 Connecticut Ave NW Suite 1000, Washington, DC 20036, **Business Phone:** (202)772-3177.

**MILLER, GWENDOLYN MARTIN**
Government official. **Personal:** Born Aug 2, 1934, Tampa, FL; daughter of Nathaniel (deceased) and Wilma Rivers; married Lesley J Jr; children: James Jones, Arthur Jones, Le & Lesley. **Educ:** Fla A&M Univ, BS, educ, 1957, MS, educ, 1966. **Career:** Hillsborough County Sch Dist, human rels specialist, 1951-94; Miller Miller & Assocs Inc, chair, pres & chief exec officer, 1994-; City Tampa City Coun, councilwoman, 1995-2003, chairperson, 2004-08, chairwoman, 2008-11. **Orgs:** Nat pres, Charmettes Inc, 1971-; 1st nat vpres, Kappa Alpha Psi Fraternity Silhouettes Inc, 1982-; pres, Nat Coalition 100 Black Women Inc, Tampa Bay Chap, 1982-; bd dir, Tampa Hillsborough, 1990-; Alpha Kappa Alpha Sorority, 1998-; New Mt Zion MB Church. **Special Achievements:** First black woman to serve as Chair of Tampa City Council, 1995; First black woman to be elected to an at-large City Council seat. **Home Addr:** 2505 E 38th Ave, Tampa, FL 33610-7617, **Home Phone:** (813)239-2719. **Business Addr:** Councilwoman, Chairwoman, City of Tampa City Council, 315 E Kennedy Blvd, Tampa, FL 33602, **Business Phone:** (813)274-7072.

**MILLER, HELEN SULLIVAN**
Nurse, college teacher. **Personal:** Born Mar 29, 1917, Atlanta, GA; daughter of Ola Sullivan and Floyd Sullivan; children: Ronald. **Educ:** Univ Hosp, dipl nursing; Med Col Va, BS, nursing; Tuskeegee Inst, Sch Midwifery, CNM; Yale Univ Sch Nursing, MSN. **Career:** Nurse, college teacher (retired); Ga Dept Pub Health, staff nurse, 1947-49; US Pub Health Serv, area supvr, 1949-51; Army Nurse Corps, admin nurse, 1951-53; City Philadelphia Dept Health, dist suprv, 1953-54; Fla Agr & Mech Univ, pub health coord sch nursing, 1954-56; NC Cent Univ, Dept Nursing, chmn, 1956-82, assoc prof nursing resident, 1977-82; Fla A&M Univ, coordr; Ga Dept Pub Health, staff nurse; Maternal Child Health, area supvr. **Orgs:** Secy, Undergrad Coun, NC Cent Univ; fac exec comn, NC Cent Univ; Long Range Planning Comt, NC Cent Univ; NC State Nurses Asn; Am Nurses Asn; comt mem, Write Hist Nursing; Yale Univ Alumnae Asn; Am Asn Univ Women; Adv Com Cont Educ Sch Nursing Univ NC, Chapel Hill; Youth Women's Christian Asn; former bd mem, Local Chap ARC; exec comt, NC Lung & Resp Asn; Health Careers Comt; chair, NC Cent Univ; Gubernatorial appt, NC Bd Nursing, 1966-70; nat pres, Chi Eta Phi Sor, 1969-73; bd dir, vpres, NC League Nursing, 1971-75; life mem, Nat Coun Negro Women; life mem, Chi Eta Phi Sor. **Honors/Awds:** Mary Mahoney Award, Am Nurses Asn, 1968; Historical Preservations America, 1975-76; listed inMinority Groups in Nursing, Am Nurses Asn, 1976; Distinguished Alumnae Award, Yale Univ, 1978; Miller Morgan Health Sci Building, named in honor. **Special Achievements:** First African-American nurse elected the president of a district nursing association; First African-American to receive a gubernational appointment to the North Carolina Board of Nursing; author, two abstracts in Abstracts of Nursing Research in the South, Vol 1, 1979; The History of Chi Eta Phi Sorority Inc, Associationn forthe Study of Afro-American Life & History, 1968; co-author, Contemporary Minority Leaders in Nursing, American Nurses Association, 1983; Auth: Mary Eliza Mahoney, 1845-1926: America's First Black Professional Nurse. **Home Addr:** 6000 Fayetteville Rd, PO Box 810, Durham, NC 27713.

**MILLER, HORATIO CABRERE**
Educator, pianist, musician. **Personal:** Born Jan 8, 1949, Birmingham, AL; children: Allison. **Educ:** Univ Pa, BA, musicol, 1970; Temple Univ, MM, piano performance, 1973. **Career:** Cheyney State Col, instr, 1973-74; Community Col Philadelphia, asst prof music, 1974-. **Orgs:** Found Study Cycles. **Honors/Awds:** Acad Music Philadelphia, Inaugural Concert President Carter Washington, DC, 1976; Timer Digest, rated top 10 market timers in the gold market, 1988; Timer Digest, Rated No 3 gold market timer, 1990; Article, EliottWave & Gold, Stocks & Commodities Magazine, 1991. **Home Addr:** 7740B Stenton Ave Apt 110, Philadelphia, PA 19118-3141. **Business Addr:** Assistant Professor, Community College of Philadelphia, 1700 Spring Garden St, Philadelphia, PA 19130, **Business Phone:** (215)751-8010.

**MILLER, INGER**
Athlete, executive. **Personal:** Born Jun 12, 1972, Los Angeles, CA; daughter of Lennox. **Educ:** Univ Southern Calif, attended 1994. **Career:** Brad tomasini, track & field athlete; Miller-Hawkins Productions, partner, owner, 2002-; Olympic Games, gold, 1996, World Championships, gold, 1997, 1999, 2001, silver, 1999, 2003, Altadena Chamber Com, pres, 2011-12; Arbonne Int, Independent Consult, 2010-. **Orgs:** HSI, Tournament Roses, 2009-. **Home Addr:** 871 E Mariposa St, Altadena, CA 91001-2420. **Business Addr:** Owner, President, Miller-Hawkins Productions, 61 S Baldwin Ave Suite 1658, Sierra Madre, CA 91025, **Business Phone:** (626)791-1225.

**MILLER, DR. INGRID FRAN WATSON**
Educator. **Personal:** Born Jul 4, 1949, Washington, DC; daughter of Dempsey and Matilda; married George E III; children: Sean Gregory & Simon Geoffry. **Educ:** NC Cent Univ, BA, span, 1971; Howard Univ, MEd, curric develop, 1983; Cath Univ Am, MA, span lit, 1993; Univ Md, College Park, 1996. **Career:** T Roosevelt S High Sch, Washingon, DC, span teacher, 1973-88; Jackson State Univ, asst prof span, 1983-85; Hampton Univ, asst prof span, 1988-96; Norfolk State Univ, asst pro span, 1996-99; Johnson C Smith Univ, asst prof span, 1999-2000; Bowie State Univ, Dir, off-campus Advisement, 2001-. **Orgs:** Alpha Kappa Alpha Sorority Inc, pres, vp, parl, reporter, grand advisor, 1968-; Am Coun Teachers Fa, 1975-; Am Asn Teachers Span & Port, 1980-, workshop chair, 1991; Col Lang Asn, 1985-, const comm, 1994-95; Phi Delta Kappa Educ Frat, 1987-; Jack & Jill Am Inc, rec sec, pres, regional dir, nat ed, nat pres, 1998-2000; Nat Coun Negro Women; Cafriz Found. **Home Addr:** 3315 Dunwood Crossing Dr, Bowie, MD 20721, **Home Phone:** (240)599-8366. **Business Addr:** Director, Bowie State University, 14000 Jericho Pk Rd, Bowie, MD 20715, **Business Phone:** (301)860-4000.

**MILLER, JACQUELINE ELIZABETH**
Executive, library administrator, educator. **Personal:** Born Apr 15, 1935, New York, NY; daughter of Lynward Roosevelt and Sarah Ellen Grevious Winslow (deceased); children: Percy Scott. **Educ:** Morgan State Col, BA, 1957; Pratt Inst, MLS, 1960. **Career:** Educator, library administrator (retired); Brooklyn Pub Libr, 1957-68; New Rochelle Pub Libr, head exten serv, 1969-70; Yonkers Pub Libr, br admin, 1970-75, dir, 1975-96; Queens Col, NY, adj prof, 1989-90. **Orgs:** Comnr Comn State-wide Libr Develop, 1980; Yonkers Black Women's Polit Caucus, 1987; NYS Govs CMS Libr, 1990-91; pres, bd, Literacy Vols Westchester County, 1991-92; mem fair campaign practices com, LWV, 1996; Rotary Yonkers; Numerous other nat, state, county prof libr org. **Honors/Awds:** Honored Citizen of Yonkers, Church Our Saviour, 1980; Annual Award West County Club, Nat Asn Negro Bus & Prof Womens Clubs, 1981; Mae Morgan Robinson Award, 1992; Womens Equality Day Award, 1992. **Home Addr:** 410 Benedict Ave Apt 4H, Tarrytown, NY 10591-4913, **Home Phone:** (914)631-9381.

**MILLER, JAMES**
Banker. **Educ:** E Tenn State Univ, BS; Univ Tenn, MBA. **Career:** First Tenn Bank, vice chmn, vpres com banking, currently. **Orgs:** Pres, 100 Black Men Chattanooga; Chattanooga African Am Chamber; chmn, Greater Chattanooga Sports & Events Comn; vice chmn, Sports Comt, chmn. **Honors/Awds:** Eagle Scout Award, 1968; Highest District Award, Boy Scouts Am Scout Reach Comt. **Home Addr:** 4919 Shoreline Dr, Chattanooga, TN 37416. **Business Addr:** Vice President, First Tennessee Bank, 701 Mkt St Suite 1128, Chattanooga, TN 37402, **Business Phone:** (423)757-4011.

**MILLER, JAMES S.**
Educator. **Personal:** Born Feb 20, 1923, Gastonia, NC; married Anne E Grier. **Educ:** Howard Univ, BS, 1949; A&T State Univ, MS, 1956; Appalachian State Univ; Univ NC, Exten Prog. **Career:** Educator (retired); CF Gingles Elem Sch, prin, 1952-70; Arlington Elem Sch, prin, 1970-88. **Orgs:** Nat Educ Asn; NC Asn Educrs; Gaston Co Educ Asn; Elder Loves Chapel Press; Omega Psi Phi Frat; treas, Local Chap; treas, Gaston Co Prin Asn; Excelsior Credit Union; Gastopn Boys Club; Gaston Co Red Cross; Gaston Co Bicentennial; Catherine's House; Community Share Food Prog; Mayors Task Force Against Crime; Presbytery Western NC Comt Ministry; comnr, Gen Assembly Witicka Kans, 1994. **Home Addr:** 202 Cedar St, Belmont, NC 28012-3004, **Home Phone:** (704)825-8860.

**MILLER, JAMIR MALIK**
Football player, social worker. **Personal:** Born Nov 19, 1973, Philadelphia, PA; son of John and Rhonda Hardy; married Racquel; children: Ashlynn & Amara. **Educ:** Univ Calif, Los Angeles. **Career:** Football player (retired); Ariz Cardinals, 1994, right linebacker, 1995-96, left linebacker, 1997-98; Cleveland Browns, linebacker, 1999-2002, left outside linebacker, 1999, defensive end, 2001. **Orgs:** Founder, Jamir Miller Foundn. **Special Achievements:** NFL Blitz 2003, 2002. **Business Addr:** Founder, Jamir Miller Foundation, Hercules, CA 94547-0000, **Business Phone:** (510)245-7950.

**MILLER, DR. JEANNE-MARIE ANDERSON**
Educator, writer, association executive. **Personal:** Born Feb 18, 1937, Washington, DC; daughter of William (deceased) and Patricia Ann Wood; married Warren Lascar; children: Patrick. **Educ:** Howard Univ, BA, 1959, MA, 1963, PhD, 1976. **Career:** Howard Univ, instr, Eng, 1963-76, Inst Arts & Humanities, asst dir, 1973-75, Acad planning off vpres acad affairs, asst, 1976-90, Dept Eng, from grad asst prof to grad prof, 1977-97, prof emer, Eng, 1997-; Auth: "The Howard University Institute for the Arts and the Humanities", 1974, "Images of black women in plays by black playwrights", 1977. **Orgs:** Adv bd, WETA-TV Ed prog, Black Folklore, 1976-77; Ed Black Theatre Bull Am Theatre Assoc, 1977-86; exec coun, Black Theatre Prog, Am Theatre Assoc, 1977-86; proposal reviewer Nat Endowment Humanities, 1979-; Friends JF Kennedy Ctr Performing Arts, Am Theatre & Drama Soc, Asn Theatre Higher Edu; Am Assoc Univ Women, Am Civil Liberites Union, Am Film Inst; assoc mem, Arena Stage, Wash Performing Arts Soc, Langston Hughes Soc, Zora Neale Hurston Soc, Eugene O'Neill Mem Theatre Ctr, Am Soc Bus & Exec Women; assoc, Art Inst Chicago, Boston Mus Fine Arts, Studio Mus Harlem, Nat Mus Women Arts; Metrop Mus Art, Corcoran Gallery Art, Smithsonian Inst, Wash Performings Arts Soc, Wash Opera Guild, World Affairs Coun Wash DC, Drama League New York, Mod Lang Assoc, Am Studies Assoc, Col Lang Assoc, Nat Coun Teachers Eng, Am Assoc Higher Educ; Nat Women's Studies Assoc; Hist Soc Wash, DC, DC Preserv League, Ibsen, SocAm, Nat Trust Hist Preserv, Folger Shakespeare Libr; Shakespeare Theatre; Metrop Opera Guild; Winterthur Guild. **Honors/Awds:** Adv Study Fel Ford Found, 1970-72; Fel So Fel Fund, 1972-74; Grantee, Am Coun Learned Societies, 1978-79; Grantee Nat Endowment for the Humanities, 1981-84; Grantee, Howard Univ Fac Res Fund, 1975-76, 1994-95, 1996-97; PiLambda Theta Nat Honor & Prof Asn Educ, 1987. **Special Achievements:** Edited book From Realism to Ritual: Form & Style in Black Theatre, 1983; The Journal of Negro History, Vol. 57, No. 4, 429-431, Oct., 1972;

Published over 80 articles in various books, journals & magazines. **Home Addr:** 504 24th St NE, Washington, DC 20002-4818, **Home Phone:** (202)388-5038. **Business Addr:** Professor Emerita, Howard University, 2400 6th St NW, Washington, DC 20059-0002, **Business Phone:** (202)806-6730.

### MILLER, JONES SANDY (SANDRA MILLER JONES)

Association executive, founder (originator), publisher. **Personal:** Born Aug 6, 1946, Winston Salem, NC; married Lafayette; children: Bridgette. **Educ:** Northwestern Univ BA, sociol, 1968; Kellogg Sch Mgt, MBA, 1971. **Career:** Quaker Oats Co, mkt mgr, 1978; Segmented Mkt Serv Inc, founder, exec partners & chmn, 1978-; Urban Call, publishers, founded, Health Ins Solutions, 2013; Wake Forest Univ, adj prof mkt. **Orgs:** Nat Black MBA Asn; Chicago Minority Purchasing Coun; bus initiative League Black Women Chicago; bd chair, Jack & Jill Am Found; Family Serv Inc; Summit Sch Winston-Salem; bd chair, Winston-Salem YWCA; Youth Active, Goler Memorial AME Zion Church Winston-Salem; Alpha Kappa Alpha Sorority. **Special Achievements:** First African American woman manager. **Business Addr:** Founder, Chairman, Segmented Marketing Services Inc, 4265 Brownsboro Rd Suite 225, Winston Salem, NC 27106-3425, **Business Phone:** (336)759-7477.

### MILLER, JOSEPH HERMAN, JR.

Insurance executive, chief executive officer, president (organization). **Personal:** Born Mar 5, 1930, Port Gibson, MS; married Cleo L Baines; children: Darryl, Stephen, Carrington, Vicki & Scott. **Educ:** Talladega Col, AB, 1950; Howard Univ, JD, 1957. **Career:** Miller Funeral Homes Inc, pres, 1972-; Freedom Nat Ins Co, pres, 1976-; Nat Inst Assoc, pres, 1976-; Reliable Life Ins Co, pres & chief exec officer, currently. **Orgs:** Bd dir, Monroe LA C C, 1976. **Special Achievements:** Black Enterprise's list of Top Insurance Companies, ranked no 10, 1999. **Home Addr:** PO Box 1157, Monroe, LA 71210, **Home Phone:** (318)323-5028. **Business Addr:** President, Reliable Life Insurance Co, 2932 Renwick St, Monroe, LA 71210, **Business Phone:** (318)387-1000.

### MILLER, JUANITA ELIZABETH JACKSON. See Obituaries Section.

### MILLER, KEVIN

Media executive, association executive, army officer. **Personal:** Born Dec 17, 1957, St. Louis, MO; son of Leroy A and Martha E; married Alyson; children: Chase T & Kathryn. **Educ:** US Mil Acad-Westpoint, BS, engineering, 1979. **Career:** Leo Burnett Usa, acct exec, 1986-89; Coca Cola Usa, mkt mgr, 1989-91; Hal Riney & Partners, vpres mgt supvr, 1991-94; Pizza Hut Inc, vpres nat mkt, 1994-98; ABC Radio Networks, sr vpres bus develop & chief mkt officer, 1998-2009; Citadel Media, chief internet officer, 2009; Kmmp Media Group Llc, pres, 2009-16; Natural Grocers by Vitamin Cottage, vpres mktg, 2016-. **Orgs:** USMA Asn Grad, 1979-; Exec Leadership Coun, 2001; Advert Awards Comt judge, Asn Nat Advertisers; bd mkt & commun comt mem, Nat Urban League. **Honors/Awds:** Corporate Executive of the Year, Am Diabetes Asn, 2003. **Home Addr:** 2721 Shoal Creek Cir, Plano, TX 75093, **Home Phone:** (972)306-2120. **Business Addr:** Vice President of Marketing, Natural Grocers by Vitamin Cottage, 12612 W Alameda Pkwy, Lakewood, CO 80228, **Business Phone:** (303)986-5700.

### MILLER, REV. KEVIN D.

Manager, clergy. **Personal:** Born Apr 9, 1966, New York, NY; son of Lawrence and Viera McAfee; married Myra Y. **Educ:** Syracuse Univ, Syracuse, NY, tv prod, 1988; Fordham Univ, Grad Sch Arts & Sci, MA, lib Studies, 1994; Drew Theol Sch, Madison, NJ, divinity degree, DMIN. **Career:** Wash Arms, Syracuse, NY, work study, 1984-87; Salt City Productions, Syracuse, NY, producer, 1985-89; Roberto Clemente Pk, Bronx, NY, filter room, summer, 1987; Campus Convenience, Syracuse, NY, work study, 1987-88; Time Warner Cable, assoc producer, 1988-89, access & com use mgr, 1989-93; Paragon Cable Manhattan, New York, NY, assoc producer & producer, 1988-89, access mgr, 1989-92, com use mgr, 1992-93; Expressive People Prod, New York, NY, producer, 1992-94-; ABC Sports, prod assoc, 1994-95, ABC Sports Div, graphic prod asst, 1995-98, ESPN, assoc producer, 1998-2001, pdir admis; Chosen Serv Enterprises, co-founder, 2001-; Drew Theol Sch, Theol Admis, Co-Founder, dir, 2003-; Bethel African Methodist Episcopal Church, pastor, 2005-10; Carter Community AME Church, pastor, 2010-. **Orgs:** Vpres, Phi Beta Sigma Fraternity Inc,1985-, comt chairperson, 1990-; Black Filmmakers Found, 1989-; liason, Harlem Week Inc, Uptown Chamber Com, 1990-; Nat Acad Cable Programming, 1990-; Prince Hall FM & AM, 1990-; bd mem, Am Cancer Soc, NYC, 1991-; bd mem, Morristown Community Develop Corp; Asn Doctor Ministry Educ. **Honors/Awds:** Sigma Man of the Year, Phi Beta Sigma-Theta Xi, 1985; Brotherhood Award, Theta Xi Chap, 1988; President's Award, Nat Pan-Hellenic Coun, 1988; Service Award, Beta Psi Sigma Chap, 1989. **Home Addr:** 240 Nagle Ave, New York, NY 10034, **Home Phone:** (212)569-2241. **Business Addr:** Pastor, Bethel African Methodist Episcopal Church, 140 Plane St, Boonton, NJ 07005, **Business Phone:** (973)334-3142.

### MILLER, DR. LAMAR PERRY

Educator. **Personal:** Born Sep 1, 1925, Ypsilanti, MI; married Deborah F Fox; children: LaMar Jr & Arianne E. **Educ:** Eastern Mich Univ, BA, 1954; Univ Mich, MA, 1958, EdS, 1965, PhD, 1968. **Career:** New York Univ, Metrop Ctr Urban Educ, founder, 1978-, exec dir, currently, sec ed & prof metro studies present, Inst Afro-Am Affairs, educ res dir, prof educ, Sec Educ Dept, Steinhardt Distinguished Fel, chair; Inst Teachers Disad Youth, dir; Educ Ypsilani MI, asso prof; Eng Dept Willow Run, chmn; dir forensic activ; Touro Col, fac, 2006-, Lander Ctr Educ Res, founding dir, Grad Sch Educ, dean emer, currently; U.S. Dept Educ, chief architect & dir. Publications: "Equality of education opportunity a handbook for research", 1974; "The testing of black students a symposium", 1974; "education for an open society", 1974. **Orgs:** Chief consult, Nat Inst Educ Dept HEW; dir, Teachers Corps; ons Union Carbide Corp; NY Urban League; secy, Div G Am Educ Res Asn, 1972-74; edbd, NY Univ Quart, 1972-75; Nat Alliance Black Sch Educ, 1975-; publ comn AsnSuper & Curric Devel, 1975-77; asso ed, Am Educ Res Jour AERA. 1975-78. **Home Addr:** 245 E 93rd St Apt 12G, New York, NY 10128-3956, **Home Phone:** (212)876-2048. **Business Addr:** Dean Emeritus, Touro College, 43 W 23 St, New York, NY 10010, **Business Phone:** (212)463-0400.

### MILLER, LAWRENCE A., JR.

Government official, manager, educator. **Personal:** Born Aug 17, 1951, Bronx, NY; son of Lawrence A and Adella B Williams King; married Shirley; children: Keisha Yvette & Dahra Ayanna. **Educ:** York Col, BA, pub admin, 1974; Brooklyn Col, MA, polit sci & govt, 1989; Union Inst & Univ, PhD, polit sci & pub policy, 2000. **Career:** Dept Juv Justice, juv counr, 1973-76; New York Youth Brd, eval consult, 1976-79; NY Div Youth, prog mgt specialist, spec projs coord, 1980-89; New York Health Hosp Corp, dir equal employ opportunity & affirmative action, 1989-94; Suffolk County Human Rights Comn, exec dir, 1994; MTA/NYC Transit, vpres, 1997-98; Elmcor Youth & Adult Activ Inc, exec dir, 1998-2006; City Sarasota, interim asst city mgr, 2006-08; City Arcadia, city adminr, 2010-12; St Petersburg Col, adj prof, 2010-; Keiser Univ, polit sci instr, 2012-. **Orgs:** Bd mem, Community Sch Brd 28, 1983-86; Comm Planning Brd 12, 1983-; Rochdale Village Inc, 1985-; vpres, Fred Wilson Regular Dem Club, 1987; chmn brd, Youth Advocates Edn & Sports, 1987; exec dir, Community Advocates Better Living Environ, 1989; Nat Asn Advan Colored People; chmn, Sarasota City Parks Found, 2007-. **Honors/Awds:** Certificate of Appreciation, New York City Off Serv Cord, 1975; Outstanding Young Men America, US Jaycees, 1980; Outstanding Service Award, New York State Div Youth, 1981; Community Service Award, Elmcor Youth & Adult Activites, 1984; Certificate of Apppreciation, Brd Edn New York City, 1986; Chancellor's Award Outstanding Alumni, 1986; Outstanding Community Service Award, York Col, 1986; Community Service Award, Nat Asn Negro Bus & Prof Women's Club, 1987; Honor Service Award, Asn Black Educators New York, 1988; Columnist, New York Voice Newspaper, 1988; Central Islip Branch, Community Service Award, Nat Asn Advan Colored People, 1997. **Special Achievements:** Producer/Host, Community Affairs Talk Show, Radio 91.5 FM & Cable TV, 1986& 1989; Producer and host of radio program WNYE Comm Trustees Report for the Borough of Manhattan. **Home Addr:** 12 Barrington Dr, Jamaica, NY 11434, **Home Phone:** (718)712-5371. **Business Addr:** Political Science Instructor, Keiser University, 1500 NW 49th St, Ft. Lauderdale, FL 33309, **Business Phone:** (954)776-4456.

### MILLER, LAWRENCE ANTHONY (ANTHONY MILLER)

Football player. **Personal:** Born Apr 15, 1965, Los Angeles, CA. **Educ:** San Diego State Univ, Pasadena City Col; Univ Tenn. **Career:** Football player (retired); San Diego Chargers, wide receiver, 1988-93; Denver Broncos, wide receiver, 1994-96, free agt, 1994; Dallas Cowboys, wide receiver, 1997. **Honors/Awds:** Pro Bowl, 1989-90, 1992-93, 1995. **Special Achievements:** Film: 1988 NFL Draft, 1988. **Home Addr:** 300 Esplanade Dr Suite 1760, Oxnard, CA 93030.

### MILLER, LOREN, JR.

Judge. **Personal:** Born Mar 7, 1937, Los Angeles, CA; married Gwen Allain; children: Pamela Allain, Michael, Stephanie Allain, Robin, Nina & Gregory Allain. **Educ:** Univ Ore, BS, 1960; Loyola Law Sch Los Angeles, LLB, 1962. **Career:** Judge (retired); State Calif, Dept Justice, dep atty gen, 1962-69; McLaren, Miller & Monet, partner, 1969-73; Western Ctr Law & Poverty, dir litigation, 1969-70; Model Neighbor Legal Prog, exec dir, 1972-73; Pac Lighting Corp, asst gen coun, 1973-75; Los Angeles Munic Ct, judge, 1975-77; Super Ct La County, super ct judge, 1977-96. **Orgs:** Calif State Senate, 1973-75; exe comt, Los Angeles County Super Ct, 1993-94. **Home Addr:** 836 S Ridgeley Dr, Los Angeles, CA 90036-4727, **Home Phone:** (323)935-0184.

### MILLER, LORRAINE C.

Government official. **Personal:** Born Ft. Worth, TX; daughter of Lena Marie and Johnnie. **Educ:** N Tex State Univ, BA, polit sci, 1975; Georgetown Sch Bus, MA. **Career:** White House, dep asst pres legis affairs, White House Community Empowerment Bd, 1994-96; Am Fed Teachers, lobbyist; Speaker Jim Wright, D-Texas, aide; Speaker Tom Foley, D-Wash, aide; John Lewis, D-Ga, aide; US House Minority Leader Pelosi's Off, sr advisor; Wash D.C. chap NAACP, pres, 2004, Interim Pres & chief exec officer, 2013; Intergovernmental Rels, sr advisor, dir; US House Reps, clerk, 2007-. **Orgs:** Pres, bd dir, Nat Asn Advan Colored People, Wash, 2004-; Shiloh Baptist Church Wash; found bd dir, Shiloh's Henry C Gregory Family Life Ctr; Fed Communication Comn; Fed Trade Comn; bd dir, Nat Asn Advan Colored People, 2008. **Special Achievements:** First African-American clerk of the U.S; First African American to serve as an official of the United States House of Representatives. **Business Addr:** Clerk, US House of Representatives, Office of the Clerk, Washington, DC 20515-6601, **Business Phone:** (202)225-7000.

### MILLER, LOUISE T.

Educator. **Personal:** Born Mar 2, 1919. **Educ:** Univ Mich, BS, 1949; Syracuse Univ, MS, 1951; Yale Univ, MPH, 1961; Univ RI, PhD, 1970. **Career:** Syracuse Univ, res asst, 1951-60; Univ RI, res asst, 1962-63, res assoc animal pathol, 1963-72; Spelman Col, assoc prof biol, 1973-. **Orgs:** Instr educ, 900 Bio Workshop Elem Sch Teachers, 1965-66, 1968, 1972; Ad Hoc Comn Disabled Stud, 1968-69; Coun Spec Prog Talent, 1970. **Honors/Awds:** USPHS Trainee Grant Yale Univ, 1960-61. **Home Addr:** 307 Adair St Apt H2, Decatur, GA 30030.

### MILLER, DR. M. SAMMYE

Educator, administrator. **Personal:** Born Feb 23, 1947, Philadelphia, PA; son of Herman S and Sammye Elizabeth Adams; married Gloria J. **Educ:** Del State Univ, BA, hist, 1968; Trinity Univ, WA, MAT, hist, 1970; Cath Univ Am, PhD, legal hist, 1977; Stanford Univ, post-doctoral study, const law & hist. **Career:** Negro Hist Bull, ed; Learned Soc, guest lectr; Fed Agencies, guest lectr; Community Orgn, guest lectr; Nat Endowment Humanities, humanist admin & policy analyst, 1978-80; Asn Study Afro-Am Life & Hist Inc, exec dir, 1983-84; Bowie State Univ, dept chmn & prof hist, dean sch arts & sci & spec asst provost, currently. **Orgs:** Southern Hist Asn; Org Am Historian; Am Hist Asn; life mem, Kappa Alpha Psi Fraternity; Phi Alpha Theta Int; Hon Soc Hist; Asn Study African Am Life & Hist; Knights Columbus fel 1970; Penfield fel Bd trustee Scholar, Cath Univ; Nat Asn Equal Opportunity Higher Educ; post doc fel Stanford Univ, 1983; Walter J Leonard fel Ctr Socio-Legal Studies, Wolfson Col, Oxford Univ. **Home Addr:** 7709 Wingate Dr, Glenn Dale, MD 20769. **Business Addr:** Professor of History, Chairman, Bowie State University, 14000 Jericho Pk Rd, Bowie, MD 20715, **Business Phone:** (301)860-3664.

### MILLER, DR. MAPOSURE T.

Dentist. **Personal:** Born Jul 17, 1934, Wadesboro, NC; son of Wade H and Mary R; married Bobbie J Grubbs; children: Teresa, Vickie & Gail E. **Educ:** Bluefield State Col, BS, 1956; WV Univ Sch Dent, DDS, 1965. **Career:** Dr MT Miller Inc, pres, currently; pvt pract, dentist, currently. **Orgs:** Beta Kappa Chi hon soc, 1955-56; Nat Dent Asn; Am Dent Asn; Buckeye State Dent Asn; Ohio State Dent Asn; Cleveland Dent Soc; pres, Forest City Dent Study Club, 1975-76; sec-treas, Lee rd Dent Centres Inc; bd trustee, Olivet Inst Bapt Ch; chmn, Health & Welfare E Cleveland Bus Men Asn; Urban League; Nat Asn Advan Colored People; bd mem, Health Legacy Cleveland. **Honors/Awds:** Provincial Man of the Year, Kappa Alpha Psi, 1956. **Home Addr:** 22076 Calverton Rd, Shaker Heights, OH 44122-2020. **Business Addr:** Dentist, 13944 Euclid Ave Suite 206, East Cleveland, OH 44112-3832, **Business Phone:** (216)761-0500.

### MILLER, DR. MARGARET ELIZABETH BATTLE

Executive. **Personal:** Born Nov 19, 1934, Chapel Hill, NC; daughter of Johnnie M Battle and Ivy Battle; children: Lisa, Monica & William II. **Educ:** NC Cent Univ, AB, 1955, JD, 1982; Univ NC, MSLS, 1961. **Career:** Highland Jr & Sr HS, librn, 1955-59; Swannee River Jr Col, librn, 1959-66; Borgess Med Ctr, librn, 1968-79; Whitaker Sch, DHR adminr II, 1981-90; MLM Serv, pres, 1986-89; Miller's ARTrium, owner, 1989-. **Orgs:** Asst ed, Commnty Courier Newspaper, 1971-73; columnist, Kalamazoo Gazette Newspaper, 1973-75; comnr, Kalamazoo Co Bd Commns, 1975-78; chmn, Orange Co Rainbow Coalition Educ Comm, 1984-85; Nat Asn Advan Colored People; Am Re-Educ Asn. **Honors/Awds:** Newspaper Fund Fellowship, 1965; US HEW Fellowship, 1967; recep Mary MBethune Award, Delta Sigma Theta Sor, 1978; Liberty Bell Award, 1978. **Home Addr:** 515 Hillsborough St, Chapel Hill, NC 27514. **Business Addr:** Owner, Millers ARTrium, PO Box 413, Chapel Hill, NC 27514.

### MILLER, DR. MARGARET GREER

School administrator. **Personal:** Born Jan 25, 1934, Indianapolis, IN; married Charles E; children: Gregory Charles & Jennifer Charmaine. **Educ:** Ind State Univ, BS, music & speech, 1955, MS, speech ther & music, 1965; Univ Fla, except child educ, emotional dis & speech path, 1978. **Career:** School administrator (retired), consultant; Orange County Pub Schs, speech clinician, 1957-70, asst supt planning, res & testing, 1981-83, assoc supt for personnel & off serv, 1983; Univ Cent Fla, faculty, asst prof, 1971-81, assoc prof except educ, 1987, dir teacher educ ctr & extended studies, 1989-91, dir off multicultural issues, 1991-93, asst dean undergrad progs & cline experiences, 1993-2002, adj prof. **Orgs:** Alpha Kappa Alpha Sorority; Am Speech & Hearing Asn; Am Soc Training & Develop; Fla Asn Sch Admin, Coun Except C; Nat Sorority Phi Delta Kappa; Asn C Learing Disabilities; Ment Health Asn; Asn Supervised Curric & Develop; Phi Delta Kappa; Am Educ Res Asn, Am Asn Sch Personnel Admin; Fla Asn Sch Personnel Admin; comn secy, Orange County Adv Comn Bd Educ; comt mem, Walt Disney Community Awards, 1990; Howard Phillips Fund Eval Comt, 1986-90, bd mem, 1991-; pres, Fla Asn Staff Develop, 1994-95; Orlando Leadership Coun; bd dir, Dr P Phillips Found; bd dir, Dr Phillips Inc; Fund Distrib Comt Heart, Fla United Way, Cent Fla Presbyterys Comn, Ministry, Orlando Leadership Coun. **Honors/Awds:** Dr Emory O Jackson Memorial Journalism Award, S Atlantic Regional Conf, Alpha Kappa Alpha Sorority, 1983; Univ Cent Fla, Pioneer Award, First Minority Full Time Instr & Outstanding Leadership, 1985, Distinguished Black Educator, 1991-94; State Health, Rehabilitation Service Award for Outstanding Work in Child Abuse, 1987; Certificate of Appreciation for Outstanding Work and Contributions to the Community and State, Gov Robert Graham, 1987; Summit Award, Pioneering Work in Community Services & Volunteerism, Women's Resource Ctr, 1991; I Dream a World Community Award, Outstanding Pioneer in Education & the Arts, County Commission & Orlando Hist Soc, 1992; Outstanding Black Achiever, 1996; Central Florida Women's Resource Center's 20th Anniversary Summit Awards; Summit Award, Cent Fla Women's Resource Ctr; Distinguished Citizen Award, Onyx mag, 2011. **Special Achievements:** Published "Multicultural teaching modules: A source of multicultural experiences for pre-school through high school curriculum", Col Educ, Univ Cent Fla, 1992. **Home Addr:** 10993 Piping Rock Cir, Orlando, FL 32817-2946, **Home Phone:** (407)384-6747. **Business Addr:** Board Director, Dr P Phillips Foundation, 7400 Dr Phillips Blvd, Orlando, FL 32819-5146, **Business Phone:** (407)422-6105.

### MILLER, MARQUIS DAVID

School administrator, executive director. **Personal:** Born Jan 22, 1959, Charleston, WV; son of Fredericka Inez Sherrill and Manuel Thurston; married Jennifer Jean Kee; children: Janae Latise. **Educ:** Ohio State Univ, BA, social & behav sci, 1981. **Career:** Buckeye Fed Savings & Loan, proj specialist, 1981-83; Continental Off, acct exec, 1983-90; Karlsberger Co, bus develop rep, 1990-91; Ohio State Univ, assoc dir, Corp Found, 1991-95, asst vpres, 1995-97; UNCF, nat dir corp gifts, 1994-98, vpres, field opers, 1997-2001, vpres, corp scholars prog, 2001-02; Chicago Urban League, External Affairs, vpres, 2002-05; Chicago State Univ Found, exec dir, 2005-08; Chicago State Univ, interim vpres instnl advan, 2006-08; SBLI Mutual Life Ins Co, vpres bus develop, 2008-10; Nat Minority Supplier Develop Coun, vpres field opers, 2011-; Inst Adv, interim vpres, currently; Corp Scholars Prog United Negro Col Fund, vpres. **Orgs:** Ohio State Univ Alumni Asn, 1981-; OH State Univ Black Alumni Soc, 1987-; Varsity "O", 1981-; bd mem, Columbus Focus Comt, 1989-91; Omega Psi Phi Fraternity, 1990-; bd mem, Prevent Blindness Ohio, 1995-97; bd mem, Mercy Housing Lakefront, 2002-06; assoc mem, Nat Black MBA Asn, 2003-05; bd mem, GRANDFamilies Prog Chicago, 2004-13; bd mem, Trinity United Church Christ, 2004-11; chicago chap bd mem, Asn Fundraising Professionals, 2005-08; leaders coun, Chicago United,

2005-08; chicago chap mem, Urban Financial Serv Coalition, 2008-10; nat bd mem, Nat African Am Ins Asn, 2009-10; bd trustee, Mus Contemp Art Chicago, 2010-; Nat Urban Fellows, Am's Leaders Chg Partic, 2010-11; diversity adv bd, Uhlich Childrens Advantage Network, 2011-; bd mem, Int Soc Hypertension Blacks, 2011-12; co-chair, diversity 2.0 taskforce, Mus Contemp Art Chicago, 2014-; bd dir, Asn Fundraising Profs Chicago Chap; co-chair, Diversity & Fels Comt; Philanthropy Day Luncheon Comt; Trinity Higher Educ Corp; Mus Contemp Art; Nat Asn Securities Professionals; Assoc Fundraising Officers Inc; Asn Fundraising Professionals; United Negro Col Fund; City Club Chicago; Nat Alliance Mkt Developers. **Honors/Awds:** Ten Outstanding Young Citizens Award, Columbus Jaycees, 1987. **Home Addr:** 1200 N Veith St Suite 819, Arlington, VA 22201, **Home Phone:** (703)527-4465. **Business Addr:** Vice President of Field Operations, National Minority Supplier Development Council, 1359 Broadway 10th Fl Suite 1000, New York, NY 10018, **Business Phone:** (212)944-2430.

### MILLER, MATTIE SHERRYL

School administrator, association executive. **Personal:** Born Jun 19, 1933, Adams, TN; daughter of George Washington and Luetta Carney Washington; married William Edward; children: Kori Edwin. **Educ:** Tuskegee Inst, Ala, BS, 1955; Ind Univ, MS, 1965, reading specialist, 1970; Univ Evansville, coun & admin cert, 1975. **Career:** School administrator (retired); Evansville-Vanderburgh Sch Corp, teacher, 1959-71, reading clinician, 1971-72, proj dir right read, 1972-75, guid counr, 1975-85; Harper Sch, prin, 1985; Univ Evansville, adj instr, 1967; Ind Univ, practicum supvr, 1970-73; Vincennes Univ, field couns-upward bound, 1975-77; Ball State Univ, Muncie, Ind, instr; Ivy Tech Community Col, adj instr eng. **Orgs:** Bd dir, Channel 9 WNIN, 1975-; sec bd dir, Leadership, Evansville, 1976-; bd dir & pres, Ind State Teachers Asn & Evansville Teachers Asn; Rotary Club Am, 1988; dir, Nat Educ Asn; bd mem, Univ Southern Ind; pres, Vanderburgh Co Retired Educr chap; bd chair, US Selective Serv Draft Appeals Bd Dist 43; Lilly Endowment Leadership Educ Fel. **Honors/Awds:** Woman of the Year in education, Evansville YWCA Leadership Award, 1975; staff rep 8th dist Congressional Appointment, 1975-78; Black woman of the Year in education, Evansville Comn Action Award, 1978; Rep W African Countries, 1984; Rep France Sec Ed Schs, 1985; LLD, University Southern Ind, 2006; Sagamore of the Wabash Award. **Special Achievements:** Mattie Miller was the first African woman teacher at Evansville Harper Elementary School in 1960. **Home Addr:** 517 S Boeke Rd, Evansville, IN 47714-1617, **Home Phone:** (812)477-7927. **Business Addr:** President, Indiana State Teachers Association, 150 W Mkt St Suite 900, Indianapolis, IN 46204, **Business Phone:** (317)263-3400.

### MILLER, MELVIN ALLEN

Executive director, public relations executive, manager. **Personal:** Born Nov 24, 1950, Hattiesburg, MS; married Alfredia Dampier. **Educ:** Univ So Miss, BS, 1972; Jackson State Univ, MS, 1978. **Career:** Jackson Plant DeSoto Inc, commun asst, 1975-76; Jackson State Univ, staff writer, 1976-77, asst to dir pub info, 1977, actg dir pub info, 1977-78, dir pub info, 1978-86, dir develop, 1987; W Jackson Community Develop Corp, exec dir, 2004. **Orgs:** Dean's list scholar, Univ So Miss, 1970-72; Delta Omicron Hon Soc, Univ Miss, 1972; trustee, New Hope Baptist Church, Jackson, 1978-, bus mgr; Phi Kappa Phi Natl Hon Soc, Jackson State Univ, 1978; pres, Coll Pub Rels Asn Miss, 1979-80; 1st vpres, Cystic Fibrosis Found, Miss Chap, 1980; unit commr, Boy Scouts Am, 1980; bd mem, Jackson Chap March Dimes. **Home Addr:** 500 Heatherstone Ct, Ridgeland, MS 39157-2908, **Home Phone:** (601)605-3888. **Business Addr:** Executive Director, West Jackson Community Development Corp, 1060 Jorhn R Lynch St, Jackson, MS 39217, **Business Phone:** (601)352-6993.

### MILLER, MELVIN B.

Television journalist, executive. **Personal:** Born Jul 22, 1934, Boston, MA; son of Louis C and Jennie; married Mildred; children: Louis C, Peter W & Edward G. **Educ:** Harvard Col, BA, 1956; Columbia Law Sch, JD, 1964. **Career:** US Justice Dept, Dist Massachusetts, asst US atty, 1965-66; Bay State Banner, founder, publ & ed, 1965-; Boston Bank Com, dir; Unity Bank & Trust Co, conservator, 1973-77; WHDH-TV Inc, vpres & gen coun, 1982-93; Fitch Miller & Tourse, founding partner, 1981-91; OneUnited Bank, bd dir, currently. **Orgs:** Trustee, Boston Univ, Milton Acad; trustee, Wang Ctr; New Eng Conserv Music; James Jackson Putnam C's Ctr; Family Serv Asn Greater Boston; Family Couns & Guid Ctr; dir, Greater Boston C C; dir, Mass Counc Crime & Correction; chmn, Boston Comn Media Com; Overseers Harvard Univ; Mass Small Bus Adv Coun; NE Reg Area One Exec Com BSA; exec bd, Minority Bus Opportunity Comn; trustee, Huntington Theatre Co; trustee, Boston Med Ctr; dir, US SAfrica Leadership Exchange Prog. **Home Addr:** 74 Harold St, Boston, MA 02119-1625, **Home Phone:** (617)442-1296. **Business Addr:** Board of Director, OneUnited Bank, 133 Federal St, Boston, MA 02110, **Business Phone:** (617)457-4400.

### MILLER, MITZI

Writer, publishing executive. **Educ:** Fla Agr & Mech Univ, BA, Eng, 1997. **Career:** CMP Media, sales & mkt asst.; "Honey", Mag, ed internship, entertainment ed, 2000-03; "Jane", mag, assoc ed, 2003-05; "Essence", Mag, contrib writer; freelance writer for "Elle" (U.K.), "Vibe" & "Upscale", 2007-11; My Mother's Child Productions, chief exec officer, pres, 2005-; "Jet", Mag, ed-in-chief, 2011; EBONY Mag, ed-in-chief, 2014. **Orgs:** Bd, Black Girls Rock Inc. **Special Achievements:** Author of "The Angry Black Woman's Guide to Life," Plume/Dutton (April 2004); "The Vow," Harper Collins (October 2005); "Hotlanta," Scholastic (April 2008).

### MILLER, NATE (NATHAN UDELL MILLER)

Football player. **Personal:** Born Oct 8, 1971, Tuscaloosa, AL. **Educ:** La State Univ, gen bus. **Career:** Offensive lineman, 1995-99; Atlanta Falcons, free agt, 1995, tackle, 1997, 1998; Frankfurt Galaxy, 1997; New York Giants, 1998-99; Los Angeles Xtreme, 2001. **Special Achievements:** Poetry: "Heart of a Man" & "love".

### MILLER, NORMA ADELE

Dancer, writer. **Personal:** Born Dec 2, 1919, New York, NY; daughter of Alma and Norman. **Career:** Jr high sch, 1932; Whitey's group, 1938; Al Minns, 1985; Frankie Manning, 2009. Movies: Lindy Hop; A Day at the Races, 1937; Hellzapoppin, 1941; Malcolm X, 1992; Dancer, writer, auth, choreographer, actor, "Queen of Swing", comedian, currently. **Orgs:** Soc Singers; Whiteys Lindy Hoppers. **Home Addr:** 4325 Bruce, Las Vegas, NV 89119, **Home Phone:** (702)734-9438. **Business Addr:** Dancer, Author, Carsey-Werner Co, 4024 Radford Ave, Studio City, CA 91604, **Business Phone:** (818)655-5598.

### MILLER, OLIVER J.

Basketball player. **Personal:** Born Apr 6, 1970, Ft. Worth, TX; children: Xavier & Amman. **Educ:** Univ Ark, attended 1992. **Career:** Basketball player (retired); Phoenix Suns, ctr, 1992-94, 1999-2000; Detroit Pistons, power forward, 1994-95; Toronto Raptors, power forward, 1995-96, 1997-98; Dallas Mavericks, ctr, 1996-97; Iraklio, Greece, 1998-99; Sacramento Kings, ctr, 1999; Harlem Globetrotters, 2000-01; Znicz Pruszkow, Poland, 2000-01; Roseto, Italy, 2002; Gary Steelheads, IBL, 2002-03; Southern Calif Surf, ABA, 2002; Dodge City Legend, USBL, 2002; Dakota Wizards, CBA, 2003, 2004; Fujian Xunxing, China, 2003; Minn Timberwolves, ctr, 2003-04; Indios de Mayaguez, Pr, 2003; Tex Tycoons, ABA, 2004-05; Ark RimRockers, ABA, 2005; Ark Rivercatz, ABA, 2006-07; Lawton-Ft Sill Cavalry, PBL, 2010.

### MILLER, OLIVER O.

Executive. **Personal:** Born Jul 23, 1944, Battle Creek, MI; son of Oliver and Edith; married Jeannette Claire Walker. **Educ:** Dartmouth Col, BA, 1966; Stanford Univ, MBA, 1968. **Career:** Mc-kinsey & Co, mgt consult, 1973-75; Seagram; McGraw-Hill Broadcasting Co, dir planning, 1974-84, dir acquisitions, 1977-79; MECCO, vpres, 1975-77; Bus Week, ad sales, 1984-. **Home Addr:** 50 E 89th St, New York, NY 10128-1225, **Home Phone:** (631)324-9137. **Business Addr:** Sales Staff, Business Week, 1221 Avenue of the Americas, New York, NY 10020, **Business Phone:** (212)512-4879.

### MILLER, PATINA

Singer, actor. **Personal:** Born Nov 6, 1984, Pageland, SC. **Educ:** South Carolina Governor's School for the Arts & Humanities, Attended; Carnegie Mellon University, Bachelor's in Musical Theatre, 2006. **Career:** ABC soap opera, "All My Children," 2007-08; Musical "Hair," 2008 (Central Park); Musical "Sister Act" as Deloris Van Cartier, 2009 (West End) and 2011-12 (Broadway); Musical "Pippin" as Leading Player, 2012-13 (American Repertory Theater) and 2013- (Music Box Theatre); Feature films "The Hunger Games: Mockingjay--Part 1" and "The Hunger Games: Mockingjay--Part 2," as Commander Paylor, 2014 and 2015. **Honors/Awds:** Theatre World Award (for "Sister Act"), 2011; Outer Critics Circle Award, Outstanding Actress in a Musical (for "Pippin"), 2013; Tony Award, Best Performance by a Leading Actress in a Musical (for "Pippin"); "The Root" Magazine, The Root 100 Honorees, 2013. **Special Achievements:** Performed song "Raise Your Voice" at The 65th Annual Tony Awards, 2011.

### MILLER, PATRICIA LEE

Executive director. **Personal:** daughter of Queen E; married Alfred Warren Zollar Sr. **Educ:** NC A&T State Univ, BA; Harvard Bus Sch, MBA. **Career:** Nations Bank, investment banker; Goldman Sachs, vpres instnl bus develop; Partnership Solutions Group, co-founder & co-head; Lehman Bros Inc, managing dir, 2004; Neuberger Berman, managing dir. **Orgs:** Co-chair, Women's Initiatives Leading Lehman (WILL); Exec Leadership Coun; bd mem, Women's Venture Fund, Uth Turn; Nc A&T State Univ, Exec Adv Coun; nat bd mem, Better Chance; bd dir, Nat Asn Investment Co, Apollo Theater. **Business Addr:** Managing Director, Neuberger Berman, 605 Third Ave 41st Fl, New York, NY 10158, **Business Phone:** (800)223-6448.

### MILLER, PERCY ROBERT

Rap musician, entrepreneur, actor. **Personal:** Born Apr 29, 1967, New Orleans, LA; married Lisa; children: 4; married Sonya; children: 6. **Educ:** Merritt Col. **Career:** No Limit Entertainment, founder & chief exec officer; No Limit Sports Mgt, founder; Wayne Fury, player, 1998; No Limit Rec, owner & chief exec officer, currently; Albums: Get Away Clean, 1991; Mama's Bad Boy, 1992; The Ghetto's Tryin' to Kill Me, 1994; 99 Ways to Die, 1995, Ice Cream Man, 1996; Ghetto D, 1997; MP the Last Don, 1998; Only God Can Judge Me, 1999; Ghetto Postage, 2000; Game Face, 2001; Good Side, Bad Side, 2004; Ghetto Bill, Living Legend: Certified D-Boy, 2005; America's Most Luved Bad Guy, 2006; The Gift, 2013; Ice Cream Man 2, 2014; Boss of All Bosses, 2014. Films: I'm Bout It, 1997; I Got the Hookup, 1998; Foolish, actor, exec producer & writer, 1999; No Tomorrow, actor, dir & exec producer, 1999; Hot Boyz, 1999; Track down, Gone in 60 Seconds, Lock down, actor & exec producer, 2000; Popcorn Shrimp, 2001; Undisputed, 2002; Dark Blue, Hollywood Homicide, 2003; Scary Movie 3, 2004; Still Bout It, 2005; Repos, 2006; Paroled, 2007; Uncle P, actor, exec producer & writer, 2007; Toxic, 2008; Soccer Mom, 2008; The Mail Man, actor & exec producer, 2009; The Pig People, 2009; Down and Distance, 2010; Knock Knock Killers, 2011; Get Money, 2011; TV series: "Oz", 2001; "Romeo!", 2003-06; "Nickelodeon", 2003; "Dancing With the Stars: Season 2", 2006; "Robot Chicken", 2008; "No Excuses", actor & exec producer, 2009; "Uncle Willy's Family", exec producer, dir & writer, 2014. **Orgs:** Las Vegas Rattlers, Am Basketball Asn, 2003. **Honors/Awds:** American Music Awards, Award for Favorite Artist, R & B/Hip-Hop, 1998; Black Star Award, 2000. **Special Achievements:** Forbes list of top 10 most highly paid entertainer for 1998; five gold and platinum albums; Black Enterprise Top 100 Industrial/Service companies, No Limit Enterprises ranked #25, 2000. **Business Addr:** Owner, Chief Executive Officer, No Limit Records, PO Box 12175, Baton Rouge, LA 70812, **Business Phone:** (225)291-8282.

### MILLER, PERCY ROMEO, JR. (LIL ROMEO)

Rap musician, baseball player, actor. **Personal:** Born Aug 19, 1989, New Orleans, LA; son of Master P and Sonya. **Career:** Albums: We can make it right; Take my pain away, 1999; My Baby; Li'l Romeo, 2001; Game Time, 2002; Romeoland, 2004; Romeo, 2005; Young Ballers: The Hood Been Good To Us, 2005; Lottery, 2006; God's Gift, 2006; Hip Hop History, 2007; Get Low LP, 2009; Patience Is A Virtue, 2009; The College Boy, 2010; Spring Break, 2010; Next Generation & Intelligent Hoodlum, 2010; Inception, 2012; Films: Max Keeble's Big Move, 2001; Honey, 2003; Crashing with Master P, 2003; Decisions, 2004; Still 'Bout It, 2004; Don't Be Scared, 2006; Gods Gift, 2006; Uncle P, 2007; Crush on U, 2007; Black Supaman, producer, 2007; Sweetwater, 2008; The Pig People, 2009; The Mailman, 2009; Down & Distance, 2010; TV Series: "The Brothers Garcia", 2001; "Oh Drama!", 2001; "The Hughleys", 2001; "Michael Jackson: 30th Anniversary Celebration", 2001; "The 29th Annual American Music Awards", 2002; "Raising Dad", 2002; "Proud Family", 2002; "Romeo", Nickelodeon", 2003; "One on One", 2003; "All Grown Up", 2004; "The Team", 2005; "Out of Jimmy's Head", 2008; "The Defenders", 2010; "The Bad Girls Club: Season 6", 2011; "The Cape", 2011; "Charlie's Angels", 2011; "Single Ladies", 2012; "The Choice", 2012. **Business Addr:** Actor, Priority Records, 1581 Phoenix Blvd, Atlanta, GA 30349.

**MILLER, PETE. See MILLER, DR. WARREN F, JR.**

### MILLER, PHILLIP M.

President (organization), executive. **Educ:** Am Univ, Wash, DC, BS, mkt & mgt, MBA, int bus & finance. **Career:** Am Express, dir, 1983-87; Citibank's Int Pvt Bank, vpres int prod develop, 1985-95; GE Money, sr vpres global mkt, 1995-2001; JPMorgan Chase, Chase Merchant Serv, pres & chief exec officer, 2001-02; Teleglobal Int Ltd, exec chmn, 2003-05; MasterCard Advisors Consult, Global Solution Leader, 2005-10, Global Head-Acquirer Knowledge Ctr, 2012-, MasterCard Worldwide, Sr vpres Mkt Develop, 2010-12. **Orgs:** Exec Leadership Coun; bd dir, Pebblebrook Hotel Trust, 2011-. **Business Addr:** Global Head, MasterCard Advisors Consulting, 2000 Purchase St, New York, NY 10577, **Business Phone:** (914)249-6524.

### MILLER, RAY

Executive. **Personal:** Born Apr 6, 1949, Hampton, VA; son of Inus Ray and Inez Smith; married Marlene Rose; children: Inus Ray III. **Educ:** Ohio State Univ, BA, polit sci, 1972, MA, pub admin, 1974. **Career:** Ohio Legis Serv Comm, res assoc; State Rep Richard F Celeste, legis asst; Rep CJ McLin Jr, admin asst; Correctional Inst Inspect Comm, exec dir; Am Fedn State, County, Munic Employees, asst dir; White House Staff Pres Jimmy Carter, dep spec asst; Columbus State Community Col, vpres minority affairs; Columbus Area Chamber Com, vpres community develop; Ohio House Rep, state rep, 29th dist, 1983-93, 1999-2002; Nat Urban Policy Inst, pres, 1993-; Ohio State Senate, sen, 2003-10; Prof Employ Servs Am, pres & chief exec officer, currently; Minority Affairs Columbus State Community Col, vpres. **Orgs:** Second Baptist Church; life mem, Nat Asn Advan Colored People; life mem, Alpha Phi Alpha Fraternity; Ohio Comn African-Am Males; pres, AfriCare, Columbus Chap; bd dir, King Cult Arts Complex; bd mem, Childrens Hunger Alliance; Ohio Comn African-Am Males; bd dir, Health Coalition Cent Ohio; bd dir, Int Health Comn African, African-Am Summit; founder & chmn, Ohio Comn Minority Health; pres, Legis Black Caucus; chair, Int Inst Democracy; bd trustee, Cent State Univ; founder & chmn, Ohio Comn Minority Health. **Honors/Awds:** Inter Nat Pathfinder Award, World Congress on the Family; Dr Martin Luther King Jr Humanitarian Award, Columbus Educ Asn; Chairman's Award, Ohio Comn Minority Health; Hubert H Humphrey Humanitarian Award, Akron Summit Community Action Asn; President's Award, Alpha Phi Alpha Fraternity; Award of Excellence, Columbus Urban League; Distinguished Service Award, Black Elected Democrats of Ohio; Distinguished Legislator of the Year Award, AmPub Health Asn, 2004; Community Leader of the Year Award, Columbus Works Inc, 2004; District Legislative Award, Am Asn Counseling Develop; Trailblazer Award, Ohio Legislative Black Caucus; CJ Mclin, Jr Award, Drug Abuse Outreach Programs of Ohio. **Special Achievements:** Chief sponsor of legislation which established first time state funding for the Head Start program in Ohio; chief sponsor of some of the most significant health care legislation ever enacted in the state of Ohio, including the Indigent Health Care Act, Health Data Act, and the Mental Health Act of 1988. **Home Addr:** 3040 Elbern Ave, Columbus, OH 43209. **Business Addr:** Senator, Ohio State Senate, Senate Bldg, Columbus, OH 43215, **Business Phone:** (614)466-5131.

### MILLER, REGINALD WAYNE (REGGIE MILLER)

Basketball player, entrepreneur. **Personal:** Born Aug 24, 1965, Riverside, CA; son of Saul and Carrie; married Marita Stavrou. **Educ:** Univ Calif, Los Angeles, CA, BA, hist, 1987. **Career:** Basketball player (retired), entrepreneur; Ind Pacers, guard, 1987-2005; Turner Sports, basketball analyst, 2005-; Boom Baby Productions, owner, currently; TNT, NBA commentator, currently. Films: He Got Game, producer, 1998; NBA TNT, producer, 1988; Pardon Interruption, producer, 2001; Thunderstruck, actor, 2012. TV Series: "Hangin' with Mr. Cooper", 1994; "Forget Paris", actor, 1995; "Hercules", actor, 1998; "Arli", actor, 2002; "Pardon the Interruption", 2005-10; "Fashion News Live", 2005-13; "Beautiful Ohio", exec producer, 2006; "Rome Is Burning", 2009; "30 for 30", producer, 2010; "Lopez Tonight", 2010; "NBA All-Star Game", announcer, 2015. **Business Addr:** Basketball Analyst, Turner Sports, 1010 Techwood Dr NW, Atlanta, GA 30318, **Business Phone:** (404)885-4538.

### MILLER, RICHARD CHARLES

School administrator, educator. **Personal:** Born Jul 26, 1947, Ithaca, NY; son of Richard (deceased) and Marjory; married Doris Jean Boyd; children: Carin Lea & Courtney Alison. **Educ:** Ithaca Col, BS, health & phys educ, 1969, MS, health & phys educ, 1971; Springfield Col, PhD, exercise physiology, 1975. **Career:** Educator, school administrator (retired); Tompkins Co Trust Co, bank teller, 1965-70; San Francisco Giants Baseball Club, prof baseball player, 1969-70; Springfield Col, instr, 1974-75; Bowie State Univ, from asst prof, 1975-90, Dept Health & Phys Educ, chair, 1976, dir, health & phys educ, 1976-90, prof, 1984, actg dir intercollegiate athletics, 1986-88; Ithaca Col, Ithaca, NY, Sch Health Sci & Human Performance, founding dean, 1990-2001; Benedict Col Columbia, sr vpres acad affairs, 2001-05, Dean, Anat & Physiology, 2005-06; Western Ky Univ, Bowling Green, assoc vpres, acad affairs, 2006-, chief diversity officer, 2007-. **Orgs:** Am Alliance Health, Phys Educ, Recreation & Dance; Nat Asn Sport Physl Educ; Asn Res, Admin, Prof Couns & Socs; Asn Schs Allied

Health Professions; bd dir, Ithacare Sr Ctr; bd dir, Cayuga Med Ctr; from Vpres to Pres, Md PartnersAmericas, 1986-90; bd trustee, Ithaca Col, 1987-90; bd dir, Tompkins County Pub Libr, 1991-96; bd dir, spec C's Ctr, Ithaca, NY, 1992-98; Pres, Ithaca-Cayuga Rotary Club, 1995-01; bd trustee, Nat Sr Games Asn, 2000-; bd trustee, Lebanon Valley Col, 2001-03; inst's liaison, Southern Asn Cols & Schs. **Honors/Awds:** Sports Hall of Fame Ithaca Col, 1979; Hall of Fame, NY State Pub High Sch Athletic Asn, 1998. **Special Achievements:** First dean of the Ithaca College's School of Health Sciences and Human Performance in 1990. **Home Addr:** 164 Journey Dr, Bowling Green, KY 42104, **Home Phone:** (270)781-9785. **Business Addr:** Chief Diversity Officer, Associate Vice President for Academic Affairs, Western Kentucky University, 1906 Col Heights Blvd Bldg 224, Bowling Green, KY 42101, **Business Phone:** (270)745-0111.

### MILLER, ROBERT, JR.

Librarian. **Personal:** Born Feb 27, 1947, New York, NY; son of Robert and Edythe Kitchens; children: Nova Jean, Jennifer Ann & Robynn Marie. **Educ:** Wagner Col, BA, 1972; Columbia Univ, MLS, 1974. **Career:** NY Pub Lib, community liaison asst, 1972-74, librn I, 1974-75; Nat Col Educ, ref librn, 1975-79; Memphis & Shelby County Pub Libr & info Ctr, first asst, 1979-81; Memphis old & new, Tenn librn, 1980; Atlanta-Fulton Pub Libr, communs officer, 1981-86; Chicago Pub Libr, cur, 1986-. **Orgs:** Am Libr Asn, 1972; Black Caucus Am Libr Asn, 1987-91. **Home Addr:** 1814 W 79th St, Chicago, IL 60620-5252, **Home Phone:** (312)488-7195. **Business Addr:** Curator, Chicago Public Library, 400 S State St, Chicago, IL 60605, **Business Phone:** (312)747-4999.

### MILLER, ROBERT LAVERNE

Administrator, football player. **Personal:** Born Jan 9, 1953, Houston, TX; married Lennie; children: Robert II, Samuel & Tiffanie. **Educ:** Univ Kans, Lawrence, bus admin, 1978. **Career:** Football player (retired), administrator; James D Ryan Jr High, 1967; Jack Yates Sr High, 1968-70; Minn Vikings, running back, 1975-80; CDC, admin, 1981. **Orgs:** Nineth St Missionary Baptist Church; deacon Church Org; asst teacher Sunday Sch; Campus Crusade Christ; fel Christian Athletes; bd ref, Hospitality House. **Honors/Awds:** Most Valuable Player, 1969-70; most determined & inspirational player, 1973; Jayhawk, 1974. **Home Addr:** 285 Holyoake RR 3, PO Box 200A, Northfield, MN 55057.

### MILLER, RODNEY M., SR.

Consultant, executive. **Educ:** Ind Univ, BS, acct; Univ Chicago Grad Sch Bus, MBA, 1986. **Career:** JP Morgan Chase & Co, Mergers & Acquisitions Group, head, N Am, co-head global energy, head financial sponsors, sr managing dir, 2007-; Credit Suisse, mergers & acquisitions N Am, head, financial sponsor mergers & acquisitions, head; Credit Suisse Global Energy Group, cohead, managing dir election comt chair; Touche, Ross & Co; Rand McNally & Co, consult. **Orgs:** Trustee, Coun Univ Chicago Grad Sch Bus; bd, Legal Information for Families Today (LIFT); dean's adv coun mem, Kelley Sch Bus Ind Univ; mem bd trustees, Studio Mus Harlem; mem bd trustees, Prep Prep; mem bd trustee, Gordon A. Rich Found; mem bd trustees, Credit Suisse Found. **Honors/Awds:** "Black Enterprise", 75 Most Powerful Blacks on Wall Street, 2011. **Business Addr:** Senior Managing Director, JPMorgan Chase & Co, 270 Pk Ave, New York, NY 10017, **Business Phone:** (212)270-6000.

### MILLER, DR. RONALD BAXTER

Educator. **Personal:** Born Oct 11, 1948, Rocky Mount, NC; son of Elsie Bryant and Marcellus C; married Jessica Garris; children: Akin Dasan; married Diana L Ransom. **Educ:** NC Cent Univ, BA, 1970; Brown Univ, AM, 1972, PhD, 1974. **Career:** State Univ Col NY, lectr, 1974; Haverford Col, asst prof eng, 1974-76; Univ Tenn, assoc prof, 1977-81, prof eng, 1982-92, dir & prof, Black Lit Prog, Lindsay Young Chair, 1986-87; LeMoyne Col, Black Scholar Prof, 1985; Univ Ga, prof sr teaching fel, Head African Am studies, 1994-95, Dept Social Justice & Civil Rights Studies, Interim Donald L. Hollowell distinguished prof, currently, Dept African Am Studies, prof, currently; Inst African Am Studies, dir, currently; Franklin Col Arts & Sci, prof eng, currently. TV Series: "The South", 1977-78; "WATU: A Cornell Journalin Black Writing", adv & contributing ed, 1978-79; "Obsidian: Black Literature in Review", 1979-; "Callaloo", 1981-; "Black American Literature Forum", African Am Review, 1982-, "Middle Atlantic Writers Asn Review", 1982-; "Langston Hughes Review", 1982-. **Orgs:** Consult, Nat Endowment Humanities; sponsor, partic & consult, Black Writers S, Ga Coun Arts & Humanities, 1980; exec, Comn Afro-Am Lit Discuss Group MLA, 1980-83; vpres, Black Hist Month Lect Ser, 1980; reader, Univ Tenn Press, 1980-; chmn, Black Studies CLA, 1982-83; founder & chmn, Div Black Am Lit & Cult, 1982-84; deleg, Mod Lang Asn Assembly, 1984-86, 1994-99; pres, Langston Hughes Soc, 1984-88; Zora Neale Hurston Rev, 1986-; sr fel Nat Res Coun, Ford Found, 1986-87; vis scholar, Irvine Found, Univ San Francisco, 1991; evaluator, Div Pub Progs Harlem Renaissance, Nat Endowment Humanities; chmn, Comm Lang & Lit Am, 1997. **Honors/Awds:** ACLS Conf Grant, Black Am Lit & Humanism Res, 1978; NEH Summer Res, 1975; Haverford Col Res, 1975; National Fellowships Fund Dissertation Grant, 1973-74; Univ of Tennessee Committee Awards for Excellence in Teaching of English, 1978-79; Nat Res Coun sr Fellowship, Univ NC, 1986-87; Distinguished Scholar, United Negro Col Fund, Xavier Univ, 1988; Honored teacher, Alpha Delta Pi, 1988; Golden Key Award for Excellence, Univ Tenn, 1990; American Book Award, 1991; Irvine Foundation Visiting Scholar, Univ San Francisco, 1991; Regional Designation Humanities Award, ACOG, 1994; Regional Designation Humanities Award, Am Col Obstetricians & Gynecologists Cultural Olympiad & Southern States Humanities Coun Black & White Perspectives Am S, 1994; Golden Key Award for Excellence, Univ Ga, 1995; Sr Lilly Teaching Fellowship, 1994-95; Who's Who in America, Who's Who in Education, Who's Who in the World, 1996; Davis Fel Lect, Univ, San Francisco, 1999; Langston Hughes Prize, 2000; Langston Hughes Prize, 2001; Love of Learning Award, Phi Kappa Phi, 2003; Who's Who Among America's Teachers, 2004; Student Government Asn Teacher Award, 2005-06; Ford-Turpin Award, 2010; Albert Christ Janer Award, 2013. **Special Achievements:** Author of Reference Guide to Langston Hughes and Gwendolyn Brooks, 1978, Editor and Contributor of Black American Literature and Humanism, 1981, author of Black American Poets Between Worlds, 1986, Tennessee Studies In Literature, 1988, Art and Imagination of Langston Hughes, 1989, Southern Trace of Black Critical Theory, 1991, co-author of Call and Response: Riverside Anthology in African American Literary Tradition, 1998, editor of "The Short Stories", The Collected Works of Langston Hughes, 2002, has given Black Scholar Lectures in LeMoyne College in 1985, has written scores of chapters, articles and reviews for professional journals; Author: The Art and Imagination of Langston Hughes, 2006. **Home Addr:** 279 Imperial Way, Bogart, GA 30622-1794, **Home Phone:** (706)548-9689. **Business Addr:** Professor, Interim Donald L Hollowell Distinguished Professor, University of Georgia, Hunter Acad Bldg 312 Holmes Tucker Hall 205, Athens, GA 30602, **Business Phone:** (706)542-5197.

### MILLER, DR. RUSSELL L., JR.

Physician, educator, administrator. **Personal:** Born Jun 30, 1939, Harvey, WV; son of Russel and Corinne; married Daryl Lawson; children: Steven & Laura. **Educ:** Howard Univ Col Lib Arts, BS, 1961; Howard Univ Col Med, MD, 1965; Nat Bd Med Examrs, dipl, 1966. **Career:** NIH, Bethesda, Md, summer fel, Nat Insts Health, 1961-63; Univ Mich Med Ctr, Ann Arbor, Mich, summer fel, internal med res, 1965-68; Univ Calif, Cardiovasc Res Inst, Dept Internal Med, San Francisco Div Clin Pharm, res fel, 1968-69, 1971-73; Roche Inst Molecular Biol, Dept Cellular Biol Div Pharm & Immuno pharamacol, Nutley, NJ, vis scientist, 1973-74; Howard Univ, Internal Med & Pharm, assoc prof, dir, sect clin pharm, 1974-79, dean colmed, 1979-88, prof internal med & pharm, 1979-93, vpres health affairs, 1988-90, sr vpres & vpres health affairs, 1990-93; NIH, vis scientist, 1984; State Univ New York Syst, Health Sci Ctr, Brooklyn, NY, pres, 1994-97. **Orgs:** Phi Beta Kappa, 1961; Alpha Omega Alpha Hon Med Socs, 1964; Med Corps Aus Res, 1969-71; DC Gen Hosp Community, 1984-88; Mayor's Adv Comn Post Sec Educ, 1987-89; chmn, Coun Southern Deans, 1987-88; Nat Adv Coun Aging, 1988-91; bd dir, Nat Res Matching Prog, 1988-91;mem at large, Nat Bd Med Examr, 1988-91; bd trustee, Educ Community Foreign Med Grad, 1991-92; exec bd mem, 1991-, chmn, 1995-99; DC Med Soc; AAAS; Am Fed Clin Res; Am Soc Internal Med; Am Soc Clin Pharm & Therapeut; DC Nat Med Asn; Med Chirurgical Soc; Baileys Harbor Symp, Dist Columbia Formulary Comn; Med Chirurgical Soc DC. **Honors/Awds:** Certified, Am Bd Internal Med, 1971; Scholar, Clin Pharm Burroughs Welcome Fund, 1977-82; Awarded grants, Dept Health Educ & Welfare Res Grant 1977-80; Certificate of honor, National Med Fel, 1988; National Competitive Scholarship.

### MILLER, SAUNDRA C.

Consultant. **Personal:** Born Jul 4, 1943, New York, NY; daughter of Vivian Hedgepeth; children: Rodney, Anthony M & Yvette. **Educ:** John Jay Col Criminal Justice, social sci, criminal law cert; Col New Rochelle, BA, lib arts, 1982. **Career:** City New York Police Dept, invest counr, 1973-97, sr spec investr; travel consult, currently. **Orgs:** Better Chance, NY-NJ Chap, 1980-; deleg, Nat Orgn Black Law Enforcement Exec, 1988-; trustee, Nat Black Police Asn, 1989-; 100 Black Women, 1992-; rec secy, New York NOBLE Chap; Nat Asn Social Workers Found, 2008. **Home Addr:** 353 Beach 57th St Suite 5A, Arverne, NY 11692-1661, **Home Phone:** (718)474-1614.

### MILLER, HON. SHEILA

Judge, lawyer. **Personal:** Born Jan 1, 1960. **Educ:** Mich State Univ, BA, polit sci & pub admin, 1984; Thomas Cooley Law Sch, JD, 1990. **Career:** Mich House Rep, legis asst, 1986-92; Mich Senate, admin asst, 1988-92; Cooley Law Sch, sr instr trial workshop, 2003-04; Macomb County Prosecutor's Off, asst prosecuting atty, 1992-2006; Macomb Co, asst prosecuting atty, 1992; 41B Dist Ct, judge, 2006-10; Thomas M. Cooley Law Sch, vis prof & assoc prof, 2011; Wayne County Prosecutor's Off, asst prosecuting atty, 2012; Sheila A Miller PLLC, atty, counr, mediator, solo practr, 2012-; asst co prosecutor. **Orgs:** State Bar Mich, 1991-; Macomb Co Bar Asn; Macomb Co Dist Judges Asn; Wolverine Bar Asn; Mich Dist Judges Asn; Asn Black Judges Mich. **Honors/Awds:** Pioneer Award, Macomb Co NAACP, 2006; Comcast Pioneer Award, 2007; Trailblazer Award, Straker Bar Asn, 2008; Women of Achievement Award, Vista Maria, 2009. **Special Achievements:** First African American to serve on any bench in Macomb County. **Business Addr:** Attorney, Counselor, Sheila A Miller PLLC, 55 Southbound Gratiot Ave, Mount Clemens, MI 48043, **Business Phone:** (586)307-5202.

### MILLER, SHERRE. See BISHOP, SHERRE WHITNEY.

### MILLER, STEPHEN DEJUAN. See MILLER, BUBBA.

### MILLER, TANGI

Actor, entertainer, dancer. **Personal:** Born Feb 28, 1974, Miami, FL. **Educ:** Ala State Univ, mkt; Univ Calif, Irvine, MFA; Royal Nat Theater, London, Ala Shakespeare Festival. **Career:** Films: Rhinos, 1998; Actress, 1999; The Other Brother, 2000; The Other Brother, 2002; Leprechaun: Back 2 the Hood (voice), 2003; Forever Is a Long, Long Time, 2004; Madea's Family Reunion, 2006; Hurricane in the Rose Garden, 2006; Madea's Family Re union, 2006; Love. & Other 4 Letter Words, writer, 2007; After School, 2008; Hurricane in the Rose Garden, 2009; My Girlfriend's Back, 2010; Drones, 2010; Fanaddict, 2011; The Good Life, 2012; Guardian of Eden, 2012; The Love Section, 2012; The Trace, 2012; TV series: "Felicity", 1998-2002; "Playing with Fire", 2000; "The Enforcers", "Too Legit: The MC Hammer Story", 2001; "All the News" (voice); "The Twilight Zone"; "Time Will Tell"; "The Shield"; "Throw away";"The Power of the Ex"; "Spin the Bottle"; "Felicity Interrupted"; "Back to the Future"; "Girls Own Juice"; "Fast lane"; "Harsh Mistress"; "Kim Possible", ed, 2002; "The District", "Blind Eye", "In God We Trust", 2003; "Cold Case", "The Division", "Hail, Hail, the Gang's All Here", "Class Actions", "The Badlands", 2004; "Half & Half", "The Big Sexism in the City Episode", "Living with Fran", 2005; "The Reunion", "Half & Half", 2005. TV movies: "The Enforcers", "Too Legit: The MC Hammer Story", 2001, "Phantom Force", 2004; Producer: Hurricane in the Rose Garden, 2006; After School, Love. & Other 4 Letter Words, 2007; Los Angeles based African dance troupe, mem, currently. **Honors/Awds:** Nat Asn Advan Colored People Image Award, 2002; One of the Most Beautiful People of the Millennium, Ebony Mag. **Business Addr:** Actress, c/o Warner Bro TV, 15303 Ventura Blvd Suite 1200, Sherman Oaks, CA 91403, **Business Phone:** (818)977-8700.

### MILLER, REV. DR. TELLY HUGH

Educator, clergy, association executive. **Personal:** Born Jun 18, 1939, Henderson, TX; married Glory D Bennett; children: Alanna Camille. **Educ:** Wiley Col, BA, 1962; Interdenom Theol Ctr, MDiv, 1965; Vanderbilt Univ, Tenn, DMin, 1973; Prairie View A&M Univ, EdM, 1980. **Career:** St Paul Baptist Church, St Albans, WV, pastor, 1965; WV State Col, relig counr, 1967; Wiley Col, Marshall, Tex, col minister, 1968, financial aid dir, 1970, assoc prof & chmn, dept relig, 1973, vpres stud affairs, 1974, prof & chmn, dept relig & philos, 1976-. **Orgs:** YMCA St Albans, 1966-67; Mt Olivet Asn, 1966-67; relig consult, Bapt WV St Col Inst, 1967; Am Asn Univ Profs; chmn, Christmas Baskets Needy St Albans, 1967; Nat Asn Advan Colored People, 1967; Kanawha Co chap, 1967; George Wash Carver Elem Sch PTA, 1977; Gamma Upsilon Lambda Chap Alpha Phi Alpha Frat Inc, 1977; Christian Athletes; Harrison County United Way Fund Dr, 1983; Harrison Co Red Cross. **Honors/Awds:** East Texas Educational Opportunities Center Award, 1980; Kappa Alpha Psi Achievement Award, 1980; Omega Psi Phi Man of the Year Award, 1983; Gov of TX, East TX Regional Review Comm for the State's Comm Develop Block Grant Prog. **Special Achievements:** First Black Comnr for Harrison County 1983. **Home Addr:** 8025 70th St, Paramount, CA 90723-5439, **Home Phone:** (562)531-6667. **Business Addr:** Professor, Chairman, Wiley College, 711 Wiley Ave, Marshall, TX 75670, **Business Phone:** (903)927-3300.

### MILLER, THOMASENE

Administrator, association executive. **Personal:** Born Dec 6, 1942, New Castle, PA; daughter of Thomas Respress and Telitha Brunzel; married David Lamar; children: David. **Educ:** DePaul Univ. **Career:** City Chicago, commndg adminstr; Model Cities, asst comndg adminstr, 1970-76; Chicago Com on Urban Oppty, asst chief clk, 1968-70, sec, 1965-68. **Orgs:** Rua Consult Firm; Metro Home Hlth Adv Com; Chicago Boys Club Martin Luther King Unit, 1977; Nat Asn Advan Colored People; mem Nat AsnComm Devel; Soc Pub Admin. **Honors/Awds:** Recog of merit, Chicago Com on Urban Oppty; Englewood Childrens Club Award, 1970; recog of merit, Chicago State Univ, 1970; recog of achvmt Model Cities/CCUO, 1975. **Home Addr:** 8748 S Luella Ave, Chicago, IL 60617.

### MILLER, WADE THOMAS

Baseball player. **Personal:** Born Sep 13, 1976, Reading, PA. **Educ:** Alvernia Univ, PA, 1996. **Career:** Houston Astros, 1999-2004; Boston Red Sox, pitcher, 2005; Chicago Cubs, pitcher, 2006-07; Toronto Blue Jays, 2009-; Alvernia Univ, pitching coach, 2012-. **Home Addr:** 12 Woods Way, Reading, PA 19610-1199, **Home Phone:** (610)898-1569. **Business Addr:** Pitching Coach, Alvernia University, 400 St Bernardine St, Reading, PA 19607, **Business Phone:** (610)796-8269.

### MILLER, WARD BEECHER

Manager, vice president (organization), banker. **Personal:** Born Jun 22, 1954, Kingstree, SC; son of Clifton and Bertha McCray; married Vicki Smith. **Educ:** Col Charleston, BA, 1976. **Career:** Wachovia Bank, personal banker, 1977-79, br mgr, 1979-81, field analyst, 1981-83, br mgr, 1983-85, exec banker, 1985-88, Main Office br mgr, 1988-92, E & S Office mgr, 1992-; NewBridge Bank, sr vpres, 2009-. **Orgs:** Steward St James AME Church, 1979-; bd mem, Big Brothers/Big Sisters, 1982-; March Dimes, 1983-; fin partner, Forsyth Investment Partners, 1985-; Juv Justice Coun, 1986-; Lift Inc 1986-; Inner City Coun, Boy Scouts Am; Forsyth County Zoning Bd. **Home Addr:** 2520 Treetop Lane, Winston Salem, NC 27101, **Home Phone:** (336)727-1061. **Business Addr:** Vice President, Wachovia Bank & Trust Co, 701 Martin Luther King Jr Dr, Winston Salem, NC 27101, **Business Phone:** (910)777-1898.

### MILLER, DR. WARREN F., JR. (PETE MILLER)

Educator. **Personal:** Born Mar 17, 1943, Chicago, IL; son of Warren F Sr and Helen Robinson; married Judith Hunter; children: David & Jonathan. **Educ:** US Mil Acad, W Pt, NY, BS, engineering sci, 1964; Northwestern Univ, Evanston, IL, MS, engineering sci, 1970, PhD, nuclear engineering sci, 1973. **Career:** Northwestern Univ, Evanston, Ill, asst prof, 1972-74; Los Alamos Nat Lab, Los Alamos, NM, staff mem, 1974-76, group leader, 1976-79, assoc dir, 1979-86, dep dir, 1986-90, sr admin, 2001; Univ Calif, Berkeley, Calif, Pardee prof, 1990-92; Sci & Technol Base Progs, Los Alama Nat Lab, dir, 1992-2001; Nuclear Energy Res Adv Coun, US Dept Energy, bd mem, 1997-; Nuclear Technol Adv Group, Los Alamos Nat Lab, bd mem, 2001; Tex A&M Univ, Tex Eng Exp Sta, res prof, 2005, Nuclear Security Sci & Policy Inst, assoc dir, 2006, adj prof; US Dept Energy, asst secy nuclear energy, 2009-. **Orgs:** US Mil Acad, 1964; Nuclear Eng Educ Disadvantaged Comt, 1972-90, chmn, 1979-80; fel Am Nuclear Soc, 1982; Prof Devel & Accreditation Comt, 1988-93; adv ed, Nuclear Sci & Eng, 1989-; gen chmn, Math & Comput Div, Topical Meeting, 1989; Math & Comput Div Exec Comt, 1990-93, chmn, 1979-80; Nat Acad Eng, 1996; Nat Soc Black Engrs, 2004; Nuclear & Radiation Studies Bd, Nat Res Coun, 2005-. **Home Addr:** 5 Erie Lane, Los Alamos, NM 87544, **Home Phone:** (505)672-9503. **Business Addr:** Assistant Secretary for Nuclear Energy, Director, US Department of Energy, 1000 Independence Ave SW, Washington, DC 20585, **Business Phone:** (202)586-5000.

### MILLER, WILLIAM NATHANIEL

Executive director, association executive. **Personal:** Born Mar 15, 1947, Perry, GA; married Shirley Jones; children: Corbett Burgess & William Franklin. **Educ:** Ft Valley State Col, BA, econ, 1969; Amican Inst Banking, attended 1971. **Career:** Nat Bank Ga, banking officer, 1972-77; US Small Bus admin, disaster loan specialist, 1977-78; Atlanta Regional Minority Purchasing Coun, exec dir, 1978-. **Orgs:** Phi Beta Sigma Fraternity; life mem, Atlanta Chamber Com; chmn bd, John Harland Boys Club, 1976; Ft Valley State Col Alumni Asn; Atlanta & Nat Bus League; Nat Asn Advan Colored People; chmn, bus com, United Negro Col Fund, 1982; Nat Asn Exhib Mgrs, 1985; grad, Leadership Atlanta, 1986. **Honors/Awds:** Nat Top Achiever Atlanta Chamber Com, 1976; Bus Develop Honors Collections Life & Heritage, 1984. **Home Addr:** 2995 Dodson Dr, East Point, GA 30344-3949. **Business Addr:** Executive Director, Atlanta Regional Minority Purchasing Council, 235 Int Blvd, Atlanta, GA 30303, **Business Phone:** (404)586-8516.

**MILLER, WILLIAM O. See Obituaries Section.**

**MILLER-HOLMES, CHERYL**
Manager, media executive. **Personal:** Born Sep 15, 1958, Detroit, MI; daughter of Hubert and Elzenia. **Educ:** Specs Howard Sch Brdcst Arts, Southfield, Mich; Oakland Community Col, Farmington Hill, Mich, AA; Spring Arbor Col, Spring Arbor, Mich, BA, 1988; Wayne State Univ, Detroit, Mich, MLS, 1990. **Career:** Manager (retired); Wayne County Dept Soc Servs, caseworker, 1981; Mich Dept Corrections, libr dir, 1993; Wayne County Community Col, libr dir; Univ Park Creative Arts, media specialist; S Fulton, mgr, 2004. **Orgs:** Bd dir, African Am Reparations Comt; Wayne County Dept Soc Serv; Affirmative Action Adv Comt. **Honors/Awds:** Paul Laurence Dunbar Award; Detroit Black Writers Guild; First Prize, Poetry Contest. **Home Addr:** 144 E Red Fox Ct, Midway, GA 31320, **Home Phone:** (912)884-9313.

**MILLER-JONES, DR. DALTON**
Psychologist, educator. **Personal:** Born Jul 6, 1940, St. Louis, MO; married Cynthia L Miller; children: Dalton A, Julie K, M Luke & Marcus N. **Educ:** Rutgers Univ, BA, BS, psychol & biol sci, 1962; Tufts Univ, MS, exp psychol, 1965; Cornell Univ, PhD, devel psychol, 1973. **Career:** Cornell Univ Africana Studies, lectr & res assoc, 1969-73; Univ Mass, Am herst, asst prof, 1973-82; Rockefeller Univ, New York, Inst Comparative Human Cognition, adj prof & fel, 1974-76; Williams Col, Henry Luce assoc prof, 1982-84; City Univ NY Grad Sch, assoc prof & dep exec officer PhD prog psychol, 1984, head psychol subprogram, 1988-91; Portland State Univ, vice provost acad affairs, 1991-96, prof psychol, 1991-, chair, Black Studies Dept, 2004-10, prof emer, develop psychol. **Orgs:** Fel NSF & Off Educ, 1966-69; Soc for Res in Child Devel, 1978-; empirical res consult in Black psychol; New York Bd Educ; Am Can Co & Black community orgns, 1980; Jean Piaget Soc, 1981-; Am Educ Res Asn, 1981-; Am Psychol Asn, 1982-; Nat Asn Res in Sci Teaching; Asn Black Psychologist; Am Psychol Asn; Jean Piaget Socs; Socs for Res in Child Develop; bd mem, Ore State Bd Higher Educ, 2006-; Native Am Community Adv Comt. **Home Addr:** 85 Edgemont Rd, Montclair, NJ 07043. **Business Addr:** Professor Emeritus, Portland State University, 317 Cramer Hall, Portland, OR 97207-0751, **Business Phone:** (503)725-5250.

**MILLER-LEWIS, S. JILL**
Art patron, machinist. **Personal:** Born Detroit, MI; daughter of Ruben H and Margie K; married James A; children: Davida, Alake, Bakari & Mekeda; married Olayami Dabls. **Educ:** Howard Univ, BS; Mich State Univ, post-grad studies; Wayne State Univ. **Career:** Nat Day Care Asn, Wash, DC, educ consult, 1978-80; Detroit Bd Educ, Detroit, Mich, teacher, 1980-82; Rosa Parks Ctr Mus, Detroit, Mich, prog dir & designer, 1983-84; Charming Shoppes Inc; Fashion Bug, Royal Oak, Mich, asst mgr, 1985-86; Detroit Bd Educ, Detroit, Mich, teacher; Jill Perette Gallery, Detroit, Mich, owner; Aida-Akante Designs & Mfg, owner; Dabl's & Perette's African Bead Gallery, owner, 1982-. **Orgs:** Prog dir, Rosa Parks Ctr Mus, 1983-84; chairperson, Walk-a-thon, 1984; Conv Bur Detroit, 1990-91; Mich Retailers Asn, 1992; network dir, Nat Asn Female Execs, 1992. **Honors/Awds:** Spirit of Detroit, City Coun Detroit, 1988; Certificate of Apppreciation, Childrens Ctr Wayne Co, 1982-83. **Special Achievements:** Author of Dressing Successfully, 1984-85, AFR Pattern Design, 1993, Scrapbook Styles, 2004. **Business Addr:** Owner, Dabl's & Perette's African Bead Gallery, 6559 Grand River Ave, Detroit, MI 48208, **Business Phone:** (313)898-3007.

**MILLER-PERRY, ROSETTA**
Newspaper publisher, periodical publisher, founder (originator). **Personal:** Born Jul 7, 1934, Coraopolis, PA; daughter of Anderson Irvin and Mary Hall Irvin; children: 3. **Educ:** Univ Memphis, BS, 1956; John A Gumpston Sch Mortuary Sci, attended 1957. **Career:** US Equal Employ Opportunity Comn, Nashville area dir, 1975-90; Perry & Perry Assocs Inc, founder, 1990; Contempora Mag, pres & publ, 1990-; Tenn Tribune Newspaper, pres & publ, 1992-. **Orgs:** Greater Nashville Black Chamber Com, founder, 1998; Anthony J Cebrun Journalism Ctr, founder, 1998. **Special Achievements:** Selected as member of "HistoryMakers".

**MILLER-POPE, CONSUELO ROBERTA**
Association executive, president (organization), chief executive officer. **Personal:** Born Ayer, MA; daughter of Harold G and Consuelo D; children: Alexis Michelle-Dale Williams. **Educ:** Pa State Univ, BA, 1965; Univ Chicago, MA, 1969; Chicago-Kent Col Law. **Career:** Chicago Econ Develop Corp, vpres, 1969-81; Cosmopolitan Chamber Com, pres & chief exec officer, 1982-; Inst Urban Econ Develop, vpres. **Orgs:** Bd mem, Univ Ill Ctr Urban Bus; Nat Asn Advan Colored People. **Business Addr:** President, Chief Executive Officer, Cosmopolitan Chamber of Commerce, 30 E Adams St Suite 1050, Chicago, IL 60603, **Business Phone:** (312)499-0611.

**MILLER-RYCRAW, EUGENIA. See RYCRAW, EUGENIA.**

**MILLETT, DR. KNOLLY E.**
Physician. **Personal:** Born Aug 15, 1922; married Mavis DeBurg; children: Eileen, Mercedes, Denise, Maria & Jacques. **Educ:** Long Island Univ, BS, 1947; Univ Paris Fac Med, MD, 1959. **Career:** Pvt pract, physician, currently. **Orgs:** Nat Med Asn; AMA; Kings Col Med Soc; Provident Clin Soc Brooklyn; Phi Beta Sigma; Gamma Rho Sigma; Brooklyn-Cumberland Med Ctr Jewish Hosp Brooklyn; Urban League; NY Civil Liberties Union; Manhasset C C; dipl, Am Bd Family Pract. **Business Addr:** Physician, Private Practice, 453 Franklin Ave, Brooklyn, NY 11238-2633, **Business Phone:** (718)622-3113.

**MILLETT, DR. RICARDO A.**
Association executive, consultant, executive director. **Personal:** Born May 10, 1945, Panama City; son of William G and Ometa Trowers; married Jan Stepto; children: Sundiata Madoda, Miguel Stepto & Maya Alegre. **Educ:** Brandeis Univ, BS, econ, 1968, Florence Heller Sch Brandeis Univ, MSW, social policy, 1971, PhD, social policy planning & res, 1974. **Career:** ABT Assocs, analyst, 1971-73, sr analyst, 1977-80; Atlanta Univ, Sch Social Work, assoc prof, 1973-76; Mass Dept Social Serv, Boston, Mass, dep asst comnr, 1980-81; Martin Luther King Jr Ctr Career Educ & Coun Serv, Boston Univ, dir, 1981-83; Roxbury Multi-Serv Ctr, exec dir, 1983-85; Boston Redevelop Authority, asst dir neighborhood housing & develop, 1985-88; United Way Mass Bay, sr vpres planning & resource mgt, 1988-93; WK Kellogg Found, dir eval, 1993-2001; Woods Fund Chicago, pres, 2001-06; Ricardo Millett & Assocs, prin & founder, 2006-08; TCC Group, affil, 2007; Community Sci, Gaithersburg, MD, prin assoc, 2008-. **Orgs:** Asst dir, Boston Redevel Auth, 1985-; Mus Afro-Am Hist, African Meeting House Comt, 1987; Brandeis Univ; bd dir, Heller Grad Sch, 1992-05; chair, Am Eval Asn, 2000; trustee, ABFE, 2000-08; Am Eval Asn, 2000-; treas & bd mem, Ctr Effective Philanthropy, 2003-; treas & bd mem, Asn Black Found Execs, 2004-; nat adv bd mem, Hispanics Philanthropy, 2004-; co-chair, Gov Ill New Americans Policy, 2005-; Govs Community Safety & Re-Entry Comn, comnr, 2005-; Investing Safricas Future, bd mem, 2006-; Nat Network Consults to Grantmakers, 2006-; bd dir, Shared Interest, 2006-; bd mem, chmn, Hillside Pre-Release Prog; pres, Black Polit Task Force; bd overseers, Florence Heller Sch, Brandeis Univ; bd dir, Thomas Jefferson Forum; New Directions Prog Eval; Grantmakers Effective Orgn; bd dir, Social Policy Res Group. **Honors/Awds:** Special Boston Redevelopment Authority Achievement Award, 1986; Outstanding Immigrant of African Descent, Ethiopia Soc Boston, 1992; Alva & Gunnar Myrdal Evaluation Practice Award, Am Evaluators Asn, 2001. **Special Achievements:** St Corner Alcoholics, Alton Childs Publ, 1976; "Widespread Citizen Participation in Model Cities and the Demands of Ethnic Minorities for a Greater Decision Making Role in Amer Cities", 1977; "Simmering on the CalmPresence and Profound Wisdom of Howard Thurman", 1981-82; "Racism andRacial Relations in Boston", 1982-83; "Movements for Social Justice: A Commentary from the Black Perspective", Toward Social & Econ Justice, 1985; "Faces to Watch in 1986", Boston Mag, 1986; "Urban Renewal and Residential Displacement in the South End", Boston Univ Afro-Am Studies Dept, 1987; "Enterprise Zones and Parcel to Parcel Linkage, The Boston Case", Univ Mass Sch Pub & Community Serv, 1987; "New Players in Urban Development", Boston Redevelop Authority, 1989; "elopment & Displacement in the Black Community", J Health & Social Policy, Vol I, No 4, 1990; "mpowerment Evaluation and the W.K. Kellogg Foundation", Empowerment Eval; Knowledge & Tools Self-Assessment & Accountability, 1996; "Information as a Management Tool", Eval with Power, 1997; "Evaluation as a Democratizing Practice", Green & Hopson Foundations & Eval: Context & Pract Effective Philanthropy, 2002. **Home Addr:** 72 Woodland Rd, Jamaica Plain, MA 02130, **Home Phone:** (617)524-0505. **Business Addr:** Principal Associate, Community Science, 438 N Frederick Ave Suite 315, Gaithersburg, MD 20877, **Business Phone:** (301)519-0722.

**MILLIARD, RALPH GREGORY**
Baseball manager, baseball player. **Personal:** Born Dec 30, 1973, Willemstad. **Career:** Baseball player (retired), baseball coach; Fla Marlins, infielder, 1996-97; New York Mets, infielder, 1998; Summer Olympics, Neth, 2000, 2004; baseball coach, currently.

**MILLIGAN, RANDY (RANDALL ANDRE MILLIGAN)**
Baseball player, baseball executive. **Personal:** Born Nov 27, 1961, San Diego, CA. **Career:** Baseball player (retired), baseball executive; New York Mets, first baseman, 1987, Pittsburgh Pirates, first baseman, 1988, Baltimore Orioles, first baseman, 1989-92, scout, currently; Cleveland Indians, first baseman, 1993; Cincinnati Reds, first baseman, 1993-94; Montreal Expos, first baseman, 1994. **Honors/Awds:** The Sporting News Minor League Player of the Year, Tidewater Tides Int League, 1987. **Special Achievements:** First baseman in Major League Baseball, 1987-94. **Business Addr:** Scout, Baltimore Orioles, 333 W Camden St Suite 1, Baltimore, MD 21201, **Business Phone:** (410)685-9800.

**MILLINER, DAVID M.**
Editor, publisher. **Educ:** Drake Univ, 1979. **Career:** DMMI World Commun, chief exec officer, 1989-; Mkt exec; Chicago Defender, ed & publ, 2003-04, Pub Media Works, vpres, Real Times Inc, co-owner & bd mem, currently. **Orgs:** Daily Gazette; African Am Chamber Com; bd mem, Real Times Inc. **Business Addr:** Chief Executive Officer, DMMI World Communications, 17119 Bennett Ave, South Holland, IL 60473, **Business Phone:** (708)339-6312.

**MILLNER, DIANNE MAXINE**
Executive director, lawyer. **Personal:** Born Mar 21, 1949, Columbus, OH; daughter of Charles and Barbara Johnson; married Herbert L Anderson; children: Ashley Anderson & Tori Anderson. **Educ:** Pasadena City Col, AA, 1969; Univ Calif, Berkeley, AB, 1972; Stanford Univ, JD, 1975. **Career:** Pillsbury Madison & Sutro Law Firm, atty, 1975-80; Hastings Col Law, instr, 1977-78; Harvard Law Sch, fel, 1978; Alexander, Millner & McGee, atty, 1980-91; Steefel, Levitt & Weiss, atty, 1991-94; Calif Continuing Educ Bar, atty; Protection & Advocacy Inc, bd dir, chair, currently; City Oakland, supv dep city atty, 2000-. **Orgs:** Phi Beta Kappa, Univ Calif, Berkeley, 1975; dir, Youth Serv, 1978-80, bd mem; Community Redevel Agency Asn, 1983-94; Nat Bar Asn; Urban Land Inst; comt chmn, Parents Div, Nat Fedn Blind, 1988-; Black Woman Lawyers Asn; Charles Houston Bar Asn; Am Asn Univ Women, 1990-92; Am Bar Asn; Calif State Bar; pres, Calif Sch Blind, Parents & Friends Asn; Nat Fed Blind; Better Chance Inc; bd dir, Disability Rights Calif, 2008-2009. **Home Addr:** 32 Sequoyah View Ct, Oakland, CA 94605-4905, **Home Phone:** (415)836-3630. **Business Addr:** Board Director, Chair, Protection Advocacy Inc, 100 Howe Ave Suite 185N, Sacramento, CA 95825, **Business Phone:** (916)488-9955.

**MILLOY, LAWYER MARZELL**
Football player, actor. **Personal:** Born Nov 14, 1973, St. Louis, MO; son of Larry and Mae; married Claudine; children: Amirah & Kiara. **Educ:** Univ Wash, sociol. **Career:** Football player (retired); New Eng Patriots, strong safety, 1996-2002; Buffalo Bills, safety, 2003-05; Atlanta Falcons, linebacker & strong safety, 2006, free safety & strong safety, 2007, strong safety, 2008; Seattle Seahawks, safety, 2009, strong safety, 2010. Films: 1996 NFL Draft, 1996; 1996 AFC Championship Game, 1997; Super Bowl XXXI, 1997; 2001 AFC Championship Game, 2002; Super Bowl XXXVI, 2002. TV Ser: "ESPN SportsCentury", 2005; "NBC Sunday Night Football", 2011; "Husky Loyal", 2012. **Orgs:** Founder, Lawyer Milloy Found. **Honors/Awds:** Jim Thorpe Award, 1995; Pardade All Am Honors, Assoc Press, Walter Camp, 1995; Pro Bowl, 1998, 1999, 2001, 2002; AFC Def Player of the Week, 1998; Super Bowl champion XXXVI. **Home Addr:** , GA.

**MILLS, AISHA. See MOODIE-MILLS, AISHA.**

**MILLS, ALAN BERNARD**
Baseball player, baseball executive. **Personal:** Born Oct 18, 1966, Lakeland, FL; married Shareese; children: Tyson. **Educ:** Ashford Univ, BA, psychol, 2009; Polk Community Col, assoc degree; Tuskegee Univ. **Career:** Baseball player (retired), coach; New York Yankees, pitcher, 1990-91; Baltimore Orioles, pitcher, 1992-98, 2000-01; Los Angeles Dodgers, pitcher, 1999-2000; Minor League Baseball, Erie Sea Wolves, pitcher, 2007-; Oneonta Tigers, pitching coach, 2008; Kathleen High Sch, phys educ teacher & head coach, 2009-11; Aberdeen IronBirds, pitching coach, 2012. **Business Addr:** Pitcher, Minor League Baseball, 110 E 10th St, Erie, PA 16501, **Business Phone:** (814)456-1300.

**MILLS, ALAN KEITH**
Lawyer, association executive. **Personal:** Born Sep 5, 1957, Savannah, GA; son of Warne and Shirley; married Sally A; children: Alexis K & Adam K. **Educ:** Carthage Col, BA, magna cum laude, 1979; Ind Univ Sch Law, JD, summa cum laude, 1982. **Career:** Barnes & Thornbury LLP, staff, 1982, partner, 1990-; US Dist Courts Southern Dist Ind, fed judge; Govt Mex, off financial insts coun, currently. **Orgs:** Pres, Marion County Bar Asn, 1988-89; chairperson, State Election Bd, 1988-92; bd mem, Madame C J Walker Urban Life Ctr, 1988-00; co-chairperson, Marion County Judicial Study Comn, 1990; bd visitor, Ind Univ Sch Law, 1990-; bd mem, Ind Black Expo, 1993-96; bd mem, Indianapolis Opera, 1993-96; bd mem, St Mary Woods Col, 1998-02; Ind Univ, Pres's Coun; bd dir, Am Pianists Asn; bd dir, Starfish Initiative. **Honors/Awds:** Harry S Truman Scholar, Truman Found, 1977; Faculty Prize, Ind Univ Sch Law, 1982; Minority Achiever of the Year, Ctr Leadership Develop, 1990; Distinguished Alumni Award, Carthage Col, 1996. **Special Achievements:** Publications: Auto Supplier Newsletter, Vol. 1, 2006; Auto Supplier Newsletter, Vol. 2, 2007; Indiana Business - Opportunities in Cuba? Fidel Castro's exit opens doors for Hoosier businesses, 2008; Commercial Finance & Insolvency Bulletin, 2009. **Home Addr:** 6818 Antietam Pl, Indianapolis, IN 46278-2808, **Home Phone:** (317)293-4222. **Business Addr:** Partner, Barnes & Thornburg LLP, 11 S Meridian St, Indianapolis, IN 46204-3535, **Business Phone:** (317)231-7239.

**MILLS, BILLY G.**
Judge. **Personal:** Born Apr 5, 1929, Waco, TX; married Rubye Maurine Jackson; children: Karol, Karen, William Karl & John Stewart. **Educ:** Compton Col, AA, 1949; Univ Calif Los Angeles, BA, 1951, LLB, 1954, JD, 1958. **Career:** Judge (retired); Los Angeles Co, dep probation officer, 1957-60; pvt prac, atty, 1957-74; Los Angeles City Coun, city councilman, 1963-74; Sup Ct, State Calif, judge, 1974; Los Angeles Super Ct, Fam Law Dept, supv judge, 1979-87, judge Super Ct, 1989. **Orgs:** Chmn, Los Angeles Co Dem Control Comt; Dept Justice Adv Com; exec bd, Los Angeles Co Bar Asn; Calif State Bar Asn; Am Bar Asn; Am Judicature Soc; bd trustee, United Church Rel Sci; League Calif Cities; United Negro Col Fund; Sickle Cell Found; Calif Black Correction Coalition; Calif Fed Black Leadership; Crippled Child Soc; Kiwanis Club; bd mem, UCLA Found. **Business Addr:** Board Member, The UCLA Foundation, UCLA Wilshire Ctr, Los Angeles, CA 90024-6519, **Business Phone:** (310)794-3193.

**MILLS, DR. CHERYL D.**
Government official. **Personal:** Born Jan 1, 1965?; daughter of LaVerne. **Educ:** Univ Va, BA, 1987; Stanford Law Sch, JD, 1990. **Career:** Pres Clinton, dep coun; Gore Transition Planning Found, assoc coun pres; Wash, DC law firm, Hogan & Hartson, assoc; DC Works, co-owner, 1990-99; Oxygen Media, sr vpres corp policy & pub programming, 1999-2001; White House, Assoc Coun, 1993; NY Univ, Off Pub Affairs, sr vpres, gen coun, secy, actg sr vpres opers & admin, 2001-09; New York Univ, sr vpres, 2002-09; US Dept State, counr, 2009-, US Secy State, chief staff, 2009-. **Orgs:** Prin liaison, Univ Bd Trustee; See Forever Found; Nat Partnership Women & Families; Leadership Conf Civil Rights Educ Fund; Jackie Robinson Found; Cent Am Progress & William J Clinton Presidential Libr Found; bd dir, Cendant Corp; Phi Beta Kappa Soc; Stanford Law Rev; counr, Secy State Hillary Clinton. **Business Addr:** Counselor, US Department of State, 2201 C St NW, Washington, DC 20520, **Business Phone:** (202)647-4000.

**MILLS, CHRISTOPHER LEMONTE**
Basketball player, business owner. **Personal:** Born Jan 25, 1970, Los Angeles, CA; son of Claude. **Educ:** Univ KY, attended 1990; Univ Ariz, BA, commun & sociol, 1993. **Career:** Basketball player (retired), business owner; Cleveland Cavaliers, small forward, 1993-97; NY Knicks, small forward, 1997-98; Golden State Warriors, small forward, 1998-2002, power forward, 2002-03; 310 Auto, owner, currently. **Orgs:** Founder, Chris Mills Found; Alpha Phi Alpha. **Honors/Awds:** McDonald's All American, 1988; Great Alaska Shootout Most Outstanding Player, 1989; NIT Season Tip-Off Most Outstanding Player, 1991; Pac-12 Conference Player of the Year, 1993. **Special Achievements:** Cameo appearance: Blue Chips, 1994; Da Game of Life, 1998. Album: B-Ball's Best Kept Secret, 1994; Sumptin' to Groove To. **Business Addr:** Owner, 310 Auto, Los Angeles, CA 90755.

### MILLS, DOREEN C.

Executive. **Personal:** Born Jan 5, 1959, New Haven, CT; daughter of Marcus and Dolores Tyson. **Educ:** Hampton Univ, BA, psychol, hospitality mkt, pub rels & brand mkt, psychol. **Career:** Ramada Renaissance Hotel, sales mgr, 1985-88; Philadelphia Conv & Visitors Bur, conv sales mgr, 1988-90; Los Angeles Conv & Visitors Bur, dir, conv sales, 1993-2000; Continental Plaza Hotel, dir sales & mkt, 1998-2000; Los angeles marriott downtown, Sales mgr, 2000-05; Sheraton gateway hotel los angeles, dir bus travel sales, 2005-09; Hilton los angeles airport, asst dir sales & mkt, 2009-10; Holiday inn los angeles, dir sales & mkt, 2011; Westin pasadena, assoc dir sales, 2011-12; Packard Hotel Group, dir sales, 2011; Task Force Hotel Sales, 2012; Maison 140 & Mosaic Hotels Beverly Hills, Sales & Catering Mgr, 2012-14; Residence Inn, Dir Sales, 2014-. **Orgs:** Delta Sigma Theta, 1982-; La Chap Urban League, 1990-; pres, Nat Asn Black Hospitality Profs, 1995-; Am Soc Asn Exec, 1996-; Meeting Profs Inst, 1997-; Relig Conf Mgt Asn, 1998-; exec chair, Southern Calif Soc Asn. **Home Addr:** 421 S Lafayette Pk Pl Suite 211, Los Angeles, CA 90057, **Home Phone:** (213)380-5971. **Business Addr:** Director Sales, Marketing, Continental Plaza Hotel, 9750 Airport Blvd, Los Angeles, CA 90045-5404, **Business Phone:** (310)645-4600.

### MILLS, ERNIE (ERNEST LEE MILLS, III)

Football player, football coach, president (organization). **Personal:** Born Oct 28, 1968, Dunnellon, FL. **Educ:** Univ Fla, BS, sports admin, exercise & sport sci, health & human performance, 1990. **Career:** Football player (retired), coach, executive; Pittsburgh Steelers, wide receiver, 1991-96; Carolina Panthers, 1997-98; Dallas Cowboys, wide receiver, 1998-2000; Miami Dolphins, intern wide receivers coach; Johnson C Smith Univ, wide receivers coach; Phillip O'Berry Acad, asst head coach, defense & spec teams cord; Off & Home Concepts, pres, 2002-05; Jacksonville Dolphins, wide receivers asst coach, 2007-13; Fla A&M Univ, wide receiver asst coach, 2013-15; Transition, Career, currently. **Orgs:** Nat Alliance African Am Athletes. **Business Addr:** Wide Receiver Coach, Florida A&M University, H Manning Efferson Bldg 1668 S MLK Blvd, Tallahassee, FL 32307, **Business Phone:** (850)599-3723.

### MILLS, JOEY RICHARD

Beautician. **Personal:** Born Apr 2, 1950, Philadelphia, PA. **Educ:** Temple Univ, BA, 1970. **Career:** Vogue, Make-up artist: Harper's Bazaar; Glamour; Red Book; Mccalls; Ladies Home Journal; Family Circle; Essence; Town & Country; The Next Man; Eyes of Laura Mars, make-up person, 1978; record album covers: Valerie Harper. **Special Achievements:** Guest appear WNBC Not For Women Only; For You Black Woman; appeared "Kenneth" Beauty Talk Show; appeared "AM New York"; appeared "PM New York"; appeared "The Morning Show" w/Regis Philbin; appeared "Today in New York"; appeared "The Barbara Walters Special" with Brooke Shields; 3 beauty books; cosmetic line 1978; author of best seller, "New Classic Beauty"; introduced & created, The Joey Mills Makeup System, beauty compacts and sets in skin palettes of Ivory, Suntan, Bronze & Mahogany, 1994; appearances on BET; First noted African American Male Makeup Artists in his time. **Home Addr:** 20 W 64th St, New York, NY 10023-7104, **Home Phone:** (212)769-2023.

### MILLS, JOHN HENRY

Football player, football coach. **Personal:** Born Oct 31, 1969, Jacksonville, FL. **Educ:** Wake Forest Univ. **Career:** Football player (retired), coach; Houston Oilers, linebacker, 1993-96; Oakland Raiders, 1997-98; SKILLS Enterprise Inc, golf classic coordr, 1998-; Minn Vikings, 1999; Pin Oak Youth Football Camp, coordr, 2002; Bellaire Cardinals, coach defensive coordr, 2003; Clear Lake High Sch, outside linebacker coach, currently. **Orgs:** Skills Inc; Alpha Sigma Phi. **Honors/Awds:** Pro Bowl, 1996; Hall of Fame Youth Football, 2004-06. **Business Addr:** Outside Linebacker Coach, Clear Lake High School, 2929 Bay Area Blvd, Houston, TX 77058, **Business Phone:** (281)284-1900.

### MILLS, REV. DR. LARRY GLENN

Executive, clergy. **Personal:** Born Oct 6, 1951, Monroe, LA; son of Catherine; married Bernice Perry; children: Erma, Larry, Larita, Larnell, Yolando, Larone, Lantz, Tracie & Milania. **Educ:** Wayne State Univ, BS, bus mgt & relig educ, spec educ & teaching, 1974; Bethany Col, BRE, 1990; Bethany Theol Sem, MA, orgn mgt & sacred theol, 1992; Bethany Bible Col, attended 1994, THD, 1999; Univ Phoenix, BSBM, 2000, MA, orgn leadership, 2002. **Career:** Executive (retired), clergy, pastor; OXY Metal Ind, mgr, pc, 1971-77; Portec Rail Car, supvr, pc, 1977-82; Gen Dynamics, mgr, pc, 1982-84; Lockheed Martin, vpres hr & bus conduct corp oper, 1984-2007; Mt Sinai Baptist Church, pastor, 1988-; LGM enterprises, chief exec officer, 2012-. **Orgs:** Vpres, SCLC Greater Orlando Chap; chmn, Pvt Indus Coun; TASTD; moderator, pres, W Coast Baptist Asn; YMCA Black Achievers; Citizen's Rev Bd; APICS, 1973-90; Phi Beta Sigma Fraternity, 1974-; exec bd dir, Boy Scouts; exec bd dir, Inroads, currently; fac mem, Nat Baptist Cong Educ; nat chair, Nat Baptist Cong M Couples Div; dir fin, Fla Gen Baptist Asn; moderator, W Coast Baptist Asn; tutoring, Orange County Jail Ministry; Good News Ministry; bd mem, Boy Scouts Exec Coun; exec bd dir, INROADS; Metrop Orlando Urban League; Nat Asn Advan Colored People; Orange County Citizens Rev Bd; Region III Sch Bd Dist; Girl Scouts Exec Coun. **Home Addr:** 6632 Crenshaw Dr, Orlando, FL 32835-5748, **Home Phone:** (407)297-4148. **Business Addr:** Pastor, Mt Sinai Missionary Baptist Church, 5200 W S St, Orlando, FL 32811, **Business Phone:** (407)299-8820.

### MILLS, LOIS TERRELL

Industrial engineer, executive, association executive. **Personal:** Born Sep 24, 1958, San Francisco, CA; daughter of Warren C and Lois M Terrell Clark; married Roderick L. **Educ:** Univ Valencia, Valencia, Spain, 1978; Stanford Univ, Stanford, Calif, BS, ind engineering, 1980; Webster Univ, MA, hr develop, 1995. **Career:** Procter & Gamble, Albany, Ga, line & staff mgmt, 1980-82, ind engr dept mgr, 1983-85; Procter & Gamble, Cincinnati, OH, corp plng mgr, 1985-88, corp distrib plng mgr, 1989-90; Ethicon Endo-Surg, Johnson & Johnson, indust engr, 1990-93, hr dir, 1990-2007, leadership develop mgr, 2001-02; Ethicon Inc, div Johnson & Johnson, Albuquerque, NMex, ind engr, 1990-93; Total Assoc Involvement, coordr, 1992, hr adminr, 1993-97; Ethicon Endo-Surg, hr team mem, 1997-2001, hr dir, 2002-06, leadership develop mgr, 2001-02; Johnson & Johnson Co, hr dir, 1990-2007, talent mgt, hr dir, 2006-07; Forte, hr dir, 2008-09; Otterbein Retirement Living Communities, vpres, hr, chief people officer, 2009-. **Orgs:** Univ Black Alumni, 1982-; Toastmasters Int, 1987-90; Nat pres, Am Bus Women's Asn, 1990-91; bd dir, Albuquerque Chamber Com, 1991-92; Stanford Nmex Network Women Sci & Engrg, 1991-; Otterbein Retirement Living Communities, chief people officer & vpres hr, 2009-. **Honors/Awds:** Top Ten Business Woman, Am Bus Women's Asn, 1985; Highest Fund Raiser, Boys Club Am, Albany, Ga, 1985; YMCA Black Achiever, YMCA, 1987; J & J Standards of Leadership Awards; Women of Color Technology Awards. **Special Achievements:** first black national president of the American Business Women s Association. **Home Addr:** PO Box 181, Cedar Crest, NM 87008-0181, **Home Phone:** (505)897-9136. **Business Addr:** Vice President HR, Chief People Officer, Otterbein Retirement Living Communities, 580 N State Rte 741, Lebanon, OH 45036, **Business Phone:** (513)933-5400.

### MILLS, MARY ELIZABETH

Educator, government official. **Personal:** Born Jul 4, 1926, Franklin, TN; daughter of Daisy Johnson Knowles; married Latham L; children: Latham L & Joycelin M Blackman. **Educ:** Tenn State Univ, Nashville, TN, BS, 1946, MS, cert admin & supv, 1965. **Career:** Williamson Co Sch Syst, Franklin Tenn, teacher, 1953-55; Franklin Spec Sch Dist, Franklin Tenn, teacher, 1955-77, asst prin, 1977-80, prin, 1980-; Williamson County Conv & Visitors Bur, Dist 11, bd comnr, currently. **Orgs:** Pres, Franklin City Teachers Asn, 1977; bd trustee, William Med Ctr, 1983-; chmn, Community Child Care Ctr, 1983-; secy, Williamson County Tourism, 1983-; Nat Educ Asn; Tenn Educ Asn; Asn Elem Sch Prin; Asn Prin & Supvr; Franklin Spec Sch Dist Educ Asn; Phi Delta Kappa; reg dir, Nat Sorority Phi Delta Kappa. **Home Addr:** 1776 W Main St, PO Box 486, Franklin, TN 37064, **Home Phone:** (615)794-2270. **Business Addr:** Member of Board of Commissioner, Williamson County Convention & Visitors Bureau, 400 Main St Suite 200, Franklin, TN 37064, **Business Phone:** (615)791-7554.

### MILLS, STEPHANIE

Actor, singer. **Personal:** Born Mar 22, 1957, New York, NY; married Michael Saunders; married Jeffrey Daniels; married Ebony; children: Down Syndrome. **Educ:** Juilliard Sch Music. **Career:** Appeared in: The Wiz, 1975, 1984; Maggie Flynn; To Sir With Love; Singles: "What Cha Gonna Do with My Lovin", 1979; "You Can Get Over", 1979; "Sweet Sensation", 1980; "Never Knew Love Like This Before", 1980; "Two Hearts", 1981; "Night Games", 1981; "Last Night", 1982; "Keep Away Girls", 1982; "You Cant Run From My Love", 1983; "Pilot Error", 1983; "How Come U Don't Call Me Anymore?", 1983; "The Medicine Song", 1984; "Edge of the Razor", 1984; "Bit by Bit", 1985; "Stand Back", 1985; "I Have Learned to Respect the Power of Love", 1986; "Rising Desire", 1986; "I Feel Good All Over", 1987; "A Rush on Me", 1987; "Secret Lady", 1987; "If I Were Your Woman", 1988; "Where Is The Love", 1988; "Something in the Way", 1989; "Home", 1989; "Comfort of a Man", 1990; "Heart to Heart", 1991; "All Day, All Night", 1992; "Never Do You Wrong", 1993; "Latin Lover", 1999; "We Are Family", 2001; "Can't Let Him Go", 2003; "Free", 2005; "So in Love This Christmas", 2012. Films: The Wiz, 1978; TV Series: "Miss Black America Page ant", 1985; "My Dad the Rock Star", Nick Toons, voice, 2004-06. Albums: Movin' in the Right Direction, 1974; For the First Time, 1976; What-cha Gonna Do With My Lovin', 1979; Sweet Sensation, 1980; Stephanie, 1981; Tantalizingly Hot, 1982; Merciless, 1983; Stephanie Mills, 1985; If I Were Your Woman, 1987; Home, 1989; Something Real, 1992; Personal Inspirations, 1995; The Best of Stephanie Mills, 2000; Born For This, 2004; Gold, 2006; Breathless, 2010; "NBC live musical production", 2015. **Honors/Awds:** Drama Desk Award, 1974; American Music Award, 1979, 1980, 1981; 2 Gold Albums; Grammy Award for Best Female R&B Vocal, 1980; American Music Award for Best Female R&B Vocal, 1981; Nat Asn Advan Colored People Image Awards. **Home Addr:** PO Box K-350, Tarzana, CA 91356. **Business Addr:** Singer, Actor, Wenig-La Monica Associates Agency, 580 White Plains Rd Suite 130, Tarrytown, NY 10591, **Business Phone:** (914)631-6500.

### MILLS, STEVE

Executive. **Personal:** Born Oct 6, 1959, Roosevelt, NY; married Beverly; children: Kristen & Danielle. **Educ:** Princeton Univ, BA, sociol, 1981. **Career:** Ecuador, prof basketball, 1981-82; Chem Bank NY, mgr new bus develop, 1982-83; NBA Properties, acc exec, 1984-87, nat prog mgr, 1986; NBA spec events dept, 1987-93, vpres, 1989; NBA comnrs off, vpres corp develop, 1993-95; NBA, sr vpres basketball & player develop, 1994-2000; NY Knickerbockers, exec vpres franchise opers, 2000-02; Madison Sq Garden sports team opers, pres, 2001-03; Madison Sq Garden Sports, pres & chief exec officer, 2003-08; MSG Sports Teams, pres bus opers & chief operating officer, 2008-09; Magic Johnson Enterprises, consult, 2009-10; Princeton Univ, course contribr, 2009-10; Athletes & Entertainers Wealth Mgt LLC, chief exec officer & partner, 2010-13; New York Knicks, pres & gen mgr, 2013-. **Orgs:** Co chmn, Madison Square Garden Cheering C Found, 2003; bd bir, Salvation Army Greater NY; Arthur Ashe Inst Urban Health & Econ Comn Nassau Co; bd trustee, Basketball Hall Fame; bd dir, USA Basketball. **Home Addr:** , South Orange, NJ 07079. **Business Addr:** President, General Manager, New York Knicks, 2 Penn Plz Suite 15, New York, NY 10121.

### MILLS, TERRY RICHARD

Basketball player, basketball coach. **Personal:** Born Dec 21, 1967, Romulus, MI; son of Emma. **Educ:** Univ Mich, BS, kinesiology, 1990. **Career:** Basketball player (retired), basketball coach; Denver Nuggets, forward, 1990-91; NJ Nets, 1991-92; Detroit Pistons, 1992-97, 1999-2000; Miami Heat, 1997-99; Ind Pacers, forward, 2000-01; Intl Basketball League, Macomb County Mustangs, head coach, 2005-06; Henry Ford Community Col, asst basketball coach, 2009-13; IMG Media, radio analyst, 2013-. **Home Addr:** , MI. **Business Addr:** Radio Analyst, IMG Media, 200 5th Ave 7th Fl, New York, NY 10010, **Business Phone:** (212)489-8300.

### MILNER, MICHAEL EDWIN

Executive director, banker. **Personal:** Born Mar 16, 1952, Atlanta, GA; son of Edwin R and Ethel M Minor; married Ocie Stiggers; children: Kimberly, Michaelyn, Therron & Tasha. **Educ:** Morehouse Col, BA, bus admin, 1974. **Career:** Gen Finance Corp, mgr, 1974-78; Fed Res Bank Atlanta, fed bank examr, 1978-90; S Trust Corp, corp vpres, dir, community reinvestment, 1990-99; Fed Res Bank Atlanta, Regional Community develop dir, sr community develop mgr, 1999-2010; Ala Asset Bldg Coalition, exec dir, 2010-. **Orgs:** Brotherhood St Andrews; Birmingham Asn Urban Bankers; bd dir, Ala Non-profit Resource Ctr. **Home Addr:** 812 Jeffery Cir, Birmingham, AL 35235. **Business Addr:** Executive Director, Alabama Asset Building Coalition, 601 19th St N, Birmingham, AL 35203, **Business Phone:** (205)731-4000.

### MILNER, THIRMAN L.

Writer, executive, mayor. **Personal:** Born Oct 29, 1933, Hartford, CT; son of Henry Marshall and Grace Allen; children: Theresa, Gary & Thirman Jr. **Career:** Executive (retired); All State Ins Co, acct rep; Gen Elec Bus Div, acct rep; New York Coun Against Poverty CAA, exec asst; Comn Develop NYC, dep asst admin; Comn Renewal Team Community Action Agency, pub rels dir; State CT, rep; House Reps, asst maj leader, 1978-81; City Hartford, mayor, 1981-87; First Nat Supermarkets Inc, dir, govt affairs, 1987; State sen, asst majority leader, 1993-94; Food Mkt Inst, chmn govt rel. **Orgs:** Sub-comm chmn, Finance Revenue & Bonding legis Comm, 1979-80; sub-comn chmn, Planning & Devel legis Comm, 1979-80; northeast region liaison, Minority Energy Tech Asst Prog, 1979-81; bd dir, Hartford Br Nat Asn Advan Colored People, 1979-81, pres, 2001-; regional coordr, Nat Caucus Black State Legislators, 1979-81; Nat Conf Black Mayors, first vpres, 1985-86, assoc mem, 1987-; bd dir, Massachusetts Food Assoc, 1989-; bd mem, Conn Food Assoc, 1989-; life mem, Nat Asn Advan Colored People; bd dirs, Ny Food Merchants Asn; Sons Am Revolution. **Honors/Awds:** Community Service Award, Omega Phi Epsilon Frat, 1980; Community Service Award, Guardians Af-Am Police, 1980; Community Service Award, NAACP, 1980; Community Service Award, Gr Hartford Black Soc Workers, 1980; Jewish Tree of Life Award, 1986; Univ of Hartford Chair-Establishing Thirman L Milner Scholar, 1987; dedication of Thirman L Milner Public Elementary School, 1989. **Special Achievements:** Book: "Up From Slavery"; First African Amer mayor, New England popularly elected, 1981. **Home Addr:** 54 Myrtle St Apt E, Hartford, CT 06105-2102, **Home Phone:** (860)246-4656.

### MILTON, DELISHA LACHELL. See JONES, DELISHA MILTON.

### MILTON, LEROY

Research scientist. **Personal:** Born Apr 7, 1924, Los Angeles, CA; married Alma M Melonson; children: James E & Angela H. **Educ:** Pepperdine Univ, BS, 1949. **Career:** Real estate investor, 1950-96; Secured Div LA Co, chief, 1961-63; LA Co, head col invest, 1963-68; exec asst, bldg serv, 1968-69; LA Co, admin dep coroner, 1969-70; Ment Health Dept, LA County, chief admin serv, 1976-96; Avacaclo Grower, 1985-; Potomac View Prop, financial consult, currently. **Orgs:** Pres, Milton Enterprise, 1960-; pres & dir, Pub Ser Credit Union, 1960-73; dir, Eye Dog Found, 1966-73; dir, Beverly Hills Hollywood Nat Asn Advan Colored People, 1969-77; pres & mem, Cosmos Club, 1946-; Alpha Phi Alpha. **Business Addr:** Financial Consultant, Potomac View Properties, 17437 Tarzana St, Encino, CA 91316-3824.

### MIMMS, DR. MAXINE BUIE

Educator, social worker. **Personal:** Born Mar 4, 1928, Newport News, VA; married Jacques; children: Theodore, Tonie & Kenneth. **Educ:** Va Union Univ, BA, 1950; Union Grad Sch, PhD, 1977. **Career:** Seattle Pub Schs, teacher, 1953-61; Kirkland Pub Schs, teacher, 1961-64, adminr, 1964-69; Women's Bur Dept Labor, 1969-72; Evergreen State Col, prof, 1972-91; prof emer; Antioch Univ, Seattle, fac; Maxine Mimms Academies, founder, 2004-. **Orgs:** Nat Consultances Educ; New Approaches Higher Educ; Nat Asn Advan Colored People; Urban League; Nat Educ Asn. **Honors/Awds:** Women of the Year, Seattle St Louis Tacoma; First Annual Sustainable Community Outstanding Leadership Award, 2001. **Special Achievements:** first Director of the Tacoma Campus. **Home Addr:** 140 SE Oyster Beach Rd, Shelton, WA 98584-7783, **Home Phone:** (360)426-5515. **Business Addr:** Founder, Maxine Mimms Academies, 1602 Martin Luther King Jr Way, Tacoma, WA 98405-0678, **Business Phone:** (253)591-5321.

### MIMS, BEVERLY CAROL

Educator. **Personal:** Born Jan 29, 1955, Washington, DC; daughter of Oscar L Sr and Barbara Crockett; children: Michael Armwood-Phillips Jackson. **Educ:** Howard Univ, BS, pharm, 1977, PhD, pharm, 1987. **Career:** Prof Pharm, pharmacist, mgr, 1978-80; DC Gen Hosp, staff pharmacist, pharmacist-in-charge, 1980-85; Howard Univ, asst prof, pharm pract, 1987-, assoc prof, Clin & Admin Pharm Scis, fac advisor, currently; Wash Ctr Aging Serv, Wash, DC, Consult Pharmacist; Pharamacol Nursing & Health Sci Students, Montgomery Col, Takoma Pk, MD, instr; Permanente Health Plan, Wash, DC, Pharmacist Kaiser; Humana/Group Health Plan, Wash, DC, Pharmacist; Howard Univ Col Pharm & Pharmaceut Sci, Wash, DC, Teaching Asst; Northwest Pharm, Wash, DC, Pharm Grad Intern. **Orgs:** Am Soc Hosp Pharmacists, 1980-; Wash Metrop Soc Hosp Pharmacists, 1980-; Rho Chi Soc Nat Pharm Hon Soc, 1986-; Nat Pharmac Asn, 1990-; Antibiotics & Adverse Drug Events Sub-Comms; Am Soc Health-Syst Pharmacists; Am Soc Consult Pharmacists; Wash D.C. Pharmaceutical Asn. **Home Addr:** 655 Kensington Pl NE, Washington, DC 20011. **Business Addr:** Associate Professor, Clinical & Administrative Pharmacy Sciences, Faculty Advisor, Howard University, 2300 4th St NW, Washington, DC 20059, **Business Phone:** (202)806-7232.

### MIMS, DR. GEORGE L.

School administrator, association executive. **Personal:** Born Feb 27, 1934, Batesburg, SC; son of George W and Mary Aletha Corley; married Clara Ann Twigg; children: Cheryl Ann & Carla Aletha. **Educ:** Fla A&M Univ, BS, 1955; Teachers Col, Columbia Univ, MA,

1957, prof dip, 1967; Rutgers Univ, EdD, 1976. **Career:** School administrator (retired); Fisk Univ, head res counr, 1959-61; Volusia Co Community Col, Fla, dean stud, 1961-63; Hunter Col, New York, asst placement dir, 1963-67; Pace Univ, dir spec progs, 1968, sch law; Argosy Univ, Col Educ, asst prof; Community aids network, secy. **Orgs:** Proposal reader, US Off Educ, New York, 1974-; pres, Eta Theta Lambda Chap, Alpha Phi Alpha, 1980-87, 1996-97; res, Ny Div AACD, 1982-83; pres AERA, Spec Int Group Black Educ, 1982-86; ed bd Jour, Educ &Psych Res, 1983-86; adv comt, Merck Sharp & Dohme, 1983-; chmn AERA, ComnSpec Int Groups, 1984-87. **Honors/Awds:** Cert Merit, Big Bro New York, 1969; Leadership Award HEOP, 1975; HEOP Award, 1980; Minority Alumni Award, Pace Univ, NY, 1983; Brothers Award, Eta Theta Lambda Chap, 1987; Community Service Award, Cent Nassau Club, 1989; Humanitarian Award, Howard Univ LI Alumni, 1990; Youth Community Educ Award, Ministerial Alliance N Amityville & Vicinity (LI), 1991; African Am Youth Award, African Am Heritage Asn Long Island, 1993; Distinguished Community Service Award, Nat Hampton Univ Alumni Asn, 1993; Distinguished Service Award, Lakeview Branch, Nat Asn Advan Colored People, 1994; Jr League LI, 1994; Community Service Award, Eta Theta Lambda Chap, Alpha Phi Alpha Frat Inc, 1995; Humanitarian Award, Lakeside Family & C Serv, Spring Valley, New York, 1996; Gentleman of Distinction Award, Holy Trinity Baptist Church, Amityville, New York, 1996; Appreciation Award, Hempstead Sch Dist, Hempstead, New York, 1996; Jewel Founders Award, Chapter NYACOA, Alpha Phi Alpha Frat, 1996; Founder's Award, Coalition Diversity, Pace Univ, 1998; Outstanding Senior Vol, Sch Bd Sarasota County, Fla, 1999-2000; Dr. George L. Mims Oratorical Contest; The African Hall of Fame, Mt Pleasant Bapt Church; Outstanding Service Award, Dedication Higher Educ. **Home Addr:** 113 Shady Pkwy, Sarasota, FL 34232-2370, **Home Phone:** (941)379-2934. **Business Addr:** Secretary, Community Aids Network, 1231 N Tuttle Ave, Sarasota, FL 34237, **Business Phone:** (941)366-0134.

## MIMS, MARJORIE JOYCE

President (organization), association executive. **Personal:** Born Sep 14, 1926, Chicago, IL; married Thomas S; children: John & Raleigh. **Educ:** Univ IL, BS, LAS, 1949, MS, admin, 1974; Univ Chicago, advan study, 1976; De Paul Univ, advan study, 1981. **Career:** Jack & Jill Am Chicago Chapt, pres, 1974-78; Moles, nat vpres, 1978-82; Links Inc, cent area dir, 1983. **Orgs:** Am & Guid Asn, 1970-; bd mem, Ada S McKinley Asn, 1972-82, Asn Family Living, 1973-81; chmn, Nat Nominating Comt Jack & Jill Am, 1978. **Honors/Awds:** Woman of the Year, Radio Station WAIT, 1974; Anti-Basielus Theta Omega Chap Alpha Kappa Alpha Sor. **Home Addr:** 7016 S Constance Ave, Chicago, IL 60649, **Home Phone:** (773)752-1184.

## MIMS, PASTOR RAYMOND EVERETT, SR.

Manager, clergy. **Personal:** Born Apr 10, 1938, Bogalusa, LA; son of Edward A and Hattie L; married Shirley Humbles; children: Raymond E Jr. **Educ:** Southern Univ, BS, 1961; United Theol Sem, BTh, 1984, MTh, 1987. **Career:** Crown Zellerbach Corp, asst safety & supvr, 1969-74, schedule coordr prod, 1974, logging foreman, 1974-79, supvr employee rels, 1979-82, employee rels mgr, 1982-86; Gaylord Container Corp, personnel supvr, 1986-; Greater Ebenezer Baptist Church, pastor, currently. **Orgs:** Am Pu lpwood Asn, 1974-86; bd mem, Zellco Fed Credit Union, 1980-91; bd mem, Habitat Humanity, 1986-; Am Paper Inst, 1986-; bd chair, Good Samaritans Nursing Home, 1987-92; Bogalusa City Sch Bd, 1992-; chmn, Finance Comt & Transp Comt; La Home & Foreign Mission Baptist State Conv Inc. **Honors/Awds:** HH Jefferson Memorial Safety Award, Am Pulpwood Asn, 1981. **Home Addr:** 1714 St Louis St, Bogalusa, LA 70427-5248, **Home Phone:** (985)735-5146. **Business Addr:** Pastor, Greater Ebenezer Baptist Church, 2301 Medora St, Lake Charles, LA 70601, **Business Phone:** (337)436-3999.

## MIMS, RHONDA

President (organization). **Personal:** daughter of Robert and Annie Mims; married James Simpson. **Educ:** Univ SC, BS, criminal justice, 1992, JD, 1992. **Career:** State S Carolina Off Atty Gen, head, prosecution Div, 1995-97; Nat Dist Atty Asn's Am Prosecutor's Res Inst, sr atty, 1997-98; US Dept Justice, litigation atty, 1998-2000; ING territorial sales mgr, 2000-01, vpres, 2001-02, vpres & coun, 2002-05; ING Am/Voya Financial, head corp responsibility, 2003-14; ING Americas, sr vpres, 2003-14; Paul Hastings LLP, managing dir, corp social responsibility, 2014-. **Orgs:** Pres, ING Found/Voya Found; dir-elect, Northeast Regional Bd dir Oper HOPE; Found Ctr; Links Inc; Alpha Kappa Alpha Sorority Inc; sitting bd dir, Thurgold Marshall Col Fund; chmn, Exec Leadership Found, currently; S Carolina Bar Asn; bd dir, Asn Corp Contrib Professionals; bd dir, US Chamber Coms Bus Civic Leadership Ctr; trustee, Ams Promise; bd dir, Woodruff Arts Ctr; bd dir, Harlem Sch Arts, currently; bd dir, Citizens Comt C New York, currently. **Business Addr:** Managing Director, Paul Hastings, 75 E 55th St, New York, NY 10022, **Business Phone:** (212)318-6000.

## MIMS, DR. ROBERT BRADFORD

Physician, educator, scientist. **Personal:** Born Mar 24, 1934, Durant, MS; son of Dawson and Laura; married Eleanor Veronica Meeseburgh; children: Sharon Beverly, Valerie Tracy, Robin Eleanor & Bari Allen. **Educ:** Shorter Col, attended 1954; Philander Smith Col, BS, 1956; Univ Ark, Sch Med, MD, 1960; Univ SC Med Sch, attended 1964. **Career:** Univ SC Sch Med, intern, 1960-61, resident, 1961-64, 1968-69, acad prof, 1964-77, Internal Med & Endocrinol, assoc clin prof, 1978-86, Internal Med Residency Prog, supvr; John Wesley County Hosp, assoc med dir, 1970-74; Univ SC LAC Med Ctr, Home Health Servs, assoc med dir, 1974-78, chmn; Found Med Ctr, pres & bd dir, 1978-82; Endocrine Metab Clin Santa Rosa, dir, 1984-2006; Thyroid Educ Inst, fac, 2001; Mims Enterprise Diversified, chief exec officer; ACE, co-founder; Peoples Network, independent sr exec; Endocrine Teaching Clin Family Pract Residents, founder & dir. **Orgs:** Med lectr, var pub educ meeting, 1977-; bd dir, Vis Nurses Asn, 1978-83; vpres & bd dir, Health Plan Redwoods, 1978-80; bd dir, Sonoma Co Diabetic Asn, 1978-88; dir, BSA, 1979-81; dir, Dept Internal Med Family Pract Sonoma County Hosp, 1984-86; Calif Polit Action Asn, 1984; dir, Dept Internal Med Santa Rosa Memorial Hosp, 1984-86; vpres, bd dir, Laura & Dawson Mims Educ Found & Mims Res Inst, 1985-; pres, N Calif Am Diabetic Asn, 1985-86; founder & pres, Endocrine Soc Redwoods, 1987-; bd dir, exec comt, Calif Affil Am Diabetes Asn, 1986-89; Felon Col Endocrinol, 1986; AACE, 1992; Am Asn Clin Endocrinologists; N Am Menopause Soc, 2001; bd dir, Tri-Co Found Med Care; bd dir, VNA Sonoma Co; Calif Asn Health Care Home; Am Diabetes Asn; Altadena Family Serv; Altadena Neighbors; Pasadena Integration Plan; med admin advr, Southwest La Comity Med Corp; served numerous community & hosp comts; Pasadena Unified Sch Dist; Calif Med Asn; Endocrinol Soc; AAAS; Am Fedn Clin Res; Am Col Phys; Am Geriat Asn; Nat Asn Home Health. **Honors/Awds:** Nat Honor Soc Philander Smith Col, 1952-56, Summa Cum Laude, 1956; Award & Scholarship Pasadena Unified School Dist, Calif Congress Parents & Teachers Inc, 1971; Award for Med-Cor Affairs, Univ SC, Sch Med, 1972-74; Nat Sci Soc; Hon Life Membership Calif & Nat Congress PTA, 1973; numerous Collegiate Awards & Honors; numerous scientific presentations & publications; Outstanding Service Award, Am Asn Clin Endocrinologists. **Home Addr:** 5500 Wilshire Dr, Santa Rosa, CA 95404-1056, **Home Phone:** (707)545-3801. **Business Addr:** Director, Endocrine Metabolic Clinic, 5202 Old Redwood Hwy, Santa Rosa, CA 95403, **Business Phone:** (707)545-3856.

## MIMS, TERRENCE

Executive. **Educ:** Univ SC; Benedict Col. **Career:** New World Group Inc, pres, currently. **Business Addr:** President, New World Group Inc, 1117 Peachtree Walk NE Suite 123, Atlanta, GA 30309-3950, **Business Phone:** (404)876-6366.

## MINAJ, NICKI (ONIKA TANYA MARAJ)

Singer. **Personal:** Born Dec 8, 1982. **Educ:** La Guardia High School of Music and Art. **Career:** "Pink Friday" album, released 2010; "American Idol," Judge, 2012-13; "Pink Friday: Roman Reloaded" album, 2012. **Honors/Awds:** Black Entertainment Television (BET) Awards, Best Hip-Hop Female, Best New Artist, 2010, Best Female Hip-Hop Artist, 2011, 2012, and 2013; MTV Video Music Awards, Best Hip-Hop Video, 2011, Best Female Video, 2012; American Music Awards, Favorite Rap/Hip-Hop Artist, Favorite Rap/Hip-Hop Album, 2011, Favorite Rap/Hip-Hop Artist, Favorite Rap/Hip-Hop Album, 2012; Billboard Music Awards, Top Rap Album, 2013; People's Choice Award, Favorite Hip-Hop Artist, 2013. **Special Achievements:** Performed at the 2012 Super Bowl; "Pink Friday" album peaked at number one on Billboard's charts and is Recording Industry Association of America (RIAA)-certified platinum; set a record for the number of appearances on the Billboard Hot 100 chart by a female rapper (44 as of 2013).

## MINCEY, KAREN

Vice president (organization), information scientist. **Personal:** married Earl; children: Lauren. **Educ:** Univ New Orleans, BS, elec engineering, 1982; Loyola Univ, MBA, 1988. **Career:** Entergy, 1982-90; TECO Energy, engr, distrib engineering; Telecommunications & Info Technol, vpres, chief info officer, 1990-. **Orgs:** Chairperson, Hillsborough Community Col Found; bd mem, Crisis Ctr Tampa Bay; bd mem, Tampa Club; bd mem, Boys & Girls Club Tampa Bay. **Honors/Awds:** Tampa Bay's "40 Under 40" Award; Woman in Color in Technology, "Chairman's Award"; "Black Enterprise", 75 Most Powerful Women in Business, 2010. **Business Addr:** Vice President, TECO Energy, 702 N Franklin St, Tampa Bay, FL 33602.

## MINCEY, W. JAMES, JR.

Administrator. **Personal:** Born Feb 27, 1947, Statesboro, GA. **Career:** NC Mut Life Ins, emp; Kroney-Mincey Inc, ins designer, currently. **Orgs:** Pres, Bulloch Co Chapt; SCLC, 1970-; co-chmn, Mcgovern campaign Bulloch Co, 1972-72; pub dir, Nat Asn Advan Colored People, 1969-70; youth coun pres, Nat Asn Advan Colored People, 1967-68; mem Wesley Lodge 161; Mason; Ins Underwriters Asn; Thomas Grove Bapt Church. **Honors/Awds:** Semi-finalist, Ford Found Leadership Develop Prog. **Home Addr:** 28 Carver St, Statesboro, GA 30458, **Home Phone:** (912)764-6511. **Business Addr:** Insurance Designer, Kroney MIncey Inc, 12221 Merit Dr Suite 1210, Dallas, TX 75251, **Business Phone:** (214)386-8500.

## MINCY, CHARLES ANTHONY (CHUCK MINCY)

Football coach, executive, football player. **Personal:** Born Dec 16, 1969, Los Angeles, CA. **Educ:** Pasadena City Col, AA, gen studies, 1989; Univ Wash, BA, African Am studies, 1991; Azusa Pac Univ, BA, orgn leadership, 2005; Univ Southern Calif, MA, teaching, 2015. **Career:** Football player (retired), executive, coach; Kans City Chiefs, defensive back, 1991-95; Mincy Investments, real estate investor, 1993-; Minn Vikings Football LLC, prof athelete, 1995-96; Tampa Bay Buccaneers, prof athlete, 1996-99; Oakland Raiders, prof athlete, 1999-2000; Dorsey High Sch, defensive backs coach, 2001-02, head football coach & defensive coordr, 2016-; Prudential Calif Realty, John Aaroe, realtor, 2004-05; Digital Command Post, non-linear video ed, producer, 2005-07; Inglewood High Sch, head football coach, 2005-10; Hathaway-Sycamores Child & Family Serv, crisis counr & asst teacher, 2008-10; Inglewood Blackhawks, defensive coordr, 2010-11; Nottingham Ventures, real estate mgr, 2009-12; Under Radar Sports Media, partner, 2010-. **Honors/Awds:** All Pac-10, 1990. **Special Achievements:** Films: 1991 Rose Bowl, 1991; 1993 AFC Championship Game, 1994. TV Series: "TNT Sunday Night Football", 1992; "ESPN's Sunday Night Football", 1992-98; "NFL Monday Night Football", 1992-98; "NFL on FOX", 1998. **Business Addr:** Partner, Under Radar Sports Media, 15727 S Western Ave Suite 108, Gardena, CA 90250.

## MINER, HAROLD DAVID

Basketball player, real estate executive. **Personal:** Born May 5, 1971, Inglewood, CA; children: 2. **Educ:** Univ Southern Calif, attended 1992. **Career:** Basketball player (retired), real estate executive; Miami Heat, shooting guard, 1992-94, point guard, 1995; Cleveland Cavaliers, shooting guard, 1995-96; real estate investor, currently. **Honors/Awds:** Pac-10 Freshman of the Year, 1990; Pac-10 Player of the Year, 1992; College Basketball Player of the Year, Sports Illus; NBA Slam Dunk Contest champion, 1993, 1995. **Home Addr:** , Las Vegas, NV.

## MINER, WILLIAM GERARD

Educator, architect. **Personal:** Born May 12, 1950, Washington, DC; son of George and Charlotte. **Educ:** Princeton Univ, AB, 1972; Mass Inst Tech, 1974. **Career:** US Dept State, Foreign Bldgs Opers, chief, engineering support br, 1990-, prog mgr, 1985-90; CRS Sirrine Int Group, training & res coordr, 1983-85; Am Inst Architects, dir pract publ, tech ed archit graphic stand, 1978-83; Univ Md Sch Archit, asst prof archit, 1977-81; Keyes Lethbridge & Condon, proj archit, 1974-77; MIT Sch Archit & Urban Planning, teaching asst, 1973-74; Keyes Lethbridge & Condon, intern archit, 1973; MIT Sch Archit, rehab consult, 1973; Keene Interior & Systs, designer draftsman, 1972; Peoples' Workshop, co-founder, designer, 1972-72; Irving Wasserman Gulf Reston Inc, asst head planner, 1971; Princeton Univ Sch Archit & Planning, res asst, 1970-71; Princeton Alumni Coun, travelling res, 1970; Joseph Minor Nat Capital Housing Authority, asst sr archit, 1970; OBOs design & engineering off, dir, 2012. **Orgs:** Stud Planning Team Metro Dist Comn, 1972; instr, Trenton Design Ctr, 1970-71; stud rep, bd dir, AIA, 1972; Am Inst Architects; Assoc Gen Contractors Am; Construct Indust Inst. **Honors/Awds:** Design competition finalist, Nat Granite Quarry Asn, 1974. **Home Addr:** 363 Aragon Ave Apt 711W, Coral Gables, FL 33134. **Business Addr:** Chief, US Department of State, Foreign Buildings Operations, SA-6 Rm 326, Washington, DC 20520.

## MINES, RAYMOND C.

Executive. **Personal:** Born Somerville, NJ; son of Raymond C Sr and Helen M Miller; children: 2; married Joyce; children: Sean M & Kimara L. **Educ:** Rutgers Univ, Acad Advan Traffic & Transp, traffic transp mgt. **Career:** McDonald's Corp, restaurant mgr, 1975, dir opers & training, 1982-84, regional mgr, 1984-85, sr regional mgr, 1985-86, regional vpres, 1986-91, zone vpres, 1991-93, sr vpres & zone mgr, 1993-98, exec vpres, system rels, 1998-. **Orgs:** Bd dir, Children's Mem Hosp; bd dir, Daniel Murphy Scholar Found; bd dir, Chicago Urban League; bd, Chipotle Mexican Grill; adv bd, United Negro Col Fund; adv bd, Northern Trust Bank, Naperville; adv bd, Nat Coun LaRaza; adv bd, Hispanic Asn on Corp Responsibility; adv bd, Nat Puerto-Rican Coalition. **Home Addr:** 1612 Winberie Ct, Naperville, IL 60564-5691, **Home Phone:** (630)369-9291. **Business Addr:** Executive Vice President, McDonald, 2915 Jorie Blvd, Oak Brook, IL 60523, **Business Phone:** (630)623-6230.

## MINION, MIA

Computer scientist. **Personal:** Born Nov 5, 1960, Washington, DC; daughter of Jackson and Katherine; children: Daryn A. **Educ:** Coppin State Col, BS, MD, mgt sci, 1985. **Career:** Coppin State Col, clerk-typist, 1981-85; US Department of Health and Human Services, Social Security Admin, comput syst analyst, IT proj mgr, 1985-. **Orgs:** Alpha Kappa Mu Nat Honor Soc, 1983; vpres, Zeta Phi Beta Sor Inc, 1984-85; Nat Deans List, 1983, 1984, 1985. **Home Addr:** 2816 Claybrooke Dr, Windsor Mill, MD 21244-2014, **Home Phone:** (410)578-8473. **Business Addr:** Computer Systems Analyst, U.S. Department of Health and Human Services Social Security Admin, 6401 Security Blvd, Baltimore, MD 21235, **Business Phone:** (410)594-6991.

## MINOR, BILLY JOE

Educator, physiologist. **Personal:** Born Nov 10, 1938, Pine Bluff, AR; married Mary McMillian; children: Billy, Devron & Darius. **Educ:** Calif State Col, Hayward, BA, 1968, MS, 1969; Ind Univ, PhD, 1974. **Career:** San Francisco Sch, sch psychologist, 1969-71; Oakland Univ, assoc prof, 1974, Human Resource Develop Dept, chair, prof emer, currently. **Home Addr:** 2160 Odette, Waterford, MI 48328. **Business Addr:** Chairperson, Professor Emeritus, Oakland University, 435B Pawley Hall, Rochester, MI 48309, **Business Phone:** (248)370-4186.

## MINOR, DALE MICHAEL

Counselor, educator. **Personal:** Born Jul 31, 1949, Cleveland, OH; son of James H and Emma Lucille; married Elizabeth; children: Ethan. **Educ:** Ohio Univ, BS, 1973, MED, 1999. **Career:** Hocking Col, Minority Affairs, Alcohol & Drug Educ Prog, judiciary sanction officer, coordr, currently; D M C & Assoc, counr, currently. **Orgs:** Chief instr, Am Bando Asn, 1973-2002; Ohio Asn Multicultural Counr Develop, 1998-99; Chi Sigma Iota Hons Soc, 1998-2000; Am Coun Asn, 1998-2001. **Honors/Awds:** Spec Serv & Achievement, King Hussein of Jordan, 1988; 6th Degree Black Belt, Am Bando Asn, 1997. **Business Addr:** Counselor, D M C & Associates, 8699 Terrell Rd, Athens, OH 45701, **Business Phone:** (740)594-2051.

## MINOR, DEWAYNE

Racehorse trainer, horseman or horsewoman. **Personal:** Born Nov 4, 1956, Detroit, MI; son of Thomas and Arleathier; married Annemette Christiansen. **Career:** Harness racing trainer & driver, 1976-. **Honors/Awds:** Dan Rathka Horseman of the Year, Mich Harness Horsemans Asn, 1996; Won 470 races in 3, 200 drives, 2000. **Special Achievements:** First African-American driver and trainer to compete in the 75-year history of the Hambletonian. **Home Addr:** 3640 Village Dr Suite D, Delray Beach, FL 33445-2956, **Home Phone:** (561)637-2503. **Business Addr:** Horse Race Driver, Odds On Racing, 1550 E Bemes Rd, Crete, IL 60417, **Business Phone:** (708)672-3438.

## MINOR, EMMA LUCILLE

Educator. **Personal:** Born Mar 16, 1925, Pollard, AL; daughter of Berry Walton and Estella Dowell Walton; married James H; children: Dale Michael, Gail Christopher & Valerie E Alloy. **Educ:** Kent State Univ, Kent, OH, BS, 1971; Cleveland State Univ, Cleveland, OH, MA, educ admin, 1974. **Career:** Cleveland Pub Schs, Cleveland OH, cadet teacher, 1968-72, consult teacher, admin intern, asst prin, 1972-75, prin, 1975-85. **Orgs:** Nat Asn Reading & Lang Educ, 1975-85; Phi Delta Kappa Educ Frat, 1976-89; Nat Alliance Black Sch Educ, 1977-89; supreme basileus, nat officer, Nat Sorority Phi Delta Kappa Inc, 1977-89; Nat Asn Advan Colored People, 1977-89; local officer, Ohio Asn Sch Admin, 1980-85; Delta Sigma Theta Sorority, 1982-89; affil rep, Nat Urban League, 1985-89, Legal Coun Civil Rights, 1986-89, United Negro Col Fund, 1986-89; affil pres, Nat CounNegro Women, 1986-89; co-chairperson, Assault Illiteracy, Prof Educ Comt, 1986-89; pres, Nat Sorority Phi Delta Kappa Perpetual Scholar Found Inc, 1997-2001. **Home Addr:** 310 Autumn Glenn Cir, Fayetteville, GA 30215, **Home Phone:** (770)460-9960.

### MINOR, GREG MAGADO
Basketball coach, basketball player. **Personal:** Born Sep 8, 1971, Sandersville, GA; son of Twiggs and Charley R Brown; married Stephanie; children: Kira, Greg Jr, Khalid & Chloe. **Educ:** Univ Phoenix, BA, criminal justice admin, 2006. **Career:** Basketball player (retired), basketball coach; Los Angeles Clippers, 1994; Boston Celtics, guard, shooting guard, 1995, 1997-99, small forward, 1996; Ind Pacers, 2004; Okla Cavalry, asst coach, currently; Nat Basketball Asn, 2007-09; Continental Basketball Asn's Lawton-Ft Sill Calvary, asst coach, 2008; Bakersfield Jam, asst coach, 2009-10; Idaho Stampede, asst coach, 2010. **Orgs:** Platinum mem, Nat Basketball Retired Players Asn. **Special Achievements:** First round pick, No 25, NBA Draft, 1994. **Business Addr:** Assistant Coach, Oklahoma Cavalry, 629 SW C Ave 3rd Fl, Lawton, OK 73502, **Business Phone:** (580)353-2287.

### MINOR, JESSICA
Executive. **Personal:** Born Chicago, IL. **Educ:** Wittenberg Univ, BA, 1962; Univ Chicago, MA, 1964; Univ Calif, JD, 1988. **Career:** Mgt consult, corp exec & psychotherapist, 1969-; Minor & Co, pres, currently. **Orgs:** Phi Alpha Delta Law Frat Un Asn; Commonwealth Club Calif; Am Women Int Understanding; Planning Forum, Int Visitors Ctr; San Francisco Opera Guild; Founders Comt, Un World Ctr San Francisco; charter mem, San Francisco Symphony League. **Business Addr:** President, Minor & Co, 2060 Ofarrell St Suite 304, San Francisco, CA 94115, **Business Phone:** (415)563-5767.

### MINOR, KEIJA
Periodical editor. **Educ:** Harvard University Law School, Graduate. **Career:** Niche Media "Aspen Peak" and "Los Angeles Confidential," Managing Editor, 2003-05; "Gotham Magazine," Editor-in-Chief, 2005-07; "Uptown Magazine," Editor-in-Chief, 2008-11; Conde Nast "Brides" Magazine, Executive Editor, 2011-12, Editor-in-Chief, 2012-. **Honors/Awds:** TheGrio.com, 100 Making History Today, 2012. **Special Achievements:** First African American woman in Conde Nast's history (publisher of "Brides") to hold position of Editor-in-Chief for any of its magazines.

### MINOR, TRACEY L. (TRACEY DE MORSELLA)
Publisher. **Personal:** Born Nov 9, 1963, Philadelphia, PA; daughter of C Wes and Evie R. **Educ:** Temple Univ, BA, commun, 1988. **Career:** Expression Modeling Agency, model, 1982-87; Ctr Social Policy, newsletter ed, intern, 1985-86; Click Modeling Agency, model, 1985-87; Horizon House, newsletter ed, intern, 1986-87; Atlantic Tech, newspaper assoc ed, 1987-88; St Benedict's Day Care Ctr, asst dir, 1988-89; EMSCO Sci Enterprises, sales rep, 1989-91; Del Valley Network, publ; Multicultural Advantage, pres, 2003, managing producer, currently. **Orgs:** Harriet Tubman Hist Preserv Soc, 1980-81; Screen Actor's Guild, 1983-87; Pub Rels Soc Am, 1987-89; Nat Asn Black MBA's, 1992-; Poor Richard Club, 1992-; New Penn Del Many Bus Coun, 1992-; Women Communs, 1992-. **Honors/Awds:** Entrepreneur of the Year, Nat Black MBA Asn, 1992; Urban Profiles Mag, Honored in 30 Under 30, Thirty Top Bus Owners, 1992; Woman of the Year, ZPB, 1992. **Business Addr:** Managing Producer, The Multicultural Advantage, 8345 NW 66th St Suite 8916, Miami, FL 33166-2626, **Business Phone:** (425)296-6109.

### MINOR, WILLIE
School administrator. **Personal:** Born Jan 31, 1951, Navasota, TX; son of Carl Jr and Marjorie Williams. **Educ:** Prairie View A&M Univ, BS, 1973, MS, 1974; Univ Phoenix, MA, 1980; Ariz State Univ, EdD, 1976. **Career:** Fac Asn, secy, 1984-85; Admin Mgmt Soc, pres, 1984-85; Phoenix Col, admin intern, 1989-97, assoc dean instr, fac exec coun, pres, 2003-04; Rio Salado Col, emer fac, currently; Rio Salado Col, fac chmn bus & appl progs; Phoenix Col, prof bus. **Orgs:** Mem & sec, Delta Mu Delta, 1972; grad co-op, NASA Space Ctr, 1974; sponsor, Afro Am Club, 1977; mem & sponsor, Phi Beta Lambda, 1972-; Bus Comm Asn, 1976-85; mem & officer Delta Pi Epsilon, 1976-; pres, Admin Mgt Soc, 1977-; Phi Delta Kappa, 1980-; arbitrator, Better Bus Bur, 1984-; pres, Maricopa Community Col Dist Retirees Asn Allied Health/Health Related Professions Bus. **Honors/Awds:** Academic Recognition, Prairie View Fac, 1976. **Home Addr:** 6442 W Fremont Rd, Laveen, AZ 85281-8519. **Business Addr:** Emeritus Faculty, Rio Salado College, 2323 W 14th St, Tempe, AZ 85281, **Business Phone:** (480)517-8283.

### MINTER, BARRY ANTOINE
Football player. **Personal:** Born Jan 28, 1970, Mount Pleasant, TX; married Shawyna; children: Gia & Bari. **Educ:** Tulsa Univ, grad. **Career:** Football player (retired); Dallas Cowboys, 1993; Chicago Bears, 1993, linebacker, 1994-95, mid linebacker, 1996, 1998-99, right linebacker, 1997, left linebacker, 1999; Cleveland Browns, 2001; S D J Properties Llc; Rd Housing Llc. **Honors/Awds:** Strength and Conditioning All-America, 1992. **Business Addr:** S D J Properties LLC, 2626 Garcitas Crk, Richmond, TX 77406.

### MINTER, MICHAEL CHRISTOPHER
Football player. **Personal:** Born Jan 15, 1974, Cleveland, OH; married Kim; children: 4. **Educ:** Nebr Univ, BE, 1996. **Career:** Football player (retired), football coach; Carolina Panthers, free safety, 1997, 1999, 2005-06, defensive back, 1998, strong safety, 2000-04; Johnson C. Smith Univ, asst head football coach & coordr, 2011; Liberty Univ, coach, 2012; Campbell Univ, head coach, 2013-. **Orgs:** Spokesperson, Salvation Army Boys & Girls Club. **Business Addr:** Head Coach, Campbell University, 143 Main St, Buies Creek, NC 27506, **Business Phone:** (800)334-4111.

### MINTER, STEVEN ALAN
Foundation executive. **Personal:** Born Oct 23, 1938, Akron, OH; son of Lawrence L and Dorothy Knox; married Dolores Kreicher; children: Michele, Caroline & Robyn. **Educ:** Baldwin Wallace Col, BA, educ, 1960; Case Western Res Univ, MA, soc admin, 1963. **Career:** Cuyahoga Co Welfare Dept, dir, 1969-70; Commonwealth MA, comnr pub welfare, 1970-75; US dept educ, under secy, 1980-81; Cleveland found, prof officer & assoc dir, 1975-84, pres & exec dir, 1984-2003; Cleveland State Univ, Maxine Goodman Levin Col Urban Affairs, exec-in-residence, 2003-16. **Orgs:** Dir, Goodyear Tire & Rubber co; trustee, Col Wooster; dir, Key Corp; life mem, Nat Asn Advan Colored People; dir, Soc Corp; dir, Consol Natural Gas; dir, Rubbermaid Inc; bd overseers, Florence Heller Grad Sch Advan Studies Social Welfare, Brandeis Univ; bd trustee, Found Ctr; bd trustee, Leadership Cleveland; N Coast Harbor Inc; fel Ctr Nonprofit Policy & Pract, currently; Community Foundations Am; Am Pub Welfare Asn; Nat Community AIDS Partnership; bd mem, Dom Resources. **Honors/Awds:** Distinguished Service Award, The Sch Applied Social Sci, Case Western Reserve Univ, 1979; Social Worker of Year, OH Chap Nat Asn Soc Workers, 1984; Black Prof Year, Black Professional Asn Cleveland, 1985; Hon PhD Humane Letters, Kent State Univ, 1988; Hon PhD Humane Letters, Case Western Reserve Univ, 1989; Ohio Governor's Award, 1991; Honorary Doctorate, Baldwin-Wallace Col, Oberlin Col, Lake Erie Col & Findlay Col; Distinguished Grantmaker Award, Coun Foundations, 2003. **Home Addr:** 2878 Woodbury Rd, Shaker Heights, OH 44120-2426, **Home Phone:** (216)283-8515. **Business Addr:** Executive in Residence, Cleveland State University, 2121 Euclid Ave, Cleveland, OH 44115-2214, **Business Phone:** (216)687-5495.

### MINTER, WILBERT DOUGLAS, SR.
Administrator. **Personal:** Born Nov 17, 1946, Knoxville, TN; children: Wilbert Douglas Jr. **Educ:** Knoxville Col, attended 1967; Univ Tenn, attended 1970. **Career:** Asn Rec Managers & Adminr, pres, 1974; Admin Mgt Soc, pres, 1982; Martin Marietta Corp, suprvr eng rec; coun mem-at-Large. **Orgs:** Pres, Oak Ridge Comn Rels Coun, 1972-73; Atomic City Sportsmen Club Oak Ridge, 1975; Human Resources Bd Oak Ridge, 1980-82; Oak Ridge Sch Bd, 1983; State Advert Comn US Civil Rights Comn, 1983-85; Dept Energy Contractors & Micrographics Asn, 1985; Nat conf speaker Asn Rec Mgrs & Admin. **Honors/Awds:** Distinguished Service Award, Shriners Knoxville, 1973; outstanding chapmem Records Mgrs & Adminrs, 1975; outstanding cert records mgr, 1982. **Home Addr:** 133 LaSalle Rd, Oak Ridge, TN 37830, **Home Phone:** (615)483-5184.

### MINUS, DR. HOMER WELLINGTON
Dentist. **Personal:** Born Mar 21, 1931, Wyoming, DE; son of George Greenfield and Luvenia Roberts; married Barbara S; children: Carla Michele Lewis & Felicia Yvette Lewis. **Educ:** Univ Del, BS, biol, 1953; Temple Univ Sch Dent, DDS, 1959; Howard Univ Sch Div, MDiv, 1987. **Career:** Pvt pract, dentist, currently; United Methodist Church, pastor. **Orgs:** Vestryman Dioc Coun Conv DE Protestant Episcopal Church; sch bd mem, Dover DE, 1967-70; life mem, Nat Asn Advan Colored People; life mem, Alpha Phi Alpha Fraternity Inc. **Home Addr:** 577 Plymouth Rd, Felton, DE 19943-6152, **Home Phone:** (302)284-4010. **Business Addr:** Dentist, Private Practice, 446A S New St, Dover, DE 19904, **Business Phone:** (302)674-3303.

### MINYARD, HANDSEL B.
Business owner, executive. **Personal:** Born Mar 11, 1943, Phoenix, AZ; son of Richard (deceased) and Vivian; married Karen Flavell; children: Stacey B & H Blair. **Educ:** Stanford Univ, AB, 1964; Yale Law Sch, LLB, 1967. **Career:** NLRB San Francisco, law clerk, 1967-68; Fordham Univ NY, asst exec, 1968-69; Sullivan & Cromwell NY, pvt pract, assoc coun, 1969-72; Temple Univ Sch Law Philadelphia, prof law, assoc dean, 1972-84; City Philadelphia, dep city solicitor, 1984-86, city solicitor, 1986-88; Graimark Realty Adv Inc, exec vpres & founder, 1989-2006, co-owner, currently; MIG Realty Advisors Inc, sr vpres; Temple Univ Beasley Sch Law, prof law & assoc dean. **Orgs:** Calif Bar Asn, 1968; NY Bar Asn, 1970; bd mem, N Pa Sch Dist Authority, 1975-79; dir, N Pa Chap ARC, 1975-79; Philadelphia Bar Asn, 1979; chair, finance comt, Friends Hosp, 1981-; bd overseers, Widener Law Sch, 1986-93; bd mem, Franklin Inst, 1988-98; dir, Penns Landing Corp, 1989-92; bd mem, Palnter govt Coop Authority, 1992-94; bd, Crime Prev Asn, 1993-98; trustee, Philadelphia Univ, 1996-; bd mem, Young Scholars Charter Sch, 1999-; dir, Health Ins Processors Inc, 2000-; asst secy, Temple's Bd Trustees; bd dir, Thomas Scattergood Behav Health Found; asst secy to bd trustee, Temple Univ Beasley Sch Law. **Home Addr:** 3400 Warden Dr, Philadelphia, PA 19129-1418, **Home Phone:** (215)790-1660. **Business Addr:** Co-Owner, Executive Vice President, Graimark Realty Advisors, 500 River Pl Dr Suite 5105, Detroit, MI 48207-5046, **Business Phone:** (313)259-9479.

### MITCHAL, SAUNDRA MARIE
Manager, marketing executive. **Personal:** Born Jun 3, 1949, Massillon, OH; daughter of Clyde and Betty Jones Brown; married John Higginbotham. **Educ:** Kent State Univ, Kent, Ohio, BBA, indust rels, 1969; Ind Univ, Kelley Sch Bus, Bloomington, IN, MBA, mkt, 1973. **Career:** Bristol Myers Co, New York, NY, prod mgr, 1973-81; Hunt Wesson Foods, Fullerton, Calif, mkt mgr, 1981-84; Neutrogena Corp, Los Angeles, Calif, vpres mkt, 1984-93; Avco Financial, vpres mkt, 1994-97; Fannie Mae, dir consumer mkt, 1998-2000; DC Lottery, chief mkt, 2005-; Ind Univ, Consortium Grad Studies fel. **Orgs:** Pres, Delta Sigma Theta Sorority, 1968-; Motor Bd Hon Soc, Kent State Univ, 1971; Corp Women's Network. **Honors/Awds:** Women of Achievement, Essence Mag, 1990. **Home Addr:** 4664-C Don Lorenzo Dr, Los Angeles, CA 90008, **Home Phone:** (213)293-9858. **Business Addr:** Chief Marketing, DC Lottery, 2101 Martin Luther King Jr Ave SE, Washington, DC 20020.

### MITCHELL, ARTHUR
Artistic director, dancer, actor. **Personal:** Born Mar 27, 1934, New York, NY. **Educ:** Katherine Dunham Sch Dance; Sch Am Ballet. **Career:** New York Ballet, dancer, 1955-70. Films: The Day the Fish Came Out, actor & choreographer, 1967; The Day the Fish Came Out, choreographer, 1967; The Cotton Club, choreographer, 1984; Creole Giselle, choreographer, 1987; Afternoon of a Faun: Tanaquil Le Clercq, 2013. Miscellaneous Crew: The Cotton Club, 1984; Creole Giselle, 1987. Dance Theater Harlem, co-founder, 1969. Writer: Creole Giselle, 1987. **Orgs:** Nat Conf Soc Welfare, 1973; adv panel, US Dept State Dance, 1973; Nat Soc Lit & Arts, 1975; coun mem, NY Coun Arts; coun mem, Nat Endowment Arts. **Honors/Awds:** Certificate of Recognition, Harold Jackman Mem Comt, 1969; Special Tribute to Arthur Mitchell & Dance Theatre of Harlem, North side Ctr Child Develop Inc, 1969; The Changers Award, Mademoiselle Mag, 1970; North Shore Commercial Arts Center Award, 1971; 20th annual Capezio Dance Award, 1971; MacArthur Fellow, 1981; Laurence Olivier Theatre Award, 1984; Lifetime Achievement Award, Sch Am Ballet, 1995; United States National Medal of Arts, 1995; John W Gardner Leadership Award, 1996; inducted into the Cornelius Vanderbilt Whitney Hall of Fame, National Museum of Dance, 1998; Americans for the Arts Education Award, 1997; Dance Hall of Fame, 1999; Governor's Martin Luther King Award, 2000; Heinz Award, 2001; honorary Doctorates from Harvard, Princeton & 11 other institutions; featured in the 2004 documentary Balanchine. **Special Achievements:** First African American dancer to become a principal artist in the New York City Ballet; First male recipient Dance Award High School of Performing Arts, 1951; First black dancer for the New York City Ballet. **Business Addr:** Artistic Director, Founder, Dance Theatre of Harlem, 466 W 152nd St, New York, NY 10031-1814, **Business Phone:** (212)690-2800.

### MITCHELL, BASIL MUCKTAR
Football player. **Personal:** Born Sep 7, 1975, Pittsburg, TX; married Sharay Traylor; children: 5. **Educ:** Tex Christian Univ, BS, psychol, 2004. **Career:** Football player (retired); Green Bay Packers, running back, 1999, 1998-2000; Memphis Maniax, Xtreme Football League, running back, 2001; Hillwood, retail real estate mkt mgr, 2004-07; Weitzman Group, leasing assoc, 2007-08; Player Made Motivation, speaker, 2012-; Prowess Sports Performance, sports performance coach, 2013-; Mpisd, asst coach recruiting coordr dir player develop, 2013-; NAI Robert Lynn, mkt dir, 2015-. **Orgs:** Int Coun Shopping Centers; N Tex Com Asn Realtors. **Honors/Awds:** Norwest Sun Bowl, 1998. **Home Addr:** 808 Meadow Creek Dr Suite 103, Irving, TX 75038. **Business Addr:** Market Director, NAI Robert Lynn, 4851 LBJ Freeway 10th Fl, Dallas, TX 75244, **Business Phone:** (214)256-7154.

### MITCHELL, BERT NORMAN
Consultant, administrator, auditor. **Personal:** Born Apr 12, 1938; son of Joseph and Edith; married Carole Harleston; children: Tracey, Robbin & Ronald. **Educ:** Baruch Col City Univ NY, BBA, 1963, MBA, 1968; Harvard Grad Sch Bus, attended 1985. **Career:** JK Lasser & Co, CPA'S, sr auditor, 1963-66; Interam Ins Co, controller, 1966-67; Ford Found, asst controller, 1967-69; Lucas Tucker & Co CPA'S, partner, 1969-73; Mitchell & Titus & Co, chief exec officer; Mitchell & Titus LLP, founder, chief exec officer, 1974-2008, chmn, 2008-10, chmn emer, currently. **Orgs:** Dir, Greater New York Fund; treas, 100 Black Men Inc; trustee, Baruch Col Fund; Asn Better NY; pres, NY Soc CPA'S; dir & chmn, State bd pub acct; dir, AICPA; dir, NYSS-CPA; chmn emer, Ariel Investment Trust, 1986-2006; former independent dir, mem audit comt & mem exec compensation committe, Bj's Wholesale Club Inc, 1986-2006; pres, dir & chmn, NY State Soc CPA's, 1987; pres, Accountants Club Am, 1991-93; bd dir, Harvard Bus Sch; comn mem, Consol CRE Fund Lincoln Ctr; Asn BlacK CPA Firms; bd dir, BJ's Wholesale Club Inc, 1998; adv bd, Sch Accountancy at Univ Southern Calif; dir & mem audit comt, Rouse co, 2004-. **Honors/Awds:** Outstanding Achievement Award, Nat Asn Black Accountants, 1977; Outstanding Alumnus Award, City Col New York, 1982; Hon Dr Laws, Baruch Col, 1988; CPA New York, NJ & DC; Townsand Harris Medal, City Col, New York, 1991; DHL, Western New England Col, 1991; Human Relations Award, Anti-Defamation League B'NaiB'Rith, 1991; DHL, State Univ New York, 1993; Alumni Achievement Award, Harvard Univ Bus Sch, 1995; Gold Medal for Distinguished Service, AICPA, 1996; Marcus Garvey Lifetime Achievement Award, Inst Caribbean Studies, 1996; DL, Adelphi Univ, 2013. **Special Achievements:** Published over 50 articles in professional journals. **Home Addr:** 5 Renaissance Sq Apt 30C, White Plains, NY 10601-3050, **Home Phone:** (561)995-8043. **Business Addr:** Chairman Emeritus, Founder, Chief Executive Officer, Mitchell & Titus LLP, 1 Battery Pk Plz 27th Fl, New York, NY 10004-1405, **Business Phone:** (212)709-4500.

### MITCHELL, BRANDON
Football player. **Personal:** Born Jun 19, 1975, Abbeville, LA. **Educ:** Tex A&M Univ. **Career:** Football player (retired); New Eng Patriots, 1997, defensive end, 1998-2000, defensive tackle, left defensive tackle, nose tackle, 2001; Seattle Seahawks, 2004, right defensive tackle, 2002, defensive end, 2003; Ark Razorbacks, guard, 2010-12.

### MITCHELL, BRENDA K.
Government official. **Personal:** Born Jan 9, 1943, New York, NY; daughter of William Franklin (deceased) and Ola Mae; married William Nelson; children: Corrie Nelson. **Educ:** Fordham Univ, New York, NY, BA, lib arts, 1973; Hunter Col, New York, NY, MS, urban affairs, 1974; Nova Univ, Ft Lauderdale, FL, PhD, pub admin, 1981. **Career:** Addictive DisAgency, Dir Manpower Planning, NY, dir, 1973-77; Pub & Pvt Ventures Corp, Philadelphia, mgr proj & contract, 1978-80; City Venture Corp, Minneapolis, Econ Develop, exec dir, 1980-84; Control Data Corp, Minneapolis, MN, dir control data bus & technol ctr, 1983-87; Control Data Corp, Minneapolis, bus mgr, 1984-87; Commonwealth Pa, Dept Com, Harrisburg, PA, dep secy com, 1987-90, Gov's Off, spec asst, 1990-91; Dept State, PA, secy commonwealth, 1991-94; African Am Port Corp, Philadelphia, pres, 1994-95; Mgmt & Environ Technologies Inc, pres, chief exec officer, 1995-; pres & chief exec officer, Mgt & Environ Technol Inc; CDAC, bus mgr. **Orgs:** Vpres, Philadelphia Regional Port Authority; co-founder, former vpres, Capitol Chap, Nat Forum Black Pub Adminrs; bd trustee, United Way Southeastern Pa; bd dir, W Philadelphia Chamber Com; vpres, W Parkside Philadelphia Bus Asn; bd dir, Ben Franklin Partnership Advan Technol Ctr Southeastern Pa; Greater Philadelphia First Neighborhood Econ Develop Task Force; bd dir, Philadelphia Fund CommunityDevelop; bd trustee, Lincoln Univ; bd fin & revenue, PA Munic Retirement Syst; PSU Econ Develop Coun; PA Econ Educ Coun; New York Addiction Agency, dir manpower planning; Richard Allen Prep Charter Sch, founder; PA Dept Com, dep secy. **Home Addr:** 792 Brentwater Rd, Camp Hill, PA 17011. **Business Addr:** President, Chief Executive Officer, Management & Environmental Technologies Inc, 1315 Walnut St Suite 1108, Philadelphia, PA 19107, **Business Phone:** (215)546-7991.

### MITCHELL, BRIAN KEITH
Football player, entertainer. **Personal:** Born Aug 18, 1968, Fort Polk, LA; married Monica; children: 4. **Educ:** Southwestern La Univ, grad.

**Career:** Football player (retired), host; Wash Redskins, 1990, 1999, kick returner & punt returner, 1991-98, fullback, 1994; Philadelphia Eagles, running back, 2000, 2001-02; New York Giants, 2003; WUSA-TV, Nat Football League Analyst, co-host, currently; Brian Mitchell Show, WTEM 980, host; John Thompson Show, co-host; Brian Keith Mitchell Comcast Sports Net, co-host; Sports Junkies, frequent guest & guest host; Mike Wise Show, frequent guest & guest host; Comcast SportsNet, co-host. **Orgs:** Founder, Brian Mitchell Found, 2001. **Honors/Awds:** NFL Alumni Kick Returner of the Year, 1995; Special Teams Player of the Year, Nat Football League Alumni, 1996; USL Hall of Fame; Hall of Fame, La Sports, 2007; Washington Redskins Ring of Fame. **Special Achievements:** Films: 1991 NFC Championship Game, 1992; Super Bowl XXVI, 1992. TV Series: "TNT Sunday Night Football", 1990-92; "NFL Monday Night Football", 1990-2003; "ESPN's Sunday Night Football", 1993-2003; "NFL on FOX ", 1995-96. First player in NCAA history to rush for 3, 000 yards and pass for 5,000 yards in a career in leading USL to four straight winning seasons; One of the 70 Greatest Redskins, 2002. **Business Addr:** Co-Host, WUSA-TV, 4100 Wis Ave NW, Washington, DC 20016, **Business Phone:** (202)895-5999.

### MITCHELL, BRIAN STOKES
Actor, singer. **Personal:** Born Oct 31, 1957, Seattle, WA; son of George and Lilian Frances(deceased); married Allyson Tucker; children: Ellington. **Career:** Films: Ghost Dad, 1990; Edward II, 1991; One Last Thing, 2005; Jumping the Broom, 2011. TV series: "Roots: The Next Generations", 1979; "The White Shadow", 1979; "The Next Generations", 1979; "Trapper John MD", 1979; "The Love Boat", 1983; "Hotel", 1985; "227", 1987; "ALF", 1987; "Houston Knights", 1987; "Night Court", 1988; "A Pup Named Scooby-Doo", 1988; "Scooby-Doo and the Reluctant Werewolf", 1988; "Generations", 1989; "Roots: The Fresh Prince of Bel-Air", 1990; "Captain Planet & the Planeteers", 1990; "Raisins Sold Out: The California Raisins II", 1990; "New Kids on the Block", 1990; "Kid 'n' Play", 1990; "Tiny Toon Adventures", 1990; "Midnight Patrol: Adventures in the Dream Zone", 1990; "Mancuso, FBI", 1990; "James Bond Jr.", 1991; Defenders of Dynatron City, 1992; "1992 Batman", 1992; "Capitol Critters", 1992; "Tom & Jerry Kids Show", 1991-93; "The Fresh Prince of Bel-Air", 1992-93; "The Ernest Green Story", 1993; "I Yabba-Dabba Do!", 1993; "Hollyrock-a-Bye Baby", 1993; "Animaniacs", 1993; "Double Platinum", 1999; "Too Rich: The Secret Life of Doris Duke", 1999; "Call Me Claus", 2001; "Ruby's Bucket of Blood", 2001; "Crossing Jordan", 2002; "Frasier", 2002; "Great Performances", 2006; A Capitol Fourth, 2008; Singer: "Kiss Of The Spider Woman", 1994; "Lunch: A Modern Musical Myth", 1994; "In the House", 1996; "Ragtime", 1998; "The Angry Beavers", 1998; "Kiss Me Kate", 1999; "Christmas with the Mormon Tabernacle Choir Featuring Brian Stokes Mitchell and Edward Herrmann", 2009; "Ugly Betty", 2010; "Glee", 2012-; "Madam Secretary", 2014. Brian Stokes Mitchell, 2006; Singing Voice: The Prince of Egypt, 1998; Composer: Trapper John, M.D, 1985; Through Heaven's Eyes, performer, 1998; The Impossible Dream The Quest, performer, 2003. **Honors/Awds:** Tony Award as Best Actor, 2000; Nominated Three times, Best Actor (musical), 1998, Portarying Colemen, Walker, 2003. **Home Addr:** 243 W 98th St, New York, NY 10025. **Business Addr:** Actor, c/o Roland Scahill, 1325 Ave of the Americas, New York, NY 10019, **Business Phone:** (212)903-1327.

### MITCHELL, DR. BYRON LYNWOOD
Dentist. **Personal:** Born Mar 2, 1936, Miami, FL; son of Robert and Lemmie Wilson; children: Vanessa, Lynita, Patricia & Michael. **Educ:** Savannah St Col, BS, 1959; Howard Univ, DDS, 1966; Howard Univ, orthod, 1969. **Career:** Pvt pract gen dentist, 1966-69; Family Health Ctr, chief family dentist, 1969-70, dent dir, 1971-72; pvt pract orthod, 1970-. **Orgs:** Alpha Phi Alpha Frat; Kiwanis Club, Elks; Dade Co Dent Soc; Dade Co Acad Med; Greater Miami Acad Orthod; Miami, E Coast, Fla Dent Socs; Southern Soc Orthod; Am Asn Orthod. **Special Achievements:** First African-American specialist in dentistry to practice in state of Florida; First African-American orthodontist to practice in Florida; 2nd African-American orthodontist to practice in entire South. **Home Addr:** 1401 NW 138th St, Miami, FL 33167-1210, **Home Phone:** (305)688-9516. **Business Addr:** Dentist, Byron L Mitchell Dds, 4885 NW 7th Ave, Miami, FL 33127, **Business Phone:** (305)751-4889.

### MITCHELL, CARLTON S.
Banker. **Personal:** Born Sep 7, 1950, New York, NY. **Educ:** Bucknell Univ, attended 1972; Howard Univ, BA, econs, 1972; Columbia Univ, Grad Sch Bus, MA, bus policy, 1984. **Career:** Chem Bank, asst br mgr, 1974-76; Marine Midland Bank, vpres, 1976-82; Community Develop, Dept Youth & Community Develop, City NY, dep commnr, 1995-2003; Int Ctr New York Inc, exec dir, 2003-06; Educr C, Youth & Families Inc, executive dir interim actg, 2006-07; Families First New York, interim pres & chief exec officer, 2008-10; Family Serv New York, exec dir & chief admin officer, 2010-11; Turning Pt Brooklyn, interim exec dir, 2012-14; Inwood House, interim exec dir, 2014-. **Orgs:** Nat Asn Urban Bankers; Nat Bankers Asn; Long Island Asn; vpres, Union Black Episcopalians; New York-based Support Ctr; pres & chief exec officer, Families First New York, currently; International Center, Civilian Conserv Corps. **Home Addr:** 21752 100th Ave, Queens Village, NY 11429-1207, **Home Phone:** (718)468-1785.

### MITCHELL, CAROL GREENE
Marketing executive, manager. **Personal:** Born Jul 22, 1960, Baltimore, MD; daughter of Thelma Stewart Greene Clardy; married A Stanley. **Educ:** Fisk Univ, Nashville, Tenn, BA, econs & mgt, 1982; Univ Wis, Madison, Wis, MBA, mkt, 1983. **Career:** Gen Mills, Minneapolis, Minn, mkt res asst, 1983; RJ Reynolds Tobacco Co, Winston-Salem, NC, mkt res analyst, 1984-85, sr mkt res analyst, 1986-87, asst mkt res mgr, 1987-88, mkt res mgr, 1988-89, mgr bus info & anal, 1989-91, sr mgr bus info & anal, 1991-2004, sr mgr II bus info & anal, 2004-05, dir bus info & anal, 2006-07, dir bus info anal & innovation res, 2007-08, dir strategy & planning, 2008-15, dir hr strategic insights, 2015-. **Orgs:** Alpha Kappa Alpha sorority, 1979-; Nat Asn Advan Colored People, 1984-; Nat Black MBA Asn, 1984-; Barrister's Wives, 1987-. **Honors/Awds:** Outstanding Business & Professional Award, Dollars & Sense Magazine, 1992. **Special Achievements:** Who's Who in the Beverage and Tobacco Industries, Dollars and Sense Magazine, 1990-92. **Home Addr:** 4440 Gatlin Knoll Lane, Clemmons, NC 27012, **Home Phone:** (336)766-9084. **Business Addr:** Director - HR Strategic Insights, R J Reynolds Tobacco Co, 401 N Main St, Winston-Salem, NC 27102-2959, **Business Phone:** (336)741-5000.

### MITCHELL, CHARLES, JR.
School administrator. **Personal:** Born Apr 21, 1938, Detroit, MI. **Educ:** Western Mich Univ, BS, phys educ, 1959; Wayne State Univ, MEd, spec educ, 1965, EdS, admin & supv, 1968, EdD, curric develop, 1972; Mass Inst Tech, MS, mgt sci, 1970. **Career:** School superintendent, vice president, public finance department (retired); Fed & St Prog, div dir, 1976-; Phys Edn, consult, 1959-60; Detroit, teacher, 1960-65; Highland Pk, coordr, 1965-67; Highland Pk, dir spec proj, 1967-69, asst supt personnel, 1970-72; supt sch, 1972-; Highland Pk Community Col, pres, prin dir; Mitchell Group Inc, founder, 1992, owner & chief exec officer; Eastern Mich Univ, assoc prof; Univ Manchester, Ford Found Fel Urban Systs Develop; State, Fed & Int Laws, US off educ fel compliance; Mass Inst Technol, Sloan Fel Mgt Sci; Univ Mo, Sch Finance & Law, Danforth Fel; Raymond James & Assocs, vpres, 2007, advisor, currently. **Orgs:** Asn Sch Col Univ Staffing; Am Asn Sch Adminrs, Personnel Adminrs; Asn Supv Curric Devel; Acad Mgt; Booker T Wash Bus Asn; Mich Asn Sch Adminrs; Mich Asn Sch Bds; Mich Asn Supv Curric Devel; Nat Community Sch Educ Asn; Nat Alliance Black Sch Adminrs; Black Causes Asn Inc; Nat AsnAdvan Colored People; YMCA; Rotary Internat; Civic League; Human RelationsCom; Civic & Indust Com; Jaycees; Caucus Club; Alumni Asn; Mich Inst TechWestern Mich Univ Wayne State; Varsity Club Inc; adv Mothers Club; founder, fOppenheimer's Educ Finance Group, 1997; co-chair, Audit Comt, 2005-07; sr consult & vpres, Nat City Investments. **Honors/Awds:** Outstanding young man of the Year, 1968; sloan fellow, MA Inst Tech, 1969-70; Danforth NAES fellow, 1975; Ford Found fellow, 1973. **Home Addr:** 1130 3 Ave Apt 1703, Oakland, CA 94606. **Business Addr:** Owner, Chairman of the Board, The Mitchell Group Inc, 1816 11th St NW, Washington, DC 20001.

### MITCHELL, CHARLES E.
Lawyer. **Personal:** Born Jul 7, 1925, Seymour, IN; married Julia Sarjeant; children: Charles L & Albert B. **Educ:** Temple Univ Sch Law, JD, 1954; Brooklyn Law Sch; NY Univ, BA, 1949; Morehouse Col. **Career:** Philadelphia Sch Dist, teacher, 1954-55; Financial Dept Philadelphia, mgt trainee, 1955-56; Atty Philadelphia, legal asst, 1956-60; Off Dist Atty Philadelphia, legal asst, 1956-60; US Dept Health, Educ & Welfare, Social Security Admin, claim rep, 1960-64, atty; Labor Mgt Rel Exam Nat Labor Rel Bd Phila, atty, 1964-72; E I DuPont DeNemours & Co Inc, att labor mgt, 1972-92; Heritage Capital Credit Corp, bd dir, Human Resources Comt, chmn, currently. **Orgs:** Am Bar Asn; Nat Labor Rel Act; Corp Banking & Bus Law; Legal Educ & Admin Bar; Philadelphia Bar Asn; Pa Bar Asn; pres, Fed Bar Asn, DE Chap; Am Judge Soc; Barristers Club Philadelphia; Lawyers Club Philadelphia; DE St Bar Asn; Com Promote Equal Opportunity Entry Legal Prof DE; PhiladelphiaInter-alumni Coun; United Negro Col Fund; Indust Rel Res Asn; Philadelphia Chap; W Mt Airy Neighbors Asn; sub chmn, Zoning; Morehouse Col Club Phila; YMCA fund raiser; United Way DE solicitor; Interested Negroes Inc; Nat Asn Advan Colored People; Rotary Club Wilmington. **Home Addr:** 3433 Midvale Ave, Philadelphia, PA 19129, **Home Phone:** (215)844-3936. **Business Addr:** Board Director, Heritage Capital Credit Corp, 200 W 9th St Suite 3, Wilmington, DE 19801, **Business Phone:** (302)778-4222.

### MITCHELL, CHILL. See MITCHELL, DARYL.

### MITCHELL, CLARENCE MARQUIS. See MITCHELL, KEITH.

### MITCHELL, CONNIE R COHN
Educator. **Personal:** Born Jun 30, 1947, Memphis, TN; daughter of Joseph R Sr and Cleopatra Evans; married George; children: George C Jr & Carlotta. **Educ:** Cent State Univ, BA, 1969; Dartmouth Col, MA, 1993. **Career:** Detroit Pub Schs, teacher, 1969-95, teacher advocate & human resources, 1995-, dir, Off Teacher Develop, currently. **Orgs:** Top Ladies Distinction Inc, status women chair, 1983-; Alpha Kappa alpha, 1995-; bd dir, Nat Bd Prof Teaching Stand, 1995-; bd dir, Inkster Community Partnership, 1998-; exec bd, Young Educrs Soc Mich, 1999-; bd dir, Methodist C's Home Socs, 1999-; bd advr, Inkster Human Develop Agency, 2000-; Univ Mich, LUCY Initiative, bd advr, 2001-. **Home Addr:** 1414 Magnolia Dr, Inkster, MI 48141-1783, **Home Phone:** (313)274-0328. **Business Addr:** Director, Teacher Advocate, Detroit Public Schools, 5057 Woodward Ave Rm 708, Detroit, MI 48202-4050, **Business Phone:** (313)494-7860.

### MITCHELL, CRANSTON J.
Law enforcement officer, city commissioner. **Personal:** Born Aug 25, 1946, St. Louis, MO; son of Monroe M and Elizabeth; married Aleta Grimes; children: Leslie Barnes, Catherine J & Christie J. **Educ:** Univ Mo, St Louis, Mo, BS, polit sci, 1973; Harvard Univ, Boston, MA, prog sr exec state & local govt, 1988. **Career:** City St Louis, Mo, police officer, 1967-74; Mitchum-Thayer Inc, St Louis, Mo, mkt rep, 1974-75; State Mo, St Louis & Kans City, Mo, voc rehab counr, adminr & supvr, 1975-83; Jobs Mo Grads, St Louis, Mo, regional supvr, 1983-84; State Mo, Mo Bd Probation & Parole, Jefferson City, Mo, dir bd govt & chmn, 1984; Nat Inst Corrections, Dept Justice, correctional prog specialist; US Parole Comn, comnr, 2003; US Parole Comn, comnr, 2009-; Dept Elem & Sec Educ, Div Voc Rehab, counr & supvr; US Parole Comn, vice chmn, currently. **Orgs:** Am Probation & Parole Asn; Am Corrections Asn; charter vpres, Nat Asn Blacks Criminal Justice, 1984-; regional vpres, Asn Paroling Authorities Int, 1988-90; comnr, Jefferson City Housing Authority. **Honors/Awds:** Vincent O'Leary Award, Asn Paroling Authorities; Ben Baer Award, Asn Paroling Authorities; Jonathan Jasper Wright Community Leadership Award, Nat Asn Blacks Criminal Justice; Outstanding Alumni Award, Univ Missouri-St. Louis. **Home Addr:** PO Box 105811, Jefferson City, MO 65110-5811, **Home Phone:** (314)634-4918. **Business Addr:** Vice Chairman, United States Parole Commission, 950 Pa Ave NW, Washington, DC 20530-0001, **Business Phone:** (202)346-7000.

### MITCHELL, DANA S.
Architect. **Educ:** Ga Inst Technol, BS, 1990, MArch. **Career:** Skidmore Owings & Merrill, Chicago, staff architect; URS Corp, mgr, vpres archit. **Orgs:** Nat Coun Archit Regist Bds, res assoc. **Business Addr:** Vice President, URS Corp, 1375 Euclid Ave Suite 600, Cleveland, OH 44115-1808.

### MITCHELL, DARYL (CHILL MITCHELL)
Actor, executive. **Personal:** Born Jul 16, 1965, Bronx, NY; married Carol; children: Kamari, Desmin & Justin. **Career:** Films: House Party, 1990; House Party 2, 1991; Boomerang, 1992; Fly by Night, 1993; Cosmic Slop, 1994; Quiet Days in Hollywood, 1995; Sgt. Bilko, 1996; A Thin Line Between Love and Hate, 1996; Med sikte pa karleken, 1996; Rebound: The Legend of Earl The Goat Manigault, 1996; White Lies, 1997; Toothless, 1997; Home Fries, 1998; 10 Things I Hate About You, 1999; Galaxy Quest, 1999; Prinsen och strykarhunden, 1999; The Pooch & the Pauper, voice, 1999; Lucky Numbers, 2000; Black Knight, 2001; 13 Moons, 2002; The Country Bears, 2002; Nalles stora aventyr, 2002; Inside Man, 2006; Playback, 2011; TV series: "The Cosby Show:", 1985-91; "Law & Order", 1992; "Here and Now", 1992-93; "Queen", 1993; 'Kalifornia", intern: Atlanta, 1993; "The John Larroquette Show", 1993-96; "Cosby", 1997; "The Fresh Prince of Bel-Air", 1994; "In the House", 1996; "Veronica's Closet", 1997-2000; "Ed", 2002-04; "Law & Order: Criminal Intent", 2004; "Eve", 2005; "I Love The 80's", 2005; "Hex", asst acct, 2005; "Sinchronicity", asst acct, 2006; "Sugar Rush", asst acct, 2006;"The Suite Life of Zack and Cody", 2007; "The Game", 2007; "Brothers", producer, music, 2009; "22 Years from Home", exex producer, 2009; "Desperate Housewives", 2010; "Wizards of Waverly Place", 2010; "Traffic Light", 2011; "The Cleveland Show", 2012; "NCIS: New Orleans", 2014-; Daryl Mitchell Found, prin, currently. **Business Addr:** Actor, William Morris Agency, 151 El Camino Dr, Beverly Hills, CA 90212, **Business Phone:** (310)859-4000.

### MITCHELL, DEAN LAMONT
Artist, painter (artist). **Personal:** Born Jan 20, 1957, Pittsburgh, PA; son of Hazel. **Educ:** Columbus Col Arts Design, BFA, 1980, hon masters degree. **Career:** Hallmark Cards, illusr, 1980-83; artist, currently; Voice123 LLC, dean. **Orgs:** Am Watercolor Soc; Nat Watercolor Soc; Allied Artist Am; Nat Soc Painters Casein, Acrylic; Knickerbocker Artist. **Honors/Awds:** Won over 400 awards for his painting; Top Prize, TH Saunders Int Artist in Watercolor, London, 1980; Allied Artist of Am, Gold Medal, Oil, 1992, Gold Medal, Watercolor, 1990; Hardie Gramatky Award, Am Watercolor Soc, 1990; Hon Masters Degree, Columbus Col Art Design, 1994; Gold Medal, Am Watercolor Soc, 1998; Grand Prize, Arts for the Park, 1999; Virtual Mod-Day Vermeer, New York Times, 2002; Newington Award for Best Painting, Am Artist Prof League; Thomas Moran Award, Salmagundi Club New York. **Home Addr:** 11918 England, Overland Park, KS 66213, **Home Phone:** (913)338-4470. **Business Addr:** Artist, c/o Gadsen Arts Center, 13 N Madison St, Quincy, FL 32351, **Business Phone:** (850)875-4866.

### MITCHELL, DENNIS ALLEN
Athlete, executive. **Personal:** Born Feb 20, 1966, Havelock, NC; son of Edward and Lenora; married Damu J Cherry; children: 3. **Educ:** Univ Fla. **Career:** US Olympic Team, Barcelona, track & field athlete, 1992; Mind, Body & Soul Inc, pres, currently; Nat Training Ctr, Star Athletics, head coach, sports performance coordr, currently. **Honors/Awds:** NCAA championships, 1989; Bronze Medalist, Tokyo Olympics 100 m, 1991; Gold Medalist, Tokyo Olympics 4x100 m relay, 1991; Gold Medalist, Barcelona Olympics 4 x 100 relay, 1992; Am Champion 100 m, 1992; Second in the World 100 m, 1992; Us Nat Championships, 1992, 1994, 1996; Bronze Medalist, Barcelona Olympics 100 m, 1992; Bronze Medalist, Stuttgart Olympics 100 m, 1993; Gold Medalist, Stuttgart Olympics 4x100 m relay, 1993; ESPY Award, 1994; Silver Medalist, Atlanta Olympics 4 x100 Relay, Olympic Games, 1996; Athletic Hall of Fame, Univ Fla. **Special Achievements:** Seven Time World Championship Team Member; 3-Time Olympic Competitor; World Record Holder in the 4 X 100 Meter Relay; Voted Best Male Track & Field Athlete in the World by IAAF, 1994. **Home Addr:** 7818 NW 22nd Lane, Gainesville, FL 32605, **Home Phone:** (352)371-1470. **Business Addr:** Sports Performance Coordinator, National Training Center, 1099 Citrus Twr Blvd, Clermont, FL 34711, **Business Phone:** (352)241-7144.

### MITCHELL, DOUGLAS
Technician, government official. **Personal:** Born Apr 10, 1948, Leslie, GA; son of Albert Joe and Lula Mae Jenkins Winbush; married Velma Jean Floyd; children: Rodney Purcell. **Career:** Procter & Gamble, Albany, Ga, line technician, 1975-82, team leader, 1982-84, elec technician, 1984-; City Smithville, Smithville, Ga, mayor. **Orgs:** Albany Area Primary Health Bd dir, 1985-86; Lee County Chamber Com Task Force, 1989; Hwy 19 Improv Task Force, 1989. **Home Addr:** 101 W Westerlee Dr, Leesburg, GA 31763-5827, **Home Phone:** (912)846-2905. **Business Addr:** GA.

### MITCHELL, DR. EARL DOUGLASS, JR.
Educator. **Personal:** Born May 16, 1938, New Orleans, LA; son of Earl Douglass Sr and Mary Duncan; married Bernice Compton; children: Karen, Doug & Mike. **Educ:** Xavier Univ La, BS, chem, 1960; Mich State Univ, MS, org chem, 1963, PhD, biochem, 1966. **Career:** Mich State Univ, Dept Chem, grad teaching asst, 1960-63, Dept Hort, Plant Anal Lab, lab technician, 1962-63, Dept Biochem, grad res asst, 1963-66, res assoc, 1966; Okla State Univ, res assoc, 1967-69, from asst prof to assoc prof, 1969-78, Grad Col, prof & asst dean, 1978-82, Dept Biochem, prof, 1982-94, Dept Biochem & Molecular Biol, from interim assoc vpres to assoc vpres multicultural affairs, 1994-2004, prof biochem & molecular biol, 1994-2004, interim head & prof, 2004-07, prof emer, 2007-; Nat Heart & Lung Inst, NIH, res chemist, 1978-79; NSF Louis-Stokes Okla Alliance Minority Participation, proj dir, 1994-2007; Louis Stokes Alliance Minority Participation, okla dir; OSU Talent search, proj dir, 2001-04. **Orgs:** Am Chem Soc, 1961; Okla State Adv Comt, US Comn Civil Rights, 1969-2007; res proposal reviewer, NSF, 1978-; mem comt, Am Soc Bio chem & Molecular Biol, 1979-81, Minority Affairs Comt, 1983-87; chmn, Okla State Personnel Bd, 1980-82; chmn, Okla Ethics & Merit Comn, 1982-84; mem consult, Biochem Study Sect, Nat Insts Health, 1984-87, Minori-

ty Biomed Res Support Prog, 1988-92, chmn, 1991-92; chmn, Okla Merit Protection Comn, 1985-91; chmn, Merit Protection Comn, 1986-88; mem bd trustee, Okla Sch Sci & Math, 1986-; chmn, Okla State Adv Comt, US Comn Civil Rights, 1989-; vpres, Soc Sigma Xi, 1991-93; Am Asn Univ Prof, Okla State Univ, 1991-95; Okla Acad Sci; AAAS. **Home Addr:** 3 Summit Cir, Stillwater, OK 74075-8234, **Home Phone:** (405)372-6873. **Business Addr:** Professor Emeritus, Oklahoma State University, 246 NRC 408 Whitehurst, Stillwater, OK 74078-0117, **Business Phone:** (405)744-2009.

## MITCHELL, GEORGE L.

Consultant, executive, association executive. **Personal:** Born Greenwood, MS; married Carolyn A; children: Cicely Elane & Cydni N. **Educ:** Morehouse Col, BA, bus admin, 1971. **Career:** Ford Motor Co, Milwaukee, Wis, mkt analyst; Dyersburg Ford Inc, Dyersburg, Tenn, chief exec, pres, 1985-2002; nowhalf, llc, consult, currently. **Orgs:** Ford Lincoln Mercury Minority Dealers Asn, pres, 2000-. **Business Addr:** President, Dyersburg Ford-Lincoln-Mercury, 920 US Hwy 51 By-Pass W, Dyersburg, TN 38024, **Business Phone:** (731)285-2500.

## MITCHELL, REV. DR. HENRY HEYWOOD, JR.

Clergy, theologian. **Personal:** Born Sep 10, 1919, Columbus, OH; son of Orlando W (deceased) and Bertha Estis (deceased); married Ella Muriel Pearson; children: Muriel M Lawrence, Elizabeth M Clement & Kenneth. **Educ:** Lincoln Univ, AB, cum laude, 1941; Union Theol Sem, MDiv, 1944; Calif State Univ, MA, ling, 1966; Claremont Sch Theol, ThD, 1973. **Career:** NC Cent Univ, dean chapel & instr, 1944-45; Am Bapt Northern Calif, area staffer & ed, 1945-59; Second Bapt Church Fresno, pastor, 1959-66; Calvary Bapt Church Santa Monica, pastor, 1966-69; Colgate Rochester & Bexley Hall & Crozer, black church studies, 1969-74; Fuller Theol Sem Pasadena & Am Bapt Sem W Berkeley & LaVerne Col, adj prof sch theol; Ecumenical Ctr Black Church Studies, prog dir, 1974-82; Martin Luther King Fels Press, lit ed, 1975-; Calif Stat Univ Northridge, prof rel & pan-African studies, 1981-82, acad dean; Va Union Univ, Samuel Proctor Sch Theol, acad dean & prof, 1982-87, prof hist & homiletics, 1986-87; Interdenominational Theol Ctr, vis prof homiletics, 1988-2001, emer prof, 1992-; United Theol Sem, Doctor Ministry Prog, mentor. **Orgs:** Dir, ML King Prog Black Church Studies, 1972-75; Soc Study Black Relig, 1972; pres, N Calif Bapt Conv, 1963, chmn bd, Fresno Co Econ Oppor Community, 1964-65, pres, 1966; Nat Comn Black Churchmen, 1968-75; Second Baptist Church Fresno, 1959-66; Lyman Beecher lectr Divinity Sch Yale Univ, 1974; founding dir, Ecumenical Ctr Black Church Studies. **Honors/Awds:** Hon DD, Am Baptist Sem; hon LHD, Lincoln Univ. **Special Achievements:** Co-author: Together For Good, 1999; Fire in the Well, 2003; Author: Black Preaching 1970, Black Belief 1975, The Recovery of Preaching 1977, Soul Theology with Nicholas Cooper Lewter, 1986, Celebration and Experience in Preaching, Abingdon Press, 1990, Black Preaching: The Recovery of a Powerful Art, Abingdon Press, 1990; Preaching for Black Self-Esteem, with Emil M Thomas, 1994; numerous articles in books magazines & journals; First Martin Luther King Jr Professor of Black Church Studies at the consortium of Colgate Rochester Divinity School, 1969. **Home Addr:** 411 Angier Ct NE, Atlanta, GA 30312, **Home Phone:** (404)873-9778. **Business Addr:** Emeritus Professor, Union Theological Seminary in the City of New York, 3041 Broadway 121st St, New York, NY 10027, **Business Phone:** (212)662-7100.

## MITCHELL, DR. HORACE

Educator. **Personal:** Born Oct 4, 1944, Lambert, MS; married Barbara J; children: 3. **Educ:** Wash Univ, AB, psychol, 1968, MEd, coun, 1969, PhD, coun psychol, 1974. **Career:** Wash Univ, St Louis, asst dean col arts & sci, 1968-73, asst prof educ & black studies, 1973-78, chair black studies prog, 1976-78; Univ Calif, Irvine, spec asst vice chancellor stud affairs, 1978-80, lectr educ, 1978-79, lectr social sci, 1979-80, from asst clin prof to assoc clin prof psychiat & human behav, 1980-95, Col Med, assoc dean stud & curricular affairs, 1980-84; Stud Affairs & Campus Life, vice chancellor, 1984-95; Univ Calif, Berkeley, Bus & Admin Servs, vice chancellor, 1995-2004, African Am Studies, affil prof, 1996-2004; Calif State Univ, Bakersfield, pres, 2004-. **Orgs:** Am Asn Higher Educ; Am Coun Asn, 1973-78; consult, Midwest Ctr Equal Educ Opport, Kans State Univ, 1974-80; AAAS; Am Col Personnel Asn; Am Psychol Asn; exec bd, Asn Multicultural Coun & Develop, 1981-84; nat pres, 1982-83; Asn Am Med Col; life mem, Asn Black Psychologists; Nat Forum Black Pub Adminrs, 1995-; APGA Com Standardized Testing Poten Disad; Kappa Delta Ph; Phi Delta Kappa; Phi Beta Sigma; Am Person & Guid Asn; Asn Black Psychol Asn; Non-White Concerns Person & Guid; comnr & past vice chair, Western Asn Schs & Cols; bd dir, Cent Valley Higher Educ Consortium; bd dir, Am Coun Educ. **Honors/Awds:** Distinguished Psychologist Award, Asn Black Psychologists, 2002; Robert C Maxson President of the Year Award, Calif State Stud Asn, 2006; Distinguished Alumnus Award, Wash Univ, 2008; President's Award, Nat Asn Stud Personnel Adminr Region VI, 2010. **Special Achievements:** Published numerous articles which incl, "The Testing Game", in Jones,R.L. (ed), Black Psychol, 3rd ed, Berkeley, CA, Cobb and Henry, 1991. **Home Addr:** 6681 Brentwood Dr, Huntington Beach, CA 92648-6655. **Business Addr:** President, California State University, 401 Golden Shore 6th Fl, Long Beach, CA 90802-4210, **Business Phone:** (562)951-4800.

## MITCHELL, HUEY P.

Judge, lawyer. **Personal:** Born Dec 10, 1935, Bivins, TX; married Nelvia G; children: Huey Jr & Janet H. **Educ:** Tex Southern Univ Sch Law, LLB, 1960. **Career:** Off Judge Advocate Gen; AUS Ft Hood, 1960-62; City Houston, asst city atty, 1964-67; Law Firm Mitchell & Bonner, atty; Reg Coun US Dept HUD, asst, 1967-73; Tex Christian Univ, teacher, Bus Law, 1968-73; Munic Ct Ft Worth, sub judge, 1973; Huey P. Mitchell PC, pvt pract atty, currently. **Orgs:** Mem chmn bd, Tarrant Co Legal Aid Found, 1972; mem & vpres, Ft Worth Chap Fed Bar Asn; Nat Bar Asn; Ft Worth Tarrant Co Sr Bar Asn; partner, Hex Learning Ctr; owner & org, HPM Mgt Develop & Co; Nat Bd Dir Planned Parenthood Fedn Am; Tarrant Co Health Planning Coun; organizing comt, Ft Worth Tarrant Community Develop Fund. **Special Achievements:** First African American Assistant City Attorney In History Of Houston, 1964; First African American Municipal Judge in Ft Worth, 1973. **Home Addr:** 4005 Lake Powell Dr, Arlington, TX 76016-4147, **Home Phone:** (817)572-6109. **Business Addr:** Attorney, Huey P Mitchell PC, 400 E Weatherford St, Ft. Worth, TX 76102-2200, **Business Phone:** (817)335-1301.

## MITCHELL, IVERSON O., III

Association executive, lawyer. **Personal:** Born Dec 20, 1943, Washington, DC. **Educ:** Georgetown Univ, BSFS, 1965; Wash Col Law, Am Univ, JD, 1968. **Career:** DC Corp Coun, asst, 1971-76; Wilkes & Artis, atty, 1976-85; pvt pract atty, 1985; Speights & Mitchell, partner, 1986-. **Orgs:** DC Bar Asn, 1969-; Wash Bar Asn, pres, 1982-84; Nat Bar Asn; DC Bd Labor Rels, 1977-79, chair, 1978-79; DC Bd Equalization & Review, 1987-93, chair, 1991-93. **Honors/Awds:** Certificate of Appreciation, Young Men's Christian Asn, 1973. **Business Addr:** Partner, Speights & Mitchell, 1819 Pa Ave NW 5th Fl, Washington, DC 20033, **Business Phone:** (202)296-6656.

## MITCHELL, JACOB BILL

Executive. **Personal:** Born Jun 19, 1932, Boswell, OK; married Erma Jean Davis; children: Waymon, Victor, Erik, Mark & Kayla. **Educ:** Armed Forces Inst, AE, 1953; Univ Calif, Los Angeles, BSEE, 1958, MSEE, 1963; City Univ, Los Angeles, Wichita State, PhD, 1979. **Career:** Librascope Inc, sr engr analyst, 1956-60; N Am Aviation, syst design engr, 1960-62; Hughes Aircraft Co, sr electronic engr, 1962-64; NASA, sr res engr, 1964-68; Beech Aircraft, design engr, 1968-73; Cessna Aircraft, design engr, 1973-75; Jacob B Mitchell Assoc, eng consult, 1975-79; NCR, sys engr, 1979-81; Mitchell Enterprises, owner, 1981-89; Learjet Inc, systs engr, 1989-, aviation consult, currently. **Orgs:** Inst Elec & Electronics Engrs, 1963-. **Honors/Awds:** NASA consult; Learjet Mgt. **Special Achievements:** First group of black engineers ever hired by NASA. **Home Addr:** 1456 N Madison Ave, Wichita, KS 67214, **Home Phone:** (316)262-8450. **Business Addr:** Aviation Consultant, Learjet Inc, 1 Learjet Way, Wichita, KS 67209, **Business Phone:** (316)946-2000.

## MITCHELL, JAMES H.

Chief executive officer, automotive executive. **Personal:** Born Sep 15, 1948, Danville, VA; married Linda T. **Educ:** Va State Univ, BS, 1972. **Career:** Detroit Lions Inc, pro football, 1970-78; Appomatox Ford-Mercury Inc, Appomatox, VA, pres, 1988-; Lynchburg Ford Inc, owner, chief exec, pres, 1981-; Mel Farr Ford, used car mgr; Pk Motor Sales, asst used car mgr; Crest Lincoln-Mercury, asst used car mgr; Ford Motor Dealer Training Prog. **Orgs:** Bd dir, United Way Lynchburg & Jr Achievement; C's Miracle Network; pres, Ford Lincoln Mercury Minority Dealers Asn. **Home Addr:** 120 Twin Creek Terr, Forest, VA 24551-1328, **Home Phone:** (434)525-0412. **Business Addr:** President, Lynchburg Ford Inc, 2123 Lakeside Dr, Lynchburg, VA 24501-6803, **Business Phone:** (434)385-5012.

## MITCHELL, DR. JAMES WINFIELD (JIM MITCHELL)

Dean (education), scientist. **Personal:** Born Nov 16, 1943, Durham, NC; son of Willie and Eunice Hester; married Alice J Kea; children: Veronica, Duane & Tonya. **Educ:** NC A&T State Univ, Greensboro, BS, chem, 1965; Iowa State Univ, PhD, anal chem, 1970. **Career:** AT&T Bell Labs, mem tech staff, 1970-72, supvr, Inorg anal chem res group, 1972-75, head, analyst chem res dept, 1975-85, nat acad engineering, mat engineering sect, 1989, head, process chem engineering res dept, 1994, Lucent Technologies, Bell Labs, dir, mat reliability & ecol res lab, 1995, dir, mat technol res lab, 1997, vpres, communs mat technol res lab, 2001; Howard Univ, david & lucille packard prof mat sci, adj, 2002, dir crest nanomaterials characterization sci & processing technol ctr, 2003, prof dept chem engineering, 2005, dir crest nanoscale anal sci res & educ ctr, 2009, dean, 2010-. **Orgs:** Omega Psi Phi Frat, 1963-; bd dir, Essex County Community Col, NJ, 1972-74; ed adv bd, Anal Chem, 1977-80; ed bd, Talanta, 1978; ed adv bd, Mikro Chim Acta, 1978-82; bd dir, Plainfield Sci Ctr, NJ, 1972-; bd, NRC, Chem Sci & Math, 1992-95; fel AT & T Bell Labs, 1985; NIST Vis Comt Advan Technol, 1999-2002; Mat Res Soc; Am Chem Soc; dir, Anal Chem Group; New York Acad Sci; Nat Soc Black Engrs; bd trustee, State Univ Nj; bd trustee, Drexel Univ, Philadelphia, Pa; indust adv bd, New York Tech Col; Army Res Lab Tech Assessment Bd; Nat Res Coun Bd Chem Sci & Technol; fel African Sci Inst; Lab Affirmative Action Comt. **Home Addr:** 17 Kingsbridge Rd, Somerset, NJ 08873, **Home Phone:** (908)828-8231. **Business Addr:** Dean, Director, Howard University, L K Downing Hall 2300 6th St Rm 1107A, Washington, DC 20059, **Business Phone:** (202)806-4398.

## MITCHELL, JOANN

College administrator, vice president (organization). **Personal:** Born Sep 2, 1956, Augusta, GA; daughter of Earl and Alice King. **Educ:** Davidson Col NC, AB, psychol, 1978; Vanderbilt Univ Sch Law, JD, 1981. **Career:** Manson Jackson & Asn, assoc atty, 1981-86; Fisk Univ, gen coun, law clerk, 1983-84; Tenn Human Rights Comn, law clerk, 1983-84; Vanderbilt Univ Opportunity Dev Ctr, asst dir, 1983-86; Univ Pa, dir affirmative action, 1986-93, vpres & chief staff, 2004-06, vpres instnl affairs, 2006-; Princeton Univ, assoc provost & affirmative action officer, 1993-2001, vice provost admin, 2001-04. **Orgs:** Am Bar Asn, 1981-; treas, bd dir, Napier-Lobby Bar Asn, 1985-86; adv bd mem, Vanderbilt Univ Women's Ctr, 1985-86; bd dir, Asn Vanderbilt Black Alumni, 1985-86; financial secy, Usher Bd Mt, Oliver Miss Baptist Church, 1985-86; deacon, Mt Oliver Miss Baptist Church, 1986-; pres, Bd McCarter Theatre Ctr; bd mem, Int Schs Serv Inc; pres, Asn Black Women Higher Educ; Women's Law Proj; Comn Minority Concerns, NJ Supreme Ct. **Home Addr:** 306 Wimbledon Way, Blackwood, NJ 08012, **Home Phone:** (609)232-2186. **Business Addr:** Vice President of Institutional Affairs, University of Pennsylvania, 200 Sansom Pl E 3600 Chestnut St, Philadelphia, PA 19104-6106, **Business Phone:** (215)898-6630.

## MITCHELL, JOANNE M.

Social worker. **Personal:** Born May 30, 1938, Evansville, IN; married Robert Bright; children: Howard & Karen. **Educ:** Roosevelt Univ Chicago, BA, sociol, 1971; Univ Chicago, Sch Social Serv Admin, AM SSA, 1973. **Career:** Brunswick Chicago Job Corps Ctr, admin asst, 1966-69; Ill Dept Corrections, community worker, 1969-73; Ill Dept Educ & Regist, social worker, 1973; Ill Dept Fin Inst, asst dir; Ill Comn Deliquency Prev, exec dir; Ill Law Enforcement Comn, assoc dir, juv justice, 1973-78; Banks & Trusts, dep comnr. **Orgs:** Acad Cert Social Workers; Nat Asn Social Workers, 1973; League Black Women, 1976; Panelist Assembly Behav & Social Sci Nat Acad Sci, 1979; Nat Asn Advan Colored People; Nat Urban League. **Honors/Awds:** Appointment Gov Adv Coun Criminal Justice Legis, 1978; Outstanding Leadership & Dedicated Service, Ill Health & Human Serv Asn, 1978. **Home Addr:** 20 Graymoor Lane, Olympia Fields, IL 60461-1210, **Home Phone:** (708)747-8627.

## MITCHELL, JUDSON, JR.

Auditor. **Personal:** Born Oct 26, 1941, Jersey City, NJ; son of Judson (deceased) and Lucy Barnes; married Patricia Roberts; children: Mark A, Judson (deceased), Steven C & Guy (deceased). **Educ:** Rutgers Univ Col, BS, acct, 1975; Rutgers GSBA, MBA, 1979. **Career:** Pub Serv Elec & Gas Co, sr plant analyst, 1980-81, assoc acct, 1981-82, internal auditor, 1982-, Internal Auditing Dept, sr staff auditor, 1994. **Orgs:** Pres, Northern NJ Chap Nat Asn Black Accountants, 1987-88; Nat Black MBA Asn; Am Inst CPA's, NJ Soc CPA's; Inst Internal Auditors, Minority Interchange; Nat Asn Cert Fraud Examr; Nat Asn Black Accountants. **Honors/Awds:** Cert Pub Accountant NJ, 1982; Cert Internal Auditor, Inst Internal Auditors, 1986; Black Achiever Bus & Educ, YMWCA Newark & Vicinity, 1988; Cert Fraud Examr, Nat Asn Cert Fraud Examr, 1989; Outstanding Mem of the Year, 1992. **Home Addr:** 15 Holly St, Jersey City, NJ 07305, **Home Phone:** (201)332-4839. **Business Addr:** Senior Staff Auditor, Public Service Electric and Gas Co, 80 Pk Plz, Newark, NJ 07101-0570, **Business Phone:** (973)430-7000.

## MITCHELL, DR. JUDY LYNN

School administrator. **Personal:** Born Aug 19, 1951, Salisbury, MD; married Fred; children: Cortni Lee-Lynn. **Educ:** Bowie State Col, BS, 1972; Bowling Green State Univ, MEd, 1974; Nova Univ, EdD, 1985. **Career:** Salisbury State Col, acad counr, 1974-79, proj dir, 1980-82, progs pecialist, 1982-83; Wicomico Co Pub Schs, supvr elem elem multi cult educ & media serv. **Orgs:** Asn Study Afro Life & Hist; bd trustee, Wicomico Co Lib; bd dir, Eastern Seals Soc; Wicomico Co Hist Soc; Ctr Human Serv, educ specialist, 1983-84, residential admin. **Honors/Awds:** Outstanding Young Women of the Year, 1982-83. **Special Achievements:** Black Heritage Articles, "Salisbury Sunday & Daily Times" Salisbury, Md, 1979; religious black hist play, "Yester-Days Women, Gone But Not Forgotten", 1983; Community Service Award, Md State Educ Asn, 2012. **Home Addr:** Rt 5 106 Southbury St, Salisbury, MD 21801, **Home Phone:** (410)677-4401. **Business Addr:** Elementary Supervisor of English, Wicomico County Public Schools, 101 Long Ave, Salisbury, MD 21802, **Business Phone:** (410)677-4400.

## MITCHELL, DR. JULIUS P.

Army officer, educator, school administrator. **Personal:** Born Nov 5, 1941, Rome, GA; son of Carrie and Pryor; married Gwendolyn McLeod; children: Toni L & Shaune. **Educ:** Clarkson Univ, Potsdam NY, BA, 1984; St Lawrence Univ, Canton NY, MED, 1987. **Career:** AUS, spec forces, 1959-81; St Lawrence Univ, dir HEOP & pres, HEOP-PO; Clarkston Univ, Potsdam NY, dir, minority affairs, 1988-, assoc vpres. **Orgs:** Pres, Higher Educ Opportunity Prog Prof Orgn New York, 1984. **Honors/Awds:** Bronze Star; Meritorious Service Award. **Home Addr:** 708 Golf House Rd, Whitsett, NC 27377, **Home Phone:** (336)449-5547. **Business Addr:** Director, Associate Vice President, Clarkson University, 101 Camp, Potsdam, NY 13676, **Business Phone:** (315)268-7615.

## MITCHELL, DR. KATHERINE PHILLIPS

Educator, administrator. **Personal:** Born Apr 16, 1943, Hope, AR; daughter of Parthenia Phillips and Clem Phillips; children: Jeffrey Allen. **Educ:** Philander Smith Col, BA, eng educ; Univ Wis, 1966; Cleveland State Univ, MEd, reading educ; Univ Ark, EdD, higher educ. **Career:** Cleveland Pub Sch, teacher, 1967-73; Univ Cent Arks, asst prof, 1977-78; City Little Rock, grant mgr, 1978-79, proj dir, 1979-81; Storer Cable, coord Channel 14, 1981-89; Independent Community Consult, 1982-; Philander Smith Col, div chair, educ, 1986-89, dean develop studies; Shorter Col, pres, 1990-97; Little Rock Sch Bd Edu, pres, currently. **Orgs:** Immediate pres & bd dir, Little Rock Sch Bd, 1988-2011; Prof Coun Assoc, 1986-, secy; Cent Ark Libr Syst, 1988-; chap pres, Delta Sigma Theta, 1962-; Ouachita Coun Girl Scouts, 1987-; Minority AIDS Task Force, 1987-; Am Asn Univ Women; Ark Acad Advising Network, 2005-. **Home Addr:** 1605 Welch St, PO Box 547, Little Rock, AR 72202, **Home Phone:** (501)375-6957. **Business Addr:** President, Little Rock School Board, 2700 Poplar St N, Little Rock, AR 72114, **Business Phone:** (501)771-8000.

## MITCHELL, KEITH (CLARENCE MARQUIS MITCHELL)

Football player. **Personal:** Born Jul 24, 1974, Garland, TX. **Educ:** Tex A&M Univ. **Career:** Football player (retired); New Orleans Saints, linebacker & left line backer & left outside linebacker, 1997-2001; Houston Texans, linebacker, right outside linebacker, 2002; Jacksonville Jaguars, linebacker, 2003. **Honors/Awds:** Pro Bowl Selection, 2000.

## MITCHELL, LEMONTE FELTON

Labor relations manager, teacher. **Personal:** Born Feb 19, 1939, Wake Forest, NC; married Emma Jean Hartsfield; children: LaMarsha, Muriel & Andrea. **Educ:** Johnson C Smith Univ, BA, 1960; Loyola Univ Chicago, grad study, 1964; Govt Exec Inst, Univ NC, Sch Bus Admin, 1979. **Career:** Executive (retired); jr & sr high sch teacher, 1960-69; NC Dept Admin, personnel analyst, 1969-77; NC Dept Correction, personnel dir, 1977; Classification Spec NC Dept Human Res NC Dept Transp, 1980-92; Raleighs Davie St Presby Church, choir dir. **Orgs:** NC Chap IPMA; pres, Wayne & Co Tchr Asn; Omega Psi Phi Fraternity; minister music, Davie St Presby Church, Comt Ministries New Hope Presbytery. **Home Addr:** 2501 Firelight Rd, Raleigh, NC 27610-5813, **Home Phone:** (919)829-9454.

**MITCHELL, LEONA PEARL**
Opera singer. **Personal:** Born Oct 13, 1948, Enid, OK; daughter of Hulon and Olive Leatherman; married Elmer Bush III; children: Elmer IV. **Educ:** Okla City Univ, BA, music, 1971; Juilliard Sch Music, New York. **Career:** Kurt Herbert Adler Award, 1972; San Francisco Opera, soprano, 1973-74, 1977; Europ debut, BarcelonaSpain, 1974; Met Opera debut, 1974; Edinburgh Scotland Festival, 1977; Sacria-Umbria Festival, Australia, 1978. **Orgs:** Am Guild Musicians Asn; Sigma Alpha Iota; Alpha Kappa Alpha; Church God Christ; honorary chair, Black Heritage Month. **Honors/Awds:** James H Schwabacher Award, San Francisco Opera Auditions, 1971; Outstanding Oklahoman citation, 1975; named Ambassadress of Enid, 1978; honorary doctorate, Okla City Univ, 1979; Okla Hall of Fame, 1983; honorary doctorate, Univ Okla. **Special Achievements:** Performed for Pres Ford, 1976, Pres Carter, 1978, 1979, Pres Clinton, 1998. **Business Addr:** Singer, c/o Columbia Artists Management LLC, 1790 Broadway Suite 16, New York, NY 10019, **Business Phone:** (212)841-9527.

**MITCHELL, MARTHA MALLARD**
Chairperson, executive director. **Personal:** Born Jan 1, 1940, Gary, IN; daughter of Louis B and Elizabeth Allen. **Educ:** Mich State Univ, E Lansing, Mich, BA, 1963, MA, 1968. **Career:** Univ DC, Wash, DC, dir continuing educ women, 1970-74; Drug Abuse Coun, dir info servs, 1974-77; US Govt Exec Off Pres, spec asst to pres, 1977-79, Dept Com, assoc dir, 1979-81; self-employed bus consult, 1981-84; Fleishman-Hillard Inc, St Louis, Mo, vpres, 1985-87, sr vpres, 1987-93, partner, 1993-98; sr partner, 1998-2005; CBRL Group Inc, independent dir, 2005, Chair, currently. **Orgs:** Bd trustee, Nat Urban League; MO Women's Forum; bd dir, vpres, Fair Found; bd dir, Eugene Field House & Toy Mus; exec comt, St Louis Br, Nat Asn Advan Colored People; Links Inc. **Honors/Awds:** Public Service Award, Capital Press Club, 1978; Distinguished Achievement Award, Nat Asn Advan Colored People, Gary Ind Br, 1985. **Special Achievements:** Hundred Top Black Business & Professional Women, Dollar & Sense Magazine, 1988. **Business Addr:** Independent Director, CBRL Group Inc, 305 Hartmann Dr, Lebanon, TN 37088-0787, **Business Phone:** (615)444-5533.

**MITCHELL, MELVIN LESTER**
Architect, educator. **Personal:** Born Aug 11, 1939, New Orleans, LA; married Geraldine Vaughan; children: Marcus Quintana & Michelle Violet. **Educ:** Howard Univ, BArch, 1967; Harvard Grad Sch Design, MArch, 1970. **Career:** Howard Univ, asst prof archit, 1970-75, prof, 1972-92; Univ DC, prof, 1972-92; Melvin Mitchell Architects, Wash DC, prin & owner, 1972; Grad Archit Prog Morgan, Baltimore, dir, 1997-2002; Am Inst Architects, fel, currently; Bryant Mitchell PLLC, pres & chief exec officer, currently; Morgan State Univ, Sch Archit & Planning, dir; Bryant & Bryant Architects & Planners Inc, pres & chief exec officer, 1965-; Book: The Crisis of the African American Architect, author. **Orgs:** Chmn, pres, DC Bd Architects; mem, DC Hist Preserv Rev Bd; Am Inst Architects; Nat Orgn Minority Architects. **Home Addr:** 413 Van Buren St NW, Washington, DC 20012-2727, **Home Phone:** (202)723-4958. **Business Addr:** President, Chief Executive Officer, Bryant Mitchell PLLC, 7826 E Ave NW Suite 408, Washington, DC 20012, **Business Phone:** (202)669-3694.

**MITCHELL, MICHELLE BURTON**
Law enforcement officer. **Personal:** Born Jun 30, 1963, Richmond, VA; daughter of Arthur Burton and Claudette Moore; married William Thomas; children: Michael. **Educ:** Va Commonwealth Univ, BS, 1984. **Career:** Va Dept Corrections, 1983-86; Richmond City Sheriff's Off, 1986-, sheriff. **Orgs:** Va Sheriff's Asn; Willing Workers Ministry; Bd Corrections Liaison Comn; Nat Sheriff's Asn; Nat Orgn Black Law Enforcement Exec. **Home Addr:** 2618 Q St, Richmond, VA 23223-5370, **Home Phone:** (804)780-8630. **Business Addr:** VA.

**MITCHELL, DR. NELLI LOUISE**
Psychiatrist. **Personal:** Born Feb 11, 1926, Jersey City, NJ; daughter of Eloise Casey and Cullie; married Edward Henry Chappelle; children: Edward H Chappelle Jr. **Educ:** NY Univ, BA, 1945; Columbia Univ, MA, 1949; Howard Univ, MD, 1950; Am Bd Psychiat & Neurol, Psychiat, dipl, 1961. **Career:** Freedmen's Hosp, resident, 1956; St Elizabeth's Hosp, staff psychiat, 1956-57; Rochester Chld Guid Ctr, fel, 1960; Ment Health Ctr, med dir, youth consult serv, 1963-65; Rochester Ment Health Ctr, training dir/child psychiat, 1965-89, supv psychiatrist, 1983-89; Hillside C's Ctr, psychiat consult, 1970-; Rochester, NY, pvt pract psychiatrist, 1989-; Anthony Health Ctr, consult, 1989-90; Univ Rochester Med Ctr, dept psychiat, asst prof. **Orgs:** Fel Am Psychiat Asn, 1956; Nat Med Asn, 1956; Am Ortho psychiat Asn, 1960; Hudson City Med Asn, 1960; bd mem, Camp Fire Girls Inc, 1967-73; Am Acad Child & Adolescent Psychiat, 1970; YWCA, 1974-75; Synod Nebr; UPC US, 1975-79; Monroe Co Bd Ment Health, 1976-80; NY State Bd Visitors Monroe Develop Ctr, 1977-; Am Bd Psychiat & Neurol, Child Psychiat; Am Coun Psychiatrists, 1999; Am Col Psychiat. **Honors/Awds:** Psi Chi Hon Soc Psychol; Distinguished Fellow, American Psychiatric Association, 2006. **Home Addr:** 345 Highland Ave, Rochester, NY 14620-3027, **Home Phone:** (585)271-8874. **Business Addr:** Psychiatrist, 345 Highland Ave, Rochester, NY 14620-3027, **Business Phone:** (585)244-9068.

**MITCHELL, DR. ORRIN DWIGHT**
Dentist, president (organization). **Personal:** Born Oct 1, 1946, Jacksonville, FL; son of Arthur O (deceased) and Ella Mae (deceased); married Patricia Hill; children: Derrick & Kia. **Educ:** Howard Univ, BS, 1969, DDS, 1973, cert orthod, 1975. **Career:** Orrin D Mitchell DDS, Pa, orthodontist, 1975-. **Orgs:** Am Asn Orthodontists; Am Dent Asn; Nat Dent Asn; Acad Gen Dent; Continental Orthod Study Club; Jacksonville Dent Soc; NE Dist Dent Asn; Fla Med, Dent & Pharmaceut Asn; Southern Soc Orthodontists; Jacksonville Med Dent & Pharmaceut Asn; Jacksonville Urban League; life mem, Alpha Phi Alpha Fraternity; Chi Delta Mu Fraternity; Howard Univ Alumni Asn; Sigma Pi Phi Fraternity; life mem, Nat Asn Advan Colored People; adv bd dir, First Union Nat Bank Fla; Fla Asn Orthodontists; trustee, bd New Bethel AME Church; Fla Bd Dent; bd dir, Jacksonville Urban League, 1988-90; bd govs, Jacksonville Chamber Com, 1989; Stewart Bd New Bethel AME Church; secy, Howard Univ Orthod Alumni Asn; Pvt Indus Coun Jacksonville; pres, NW Coun, Jacksonville Chamber Com; bd dir, Midas Touch Day Care Ctr; pres, Continental Orthod Study Club; fel Am Col Dentists; fel World Fedn Orthodontists; bd dir, United Way Northeast Fla. **Home Addr:** 5365 Oak Bay Dr E, Jacksonville, FL 32277-1028, **Home Phone:** (904)744-4651. **Business Addr:** Orthodontist, Jacksonville Orthodontics, 1190 W Edgewood Ave Suite A, Jacksonville, FL 32208-3419, **Business Phone:** (904)766-6000.

**MITCHELL, QUITMAN J., JR.**
Mayor. **Personal:** married Claire L. **Career:** Twentieth Century Barbershop, staff, 1964-98; City Bessemer, AL, mayor, 1998-2002. **Orgs:** Bessemer Area Chamber Com. **Honors/Awds:** First African American mayor of Bessemer. **Home Addr:** 948 Posey Ave, Bessemer, AL 35022-4546, **Home Phone:** (205)424-0430.

**MITCHELL, RHONDA ALMA**
Writer, painter (artist), illustrator. **Personal:** Born Feb 22, 1954, Cleveland, OH; daughter of Melvin and Beatrice. **Educ:** Kent State Univ, BA, 1992. **Career:** Orchard Bks, illusr & writer, 1992-97; Writer, illusr & artist, currently. Books: Joshua by the Sea, illusr, 1994; Rain Feet, illusr, 1994, 2001; Joshua's Night Whispers, illusr, 1994; Mama Bird, Baby Birds, illusr, 1994; Sleep Song, pictures, 1995; Talking Cloth, story & pictures, 1997; Daddy Call Me Man, illusr, 1997; Little Red Ronnika, illusr, 1998. **Orgs:** Hudson Soc Artist, 1980-99; Cuyahoga Art Ctr, 1998-99; Authors League Am. **Home Addr:** 3882 Lovers Lane, Ravenna, OH 44266-1801, **Home Phone:** (330)296-0401. **Business Addr:** Writer, Artist, PO Box 922, Ravenna, OH 44266, **Business Phone:** (330)296-0401.

**MITCHELL, ROBERT CORNELIUS**
Football executive. **Personal:** Born Jun 6, 1935, Hot Springs, AR; son of Albert James Jr and Avis; married Gwendolyn E Morrow; children: Terri Sue & Robert Jr. **Educ:** Univ Ill, BS, 1958. **Career:** Football palyer, executive (retired); Cleveland Browns, kick returner, 1958-61, punt returner, 1959, 1961, half back, 1960-61; Wash Redskins, flanker, 1962-68, front off exec, 1969, dir pro scouting, 1972-78, exec asst pres, 1978, asst gen mgr, 1981-2003; Pepsi Cola, mkt rep, 1963-69; Bobby Mitchell Ins Agency, owner, 1967-72; pro football scout, 1969-72. **Orgs:** Pigskin Club Wash; Univ Ill Presidents Coun; Univ Ill Found; chmn, Metrop Wash DC Area Leadership Coun; bd mem, Am Lung Asn; Martin Luther King Fed Holiday Comn; NFL Alumni Exec Comt; Boys Club Wash; bd mem, Bike Found; adv coun, Variety Club Greater Wash; adv bd, UNCF; adv bd, Univ Ill Libr; adv bd, Provident Bank Va; bd trustee, Plymouth Church Unified Church Christ; Howard Univ Cancer Res Adv Comt; Am Lung Asn; Nat Urban League; Jr Chamber Com; Univ Ill Presidents Coun; Univ Ill Found; Nat Asn Advan Colored People. **Honors/Awds:** Numerous honors & awards including: Rookie of the Year, 1958; NFL Receiving Title, 1962; Arkansas Hall of Fame, 1977; DC Stars Hall of Fame, 1979; NFL Pro Football Hall of Fame, 1983; Washington Touchdown Hall of Fame, 1983; Hot Springs School District Hall of Fame, 1989; Illini of the Year, Ill Varsity, 1995; Outstanding Leadership Award, Univ Ill Found, Nat Network; Lifetime Achievement, Pigskin Club DC; Bobby Mitchell Hall of Fame, Golf Classic Leukemia Found Charity; Nat Intercollegiate All-Am Football Players. **Special Achievements:** First African-American to play for Washington Redskins 1962. **Home Addr:** 1561 Locust Rd NW, PO Box 55283, Washington, DC 20012.

**MITCHELL, DR. ROBERT L.**
School administrator. **Educ:** Fla State Univ, Tallahassee, FL, PhD, educ admin & supv. **Career:** Univ N Fla's Downtown Campus, assoc vpres, acad affairs/chief admin officer, assoc prof, 1984-88; Edward Waters Col, Jacksonville, Fla, interim pres, 1990-95.

**MITCHELL, ROBERT LEE, SR.**
Executive. **Personal:** Born Nov 18, 1932, West Palm Beach, FL; son of Hezekiah and Grace; children: Verdette L, Marc A & Robert Jr. **Career:** Executive (retired); Pratt & Whitney Aircraft, utility, 1964-93. **Orgs:** Founder, Afro-Amer Civ Action Unit Inc, 1960-69; Palm Beach co Repub Exec Comm, 1970-80; Policy Comm & Platform Com Rep Party FL, 1975-77; organz & chmn, FL black Repub Councl, 1975; del, GOP Conv, 1976; bd dir, Palm Beach Co Comm Ment Health Ctr, 1979-81; pres, Frederick Douglass Repub Club, 1979-81; state chmn, FL Minority Conf Repub Clubs, 1980-82; Black Citizen's Coalition PB Co, 1979-84; Nat Asn Advan Colored People; gen bd mem, Urban League; Black Prof Caucus; bd mem, Concerned Alliance Progressive Action Inc; bd mem, Tri-Cnty Chap Nat Bus League, 1984-; Palm Beach Cnty Reagan-Bush Campaign; co-chmn, Blacks Reagan, 1984; Nat coordr, Commun Network Negro League Players, 1996-; Crime Prev Task Force; Tampa-Hillsborough Urban League Inc; Brotherhood St. Andrews, St. James Episcopal House Prayer; vol, YWCA, 2000; Yesterday Negro League Baseball. **Honors/Awds:** Community Serv Award, Tri-Cnty Nat Bus League, 1984; Accomp Pres Ford on hist riverboat trip down the MS river, 1975; Man of the Year, Prof Men's Bus League, 1966; Off Particip, FL Human Rel Conf, 1977; Player KC Monarchs Baseball Team, 1954-57; Man of the Year, Omega Si Phi, 1967. **Special Achievements:** Successfully lobbied for some 155 Negro League legends who had been excluded from receiving a suppl pension from Maj League Baseball. **Home Addr:** 2009 Elmwood Ave, Tampa, FL 33605-6625, **Home Phone:** (813)247-3357.

**MITCHELL, RODERICK BERNARD (ROCKY MITCHELL)**
Executive, president (organization). **Personal:** Born Aug 14, 1955, Reidsville, NC; son of Hunter Lee and Christine Odessa Dixon; married Monica Boswell; children: Marcus Galen & Akia Lee. **Educ:** Univ Calif, Los Angels, CA, BA, econs, 1977; Columbia Univ, New York, NY, MBA, 1980. **Career:** Collins & Aikman Corp, Charlotte, NC, indust engr, 1977-79; Celanese Corp, New York, NY, sr financial analyst, 1981-83; Bedford Stuyvesant Restoration Corp, Brooklyn, NY, 1984-85, dir opers, 1985-86, vpres phys develop, 1987-88, pres & chief exec officer, 1984-00; Bethel Gospel Assembly, Adult Sunday Sch, teacher, 1989; Pentagon Fed Credit Union, chief exec officer, founding pres, 2001-08, chief admin officer, 2006-08, exec vpres, chief opearting officer, 2008-11, exec vpres, chief financial officer, 2012-14, exec vice pres global fixed assets, 2015-. **Orgs:** Treas, Men 'N' Ministries, 1986-; bd dir, Brooklyn Acad Cult Affairs, 1988-; bd dir, Brooklyn Chamber Com, 1988-; bd dir, Brooklyn Bur Community Serv, 1989; 100 Black Men Manhattan, 1989. **Home Addr:** 548 Riverside Dr Apt 3B, New York, NY 10027, **Home Phone:** (212)662-6752.

**MITCHELL, REV. DR. SADIE STRIDIRON**
Clergy. **Personal:** Born Jan 4, 1922, Philadelphia, PA; daughter of Joseph Alfonso Stridiron and Lucinda Clifton; married Charles Jr; children: Sadye Lawson, Chas T III & Charlene Wiltshire. **Educ:** Temple Univ, BS, educ, 1942; Univ Penn, MS, 1968; Nova Univ, EdD, 1978; Lutheran Theol Sem, MDiv, 1990. **Career:** Clergy (retired); Philadelphia Bd Edu, teacher, 1945-68, prin, 1968-81; sem, 1981-83; St Luke's, deacon & deacon training, 1983-89; St Luke's, asst rector, 1984-91; Christ Church, priest in-chg, 1989-90; African Episcopal Church, St Thomas, asst rector. **Orgs:** Nat Asn Advan Colored People, 1944-; Union Black Episcopalians, 1961-; secy, Philadelphia Asn Sch Adv, 1968-81; founder, vpres, Black Women's Ed Alliance, 1975-; Diocesan Christian Ed Comn, 1981-92; Diocesan Phia Theol Inst; bd coun, Episcopal Comm Serv, 1990-. **Honors/Awds:** Highest Achievement Award, Administrative, PASA, 1981; Community Service, Mill Creek Comm Ctr, 1978; Achievement Award Women Clergy, 1994. **Home Addr:** 3600 Conshohocken Ave Apt 508, Philadelphia, PA 19131-5309, **Home Phone:** (215)877-4703.

**MITCHELL, SALLY RUTH**
Executive. **Personal:** Born Oct 5, 1960, Dallas, TX; daughter of David and Cerenia. **Educ:** Southern Methodist Univ, BBA, 1982. **Career:** Mitchell's Floor Covering Co, off asst, 1978-83; Internal Revenue Serv, taxpayer serv rep, 1983-85; EDS, employee rels specialist, 1985-91, 1994-; EGG Inc, hr adminr, eeo coord, 1991-94. **Orgs:** Alpha Kappa Alpha Sorority Inc; Dallas Human Resource Mgt Asn. **Special Achievements:** Accreditation, Professional in Human Resources (PHR), Human Resources Cert Inst (HRCI), 1994-; Performed on TV: commercial, lead vocalist; shows, Insight, Good Day Dallas. **Home Addr:** 5014 Waneta Dr, Dallas, TX 75398, **Home Phone:** (214)470-6835. **Business Addr:** Employee Relations Specialist, Electronic Data Systems Corp (EDS), 5400 Legacy Dr, Plano, TX 75024, **Business Phone:** (800)566-9337.

**MITCHELL, SAM, JR. (SAMUEL E MITCHELL, JR.)**
Basketball executive, basketball player, basketball coach. **Personal:** Born Sep 2, 1963, Columbus, GA; married Anita; children: Morgann, Maya, Rhagan & Rhana. **Educ:** Mercer Univ, attended 1985. **Career:** Basketball player (retired), basketball coach, basketball executive; Wisc Flyers, CBA, forward, 1985-86; Tampa Bay Flash, guard, 1986; Rapid City Thrillers, CBA, 1986-87; Montpellier, 1987-89; Minn Timber wolves, 1989-92, 1995-2002, head coach, 2015-; Ind Pacers, 1992-95; Milwaukee Bucks, asst coach, 2002-04; Charlotte Bobcats, asst coach, 2004; Toronto Raptors, head coach, 2004-08; Nj Nets, asst coach; TSN, sports announcer, currently; NBA TV, analyst, currently. TV Series : "Eddie", 1996; "ESPN Sports Country", 2002; "Quite Frankly With Stephen A. Smith", 2006; "Rome Is Burning", 2007, actor. **Orgs:** Spec Olympics. **Business Addr:** Analyst, NBA TV, Olympic Tower 645 5th Ave, New York, NY 10022, **Business Phone:** (212)688-9622.

**MITCHELL, SHANNON LAMONT**
Football player. **Personal:** Born Mar 28, 1972, Alcoa, TN. **Educ:** Ga Univ, attended. **Career:** Football player (retired); San Diego Chargers, tight end, 1994-97. **Special Achievements:** Hall of Fame, Great Am Rivalry Ser, 2011.

**MITCHELL, SHARON**
Writer, psychologist, educator. **Personal:** Born Oct 27, 1962, Ft. Deposit, AL; daughter of Curtis and Bertha. **Educ:** Carleton Col, BA, 1984; Ohio State Univ, MA, 1987, PhD, coun psychol, 1990. **Career:** Boston Univ, psychologist, 1989-94; Univ Del, psychologist & asst prof, 1994-, asst dir, 1994-2003; State Univ New York, Buffalo, NY, dir coun serv, 2003-; Books: Nothing But Rent, 1998; Sheer Necessity, 1999; Near Perfect, 2001. **Orgs:** Am Psychologist Asn, 1988-; Am Coun Asn, 1997-; pres, Examiners Psychologists, 2001-; Nat Asn Advan Colored People; Asn Univ & Col Coun Ctr; Am Col Stud Personnel Asn. **Home Addr:** 13 Tarcote Turn, Newark, DE 19702, **Home Phone:** (302)836-2046. **Business Addr:** Director of Counseling Services, State University of New York, 120 Richmond Quad, Buffalo, NY 14261, **Business Phone:** (716)645-2720.

**MITCHELL, STANLEY HENRYK**
Lawyer, executive director. **Personal:** Born Sep 28, 1949, St. Louis, MO; children: Stanley J P. **Educ:** Univ Mo, BS, 1974; Wash Univ, MSW, 1976; Temple Univ Sch Law, JD, 1979. **Career:** Pvt law pract, 1980; Solo Practicioner, atty, 1980-; Pa House Reps, exec dir, 1981-83; Elizabeth Town Col Soc Welfare, adj prof, 1982-84; City Harrisburg, solicitor, 1984-; Pa House Reps, chief coun; Shippens Burg Univ, adj prof criminal law, 1991-96. **Orgs:** Chmn, Pro Bono Legal Redress City Harrisburg, Nat Asn Advan Colored People, 1981-; Omega Psi Phi Fraternity, 1984-; Dem Nominee City Harrisburg City Coun, 1985; comt man, 11th Ward City Harrisburg; City Coun Harrisburg, Pa, 1986-90. **Honors/Awds:** American Jurisprudence Award Conract Remedies, 1976-77. **Business Addr:** Attorney, 600 N 2nd St Suite 305, Harrisburg, PA 17101, **Business Phone:** (717)233-3339.

**MITCHELL, TEX DWAYNE**
Manager, president (organization). **Personal:** Born Nov 19, 1949, Houston, TX; married Deborah Ann Earvin; children: Tonya DiBonne & Tess Dionne. **Educ:** Lee Jr Col, attended 1970; Tex Southern Univ, BA, 1971. **Career:** Courtesy Ford, parts delivery, 1968-69; Petro-Tex Chem Corp, plant oper, 1969; TX Petrochem, pumping suprv; Crosby ISD Trustee Bd, vpres. **Orgs:** Pres, Barrett-Crosby Civic League, 1976; Tenneco vols, 1979-83. **Home Addr:** 407 Red Oak, Crosby, TX 77532.

### MITCHELL, THEO W.

State government official, lawyer. **Personal:** Born Jul 2, 1938, Greenville, SC; son of Clyde D and Dothenia E Lomax; married Greta Jo-Anne Knight; children: Emily Kaye, Tamara JoAnne & Megan Dawn. **Educ:** Fisk Univ, AB, biol, 1960; Howard Univ Law Sch, JD, 1969. **Career:** Clemson Univ, Greenville Tech Col, adj prof; Greenville Inc, atty, 1969; SC House Representatives, rep, 1974; SC Gen Assembly, sen & atty, 1975-95; Sc Senate, Dist 7, sen, 1984; Greenville County Legis Deleg, vice-chmn, 1984; Theo W Mitchell & Assocs, atty, currently. **Orgs:** Pres, Greenville Urban League Inc, 1971-73; chmn, SC Legis Black Caucus; chmn, SC House Reps Task Force Struct & Authority State Agencies; vice chmn, House Judiciary Comt; SC adv comt, US Comn Civil Rights; Health Care Planning & Oversight Comt; chmn, Region 5 Nat Black Caucus State Legislators; Omega Psi Phi Fraternity Inc; bd dir, Schiller Inst; life mem, Nat Asn Advan Colored People; Allen Temple AME Church; chmn, Senate Corrections; chmn, Penol comt;Nat Asn Advan Colored People; Adv Committes Intergovernmental Rels; Exec Comt; County's Recreation Comn. **Home Addr:** 522 Woodland Way, Greenville, SC 29607, **Home Phone:** (803)232-3021. **Business Addr:** Attorney, Theo W Mitchell & Associates, 9 Bradshaw St, Greenville, SC 29601, **Business Phone:** (864)235-6361.

### MITCHELL, WILLIAM GRAYSON

Editor. **Personal:** Born Mar 8, 1950, Mobile, AL; married Renee Grant; children: 2. **Educ:** Univ Ill, BS, econs, 1971. **Career:** Chicago Sun Times, polit reporter, 1970-72; Wash Post, gen assignment reporter, 1972-73; Ebony Jet Mag, 1973-74; Black Enterprise mag, columnist, 1975-79; Nat Endowment Humanities Journ, fel, 1975-76; Johnson Prod, Chicago, dir corp commun, 1980; Chicago's first African Am Mayor, press secy, 1983-85; Summit Consult Inc, founder, chmn & chief exec officer, currently; Johnson Pub Co, assoc ed. **Orgs:** Bd dir, Lakefront Supportive Housing; bd dir, Ill Humanities Coun; bd dir, Fedn State Humanities Coun; Econ Club Chicago. **Special Achievements:** First African American Mayor. **Business Addr:** Chairman & Chief Executive Officer, Founder, Summit Consulting Inc, 50 N Mich Ave Suite 1000, Chicago, IL 60601, **Business Phone:** (312)201-8700.

### MITCHELL-KERNAN, DR. CLAUDIA IRENE

School administrator, educator. **Personal:** Born Aug 29, 1941, Gary, IN; daughter of Joseph Henry Mitchell and Claudia; married Keith; children: Claudia L & Ryan J. **Educ:** Ind Univ, BA, anthrop, 1963, MA, anthrop, 1965; Univ Calif, Berkeley, PhD, anthrop, 1969. **Career:** Harvard Univ, asst prof anthrop, 1969-73; Univ Calif, Los Angeles, from asst prof anthrop to assoc prof anthrop, 1973-89, Ctr Afro-Am Studies, dir, 1977, vice chancellor & dean, grad studies, 1994, Semel Inst Neuroscience & Human Behav, prof, Dept Anthrop, prof, prof emer; Coun Grad Schs & Nat Sci Found, dean residence, 2005. **Orgs:** Fel Nat Inst Ment Health, 1965-66; fel Social Sci Res Coun, 1966-68; fel Ford Found, 1968-69; researcher, Nat Inst Ment Health, 1971-75; consult, Nat Urban League, 1973; fel rev commn, Nat Sci Found, 1974; bd trustees, Ctr Appl Ling, Wash, DC, 1979-81; bd mem, Crystal Stairs Inc, 1980-; vice chancellor, Acad Affairs & Dean Grad Div, Univ Calif, Los angeles, 1994-; Nat Sci Bd, 1994; Grad Rec Exam Bd, 1994-2000, chmn, 1999-2000; Nat Sci Bd, 1994-2000; chmn, Sci & Engineering Indicators Sub comt, 1996-2000; bd dir, Consortium Social Sci Associations; adv bd, Nat Security Educ Prog; bd dean Africa Am Inst; mem & bd dir, Golden State Minority Found; bd dir, Venice Family Clin. **Honors/Awds:** President's Achievement Award of the Greater Los Angeles African American Chamber of Commerce, 1996, Distinguished Service Award, Caribbean Studies Asn, 1997; Distinguished Alumni Service Award, Ind Univ. **Special Achievements:** Books: "The Decline in Marriage Among African Americans". **Home Addr:** 3960 Hayvenhurst, Encino, CA 91316. **Business Addr:** Professor, University of California, 375 Portola Pz, Los Angeles, CA 90095-1553, **Business Phone:** (310)825-2918.

### MITCHELL-RANKIN, ZINORA M.

Judge, lawyer. **Personal:** Born Jan 1, 1956, Washington, DC; married Michael L; children: John Michael, Everett, Michael Joseph & Lee Elliott. **Educ:** Spelman Col, BA, polit sci, 1976; George Washington Univ, Nat Law Ctr, JD, 1979. **Career:** Civil Div, Com Litigation Br, US Dept Justice, trial atty; US Atty's Off, asst US atty, 1982-87, admin asst, 1987-88, exec asst mgt, 1988-90; DC Super Ct, Wash, assoc judge, 1990-, Family Div, dep presiding judge, presiding judge, 1999-2000, Super Ct Drug Ct, assoc judge, 2003, Criminal Div, Misdemeanor Br, judge, 2004-07, Domestic Rels Br, assoc judge, currently, sr judge, 2012-. **Orgs:** Nat Asn Women Judges; Nat Bar Asn; Am Bar Asn; bd trustee, Black Stud Fund. **Business Addr:** Senior Judge, Superior Court of the District of Columbia, Rm 2500 500 Ind Ave NW, Washington, DC 20001, **Business Phone:** (202)879-7846.

### MITCHEM, DR. ARNOLD LEVY

President (organization), school administrator. **Personal:** Born Sep 17, 1938, Chicago, IL; son of DeV Levy and Archie; married Freda Kellams; children: Nichelle, Adrienne, Michael & Thea. **Educ:** Pueblo Jr Col, AA, 1959; Univ Southern Colo, BA, 1965; Haverford Col, attended 1966; Univ Wis, attended 1968; Marquette Univ, PhD, found educ, 1981. **Career:** Marquette Univ, hist dept instr, 1968-69, educ opportunity prog, dir, 1969-86; Coun Opportunity Educ, pres, 1986-, pres emer. **Orgs:** Fel hon Woodrow Wilson, 1965-66; fel, spec Woodrow Wilson fel, 1966-67, 1967-68; pres, Mid-Am Asn Educ Opportunity Prog Personnel, 1974-76; bd dir, First Nat Inroads Inc, 1975-77; chairperson, Nat Coord Coun Educ Opportunity Asn, 1977-81; bd dir & trustee, Col Bd; Europ Access Network; pres, Comt Educ Funding; bd trustee, Marquette Univ. **Home Addr:** 3901 Woodlawn Rd, Chevy Chase, MD 20815. **Business Addr:** President, Founder, Council Opportunity Education, 1025 Vermont Ave NW Suite 900, Washington, DC 20005-3516, **Business Phone:** (202)347-7430.

### MITCHUM, DOROTHY M.

Media executive. **Personal:** Born Oct 7, 1951, Moncks Corner, SC; daughter of Frank Simmons and Laura Simmons; married Ronnie; children: Ronnie L & Melody. **Educ:** Denmark Tech Col, Assoc's degree, admin asst & secretarial sci, gen 1969; Charleston Southern Univ, BS, bus admin & speech & dramatic arts, 1990; Primerica, regional vpres, 1999-; Univ SC, MA, mass commun, radio & TV, 1995. **Career:** Primerica, regional vpres, 1999-; Dotty Sims Graphic Designs, owner, currently; WMCJ Radio, vpres & gen mgr, currently. **Orgs:** Kids Who Care. **Home Addr:** PO Box 1483, Moncks Corner, SC 29461. **Business Addr:** Regional Vice President, Primerica, 314 Rembert Dennis Blvd, Moncks Corner, SC 29461, **Business Phone:** (803)899-7746.

### MIX, BRYANT LEE

Football player. **Personal:** Born Jul 28, 1972, Water Valley, MS; married Tonette. **Educ:** NW Ms Comm Col; Alcorn State Univ. **Career:** Football player (retired); Houston Oilers, defensive end, 1996; Tenn Oilers, 1997; Tampa Bay Buccaneers, 1998. **Business Addr:** Tampa Bay Buccaneers, 1 Buccaneer Pl, Tampa, FL 33607, **Business Phone:** (813)870-2700.

### MIXON, KENNETH JERMAINE

Football player. **Personal:** Born May 31, 1975, Sun Valley, CA. **Educ:** La State Univ, grad. **Career:** Football player (retired); Miami Dolphins, left defensive end & right defensive tackle, 1998, 2000-01, defensive end, 1999; Minn Vikings, left defensive end, 2002, 2004, right defensive end, 2003. **Honors/Awds:** Rookie of the Year, 1998.

### MIXON, VERONICA

Writer, editor. **Personal:** Born Jul 11, 1948, Philadelphia, PA; daughter of William and Bertha Goodwine. **Educ:** Long Island Univ, BA, 1974. **Career:** Food Fair, bookkeeper, 1966-68; Social Sec Admin, admin asst, 1968-70; Doubleday & Co Inc, Starlight romance ed, 1974-88; DVDivas, Film Gazette, ed; E! Online, feature writer; New York Trends, film critic; New York Carib News, film ed, currently; Austin Times, film ed; Filmgazette, founder, ed-in-chief. **Orgs:** VM Media Serv, 1985-; film reviewer, Carib News, 1983- New York Online Film Critics. **Honors/Awds:** Co-ed, Freshstones, Women's Anthology, 1979; author, " The World of Octavia Butler, " Essence Mag, 1979; " black agents, " Emerge Mag, 1993; "Nick Gomez, " The Independent Film & Video Mag, 1995. **Home Addr:** PO Box 694 Grand Cent Sta, New York, NY 10163-0694, **Home Phone:** (212)862-8487. **Business Addr:** Editor-in-Chief, The Filmgazette, 51 N Third St Suite 176, Philadelphia, PA 19106-4597.

**MO, KEB. See MOORE, KEVIN.**

### MOANEY, ERIC R.

Educator, association executive. **Personal:** Born May 16, 1934, Easton, MD; children: Sara Elizabeth & Lucinda Jennifer. **Educ:** RI Sch Design, BFA, 1956; Syracuse Univ, MFA, 1965; San Diego State Univ, MS. **Career:** Educator (retired); Rustcraft Greeting Cards, designer, 1956-57; Darrel Prutzman Assoc, asst art dir, 1957-62; freelance artist, 1962-63; Syracuse Univ, designer asst dir graphic arts, 1963-65; Benton & Bowles Advert Agency, asst art dir, 1965-66; New Frontiers Corp, 1965; NJ area libr, 1966-70; Calif State Univ, San Diego, Dept Art, asst prof, 1968-98; Motown Rec Corp, design consult, 1968; Terry Phillips Enterprises, 1968-69; Four Guys Stores, 1969; Thomas Corp, 1970; Core Fac Calif, Sch Prof Psychol, ser coordr humanities, 1973-76. **Honors/Awds:** Commission sculpture bust of Beethoven to be completed for BeethovenBi-centennial NJ, 1970; Certificate of merit, CA Governor's comt, 1971. **Home Addr:** 3683 Paul Jones Ave, San Diego, CA 92117-5633, **Home Phone:** (858)270-0246. **Business Addr:** Assistant Professor, San Diego State University, 5500 Campanile Dr, San Diego, CA 92182-4805, **Business Phone:** (619)594-6511.

### MOANEY, GAIL L.

Vice president (organization). **Educ:** Howard Univ, BFA, art educ, 1972; Am Univ, MA, commun, 1975. **Career:** NBC/WRC-TV, exec producer; Pub Broadcasting Syst, exec producer; Warner Amex Cable Commun, exec producer; Manning Selvage & Lee, sr vpres, 1989-98; Ohio's Dept Econ Develop, chief commun; Mt Carmel Health; Ruder Finn, exec vpres, 1998-, dir travel & econ develop, 2011-; New York Univ Sch Continuing & Prof Studies, adj prof, 2009-. **Orgs:** New York Urban League, bd mem; Am Found Univ W Indies Partnership, bd mem; Caribbean Media Exchange, bd mem; Counterpart Int & Opportunities Industrialization Centers Am, bd mem; bd dir, Pub Rels Soc Am, 1995-; Travel & Tourism Res Asn; Women Commun Inc; allied mem, Am Soc Travel Agents; N Am Airlines Pub Rels Asn; Hotel Sales & Mkt Asn Int; bd, Lagrant Found, 2004-09. **Business Addr:** Adjunct Professor, New York University School of Continuing & Professional Studies, 7 E 12th St Suite 11, New York, NY 10003, **Business Phone:** (212)998-7070.

### MOBLEY, EMILY RUTH

Librarian, educator. **Personal:** Born Oct 1, 1942, Valdosta, GA; daughter of Ruth Johnson and Emmett. **Educ:** Univ Mich, AB, educ, 1964, AM, libr sci, 1967, postgrad, 1976. **Career:** Teacher Ecorse, Mich, Pub Schs, 1964-1965; Chrysler Corp, engr librn, 1965-69; Wayne State Univ, librn, 1969-75; Libr Sci Comm Inst Coop, CIC Doctoral fel, 1973-76; Univ Mich Sch Libr, adjust lectr, 1974-75, 1983-86; Gen Motors Res Labs, 1976-81; Univ Mich, adj lectr, 1974-75 & 1983-85; GMI Engr & Mgt Inst, libr dir, 1982-86; Purdue Univ, assoc dir libr, 1986-89, dean libr, 1989-2004, Esther Ellis Norton Distinguished prof libr sci, prof, 1997-2008; Am Libr Assn, ACRL prof educ comm, 1990-92. **Orgs:** Resolutions Comt, 1969-71; Comn Positive Action, 1972-74; Mich Chap Bull ed, 1972-73; Ed Comt, 1974-76; Prog Comt, 1976-80; Res Comt, 1977-80; pres elect, 1979-81; pres, Prog Comt, 1980-81, 1981-82; Career Adv, 1980-83; chmn, Long Range Planning Comt, 1981-82; chmn, Nominating Comt, 1982-83; Libr Mgt Div Sec, 1983-85; pres, Spec Libr Asn, 1987-88; bd trustee, Libr Mich, 1983-86; chap cabinet chmn elect, 1984-85; chap cabinet chmn, 1985-86; pres-elect, 1986-87; pres, Awards Comt, 1987-89, chmn, 1989-90; fel, Spec Libr Asn, 1991; rep, Int Fed Libr Asn, 1989-93; Alpha Kappa Alpha Sorority; bd dir, Asn Res Libr, 1990-93; Gen Motors Pub Affairs Subcomt; Phi Kappa Phi; Sigma Xi; Mass Inst Technol, 1990-2004. **Special Achievements:** Author: Special Libraries at Work, 1984. **Home Addr:** 10010 Lost Hollow Lane, Missouri City, TX 77459-2490, **Home Phone:** (281)778-7646. **Business Addr:** Director, Purdue University, G938, West Lafayette, IN 47907, **Business Phone:** (765)494-2900.

### MOBLEY, DR. JOAN THOMPSON

Physician, health services administrator. **Personal:** Born Jun 2, 1944, New York, NY; daughter of Alfonso and Gertrude Porcher; married Stacey J; children: Michele T. **Educ:** Fisk Univ, BA, 1966; Howard Univ Col Med, MD, 1970. **Career:** Pathologists (retired); Thomas Jefferson Univ Hosp, resident, 1971-75, staff pathologist, 1975-77; Howard Univ Hosp, asst prof, 1977-79; HHS Indian Health Serv, dir labs, 1979-83; St Francis Hosp, dir labs, 1983-; PNC Bank, bd mem; pvt pract. **Orgs:** Fel Col Am Pathologists; dir, Girls Clubs DE; dir, Blood Bank Del, 1991; State Arts Coun, 1989-; dir, Neumann Col, 1991; Bd Prof Responsibility Supreme Ct Del; bd trustee, Fisk univ; secy, treas & trustee, Univ Del; trustee, Del Art Mus. **Home Addr:** 10 Stone Tower Lane, Wilmington, DE 19803, **Home Phone:** (302)656-1973. **Business Addr:** Trustee, Delaware Art Museum, 2301 Kentmere Pkwy, Wilmington, DE 19806, **Business Phone:** (302)571-9590.

### MOBLEY, JOHN ULYSSES

Football player. **Personal:** Born Oct 10, 1973, Chester, PA; married Rebecca; children: Jasmine, Kameron Yvonne & Tyson Lee. **Educ:** Kutztown State Univ, grad. **Career:** Football player (retired); Denver Broncos, right linebacker, 1996-98, linebacker, 1999-2003. **Honors/Awds:** All-Pro, 1997; Super Bowl Champion. **Special Achievements:** Films: 1996 NFL Draft, 1996; 1997 AFC Championship Game, 1998; Super Bowl XXXII, 1998; 1998 AFC Championship Game, 1999; Super Bowl XXXIII, 1999; The European Kid, 2007.

### MOBLEY, SINGOR A.

Football player, football coach. **Personal:** Born Oct 12, 1972, Tacoma, WA; children: Aliyah. **Educ:** Wash State Univ. **Career:** Football player (retired), coach; Can Football League, Edmonton Eskimos, linebacker, 1995-96, 2000-07; Dallas Cowboys, defensive back, 1997-99; Football Univ, defensive back coach, currently; Bonney Lake High Sch, sec coach, currently. **Orgs:** Hon chair, Kid Sport. **Honors/Awds:** Defensive Player of the Week, Canadian Football League, 2003; Champion, Grey Cup, 2003, 2005. **Home Addr:** 8620 Jasper Ave Suite 601, Edmonton, AB T6H 3S6. **Business Addr:** Defensive Back Coach, Football University, 175 N Main St, Wharton, NJ 07885, **Business Phone:** (973)366-8448.

### MOBLEY, STACEY J.

Lawyer. **Personal:** Born Nov 19, 1945, Chester, PA; married Joan C Thompson; children: Michele. **Educ:** Howard Univ Col Pharm, BPharm, 1968; Howard Univ Sch Law, JD, 1971. **Career:** Del Co Legal Asst Asn, atty, 1971-72; EI DuPont DeNemours & Co, atty, 1972-76, Wash Coun, 1977-82, dir fed affairs, 1983-86, vpres, fed affairs, 1986-92, vpres commun external affairs, 1992, sr vpres, 1992-2008, chief admin officer, 1999-2008, gen coun, 1999-2008; Dickstein Shapiro LLP, sr coun, 2008-15. **Orgs:** DC Bar, 1977; chmn, Del Strategic Econ Coun, 2001; chmn, Nat Asn Advan Colored People, 2003; trustee, Howard Univ Hosp, 2005-; dir, Int Paper Italia S.r.l., 2008-; independent dir, chmn governance comt, mem exec comt & mem pub policy & environ comt, Int Paper Co, 2008-;independent dir & mem governance comt, Nuclear Elec Ins Ltd, 2015-; independent dir, mem hr & compensation comt & mem nominating, governance & social responsibility comt, HP Inc, 2015-; mem bd dirs, Int Paper do Brasil Ltd; dir, Am Chem Coun, Inc; bd dir, Wilmington Trust Co; Wilmington Club; bd trustee, Howard Univ; Pa, DC & US Supreme Ct bars; Nat Asn Corp Dir. **Honors/Awds:** Distinguished Alumni Award, Nat Asn Equal Opportunity Higher Educ, 1987; Trail Blazer Award, MC Calif, 2000; Distinguished Service Award, United Way Delaware, 2001; Howard University Distinguished Alumni Award, Law, 2002; Gerald Kandler Award, Am Civil Liberties Union Del, 2006; Association of Corporate Counsel Award, 2006. **Special Achievements:** First African American attorney at E.I. du Pont de Nemours and Company, was named a senior vice president in 1992. **Home Addr:** 141 Deer Valley Lane, Wilmington, DE 19807. **Business Addr:** Senior Counsel, Dickstein Shapiro LLP, 1825 Eye St NW, Washington, DC 20006-5403, **Business Phone:** (202)420-2200.

**MOBLEY, DR. SYBIL COLLINS. See Obituaries Section.**

### MOCK, JAMES EDWARD, SR.

Educator. **Personal:** Born Oct 26, 1940, Tuscaloosa, AL; son of Christopher and Elizabeth Jemison Jackson; married Lorna Thorpe; children: Che & Tekalie. **Educ:** Univ Memphis, Memphis, TN, BBA, econ, 1972; Univ Tenn, Nashville, TN, MPA, 1977; Univ Tenn, Knoxville, TN, PhD, 1981. **Career:** Austin Peay State Univ, Clarksville, Tenn, chairperson, prof polit sci, Pub Mgt & African Studies, prof emer, currently; Cuttington Univ, vpres. **Orgs:** Chairperson, Dept Pub Mgt, 1994-97; dir, Pub Mgt Progs, 1981-91; chair, Polit Sci, 1991-94; Africorps. **Home Addr:** 138 Queens Ct, Clarksville, TN 37043-5432, **Home Phone:** (931)358-9964. **Business Addr:** Member, AfriCorps, 1711 S 21 St, Philadelphia, PA 19146, **Business Phone:** (267)519-3825.

### MOHAMED, GERALD R., JR.

Accountant, manager. **Personal:** Born Oct 3, 1948, New York, NY; son of Gerald R Sr and Helen Brown; children: Gerald R III. **Educ:** Duquesne Univ, BS, acct, 1970; Univ Pittsburgh, MBA, finance, 1979. **Career:** Westinghouse Elec Corp, mgr gen acct, 1971-84, staff asst corp, financial planning & procedures, 1984-88, mgr financial planning, 1989-92; Ad Value Network, comptroller, 1992-95; UAAI, staff acct, 1996-99; Signal Apparel Comp, acct mgr, 1999-2001; Emsig Mfg Corp, dep chief financial officer, 2001-, sr acct, 2001-. **Orgs:** Black MBA Asn, 1983-86; 1968-, basilius, 1969-70, treas, 1985-87, Omega Psi Phi Frat; Masonry PHA, 1985-. **Honors/Awds:** Omega Man of the Year, 1987. **Home Addr:** 4 Suttie Ave, Piscataway, NJ 08854. **Business Addr:** Senior Accountant, Deputy Chief Financial Officer, Emsig Manufacturing Corp, 263 W 38th St 5th Fl, New York, NY 10018, **Business Phone:** (800)364-8003.

### MOHAMMAD, SANDRA B.
Librarian. **Personal:** Born Nov 10, 1947, Chicago, IL; daughter of Mattie McGuire Matthews and Aubrey D Matthews; married Ali S; children: Nena & Christopher. **Educ:** Chicago State Col, Chicago, IL, BA, 1971; Univ Ill Urbana Champaign, Urbana, IL, MS, 1973. **Career:** Chicago Pub Libr, Chicago, IL, librn I, first asst, 1976-77, librn I, br head, 1977-80, librn I, unit head, 1980-82, librn II, ref asst, 1982-93, librn II, ref asst, 1993-02, librn III, ref asst, 2002-04, librn IV, br mgr, 2004-. **Orgs:** Chair, Black Caucus Ala, Chicago Chap, 1979, chair-elect, 1981-82, chair, 1983, scholar chair, 1994. **Home Addr:** 6612 S Kenwood Ave Apt 110, Chicago, IL 60637. **Business Addr:** Branch Manager, The Chicago Public Library, 400 S State St, Chicago, IL 60605, **Business Phone:** (312)747-5281.

### MOHAMMED, NAZR TAHIRU
Basketball player. **Personal:** Born Sep 5, 1977, Chicago, IL; son of Tahiru Abdul; married Mandy; children: Amani, Sanaa & Nasir. **Educ:** Univ Ky, BA, 1998. **Career:** Utah Jazz, 1998; Philadelphia 76ers, ctr, 1998-2001; Atlanta Hawks, 2001-04; New York Knicks, 2004-05; San Antonio Spurs, 2005-06; Detroit Pistons, 2006-07; Charlotte Bobcats, 2007-11; Okla City Thunder, 2011-12; Chicago Bulls, ctr, 2012-. **Orgs:** Wildcats NCAA Championship teams, 1996, 1998. **Business Addr:** Center, Chicago Bulls, 1901 W Madison St, Chicago, IL 60612, **Business Phone:** (312)455-4000.

### MOHR, DIANE LOUISE
Library administrator. **Personal:** Born Nov 24, 1951, Fairbanks, AK; daughter of Dean Burgette and Mary Louise Leonard. **Educ:** Alliance Francais Brussels Belg, Deuxieme deg, 1971; Calif State Univ, Long Beach, CA, BA, black studies, 1977; Univ S Calif, Los Angeles, CA, MSLS, 1978; George Washington Univ, Wash, DC, cert pub admin, 1999. **Career:** Getty Oil Co, indexer reviewer, 1978-79; Woodcrest Pub Libr, librn in-charge, 1979-82; View Pk Pub Libr, librn in-charge, 1982-83; Compton Pub Libr, sr librn in-charge, 1983-87; DC Pub Libr, Martin Luther King Jr Br, sociol librn, 1987-89, W End Br, br librn, 1990, asst coordr, adult serv, 1991-2000, adult collection coordr, 2001-. **Orgs:** Phi Kappa Phi Hon Soc, Calif State Univ, 1977-; Univ S Calif, Alumni Asn, 1978-; Am Libr Asn, 1978-; Calif Libr Asn, 1980-87; bd, Vesta Bruner Scholar, 1980-83; Calif Black Librn, Caucus, Calif, 1981-87; Alpha Kappa Alpha Sor Inc, 1981-; Links Inc, 1985-87; DC Libr Asn, 1989; E Coast Chap Tuskegee Airmen Inc, 2005-. **Home Addr:** 14805 Flintstone Lane, Silver Spring, MD 20905, **Home Phone:** (301)879-0407. **Business Addr:** Adult Collection Coordinator, District of Columbia Public Library, Rm 416 901 G St NW, Washington, DC 20001, **Business Phone:** (202)727-1117.

### MOHR, DR. PAUL B., SR.
Educator. **Personal:** Born Aug 19, 1931, Waco, TX; married Rebecca Dixon; children: Paul & Michelle. **Educ:** Fla A&M Univ, BS, 1954; Univ NMex, MS, 1969; Okla State Univ, EdD, 1969. **Career:** St Petersburg Jr Col, FL, instr, 1954-55; Fla A&M Univ, Tallahassee, acad dean, 1969; Norfolk State Univ, VA, acad affairs vpres & prof; SREB Doctoral Fel prog, dir; Talladega Col, AL, pres & prof, 1984-88; Ala Comn Higher Educ, dir spec progs, currently. **Orgs:** Consult, S Asn Cols & Schs, 1971-; evalr proposals, Nat Inst Educ & Dept HEW, 1975-; S Reg Educ Bd, 1975-, Fla Coun Teacher Educ, 1976-; Am Asn Univ Profs; bd dir, Ala MathSci & Technol Educ Coalition. **Business Addr:** Director of Special Programs, Alabama Commission on Higher Education, 100 N Union St, Montgomery, AL 36104-3758, **Business Phone:** (334)242-2209.

### MOLAIRE, MICHEL FRANTZ
Chemist. **Personal:** Born Jul 8, 1950, St. Marc; son of Marcel and Marie Therese; married Tulienne; children: Alexandra & Melissa. **Educ:** New York Tech Col, AAS; chem technol; Univ Rochester, BS, chem, 1977, MS, chem Engineering, 1982, MBA, exec develop, 1986. **Career:** Eastman Kodak Co, proj mgr, res assoc, 1974-99, Imaging Res Develop Group, sr res assoc, currently; NexPress Solutions LLC, res assoc, 1999-; houseKALLfotography, photogr, currently. **Orgs:** Hillside C Ctr, Pub Rels Comn; past pres, African Am Leadership Develop, Rochester, NY; past pres, Rochester Nat Orgn Black Chem Engrs; Leadership Rochester; bd mem, Threshold Alternative Youth Serv Inc, 1993-96; corp mem, Hillside's C Ctr, 1995-2000; Greater Rochester United Way, Kids Track Comn, 1997-2005; corp mem, United Way Rochester, 2000-05; Socs Imaging Sci & Technol Rochester sect, vpres, 2007-, pres, 2008-; chair, counr, Am Chem Soc, Minority Affairs Comt, 2007-; Fedn Soc Coatings Technol; Rochester Prof Consults Network. **Honors/Awds:** CEK Mees Award for Scientific Research Excellence, Eastman Kodak Co Res Lab, 1984; Distinguished Inventor's Award, Inventor's Hall of Fame, Eastman Kodak Co, 1994; Modern Black Inventor, Ebony Mag; Inducted, African Scientific Institute Fellowship, 2006. **Special Achievements:** Thirty Four US patents and over 75 foreign patents; numerous scientific publications; Shadow of Dreams, poems, 1995; author, African-American Who's Who, Past & Present-Greater Rochester Area, first and second editions, 1996; publisher, Blackfirsts.com, Blackshoppersclub.com; Poetry: La Vie Des Oiseaux Morts, The Life of The Dead Birds, 1965; Plus Pres, 1968. **Home Addr:** 16 Cardogan Sq, Rochester, NY 14625, **Home Phone:** (585)671-3427. **Business Addr:** Senior Research Associate, Imaging Research and Development Group, 1999 Lake Ave, Rochester, NY 14650-2110, **Business Phone:** (585)722-9104.

### MOLAND, WILLIE C.
Consultant, president (organization), school administrator. **Personal:** Born Jan 19, 1931, Shamrock, OK; married Marianne; children: Charlotte, Debbie, Gary, Brent & Bryan. **Educ:** Denver Art Acad Denver Colo, cert, 1958. **Career:** Martin Luther King Young Adults Ctr, dir, 1955-68; Metrop State Col, coordr resources & support, 1968-69, affirmative action staff officer, 1971; Denver Community Comn rels, consult, 1970; Air Force Acct & Finance ctr, data devel technician. **Orgs:** Chmn, Black Fac Staff Caucus Metro State Col; state dir, Youth Prince Hall Grand Lodge Co; co-pres, Phillips Elem PTSA; secy, Syrian Temple 49 Chanters Group; pres, Syrian Temple 49 Arabic Patrol; exec bd mem, dir, youth prog, Greater Pk Hill Community Inc; youth dir, Worshipful Grand. **Home Addr:** 2291 Krameria St, Denver, CO 80207, **Home Phone:** (303)355-4174. **Business Addr:** Coordinator, Metropolitan State College, 250 W 14 Ave Rm 208, Denver, CO 80204.

### MOLDEN, ALEX M.
Football player, executive. **Personal:** Born Aug 4, 1973, Detroit, MI; married Christin; children: Isaiah & Elijah. **Educ:** Univ Ore, BS, psychol, 1995; Int Sports Sci Asn, cert; Youth Fitness Trainer, cert; SPARQ, cert. **Career:** Football player (retired); Univ Ore, corner back, 1991-95; New Orleans Saints, corner back, 1996-2000; San Diego Chargers, 2001-02; Detroit Lions, 2003; Wash Redskins, corner back, 2003; Sports performance specialist, Nike world HQ, currently; All-star performance athletics, dir, currently. **Business Addr:** Director, All-Star Performance Athletics, 1980 Willamette Falls Dr Suite 120, West linn, OR 97068, **Business Phone:** (503)344-4619.

### MOLETTE, BARBARA J.
Educator. **Personal:** Born Jan 31, 1940, Los Angeles, CA; daughter of Baxter R Roseburr and Nora L Johnson; married Carlton W; children: Carla E & Andrea R. **Educ:** Fla A&M Univ, BA, 1966; Fla State Univ, Tallahassee, FL, MFA, 1969; Univ Mo, Columbia, MO, PhD, 1989; Univ Md, theatre educ, 1990. **Career:** Fla State Univ, grad fel, 1967-69; Spelman Col, Atlanta GA, instr, 1969-75; Tex Southern Univ, Houston TX, asst prof, 1975-85; Univ Mo, grad fel, 1986-87; Mayor's Adv Comt Arts & Cult, Baltimore, Md, dir arts educ prog, 1988-90; Baltimore City Col, prof, 1990-93; Eastern Conn State Univ, assoc ed, prof, 1993-2002, prof emer, 2002-; consult, workshops, theatre & mass commun; Mid-Mo Assoc Cols & Univs, adminr; Black Theatre: Premise and Presentation & Afrocentric Theatre. Plays: Arosalee Pritchett, Noah'S Ark (published in Center Stage), Booji, Out of Time, 2011; Move the Car, 2012; Tee Shirt History, 2012; Last Supper, 2013; Kin Ship, 2014. **Orgs:** Dramatist Guild Am, 1971-; pres, Nat Asn African-Am Theatre, 1989-91; Black Theatre Network; English dept chair, Eastern Conn State U. **Home Addr:** 3 Nutmeg Ct, Mansfield, CT 06250, **Home Phone:** (860)423-9174. **Business Addr:** Professor Emeritus, Eastern Connecticut State University, 83 Windham St, Willimantic, CT 06226, **Business Phone:** (860)465-4570.

### MOLETTE, DR. CARLTON WOODARD
College teacher, playwright. **Personal:** Born Aug 23, 1939, Pine Bluff, AR; son of Carlton William Sr and Evelyn Richardson; married Barbara Roseburr; children: Carla & Andrea. **Educ:** Morehouse Col, BA, 1959; Univ KC, grad study, 1960; Univ Iowa, MA, 1962; Fla State Univ, PhD, 1968. **Career:** Educator, African-Am Theatre, Dramatic Lit, prof, producer, playwright, director, designer/stage mgr; Univ KC, grad fel theatre; Little Theatre Div Humanities, Tuskegee Inst, asst dir, 1960-61; Des Moines Comm Playhouse, designer tech dir, 1962-63; Howard Univ Dept Drama, asst prof tech prod & design, 1963-64; Fla A & M Univ, asst prof & tech dir, 1964-67, assoc prof, 1967-69; Spelman Col, assoc prof drama, 1969-75, Div Fine Arts, chmn, 1974-75; Atlanta Univ Summer Theatre, Dir, 1972-75; Univ Mich, guest dir, 1974; Tex Southern Univ, dean, 1975-84; Lincoln Univ, Col Arts & Sci, dean, 1985-87; Coppin State Col, Acad Affairs, vpres, 1987-91; Univ Conn, Dept Dramatic Arts, prof and sr fel, Inst African Am Studies, 1992-2008; Univ Conn, prof emer 2009-; Plays: Dr B S Black; Rosalee Pritchett, Negro Ensemble Co, 1971; Booji; Noah's Ark; Fortunes of the Moor, Frank Silvera Writers' Workshop, 1995; Presidential Timber, 2001; Our Short Stay, M Ensemble, 2005; Prudence, Conn Repertory, 2006; Legacy 2013. Ten minute plays: Out of Time, Turtle Prod, NY 2011; Move the Car, 2012, Warehouse Perf Arts Ctr NC, Tee Shirt History, Essential T GA, 2012; Last Supper, 2013; A Fond Farewell, Greenbrier Valley, WVA 2014; Kin Ship, 2014, Fade to Black, TX. **Orgs:** Dramatists Guild; Black Theatre Network; pres, Natl Conf African Am Theatre; Natl Asn Dramatic & Speech Arts; ed, Encore; mem bd dir, Atlanta Arts Festival; vpres, Greater Atlanta Arts Coun; Nat Endowment Arts; US Nat Comn Un Educ, Sci & Cult Orgn; chmn bd trustee, Neighborhood Arts Ctr, Miller Theatre Adv Coun; bd dir, Young Audiences Md, 1990-93. **Home Addr:** 103 Cascade Pk Dr, Atlanta, GA 30331, **Home Phone:** (404)344-4843. **Business Addr:** Professor Emeritus, Dramatic Arts and Africana Studies, University Conn School Fine Arts, 802 Bolton Rd Unit 1127, Storrs, CT 06269-1127.

### MOLETTE-OGDEN, CARLA
Executive. **Personal:** married Christopher; children: Courtney & Conrad. **Educ:** Spelman Col, BA, Span, 1991; Wash Univ, St. Louis, Mo, PhD, polit sci, 1998. **Career:** Wash Univ, St. Louis, teaching asst, 1992-95; State Univ NY, Stony Brook, asst prof, 1997-2003; JWT Atlanta, partner, bus develop mgr & sr strategic planner, 2000-04; JWT Commun, Entertainment & Technol, dir strategic plng, 2004-07; Fitzgerald Co, vpres & sr brand planner, 2007-09; Neenah Paper, freelance creative strategist; Richards Grp, dir brand plng, 2009-10; Eric Mower & Assocs, sr acct planner, 2011-15; Big Red Rooster, vp, strategy, 2015-. **Business Addr:** Strategy, Big Red Rooster, 121 Thurman Ave, Columbus, OH 43206, **Business Phone:** (614)255-0200.

### MOLETTE-OGDEN, DR. CARLA
Marketing executive, advertising executive, research administrator. **Personal:** Born Apr 11, 1970, Atlanta, GA; daughter of Carlton W Molette II and Barbara J Molette; married Christopher A; children: Courtney & Conrad M. **Educ:** Spelman Col, BA, 1991; Wash Univ, PhD, 1998. **Career:** State Univ New York, asst prof, 1997-2000; J Walter Thompson, partner, sr strategic planner & bus develop mgr, 2000-04, dir, Strategic Planning, 2004-07; Fitzgerald + Co, vpres, sr brand planner, 2007-09; Richards Group, brand planning dir, 2009-10; Eric Mower + assocs, sr acct planner, 2011-15; Big Red Rooster, vp, strategy, currently. **Home Phone:** (678)662-5341.

### MOLOCK, REV. GUIZELOUS O., JR. (GUY MOLOCK)
Lawyer, religious leader. **Personal:** Born Apr 10, 1958, Wilmington, DE; son of Inez and Guy; married Sherry Davis; children: Amber N, Jelani L & Diarra M I. **Educ:** Bethune-Cookman Col, BA, Eng, 1980; Howard Univ, Sch Law, JD, 1983, MDiv, 2007. **Career:** USAF, asst judge advocate gen, 1985-89; US Atty Off, asst US atty, 1989-92; US Senate, Comt Judiciary Chief Nominations, coun, 1992-94; Admin Off US Ct, Article III Judges Div, sr atty, 1994-98, Bankruptcy Judges Div, spec coun, 1998-2003, br chief, safety, security & emergency preparedness, 2003-; NASA, Sr Equal Employmen Specialist, att. **Orgs:** Am Bar Asn; Dist Columbia Bar Asn; Nat Bar Asn; J Franklyn Bourne Bar Asn; Am Bankruptcy Inst; Apa Fraternity Inc; Bethune-Cookman Col Nat Alumni Asn; Ft Foote Baptist Church; Alpha Phi Alpha fraternity. **Honors/Awds:** Outstanding Young Man America, 1982; International Science Award, Optimist Club, 1987; Commendation Medal, USAF, 1989; Administrative Office Special Act Awards, 1994-99; Certificate of Appreciation, 1994; Distinguished Alumni Award, Nat Asn Equal Opportunity Higher Educ, 1994. **Home Addr:** 9007 Doris Dr, Ft. Washington, MD 20744-2414. **Business Addr:** Special Council, Administrative Office of US Courts, 1 Columbus Cir NE Suite 4-250, Washington, DC 20544, **Business Phone:** (202)502-2600.

### MONAE, JANELLE
Singer, songwriter. **Personal:** Born Dec 1, 1985, Kansas City, KS. **Educ:** Am Musical & Dramatic Acad, attended. **Career:** R&B Singer/Songwriter, "The ArchAndroid", 2010, "The Electric Lady", 2013. **Orgs:** Wondaland Arts Soc, co-founder. **Honors/Awds:** ASCAP Awards, Vanguard Award, 2009; Soul Train Awards, Centric Award - Best Dance Performance, 2010; Essence Awards, Black Women in Music Award, 2010; NME Awards, Best Track ("Tightrope"), 2011; MTV Video Music Awards, Best Art Direction ("Q.U.E.E.N."), 2012; Soul Train Awards, Video of the Year ("Q.U.E.E.N."), 2013; Billboard's Women in Music, Rising Star Award, 2013; Variety Breakthrough of the Year Awards, Breakthrough in Music Award, 2014; NAACP Image Awards, Outstanding Music Video ("Q.U.E.E.N."), 2014; 18th Hollywood Film Awards, Hollywood Song ("What is Love?"), 2014; Trumpet Awards, Honoree, 2015.

### MONAGAN, DR. ALFRIETA PARKS
Educator. **Personal:** Born Nov 27, 1945, Washington, DC; daughter of Frances Gordon Parks and Claude E; children: Venice Frances & Agra Charlotte. **Educ:** George Washington Univ, BA, 1969; Princeton Univ, MA, 1971, PhD, 1981. **Career:** Princeton Univ, fel, 1969-70, 1973-74; Hamilton Col, vis asst prof, 1974-75; Univ Erlangen-Nuremberg, Am Studies, Fulbright Jr lectr, 1975-76; Univ Iowa, from instr to asst prof, 1976-86, from adj asst prof to adj assoc prof, 1986-90; Cornell Col, Dept Social & Anthrop, lectr, 1990-98, vis fac, 1999-2000, assoc prof, 2000-07, prof 2007-. **Orgs:** Am Anthrop Asn; Asn Black Anthropologists; Soc Appl Anthrop; Cult Survival Asn; Asn Princeton Grad Alumni; Citizens Police Acad Alumni; fel Soc Women Geogr. **Home Addr:** 806 Clark St, Iowa City, IA 52240, **Home Phone:** (319)351-3044. **Business Addr:** Professor, Professor of Anthropology, Cornell College, 600 1st St W, Mount Vernon, IA 52314-1098, **Business Phone:** (319)895-4482.

### MONCRIEF, SIDNEY A.
Executive, basketball player, basketball coach. **Personal:** Born Sep 21, 1957, Little Rock, AR; married Debra; children: Brett. **Educ:** Univ Ark, BS, phys educ, 1979. **Career:** Basketball player (retired), coach, president, executive; Welch One Competition, spokesman; Milwaukee Bucks, 1979-89; Sidney Moncrief Pontiac Buick GMC Truck Inc, pres, 1987-; Atlanta Hawks, 1990-91; Univ Ark, Little Rock, head coach, 1999-2000; Ft Worth Flyers, head coach, 2006; Golden State Warriors, shooting coach, 2007; Milwaukee Bucks, asst coach, 2011; Glendale Mitsubishi, pres, currently. **Orgs:** Bd dir, Arkla Corp. **Business Addr:** President, Partner, Sidney Moncrief Pontiac-Buick-GMC Truck Inc, PO Box 4357, Troy, MI 48099-4357, **Business Phone:** (501)945-1601.

### MONCRIEFFE, PETER
Executive. **Career:** Executive (retired); Citywide Broadcasting, KQXL-FM, pres; Citadel Broadcasting Corp, staff.

### MONDAY, SABRINA GOODWIN
Sales manager. **Personal:** Born Aug 7, 1961, Tulsa, OK; daughter of Alquita Parker and Edward Goodwin Jr; married Kenny; children: Sydnee, Kennedy & Quincy. **Educ:** Tenn State Univ, BS, 1983; Boston Univ, MA, broadcast jour, 1985. **Career:** Boston Globe Newspaper, ed asst, 1989-92; Mary Kay Cosmetics, sr sls dir, 1989-2000, nat sls dir, currently; Inner Circle Elite Exec, recruit & nat sales dir; Gloria Mayfield Banks, nat sales dir. **Orgs:** Beta Sigma Theta, 1982-; Nat Asn Advan Colored People, 1985-; Moteis Grp, 1996-; Community Serv Coun, 1997-99; Black Women's Adv Comt, 1998-. **Home Addr:** 2210 Shari Lane, Garland, TX 75043-1641, **Home Phone:** (972)240-3387.

### MONET, JERZEE (TANISHA MONET CAREY)
Singer. **Personal:** Born Bordentown, NJ. **Career:** Hair stylist; Big Daddy's Northern Style Cuisine, chef; Album: Love & War, 2002. Singles: "Most High", 2002; "Work It Out". **Business Addr:** Recording Artist, c/o Universal Music Group, 1755 Broadway, New York, NY 10019-3743, **Business Phone:** (212)841-8000.

### MONK, ART (JAMES ARTHUR MONK)
Football player, executive, business owner. **Personal:** Born Dec 5, 1957, White Plains, NY; son of Arthur and Lela; married Desiree; children: James Arthur Jr, Danielle & Monica. **Educ:** Syracuse Univ, BA, commun, 1980. **Career:** Football player (retired), businessperson; Wash Redskins, wide receiver, 1980-93; New York Jets, 1994; Philadelphia Eagles, wide receiver, 1995; Rec Den Inc, dir outside sales; Rich Walker's Scoreboard Restaurant, Herndon, VA, co-owner; WRC-TV, broadcaster; Cactus Advert Assocs, prin owner; Alliant Merchant Serv LLC, co-founder & partner; Art Monk Enterprises LLC, founder; Art Monk Ventures LLC, founder; 3-Pillar Serv LLC, founder; Alliant Payment Solutions LLC, founder; Art Monk Football Camp Inc, founder; Cactus Commun Inc, partner; Monk's Graphics & Design Inc, founder; Redskins Basketball Team, mgr; Youth Power Ctr Inc, co-founder. **Orgs:** Bd dir, Nat Capital Bank Wash; founder, Good Samaritan Found, 1992-; bd dir, Football Am Inc; bd dir, Greater Wash Sports Alliance; bd trustee, Loudoun Healthcare Found; bd trustee, Syracuse Univ; bd trustee, Wash Redskins Exec Leadership Coun; co-founder, bd dir, Youth Power Ctr; Football Am Inc, bd dir; Greater Wash Sports Alliance, bd dir. **Honors/Awds:** Received numerous awards including: Player of the Year, Wash Touchdown Club & Quarterback Club; Offensive Player of the Game; Elected to Syracuse University Board of Trustees; Redskins Most Valuable Player, 1984; Pro Bowl, 1984-86; Redskins Quarterback Club Player of the

Year, 1984, 1985; NFL Alumni Player of the Year, 1984; NFLPA John Mackey Award, 1985; Timmie Award Redskins Offensive Player of the Year, 1989;NFL Quarterback Club Player of the Year, 1990, 1995; Nike Walk of Fame, 1990; Nike Player of the Year, 1992; Redskins Alumni Nate Fine Memorial Award, 1993; Ed Block Courage Award, 1993; Schering Asthma Athlete of the Year, 1993; Golden Timmie Award Outstanding Performance in NFL, 1994; NFLPA Ken Houston Humanitarian Award, 1994; Syracuse University Hall of Fame, 1995; Sales & Marketing Executives of Washington Community Service Award, 1997; The National Conference Humanitarian Award, 1997; Senior Bowl Hall of Fame, 1999; Independence Bowl Hall of Honor, 2000; Redskins Circle of Honor, 2000; Westchester Sports Hall of Fame Award, 2001; Congressional Horizon Award, 2003; Pigskin Club Award of Valor, 2008; Pro Football Hall of Fame inductee, 2008; Redskins' Ring of Fame; College Football Hall of Fame, 2012; WPHS Sports Hall of Fame Inductee, 2015. **Special Achievements:** First and only player to record over 100 receptions. Films: 1983 NFC Championship Game, 1983; First player to record back to back seasons on 1,200 yards and 90 receptions 1984, 1985; Super Bowl XVIII, 1984; 1986 NFC Championship Game, 1987; Super Bowl XXII, 1988; Super Bowl XXVI, 1991; 1991 NFC Championship Game, 1992; Jerry Maguire, 1996; First NFL player to reach 820 receptions in a career; First NFL player to surpass 900 career receptions, finishing career with 940 (all-time record at the time); First player to record at least one reception in 180 consecutive games; First player to record a touchdown reception in 15 consecutive seasons. **Business Addr:** Co-Founder, Partner, Alliant Merchant Services LLC, 8133 Leesburg Pke Suite 600, Vienna, VA 22182-2706, **Business Phone:** (703)448-2510.

### MONK, JAMES ARTHUR. See MONK, ART.

### MONROE, ANNIE LUCKY
Educator, association executive. **Personal:** Born Dec 6, 1933, Milledgeville, GA; married Semon V; children: Angela V & Michael V. **Educ:** Paine Col, BA, 1953; GA Col, MEd, 1977. **Career:** Boddie High Sch, teacher, 1953-68; Baldwin High Sch, teacher, 1968-76, asst prin, 1976-77; GA Col, instr eng, 1977-80. **Orgs:** Ga Libr Asn, 1976-80; Ga Col Alumni Asn, 1977-80; Ga Col Women's Club, 1978-79; trustee, Mary Vinson Libr, 1976-80; asst pianist, Trinity CME Church. **Honors/Awds:** Teacher of the Year, Boddie High Sch, 1967; Most Effective Teacher in Classroom Study, Baldwin High Sch, 1977. **Special Achievements:** First Black Instr of Eng, Baldwin High Sch, 1968; First Black Woman chosen Bd of Trustees, Mary Vinson Libr, 1976; First Black Instr of Eng, GA Col, 1977; First Black Woman asst prin, Baldwin High Sch, 1976-77. **Home Addr:** 272 Old Plantation Trl NW, Milledgeville, GA 31061-9433, **Home Phone:** (478)968-7517. **Business Addr:** Instructor, Georgia College, 231 W Hancock St, Milledgeville, GA 31061, **Business Phone:** (478)445-5004.

### MONROE, DR. ANTHONY E.
President (organization). **Personal:** Born Bronx, NY. **Educ:** Excelsior Col, UG; Northwestern Univ, Kellogg Grad Sch Mgt, MBA, 2001; Columbia Univ, NY, MPH, health policy & mgt, 2003, Teachers Col, NY, EdD, health educ; Univ Mich, LEAN, healthcare; Am Col, Healthcare Execs, FACHE. **Career:** Econ Opportunity Family Health Ctr, pres & chief exec officer, 1998-2003; St John Detroit Riverview Hosp & St. John Conner Creek Campus, St. John Health Syst, pres, 2003-05; Advocate Trinity Hosp, pres & serv area leader, 2005-07; Munroe mgt grp LLC, chmn, pres, chief exec officer, 2007-; Ross Univ Sch Med, assoc vpres, health syst affairs, assoc dean, clin network opers, 2009-10; City Cols Chicago, Malcolm X Col, pres, 2011-15. **Orgs:** Fel & bd cert healthcare exec, ACHE; Nat Asn Health Serv Execs; life mem, Alpha Phi Alpha Fraternity Inc; chmn, CEO Comt, 1986; fel Pub Health, Kellogg Found, 1998.

### MONROE, BRYAN K.
Newspaper executive. **Personal:** Born Aug 22, 1965, Munich; son of James W and Charlyne W; married Tahirah; children: Seanna & Jackson. **Educ:** Univ Wash, BA, commun, 1987; Harvard Univ, Nieman Fel, 2003. **Career:** United Press Int, photojournalist, 1985; Seattle Times, photog intern, 1986-87; Roanoke Times & World News, photojournalist, 1986; Univ Wash Daily, ed; Poynter Inst Media Studies, vis lectr; Myrtle Beach Sun News, dir photog & graphics ed, 1987-91; Sun News, graphics ed, dir photog, 1988; Knight-Ridder Inc, dep dir, 25/43 Proj, 1989-91, asst proj dir, asst vpres news, 2002-06; Harvard Univ, Nieman fel, 2002-03; San Jose Mercury News, duputy managing ed, design dir, 1991-2002; Johnson Publ Co, Ebony & Jet Mag, vpres, ed dir, 2006-09; Urban Access Media Group, bd mem, 2009-10; Northwestern Univ, Medill Sch Journalism, vis prof, 2009-11; CNN, ed, 2011-13, Wash ed & opinion, 2013-15; Temple Univ, verizon chair & prof, 2015-. **Orgs:** Co chmn, Bay Area Black Journalists Asn; bd dir, Hillcrest Homeowners Asn; 100 Black Men Silicon Valley Inc; pres, Nat Asn Black Journalists, 2005-07; bd dir, Unity: Journalists Color. Seattle Times; Roanoke Times & World News; United Press Int; Soc News Design. **Honors/Awds:** Numerous journalism awards: The Society of Newspaper Design; Nat Press Photographers Asn; The South Carolina Press Asn; The Florida Press Asn; The Washington Press Asn; Award of Valor, Nat Asn Minority Media Exec; Media Elite, MediaWeek Magazine; Hall of Fame, Univ Wash Sch Commun Alumni. **Special Achievements:** Guest speaker on topics including newspaper design, graphics, photojournalism, technology, innovation and the future of American newspapers. First African-American editor of the University of Washington DAILY. **Home Addr:** 1387 Alder Lake Ct, San Jose, CA 95131, **Home Phone:** (408)437-3118. **Business Addr:** Verizon Chair, Professor, Temple University, 1801 N Broad St, Philadelphia, PA 19122, **Business Phone:** (215)204-7000.

### MONROE, DR. CHARLES EDWARD, SR.
School administrator. **Personal:** Born Dec 9, 1950, Laurel Hill, NC; married Edwina Williams; children: Jarrod, Keisha & Charles Jr. **Educ:** Johnson C Smith Univ, BA (cum laude), 1978; Univ NC, MEd, 1980, EdS, 1989. **Career:** Greensboro City Schs, teacher, 1980-84, asst prin, 1984-86, prin, 1986-; Hugh M Cummings High Sch, asst supt sch admin, currently; Alamance Burlington Sch Syst, asst supt sch admin/ stud serv. **Orgs:** NC Asn Educr, 1981-, Nat Asn Elem Sch Principals, 1986-, NC Asn Adminrs, 1986-; Cedar Grove Baptist Church, 1985-; pres, Alpha Kappa Mu Nat Honor Soc; vpres, Alpha Chi Nat Honor Soc; Pi Delta Tau Educ Honor Soc, Hon Prog. **Home Addr:** 23 Woodstream Lane, Greensboro, NC 27410-6363, **Home Phone:** (336)856-2077. **Business Addr:** Assistant Superintendent for School Administration, Hugh M Cummings High School, 1712 Vaughn Rd, Burlington, NC 27217-2916, **Business Phone:** (336)570-6060.

### MONROE, EARL (VERNON EARL MONROE)
Executive, basketball player, television show host. **Personal:** Born Nov 21, 1944, Philadelphia, PA; married Marita Green; children: Rodney. **Educ:** Winston Salem State Univ, attended 1967. **Career:** Basketball player (retired), executive, commentator; Baltimore Bullets, 1967-71, NY Knicks, 1971-80; US Basketball League, comnr, 1985; ABC Radio, commentator; Pretty Pearl Recs, founder; Pretty Pearl Entertainment Co, pres; Madison Sq Garden, tv commentator, currently; NJ Urban Develop Corp, comnr, currently; Earl Monroe's Restaurant & Pearl Club, owner; The River Room Restaurant, owner, 2005-; Reverse Spin Rec, pres, currently. **Orgs:** Groove Phi Groove Fraternity; spokesman, Am Heart Asn; President Coun Physical Fitness & Health; Crown Heights Youth Collective; Lit Assistance Fund; Harlem Jr Tennis Prog. **Home Addr:** 113 W 88th St, New York, NY 10025. **Business Addr:** TV Commentator, Madison Square Garden, 4 Pa Plz btwn 7th & 8th, New York, NY 10001, **Business Phone:** (212)465-6000.

### MONROE, KEVIN A.
School administrator. **Personal:** Born Oct 29, 1951, Canton, OH; son of Joseph and Bettye; married Francine J; children: Kevin, Patrice & Candice. **Educ:** Mount Union Col, BA, 1974; Univ Akron, MPA, 1994. **Career:** City Canton Income tax auditor III, 1974-77, dep personnel dir, 1987-88, supt pub works, 1988-2014; Brown & Williamson Tolo, sales rep, 1977-88; Consol Freightways, dock supvr, 1979-87. **Orgs:** Steering comt, Am Soc Pub Admin, 1993-; Am Pub Works Asn, 1996-; Int City & County Mgt Asn, 1998-; Water Environ Fedn, 1998-. **Home Addr:** 5971 Drenta Cir SW, Navarre, OH 44662, **Home Phone:** (330)484-6443. **Business Addr:** Superintendent of Public Works, City of Canton, City Service Ctr Bldg C, Canton, OH 44705, **Business Phone:** (330)489-3030.

### MONROE, MARY
Writer. **Personal:** Born Dec 12, 1951, Toxey, AL; daughter of Otis Sr and Ocie Mae; married Joseph; children: Michelle & Jacquelyn. **Career:** Writer; Novels: The Upper Room, 1985; God Don't Like Ugly, 2000; Gonna Lay Down My Burdens, 2002, God STILL Don't Like Ugly, 2003; Red Light Wives, 2004; In Sheep's Clothing, 2005; Borrow trouble, 2006; God don't play, 2006; Deliver me from evil, 2007; She Had It Coming, 2008, The Company We Keep 2009; God Ain't Blind, 2009; God Ain't Through Yet 2010; Mama Ruby, 2011; God Don't Make Mistakes; Lost Daughters. **Honors/Awds:** Oakland Pen Award, 2001; Best Southern Author Award, 2004. **Special Achievements:** Nomination for the Black Writers Alliance's Golden Pen Award; New York Times bestselling African-American fiction author. **Business Addr:** Author, Kensington Publ Corp, 119 W 40th St, New York, NY 10018, **Business Phone:** (212)407-1500.

### MONROE, ROBERT ALEX
Businessperson, salesperson, executive. **Personal:** Born Somerville, NJ; married Victoria; children: 3. **Educ:** Westchester Community Col, Hofstra Univ, BA, bus admin, 1964. **Career:** Joseph E Seagram & Sons Inc, mkt res analyst, 1964; Calvert Distillers Co, asst eastern div sales mgr, 1971, eastern div mgr, vpres/dir mkt; Gen Wine, mgr, NY mgr, nat brand mgr, sales mgr, eastern div sales rep; Summit Sales Co, pres, 1980; Perennial Sales Co, pres, 1985; Leonine Workshop Inc, pres, 1995-; Bay Cities Bank, dir; Fla Bus Banc Group Inc, dir & chmn audit comt, 2000-. **Orgs:** Bd dir, Joseph E Seagram & Sons Inc, 1982; Polit Action Comt. **Honors/Awds:** Outstanding Business & Professional Award, Blackbook Mag, 1983; Man of the Year Award, Anti-Defamation League, 1985; George M Estabrook Award, Hofstra Univ Alumni Asn, 1987. **Special Achievements:** First black to lead a major firm in the liquor industry. **Home Addr:** 1206 Parrilla De Avila, Tampa, FL 33613, **Home Phone:** (813)968-9091. **Business Addr:** Director, Chairman, Florida Business Banc Group Inc, 2202 N Westshore Blvd Suite 150, Tampa, FL 33607, **Business Phone:** (813)281-0009.

### MONROE, VERNON EARL. See MONROE, EARL.

### MONROQUE, SHALA
Fashion consultant, writer, fashion model. **Personal:** Born Jul 25, 1979. **Career:** Pop Mag, art consult, 2009-11; Garage Mag, fashion consult, creative dir, 2011-; Freelance art consult & writer; "Shala's Rabbit Hole", Blog Writer; "Net-a-Porter", Magazine, model. **Special Achievements:** Contributor to American "Vogue" and "Harper's Bazaar"; featured in Japan's "Vogue," "Chicago Society Magazine," and "New York Magazine". **Business Addr:** Creative Director, Garage Magazine, 51 Holland St, London, GL W8 7JB.

### MONSON, ANGELA ZOE
Government official. **Educ:** Okla City Univ, BS, corrections; Univ Okla, MPA. **Career:** Okla House Representatives, 1990; Okla Health Proj, exec dir; Okla Dept Corrections, Probation & Parole Off; Oklahama State Senate, asst senate majority leader, 1993-2005; Univ Okla Health Sci Ctr, sr vpres; Community Partnerships & Health Policy, assoc provost, currently; Okla City Sch Bd, chmn, 2009; Dept Family & Prev Med, adj assoc prof. **Orgs:** Pres, Nat Conf State Legislatures; bd mem, Families USA Found; exec comt mem, Nat Black Caucus State Legislatures; trustee, Praise Baptist Church; bd chair, Lennie Marie Tolliver Alternative Care Ctr; Mary Mahoney Community Health Ctr; bd mem, Neighborhood Serv Orgn; pres, chair, Nat Conf State Legislatures; bd mem, Girl Scouts Redland Coun; bd trustee, OU Med Ctr; County Bd Health; bd dir, Ctr Health Policy Develop; Robert Wood Johnson Found Nat Adv Comt; bd dir, nat consumer health advocacy orgn; bd mem, Pub Health Law Asn. **Business Addr:** Associate Provost, Community Partnerships & Health Policy, Rm 21 801 NE 13th St, Oklahoma City, OK 73104.

### MONTAGUE, CHRISTINA P.
County commissioner, educator, government official. **Personal:** Born Dec 25, 1952, Inkster, MI; daughter of Romo Watson and Mattie Lee Watson; married Larry; children: Teesha Fanessa. **Educ:** Washtenaw Community Col, criminal justice, 1974; Eastern Mich Univ, BSW, 1984; Univ Mich, MSW, 1988. **Career:** Ann Arbor Pub Sch, community agt, 1974-87, res asst, 1987-88; Joint Ctr Polit & Econ Studies, exec dir, 1984-85; Ann Arbor Pub Sch, social worker, 1988-90, child & family therapist, 1990-91, family serv supt, 1991-; Franklin Wright Settlement, case mgr, 1989-90; Michiganders Obama, state coordr, currently; Lawton Elem Sch, sch social worker, currently; Ann Arbor Pub Schs, social worker; Univ Mich, Sch Social Work, fac liason, currently. **Orgs:** Judge, State Mich Lic Prof & Amateur Boxing, 1984-88; vpres, Ann Arbor NCP, 1987-89; cent comt mem, Mich Dem Party, 1988-; founding pres, Nat Polit Cong Black Women, Washtenaw Co Chap, 1989; host, women Ann Arbor Mich; Nat Taxation & Finance Steering Comt Co Officials; nat pres, Terry Scholar Found; Sheriff's Community Rels Adv Bd; Drug Forfeiture Comt; Property Tax Foreclosure Prev Task Force; Workforce Develop Bd; Community Action Bd; Drainage Bd; Emergency Tel Dist Bd. **Honors/Awds:** Polit & Educ Award, Nat NCP, 1985; Outstanding Achievement, Nat Polit Cong Black Women, 1989; Cert of Appreciation, African Am Youth Acad, 1991; Serv to Washtenaw County Award, Washtenaw Co Dem Party. **Special Achievements:** First black to chair Ann Arbor Democratic Party, 1988-90; First African American woman ever elected Washtenaw County Commissioner, 1990. **Home Addr:** 1245 Island Dr Suite 201, Ann Arbor, MI 48105-2065, **Home Phone:** (734)434-4611. **Business Addr:** School Social Worker, Lawton Elementary School, 2250 S 7th St, Ann Arbor, MI 48103, **Business Phone:** (734)994-1947.

### MONTAGUE, NELSON C.
Scientist, clergy. **Personal:** Born Jul 12, 1929, Washington, DC; son of Nelson R and Rosmond P; married Nancy L; children: Lennis Lee. **Educ:** BS, elec engr, 1952. **Career:** Electical engineer (retired); Nat Bur Stand, elec engr, 1951-68; Defense Doc Ctr, Defense Logistics Agency, phys scientist, elec engr, 1984; VIR, marriage celebrant. **Orgs:** Inst Elec & Electronics Engrs Inc, 1950; Fairfax Nat Asn Advan Colored People; treas, N VA Baptist Asn, 1968-; exec bd, NVB Asn; vpres Comn Human Rights & Community Rels, Vienna VA; Mayor's Adv Comt, 1966-70; coach Little League VA, 1972-73; final sec Northern VA Baptist Ministers & Laymen's Union, 1985-94; life mem, Nat Asn Advan Colored People, 1994. **Honors/Awds:** Recipient Group Award, Nat Bur Stand, 1964; Outstanding Performance Rating QSI, Def Doc Ctr, 1974; finished 4 7 man race for 3 seats Vienna Town Coun, 1968; Achievement Award, Arlington Br, Nat Asn for the Advan of Colored People, 1986; Faithful Service Award, Fairfax Nat Asn for the Advan of Colored People Br, 1988. **Home Addr:** 1324 Westhills Lane, Reston, VA 20190, **Home Phone:** (703)742-9576.

### MONTEIRO, DR. THOMAS
College teacher. **Personal:** Born Oct 6, 1939, New York, NY; son of John and Lovely Peters; married Joy Williams; children: Thomas & Tod. **Educ:** Winston-Salem State Univ, NC, BS, 1961; City Univ NY, Queens Col, NY, MA, 1966; Fordham Univ, NY, prof dipl, 1969, EdD, 1971, PhD, 1974. **Career:** Bd Educ, New York, NY, teacher, 1961-68, dist curric dir, 1969-70; Brooklyn Col, City Univ New York, New York, prof, 1970-85, City Univ New York, Brooklyn Col, Dept Educ Admin & Supv, chairperson & dir prin's ctr, 1985-95, prof emer, currently. **Orgs:** Educ co-chairperson, Ny, Nat Asn Advan Colored People, 1976-80; pres, New York Jamaica Br, Nat Asn Advan Colored People, 1977-78; New York Task Force on Minorities, Equity & Excellence; Winston-salem State Univ Found. **Home Addr:** 110-29 176 St, Jamaica, NY 11433, **Home Phone:** (718)380-2383. **Business Addr:** Professor Emeritus, Brooklyn College, 2900 Bedford Ave, Brooklyn, NY 11210, **Business Phone:** (718)951-5209.

### MONTEITH, DR. HENRY C.
Nuclear engineer, educator. **Personal:** Born May 10, 1937, Columbia, SC; son of Frank Hull and Susie Elizabeth. **Educ:** Univ Pa, physics, 1957; Milwaukee Sch Engineering, BS, elec & electronics engineering, 1967; Purdue Univ; Univ N Mex, MS, elec engineering, 1970, PhD, 1975. **Career:** Educator (retired), nuclear engineer; self-employed spiritual cosmologist, 1959-; RCA Indianapolis, elec engr, 1965-67; Sandia Natl Labs, Albuquerque, NMex, math, comp programmer, elec engr, tech staff mem, 1967-80, engineering physicist, 1968-89, nuclear engr, 1976-88; ITT Tech Inst, instr, 1990-92; Albuquerque Acad, math instr, 1992-93; Eastern NMex Univ, mathinstr, 1993-2003. **Orgs:** AAAS; Soc Physics; Int Asn Math Physicists. **Honors/Awds:** Sigma Pi Sigma Physics Honor Soc. **Special Achievements:** Computer Determination of Decoder Parameters for Color Television, 1967; "The Time Theory of Nikolai A. Kozyrev", 1971; "Stimulated Emissions from Living Forms May Provide Clues to Novel Medical Techniques of the Future"; Dynamic Gravity and Electromagnetic Processes, 1987; Psychotronics: Yesterday, Today and Tomorrow, 1988; Preliminary design of the cooling system for a gas-cooled, high-fluence fas pulsed reactor; "Applications of Scalar Technology: The Liatronics Microscope", 1991. **Home Addr:** 1514 S Kansas Ave, Roswell, NM 88203, **Home Phone:** (505)623-1877.

### MONTEVERDI, MARK VICTOR
Vice president (organization), executive, executive director. **Personal:** Born Jun 19, 1963, New York, NY; son of Monahan and Marcella F. **Educ:** Hiram Col, Hiram OH, BA, polit sci, Span, 1985; NY Univ, MA, polit sci. **Career:** Small Bus Admin, New York, New York, pub affairs specialist, 1985-87; Black Enterprise Mag & Earl G Graves, Ltd, New York NY, nat networking forum coord, 1987-88; Mayors Off, New York, New York, mgr pub communs & outreach, 1988-89; Thurgood Marshall Col Fund, chief mkt officer, sr vpres, chief develop & mkt officer; Westchester Minority Com Asn, exec dir, 1989-90; Phillip Morris Co Inc, pub affairs coord, 1990-91, mgr pub prog, 1991-96; AT&T, dir corp affairs, 1996-. **Orgs:** Alpha Lamda Delta, 1981-; jr fel, US Small Bus Admin, 1981-85; Omicron Delta Kappa, 1983-; Asn Minority Enterprises New York, 1985-; Caribbean-Am Chamber Com, 1985-; Nat Minority Bus Coun, 1985-; adv bd mem, Self-Help Group, 1988-; vice chmn, New Prof Theatre; Prog develop vip, Bus Policy Rev Coun; adv bd secy, Latin Am Mgt Asn; vpres mkt & commun, ctr so-

cial Inclusion; bd mem, Manhattanville Col Ential Coun; vpres, BEEP & Vol Progs, Nat Urban League's Black Exchange Prog, dir Black Exec Exchange Prog; Nat Asn Mkt Developers; Proj prize mentor, Queensborough Community Col; bd mem, chair mkt commun comt, NAT Coalition Black Meeting Planners; nat trustee, Nat Asn Advan Colored People; vpres, alumni exec bd Hiram Col; chmn & pres, Harlem Dowling; chmn, Jamaica Ctr Arts Learning. **Home Addr:** 23 S Elliot Pl, Brooklyn, NY 11217, **Home Phone:** (718)243-1887. **Business Addr:** Director Corporate Affairs, AT&T, 175 E Houston, San Antonio, TX 78299-2933, **Business Phone:** (210)821-4105.

### MONTGOMERY, ANNETTE

Archivist, educator. **Personal:** Born Jan 9, 1961, Suffolk, VA; daughter of Raymond Jones Jr and Edna M. **Educ:** Norfolk State Univ, BA, sociol, 1984, MA, urban affairs, 1992. **Career:** Norfolk State Univ Urban Affairs Grad Prog grad fel, 1990-91, asst archivist, 1996-, instr, 1999-, asst dir, currently. **Orgs:** Norfolk State Univ Asn Educ Off Profs, 1993-; Va Asn Govt Archivists & Rec Adminstrators, 1998-; Mid-Atlantic Regional Arch Conf, 1999-; Millionaire Mommie. **Honors/Awds:** Employee of the Quarter, Norfolk State Univ Cluster, 1993, 1994; participant, res conf, Nat Endowment Humanities, 1995; Carter G Woodson Inst Afro-Am Studies, UVA, Scholars Summer Seminar in African Am Studies, 1999. **Special Achievements:** Co-author: Policy and Guidelines for Records Management at Norfolk State Univ, revised 2008; A Guide to the Manuscript Collection in the Harrison B Wilson Archives at Norfolk State Univ, 1997; Black America Series, Suffolk, Arcadia Publishing 2005. **Home Addr:** 622 Spruce St, Suffolk, VA 23434, **Home Phone:** (757)923-1132. **Business Addr:** Assistant Archivist, Norfolk State University, Rm 115A 700 Pk Ave Suite 2851, Norfolk, VA 23504, **Business Phone:** (757)823-2003.

### MONTGOMERY, CATHERINE LEWIS

Executive, government official, association executive. **Personal:** Born Washington, DC; daughter of Lloyd Lewis (deceased) and Catherine Branch Lewis Laster (deceased); married Alpha LeVon Sr; children: Alpha Jr. **Educ:** Howard Univ, attended 1946; Univ Calif, attended 1949; Nat Inst Pub Affairs, attended 1968. **Career:** USN Elect Lab, San Diego, Calif, admin asst to tech dir, 1950-62; Republican State Cent Comn, admin asst field dir, 1966; Econ Opportunity Comn, San Diego County, personal dir admin serv, 1966-69; State Calif Fair Employ Prac Comn, comnr, 1969-75; USN Dept, consult urban affairs, 1972-, mgt consult equal opportunity spec, 1978-90. **Orgs:** San Diego Planning Comnr, 1966-73; adv bd, Ment Health Serv, 1968-72; Pres's Adv Coun Minority Bus Enterprise, 1972-75; founder, bd mem, Women's Bank, 1974-78; Western Gov Res Asn; Nat Asn Planners; Am Soc Planning Officials; Commonwealth Club Calif; pres, Soroptimist Int San Diego, 1979-80; Nat Girls Clubs Am Inc; Urban League San Diego Inc; Univ Hosp Adv Bd; life mem, Nat Asn Advan Colored People; life mem, Nat Coun Negro Women; League Women Voters; San Diego Girls Club Inc; San Diego Links Inc; bd mem, SE Econ Devlop Corp, 1987-94; govt & community rels comn, San Diego Conv Tourist Bur, 1989-90; life mem, Friends VP Pub Libr, 1990. **Honors/Awds:** Essence Women of the Month, 1974; National Recognition Award, Lambda Kappa Mu, 1978; Woman of Dedication, Salvation Army Door Hope, 1994; Humanitarian Service Award, Catfish Club, 1994; Unsung Hero Award, San Diego Nat Asn Adavn Colored People, 1994; San Diegan of the Year, San Diego Home-Garden Mag, 1994; Making a Difference Award of Excellence, San Diego City Mayor Susan Golding, 1995; Appreciation Award, SE San Diego Develop Comn, 1996. **Home Addr:** 5171 Roswell St, PO Box 740041, San Diego, CA 92114-1704, **Home Phone:** (619)264-1738. **Business Addr:** Urban Consultant, 5171 Rosewell St, San Diego, CA 92114-1704, **Business Phone:** (619)264-1738.

### MONTGOMERY, DR. CLYDE, JR.

Educator. **Educ:** Miss Valley State Col, BS; Miss State Univ, MME; Univ Okla, PhD, 1972. **Career:** Langston Univ, Sch Arts & Scis, dean & prof music, assoc vpres acad affairs, actg vpres acad affairs, vpres acad affairs, currently, chief acad officer, currently. **Orgs:** Okla Asn Col Teacher Educ; N Cent Asn Col & Sch. **Business Addr:** Vice President Academic Affairs, Langston University, Page Hall 128 219 Sanford Hall, Langston, OK 73050, **Business Phone:** (866)829-3364.

### MONTGOMERY, DEBBIE

City council member, police officer. **Educ:** Univ Minn. **Career:** State Dept Pub Safety, asst comnr; St Paul Police Dept, comdr, City Planner, Grants Specialist & Aide to Mayor; St Paul City Coun, councilwoman & rep, currently. **Orgs:** Family Housing Fund Bd; Landmark Ctr Bd; Workforce Investment Bd, 2006; St Paul Water Comn Bd; Hallie Q Brown Bd; YWCA St Paul Bd; Ctr Excellence Urban Teaching Bd, Hamline Univ; Adv Bd, Lao Family Ctr; African Am Leadership Coun. **Business Addr:** Councilwoman, Representative, St Paul City Council, Ward 1 Rm 310-A City Hall 15 West Kellogg Blvd, St. Paul, MN 55102-1615, **Business Phone:** (651)266-8610.

### MONTGOMERY, DELMONICO LAMONT. See MONTGOMERY, MONTY.

### MONTGOMERY, REV. DWIGHT RAY

Clergy. **Personal:** Born Apr 8, 1950, Memphis, TN; son of Howard and Elizabeth; children: Gamal. **Educ:** Lane Col, BA, 1972. **Career:** Reg Sickle Cell Coun, dep dir, 1973-76; Goodwill Indust, counr, 1977; Annesdale Cherokee Baptist Church, pastor, minister, 1985-. **Orgs:** Kappa Alpha Psi Alumni Chap, 1969; Masonic Lodge; 32 deg Scotish Rite; Elks; Shriners, 1969-71; found & dir, Coalition Benevolent Youth, 1974; chmn, Memphis Baptist Ministerial Asn; bd mem, Memphis Housing Authority; pastor, New Zion Missionary Baptist Church; pres, Southern Christian Leadership Conf; Nat Civil Rights Mus; Tenn Justice Ctr; Oper Safe Community. **Honors/Awds:** Memphis Hall of Fame, Alpha Kappa Alpha Sor, 1973-75; Outstanding Young Men Am, 1975; Outstanding Citizen Memphis, Tri-St Def Newspaper, 1976; 50 Future Black Leaders, Ebony Mag Chicago, 1978. **Home Addr:** 1846 Edmondson Ave, Memphis, TN 38114-2805. **Business Addr:** Pastor, Annesdale Cherokee Baptist Church, 2960 Kimball Ave, Memphis, TN 38114, **Business Phone:** (901)743-2057.

### MONTGOMERY, DR. EDWARD B.

Dean (education), educator. **Personal:** Born Jul 3, 1955, NY; married Kari; children: Lindsay, Elizabeth & Edward. **Educ:** Pa State Univ, BA, econs, 1976; Harvard Univ, MA, AM, econs, 1980, PhD, econs, 1982. **Career:** Eastman Kodak Co, 1976-77; Harvard Univ, fel, 1977-79; Carnegie Mellon Univ, fac, assoc prof, 1981-86; Mich State Univ, asst & assoc prof, 1986-90; Ameritech Found fel, 1988; Ford Found, fel, 1989; NJ Gov's Study Comn Discrimination Pub Works, consult; State Ct Child Support Admin Off Mich, consult; Fed Res Bank, bd govs; Fed Res Bank Cleveland, consult; Urban League Pa, consult; Univ Md, Col Behav & Social Scis, assoc prof, 1990-92, prof econs, 1992-2010, dean, 2003-09, affil prof, 2002-10; Md Pop Res Ctr, fac assoc, 2002-10; US Dept Labor, chief economist, 1997-99, dep secy, asst secy policy, 1999-2001; Ctr Study Poverty & Inequality, Univ Stanford, fel, 2006-; Presidential Task Force Auto Indust, fel, 2009; Recovery Auto Communities & Workers Barack Obama admin, dir, 2009-10; Georgetown Univ, Georgetown Pub Policy Inst, dean, 2010-; exec dir, White House Coun Auto Communities & Workers. **Orgs:** Fel Bd Gov Fed Res Syst, 1979-81; Vis scholar, Bd Govs Fed Res & Fed Res Bank Cleveland, 1983-84; res assoc, Nat Bur Econ Res, 1989-; US Dept Labor's Adv Coun Employee Welfare & Benefits, 1994-96; Nat Partnership Coun, 2000-01; W.E. Upjohn Inst Employ Policy, res adv bd, 2001-03; trustee, Coun Excellence Govt, 2004-09; bd visitors, Soc & Econs Scis Directorate; bd Visitors, Adv Panel Econs Nat Sci Found, 1995-96, 2004; Urban Inst; Upjohn Inst Employ; Joint Ctr Polit & Econ Studies; Econ Domain Design Grp, Key Nat Indicators Initiative, 2005; affliate, Ctr Integrate Environ Res, 2007-; fel Nat Acad Pub Admin, 2011; Gen Accountability Off, 2011-. **Honors/Awds:** Teacher-Scholar Award, Mich State Univ, 1989. **Special Achievements:** First African American chief economist at the US Dept of Labor; Publications: "Pensions and Wage Premia" (with Kathryn Shaw), Economic Inquiry, 1997, "Do Workplace Smoking Bans Reduce Smoking," (with William Evans and Matthew Farrelly), American Economic Review, September 1999, Affirmative Action and Reservations in the American and Indian Labor Markets: Are They Really That Bad? in A Not So Dismal Science, edited by Mancur Olson, 2000, "Cross State Variation in Medical Programs and Female Labor Supply (with John Navin), Economic Inquiry, July 2000. **Business Addr:** Dean, Professor, University of Maryland, 2141 Tydings Hall, College Park, MD 20742, **Business Phone:** (301)405-1691.

### MONTGOMERY, ETHEL CONSTANCE

Executive. **Personal:** Born Jul 10, 1931, Morristown, NJ; daughter of Arnold and Aletha; children: Byron & Lisa. **Educ:** Fairleigh Dickinson Univ. **Career:** Executive (retired); Morristown Neighborhood House, prog dir, coordr, vol, group worker, secy, 1951-64; Warner Lambert Inc, coder, 1965; Silver Burdette, Morristown Ship, 1967; Bell Tel Co, typist, 1968; Western Elec Co, salaried personnal rels, personnal results investr, tech clerk, sec, steno secy, 1968-75; AT&T Bell Labs, affirm act coordr, 1975, group supvr, 1978, supvr, 1985-87, employment rep, 1987-90. **Orgs:** Leader Girl Scout, 1952; pres, Parent Teacher Asn, 1957; Carettes Inc, 1959; sec, treas, vp, corrs sec, Carettes Inc, 1959-76; vp, pres, Morristown Bd Ed, 1966-70; corrs sec Morris Co Sch Bd Asn, 1969; Morristown Civil Rights Comn, 1969; Morristown Community Act Comn, 1969; Urban Leag & Family Serv, 1970; Youth Empl Serv, 1970; United Fund Adv Bd, 1970; vpres, Morris Sch Dist Bd Ed, 1972-74; St Bd Ed, 1975; Juv Conf, 1977; adv com, Memorial Hosp, 1977; Gov Byrn's Govt Cost & Tax Policy Com, 1977; 1982-, pres, 1984, 1986-87; Morristown Coun; newsletter chairperson, Concerned Citizens second Ward, 1989-90; Morris Count Dem Comn, 1986-90; bd mem, Morristown Neighborhood Watch, 1987-90. **Honors/Awds:** Morris Co Urban League Award, 1953, 1963; Outstanding Women New Jersey, Fairleigh Dickinson Univ, 1964; Morris Co NAACP Award, 1970; Lambda Kappa Mu Sor Award, 1970; Transcendental Meditation Award, 1977; Nat Black Achiever, 1979. **Home Addr:** 17 Liberty St, Morristown, NJ 07960, **Home Phone:** (973)539-3091.

### MONTGOMERY, EVANGELINE JULIET

Painter (artist), artist, executive. **Personal:** Born May 2, 1933, New York, NY. **Educ:** Los Angeles City Col, AA, 1958; Calif State Univ, Los Angeles, attended 1962; Calif Col Arts & Crafts, BFA, 1969; Univ Calif, Berkeley, attended 1970. **Career:** Painting faces dolls & relig statues, 1951-54; Freelance artist, 1960-62; EJ Assocs, art consult to mus, comm orgns & cols, 1967-; Ethnic art consult Oakland Mus, 1968-74; independent cur, 1967-79; Montgomery & Co, exhibs specialist, freelance art consult, 1969-73; Rainbow Sign Gallery, cur, 1971-76; ARK Urban Systs Inc, vpres & dir, 1973-77; San Francisco Art Comn, art comnr, 1976-79; Am Asn State & Local Hist, exhib workshop coordr, 1979; WHMM TV Wash, DC Community Affairs, dir, 1980; African Am Mus Asn, exhib workshops coordr, 1982; Art Consults & Gallery, Unity Works, Los Angeles, Calif, freelance artist; UFA Gallery, New York, artist; Dist W Fine Art Gallery, artist; Mich Chap NCA Gallery, Detroit, artist; Stella Jones Gallery, artist; Parish Gallery, artist; USIA, Arts Am, prog officer, 1983-99, US Dept State, Cult Prog, prog officer, 1999-; Us Info Agency, Arts Am Prog, prog develop officer. **Orgs:** Pres, Art W Asn N Inc, 1967-78; Am Mus Asn, 1970-; pres, Metal Arts Guild, CA, 1972-74; nat coordr regions, Nat Conf Artists, 1973-81; bd mem, Mus Nat Ctr Afro-Am Artists, 1974-85; nat fine arts & cult dir, Nat Asn Negro Bus & Prof Women Clubs Inc, 1976-78; adv bd, Parting Ways Ethnohistory Mus, Plymouth, MA, 1977-85; co-chairperson, DC chap, Fine Arts & Cult Comm; Col Art Asn, 1983-; Coalition 100 Black Women, 1984-91; honorary life mem, Womens Art Caucus, 1988-; bd dir, DC Arts Ctr, 1989-99; Brandywine Workshop, 1990-; Mich Chap Nat Conf Artists, 1990-; bd mem, Yr Craft Celebration, Am Craft Coun, 1993; Am Asn State & Local Hist, 1973-79; Los Angeles Bd Educ; Oakland Mus; Mus Nat Ctr African Am Artists; Am Asn Mus. **Honors/Awds:** Service Awards, Nat Conf Artists, 1970, 1974, 1976; Museum Grant, Nat Endowment Arts, 1973; Nat Program Award, NANB & P W Clubs Inc, 1977; Grant, Third World Fund San Francisco, 1974; Special Achievement Award, USIA Arts Am, 1989; Outstanding Woman Artist of the Year Award, Nat Womens Art Caucus, 1999; Outstanding Women on the Move in the Arts Award, IAM, 2001; Outstanding Woman Artist Award, Women's Caucus, 2003. **Home Addr:** 1325 15th St NW Suite 809, Washington, DC 20005. **Business Addr:** Program Officer, US Information Agency, 301 Fourth St SW, Washington, DC 20547, **Business Phone:** (202)619-4355.

### MONTGOMERY, ESQ. GREGORY B.

Lawyer, air force officer. **Personal:** Born Mar 23, 1946, McKeesport, PA; married Patricia A Felton. **Educ:** Rutgers Col, AB, 1968; Rutgers Law Sch, JD, 1975. **Career:** Matah Network, exec vpres; pvt pract atty, 1985-; Forrestal Village Inc, corp sec, 1978-79; S & E Const Corp, corp sec, 1977-79; Fidelity First Corp, vpres, 1975-79; Am Real Estate Develop Inc, vpres & gen coun. **Orgs:** Mem Nat Bar Asn; Kappa Alpha Psi Fraternity; secy, Lawnside Educ Found Inc. **Home Addr:** 361 Independence Blvd, Lawnside, NJ 08045-1033, **Home Phone:** (609)546-1446. **Business Addr:** Secretary, Lawnside Education Foundation Inc, PO Box 122, Lawnside, NJ 08045, **Business Phone:** (856)323-7573.

### MONTGOMERY, JAMES C.

Clergy. **Personal:** Born Feb 8, 1918, Lake, MS; married Mary I Roberts. **Educ:** Rust Col, Holly Springs, MS, 1952. **Career:** Mt Sinai Missionary Bapt Ch, pastor; Radio Shop, owner. **Orgs:** Nat Asn Advan Colored People. **Honors/Awds:** Award of Appreciation, Metro Bapt Church, 1954; Award for Common School Improvement Program, 1961; Service Award, Dept of Christine Ed Nat Coun Churches. **Home Addr:** 760 Edmund St, Flint, MI 48505, **Home Phone:** (810)787-7099. **Business Addr:** Pastor, Sinai Missionary Baptist Church, 1215 Downey Ave, Flint, MI 48505.

### MONTGOMERY, JOE ELLIOTT

Government official. **Personal:** Born Jul 10, 1942, Hemingway, SC; son of Elliott and Emma Jane; married Phyoncia; children: Charles. **Educ:** Allen Univ, Columbia, SC, BA, 1965; Univ SC. **Career:** City NY, counr, 1965-66; Horry County Dept Educ, teacher, 1966; Town Atlantic Beach, Atlantic Beach, SC, mayor. **Orgs:** SC Educ Asn; Nat Educ Asn; Horry County Educ Asn; Nat Coun Black Mayors; SC Coun Black Mayors. **Home Addr:** 807 31st Ave S, PO Box I374, Atlantic Beach, SC 29582, **Home Phone:** (843)272-5569.

### MONTGOMERY, JOSEPH, JR. (JOE MONTGOMERY)

Football player, broadcaster. **Personal:** Born Jun 8, 1976, Robbins, IL; son of Joe and Renee. **Educ:** Ohio State Univ, attended 2005. **Career:** Football player (retired), analyst; New York Giants, running back, 1999-2001; Carolina Panthers, 2002; WBNS-AM & NBC Channel 4, broadcaster, col football analyst, currently. **Business Addr:** College Football Analyst, NBC Channel 4, 4001 Nebr Ave NW, Washington, DC 20016, **Business Phone:** (202)885-4111.

### MONTGOMERY, MONTY (DELMONICO LAMONT MONTGOMERY)

Football player. **Personal:** Born Dec 8, 1973, Dallas, TX. **Educ:** Univ Houston, attended. **Career:** Football player (retired); Indianapolis Colts, defensive back, 1997-99; San Francisco 49ers, left cornerback, 1999-2000, cornerback, free safety, right cornerback, 2000; Philadelphia Eagles, 2001; New Orleans Saints, 2004; New Orleans VooDoo, 2005; Nashville Kats, 2006-07; New York Dragons, 2008; Kans City Brigade, 2008.

### MONTGOMERY, OLIVER R. See Obituaries Section.

### MONTGOMERY, ELDER OSCAR LEE

Educator, clergy, association executive. **Personal:** Born Jul 19, 1949, Chapman, AL; married Alfredia Marshall; children: Paula Onese, Renita Falana, Christa Ivana & Oscar Lee Jr. **Educ:** Ala A&M Univ, BS, 1972; Purdue Univ, MS, 1974, PhD, 1976; Trinity Theol Sem, DMin, 1997. **Career:** Ala A&M Univ, asst prof, 1976-81, assoc prof, 1981, vpres, prof; Union Hill Primitive Baptist Church, pastor, sr pastor, 1977-. **Orgs:** Pres, Ala A&M Univ Stud Govt Asn; Ala Ctr Applications Remote Sensing, 1980-; pres, GHIMF-Ministerial Fel, 1980-88; Nat Asn Advan Colored People, 1982-84. **Home Addr:** 3800 Milbrae Dr, Huntsville, AL 35810, **Home Phone:** (256)852-3355. **Business Addr:** Senior Pastor, Union Hill Primitive Baptist Church, 2115 Winchester Rd NW, Huntsville, AL 35810, **Business Phone:** (256)852-0170.

### MONTGOMERY, DR. PATRICIA ANN FELTON

Educator, school administrator. **Personal:** Born Sep 11, 1946, Greenville, SC; daughter of Clifton Howard Felton and Ruth Elizabeth Beal; married Gregory Byron; children: Gregory Hassan & Clifton Amir. **Educ:** Douglas Col, Rutgers State Univ, BA, 1968; Syracuse Univ, MEd, educ, 1971; Teachers Col-Columbia Univ, EdD, 1994. **Career:** Lawnside Pub Sch, stud-personnel Serv, 1975-79; Acad Advan, Teaching, mgt, educ prog specialist, 1984-89; Winslow Twp Sch, prin, 1989-93; Camden City Pub Sch, dir regional schs, 1993-97; W Dept ford Twp Sch, asst supt, 1997-99; Willingboro Pub Sch, asst supt, 1999-2001; Montgomery Educ Assocs Group, pres & chief exec officer, 2000-; Temple Univ, lab stud success, dir, 2001-; Bridgeton Pub Schs, Bridgeton, NJ, asst supt, 2004-08; US Dept Educ, Mid-Atlantic Regional Educ Lab, dir educ leadership lab stud success; Int Ctr Leadership Educ, consult, 2011-12. **Orgs:** Am Asn Univ Women; Asn Curric & Supv; NJ Asn Curric & Supv; exec bd, NE Coalition Edu, Southern NJ Chap; NJ Chap, Black Sch Educrs; NJ Chap, Phi Delta Kappa; Rowan Univ Leadership NJ, Zeta Nu Chap; asst vpres, Big Bros & Big Sisters Am, 1979-82; Coalition 100 Black Women, S Jersey Chap; Jack & Jill Am, S Jersey Chap; Camden Co Girl Scout Coun Bd; Continental Socs Inc; Delta Sigma Theta, S Jersey. **Home Addr:** 183 Echelon Rd, Voorhees, NJ 08043, **Home Phone:** (856)772-1955. **Business Addr:** Assistant Superintendent, Bridgeton Public Schools, 41 Bank St, Bridgeton, NJ 08302, **Business Phone:** (856)455-8030.

### MONTGOMERY, REV. PAYNE

Educator, government official, basketball coach. **Personal:** Born Nov 24, 1933, Bernice, LA; married Rosemary Prescott; children: Janice, Eric & Joyce. **Educ:** Grambling Col, BS, 1956; Tuskegee Inst, MS, 1969; NE La Univ, attended 1969. **Career:** Morehouse Par Sch Bd, hum rel cnsl; City Bastrop, city coun man; Morehouse High Sch, basketball coach, 1959-69; Delta High Sch, soc stud teacher, 1969-72. **Orgs:** La Ed Asn; Nat Educ Asn; Parish Rec Bd; C C; Am Leg; bd dir, Headstart; pres, Morehouse Community Improv Orgn, 1965; City Coun, 1973. **Honors/Awds:** Special recognition Coaching Record; Coach of the Year, 1961. **Home Addr:** 181 Margaret Pl, Grambling, LA 71245-9201, **Home Phone:** (318)247-8715. **Business Addr:** Government Officer, Human Relations Office, Bastrop HS, Bastrop, LA 71220.

### MONTGOMERY, ROBERT E.
Automotive executive, consultant, president (organization). **Personal:** Born Feb 1, 1948, Lake Wales, FL; son of Annie L Gadson; married Valorie A; children: Ryan & Raven. **Educ:** John B Stetson Univ, BBA, 1970; Columbia Univ, Grad Sch Bus, MBA, 1972. **Career:** Ford Motor Co, analyst, 1972-73; Chevrolet Motor Co, analyst & supvr, 1973-80; Gulf & Western, dir bus planning, 1980-85; GM Dealer Sch, trainee, 1985-86; consult, 1986-88; Mountain Home Ford, vpres, pres, chief exec, 1988-; Flagler Ford Inc, pres & owner, currently. **Orgs:** Alpha Phi Alpha; bd dir, Ford-Lincoln Mercury Minority Dealers Asn. **Business Addr:** Chief Executive, President, Mountain Home Ford-Lincoln mercury Inc, 491 W 6th S, Mountain Home, ID 83647-3483, **Business Phone:** (208)587-3326.

### MONTGOMERY, SONCEREY L.
College administrator, writer, advocate. **Educ:** NC State Univ, BA; Univ NC, Chapel Hill, MA; Univ NC, Greensboro, PhD. **Career:** Winston-Salem State Univ, dir Hons Prog, assoc prof, 1996-; motivational speaker; "Success with Soncerey", founder; THE LIGHT radio station, "Sound Waves of Success" show, host. **Orgs:** Nat Col Hons Coun (NCHC), bd dirs; State Employees Credit Union, adv bd; Pink Gem Team Found, exec bd. **Honors/Awds:** MLK Jr. Building the Dream Award, Recipient; Wilma Lassiter Master Teacher Award, recipient. **Special Achievements:** Author of "The Heart of a Student: Success Principles for College Students" (Pendium, 2011); numerous presentations at worldwide conferences. **Business Addr:** Director of Honors Program, Winston-Salem State University, 601 S Martin Luther King Jr Dr, Winston-Salem, NC 27110, **Business Phone:** (336)750-2182.

### MONTGOMERY, SONSYREA TATE
Journalist, educator, writer. **Personal:** Born Apr 22, 1966, Washington, DC; daughter of Joseph Tate and Meauvelle. **Educ:** Univ DC, BA, mass media, 1985; Regent Univ, MA, jour, 2003. **Career:** Wash Post, ed aide, writer, 1986-89; Wash Times Newspaper, reporter, 1989-91; Va-Pilot Newspaper, reporter, 1991-93; US House Representatives, off Eleanor Holmes Norton, asst, commun dir, 2008-2010; Publ Indust, auth, 1993-2010; Sylvan Learning Syst, instr, 1997-; Wash Informer Newspaper, managing ed, 2003-05; Prince Georges Gazette, sr polit reporter, 2003-05; Univ Tenn Press, auth, 2004-; Strebor Bks int/Simon & Schuster, auth, 2005-; Literacy Coun Prince George's County, ESl instr, 2012-; Publications: Little X: Growing up in the Nation of Islam, author, 1997; Do Me Twice: My Life After Islam, 2006; Soul Food: Inspirational Stories for African Americans/edited by Eric Copage; Prayers for a Thousand Years/edited by Elizabeth Roberts and Elias Amidon, 1999; It's All Love: Black Writers on Soul Mates, Family and Friends/edited by Marita Golden, 2009. **Orgs:** Nat Asn Black Journalists, 1987-94. **Home Addr:** 339 17th St SE Apt 1, Washington, DC 20003, **Home Phone:** (202)396-7612. **Business Addr:** ESL Instructor, Literacy Council of Prince George's County, 6532 Adelphi Rd, Hyattsville, MD 20782, **Business Phone:** (301)699-9770.

### MONTGOMERY, DR. TONI-MARIE
Pianist, school administrator, educator. **Personal:** Born Jun 25, 1956, Philadelphia, PA; daughter of Milton and Mattie Drayton. **Educ:** Philadelphia Col Performing Arts, Philadelphia, PA, BM, piano, 1980; Univ Mich, Ann Arbor, MI, MM, piano chamber music, 1981, DMA, piano chamber music, 1984. **Career:** Pianist, music professor; Western Mich Univ, Sch Music, Kalamazoo, Mich, asst dir & artistic dir, 1985-87; Univ Conn, Storrs, CT, Sch Fine Arts, asst dean, 1987-89; Ariz State Univ, Tempe, AZ, assoc dean, asst prof, 1990-96, Sch Music, dir, 1996-2000; Univ Kans, Sch Fine Arts, dean, 2000-03; Northwestern Univ Sch Music, dean, 2003-, prof piano, currently; Albums: Music for Cello & Piano by African American Composers; TV Show/series: "Today Show", Cable News Network; "Performance Today", National Public Radios; "African-American Music Tree", Public Radio Internationals. **Orgs:** Founding mem, Columbia Col Chicago, Black Music Repertory Ensemble, 1987; pres, Sister Friends, African-Am Women, 1990-; bd dir, pres, Fac Womens asn, 1990-; Tempe Arts Comn, 1991-93; Phoenix Symphony Bd, 1998-; jury mem, Sphinx Orgn, 2015; treas, Nat Asn Schs Music. **Special Achievements:** First African American academic dean in University of Kansas School of the Fine Arts, 2000; First African American and first female dean of the Bienen School of Music. **Business Addr:** Dean, Professor, Northwestern University, 711 Elgin Rd, Evanston, IL 60208-1200, **Business Phone:** (847)491-7552.

### MONTGOMERY, DR. V. TRENT
Dean (education), educator, college administrator. **Educ:** Southern Univ, BSEE, 1969; Univ Ill, MSEE, 1971; Univ Tex, PhD, 1976. **Career:** Univ Ill, fac; Univ Tex, fac; Southern Univ, Baton Rouge, LA, dean col eng & prof elec eng & comput sci; Ala A&M Univ, fac, 1996; Ala A&M Univ, Dept Elec eng, prof & Sch Eng & Technol, interim dean, dean, currently; staff, AT & T Bell Labs; staff, Int Bus Mach. **Orgs:** Inst Elec & Electronics Engrs; Eta Kappa Nu; Am Soc Eng Educ; Nat Soc Prof Engrs; La Eng Soc; HKN Hon Soc; Asn Comput Mach, Am Soc Engineering Educ, La Engineering Soc, Nat Soc Black Engrs. **Business Addr:** Professor, Dean, Alabama A&M University, 222 Carver Complex N Rm 226, Normal, AL 35762, **Business Phone:** (256)372-5463.

### MONTGOMERY, VELMANETTE
State government official, teacher. **Personal:** Born Jan 1, 1942?, TX; married William Walker; children: William. **Educ:** NY Univ, BA, MS, educ, 1975; Univ Accra, Ghana; St Josephs Col, LLD, 1991. **Career:** NY City Dist 13 Sch Bd, mem, 1977-80, pres, 1977-84; Child Care Inc, Advocacy Group, co-dir; Day Care Forum, NY, teacher, adj prof, co-founder & dir; State NY Senate, 18th Sen Dist, state sen, 1984-; Ny 22nd Dist, senate, 1985-1992, 18th Dist, senate, 1993-2012, 25th Dist, senate, 2013-. **Orgs:** Crime Victims, Crime & Correction; Consumer Protection; Housing & Community Develop; Ment Health & Develop Disabilities Educ & Health; chief dem, C & Families; chair, Dem Task Force Primary Health Care; co-chair, Dem Task Force Criminal Justice Reform; Robert Wood Johnson Found, Nat Adv Comn; revson fel, Columbia Univ; dem mem, Ny Senate; Asst Majority Whip;co-founder, Day Care Forum New York; fel Inst Educ Leadership, 1981; revson fel Columbia Univ, 1984; chairwoman, Comt Social Serv, 2009; chairwoman, Comt C & Families, 2009-10. **Home Addr:** 30 3rd Ave 11th Fl Rm 615, Brooklyn, NY 11217, **Home Phone:** (718)643-6140. **Business Addr:** State Senator, State of NewYork, 188 State St Rm 711 Legis Off Bldg, Albany, NY 12247, **Business Phone:** (518)455-3451.

### MOO-YOUNG, LOUISE L.
Educator, nurse, association executive. **Personal:** Born Dec 29, 1942, Lexington, MS; married Ervin; children: Troy, Tiffany & Tricia. **Educ:** Gov's State Univ, BS; St Mary Nazareth, attended 1963; Roosevelt Univ, BS, 1974, MPA, 1975. **Career:** Mich Ave Hosp Chicago, staff nurse head nurse, 1963-64; Chicago Bd Health, pub health field nurse, 1964-70, pub health nurse supvr, 1970-72; Ryerson Stell, part-time indust nurse; Woodlawn Hosp, staff nurse; State Univ, instr; Marion Adult Educ Ctr, prof; Oak Forest Hosp, dir. **Orgs:** Chicago Bd Health Claude WB Holman Neighborhood Health Ctr, 1972-; chmn, Health Task Force Chicago Urban League, 1973-74; Pub Health Sect Ill Nurses Asn, 1975; off mgr, Chicago Campaign Off, 1975; St Margaret Epis Church Vestery, 1976-77; Gov Adv Coun Develop Disabilites, 1976-77; pres, Faulkner Sch Asn, 1977-78; bd trustee, Faulkner Sch, 1977-78; beat rep, 21st Dist Police; Comprehensive Sickle Cell Anemia Community Adv Coun; Univ Chicago Neighborhood Health Ctr; past mem, Am Nurses Asn; Econ & Gen Welfare Com; Ill Nurses Asn; ARC Nurse Active Church & Comm Affairs; peer group educ comt, Loop Jr Col; adv bd, Claude WB Holman Neighborhood Health Ctr; Am Soc Pub Adminr; St Mary's Alumni Asn; Roosevelt Univ Alumni Asn. **Honors/Awds:** One of Chicago's Ten Outstanding Young Citizens, Jr Asn Commerce Indus, 1973-74; Outstanding Achievement Award, Fourth Ward Dom Orgn; The Emerging Women in Management Workshop. **Home Addr:** 1063 W 108th St, Chicago, IL 60643.

### MOODIE, DANIELLE. See MOODIE-MILLS, DANIELLE.

### MOODIE-MILLS, AISHA (AISHA MILLS)
Activist, administrator. **Personal:** married Danielle Moodie-Mills. **Educ:** Univ Md, College Park, BA, 1999, MBA, 2008. **Career:** Ctr Educ Reform, policy analyst, 2000-01; Ron Kirk US Senate, fundraiser, 2002; Dem Sen Campaign Comt, regional finance dir, 2003-04; Cong Black Caucus PAC, exec dir, 2004-06; Synergy Strategy Group, pres & chief exec officer, 2006-10; Campaign All DC Families, pres bd, 2009-11; Ctr Am Progress, sr fel & dir Fighting Injustice to Reach Equality initiative, 2010-15; threeLOL strategies LLC, chief catalyst, 2013-; Politini Media, exec producer & host, 2013-; Victory Fund & Inst, pres & chief exec officer, 2015-. **Orgs:** Choice USA, bd mem; mem, Human Rights Campaign, Dem Nat Comt, Nat Black MBA Asn, Inspiring Am, Net Impact, WIN Network, GLAAD, Dingman Ctr Entrepreneurship. **Special Achievements:** Contributor, The Atlantic, Black Enterprise, Washington Post, Essence, Politico, Ebony, Huffington Post, Uptown Magazine; political commentator, Melissa Harris-Perry Show, MSNBC, MSNBC Live, Jansing & Co., and The Daily Rundown; co-writer, three LOL (Living, Loving, and Laboring OUT Loud) blog. **Business Addr:** Victory Fund & Institute, 1133 15th NW Suite 350, Washington, DC 20005, **Business Phone:** (202)251-6763.

### MOODIE-MILLS, DANIELLE (DANIELLE MOODIE)
Activist, executive. **Personal:** married Aisha Moodie-Mills. **Educ:** Marymount Univ, BS, 2001; George Mason Univ, MEd, special educ & early childhood, 2006. **Career:** Nat Orgn Women, community outreach, 2002; Off Congresswoman Yvette Clarke, CBCF fel, 2007-08; New York Dept Educ, dir fed govt rels, 2008-10; Nat Wildlife Fedn, dir environ educ, 2010-13; NBCUniversal Inc, theGrio personality, 2014; Ctr Am Progress, advisor LGBT policy & racial justice, 2010-; Poltini Media, chief creative officer, 2013-; Politini podcast, exec producer & host, 2013-; wrote and produced the miniseries "Politini on theGrio", MSNBC's African American website. **Special Achievements:** Contributor, xoJane, Essence, The Atlantic, Ebony, and Huffington Post; appearances on MSNBC, Fox News, PBS, and BBC America; coauthor, three LOL (Living, Loving, and Laboring OUT Loud) blog. **Business Addr:** Center for American Progress, 1333 H St NW 10th Fl, Washington, DC 20005, **Business Phone:** (202)445-5210.

### MOODY, ANNE
Writer. **Personal:** Born Sep 15, 1940, Wilkinson County, MS; daughter of Elmire Williams and Fred; married Austin Straus; children: Sascha. **Educ:** Natchez Jr Col, attended 1961; Tougaloo Col, BS, 1964. **Career:** Cong Racial Equality, Wash, DC, organizer, 1961-63, fundaraiser, 1964; Cornell Univ, Ithaca, NY, civil rights proj coord, 1964-65; Coming of Age in Miss, auth, 1968; Mr.Death, auth, 1975; New York Poverty Prog, coun, currently; The Clay Gully, writer. **Orgs:** National Association for the Advancement of Colored People; Cong Racial Equality; Int PEN; Stud Nonviolent Coord Comt. **Honors/Awds:** Brotherhood Award, Faulkner Awards, Nat Coun Christians & Jews, 1969; Acad scholar, Tougaloo Col; Best Book of the Year Award, Nat Libr Asn, 1969; Coming of Age in Mississippi, 1969; Silver Medal, Mademoiselle, 1970. **Business Addr:** c/o Harper & Row, New York, NY 10022.

### MOODY, C. DAVID, JR.
Executive, president (organization). **Personal:** Born May 21, 1956, Chicago, IL; married Karla Lynn; children: Charles & Karia Lynn. **Educ:** Morehouse Col, BS, psychol, 1978; Howard Univ, BA, 1981. **Career:** Citizens Bancshares Corp, bd dir, 2000-; Theragenics Corp, bd dir, 2007-; Citizens Trust Bank, dir; CD Moody Construct Inc, pres & chief exec officer, currently. **Orgs:** Fel Loan Comt, fel Exec Comt, chmn, Asset & Liability Comt, OTC Bull Bd; fel Atlanta Bus League; fel Atlanta Chamber Com; fel Nat Asn Minority Contractors. **Business Addr:** Chief Executive Officer, President, CD Moody Construction Co Inc, 6017 Redan Rd, Lithonia, GA 30058, **Business Phone:** (770)482-7778.

### MOODY, CAMERON DENNIS
Engineer, executive. **Personal:** Born Jun 17, 1962, Chicago, IL; son of Charles and Christella. **Educ:** NC Agr & Tech State Univ, BS, indust engineering, 1986; Morehouse Col, 1987. **Career:** Ford Motor Co, engr, 1986-91; CD Moody Const, engr, 1991-92; Atlanta Olympic Comt, regional logistics mgr, 1994-96; Dem Nat Conv, dep dir transp; olumpics, 1996, 2000 & 2002; Denver Summit Eight, dir transp, 1997; Sinbad Soul Music Festival, Aruba, transp coordr, 1997; DJ Miller & Assocs, chief info officer, 1997-; CD Moody Const Co, chief info officer, 1998-99; Dem Nat Conv, dep dir transp, 1996, dep dir logistics, 2000, dir opers, dep chief exec officer opers comt, 2004-; Am Cancer Soc, dir strategic planning & opers; Dem Nat Conv Comt, dep chief exec officer, opers, 2007-08, sr advisor, 2011-; exec off pres, dir off admin, 2009-11; Fed Agency, dir admin, 2009-11. **Orgs:** Omega Psi Phi; Nat Alliance Black Sch Educr. **Home Addr:** 33 Chestnut Dr Suite 3, Chelsea, MI 48110-9416, **Home Phone:** (313)434-2294. **Business Addr:** Senior Advisor, Democratic National Committee, 430 S Capitol St SE, Washington, DC 20003, **Business Phone:** (202)863-8000.

### MOODY, CAROL BALDWIN
Vice president (organization). **Educ:** Wharton Sch Univ Pa, BSE, finance, 1978; Columbia Univ Sch Law, LLB, JD, 1982. **Career:** Debevoise & Plimpton, corp assoc, 1982-88; Citibank, chief compliance officer, 1988-2000; TCW/Latin Am Partners LLC, managing dir & gen coun, 2000-04; Carver Bancorp Inc, dir, 2003-10; TIAA-CREF, chief compliance officer, 2004-05; Nationwide Mutual Ins Co, sr vpres & chief compliance officer, 2005-10; Germantown Friends Sch, sch comt, 2006-10; CalPERS, investment compliance & oper risk, sr portfolio mgr, 2011-; Wilmington Trust, sr vpres & chief risk officer, 2010-11; CAB Moody LLC, prin, currently. **Orgs:** Brister Soc Univ Pa. **Business Addr:** Senior Portfolio Manager, CalPERS, 400 Q St, Sacramento, CA 95811.

### MOODY, DR. CHARLES DAVID, SR.
Executive director, association executive, educator. **Personal:** Born Aug 30, 1932, Baton Rouge, LA; son of James Nathaniel and Rosetta Ella Hall; married Christella Delois Parks; children: 8. **Educ:** Cent State Univ, BS, chem, 1954; Chicago Teachers Col, MS, educ, 1961; Univ Chicago, cert adv study, 1969; Northwestern Univ, PhD, educ admin, 1971. **Career:** Ment Handicapped Chicago Schs, educ teacher, 1959-62; Posen-Robbins Jr High Sch, asst teacher to asst prin, 1963-68; Schs Harvey, Il, supt, 1968-70; Northwestern Univ, TTT fel, 1969-70; Nat Alliance Black Sch Educr, founder, 1970-; Univ Mich, Sch Educ, dir prog educ opportunity, 1970-73, Div Educ Specialist, chmn, 1973-77, Proj Fair Admn Stud Disc, dir, 1975-80, prof educ, dir prog educ oppor, 1970-87, vice provost minority affairs, 1987-96, vice provost emer minority affairs & prof emer, 1996-, Psychol & Educ, sr col professorship, 2011; Ctr Sex Equity Schs, dir, 1981-87; Safrica Initiative Off, exec dir, 1993-. **Orgs:** Ex bd, Nat Alliance Black Sch Educr, 1970-; bd dir, Nat Asn Advan Colored People, Ann Arbor, 1983-85; bd dirs, Network Instrnl TV Inc; Phi Delta Kappa; Sigma Pi Phi; Omega Psi Phi Fraternity; supt, Hazard Young & Attea Assocs, 1987-2002; Moody S African Initiative Fund. **Honors/Awds:** Community Leader Award, Ann Arbor Veterans Admn Med Ctr, 1980; Doctorate of Laws Degree, Cent State Univ, 1981; Award of Respect, Washtenaw Comn Col, Ann Arbor, MI, 1984; Professional of the Year Award, Ann Arbor; Charter Inductee, Cent State Univ, Wilberforce, OH, 1989; Alumni Merit Award, Northwestern Univ; Living Legend Designation Award, Nat Alliance Black Sch Educr; President's Medallion, 1996; received various awards and honors. **Home Addr:** , Ann Arbor, MI, **Home Phone:** (313)663-7508. **Business Addr:** Founder, National Alliance of Black School Educators, 310 Pa Ave SE, Washington, DC 20003, **Business Phone:** (202)608-6310.

### MOODY, DOMINIQUE FAYE
Artist. **Personal:** Born Dec 14, 1956, Augsburg; daughter of Theodore Robert and Barbara Spurlock Bundage; married Phillip Bannister III. **Educ:** Philadelphia Col Art, Philadelphia, PA, attended 1972; Pratt Univ, Brooklyn, NY, attended 1975; Univ Calif, Berkely, BFA, 1991. **Career:** Art ed, 1991-95; artist. **Orgs:** Nat Conf Artists, 1993-95; Mus C's Art, Oakland CA, 1993-95; Pro Arts, Oakland, CA, 1994; Southern Exposure, San Francisco, 1994; Calif African Am Mus, 1997-; Friends Watts Towers, 1998-99; La County Mus Art, 1999. **Honors/Awds:** Univ Calif Berkely Hons, 1987-91; Fine Arts Award, Gordon Heinz, 1990; Fine Arts Award, Maybelle Toombs, 1990, 1991; Fine Arts Honor, Phi Beta Kappa, 1991; Seagram's Gin, Perspectives in African American Art, 1997; Grantee, Calif Community Found. **Special Achievements:** Commissioned work through Seagram's Perspectives in African American was donated to the CA African American Museum, 1997; Publications: Ramsey Bell Breslin, The Figured identified (unpublished review from Bay GuardianWeekly), Oakland, CA James Brzezinski, Reassurance: The Figure Identified, Review Art Week, Richmond, CA, 1991; G. Shontell, Multimedia Show, The Figure Identified, West County Times, Richmond, CA, 1991; Jocelyn Stewart "Walkin on Water", Ramsess Publications, Los Angeles, CA, 1994; David Pagel Reviews Into the Dream Box Exhibit at Watts Towers Arts Center, Calendar Section, Los Angeles Times, 1996; Angela Johnson Interview, Los Angeles Watts Times, June 20, 1996; Adrienne Johnson, feature article, "A Matter of Perception" Life & Style Section, Los Angeles Times, 1997; Donald James "Artist Weaves a Different Kind of Vision", first column, Los Angeles Watts Times, 1997; Jocelyn Stewart self-published book of poetry "Walkin on Water" in collaboration with D. Moody in stallation"Walking on Water", 1998; Sharon Banister Arts Viewing Points: Art takes many forms Review for the Hanford Sentinel Carousel Weekly Mag a zine, Hanford, CA (February); American Visions Magazine" Perspectives in African American Art (Teamsheet) Spring, 1998; Emerge Magazine "Perspectives in African American Art", 1998. **Home Addr:** 1784 E 107th St, Los Angeles, CA 90002-3650.

**MOODY, ERIC ORLANDO**
Lawyer. **Personal:** Born Jul 16, 1951, Petersburg, VA; married Sherrie Y Brown. **Educ:** Lafayette Col, AB, philos, 1973; Univ Va Sch Law, JD, 1976. **Career:** Va Beach Police Dept, uniformed police officer, 1974; WINA/WOMC Radio, reporter & announcer, 1974-75; Neighborhood Youth Corps, client counr, 1975-76; Eric O Moody & Assoc, sr partner, 1976-; Norfolk State Col, instr, 1977-78; City Chesapeake, comnr econ develop authority; Chesapeake Gen Dist Ct, chmn, substitute Judge, 1983-2007; S Hampton Roads Bar Asn, pres. **Orgs:** Va State Bar; Portsmouth Bar Asn; Old Dom Bar Asn; Am Bar Asn; Va Trial Lawyers Asn; NAACP; Chesapeake Bar Asn; Twin City Bar Asn; bd dir, Chesapeake YMCA; Nat Asn Advan Colored People; Chesapeake Men Progress; Chesapeake Forward; BoyScouts Am; fel United Church Christ. **Honors/Awds:** Dean's List; George F Baker Scholar; Substitute Judge City Chesapeake; Indust Develop Authority. **Special Achievements:** He offers legal commentary for the NBC Hampton Roads affiliate WAVY TV 10 NEWS; He is a guest host for Hampton University's radio station, WHOV 88.1 FM; He is a legal expert for Clear Channel Communications WKUS 92.1 and 103 JAMZ. **Home Addr:** 2124 Burnside Pl, Chesapeake, VA 23325. **Business Addr:** Senior Partner, Eric O Moody & Assoc, 355 Crawford St Suite 810, Portsmouth, VA 23704-2825, **Business Phone:** (757)399-7683.

**MOODY, DR. WILLIAM DENNIS**
Dentist. **Personal:** Born Jun 6, 1948, White Plains, NY; son of William Jr and Ellen Rebecca. **Educ:** N Cent Col, BA, 1970; State Univ NY, Buffalo, DDS, 1974. **Career:** Pvt pract, dentist, currently. **Orgs:** Prog chmn, Greater Metrop Dent Soc, 1977-78; bd dir, Greenburgh Neighborhood Health Ctr, 1979-81, Greenburgh Community Ctr, 1982-83; Thomas H Slater Ctr, 1984-91; White Plains Dent Forum, Scarsdale Dent Soc; bd dir, Union Child Day Care Ctr; Am Dent Asn; Alpha Omega Frat; Nat Dent Asn; Greater Metro NY Dent Soc; pres, Greater Metrop Dent Soc, 1987-89; corresp secy, Greater Metrop NY Dent Soc, 1990-91. **Home Addr:** 18 Robert Lane, White Plains, NY 10601, **Home Phone:** (914)428-7394. **Business Addr:** Dentist, Private Practice, 48 Mamaroneck Ave 65 Ct St Suite 42, White Plains, NY 10601-4200, **Business Phone:** (914)428-7394.

**MOON, HAROLD WARREN.** **See MOON, WARREN.**

**MOON, REV. WALTER DEAN**
Government official, clergy. **Personal:** Born Aug 10, 1940, Marietta, GA; married Winford G Strong; children: Sonja & Sonita. **Educ:** Kennesaw Jr Col; Savannah State Col; Inst Comput Technol, attended 1967. **Career:** Mails US Postal Serv, Marietta, Ga, lett carrier; USPS, Ala, cust serv mgr; part-time bldg contractor; Word Faith AME Church, Mableton, Ga, sr pastor, currently. **Orgs:** Treas, Future Develop Asn Inc; pres, Concerned Citizens Marietta; Nat Asn Advan Colored People; Marietta Cobb Bridges Prog; vice chmn, Marietta Bd Educ; Marietta Civil Serv Comn; USN Manpower Speakers Team Freshman Scholastic Savannah State Col, USN, 1960-64; Atlanta E Dist, African Methodist Episcopal Church, 2005-. **Home Addr:** 331 Hermitage Ct SW, Marietta, GA 30064-2915, **Home Phone:** (770)428-6744. **Business Addr:** Senior Pastor, Word of Faith AME Church, 5719 Garner Rd, Mableton, GA 30126-3421.

**MOON, WARREN (HAROLD WARREN MOON)**
Football player, television broadcaster. **Personal:** Born Nov 18, 1956, Los Angeles, CA; son of Harold (deceased) and Pat; married Felicia Hendricks; children: Joshua, Chelsea, Blair & Jeffrey; married Mandy Ritter; children: Ryken. **Educ:** Univ Wash. **Career:** Football player (retired), owner; Edmonton Eskimos, Can Football League, quarterback, 1978-83; Houston Oilers, quarterback, 1984-93; Minn Vikings, 1994-96; Seattle Seahawks, quarterback, 1997-98, Seahawks radio team, broadcast analyst, currently; KansCity Chiefs, quarterback, 1999-2000; Warren Moon's Chocolate Chippery, Edmonton, owner; Sports 1 Mkt, pres & founder, 2010-. **Orgs:** Founder, Crescent Moon Found. **Honors/Awds:** Most Valuable Player, Rose Bowl, 1978; Most Valuable Player, Grey Cup, 1980, 1982; Most Outstanding Player, Can Football League, 1983; Jeff Nicklin Memorial Trophy, 1983; All NFL Rookie Team, Pro Football Writers, UPI & Pro Football Weekly; Football Digest's Rookie All-Star Team; Man of the Year, Nat football League, 1989; Travelers NFL Man of the Year, 1989; Most Valuable Player, Newspaper Enterprise Asn, 1990; Offensive Player of the Year, Nat Football League, 1990; Player of the Year, Am Football Club, 1990; Walter Camp Man of the Year, Walter Camp Football Found, 1993; Bart Starr Man of the Year, 1994; Most Valuable Player, Pro Bowl, 1997; Am Football Club Passing Leader, 1992; Canadian Football Hall of Fame, 2001; Pro Football Hall of Fame, 2006; Edmonton Eskimos Wall of Honour. **Special Achievements:** One of nine African-American quarterbacks, largest number in NFL history, 1997; First modern African-American quarterback to be elected to the Pro Football Hall of Fame; Film: Any Given Sunday. **Business Addr:** President, Founder, Sports 1 Marketing, 2 Venture, Irvine, CA 92618, **Business Phone:** (949)336-6380.

**MOONE, WANDA RENEE**
Consultant, social worker, manager. **Personal:** Born Oct 12, 1956, Greensboro, NC; daughter of Connell and Beulah M; children: Dedrick L. **Educ:** NC Agr & Tech State Univ, BSW, 1982; Univ NC Chapel Hill, MSW, 1983. **Career:** Bowman Group Sch Med, Amos Cottage Rehab Hosp, social worker, 1983-85; St James Nursing Ctr Inc, dir social serv, 1985-87; Rockingham Coun Aging, case mgr, 1987-89; Piedmont Triad Coun Govts, reg long term careom budsman, 1989-90; Youth Focus Psychiat Hosp, dir social work, 1990-94; Guilford Co Dept Soc Serv, child protection servs supvr, 1995-2006, Child welfare supvr, 1996-2009, qual assurance evaluator/child welfare trainer, 2009. **Orgs:** NASW, 1982-; Alpha Delta Mu, 1982-; field instr, Bennett Col, 1985-86; NC A&T State Univ & Univ NC, 1986-; NC Asn Black Social Workers, 1987-90; Nat Asn Advan Colored People, 1987-; NC Asn Health Care Facil, 1987-88; Acad Cert Social Workers, 1988; Alzheimer's Asn, 1989; adv comt mem, United Servs Older Adults, 1989-90. **Honors/Awds:** NC Dean's List, 1979-80; Certificate, Alpha Delta Mu; Nat Social Work Hon, Soc Rho Chap, 1982-. **Home Addr:** 527 Foxridge Rd, Greensboro, NC 27406-8233, **Home Phone:** (336)297-1012. **Business Addr:** Supervisor, Guilford Co DSS, 1203 Maple St, Greensboro, NC 27405, **Business Phone:** (336)641-3056.

**MOORE, ACEL**
Editor. **Personal:** Born Oct 5, 1940, Philadelphia, PA; son of Jarry A and Hura Mae; married Carolyn Weaver, Jan 1, 1964, (divorced 1974); married Cheryl Rice, Jan 1, 1975; children: Acel Jr; married Linda Wright Avery, Jan 1, 1988. **Educ:** Settlement Music Sch, attended 1958; Charles Morris Price Sch, advert & jour, 1966. **Career:** Philadelphia Inquirer, copy clerk, 1962, ed clerk, 1964-68, copy boy, 1965, staff writer, 1968-81, assoc ed & dir recruiting, columnist & mem ed bd, 1981-05, assoc ed emer, 1981-2005; Univ Calif, Berkeley, fac, 1980-89; Temple Univ, journalism instr; Fla A&M Univ, journalism instr; Northwestern Univ, journalism consult; Duquesne Univ, journalism consult; Univ Kans, journalism consult; Norfolk State Univ, journalism consult. **Orgs:** Pres, Philadelphia Asn Black Journalists; founding mem, Nat Asn Black Journalists Sigma Delta Chi; Am Soc Newspaper Ed; Pulitzer Prize Juror. **Business Addr:** Associate Editor Emeritus, The Philadelphia Inquirer, 400 N Broad St, Philadelphia, PA 19101, **Business Phone:** (215)854-4975.

**MOORE, ALBERT**
Public relations executive, school administrator. **Personal:** Born Feb 17, 1952, Johnsonville, SC; married Marie Durant; children: Porchia Atiya & Chelsey Maria. **Educ:** Friendship Jr Col, attended 1971; Benedict Col, BA, polit sci, 1974; Univ SC, pub admin, 1979; SC Criminal Justice Acad, cert correction officer, 1981. **Career:** Crayton Mid Sch, sub teacher, 1974-75; Sq D Co, prod coordr, 1975-76; US Auto Assoc, vpres mktg & pub rels, 1976-77; Al's Dr Restaurant, owner, 1976-77; Benedict Col, equip mgr, 1977-79, tech asst, dean acad affairs, 1979-82; Nat Conf Black Mayors Prog, asst dir, 1979-82; Cent Correctional Inst, correction officer II, 1981-83; Benedict Col, coordr spec servs, pub rels, 1982-84; St Augustines Col, dir pub rels, 1984; Florence County, treas, 1999-2000. **Orgs:** Sem, Robert R Morton Mem Inst, 1980; panalist, Am Census Bur Workshop, 1980; partic, Assoc Rec Mgrs, 1981; Benedict Col Jr Alumni Club; Drexel Lake Residents Civic Org, Nat Asn Advan Colored People; SCARMA, SC Correction Officers Asn; charter mem, Benedict Col Tiger Club. **Home Addr:** 632 N Myrtlebeach Hwy, Johnsonville, SC 29555, **Home Phone:** (843)380-1062.

**MOORE, ALFRED**
Chief executive officer, executive director. **Personal:** Born Feb 24, 1956, Detroit, MI. **Educ:** Adrian Col, BA, acct, 1978; State Mich, cert, pub acct; Wright Leadership Inst, cert yr more & self improv, 2008. **Career:** PricewaterhouseCoopers, staff acct, 1978-80; George Johnson & Co, sr auditor, 1980-81; Alternative Inc, fiscal officer residential care, 1981-84; Champion Homes Inc, internal auditor, 1984-85; Cent City Health Serv Inc, Detroit, Mich, exec dir, 1984; New Ctr Hosp, Detroit, Mich, chief exec officer, 1984-93; Alfred Moore & Co, pres, 1984-2005; Residential Care Alternatives Inc, chief financial officer, 1997-2000; CHAN Healthcare Auditors, syst corp internal audit mgr, 2005-10; Community Found Northwest Ind Inc, acct mgr, 2011-12; Alfred Moore CPA LLC, pres, 2010-; Discover Financial Serv, sr assoc mkt bus risk, 2014-. **Orgs:** Life mem, Nat Asn Advan Colored People; pres, Block Club; Healthcare Financial Mgt Asn. **Home Addr:** 18401 Annchester, Detroit, MI 48219, **Home Phone:** (313)532-9752. **Business Addr:** President, Alfred Moore CPA LLC, 637 E Woodland Pk Ave, Chicago, IL 60616, **Business Phone:** (630)405-8514.

**MOORE, ALICE EVELYN**
Educator, secretary (organization). **Personal:** Born Feb 16, 1932, Washington, NC; daughter of Willie B and Lillie Bell Barrow (deceased). **Educ:** Tuskegee Inst, social studies, 1955; NMex Highlands Univ, hist educ, 1962; Johns Hopkins Univ, cert negro & sou hist, 1970; N Tex State Univ, cert aging specialist, 1979. **Career:** Young Women's Christian Asn, teen-age dir, 1955-56; Emerson Settlement House, group awork, 1957-58; Friendship Jr Col, instr social sci, 1962-71; Elizabeth City State Univ, instr social sci, 1971-73; Claflin Col, asst prof social sci, 1974-80; Allen Univ, assoc prof social sci, 1981-, coordr geront prog, 1981-, interim dir acad affairs, 1985-86. **Orgs:** Counr, Ep worth C's Home, 1981; secy, Resource Mobilization Adv Coun Dept Social Serv Richland Co, 1981-84; founder, secy & treas, Orangeburg Br Asn Study Life Hist. **Business Addr:** Coordinator Gerontology Program Social Science, Allen University, 1530 Harden St, Columbia, SC 29204, **Business Phone:** (803)254-4165.

**MOORE, ALLYN D.**
Automotive executive. **Personal:** Born Aug 9, 1960, Chicago, IL; son of Buck and Elizabeth; married Cheryl; children: Cydney, Zackery & Camryn. **Educ:** Bradley Univ, Peoria, IL, BA & MBA, gen, 1982. **Career:** Ford Motor Co, Ford Div Chicago, St Louis, field mgr, 1982-88; Qual Ford Mercury Inc, owner, 1989-2011; Allyn Moore Lincoln Mercury, pres, 1999-2002; Paducah Ford Lincoln Mazda, sales consult, 2011-15; Volvo Southborough, prod specialist, 2015-. **Orgs:** Bus comn, long range planning comt, Southside Bapt Church; Ford Lincoln mercury Minority Dealers Asn; secy, Nat Automobile Dealers Asn; bd mem, Princeton Chamber Com; Optimist Club; bd mem, United Way; bd mem, St Charles Community Col; St Charles Chamber Com; St Peter's Optimist Club; Corridor 9 & MetroWest Chamber Com, 2015-. **Home Addr:** 1159 Charter Oak, Creve Coeur, MO 63141. **Business Addr:** Owner, Quality Ford Mercury, 311 US Hwy 62 W, Princeton, KY 42445, **Business Phone:** (270)365-3673.

**MOORE, ANNIE JEWELL**
Fashion designer. **Personal:** Born Sep 20, 1919, Daytona Beach, FL; daughter of James (deceased) and Ora Lee Hall (deceased). **Educ:** Spelman Col, BA, 1943; Fashion Acad, golden pen cert, 1952; Ecole Guerre-Lavigne, Paris, France, cert, 1954; Marygrove Col, cert, 1976. **Career:** Ann Moore Couturiere Inc, fashion designer & pres, 1952-70; Detroit Pub Sch Syst, teacher, 1972-82; Spelman Col, Drama Dept, fac costume design, 1983-84; Atlanta Pub Sch Syst, teacher, 1985-86; Richs Acad, couturiere teacher, 1986-91; Mil Justice Clin Inc, receptionist, 1991; Dekalb & Futton Housing Coun, off asst, 2000-03; Social Security, clerical asst, 2003. **Orgs:** Pres, Mich Womens Civic Coun; vpres, Detroit Chap, Nat Alumnae Asn Spelman Col, 1980-82; chairperson, comm Atlanta Chap, Nat Alumnae Asn Spelman Col, 1986-87; Ad Hoc Comm Clothing & Textile; founder, Benefactors Educ, 1990. **Honors/Awds:** Michigan Women Civic Council Award, 1982; Honoree, Military Justice Annual Banquet, 1999; Certificates of recognition, Detroit Chap Nat Alumnae Asn Spelman Col; Honoree, Nat Black Arts Festival Event, 2006. **Home Addr:** 988 Palmetto Ave SW, Atlanta, GA 30314-3128, **Home Phone:** (404)753-3417.

**MOORE, ANTHONY LOUIS**
Executive. **Personal:** Born Jan 10, 1946, Chicago, IL; married Joyce M Watson; children: Jason A. **Educ:** Southern Ill Univ, BS, 1971; DePaul Univ, attended 1976; Univ Ill Chicago, attended 1978. **Career:** Vince Cullers Advert, media buyer, 1971-73, media planner, 1973-74; Proctor & Gardner Advert, from assoc media dir to media dir, 1974-78, vpres advert serv, sr vpres advert serv, 1990. **Orgs:** Alpha Delta Sigma, 1970-; Am Advert Fed, 1971-; Nat Asn Mkt Develop, 1975-; Am Mgt Asn, 1976-; adv bd, Chicago YMCA, 1976-; bd mem, Faulkner Sch, 1984-; Chicago Media Dirs Coun, 1986; Target Adv Pros; Stepp Sch. **Honors/Awds:** Creative Advertising Certificate, Asn Nat Advertisers; Black Media Merit, Black Media Inc; Employee of the Year, Proctor & Gardner; Achievement Award, YMCA. **Home Addr:** 7236 Oglesby Ave, Chicago, IL 60649, **Home Phone:** (773)288-5362. **Business Addr:** Senior Vice President, Proctor Communications Network, 980 N Michigan Ave, Chicago, IL 60611.

**MOORE, BARBARA CROCKETT**
Association executive, vice president (organization). **Personal:** Born Dec 27, 1949, Columbia, SC; daughter of Albert Crockett (deceased) and Wilhelmina; married Norman; children: Walletta. **Educ:** Benedict Col, BS, biol, 1971; Univ Chicago, MS, educ, 1986. **Career:** Benedict Col, Columbia, SC, admis counr, recruiter, dir alumni affairs, vpres instnl advan, 1975-. **Orgs:** Midlands YWCA; Nat Asn Female Execs; chmn, Nat Capital Campaign; Richland County Nat March Dimes Found; Nat Asn Female Execs; Coun Advan Support Edu; Zeta Phi Beta Sorority Inc, int pres, 2002-; Nat Polit Cong Black Women Inc; Top Ladies Distinction Inc. **Honors/Awds:** Zeta's SC Hall of Fame; Zeta's Southeastern Regional Hall of Fame; Living the Legacy Award, Nat Coun Negro Women, 1983; Hall of Fame, Zeta Phi Beta Southeastern Region, 2000. **Business Addr:** International President, Zeta Phi Beta Sorority Inc, 1734 New Hampshire Ave NW, Washington, DC 20009, **Business Phone:** (202)387-3103.

**MOORE, BEVERLY**
School administrator, mayor. **Personal:** married Larry; children: Bryan & Craig. **Educ:** Ohio State Univ, BS, social welfare, 1966; Western Mich Univ, MSW, social work, 1984. **Career:** City Kalamazoo, vice mayor, 1989-93, mayor; Western Mich Univ, Sch Social Work, dir admin, currently; Kalamazoo Pub Sch, Bd Educ, pres; Western Mich Univ, admin; Health Connect, exec dir. **Orgs:** Greater Kalamazoo United Way Bd, pres; Kalamazoo Pub Educ Found; trustee, Bronson Hosp; founding mem, WMU; Community Access Ctr Bd; Vol Ctr Bd; Planned Parenthood Southwest Mich Bd; Rotary Club Kalamazoo; Forum Kalamazoo; Irving S Gilmore Keyboard Festival Bd; League Women Voters; Nat Asn Advan Colored People; Alpha Kappa Alpha Sorority; Saturday Eves Bk Club. **Business Addr:** Adminstration Director, Western Michigan University, 1903 W Michigan Ave, Kalamazoo, MI 49008-5433, **Business Phone:** (269)387-8400.

**MOORE, CARMAN LEROY**
Music critic, composer, educator. **Personal:** Born Oct 8, 1936, Lorain, OH; son of Claude Leroy and Jessie Lee Franklin; married Susan Stern; children: Martin Douglass & Justin Charles. **Educ:** Ohio State Univ, BA, music, 1958; Juilliard Sch Music, MS, 1966. **Career:** Village Voice, music critic, 1965-; Harlem Theatre Workshop, assoc artistic dir; Sunday New York Times, staff, 1969; Manhattanville Col, asst prof music & composer, 1968-71; Univ Yale Grad Sch Music, asst prof, 1969-71; New Sch Soc Res, Queens Col, NY, asst prof, 1970-72; Saturday Rev; Am Dance Festival, master composer, 1986-; Sky music Inc, dir, founder & conductor, 1972-; Brooklyn Col, asst prof, 1972-74; Compositions: Mass 21st Century, Lincoln Ctr Performing Arts; African Tears; Drum Maj; Wildfires & Field Songs; Gospel Fuse; Hit, A Concerto Percussion & Orchestra Wild Gardens Loup Garou music theatre work Paradise-Lost Musical & Journey to Benares; Opera, Last Chance Planet & Gethsemane Pk (libretto by Ishmael Reed); Songs: Wellness All; Zen Garden; Gratitude; Garden Time; Healing Music; Home Galaxy; Star music; Spirit Kamakura; Dream Time; At Peace; With Thee Conversing; Lots Love; Oakland Blues; You Promised; BLUE..RED..GREEN, 2007. **Orgs:** Am Soc Composers, Authors & Publ; founder & secy-treas, Soc Black Composers. **Honors/Awds:** Meet-the-Composer Readers Digest Composer / Choreographer Award. **Special Achievements:** Composer: The Other Side of the Moon, 1990; Our Planet Earth, 1991; Personal Problems, 1980; Fixed Do, Moveable Sol, Goddess of the Waters; Author: Somebody's Angel Child, The Story of Bessie Smith, 1970. **Home Addr:** 152 Columbus Ave, New York, NY 10023-5918, **Home Phone:** (212)580-0825. **Business Addr:** Composer, Conductor, Sky Music Inc, 148 Columbus Ave, New York, NY 10023-5918, **Business Phone:** (212)633-1456.

**MOORE, CHANTE TORRANE**
Singer. **Personal:** Born Feb 17, 1967, San Francisco, CA; married Kadeem Hardison; children: Sophia Milan Hardison; married Kenny Lattimore; children: Kenny Jr. **Career:** Albums: Precious, 1992; A Love Supreme, 1994; This Moment Is Mine, 1999; Exposed, 2000; The Millennium Collection: The Best Chante Moore; play Things That Lovers Do, 2003; Uncovered & Covered, 2006; Love The Woman, 2008, Moore Is More, 2013. TV apperences: "Soul Train", 1992-2003; "The Tonight Show with Jay Leno", 1993; "New York Undercover", 1995; "Girlfriends", 2002; "The Young & the Restless", 2003; "The Tom Joyner Show", 2005; "In the Mix", 2006. Soundtrack: House Party 2, 1992; Beverly Hills Cop III, 1994; Waiting to Exhale, 1995; Drive, 1997; How Stella Got Her Groove Back, 1998; Shake, Rattle & Roll: An American Love Story, 1999; Romeo Must Die, 2000; Treated Like He, 2000; Contagious, 2001; Feeling The Way, 2002; One More Time, 2002; Shes Amazing, 2003; Till You Come Back To Me, 2005; Santa Baby, 2007; Where is the Love, 2013. **Business Addr:** Singer, MCA Records, 2220 Colorado Ave Suite 1, Santa Monica, CA 90404-3506, **Business Phone:** (310)865-4500.

### MOORE, DR. CHARLES W.
School administrator, executive. **Personal:** Born Nov 2, 1923, Macon, GA; son of Henry and Rose Bud Cornelius; married Mary Agnes DuBose; children: Tallulah Ragsdale. **Educ:** Morris Brown Col, AB, 1950, LLD, 1980; NY Univ, MBA, 1952; Daniel Payne Col, DHL, 1971; Univ Utah, MS, human resources mgt, 1975. **Career:** Morris Brown Col, bus mgr, 1951-66, vpres fin, 1985-91, chief fiscal officer; US Dept HEW, educ prog officer, 1966-78; US Dept Health & Human Serv, fin mgr, 1978-85; Brown & Moore Fin Serv LLC, founder, 1992-, vpres, currently, tournament co-chair, currently; B&M Financial Serv, partner, currently. **Orgs:** Bd mem, Stewards Big Bethel AME Church, 1955; treas, Atlanta Invest Asn Inc, 1956-; treas, Am Asn Col & Univ Bus Off, 1960-66; nat treas, Phi Beta Sigma Fraternity Inc, 1970-93; chmn, bd dir, Butler St Young Mens Christian Asn, 1979-81; Asn Govt Acct, 1983-; pres, Nat Alumni Asn Morris Brown Col, 1984-85. **Home Addr:** 734 Flamingo Dr SW, Atlanta, GA 30311. **Business Addr:** Vice President, Tournament Co-Chair, Brown & Moore Financial Services LLC, 34 Peachtree St NW Suite 2480, Atlanta, GA 30303, **Business Phone:** (404)522-7431.

### MOORE, CHRISTINE JAMES
Consultant, social worker, school administrator. **Personal:** Born Windsor, NC; daughter of Henry and Maude Boxley; married Marcellus; children: Lisa M Barkley. **Educ:** Morgan State Univ, Baltimore, BA, eng & hist, 1952; Columbia Univ, Teachers Col, New York, NY, MA, guid & stud personnel admin, 1962; Johns Hopkins Univ, advan grad study; Syracuse Univ, advan grad study. **Career:** Social worker, consultant, educational administrator (retired); Booker T Wash Jr High Sch, teacher 1952-59, counr, 1959-64; Balt Sec Schs, specialist guid, 1965-69; Workshop Employ Opportunities Disadvantaged Youth, Johns Hopkins Univ, asst dir, 1966, instr, 1969-70; Community Col Baltimore, Md, dir develop studies, 1969-74, Stud Serv, Harbor Campus, dean, 1974-79, dean staff develop & urban resources, 1980-81, exec asst pres, 1981-83; House Delegates Gen Assembly State Md, reader, 1986-87; Morgan State Univ, acad adv, 1988-92. **Orgs:** Regional dir, Delta Sigma Theta, 1968-70; bd dir, Mun Employees Credit Union Baltimore, 1975-83; Mayor's Steering Com Baltimore Best Promotional Com, 1976-87; Mid States Asn Col & Sec Schs, 1977-83; Am Personnel & Guid Asn; Am Col Personnel Asn; bd dir, Arena Players Community Theater; bd dir, 4th Dist Dem Org, 1980-82; Am Fed Tv & Radio Artists, 1983-; Nat Asn Advan Colored People; Nat Coun Negro Women; Coun&human rels, Urban League Consult; bd dir, Baltimore Md Metro YWCA, 1983-86; bd dir, Baltimore Md Metrop, YWCA, 1983-86; bd examr, Speech Pathol, 1983-85; comnr, Comn Med Discipline Md, 1984-88; Comn Med Discipline State Md, 1985-88; bd trust, City Temple Baltimore Baptist Church, 1986-87; bd mem, Physicians Qual Assurance State Md, 1988-98; Md Stat eBd Physicians Qual Assurance, 1988-98; Screen Actors Guild, 1991-; Nat Coalition 100 Black Women; Links Inc; steering comt, Rev Characteristics Excellence Higher Educ: Stand Accreditation Mid States Asn Cols & Schs Comn Higher Educ, 1992-93. **Home Addr:** 3501 Hilton Rd, Baltimore, MD 21215-7408, **Home Phone:** (410)367-0897.

### MOORE, CHRISTOPHER PAUL
Writer, playwright, actor. **Personal:** son of Willard and Norma K D; married Kim Yancey; children: 2. **Educ:** Northeastern Univ, attended 1974. **Career:** Author, playwright, actor, historian, journalist; ABC Radio News, ed; Nat Black Network News, ed; NY Pub Libr, Schomburg Ctr Res Black Cult, cur & res historian, currently; writer, currently; Books: Santa & Pete: A Novel of Christmas Present & Past, 1998; The Black New Yorkers: 400 Years of African-American History, 1999; Jubilee: The Emergence of African-American Culture, 2003; Standing in the Need of Prayer: A Celebration of Black Prayer; 2003; Fighting for America: Black Soldiers, The Unsung Heroes of World War II, 2005; Plays: The Last Season, 2004; TV: "The African Burial Ground: An American Discovery"; "Santa & Pete". "Black Soldiers Blue", 2005. **Orgs:** Northeastern Univ Alumni Asn; New York Landmarks Preserv Comt. **Special Achievements:** Interviewed every American president from Jimmy Carter to Bill Clinton. **Business Addr:** Writer, c/o Random House Inc, New York, NY 10019, **Business Phone:** (212)782-9000.

### MOORE, CLEOTHA FRANKLIN
Teacher, association executive, social worker. **Personal:** Born Sep 16, 1942, Canton, MS; son of Sam A and Luevenia Lee McGee; married Normajo Ramsey; children: Faith Veleen & Sterling Kent. **Educ:** Ind Cent Univ, BS, 1964; Ball St Univ, Ed, 1965; Ind Univ Purdue Univ, bus studies, 1975. **Career:** Wood HS Indianapolis Pub Sch Syst, teacher, coach, 1964-69; Nat Bank, personnel admin, 1969-74; RCA & Consumer Electronics, emp rels mgr, 1974-90; United Way Cent Ind, dir human res, 1990. **Orgs:** First vp, newsletter edSt Missionary Bapt Conv, 1968-79; Nat Asn Advan Colored People, 1969-; trustee, asst treas, S Calvary Bapt Church, 1977-; pres, Audubon Terr Neighborhood Asn, 1978-85; mem Mayor's Ridesharing Work Rescheduling Task Force, 1979; bd mem, Metro Sch Dist Warren Twp; bd dir, Near E Side Multi Serv Ctr, 1983-89; bd dir, Indianapolis Day Nursery Asn, 1988-90; mentor, Bus Encouraging SuccessTomorrow, 1990-; mentor, Indianapolis Pub Sch Syst, 1990-. **Honors/Awds:** Work study Grant IN Central Col, 1960-64; IN St HS Wrestling Champion in HS Athletic Assoc, 1960; Col Wrestling Championship Awards, IN Little State Col Conf, 1962, 1964; Spoke Aws Indianapolis Jaycees, 1971; Spark Award Indianapolis Jaycees, 1972; Service Award Indianapolis Head start Prog, 1974. **Home Addr:** 3625 N Audubon Rd, Indianapolis, IN 46218, **Home Phone:** (317)547-1443. **Business Addr:** Human Resources Director, United Way Cent Ind, 3901 N Meridian St, Indianapolis, IN 46208, **Business Phone:** (317)921-1274.

### MOORE, COLIN A.
Lawyer. **Personal:** Born Apr 24, 1944, Berbice; son of Victor Emmanuel and Olive Muriel; married Ela Babb; children: Simone. **Educ:** Univ Wis, Kingston, Jamaica, BSc, 1963; Univ London, MA, 1968; Brooklyn LawSch, attended 1978; Princeton Univ. **Career:** Douglas Col, Rutgers Univ, Nb, NJ, lectr, 1971-75; Wachtell Lipton Rosen Katz, NY, paralegal, 1975-76; Atty Gen, St NY, law clerk, 1976-78; Bronx County, NY, asst dist atty, 1978-79; Brooklyn, NY, self employed atty, 1979-. **Orgs:** Chmn, Legal Redress Comt, Nat Asn Advan Colored People, Jamaica Chap, 1978-81; St Albans Local Develop Corp, 1979-82; pres, Macon B Allen Bar Asn, 1980-83; pres, Carribean Action Lobby, 1981-82; bd mem, Nat Bar Asn, 1981-83; Nat Conf Black Lawyers, 1982-84; bd mem, Medgar Evers Ctr Law & Social Justice, 1986-. **Honors/Awds:** Am Jurisp Award, Lawyers Coop Publ House, 1976; Leadership Award, Sesame Flyers Int, 1987; Achievement & Community Serv Award, Medgar Evers Col, 1987; Distinguished Service Award, Jamaica Nat Movement, 1988; Humanitarian Award, Vidcap Inc, 1989. **Special Achievements:** Author of The Simpson-Mazzoli Bill: Two Steps Forward, One Step Backward, 1984; Author of The History of African Liberation Movements from Os Palmares to Montgomery, 1989; Author of collection of articles, 1989. **Home Addr:** 47 Remsen St Apt 2, Brooklyn, NY 11201-4175, **Home Phone:** (718)643-0285. **Business Addr:** Attorney, Private Practice, 15 Ct St Suite 1212, Brooklyn, NY 11241, **Business Phone:** (718)330-9110.

### MOORE, CORNELL LEVERETTE
Lawyer, president (organization). **Personal:** Born Sep 18, 1939, Tignall, GA; son of Luetta T and Jesse L; married Wenda Weekes; children: Lynne M, Jonathon C & Meredith L. **Educ:** Va Union Univ, AB, socio-econs, 1961; Howard Univ Law Sch, JD, 1964. **Career:** US Treas, staff atty, 1962-64; Crocker Bank, trust admin, 1964-66; Comptroller Currency, US Treas, regional coun, 1966-68; NW Nat Bank Minneapolis, asst vpres & legal officer, 1968-70; Shelter Mortgage Co Inc, exec vpres & dir, 1970-73; Shelard Nat Bank, dir, 1973-78; Lease More Equip Inc, pres & chief exec officer, 1977-86; Marquette, Golden Valley Bank, dir, 1978-2002; Miller & Schroeder Financial Inc, sr vpres & gen coun, 1987-95; Dorsey & Whitney, partner, 1995-; Howard Univ, chair. **Orgs:** Trustee, Dunwoody Inst; dir, Greater Minneapolis Housing Corp; trustee, Va Union Univ; trustee, Howard Univ; dir, Greater Minneapolis Visitors & Conv Asn; trustee, Johnson C Smith Univ; chmn, Minneapolis Pub Housing Authority; co-chair, Firm-Wide Diversity Steering Comt; Firm's Minneapolis Recruiting Comt; pres, Hennepin Co Bar Found, 1975-78; Minn Twins, 1986-95; co-chair, Minneapolis African Am Family Serv Capital Campaig, 1997-2001; Minneapolis Aquatennial Commodore, 1998; Sigma Pi Phi; Grand Sire Archon-elect, 2004. **Honors/Awds:** Whitney Young Award, Boy Scouts Am, Minneapolis; Silver Beaver Award, 2005; Kappa Alpha Psi Distinguished Citizen Award, 2007; Legacy Award, Pan African Community Endowment; Child of America Award. **Special Achievements:** First African American Greek-lettered organization. **Home Addr:** 6105 Lincoln Dr Suite 335, Edina, MN 55436. **Business Addr:** Counsel, Dorsey & Whitney LLP, 50 S 6th St Suite 1500, Minneapolis, MN 55402-1498, **Business Phone:** (612)340-2600.

### MOORE, CYNTHIA M.
Journalist. **Personal:** Born Nov 11, 1963, Columbus, OH; daughter of Jackie and Barbara Price Hughes. **Educ:** Ohio State Univ, Columbus, OH, BA, 1990. **Career:** WSYX, TV 6, ABC, Good Morning Columbus, producer, currently. **Orgs:** Nat Asn Black Journalists. **Honors/Awds:** American Heart Association Media Award, 1992. **Home Addr:** 3751 Rosewell Dr, Columbus, OH 43227, **Home Phone:** (614)237-8975. **Business Addr:** Producer, WSYX-TV 6 ABC, 1261 Dublin Rd, Columbus, OH 43215, **Business Phone:** (614)481-6659.

### MOORE, DAMON E.
Football player. **Personal:** Born Sep 15, 1976, Fostoria, OH; son of Cleo (deceased) and Addie. **Educ:** Ohio State Univ. **Career:** Football player (retired); Philadelphia Eagles, defensive back & strong safety & free safety, 1999-2001; Chicago Bears, free safety, 2002.

### MOORE, DAVID BERNARD, II
Educator. **Personal:** Born Jul 13, 1940, Uniontown, AL. **Educ:** Ala State Univ, BS, 1960; Fordham Univ, spec educ, 1962; Univ AL, MA, 1972. **Career:** Educator (retired); Super Graphics, dir, 1973-79; RC Hatch HS, teacher, 1981-90. **Orgs:** Pres, Union Town Civic League, 1970-; city coun man, 1972-. **Honors/Awds:** Versality Award, 1975. **Home Addr:** Forniss St, PO Box 635, Uniontown, AL 36786-0635, **Home Phone:** (334)628-9207.

### MOORE, DAVID M.
Executive. **Personal:** Born May 2, 1955, Chattanooga, TN; son of David and Clara S. **Educ:** Univ Wis, Eau Claire, WI, BA, mkt & mgt, 1978. **Career:** Miller Brewing Co, Milwaukee, Wis, group mgr, 1977-82, area mgr, 1982-85, mkt develop mgr, 1987; Quali Croutons Inc, Chicago, Ill, founder, pres, gen mgr, 1986-2008; Moore Holding Group LLC, managing partner, 2011-. **Business Addr:** Founder, Quality Croutons Inc, 825 W 37th Pl, Chicago, IL 60609, **Business Phone:** (773)927-8200.

### MOORE, DERRICK C.
Writer, football player, football coach. **Personal:** Born Oct 13, 1967, Albany, GA; married Stephanie; children: 2. **Educ:** Northeastern Okla State Univ. **Career:** Football player (retired), author, motivational speaker; Atlanta Falcons, running back, 1992; Detroit Lions, running back, 1993-94; Carolina Panthers, running back, 1995; Ariz Cardinals, running back, 1996-2001; Ga Tech, Athletic Dept, adv & counr, campus dir, develop coach & chaplain; Books: The Great Adventure, 2003; Going the Distance, 2011; Winning the Battle, 2011; Learning the Rules, 2011; Making the Team, 2011; Taking the Lead, 2012; Tv: The Big 4-0, Tv land; Editor: Strength & Honor Bible. **Orgs:** Fel Christian Athletes; Best Friends Found. **Honors/Awds:** AIA All-American; Most Valuable Player, 1992; Hula Bowl. **Business Addr:** Member, Fellowship of Christian Athletes, 8701 Leeds Rd, Kansas City, MO 64129, **Business Phone:** (770)316-5273.

### MOORE, DOROTHY RUDD
Composer, singer. **Personal:** Born Jun 4, 1940, New Castle, DE; married Kermit. **Educ:** Howard Univ Sch Music, BMus, music theor & compos, 1963; Am Conserv Fontainebleau, France, dipl, 1963. **Career:** Best works: Twelve Quatrains from the Rubaiyat, song cycle, 1962; Symphony No. 1, 1963; Harlem Sch Arts, teacher piano & music theory, 1965-66; pvt piano, voice, sight-singing & ear-training teacher, 1968-; New York Univ, teacher music hist appreciation, 1969; Dark Tower, 1970; Bronx Community Col, teacher music histappreciation, 1971; Dream & Variations piano, 1974; Transencion, 1986. **Orgs:** Founder, Soc Black Composers, 1968; bd mem, 1986, mem, Am Composers Alliance, 1972-; Broadcast Music Inc, 1972-; composer mem rec panel, Nat Endowment Arts, 1986 & 1988; Ny Coun Arts, 1988-90; New York Singing Teachers Asn; New York Women Composers. **Honors/Awds:** Lucy Moten Fellowship, 1963; Grant, Am Music Ctr, 1972; Grant, NY State Coun Arts, 1985. **Home Addr:** 33 Riverside Dr, New York, NY 10023, **Home Phone:** (212)787-1869. **Business Addr:** Composer, c/o Rud/Mor Publishing Co, 33 Riverside Dr, New York, NY 10023, **Business Phone:** (212)787-1869.

### MOORE, EDDIE N., JR.
School administrator, president (organization). **Personal:** Born Jan 1, 1947; married Elisia Almendarez; children: 5. **Educ:** Pa State Univ, BS, acct, 1968; Katz Bus Sch, Univ Pittsburgh, MBA, 1975. **Career:** Gulf Oil Corp, var positions, 1971-85; Commonwealth Va, asst controller, 1985-88, controller, Col William & Mary, 1988-90; Dept Treas, state treas, 1990-93; Va State Univ, pres, 1993-2010; St Pauls Col, pres, currently. **Orgs:** Omega Psi Phi Fraternity Inc; Forum Club; Va Heroes Inc; chmn, Finance Comn Cent Intercollegiate Athletic Asn; Va Bd Agr, Va Ctr Innovative Technol, Va Hist Soc & Am Asn Col Teacher Educ; chair, Vantagepoint Funds Bd; bd, Universal Corp; St James Baptist Church; Joint Comn Reporting Req; United Way Servs; Greater Richmond Chamber Com. **Business Addr:** President, Saint Pauls College, 115 Col Dr, Lawrenceville, VA 23868, **Business Phone:** (434)848-6412.

### MOORE, DR. ELIZABETH D. (LIZ MOORE)
Lawyer, executive director. **Personal:** Born Jul 29, 1954, Queens, NY; daughter of William A and M Doreen; married Jimmy L Miller. **Educ:** NY State Sch Indust & Labor Rels; Cornell Univ, BS, indust & labor rels, 1975; St John's Univ Sch Law, JD. **Career:** Consol Edison Co New York, atty, 1978-79, sr vpres & gen coun, 2009-; Am Express Co, atty, 1979-80; Equitable Life Assurance Soc, mgr, equal opportunity, 1981; Off Coun Gov, asst coun, 1981-83, first asst coun, 1983-87; Gov Off Employee Rels, dir, 1987-90; NY Ethics Comn, chairperson, 1988-90; NY Gov, Off Coun Gov, coun gov, 1991-94; Gov Off, dir; Nixon Peabody LLP, partner, 1995-2004; Burke Rehab Hosp, dir, 2005-12. **Orgs:** Bd dir, Ctr Women GOV; co-chair, Task Force NYS Pub Workforce 21stCentury; ch-chair, NYS/CSEA COM Work Environ & Productivity; bd trustees, Cath Interracial Coun; Govs Exec Comn Affirmative Action; Int Personnel Mgt Asn; Nat Asn State DRRs Employee Rels; Nat Forum Black Pub ADRs; Nat Pub Employer Labor Rels Asn; New York Joint Labor/Mgt Coms; State Acad Pub Admin; Women Exec State Gov; Gov Task Force Work & Family; Gov's Spec Prosecutor Screening Com; Govs Task Force Bias-Related Violence; bd trustee, Rochester Inst Technol; gov, Ny Second Dept Judicial Screening Comt; adv coun mem, Sch Indust Labor Rels, 1989-; Pres Coun Cornell Women, 1992; bd trustee, Cornell Univ; bd trustee, Burke Rehab Hosp. **Honors/Awds:** Hon JD, St John's Univ Sch Law, 1978; Governor Mario M Cuomo, nominated for the 9th Annual Salute to Young Women Achievers Award, 1985; Legislative Mobilization Appreciation Award, Nat Asn Advan Colored People, 1986; Toll fel, Nat Coun State Govs, 1987; Westchester County Black Women's Political Caucus Leadership Award, 1989; John E Burton Award, State Univ NY, 1990; Honorary Doctor of Civil Law, St John's Univ; Judge William B. Groat Award, ILR School, 2003; Diversity Champion Award, New York City Bar Asn, 2006; Groat Award, Cornell Univ Sch Indust Rels; Leaders for a New Century Legal Community Award, Asn Black Women Atty; Distinguished honor Award, Girl Scout Council of Greater, 2007. **Business Addr:** Senior Vice President, General Counsel, Consolidated Edison Company of New York, 4 Irving Pl, New York, NY 10003, **Business Phone:** (212)460-4600.

### MOORE, ESQ. EMANUEL A.
Lawyer, real estate agent. **Personal:** Born Nov 22, 1941, Brooklyn, NY; son of Hubert and Hilda Waterman; married Hilda Rosa Garcia. **Educ:** NY Univ, BS, Willard J Martin Scholar, James Talcott Scholar, 1963; NY Law Sch, JD, Thurgood Marshall Scholar, 1966. **Career:** Justice Dept, Civil Rights Div, atty, 1966-68; Queens Co NY, asst dist atty, 1968; Off Gen Coun AID Wash, legal adv, 1968-70; Eastern Dist NY, US atty, 1970-72; US Atty Off Eastern Dist NY, chief consumer protect secy, 1972-74; US Fed Energy Admin, dir compliance & enforcement, 1974-77; pvt pract atty, 1977-; Sunshine Quest R ealty Inc, atty law, currently, Law Off Emanuel Moore Esq, owner, currently. **Orgs:** Ed, NY Law Forum, 1965-66; Chinese Am Lions Club, NY, Knighted Order St George & Constantine, 1986; pres, Atlantic Palace Condo Asn, 1989-; app US magistrate, Selection Com, Eastern Dist, NY, 1992-; dir, Nat Macon B Allen Black Bar Asn; dir, NY Law Sch Alumni Asn. **Honors/Awds:** American Jurisprudence Award Academic Excellence in Law of Evidence, 1965; Vice President Award Academic Excellence, 1966. **Home Addr:** 125-10 Queens Blvd, Kew Gardens, NY 11415, **Home Phone:** (718)793-5535. **Business Addr:** Attorney at Law, Real Estate Broker, 12 S Clyde Ave, Kissimmee, FL 34741, **Business Phone:** (407)301-8061.

### MOORE, ETTA R.
Manager, executive, sales manager. **Personal:** Born Jan 9, 1957, Oklahoma City, OK; daughter of Myrtle Holloway; children: DeAngelo. **Educ:** Okla State Univ, BS, bus & mkt, 1979. **Career:** Woolco Dept Store, asst div mgr, 1979-81; Pan Okla Commun, sales admin, 1981-83. **Orgs:** Grad adv, AKA Sorority Inc, 1981-83; field dir, Red Lands Girl Scout Coun, 1984-89; treas, High Sch Alumni Class, 1985-; bd mem, exec staff, Asn Girl Scout; Am Bus Women's Asn, 1987-89; Urban League, 1987; YWCA Leader Luncheon Comt, 1989-93; Austin Independent Sch Dist Vol Adv Comt, 1989-92, chmn, 1991-92; Regist Prof Camp Planner, 1990; Capital Area Chamber Com, 1990-; St Stephen's Missionary Baptist Church: Sunday Sch Teacher, Vacation Bible Sch Worker, 1990-; vol, Dessau Elem Sch, 1991-93; bd dir, Adopt-A-Sch, 1992-, comt chmn, 1993, treas; vol, Hyde Pk Baptist Elem Sch, 1993-95; dir mem & prog, vol, Girl Scouts-Lone Star Coun, 1989-92, asst exec dir, 1992-93, exec dir & chief exec officer, 1993-2007; E Austin Rotary Club Charter; Women's Chamber Com; exec coun chmn, United Way & Capital Area; bd dir, comt co-chmn, prog partic & alum, Leadership Austin, 1993-2013; bd dir, agency rep, UW & CA; County Invest Comt; Leadership Tex; Alpha Kappa Alpha Sorority; Trinity Episcopal Sch Bd; Trinity Episcopal Head Sch Search Comt; bd dir, Partners Educ; chief exec officer, Girl Scouts Cent Tex, 2007-12; exec dir, 100 Club Cent Tex, 2013-. **Honors/Awds:** Appreciation

Pin, Girl Scouts-Lone Star Coun, 1992; Honor Pin, Girl Scouts-Lone Star Coun, 1993; Thanks Badge, Girl Scouts-Lone Star Coun, 1994; Ring of Honor, Ment Health Asn Tex, 2005; H. L. Gaines Human Relations Award, AISD, 2006; Sheffield Award, Austin Community Found. **Home Addr:** 901 Tayside Dr, Pflugerville, TX 78660-8853, **Home Phone:** (512)251-3228. **Business Addr:** Executive Director, The 100 Club of Central Texas, 3200 Steck Ave Suite 240, Austin, TX 78757, **Business Phone:** (512)345-3200.

**MOORE, EVELYN K.**
Executive. **Personal:** Born Jul 29, 1937, Detroit, MI. **Educ:** Eastern Mich Univ, BS, 1960; Univ Mich, MA, 1960. **Career:** Nat Black Child Develop Inst, DC, exec dir, 1988-99, pres & chief exec officer, 1999-2013, pres emer, 2013-. **Orgs:** Bd dir, C's Lobby; N Am Adoption Bd; adv, comt DC Citizens Pub Educ; consult, US Off Educ; Nat Asn Educ Young C; dir emer, Child Trends Inc. **Honors/Awds:** Outstanding Young Woman of State of MI, 1970. **Business Addr:** President Emeritus, National Black Child Development Institute, 1313 L St NW Suite 110, Washington, DC 20005-4110, **Business Phone:** (202)833-2220.

**MOORE, EVIA BRIGGS**
Educator, librarian. **Personal:** Born Jan 18, 1943, Ripley, MS; daughter of Vance and Ruby Simelton; married Jones Ambrose Jr; children: Robert Vance; married Henry Earl Briggs. **Educ:** Tougaloo Col, BA, 1965; Syracuse Univ, MSLS, 1970; Univ Wis-Madison, cert libr admin; Univ Pac, doctoral, cand. **Career:** Jackson Pub Schs, elem teacher, 1965-66; Tougaloo Col, acquisitions librn, 1966-74; Jackson State Univ, asst prof libr sci, 1974-75; San Joaquin Delta Col, periodicals & ref librn, 1977-90, librn & coordr pub serv, 1990-91, interim dir affirmative action, 1991-92, librn & coordr pub serv, 1992-95, interim dir affirmative action, 1995-96, dir libr serv, Goleman Libr, div dean, currently; Delta Col, Acad Sen, pres, 1990-91. **Orgs:** Am Libr Asn; Calif Libr asn; Phi Delta Kappa (Univ Pac Chap); Am Asn Univ Women, 1975-2003; Delta Sigma Theta Sorority, 1976-88; Links Inc, Stockton Chap, 1977-2003, pres, 1984-86; Stockton Symphony League, 1980-93; Jack & Jill Am, 1988-94; Stockton Seaport Rotary, 2001-03; Delta Kappa Gamma. **Home Addr:** 4344 Spyglass Dr, Stockton, CA 95219-1924, **Home Phone:** (209)957-2034. **Business Addr:** Division Dean, San Joaquin Delta College, 5151 Pacific Ave, Stockton, CA 95207, **Business Phone:** (209)954-5139.

**MOORE, FLOREESE NAOMI**
Educator, school administrator. **Personal:** Born Mar 15, 1940, Wilson, NC; daughter of Naomi Jones Lucas and Wiley Floyd Lucas; children: Lemuel Wiley & Lyndon Benjamin. **Educ:** W Chester State Univ, BS, 1974; Univ Del, MI, 1979; Nova Univ, EdD, 1984; Ohio State Univ. **Career:** Red Cross, Japan, gen off worker, 1961-63; Vita Foods Inc, bookkeeper, 1963-64; Chesapeake Potomac Tel Co, operator, 1964-66; Doctors Bk keeping, secy, 1966-68; New Castle Co, Del Pub Sch, human rels sp, teacher, 1968-79; Sch Bd Alachua, teacher, adminr, prin, asst supt, 1979-90; Fla Asn Except Sch Adminrs, founder, 1984; Columbus Pub Sch, asst supt, 1990-96, elem prin, 1996-2005; LB HandiCare Inc, vpres, 2007-08. **Orgs:** Exec bd, Coun Except C, 1980-84; Delta Sigma Theta Sorority int comn, 1982; secy, Phi Delta Kappa, 1983; Altrussa Club Gainesville; Fla Orgn Instrnl Leaders, 1984-90; arts comn, teens comn, Links Inc, 1985-; Am Asn Sch Adminrs, 1985-; Buckeye Asn Sch Adminrs, 1990-; Delta Sigma Theta. **Home Addr:** 6298 Bidwell Lane, Columbus, OH 43213, **Home Phone:** (614)868-2658. **Business Addr:** Principal, Columbus Public Schools, 4767 Northtowne Blvd, Columbus, OH 43229.

**MOORE, FRED HENDERSON**
Lawyer. **Personal:** Born Jul 25, 1934, Charleston, SC; married Louise Smalls; children: Fredena, Melissa, Fred, Louis & Rembert. **Educ:** SC State Col, attended 1956; Roosevelt Univ, Chicago, attended 1956; Allen Univ, BS, 1957; Howard Episcopal, JD, 1960; Teamers Sch Relig, DD, 1976; Stephens Christian Inst, 1976; Reform Episcopal Sem. **Career:** Self-employed atty, 1977; Payne RMUE Church, assoc pastor. **Orgs:** Corp coun, Nat Advan Asn Colored People, 1960; Black Rep Party; Silver Elephant Club; first Dist Coun SC Conf Nat Advan Asn Colored People; assoc coun, NC Mutual Ins Co; Omega Psi Phi Frat. **Honors/Awds:** Youth Award, Nat Advan Asn Colored People, 1957; Memorial Award, Charles Drew, 1957. **Special Achievements:** Co-authored a book: "Angry Black South", 1960. **Home Addr:** 115 St Margaret St, Charleston, SC 29403-3637, **Home Phone:** (502)231-8088. **Business Addr:** Attorney, 115 St Margaret St, Charleston, SC 29403-3637, **Business Phone:** (843)579-0730.

**MOORE, GARY**
Chief executive officer. **Educ:** Tyler Jr Col, assoc bus, 1979. **Career:** Highline Autoplex, pres; Texoma Ford, chief exec officer & pres, 1999-2007; Moore Transp LLC, pres, chief exec officer, 2005-. **Orgs:** Sherman Chamber Com; Ford Motor Minority Dealers Asn; Pottsboro Area Chamber Com; Dension Chamber Com. **Business Addr:** Chief Executive Officer, President, Moore Transport of Tulsa LLC, 661 N Plano Rd Suite 319, Richardson, TX 75081, **Business Phone:** (972)578-0606.

**MOORE, GARY E.**
School administrator, manager. **Personal:** Born Dec 8, 1962, Rochester, NY; son of Frank Lewis and Christine Enge; married Marva Elaine. **Educ:** Clarion Univ Pa, BS, acct, 1985, MS, commun, 1988. **Career:** Clarion Univ, grad asst; 1985, admis recruiter, 1987, proj dir; Univ Pa, asst dir admissional, dir grad progs; 332nd Eng Co (DT), Kittanning Pa, Co comdr; GEM Presentation Graphics, pres, owner, currently. **Orgs:** Grad adv, Black Stud Union, 1985-87; chair, ed, Am Mktg Asn Newsletter, 1986-87; chmn, educ, Black Stud Union Newsletter, 1987; human rels sub comm, Clarion Univ; Acct Club, Am Mkt Asn; Soc Mil Engrs, 1987; Res Officers Asn, 1989. **Honors/Awds:** Black Stud Union Academy Achievement Award; Grad Assistantship, Clarion Univ Pa, 1985-87. **Home Addr:** 512 Clermont Dr, Harrisburg, PA 17112. **Business Addr:** Project Director, Clarion University of Pennsylvania, PO Box 250, Clarion, PA 16214, **Business Phone:** (814)226-2306.

**MOORE, GEORGE THOMAS**
Scientist. **Personal:** Born Jun 2, 1945, Owensboro, KY; married Peggy Frances Jouett. **Educ:** Ky State Univ, BS, chem & math, 1967; Univ Dayton, MS, inorg chem, 1971; Environ Health Univ Cincinnati Med Ctr, PhD, 1978. **Career:** Monsanto Res Corp Mound Lab, res chemist, 1967-72; US DOE Pittsburgh Energy Tech Ctr, res indust hygienist, 1978-79, chief occup health br, 1979-; US Environ Protection Agency, indust hygenist, task order mgr, currently. **Orgs:** Unity Lodge 115 Price Hall affil, 1963-; Omega Psi Phi Fraternity, 1964-; Am Chem Soc, 1975-; Air Pollution Control Asn, 1977-; Am Indust Hyg Asn, 1978-; supt, Ebenezer Baptist Church Sunday Sch, 1980-. **Home Addr:** 6574 Bluebird Ct, Mason, OH 45040-9725, **Home Phone:** (513)398-8968. **Business Addr:** Task Order Manager, US Environmental Protection Agency, 26 W Martin Luther King Dr, Cincinnati, OH 45268, **Business Phone:** (513)569-7991.

**MOORE, GREGORY B.**
Electronics engineer, manager. **Personal:** Born Mar 27, 1962, New York, NY; son of Vera. **Educ:** Norfolk State Univ, BS, ind educ, elec & electronics engineering, 1987. **Career:** Norfolk State Univ, head resident asst, 1982-86, elec lab asst, 1986-87; Cox Cable Hampton Roads, repair dispatch oper, 1987-88, radio dispatcher, 1988-89; signal leakage auditor, 1989-91; telecommunicator I, 1992-97, help desk tech, 1997-99, network monitoring coordr, 1999-2000, systs opers specialist II (residential), 2000-02; Cox Commun, com test desk tech, 1987-2011, test desk tech, 2000-11, sr systs support opers specialist II (com), 2002-03, sr tech support specialist (telephony), 2003-; Verizon Wireless, govt tech support coordr, 2012-. **Orgs:** Nat Tech Asn, bd dir, 1984-85, stud dir, 1982-88, 1987-89; Stud Nat Asn, pres, 1984-85, 1987-89, stud adv, 1985-86; Norfolk State Univ, SNTA; Stud Asn Norfolk State Univ, cofounder, 1982-86; Concerned Citizens for Polit Educ Norfolk, treas, 1988-; 3rd Dist Deleg, Norfolk City Dem Comt Va, 1996-97; 89th Precinct Chairmen, Norfolk City Dem Comt Va, 1996-99; 89th House Dist Norfolk City Dem Comt, vchair, 1998-2001; 5th Senate Dist Norfolk City Dem Comt Va, vchair, 2001-; Soc Cable Telecommunications Engrs. **Honors/Awds:** Outstanding Young Men of America, 1989; Outstanding Person of the 20th Century, 1998-01. **Special Achievements:** Nominee of Black Engineer of the Year Award, 1989. **Home Addr:** 645 34th St, Norfolk, VA 23508, **Home Phone:** (757)627-2892. **Business Addr:** Senior Technical Support Specialist, Commercial Test Desk Telephony Services, Cox Communications, 4585 Village Ave, Norfolk, VA 23502-2034, **Business Phone:** (757)369-4584.

**MOORE, GWEN**
Chief executive officer, legislator (U.S. state government). **Personal:** Born Detroit, MI; married Ronald Dobson; children: Ronald Dobson II. **Educ:** Calif State Univ, LA, BA, teaching, 1963; Univ Southern Calif, MPA. **Career:** LA County, dep probation officer, 1963-69; Gr LA Comm Action Agency, dir pub affairs & dir personnel, 1969-76; Social Action Res Ctr, LA, consult, 1970-72; LA Community Col, bd trustees, 1975; Compton Community Col, instr, 1975; Inner City Info Syst LA, consult, 1976-77; Calif State Assembly, 1978-94, chairperson assembly subcomm cable TV, 1982, chair assembly utilities & com comm, 1983-94; G & M Commun Group, chief exec officer, currently. **Orgs:** Chmn, Western region, Nat Black Caucus State Legislators; Nat Exec Bd; regional vice chairperson, Nat Conf Legis; Calif Pub Broadcasting Task Force; Common State Govt Orgn & Econ; platform comm, Dem Nat Comm; Calif Elected Women's Asn Educ & Res; Dem Women's Forum; LA Coalition 100 Black Women; Nat Women's Polit Caucus; YWCA; United Negro Col Fund; Calif Legis Black Caucus; regional dir, Women's Network Nat Caucus State Legis; secy, Nat Orgn Black Elected Legis Women; Calif Assembly, 1978-94; chmn, prestigious Assembly Utilities & Com Comt; Nat Conf State Legislatures; chmn, State-Fed Assembly; chmn, Nat Conf State Legislatures Nat Comt Telecommunications; Nat Asn Advan Colored People 1st vpres CA/HI State Conf; bd dir, LAAAW Pub Policy Inst; Nat Asn Minorities Cable's; US Dept Com;Nat Asn Advan Colored People Legal Defense Fund; Prof Commun Asn; Calif Independent Gas Producers Asn; Calif Trucking Asn; Calif Hunger Action Coalition; S Coast Air Qual Mgt Dist. **Special Achievements:** Member of National Board of Directors National Association for the Advancement of Colored People; Member of California State Bar Board of Trustees. **Home Addr:** 1089 S Redondo Blvd, Los Angeles, CA 90008. **Business Addr:** President, GEM Communications Group Goverment Affairs Firm, 4201 Wilshire Blvd Suite 615, Los Angeles, CA 90010, **Business Phone:** (323)954-3777.

**MOORE, DR. HAROLD EARL, JR.**
Physician, educator, association executive. **Personal:** Born Sep 5, 1954, San Antonio, TX; son of Harold Earl Sr and Barbara Stewart. **Educ:** Fla A&M Univ, attended 1976; Morehouse Col, BS, pre-med & biol, 1979; Morehouse Sch Med, attended 1983; Howard Univ, Col Med, MD, 1985; Morehouse Sch Med, Dept Family Med, fac develop fel, 1995. **Career:** Fla State Univ, Dept Psychol & Neuro-Histol, lab technician, res, Dr Karen Berkley, 1974-75; Cornell Univ Col Pharmacol, lab technician, 1979-80; Harlem Hosp, Gen Surg Internship, 1985-86; Morehouse Sch Med, family pract residency, 1986-88, physician, 2000-15; Ga Reg Hosp, Atlanta, ER physician, 1988-89; Fulton County Teen Clinics, physician, 1988-89; Sterling Grp, ER physician, 1989-95; Stewart Webster Rural Health Inc, physician, 1989-91; Southeastern Health Servs Inc, physician, 1991; Emory Healthcare, physician, 1994-, asst prof, currently; pvt pract, currently; GNLD, physician, 2000-12. **Orgs:** Am Acad Family Physicians, 1987-; Ga State Med Asn, 1988-; Am Med Asn, 1989-; Ga Acad Family Physicians, 1983-; Nat Med Asn, 1987-; Morehouse Sch Med Nat Alumni Asn, 1983, pres, 1993; Howard Univ Col Med Alumni Asn, 1985-; Kappa Alpha Psi Fraternity, 1989-. **Honors/Awds:** Deans Leadership Award, Morehouse Sch Med, 1982; Fellow of American Academy of Family Physicians, 1994; Outstanding Young Doctor Award, Dollar & Sense Mag, 1991; Honorary doctor of medicine, Morehouse Sch Med, 2000. **Home Addr:** 11 Dunwoody Pk Suite 150, Atlanta, GA 30338, **Home Phone:** (404)778-6920. **Business Addr:** Physician, Emory Healthcare, 2764 Candler Rd, Decatur, GA 30034, **Business Phone:** (404)778-8669.

**MOORE, HAZEL STAMPS**
Librarian. **Personal:** Born Jan 10, 1924, Learned, MS; daughter of Andrew Stamps and Seretha Hicks Stamps; married Wilbur D; children: Wibur Dexter & Debra M Carter. **Educ:** Southern Christian Inst Jr Col, cert, 1945; Tougaloo Col, BA, 1947; Atlanta Univ, MS, libr sci, 1955; Wash Univ, St Louis, Mo; Xavier Univ; La State Univ; Univ New Orleans; Tulane Univ. **Career:** Librn (retired); Tougaloo Col, librn, 1947; Oakley Trng Sch, teacher, librn, 1947-49; Tougaloo Col, Prep Sch, teacher & from asst librn to librn, 1949-57; Booker T Wash High Sch, head librn, 1957-61, 1962-66 & 1967-72; St Louis Pub Libr, sr ref librn, 1961-62; New Orleans Pub Schs, Proj 1089-B, 1095-A & 1200-G, asst supvr, 1966-67; Marion Abramson High Sch, head librn, 1972-91; New Orleans Pub Schs, Adult Educ Ctr, intern; One Church One Sch, Cent Congregational United Church Christ, dir, 1990-93; Wider Church Ministry, Global Ministries, bd mem; United Church Christ, leader. **Orgs:** Numerous memberships in various organizations including Am Libr Asn; Am Asn Sch Librarians; La Libr Asn; La Asn Sch Librarians; Catholic Libr Asn, Greater New Orleans Unit, 1958-91; La Asn Educ Commun & Technol; La Asn Comput Users Educr; United Teachers New Orleans Retired Chap; Southern Asn Cols & Schs Teams; Nat Coun Negro Women; Tougoloo Alumnae Club; Snacirema Club. **Honors/Awds:** PTA Outstanding Service Award, Abramson; Guidance Department Award, Landry; Modisette Award, La Libr Asn; Spec Citation, US Dept Educ. **Special Achievements:** Author, How to Conduct a Dial-an-Author Program, LLA Bulletin, 1989. **Home Addr:** 5931 Cong Dr, New Orleans, LA 70126, **Home Phone:** (504)282-0184.

**MOORE, HELEN D. S.**
Educator, founder (originator). **Personal:** Born Jan 21, 1932, Baldwyn, MS; married Elijah; children: Michelle, Pamela & Elijah. **Educ:** Miss Indust Col, BA, 1951; Tenn State Univ, MS, 1957; Delta State Univ, educ specialist, 1977. **Career:** Teacher (retired), clergy; Eastern Mich Univ, NSG grant, 1963; Greenville Munic Sch Dist, elem prin, 1975-90; AME Church, ordained minister, 1994; Day spring Ministries Inc, founder & pres, currently. **Orgs:** Voter Reg; Polit Camp; Ad Hoc Comm; lectr, Wash Co Polit Action Comm; pres, YWCA, 1950-51; pres, Greenville Teacher Asn; pres, Miss Asn Educ, 1978-79; youth adv, St Voter Reg; Polit Camp; Ad Hoc Comm; youth adv, St Matthew AME Church, 1977; adv, Teenette Art & Civic Club; Mod Art & Civic Club, Nat Asn Advan Colored People, Nat Fed Colored Womens Club; bd dir, NEA, 1984-88; pastor, Disney Chapel AME Church; Greenville Area Chamber Com. **Home Addr:** 3583 Forest Dr, Greenville, MS 38703, **Home Phone:** (662)334-9914. **Business Addr:** Founder, President, Dayspring Ministries Inc, 3583 Forest Dr, Greenville, MS 38703, **Business Phone:** (662)334-9914.

**MOORE, HERMAN JOSEPH**
Actor, football player, president (organization). **Personal:** Born Oct 20, 1969, Danville, VA; married Angela; children: Aaron & Ashton. **Educ:** Univ Va, BA, rhet & communs studies, 1991. **Career:** Football player (retired), executive, actor; Detroit Lions, wide receiver, 1991-2000; HJM Enterprises, pres & chief exec officer, 2001-; NY Giants, wide receiver, 2002; AH!MOORE Int Caf, owner, 2002-; Films: Jerry Maguire, 1996; Wahoowa: The History of Virginia Cavalier Football, 2010. **Orgs:** Founder, Catch 84 Found. **Honors/Awds:** Second-Team All-Pro, 1994; Pro Bowl Selection, 1994-97; Offensive Most Valuable Player, Detroit Lions, 1995; True Value & NFL Man of the Year, Detroit Lions, 1995-96; First Team All-Pro, 1995-97; All-Iron Award, 1998. **Special Achievements:** He was the second player to have three 100-catch seasons. **Business Addr:** President, Chief Executive Officer, HJM Enterprises, 2600 Auburn Rd, Auburn Hills, MI 48326, **Business Phone:** (248)853-3945.

**MOORE, HOWARD, JR. (HOWARD T MOORE)**
Lawyer. **Personal:** Born Feb 28, 1932, Atlanta, GA; son of Howard Sr and Bessie Sims; married Jane Bond; children: Grace, Constance & Kojo. **Educ:** Morehouse Col, BA, polit sci 1954; Boston Univ, LLB, 1960. **Career:** Moore & Lawrence, atty; Hollowell, Ward, Moore & Alexander, partner; Nat Asn Advan Colored People, lawyer; Angela Davis, atty, 1971-77; Nat Bar Asn, 1986. **Orgs:** Nat Conf Black Lawyers; Charles Houston Law Club; Nat Lawyers Guild; Nat Emergency Civil Liberties Com; Am Civil Liberties Union; Fedn Southern Co op; gen counr, Stud Nonviolent Coord Comt; State Bar Ca, 2009. **Honors/Awds:** Martin Luther King Jr Award, Howard Univ, 1972; Distinguished Son Morehouse Col, 1973; Centennial Award, Boston Univ, 1973; Distinguished Service, Nat Col Advocacy, Asn Am Trial Lawyers, 1975. **Home Addr:** 1880 San Pedro Ave, Berkeley, CA 94707, **Home Phone:** (510)525-7249. **Business Addr:** Attorney, Moore & Moore, 445 Bellevue Ave 3rd Fl, Oakland, CA 94610-4923, **Business Phone:** (510)451-0104.

**MOORE, JANE BOND**
Lawyer. **Personal:** Born Sep 1, 1938, Nashville, TN; daughter of Horace Mann and Julia Hynes Washington; married Howard Jr; children: Grace, Constance & Kojo. **Educ:** Spelman Col Atlanta, BA, psychol, mathematics, 1959; Boalt Hall Univ Calif, JD, 1975. **Career:** So Regional Coun, res asst, 1961-63; So Christian Leadership Conf, res asst, 1963-64; Moore & Bell, assoc atty, 1975-76; Open Rd, admin, 1976-77; Bank Calif, asst coun, 1977-80; Fed Trade Comn, San Francisco, Calif, atty, 1990-2001; Moore & Moore Attorneys Law, Oakland, Calif, partner, 1983-90, owner; Oakland Unified Sch Dist, Oakland, Calif, assoc coun, 1990-2001, dep gen coun, 1995-2001; pvt pract, 2001-; John F Kennedy Sch Law, fac, currently; Notre Dame de Namur Univ, lectr hisotry & polit sci, 2004-. **Orgs:** Southern Regional Coun; Stud Nonviolent Coord Comt; Charles Houston Bar Asn; Labor & Employ Sect State Bar Calif; Calif Law Asn; Nat Law Asn, Alameda County Bar Asn. **Home Addr:** 1880 San Pedro Ave, Berkeley, CA 94707. **Business Addr:** Lecturer, Notre Dame de Namur University, 1500 Ralston Ave Ralston Hall 307, Belmont, CA 94002, **Business Phone:** (650)508-3796.

**MOORE, DR. JEAN E.**
Television producer, educator, radio host. **Personal:** Born New York, NY; daughter of Hugh Campbell and Theodora Campbell; married Robert M Jr; children: Robert III & Doreen Moore-Closson. **Educ:** Hunter Col, BA; Bryn Mawr Col, MSS; Temple Univ, EdD, 1978.

**Career:** Vet Admin, Pa, Clin Social Work Serv, asst chief; Redevelop Auth City Philadelphia, social work specialist; Model Cities US Dept Housing & Urban Develop, human serv adv; Temple Univ, Sch Soc Admin, assoc prof, 1969-89, assoc prof emer, currently; Cheyney Univ, Pa, exec asst to pres, 1985-91; Univ Md Eastern Shore, Princess Anne, MD, vpres inst advan, 1991-97; WESM-FM, radio host, 1994-97; WRTI-Temple Univ, Univ Forum, creator, host & exec producer, 1997-. **Orgs:** Nat Asn Social Workers; Acad Cert Soc Workers; Coun Soc Work Educ; Pa Black Conf Higher Educ; team chairperson & team mem, Comn Higher Educ, Mid States Asn Col & Schs; Act 101 reviewer & eval Commonwealth Pa; US Dept Educ; reviewer & pres, Spectrum Health Serv; bd dir comm, Y Eastern Del County; chairperson, Fair Housing Coun Suburban Philadelphia; elder, Lansdowne Presby Church; Delta Sigma Theta Sorority; Phi Delta Kappa; Phi Beta Kappa; bd trustee, Community Col Philadelphia; LackawannaJr Col; bd, C's Serv Inc; int bd adv, Radio Peace Int; Alpha Chi Alpha. **Home Addr:** 10 Hemlock Rd, Lansdowne, PA 19050, **Home Phone:** (610)259-3080. **Business Addr:** Host, Executive Producer, Temple University Public Radio-WRTI, 1509 Cecil B Moore Ave 3rd Fl, Philadelphia, PA 19121-3410, **Business Phone:** (215)204-8405.

## MOORE, JERALD CHRISTOPHER

Football player. **Personal:** Born Nov 20, 1974, Houston, TX. **Educ:** Univ Okla. **Career:** Football player (retired); St Louis Rams, running back, 1996-98; New Orleans Saints, running back, 2000.

## MOORE, REV. DR. JERRY ALEXANDER, JR.

Executive, clergy. **Personal:** Born Jun 12, 1918, Minden, LA; son of Jerry Alexander Sr and Mae Dee; married Ettyce Hill; children: Jerry III & Juran D. **Educ:** Morehouse Col, BA, 1940; Howard Univ, BD, 1943, MA, 1957. **Career:** Clergy (retired), executive; Nineteenth St Baptist Church, pastor, 1946-94, pator emer; Howard Univ, Baptist chaplain, 1958; Wash Baptist Sem, 1964; Conf Minority Transp Officials, co-founder, 1971; DC, councilman, 1975-85; Home Mission Bd, NBC, exec secy, 1985-97; Home Mission Bd, Nat Baptist Conv, exec secy, 1985-97. **Orgs:** Co-founder, Conf Minority Transp Officials, 1971; pres, Baptist Conv Wash DC & Vincinity; pres, Int Soc Christian Endwavor; pres, Wash Metro Area Coun Govts; chair, Pub Works Com DC Coun; Rock Creek E Civic Asn; Nat Asn Advan Colored People; Pigskin Club; Urban League; Capitol City Rep Club; mem-at-large, Coun Dist Columbia. **Honors/Awds:** Washington Area Contractors Award, 1971; Nat Asn Advan Colored People Service Award, 1972; Capitol City Rep Club Lincoln Award, 1974; Minority Transportation Officials Award, 1986. **Home Addr:** 1612 Buchanan St NW, Washington, DC 20011-4216, **Home Phone:** (202)882-3127. **Business Addr:** Pastor Emeritus, Nineteenth Street Baptist Church, 4606 16th St NW, Washington, DC 20011, **Business Phone:** (202)829-2773.

## MOORE, JESSE A.

Automotive executive, business owner, chief executive officer. **Educ:** Wayne State Univ, BA, bus admin & mgt, 1967. **Career:** Moores Auto Body & Paint Inc, pres, 1972-; Warner Robins Olds-Cadillac-Pontiac-GMC, chief exec officer & owner, 1991-. **Orgs:** Metropolitan Bus League; Gen Motors Minority Dealer Develop prog. **Business Addr:** President, Moore's Auto Body & Paint Inc, 401 W Broad St, Richmond, VA 23220, **Business Phone:** (804)649-2671.

## MOORE, JOHN BRIAN (JOHNNY MOORE)

Basketball player. **Personal:** Born Mar 3, 1958, Altoona, PA; married Natalie. **Educ:** Univ Tex, Austin, TX, phys educ, 1979. **Career:** Basketball player (retired), basketball coach; San Antonio Spurs, 1980-87; NJ Nets, 1987; San Antonio Spurs, 1989-90; Tulsa Fast Breakers, 1989; Girona, 1992; Austin Ice, coach, currently; Fresno Heatwave, coach, 2004-05; NBA D-League, asst coach, 2010-11; S Tex Stingrays, head coach, 2013; Am Basketball League, Corpus Christi Clutch, head coach, currently. **Business Addr:** Coach, Austin Ice, Austin, TX 78701, **Business Phone:** (704)855-7795.

## MOORE, JOHN WESLEY, JR.

Executive, vice president (organization). **Personal:** Born Mar 10, 1948, Martins Ferry, OH; married Brenda Scott; children: Kelly Shannon, Ryan Wesley, Johnathan Morgan & Nicholas Patrick. **Educ:** W Liberty State Col, BA, 1970; WVa Univ, Morgantown, MA, 1972. **Career:** Bridgeport High Sch, teacher, 1970-71; W Liberty State Col, dir coun ctr & asst dir financial aids, adj instr, 1971-76; WesBanco Inc, dir personnel, 1976-80, vpres personnel human resources, 1980-86, vpres personnel, 1986-93, sr vpres personnel & human resources, 1993-2002, exec vpres human resources, 2002-. **Orgs:** Consult, Ctr Creative Comm, 1974-75; bd dir, Big Bros Big Sisters Wheeling, 1976-77; consult, No Panhandle Ment Health Ctr Wheeling, 1977-79; adv bd, Ohio County Bd Voc Educ, 1977-; bd trustee, OH Valley Med Ctr, 1979; bd dir, Am Inst Banking Wheeling Chap, 1979-; Ambassadors Club Wheeling Area C C, 1979-; adv comn, Upper Ohio Valley Employer Wheeling, 1979-80; pres & bd mem, Salvation Army, 1980; bd mem, Ohio Valley Bus Indust CMS. **Home Addr:** 7 Forest Hills, Wheeling, WV 26003. **Business Addr:** Executive Vice President Human Resources, WesBanco Inc, 1 Bank Plz, Wheeling, WV 26003, **Business Phone:** (304)234-9000.

## MOORE, JOHNNIE ADOLPH

Government official. **Personal:** Born Sep 28, 1929, Cuero, TX; son of Nelson and Eva Jones; married Tommye Dalphine Jordan; children: Carmalie Budgewater. **Educ:** Tuskegee Inst, AL, BS, 1950; George Williams Col, MS, 1957. **Career:** Int Personnel Mgt Asn, Chicago, IL, ed, 1963-66; US Dept Labor Chicago, IL, pub affil officer, 1966-67; US Civil Serv Comn, Wash, DC, pub affil officer, 1967-79; Bowie State Col, Bowie, MD, asst pres, 1980-82; US Off Personnel Mgt Wash, DC, pub affil officer, 1979-83; Am Nurses Asn, dir mkt & pub affil div, 1984-85; US Nuclear Regulatory Comn, pub affairs officer, 1985-90; US Dept Treas, Bur Engraving & Printing, Wash, DC, pub affairs mgr, 1990-93, pub rels consult. **Orgs:** Bur ed, Norfolk J & Guide, 1958-59; night ed, Chicago Daily Defender, 1959-61; info specialist, Pres Comn Gov't Contracts, 1960-61; asst exec dir, Nat Ins Asn, 1961-62; pres, Capital Press Club, Wash, DC, 1972-74; Pub Rel Soc Am, 1977-; vis prof, NUL Black Exec Exchange Prog, 1978-; state coordr, Am Asn Retired Persons, 1997-; Kappa Alpha Psi Fraternity. **Honors/Awds:** Pearlie Cox Harrison Award, Capital Press Club, 1974; Image Maker Award, Nat Asn Media Women, 1976; Albert Gallatin Award, Treasury Dept, 1993. **Home Addr:** 2212 Westview Ct, Silver Spring, MD 20910-1325, **Home Phone:** (301)587-6825.

## MOORE, JOHNNY BELLE

Guitarist, singer, songwriter. **Personal:** Born Jan 24, 1950, Clarksdale, MS; son of Floyd. **Career:** Delmark Rec, singer & guitarist, currently; Albums: The Earthshaker, 1978; Hard Times, 1987; Lonesome Blues Chicago Blues Session, 1993; Johnny B Moore, 1996; Live at Blue Chicago, 1996; Troubled World, 1997; 911 Blues, 1997; Acoustic Blue Chicago, 1999; Born in Clarksdale, 2001; Rockin in the Same Old Boat, 2003. **Orgs:** Koko Taylor's backing band, 1970. **Business Addr:** Singer, Guitarist, Delmark Records, 4121 N Rockwell St, Chicago, IL 60618, **Business Phone:** (773)539-5001.

## MOORE, DR. JOSSIE A.

Educator, chairperson. **Personal:** Born Aug 20, 1947, Jackson, TN; married Jimmy L; children: Juan & Jerry. **Educ:** Lane Col, BA, 1971; Memphis State Univ, ME, 1975, EdD, 1986. **Career:** Lane Col, secy & dir AV, 1970-74; Memphis State Univ, Memphis City Sch, teacher corps intern, 1974-75; Lauderdale Co Sch, resource teacher, 1975-76; Covington City Sch, spec educ teacher, 1976-77; State Tech Inst, chmn, develop reading & writing, prof reading, 1999-2002; Southwest Tenn Community Col, prof develop studies & reading, currently. **Orgs:** Secy, PTA Lincoln Sch, 1973-74; NEA, 1977-83; secy, adminr, vpres, Stimulus Toastmasters, 1978-84; consult, Fed Corrections Inst, 1978-79; rep, Parent Adv Comn, 1979-82; consult, Expert Secretarial Serv, 1981-84; Sigma Gamma Rho; AUA; TEA, SCETC; CRLA. **Honors/Awds:** Hon Mention, Third World Writer's Contest, 1979; Best Regional Bullet, Toastmasters Regional, 1981-82. **Special Achievements:** Book: "Practical Reading", 2002. **Home Addr:** 2073 Leichester Lane, Bartlett, TN 38134-6961, **Home Phone:** (901)386-8016. **Business Addr:** Professor Developmental Studies & Reading, Southwest Tennessee Community College, 5983 Macon Cove, Memphis, TN 38134, **Business Phone:** (901)333-5000.

## MOORE, JULIETTE R.

School administrator. **Personal:** Born Sep 30, 1953, New Orleans, LA; daughter of Frank G. **Educ:** Xavier Univ, New Orleans, BS, health & phys educ/fitness, 1975; Univ W Fla, MS, leisure studies, 1977. **Career:** Educator (retired); Univ W Fla, grad teaching asst, 1975-76, sports club coordr, 1975-76, asst dir recreation & sports, 1976-84; Ariz State Univ, asst dir recreation, intramural sports & sports clubs, 1985-89; James Madison Univ, assoc dir stud activ prog & recreation, 1989-91; Northern Ill Univ, dir campus recreation, 1991-97; Ariz Univ, dir, Campus Recreation, 1997-10; Univ W Fla, sr off specialist, 2012-. **Orgs:** Ariz Coll Personnel Asn, 1988-89; Nat Asn Campus Activ, 1989-91; Nat Asn Stud Personnel Admin, 1989; fac adv, Zeta Phi Beta Sorority Inc, 1991-. **Home Addr:** 209 Pardridge Pl Apt 1, DeKalb, IL 60115-4638. **Business Addr:** Senior Office Specialist, University of West Florida, 11000 Univ Pkwy, Pensacola, FL 32514, **Business Phone:** (850)474-2000.

## MOORE, KATHERINE BELL

Executive, government official. **Personal:** Born Nov 30, 1941, Norfolk, VA; daughter of William Grant Bell and Katherine Scott Bell-Weller; children: Ira Braswell IV & Katherine Larilee. **Educ:** Univ NC, Wilmington, BA, eng, speech & theater, 1973. **Career:** Mecklenberg & Cent Piedmont Community Col, prof, 1972-73; Cape Fear Community Col, teacher, 1973-74; Fairfax County Schs, teacher, 1974-77; Eastern Transp Serv Inc, pres, chief exec officer, 1977-2002; City Wilmington, mayor pro-tem, 1992-2002; freelance writer, 2002-09; Writing For Others, freelance writer, 2007-. **Orgs:** Numerous mem incl chair, New Hanover County Human Rels Comt, 1980-83; vice chair, New Hanover Dept Social Serv, 1980-82; adv bd, Duke Univ LEAD Prog, 1980-82; bd mem, Govs Comn Econ Develop, 1982-84; bd mem, Lt Gov's Comn Jobs, 1984-86; trustee, Univ NC Ctr Pub Tv, 1990-; bd dir, Carolina Savings Bank, 1986-; Wilmington City Coun. **Home Addr:** 4311 Appleton Way, Wilmington, NC 28412, **Home Phone:** (910)395-1510.

## MOORE, KENYA SUMMER

Actor, fashion model. **Personal:** Born Jan 24, 1971, Detroit, MI; daughter of Ronald Grant and Patricia. **Educ:** Wayne State Univ, Detroit, Mich, child psychol. **Career:** Actress & producer, currently; Moore Vision Media, founder, 2008. Films: Waiting to Exhale, 1995; Senseless, 1998; Trois, 2000; No Turning Back, 2001; Hot Parts, 2003; Deliver Us from Eva, 2003; Nas: Video Anthology Vol. 1, 2004; Resurrection: The J.R. Richard Story, 2005; Brothers in Arms, 2005; Cloud 9, 2006, I Know Who Killed Me, 2007; Haitian Nights, dir, writer, 2009; Trapped: Haitian Nights, producer, actress, 2009, 2010; The Confidant, producer, actress, 2010; Dolls of Voodoo, 2013; Sharknado: The 4th Awakens, 2016. TV episodes: "The Fresh Prince of Bel-Air", 1994; "Martin", 1996; "Homeboys in Outer Space", 1996; "Sparks", 1997; "Smart Guy", 1997; "Living Single", 1997; "Damon", 1998; "The Steve Harvey Show", 1998; "Nubian Goddess", 1997; "The Parent Hood", 1998-99; "The Jamie Foxx Show", 1999; "In the House", 1999; "Men, Women & Dogs", 2001; "The Parkers", 2002; "Girlfriends", 2004; "Brothers in Arms", 2005; "Under One Roof", 2008; "Meet The Browns", 2009; "The Real Housewives of Atlanta", 2012-; "Walk This Way", 2013; "Celebrity Apprentice", 2014-15; "The Millionaire Matchmaker", 2015. **Orgs:** Founder, Kenya Moore found. **Honors/Awds:** Miss Michigan USA, 1993; Miss USA, 1993. **Special Achievements:** Second African-American to gain both Miss Mich & Miss USA titles, 1993. Book: Game, Get Some, Dark Horse Productions, 2007. **Business Addr:** Actress, SMS Talent, c/o lan, Los Angeles, CA 90069.

## MOORE, KERWIN LAMAR

Baseball player. **Personal:** Born Oct 29, 1970, Detroit, MI. **Career:** Baseball player (retired); Kans City Royals, outfielder, 1988-92; Fla-Marlins, 1993; Oakland Athletics, outfielder, 1996. **Honors/Awds:** Rookie of the Year, 1996.

## MOORE, KEVIN (KEB MO)

Writer, singer, guitarist. **Personal:** Born Oct 3, 1951, Los Angeles, CA; children: one son. **Career:** Albums: Rainmaker, 1980; Keb'Mo', 1994; Just Like You, 1996; Slow Down, 1998; The Door, 2000; Big Wide Grin, 2001; contributor, When Love Speaks: Sonnets of Shakespeare, 2002; The Blues, 2003; Keep It Simple, 2004; Peace Back by Popular Demand; Suitcase, 2006; Live & Mo, 2009. **Honors/Awds:** Blues Artist of the Year, 1996; Grammy Award, Best Contemporary Blues Album, 1996, 1998, 2004. **Business Addr:** Singer & Songwriter, Guitarist, Keb' Mo' Music Merchandise, PO Box 210023, San Francisco, CA 94121.

## MOORE, LARRY LOUIS

Educator. **Personal:** Born Jul 21, 1954, Kings Mountain, NC. **Educ:** Western Carolina Univ, BA, 1978; Grad Sch Univ NC, Charlotte, NC, attended 1980. **Career:** Cleveland Tech Col, instr black hist & world civilization, 1979-81; S W Jr High Sch, teacher chmn & foreign lang dept. **Orgs:** NEA & NCEA 1982-84; Nc Coun Teachers Mathematics, 1983-84; chmn, Stud Activ Comn, 1984-85; sec, Parents & Teachers Org, 1985-87; Nat Asn Advan Colored People, 1987. **Home Addr:** 808 Phillips Dr, Kings Mountain, NC 28086, **Home Phone:** (704)739-8640.

## MOORE, LARRY MACEO

Football coach, football player. **Personal:** Born Jun 1, 1975, San Diego, CA. **Educ:** Grossmont Col, El Cajon, grad; Brigham Young Univ, bus mgt. **Career:** Indianapolis Colts, right guard & left guard, 1998, 2000-01, corner, 1999; Wash Redskins, corner & left guard, 2002-03; Cincinnati Bengals, corner & left guard, 2004, 2005; Univ Incarnate Word, offensive asst coach, currently. **Honors/Awds:** Rookie of the Year, 1998. **Business Addr:** Offensive Assistant Coach, University of the Incarnate Word, 4301 Broadway St, San Antonio, TX 78209, **Business Phone:** (210)829-6000.

## MOORE, LENARD DUANE

Consultant, educator, poet. **Personal:** Born Feb 13, 1958, Jacksonville, NC; son of Rogers Edward and Mary Louise Pearson; married Marcille Lynn; children: Maiisha. **Educ:** Coastal Carolina Community Col, attended 1978; Univ Md, attended 1981; Shaw Univ, BA, lib studies, 1995; NC A&T State Univ, MA, eng, 1997. **Career:** Freelance, lectr & workshop conductor, 1981-; Black Writer Chicago, mag consult, 1982-83; Pac Quart Moana Hamilton Nz, actg adv, 1982-83; Int Black Writers Conf Inc, Chicago, regional dir, 1982-83; Mira Mesa Br Libr, San Diego, Calif, poet-in-residence, 1983; NC Dept Pub Instr, educ media technician, 1984-95; United Arts Coun, Raleigh, NC, writer residence, 1987-93; Enloe High Sch, Raleigh, NC, eng teacher, 1995-96; NC State Univ, Eng Dept, vis lectr, 1997, prof eng, currently; Mt Olive Col, asst prof, assoc prof, currently; Shaw Univ, adj prof, currently; NC State Univ Raleigh; NC A&T State Univ-Greensboro. Poets: Poems of Love & Understanding, 1982; The Open Eye, 1985; Forever Home, 1992; Desert Storm: A Brief History, 1993. **Orgs:** Kuumba Festival Community; Nat Asn Advan Colored People; Onslow Co Br, 1982; bd dir, Int Black Writers Conf Inc, 1982; Toastmasters Int, 1982-84; exec comt, NC Haiku Soc 1983-; bd mem, Marshall Chapel Missionary Baptist Church, 1984-85; Poetry Soc Am; Acad Am Poets; World Poetry Soc; NC Poetry Soc; Poets Study Club Terra Haute, NC Writers Network; Int Platform Assoc; Poetry Coun NC Inc; pres, Haiku Soc Am; WV Poetry Soc; Raleigh Writing Alliance; NC Writers Conf, 1989-; Nat Bk Critics Cir, 1989-; founder & exec dir, Carolina African Am Writers Collective, 1992-; exec chmn, NC Haiku Soc, 1995-96; bd dir, La Jan Productions, 1995-; Alpha Chi Nat Col Hon Scholar Soc, 1995; co-founder, Wash St Writers Group. **Special Achievements:** First African American president of the Haiku Society of America. **Home Addr:** 5625 Continental Way, Raleigh, NC 27610, **Home Phone:** (919)231-8536. **Business Addr:** Associate Professor, University of Mount Olive, 634 Henderson St, Mount Olive, NC 28365, **Business Phone:** (919)658-2502.

## MOORE, LENNY EDWARD (LEONARD EDWARD MOORE)

Administrator, football player. **Personal:** Born Nov 25, 1933, Reading, PA; son of George and Virginia; married Francis; married Erma; children: Lenny, Leslie, Carol, Toni & Terri; married Edith. **Educ:** Pa State Univ, attended 1956. **Career:** Football player (retired), administrator; Nittany Lions, hon capt, 1953-55; WSID-RADIO, disc jockey sports dir, 1956-58; Baltimore Colts, prof football, kick return, 1956-67; pub rels nat brewery, 1958-63; WWIN Radio, sports dir, 1962-64; NW Ayer & Sons, field rep, 1970-74; Baltimore Colts Football Inc, prom dir, 1975-84; resource consult, 1984-; Juvenile Serv Admin State Md, staff, 1984-; prog specialist, 1989; crisis intervention counr, 1991. **Orgs:** Chmn, Heart Asn; Camp Concern; analyst, CBS Pro-Football, 1968; assoc Leukemia, Kidney Found, Mult Sclerosis, Muscular Dystrophy, Spec Olympics, 1975-; adv coun Juv Justice, 1985; bd dir, Door, 1991; Gov's Adv Comt Violence Schs, 1994; Pigskin Club Wash. **Honors/Awds:** NFL Rookie of The Year, 1956; Pro Bowl, 1956, 1958-62, 1964; First-team All-Pro, 1958-61, 1964; NFL champion, 1958, 1959; NFL Most Valuable Player, 1964; NFL Comeback Player of the Year, 1964; Pro Football Hall Fame, 1975; PEN, Hall Fame, 1976; East-West Shrine Game Hall of Fame, 2009. **Special Achievements:** Moore was ranked number 71 on The Sporting News' list of the 100 Greatest Football Players, 1999; The only player to have at least 40 receiving touchdowns and 40 rushing touchdowns. **Home Addr:** 8815 Stonehaven Rd, Randallstown, MD 21133-4223, **Home Phone:** (410)655-6239. **Business Addr:** Worker, Maryland Department Juvenile Justice, Liberty & Fayette St, Baltimore, MD 21203, **Business Phone:** (410)230-3268.

## MOORE, LEWIS CALVIN

Labor activist, president (organization). **Personal:** Born Jun 22, 1935, Canton, MS; son of Sam A and Louvenia McGee; married Delores Thurman; children: Kelly, Thurman & Anderson. **Educ:** Manual HS Indianapolis, IN, 1954. **Career:** Oil Chem & Atomic Workers Local 7-706, pres, 1970-75; Oil Chem & Atomic Workers Dist Coun 7, pres, 1970-75; OCAW Dist 4 Houston, int rep, 1975-77; Oil Chem & Atomic Workers Wash Off, citizenship-legis dir, 1977-79; Oil Chem & Atomic Workers Int Union, legis dir & sr vpres. **Orgs:** Labor instr,

Univ Ind; charter mem, Nat bd mem, A Philip Randolph Inst; Nat Asn Advan Colored People; bd mem, Big Brothers Am; leader Boy Scouts Am; Tex Black Alcoholism Coun; instr, Health & Safety Seminars Kenya, 1984-88; Drugs in Contemporary Soc. **Home Addr:** 4177 S Sebring Ct, Denver, CO 80237-2164, **Home Phone:** (303)779-8789. **Business Addr:** Vice President, OCAW International Union, PO Box 2812, Denver, CO 80201, **Business Phone:** (303)987-2229.

**MOORE, LIZ. See MOORE, DR. ELIZABETH D.**

## MOORE, DR. LOIS JEAN

Executive. **Personal:** Born Oct 12, 1935, Bastrop, TX; daughter of Coronza and Cecelia; married Harold; children: Yolanda E. **Educ:** Prairie View A&M Univ, Sch Nursing, Prairie View, TX, nursing dipl, 1957; Tex Woman's Univ, Houston, TX, BS, nursing, 1970; Tex Southern Univ, Houston, TX, MEd, 1974. **Career:** Harris County Hosp Dist-Ben Taub Gen Hosp, Houston, Tex, shift supvr, 1962-68, asst dir nursing serv, 1968-77, adminr, 1977-87, exec vpres, 1987-89, chief exec officer, 1987-99, pres, 1989-99; Jefferson Davis Hosp, chief exec officer, 1988-2001; Univ Tex, Harris County Psychiat Hosp, chief adminr, 2000-13; Prairie View A&M Univ, Prairie View, interim dean. **Orgs:** Bd dir & fel, Am Col Healthcare Exec, 1987-; bd mem, Nat Asn Pub & Non Profit Hosps; bd mem, Tex Asn Pub Hosp; bd mem, March Dimes Gulf Coast; chairperson, Houston Crackdown Treat & Res Comt; Am Red Cross; United Way; bd dir, Brit Socs for Neuroendocrinology; bd dir, Med Socs; bd dir, Learning House for Develop; bd mem, chair, audit & prog comt, bd trustee, MHMRA, 2013-; adv bd, Frost Bank; Houstan C Charity. **Home Addr:** 3730 S Macgregor Way, Houston, TX 77021-1506, **Home Phone:** (713)523-2272. **Business Addr:** Board Of Trustee, Chair, Audit Committee & Program Committee, MHMRA of Harris County, 9401 SW Freeway, Houston, TX 77074, **Business Phone:** (713)970-7000.

## MOORE, M. ELIZABETH GIBBS

Librarian. **Personal:** Born Boston, MA; daughter of Warmoth T and Marece A Jones (deceased). **Educ:** NC A&T State Univ, attended 1940; Univ Chicago, BLS, 1945, grad study, 1949. **Career:** Librn (retired); NC A&T State Univ, instr, 1940-43; NC A&T State Univ, asst librn, 1943-44; Fisk Univ, cataloger, 1945-48, Libr Sci, instr, 1945-46; Detroit Pub Libr, cataloger, 1945-53; Detroit Pub Libr, ref librn, 1953-54, cataloging supvr, 1955-67; Burroughs Corp, Detroit area librn, 1967-71; Corp Libr Burroughs Corp, 1971-79; Libr MI Bell, hr supvr, 1979-82, libr consult, 1982-85. **Orgs:** Women's Econ Club Detroit, 1967-82; Women's Econ Club, Spec Librs Asn; Am Libr Asn, YWCA, Womens Nat Bk Asn; Your Heritage House, 1969-; Friends Detroit Pub Libr, 1970-76, 1980-82; bd dir, Delta Home Girls, 1974-76; Ctrl Adv Comn Re-Accreditation Wayne State Univ, div Libr Sci, 1975-76; Adv Grp Selection Head Sci Libr, Wayne State Univ, 1976-77; bd dir, Spec librs Asn, 1981-84; Delta Sigma Theta, Nat Asn Advan Colored People; adv coun, NC Cent Univ, Sch Libr & Info Serv, 1981-88, mem, 1988-, rec secy, 1990-; Friends Sch Educ, NC A&T State Univ; Guilford County, Bd Soc Serv, 1984-87, 1988-90; bd dir, Charlotte Hawkins Brown Hist Found, 1985-; Libr Serv & Construct Act Adv Coun NC State Libr, 1988-89; bd dir, Guilford Women's Network, 1989-90. **Home Addr:** 1000 Ross Ave, Greensboro, NC 27406.

## MOORE, DR. MARIAN J.

Historian, executive director. **Personal:** Born Saginaw, MI; daughter of Eugene and Ann. **Career:** Nat Afro-Am Mus & Cult Ctr, dir; Mus African Am Hist, Detroit, MI, dir, 1988-93; Birmingham Civil Rights Inst, exec dir, 1994.

## MOORE, MELBA (BEATRICE MELBA HILL)

Singer, actor. **Personal:** Born Oct 29, 1945, New York, NY; daughter of Melba Smith Hill and Bonnie Davis; married George Brewingston; children: 1; married Charles Huggins. **Educ:** Montclair State Col, BA, music educ. **Career:** Films: The Sidelong Glances of a Pigeon Kicker, 1970; Cotton Comes to Harlem, 1970; Lost in the Stars, 1974; Hair, 1979; Def by Temptation, 1990; The Fighting Temptations, 2003; TV series: "The Melba Moore-Clifton Davis Show", 1972; Opryland, 1973; "NBC Special Treat", 1975; The American Woman: Portraits of Courage, 1976; "The Love Boat", 1979-84; "The Tim Conway Show", 1980; Flamingo Road, 1980; Purlie?, 1981; "Ellis Island", 1984; Charlotte Forten's Mission: Experiment in Freedom, 1985; "ABC Weekend Specials", 1985; "Hotel", 1985; "Melba", 1986; "Falcon Crest", 1987; "ABC After school Specials", 1987; "The Cosby Show", 1988; Mother's Day, 1989; "Monsters", 1989; "Mathnet", 1992; "Square One TV", 1992; "Loving", 1983; Albums: I got Love, 1970; Look What You're Doing to the Man, 1971; Live, 1972; Peach Melba, 1975; This is it, 1976; Melba, 1976; A Portrait of Melba, 1977; Burn, 1979; The Other Side of the Rainbow, 1982; A Lot of Love, 1986; I'm in Love, 1988; Soul Exposed, 1990; Solitary Journey, 1990; A Very Special Christmas Gift, 2001; A Night in St. Lucia, 2002; I'm Still Here, 2003; Nobody But Jesus, 2004; The Gift Of Love, 2009. Singles: "Look What You're Doing To The Man", 1970; "I Am His Lady", 1975; "This Is It", 1976; "You Stepped Into My Life", "Lean On Me", 1976; "Free", 1976; "Make Me Believe In You", 1976; "Play Boy Scout", 1976; "Good Love Makes Everything Alright", 1977; "The Long and Winding Road", 1977; "The Way You Make Me Feel", 1977; "You Stepped Into My Life", 1978; "Standing Right Here", 1978; "Miss Thing", 1979; "Pick Me Up, I'll Dance", 1979; "Let's Stand Together", 1981; "Take My Love", 1981; "Love's Comin' At Ya"; "Keepin' My Lover Satisfied", 1983; "Mind Up Tonight", 1983; "Underlove", 1983; "Livin' for Your Love", 1984; "I Can't Believe", 1985; "Read My Lips", 1985; "When You Love Me Like This", 1985; "A Little Bit More", 1986; "Love the One I'm With", 1986; "Falling", 1986; "I'm Not Gonna Let You Go", 1987; "It's Been So Long", 1987; "I Can't Complain", 1988; "I'm in Love", 1988; "Love & Kisses", 1988; "Do You Really", 1990; "Lift Ev'ry Voice and Sing", 1990; "Love Is", 2011; Legends Ball, 2006; Melba Moore: Live in Concert, 2007; Hair, Let the Sun Shine In, 2007; Unsung, 2009. **Honors/Awds:** Tony Award, Best Supporting Actress, Purlie, 1970; Drama Desk Award, Purlie, 1970; Antoinette Perry Award, Purlie, 1970; New York Drama Critics Award, Purlie, 1970; Grammy Award, nomination, Read My Lips, 1985. **Special Achievements:** First African American to perform solo, Metro Opera House, 1977.

## MOORE, DR. MILTON DONALD, JR.

Dermatologist, pharmacist, pharmacist. **Personal:** Born Aug 16, 1953, Aberdeen, MD; son of Dora Lee; children: Rahmon & Justin. **Educ:** Xavier Col Pharm, RPh, 1976; Meharry Med Col, MD, 1980. **Career:** Hubbard Hosp, pharmacist, 1976-80; Howard Univ Hosp, Wash, DC, physician, 1980-84; Dc Gen Hosp, resident dermat, 1981-84; Suburban Hosp, advisor to chief pharmacist pharamacol, 1982-83; City Houston Dept, Riverside Health Ctr, 1984-87; Baylor Col Med, Dermat Dept, asst prof, 1985-; pvt practr, physician, 1985-; Moore Unique Skin Care, founder, chief exec officer & pres, 1993-; St Lukes Episcopal Hosp, physician, currently; Hermann Hosp, physician, currently. **Orgs:** Bd mem, Ensemble Theatre, 1986; Ama; Nat Med Asn; Am Soc Dermat Surg; Am Bd Cosmetic Surgeons; Am Acad Dermat. **Honors/Awds:** Outstanding Young Men of America, Am Acad Dermat. **Home Addr:** 9350 Kirby Dr Suite 100A, Houston, TX 77054, **Home Phone:** (713)741-3376. **Business Addr:** President, Chief Executive Officer, Moore Unique Skin Care LLC, 2525 W Bellfort Ave Suite 105, Houston, TX 77054, **Business Phone:** (713)741-9422.

## MOORE, MINYON

Association executive, executive. **Personal:** Born May 16, 1958, Chicago, IL. **Educ:** Univ Ill, BS, sociol, 1982. **Career:** Enclopedia Britannica Educ Corp, promotional serv dir, 1982-85; Oper PUSH Inc, exec asst, 1985-87; Jackson 88 Campaign, nat dept field dir, 1988; Dukakis-Bentsen Gen Election Campaign, nat dept field dir, 1988; Nat Rainbow Coalition, sr adv, nat dep polit dir, 1988-93; DNC Voter Proj, proj dir, 1992, chief exec officer, 2001-02; Dem Nat comt, dep chief staff, asst chair, dir Pub Liaison, Training, Voter Contact, Constituency Outreach, 1993-95, nat polit dir, 1995-97; 2008 Hillary Rodham Clinton presidential campaign, sr polit consult; White House, dep asst to Pres, dep pol dir, 1996-98, asst to Pres, dir Pub Liaison, 1998-99, asst pres, pol dir, 1999-2001; Dewey Sq Group's, prin, partner, 2001-; Am Coming Together, founder; Sen Hillary Clinton's, sr polit consult, currently; Harvard Univ Kennedy Sch Gov, guest lectr; Yale Univ, guest lectr. **Orgs:** Bd mem, Nat Coun Negro Women, currently; Push/Rainbow Coalition; Nat Polit Caucus Black Women; bd mem, Writers Guild Found, currently; bd mem, Sch Global Journalism & Commun at Morgan State Univ, currently. **Honors/Awds:** Mothers in Action Lifetime Award; Rainbow Push, Women on the Rise Award; ACE Award, 1998. **Special Achievements:** First African American political director of the Democratic Natl Committee; First African American political director in White House. **Business Addr:** Principal, Dewey Square Group, 607 14th St NW Suite 500, Washington, DC 20005, **Business Phone:** (202)638-5616.

**MOORE, DR. NATHAN. See Obituaries Section.**

## MOORE, NATHANIEL (STEVON NATHANIEL MOORE)

Executive, football player, philanthropist. **Personal:** Born Sep 19, 1951, Tallahassee, FL; son of Julia Mae Gilliam; married Patricia; children: Trellanee, Natalie, Melanie, Tiffanie & Maurice. **Educ:** Univ Fla, exercise & sport sci, 1975. **Career:** Football player (retired), executive; Miami Dolphins, wide receiver, 1974-86, kick returner, 1974; Superstar Rollertheque, owner; Inferno Lounge, owner; L&S Builders, partner; Nat Moore & Assocs Inc, pres, currently; Sunshine Network, Sun Sports, football broadcaster; NFL Super Bowl Football Clin, exec dir, currently. **Orgs:** Bd dir, Orange Bowl Comt; bd dir, Genuity Championship; bd dir, Sun Trust Bank; bd dir, Doral Golf Resort & Spa; bd mem, Univ Fla Found; founder, Nat Moore Found, 1998; vpres, Miami Dolphins Orgn; Miami Dolphins Alumni Asn. **Honors/Awds:** First-team All-SEC, 1972; Tommy Fitzgerald Award Outstanding Rookie, 1974; All NFL Honors AP Pro-Football Writers, 1977; University of Florida Athletic Hall of Fame, 1978; All AFC Recognition; Man of the Year, NFL, 1984; Byron "Whizzer" White Humanitarian Award, NFL Players Asn, 1986; Miami Dolphins Ring Honor, 1999; Florida Hall Fame, Sports Hall Champions; Florida Georgia Hall of Fame. **Special Achievements:** TV Movie: 1978 AFC Wild Card Playoff Game, 1978; Super Bowl XVII, 1983; 1985 AFC Championship Game, 1986. **Home Addr:** 20041 E Oakmont Dr, Hialeah, FL 33015-2048. **Business Addr:** Football Broadcaster, Sun Sports/FSN, 1000 Legion Pl Suite 1600, Orlando, FL 32801-1060, **Business Phone:** (407)648-1150.

## MOORE, NINA HENDERSON

Executive. **Personal:** married Greg; children: Jasmine Henderson & Jaden Henderson. **Educ:** Harvard Univ, BA, econs, 1985; Harvard Bus Sch, MBA, bus, 1991. **Career:** Griot Group, pres, 1995-97; Starz, vpres, 1997-99; BET Pictures, vpres Mkt & Distrib, 1999-2000; pres & chief operating officer, 2000-01; Black Entertainment Tv, exec vpres, news, pub affairs & prog acquisitions, 2001-06; Griot Productions, pres, 2009-; RLJ Entertainment Inc, pres, 2013-14; Fire & Ice, prod mgr, 2001; Commitments, prod mgr, 2001; One Special Moment, prod mgr, 2001; Woman Thou Art Loosed: On the 7th Day, producer, 2012; The Hot Flashes, producer, 2013. **Orgs:** Walter Kaitz fel, 1991-92; Women in Cable & Telecom Betsy Magness fel, 1998-99; bd dir, Nat Asn Minorities Cable; bd dir, Women Cable & Telecommunications; bd dir, Mkt Opportunities Blacks Entertainment; bd dir, S Fla Black Film Festival; bd dir, Martha's Flavor Festival. **Business Addr:** President, Griot Productions.

## MOORE, DR. OSCAR JAMES, JR.

Physician, educator. **Personal:** son of Oscar Sr and Minnie B; children: Frederick & Elna. **Educ:** Morehouse Col, BS, 1955; Atlanta Univ, 1956; Howard Univ, MD, 1962, intern, 1963. **Career:** Harvard Univ, Thorndike Mem Lab, Boston City Hosp, resident, 1963-66; USn Submarine Base Hosp, dir med, 1966-68; St Francis Hosp, Hartford, Conn, physician, 1968-69; Mt Sinai Hosp, physician, 1968-69; Mile Sq Ctr, Chicago, Ill, physician, 1969-72; Michael Reese Hosp, Chicago, Ill, physician, 1969-80; Presby St Lukes Hosp, Chicago, Ill, physician, 1969-80; Rush Med Col, asst prof, 1969-79; Cedar Sinai Hosp, LA, Calif, physician, 1970-99; Univ Calif Sch Med, asst clin prof, 1970, clin prof; Ko Med Ctr, med dir, 1972-80; Univ Chicago Pritzker Sch Med, assoc prof; Calif Hosp, Loa Angeles, physician, 1990; pvt pract, physician, currently. **Orgs:** Bd dir, Hoover Inst, Stanford Univ, 1990-; bd dir, Chicago Urban League; bd dir, Olive Harvey Col; Chicago Jr Col Bd; bd dir, Mid S Health Planning Orgn; consult, HEW Regional Planning; bd dir, Abraham Lincoln Ctr, Chicago, Ill; Omega Psi Phi; Beta Kappa Chi; 33 Scotish Rite Mason. **Honors/Awds:** Citizen of the Year Award, Olive Harvey Col, Junior Col Bd, 1976. **Business Addr:** Physician, Metro Medical Association, 8306 Wilshire Blvd Suite 21B, Beverly Hills, CA 90211, **Business Phone:** (213)386-9970.

## MOORE, OSCAR WILLIAM, JR.

Clergy, educator. **Personal:** Born Mar 31, 1938, White Plains, NY; son of Oscar Sr and Helen; married Vicki Renee Bransford; children: Derrick, John, Sean, Mahla & William. **Educ:** Southern Ill Univ, BS, recreation, 1968, MS, 1970; Philadelphia Col Bible; Trinity Col Bible; Trinity Theol Sem. **Career:** Coach (retired); Southern Ill Univ, asst dir, 1969-71; womens track & field team, head coach; Mens & Womens Cross County, asst coach, 1971-92; Rowan Univ, mens track & field prog, 1971, asst prof, head track & field coach, 1976-2003, teacher & dir recreation; Mt Olive Baptist Church, Glassboro, NJ, assoc minister. **Orgs:** Secy & treas, NJ Track Coaches Asn, 1975-; fac sponsor, Alpha Phi Alpha, Sigma Sor; dir, Glassboro Summer Martin Luther King; dir, Manna Bible Inst, Glassboro campus; US Track & Field Cross Country Coaches Asn Hall Fame; Nat Col Athletic Asn; Southern Ill Univ Gloucester County; Rowan-Glassboro State Sports Hall Fames. **Home Addr:** 6 Harrell Ave, Williamstown, NJ 08094.

## MOORE, PENNY

Basketball player. **Personal:** Born Jan 25, 1969. **Educ:** Long Beach State Univ, attended 1991. **Career:** Basketball player (retired); Charlotte Sting, forward, 1997; Wash Mystics, forward, 1998-99, 2002.

## MOORE, DR. QUINCY L., SR.

School administrator. **Personal:** Born Dec 31, 1949, Chicago, IL; son of N L and Hannah. **Educ:** Culver-Stockton Col, BA, 1972; Univ Nev, Las Vegas, NV, MS, coun, 1975; Univ Iowa, PhD, counr educ, 1983; Harvard Grad Sch Educ, MDP, dipl, 1992. **Career:** Univ Nev, Upward Bound Prog, dir, 1973-76; Clark County Community Col, CETA consult, 1976-77; Univ Nev, Spec Servs Prog, dir, 1977-78; Va Commonwealth Univ, Educ Support Prog, dir, 1985-89, pres's off admin asst, 1991, Off Acad Support, dir, 1989-98, Acad Success Ctr, exec dir, 1998-2001; W Chester Univ, dean undergrad studies & stud support serv, 2001-06; Palm Beach Community Col, vpres stud serv, 2006-. **Orgs:** Concerned Black Men Richmond, 1990-94; chmn, Am Coun Asn, Task Force Black Males, 1991-92; Leadership Metro Richmond, 1991-92; adv bd mem, Richmond Jazz Soc; adv Bd mem, Richmond Community High Sch, 1991-94; pres, Asn Multicult Coun & Develop, 1992-93; vice chmn, Coalition Access, Affordability & Diversity Higher Educ, 1992-93; adv bd, Richmond Javeline & Domestic Courts, 1993-. **Home Addr:** 3809 Cedar Grove Rd, Richmond, VA 23235-1205, **Home Phone:** (804)323-0585. **Business Addr:** Vice President of Student Services, Palm Beach Community College, 4200 Congress Ave, Lake Worth, FL 33461-4796, **Business Phone:** (561)868-3122.

## MOORE, RALPH G.

President (organization), businessperson. **Personal:** Born Jul 4, 1949, Evanston, IL; son of William and Alberta. **Educ:** Southern Ill Univ, BS, acct, 1971. **Career:** Arthur Andersen & Co, acct staff; Minority Enterprise Small Bus Investment Co, vpres; Parker House Sausage Co, controller; Ralph G Moore & Assocs, founder & pres, 1979-; Hamton Roads MBDC, engagement partner, 1992-2000. **Orgs:** Co founder & pres, Alliance Bus Leaders & Entrepreneurs; consult, Nat Minority Supplier Develop Coun, 1992-; trustee, Univ Chicago Hosps & Health Syst; trustee, City Col Chicago, 1994; Jr Achievement Chicago; Chicago Minority Bus Develop Coun; contrib, Harvard Bus Rev Mag & MBE Mag. **Business Addr:** President, Ralph G Moore & Associates, 401 S LaSalle St Suite 1401, Chicago, IL 60605, **Business Phone:** (312)419-1911.

## MOORE, REV. RICHARD

Clergy, educator. **Personal:** Born Oct 19, 1956, Chicago, IL. **Educ:** Bishop Col, BA; Union Theol Sem, MDiv; Tenn Sch Relig, DDiv. **Career:** Holy Unity Christian Acad & Day Care, owner, exec dir & founder, 1977-; Holy Unity Baptist Church, clergy, founder & pastor, 1997-. **Orgs:** Nat Asn Advan Colored People; pres, Youth Unlimited Inc. **Home Addr:** 13742 Guy R Brewer Blvd, Jamaica, NY 11434, **Home Phone:** (718)723-7353. **Business Addr:** Pastor, Holy Unity, 167 10 137th Ave, Jamaica, NY 11434, **Business Phone:** (718)712-8515.

## MOORE, RICHARD BAXTER

Lawyer. **Personal:** Born May 26, 1943, Erie, PA; son of Lewis Tanner and Jean; children: Leonard, Richard Jr & Tiffiny. **Educ:** Cent State Col, BS, 1965; Howard Univ Sch Law, JD, 1969. **Career:** City Philadelphia, asst jury comnr, 1979-91; Philadelphia, Pa, asst dist atty, 1971-77; pvt pract atty, currently. **Orgs:** Improved Benevolent Protective Order Elks World; Phi Alpha Delta Law Fraternity; Omega Psi Phi Fraternity Inc; Nat Asn Advan Colored People; chmn, Veterans Comn; vice chmn, United Negro Col Fund, City Philadelphia; vice chmn, Juv Serv Sub Comn Pub Serv, 1973-74; Compensation Victims Crimes Comn, 1974-75; vpres, bd dir, Nat Bar Found, 1975-78; Philadelphia Bar Asn; Sigma Pi Phi Fraternity. **Honors/Awds:** Service Award Chapel of Four Chaplains; Citation, United Negro Col Fund; Service Award, Boys & Girls Clubs Am. **Business Addr:** Attorney, 406 S 16th St, Philadelphia, PA 19146, **Business Phone:** (215)545-2781.

## MOORE, RICK

Executive. **Personal:** Born Jun 16, 1951, Dayton, OH; son of Jessie and Dorothy; married Judi; children: 4. **Educ:** Wright State Univ; Sinclair Col; Wilberforce Univ, BS, 2002, MBA, orgn mgt. **Career:** Griffin Blosser Color Labs, 1969-72; Wolpent Engineering, 1972-76; Price Bro's Co, 1976-83; Dayton Metrop Housing Authority, mgr, dir, 1983-2004; Housing Authority City Bridgeport, dep exec dir, 2006-10; Housing Authority Baltimore, dep exec dir, 2010-11; Evansville Housing Authority, exec dir, 2011-. **Orgs:** Bd mem, Buckeye Trails Girl Scouts, 1995-2001; City Dayton Citizens Awareness Comt, 1996-; Nat forum Black Pub Admin, 1998-; bd mem, Big Bro Big Sisters, 1998-;

Rotary Int; First Tee Nat Golf Orgn; Martin Luther King Develop Ctr. **Home Addr:** 212 W Norman Ave, Dayton, OH 45405, **Home Phone:** (937)274-5334. **Business Addr:** Executive Director, Housing Authority of the City of Evansville, 500 Ct St, Evansville, IN 47708, **Business Phone:** (812)428-8500.

### MOORE, ROB (ROBERT SEAN MOORE)
Football player, football coach. **Personal:** Born Sep 27, 1968, Hempstead, NY; married Drucilla; children: Dakota & Savoy. **Educ:** Syracuse Univ, BS, psychol, 1990. **Career:** Football player (retired), coach; New York Jets, wide receiver, 1990-94; Ariz Cardinals, wide receiver, 1995-2001; Denver Broncos, wide receiver, 2002; Montclair High Sch, wide receivers coach, 2002-03; Syracuse Univ, wide receiver coach, 2009; Phoenix Bears, wide receivers coach, 2009; Syracuse Orange, wide receivers coach, 2010-13; Buffalo Bills, wide receivers coach, 2014; Oakland Raiders, wide receivers coach, 2015-. **Honors/Awds:** Role Model of the Year, New York City Coun, 1991; Marty Lyons Award, 1992; Edge Man of the Year, 1992; Pro Bowl, 1994, 1997; NFL Receiving Yards Leader, 1997. **Special Achievements:** Film: Jerry Maguire, 1996. **Business Addr:** Wide Receivers Coach, Oakland Raiders, 1220 Harbor Bay Pkwy, Alameda, CA 94502, **Business Phone:** (510)864-5000.

### MOORE, ROBERT EARL. See RASHAD, DR. AHMAD.

### MOORE, DR. ROBERT FRAZIER
Socialist, educator. **Personal:** Born Jan 30, 1944, Tuskegee, AL. **Educ:** Fisk Univ, BA, psychol, 1965; Ind Univ, MEd, spec educ, 1966, EdD, spec educ, 1969. **Career:** Coppin State Col, asst prof, 1968-70; John Hopkins Univ, John F Kennedy Sch, teacher, 1968-69; Fisk Univ, Nashville, from asst prof to assoc, prof educ, 1970-75; Tenn State Univ, assoc prof, 1975; Univ Miami, assoc prof, 1975-2000, assoc dean, 1981-94, Dept Teaching & Learning, assoc prof & assoc chair, 1994-, Undergrad Educ, asst provost, Off Acad Enhancement, dir, Undergrad Spec Educ Prog, coord, currently; Milwaukee Pub Schs, Div Except Stud Educ, Early Childhood Audit, consult, 1985; Silny & Assocs, Coral Gables, Fla, consult, 1988-; Dade Co Pub Schs, Fla, consult, 1994-; Mahoney Residential Col, master, currently; Bel-Aire Elem Sch, prof resident, currently. **Orgs:** Miami Fisk Club, 1975-2000; Golden Key Nat Hon Soc Iron Arrow; Coun Except C; bd dir, Tenn Asn Retarded Citizens; Davidson Co Asn Retarded Citizens; Tenn Foster Grandparents Asn; Grace Eaton Day Home; Phi Delta Kappa; Am Asn Ment Retardation; Asn Supv & Curric Develop; bd trustee, Bertha Abess Childrens Ctr; Phi Kappa Phi; honarary mem, Golden Key Nat Hon Soc; bd trustee, Canterbury Preschool Bd Dirs; Southern Asn Cols & Schs. **Honors/Awds:** Professor of the Year & Golden Apple Award, Panhellenic Coun, Univ Miami, 1999; Received Numerous Honors. **Business Addr:** Associate Professor, University of Miami School of Education, 222 Merrick Bldg 5202 University Dr, Coral Gables, FL 33124, **Business Phone:** (305)284-3187.

### MOORE, RODNEY GREGORY
Lawyer. **Personal:** Born Sep 1, 1960, Birmingham, AL; son of Tommie and Jethroe (deceased); married Yaslyn; children: Nyosha, Rodney G II & Imari. **Educ:** Univ Wash, BA, polit sci, 1982; Santa Clara Univ Sch Law, JD, 1985. **Career:** Wash State Atty Gen's Off, consumer protection claims rep, 1980-82; Bancroft Whitney Legal Publ, Am Law Rev Ser, assoc ed, 1984-85; Law Offices Williams, Robinson & Moore, partner, atty, 1987-89; Moore Law Firm, pres & chief exec officer, 1989-97; Lincoln Law Sch, pro, 1991-93; Santa Clara Co Black Chamber Com, gen coun, 1992-98; E Side Union High Sch Dist, sch bd mem, 1994-97; Eastside Union High Dist, gen coun, 1997-2000; Atlanta Pub Schs, gen coun, 2000-05; Greenberg Traurig LLP, gen coun, atty, 2005-09; Adorno & Yoss, 2009-10, partner; Baker Donelson Bearman, Caldwell & Berkowitz, PC, atty, partner, 2010-13; Moore Sparks LLC, atty, mem, 2013-14; Lewis Brisbois Bisgaard & Smith LLP, partner, 2014-16; Shelby County Schs, gen coun & chief legal officer, 2016-. **Orgs:** Pres, Univ Wash, Black Stud Union, 1980-82; assoc ed, Santa Clara Comp & High TEC Law J, 1984-85; treas, Stud Bar Asn, 1984-85; Nat Black Law Students Asn, western regional dir, 1984-85; Calif State Bar Asn, 1987-; pres, Santa Clara Co Black Lawyers Asn, 1989-91; bd trustees, Santa Clara Co Bar Asn, 1989-91; chief coun, Santa Clara Co Black Chamber Com, 1991-97; bd visitor, Univ Santa Clara Law Sch, 1993-01; pres, Calif Asn Black Lawyers, 1993-94; alumni bd mem, Santa Clara Univ Law Sch, 1993-95; dir region IX, Nat Bar Asn, 1993-94, gen coun, 1997-99; bd mem, Hampton-Phillips Track & Field Classic, 1993-99; San Jose Libr Vision Comt, 1994-96; bd mem, 100 Black Men Am, Atlanta Chap; bd mem, Metrop Edu Dist, 1994-97, pres, 1996-97; chair, ed bd, Nat Bar Asn J, 1997-99, vpres, 2002-04, pres, 2008-; bd dir, Nat Sch Bd Asn, Coun Sch Atty, 2002-06; chair, Urban Law Comn, 2003-06; pres, Nat Bar Asn, 2008-09, chair, judicial selection comt, 2012-13; Atlanta Bar Asn; Gate City Bar Asn; State Bar Calif; State Bar Ga. **Honors/Awds:** Order of the Golden Hand, Santa Clara Co Black COC, 1991; Proclamation, City San Jose, 1994; Certificate of Recognition, Entreprenurial Spirit, Calif Legis, 1994; Loren Miller Award-Attorney of the Year, CA Asn Black Lawyers, 1997; Special Award of Merit, Nat Bar Asn, 1998; Best Lawyers in America, 2007, 2008; The 50 Most Influential Minority Lawyers in America, National Law Journal, 2008. **Special Achievements:** Int Monitor, Independent Elections CMS, Republic of South Africa, 1994; chair, Nat Bar Asn, Int Delegation to United Nations Int Criminal Tribunal for Rwanda; first Georgia lawyer to serve as NBA President, 2008. **Home Addr:** 6243 High Meadow Ct, San Jose, CA 95135. **Business Addr:** General Counsel, Chief Legal Officer, Shelby County Schools, 160 S Hollywood St, Memphis, TN 38112, **Business Phone:** (901)416-5300.

### MOORE, RONALD
Football player, public utility executive. **Personal:** Born Jan 26, 1970, Spencer, OK; married Tammy; children: Ashlynn & Allison. **Educ:** Pittsburg State Univ. **Career:** Football player (retired); Phoenix Ariz Cardinals, running back, 1993-94, 1997; New York Jets, running back, 1995, 1996; St Louis Rams, running back, 1997; Miami Dolphins, running back, 1998; police officer & minister, currently. **Orgs:** Pres, PSU's Fellowship Christian Athletes; Alpha Phi Alpha Fraternity. **Honors/Awds:** Harlon Hill Trophy winner, 1992; National Player of the Year, 1992; Hall of Fame, Nat Col Athletic Asn, 2005. **Home Addr:** 3705 Glen Alpine Rd, Kingsport, TN 37660-7862.

### MOORE, DR. ROSCOE MICHAEL, JR.
Veterinarian, chief executive officer. **Personal:** Born Dec 2, 1944, Richmond, VA; son of Roscoe Michael Sr and Robnette Johnson; married Patricia Ann Haywood; children: Roscoe III & John H. **Educ:** Tuskegee Univ, BS, 1968, DVM, 1969, DSc; Univ Mich, MPH, epidemiol, 1970; Johns Hopkins Univ, MHS, 1982, PhD, epidemiol, 1985. **Career:** Nat Insts Health, vet, 1970-71; Ctrs Dis Control, epidemic intelligence serv officer, 1971-73; Ctr Vet Med, sr vet, 1973-74; Nat Inst Occup Safety & Health, sr epidemiologist, 1974-81; Ctr Devices & ad Health, sr epidemiologist, 1981-92; Univ Wash, Seattle, assoc prof, 1989-; Pub Health Serv, chief vet med officer, 1989-93; US Pub Health Serv, assoc dir, Off Int & Refugee Health, 1992, surgeon gen & rear adm; Potomac Inst Policy Studies, srfel & staff, 2003-; Global Flu Consortium, chief exec officer & vice chmn, currently; US Food & Drug Admin, chief epidemiologist; Cannabis Sci, pres & chief exec officer. **Orgs:** Am Vet Med Asn, 1969-; bd dir, FONZ, 1979-; pres, bd dir, Friends Nat Zoo, 1984-87; fel Am Col Epidemiol, 1984-; adv comn, Howard Univ Col Med, 1985-; consult, Sch Vet Med, Tuskegee Univ, 1988-; bd govr, Univ Mich Pub Health Alumni, 1987-93; Omega Psi Phi Fraternity, 1995-; bd dir, Montgomery Gen Hosp, 1992-; assoc dir, HHS. **Home Addr:** 14315 Arctic Ave, Rockville, MD 20853, **Home Phone:** (301)871-8578. **Business Addr:** Senior Fellow, Staff, Potomac Institute for Policy Studies, 901 N Stuart St, Arlington, VA 22203, **Business Phone:** (703)525-0770.

### MOORE, SAMUEL DAVID (SAMUEL DAVID HICKS)
Actor, singer. **Personal:** Born Oct 12, 1935, Miami, FL; son of John Richard Hicks and Louise White; married Joyce McRae; children: Deborah, Nicole, Tangela, Lawanda Denise, Michelle Gayle, Vicky & JoAnn. **Career:** Singer, entertainer, actor; Singles: "You Don't Know Like I Know", 1966; "Hold On, I'm Comin", 1966; "Soul Man", 1967; "I Thank You", 1968; Albums: Sam & Dave, 1966; Best of Sam & Dave, 1969; One Trick Pony, 1980; Soul Men, 1986; Films: Tapeheads, 1988; "Rainy Night in Georgia", 1994; Blues Brothers 2000, 1998; Night at the Golden Eagle, 2001; Only the Strong Survive, 2002; "I Can't Stand the Rain", 2006; TV series: "Saturday Night Live", 1980; "Golden Age of Rock'n'Roll", 1991; "Tales of the City", 1993; The Roots of Country: Nashville Celebrates the Ryman, 1994; Elvis: The Tribute, 1994; The Life & Times of Conway Twitty, 1995; Rhythm & Blues 40: A Soul Spectacular, 2001; Sounds of Memphis, 2002; Soulsville, 2003; Soul Man: Isaac Hayes, 2003; "Late Night with Conan O'Brien", 2004-06; "Tavis Smiley", 2007; "Great Performances", 2007; "Respect Yourself: The Stax Records Story", 2007; "Ovenight Sensational"; "Plenty Good Lovin"; "Worldwide Symphony Concert Tour", 2008-09. **Orgs:** Nat Acad Rec Arts & Sci; Soc Singers; Rhythm & Blues Foun Artist Bd. **Honors/Awds:** Grammy Award, Nat Acad Recording Arts & Sci, 1967; Rhythm & Blues Found, Pioneer, 1991; Rock & Roll Hall of Fame, inductee, 1992; two Country Music Association Awards nominations; NARAS Heroes Award; Grammy Song Hall of Fame for Soul Man, inductee; ETAM Living Legend Award; MOBO Lifetime Achievement Living Legend Award, 2006. **Special Achievements:** Command performance for Queen of England, 1967; command performance for Jimmy Carter, White House, 1975; Presidential Inauguration of George Bush, 1989. **Business Addr:** Singer, Buddy Lee Attractions Inc, 38 Music Square E Suite 300, Nashville, TN 37203, **Business Phone:** (615)244-4336.

### MOORE, SHAMEIK
Actor, rap musician. **Personal:** Born May 4, 1995, Atlanta, GA; son of Errol and Sharon. **Career:** Rapper, 2011-; actor, 2011-. Television: House of Payne, 2011; Reed Between the Lines, 2011; An Elf's Story: The Elf on the Shelf, 2011; Incredible Crew, 2012-13; The Watons Go to Birmingham, 2013; The Get Down, 2016-. Film: Joyful Noise, 2013; Dope, 2013. **Special Achievements:** Albums: I Am Da Beat, 2012; 30058, 2015; child dancer in music videos and on tour with Keri Hilson, Soulja Boy, and Pop It Off Boyz. **Business Addr:** c/o We Entertain, 976 Jefferson St NW I, Atlanta, GA 30318.

### MOORE, SHEMAR F.
Fashion model, actor. **Personal:** Born Apr 20, 1970, Oakland, CA; son of Marilyn Wilson and Sherrod. **Educ:** Santa Clara Univ, commun. **Career:** Films: Hav Plenty, 1997; Butter, 1998; The Brothers, 2001; Motives, 2004; The Seat Filler, 2004; Greener, 2004; Diary of a Mad Black Woman, 2005; Short videos: Motives 2, 2007; Profile: Rossi/Mantegna, 2008; Shemar Moore: Criminal Minds' Wild Ride, 2008; The Criminal Element: The Making of 'Criminal Minds, Season 3', 2008; Criminal Minds Season 3: Killer Roles, 2008; From Script to Screen: True Night, 2008. TV Series: "The Young & the Restless", 1994-2014; "Living Single", 1995; "The Jamie Foxx Show", 1996; "Arli$$", 1997; "Chicago Hope", 1998; "Mama Flora's Family", 1998; "Moesha", 1999; "For Your Love", 1999; "Malcolm & Eddie", 1999; "Soul Train", host, 1999-2003; "How to Marry a Billionaire: A Christmas Tale, 2000"; "Celebrity", 2000; "Birds of Prey", 2002-03; "Chasing Alice", 2003; "Nikki and Nora", 2004; "Half & Half", 2004; "Reversible Errors", 2004; "Criminal Minds", 2005-; "The Nanny", 2006; True Night, 2008; A Shade of Gray, 2009; The Big Wheel, 2009; Roadkill, 2009; Amplification, 2009; To Hell... And Back, 2009. **Honors/Awds:** NAACP Image Awards, nominated, 1996; Emmy Award nomination, 1997; Oust standing Actor in a Daytime Drama Series, 1998, 2002. **Business Addr:** Actor, Craig Agency, 8485 E Melrose Pl Suite E, Los Angeles, CA 90069, **Business Phone:** (213)655-0236.

### MOORE, STEVON NATHANIEL. See MOORE, NATHANIEL.

### MOORE, THELMA LAVERNE WYATT CUMMINGS
Judge. **Personal:** Born Jul 6, 1945, Amarillo, TX; daughter of James Odis Wyatt Sr and Annie Lavernia Lott Wyatt; married Luke C; children: Khari Sekou & Ayanna Rashida; married Arthur B Cummings; children: Khari Sekou & Ayanna Rashida. **Educ:** Univ Calif, BA, zool & Fr, 1965; Ill Inst Technol, psychodynamics fel, psychodynamics, 1966; Emory Univ Sch Law, JD, 1971. **Career:** Bd educ, City Chicago, teacher, 1965-67; Atlanta Urban League, field rep, 1967-69; Thelma Wyatt, atty, 1971-74; Ward & Wyatt, atty, 1974-77; Munic Ct Atlanta, judge, 1977-80; City Ct Atlanta, judge, 1980, State Ct Fulton County, judge, 1985-90, immediate post-chief judge, 1998-2000; Fulton County Super Ct, Ga, chief judge, 1978-2008; Dellums Comn, Criminal Justice Component, co-chair; Moore Law LLC, atty & counr-at-law, 2009-. **Orgs:** Fel Ill Inst Tech, Psychodynamics, 1966; historian, Ga State Bar Asn, 1971; Am Bar Asn; Nat Bar Asn, 1977-; chmn, Nat Judicial Coun; historian, Gate City Bar Asn, 1990-; Ga Asn Black Women Atty; Atlanta Bar Asn; Am Judicature Soc; Am Judges Asn; Phi Alpha Delta; Alpha Kappa Alpha; life mem, Nat Asn Advan Colored People; bd gov, Joint Ctr Polit Studies; bd trustee, Emory Univ; bd dir, Nat Ctr State Conn, 1994-2000; Fulton Co Family Ct Proj, conceived & spearheaded, 1998; Joseph Lowery Inst; john hay whitney fel Mortgages & Admin Law. **Honors/Awds:** Distinguished Service, Nat Judicial Coun, 1982, 1983, 1986, 1988; Essence Award for Outstanding Contribution, Essence mag, 1982; Outstanding Jurist Award, Gate City Bar Asn, 1983; Outstanding Public Service Award, Ga Coalition Black Women Inc, 1984; Distinguished Alumni Award, Emory BLSA, 1986; Order of the Coif, Bryan Soc; Pi Delta Phi Appellate Advocacy; Am Jurisprudence Awards in Commission Law; Mortgages & Admin Law, John Hay Whitney Fellow; State Illinois Fellow; National Urban League Fellow; Gate City Bar Association President Award, 1990; Govt Award, Atlanta Bus League, 1990; Thurgood Marshall Award, 1991; Emory Medal, 1992; WSB Living Legend Award, 1992; Distinguished Alumni Award, Emory Law Sch, 1996; Woman of Vision Award, Atlanta Bus League, 1996-03; Emory Distinguished Law Alumni Award; Wiley Branton Award, NBA; Raymond Pare Alexander Award, NBA; US Chief Justice Award, 2001; Sojourner Truth Award, NBPW, 2002; Pinnacle Award, Delta Sigma Theta, 2003; Atlanta Bar Outstanding Jurist Award; Jondelle Johnson Legacy Award, Nat Asn Advan Colored People, 2004; Gate City Bar Judicial Section Legacy Award, 2005; Thurgood Marshall Award, Judicial Coun, Nat Bar Asn, 2006; Concerned Black Clergy President's Award, Georgia Legislative Black Caucus Pacesetter Award; Atlanta Business League Catalyst Award; Lifetime Achievement Award, 2014. **Special Achievements:** The first black woman appointed to the Superior Courts of Georgia, Moore is also Georgia's first black woman to serve on the State Court Bench and the first woman to serve full-time on the benches of the Atlanta Municipal Court & the Atlanta City Court. **Home Addr:** 850 Flamingo Dr SW, Atlanta, GA 30311-2405, **Home Phone:** (404)753-1372. **Business Addr:** Judge, Fulton County Super Court, T4905 Justice Center Twr 185 Cent Ave SW, Atlanta, GA 30303, **Business Phone:** (404)730-4305.

### MOORE, THELMA WYATT CUMMINGS
Judge. **Personal:** married Luke; children: Charles Mmarried Arthur B Cummings Sr; children: Khari Sekou & Ayanna Rashida. **Educ:** Univ Calif, Los Angeles, BA, 1965; Emory Univ, JD, 1971. **Career:** Judge (retired), attorney; fel Psychodynamics, Ill Inst Technol, 1966; Morris Brown Col; Univ Warwick, Coventry, Eng; Munic Ct, Atlanta, judge, 1977-80; City Ct, Atlanta, 1980-85; Cheif judge, Super Ct, Fulton County, 1978-2008; State Ct, Fulton County, judge, 1985-90; Atlanta Judicial Circuit, Fulton County, Super Ct, Ga, judge, 1990-2008; Moore Law LLC, atty & counr Law, 2009-. **Orgs:** Joint Ctr Polit & Econ Studies, bd govs, currently; co-chair, Criminal Justice component Health Policy Inst's Dellums Comn; Alpha Kappa Alpha Sorority Inc; Bd Joseph E. Lowery Inst Justice & Human Rights Clark Atlanta Univ. **Business Addr:** Attorney, Moore Law LLC, 3915 Cascade Rd Suite 235, Atlanta, GA 30303, **Business Phone:** (404)699-6001.

### MOORE, THOMAS L.
Executive. **Personal:** Born Jun 26, 1926, Burke County, GA; married Alma Jean Brown; children: Thomas, Yvonne, Dionne & Michael. **Educ:** Swift Meml Col; Knoxville Col. **Career:** TAM Inc Constrn Co, pres; Tommy Moore Enter, staff; Moore's Package Store, staff. **Orgs:** City & Co Bank Knox Co; charter comnr, Knox Co Bd Comnr; pres knoxville, Nat Bus League; Bus Develop Ctr C C; BSA; pres, Coun Youth Oppt YMCA. **Honors/Awds:** Cert Award Commonwealth of Kentucky, YMCA. **Home Addr:** 1940 Dardridge Ave, Knoxville, TN 37915.

### MOORE, TRUDY S.
Journalist. **Personal:** Born Jan 6, 1957, Paterson, NJ; daughter of Queen E; children: Taylor S. **Educ:** Howard Univ, Wash, DC, BS, 1979; Northwestern Univ, Evanston, IL, MS, 1980. **Career:** Chicago Sun-Times, Chicago, Ill, gen assignment reporter, l980; Jet Mag, Chicago, Ill, asst ed, l980-83, assoc ed, 1983-89, feature ed, l989; Ebony Man, Chicago, Ill, contrib ed, 1988-90; Jet Mag, Johnson Publ Co, feature ed. **Orgs:** Vol, Big Bros/Big Sisters, Chicago, Ill, l982-85; Chicago Urban League, l986-; Nat Asn Advan Colored People, Women's Auxiliary, l989; mem bd dir, Nat Asn Advan Colored People, Chicago, S Side Br, l989; Chicago Asn Black Journalists. **Home Addr:** 6910 S Oglesby Ave Suite 1, Chicago, IL 60649-1814, **Home Phone:** (773)363-7887. **Business Addr:** Feature Editor, Jet Magazine/Johnson Publishing Co, 820 S Mich Ave, Chicago, IL 60605, **Business Phone:** (312)322-9307.

### MOORE, WALTER LOUIS
Government official, mayor. **Personal:** Born Mar 14, 1946, Pontiac, MI; married Daisy Barber. **Educ:** Ferris State Col, attended 1968; Oakland Univ. **Career:** Pontiac City, Mich, firefighter; Oakland County, Mich, comnr, 1978; Pontiac City, Mich, mayor, currently. **Orgs:** Campaign mgr, Coalition Mod Charter, Pontiac City; I-75 Mayors Conf; US Conf Mayors; Nat Conf Black Mayors; dir, Pontiac Youth Assistance; charter mem, Pontiac Optimist Club; mason, Gibraltor Lodge #19 Prince Hall; bd mem, Offender Aid & Restoration. **Home Addr:** 37 Ottawa Dr, Pontiac, MI 48341-1631, **Home Phone:** (248)334-1835. **Business Addr:** Mayor, City of Pontiac, 47450 Woodward Ave, Pontiac, MI 48342.

### MOORE, HON. WARFIELD, JR.
Judge. **Personal:** Born Mar 5, 1934, Chicago, IL; son of Warfield Sr and Sally Curry; married Jeane Virginia; children: Warfield III, Sharon, Sally Anne & Janet. **Educ:** Univ Mich, BA, polit sci & eng, 1957;

Wayne State Univ, JD, LLB, 1960. **Career:** Judge (retired) Pvt Pract, atty, 1961-78; Colista Wiegle & Moore, Detroit, Mich, 1962-66; Philo Mackie Moore Pitts Ravitz Glotta Cockrell & Robb, Detroit, Mich, 1966-73; Moore Barr & Kerwin, Detroit, Mich, 1973-78; Recorders Ct, Detroit, Mich, judge, 1978-96; Recs Ct, judge, 1979; Wayne County Circuit Ct, Criminal Div, Detroit, Mich, judge, 1996-97; Wayne County Circuit Ct, Civil Div, Detroit, Mich, judge, 1997-2008, 3rd Circuit Ct, judge, 2009. **Orgs:** Mich Bar Asn; Wolverine Bar Asn; Black Judges Asn. **Special Achievements:** Did Law Review in Wayne State University, editor, 1958-60. **Home Addr:** 1561 Lincolnshire Dr, Detroit, MI 48203. **Business Addr:** Judge, Circuit Court, Rm 921 711 Coleman A Young Munic Ctr 2 Woodward Ave, Detroit, MI 48226, **Business Phone:** (313)224-5261.

### MOORE, WENDA WEEKES
Research scientist. **Personal:** Born Dec 24, 1941, Boston, MA; daughter of Leroy Randolph Weekes and Sylvia Means Weekes; married Cornell L; children: Lynne, Jonathon & Meredith. **Educ:** Howard Univ, BA, 1963. **Career:** Gov Wendell R Anderson, staff asst, 1976; Wash, DC Libr, resr; Westminster Town Hall Forum, dir, currently. **Orgs:** League Women Voters, 1964 &1974; bd regents, Univ Minn, 1973; vice chm bd regents, 1975; chmn bd regents, 1977-83; Univ Minn Found; Asn Black Found Execs; bd Minn Bd Continuing Leg Educ; dir, Gamble Skogm Inc, 1978-82; bd dir, Wickes Co; bd advisor, Gen Med Sci Coun, Nat Insts Health; leader, First Educ Exchange Deleg Univ Minn Peoples Repub China, 1979; Bd Adv US Dept Educ, 1980; Adv Coun, 1980-83; Nat Comn Foreign Lang, 1980; bd advisors, Dept Educ, pres George H. Bush, 1980; Univ Minns Weisman Mus; Alpha Kappa Alpha; Minn Orchestral Asn; pres, St Paul Chap Links, 1987-; Jacks & Jill; pres bd & chmn, Chart & Wedco 1989-90; Graywolf Press; Fed Dist Judge Selection Comt; trustee, Kellog Found, 1989-; bd, Am Judicature Soc, 1990; Womens Funding Network; chair, Budget Comt; bd trustee, WK Kellogg Found; Minneapolis Coun Churches; Graywolf Press; Nat Comt Presidential Selection & Eval; Asn Gov Boards; Adv Bd US Dept Educ, St Benedict's Col; bd mem, Ms Found Women. **Special Achievements:** University of Minnesota, First African American chairperson of the board. **Home Addr:** 2727 Dean Pkwy, Minneapolis, MN 55416. **Business Addr:** Director, Westminster Town Hall Forum, 83 S 12th St, Minneapolis, MN 55403, **Business Phone:** (612)332-3421.

### MOORE, WILL HENRY, III
Football player, executive. **Personal:** Born Feb 21, 1970, Dallas, TX; married Phyllis. **Educ:** Tex Southern Univ, BA, bus admin, mgt, 1993. **Career:** Football player (retired), exec; New Eng Patriots, wide receiver, 1995-96; Norwest Financial, sales rep & acct mgr, 1996-97; Jacksonville Jaguars, wide receiver, 1997-98; Bristol-Myers Squibb, pharmaceut sales rep, 2000-02; Novartis Pharmaceut, sr pharmaceut sales consult, 2002-11; Novo Nordisk A/S, sr diabetes care specialist, 2011-. **Honors/Awds:** Pinnacle Award, 2000, 2001; Most Valuable Player, 2006; Regional Commitment of Excellence Award, 2013; Circle of Excellence Award, 2013. **Home Addr:** , Jacksonville, FL. **Business Addr:** Senior Diabetes Care Specialist, Novo Nordisk A/S, Novo Alle, Bagsvaerd2880, **Business Phone:** (454)444-8888.

### MOORE, YOLANDA
Basketball player, television sportscaster. **Personal:** Born Jul 1, 1974, Port Gibson, MS; children: Courtney & Ashley. **Educ:** Univ Miss, BA, eng & radio & tv, 2002; Alcorn State Univ, MS, workforce educ leadership, 2009; Miss State Univ, EdS, educ & instrnl technol, 2013, PhD, instrnl systs & workforce develop, 2009-. **Career:** Basketball player (retired), basketball analyst, author, educator; Univ of Miss, 1992-96; Houston Comets, forward, 1997-98; Orlando Miracle, 1999; Miami Sol, 2000; Women's Korean Basketball League, Seoul, Korea, 2001-02; Dallas Mavericks, broadcast intern, 2004-05; Fox Sports Net, basketball analyst, 2005; Claiborne County Schs, journalism teacher & asst girls' basketball coach, 2006-07; DeSoto County Schs, Eng teacher & asst boys basketball coach, 2007; Memphis Grizzlies, post game radio analyst, 2007; Yolanda Moore 33 LLC, pres & chief impowerment officer, 2009-; Miss State Univ, grad asst, adj instr, 2009-10; Miss Sports Mag, columnist, 2009-11; Heritage Acad, head girls basketball coach, 2011; InstrucTech LLC, workforce develop consult, 2013-; La State Univ, 2013-14; Southeastern La Univ, head coach, 2014-. **Orgs:** Owner, Yolanda Moore Basketball Enterprises; owner, Yolanda Moore Motivational Training Systs. **Business Addr:** Workforce Development Consultant, InstrucTech LLC, 2301 N New Jersey St, New Jersey, IN 46205, **Business Phone:** (317)755-7896.

### MOORE-CASH, BETTYE JOYCE. See Obituaries Section.

### MOORE-POOLE, JESSICA CARE
Poet, chief executive officer, publisher. **Personal:** Born Oct 28, 1971, Detroit, MI; daughter of Thomas and Irene; married Sharrif Simmons; children: Omari. **Educ:** Mich State Univ; Wayne State Univ, jour & polit sci. **Career:** Poet, actor, publisher, Recording artist; Moore Black Press Inc, founder & chief exec officer, 1997-; Black Women Rock, founder, 2004-; jess Care moore Found, founder & dir, 2008-; Prison Performing Arts, facilitator & teacher, 2009-; Detroit Read, singer, currently; Poet, currently; Poetry collections: The Alphabet Verses The Ghetto, 2002; The Words Don't Fit in My Mouth; God is Not an American; Plays: There Are No Asylums for the Real Crazy Women; Alphaphobia!, Moore Black Press. **Business Addr:** Founder, Chief Executive Officer, Moore Black Press, PO Box 10545, Atlanta, GA 30310, **Business Phone:** (404)752-0450.

### MOORE-STOVALL, DR. JOYCE
Physician. **Personal:** Born Nov 5, 1948, Washington, DC; daughter of Joseph Samuel and Ida Barnes; married Arthur J; children: Artis Jomar, Aaron Joseph, Arthur Jr & Kelly Ann. **Educ:** Fisk Univ, BA, 1970; Meharry Medical Col, MD, 1974. **Career:** Long Island Jewish Med Ctr, USPHS Hosp, internship radiol; N Shore-Long Island Jewish Health Syst, resident; Veteran's Admin, diag radiologist; Mallinckrodt Inst Radiol, St Louis, Mo, vis fel, 1983; Va Med Ctr, Kans City, Mo, vis fel, 1984; Wash Sch Med, Mallinckrodt Inst Radiol, St Louis, Mo, vis fel, 1987; Wis Sch Med, Milwaukee, WI, vis fel, 1990; Eisenhower Veteran's Affair Med Ctr, diag radiologist, currently; pvt pract radiologist, currently. **Orgs:** NMA; Greater Kans City Radiological Soc. **Honors/Awds:** Bd Certified Radiol, 1989; A Consortium of Doctors Honoree, 1993. **Special Achievements:** Author: "Parosteal Osteosarcoma", 1982; "Anorectal Abscesses", 1983, Journal of the Kansas Medical Soc; "Pneumatosis Coli",Journal of the NMA, 1983; "CT, Detecting Intra abdominal Abscesses",Journal of the NMA, 1985;"AIDS: The Role of Imaging Modalities and Infection Control Policies,"Journal of the NMA, 1988; "Magnetic Resonance Imaging of an Adult with Dandy Walker Syndrome",Journal of the NMA, 1988; "Serial Nonenhancing Magnetic Resonance Imaging Scans of High Grade Glioblastoma Multiforme,"Journal of the NMA, 1993; "Ruptured Pancreaticoduodenal Arterial Aneurysms: Diagnosis and Treatment by Angiographic Interventional,"Journal of NMA, 1995; "Multiple Glioblastomas",-Journal of Applied Radiology, 2002. **Home Addr:** 1617 Ridge Rd, Leavenworth, KS 66048-6504, **Home Phone:** (913)651-4911. **Business Addr:** Diagnostic Radiologist, Dwight D Eisenhower Virginia Medical Center, 4101 S 4th Trafficway, Leavenworth, KS 66048-5055, **Business Phone:** (913)682-2000.

### MOOREHEAD, BOBBIE WOOTEN
Educator, meeting planner. **Personal:** Born May 26, 1937, Kelly, LA; daughter of Verdie C Wooten and Ora Lee Edwards Jones; married Erskine L; children: Eric Lyn & Jennifer Lynne. **Educ:** Tex Southern Univ, BS, 1958, MEd, 1977; cert, admin supv, 1977. **Career:** Goose Creek Consol Sch Dist, teacher, 1959-62; Houston Independent Sch Dist, teacher, 1963-; Capt Campaign, meeting planner & consult, currently. **Orgs:** Comn Admin, Young Women's Christian Asn, 1977-84; regional dir, Zeta Phi Beta Sorority, 1978-80, nat conv chmn, 1978, nat first vpres, 1980-84; Comn Accreditation Schs Tex, 1978-83; nat pres, Top Ladies Distinction Inc, 1983-87; hon bd mem, TSU Maroon & Grey Ex-Students Asn, 1983-84; nat bd conv chmn, Nat Coun Negro Women, 1985, 1987 & 1989; speakers bur, Houston Planned Parenthood Fedn, Houston Urban League Guild; nat exec Bd, Nat Coun Negro Women; nat chmn, Social & Legis Action Top Ladies Distinction Inc; nat vpres, Nat Coun Negro Women Inc, 1991-95; dir, Franchell Boswell Educ Found. **Home Addr:** 3207 Parkwood Dr, Houston, TX 77021, **Home Phone:** (713)747-1541. **Business Addr:** Meeting Planner, Consultant, Captain Campaign, 3207 Parkwood Dr, Houston, TX 77021, **Business Phone:** (713)748-3119.

### MOOREHEAD, ERIC K.
Research administrator. **Personal:** Born Jun 21, 1958, Baltimore, MD; son of Archie Clarence and Rose Marie Lewis; married Gemma Arlene Arrieta; children: Bradford & Brookelyn. **Educ:** Univ Cent Arks, BA, 1980; Univ Southern Calif, Grad Sch, jour, 1984. **Career:** Western Elec, NY, intern pub Rels, 1980; City Los Angeles, Los Angeles, intern, press Off Mayor Tom Bradley, 1982; Los Angeles Bus Jour, Los Angeles, Calif, edial intern, 1984; Arks Dem Gazette, Little Rock, copy ed & reporter, 1986-90; Ark State Press, Little Rock, Ark, reporter, 1990-91; Little Rock View Mag, Little Rock, ed, 1991; Univ Ark Med Sci, Little Rock, med rec technician, 1997-, res admin, 2002-, inst rev bd adminr, currently. **Orgs:** Nat Asn Black Journalists; Univ Cent Ark Alumni Asn; Univ Cent Ariz, African-Am Alumni Asn. **Honors/Awds:** AEJ/NYU Summer Internship, Asn Educ Journalism, New York Univ, 1980; Dean's List, Univ Cent Arks, 1979; Whos Who Among African Am; Grants Mgt Cert, 2005. **Home Addr:** 2025 Lawson Oaks Dr, Little Rock, AR 72210-5031. **Business Addr:** Institutional Review Board Administrator, Research Administration, University of Arizona Medical Science, 4301 W Markham St, Little Rock, AR 72205, **Business Phone:** (501)526-6248.

### MOOREHEAD, JUSTIN LESLIE
Banker. **Personal:** Born Oct 31, 1947, St. Thomas. **Educ:** Occidental Col, Los Angeles, CA, BA, hist, 1969; Princeton Univ, Woodrow Wilson Sch, MPA, econ devel, 1971; NY Univ Grad Sch Bus Admin, transp econ, 1974; Univ Mich Exec Acad, 1977. **Career:** Govt Kenya, rural devel planner, 1970; Govt US Vi, economist off budget dir, 1971-72; Virgin Island Dept PubWorks, admin, 1972-73; Amerada Hess Corp, analyst, 1973-75; Govt US VI, dir, off mgt & budget, 1975-79; Bank Am, Munic Credit & Money Mkt Instr, 1978; Lehman Bros Kuhn Loeb Inc, vpres, publ fin, 1979-93; City Philadelphia, dep mayor econmic develop, 1988-99; Seslia & Co, pres, prin, managing dir, 1990-; Dean Witter Reynolds Inc, sr vpres, managing dir pub finance, 1993-97. **Orgs:** Woodrow Wilson Sch Alumni Asn. **Home Addr:** 390 Highland Ave, Montclair, NJ 07042. **Business Addr:** President, Principal, Seslia & CO, 281 Locust St, Philadelphia, PA 19106, **Business Phone:** (267)671-0900.

### MOORER, LANA MICHELE. See MC LYTE.

### MOORER, MICHAEL LEE
Boxer, executive. **Personal:** Born Nov 12, 1967, Brooklyn, NY; married Bobbie; children: Michael Jr. **Career:** Professional boxer (retired), coach, bodyguard; prof boxer, 1988-2004; Tiger Woods, boxing trainer, currently; bodyguard, currently; Moorer Sports and Entertainment Management, founder, 1992; John Chapman, trainer, 2005; Wild Card Boxing Club, asst trainer, 2009. **Honors/Awds:** United States Amateur Light Middleweight champion, 1986; Bronze Medal, Goodwill Games, 1986; WBO Light Heavyweight Champion, World Boxing Orgn, 1988-91; WBO Heavyweight Champion, World Boxing Orgn, 1992-93; World Heavyweight Boxing Champion, 1994-95; IBF Heavyweight Champion, Int Boxing Fedn, 1996-97; WBC Continental Americas Heavyweight Champion, World Boxing Coun, 2004; NABA Heavyweight Champion, N Am Boxing Asn, 2004. **Business Addr:** Trainer.

### MOORING, DR. KITTYE D.S.
Educator, association executive. **Personal:** Born Mar 18, 1932, San Antonio, TX; married Leon. **Educ:** Prairie View A&M Univ, BA, 1953, MS, 1960; Univ Houston, EdD, 1969. **Career:** Carver HS, dept head, 1953-62; Prairie View A & M Univ, assoc prof, 1962-68; Bus Educ & Off Admin Tex Southern Univ, dept head; Sch Bus, assoc dean, 1990-93. **Orgs:** Nat & Tex Bus Asn; chmn, Tex Bus Teacher Educ Coun, 1973-75; Tex Asn Col Teachers; Am Asn Univ Prof; YWCA; chmn, Univ Curric Comn, 1980-; chmn, Fac Awards & Recognition Comt, 1985-; Chadwick Manor Civic Club; Community Stand, 1989-92; life mem, Delta Pi Epsilon, 2010. **Honors/Awds:** Many hon soc; State Service Youth Award; Leaders Black Am, 1974; Teacher of the Year, TBEA Col Bus, 1983; Teacher of the Year, McCleary, 1993. **Home Addr:** 2615 Hodges Bend Cir, Sugar Land, TX 77479-1406, **Home Phone:** (281)980-8168.

### MOORMAN, HOLSEY ALEXANDER
Military leader. **Personal:** Born May 18, 1938, Roanoke, VA; son of Holsey James and Grace O Walker; married Carrie Boyd; children: Gary Wayne. **Educ:** Thomas A Edison Col, AA; Hampton Univ, attended 1958; Pk Col, BS, bus admin, 1986; Command & Gen Staff Col; AUs War Col, sr res component officer course; mediation & conflict mgt skills, 2000. **Career:** Military leader (retired); US Civil Serv, training officer, 1965-68, admin officer, 1968-80, EEO officer, 1980-86; 104th's C Co Comdr, 1975; 104th's asst div engr; Head quarters State Area Command, human resource/equal opportunity officer & asst exec dir, 1981-82; Off Human Resources, Nat Guard Bur, Wash, DC, equal opportunity specialist to chief field operating agency; Off Dept Chief Staff Personnel AUs, personnel policy integrator; Nj Army Nat Guard, 50th Armored Div, platoon leader, personnel officer, & liaison officer; Off Dep Chief Staff Personnel a Personnel Policy Integrator, 1986-87; Army Res Forces & Mobilization, asst dep secy, mil asst, 1987-90; Asst Secy Army, Wa, DC, asst dep, 1990-92; Army Res Forces Policy Comt, mil exec, 1992-94, dep adj gen, 1994-98. **Orgs:** Life mem, Nat Guard Asn NJ, 1964-, life mem, Nat Guard Asn US, 1964-; PHA, F&AM, 1978-; EEO investr Nat Guard Bur, 1982-86. **Honors/Awds:** Service Award, NAACP, Roy Wilkens Renown Service, 1993; Meritorious Serv Medal, Army Commendation Medal, Army Serv Ribbon, Armed Forces Reserve Achievement Medal, Armed Forces Reserve Medal, NJ Medal Honor; Army Distinguished Service Medal; Legion Merit; National Defense Service Medal; Army Superior Unit Award; NJ Good Conduct Award; Desert Storm Ribbon; New Mexico Medal Merit; Governor's Unit Award; Unit Strength Award; National Guard Bureau Eagle Award, 1994, 2000; Army Reserve Component Achievement Medal. **Home Addr:** 56 Brookside Lane, Palm Coast, FL 32137, **Home Phone:** (386)447-3860.

### MOOSE, GEORGE EDWARD
Educator, government official. **Personal:** Born Jun 23, 1944, New York, NY; son of Robert and Ellen Amanda Lane Jones; married Judith Roberta Kaufmann. **Educ:** Grinnell Col, BA, 1966, hon doctorate law, 1990; Syracuse Univ, postgrad, 1967. **Career:** Dept State Wash DC, spec asst under secy polit affairs, 1977-78, dep dir SAfrica 1978-79; Coun Foreign Rels New York, int affairs fel, 1979-80; US Mission UN New York, dep polit counr, 1980-83; Dept State Wash DC, US ambassador Benin, 1983-86, dep dir off mgt opers, 1986-87, dir off mgt opers, 1987-88; US ambassador Senegal, 1988-91; US Alt Rep UN Security Coun, 1991-92; Dept State, asst secy African affairs, 1993-97; Europ Off UN, Geneva, US Ambassador & permanent rep, 1998-2001; Ralph J Bunche Int Affairs Ctr, Howard Univ, 2001-02; Elliott Sch Int Affairs, George Wash Univ, adj prof, currently; int health diplomacy, consult, currently; US Dept State, sr inspector, Off Inspector Gen, 2002-. **Orgs:** Am Foreign Serv Asn, 1967-; foreign affairs fel, Coun Foreign Rels New York, 1979-80; Asn Black Am Ambassadors, 1985-; Policy Coun Una Chapman Cox Found, 1986-89; Coun Foreign Rels, 1991-; bd dir, African Develop Found, 1993-97; ambassador & permanent rep, UN Off Geneva, 1998-2001; sr fel, Ralph J Bunche Int Affairs Ctr, Howard Univ, 2001-02; sr inspector, Off Inspector Gen, US Dept State, 2002-; fel, Harvard Univ, currently; vice chmn bd dir, US Inst Peace, 2007-; chair & bd dir, Search Common Ground, 2003-; sr fel LMI, 2006-. **Home Addr:** 2315 N Glebe Rd, Arlington, VA 22207-3410, **Home Phone:** (703)248-8694. **Business Addr:** Adjunct Professor, The George Washington University, 1957 E St NW, Washington, DC 20052, **Business Phone:** (202)994-6240.

### MORAGNE, LENORA
Editor, publisher. **Personal:** Born Sep 29, 1931, Evanston, IL; daughter of Joseph Sr (deceased) and Linnie Lee (deceased). **Educ:** Iowa State Univ, BS; Cornell Univ, MS, PhD, 1969. **Career:** Community Hosp, Evanston, Ill, chief dietitian, 1955-57; Cornell Univ, asst prof, 1961-63; NC Col, asst prof, 1965-67; Gen Foods Corp, nutrit publicist, 1968-71; Columbia Univ, lectr, 1971-72; Hunter Col, prof, 1971-72; Food & Nutrit Serv USDA, head nutrit, ed & trng, 1972-77; Agr Nutrit & Forestry Comn, US Senate, prof staff mem, first female, 1977-79; DHHS, nutrit policy coordr, 1979-84; Nutrit Legis Serv, founder, pres, 1985-; Nat Acad Sci, sr proj officer, Inst Med, 1988-89; Nat Rainbow Coalition, consult, 1990; Environ Protection Agency, environ officer, 1994-. **Orgs:** Bd dir, Am Dietetic Asn, 1981-84; APHA Prog Develop Bd, 1984-87; nominee bd trustee, Cornell Univ, 1984; chmn, Cornell Univ Fed Govt Rels Comt, 1985-88; adv coun, Meharry Med Col Nutrit Ctr, 1986-90; founding ed, publ, Nutrit Legis & Regulatory News, Nutrit Funding Report, 1986-; founding ed, publ, Black Cong Monitor, 1987-; pres, Soc Nutrit Educ, 1987-88; founding mem, Joseph & Linnie Lee Monagne Memorial Scholar Fund, 1992-; Am Dietetic Asn; Soc Nutrit Ed; Am Pub Health Asn; Cornell Club DC; Nat Coun Women; adv Coun, Cornell Univ; adv coun, Iowa State Univ; adv coun, Univ Del; adv coun, Univ Md. **Home Addr:** 607 4th St SW, Washington, DC 20024-2792, **Home Phone:** (202)484-3571. **Business Addr:** Environmental Officer, Environmental Protection Agency, 1200 Pa Ave NW, Washington, DC 20460, **Business Phone:** (215)814-5000.

### MORAGNE, MAURICE S. (MAURICE MO MORAGNE)
Executive, businessperson. **Personal:** Born Jan 22, 1964, Washington, DC; son of Jacquelyn D; married Dana M; children: Mitchell M & Jordan A. **Educ:** Edinboro Univ Pa, BA, polit sci & span, 1986. **Career:** Brit Am Tobacco, global dir trade mkt, 1986-99; Brown & Williamson, sales rep, Orlando, 1987-89, div mgr, Orlando, 1989-91, brand mkt assoc, Louisville KY, 1991-94, dist sales mgr, Champaign IL, 1994, dist sales mgr, Milwaukee WI, 1994-95, sect sales mgr, Baltimore, 1995-96, dir human resources, 1996-2002, dir, trade mkt, 2000-02; Moragne & Assoc, prin, 2003-04; Chiquita Brands Int, dir sales & mkt, US Food Serv Div, dir, 2004-08; L'Oreal, asst vpres sales admin & oper, 2006-07; Naturipe Foods LLC, vpres sales & mkt, 2008-10; Chiquita Fresh Exp, global dir sales, 2006-07, global dir bus develop, 2011; Chiquita Fruit

Solutions, gen mgr, 2011-15; Patagonia Foods, sr consult, 2015-16; Int Agr Group LLC, chief exec officer, 2015-. **Orgs:** Foodnews World Juice; Int Mango Orgn; Phi Kappa Psi Alumni & Undergraduates; N Am Fruit & Veg Buyers & Sellers; Phi Kappa Psi Alumni; Northwest Food Mfg; Phi Kappa Psi Fraternity Penn Xi. **Honors/Awds:** Black Achievers Award, Louisville, 1993; Who's Who In Corporate Black America Award, Dollars & Sense Mag, 1998. **Home Addr:** 17207 Mallet Hill Dr, Louisville, KY 40245, **Home Phone:** (502)244-9590. **Business Addr:** Chief Executive Officer, International Agriculture Group LLC, Charlotte, NC.

## MORAGNE, DR. RUDOLPH

Physician. **Personal:** Born Feb 5, 1933, Evanston, IL; married Kathlyn Elaine; children: Donna, Diana & Lisa. **Educ:** Univ Ill, BS, 1955; Meharry Med Col, MD, 1959. **Career:** Cook Co Hosp, intern, 1959, resident, 1961-66; Hedd Surgi Ctr, abortionist, 1986. **Orgs:** Life fel Am Col Obstet & Gynec; AMA; Nat Med Asn; Ill & Chicago MedSoc; Cook Co Physicians Asn; Univ Chicago LyingHosp staff; dir, S Side-Bank; Urban League; Oper PUSH; fel Am Cong Obstetricians & Gynecologists. **Honors/Awds:** Beautiful People Award, Chicago Urban League, 1973. **Special Achievements:** Co-author Our Baby's Early Years 1974. **Home Addr:** 5036 S Ellis Ave, Chicago, IL 60615. **Business Addr:** Abortionist, Hedd Surgi-Center, 8124 S Cottage Grove Ave, Chicago, IL 60619, **Business Phone:** (773)723-4098.

## MORAN, GEORGE H., JR.

Human services worker. **Personal:** Born Jun 30, 1941, Chicago, IL; son of George H and Wedell Johnson. **Educ:** Ind Univ-Purdue Univ, Indianapolis; Baker Col, AAS; Detroit Col, BS, comput info syst. **Career:** Instr, data processing; comput programming; Employ Serv, Durable Veteran Outreach; Mich Employ Security Comn, employ analyst, chair emer, currently; Mich Employ Security Agency, veterans coordr, currently. **Orgs:** Chair, Vietnam Veterans Monument Comn; VFW 3791; Southern Cross 39, free mason; Int Asn State Employ; Black Asn State Employers; Black Data Processing Asn, VVA, Vietnam, Vietnam Veterans Am. **Honors/Awds:** VVA Retraining Award, Veterans VVA, 1993; VFW Henry Wolfe Award, Henry Wolf Dept Mich, 1994; African Veterans Banquet, State of MI, 1994. **Home Addr:** 1055 W Harvard Ave, Flint, MI 48505-1223, **Home Phone:** (810)875-9871. **Business Addr:** Chair Emeritus, Michigan Employment Security Commission, 510 Blvd Bldg 7310 Woodward Ave, Detroit, MI 48202, **Business Phone:** (313)876-5901.

## MORAN, DR. JOYCE E.

Lawyer. **Personal:** Born May 21, 1948, Chicago, IL; daughter of Theodore E and Irma Rhyne. **Educ:** Smith Col Northampton, AB, psychol, 1969; Yale Law Sch New Haven, JD, 1972; Univ Chicago, MBA, finance, 1981. **Career:** Sidley & Austin, assoc atty, 1972-78; Sears Roebuck & Co, vpres, law, 1978-2002, asst gen coun & asst secy, 1993; gen coun bus, corp secy, vpres-law, full-line stores, 1996; Welfare Work Partnership, exec loan, 2000-02; Morityne Develop Co LLC, pres, 2002-; Latham & Watkins Chicago, coun. **Orgs:** Vpres, Smith Col Class, 1969, 1974-79; vpres, Chicago League Smith Col Clubs, 1972-; Jr Gov Bd Chicago Symphony Orchestra, 1973-85; bd dir, vpres, pres, 1980-82, Legal Asst Found Chicago, 1974-88; Chicago Symphony Chorus & Chorale Omega, 1974-78; vpres, treas, Yale Law Sch Asn, 1975-78; chmn, Lawyers Comt Chicago Urban League, 1980-82; coordr, Coppin AME Church Enrichment Prog, 1981-84; bd dir, Chicago Area Found Legal Serv, 1982-95; ed rev team leader, Mayor Wash Transition Comt Chicago, 1983; bd dir, vpres, Am Civil Liberties Union, 1983-92; bd dir, Alumnae Asn Smith Col, 1984-87; bd dir, Chicago Found Women, vice chmn, 1985-88, adv coun, 1989-92; bd dir, vpres, treas, Chicago Sch Fin Authority, 1985-93; Kennedy-King COT Chorus, 1986-99; Ill Judicial Inquiry Bd, 1987-91; dir, Am Civil Liberties Union, 1987-89; bd trustee, Smith Col, vice chmn, chmn, pres, search comnr, AD Hoc chapel comt, 1988-98; bd dir, Women's Asn Chicago Symphony Orchestra, secy, 1991-97, dir, exec leadership coun, 1997-; vol, Minority Corp Coun Asn, Inc. **Honors/Awds:** Distinguished Service Award, Coppin Am Church Chicago, 1972; Player of the Year Jr Master, Am Bridge Asn, 1977; Beautiful People Award, Chicago Urban League, 1979; YMCA of Metro Chicago Black & Hispanic Achievers of Industrial Recognition Award, 1981; Ten Outstanding Young Citizen Award, Chicago Jr Asn Com & Indust, 1985. **Home Addr:** 5831 N Sheridan Rd, Chicago, IL 60660-3835, **Home Phone:** (773)334-3157. **Business Addr:** Volunteer, Minority Corporate Counsel Association Inc, 1111 Pa Ave NW, Washington, DC 20004, **Business Phone:** (202)739-5901.

## MORANCIE, HORACE L.

Government official, management consultant. **Personal:** Born San Fernando. **Educ:** Polytech Inst Brooklyn, BS, civil engineering, 1958; Cornell Univ, MS, sanit engineering & microbiol, 1960; Brooklyn Law Sch, Harvard Univ, John F Kennedy Sch Govt, cert, 1982. **Career:** Cornell Univ, teaching fel, 1958-60; Port Authority NY & NJ, res & civil engr, 1960-68; Off Mayor, City NY, asst admin, 1968-74; Addiction Res Treat Corp, founder, 1969, chmn emer, dir, currently; Rockland Community Action Coun Inc, mgt consult, 1974-80, exec dir, 1976-80; State NY, Div Econs Opportunity, dir, 1980-82; City Harrisburg, Dept Community & Econs Develop, dir; Horace L Morancie & Assocs, develop housing & mgt consult. **Orgs:** Bd chmn, Urban Resources Inst, Addiction Res & Treat Corp; vice chmn, Harrisburg Redevelop Authority; bd mem, Nat Community Develop Asn; chmn, Harrisburg Property Reinvestment Bd. **Home Addr:** 469 Rockaway Pkwy, Brooklyn, NY 11212, **Home Phone:** (718)495-4977. **Business Addr:** Chairman Emeritus, Addiction Research & Treatment Corp, 22 Chapel St, Brooklyn, NY 11201, **Business Phone:** (718)260-2900.

## MORANT, MACK BERNARD

Publisher, educator, writer. **Personal:** Born Oct 15, 1946, Holly Hill, SC; son of Mack and Jannie Gilmore. **Educ:** Voorhees Col, Denmark, SC, BS, bus admin, 1968; Univ Mass, Amherst, MA, MEd, urban educ, 1972, CAGS, educ admin, 1973, EdD, 1976. **Career:** SC Pub Sch Syst, hist, Eng, bus teacher, 1968-71; Univ Mass, grad stud, res asst, 1971-74; Belcher Town State Sch, ment health asst, 1974-76; Dillion-Marion Human Resources Com, dep dir, 1977-81; SC State Col, Orangeburg, SC, dir small bus develop, 1982-85; Va State Univ, Petersburg, Va, placement dir, 1985-92; Augusta Col, asst prog, teacher geog, 1992-96; Voorhees Col, stud support serv prog, dir & asst prof, 1997-; Blackville Hilda High Sch, bus educ teacher, currently. Books: Insane Nigger, auth; African Americans on Stamps, auth; Teacher / Student Work Manual: A Model For Evaluating Traditional U. S. History Textbooks; A Guide For A Balanced History Curriculum, auth; Face of African Americans on US and International Stamps: A Guide to Collecting and Investing, auth. **Orgs:** Alpha Kappa Psi Fraternity, 1985-; vice-chmn, VA State Univ Assessment Comt, 1986-87; Prince Hall Mason, 1986-; Am Philatelic Soc, 1988-. **Home Addr:** , North Augusta, SC 29841. **Business Addr:** Teacher, Blackville-Hilda High School, 76 Atkins Cir, Blackville, SC 29817, **Business Phone:** (803)284-5700.

## MORDECAI, DAVID K. A.

Economist, financial manager. **Personal:** Born Sep 27, 1961, New York, NY; son of Kenneth and Vinette; married Samantha Kappagoda. **Educ:** King's Col, BA, philos/humanities, 1983; NY Univ, Stern Grad Sch Bus Admin, MBA, finance, 1987; Univ Chicago, Grad Sch Bus, PhD, econs & economet/statist, 2004. **Career:** NatWest NJ Com Credit Analyst, 1984-86; New York Univ Stern Sch/Chase Manhattan fel, 1985-86; Bankers Trust, assoc, corp finance, 1987-88; Emanuel & Co, vpres, corp finance, 1988-90; W Deutsche Landesbank, asst vp, leveraged capital group, 1990-91; Bank Montreal, consult, foreign exchange trading, 1992-93; Univ Chicago, Grad Sch Bus fel, 1993-; Credit Suisse First Boston, consult, 1995; FITCHIBCA Inc, dir, com ABS group, 1997-98; AIG Global Investments, vpres, financial eng, 1998-2001; Am Int Group, Structured Prod, vpres, financial eng/prin finance, 1998-2001; Clinton Group, managing dir, structured prod, 2001-03; Risk Econs Ltd Inc, founder, currently; Columbia Univ, guest lectr; Compass Lexecon, sr advisor, 2009-14, adv comt, 2011-14; J Risk Finance (JRF), founding Ed-in-Chief; S3 Asset Mgt, S3 Asset Funding, founding Partner. **Orgs:** Int Investment Mgt Steering Comt, New York Mercantile Exchange, 1998-; Am Econ Asn, 1998-; Am Finance Asn, 1998-; Ins Indust Working Group, Nat Bur Econ Res, 1999-; adv bd & IRC Steering Comt, Int Asn Financial Engrs, 2000-01; adv bd, Jour Alternative Investments, Euromoney/Insts Investor Jour, 2004-; co-chair, Liquidity Risk Comt, 2005-; Financial Insts Risks Working Group, 2005-; bd mem, Hudson Highlands Land Trust, 2007-; sr adv, Swiss Financial Serv, 2007; New York Asn Bus Economists, 2007-; bd mem, Hudsonia, 2008-; bd mem, Clearwater, 2008-; bd mem, Scenic Hudson, 2009-; speaker, Off Directorate Nat Intelligence, 2009; Am Bar Asn, 2010-; NYU Courant Inst Math Sci, Computational Econs & Algorithmic Data Analytics Initiative, co-exec dir, 2011-; Asn Comput Mach, 2011-; Am Statist Asn, 2012-; New York Acad Sci, 2012-; Steering Comt, Investor Risk Working Group, 2013-; Soc Bayesian Statist, 2013-; SIAM, 2013-; adv/edial bd, Int Encycl Derivatives; chief exec officer, Swiss Re Capital Mgt & Div; bd mem, Univ Chicago Grad Sch Bus Alumni Club; Beta Gamma Sigma Hons Socs; sr mem, JRF adv bd; adv bd J Alternative Investments; active mem IAFE Adv Bd; advisor to NYMEX, partic, Nat bur Econ Res, & Wharton Financial Insts Ctr. **Honors/Awds:** Stern School Dean's Service Awardd, New York Univ, 1986-87; Received Numerous Awards. **Special Achievements:** Editor in Chief, Journal of Risk Finance, Euromoney/Institutional Investor Journals, 1998-2004; Author: Emerging Market Credit Derivatives & Default Estimation, in Credit Derivatives: Applications for Investment, Portfolio Optimization & Risk Mgmt, 1998; The Use of Credit Derivatives In Credit-Enhanced & Credit-Linked Structuren Notes, The Handbook of Credit Derivatives, 1999; Alternative Risk Transfer, The Handbook of Alternate Investment Strategies, 1999: Editor of Numerous Articles/Books. **Home Addr:** 325 Fifth Ave, PO Box 76, New York, NY 10016, **Home Phone:** (917)402-1422. **Business Addr:** President/Partner, Founder, Risk Economics Ltd Inc, c/o S3 Partners, New York, NY 10022, **Business Phone:** (212)759-5222.

## MORELAND, DR. LOIS BALDWIN

Educator, school administrator. **Personal:** Born Washington, DC; daughter of Genis G and Fannie Lillian Rives; married Charlie J; children: Lisa Carol. **Educ:** Sarah Lawrence Col, BA, 1955; Howard Univ, MA, polit sci, 1957; Am Univ, WA, PhD, polit sci, 1968. **Career:** Howard Univ, asst & instr social sci, 1956-57; Libr Congress, Wash, legal advisor, 1958-59; SE reg youth field sec, 1957-58; US Sen R Vance Hartke, legis asst, 1958-59; Spelman Col, instr, 1959-65, Polit Sci Dept, asst prof & founding chmn, 1965-70, prof & chmn, 1970-90, 1991-92, actg dean instr, 1970-72, chmn soc sci div, 1980-90, prof polit sci, Int Affairs Ctr, founding dir, 1989-98, prof emer, 1999-, secy. **Orgs:** Charter mem & first treas, Nat Conf Black Polit Sci; mem, Am Asn Univ Women; Nat Asn Advan Colored People; League Women Voters; mem, Fulton Co Bd Elections; Fulton Co Jury Comn; Gov's Coun Human Rel; Am Southern & Ga Polit Sci Assoc; Assoc Polit & Life Sci; Alpha Kappa Alpha; mem, adv Coun, Nat Inst Neurol, Commun Disease & Stroke; mem, Adv Coun Deafness & Commun Dis; NIH; Prof Adv Bd, Nat Epilepsy Found, 1984-9; Am Polit Sci Asn; Am Asn Univ Prof; Am Asn Univ Women; Nat Conf Black Polit Scientists; Southern Polit Sci Asn; Ga Polit Sci Asn. **Home Addr:** 849 Woodmere Dr NW, Atlanta, GA 30318-6001, **Home Phone:** (404)799-9310. **Business Addr:** Professor Emeritus, Spelman College, 350 Spelman Lane SW, Atlanta, GA 30314-4399, **Business Phone:** (404)681-3643.

## MORELAND-YOUNG, DR. CURTINA

Educator. **Personal:** Born Mar 5, 1949, Columbia, SC; daughter of Gladys Evelyn Glover Moreland and Curtis Weldon Moreland; married James Young; children: Curtis Jamel Turner. **Educ:** Fisk Univ, Nashville, TN, BA, eng, BS, polit sci, 1969; Univ Ill, Urbana, MA, polit sci, 1970, PhD, 1976; Harvard Univ, Cambridge, MA, PhD, 1984; Univ Mich, post doctoral, pub health, 2001. **Career:** Ohio State Univ, Dept Black Studies, Columbus, Ohio, instr asst prof, 1971-78; Jackson State Univ, Miss Col & Univ Consortium Int Study, Dept Polit Sci, coordr MA prog, assoc prof, 1978-84, prof & chair, pub policy & admin dept, 1984-2006, founding chair, 1993-12; Harvard Univ, postdoctoral fel, 1983-84; Nexus Consults, chief exec officer, 1998-; Univ Mich, post-doctoral fel, 2001; Ms. Consortium Int Develop, dir int progs, 2005-10. **Orgs:** Chair, pres, Conf Minority Pub Adminr, 1989-90; exec bd, Nat Conf Black Polit Scientist, 1989; Nat Coun Am Soc Pub Adminr, 1989-90; chair, Comt Orgn Rev & Eval, ASPA, 1990-91; exec bd, Jackson Int Visitors Ctr. **Home Addr:** 5915 Huntview Dr, Jackson, MS 39206-2128, **Home Phone:** (601)366-5910. **Business Addr:** Professor, Jackson State University, 3825 Ridgewood Rd, Jackson, MS 39211, **Business Phone:** (601)432-6266.

## MORGAN, ALICE JOHNSON PARHAM

Health services administrator. **Personal:** Born Jul 17, 1943, Richmond, VA; daughter of Elmore W Johnson Jr and Fannye Mae Quarles Johnson; married Wilson M; children: Weldon Leo & Arvette Patrice. **Educ:** Va Union Univ, BA, 1965; Va Commonwealth Univ, MSW, 1967; Univ Southern Calif, Wash Pub Affairs Ctr, MPA, 1982. **Career:** Health service adminstrator (retired); Area D CMHC, supvr, soc worker, 1981; St Elizabeth's Hosp, soc work prog, 1981-82; Area D CMHC, soc worker, 1982-83, dir, spec apt prog, 1983-88, dir, Region IV Psychosocial Day Prog, 1988-91, Region 4 Housing, resource specialist, 1991-2002. **Orgs:** Bd dir, Nat Conf Christians & Jews; bd dir, Alexandria Ment Health Asn; VA, Planning Comm, 1971-79; chairperson, city Alex, VA, Martin Luther King Planning Comm, 1973-; dir, comm placement off, Area D, CMHC, 1972-79; First Black Female City Coun Cand, Alex, VA, 1979; ed & stand specialist, St Elizabeth's Hosp, 1979-80; prog analyst, Pub Health Serv, 1980-81; dir, comm placement off, AreaD, CMHC, 1980; Boys Club; Legal Aid Soc. **Special Achievements:** In 1979, she was the first African American woman to run for City Council. First African American woman to be appointed to the Planning Commission. **Home Addr:** 1513 Dogwood Dr, Alexandria, VA 22302.

## MORGAN, ALISHA THOMAS

**Personal:** Born May 9, 1978, Miami, FL; married David; children: Lailah. **Educ:** Spelman Col, BA, sociol & drama, 2000. **Career:** Ga House, Dist 39, rep, currently, educ comn, C & youth comn, info comn & audits comn, currently; 1380 WAOK, comn talk, host, currently; Morganics, prin & chief exec officer, currently. **Orgs:** Pres, Nat Asn Advan Colored People, Miami Dade Youth Coun; pres, Spelman Col Chap; state pres, Spelman Col Chap, Youth & Col Div; Destiny World Church Austell; Alpha Kappa Alpha Sorority Inc; Rho Zeta Omega Chap; bd, Joseph E LoweryInst; Steering Comn, Ga Coalition People Agenda; Austell Community askforce; Nat Coalition 100 Black Women, NW Ga Chap. **Honors/Awds:** Leadership Awards, Nat Asn Advan Colored People; Outstanding Young Woman Award, Concerned Black Clergy; Unsung Heroine Award, Anti-Defamation League; Freshman Legislator of the Year, Ga Legis Black Caucus, 2008; Flemming Fel, Ctr Policy Alternatives, 2006; s 30 Leaders who are under 30, Ebony mag; Americas Young Civil Rights Heroes, AOL Black Voices; New Power Generation, Essence mag; Brightest 40 under 40, Ga Trend Mag & Ga Informer. **Special Achievements:** First African-Am to serve in Ga House Representatives, Cobb Co, 2002; Youngest service mem entire Ga Gen Assembly; Featured in: Atlanta Tribune, Women Looking Ahead; Ga brightest 40 under 40, Ga Trend Mag; Nations 30Leaders who are under 30, Ebony mag; one ten Am Young Civil Rights Heroes, AOL Black Voices; one six women in country featured in article "I Made in By 30 & You Can Too", Marie Claire Mag; selected as a deleg to travel to S Africa with Am Coun Young Polit Leaders; Flemming Fel, Ctr for Policy Alternatives, 2006; Launched "Closing the Achievement Gap", 2009; Author of "No Apologies: Powerful Lessons in Life, Love and Politics", 2009. **Business Addr:** Representative, GA House of Representatives, 6570 Brandemere Way, Austell, GA 30168, **Business Phone:** (404)656-0109.

## MORGAN, CLYDE ALAFIJU

Educator, dance teacher. **Personal:** Born Jan 30, 1940, Cincinnati, OH; son of Lee and Harriette Young; married Marie Lais Goes; children: Clyde G, Dyuna G & Lee Young G. **Educ:** Cleveland State Univ, Cleveland, OH, BA, 1963; Bennington Col, Bennington, VT, prof cert, 1965. **Career:** Bennington Col, VT, dance fel, 1963-64; Jose Limon Dance Co; Univ Wis, Madison, WI, vis artist, 1979-80, asst prof, 1980-87; Fed Univ Bahia, Salvador, Bahia, Brazil, Group Dance, choreographer & artistic dir, Fulbright, prof, 1984-86, vis artist; State Univ NY Brockport, Sankofa African Dance & Drum Ensemble, artistic dir, 1985-, assoc prof, African dance, senate rep, currently; Cult Found, Salvador, Bahia, Brazil, vis artist; Young Audience Inc, assoc prof, 1993; Int Dance and Music Inst. **Orgs:** Cong Res Dance, 1985-; United Univ Prof, 1987-; Dance Hist Scholars, 1991-; Fulbright Alumni Asn; judge, advisor & adjudicator, Nat Found Advan Arts, Fla; bd mem, Dance Brazil Co Inc. **Home Addr:** 3871 Lake Rd N, Brockport, NY 14420, **Home Phone:** (716)637-5663. **Business Addr:** Associate Professor of African Dance, Artistic Director of Sankofa, State University of New York, Hartwell Hall 350 New Campus Dr, Brockport, NY 14420-2914, **Business Phone:** (585)395-5789.

## MORGAN, DARIAN. See TIGGER, BIG.

## MORGAN, DEBBI

Actor. **Personal:** Born Sep 20, 1956, Dunn, NC; daughter of George Jr and Lora; married Charles S Dutton, Dec 31, 1989, (divorced 1994); married Charles Weldon, Jan 1, 1980, (divorced 1984); married Jeffery Winston, Jun 6, 2009. **Career:** Soap operas: All My C, 1982-90; Generations, 1990-91; Loving, 1993-95; The City, 1995-97; Port Charles, 1997-98. TV series: "Roots", 1979; "All my Children", 1982-2008; "Loving", 1983-95; "The Jesse Owens Story", 1984; "The city", 1995; "Soul Food", 2000; "Boston Pub", recurring role, 2000; "The Runaway", 2000; "For the People", 2002; "Charmed", 2002-03; "Touching Evil", 2004; "Woman Thou Art Loosed", 2006; "Prodigal Son", 2006; "Closeto Home", 2006; "Ghost Whisperer", 2006; "Close to Home", 2006; "The Bold & the Beautiful", 2006-07; "The Young and the Restless", 2011-12; "Power", 2014; The Black Man's Guide to Understanding Black Women, 2010. Films: Mandingo, 1975; Eve's Bayou, 1997; Asunder, 1998; She's All That, 1999; The Hurricane, 1999; Love & Basketball, 2000; Woman Thou Art Loosed, 2004; Back in the Day, 2005; Relative Strangers, 2005; Coach Carter, 2005; Rel Strangers, 2006; Close to Home, 2006; Color of the Cross, 2006; The Young & the Restless, 2011; A Royal Family Holiday, 2015; Royal Family Christmas, 2015; Toni Braxton: Unbreak My Heart, 2016. **Honors/Awds:** The 14th Annual Daytime Emmy Awards, ABC, 1987; Daytime Emmy Award, Outstanding Supporting Actress in Drama Series, 1989; Daytime Emmy Award, 1989; CFCA Award, Chicago Film Critics Asn, 1998; Independent Spirit Award, 1998; OFTA Film Award & OFTA Television Award, Online Film & Tv Asn, 1998; Image Award, 2002 & 2009-10; Critics Association Award; Gracie Allen Award, 2009; Emmy Award. **Special Achievements:** First African American Actress to win the Emmy Award for Best Supporting Actress, 1989; Syndicated for 19th Annual Black Filmmakers Hall of Fame, 1992; Presenter of the 21st Annual Daytime Emmy Awards, ABC, 1994; Presenter of The 22nd

Annual Daytime Emmy Awards, NBC, 1995; Syndicated for 12th Annual Stellar Gospel Music Awards, 1997; Presenter of the 14th Annual Soap Opera Awards, NBC, 1998; Syndicated for 13th Annual Stellar Awards, 1998; Nominee for Daytime Emmy Award for Outstanding Lead Actress in a Drama Series, 2009. **Business Addr:** Actress, Stone Manners, 8436 W Third St Suite 740, Los Angeles, CA 90048-4100, **Business Phone:** (213)654-7575.

## MORGAN, DOLORES PARKER

Entertainer, musician. **Personal:** Born New Orleans, LA; daughter of Joseph and Mabel Moton; married Vernon Smith; children: Melodie Morgan-Minott; married E Gates. **Educ:** Chicago Musical Col, 1941; Wilson Col. **Career:** Earl "Fatha" Hines, singer, 1945-47; Duke Ellington, singer, 1947-49; solo performer & singer, 1949-56; Local Charity Events, singer, 1960-; Traditions, soloist, 1999; Duke Ellington Orchestra. **Orgs:** Bd mem, corres secn Ohio Ballet, 1983-87; exec bd trust, Vis Nurses Serv, 1984-; develop coun, Akron Art Mus, 1984-; exec bd, Boy Scouts Am, 1986-; bd mem, Akron Symphony, 1986-; bd dir, Kent State Found, 1987-; hon mem, Alpha Kappa Alpha Sorority, 1990. **Honors/Awds:** Hall of Fame Best Dressed Akron, Beacon Jour, 1971; Ebony Best Dressed List, Ebony Mag, 1972; Dolores Parker Morgan Endowed Scholarship, Music Kent State Univ, named in honor, 1986; EL Novotny Award, Kent State Sch Art, 1989; Dolores Parker Morgan Day, City Akron, Ohio, named in honor, 1990. **Special Achievements:** Honored by Smithsonian Museum of American History as one of the five surviving female vocalists of the Duke Ellington Orchestra. **Home Addr:** 515 Club Dr, Aurora, OH 44202-8565. **Business Addr:** Member, Duke Ellington Orchestra, 1674 Broadway 3rd Fl, New York, NY 10019, **Business Phone:** (212)293-7070.

## MORGAN, DR. GORDON DANIEL

Educator. **Personal:** Born Oct 31, 1931, Mayflower, AR; son of Roosevelt and Georgianna Madlock; married Izola Preston; children: Marsha M, Brian, Marian & Bryce (deceased). **Educ:** Ark AM & N Col, BA (cum laude), sociol, 1953; Univ Ark, MA, sociol, 1956; Wash State Univ, PhD, sociol, 1961. **Career:** Pine State Sch, teacher, 1956-59; Wash State Univ, TA/RA, 1960-63; Teachers E Africa Proj, res asst, 1963-65, vis distinguished prof sociol, 1991-; Lincoln Univ, asst prof sociol, 1965-69; Ark AM & N Col, instr, 1969-60; Ford Found, postdoc fel, Lincoln Univ, 1969; Am Col Testing, postdoc fel, Lincoln Univ, 1969; Russell Sage, post doc fel, Univ Ark, 1972; Nat Endowment Humanities, fel; Univ Ark, assoc prof & prof, 1973-91, univ prof, prof emer; Philander Smith Col, Little Rock, Ark Prog Basic Adult Educ & Nat Insts Ment Health, consult; Publications: Tilman C. Cothran: Second Generation Sociologist, 1995; Toward an American Sociology: Questioning the European Construct, 1997; Marguerite Rogers Howie: Winners Never Quit, African American Woman Sociologist, 2006; No Violence is Progress: Early African-American Student Adjustment in a Southern University, 2007; Blue Hole, 2010; The Edge of Campus and America without Ethnicity; Sixty Years a Que: Greek Letter Societies and the African American Community. **Orgs:** Fel Nat Endowment Humanities Teaching; Consult, S Regional Educ Bd; consult, SW Minn State Col; consult, Philander Smith Col; consult, Ark Prog Basic Adult Educ; consult, Ark Tech Assistance Prog; consult, Quachita Baptist Col; consult, Nat Inst Ment Health; flyprof, St Ambrose Col, 1973; expert witness before Rockefeller Comm, Pop & Future, 1971; expert witness fed judge panel onat-large voting AR, 1973; Wash Co Grand Jury, 1974; Rotary/Downtown, AR, 1980-; fel Southern Studio Miss, 1987-88; Omega Psi Phi fraternity. **Special Achievements:** First black professor hired by the University of Arkansas in 1969. **Home Addr:** 947 E Oak Manor Dr, Fayetteville, AR 72701-3519, **Home Phone:** (479)521-2809. **Business Addr:** Professor Emeritus, University of Arkansas, 224 Old Main, Fayetteville, AR 72701, **Business Phone:** (479)575-3810.

## MORGAN, HAZEL C BROWN

Educator. **Personal:** Born Oct 25, 1930, Rocky Mount, NC; daughter of Rollon Brown (deceased) and Beulah McGee Brown (deceased); married Charlie; children: Savoynne Ewell. **Educ:** A&T State Univ, BS, nursing, 1960; East Carolina Univ, MS, rehab coun, 1977, MS, nursing, 1980. **Career:** Wilson Memorial Hosp, charge nurse, 1964-66; Northern Nash High Sch, health occup teacher, 1966-73; Nash Gen Hosp, team leader, pt care, 1971-; E Carolina Univ Sch Nursing, asst prof nursing, 1973-93, asst prof emer; Veterans Admin Hosp, Richmond Va & E Orange NJ, staff nurse, 1960-62; Landis State Hosp Philadelphia Pa, asst head nurse & instr, 1963; Resurrection Ministries Christian Ctr, secy, currently. **Orgs:** Am Nurses Asn; Asn Black Educr, NC; Nurses Asn Dist 20; ECU Orgn Black Fac & Staff; Sigma Theta Tau 1988-; Asn Black Nursing Fac, 1987-; health consult, Wright Geriat Day Care Ctr, 1988-; pres, Carrie Broadfoot Nurses Club; secy, 1995, pres, Seasons Plus Srs; prof retirees, 1997-98, treas, 1997, Leisurettes Club; E Carolina Retired Fac Asn; comn mem, E Carolina Univ, Sch Nursing Emer; secy; Diabetic comn; Nash Cty Dem Comn. **Home Addr:** 913 Beal St, Rocky Mount, NC 27804, **Home Phone:** (252)446-1554.

## MORGAN, JANE HALE

Librarian. **Personal:** Born May 11, 1925, Dines, WY; daughter of Arthur Hale and Billie Wood; married Joseph C; children: Joseph Hale, Jane Frances & Ann Michele. **Educ:** Howard Univ, BA, 1947; Univ Denver, MA, 1954. **Career:** Librarian (retired); Detroit Pub Libr, staff, 1954-1987, exec asst dir, 1973-75, dep dir, 1975-78, dir, 1978-87; Wayne State Univ, vis prof, 1989-91. **Orgs:** Am Libr Asn; Mich Libr Asn; exec bd, Southeastern Mich Reg Film Libr; LSCA adv coun Lib; bd trustee, Womens Nat Bk Asn; New Detroit Inc; bd dir, Rehab Inst; vpres, United Way Southeastern Mich; bd dir, YWCA; Asn Munic & Pressional Women; Alpha Kappa Alpha; bd dir, Univ Cult Ctr Asn; Urban League; Nat Asn Advan Colored People; bd dir, Women's Econ Club; bd dir, United Community Serv; bd dir, Delta Dent Plan; bd dir, Metrop Affairs Corp; bd, New Detroit Inc; Mich Coun Humanities; Mich Womens CMS; Detroit Women's Community; Delta Dent Plan Ohio; pres, Delta Dent Fund; Detroit Exec Serv Corps; pres, Sorosis Art & Lit Club; bd mem, Mich Ctr Bk; Detroit Women's Forum. **Home Addr:** 7473 N Brynmawr Ct, West Bloomfield, MI 48322-3542, **Home Phone:** (248)539-9383.

## MORGAN, JOE LEONARD

Baseball player, broadcaster. **Personal:** Born Sep 19, 1943, Bonham, TX; married Gloria Stewart; children: Lisa & Angela. **Educ:** Calif State Univ, Hayward, CA, BA, phys educ, 1990. **Career:** Baseball player (retired), broadcaster; Houston Colt 45's (later Houston Astros), 1963-71, 1980; Cincinnati Reds, 1972-79, announcer, 1985, spec adv baseball opers, 2010-; San Francisco Giants, 1981-82, announcer, 1986-95; Philadelphia Phillies, 1983; Oakland Athletics, 1984; Joe Morgan Beverage Co, chief exec officer, 1988-95; ABC, announcer, 1988-89; Entertainment & Sports Programming Network, NBC Sports, color analyst, baseball analyst, color commentator, 1994-2000; KTVU, broadcaster. **Orgs:** Vice chmn, Nat Baseball Hall Fame, 2000; contribr, Young Am baseball prog; contribr, Oakland Unified Sch Dist Sports Prog; pres, Joe Morgan Youth Found. **Honors/Awds:** Rookie of the Year, Nat League, 1965; Most Valuable Player, All-Star Game, 1972; Gold Glove Award, Nat League, 1973-77; Most Valuable Player, Baseball Writers Asn Am, 1975-76; Most Valuable Player, San Francisco Giants, 1982; Willie Mac Award, 1982; Comeback Player of the Year, Sporting News, 1982; Silver Slugger Award, 1982; Comeback Player of the Year, Nat League, 1982; Cincinnati Reds Hall of Fame, 1987; Nat Baseball Hall of Fame, 1990; Sports Emmy, 1998, 2005; Emmy Award. **Special Achievements:** Author: Joe Morgan: A Life in Baseball; Baseball for Dummies; Two-time Sports Emmy Award winner. **Home Addr:** 5588 Fernhoff Rd, Oakland, CA 94619. **Business Addr:** Special Advisor, Cincinnati Reds, 100 Joe Nuxhall Way, Cincinnati, OH 45202, **Business Phone:** (513)765-7000.

## MORGAN, DR. JOHN PAUL

Dentist. **Personal:** Born Oct 23, 1929, Kokomo, IN; married Pauline Marie Jones; children: Angela Marie. **Educ:** Ind Univ, pre-dent studies; Meharry Med Col, DDS, 1960. **Career:** Dentist (retired); 6510 USAF Hosp Edwards AFB Calif, officer-in-charge hosp dent, 1960-64; 439th USAF Hosp Misawa, AB, Japan, oic security serv dent asst base dent surg, 1964-67; Lockbourne AFB, Ohio, chief prosthodontics, 1967-71; 377th USAF Disp Tan Son Nhut AB Vietnam, chief oral surg, 1971-72; USAF Hosp Kirtland AFB NM, asst base dent surgeon, 1972-78; USAF Hosp Hahn AB Ger, base dent surgeon, 1978-81; USAF Med Ctr SGD Scott AFB IL, dep dir dent serv, 1981. **Orgs:** Nat Dent Assoc; Acad Gen Dent; Assoc Mil Surgeons; Prince Hall Lodge; life mem, Nat Asn Advan Colored People; Alpha Phi Alpha; Tuskegee Airmen Inc; Kiwanis Club. **Home Addr:** 4 Deer Run, O Fallon, IL 62269-1209, **Home Phone:** (618)624-8250.

## MORGAN, MELI'SA

Singer, songwriter, music producer. **Personal:** Born Jan 1, 1964, Queens, NY; married Shelly Garrett. **Educ:** Juilliard Sch, New York, NY. **Career:** Albums: Do Me Baby, 1986; Good Love, 1988; The Lady in Me, 1990; Still in Love With You, 1992; Tell Me How It Feels, 1995; Do You Still Love Me, 1996; Believe in Yourself, 1998; Fools Paradise, 2001; Don't Say Love, 2003; Back Together Again, 2005; I Remember, 2005. Singles: "Do Me Baby", 1985; "Do You Still Love Me?", 1986; "Fool's Paradise", 1986; "Now or Never", 1986; "Deeper Love", 1987; "If You Can Do It: I Can Too!!", 1987; "Love Changes", 1987; "Here Comes the Night", 1988; "Good Love", 1988; "Can You Give Me What I Want", 1990; "Don't You Know", 1990; "Still in Love with You", 1992; "Through the Tears", 1992; "I'm Gonna Be Your Lover", 1992; "How", 2000; "Back Together Again", 2005; "I Remember...", 2006; High Maintenance, 2007. **Business Addr:** Singer, c/o Capitol Records, 1750 Vine St Suite 6252, Los Angeles, CA 90028, **Business Phone:** (323)462-6252.

## MORGAN, MICHAEL

Music director, conductor (music). **Personal:** Born Jan 1, 1957, Washington, DC. **Educ:** Oberlin Col Conserv Music; Berkshire Music Ctr. **Career:** St Louis Symphony Orchestra, asst conductor; Buffalo Philharmonic, apprentice conductor; Chicago Symphony Orchestra, asst conductor, 1986-92; Civic Orchestra Chicago, conductor; Oakland Youth Orchestra, artistic dir; Festival Opera, artistic dir; San Francisco Conserv Music, music teacher; Tanglewood Music Ctr, conducting teacher, 2002 & 2003; New York Opera, guest conductor; St. Louis Opera Theater, guest conductor; Wash Nat Opera, guest conductor; Oakland E Bay Symphony, music dir, 1990, conductor, currently; Sacramento Philharmonic Orchestra, music dir, currently; Bear Valley Music Festival, music dir, 2012. **Orgs:** Bd mem, ASOL; Rec Acad; Am Soc Composers; Purple Silk Music Educ Found; League Am Orchestras; Int House at Univ Calif; Nat Guild Community Schs Arts; Oaktown Jazz Workshops; bd trustee, Math Sci Res Inst. **Honors/Awds:** First Prize, Hans Swarowsky Inter Nat Conductors Competition, Vienna, Austria, 1980; Two Nat Awards, 2005; Governors Award, San Francisco Chapter, Recording Acad, 2005; Concert Music Award, Am Soc Composers, Authors & Publ, 2005; Community Leadership Award, San Francisco Found; Honorary Doctorate, Holy Names Univ. **Business Addr:** Music Director, Conductor, Oakland East Bay Symphony, 1440 Broadway Suite 405, Oakland, CA 94612, **Business Phone:** (510)444-0801.

## MORGAN, MONICA ALISE (MONICA MORGAN)

Photojournalist. **Personal:** Born May 27, 1963, Detroit, MI; daughter of Barbara Jean Pace. **Educ:** Wayne State Univ, Detroit MI, BA, 1985. **Career:** Domino's Pizza, Ann Arbor, Mich, promotional coordr; Detroit Pub Schs, Detroit, Mich, pub rels coordr; WDIV-TV, Detroit, Mich, prod asst; Palmer St Productions, Detroit, Mich, host & pub rels dir; WQBH-radio, talk show host; Ebony Mag; jet Mag; NY Daily News; AOL; ESPN; New week-Japan; touch weekly, Entertaiment weekly; US weekly mag; Sister2sister; Black Enterprise mag; Essence; TV Guide can; Scholastic mag; Detroit News; Detroit Free Press; Mich Chronicle, Detroit, Mich, columnist & photojournalist, 1987-; US Dept Census, Detroit, Mich, Community Awareness Specialist, 1988-90; Monica Morgan Photog, owner & photojournalist, currently. **Orgs:** Secy, Nat Asn Black Journalists, 1981-; Optimist Club, 1987-; bd mem, Manhood Inc, 1988-; Elliottorian Bus Women Inc, 1988-; Nat Asn Broadcasters; Nat Asn Female Execs; Nat Press Photogr; Kindred Souls. **Honors/Awds:** Numerous awards & honors including Outstanding Young Woman of America, 1986 & 1987; Civic & Community Award, Wall Street Inc, 1989; Certificate of Appreciation, Rosa & Raymond Parks Inst Self Develop; SBC Ameritech African American Excellence Award, 2003; Detroit's Most Influential Woman; Leader of the 21st Century. **Home Addr:** 3552 S Ethel, Detroit, MI 48217-1538, **Home Phone:** (313)928-3270. **Business Addr:** Owner, Photojournalist, Monica Morgan Photography, 500 River Pl Suite 5109, Detroit, MI 48207, **Business Phone:** (313)259-7005.

## MORGAN, RICHARD H., JR.

Lawyer. **Personal:** Born Feb 12, 1944, Memphis, TN; married Olga Jackson; children: Darrin Allan, Heather Nicole, Nia Abena, Amish Adzua & Erica. **Educ:** Western Mich Univ, BA, 1967, MA, 1968; Univ Detroit Law Sch, JD, 1973. **Career:** Western Mich Univ, counr; Oakland Univ Proj Pontiac, dir; Stud Ctr, asst dir, asso dir, dean Stud asst; Community Serv Prog Urban Affairs Ctr, dir; Hatchett Mitchell Morgan & Hall, atty; Morgan & Hall, sr partner; Oakland Univ, asst vpres, 1969-75; Law Offices William Waterman, atty, 1975-77; Law Offices Elbert Hatchett, atty, 1978-83; Morgan & William, sr partner, 1983; pvt practr, currently. **Orgs:** Am Pub Gardens Asn, Maine Prof Guides Asn; Mich State Bar; Oakland Co Bar; Wolverine Bar; Am Bar & Wayne Co Bar; Kappa Alpha Psi Frat; Big BroKalamazoo; Pontiac Area Urban Force dropouts; treasure & vpres, Black LawStud Alliance Univ Detroit Law Sch; bd mem, Heritage Cult Ctr; Akan Priest; pres, Walton Acad Bd. **Home Addr:** 19105 Addison, Southfield, MI 48075. **Business Addr:** Attorney, Private Practitioner, 485 Orchard Lake Rd, Pontiac, MI 48342-2153, **Business Phone:** (248)334-8970.

## MORGAN, ROBERT, JR.

Transportation consultant, military leader, association executive. **Personal:** Born May 17, 1954, Donaldsonville, LA; son of Robert Sr and Ruby Fields; married Rowena Guanlao; children: Robyn Talana, Ryan Guanlao & Rubi Guanlas. **Educ:** Southern Univ, BS, acct, 1976; Univ RI, int studies, 1976; Old Dom Univ, oceanog, 1978; Human Resources Mgt Sch, teacher cert, leadership, mgt & educ training, 1981; Nat Univ, MBA, mgt, 1982; San Diego State Univ, finance, 1983; Univ Md, comput sci, 1984; Cent Tex Col, taxation, 1984; Univ S Fla, foreign lang, 1986; Armed Forces Staff Col, cert, 1986; Univ Ariz, human resources, 1987; Ft Gordon Signal Sch, Augusta, GA, cert, 1987; Fla State Univ, comput sci, 1989; Univ Md, foreign lang studies, 1989; Panama Canal Col, AS, bus data processing, 1993; Tex Southern Univ, MS, transp palanning & mgt, 1996; Maritime Inst Technol & Grad Studies, marine terminal mgt cert, 1998; Grand Canyon Univ, DBA, mgt, 2015. **Career:** USN, lt cmdr, 1976-94; USS Am CV 66, Norfolk, VA, deck/ASW officer, 1977-79; USS Cleveland LPD 7, San Diego, CA, navigator/weapons officer, 1979-80; Surface Warfare Officer Sch, Coronado, CA, instr, 1981-83; USNS Ponchatoula FAO 108, Philippines Island, officer in-chg, 1983-84; USN, human resource mgr instr, 1983; Naval Sta Guam, Guam MI, opers officer, 1984-85; Cent Tex Col, Guam MI, instr, 1984-85; Cent Tex Col, mgt prof, 1985; HQ Cent Command, Macdill AFB FL, comm staff officer, 1986-88; MSCO Korea, Pusan Korea, comndg officer, 1988-90; HQ US Southern Command, Quarry Heights, Panama, logistics staff officer, 1990-92; MSCO Panama, comndg officer, 1992-94; Tex Southern Univ, instr, vis prof, 2002-; Univ Houston, instr, adj prof & lectr, 1999-; Houston Port Authority, opers mgr, trade develop mgr cust serv, asst oper mgr, 1994-96, midwest sales mgr, 1996-97, trade develop mgr, 1997-2010, maritime acad mgr, 2010-12. **Orgs:** Life mem, Alpha Phi Omega Frat, 1973-; life mem, Omega Psi Phi Frat, 1980-; Asn MBA Execs, 1981, Acct Soc, 1982; St Joseph Masonic Lodge, 1982; master scuba diver, Micronesian Diver Asn, 1985; Nat Defense Transp Asn, 1987; Cert PADL & NAUL diver; Nat Naval Officers Asn; Nat Asn Advan Colored People; Armed Forces Commun & Electronics Asn, 1988-; Am Chamber Com, Korea, 1988-; bd mem & treas, Transp Club Houston; Ord Soc. **Honors/Awds:** Outstanding Black American Award, Comnav Marianas, 1985; Outstanding Citizens of the Year, 1992, Omega Man of the Year, 1993. **Home Addr:** PO Box 890263, Houston, TX 77289-0263, **Home Phone:** (713)997-9143. **Business Addr:** Visiting Professor, Texas Southern University, 3100 Cleburne St, Houston, TX 77004, **Business Phone:** (713)313-7011.

## MORGAN, ROBERT LEE

Architect. **Personal:** Born Mar 6, 1934, Yazoo City, MS; married Janet Rogers; children: Allyson, Whitney & Peter. **Educ:** Kans State Univ, BA, archit, 1964; Lincoln Univ, Jefferson City, Mo. **Career:** Architect (retired); Opus Architects & Engrs, 1984-99; Adkins-Jackels Asn Architects, exec vip partner, stockholder, architect, 1968-84; Hammel, Green & Abrahamson, architect, 1966-68; Cavin & Page Architects, architect, 1964-66. **Orgs:** Soc Architects Am Inst Architects; Nat Orgn Minority Architects; bd, Minn Comt Urban Environ, 1993-95, secy, 1968-76; Minn Schs Long-Range Facil Planning Comn; pres, Minn CDC, 1971; Comt Archit Arts & Recreation, Am Inst Architects, 1974-77; Minn Bd Architect, Engrs, Land Surv & Landscape Architect, 1983-91; Nat Coun Architect Regist Bds, 1991-95. **Honors/Awds:** Invested Col Fels, Am Inst Architects, 1995. **Home Addr:** 220 Oakshore Dr, Port Townsend, WA 98368.

## MORGAN, STACEY EVANS (STACEY LYN EVANS)

Television producer, television writer. **Career:** Warner Bros, comedy writer training prog; BET, producer spec proj; TV ser: "The Parkers", producer & writer, exec story ed & writer, 1999-2004; "After All", writer, 1999; "One on One", writer; Jamie Foxx Show, writer; "Judge Not a Book", producer, 2004; "Practice What You Preach", producer, 2004; "Could It Be You", co-producer, 2004; "A Little Change Never Hurt Anybody", co-producer, 2004; "At Last", producer, 2004; Nu Urban Audio LLC, ceo & partner, 2008-; "My Sister's Keeper", supv producer, 2010; "Keep It in the Closet", supv producer, 2010; "My Guy Friend", supv producer, 2010; "Pilot", supv producer, 2010; "Love That Girl!", supv producer & writer, 2013; "Teach Me Tonight", exec story ed, 2002; "It's Showtime ", exec story ed, 2002; "Mother's Day Blues ", exec story ed, 2002; "The Crush ", exec story ed, 2002; "Make a Joyful Noise", exec story ed, 2002; Writer: "The Parkers", 1999-2004; "36th NAACP Image Awards", 2005; "37th NAACP Image Awards", 2006; "One on One", 2006; "39th NAACP Image Awards", 2008;"The 40th NAACP Image Awards", 2009; "House of Payne", 2009; "Meet the Browns", 2009-10; "41st NAACP Image Awards", 2010; "Family Time", 2012; Strut Entertainment, pres & ceo, 2013-; SEM PRO Inc, pres & chief exec officer, 2013-. **Business Addr:** c/o Television Producer, United Paramount Network, 11800 Wilshire Blvd, Los Angeles, CA 90025, **Business Phone:** (310)575-7000.

## MORGAN, STANLEY DOUGLAS

Football player, executive, president (organization). **Personal:** Born Feb 17, 1955, Easley, SC; married Rholedia; children: Sanitra Nikole & Monique. **Educ:** Univ Tenn, BS, educ, 1979. **Career:** Football player (retired), president; Industrial Nat Bank; New England Patriots, wide receiver, 1977-89; SC Shrine Bowl Team; Pro Bowl, player, 1979-80, 1986-87; Nat Football League All Rookie team; Indianapolis Colts, wide receiver, 1990; Denver Broncos, wide receiver, 1992; Mid-S Sports Mgt, pres, currently. **Orgs:** AFC Champion New Eng Patriot, 1985. **Business Addr:** President, Mid-South Sports Management, 22 N Front St Suite 780, Memphis, TN 38103, **Business Phone:** (901)523-2535.

## MORGAN, TRACY JAMAL

Actor, painter (artist). **Personal:** Born Nov 10, 1968, Bronx, NY; son of James (deceased) and Alicia Warden; married Sabrina; children: Gitrid, Malcomb & Tracy Jr. **Career:** L&L Painting & Rose Co, painter: Films: A Thin Line Btwn Love & Hate, 1996; Half Baked, 1998; Bamboozled, 2000; 30 Years to Life, 2001; WaSan Go, 2001; Jay & Silent Bob Stike Back, 2001; How High, 2001; Frank McKlusky, C.I., 2002; Head of State, 2003; The Longest Yard, 2005; Little Man, 2006; First Sunday, 2008; Superhero Movie, 2008; Deep in the Valley, 2009; G-Force, 2009; Nailed, 2010; Cop Out, 2010, Death at a Funeral, 2010; The Other Guys, 2010; Rio, 2011; Son of No One, 2011; Rio, 2011; Why Stop Now?, 2012; Rio 2, 2014; The Boxtrolls, 2014; Top Five, 2014; TV series: "Martin", 1994-96; "Saturday Night Live", 1996-2006; "Crank Yankers", 2002; "Comic Groove", 2002; "The Tracy Morgan Show", 2003-04; Saturday Night Live Weekend Update Halftime Special, 2003; "Where My Dogs At?", 2006; "Mind of Mencia", 2006; "Totally Awesome", 2006; Human Giant, 2008; "30 Rock", 2006-13. **Honors/Awds:** Nominee, Image Award, 2008 & 2009; nominee, Emmy Award, 2009; Screen Actors Guild Award, 2009; Vision Award, NAMIC Vision, 2010; Golden Nymph Award, Monte-Carlo TV Festival, 2011. **Business Addr:** Actor, c/o NBC, 30 Rockefeller Plz Suite 2, New York, NY 10112, **Business Phone:** (212)315-9016.

## MORGAN, WAYNE

Basketball player, basketball coach, executive. **Personal:** Born Oct 7, 1950, Brooklyn, NY; married Maribeth; children: Jerusha, Shayne & Ciara. **Educ:** St Lawrence Univ, BS, phys educ, teaching & coaching, 1973; Ithaca Col, MS, motor learning & physiol sport, 1974. **Career:** Basketball player(retired), basketball coach, executive; Westchester Community Col, basketball player, 1968-70; St Lawrence, asst coach, 1972-73; Ithaca Col, asst coach, 1973-74; Dutchess Community Col, head coach, 1974-75; Dartmouth Col, asst coach, 1975-79; Xavier, asst coach, 1979-84; Syracuse Orange men, asst coach, 1984-96; Long Beach State Univ, head coach, 1996-2002; WM Enterprises LLC, pres, 1996-2010; Iowa State Univ, from asst coach to head coach, 2002-06; Installation Co / Mid-Iowa Satellite, owner, 2007-10; Hofstra Univ, asst coach, 2010-13; New York Life Ins Co, LIC agt, 2013-. **Orgs:** Nat Asn Basketball Coaches. **Special Achievements:** First African American head basketball coach of Iowa State University. **Business Addr:** Licensed Agent, New York Life Insurance Company, 51 Madison Ave Rm 251, New York, NY 10010-1603, **Business Phone:** (800)695-4785.

## MORGAN-CATO, PROF. CHARLOTTE THERESA

Educator, college teacher. **Personal:** Born Jun 28, 1938, Chicago, IL; daughter of Eleazar Jack and Helen Juanita Brewer; married John David Cato; children: 1. **Educ:** Univ Chicago, BA, 1960; Haile Selassie Univ Addis Ababa, cert, 1965; Columbia Univ, Sch Int Affairs, master, int affairs, 1967, Teachers Col, MEd, 1976 & EdD, 1979. **Career:** Professor (retired), professor emeritus; Chicago Bd Educ, high sch social studies teacher, 1961-65; African-AmInst, teacher Kurasini Sch, 1967-70; Phelps-Stokes Found, asst African progs, 1970-71; Lehman Col CUNY, assoc prof, 1972-02, dir, Women's Studies Prog, 1996-2002, prof emer, currently. **Orgs:** Adv comt adult learning, Follett Publ Co, 1982-83; nat treas, African Heritage Studies Asn, 1984-88; alt rep, Un NGO, Alpha Kappa Alpha Sor Inc, 1985-86; Am Asn Adult & Cont Educ; Asn Study African-Am Life & Hist; Nat Coun Black Studies; Alpha Kappa Alpha Sor; Links Inc; bd mem, Free Rein Therapeut Riding & Educ Ctr. **Home Addr:** 2385 Rosemont Ct, Hendersonville, NC 27891, **Home Phone:** (828)692-6937. **Business Addr:** Professor Emeritus, Lehman College, 250 Bedford Pk Blvd W, Bronx, NY 10468, **Business Phone:** (718)960-8000.

## MORGAN-PRICE, HON. VERONICA ELIZABETH

Judge. **Personal:** Born Nov 30, 1945, Charleston, SC; daughter of Robert and Mary Cross; married Jerome Henry; children: Jerome Marcus. **Educ:** Tenn State Univ, BS, eng, 1969; Univ Cincinnati Summer Law Scholar, cert; Tex Southern Univ, JD, 1972; Univ Nev, Nat Col Juv Judges, cert, 1980. **Career:** Judge (retired); Wade Rasmus & Wash, law clerk & atty, 1970-72; Baylor Col Med Alcoholism Prog, chief counr coord, 1972-75; Houston Community Col, law prof, 1972-78; Harris Co Dist Atty Off, asst dist atty, 1975-80; TX Paralegal Sch, prof law; Harris Co Juv Ct, assoc judge, judge; Juv Ct Judge, Houston Tex. **Orgs:** Tex State Bar, 1973-; Houston Lawyers Asn, 1973-; Nat Bar Asn, 1975-; adv bd, Safety Coun Great Houston, 1979-; chairperson, Med Legal Child Advocacy Comn, 1980; adv bd, Criminal & Juv Justice Educ Prog, 1980; Cs Defense Fund/Black Community Crusade C, 1997; Ford Found Coun Legal Educ; bd dir, Asn Community TV Channel 8; Nat Coun Juv & Family Ct Judges; Metro Ct Judges; comt mem, Learning Disabilities & Juv Delinquincy; Nat Coun Juv & Family Ct Judges; chair, Judicial Leadership Coun; Black Women Lawyers Asn; Thurgood Marshall Sch Law Alumni Asn. **Home Addr:** 11601 Shadow Creek Pkwy Suite 111-113, Pearland, TX 77584, **Home Phone:** (713)562-2951.

## MORGAN-SMITH, DR. SYLVIA

Executive. **Personal:** Born AL; married William F II; children: Shiva, Andre, Melody & Ramon Morgan. **Educ:** Technol Community Col, nursing, 1959; Univ Colo-Denver, jour, 1970; Signal Broadcasting, dipl, 1971; Real Estate Col, dipl, 1976; Omaha Univ. **Career:** BPI-FM Radio, radio producer & announcer, 1970-72; KWGN-TV 2, anchorwoman, 1972-77; Denver Comn Community Rels, comnr & chmn, 1973-79; Champion Realty, realtor, 1975-; Rockwell Int Rocky Flats, mgr pub affairs, 1977-81; First Interstate Bank Golden, dir, 1979-95; Jefferson Co Priv Indstry Coun, Exec comt, mem, 1980-97; Childrens Hosp, dir, 1981-85; Nat Solar Energy Res Inst, mgr communs, 1981-91; KOA-TV, announcer, 1981-92; Nat Renewable Energy Lab, Midwest Res Inst, dir pub rel, dir creative communs, 1991-, Colo Govt Rels, mgr, currently; Colo Gospel Music Acad & Hall Fame, founder & pres, currently. **Orgs:** Pres, Police Retirement Comn & Citizens Appreciate Police, 1981-; vice chmn, Nat Small Bus Admin Adv Coun, 1990-92; Asn Blacks Energy; bd mem, Denver Zoo & First Nat; bd mem, Denver C; civilian mem pension fund bd, Denver Police & Firemen. **Honors/Awds:** Trailblazer Award, Colo Martin Luther King Comn, 2001; Shaka Franklin Foundation for Youth Award; Award, Colo Asn Black Journalists; President's Special Award, Denver Ministerial Alliance; Chairman's Cup, Am Asn Blacks Energy, 2005; Outstanding Community Service Award, Urban League Metrop Denver, 2006. **Home Addr:** 102 S Balsam St, Denver, CO 80226, **Home Phone:** (303)233-3321. **Business Addr:** Director Public Relations, National Renewable Energy Laboratory, 15013 Denver W Pkwy, Golden, CO 80401.

## MORGAN-WASHINGTON, DR. BARBARA

Dentist. **Personal:** Born Nov 9, 1953, Richmond, VA; daughter of Calvin T Sr and Florence Brown; married Fredica Samone Jr; children: Bria Renee & Fredrica Samone II. **Educ:** Va State Univ, BS, 1976; Med Col Va Sch Dent, DDS, 1980. **Career:** USPHS, sr asst dent surgeon, 1980-82; pvt pract, assoc, 1983-86; Beaufort Jasper Community Health Servs, staff dentist, 1982-97; pvt pract, 1997-. **Orgs:** Acad Gen Dent, 1980-; Tabernacle Baptist Church, 1981-; Am Dent asn, 1982-, SC Dent Asn, 1982-; Nat Asn Advan Colored People, 1986-; Alpha Pi Alpha Sorority; Beaufort Regional Chamber Com; Tings fa Tek. **Home Addr:** 804 W St, Beaufort, SC 29902-4663, **Home Phone:** (843)524-8404. **Business Addr:** Dentist, 102 Sea Island Pkwy Suite J, Lady's Island, SC 29907, **Business Phone:** (843)986-0157.

## MORGAN-WELCH, BEVERLY ANN

Executive, executive director, president (organization). **Personal:** Born Sep 15, 1952, Norwich, CT; married Mark RP Welch Jr; children: Michael, Dominique & Alexandra. **Educ:** Smith Col, BA, 1974. **Career:** Creative Arts Comn, admin asst, 1975-76; Amherst Col, asst dean, 1976-77, asst dean admis, 1977-78; Conn Mutual Life, consult corp responsibility, 1979-83; Avery Theater, gen mgr; Wadsworth Atheneum, corp & mus serv officer, 1983-86; Wads Worth Atheneum, develop officer, 1986-87; Greater Hartford Arts Coun, exec dir, 1987-1993; Bank Hartford, dir, 1988-94; Kemsit Consult Inc, pres, 1993-1996; Efficacy Inst, dir, 1996-97; Patrick Inauguration, co-chair, 2007-11; Raytheon, mgr community rels; Mus Afro-Am Hist, exec dir, 1999-. **Orgs:** Chair, Urban Affairs Coun, 1981-82; secy, Conn Mutual Life Found, 1981-83; charter bd mem, Conn Coalition 100 Black Women, 1982-85; United Way Allocations Com Capitol Area, 1982-86; bd dir, Newington C Hosp, 1983-86; bd dir, sec Jazz Inc, 1983-86; bus assoc, Greater Hartford C C, 1983-86; bd dir, Am Red Cross, Greater Hartford Chap, 1985-86; pres, Goodwin Track Conservancy, 1986-88; vpres, Horace Bushnell Mgt Resources Inc, 1985; exec comt, Hartford Downtown Coun, 1988-; vpres, Amistad Found, 1987-; corporator & dir, Inst Living, 1988-; Diaconate, First Church Christ, Hartford, 1989-; regional adv coun, Capitol Community Tech Col Found, 1991-; corporator, Hartford Sem, 1991-; Antiqn Soc., Colonial Soc Massachusetts; Massachusetts Hist Soc; bd dir, Bank Hartford; secy, Conn Mutual Life Found. **Home Addr:** 10 Pk Pl, Hartford, CT 06106. **Business Addr:** Executive Director, Museum of Afro-American History, 14 Beacon St Suite 719, Boston, MA 02108, **Business Phone:** (617)725-0022.

## MORIAL, DR. MARC HAYDEL

President (organization), mayor, chief executive officer. **Personal:** Born Jan 3, 1958, New Orleans, LA; son of Ernest Dutch and Sybil Haydel; married Michelle Miller; children: Mason & Margeaux. **Educ:** Univ Pa, BA, econs, 1980; Georgetown Univ, JD, 1983. **Career:** Barham & Churchill Law Firm, assoc, 1983-85; Harare Inc, chmn, 1983-86; Marc H Morial Prof Law Corp, managing partner, 1985-; Off Civil Sheriff, Orleans Parish, LA, legal coun auctioneer; Xavier Univ, adj prof polit sci, 1988; State La, sen; City New Orleans, mayor, 1992-98; Nat Urban League Inc, pres & chief exec officer, 2003-. **Orgs:** Dem campaign coord, Morial Mayor New Orleans, 1977; dep campaign mgr, Russell Long Sen, 1980; Jesse Jackson Pres, 1984; La Voter Regist Educ Crusade Inc, 1986-; deleg, Dem Nat Conv, 1988; bd dir, La Spec Olympics, 1991-; Milne Boys Home, 1991-; pres, US Conf Mayors, 2001-02; pres, US Conf Mayors, 2001-02; Am Bar Asn; Nat Bar Asn; La Trial Lawyers Asn; Nat Conf Black Lawyers; La State Bar Asn; Gen coun, La Asn Minority & Women Owned Bus Inc; exec comt mem, Black Leadership Forum; exec comt mem, Leadership Conf Civil Rights; exec comt mem, Leadership 18; bd mem, Nj Performing Arts Ctr; bd mem, Muhammad Ali Ctr; New Orleans Asn Independent Cab Drivers Inc; La Am Civil Liberties Union; Debt Reduction Task Force; Pres Adv Coun Financial Capability, 2012. **Business Addr:** President, Chief Executive Officer, National Urban League Inc, 120 Wall St, New York, NY 10005, **Business Phone:** (212)558-5300.

## MORIAL, SYBIL HAYDEL

College teacher, educator. **Personal:** Born Nov 26, 1932, New Orleans, LA; daughter of Eudora Arnaud and Clarence C; married Ernest Nathan; children: Julie, Marc, Jacques, Cheri & Monique. **Educ:** Boston Univ, BS Ed, 1952, MEd, 1955. **Career:** Educator, college teacher (retired); Newton Pub Sch, teacher, 1952-55; Baltimore Pub Sch, teacher, 1955-56; New Orleans Pub Sch, teacher, 1959-71; Xavier Univ, dir spec serv, 1977-85, Drexel Ctr Extended Learning, assoc dean, 1985-93, assoc vpres, pub & commun affairs, 1993-2005. **Orgs:** Founder, La League Good Govt, pres, pres emer, 1963-; pres, New Orleans Chap Links Inc, 1976-78; dir, Liberty Bank & Trust Co, 1979-; bd dir, WLAE-TV, 1979-81, adv bd, 1984-; bd trustee, Amistad Res Ctr, 1980-; founder, I've Known Rivers Afro-Amer Pavilion La World Expos, pres, chmn, 1982-85; Nat Conf C Having C, Black Women Respond, 1983; co-chair, Yr Healthy Birth, 1983; trustee, Nat Jewish Hosp, Nat Asthma Ctr, 1983-; pres, Women's Forum La, 1985-; vpres, Int Women's Forum, 1987-; Tulane Univ Press Fund, 1988-; adv bd, Tulane Med Ctr, 1990-; bd dir, Greater New Orleans Found, 1993-; bd dir, Leadership Found, 1993; chair, Ernest N Morial Asthma & Respiratory Dis Ctr, La State Univ Med Ctr, 1994; Nat Hon Soc; Ed Pi Lambda Theta; bd dir, Blue Cross & Blue Shield La. **Honors/Awds:** Torch of Liberty Award, Anti-Defamation League of B'nai B'rith, 1978; Whitney M Young Brotherhood Award, Urban League Greater New Orleans, 1978; Zeta Phi Beta Finer Women hood Award, 1978; Arts Council Medal, La Coun Music & Performing Arts Co, 1979; Weiss Award, Nat Conf Christians & Jews, 1979; Woman of the Year, Links Inc, 1981; Citizen of the Year, Spectator News J, 1984; Lifetime Achievement Award, Martin Luther King Jr, 1995; DHL, Xavier Univ, 2014; The Women Of Power Award, Nat Urban League; A Legend in Her Own Time Award, Faulkner Soc; New Orleans Legend Award, New Orleans. **Home Addr:** 5051 Bancroft Dr, New Orleans, LA 70122, **Home Phone:** (504)288-8784.

## MORISEY, DR. PATRICIA GARLAND

Educator, executive director. **Personal:** Born Aug 1, 1921, New York, NY; daughter of Arthur L Williams and Dagmar Cheatum; children: Paul, Jean, Carroway Muriel Spence & Alex. **Educ:** Hunter Col, BA, 1941; Columbia Univ Sch Social Work, MSS, 1947, DSW, 1970. **Career:** Comm Serv Soc & NYANA, caseworker, 1944-51; Louise Wise Adoption Serv, caseworker consult, 1951-59; Bur Child Welfare NY Dept Social Serv, proj dir, dir training, 1959-63; Youth & Corrections, Community Serv Soc, staff consult, 1963-64; Family & Child Welfare Fedn Protestant Welfare Agency, dir, div family & child welfare, 1966-68; Cath Univ Am, Wash, DC, assoc prof, 1968-69; Lincoln Ctr Fordham Univ, Grad Sch Social Sci, prof emer, 1970-, asst dean, 1975-86. **Orgs:** Pres, Comm Men Health, 1977-78; Mayor's Task Force Child Abuse & Mayor's Task Force Foster Care, 1980; Greater NY Comn, Nat Coun Negro Women, 1984-; vpres, Leake & Wahs C's Serv, 1985-91; secy, Fedn Protestant Welfare Agencies, 1988-91, prof emer; New York Dept Ment & Retardation-Task Force Youth & Law, Coun Social Work Educ, Nat Asn Social Workers; vpres, Leake & Watts C Svc; mem bd, Citizens Comm C; bd dir, Fedn Protestant Welfare Agencies; Subpanel Spec Pops. **Honors/Awds:** Hall of Fame, Hunter Col, 1975; Honoree, Nat Asn Women's Bus & Prof Club, 1975; Bene Merente, Fordham Univ, 1989; Ninth Ann Award, Coun Adoptable C, 1992; Keystone Award, Fedn Protestant Welfare Agencies, 1993; Josephine Shaw Lowell Award, Community Serv Soc, 1996; Louise Wise Service Award, 1996; Outstanding Mentor Award, Highbridge Advising Coun, 1997. **Home Addr:** 10 W 135th St Apt 16F, New York, NY 10037, **Home Phone:** (212)283-7789. **Business Addr:** Professor Emeritus, Fordham University, Rose Hill Campus 113 W 60th St, New York, NY 10023, **Business Phone:** (718)817-1000.

## MORMAN, ALVIN

Counselor, baseball player. **Personal:** Born Jan 6, 1969, Rockingham, NC; son of Hettie F; married Pamela; children: Latydra Janae. **Educ:** Wingate Univ, BS, bus admin, mgt & opers, 1991; NC Cent Univ, MS, counr educ, 2003. **Career:** Baseball Player (retired), counr; Houston Astros, pitcher, 1996; Cleveland Indians, 1997-98; San Francisco Giants, 1998; Kans City Royals, 1999; Fuquay Varina Mid Sch, stud counr, 2002-. **Home Addr:** 52 Woodhart Cir, Fuquay Varina, NC 27526-4916, **Home Phone:** (919)577-2267. **Business Addr:** Student Counselor, Fuquay Varina Middle School, 109 N Ennis St, Fuquay Varina, NC 27526, **Business Phone:** (919)557-2727.

## MORNING, JOHN

Executive, financial manager, association executive. **Personal:** Born Jan 8, 1932, Cleveland, OH; son of John Frew Sr and Juanita Kathryn (Brannan) M; married Carole Ann Coleman; children: Ann Juanita & John Floyd. **Educ:** Wayne State Univ, attended 1951; Pratt Inst, BFA, 1955. **Career:** McCann-Erickson Inc, art dir, 1958-60; pvt pract design, 1960; John Morning Design Inc, pres, 1960-; Dime Savings Bank, dir, 1979-; Anchor Bancorp, dir; Anchor Savings Bank FSB, dir, 1979. **Orgs:** Dir, Henry St Stlmnt, 1973-, chmn, 1979-86; dir, NY Landmarks Conservancy, 1985-; trustee, Wilberforce Univ, 1987-; chmn, Pratt Inst Brd Trustees, 1989-92; trustee, Mus African Art, 1990-98; dir, Charles E Culpeper Found, 1991-99; trustee, Brooklyn Acad Music, 1993-; dir, Dime Bancorp Inc, 1994-; dir, Lincoln Ctr Theater, 1995-, trustee; trustee, City Univ NY, 1997-2002; chair, Asn Gov Boards Univs & Cols, 1998-2000, vice chair; trustee, Rockefeller Bros Fund, 1999-; trustee, C S Mott Found, 2000-; trustee, Pratt Inst; found trustee, Inter Nat Print Ctr New York; dir & trustee, New York Landmarks Conservancy; trustee & bd dir, Charles Stewart Mott Found; vice chmn, New York Adv Comn Cult Affairs. **Honors/Awds:** Alumni Medal, Pratt Inst, 1972; Presidential Recognition Award, White House, 1984; Lillian D. Wald Humanitarian Award of Henry Street Settlement, 1992. **Business Addr:** Trustee, Charles Stewart Mott Foundation, 503 S Saginaw St, Flint, MI 48502-1851, **Business Phone:** (810)238-5651.

## MORRIS, DR. ARCHIE M., III

Educator, manager. **Personal:** Born Mar 24, 1938, Washington, DC; married Irene Beatrice Poindexter; children: Giovanni & Ottiviani. **Educ:** Howard Univ, BA, sociol & econs, 1968, MUS, 1973; Nova Southeastern Univ, MPA, DPA, 1976. **Career:** US Dept Com, dep asst dir admin, 1972-73; US Dept Com, OMBE, R& D spec, 1973-74; DC Govt, rent admin, 1974-76; MATCH Inst, proj dir, cons, 1976-79; US Dept Agr, chief facil mgt, 1979-82; US Dept Agr, chief mail & reproduc mgt, 1982-; Bowie State Univ, Dept Mgt, Mkt & Pub Admin, asst prof, prog coord, 2008-. **Orgs:** Bd dir, HUD Fed Credit Union, 1971-76; instr, WA Ctr Learning Alternatives, 1976; instr, Howard Univ Dept Publ Admin, 1976-77; pres, Nat Capital Area Chap Nova Univ Alumni, 1980-81; dir social servs, Alexandria Redevel & Housing Authority, 1999-2006; Am Soc Publ Admin; Nat Urban League. **Honors/Awds:** Honors & Plaque HUD Task Force Against Racism WA, 1972; Spec Achievement Award, OMBE Dept Com WA, 1973; Outstanding Service Award, HUD Fed Credit Union WA, 1976; Cert Appreciation, Mayor WA, 1976. Publication: "Race, Class, and the Culture of Poverty", 2007, "Black Education in a Segregated Setting: Dunbar High School", 2008. **Home Addr:** 4918 43rd St NW, Washington, DC 20016-4021. **Business Addr:** Assistant Professor, Bowie State University College of Business, 14000 Jericho Park Rd, Bowie, MD 20715, **Business Phone:** (301)860-4155.

## MORRIS, BERNARD ALEXANDER

Consultant, executive, college teacher. **Personal:** Born Jun 25, 1937, New York, NY; son of Herbert Anthony and Beryl Bernice Berry; married Margaret Mary Taylor; children: Myron, Michael, Loree V Smith & Quincy. **Educ:** Boston State Col, BS, 1975; Harvard Univ,

EdM, 1983; Univ Mass Boston, BS, polit sci & govt, 1985. **Career:** Mass Inst Technol, acad admin, 1971-77; NY City Bd Educ, sr policy-analyst, 1979-80; Nolan Norton & Co, MIS consult, 1980-85; Morris Assocs, pres & consult, 1985-; Peripheral Mfg Inc, sr proj mgr, 2004-12; Parker Fire Systs LLC, consult, 2012-; Denver Pub Schs, denver math fel, 2013-. **Orgs:** Transafrica; Pi Sigma Alpha; Phi Delta Kappa. **Home Addr:** PO Box 358, Littleton, CO 80160-0358, **Home Phone:** (617)354-2293. **Business Addr:** Senior Project Manager, Peripheral Manufacturing Inc, 4775 Paris St, Denver, CO 80239, **Business Phone:** (303)371-8651.

## MORRIS, DR. CAROLE V.

Educator. **Personal:** Born May 1, 1945, Conway, NC; daughter of Roland C Lassiter Sr; children: Diallo Kobie. **Educ:** Elizabeth City State Univ, BS, 1967; Antioch Col, MPh, 1973; Univ Miami, EdD, 1988. **Career:** Educator (retired); City Univ NY, instr, 1968-69; Rutgers State Univ, instr, 1969-72; Norfolk State Univ, assoc prof, dept chair, spec educ, prof spec educ, prof emer, 1973-2006; Eastern VA Med, consult, 1980; Univ Miami, grad teaching, 1986-88; Leadership in Educ, VA Educ Policy, fel, 1990-92. **Orgs:** Bd chair, Speer Trust Fund, 1996-2000; bd mem, Nat Asn Investment Clubs, Hampton Roads Chap, 1997-; co-dir, Rehabil Servs Proj, 1998-2004; bd mem, Ecumenical Family Shelter, 1998-2003, vpres, 2004-. **Home Addr:** 802 Rivanna River Reach, Chesapeake, VA 23320-9234, **Home Phone:** (757)436-7459.

## MORRIS, CAROLYN G.

President (organization), executive. **Educ:** NC Cent Univ, BS, math, 1960; Harvard Univ, MS, math. **Career:** Fed Bur Invest, Systs Develop Sect, chief, dep asst dir info technol, 1984-95, asst dir info resources div, 1995-2000; Innovative Mgt & Technol Approaches Inc, pres, 2000-. **Business Addr:** President, Innovative Management & Technology Approaches Inc, 1522 K St NW Suite 704, Washington, DC 20005-1210, **Business Phone:** (202)962-0000.

## MORRIS, CELESTE

Publisher, political consultant. **Personal:** Born Oct 7, 1949, Brooklyn, NY; daughter of Edith Harding and Cuthbert Allsop; children: Oji & Kimya. **Educ:** Howard Univ, attended 1968; Brooklyn Col, BS, 1980; Columbia Univ, revson fel, 1994. **Career:** BHRAGS Home Care Progs, prog dir, 1980-85; dir, New York funded training employ; NY City Transit Authority, govt rels specialist, prog dir, 1986-87; Congressman Maj Owens, community specialist, 1987; Unlimited Creative Enterprises Inc, pres & founder, 1987; State Sen Malcolm Smith, chief staff; Albany State Sen, chief staff, 2000-02; NY Dept Small Bus Serv, dir minority woman & local bus enterprise progs, 2002-03; MTA, dep dir, 2004-06; Campaign Consult, consult, 2005; MorrisAllsop Pub Affairs, founder, pres, 2007-; New York Foreclosure Defense Bar, govt rels consult, 2013-16. **Orgs:** Nat Minority Bus Coun; Caribbean Am Chamber Com; vpres, bd dir, Nat Asn Mkt Developers; pres, Black Pages Pub Asn; bd mem, Workshop Bus Opportunities; Ny Coun Black Elected Dem; coun mem, Una Clarke Yvette Clarke; bd dir, Bedford Stuyvesant Legal Serv Corp; treas, Nat Orgn; mem & chairperson, Bedford Stuyvesant Legal Serv Bd Dirs, 2009-12. **Honors/Awds:** Comm Serv Award, Mosaic Coun, 1990; Women of Color Entrepreneurs Award, Medgar Evers Col, 1991; NAMDer Award, Nat Asn Market Developers, 1992; Outstanding Minority Bus, Nat Minority Bus Coun, 1992; Communicators Award, Councilwoman Annette Robinson, 1992; Charles H Revson fel, Columbia Univ, 1993-94; Commendation, NY City, Controller, 1996; Prestigious Revson Fellowship, Columbia University. **Special Achievements:** The Big Black Book, 1987-95; NY's Black Pages, 1987-. **Business Addr:** Founder, President, MorrisAllsop Public Affairs, 14 Wall St 20th Fl, New York, NY 10005, **Business Phone:** (212)563-5555.

## MORRIS, DR. CHARLES EDWARD, JR.

School administrator, president (organization). **Personal:** Born Sep 30, 1931, Big Stone Gap, VA; son of Charles E and Verta Edith Warner; married Jeanne A Brown; children: David & Lyn Elizabeth. **Educ:** Johnson C Smith Univ, BS, 1952; Univ Ill, MS, math, 1959, PhD, math, 1966. **Career:** William Penn High Sch, teacher, 1954-58; Univ Ill-Urbana, teaching & res assoc, 1959-66; High Potential Students Prog, actg dir, 1968-70; Undergrad Instr at ISU, internship acad admin, 1972-73; Ill State Univ, fac, assoc prof math, sec univ, 1973-80, vpres admin, 1980-90, emer assoc prof math & emer vpres admin serv, 1995-; Ill Bd Regents, Springfield, Ill, from interim vchancellor acad affairs to vchancellor, 1990-95; CEM Assoc Inc, pres, currently. **Orgs:** Bd dirs, Presby Found, 1974-83, Presby Econ Develop Corp, 1975-85, Western Ave Comm Ctr, 1978-86; chairperson, Ill Community Black Concerns Higher Educ, 1982-88, chmn emer, 1988-; adv bd, Col Potential Prog Coun Advan Experiential Learning, 1984-; chairperson, Ill Consortium Educ Oppor Bd, 1986-90; trustee emer, Monmouth Col, currently; Am Math Soc; Pi Mu Epsilon; Sigma Xi; Omicron Delta Kappa; Am Asn Univ Professors. **Honors/Awds:** Distinguished Alumnus Johnson C Smith Univ, 1976; Citizen's Awd for Human Rel Town Normal, 1979; Distinguished Alum of the Year Citation Nat Asn for Equal Oppor in Higher Educ, 1979; numerous speeches and articles on topics including mathematics educ, univ governance, blacks in higher educ; Doctor of Humane Letters, Monmouth Col, 1991. **Special Achievements:** He has published articles which appeared in the Illinois Journal of Education and in the Illinois State University Statesman. **Home Addr:** 1023 Barton Dr, Normal, IL 61761-4240, **Home Phone:** (309)452-3161. **Business Addr:** President, CEM Associates Inc, 1023 Barton Dr, Normal, IL 61761-4240, **Business Phone:** (309)454-5459.

## MORRIS, CHRISTOPHER VERNARD (CHRIS MORRIS)

Basketball player. **Personal:** Born Jan 20, 1966, Atlanta, GA; son of John and Patricia Ann Pittman Walton; married Felicia Michelle Hammonds; children: Micheal Christopher & Brenden Re. **Educ:** Auburn Univ, attended 1988. **Career:** Basketball player (retired); NJ Nets, forward, 1988-95; Utah Jazz, 1995-98; Orlando Magic, 1997; Phoenix Suns, 1998-99; Olympiacos B.C., Greece, 1999-2001; Harlem Globetrotters, 2001; Southern Calif Surf, 2002; Purefoods Tender Juicy Hotdogs, Philippines, 2002; Gaiteros del Zulia, Venezuela, 2003-04. **Orgs:** Philippine Basketball Asn. **Home Addr:** 1419 Kelliwood Oaks, Katy, TX 77450, **Home Phone:** (713)957-0600.

## MORRIS, DR. DOLORES ORINSKIA

Clinical psychologist. **Personal:** Born New York, NY; daughter of Joseph and Gertude Elliott. **Educ:** City Univ NY, MS, 1960; Yeshiva Univ, PhD, clin psychol, 1974; NY Univ, cert, psychoanalysis, psychother post doctoral prog, 1980. **Career:** C's Ctr, Dept Child Welfare, psychologist, 1959-62; Urban League Greater New York, staff psychologist, 1962-65; Bur Child Guid New York city, sch psychologist, 1965-74, supvr sch psychologists, 1974-78; Urban Res Planning Conf Ctr, tech asst, 1976; Bedford Stuyvesant St Acad, consult, 1977; Fordham Univ, asst prof, 1978-87; pvt pract, 1980-; New York Pub Schs Div Spec Educ, Clin Prof Develop, educ admin, 1987-92, supvr sch psychologists, clin adminr, 1992-95; New York Univ Postdoctoral Prog, supvr, sychoanalysis, psychother, supvr, currently; New Hope Guild Ment Health Servs, supvr, 1994-2001. **Orgs:** Treas, New York Asn Black Psychologists, 1967-75; co-chair, prof develop New York Asn Black Psychologists, 1975-77; chair, Schs & Ment Health Am Orthopsychiat Asn, 1978-81, 1986-87; Nat Asn Sch Psychol; Ny Psychol Asn pres Div Sch Psychol, 1985-86; vice chairperson, Psychol New York Educ Dept, 1988-2000; Diplte PsychoanalPsychol, 1996-; Div 39, 1998-; bd mem, Am Psychol Asn. **Honors/Awds:** Yeshiva Fellowship, NIMH, 1970-72; fellowship, Black Analysis Inc, 1972-74. **Special Achievements:** Books Published: "Race in the analytic situation: Reflections of an African American therapist"; Creative Dissent: Psychoanalysis in Evolution, Westport, Connecticut: Praeger, 2003; "The supervision of psychotherapy for African American and culturally diverse patients"; Personality development and psychotherapy in our diverse society: A source book. New York: Jason Arson, 1998; "African American students and their families"; A Handbook for school professionals, Teacher's College Press, Columbia University, 1992. **Home Addr:** 290 Riverside Dr Apt 11B, New York, NY 10025-5200, **Home Phone:** (212)222-1060. **Business Addr:** Supervisor, Postdoctoral Program in Psychotherapy & Psychoanalysis, 240 Greene St 3rd Fl, New York, NY 10003, **Business Phone:** (212)998-7890.

## MORRIS, EARL SCOTT

Fashion designer. **Personal:** Born May 24, 1966, Waukegan, IL; son of Velma D and Earle. **Educ:** Mich State Univ, BA, indust design, 1989. **Career:** Hasbro Inc, toy designer, 1990; Reebok Int, sr footwear designer, 1990-98; Nike Inc, sr level footwear designer, dir, 2003-09; Nike, design mgr, 2009-. **Orgs:** Mich State Alumni Group, 1990; Werner Icking Music Archive, Cult Diversity Group Reebok Int, 1992; Asn Black Sporting Goods Prof, 1992. **Honors/Awds:** Hasbro Inc, GI Joe action figure, codenamed Bulletproof, named after self, 1992; Fifth highest honor in the United States Marine Corps for team work, combat environ; Southwest Asia Campaign Medal, 4th Marine Div, 5th Motor Transp Battalion, Providence RI; Southwest Asia Campaign Medal; National Defense Medal; Naval Achievement Medal. **Special Achievements:** Spoke as rep for Reebok at Association of Black Sporting Goods Professional's Career Awareness Program, 1992. **Business Addr:** Design Manager, Nike Inc, 1 Bowerman Dr, Beaverton, OR 97005.

## MORRIS, ELISE LENOIR

Educator. **Personal:** Born Oct 25, 1916, Deridder, LA; daughter of York Alonzo and Ivy Darensbourgh; married John; children: Monica Wilson, John T & Gabriella Coleman. **Educ:** Xavier Univ, BA, lib arts, 1937; Prairie View A&M Univ, MEd, 1965; Tex S Univ, post grad study; Univ Houston, post grad study; Southwestern Univ, post grad study; Univ St Thomas, relig educ. **Career:** Archditoches Parish Training Sch, teacher, 1973; Our Mother Mercy Sch, 1942; Our Lady Star Sea Day Sch, dir, 1956; Galena Park Ind Sch Dist, teacher, 1962-. **Orgs:** Nat Educ Asn; Nat PTA & TX PTA; Delta Sigma ta Sorority; TX State Teacher Asn; Nat Asn Univ Women; Nat Asn Univ Women Houston, 1965; HarrisCo Grand Jury Adv Com, 1974-75; Supreme Lady Knights Peter Claver, 1970-75; steering comt, black participation 41st Int Eucharistic Congress, 1975; pres emer, founder, Drexel Soc, 1978; Voc Guid & Clinton Park Civic Asn. **Home Addr:** 16503 Rock W Dr, Houston, TX 77073, **Home Phone:** (281)443-0115.

## MORRIS, ELIZABETH LOUISE

Nurse. **Personal:** Born Dec 3, 1924, Cincinnati, OH; daughter of Malcolm and Ethel Ruth Brown; married Laurence; children: Donna Louise Higgins. **Educ:** Practical Sch Nursing, lic practical nurse, 1954, pharmacol course, 1968. **Career:** Nurse (retired); Jewish Hosp Cincinnati, staff develop, 1978-89. **Orgs:** Am Bridge Asn; Gaines United Methodist church. **Home Addr:** 3469 Ruther Ave, Cincinnati, OH 45220-1809, **Home Phone:** (513)751-2001.

## MORRIS, ERNEST ROLAND

School administrator. **Personal:** Born Dec 15, 1942, Memphis, TN; son of Benjamin C and Ernestine Edwards; married Freddie Linda Wilson; children: Ernest Jr & Daniel. **Educ:** Rocky Mountain Col, BS, 1967; Eastern Ill Univ, MS, educ, 1968; Univ Ill, Urbana-Champaign, PhD, 1976. **Career:** School administrator (retired); Minneapolis Pub Sch, hist teacher, 1968-69; Eastern Ill Univ, admis counr, 1969-71; Univ Ill Urbana-Champaign, asst dean, 1971-75, assoc dean, 19715-78, exec asst chancellor, 1978-80; Univ Wash, spec asst pres, 1979-82, vpres stud affairs, 1982-2005. **Orgs:** Chmn, educ div, 1983-84; admis & rev community, 1984-85, vice chmn bd dir, 1985-88, chmn elect, 1990, chmn, 1991, Residential Care & Family Serv Conf Panel, 1984-; chmn, Fed Emergency Mgt Agency Local Bd Seattle/King Co, 1984-86; founding trustee, Seattle/King Co Emergency Shelter Found, 1984-86 bd trustee, First Funds Am, 1990-93; vice chmn, planning & distrib comt, 1985-86, chmn, planning & distrib comt, 1987-, first vice chair, 1989, finance comt, 1993-, United Way Seattle/King Co; class, 1983-84, bd dir, 1985-96, exec comt, 1986-96, chmn, selection comt, 1987, vpres, 1992, pres, 1993, exec comt, 1992-94, chair bd dir, 1994-95, bd dr, United Way/Chamber Com Leadership Tomorrow Prog, 1984-; bd dir, Cent Puget Sound Coun Campfire, var bd comts, 1993-98; YWCA Isabel Colman Pierce Award Comt, 1992-98; King County Redistricting Comt, chair (nonpartisan), 1996; bd dir, Consumer Credit Coun Serv Seattle, 1997-2000; bd dir, chmn, United Way King County, 1998-; endowment Bd, United Way King County, 1999-2000; Nat Asn State Univ; Am Asn Higher Educ; Nat Asn Stud Personnel Admin. **Honors/Awds:** Cark Mem Scholar, 1966; Outstanding History Student Award, 1966; Alumni Distinguished Achievement Award, Rocky MT Col, 1982; Nat Assoc Stud Personnel Adminr; Nat Assoc State Univ & Land Grant Cols; Outstanding Alumnus Award, Leadership Tomorrow, 1988; Ernest Thompson Seton Award, Cent Puget Sound Coun Camp Fire Boys & Girls, 1998.

## MORRIS, EUGENE, JR.

Advertising executive, president (organization), chief executive officer. **Personal:** Born Jul 25, 1939, Chicago, IL; son of Eugene Sr and Willie Mae Mitchell. **Educ:** Roosevelt Univ, Chicago, BA, bus admin, 1969, MBA, 1971. **Career:** Foote, Cone & Belding, Chicago, Ill, acct exec, 1968-74; Burrell Advert, Chicago, Ill, acct supvr & sr vpres, 1974-86; Morris & Co, Chicago, Ill, pres, 1986-87; Morris & Randall Advert, Chicago, Ill, pres, 1987-88; E Morris Commun Inc, Chicago, Ill, chmn, founder, pres & chief exec officer, 1987-. **Orgs:** Bd mem, Bethune Mus, 1989-; vice chmn, Sickle Cell Dis Asn Ill; dir, Cosmopolitan Chamber Com; bd dir, Jr Achievement, Chicago; ABLE, Alliance Bus Leaders & Entrepreneurs. **Honors/Awds:** Blackbook Business & Professional Award, Nat Pub, 1984; Citizen Professional Award, Citizen Newspapers, 1985; Entrepreneur of the Year Award, State Ill, 2000; Asn Fundraising Professionals Outstanding Volunteer Award, 2001; Martin Luther King Legacy Award, Martin Luther King Boys & Girls Club, 2005; Illinois Governor's Small Business Person of the Year Award, 2006; Distinguished and Honored Guest Award, 2008; MAAX Advertising Executive of the Year Award; Business Leaders of Color Award; ABLE Leadership Award; Diversity In Advertising Leadership Award; Monarch Foundation Award for Communications; Moss Kendrix Marketer of the Year Award, Nat Alliance Mkt Developers. **Special Achievements:** Black Enterprise's List of Top Advertising Agencies, ranked 10th, 1999, ranked 8th, 2000, ranked 8th, 2001. **Home Addr:** 5555 S Everett Ave, Chicago, IL 60637-1968, **Home Phone:** (773)493-8244. **Business Addr:** President, Chief Executive Officer, E Morris Communications Inc, 820 N Orleans St Suite 402, Chicago, IL 60610, **Business Phone:** (312)943-2900.

## MORRIS, DR. FRANK LORENZO, SR.

School administrator. **Personal:** Born Jul 21, 1931, Cairo, IL; son of Lorenzo Richard Jr and Frankie Mae Taylor (Honesty); married M Winston Baker; children: Frank Jr, Scott, Rebecca & Kristina. **Educ:** Colgate Univ, BA, 1961; Syracuse Univ, MPA, 1962; MIT, PhD, polit sci; Georgetown Univ, MS, int affairs, 1976. **Career:** Professor, dean (retired); US Dept Housing & Urban Devel, Seattle WA, urban renewal rep, 1962-66; US State Dept, staff, 1966, Latin Am Off Prog & Policy Coord, dep regional coord, 1969-72; Northwestern Univ, assoc prof polit sci, 1972-77; US Community Serv Admin, chief planning & policy, 1978; US Foreign AID Prog, dep dir chief opers, 1979-83; Colgate Univ, O'Connor prof, 1986; Univ MD Sch Pub Affairs, assoc dean, 1986-88; Morgan State Univ, Baltimore MD, dean grad studies & res, 1988-96; Univ Md, prof; W Valley View, staff writer, currently; Univ Tex Dallas, Sch Social Sci, vis prof govt & polit, 1997-99; consult. **Orgs:** Pres, Nat Asn Advan Colored People Tacoma, 1963-66; vpres, Nat Asn Advan Colored People Montgomery County, 1977-79; exec dir, chmn & dir, Cong Black Caucus Found, 1983-85; trustee, Lincoln Temple UCC, 1984; moderator Potomac Asn, United Church Christ, 1987-; treas, bd dir, Global Tomorrow Coalition, 1987-; Alpha Phi Alpha; bd dir, Ctr Immigration Studies, 1988-; bd homeland ministries, United Church Christ, 1988-; pres, Coun Historically Black Grad Schs, 1992-94; Grad Rec Exam, minority adv com, 1992-94; exec dir, chmn, Diversity Alliance for a Sustainable Am, currently; trustee, Huston Tillotson Univ, currently; bd dir, 911 Families a Secure Am, currently; AARP Nat Policy Coun; vpres, Progressives Immigration Reform. **Honors/Awds:** NDEA Fel MIT, 1971; Dissertation Fel Russel Sage Found, 1972; Father of the Year, Chicago Defender, 1975; Education Policy Fel Inst Educ Leadership, 1977; Three Awards NAACP Evanston, Ind, Mont City, Md; Superior Honor Award, Dept State, 1982. **Home Addr:** 1212 Hidden Rdg Apt 1048, Irving, TX 75038-3758. **Business Addr:** Chairman, Diversity Alliance for a Sustainable America, 1904 Franklin St Suite 517, Oakland, CA 94612, **Business Phone:** (510)835-5017.

## MORRIS, GARRETT GONZALEZ

Actor. **Personal:** Born Feb 1, 1937, New Orleans, LA; married Freda. **Educ:** Dillard Univ, BA, 1958; Juilliard Sch Music, Manhattan Sch Music. **Career:** Plays: Bible Salesman, 1960; Porgy and Bess, 1964; Show Boat, 1966; Hallelujah, Baby!, 1967; I'm Solomon, 1968; Slave Ship, 1969-70; Transfers, 1970; Operation Sidewinder, 1970; In New England Winter, 1971; The Basic Training of Pavlo Hummel, 1971; What the Wine-Sellers Buy, Don't Bother Me, I Can't Cope, Sweet Talk, 1974; The World of Ben Caldwell, 1982; The Unvarnished Truth, 1985; Films: Where's Poppa (also known as Going Ape), 1970; The Anderson Tapes, 1971; Cooley High, 1975; Car Wash, 1976; How to Beat the High Cost of Living, 1980; The Census Taker, 1984; The Stuff, 1985; Critical Condition, 1987; The Underachievers, Critical Condition, 1987; Dance to Win; Husbands, Wives, Money, and Murder, 1989; Blackbird Fly, Children of the Night, Motorama, 1991; Severed Ties, Almost Blue, 1992; Coneheads, 1993; Black Rose of Harlem, Santa with Muscles, 1996; Black Scorpion II: Aftershock, 1997; Graham's Diner, Palmer's PickUp, Twin Falls Idaho, 1999; Little Richard, 2000; Jackpot, How High, 2001; Connecting Dots, 2003; The Salon, 2005; Frank, 2007; Implanted, 2007; Who's Your Caddy?, 2007; Amenic, 2007; Dog Gone, 2008; The Longshots, 2008; Bed Ridden, 2009; Just Like Family, 2009; Sonny Dreamweaver, 2009; Pickin & Grinnin, 2010; Valley of the Sun, 2011; Let Go, 2011; Pawn Shop, 2012; Freeloaders, 2012; TV series: "General Hospital", 1963; "Roll Out", 1973-74; "Change at 125th Street", 1974; "Saturday NightLive", regular, 1975-80; "ABC Weekend Specials", 1978; "Diff'rent Strokes", 1982; "The Invisible Woman", 1983, 1984; "True Confessions", 1983, 1984; "The Jeffersons", 1983, 1984; "It's Your Move", 1984-85; "Murder, She Wrote", 1985; "Hill Street Blues", 1985; "The Twilight Zone", 1985; "Scarecrow and Mrs. King", 1985; "Hunter", 1986-89; "227", 1987; "Married With Children", 1987, 1989; "Who's the Boss?", 1988; "Earth Angel", 1991; "Roc", 1991-92; "Maid for Each Other", 1992; "Martin", 1992-95; "ER", 1994; "The Wayans Bros.", "Black Scorpion", 1995; "Minor Adjustments", 1995; "Cleghorne!", 1995-96; "The Jamie Foxx Show", 1996; "Boston Common", 1997; "G vs E", 1999; "City of Angels", 2000; "Little Richard", 2000; "Static Shock", 2000; "Justice League", 2001; "The Hughleys", 2001; "Maniac Magee", 2003; "Noah's

Arc", 2005; "All of Us", 2005; "2 Broke Girls", 2011-14; "Shameless", 2011; "Psych", 2013; "CBS Cares", 2014; "Tom Green Live", 2014; Harry Belafonte Folk Singers, singer & musical arranger; Books: The Secret Place, 1972; aturday Night Live, 1975; Daddy Picou and Marie LeVeau, 1981; Downtown Comedy Club, Los Angeles, owner, currently. **Orgs:** Am Soc Composers, Authors & Publishers, 1963-; Am Fedn TV & Radio Artists. **Honors/Awds:** Tanglewood Conductors Award, 1956; National Singing Contest Winner, Omega Psi Phi; Garrett Morris Day, Los Angeles mayor Antonio Villaraigosa, named in honor, 2007. **Special Achievements:** Nominated, Independent Spirit Award, 2001; Nominated, Emmy Award, 1979; Declared February 9, 2007 as Garrett Morris Day in Los Angeles. **Business Addr:** Actor, Stone Manners Agency, 6500 Wilshire Blvd, Los Angeles, CA 90048, **Business Phone:** (323)655-1313.

### MORRIS, HERMAN, JR.
Lawyer, president (organization). **Personal:** Born Jan 16, 1951, Memphis, TN; son of Herman and Reba Garrett; married Brenda Partee; children: Amanda Elizabeth, Patrick Herman & Geoffrey Alexander. **Educ:** Southwestern Univ, Rhodes Col, BA, econs, 1973; Vanderbilt Univ Sch Law, JD, 1977. **Career:** Dixie Homes Boys Club Inc, Memphis, TN, counr, 1969; Porter Leath C Ctr, Memphis, TN, counr, 1970-73; RLS Assoc, Charleston, SC, dir minority recruiting, 1973-74; Sears, Nashville, TN, retail salesman, 1975; Tenn Comn Human Develop, Nashville, Tenn, law clerk, 1976; Ratner, Sugarmon & Lucas, Memphis, TN, law clerk, 1976; Ratner & Sugarmon, Memphis, TN, assoc atty, 1977-82, partner, 1982; Sugarmon, Salky & Morris, Memphis, TN, managing partner, 1982-86; Herman Morris & Assocs, Memphis, Tenn, 1986-88; Morris & Noel Attorneys Law, Memphis, TN, partner, 1988-89; Memphis Light, Gas & Water Div, gen coun, 1989-96, pres & chief exec officer, 1997-2003; Baker, Donelson, Bearman, Caldwell & Berkowitz PC, partner, 2004-06; Pinnacle Airlines, vpres & Gen Coun, 2006; Gen Atty Law, pvt pract, 2006-; City Memphis, atty, 2009-. **Orgs:** Chmn, Shelby County Homerule Charter Comn; chmn bd, Memphis Health CtrInc; chmn, Dixie Home Boys Club; exec bd, Southwestern Memphis Alumni Asn; Primary Health Care Adv Bd; pres, Ben Jones Chap, Nat Bar Asn; Memphis Pub Educ Fund; Nat Conf Christians & Jews; pres, Memphis Br, Nat Asn Advan Colored People; Am Bar Asn; Tenn Bar Asn; bd mem, Memphis Bar Asn; Am Trial Lawyers' Asn; bd dir, Tenn Trial Lawyer's Asn; bd dir, Judicial Criminal Justice Ctr Adv Comt; vice chmn, Tenn Bd Prof Responsibility; Tenn Judicial Selection Comt, 1997; adv bd, Bank Am, 1998-; dir, Am Gas Asn, 1998-; dir, Perrigo Co, 1999-; dir, Tenn Valley Auth Reg Resource Adv Coun, 2000-; Am Asn Blacks Energy, 2000-; dir, Tenn Qual Award, 2000-; Nat Petrol Coun, 2000-01; treas, Am Pub Power Asn, 2000-; bd trustee, Rhodes Col, 2003-; bd dir, Soulsville Found, 2006-; vice chmn, Miss River Recreational Corridor Task Force, 2006-; dir, UT Med Group Inc; dir, Tri-State Bank Memphis; dir, Univ Tenn Med Group, currently; Boy Scouts Am; campaign chmn, United Way Mid-S; dir, Tenn Valley Pub Power Asn, currently. **Business Addr:** Attorney, City of Memphis, 125 N Main St Rm 336, Memphis, TN 38103, **Business Phone:** (901)576-6614.

### MORRIS, HORACE W. See Obituaries Section.

### MORRIS, JAMES WALTER (JAMIE MORRIS)
Football player, football executive. **Personal:** Born Jun 6, 1965, Southern Pines, NC; son of Earl. **Educ:** Univ Mich, attended 1987. **Career:** Football player (retired), football administrator; Wash Redskins, running back, kick returner, 1988-89; New Eng Patriots, running back, 1990; Hamilton Tiger-Cats, 1991; Univ Mich, Athletic Dept, asst dir develop, develop mgr, 1998-2010; Randy Wise Chevrolet Buick Milan, dir customer develop, currently; Telemus Capital Partners, relationship mgr. **Honors/Awds:** All-Big Ten, 1986-87; Fiesta Bowl Co-MVP, 1986; Michigan Wolverines team MVP, 1987; Big Ten rushing champion, 1987; Hall of Fame Bowl MVP, 1988. **Special Achievements:** His career rushing total was once third in Big Ten Conference history. He continues to hold the career receptions record for Michigan running backs. He also still holds the all-time NFL record for most rushing attempts in a game with 45. **Business Addr:** Director of Customer Development, Randy Wise Chevrolet Buick, 1250 Dexter St, Milan, MI 48160.

### MORRIS, JOE (JOSEPH EDWARD MORRIS)
Football player, business owner. **Personal:** Born Sep 15, 1960, Ft. Bragg, NC; married Linda; children: Samantha & Blake. **Educ:** Syracuse Univ, BS, 1982. **Career:** Football player (retired), business owner; New York Giants, running back, 1982-88; Cleveland Browns, running back, 1991; AFL, NJ Red Dogs, co-owner, 1997-2000; real estate & ins bus, owner, currently. **Honors/Awds:** Independence Bowl Outstanding Offensive Player, 1979; Mark Hoffman Outstanding Back Award, 1981; Pro Bowl selection, 1985-86; Super Bowl XXI champion. **Special Achievements:** Films: 1982 NFL Draft, 1982; 1986 NFC Championship Game, 1987; Super Bowl XXI, 1987. **Home Addr:** , NJ.

### MORRIS, JOHN P., III
Shipping executive, business owner. **Personal:** son of John P Sr (deceased). **Career:** Red River Shipping Corp, owner, 1993-. **Special Achievements:** Red River Shipping is the first African-American controlled company to own and operate an oceangoing motor vessel under the US flag. **Business Addr:** Owner, Red River Shipping Corp, 6110 Executive Blvd Suite 620, Rockville, MD 20852, **Business Phone:** (301)230-0854.

### MORRIS, LATICIA
Basketball player. **Personal:** Born May 26, 1974, Detroit, MI. **Educ:** Auburn Univ. **Career:** Auburn Tigers, 1995-97; Portland Power, forward, 1997-98.

### MORRIS, LEIBERT WAYNE
School administrator. **Personal:** Born Nov 20, 1950, Cleveland, OH; married Cathy L. **Educ:** Ohio Univ, BGS, 1973, MEd, 1980. **Career:** OH State Univ Off Minority Affairs, coord recruitment, 1974-75; Oberlin Col, asst dir admin, 1975-77; Col Osteop Med, OH Univ, assoc dir admis, 1977-79, asst regional dean, 1979-85; Doctors Hosp Columbus, asst dir GME, 1979-85; OH State Univ Col Med, assoc dean, 1985-90, dir admin, 1985-98; Columbus State Community Col, dir admin, 1996-98, coord admin enrollment serv, 1998; Mayo Sch Med, asst dean stud affairs, 1998-2001; Loyola Univ, Chicago Stritch Sch Med asst dean stud affairs, 2001-07. **Orgs:** Adv bd, Staff Builders Home Health Care Agency, 1983-85; keeper rec & seal, Omega Psi Phi Fraternity, Life Mem, 1984-; bd trustee, Triedstone Missionary Baptist Church, 1985-88; nat nominations chair, Nat Asn Med Minority Educr, 1989-91; Ohio Comn Minority Health, comnr, 1989-92; New Salem Missionary Baptist Church; Triedstone Missionary Baptist Church, trustee; DuPage AME Church, 2010-11. **Home Addr:** 1419 Glendale Hills Dr NE, Rochester, MN 55906-8342, **Home Phone:** (507)340-8177.

### MORRIS, MAJOR
Educator, photographer. **Personal:** Born May 12, 1921, Cincinnati, OH; son of Ellen; married Anne Grethe Jakobsen; children: Lia Jacqueline. **Educ:** Boston Univ, attended 1951; Harvard Univ, Grad Sch Educ, EdM, 1976. **Career:** Educator (retired), photogr; Mass Inst Technol, res technician, 1953-66; Tufts Univ, prog dir officer, 1969-76; Southeastern Mass Univ, affirmative action officer, 1977-79; Portland State Univ, dir equity progs, 1979-87; photogr, currently. **Orgs:** Photogr/adminr, Educ Develop Ctr, 1966-68; dir, Deseg Training Inst, Univ Del, 1976-77; state coordr, Mass Region I AAAA, 1977-79; vice chair, Tri-County AA Assoc, Portland, 1981-83; state coordr, Ore Region XAAAA, 1983-; Willamette Valley Racial Minority Consortium; dir/photogr, Foto MaJac, 1987-; bd mem, Beaverton Ore Arts Comn, 1989-91; Retirement Asn Portland State Univ. **Home Addr:** 9521 High Pk Lane, San Diego, CA 92129, **Home Phone:** (619)484-7007. **Business Addr:** Photographer, 9521 High Pk Lane, Escondido, CA 92025.

### MORRIS, MARGARET LINDSAY
Educator, association executive. **Personal:** Born Dec 23, 1950, Princess Anne County, VA; daughter of George Alfred and Lillie Mae Phelps; married Richard Donald; children: Kristin Richelle & Tyler Donald. **Educ:** Norfolk State Univ, BA, 1973; Iberian Am Univ Mex City, 1975; Univ Ill, Urbana-Champaign, MA, 1974; PhD, 1979; Univ Madrid, attended 1982; Mich State Univ, attended 1991. **Career:** Univ Ill, fel, 1973-74; Grad Col Univ Ill, fel, 1975; Lincoln Univ, asst prof span, 1980; Cent State Univ Wilberforce Ohio, lang lab dir, 1980; Livingstone Col Salisbury NC, asst prof, 1981-85; Portsmouth City Schs, teacher, 1986; Ford Found, fel, 1992; Hampton Univ, asst prof span; Smith Univ, educr; SC State Univ, assoc prof span, 2011-. **Orgs:** Alpha Gamma Mu Span Hon Soc, 1972-; Alpha Kappa Mu Hon Soc, 1972-; Sigma Delta Pi Span Hon Soc, 1974-; Am Asn Teacher Span & Port, 1976-80; Am Asn Univ Prof, 1976-80; founder, Omega Iota Chap Sigma Delta Pi Span Nat Hon Soc; Col Lang Asn, 1980; Alpha Kappa Alpha Soc, 1983-. **Special Achievements:** First Black received PhD Span from Univ of Ill, 1979. **Home Addr:** 1021 Great Bridge Blvd, Chesapeake, VA 23320-6615, **Home Phone:** (804)543-3908. **Business Addr:** Associate Professor of Spanish, South Carolina State University, 300 Col St NE, Orangeburg, SC 29115, **Business Phone:** (803)536-8847.

### MORRIS, MARLENE C.
Chemist. **Personal:** Born Dec 20, 1933, Washington, DC; daughter of Richard Cook and Ruby Cook; married Kelson B; children: Gregory A, Karen D & Lisa F. **Educ:** Howard Univ, BS, 1955; Polytech Inst NY, postgrad. **Career:** Chemist (retired); AUS, res assoc, High Temp Res Proj, 1953-55; NBS JCPDS Associateship, res assoc, 1955, dir & res assoc, 1975; Int Ctr Diffraction Data, res chemist, 1986-90. **Orgs:** Am Chemist Soc; Am Crystallog Soc; AAAS; Joint Comn Powder Diff Stand; Int Union Crystallog; NBSSR Lunch Club; fel Wash Acad Sci Sigma Xi; Beta Kappa Chi Hon Sci Soc; Unitarian Church. **Special Achievements:** Published 69 articles in professional periodicals; author of 4 books. **Home Addr:** 1448 Leegate Rd NW, Washington, DC 20012-1212, **Home Phone:** (202)829-1256.

### MORRIS, MELVIN
Lawyer. **Personal:** Born May 7, 1937, Chicago, IL. **Educ:** Univ Wis, BS, 1959; John Marshall Law Sch, JD, 1965. **Career:** Pvt pract atty, currently. **Orgs:** Ill State Bar. **Home Addr:** 4435 Lane of the Roses, East Chicago, IL 46312-3156, **Home Phone:** (219)397-1449. **Business Addr:** Attorney, 602 E 150th St, East Chicago, IL 46312-3751, **Business Phone:** (219)398-6711.

### MORRIS, NATHAN BARTHOLOMEW (ALEX VANDERPOOL)
Singer. **Personal:** Born Jun 18, 1971, Philadelphia, PA; son of Alphonso Sr and Gail Harris. **Career:** Albums: Cooleyhighharmony, 1991; II, 1994; Evolution, 1997; Full Circle, 2002; Boys II Men, founding mem; Int Stylings, owner, 1997-; Behind the School Studios, owner, currently. Tv Appearances: The Jacksons: An American Dream (1992); Boyz II Men Motown: A Journey Through Hitsville USA Live, 2008; Soundtrack: House Party 2, 1991; Full House, 1991; White Men Can't Jump, 1992; MTV Unplugged: Ballads, 2000; Live from Studio Five, 2009. **Honors/Awds:** Grammy Award, 1992, 1995; 9 American Music Awards; 9 Soul Train Awards; 3 Billboard Awards; MOBO Award, 2011. **Business Addr:** Recording Artist, Arista Records, 6 W 57th St, New York, NY 10019, **Business Phone:** (212)489-7400.

### MORRIS, ROBERT V.
Executive, consultant. **Personal:** Born May 13, 1958, Des Moines, IA; son of James B Jr and Arlene J; married Vivian E; children: Jessica, Robert Jr & Brandon. **Educ:** Univ Iowa, attended 1982. **Career:** Iowa Bystander, ed & writer, 1968-83; Des Moines Regist, editorialist, 1990-; Morris Communs Int Inc, chief exec officer & pres, 1983-96; Future Electronic Mgt Inc, chief exec officer & pres, 1997-; Iowa State Univ, journalism instr; Ft Des Monies Memorial Pk & Educ Ctr, founder, chief exec officer; Morris Contracting Serv Inc, consult, currently; Morris Entertainment LLC, owner, managing mem, currently. **Orgs:** Kappa Alpha Psi Fraternity, 1984; pres, Iowa City Chap, Nat Asn Advan Colored People, 1979-81; Iowa Tuskegee Airmen; founder, Iowa Air Nat Guard 132rd Fighter Wing. **Honors/Awds:** Black Hall of Fame, Univ Iowa, 1980; Chairs Award, Nat Asn Advan Colored People Iowa City Chap, 1980; TSB Entrepreneur of the Year, State Iowa, 1989; Meritorious Service Award, Nat Asn Advan Colored People, Iowa & NEB Conf, 1990. **Special Achievements:** Fifty Most Influential Iowans of the New Twenty Century; Author: Tradition & Valor, Sunflower Press, 1999. **Business Addr:** President, Chief Executive Officer, Future Electronics Management Inc, 3700 SE 18th Ct, Des Moines, IA 50320-2334, **Business Phone:** (515)237-8152.

### MORRIS, STANLEY E., JR.
President (organization), college administrator. **Personal:** Born Nov 15, 1944, Brooklyn, NY; son of E Sr and Bernice Lambert; married Sandra Brito; children: Brooke Brito. **Educ:** Howard Univ, BA, 1968; Cornell Univ, pub rels bd, cert, neutral training, 1990. **Career:** Educator (retired); NY City Bd Educ, teacher, 1968-69; State Univ NY, asst dir, 1969-70, asso dean, 1970-95; Stan Morris Conceptual Engineering, owner. **Orgs:** Pres & chmn bd, Elephant Ent Ltd; pres, SE Morris Mgt Asn; NY St Personnel & Guidance Asn; Afro Am Teacher Asn; rep, Univ Negro Col Fund, 1970; rep, ASG DC Sociol Soc; Nat Asn Stud Personnel Adminr, 1990-91; Am Asn Higher Educ, 1991; trainer, Nat Coalition Bldg Inst Prejudice Reduction, 1990-91. **Home Addr:** 632 W St, Oneonta, NY 13820, **Home Phone:** (607)432-4656. **Business Addr:** owner, Stan Morris Conceptual Engineering, 907 East Broadway, Sweetwater, TX 79556-4766.

### MORRIS, STEVLAND HARDAWAY. See WONDER, STEVIE.

### MORRIS, VALERIE COLEMAN
Television news anchorperson, radio broadcaster. **Personal:** Born Nov 25, 1946, Philadelphia, PA; daughter of William O Dickerson and Vivien A Dickerson; married Robert L Jr; children: Michon Coleman & Ciara Coleman Harris. **Educ:** San Jose State Univ, BS, broadcast jour, 1968; Columbia Univ Grad Sch Jour, MS, jour, 1969. **Career:** KRON-TV, researcher; KGO-TV, gen assignment reporter, news anchor; KRON-TV, anchor; KCBS Newsradio, morning dr anchor; KCBS-TV, anchor, 1986-88; CBS Network Radio, creator & narrator, 1986-; KCBS Radio, morning dr anchor, 1988-, "With the Family in Mind" radio commentary ser, writer & narrator, 1986-; WPIX-TV Channel 11, anchor; CNN Fin Network, anchor & corresp; CNN Bus, anchor, 1994-2006; It's Your Money So Take It Personally, auth, 2011-. **Orgs:** Dd dir, Hearing Soc Bay Area. **Honors/Awds:** Three Emmy awards; Peabody Award, KCBS Radio. **Special Achievements:** American Sign Language. **Business Addr:** Writer, Narrator, CBS Network Radio, 40 W 57th St, New York, NY 10019.

### MORRIS, VALERIE DICKERSON COLEMAN
Journalist. **Personal:** Born Nov 25, 1946, Philadelphia, PA; daughter of William O and Vivien A; married Robert Lee Jr; children: Michon Allyce & Ciara Ashley. **Educ:** San Jose State Col, BA, jour, 1968; Columbia Univ, Grad Sch Jour, MA, broadcast jour, 1969. **Career:** KRON-TV, prod asst & res, 1969-73; KGO-TV, reporter, 1974-79; KRON-TV, news anchor & reporter, 1979-82; KGO-TV, news anchor & reporter, 1982-85; KCBS-Radio, news anchor, 1985-87; KCBS-TV, news anchor & reporter, 1987-89; KCBS-Radio, news anchor, 1989; WPIX-TV, reporter & anchor, 1996; CNN, fin, reporter, 1996-2007; narrator, currently; Valerie Coleman Morris, Inc, owner, currently. **Orgs:** Delta Sigma Theta Sorority, 1968-; Oakland Bay Area Links, 1989-; vpres, Hearing Soc Bay Area, 1983-; adv bd, Chronic Fatigue Fund, 1984-; bd dir, C's Hosp, 1990-92; vpres, Alumnae Resources, 1990-. **Honors/Awds:** Received three Emmy Awards, 1975 & 1988; RTNDA Best Live Coverage News Story, Class A Div, Earthquake, 1987; Soulbeat Civic Award, 1990; Award of Courage, Los Angeles Chap, Natl Org Women, 1987. **Home Addr:** 3794 W Placita Del Correca, Tucson, AZ 85745, **Home Phone:** (520)628-3182. **Business Addr:** Owner, Valerie Coleman Morris Inc.

### MORRIS, VERNON R.
Scientist, college teacher. **Personal:** Born Nov 23, 1973, San Antonio, TX. **Educ:** Morehouse Col, BS, chem & mathematics, 1985; Ga Inst Technol, PhD, geophys sci, 1990. **Career:** Univ Calif, Davis, postdoctoral fel chem dynamics, 1992-94; Howard Univ, Ctr Study Terrestrial & Extraterrestrial Atmospheres, dep dir, 1996-98; Howard Univ, Dept Chem & Grad Prog Atmospheric Sci, assoc prof, 1998-2000; NASA Goddard Earth Sci & Technol Ctr, Howard Univ Component, dir, 2000-; NOAA Ctr Atmospheric Sci, dir, 2001-; Nat Insts Health Res Ctr Minority Insts, Lab Molecular Computations & Bioinformatics, co-dir, 2003-; NASA Earth Systs Sci & Applications Adv Coun, (ESSAAC), mem, 2003-05; Nat Academies Sci Bd Atmospheric Sci & Climate (BASC), 2004-07; Howard Univ, Dept Chem, chair, 2006-08. **Orgs:** Nat Acad Sci Bd Atmospheric Sci & Climate (BASC); Adv Bd Benjamin Banneker Inst Sci & Technol; Am Meteorol Soc; Nat Orgn Prof Advan Black Chemists & Chem Engrs; Am Geophys Union; N Atlantic Treaty Orgn (NATO) Advan Study Inst; bd dirs, Penn Sch Community Serv Ctr. **Honors/Awds:** NATO/ASI Travel Award and Scholarship, 1991; University of California President's Postdoctoral Fellowship, 1992-94; Mordecai W. Johnson New Faculty Research Support Grant, 1994; University Merit Award 1996-2005, IBM SUR Award 1996; NSF CAREER Award 1997-2001; PKAL Faculty for the 21st Century 1997-; NASA Administrator's Fellowship 1998-2000, Howard University Faculty Merit Award 1996-2002, Howard University Most Productive Faculty Researcher in Natural Sciences 2004-06.

### MORRIS, WANYA JERMAINE
Singer, business owner. **Personal:** Born Jul 29, 1973, Philadelphia, PA; son of Carla and Dallas Thornton; married Traci Nash; children: 4. **Career:** Boys II Men, founder & singer, currently; The Co Entertainment Inc, owner, 2005-; Arista Rec, rec artist. Albums with Boys II Men: Cooleyhighharmony, 1991; II, 1994; Evolution, 1997; Full Circle, 2002; Motown: A Journey Through Hitsville USA, 2007; Love, 2009. Film: UnInvited Guest, 1999. **Orgs:** Omega Psi Phi fraternity. **Home Addr:** 1 Elena Ct, Voorhees, NJ 08043-4819. **Business Addr:** Recording Artist, Arista Records, 888 7th Ave, New York, NY 10019, **Business Phone:** (212)489-7400.

**MORRIS, WAYNE LEE**
Rancher, contractor, football player. **Personal:** Born May 3, 1954, Dallas, TX; children: 1. **Educ:** Southern Methodist Univ, BA, 1976. **Career:** Rancher, contractor, football player (retired); St Louis Cardinals, running back, full back, 1976-83; Landmark Northwest Plz Bank, loan officer, 1978; Wayne Morris Quarter Horse Ranch, owner, 1979; San Diego Chargers, running back, 1984. **Orgs:** Co-chmn, YMCA; chmn bd, Wayne Morris Enterprises Inc. **Honors/Awds:** Player of Year, Golden Knights, 1975-76; Most Valuable Player, Shriners C's Hosp, 1976; Most Improved Player, St Louis Quarterback Club, 1977. **Home Addr:** 5715 Old Ox Rd, Dallas, TX 75241-2118.

**MORRIS, WILLIAM HOWARD**
Executive, educator. **Personal:** Born Sep 7, 1960, Detroit, MI. **Educ:** Northwood Inst, BBA, acct, 1981; State Mich, CPA, 1985; Wharton Sch Univ Pa, MBA, finance, 1988; CFA Inst, chartered financial analyst, 1995; Am Inst Cert Pub Accts, personal financial specialist, 2003. **Career:** Peat Marwick, supvr sr acct, 1982-86; Chrysler Corp, sr treas analyst, 1988-91; Wilmoco Capital Mgt, pres & chief invest officer, 1990-98; Hillsdale col, asst prof, 1991-98; Prairie & Tireman, pres & chief investment officer, 1998-; Detroit Pub Schs, chief financial officer, 1999-2001; Inkster Pub Sch Dist, chief exec officer & emergency financial mgr, 2002-05; Comerica Bank, vpres & sr portfolio mgr, 2006-07; Fed-Mogul Corp, bd dir, 2007-08; Owens Corning, bd dir, 2007-; Mich Strategic Fund, bd dir, 2011-; City Detroit Financial Adv Bd, bd dir, 2012-. **Orgs:** Nat Black MBA Asn, 1987-; Mic Asn Cpa's, 1988; Fin Analysts Soc Detroit, Acct Comt, 1989-; secy & treas, State MIC Accountancy Bd, 1991-; Am Inst CPAs, invest comt, 1992-93; Nat Asn St Bd Accts, finance & admin comt, 1992-93. **Home Addr:** , Hillsdale, MI 49242. **Business Addr:** Board of Director, Owens Corning, 1 Owens Corning Pkwy, Toledo, OH 43659, **Business Phone:** (419)248-8000.

**MORRISON, BOB, JR.** See MORRISON, ROBERT B, JR.

**MORRISON, CHARLES EDWARD (CHUCK MORRISON)**
Executive, manager. **Personal:** Born Jul 18, 1943, Longview, TX; married Geri Brooks; children: Constance, Rani, Kristi & Jennifer. **Educ:** Bishop Col, BS, 1964; Wichita State Univ; Rust Col, Hon Dr, 1988; Grambling State Univ, Hon Dr, 1989. **Career:** Gen Motors, acct, 1965-70; Procter & Gamble, sales, mkt, 1970-72; Schlitz Brewing Co, sales, mkt, 1972-77, 1979-81; Burrell Advert Inc, advert acct sup, 1977-79, acct dir; Coca-Cola USA, vpres multicultural mkt, 1981; Don Coleman Advert, exec vpres & partner, 2000; Ford Motor Co, package engr; Uniworld Group Inc, exec vpres & gen mgr client serv, 1995-. **Orgs:** Consult, WCLK Adv Bd, 1985-86; consult, Southern Arts Fedn, 1985; trustee, Bishop Col, 1985-86; bd mem, S DeKalb YMCA, 1986; life mem, Nat Asn Advan Colored People, Urban League; bd mem, Atlanta Boys Club; Grambling State Univ Indust Cluster; chmn, Nat Asn Mkt Develop, 1991-92; trustee, Rust Col; bd mem, Jackie Robinson Found; bd mem, Grambling Black & Gold Found Inc; Boys & Girls Clubs; US Youth Games. **Honors/Awds:** Top 10 Black Businessperson Dollar & Sense Magazine, 1985; Beverage Executive of Year, Cal-PAC Org, 1986; Communications Excellence to Black Audiences Award; CLIO's, Addy's. **Home Addr:** 3614 Greentree Farms Dr, Decatur, GA 30034. **Business Addr:** Executive Vice President, General Manager of Client Service, Uniworld Group Inc, 1 MetroTech Ctr N 11th Fl, Brooklyn, NY 11201, **Business Phone:** (212)219-1600.

**MORRISON, GARFIELD E., JR.**
Law enforcement officer. **Personal:** Born Apr 13, 1939, Boston, MA; son of Iona Blackman and Garfield E Sr; married Pearl P Johnson; children: Garfield E III & Melissa E. **Educ:** Mass Bay Community Col, Wellesley, MA, AS, 1978; Boston State Col, Boston, MA, BS, 1981; Anna Maria Col, Paxton, MA, 1982. **Career:** Law enforcement officer (retired); US Post Off, Boston, Mass, lett carrier, 1966-74; Cambridge Police Dept, Cambridge, Mass, police officer, 1974-84, sgt, 1984-94, lt, 1994-2001, dep supt, 2001-04. **Orgs:** Chmn, usher bd, Mass Ave Baptist Church, 1966-70; secy, Men's Club, Mass Ave Baptist Church, 1965-68; trustee, Mass Ave Baptist Church, 1968-72; treas, Cambridge Afro-Am Police Asn, 1977-86, pres, 1990 & 1992. **Home Addr:** 14 Pawnee Dr, Arlington, MA 02474, **Home Phone:** (781)646-5783.

**MORRISON, HAROLD L., JR.**
Executive, vice president (organization). **Educ:** Duke Univ, BA, hist. **Career:** Chubb Corp, 1984-96, Northwest Regional Off Seattle, mgr, 1996-2001, New York brokerage zone officer, 2001-03, US field opers mgr, 2003-08, exec vpres, 2008-; chief global field officer, 2008-; chief admin officer, 2011-.

**MORRISON, JACQUELINE**
Association executive. **Personal:** Born Aug 9, 1951, Plainfield, NJ; daughter of Wisteria Ingram McKnight and Caldwell; married Curtis Sr; children: Curtis Jr (deceased). **Educ:** San Diego State Univ, BA, 1978; Univ Mich Sch Pub Health, MPH, 1983. **Career:** Pub health consult, 1984-86; Wayne State Univ, pub health consult, 1986-88; Detroit Urban League, sr vpres progs, 1988-98; Am Asn Retired Persons, Mich, interim state dir, assoc state dir & sr mgr state opers, state dir, 2005-15; Planned Parenthood SE Mich, pres & chief exec oficer; Transformation Mgt Consults, pres. **Orgs:** Bd mem, Life Directions, 1990-91; adv bd mem, Literacy Vols Am; New Detroit Inc; bd mem, Sickle Cell Dis Asn; Brush pk Develop Corp; Workforce Develop Bd; Am Pub Health Asn. **Honors/Awds:** Community Service Award, Nat Coun Negro Women, 1994. **Business Addr:** State Director, American Association of Retired Persons, 601 E St NW, Washington, DC 20049, **Business Phone:** (888)687-2277.

**MORRISON, JAMES W., JR.**
President (organization), consultant. **Personal:** Born Jan 14, 1936, Bluefield, WV; son of James W Sr and Winnie E; married Jean M; children: Traquita Renee, James W III & Susannah Myerson. **Educ:** WVa State Col, BA, 1957; Univ Dayton, MPA, 1970. **Career:** Dayton AF Dept Def Electronics Supply Ctr, Ohio, inventory mgr, 1959-63; AF Logistics Command, Dayton, Ohio, mgt spec, 1963-72; Nat Aeronaut & Space Admin, Wash, DC, execasst dir mgt systs, 1972-74; Exec Off Pres Off Mgt & Budget, Wash, DC, sr mgt assoc, 1974-79; Exec Proj State Univ New York, Albany, NY, vis lectr publ, 1974-76; US Off Personnel Mgt, Wash, DC, asst dir econ & govt, 1979, dir congional rel, 1979-81, assoc dir compensation, 1981-87; CNA Ins Co, Rockville, Md, sr mgr prog support, 1987-88; Morrison Assocs, Wash, DC/Scottsdale, Ariz, pres, 1988-. **Orgs:** Adv comt mem, Dayton Bd Educ, 1971; Alpha Phi Alpha; Pi Delta Phi; Pi Alpha Alpha. **Home Addr:** 7078 E Chipmunk Ct, Tucson, AZ 85750. **Business Addr:** AZ.

**MORRISON, HON. JOHNNY EDWARD, JR.**
Lawyer, judge. **Personal:** Born Jun 24, 1952, Portsmouth, VA; son of Mary Bernard; married Cynthia L Payton; children: Melanie Yvette & Camille Yvonne. **Educ:** Wash & Lee Univ, grad, 1974; Wash & Lee Univ Sch Law, grad, 1977. **Career:** Legal Aid Soc Roanoke Valley, staff atty, 1977-78; Wash & Lee Sch Law, Reginald Heber Smith fel, 1977; Norfolk Commonwealth Attys Off, prosecutor, 1978-79; Portsmouth Commonwealth Atty's Off, prosecutor, 1979-82; Overton, Sallee & Morrison, partner, 1982; Portsmouth Commonwealth Atty's Off, atty, 1982-91; Portsmouth Circuit Ct, 3rd Judicial Circuit Va, judge, 1991-, chief judge, 1992-94, 1996-98. **Orgs:** Va State Bar Asn; VA Asn Commonwealths Attys; Kiwanis Int; bd mem, Tidewater Legal Aid Soc, United Way, Effingham St Br YMCA; pres, Tidewater Legal Aid Soc; bd dir Wash & Lee, Tidewater Alumni; Va Black Caucus; Cent Civic Forum; Old Dom Bar Asn; Twin City Bar Asn; Nat Criminal Justice Asn; Nat Black Prosecutors Asn. **Home Addr:** 4320 Midfield Pkwy, Portsmouth, VA 23703-3944, **Home Phone:** (804)483-1943. **Business Addr:** Chief Judge, Portsmouth Circuit Court, 801 Crawford St, Portsmouth, VA 23705-1217, **Business Phone:** (757)393-8000.

**MORRISON, DR. REV. JUAN LARUE, SR.**
Educator, clergy, administrator. **Personal:** Born Mar 22, 1943, Springfield, IL; son of Farries Sr and Margaret; married Clementine Lorraine; children: Juan L Jr, Daryl G & Cheryl L. **Educ:** IL State Univ, BS, educ, 1969, MA, ed admin, 1972, PhD, higher educ admin, 1980; Sangamon State Univ, MA, human dev & coun, 1975. **Career:** Springfield Sch Dist No 186, elem teacher, 1969-70, sec teacher, 1970-72; Prayer Wheel Church God Christ, co-pastor, 1980-84; Emmanuel Temple Church God Christ, founding pastor, 1984-; Lincoln Land Comm Col, counr, coordr, prof phsycol; Charles Harris Mason Bible Col, instr; Ill S Cent Fel Church God Christ, supt, 1st admin asst, founding overseer, currently. **Orgs:** Test admin Am Col Test, 1979-; test admin, Am Registry Radiologic Technologists, 1982-; test admin, Nat BdRespiratory Care Mgmt Servs Inc, 1982-; publicity chmn, Springfield Ministerial Alliance, 1983-; test admin, Educ Testing Serv, 1984-; pres music Dept Cent Ill Jurisdiction Church God Christ, 1984-. **Honors/Awds:** IL Guidance and Personnel Asn, 1982; Community Service Award, Nat Asn Advan Colored People, 1996. **Home Addr:** 260 Maple Grove, Springfield, IL 62707-9527. **Business Addr:** Founding Pastor, Emmanuel Temple Church Of God In Christ, 2401 E Ash St, Springfield, IL 62703, **Business Phone:** (217)525-0156.

**MORRISON, DR. K. C (MINION KENNETH CHAUNCEY)**
Educator. **Personal:** Born Sep 24, 1946, Edwards, MS; son of Elvestra Jackson and Minion; married Johnetta Bernadette Wade; children: Iyabo Abena. **Educ:** Tougaloo Col, BA, 1968; Univ WI, Madison, MA, 1969, cert African studies, 1974, PhD, 1977; Univ Ghana, cert African studies, 1972. **Career:** Tougaloo Col, instr, 1969-71, co dir freshman studies, 1970-71, asst prof polit sci, 1974-77; Hobart Col, asst prof polit sci & coordr, 1977-78; Syracuse Univ, assoc prof afro-am studies & polit sci, 1978-89, chair afro am studies, 1982-87; Univ Mo, Columbia, vice provost, 1989-97, prof polit sci, 1989-2009, Frederick Middlebush prof of polit sci, 2005-08; Miss State Univ, Dept Polit Sci & Pub Admin, prof & head, 2009-, sr assoc african am studies, 2009-. **Orgs:** Consult, fel Ford Found, Danforth Frost & Sullivan Huber Found, 1968-84; African Studies Asn; pres, Nat Conf Black Polit Scientists; Am Pol Sci Asn; Nat AsnAdvan Colored People; bd dir, United Way; Grad Asst Prog Bd; chair, Midwest Polit Sci Asn; Am Asn Univ Professors; Int Polit Sci Asn; pres, African Asn Polit Sci; bd dir, Third World Conf Found; Am Polit Sci Asn. **Honors/Awds:** Faculty Alumni Award, Univ Mo; Martin Luther King Community Award; Univ of Missouri Diversity Enhancement Award; Black Alumni Kwanzaa Recognition Award, Univ Mo; Barbara Jordan Leadership Award; Directory of Distinguished Americans; Outstanding Young Men of America; Teacher of the Year, Tougaloo Col. **Special Achievements:** The African Voter: Survey Evidence from Ghana in Comparative Perspective; Author: Housing Urban Poor Africa, 1982; Ethnicity & Political Integration, 1982; Black Political Mobilization, 1987; Political Parties in Ghana through Four Republics: A Path to Democratic Consolidation, 2004; Exploring Voter Alignments In Africa: Core and Swing Voters In Ghana, 2005; Ghana's Political Parties: How Ethno/Regional Variations Sustain the National Two-Party System, 2006. **Home Addr:** 1312 Overhill Rd, Columbia, MO 65203-1523. **Business Addr:** Professor & Senior Fellow, Head of Political Science & Public Administration, University of Missouri, 105 Bowen Hall 456 Hardy Rd, Mississippi State, MO 39762, **Business Phone:** (662)325-2711.

**MORRISON, PROF. KEITH ANTHONY**
Artist, educator. **Personal:** Born May 20, 1942, Linstead; son of Noel and Beatrice McPherson; married Susan Alunan. **Educ:** Sch Art Inst Chicago, BFA, 1963, MFA, 1965; Univ Chicago, attended; DePaul Univ, attended; Loyola Univ, attended. **Career:** Fisk Univ, asst prof art, 1967-68; DePaul Univ, Dept Art, chmn & assoc prof art, 1969-71; Univ Ill, assoc prof art, 1971-79, Col Art, assoc dean, 1974-78; Univ Md, Dept Art, prof art, 1979-92, chmn, 1987-92, art studio coordr, 1987; Md Inst Art, grad lectr, 1989-90; Sch Art & Inst Humanities, fac, 1990; San Francisco Art Inst, prof art, 1992-93, dean, 1993-94; San Francisco State Univ, Col Creative Arts, dean, 1994-96, 1997-2005; Univ Mich, King-Chavez Distinguished Vis Scholar; Temple Univ, Tyler Sch Art, dean, 2005-08, prof painting, drawing & sculpture, 2008-; Sichuan Fine Arts Inst, vis prof, 2008; Pub Sch Syst, Gary, Ind, instr art. **Orgs:** Danforth Found Teaching Asn, 1970-71; adv bd, New Art Examr, 1983-; chmn bd, Wash Proj Arts, 1984-85. **Honors/Awds:** Danforth Foundation Award for Teaching; Bicentennial Award for Painting, City Chicago, 1976; International Award for Painting, OAU Monrovia, Liberia, 1979; Distinguished Achievement Award for Painting, Nat Asn Equal Opportunity Educ, 1984; US Cultural Envoy to Shanghai Biennale, 2008; Fulbright to China, 2009; Lifetime Achievement Award, 2013. **Special Achievements:** Paintings and prints exhibited in such as the Art Institute of Chicago; Museum of Contemporary Art, Chicago; Corcoran Gallery of Art; Smithsonian American Museum of Art; Smithsonian Anacostia Museum of Art; Bronx Museum; The Studio Museum of Harlem; The Wadsworth Atheneum; Cincinnati Museum of Art; The duSable Museum; The de young Museum; The Museum of Modern Art; The National Gallery of Art; The Philadelphia Museum; The Pennsylvania Academy of Art; The High Museum; The Venice Biennale; The Caribbean Biennale. Numerous other exhibitions worldwide, including solo exhibitions at the Cavin Morris Gallery; Miller/Geisler Gallery; 611 Gallery; Bomani Gallery; Liz Harris Gallery; Brody's Gallery; Jan Cicero Gallery; Contributed articles to numerous publications & organizations, including The New Art Examiner, American Visions, The Washington Post, the USIA, the University of Chicago, & the Smithsonian Institution; written catalog essays for museums such as the Baltimore Museum of Art, the Corcoran Gallery of Art, the MH de Young Memorial Museum, the Getty Museum & the Alternative Museum; Art in Washington & Its Afro-American Presence: 1940-1970. Curated many exhibitions including: "Jacob Lawrence's Toussaint L'Ouverture," DePaul University; African American Art, Bergman Gallery, University of Chicago; "Art In Washington and It's African American Presence", WPA; Art in Washington, Foundation for Today's Art; "Contemporary Art of Cuba," San Francisco State University. **Home Addr:** 911 Dale Rd, Meadowbrook, PA 19046-2513, **Home Phone:** (215)886-1362. **Business Addr:** Professor of Painting, Drawing & Sculpture, Temple University, 2001 N 13th St, Philadelphia, PA 19122, **Business Phone:** (215)777-9000.

**MORRISON, PAUL-DAVID**
Executive, entrepreneur. **Personal:** Born Apr 28, 1965, Boston, MA; son of Paul E and Carole Vitale-Chase; married Nancy. **Career:** Digital Equip Corp, mech engr tech, 1983-88; Raytheon, supvr, 1988-91; Motorola, sr pkg engrg tech, 1991-94; P D Morrison Enterprises Inc, pres & chief exec officer, 1995-; Hurricane Off Supply, Cedar Pk, TX, sls mgr & owner. **Orgs:** Bd mem, Cent & S Tex Minority Bus Coun; bd dir, Capital City African-Am Chamber Com. **Home Addr:** 205 Cherry Laurel Dr, Cedar Park, TX 78613-2854. **Business Addr:** President, Chief Executive Officer, PD Morrison Enterprises Inc, 1120 Toro Grande Blvd Bldg 2 Suite 208, Cedar Park, TX 78613, **Business Phone:** (512)335-7173.

**MORRISON, PEARL PATTY**
School administrator, educator. **Personal:** Born Oct 11, 1938, Boston, MA; daughter of Annie Lenox and Harry Samuel Johnson; married Garfield E III & Melissa E. **Educ:** State Teachers Col, Boston, MA, BSED, 1960; State Col Boston, ME, 1967. **Career:** Educator, school principal (retired); City Somerville, teacher, 1960-87, vice prin, 1987-95, prin. **Orgs:** Treas, Mass Ave Baptist Church, 1970-; pres, African-Am Soc Arlington; pres, Arlington Civil Right Comt Arlington; sec, Somerville Racial Understanding Comm, 1970-80; bd mem, Somerville YMCA, 1990-; bd mem, Elizabeth Peabody House, 1990-; Delta Kappa Gamma, MA Chap. **Home Addr:** 14 Pawnee Dr, Arlington, TX 02474, **Home Phone:** (781)646-5783.

**MORRISON, ROBERT B., JR. (BOB MORRISON, JR.)**
Government official, consultant. **Personal:** Born Jul 9, 1954, Orlando, FL; son of Robert B Sr. **Educ:** Loyola Univ, BA, polit sci, bus admin, 1975; Univ Fla, JD, 1978. **Career:** Law Off Warren H Dawson, atty, 1978-79; City Tampa, exec asst mayor, 1979-87; Morrison Gilmore & Clark, Pa, partner, 1986-96; State Fla Lottery Comn, staff, 1987-94; Morrison & Assoc Inc, chief exec officer & pres, 1996-. **Orgs:** Am Bar Asn; Nat Bar Asn; Fla Bar Asn; Fla Chap Nat Bar Asn, 1979-; chmn, Bi-Racial Adv Comn Hills bor City Sch Bd, 1978-81; chmn, Mayor's CableTV Adv Comn, 1979-83; pres, St Peter Claver Parish Coun, 1979-83; Franklin St Mall Adv Comn, 1979-; Tampa Orgn Black Affairs, 1979-; mediator Citizen Dispute Settlement Prog, 1979-80; bd dir, Tampa Urban League, 1980-; March Dimes Hillsborough City, 1980-; Nat Advan Asn Colored People, 1981; bd dir, Boy Scouts Am, 1982-; State Job Training Coordr Coun, 1983-; Rotary Club Tampa, 1983-; pres, Fla Chap Nat Bar Asn, 1986-87; Bi-Racial Comn, 1987; exec dir, Hillsborough Co Hotel & Motel Asn, 1989-. **Home Addr:** 3613 Lindell Ave, Tampa, FL 33610-7950, **Home Phone:** (813)247-2394. **Business Addr:** President, Chief Executive Officer, Morrison & Associates Inc, 201 E Kennedy Blvd, Tampa, FL 33602, **Business Phone:** (813)833-8311.

**MORRISON, SAMUEL F. (SAM MORRISON)**
Librarian, executive. **Personal:** Born Dec 19, 1936, Flagstaff, AZ; son of Travis B (deceased) and Ruth Morrison Genes; married Judith Moore. **Educ:** Compton Jr Col, AA, 1955; Calif State Univ, Los Angeles, BA, eng, 1971; Univ Ill, Champaign, MS, libr sci, 1972; Harvard Univ, Kennedy Sch Govt, attended 1989. **Career:** Frostproof Living Learning Libr, Frostproof, FL, dir, 1972-74; Broward County Libr Syst Ft Lauderdale, FL, asst to dir & dep dir, 1974-87; Chicago Pub Libr, Chicago, IL, dep comnr & chief librn, 1987-90; Broward County Libr Syst, Ft Lauderdale, dir, 1990-2003; Southeastern Consult Grp, Boca Raton, FL, assoc, 2003-. **Orgs:** Am Libr Asn, 1971-; Nat Urban League, 1972-; Nat Asn Advan Colored People, 1972-; bd mem, Broward County Libr Found, 1990; bd mem, Urban League Broward County; bd mem, Nat Forum Black Pub Adminr, S Fla Chap, 1990; steering comt, Ctr Bk; plng comn, Fla Libr Asn; Fontaneda Soc, Ft Lauderdale, FL; bd mem, United Way, 1995-97; bd mem, Nat Conf; bd mem, Gold Coast Jazz Soc; bd mem, Fla Humanities Coun; bd mem, Urban Libr Coun; SE Fla Libr Info Network; Bonnet House; Boys & Girls Clubs Broward County. **Home Addr:** 1317 NE 2nd St, Ft. Lauderdale, FL 33301, **Home Phone:** (954)763-7430. **Business Addr:** Associate, Southeastern Consulting Group LLC, 21218 St Andrews Blvd Suite 307, Boca Raton, FL 33433.

**MORRISON, TONI (CHLOE ANTHONY WOF-**

FORD)
Writer, educator, editor. **Personal:** Born Feb 18, 1931, Lorain, OH; daughter of George Wofford and Ramah Willis; married Harold; children: Harold Ford & Slade Kevin. **Educ:** Howard Univ, BA, 1953; Cornell Univ, MA, 1955; Oxford Univ, DLitt, 2005. **Career:** Tex Southern Univ, instr, 1955-57; Howard Univ, instr, 1957-64; Random House Publ Co, ed, sr ed, 1965-; auth, 1969-; State Univ NY, Purchase, assoc prof, 1971-72; Yale Univ, vis prof, 1976-77; State Univ NY, Albany, Schweitzer prof humanities, 1984-89, Albert Schweitzer chair, 1984; Bard Col, vis prof, 1986-88; Princeton Univ, Robert F Goheen prof humanities, 1989-2006, chair, 1989-, prof emer, 2006-, Robert F. Goheen Prof Emer, currently; Rutgers Univ; Princeton Atelier, founder; Novels: The Bluest Eye, 1970; Sula, 1974; Song of Solomon, 1977; Tar Baby, 1981; Beloved, 1987; Jazz, 1992; Paradise, 1998; The Big Box, 1999; The Book of Mean People, 2002; Love, 2003; A Mercy, 2008; Playwright: Dreaming Emmett, 1986; Non fiction: Black Book, 1974; ed, Race-ing Justice, En-gendering Power, 1992; Playing in the Dark, 1992; Remember, 2004; What Moves at the Margin, 2008; Burn This Book, 2009. **Orgs:** Toni Morrison Soc, 1993; Am Acad & Inst Arts & Letters; Nat Coun Arts; Authors Guild; Authors League Am; mem ed bd, Nation mag. **Honors/Awds:** Ohoana Book Award for Sula, 1975; Nat Book Critics Circle Award; Award for Song of Solomon, Am Acad & Inst Arts & Letters, 1977; Am Acad Arts & Lett, 1981-; New York State Governor's Art Award, 1986; Robert F. Kennedy Book Award, 1987-88; American Book Award, 1988; Helmerich Award, 1988; Pulitzer Prize for Fiction, 1988; Robert FKennedy Award, 1988; Pulitzer Prize for Beloved, 1989; MLA Commonwealth Award in Literature, 1989; Nobel Prize, lit, 1993; Elizabeth Cady Stanton Award, Nat Orgn Women; Pearl Buck Award, 1994; Condorcet Medal, Paris, 1994; Rhegium Julii Prize for Literature, 1994; Nat Book Foundation Medal, 1996; Nat Arts & Humanites Medal, presented by President Clinton, 2000; nominee, National Book Award; 30 Most Powerful Women in America; DHL, Oxford Univ, 2005; DHL, Rutgers Univ, 2011; DHL, 2011; Presidential Medal of Freedom, 2012; Ivan Sandrof Lifetime Achievement Award, Nat Bk Critics Circle, 2014; PEN/Saul Bellow Award for Achievement in American Fiction, 2016. **Special Achievements:** First African-American to win a Nobel Prize in literature, 1993. **Home Addr:** , NJ. **Business Addr:** Robert F. Goheen Professor Emeritus, Princeton University, 58 Prospect Ave, Princeton, NJ 08544-1099, **Business Phone:** (609)258-3000.

## MORRISON, DR. TRUDI MICHELLE
Presidential aide, lawyer. **Personal:** Born Jul 25, 1950, Denver, CO; daughter of George and Marjorie; married Dale Saunders. **Educ:** Colo State Univ, BS, 1971; Univ Mich, MA, polit theory, PhD, polit sci. **Career:** States Atty Off, Rockville, Md, asst states atty, 1975-76; Gorsuch Kirgis Campbell Walker & Grover, atty, 1977; Denver Dist Atty Off, atty, 1977-78; Colo Div Criminal Justice, criminal justice admin, 1978-81; US Dept HUD, actg dep asst secy, policy & budget, 1981-82; US Dept Health & Human Serv, reg dep dir, 1982-83; White House, assoc dir off pub liaison; US Sen, dep sgt arms; US Courts, chief fair employ pract, chief employ rels off, currently. **Orgs:** Exec secy stud body, Colo State Univ, 1969-71; bd dir, Nat Stroke Asn, 1983-87; Nat Coun Negro Women; founder, Colo Black Repub Coun; Nat Urban League; Nat Asn Advan Colored People. **Honors/Awds:** Outstanding Young Women of America, 1978, 1979, 1982; Young Careerist, Nat Org Bus & Prof Women, 1978; Highest Ranking Black Woman White House, 1983-; Black Republican of the Year, 1984; William E Morgan CSU Alumni Achievement Award, 1984. **Special Achievements:** First African American Homecoming Queen Colo State Univ, 1970-71; first woman and the first African American to serve as chief of the Fair Employment Practices Office at the Administrative Office of the United States Courts; First Recipient of the William E. Morgan Alumni Achievement Award. **Business Addr:** Chief Employment Relations Office, Administrative Office of the US Courts, Rm 5265 1 Columbus Cr, Washington, DC 20544, **Business Phone:** (202)502-1380.

## MORRISON, VANESSA (VANESSA MORRISON MURCHISON)
Movie producer, president (organization). **Personal:** married John Murchison; children: Julian Murchison. **Educ:** UC Berkeley, Bachelor's in Rhetoric. **Career:** Black Filmmakers Hall of Fame; Fox Studio, Sr. VP Production, VP Production, Executive VP; Fox Animation Studios, President, 2007-. **Honors/Awds:** "Hollywood Reporter," Women in Entertainment Power 100, 2011, 2012, 2013. **Special Achievements:** First woman to head a studio animation division.

## MORROW, CHARLES G., III
Manager, educator, government official. **Personal:** Born Jul 21, 1956, Chicago, IL; son of Lillian; married Sherri H; children: 3. **Educ:** De LaSalle Inst; Ill Inst Technol. **Career:** Sch Dist, drivers educ instr, 1971-74; Metro Sanit Dist, bookkeeper, 1975-76; Peoples Gas, customer serv rep, 1977; Ill Gen Assembly, 32ndDist, rep, 1987-2005. **Orgs:** Boy Scouts Am; Nat Asn Advan Colored People; Urban League; chairperson, Appropriations Pub Safety; vchairperson, Pub Utilities; Financial Insts. **Home Addr:** 7215 S Prairie Ave, Chicago, IL 60619-1731, **Home Phone:** (773)483-2215.

## MORROW, HON. DION GRIFFITH
Judge. **Personal:** Born Jul 9, 1932, Los Angeles, CA; son of Anna Griffith and Virgil; married Glynis Ann Dejan; children: Jan Bell, Kim Wade, Cydney, Carla Cavalier, Melvin Cavalier & Dion Jr. **Educ:** Loyola Univ Law Sch, JD, 1957; Pepperdine Col, Malibu, CA. **Career:** Judge (retired); La City Atty, asst city atty, 1973-75; La, atty law, 1957-73; Munic Ct Compton, CA, judge, 1975-78; Super Ct, judge, 1978-95; Nat Judicial Col; Calif State Univ, Dept Criminal Justice, asst prof. **Orgs:** Vpres, Gen Coun dir, Enterprise Savings & Loan, 1962-72; pres, John M Langston Bar Asn, 1969-71; life mem, Nat Asn Advan Colored People; Nat Bar Asn, 1969-; dir, Mercantile Nat Bank; Los Angeles Co Bar Asn; Presenter & lectr, MCLE, Rutter Group; Presenter & lectr, Calif Judges Asn, Presenter & lectr, CJER; Nat Judicial Col & Calif State Univ, instr; BAJI Comt, 1983-89. **Home Addr:** 5101 Bedford Ave, Los Angeles, CA 90056-1002, **Home Phone:** (310)641-6276.

## MORROW, HAROLD, JR.
Executive, football player. **Personal:** Born Feb 24, 1973, Maplesville, AL. **Educ:** Auburn Univ, BS, lib arts, bus mkt & interdisciplinary studies, 1995. **Career:** Football player (retired), exec; Minn Vikings, running back & fullback, 1996-2002; Baltimore Ravens, 2003-04; Ariz Cardinals, running back & fullback, 2005; Anheuser-Busch, nat acct mgr, 2007-09; Lee County Boys & Girls Club, prog co-dir, 2010-11; Auburn Univ, Tiger 4 Life Prog Dir & Founder, 2011; Auburn Football Letterman Club, bd dir, 2011-12; TILT Theory, promotions mgr & brand ambassador, 2012; Final Phase Mkt, pres, 2013-. **Business Addr:** President, Final Phase Marketing Inc, 6151 Palm Trace Landings Dr, Davie, FL 33314.

## MORROW, JESSE
Executive. **Career:** Leader Lincoln-Mercury-Merkur Inc, St Louis, Mo, chief exec officer, pres & owner, 1983-. **Home Addr:** 13345 Buckland Hall Rd, St. Louis, MO 63131-1214, **Home Phone:** (210)320-7576. **Business Addr:** Owner, Chief Executive Officer, Leader Lincoln-Mercury-Merkur Inc, 6160 S Lindbergh Blvd, St. Louis, MO 63123, **Business Phone:** (314)487-3900.

## MORROW, DR. JOHN HOWARD, JR.
Educator. **Personal:** Born May 27, 1944, Trenton, NJ; son of John H Sr (deceased) and Ann Rowena; married Diane Batts; children: Kieran & Evan. **Educ:** Swarthmore Col, BA, hist, 1966; Univ Pa, Philadelphia, PhD, hist, 1971. **Career:** Univ Tenn, Knoxville, from asst prof to prof & dept head, 1971-; Nat Air & Space Mus, Wash, DC, Charles A. Lindbergh vis prof hist, 1988-89; Univ Ga, Athens, GA, Franklin prof hist, 1988-, hist dpt chmn, 1991-93, assoc dean arts & sci, 1993-95; US Mil Acad, vis prof, 2005. **Orgs:** Am Hist Asn, 1971-; consult, Col Bd & Ed Testing Serv, 1980-84, 1990-; AHA Comn Comm, 1982-85, AHA Prog Comm 1984 Meeting, 1983-84; mem edit adv bds, Aerospace Historian, 1984-87, Mil Affairs 1987-90; Smith sonian Inst Pr, 1987-93; chmn, Hist Adv Comm Secy Air Force, 1988-92; chmn, Col Bd Nat Acad Asn, 1993-95, mem col bd, bd trustee, 1993-; Dept Army Hist Adv Comm, 1999-2001; Res Adv Comt Nat Mus Am Hist; Search Comt Dir NMAH; Dwight D. Eisenhower Mem Comns Legacy Comt; First Flight Centennial Fed Adv Bd; Presidential Counors, Nat World War II Mus; adv bd, Ctr Oral Hist US Mil Acad. **Special Achievements:** Books: "Building German Airpower, 1903-1914", 1976; German Airpower in World War I, 1982; The Great War in the Air, 1993; A Yankee Ace In The Raf: The World War I Letters Of Captain Bogart Rogers, 1996; The Great War: An Imperial History, 2005. **Home Addr:** 130 Pine Tops Dr, Athens, GA 30606. **Business Addr:** Franklin Professor of History, Head, University of Georgia, 220 LeConte Hall Baldwin St, Athens, GA 30602-1602, **Business Phone:** (706)542-2053.

## MORROW, LAVERNE
Business owner, executive. **Personal:** Born Mar 2, 1954, Kankakee, IL; daughter of George and Shirley Jackson Watson. **Educ:** Ill State Univ, BS, 1976; Wash Univ, St Louis, MA, 1978. **Career:** Urban League, specialist, 1978-79; Mid town Pre Apprenticeship Ctr, dir, 1979-82; Coro Found, trainer, 1983-85; Emprise Designs Inc, pres founder, 1985-. **Orgs:** First vpres, Coalition 100 Black Women Prog, 1981-84; Nat chap, White House Conf Small Bus Minority Caucus, 1986, 1995, rules comt, 1995; comm chmn, Jr League St Louis, 1986. **Honors/Awds:** Appointed to the US Senate, Small Bus Nat Adv Coun. **Special Achievements:** Featured and profiled as an Outstanding Business Woman in the September 1988, St Louis Business Journal. **Home Addr:** 3720 Marietta Dr, Florissant, MO 63033. **Business Addr:** President, Emprise Designs Inc, 3622 Cypress Creek Dr, Florissant, MO 63031-8928, **Business Phone:** (314)972-8521.

## MORROW, PHILLIP HENRY
Administrator, president (organization), chief executive officer. **Personal:** Born Sep 30, 1943, New Haven, CT; son of Benjamin and Viola English; married Ann Jordan; children: Nicole, Haleema & Germaine. **Educ:** Univ Conn, Storrs, BA, 1965, MA, 1967; Mass Inst Technol, min developers prog, 1992. **Career:** Poor Peoples Fed, Hartford, CT, exec dir, 1968-71; Greater Hartford Process, dir social dev, 1971-75; Upper Albany Community Orgn, Hartford, CT, exec dir, 1975-79; US Dept Housing & Urban Develop, Wash, DC, dir off pub pri, 1979-81; Harlem Urban Develop Corp, New York, NY, dir dev, 1982-95; S Bronx Overall Econ Develop Corp, exec dir, 1994, pres & chief exec officer, 1996-. **Orgs:** Pres, 260-262 Corp, 1985-; bd mem, N Gen Attend Proj, 1986-; vice chair, 125st LDC, 1986-; bd mem, Int Downtown Asn, 1987-94; treas, PACC Housing Asn, 1988-; vice chair, Pratt Area Community Coun; Housing & community develop; Greenhouse Roof Oper. **Home Addr:** 301 W 115th St Apt 4C, New York, NY 10026-1590, **Home Phone:** (212)795-9720. **Business Addr:** President, Chief Executive Officer, South Bronx Overall Economic Development Corp, 555 Bergen Ave, Bronx, NY 10455, **Business Phone:** (718)292-3113.

## MORROW, W. DERRICK
Executive. **Personal:** Born May 26, 1964, Philadelphia, PA; son of Tammy and Ward; children: 2. **Educ:** Howard Univ, bus, hotel mgt, 1987. **Career:** Wash Hilton & Towers, sales mgr, 1987-92; Hyatt Regency Atlanta, assoc dir sales, 1991-93; Hyatt Regency Bethesda, dir sales, 1994; Hyatt Regency Baltimore, dir sales & mkt, 1995-99; Hyatt Regency O'Hare, Rosemont, Ill, dir mkt, 1999-2002; Hyatt Regency Chicago, dir mkt, 2002-04; Hyatt Hotels Corp, regional vpres sales, 2004-07; Grand Hyatt Tampa Bay, resident mgr, 2007-08; Hyatt Regency Tampa, gen mgr, 2008-12; Hyatt Regency Crystal City, Reagan Nat Airport, gen mgr, 2012-, area vpres, 2015-. **Orgs:** Black Prof Men Inc; Prof Conv Managers Asn; bd dir, Hillsborough County Hotel & Motel Asn; bd mem, Tampa Bay Sports Comn; Hyatt Hotels & Resorts Diversity Coun; bd mem, Tampa Downtown Partnership; bd dir, Tampa Bay & Co. **Honors/Awds:** Nominee for Director of Sales of the Year, Hyatt Hotels, 1994 & 1995; Director of Sales of the Year, Hyatt Hotels, 1997. **Business Addr:** General Manager, Area Vice President, Hyatt Regency Crystal City, 2799 Jefferson Davis Hwy, Arlington, VA 22202, **Business Phone:** (703)418-1234.

## MORSE, BARBARA LYN
Television journalist. **Personal:** Born Nov 15, 1958, Zanesville, OH; daughter of Stanley LaVerne and Sylvia Barbara Yancich; children: Maryssa Ann, David Marko & Sydney Elaine. **Educ:** Ind Univ Indianapolis, Indianapolis, IN, BA, 1983. **Career:** Indy Today Newspaper, Indianapolis, Ind, columnist, 1984-86; Visions Mag, Indianapolis, Ind, staff writer, 1985-86; WNDE-AM, Indianapolis, Ind, news anchor & reporter, 1986; WAND-TV, Decatur, Ill, news reporter, 1987-88; WLNE-TV 6, Providence, RI, news reporter, 1988-89; WLVI-TV 56, Boston, Mass, news reporter, 1989-94; WLVI-TV, "Beyond Hate", "Easter Seals Telethon", co-host, 1993. WISH TV 8, Indianapolis, Ind, reporter, 1994-95; WJAR TV 10, Providence RI, anchor & health reporter, news reporter, 1995-. **Orgs:** Nat Asn Black Journalists, 1987-. **Honors/Awds:** Emmy Nominations, 1993, 1999, 2001; American Heart Asn's First Annual Media Awards. **Home Addr:** 89 Woodhaven Blvd, North Providence, RI 02911. **Business Addr:** News Reporter, WJAR-TV, 23 Kenney Dr, Cranston, RI 02920.

## MORSE, HON. JOHN E., JR.
Judge. **Educ:** Ga State Univ, BA; Mercer Law Sch, JD, 1982. **Career:** Chatham Co State Ct, state ct judge, 1992-; super ct judge, 1995. **Orgs:** Standing Comt mem, State Bar Ga, currently. **Business Addr:** Judge, Chatham County Court, 133 Montgomery St Rm 213, Savannah, GA 31401, **Business Phone:** (912)652-7236.

## MORSE, DR. LAURENCE C.
Founder (originator), manager, chief executive officer. **Educ:** Howard Univ, BA, econ, 1963; Princeton Univ, MA, econ, PhD, econ, 1978. **Career:** Harvard Univ, fel; UNC Ventures, mgr, 1983-87; Equico Capital Corp, vpres, 1988-91; TSG Ventures, founding prin, 1992; Coopers & Lybrand Int, sr venture capital adv, 1993; Fairview Capital Partners Inc, co-founder & managing partner, chief exec officer, 1994-; Webster Bank, dir, 2004-; Webster Bus Credit Corp, dir, currently. **Orgs:** Syndicated Commun Venture Partners; Opportunity Capital Partners; MedVenture Assocs; Ascend Venture Group; chmn & bd dir, Nat Asn Investment Co; Phi Beta Kappa; US Venture Partners; Battery Ventures; Sierra Ventures; Trinity Ventures; vpres, Equitable Life Assurance Socs Us; Nat Bd Eng Speaking Union Us; bd trustee, Princeton Univ; fel Harvard Univ; Princeton Univ Investment Co; bd dir, Webster Financial Corp, 2004-; trustee, Oakmark Int Fund, 2013-; bd trustee, Inst Int Educ, currently; bd trustee, Howard Univ, currently. **Business Addr:** Co-Founder, Managing Partner, Fairview Capital Partners Inc, 75 Isham Rd Suite 200, West Hartford, CT 06107, **Business Phone:** (860)674-8066.

## MORSE, DR. LAURENCE C.
Founder (originator), executive, association executive. **Educ:** Howard Univ, BA, econs; Princeton Univ, MA & PhD; Harvard Univ, postdoctoral fel. **Career:** UNC Ventures, 1983-88; Equico Capital Corp, vpres, 1988-92; TSG Ventures, founding prin, 1992-94; Fairview Capital Partners Inc, co-founder & managing partner, 1994-; Webster Bank, dir, 2004-. **Orgs:** Bd dir, Webster Financial Corp; bd dir, Inst Int Educ; bd mem, Princeton Univ Investment Co. **Honors/Awds:** "Fortune Small Business," Top Ten Minds in Small Business, January, 2003; "Black Enterprise," 75 Most Powerful Blacks on Wall Street, 2011. **Business Addr:** Co-founder, Managing Partner, Fairview Capital Partners Inc, 75 Isham Rd Suite 200, West Hartford, CT 06107, **Business Phone:** (860)674-8066.

## MORSE, MILDRED S.
Executive, founder (originator), executive director. **Personal:** Born Oct 20, 1942, Dermott, AR; daughter of John Sharpe and Helen Wilson Sharpe; married Oliver; children: Stacey & Kasey. **Educ:** Bowling Green State Univ, attended 1962; Univ Ark, BA, 1964; Howard Univ, JD, 1968. **Career:** Civil Rights, specialist, 1968-71; HEW, staff asst dir, 1971-73; HUD, dir 1973-77, 1979-80; Phase II White House Task Force Civil Rights Presidents Reorganization Proj, dep dir, 1977-79; Corp Pub Broadcasting, Wash, DC, asst pres, 1980-89; Morse Enterprises Inc, Silver Spring, MD, pres & chief exec officer, 1989-. **Orgs:** Nat Bar Asn; Nat Civil Rights Asn; steering comt, Dept Justice Title VI Proj; Blacks Pub Radio, 1980-90; Arcousa Sigma Phi Pi Frat, 1980-; Am Women Radio & TV, 1980-90; Capital City Links Inc, 1981-; Nat Black Media Coalition, 1982-; bd dir, Am Indians Media Asn, 1982-91; Delta Sigma Theta Sorority, 1983-; Ams Indian Opportunity, 1989-91; adv bd, Channel 32, 1990-95; Adv Comn Minority Stud Educ, Montg County Sch Bd, 1990-92, vice chair, 1991-92; life mem, Nat Asn Advan Colored People; Nat Smoking Cessation Campaign African Am Women; bd mem, founder & dir, Nat Tobacco Independence Campaign. **Home Addr:** 98 Delford Ave, Silver Spring, MD 20904. **Business Addr:** President, Chief Executive Officer, Morse Enterprises Inc, 510 Wolf Dr Fl 1, Silver Spring, MD 20904-3467, **Business Phone:** (301)879-7933.

## MORSELL, FREDERICK ALBERT (FRED MORSELL)
President (organization), educator, entertainer. **Personal:** Born Aug 3, 1940, New York, NY; son of John Albert and Marjorie Ellen Poole. **Educ:** Dickinson Col, BA, 1962; Wayne State Univ, MA, theatre arts, 1974. **Career:** Educator, actor; Terry Schreiber Studio, New York, actor, dir, teacher, 1970-; Fremarjo Enterprises Inc, pres, currently; Plays: Hill St. Blues; LA law; Scarecrow & Mrs.King; Presenting Mr. Frederick Douglass; General Hosp; Another World; One Life To Live TV Appearances: "We"; "The Women"; Films: Wilson's Reward, 1980; Q, 1982; Fatal Vision, 1984; Delirious, 1991. **Orgs:** Actor's Equity Asn; Screen Actor's Guild; Am Soc Composers, Auth & Publ; Am Fedn TV & Radio Artists; Dramatists Guild. **Home Addr:** PO Box 394, Emigrant, MT 59027, **Home Phone:** (406)333-4970. **Business Addr:** President, Fremarjo Enterprises Inc, PO Box 382, Emigrant, MT 59027, **Business Phone:** (406)333-4970.

## MORSTON, GARY SCOTT
Educator. **Personal:** Born Oct 20, 1960, Queens, NY; son of Thelima; married Margaret E; children: Jared & Jessica. **Educ:** City Univ NY, AAS, child care, 1983, BS, spec educ, 1985, MS, spec educ, 1990; Bank St Col, educ leadership, 1992. **Career:** United Cerebral Palsy, health aide, 1983-91; NY Bd Educ, Cent Pk E II, kindergarten teach-

er, 1985-. **Orgs:** Educ adv, Scholastic, 1992-; City Univ Track Team; Mustang Track Club; NY Tech Col Theatre Works Performing Arts Group. **Home Addr:** 468 W 141st St, New York, NY 10031, **Home Phone:** (212)281-7815. **Business Addr:** Kindergarten Teacher, Central Park East, 19 E 103rd St, New York, NY 10029, **Business Phone:** (212)860-5992.

### MORTEL, DR. RODRIGUE M.
Physician, educator, association executive. **Personal:** Born Dec 3, 1933, St. Marc; married Cecilia H; children: Ronald, Michelle, Denise & Renee. **Educ:** Lycee Stenio Vincent, BS, 1954; Med Sch Port Au Prince Haiti, MD, 1960. **Career:** Educator (retired), physician; Pvt Pract, physician; Pa State Univ, consult, chmn, dept Ob-gyn, Col Med, univ chair emer & assoc dean; Lancaster Gen Hosp, prof; Pa State Geisinger Cancer Ctr, dir; Pa State Cancer Ctr, assoc dean & dir, prof dept obstet & gynec, chmn dept; Mortel Family Charitable Found, founder, currently. **Orgs:** AMA; Pa Med Soc; James Ewing Soc; Soc Synecologic & Oncologist; Amer Col Ob-Gyn; Amer Coll Surgeons; Amer Radium Soc; NY Acad Sci OB Soc Phila; Missions Off Archdiocese Baltimore; health policy fel Robert Wood Johnson Found, 1988. **Honors/Awds:** USPHS Award, 1968; Horatio Alger Award, 1985; Pennsylvania State Univ Faculty Scholar Award for Outstanding Achievement in the Area of Life and Health Sciences, 1986. **Home Addr:** 1229 Sand Hill Rd, Hummelstown, PA 17036-9791, **Home Phone:** (717)533-4909. **Business Addr:** Founder, The Mortel Family Charitable Foundation, PO Box 405, Hershey, PA 17033-0405, **Business Phone:** (888)355-6065.

### MORTIMER, DELORES M.
College administrator. **Educ:** Howard Univ, Macalester Col, BA, 1971; Cornell Univ, MA, prof studies, 1973; Univ Mich, Int Educ, PhD, 1994. **Career:** Cornell Univ, grad asst, 1971-72; African Bibliog Ctr, res coordr & proj supvr, 1972-75, tech resource person & broadcaster, 1973-76; freelance consult, 1973-89; Phelps-Stokes Fund Wash, adminr, 1974-75; Smithsonian Inst, Res Inst Immigration & Ethnic Studies, social sci analyst, 1975-79; US Comn Civil Rights, social sci analyst, 1979-81; US Info Agency, sr int acad exchange specialist, 1981-89; Univ Mich Ctr Afro-Am & African Studies, asst dir, 1988-90; Univ Mich Rackham Sch Grad Studies, sr financial aid officer, 1990-94; US Dept State, Am Embassy Pretoria, foreign serv officer, currently. **Orgs:** Nat Asn Female Exec, 1981-; vpres, Thursday Luncheon Group, 1985-89; Int Studies Asn, 1987; Black Prof Int Affairs, 1988-. **Business Addr:** Foreign Service Officer, Am Embassy Pretoria (USIS), Washington, DC 20521-9300.

### MORTON, CAPT. BENJAMIN
Lawyer, executive. **Personal:** Born Jan 2, 1966, Detroit, MI; son of McClenton and Ella Lee; married Brigette Monique. **Educ:** Eastern Ariz Col, AA, 1986; Univ Cent Fla, BA, polit sci, 1989; Touro Law Ctr, JD, 1996. **Career:** US Atty's off, Dayton, Ohio, spec asst us atty, 1999-2001; USAF, asst staff judge advocate, 1999-2001, trial atty, Air Force litigation team, 2001-05; Verizon, contracts atty, 2005-08; Morton Law Group LLC, owner & managing atty, 2008-; Gordon & Rees LLP, partner; Legal Info-Graphics LLC, founder, pres & chief exec officer, currently. **Orgs:** Am Bar Asn; Nat Inst Trial Advocacy; Nat Bar Asn; Kappa Alpha Psi Fraternity Inc. **Honors/Awds:** Outstanding Young American, 1996; Air Force Commendation Medal. **Special Achievements:** Author: The Federal Rules of Evidence-Simplified, 2003; Criminal Procedure-Simplified, 2004. **Business Addr:** Owner, Managing Attorney, The Morton Law Group LLC, 744 Broad St Suite 1600, Newark, MN 07102, **Business Phone:** (973)947-7460.

### MORTON, JAMES A, II. See Obituaries Section.

### MORTON, JOE, JR. (JOSEPH THOMAS MORTON)
Actor. **Personal:** Born Oct 18, 1947, Bronx, NY; son of Joseph Thomas and Evelyn; married Nora Chavooshian; children: Hopi, Ara & Seta; children: Ara & Seta. **Educ:** Hofstra Univ, drama. **Career:** Stage: A Month of Sundays, off broad way, 1968; Hair, broad way; Salvation, 1969; Pretty belle, 1971; Charlie Was Here & Now He's Gone, 1971; Two if By Sea, 1972; Tricks, 1973; Raisin, 1973-75; Oh, Brother!, 1981; Honky Tonk Nights, 1986; Art, 1998-99. Films: And Justice for All, 1970; The Brother From Another Planet, 1984; Crossroads, 1985; Zelly & Me, 1988; There's City of Hope, 1991; Terminator 2, 1992; The Astronaut's Wife, 1999; Blues Brothers, 1997, 2000; What Lies Beneath, Bounce, 2000; Ali, 2001; Dragonfly, Crossing, 2002; Paycheck, 2003; Lenny the Wonder Dog, 2004; Stealth, 2005; The Night Listener, 2006; Badland, 2007; American Gangster, 2007; La Linea, 2009; The Mulberry Tree, 2010; Home, 2013. TV series: "Another World"; "MASH", 1976; Jack Reed: Death& Vengeance, 1996; "Y2K", 1999; "Law & Order", 1992-2005; "Touched by an Angel", 1996-2002; "Smallville", 2001-02; "All My Children", 2002; "Texas Jasper", 2003; "The Jury", 2004; "E-Ring", 2005-06; "CSI: NY", 2005; "Numb3rs", 2007; "Eureka", 2006-12; "The Good Wife", 2009-11; "White Collar", 2010; "Scandal", 2013-14; "Proof", 2014. **Honors/Awds:** Theatre World Award, Best Actor Musical Raisin, 1974; nomination, Antoinette Perry Award, Best Actor Musical Raisin, 1974; Caixa de Catalunya Award, Catalonian Int Film Festival, 1984; Image Award, Nat Asn Advan Colored People, 1990, 1993 & 2014; Primetime Emmy, 2014. **Business Addr:** Actor, Judy Schoen & Associates, 606 N Larchmont Suite 309, Los Angeles, CA 90004-1309, **Business Phone:** (213)962-1950.

### MORTON, JOHNNIE JAMES, JR.
Football player, football coach. **Personal:** Born Oct 7, 1971, Inglewood, CA. **Educ:** Univ Southern Calif, grad. **Career:** Football player (retired); Detroit Lions, wide receiver, punt returner, 1994-2001; Kans City Chiefs, wide receiver, 2002-04; San Francisco 49ers, wide receiver, tight end, 2005; Glenville State, asst coach, 2012-. **Orgs:** Screen Actors Guild; Am Fed Radio & TV Asn; DARE; Athletes & Entertainers Kids; Big Bros Am. **Honors/Awds:** All-American, 1993; Pop Warner Trophy (1993. **Special Achievements:** Appeared in numerous episodes of "The Young and the Restless", 1996; Films: Jerry Maguire, 1969; Dynamite!! USA, 2007. TV Series: "Moesha", 1999; "Sports Geniuses", 2000; "The Tonight Show with Jay Leno", 2002. **Business Addr:** Assistant Coach, Glenville State Col, 200 High St, Glenville, WV 26351, **Business Phone:** (304)462-7361.

### MORTON, KAREN VICTORIA (KAREN V MORTON-GROOMS)
Executive, lawyer, vice president (organization). **Personal:** Born Jun 16, 1956, Plainfield, IL; daughter of Edward N and Eva S; married Kenneth B Grooms; children: Kya Nicole & Keenen Edward. **Educ:** Tufts Univ, Medford, MA, BA, polit sci & govt, 1977; Northeastern Univ Law Sch, Boston, MA, JD, 1980. **Career:** City Boston, asst corp coun, 1980-81; Mass Comn against Discrimination, sr staff atty, 1981-83; US Equal Employ Opportunity Comn, spec asst atty adv, 1984-86; Delaney, Siegel, Zorn & Assocs Inc, sr staff coun & dir training, 1986-87; Dukakis, pres, admin coordr, 1987-88; John Hancock Mutual Life Ins Co, from asst coun to coun, 1988-97, sr coun, 1997, Employ & Labor Rels Law, second vpres & asst gen coun, 1998-2006, vpres & coun, 2001-06; Liberty Mutual Group, vpres & asst gen coun-employ, benefits & corp serv, 2006-, sr vpres & dep gen coun-corp litigation, 2014-. **Orgs:** Mass Black Women Atty, 1987-89; bd mem, Ecumenical Soc Action Coun, 1988-91; bd mem, Int Inst Boston, 1991-93; bd mem, Am Corp Coun Asn, Northeast Chap, 1993-97; bd dir, Generations Inc. **Honors/Awds:** Hundred of the Most Promising Black Women in Corporate America, Ebony Mag, 1991. **Home Addr:** 41 Janet Rd, Newton, MA 02459, **Home Phone:** (617)965-0201. **Business Addr:** Senior Vice President, Deputy General Counsel, Liberty Mutual, 175 Berkeley St, Boston, MA 02116, **Business Phone:** (617)574-5669.

### MORTON, LORRAINE H.
Government official, mayor. **Personal:** Born Winston-Salem, NC; daughter of William Patrick and Keziah; married James T; children: Elizabeth Morton Brown. **Educ:** Winston-Salem State Univ, BS, 1938; Northwestern Univ, MA, 1942. **Career:** Educator (retired), Mayor (retired); Foster Sch, Nichols Mid Sch, Chute Mid Sch, teacher, 1953-77; Dist 65 sch syst, educr, 1953-89; Haven Middle Sch, prin, 1977-89; Fifth Ward, alderman, 1982-91; US Conf Mayors, chair humanities comn; Northwestern Munic Conf, legis comm; Workforce Develop Coun Northern Cook Co, exec bd inventure; City Evanston, mayor, 1993, 1997, 2001, 2005-09; Tuskegee Inst, teacher. **Orgs:** Deacon, Second Baptist Church; adv comn, Kellogg Grad Sch Mgt; Nat Asn Univ Women; life mem, Nat Asn Advan Colored People; N Shore Ill Chap; Alpha Kappa Alpha Sorority; Delta Chi Omega Grad Chap; vpres, Evanston Hist Soc; bd mem, Sr Action Serv; bd mem, Foster Reading Ctr; bd mem, Family Coun Serv; bd mem, Leadership Evanston Steering Comn; Evanston Township High Sch Comn Serv Comm; deleg, White House Conf on Libr & Info Serv; life mem, Ill Cong; Evanston City Coun, Housing & Community Develop; Police Serv; Planning & Develop; Human Serv & Rules; Unified Budget Panel. **Home Addr:** 2102 Darrow Ave, Evanston, IL 60201-3019, **Home Phone:** (847)328-4222. **Business Addr:** IL.

### MORTON, MARILYN M.
Executive, manager. **Personal:** Born Jan 20, 1946, New York, NY; daughter of William Gaitha Pegg (deceased) and Wilma Hayes Pegg (deceased); children: Louis-Hale, Khaim & Micah. **Educ:** Howard Univ, Wash, DC, BA, 1967; Univ Calif Ext, Los Angeles, CA, 1977; Calif State Univ, Dominquez Hills, MBS, negotiation & conflict mgt, 1999; Orgn Leadership Acad, cert; Univ Calif, Los Angeles, Anderson Grad Sch Mgt, cert; Straus Inst Dispute Resolution. **Career:** Los Angeles 200 Bicentennial Comt, Los Angeles, Calif, dir, pub rels, 1979-81; Mixner, Scott & Assocs, Los Angeles, Calif, assoc, pub affairs, 1981-83; Times-Mirror Cable TV, Irvine, mgr pub affairs, 1983-84; Parsons Corp, Los Angeles, mgr community affairs, 1984-96, reg mgr, gov't rels, 1987-96; Jasmine Consult Llc; Customer Arbit Bd, arbitrator, 2002; Metro Transp Authority, mgr external rels, Pub Affairs, ADA compliance officer, currently; Los Angeles County C, dir mgt serv, currently. **Orgs:** Co-founder, Women Color Inc, 1985-98; pres, Environ Affairs Comn, app by Mayor Tom Bradley, 1987-93; bd dir, co-chair, founder, Ethnic Coalition, 1989-; bd dir, Southern Calif Econ Partnership, 1994-; Dispute Settlement Bd, 1997-2001; Pac Enterprises Community Adv Panel; dir mgt serv, First 5 LA; Adopt-A-Sch Bus Found. **Home Addr:** 740 S Burnside Ave Suite 303, Los Angeles, CA 90036, **Home Phone:** (323)936-1802. **Business Addr:** Manager, Public Affairs/ADA Compliance Officer, Metro Transportation Authority, 1 Gateway Plz, Los Angeles, CA 90012, **Business Phone:** (213)922-2000.

### MORTON, NORMAN
Computer scientist. **Personal:** Born Jul 27, 1938, Washington, DC; son of Matthew and Bertha; married Robbie Clark; children: Norman Jr & Mark. **Educ:** Grantham Col Eng, Aset, 1989; Univ Mar, BS, mathematics; George Mason Univ, MA, mathematics. **Career:** Self-employed, prof tutor, 1965-; USY, Fin & Acctg Off, comput programmer, 1966-68; Small BUS ADMIN, comput programmer, 1968-74; Minority Bus Develop Admin, comput systs analyst, 1974-75; Econ Develop Admin, comput systs analyst, 1975-88; Dept Com, Census Bur, comput programmer, systs analyst. **Orgs:** Mensa, 98th percentile, IQ, 1992-; Intertel, 99th percentile, IQ, 1993; Boy Scouts AME, den leader, 1977-81, 1984-88; Good Shepherd Church, homeless shelter vol helper, 1986-87; Intl Soc Philos Enquiry, 99.9th percentile IQ, 1994-; Prometheus Soc, 99.9th percentile IQ, 1994-. **Honors/Awds:** DC TCRs COL, BKX SCI Honor Fraternity, 1963; PRES of the Math Club, 1963; Small BUS ADMIN, PRES of the SBA Statistical Club, 1972. **Special Achievements:** Volunteer tutor: Census Bureau, 1992-93; Crossland High School, 1991; Inr: COBOL programming class, SBA, 1973; Copyrights: "CLOAK", cryptographic software, TX 1675827, 1985; "Large Scale Number Manipulations on the PC", TX 1705169, 1985; "Hide It Find It", TX 4-332-687; Author: "Why Does Light Disappear in a Closed Room after the Switch is Turned Off", Capital M, MENSA Publishing, 1993; Scored at 99th percentile, IQ test, INTERTEL, 1993; Scored at 98th percentile, IQ test, MENSA, 1993; IQ percentile of 99.997 ranks at 1 in 33, 000 of the general population. **Home Addr:** 1600 S Eads St Suite 302, Arlington, VA 22202, **Home Phone:** (703)920-2678.

### MORTON, PATSY JENNINGS
Advertising executive. **Personal:** Born Oct 2, 1951, Fauquier County, VA; daughter of Thomas Scott and Louise Dickson; married Allen James Jr; children: Valerie, Allen Christopher & Douglas. **Educ:** Jersey Acad, Jersey City, 1969; Oberlin Col, Oberlin, BA, 1973; Columbia Univ, New York, 1975. **Career:** Earl G Graves Publ, New York, NY, mkt mgr, 1973-75; The New York Times Co, New York, sales rep, 1975-81, assoc group mgr, 1981-83, group mgr, 1983-87, advert mgr, 1987-, classified advert dir, 1989-92, advert managing dir, 1992-96; Educ Allicances, dir, 1997-. **Orgs:** Bus Comm, Admis Comn, Oberlin Col, 1986; task force, Five Star Newspaper Network, 1988; bd dir, Ny Food Merchants, 1989; Asn Newspaper Classified Advert Mgrs; exec coun, NYU Metro Ctr, 1993-. **Honors/Awds:** Rookie of the Year, Jersey Acad, 1965; Black Achievers Award, YMCA, 1989; Publisher's Award, 1994. **Home Addr:** 692 Croton Lake Rd, Mt Kisco, NY 10549, **Home Phone:** (914)241-9488. **Business Addr:** Education Programs, The New York Times, 229 W 43rd St, New York, NY 10036, **Business Phone:** (212)556-8843.

### MORTON, WILLIAM STANLEY
Lawyer, legal consultant. **Personal:** Born Jul 18, 1947, White Plains, NY; son of Clara E and William; married Mary; children: William Stanley Jr & Sydney Elaine. **Educ:** Col Arts & Sci, BS, 1969; Ohio State Univ, Col Law, JD, 1974. **Career:** Procter & Gamble Co, sr coun, 1974-88, div coun, 1988-, assoc gen coun, currently. **Orgs:** Cincinnati Bar Asn; Am Bar Asn; Ohio Bar Asn, 1974-; Omega Psi Phi Fraternity; bd dir, Pro Kids, 1985-87; bd mem, Housing Opportunities Made Equal, 1990-94; vpres & bd mem, Cincinnati Opera, 1991-01, bd trustee, 2016; bd dir, Cincinnati Better Bus Bur, 2000-; bd dir, Nat Coun Better Bus Bur Exec Comn, 2000-. **Home Addr:** 8429 Preakness Lane, Cincinnati, OH 45249-1319, **Home Phone:** (513)469-7180. **Business Addr:** Associate General Counsel, Procter & Gamble Co, 7250 Poe Ave, Dayton, OH 45415, **Business Phone:** (937)898-7387.

### MORTON-GROOMS, KAREN V. See MORTON, KAREN VICTORIA.

### MOS DEF (DANTE TERRELL SMITH)
Rap musician, actor. **Personal:** Born Dec 11, 1973, Brooklyn, NY; son of Sheron and Abdul Rahman; married Maria Yepes; children: 6. **Career:** Albums: Black Star, 1998; Black on Both Sides, 1999; Jam on It, 2001; Urban Renewal Program, 2002; The New Danger, 2004; True Magic, 2006; Mos Definite, 2007; The Ecstatic, 2008; Films: Monster's Ball, 2001; Showtime, 2002; Brown Sugar, 2002; The Italian Job, 2003; The Sky Is Green, 2003; From the Outside Looking In, 2003; 16 Blocks, 2006; Talladega Nights: The Ballad of Ricky Bobby, 2006; Prince Among Slaves, 2007; Be Kind Rewind, 2008; Stringbean & Marcus, 2008; Toussaint, 2008; Next Day Air, 2009; Theater: Topdog & Underdog, Broadway prod, 2002; TV series: "Chappelle's Show", 2003-06; "The Boondocks", 2005, "House", 2009; "Locked In", 2009. **Business Addr:** Recording Artist, Rawkus Records, 676 Broadway Fl 4, New York, NY 10012, **Business Phone:** (212)358-7890.

### MOSBY, DR. CARLA MANE (CARLA MOSBY WARD)
Physician, immunologist. **Personal:** Born Apr 16, 1974, Heidelberg; daughter of Charles and Bennell; married Lance Ward; children: 2. **Educ:** Univ Md, BS, physiology, neurobiology, 1996, Sch Med, MD, 2000. **Career:** Beth Israel Deaconess Med Ctr, resident, 2000-03; Kaiser Permanente, physician, internal med, 2003-04; Allergy & Immunol, Univ Med & Dent, fel, NJ; Univ Community Hosp, Allergy & Immunol consult, currently; Hayward/Fremont Med Centers, Dept Internal Med, facil; St Josephs Childrens Hosp, physician; St Josephs Hosp, physician; Fla Hosp Carrollwood, physician. **Orgs:** Alpha Kappa Alpha Sorority; Nat Med Asn; Med Alumni Asn, 2000; Ama; Mass Med Soc. **Home Addr:** 100 Dudley St 2340, PO Box 99, Jersey City, NJ 07302, **Home Phone:** (201)209-0088. **Business Addr:** Consultant in Allergy & Immunology, University Community Hospital Medical Center, 3645 Madaca Lane, Tampa, FL 33618, **Business Phone:** (813)969-0116.

### MOSBY, CAROLYN ELIZABETH
Manager. **Personal:** Born Nov 27, 1967, Gary, IN; daughter of John O (deceased) and Carolyn (deceased). **Educ:** Ind State Univ, BS, radio, tv & film commun, 1990. **Career:** Ind State Dept Admin, minority bus develop div, commun mgr, 1990-94, mgr, 1994-95; Ind Black Expo, chair bd, 1992-94, pub rels mgr, 1997-98, regional community rels dir, 2000-01; Nicor Gas, regional community rels dir, 2000-01; Ameritech Advert Serv, mkt rels mgr, 1996-97; AT&T, mkt rels & develop mgr, 1996-97; USX Corp, mgr community & govt affairs, 1997-2000; govt affairs rep, 2000-02; US Filter Indianapolis Water LLC, dir commun & community affairs, 2002-03, vpres commun & community affairs, 2003-04; Veolia Water Indianapolis LLC, mkt commun & community affairs, vpres, 2002-05; consult, 2005-07; Dell, Consult, 2007-08; Kiwanis Int, chief mkt officer, 2008-10; Cole Brown, pres, 1997-2011; Mid-States Minority Supplier Develop Coun, pres & chief exec officer, 2011-. **Orgs:** Pres, Soc Govt Meeting Planners, 1994; Nat Asn Female Exec, 1994; mem exec comt, Circle City Classic, 1995-96; mem pub rel comt, NCAA Final Four, 1996-; adv bd, Salvation Army, 1997-; mem bd, Hoosier Boystown, 1997-; vpres, Gary Police Found, 1997-; bd mem, Indianapolis Prof Asn; bd mem, Ind State Univ Black Alumni Coun; bd mem, Cent Ind Womens Bus Coun; bd mem, Urban League Indianapolis; bd pres, Trusted Mentors; bd mem, Hisp Bus Coun. **Honors/Awds:** Vanguard Award, Nat Minority Supplier Develop Coun, 2014. **Home Addr:** 2606 W 63rd Ave Suite 2A, Merrillville, IN 46410, **Home Phone:** (219)985-2023. **Business Addr:** President, Chief Executive Officer, Mid-States Minority Supplier Development Council, 2126 N Meridian St, Indianapolis, IN 46202, **Business Phone:** (317)921-2675.

### MOSBY, DR. CAROLYN LEWIS
Educator. **Personal:** Born Mar 6, 1937, Lynchburg, VA; daughter of William and Nannie Jackson; married Alexander. **Educ:** Va Union Univ, Richmond, VA, BS, math, 1958; Morgan State Univ, Baltimore, MD, MA, math, 1970; Col William & Mary, Williamsburg, VA, EdD, higher educ, 1983. **Career:** Educator (retired); E High Sch, Buffalo, NY, teacher, math, 1959-61; Blackwell Jr High Sch, Richmond, Va, teacher, math, 1961-65; John Marshall High Sch, Richmond, Va, teacher & asst prin, 1965-74; Va Union Univ, Richmond, Va, dir learning skills & gen educ, 1974-76; John Tyler Community Col,

Chester, Va, dean, math, natural sci allied health, 1978-91; Richmond Pub Schs, staff dev & officer, part-time; Va State Univ, adj prof, math. **Orgs:** Charter mem, James River Chap, Links Inc, 1983-; Girl Friends Inc, Richmond, Va, 1984-; Delta Sigma ta Sorority, 1955-; nat pres, Nat Epicureans Inc, Richmond, Va, 1984-86; charter mem, Coalition 100 Black Women, Richmond, Va, 1984-; chair, Comn, pupil reassignment, Richmond Pub Schs, 1985; bd mem, State Health Regulatory bd, Commonwealth Va, 1978-82; bd mem, United Giver's Fund, 1970; bd dir, Girl Scout Commonwealth Coun Va Inc, 1995; chair, Strategic Planning; bd mem, Va League Planned Parent Hood, 1998; bd mem, J. Sargeant Reynolds Commun Col, 2005. **Home Addr:** 3524 Bathgate Rd, Richmond, VA 23234-3564, **Home Phone:** (804)271-0565.

### MOSBY, CHARLES
Hotel executive. **Career:** Marriott Hotels, corp exec. **Business Addr:** Corporate Executive, Marriott Hotels, 10400 Fernwood Rd, Bethesda, MD 20817-1102, **Business Phone:** (301)380-3000.

### MOSBY, MARILYN (MARILYN JAMES)
Lawyer. **Personal:** Born Jan 22, 1980, Boston, MA; daughter of Alan C James and Linda Thompson; married Nick J Mosby; children: Nylyn & Aniyah. **Educ:** Tuskegee Univ, BA, polit sci & govt, 2002; Boston Col Law Sch, JD, 2005. **Career:** Liberty Mutual Ins, paralegal coordr & legal dept intern, 2001-02; Us Atty's Off, Boston, MA, legal intern, 2003, Wash, D.C., legal intern, 2004; Boston Col Legal Assistance Bur, stud civil litigation atty, 2003; Suffolk County Dist Atty's Off, legal intern, 2004; Dorchester Dist Ct, stud criminal defense atty, 2004-05; Baltimore City State Atty's Off, law clerk, 2005-06, asst state's atty, 2006-11, Baltimore City State's Atty, 2015-; Liberty Mutual Ins, Baltimore, MD, field coun, 2011-14. **Orgs:** Empowering Minds Md's Youth, pres & bd advisor, 2010-; Psalms Motion, treas & bd advisor, 2011-; Monumental Bar Asn, Judicial Nomination Comt, 2012-; Md Atty Grievance Comn, Peer Rev Comt, 2012-; Reservoir Hill Improv Coun, bd mem & advisor, 2013-; mem, Alliance Black Women Attorneys, Md State Bar Asn. **Special Achievements:** The youngest chief prosecutor of any major city in the United States, 2015. **Business Addr:** Office of the State's Attorney for Baltimore City, 120 E Baltimore St 9th Fl, Baltimore, MD 21202.

### MOSEBY, LLOYD ANTHONY
Baseball player. **Personal:** Born Nov 5, 1959, Portland, AR; children: Lydell. **Career:** Baseball player (retired), coach; Med Hat Blue Jays, 1978; Dunedin Blue Jays, 1979; Syracuse Chiefs, 1980; Toronto Blue Jays, outfielder, 1980-89; Detroit Tigers, outfielder, 1990-91; Tokyo Giants, outfielder; Yomiuri Giants, 1992-93; Blue Jay, first base coach, 1998-99; Duane Ward Baseball Clin, fielding instr, currently. **Home Addr:** 9140 Los Lagos Cir S, Granite Bay, CA 95746-5842. **Business Addr:** Fielding Instructor, Duane Ward Baseball Clinic, PO Box 371085, Las Vegas, NV 89137.

### MOSELEY, FRANCES KENNEY
Association executive, chief executive officer. **Personal:** Born Mar 20, 1949, Cleveland, OH; married Monroe Avant; children: Gavin. **Educ:** Univ Denver, BA, psychol, 1971. **Career:** St Bank & Trust, security analyst, 1974-77; Bank Boston, trustofficer, 1977-79; WGBH-TV, dir promo, 1979-80; Boston Edison Co, sr pub info rep; John Hancock Financial Serv Inc, sr mgr retail mkt & consumer affairs, through 1993; Boys & Girls Clubs Boston, pres & chief exec officer, 1992-98; Boston Partners, owner, educ, pres & chief exec officer; One Family Inc, chief develop officer, currently; State St Global Advisors, prin; Pathfinder Int, vpres Resource Develop; Friday Forum, clerk; State St Corp, prin & managing dir; Empowered Philanthropy, managing dir. **Orgs:** Former officer, Boston Br Nat Asn Advan Colored People, 1976; Am Assoc Blacks Energy, 1980-88; chmn, bd Big Sister Assoc Greater Boston, 1984; pres, bd BigSisters Asn Greater Boston, 1982; bd mem, since, 1979; trustee, Huntington Theatre; New Eng Aquarium; dir, PNC Bank, New Eng, 1996; dir, Tufts Assoc Health Plans Inc, 1996; Beth Israel Deaconess Med Ctr; Wang Ctr Performing Arts; C's Hosp Bd Overseers; founding mem, Boston Chap Coalition 100 Black Women; chair Bell Atlanta Consumer Adv Panel; bd mem, Mass Sports Partnership; bd trustee, Pine Manor Col; trustee, Belmont Hill Sch; Friday Forum; Empowered Philanthropy; Port Financial Corp. **Honors/Awds:** The Urban League, 75th Anniversary President's Award; The College Club 1993 Career Award, Soc Serv; Honorary Doctorate of Public Service, Bridgewater State Col, 1998; Named 1 of Boston's Most Powerful 100 Peopleby Boston Magazine, 1997. **Home Addr:** 180 Pond St, Jamaica Plain, MA 02130. **Business Addr:** Chief Development Officer, One Family Inc, 186 S St 4th Fl, Boston, MA 02111, **Business Phone:** (617)423-0504.

### MOSELEY-DAVIS, BARBARA M.
Executive, manager. **Personal:** Born Feb 12, 1938, New York, NY. **Educ:** Morgan State Univ, BS, math, 1960; Johns Hopkins Univ, MS, comput sci, 1985. **Career:** M-Cubed Info Systs Inc, strategic planning mgr, 1992-2000; Delta Res & Educ Found, Sci & Everyday Experiences, nat proj mgr, 2004-07. **Orgs:** Regional corresp secy, Eastern Region, Delta Sigma Theta Sorority; First Combined Community Fed Credit Union; pres, Wash DC Alumnae Chap, Delta Sigma Theta Sorority; Alpha Gamma Chap; Morgan State Alumni Asn; Nat Prog Planning & Develop Comt, Delta Sigma Theta Sorority Inc, 2004-; victims advocate/ grant writer, Community Advocates Family & Youth, 2010-. **Honors/Awds:** Eliza P. Shippen Award, Delta Sigma Theta Sorority, 1993. **Home Addr:** 1506 Kingsgate St, Bowie, MD 20721-2033, **Home Phone:** (301)249-2778. **Business Addr:** Victims Advocate, Grant Writer, Community Advocates for Family & Youth, PO Box 4419, Capitol Heights, MD 20791, **Business Phone:** (301)390-4092.

### MOSELY, DR. KENNETH D.
Educator. **Personal:** Born Baltimore, MD. **Educ:** Morgan State Univ, BS, Phd, 1970; Kans State Univ, MS, PhD, 1973; Ind Univ, PhD, phys educ, 1976. **Career:** Educator (retired); SC State Univ, Dept Health & Phys Educ, prof & chmn, 1989-2004, Nat Youth Sports Prog, proj dir, 1988-2002. **Orgs:** Phi Delta Kappa; Am Alliance Health; Phys Educ; Recreation & Dance; Red Cross. **Home Addr:** 2480 Hickory Dr, Orangeburg, SC 29115-2611, **Home Phone:** (803)536-9689.

### MOSES, DR. CHARLES T.
Government official, executive director. **Personal:** Born Oct 2, 1952, New York, NY; son of Grace and Charles T. **Educ:** Howard Univ, BS, psychol, 1975; City Univ NY, Baruch Col, MBA, 1985; Case Western Res Univ, PhD, 2004. **Career:** Newsday, reporter, asst bus ed, strategic planning dir, 1978-88; Bristol Myers-Squibb, commun exec, 1988-89; State New York, Gov's Off, exec dir, 1989-2003; City New York, Comptroller's Off, dep press secy, 1991; Labat Africa, managing dir, 1997-99; Deloitte & Touche, consult, 1998-99; Earth Gazer Pty Ltd, founder & chief exec officer, 1999-2004; Univ Wi, Mona Sch Bus, vis lectr, 2007-09, fel, 2010-11; Clark Atlanta Univ, assoc prof, 2011-, interim dean, 2012-15; Black Col & Univ bus sch, chief acad officer; Bentley Univ, adj prof. **Orgs:** Nat Asn Black Journalists, 1976-88; bd mem, Spec Olympics Nj, 1982-84. **Home Addr:** 3 Pope Rd, Paterson, NJ 07514, **Home Phone:** (201)977-8636. **Business Addr:** Associate Professor, Clark Atlanta University, 223 James P Brawley Dr SW, Atlanta, GA 30314, **Business Phone:** (404)880-8000.

### MOSES, EDWIN CORLEY
Chairperson, athlete. **Personal:** Born Aug 31, 1955, Dayton, OH; son of Irving S and Gladys H; married Myrella Bordt; children: Edwin Julian. **Educ:** Morehouse Col, BS, physics, 1978; Pepperdine Univ, MBA, bus mgt, 1994. **Career:** Olympic hurdler (retired); Montreal, 1976; Los angeles, 1984; Seoul, 1988; World Championships, Helsinki, 1983; Rome, 1987; IAAF World cup, Dusseldorf, 1977; Montreal, 1979; Rome, 1981; Goodwill Games, Moscow, 1986; Platinum Group, partner; Robinson-Humphrey Co, financial consult; Film: Australian Geography, 1971; Our Land Australia, 1972; TV: The 6th Annual Black Achievement Awards, 1985. **Orgs:** Intl Olympic Comt, Athletes Comn, 1982-96, Med Comn, 1994-96; pres, Int Amateur Athletic Asn, 1982-; bd dir, USOC, Substance Abuse Comt, chmn, 1986-96, exec comn, 1994-96; Comn White Fels, 1992-; vice chair, US Olympic Found, 1996-; 100 Black Men Atlanta, 1997-; Laureus World Sports Acad, Laureus Sport Good Found, chmn, 2000-. **Home Addr:** 1184 Daventry Way NE, Atlanta, GA 30319-4547. **Business Addr:** Chairman, Laureus World Sports Academy, 460 Fulham Rd, LondonSW6 1BZ, **Business Phone:** (440)207514-2.

### MOSES, DR. HAROLD WEBSTER
Educator. **Personal:** Born Jun 6, 1949, Little Rock, AR; son of Tracie and Bishop; children: Harold & Corye. **Educ:** Univ Ark, Little Rock, AR, BA, 1973, MPA, 1984; Southern Ill Univ, Carbondale, IL, PhD, 1995. **Career:** Ark Int Lang Prog, Russellville, AR, Fr tutor, 1985-88; Ill Legis Res Unit, Springfield, Ill, res asst, 1985-86; Southern Ill Univ, Carbondale, Ill, grad admin asst to Ill Minority Fels, 1990, instr, 1991-92, Bethune Cookman Col, Daytona Beach FL, asst prof, Politl Sci; Cent Fla Legal Serv, Daytona Beach, Fla, acct asst, 1997-98; Little Rock Pub Sch Dist, Little Rock, Ark, teacher, 1998-. **Orgs:** Chair, Awards Comt, Southern Ill Univ Polit Sci Dept, 1985-91; Secy, Grad Assistant ship Prog, Nat Conf Black Polit Scientists, 1989-91; African Studies Asn, 1991; Grad Politl Sci Comt; Nat Conf Black Polit Scientist. **Home Addr:** 2900 Gribble St, North Little Rock, AR 72114, **Home Phone:** (501)945-4350.

### MOSES, DR. HENRY A.
Educator, school administrator. **Personal:** Born Sep 8, 1939, Gaston County, NC; son of Roy and Mary. **Educ:** Livingstone Col, BS, 1959; Purdue Univ, MS, biochem, 1962, PhD, biochem, 1964; Meharry Med Col, MD; Fisk Univ. **Career:** GW Hubbard Hosp, Meharry Med Col, asst prof, biochem, 1964-69, consult clin chem, 1968-74, assoc prof biochem nutrit, 1969-81, provost internal affairs, 1976-83, dir continuing educ 1981-, prof biochem, 1981-, asst vpres acad support, 1983-95, dir continuing educ area health educ ctrs, 1984-99, Meharry Med Col, prof emer biochem; TN State Univ, vis lectr biochem, 1966-70; Col Rels & Lifelong Learning, assoc vpres, 1995-99, consult, Alumni Rels, currently; Fisk Univ, distinguished prof, chem & biol, currently; Mehary Med Col, interim exec dir, currently. **Orgs:** Aaas; Am Chem Soc; Alpha Chi Sigma Frat Chemists; Am Asn Univ Profs; Beta Kappa Chi Sci Hon Soc, 1972-; chmn, Hons & Awards Comm; Sch Med, 1976-99; Alpha Omega Alpha Hon Med Soc, 1980; adv, Meharrian Stud Yr bk, 1980-99; chmn, Acad Policy Comm, Sch Med, 1985-97; McKendree United Methodist Church. **Home Addr:** 4220 Drakes Hill Dr, Nashville, TN 37218, **Home Phone:** (615)238-5344. **Business Addr:** Professor Emeritus, Executive Director MNAA, Meharry Medical College, Henry A Moses Bldg 1005 Dr DB Todd Jr Blvd, Nashville, TN 37208-3599, **Business Phone:** (615)327-6266.

### MOSES, MACDONALD
President (organization), school administrator, bishop. **Personal:** Born May 20, 1936, Bailey, NC; married Marie Biggs; children: Alvin, Jacqueline, Reginald & Kenneth. **Educ:** Westchester Community Col; Alexander Hamilton Brooklyn Tech; IBM Educ Ctr. **Career:** Gen Assembly, bishop; Church Christ, Disciples Christ, gen bishop, pres; Mt Hebron Church Christ, pastor. **Orgs:** Mgr, MI Botway Media Assocs; Am Mgt Asn. **Home Addr:** 14 Granada Cres Apt 13, White Plains, NY 10603-1230, **Home Phone:** (914)667-8234. **Business Addr:** Bishop, Disciples of Christ, 330 Warwick Ave, Mount Vernon, NY 10553.

### MOSES, MILTON E.
Chief executive officer. **Personal:** Born Aug 5, 1939, Chicago, IL; son of Jeffery and Mary; married Shirley C; children: Timothy E, Melody L & Milton E Jr. **Educ:** DePaul Univ, attended 1965. **Career:** Supreme Life Ins Co Am, agt, 1963; Robbins Ins Agency Inc, underwriter, 1965; Community Ins Agency Inc, pres, 1965-, chief exec officer, currently; Prof Independent Ins Agts Ill, regional dir, 2002. **Orgs:** Pres, Men Provident Hosp, 1971; bd mem, Ind Ins Agts Am, 1980; Chicago Bd Underwriters, 1980; Ins Inst Am, 1980; chmn bd, Human Resources Develop Inst, 1980; pres, We Can Found Inc, 1980; chmn, Minority Agents Comt; bd mem, Bernie Mac Found; bd mem, Prof Independent Ins Agents Ill. **Home Addr:** 1812 S Fed St Apt 9, Chicago, IL 60616-1650, **Home Phone:** (773)994-2856. **Business Addr:** President, Chief Executive Officer, Community Insurance Center Inc, 526 E 87th St, Chicago, IL 60619, **Business Phone:** (773)651-6200.

### MOSES, YOLANDA T.
School administrator, president (organization), anthropologist. **Personal:** Born Sep 27, 1946, Los Angeles, CA; married James F Bawek; children: Shana & Antonia. **Educ:** Perris High Sch, Valley Col, attended 1966; San Bernardino Valley Col, BA, 1968; Calif State Univ, San Bernardino, attended; Univ Calif, Riverside, MA, 1974, PhD, anthropol, 1976; Bloomfield Col NJ, PhD, 1998. **Career:** Calif State Poly tech Univ, fac, 1985-88, Ethnic & Women's Studies Dept, chair, Sch Lib Arts, dean; Calif State Univ, Dominguez Hills, anthropol prof & vpres acad affairs, 1988-93; City Univ NY, City Col, pres, 1993-99, prof anthrop, 1993-2000; Am Coun Educ, sr scholar; Am Asn Higher Educ, pres, 2000-03; anthropologist; Ctr Adv Studies, Behav Sci, Andrew Mellon postdoctoral fel; calif univ, prof anthrop, vice provost conflict resolution & spec asst to chancellor excellence, currently; Salzburg Sems ISP Prog, fac mem, currently; Univ Calif Ctr New Racial Studies, co-founder, currently; Books: How Real is Race: A Sourcebook on Race, Culture and Biology, 2007; Race: are we so different?, 2012. **Orgs:** Free Angela Davis Comt, 1970; pres, Am Anthro pol Asn, 1995-97; Women's Forum; Ford Found Bd trustee, 1996-2008; bd chair, Am Cols & Univs, 2000; Nat Coun Res Women; Campus Women Lead; Women Color Res Collective; chair, Nat Adv Bd; fel AAAS, 2009; consult, Am Coun, currently. **Home Addr:** 75 W End Ave C17I, New York, NY 10023. **Business Addr:** Professor of Anthropology, Associate Vice Chancellor for Diversity, Excellence and Equity, University of California Riverside, 365 Surge Bldg, Riverside, CA 92521, **Business Phone:** (951)827-6224.

### MOSLEY, BENITA FITZGERALD (BENITA FITZGERALD-BROWN)
Athletic director, president (organization). **Personal:** Born Jul 6, 1961, Warrenton, VA; daughter of Roger and Fannie; married Ron; children: Isaiah & Maya. **Educ:** Univ Tenn, Knoxville, TN, BS, indust engineering, 1984. **Career:** Athlete (retired); PRO, athlete, 1980-88; med spokesperson, 1988; Tracor inc & MHP Fu-Techinc, indust systs & software engr, 1991-95; Spec Olympics Int Inc, reg dir, 1991-92, sports mktg mgr, 1992-93; Atlanta Comt Olympic Games, prog dir mkt div, 1993-95; Atlanta Centennial Olympic Properties, prog dir, 1993-95; ARCO Olympic training ctr, San Diego, dir, 1995-97, dir pub rels prog, 2000-01; US Olympic Comt, Olympic Training Centers, dir, 1997-2000, chief orgn excellence, 2013-; Women Cable Telecommunications, pres & chief exec officer, 2001-09; USA Track & Field, chief sport performance, 2009-13. **Orgs:** Pres & bd trustee, Womens Sports Fed; dir, US Olympics Comt, 1995-2001; chair, diversity comt, 2000-01; athletes adv coun; bd mem, USA track & field; Delta Sigma Theta Sorority Inc; women sports & events; trustee & pres, bd trustee, Womens Sports found, currently. **Honors/Awds:** Gold Medal, Pan Am Games, 1983; Olympic Gold Medalist, 100 Meter Hurdles, 1984; Va Sports Hall Fame, 1988; Hall of Fame, Univ Tenn, 1994; Distinguished Service Award, US Sports Acad, 1996; Hall of Fame, VIR Sports, 1998; Hall of Fame, Penn Relays; Hall of Fame, UT Lady Vols, 2001; Cable TV Executive of the Year, Television Week Mag, 2004; Hall of Fame, Va Sports; Hall of Fame, Va High Sch. **Special Achievements:** Named "Hurdler of the Decade" for the 1980s by Track and Field News, she was honored with a street named Benita Fitzgerald Drive in her hometown of Dale City, VA, 1987; First African American woman to win a gold medal in the 100-meter hurdles. **Business Addr:** Chief of Organizational Excellence, United States Olympic Committee, 1 Olympic Plz, Colorado Springs, CO 80909, **Business Phone:** (719)632-5551.

### MOSLEY, BRUCE
Executive. **Career:** Unity Church, chief financial officer. **Business Addr:** AZ.

### MOSLEY, CAROLYN W.
Educator. **Personal:** Born Nov 2, 1952, New Orleans, LA; daughter of Johnny Washington Sr and Lillie Lee Washington; married Shantell Nicole; children: Shantell Nicole. **Educ:** La State Univ, BSN, 1974, MN, 1980; Tex Woman's Univ, Houston, PhD, nursing, 1994. **Career:** Charity Hosp New Orleans, staff nurse, 1974-75 & 1987-91; Vet ADM New Orleans, head nurse, 1975-81; La State Univ, Med Ctr, Sch Nursing, asst prof, 1981-87, bd regents fel, 1987-90 & 1989, assoc prof, prof, assoc dean acad admin; Tex Woman's Univ, Mary Gibbs fel, 1988; J Nursing Educ; Univ Ark, Ft Smith, prof & dean, currently; Ark Minority Health Comn, comnr. **Orgs:** Chi Eta Phi Sorority Blacks, 1976-; pres, Sigma Theta Tau, Epsilon NU, 1982-; Am Nurses Asn, 1990-; New Orleans Dist Nurses Asn, 1990-; bd gov mem, Nat League Nursing, 1990-; pres, La League Nurses, 1990-; Asn Black Nursing Fac, 1990-; vol, Cope-line, 1992-; ANA Coun Nursing, Res Exec Comt; fel Am Acad Nursing; Int Coun Nursing; founder, Citizens Ensuring Access Healthcare; Nat Inst Health; Nat Kidney Dis Educ Prog, consult, Med Team Home Health Agency; ed bd mem, Nursing Leadership Network Nursing & Health Perspective; ed bd mem, J Nursing Educ; fel Am Acad Nursing; pres, Chi Eta Phi Sorority Inc; fel Acad Nursing Educ. **Home Addr:** 1812 S 70th St, Fort Smith, AR 72903. **Business Addr:** Professor, Dean, University of Arkansas, 113 Pendergraft Health Sci Ctr 5210 Grand Ave, Fort Smith, AR 72901-3649, **Business Phone:** (479)788-7840.

### MOSLEY, CHRISTOPHER D.
Financial manager, association executive. **Personal:** Born Jul 12, 1960, Atlanta, GA; son of Lamar T and Annie B. **Educ:** W Geo Col, BS, 1983. **Career:** Nations Banc Securities Inc, investment specialist, 1986, margin specialist, 1986-89, retirement plan dir, 1989-. **Orgs:** Toastmasters Int; bd mem & treas, Rehab Exposure; vol, Income Tax Assistance; pres, Mays Manor Neighborhood Asn, currently. **Honors/Awds:** Outstanding Young Men of America, US Jaycees, 1983; External Client Services Award, Nations Banc Securities Inc, 1992; Americas Best & Brightest Professional Men, Dollars & Sense Mag, 1992. **Home Addr:** 3796 Benjamin Ct, Atlanta, GA 30331. **Business Addr:** President, Mays Manor Neighborhood Association, 3796 Benjamin Ct SW, Atlanta, GA 30331, **Business Phone:** (404)505-8687.

**MOSLEY, EDNA WILSON.** **See Obituaries Section.**

**MOSLEY, ELWOOD A.**
Government official. **Personal:** Born May 12, 1943, Philadelphia, PA; son of John and Ethel Glenn; married Eileen Carson; children: Danielle. **Educ:** St Joseph's Univ, Philadelphia Pa, bus admin, 1972; Harvard Univ, Cambridge, MA, 1989. **Career:** Chase Manhattan Bank, New York NY, asst treas, 1972-76; CIGNA Ins, Philadelphia Pa, vpres, 1976-82; USF & G Ins, Baltimore Md, vpres, 1982-85; Huggins Financial, Philadelphia Pa, vpres, 1985-87; US Postal Serv, Wash, DC, n, trasst postmaster geaining & devel, 1987, S Jersey Dist, dist mgr; MBNA Am Bank Nat Assn, exec vpres, currently. **Home Addr:** 1684 Kingsbridge Ct, Annapolis, MD 21401-6408, **Home Phone:** (410)849-2261. **Business Addr:** Executive Vice President, MBNA America Bank National Association, 1100 King St, Wilmington, DE 19884.

**MOSLEY, JAMES EARL, SR.**
Law enforcement officer. **Personal:** Born Jan 19, 1939, Hackensack, NJ; son of Charles E and Hattie Mae; married JoAnn; children: James Jr (deceased), Paulette & Beverly Allen. **Educ:** Bergen Community Col, AAS, 1975. **Career:** Law enforcement officer (retired), patrolman, sergeant, lieutenant; NJ Police Dept, City Englewood, from dep police chief to chief force, 2003. **Orgs:** MT Zion Baptist Church, 1953-; dean instrn, Shiloh Masonic Lodge No 53-F & AM, 1983-; Nat Orgn Black Law Enforcement Execs, 1990-; NJ State Police Chief's Asn, 1994-; Holy Royal Arch Masons, Joshua Chap No 15, 1994-. **Home Addr:** 71 Fairfield St, Englewood, NJ 07631-1504.

**MOSLEY, MARIE OLEATHA PITTS**
Educator, nurse. **Personal:** Born Jul 14, 1941, Miami, FL; daughter of Jimmie Pitts and Bertha Lee Pitts; children: DaShawn Lynette Young. **Educ:** Hunter Col Bellevue Sch Nursing, BSN, 1976, MSN, 1983; Columbia Univ Teachers Col, EdM, 1986, EdD, 1992. **Career:** Educator (retired), nurse, executive; Jackson Memorial Hosp; Boone Munic Hosp Ctr, head nurse, 1971-80; Staff Builders, staff relief, 1980-82; Hunter Col Bellevue Sch Nursing, asst prof, 1983, assoc prof; La Guardia Community Col, asst prof, 1985-86; AUSR, Army Nurse Corp, asst med officer, 1989-. **Orgs:** Rep, Nurses Polit Action; chairperson, nominating comt, Sigma Theta Tau, Alpha Phi Chap, 1984-; prog comnr, Asn Black Nursing Fac Higher Educ, 1987-; New York Nurses Asn, educ comt, 1988-; Civil Affairs Officers Asn, New York/NJS Chap, 1989-; Nat Black Nurses Asn, 1991-; Am Asn Hist Nursing, 1992-; educ comt, NYSNA Dist 13. **Home Addr:** 2541 7th Ave Suite 17B, New York, NY 10039, **Home Phone:** (212)926-1647.

**MOSLEY, MAURICE B.**
Lawyer, judge, executive. **Personal:** Born Jun 4, 1946, Waterbury, CT. **Educ:** SC St Col, BS, 1968; Cent Conn St Col, MS, 1972; Univ Conn, Sch Law, JD, 1975. **Career:** Teacher, 1968-72; Urban Leag, legis consult, 1974; Conn St Treas, exec asst, 1975-77; Conn, legis, 1976-; State Conn, Rep, Atty; Mosley & Sinclair LLP, owner & managing partner; Super Ct, judge, 2013-. **Orgs:** Adv bd, Colonial Bank & Trust Co; chmn, Legis Black Caucus; bd trustee, Waterbury Hosp; exec bd, Nat Asn Advan Colored People, 1974-77; pres & chief exec officer, Granville Acad Waterbury Inc. **Honors/Awds:** Business Award, SC St Dist, 1968; "Citizen of the Law" Award, Conn Bar Asn ann awards celebration, 2016. **Home Addr:** 66 Redcoat Rd, Waterbury, CT 06704, **Home Phone:** (203)574-8044. **Business Addr:** Judge, Connecticut Superior Court, 400 Grand St, Waterbury, CT 06702, **Business Phone:** (203)236-8100.

**MOSLEY, ROOSEVELT CHARLES, JR.**
Insurance executive. **Personal:** Born Jul 29, 1972, Saginaw, MI; son of Roosevelt and Evelyn; married Yashica; children: Tanisha & Bria. **Educ:** Univ Mich, Ann Arbor, BS, actuarial sci, 1993, BS, statist, 1993. **Career:** State Farm, sr asst actuary, actuarial analyst, 1994-98; Vesta Ins, actuarial mgr, 1998-99; Miller, Herbers, Lehmann & Assocs Inc, 1999-2002; State Farm Mutual Automobile Ins Co, pricing actuary; Vesta Ins Group, pricing actuar, actuarial mgr, 2008-09; Pinnacle Actuarial Resources Inc, sr consult, 2003-, prin, 1999-. **Orgs:** Kappa Alpha Psi Fraternity Inc, 1991-; Am Acad Actuaries, 1996-; fel & assoc mem, Casualty Actuarial Soc, Prog Planning Comt, Strategic Planning Comt, 1996-, Mkt & Commun, vpres, 2013-; Midwestern Actuarial Forum, 1996-; Joint CAS/SOA Comt Minority Recruiting, 1999-2003; CAS Comt Profism Educ, 1999-2005; vpres, InterNat Asn Black Actuaries Found, 2003-04, bd dir, 2004-; CAS Exam Comt, 2003-05; CAS Ratemaking Sem Comt, 2004-05; CAS Bd dir, 2005-; CAS Long Range Planning Comt, 2005-; bd dir, AAA Governance Task Forces. bd dir, Int Asn Black Actuaries; Kappa Alpha Psi. **Special Achievements:** Estimating Claim Settlement Values Using GLM, 2004 CAS Discussion Paper Program? Applying and Evaluating Generalized Linear Models; Detecting a Pattern, Best's Review, May, 2005, pp. 68-70. **Home Addr:** 4114 Colony Pk Dr, Birmingham, AL 35243. **Business Addr:** Principal, Consultant, Pinnacle Actuarial Resources Inc, 2817 Reed Rd Suite 2, Bloomington, IL 61704, **Business Phone:** (309)807-2330.

**MOSLEY, SHANE DANIEL DONTE**
Boxer. **Personal:** Born Sep 7, 1971, Lynwood, CA; son of Jack and Clemmie; married Jin; children: Najee Jamarr, Taiseki Justin, Mee-Yon Jinae, Shane Jr & Norman. **Career:** Boxer (retired), 2005; Sugar Shane Inc, owner, currently. **Honors/Awds:** US Championship winner, 1989; United States Amateur Champion, Lightweight, 1989; Jr Worlds champion Silver Medalist, 1989; United States Amateur Champion, Lightweight, 1990; Goodwill Games Bronze Medalist, 1990; US Amateur Champion, 1992; US Olympic Team, 1992; Int Boxing Fedn Champion, 1997; Fighter of the Year, Boxing Writers Asn, 1998; World Boxing Coun Champion, 2000; Champion, World Boxing Asn; Champion, World Boxing Coun, 2003; Junior Middleweight Champion, The Ring Mag, 2003-04; Welterweight Champion, World Boxing Coun, 2007; Welterweight Super Champion, World Boxing Coun, 2009-10. **Special Achievements:** Number five pound-for-pound boxer in the world, Ring Mag. **Home Addr:** 1118 Loma-Vista St, Pomona, CA 91768, **Home Phone:** (909)865-6979. **Business Addr:** Owner, Sugar Shane Inc, PO Box 8318, La Verne, CA 91750.

**MOSLEY, TIMOTHY ZACHERY. See TIMBALAND.**

**MOSLEY, VALERIE**
Vice president (organization). **Educ:** Duke Univ, BA, Hist; Univ Pa, Wharton Sch Bus, MBA. **Career:** Chase Manhattan Bank, com lending officer, 1982-84; Kidder Peabody, Instnl Corp Bond Sales, 1986-90; PG Corbin Asset Mgt, chief investment officer, 1990-92; Chase Manhattan Bank; Kidder Peabody; PG Corbin Asset Mgt; Wellington Mgt Co LLP, sr vpres, partner, investment strategist, fixed income portfolio mgr, 1992-2012; Valmo Ventures, chairwoman & chief exec officer, currently. **Orgs:** Corp Strategies Inc; bd mem, Nat Asn Securities Professionals; Core Bond Strategy Group; Duke Univ's Trinity Col Arts & Sci, Bd Advisors & Capital Campaign Adv Bd; Mus Sci Boston; NASP Boston Bd. **Honors/Awds:** "Black Enterprise", Top 75 Blacks on Wall Street, 2006; "Black Enterprise", 50 Most Powerful Women in Business, 2006; "Black Enterprise", 75 Most Powerful Women in Business, 2010. **Business Addr:** Chairwoman, Chief Executive Officer, Valmo Ventures Inc, 130 Summer St, Weston, MA 02493.

**MOSLEY, WALTER**
Writer, educator. **Personal:** Born Jan 12, 1952, Los Angeles, CA; son of LeRoy and Ella; married Joy Kellman. **Educ:** Goddard Col; Johnson State Col, polit theory; City Col NY, grad writing prog. **Career:** Publ: New Yorker; GQ; Esquire; USA Weekend; Los Angeles Times Mag; Savoy; Black Betty; A Little Yellow Dog Cinnamon Kiss; NY Times bestsellers; Bks: Devil a Blue Dress, 1990; A Red Death, 1991; White Butterfly, 1992; Black Betty, 1994; Norton, 1994; RL's Dream, 1995; A Little Yellow Dog, 1996; Always Out gunned, Gone Fishin', 1997; Blue Light, 1999; Walkin' Dog, 1999; RL's Dream; A Yellow Dog; Always Out numbered; Workin' Chain Gang: Shaking off Dead Hand Hist, 2000; Fearless Jones; What next, 2003; Man My Basement, 2004; Little Scarlet, 2004; Wave, 2006; Fortunate Son, 2006; Blonde Faith, 2007; The Tempest Tales, 2008; The Last Days of Ptolemy Grey, 2010; Parishioner, 2012; Little Green, 2013; Debbie Doesn't Do It Anymore, 2014; Inside a Silver Box, 2015; Rose Gold, 2015; Black Genius, ed & contribr; NY Univ, prof Eng, currently; auth, currently. **Orgs:** Bd dir, Nat Book Awards; bd, Full Frame Doc Film Festival; Poetry Soc Am; Trans Africa; pres, Mystery Writers Am. **Business Addr:** Author, Time Warner Book Group, 1271 Avenue of the Americas 9th Fl, New York, NY 10020, **Business Phone:** (212)522-7200.

**MOSS, ALFRED A., JR.**
Educator, clergy. **Personal:** Born Mar 2, 1943, Chicago, IL; son of Alfred Alfonso Sr and Ruth Watson; married Alice E Foster; children: Daniel Clement. **Educ:** Lake Forest Col, Lake Forest, IL, BA, hon, 1965; Episcopal Divinity Sch, Cambridge, MA, MA, divinity, 1968; Univ Chicago, Chicago, IL, MA, 1972, PhD, hist, 1977. **Career:** Episcopal Church Holy Spirit, Lake Forest, Ill, asst minister urban ministry, 1968-70; Univ Chicago, Episcopal Chaplaincy, Chicago, Ill, assoc chaplain, 1970-75, assoc prof, 1977; Univ Md, Dept Hist, Col Park, Md, lectr, 1975-77, asst prof hist, 1977-83, assoc prof hist, 1983-, assoc prof emer, currently. Books: The American Negro Academy: Voice of the Talented Tenth, auth; Looking At History, A Review of Major United States History Textbooks, co-auth; The Facts of Reconstruction: Essays in Honor of John Hope Franklin, co-ed; Dangerous Donations: Northern Foundations and Southern Black Schools, 1902-1930, co-auth, 1999. **Orgs:** Hon mem, Phi Beta Kappa, 1999; mem ed bd, Wash Hist & Studies Anglican & Episcopal Hist; trustee & first vpres, Hist Soc Episcopal Church; asst Minister & dir, Adult Educ Prog Urban Life Cult Ethnic & Racial Diversity Church Holy Spirit Lake Forest Ill, 1968-70; assoc chaplain & co-dir, Inst Inter-Group Commun Episcopal Chaplaincy Univ Chicago, 1970-75; co-chair bd trustee, African Am Hist Collection Episcopal Church; mem comt scholars, Smithsonians Nat Mus African Am Hist Cult. **Home Addr:** 1500 N Lancaster St, Arlington, VA 22205, **Home Phone:** (703)237-8454. **Business Addr:** Associate Professor, University Maryland College Park, 2101H Francis Scott Key Hall, College Park, MD 20742-7315, **Business Phone:** (301)405-4317.

**MOSS, ANNI R.**
Actor, writer, fashion model. **Personal:** Born AL; daughter of Samuel D and Rebecca C. **Educ:** WVa State Col, BS, educ, math, fr, 1966; Boston Univ, Theatre Inst, 1988; State Univ NY, 1984, 1991. **Career:** NASA Lewis Res, math asst, 1965; IBM CRP, syst engr, 1966-74, instr, 1974-75, IBM Ger, consult & writer, 1976, prod planner, 1976-81, syst req specialist, 1981-82; IBM Worldwide, auditor, 1983-84, systeng mgr, 1984-89, hq mkt planner, admnr, 1989-92; SabbyLewis Band, Charlie Bateman Band, jazz singer, 1991-92, concert producer; ARM Int, pres, 1992-; actress, Films: Bed of Roses, The Last Good Time; Movin' Up, Boston Cable; Mountain Don't Move for Me; Television Series: Law & Order; The CosbyMysteries; NY Undercover; Nat & Reg TV commercials; Press Coun PhysFitness PSA, corporate videos; Community Scene, WICZ-TV; Black HistVignettes, WBNG-TV; Black Women's Spec, WSKG-TV; Host producer: dreamUpwith Anni, cable TV show; radio show dream Sounds, WRTN/WVOX; GospelRenaissance Music, WENE/WMRV; Theatrical appearances: Joe Turner'sCome & Gone, Huntington Theatre, Boston; Antigone, Boston Univ; Over theDamn, Playwright's Platform; Concert soloist of gospel, jazz, & pop. **Orgs:** AFTRA, 1988-; Screen Actors Guild, 1992-. **Honors/Awds:** Black Achievers Award, 1985; IBM Hundred Percent Club & Golden Circle, 1985-88. **Special Achievements:** Unex corporate video, spokesperson, 1992; Nat Fire Protection Asn Int MagPubl, first female & first AFA to appear on the cover, 1992; IBM's System, 390: originator, planner, producer, & executor of worldwide photography & videos for the system, 1990; Author of Marketing publications for the system, 1990-92; Published writer: Women's News, Mentor Magazine, numerous others. **Business Addr:** President, ARM International, PO Box 1272, White Plains, NY 10602, **Business Phone:** (212)724-2800.

**MOSS, DELRISH**
Police detective, police officer, police chief. **Personal:** Born Jan 1, 1965?, Miami, FL. **Career:** Miami Police Dept, pub serv aide, 1984-87, patrol officer, 1987-89, homicide investr, 1989-96, pub info officer, 1996-2008, sr exec asst to police chief, 2008-11, comdr community rels sect & pub info officer, 2011-16; Ferguson Police Dept, Ferguson, MO, 2016-. **Orgs:** Urban League Greater Miami bd dirs, Safe Haven New Bornsboard dirs, Do Right Thing Prog bd dirs, Miami Police Athletic League (pres) & NAACP. **Special Achievements:** First black police chief of Ferguson, MO; represented Rotary International in Group Study Exchange in the Philippines, 2009. **Business Addr:** Ferguson Police Department, 222 S Florissant Rd, Ferguson, MO 63135, **Business Phone:** (314)522-3100.

**MOSS, ERIC**
Football player. **Personal:** Born Sep 25, 1974, Belle, WV. **Educ:** Ohio State Univ, grad. **Career:** Football player (retired); Fork Union Mil Acad, tight end; Minn Vikings, offensive tackle, 1997-98; Columbia Lions, quater back, 1999; Scottish Claymores, guard, 1999; Jacksonville Jaguars, 2000.

**MOSS, ESTELLA MAE**
Government official, commissioner, executive. **Personal:** Born Sep 15, 1928, Providence, KY; daughter of Eugene Jones and Odessa; married Charles E Moss Sr; children: Phyllis Johnson, Ardell, Sheila Spencer, Deborah L Ray, Charles E Jr & Angie V. **Educ:** Ind State Univ, Sch Pub & Environ Affairs, attended 1975. **Career:** Government official (retired); Super Ct, clerk probate; Pigeon Twp Assessor; chief dep, 1974-76; Vanderburgh Co, recorder, comnr human rels omn, 1976-84; City Cemeteries, supt, 1987-91. **Orgs:** Vpres, Comm Action Prog, 1969-77; bd dir, Carver Comm Day Care, 1970-76; Nat Asn Advan Colored People Coalition 100 Black Women Polit Black Caucus, 1978-85; bd dir, Liberty Baptist Housing Authority. **Honors/Awds:** Community Leadership Award, Young Women's Christian Asn, 1976; Black Woman of the Year, Politics Black Women Task Force, 1977; State of Ind Black Expo, 1978; Selected & Honored as one of 105 Outstanding Black Women of Ind, Natl Coun of Negro Women, 1983; Spec Recognition Community Service Award, Black Women Task Force, 1990; Jefferson Award, 2004. **Special Achievements:** First African-American elected to Vanderburgh County-Wide office. **Home Addr:** 804 E Mulberry St, Evansville, IN 47713-2359, **Home Phone:** (812)425-8789.

**MOSS, JAMES EDWARD**
Police officer. **Personal:** Born Jan 8, 1949, Columbus, OH; son of Frank P and Ernestine Coggins; married Andria Felder; children: Shondrika, Marquai, Jamarran & Jamelah; children: Jamelah. **Educ:** Columbus Bus Univ, AA, bus admin, 1973; OH Dominican Col, BA, bus admin, 1975; Capital Univ, attended 1978; OH State Univ, MA, black studies, 1989, MA, US hist, 1993, PhD, cand hist, 1994. **Career:** Police officer (retired); Columbus Police Dept, Columbus, OH, sgt, 1970-94; Voice People, Z103 FM radio sta, co-host, 1999-; US Dept Justice; Moss & Assocs, founder & pres; Fulton County Pub Schs, hist teacher. **Orgs:** Pres, Police Officers Equal Rights, 1988-; Am Hist Asn, 1990-; Orgn Am Historians, 1990-; bd mem, Columbus Police Athletic League; OH Guardians, 1988-; pres, Nat Black Police Asn, 1993-; columbus chap, Nat Asn Advan Colored People, 1994-; Nat Coun Black Studies; Asn Study Afro Am Life & Hist; head tutor, YMCA. **Honors/Awds:** Jefferson Award, 1985; Coach of the Year, Police Athletic League, 1983; Service Award, Police Athletic League, 1986, 1987, 1990; Police Officer of the Year, Nat Black Police Asn, 1993; Chief of Police Award. **Home Addr:** 295 Vickery Lane, Fayetteville, GA 30215-4680. **Business Addr:** Founder, President, Moss & Associates, 8720 Orion Pl Suitte 120, Columbus, OH 43240-2118, **Business Phone:** (614)540-1889.

**MOSS, LESIA BATES**
President (organization). **Educ:** Univ Va, BA, Am govt, 1987; NY Univ, MS, real estate investment anal & finance, 1996. **Career:** JP-Morgan Chase & Co, relationship mgr, 1987-91; New York Housing Authority, mgr bus develop, 1991-92; New York Dept Gen Serv, dir off contract opportunity, 1992-94; Mario Cuomo's 1994 Gubernatorial Campaign;Lesia, pres; Moody's Investors Serv, vpres, sr vpres, 1997-2004; Ny Ins Dept Liquidation Bur, dir admin serv, 1994-95; Glaves & Assocs, assoc, 1996-97; Family Mae, vpres & head Risk Mgt, 2005-07; LBM & Assocs, pres & chief exec officer, consult, 2008. **Orgs:** Exec Leadership Coun; Bedford-Stuyvesant Restoration Corp, currently; Seedco Financial Serv, exec vpres, pres, 2009-10; adv bd mem, Ron Brown Scholar Prog; dir, Walter Ridley Scholar Fund Bd. **Business Addr:** Advisory Board Member, Ron Brown Scholar Program, 1160 Pepsi Pl Suite 206, Charlottesville, VA 22901, **Business Phone:** (434)964-1588.

**MOSS, NIKKI**
Labor relations manager. **Personal:** married Gary; children: Jelani & Shomari. **Educ:** Oakland Univ, BS & MBA, orgn leadership. **Career:** Detroit Edison, col recruiter, 1977; Ford Motor Co, panelist; DTE Energy's Diversity Leadership Coun, mem, hr prof; DTE Energy, human resource prof, supvr, orgn learning, currently. **Orgs:** Leader, Youth Fel; chairperson, Black Hist Month Celebration; Women's Retreat Comt; DTE Energy's Diversity Leadership Coun; Hope United Methodist Church, Southfield, MI; trustee, Southfield Community Found, 2011-14; trustee, Heritage Works, 2014-. **Honors/Awds:** Sarah Sheridan Award, 1997; Walter J McCarthy Award of Volunteerism, DTE Energy. **Business Addr:** Supervisor of Organizational Learning, DTE Energy, 2000 2nd Ave, Detroit, MI 48226-1203, **Business Phone:** (313)235-4000.

**MOSS, REV. DR. OTIS, JR.**
Clergy. **Personal:** Born Feb 26, 1935, LaGrange, GA; son of Otis Sr and Magnolia; married Edwina Hudson; children: Kevin, Daphne (deceased) & Otis III. **Educ:** Morehouse Col, BA, 1956, DD, 1977; Morehouse Sch Relig, BD, 1959; Interdenominational Theol Ctr, spec studies, 1961; United Theol Sem, PhD, 1990; Temple Bible Col, DD. **Career:** Raymond Walters Col, instr; Old Mt Olive Baptist Church, Los Angeles Grange, pastor, 1954-59; Providence Baptist Church, pastor, 1956-61; Mt Zion Baptist Church, minister, 1961-75; Ebenezer Baptist Church, co-pastor, 1971; Mt Olivet Instnl Church, pastor, 1975-, pastor emer, currently. **Orgs:** Bd dir, Morehouse Sch Relig & Morehouse Col; bd dir, ML King Jr Ctr; bd dir, vice chmn, Oper PUSH; Alpha Phi Alpha; vpres, Nat Asn Advan Colored People; pres & founder, Cincinnati Chap SCLC; bd trustee, Leadership Cleveland Civil Right Activist; former columnist, Atlanta Inquirer, 1970-75;

mem rev comn, Harvard Divinity Sch Harvard Univ, 1975-82; mem bd trustee, Morehouse Col, 1979-; delivered speeches, sermons & addresses, Atlanta Univ, Colgate Rochester Divinity Sch, Col Mt.St Joseph, Dillard Univ, Eden Theol Ctr, Howard Univ, Kalamazoo Col, Miami Univ, Fisk Univ, Univ Cincinnati, Vanderbilt Univ, Wilberforce Univ, Wright State Univ, Morehouse Col. **Honors/Awds:** Keynote speaker March, Cincinnati, 1963; served as part of clergy mission to the Far E Hong Kong, Taiwan & Japan, 1970; invited to act as deleg to World Bapt Conf in Beirut; twice honored by Ohio House of Reps, Resolutions, 1971, 1975; sermon Gg, Disgrace to Dignity Best Black Sermons, 1972; Human Relations Award, Bethune Cookman Col, 1976; consult with govt officials as part of clergy mission to Israel, 1977-78; Consult with Pres Carter Camp David, 1979; Ranked as one of Clevelands 10 Most Influential Ministers, Cleveland Press, 1981; Govs Award in Civil Rights Gov Richard F Celeste; Spec Award in Leadership, Cent State Univ, 1982; Black Prof of the Year, Black Prof Asn, Cleveland, OH, 1983; Greatest Black Preachers, Ebony Mag, 1984; invited as part of clergy mission to Repub of China Taiwan, 1984; Role Model of the Year Award, Nat Inst for Responsible Fatherhood and Family Develop, 1992; Leadership Award, Cleveland Chap of the Am Jewish Comt, 1996; University Hospitals Health medical centre named in honor, 1997; essays "Black Church Distinctives", "Black Church Revolution" The Black Christian Experience; listed in Ebony Success Libr; Hon DD, LaGrange Col, 2004; Int Civil Rights Walk of Fame, 2007. **Home Addr:** 87 Haskell Dr, Cleveland, OH 44108-1177, **Home Phone:** (216)268-3513. **Business Addr:** Emeritus Pastor, Olivet Institute Baptist Church, 8712 Quincy Ave, Cleveland, OH 44106, **Business Phone:** (216)721-7729.

## MOSS, OTIS, III

Minister (clergy). **Personal:** son of Otis Moss Jr.; married Monica Brown Moss; children: Makayla Elon and Elijah Wynton. **Educ:** Morehouse College, B.A. in Religion and Philosophy, 1992; Yale Divinity School, Master of Divinity, 1995; Chicago Theological Seminary, Doctor of Ministry. **Career:** Tabernacle Baptist Church (Augusta, GA), Pastor; Trinity United Church of Christ (Chicago), Asst. Pastor, 2006-08, Senior Pastor, 2008-. **Orgs:** Progressive National Baptist Convention, Ordained Minister and Board Member; United Church of Christ, Ordained Minister; "Christian Century" Magazine, Board Member; Children's Defense Fund's Samuel DeWitt Proctor Child Advocacy Conference, Chaplain. **Honors/Awds:** "The African American Pulpit Journal," 20 To Watch. **Special Achievements:** Author of "Redemption in a Red Light District," 1999; co-author of "The Gospel Re-mix: How to Reach the Hip-Hop Generation," 2006. **Business Addr:** Senior Pastor, Trinity United Church of Christ, 400 W. 95th St., Chicago, IL 60628, **Business Phone:** ((77)3)962-56.

## MOSS, RANDY (RANDY GENE MOSS)

Broadcaster, football player. **Personal:** Born Feb 13, 1977, Rand, WV; son of Randy Pratt and Maxine; children: Sydney, Senali, Thaddeus, Montigo & Sylee. **Educ:** Marshall Univ, grad. **Career:** Football player (retired), analyst; Minn Vikings, wide receiver, 1998-2004, 2010; Oakland Raiders, wide receiver, 2005-06; New Eng Patriots, wide receiver, 2007, 2008-10; Randy Moss Motorsports, founder, 2008; Tenn Titans, wide receiver, 2010; San Francisco 49ers, wide receiver, 2012; Victory Christian Ctr High Sch, assoc head coach, defensive coordr, 2014; Fox Sports 1, analyst, currently. **Orgs:** Randy Moss Found; founder, Learning Links Found, 2008. **Honors/Awds:** West Virginia Player of the Year, 1993, 1994; Paul Warfield Trophy, 997; Best at Each Position Award, Nat Football League, 1998; Alumni Wide receiver of the Year, Nat Football League, 1998; Offensive Rookie of the Year, Associated Press, 1998; Seven times Pro Bowl, 1998, 1999, 2000, 2002, 2003, 2007, 2009; Pro Bowl Most Valuable Player, 1999; Player of the Year, Nat Football League, 2003; Player of the Month, Am Football Conf, 2007; Comeback Player of the Year, Prof Football Writers Am, 2007; Champion, Am Football Conf, 2007; Champion, Nat Football Conf, 2012. **Special Achievements:** National Football League Record Most TD Receptions in One Season; National Football League Record Most TD Receptions in One Season by a Rookie. **Business Addr:** Wide Receiver, New England Patriots, Gillette Stadium 1 Patriot Pl, Foxboro, MA 02035, **Business Phone:** (508)543-8200.

## MOSS, ROBERT C., JR.

Consultant, baseball umpire. **Personal:** Born May 30, 1939, San Diego, CA; son of Robert C Sr and La Verne; married Edna Jean; children: Anita Louise & Parry Donald. **Educ:** San Diego State Univ, BA, 1961, MS, 1975; US Int Univ, teaching cred, 1965. **Career:** Lincoln High Sch, biol teacher, 1965-66; Mission Bay High Sch, biol instr, football, baseball coach, 1966-69; prof baseball umpire, 1969-71; San Diego High Sch, black studies teacher, black stud motivation counr, 1969-71; Phys Educ Dept Univ Calif San Diego, supvr, 1971-92; Moss-Cess Unlimited, founder & dir, 1973. **Orgs:** Kappa Alpha Psi Fraternity; Am Alliance Health, Phys Educ Recreation &Dance; Am Coun Asn; Calif Asn Health, Phys Educ Recreation & Dance; Calif Asn Couns & Develop; Calif & Am Asn Multicultural Coun & Develop; vpres, San Diego County Baseball Umpires Asn. **Honors/Awds:** Ted Williams Award, 1960; Byron Chase Memorial Award, 1960; Most Outstanding San Diego State University Senior Athlete, 1961; Associated Students Man of the Month, San Diego State Univ, 1961; Blue Key Honorary Soc, 1961; Ashanti Weusi Award, Southeast San Diego community; Unit Meritorious Service Award, Calif Asn Health Phys Educ Recreation & Dance, San Diego, 1975; Calif Asn Health Phys Educ Recreation & Dance President's Citation, 1981; Oustanding Teacher Award, Univ Calif, San Diego African Am graduates, 1985; Calif Asn Health Phys Educ Recreation & Dance Emmett Ashford Community Spirit Award, 1986; Am Asn Cosmetic Dentist President's Citation, 1986; CACD Black Caucus Service Award, 1986; Calif Asn Health Phys Educ Recreation & Dance Honor Award, 1987; Special Recognition Award, Univ Calif San Diego Athletics Prog; Special Recognition Award, US Int Univ basketball team, 1988; CACD Black Caucus Dedicated Service Award, 1989; CACD-CAMC President's Outstanding Professional Service Award, 1989; Outstanding Service Award, Camperd Multicultural Dynamics Section, 1991; CACD Human Rights Award, 1993; ACA-AMCD Professional Development Award, 1994. **Special Achievements:** Author: booklet on positive uses of laughter. **Home Addr:** 2409 Fleetwood St, San Diego, CA 92111, **Home Phone:** (858)279-4376.

## MOSS, SHAD GREGORY. See WOW, BOW.

## MOSS, THYLIAS

Poet, educator. **Personal:** Born Feb 27, 1954, Cleveland, OH; daughter of Calvin Brasier and Florida Brasier; children: 2. **Educ:** Oberlin Col, grad, 1981; Univ NH, MA, eng. **Career:** May Co, order checker, 1973-74, jr exec auditor, 1975-79, data entry supvr, 1974-75; Phillips Acad, instr, 1984-92; Univ Mich, asst prof, 1993-94, assoc prof, 1994-98, prof eng & poet, art & design, 1998-; Univ NH, Durham, vis prof, 1991-92; Brandeis Univ, Fannie Hurst Poet, 1992; Poetry: Hosiery Seams on a Bowlegged Woman, 1983; Pyramid of Bone, 1989; At Redbones, 1990; Rainbow Remnants in Rock Bottom Ghetto Sky, 1991; Small Congregations: New & Selected Poems, 1993; Last Chance for the Tarzan Holler, 1998; Slave Moth: A Narrative in Verse, 2004; Tokyo Butter: Poems, 2006; Prose: Talking to Myself, 1984; The Dolls in the Basement, 1984; I Want to Be, 1995; Someone Else Right Now, 1997; Tale of a Sky-Blue Dress, 1998; Pyramid of Bone, 1989; At Redbones, 1990; Rainbow Remnants in Rock Bottom Ghetto Sky, 1991; Last Chance for the Tarzan Holler, 1998; A Narrative in Verse Persea Books, 2004; Limited Fork weblogs, 2007. **Orgs:** Fel, MacArthur Genius; fel, Guggenheim; grant, Nat Endowment Arts; artist fel, Mass Arts Coun. **Business Addr:** Poet, Professor, University of Michigan-Ann Arbor, 3247 Angell Hall 435 S State St, Ann Arbor, MI 48109-1003, **Business Phone:** (734)764-0443.

## MOSS, WAYNE B.

Manager, executive director, association executive. **Personal:** Born Jul 28, 1960, Cleveland, OH; son of Ceasar and Earlene Hill. **Educ:** Howard Univ, Wash, DC, BA, jour, 1982; Ohio Univ, Athens, OH, MA, sports admin & facil mgt, 1988. **Career:** Cleveland Browns, pub rels asst, 1988; Detroit Lions, dir, pub rels, 1988-91; Baltimore Orioles, asst dir community rels, 1989; City Cleveland, comnr recreation, 1991-95; Dekalb County, dep dir recreation, 1996-2001; Mossman Consult, pres, 2001-03; Boys & Girls Clubs Am, dir prog plng, 2003, sr dir sports, fitness & recreation, 2004-. **Orgs:** Acct exec, Bur Employ Serv, Maple Heights, OH, 1983-2008; Career Beginnings, 1988; United Negro Col Fund, 1989. **Home Addr:** 1490 Oglethorpe Run Lane, Suwanee, GA 30024-3645, **Home Phone:** (770)623-4933. **Business Addr:** Senior Director of Sports, Fitness and Recreation, Boys & Girls Clubs of America, 1230 W Peachtree St NW, Atlanta, GA 30309, **Business Phone:** (404)487-5761.

## MOSS, WILMAR BURNETT

Educator, commissioner. **Personal:** Born Jul 13, 1928, Homer, LA; married Orean Sanders; children: Dwight, Victor, Gary & LaDonna. **Educ:** Ark Baptist Col, attended 1949; Southern State Col, attended 1957; AM&N Col, Pine Bluff, BS, bus admin, 1960; Univ Ark, Fayetteville, MEd, educ admin, 1970. **Career:** McNeil Cleaners, cleaner spotter presser; McNeil Lumber Co, tractor truck driver lumber grader; Partee Lumber Co, tractor driver; Navel Ord Plant Camden, light mach oper; Stuttgard, teacher, 1960; E Side Lincoln Elem Schs Stuttgart, head teacher, 1961-63; E Side Lincoln Holman, prin, 1964-69; Holman Northside Elem Schs, prin, 1969-72; Walker Sch Dist No 33, supt schs, 1972-; Ark Fair Housing Comn, comnr, 2002-04. **Orgs:** Ark Sch Admin Asn; Ark Educ Asn; S Ark Admins Asn; Columbia County Educ Asn; Nat Educ Asn; Nat Asn Advan Colored People; Nat Alliance Black Sch Supts; Phi Delta Kappa; Bethany Baptist Church McNeil; Golden Diadem Lodge No 41; McNeil Jaycees; bd mem, Pres Johnson Concentrated Employ Prog, 1971-72; Stuttgart Civic League; Walker Alumni Asn, 1974. **Special Achievements:** First African American to Attend Southern State College. **Home Addr:** PO Box 723, Magnolia, AR 71753.

## MOSS, WINSTON

Writer. **Personal:** Born Selma, AL. **Educ:** Bellarmine Col, KY, 1964; Western Ky Univ, attended 1968. **Career:** Wilson Show staff writer, 1970; Laugh, staff writer, 1972; Love, Am Style, 1973; "Sanford & Son", 1973-74; "That's My Mama", story ed, 1975-76; "Barney Miller"-Community Rels, 1977; "Jacksons"-5 Shows, staff writer, 1977; Writers Guild Am/WST, freelance writer; Staff writer: Clifton Davis Spec, 1977; "Whats happening"-If I'm Elected, 1977; "All in the Family", 1977-79; Archie Bunkers Pl, 1979-80; "One Day at a Time"-Male Jealousy, 1979; "Sanford"-Cissy & Nephew, 1980; "Jeffersons"-Bobbles, Bangles & Booboos, 1984; "227"-Mary's Bro, 1985. **Orgs:** Vice chmn, Black Writers Comt, 1979-81; Hollywood Br mem, Nat Asn Advan Colored People. **Home Addr:** 4714 Rodeo Lane Apt 3, Los Angeles, CA 90016, **Home Phone:** (323)291-9391.

## MOSS, WINSTON N., SR.

Football player, football coach. **Personal:** Born Dec 24, 1965, Miami, FL; married Zoila; children: Winston Jr, Robert, Marcus, Victoria & Isabella. **Educ:** Univ Miami. **Career:** Football player (retired), coach; Tampa Bay Buccaneers, right outside linebacker, 1987-90, right inside linebacker, 1990; Los Angeles Raiders, right linebacker, 1991-94; Seattle Seahawks, left linebacker, 1995-97, defensive qual control coach, 1998-2000; New Orleans Saints, defensive asst & qual control coach, 2000-01, linebackers coach, 2001-05; Green Bay Packers, linebackers coach, 2006-07, asst head coach & defensive, 2007-. **Honors/Awds:** Ed Block Courage Award, 1993; Unsung Hero Award, Nat Football League Players Asn, 1996. **Home Addr:** 937 Thornberry Creek Dr, Oneida, WI 54155-8621. **Business Addr:** Assistant Head Coach, Defensive Coach, Green Bay Packers, 1265 Lombardi Ave, Green Bay, WI 54304, **Business Phone:** (920)569-7500.

## MOSS, YOLANDA M.

School principal. **Personal:** married Kerry. **Career:** St Louis Bd Elections, republican comnr; Pierre Laclede Elem St Louis Pub Schs, prin. **Orgs:** St Louis Bd Elections; St Louis Election Bd. **Business Addr:** Principal, Pierre Laclede Elementary St Louis Public Schools, 5821 Kennerly Ave, St. Louis, MO 63112-3821, **Business Phone:** (314)385-0546.

## MOSS, ZEFROSS P.

Football player, football coach, business owner. **Personal:** Born Aug 17, 1966, Tuscaloosa, AL. **Educ:** Ala State Univ, grad. **Career:** Football player (retired); Dallas Cowboys, 1988; Indianapolis Colts, 1989, left tackle, 1990-92, right tackle, 1993-94; Detroit Lions, right tackle, 1995-96; New Eng Patriots, right tackle, 1997-99; Housing construct; Ice cream shops; Madison Patriots, coach. **Home Addr:** , Madison, AL.

## MOSS-BUCHANAN, TANYA JILL

Government official, association executive, lawyer. **Personal:** Born Dec 20, 1958, Chicago, IL; daughter of Hiawatha and Arzelia. **Educ:** Univ Chicago, BS, 1983. **Career:** Carson Pirie Scott & Co, personnel asst, 1980-83; Quaker Oats, acct rep, 1983-84; City Chicago, proj coordr, 1987-02; atty. **Orgs:** Alpha Kappa Alpha Sorority Inc, 1979-; Order Eastern Star, 1982-; Nat Asn Female Execs, 1984-; Nat Forum Black Pub Admins, 1985-; bd mem, ETA Creative Arts Found; exec bd mem, Polit Action League. **Home Addr:** 8910 SE End Ave, Chicago, IL 60617-2807, **Home Phone:** (312)747-1127. **Business Addr:** IL.

## MOTEN, EMMETT S., JR.

Executive. **Personal:** Born Feb 6, 1944, Birmingham, AL; son of Emmett S Sr and Marie Creighton; married Loran Williams; children: Eric & Alicia. **Educ:** Grambling State Univ, Grambling, LA, BS; La State Univ, New Orleans, LA, MA, educ. **Career:** St Augustine High Sch, New Orleans, La, athletic dir, football coach, 1966-70; City New Orleans, New Orleans, La, rec dept dep dir, 1970-73, dir policy plng & anal, 1973-75, asst chief admin officer, 1975-78; Detroit Econ Growth Corp, Detroit, Mich, exec vpres, downtown develop authority, 1978-79; Moten Group, pres & chief exec officer; City Detroit, Detroit, Mich, dir, community & econ develop, 1979-88; Little Caesar Enterprises Inc, vpres, develop, 1998-96; Detroit Tigers Inc, vpres, develop; John D Moten Inc, pres; Morton Group Inc, pres, 1996; Twinpines Paper Corp, chmn; United Am Healthcare Corp, secy & dir, currently. **Orgs:** Chmn, Boys Hope; bd mem, Orchard Childrens Serv; bd mem, Inst Bus; bd mem, Detroit Downtown Develop Authority; bd mem, Detroit Econ Develop Authority; pres, Joint Fraternal Devt Corp; Kappa Alpha Psi, Detroit chap; bd dir, United Am Healthcare Corp. **Home Addr:** 17526 Warrington Dr, Detroit, MI 48221-2769. **Business Addr:** Secretary, Independent Director, United American Healthcare Corp, 300 River Pl Suite 4950, Detroit, MI 48207-4291, **Business Phone:** (313)393-4571.

## MOTHERSHED, SPAESIO WILLAR

Librarian. **Personal:** Born Jun 30, 1925, Bloomburg, TX; married Juliene Craven; children: Spaesio Jr & Willa Renee. **Educ:** Jarvis Christian Col, BA, 1952; Syracuse Univ, MS, 1956; N Tex State Univ, attended 1963. **Career:** Syracuse Univ Libr, grad asst, 1954-56; State Libr Mich, cataloger, 1956-60; Jarvis Christian Col, head librn, 1960-66; Tex Southern Univ, dir librn. **Orgs:** Tex Libr Asn; SW Libr Asn; Houston Met Archives; ed, News Notes, 1968-72; Comt Sci & Tech Info Sub-com Negro Res Libr, 1970-73. **Home Addr:** 19700 Hickory Twig Way, Spring, TX 77388, **Home Phone:** (713)529-0203.

## MOTLEY, DAVID LYNN

Manager. **Personal:** Born Sep 11, 1958, Pittsburgh, PA; son of Thomas A and Lillie M Law; married Darlene Gambill; children: Renee & Carrington. **Educ:** Univ Pittsburgh, BSME, 1980; Harvard Bus Sch, MBA, 1988. **Career:** PPG Indust Inc, dir sales & mkt, dir sales & com glass, Pittsburgh, PA, design engr, analyst, 1980-82, dir corp invest, 1989-99, St Louis, Mo, sls rep, 1982-84, New York, NY, res sls rep, 1984-86; MBA Develop, Wash, DC, consult, 1988-89; MicroCoating Technologies, exec vpres, 1999; Alcoa Inc, dir mkt & vpres, 2002-05; Alcoa Advan Transp Systs, strategy develop, dir, 1999-2002, global vpres, 2004; Respironics, vpres & gen mgr, 2006-08, Covidien Surg Devices, vpres, gen mgr, 2009; Sleep Well Ventures, Philips Home Healthcare Solutions, dir corp strategic plng, vpres & gen mgr, currently; Headwaters SC LP, sr managing dir; BlueTree Venture Fund, co-founder & gen partner. **Orgs:** Chmn, Langley High Sch Future Jobs, 1989-; bd dir, E Liberty Develop Corp, 1989-; alumni steering comn, NEED, 1990-; bd dir, Urban League Pittsburgh, 1990-; treas, Harvard Sch Club, Pittsburgh, 1990-; Pittsburgh C's Mus; bd trustees, Sewickley Acad; Bd Pittsburgh Zoo; Bd PPG Aquarium; exec dir, Inner City Jr Tennis Prog; founder, Univ Pittsburgh Eng Endowed Scholar Fund; Pittsburgh Found. **Home Addr:** , Pittsburgh, PA. **Business Addr:** Senior Managing Director, Headwaters SC LP, Blaymore 1 Suite 300, Sewickley, PA 15143, **Business Phone:** (724)933-6600.

## MOTLEY, J. KEITH

Chancellor (education). **Personal:** married Angela; children: Keith Allyn Jr, Kayla Iman & Jordan Kiara. **Educ:** Northeastern Univ, BS, MS; Boston Col, PhD, philos. **Career:** Univ Mass, Boston, vice chancellor stud affairs, vpres bus mkt & pub affairs, interim chancellor, vice chancellor stud affairs, chancellor, 2007-; Newbury Col, bd trustee, chair; Concerned Black Men Mass Inc, founder & educ chair; Paul Robeson Inst, founder & educ chair; Northeastern Univ, dean stud serv. **Orgs:** Iota Phi Theta Fraternity; Sigma Pi Phi Fraternity; Beta Beta Boule; Am Red Cross; Freedom House; United Way Mass Ba; Boston Pvt Indust Ctr; Dimock Community Health Ctr; founder, Roxbury Prep Charter Sch; Carney Hosp; Boston World Partnership; Boston Munic Res Bur; Boston Sports Mus; Commonwealth Corp; John F Kennedy Libr Found; Boston Comt; Chair Emer Schs Bd Trustees; Am Coun Educs; chair, Newbury Col Bd Trustees; Asn Pub & Land Grant Univs, Am Asn State Cols & Univs; Asn Pub & Land Grant Univs. **Honors/Awds:** Honorary degree award, Northeastern University. **Business Addr:** Chancellor, University of Massachusettes, Rm 0054A Quinn Admin Bldg 3, Boston, MA 02125-3393, **Business Phone:** (617)287-6800.

## MOTLEY, DR. RONALD CLARK

Physician, educator. **Personal:** Born Jan 25, 1954, Dayton, OH; son of Claude L Dunson (stepfather) and Birdella M Rhodes Dunson; married Charlyn Coleman; children: Melissa Charon. **Educ:** Northwestern Univ, BA, 1976; Howard Univ, Col Med, MD, 1983. **Career:** Northwestern Univ, lab tech, 1972-74; Ind Bio test Labs, toxicologist & group leader skin sensitization, 1976-77; Avon Products Inc, process control chemist, 1977-78; Southern Ill Univ, Sch Med, vis asst instr, 1978-79; Howard Univ, Col Med, instr & tutor, 1980-81; Howard Univ, Col Med, Health Scis Acad, gen coordr, 1981-83; Mayo Clin, gen surg internship, 1983-84, urol residency, 1984-88; pvt pract, currently. **Orgs:** Equal opportunity comm, Mayo Clinci, 1985-; assoc mem, Minority Fellows Mayo Clinic, 1985-; Nat Med Asn, 1985-; educ comn, Dept Urol Mayo Clinic, 1987-88; bd dir, Family Serv Agency San Bernardino, CA, 1989-. **Home Addr:** 7231 Boulder Ave Suite 513, Highland, CA 92346, **Home Phone:** (714)862-9384. **Business Addr:** Physician, 245 Terracina Blvd, Redlands, CA 92373, **Business Phone:** (909)335-9373.

### MOTT, STOKES E., JR.
Lawyer. **Personal:** Born Mar 11, 1947, Tifton, GA; son of Stokes E Sr and Kathleen M; married Neilda E Jackman; children: Ako K & Khari S. **Educ:** Ohio State Univ, attended 1965; Long Island Univ, BA, sociol & econs, 1968; NY Univ, MS, urban regional planning & pub admin, 1971; Seton Hall Law Sch, JD, 1978. **Career:** NYC Dept Educ, social studies teacher, 1968-71; New York Dept City Planning, urban & regional planning consult, 1972-77; Essex Co Col, urban studies & urban planning prog dir, 1971-80; Equal Employ Opportunity Comn, atty, 1979-81; Law Clins Mott & Gray PC, managing partner & atty, 1981-82; Stokes E Mott Jr PC, atty, 1979-81; Law Clins Mott & Gray, atty, 1981-84; Mott Law Group LLC, atty & owner, 1982-. **Orgs:** Nat Asn Advan Colored People Media; Del Co Nether Providence Community Asn; Alpha Phi Alpha; Pa Bar Asn; Philadelphia Bar Asn; pres, Alpha Phi Alpha; Zeta Omicron Lambda Chap; Legis & Const Comts; Chap Parliamentarian. **Home Addr:** 1749 Ashbrooke Ave, Garnet Valley, PA 19060-6821, **Home Phone:** (484)483-9485. **Business Addr:** Attorney, Owner, Mott Law Group LLC, 210 W Front St Suite 210, Media, PA 19063, **Business Phone:** (610)891-0900.

### MOULDS, ERIC SHANNON
Football player. **Personal:** Born Jul 17, 1973, Lucedale, MS. **Educ:** Miss State Univ, psychol. **Career:** Football player (retired); Buffalo Bills, kick returner, wide receiver, 1996-97, wide receiver, 1998-2005; Houston Texans, wide receiver, 2006; Tenn Titans, wide receiver, 2007. **Orgs:** Nat Asn Advan Colored People. **Honors/Awds:** Rookie of the Year, Buffalo Bills, 1996; Receiving Yards Leader, Am Football Conf, 1998; Pro Bowl, 1998, 2000, 2002. **Business Addr:** New York, NY.

### MOURNING, ALONZO HARDING, JR.
Basketball player, executive. **Personal:** Born Feb 8, 1970, Chesapeake, VA; married Tracy; children: Alonzo III, Myka Sydney & Alijah. **Educ:** Georgetown Univ, BA, sociol, 1992. **Career:** Basketball player (retired), executive; Charlotte Hornets, ctr, 1992-95; Miami Heat, 1995-2002, 2005-08; NJ Nets, ctr, 2003-04; Miami Heat front off, exec, currently. **Orgs:** C's Home Soc; founder, Zo Fund Life; founder, Alonzo Mourning Charities, 1997-; co-founder, Athletes Hope. **Honors/Awds:** Naismith Prep Player of the Year, 1988; McDonald's All-American MVP, 1988; silver medal, Goodwill Games, Seattle, 1990; bronze medal, FIBA World Championship, Argentina, 1990; USA Basketball Male Athlete of the Year, 1990; Big East Tournament MVP, 1992; Big East Conference Player of the Year, 1992; Miami Heat all time Leader in Blocks; NBA All-Rookie First Team, 1993; gold medal, FIBA World Championship, Canada, 1994; All-NBA First Team, 1999; NBA Defensive Player of the Year, 1999, 2000; All-NBA Second Team, 2000; gold medal, Olympic Games, Sydney, 2000; J WalterKennedy Citizenship Award; NBAOCOs J Walter Kennedy Sportsmanship Award, 2002; Hometown Hero, Fla Sports Awards, 2002; Good Guy, The Sporting News, 2002; Silver Medallion Community Service Award, Nat Conf Community & Justice, 2003; Outstanding Community Service Award, Nat Urban League, 2003; NBA Champion, 2006; Naismith Memorial Basketball Hall of Fame, 2014. **Special Achievements:** First round pick, No 2, NBA Draft, 1992; Book: Resilience, 2008. **Home Addr:** , Pinecrest, FL. **Business Addr:** Founder, Alonzo Mourning Charities Inc, 100 S Biscayne Blvd 3rd Fl, Coconut Grove, FL 33131, **Business Phone:** (305)476-0095.

### MOUTON, JAMES RALEIGH
Baseball player, baseball manager. **Personal:** Born Dec 19, 1968, Denver, CO; children: 3. **Educ:** St Mary's Col, Calif. **Career:** Baseball player (retired), baseball coach; Houston Astros, outfielder, 1994-97; San Diego Padres, 1998; Montreal Expos, 1999; Milwaukee Brewers, 2000-01; Fort Bend Texans Sports Asn, hitting & fielding coach, 2006-; Arizona Diamondbacks, area scout, 2010-. **Business Addr:** Hitting and Fielding Coach, The Fort Bend Texans Sports Association, 8523 Old Quarry Dr, Sugar Land, TX 77479, **Business Phone:** (832)444-2307.

### MOUTON, LYLE JOSEPH
Baseball player, executive. **Personal:** Born May 13, 1969, Lafayette, LA; married Aimee Churchill; children: Alexis Leigh, Kayla Lynn & Cameron. **Educ:** La State Univ, BA, mkt, 1991. **Career:** Baseball player (retired) executive, partner; All-Tournament Col World Ser, 1990-91; La State Univ Tigers, outfielder, 1989-91; Chicago White Sox, outfielder, 1995-97; Yakult Swallows, 1998; Baltimore Orioles, 1998; Milwaukee Brewers, 1999-2000; Fla Marlins, 2001; Montreal Expos, free agt, 2002; Philadelphia Phillies, free agt, 2003; Cleveland Indians, 2003; Life Brokerage Partners, Brokerage dir, 2004-08; Ins Claims Unlimited, dir bus develop, 2011; RSC Southeast, dir bus develop, 2011-12; Mouton Emergency Serv, owner, 2012; Enviro-Clean Serv Inc, partner, 2013-. **Business Addr:** Partner, Enviro-Clean Services Inc, PO Box 2818, Holland, MI 49422-2818, **Business Phone:** (888)672-9060.

### MOUTOUSSAMY-ASHE, JEANNE
Photographer. **Personal:** Born Jul 9, 1951, Chicago, IL; married Arthur Ashe; children: Camera. **Educ:** Cooper Union, NT, BFA, photog, 1975. **Career:** Prof photogr, 1975-; Arthur Ashe Found Defeat AIDS, chairwoman, currently. **Honors/Awds:** CEBA Award for IBM Advertisement, 1979; City of Chicago, Mayoral Citation for Viewfinders, 1986; Distinguished Alumni Citation, The Cooper Union, 1990; LISC Award for Art, 1999; Hon Dr of Fine Arts, Long Island University, C.W. Post Campus, 2001; Hon Dr of Fine Arts, Queens Cil, 2002; Essence Photography Literary Award, 2007. **Special Achievements:** Books: "Daddy and Me", Knopf, 1993; "Viewfinders: Black Women Photographers, 1839-1985",New York: Dodd, Mead and Company, 1986; "Daufuskie Island: A Photography Essay",Columbia, SC: University of South Carolina Press, 1982. Exhibitions: "America: Another Perspective",New York University, 1986; "Three Photographers",Black Gallery, Los Angeles, CA, 1985; "Art Against Apartheid: 3 Perspectives",Schomburg Center for Research in Black Culture, New York Public Library, 1984; "Image and Imagination",Jazzonia Gallery, Detroit, MI, 1982; one woman shows, NY, Chicago, Florence, Paris; one woman exhibition, Leica Gallery, 1996-97; work appears in Columbia Museum of Art & Sci, Natl Portrait Gallery, Studio Museum of Harlem; "Reflections In Black, A History of Black Photographers, Debroah Willis", WW Norton & Co, 2000; Committed to Image Contemporary Black Photographers, Merril Publ, LTD, 2001. **Business Addr:** Photographer, The Leica Gallery, 670 Broadway 5th Fl, New York, NY 10012.

### MOWATT, EZEKIEL. See MOWATT, ZEKE.

### MOWATT, DR. OSWALD VICTOR
Surgeon. **Personal:** Born Spanish Town; married Glenda; children: Cecilia, Oswald Jr, Cyril, Raoul, Enrico & Mario. **Educ:** Roosevelt Univ, BS, 1959; Loyola Univ Med Sch, Md, 1963; Am Bd Surg, dipl, 1976. **Career:** Cook Co Hosp, intern, 1963-64; Michale Reese Hosp, resident surg, 1964-65; gen pract, 1965-67; Univ Ill, 1967-60, chief, resident surg; Westside Va Hosp, 1969-76; instr surg, 1969-76; Westside Va, resident surg, 1969-70; St Bernard Hosp, attend surg, 1970-73; Provident Hosp, sr attend surg, 1971-; Proficent Hosp, chief emer serv, dir med affairs, 1972-74; St Bernard Hosp, Dept Surg, chmn, 1976-, consult surg 1973-; Vet Affairs Westside M C, physician; Self-employed, surgeon, currently. **Orgs:** Am Med Asn, 1965-; Ill State Med Soc, 1965-; Chicago Med Soc, 1965-; Asn Hosp Med Educ, 1973-74; Nat Med Asn; chmn, Bylaws com Cook Co Physicians Asn, 1974-76; Judicial Coun Nat Med Asn, 1975-; nominating comt, Nat Med Asn, 1977-; chmn bd dir, Martin L King Boys Club, 1977; pres, Cook Co Physicians Asn, 1977; fel Am Col Surgeons, 1977. **Home Addr:** 8715 Kenwood Ave, Chicago, IL 60619. **Business Addr:** Surgeon, 2011 E 75th St, Chicago, IL 60620.

### MOWATT, ZEKE (EZEKIEL MOWATT)
Founder (originator), football player. **Personal:** Born Mar 5, 1961, Wauchula, FL. **Educ:** Fla State Univ. **Career:** Football player (retired); New York Giants, tight end, 1983-89, 1991; New Eng Patriots, tight end, 1990; Mowatt Inc, founder, currently. **Honors/Awds:** Post-season play, 1986: NFC Championship Game; NFL Championship Game. **Business Addr:** Founder, Mowatt Inc, 194 Passaic St Suite 2A, Hackensack, NJ 07601, **Business Phone:** (201)968-9860.

### MOYO, YVETTE JACKSON
Publishing executive, founder (originator). **Personal:** Born Dec 8, 1953, Chicago, IL; daughter of Rudolph and Pauline; married Karega Kofi; children: Angela Saunders, Kweli, Ki-Afi, Kilolo Shalomeet, Rael, Yosheyah Gavriel, Kush & Kevani Zelpha (deceased). **Educ:** Eastern Ill Univ, BA, Afro-Am studies, 1974. **Career:** Black United Fund, local conv coordr, 1976-77, prog & commun officer, 2014-15; Nat Pub Sales Agency, acct exec, 1977-79, sales mgr, 1979-81, vpres dir sales, 1984-84, sr vpres, dir sales, 1984-88; Dollars & Sense Mag, sr vpres sales & prom, 1977-88; Resource Assocs Int, pres & co-founder, 1988-; Real Men Cook/MOBE, pres, 1988-2013, co-founder, 2004-; US Postal Serv, Black Heritage Ser, pr & mktg consult, 1994-2000; Time Warner Inc, Mkt Opportunities Bus & Entertainment, consult, 1992-2000; Real Men Charities Inc, co-founder, exec dir, 2003-13; Landmark Educ, introd leader, 2006-08; Bonus Life Health, Wellness & Simple TV, master bus builder, 2008; Ryan Mag, S Shore Current & W, Binamu Media, publ, 2014-. **Orgs:** Life mem, Nat Asn Advan Colored People, 1985; Oper PUSH, 1987; League Black Women, 1987. **Honors/Awds:** Black Achievers Award, YMCA, 1983; Kizzy Award Black Womens Hall of Fame, 1985; Todays Chicago Woman, 1988; Public Relations Advertising & Marketing Excellence Award, 1998; 100 Women to Watch, Todays Chicago Woman, 1988; Women in Entertainment Pioneer Award, 2002; 50 Women of Excellence Award; Fatherhood Movement Award. **Special Achievements:** Author: Health and Fitness Enthusiast, Healthy Family Advocate and Coach: Real Women Cook: Building Healthy Families with Recipes that Stir the Soul, 2012-. **Home Addr:** 7425 S Mich Ave, Chicago, IL 60619, **Home Phone:** (312)783-2882. **Business Addr:** Co-Founder, President, Real Men Cook, 7425 S Mich Ave, Chicago, IL 60619, **Business Phone:** (773)651-8008.

### MSHONAJI, BIBI TALIBA. See BELLINGER, REV. MARY ANNE ALLEN.

### MUCKELROY, WILLIAM LAWRENCE
Lawyer, counselor. **Personal:** Born Dec 4, 1945, Los Angeles, CA; son of John and Josie; children: William Jr, William II, William III & Heather. **Educ:** Univ Tex, BA, math, 1967; Am Univ, MS, solid state physics, 1970, JD, 1974. **Career:** Muckelroy & Assoc, patent atty, 1975-; Litton Indust, div patent & licensing coun, 1977-78; Prothon Cyber Ltd, dir & pres; Riggs Liquor, dir & pres; Iram Am Invests Ltd, dir, pres & chmn bd; Dow Chem Co, electronic physicist; Am Univ, teaching asst; Harry Diamond Labs, Wash, patent adv; RCA Corp, David Sarnoff Res Ctr, patent coun; William Lawrence Muckelroy PC, atty, currently. **Orgs:** Trustee, Montclair State Col, NJ, 1982-88; pres, Int Soc Hybrid Micro electronics Capital Chap; pres & dir, Nat Patent Law Asn; NJ, Am Bar Asn; trustee, Montclair State Col; dir, Trenton Bus Asst Corp; fel Wash Col Law Am Univ; Teaching fel Am Univ; chmn, NJ Patent Law Asn Ethics Comt; dir, Trenton Bus Assistance Corp; dir & patent coun, US Patent Soc Inc; Int Intellectual Property Law Soc; Am Intellectual Property Law Asn; NJ Intellectual Property Law Asn; Tex Acad Sci; Mercer County Bar Asn; US Ct Appeals DC; Third, & Tenth Circuits; US Ct Customs & Patent Appeals; Fed Circuit Ct; DC Ct Appeals; NJ Supreme Ct; James E. Carty III P.C. **Honors/Awds:** Honors Univ, 1963-64; Apa Scholar; NSSFNS Scholar; Lawrence D Bell Scholar; 70 patents granted; Lawrence D Bell Advanced Mathematics Fellowship Award. **Home Addr:** PO Box 514, Yardley, PA 19067-8514, **Home Phone:** (215)321-0818. **Business Addr:** Attorney, William Lawrence Muckelroy PC, 1901 N Olden Ave Ewing Prof Bldg Suite 3A, Trenton, NJ 08618-2101, **Business Phone:** (609)882-2111.

### MUDIKU, MARY ESTHER GREER (MAESGARA MUDIKU)
Educator. **Personal:** Born Jan 1, 1943?, Greenville, MS; daughter of Cornelius Members and Rose Esthers Jones; children: Mark K Greer & Masavia N Greer. **Educ:** Memphis State Univ, BFA, 1968; Memphis Acad Art, attended 1971; Howard Univ, MFA, painting. **Career:** DC Pub Schs, art teacher, 1986-89; Carter Global, art ther consult, 1990-92; DC Dept Corrections, art therapist, 1992-97; CCA Corrections Corp Am, art therapist, 1997-; Season Rebirth, founder; African Wholistic Health Asn, wholistic health practr & founder & dir; DC Correctional Treat Facil, art therapist. **Orgs:** Nat Conf Artists, 1990-97; GABA, 1990-2000; co-founder, New Age African Elders, 1995-2001; founder, Sacred Sisterhood, 1997-2001; African Diaspora Ancestral Commemoration Inst. **Home Addr:** PO Box 48153, Washington, DC 20002-0153, **Home Phone:** (202)388-0951. **Business Addr:** Art Therapist, Corrections Corp of America, 1901 E St SE, Washington, DC 20003, **Business Phone:** (202)698-3000.

### MUHAMMAD, AKBAR A.
Association executive, business owner, foreign correspondent. **Personal:** Born Jun 9, 1942, Hampton, VA; son of Celeste Brown-Prescott; married Maryam Aziz; children: 7. **Educ:** Hunter Col. **Career:** NY Minister Louis Farrakhan, top asst, 1965-75; Imam Muhammad, spec asst, 1976; own bus, 1977-82; Nation Islam, int rep, Louis Farrakhan, 1982-; Adventure Africa Tours, founder & owner, currently. **Orgs:** Rep, Nation Islam. **Special Achievements:** One of the most historical trips of any Black leader in the history of the United States; coordinated the publishing of Minister Farrakhan's book, "7 Speeches", published in 1973; responsible for producing four albums by Minister Farrakhan titled "Black Family Day", "Our Time Has Come", "Let Us Unite" with Rev. Jesse Jackson and "Heed the Call"; featured in weekly in more than 100 African-American newspapers nationally and also in several newspapers internationally; currently working on Minister Farrakhan's biography and a book on the history of the Nation of Islam, 1930-85. **Home Addr:** 8920 Madge Ave Suite 117, St. Louis, MO 63144. **Business Addr:** Speaker, Ghana Mission - Nation of Islam, 8816 Manchester Rd Suite 117, St. Louis, MO 63144, **Business Phone:** (314)963-0913.

### MUHAMMAD, ALI SHAHEED
Rap musician. **Personal:** Born Aug 11, 1970, Brooklyn, NY. **Career:** A Tribe Called Quest, mem; The Ummah, mem; Lucy Pearl, mem; D'Angelo, mem; Albums: People's Instinctive Travels & the Paths of Rhythm, 1990; The Low End Theory, 1991; Midnight Marauders, 1993; Kids, writer, 1995; Beats, Rhymes & Life, 1996; The Love Movement, 1998; The Anthology; Hits, 1999; Lucy Pearl, 2000; Rarities & Remixes, 2003; Shaheedullah & Stereotypes, 2004; Singles: "Bonita Applebum", "I Left My Wallet in El Segundo", "Can I Kick It?", "Check the Rhime", "Jazz (We've Got)", "Scenario", "Hot Sex", "Award Tour", "Electric Relaxation", "Oh My God", "1nce Again", "Stressed Out", "Find a Way" & "Like It like That". **Honors/Awds:** ASCAP Song writer Award. **Business Addr:** Musician, c/o BMG Entertainment Inc, 1540 Broadway Suite 9W, New York, NY 10036, **Business Phone:** (212)930-4000.

### MUHAMMAD, ASKIA
Journalist, poet, radio producer. **Personal:** Born Mar 28, 1945, Yazoo City, MS; married Alverda Ann; children: Nadirah I & Raafi. **Educ:** Los Angeles State Univ, attended 1963; Los Angeles City Col, attended 1965; San Jose State Univ, attended 1970. **Career:** Newsweek Mag, corresp, 1968; Multi-Cult Prog Foothill Col, dir, 1970-72; Muhammad Speaks News, ed chief, 1972-75; Chicago Daily Defender, Wash, corresp, 1977-78; Black Journ Rev, founder, Pac Radio Nat News Bur, diplomatic corresp, 1978-79, reporter, 1979-80; Nat Sci Mag, ed, 1978-80; Nat Pub Radio, commentator, 1980-93; WPFW Paper, ed, news dir, 1991-93, prog dir, 1994, photojournalist, currently; Christian Sci Monitor Radio, 1993-; Final Call Newspaper, White House, sr corresp & Wash bur chief, 1996-97; Author: "Behind Enemy Lines". **Orgs:** Nat Press Club; Sigma Delta Chi; Wash Automotive Press Asn; Capital Press Club; Nat Asn Black Journalists; Soc Profl Journ; Trotter Group Black opinion writers. **Home Addr:** 3636 16th St NW Apt B966, Washington, DC 20010-1124, **Home Phone:** (202)234-7437. **Business Addr:** White House Correspondence Reporter, Senior Correspondent, Final Call Newspaper, 236 Mass Ave NE Suite 610, Washington, DC 20002, **Business Phone:** (202)543-7796.

### MUHAMMAD, AVA
Clergy. **Personal:** Born Jan 1, 1951, Columbus, OH; married Darius. **Educ:** Georgetown Univ Law Ctr, Wash, DC, JD, 1975. **Career:** Muhammad Mosque No 15, head, 1998; Nat Islam, southern region rep, 1998, Southern Regional Minister, nat spokesperson to Louis Farrakhan minister, 1998; Elevated Places, radio talk show, host; Author: Real Love; Queens Planet Earth: Birth & Rise Original Woman. **Orgs:** New York Bar Asn; Muslim Girls Training. **Special Achievements:** First female Minister to preside over a mosque and region in the history of the Nation of Islam. **Business Addr:** Minister, National Spokesperson, Nation of Islam, 734 W 79th St, Chicago, IL 60620, **Business Phone:** (866)602-1230.

### MUHAMMAD, BENJAMIN CHAVIS (BENJAMIN FRANKLIN CHAVIS, JR.)
Association executive, talk show host. **Personal:** Born Jan 22, 1948, Oxford, NC; married Martha; children: 8. **Educ:** Univ NC, BA, chem, 1969; Duke Univ Divinity Sch, MA, divinity, 1980; Howard Univ, PhD, theol, 1982. **Career:** United Church Christ, Comn Racial Justice, southern regional prog dir, 1972, minister, 1972-, dep dir, exec dir; polit prisoner, NC, 1976-80; Nat Asn Advan Colored People, exec dir, 1993-94, chief exec officer; WOL-AM, Wash, DC, talk show host, 1995-97; Hip-Hop Summit Action Network, pres & chief exec officer, 2001; Nation Islam, E coast regional minister, Million Family March, nat dir, currently. **Orgs:** Civil rights organizer, Southern Christian Leadership Conf, 1967-69, youth coordr; labor organizer, AFSCME, 1969; co-chmn, Nat Alliance Against Racism & Polit Repression, 1977-; co-chmn, Southern Organizing Comn Econ & SocialJustice, 1977; chmn, Nat Coun Churches, Prophetic Justice Unit; chairperson, Southern Organizing Comt Econ & Social Justice; pres,

Angola Found; pres bd, Wash Off Africa; Phi Beta Sigma Fraternity; chief exec officer & founder, Nat African Am Leadership Summit; co-founder, Nat Black Independent Polit Party; Nat Newspaper Publishers Asn, Pres, 2014. **Honors/Awds:** George Colins Community Service Award, Congressional Black Caucus, 1977; William L Patterson Award, Patterson Found, 1977; Shalom Award, Eden TheolSem, 1977; Gertrude E Rush Distinguished Service Award, Nat Bar Asn; J E Walker Humanitarian Award, Nat Bus League; Martin Luther King Jr Freedom Award, Progressive Nat Baptist Conv. **Special Achievements:** Author, An American Political Prisoner; Appeals for Human Rights; Psalms From Prison, Pilgrim Press, 1983; United Church of Christ Commission on Racial Justice, 1979; First African Americans to attend Princeton University. **Business Addr:** East Coast Regional Minister, National Director of the Million Family March, Nation of Islam, 106-108 W 127th St Muhammad Mosque Suite 7, New York, NY 10027, **Business Phone:** (212)865-1200.

## MUHAMMAD, IBTIHAJ

Entrepreneur, athlete. **Personal:** Born Dec 4, 1985, Maplewood, NJ; daughter of Eugene and Denise. **Educ:** Duke Univ, BA, 2007. **Career:** Fencing athlete, 2003-; member of U.S. teams for Pan American Championships, 2010-16, Senior World Championships, 2010-16, Pan American Games, 2011, 2015, and the Summer Olympics, 2016; Louella, founder, 2014-. **Orgs:** Peter Westbrook Found. **Honors/Awds:** NCAA All-American, 2004, 2005, 2006; USA Fencing Junior Olympic Championships, gold medal, 2005; Pan American Championship, bronze medal (individual), gold medal (team), 2010; Pan American Championship, gold medal (team), 2011, 2012, 2013, 2015, 2016, bronze medal (team), 2014, and gold medal (individual), 2016; Pan American Games, gold medal (team), 2011, 2015; Senior World Championships, bronze medal (team), 2011, 2012, 2013, and gold medal (team), 2014, 2015; Muslim Sportswoman of the Year, 2013; Summer Olympics, bronze medal (team), 2016; Time's 100 Most Influential People of 2016 list. **Special Achievements:** The first U.S. female athlete to wear a hijab at the Olympic Games, 2016; sports ambassador, U.S. Department of State's Empowering Women and Girls Through Sport Initiative. **Business Addr:** USA Fencing, 4065 Sinton Rd Suite 140, Colorado Springs, CO 80907, **Business Phone:** (719)866-4511.

## MUHAMMAD, JAMES A.

Executive. **Personal:** Born Sep 11, 1970, Columbia, SC; son of James Arthur Williams; married Shelia Culpepper; children: Salih Rafiq. **Educ:** Stillman Col, BA, mass commun, 1992. **Career:** Ala Pub Radio, intern, reporter, producer, class host & opers mgr; Bradley Univ, WCBU-FM, prog dir, 1998-2001; WVa Pub Broadcasting, dir radio programming, 2001-; Pub broadcasting, consult; The Ctr for Pub Tv, prod asst & narrator; Lakeshore Pub Media, pres & chief exec officer, 2013. **Orgs:** Alpha Phi Alpha Fraternity; Sigma Pi Phi Fraternity; Pub Radio Prog dir Asn; Eastern Region Pub Radio; bd mem, Wva Music Hall Fame; Nat Pub Radio's Comt. **Home Addr:** 600 Capitol St, Charleston, WV 25301, **Home Phone:** (304)556-4921. **Business Addr:** Director of Radio Programming, West Virginia Public Broadcasting, 600 Capitol St, Charleston, WV 25301, **Business Phone:** (304)556-4900.

## MUHAMMAD, KHALIL GIBRAN

Scholar, writer, executive director. **Personal:** Born Apr 1, 1972?, Chicago, IL; son of Ozier Muhammad. **Educ:** University of Pennsylvania, B.A. in Economics, 1993; Rutgers University, Ph.D. in History, 2004. **Career:** Andrew W. Mellon, Postdoctoral Fellow at Vera Institute of Justice, 2003-05; Indiana University, Asst. Professor of History, 2005-11; "Journal of American History," Associate Editor, 2010-11; Schomburg Center for Research in Black Culture, Director, 2011-. **Orgs:** John Hope Franklin Publication Prize for "The Condemnation of Blackness"; "Crain's New York Business," 40 Under Forty, 2011; "The Root" Magazine, The Root 100 Honorees, 2012, 2013. **Honors/Awds:** A great-grandson of Nation of Islam founder Elijah Muhammad; author of "The Condemnation of Blackness: Race, Crime and the Making of Modern Urban America," Harvard University Press (2010); regular appearances on news program "Melissa Harris-Perry Show".

## MUHAMMAD, MARIAN

President (organization), vice president (organization). **Personal:** Born Wilson, NC; daughter of Marvin Wilkins Sr and Helen (deceased); children: Dawn, Mahasin, AlNissa, Mikki, Nicole, Ali, Omar & Kato. **Educ:** BS, socio-econs; BBA, bus admin. **Career:** NJ Div Consumer Affairs, dir, 1971; Int Boxing Fedn/Us Boxing Asn, assist pres, exec secy, 1983-2001; exec secy & treas, 1999-2001, pres, 2001-; Combative Sports Fedn, vpres. **Orgs:** Am Cancer Soc; Schomburg Ctr Res Black Cult; Abandoned Babies Ctr; Essex County Educ Servs Comn; Nat HIV-AIDS Found; Peoples Org Progress; silver life mem, Nat Asn Advan Colored People; Nat Campaign Tolerance; Nat Asn Female Execs; Juv Diabetes Found; Feed C; world boxing sanctioning orgn. **Home Addr:** 3509 Appleberry Ct, Wilson, NC 27896-1874. **Business Addr:** President, International Boxing Federation, 899 Mountain Ave Suite 2C, Springfield, NJ 07081, **Business Phone:** (973)564-8046.

## MUHAMMAD, MUHSIN, II (MELVIN DARNELL CAMPBELL, JR.)

Football player, executive. **Personal:** Born May 5, 1973, Lansing, MI; married Christa; children: Jordan Taylor, Chase Soen, Muhsin III & Kennedy. **Educ:** Mich State Univ, BS, telecommunication, 1995. **Career:** Football player (retired), exec, color commentator; Carolina Panthers, wide receiver, left guard, 1996-2005, 2008-09; Fox, NFL Europe, color commentator, 2002, 2003, corresp; Big Ten Network, color commentator; Chicago Bears, wide receiver, 2005-08; NFL Players Asn, team rep, 2006-10; Ruckus House Learning Ctr, owner & mgr, 2005-11; Axum Capital Partners, managing partner, 2008-. **Orgs:** Founder, M2 Found Kids; spokesperson, Muscular Dystrophy Asn. **Honors/Awds:** Panthers Man of the Year; Pro Bowl, 1999, 2004; All-Pro, 2004; NFC champion, 2003, 2006; Alumni Wide Receiver of the Year, Nat Football League, 2004; Yards Leader, Nat Football League, 2004; Touchdowns Leader, Nat Football League, 2004; Super Bowl, XXXVIII; Emmy Award, Acad Tv Arts & Sci, Nat Acad Tv Arts & Sci, 2005. **Business Addr:** Managing Partner, Axum Capital Partners, 6100 Fairview Rd Suite 1156, Charlotte, NC 28210, **Business Phone:** (704)334-3334.

## MUHAMMAD, SHIRLEY M.

Executive. **Personal:** Born Apr 28, 1938, Chicago, IL; married Warith Deen; children: Laila, Ngina, Warithdeen & Sadrud-Din. **Educ:** Cortez Peters Bus Col, attended 1957; Wilson Jr Col, attended 1958. **Career:** Clara Muhammad Memorial Fund, pres, 1976-. **Orgs:** Pres, CMMEF, 1976-; bd dir, Pkwy Comm House, 1982; Provident Hosp, 1983. **Home Addr:** 8752 Cornell Ave, Chicago, IL 60617-2704, **Home Phone:** (773)731-8990. **Business Addr:** President, Clara Muhammad Memorial Education Foundation Inc, 1625 E 74th St, Chicago, IL 60649, **Business Phone:** (312)487-9709.

## MUHAMMAD, DR. TIY-E

Sex therapist, entertainer, athlete. **Educ:** Eastern Ill Univ, BA, polit sci & hist, 1992, MS, psychol, 1993; Southern Ill Univ, Carbondale, IL, PhD, psychol, 1999; Fla Coastal Sch Law, JD, 2013. **Career:** Morris Brown Col; Clark Atlanta Univ, prof psychol; Hot 107.9 FM, host; life coach; sex therapist; playwright; radio/tv personality; dancer & athlete; Man II Man Develop Inc, founder & chief exec officer, 1998-. **Orgs:** Phi Beta Sigma Fraternity Inc; Prince Hall affiliated Mason; founder, 1-Step Above; founder, Men Against Molestation. **Honors/Awds:** Most Eligible Bachelor, Ebony Magazine. **Special Achievements:** First black professor on the TBS reality series; Book: Secrets Men Keep; My Mind, My Body, My Spirit. **Home Addr:** 604 Beckwith St, Atlanta, GA 30314. **Business Addr:** Chief Executive Officer, Founder, Man II Man Development Inc, 659 Auburn Ave NE, Atlanta, GA 30312, **Business Phone:** (404)221-9003.

## MULLEN, HARRYETTE

Poet. **Personal:** Born Jul 1, 1953, Florence, AL. **Educ:** Univ Tex, Austin, BA, 1975; Univ Calif, Santa Cruz, MA, 1989, PhD, 1990. **Career:** Austin Community Col, TX, Instrnl Asst, instr, 1975-77; Manpower, Austin, TX, temp off worker, 1977-79; Tex Comn Arts, Beaumont & Galveston, artist schs, 1978-81; Dobie-Paisano writer's fel, Tex Inst Lett & Univ Tex, 1981-82; Univ Calif, Santa Cruz, teaching asst, 1985-89, vis lectr/dissertation fel, 1988-89; Cornell Univ, Ithaca, NY, asst prof, 1989-95; Univ Calif, Los Angeles, assoc prof, 1995-03, prof 2003-; Poems: Tree Tall Woman, 1981; Trimmings, 1991; Spermkt, 1992; Muse & Drudge, 1995; Sleeping with the Dictionary, 2002; Blues Baby, 2002; Recyclopedia: Trimmings, Spermkt, and Muse and Drudge, 2006; Short stories: Bad Girls and Pica", 1982; What Can't Be Measured, 1986; Sugar Sandwiches, 1987; Tenderhead, 1990. **Honors/Awds:** Artist grant, Helene Wurlitzer Found NMex, 1981-82; Literature Award, Black Arts Acad, Dallas, 1986; Rockefeller Fel, Susan B Anthony Ctr for Women's Studies, Univ Rochester, NY, 1994-95; Katherine Newman Award for Best Essay, MELUS, 1996; artist residency, Va for the Arts, 1999; Nat Book Award, poetry finalist, 2002; Los Angeles Times Book Prize, poetry finalist, 2003; Nat Book Critics Circle Award, poetry finalist, 2003; Award in poetry, Found for Contemporary Arts, 2004; fel award, John Simon Guggenheim Mem Found, 2005; PEN Beyond Margins Award, 2007. **Special Achievements:** Poetry collection: Sleeping with the Dictionary (2002), was a finalist for a National Book Award, National Book Critics Circle Award, and Los Angeles Times Book Prize; Blues Baby, 2002; Dim Lady, 2003; Recyclopedia: Trimmings, S*PeRM**K*T, and Muse and Drudge, 2006. **Business Addr:** Professor, University of California at Los Angeles, 149 Humanities Bldg, Los Angeles, CA 90095-1530, **Business Phone:** (310)825-7553.

## MULLEN, RODERICK LOUIS

Manager, football player. **Personal:** Born Dec 5, 1972, Baton Rouge, LA; married Deneca; children: Roderick M J II, Meagan & Layla. **Educ:** Grambling State Univ, BS, criminal justice. **Career:** Football player (retired), adminr; Green Bay Packers, defensive back, 1995-98; Carolina Panthers, corner back, 1999; Minn Vikings, safety, 2000; Las Vega prop, investor, 2001-02; Bally Total Fitness, gen mgr, 2002-; Cintas, capt-sales rep, 2009-14; Cintas Corp, mkt sales mgr, 2009-currently. **Honors/Awds:** Rookie of the Year, 1995; Elite Performer Award; President's Club, David Montgomery, 2013 & 2015; President's Club, Diamond Level, David Montgomery, 2014. **Business Addr:** General Manager, Bally Total Fitness, 3232 McKinney Ave, Dallas, TX 75204-7414, **Business Phone:** (214)871-7700.

## MULLENS, DELBERT W.

Executive. **Personal:** Born Nov 14, 1944, New York, NY; son of Edythe J; married Lula Sweat; children: Dorian & Mandy. **Educ:** Tenn State Univ, Nashville, TN, BS, 1968; Univ NY, Buffalo, NY, MS, 1974. **Career:** Flint Coatings Inc, Flint, Mich, pres, dir, chief exec officer, 1983-98; Wesley Financial Corp, pres & chief exec officer, 1990-; Margate Industs Inc, dir, 1990-2001; NHF, pres, 1992-; Prod-SDL Chem Inc, chmn, currently. **Orgs:** Omega Psi Phi Fraternity, 1965-; pres, Nat Asn Black Automotive Suppliers, 1990-; sr mem, Soc Mfg Engrs, 1984-; trustee, Univ Buffalo; chair Grad Sch Educ comt. **Home Addr:** 2888 Bloomfield Crossings, Bloomfield Hills, MI 48013. **Business Addr:** Chief Executive Officer, President, Wesley Financial Corp, 2100 N Woodward Ave Suite 395, Bloomfield Hills, MI 48340, **Business Phone:** (248)203-9906.

## MULLINGS, PAUL

Executive. **Educ:** Inst Acct Staff, London, eng. **Career:** Int Tel & Tel (ITT), manger, budgets & financial anal, 1976-79; Glendale Fed Bank, exec vpres, mgr retail lending, 1979-92; First Interstate Bank, pres & chief exec officer1992-96; Mortgage Electronic Regist Systs Inc, pres & chief exec officer, 1996-97; JP Morgan Chase & Co, Home Finance, sr vpres, mgr mortgage finance chase home, 1997-2005; Freddie Mac, sr vpres single family mortgage sourcing, 2005-, Strategic Bus Initiatives, Head Sourcing & Securitization Single Family Bus, Head Sourcing Single Family Bus, interim head Single-Family Bus, 2012-; Chase Home Finance, fair lending exec. **Business Addr:** Senior Vice President, Freddie Mac, 8200 Jones Br Dr, McLean, VA 22102, **Business Phone:** (703)903-2000.

## MULLINS, JARRETT R.

Executive. **Personal:** Born Nov 16, 1957, South Bend, IN; son of Ralph and Mary; married Kathy; children: Kevin & John. **Educ:** Auburn Univ, BS, 1980. **Career:** Fed Express Corp, sr mgr, cust serv, 1984-88; US Sprint, group mgr sales, 1988-91; Purator Courier, managing dir, customer serv & sales, 1991-93; TLI, dir, customer serv, 1993-94; Zenith Electronics, vpres sales, 1994-. **Orgs:** Kappa Alpha Psi; Nat Asn Minorities in Cable; CTAM. **Home Addr:** 704 Old Oak Rd, Livermore, CA 94550-8657.

## MUMFORD, ESTHER HALL

Writer, editor, publisher. **Personal:** Born Jan 20, 1941, Ruston, LA; daughter of Nona Mae and Shellie O; married Donald Emerson; children: Donald Toussaint & Zola Marie. **Educ:** Southern Univ, 1959; Univ Wash, BA, polit sci, 1964. **Career:** Wash State Arch, oral hist interviewer; Ananse Press, co-publ, writer & researcher, 1980-, managing ed; Off Archaeol & Hist Preserv, researcher; King Co Hist Preserv Off, oral hist interviewer; Wash Comn Humanities, lectr; Yesler Terr Comn Coun, outreach worker; assoc cur, Mus Hist & Indust; Douglass-Truth Libr, African Am Mus, Tacoma; proj consult, State Centennial Exhibs; African Americans Northwest, lectr; Ananse Press, founder, ed, currently; Publ: Seattle's Black Victorians 1852-1901, 1980; Seven Stars & Orion: Reflections of the Past, editor, 1986; The Man Who Founded A Town; Calabash: A Guide to the History, Culture & Art of African-Am in Seattle & King Co, 1993; independent researcher & writer, currently. **Orgs:** Founding mem, Black Heritage Soc Wash State; Nat Trust Hist Preserv; Asn King County Hist Orgns; Episcopal Women's Hist Proj; bd dir, Raven Chronicles; Festvial Sundiata Prog Comm; adv bd mem, Wash Women's Hist Consortium. **Honors/Awds:** Aspasia Phoutrides Pulakis Award, Ethnic Heritage Council NW; Wash Living Treasure, Wash State Centennial Comn; Peace & Friendship Medal, Wash State Capital Museum; Award for Outstanding Scholarly Achievement in Black Studies, Natl Coun For Black Studies, Pacific NW Region; Voices of Kuumba Award, NW African Am Writers Workshop; Seattle Heritage Award, Museum of History & Industry; Cert of Recognition for Preservation of King Co, WA, History; Black Heritage Society Award, First African Methodist Episcopal Church; Heritage Organizations Award, Asn King County. **Home Addr:** 1504 32nd Ave S, Seattle, WA 98144-3918, **Home Phone:** (206)325-8205. **Business Addr:** Editor, Ananse Press, 1504 32nd Ave S, Seattle, WA 98144-3918, **Business Phone:** (206)325-8205.

## MUMFORD, PROF. JEFFREY CARLTON

Educator, composer. **Personal:** Born Jun 22, 1955, Washington, DC; son of Thaddeus Q and Sylvia J; married Donna Coleman; children: Blythe Coleman. **Educ:** Univ Calif, Irvine, BA, 1977; Univ Calif, San Diego, MA, 1981. **Career:** Settlement Music Sch, theory, comp inst, 1985-89; Westchester Conserv Music, theory instr, 1986-89; Wash Bach Consort, asst dir, 1989-90; Wash Conserv Music, theory, comp instr, 1989-99; Concert Soc, MD, sem coordr, prod supvr, 1990-95; Guggenheim Found Fel, 1995; Bowling Green State Univ, artist-in-residence, 1999-2000; Oberlin Col, asst prof compos music, composer-in-residence, 2003-06; Lorain County Community Col, Distinguished vis prof, 2008-; Recordings: Fragments From Surrounding Eve; Focus Blue Light; A Window Resonant Light; promise far horizon; Dark Fires; wending; A landscape interior resonances; Milliner's Fancy, barbaglio dal manca; a Fel to Composers' Conf, Johnson, Vt. **Orgs:** Bd dir, League Composers, Int Soc Contemp Music, US Chap, 1990-; bd dir, Nat Acad Rec Arts & Sci, 1997-99; adv bd, Bascom Little Fund, 2005-. **Home Addr:** 108 E Col St, Oberlin, OH 44074-1609, **Home Phone:** (440)774-1583. **Business Addr:** Composer, Carlson & Carlson Arts Contractors, 10208 Lake Gardens Dr, Dallas, TX 75218.

## MUMFORD, THADDEUS QUENTIN, JR. (THAD MUMFORD)

Television producer, writer. **Personal:** Born Feb 8, 1951, Washington, DC. **Educ:** Hampton Univ, attended 1969; Fordham Univ, attended 1971. **Career:** TV series: "That's My Mama", script consult, 1975; "What's Happening!!", story ed, 1976, 1977-78; "Maude", story ed, 1976-77; "Sesame Street", actor, 1978-92; "Angie", exec story ed, 1979; The Electric Company, 1971; Twentieth Century Fox, Los Angeles CA, "MASH"; writer & producer, 1979-83; "The Duck Factory", producer, 1984; Alien Prod, "ALF", writer & supv producer, 1986-87; "The Cosby Show", writer, 1986; Carsey-Werner, Studio City CA, "A Different World", writer & supv producer, 1987-88, head writer & co-exec producer, 1988-90; CBS Entertainment, "Bagdad Cafe", head writer & co-exec producer, 1990; "Time Out: The Truth About HIV, AIDS & You", 1992; "Home Improvement", writer, 1995; "Judging Amy", writer, 2001. **Orgs:** Writers Guild Am, 1971-; Am Soc Composers, Artists & Performers, 1973-; Humanitas Comt, 1984; Nat Asn Advan Colored People, 1984; SaveC, 1986-; Friends Friendless, 1986-; Los Angeles Partnership Homeless, 1986-. **Honors/Awds:** Primetime Emmy Award, 1973; Writers Guild Award, 1974, 1980. **Home Addr:** 3130 Oakshire Dr, Los Angeles, CA 90068. **Business Addr:** Writer, c/o Ronald Koblin, 9478 W Olympic Blvd Suite 300, Beverly Hills, CA 90212.

## MUMPHREY, JERRY WAYNE

Baseball player. **Personal:** Born Sep 9, 1952, Tyler, TX; married Gloria; children: Tamara & Jerron. **Career:** Baseball player (retired); St Louis Cardinals, outfielder, 1974-79; San Diego Padres, outfielder, 1980; NY Yankees, outfielder, 1981-83; Houston Astros, outfielder, 1983-85; Chicago Cubs, outfielder, 1986-88. **Home Addr:** 7709 FM 850, Tyler, TX 75706.

## MUNDAY, DR. CHERYL CASSELBERRY

Clinical psychologist, educator. **Personal:** Born Jan 20, 1950, Osaka; married Reuben Alexander; children: Reuben Ahmed. **Educ:** Cornell Univ, BA, 1972; Univ Mich, MA, 1978, PhD, 1985. **Career:** Detroit Psychol Inst, dir psychol; Birmingham, Mich, pvt pract; Sinai Hosp, consult/fac; Univ Detroit Mercy, asst prof, assoc prof psychol, 1997-, Psychol Clin, dir, currently. **Orgs:** Am Psychol Asn; Mich Psychol Asn. **Home Addr:** 18994 Birchcrest Dr, Detroit, MI 48221-2227. **Business Addr:** Director, University of Detroit Mercy, Reno Hall 142

4001 W McNichols Rd, Detroit, MI 48221-3038, **Business Phone:** (313)578-0518.

### MUNDAY, REUBEN A.
Lawyer. **Personal:** Born Mar 2, 1947, East Orange, NJ; married Cheryl Casselberry; children: Reuben Ahmed. **Educ:** Cornell Univ, Ithaca, NY, BA, eng, 1971, MPS, 1974; Univ Mich Law Sch, Ann Arbor, MI, JD, law, 1976. **Career:** Cornell Univ, staff writer, 1972-74; Coun Real Property Law Sect State Bar Mich, mem, officer; Lewis & Munday Law Firm, atty, partner & shareholder, 1977-, pres & chief exec officer, 1994-2003, chmn & shareholder, currently; Real Estate Pract Group, pract group leader. **Orgs:** Detroit Bar Asn; Wolverine Bar Asn; life Mem Nat Bar Asn; Am Bar Asn; bd dir, Fund Detroits Future; bd dir, City Detroit Bd Ethics, 2001-; bd dir, St John Detroit Macomb Hosp Corp, Big Bros Big Sisters Am, Leadership Detroit Prog Detroit Regional Chamber Com; bd dir, Wyo Sem Col Prep Sch; Mich bar asn; Cornell Univ Coun; Mich Roundtable Diversity & Inclusion; bd dir, Greening Detroit; bd dir, Mosaic Youth Theatre; bd dir, Detroit Inst Arts; bd dir, Detroit Econ Growth Corp; bd mem, City Yr Detroit. **Business Addr:** Chairman, Attorney, Lewis & Munday Law Firm, 535 Griswold St Suite 2300, Detroit, MI 48226, **Business Phone:** (313)961-2550.

### MUNOZ, ANTHONY (MICHAEL ANTHONY MUNOZ)
Football player, social worker, television show host. **Personal:** Born Aug 19, 1958, Ontario, CA; married DeDe; children: Michael & Michelle. **Educ:** Univ Southern Calif, BS, pub admin, 1980. **Career:** Football player (retired), social worker, color commentator; Cincinnati Bengals, offensive tackle, 1980-92; Tampa Bay Buccaneers, 1993; Fox Sports, Nat Football League Telecasts, color commentator, 1994-95. Films: "Borderline"; "The Right Stuff". **Orgs:** Founder & pres, Anthony Munoz Found, 2002-; Crusade life; United Appeal; chmn, Billy Graham Mission, 2002. **Honors/Awds:** Man of the Year, Cincinnati Bengals, 1981; Three times Offensive Lineman of the Year, Nat Football League, 1981, 1987, 1988; Bart Starr Man of the Year Award, 1989; Man of the Year, Nat Football League, 1991; Walter Payton Man of the Year Award, 1991; Pro Football Hall of Fame, 1998; Allstate dedicated a Hometown Hall of Famers plaque at Chaffey High School, 2012. **Special Achievements:** Only Pro Football Hall of Fame inductee in Cincinnati Bengals history; Motion Pictures: Borderline, 1980, The Right Stuff, 1983. **Business Addr:** Founder, President, Anthony Munoz Foundation, 8919 Rossash Rd, Cincinnati, OH 45236, **Business Phone:** (513)772-4900.

### MUNOZ, MICHAEL ANTHONY. See MUNOZ, ANTHONY.

### MUNROE, DR. ANTHONY E.
Chief executive officer. **Personal:** Born Bronx, NY; married Michelle Marie Francis. **Educ:** Excelsior Col, Albany, NY, lib arts; Columbia Univ, NY, MA, pub health; Northwestern Univ, Evanston, IL, MBA, bus admin. **Career:** Brookdale Hosp Med Ctr, Brooklyn, NY, adminr; pres & chief exec officer, Econ Opportunity Family Health Ctr, Miami, FL, 1998-2003; St John Detroit Riverview Hosp, St John Health Syst, Warren, Mi, pres, 2003-05; Advocate Trinity Hosp, pres, 2005-07; Munroe Mgt Group LLC, chmn & chief exec officer, 2007-; Ross Univ, Bahamas, exec admin, 2009-10; City Cols Chicago, pres, currently; Malcom X Col, pres, 2011-15. **Orgs:** Fel, ACHE; Memorial Sloan-Kettering Cancer Ctr; NY City Health & Hosps Corp; New York Dept Health; dir Community Health Prom, DeKalb County Bd Health, Decatur, GA; Missionary Baptist Church, Ill; life mem, vice chmm, Alpha Phi Alpha Fraternity Inc; bd dir, Health Choice Network; advisor, Miami Fels Prog; community adv bd, Brooklyn Med Ctr; Int Scholar Exchange. **Business Addr:** President, Chief Executive Officer, Munroe Management Group, Chicago, IL.

### MUNSON, CHERYL DENISE
Executive. **Personal:** Born Aug 3, 1954, Milwaukee, WI; daughter of John and Mattie Waldon. **Educ:** Univ Wis, Madison, WI, BA, jour, 1975. **Career:** Leo Burnett Advert, Chicago, Ill, intern, 1975; Kloppenberg, Switzer & Teich Advert, Milwaukee, Wis, writer/producer, 1976-80; Foote, Cone & Belding Advert, San Francisco, Calif, copywriter, 1980-84; Leo Burnett USA; Visions USA; Saatchi & Saatchi X; Love Auntie Cheryl Greetings Inc, San Francisco, Calif, chief exec officer & founder, 1985-96; Mason, advert creative dir & insight & shopper mkt expert, currently. **Orgs:** Greeting Card Asn Am, 1985; Third Baptist Church, 1980-. **Home Addr:** 910 Forest Overlook Trail, Atlanta, GA 30331, **Home Phone:** (404)806-9211. **Business Addr:** Advert Creative Director, Insight & Shopper Marketing Expert, MUNSON, 910 Forest Overlook Trail, Atlanta, GA 30331, **Business Phone:** (404)567-5796.

### MUNSON, EDDIE RAY
Certified public accountant. **Personal:** Born Aug 4, 1950, Columbus, MS; son of Ray and Rosetta Moore; married Delores Butler; children: Eddie III & Derek. **Educ:** Jackson State Univ, BS, acct, 1972. **Career:** Peat Marwick Main & Co, partner, 1972, audit partner, 1983; KPMG Detroit Off, managing partner, 1993-2003; KPMG LLP, chmn, 2003-06; Bearingpoint Inc, dir, 2007-, chief financial officer, 2008; Caraco Pharmaceut Labs Ltd, dir, 2010-. **Orgs:** MS Soc CPAs, 1977-, Am Inst CPAs, 1980-, Mich Asn CPAs, 1980-; bd dir, Acct Aid Soc, 1984-, Black Family Develop Inc, 1984-, Boys & Girls Clubs, 1989-; bd dir, YMCA, Detroit, MI; bd dir, Urban League, Detroit, MI; Nat Asn Black Acct; dir, United Am Healthcare Corp, 2006-; bd trustee, Skillman Found; Detroit Financial Adv Bd; trustee, Henry Ford Health Syst finance comt; trustee, Jackson State Develop Found. **Home Addr:** 5879 Murfield Dr, Rochester Hills, MI 48306, **Home Phone:** (313)357-4116. **Business Addr:** Chief Financial Officer, Board of Director, BearingPoint Inc, 1050 Wilshire Dr Suite 345, Troy, MI 48084, **Business Phone:** (248)430-3030.

### MUNSON, ROBERT H.
Engineer, executive director. **Personal:** Born Jan 15, 1931, Detroit, MI; married Shirley C Segars; children: Renee Angelique & Rochelle Alicia. **Educ:** Detroit Inst Technol, BS, chem, 1966; Mich State Univ, MBA, 1977. **Career:** Ford Sci Lab, metall engr, 1956; Ford Motor Co, mats design engr, sect supvr front end sect, bumper sect, body engineering off, dept mgr elec components lighting dept body & elec engineering off, exec engr paint corrosion & mats engineering body & elec engineering off, exec engr lighting bumpers & grills, exec engr advan & pre-prog engineering, exec engr instrument panels & elec systs, chief engr N Am design, chief plastics engr plastics prods div, dir automotive safety off environ & safety engineering staff; Automotive Safety & Engineering Stand Off, dir, currently. **Orgs:** Am Soc Body Engineering; Am Metals Soc; Ford Col Recruiting Prog; Adv Bd Col Engineering, Univ Detroit; engineering sch sponsor, NC A&T State Univ; Engineering Soc Detroit, Soc Automotive Engrs; Motor Vehicle Safety Res, adv comt; life mem, Nat Asn Advan Colored People. **Honors/Awds:** Blue Ribbon Award, Am Soc Metals, 1963; Congress & Exposition Detroit. **Special Achievements:** Co-author, A Modified Carbide Extraction Replica Technique in Transactions, Quart, 1963; Metallographis Examination of the Corrosion Mechanism of Plated Plastics, 1969; SAE Int Automotive Engr; Air Bag Supplemental Restraint Systems: Progress to Date and Future Challenges. **Home Addr:** 1668 Sweetwater West Cir, Apopka, FL 32712-2485, **Home Phone:** (407)880-2746. **Business Addr:** Director, Automotive Safety Engineering Standards Office, 330 Town Ctr Dr Suite 400, Dearborn, MI 48126, **Business Phone:** (313)845-4320.

### MURDOCK, ERIC LLOYD
Basketball coach, executive, basketball player. **Personal:** Born Jun 14, 1968, Somerville, NJ. **Educ:** Providence Col, BA, 1991. **Career:** Basketball player (retired), coach, executive; Utah Jazz, pt guard, 1991-92; Milwaukee Bucks, pt guard, 1992-95; Vancouver Grizzlies, pt guard, 1995-96; Fortitudo Bologna, Italy, pt guard, 1996-97; Denver Nuggets, pt guard, 1996; Teamsystem Bologna, Italy, pt guard, 1996-97; Miami Heat, pt guard, 1997-98; NJ Nets, pt guard, 1999; Los Angeles Clippers, pt guard, 1999-2000; Grand Rapids Hoops, 2002; Virtus Bologna, 2002-03; Kinder Bologna, Italy, 2002-03; Jersey Squires, 2003; Pingry Sch, coach, 2007-08; Rutgers Univ, Dir Player Develop, 2010-12; Stapleton's Restaurant & Lounge, owner, 2013-. **Orgs:** March Dimes, Blue Jeans For Babies; Bucks/YMCA Basketball Clin, Athletes For Youth Prog. **Home Addr:** 539 N Bridge St, Bridgewater, NJ 08807-2109, **Home Phone:** (908)722-7240. **Business Addr:** Owner, Stapleton's Restaurant and Lounge, 122 Thompson St, Raritan, NJ 08869, **Business Phone:** (908)707-2400.

### MURDOCK, DR. NATHANIEL H.
Health services administrator. **Personal:** Born Texas City, TX; married Sandra Lee; children: 2. **Educ:** Howard Univ, Wash DC, BS, chem, 1958; Meharry Medical Col, Nashville, TN, MD, 1963. **Career:** Professor (retired), physician; Homer G. Phillips Hosp, St. Louis; Wash Univ, fac, 1969-; Wash Univ, obstet & gynec clin asst prof, assoc prof, resident asst path, exec vice chancellor med affairs, Sch Med, dean; Barnes-Jewish Hosp, asst prof; Nathaniel H Murdock Md Inc, physician. **Orgs:** Cent Eastern Mo Prof Rev Org Comt; Mo State Med Asn; Mound City Med Forum; St. Louis Gynec Soc; St. Louis Metrop Med Soc; St. Louis Gynec Soc; pres, Nat Med Asn, 1997; bd mem, Primaris; Am Col Obstetricians-Gynecologists. **Business Addr:** Physician, Nathaniel H Murdock Md Inc, 1 Barnes-Jewish Hosp Plz, St. Louis, MO 63110, **Business Phone:** (314)361-0313.

### MURDOCK, PATRICIA GREEN
Educator, school administrator. **Personal:** Born Dec 12, 1949, Richmond, VA; daughter of William and Josephine Evelyn; married Hugh Jr; children: Elwin Michael & Patrice Michelle Cotman. **Educ:** Va Union Univ, BA, 1972; Va Commonwealth Univ, MSW, 1974; Am Univ, WA, DC, MSPR, 1980. **Career:** Va Union Univ, Richmond Va, dir practicum, dir urban studies, 1974-76; Nat Coun Negro Women-Opn Sisters United, Nat resource developer, nat dir, nat prog vol coordr, 1977-81; Women's Ctr & Shelter Greater Pittsburgh, community outreach cordr, 1983-87; Community Col Allegheny County, Pittsburgh, adj prof sociol, 1988-89; Partnerships Educ, cordr, opendoors, 1991; La Roche col, dir pub rels, adj prof, 1992-; Duquesne Univ, adj prof, 1995-. **Orgs:** Nat Coun Negro Women, pres, Pittsburgh secy, 1989-92; YWCA NominatingComt, 1992; bd dir, Am Wind Symphony Orchestra, 1992; bd dir, MyastheniaGravis Asn Western Pa, 1991-; Pub Rels Soc Am, 1996; Pa Black ConfHigher Educ, 1993; bd dir, Beginning with Bks, 1996. **Home Addr:** 4828 Mossfield Ct, Pittsburgh, PA 15224, **Home Phone:** (412)367-9299. **Business Addr:** Assistant to the President for Community Relations, La Roche College, 9000 Babcock Blvd, Pittsburgh, PA 15237-5898, **Business Phone:** (412)536-1272.

### MURFREE, DR. JOSHUA, JR.
Civil rights activist. **Educ:** Ft Valley State Col, psychol, BA, 1978; Valdosta State Col, MS, clin coun psychol, 1980; Howard Univ, Grad Sch Arts & Sci, PhD, coun psychol, 1987; Albany State Univ, educ, educ leadership & admin, gen, 2012. **Career:** Valdosta State Col, Dept Psychol, grad asst, 1979-80; Nursing homes Montgomery, consult, 1980-82; Community Ment Health Ctr, behav specialist, 1980-83; Sutton Plaza Dormitory, grad asst, 1983-86; Northwest Ga Regional Hosp, staff psychologist, 1988-98; Berry Col, Dept Educ & Psychol, Adj Prof, 1988-98; Shorter Col, Dept Psychol, Adj Prof, 1990-98; Ment Health, 1990-94; Regional Nat Col Athletic Asn championship selection comt, interim athletics dir, 2006-; Albany State Univ, Dept Psychol, Sociol & Social Work, chmn, 1999-, exec asst, admin chief staff, dir athletics, 2006-. **Orgs:** Nat/int chmn & vice chmn prog, 100 Black Men Am; adv group mem, Reading Fundamental Multicultural Literacy Campaign; chmn, Albany State Univ, 1999-; pres, Albany State Univ, 2006-; Am Educ Res Asn; Am Asn Coun & Develop; Asn Black Psychologist; Am Psychol Asn; Phi Beta Sigma Fraternity Inc; Beta Kappa Chi Sci Hon Soc; Kappa Delta Pi Hon Soc Educ; Nat Asn Personnel Workers; Am Bd Forensic Examiners; Chmn, Ethnic Minority Affairs Comt; bd dir, Ethnic minority Success Comt Floyd Col; bd dir, Mercy Sr Care; bd dir, Am Red Cross; chmn, vice chmn Progs, Nat Mentoring Comt 100 Black Men Am; pres, 100 Black Men Rome Inc; dir, Ctr African-Am Male; Grad Stud Coun. **Home Addr:** 2301 Andrews Garden Ct, Albany, GA 31721, **Home Phone:** (229)446-6657. **Business Addr:** Member, President's Cabinet, Albany State Univ, 504 College Dr, Albany, GA 31705, **Business Phone:** (229)430-4896.

### MURPHY, CALVIN JEROME
Basketball player, radio host. **Personal:** Born May 9, 1948, Norwalk, CT; married Vernetta; children: 3. **Educ:** Niagara Univ, NY, attended 1970. **Career:** Basketball player (retired), radio host; Purple Eagles, 1967-68; San Diego Rockets, guard, point guard, 1970-71; Houston Rockets, guard, point guard, 1970-83, 1976-77; Tv broadcaster, currently; ESPN, Calvin Murphy Show, host, 2007-10. **Orgs:** Conn Coaches Asn; fel Basketball Hall Fame; fel Rockets Broadcast Team; Rockets Orgn; Iota Phi Theta fraternity. **Honors/Awds:** NBA All-Rookie Team, 1971; NBA All-Star Game, 1979; Conn Coaches Asn Hall of Fame; Conn Sportswriters Gold Key Award; J. Walter Kennedy Citizenship Award, 1979; Naismith Basketball Hall of Fame, 1993. **Special Achievements:** Used his voice as a color commentator for Play Station NBA Live, 2003. **Business Addr:** Show Host, ESPN Ticket FM 97.5, 9801 Westheimer Suite 700, Houston, TX 77042, **Business Phone:** (713)266-1000.

### MURPHY, DANIEL HOWARD (DAN MURPHY)
Marketing executive, manager, association executive. **Personal:** Born Aug 13, 1944, Washington, DC; son of John Henry and Alice Adeline Quivers; married Bernadette Francine Brown; children: Brett Nicole & Lynn Teresa. **Educ:** Wharton Sch, Univ Pa, Philadelphia, Pa, BS, econs, 1966; Phillips Exeter Acad, BS, econs. **Career:** McCormick Spice Co, Baltimore, Md, proj supvr mkt res, 1966-70; Gen Foods, White Plains, New York, brand res supvr, 1970-73; Hunt Wesson Foods, Fullerton, Calif, prod res mgr, 1973-76; RJ Reynolds Tobacco Co, Winston-Salem, NC, bd res mgr, 1976-80, brand mgr, 1980-85, sr grp mkt res mgr, 1985-; Insights Mkt Group, vpres; Quirks.com, contribr; Diag Res Inc, vpres & gen mgr; Babcock Grad Sch Mgt Wake Forest Univ, guest lectr; NorthCarolina.com, vpres & gen mgr off diag res; Afro Am Newspaper, bd mem. **Orgs:** Bd dir, Winston-Salem Tennis Inc, 1986-; grammateus, Sigma Pi Phi Fraternity, 1986-; bd mem, YMCA, Winston Lake, 1988-; Alpha Phi Alpha Fraternity, 1990-. **Home Addr:** 321 Stanaford Rd, Winston-Salem, NC 27104, **Home Phone:** (336)765-8407. **Business Addr:** Senior Manager of Communications Research, RJ Reynolds Tobacco Co, 401 N Main St, Winston-Salem, NC 27102, **Business Phone:** (336)741-5000.

### MURPHY, DR. DONALD RICHARD, II
Lawyer, manager. **Personal:** Born Aug 1, 1938, Johnstown, PA; married Carol Handy; children: Steven, Michael & Richard. **Educ:** Wilberforce Univ, BA, econ, 1958; NY Law Sch, JD, 1969. **Career:** IBM Corp, acct supvr, 1963-66; Chem Bank NY, oper mgr, 1966-69; Soc Nat Bank, vpres, 1969-73; Sherwin Williams Co, staff atty & asst dir laborrel, 1973-83; Forest City Enterprises Inc, atty, currently. **Orgs:** Cleveland Comn OH Fund Independent Col, 1970-; Cuyahoga City Bar Asn, 1972-; adv mem, United Negro Col Fund, 1974-82; EEO Sub Comt, Am Bar Asn, 1974-; bd trustee, United Way Serv, 1980-. **Honors/Awds:** Distinguished Service Award, Wilberforce Univ, 1972; Outstanding Alumnus of Year, Wilberforce Univ, 1972. **Special Achievements:** First Black recruited for IBM Management & Training Course in 1963. **Home Addr:** 24284 Halburton Rd, Beachwood, OH 44122, **Home Phone:** (216)464-1029. **Business Addr:** Attorney, Forest City Enterprises Inc, 10800 Brookpark Rd, Cleveland, OH 44130-1199, **Business Phone:** (216)267-1200.

### MURPHY, EDDIE (EDWARD REGAN MURPHY)
Singer, comedian, actor. **Personal:** Born Apr 3, 1961, Brooklyn, NY; son of Charles Edward (deceased) and Lillian Murphy Lynch; married Tracey Edmonds; married Nicole Mitchell; children: Bria, Myles Mitchell, Shayne Audra, Zola Ivey & Bella Zahra. **Educ:** Nassau Community Col. **Career:** Stand-up comedian, 1978-; show host, currently; Panda Merchandising, owner, currently; TV: Saturday Night Live, cast mem, 1980-84; The PJs, 1999; The Jeffersons, voice, 2000; Robbin' HUD, voice, 2000; The Last Affirmative Action Hero, voice, 2000; Shrek the Halls, voice, 2007; Clip Show, voice, 2008; Donkey's Christmas Shrektacular, 2010; Films: 48 Hours, 1982; Trading Places, 1983; Best Defense, 1984; Beverly Hills Cop, 1985; The Golden Child, 1986; Beverly Hills Cop II, 1987; Eddie Murphy Raw, 1987; Coming to Am, 1988; Another 48 Hours, 1990; Harlem Nights, 1990; Boomerang, 1992; Beverly Hills Cop III, 1994; Vampire in Brooklyn, 1995; The Nutty Prof, 1996; Metro, 1997; Dr Doolittle, 1998; Holy Man, 1998; Mulan, 1998; Bowfinger, 1999; Life, 1999; Nutty Prof II: The Klumps, 2000; Shrek, 2001; Dr Doolittle 2, 2001; Showtime, 2002; The Adventures of Pluto Nash, 2002; I Spy, 2002; Daddy Daycare, 2003; Haunted Mansion, 2003; Shrek 2, 2004; The Incredible Shrinking Man, 2005; Dreamgirls, 2006; Norbit, 2007; Shrek the Third, 2007; Shrek the Halls, 2007; Meet Dave, 2008; Imagine That, 2009; Shrek Forever After, 2010; Tower Heist, 2011; A Thousand Words, 2012; Mr. Church, 2016. Album: Eddie Murphy, 1982; Comedian, 1983; How Could It Be, 1985; So Happy, 1989; Harlem Nights, 1990; Remember the Times, 1992; Love's Alright, 1993; Greatest Comedy Hits, 1997; All I Fuckin' Know, 1998; Writer: Saturday Night Live, 1982-84; Eddie Murphy Delirious, 1983; Beverly Hills Cop II, 1987; Eddie Murphy Raw, 1987; Another 48 Hrs, 1990; Boomerang, 1992; Vampire in Brooklyn, 1995; The PJs, 1999; Norbit, 2007; Producer: Eddie Murphy Delirious, 1983; Eddie Murphy Raw, 1987; What's Alan Watching, 1989; The Royal Family, 1991; Vampire in Brooklyn, 1995; Life, 1999; Nutty Professor II: The Klumps, 2000; Norbit, 2007; Dir: Harlem Nights, 1989. **Honors/Awds:** Emmy Award nomination for outstanding comedy performance and outstanding comedy writing, for Saturday Night Live; Grammy Award nomination for best comedy album, 1982; Image Award, Nat Asn Advan Colored People, 1983; Golden Globe Foreign Press Award, 1983; Grammy Award for best comedy album, 1984; Golden Globe Award nomination for best actor, 1985; Star of the Year Award, 1985; People's Choice Award, 1985; Golden Raspberry Award, 1990, 2008, 2010; Natl Soc of Film Critics, Best Actor, The Nutty Prof, 1996; Saturn Award, Acad Sci Fiction, Fantasy & Horror Films, 1997; Blockbuster Entertainment Award, 1997; NSFC Award, Nat Soc Film Critics Awards, USA, 1997; Kids Choice Award, 1998, 2008, 2011; Annie Awards, 2001; People's Choice Award, Best Motion Picture Star in a Comedy, 2002; Critics Choice Award, Broadcast Film Critics Asn, 2007; COFCA Award, Cent Ohio Film Critics Asn, 2007; Golden Globe Award, 2007; Actor Supporting Role, Screen Actors Guild Awards, 2007; Blimp Award, Kids Choice Awards USA, 2008. **Home Addr:** , Englewood, NJ. **Business Addr:** Actor, Singer, ML Management Assoc Inc, 250 W 57th St, New York, NY 10019, **Business Phone:** (212)333-5500.

**MURPHY, HON. HARRIET LOUISE M.**
Judge, educator, lawyer. **Personal:** Born Atlanta, GA; married Patrick H; children: Charles Wray. **Educ:** Spelman Col, AB, 1949; Clark Atlanta Univ, MA, 1952; Johns Hopkins Sch, attended 1954; Univ Tex Law Sch, JD, 1969; Univ Gratz, Austria, 1971. **Career:** Educator, judge (retired), lawyer; Fulton Co, Ga, high sch teacher, 1949-54; Southern Univ, teacher, 1954-56; Prairie View A&M Univ, teacher, 1956-60; Womack Sr High, high sch teacher, 1960-66; Houston-Tillotson Col, prof gov, 1967-78; US State Dept Adv Coun African Affairs, 1970-72; State Tex, goodwill ambassador, 1976; City Austin, assoc judge, 1978-88, presiding judge, 1988-94; pvt pract lawyer, currently. **Orgs:** Delta Sigma Theta Sorority, 1964-; bd mem, Greater Austin Coun Alcoholism, 1970-93; Links Inc, 1982; bd mem, Judicial Coun Nat Bar Asn; bd mem, Tex Munic Ct Found; Nat Bar Asn; Tex Bar Asn; Austin Black Lawyers Asn; J Travis Co Women Lawyers Asn; Travis County Bar Asn; financial secy, Judicial Coun; financial secy bd, Habitat Humanity; Int Hosp Coun Austin; Gender Bias Implementation Task Force; Munic Ct Found; Austin Black Lawyers Asn; Travis Co Women Lawyers Asn; Austin Urban League. **Honors/Awds:** Outstanding Sorority Woman, Delta Sigma Theta Sorority, 1974; U T Award, Thurgood Marshall Legal Soc, 1986; Judicial Coun, 1987; De Witty Award Civil Rights, Austin Nat Asn Advan Colored People, 1989; Distinguished Service Chairman's Award, Greater Austin Coun Alcoholism, 1990; Hall of Fame, Spelman Col, 1993; Hall of Fame, Nat Women Achievement, Austin Chap, 1996; National Meril Award, Spelman Col, 1999; Gertrude E Rush Award, Nat Bar Asn, 2003; Raymond Pace Alexander Award, Judicial Coun Nat Bar Asn, 2005. **Special Achievements:** First African American woman to be app a permanent judge in Tex, 1974; First black woman dem presidential elector for Tex, 1976; Most outstanding class mem, Spelman Col, 1984; Selected as one of the 10 Legal Legends of Austin, TX, Travis County Bar Asn, 2001. **Home Addr:** 3638 Quictte Dr, Austin, TX 78754-4927, **Home Phone:** (512)928-2045. **Business Addr:** Attorney, 6635 Greensboro Dr, Austin, TX 78723-3919, **Business Phone:** (512)928-2045.

**MURPHY, DR. JOHN MATTHEW, JR.**
Dentist, executive. **Personal:** Born Mar 12, 1935, Charlotte, NC; son of John Sr and Elizabeth Benton; married Claudette Owens; children: Alicia Williams, Snowden Williams, John Matthew III & Brian Keith. **Educ:** Morgan St Col, BS, 1959; MeHarry Med Col Sch Dent, DDS, 1965; Va Hosp, cert, 1966. **Career:** Meharry Med Col Sch Dent, res assoc dept orthod, 1966; VA Ctr, Dayton, OH, staff dentist, 1967-70; Charles Drew Health Ctr, Dayton, clin dir dent, 1971-73; pvt pract gen dentist, 1973-; Metrolina Urban Health Initiative, originator & co-founder, 1979. **Orgs:** Pres, Dayton Hosp Mgt Asn, 1970-73; fel Royal Soc Health, 1974-; bd trustee, Little Rock AME Zion Church, 1975-; Charlotte C C, 1975-; treas, Martin Luther King Mem Comn, 1976-; life mem, Nat Asn Advan Colored People, 1977-; life mem, Omega Psi Phi Fraternity, 1978-; coun comm chmn, Boy Scouts Am, 1978; Charlotte Bus League, 1979-; Sigma Pi Phi, 1980; fel Acad Gen Dent, 1980; NC Chap Guardsmen, 1983-; pres & founder, A J Williams Dent Study Club, 1985-. **Honors/Awds:** Scroll of Honor, Omega Psi Phi, 1970; Certificate of Appreciation, Boy Scouts Am, 1972. **Home Addr:** 1113 Auten Rd, Charlotte, NC 28216-2909. **Business Addr:** Dentist, Private Practice, 11535 Carmel Commons Blvd Suite 200, Charlotte, NC 28226, **Business Phone:** (704)540-2443.

**MURPHY, LAURA W.**
Association executive, consultant. **Personal:** Born Oct 3, 1955, Baltimore, MD; daughter of William H and Madeline; children: Bertram M Lee Jr. **Educ:** Wellesley Col, AB, 1976. **Career:** Off Congressman, Parren Mitchell, legis asst, 1976-77; Off Congresswoman, Shirley Chisholm, legis asst, 1977-79; ACLU, legis rep, 1979-82, Am Civil Liberties Union Found Southern Calif, dir develop & planning giving, 1982-84; Mixner ScottInc, proj mgr, 1984-87; Pub Affairs Consult Firm, acct exec, 1985; Assembly Speaker, Willie L Brown Jr, chief staff, 1986-87; Jesse Jackson Pres Campaign, nat finance dir, 1987-88; Fundraising consult, 1988-90; Exec Off Mayor Sharon Pratt Kelly, mayor'stourism consult, 1990-92; DC Govt, Off Tourism, dir, 1992-93; Am Civil Liberties Union, Wash Legis Off, dir, 1993-2005, 2010-; Laura Murphy & Assocs LLC, founder, pres, 2007-10, 2015-; Harvard Univ, Fel, Harvard Advan Leadership Initiative, 2016-. **Orgs:** DC Comt Promote Wash, actg chair, 1993-95; exec comt, Leadership Conf Civil Rights, 1993-; bd mem, Pub Defenders Serv Wash, 1993-95; bd dir, Afro-Am Newspapers; numerous past memships; Mayor Dc; Baltimore's Cherry Hill neighborhood; Women's Foreign Policy Group; Exec Comt Leadership Conf Civil Rights; chmn, Criminal Justice Task Force. **Honors/Awds:** State Md, Citation Public Service, 1980; ACLU, Wash Off, Human Rights Award, 1982; NAACP Legal Defense & Educ Fund Inc, Black Women Achievement Award, 1987; Capital Entertainment Servs, Honorary Tour Guide DC, 1992; Mayor Sharon Pratt Kelly, Distinguished Public Service Award, 1994; Congressional Black Caucus, William L Dawson Award, 1997; Presidents Award, Leadership Conf on Civil Rights, 2007; received numerous awards and recognition. **Special Achievements:** First African American and first female director of ACLU. Authored Numerous Publications. **Home Addr:** 2716 Unicorn Lane NW, Washington, DC 20015-2234, **Home Phone:** (202)244-5949. **Business Addr:** Director, American Civil Liberties Union, 125 Broad St 18th Fl, New York, NY 10004, **Business Phone:** (212)549-2500.

**MURPHY, MARGARET HUMPHRIES (MARGARET PEGGY MURPHY)**
Government official, administrator. **Personal:** Born Baltimore, MD; married Arthur G; children: Terry M Bailey, Arthur G Jr & Lynn M Press. **Educ:** Coppin State Col, BS, 1952, MA, 1977; Morgan State Col. **Career:** Education associate (retired); Baltimore City Pub Sch, teacher, 1952-78, educ asn, 1978; Md State, deleg, 1978-95. **Orgs:** Pub Sch Teachers Asn, 1952-; Md St Teachers Asn, 1952-; Nat Educ Asn; Nat Asn Advan Colored People; Lambda Kappa Mu; Red Cross; treas, Orgn Women Legislators; Delta Sigma Theta; Forest Pk Neighborhood Asn; chmn, Baltimore City Health Sub-Comm; bd mem, Threshold Inc; Baltimore City Dem State Cent Comt, 1978-; Environ Matters Comt; Med Transplant Study Comn, 1984-85; Gov's adv coun, Acquired Immune Deficiency Syndrome (AIDS), 1987-91; Joint Comt Fed Rels; chair, Baltimore City Deleg, 1989-92; gov's coun, Substance Abuse, Tuberc, & AIDS, 1994-95; chair, Vanguard Polit Orgn Inc; Ethland Ave Neighborhood Asn; Delta Sigma Theta Sorority Inc; Ten Plus Social Club; Joyettes Social Club; secy, MD Leg Black Caucus; Women Legislators Md. **Special Achievements:** First African-American chairman of the Baltimore City Delegation. **Home Addr:** 4811 Liberty Heights Ave, Baltimore, MD 21207, **Home Phone:** (410)367-5811.

**MURPHY, MICHAEL MCKAY**
Executive. **Personal:** Born Aug 13, 1946, Fayetteville, NC; son of Charles L (deceased) and Eleanor (deceased); married Gwendolyn Ferguson; children: L Mark. **Educ:** St Louis Univ, BS, com, 1968. **Career:** John Hancock Ins Co, life underwriter, 1968-71; Ford Motor Co, bus mgt specialist, 1971-75; Dunkin Donuts, purchasing mgr, 1975-79, dir qual control beginning, 1979-, dir consumer affairs; Renewal Inc, pres & gen mgr. **Orgs:** Zeta Kappa Sigma Chap, 1988-89; clerk, Canton, MA Bd Health, 1996; pres, Phi Beta Sigma Fraternity Inc; pres, Blue Hill Civic Asn; Nat Restaurant Asn. **Honors/Awds:** Governors Coun, Republican, elected, 1990; Congressional Candidata, MA Dist 9, 1994. **Home Addr:** 5715 Glandor Dr SE, Mableton, GA 30126, **Home Phone:** (404)791-0207. **Business Addr:** President, Renewal Inc, 100 Boylston St No 300, Boston, MA 02116, **Business Phone:** (617)338-1904.

**MURPHY, PAULA CHRISTINE**
Librarian. **Personal:** Born Dec 15, 1950, Oberlin, OH; daughter of Paul Onieal and Vivian Chiquita Lane. **Educ:** Rosary Col Dominican Univ, River Forest, IL, BA, 1973; Dominican Univ, Sch Libr Sci, MALS, 1975; Northern Ill Univ, Dekalb, IL, MA, 1982; Triton Col, cert, 2003. **Career:** Chicago Pub Libr, Chicago, IL, libr I, 1974-76; Gov's Libr State Univ, Univ Pk, IL, circulation/media librn, 1976-80; Columbia Col Libr, Chicago, IL, head av servs, 1980-89; Loyola Univ Libr, Chicago, IL, head av servs, 1989-96; Dominican Univ, head access servs, 1996-98; Univ Pittsburgh Semester At Sea, 1998; Chicago Hist Soc, Res Serv, libr, 1998-03; Paula Murphy Consult, 2003-; Proviso Twp High Sch, teacher, 2005-07; Huntington Learning Ctr, teacher, 2007-. **Orgs:** Tutor, Cleveland Bd Educ, 1971; Ohio Bell Tel, 1969-74; Am Libr Asn Divs & Roundtables, 1975-; Ill Libr Asn, 1975-90; treas, Jr Mem Roundtable Am Libr Asn, 1980-82; Black Caucus Am Libr Asn, 1985-; chair, arts sect, Asn Col & Res Libr Am Libr Asn, 1989-90; exec bd mem, Am Film & Video Asn, 1976-80 & 1989-95; chair, ACRL New Publs Adv Bd, 1993-95; chair, ACRL Arts Dance Subcomt Inter libr Loan Video, 1994-96; Ala Elections Comt, 1994-96; chair, Video Roundtable, Am Lib Asn, 1997-98; chair, ACRL Arts Dance Comt, 1999-2002; chair, ACRL Arts Stand Comt, 2001-04; Midwest Arch Conf, 2005-. **Honors/Awds:** Elected Mem in Beta Phi Mu, 1973; 3M/JMRT Prof Develop, 3M Co & JMRT; Grant, Am Libr Asn, 1977; Speaker, Art Libr Soc NA & Consortium Col & Univ Media Ctrs, 1986, 1989; African-American Women's Achievement Award, African-American Alliance, 1989; Judge, Am Film Festival, 1989-92; Speaker, Charleston Conf Bk & Ser Acq, 1991; Nat Conf African Am Librns, 1994; Speaker 6th Biennial Symp of Arts & Technol, 1997. **Special Achievements:** Author "Visual Literacy, Libraries & Community Development in Collection Building," March 1981; Films for the Black Music Researcher in Black Music Research Journal, Center for Black Music Research, 1987; "Audio Visual Services for the Performing Arts Programs at Columbia Coll, Chicago," in Performing Arts Resources, Vol 15, 1990; "Documentation of Performance Art," Coll and Research Libraries News, Apr 1992; Senior Advisory Viewing Race Project, 1997-; "What Classroom Teachers Should Know About Using Interactive Multi Media Materials," Media Horizons, vol 13, Spring 1997; contributor, Int Dictionary of Modern Dance, 1998; grant panelist, Nat Initiative to Preserve America's Dance, 1998-2002; speaker, Am Libr Asn Conf, 2000; speaker, Dancing in the Millennium Conf, 2000; contributor, Amer Women Writers; advisor, Nat Video Resources Viewing Races project; speaker, 5th Nat African Am Librarians Conf, 2002. **Home Addr:** 423 Southeast Ave, Oak Park, IL 60302, **Home Phone:** (708)383-4591. **Business Addr:** Teacher, Huntington Learning Center, 496 Kinderkamack Rd, Oradell, NJ 07649, **Business Phone:** (201)261-8400.

**MURPHY, RAYMOND M., JR.**
State government official. **Personal:** Born Dec 13, 1927, St. Louis, MO; married Lynette; children: Clinton, Krystal, Leslie, Raymond, Anita, James, Brandon & Alicia. **Educ:** Detroit Inst Tech, Wayne State Univ. **Career:** Mich State House Representatives, state rep, 1983-98; D-3rd Senate Dist, state sen; 36th Dist Ct, ct officer; real estate agt; Young Dem Clubs Am, rep. **Orgs:** Mem, Nat Black Caucus State Legislators; lifetime mem, Nat Asn Advan Colored People; imp grandcncl, Ancient Arabic Orders; Nobles Mystic Shrine; Mich Legis Black Caucus; exec bd mem, Detroit Transit Alternative; mem Metro Elks Lodge; Eureka Temple No 1; Lions Club; Optimist Club; chmn, 13th Dist Dem Orgn; pub affairs dir, Wayne County Bailiffs Asn; chmn, 13th Cong Dist Young Dems; High Speed Rail Comn; UAW. **Honors/Awds:** Legislator of the Year Minority Women Network, 1987. **Home Addr:** 610 Chicago Blvd, Detroit, MI 48202-1415, **Home Phone:** (313)931-0601. **Business Addr:** Representative, Michigan State House, Rm 715 Farnum Bldg, Lansing, MI 48909, **Business Phone:** (517)373-0990.

**MURPHY, DR. VANESSA A.**
Fashion model, educational consultant, executive director. **Educ:** Mobile Univ, BS; Al Univ, MS. **Career:** Model; Jefferson Davis Community Col, Brewton, AL, counr & coordr stud activ; H Councill Trenholm State Tech Col, asst dir stud support serv, dir stud support serv. **Honors/Awds:** Ms Plus USA, 1997. **Business Addr:** Director of Student Support Services, H Council Trenholm State Technical College, PO Box 10048, Montgomery, AL 36108, **Business Phone:** (334)420-4200.

**MURRAIN, GODFREY H.**
Association executive, lawyer. **Personal:** Born Mar 14, 1927, New York, NY; son of Walter Herbert and Ellouise Pearl Jones; married Peggy Gray; children: Michelle Pearl. **Educ:** Howard Univ, attended 1949; NY Univ, BS, 1951; Brooklyn Law Sch, LLB, JD, 1955. **Career:** Treas Dept, IRS agt, 1953-58; New York, pvt prac; Godfrey H Murrain Esq, atty coun, law tax consult advising & coun individual corp estates, 1958-; Self-employed, Atty, 1965-. **Orgs:** Am Arbitration Asn; NY Co Lawyers Asn; Metrop Black Bar Asn; Nat Bar Asn; Am Civil Liberties Union; elder, Hollis Presbyterian Church; Task Force Justice Presbytery City NY; adv bd, Borough Manhattan Community Col, 1970; secy gen, coun, One Hundred Black Men Inc; bd trustee, Great Neck Libr; bd mem, Nat Asn Advan Colored People, Great Neck Manhasset Port Wash Br; Dept Disciplinary Comn, First Judicial Dept Supreme Ct, State NY; NY Surrogate's Ct Adv Comt; grand gammateus & exec sec, Grand Boule Sigma Pi Phi; bd dir, One Hundred Black Men New York Inc. **Home Addr:** 240 Shoreward Dr, Great Neck, NY 11021, **Home Phone:** (516)482-4039. **Business Addr:** Attorney at Law, Godfrey H Murrain Esq, Rm 613 225 Broadway, New York, NY 10007-3001, **Business Phone:** (212)619-1250.

**MURRAY, ALBERT R.**
Law enforcement officer. **Personal:** Born Jan 25, 1946, Ripley, TN; son of Rossie G and Pearl L; married Connie Graffread; children: Andrea & Camille. **Educ:** Tenn State Univ, Nashville, TN, BS, eng, 1969; Middle Tenn State Univ, Murfreesboro, TN, MA, educ, 1973; Tenn Govt Exec Inst, grad, 1988. **Career:** Spencer Youth Ctr, Nashville, TN, counr, 1970-76; Tenn Youth Ctr, Nashville, TN, asst supt, 1976-81, supt, 1981-; Tenn Dept C Servs, Nashville, TN, asst comnr; Kans Juv Justice Authority, comnr, 1997-2003; Ala Dept Corrections, dep comnr prog, 2003; Ga Dept Juv Justice, comnr, 2004-10. **Orgs:** Phi Beta Sigma Fraternity, 1968-; Govs Adv Coun Voc Ed, 1984; bd Mgrs, YMCA, 1987-; auditor, Am Correctional Asn, 1988-; bd Govs, Tenn Correctional Asn, 1990; Comn Accreditation, Tenn Correctional Asn, currently; chmn, Peoples Action Party; from vice chair to chmn, Pardons & Paroles, 2010-14; Pardons & Paroles, 2010-. **Home Addr:** 109 Bella Ct, Nashville, TN 37207, **Home Phone:** (615)865-6054.

**MURRAY, ANNA MARTIN**
Educator. **Personal:** Born Oct 31, 1910, Birmingham, AL; married Willie Alca. **Educ:** AL State Col, BS, 1952; Samford Univ, cert early childhood educ, 1975; CA Inst Metaphys, 1952; A&M Univ, attended 1964; George Peabody Col. **Career:** Educator (retired); St Clair Bd Educ, teacher, 1944-46; Birmingham City Bd Educ, teacher, 1947-72, substitute teacher, 1977-87; Helping Hand Day Care, teacher, 1976-77. **Orgs:** Ultra Mod Club, 1930-87; Gamma Phi Delta Alpha Mu Chap, 1968-; vpres, Deaconess Bd Macedonia Baptist Church, 1970-85; sec, Alert Prof Club, 1980-85; sec, Tyree Chap 77 OES, 1981-85; AL Retired Teachers Asn Montgomery AL; Am Asn Retired Persons Long Beach CA; Nat Ed Asn WA DC; Fraternal OES, Alert Twelve Profl, Alpha Mu Gamma Phi Delta Sor; Macedonia Missionary Baptist Church, Ensley, AL. **Honors/Awds:** Meritorious Service Award, Birmingham Educ Asn, 1973; New verses in American Poetry, Vantage Press NY, 1976; Inspiration from a Save in Action Vantage Press NY, 1977; Award Nat Black Women's Polit Leadership Caucus, 1978; Meritorious Service Award Field Jour, 1980; Dipl The Inst Mental physics; Outstanding Service Award, Supreme Chap Zeta Phi Lambda Sor, 1983. **Special Achievements:** Author: "From A Soul In Action". **Home Addr:** 2112-18th St, Birmingham, AL 35218, **Home Phone:** (205)785-2879.

**MURRAY, CALVIN DUANE**
Baseball player. **Personal:** Born Jul 30, 1971, Dallas, TX; son of Kevin; married Kelli Nichols. **Educ:** Univ Tex, Austin, attended. **Career:** Baseball player (retired); San Francisco Giants, outfielder, 1999-2002; Tex Rangers, 2002; Chicago Cubs, outfielder, 2004.

**MURRAY, REV. CECIL LEONARD**
Clergy. **Personal:** Born Sep 26, 1929, Lakeland, FL; son of Edward Wilder and Minnie Lee (deceased); married Bernadine Cousin; children: Drew David. **Educ:** Fla A&M Univ, BA, 1951; Sch Theol, Claremont Col, PhD, 1964. **Career:** Clergy (retired); USF, capt, jet radar interceptor & navigator; Trinity AME, 1966-71; First African Methodist Episcopal Church, minister & sr pastor, 1977-2004; Film Producer: Carry Me Home, 2009; Clash of Colors: LA Riots of 1992, 2012. **Orgs:** Gen bd, African Methodist Episcopal Church, 1972-92; gen bd, Nat Coun Churches, 1972-92; Alpha Phi Alpha Fraternity, 1948-; NCP; Southern Christian Leadership Conf; CORE; Urban League; Un Asn, USA; gen bd, Nat Coun Aging, 1988-93; founder, FAME Renaissance; sr fel Ctr Relig Civic Cult; Nat Asn Advan Colored People; bd dir, The Ray Charles Foundation. **Honors/Awds:** Ralph Bunche Peace Prize Award, United Nations Asn, 1992; Alpha Man of the Year, Alpha Phi Alpha, 1951; Daniel Alexander Payne Award, African Methodist Epicopal Church, 1992; Community Achievement Award, NCP, Los Angeles, 1986; Outstanding Role Model, Nat Asn Univ Women, 1992. **Special Achievements:** Sermon in Dreams of Fire, compendium of sermons after Los Angeles riots; Named by PRS George Bush: 177th Point of Light, First AME Church; Excerpts in Time Mag, Wall St J, BBC, CNN. **Home Addr:** 5858 S Citrus, Los Angeles, CA 90043, **Home Phone:** (213)294-4407.

**MURRAY, DESMOND.** **See ADEYEMI, BAKARI.**

**MURRAY, EDDIE CLARENCE**
Baseball player, athletic coach. **Personal:** Born Feb 24, 1956, Los Angeles, CA; son of Charles and Carrie; married Janet; children: Jordan & Jessica. **Educ:** Calif State Univ. **Career:** Baseball player (retired), athletic coach; Baltimore Orioles, infielder, 1977-88, 1996; Los Angeles Dodgers, infielder, 1989-91, 1997, bench coach, hitting coach, 1997, 2006-07; New York Mets, infielder, 1992-93; Cleveland Indians, 1994-96, hitting coach, 2002-05; Anaheim Angels, 1997. **Orgs:** United Cerebral Palsy; Am Red Cross; United Way; Johns Hopkins C's Ctr; New Holiness Refuge Church & Pk Heights Acad. **Home Addr:** 13401 Blythenia Rd, Phoenix, MD 21131.

**MURRAY, GARY S., SR.**
Computer executive, manager, business owner. **Personal:** children: Gary II. **Educ:** Howard Univ, BBA. **Career:** Arthur Young & Co, cert pub acct; Falcon Microsystems, chief operating officer; Sylvest Mgt Syst Corp, vpres & chief exec officer; Integrated Spatial Inform Solutions, chmn & bd dir, 2003; Greater Wash Bd Trade, bd mem; Md Sci Ctr, bd mem; Hi-Tech Coun, Prince George's County, founder & chair; Greater Prince George's Bus Round table, founding chmn; Prince Georges County Econ Develop Corp, chmn; Bio Tech Inst,

Univ Md, bd mem; Greater Wash Bd Trade Mem Pappas Comn; Human Vision LLC, founder & managing dir, prin, currently; WiSE Technologies, founder, chief exec officer, dir bus develop; Murray Financial Solutions, founder & amp, chief operating officer; Plan-Graphics Inc; Md Econ Develop Comn; real estate. **Orgs:** Chmn, Md Econ Develop Comn; Md Chamber Com; Md Sci Ctr; Reginald F Lewis Mus Md African Am Hist & Cult; Coun Md. **Honors/Awds:** Executive of the Year, Bus Gazette, 2003; Business Gazette Newspaper Executive of the Year, 2004; Volunteer of the Year, Md Econ Develop Asn, 2005. **Business Addr:** Founder, Human Vision LLC, 8181 Prof Pl Suite 200, Landover, MD 20785, **Business Phone:** (301)577-3300.

### MURRAY, FR. J-GLENN
Educator, clergy. **Personal:** Born Apr 22, 1950, Philadelphia, PA; son of James Albert and Lillian Marie Hilton. **Educ:** St Louis Univ, BA, philos & commun, 1970; Jesuit Sch Theol, Berkeley, CA, Mdiv, liturgy, 1983; Aquinas Inst, MA, 1996; Cath Theol Union, Chicago, IL, DMin, 1996; Cath Theol Union, Chicago, IL, DMin, 2006. **Career:** Holy Cross Church, Durham, assoc pastor, 1979; Duke Univ, campus minister, 1981-88; St Frances Acad, vice prin, 1981-88; Off Pastoral Liturgy, asst dir, 1989-95, dir, 1995-2007; St Mary Sem, homiletics prof, 1992-; St Aloysius Gonzaga Church, parochial vicar, currently; Jesuit Sch Theol, teacher. **Orgs:** Nat Black Cath Clergy Caucus, 1979-; Cath Asn Teachers Homiletics, 1992-; Acad Homiletics, 1992-; N Am Acad Liturgy, 1993-; Black Cath Theol Symp, 1994-; Cath Asn Liturgy; Jungmann Soc; Md Prov Jesuits. **Home Addr:** St Henry Church 18200 Harvard Ave, Cleveland, OH 44128, **Home Phone:** (216)921-0725. **Business Addr:** Parochial Vicar, St Aloysius Gonzaga Church, 4366 Bridgetown Rd, Cincinnati, OH 45211, **Business Phone:** (513)574-4840.

### MURRAY, J. RALPH
Insurance executive, business owner. **Personal:** Born Oct 4, 1931, Manatee, FL; married Alaine; children: James, Janmarie & Jodi. **Educ:** BS, 1960. **Career:** Am Cyanamid Co Res Labs; Travelers Ins Co, 1967; Ins & Fin Serv Inc, owner, currently. **Orgs:** Bd fin dir, Liberty Nat Bank, 1970; SW CT Life Underwriters Asn; bd dir, St Lukes Infant Child Care; secy, Stamford Ctr Arts, currently. **Honors/Awds:** Civic Award, Planning Bd City Stamford, 1970; Travelers Inner Circle Award, 1970; Outstanding Political Service Award, Afro-Am Club, 1972. **Home Addr:** 15 Butternut Pl, Stamford, CT 06903-3829. **Business Addr:** Owner, Insurance & Financial Services Inc, 832 Bedford St Suite 2, Stamford, CT 06901, **Business Phone:** (203)359-1326.

### MURRAY, DR. JAMES HAMILTON
Educator, dentist. **Personal:** Born Nov 22, 1933, Washington, DC; married Joan; children: Christina & Michelle. **Educ:** Howard Univ, BS, 1956; Meharry Med Col, DDS, 1960; Johns Hopkins Sch Hyg & Pub Health, MPH, 1969. **Career:** Educator, dentist (retired); Jersey City Med Ctr, rotating dent internship, 1961; VIR Pub Health Dept, clin dentist, 1964-68; Howard Univ Col Dent, Dept Prostho dontics, asst prof, 1964-68, Dept Community Dent, asst prof, 1968-69, Dept Clin Dent, assoc prof, 1975-92; Nat Med Asn Found, Shaw Community Health Proj, dent dir, 1969-70; Meharry Med Col, Matthew Walker Health Ctr, proj dir, Dept Family & Community Health, prof, 1970-71; Dept Health Educ & Welfare Family Health Serv, Rockville MD, health adminr, 1972-74; Dept Human Resource Comt Health & Hosp Admin, Wash, DC, 1974-75. **Honors/Awds:** Award, Am Soc Dent C, 1960; Award for Clinical Dentistry, Nashville Dent Supply Co, 1960; US Public Health Traineeship Grant, 1968-69; DC Dental Soc Award, 1969; Dental Alumnus of the Year, Meharry Med Col, 1970-71; Honorary Dental Society Award, Omicron Kappa Upsilon, 1960. **Special Achievements:** Published articles for dental journals. **Home Addr:** 1433 Locust Rd NW, Washington, DC 20012.

### MURRAY, JAMES P., JR.
Writer, executive, manager. **Personal:** Born Oct 16, 1946, Bronx, NY; son of Eddie and Helena; married Mary; children: Sean Edward, Sherron Anita & Angela Dawn. **Educ:** Syracuse Univ, BA, 1968. **Career:** White Plains Reporter Dispatch, copy ed, 1968; ABC-TV News, news trainee, 1968-71; Western Elec Co, pub rels assoc, 1971-72; freelance writer, 1972-73; NY Amsterdam News, arts & entertainment ed, 1973-75; Nat Broadcasting Co, press rep, 1975-83; Black Creation Mag, ed chief, 1972-74; free lancewriter, 1983-85; USA Network, mgr pub rels, 1985-90, dir corp rels, 1990-91, freelance publicist, 1991-93; Terrie Williams Agency, acct supvr, 1993, publicity consult, 1993-94; Valley Youth Agency, dep dir, fund dev & pub rels, 1994-. **Orgs:** Vol Fire Co, 1968; judge, Newspaper Guild Page One Award, 1976-86; cont ed, Afro-Am Almanac, 1976, 1989; pres, Fairview Engine Co #1, 1980. **Honors/Awds:** Man of the Year, Fairview Engine Co #1 1971; Humanitarian Achievement Award MLK Players, 1975; ordained elder Christs Temple White Plains NY, 1978; judge Gabriel Awards, 1986. **Special Achievements:** First African American Member in Fairview Engine Co #1 Greenburgh NY; first Black elected to New York Film Critics Circle, 1972; Author, "To Find An Image", 1974. **Home Addr:** 617 Woodland Hills Rd, White Plains, NY 10603, **Home Phone:** (914)761-4439. **Business Addr:** Deputy Director, The Valley Inc, 1047 Amsterdam Ave, New York, NY 10025, **Business Phone:** (212)665-2607.

### MURRAY, LAMOND MAURICE
Basketball player. **Personal:** Born Apr 20, 1973, Pasadena, CA; married Carmen; children: Lamond Jr & Ashley. **Educ:** Univ Calif, Berkeley, attended 1994. **Career:** Basketball player (retired); Los Angeles Clippers, forward & small forward, 1994-99, 2006-07; Cleveland Cavaliers, small forward, 1999-2002; Toronto Raptors, forward & small forward, 2003-05; NJ Nets, forward, 2005-06; Santa Barbara Breakers, 2007; Long Beach Breakers, Am Basketball Asn, 2007-08; Guangdong Southern Tigers, China, 2008-09; Los Angeles Lightning, Int Basketball League, 2009; Al-Muharraq, Bahrain, 2010-11; Los Angeles Slam, 2011-12. **Business Addr:** Professional Basketball Player, Guangdong Southern Tigers510620, **Business Phone:** (861)06711-14.

### MURRAY, DR. MABEL LAKE
Educator. **Personal:** Born Feb 24, 1935, Baltimore, MD; daughter of Moses Oliver Lake (deceased) and Iantha Alexander Lake; married Elmer R; children: Mark Alfonso Butler & Sarita. **Educ:** Coppin State Teachers Col, Baltimore, MD, BS, 1956; Loyola Col, Baltimore, MD, EdM, 1969; Va Polytech Inst, Blacksburg, VA, case, 1981, EdD, 1982. **Career:** Educator (retired); Baltimore City Pub Schs, teacher, 1956-68; Prince Georges County Pub Schs, reading specialist, 1968-70; Proj KAPS, Baltimore, Md, reading coordr, 1970-72; Univ Md, reading coordr, 1972-76; Johns Hopkins Univ, adj prof, 1972-76; Carroll County Pub Schs, supvr, 1976-87; Baltimore City Schs Spec Educ, guest lect, 1979; Sojourner Douglass Col, Baltimore, Md, prof, 1987, supvr, Stud Teaching, chair dept educ, coordr human growth & develop. **Orgs:** Delta Sigma Theta Sorority, 1972-; Baltimore County Alumnae Chap, Delta Sigma Theta; adv, Lambda Kappa & Mu Psi Chapters, Delta Sigma Theta; consult, Piney Woods Sch, 1984-89; comn chair-instr, 1987-96, exec bd, 1987-, Nat Alliance Black Sch Educr; consult, AIDS Proj MSDE, 1988; consult, Dunbar Mid Sch, 1989; Congressman Louis Stokes Comt Black Health Issues, 1989; consult, Des Moines Iowa Schs; Nat Coun Educating Black C; pres, Md Coun Deltas; nat pres, Pinochle Bugs Social & Civic Club; nat treas, Societas Doctas; Baho Chap, Soc; Coalition 100 Black Women; Nat Coalition Black Women; Soc Inc Pinochle Bugs; bd dir, Nat Asn Advan Colored People Educ Dept, nat. **Home Addr:** 3 Kittridge Ct, Randallstown, MD 21133-2409, **Home Phone:** (410)655-0269.

### MURRAY, SYLVESTER
School administrator, educator. **Personal:** Born Aug 15, 1941, Miami, FL; son of Tommy Lee and Annie Anderson; children: Kimberly & Joshua. **Educ:** Lincoln Univ Pa, BA, hist, 1963, LLD, 1984; Univ Pa, MGA, govt admin, 1967; Eastern Mich Univ, MA, econ, 1976. **Career:** City Inkster Mich, city mgr, 1970-73; City Ann Arbor Mich, city admin, 1973-79; City Cincinnati Ohio, city mgr, 1979-85; Jackson State Univ, vis prof pub policy & admin, 1981-; City San Diego Calif, city mgr, 1985-87; Coopers & Lybrand, mgr; Am Soc Pub Admin & Int City Mgt Asn; Cleveland State Univ, educ adminr, prof urban studies & pub admin, prof emer, currently; Maxine Goodman Levin Col Urban Affairs, prof; Savannah State Univ, master pub admin prog, prof & coordr. **Orgs:** Pres, Int City mgt Asn, 1984; pres, Am Soc Pub Admin & Int City Mgmt Asn, 1987; fulbright sr specialist, fel treas & dir, Nat Acad Pub Admin; bd mem, Nat Civic League Stand Rev Steering Comt. **Honors/Awds:** National Public Service Award, Am Soc Pub Admin, 1984, Staats Lifetime Achievement Award. **Special Achievements:** First African-American President of ICMA, 1983-84. **Business Addr:** Professor Emeritus, Cleveland State University, 2121 Euclid Ave, Cleveland, OH 44115-2214, **Business Phone:** (216)687-2254.

### MURRAY, DR. THOMAS AZEL, SR.
Educator, consultant, government official. **Personal:** Born Jan 15, 1929, Chicago, IL; son of Arnette Bedford Francis and Hazel Marie Lumpkins; married Gale Patricia Roberts. **Educ:** Ohio State Univ, BA, bus, 1974; Univ Ill, MA, coun, 1976, MA, interpersonal commun, 1979; Southern Ill Univ, PhD, edu, 1981. **Career:** Military official, government official (retired), educator, consult; Univ Ill, Chicago, proj coordr, 1959-72; Chicago Baptist Asn, dir, 1971-72; Fed Civil Serv, US Dept Housing & Urban Develop, supvry equal opportunity specialist, 1973-75, 1984-87; Fed Hwy Admin, civil rights officer, 1975-78; Ill State Bd Educ, officer & parliamentarian, 1978-84 & 1994-96; Ill State Bd Educ, affirmative action officer, 1978-85; Sangamon State Univ Alumni Asn, dir, 1979-85; US Dept HUD Region V, dir compliance, Off Civil Rights, dep dir, 1984-85, prog opers div, dir, 1985-87; US Off Personnel Mgt; Prof Serv Corps, Ill State Bd Educ, 1989; NMex State Univ-Grants, consult, assoc prof, 1999-; US Dept Transp, supvr & complaint investigators; State Ill & Chicago Bd Educ, consult. **Orgs:** Dir, Springfield Sangamon Co Youth Serv Bur, 1974-75; adv comt mem, Land Lincoln Legal Act Found, 1978-80; adv coun mem, Region IV Career Guid Ctr, Springfield, Ill, 1982-83; Prof Serv Corps, Ill State Bd Educ, 1989-96; Chicago Bd Educ, Admin Acad, 1989-96; presenter, Educ Serv Ctr VI, 1989-96. **Honors/Awds:** Black Affiliate Council Award of Merit, Southern Ill Univ, 1981; HE Honor, Phi Kappa Phi Soc, Southern Ill Univ. **Home Addr:** PO Box 430, Ramah, NM 87321, **Home Phone:** (505)775-3634. **Business Addr:** Associate Professor, New Mexico State University, 1780 E University Ave, Las Cruces, NM 88003, **Business Phone:** (575)646-0111.

### MURRAY, TRACY LAMONT
Basketball player, basketball executive, basketball coach. **Personal:** Born Jul 25, 1971, Los Angeles, CA. **Educ:** Univ Calif, Los Angeles, BA, hist, 1992. **Career:** Basketball player (retired), coach, executive; Portland Trail Blazers, forward, 1992-95, 2003; Haynes Boys Home, mentor, 1992-; Houston Rockets, 1995; Toronto Raptors, 1995-96, 2001-02; Wash Wizards, 1996-2000; Denver Nuggets, 2000-01; donator, Shoes that Fit, 2000-; Los Angeles Lakers, 2002-03, asst coach & shooting coach, 2015-16; NY Knicks, forward, 2004-05; Panathinaikos, Greece, 2004-05; PAOK, Greece, 2005-06; Elan Chalon, France, 2006-07; Prodigy Athletic Inst, asst coach, mentor & trainer, 2006-; Univ Calif, Los Angeles, IMG Col, color commentator, 2007-15; Bakersfield Jam, mentor, asst coach, 2007-09; Ball Up Streetball, coach, 2011-15; Campus Insiders, broadcast analyst, 2012-14; Univ Calif, Los Angeles, Sports Network, analyst, currently. **Orgs:** Co-chmn, Toshiba Celebrity Golf Classic; founder, Tracy Murray Summer Basketball Camp; Nat Basketball Asn; bd mem, Boys & Girls Clubs, 2010-15. **Honors/Awds:** Bronze Medal, Pan American Games, 1991; Most Improved Player, 1995, 1996; NBA champion, Houston Rockets, 1995. **Business Addr:** Assistant Coach, Mentor, Prodigy Athletic Institute, 870 Cienega Ave Suite 5, San Dimas, CA 91773, **Business Phone:** (951)314-3375.

### MURRAY, VIRGIE W.
Editor. **Personal:** Born Sep 4, 1931, Birmingham, AL; daughter of Virgus Williams and Martha Miller Reese (deceased); married McKinley C; children: Charles. **Educ:** Miles Col; Booker T Wash Bus Col. **Career:** Editor (retired); Dr John W Nixon, bookkeeper, 1954-58; Thomas Floorwaxing Serv, bookkeeper, 1954-64; Birmingham World, clerk/reporter, 1958-64; Long Time Sentinel Relig Ed; First Baptist Church Graymont, secy, 1960-64; Los Angeles Sentinel Newspaper, relig ed, 1964-06. **Orgs:** Pres, Nat Baptist Conv USA INC; Secy, Relig Newswriters Asn, 1971; W Coast PR Dr Frederick Eikerenkoetter, 1974-; bd mem, Inst Sacred Music, 1979-; bd mem, Ecumenical Black Campus Ministry Univ Calif Los Angeles, 1982-; Trinity Baptist Church; Nat Asn Advan Colored People; Urban League; Angeles Mesa; Young Men's Christian Asn; Boy Scouts Am; Los Angeles Chap Bus & Prof Women's Club Inc; spec task force, UN Asn USA's Ralph Bunche Awards; Los Angeles chap Lane Col & Mileans & Parker High Sch Alumni; Relig Heritage Am, 1989-90; bd dir, Los Angeles Sentinel Inc; Bertha Whitterson Circle & Pub Rels; Los Angeles Chap Nat Asn Advan Colored People. **Home Addr:** 1112 E 43rd St, Los Angeles, CA 90011, **Home Phone:** (213)232-3261.

### MURRELL, ADRIAN BRYAN
Football player, president (organization), chief executive officer. **Personal:** Born Oct 16, 1970, Fayetteville, NC; son of Angelo and Patricia; married Tonia Peck; children: 3. **Educ:** West Va Univ. **Career:** Football player (retired), president, chief executive officer; NY Jets, running back, 1993-97; Ariz Cardinals, 1998-99; Wash Redskins, 2000; Dallas Cowboys, running back, 2003; Water Eng Serv Inc, owner, pres & chief exec officer, 2003-07; Vector Supply Group, owner, 2007-; Murrell Contracting Inc, pres & chief exec officer, 2009-. **Orgs:** Alpha Phi Alpha Fraternity; Nat Football League Alumni Asn; Nat Football League Players Asn; Metrolina Minority Contractors Asn. **Business Addr:** President, Chief Executive Officer, Murrell Contracting Inc, 17236 Green Dolphin Lane, Cornelius, NC 28031-7693, **Business Phone:** (704)941-9930.

### MURRELL, DR. BARBARA CURRY
Founder (originator), school administrator. **Personal:** Born Jan 12, 1938, Starkville, MS; married Robert N. **Educ:** Tenn State Univ, BS, 1960, MS, 1963; Univ Ill, post grad cert, 1970. **Career:** Tenn State Univ, dir, stud activ, 1965-75, asst vpres, stud affairs, 1975-81, vpres, stud affairs, 1981; Fisk Univ, adj prof social sci, currently, Real Sports Leadership Acad, founder & exec dir, currently, vpres Stud Life, 2007-. **Orgs:** Task Force Human Resources Asn Col Unions Int, 1968-79; state coordr, Nat Asn Stud Personnel Admins, 1973; Harvard Univ Inst Educ Mgrs Prog, 1984; consult, Prof Develop Workshop Asn Col Unions Int; bd dir, Bordeaux YMCA; Asn Col Unions Int; Nat Entertainment & Campus Activ Asn; Beta Kappa Chi Nat Hon Soc; Delta Sigma Theta Sorority Inc. **Home Addr:** 4216 Kings Ct, Nashville, TN 37218, **Home Phone:** (615)876-1878. **Business Addr:** Founder & Executive Director, Vice President for Student Life, Fisk University, 1000 17th Ave N, Nashville, TN 37208-3051, **Business Phone:** (615)329-8854.

### MURRELL, DR. PETER C., SR.
Dentist. **Personal:** Born May 14, 1920, Glasgow, KY; son of Samuel and Nellie; married Eva Ruth Greenlee; children: Peggy, Peter Jr, Linda & James. **Educ:** Ky State Col, BS, gen sci, 1943; Marquette Univ, DDS, 1947. **Career:** Dentist (retired); Howard Univ Col Dent, instr, 1947-48; pvt pract dentist, 1948-51, 1953-92. **Orgs:** Pres, Cream City Med Socs, 1954-57; co-founder, Frontiers Int-local chap, 1956; Am Wisc & Gr Milwaukee Dent Asn; pres, Greater Milwaukee Dent Asn; Am Soc Prev Dent; Am Acad Gen Pract; treas, bd mem, Childrens Serv Soc, 1962-77; bd dir & chmn, YMCA; Garfield Found; former mem, Frontiers Int; past pres, Delta Chi Lambda; founding mem, pres, Alpha Phi Alpha Fraternity; fel Int Col Dentists, 1978; Acad Gen Dent, 1981; trustee, Wis Dent Asn, 7th Dist, 1983-84; adv coun, Marquette Univ Sch Dent, 1988; Wis State Med Asst Adv Comt; Pierre Fauchard Acad, 1989; fel Am Col Dentists, 1989. **Honors/Awds:** Distinguished Service Award, Opportunity Industrialization Ctr, 1971; Service to Dent, Greater Milwaukee Dent Asn, 1987; Lifetime Achievement Award, Wisc Dent Asn, 1993; Founders Plaque, Frontiers Int, 1995. **Home Addr:** 1302 W Capitol Dr, Milwaukee, WI 53206, **Home Phone:** (414)562-6990.

### MUSE, J. MELVIN (JO MUSE)
Advertising executive, association executive. **Educ:** Mich State Univ, East Lansing, attended 1972. **Career:** Olin Corp, pub rels mgr, 1972-78; Reid Advert, copywritter, 1978-70; Hubbert Advert, creative dir, 1980-82; Mcc, Creative Develop Advert, mgr; Muse Cordero Chen & Partners, chmn, exec creative dir, chief exec officer; J Melvin Muse & Co, owner, 1985-86; Muse Commun Inc, exec creative dir, chmn, 1982-, chief exec officer, 2000-; Muse Creative Holdings, chmn & chief exec officer. **Orgs:** Bd dir, Am Asn Advert Agencies; Am Asn Advert Agencies. **Business Addr:** Chief Executive Officer, Chairman, Muse Communications Inc, 9543 Culver Blvd, Culver City, CA 90232, **Business Phone:** (310)945-4100.

### MUSE, MARIE FRANKIE. See FREEMAN, FRANKIE MUSE.

### MUSE, DR. WILLIE L.
School administrator, president (organization). **Educ:** Selma Univ, ThB; Ala State Univ, BA, educ; Interdenominational Theol Ctr, Atlanta, GA, Mdiv. **Career:** Selma Univ, prof relig pres, interim pres, pres, 1994-. **Orgs:** Prof religion, Selma Univ Asn. **Business Addr:** President, Selma University, 1501 Lapsley St, Selma, AL 36701, **Business Phone:** (334)872-2533.

### MUSGROVE, DR. MARGARET WYNKOOP
Writer, teacher. **Personal:** Born Nov 19, 1943, New Britain, CT; daughter of John T and Margaret Holden; married George Gilbert; children: Taura Johnene & George Derek. **Educ:** Univ Conn, BA, 1966; Cent Conn State Univ, MS, 1970; Univ Mass, EdD, 1979. **Career:** Hartford, Conn, high sch eng teacher, 1967-69, 1970; W Bershireshire Community Col, Pittsfield, Mass, teacher; Community Col Baltimore, Md, eng teacher, dir develop studies, coordr ctr educ develop & coordr early childhood educ, 1981-91; Loyola Col, writing media dept & writing teacher, 1991-, Women's Ctr, dir, currently; Books: The Spider Weaver: A Legend of Kente Cloth, 2001; Ashanti to Zulu: African Traditions, 1977. **Orgs:** Soc Children's Book Writers, Md Writer's Proj & Int Women's Writers Guild. **Home Addr:** 6304 Wallis Ave, Baltimore, MD 21215. **Business Addr:** Director, Loyola College, 4504A-3 Seton Court, Baltimore, MD 21210-2699, **Business Phone:** (410)617-5844.

**MUTCHERSON, DR. JAMES ALBERTUS, JR.**
Physician. **Personal:** Born Mar 22, 1941, Tampa, FL; married Katherine; children: Rovenia & Kimberly. **Educ:** Fla Agr & Mech Univ, attended 1962; Am Int Col, BA, 1965; Howard Univ Col Med, attended 1971. **Career:** Childrens Hosp, DC, pediat resident, 1971-73; Howard Univ Hosp, resident, 1973-75, pediat allergy fel, 1973-75, clin instr, 1975; pvt pract, physician, currently. **Orgs:** DC Med Soc; DC Social Asthma & Allergy; Am Acad Allergy Asthma & Immunol; fel Pediat Allergy, 1973-75. **Home Addr:** 2041 Martin Luther King Jr Ave SE, Washington, DC 20020-7024, **Home Phone:** (202)678-5644. **Business Addr:** Physician, Private Practice, 1140 Varnum St NE Suite 30, Washington, DC 20017-2152, **Business Phone:** (202)269-4223.

**MUTOMBO, DIKEMBE (DIKEMBE MUTOMBO MPOLONDO MUKAMBA JEAN JACQUE WAMUTOMBO)**
Basketball player, business owner. **Personal:** Born Jun 25, 1966, Kinshasa; son of Samuel and Biamba Marie; married Rosario; children: Carrie Biamba, Jean Jr, Ryan, Reagan, Harouna, Pearla & Nancy. **Educ:** Georgetown Univ, BA, linguistics & diplomacy, 1991. **Career:** Basketball player (retired), global ambassador, business owner; Denver Nuggets ctr, 1991-95; Atlanta Hawks, ctr, 1996-2001; Philadelphia 76ers, ctr, 2001-02; NJ Nets, ctr, 2002-03; New York Knicks, ctr, 2003-04; Chicago Bulls, ctr, 2004; Houston Rockets, res ctr, 2004-09; Africa Channel, owner, currently; Nat basketball Asn, global ambassador, currently; BuzzFeed, creative consult, 2013-. **Orgs:** Founder, chmn, pres & bd dir, Dikembe Mutombo Found, 1997-; Bd Trustees, Nat Const Ctr; Spec Olympics Int; Luba Ethnic Group. **Honors/Awds:** NBA All-Star, Nat Basketball Asn, 1992, 1995-98, 2000-02; Defensive Player of the Year Award, Nat Basketball Asn, 1995, 1997, 1998, 2001; Henry P. Iba Citizen Athlete Award, 1999; IBM Award, Nat Basketball Asn, 1999; NBA's Humanitarian Award, Nat Basketball Asn, 2001; J. Walter Kennedy Citizenship Award, 2001, 2009; Nat Civil Rights Museums Sports Legacy Award, 2007; Goodermote Humanitarian Award, Johns Hopkins Bloomberg School of Public Health, 2011; Most Caring Athlete Award, USA Weekend Magazine; hon Doctor Humane Lett, State Univ New York Col. **Special Achievements:** Passed Kareem Abdul-Jabbar as the second highest shot blocker of all time, behind only Hakeem Olajuwon. Films: 1992 NBA All-Star Game, 1992, 2002 NBA All-Star Game, 2002, The 2003 NBA Finals, 2003. **Home Addr:** 4787 Northside Dr NW, Atlanta, GA 30327-4551, **Home Phone:** (404)303-0932. **Business Addr:** Founder, Dikembe Mutombo Foundation Inc, PO Box 250225, Atlanta, GA 30325-1225, **Business Phone:** (404)262-2109.

**MUWAKKIL, SALIM (ALONZO JAMES CANNADY)**
Writer, editor. **Personal:** Born Jan 20, 1947, New York, NY; son of Alonzo and Bertha; married Karimah; children: Salimah & Rasheeda. **Educ:** Rutgers Univ, BA, polit sci; Newark Col Arts & Sci, attended 1973. **Career:** Black-owned publ, copy ed, 1970; Livingston Neighborhood Educ Ctr, co-founder educ, 1971; Addiction Planning & Coordr Agency Newark, res specialist, 1972; AP, bur newsman, 1972-74; copy ed, 1974; Muhammad Speaks, news ed, 1974-75; Bilalian News, managing ed, 1975-77; US Dept Housing & Develop, writer & ed, 1980; In These Times Mag, Chicago, Ill, sr ed, 1984-; Black Journalism Rev, consult ed bd; Columbia Col, Chicago, Ill, journalism lectr, 1986-90; Assoc Col Midwest, Chicago, Ill, part-time fac, 1990-; "The Salim Muwakkil", host; CHI Suntimes, contrib columnist, 1993-97; Columbia Col, adj Profession; CHI Tribune, contrib columnist, 1998-. **Orgs:** Pres, Black Students Union, 1970-72; consult, Livingston Col Neighborhood Educ Ctr, 1972-74; bd, Gov S Shore Community Ctr Several Publ; Spl Observer Orgn African Unity, 1975; bd mem, Progressive Media Proj & Chicago-based Pub Sq; fac mem, Assoc Cols Midwests Urban Studioes Prog; Crime & Communities Media Fel, Open Soc Inst. **Honors/Awds:** International Reggae Music Awards, Outstanding Music Criticism, 1983-84; Article of the Year, Int Black Writers Conference, 1984; Outstanding Service Award, African-American Alliance Columbia Col, Chicago, 1990; Top Ten Media Heroes, IST Alternative Journalism, 1994; Black Rose Achievement Award, League Black Women, 1997; Studs Terkel Award for Journalistic Excellence, COT Media Workshop, 2001; Lillian Award, Delta Sigma Theta Sorority, 2004. **Home Addr:** 5311 S Cornell St, Chicago, IL 60615. **Business Addr:** Senior Editor, In These Times Magazine, 2040 N Milwaukee Ave, Chicago, IL 60647, **Business Phone:** (773)772-0100.

**MWAMBA, DR. ZUBERI I.**
Educator, government official, association executive. **Personal:** Born Jan 3, 1937. **Educ:** Univ Wis, BA, 1968; Univ Pitts, MA, 1968; Howard Univ, PhD, 1972. **Career:** Govt Tanzania, radio announcer, ct clerk, interpreter, info asst, 1957-62; Fulbright, fel, 1965-68; Howard Univ, from instr to asst prof, 1968-82; US State Dept, staff, 1969-70; Tex Southern Univ, African Studies Prog, dir, 1972-2004, prof, currently; Univ Houston, Downtown Col, instr, 1975-76; Tex Southern Univ, African Studies, prof pub admin & dir, 1982-; Gen Elections, S Africa, int election observer, 1994. **Orgs:** Pres, Pan African Stud Orgn, 1965-67; Tanzania Stud Union, 1968-70, 1971-72; exec comt, E African Stud Orgn, 1968-70; Howard Univ Trust, 1969-70; Am Polit Sci Asn, 1971-; Nat Coun Black Polit Scientists, 1971-; Educr Africa Asn, 1972-; adv, Tex Southern Univ, Stud Govt Asn, 1974-75; fac, TSU Young Demo, 1974-75; adv bd, Southern Conf African Am Studies Inc. **Honors/Awds:** Distinguished Service of the Year Award, Tex Southern Univ, 1997. **Home Addr:** 7211 Castleview Lane, Missouri City, TX 77489-2422, **Home Phone:** (281)438-0240. **Business Addr:** Professor of Public Administration, Texas Southern University, 3100 Cleburne Ave, Houston, TX 77004, **Business Phone:** (713)313-7332.

**MYATT, HON. GORDON J., SR.**
Judge. **Personal:** Born Jan 2, 1928, Brooklyn, NY; son of Carlton O Sr and Frances Simons; married Evelyne E Hutchings; children: Gordon Jr, Kevin M & Craig. **Educ:** NY Univ, BS, 1950, Sch Law, LLB, 1956. **Career:** Pvt Pract, atty, 1956-60; US Dept Justice, Nat Labor Rels Bd Chicago, trial atty, 1960-62, supv atty, 1962-64, legal adv, admin law judge, 1989. **Orgs:** Nat Bar Asn; Nat Bar Judicial Coun; Am Bar Asn; Alpha Phi Alpha Fraternity, 1945-; chmn, Conf Admin Law Judges; Alpha Gamma Boule Sigma Pi Phi, 1989-. **Home Addr:** 4100 E Fletcher Ave Ste Al, Tampa, FL 33613-4831.

**MYERS, ANDRE**
Insurance executive, consultant. **Personal:** Born Aug 2, 1959, Philadelphia, PA; son of George and Pauline. **Educ:** Community Col, Philadelphia, PA, AS, retail mkt mgt, 1984; Eastern Univ, St Davids, PA, BA, orgn mgt, MS, nonprofit mgt, 1996. **Career:** Independence Blue Cross, enrollment specialist, 1998, electronic data interchange specialist, 1998-2004; Kintock Group, case mgr, 2004-05; Pa Prison Socs, human resource coordr, 2005-06; United Communities Southeast Philadelphia, asst dir mentoring matters, 2006; Church Mentoring Network, coordr & comnr, consult, 2006-; Myers Non-Profit Consult LLC, prin consult & founder, 2006-; Ins Overload Staffing, case assoc, 2007-09, enrollment specialist, 2007-13; Del Valley Financial Group, acct adminr, 2007; Community Integrated Serv, employ training specialist, 2010; Ingerman Group, community & supportive serv coordr, 2012-13. **Orgs:** Enon Tabernacle Baptist Church; vpres, Young Dem Pa, 1992-94; life mem, Nat Asn Advan Colored People; coordr, comnr, Church Mentoring Network, 1996; Philadelphia Prison Ministry. **Honors/Awds:** Bulldog Award & MUP Award, Independence Blue Cross; Regional Outreach Award, 2002. **Home Addr:** 23 E Slocum St, Philadelphia, PA 19119, **Home Phone:** (215)849-1075. **Business Addr:** Electronic Data Interchange Specialist, Independence Blue Cross, 1901 Mkt St 38th Fl, Philadelphia, PA 19103-1480, **Business Phone:** (215)241-2400.

**MYERS, DR. BERNARD SAMUEL**
Veterinarian, administrator. **Personal:** Born Jun 2, 1949, Moultrie, GA. **Educ:** Rollins Col, BA, 1970; Cornell Univ, DVM, 1974. **Career:** Harvard Sch Pub Health, res asst, 1973; Bruce Animal Hosp, assoc vet, 1974-75; Stoneham Animal Hosp, asso vet, 1975-77; Needham Animal Hosp, assoc vet, 1977-80; Lynn Animal Hosp, vet, 1985; Williamsburg Vet Clin, owner, veterinarian, currently. **Orgs:** Am Vet Med Asn, 1974-80; Mass Vet Med Asn, 1974-80; asst moderator, Shiloh Bapt Church, 1980; Vet Emergency Clin Cent Fla. **Honors/Awds:** Acad Scholar, Rollins Col, 1966-70; Algernon Sidney Sullivan Award, Rollins Col, 1969; Health Professions Scholarship, Cornell Univ, 1970-74. **Home Addr:** 1320 Crooms Ave, Orlando, FL 32805. **Business Addr:** Owner, Veterinarian, Williamsburg Veterinary Clinic, 5518 Cent Fla Pkwy, Orlando, FL 32821, **Business Phone:** (407)239-7606.

**MYERS, DEXTER**
Accountant. **Home Addr:** 228 W Poppyfields Dr, Altadena, CA 91001, **Home Phone:** (626)794-6927.

**MYERS, EMMA MCGRAW**
Chief executive officer, educator. **Personal:** Born Nov 15, 1953, Hartsville, SC; married Kenneth E. **Educ:** Fl State Univ, BA, 1974, MSW, social work admin, 1975. **Career:** United Way Am, united way intern, 1976-77, consul planning & allocations div, 1979-80; United Way Tarrant Co, mgr vol training, 1977-78, campaign div dir, 1978-79; UWA, assoc dir nat rels, 1980-83; United Way Midlands, dir planning & allocations div; United Way Aiken County AikenSC, pres & chief exec officer, 1988-92; United Way Richland County Aiken SC, pres & chief exec officer, 1992-94; EM Consults, pres & chief exec officer, 1994-; USC Inst Families soc, res assoc, 1999-2003; DeSaussure Col Social Work, adj fac, 2001-. **Orgs:** Pres & bd dir, Alpha Kappa Alpha Sorority, 1972; Parlimentarian Episcopal Ch Women, 1985; treas, FSU Black Alumin Asn; bd dir, secy, Nat Asn Black Social Workers; bd dir, Nat Asn Social Workers; pres, Dutch Fork Citivans; Leadership Aiken, 1995; Nat Asn Advan Colored People; chmn, Woman Yr Pageant Aiken Br, 1995, 1997; pres, Watkins Elem Sch PTA, 1996-2000; Rotary Club Aiken, 1996-97; Paul Harris, 1997; Richland Sch Dist One Blue Ribbon Comt, 1999-; pres, Rich Land Found, 2001-; pres, Columbia Luncheon Club, 2000-01; Richland Sch Dist One Calendar Comt, 2001, 2004; pres, WA Perry Mid Sch PTA, 2001-04; Ctr Relig S, 2002-05; vpres, CA Johnson Prep Acad PSTA, 2002-; dir develop, Communities Schs Midlands, 2003-05; pres, Asn Fundraising Prof, Cent SC Chap; Comt 100 Black Women, 2005-; pres, Parliamentarian, 2005-; pres, Jones McDonald Community Club, 2005; City Columbia Community Promotions Comt, 2005-; bd dir, Gamma Nu Omega; bd dir, Benedict-Allen Community Develop Corp. **Home Addr:** 3508 Hazelhurst Rd, Columbia, SC 29203, **Home Phone:** (803)252-1252. **Business Addr:** Adjunct Faculty, DeSaussure College of social Work, 920 Sumter St, Columbia, SC 29208, **Business Phone:** (803)777-7000.

**MYERS, DR. ERNEST RAY.** **See Obituaries Section.**

**MYERS, DR. JACQUALINE DESMONA**
Educator, college teacher. **Personal:** Born Jan 5, 1951, Charleston, SC; daughter of William Nicholas and Daisy Elouise Brown. **Educ:** Benedict Col, Columbia, SC, BS, 1971; Ind Univ, Bloomington, MS, 1972; Univ Wis, Madison, PhD, 1980. **Career:** Benedict Col, work study secy, 1968-71; Med Univ SC, clin acct, 1971; Ind Univ, asst instr, 1971-72; Ala State Univ, asst prof, 1973-86, assoc prof, bus educ, co dir, 1986-. **Orgs:** Asn, 1971-; Am Educ Res Asn, 1980-; asst corresp secy, Delta Sigma Theta Montgomery Alumnae, 1983-84; fac staff alliance, Am Fed Teachers; Phi Delta Kappa, AL; Southern Bus Educ Asn, 1989-91; fac senate, Ala State Univ; bd mem, Consortium Doctors Ltd. **Home Addr:** 501 Deerfield Dr, Montgomery, AL 36109-3312, **Home Phone:** (334)272-1271. **Business Addr:** Associate Professor of Business Education, Alabama State University, 206 McGehee Hall, Montgomery, AL 36101-0271, **Business Phone:** (334)229-4447.

**MYERS, L. LEONARD**
Chief executive officer, executive. **Personal:** Born Jan 25, 1933, Aliquippa, PA; son of Joseph and Eddie Mae Ham; married R Elizabeth; children: Linda Ann & Larry Leonard. **Educ:** Univ Pittsburgh, BA; Life Underwriter Training Coun LUTC; Calif Lutheran Univ, chartered life underwriters; Am Col Am Inst, property & liability underwriter. **Career:** First Summit Agency Inc, chief exec officer, pres, currently. **Orgs:** Pres, Long Island Chap, Casualty & Property Ins Underwriters; Long Island Chap, Calif Lutheran Univ; Hempstead Chamber Com; pres, Nat Inst Ind Asn; Lakeview Lions Club. **Home Addr:** 19 Surrey Lane, Hempstead, NY 11550-3521, **Home Phone:** (516)485-7067. **Business Addr:** President, First Summit Agency Inc, 100 Main St Unit D, Hempstead, NY 11550-2427, **Business Phone:** (516)483-3300.

**MYERS, DR. LENA WRIGHT**
Educator. **Personal:** married Julius Jr; children: Stanley. **Educ:** Tougaloo Col, BA, sociol & psychol; Mich State Univ, MA, social & cult anthropol, 1964, PhD, sociol, 1973. **Career:** Utica Jr Col, instr, sociol & psychol, 1962-68; Washtenaw Comm Col, asst prof psychol, 1968; Mich State Univ, Ctr Urban Affairs, urban res, 1970-73; Jackson State Univ, prof social, 1973-; Ohio Univ, prof sociol & anthropol, res agenda, prof emer, currently. Books: Black Women: Do They Cope Better?, 1981; Black Male Socialization Revisited in the Minds of Respondents. **Orgs:** Community Status Women Sociol Am Sociol Assoc, 1974-77; res consult, TIDE, 1975-78; pres, Asn Social Behav Scientists Inc, 1976-77; res consult, KOBA, 1979-80; bd dir, Soc Study Social Probs, 1980-83; res consult, Nat Sci Found, 1983; pres, Asn Black Sociologists, 1983-84; mem ed bd, Nat JAfrican Am Men. **Home Addr:** 2320 Queensroad Ave, Jackson, MS 39213. **Business Addr:** Professor Emeritus, Ohio University, Bentley Annex 162, Athens, OH 45701-2979, **Business Phone:** (740)593-1375.

**MYERS, LEWIS HORACE**
President (organization), executive. **Personal:** Born Apr 28, 1946, Carlisle, PA; married Cheryl; children: Donnell L, Marrielle & Lewis H III. **Educ:** Franklin & Marshall Col, BA, 1968; Univ NC, MBA, 1974; Univ NC, Basic Ind Dev Course, cert, 1979; Govt Exec Inst, attended 1980. **Career:** Off Spec Progs Franklin & Marshall Col, assoc dir, 1968-69; Upward Bound Prog Harvard Univ, exec dir, 1969-71; Soul City Found Inc, assoc dir, 1971-76; Soul City Co, vpres, 1976-79; NC Minority Bus Dev Agency, dir, 1980-82; NC Dept Com Small Bus Develop Div, asst sec, 1980-88; Construct Control Serv Corp, vpres mkt, 1988-91; LHM Assocs, pres, 1991-2003; Freelon Group, dir bus develop, currently. **Orgs:** NC Econ Develop Asn, 1979-; founder & mem, NC Asn Minority Bus; life mem, Nat Asn Advan Colored People; chair, NC Citizens Bus & Indus; chair, Econ develop Comn; 100 Black Men, Triangle E Chap; NCM/WBE Coordinators Network; Socs Mkt Prof Serv; Socs Col & Univ Planning; Asn African Am Mus; chair bd advisors, NC State Univ Indust Exten Serv; chair bd dir, Ctr Community Self Help; bd mem & founder, NC Inst Minority Econ Develop; vice chair, Mus Durham Hist. **Home Addr:** 5119 Shady Bluff St, Durham, NC 27704, **Home Phone:** (919)971-5680. **Business Addr:** President, LHM Associates, 5119 Shady Bluff St, Durham, NC 27704, **Business Phone:** (919)971-5680.

**MYERS, MICHAEL**
Football player, executive. **Personal:** Born Jan 20, 1976, Vicksburg, MS; married Brandy; children: Mykayla. **Educ:** Ala Univ. **Career:** Football player (retired), executive; Dallas Cowboys, defensive tackle, 1998, 2001, 1999, 2002, left defensive tackle, 2000, 2003; Cleveland Browns, right defensive tackle, 2003, defensive tackle & left defensive tackle, 2004; Denver Broncos, left defensive tackle, 2005-06; Cincinnati Bengals, right defensive tackle, 2007, 2008; Hinds Community Col, coaching defensive side.

**MYERS, PETER EDDIE (PETE MYERS)**
Basketball player, basketball coach. **Personal:** Born Sep 15, 1963, Mobile, AL. **Educ:** Faulkner State Community Col, attended 1983; Univ Ark, Little Rock, attended 1986. **Career:** Basketball player (retired), basketball coach; NBA Chicago Bulls, 1986-87, 1993-95; CBA Rockford Lightning, 1987-88, 1998; San Antonio Spurs, 1988, 1990; Philadelphia 76ers, 1988; Zaragoza, Spain, 1988; New York Knicks, 1988-90, 1997-98; Nj Nets, 1990; Ital League Mang Bologna, 1991-92; Albany Patroons, 1991; Scavolini Pesaro, Italy, 1992-93; Wash Bullets, 1992; Scavolini Pesaro, 1992-93; Miami Heat, 1995-96; Charlotte Hornets, 1996; Pallacanestro Cantu, 1997; Quad City Thunder, 1999; Chicago Bulls, asst coach, 2001-10, 2015-; Golden State Warriors, asst coach, 2011-14. **Business Addr:** Assistant Coach, Chicago Bulls, 1901 W Madison St, Chicago, IL 60612-2459, **Business Phone:** (312)455-4000.

**MYERS, DR. SAMUEL L., SR.**
Educator, association executive. **Personal:** Born Apr 18, 1919, Baltimore, MD; son of David and Edith; married Marion R Rieras; children: Yvette M, Tama M Clark & Samuel L Jr. **Educ:** Morgan State Col, AB, social sci, 1940, LLD, 1968; Boston Univ, MA, 1942; Harvard Univ, MA, 1948, PhD, econs, 1949; Univ Md, LLD, 1983; Sojourner & Douglass Col, DH, lit, 1992; Shaw Univ, DHL, 1994; Univ DC, LLD, 1997. **Career:** Harvard Univ, res assoc, 1949; Bur Statist US Dept Labor, economist, 1950; Morgan State Col, prof & div chmn soc sci, 1950-63; Inter-Am Affairs US Dept State, adv, 1963-67; Bowie State Col, pres, 1967-77, pres emer, 1977-; Nat Asn Equal Opportunity Higher Educ, pres; Nat Asn Equal Opportunity, 1977-95, pres emer, 1995-; Minority Access Inc, chair & sr educ advisor, 1998-. **Orgs:** Md Tax Study Comn, 1958; Gov Comn Prevailing Wage Law Md, 1962; vice chmn, Md Community Humanities & Publ Policy; Alpha Kappa Mu, State Scholar Bd, 1968-77; vice chmn, Gov Community Aide Educ, 1969-70; pres, MD Asn Higher Educ, 1971-72; chmn, Comn Int Prog, Am Asn State Col & Univ; rep, Nat Adv Coun Int Teacher Exchange; steering comt, Comn Future Int Studies; vpres & bd dir, Nat Asn Equal Opportunity Higher Educ; pres comn, Foreign Lang & Int Studies, 1978-80; mem bd dir, Rassias Found, 1980; Baltimore Urban League; res fel Rosenwald; Fel Harvard Univ; Julius Rosenwald Fel, 1948; lifetime mem, Alpha Phi Alpha fraternity. **Honors/Awds:** Commandeur de L'Ordre National de Cote d Ivoire; Samuel Z Westerfield Award, Nat Econ Asn, 1995; Hall of Fame, Morgan State Univ Alumni, 1998. **Home Addr:** 9707 Old Georgetown Rd Suite 1213, Bethesda, MD 20814-1747, **Home Phone:** (301)571-8949. **Business Addr:** Chairman, Senior Education Advisor, Minority Access Inc, 5214 Baltimore Ave, Hyattsville, MD 20781, **Business Phone:** (301)779-7100.

**MYERS, DR. SAMUEL L., JR.**
Economist. **Personal:** Born Mar 9, 1949, Boston, MA; son of Samuel L and Marion; married Sheila Ards; children: Andrea Mari & Angela

Rose. **Educ:** Morgan State Univ, BA, econ, 1971; Mass Inst Technol, PhD, econs, 1976. **Career:** Bowie State Col, vis instr, 1972; Boston Col, instr, 1973; Cuttington Univ Col, Liberia, W Africa, Fulbright Lectr, 1975-76; Univ Tex, Dept Econ, asst prof, 1976-80; Urban Inst, vis res assoc, 1977; Univ Wis-Madison, vis res fel, 1979-80; Nat Inst Justice. **Orgs:** Alpha Kappa Mu Nat Hon Socs; ed adv bd, J Pub & Int Affairs, 1982-86; bd ed, Rev Black Polit Econ, 1983-98; consult, Pa Food Merchants Asn, 1985; assoc ed, Eval Rev, 1986-89; consult, Pittsburgh Urban League, 1986; ed bd, Social Sci Quart, 1986-; consult, Nat Acad Sci, 1987; consult, NJ State & Local Expenditures & Revenue Policy Comn, 1987; consult, Baltimore Urban League, 1987; consult, US Civil Rights Comn, 1989; consult, Nat Drug Policy Comt, 1992; Pres, Asn Pub Policy Anal & Mgt, 2000-01; chair, Comt Equal Opportunity Sci & Engineering; Am Econ Asn; Nat Econ Asn; Am Acad Polit & Social Sci; Am Asn Advan Sci; Alpha Phi Alpha; co-coordr, Black Grad Econ Asn, 1973; Asn Pub Policy Anal & Mgmt, vp, 1997-99; Assessment Space Needs Juv Detention & Corrections, Prog Law & Behav, The Urban Inst, 1999; exec coun, Nat Asn Schs Pub Affairs & Admin, 2000-03; Asn Pub Policy Anal & Mgt, pres, 2000-01, vpres, 1997-99, policy coun, 1983-86; adv bd, Nat Forum Black Pub Adminr; bd dir, Nat Coun Black Studies; ed boards, J Policy Anal & Mgt, Social Sci Quart & Black Polit Econ; Cath Community Found, bd mem, 1995-2003, exec comt, 2000-03; Nat Acad Pub Admin, 2001-; Asn Pub Policy Anal & Mgt, 2001-; bd trustee, Breck Sch, Minneapolis, Minn, 2007-; NSF, 2006-08, chair, 2006-07, vice chair, 2005-06; coun mem, Inter Univ Consortium Polit & Social Res, 2004-09; Chinese Acad Social Sci, Vis Scholar, 2008-09; bd mem, Cath Charities Minneapolis, 2009-. **Honors/Awds:** Alpha Kappa Mu Merit Award, 1970; Inst Fel, MIT, 1971-73; National Fel Fund Fel, 1973-75; Fulbright Lectr Econ, Cuttington Col, Liberia, 1975-76; Top twenty US black economists, Black Polit Econ, 1990; Fulbright Scholar, Univ S Australia, Fac Aboriginal & Islander Studies, 1997; Insight Award, Inst Domestic Violence African Am Community, 2004; Elected Fel, Nat Acad Publ Adm, 2007; Sr Fulbright Scholar, Chinese Acad of Social Sci, Beijing, 2008-09. **Special Achievements:** Co-editor: Economics of Race and Crime, Transaction Press, 1988; The Black Underclass: Critical Essays on Race and Unwantedness, 1994; Editor: Civil Rights and Race Relations in the Post Reagan-Bush Era 1997; Co-author, Faculty of Color in Academe; Persistent Disparity: Race & Economic Inequality in the US 1998; Expert Testimony, Civil Action No. 04 2425, GEOD v NEW JERSEY TRANSIT; Co-author, Estimation of Race Neutral Goals in Public Procurement and Contracting, Applied Economics Letters, 2009; author, editor, and contributor of articles, chapters, and reviews to newspaper, periodicals, books, and journals. **Home Addr:** 9 Island View Lane, North Oaks, MN 55127-2614, **Home Phone:** (651)482-8749. **Business Addr:** Roy Wilkins Center for Human Relations & Social Justice, University of Minnesota, 130 Humphrey Sch 301 19th Ave S, Minneapolis, MN 55455, **Business Phone:** (612)625-9821.

### MYERS, VICTORIA CHRISTINA

Human services worker, parole officer, executive. **Personal:** Born Nov 23, 1943, Indianapolis, IN; daughter of Stanley Louis Porter and Victoria Knox Porter; married Albert Louis; children: David, John & Matthew. **Educ:** Ind Univ, Bloomington, IN, AB, sociol, 1966; Webster Univ, Webster Groves, MO, MA, corrections, 1975. **Career:** Marion County Juv Ct, Indianapolis, Ind, juv probation officer, 1967-69; Mo Bd Probation & Parole, St Louis, Mo, probation & parole officer, 1970-73; Mo Bd Probation & Parole, St Louis, Mo, unit supvr, 1973-78, dist supvr, 1978-84; Mo Bd Probation & Parole, Jefferson City, Mo, bd mem, 1984-96, probation & parole adminr, 1996-2000, dir parole serv, 2000-01; Mo Dept Corrections, dir human serv, 2001-. **Orgs:** Pres, Mo Corrections Asn, 1978-79; bd mem, Am Probation & Parole Asn, 1982-88; bd mem, Nat Asn Blacks Criminal Justice, 1982-88, nat secy, 1983-88, nat prog chair, 1989-; chmn, Am Correctional Asn, Ethics Comt, 1990-92, prog chair, 1994-96, vpres, 1996-98, bd gov, deleg assembly; comnr, Comn Accreditation Corrections, 1982-94, exec comt, 1988-92; treas, Alpha Kappa Alpha. 1992-95, pres, 1996-99, financial secy, 2000-04; vestry, Grace Episcopal Church, 1992-95 & 2000-03, sr warden, 1993-95; coordr int/nat conf, Asn Paroling Authorities, 1994-; Episcopal Diocese Mo, diocesan coun, 1995-2000 & 2003-06; bd dir, United Way Cent Mo, 1994-99, secy, 1999-2000; Gamma Epsilon Omega. **Honors/Awds:** Outstanding Employee, Mo Bd Probation & Parole, 1975; Dedicated Service Award, Nat Asn Blacks Criminal Justice, St Louis Chap, 1985; Chairman's Award, Nat Asn Blacks Criminal Justice, 1987; ER Cass Correctional Achievement Award, Am Correctional Asn, 1994; Ben Baer Award, Asn Paroling Authorities Int, 2001. **Home Addr:** 2408 Parkcrest Dr, Jefferson City, MO 65101-5152, **Home Phone:** (573)634-7159. **Business Addr:** Director of Human Services, Missouri Department of Corrections, 2729 Plz Dr, Jefferson City, MO 65109, **Business Phone:** (573)526-6472.

### MYERS, DR. WOODROW AUGUSTUS, JR.

Health services administrator. **Personal:** Born Feb 14, 1954, Indianapolis, IN; son of Woodrow and Charlotte; married Debra Jackson; children: Kimberly Leilani & Zachary Augustus. **Educ:** Stanford Univ, BS, biol sci, 1973; Harvard Med Sch, MD, 1977; Stanford Univ Grad Sch Bus, MBA, primary sector & health care mgt, 1982. **Career:** US Senate Comt Labor & HR, physician health adv, 1984; Univ Calif, asst prof, 1982-84, prof; San Francisco Gen Hosp Med Ctr, qual assurance prog chmn, 1982-84, cost containment task force chmn, qual assurance dept med-comput syst mgr, dept med gen internal med div-attend physician, med surg intensive care unit-assoc dir; Univ Calif Inst Health Policy Studies, affiliated fac; Ind Univ Med Ctr, asst prof med; Stanford Univ Med Ctr, physician specialist surg, attend physician, Bd Dirs, 2005-14; St IN, st health comnr; City New York, health comnr; Assoc Group, sr vpres, corp med dir; Ford Motor Co, dir, 1996-2000; Wellpoint Health Networks, exec vpres & chief med officer, 2000-05; Estes Pk Inst, fac, 2005; Genomic Health Inc, dir, 2006-; Express Scripts, 2007-; Mozambique Healthcare Consortium, 2007-; LipoScience, Bd Dirs, 2011-12; Corizon Health, chief exec officer, 2013-16, vice chmn, currently; Myers Ventures LLC, managing dir. **Orgs:** Am Col Physicians; AMA; Nat Med Asn; Soc Critical Care Med; State MedAsn; Marion County Med Soc; dipl, Am Bd Internal Med, 1980; bd trustee, Stanford Univ, 1987-92; bd overseer, Harvard Univ; chmn Vis Comt Harvard Sch Pub Health; Ind State Off, 1985-; Genomic Health, 2006-; Express Scripts, 2007-. **Honors/Awds:** Dr Charles F Whitten Award, The Sickle Cell Found NW Ind, 1985; Sagamore of the Wabash, Gov Robert D Orr, 1986; Hoosier Freedom Award, Ind Trial Lawyers Asn, 1986; US Public Health Service Award, US Surgeon Gen CEverett Koop, 1989; Distinguished Mentor Award, Stud Nat Med Asn, RegionV, 1990; Sagamore of the Wabash, Gov Evan Bayh, 1990; Above & Beyond Award, Indiana Black Expo, Ind St Sen Carolyn B Mosby, 1990; Key to the City of Indianapolis, Indiana, Mayor William Hudnut, 1990; Spirit of the Heartland Award, Gov Evan Bayh, IN, 1990; Living Legend Award, Hoosier Minority Chamber Com, 1992. **Special Achievements:** Author: Problems of Minorities at Majority Institutions: A Student's Perspective; 23 articles; medical licenses in states of Indiana, California and DC; appointed by President Reagan to 13 member committee to find a strategy for battling AIDS, 1987. **Home Addr:** 120 Monument Cir, Indianapolis, IN 46204, **Home Phone:** (317)488-6295. **Business Addr:** Director, Genomic Health Inc, 301 Penobscot Dr, Redwood City, CA 94063, **Business Phone:** (650)556-9300.

### MYLES, DESHONE J.

Football player. **Personal:** Born Oct 31, 1974, Las Vegas, NV. **Educ:** Univ Nev, Reno, grad. **Career:** Football player (retired); Seattle Seahawks, 1999, linebacker, middle linebacker, 1998; New Orleans Saints, 2001. **Honors/Awds:** Defensive Player of the Year, 1996.

### MYLES, STAN, JR.

Television show host, television producer. **Personal:** Born May 2, 1943, Los Angeles, CA. **Educ:** Calif State Univ, BA, 1966. **Career:** KABC-TV, La, host-producer; manpower develop specialist, 1969-71; Mich Mining Mfg Co, sls rep, 1968-69; La Hair Co, pub rels rep, 1968-69; Ala Locke HS, La, teacher, 1968; TV movie: "Louis Armstrong-Chicago Style", producer, 1976. **Orgs:** Dir pub info, Westminister Neighborhood Asn, LA, 1965-68; Nat Asn Mkg Developers; Am Fedn TV & Radio Artists; Kappa Alpha Psi; YMCA; life-time mem, Nat Asn Advan Colored People; Urban League. **Honors/Awds:** John Sweat Award, Calif Teachers Asn; Urban Affairs Community Relations Award, La City Schs; Man of the Year Award, Bahai Faith. **Home Addr:** 1310 S Catalina Ave Apt 217, Redondo Beach, CA 90277-5090. **Business Addr:** TV Executive, CBS-TV, 7800 Beverly Blvd, Los Angeles, CA 90036.

### MYLES, TOBY L. (TOBIATH L MYLES)

Football player. **Personal:** Born Jul 23, 1975, Jackson, MS. **Educ:** Miss State Univ; Jackson State Univ, attended 2001. **Career:** Football player (retired); New York Giants, offensive tackle, 1998-99; Oakland Raiders, 2000, 2001; Cleveland Browns, 2001.

### MYLES, WILBERT

Executive, vice president (organization). **Personal:** Born Aug 28, 1935, Winnsboro, LA; son of John and Armeather; married Geraldine C Pinkney; children: Wilbert Anthony Jr & Nicole Denise. **Educ:** Am Inst Banking; Pace Univ. **Career:** Baltman & Co, nyc porter, 1961; Mail Clerk Home Ins Co, clerk typist, 1962-64, asst cashier, 1968-73; Corp Trust Dept Nat Bank North Am, asst vpres, 1973-. **Orgs:** Stock Transfer Asn, 1968; BANWYs Black Non-white YMCAs Black Comn; Black Achievers Comt, Harlem YMCA, Greater New York, 1974-; Reorganization Group, Securities Industries Asn, 1975; bd mgrs, Harlem Br YMCA, 1975; Nat Task Force Steering Comt, YMCA Black Comt, 1975. **Home Addr:** 32 Sutin Pl, Chestnut Ridge, NY 10977-6424, **Home Phone:** (845)356-2646.

### MYLES, WILLIAM, JR.

Athletic director. **Personal:** Born Nov 21, 1936, Kansas City, MO; son of William Sr and Vera L Phillips; married Lorita Thompson; children: Debbie & Billy. **Educ:** Drake Univ, Des Moines, Iowa, BS, 1962; Cent Mo State, MS, 1967. **Career:** Manual High Sch, Kansas City, Mo, asst football & basketball coach, 1962-63; Lincoln High Sch, Kansas City, Mo, asst football & basket ball coach & head football coach, 1963-69; SE High Sch, Kansas City, Mo, head football coach, 1969-72; Univ NE, Lincoln, Nebr, asst football coach, 1972-77; OH State Univ, Columbus, OH, asst football coach, 1977-85, assoc dir athletics, 1985-2007. **Orgs:** Christian Science Church, Fel Christian Athletes, 1964-, Am Football Coaches Asn, 1972-; dir Athletics, Nat asn col, 1985-; Boy Scouts Am. **Honors/Awds:** Kansas City Area Man of the Year; Greater Kansas City Coach of the Year, 1971; Double D Award, Drake Univ, 1981; Drake National Distinguished Alumni Award, Drake Univ, 1988; Ohio Glod Award, Nat Football Found. **Home Addr:** 1100 Kirk Ave, Worthington, OH 43085, **Home Phone:** (614)885-1122.

### MYRICK, BISMARCK

Diplomat. **Personal:** Born Dec 23, 1940, Portsmouth, VA; married Marie Pierre Mbaye; children: Bismarck Jr, Wesley Todd & Allison Elizabeth. **Educ:** Univ Tampa, BA, 1972; Syracuse Univ, MA, 1973; postgrad, 1980. **Career:** US Dept State, Off E African Affairs, Somalia, desk officer, 1980-82; Monrovia, Liberia, polit officer, 1982-84; Off Strategic Nuclear Policy, action officer, 1985-87; Interagency Nuclear Testing Arms Control Working Group, chmn, 1986-87; Policy Plans & Coord Bur, dep dir, 1987-89; US-African Policy, Una Chapman Cox fel, 1988-90; Durban, SafricA, prin officer, 1990-93; Capetown, SafricA, prin officer, 1993-95; Kingdom Lesotho, ambassador, Maseru, 1995-98; Spelman Col, dipl residence, 1998-99; Repub Liberia, ambassador, 1999-2002; Old Dom Univ, ambassador-in-residence, adj fac, currently; Goree Island, Senegal, goodwill ambassador, 2008-; polit officer, Liberia. **Orgs:** Sr Foreign Serv, career mem. **Honors/Awds:** Most Meritorious Order of Mohlomi, Gov Lesotho; Department of State's Superior Honor Award; Four Meritorious Honor Awards; AUS Hall of Fame, 1996; Doctor of Humane Letters degree award, Spelman Col; Portsmouth Notable, 2006; The Citizen of Chesapeake, 2013. **Special Achievements:** Author: Three Aspects of Crisis in Colonial Kenya, 1975, The United States and Liberia; Vietnam War hero; named "Diplomat of the Year", "Man of the Year". **Business Addr:** Adjunct Faculty, Old Dominion University, Dept Polit Sci 5115 Hampton Blvd, Norfolk, VA 23529, **Business Phone:** (757)683-3000.

### MYRICK, DR. HOWARD A.

Educator, television broadcaster. **Personal:** Born Jun 22, 1934, Dawson, GA; son of Howard and Lenora Pratt; married Roberta Bowens; children: Kyl V & Keris J. **Educ:** Fla A&M Univ, Tallahassee, FL, BS, 1955; Univ Southern Calif, Los Angeles, MA, cinema commun & educ technol, 1966, PhD, cinema commun & educ technol, 1967. **Career:** Media specialist, Motion picture, Tv producer & Broadcast mgr; Corp Pub Broadcasting, Wash, DC, dir, res, 1977-82; Am Forces Radio-TV Network, Repub Korea, dir & gen mgr; Clark Col, Atlanta Univ Ctr, Atlanta, GA, Mass Commun, prof, 1982-83; WCLK-FM, gen mgr; Howard Univ, Sch Commun, Radio, Tv & Film, chmn & prof; Temple Univ, chmn radio, tv & film dept, 1983-89; Educ TV Div, AUS Command & Gen Staff Col, Ft Leavenworth, dir & gen mgr; Off Asst Secy Defense Pub Affairs, audio visual officer; Temple Univ, Sch Commun & Theater, Philadelphia, prof commun, currently; Youth & Violence Prev Proj, Philadelphia Comnr Health, consult; Nat Telecommunications & Info Admin, consult; Nat Endowment Arts, consult, 1988-91. **Orgs:** Consult, Nat Telecom & Info Agency, 1986-90; ed bd, J Nat Acad TV Arts & Sci, 1989-91; chmn, comn minorities, Broadcast Educ Asn, 1988-90; bd dir, Int Asn Knowledge Engrs, 1988-91; bd experts, Nat Endowment Arts, 1988-91; Now Defunct Pa Pub Tv Network Comn; consult, Media Experts, US Off Educ & HEW. **Home Addr:** 630 W Allens Lane, Philadelphia, PA 19119-3309, **Home Phone:** (215)248-5382. **Business Addr:** Professor, Temple University, 1301 W Norris St Tomlinson Theater Rm 212, Philadelphia, PA 19122, **Business Phone:** (215)204-8431.

### MYRICK, SVANTE L.

City council member, mayor. **Personal:** Born Mar 15, 1987, Earlville, NY. **Educ:** Cornell University, Bachelor's in Communications, 2009. **Career:** Cornell Cooperative Extension, Reality Check, Asst. Program Coordinator, 2006-08; The Learning Web, Coordinator-Career Exploration and Apprenticeship Coordination, 2009-10; Cornell University, Asst. Director of Student and Young Alumni Programs, 2010-11; City of Ithaca, NY, Councilperson, 2008-11, Mayor, 2012-. **Honors/Awds:** TheGrio.com, 100 Making History Today, 2012. **Special Achievements:** Ithaca's youngest mayor and one of the youngest in U.S. history; youngest councilperson for Ithaca; first African American mayor in Ithaca's history. **Business Addr:** Fourth Fl., City Hall, Ithaca, NY 14850, **Business Phone:** ((60)7)274-65.

### MYRICK-HARRIS, CLARISSA

Dean (education), vice president (organization), college teacher. **Educ:** Morris Brown Col, BA, Eng, 1976; Ohio State Univ, MA, news ed journalism, 1977; Emory Univ, PhD, Am studies. **Career:** One-WorldArchives, co-founder, vpres, 1998-; Morris Brown Col, African Studies, Hist & World Lang Dept, chair, 1998-2001; Southern Black Communities Oral Hist Ctr, founding dir, 2001-03; Interdisciplinary Ctr Study Global Chg, distinguished res & teaching fel, 2006-08; Global Issues Hons Consortium, nat dir, 2006-08; United Negro Col Fund (UNCF), dir curric & fac Enhancement Prog, 2007-12; UNCF, Inst Capacity Bldg, interim exec dir, 2010-12; Morehouse Col, dean humanities & social sci & prof African studies, 2012-. **Orgs:** Coalition to Remember 1906 Atlanta Riot, Pub Educ Comt, co-chair, 2004-; Ga Trust Hist Preserv, Higher Educ Comt, mem, 2005-. **Special Achievements:** Co-author of "All Day and All Night: The History of the Atlanta Media Association" (2010); author of various publications, articles, and papers; has made numerous media appearances.

### MYRICKS, DR. NOEL

President (organization), lawyer, educator. **Personal:** Born Dec 22, 1935, Chicago, IL; son of Wyman and Mollie Palmer; children: Toussaint L & Mollie; married Sherralyn L Faine. **Educ:** San Francisco State Univ, BA, 1965, MS, 1967; Howard Univ, JD, 1970; Am Univ, EdD, coun psychol & higher educ, 1974. **Career:** Professor (retired), professor emeritus; Howard Univ, prof, 1967-69; Univ DC, educ adminr, 1969-72; pvt pract atty, 1973-; Univ Md, prof, assoc prof, assoc prof emer, 2004-; Noel Myricks & Assocs Inv, pres, currently. **Orgs:** Assoc ed, Family Rels J, 1978-82; NFL Players Asn, 1984-; Kappa Upsilon Lambda; Alpha Phi Alpha, 1984-; Am Bar Asn; Groves Asn; educr, atty coach, Nat Intercollegiate Mock Trial Champions, UMCP, 1992; Omicron Delta Kappa Hon Soc, 1992. **Home Addr:** 2000 Golf Course Dr, Reston, VA 20191-3802. **Business Addr:** Associate Professor Emeritus, University of Maryland, 1204 Marie Mt Hall, College Park, MD 20781, **Business Phone:** (301)405-4007.

# N

### N'DIAYE, MAKHTAR. See NDIAYE, MAKHTAR VINCENT.

### N'NAMDI, CARMEN ANN

Educator, school principal. **Personal:** Born May 13, 1949, Cincinnati, OH; daughter of Carl and Dorothy Jenkins; married George N; children: Kemba, Nataki (deceased), Jumaane & Izegbe. **Educ:** Ohio State Univ, Columbus, OH, BS, educ, 1971; Wayne State Univ, Detroit, MI, MA, educ, 1978. **Career:** Educator (retired); Nataki Talibah Schhouse, Detroit, MI, co-founder & headmistress, 1978-95, prin, 1995-2008. **Orgs:** Founder & bd dir, Nataki Talibah Schhouse, Detroit, MI, 1978; bd mem, Detroit C's Mus Friends; exec bd, Detroit Chap Jack & Jill, 1987-; Greater Wayne County Links, 1990-, pres, 1997-99; chair bd, Nat Charter Sch Inst; mem bd, Mich Asn Pub Sch Academies. **Home Addr:** 43885 S Interstate 94 Serv, Belleville, MI 48111, **Home Phone:** (734)697-5474.

### N'NAMDI, DR. GEORGE RICHARD

Art museum director. **Personal:** Born Sep 12, 1946, Columbus, OH; son of George Richard Johnson and Ima Jo Winson Watson; married Carmen Ann Kiner; children: Kemba, Nataki (deceased), Jumaane & Izegbe. **Educ:** Ohio State Univ, Columbus, BS, 1970, MS, 1972; Univ Mich, Ann Arbor, 1974, PhD, psychol, 1978. **Career:** Univ Cincinnati, Ohio, dir head start training, 1970-72; Univ Mich, Ann Arbor, instr, 1973-76; Wayne State Univ, Detroit, Mich, asst prof, 1976-86; Wayne Co Health Dept, Detroit, Mich, psychologist, 1978-82; Nataki Talibah Schoolhouse of Detroit, founder, 1978; Jazzonia Gallery, Detroit, Mich, dir, 1981-84; G R N'Namdi Gallery, Birmingham, Mich, owner, 1981-; Milan Fed Prison, therapist. **Orgs:** Chmn bd, Cass Food Co-op, 1983-86; Paradigm Dance Co, 1986-88; treas, Nataki Talibah Sch house, 1989-; Birmingham Bloom field Cult Coun, 1990-; Friends African & African Am Detroit Inst Art; Detroit Artist Mkt; Mich coun Arts & Cult; founder, N'Namdi Ctr Contemp Art; Black Stud Psychol Asn. **Home Addr:** 43885 S 94 Serv Dr, Belleville, MI 48111, **Home Phone:** (734)697-5474. **Business Addr:** Founder, G R N'Namdi Gallery, 1435 Randolph St, Detroit, MI 48226, **Business Phone:** (313)831-8700.

## NABORS, JESSE LEE
Counselor, president (organization), educator. **Personal:** Born May 17, 1940, Columbus, MS; married Rebecca Gibson; children: Sherri, Tejia, Jesse Jr & Marcellus III. **Educ:** Tuskegee Inst, BS, 1965, MEd, 1968. **Career:** Tuskegee Inst, coordr, 1966; Tuskegee Inst, residence hall counr, 1967-68; Sanders Unified Sch Dist, teacher, 1968; Stockton Unified Sch Dist, child welfare attendance, 1971, asst prin, 1993; City Stockton, vice-mayor, 1975; Amos Alonzo Stagg High Sch, head security team, currently. **Orgs:** Pres, Stockton Br Nat Asn Advan Colored People, 1971-73; pres, BTA, 1972-73; Stockton Alumni Chap, 1975-77; polemarch, Kappa Alpha Psi Frat; Stockton City Coun; bd educ, Stockton Unified Sch Dist. **Home Addr:** 138 W 8th St, Stockton, CA 95206-2617, **Home Phone:** (209)943-5834. **Business Addr:** Head of Security Team, Amos Alonzo Stagg High School, 1621 Brookside Rd, Stockton, CA 95207, **Business Phone:** (708)974-7400.

## NABORS, REV. DR. MICHAEL C.R.
Clergy, president (organization). **Personal:** Born Nov 12, 1959, Kalamazoo, MI; son of Clarence Lee and Kathleen Whaling; married Sydni Craig; children: Simone Charice, LaNez Domimic, JaRell Desmond, Spencer Alexandria & Pierce Alexander. **Educ:** Western Mich Univ, BS, eng & creative writing, 1982; Princeton Theol Sem, MDiv, 1985, ThM, 1986; United Theol Sem, DMin, 1992. **Career:** Galilee Missionary Baptist Church, youth minister, 1980-82; First Baptist Church, interim pastor & pastor, 1983-92; Joint Action Community Serv Inc, regional dir, 1993; C's Home Soc, prog dir, 1994-96; Shiloh Baptist Church, asst pastor, 1994-98; Bor & Twp Princeton, civil rights dir, 1996-98; New Calvary Baptist Church, sr pastor, 1997-; Ashland Theol Sem, adj prof; Marygrove Col & Ecumenical Theol Sem, adj prof preaching, currently; Gateway Community Health, bd chmn, 2013-. **Orgs:** Pres, Nat Asn Advan Colored People, Cent NJ br, 1986-89, Trenton br, 1995-97; pres, Princeton Clergy Asn, 1987-88; co chair, NJ Relig Task Force; bd mem, NJ Health Dept's Cardiac Surg Adv Comt; chair, Urban Agenda Comt Black Ministers Coun NJ; dir, Cong Christian Educ Eastern Region PNBC Inc; first vpres, Mich Progressive Baptist Conv Inc, 2000-; bd mem, Nat Asn Advan Colored People, Detroit br, 2000-; bd mem, United Way, Oakland County, 2001-; bd mem, St John's Health Systs; bd mem, Detroit Area Agency on Aging; bd mem, Nat Conf Community Justice; Birmingham-Bloomfield Task Force Race Rels & Ethnic Diversity; Clergy Task Force Skillman Found Detroit; exec dir, Joint Comn Civil Rights, Princeton, NJ; bd dir, Gateway Detroit East. **Honors/Awds:** Outstanding Youth of the Year, Kalamazoo Rotary Club, 1977; Princeton, NJ, Oct 12, 1991 declared Michael CR Nabors Day; Samuel DeWitt Proctor Fellow, United Theol Sem Dayton. **Business Addr:** Pastor, New Calvary Baptist Church, 3975 Concord Ave, Detroit, MI 48207, **Business Phone:** (313)923-1600.

## NABORS, ROB
Government official. **Personal:** Born Jan 1, 1971, Ft. Dix, NJ; son of Robert L. **Educ:** Univ Notre Dame, BA, 1993; Univ NC-Chapel Hill, MA, 1996. **Career:** US Gov, sr advisor to chief staff Rahm Emanuel, dep chief staff to US Pres Barack Obama; Off Mgt & Budget (OMB), prog examr, 1996-98, spec asst, 1998, asst dir & exec secy, 2000, minority staff dir, 2004, dep dir off mgt & budget, 2009-, majority staff dir; asst to dir legis affairs; House Appropriations Comt, clerk & staff dir comt. **Special Achievements:** Recognized as a "budding wunderkind" by OMB Director Jacob Lew; as a graduate, co-authored a paper political scientist Thomas Oatley, published in journal Intl Organization, 1996. **Business Addr:** Deputy Director, The Office of Management and Budget, 725 17th St NW, Washington, DC 20503, **Business Phone:** (202)395-3080.

## NAEOLE, CHRIS
Football coach, football player. **Personal:** Born Dec 25, 1974, Kailua, HI; married Tara; children: Azure Ke'alohilani & Christian Kaiwikani. **Educ:** Univ Colo, BA, sociol. **Career:** Football player (retired), coach; New Orleans Saints, 1997, right guard, 1998-2001, guard, 1999; Jacksonville Jaguars, right guard, 2002-09; Iolani Sch, defensive line coach, 2010-12; Univ Hawaii, offensive line coach, 2013-15, Hawaii Warriors, asst head coach & offensive line coach, 2015-. **Honors/Awds:** First team All Big 12, 1995-96; First team All American, 1996; All Am first team, Assoc Press, Am Football Coaches Asn; Walter Camp & Football News; second-team hons, The Sporting News; John Mack Award. **Home Addr:** , Honolulu, HI. **Business Addr:** Assistant Head Coach, Offensive Line Coach, University of Hawaii, 1337 Lower Campus Rd, Honolulu, HI 96822, **Business Phone:** (808)956-6508.

## NAGAN, WINSTON PERCIVAL
Educator. **Personal:** Born Jun 23, 1940, Port Elizabeth; married Judith Mattox(deceased); children: Jean, Catherine & Arthur. **Educ:** Univ SAfrica, BA, 1965; Oxford Univ, Brasenose Col, BA, jurisp, 1966, MA, jurisp, 1970; Duke Univ, LLM, 1970, MCL, 1970; Yale Univ, JSD, 1977. **Career:** Duke Sch Law, Rule Law Res Ctr, res asst, 1967-68; Ross Arnold atty-at-law, law clerk, 1967; African-Am Inst, fel, 1967-68; Va Polytech Inst & State Univ, asst prof polit sci, 1968-71; Duke Law Sch, res asst, 1968; AALS Law Teachers Clin, 1971; Valparaiso Univ Sch Law, asst prof, 1971-72; De Paul Univ Col Law, from assoc prof to asst prof, 1972-75; Expedited Arbit Proc, arbitrator, 1972-74; Yale Univ, lectr, 1974-75; CLEO Inst, assoc prof, 1974; Univ Fla Law Sch, assoc prof, 1975-77, prof, 1978-, affil prof anthrop, 1989-, Inst Human Rights & Peace Develop, founder & dir, 1994-, affil african studies & latin am studies, 2006-, Samuel T Dell Res Scholar prof law, currently, Inst Human Rights & Peace Develop, founding dir, currently; Monash Univ Sch Law Australia, vis prof, 1979; Brit PEN, mem, 1993-; Int Com Arbit Moot, arbitrator, 1996-; Makerere Univ, Human Rights & Peace Ctr, co-founder & principle investr, 1997; Univ Cape Town, dir, 1998-2005; Shuar Bill Fundamental Rights, co-drafter, 2002; Shuar Nation Ecuador, procurador judicia & abogado defensor, 2002-; Eritrea Ministry Justice, legal consult, 2003; World Bank, consult, 2004-05; High Ct Repub S Africa, Western Cape Div, actg justice, 2006-07; Univ Frankfurt Law Sch, vis prof, 2008; CADMUS J World Acad Art, ed, 2010-; Eruditio, Electronic J World Acad Art & Sci, ed chief, 2012-; Univ Warsaw Law Sch, Poland, vis prof, 2012. **Orgs:** Fel African-Am Inst, 1967-68; fel Am Soc Int Law; test UN, 1968-73; ed, Soviet Pub Int Law, 1970; trustee, Int Def Aid Fund, 1971-74; secy, Int Campaign vs Racism Sports, 1972-74; Int Def & Aid Fund S Africa, 1972-74; James B Warburg fel ConsortiumWorld Order Studies, 1974-75; fel James B Warburg, 1974-75; consult, Am Bar Asn, 1976; African Stud Asn; Asn Am Law Sch; Ctr Study Dem Inst; Am Soc Social Philos & Philos Law; Arts & Civil Sem Univ Fla; Am Civil Sem Univ Fla; Minority Comt; Prom Tenure Comt; Libr Comt; fac, Recruit Comt; chmn, Admin Foreign Lawyers Comt, Univ Senate; Amnesty Int USA, 1986-92; pres, bd dirs, Policy Sci Ctr Yale Law Sch, 1986-91; S Africa Const Watch Comn, 1989-90; adv, Nat Coalition Against Capital Punishment; bd dir, Prog Interdisciplinary Res Causes Human Rights Violations, 1994-; bd, co-founder, ed, E African J Peace & Human Rights, 1994-; fel World Acad Art & Sci, 1998-, bd dir, 2009-, secy gen, 2011-; trustee res fel Univ Fla, 1998; bd dir, Inst Victims Trauma, 2001-; vis fel Brasenose Col, 2002-03; fel Royal Soc Arts, 2003-; int ed advisor, J Law Polit, 2005-; bd dir, Shuar Nation Corp, 2005-; plenary chair, Dag Hammarskjold Found, 2005; adv bd, Princeton Ctr Prev Crimes Against Humanity, 2006-; bd dir, World Acad Art Sci, 2009-; ed bd, CADMUS Publ, 2009-; Am Soc Social Philos & Philos Law; Am Bar Asn; Nat Dem Lawyers Asn; African Studies Asn; chair, World Acad Art Sci, 2011-; pres, organizing comt, XII Int Colloquium Visions Sustainable Develop, Theory & Action, UF, 2015. **Honors/Awds:** English Dept Prize, Univ S Africa, 1962; Faculty of Law prize, Ft Hare, 1963; Princess Beatrix Inter Nat Scholarship Award, 1964; Brasenose Oxford Overseas Scholar, 1964-67; Senior Fulbright Scholar, Monash Univ, 1979; Bahai Human Rights Award, 1990; Rosa Parks Award, Accepted on behalf of AIUSA, 1990; Senior Fulbright Law Scholar Award, 1993; Professorial Excellence Award, 1997, Unviersity Step Award, 2001; Honorary Professor, Univ Cape Town, State Fla, 2002-; Distinguished Int Educr, Univ Fla, 2005. **Special Achievements:** Numerous appearances on radio & television, numerous publications of papers & speeches. **Home Addr:** 8966 SW 44th Lane, Hale Plantation, Gainesville, FL 32608, **Home Phone:** (352)376-1719. **Business Addr:** Affiliate Professor, Professor of Law Sam T Dell Research Scholar, University of Florida, 312L Holland Hall, Gainesville, FL 32611, **Business Phone:** (352)273-0935.

## NAGIN, CLARENCE RAY, JR.
Mayor. **Personal:** Born Jun 11, 1956, New Orleans, LA; married Seletha Smith; children: Jeremy, Jarin & Tianna. **Educ:** Tuskegee Univ, BS, acct, bus & mgt, 1978; Tulane Univ, MBA, bus admin, mgt & opers, 1994. **Career:** Gen Motors, Detroit, MI, 1978-81; Assoc Corp, Dallas, TX, 1981-85; Cox Commun, New Orleans, LA, controller, 1985-89, vpres & gen mgr, 1989-2002; City New Orleans, mayor, 2002-10; CRN Initiatives LLC, owner, pres, 2010-. **Orgs:** Pres, founder, 100 Black Men Metro New Orleans; pres, LA Cable TV Asn; chmn, UNCF Walkathon; bd mem, Greater New Orleans Educ Found; Orleans & Jefferson Parish Bus Coun; bd mem, United Way; bd mem, Covenant House; Nat Conf Dem Mayors; Nat Black MBA Asn. **Home Addr:** 28 Pk Island Dr, New Orleans, LA 70122.

## NAILS, JAMIE MARCELLUS
Football player, football coach. **Personal:** Born Jun 3, 1977, Baxley, GA. **Educ:** Fla A&M Univ, 1997. **Career:** Football player (retired), football coach; Buffalo Bills, 1997, guard, 1998-99, right guard, 1999-2000; Miami Dolphins, left guard, 2002-03; Miami Morays, Nat Indoor Football League, offensive line coach. **Business Addr:** Offensive Line Coach, Miami Morays, Miami Arena, Miami, FL 33136, **Business Phone:** (305)530-4400.

## NAILS, JOHN WALKER
Lawyer. **Personal:** Born Sep 5, 1947, Florence, AL; son of Rudolph Jr and Mary Ester; married Phyllis Johnson, Mar 9, 1974; children: Tanique Yvette & Rudolph IV. **Educ:** Howard Univ, BA, 1969; Villanova Law Sch, JD, 1972. **Career:** Community Assistance Proj, legal rep, 1972-75; pvt pract atty, 1975-; City Chester, asst city solicitor, 1978-87, city solicitor, 1988-91. **Orgs:** PA Bar Asn, 1972-; boards community assistance proj, Del County Bar Asn, 1975-; Nat Bar Asn, 1985-; trustee, Calvary Baptist Church, 1987-. **Honors/Awds:** Outstanding Community Service, Chester Scholar Fund, 1983; co-winner Riemel Moot Court Competition, Villanova Law Sch, 1972. **Special Achievements:** City of Chester, first black city solicitor, 1988. **Home Addr:** 914 Highland Ave, Chester, PA 19013-1610, **Home Phone:** (302)464-2521. **Business Addr:** Attorney at Law, 511-513 Welsh St Suite 101, Chester, PA 19013-4413, **Business Phone:** (610)876-0306.

## NAJEE, J. (JEROME NAJEE RASHEED)
Musician. **Personal:** Born Nov 4, 1957, NY; children: Noah & Jamal. **Educ:** Bronx Community Col, attended 1978; New Eng Conserv Music, attended 1982. **Career:** Recordings include: Najee's Theme, 1987; Day By Day, 1988; Tokyo Blue, 1990; Just An Illusion, 1992; Share My World, 1995; Best Najee, 1998; Morning Tenderness, 1998; Embrace, 2003; My Pt View, 2005; Songs from Key Life; Love Songs; Rising Sun, 2007; Mind Over Matter, 2009; Not a Day Goes By; Indian Summer; FAN Entertainment Grp, jazz artist. **Honors/Awds:** Soul Train Music Award, 1993, 1995; NAACP Image Award, 2006; Trumpet Award, 2008. **Special Achievements:** Plays soprano, alto & tenor sax & flute; Performed as a spec guest artist on Hit & Run tour with Prince; Nominated for Grammy music award, 1987; Performed for Nelson Mandela for the S African leaders birthday celebration, 1998; Guest of Bill Clinton in a spec performance, 1999. **Home Addr:** PO Box 14568, Oakland, CA 94614, **Home Phone:** (510)430-0392. **Business Addr:** Jazz Artist, FAN Entertainment Group, 3940 Laurel Canyon Blvd Suite 689, Studio City, CA 91604.

## NALL, ALVIN JAMES, JR.
Photojournalist, accountant. **Personal:** Born Nov 27, 1960, New York, NY; son of Alvin J and Emma. **Educ:** Cayuga Community Col, AAS, 1995; Ithaca Col, Roy H Park Sch Communs, BS, tv & radio studies, 1997, MS, communs, 1998. **Career:** Portrait Photogr, 1981-82; WTVH-TV, Syracuse, NY, photojournalist/ed, 1982-93, prod tech, 1993, 1995; USF, tech sgt, 1990-91; NY Air Nat Guard, media specialist, master sgt, 1998-, human resources advr, 1998-; Sen Hoffmann, commun dir; Eric Mower & Assocs, Pub Rels Servs Group, sr acct exec, currently. **Orgs:** Nat Press Photogrs Asn, 1988-94; Nat Asn Broadcasters, 1989-; mentor, coach, NCP, ACT-So Prog, 1989-; Syracuse Asn Black Journalists, 1991-; bd mem, Nat Asn Advan Colored People's Afro-Cult Technol Sci Olympics prog. **Home Addr:** 2323 Eastchester Rd, Bronx, NY 10469, **Home Phone:** (718)653-6521. **Business Addr:** Senior Account Executive, Eric Mower & Associates, 50 Fountain Plz Suite 1300, Buffalo, NY 14202, **Business Phone:** (716)842-2233.

## NALLS, PATRICIA
Founder (originator), chief executive officer. **Personal:** children: Alana & Shawn. **Career:** The Women's Collective, founder & exec dir, currently. **Orgs:** Consult, Health Resources & Servs Admin; Ryan White Title I Planning Coun; DC HIV Housing Planning Coun; Nat Conf Women & HIV/AIDS. **Home Addr:** 8813 Providence Ridge Ct, North Chesterfield, VA 23236-2172, **Home Phone:** (804)590-1389. **Business Addr:** Founder, Executive Director, The Womens Collective, 1436 U St NW Suite 200, Washington, DC 20009, **Business Phone:** (202)483-7003.

## NAMPHY, DR. ANDRE C.
Executive, lawyer. **Educ:** Harvard Univ, AB, hist, 1994; Univ Oxford, DPhil, 1998; Yale Law Sch, JD, law, 2001. **Career:** Sullivan & Cromwell LLP, assoc, 2001-09; Mubadala Develop Co, gen coun, corp finance & treas, 2010-. **Home Addr:** 692 Longview Rd, South Orange, NJ 07079-1109. **Business Addr:** Associate, Sullivan & Cromwell LLP, 125 Broad St, New York, NY 10004, **Business Phone:** (212)558-4000.

## NANCE, BOOKER JOE, SR.
Government official, association executive, mayor. **Personal:** Born Apr 10, 1933, Crockett County, TN; married Everlena Lucas; children: Alice Eison, Booker J Jr, Mary, Phyllis, Gladys & Marvin. **Career:** Gates City, town board, alderman, 1973, mayor, currently; Nance's Construction & Contracting, pres, 1984-. **Orgs:** Chmn, Parents Adv Comt Halls Elem. **Home Addr:** 1191 7th St, PO Box 99, Gates, TN 38037-0099, **Home Phone:** (731)836-5205. **Business Addr:** Mayor, City of Gates, Second St, Gates, TN 38037, **Business Phone:** (731)836-7501.

## NANCE, FREDERICK R.
Executive. **Personal:** Born OH; married Jacquelyn Jones; children: Melanie & Ricky. **Educ:** Harvard Univ, BA, 1975; Univ Mich, Law Sch, JD, 1978. **Career:** City Cleveland, primary outside coun; fed & state courts, jury trial litigator; RPM Int Inc, bd dir, 2007-; Bio Enterprise Inc, bd dir; McDonald & Co Investments Inc, audit & compensation comt; Nat Football League, comnr; Squire Sanders & Dempsey, Cleveland, OH, 1978-, managing partner, 1987-; KeyBanc Capital Markets Inc, bd dir; Cleveland Browns, sr advisor & spec coun, currently; Cleveland Mayor Frank Jackson. **Orgs:** Chmn, advocacy, exec comt Greater Cleveland Partnership; Cleveland's 16, 000 plus; Exec Comt 50 Club Cleveland; chmn, Cleveland Defense Ind Alliance; bd dir, Cleveland Found; Cleveland Clin; bd trustee, United Way Greater Cleveland; Cath Charities Found; US Ct Appeals Sixth Circuit Judicial Conf; adv bd, Nat Asn Black Sports Professionals, currently; bd mem, Cleveland Mus Art; bd mem, Cath Diocese Cleveland Found; Ohio State Legal Serv Asn; Parmadale & Cleveland State Univ Found; co-chmn, NCAA Womens Final Four; adv bd, Nat Asn Black Sports Professionals. **Business Addr:** Managing Partner, Squire Sanders & Dempsey LLP, 4900 Key Tower 127 Pub Sq, Cleveland, OH 44114-1304, **Business Phone:** (216)479-8623.

## NANCE, HERBERT CHARLES, SR.
Lawyer, auditor, educator. **Personal:** Born Dec 30, 1946, Taylor, TX; son of Henry Jr and Alice Lavern Sanford; married Linda Lee Brown; children: Charlinda Audlice & Herbert Jr. **Educ:** Huston Tillotson Col, BA, 1969; Univ Tex, San Antonio, MA, 1979. **Career:** Ross Jr High Sch, teacher & coach, 1974-76; Kitty Hawk Jr High Sch, teacher & coach, 1976-80; Vietnam Era Veterans Outreach Prog, counr, 1980-81; Kelly AFB, Base Educ Serv Off, guid counr; Base Educ Serv SA-ALC & DPE, Tex, Educ Serv Specialist; Sam Houston High Sch, San Antonio, TX, col counr, 2003; San Antonio Indep Sch Dist, sch attendance auditor, non-traditional prog, currently. **Orgs:** Am Asn Coun; bd trustee, Lackland Indep Sch Dist; adv coun, Comn Col Air Force, 1986; asst keeper rec, Omega Psi Phi Frat, San Antonio Chap, 1986; bd mem, Bexar County Sickle Cell Anemia; vBasileus, Psi Alpha Chap; Omega Psi Phi Fraternity. **Home Addr:** 2942 Lakeland Dr, San Antonio, TX 78222, **Home Phone:** (210)648-2636. **Business Addr:** Attendance Auditor, San Antonio Independent School District, 141 Lavaca St, San Antonio, TX 78210, **Business Phone:** (210)299-5500.

## NANCE, JESSE J., JR.
Educator. **Personal:** Born Aug 2, 1939, Alamo, TN; son of Jesse J and Lillie L Nunn. **Educ:** Tenn State Univ, Nashville, BS, 1961; Univ Wis Madison, MS, 1971; Univ Tenn, addn grad studies. **Career:** Tenn High Sch, teacher, 1961-67; Oak Ridge Assoc Univ, special training in atomic energy, 1967, instr nuclear sci, 1967-69; Atlantic Comm Col, asst prof biol, 1971-76; Univ Tenn Med Units Memphis, special training, 1972; Jackson St Comm Col, instr biol, 1976-78; Vol Comm Col, assoc prof biol, 1978. **Orgs:** Phi Beta Sigma, 1959; Int Wildlife Fed, 1972; church choir mem, dir malechorus, minister educ, church sch teacher. **Home Addr:** 37 Nolan Dr, Gates, TN 38037-4115.

## NANCE, LARRY DONELL, SR.
Basketball player, race car driver. **Personal:** Born Feb 12, 1959, Anderson, SC; married Jaynee; children: Casey, Larry Jr & Pete. **Educ:** Clemson Univ, attended 1981. **Career:** Basketball player (retired), race car driver, executive; Phoenix Suns, 1981-88; Cleveland Cavaliers, 1988-94; US Marine Corps, driver; Black Dragracers.com Inc; Catch-22 Racing, NHRA, prof stock car racer, owner & driver, 1986-.

**Orgs:** Int Hot Rod Asn; Athletes Hope. **Home Addr:** , OH. **Business Addr:** Stock Car Racer, NHRA, 2035 Financial Way, Glendora, CA 91741, **Business Phone:** (626)914-4761.

**NANULA, RICHARD D.**
Executive, vice president (organization), chief financial officer. **Personal:** Born May 9, 1960, Los Angeles, CA; married Tracey; children: Anthony & Samantha. **Educ:** Univ Calif, Santa Barbara, CA, BA, econ, 1982; Harvard Sch Bus, MBA, 1986. **Career:** Deloitte, Haskins & Sells, Atlanta, staff, 1980; Walt Disney & Co, sr planning analyst, 1986-87, strategic planning mgr, 1987, dir strategic planning, 1988-89, vpres & treas, 1989-91, sr vpres & chief financial officer, 1991-95; Disney Stores, pres, 1995-96, sr exec vpres & chief financial officer, 1996-98; Starwood Hotels & Resorts Worldwide Inc, pres, bd dir & chief operating officer, 1998-99; Broadband Sports Inc, dir, chmn & chief exec officer, 1999-2001; Amgen Inc, exec vpres & chief financial officer, 2001-07; Colony Capital LLC, prin, 2008-. **Orgs:** Bd dir, Boeing Co, 2005-07; bd mem, Amateur Athletic Found, LA; bd trustee, Univ Calif Santa Barbara; mem adv bd, Zuma Beach Entertainment Inc; dir, Expedia; SBE Entertainment Group LLC; dir, El Silencio Holdings Inc; chmn, Sonifi Solutions Inc; chairman, LodgeNet Interactive Corporation, 2013-. **Home Addr:** 6574 Dume Dr, Malibu, CA 90265. **Business Addr:** Principal, Colony Capital LLC, 2450 Broadway 6th Fl, Santa Monica, CA 90404, **Business Phone:** (310)282-8820.

**NAPOLEON, BENNY NELSON**
Educator, police chief, lawyer. **Personal:** Born Sep 10, 1955, Detroit, MI; son of Harry N and Betty Lee Currie; children: Tiffani Chanel. **Educ:** Mercy Col Detroit, AA, cum laude, 1980, BA, cum laude, 1982; Detroit Col Law, JD, 1986; FBI Nat Acad, US Secret Serv Dignitary Protection Sch, Northwestern Univ Sch Police Staff & Command, Aresty Inst Exec Develop Wharton Sch Univ PA. **Career:** Police chief (retired), attorney; Sibley's Shoes; Detroit Police Dept, trainee police officer, 1975, sgt, 1983, lt, 1985, inspector, 1987, comdr, 1993, dep police chief, 1994, asst chief, 1995, chief police, 1998-2001; self-employed, atty, 1987-; Capri Capital, exec vpres, 2001; pvt pract atty; Univ Phoenix, adj prof criminal justice; Detroit Police Athletic League, basketball coach; Wayne County, sheriff; Dozier Turner & Braceful PC, atty, currently. **Orgs:** Noble, 1985-; Am Bar Asn, 1986-; FBI NAA, 1987-; State Bar Mich, 1987-; bd dir, GDIRT, NCCJ, 1990-; secy, Coalition DEMH, 1990-91; IAATI, 1990-; stud mentor, Detroit Pub Schs; baseball coach, Boys & Girls Clubs Mich; chair, Mich Civil Rights Comn, currently; Nat Asn Advan Colored People, currently; Cass Tech Hall Fame, currently. **Honors/Awds:** Trustee Scholar, DCL, 1982; Dean's Award for Outstanding Scholar, DCL, 1983; Distinguished Alumni Award, MCD, 1988; Police Community Service Award, Greater Detroit Chamber Com, 1990; Distinguished Alumni Award, Wolverine Stud Bar Asn, Detroit Col Law, 1991. **Home Addr:** 12210 Monica, Detroit, MI 48204, **Home Phone:** (313)224-2222. **Business Addr:** Attorney, Dozier Turner & Braceful PC, 1110 1st Natl Bldg, Detroit, MI 48226-3516, **Business Phone:** (313)226-0260.

**NAPPER, HYACINTHE T.**
Government official, ice skater. **Personal:** Born Feb 26, 1928, New York, NY; daughter of Georgiana Bergen Tatem and Charles A; married Guy T; children: Cynthia, Guy & Geoffrey. **Educ:** Fisk Univ, attended 1947; Howard Univ, AB, 1951. **Career:** Government Official (retired); US Dept Labor, Sec Thomasina Norford Minority Groups, consult, 1951-53; Hon John Conyers Jr, admin asst; self employed financial mgr; Wash Figure Skating Club, The Blade newsletter, ed, 1990-97. **Orgs:** Alpha Kappa Alpha Sor; interestbringing greater polit awareness to African Am comm improve voter turnout; US Figure Skating Asn; Ft Dupont Skating Club; Cong Staff Club, 1965-95; Wash Figure Skating Club; bd gov, 1992-96; DC Specl Olympics, ice skating coach; DC Police Boys & Girls Club. **Honors/Awds:** DC Spec Olympics Figure Skating Coach Award; Miscellaneous figure skating Awards. **Home Addr:** 13901 Amberfield Ter, Upper Marlboro, MD 20772, **Home Phone:** (301)574-0353.

**NAPPER, JAMES WILBUR. See Obituaries Section.**

**NARCISSE, COLBERT**
Executive. **Educ:** NY Univ, BS, finance, 1987; Harvard Bus Sch, MBA, bus admin & mgt, gen, 1992. **Career:** Fed Res Bank, bank examr, 1987-90; Merrill Lynch, chief operating officer, 1990-2009, managing dir; Gold Bullion Int LLC, chief exec officer, 2009-11; Carver Fed Savings Bank, dir, 2010-11; Morgan Stanley, head alternative investment group & head corp equity solutions group, managing dir, Client Solutions Div, head global alternative investments, chief operating officer investment strategy, 2011-; Fairfield Futures Fund LP II, dir, gen partner, 2011-; Carver BanCorp Inc, dir, 2011-15; Montclair Coop Sch, vice chmn finance; People Capital Inc, advisor; Harlem RBI, dir; Ceres Managed Futures LLC, dir. **Orgs:** Mem, Exec Leadership Coun; Econ Club New York; chmn, Americas Clean Energy Group; chmn, Environ Sustainability Adv Panel; trustee, Montclair Coop Sch; investment adv comt, New York Investment Fund; audit comt mem, New York Housing Authority. **Honors/Awds:** "Black Enterprise," 75 Most Powerful Blacks on Wall Street, 2011. **Business Addr:** Managing Director, Head of Global Alternative Investments, Morgan Stanley, 1585 Broadway, New York, NY 10036, **Business Phone:** (212)761-4000.

**NASH, BOB J.**
Government official. **Personal:** Born Sep 26, 1947, Texarkana, AR; married Janis F Kearney; children: 3. **Educ:** Univ Ark, Pine Bluff, BA, sociol, 1969; USDA, grad prog, cert mgt, 1971; Howard Univ, MA, urban studies, 1972. **Career:** US Dept Agr, under secy agr, 1993-95; City Wash, DC, asst dep mayor; City Fairfax Va, asst city mgr; Nat Training & Develop Serv, admin officer; Ark State Dept Planning, dir, community & regional aff; Winthrop Rockefeller Found, vpres; Off Ark, Gov Bill Clinton, sr exec asst, econ develop; Ark State Develop Fin Authority, pres; White House Personnel, assoc dir, personnel chief, 1995-2001; Shore Bank Corp, vice chmn, 2001-07; James Lee Witt Assocs, sr advisor, 2008-; Bob J. Nash & Assocs, chief exec officer, 2013-. **Orgs:** Chmn, bd dir, Shore Bank Enterprise Group, Cleveland; chmn, bd dir, Shore Bank Enterprise, Detroit; Chmn, bd dir, Winthrop Rockefeller Found, Little Rock; Mercy Housing bd, Denver; Chicago C's Advocacy Ctr; S Side YMCA, Chicago; Mercy Housing Bd Denver; bd, Ill Med Dist Comn; bd, Environ Law & Policy Ctr; bd, Jobs Future. **Home Addr:** 5276 Chillum Pl NE, Washington, DC 20011. **Business Addr:** Senior Advisor, James Lee Witt Associates, 1501 M St NW, Washington, DC 20005, **Business Phone:** (202)585-0780.

**NASH, CURTIS**
Lawyer. **Personal:** Born Jul 11, 1946, Tallulah, LA; married Betty Jean Gordon. **Educ:** Southern Univ, Baton Rouge, BA, 1969; Univ Col Law, JD, 1972. **Career:** Firm Kidd & McLeod Monroe, La, law clerk, 1971; Vermillion Co Legal Aid Soc Danville, Ill, law clerk, 1972; Corp Tax Br IRS Nat Off, tax law spec, 1972-75; Tax Div Criminal Enforcement Section Northern Region, Justice Dept, DC, trial atty, 1975-. **Orgs:** Vpres, Fairfax Co Wide Black Citizens Asn, 1980; Pi Gamma Mu; Omega Psi Phi Frat. **Home Addr:** 6595 Braddock Rd, Alexandria, VA 22312-2101, **Home Phone:** (703)354-6163. **Business Addr:** Trial Attorney, Tax Division Criminal Enforcement Section Northern Region, 950 Pa Ave NW, Washington, DC 20530-0001, **Business Phone:** (202)514-2000.

**NASH, DR. DANIEL ALPHONZA, JR.**
Physician. **Personal:** Born Jul 15, 1942, Washington, DC; son of Daniel A Sr and Ruby I; married Bettie Louise Taylor; children: Cheryl L & Daniel E. **Educ:** Syracuse Univ, BS, 1964; Howard Univ, MD, 1968. **Career:** Georgetown Med Serv DC Gen Hosp, internship first Yr res, 1968-70; Brooke Army Med Ctr, resd nephrol fel, 1970-73, asst chief, 1973-76; Walter Reed Army Med Ctr, asst chief, 1976-77, chief nephrol serv, 1977-83; pvt pract physician, 1983-. **Orgs:** Med licensure Wash, DC, 1969; diplomat, Am Bd Int Med, 1973; subspecialty, Bd Nephrol, 1974; Am Col Physicians, 1974, fel 1976; Nat Med Asn, 1974; Am Med Asn, 1975; Am Soc Nephrol, 1975; Int Soc Nephrol, 1975; MD, 1977; assoc prof, med Howard Univ Col Med, 1978. **Honors/Awds:** Ten major medical publications; Twelve publ abstracts; Four sci presentations. **Home Addr:** 831 Ramsay St, Baltimore, MD 21230-2102, **Home Phone:** (410)878-0201. **Business Addr:** Physician, 6192 Oxon Hill Rd Suite 207, Oxon Hill, MD 20745, **Business Phone:** (301)412-0715.

**NASH, DIANE**
Civil rights activist. **Personal:** Born May 15, 1938, Chicago, IL; daughter of Leon Nash and Dorothy Bolton Nash; married James Bevel; children: Sherri Bevel, Douglass Bevel. **Educ:** Fisk University, Attended; Howard University, Attended; Fisk University, Honorary Degree, 2009. **Orgs:** Student Nonviolent Coordinating Committee (SNCC), Founding Member, 1960. **Honors/Awds:** Rosa Parks Award; John F. Kennedy Library and Foundation, Distinguished American Award, 2003; Lyndon Baines Johnson Library and Museum, LBJ Award for Leadership in Civil Rights, 2004; National Civil Rights Museum, Freedom Award, 2008. **Special Achievements:** Student leader during the 1960s Movement: significant participant in the Birmingham, Alabama, de-segregation campaign in 1963, as well as the Selma Voting Rights Campaign in 1965; appears in the award-winning documentary series, "Eyes on the Prize," and in PBS's "American Experience" documentary on freedom riders, 2011; featured in David Halberstam's book, "The Children," Random House (1998) and Lisa Mullins' "Diane Nash: The Fire of the Civil Rights Movement," Barnhardt & Ashe Pub Inc. (2007).

**NASH, EVA L.**
Executive. **Personal:** Born Jul 25, 1925, Atlantic City, NJ; children: Michele & Sharon. **Educ:** Howard Univ, AB, 1945; Univ Chicago, Sch Soc Serv Admin, 1946; Univ Pgh Sch Soc Work, MSW, 1959. **Career:** Hubbard Hosp, med soc worker, 1947-49; Atlantic City NJ, sub teacher, 1954-55; City Pgh, mkt survr, 1956-57; Travelers Aid, 1957; Freedman's Hosp, 1961-64; Child Guid Clin, clin soc worker, 1964-67; DC Develop Serv, chief soc worker, 1967-69; DC Model Cities Prog, health planner, 1969; HUD, comm serv officer, 1969-72, asst dir, admin on aging. **Orgs:** Comn Chest Area Capt Nashville, 1951; World & Polit Disc Grp Pgh, 1955-57; Bunker Hill Sch PTA, 1959-64, chmn, nominating comn, 1960; chmn, Sch Fair, 1961; Marriage Prep Inst Bd, 1963-64; V St Proj Com, 1963-64; Ment Health Sub-Comn Urban League, 1963-64; Howard Univ & Interdisciplinary Fac Sem, 1963-64; Western HS PTA, 1965-66; Am Orthopsychiatric Asn, 1965; Nat Asn Advan Colored People; Nat Coun Negro Women; workshop ldr Howard Univ Sch Soc Work Sch Agency Inst, 1967; Nat Comn Support Pub Sch; consult, Group Coun Prog Model Sch Div Sec Sch, 1967-68; bd dir, DC Planned Parenthood, 1968; NASW Regional Conf Buffal, 1968; conslting sem ldr, Wash Sch Psychiat, 1968-69; staff, DC Pub Sch Model Sch Div sum, 1968; Educ Working Party Ment Retardation Planning Comn DC, 1968; co-chmn spec serv comm, DC Citizens Better Pub Sch Educ, 1968-70; Nat Asn Soc Workers; Acad Cert Soc Workers; pres, NW settlement House Aux, 1972-73; Budget Comn Wash Coun Planned Parenthood. **Honors/Awds:** Urban League Voluntary Service Award, 1967.

**NASH, HENRY GARY**
Executive, president (organization). **Personal:** Born May 3, 1952, Macon, GA; son of Henry and Elizabeth Cason; children: David & Gary Alton. **Educ:** Savannah State Col, Savannah, GA, BSEE, 1974; Univ Southern Calif, Los Angeles, MS, 1979. **Career:** Automation Industs, Silver Spring, Md, systs engr, 1974-77; Raytheon Co, Burlington, MA, sr proj engr, 1977-81; Gen Elec Co, Arlington, Va, sr systs engr, 1981-85; Tracor Appl Sci Inc, Arlington, Va, prog mgr, 1985-87; Gen Sci Corp, Arlington, Va, pres, chief exec officer, chmn, 1987-. **Orgs:** Kappa Alpha Psi Fraternity, 1972; Arlington County Chamber Com, 1987; chmn, SSU Athletic Found. **Business Addr:** President, Chief Executive Officer, General Scientific Corp, Maritime Plz I 1201 M St SE Suite 120, Washington, DC 20003-3711, **Business Phone:** (202)547-4299.

**NASH, JOHN LESTER, JR. (JOHNNY NASH)**
Singer, business owner. **Personal:** Born Aug 19, 1940, Houston, TX; son of John; married Carlie; children: 2. **Career:** Songs: "A Teenager Sings The Blues", 1957; "A Very Special Love", 1958, "Stir It Up"; Albums: Johnny Nash, 1958; I Got Rhythm, 1959; Quiet Hour, 1959; Let's Get Lost, 1960; Starring Johnny Nash, 1961; Composer's Choice, 1964; Hold Me Tight, 1968; Prince of Peace, 1969; Let's Go Dancing, 1969; I Can See Clearly Now, 1972; Celebrate Life, 1974; What a Wonderful World, 1977; The Johnny Nash Album, 1980; Here Again, 1986; Tears on My Pillow, 1987; The Reggae Collection, 1993; Movie: Take A Giant Step, 1959; Key Witness, 1960; Johnny Nash Indoor Arena, owner & operator, 1980-. **Business Addr:** Owner, Johnny Nash Indoor Arena, 6200 Willardsville Rd, Houston, TX 77048, **Business Phone:** (713)991-0671.

**NASH, MARCUS DELANDO**
Football player. **Personal:** Born Feb 1, 1976, Tulsa, OK; married Lorie. **Educ:** Univ Tenn. **Career:** Football player (retired); Denver Broncos, wide receiver, 1998-99; Miami Dolphins, 1999; Baltimore Ravens, 1999-2000; Detroit Fury, 2003; Las Vegas Gladiators, 2004-06; Dallas Desperados, 2007-08. **Honors/Awds:** All-American, 1997; Champion, Super Bowl, XXXIII, XXXV; Offensive Player of the Year, Australian Football League, 2004. **Home Addr:** 2660 Churchill Downs Cir, Chattanooga, TN 37421-1489. **Business Addr:** Wide Receiver, Dallas Desperados, Cowboys Ctr 1 Cowboys Pkwy, Irving, TX 75063-4999, **Business Phone:** (972)785-4900.

**NASH, NIECY (CAROLE DENISE ENSLEY)**
Actor, television show host, television producer. **Personal:** Born Feb 23, 1970, Palmdale, CA; daughter of Margaret Ensley; married Don, Jan 8, 1994?, (divorced 2007); children: Dominic, Donielle & Dia; married Jay Tucker, May 28, 2011; children: Romallis Tucker. **Educ:** Calif State Univ, BA, theater arts. **Career:** Style Network, "Clean House", host, 2004-11; Actress, TV series, "Reno 911!", 2003-09, "American Dad!", 2007-12; movie "Horton Hears a Who", 2008; "Dancing with the Stars", contestant, 2010; TV movie, "Niecy Nash Wedding Blast", self, 2011; Actress TV series, "The Soul Man", 2012-14, "Getting On", 2013-14; movie "Selma", 2014. **Orgs:** Mothers Against Violence Schs (MAVIS), spokesperson. **Honors/Awds:** Gracie Allen Award, Outstanding Supporting Actress in a Comedy Series ("Reno 911!"), 2010; Daytime Emmy Award, Outstanding Special Class Special ("Clean House"), Producer/Host, 2010. **Special Achievements:** MAVIS was founded by her mother; author of "It's Hard to Fight Naked" (Gallery Books, 2013).

**NASH, TROY**
Government official, executive. **Personal:** Born Apr 10, 1969, Kansas City, MO. **Educ:** Wesley Col, BS, econs, 1994; Univ Mo, Sch Law, JD, 1997; Univ Mo, Kans City, MA, econs, 2005, polit sci, 2011, MBA, finance, 2013, PhD, econs; St Louis Univ, EdD, educ, 2015. **Career:** Lathrop & Gage; Univ Mo Bd Curators, cur; City Coun, Kans City, admin asst; Mayor Emanuel Cleaver, spec asst; Econ Develop Corp Kans City, bd mem, 1999-2007; Mo City Coun, Kans City, mem, 1999, 2003-07; Greater Downtown Develop Authority, mem, 2003-07; Zimmer Real Estate Serv Inc, Pub Sector Consult, dir & vpres, 2007-; Am Jazz Mus, Bd Dir, vice chmn, 2007-. **Orgs:** Vice chmn, Planning, Zoning & Econ Develop Comt, 1993-03; bd mem & vice chair, Samuel U. Rodgers Health Ctr, 1996-99; chmn bd trustee, People to People Int, 2006-, bd dir, 1998-; Mid-Am Regional Coun, 1999-2003; Jazz Dist Redevelop Corp, 1999-; Greater Downtown Develop Authority, 2003-07; vice chmn, Budget & Audit Comt, 2003-05; Downtown Minority Develop Corp, 2005-; chmn, Int Comt, 2006-07; Neighborhood Develop & Housing Comt; Legis, Rules, & Ethics Comt; Pub Interest & Int Law Asn; Am Royal Bd Gov, 2008-; bd mem, Hawthorn Found, 2012-; Econ Develop Corp Kans City, 1999-2007; regional bd mem, Arvest Bank, 2013-; bd mem, Cong Black Caucus Found, 2015-. **Business Addr:** Vice President of Public Sector Consulting & Development, Zimmer Real Estate Services Inc, 1220 Wash St Suite 200, Kansas City, MO 64141-1299, **Business Phone:** (816)474-2000.

**NATHAN, REV. TIMOTHY ERIC**
Clergy. **Personal:** Born Oct 12, 1970, Columbus, GA; son of Thomas L and Hattie F. **Educ:** Ala Agr & Mech Univ, BS, art educ, 1994; Turner Theol Sem, MDiv, christian edu, 1998. **Career:** Oak Grove AME Church, Newell, Ala, pastor, 1993-98; St Paul AME Church, Lanett, Ala, pastor, 1996-98; Greater St Paul AME Church, pastor; African Methodist Episcopal Church, pastor, 2005-. **Orgs:** Nat Art Educrs Asn; United Asn Visual Arts; exec bd, Univ N Ala, Campus Ministry; Coop Task Force City Florence; Alpha Phi Alpha; asst dir, Christian Educ, Ninth Episcopal Dist-AMEC; exec bd, N Ala Habitat Humanity. **Honors/Awds:** The Bishop WD Fountain Award AME, The Interdenominational theol Ctr; The Issac Clark Preaching Award, 1998. **Home Addr:** 454 N Locust St, Florence, AL 35630, **Home Phone:** (256)764-3900.

**NATHAN, TONY CURTIS**
Legal consultant, football coach, football player. **Personal:** Born Dec 14, 1956, Birmingham, AL; son of William and Louise; married Johnnie F Wilson; children: Nichole, Natalie & Nadia. **Educ:** Univ Ala. **Career:** Football player (retired), coach, bailiff; Miami Dolphins, kick returner, running back, punt returner, 1979-87, asst coach, 1988-95, running backs coach, 1993; Tampa Bay Buccaneers, asst coach, 1996-2001; Dade Christian Sch, 2002; Fla Int Univ, coach running backs, 2003-05; Baltimore Ravens, running backs coach, 2006-08; San Francisco 49ers, running backs coach, 2008; Miami-Dade County court, bailiff, currently. **Orgs:** FCA; Am Football Coaches Asn. **Honors/Awds:** All-Pro, 1979; Alabama Sports Hall of Fame, 1999; Senior Bowl Hall of Fame, 2006. **Special Achievements:** First black football players at Woodlawn High School in Birmingham, Alabama. **Home Addr:** 15110 Dunbarton Pl, Hialeah, FL 33016, **Home Phone:** (305)820-1490. **Business Addr:** Bailiff, Miami-Dade County Court, 73 W Flagler St, Miami, FL 33130, **Business Phone:** (305)275-1155.

**NATT, KENNY (KENNETH WAYNE NATT)**
Basketball player, basketball coach. **Personal:** Born Oct 5, 1958, Monroe, LA; married Jolene; children: Ki & Yazmine. **Educ:** Northeast La Univ, BA, bus admin, 1980. **Career:** Basketball player, basketball coach (retired), exec; IMinor League Basketball, Albuquerque, Leth bridge, Can, Las Vegas, Lancaster, Pa, Casper, Wyo; Ind Pacers, 1980; Alta Dusters, 1981-82; Utah Jazz, 1983, asst coach, 1984, scout, 1995-96, asst coach, 1996-2004; Albuquerque Silvers, 1983-84; Kans

City Kings, head coach, 1984; Lancaster Lightning, 1984; Albany Patroons, 1985-87; Wyo Wildcatters, 1987-88; Fresno Flames, 1988; Rockford Lightning, 1988-89; Youngstown Pride, 1989; World Basketball League, Fresno, Youngstown, pro player, player personnel dir, scout, 1989; CBA, Columbus Horizon, asst coach, 1992; Columbus Horizon, asst coach & dir, 1992-94; Natl Basketball League, Can, Cape Breton Breakers, head coach, 1992-93; Youngstown State Univ, asst coach, 1994-95; Cleveland Cavaliers, asst coach, 2004-07; Sacramento Kings, asst coach, 2007-08, interim head coach, 2008-09; Basketball Fedn India, head coach; India Nat Basketball Team, head coach, 2011-12; IMG Acad, dir, 2012-. **Orgs:** Continental Basketball Asn. **Home Addr:** , Oxford, GA. **Business Addr:** Director, IMG Academy, 5500 34th St W, Bradenton, FL 34210, **Business Phone:** (941)752-2600.

## NATTA, CLAYTON LYLE

Educator, physician. **Personal:** Born Nov 17, 1932, San Fernando; son of Samuel and Leonora; married Stephenie Lukowich; children: Laura & Andrea. **Educ:** McMaster Univ, BA, 1957; Univ Toronto, MD, 1961; Royal Col Physicians, Can, FRCP, 1972; Royal Col Pathologists, FRC, path, 1990. **Career:** Ottawa Civic Hosp, 1965-66; NY Univ Med Ctr, fel clin hematol, 1966-68; Columbia Univ, instr, assoc, 1970-73, asst prof med & pathol, 1973-81, assoc prof clin med & internist, 1981, spec lectr med, currently. **Orgs:** AAAS, 1969-; Am Soc Hematol, 1969-; fel Royal Col Physicians Can, 1972; NY Acad Sci, 1973-; NY State Soc Internal Med, 1974-; chair, Soc Study Blood, 1977; fel Am Col Nutrit, 1980; Int Soc Hematol, 1983-; Biochem Soc London, 1983-; Nutrit Soc London, 1985-; Am Soc Clin Nutrit, 1987-; Fel Royal Col Pathologists London, 1992; trustee, Columbia Univ. **Home Addr:** 300 W 55th St Suite 14B, New York, NY 10019, **Home Phone:** (212)245-7607. **Business Addr:** Special Lecturer in Medicine, Columbia University, 630 W 168th St, New York, NY 10032, **Business Phone:** (212)305-2645.

## NATTIEL, RICHARD RENNARD (RICKY NATTIEL)

Football coach, football player. **Personal:** Born Jan 25, 1966, Gainesville, FL. **Educ:** Univ Fla, rehab coun, 1987. **Career:** Football player (retired), coach; Denver Broncos, wide receiver, 1987-88, 1990, punt returner, 1988, 1989, 1991-92; Trinity Cath High Sch, coach, 2007; Celtics football team, head coach. **Honors/Awds:** Post-season play, 1987-89: AFC Championship Game, NFL Championship Game; Hall of Fame, Univ Fla Athletic; Gators' Fergie Ferguson Award.

## NAVES, LARRY J.

Judge. **Personal:** Born Birmingham, AL; children: 3. **Educ:** Univ Denver, BA, econs, attended 1968; Univ Colo Sch Law, JD, 1974. **Career:** Pvt pract, atty; Colo Pub Defender, dep state pub defender, 1974-79; US Pub Defender, asst fed pub defender, 1979-84; Denver Dist Ct, judge, 1987-10; Denver Dist Ct, Second Judicial Dist, judge, chief judge, 2006-10; Judicial Arbiter Group Inc, arbiter, 2010-; Col Com Arbitrators, fel, 2014. **Orgs:** Bd trustee, Denver Bar Asn, 1992-94; bd trustee, Colo C Chorale, 1999-2005; Childrens Chorale; Colo Bar Asn; Sam Carey Bar Asn; Colo Supreme Courts Civil Jury Instr Comt; chair, Colo Supreme Ct Criminal Rules Comt; Colo Comn Judicial Discipline; Denver County Ct Comn Judicial Discipline; Supreme Ct Comt Revisions to Colo Code Judicial Conduct; bd mem, Colo C's Chorale. **Business Addr:** Arbiter, Judicial Arbiter Group Inc, 1601 Blake St Suite 400, Denver, CO 80202, **Business Phone:** (720)932-3426.

## NAYLOR, GLORIA

Novelist, writer. **Personal:** Born Jan 25, 1950, New York, NY; daughter of Roosevelt and Alberta McAlpin. **Educ:** Brooklyn Col, BA, Eng, 1981; Yale Univ, MA, Afro-Am Studies, 1983. **Career:** George Washington Univ, vis lect, 1983-84; New York Univ, vis prof, 1986; Princeton Univ, vis lectr, 1986; Boston Univ, vis prof, 1987; Cornell Univ; US Info Agency, cultural exchange lectr; One Way Productions, founder & pres, 1990-, Univ Kent, Eng, vis prof; Novels: The Women of Brewster Place, 1982; Linden Hills, 1985; Mama Day, 1988; Bailey's Cafe, 1992; The Best Short Stories by Black Writers, volume II, editor, Sept, 1995; The Men of Brewster Place, 1996, 1998, 2005; Univ Kent, vis prof. **Orgs:** Sr fel Soc Humanities, Cornell Univ, 1988; Exec bd mem, BookMonth Club, 1989-94. **Honors/Awds:** National Book Award, 1983; American Book Award, 1983; National Endowment for the Arts fellowships, 1985 Candace Award, Nat Coalition One Hundred Black Women, 1986; Lillian Smith Award, 1989; scholar-in-residence, Univ Pa; President's Medal, Brooklyn Col; Guggenheim fellowship, 1988; Distinguished Writer Award, Mid-Atlantic Writers Asn. **Business Addr:** Founder, President, One Way Productions, 638 2nd St, Brooklyn, NY 11215, **Business Phone:** (718)965-1031.

## NAYMAN, DR. ROBBIE L.

Executive, educator, psychologist. **Personal:** Born , 1937, Dallas, TX; married Oguz B. **Educ:** Univ Wis, BS, 1960; MS, 1962; PhD, 1973. **Career:** S IL Univ, cnslr, 1960-62; Col State Univ, asst dean studs, 1962-64; Univ Wis, teaching asst, 1964-69; Wis St Dept Health & Soc Servs, affirm acct coord, 1969-70; Ariz State Univ, dir coun, vpres stud serv, 1983-88; Skidmore Col New York, assoc prof psychol, dean, 1988; Calif State Univ Fullerton, sr counr Univ Counselling Ctr, dir Univ Learning Lab, vpres stud affairs; Colo State Univ, Dept Psychol, Dept Edu, asst prof. **Orgs:** Am Personnel & Guid Asn; Am Psychol Asn; Pi Lambda Theta; Urban League, Nat Advan Asn Colored People; chmn, Comn XI; chmn, ACPA. **Home Addr:** 1601 Germantown Ct, Ft Collins, CO 80526. **Business Addr:** Vice President of Student Affairs, California State University, 800 N State Col Blvd, Fullerton, CA 92831-3599, **Business Phone:** (714)773-3221.

## NDIAYE, MAKHTAR VINCENT (MAKHTAR N'DIAYE)

Basketball player. **Personal:** Born Dec 12, 1973, Dakar. **Educ:** NC State Univ, attended 1998. **Career:** Basketball player (retired); Oyak Renault, 1998; BC Lietuvos rytas, 1998-99; Vancouver Grizzlies, forward, 1998-99; Chorale Roanne Basket, 1999-2000; Besancon BCD, 2000-01; Chorale Roanne Basket, 2001; N Charleston Lowgators, 2001-02; JA Vichy, 2002-03; JDA Dijon Basket, 2003-04; Chorale Roanne Basket, 2004; Edimes Pavia, 2004; TBB Trier, 2004; ASVEL Basket, 2005; Levallois, 2005-07; AEK Larnaca, 2007-08.

## NDIAYE-DIATTA, ASTOU

Basketball player, basketball coach. **Personal:** Born Nov 5, 1973, Kaolack; married Ousman; children: Boubacar, Bineta & Ndiaysse. **Educ:** Southern Nazarene Univ, BA, bus, 1997. **Career:** Basketball player (retired), basketball coach; Detroit Shock, 1999-2003; Indiana Fever, 2004; Houston Comets, 2006; Seattle Storm, 2007; Utah State Univ, asst coach, 2008-. **Business Addr:** Assistant Coach, Utah State University, 1400 Old Main Hill, Logan, UT 84322-1400, **Business Phone:** (435)797-1162.

## NEAL, BRANDON

Executive. **Educ:** Howard Univ, BA, African-Am studies, 2000; Am Univ, Sch Pub Affairs, MPA, pub admin. **Career:** Nat Asn Advan Colored People, nat youth & col div, 2000-05, Nat Off, mid-atlantic youth field dir, Youth & Col Div, nat dir, 2003-, asst dir, currently; Dem Gov Asn, dep polit dir, 2005-06, dir external affairs, 2006-07; 2009 Presidential Inaugural Comt, mid atlantic finance dir, 2008-09; African-Am Affairs Obama Am, finance dir; US Secy Transp, Off Small & Disadvantaged Bus Utilization, dir, 2009-, sr advisor. **Orgs:** Nat Finance Comt; Alpha Phi Alpha Fraternity Inc; Howard Univ Alumni Asn; Urban League Young Prof Network; Young Dem Am; Peoples Community Baptist Church; life mem, Nat Asn Advan Colored People; advisor, Teen Choir; mentor, Mens Rites Passage Prog; Sr Exec Serv. **Honors/Awds:** Distinguished Alumni of the Year Award, Nat Asn Equal Opportunity Educ, 2005. **Special Achievements:** Featured in EBONY magazine as a "top thirty leader in America under thirty". **Business Addr:** Director, U S Department of Transportation, 1200 New Jersey Ave SE W56-485, Washington, DC 20590, **Business Phone:** (202)366-1930.

## NEAL, BRENDA JEAN

Manager, social worker. **Personal:** Born Jan 3, 1952, Greenville, SC; children: Damon Yusef. **Educ:** NMex State Univ; Onondaga Community Col, AA, social work, 1976; Le Moyne Col, BA, sociol, 1978. **Career:** Lincoln First Bank, teller, 1974; Syracuse City Sch Dist, sch social worker, 1982-83; Xerox Corp, internal control mgr, customer serv mgr, 1983. **Orgs:** YWCA. **Honors/Awds:** Black Achievers Award, 1490 Enterprise Buffalo, 1983; Special Merit Award, Xerox Corp, 1984. **Home Addr:** 114 Kay St, Buffalo, NY 14215.

## NEAL, CHARLIE

Broadcaster. **Personal:** Born Oct 28, 1944, Philadelphia, PA; son of Robert Parrish and Elizabeth. **Educ:** Villanova Univ, attended 1966. **Career:** Greyhound Lines Inc, safety instr, 1971-; BET TV, sports broadcaster, 1980; CBS TV, sports broadcaster, 1982-85; TBS TV, sports broadcaster, 1986-88; Premier Basketball League, supvr officials, 2007-; ESPN, play-by-play announcer, currently; ABL, off; IBL, off; USBL, off; ABA, off; NCAA Div I Games, off; MBC; TNT; Historically black cols & univs, commentator; Del Magic, pres, currently. **Orgs:** Am Fedn TV & Radio Artists, 1982-; Blue Knights Safety Comt, 1985-; spec oper sect, Arlington Co Police, 1986-. **Honors/Awds:** Numerous broadcasting awards including Sportcaster of the Year, 100% Wrong Club, 1989; Outstanding Volunteer, Arlington Co, Va, 1991. **Home Addr:** 15105 Jennings Lane, Bowie, MD 20721, **Home Phone:** (301)390-0990. **Business Addr:** Supervisor of Officials, Premier Basketball League, 4958 W Irving Pk Rd, Chicago, IL 60641, **Business Phone:** (773)844-7251.

## NEAL, CURTIS EMERSON, JR.

Consulting engineer. **Personal:** Born Feb 20, 1931, Yoakum, TX; son of Ellie and Curtis Emerson Sr (deceased); married Evelyn V Spears. **Educ:** Prairie View A&M Univ, BS, archit engineering, 1958; Dept Defense Fallout Shelter Anal, cert; Dwyer Sch Real Estate. **Career:** St Philip's Col, instr, 1958-63; Wash Moore Eng Co, vpres, 1963-71, vpres, 1973-75; GW Adams Mfg Co, pres, 1971-73; Curtis Neal Assoc, prin, 1975-; St Philips Col, Drafting Dept, San Antonio, Tex, instr. **Orgs:** Tex Soc Prof Engrs; Nat Soc Prof Engrs; Prof Engrs Pvt Pract; Nat Asn Black Consult Engrs; bd mem, Alamo City Chamber Com; bd mem, San Antonio Water Serv Bd; San Antonio Energy Study Tech Adv Panel; Waste water Adv Comt, City San Antonio; trustee & secy, San Antonio Water Syst; bd mem, San Antonio Coun Eng Educ; vice chmn, Alamo Conserv & Reuse Dist; asst Dist Comnr, Polaris Dist Boy Scouts Am; Prof Engr State Tex; Nat Asn Black Consult Engrs. **Honors/Awds:** The United Negro Col Fund, Leadership in the Minority Community, 1980; Legislative Black Caucas, State of Texas, Outstanding Contribution to the Business Field, 1983; Community Award Prof Bus, Alamo City Chamber Com; Outstanding Serv Community, City of San Antonio; Outstanding Serv Community, Legis Black Caucus State Tex; Rotary Club Merit Award, Northwest San Antonio; Scouter's Training Award, Alamo Area Coun Boy Scouts of Am. **Home Addr:** 949 Aransas Ave, San Antonio, TX 78210, **Home Phone:** (210)534-8774. **Business Addr:** Principal, Curtis Neal & Associates, 405 N St Marys Suite 550, San Antonio, TX 78205, **Business Phone:** (210)579-0913.

## NEAL, ELISE

Actor. **Personal:** Born Mar 14, 1966, Memphis, TN. **Educ:** Univ Arts, PA; Am Acad Dramatic Arts. **Career:** Stage: Oh, Kay!, 1991; TV series: "Law & Order; Family Matters", 1993; "Loving", 1994; "Sea Quest", 1995-96; "Chicago Hope", 1995; "The Steve Harvey Show", 1996; "The Hughley's", 1998; "Fantasy Island", 1998; "Brian's Song", 2001; "All of Us", 2003; AUSA, 2003; "Something About Brenda", 2004; "Bodies in Motion", 2005; "CSI: Crime Scene Investigation", 2005; "K-Ville", 2007; "My Manny", 2009; "Private Practice", 2009; A N T Farm, 2011; "The Soul Man", 2013; "The Fright Night Files", 2014; "Aaliyah: The Princess of R&B", 2014. Films: Malcolm X, 1992; Rosewood, 1997; How to Be a Player, 1997; Money Talks, 1997; Scream 2, 1997; Restaurant, 1998; Mission to Mars, 2000; Sacred Is the Flesh, 2001; Paid in Full, 2002; The Rising Place, 2002; Playas Ball, 2003; Hustle & Flow, 2005; 4 Life, 2007; Who's Deal?, 2008; Jack & Janet Save the Planet, 2009; Love Ranch, 2010; Gun, 2010; N-Secure, 2010; Lord, All Men Can't Be Dogs, 2011; The Perfect Man, 2011; Poolboy: Drowning Out the Fury, 2011; Breathe, 2011; The Undershepherd, 2012; School of Hard Knocks, 2012; Preaching to the Pastor, 2012; Who's Watching the Kids, 2012; 1982, 2013; First Impression, 2014; Aaliyah: The Princess of R&B, 2014; Ransum Games, 2014; The White Sistas, 2016; Ladies Book Club, 2016; What Are the Chances?, 2016; 36 Hour Layover, 2016; Tragedy Girls, 2017; Wolverine Sequel, 2017. **Honors/Awds:** Best Ensemble Cast, SAG Awards, 2006; Best Supporting Actress in Film, Nat Asn Advan Colored People, 2006; Hottest Ensemble Cast, 2006; Trailblazer Award, 2006. **Business Addr:** Actress, Star File Photo Agency Ltd, 11 W 20th St Fl 7, New York, NY 10011, **Business Phone:** (212)929-2525.

## NEAL, FREDERIC DOUGLAS (FRED NEAL)

Basketball player, public relations executive, basketball coach. **Personal:** Born May 19, 1941, Greensboro, NC; son of Katie C Carter and Alfonza Lowdermilk; married Rose Allen; children: Lavern, Frederic Jr, Pamela, Toi & RoCurl. **Educ:** Johnson C Smith Univ, attended 1963, BS, 1975. **Career:** Basketball player, basketball executive, public relations executive (retired); Harlem Globetrotters, Los Angeles, Calif, basketball player, coach & pub rels exec, 1963-85; Cernitin Am, Yellow Springs, Ohio, pub rels exec, 1985; Orlando Magic, Orlando, Fla, ticket chmn & dir spec proj, 1986-; Celebrity Golf Asn, PGA, prof golfer, 1990.TV Series : "The Harlem Globetrotters Popcorn Machine", 1974; "The Goldie Hawn Special", 1978; "The White Shadow", 1979-80; "The John Davidson Show", 1980; "The Harlem Globetrotters on Gilligan's Island ", 1981; "The Love Boat", 1984; "Biography", 1987; "Superboy", 1988; "The Howard Stern Show", 1991; "ESPN 25: Who's #1? ", 2005; "Best Friends Forever", 2012; "30 for 30", 2012; "Unsung Hollywood", 2014, actor. **Orgs:** Screen Actors Guild; Am Fedn Television & Radio Artists. **Home Addr:** , Greensboro, NC.

## NEAL, DR. GREEN BELTON, II

Physician. **Personal:** Born Sep 4, 1946, Hopkins, SC; married Linda Mattison; children: Green II, Tiffany & Marcus. **Educ:** Benedict Col, BS, 1966; Meharry Med Col, MD, 1971. **Career:** Providence Hosp, med staff; Columbia; SC Richland Memorial Hosp; Meharry Med Col, asst prof med; GW Hubbard Hosp, resident, 1973, dir cardiac catherization lab, 1975-76; pvt pract, physician, currently. **Orgs:** Fel Vanderbilt Univ Med Sch, 1973; GA St Med Asn, 1975; LA St Med Asn, 1975; Nat Med Asn; AMA; bd mem, Boys Club Greater Columbia; Columbia Med Asn; Am Heart Asn; Congaree Med Dent & Pharm Asn. **Honors/Awds:** Fel Grant Cardiol, Nat Insts Health. **Home Addr:** 3010 Farrow Rd Suite 230, Columbia, SC 29203-7606, **Home Phone:** (803)256-7985. **Business Addr:** Physician, Private Practice, 1415 Barnwell St, Columbia, SC 29201, **Business Phone:** (803)318-8277.

## NEAL, DR. HOMER ALFRED

Educator, scientist. **Personal:** Born Jun 13, 1942, Franklin, KY; married Donna Jean; children: Sharon & Homer Jr. **Educ:** Ind Univ, BS, physics, 1961; Univ Mich, MS, physics, 1963, PhD, physics, 1966. **Career:** Ind Univ, from asst prof to prof, 1967-81, dean, res & grad develop, 1976-81; State Univ New York, Stony Brook, provost, 1981-86; Univ Mich, prof, 1987-97, dept Physics, chmn, 1987-93, emer vpres res, 1993-97, interim emer pres, 1996-97, UM-ATLAS Proj, dir, 1997-2015, Samuel AGoudsmit prof, 2000-; Europ Lab Particle Physics, res, currently. **Orgs:** Sloan Found; fel Am Phys Soc; US Dept Energy, High Energy Physics Adv Panel, 1977-81; Nat Sci Bd, 1980-86; Guggenheim Fel, 1980-81; JS Guggenheim Found; New York Seagrant Inst, 1982-86; AAAS, 1983; Univ Res Asn Bd, trustee, 1983; DSc, Ind Univ, 1984; Covanta Corp, 1985; chmn physics adv comt, Nat Sci Found Physics Adv Panel, 1986; Smithsonian Inst, 1989-2001; Ind Univ, Inst Adv Study, 1992; bd, Ford Motor Co, 1997-, chmn, Comt Sustainability, currently; Sloan Found Fel; External Adv coun Nat Computational Sci Alliance, 1997-; Appln Stategy Coun, Univ Corp Advan Internet Develop, 2000-; Smithsonian Coun Nat Mus African Am Hist & Cult; Adv Bd, Oak Ridge Nat Lab; Trustee, Richard Lounsbery Found; Nat Res Coun Bd Physics & Astron; APS, vpres, fel, Panel Pub Affairs; fel, AAAS; fel, Am Acad Arts & Sci; Hon Doctorates, Ind Univ, Notre Dame Univ & Mich State Univ; Bd Ctr Strategic & Int Studies; MIT Vis Comt Sponsored Res; Lawrence Berkeley Lab; Argonne Nat Lab; Fermilab; bd Regents, Smithsonian Inst; pres, APS. **Home Addr:** PO Box 130620, Ann Arbor, MI 48113-0620. **Business Addr:** Samuel A Goudsmit Professor, University of Michigan, 1440 Randall Lab, Ann Arbor, MI 48109-1040, **Business Phone:** (734)764-4375.

## NEAL, DR. IRA TINSLEY

School administrator, educator. **Personal:** Born Nov 14, 1931, Memphis, TN; son of James and Ogie; married Jacqueline Elaine Wiley. **Educ:** Evansville Col, Ind, BS, 1960; Ind Univ, Bloomington, MS, 1964; Nova Southwestern Univ, EdD; Univ Southern Ind, Hon Doctor Laws. **Career:** Evansville-Vanderburgh Sch Corp, Chestnut Walnut Sch, teacher, 1960-65, exec dir, 1966-70, Lincoln Elem Sch, supr, 1970-77, dir fed projs, 1977-; Neighborhood Youth Corps, dir, 1965-66; Univ Southern Ind, adj prof. **Orgs:** Kappa Alpha Psi Fraternity, 1966-80; Community Action Prog Evansville; pres, Pride Inc, 1968-78; bd mem, Vanderburgh Co Judiciary Nominating Com, 1971-80; bd mem, Inner City Cult Ctr, 1977-80; sec-treas, New Hope Housing Inc, 1979-80; ctr assoc, Ill /Ind Race Desegregation Assistance Ctr, 1979-80; EVSC's African Am Choral Ensemble; African Am Acad; trustee, Vincennes Univ; Police Merit Comn; IU Med Adv Comt; Vanderburgh County Judicial Nominating Comt; City-County Human Rels Comn; bd dir, USI Found. **Special Achievements:** Nominated NEA's Carter G Woodson Award, Local Black Teachers, 1978; Black Community Award, Black Community Evansville, 1978; Plaque Service Rendered Head Start Evansville, Ind, 1979. **Home Addr:** 329 Holly Hill Dr, Evansville, IN 47710, **Home Phone:** (812)437-9944. **Business Addr:** Director of Field Projects, Evansville-Vanderburgh School Corp, 1 SE 9th St, Evansville, IN 47708, **Business Phone:** (812)435-8159.

## NEAL, DR. JOSEPH C., JR.

Insurance agent, financial manager, chief financial officer. **Personal:** Born Mar 23, 1941, Memphis, TN; son of Joseph C Sr and Hattie Counts Owens; children: Lisa M & Thomas Joseph. **Educ:** Trade Tech Col LA, AA, 1960; Calif State Col LA, BA, 1973. **Career:** Phoenix Life Ins Co & WS Griffith, 1969-; Christian Method Episcopal Church, gen secy finance & chief financial officer, currently. **Orgs:** Nat Asn Advan Colored People, 1965-; 32nd degree mason, Prince Hall Grand

Lodge, 1966-; Los Angeles Life Underwriters Asn, 1969-; La Kiwanis Club, 1972-; lic rep, Nat Asn Securities Dealers, 1974-. **Honors/Awds:** Honorary Doctor of Laws, Lane Col, 1989; Outstanding Sales, Phoenix Life Ins Co; Blue Vase Winner, Pres Club. **Home Addr:** 8325 Byrd Ave, Inglewood, CA 90305. **Business Addr:** General Secretary of Finance, Chief Financial Officer, Christian Methodist Episcopal Church, 4466 Elvis Presley Blvd, Memphis, TN 38116-7100, **Business Phone:** (901)345-0580.

### NEAL, LANGDON D.
Lawyer, association executive. **Personal:** Born Chicago, IL. **Educ:** Cornell Univ, BA, 1978; Univ Ill Law Sch, JD, 1981. **Career:** Mercy Hosp, staff; Am Inst Real Estate Appraisers, lectr; Cole Taylor Bank, bd dir; Cook Co Bar Asn, lectr; Earl L Neal & Assocs, managing partner, 1968-; Chicago Gary Regional Airport Authority, chmn, 1995-; Ill State Bd Elections, chmn, 1991-93; Chicago Bd Election Commissioners, chmn, 1997-; Neal & Leroy LLC, owner, prin & atty, 1981-; Am Inst Real Estate Appraisers, lectr; Cook County Bar Assoc, Judicial Candidates Symp, lectr; Int Network Boutique Law Firms, atty. **Orgs:** Support Group; Cook County Bar Asn; Chicago Bar Asn; Am Bar Asn; Ill State Bar Asn; Chicago Hist Soc; W DePaul Neighbors; Cs Pl Asn; Chicago Pub Educ Fund; Jane Addams Juv Ct Found; Bar Admiss Supreme Ct Ill; Int Coun Shopping Centers; US Dist Ct; Northern Dist Ill; Trial Bar; C's Pl Asn; co-chair, High Jump Orgn, Acad Enrichment Prog, 2008-; hon chair & keynote speaker, Mikva Challenge Found, 2014; moderator, Joyce Found, 2014; Jane Addams Juv Ct Found; dir, After Sch Matters Inc. **Honors/Awds:** Matthew Maloney Tradition of Excellence Award, 2010; Richard J. Almeida Award, 2010; Legendary Landmark Award, 2016. **Special Achievements:** Only the second African Am to be elected to the Chicago Bd of Election Commissioners. **Business Addr:** Attorney, Co-chair, Neal & Leroy LLC, 203 N LaSalle St Suite 2300, Chicago, IL 60601, **Business Phone:** (312)641-7144.

### NEAL, LAVELLE E., III
Writer. **Personal:** Born Sep 28, 1965, Chicago, IL; son of Lillian E and La Velle E Jr. **Educ:** Univ Ill, Champaign, 1986; Univ Ill, Chicago, BA, commun, 1989. **Career:** Chicago Illini, sports ed, 1986-89; Southtown Economist, Chicago, Ill, sports writer, 1988-89; Kans City Star, Kans City, Mo, sports writer, 1989-98; Star Tribune, baseball writer & reporter, 1998-. **Orgs:** Nab, 1987-; secy, Kans City Asn Black Journalists, 1989-; pres, Baseball Writers Asn Am. **Honors/Awds:** Chancellor's Student Service Award, Univ Ill, 1989; Kans City Assn Black Journalists, PRS's Award, 1992; First African-American president in the 105-year history of the BBWAA. **Home Addr:** 8013 N Hickory Suite 737, Kansas City, MO 64118-8338, **Home Phone:** (816)468-8748. **Business Addr:** Sports Writer, Reporter, The Star Tribune Media Co, 425 Portland Ave S, Minneapolis, MN 55488, **Business Phone:** (612)673-4000.

### NEAL, LIA
Swimmer. **Personal:** Born Feb 13, 1995, Brooklyn, NY; daughter of Jerome Neal and Siu Neal. **Career:** U.S. Olympic Women's Swim team, Member, 2012. **Orgs:** Asphalt Green Unified Aquatics in Manhattan, NY, Member. **Honors/Awds:** Junior Pan Pacific Championships, Gold in 4x100m freestyle relay, Gold in 800m freestyle relay, Gold in 400m medley relay, Silver in 100m freestyle, Bronze in 50m freestyle, 2010; World Junior Champs, Gold in 100m freestyle relay and Silver in 50m freestyle relay, 2011; 2012 Olympics, Bronze medal winner in the 4x100m freestyle relay; Swim for the Future, Scholarship Recipient; TheGrio.com, 100 Making History Today, 2012. **Special Achievements:** Second African American woman in history to qualify for the U.S. Women's Olympic Swim team, 2012; qualified for the team after surpassing the 11-12 age-group record in the 100m freestyle as a 2008 Olympic Trials Participant.

### NEAL, LORENZO LAVON
Football player, business owner. **Personal:** Born Dec 27, 1970, Hanford, CA; married Denisha; children: Lorenzo, Nylya & Mia. **Educ:** Fresno State Univ, Grad, crim justice, 1992. **Career:** Football player (retired), business owner; New Orleans Saints, full back, 1993-96; New York Jets, full back, 1997; Tampa Bay Buccaneers, full back, 1998-2000, running back, 1999; Tenn Titans, full back, 1999-2000; Cincinnati Bengals, full back, 2001-02; San Diego Chargers, full back, 2003-07, Baltimore Ravens, full back, 2008; Oakland Raiders, 2009; M & N Serv Inc, owner; 95.7 The Game, co host, currently. **Honors/Awds:** All Big-West, 1991, 1992; Champion, Am Football Conf, 1999; Pro Bowl, 2002, 2005, 2006, 2007. **Special Achievements:** Co-hosted Nat Football League Total Access on the Nat Football League Network. **Business Addr:** Owner, M & N Service Inc, Fresno, CA 93720.

### NEAL, MARIO LANZA
Banker, vice president (organization), president (organization). **Personal:** Born Aug 3, 1951, Haines City, FL; son of Warren Jr and Mary E Wolfe; married Emma L Woodward; children: Warren Keith & Jennifer Woodard. **Educ:** Fla State Univ, BS, finan & mgt, 1973; Univ Del, Stonier Grad Sch Banking, 1989. **Career:** First Union Corp, area prest/Fla panhandle, 1973; Ed, Charlotte Citizen, publ Charlotte Jaycees, 1975-76; First Union Nat Bank, sr vpres & consumer bank dir, area pres, currently. **Orgs:** Pres, Family Housing Serv, Inc, 1974-76; treas, Energy Committed to Ex-Offenders, Inc, 1978-83; Mecklenburg County Personnel Comn, 1980-85; chair-elect, United Way Big Bend Tallahassee, Fla; chair-elect, Econ Develop Coun; bd dir, Tallahassee Area Chamber Com; bd dir, March Dimes; bd dir, Regional 5 Workforce Develop Bd; bd dir, Fla State Univ Alumni; Fla State Univ Col Bus Adv Bd; comt mem, Davis Productivity Awards, Fla Tax Watch; bd dir, Capital Cult Ctr, Tallahassee; bd mem, INROADS Tampa Bay, Inc, 1989-; YMCA Black Achievers Inc, 1992; Bd mem, Ctr drug-Free Living Inc, 1992-; bd mem, Hi-Tech Learning Ctr, Inc, 1992. **Honors/Awds:** Central Florida YMCA Black Achievers Inc, 1992. **Special Achievements:** Recognized as One of Two areas within First Union Corp for top performance, 1995. **Home Addr:** 2479 Elfinwing Lane, Tallahassee, FL 32308. **Business Addr:** Senior Vice President, Consumer Bank Director, First Union National Bank, 11510 E Colonial Dr, Orlando, FL 32817, **Business Phone:** (407)273-2300.

### NEAL, RICHARD W.
Law enforcement officer, consultant. **Personal:** Born Jan 1, 1940, MI. **Career:** Police comnr(retired); Philadelphia Police Dept, patrolman, 12th dist, community rels, Internal Affairs Div, head, Housing Police, interim chief, Patrol Bur, chief inspector, comnr, 1992-98; Drexel Univ, security consult, 1998; Penn's Landing Corp, security consult.

### NEAL, SYLVESTER
Firefighter, lieutenant governor, president (organization). **Personal:** Born Sep 21, 1943, Austin, TX; son of Willis and Ima L Jenkins; married Doris Marie; children: Sylvia, Sylvester L, Keith, Todd & Angela Williams. **Educ:** Univ Alaska, Fairbanks, degree criminal justice, 1983. **Career:** Firefighter (retired); City of Austin, Tex, firefighter, 1965-68; AUS, Ft Wainwright AK, firefighter, crew chief, 1968-70; State Alaska, Dept Transp, Fairbanks AK, firefighter, security police, 1970-79, fire/security chief, 1979-83; Fire & Security Chief, Fairbanks International Airport; Dept Pub Safety, Anchorage, AK, state fire marshal, 1983; Anchorage Daily News, safety dir, 1994. **Orgs:** Bd mem, Alaska Fire Chiefs Asn, 1976-; Alaska Peace Officers Asn, 1979-; secy, Fairbanks Kiwanis Club, 1982-83; Int Fire Chiefs Asn, 1983-; Fire Marshals Asn N Am, 1984-; consult, Alaska Asn Pub Fire Educ, 1985-; pres, Anchorage Kiwanis Club, 1987-88; bd dir, Community Action Drug Free Youth, 1988-; Kiwanis/Alaska-Yukon Div, lt gov elect, 1989-90, gov-elect, 2001-02, gov, 1989-90, 2002-03; hon chair, Pac Northwest Dist Kiwanis/SIGN proj; Kiwanis Int Inc, pres, 2009-; Fel Kiwanis Int Found. **Honors/Awds:** Student of the Year Justice Dept, Univ of Alaska Fairbanks, 1982; Kiwanian of the Year, Fairbanks Kiwanis Club, 1983; Outstanding President, Kiwanis/Pacific Northwest Dist, 1989; Citizen Volunteer Award, Anchorage Sch Dist. **Home Addr:** 1720 64th St SE, Auburn, WA 98092-8022, **Home Phone:** (253)735-0139.

### NEAL-BARNETT, DR. ANGELA M.
Educator, business owner. **Personal:** Born Feb 13, 1960, Youngstown, OH; daughter of Andrew and Doris L; married Edgar J Jr; children: Reece L. **Educ:** Mt Union Col, BA, psychol, 1982; De Paul Univ, MA, 1985, PhD, clin psychol, 1988. **Career:** Englewood Community Health Orgn, clin therapist, 1985-87; Univ Pittsburgh Sch Med, Western Psychiat Inst & Clin, intern, 1987-88, fel, 1988-89; Kent State Univ, asst prof, 1989-95, res fel, 1991-, assoc prof, 1995-, Summa Health Systs, sci med staff, 1996-, PRADAA, dir, currently; Rise Sally Rise Inc, founder & chief exec officer, 2000-; Soothe Your Nerves Inc, chief exec officer. Books: Family and peers: Linking two worlds, ed, 2000; Forging Links: African American Children Clinical Developmental Perspectives, ed, 2001; Soothe Your Nerves: The Black Womans Guide to Understanding and Overcoming Anxiety, Panic and Fear, auth. **Orgs:** Am Psychol Asn, 1989-; Anxiety Disorder Asn Am; Trichotillamania Learning Ctr; Asn Black Psychologist; Arlington Church God; adv comm, Am Psychol Asn Minority Fel Prog, 2003-06; Asn Advan Behav Ther; Soc Res Child Develop. **Home Addr:** 361 Starr Lane, Tallmadge, OH 44278, **Home Phone:** (330)633-5990. **Business Addr:** Chief Executive Officer, Founder, Rise Sally Rise Inc, PO Box 514, Tallmadge, OH 44278, **Business Phone:** (330)630-5792.

### NEALS, FELIX RAMON
Judge. **Personal:** Born Jan 5, 1929, Jacksonville, FL; married Betty Harris; children: Felice, Felix & Julien. **Educ:** Idaho State Univ, BS; Washburn Univ, LLB, JD, 1958. **Career:** Judge (retired); Appellate Law NY, pvt pract, 1960-64; ITT & RCA, mgt positions, 1965-69; NY Dept State, supv admin law judge; pvt pract, corp law. **Orgs:** Arbitrator Community Dispute Serv, Am Arbit Asn, NY; founder, "Psycho-Systs"; authority & collector mats Black Magic; bd mem, State Coun Soc Prev Cruelty C Inc, 1988-; exec vpres, NY State Admin Law Judges Asn; Nat Asn Admin Law Judges; Ny Bar, 1961-. **Honors/Awds:** US Nat Intercoll Oratorical Champion, 1954-55. **Home Addr:** 134 Roosevelt Ave, East Orange, NJ 07017. **Business Addr:** Supervising Administrative Law Judge, NY State Department of State, 123 William St 19th Fl, New York, NY 10038, **Business Phone:** (212)417-5776.

### NEARN, ARNOLD DORSEY, JR.
Secretary general, executive. **Personal:** Born Jun 7, 1949, Philadelphia, PA; son of Arnold Dorsey Sr and Isabelle Lawrence; married Sharon Anderson. **Educ:** Del State Col, BS, bus admin, 1971; Temple Univ Law Sch, attended 1972; Rutgers Univ, Grad Bus Sch, attended 1976; Fairleigh Dickinson Univ, attended 1981. **Career:** Allstate Ins Co, casualty claims adjuster, 1971-82; Ethicon Inc, head prod supvr, 1972-76; Monsanto Co, mfg foreperson, 1976-77; Calgon Corp, prime prod foreperson, 1977-78, asst mgr, 1978-81; Schering-Plough Corp, Warehouse Opers, mgr, 1981-82, mgr, 1983; Belle-Sue Assocs, pres, 1983-87; Millennium Fire & Safety Equip, secy, owner, currently. **Orgs:** Dania coun, exec comt, 1988-; Coun Black Econ Develop, 1985-; Broward County Boys & Girls Clubs, 1989-; Fla Reg Purchasing coun; bd dir, Fla Fire Equip Dealers Asn; alumni leadership coun, DE State Univ. **Home Addr:** 425 SE 6th St, Dania, FL 33004, **Home Phone:** (954)925-7162. **Business Addr:** Secretary, Owner, Millennium Fire & Safety Equipment, 1496 W Dixie Hwy, Dania, FL 33004-3802, **Business Phone:** (954)922-9136.

### NEAVON, JOSEPH ROY
Clergy. **Personal:** Born Dec 4, 1928, New York, NY. **Educ:** Manhattan Col, BA, 1950; Gregorian Univ, STD, 1973. **Career:** John Carroll Univ, fac fel, 1980-81; Blessed Sacrament Fathers, rev, dr, prof, 1985. **Orgs:** Parliamentarian Cath Theol Soc Am, 1970-; Black Cath Clergy Caucus, 1978-.

### NEDD, CATHY
Business owner. **Educ:** Spring Arbor Univ, BA, mgt & orgn develop. **Career:** Nedd Detroit Pub Rels, owner & pres, 1994-04; Hass Assocs-Nedd; The Hair Network, founder & owner, 2005-. **Business Addr:** Founder, Owner, The Hair Network, 703 Livernois, Ferndale, MI 48220, **Business Phone:** (313)350-4241.

### NEELY, DAVID E.
School administrator, educator, lawyer. **Personal:** Born Chicago, IL. **Educ:** Fayetteville State Univ, BA, sociol, 1975; Univ Idaho, MA, sociol, 1978; Univ Iowa, Sch Law, JD, 1981; Univ Ill, Chicago, PhD, educ, 1997. **Career:** Univ IA, Univ Ombudsman, 1979-81; Ill State Univ, assoc prof, Polit Sci, 1981-83, dir affirm action, 1981-83; John Marshall Law Sch, practicing atty, prof law, consult, K-12, col & univ, asst dean, 1983; Cabrini Green Legal Aid, exec dir, 2000-01; Elmhurst Col, assoc dean, 2000-02; Criminal & Civil Law-Pvt Pract, atty, 2001-; David E. Neely & Assocs, atty, 2001-; N Dahoz Entertainment, legal coun, 2004-; Nat Bar Asn, reg dir. **Orgs:** Legal coun, Ill Affirm Action Officer Asn; Ill Human Rels Asn; Ill Comn Black Concern Higher Ed; Chicago Southside Br; Nat Asn Advan Colored People. **Special Achievements:** Works: Capital punishment discrimination An Indicator of Inst Western Jrnl of Black Studies, 1979; innovative approach to recruiting minority employees in higher ed EEO Today, 1982; Blacks in IL Higher Ed A Status Report Jrnl for the Soc of Soc & Ethnic Studies, 1983; The Social Reality of Blacks Under representation in Legal Ed Approach Toward Racial Parity, 1985. Author of articles, "Pedagogy of Culturally Biased Curriculum in Public Education," 1994; "Social Reality of African American Street Gangs," 1997. **Home Addr:** 8401 S Luella Ave, Chicago, IL 60617, **Home Phone:** (312)315-8241. **Business Addr:** Attorney, David E Neely & Associates, 8401 S Luella Ave, Chicago, IL 60617, **Business Phone:** (312)315-8241.

### NEIGHBORS, REV. DOLORES MARIA
Clergy. **Personal:** Born Aug 29, 1929, Chicago, IL; daughter of Roscoe Cokiegee and Ruth Smith; children: Deborah Ann, Eric Chanlyn & Lori Dee. **Educ:** Seabury Western Theol Sem, MDiv, 1988; advan sem, psychiat & pastoral coun, 1992; Claret Ctr, internship, spiritual direction, 1997. **Career:** Clergy (retired); Univ Chicago, Nat Opinion Res Ctr, area supvr, 1967-78; Ill Human Rights Dept, human rights investr, 1978-86; Seabury Western Theol Sem, seminarian, 1985-88; St George & Matthias Episcopal Church, seminarian asst, 1988; Church Epiphany, assoc priest, 1988-90; St Edmund Episcopal Church, asst priest, 1990-96, spiritual dir, 1996; St James Episcopal Cathedral, canon, 1997-2000; St Chrysastoms Episcopal Church, assoc priest, 2000-01. **Orgs:** Nat Alliance Mentally Ill, 1981-89; Alliance Mentally Ill, 1981-90; Black Union Episcopalians, 1985-; Chicago Episcopal Diocese, 1990-97; Clergy Family Proj Comt, 1993-96; Standing Comn, Diocese Chicago, 1999-2001; Network Biblical Storytellers, 2000-01; pres, Standing Comn, 2001; Pastoral Asn St Paul & The Redeemer Episcopal Church, 2001. **Special Achievements:** Ordained to the Diaconate, Deacon, 1988; Ordained to the Sacred Order of Priests, 1988. **Home Addr:** 5555 S Everett Ave C4, Chicago, IL 60637-1968, **Home Phone:** (773)493-3429.

### NEIL, REV. EARL ALBERT
Clergy. **Personal:** Born Dec 17, 1935, St. Paul, MN; son of Earl Willus and Katherine Louise Martin; married Angela; children: Latoya. **Educ:** Carleton Col, Northfield, Minn, BA, 1957; Seabury-Western Theol Sem, MDiv, 1960, DDiv, 1989; Univ Calif-Berkeley, MSW, 1973. **Career:** Clergy (retired); St Augustine's Wichita, Kans, vicar, 1960-63; Christ Church, Chicago, Ill, vicar, 1964-67; St Augustine's, Oakland, Calif, rector, 1967-74; Episcopal Church Ctr, New York, NY, prog exec & officer, 1974-90; Church Prov Southern Africa, Safrica, 1990-93; Wash Nat Cathedral, WDC, canon missioner, 1994-97; Calvary Episcopal Church, WDC, interim rector, 1997-2000; Black Panther Party. **Orgs:** Exec coun, Episcopal Church; chap pres, Episcopal Soc Cult & Racial Unity; Woodlawn Orgn. **Honors/Awds:** Alumni Award, Carleton Col, 1971. **Home Addr:** 4545 Conn Ave NW Suite 929, Washington, DC 20008, **Home Phone:** (202)244-0579.

### NEIZER, MEREDITH ANN
Vice president (government), president (organization). **Personal:** Born Jul 24, 1956, Chateauroux; daughter of Donald and Roberta Marie Faulcon Neizer. **Educ:** US Merchant Marine Acad, Kings Pt, NY, BS, marine transp, 1978, USCG Third Mate Lic, 1978; Stanford Grad Sch Bus, Stanford, Calif, MBA, bus admin, mgt & opers, 1982. **Career:** Arco Marine, Long Beach, Calif, third mate, 1978-80; Exxon Int, Florham Pk, NJ, sr analyst & fleet personnel adminr, 1982-86; US Dept Defense, Wash, DC, spec asst, 1986-87; Port Authority New York, bus mgr, 1987-90; Sea-Land Serv Inc, 1992-95, port mgr, 1995-97, gen mgr & country mgr Philippines, 1997-99; Martin-Brower, Pr & Cent Am, vpres, 2000-02, Can vpres opers, 2002-05, Mbx Logistics, pres, 2005-08; US Foodservice, Alliant Logistics, pres, 2008-09, sr vpres opers, 2008-11; iGPS, chief operating officer, 2012-13; ARMADA Supply Chain Solutions, vpres transp opers, 2014-; FedEx Logistics. **Orgs:** Kings Pt info rep, Kings Pt Alumni Asn, 1979-91; minority rep, Stanford Grad Sch Bus Admis, 1982-89; corp liason comm, Nj Black MBA Asn, 1983-89; consult, Morris Co Bus Vol Arts, 1986; US Dept Defense, white house fel, 1986; chair sub comt no 1; Defense Adv Comm WomenServ, 1988-90, Navy League, 1988-89; young exec fel FundCorp Initiatives, 1989; Transp Res Forum, 1989-; Leadership NJ, 1991-; Press Comn Women Mil, 1991-; Bd Pilot Commissioners Bays San Francisco, San Pablo & Suisun, 1996-97; bd dir, Philippine Asn Int Shipping Lines, 1998-99; bd dir, Marcus A Foster Educ Inst, 1998-99; bd dir, Navy League Us Panama Coun, 2002-; bd mem, US Dept Transp Adv Bd USMMA, 2002-11; bd dir, Eno Transp Found, bd advisor, 2008-11; Coun Supply Chain Mgt Professionals; Univ Chicago Women's Bd, 2011-; bd dir, Cent Fla Urban League, 2013-. **Honors/Awds:** Partner, Creative Renovations Assoc, 1984-85; White House Fel, Press Commn on White House Fel, 1986, 1987; Leadership Award, New Jersey Black MBA Asn, 1986; Woman Pioneer, Kings Point Asn, 1988; Secy Defense Medal for Outstanding Pub Serv, 1990. **Home Addr:** 75-38 Liberty Ave, Jersey City, NJ 07306, **Home Phone:** (201)656-6744. **Business Addr:** President, Mbx Logistics LLC, 9500 West Bryn Mawr Ave, Rosemont, IL 60018, **Business Phone:** (847)227-6500.

### NELLUMS, MICHAEL WAYNE
School administrator, businessperson. **Personal:** Born Jan 1, 1965, England, AR; son of Silas and Shirley; married Brenda Kay Clipper; children: Michael B. **Educ:** Univ Cent Ark, BSE, 1985, MSE, 1991; UALR, ABD. **Career:** Little Rock City, pool mgr, 1983-; Pulaski Co Spec Sch Dist, prin, admin ranks position, teacher, adr, 1985; Mills Univ Studies High Sch, asst prin, prin, 2011; Sigma One Productions,

owner, 1985-; Power 92-Radio, on-air announcer, 1990-; Jacksonville Mid Sch, prin; Sylvan Hills High Sch, prin; Jack Robey Jr High Sch. **Orgs:** Educ comt, Phi Beta Fraternity, Mu Beta Sigma, 1983-; bd mem, Ark Asn Mid Level Educ, 1985-; Nat Educ Asn, 1985-; curric develop, Asn Supv & Curric Develop, 1989-; dir, Teachers Tomorrow Acad, 1992-. **Business Addr:** Principal, Wilbur D Mills University Studies High School, 1205 E Dixon Rd, Little Rock, AR 72206, **Business Phone:** (625)078-3655.

### NELLY (CORNELL IRAL HAYNES, JR.)

Rap musician. **Personal:** Born Nov 2, 1974, Austin, TX; son of Cornall Haynes Sr and Rhonda Mack; children: Chanel Haynes & Cornell Haynes III. **Career:** Albums: Country Grammar, 2000; Free City, 2001; Nellyville, 2002; Da Derrty Versions: The Reinvention, 2003; Iz U, 2004; Sweat, 2004; Suit, 2004; Sweatsuit, 2005; Who's The Boss, 2006; Brass Knuckles, 2008; TV: "Cedric the Entertainer Presents", 2003; Fuse's Summer Jam X, 2003; Turbulence, 2008; My Name Is Mac Taylor, 2008; Pay Up, 2009; Cuckoo's Nest, 2009; M.O., 2010; Films: The Longest Yard, 2005; Singles: "Country Grammar", 2000; "E.I.", 2000; "Ride wit Me", 2001; "Batter Up", 2001; "#1", 2001; "Hot in Herre", 2002; "Dilemma", 2002; "Air Force Ones", 2002; "Work It", 2003; "Pimp Juice", 2003; "Iz U", 2003; "Na-Nana-Na", 2004; "My Place", 2004; "Flap Your Wings", 2004; "Tilt Ya Head Back", 2004; "Over & Over", 2004; "N Dey Say", 2005; "Errtime", 2005; "Fly Away", 2005; "Grillz", 2005; "Wadsya name", 2007; "Party People", 2008; "Kill YaSelf", 2008; "Hey Porsche", 2010; "Get Like Me", 2010; "The Next: Fame Is at Your Doorstep", 2012. **Business Addr:** Recording Artist, Universal Records, 1755 Broadway, New York, NY 10019, **Business Phone:** (212)373-0600.

### NELOMS, HENRY

Executive. **Career:** Premium Distribr Inc, chief exec officer, currently. **Business Addr:** President, Chief Executive Officer, Premium Distributors Inc, 3500 Ft Lincoln Dr NE, Washington, DC 20002, **Business Phone:** (202)526-3900.

### NELSON, DARRIN MILO

Football player, executive director. **Personal:** Born Jan 2, 1959, Sacramento, CA; married Camilla; children: Jordan. **Educ:** Stanford Univ, BS, urban & environ planning, 1981. **Career:** Football player (retired), exec dir; Minn Vikings, running back, 1982-89 & 1991-92; San Diego Chargers, 1989-90; Piper Capital Mgt; Stanford Univ Cardinal, asst athletic dir community rels, 1997-99, sr assoc athletic dir external rels, 2005-. **Orgs:** Acad All-Am; Nat Football Found Scholar Athlete. **Business Addr:** Senior Associate Athletic Director, Stanford University, Arrillaga Family Sports Ctr, Stanford, CA 94305-6150, **Business Phone:** (650)723-4591.

### NELSON, DEBRA J.

Manager, vice president (organization), educator. **Personal:** Born Birmingham, AL; daughter of James. **Educ:** Univ Ala, Tuscaloosa, BA, commun, 1980. **Career:** WSGN Radio, Birmingham, dir pub affairs, 1980-84; WBRC-TV, Birmingham, dir community affairs, 1984-88, news anchor, noon show, 1987-88; Univ Ala, Birmingham, spec studies instr, 1988-; Univ Ala Syst, Tuscoosa, dir media rels, 1994; Mercedes-Benz, mgr corp diversity, Daimler Chrysler, sr mgr, human resources, diversity & extern commun, adminr Extern Affairs, 1998-2000; Daimler Chrysler sr mgr, 2000-05; Group Mkt & Diversity Commun, sr mgr, Human Resources, labor, mfg Gov Affairs Commun, 2001; MGM Resorts Int, vpres corp diversity & community affairs, 2005-; Great Women Gaming, Judging Comt, mem, currently. **Orgs:** Convener, Birmingham Literacy Task Force, 1987-88; US Libr Literacy Rev Panel, 1988-91; dir, Am Heart Asn, Ala Affil, 1986-; commun chmn, Am Heart Asn, 1986-; Ala Japan Leadership Prog, 1988-89; Mil Acad Rev Comt, 6th Cong Dist, 1999; Ed Davis Edu Found Bd; bd mem, William Paterson Univ Found; chmn, Edward Davis Edu Found, 2002; chmn, Edward Davis Edu Found bd, 2003; pres, bd mem, Urban Chamber Com; bd mem, Chief Diversity; bd mem, Nev HAND Inc. **Honors/Awds:** Distinguished Leadership Award, United Negro Col Fund, 1985, 1987, 1988; Award of Distinction, Int Asn Bus Communicators, 1985; Hon Lt Col, Ala Militia Gov's Off, 1987; Woman of Distinction, Iota Phi Lambda Serv Sorority, 1985; Outstanding Leadership Award, Am Heart Asn, 1987-89; Outstanding Vol Serv Award, Am Red Cross, 1985; Human Rights Award, Southern Christian Leadership Conf; Outstanding Corp & Comm Rels Award, Human Resources Develop IST; Woman of the Yr, African Am Wheels Mag, 2001; Prism Award, 2002; Women to Watch, Bus Las Vegas, 2008; Great Women of Gaming Rising Star, Casino Enterprise Mgt Mag, 2007; Professional Services Award, Latin Chamber of Commerce; Hall of Fame inductee Women's Chamber Com Nev. **Business Addr:** Vice President of Corporate Diversity & Community, MGM Resorts International, 4886 Frank Sinatra Dr, Las Vegas, NV 89158, **Business Phone:** (702)692-1888.

### NELSON, DR. DOROTHY J. SMITH

Educator. **Personal:** Born Jun 24, 1948, Greenville, MS; daughter of Dorothy J and Jim M; married Jim Sr; children: Jim Jr, Gwendolyn (Cornelius), Janice (Birlette), Brendra Anderson & Cheryl (Morris Sr). **Educ:** Tufts Univ, BA, 1970, MEd, 1971; Southern Ill Univ, Carbondale, PhD, higher educ, acad admin, 1981. **Career:** Miss Valley State Univ, acad affairs, asst vpres, interim vpres acad affairs, assoc prof & dir acad skills parlor, 1971-99; Southern Ill Univ, Carbondale Off Stud Develop, coordr stud develop, 1979-81; Frisby-Smith-Nelson Rentals, property mgr, 1999-. **Orgs:** Post Doctoral Acad Higher Educ, 1979-; bd mem, Nat Asn Advan Colored People, 1982-84; fin sec, Les Modernette Social Club; Int Reading Asn; Southern Ill Univ Alumni Asn; Concerned Educrs Black Students; SE Regional Reading Conf; Alpha Kappa Alpha; Progressive Art & Civic Club, Miss Reading Asn; Nat Asn Develop Educrs; Miss Asn Develop Educrs; State Bd Community & Jr Cols, 2002-08; Am Asn Higher Educ; Miss Associations Cols. **Honors/Awds:** Clark Doctoral Scholar Award for Research, Southern Ill Univ; Education Award, Nat Asn Advan Colored People; Education Achievement Award, Progressive Art & Civic Club; Outstanding Young Women of America; MVSA Presidential Citation for Outstanding Services and Financial Support, 1998; Diversity Award & Black History Month, 1998; Preeminence Award, Miss Valley State Univ, 2003. **Home Addr:** 18 Bonda Dr, Greenville, MS 38701, **Home Phone:** (662)332-7075.

### NELSON, EDWARD O.

Engineer. **Personal:** Born Feb 2, 1925, Johnsonville, TN; son of Edgar and Lucille; married Pauline; children: Stanley, Michael, Michelle, Cozetta, Richard & Viola. **Educ:** Wash Univ, St Louis, Mo, BS, Eng, 1975; St Louis Univ; Rankin Tech Inst. **Career:** Engineer (retired); Rockwell Int Environ Monitoring Serv Ctr, tech staff; US Environ Protection Agency St Louis, engr technician; Radio Broadcast Engr. **Orgs:** Am Radio Relay Leag; Am Asn Retired Persons; IBEW-LU Suite 4; Am Legion; Disabled Am Vet. **Special Achievements:** First black admitted to the International Brotherhood of Electrical Workers. **Home Addr:** 4614 Elmbank Ave, St Louis, MO 63115, **Home Phone:** (314)383-0107. **Business Addr:** .

### NELSON, EILEEN F.

Artist. **Personal:** Born Chicago, IL; daughter of Frances Irons Anderson and Summers Anderson; married Alphonzo George; children: Maisha Eileen. **Educ:** Art Inst Chicago, attended 1964; Ill Inst Technol, attended 1969; Los Angeles City Col, attended 1974; Indian Valley Col, attended 1979. **Career:** Studio F, artist & designer; self employed artist & designer, currently. **Business Addr:** Designer, Artist, Studio F, 7 Regent Ct, Novato, CA 94947, **Business Phone:** (415)892-4471.

### NELSON, FLORA SUE

Administrator. **Personal:** Born Dec 14, 1930, Chicago, IL; daughter of William Jarrett Martin (deceased) and Clara Payne Martin (deceased); married Herman; children: Lisa & Tracey. **Educ:** Univ Wis-Madison, WI, attended 1949; Roosevelt Univ, Chicago, BA, 1951; Univ Chicago, Chicago, IL, MA, 1957. **Career:** Administrator (retired); Cook County Juv Ct, Chicago, Ill, 1951-58; Dept Housing, Chicago, Ill, specialist, 1958-67, asst relocation, 1967-76, dir relocation, 1976-80, dep comnr, 1980-92. **Orgs:** Delta Sigma Theta Sorority, 1951-. **Home Addr:** 6707 S Bennett Ave, Chicago, IL 60649, **Home Phone:** (773)947-7095.

### NELSON, DR. IVORY V.

President (organization), college administrator, educator. **Personal:** Born Jun 11, 1934, Curtis, LA; son of Elijah and Mattie; married Patricia Ann; children: Cherlyn, Karyn, Eric Beatty & Kim Beatty. **Educ:** Grambling State Univ, BS, chem, 1959; Univ Kans, PhD, anal chem, 1963. **Career:** Union Carbide, res chemist; Am Oil Co, res chemist; Southern Univ Baton Rouge, chair, natural sci div, 1966-68; Prairie View A & M, asst acad dean, prof chem, 1968-72, vpres res, prof chem, 1972-82, actg pres, prof chem, 1982-83; Tex A&M Univ Syst, exec asst chancellor, 1983-86; Alamo Community Col Dist, chancellor, 1986-92; Cent Wash Univ, pres, 1992-99; Lincoln Univ, pres, 1999-2011. **Orgs:** AAAS, 1963-; Am Chem Soc, 1963-; Tex Acad Sci, 1968-; Africult Res Inst; Am Asn Col Teachers; Nat Asn Fed Rel Officers, 1975-83; Nat Asn State Univ & Land Grant Col, exec comm; Nat Coun Univ Res Admin, 1976-83; bd dir, Key Bank Wash; Wash State Comn; NY Acad Sci, 1976-83; Western Interstate Regional Policy Comm Higher Ed, 1986-88; Kappa Delta Phi educ hon soc; Southeast Consortium Int Develop; exec comm, TexPub Community, Jr Col Asn, 1989-91; exec comm, Nat Jr Col Athletic Asn, 1991; Nat Asn Intercollegiate Athletics, 1993-98; Am Coun Ed Comm Int Ed, 1995-98; Pres Coun Div III, NCAA, 2001-; Sigma Xi; Sigma Phi Sigma physics hon soc; Phi Kappa Phi; Phi Lamda Upsilon hon chem soc; dir, Greater Philadelphia Chamber Com; Gov Blue Ribbon Task Force Arts; Phi Beta Kappa hon soc; Wash State Comn Stud Learning. **Home Addr:** 1570 Baltimore Pke, Lincoln University, PA 19352-9141. **Business Addr:** Director, Greater Philadelphia Chamber of Commerce, 200 S Broad St Suite 700, Philadelphia, PA 19102, **Business Phone:** (215)545-1234.

### NELSON, JILL

Writer, journalist. **Personal:** Born Jun 14, 1952, Harlem, NY; children: Misu. **Educ:** City Col NY; Columbia Sch Journalism, MA, 1975. **Career:** Wash Post Mag, journalist, 1986-; City Col New York, prof jour, 1998-03; USA Weekend, contrib ed; MSNBC.com, columnist; Volunteer Slavery: My Authentic Negro Wash Post Mag, journalist, 1986-; City Col New York, prof jour, 1998-03; USA Weekend, contrib ed; MSNBC.com, columnist; City Col New York, prof journalism, currently; Books: Volunteer Slavery: My Authentic Negro Experience, 1993; Straight, No Chaser: How I Became A Grown-Up Black Woman, 1997; Police Brutality: An Anthology, ed, 2000; Sexual Healing, 2003; Finding Martha's Vineyard: African Americans at Home on an Island, 2005; Sequel to Sexual Healing, Let's Get It On, 2009. **Honors/Awds:** Washington DC Journalist of the Year Award; American Book Award. **Special Achievements:** Writings have appeared in numerous publications including The New York Times, Essence, The Nation, Ms, The Chicago Tribune and The Village Voice. **Business Addr:** Professor, The City College of New York, 160 Convent Ave, New York, NY 10031, **Business Phone:** (212)650-7000.

### NELSON, JONATHAN P.

Executive. **Personal:** Born Jun 5, 1939, New York, NY; married Dorothy Higgins. **Educ:** Howard Univ, BSEE, 1963; St John's Univ, MBA, 1974. **Career:** Nat Bur Stand, stand trainee, 1961-63; ACF Ind Inc, electronics design engr, 1963-67; EG & G Inc, electronics engr, 1967-68; Pfizer Inc, mgr oral prod pkg dept, 1968-94; Haagen Dazs Co, eng mgr, 1994; Strategic Mfg Initiatives Inc, proj dir, 1995-. **Orgs:** Inst Elec & Electronics Engrs; Nat Mgt Asn; exec bd, Brooklyn BSA; Omega Psi Phi; Nat Black MBA Asn; Am Fin Asn. **Honors/Awds:** Recipient Achievement Award, Nat Asn Negro Bus & Prof Women, 1969; Black Achiever Ind Harlem YMCA, 1972, 1974. **Home Addr:** 232 Hancock St, Brooklyn, NY 11216-2201, **Home Phone:** (718)622-1737. **Business Addr:** Project Director, Strategic Manufacturing Initiatives Inc, 242 Old New Burnswick Rd Suite 100, Piscataway, NJ 08854.

### NELSON, KIMBERLY A.

President (organization). **Educ:** Georgetown Univ, BS, int rels, 1984; Columbia Univ, MBA, 1988. **Career:** Gen Mills, corp officer, 2000, external rels, sr vpres, 2010-, Snacks Unlimited Div, pres, 2011-. **Orgs:** Cong Black Caucus Found Bd; Exec Leadership Coun; Nat Exec Women Network; chairperson, Minneapolis Young Women's Christian Asn Bd; founding mem, Black Champions Network; founding mem, Women Mkt Network; Gen Mills Community. **Business Addr:** President, Senior Vice President, General Mills Inc, 1 General Mills Blvd, Minneapolis, MN 55426, **Business Phone:** (800)248-7310.

### NELSON, LARRY

Vice president (organization). **Personal:** married Theresa; children: Eric & Danielle. **Educ:** Rutgers Univ, BS; Univ Pittsburgh Sch Law, JD, 1976. **Career:** Wendy's legal dept, 1978; Wendy's Int Inc, officer, vpres & asst gen couns, sr vpres & assoc gen coun develop, 1991. **Orgs:** Bd dir, Big Brother/Big Sister Asn Greater Columbus; bd, King Arts Complex Columbus. **Business Addr:** Senior Vice President, Associate General Councel of Development, Wendy's Intl, 4288 W-Dublin-Granville Rd, Dublin, OH 43017, **Business Phone:** (614)764-3100.

### NELSON, MARIO

Marketing executive. **Personal:** Born Jan 19, 1955, Los Angeles, CA; son of George and Martha; married Cheryl; children: Mario Umjamo & Ahree Kashawn. **Educ:** Kans State Univ, econs, 1977; Riverside City Col, AA, 1980; Calif State Col, San Bernardino, BA, 1983; Calif State Univ, San Bernardino, MBA, mkt mgt, 1986. **Career:** Ft Riley, Kans, stock control & acounting specialist, 1974-77; Jerry L Pettis, Loma Linda, property mgr, 1977-83; BF Spirits, merchandiser, 1983-84, asst regional dir, 1984-86; Brown-Forman Beverages Worldwide: merchandiser, sales rep, asst to reg mgr, convenient store mgr, 1986-87, reg sales mgr, 1987-94, div mkt mgr, 1994-98, chain channel mgr, 1998-2000, mkt mgr, Va, 2002-06, mkt brand mgr, 2006-08; Spirits Americas, bus develop mgr, 2000-02; Strayer Univ, prof mkt, 2009-10; The Art Inst Atlanta, prof mkt, advert dept, 2009-15; Gwinnett Tech Col, adj instr mkt mgt, 2015-. **Orgs:** Nat Black MBA Asn, 1987-; leader, Money Matters Ministry, Friendship Baptist Church, Duluth, 2007-; founding mem, Black Alumni Asn; life mem, NBMBAA Asn. **Honors/Awds:** Top Sales Team, 1991; National Award, 1995; National Award, Brown Forman Corp; Fleet Owner Graphics Award, 1997; Best in Nation, 2003. **Special Achievements:** Featured in National publications of "Jet" & 'Black Enterprize" Magazines. **Business Addr:** Adjunct Instructor, Gwinnett Technical College, 5150 Sugarloaf Pkwy, Lawrenceville, GA 30043, **Business Phone:** (770)962-7580.

### NELSON, MARY ELIZABETH

Lawyer, president (government), government official. **Personal:** Born Feb 6, 1955, St. Louis, MO; daughter of Clyde H and Kathryn E. **Educ:** Princeton Univ, BA, polit philos, 1977; Univ Miss-Columbia Sch Law, JD, 1981. **Career:** Wilson Smith & Mc Cullin, assoc, 1981-82; Mary E Nelson LLC, pvt pract; Off Bus Develop, minority bus develop dir, 1982-86; St Louis Develop Corp, gen coun, 1993-96; City St Louis, gen coun, 1993-96; Vickers Moore & Wiest, PC, assoc, 1986-88; Lashley & Baer PC, assoc, 1987-93, partner, 1992; Mound City Bar Asn, pres, 1994-95; Law Offices Mary E Nelson LLC, prin, 2000-06; House Redistricting & Reapportionment Comn, comnr, 2000-01; St Louis Police Bd Comnrs, vpres, pres, 2002-04; Speaker Miss House Reps, gen coun; Kwame Bldg Group Inc, gen coun, 2006-08; Greensfelder, Hemker & Gale PC, officer, 2008-09; Off Gov Jeremiah W (Jay) Nixon, bd dir & comns, 2009-10; Admin Hearing Comn, comnr, 2010-14; St. Louis Community Col, gen coun & chief legal oficer, 2014-. **Orgs:** Vpres, Mound City Bar Asn, 1988, corresp secy, 1985-87; Bar Asn Metrop St Louis, long-range planning comn, 1989-; bd dir, Bar Found St Louis, 1990-; bd dir, Peoples Health Ctr, 1991-; bd comnrs, Regional Arts Comn, 1991-96; bd dir, Opera Theatre St Louis, 1992-; Nat Bar Asn, entertainment law comn, 1992; Black Entertainment & Sports Lawyers Asn, 1992; bd mem, Doorways, 2002-; St Louis Forum, 2008-2009. **Home Addr:** 4100 Laclede Ave Apt 202, St. Louis, MO 63108-2854. **Business Addr:** Commissioner, Administrative Hearing Commission, Truman State Off Bldg, Jefferson City, MO 65101, **Business Phone:** (573)751-2422.

### NELSON, NATHANIEL W.

Podiatrist. **Personal:** Born Nov 28, 1921, Birmingham, AL; married Lee E; children: Altamease, Beth, Nolita W (Rice), Stanley, Pierre & Milford. **Educ:** Wayne Univ Detroit; Detroit Inst Technol. **Career:** Podiatrist, foot & ankle surg; podiatrist admitted hosp surg staff; Old Kirwood Hosp, chief podiatry serv. **Orgs:** Mich Podiatry Asn; Am Podiatry Asn; Nat Podiatry Asn; Ohio Col Podiatric Med Alumni Asn; Bethal AME Ch BTA. **Special Achievements:** First African American podiatrist to be appointed as examiner & consult in Detroit area of Aetna Life & Casalty Ins Co for foot & ankle disabilities Quarter Master Serv & Corp, 1943-46. **Home Addr:** 18000 Indiana St, Detroit, MI 48221-2419, **Home Phone:** (313)861-7668. **Business Addr:** 11477 E 12 Mile Rd, Warren, MI 48093, **Business Phone:** (586)751-0200.

### NELSON, NOVELLA C.

Actor, singer, administrator. **Personal:** Born Dec 17, 1939, Brooklyn, NY; daughter of James and Evelyn Hines; children: Alesa Novella Blanchard. **Educ:** Brooklyn Col. **Career:** J Papp, consult; Sundance Theatre Prog, dir; Lincoln Ctr Dirs prog, dir; Hartford Stage, dir; Ky Humana Fest, dir; Eugene O'Neill Ctr, dir; MTC, dir; Pub Theatre, dir; Negro Ensemble Co, dir; New Fed Theatre, dir; Films: Seattle Rep; ACT; Alliance; Mark Taper Forum; Long Wharf Theatre; Caucasian Chalk Circle; He Doctor's Story; One Life to Live; You Are There; All My C; As The World Turns; The Equalizer; Orphans; The Cotton Club; The Flamingo Kid; An Unmarried Woman, 1978; The Seduction of Joe Tynan; Green Card; The Devil's Advocate; A Perfect Murder; Clockers; Girl Six; Performed in: Purlie; Hello Dolly; The Little Foxes; Caesar & Cleopatra; Having Our Say; Passing Game; Div St; A Piece of My Heart; Trio; The Skin of Our Teeth; In New Eng Winter; S Pac; Widows; Mecuba; Judy Berlin, 2000; Antwone Fisher, 2002, Taboo; Death, 2002, Head of State, 2003; Birth, 2004; Dear Wendy, 2005; Preaching to the Choir, 2005; Stephanie Daley, 2006; Premium, 2006; Griffin & Phoenix, 2006; King, 2007; The Ten, 2007; The Toe Tactic, 2008; Sweet Kandy, 2009; My Pl in the Horror, 2009; Night Catches Us, 2009; TV series: "100 Centre St, " 2001; "Things Chg, " 2001; "Third Watch", 2003; "Whoopi", 2003; "The W Wing", 2004; "The Starter Wife", 2007; "Oedipus", 2009; "Law & Order: Spec Victims Unit", 1999-2008; Voice-over actors, instructor; Le Femme Noir, dir. **Orgs:** ACT;

Alliance Theatre; Nat Counc Negro Women; Delta Sigma Theta; mem bd, DST Community Arts & Letters; Harlem C Theatre; New Heritage Theatre; bd mem, Studio WIS; NY State Coun Arts Theatre panelist, Young Playwrights Festival Selection Comt. **Honors/Awds:** Mary M Bethune Lifetime Achievement Award, Nat Coun Negro Women; Image Award, Nat Asn Advan Colored People. **Special Achievements:** DRR, Hunana Festival, ATL; Appeared in Hawk; Law & Order; The Littlest Victim; He's Hired She's Fired; Chiefs; album, Novella Nelson; numerous singing engagements. **Home Addr:** 43 Midwood St, Brooklyn, NY 11225-5003, **Home Phone:** (718)282-5614. **Business Addr:** Producer, DBA, 10 E 44th St, New York, NY 10012.

### NELSON, OTHA CURTIS, SR.
Lawyer. **Personal:** Born Feb 28, 1947, Marion, IN; son of Jeremiah and Wilma Pearson; married Vernita Moore, Sep 1, 1968; children: Otha Curtis Jr. **Educ:** Southern Univ, Agr & Mech Col, BA, 1969; Southern Univ, Sch Law, JD, 1972. **Career:** Capital Area Legal Serv Corp, law clerk, 1971-72, staff atty, 1973-74; Off Gen Coun, staff atty, state La, 1974-82; Simmons & Nelson Law Firm, founding partner, 1974-80; Otha Curtis Nelson Sr, atty-at-Law, notary pub, 1980-; Southwest La Legal Serv Corp, staff atty. **Orgs:** Chaplain, Louis A Martinet Soc, 1972-92; co-pastor, Pentecostal Assembly Christ, 1975-78; pres, Pentecostal Assemblies World La State Choir, 1975-76; Sunday Sch supt, Holy Ghost Temple Church God Christ, 1979-91, asst pastor, 1985-; founder, Christians Basketball Teams, sponsor, coach, 1982-87; chmn bd dirs, Martinet Fin Serv, 1991-; co-chaplain, Southern Univ Law Sch Alumni, 1992-; Nat Asn Coun C. **Honors/Awds:** Valuable Services Rendered, Louis A Martinet Soc, 1991; Honorary Secretary of the State of Louisiana Award, 1980. **Special Achievements:** Coach, Basketball Champion teams, First Place, 1985-86. **Home Addr:** 2225 Moeling St, PO Box 3002, Lake Charles, LA 70602. **Business Addr:** Attorney, Lawyer, Simmons & Nelson, 1606 Scenic Hwy, Baton Rouge, LA 70802, **Business Phone:** (225)383-3675.

**NELSON, PRINCE ROGERS.** See Obituaries Section.

### NELSON, RAMONA M.
Broker, executive. **Personal:** Born Mar 23, 1950, Pittsburgh, PA; daughter of Ramona L Collie and Pronty L Ford; children: Tawana R Cook & John. **Educ:** Knoxville Col, BA, psychol, 1972; Univ Pa, MGA, govt admin, 1984. **Career:** PEN Housing Finance Agency, sr mgt rep, 1979-84; Cert Property Mgr, 1984; Remanco Inc, regional mgr, 1985-87; Nelson & Assoc Inc, pres & chief exec officer, 1987-; Lic Real Estate Broker. **Orgs:** Greater Cincinnati Chap IREM, past pres, 1991; Nat Asn Realtors; Nat Asn Real Estates Brokers; Greater Cincinnati Chamber Com; Delta Sigma Theta Sorority; Inst Real Estate Mgt; Fla Coun Affordable & Rural Housing; Nat Asn Housing & Redevelop Officials; Nat Asn Realtors. **Honors/Awds:** Black Achiever, YMCA, 1992. **Home Addr:** 10632 Merrick Lane, Cincinnati, OH 45242, **Home Phone:** (513)489-2707. **Business Addr:** President, Chief Executive Officer, Nelson & Associates Inc, 5181 Natorp Blvd Suite 140, Mason, OH 45040, **Business Phone:** (561)504-2110.

### NELSON, REX
Sports manager, executive director. **Educ:** Mich State Univ, BA, commun arts & sci, 1983-. **Career:** M&M Mars, territory sales supvr, 1986-88, sales trainer, 1989; Detroit Pistons, dir community rels, 1989-96, vpres, community develop & player progs, 1996-2000; Pistons-Palace Found, exec dir, 1989-2000; Skillman Found, prog off, 2000-03; Lilly USA, sr sales rep, 2004-08, exec sales rep, 2008-. **Orgs:** Exec dir, Pistons Palace Found; ABFE, 2003-04; Asn Black Found Exec; Mich Col Found; pres, Rosa Parks Found; City Yr Community. **Business Addr:** Executive Sales Representative, Lilly USA, Lilly Corp Ctr, Indianapolis, IN 46285-0001, **Business Phone:** (317)276-2000.

### NELSON, RICHARD Y., JR. (RICK NELSON)
Executive director, government official. **Personal:** Born Aug 27, 1939, Atlantic City, NJ; married Nancy Allen; children: Michael, Michele, Cherie, Gregg & Nancy. **Educ:** San Fran State Univ, BA, 1961; Temple Univ Law Sch, JD, 1969. **Career:** Def Support Agency, Philadelphia, pur agt, 1961-65; Philadelphia Reg off, Dept Housing & Urban Develop, area coord, 1965-70; NJ Bar, admitted, 1969; Nat Asn Housing & Redevelop officials, dep exec dir, 1970-2001; Housing Opportunities Comn Montgomery County, comnr, 1991, chair, 2003-; Univ Md, Sch Pub Policy, sr fel; Dept Housing & Community Affairs, Montgomery County, dir, currently. **Orgs:** Am Soc Asn Exec; Alpha Phi Alpha Frat; Nat Asn Advan Colored People; officer, Local PTA; bd mem & vice chair, Camp Hill Sq Housing Develop Corp; emer mem, Housing & Develop Law Inst; bd mem, Housing & Develop Reporter; life dir, Nat Housing Conf; bd mem, Town Ctr Housing Corp; hon mem, Chartered Inst Housing UK; mem adv bd, Md Dept Housing & Community Develop; US China Residential Bldg Coun; Affordable Housing Coun, Fed Home Loan bank, 2015. **Home Addr:** 12521 Kuhl Rd, Silver Spring, MD 20902-1443, **Home Phone:** (301)949-6307. **Business Addr:** Director, Montgomery County Department of Housing and Community Affairs, 100 Md Ave 4th Fl, Rockville, MD 20850, **Business Phone:** (240)777-0311.

### NELSON, RICKY LEE
Baseball player, manager, police officer. **Personal:** Born May 8, 1959, Eloy, AZ; son of Ebb Corelius and Willie Pearl Whitehead; married Deanna Christina Perez; children: Alexis, Ashley & Austin. **Educ:** Ariz State Univ, Tempe, BA, 1991. **Career:** Police officer, baseball player (retired); Seattle Mariners, outfielder & right fielder & left fielder & designated hitter & ctr fielder, 1983-86; NY Mets, outfielder, 1986; Cleveland Indians, outfielder, 1987; A L Williams Financial Serv, Phoenix, regional mgr, 1985-91; Durango Juv Ct, youth supvr, probations officer. **Orgs:** Calif All-Star Team, 1982. **Honors/Awds:** Bob Feller Man of the Year Award; Baseball Digest Pitcher of the Year Award; Babe Ruth Award; American Legion Player of the Year; All-Star Game Most Valuable Player Award. **Special Achievements:** Attended Arizona state univ winning All-Pac 10 honors while playing for the 1981 College World Series champions. **Home Addr:** 7250 S 46th St, Phoenix, AZ 85040, **Home Phone:** (602)438-2733.

### NELSON, DR. ROBERT WALES, SR.
Physician. **Personal:** Born Mar 26, 1925, Red Bank, NJ; married Pamela Diana Fields; children: Debra C, Renae V, Desiree M, Jason D, Roxanne W & Robert W. **Educ:** Howard Univ, attended 1951; Howard Med Sch, attended 1956; Univ SC Med Ctr, attended 1957. **Career:** Pvt pract, 1957-65; Los Angeles County Bd Educ, 1959-60, Health Dept, 1965-66; Gardena Med Ctr, physician; W Adams Emergency Med & Group, emergency physician, 1967-80. **Orgs:** Am Col Emergency Physicians; Am Arabian Horse Asn, 1974-77; Int Arabian Horse Asn, 1974-77; Breeder Arabian Horses, 1974-; Breeder Black Angus, 1975-.

**NELSON, RONALD DUNCAN.** See Obituaries Section.

### NELSON, RONALD J.
Automotive executive. **Career:** Gen Motors, dealer; Bill Nelson Chevrolet Inc, pres & chief exec officer, currently. **Business Addr:** Chief Executive Officer, President, Bill Nelson Chevrolet Inc, 3233 Auto Plz, Richmond, CA 94806-1994, **Business Phone:** (510)222-2070.

### NELSON, TANYKA SHINELL
Psychologist. **Personal:** married Reginald Lee Robinson. **Educ:** Ala State Univ; Calif State Univ, Northridge, CA. **Career:** Los Angeles Unified Sch Dist, sch psychologist, currently. **Home Addr:** 27803 Summer Grove Pl, Valencia, CA 91354-1896, **Home Phone:** (661)263-0889. **Business Addr:** School Psychologist, Los Angeles Unified School District, 333 S Bleaudry Ave, Los Angeles, CA 90001, **Business Phone:** (213)241-4262.

### NELSON, DR. WANDA JEAN
Association executive, business owner, beautician. **Personal:** Born Jul 5, 1938, Kingfisher, OK; married Earl Lee Sr; children: Marie, Stephen A & Earl Lee Jr. **Educ:** Madam CJ Walker's Beauty Col, attended 1958; Nat Inst Cosmetology, Wash DC, BA, 1966, MA, 1968, PhD, 1973; Pa Valley Community Col Sci, attended 1973; Univ Ottawa, Ottawa, KS, BS, 1979. **Career:** Le Conte Cosmetics, tech hairstylist & instr; Air Cargo TWA, supvr; USDA, keypunch & verifier; US Postal Servs, guard, 1979-80; Ms Marie Cosmetics, owner; Assoc Hairdresser Cosmetologist, Mo, pres. **Orgs:** Founder & first pres, Young Progressors Beauty & Barbers; MO State Asn Cosmetology; pres, Nat Beauty Culturist League Inc, vpres; Women's Polit Caucus; parliamentarian, Black Chamber Com, 1987-. **Honors/Awds:** Certificate, Jackson Co State Sch Retarded C; Top 100 Influential Black Americas in Greater Kansas City, 1985; Woman of the Year, Theta Nu Sigma Nat Sorority, 1986; Woman of the Year, Alpha Beta Local Chap, 1986. **Home Addr:** 12375 Hardy St, Overland Park, KS 66213, **Home Phone:** (913)469-4389. **Business Addr:** Executive Vice President & Founder, National Beauty Culturists, 25 Logan Cir NW, Washington, DC 20005, **Business Phone:** (202)332-2695.

### NELSON, DR. WANDA LEE
School administrator, association executive, musician. **Personal:** Born Nov 16, 1952, Franklin, LA; daughter of James Green and Geraldine Minor Green; married Elridge; children: Michael & James. **Educ:** Grambling State Univ, BA, 1973; Ball State Univ, MA, 1975; Nat cert Counr, 1984; La State Univ, EdS, 1985; Northern Ill, Univ DeKalb, Ill, EdD, 1989. **Career:** La State Univ Eunice, counr; Bicester Am Elem Sch, Eng, learning specialist, 1974-76; Summer Enrichment Prog LSUE, music teacher, 1984; Northern Ill Univ, counr & minority prog coordr, 1985-89; Univ Tex, Austin, Tex, assoc dean students, 1989-92, assoc dean students, 1992-95, exec dir, Univ Outreach Centers, 1995-, asst vpres, assoc vpres, currently. **Orgs:** Adv, Awareness Cult, Educ & Soc Stud Club, 1978-85; Anti-Grammateus Epsilon Alpha Sigma Chap, 1979-80; adv, Zeta Nu Chap, 1984-89; organized Mu Upsilon Chap, 1992; Basileus Alpha Kappa Sigma, Chap, 1994-98; adv, Innervisions Gospel Choir, Univ Tex, 1993-95; life mem, Sigma Gamma Rho Sorority Inc; Jack & Jill AME Inc, 1996-99; life mem, Grambling State Univ Alumni asn; Am Asn Coun & Develop; Am Asn Higher Educ; Am Col Personnel Asn; founder, Univ Tex Black Fac Staff Asn. **Honors/Awds:** Magna Cum Laude, Grambling State Univ, 1973; President's Award, Little Zion BC Matrons, Opelousas, La, 1985; Alpha Kappa Mu Honor Soc, Grambling State Univ; Kappa Delta Pi Hon Soc, Northern Ill Univ, 1988; Best Advisorof the Year, 1989; Alpha Golden Image Award, Northern Ill Univ; Outstanding Educr, Tex Employees Retirement System, 1991; AfricanFac & Staff of the Year, 1995; Pan-Hellenic Image Award, Univ Tex; Leadership Austin Class, 1997-98; Governor's Exec Develop Prog, 1998. **Home Addr:** 11100 Long Winter Dr, Austin, TX 78754-5859, **Home Phone:** (512)835-9059. **Business Addr:** Associate Vice President, Executive Director, The University of Texas at Austin, 1301 E 7th St, Austin, TX 78702, **Business Phone:** (512)232-4630.

### NELSON-HOLGATE, GAIL EVANGELYN
Singer, educator, actor. **Personal:** Born Mar 29, 1944, Durham, NC; daughter of William Tycer (deceased) and Jane Avant (deceased); married Daniel A. **Educ:** Mozarteum Conserv, Salzburg Austria, 1964; Oberlin Col, MusM, 1965; New Eng Conserv Music, MusM, 1967; Metrop Opera Studio, attended 1972; Am Inst Musical Studies, Graz Austria, 1972. **Career:** Henry St Music Settlement, priv vocal teacher, 1986-87; New York Col, adj prof contemp pop-vocal music, 1986-89; Acad Music and Dramatic Arts, vocal instr; D & G Productions Inc, vpres, prof vocalist, currently. Films: The Way We Live Now, I Never Sang for My Father, Cotton Comes to Harlem; Recordings: Gail Nelson Sings! (on cassette), That Healin' Feelin & Phase III from the US of Mind w/Horace Silver, Blue Note Label, the original broadway cast album of Tap Dance Kid; Lady Day at Emerson's Bar & Grill (Cast Recording Starring Gail Nelson as Billie Holiday); many television & radio commercials, voice overs, indust films & shows; numerous operas; orchs: The Maggio Musicale Orch Florence Italy, The Ball of the Silver Rose Deutsches Theatre, Munich, Germ, The Madame Mag Ball Baden Baden, Detroit Symph Gala, Buffalo Philharm, Philadelphia Pops, St Louis, Hartford, Tulsa, Chicago Ravinia Fest, Wmsburg Fest; Omaha, Oklahoma City Philharmonic, Edmonton, Calgary Philh, Indianapolis; One Life to Live (ABC); Another World (CBS), Guiding Light (NBC); Maya Angelou's "King", as Coretta Scott King, Jan, 1997; Broadway theatre, Hello Dolly, Applause, On The Town, Music Music, Eubie; Tap Dance Kid; Porgy and Bess (as Bess) with Houston Grand Opera, tour, 1977; Bubbling Brown Sugar; (as Irene Page) 1986; Lady Day at Emerson's Bar & Grill, on tour, 1994-2003; AMR Symphony at Carnegie Hall, debut, London Philharmonic, debut, guest artist Queen Elizabeth II Cruise Ship, Holland America CruiseLines; New Jersey Symphony, debut, Buffalo Philharmonic New York, soloist; Indianapolis Symphony, debut, 1992; "Lady Day at Emerson's Bar & Grill, "An Evening of the Life and Music of Billie Holiday (as Billie Holliday), Seabourn Spirit Cruise Ship thru Asia, guest artist, Soloist: Connecticut Symphony; New Jersey Symphony; Portland Maine Symphony; Indianapolis Symphony; "Funny, You Don't Look Like A Grandma", "By Strouse", Talking Books Inc, narrator for the American Foundation for the Blind, NY; Boston "Pops", Orchestra, Brevard Music Festival; Carnegie Hall Soloist for Nicholas Brothers tribute, 1998; the Palm Beach Pops, soloist; "Gershwin and Friends", "this Joint is Jumpin!" and "Puttin' on the Ritz "; television commercials; teaches voice privately in New York City. **Orgs:** AGMA, 1967; Mu Phi Epsilon, 1967-; AEA, 1968; Am Fed Tv & Radio Artists, 1968; SAG, 1968; Oberlin Alumnae; New Eng Conserv Alumnae; Am Cancer Soc, 1975-; Black Women Theatre, 1985-87. **Honors/Awds:** Lucretia Bori Award, NY Metro Opera Studio Performance Scholar, 1970-72; Humanitarian Plaque, Oakwood Col, 1977; Stone Soul Festival "97", 1995; In Recog of Your Valuable Contrib to Human Life & Dignity and to Black Cultural Enrichment in Particular United Student Movement, 1977. **Home Addr:** 160 W 73rd St Suite 9B, New York, NY 10023-3058, **Home Phone:** (212)580-8116. **Business Addr:** Vice President, D & G Productions Inc, 160 W 73rd St Studio 9B, New York, NY 10023, **Business Phone:** (212)580-8116.

### NENGUDI, SENGA (SENGA NENGUDI FITTZ)
Artist. **Personal:** Born Sep 18, 1943, Chicago, IL; daughter of Samuel Irons and Elois Jackson Irons; married Ellioutt; children: Sanza & Oji. **Educ:** Calif State Univ, Los Angeles, BA, art, 1966, MA, sculpture, 1971; Waseda Univ Tokyo, Japan, studies japanese cult, 1967. **Career:** Watts Tower Art Ctr, Watts, Calif, art instr, 1965-66 & 1978; MacLaren Hall-County Juv Detention Ctr, art instr, 1968; Los Angeles County Dept Pub Social Serv, social worker, 1968-69; Pasadena Art Mus, art instr, 1969-71; Fine Arts Community Workshop, art instr, 1970-71; C's Art Carnival, NYC, art instr, 1971-74; Calif State Univ, substitute instr, 1980; Comm Artists Prog, LA, prog coordr & art instr, 1982-86, arts prog developer, 1990-, dance instr comm & pvt classes, 1992-98; Fairburn Elem Sch, coordr, 1985-86; Univ Southern Calif, asst slide cur, 1986-88; "Mouth to Mouth Conversations on Being", creator & independent radio producer, 1988-; Kennedy Ctr Imagination Celebration Community Liaison, artist residence, 1991-93; African Dance & Diaspora, Colo Col & Pikes Peak Comm Col, Colo Springs, guest dance instr, 1993-98; Univ Colo, Afro Am Art Studies, art hist lectr, 1998-; Art Space Community Gallery, owner, 2001; Sante Fe Art Inst, vis artist, 2005; Chicago Art Inst, guest artist, 2006; Tufts Univ, guest artist, 2007; Art Works: Art as a Verb, Group Travelling Exhib, 1988-89; "Coast to Coast, " Group Travelling Exhib, A Women Color Artists Box and Bks Exhib, 1988-92; Shaping the Spirit, Exhib CAP St Proj & AVT-Exp Proj Gallery, San Francisco, Calif, 1990; "Whisper! Stomp! Shout! A Salute to African-Am Performance Art, cur; Solo Exhib: "Wet Night Early Dawn Seat Chant Pilgrims Song, " Thomas Erben Gallery, NYC, 1996, "Populated Air" Thomas Erben Gallery, 1997. **Orgs:** Curatorial comm perf art, Womans Bldg, LA, 1984-85; bd dir, Performing Arts Youth, 1990-; co-pres, Performing Arts Youth, 1991-92; Bus Arts Ctr, 1990-92; Nat Black Women's Health Proj; Black Life Support Sisterhood, 1990-94; founding mem, Sankofa African Dance & Cult Orgn, 1992-95; community liaison, Kennedy Ctr Imagination Celebration, 1992-95; adv bd mem, Performing Arts Youth, 1995-2000; Grants Rev Selection Comt Colo Coun Arts, 1995-96; Tutmose Acad, 1998-2002; Selection Comt Dir Ethnic Studies Dept, 1999; bd trustee, Tutmose Acad Sch, 1996-; Col Art Asn; Toni Morrison Soc, 2003; Col Art Asn, 2005-; bd mem, Kennedy Ctr Imagination Celebration, 2006-. **Honors/Awds:** Dance scholarship, Orchesis Calif State Univ, 1965; CAPS Grant Sculpture, Creative Artists Pub Serv Prog, 1972; Distinguished Service Award, Bd Regents Univ Colo, 1994; Anonymous Was A Woman Award, 2005; Louis Comfort Tiffany Foundation Award, 2005; Penny McCall Foundation Ordway Prize, 2005. **Home Addr:** PO Box 10255, Colorado Springs, CO 80932-1255, **Home Phone:** (719)640-1621. **Business Addr:** Artist, University of Colorado, 1420 Austin Bluffs Pkwy, Colorado Springs, CO 80918, **Business Phone:** (719)262-4360.

**NERO, MARIE ELOISE.** See TARVER, MARIE NERO.

### NESBITT, PREXY-ROZELL WILLIAM
Educator, government official, consultant. **Personal:** Born Feb 23, 1944, Chicago, IL; son of Rozell Rufus and Sadie Alberta Crain; children: Samora. **Educ:** Antioch Col, BA, polit sci, 1967; Columbia Univ, PhD, polit sci & African hist, 1968, Cert, African studies, 1968; Univ Chicago, PhD, social thought & African hist, 1971; Northwestern Univ, MA, hist, 1974, cert, African studies, PhD, African hist, 1975. **Career:** Educator, Speaker, Consult: Amilcar Cabral Comm Organizers Training Inst, dir, 1970-72; SEIU, Chicago, Ill, organizer, 1972-74; Univ Ill, Champaign Urbana Ill, nat coordr & field organizer, 1976-79; Africa Proj, Inst Policy Studies, Wash, DC, dir, 1978-79; World Coun Churches, dir & secy, 1979-84; Dist 65 United Auto Workers Union, adminr 1983-86; Sch Art Inst Chicago, lectr african Lit, 1983-90; Mayor Harold Wash, Chicago, Ill, spec asst, 1986-87; City Chicago Mayor's Off, asst dir comm rels, 1986-88; Govt Mozambique, sr consult, 1987-92; Assoc Col Midwest, Multiculturalism coord & hist lectr, 1990-93; John D & Catherine T Mac Arthur Fndn, Prog Peace & Int Cooper, sr prog officer, 1993-96; ed bd Chicago Reporter, 1995-2000 & 2002-04; Francis W Parker Sch, dean, 1996-2001, consult; Am Ctr Int Labor Solidarity, Southern African, rep, 2001-03; Am Friends Serv Comt, interim dir, 2001-03; Chicago Teachers Ctr, Northern Ill Univ, sr multiculturalism & diversity specialist, 2003-; Columbia Col, instr african hist, adj fac, 2003-; Francis W Parker Sch, consult, 2003-; Univ Chicago Lab Sch, consult, 2003-; speaker & Educator pvt pract, currently. **Orgs:** Nat Asn Advan Colored People, 1970-; Asn Concerned African Scholars, 1980-; bd dir, CA Newsreel, 1980-; consult, Am Comn Africa, 1980-; bd dir, Trans Africa, 1981-86, Inst Food & Devel Policy, 1994-; Anti-Racism Inst, Chicago, consult, 1994-; bd dir, Shared Interest, 1996-00, 2002-06; Nat Asn Independent Sch; African Activist

Archive Adv Comt, E Lansing, Mich, currently; Changing Worlds, Chicago, IL, currently; S African Exchange Prog Environ Justice, Boston, MA, currently. **Home Addr:** 502 W Jackson Blvd, Oak Park, IL 60304-1402, **Home Phone:** (708)445-7359. **Business Addr:** Adjunct faculty, Columbia College Chicago, 600 S Michigan Ave, Chicago, IL 60605, **Business Phone:** (312)663-1600.

**NESBITT, ROBIN ANTHONY**
Lawyer. **Personal:** Born May 17, 1956, New York, NY; son of Robert and Vivian Nimmo; married Michelle Ponds; children: Robin Anthony Jr & Christine Michelle. **Educ:** Morehouse Col, BA, econ, 1977; Atlanta Univ Sch Bus, MBA, 1980; Southern Univ Sch Law, JD, 1984. **Career:** First Fed Savings & Loan, managing atty, 1984-87; Southern Univ, asst prof, 1984-89; Nesbitt & Simmons, atty, partner, 1984-. **Orgs:** Kappa Alpha Psi, 1974; Toastmasters, 1977; Phi Alta Delta, 1982; Community Asn Welfare Sch Age C, 1989; O'Brien House, 1990. **Honors/Awds:** Licensed registered rep, series No 6, Nat Asn Securities Dealers. **Home Addr:** 7928 Wimbledon Ave, Baton Rouge, LA 70810-1774, **Home Phone:** (225)767-3107. **Business Addr:** Attorney, Nesbitt & Simmons, 118 S 19th St, Baton Rouge, LA 70806-3636, **Business Phone:** (225)336-1296.

**NESBY, ANN (ANN BENNETT)**
Singer. **Personal:** Born Jan 1, 1955, Joliet, IL; married Timothy Lee; children: 3. **Career:** Sounds Blackness, vocalist; solo, 1996; Albums: I'm Here for You, 1996; Love Is What We Need: The Essentials, 2001; Put It on Paper, 2002; Make Me Better, 2003; In the Spirit, 2006; This Is Love, 2007; The Lula Lee Project, 2009; Living My Life, 2014. Films: Gigli, 2003; The Fighting Temptations, 2003; Other Contributions: "Keep Ya Head Up", 2001; "Praisin His Name", 2002; "Spread Love", 2004; "Best Friends", 2007, "Its so Easy", 2007. **Honors/Awds:** Two Grammy Awards as part of Sounds of Blackness; Has been nominated for three solo Grammys.

**NESMITH, DR. KIMBLIN E.**
Educator. **Personal:** married Winifred L Acosta. **Educ:** Morehouse Col; Univ Miami Sch Law, JD. **Career:** Edward Waters Col, Dept Criminal Justice & Study Law, asst prof & chair, currently; Tallahassee Community Col, exec dir & chief exec officer, adj fac; Gadsden Leadership & Law Acad, exec dir & chief exec officer, 2007-. **Orgs:** Bd trustee, Edward Waters Col, 2004; Our Family Investment Club, currently. **Business Addr:** Assistant Professor, Chair, Edward Waters College, 1658 Kings Rd, Jacksonville, FL 32209, **Business Phone:** (904)470-8000.

**NESMITH, WINIFRED L. ACOSTA**
Lawyer, association executive. **Personal:** married Kimblin. **Educ:** Univ Fla, BA, 1992, JD, 1995. **Career:** Fla Atty Gen Off, Jacksonville, asst state wide prosecutor; Third Judicial Circuit Lake City, asst state atty; US Attys Off Northern Dist Fla, asst US atty. **Orgs:** Vpres planning, Nat Black Prosecutors Asn, regional dir. **Honors/Awds:** Received numerous awards from high school, church, family & civic organizations; executive board member of the year. **Special Achievements:** First African American to receive the honor from Mayor Garth "Sonny" Nobles with the Live Oak "key to the city? and a proclamation; recognized as the "Executive Board Member of the Year" for outstanding service. **Business Addr:** Attorney, Private Practice, 111 N Adams St Suite 4, Tallahassee, FL 32301-7730, **Business Phone:** (850)942-8430.

**NETTERS, REV. TYRONE HOMER**
Secretary (office), consultant. **Personal:** Born Oct 11, 1954, Clarksdale, MS; married Beverly Bracy; children: Malik & Toure. **Educ:** Calif State Univ, Sacramento, BS, 1976. **Career:** Off Majority Consults, campaign specialist, 1979-82; Assembly Ways & Means, consult, 1982-83; Sacramento Valley Organizing Community, organizer, currently; Off Assemblywoman Moore, legis asst. **Orgs:** Bd dir, Magalink Corp, 1984-; Philip Randolph Inst, 1985; founding mem, Fannie Lou Hamer Demo Club, 1985; first vpres, pres, Nat Asn Advan Colored People, Sacramento, Calif. **Honors/Awds:** SABC Community Service Award, 1980; National Black Child Development Merit Award, 1981. **Home Addr:** 8767 Carissa Way, Elk Grove, CA 95624-3887. **Business Addr:** First Vice President, National Association for the Advancement of Colored People, PO Box 188231, Sacramento, CA 95814-2611, **Business Phone:** (916)447-8629.

**NETTLES, WILLARD P., JR.**
Educator, executive, government official. **Personal:** Born Jan 17, 1944, Hooks, TX; son of Willard and Gladys Hammick; married Rosemary. **Educ:** Lewis & Clark Col, BA, 1967, MAT, 1973. **Career:** Vancouver, WA, city councilman; Portland Sch Dist, teacher; Crown Zellerbach Corp, prod planner, 1967-70; Vancouver Pub Sch, teacher math & span, 1978-91; Trailblazer Fence Co, owner, 1982-91. **Orgs:** Nat Asn Advan Colored People. **Honors/Awds:** Washington State Athletic Association of Community Colleges Championship. **Special Achievements:** First African American Councilman of Vancouver, WA. **Home Addr:** 14402 NE Piper Rd, Vancouver, WA 98684-7439, **Home Phone:** (360)254-0441.

**NEUFVILLE, DR. MORTIMER H.**
Vice president (organization), school administrator, educator. **Personal:** Born Dec 10, 1939, Portland; married Masie Brown; children: Sonetta, Nadine & Tisha. **Educ:** Tuskegee Inst, BSc, 1970, sci, 2001; Univ Fla, MSc, 1971, PhD, 1974. **Career:** Univ Fla, grad asst, 1971-74; Prairie View A&M, head dept animal sci, 1974-78; Lincoln Univ Sch Appl Sci MO, assoc dean, 1978-83; Univ MD Eastern Shore, dean agr, res dir, 1983-91, assoc vpres, 1991-93, Acad Affairs, vpres, 1994-96; Nat Asn State Univ & Land-Grant Cols, exec vpres, 1997-. **Orgs:** Agr rsch asst, Ministry Agri-Jamaica, 1961-68; Gamma Sigma Delta Hon Soc, 1970, Alpha Zeta Hon Soc, 1971, bd dir, N Cent R&D Ctr, 1982-83; Sigma Pi Phi, 1984; Nat Higher Ed Comm, 1985; N E Regional Coun, 1986; Govs Comn Educ Agr, 1987; Int Sci & Educ Coun, 1987; vice chmn, chmn, Asn Res dir, 1989-90; chair, JCARD-CSRP Rev Comt, 1990; ACOP, 1993, Budget Comt, chair, 1992; Northeast Regional Ctr Rural Develop, 1990; Dir, Fed Rels Food, Environ & Int Affairs, NASULGC, 1997; Dean, Agr Sci, 1998-91; bd dir, Bd Agr Assembly, 2004; Govt Repub Cameroon; HBCU Int Liaison Officers Comt; W K Kellogg Found; fac mem, Prairie View A&M. **Home Addr:** 14844 Poplar Hill Rd, Darnestown, MD 20874-3622, **Home Phone:** (240)246-7323. **Business Addr:** Executive Vice President for Academic Affairs, National Association of State Universities & Land-Grant Colleges, 1307 New York Ave NW Suite 400, Washington, DC 20005-4722, **Business Phone:** (202)478-6040.

**NEVERDON-MORTON, DR. CYNTHIA**
Educator, writer. **Personal:** Born Jan 23, 1944, Baltimore, MD; daughter of James Neverdon and Hattie Neverdon; married Lonnie George. **Educ:** Morgan State Univ, BA, 1965, MS, 1967; Howard Univ, PhD, hist, 1974. **Career:** Baltimore Pub Sch Syst, teacher hist, 1965-68; Peale Mus, researcher & jr archivist, 1965; Univ Minn, admis assoc, 1968-69, coordr spec progr, 1969-71; Inst Afro-Am Studies, instr curric develop, 1968; MN Lutheran Synod Priority Prog, consult, 1969; Coppin State Univ, asst dean stud & asst prof hist, 1971-72, assoc prof hist, 1972-81, Dept Hist & Geog Int Studies, chmn, 1978-81, prof hist, 1981-; Historically Black Col & Univ fel, Dept Defense, EEO & Spec Emphasis Prog, 1989-93, Fiftieth Anniversary WWII Commemoration Comt, 1993-95; Mich St Univ, Res CD-ROM Immigration & Migration US 1900-2000, consult, 1996; Md Mus African Am Hist & Cult, head acad team, 1998-. **Orgs:** Study grant to selected W African Nations, 1974; partic, Caribbean-Am Scholars Exchange Prog, 1974; adv bd, Md Comn Afro-Am Life, 1977-; Asn Black Female Historians, 1979-; adv bd, Multicultural Educ Coalition Comt, 1980-; Asn Study Afro-Am Life & Hist; reader & panelist, Nat Endowment Humanities Smithsonian Inst Fel, 1986; Nonstandard Eng & Sch Environ TaskForce, Baltimore County Pub Sch, 1990; Md St Dept Educ Task Force Teacher Social Studies, 1991; Accreditation Team; Nat Forum Hist Stand, 1992-94; reviewer, hist dept, Howard Univ, 1995; bd ed, Twentieth Century Black Am Officials & Leaders; bd mem, Great Blacks Wax. **Special Achievements:** Book: Afro-American Women of the South and the Advancement of the Race, 1895-1925, 1991. **Home Addr:** 23 Deep Powder Ct, Woodstock, MD 21163-1110, **Home Phone:** (410)521-4924. **Business Addr:** Professor, Coppin State University, 2500 W N Ave, Baltimore, MD 21216-3698, **Business Phone:** (410)951-3433.

**NEVILLE, AARON**
Singer. **Personal:** Born Jan 24, 1941, New Orleans, LA; son of Arthur (deceased) and Amelia (deceased); married Joel Roux; children: Ivan, Aaron Jr, Ernestine & Jason; married Friedman. **Career:** Albums: Aaron Neville Greatest Hits, 1967; Orchid in the Storm, 1985; The Classic Aaron Neville - My Greatest Gift, 1990; Tell It Like It Is, 1991; Warm Your Heart, 1991; Aaron Neville's Soulful Christmas, 1993; The Grand Tour, 1993; The Tatoo ed Heart, 1995; Can't Stop My Heart, 1995; Doing It Their Own Way, 1996; To make Me Who I Am, 1997; The Very Best of Aaron Neville, 2000; Devotion, 2000; Aaron Neville - The Ultimate Collection, 2001; The Best of Aaron Neville - The Millennium Collection, 2002; Humdinger, 2002; Gospel Roots, 2003; Love Songs, 2003; Believe, 2003; Orchid in the Storm [Bonus Tracks], 2003; Nature Boy: The Standards Album, 2003; Christmas Prayer, 2005; Bring It On Home, 2006; Mojo Soul, 2006; I Know I've Been Changed, 2010; My True Story, 2013. Singles: "Over You", 1960; "Tell It Like It Is", 1966; "She Took You for a Ride", 1967; "Everybody Plays the Fool", 1991; "Somewhere Somebody", 1991; "Close Your Eyes", 1992; "Don't Take Away My Heaven", 1993; "The Grand Tour", 1993; "Don't Fall Apart on Me Tonight", 1993; "I Owe You One", 1994; "I Fall to Pieces", 1994; "Even If My Heart Would Break", 1994; "Betcha By Golly, Wow", 1994; "Can't Stop My Heart from Loving You", 1995; "For the Good Times", 1995; "Use Me", 1996; "Crazy Love", 1996; "Say What's in My Heart", 1997; "It's All Right", 2006. **Honors/Awds:** Numerous honors & awards including 14 Grammy Awards, 3 Big Easy Awards & Rolling Stone Critics' Poll. **Business Addr:** Singer, c/o William Morris Agency, 151 El Camino Dr, Beverly Hills, CA 90212, **Business Phone:** (310)859-4000.

**NEWBERRY, CEDRIC CHARLES**
Manager, biologist, executive. **Personal:** Born Aug 10, 1953, Perry, GA; son of Charlie C and Rubye L Allen; married Lillie Ruth Brown; children: Carnice, Candice & Clayton. **Educ:** Ft Valley State Univ, BS, agron & crop sci, 1975; Univ Wis-Madison, MS, agron & crop sci, 1977; Southern Ill Univ, Edwardsville, MBA, mkt, 1982. **Career:** Monsanto Co, sr res biologist, 1977-83; Meineke Discount Mufflers, Meineke Car Care, CC Newberry Automotive Corp, owner, pres, gen mgr, 1983-. **Orgs:** Am Soc Agron, 1977-83; Comm Support Black Bus & Prof, 1983-; chmn educ comn, Nat Black MBA Assoc, 1986-87. **Home Addr:** 135 Springfield Pke, Cincinnati, OH 45215-4261, **Home Phone:** (513)821-8363. **Business Addr:** Owner, General Manager, Meineke Car Care, 7760 Reading Rd, Cincinnati, OH 45237, **Business Phone:** (513)761-9900.

**NEWBERRY, TRUDELL MCCLELLAND**
School administrator. **Personal:** Born Jan 30, 1939, Junction City, AR; daughter of Roosevelt and Margaret Knighten; children: Fe Lesia Michelle & Thomas Walter III. **Educ:** Univ Ariz, Pine Bluff, BA, 1962; Roosevelt Univ, Chicago, MA, 1980; Gov State, post grad Work, 1984; Northern Ill Univ, post grad work, 1989. **Career:** Almyra Pub Sch Syst, teacher, 1962-65; Franklin-Wright Settlement, social worker, 1965-69; N Chicago Grade Sch, teacher, 1970-93; Foss Park Dist N Chicago, recreational supvr, 1982-83; City Coun N Chicago IL, alderwoman fifth ward, 1983-87; N Chicago Unit Sch Dist, N Chicago, Ill, dean students, 1990-92; Neal Elem Sch, teacher, 1992-93. **Orgs:** Eureka Temple no 1172, 1972-; UAPB Alumni Asn, 1982-; N Chicago Teachers Asn, 1982-87; N Chicago High Sch PTO, 1984-88; N Chicago Booster Club, 1984-; bldg rep, NCTA, 1985-87; N Chicago Libr Bd, 1986-87; exec bd, Coun Rep Lake Co Fed Teachers, 1987-89; Comt Ten Unification N Chicago Sch Sys, 1988-89; pres, N Chicago Elemen Coun Federated Teachers, 1989-90; N Chicago Unit Dist Coun, 1992-; Am Fedn Teachers; Am Fedn Labor & Cong Indust Orgn. **Honors/Awds:** Ark Travelers Award, Ambassador of Goodwill, signed by Governor BillClinton, 1992. **Home Addr:** 2111 S Lewis Ave, North Chicago, IL 60064-2544, **Home Phone:** (708)473-9094.

**NEWBILLE, CYNTHIA I.**
Manager, association executive. **Educ:** State Univ NY, BA, psychol & ling, 1974, MA, psychol, 1983; Va Commonwealth Univ, PhD, pub policy & admin, 2010. **Career:** Charles Drew Univ Med & Sci, head start, prog dir; Nat Black Women's Health Proj, exec dir; City Richmond, Va, dist mgr & chief staff, currently; Richmond City Coun, rep, 2009-12, 2013-; Orgn Mgt & Admin, consult. **Orgs:** Founder, Parent Policy Coun; actg dir, E End Family Res Ctr; bd dir, Sports Backers. **Business Addr:** Representative, Richmond City Council, Rm 201 900 E Broad St Suite 200, Richmond, VA 23219, **Business Phone:** (804)646-3012.

**NEWBOLD, REV. SIMEON EUGENE, SR.**
Clergy. **Personal:** Born Sep 4, 1954, Miami, FL; son of David Jerome Sr and Catherine Melvina Armbrister; married Audrea Stitt; children: Simon Eugene Jr & Krishna Alanna. **Educ:** Tuskegee Inst, BS, social work, 1977, MEd, personnel admin, 1979; Seabury-Western Theol Sem, MDiv, 1989; Va Union Univ, Samuel Dewitt Proctor Sch Theol, DMin. **Career:** Barnett Bank, credit analyst; Oper PUSH Nat, financial analyst; Messiah-St Bartholomew Episcopal Church, asst; St Simon's Episcopal Church, rector; Hampton Univ, prof; St Peter's Episcopal Church, vicar, currently. **Orgs:** Union Black Episcopalians; Opp Fraternity Inc; Nat Asn Black Suba Divers Inc; Omega Psi Phi Fraternity Inc. **Honors/Awds:** Lectured, Ala State Univ, Miami Dade Community Col & Elizabeth City State Univ. **Business Addr:** Vicar, St Peter Episcopal Church, 1719 N 22nd St, Richmond, VA 23223, **Business Phone:** (804)643-2686.

**NEWBORN, DR. ODIE VERNON, JR.**
Physician. **Personal:** Born Nov 5, 1947, Nashville, TN; married Trina. **Educ:** Tenn State Univ, BS; Meharry Med Col, MD, 1973. **Career:** Flint Mich, intern, residency; Genesys Reg M C-St Joseph Cp, residency; Hurley Med Ctr, resident; physician, family practr, currently. **Orgs:** NMA; Ga State Med Soc; Colquitt Co Med Soc; NCP. **Home Addr:** 116 Southlake Ct, Columbia, SC 29223, **Home Phone:** (912)985-9660. **Business Addr:** Physician Family Practitioner, 1315 S Main St, Moultrie, GA 31768.

**NEWELL, DARYL**
Banker, executive, association executive. **Personal:** Born Oct 5, 1963, Chicago, IL; son of Hallie and Eli; married Verlena Mooney; children: Daryl Isaac & Grant Eli George. **Educ:** Northwestern Univ, BA, sociol, 1986; DeVry Univ, Keller Grad Sch Mgt, MBA, gen mgt, 1991; Northwestern Univ, Kellogg Sch Mgt, cert mgt, 2007. **Career:** Green Bay Packer Football Club, free agt profl athlete, 1986; Dean Foods, mgt trainee, 1986-89; Harris Trust & Savings Bank, unit mgr & opers officer, 1989-92, sect mgr & asst vpres, 1992-95, br mgr & vpres, 1995-97, financial consult & vpres & client advisor, 1997-2003; ShoreBank Corp, sr vpres retail banking, 2003-10; Harris Urban Partnership Bank, sr vpres, dir, 2010-13; Fifth Third Bank, vpres, retail regional mgr, 2014-15; Seaway Bank & Trust Co, chief retail banking officer, 2015-. **Orgs:** Bd mem & vpres develop, 100 Black Men Chicago, 1995-; treas, Northwestern Black Alumni Asn, 1995-; NFL Retired Players Asn, 1996-; dir, S E Chicago Comn, 1996-; Big Ten Av Comn, 1998. **Honors/Awds:** 1st Tean All State Defensive Tackle, Bloomington Herald, 1981; First Team Defense Freshman All-America, Football News, 1982; Best Conditioned Athlete, Northwestern Athletic Dept, 1984; Illuminati Honoree, Inst Positive Learning Open Book Prog, 2002. **Special Achievements:** Author: International Banks Initiate Strategic, 1998; co-auth, Partnerships with Small and Medium Size Enterprises in the Emerging Global Market Place. **Home Addr:** 5313 S Drexel Ave, Chicago, IL 60615, **Home Phone:** (773)955-1481. **Business Addr:** Chief Retail Banking Officer, Seaway Bank and Trust Co, 645 E 87th St, Chicago, IL 60619, **Business Phone:** (773)487-4800.

**NEWELL, JULIE ANGELYN.** See SCOTT, JULIE.

**NEWELL, KATHLEEN W.**
Judge, lawyer. **Personal:** Born Aug 30, 1943, Alexandria, LA; daughter of Leroy and Juanita Mandebourgh; children: Oliver Joseph. **Educ:** Univ Calif, Los Angeles, BA, biol, gen, 1965; Wayne State Univ Sch Law, JD, 1973. **Career:** Mich Dept Treas-Revenue Div-Hearings/Appeals, admin law judge, 1973-2002; Oakland County Prosecutors' Off, asst prosecuting atty, 1974-76; Ernst & Young LLP, sr tax mgr, 1997-99; Atty & Counr at Law solo practr, 2002-; Wayne State Univ-Bd Visitors-Inst Geront, vol mem, 2013-16; pvt pract, atty, 2015-. **Orgs:** Probate & Estate Plng & Taxation Sect, 1985-88; pres, New Home Community Develop & Non-Profit Housing, 1995-96; chair, elder law & advocate secy, State Bar Mich, 1996-97; adv coun, Denby Home/Salvation Army, 1995-, pres, 1998-2001; bd mem & treas, Family Defense Attorneys Mich, 2014; bd mem, St Christine Christian Serv, 2014. **Business Addr:** Attorney, 22433 Chippewa St, Detroit, MI 48219-1112, **Business Phone:** (313)592-1187.

**NEWELL, KEVIN**
Executive, vice president (organization). **Educ:** Univ Kans, BS, jour. **Career:** Leo Burnett Worldwide; Burrell Commun; McDonald's Corp, Int Mkt Dept, field media mgr, 1989-, staff, 1990-2001, mkt div officer cent div, 2001-04; Viacom's BET Cable Network, vpres, 2004-05; McDonald's Corp, US vpres & gen mgr great Southern region, 2006-09, US sr vpres & restaurant support officer W div, 2009-11, exec vpres & global chief brand officer, 2011-13, chief brand officer, 2013-14, pres, 2014-. **Orgs:** Bd mem, Ronald McDonald House Memphis, Tenn; bd mem, Louis Carr Internship Found; bd mem, Hist Makers Tomorrow; founding bd mem, Ronald McDonald House, Loyola, Chicago; bd mem, Off Street Club, 2012-.

**NEWELL, VIRGINIA K.**
Executive, educator. **Personal:** Born Advance, NC; daughter of William S Kimbrough (deceased) and Dinah; married George; children: Virginia D Banks & Glenda Harris. **Educ:** Talladega Col, BA, math, 1940; NY Univ, MA, math, 1956; Univ Sarasota, PhD, 1976; Winston-Salem State Univ, LHD, 1989. **Career:** Educator (retired), executive; Winston-Salem City, Councilwoman; Winston-Salem State Univ, assoc prof, math & comput sci, chairperson; Va Newell Real-

ty, pres, broker, currently. **Orgs:** ASF fel Univ Chicago, 1959; Winston-Salem Chap Links Inc; pres, NC Coun Teachers Math; life mem, Nat Educ Asn; ed, newsletter Nat Asn Math; Am Math Sci; Math Asn Am; NCTM; life mem, Nat Asn Advan Colored People; State Comnr Nat Coun Negro Women; Alpa Kappa Alpha Sorority; Phi Omega Chap; bd dir, Chamber Com; bd dir, Arts Coun; bd dir, Winston-Salem Symphony; bd dir, Marshall B. Bass C's Fund, currently. **Home Addr:** 2429 Pickford Ct, Winston-Salem, NC 27101, **Home Phone:** (336)722-3480. **Business Addr:** President, Broker, Virginia Newell Realty, 402 Laura Wall Blvd, Winston-Salem, NC 27101, **Business Phone:** (336)722-3480.

### NEWFIELD, MARC ALEXANDER

Baseball player. **Personal:** Born Oct 19, 1972, Sacramento, CA; son of Ross Newhan. **Career:** Baseball player (retired); Ariz League, Ariz Mariners, player, 1990; Seattle Mariners, 1990, outfielder, 1993-95; Calif League, San Bernardino, player, 1991; Southern League, Jacksonville Suns, player, 1992-93; Pac Coast League, Calgary, player, 1994, Tacoma Rainers, player, 1995, Las Vegas 51s, player, 1995; San Diego Padres, player, 1995-96; Milwaukee Brewers, player, 1996-98; Eastern League, Trenton Thunder, player, 1999; Vancouver, 1999; Oakland Athletics, player, 1999.

### NEWHOUSE, MILLICENT DELAINE

Lawyer, educator. **Personal:** Born May 28, 1964, Detroit, MI; daughter of Benjamin and Janette. **Educ:** Univ Mich, BA, 1986; Howard Univ, JD, 1989. **Career:** State Atty Gen Off, asst atty gen, 1989-98, legal assistance, 1998; Nat Acad Para legal Studies, teacher, 1992; Univ Wash Sch Law, Career Planning & Pub Serv Ctr, dir, 2000-03; Off Admin Hearings, admin law judge, 2003-06; Northwest Justice Proj, statewide legal advocacy coordr, 2006-10; Columbia Legal Serv, dir prog admin, 2012-; Univ Baltimore Sch Law, dir externships, 2014-. **Orgs:** Mentor, Boys & Girls Club, 1990-91; Maddona Presby Church, tutor, 1990-92; secy, Loren Miller Bar Asn, 1992-93; vol, atty coordr, Neighborhood Legal Clin, 1992-; Equality Pract Comn; Munic League Cand Comn, 1992; Howard Univ Alumni Asn; Wash Women Lawyers Orgn Pres, 1997-98; Leadership Tomorrow, alumni, 2000-. **Home Addr:** 1511 Cherrylane Ave S, Seattle, WA 98144-3521, **Home Phone:** (206)709-9485. **Business Addr:** Director of Externships, University Of Baltimore Law School, 1401 N Charles St, Baltimore, MD 21201, **Business Phone:** (410)837-5890.

### NEWHOUSE, DR. QUENTIN, JR.

Psychologist, college administrator, educator. **Personal:** Born Oct 20, 1949, Washington, DC; son of Quentin Sr and Berlene Byrd; married Debra Carter; children: Alyse Elizabeth Belinda. **Educ:** Marietta Col, BA, psychol, 1971; Howard Univ, MS, gen exp psychol, 1974, PhD, exp social psychol, 1980. **Career:** Antioch Univ, asst prof social scis, 1976-79; Quentin Newhouse Jr & Assocs, pres, 1981-; Howard Univ, asst prof social sci, 1982-88; United Synagogue Youth, comput syst analyst, 1984-85; Univ DIS, adj prof psychol, 1984, 1991-; US Census Bur, 21th Century staff, comput supt, 1988-91, Ctr Surv Methods Res, statistician, 1991-93; Bureautots Inc, adv bd, vpres, 1990-91; Prepare Our Youth Inc, adv bd, 1990-94; Mkt Res Analyst, 1994; PG Pvt Ind Coun, job developer, 1994; Bowie State Univ, Bowie Md, Dept Behav Scis & Human Servs, asst prof, 1995-, Interim chmn, 1996-; Strayer Univ, Nasville Campus, dean, currently. **Orgs:** Life mem, Tau Epsilon Phi, 1980-; Am Psychol Asn, 1981, 1993-; affil, Social Sci Comput Asn, 1990-94; PG County CMS C & Youth, 1991-92; PGCounty C's Comn C & Families, 1992-95; P G County rep, State Adv CMS C, Youth, & Families, 1992-95; co-chmn, CENSUG, Census SAS User's Group, 1992-; Am Statist Asn, 1993; Asn Black Psychols, 1994-; bd dir, Ment Health Asn PG County, 1994-95; Regional Adv Bd, United Way PGCounty, 1994-; bd dir, Metrop Police Boys & Girls Clubs, 1994-; Int Coaching Fedn, 2001-; Can Psychol Asn, 2011; Biz Montreal, 2014-; Montreal Bd Trade, 2015-. **Home Addr:** 971 Davaar Ave, Madison, TN 37115, **Home Phone:** (514)271-4980. **Business Addr:** Vice President for Institutional Advancement, Emmanuel Christian Institute, 3723 Medford Dr, Nashville, TN 37211, **Business Phone:** (438)333-1590.

### NEWKIRK, DR. GWENDOLYN

School administrator, educator. **Personal:** Born Washington, DC; daughter of Rachel Cornelia Polk and William Henry. **Educ:** Tillotson Col, Austin, TX, BS, 1945; Columbia Univ, Teachers Col, New York, NY, MA, 1946; Cornell Univ, Ithaca, NY, EdD, 1961. **Career:** Professor (retired), professor emeritus; Bennet Col, Greensboro, NC, instr, 1946-50; Lincoln Univ, Jefferson City, Mo, prof, 1950-62; Cornell Univ, Ithaca, NY, grad teaching & res asst, 1960-61; NC Col, Durham, NC, prof, 1962-69; Univ Minn, assoc prof, 1969-71; Univ Nebr, Lincoln, NE, Dept Consumer Sci & Educ, dept chmn & prof, prof emer, currently; Univ Okla, Home Econs Women's Scholars Prog, vis scholar, 1976; Ind Univ, Pa, vis scholar, 1982. **Orgs:** Life mem & pres, Am Home Econs Asn; Nebr Home Econs Asn; life mem, Am Voc Asn; Nebr Voc Asn, 1971-; Nebr Educ Asn; bd dir, Child Guidance Ctr, currently. **Business Addr:** Professor Emeritus, University of Nebraska Lincoln, 135 Mabel Lee Hall, Lincoln, NE 68588-0236, **Business Phone:** (402)472-2957.

### NEWKIRK, DR. PAMELA

Journalist. **Personal:** Born Nov 13, 1957, New York, NY; daughter of Louis and Gloria; married Michael Nairne; children: Marjani & Mykel. **Educ:** NY Univ, BA, jour, 1983; Columbia Univ, MS, jour, 2001, PhD, 2012. **Career:** Knickerbocker News, reporter, 1984-89; Gannett News Serv, Capitol Hill, corresp, 1988-89; New York Post, reporter, 1989-90; New York Newsday, reporter, 1991-93; New York Univ, adj prof, 1991-93, asst prof, 1993-2000, dir undergrad studies, 1994-96, assoc prof, 2000-09, prof, jour, 2009-. Books: Within the Veil: Black Journalists, White Media, auth, 2000; A Love No Less: More Than Two Centuries of African American Love Letters, ed, 2004; Letters from Black America, ed, 2011; Spectacle: The Astonishing Life of Ota Benga, auth, 2015. **Orgs:** Exec bd mem, Support Network, 1993-; adv bd mem, Annenberg Found Comn Press, 2003; adv bd mem, Press Am, Pub Broadcasting Serv; co-dir, Urban Jour Workshop, New York Univ, 2003-; fel Nation Inst, 2004-. **Home Addr:** 1 Wash Sq Village, New York, NY 10012. **Business Addr:** Professor of Journalism, New York University, 20 Cooper Sq 6th Fl, New York, NY 10003, **Business Phone:** (212)998-7980.

### NEWKIRK, THOMAS H.

School administrator, executive. **Personal:** Born New York, NY; son of Climith J Sr and Esther; children: Kori, Kisan, Kamila & Tori. **Educ:** Univ Mas, Amherst, MEd, 1974, EdD, 1985. **Career:** Consult Newkirk Assoc Tax & Bus, pres, 1958-; educ consult, 1958-; ins broker, 1959-63; State Univ NY, Corland, dir emer, educ opportunity prog, 1979; Haryou-Act NYC, coord training testing youth div, dir mgt training. **Orgs:** Founding mem, Holcombe Rucker Scholar Fund, 1967; consult, State Ed Dept, 1967-72; vpres, United Black Ed, 1969; founding mem, NYS Spec Prog Personnel Assoc, 1973; chmn, Spec Prog Inst on Teaching & Coun, 1979; Mayors Adv Comt Cortland; swimming instr, Cortland; lectr, Social Found Ed; past vpres, Spec Progs Pers Assoc State NY. **Honors/Awds:** Superlative Community Service Award, Int Key Women, 1974; Chancellors Award for Excellence in Professional Service, State Univ NY, 1979; Arthur Eve Award, Outstanding Public Service, 1991. **Special Achievements:** Publisher of books and articles. **Home Addr:** 2628 7th Ave, New York, NY 10039. **Business Addr:** President, Newkirk Associates, 2628 7th Ave, New York, NY 10039-2601, **Business Phone:** (212)926-4103.

### NEWLAND, DR. ZACHARY JONAS

Podiatrist. **Personal:** Born Dec 15, 1954, Ft. Lee, VA; son of Archie J and Adeline M; married Camillia Sutton; children: Yolanda. **Educ:** SC State Col, BS, chem, 1975; Med Univ SC, BS, pharm, 1978; Pa Col Podiatric Med, DPM, 1984. **Career:** Thrift Drugs, asst mgr pharmacist, 1978-80; SC Army Nat Guard, med platoon leader, 1978-80; Laurel Pharm, pharmacist, 1982-84; Lindell Hosp, resident podiatric surg, 1984-85; Lindell Hosp, chief resident podiatric surg, 1985-86, resident teaching staff & lectr, 1986-; Metro Community Health Ctr, dir podiatric med & surg, 1986-88; People's Health Ctr, staff podiatrist, 1988-; pvt med pract, 1990-. **Orgs:** SC Pharmaceut Asn, 1978-, Nat Health Serv Corps, 1980-, Am Podiatric Med Asn, Omega Psi Phi Frat. **Honors/Awds:** Article published in Journal of Foot Surgery, 1984. **Home Addr:** 4106 Sheridan Meadows Dr, Florissant, MO 63034-3484, **Home Phone:** (314)968-8999. **Business Addr:** Podiatrist, Private Practice, 4585 Washington St Suite A2, Florissant, MO 63033, **Business Phone:** (314)972-1040.

### NEWMAN, ANTHONY Q.

Football player, administrator, football coach. **Personal:** Born Nov 21, 1965, Bellingham, WA; married Teri; children: 3. **Educ:** Univ Ore. **Career:** Football player (retired), football coach, TV host, executive; Los Angeles Rams, defensive back, 1988-94; New Orleans Saints, 1995-97; Oakland Raiders, 1998-99; Ore Sports Network, show host, currently; Anthony Newman Sports Camps, chief exec officer & owner, currently; Cent Catholic High Sch, Portland, Ore, defensive back coach, currently. **Orgs:** Founder, Anthony Q Newman Found. **Business Addr:** Chief Executive Officer, Owner, Anthony Newmans Sports Camps, PO Box 3364, Clackamas, OR 97015, **Business Phone:** (503)329-4899.

### NEWMAN, CONSTANCE ERNESTINE BERRY

Government official. **Personal:** Born Jul 8, 1935, Chicago, IL; daughter of Joseph Alonzo and Ernestine Siggers; married Theodore. **Educ:** Bates Col, Lewiston, ME, BS, polit sci, 1956; Univ Minn, Sch Law, Minneapolis, MN, JD, 1959. **Career:** Vol Serv Am, Wash, DC, dir, 1971-73; Consumer Prod Safety Comn, Wash, DC, dir & comnr, 1973-76; US Dept Housing & Urban Develop, Wash, DC, asst secy, 1976-77; Newman & Hermanson Co, Wash, DC, pres, co-founder, 1977-82; Govt Lesotho, Ministry Interior, consult, 1987-88; Bush-Quayle 1988 Campaign, Wash, DC, dep dir, Nat voter coalitions, 1988; Presial Transition Team, Wash, DC, co-dir outreach, 1988-89; US Off Personnel Mgt, Wash, DC, dir, 1989-92; US Dept State, Bur African Affairs, asst secy, 2004-05; Smithsonian Inst, Wash, DC, under secy; World Bank Safrica, consult; World Bank Govt Lesotho, consult; Safrican leaders affirmative Action & Diversity, consult; UpStart Partners, co-founder & partner; Carmen Group, Spec Coun African Affairs, currently. **Orgs:** Pres, Inst Am Bus, 1982-84; bd trustee, Brookings Inst; bd trustee, Bates Col; vice chair, bd mem, DC Financial Responsibility & Mgt Asst Authority; bd mem, Int Republican Inst; vchmn, Consumer Prod Safety Comn; chair, Personal Search Rev Comn, US Customs Serv. **Honors/Awds:** Hon Doctors Laws, Amherst Col, 1980; Hon Doctors Laws, Bates Col, 1972; Secy Defense Medal for Outstanding Pub Serv, 1985; Secy's Award for Excellence, US Dept Housing & Urban Develop, 1977; Washingtonian of the Year, 1998; Smithsonian Institution Joseph Henry Medal, 2000. **Home Addr:** 114 Duddington Pl SE, Washington, DC 20003, **Home Phone:** (202)546-7013. **Business Addr:** Special Counsel African Affairs, Carmen Group Inc, 505 9th St NW Suite 700, Washington, WA 20004, **Business Phone:** (202)785-0500.

### NEWMAN, DR. GEOFFREY W.

Artistic director, dean (education), educator. **Personal:** Born Aug 29, 1946, Oberlin, OH; son of Arthur Eugene and Bertha Battle. **Educ:** Howard Univ, Wash, DC, BFA, 1968, PhD, 1978; Wayne State Univ, MI, MA, 1970. **Career:** Howard Univ, Wabash Col, Owen Duston distinguished prof, Drama Dept, chmn; World Premiere Owen Dodson's Sound Soul & Europ Premiere Robert Nemiroff's Raisin, dir; Pk Pl Productions, DC, artistic dir; Young Audiences Dist Columbia, artistic dir; Ira Aldridge Theatre, Howard Univ, Wash, DC, artistic dir; Takoma Players, Takoma Theatre, Wash, DC, artistic dir, co-founder; Montclair State Univ, Sch Fine & Performing Arts, dean, 1988-, dean emer, currently. **Orgs:** Grant screening panels, Dist Columbia Comn Arts & Humanities, Penn State Coun Arts & Ill State Arts Coun; nominator, Wash Awards Soc Helen Hayes Awards. **Home Addr:** 49 Northview Ave, Upper Montclair, NJ 07043, **Home Phone:** (201)744-0956. **Business Addr:** Dean, Dean Emeritus, Montclair State University, 1 Normal Ave, Montclair, NJ 07043-1624, **Business Phone:** (973)655-5104.

### NEWMAN, JOHN SYLVESTER, JR. (JOHNNY NEWMAN)

Basketball player. **Personal:** Born Nov 28, 1963, Danville, VA; married Tina; married Dawn Lewis. **Educ:** Univ Richmond, attended 1986. **Career:** Basketball player (retired); Cleveland Cavaliers, forward, 1986-87 & 1998-99; New York Knicks, 1987-90; Charlotte Hornets, 1990-93; NJ Nets, 1993-94, 2000-01; Milwaukee Bucks, 1994-97; Denver Nuggets, 1997-98; Dallas Mavericks, forward-guard, 2001-02; Panionios, Greece, 2002-03. **Orgs:** Kappa Alpha Psi Fraternity; Sickle Cell Anemia Found; chmn youth coun workforce investment bd & prog chmn, Henrico Police Athletic League!. **Home Addr:** PO Box 17754, Richmond, VA 23226.

### NEWMAN, KENNETH J., SR.

Accountant, auditor, executive director. **Personal:** Born Nov 7, 1944; married Barbara B; children: Kenneth J Jr & Eric J. **Educ:** Grambling Col, BS, 1967. **Career:** Grambling Col, asst dir comput ctr, 1967; Veteran Admin Data Processing Ctr, acct trainee, 1967-68, data processor, 1968-69, asst auditor, 1969-70; Grambling State Univ, bus mgr, 1970-73; Mary Holmes Col, bus mgr, 1974-79; City Monroe, prog auditor, 1979-81, dir planning & urban develop. **Orgs:** Vis comt, S Asn Col & Schs Atlanta, 1976; Alpha Phi Alpha Fraternity, 1979; bd trustee, Zion Travelor Baptist Church, 1979-; bd mem, Tri Dist Boys Club; United Way, 1981-; PIC mem, Job Training Partnership Ac, 1984-90; Indust Develop Bd, 1986-92; pres, Carroll HS PTA, 1986; Monroe Chamber Com; adv bd mem, SpecServ Mary Holmes Col; adv bd, Gourmet Serv. **Home Addr:** 5712 Bay Oaks Dr, Monroe, LA 71203-3206, **Home Phone:** (318)343-8092.

### NEWMAN, MILLER MAURICE

Salesperson. **Personal:** Born Oct 31, 1941, Terrell, TX; son of Miller and Lillie Vee Coleman Whestone; married Alice Faye Keith; children: Keith, Donald & Mark. **Educ:** Eastern Okla State Col, attended 1971. **Career:** Hunt's Dept Store, Shipping & Receiving, staff, 1960-66; Rockwell Int, mach oper, 1966-83, stock clerk, 1983-; B & B Skelly Sta, staff, 1968-76; Eastside Exxon, owner, 1970-75; Eastside Supperette, owner, 1976-81; Teen's Vill USA, co-owner. **Orgs:** Model Cities, 1971-76; scoutmaster, Boy Scouts Am, 1971-73; mem bd trustee, Keddo, 1973-; pres, Pitts Co Nat Asn Advan Colored People, 1973-; pres, UAW Local Suite, 1558, 1985-91; Pitts County Holiday Comn, 1985-; chmn, McAlster Housing Auth, 1989-92; rec secy & chair trustees, Okla State UAW CAP/PAC, 1992-. **Honors/Awds:** Martin Luther King Jr Award, Nat Alliance Against Racism, 1984. **Home Addr:** 1107 E Pierce Ave, PO Box 13, McAlester, OK 74501, **Home Phone:** (918)423-6396.

### NEWMAN, NATHANIEL

Government official, clergy. **Personal:** Born Aug 6, 1942, Altheimer, AR; son of Abraham Henry and Marguerite Ruth Gordon; married Norma; children: Mia Ruth & Angelique Marie. **Educ:** Merritt Col, Oakland, CA, AA, 1971; San Jose State Univ, BS, 1974, MS, 1976; Spring Valley Bible Col, Alameda, CA, BA, 1983; Fuller Theol Sem, Pasadena, CA, cert, relig studies, 1985; FBI Nat Acad, US Dept Justice, grad; Pac Western Univ, PhD, criminol, 2001. **Career:** Oakland City, Oakland, Calif, patrolman, 1968-74; Santa Clara County, San Jose, Calif, inspector; Antioch Baptist, San Jose, Calif, assoc minister, 1981-86; Concord Missionary Baptist, San Francisco, Calif, youth minister, 1986-90; Santa Clara County Dist Atty's Off, 1990-, asst chief bur invest, currently; Good News Missionary Baptist Church, pastor, 1991-. **Orgs:** Chaplain, Alpha Phi Alpha, 1973-; life mem, Alpha Phi Alpha Fraternity, 1975-; pres, Black Peace Officers Asn, 1980-88; vice chmn, Minority Citizens Adv Coun, Metro Transp Comn, 1980-; pres, Dist Atty's Investigators Asn, 1982-84; pres, Frank Sypert Afro-Am Community Serv Agency, 1982-88, ceo, 1982-88; chaplain, Nat Black Police Asn, 1982-; chmn, Pack Comy, Boy Scouts Am, 1986-; bd mem, Santa Clara County Dist Atty's Investigators Asn, 1990-; pres, 1991-92, Nat Asn Advan Colored People, San Jose Br, 1993-, exec comt mem; vice chmn, San Jose Traffic Appeals Comnr, 1991-; Mayor's Citizens Adv Group, 1992-. **Honors/Awds:** Doctor of Divinity, School of Gospel Ministry, 1982; Peace Officer of the Year, Santa Clara County Black Peace Officers, 1983, 1985, 1988; Community recognition, Omega Psi Phi, 1985; Community Service Award, San Jose Black Chamber Commerce, 1986; Humanitarian Award, Ministers Alliance of San Jose, 1986; Brother of the Year, Alpha Phi Alpha Fraternity, Western Region, 1990; Certificate of Appreciation, Calif Dist Atty Investrs Asn, 1992; Good Neighbor Award, Martin Luther King Jr Asn Santa Clara County, 1993; Outstanding Service Award, San Jose State Univ, 1996; Certificate of Appreciation, San Jose African Am Parents Group, 1997; Certificate of Appreciation, San Jose Traffic Appeals Commission, 1998. **Home Addr:** 207 Quail Creek Rd, Hot Springs, AR 71901-7307, **Home Phone:** (501)318-2103.

### NEWMAN, PAUL DEAN

Automotive executive. **Personal:** Born Dec 15, 1938, Zanesville, OH; son of Sarah Margaret and Delbert F; married Norma Jean Guy; children: Vicki, Paula, Valerie, Paul II, Scott & Sharri. **Educ:** Tri State Univ, BS, 1966; Univ Va, dipl, exec develop prog, 1985; Univ Mich, dipl, exec develop prog, 1986; Baker Col, DHL, 2013. **Career:** Executive (retired); Gen Motors Corp, dir urban affairs. **Orgs:** Exec leadership coun, Mich League Human Serv; insight bd mem, Bus Policy Rev Coun; chair, Flint Mass Transp Bd, Genesee Intermediate Sch Dist Bd Educ. **Honors/Awds:** Distinguished Service Award, Tri State Univ, 1986. **Special Achievements:** Genesee Library District, honoree of black history. **Home Addr:** 3020 Westwood Pky, Flint, MI 48503, **Home Phone:** (810)233-6897.

### NEWMAN, TERENCE

**Personal:** Born Sep 4, 1978, Salina, KS; son of Wanda. **Educ:** Kans State Univ, grad. **Career:** Dallas Cowboys, corner back, 2003-11; Cincinnati Bengals, left corner back, 2012-. **Orgs:** Breakfast Buddy prog; Cowboys Rookie Club, 2003. **Honors/Awds:** Jim Thorpe Award, 2002; NFC Defensive Rookie of the Year, 2003; Nagurski Award; Co-All Iron Award, 2007; Pro Bowl, 2007, 2009. **Special Achievements:** TV Series: "ESPN's Sunday Night Football", 2003-06; "NFL Monday Night Football", 2003-10; "NBC Sunday Night Football", 2006-09; "The Biggest Loser", 2009. **Business Addr:** Corner Back, Cincinnati Bengals, 1 Paul Brown Stadium, Cincinnati, TX 45202, **Business Phone:** (513)621-3550.

### NEWMAN, DR. THEODORE ROOSEVELT, JR.
Air force officer, judge. **Personal:** Born Jul 5, 1934, Birmingham, AL; son of Theodore R Sr and Ruth O. **Educ:** Brown Univ, AB, philos, 1955, LLD, 1980; Harvard Law Sch, JD, 1958. **Career:** Judge (retired); Dept Justice, Civil Rights Div, atty, 1961-62; pvt pract, Wash, DC, 1962; Houston, Bryant & Gardner, 1962-68; Pratt, Bowers & Newman, partner, 1968-70; DC Super Ct, assoc judge, 1970-76; DC Ct Appeals, chief judge, 1976-84, assoc judge, 1984-91, sr judge, 1991-; Brown Univ, trustee, 1979-83; Harvard Law Sch, lectr; Howard Univ, adj prof, Law Sch, vis lectr; Georgetown Law Ctr, adj prof. **Orgs:** Fel Am Bar Found; Am Bar Asn; pres, Nat Ctr State Cts, 1981-82; chair, Nat Bar Asn; chmn, Judicial Coun Nat Bar Asn; Ala Bar Asn; DC Bar Asn; Kappa Alpha Psi; Nat Ctr State Courts. **Honors/Awds:** LLD, Brown Univ, 1980; C Francis Stradford Award, Nat Bar Asn, 1984; William H Hastie Award, Judicial Coun, Nat Bar Asn, 1988.

### NEWMAN, HON. WILLIAM THOMAS, JR.
Lawyer, government official. **Personal:** Born Sep 11, 1950, Richmond, VA; son of William T and Geraldine Nunn; married Sheila C Johnson; children: 2. **Educ:** Ohio Univ, Athens OH, BA, 1972; Cath Univ Am, Catholic Univ Sch Law, Wash, DC, JD, 1977. **Career:** US Dept Com, Washington, DC, atty, 1977-80; Self-Employed, Arlington VA, atty, 1980-; Arlington County Bd, 1988-, chr, 1991-, judge, 1993-; Arlington County Circuit Ct, chief judge, currently. **Orgs:** Va State Bar Asn, 1977-; DC Bar Asn, 1978-; bd dir, Northern Va Black Atty's Asn, 1984-88; chmn, Arlington County Fire Trial Bd, 1985-87; trustee coun, Nat Capital Area YMCA, 1985-; bd dir, Arlington County United Way, 1985-86; Arlington Com PO, 1985-; Northern Va Urban League Adv Com, 1985-; vpres, Old Dominion Bar Asn, 1986; Va Med Malpract Review Panel, 1986-; comn chancery, Arlington County Circuit Ct, 1986-; vice chmn, Arlington Civic Coalition Minority Affairs, 1986-88; Founder & President Emeritus, Arlington Community Found. **Home Addr:** 2912 13th Rd S Apt 103 Arlington, Arlington, VA 22204-4929. **Business Addr:** Chief Judge, Arlington County Circuit Court, 1425 N Courthouse Rd Suite 6700, Arlington, VA 22201, **Business Phone:** (703)228-7010.

### NEWSOME, REV. BURNELL, SR.
Manager, clergy, accountant. **Personal:** Born Apr 13, 1938, Wesson, MS; son of James; married Gloria J Wilson; children: Burnell Jr (deceased) & Kenneth. **Educ:** Marion Col, cert bus admin, 1962; Copiah Lincoln Jr Col Wesson MS, cert carpentry, 1977; MS Baptist Sem Jackson MS, BTh. **Career:** Towne Shoes, store mgr, 1965; Com Credit Corp, dist rep, 1968; St Regis Paper Co, acct, 1973; BF Goodrich, budget control mgr; St. James United Methodist Church, eulogy, pastor; St Mary's United Methodist Church, pastor, currently; Mt Salem United Methodist, pastor, currently; Evergreen United Methodist Church, pastor, currently. **Orgs:** Trustee, Hazlehurst MS Separate Sch Dist, 1982; adv comt, SW MS Elec Power Asn, 1983; bd mem, MS Dept Educ Comn Accreditation, 1984; chmn steering comt, Copiah County CrusadeChrist, 1985; secy, Copiah County Interdenomi Nat Ministerial Alliance. **Honors/Awds:** FHA Farm Family of the Year, USDA Farmers Home Admin, 1977. **Home Addr:** PO Box 268, Hazlehurst, MS 39083-0268, **Home Phone:** (601)695-0547. **Business Addr:** Pastor, St Mary United Methodist Church, 3009 Harmony Rd, Crystal Springs, MS 39059, **Business Phone:** (601)892-4483.

### NEWSOME, DR. CLARENCE GENO
Educator. **Personal:** Born Mar 22, 1950, Ahoskie, NC; son of Annie Butler Lewis and Clarence Shaw; married Lynne DaNean Platt; children: Gina Lynn & Brittany Ann Byuarm. **Educ:** Duke Univ, BA, 1972, PhD, 1982; Duke Divinity Sch, Mdiv, 1975. **Career:** Duke Univ, Dept Minority Affairs, asst prof, dean, 1973-74, Am relig thought, asst prof; Mt Level Baptist Church, Durham, NC Dem Nat Comn, asst staff, dir, demo charter comn, 1974-75; Duke Divinity Sch, instr, 1978-82, asst prof Am Christianity, 1978-86; James B. Duke Dissertation Yr, Fel; Howard Univ, DC, Divinity Sch, from asst dean to assoc dean, 1986-91, from actg dean to dean, 1991-2003; Duke Univ Bd Trustee, Trustee, 2002-; Shaw Univ, pres, 2003; Nat Underground Rr Freedom Ctr, pres. **Orgs:** Am Soc Church Hist, 1980-; Finance Comt Creative Ministries Assoc, 1981; chmn bd, NC Gen Baptist Found Inc, 1982; bd dir, Divinity Sch Bd Visitors; Alumni Asn; Comt Educ Durham Comm Affairs Black People, 1983; co-chmn, Comt Educ Durham Interdenomi Nat Ministerial Alliance, 1983-84; planning coord, Euro-Am Theol Consult Group; Am Acad Relig, 1987-; pres, Soc Study Black Relig, 1989-. **Home Addr:** 6761 Sewells Orchard Dr, Columbia, MD 21045, **Home Phone:** (301)596-7053. **Business Addr:** President, Shaw University, 118 E S St, Raleigh, NC 27601, **Business Phone:** (919)546-8300.

### NEWSOME, DR. EMANUEL T.
Educator, association executive, executive. **Personal:** Born Mar 21, 1942, Gary, IN; married Nellie Smith; children: Kim, Eric & Erika. **Educ:** Western Mich Univ, BS, 1964; MA, 1965; Ind State Univ, PhD coun guid & psychol serv, 1976. **Career:** Grad asst phys educ, 1964-65; head scout & asst basketball coach, 1964-65; St Univ, asst dean stud life stud activ; financial aid couns & field rep, 1965-66; dir coordr st educ talent search search prog, 1966-68; Univ Toledo, dir stud activ, 1976-, dean stud affairs, currently; Fla Atlantic Univ, Sr vpres stud affairs, 1988; Palm Beach Atlantic Col, adj prof, 1990. **Orgs:** Nat Asn Advan Colored People, 1960-; bd dir, Big Bro Orgn Kalamazoo, Mich, 1965-66; Midwest Stud Financial Aid Asn, 1965-68; Urban League, 1967-; Nat Asn Stud Personnel Asn, 1969-; bd dir, Hyte Comn Ctr, 1973-; basketball coach, Terre Haute Boys Club, 1973-; Gov Steering Comt Volunteerism, 1975; adv bd, Toledo March Dimes; Western Mich Univ Athletic Hall Fame, 1974. **Honors/Awds:** IN All-star Basketball Team, 1960; All Mid-am Conf basketball 3 yrs, 1961-64; All American in basketball, 1964; 2nd leading scorer nation majorcol, 1964; Participant Olympic Trials basketball; Athletic Hall of Fame, 1980. **Special Achievements:** Wall of Distinction, Western Mich Univ, 1989. **Home Addr:** 1501 SW 21st Lane, Boca Raton, FL 33486-6527, **Home Phone:** (561)368-3895. **Business Addr:** Dean of Student Affairs, University of Toledo, 2801 W Bancroft St, Toledo, OH 43606, **Business Phone:** (419)530-1470.

### NEWSOME, DR. MOSES, JR.
School administrator. **Personal:** Born Sep 6, 1944, Charleston, WV; son of Rev Moses and Ruth G Bass; married Barbara; children: Ayanna & Mariana. **Educ:** Univ Toledo, BA, sociol, 1966; Univ Mich, MSW, 1970; Univ Wis, PhD, social work, 1976. **Career:** Howard Univ Human Serv Eval Design Div, asst dir, 1977-78; Howard Univ Sch Social Work, asst dean, 1979-80, assoc prof, 1978-84, assoc dean, 1980-84; Norfolk State Univ, Ethelyn R. Strong Sch Social Work, dean, prof, 1984-99, asst vpres acad affairs, 1999; Jackson State Univ, vis prof, 2000; Rutgers, Univ NJ, vis prof, 2000-01; Medgar Evers Col City Univ New York, distinguished higher educ adminr & prof, vpres econ develop & pub serv, vpres external rels, 2010-12, interim assoc dean, 2012-; Optimum Inst Empowerment, consult, 2012-; Howard Univ Wash, assoc dean sch social work; Miss Valley State Univ, vpres res, planning, community & econ develop, currently. **Orgs:** Nat Assoc Black Soc Workers, 1979; Deleg Assembly Nat Assoc Soc Workers, 1983-84; vchmn, Norfolk Area Health Study, Adv Bd, 1987-88; Planning Coun, Norfolk, Va, bd, 1987-90; Bd Accreditation Coun Social Work Educ, 1988-90; chmn, Norfolk City Counl Task Force ChildrenNeed Serv, 1988-89; distchmn, Va Chap Nat Asn Social Workers, 1989-90; State Bd Va Coun Social Welfare, 1989-91; chmn, Greenwood-Leflore Chamber Com, 2006-09; Greenwood-Leflore County United Way, 2009-10; Brooklyn Chamber Com, 2010-; Caribbean Am Chamber Com, 2010-; Nat Steering Comt; chmn, Va Social Work Educ Consortium; Alpha Phi Alpha Fraternity Inc; 100 Black Men Inc; Sigma Pi Phi Fraternity, Beta Lambda Boule; Concord Baptist Church; Am Pub Welfare Asn; VA Pub Coun Welfare. **Honors/Awds:** Outstanding Young Man in Am US Jaycees, 1977; Outstanding Macro Faculty Member, Howard Univ Sch Soc Work, 1978; "Frequency and Distribution of Disabilities Among Blacks, " in Equal to the Challenge, Bureau Educ Res, Washington, DC, 1986; "Job Satisfaction and Work Relationships of Social Service Workers, " Dept Human Resources, Norfolk, Va, 1987. **Special Achievements:** Numerous Publications. **Home Addr:** 513 Cheswick Arch, Virginia Beach, VA 23455. **Business Addr:** Interim Associate Dean, Mississippi Valley State University, 14000 Hwy 82 W, Itta Bena, MS 38941, **Business Phone:** (662)254-9041.

### NEWSOME, OZZIE, JR.
Manager, football player, executive. **Personal:** Born Mar 16, 1956, Muscle Shoals, AL; son of Ozzie Sr and Ethel; married Gloria Jenkins; children: Michael Ryan. **Educ:** Univ Ala, BS, recreation admin, 1978. **Career:** Football player (retired), executive; Cleveland Browns, tight end, 1978-90, spec assignment scout, 1991-93, asst, 1993-94, dir pro personnel, 1994-95; Baltimore Ravens, vp player personnel, 1996-2002, sr vpres football opers, gen mgr, 2002-, exec vpres, 2003-; Active Fel Christian Athletes, Big Bros, Athletes Action. **Orgs:** Bd dir, Police Athletic League; Omega Psi Phi; Cleveland Browns Ring Hon, 2010. **Honors/Awds:** Alabama Amateur Athlete of the Year, Ala Sportswriters Asn, 1977; Teams Outstanding Player, 1981; All-Pro, 1979, 1981, 1983, 1985; Pro Bowl, 1981, 1984, 1985; AP first-team All-Pro, 1984; Ed Block Courage Award, 1986; Byron "Whizzer" White Man of the Year, Nat Football League, 1989; College Hall of Fame, Nat Football Found, 1994; Hall of Fame, Nat Col Athletic Asn, 1994; State of Alabama Hall of Fame, 1995; Pro Football Hall of Fame, Nat Football League, 1999; Offensive Player of the Year, Cleveland Touchdown Club, 1978, 1981, 1983, 1984; Executive of the Year, Nat Football League, 2000; The Eagle Award, US Sports Acad, 2003; Paul "Tank" Younger Award, Fantasy Points Against, 2007; Baseball Hall of Fame, Little League, 2008; Francis J. "Reds" Bagnell Award, Maxwell Football Club, 2012; Hometown Hall of Fame, Colbert County High Sch, 2012; National High School Hall of Fame, Nat Fedn State High Sch Asn, 2014. **Special Achievements:** First African American general manager in NFL history. **Home Addr:** 6 Padonia Woods Ct, Cockeysville, MD 21030-1744. **Business Addr:** General Manager, Executive Vice President, Baltimore Ravens, 1 Winning Dr, Owings Mills, MD 21117, **Business Phone:** (410)701-4000.

### NEWSOME, DR. PAULA RENEE
Optometrist, president (organization). **Personal:** Born Jul 3, 1955, Wilmington, NC; daughter of Mercedes and Carter; children: Ayana Renee. **Educ:** Univ NC-Chapel Hill, BA, 1977; Univ Ala, Birmingham Med Ctr, OD, 1981, MS, 1981. **Career:** Eye Inst Philadelphia, residency, 1982; Univ Mo, St Louis Sch Optom, asst prof, 1982-84; VA Hosp St Louis, optom consult, 1983-84; pvt pract optom, 1984-; Advantage Vision Ctr, pres, currently, optometrist, currently. **Orgs:** Delta Sigma Theta Sorority, 1974-; Am Optom Asn, 1981-; Nat Optom Asn, 1981-; NC State Optom Soc, 1982-; Mecklenburg Co Optom Soc, 1984-; Charlotte Med Soc, 1984-; state legis affairs adv comm Scope Prac AOA, 1984-; free visual screening area churches, 1984-; speaker, Role Model Ser Charlotte-Mecklenburg Sch Syst, 1985-; urban optom, Am Optom Asn, 1986-; bd mem, Charlotte Women Bus Owners, 1986-87; charter mem, Doctors Heart, 1986-90; free visual screenings Mecklenburg Co Parks & Recreation, 1986; Leadership Charlotte, 1986-; pres, bd dir, Focus Leadership, 1986-90; Mecklenburg Co, YWCA, 1988-90; Coalition Lit, 1988-90; bd dir, Charlotte Chamber Comn, 1990-96; bd dir, Cent Piedmont Community Col, 1991-95; chmn, Discovery Pl, 2000-01; bd dir, Univ NC-Chapel Hill, Gen Alumni Asn; Crown Jewel Chap; Delta Sigma Theta Sorority; treas, Charlotte Chap; Jack & Jill Am; Friendship Missionary Baptist Church; Crown Jewel Chap Links Inc. **Special Achievements:** First African American female optometrist to practice in the state of North Carolina. The country's first African American Female fellow in the prestigious American Academy of Optometry. **Home Addr:** 1314 S Kings Dr, Charlotte, NC 28207. **Business Addr:** President, Optometrist, Advantage Vision Center, 1016 S Church St, Charlotte, NC 28203, **Business Phone:** (704)375-3935.

### NEWSOME, RONALD WRIGHT
Banker, vice president (organization). **Personal:** Born Jan 21, 1949, Charleston, WV; son of Moses and Ruth; married Toni; children: Nicole & Kristine. **Educ:** Philander Smith Col, BA, bus admin, 1971; Clark/Atlanta Univ, MBA, 1973. **Career:** Nat Bank Detroit, asst br mgr, credit officer, commerical loan officer, 1973-81; Bank One, Columbus, NA, com loan officer, sr loan officer, asst vpres res, 1981-86, asst vpres res, unit mgr, vpres, 1988-; Huntington Nat Bank, asst vpres/com lender, 1986-88, asst vpres & unit mgr, vpres & group mgr, 1988-98; Franklin Univ, adj prof, 1986-96; Bank One COT Develop Corp, vpres & mgr small bus group, sr vpres & mgr small bus group, 1998-; Wilberforce Univ, adj prof, 1999; Small Bus Investment Alliance Inc, dir & mgr, Bank One CDC, sr vpres, currently; JPMorgan Chase Community Develop Corp, sr vpres; Banc One Community Develop Corp, sr vpres; Stonehenge Capital Co LLC, dir, currently. **Orgs:** Univ Club Columbus, 1983-; bd dir, exec comt mem & secy, Columbus Urban League, 1989-; bd mem & vice chmn, Pvt Indust Coun Columbus & Franklin County Inc, 1991-; bd mem & second vpres, Columbus Metrop Area Community Action Org, 1990-; pres, Mark D Philmore Urban Bankers Forum Cent Ohio Inc, 1994-; Univ Club; Columbus Regional MNY Supplier Develop Coun; OH Found Entrepeneurship Ed; chair, Pvt Indus CNL Columbus & Franklin County; APA. **Honors/Awds:** Philander Smith Col Distinguished Alumni Award; UNCF Inter-Alumni C James E Stamp Alumni Recognition Award. **Home Addr:** 1020 Zodiac Ave, Gahanna, OH 43230, **Home Phone:** (614)855-0120. **Business Addr:** Director, Stonehenge Capital Co LLC, 6 Landmark Sq 4th Fl, Stamford, CT 06901, **Business Phone:** (203)359-5718.

### NEWSOME, RUTHIE B.
Educator. **Personal:** Born Mar 16, 1940, Marvell, AR; daughter of Sam and Josephine. **Educ:** Ark Baptist Col, BA, 1962; Webster Univ, attended 1976; Northeast State Univ, attended 1986. **Career:** St Louis Pub Sch, teacher. **Orgs:** Antioch Bapt Church; Stevens Mid Sch Community Coun; secy, Ark Baptist Col Alumni, St Louis Chap; nat pres, Ark Bapt Col Alumni; St Louis Teacher Union; YWCA, Phyllis Wheatley Br; group leader, ABC Alumni Club, currently. **Home Addr:** 7720 Nacomis Dr, St. Louis, MO 63121, **Home Phone:** (314)382-7681. **Business Addr:** Group Leader, ABC Alumni Club, 7720 Nacomis Dr, St. Louis, MO 63121, **Business Phone:** (314)382-7681.

### NEWSOME, VINCENT KARL
Football executive, football player. **Personal:** Born Jan 22, 1961, Braintree; married Tasha; children: Candace, Emerald & Victoria. **Educ:** Univ Wash, psychol. **Career:** Football player (retired), football executive; Los Angeles Rams, defensive back, 1983, 1985, strong safety, 1984, 1987-88, 1990, free safety, 1986, 1989; Cleveland Browns, free safety, 1991-92, spec assignment scout, 1993-95; Baltimore Ravens, W area scout, 1996-99, front office staff, currently; Western Col, supvr, 2000-02, asst dir pro personnel, 2003-08, dir pro personnel, 2009-. **Orgs:** Pres, Alpha Phi Alpha, Alpha Xi Chap. **Honors/Awds:** Ed Block Courage Award, 1988. **Business Addr:** Director of Pro Personnel, Baltimore Ravens, 1 Winning Dr, Owings Mills, MD 21117, **Business Phone:** (410)701-4000.

### NEWTON, ANDREW E., JR.
Lawyer, executive. **Personal:** Born Mar 9, 1943, Boston, MA; married Joan Ambrose. **Educ:** Dartmouth Col, BA, 1965; Columbia Univ Sch Law, JD, 1969. **Career:** Winston A Burnett Construct Co, asst gen coun, 1969-70; Amos Tuch Sch Bus Admin, Dartmouth Col, 1970-71; Burnett Int Develop Corp, gen coun, 1971-72; Honeywell Info Systs Inc, opers coun, 1972-74, staff coun, 1974-75, Western Region, regional coun, 1975-77; Amdahl Corp, dir mkt opercoun, 1977, gen coun; Digital Res Inc, gen coun; Frame Technol Corp, vpres & gen coun, 1989-93, secy; Infoseek Corp, co-founder, vpres, gen coun & secy, 1994-; Propel Software Corp, co-founder, vpres, gen coun & secy, 1999-; Abaca Technol Corp, co-founder, vpres, gen coun & secy, currently; OneID Inc, vpres, gen coun & secy. **Orgs:** Am Bar Asn; Boston Bar Asn; Fed Bar Asn; Mass Bar Asn; Nat Bar Asn; NY Bar; Mass Bar; Peninsula Asn Gen Coun; Comput Lawyers Asn; Nat Contract Mgt Asn. **Home Addr:** 227 Peter Pan Rd, Carmel, CA 93923-9746. **Business Addr:** Co-founder, Vice President, Propel Software Corp, 2216 O'Toole Ave, San Jose, CA 95131-1326, **Business Phone:** (408)571-6300.

### NEWTON, CAM (CAMERON NEWTON)
Football player. **Personal:** Born May 11, 1989, Atlanta, GA; son of Cecil Sr and Jackie. **Educ:** Univ Fla, attended 2008; Blinn Col, Tenn, attended 2009; Auburn Univ, attended 2015. **Career:** Univ Fla Football Team, quarterback, 2007-08; Blinn Col (Tenn) Football Team, quarterback, 2009; Auburn Univ Football Team, quarterback, 2009-10; Carolina Panthers, quarterback, 2011-. **Honors/Awds:** Heisman Trophy, 2010; AP Player of the Year, 2010; BCS National Champion, 2009 and 2011; SEC Offensive Player of the Year, 2010; Consensus All-American, 2010; Maxwell Award, 2010; Chic Harley Award, 2010; Walter Camp Award, 2010; Manning Award, 2010; Davey O'Brien Award, 2010; AP College Player of the Year, 2010; Sporting News College Player of the Year, 2010; AP Offensive Rookie of the Year, 2011; Pepsi NFL Rookie of the Year, 2011; Pro Bowl, 2011 & 2013 & 2015 ; Sporting News Rookie of the Year, 2011; NFL AP Most Valuable Player, 2015; NFL AP Offensive Player of the Year, 2015; NFL PFWA Most Valuable Player, 2015; NFL Bert Bell Award, 2015. **Special Achievements:** First overall pick in the 2011 NFL draft; first rookie to throw more than 400 yards in his first NFL game and 4,000 yards in his first season; first quarterback in history to run for 14 touchdowns in a season. **Business Addr:** Carolina Panthers, 800 S Mint St, Charlotte, NC 28202, **Business Phone:** (704)358-7000.

**NEWTON, ERIC CHRISTOPHER.** **See Obituaries Section.**

### NEWTON, ERNEST E., II
Government official, executive, association executive. **Personal:** Born Feb 21, 1956, Ft. Belvoir, VA; married Pamela A; children: Ernest E III, Chad J, Enrico & Kayla. **Educ:** Winston-Salem State Univ, BA, 1978; Univ Bridgeport, grad prog, 1980. **Career:** Bridgeport Sch Syst, teacher; Bridgeport Bd Educ, music teacher, 1980-84; Bridgeport City Coun, pres, mem, 1981-85; Conn Nat Bank, personal banking rep, 1984; Peoples Bank, admin supv, 1986; Conn State House Representatives, mem, 1989-2003, asst majority leader, 1995-96; 23rdDist Spec Election, state sen, 2003-06, dep pres pro tempore. **Orgs:** Pres, Bridgeport bd alderman, mem Bd, 139th Dist; Alpha Phi Alpha Frat; bd mgrs, YMCA; policy coun Head Start; adv bd, Greater Bridgeport Regional Narcotics Prog; comn Sikorsky Mem Airport; coun pres Red Cross; vice chmn, 150th Anniversary Bridgeport; Alpha Phi Alpha; Mt Airy Baptist Church; Bridgeport Chap Nat Asn Advan Colored

People; Prince Hall Masons; chmn exec, Legis Nominations Comt; Fire Sprinkler Syst Comn; Bridgeport Dem Town Comt, 1982-84; chmn, legis Black & Puerto Rican Caucus, Conn, 1991-92; pres, Nat Black Caucus State Legislators, 1995. **Honors/Awds:** Outstanding Merit Award, Nat Bulk Teachers Asn, 1974; Scholarship Award, Alpha Phi Alpha Grad Chap, 1976; Outstanding Young Men of America Award, Nat Jaycees, 1983; Commission Service Award, Bus & Prof Women Youth Dept; Heritage Award, Alpha Kappa Alpha Sor, 1983; City Govt Award, Omega Psi Phi Frat, 1983; Outstanding Achievement Award, Nat Asn Negro Bus & Prof Women, 1983; TGBOIC Proj Saga Sponsorship Award; has received a number of awards. **Special Achievements:** Becoming the youngest age 25 and first black person to ever hold the position as council president. **Home Addr:** 190 Read St, Bridgeport, CT 06607.

### NEWTON, JACQUELINE L.
Counselor, educator. **Personal:** Born Oklahoma City, OK; daughter of Jack Jefferson and Josephine; children: Jeffrey & Richard. **Educ:** Univ Okla, BBA, MEd, 1974; Southern Univ Lab Sch, Grad. **Career:** Univ Okla, acad adv, 1972-78, financial aids couns; Univ Nev, athletic acad counr, 1978-, acad advisor; Apco Oil Corp, from clerk to acct; Okla City Law Firm, bookkeeper; Mobil Oil Co, admin phys res coun, equal employee Com. **Orgs:** Chaired Employee Orgn, 1972-73; Active Okla Univ Prof Employee Group; pres, Okla Univ Asn Black Personnel, 1975-76; Nat Asn Advan Colored People; supr training sem, Jan, 1974; secy, Univ Nev Las Vegas Alliance Black Prof, 1984-; Nat Asn Acad Adv Athletics, 1988-93; Alpha Kappa Alpha Sor; chmn, Comt Okla Black Coalition Educ; chair, Stud Athlete Recognition Comn; chair, Univ Okla Staff Senate. **Honors/Awds:** Voted outstanding achievement Award. **Home Addr:** 2368 Pickwick Dr, Henderson, NV 89014-3762, **Home Phone:** (702)458-3053. **Business Addr:** Athletic Academy Councilor, University of Nevada, 4505 S Maryland Pkwy, Las Vegas, NV 89154, **Business Phone:** (702)895-0655.

**NEWTON, JAMES DOUGLAS, JR.** **See Obituaries Section.**

### NEWTON, JAMES DOUGLAS, JR.
Government official, nurse. **Personal:** Born Sep 3, 1929, Malakoff, TX; son of Hillary Cook and Mary Glenn Cook; children: Carolyn Andrenia Barron & Audry Laverne. **Educ:** Henderson City Jr Col, LVN, 1963; Navarro Col, attended 1975; El Centro Col, attended 1975. **Career:** Nurse, Government official (retired); Lakeland Med Ctr, lic voc nurse, 1979-93. **Orgs:** Youth counr, Cedar Forks Baptist Church, 1970; counr, Galilee Griggs Mem Dist Youth Conf, 1975-; nursing fac, Lakeland Med Ctr, 1979-87; E Tex Coun Governments, 1980-; Trinidad Chamber Com, 1980; app mem, State Task Force Indigent Health Care, 1984. **Honors/Awds:** Outstanding Black Henderson Countian Award; Black History Committee, 1989; Attended & participated in the inauguration of President George Bush, 1989. **Home Addr:** 830 Pinoak, Trinidad, TX 75163.

### NEWTON, DR. JAMES ELWOOD
College teacher, school administrator. **Personal:** Born Jul 3, 1941, Bridgeton, NJ; son of Charles C Sr and Hilda H; married LaWanda Williams; children: Regina, Walidah & KaWansi. **Educ:** NC Cent Univ, BA, 1966; Univ NC, Chapel Hill, NC, MFA, 1968; Ill State Univ, PhD, 1972. **Career:** Univ NC, art instr, 1967-68; W Chester State Col, asst prof art, 1968-69; Ill State Univ, asst prof art, 1969-71; Western Ill Univ, asst prof art, 1971-72; Univ Del, asst prof educ, 1972-73, Black Am Studies, prof, 1973-2005, emer prof, 2005-. Book:The Principles of Diversity: Handbook for a Diversity-Friendly America, The Other slaves: Mechanics, artisans and craftsmen. **Orgs:** Ed bd, Nat Art Ed Assoc; ed bd educ, 1974-; exec counr, Assoc Study Afro-Am Life & Hist, 1976-77; bd mem, Western J Black Studies, 1983-; bd mem, chmn, Walnut St Youth Men's Christian Asn, 1983-; Del State Arts Coun; Del Art Mus; Youth Men's Christian Asn Del & Pub Allies; state dir, Asn Study Afro-Am Life & Hist, 1988-; sr fel Ctr Community Res & Serv. **Home Addr:** 217 Harris Cir, Newark, DE 19711-2430, **Home Phone:** (302)239-6579. **Business Addr:** Professor Emeritus, University of Delaware, 401 Acad St, Newark, DE 19716, **Business Phone:** (302)831-2392.

### NEWTON, GEN. LLOYD W.
Executive, military leader. **Personal:** Born Dec 24, 1942, Ridgeland, SC; son of John and Annie; married Elousie M Morning. **Educ:** Tenn State Univ, BS, aviation educ, 1966; Armed Forces Staff Col, 1978; Indust Col Armed Forces, 1985; George Washington Univ, MS, pub admin, 1985; Harvard Univ, nat security sr exec course, MA, 1987. **Career:** Air force officer (retired), executive; USAF, second lt, 1966, first lt, 1967, capt, 1969, maj, 1978, lt col, 1990, col, 1983, brig gen, 1991, maj gen, 1993, lt gen, 1995, gen, 1997; Williams AFB, AZ, pilot training, 1966-67, Luke AFB, Ariz, F-4D flight instr pilot, 1973-74; USAF Thunderbirds, Nellis Afb, Nev, narrator & slot pilot, 1974-78, right wingman & narrator, 1978; US House Representatives, cong liaison officer, 1978-82; 8th Tactical Fighter Wing, Kunsan Air Base, S Korea, asst dep comdr opers, 1982-83; 388th Tactical Fighter Wing, Hill AFB, Utah, asst dep comdr opers, 1983-84; USAF, Wash, DC, asst dep dir opers & training, 1985-86, asst dir spec proj directorate plans, 1986-88; 71st Air Base Group, Vance AFB, Okla, comdr, 1988-89; 71st Flying Training Wing, Vance AFB, Okla, comdr, 1989-90; Twelfth Flying Training Wing, Randolph AFB, TX, comdr, 1990-91; 833rd Air Div, Holloman AFB, NMex, comdr, 1991; 49th Figher Wing, Holloman AFB, NMex, comdr, 1991-93; J-3 US Spec Opers Command, MacDill AFB, Fla, dir opers, 1993-95; HQ USAF, Wash, DC, asst vice chief staff, 1995-97; HQ Air Educ & Training Command, Randolph AFB, comdr, 1997-2000; Pratt & Whitney, vpres int mil progs, 2000-, exec vpres; TSU Air Force Res Officer Training Corp, group wing comdr. **Orgs:** Bd dir, Goodrich Corp; bd dir, Torchmark Corp, 2006-; bd mem, Sonoco Prod, 2008-; bd dir, Air Force Asn; trustee, Nat Air & Space Mus; trustee, Nat Mus USAF; vpres, Pratt & Whitney, 2000-06. **Honors/Awds:** Distinguished Service Medal; Legion of Merit with oak leaf cluster; Distinguished Flying Cross with oak leaf cluster; Meritorious Service Medal with oak leaf cluster; Air Medal with 16 oak leaf clusters; Air Force Commendation Medal; Air Force Outstanding Unit Award with "V" device and two oak leaf clusters; Vietnam Service Medal; Philippine Presidential Union Citation; Republic Vietnam Campaign Medal; Hon doctorate aeronaut sci, Embry-Riddle Aeronaut Univ, Daytona Beach, Fla, 1997; Hon doctor sci degree, Benedict Col, Columbia, Sc, 1999. **Special Achievements:** First African American to fly with US Air Force Aerial Demonstration Squadron, the Thunderbirds; 1 of 12 Four Star Generals in the US Air Force. **Business Addr:** Board Director, Torchmark Corp, 3700 S Stonebridge Dr, McKinney, TX 75070-8080, **Business Phone:** (972)569-4000.

### NEWTON, NATE, JR. (NATHANIEL NEWTON, JR.)
Football player, radio host. **Personal:** Born Dec 20, 1961, Orlando, FL; married Dorothy; children: Nathaniel Tre III & Nate King. **Educ:** Fla A&M Univ, grad. **Career:** Football player (retired); Tampa Bay Bandits, United States Football League, 1984-85; Dallas Cowboys, guard, 1986-98; Carolina Panthers, 1999-2000; ESPN radio, commentator; ESPN Dallas 103.3 FM, co-host, 2013; BET television, analyst. **Orgs:** Mem, N Dallas Community God. **Honors/Awds:** NFL Offensive Lineman of the Year, Nat Football League Alumni Asn, 1994; six time Pro Bowler, 1992, 1994-97. **Home Addr:** , TX.

### NEWTON, OLIVER A., JR.
Educator, air force officer, association executive. **Personal:** Born Jan 31, 1925, Long Branch, NJ; married Eleanor M Simmons; children: Martha Louise. **Educ:** Howard Univ, BS, 1949, MS, 1950. **Career:** Educator (retired); Inter-Am Inst Agr Sci Turrialba, Costa Rica, res, 1950-52; Pan Am Union, fel, 950-52; Univ So CA, lab assoc, 1952-56; Howard Univ, instr bot, 1956-58; William Paterson Col, NJ, assoc prof, 1958-90; Rutgers Univ, Nat Sci Found Col Fac fel, 1964. **Orgs:** AAAS, Am Asn Univ Professors; Am Inst Biol Sci; Bot Soc Am, Alpha Phi Alpha, Ridgewood Glen Rock Coun Boy Scouts Am, Soc Econ Bot, Glen Rock Adult Sch Coun, Glen Rock Civic Asn; dir, Glen Rock Human Rels Coun, Cits Comn Sch Plant & Classroom Eval; local asst bd, Glen Rock, 1966-74; Glen Rock Bd Ed, 1969-75; State Comn Study Stud Activism & Involvement Ed Progs, 1970; Community Rels Bd Ridgewood & Glen Rock, 1991. **Home Addr:** 20 Henry St, Glen Rock, NJ 07452-1419, **Home Phone:** (201)445-7758.

### NEWTON, DR. PYNKERTON DION
Physician. **Personal:** Born Nov 9, 1960, Marion, IN; son of John W and Olivia McNair. **Educ:** Ball State Univ, BA, 1983, MA, 1986; Logan Col Chiropractic, DC, 1992. **Career:** Oper Crossroads Africa, group leader, 1986; Ball State Univ, asst dir, 1986; Marine Midland Bank, corp analyst, 1986-87, mgr, 1987-89; Logan Col Chiropractic, corr, admis dept, 1989-92, consult, 1992-; Pynkerton Chiropractic Group, PC, clin dir, 1992-. **Orgs:** Am Black Chiropractic Asn, exec dir, 1995-96; Am Chiropractic Asn, 1989-; Nat Asn Med Minority Educrs, 1990-91; Ind State Chiropractic Asn, 1989-; Nat Asn Advan Colored People. **Honors/Awds:** Meritorious Award, Logan Col Chiropractic, 1992. **Business Addr:** Clinic Director, Pynkerton Chiropractic Group, 2102 E 52nd St Suite E, Indianapolis, IN 46205-1497, **Business Phone:** (317)257-7463.

### NEWTON, ESQ. ROBERT
Lawyer. **Personal:** Born Nov 13, 1944, Fairfield, CA; married Ruth Ann Boles; children: Robert Wade & Reginald Alan. **Educ:** Harvard-Yale-Columbia, intensive summer studis cert summer, 1966; Lincoln Univ, Jefferson City, Mo, BS, 1968; Howard Univ Sch Law, JD, 1971. **Career:** Mo Comn Human Rights, spec field rep, 1968; Econ & Opportunity Wash, legal asst ofc, 1969; US Atomic Energy Comn, Off Gen Coun, staff atty, 1971-74; Erda, Off Gen Coun, 1976-78; Dept Energy, 1978-, Off Asst Gen Coun Int & Nat Security Progs, atty adv, currently; Newton Coar Newton & Tucker Law Firm, atty. **Orgs:** Jeff City Mo Comn Fiar Housing, 1966-67; Omega Psi Phi Fraternity Inc; pres, Lincoln Univ Stud Govt Asn, 1966-67; Law J Howard Univ Law Sch, 1969-70; Earl Warren Legal fel Nat Asn Advan Colored People, 1974-75; Am Bar Asn; Ala Bar Asn; Nat Asn Advan Colored People; Legal Defense Fund Earl Warren fel. **Honors/Awds:** Man of the Year, Lincoln Univ, 1966-67; Cobb-trustee Scholar, Howard UnivLaw Sch, 1969-71. **Home Addr:** 3524 Squire Lane, Birmingham, AL 35211, **Home Phone:** (205)969-7494. **Business Addr:** Attorney-Adviser, US Department of Energy, 1000 Independence Ave SW, Washington, DC 20585, **Business Phone:** (202)586-5000.

### NEYLAND, LEEDELL WALLACE
Educator, school administrator. **Personal:** Born Aug 4, 1921, Gloster, MS; son of Sam Matthew and Estella McGehee; married Della Louise Adams; children: Beverly Ann, Keith Wallace & Katrina Denise. **Educ:** Va State Col, AB, 1949; NY Univ, MA, 1950, PhD, 1959. **Career:** School administrator (retired); Leland Col Baker LA, prof social sci, dean Col, 1950-52; Grambling Col, assoc prof social sci, 1952-58; Elizabeth City Col, dean, 1958-59; Fla A&M Univ, prof hist, dean humanities/social sci, 1959-84, Col Arts & Sci, dean, 1968-82, vpres, acad affairs, 1982-85, consult, lectr Black hist & educ. **Orgs:** Fla Interscholastic Athletic Asn, 1932-68; bd dir, Leon County/Tallahassee Chamber Com, 1984-86; vice chmn, Tallahassee Preserv Bd, 1984-88; co-chmn, Gov Dr Martin Luther King Jr Com memorative Celebration Comn, 1985-87; Presby Nat Comt Self-Devel People; Fla Hist Rec Adv Bd; Phi Beta Sigma; Sigma Pi Phi; 32 Degree Mason, Mod Free & Accepted Masons World; Fla State Teachers Asn Collection. **Home Addr:** 2522 Blarney Dr, Tallahassee, FL 32309, **Home Phone:** (850)893-4333.

### NGONGBA, TAJAMA ABRAHAM
Basketball player, basketball coach. **Personal:** Born Sep 27, 1975, St. Croix, VI; married Patrick; children: Naja & Patrick II. **Educ:** George Washington Univ, BA, sociol, 1997. **Career:** Basketball player (retired), basketball coach; George Wash, 1994-97; Sacramento Monarchs, ctr, 1997; Colonials' Women's Basketball Prog, asst coach, 1997; Detroit Shock, 1998; Nice Cavigal, 1998-99; George Wash Univ, admin asst, 1999-2001, US VI Women's Sr Nat Team, 2001 & 2003; US VI Jr Nat Team, asst coach, 2001; Univ Richmond, asst coach, 2001-02; Va Commonwealth Univ, coach, 2002-04; US VI Nat Team, team capt & asst coach, 2002; George Wash, asst coach, 2004-08; Radford Univ, head coach, 2008-; US VI Sr Nat Team, head coach, 2011 & 2012. **Business Addr:** Head Coach, Radford University, 801 E Main St, Radford, VA 24142, **Business Phone:** (540)831-5000.

### NIBBS, ALPHONSE (ALLIE), SR.
Executive, government official. **Personal:** Born Nov 10, 1947, Charlotte Amalie; son of Elenora Charles and Ernest Albert; married Paulette E Shelford; children: Berecia Nibbs-Cartwright, Alphonse Jr, Antoninette, Annette Garces, Anthony & Alyssa. **Educ:** Col VI, attended 1980; Cert Labor Rels, Pub Admin, Personnel Mgt, 1980; Inst Prof & Econ Develop, attended 1981; Ga Inst Technol, Atlanta, Ga, Contract Admin, 1986. **Career:** Water & Power Authority, distrib engr, 1967-76; Nibbs Bros Inc, secy, treas, 1974-; ICM, Dept Housing, asst comnr of housing & community renewal, 1976-84; Lt Gov Off, temp housing off hd-gar team, terr coord off, 1979-86; VI Housing Authority, exec dir, 1985-87; Legisl VI, exec dir, 1991-93; VI Cong Off, dist chair staff, 1995-97. **Orgs:** Comn Aging, 1977-87; VI Soc Pub Admin, 1980-87. **Honors/Awds:** Lt Col/AIDE DeCamp, State Ga Nat Guard, Civilian Appointment. **Home Addr:** Annas Retreat 3AB Charlotte Amalie, St Thomas00801, **Home Phone:** (809)775-1704. **Business Addr:** Secretary, Treasurer, Nibbs Bros Inc, 4A Estate Thomas, St. Thomas00801, **Business Phone:** (809)774-2108.

### NICCO-ANNAN, LIONEL
Executive. **Career:** Clipper Int Corp, Detroit, chief exec, 1963-. **Business Addr:** Chief Executive, Clipper International Corp, 8651 E 7 Mile Rd, Detroit, MI 48234, **Business Phone:** (313)366-6210.

### NICHOLAS, BOB
Chairperson, executive. **Personal:** married Arita. **Educ:** NY Univ, attended 1961. **Career:** Channel 2 News, Houston, TX, anchorperson; BNE Fine Printing, founder & chmn, 1999-; Nicholas Earth Printing LLC, pres, 2003-; Crime Stoppers Houston Inc, adv bd, mem, currently. **Orgs:** Bd mem, Ment Health Asn; bd mem, Houston Citizens Chamber Com; Super Bowl Host Comt; bd mem, Greater Houston Partnership; Strake Found. **Honors/Awds:** Best printing among medium-sized facil, Printing & Imaging Asn, 2001; Emerging E-10 Award, 2002. **Special Achievements:** First African American TV news reporter in the south in Charlotte, NC; first African American TV news anchor in Houston at KHOU-TV, 1971. **Business Addr:** President, Nicholas Earth Printing, 7021 Portwest Dr Suite 100, Houston, TX 77024, **Business Phone:** (713)880-0195.

### NICHOLAS, BRENDA L.
Gospel singer. **Personal:** Born Dec 16, 1953, Salem, NJ; daughter of John H Watson and Janette Coleman; married Philip; children: Jennifer & Philip Jr. **Educ:** Career Educ Inst, AS, 1974. **Career:** Command recs, gospel singer; Nicholas Ministries Int, gospel vocalist, currently; Song: "God's Woman"; "A Love Like This"; "The Closer I Get To You"; "Dedicated"; "I Do"; "The Love CD"; "Just Dance"; "Hes Been Good"; "Our Love "; "Dedicated". **Honors/Awds:** Excellence Awards, Gospel Music Workshops Am, 1983; Dove Award, 1987; Grammy Award, ARAS, 1986; Golden Eagle Award, Southern Cal Motion Picture, 1986; Halo Award, Best Foreign Rec, 1988. **Home Addr:** PO Box 1869, Van Nuys, CA 91401, **Home Phone:** (818)995-6363. **Business Addr:** Gospel Singer, Nicholas Ministries International, PO Box 10151, Palm Desert, CA 92255, **Business Phone:** (760)836-0776.

### NICHOLAS, DONNA DENISE (DONNA HILL)
Socialist, actor, writer. **Personal:** Born Jul 12, 1944, Detroit, DE; daughter of Otto and Louise Carolyn Burgen; married Bill Withers, Jan 1, 1973, (divorced 1974); married Gilbert Moses, Jan 1, 1964, (divorced 1965); married Jim Hill, Jan 1, 1981, (divorced 1984). **Educ:** Univ Mich, 1965; Univ Southern Calif, BA, drama, 1985. **Career:** Negro Ensemble Co, actress, 1967-69; TV series: "It Takes a Thief", 1968; "The F.B.I.", 1969; "N.Y.P.D.", 1967-69; "The Flip Wilson Show", 1970; "Love, American Style", 1972; "Room 222", actress, 1969-74; "Baby I'm Back", actress, 1978; The Paper Chase, actress, 1979; Jacqueline Susann's Valley of the Dolls, actress, 1981; "In the Heat of the Night", actress, 1988; "My Wife & Kids", actress, 2002; Films: The Soul of Nigger Charley, actress, 1973; Blacula, actress; Let's Do It Again, actress, 1975; Mr Ricco, actress, 1975; A Piece of the Action, actress, 1977; Media Forum Inc, producer, 1980-; Ghost Dad, actress, 1990; Ritual, actress, 2000; Proud, actress, 2004; Author: Freshwater Road, 2005; producer. **Orgs:** Neighbors Watts Inc, 1976-; bd dir, Communs Bridge Video Sch, 1983-; fund raiser, Artists & Athletes Against Apartheid; Mus African Am Art, LA; Mus Afro-Am Hist & Cult. **Honors/Awds:** Author, The Denise Nicholas Beauty Book, 1971; Two LA Emmy Awards producer/actress Voices of our People in Celebration of Black Poetry, 1981; 2 CEBA Awards Excellence for Advertising & Communications to Black Comn, 1981, 1982; 3 Emmy nominations Room 222; Black Filmmakers Hall of Fame, 1992; Zora Neal Hurston/Richard Wright Award, 2006; American Library Asns Black Caucus Award, 2006. **Business Addr:** 9300 Wilshire Blvd Suite 555, Beverly Hills, CA 90212, **Business Phone:** (310)550-1060.

### NICHOLAS, GWENDOLYN SMITH
Government official. **Personal:** Born Jan 27, 1951, San Francisco, CA. **Educ:** Univ San Francisco, BA, sociol, 1972; Clark Atlanta Univ, MSW, 1974. **Career:** Fireman's Fund Ins Co, bus syst analyst, 1976-77; W Oak Ment Health Dept, psychiat social worker, 1977-78; State Calif Dept Ment Health, psychiat social worker, 1978-81, ment health prog specialist, 1981-83, Dept Social Serv, lic prog analyst II, 1984-91, Calif Pub Utilities Comn, 1991-95, Dept Alcohol Drug Progs, analyst, 1995-2010. **Orgs:** Alpha Kappa Alpha, 1972; area pub info officer, chap rec sec, Nat Nominating Comn SF Chap Links Inc, 1975-; Links Inc, 1975-; Bay Area Asn Black Social Workers, 1977-; contribr, United Negro Col Fund, 1978-; contribr, Bay Area Black United Fund, 1980-; Soroptimist Int Oak Founder Club, 1986-91; Black Advocates State Serv, Bay Area Heath Consortium. **Home Addr:** PO Box 1175, Sacramento, CA 95812-1175. **Business Addr:** Analyst, California Department of Alcohol & Drug Programs, 1700 K St, Sacramento, CA 95811-4022, **Business Phone:** (916)445-0834.

### NICHOLAS, PHILIP
Gospel singer, executive. **Personal:** Born Feb 18, 1954, Chester, PA; son of Julia B Shade and Ross B; married Brenda L Watson; children: Jennifer & Phil Jr. **Educ:** Drexel Univ, BS, 1977. **Career:** Command Rec, Nicholas Ministries, pres, gospel vocalist, 2009-; Albums: Tell the World, 1981; Words Can't Express, 1983; Songs: God's Woman,

1985; A Love Like This; The Closer I Get To You'; Dedicated; I Do; Fired Up-God Will See you Through; The Nicholas Love Cruise, 1998, BreakThrough, 2014; Nicholas' Classic Wedding & Love Songs. **Honors/Awds:** Excellence Awards, Gospel Music Workshops Am, 1983; Grammy Award, nomination, ARAS, 1986; Golden Eagle Award, Southern CAL Motion Picture, 1986; Dove Award, nomination, 1987; Halo Award, Best Foreign Recording, Can, 1988. **Business Addr:** President, Nicholas Ministries Int, PO Box 10151, Palm Desert, CA 92255, **Business Phone:** (760)836-0776.

### NICHOLS, ALFRED GLEN

Printer. **Personal:** Born Mar 20, 1952, Jackson, MS; married Sylvia Lauree Robinson; children: Derek Allen & Shaunte Latrice. **Educ:** Purdue Univ, BS, 1975; Univ Chicago, MBA, 1985. **Career:** RR Donnelley & Sons Co, price admin estimator, 1975-78, indust engr, 1978-80, proj engr, 1980-86, supvr planning & facil engr, 1986-. **Orgs:** Dir, Hazel Crest Jaycees, 1982-85. **Honors/Awds:** Outstanding Young Men in America, 1985; Black Achiever of Industry, Young Mens Christian Asn, Chicago, 1986. **Home Addr:** 2918 Greenwood Rd, PO Box 315, Hazel Crest, IL 60429, **Home Phone:** (312)335-3422. **Business Addr:** Supervisor Planning, Facility Engineer, RR Donnelley & Sons Co, 111 S Wacker Dr, Chicago, IL 60606-4301, **Business Phone:** (312)326-8000.

### NICHOLS, CRYSTAL FAYE

Office worker, manager. **Personal:** Born Apr 11, 1969, Lansing, MI; daughter of Charles and Dorthy. **Educ:** Brook Col, AA, 1982; Lee Strasburg Actg Sch. **Career:** Ashford Properties, apt mgr, 1987-; bartender; Prof Int Basketball League, basketball off, 1989-; La Unit, football off, line judge, 1994-; IFAF Women's World Championship, off, 2010. property mgr. **Special Achievements:** First woman to officiate high school football playoff games in Los Angeles, 1999. **Home Addr:** 3865 Nicolet Suite 19, Los Angeles, CA 90008, **Home Phone:** (323)293-4198. **Business Addr:** Apartment Manager, Ashford Properties Inc, 5126 Clareton Dr Suite 206, Agoura Hills, CA 91301, **Business Phone:** (818)865-1088.

### NICHOLS, DR. DAVID G.

Dean (education), physician, educator. **Educ:** Yale Univ, BA, molecular biophys & biochem, 1973; NY Mt Sinai Sch Med, MD, 1977; Johns Hopkins Univ Sch Prof Studies Bus & Educ, MBA, 2000. **Career:** C's Hosp Philadelphia, resident, 1977-80, chief resident, 1980-81, Pediat Anesthesia & Critical fel, 1983; Univ Pa Sch Med, instr, 1980-81; Hosp Univ Pa, residency anesthesiol, 1981-83; Johns Hopkins Sch Med, from asstprof to assoc prof anesthesiol/critical care med & pediat, 1984-91, Residency Educ Prog, assoc dir, 1984-87, Pediatric Intensive Care, from assoc dir to dir, 1987-97, assoc prof anesthesiol/critical care med, 1991-98, Div Pediat Anesthesia & Critical Care Med, 1997-2001, prof anesthesiol/critical Care Med & Pediat, 1998-, vice dean educ, 2000-, Mary Wallace Stanton Prof Educ, 2005-, Johns Hopkins Dr Mohan Swami Inst Int Med Educ, dir, 2011-; Editor: Golden Hour: The Handbook for Advanced Pediatric Life Support, 3rd Edition. **Orgs:** Alpha Omega Alpha Hon Med Soc, 1976; chair, Intermediate Care Unit Comt, 1984-88; pres, chief exec officer, dir, chair, bd dir, Am Bd Pediat, 1988-2011; dir, Md Int Health Task Force, 1991; fel Am Acad Pediat, 1991; fel Am Col Critical Care Med, 1992; Am Soc Anesthesiol, 1992-93; Nat Head Injury Found, 1993-97; Int Anesthesia Res Soc; bd mem, chair, Soc Pediat Anesthesia, 1995-98; chair, Fac Compensation Comt, 1996; World Fedn Pediat Intensive Care, 1997-2003; Pediat Critical Care Med, 1999-2000; bd dir, Hopkins-Dunbar High Sch Scholars Prog, 2000-; chair, Educ Policy & Curric Comt, 2000-; chair, Robert Wood Johnson JHSOM Clin Scholars Adv Bd, 2002-05; bd trustee, Horizon Found Howard County, 2003-07; chair, Financial Aid Adv Bd, 2006-; chair, Search Comt, 2007; Nat Adv Coun, 2007-11; Am Thoracic Soc; Soc Pediat Res; Asn Univ Anesthesiologists; Phi Beta Kappa, 2009; Soc Critical Care Med, 2010; bd dir, E Baltimore Develop Initiative, 2010-12; chair, E Baltimore Community Sch Bd dir, 2011-; pres, E Baltimore Community Sch, 2011-. **Business Addr:** Professor, Vice Dean, Johns Hopkins University School of Medicine, Blalock 941 600 N Wolfe St, Baltimore, MD 21287-4904, **Business Phone:** (410)955-8401.

### NICHOLS, DIMAGGIO

Executive. **Personal:** Born May 8, 1951, Byhalia, MS; son of Emmitt Jr and Lucille Bougard; married Lizzie Emma Shelton; children: Dimeka W & Dondra O. **Educ:** Rust Col, Holly Spring, BS, 1973; Gen Motor Inst, Flint, dealer develop, 1983. **Career:** Buick Motor Div, Flint Mich, dist sales mgr, 1974-83; Gen Motor Inst, Flint Mich, trainee, 1983-84; Sentry Buick, Omaha, salesperson, 1984-85; Noble Ford-Mercury Inc, Indianola, owner, pres & founder, 1985-; Noble All Am, pres & founder. **Orgs:** Bd mem, Chamber Com, Indianola, 1987-; bd mem, Black Ford Lincoln Mercury Asn, 1988-. **Home Addr:** 923 Hwy 65-69 N, Indianola, IA 50125, **Home Phone:** (515)961-7850. **Business Addr:** President, Owner, Noble Ford-Mercury Inc, 947 Hwy 65-69 N, Indianola, IA 50125, **Business Phone:** (515)961-8151.

### NICHOLS, DR. EDWIN J.

Executive, consultant, physiologist. **Personal:** Born Jun 23, 1931, Detroit, MI; married Sandra; children: Lisa & Edwin. **Educ:** Assumption Col, attended 1955; Windsor Can; Eberhardt Karls Univ, Ger, attended 1957; Leopoline-franciscea Univ, PhD, psychol & psychiat, 1961. **Career:** ACA, Clin, Indust Psychologist, 1961-; Nat Inst Ment Health, Rockville, Md, chief Appl & Social Proj Rev Br, 1969-89; Kans Neurol Inst, psychologist; Cleveland Job Corps Ctr Women, psychologist; Meharry Med Col, psychologist; Fisk Univ, psychologist; Univ Ibadan Nigeria, dir Childs Clin, 1974-77; Ctr Mgt Develop Lagos Nigeria, mgt consult, 1974-77; Harvard Univ Found, distinguished clin psychologist; Bellagio Study Ctr, Italy, Rockefeller Found, vis scholar; George Washington Univ, Ctr Excellence Pub Leadership, fac, currently; Nichols & Assocs Inc, dir, 1968-. **Orgs:** Fel Austrian Ministry Educ, 1961. **Honors/Awds:** Public Service Award, US Gen Serv Admin; Public Service Award, Dept Justice; Public Service Award, Social Security Admin. **Business Addr:** Director, Nichols & Associates Inc, 5521 Sixteenth St NW, Washington, DC 20011, **Business Phone:** (202)291-3574.

### NICHOLS, ELAINE

Archaeologist. **Personal:** Born Oct 5, 1952, Charlotte, NC. **Educ:** Univ Nc, Charlotte, BA, polit sci, 1974; Case Western Res Univ, MS, social admin, 1980; Univ Sc, MA, pub serv archaeol, 1988. **Career:** Planned Parenthood Charlotte, crisis intervention counr, 1974-75; Big Bros Big Sisters, social caseworker, 1975-78; City Cleveland, neighborhood planner, 1980-81, asst mgr planners, 1981-82; Univ NC, Charlotte, lectr, 1982-85; Univ SC, grad stud, dept anthrop, 1985-88; SC State Mus, guest cur hist, 1987-90, cur hist, 1989; Mus Marines, consult; Underground Rr Mus, consult; Bettis Acad Mus, consult; Penn Ctr Mus, consult; Lucy Craft Mus, Augusta, Ga, consult; Smithsonian Inst, Mus African Am Hist & Cult, sr cur, currently. **Orgs:** Charter mem, Afro-Am Serv Ctr, 1974; Delta Sigma Theta Sor, 1977-; Co-chairperson, Afro-Am Hist Soc, Charlotte, 1982-83; bd mem, Metrolina Asn Blind, 1983-85; researcher, Am Heart Asn, Charlotte, 1985. **Honors/Awds:** Pulse of Black Charlotte, Urban Inst Grant UNCC, 1984; Research Assistant, Dept Anthrop, USC, 1985-; Service Award, Alpha Kappa Alpha Sorority, 1986; Sigma Xi Science Award, 1987; YMCA Family Center Award; Fulbright-Hays, 2008. **Special Achievements:** Author: The Last Mile of the Way: African-American Home going Traditions, 1890-; African-American Inventors, Mathematicians, Scientists & Physicians Association. **Home Addr:** PO Box 3536, Columbia, SC 29230. **Business Addr:** Senior Curator, Smithsonian Institution, PO Box 37012, Washington, DC 20013-7012, **Business Phone:** (202)633-9511.

### NICHOLS, GRACE DELL. See NICHOLS, NICHELLE.

### NICHOLS, NICHELLE (GRACE DELL NICHOLS)

Actor, singer. **Personal:** Born Dec 28, 1932, Robbins, IL; daughter of Samuel Earl and Lishia Parks; married Foster Johnson; children: Kyle Johnson; married Duke Mondy. **Educ:** Chicago Ballet Acad, Chicago, attended 1956; Columbia Law Sch. **Career:** Actress, singer, dancer; Duke Ellington; Women In Motion, pres; NASA, minority recruitment officer; Films: Star Trek; A-R Way Productions, pres, 1979-; Films: Porgy & Bess, 1959; Made in Paris, 1966; Mister Buddwing, 1966; Doctor, You've Got to Be Kidding!, 1967; Truck Turner, 1974; StarTrek: The Motion Picture, 1979; Star Trek II: The Wrath of Khan, 1982; StarTrek III: The Search for Spock, 1984; The Supernaturals, 1986; Star Trek IV: The Voyage Home, 1986; Star Trek V: The Final Frontier, 1989; StarTrek VI: The Undiscovered Country, 1991; Captain Zoom in Outer Space, 1995; Trekkies, 1997; Snow Dogs, 2002; The Adventures of Surge of Power, 2004; Are We There Yet?, 2005; Mirror Universe: Part 1, 2008; Lady Magdalene's, actress & exec producer, 2008; Tru Loved, 2008; The Torturer, 2008; This Bitter Earth, 2012. TV series: Great Gettin' Up Mornin', 1964; "Tarzan", 1966; "Star Trek", 1966-69; "Star Trek", 1973-74; Antony & Cleopatra, 1983; "Inside Space", 1992; "Gargoyles", 1994-96; "Renunciation", 2000; "Futurama", 2000; "Buzz Light year of Star Command", 2000; "Heroes", 2007; "The Cabonauts", 2009; "Scooby-Doo! Curse of the Lake Monster", 2010. Albums: Uhura Sings & Hauntingly. **Orgs:** Kwanza Found, 1973-; bd gov, Nat Space Soc; Nat bd adv, SEDS-MIT; Hon mem, Alpha Kappa Alpha Sorority. **Honors/Awds:** Women of the Year, Nat Educ Asn, 1978; Distinguished Pub Service Award Agency, 1989; ACTSO Award Performing Arts, Acad Olympics, 1991; Hollywood Walk of Fame, 1992; Los Angeles Mission Col; Golden Camera Award, 1999. **Special Achievements:** First African-American to place her handprints in front of Hollywood's Chinese Theatre. Books: Beyond Uhura: Star Trek & Other Memories, 1994; (With Margaret Wander Bonanno) Saturn's Child, 1995; Played prominent role in the recruitment of minorities and women by NASA. **Home Addr:** 23281 Leonora Dr, Woodland Hills, CA 91367, **Home Phone:** (818)704-6017. **Business Addr:** President, AR-Way Productions, 22647 Ventura Blvd Suite 121, Woodland Hills, CA 91364, **Business Phone:** (818)340-7929.

### NICHOLS, DR. OWEN DOUGLAS

Educator, association executive, administrator. **Personal:** Born Apr 8, 1929, Raleigh, NC; son of William and Pearl; married Delores Tucker; children: Bryan K & Diane Maria. **Educ:** Shaw Univ, BS, 1955; Howard Univ, MS, phy chem, 1958; HIghland Univ, EdD, educ admin & supv, 1975. **Career:** Educator (retired); SC State Col, assoc prof, 1958-59; US Naval Res Lab Wash DC, res chemist, 1959-62; Dept Defense Alexandria VA, phys sci analyst, 1962-66; Air Pollution Tech Info Ctr, Nat Air Pollution Control Admin Wash DC, dep dir, 1966-68; Off Tech Info & Pub Nat Air Polllution Control Admin Wash DC, dir, 1968-69; Howard Univ Wash DC, exec asst to pres, 1969-71; Howard Univ, vpres admins & secy, 1971-88, chair, 2001-03. **Orgs:** Alpha Kappa Mu Soc; Beta Kappa Chi Sci Soc; Am Chem Soc; Air Pollution Control Asn; Soc Sigma XI; Int Platform Asn; Am Mgt Asn; Am Asn High Educ; Am Asn Univ Admin; Comn Educ Statis & Admin Affairs, Am Coun Educ MD Cong; PTA; Adv Con Hosp Construct MD; town Counman, Seat Pleasant MD; advisor, coordr, organizer, African Am Festival Acad Achievement, 1989-; Prince Georges County Housing Authority; legis chmn, 2nd vpres Prince Georges Co Coun, PTA; Lay Speaker United Methodist Church; montgomery col, bd trustee, 2001-03, bd mem. **Honors/Awds:** Comn Campus Ministry & Higher Educ; Baltimore Washington Conf United Methodist Church. **Special Achievements:** Author: Things My Father Taught Me, 1998. **Home Addr:** 12713 Eldrid Pl, Silver Spring, MD 20904-3514, **Home Phone:** (301)622-6574.

### NICHOLS, DR. RONALD AUGUSTUS

Hospital administrator. **Personal:** Born Jun 4, 1956, Louvain; son of Rufus and Janet Watson; married Sati Harris; children: Aaron. **Educ:** Boston Univ, Boston, Mass, BA, 1978; Brown Univ, Providence, RI, MD, 1982; Harvard Univ, Boston, Mass, MPH, 1982; Am Bd Obstet & Gynec, cert. **Career:** Mt Sinai Hosp, New York, residency in Obstet & Gynec, 1982-86; Univ Cincinnati, Cincinnati, Ohio, dir, univ obstet practice, 1987-88; Mich State Univ, Sparrow Hosp, Lansing, Mich, dir, perinatal ctr, 1988-; Obstetrician & Gynecologist, currently. **Orgs:** Mt Sinai Hosp, New York, obstet & gynec, 1982-86; Univ Cincinnati, Cincinnati, OH, dir & univ obstet pract, 1987-88; Mich State Univ, Sparrow Hosp, Lansing, Mich, dir perinatal ctr, 1988-. **Honors/Awds:** Fel maternal-fetal med, Univ Cincinnati, Cincinnati, OH; Sigma Xi Hon Socs Res, 1980-81. **Home Addr:** 4250 Marmoor Dr, Lansing, MI 48917, **Home Phone:** (517)712-5837. **Business Addr:** Chief Doctor in Obstetrics and Gynecology, Abortion Clinic of Grand Rapids, 3212 Eastern Ave SE, Grand Rapids, MI 49508, **Business Phone:** (616)361-8800.

### NICHOLS, DR. WALTER LAPLORA

Educator, athletic coach. **Personal:** Born Aug 31, 1938, Bolton, MS; married Louise Faye Harris; children: Anthony & Kala Faye. **Educ:** Miss Valley State Univ, BS, phys educ, 1964; Northern Ill Univ, MS, admin, 1978; Independence Univ, DEd, recreation admin, 1979. **Career:** Sheridan Ind Boys, teacher, 1965-67; Fairmont Jr High Sch, teacher, coach, 1967-71, athletic dir & head coach; Argo Comm High Sch, teacher, coach, 1971-, athletic dir & head coach; United Football League, athletic dir & head coach; Prof Football League, athletic dir & head coach; Sumner Hill High Sch, athletic dir & head coach. **Orgs:** Vpres, Dist 86 Sch Bd, 1981-; Nat Sch Bd Asn, 1981-; mem & pres, Ill Sch Bd Asn, 1981-; consult, Joliet Job Corp, 1982-83; bd mem, PUSH, 1983-; Marquette Joliet Consistory, 1983; Shriner, 1984; founder, Cent Miss Walker Horse Asn, currently. **Honors/Awds:** MVSU Hall of Fame, 1985. **Special Achievements:** Article "You Either Move Up or Move Out" Chicago Tribune, 1967, "Title Triumph by Charger Something Special, Walt", 1967, "Remember Walter Nichols Offensive Tackle", Joliet Herald newspaper, 1964-67, "Stand by Valley State Alumni Urge Official" Clarion Ledger Paper, 1983. **Business Addr:** Founder, Central Mississippi Walker Horse Association, 406 Church St, Clinton, MS 39056-5308, **Business Phone:** (601)925-9941.

### NICHOLSON, REV. ALEATHIA DOLORES

Educator, clergy. **Personal:** Born Apr 10, 1937, Salisbury, NC; daughter of John Wadsworth and Leathia Williams. **Educ:** Hampton Univ, BS, 1959; Univ Conn, MA, 1965; Vanderbilt Univ, George Peabody Col, EdS, 1968; Episcopal Theol Sem Ky, licentiate servant ministry, 1989. **Career:** Educator (retired), deacon: Pub Pvt Schs, music specialist, 1959-78; Meharry Med Col, stud affairs dir & nursing educ, 1978-81; Tenn State Univ, stud affairs dir & sch nursing, 1981-85; Fisk Univ, dir teacher educ progs, 1985-92; Episcopal Diocese Tenn, voc deacon, 1989; Teach Am, curric consult, 1990-92; Metro Bd Educ, music specialist, 1992-2002; Christ Church Cathedral, episcopal deacon, 2007-. **Orgs:** Zeta Phi Beta Sorority Inc, 1960-; N Am Asn Diaconate, 1989-2001; bd mem, Neighborhood Educ Proj, 1989-91; bd trustee, Dubose Scholar Fund, 1998; Nat Educ Asn Affil. **Home Addr:** 3729 Creekland Ct, Nashville, TN 37218-1803, **Home Phone:** (615)876-7914. **Business Addr:** Deacon, Christ Church Cathedral, 900 Broadway, Nashville, TN 37203, **Business Phone:** (615)255-7729.

### NICHOLSON, ALFRED

Educator. **Personal:** Born Jun 3, 1936, Edgefield, SC; children: Sharon Michell & Althea Gail. **Educ:** Community Col, Philadelphia, AAS, 1968; La Salle Univ, BS, 1974. **Career:** AAA Refinishing Co, tanner & inspector, 1956-59; Strick Corp, elec wireman, 1961-68, personnel asst, 1968-69; Community Col Philadelphia, personnel officer & aa dir, 1974-. **Orgs:** Treas, Col & Univ Personnel Asn, 1972-74; bd trustee, United Way Southeastern, PA. **Home Addr:** 910 Summit Lane, Oreland, PA 19075. **Business Addr:** Personnel Officer, AA Director, Community College of Philadelphia, 1700 Spring Garden St, Philadelphia, PA 19130, **Business Phone:** (215)751-8010.

### NICHOLSON, GEMMA

Executive, educator. **Personal:** Born Jul 28, 1959, Port-au-Prince; daughter of Jean-Pierre Gaetjens (deceased) and Rachel Gaetjens; children: Felicia & Carlos. **Educ:** Univ VI, attended 1994; Univ Md, BS, bus, 1996; George Washington Univ, MTA. **Career:** Davenport Univ, instr; Horizons Conf Ctr, food & beverage dir; Ritz Carlton, proj mgr; Dona Ana Community Col, instr, asst prof, currently. **Orgs:** Horizon's Conf Ctr. **Business Addr:** Assistant Professor, Instructor, Dona Ana Community College, 2800 N Sonoma Ranch Blvd, Las Cruces, NM 88011, **Business Phone:** (575)528-7264.

### NICHOLSON, DR. JESSIE R.

Lawyer. **Personal:** Born Waterloo, IA; married Charles E; children: Ephraim C. **Educ:** Univ Northern Iowa, BA, sociol, 1974, MA, Span, 1975; William Mitchell Col Law, JD, 1985. **Career:** Ramsey County, sr leadership atty. **Orgs:** Am Bar Asn, 1985-90; conciliator, Due Process Bd, Conciliator Minneapolis-St Paul Archidocese, 1988-; bd mem, Housing Trust Adv Comn, 1989-91; Ramsey & Wash Co Bar Asn, 1989-; Minn Asn Black Lawyers, 1996; bd gov, Minn State Bar Asn, 1998-; legal asst, Disadvantage Comn, Minn State Bar Asn, 1998-; dep exec dir, Southern Minn Regional Legal Servs, 2001-07; exec dir & chief exec officer, Southern Minn Regional Legal Servs, 2007-; exec dirs, African Am Proj Dirs Asn. **Honors/Awds:** Service Recognition Award, Minn State Housing Finance Agency, 1991; Distinguished Service Award, William Mitchell Col Law, 2000; 15 Year Recognition Award for distinguished service, Southern Minn Regional Legal Serv, 2000; Anderson Trailblazer Award, William Mitchell Col Law, 2008; Ronald E. Hachey Outstanding Alumni Award, William Mitchell Col Law, 2009; MN Black Women Lawyers Network Achievement Award, 2013; Advocate Award, 2014. **Special Achievements:** First African-American woman to head a legal aid organization in the Midwest. **Home Addr:** 3302 Commonwealth Ct, Saint Paul, MN 55125-4312. **Business Addr:** Executive Director, Chief Executive Officer, Southern Minnesota Regional Legal Services Inc, 1000 Alliance Bank Ctr 55 E 5th St, St. Paul, MN 55101, **Business Phone:** (651)228-9823.

### NICHOLSON, TINA

Basketball player. **Personal:** Born Sep 27, 1973. **Educ:** Pa State Univ, BS, exercise & sports mgt, 1996. **Career:** Basketball player (retired), coach; Cleveland Rockers, guard, 1997; Lady Lions, asst coach.

### NICKERSON, JUDGE DON CARLOS

Judge, lawyer. **Personal:** Born Aug 24, 1951, Wilmington, DE; son of David B and Floretta W; children: Christen, Jordan & Dariann. **Educ:** Iowa State Univ, BS, sociol, jour, 1974; Drake Univ Law Sch, JD, 1977. **Career:** Judge, (retired); WHO Radio & TV, news reporter, 1972-74; Parrish & Del Gallo, assoc atty, 1977-78; Des Moines, Iowa, asst US atty, 1978-80; Babich & Nickerson, partner, atty; Wellmark Blue Cross & Blue Shield Iowa, assoc gen coun, 2001-03; Southern Dist Iowa, US atty, 1993-2001; Iowa Dist Ct, Polk Co Dist Ct, Dist Ct 5C, judge, 2003-11; Babich Goldman, staff, currently. **Orgs:** Iowa Comn Aging, 1983-85; United Way Cent Iowa, 1985-88; Drake Univ Law Sch Bd Counrs, 1989-92; Nat Bar Asn, 1991-; pres, Iowa Nat Bar Asn, 1991-92; Nat Asn Criminal Defense Lawyers, 1991-; Atty Gen's Health Care Fraud Adv Comm, 1994; Iowa State Bar Asn; pres, Black Am Law Students Asn; Moot Ct; Legal Res Teaching Asst. **Honors/Awds:** Iowa Governor's Volunteer Award, 1984-85, 1992; Des Moines Register, Up & Comer, 1989; Certificate Recognition, Amnesty Int, 1991; Top lawyer rating, Martindale-Hubbell, AV, 1992; Medal of Honor, Drake Univ; SBA Community Service Award. **Special Achievements:** Conference presenter, first annual state conference on the Black Male, Criminal Justice, 1992. **Home Addr:** 3416 SW Rose, Des Moines, IA 50321, **Home Phone:** (515)222-9617. **Business Addr:** Staff, Babich Goldman, 501 SW 7th St Suite J, Des Moines, IA 50309, **Business Phone:** (515)244-4300.

**NICKERSON, HARDY OTTO**
Football player, executive, football coach. **Personal:** Born Sep 1, 1965, Compton, CA; son of Hardy Sr; married Amy; children: Ashleigh, Hardy & Haleigh. **Educ:** Univ Calif, Berkeley, BA, sociol, 1989. **Career:** Football player (retired), coach, executive; Pittsburgh Steelers, right inside linebacker, 1987-89, left inside linebacker, 1990-92; Tampa Bay Buccaneers, mid linebacker, 1993-99, linebackers coach, 2014-15; Jacksonville Jaguars, linebacker, 2000, mid linebacker, 2000-01; Green Bay Packers, mid linebacker, 2002; Nickerson Realty Group, founder & chief exec officer, 2005-; Buccaneer Radio Network, color analyst, 2006; Chicago Bears, linebackers coach, 2007-08; Bishop O'Dowd High Sch, head football coach, 2010-13; San Francisco 49ers, linebackers coach, 2016; Univ Ill, defensive coordr, 2016-. **Honors/Awds:** Pro Bowl, 1993, 1996-99; All-Pro, 1993, 1996-99; White Man of the Year Award, Nat Football League, 1997. **Special Achievements:** TV appearance: 1987 NFL Draft, 1987; The NFL on NBC, 1988; NFL on FOX, 1997; ESPN's Sunday Night Football, 1993-99; NFL Monday Night Football, 1992-99; The Jersey, 2000. **Home Addr:** 1820 Melvin Rd, Oakland, CA 94602-2025. **Business Addr:** Founder, Chief Executive Officer, Nickerson Realty Group, 14120 Ballantyne Corp Pl Suite 160, Charlotte, NC 28277, **Business Phone:** (704)295-0093.

**NICKSON, SHEILA JOAN**
College administrator. **Personal:** Born May 20, 1936, Buffalo, NY; daughter of William Harris and Genevieve Martha Briggs; children: Stephen Dwight & Roderick Matthew. **Educ:** Buffalo State Col, attended 1953; Erie County Col, attended 1966. **Career:** College administrator (retired); State Univ New York, Buffalo, Dept Chem, asst to chmn, 1966-75, Human Resources Off, dir affirmative action, 1975-80, pres, 1984; State Univ New York, Albany, Cent Admin, dir affirmative action, 1980-84, co-chmn, 1972-76; founding mem, Northern Region Black Polit Caucus. **Orgs:** Exec bd, State Univ NY Black Fac & Staff Asn, 1980; educ adv comt, Nat Urban League, 1983; bd dir, YWCA, Buffalo, 1983; vice chair, NY State Human Rights Adv Coun, 1984-; pres, Nat Org Am Asn Affirmative Action, 1981-; bd mem, vpres, Girl Scouts Am; Nat Asn Advan Colored People, 1987; bd mem, Sheehan Mem Hosp, 1988; Nat Women's Polit Caucus; founding mem, Afro-Am Hist Asn Niagara Frontier. **Home Addr:** 151 Sanders Rd, Buffalo, NY 14216, **Home Phone:** (716)871-1810.

**NIGHTINGALE-HAWKINS, MONICA R.**
Marketing executive, president (organization), vice president (organization). **Personal:** Born Feb 6, 1960, Topeka, KS; daughter of Floyd Nightingale and Carol Lawton; married Thomas. **Educ:** Pa Valley Community Col, attended 1991; Avila Col, attended 1995. **Career:** Off Mayor, opers mgt engr, 1980-85; job training prog mgr, 1982-83; KSNT-TV 27, news producer & opers engr, 1984-85; KSNW-TV 3, music dir & on-air boardcaster, 1985-87; KPRS/KPRT Radio FM, mkt Promotions dir, proj mgr, music dir, 1987-89; AA Productions, vpres mkt & promotions, exec dir, 1989-2000; Church Ascension, youth minister, 1989-; Wyandotte County Youth Commun, exec dir, 1990-93; KXTR 96.5, on-air boardcaster, asst music dir, 1994-; KMXV 93.3FM, tv host & producer, 1994-95; KUDL 98FM, tv host & exec producer, 1994-95; Time Warner Cable & Am Cablevision, asst managing ed-in-chief & news reporter, 1995-97; KGGN & WREN, gen mgr, 1998-99; Mortenson Broadcasting, mgr & ed-in-chief, 1998-99; The Gospel Truth Newspaper, community affairs & news dir, 1998-2000; KMJK 107.3FM, Commun Dir & Proj Coordr & Grant writer, 2004-06; TYCOR Community Develop Corp Inc, morning ed host & news anchor, 2009-. **Orgs:** Bd mem, Turner House Episcopal Social Serv, 1987-90; State Kans, Comn AIDS Black, 1988-89; artist educ, Gov Artist Residence, 1988-; pres, Episcopal Church Women, 1989-91. **Honors/Awds:** Salute to Women, Am Bus Women, 1988; Mayor Richard Berkey, Key to The City, 1989; Outstanding Female Broadcaster, A & M Records, 1989; $32k grant to train inner-city youth, State Kans. **Special Achievements:** Appeared in local, state, and national A music trades magazines for involvement & work in the inner-city, 1989-92; Appeared on "Mass Communications Project for Youth Intervention and Training", NBC television, Aug, 1992; "President's Glass Ceiling" Witness, 1992. **Home Phone:** (816)213-3787.

**NILES, ALBAN I.**
Judge. **Personal:** Born Jun 10, 1933, St. Vincent; son of Isaac and Elsie; children: Maria, Gloria & Angela. **Educ:** Univ Calif, Los Angeles, BS, 1959, JD, 1963. **Career:** Judge (retired); State Bar Ct, hearing judge; Ernst & Ernst, auditor, 1963-64; Whitaker & Niles, co-founder; Pvt pract, atty, 1964-82; Kedren Comm Health Ctr Inc, pres, 1968-79; LA Cty Civil Serv Comm, pres comn, 1980; La Munic Ct, judge, 1982, asst presiding judge, 1992-94, presiding judge, 1994-95; La Super Ct, judge, 2002; Parliamentarian 100 Black Men Inc, Los Angeles; Urban Exec Leadership, Carnegie Found fel; bd dir, Kedren Ment Health Serv; Arbitrator, Mediator & Consult. **Orgs:** Langston Bar Asn; chmn bd, Bus Devel Ctr S CA, 1978-91; Nat Asn Advan Colored People, Urban League; Comdr Post 116 Am Legion; chmn, Munic Ct Judges Asn, 1992-93; treas, Judicial Div, Nat Bar Asn, 1991-93; 33 degree Mason & Hon Potentate Shriners rank Ambassador Large; pres, Los Angeles County Civil Serv Comn. **Honors/Awds:** Passed the CPA examination, 1960; Selected as person of Caribbean birth to make signif contrib, 1976; Univ Calif Los Angeles Law Reviewappointed to the bench Feb 3, 1982; Honored by the State Legislature, The County Bd of Supervisors, The Los Angeles City Council, 1996. **Home Addr:** 3859 Lenawee Ave, Culver City, CA 90232.

**NILES, PROF. LYNDREY ARNAUD**
Chairperson, educator. **Personal:** Born May 9, 1936; married Patricia Aqui; children: Kathryn Arlene & Ian Arnaud. **Educ:** Columbia Union Col, BA, 1963; Univ Md, MA, 1965; Temple Univ, PhD, 1973; Caribbean Union Col, AA. **Career:** Columbia Union Col, lectr, 1964-65; Univ DC, instr, 1965-68, asst prof, 1968-74; Univ Md, lectr, 1971-75; Leadership Resources Inc, mgt consult, 1974-75; Howard Univ, Annenberg Hons Prog, dir, Commun, prof, 1975-79, Sch Commun, Grad Sch Arts & Sci, assoc dean, Sch Commun, assoc dean, Commun Arts & Sci Dept, chmn, 1979-2005, Human Commun Studies, prof emer, currently. **Orgs:** Pres, Met Wash Commun Asn, 1974-75; Speech Commun Asn; Int Commun Asn; Am Soc Training & Develop; Nat Asn Advan Colored People. **Honors/Awds:** Outstanding Teacher of the Year Award, Nat Speech Commun Asn, 1996. **Special Achievements:** Published article: "Listening & Note TakingMethods", 1965; Published dissertation: "The Defel of Speech Educ Problems at Predominately Black Colls", 1973; "black rhetoric five years of growth, Encoder", 1974; "Communication in Dental Office", article in Encoder 1979; "The Relative Effectivenesss of Note-taking Methods in Listening". Editor: Toward an Afrocentric For the Critical Assessment of Rhetoric, ed, 1995. **Home Addr:** 6609 16th St NW, Washington, DC 20012. **Business Addr:** Professor Emeritus, Howard University, 2400 6th St, Washington, DC 20059, **Business Phone:** (202)806-7692.

**NIMMONS, DR. JULIUS F., JR.**
School administrator, college president, dean (education). **Educ:** Morehouse Col, BA, am hist/educ; Am Coun, cert, educ felsin acad admin; Atlanta Univ, MA, europ hist; Howard Univ, PhD, US hist. **Career:** Jarvis Christian Col, Hawkins, Tex, pres; Harford Community Col, Bel Air MD, dean arts & scis, 1990-93; Univ DC, provost & vpres acad affairs, 1993-96, actg pres, 1996-98, pres, 1998-2001, prof urban affairs. **Orgs:** Nat Asn Equal Opportunity, Washington, DC; trustee, Fed City Coun, DC; Wash Econ Coun, DC; Leadership Wash, DC; DC Pvt Indust Coun; DC Sch Careers Gov Coun; bd dir, DC Workforce Investment Coun. **Home Addr:** 3520 Rittenhouse St NW, Washington, DC 20015. **Business Addr:** Professor of Urban Affairs, University of the District of Columbia, 4200 Conn Ave NW, Washington, DC 20008, **Business Phone:** (202)274-5000.

**NISSEL, ANGELA**
Writer, television producer. **Personal:** Born Dec 5, 1978, Philadelphia, PA; daughter of Jack and Gwen. **Educ:** Univ Pa, BA, med anthrop, 1998. **Career:** Okayplayer.com, co-founder, site mgr, 1999; TV series: "Scrubs", staff writer, co-producer, 2002; "Til Death", consult producer, writer, 2010; "The Boondocks", consulting producer, writer, 2014; "New York Goes to Hollywood", consult. Books: The Broke Diaries: The Completely True & Hilarious Misadventures of a Good Girl Gone Broke, 2001; Mixed: My Life in Black & White, 2006; c/o Author Mail, Author & Television writer, Currently. **Business Addr:** Author, Television writer, c/o Author Mail, 299 Pk Ave, New York, NY 10171.

**NIVENS, BEATRYCE THOMASINIA.** **See Obituaries Section.**

**NIX, RICK (JAIME RICARDO)**
Administrator. **Personal:** Born Jan 6, 1950, Toledo, OH; son of Ulysesses S and Viola Crane (deceased); children: Noel. **Educ:** St Joseph's Col, Rensselaer, IN, BS, philos, 1972. **Career:** Ohio Civil Rights Comn, Toledo, Ohio, field rep, 1973; City Flint, Mich, mgt intern, 1974, community develop, 1975; Genesee Co, Flint, Mich, community coord specialist, 1974-75; Gen Motors Corp, Flint, Mich, inspector, 1976-82; Cath Diocese Saginaw, Mich, Off Black Cath Concerns, dir, Mission Off, assoc dir, 1982-. **Orgs:** Vice chmn, City-Wide Adv Comt Community Develop, 1974-; Nat Asn Black Cath Adminrs, Communs Comt, 1982-; Knights St Peter Claver, 1989-; founder & chmn, Black Fathers Day March Against Drugs & Crime, 1989-; co-chair & co-founder, First Ann Bridge Walk (Bridging Gap); United Saginaw Against Crime, 1993; pres & founder, Ministry Black Cath Men, 1995-; US Conf Cath Bishops; pres, Nat Ministry Black Cath Men; dir, Saginaw Cath diocese's Off Black Concerns. **Home Addr:** 5800 Weiss St, Saginaw, MI 58607, **Home Phone:** (517)797-6635. **Business Addr:** MI.

**NIX, DR. THEOPHILUS RICHARD, JR.**
Association executive, lawyer, government official. **Personal:** Born Oct 12, 1953, Washington, DC; son of Theophilus R (deceased) and Lulu Mae; married Myrtice Servance. **Educ:** Cincinnati Col Mortuary Sci, 1975; Ithaca Col, BFA, 1979; Howard Univ Sch Law, JD, 1982. **Career:** Funeral dir & embalmer; Bechtel Corp, sr contract formation specialist procurement; Boston Housing Authority, construct & contract atty; pvt pract, currently; EI Du Pont De Nemours & Co, corp coun, currently; Red Orange USA, gen coun & vpres develop, currently. **Orgs:** Philadelphia Contractors Asn, 1984-87; bd dir, Bd DE Contractors Asn, 1985-86; Philadelphia Barristers Asn, 1986-87; Nobles Mystic Mason Shrine; Am Arbit Asn; Nonprofit Develop Inst. **Home Addr:** 26 Bayes Hill Rd, PO Box 2298, Vineyard Haven, MA 02568, **Home Phone:** (508)693-8658. **Business Addr:** Corporate Counsel, E I du Pont de Nemours & Co, DuPont Bldg, Wilmington, DE 19805.

**NIXON, DR. HAROLD LEWIS**
Educator, administrator. **Personal:** Born May 31, 1939, Smithfield, NC; son of Mark A and Lizzie O; married Brenda Flint; children: Eric F & Leah. **Educ:** Fisk Univ, BS, biol, 1962; NC Cent Univ, MA, stud personnel, 1976; Univ NC, Chapel Hill, PhD, higher educ admin, 1988. **Career:** Food & Drug ADM, res biologist, 1963-64; Nat Inst Health, res biologist, 1966-69; Fayetteville State Univ, dir financial aid, 1969-80, assoc dean spec progs & stud life, 1980-83, vice chancellor stud develop, 1983-88; Wright State Univ, vpres stud affairs, pro edu, 1988; Urban Develop, partner, currently; Univ S Fla, vpres student affairs; Hln Enterprises LLC, pres. **Orgs:** Chr, legis comt, NCA Asn Fin Aid ADRs, 1975, pres, 1976; exe bd, Southern Asn Fin Aid ADRs, 1976; nat mem-at-large, Nat Asn Fin Aid ADRs, 1977; Nat Asn Stud Personnel ADRs, 1983-; Ohio Asn Stud Personnel ADRs, 1988-; Ohio Col Personnel Asn, 1988-; Mid-Western Res Asn, 1990-. **Home Addr:** 15916 Ellsworth Dr, Tampa, FL 33647-1326, **Home Phone:** (813)278-5054. **Business Addr:** Partner, Urban Development Partners, 8630 M Guilford Rd Suite 409, Columbia, MD 21046.

**NIXON, JAMES I., JR. (JIM NIXON)**
Executive, business owner, automotive executive. **Personal:** Born Jun 21, 1933, Pittsburgh, PA; son of James I Sr and Annie Forest; married LaRue Saunders Howard; children: GiAnna Watkins & Edward T IV; married Lea Young Hair; children: James I Nixon III, Danita Hair Brown, James Hair Jr & Janette Hair Dent. **Educ:** Carnegie-Mellon Univ, BS, mech engineering, 1956; Univ Cincinnati, 1959; Union Col, Schenectady, NY, nuclear plant technol & bus admin, 1964. **Career:** Gen Elec Corp, dist sales mgr, 1956-74; ITT Corp, vpres Equal Opportunity Opers, dir, 1974-87; N Am Venture Develop Group, founder, 1987-; Metrop Transp Authority, dir affirmative action, 1989-91; Inline Brake Mfg Corp, pres & chief exec officer, 1991-97; York Col, Queens, NY, adj prof; Beacon Partners Inc, managing dir, 1997-. **Orgs:** Bd mem, Nat Urban Affairs Coun, 1980-81; bd mem, Equal Employ Adv Coun, 1981-82; bd mem & chair policy comt, Asn Black Charities Inc, 1984-96; Urban Redevelop Comn Stamford, 1994-2012, pres, 2012; small bus adv coun, Fed Res Bank NY, 1995-97; regional adv bd, Bank Boston & Conn, 1997-; adv coun, Employ Policy Found; bd dir, Vis Nurse & Hospice Care; bd representatives, City Stamford. **Home Addr:** 337 Mayapple Rd, Stamford, CT 06903-1310, **Home Phone:** (203)329-3515. **Business Addr:** Managing Director, Beacon Partners Inc, 97 Libbey Pkwy Suite 310, Weymouth, MA 02189, **Business Phone:** (781)982-8400.

**NIXON, JAMES MELVIN**
Association executive. **Career:** C C, assoc exec prof dir. **Orgs:** Nat Ctr Youth Outreach Workers; Omega Psi Phi. **Home Addr:** 1700 Lansing Ave, Portsmouth, VA 23704, **Home Phone:** (757)393-6714.

**NIXON, NORMAN ELLARD**
Executive, basketball player. **Personal:** Born Oct 11, 1955, Macon, GA; son of Elmer and Mary Jo; married Debbie Allen; children: Vivian Nichole & Norm Jr. **Educ:** Duquesne Univ, attended 1977. **Career:** Basketball player (retired), Exec, Analyst; Los Angeles Lakers, 1978-83, San Diego Clippers, 1984, Los Angeles Clippers, 1985-86, 1989; Scavolini Pesaro, 1989; Nixon-Katz Assocs, personal mgr/sports agents; Ga Restaurant, owner; KABC-TV, analyst, 2005-07; FSN West, studio color analyst, currently; Debbie Allen Dance Acad, Culver City, Calif, founder. **Orgs:** Bd dir, MM VII Oper Hope, 1995-97. **Home Addr:** 4151 Prospect Ave, Hollywood, CA 90027, **Home Phone:** (310)557-7777. **Business Addr:** Studio Color Analyst, FSN West, 10000 Santa Monica Blvd, Los Angeles, CA 90067, **Business Phone:** (310)286-3800.

**NIXON, OTIS JUNIOR, JR.**
Baseball player, minister (clergy). **Personal:** Born Jan 9, 1959, Evergreen, NC; married Pebbles, Jan 1, 2000?, (divorced 2004); married Juanita Leonard, Dec 24, 1992; married Candi Staton, Jan 1, 2010, (divorced 2012). **Educ:** Mdiv. **Career:** Baseball player (retired), minister; New York Yankees, centerfielder, 1983; Cleveland Indians, centerfielder, 1984-87; Montreal Expos, centerfielder, 1988-90; Atlanta Braves, centerfielder, 1991-93, 1999; BostonRed Sox, centerfielder, 1994; Tex Rangers, centerfielder, 1995; Toronto Blue Jays, centerfielder, 1996-97; Los Angeles Dodgers, centerfielder, 1997; Minn Twins, centerfielder, 1998; On-Track Ministries, minister, currently. **Home Addr:** 3710 Vly NE, Sandy Springs, GA 30328, **Home Phone:** (770)837-0337. **Business Addr:** Minister, ON-Track Ministries, 61 Bill Wigington Pkwy Suite 101-102, Jasper, GA 30143, **Business Phone:** (770)987-6159.

**NKONYANSA, OSAFUHIN KWAKU.** **See PRESTON, GEORGE NELSON.**

**NNAJI, PROF. BARTHOLOMEW O.**
College teacher. **Personal:** Born Jul 13, 1956, Oruku Enugu; son of Emmanuel and Nev; married Patricia; children: Chik & Nev. **Educ:** St John's Univ, NY, BS, physics, 1980; Va Poly tech Inst & State Univ, MS, 1982, PhD, indust & systs engineering, 1983. **Career:** Univ Mass, asst prof, 1983-91, prof, 1991, dir & founder, automation & robotics lab, prof, mech & indust engineering, 1992; Fed Repub Nigeria, hon minister, 1993; Univ Pittsburgh, Mfg Eng, ALCOA found chair, 1996-2002; William Kepler Whiteford prof engr, 2002-07; Geom Power Ltd, chief exec officer & chmn, currently. **Orgs:** Fel, Int Soc Productivity Enhancement, 1994; sr mem, Inst Indust Eng; srmem, Soc Mfg Engrs; bd mem, Robotics Int; Am Inst Physics; dir, US Nat Sci Found Ctr, 2002-; founder, Geom Power Ltd. **Business Addr:** Chairman & Chairman, Chief Executive Officer, Geometric Power Ltd, 8 Mary Slessor St, Abuja23409.

**NNOLIM, CHARLES EKWUSIAGA**
Educator, association executive, writer. **Personal:** Born May 10, 1939, Umuchu; son of Lolo Ezelibe and Obidegwu; married Virginia Onwugigbo; children: Emeka, Chinyere, Amaeze & Azuka. **Educ:** Benedictine Col, Atchison, KS, BA, Eng, 1966; Bemidji State Univ, Bemidji, MN, MA, Eng, 1968; Cath Univ Am, Wash, DC, PhD, Eng, 1975. **Career:** St Brigid's Primary Sch, Ogui, Enugu, Nigeria, teacher, 1956-57; Holy Ghost Primary Sch, Ogui, Enugu, Nigeria, 1960-62; Ferris St Col, Big Rapids, MI, asst prof eng, 1969-70; Babson Col, Wellesley, MA, asst prof eng, 1970-76; Alvan Ikoku, Owerri, fac, sr lectr, 1976-78; Polytech, Owerri, Imo State, founding head-dept humanities & social sci, 1978-80; Univ Port Harcourt, Sch Humanities, Port Harcourt, Nigeria, Dept Eng Studies, founding head, 1980-82, prof eng lit, 1980, fac humanities, dean, 1997-99, 1999-2001, emer prof, currently; Ahmadu Bello Univ, vis prof eng, 1989-90; Imo State Univ, founding dean humanities & social sci & coord dean educ & legal studies, 1992-93; Univ Md Shore, vis prof eng, 1993-95. **Orgs:** African Lit Asn, 1974-; African Studies Asn; Mod Lang Asn Am; Nat Soc Lit & Arts; pres, Lit Soc Nigeria, 1986-; regional vpres, W African Sub-Region Lit Soc Nigeria, nt pres, 1986-2004; W African Asn Common wealth Lit & Lang Studies, 1988-; Univ Port Harcourt, Univ Port Harcourt Teaching Hosp; Univ Orator; African Lit Asn; W African Asn Commonwealth Lit & Lang Studies; Nigeria Acad Lett, 1998-; World Acad

Lett; fel World Lit Acad; fel Int Biog Asn; Int Who Who Intellectuals; 2000 Outstanding Scholars 21st Century; Men Achievement; Nat Soc Lit & Arts; Int Bk Honour; fel Nigerian Acad Lett. **Honors/Awds:** Doctoral Fellowship, Catholic Univ Am, 1968-72; Voted Dean of the Year, 1998; Nigerian National Order of Merit Award, 2006. **Special Achievements:** Author of Melville's Benito Cereno: A Study in Mng of Name-Symbolism, 1974, author of Pessimism in Conrad's Heart of Darkness, 1980, author of critical essays on African literature published in US and British journals, author of the book-Justice of the Jungle; Issues in African Literature, 2010; First and only Dean in the University of Port Harcourt; First Chairman, Board of Directors, College of Continuing Education. **Business Addr:** Professor Emeritus, University of Port Harcourt, East/West Rd, Rivers State00000, **Business Phone:** (208)03340-00.

### NOAH, LEROY EDWARD

Government official. **Personal:** Born Jul 25, 1934, Clarksdale, MS; son of Jesse and Lilliam Mae White; married Grace Fulghum; children: Sharon Davis, Carolyn Mann & Brenda. **Educ:** Forest Pk Community Col, AAS, 1975; Nat Inst Cosmetology, PhD, 1987. **Career:** Government official (retired); City Kinloch, pres, bd aldermen. **Orgs:** Pres, Sch Bd, 1963-75; financial secy, Assoc Hairdresser, Cosmetologist Mo, 1980-94; United Beautician, 1991-; first vpres, Sigma Nu Theta Fraternity; pres, United Beauticians, 1992-2000; pres, Assoc Hairdressers & Cosmetologist MO, 2001-; Nat Beauty Culturist League, 2003-. **Honors/Awds:** Citizen of the Year, Ward Chapel AME Church, 1981; Nat King, Nat Beauty CulturistLeague, 1987-88; Man of the Year, AssocHairdresser, Cosmetologist Mo, 1988-; Dr John Bryant Memorial Award, 1988. **Home Addr:** 11849 Northport Dr, Florissant, MO 63033-6736, **Home Phone:** (314)921-0021.

### NOAH, TREVOR

Comedian, actor, television show host. **Personal:** Born Feb 20, 1984, Johannesburg; son of Robert Noah and Patricia Noah. **Career:** Actor, 2002-; stand-up comedian, 2006-. TV series: "Isidingo", 2002; "Tonight with Trevor Noah", 2010-12; "The Tonight Show with Jay Leno", 2012; "Funny Business", 2013; "Comedy Up Late", 2013; "Late Show with David Letterman", 2013; "Totally Biased with W. Kamau Bell", 2013; "Trevor Noah: African American", 2013; "QI", 2013; "The Royal Variety Performance 2014", 2014; "The Daily Show", contributor, 2014-15, host, 2015-; "Trevor Noah: Nationwild Comedy Tour", 2015; "Red Nose Day", 2015; "Comedians in Cars Getting Coffee: Single Shot", 2015; "Trevor Noah: Lost in Translation", 2015. Films: "Trevor Noah: The Daywalker", 2009; "Trevor Noah: The Daywalker Revisited", 2010; "Trevor Noah: Crazy Normal", 2011; "You Laugh But It's True", 2011; "Taka Takata", 2011; "WROARF Public Service Announcement", 2011; "Mad Buddies", 2012; "Trevor Noah: That's Racist", 2012; "Trevor Noah: It's My Culture", 2013. Stage: "The Racist", Edinburgh Fringe, 2012. **Special Achievements:** Toured the world as a stand-up comedian; hosted numerous music, television, and film awards in South Africa; South African Comedy Festival, host; first South African stand-up comedian to appear on "The Tonight Show with Jay Leno" and "The Late Show with David Letterman".

### NOBLE, JOHN CHARLES

School administrator, school superintendent, association executive. **Personal:** Born Sep 21, 1941, Port Gibson, MS; married Colleen L; children: Michaelle, Leketha, Carlos, Tracy & Stephanie. **Educ:** Claiborne Co Training Sch, attended 1959; Alcorn State Univ, BS, 1962; Tenn A&I State Univ, MA, 1971; Jackson State Univ. **Career:** MS Chicago, teacher; Chicago, juv probation officer; Medgar Evers Comprehensive Health Ctr, dir res & eval; Opportunity Industrialization Ctr, instr; Claiborne County Pub Schs, supt educ. **Orgs:** Omega Psi Phi; Am Asn Sch Admins; fel Inst Polit; Rising Sun MB; chmn, Bd Trustees Hinds Jr Col; bd trustee, Utica Jr Col; advan ind instr, Dr Thomas Gordons Parent Effectiveness Training & Teacher EFfective Training; Claiborn Co Chap, Nat Asn Advan Colored People; Port Gibson Masonic Lodge 21; bd dir, Miss Action Prog; bd dir, Urban League LEAP Prog. **Home Addr:** 306 Anthony St, Port Gibson, MS 39150. **Business Addr:** Superintendent, Claiborne County Public Schools, PO Box 337, Port Gibson, MS 39150.

### NOBLE, JOHN PRITCHARD

Administrator, executive director. **Personal:** Born May 31, 1931, West Palm Beach, FL; son of Floyd Grafton and Aurelia; married Barbara Norwood; children: John Jr & Michael. **Educ:** Fla A&M Univ, BS, 1959; Columbia Univ NYC, MA, hosp admin, 1963; Cornell Univ, Ithaca, attended 1969. **Career:** Administrator (retired); Arabian Amer Oil Co Dhahran Saudi Arabia, hosp admin, 1962-69; Arabian Amer Oil Co, dir & chief exec officer, 1969-71; Forsyth Hosp Authority Winston-Salem, vpres, planning & develop, 1971-73; Homer G Phillips Hosp St Louis, admin, 1973-78; Acute Care Hosp City St Louis, dir, 1978-79; Dept Health & Hosp, City St Louis, hosp com; Lambert-St Louis Int Airport, asst dir. **Orgs:** Am Col Hosp Admins, 1965-; Am Pub Health Asn, 1976-; chmn, Nat Asn Health Serv Exec, 1978-80; bd mem, Family & Children Serv, 1977-; bd mem, King Fanon Mental Health, 1978-; life mem, Alpha Phi Alpha Frat; bd mem, Tower Village Nursing Home, 1978-; Nat Asn Guardsmen, 1994-; Sigma Pi Phi Frat, 1994-. **Honors/Awds:** Meritom Citation. **Home Addr:** 49 Kingsbury Pl, St Louis, MO 63112-1824, **Home Phone:** (314)367-6324. **Business Addr:** .

### NOBLE, REGINALD (REGGIE). See REDMAN, R.

### NOBLE, RONALD KENNETH

Educator, police officer, judge. **Personal:** Born Jan 1, 1956?, Ft. Dix, NJ; children: 1. **Educ:** Univ New Hampshire, BA, econ & bus admin, 1979; Stanford Univ, Law Sch, JD, 1982. **Career:** US Ct Appeals Third Circuit, law clerk judge, 1982-84; US Dept Justice, asst US atty & dep asst atty gen, 1984-89; NY Univ Law Sch, from asst prof to assoc prof, 1990-99, prof, 1999-, fac dir Root-Tilden-Kern scholar prog, currently; 26-nation Financial Action Task Force, pres; US Dept Treas, asst secy enforcement, undersecretary enforcement, 1993-96; Int Crim Police Orgn, chief; Interpol, 69th Gen Assembly, secy gen, 2000; Interpol, 70th Gen Assembly, secy gen, 2005-. **Orgs:** Int Crim Police Orgn Exec Comt; pres, 33-mem Financial Action Task Force. **Special Achievements:** First American to lead a 76 year old organization. **Business Addr:** Professor, New York University School of Law, 40 Wash Sq S 302B, New York, NY 10012, **Business Phone:** (212)998-6702.

### NOBLES, DR. PATRICIA JOYCE

Executive, lawyer. **Personal:** Born Jun 3, 1955, St. Louis, MO; daughter of Henry Stovall and Gwendolyn Bell Stovall. **Educ:** Southwest Baptist Col, BA, speech commun & rhet, 1976; Univ Alaska, JD, 1981. **Career:** Attorney (retired); US Dist Judge, law clerk, 1981-83; Southwestern Bell Tel Co, atty to sr atty to gen atty, 1983-2005; SBC Commun Inc, sr coun, 2000-05; SuperMedia LLC, proj contract mgr, 2006-07; Catalyst Corp FCU, asst gen coun, 2007-11; CHRISTUS Health, corp secy, 2012-15; J. Hilburn, style advisor, 2015-; Privately Pract, atty. **Orgs:** Exec bd, Urban League, 1981-84; Am Asn Trial Attys, 1983-87; Alaska Bar Asn, 1983-87; pres, Alaska Asn Women Lawyers, 1985-86; bd mem, KLRE Pub Radio Sta, 1986-87; Nat Advan Asn Colored People; Mo Bar Asn; Tex Bar Asn; bd mem, Literacy Instr Tex; CHRISTUS Health. **Honors/Awds:** Edwin Lightfoot Distinquished Alumni Award, Southwest Baptist Univ, 2005; Life Service Award, Southwest Baptist Univ, 2015. **Home Addr:** 7310 Lizshore Ave, Dallas, TX 75231, **Home Phone:** (214)221-2160. **Business Addr:** Style Advisor, J Hilburn Inc, 12700 Pk Cent Dr Suite 2000, Dallas, TX 75251, **Business Phone:** (866)789-5381.

### NOEL, DR. PATRICK ADOLPHUS. See Obituaries Section.

### NOGUERA, DR. PEDRO ANTONIO

Sociologist, educator. **Personal:** Born Aug 7, 1959, New York, NY; son of Felipe Carl and Millicent Yvonne Brooks; married Patricia Vattuone (deceased); children: Joaquin, Amaya, Antonio & Naima. **Educ:** Brown Univ, BA, sociol, hist, 1981, MA, sociol, 1982; Univ Calif, Berkeley, PhD, sociol, 1989. **Career:** Univ Calif, Berkeley, Dept Ethnic Studies, course instr, 1983-84, Dept Sociol, course instr, 1984-85, res specialist, 1985-86, asst to vice chancellor, 1988-89, coordr multicultural action team, 1989-90, asst prof, 1990-94, assoc prof, 1994-2000, dir Inst Study Social Chg, 1990-2000; Goldberg & Assocs, consult, 1985; S Berkeley Youth Proj, dir, 1985-86; City Berkeley, exec asst & mayor, 1986-88; Fulbright fel, 1987-88; Harvard Univ, Judith K Dimon prof, 2000-03; NY Univ, Steinhardt Sch Educ, prof teaching & learning, currently; Author: The Imperatives of Power: Political Change and the Social Basis of Regime Support in Grenada, 1997; City Schools and the American Dream, 2003; Unfinished Business: Closing the Achievement Gap in Our Nations Schools, 2006; The Trouble With Black Boy and Other Reflections on Race, Equity and the Future of Public Education, 2008; Creating the Opportunity to Learn: Moving from Research to Practice to Close the Achievement Gap with A. Wade Boykin, 2011; Schooling for Resilience: Improving the Life Trajectories of African American and Latino Boys, 2014. **Orgs:** Vpres, Berkeley Black Caucus, 1985-; bd mem, Daily Calif Newpaper, 1985-88; mem congressman, Dellums Exec Comt, 1986-; pres, Black Men United Chg, 1987-90; bd mem, YMCA, Berkeley, 1988-; bd dir, Berkeley Unified Sch Dist, 1990-94; pres, Caribbean Studies Asn, 2006; Am Sociol Asn; bd dir, S African Educ Fund; bd dir, S Berkeley Neighborhood Develop Corp; Caribbean Studies Asn; bd dir, Berkeley Community Found; pres, Berkeley Sch Bd Orgn; trustee, State Univ New York; bd dir, S African Educ Fund. **Home Addr:** 726 Broadway, New York, NY 10003, **Home Phone:** (510)653-3977. **Business Addr:** Professor of Teaching & Learning, New York University, 82 Wash Sq E, New York, NY 10003, **Business Phone:** (212)998-5787.

### NOLAN, DANIEL KAYE

School administrator, educator. **Personal:** Born May 20, 1949, Newbern, TN; married Margaret M; children: Richard A Owens, Kyra D & Daniel M. **Educ:** Ball State Univ Admin; Butler Univ, BSEd; St Frances Univ, MS Coun. **Career:** S side High Sch, guid counr, 1974-79; YMCA, br exec, 1979-89; Magnavox Corp, eng coordr, 1989-93; NBS-Imaging, purchasing mgr, 1993-93; FWCS, vice prin, 1993-95, admin intern, 1995; Elmhurst High Sch, asst prin, 2006; Northrup High Sch, counr & spec assignment adminr, 1996-, asst prin, currently. **Orgs:** Omega Psi Phi. **Honors/Awds:** Omega Man of the Year, 1999. **Home Addr:** 7001 Coldwater Rd, Ft Wayne, IN 46806, **Home Phone:** (260)744-9302. **Business Addr:** Assistant Principal, Northrop High School, 7001 Coldwater Rd, Ft Wayne, IN 46825, **Business Phone:** (260)467-2329.

### NOLAN, DEANNA (DEANNA TWEETY NICOLE NOLOAN)

Basketball player. **Personal:** Born Aug 25, 1979, Flint, MI; daughter of Philip Murray (deceased) and Virginia. **Educ:** Ga Univ, BA, child & family develop, 2001. **Career:** Detroit Shock, guard & forward, 2001-09; Ekaterinburg club, 2009-10. **Business Addr:** Basketball Player, Detroit Shock, 6 Championship Dr, Auburn Hills, MI 48326, **Business Phone:** (248)377-0100.

### NOLES, EVA MALINDA. See Obituaries Section.

### NOLOAN, DEANNA TWEETY NICOLE. See NOLAN, DEANNA.

### NOONAN, DR. ALLAN S.

Dean (education), physician, administrator. **Personal:** Born Dec 10, 1942, Providence, RI; son of Herbert and Agnes; married Martha Prescod. **Educ:** Tufts Univ Sch Med, MD, 1968. **Career:** Pub health progs, developer & implementor; Ny Health Dept, assoc comnr; Commonwealth Univ, Pa, secy health, chief health officer; Morgan State Univ, Sch Pub Health & Policy, prof & dean, 2005-12; Dept Health DC, dir, chief health officer; US Pub Health Serv, Off Surgeon Gen, sr advisor, 2005-12; six Midwestern states, pub health serv progs, reg health adminr & asst surgeon gen. **Orgs:** US Public Health Service. **Home Addr:** 603 Nicholas Lane, Cockeysville, MD 21030-1326, **Home Phone:** (410)785-1919. **Business Addr:** Professor, Dean School Public Health & Policy, Morgan State University, 1700 E Cold Spring Lane, Baltimore, MD 21251, **Business Phone:** (443)885-3238.

### NORFLEET, JANET

Postmaster general. **Personal:** Born Aug 14, 1933, Chicago, IL; daughter of Willis Richards and Blanche Gilbert Richards; married Junious; children: Cedric Williams. **Educ:** Olive Harvey Col, AA, 1977; Duke Univ, FUQA Sch Bus, exec develop prog, 1998; Univ Va Grad Sch Bus Admin, Prog Postal Exec, 1988; Chicago State Univ, BA, 1997. **Career:** Postmaster general (retired); US Postal Serv, supt customer serv reps, customer relations officer, pub affairs officer, mgr retail sales & serv, mgr delivery & collection, mgr N Suburban Ill mgt sect ctr, field div mgr, postmaster S Suburban Ill div, 1986-87; field div gen mgr; postmaster Chicago Ill Div, 1987-90. **Orgs:** Bd dir, Carson Pirie Scott & Co, 1988-; bd mem, Red Cross; bd mem, Fed Exec; Chmn's Leadership Group, Nat Asn Advan Colored People. **Honors/Awds:** Partnership For Progress Award Postmaster General TISCH, 1986; Appointment Congressional Records by Congressman Savage, 1987; Proclamation by Mayor Washington Janet Norfleet Day in Chicago, 1987; American Black Achievement Award, Bus & Prof, Johnson Publ, 1987; African-American Award, Bus & Prof Women, Dollars & Sense Mag, 1989; Women's Hall of Fame, City of Chicago, 1990. **Special Achievements:** First Woman Postmaster of the US Postal Service Chicago Div, 1987. **Home Addr:** 8217 S Evans Ave, Chicago, IL 60619-5305, **Home Phone:** (773)224-9442.

### NORMAN, BOBBY DON

Artist, geologist. **Personal:** Born Jun 5, 1933, Dallas, TX; son of Ruben and Bessie Taylor Gregory; children: Parette Michelle Barnes. **Educ:** San Francisco City Col, attended 1951; USAF, Radio Electronics Tech, attended 1955; SW Sch Bus Admin, cert, 1959. **Career:** Artist, writer & scientist, 1955-; Mile High Club Restaurant & Cabins, gen mgr, 1955-57; D H Byrd Properties, property mgr, 1957-65; US Post Serv, city distro clerk, 1959-66; Univ Chicago-Dallas, Nat Opinion Res Ctr, field eval researcher, 1969-70; AAAW Inc Cult Gallery, dir, 1972; SCLC Dallas, Tex, co-founder, off mgr & co-dir, 1970-72; Planned Parenthood NETex, community liaison, 1974-76; Davis Norman Zanders Inc, vpres & gen mgr, 1976-77, exec vpres, 1977-78; Halfway House Tex Dept Corrections, supvr, 1983-84; free-lance artist & inventor anti-collision car; bibl geologist, 1987-; self-employed tectonic analyst, 1988-; Bks: 500 Shaft Tbl-Sports, 1973; Time Babel: Bibl Geol & Tectonics, 1998; Bibl Geol & Tectonics, 1998; Tectonic Analyses & Notes Mod Bibl Geol & Earth Sci, 1998; Tectonic Fundamentals Bibl Geol, 1998; Tectonic Verbal Posturing & Var Advan Studies Earth Sci, 1998; Relig Art & Artistic Evangelism, 1998; Glossary & Cross Ref Bibl Geol & Tectonics, 1999; Bibl Geol: Events, Writings & Geo-Morality, 2003. **Orgs:** Vpres, Forest Lakes Sportsmans Club; hunter safety instr, NRA, 1963; pres & founder, Asn Advancing Artists & Writers, 1969-74; Citizenship training, SCLC, 1969; founder & off mgr, Southern Christian Leadership Conf DallasBr, 1969-73; comnr, Greater Dallas Comm Rels Comn, 1970-73; organizer & tech consult, Greater DFW Coalition FFI, 1971-74; alumnus Chi Rho Int Bus Fraternity; comtman, Block Partnership Comm Greater Dallas Coun Churches, 1971-72; serv, GDCRC, 1973; fine arts, Dallas Black Chamber Com, 1973; Int Platform Asn Pub Speakers, 1977-78. **Honors/Awds:** Citizenship Training Award, SCLC, 1969; Art Award, Dallas Black Chamber Commerce, 1973. **Special Achievements:** Author: 500 Shaft Table-Sports, 1973; Artistic Theological Science, 1998; Biblical Geology, 1998. **Home Addr:** 2802 N Carroll Ave Apt 1308, Dallas, TX 75204-3064, **Home Phone:** (214)534-2584. **Business Addr:** Artist, Art Religious, PO Box 191904, Dallas, TX 75219-8509.

### NORMAN, CHRISTINA

Chief executive officer. **Educ:** Boston Univ, film prod. **Career:** MTV Networks, prod mgr, 1991-97, sr vpres, Mkt & On-Air Promotions, 1997-2002, pres, 2005-08; VH1, exec vpres & gen mgr, 2002-05; MTV Networks, pres, 2005-08; OWN: Oprah Winfrey Network, chief exec officer, 2009-11; Water Cooler Group LLC, chief exec officer, 2015- . **Orgs:** Mt Sinai Adolescent Health Ctr Adv Bd; BRIC Arts Media Brooklyn Bd. **Business Addr:** Chief Executive Officer, Water Cooler Group LLC, 99 Wash St S Norwalk, Norwalk, CT 06854, **Business Phone:** (203)299-0802.

### NORMAN, CLIFFORD P.

Executive. **Personal:** Born Mar 22, 1943, Detroit, MI; son of Leavi and Claudia Cloud; married Pauline C Johnson; children: Jays S & Rebecca L. **Educ:** Wayne State Univ, BA, 1974, MA, 1980. **Career:** Fisher Body Div GM, engr test, 1967-71, sr analyst qc, 1971-72, sr serv & tool spec, 1972-74, div process engr, 1974-76; Ford Motor Co, div staff engr, 1976-80; Glasurit Amer Inc, acct exec; BASF Corp, acct exec, mkt coordr, currently. **Orgs:** ESD, 1975-; Soc Engr & Appl Scis, 1975-82; Budget & Allocation Comn, UCS, Detroit, 1981-84, 1995-; u-f Speakers Bur, 1985-; exec comt, Metro Detroit, Big Bros Big Sisters, 2000-, Region IV, pres, 2000-. **Home Addr:** 19703 Steel Rd, Detroit, MI 48235-1151, **Home Phone:** (313)341-2425. **Business Addr:** Marketing Coordinator, BASF Corp, 26701 Tel Rd, Southfield, MI 48034-2442, **Business Phone:** (248)304-5771.

### NORMAN, GEORGETTE M.

Educator. **Personal:** Born Jan 27, 1946, Montgomery, AL; daughter of George J Jr and Thelma Juliette Graham. **Educ:** Fisk Univ, Nashville, TN, BA, hist, 1967; Hampton Inst, Hampton, VA, MA, educ, 1970; Univ Miami, cert humanistic educ. **Career:** Troy Univ Rosa Parks Museum, dir; Auburn Univ, Dept Communication & Dramatic Arts Montgomery, adj instr. **Orgs:** Leadership Montgomery Alumni Asn, 1987-2014; bd dir, chair, Homeowner Asn Montgomery Habitat Humanity, 1987-2014; panel mem, Lit & Rural Initiative Ala State Coun Arts, 1988-2014; bd dir, secy, Springtree/Snowhill Inst for Performing Arts, 1991; adv bd, multicultural chair, Armory Learning Ctr for performing Arts, 1991; founder, Am Arts Alliance, 1992-99; dir, Ala Mus Asn. **Home Addr:** 1273 Rosa Parks, Montgomery, AL 36108-3070, **Home Phone:** (334)263-3210. **Business Addr:** Director, Troy University Rosa Parks Museum, 252 Montgomery St, Montgomery, AL 36103-4419, **Business Phone:** (334)241-8615.

### NORMAN, JAMES H.
Administrator. **Personal:** Born Aug 14, 1948, Augusta, GA; son of Silas Sr (deceased) and Janie M King (deceased); children: James H Jr. **Educ:** Mercer Univ, Macon, Ga, BA, psychol, 1970; Western Mich Univ, Kalamazoo, MSW, 1972; leadership & exec coaching cert, 2009. **Career:** Western Mich Univ, Full Univ Grad fel, 1970-72; Douglass Community Asn, Kalamazoo, Mich, coordr job develop & placement, 1972-74; Kalamazoo Mich Pub Schs, parent consult, 1974-75; Oakland Livingston Human Serv, Pontiac, Mich, div mgr community develop, 1974-78; Mich Dept Labor, dir bur community serv, 1978-87, dep dir, 1987-92; Action Better Community Inc, exec dir, pres & chief exec officer, 1992-; Monroe Community Col, adj fac, 1999-; Rochester Inst Technol, Distinguished Minett Prof, 2010-11. **Orgs:** Chmn & legis comn chair, Nat Asn State Community Serv Prog, 1981-82 &1985-87; exec secy, Mich Econ & Social Opp Comn, 1983-87; Am Soc Pub Admin, 1984-; Assoc State Govt Execs, 1986-92; Nat Coun State Bldg Code Officials, 1988-90; Int Asn Personnel Employ Security, 1988-90; bdmem, Mich Asn Black Orgn, 1988-92; Greater Lansing Urgan League, 1989-92; adv coun mem, EOC, State Univ New York, 1993-; adv coun, Leadership Rochester, 1993-; life mem, Nat Asn Advan Colored People; Asn Black Social Workers; Phi Mu Alpha Nat Music Frat; Omega Psi Phi Frat Inc; life mem, Western Mich Univ Alumni Asn; ABC Found Bd; Ny Community Action Asn Bd. **Honors/Awds:** Community Service Award, Nat Alliance Businessmen, 1973 & 1974; Outstanding Young Man of America, US Jaycees Pub, 1978 & 1979; Hall of Distinction, Western Mich Univ, 1980; Service Award, Nat Asn State Community Serv Prog, 1983. **Home Addr:** 103 Rosebud Trail, Webster, NY 14580-2571. **Business Addr:** President, Chief Executive Officer, Action For a Better Community Inc, 550 E Main St, Rochester, NY 14604, **Business Phone:** (585)325-5116.

### NORMAN, JESSYE MAE
Opera singer. **Personal:** Born Sep 15, 1945, Augusta, GA; daughter of Silas Sr and Janie King. **Educ:** Howard Univ, BM, 1967; Peabody Conserv Music, attended 1967; Univ Mich, MMus, 1968. **Career:** Deutsch Opera, Berlin, debut, 1969; Deutsch Opera, Italy, 1970; Opera: Die Walkure, Idomeneo, L'Africaine, Marriage of Figaro, Aida, Don Giovanni, Tannhauser, Gotterdammerung, Ariadne auf Naxos, Les Troyens, Dido & Aeneas, Oedipus Rex; La Scala Milan, Italy, 1972; Hollywood Bowl, US debut, 1972; Salzburg Festival, 1977; appeared with Tanglewood Festival MA, Edinburgh, Scotland Festival; Covent Garden, 1972; appeared in first Great Performers Recital Lincoln Ctr, New York, 1973; guest performances: LosAngeles Philharmonic Orch, Boston Symphony Orch, Am Symphony Orch, Chicago Symphony Orch, San Fran Symphony Orch, Cleve Orch, Detroit Symphony, New York Philharmonic Orch, London Symphony Orch, London Philharmonic Orch, BBC Orch, Israel Philharmonic Orch, Orchestre de Paris, National Symphony Orch Australia; Das Lied von der Erde; Albums: Brava, Jessye!; Sacred Song: "With a Song in My Heart"; "Christmastide", 1990; "Amazing Grace", 1991; "Jessye Norman at Notre Dame", 1991; "Lucky to Be Me", 1992; "In the Spirit", 1996; "Jessye Norman", 1999; "I Was Born in Love With You", 2000; Soundtrack: Revolution francaise, La, 1989; Wild at Heart, 1990; The Hours, 2002. **Orgs:** Gamma Sigma Sigma; Sigma Alpha Iota Pi Kappa Lambda; Royal Acad Music. **Honors/Awds:** Numerous recordings Columbia, EMI, Philips Records; recip first Prize Bavarian Radio Corp Intl Music Competitor; Grand Prix du Disque Deutsch Schallplatten; Preis Alumniat MI, 1982; Musician of the Year, High Fidelity Musical/America, 1982; Outstanding Musician of the Year Award, Musical Am, 1982; 5 Grand Prix du Disque, Acad du Disque Francais; thirty hon doctorates from col & universities, decorations and distinctions from governments around the world including Hon Doctor Music, Howard Univ, 1982; Grand Prix du Disque, Academie Charles Cros, 1983; hon Doctor Humane Letters, Am Univ Paris, 1989; Honorary Doctorate Music, Cambridge Univ, 1989; Hon fel, Newnham Col, Cambridge, 1989; Honorary Fellow, Jesus Col, Cambridge, 1989; Grammy Awards for Best Opera Recording for Wagner: Lohengrin, 1984; Grammy Award for Best Classical Vocal Soloist Performance for Ravel: Songs of Maurice Ravel, 1988; appointment in 1990 as an hon United Nations ambassador; Women of the Arts Award, Coun Fashion Designers Am, 1992; Youngest Recipient of the US Kennedy Ctr Honor, 1997; Awarded hon doctorate for services to music from the Univ PA, 1998; Grammy Award for Best Opera Recording for "Bartok: Bluebeard's Castle, 1998; Georgia Music Hall of Fame, 1999; Outstanding Alumnae by Howard Univ, 2000; Eleanor Roosevelt Val-Kill Medal, 2000; Hammond Award, 2002; Grammy Lifetime Achievement Award, 2006; Named in honor, The Amphitheatre & Plz, Augusta, GA; Ace Award, Nat Acad Cable Programming; Amsterdam's Edison Prize; National Medal of Arts, 2009; Edison Award; Ace Award, Nat Cable Tv Asn; National Medal of Arts, 2010; Honorary Doctorate, Northwestern Univ, 2011; Received honorary doctorates from more than 30 colleges, universities; Spingarn Award, Nat Asn Advan Colored People, 2013. **Special Achievements:** The youngest recipient of the US Kennedy Ctr Honor, 1997; In Augusta, Georgia, the Amphitheatre and Plaza overlooking the tranquil Savannah River have been named for Jessye Norman; Houghton Mifflin Harcourt, 2014. **Home Addr:** , NY. **Business Addr:** Opera Singer, Grabow Entertainment, 4219 Creekmeadow Dr, Dallas, TX 75287-6806, **Business Phone:** (972)250-1162.

### NORMAN, KENNETH DARNEL (KEN NORMAN)
Basketball player. **Personal:** Born Sep 5, 1964, Chicago, IL. **Educ:** Wabash Valley Col, attended 1983; Univ Ill Urbana-Champaign, attended 1987. **Career:** Basketball player (retired); Illini Men's Basketball All-Century Team, 1985-87; Los Angeles Clippers, forward, 1987-93; Milwaukee Bucks, 1993-94; Atlanta Hawks, 1994-97. **Home Addr:** 19020 Kedzie Ave, Homewood, IL 60430-4359.

### NORMAN, DR. MOSES C., SR.
Educator. **Educ:** Clark Col, BA, 1957; Univ Mich, MA, eng lang & lit, 1963; Ga State Univ, PhD, educ leadership & mgt, 1978. **Career:** Luther Judson Price High Sch, eng dept chair, humanities proj leader, area supt & asst supt sec educ; Clark Atlanta Univ, dir alumni rels, Sch Educ, assoc prof & chmn educ leadership, currently; MASTER Inst, assoc dir, currently. **Orgs:** Grand basileus, Omega Psi Phi, Wash, DC, 1984-88; bd mem, Am Asn Sch Adminr. **Business Addr:** Associate Professor, Chair, Clark Atlanta University School of Education, Rufus E Clement Hall 317 223 James P Brawley Dr SW, Atlanta, GA 30314, **Business Phone:** (404)880-8495.

### NORMAN, DR. PHILLIP ROOSEVELT
Dentist, air force officer. **Personal:** Born Sep 8, 1933, Mound Bayou, MS; son of Oscar Clifton and Phillipa L'Estrange; married DeLois Williams; children: Philippa J & David W. **Educ:** Tougaloo Col, BS, 1955; Meharry Med Col, DDS, 1959. **Career:** Va Hosp Tuskeegee, rotating dent internship; Pvt Pract, dentist; Babe Ruth League, baseball coach; Mound Bayou Community Hosp, dent consult; Frances Nelson Health Ctr, adv consult; Union Med Ctr Dent Serv, co-dir; Gen Dent Malcom Grow Reg Med Ctr USAF, officer in-chg; Sheppard AFB TX, prev dent officer; Misawa AFB Japan, air base oral surg. **Orgs:** Nat Dent Asn; Am Dent Asn; Acad Gen Dent; Am Soc Prev Dent; Lone Star Masonic Lodge; Am Endodontic Soc; Mil Surgeons Asn; LicensedPrac Ill, TX, DC, Md, NH, Pa, Miss; Omega Psi Phi Frat; Champaign Co C C; Neighborhood Comdr Boy Scouts Am; Career Couning HS; bd dir, Boys Club Am Champaign Co; Univ Dent Res Team; Sigma Xi Chap Omega Psi; Air Nat Guard Res. **Home Addr:** 501 S 6th St Suite 207, Champaign, IL 61820. **Business Addr:** DENTIST, PO Box 2808, Champaign, IL 61820.

### NORMAN, WALLACE
Controller, manager. **Personal:** Born Jan 1, 1961, Atlanta, GA. **Educ:** Univ Ga, polit sci, MBA, finance; Ga State Univ, master's prog, acct. **Career:** Fed Express, assoc financial analyst; Atlanta Falcons, asst treas, controller, payroll & benefits mgr, 1989-. **Honors/Awds:** First minority controller, Nat Football League. **Business Addr:** Payroll & Benefits Manager, Atlanta Falcons, Suwanee Rd & I-85, Flowery Branch, GA 30542, **Business Phone:** (770)965-3115.

### NORMAN, DR. WILLIAM H.
Psychologist. **Personal:** Born Dec 14, 1946, Sharon, PA; married Belinda Ann Johnson; children: Monica & Michael. **Educ:** Youngstown State Univ, BA, 1968; Howard Univ, MS, 1971; Penn State Univ, PhD, 1975. **Career:** Duke Univ Med Ctr, psychol internship, 1974-75; Butler Hosp, dir psychol consult prog, 1976-93, dir psychol, 1982-91, coordr, eating dis prog, 1987-; Brown Univ Internship Consortium, coordr adult clin psychol track comn, 1983-92; Brown Univ Med Sch, assoc prof psychiat & human behav, 1986-. **Orgs:** Am Psychol Asn, 1975-; Asn Advan Behav Ther, 1975-; Soc Psychother Res, 1986-. **Honors/Awds:** Reviewer for several journals; J Abnormal Psychol & J Consulting & Clin Psychol; Master Arts ad eundem, Brown Univ, 1987; recipient/co-recipient, NIH grants, 1979, 1981, 1983, 1990, 1992. **Home Addr:** 580 Ten Rod Rd, North Kingstown, RI 02852-4220, **Home Phone:** (401)294-6170. **Business Addr:** Coordinator, Butler Hospital, 345 Blackstone Blvd, Providence, RI 02906, **Business Phone:** (401)455-6200.

### NORMAN, WILLIAM STANLEY
Executive, president (organization), chief executive officer. **Personal:** Born Apr 27, 1938, Roper, NC; son of James Colbitt and Josephine Cleo Woods; married Elizabeth Patricia Patterson; children: Lisa Renee & William Stanley II. **Educ:** WVa Wesleyan Univ, BS, chem & math, 1960; Am Univ, MA, int rel, 1967; Stanford Univ Grad Sch Bus, exec prog, 1976. **Career:** Exec (retired); Wash High Sch, Norfolk, Va, teacher, mathematics, 1961; Cummins Engine Co Inc, Columbus, Ind, dir corp action, 1973-74, exec dir corp responsibility, 1974-76, exec mkt mgr, 1976-77, exec dir distrib & mkt, 1977-78, vpres eastern div, 1978-79; Amtrak, Nat RR Passenger Corp, Wash, DC, vpres sales & mkt, 1979-81, group vpres, 1981-84, exec vpres, 1984-94; Travel Indust Asn Am, Wash, DC, pres & chief exec officer, 1994-2005. **Orgs:** Bd dir, USN Mem Found, 1980-2003; bd dir, Travel Indust Asn Am, 1980, bd chmn, 1987-89, chmn, bd dir found, 1990-92; bd dir, UN Asn US, 1983, bd gov, 1985; bd adv, Am Univ Kogod Col Bus Admin, 1990; Int Consortium Health Effects Radiation, 1993-2003; An-Bryce Found, 1993; bd dir, Best Foods Inc, 1993; bd trustee, chmn, Logistics Mgt Inst, 1993; bd dir, An-Bryce Found, 1994; bd trustee, Wva Wesleyan Col, 1996; bd dir, Corn Prod Int Inc, 1997. **Home Addr:** 1308 Timberly Lane, Mc Lean, VA 22102-2504.

### NORMENT, LYNN AURELIA
Editor, writer, media executive. **Personal:** Born Feb 14, 1952, Bolivar, TN; daughter of Alex and Esther Morrow. **Educ:** Univ Memphis, BA, jour, 1973. **Career:** Com Appeal, gen assignment reporter, relig ed & investigative reporter, 1973-77; Johnson Publ Co, managing ed; Ebony Mag, mem ed bd, managing ed, sr writer, photog producer, 1977-2009; Carol H Williams Advert, writer, ed, media consult, events planner, 2009-12; Publicity Club Chicago, panelist; Lynn Norment Media, journalist, writer, ed, events planner, media rels, pres, 2012-. **Orgs:** Vpres print, Nat Asn Black Journalists, chair, 2009-, bd mem; Beta Club; bd mem, Habilitative Systs Inc; Nat Asn Black Journalists; chair, Nat Asn Black Journalists Develop Comt, 2009-; chair, Nat Asn Black Journalists Hall Fame Reception & Induction Ceremony Newseum Wash, DC 2011; nat bd mem, Nat Asn Black Journalists; chaired, Nat Asn Black Journalists 25th Anniversary Celebration 2000; chair, Nat Asn Black Journalists Conv Chicago 1997; bd mem, Nat Asn Black Journalists Chicago; co-chair, Nat Asn Black Journalists Chicago Prog Comt; Habilitative Systs Inc; adv bd, Columbia Links, currently. **Home Phone:** (312)427-3121. **Business Addr:** Managing Editor, Ebony Magazine, 820 S Mich Ave, Chicago, IL 60605, **Business Phone:** (312)322-9200.

### NORRELL-NANCE, ROSALIND ELIZABETH
Government official. **Personal:** Born May 17, 1950, Atlantic City, NJ; daughter of Albert V Norrell Jr and Vivian M Rhoades-Norrell; married Nelson W; children: Kimberly, Alisha, Nelson Jr, Antonio, Noel & Patrick. **Educ:** Hampton Inst, 1969; Atlantic Comm Col, AS, 1976; Glassboro State Col, BA, 1978. **Career:** Pleasantville Sch Dist, educr, 1976-84; City Atlantic City, mayoral aide, 1984-90; Atlantic City Pub Sch, Drug & Weapon Free Schs Prog, 1991-96; Atlantic City, councilwoman, 1992-, pres, 1994-2000; Atlanticare Family Ctr, dir, 1997; State NJ, Dept Educ, AtlantiCare Behav Health Family Centers, proj dir, currently. **Orgs:** Exec bd/youth adv, Atlantic City Nat Asn Advan Colored People, 1969-95; bd dir, Atlantic Human Resources Inc, 1981-97; Nat Sorority Phi Delta Kappa Delta Lambda Chap, 1982-; govt affairs chairperson, 101 Women Plus, 1982-85; bd dir, Minority Entrepreneur Develop Co, 1984-85; bd dir, United Way S Jersey, 1984-85; vpres, bd dir, Inst Human Develop; NJ State Bus & Prof Women; bd dir, Atlantic Human Resources; chairperson, Atlantic County Comprehensive Network Task Force Homeless Serv; Atlantic City Pub Rel Adv Bd; Nat Coun Colored Women's Clubs; bd dir, Atlantic Community Concerts, 1984-87; bd dir, Atlantic City Coastal Mus, 1985-89; Ruth Newman Shapiro Cancer Fund; bd dir, Atlantic City Local Assistance; Healthy Mothers/Healthy Babies Coalition Atlantic City Hampton Alumni Asn; pres, mayor's youth adv bd, chair educ task force Cong Black Caucus; NJ State Div Youth & Family Servs Adv bd, 1985-; bd dir, Atlantic County Transp Authority, 1986-92; bd dir, Coalition 100 Black Women, 1987-; bd dir, Black United Fund, NJ, 1987; Atlantic County Red Cross, 1988-92; Atlantic City Drug Alliance, 1990-; founder, Atlantic County Welfare Mothers Support Group, 1992-; Atlantic County Human Serv Adv Bd; Atlantic City Inc, 1994-; Links Inc, 1995-; Uptown Family Ctr. **Honors/Awds:** Community Service Award, W Side Parent Adv Coun, 1976; Outstanding Leadership Award, Black Atlantic City Mag, 1983; Phi Delta Kappa-Leadership, NJ Div Youth & Family Serv, 1995; Dr Martin Luther King Award, 2006. **Special Achievements:** First women City Council President in the history of Atlantic City. **Home Addr:** 101 Cherry Dr, Egg Harbor Township, NJ 08234-5344, **Home Phone:** (609)677-1340. **Business Addr:** Project Director, Atlanticare Behavioral Health, Uptown School Complex 323 Madison Ave, Atlantic City, NJ 08401, **Business Phone:** (609)345-1994.

### NORRELL-THOMAS, SONDRA L.
Athletic director, teacher. **Personal:** Born May 31, 1941, Richmond, VA; daughter of Faith Morris Norrell and Edinboro A Norrell; married Chauncey S. **Educ:** Hampton Inst, BS, phys educ & biol, 1961; Howard Univ, MS, 1973. **Career:** Charlottesville Schs, teacher 1961-63; Richmond Pub Schs, teacher, 1963-64; Howard Univ, teacher 1964-77, womens athletics coordr, 1972, assoc dir athletics, 1974-86, asst athletic dir, exec asst to vpres stud affairs, 1986-2000, dir athletics, 2000, interim athletics dir, exec asst to vpres Stud Affairs, sr womens adminr athletics, dir athletics, 2001-04, swimming coach. **Orgs:** Spec Comn Womens Interest Nat Col Athletic Asn, 1983-86, 1995-96; coun, Nat Col Athletic Asn, 1983-87; Div I Steering Comt, Nat Col Athletic Asn, 1983-87; spec liaison, 1983-, chair SWAs, consult, coun pres & chancellors, Mid Eastern Athletic Conf; pres, Capital City Chap, Links Inc, 1987-89; Nat Col Athletic Asn Coun, 1995-99; Alpha Kappa Alpha Sor; Just Good Friends Inc; HUAA; Nat Coun Negro Women; Nat Asn Advan Colored People; United Way Dist Columbia Bd; Acad-Eligibility &Compliance Cabinet & Nat Col Athletic Asn; Championships & Competition Cabinet, Nat Col Athletic Asn1997-2000; nominating comt, Nat Asn Col Women Athletic Adrs. **Special Achievements:** First female to be inducted into the Mid-Eastern Athletic Conference Hall of Fame; First female member of the Mid-Eastern Athletic Conference that selected the conferences first full-time commissioner. **Home Addr:** 1611 Webster St NW, Washington, DC 20011, **Home Phone:** (202)726-5647.

### NORRIS, REV. CHARLES L., SR.
Clergy. **Personal:** Born Aug 14, 1926, Williston, SC; married Ruby Dent; children: Keith Alexander & Charles Jr. **Educ:** Nat Theol Sem, BS, 1979, MDiv, 1984; Blanton Peale Inst, cert coun. **Career:** Pastor (retired); Kitchen Modernization, prod mgr, 1950-69; Bethesda Missionary Baptist Church, pastor, 1973, sr pastor. **Orgs:** New York Mission Soc Urban Ministries, 1981-; United Negro Col Fund Clergy Consortium, Queens County, 1985-; co-chair, Concerned Citizens S Queens, 1986-; City New York Comn Human Rights, 1993-; vice moderator, Eastern Baptist Asn, Long Island Inc; dir, United Black Men Queens County Inc; exec secy, Clergy United Community Empowerment, currently. **Honors/Awds:** Leadership & Dedication Award, Inwood-Nassau Community Health Comt, 1981; Outstanding Clergy Award, Nat Asn Negro Bus & Prof Women Queens Borough Club, 1983; Meritorious Service Award, 1985; Outstanding Leadership & Dedicated Service, 1986; United Negro College Fund. **Home Addr:** 831 Meechan Ave, Far Rockaway, NY 11691, **Home Phone:** (718)327-1557. **Business Addr:** Co-chair, Concerned Citizens of Southern Queens, 40-06 Warren St, Elmhurst, NY 11373, **Business Phone:** (718)478-1600.

### NORRIS, DR. DONNA MARIE
Psychiatrist. **Personal:** Born May 28, 1943, Columbus, OH; married Lonnie H; children: Marlaina & Michael. **Educ:** Fisk Univ, Nashville, BA, 1964; Ohio State Univ, Col Med, MD, 1969. **Career:** Mt Carmel Med Ctr, Columbus, Ohio, intern, 1969-70; Boston Univ Med Ctr, resident, 1970-72; Mass Rehab Community Roxbury & Quincy MA, psychol consult, 1974-79; pvt pract psychiat, 1974-; Childrens Hosp Med Ctr, Boston, med staff, 1974-, asst psychiat, 1974-82, attend psychiatrist, 1981-94, sr assoc psychiat, 1983-2006, adj fac, dept psychiat, 2006; Boston Juv Ct Clin, sr psychol, 1974-88; Judge Baker Guid Ctr, mem, 1979-90; Harvard Univ Med Sch, instr psychol, 1974-2001, asst psychol, 1974-83, clin instr, 1974-2001; Harvard Longwood Psychiat, asst clin prof, 2001-; Family Serv Assoc Greater Boston, med dir, 1981-89. **Orgs:** Am Acad Child Psychol, 1974-; Am Psychol Asn, fel speaker assembly; Black Psychol Am; Soroptomist Asn, 1985-89; Links Inc, Mid Clearwater Chap, 1988-; Jack & Jill Am, 1978-; staff consult, Levison Inst, 1981-; Falk Fel, 1973-75; Exec Comt & Steering Comt to plan Conf Psychol Educ, 1974-75; Task Force Films, 1975-77; ed bd, Psychol Educ, Prologue to1980s, 1976-; Comn Women, 1976-79; ed newsletter, Comn Women, 1977-79; Spouses Sub-comn, 1977-78; Dep Rep to Leg Assembly Am Psychol Asn, 1981-83; Rep to Leg Assembly Am Psychol Asn, 1983-; Task Force mem, Non-participation, 1983-85; Comn Black Psychol, Am Psychol Asn, 1984-; Site Visitor Ach Awards Bd, 1984; Mass Psychol Soc Boston, 1973-; Ethic Comn, 1978-88; Am Acad Child Psychol, 1974-; Rep to Mass Comrtho psychiat Asn Inc, 1983-; sr Mass rep, leg AssemblyAm Psychiat Asn, 1986-; chp, mem comt, Am Psychiat Asn, 1990-91; Mass Bd Regn Med, 1988-91; bd trustee, Univ Lowell, 1987-88; Secy-Treas, APA; asoc mem, Indo-Am Psychiat Asn, 2009-. **Honors/Awds:** Falk Found, Am Psychol Asn, 1973-75; Am Bds Psychol & Neurol, 1978; Excellence in Residency Advocacy Award, Children's Psychiatric Hosp, 1994; Women of Courage and Conviction Award, Nat Coun of Negro Women, 1996; Special Lecturer, Inst on Psychiat Serv Ann Meeting, New Orleans, LA, 1999; Outstanding Psychiatrist Award for

the Advancement of the Profession, Mass Psychiat Socs, 2001; Special Presidential Commendation, Am Psychiat Asn, 2002 & 2008; Special Presidential Commendation, Mass Psychiat Asn, 2008. **Special Achievements:** First woman and first African American to be named speaker of the American Psychiatric Asn. **Home Addr:** 54 Cartwright Rd, Wellesley, MA 02482. **Business Addr:** Assistant Clinicial Professor of Psychiatry, Harvard Longwood Psychiatry, 330 Brookline Ave, Boston, MA 02215, **Business Phone:** (617)667-4630.

### NORRIS, FRED ARTHUR, JR.

Administrator. **Personal:** Born Nov 25, 1945, Ecorse, MI; son of Fred Arthur and Annie B Davis; married Betty Sue Graves; children: Tracy M Graves & Shawna L. **Educ:** Wayne City Community Col; Wayne State Univ; Ind Univ; Univ Wis; Mich State Univ; George Meany Sch Labor. **Career:** City Ecorse, coun mem, 1974-87; Local 616 Allied Ind Workers, pres, beginning, 1977; Metrop Detroit AFL-CIO, trustee, pres, currently. **Orgs:** United Black Trade Unionist, 1976; SPIDER, 1979; bd mem, Mich Downriver Comn Conf, 1979-; bd mem, Metro Detroit Chap A Philip Randolph Inst, 1984; Elder Ecorse Seventh Day Adventist Church, 1989; Allied Indust Workers Human Rights; pres, Independence Alliance; Nat Black Elected Officials; secy, treas, New Ctr Med CLin; personal ministry dir, Ecorse Seventh Day Adventist Church. **Honors/Awds:** Community Service Award, Ecorse, 1981; Community Service Award, Wayne County, 1982; Little League Award, Ecorse Little League, 1982. **Home Addr:** 3907 10th St, Ecorse, MI 48229-1616, **Home Phone:** (313)928-8264. **Business Addr:** President, Metropolitan Detroit AFL-CIO, 600 W Lafayette Suite 200, Detroit, MI 48226, **Business Phone:** (313)389-7038.

### NORRIS, DR. JAMES ELLSWORTH CHILES

Surgeon. **Personal:** Born May 12, 1932, Kilmarnock, VA; son of Morgan E Sr and Theresita Chiles; married Motoko Endo; children: Ernest Takashi. **Educ:** Hampton Inst Va, BS, 1953; Case Western Res Univ, Cleveland, Ohio, MD, 1957. **Career:** Grasslands Hosp, internship, 1958; Queens Hosp Ctr Jamaica, gen surg res, 1966; Univ Mich Med Ctr, plastic surg res, 1974; Kilmarnock Va & Melbourne, Fl, gen practr, 1958-62; Va Hosp, Tuskegee, chief Surg serv & dir surg res prog, 1969-72; Burn Unit Div Plastic Surg Harlem Hosp Ctr, chief, 1974-77; Hosp Joint Dis & Med Ctr, assoc attend plastic surg, 1975-88; Jamaica Hosp, Jamaica, attend & chief plastic surg, 1975-88, consult plastic surg, 1988-90; Col Physicians & Surgeons, Columbia Univ, asst prof, clin surg, 1976-87; Div Plastic Surg Harlem Hosp Ctr, attend, 1977-87; St Lukes-Roosevelt Hosp Ctr, Manhattan, assoc attend plastic surg, 1981-97; Pvt pract, physician; Jamtak Int, consult & founder, currently. **Orgs:** Reed O Dingman Soc, 1974; Am Burn Asn, 1975-94; NY County Med Soc, 1975; NY State Med Soc, 1975; Am Soc Plastic & Reconst Surgeons, 1975, NY Regional Soc ASPRS, 1976, Lipoplasty Soc N Am, 1987-97, Am Cleft Palate Asn, 1988-94, Am Soc Laser & Med & Surg Inc, 1987-97; NY Acad Med, 1992-; vol surgeon, Juazerio do Norte, Brazil, 1999, Phillipines, Vietnam, 2001; Vietnam, 2002, 2003; Nat Asn Advan Colored People State bd Prof Med Conduct, 2004-09. **Honors/Awds:** Certified Nat Board of Medical Examiners, 1958; Certified American Board of Surgery, 1967; Certified American Board of Plastic Surgery, 1975. **Special Achievements:** Numerous med articles in various med journals. **Home Addr:** 115 E 87th St Apt 19D, New York, NY 10128-1139, **Home Phone:** (212)876-6936. **Business Addr:** President, Jamtak International Inc, 144 E 90th St, New York, NY 10128-1139, **Business Phone:** (212)831-9313.

### NORRIS, LAVENA M.

Real estate agent. **Personal:** Born Chicago, IL; daughter of Robert W Collins and Annie M Collins; married Alvin. **Educ:** De Paul Univ, BS, 1981. **Career:** LaVena Norris Real Estate, broker, pres, 1986-; US Bur Census, Minority Bus Opportunity Comt, exec dir, 1991-. **Orgs:** Rho Epsilon, Prof Real Estate Fraternity, 1980-; C & Adolescents Forum, 1984-; pres, Dearborn Real Estate Bd, 1991-; Physicians Nat Healthcare Prog, 1991-; Nat Asn Real Estate Brokers, Invest Div, 1991-; bd dir, Chicago Gray Panthers, 1992-; adv bd mem, Health & Med Res Grp, 1992-. **Honors/Awds:** Unsung Herione Award, Nat Asn Advan Colored People, 1983; Dedicated Service Award, Dearborn Real Estate Bd, 1985; Fair Housing Advocate Award, Nat Asn Real Estate Brokers Region IX, 1988; Presidential Service Award, Nat Asn Real Estate Brokers, 1989; Kellogg National fel, WK Kellogg Found, 1991. **Special Achievements:** Author of "House Hunting", Black Family Magazine, 1982. **Home Addr:** 2772 E 75th St, Chicago, IL 60649, **Home Phone:** (773)978-0550. **Business Addr:** President, LaVena Norris Real Estate, 27 E Monroe St 11th Fl, Chicago, IL 60602, **Business Phone:** (312)641-0084.

### NORRIS, DR. LONNIE H.

Dentist. **Personal:** Born Houston, TX; married Donna M. **Educ:** Fisk Univ, BA; Harvard Dent Med, DMD; Harvard Pub Health, MPH; Tufts Dent Med, Residency Cert Oral & Maxillofacial Surg. **Career:** Tufts Univ Dent Sch, interim dean, 1995-96, dean, 1995-2011, dean emer, currently, tenured prof oral & maxillofacial surg, currently. **Orgs:** Am Bd Oral & Maxillofacial Surg; Phi Beta Kappa; Am Dent Educ Assn; Am Acad Dent Sci; Am Col Dentists; Int Col Dentists; Pierre Fauchard Acad; fel Am Asn Oral & Maxillofacial Surg. **Home Addr:** 54 Cartwright Rd, Wellesley, MA 02481. **Business Addr:** Medford, MA.

### NORRIS, WALTER

Government official. **Personal:** Born Jan 9, 1945, Jackson, MI; son of Walter Sr and Willie Mae Glaspie-Neely; married Rosie Hill; children: Gloria J, Anthony W, Vernon D & Shannon D. **Educ:** Spring Arbor Col, Spring Arbor, MI, BS, 1970; Mich State Univ, E Lansing, MI, Grad Study Educ Admin, 1979. **Career:** Jackson Community Col, Jackson, MI, fin aid dir, 1968-70; Norris Real Estate, Jackson, MI, owner & broker, 1970-76; Jackson Pub Sch, Jackson, MI, dir, minority affairs, 1970-76; Jackson Housing Comn, Jackson, MI, exec dir, 1976-79; Lansing Housing Comn, Lansing, MI, exec dir, 1978-88; Ypsilanti Housing Comn, exec dir, 1988-. **Orgs:** Nat Asn Housing & Redevelop Officials; Mich Chap NAHRO; chmn & bd dir, Legis Comn; cert trainer, HAHRO Pub Housing Mgt; Pub Housing Authority Dirs Asn; Tex Housing Asn; assoc mem, Galveston Hist Found, 1988-, Galveston Chap, Nat Asn Advan Colored People, 1988-; bd mem, Galveston Boys Club, 1988-, Galveston Chamber Com, 1988-, Rotary Club Galveston, 1988-; bd dir, SOS community serv; exec dir, Galveston Housing Authority. **Honors/Awds:** Mens Union Award, Most Outstanding Young Man of the Year, Jackson Community Col, 1965; Sophomore Class Pres, Jackson Jr Col, 1965; Outstanding Young Man of the Year, Jackson Jaycees, 1968; Service Award, Outstanding Service & Contribution, HUD Prog, 1982; NAHRO Pub Housing Mgmt Cert. **Home Addr:** 132 Franklin Blvd, Pontiac, MI 48341. **Business Addr:** Executive Director, President, Ypsilanti Housing Commission, 601 Armstrong Dr, Ypsilanti, MI 48197, **Business Phone:** (734)482-4300.

### NORRIS, WILLIAM E.

Automotive executive, chief executive officer. **Career:** Utica Chrysler Plymouth Inc, chief exec officer, currently. **Business Addr:** Chief Executive Officer, chairman, Utica Chrysler Plymouth Inc, PO Box 214, Yorkville, NY 13495, **Business Phone:** (315)736-0831.

### NORTHCROSS, DEBORAH AMETRA

School administrator. **Personal:** Born Jun 27, 1951, Nashville, TN; daughter of Theron and Nell. **Educ:** Mt Holyoke Col, BA, fr, 1973; Memphis State Univ, MEd, spec educ, 1975. **Career:** School administrator (retired); Shelby St Comm Col, counr, 1973-76, dir spec serv prog, 1976-79, coordr fed affairs, 1979-81, asst dir, stud develop, 1981-83, dir stud retention, 1982-83, grants officer, 1983-84, dir develop 1984; Univ Tenn Health Sci Ctr, Enrichment Programs, coordr, Community Outreach, dir, Ronald E McNair Post bacca laureate Achievement Prog, dir, 2004-. **Orgs:** Field reader, US Dept Educ; pres, Tenn Asn Spec Prog, 1977-79; secy, vpres & pres, Southeastern Asn Educ Opportunity Prog Personnel, 1978-79; tutor, Memphis Literacy Coun, 1983-87; chairperson, Christian Educ Comn MS Blvd Christian Church, 1984-; chair nominating comt, YWCA, 1985, bd dir, 1986-, vpres, 1987, chair, Fin Develop Comt, 1988-; eval consult, US Dept Educ Spec Prog Training Grant, 1986-; vpres alumni asn, Leadership Memphis, 1987-88, bd mem, 1987-89, vice chair bd trustee, 1989-; bd trustee, Campaign Steering Comt, Mt Holyhoke Col, currently; Pres Comn, Diverse Community; Bd Educ Memphis City Schs; bd dir & bd trustee, Mt Holyoke Col Alumni Asn; bd dir chair, Coun Opportunity Educ, currently; Presidential Comn Diverse Community. **Home Addr:** 1832 S Pkwy E, Memphis, TN 38114-1911, **Home Phone:** (901)274-4127. **Business Addr:** Board of Directors Chair, Council of Opportunity in Education, 1025 Vt Ave NW Suite 900, Washington, DC 20005-3516, **Business Phone:** (202)347-7430.

### NORTHCROSS, WILSON HILL, JR.

Lawyer. **Personal:** Born Dec 8, 1946, Detroit, MI; son of Wilson H Sr and Gwendolyn Pinkney; married Winifred C Wheelock; children: Jill Inez & Christopher Wilson. **Educ:** Wayne State Univ, BS, 1969; Harvard Univ, Law Sch, JD, 1972. **Career:** Vice chmn, First Dist Young Dem, Detroit, 1967; Miller, Canfield, Paddock & Stone, assoc, 1973-75, atty, 1975-77; pvt law pract, 1975-77, 1981-83, 1987-; Mich Supreme Ct, assoc comnr, 1977-78; UAW Legal Serv Plan, Detroit, sr atty, 1978-81; Sr Citizens Law Prog, Legal Serv Southeastern Mich, dir, 1983-87. **Orgs:** Am Bar Asn; Mich State Bar Asn; bd dir, Wolverine Bar Asn, 1973-74; Church Christ. **Special Achievements:** Publication of "The Limits on Employment Testing," University of Detroit Journal of Urban Law, Vol 50, Issue 3, 1973. **Business Addr:** Attorney, 801 Sunrise Ct, Ann Arbor, MI 48103-3544, **Business Phone:** (313)622-9087.

### NORTHERN, BOB. See NORTHERN, ROBERT A.

### NORTHERN, CHRISTINA ANN

Executive, lawyer. **Personal:** Born May 21, 1956, Kansas City, KS; daughter of Emanuel and Christine. **Educ:** Wash Univ, BA, polit sci, 1978; Univ Dc, David A. Clarke Sch Law, JD, gen law, 1981; Antioch Sch Law, JD. **Career:** Christina Northern Esq, owner, 1989-, atty, 1992-, prin, 2002-; DC Consumer & Regulatory Affairs, rent adminr dc, 1999-2002. **Orgs:** Nat Bar Asn, 1981-; Am Friends London Econs, 1989-; bd mem, chair fund raising & asst treas, New Columbia COT Land Trust, 1990-; Dc Consumer & Regulatory Affairs, rent adminr, 1999-2002; Delta Sigma Theta Sorority; Md State Bar Asn; New Columbia Community Land Trust. **Honors/Awds:** Outstanding Young Woman of the the Year, 1984. **Home Addr:** 1822 11th St NW, Washington, MD 20001-5015, **Home Phone:** (202)234-1722. **Business Addr:** Attorney, Owner, Christina Northern Esq, 8455 Colesville Rd Suite 1080, Silver Spring, MD 20910-3319, **Business Phone:** (301)562-9212.

### NORTHERN, DAVID A., SR.

Executive, association executive. **Personal:** Born Sep 4, 1973, Lake County; children: Dasanie & David Jr. **Educ:** Ball State Univ, BS, acct, 1997; Ind Univ Northwest, MPA, pub admin, 2003; Univ MD, cert, exec educ prog; Harvard Univ, John F Kennedy Sch Govt, achieving excellence community develop cert, housing & community develop, 2014-. **Career:** City E Chicago Housing & Community Develop, dir capital improv, 1997-2002; Lake Co Housing Authority, chief exec officer, exec dir, 2002-; Philadelphia Housing Authority, exec vpres-housing opers, 2013. **Orgs:** Lake Co Affordable Housing Team; adv bd, Nicasa Women Servs; adv bd, Youth Build Lake Co; Allocations Comt, Lake Area United Way; life mem, Irish Univs Athletics Asn; Neal-Marshall Alumni Club NWI; Hoosiers Higher Educ; Ind Univ Alumni Club Chicago; Inst Innovative Leadership; Pi Alpha Alpha; Nat Hon Soc; Omega Psi Phi Fraternity; Alumni Asn Ind Univ; Northeast Ill Boy Scouts; Community Consol Sch Dist 46, 2015. **Honors/Awds:** Last Decade Award, ball state univ, 2004; African Americans of Lake County Award, 2007, 2010; Housing Award, 2010. **Home Addr:** 768 S Vintage Lane, Round Lake, NY 12151. **Business Addr:** Chief Executive Officer, Executive Director, Lake County Housing Authority, 33928 N US Hwy 45, Grayslake, IL 60030-1714, **Business Phone:** (847)223-1170.

### NORTHERN, GABRIEL O' KARA (GABE NORTHERN)

Football player, football coach, business owner. **Personal:** Born Jun 8, 1974, Baton Rouge, LA. **Educ:** La State Univ. **Career:** Football player (retired), football coach; Buffalo Bills, linebacker & defensive end, 1996-99; Minnesota Vikings, linebacker & defensive end, 2000; Anytime Fitness, owner, 2000-, defensive line coach, Prairie View A&M Univ, currently. **Business Addr:** Owner, Anytime Fitness LLC, 12181 Margo Ave S, Hastings, MN 55033, **Business Phone:** (800)704-5004.

### NORTHERN, ROBERT A. (BOB NORTHERN)

Educator, musician, lecturer. **Personal:** Born May 21, 1934, Kinston, NC; son of Ralph and Madie. **Educ:** Manhattan Sch Music, attended 1953; Vienna State Acad Music Vienna, Austria, attended 1958; Howard Univ, grad. **Career:** Musician; Sym Air Orchestra, NYC, stage band, 1958-70; Metro Opera, NYC, 1958-59; Radio City Music Hall, Orchestra, 1963-66; Brass Instruments Pub Sch Syst, NYC, instr, 1964-67; Broadway Theatre Orchestra, NYC, staff, 1969-71; Jazz Composer Orchestra, NYC, staff, 1969-71; Dartmouth Col, Music Dept, artist-in-residence, lectr, 1970-73; Ti-Jean Dartmouth Col, 1971; Recordings: Ode Creation, 1971; Confrontation & Commun Dartmouth Col, 1971; Magical Mode Dartmouth Col, 1971; Symbols Dartmouth Col, 1972; Child Woman Brown Univ, 1973; Brown Univ Afro Am Studies Prog, lectr, 1973-82; Umoja Music Publ Co, owner & founder, 1973-; Forces Nature Brown Univ, 1974; Levine Sch Music; Divine Recs, owner, 1975-; Move Ever Onward, 1975; World Music Ensemble, founder & dir, 1986; World Community Sch Music, founder & exec dir, 1986-; Open Sky, 1986; WPFW-FM, Wash, DC, founder & producer, 1993; Celebration, composer, dir & producer, 1993; Meditation; Light from Womb; Key to Nowhere; Smithsonian Inst, lectr, currently. Albums: Sound Awareness, 1974; Move Ever Onward, 1975; Key to Nowhere, 1983; Open Sky, 1986; Celebration!, 1993. **Orgs:** Charter mem, Soc Black Composers, 1965; founder, NY Wind Octet, 1966; founder, World Music Ensemble; founder, Sound Awareness Ensemble, 1968; founder, Radio Ser Dimensions Black Sounds WBAI-FM, New York, 1970; Sound Awareness Vol Move Ever Onward III, 1975; New World Vol III, 1980; founder, World Community Sch Music; music dir, Black Fire Performing Arts Co, Birmingham. **Home Addr:** 6101 4th St NW, Washington, DC 20011, **Home Phone:** (202)829-5345. **Business Addr:** Founder, Chief Executive Officer, World Community School of Music, 6101 4th St NW, Washington, DC 20011, **Business Phone:** (202)829-5345.

### NORTON, DR. AURELIA EVANGELINE

**Personal:** Born Feb 14, 1932, Dayton, OH; daughter of Joseph Turner and Aurelia DeMar. **Educ:** Wayne State, BA, 1961, MA, PhD; Cent State Univ, Dayton. **Career:** Wayne State, res psychologist; C & Emergency Psychiat Clin Detroit Gen Hosp, staff psychologist; Oak Pk Sch Syst, psychologist; Chrysler Corp, psychologist; C Hosp Consult Psychologist, res psychologist; Univ Cincinnati Multi Ethnic Br Psychol Serv, assoc prof psychol; Univ Cincinnati, Psychol Serv Ctr, dir training, emer fac, 2005-. **Orgs:** Am Psychol Asn; Asn Black Psychologists; Nat Asn Advan Colored People; Mt Zion Baptist Church. **Home Addr:** 1129 Towanda Ter, Cincinnati, OH 45216-2248, **Home Phone:** (513)242-2492. **Business Addr:** Emeritus Faculty, University of Cincinnati, 316 Dyer Hall, Cincinnati, OH 45221-0037, **Business Phone:** (513)556-0648.

### NORTON, CHERYL WEEK

Singer, songwriter. **Personal:** Born Oct 13, 1958, Los Angeles, CA. **Career:** Tabu Rec, rec artist, 1984-88; CBS Rec Inc, singer, currently; Albums: Fragile, 1984; High Priority, 1986; Affair, 1988; The Woman I Am, 1991; The Best Of Cherrelle, 1995; The Right Time, 1999; Greatest Hits, 2005; Icon, 2011; Songs: "I Didn't Mean to Turn You On", 1984; "Fragile Handle with Care", 1984; "Like I Will", 1984; "You Look Good to Me", 1985; "Saturday Love", 1985; "Will You Satisfy?", 1986; "Artificial Heart", 1986; "Oh No It's U Again", 1986; "Never Knew Love Like This", 1988; "Everything I Miss at Home", 1988; "Affair", 1989; "What More Can I Do for You", 1989; "Saturday Love", 1990; "Never in My Life", 1991; "Tears of Joy", 1992; "Still in Love with You", 1992; "Baby Come to Me", 1997; "The Right Time", 1999; "Just Tell Me", 1999; "I Wanna Get Next To You", 1999. **Business Addr:** Singer, c/o CBS Records Inc, 51 W 52nd St, New York, NY 10019, **Business Phone:** (212)975-4321.

### NORTON, ELEANOR HOLMES

Government official, educator. **Personal:** Born Jun 13, 1937, Washington, DC; daughter of Coleman Holmes and Vela Holmes Nee Lynch; married Edward; children: Katherine & John. **Educ:** Antioch Col, BA, 1960; Yale Univ, MA, Am studies, 1963; Yale Law Sch, JD, 1964. **Career:** Judge A. Leon Higginbotham Jr, law clerk, 1964-65; Am Civil Liberties Union, asst legal dir, atty, 1965-70; NY Univ Law Sch, adj asst prof law, 1970-71; Mayor NY, exec asst, 1971-74; Georgetown Univ Law Ctr, prof law, 1982-90; US House Rep, congresswoman, 1991-, deleg, currently; Women's Rights Law Reporter, founder. **Orgs:** Rockefeller Found; Bd Gov, DC Bar Asn; chair, NY Human Rights Comn, 1970-77; chair, US Equal Employ Opportunity Comn, 1977-81; sr fel Urban Inst, 1981-82. **Honors/Awds:** Outstanding Alumna, Yale Law Sch; Yale Wilbur Cross Medal, Yale Grad Sch; Distinguished Public Service Award, Ctr Nat Policy, 1985; 60 honorary doctorates; Louise Waterman Wise Award; Foremother Award, Nat Res Ctr Women & Families, 2011. **Special Achievements:** First woman to chair the Equal Employment Opportunity Commission; published articles: "Public Assistance, Post New-Deal Bureaucracy and the Law: Learning from Negative Models," Yale Law Jour, 1983; "The Private Bar and Public Confusion: A New Civil Rights Challenge," Howard Law Jour, 1984; "Equal Employment Law: Crisis in Interpretation, Survival against the Odds," Tulane Law Rev, 1988; author, Sex Discrimination and the Law: Causes and Remedies; listed in "100 Most Important Women", Ladies Home Jour, 1988; listed in "100 Most Powerful Women in Washington", The Wash Mag, 1989; featured on "Better Know A District" segment of Comedy Central's "The Colbert Report", 2006. **Business Addr:** Congresswoman, US House of Representatives, National Press Bldg, Washington, DC 20045, **Business Phone:** (202)783-5065.

### NORTON, KENNETH HOWARD, JR.

Football player, football coach. **Personal:** Born Sep 29, 1966, Jacksonville, FL; son of Ken Sr; married Angela; children: Brittney, Sabrina Brooke & Ken III. **Educ:** Univ Calif, Los Angeles, BS, sociol, 1999. **Career:** Football player (retired), football coach; Dallas Cowboys, linebacker, 1988, right linebacker, 1989-90, 1992, left linebacker, 1991, middle linebacker, 1993; San Francisco 49ers, linebacker & right linebacker, 1994, 1997-98, middle linebacker, 1995-96, linebacker & Right Inside Linebacker, 1999, left Inside Linebacker & middle linebacker, 2000; radio & TV commentator & analyst; Hamilton High Los Angeles, defensive coordr, 2003; Univ Southern Calif Trojans, linebackers coach, 2004-08, asst head coach/defense, 2009; Seattle Seahawks, linebackers coach, 2010-; Oakland Raiders, defensive coordr, 2015-. **Honors/Awds:** Linebacker, Sporting News Col, All-Am Team, 1987; Super Bowls XXVII-XXIX, 1992-94; Pro Bowl appearances, 1993, 1995 & 1997; UCLA Hall of Fame, 1998, All Pro, 1993-95. **Special Achievements:** Autobiography: Going The Distance: The Ken Norton Story; Only player inNFL history to win three consecutive Super Bowl rings, 1992-94. **Business Addr:** Line Backers Coach, Seattle Seahawks, 12 Seahawks Way, Renton, WA 98056, **Business Phone:** (425)203-8000.

### NORVEL, REV. WILLIAM LEONARD
Clergy. **Personal:** Born Oct 1, 1935, Pascagoula, MS; son of William L Sr and Velma H. **Educ:** Epiphany Apostolic Col, attended 1956; St Joseph's Sem, BA, 1959; St Michael's Col, attended 1961; St Bonaventure Col, attended 1963; Marquette Univ, attended 1967. **Career:** Holy Family, asst pastor, 1965; St Augustine HS, teacher, 1965; Josephite Training Ctr, dir, 1968; St Joseph's Sem, staff asst, 1970; St Benedict Moor, pastor, 1971; St Brigid, pastor, 1979-83; consult Black Cath Parishes USA, 1983-; Josephite Soc, consultor gen, 1983; Most Pure Heart Mary Church, pastor, 1987-91; St Peter The Apostle Parish, Pascagoula, pastor, currently . **Orgs:** Bd mem, Lithurgical Conf, 1978-82; bd mem, Southern Christian Leadership Conferenc, 1979, 1983; Nat Asn Advan Colored People, 1983-85; pres, Black Cath Clergy Caucus, 1985-87; trustee, bd Nat Black Cath Cong, 1987. **Home Addr:** 1402 E Dupont Ave, Pascagoula, MS 39567. **Business Addr:** Pastor, St Peter The Apostle Parish, 1715 Telephone Rd, Pascagoula, MS 39567, **Business Phone:** (228)762-1759.

### NORVELL, DR. MERRITT J., JR.
Executive, athletic director, dean (education). **Personal:** children: 2. **Educ:** Univ Wis, Madison, BS, 1963, MS, 1966, PhD, higher educ. **Career:** City Madison, dir community serv, 1966-69; Madison Mustangs Football Team, head football coach, 1966-70; Univ Wis, asst dean, 1969-77, asst vice chancellor; IBM Corp, nat mgr mkt support servs & col merchandising progs mgr, 1977-95; Mich State Univ, athletic dir, 1995-2000; TV & radio; officer & psychiat social worker; educ pract group, leader; Norvell Group mkt firm, founder; DHR Int, exec vpres & managing dir & global leader educ pract group, 2000-; NCAA Minority Male Leadership Inst, lectr, currently; Black Coaches Asn's Prof Develop Prog, lectr, currently; Div 1A Athletic Dirs & Minority Opportunities Athletic Asn Inc, consult, currently; TNG & Assocs, pres prin, currently. **Orgs:** Bd mem, United Negro Col Fund; Univ Wis Big Ten Championship, 1962; NCAA Budget & Finance Cabinet; Big Ten Conf Budget Comt; chair, Madison Urban League; bd mem, Wis Spec Olympics & Madison Wis Community Found Boar; Kappa Alpha Psi Fraternity; 100 Black Men Inc; Rotary Int; Capital City Masonic Lodge. **Home Addr:** 4236 Pine Tree Lane, Lansing, MI 48911-1155, **Home Phone:** (517)272-0463. **Business Addr:** Executive Vice President, Managing Director, DHR International, 6639 Centurion Dr Suite 140, Lansing, MI 48917, **Business Phone:** (517)886-9010.

### NORWOOD, BRANDY
Actor, singer. **Personal:** Born Feb 11, 1979, McComb, MS; daughter of Willie Ray Sr and Sonja Bates; married Robert Smith; children: Sy'rai. **Educ:** Pepperdine Univ. **Career:** Singer, actor, currently; Albums: Brandy, 1994; Never Say Never, 1998; Full Moon, 2002; Afrodisiac, 2004; The Best of Brandy, 2005; Human, 2008; Two Eleven, 2012; TV: "Thea", 1993-94; "Moesha", 1996-2001; "The Parkers", 2001; "Sabrina, the Teenage Witch", 2002; "Reba", 2002; "American Dreams", 2004; "House", 2005; "One on One", 2006; "I Love LA", 2006; "The Hills", 2008; "This Little Piggy", 2009; "Brandy & Ray J: A Family Business", 2010-11; "90210", 2011; "Drop Dead Diva", 2011-12; "The Game", 2012-15; "The Soul Man", 2014; "Zoe Ever After", forthcoming, 2016; TV movies: Cinderella, 1997; Double Platinum, 1999; Films: Arachnophobia, 1990; I Still Know What You Did Last Summer, 1998; Osmosis Jones, voice, 2001, Temptation: Confessions of a Marriage Counselor, 2013; The Perfect Match, forthcoming, 2016; Producer: Double Platinum, 1999, "Moesha", 1996-2001; "Brandy & Ray J: A Family Business", 2011. **Special Achievements:** First African American woman to portray Cinderella in a major TV movie. **Home Addr:** 23463 Pk Colombo, Calabasas, CA 91302. **Business Addr:** Vocalist, c/o Atlantic Recordings, 1290 Ave of the Americas, New York, NY 10104, **Business Phone:** (212)275-2000.

### NORWOOD, CALVIN COOLIDGE
Association executive. **Personal:** Born Apr 1, 1927, Tunica, MS; son of Hester and Willie; married Ida Williams; children: Doris Norwood Jernigan, Deloris Norwood Sanders, Demetrice Norwood Burnette & Regina. **Educ:** Coahoma Jr Col, GED, 1979. **Career:** Co Rd Dept Co Turstee Bd Rosa Ft Sch, foreman; Miss St Hwy Dept, Tunica County, black jury comn supvr, Miss Dept Transp, rd supvr. **Orgs:** Pres, Nat Asn Advan Colored People, 1966-97; EDA Bd; Co Dem Party; Legal Aide Bd Joint Commun Activ & Job Care; Nat Asn Advan Colored People; VFW. **Honors/Awds:** Job Core Cert Job Core, 1979; Politician Action Award, Ed Award, Nat Asn Advan Colored People, 1980, Programmatic Award, 1985-86, 1990; Recognition Appreciation, Miss State Highway Dept, 1989. **Home Addr:** PO Box 1829, Tunica, MS 38676.

### NORWOOD, FELICIA
Chief executive officer, president (organization). **Educ:** Valdosta State Univ, BA, polit sci, 1981; Univ Madison-Wis, MA, polit sci, 1982; Yale Law Sch, JD, 1989. **Career:** Hopkins & Sutter, assoc, 1989-91; State Ill, Off Gov, sr policy advisor, 1991-94; Aetna, govt rels coun 1994-97, regional gen coun, 1997-99, mkt pres, 1999-2000, regional mgr, mid-atlantic region, 2000-01, regional mgr/mid mkt accounts & head healthcare delivery, mid-atlantic region, 2001-02, pres, aetna govt health plans, 2002-03, nat head small group & individual mkt segments, 2003-05, head medicaid, 2005-06, Mid-Am Region, pres, 2010-13; ActiveHealth Mgt Inc, chief operating officer & pres, 2007-10; State Ill, dept healthcare & family serv, dir, 2015-. **Business Addr:** Director, Illinois Department Healthcare and Family Services, 201 S Grand Ave E, Springfield, IL 62704, **Business Phone:** (217)782-1200.

### NORWOOD, KIMBERLY JADE
Educator. **Personal:** Born Aug 18, 1960, New York, NY; daughter of Ahmad Akbar and Marietta Holt; married Ronald Alan; children: Candice Jade, Ellis Grant & Donnell Bussey. **Educ:** Fordham Univ, BA, 1982; Univ Mo, JD, 1985. **Career:** Hon Clifford Scott Green, law clerk, 1985-86; Bryan Cave LLP, litigation assoc, 1986-90; Wash Univ Sch Law, adj prof, 1987-89, prof law, 1990-, prof African & African Am Studies, currently; Univ Mo, Columbia, vis lectr, Cleo Prog, 1990, lectr, 2010; Aoyama Gakuin Univ, vis prof, 2008; Fudan Univ, vis lect, 2010; Univ Utrecht-Summer Inst Global Justice Prog, 2011. Workshop: "The Struggle for Education in Black America: From Slavery through the Reconstruction", St. Louis pub sch. Book: "Color Matters: Skin Tone Bias & the Myth of a Post-Racial America", ed & contribr, 2014; "Ferguson's Fault Lines: The Race Quake That Rocked A Nation", 2016; Global Perspectives on Colorism, organizer, 2015. **Orgs:** Am Bar Asn, 1986-; gen con, Mound City Bar Asn, 1986-; Bar Asn Metro St Louis, 1986-; Ill Bar Asn, 1987-; bd mem 7 secy, St Louis Women Lawyers Asn, 1993-2000; bd mem, Greeley Comn Asn, 1993-94; Am Asn Law Sch, 1993-; Jack & Jill Am, 1994-96; bd mem, Girls Inc, 1994; bd mem, Am Civil Liberties Union Eastern MO; Nat Bar Asn; Soc Am Law Teacher; vice chair, 1994-95, chair, 1996-97, Asn Am Law Sch; bd mem, Sheldon Arts Found; comnr, Mo Civil War Sesquicentennial Comn; Legal Educ Opportunity coun; co chair, Implicit Bias Comt; Mo Supreme Ct. **Home Addr:** 8231 Glen Echo Dr, St. Louis, MO 63121, **Home Phone:** (314)935-6416. **Business Addr:** Professor of Law, Professor of African & African American Studies, Washington University School of Law, 1 Brookings Dr Anheuser-Busch Hall Rm 561, St. Louis, MO 63130, **Business Phone:** (314)935-6416.

### NORWOOD, DR. TOM
School administrator, lecturer. **Personal:** Born Jul 19, 1943, Baton Rouge, LA; son of Edward A Sr and Corinne Burrell; married Marjorie Marshall; children: Teri Lynn & Tony. **Educ:** Southern Univ A&M Col, BS, art & eng, 1964, MEd, educ admin, 1969; Univ Nebr, Lincoln, PhD, educ admin, 1975. **Career:** Dean (retired); Omaha Pub Sch, traveling art teacher, 1964-65, jr high art teacher, 1965-68, jr high coun, 1968-70; Col Educ Univ NE Omaha, asst dean, 1970-83, assoc prof, 1983-88; Univ Wisc-River Falls, asst dean & prof. **Orgs:** Vpres, Greater Omaha Comm Action, 1975; Appointedby US Dist Court Judge Albert Schatz, 1976; workshop dir, Sioux Falls SD City Dept Heads, "Racism & Sexism" 1979; pres, vpres, NE Coun Teacher Educ, 1981-83; workshop dir, Joslyn Art Mus "Forever Free Exhibit" 1981; Urban League NE, 1983-84; consult Omaha Pub Sch re Implementing Discipline Based Art Educ Prog, 1987-87. **Honors/Awds:** Phi Delta Kappa Southern Univ & A&M Col, 1964; hon mention Water color Coun Bluffs IA Art Fair, 1972; "Contemp Nebr Art & Artists" Univ Nebr, Omaha, 1978; Article "Facilitating Multicultural Educ Via the Visual Arts" Nebr Humanist, 1980; 1st pl Award Nebr Art Educ Competition, 1982; paintings selected nat & int juried competitions, Nat Miniature Competition, 1983, Nat Exhib Contemp Realism, 1983, Mo Int Miniature Competition, 1983, Int Small Fine Art Exhib, 1984, Int Miniature Competition, 1984, Biennial Juried Competition, Nat, 1984, Tenth Int Miniature Competition, 1985; Comn St Nebr create poster design for first state observance of Martin Luther King, Jr holiday, 1986; First Ann Nat NC Miniature Painting Show Cert of Merit, 1985; participated in 17 exhib, 1985-87; Second Ann NC Nat Miniature Painting Show Second Pl Watercolor, 1986; Comn by Chancellor of UW-RF to produce painting "Celebration of Diversity", 1990; Achiever of the Year, Greater St Paul YMCA Black Achievers Prog, 1991; Arts W juried Competition, Eau Claire, Wis, 1993-94. **Home Addr:** 1520 8th St, Pueblo, CO 81001, **Home Phone:** (719)542-1693.

### NORWOOD, WILLIAM R.
Pilot. **Personal:** Born Feb 14, 1936, Centralia, IL; son of Sam and Allingal; married Molly F Cross; children: William R & George A. **Educ:** Southern Ill Univ, BA, chem, 1959; Univ Chicago, MBA, 1974. **Career:** Pilot (retired); Airline pilot first officer, 1968-83; second officer, 1965-68; United Airlines, capt, 1983-96; Phoenix Chap Tuskegee Airmen, Inc, vpres, currently. **Orgs:** Bd trust, Southern Ill Univ, 1974-01; commencement speaker, Shawnee Community Col, 1975; National Association for the Advancement of Colored People, 1985-; Airline Pilots Asn; United Air Lines Speakers Panel; charter mem, Org Black Air Line Pilots; bd dir, Suburban Chap, SCLC; pres, bd trustee, State Univ Retirement Syst; Ill Comt Black Concerns Higher Educ; Southern Ill Univ Alumini Asn. **Honors/Awds:** United Airlines Corp Community Rels Award, 1991; O'Hare Capt of the Year, United Airlines, 1995; Chicagoan of the Year, 1995; Southern Ill Reunion Coun Founders Award, 1996; United Airlines Black Prof Orgn Outstanding Achievement & Leadership Award, 1996; Alpha Kappa Alpha Monary Award Winner, 1997; Destiny Church Community Serv Award, 1997; Southern Ill Univ Distinguished Alumni Award; Ill Educ Asn Friend of Educ Award; Flight Opers Div Spec Achievement Award; Carbondale ROTC Hall of Fame, Southern Ill Univ; Carbondale Athletic Hall of Fame, Southern Ill Univ; Boeing 727 Aircraft Named in Honor of Capt William R Norwood; Black Wings, Smithsonian Inst Nat Air & Space Mus, Washington. **Special Achievements:** First African-American Pilot with United Air Lines; First African-American Quarterback SIU. **Home Addr:** PO Box 3100, Carbondale, IL 62901, **Home Phone:** (618)351-0315.

### NORWOOD, WILLIE RAYMOND, JR. See J., RAY.

### NOWLIN, BETTYE J ISOM
Teacher, manager, publicist. **Personal:** Born Knoxville, TN; daughter of Jettie Isom and Elizabeth; married Thomas A III; children: Thomas IV, Mark & Brett. **Educ:** Tenn A & I State Univ, BS, 1956; Univ Calif, Los Angeles, CA, MPH, 1971. **Career:** Pepperdine Univ, community nutrit teacher; St Lukes Hosp & Med Ctr, dietetic intern, 1957; Cook County Hosp, therapeut dietitian, 1957-59; Michael Reese Hosp, admin dietitian, 1959-61; Chicago Bd Educ, teacher, 1961-63; Chicago Bd Health, pub health nutritionist, 1962-68; Delta Sigma Theta, Head Start, nutritionist, 1968-70, dietitian; Dairy Coun Calif, mgr, adult nutrit prog, 1970-90, pub affairs mgr, 1990-. **Orgs:** Alpha Kappa Alpha Sorority, 1952-56; deleg, Am Dietetic Asn, 1957-, media spokesperson, 1982-, pub health, Dietitians Bus & Comm, regist dietitian; deleg, Calif Dietetic Asn, 1968-; Calif Nutrit Coun, 1970-; Soc Nutrit Educ, 1971-; Am Pub Health Asn, 1972-; Nutrit Educ Pub, 1980-; Nat Asn Female Exec, 1995-; Am Sch Food Serv Asn, 1993-. **Honors/Awds:** Distinguished Service Award, Excellence Community Nutrition, 1990; Medallion Award, Am Dietetic Asn, 1994. **Special Achievements:** Publications: Development of a Nutrition Educ Program for Homemakers; Society for Nutrition Educ Journal; Leader-Led & Self Instruction Work Site Programs; Keep It Short & Simple, Journal of American Dietetic Association; Marketing Social Programs, The Competetive Edge, ADA Mkting Manuel, 2ndEditon. **Home Addr:** 22556 Liberty Bell Rd, Calabasas, CA 91302, **Home Phone:** (818)222-2582. **Business Addr:** Public Affairs Manager, Dairy Council of California, 1101 Nat Dr Suite B, Sacramento, CA 95834-1901, **Business Phone:** (916)263-3560.

### NOWLIN, FRANKIE L.
Foundation executive, executive, association executive. **Personal:** Born Huntington Beach, CA. **Educ:** Marshall Univ, grad; WVa Univ, grad sch; Ohio State Univ, grad sch; McGregor Sch Antioch Univ. **Career:** Tri-State Opportunities Industrialization Ctr Inc, exec dir, 1973-84; Pvt Indust Coun Columbus & Franklin Co, Prog Oper Dept, dir, 1984-89; Borden Found, adminr, 1989-91, exec dir, 1991, pres, dir social responsibility, 1996-2001. **Orgs:** Marshall Univ Found; United Way, Safety Vision Coun; adv, The Col Fund/UNCF; trustee, Keystone Col; trustee, secy, Mt Carmel Col Nursing; trustee, pres, Ctr New Directions; trustee, vpres, Martin Luther King Arts Complex; trustee, The Conf Bd, Contribs Coun II; dir anti-racism & race rels, vpres racial justice, YWCA, Columbus. **Business Addr:** President, Borden Foundation Inc, 180 E Broad St 30th Fl, Columbus, OH 43215, **Business Phone:** (614)225-4340.

### NUNER, DR. LEE
Administrator. **Career:** Univ Pa, vpres bus. **Business Addr:** PA.

### NUNERY, DR. LEROY DAVID, II (LEE NUNERY)
Vice president (organization), administrator. **Personal:** Born Dec 22, 1955, Jersey City, NJ; son of Leroy C and Thelma Jones; married Carolyn Thomas; children: Leroy David III & Dorothy Jacqueline. **Educ:** Lafayette Col, BA, hist, 1977; Wash Univ, MBA, finance, 1979; Univ Pa, EdD, 2003. **Career:** Leroy Nunery & Sons Inc, vpres, 1973; Edward D Jones & Co, res analyst, 1978-79; Northern Trust Co, com banking officer, 1979-83; First Nat Bank Chicago, vpres, 1983-87; Swiss Bank Corp, vpres, 1987-93; Nat Basketball Asn, vpres, human & info resources, 1993-97; LSP Inc, co-owner, 1998; Univ Pa, vpres bus serv, 1999-2005; Edison Schs, Charter Sch Div, pres, 2005-07; PlusUltre LLC, prin & found, 2007-; Global Corp Investment Bank, managing dir; Gilfus Educ Group, educ advisor, 2012-13; Gerson Lehrman Group, subj matter expert, 2013-; Nj Dept Educ, spec asst, 2014-15; ECRA Group, vpres, 2014-. **Orgs:** Nat pres, life mem, Nat Black MBA Asn, 1979-2012; bd dir, Chicago Community Ventures, 1980-83; nat pres, Nat Black MBA Asn, 1986-89; dir, Family Resource Coalition, 1988-90; trustee, Lafayette Col, 1987-; bd dir, Pitney Bowes, 1991-97; Nu Beta Beta Chap, Omega Psi Phi Fraternity; dir, 1997-99; Fin Performance & Stand Comt Blue Cross Blue Shield Asn; dir, WXPN-FM; dir, Enterprise Ctr W Philadelphia; dir, Enterprise Ctr CapitalCorp; dir, W Philadelphia Partnership; dir, Univ City Dist; Philadelphia Conv & Visitors Bur; dir, Philadelphia Sports Cong; bd mem, Please Touch Mus, 2001-09; bd mem, Springside Sch, 2003-09; Savoy Bank, 2007-2009; chief, 2010, dep supt, dep ceo, 2010-11, spec advisor, 2012, Sch Dist Philadelphia; Anchor Insts Task Force, 2010-12. **Home Addr:** 56 Hawthorne Pl, Montclair, NJ 07042-2604, **Home Phone:** (201)509-9040. **Business Addr:** Vice President, ECRA Group, 5600 N River Rd, Rosemont, IL 60018, **Business Phone:** (847)318-0072.

### NUNES KIRBY, MIZAN ROBERTA PATRICIA (MIZAN ROBERTA PATRICIA KIRBY)
Actor. **Personal:** daughter of Joe and Bertina. **Educ:** Colby Col, Waterville, ME, 1970; Univ Chicago Divinity Sch, attended 1974; Franklin & Marshall Col, AB, 1973; Am Conserv Theatre, San Francisco, attended 1978. **Career:** Director & Actress; Plays: Othello; Hamlet; Antony; King Lear; Elizabeth & Will; Bridge Party; Faith, Hope & Charity; Hot Snow; Only Sky Free; Alice Childress's Mojo; When Eagle Screams; I Marcus Garvey; Films: voice of "Midnight Ravers; Ethnic Bacchanal; Occultist; Crooklyn, dir, 2009; M To Mob, dir; Fortunes Moor; Shakin' Mess Outta Misery; Ctr Theatre Tech Educ, actor & teacher, 1983-85; NY Univ Creative Arts Team, Crisis Resolution Through Drama, co-creator, 1985-87, Schomburg Ctr Res Black Cult Tribute Langston Huges I've Known Rivers Ceremonial Actor, 1991; Frank Silver Writers Workshop, am reporter, 1992; Almas Rainbow, actor & contrib feature film, 1994; Angel Child Prods, LLC, founder & chief exec officer, 1997-2002; NY Univ & Actors Equity Asn, CAGE Afro Centric, writer & performer, 1998-2000; Lock Down, 2000-01; campaign rep, 2001; Taking Back New York, reading ser, 2001; INN Report, anchor, 2002-. **Orgs:** Nat Asn Advan Colored People, 1970-; Screen Actors Guild, 1988-2000; dist coordr, Nichiren Shoshu Temple, 1998-2002; judge, Nat Acad Arts & Sci, 1996-2000. **Honors/Awds:** Award in the Arts, Lincoln Ctr, 1969; Actress Extra ordinaire, State NY, 1981; Nominee, Recognition Award, Audience Develop Comt Inc, 1990; Clifford A Ridley Citation for Notable Achievement in Theater, Philadelphia Inquirer, 1992-93; Golden Reel Award, 2003. **Special Achievements:** Awarded one year course of study in African political studies at Univ of Lagos, Nigeria, 1971, History of Religions, co-presenter, Univ of Chicago, 1974, Theatre for the Forgotten, 1981, United Nations, "I, Marcus Garvey", benefit performer, 1990, Abysinnian Baptist Church, "The Glory of the African Diaspora", commentator, 1991, WBAI, Pacifica Public Radio, "Tribute to the Martyrs", presenter, 1991, "Tribute to Nestor Robert Marley", guest speaker, 2000, wrote and acted in "Incidents" at Playwrights Horizons Voice & Vision Production: 1, 000 years of women playwrights, 1997. **Business Addr:** Actor, Andreadis Talent Agency, 119 W 57th St Suite 711, New York, NY 10019, **Business Phone:** (212)315-0303.

**NUNEZ, MIGUEL A., JR.**
Actor, movie producer, movie director. **Personal:** Born Aug 11, 1964, New York, NY; married Yulanda Simon; children: Mia & Micole. **Career:** TV Series: "Automan", 1984; "Tour of Duty", 1987; "Rhythm & Blues", 1992; "Martin", 1993; "Living Single", 1993-94; "Babylon 5", 1994; "My Wildest Dreams", 1995; "Sparks", 1996; "The Faculty", 1996; "Homeboys in Outer Space", producer, 1996; "Sparks", 1996-98; "The Hughleys", 1999; "The Parkers", 2000; "The Bernie Mac Show", 2002; "Boomtown", 2002; "Andy Richter Controls the Universe", 2002; "My Wife & Kids", 2003; "Tarzan", 2003; "The Tracy Morgan Show", 2004; "Flip the Script ", 2005; "Joey", 2005-06; "Joey & the Critic", 2006; "Joey & the Wedding", 2006; "The PTA", 2006; Black Poker Stars Invitational, 2008; Episode dated 5 November 2009; "Belle's", exec producer, writer; "Dolls of Voodoo", 2013. TV Films: Secrets, 1992; WEIRD World, 1995; For Richer or Poorer, 1997; Why Do Fools Fall in Love, 1998; Life, 1999; If You Only Knew, 2000; Nutty Professor II, 2000; Mac Arthur Park, 2001; Flossin, 2001; Zig Zag, 2002; Scooby Doo, 2002; Juwanna Man, 2002; Pluto Nash, 2002; Up Against the 8 Ball, dir, 2004; Bathsheba, 2005; Flip the Script, producer, 2005; Clean Up Men, 2005; Kickin It Old Skool, 2007; All Lies on Me, co-producer, 2007; Meet Dave, 2008; Black Dynamite, 2009; Diamond Dawgs, 2009; Haitian Nights, 2009; Back Nine, 2010; Blue Mountain State, 2010; Double Crossed, producer, 2010; Hollywood & Wine, 2010; Mad Love, 2011; Breathe, 2011; Nice Guy, assoc producer, 2012; School Dance, producer, 2014; Fair Chase, forthcoming, 2015; The Griddle House, forthcoming, 2015; Only You & Me, forthcoming, 2015. **Business Addr:** Actor, Abrams Artists Agency, 9200 Sunset Blvd Suite 1130, West Hollywood, CA 90069, **Business Phone:** (310)859-0625.

**NUNN, CLARENCE**
Marketing executive, executive, football player. **Personal:** Born Dec 29, 1964, Los Angeles, CA. **Educ:** San Diego State Univ, BS, bus, mgt, mkt, & related support serv, 1988; Rensselaer Polytech Inst, MBA, 2000. **Career:** Football player (retired), executive; New Orleans Saints, defensive back, 1988-89; Los Angeles Rams, football player, 1989-90; James River Corp, acct mgr, 1990-92; GE Polymerland, acct mgr, 1992-94, Americas qual leader, 2000-02; GE Plastics, sr acct mgr, 1994-96, global media mkt mgr, 1996-99, com dir, 1999-2001; GE Capital, sr vpres; GE Com Equip Finance, chief sales & mkt officer, 2002-04; GE Vendor Financial Serv, sr vpres & gen mgr, 2004-06; GE Capital Com Distrib Finance, chief com officer, 2005-06; GE Capital Fleet Serv, chief exec officer & pres, 2008-12; GE Capital Americas, GE vpres & chief com officer, 2012-14; GE Capital Franchise Finance, pres & chief exec officer, 2014-. **Orgs:** Mem, Exec Leadership Coun. **Special Achievements:** The 100 Most Powerful Executives in Corporate America, Black Enterprise, 2012. **Business Addr:** President, Chief Executive Officer, GE Capital - Franchise Finance, 8377 E Hartford Dr Suite 200, Scottsdale, AZ 85255, **Business Phone:** (866)438-4333.

**NUNN, GREGORY**
Chief executive officer. **Career:** Nunn & Assocs, chief exec officer, owner, currently. **Business Addr:** Chief Executive Officer, Nunn & Associates, 575 Madison Ave Suite 1006, New York, NY 10022, **Business Phone:** (212)826-1999.

**NUNN, JOHN**
Executive, vice president (organization). **Personal:** Born Sep 19, 1953, Berkeley, CA; son of John and Yvonne Hunter; married Valmere Fischer; children: Arianna M, Julian G & Micheala Y. **Educ:** St Mary's Col, Moraga, CA, BS, biol, 1976; Univ Calif, Berkeley, CA, 1975. **Career:** World Savings, Alamo, Calif, asst vpres br mgr, 1976-78; Am Savings, Oakland, Calif, asst vpres br mgr, 1979-80, El Cerrito, Calif, vpres regional mgr, 1980-85, sr vpres off chief admin officer, 1985-87, sr vpres, NC area mgr, 1987-89; Community Outreach & Urban Develop, sr vpres dir, 1989; UPS Stores, owner, 1999-2007; State Enterprise Zone Prog Mgr, calif, 2007-; Wash Mutual Bank, sr vpres, currently. **Orgs:** Alumni Bd, Bishop O'Dowd HS Prep, 1980-85; pres, Bishop O'Dowd HS Prep, 1985-87,; Stockton Chamber Com, 1987-; Stockton Black Chamber Com, 1987-; Sacramento Chamber Com, 1987-; Calif League Savings Inst, 1988-; Bus Sch Adv Bd, Calif State Univ, 1988-. **Home Addr:** 3224 Palomino Cir, Fairfield, CA 94533-7224, **Home Phone:** (707)429-3593. **Business Addr:** Senior Vice President, Washington Mutual Bank, 1301 2nd Ave, Seattle, WA 98101, **Business Phone:** (206)461-2000.

**NUNN, ROBINSON S.**
Judge, legal consultant, lawyer. **Personal:** Born Sep 29, 1944, Blytheville, AR; married Glanetta Miller. **Educ:** Mich State Univ, East Lansing, BA, social sci, 1966; Am Univ, Wash Col Law, Wash, DC, JD, 1969. **Career:** US Tax Ct, Wash, DC, legal asst, 1969, law clerk, 1973; Robinson nunn, atty, pvt law pract, little rock, ar, 1973-74; Little Rock, Ark, gen prac law, 1976; Small Bus Admin, Gen Coun Off, chief coun ethics, 1977-; US Tax Ct Bar, 1978; US Supreme Ct Bar, 1978. **Orgs:** Am Bar Asn; Nat Bar Asn, 1973-; Ark Bar Asn, 1973-; US Dist Ct, Eastern Dist Ark, 1973; US Dist Ct, Western Dist Ark, 1973; Nat Asn Advan Colored People; Kappa Alpha Psi Fraternity; pres, Mich State Black Alumni Asn, 1982-. **Home Addr:** PO Box 2204, Reston, VA 20195-0204. **Business Addr:** Chief Counsel for Ethics, Small Business Administration, 409 3rd St SW 7th Fl, Washington, DC 20416-0005, **Business Phone:** (202)205-6642.

**NUNN, RONNIE**
Basketball player, basketball coach, basketball executive. **Personal:** Born Brooklyn, NY; married Andee; children: Adena. **Educ:** George Washington Univ, phys educ; Brooklyn Tech, educ, cert, admin & supv. **Career:** Basketball player, referee (retired), basketball coach; Nat Basketball Circuit, basketball player; NY Knicks, basketball player; Houston Rockets, basketball player; NJ Nets, basketball player; Brooklyn Tech, asst coach, 1976-77; Pace Univ, asst coach, 1978-1980; Nat Basketball Asn, prof staff; Nat Pro-Am, mem; Western CT State Univ, coaching staff; Nat Basketball Asn, referee, 1984-2003; Nat Basketball Asn, dir of officials, currently. **Orgs:** Concerned Black MenYouth; Hord Found; Officiating Develop Alliance; Nat Pro-Am. **Home Addr:** PO Box 3392, Danbury, CT 06810. **Business Addr:** Director of Officials, National Basketball Association, 645 5th Ave 10th Fl, New York, NY 10022-5986, **Business Phone:** (212)407-8000.

**NUNNALLY, JONATHON KEITH**
Baseball player. **Personal:** Born Nov 9, 1971, Pelham, NC; married Tammy; children: Kristen,Josie & Jonathan. **Educ:** Miami-Dade Community Col, 1992. **Career:** Baseball player (retired); baseball coach; Kans City Royals, 1995-97; Cincinnati Reds, 1997-98; Boston Red Sox, 1999; New York Mets, 2000; Orix BlueWave; 2000; Milwaukee Brewers, left fielder; Pittsburgh Pirates, outfielder, 2005; Kinston Indians, hitting coach, 2006-; Cleveland Indians, hitting coach, 2009-11; Toronto Blue Jays, hitting coach, 2013-. **Business Addr:** Hitting Coach, Toronto Blue Jays, 1 Blue Jays Way Suite 3200, Toronto, ON M5V 1J1.

**NUNNERY, WILLIE JAMES**
Lawyer, government official. **Personal:** Born Jul 28, 1948, Chicago, IL. **Educ:** Univ Kans, Lawrence, BS, 1971; Univ Wis Sch Law, JD, 1975. **Career:** Atlantic Richfield, jr anal engr, 1971; Energy Res Ctr, Univ Wis, Col Eng, asso dir; Atlantic Richfield, legal intern, 1972; Univ Wis, Col Eng, asst dean, 1972-75; State WI, dep sec energy, 1975-; Midwestern Gov Energy Task Force; Four Lakes Area Boy Scout Coun, Wis, scout master & exec dir; Univ Wis, Sch Eng, adj assoc prof, 1984-85; Stolper, Kotzinski, Brewster & Neider, atty, 1985-86; pvt prac atty, 1986-; Nunnery Law Firm, atty, currently. **Orgs:** WI State Bar, 1976-; Pres Comt, Nat Medal Sci, 1981-89; Downtown Kiwanis Club Madison & Greenfield; Baptist Church; bd dir, Young Men Christian Asn. **Home Addr:** 17 Chequamegon Bay, Madison, WI 53711-3088, **Home Phone:** (608)271-7142. **Business Addr:** Attorney, Nunnery Law Firm, Bank 1 Bldg 802 W Broadway, Madison, WI 53713-1866, **Business Phone:** (608)224-1900.

**NURSE, RICHARD A.**
Vice president (organization), executive director, school administrator. **Personal:** Born Sep 1, 1939, New York, NY; son of Reginald and Bernice Lawless; children: Allison & Richard C. **Educ:** Brown Univ, polit sci & govt, RI, BA, 1961; NY Univ, pub admin, NY, attended 1968; Univ RI, Kingston, pub admin, RI, MPA, 1973. **Career:** Vice president (retired), execurive; AUS, France & Ger, counter intelligence, 1962-64; Prudential Ins Co, Newark, NY, actuarial corresp, 1964-66; AUS Electronics Command, Ft Monmouth, NJ, contract specialist, 1966-68; Brown Univ, Providence, RI, assoc dir admis, 1968-73, col admis officer; Stockbridge Sch, Stockbridge, Mass, headmaster, 1973-76; Rutgers Univ, Nb, NJ, Educ Opportunity Fund & Veterans Affairs, univ dir, 1976-86, asst vpres, 1986-2000, Rutgers Athletics, eng writing tutor, 2011-; Stockbridge Sch in Stockbridge, Mass, head master; Crossroads Theatre Co, boarding sch headmaster & exec dir, 2004-08; Gardner Doc Group, sr producer & grant writer, 2013-. **Orgs:** Bd trustee, Princeton Friends Sch, 1986-94; coun mem, Nj Basic Skills Coun, 1978-90; state chmn, Nj Alumni Brown Univ, 1986-90; bd dir, Planned Parenthood League Middlesex County, 1989-94; co-chmn, Dance Power, 1988-; bd trustee, Princeton Ballet; treas, Ctr Health & Social Policy; bd trustee, Arbor Glen Quaker Continuing Care Retirement COT; Grad Sch Bd, New Sch Univ; contract negotiator, Fed govt; Nj's largest Educ Opportunity Fund; exec asst minority affairs, pres, Rutgers Univ; african am adminr, Ivy League alma mater; procurement specialist, AUs Electronics Command, Red Bank; AUs's 513th Mil Intelligence br; trustee emer, Crossroads Theatre Co, currently. **Home Addr:** 27 Lilac Way, Piscataway, NJ 08854-3596, **Home Phone:** (732)627-9229. **Business Addr:** Executive Director, Crossroads Theatre Co, 7 Livingston Ave, New Brunswick, NJ 08901, **Business Phone:** (732)545-8100.

**NUTT, REV. MAURICE JOSEPH**
Clergy. **Personal:** Born Dec 20, 1962, St. Louis, MO; son of Haller Levi and Beatrice Lucille Duvall. **Educ:** Holy Redeemer Col, BA, philos, 1985; Cath Theol Union, MDiv, 1989; Xavier Univ, La, MS theol, 1989; Aquinas Inst Theol, DMin, 1997; Harvard Univ, John F Kennedy Sch Govt, Leadership Prog Sr Execs State & Local Govt. **Career:** St Alphonsus Rock Church, St Louis, Mo, from assoc pastor to pastor, 1989-93; St Louis Univ, adj prof theol, 1990-91; Redemptorist priest; Bd Police Comnr, pres, St Louis, Mo; Holy Names & Mary Cath Church, pastor, currently; Hampton Univ, Relig Studies Distance Learning Prog, fac mem; Xavier Univ, Inst for Black Cath Studies, fac mem. **Orgs:** Pres, Nat Black Cath Seminarians Asn, 1986-87; mem bd dir, Nat Black Cath Clergy Caucus, 1986-89; Seminarians Asn, 1988; organizer & speaker, Redemptorist Conf Black Ministry, 1989; pres, bd dir, Better Family Life Inc, 1990-98; bd dir, St Charles Lwanga Ctr, 1990; Portfolio Art Gallery, 1993; St Louis Civil Rights Comn, 1994; exec comt, Nat Asn Advan Colored People, St Louis Br, 1994; Young Dem St Louis, 1994; vpres, bd dir, Nat Coun Drug & Alcohol Abuse, St Louis Chap, 1995; Alpha Phi Alpha Fraternity, Inc. **Honors/Awds:** Man of the Year Award, St Joseph Preparatory Col, 1980; The Fr Clarence Williams Award, Nat Black Cath Seminarians Asn, 1988; Rodel Model Award, St Louis Pub Sch, 1990; Forty Under Forty Award, St Louis Mag, 1990; Trumpet of Justice Award, Institute for Peace & Justice, 1994; Young Democrats St Louis, 1994; Finalist, Greater Preacher Award, Aquinas Inst Theol, 1995; Steller Performer Award, St Louis American Newspaper, 1996; The John Simon Civic Service Award, Maryville Univ, 1997. **Special Achievements:** The First Black pastor of the hist St Louis Parish; Publ: Black Vocations: The Responsibility and Challenge, 1987; 32nd Pastor and the First African American Pastor. **Business Addr:** Pastor, Holy Names, 3141 Sandwich St, Windsor, ON N9C 1A7, **Business Phone:** (519)253-4217.

**NWA, WILLIA L. DEADWYLER**
Educator, pianist. **Personal:** Born Cleveland, OH; daughter of Thurman and Josephine; married Umoh; children: Idara, Jakitoro, Ayama, Ifiok & Uko. **Educ:** Ohio State Univ, BS, 1971; Wittenberg Univ, attended 1974; Univ Akron, MS, 1975, PhD, 1992. **Career:** Educator; Seventh Ave COT Baptist Church, pianist, organist, 1970-71; Northeastern Local Schs, educr, 1971-74; Canton City Schs, educr, 1975-; Univ Akron, supvr, 1989, Col Educ, fac, currently; Malone Col, adj prof, 1997-. **Orgs:** Exe comt, Coun Except C, Chap 464; Nat Educ Asn; Ohio Educ Asn; Canton Prof Educr's Asn; Ohio Teachers Except C; Asn Supv & Curric Develop; Am Educ Res Asn; Kappa Delta Pi, Alpha Theta Chap; Pi Lambda Theta, Beta Lambda Chap, exec com; Nat Alliance Black Sch Educrs; Leila Green Alliance Black Sch Educrs; Nat Cong Parents & Teachers Asn; Sunday Sch; Deaconess Bd, asst soc; Missionary Soc; E Cent Ohio Educ Asn. **Home Addr:** 1618 Spring Ave NE, Canton, OH 44714, **Home Phone:** (216)452-0011. **Business Addr:** Faculty, University of Akron, Zook 210, Akron, OH 44325-4201, **Business Phone:** (330)972-7111.

**NWAGBARAOCHA, DR. JOEL O.**
School administrator, dean (education), college president. **Personal:** Born Nov 21, 1942; son of John Oluigbo and Christiana; married Patsy Coleman; children: Eric, Jason, John & Jonathan. **Educ:** Norfolk State Univ, BS, math, 1969; Harvard Univ, MEd, educ planning & mgt, 1970, EdD, educ planning & mgt, 1972. **Career:** Inst Serv, Div Acad Planning & Fac Develop, dir, 1972-74; Morgan State Univ, vpres plan & opers anal, 1978-84; Tech Systs, pres, 1982-86; Voorhees Col, vpres, acad affairs, 1985-90; Barber-Scotia Col, pres, 1990-94; Strayer Univ, from adj fac to dean grad studies, campus dean fac, 1994-2006, interim univ pres, 2006-07, provost & chief acad officer, 2007-10, provost emer & spec asst to pres, currently. **Orgs:** Bd dir, Harvard Univ Coop Soc; bd dir, Harvard Univ Phi Delta Kappa Chap; bd dir, C Inst; bd dir, Higher Educ Support Serv; bd dir, African Relief Fund Inc; Higher Educ Group Wash, DC; Am Coun Educ; Nat Coun Social Studies; Am Humanist Asn. **Home Addr:** 117 Cabarrus Ave W, Concord, NC 28025, **Home Phone:** (704)782-7630. **Business Addr:** Provost Emeritus, Special Assistant to the President, Strayer University, 8335 IBM Dr Suite 150, Charlotte, NC 28262-4329, **Business Phone:** (704)717-2380.

**NWANNA, DR. GLADSON I. N.**
Educator. **Personal:** Born May 12, 1954, Mbonge. **Educ:** Essex County Col, AS, acct, 1977, AA, 1978; Rutgers State Univ, BA, acct, 1979; St Johns Univ, MBA, finance, 1980; Fordham Univ, PhD, econ, 1984; Am Inst Banking, cert, 1985. **Career:** NJ Blood Ctr, distrib clerk, 1978-79; St Benedict High Sch, math teacher, 1979-80; Essex County Col, adj prof math & bus, 1981-84; Kean Col, NJ, asst prof fin & econ, 1983-85; Rutgers State Univ, adj prof math, 1984; Morgan State Univ, Earl Graves Sch Bus & Mgt, prof acct & finance dept, 1985-. **Orgs:** Who's Who Am, Jr Col Essex County Col, 1978; Alpha Epsilon Beta, Essex County Col, 1979; Omicron Delta Epsilon, 1980; Beta Gamma Sigma, St Johns Univ, 1981; Rutgers State Univ, Int Stud Org, 1978-79, Am Econ Asn, 1983-, Eastern Fin Asn, 1985; World Acad Devel & Coop, 1986-; Nat Asn Advan Colored People, 1986; Nat Urban League, 1986; Soc Int Devel, 1986. **Home Addr:** 8268 Streamwood Dr, Baltimore, MD 21208. **Business Addr:** Professor of Accounting & Finance Department, Morgan State University, 608 McMechen Hall 1700 E Cold Spring Lane, Baltimore, MD 21251, **Business Phone:** (443)885-3254.

**NYONG'O, LUPITA**
Movie actor, movie director. **Personal:** Born Mar 1, 1983; daughter of Peter Anyang and Dorothy. **Educ:** Hampshire Col, BA, film & theatre studies; Yale Sch Drama, MA, actg. **Career:** Actress: tv series "Shuga", 2009-12; producer/writer/director of documentary "In My Genes", 2009; theatrical movie "Non-Stop", 2014; "Star Wars: Episode VII--The Force Awakens", 2015; "The Jungle Book", 2015; stage actress in "The Winter's Tale" (Yale Repertory Theatre), "Uncle Vanya", "The Taming of the Shrew", Michael Mitnick's "Elijah". **Honors/Awds:** Winner of various award as Patsey in "12 Years a Slave"-- Academy Award for Best Supporting Actress (2014), BET Awards for Best Actress (2014), African-American Film Critics Association (2013), Boston Online Film Critics Association (2013), Chicago Film Critics Association (2013), Hollywood Film Festival (2013), Houston Film Critics Society (2013), Las Vegas Film Critics Society (2013), Los Angeles Film Critics Association (2013), Phoenix Film Critics Society (2013), Screen Actors Guild (2013), Washington DC Area Film Critics Association (2013); "People" magazine, The Most Beautiful Woman, 2014; "Glamour" magazine, Woman of the Year, 2014. **Special Achievements:** Became the sixth African American Actress to win the Best Support Actress award; featured on magazine covers of "Vogue," "New York," and "ELLE"; named "Face of Lancome" (French luxury cosmetic brand) in April 2014.

**O'BANNO, DR. DONNA M. EDWARDS (DONNA MARIA EDWARDS)**
Judge, lawyer. **Personal:** Born Jun 26, 1957, New York, NY; daughter of Theodore U (deceased) and Ione Dunkley; married Don T OBannon Jr; children: Danielle Salone & Dionne Teddie. **Educ:** Wellesley Col, BA, 1979; Univ Va Sch Law, JD, 1982. **Career:** Exxon Co USA, tax atty, 1982-85; Harris County DA, ast DA, 1985-87; US Equal Employ Opportunity Comn, trial atty, 1987-88, admin judge, 1994-2003; sr trial atty, 1988-89; FDIC, Consol Off, staff atty, 1989-90, Litigation Dept, head, 1990-92, sr regional atty, 1992-94; Thur good Marshall Recreation Ctr, vpres, 1994-96, pres, 1996-; Equal Employ Opportunity Tech Adv, US Dept Treas, Treas Complaint Ctr, Dallas, 2003-; pvt pract, currently. **Orgs:** Hundred Black Women, 1989-94; int trends chair, Links Inc, 1992-94, historian, 1994-96, cor resp secy, 1996-; Thurgood Marshall Recreation Ctr Adv Coun, vpres, 1994-96, pres, 1996-98; chair, Parish Coun, Holy Cross Cath Church; State Bar Tex; Jack & Jill Am Inc. **Honors/Awds:** Freshman Honors, Wellesley Col, 1975-76; Wellesley Scholar, 1979; Pinkston Camp Award, Mooreland YMCA, 1991; Special Achievement Award, FDIC, 1992-94; Special Achievement Award, EEOC, 1994-2002. **Special Achievements:** Tax article, UVA Tax Rev, 1982. **Business Addr:** Lawyer, Private Practice, 2122 Elderoaks Lane, Dallas, TX 75232-3309, **Business Phone:** (214)339-0309.

**O'BANNON, CHARLES EDWARD**
Basketball player. **Personal:** Born Feb 22, 1975, Bellflower, CA. **Educ:** Univ Calif, attended 1997. **Career:** Detroit Pistons, guard & forward, 1997-99; Slask Wroclaw (Poland), 1999-2000; Polonia, Polish Basketball League, Warsaw, Poland, player, 2002; Benetton Treviso (Italy), 2003; Ital League, Suns; Toyota Alvark, 2003-10; Toshiba Brave

Thunders (Japan), 2010-11; Panasonic Trians (Japan), 2011-. **Business Addr:** Professional Basketball Player, Panasonic Trians, Osaka.

**O'BANNON, EDWARD CHARLES, JR.**
Basketball coach, basketball player, car dealer. **Personal:** Born Aug 14, 1972, Los Angeles, CA; married Rosa; children: Aaron, Jazmin & Edward III. **Educ:** Univ Nev, Las Vegas; Univ Calif, Los Angeles, CA, attended 1995. **Career:** Basketball player (retired), car salesman; NJ Nets, 1995-97; Dallas Mavericks, 1997; La Crosse Bobcats, 1998; Acegas A.P.S. Trieste, Italy, 1998; CB Valladolid, Spain, 1998-99; Rethymno Aegean, Greece, 1999-2000; Boca Juniors, Arg, 1999-2000; Los Angeles Stars, 2000-01; Anwil Wloclawek, Poland, 2001-02; Polonia Warszawa, Poland, 2002-03; Ostromecko Astoria Bydgoszcz Poland, 2003-04; Green Valley High Sch, vol coach; Henderson Int Sch, head coach; Las Vegas auto dealership, car salesman, 2006, mkt dir, currently.

**O'BRIEN, MARY NELL**
Labor activist, business owner. **Personal:** Born Mar 23, 1945, Bolton, MS; married Hank; children: Edgar Whipps Jr. **Educ:** Utica Jr Col, attended 1964; Campbell Jr Col, attended 1965. **Career:** Business owner, labor activist (retired); IBEW Local Union 2262, negotiating comn, 1970, fin sec, 1971-78, int rep, pres, 2000; Hammond Jr High Sch PTA, first vpres; A Philips Randolph Conf, resource person & workshop instr; catering bus, co-owner, 2000-. **Orgs:** Corresp sec, MS A Philip Randolph Inst, 1973-76; sec, treas, Jackson Cent Labor Union, AFL CIO COPE Dir, 1974-78; labor sect chairperson, United Way Kick Off Fund Dr; secy, Ind Employee Credit Union, bd dirs; Labors' Panel on Easter Seal Telethon; vpres, pres, Ramsey Rec Ctr Alexandria, 1980-82; Nat exec bd, Coalition Labor Union Women, 1984-86; steering comt, Nat A Philip Randolph Inst, 1984; IBEW Minority Caucus, 1974-78. **Honors/Awds:** Among first Black females at Presto Mfg Co; delegate to many Union activities including MS AFL CIO Convention, Jackson Central Labor Union, MS Electrical Workers Asn, Natl Conference A Philip Randolph; Crowned Miss A Philip Randolph; 2 Outstanding Service Awards, MS A Philip Randolph Inst; Service Awards IBEW Local 2262, IBEW Syst Council EM 6. **Special Achievements:** First African American female Intl Rep of Intl Brotherhood of Elect Workers AFL CIO (IBEW); Labor's Ad Hoc Committee Natl Coun Negro Women. **Home Addr:** 10722 Castleton Turn, Upper Marlboro, MD 20774-1450, **Home Phone:** (301)350-8079.

**O'BRIEN, SOLEDAD**
Journalist, broadcaster. **Personal:** Born Sep 19, 1966, St. James, NY; daughter of Edward and Estella; married Bradley Raymond; children: Sofia Elizabeth Raymond, Cecilia Raymond, Charles Raymond & Jackson Raymond. **Educ:** Harvard Univ, BA, Eng & Am lit, 2000. **Career:** KISS-FM (Boston), reporter, 1989; WBZ-TV (Boston), assoc producer & news writer; NBC-affil KRON (San Francisco), corresp, 1988-91; NBC News, corresp, 1991-2003; CNN, corresp, 2003-13; Al Jazeera Am, corresp, 2013-; Starfish Media Group, owner, 2013-. **Orgs:** Nat Asn Black Journalists; Nat Asn Hisp Journalists; bd dirs, Harlem Sch Arts. **Honors/Awds:** People Magazine, 50 Most Beautiful People in the World, 2000; "Black Enterprise" Magazine, Hot List, 2005; Gracie Allen Award, 2007; NAACP President's Award, 2007; Morehouse School of Medicine, Soledad O'Brien Freedom's Voice Award, 2008; Johns Hopkins Bloomberg School of Public Health, Goodermote Humanitarian Award, 2008; Congressional Hispanic Caucus Institute, Medallion of Excellence for Leadership and Community Service Award, 2009; National Association of Black Journalists, Journalist of the Year, 2010; Emmy Award, Outstanding Live Coverage of a Current News Story--Long Form, 2011; Spelman College, Commencement Speaker and honorary Doctor of Human Letters, 2014. **Special Achievements:** Author: "Latinos in America" (Celebra Trade, 2009): "The Next Big Story: My Journey Through the Land of Possibilities" (New American Library, 2010).

**O'BRYANT, BEVERLY J.**
Educator. **Personal:** Born Aug 21, 1947, Washington, DC; daughter of James C and Gertrude Robb; married Michael T O; children: Kimberly Michelle & Michael Tilmon II. **Educ:** Dumbarton Col, BA, elem educ, 1969; Univ Md, MA, coun, 1972; Bowie State Univ, PhD, counr educ. **Career:** DC School Administrator (retired); James C. Jones Builders Inc, asst estimator, 1965-80; DC Pub Schs, counr, 1978-88, 1990-92, reg counr, 1986-88, Elem Div, pupil personnel team coordr, 1988-90, exec asst to supt, 1992-94, dir community serv learning progs, comnr; Mazima CRP, tech writer, ed, res analyst, 1979-80; Bowie State Univ, Dept Educ Studies & Leadership, dir & asst prof, prof, Minority Male Health Proj, res dir, asst prof, doctoral prog, dir, coordr res & Grad Studies & Res, asst to provost, fac, Dept of Coun, Dept of Supv & Admin; Coppin State Univ, Sch Prof Studies, dean, currently; Trinity Col, adj prof; Miss State Univ, adj prof. Article: A Call for National School Counselor Certification. **Orgs:** Pres, Inter prof Rels, chap, 1983-85; pres, Counr/CounImage Task Force, 1985-86; vpres, N Atlantic Region, 1985-87; pres, Leadership Develop CNF, chap, 1986; pres, Ethics Comt, chap, 1988-90; pres, Gov CNL, 1989-94; pres, Am Sch Counr Asn, 1990-91; pres, Am Coun Asn, 1993-94; Barrister's Wives Dis Columbia; Jack Jill Inc Am; Kiwanis Wives DC; Am Asn Teachers Col Edu; Nat Bd Cert Counors; Am Pub Health asn; pres, Asn Multicultural Coun & Develop; Nat Orgn Fetal Alcohol Syndrome; Asn Supv & Curric Develop; Int Roundtable Advan Coun; bd, Universalities Retention /task Force; bd, Col Bd Equity 2000 nat Guid Comt; Alpha Kappa Alpha sorority Inc; fel Wash DC Assocs Chap; Historically Black cols. **Home Addr:** 1777 Sycamore St NW, Washington, DC 20012, **Home Phone:** (202)882-4990. **Business Addr:** Dean, Coppin State University, 2500 W N Ave, Baltimore, MD 21216-3698, **Business Phone:** (410)951-2666.

**O'BRYANT, DR. CONSTANCE TAYLOR**
Judge. **Personal:** Born Apr 12, 1946, Meherrin, VA; daughter of Joseph E Taylor and Mattie Naomi Taylor; married Adgie O Bryant Jr; children: Taylora Laurece Obryant & Kristal Cherrie (Yusef Mohammed Kassim). **Educ:** Howard Univ, Col Liberal Arts, BA, 1968, Sch Law, JD, 1971. **Career:** Judge (retired); DC Pub Defender Serv, sr staff atty, 1971-81; Dept Health & Human Serv, Social Security Admin, admin law judge, 1981-83, admin appeals judge, 1983-90, Dept Appeals Bd, admin law judge, 1991, Social Security Adm, dep chief admin law judge, 1991-94; Harvard Law Trial Advocacy Workshop, vis fac, 1985-86, 1996-97; Dept Housing & Urban Develop, admin law judge, 1994; Sch Law, John Marshall Univ, vis fac, 1997-98; US Am Dept Housing & Urban Develop Off Admin Law Judges, admin law judge. **Orgs:** Secy, Friends DC Youth Orchestra, 1987-89; secy, Banneker Sch Coun, 1989-91; exec bd, Nat Asn Advan Colored People, Nat Urban League Off Hearings & Appeals, SSA Law J, 1991-94; SSA Strategic Planning Comn, 1991-94; chair, bd trustee, DC Pub Defender Serv, 1992-98; exec bd, Fed Admin Law Judge Conf, 1995-97; tutor, DC Pub Sch-Reading & Math, 1995-96; vol, Proj Champ, 1996-97; tutor & mentor, Nat Coun Negro Women, 1998; Nat Bar Asn; Judicial Coun NBA; Nat Asn Women Judges; adv bd, Joint Educal Facil. **Home Addr:** 2129 32nd St SE, Washington, DC 20020-3384, **Home Phone:** (202)582-0771. **Business Addr:** DC.

**O'CONNOR, DR. RODNEY EARL**
Dentist. **Personal:** Born Jun 25, 1950, Sharon, PA; son of Dr Lauriston E and Helena B McBride; children: Elena Moi & Candance Nicole. **Educ:** Ky State Univ, Frankfort, KY, 1971; Univ Ky, Lexington, KY, Col Dent, DMD, 1975; Eastman Dent Ctr, Rochester, NY, 1976; Rochester Inst Technol, 1983. **Career:** Rushville Clin, dent, consult, 1976-77; Rochester Health Network, dent consult, 1978-87; RE O'Connor DDS, vpres, 1978-; Anthony L Jordan Health Ctr, consult, 1981-85; Westgate Nursing Home, consult, 2006-10; Dr. Rodney O'Connor Family Dent, dent, currently. **Orgs:** Fel Strong Hosp Dent Res, 1972; Treas, Oper Big Vote, 1983; Acad Gen Dent, 1984-; Am Dent Asn; Nat Dent Asn; Northeast Regional Dent Bd; mentor, Urban League Mentorship Prog, 1990-91; Dent Soc State NY; 7th Dist Dent Soc; 19th Ward Asn; bd mem, Anthony L Jordan Health Ctr; Monroe County Dent Soc. **Honors/Awds:** Abstr & patent search, Method Ultrasonic Pyrogenic Root Canal Ther, 1976; Distinguished Service, 1991; Distinguished Chefs, 1991, 1992; Community Service Award, Ward Asn, 1999; American Top Dentists, 2000. **Special Achievements:** Recorded CD of original music, Time Traveled, 1998. **Home Addr:** 311 Aberdeen St, Rochester, NY 14619, **Home Phone:** (716)436-9518. **Business Addr:** Vice President, Dr Rodney O'Connor Family Dent, 521 Beahan Rd Gates, Rochester, NY 14624, **Business Phone:** (585)436-1640.

**O'CONNOR, THOMAS F., JR.**
Lawyer, executive. **Personal:** Born Mar 16, 1947, New Bedford, MA; married Donna L Dias; children: Jolon Thomas, Justin Kahil & Quinton Kolby. **Educ:** Roger Williams Col, AA, BA, 1975; New Eng Sch Law, JD, 1993. **Career:** War II Providence, city councilman, sch comt man, 1973-79; City Coun, 1979-89; Dept Planning, 1989-90; Port Comn, assoc dir proj mgt & construct, 1990-94; Dept Planning & Develop, spec assoc dir, dep dir. **Orgs:** ILA Local 1329; bd dir, Afro Arts Ctr; bd dir, S Providence Tutorial; pres, Omni Dev Corp; treas, RI Black Lawyers Asn. **Home Addr:** 202 Cong Ave, Providence, RI 02907.

**O'FLYNN-PATTILLO, PATRICIA**
Executive. **Personal:** Born Jul 28, 1940, St. Louis, IL; daughter of James E and Margarette Matthews; married Roland A; children: Terence (deceased) & Todd. **Educ:** Southern Ill Univ, BS, 1963; Univ Wis-Milwaukee, MA, educ admin, 1973; St Martins Acad, hon doctoral, 1983. **Career:** Nat Newspaper Publ Asn, pres, 1987-90, vpres secy, 1983-86; Milwaukee Minority C C, dir, 1986; Milwaukee Nat Asn Advan Colored People, dir, 1983; Milwaukee Community Jour Inc, newspaper publ, pres, chief exec officer, currently; MCJ Publ; pub pvt partnership Inc, pres; Speech singing group, Arrested Develop, agt, currently; MCJ weekly newspaper, founder, chief exec officer; Milwaukee Community J Inc, pres, publ. **Orgs:** Founder, Eta Phi Beta Milwaukee Chap, 1976; founder, Milwaukee Comm Pride Expo, 1976; mayoral, appt Lakefront Design Comm, 1979; founder, Milwaukee Chap Squaws, 1980; gov appt, Comm Small Bus, 1980; dir, Milwaukee Chap PUSH, 1980; deleg, White House Comm, 1980. **Special Achievements:** First female president of the National Newspaper Publishers Association. **Home Addr:** 3608 N Martin L King Dr, Milwaukee, WI 53212, **Home Phone:** (414)265-6647. **Business Addr:** Publisher, Chief Executive Officer, Milwaukee Community Journal Inc, 3612 N Martin L King Dr, Milwaukee, WI 53212, **Business Phone:** (414)265-5300.

**O'LEARY, HAZEL R.**
Government official, consultant, college president. **Personal:** Born May 17, 1937, Newport News, VA; daughter of Russell E and Hazel Palleman; married Carl G Rollins Jr; children: Carl; married Max Robinson; married John F. **Educ:** Fisk Univ; Rutgers Univ, JD, law. **Career:** State NJ, atty gen & asst prosecutor; Coopers & Ly brand, partner; Gerald Ford Admin, Community Serv Admin, gen coun; Ford Admin, dir fed energy post; Carter Admin, Dept Energys Econ Regulatory Admin, head; Northern States Power Co, Minneapolis, MN, exec vpres environ & pub affairs, pres natural gas div; O'Leary & Assocs Inc, vice pres & gen coun, 1981-89, pres, 1997-; Clinton Admin, US Dept Energy, secy, 1993-97; Blaylock & Partners LP, pres & chief oper officer, 2001-02; Fisk Univ, pres, 2002-13. **Orgs:** Bd trustee, Morehouse Col, 1998-; bd trustee, Africare; dir, AES Corp; dir, Alchemix Corp; bd trustee, Ctr Democracy; bd trustee, Keystone Ctr; dir, ICF Kaiser Inc; dir, United Continental Holdings, 1999-2005; dir, Scottish Re Group Ltd, 2001; bd trustee, World Wildlife Fund; Alpha Kappa Alpha sorority; bd trustee, Andrew Young Ctr Int Develop; bd mem, Nashville Alliance Pub Educ; bd dir, Nashville Bus Community Arts, & Arms Control Asn; Nj State Bar Asn; Dc Bar Asn; independent dir, ITC Holdings Corp, 2007; independent dir, Erin Energy Corp 2010-. **Special Achievements:** Become the second woman and third African American nominated to the Clinton Cabinet. **Business Addr:** Independent Director, Erin Energy Corporation, 1330 Post Oak Blvd Suite 2250, Houston, TX 77056, **Business Phone:** (713)797-2940.

**O'LEARY, TROY FRANKLIN**
Baseball player. **Personal:** Born Aug 4, 1969, Compton, CA. **Educ:** Chaffey Col. **Career:** Baseball player (retired); Milwaukee Brewers, outfielder, 1993-94; Boston Red Sox, 1995-2001; Montreal Expos, 2002; Tampa Bay Devil Rays, free agt, 2002; Montreal Expos, 2002; Chicago Cubs, 2003; Samsung Lions, 2004; Daikyo Dolphins; baseball leagues, S Korea.

**O'NEAL, REV. EDDIE S.**
Educator, clergy. **Personal:** Born Mar 28, 1935, Meridian, MS; son of Eddie S and Sara Lenora. **Educ:** Tougaloo So Christian Col, BA, 1963; Andover Newton Theol Sch, BD, 1967, STM, cum laude, 1969, DMin, 1972. **Career:** Clergy (retired); Rockefeller Protestant fel, 1962-66; Woodrow Wilson fel, 1963; Peoples Baptist Church, assoc minister; Clinton Ave Baptist Church, co-pastor; Myrtle Bapt, pastor; St Mark Congregational, assoc pastor; Mt Olive Baptist Church, pastor; Pine Grove Baptist Church, pastor; Andover Newton Theol Sch, william bartlet prof sacred rhet, emer, currently. **Orgs:** Chmn, Black Studies Comn Boston Theol Inst, 1970-76; Ministries Black Higher Educ; Interfaith Coun Ministry & Aging; Rockefeller Protestant Fel Prg; trustee, Andover Newton Theol Sch; auditor, United Baptist Conv Mass & RI; Nat Comn Black Chmn; Soc Study Black Relig; City Missionary Soc Boston; Am Bapt Conv; Nat Asn Advan Colored People; Omega Psi Phi Frat; consult, Women's Serv Club. **Honors/Awds:** Key to the City of Newton, MA, 1969; Andover Newton Quar, 1970. **Special Achievements:** Articles Christian Century, 1971. **Home Addr:** 239 Manning St, Needham, MA 02492, **Home Phone:** (781)449-7058. **Business Addr:** Professor Emeritus, Andover Newton Theological School, 210 Herrick Rd, Newton Centre, MA 02459, **Business Phone:** (617)964-1100.

**O'NEAL, FREDRICK WILLIAM, JR.**
Engineer, consultant, government official. **Personal:** Born Dec 8, 1948, Chicago, IL; son of Fredrick W and Essie M Reed (deceased). **Educ:** Roosevelt Univ, Chicago, IL, BS, 1985; Keller Grad Sch Mgmt, Chicago, IL, MBA, 1987. **Career:** Commonwealth Edison Co, Chicago, Ill, efficiency technician, 1966-71; Western Union Tel Co, Chicago, Ill, comput technician, 1972-88; City Chicago, Dept Fleet Mgmt, prin systs eng, 1988-96, dir, dp, 1996-; Fredrick W O'neal, Realtor, agt, currently. **Orgs:** City Chicago, Dept Fleet Mgmt, Dir Info Systs, 2002-; Telecom Profs. **Business Addr:** Agent, Fredrick W O'neal, 11440 S Bell Ave, Chicago, IL 60643, **Business Phone:** (773)925-9300.

**O'NEAL, JERMAINE LEE**
Business owner, basketball player. **Personal:** Born Oct 13, 1978, Columbia, SC; son of Angela Ocean; married Mesha; children: Jermaine Jr & Asjia. **Career:** Portland Trail Blazers, power forward, 1996-99, ctr, 1999-2000; Ind Pacers, ctr & power forward, 2000-08; Toranto Raptors, 2008-09; Miami heat, ctr, 2009-10; Boston Celtics, ctr, 2010-12; Phoenix Suns, ctr, 2012-13; Bogota Entertainment, owner, currently; Golden State Warriors, power forward, 2013-14. **Honors/Awds:** Gold Medal, Goodwill Games, 2001; All-Star, Nat Basketball Asn, 2002-07; Most Improved Player Award, Nat Basketball Asn, 2002; Gold Medal, FIBA Americas Championship, San Juan, 2003; Magic Johnson Award, Pro Basketball Writers Asn, 2004. **Business Addr:** Professional Basketball Player, Miami Heat, Am Airlines Arena, Miami, FL 33132, **Business Phone:** (786)777-4234.

**O'NEAL, LESLIE CLAUDIS**
Football player. **Personal:** Born May 7, 1964, Little Rock, AR. **Educ:** Okla State Univ. **Career:** Football player (retired); San Diego Chargers, right defensive back, 1986, 1992-95, right outside linebacker, 1989-91; St.Louis Rams, defensive back, 1996-97; Kans City Chiefs, left defensive back, 1998, defensive end & middle linebacker, 1999. **Honors/Awds:** Defensive Rookie of the Year, Nat Football League, 1986; Pro Bowl, 1989, 1990, 1992, 1993, 1994, 1995; All-Pro, 1990, 1992, 1994; Champion, Am Football Conf, 1994; Hall of Fame, San Diego Chargers, 2014; Oklahoma Sports Hall of Fame, 2014; Big Eight Defensive Player of the Year.

**O'NEAL, MALINDA KING**
Executive. **Personal:** Born Jan 1, 1929, Cartersville, GA; daughter of Dan; married Sheppard Dickerson Sr; children: Sheppard D Jr & Sherod Lynn. **Educ:** Morris Brown Col, BA, 1965; Atlanta Univ, MA, 1970; Alumni Admin Am Alumni Coun, Wash, DC, cert; Skillings Bus Col, Kilmarnock, Scotland, prof cert. **Career:** Radio Sta WERD, rec librn, disc jockey & continuity writer, 1949-50; Mammy's Shanty Restaurant Atlanta, sec bookkeeper, 1951-53; MKO Graphics & Printers, Atlanta, Ga, owner & pres, 1987-; Nat Cong Colored Parents & Teachers Atlanta, off dir; Emory Univ Ctr Res Soc Chg, field supvr spec proj; Morris Brown Col, dir alumni affairs, gov rels, dir admiss & dean stud. **Orgs:** Better Bus Bur, 1988; Atlanta Bus League, 1988; United Negro Col Fund; Nat Asn Advan Colored People; YWCA; Kappa Omega chap, Alpha Kappa Alpha; vol, Atlanta Coun Int Visitors; trustee bd, Ebenezer Baptist Church. **Home Addr:** 215 Piedmony Ave NE Apt 306, Atlanta, GA 30308-3319, **Home Phone:** (404)523-0845. **Business Addr:** President, Owner, MKO Graphics & Printers, 846 M L King Jr Dr SW, Atlanta, GA 30314, **Business Phone:** (404)523-1560.

**O'NEAL, RAYMOND W., SR.**
Executive director, lawyer. **Personal:** Born Sep 22, 1940, Dayton, OH; son of Carrie B and Henry L; married Brenda; children: Raymond Jr & Terisa. **Educ:** Ohio Univ, BA, 1968; Howard Univ, MA, 1968, JD, 1973. **Career:** US Dept Trea, financial analyst, 1971-74; Wilberforce Univ, polit sci asn prog, 1977-79; Miami Univ, econs instr, 1978-84; atty Law, sole practr, 1981-; Advan Eldercare Law Firm, lawyer, currently; 39th House Dist cand to Ohio Legis, 1992. **Orgs:** Founder, Dayton-Miami Valley Minority Chamber Com; APA Fraternity Inc, 1970-; Ohio Bar Asn, 1981-; second vpres, Cent Steering Comt, Montgomery County Republican Party, 1981-; Am Bar Asn, 1982-; bd mem, Dayton Educ & Legal Comn, Nat Asn Advan Colored People, 1987-92; bd mem, Montgomery County Arthritis Found, 1990-92; O'Neal Fund, 2000. **Honors/Awds:** Economics Honorary, Omicron Delta Epsilon, 1968; Business Leadership Award, Middletown Ohio, 1984; Citizens Volunteer Award, City Dayton, 1992; Assistance To Indigent Clients Award, Dayton Bar Asn, 1992. **Special Achievements:** The Black Labor Force in the USA: Critical Analysis (master's thesis), 1968. **Home Addr:** 2128 University Pl, Dayton, OH 45406-5965. **Business Addr:** Lawyer, Advance Eldercare Law Firm, 211 S M St Suite 1130, Dayton, OH 45402-2419, **Business Phone:** (937)222-7773.

## O'NEAL, RODNEY

President (organization), chief executive officer. **Personal:** Born Jan 1, 1954. **Educ:** Kettering Univ, BS, 1976; Gen Motors Inst, BS; Stanford Univ, MS. **Career:** Gen Motors, Inland Div, engineering & mfg, 1975-91, dir mfg engineering, GM Serv Parts, gen dir warehousing & distrib, 1994; Chevrolet-Pontiac-GM Can Group, dir, 1991-92; ACG Worldwide, dir mfg, 1992-94; Delphi, dir mfg, 1992-94, officer, 1997-98, Interior Systs Div, vpres & pres, 1997; Delphi Interior & Lighting Systs, gen mgr, 1997-98, vpres, pres, 1998; Woodward Inc, dir, 1999-2004; GM Serv Parts Opers, gen dir warehousing & distrib; Delphi Holdings Corp, exec vpres safety, 2000-03, pres Dynamics, Propulsion, Thermal, 2003-05, exec dir, 2005, pres & chief operating officer, 2005-06, chief exec officer & pres, 2007-09; Delphi Automotive PLC, chief exec officer & pres, 2009-15, dir, 2011-15; Steering Solutions Serv Corp, chief exec officer & pres; Merrick Ventures LLC, spec advisor; Wrapports LLC, dir. **Orgs:** Bd mgr, Delphi; bd dir, Goodyear Tire & Rubber Co, 2004-12; bd dir, Sprint/Nextel, 2007-13; Exec Leadership Coun, 2007-; bd dir, Inroads Inc; bd dir, Mich Manufacturers Asn; adv bd, Focus: HOPE. **Honors/Awds:** "Black Enterprise," The 100 Most Powerful Executives in Corporate America, 2010. Achievement in Industry Award, Nat Soc Black Engrs, 2002. **Business Addr:** Member, The Executive Leadership Council, 1001 N Fairfax St Suite 300, Alexandria, VA 22314, **Business Phone:** (703)706-5200.

## O'NEAL, SHAQUILLE RASHAUN

Actor, basketball player, business owner. **Personal:** Born Mar 6, 1972, Newark, NJ; son of Joseph Toney and Lucille O'Neal Harrison; married Arnetta Yardbourgh; children: Taheara; married Shaunie Nelson; children: Shareef Rashaun, Amirah Sanaa, Me'arah & Shaquir Rashaun. **Educ:** La State Univ, BA, gen studies, 2000; Univ Phoenix, MBA, 2005; Syracuse Univ, attended 2009; Barry Univ, EdD, human resource develop, 2012. **Career:** Basketball player (retired), executive, actor, musician; Orlando Magic, ctr, 1993-96; Los Angeles Lakers, 1996-2004; TWISM RecLabel, founder, 1997-; Miami Heat, ctr, 2004-08; Phoenix Suns, ctr, 2008-09; Cleveland Cavaliers, 2009-10; Boston Celtics, 2010-11; Los Angeles Port Police, res officer; Sheriff's dept, hon dep; real estate entrepreneur; TWISM Clothing Co, founder & owner, currently; Sacramento Kings, minority owner, 2013; Loyale3 Holdings Inc, owner, 2015; Big Podcast with Shaq, host, currently. Film: CB4, 1993; Blue Chips, 1994; Kazaam, 1996; Good Burger, 1997; Steel, 1997; He Got Game, 1998; Freddy Got Fingered, 2001; The Wash, 2001; The Year of the Yao, 2004; After the Sunset, 2004; The Kid & I, 2005; Scary Movie 4, 2006; The House Bunny, 2008; When in Rome, 2010; Jack and Jill, 2011; Grown Ups 2, 2013; The Smurfs 2, 2013; The Lego Movie, 2014; Blended, 2014. Rap Album: Shaq Diesel; Shaq Fu: The Return, 1994. **Orgs:** Founder, Real Model Found; spokesman, Safe Surfin' Found. **Honors/Awds:** Eddie Gottlieb Award, 1993; NBA Rookie of the Year, 1993; NBA All-Rookie First Team, 1993; NBA All-Star, 1993-98; CableACE Award, 1996; Gold Medal, US Olympic Basketball Team, 1996; NBA Most Valuable Player, 1999-01; NBA Champions, 2000; Adolph Rupp Trophy; SEC Player of the Year; Naismith Memorial Basketball Hall of Fame, 2016; LSU Hall of Fame; hon US Dep Marshal. **Special Achievements:** First pick, overall, NBA draft, first round, 1992; Nominated for Razzie Award, 1995 & 1998; Selected as one of the 50 Greatest Players in NBA Hist, 1996, was ranked No 9 on SLAM Magazine's Top 75 NBA Players of all time in 2003; Films: CB4, 1993; Blue Chips, 1994; Kazaam, 1996; Good Burger, 1997; Stell, 1997; He Got Game, 1998; Freddy Got Fingered, 2001; The Wash, 2001; The Year of the Yao, 2004; After the Sunset, 2004; The Kid & I, 2005; Scary Movie 4, 2006; The House Bunny, 2008; Jack & Jill, 2011; Albums: Shaq Diesel; Shaq Fu: Da Return; You Can't Stop the Reign; Respect. **Home Addr:** , Sudbury, MA. **Business Addr:** Founder, Owner, TWISM Promotions Inc, 500 Executive Blvd, New York, NY 10562, **Business Phone:** (845)623-9258.

## O'NEAL, STANLEY

Executive director, association executive, executive. **Personal:** Born Oct 7, 1951, Roanoke, AL; married Nancy Garvey; children: 2. **Educ:** Kettering Univ, BS, indust admin, 1974; Harvard Bus Sch, MBA, finance, 1978. **Career:** Gen Motors Corp, treas analyst, 1978-80, dir, 1980-82, Span subsid, treas, 1982-84, asst treas, NY, 1984-87; Global Markets & Investment Banking, exec vpres & co-head, 1997-98; Merrill Lynch & Co Inc, investment banker, dir investment banking, managing dir financial servs group, head client strategies group, 1987-96, chief financial officer, 1998-2000, pres & chief operating officer, 2001-02, chief exec officer, 2002; US Pvt Client, 2000-01; BAC Can Finance Co, chmn & chief exec officer, 2001; Motors Liquidation Co, dir, 2001-06; Alcoa Inc, dir, 2008-; Lighthouse Global Network Inc, dir, 2009. **Orgs:** Exec Leadership Coun & Fedn; bd mem GM Corp, 2001-06; chmn bd, Merrill Lynch & Co Inc, 2003-07; bd mem, Lower Manhattan Develop Corp; bd mem, NASDAQ Stock Exchange; bd mem, Nat Urban League; bd mem, Ronald McDonald House; bd mem, Bronx Prep Sch; trustee, Buckley Sch; trustee, Ctr Strategic & Int Studies; mem exec comt, dir, Alcoa Inc; former dir, BlackRock Inc, 2006-07; bd, Memorial Sloan-Kettering Cancer Ctr; bd, Coun Foreign Rels; dir, Am Beacon Advisors Inc, 2009-12. **Honors/Awds:** Corporate Executive of the Year, Black Enterprise, 2000; Achievement Award, Exec Leadership Coun, 2000. **Special Achievements:** first African-American to run a major Wall Street firm. **Business Addr:** Chief Executive Officer, Director, Alcoa Inc, 201 Isabella St, Pittsburgh, PA 15212-5858, **Business Phone:** (412)553-4545.

## O'NEALE, DR. SONDRA A.

School administrator, dean (education). **Educ:** Asbury Col, BA, eng lit; Univ Ky, MA, Am lit, PhD, Am lit. **Career:** Univ Ky; Emory Univ; Univ Calif, San Diego, CA; Univ Wisc-La Crosse, Dept Women's Studies, chairperson; Wayne State Univ, Col Lib Arts, dean, 1995-98, prof Eng, 1999. **Orgs:** Phi Beta Kappa. **Special Achievements:** Author, Jupiter Hammon and the Biblical Beginnings of African-American Literature, 1993; Editor, Keepers of the Flame: Power, Myth and Cultural Consciousness in Ethnic Female Identity, 1998. **Business Addr:** MI.

## O'NEILL, ANTHONY B., SR.

Lawyer. **Educ:** St Augustine Col, BA, 1969; Univ Iowa Col Law, JD, 1975. **Career:** Magistrate (retired); O'Neill & Fair Attorneys at Law, atty. **Orgs:** Nat Secy, 100 Black Men Am Inc; bd dir, Neighborhood Legal Assistance Prog Inc; Sc Black Lawyers Asn; Thurgood Marshall Law Socs; Nat Asn Advan Colored People; Nat Bar Asn. **Business Addr:** Attorney, O'Neill & Fair, 1847 Ashley River Rd Suite 200, Charleston, SC 29407-8706, **Business Phone:** (843)763-3900.

## OAKLEY, CHARLES

Basketball player, basketball coach. **Personal:** Born Dec 18, 1963, Cleveland, OH. **Educ:** Va Union Univ, Richmond, attended 1985. **Career:** Basketball player (retired), basketball coach; Chicago Bulls, forward, 1985-88, 2001-02, New York Knicks, 1988-98, 1997-98; Oaktree Entertainment, co-founder; Toronto Raptors, 1998-2001; Wash Wizards, 2002-03; Houston Rockets, forward, 2003-04; Charlotte Bobcats, asst coach, 2010-11. **Business Addr:** Assistant Coach, Charlotte Bobcats, 333 E Trade St, Charlotte, NC 28202, **Business Phone:** (704)688-8600.

## OATES, GISELE CASANOVA. See CASANOVA, DR. GISELE M.

## OATES, WANDA ANITA

Athletic director. **Personal:** Born Sep 11, 1942, Washington, DC; daughter of Robert L Sr and Ruth Dorothy. **Educ:** Howard Univ, Wash, DC, BS, 1965; George Washington Univ, Wash, DC, MA, 1967. **Career:** Athletic director (retired); F W Ballou High Sch, athletic coach, athletic dir, 1988-94. **Orgs:** Delta Sigma Theta Sorority. **Honors/Awds:** Coach of the Year, Eastern Bd Athletic Officials; Outstanding Achievement Award, Howard Univ Alumni Club; Coach of the Year, Inter High E, 1991; DCPS & DCIAA Service Award, 1997; Sports Pioneer Award, Nat Asn Black Journalists, 1998; Distinguished Service Award, DC Coaches Asn, 1999; inductee, DC Coaches Hall of Fame, 2000, Athletic Coaches Association's Hall of Fame, 2009. **Home Addr:** 5700 4th St NW, Washington, DC 20011, **Home Phone:** (202)291-3941.

## OBAMA, DR. BARACK HUSSEIN, II

President (government). **Personal:** Born Aug 4, 1961, Honolulu, HI; son of Barack Sr (deceased) and Ann Dunham (deceased); married Michelle Robinson; children: Malia Ann & Natasha. **Educ:** Occidental Col; Columbia Univ, BS, polit sci, 1983; Harvard Law Sch, JD, 1991. **Career:** Chicago, community organizer, 1983-87; Church-based Group, Develop Communities Proj, dir, 1985; Univ Chicago Law Sch, lectr, 1993-96, sr lectr const law, 1996-2004; Davis, Miner, Barnhill & Galland, assoc, 1993-96, coun, 1996-2004; Ill State Senate, 13th Cong Dist, rep, 1997-2004, US sen, 2005-08; US, pres-elect, 2008, 44th pres, 2009-; Senate's subcomt Europ Affairs, chmn. **Orgs:** Trinity United Church Christ, 1992-2008; founding mem bd dir, founding exec dir, Pub Allies; bd dir, Woods Fund Chicago, 1994-2002; bd dir, Joyce Found, 1994-2002; bd dir, Chicago Annenberg Challenge, 1995-2002; Senate Foreign Rels Comt; bd dir, Chicago Lawyers' Comt Civil Rights Under Law; bd dir, Lugenia Burns Hope Ctr; Ctr Neighborhood Technol; pres, Harvard Law Rev; Senate Health & Human Serv Comt, 2003; chair, Chicago Annenberg Challenge; found, Barack Obama Found, 2014. **Honors/Awds:** Hon Doctorates of Law, Knox Col; Hon Doctorates of Law, Univ Mass; Hon Doctorates of Law, Northwestern Univ; Hon Doctorates of Law, Xavier Univ; "Forty under Forty", Crain's Chicago Bus, 1993; News maker of the Year Award, Nat Newspaper Publ Asn, 2004; 50 Most Intriguing Blacks, Ebony, 2004; Chairman's Award, Nat Asn Advan Colored People, 2005; 10 people who could change the world, New Statesman, 2005; Best Spoken Word Album Grammy Award, 2006, 2008; Daytime Emmy Award; Person of the Year, Time magazine, 2008; Nobel peace prize, 2009. **Special Achievements:** First African American president of the Harvard Law Review; author, autobiography, Dreams From My Father, 1992; appeared on various TV shows; auth, The Audacity of Hope Crown, 2006; First African American Democratic presidential nominee, 2008; first African American president of United States, 2009; first sitting U.S. President to preside over a meeting of the United Nations Security, 2009; First sitting president to stand up for marriage equality, and is fighting for equal pay and a woman's right to make her own health decisions; First president born outside the continental United States. **Business Addr:** President, United States of America, Oval Office White House W Wing, Washington, DC 20500, **Business Phone:** (202)456-1111.

## OBAMA, MICHELLE LAVAUGHN ROBINSON

Lawyer. **Personal:** Born Jan 17, 1964, Chicago, IL; daughter of Fraser Robinson and Marian Robinson; married Barack; children: Malia Ann & Natasha. **Educ:** Princeton Univ, BA, sociol, 1985; Harvard Law Sch, JD, 1988. **Career:** Univ Chicago Med Ctr, assoc dean, stud affairs, dir, Univ Community Serv Ctr, exec dir community affairs, vpres community & external affairs, 2005-09. **Orgs:** Trinity United Church Christ S Side; bd dir, TreeHouse Foods; bd dir, Chicago Coun Global Affairs; bd trustee, Univ Chicago Lab Schs; comt mem, Mus Sci & Indust. **Special Achievements:** First African-American First Lady of the United States, 2009-.

## OBAYUWANA, DR. ALPHONSUS OSAROBO

Physician. **Personal:** Born Jul 26, 1948, Benin City; son of William and Irene Osemwegie; married Ann Louise Carter; children: Alphonsus & Anson. **Educ:** High Point Univ, BS, biol & chem, 1973; Howard Univ, MS, 1977, Col Med, MD, 1981. **Career:** S Baltimore Gen Hosp, intern, 1981-82; Harbor Hosp Ctr, resident, 1982-85; Johns Hopkins Univ, Sch Med, instr, 1985-86; Group Health Assoc, obstetrician & gynecologist, 1986-93; Univ Md, Col Med, dept obstet & gynec, clin fac position; Mitchell-Trotman Med Group, 1993-97; Kaiser-Permanente Med Group, 1997; Eastern Va Med Sch, asst prof, 2004-, Ghent Family Prac, Div Family Obstet & Gynec, physician, currently. **Orgs:** Prin investr, Inst Hope, 1982-; Am Med Asn; Nat Med Asn; Am Soc Psychosom Obst & Gynec; consult, Female Care Ctr, Silver Spring, MD, 1985-; pres, Asn Nigerian Physicians Americas, 2000. **Honors/Awds:** Dipl, Nat Bd Med Examiners; Dipl, Am Bd Obstet & Gynec; National Resident Research Paper Award; fel Am Col Obstet & Gynec. **Special Achievements:** Co-author "The Hope Index Scale", 1982; "Psychosocial Distress & Pregnancy Outcome", 1984. **Home Addr:** 613 Manorbrook Dr, Silver Spring, MD 20904. **Business Addr:** Obstetrician, Gynecologist, Eastern Virginia Medical School, 604 Fairfax Ave, Norfolk, VA 23507, **Business Phone:** (757)446-9236.

## OBEN, ROMAN DISSAKE

Football player, radio host. **Personal:** Born Oct 9, 1972; son of Marie; married Linda; children: Roman Jr & Andre. **Educ:** Louisville, BA, econ, 1995; Fairleigh Dickinson Univ, MPA, 2001; ForkUnion Mil Acad. **Career:** Football player (retired), radio host, analyst; NY Giants, 1996, left tackle, 1997-99; Cleveland Browns, left tackle, 2000-01; Tampa Bay Buccaneers, left tackle, 2002-03; San Diego Chargers, left tackle, 2004-05, 2006-07; New York Giants Radio Network, co host, currently; MSG, color analyst, currently; NFL, Youth & High Sch Football, dir, 2015-. **Orgs:** Founder, Roman Oben Found, 2002; vpres, Corporate Playbook, 2009; chmn, bd mem, local Dem Party Kinnelon, Nj, 2009; vpres, Alpha Phi Alpha Fraternity; charter mem, NFLPA Benefits Com. **Honors/Awds:** Louisville Community Service Award, 1994; four-time Athletic dir Hon Roll; offensive game ball, 1999; Metro Conf Championship; Vince Lombardi Champion, Vincent T Lombardi Found, 2003; Alumni Player of Week, 2004-05; Super Bowl XXXVII Champion, 2003; Man of the Year, Big Brothers Big Sisters San Diego, 2007; Athletic Hall of Fame at Gonzaga Col High Sch, Fork Union Mil Acad & the Univ of Louisville. **Special Achievements:** Films: 1996 NFL Draft, 1996; Super Bowl XXXVII, 2003. TV Series: "Melissa Harris-Perry", 2013; "A Football Life", 2014. Internship with US Congressmen Dennis Kucinich, OH & Bill Pascrell, NJ. **Home Addr:** 7006 40th Ave, University Park, MD 20782. **Business Addr:** Founder, The Roman Oben Foundation, 1320 Forestedge Blvd, Oldsmar, FL 34677, **Business Phone:** (727)786-2223.

## OBI, JAMES ESOMONU

Manager, chairperson. **Personal:** Born Sep 2, 1942, Lagos; son of John (deceased) and Adannaya (deceased); married Cecilia Olubosede; children: Funke, Femi, Siji & Uche. **Educ:** St Peters Col, Oxford Eng, BA, 1963; Am Col, Life Underwriters, CLU, 1973. **Career:** Equit Life Assurance Soc US, sales rep, 1967-68, dist mgr, 1968-72, agency mgr, 1972-97, dir mgt dev, 1991; The Obi Group, pres, 1992-, chair, currently; chartered financial consult, chartered life underwriter. **Orgs:** Bd mem, Nigerian-Am Friendship Soc, 1979-; past mem, Bus Adv Comn Bus Coun Un; past mem, Corp Coun Africa; Million Dollar Round Table; Bd chair, Crescent Investment Group Inc; Bd, TLC Beatrice Int Foods Inc; Glaucoma Trust Found; Forum World Affairs; Nigerian-Am Alliance; Bd, Ment Health Asn New York; Bd, Un Disarmament Comn. **Honors/Awds:** Six National Management Awards; Two Master Agency Award. **Home Addr:** 97 Fairway Dr, Stamford, CT 06903-1425. **Business Addr:** President, The Obi Group, 97 Fairway Dr, Stamford, CT 06903-1425, **Business Phone:** (203)329-7500.

## ODOM, CARLA MORGAN

Nurse. **Career:** W Jefferson Med Ctr, nurse. **Home Addr:** 84 Anchorage Dr, Marrero, LA 70072-5023, **Home Phone:** (504)347-5582. **Business Addr:** Nurse, West Jefferson Medical Center, 1101 Med Ctr Blvd, Marrero, LA 70072, **Business Phone:** (504)347-5511.

## ODOM, CLIFTON LEWIS

Football player, executive. **Personal:** Born Sep 15, 1958, Beaumont, TX; married Cynthia; children: Clifton Lewis Jr. **Educ:** Univ Tex, Arlington, BA, bus admin. **Career:** Football player (retired), owner; Cleveland Browns, linebacker, 1980-81; Baltimore Colts, linebacker, 1982-83; Indianapolis Colts, left inside linebacker, 1984-90; Miami Dolphins, left inside linebacker, right inside linebacker, 1990-94; Blockbuster Video Franchisee, owner, currently. **Orgs:** Athlete Action; Optimist Club Arlington; Nat Football Leaue Alumni; Univ Tex Alumni Asn; Fel Christian Athletes. **Business Addr:** Owner, Blockbuster Video, 1521 Marlandwood Rd, Temple, TX 76502, **Business Phone:** (254)774-8480.

## ODOM, DARRYL EUGENE

Manager, administrator. **Personal:** Born Mar 14, 1955, Houston, TX; son of Cleveland and Elizia Amboree; married Rene; children: Matthew, Crystal, Russell & Brittany. **Educ:** Morgan State Univ, BA, econs polit sci, 1977; Tex Southern Univ, Houston, TX, MPA, urban mgt, 1979; Rice Univ, attended 1986. **Career:** City Houston, Houston, Tex, ctr adminr, 1979-2003, Sunnyside Multi-Serv Ctr, asst, prog mgr, adminr, currently. **Orgs:** Am Red Cross, 1986-91; bd mem, Boy Scouts, 1989-91; literacy advan, Literacy Advan, 1989-91; Family to Family, 1990-91; bd dir, Cent Care Community Health Ctr, chairman, 2003-; Nat Asn Community Health Ctr. **Home Addr:** 4123 Heritage Trl Dr, Houston, TX 77047-2929, **Home Phone:** (713)731-0705. **Business Addr:** Chairman, Central Care Community Health Center, 8610 Martin Luther King Jr Blvd, Houston, TX 77033, **Business Phone:** (713)734-0199.

## ODOM, DR. JOHN YANCY

Consultant, writer. **Personal:** Born Sep 22, 1948, Jackson, MS; son of Corey Franklin Sr and Rosa B; married Annie S; children: Nikki Annette. **Educ:** Lane Col, BA, 1969; Univ Wis, Madison, MS, 1973, PhD, educ admin, 1978. **Career:** Teacher eng; affirmative action officer; Sch Dist Beloit, engineering teacher, 1969-72; Madison Schs, asst dir human rels, 1973-76, dir human rels, 1976-80, mid sch prin, 1980-85; Oscar Mayer Theatre, actor; Univ Wis, Madison, acad specialist, 1986-86; Edgewood Col, instr; Cardinal Strich Univ, instr; Odom & Assocs LLC, pres, 1985-. **Orgs:** Bd mem, Big Bros/Sister Dane County, 1973-82; founder, Mu Eta Lambda Chap, Alpha Phi Alpha, 1978-; bd mem, C's Theatre Madison, 1981-95; Nat Res Ctr Eng Learning & Achievement, 1996-; vpres, chair, ed comt, Nat Asn Advan Colored People-Madison, WI, 1998-; pres, Nat Asn Advan Colored People, Madison, WI, 1990-93; life mem, Nat Asn Advan Colored People, Nat Educ Task Force, 2000-01; pres, Charles Hamilton Houston Inst, 2001-; founder, OfMyDreams.com; bd mem, Urban League; bd mem, Greater Madison Conv & Visitors Bur; bd mem, Edgewood High Sch & Schs Hope; adv bd, Nat Res Ctr Improving Stud Achievement Eng; adv bd, Diversity Oversight Comt Univ Wisc, Madison; pres, Charles Hamilton Houston Inst. **Home Addr:** 309 Sauk Creek Dr, Madison, WI 53717, **Home Phone:** (608)836-5555. **Business Addr:** President, Odom & Associates, LLC, PO Box 56155, Madison, WI 53705, **Business Phone:** (608)836-5555.

## ODOM, LESLIE, JR.

Singer, actor. **Personal:** Born Aug 6, 1981, Queens, NY; married Nicolette Robinson, Dec 1, 2012. **Educ:** Carnegie Mellon Univ, BA, 2003. **Career:** Actor and singer, 1996-. Stage: Rent, 1996; Dreamgirls, 2001; Leap of Faith, 2012; Hamilton, 2015-.Television: CSI: Miami, CBS, 2003-06; The Big House, 2004; Threshold, 2006; Gilmore Girls, 2006; Vanished, 2006; Close to Home, 2006; Big Day, 2006-07; Supreme Courtships, 2007; The Bill Engvall Show, 2007; Grey's Anatomy, ABC, 2008; NCIS: Los Angeles, 2011; Zeke and Luther, 2011; Bandwagon: The Series, 2011; Supernatural, 2011; Poe, 2011; House of Lies, 2012; Smash, 2012-13; Person of Interest, CBS, 2013-14; Law & Order; Special Victims Unit, NBC, 2013-15; Gotham, Fox, 2014; The Good Wife, CBS, 2016. Film: Red Tails, 2012. **Honors/Awds:** Princess Grace Award for Acting, 2002; Astaire Award, 2012; Antoinette Perry Award, 2016. **Special Achievements:** Albums: "Simply Christmas", 2016; "Leslie Odom Jr.", 2016. **Business Addr:** CESD Talent Agency, 10635 Santa Monica Blvd Suite 130, Los Angeles, CA 90025.

## ODOM, MELANIE

Association executive. **Educ:** Western Mich Univ, BBA, accountancy; Boston Col, cert, Advan Mgt, 2004; Ind Univ, MA, 2013. **Career:** Bank Am formerly MIch Nat Bank, Investment Banking, vpres & Chief financial officer, 1989-94; JPMorgan Chase formerly NBD Bank, Retail Investments & Ins, vpres, 1994-96; Comerica Bank, vpres civic affairs, 1996-2008, prod risk mgr, 1996-2002; Banking Indust, Expertise Financial Serv Indust, progressive responsibilitiy, 1990-2007; Impact Solutions, chief strategist, 2008-11; Ind Univ, exec masters prog, 2010-13; Eli Lilly & Co, mkt consult, 2011-. **Orgs:** Treas, Impact Solutions, Belle Isle Women's Comt, vpres; bd mem, United Way; Delta Sigma Theta Sorority Inc; exec bd, Urban Financial Serv Coalition; exec bd mem & treas, Belle Isle Conservancy, 2005-11. **Business Addr:** Marketing Consultant, Eli Lilly and Co, 893 S Delaware St, Indianapolis, IN 46225, **Business Phone:** (317)276-2000.

## ODOM, STONEWALL

Executive, government official. **Personal:** Born Nov 1, 1940, Petersburg, VA; son of Stonewall Faison and Flossie; married Marlena Hines; children: Terrance, Jacqueline, Latisha, Nicole, Stonewall III, Marlena, Marcus, Malcolm, Mandela, Muhammad, Malik & Myles. **Educ:** John Jay Col Criminal Law. **Career:** Metrop Life, sales rep; City NY, police officer, 1965-73; CORE, chief coordr & interim chmn, 1989-; Black Men Opposed to Drugs & Violence, Yonkers NY, chmn; Odom & Sons Vending Co, prin owner. **Orgs:** Sammuel H Dow Am Legion Post 017; master mason, James H Farrell Lodge; Vietnam Veterans Am; coord mem, Yonkers Crack Task Force; founder & chmn, Tower Soc Citizens Responsible Govt, 1985-89; legis chmn, Sammuel H Dow Post 1017 Am Legion; Nat Asn Advan Colored People, 1986; vice chair, Petersburgh Repuban Comn, 2000-; bd comnrs, Petersburg Dinwiddie Airport, 2002; bd comnrs, resident comnr, Petersburg Redevelop & Housing Authority, 2002. **Business Addr:** Owner, Stonewall Odom Vending Co, 1844 Ft Rice St, Petersburg, VA 23805, **Business Phone:** (804)733-3049.

## ODOMES, NATHANIEL BERNARD (NATE ODOMES)

Football coach, football player. **Personal:** Born Aug 25, 1965, Columbus, GA. **Educ:** Univ Wis. **Career:** Football player (retired), football coach; Buffalo Bills, corner back & right corner back, 1987-93; Seattle Seahawks, 1994-95; Atlanta Falcons, corner back & defensive back, 1996; Columbus Wardogs, defensive back coach. **Honors/Awds:** AFC Championship Game, Post-1988 Season. One of the top Defensive Backs in the NFL during the early 1990s; won four consecutive Super Bowl appearances, & making the Pro Bowl twice, 1992 & 1993.

## OFFICER, CARL EDWARD

Mayor, vice president (organization), funeral director. **Personal:** Born Apr 3, 1952, St. Louis, MO; children: 1. **Educ:** Western Col, Miami, BS, polit sci & philos, 1974; John F Kennedy Sch Govt, Harvard Univ; Southern Ill Univ, Carbondale, mortuary sci, 1975. **Career:** Officer Funeral Home PC, E St Louis IL, vpres, 1970-; St Clair County, IL, dep coroner, 1975-77; State Ill, Drivers Servs, dep dir, 1977-79; City E St Louis, IL, mayor, 1979-91, 2003-07; AME Church, ordained elder, 2001-. **Orgs:** US Conf Mayors; Nat Conf Black Mayors; Urban League; Jaycees; Nat Asn Advan Colored People; Sigma Phi Sigma; life mem, Kappa Alpha Psi Fraternity; bd mem, E W Gateway Coun Govts; Ill Funeral Dirs Asn; St Clair County Funeral Dir Asn; Nat Funeral Dir Asn; Int Order Golden Rule. **Honors/Awds:** Certificate of Commendation, Top Ladies Distinction, 1980; Humanitarian Award, Campbell Chapel AME Church, 1980. **Special Achievements:** First African American Cadet to graduate from the Mormion Military Academy in Aurora, IL. **Business Addr:** Vice President, Officer Funeral Home PC, 2114 Missouri Ave, East St. Louis, IL 62205, **Business Phone:** (618)271-6055.

## OFODILE, DR. FERDINAND AZIKIWE

Surgeon. **Personal:** Born Oct 20, 1941, Nnobi; son of Julius and Regina Eruchalu; married Caroline Okafor; children: Uchenna, Ikechukwu, Nnaemeka & Nnamdi. **Educ:** Northwestern Univ, Evanston, IL, BS, 1964; Northwestern Med Sch, Chicago, IL, MD, 1968. **Career:** Am Asn Plastic Surgeons, fel; St Lukes & Roosevelt Hosp, New York, NY, assoc attend surg, 1982-; New York Presby Hosp-Columbia Presby Ctr, resident; Harlem Hosp Ctr, New York, NY, resident, intern, dir plastic surg, 1982-; Mayo Clin, fel plastic surg; Columbia Univ, NewYork, NY, clin prof surg, 1996-; Corona, NY, pvt pract, currently; Ofodile Plastic Surg & MedNet Technologies Inc, surgeon, currently. **Orgs:** Am Soc Plastic & Recon Surgeon, 1986; fel Am Col Surgs, 1986; Am Soc Plastic Surgeons; Int progs Comt ASPRS, 1992; New York County Med Soc, 1988-; chmn plastic surg, Am Asn Acad; fel Am Col Surgeons; New York Regional Socs Plastic & Reconstructive Surgeons. **Honors/Awds:** Author of many scientific articles; lect many intl symposiums; Fellow, Am Asn Plastic & Reconstructive Surgs; "America's Top Physicians", Consumers' Res Coun Am; "Top African American Doctor", Network Journal. **Special Achievements:** Designed the "Ofodile Nasal Implant" for augmentation Rhinoplasty AFA & Hispanic noses; Published numerous scientific articles in plastic surgery and presented scientific plastic surgery papers in many international conferences. **Home Addr:** 84 Woodmont Dr, Woodcliff Lake, NJ 07677-7655, **Home Phone:** (201)782-1666. **Business Addr:** Surgeon, Ofodile Plastic Surgery & MedNet Technologies Inc, 506 Lenox Ave, New York, NY 10037, **Business Phone:** (212)939-3537.

## OFUATEY-KODJOE, BORIS FREDERIC CECIL TAY-NATEY. See KODJOE, BORIS.

## OGBOGU, ERIC O.

Executive, football player. **Personal:** Born Jul 18, 1975, Irvington, NY; son of Louis (deceased). **Educ:** Univ Md. **Career:** Football player (retired), executive; New York Jets, defensive end, 1998-2001; Cincinnati Bengals, 2002; Dallas Cowboys, linebacker, defensive back, 2003-05; Under Armour Band, spokesperson, dir sports mkt, currently. **Honors/Awds:** Most Valuable Player, Hula Bowl, 1998; Rookie of the Year, 1998; Westchester Sports Hall of Fame, 2013. **Special Achievements:** Official star & spokesperson of the famous Under Armour brand, and is named Big E in the Under Armour commercials; Actor: The Game Plan, 2007. **Business Addr:** Director of Sports Marketing, Spokesperson, Under Armour Inc, 1020 Hull St, Baltimore, MD 21230-2080, **Business Phone:** (888)727-6687.

## OGDEN, CHRISTOPHER A.

Financial manager. **Educ:** BS, bus mgt; MBA, int bus studies. **Career:** Ogden Capital Group LLC, pres, founder & managing partner, currently; Protein Technologies Int, bus develop mgr, regional sales mgr; Merrill Lynch, NY, financial adv. **Honors/Awds:** Won numerous performance rewards. **Home Addr:** 980 Oriole Dr SW, Atlanta, GA 30311, **Home Phone:** (404)756-1780. **Business Addr:** President, Founder & Managing Partner, Ogden Capital Group LLC, 1751 Tappahannock Trl, Marietta, GA 30062-2087, **Business Phone:** (404)755-2257.

## OGDEN, JONATHAN PHILLIP

Football player. **Personal:** Born Jul 31, 1974, Washington, DC; son of Shirrel and Cassandra; married Kema Francis; children: Jayden. **Educ:** Univ Calif, Los Angeles, hist. **Career:** Football player (retired); Baltimore Ravens, left tackle & left guard & offensive tackle, 1996-2007. **Orgs:** Bd trustees, Nat Urban League; founder, Jonathan Ogden Found, 1996-; founder, Ogden Club; chmn, Beacon Inst. **Honors/Awds:** Champion, Super Bowl, XXXV; Outland Trophy, 1995; Lineman of the Year, United Press Int, 1995; Jim Parker Award, 1995; Morris Trophy, 1995; Pro bowl, 1997 & 1998 & 1999 & 2000 & 2001 & 2002 & 2003 & 2004 & 2005 & 2006 & 2007 Alumni Offensive Lineman of the Year, Nat Football League, 2002; Athletics Hall Of Fame, Univ Calif, Los Angeles, 2006; Baltimore Ravens Ring of Honor; College Football Hall of Fame, 2012; Pro Football Hall of Fame, 2013. **Business Addr:** Founder, Jonathan Ogden Foundation Inc, 10019 Reisterstown Rd, Owings Mills, MD 21117-3902, **Business Phone:** (410)998-9390.

## OGDEN, STEVEN A.

Real estate executive, president (organization). **Personal:** son of Sharon. **Educ:** Mich State Univ, BA, pub policy, 1985. **Career:** Sterling Group, vpres & dir real estate; Heritage Develop Serv LLC, pres; Next Detroit Neighborhood Initiative, exec dir, pres. **Orgs:** Bd mem, Habitat Detroit; Habitat for Humanity; Music Hall for Performing Arts; Detroit Discovery Mus; Eastside Emergency Ctr Inc; bd mem, Next Detroit Neighborhood Initiative; bd mem, Detroit Econ Growth Corp. **Home Addr:** 5736 Harvard Rd, Detroit MI, MI 48224, **Home Phone:** (313)885-8267. **Business Addr:** President, Next Detroit Neighborhood Initiative, 7310 Woodward Ave, Detroit, MI 48202, **Business Phone:** (313)394-1000.

## OGILVIE, LANA

Fashion model, television show host. **Personal:** Born Toronto, ON; children: 1. **Career:** Ford & Elite Modeling Agencies, model; paraded catwalks Dior, Gianfranco Ferre, Isaac Mizrahi, Issey Miyake, Prada, Karl Lagerfeld, Christian Lacroix, Calvin Klein & Gucci; print campaigns include: Bali, CoverGirl, Banana Republic, Gap & Tia Maria; model: Sports Illustrated, Elle, Vogue, Glamour, Flare, Mademoiselle, Essence & Harpers Bazaar; advertisements for clients including: Gap, Guess Jeans, Victoria's Secret, John Galliano & Katherine Hamnett; Macys; Napier; Revlon; Tia Maria liquor; Victorias Secret; Fashion TV Channel, "The Review", co-host, "This Week in Fashion", segment contribr, 2002-; fashion model, currently. **Orgs:** Christian Children's Fund. **Special Achievements:** First black model to sign an exclusive deal with CoverGirl cosmetics, 1992. **Business Addr:** Fashion Model, c/o Ford Models, 111 Fifth Ave, New York, NY 10003, **Business Phone:** (212)219-6500.

## OGLESBY, BORIS

Executive. **Educ:** Grambling State Univ, Grambling, LA, BS, mkt, 1984; Northwestern Univ, Kellogg Sch Mgt, MBA, mkt & mgt, 1999. **Career:** Pizza Hut, asst prod mgr, 1984-85; Miller Brewing Co, gen mgr, brand mgt, 1985-96; Kraft Foods, dir ethnic mkt, 1996-98, category bus dir, 1998-2000, dir consumer promotions, 2000-01, sr category bus dir, 2001-02; Jim Beam Brands Co, vpres premium cordials, 2002-04, vpres strategic planning, 2004-05; JohnsonDiversey Inc, vpres mkt, 2006-08; Swed Match, sr vpres mkt develop, 2008-09; MeadWestvaco, consult corp strategy, vpres global mkt & strategy, 2010-12; IRI Inc, vpres/prin client insights, 2012-. **Orgs:** Mem, Omega Psi Phi. **Business Addr:** Vice President, Principal Client Insights, IRI, 150 N Clinton St, Chicago, IL 60661-1416, **Business Phone:** (312)726-1221.

## OGLESBY, JOE

Newspaper editor. **Personal:** Born Aug 1, 1947, Tampa, FL; son of Northern and Terrie Del Benniefield Yarde; married Linda Blash; children: 2; married Bloneva McKenzie; children: Joy Denise. **Educ:** Fla Agr & Mech Univ, BA, eng & jour, 1970; Harvard Univ, attended 1985. **Career:** Editor (retired), executive; Miami Herald, day city ed, ed writer, reporter, 1972-87, asst managing ed, 1990-, ed page ed, currently; Philadelphia Inquirer, suburban ed, 1987-90; State newspaper, Columbia, SC, managing ed, 1995-97; Miami Herald, Ed Page Ed, 2001-09; Miami Herald, ASNE, NABJ, IRE, Poynter, Unity & other media groups, coordr haiti news proj, 2010-11; Financial Fed Credit Union, chmn, supvry comt, 1995; Subscriptions Success, dir, 2012-; Goodwill Industs, bd dir, 2013-. **Orgs:** Nat Asn Black Journalists, 1977-; Fla Socs Newspaper Ed; Nat Conf Ed Writers; bd trustee, Collins Ctr Pub Policy, 2010-. **Honors/Awds:** Pulitzer Prize, Columbia Univ, 1983. **Home Addr:** 2100 NE 208th St, Miami, FL 33179, **Home Phone:** (305)931-4925. **Business Addr:** Board of Trustee, Collins Center for Public Policy, PO Box 8850, Coral Springs, FL 33075, **Business Phone:** (305)842-0393.

## OGLETREE, CHARLES J., JR.

Lawyer, educator. **Personal:** Born Dec 31, 1952, Merced, CA; son of Charles J Sr and WillieMae Reed; married Pamela Barnes; children: Charles J III & Rashida Jamila. **Educ:** Stanford Univ, Stanford, CA, BA, polit sci, 1974, MA, polit sci, 1975; Harvard Law Sch, Cambridge, MA, JD, 1978. **Career:** DC Pub Defender Serv, Wash, DC, staff atty, 1978-82, dir staff training, 1982-83, dep dir, 1984-85; Am Univ, Wash Col Law, Wash, DC, adj prof, 1982-84; Antioch Law Sch, Wash, DC, adj prof, 1983-84; Jessamy, Ft & Ogletree, Wash, DC, partner, 1985-89; Harvard Law Sch, Cambridge, Mass, vprof, 1985-89, dir, introd trial advocacy workshop, 1986-, asst prof, 1989-93, prof law, 1993-; Jessamy, Ft & Botts, Wash, DC, legal coun, 1989-; Harvard Law Sch, Criminal Justice Inst, Cambridge, Mass, dir, Jesse Climenko Prof Law, currently; Charles Hamilton Houston Inst Race & Justice, founding & exec dir, 2005-; Publications: Beyond the Rodney King Story: An Investigation of Police Conduct in Minority Communities, 1995; All Deliberate Speed: Reflections on the First Half-Century of Brown v. Board of Education, 2004; From Lynch Mobs to the Killing State: Race and the Death Penalty in America, 2006; When Law Fails: Making Sense of Miscarriages of Justice, 2009; The Road to Abolition: The Future of Capital Punishment in the United States, 2009; The Presumption of Guilt: The Arrest of Henry Louis Gates, Jr. and Race, Class and Crime in America, 2010; Life without Parole: America's New Death Penalty?, 2012. **Orgs:** Am Bar Asn; Nat Conf Black Lawyers; Nat Bar Asn; Am Civil Liberties Union; Bar Asn DC; Wash Bar Asn; defender comt mem, Nat Legal Aid & Defender Asn; Asn Am Law Sch; DC Bar; chmn, Southern Ctr Human Rights Comt; nat pres, Nat Black Law Students Asn, 1977-78; St Paul African Methodist Episcopal Church. **Home Addr:** , MA. **Business Addr:** Jesse Climenko Professor of Law, Harvard Law School, Hauser 516 1575 Mass Ave, Cambridge, MA 02138, **Business Phone:** (617)496-2054.

## OGLETREE, DR. JOHN D., JR.

Clergy, lawyer. **Personal:** Born Mar 1, 1952, Dallas, TX; son of John D Sr and Marion Deckard; married Evelyn Horn; children: Johnny, Lambrini, Joseph & Jordan. **Educ:** Univ Tex, Arlington, BA, 1973; S Col Law, JD, 1979. **Career:** Fulbright & Jaworski Law Firm, messenger, 1976-77; Harris County Sheriff dept, baliff, 1977-79; Caggins, Hartsfield & Ogletree Law Firm, partner, 1979-93; mem, Bethel Instnl Baptist Church Houston, Tex, 1985; Gospel ministry, 1982; Antioch Missionary Baptist Church, minister Christian develop, 1985-86; First Metropolitan Baptist Church, pastor, founder, 1986, sr pastor, currently. **Orgs:** Nat Bar Asn, 1979-; State Bar Tex, 1979-; Nat Baptist Conv USA, 1986-; Urban Alternative, 1987-; instr, Eastern Progressive Baptist Missionary Dist Asn, 1987-; Baptist Missionary & Educ State Conv, 1987-; Evangelist Gulf Coast Asn, 1989; NE Baptist Church; bd trustee, Cypress-Fairbanks ISD; trustee secy, pres, CyFair-Independent Sch Dist Bd, moderator, Union Baptist Asn; pres, African Am Fel Asn, currently; founder, Redemption Community Develop Corp; chair & vice chair exec bd, Baptist Gen Conv Tex; pres, African Am Fel Asn of BGCT. **Special Achievements:** Keynote speaker Gulf Coast Keswick, 1990; ctr, Workshop Cooperative Baptist Fel, 1992. **Home Addr:** 8131 Sun Terrace Lane, Houston, TX 77095, **Home Phone:** (713)550-0566. **Business Addr:** Senior Pastor, First Metropolitan Baptist Church, 8870 W Sam Houston Pkwy N, Houston, TX 77040, **Business Phone:** (713)460-8000.

## OGLIVIE, BENJAMIN AMBROSIO (BENJAMIN AMBROSIO OGLIVIE PALMER)

Baseball player, athletic coach, baseball manager. **Personal:** Born Feb 11, 1949, Colon; married Tami; children: Trianni & Benjamin. **Educ:** Bronx Community Col, New York, NY; Northeastern Univ, Boston, MA; Wayne State Univ, Detroit, MI; Univ Wis, Milwaukee, WI. **Career:** Baseball player (retired), baseball coach; Boston Red Sox, outfielder, 1971-73; Detroit Tigers, outfielder, 1974-77; Milwaukee Brewers, outfielder, 1978-86; Kintetsu Buffaloes, outfielder, 1987-88; Calgary Cannons, hitting coach, 1995; Hickory Crawdads, hitting coach; San Diego Padres, coach, 1998-2006; Idaho Falls Padres, coach, 2001; Eugene Emeralds, coach, 2003-05; Vero Beach Devil Rays, coach, 2007; Montgomery Biscuits, hitting coach, 2008; Gulf Coast Rays, coach, 2009; West Michigan Whitecaps, hitting coach, 2011; Tampa Bay Rays, coach, currently. **Home Addr:** 917 Bodark Lane, Austin, TX 78745. **Business Addr:** Coach, Tampa Bay Rays, Tropicana Field 1 Tropicana Dr, St Petersburg, FL 33705, **Business Phone:** (727)825-3137.

## OGUNDE, ADEYEMI

Clergy. **Personal:** Born Oct 10, 1950, West Africa; son of Ogunde Adejoke; children: Aderonke, Adeyemi, Adeola & Adewale. **Educ:** Yoba Col Technol, Nigeria, OND, 1972, HND, printing, 1974; Univ Logos, Nigeria, BA, cosmology, 1978; Univ Norttingham, attended 1983. **Career:** Inst African Wisdom, chief priest, founder, 1988-. **Orgs:** Exec deleg, Nat African Religion Congress; The Ijebu Descendant Asn; Nat Black United Front; Nat Asn Advan Colored People. **Honors/Awds:** African Letter Excellence, Nat Black United Front, 1985; Certificate of Special Congressional Recognition, 1996; Proclamation from the City of Houston, Mayor Lee Brown, 1998, 1999, 2001; Certificate of Appreciation, Mem African Wisdom, 2001. **Special Achievements:** Presented Meditation for Unity Church Convention in Portland, Oregon, 1999; Special Presentation to Maya Angelo Ku Lamanjaro, 2001. **Home Addr:** 12054 White Cap Lane, Houston, TX 77072, **Home Phone:** (713)777-9514. **Business Addr:** Chief Priest, The Institute of African Wisdom & Ifa Orisa Educational Center, **Business Phone:** (281)776-9514.

### OGUNLESI, ADEBAYO O.
Lawyer, investment banker. **Personal:** Born Jan 1, 1953?; children: 1. **Educ:** Oxford Univ, BA, eng; Harvard Law Sch, magna cum laude; Harvard Bus Sch, JD, MBA. **Career:** Corp Pract Group New York law firm, atty; Harvard Law Rev, ed; Dist Columbia, US Ct Appeals, staff; Supreme Ct Justice Thur Marshall, staff; Cravath, Swaine & Moore, atty; Yale Sch Org, lectr; Credit Suisse First Boston Inc, 1983, managing dir, 1993, headed global energy group, 1993-2002, exec vice chmn & chief client officer, head global invest banking, 2002-, bd dir, 2002-. **Orgs:** Bd dir, Callaway Golf Co; chair, Credit Suisses Exec Bd & Mgt Coun & Chmns Bd; chmn, managing partner, Global Infrastructure Mgt LLC. **Business Addr:** Chairman, Managing Partner, Global Infrastructure Management LLC, 12 E 49th St, New York, NY 10017, **Business Phone:** (212)315-8100.

### OHENE-FREMPONG, PROF. KWAKU
Physician, medical scientist, president (organization). **Personal:** Born Mar 13, 1946, Kukurantumi; son of Kwasi Ohene Dokyi and Ernestina Odi Boafo; married Janet; children: Kwame (deceased) & Afia. **Educ:** Yale Univ, BS, biol, 1970; Yale Univ Sch Med, MD, 1875; Cornell Med Ctr, pediat, 1977. **Career:** New York Hosp-Cornell Med Ctr, residency; Univ PA Sch Med, asst prof pediat, 1986-89, emer prof pediat, 2010-; Tulane Univ Sch, asst prof; Med Nat Assn Sickle Cell Dis Inc, nat pres; C's Hosp Philadelphia, assoc prof pediat, 1989-96, prof pediat, 1996-2010, dir sickle cell prog, Comprehensive Sickle Cell Ctr, emer dir, pediat hemat, fel, currently; Sickle Cell Dis Asn Am Inc, chief med officer. **Orgs:** Founder, Treat Ctr; bd mem, Sickle Cell Ctr; pres, Sickle Cell Found Ghana; bd mem, dir, Africa Am Inst; bd mem, C's Hosp Philadelphia; mem fac, Univ PA Sch Med; chmn dir, Sickle Cell Dis Asn Am Inc. **Business Addr:** Director Emeritus, Childrens Hospital of Philadelphia, 3400 St Civic Ctr Blvd, Philadelphia, PA 19104-4399, **Business Phone:** (215)590-3423.

### OHUCHE, EMEKA
Chief financial officer, president (organization), entrepreneur. **Educ:** Univ Iowa, BS, engineering & bus; Univ Mich, MBA. **Career:** Deloitte Group, int bus consult; IKobo Inc, co-founder, pres & chief financial officer, 2001-; Babeme LLC, chief exec officer; Barklay Capital Group LLC, founder; Barklay Community Develop Inc, founder; Babeme LLC, founder; McDonald's Corp, finance oper. **Orgs:** Treas, McDonald's Corp. **Business Addr:** Co-Founder, President, Chief Financial Officer, Ikobo Inc, 2030 Powers Ferry Rd Bldg 200 Suite 222, Atlanta, GA 30339, **Business Phone:** (678)483-4562.

### OJUMU, AYODELE
Librarian. **Personal:** Born Mar 15, 1972, Buffalo, NY; daughter of Ochun and Vivian. **Educ:** Univ Rochester, BA, african-am studies, 1994; Univ Buffalo, MLS, 1997, advan studies cert, Info & Libr Studies, 2006; NY Univ, dipl paralegal studies, 2001. **Career:** New York Pub Libr, Sr Asst Librn, 1997-2000; NYC Bd Educ, sch librn, 1999-2000; SUNY Col, Fredonia, sr asst librn, 2001-04; Rochester City Sch Dist, librn, currently; Buffalo Pub Schs, 2010-, Lafayette High Sch, libr media specialist. **Orgs:** Black Caucus Am libr Asn, 1996-; Am Libr Asn, 2001-; SUNY Libr Asn, 2001-04; Asn Col 2nd Res Libr, WNY/Ont Chap, 2001-04. **Special Achievements:** Publications: "5th Natl Conf of African American Librarians: Source of Professional Rejuvenation 2nd Affirmation," Newsletter of the Black Caucus of the American Library Assn, Oct/Dec 2002. **Home Addr:** 831 Edgecreek Trail, Rochester, NY 14609. **Business Addr:** Librarian, Rochester City School District, 131 W Broad St, Rochester, NY 14614, **Business Phone:** (585)262-8100.

### OKANTAH, MWATABU S.
Writer, educator. **Personal:** Born Aug 18, 1952, Newark, NJ; son of Wilbur and Gladys Smith; married Aminah M; children: Janeia, Ta-Seti, Jamila T, Afrikiti, Ile-Ife, Sowande & Berhane. **Educ:** Kent State Univ, BA, eng & African studies, 1976; City Col NY, MA, creative writing, 1982. **Career:** Cleveland State Univ, Black Studies Prog, asst to dir, 1981-89; Author: Afreeka Brass, 1983; Collage, 1984; Legacy: Martin & Malcolm, 1987; Kent State Univ, Pan-African Studies, Assoc Prof, 1991-; Cheikh Anta Diop: Poem Living, 1997; Reconnecting Memories: Dreams No Longer Deferred, 2004; Muntu Kuntu Energy: New & Selected Poetry, 2013. **Orgs:** Leader, Muntu Kuntu Energy Ensemble, 1989-; Guest Artist, Cavani String Quartet, 1990-; Guest Artist, Vince Robinson & Jazz Poets, 2013-. **Home Addr:** 209 S Balch St, Akron, OH 44302, **Home Phone:** (330)524-4669. **Business Addr:** Associate Professor, Kent State University, PO Box 5190, Kent, OH 44242-0001, **Business Phone:** (330)672-2300.

### OKHAMAFE, DR. IMAFEDIA
Educator. **Educ:** Purdue Univ, PhD, philos, PhD, eng, 1984. **Career:** Univ Nebr, Omaha, prof, philos & eng, 1993-, Goodrich Scholar Prog & Dept Eng, prof, chmn, currently. **Orgs:** Am Asn Adv Sci; Philos Sci Asn; Am Mod Lang Asn; Am Philos Asn. **Home Addr:** 60th & Dodge CB 123E UNO, Omaha, NE 68182. **Business Addr:** Professor Philosophy & English, Chairman, Goodrich Scholarship Program, University Nebraska-Omaha, 6001 Dodge St, Omaha, NE 68182-0265, **Business Phone:** (402)554-2628.

**OKINO, BETTY.** **See OKINO, ELIZABETH ANNA.**

### OKINO, ELIZABETH ANNA (BETTY OKINO)
Gymnast, actor. **Personal:** Born Jun 4, 1975, Entebbe; daughter of Francis C and Aurelia Matei. **Educ:** Univ Okla, jour, 1998. **Career:** Gymnast (retired), actress; Olympic Team, gymnast, 1992; Jr Gym, gymnastic coach, Van Nuys; Disney Channel, Z Games, co-host; Films: The District, 2000; Creature Unknown, 2004; Eon Flux, 2005; TV series: The Phantom Menace, 1999; Undressed, 1999; The Norm Law, 2000; The Real Terrorist, 2000; Definitely Not the Cosbys, 2000; Moesha, 2000; "No Sex, No Mary, No Title", 2000; Won't You Beat My Neighbor?, 2000; One Wedding & a Funeral, 2001; What's News, 2001; Mission Im-posse-ble, 2002; Everybody Hates Food Stamps, 2005; Eon Flux, 2005; Downward Doug, 2015. **Honors/Awds:** Gold on Beam, Silver, US Nat Championships, Denver, 1990; Silver Team Medal, Bronze on Beam, World Championships, Indianapolis, 1991; Silver Medal, World Championships, Paris, 1992; Bronze, Olympic Games, Barcelona, 1992; Spec Sports Award, Chicago State Univ, 1992. **Home Addr:** 426 W Fremont Ave, Elmhurst, IL 60126, **Home Phone:** (630)941-3821.

### OKORE, CYNTHIA ANN
Social worker. **Personal:** Born Nov 15, 1945, Philadelphia, PA; daughter of William (deceased) and Jessie M; married Caleb J; children: Elizabeth A. **Educ:** Cheyney Univ, BA, 1974; Rutgers Univ, MSW, 1981. **Career:** Presby Univ Pa Hosp, Philadelphia, PA, social worker, 1977-79; John F Kennedy Community Ment Health & Ment Retardation Ctr, Philadelphia, PA, social worker, 1981-84; US Dept Veterans Affairs, Philadelphia Veterans Affairs Med Ctr, social worker, 1984-. **Orgs:** Nat Asn Social Workers, 1980-; Pa Chap Social Workers, 1980-; Philadelphia Chap Social Workers, 1980-; Nat Coun Negro Women, 1989-; Nat Black Alcoholism Coun, 1989-; Nat Black Women's Health Proj, 1990-. **Honors/Awds:** Technical Art & Publishers Competition Award of Excellence, Soc Tech Commun, Puget Sound Chapter, 1990-91. **Special Achievements:** Author: The Nurse Practitioner, The Jour of Primary Health Care, July 1990; The Cocaine Epidemic: A Comprehensive Review of Use, Abuse, & Dependence. **Home Addr:** 5543 Windsor Ave, Philadelphia, PA 19143-4724, **Home Phone:** (215)921-4562. **Business Addr:** Social Worker/Family Therapist, Philadelphia Veterans Affairs Medical Center, 3900 Woodland Ave, Philadelphia, PA 19104, **Business Phone:** (215)823-5800.

### OKOYE, CHRISTIAN EMEKA
Football coach, football player, executive. **Personal:** Born Aug 16, 1961, Enugu. **Educ:** Azusa Pac Univ, BA, athletic training & phys educ, 1987. **Career:** Football player (retired), coach, executive; Kans City Chiefs, running back, fullback, 1987-92; Golden Baseball League, investor, currently; Okoye Fitness & Nutrit Inc, pres, owner, currently; Calif Sports Hall Fame, pres & founder, 2006; Montclair High Sch, head football coach, currently. **Orgs:** Founder, Christian Okoye Found. **Honors/Awds:** Ed Block Courage Award, 1988; Sporting News All-Star Team, 1989; Led NFL in Rushing Yards, 1989; UPI AFC Offensive Player of the Year, 1989; Pro Bowl, 1989, 1991; NAIA Track & Field Hall Of Fame; KC Chiefs Hall of Fame, 2000; Arrowhead Stadium Ring of Honor, 2000; Missouri Sports Hall of Fame, 2003; Senior Bowl Hall of Fame, 2004. **Special Achievements:** TV Appearences: CBS reality show Pirate Master & Pros vs Joes. **Business Addr:** Owner, President, Okoye Fitness & Nutrition Inc, 10082 Big Pine Dr, Alta Loma, CA 91737, **Business Phone:** (909)481-3541.

### OKUNOR, REV. DR. SHIAME S.
School administrator, chairperson, educator. **Personal:** Born Jun 2, 1937, Accra; son of Benjamin and Dorothea; married Ivy; children: Dorothy Ometse. **Educ:** NY Univ, cert, 1968; Grahm Jr Col, AAS, 1971; Univ NMex, BA, speech commun, 1973, MPA, 1975, PhD, 1981; Yale Divinity Sch, Mdiv, 1995. **Career:** Univ NMex, African-Am studies, 1981-82, dir, acad affairs Afro-Am studies, 1982-, actg dean univ col, 1985-86, dean gen col, 1986-87, asst prof educ found, assoc dean, Grad Studies, 1988-89, prof, currently, Summer Inst African-Am Studies, dir, currently; Charlie Morrisey Res Hall, dir; Cult & Edu Proj, dir; Team Excellence Mentoring Prog; AME Church, Grant Chapel, assoc pastor, Howard Chapel, sr pastor; Charlie Morrisey Educ Ctr, exec dir. **Orgs:** Exec bd, Nat Asn Advan Colored People, 1975-86; Affirmative Action Policy Comm; bd dir, pres, NM Sickle Cell, 1981-91; secy, treas, NMex Endowment Humanities, 1987-92; NMex Jazz Workshop, 1991-92; chmn, Ghana Free Community Libr, currently. **Home Addr:** 1432 Summerfield Pl SW, Albuquerque, NM 87121-8356, **Home Phone:** (505)839-1381. **Business Addr:** Executive Director, The Charlie Morrisey Education Center, 310 San Pedro NE Suite 220, Albuquerque, NM 87108, **Business Phone:** (505)222-0775.

### OLAJUWON, HAKEEM ABDUL
Basketball executive, basketball player, actor. **Personal:** Born Jan 21, 1963, Lagos; son of Salim and Abike; married Lita Spencer; married Abisola Dalia Asafi; children: Rahmah & Aisha. **Educ:** Univ Houston, attended 1984. **Career:** Basketball player (retired), basketball executive, actor; Nigerian Nat Team, 1980; Houston Rockets, ctr, 1984-2001; Toronto Raptors, 2001-02; Barakaat Holdings Ltd, mgr; Big Man Camp, founder, 2006-. Films: 1987 NBA All-Star Game, 1987; Heaven Is a Playground, 1991; Arvydas Sabonis 11, 2014; The84Draft, 2014. **Orgs:** Olympic Games, 1996. **Home Addr:** 5847 San Felipe Suite 220, Houston, TX 77057.

### OLAPO, OLAITAN
President (organization), consulting engineer, founder (originator). **Personal:** Born Apr 2, 1956, Lagos; son of F A Osidele and J O Osidele; married Oluwayimika Aduloju; children: Olabamigbe & Ayoola. **Educ:** Va Community Col, AAS, 1980; Milwaukee Sch Engrg, BSc, archit engrg, 1983; Marquette Univ, MSc, struct engrg, 1986. **Career:** Wisc Dept Transp, eng, 1984-90; Toki & Assoc Inc, founder & pres, 1987-. **Orgs:** Bd dir, Int Inst Wisc, 1991-; Am Soc Civil Engr; Concrete Reinforcing Steel Inst. **Honors/Awds:** Secretary's Award, Wisc Dept Transp, 1992. **Home Addr:** W147N6945 Woodland Dr, Menomonee Falls, WI 53051, **Home Phone:** (414)250-9868. **Business Addr:** President, Toki & Associates Inc, 7100 W Fond du lac Ave Suite 201, Milwaukee, WI 53218, **Business Phone:** (414)463-2700.

### OLAWUMI, BERTHA ANN
Counselor, executive, advocate. **Personal:** Born Dec 19, 1945, Chicago, IL; married Aina M; children: Tracy & Tanya. **Educ:** Thronton Comm Col, AAS, 1979; John Marshall Law Sch, cert, 1980; Gov State Univ, BA, human justice, 1981. **Career:** Tinley Pk Ment Health Ctr, ment health tech, 1979; Robbins Juv Advocacy, juv advocate, 1979-83; John Howard Assoc Prison Watch Group, intern stud, 1984; Minority Econ Resources Corp, employ spec & instr. **Orgs:** Chairperson, Thornton Community Col Ment Health Club, 1978-79; bd dir, Worth Twp Youth Serv, 1981, 1981-83, pres, 1982; Am Criminal Justice Assoc; Blue Island Recreation Comn, 1982-84; pres, Posen-Robbins Sch Dist 143 1 & 2. **Honors/Awds:** Student Found Scholarship Award, Thornton Community Col, 1979; Cert, Cook Cty Sheriffs Youth Serv, 1980; Cert, Citizens Info Serv, 1980; Cert, Morraine Valley Community Col, 1980; Cert, St Xavier Col, 1981. **Home Addr:** 19114 Jonathan Lane, Homewood, IL 60430, **Home Phone:** (708)957-0870. **Business Addr:** President, Posen-Robbins School District 143 1/2, 14025 Harrison Ave, Posen, IL 60469, **Business Phone:** (708)388-7200.

### OLDHAM, CHRISTOPHER MARTIN (CHRIS OLDHAM)
Football player. **Personal:** Born Oct 26, 1968, Sacramento, CA. **Educ:** Univ Ore, grad. **Career:** Football player (retired); Detroit Lions, defensive back, 1990; Buffalo Bills, 1991; Phoenix Cardinals, 1991-92, strong safety, 1993; Ariz Cardinals, defensive back, 1994; Pittsburgh Steelers, 1995-97, 1999, defensive back, 1998; New Orleans Saints, 2000, cornerback, 2001. **Special Achievements:** Films: ESPN's Sunday Night Football, 1987; 1989 Independence Bowl, 1989; Super Bowl XXX, 1996; The Girl with Golden Ringlets, 2008.

### OLDHAM, JAWANN
Basketball player, executive. **Personal:** Born Jul 4, 1957, Chicago, IL. **Educ:** Seattle Univ, attended 1980. **Career:** Basketball player (retired), executive; Denver Nuggets, ctr, 1980; Mont Golden Nuggets, 1980-81; Houston Rockets, ctr, 1981-82; Chicago Bulls, ctr, 1983-86; New York Knicks, 1986-87; Sacramento Kings, 1987-88; Santa Barbara Islanders, 1989-90; Los Angeles Lakers, 1990; Orlando Magic, 1990; Ind Pacers, 1991; Tulsa Zone, 1991-92; Okla City Cavalry, 1992-93; Capitanes de Arecibo, 1993; Chicago Rockers, 1995-96; Basketball Acad Dubai, head coach & dir, 2007-. **Business Addr:** Director, Head Coach, Basketball Academy of Dubai, S Campus Raffles Int Sch St Suite 20 Jumeirah Beach Rd, Dubai, **Business Phone:** (971)50683-06.

**OLDHAM, KIMBERLY ELISE.** **See TRAMMEL, KIMBERLY ELISE.**

### OLDHAM, DR. LLOYD
Clergy. **Career:** First Church Divine, sr pastor, currently. **Orgs:** Founder, First Church Divine. **Business Addr:** Founder, Pastor, First Church Divine, 233 Central Pk, Rochester, NY 14606, **Business Phone:** (585)325-5471.

### OLDS, LYDIA MICHELLE
Administrator, manager. **Personal:** Born Aug 25, 1961, Sanford, FL; daughter of Oliver Glover Sr (deceased) and Ruth Y; children: Rashonda Jamil. **Educ:** Roberts Wesleyan Col, BS, orgn mgt, 1996. **Career:** Xerox Corp, sr commodity mgr; Am Airlines, purchasing mgr, currently. **Orgs:** Nat Asn Purchasing Mgr, 1997. **Business Addr:** Purchasing Manager, American Airlines, PO Box 582809, Tulsa, OK 74158, **Business Phone:** (918)292-2724.

### OLINGER, DAVID Y., JR.
Lawyer. **Personal:** Born Jan 8, 1948, Hazard, KY; son of David Y Sr and Zetta M; married Betty; children: Joslyn. **Educ:** Berea Col, BA, 1969; Univ Ky, JD, 1976. **Career:** Ky Dept Transp, staff atty; US Dept Justice, Eastern Dist Ky, asst US atty, currently. **Orgs:** Pres, Kiwanis Club Berea, 1987; lt gov, Ky-Tenn Div Nine, Kiwanis Club, 1992-93; gov, Kiwanis Club Berea, 2006-07; master, Ashler Lodge 49 F & AM. **Home Addr:** 307 Brown St, Berea, KY 40403-1112, **Home Phone:** (859)986-8716. **Business Addr:** Assistant US Attorney, United States Department of Justice, 260 W Vine St Suite 300, Lexington, KY 40507-1671, **Business Phone:** (859)233-2661.

### OLIVER, ALBERT, JR. (AL SCOOP OLIVER)
Baseball player, executive. **Personal:** Born Oct 14, 1946, Portsmouth, OH; married Donna; children: Felisa & Aaron. **Educ:** Ky State Univ. **Career:** Baseball player (retired), executive; Pittsburgh Pirates, outfielder & first baseman, 1968-77; Tex Rangers, outfielder & first baseman, 1978-81; Montreal Expos, outfielder & first baseman, 1982-83; San Francisco Giants, outfielder & first baseman, 1984; Philadelphia Phillies, outfielder & first baseman, 1984; Los Angeles Dodgers, outfielder & first baseman, 1985; Toronto Blue Jays, outfielder & first baseman, 1985; Al Oliver Enterprises Inc, pres, currently. **Orgs:** Vpres, Kiwanis Club, 2008; founder, Al Oliver 300 Club; Beulah Baptist Church; Int Youth Connection. **Honors/Awds:** World Series champion, 1971; Nat League All-Star Team, 1972, 1975-76, 1982-83; named to The Sporting News Natl League All-Star team, 1975, 1982; first player in history to have 200 hits & 100 RBI in same season in both leagues, 1980, Tex, 1982, Montreal; Am League All-Star Team, 1980-81; 3 Times Silver Slugger Award winner, 1980-82; Nat League batting title winner, 1982; collected the 2500 hit of his career, 1983; played 2000 major league game, 1983. **Special Achievements:** Book: "Life is a Hit, Don't Strike Out that Chronicled his Life and Career", 2014. **Business Addr:** President, Al Oliver Enterprises Inc, PO Box 1466, Portsmouth, OH 45662.

### OLIVER, BILAL SAYEED (JAZZ BILAL)
Singer. **Personal:** Born Aug 21, 1979, Philadelphia, PA. **Educ:** Mannes Music Conserv, NY. **Career:** Soul Sista; "The 6th Sense"; Appearances: Common's Like Water for Chocolate, Guru's Jazzmatazz Street Soul; UNI/Motown, mama's gun album, 2000; Soul Aquarians collective; Albums: 1st Born Second, 2001; Love for Sale, 2006; Air Tight's Revenge, 2010; A Love Surreal, 2013. Singles: "Fast Lane"; "Love It"; "Soul Sista"; "Restart"; "Little One"; "Levels"; "Back To Love". Mixtapes: "The Return of Mr. Wonderful", 2007; "The Retrospection", 2012. **Special Achievements:** Hit single "Soul Sista" on Love and Basketball soundtrack. **Business Addr:** Recording artist, Interscope Records Inc, 2220 Colorado Ave, Santa Monica, CA 90404, **Business Phone:** (310)865-1000.

### OLIVER, BRIAN DARNELL
Basketball player. **Personal:** Born Jun 1, 1968, Chicago, IL. **Educ:** Ga Inst Technol, attended 1990. **Career:** Basketball player (retired); Philadelphia 76ers, guard, 1990-92; Rockford Lightning, 1992-93, 1994-95; Wash Bullets, 1994-95; Maccabi Rishon LeZion, Israel, 1995-96; Viola Reggio Calabria, Italy, 1996-97, 1998-2000; Polti Cantu, Italy, 1997-98; Atlanta Hawks, guard, 1997-98; Apollon Patras, Greece,

1998-99; Pallacanestro Messina, Italy, 2001-03; Coop Nordest Trieste, Itlay, 2003-04; Upea Capo d'Orlando, Italy, 2004-05; Carifabriano, Italy, 2005-06; Cimberio Novara, Italy, 2006-07.

**OLIVER, CECELIA. See BLANKS, CECELIA.**

**OLIVER, DARREN CHRISTOPHER**
Baseball player. **Personal:** Born Oct 6, 1970, Kansas City, MO; son of Bob; married Melissa Welch. **Career:** Baseball player (retired), free agent; Tex Rangers, pitcher, 1993-98, 2000-01, 2010-11; St. Louis Cardinals, pitcher, 1998-99; Boston Red Sox, pitcher, 2002; Colo Rockies, pitcher, 2003; Fla Marlins, pitcher, 2004; Houston Astros, pitcher, 2004; New York Mets, pitcher, 2006; Los Angeles Angels Anaheim, pitcher, 2007-09; Toronto Blue Jays, free agt, 2011; spec asst to gen mgr, Tex Rangers, 2014. **Business Addr:** Pitcher, Texas Rangers, 1000 Ballpark Way Suite 400, Arlington, TX 76011, **Business Phone:** (817)273-5222.

**OLIVER, DONALD BYRD, SR.**
Clergy. **Personal:** Born Nov 13, 1948, New York, NY; son of Byrd and Deforest; married Marionette; children: Marlo, Donald Jr & David. **Educ:** Pt Loma Pasadena Nazarene Univ, BA, 1971; Princeton Theol Sem, MDiv, 1975; Ft Valley State Univ, MS, ment health coun & counr, 1984; Oxford Grad Sch, PhD, 1989. **Career:** Bethel Presby Church, pastor, 1976-79; Wash Ave Presby, pastor, 1979-84; Coliseum Psychiat Hosp, psychotherapist, 1984-85; Med Ctr Cent Ga, assoc dir pastoral care, 1985-92; Mercer Univ, adj asst prof-psychol, 1990-92; Hoag Memorial Hosp Presby, dir pastoral care, 1992-, chaplain, 2009; San Francisco Theol Sem, adj prof ministry, 1996-. **Orgs:** Clin mem, Asn Clin Pastoral Educ, 1985-; prof mem, InterNat Enneagram Asn, 1997-; pres, Presby Chap Black Caucus, 1998-2000; chairperson, Presby Black Adv Comt, 1998-2000; pres, Newport Mesa Irvine Interfaith Coun, 1999-; trustee, San Francisco Theol Sem, 1999-; moderator, Synod Southern CA/Hawaii, 2000-01. **Home Addr:** 13361 Wheeler Pl, Santa Ana, CA 92705, **Home Phone:** (714)838-3922. **Business Addr:** Director, Hoag Memorial Hospital Presbyterian, Rm 204 Fishback Bldg 1 Hoag Dr, Newport Beach, CA 92658-6100, **Business Phone:** (949)764-8358.

**OLIVER, EVERETT AHMAD**
Manager, executive. **Personal:** Born Nov 22, 1961, Memphis, TN; son of George Sr and Evelyn Minor; married Kim Manning; children: Trevor & Shane. **Educ:** Univ Northern Colo, BA, criminal justice, 1985. **Career:** Coors, security rep, 1985-, mgr invest recovery, currently. **Orgs:** Bd mem, Colo State Juv & Delinq Prevention Adv Coun, 1989-92; bd mem, Coors African-Am Asn; chairperson, Systems Monitoring; Colo Uplift. **Home Addr:** 2534 S Dawson Ct, Aurora, CO 80014. **Business Addr:** Manager Investment Recovery, Coors Brewing Co, 311 10th St, Golden, CO 80401, **Business Phone:** (303)279-6565.

**OLIVER, GARY DEWAYNE**
School administrator. **Personal:** Born Sep 30, 1968, Montgomery, AL; son of George and Minnie. **Educ:** Savannah State Col, BA, 1992; Ga Southern Univ, MEd, 2008, EdS, 2012. **Career:** Savannah State Univ, dir stud progs & orgn, asst adv, currently; Univ S Fla, asst dir grad stud serv, 2012. **Orgs:** Alpha Phi Alpha; Nat Asn Stud Affairs Profs; Ga Col Personnel Asn; Nat Orientation Dir Asn; Nat Asn Advan Colored People; Delta Eta Chap, Alpha Phi Alpha. **Home Addr:** 12409 Largo Dr Suite 73, Savannah, GA 31419, **Home Phone:** (912)927-1703. **Business Addr:** Director of Student Programs & Organizations, Assistant Advisor, Savannah State University, Rm 208 King Frazier Stud Ctr, Savannah, GA 31404, **Business Phone:** (912)353-3149.

**OLIVER, JAKE (JOHN JACOB OLIVER, JR.)**
Newspaper publisher, newspaper executive. **Personal:** Born Jul 20, 1945, Baltimore, MD; son of John J Sr. **Educ:** Univ Md; Fisk Univ, bachelor's degree, 1969; Columbia Univ Law Sch, JD, 1972. **Career:** Davis, Polk and Wardell, New York City, corporate attorney, 1972-78; General Electric, Rockville, MD, staff counsel, 1978-82; The Afro-American Newspapers, vice chairman & publisher, 1982, chairman & publisher, 1983-, chief operating officer. **Orgs:** Nat Newspapers Publishers Asn, pres 1999-2003; First Mariner Bank, bd mem; Md Higher Educ Comn, chair. **Special Achievements:** Great-grandson of John J. Murphy, the founder of The Afro-American Newspapers; integrated the John E. Howard Elementary School, Baltimore, MD, as a child. **Business Addr:** The Afro-American Newspapers, 2519 N Charles St, Baltimore, MD 21218, **Business Phone:** (410)554-8200.

**OLIVER, JERRY ALTON, SR.**
Law enforcement officer. **Personal:** Born Mar 2, 1947, Phoenix, AZ; son of Florine Goodman and Fred A; married Felicia; children: Jerry II, Hope, Jacob, Joshua & Jordan. **Educ:** Phoenix Col, Phoenix, AZ, AA, 1972; Ariz State Univ, BS, 1976, MPA, 1988; Fed Bur Invest, Nat Exec Ins, grad. **Career:** Phoenix Police Dept, asst police chief, 1970-90; City Memphis, TN, dir, off drug policy, 1990-91; City Pasadena, chief police, 1991-95; City Richmond, chief police, 1995-2002; City Detroit, chief police, 2002-04; State Ariz Dept Liquor Licenses & Control, dir, 2004-09; Oliver-Sage & Assocs, Proprietor, prin, 2009-. **Orgs:** Nat Orgn Black Law Enforcement, 1985-; bd pres, Valley Leadership, 1985-86; Kappa Alpha Psi Fraternity; Nat 100 Black Men, 1990; nat steering comt, Urban Youth Educ, Off Substance Abuse Prev, 1991; Phoenix Rotary 100; advisor, Ctr Alcohol Policy, 2010-. **Home Addr:** 216 E Hillcrest Ave, Richmond, VA 23226. **Business Addr:** Advisor, Center for Alcohol Policy, 1101 King St Suite 600-A, Alexandria, VA 22314, **Business Phone:** (703)519-3090.

**OLIVER, JESSE DEAN**
Government official, lawyer, school administrator. **Personal:** Born Oct 11, 1944, Gladewater, TX; married Gwendolyn Lee. **Educ:** Univ Tex, Arlington, hist & govt, 1965; Dallas Baptist Univ, BCA, mgt, 1976; Univ Tex Sch Law, JD, 1981. **Career:** Sanger Harris Dept Stores, asst dept mgr, 1971-72, dept mgr, 1972-73; Int Bus Mach Corp, admin specialist, 1973-78; Univ Tex Sch Law, stud asst assoc dean; Byron Fullerton, 1979-80; Mahomes Biscoe & Haywood, assoc atty, 1981-83; Dallas Independent Sch Dist, 1983-88; Tex legislator, 1983-87; Atty Law, pract atty, 1983-; Tex Dist Judge, 1986-89; Tex Dept Agr, gen coun, 1989-90; Tex Atty Gen, exec asst atty gen, 1991; Lannen & Oliver PC, atty, partner, 1992-; Brookhaven Col, adj prof, 1993-94; Univ Tex Southwestern Med Ctr, assoc dir human resources, 1993-2003; Lockwood Andrews & Newnam Inc, dir bus & community rels, 2005-12; Dallas Area Rapid Transit, dep exec dir, 2012-. **Orgs:** E Garland Neighborhood Serv Ctr, 1974 & 1975; Dallas Plans Progress Youth Motivation Comt, 1977; Adv Comt, Lic Voc Nurses Asn; partic, Info Sem Am Opinion LeadersHamburg & Berlin Ger, 1983; Nat Forum Excellence Educ, 1983; PlanningComt, Secretarial Initiative Teenage Alcohol Abuse Youth Treat Regional Conf, 1983; Exec Comt Mayor's Task Force Housing & Econ Develop S Dallas, 1983-84; partic, 19th Ann Women's Symp, Polit Power &Conscience, 1984; Nat Ctr Health Serv Res User Liaison Prog, 1984; speaker, Tex Pub Health Asn Conf, 1984; speaker, Nat Conf State Legislators Conf Indigent Health Care, 1984; speaker, Tex Pub Health Asn Conf; chmn, DART Bd; Tex House Rep, mem 68th & 69th Tex Legis; bd dir, Homeward Bound Inc; trustee, Tex Ct App Spec Advocates, 2004; bd dir, Am Pub Transp Asn, 2010-12; bd dir, Dallas Area Rapid Transit. **Home Addr:** 2027 Argyle, Dallas, TX 75203, **Home Phone:** (214)942-6749. **Business Addr:** Deputy Executive Director, Dallas Area Rapid Transit, 1401 Pac Ave, Dallas, TX 75202, **Business Phone:** (214)979-1111.

**OLIVER, JOHN J., JR.**
Publishing executive, publisher, chief executive officer. **Personal:** Born Jul 20, 1945, Baltimore, MD. **Educ:** Univ Md, attended; Fisk Univ, Nashville, TN, BA, 1969; Columbia Univ Sch Law, New York, NY, JD, 1972. **Career:** Davis Polk & Wardwell, corp atty, 1972-78; Assigned Components GE Co, corp counr, 1978-82; GE Info Serv Co, counr asst sec, 1980; Afro Am Newspapers, vice chmn, 1982, publ, 1982-, chmn bd dir, 1983-, chief exec officer, currently. **Orgs:** Life mem, Kappa Alpha Psi Fraternity; life mem, Nat Asn Advan Colored People; assoc mem, Mus Nat Hist; Columbia Law Sch Alum Asn; pres, Nat Newspaper Publishers Asn, 1999-2003; pres, Md-DC-Del Press Asn; chmn, Md Higher Educ Comn; bd dir, First Mariner Bank; Kennedy Krieger Inst; Charles St Develop Corp; Texaco; Coors Brewing Co. **Home Addr:** 8 Melisa Ct, Owings Mills, MD 21117-3014, **Home Phone:** (410)554-8219. **Business Addr:** Chairman of the Board, Publisher, Afro American Newspapers, 2519 N Charles St, Baltimore, MD 21218, **Business Phone:** (410)554-8200.

**OLIVER, KENNETH NATHANIEL**
Executive, association executive, government official. **Personal:** Born Mar 6, 1945, Montgomery, AL; married Thelma G Hawkins; children: Tracey, Karen & Kellie. **Educ:** Univ Baltimore, BS, bus admin, 1973; Morgan State Univ, MBA, finance, 1980. **Career:** Credit & Mkt, Develop Credit Fund Inc, sr vpres; Equitable Bank NA, sr banking officer, 1973-83; Coppin State Col, asst prof; Harbor Bank, MD, vpres commercial lending, 2003-09; Baltimore Coun County, Dist 4, councilman, 2002-14. **Orgs:** Pres, Baltimore Mkt Asn; Baltimore Cty Pvt Ind Coun; State Md Adv Bd; chair, Walter P Carter Ctr, 1983-91; State Bd Waterworks & Waste Systs Operators, 1986-90; bd mem, Baltimore Co Plng Bd, 1993-97, vice chair, 1998; treas, Investing Baltimore; adv coun, John Hopkins Univ; Dem State Cent Community; bd mem, Hannah More Sch. **Special Achievements:** First African-American elected to Baltimore County Council, 2002. **Home Addr:** 8818 Greens Lane, Randallstown, MD 21133-4206, **Home Phone:** (410)655-5891. **Business Addr:** Councilman, Member, Baltimore Council County, Old Ct House 2nd Fl, Towson, MD 21204, **Business Phone:** (410)887-3389.

**OLIVER, LOUIS, III**
Real estate executive, football player. **Personal:** Born Mar 9, 1966, Belle Glade, FL. **Educ:** Univ Fla, BS, criminal justice, law, 1989. **Career:** Football player (retired), co-founder; Miami Dolphins, safety, 1989-93; Cincinnati Bengals, 1994; Miami Dolphins, 1995-96; Sports & Entertainment Realty Advisors, co-founder, currently. **Honors/Awds:** Inductee, University Florida Athletic Hall of Fame, 2000; Honoree, SEC Academic Honor Roll; Fergie Ferguson Award. **Special Achievements:** First team in All Southeastern Conference selection, 1987-88; First team in All-American, 1987; Consensus First Team All-American, 1988; Second Team All-Pro, 1992. **Home Addr:** 5082 SW 167th Ave, Miramar, FL 33027. **Business Addr:** Co-Founder, Sports and Entertainment Realty Advisors, 846 Lincoln Rd Fl 5, Miami Beach, FL 33139-2878, **Business Phone:** (305)535-9686.

**OLIVER, DR. MELVIN L.**
Educator, dean (education). **Personal:** Born Aug 17, 1950, Pittsburgh, PA; son of Loman and Ruby. **Educ:** William Pa Col, BA, 1972; Wash Univ, St Louis, MI, MA, 1974, PhD, sociol, 1977; Univ Mich, postdoctoral work, statist, 1980. **Career:** Univ Mo, vis asst prof, 1977-78; Univ Calif, Los Angeles, from asst prof to assoc prof, 1978-92; Rockefeller Found, res fel, 1984-86; Univ Calif, Santa Barbara, dean social sci & prof sociol, 2004-. **Orgs:** Fac assoc, Univ Calif, LA, Ctr Afro-Am Studies, 1978-99; Resource Allocation Comt, 1981-86, chair 1986-; mem bd, Urban Inst, Wash; mem advbd, Div Behav & Social Sci & Educ, Nat Res Coun; mem adv bd, Gerald R Ford Sch Pub Policy, Univ Mich; vpres, Asset Bldg & Community Develop Prog, 1996-04; William T. Grant Found; vpres, Ford Found, Asset Bldg & Community Develop Prog; bd mem, Santa Barbara Inst; McCune Found; Sociol Res Asn; Coun Am Sociol Asn. **Home Addr:** 1139 N Catalina, Pasadena, CA 91104. **Business Addr:** Dean of Social Sciences, Professor of Sociology, University of California, 552 Univ Rd Rm 2217, Santa Barbara, CA 93106, **Business Phone:** (805)893-8354.

**OLIVER, PAM (PAMELA DONIELLE OLIVER)**
Broadcaster, journalist. **Personal:** Born Mar 10, 1961, Dallas, TX; daughter of John and Mary. **Educ:** Fla A&M Univ, BS, broadcast jour, 1984. **Career:** WFSU-TV, reporter/producer, 1984-85; WALB-TV, Albany, Ga, polit/news reporter, 1985-86; WAAY-TV, Huntsville, Ala, sci/mil reporter, 1986-88; WIVB-TV, Buffalo, NY, news reporter/anchor, 1988-90; WTVT-TV, Tampa, Fla, news reporter, sports anchor, 1990-91, sports reporter/anchor, 1991-92; KHOU-TV, Houston, Tex, sports anchor, reporter, 1992-93; ESPN, sportscaster, 1993-95; Fox Sports, NFL Games, sideline reporter, 1995-; TNT, NBA Playoffs, sideline reporter, 2005-. **Honors/Awds:** Outstanding Woman in Journalism, Ebony Mag, 2004. **Business Addr:** Reporter, Fox Sports, 10201 W Pico Blvd, Los Angeles, CA 90064, **Business Phone:** (310)369-1000.

**OLIVER, WINSLOW PAUL**
Football player, contractor. **Personal:** Born Mar 3, 1973, Houston, TX; married Julie; children: Christopher, Steven & Lauren. **Educ:** Univ NMex, Commun, 1996. **Career:** Football player (retired), contractor, free agent; Carolina Panthers, running back, punt returner, 1996-98; Atlanta Falcons, 1999-2000; Oliver Metro Bldg, gen contractor, currently; free agt. **Honors/Awds:** Hula Bowl Most Valuable Player, 1996.

**OLIVER-SIMON, GLORIA CRAIG**
Government official. **Personal:** Born Sep 19, 1947, Chester, PA; daughter of Lavinia C Staton and Jesse Harper; married Joseph M; children: James R Norwood. **Educ:** Prince George Community Col, AAS, 1983; Bowie State Univ, attended 1986; Univ Md, BS, 1987; Wash Col Law, JD, 1990; Am Univ, MS, 1992. **Career:** Government offical (retired); PMC Col, Widener Univ, admin asst, 1966-68; Veterans Admin, Med Ctr, personnel specialist, 1975-80, sr personnel specialist, 1980-90; Dept Vet Affairs, Recruitment & Exam Div, chief, 1990-96; sr human resources consult, 1996, adv human resource mgt. **Orgs:** Am Bar Asn, 1987-; Nat Bar Asn, 1987-; Am Univ, Stud & Fac Comt, 1987-88; vice chair, Black Law Stud Asn, AU Chap, 1988-89; Phi Delta Phi Legal Frat, 1988-; Nat Black Law Stud Asn; coordr, Mid-Eastern Region, Frederick Douglass Moot Ct Ann Competition, 1989; Pa Bar Asn, 1991-; Fed Bar Asn, 1992; Pub Employees Round table, Va, coordr, PSRW, 1991-92; Leadership Va Alumni Asn, 1992; Am Soc Law, Med & Ethics, 1992-94; Fed Circuit Bar Asn, 1993; DC Bar, 1997; DAV Auxiliary, 1993-; AKA Sorority Inc, 1995; bd chair, Promotions Comt, 1996-2000; Asn Trial Lawyers Am, 2000-; Asn Conflict Resolution, 2000-; DC Bar Asn, 2000-; Dept HAS Sharing Neutrals Prog, 2000-; fel Soc Fed Labor & Employee Rels Prof, 2001-, bd secy, 2001-; Md Asn Nonprofit Orgn, 2001-03; VFW Auxiliary, 2003-. **Honors/Awds:** Director's Commendation, Med Ctr, Philadelphia, 1980; Word Master Award, Veterans Admin, 1981; Prince George Community Col, Phi Theta Kappa Hon Frat, 1983; Appreciation Plaque, Black Law Students Asn, 1989; Special Contribution Award, 1996, 1997, 2000 & 2003; Recognition Award, 2001. **Home Addr:** 809 Braeburn Dr, Fort Washington, MD 20744, **Home Phone:** (301)203-0687.

**OLLEE, MILDRED W.**
School administrator, college president. **Personal:** Born Jun 24, 1936, Alexandria, LA; daughter of Robert L Wilkerson and Pearl Herbert Wilkerson; married Henry P Jr; children: David Michael & Darrell Jacques. **Educ:** Xavier Univ, BA, educ, Eng, & social sci, 1956; Univ SW La, grad courses, 1960; Walla Walla Col, MA, educ, 1967; Univ Wash Grad Work, attended 1978; Seattle Univ, Seattle, Wash, EdD, 1988. **Career:** President (retired); High Sch teacher, 1956-62; George Washington Carver High Sch, La, soc sci lead teacher, 1960-61; WA Asn Retarded C Walla Walla Lillie Rice Activ Ctr Youths & Adults, dir, 1964-66; Walla Walla County Sup Ct, marriage counr, therapist, 1967; Walla Walla Community Col, instr fac, 1968-70; Birdseye Frozen Foods Div Gen Foods Walla Walla WA, consult, 1968; Seattle Cent Community Col, dist VI, couns fac, 1970-73, dir spec serv to disadv stud, 1973-; AIDP SSDE FIPSE Dept HEW Off Ed, consult, 1977-80; Seattle Community Col Dist VI, assoc dean stud, 1976-, vpres stud serv, 1987-95, exec dean, 1995, dean stud develop serv, 1988-, chancellorship, pres, 2003; Portland Community Col Dist, Cascade Campus, chief exec officer, 1995. **Orgs:** Bd mem, Am Red Cross Walla Walla, 1962-64, Puget Sound Black Educ Asn, Seattle, 1970-72; chmn pres search comm, Seattle Cent Community Col, 1979; pres, NASP, NW Asn Spec Prog Regional X, 1979-81; Delta Sigma Theta, Citizens Transit Adv Comm, METRO Coun, 1979-80; area rep, Fed WayCommunity Coun, 1979-80; fin secy, Links, Inc, 1983-90; exec bd, Leadership Synthesis, 1989-91. **Honors/Awds:** Most Outstanding Young College Woman Award, Xavier Univ, 1956; Workshop Leader Compensatory Ed for the New Learner, Univ of Wash, 1975; Co-author, SSDS-TRIO Project Dir Manual Dept of HEW Office of Ed, 1978; Presented paper "3 R's for Black Students, Recruitment Requirements & Retention" 4thAnnual Conf of Council on Black Affairs. **Home Addr:** 6645 Burnside St, Portland, OR 97210, **Home Phone:** (503)297-3177.

**OLLISON, RUTH ALLEN**
Journalist. **Personal:** Born Apr 1, 1954, Mt. Pleasant, TX; daughter of Vera Lewis; married Quincy L; children: Jacob Waelder Allen. **Educ:** Univ Tex, Arlington, bus courses; Am Univ, bus courses; Univ N Tex, BA, radio-tv-film, 1975; Wesley Theol Sem, pursuing masters theol studies. **Career:** KKDA-FM, news dir, 1975-78; KRLD Radio, reporter, 1978-80; KXAS TV, news mgr, 1980-84; KDAF TV, news dir & asst news dir, 1984-86; KETK TV, news dir & anchor, 1986-87; Fox TV, asst news dir, 1987-; KEGG Radio Sta, co-owner & mgr, 1990-; Houston's Beulah Land Community Church, pastor, currently; Houston Baptist Univ, Houston Grad Sch Theol, adj prof appl theol, currently; Mt. Eden Properties, currently; Eldberg Assocs, vpres, currently. **Orgs:** Nat Asn Black Journalists; Shiloh Baptist Church. **Honors/Awds:** Best Newscast, United Press Int, 1987; Outstanding News Operation, Assoc Press, 1988; Regional Overall Excellence Award, Radio TV News Dirs Asn, 1989. **Home Addr:** 3211 N Macgregor Way, Houston, TX 77004-7803, **Home Phone:** (713)522-2344. **Business Addr:** Adjunct Instructor, Houston Baptist University, 7502 Fondren Rd, Houston, TX 77074, **Business Phone:** (281)649-3000.

**OLOWOKANDI, MICHAEL**
Basketball player. **Personal:** Born Apr 3, 1975, Lagos; son of Ezekiel; children: 2. **Educ:** Univ Pac, econ, 1998. **Career:** Baketball player (retired), free agent; Kinder Bologna, 1998; Los Angeles Clippers, ctr, 1998-2003; Minn Timberwolves, ctr, 2003-06; Boston Celtics, ctr, 2006-07; free agt, currently.

**OLUGEBEFOLA, DR. ADEMOLA**
Arts administrator, educator, artist. **Personal:** Born Oct 2, 1941, Charlotte Amalie; son of Harold Thomas II and Golda Matthias Thomas; married Pat Davis; children: Mona, Monica, Rahim, Alejandro, Tanyeni, Solar, Khari & Denise. **Educ:** Fashion Inst Tech, AA,

1961; Yoruba Acad W African Cult; Weusi Acad African Arts & studies, New York; Printmaking Workshop, New York. **Career:** Artist, designer, educator & businessman; Pomusicart's Jazz Art Develop & Res Pro, dir; Harlem Cult Coun, consult; Metrop Mus Art, New York, spec consult; Ori-Gem, founder; New Lafayette Theatre, resident designer & assoc art dir, 1969-72; Caribbean Media Assoc Inc, pres, 1975-76; Tetrahedron, founder, 1978; Gumbs & Thomas Publishers Inc, consult & partner, 1993-. **Orgs:** Vpres, NCA, 1973-77; vpres, Int Commun Asn; chmn, Educ Dept Weusi Acad Arts & Studies; Harlem Community; Nat & Int Artistic Community; bd mem, Harlem Cult Coun; bd mem, New York Arts Consortium; bd mem, Nat Conf Artists; bd mem, Black Artists US. **Honors/Awds:** Hon Doc, Weusi, 1969; Commendation, City of New York, 2000; Who's Who Among Black Americans; Who's Who in American Art; International Dictionary Biography Cambridge, Eng; 1000 Notable Americans; Who's Who in the East. **Special Achievements:** Albany International Airport hosted his paintings & a lecture as part of a landmark exhibition in October 2000. In June 2001 Poughkeepsie's Albert Shahinian Gallery presented Olugebefola & painter Helen Douglas in a critically acclaimed exhibition. **Home Addr:** , NY. **Business Addr:** Partner, Consultant, Gumbs & Thomas Publishers Inc, 142 W 72nd St, New York, NY 10023, **Business Phone:** (212)694-0602.

### OMOGBAI, MEME
Executive. **Personal:** married Christopher; children: Osi & Emike. **Educ:** Rutgers Univ, BS, accountancy, MBA, finance & mgt consultancy; J. Paul Getty Trust Leadership Inst. **Career:** NJ Dept Higher Educ, dep asst chancellor; Casino Control Comn, sr financial analyst; Newark Mus, chief operating officer, chief financial officer, dep dir, 1995-2014; Meme Omogbai & Assocs, pres, 2014-. **Orgs:** Chair, NJ Hist Trust; bd dir, Am Asn Muss; bd dir, adv bd, Montclair State Univ; Newark Regional Bus Partnership; bd dir, St Vincent Acad; bd dir, Newark Regional Bus Partnership; bd trustee, Newark Mus Asn; Chartered Inst Mgt Accountants; Am Inst Cert Pub Accountants; Finance Comt Chair & Adv Bd Trustees, St. Vincent Acad. **Honors/Awds:** Woman of the Year Award, Am Biographic Inst, 2000; NJBIZs CFO of the Year Award, Finalist, 2009; Meritorious Service Award, Nj Rehab Asn. **Special Achievements:** Highest-ranked African-American in Newark Museums history; The Network Journal: Black Professionals and Small Business Magazine, 25 Influential Black Women in Business, 2010. **Business Addr:** President, Meme Omogbai & Assocs LLC, Franklin Park, NJ 08823.

### OMOLADE, BARBARA J.
Educator. **Personal:** Born Oct 29, 1942, Brooklyn, NY; daughter of Hugh Jones (deceased) and Mamie Taylor Jones (deceased); children: Kipchamba, Ngina, Eskimo & Krishna. **Educ:** Queens Col, BA, 1964; Goddard Col, MA, 1980; City Univ NY, New York, NY, PhD, sociol, 1997. **Career:** Feminist-run domestic violence Ctr; Ctr Elimination Violence Family, co-dir, 1977-78; Women's Action Alliance, 1979-81; Empire State Col, Ctr Labor Studies, instr, 1980-81; WBAI Radio, producer & commentator, 1981-83; CCNY-CWE, higher educ officer & adjunct fac, 1981, assoc prof; freelance writer, 1979-; City Univ NY, New York, NY, coordr curric change fac develop sems, 1988-; Calvin Col, dean multicultural affairs, dean emer, 2004-. **Orgs:** Bd mem, Sisterhood Black Single Mothers, 1983-; co-founder, CUNY Friends Women Studies, 1984-; career fac mem, CCNY-CWE; Nat Asn Advan Colored People; staff mem, Student Non-Violent Coord Comt. **Home Addr:** 231 Ocean Ave Suite 4B, Brooklyn, NY 11225, **Home Phone:** (718)826-0508. **Business Addr:** Dean Emeritus, Calvin College, 3201 Burton St SE, Grand Rapids, MI 49546, **Business Phone:** (616)526-6000.

### ONASSIS, ERICK. See SERMON, ERICK.

### ONLI, TURTEL
Artist, educator, publisher. **Personal:** Born Jan 25, 1952, Chicago, IL. **Educ:** Olive-Harvey Col, AA, 1972; L'Academie De Port-Royal, attended 1977; Sch Art Inst, Chicago, BFA, 1978, MFA, art ther; Art Inst Chicago, MAAT, artists guild, 1989. **Career:** Columbia Col, instr, 1978-81; freelance illusr, 1974-98; Dysfunctioning Child Ctr, art therapist, 1978-82; Onli Studios LLC, master artist, 1979-85, dir & owner, 2010-; Black Black Love, Fine Arts Ctr, actg dir, 1984-85; Chicago's Robert Taylor Homes, art therapist, 1984-89; Chicago Pub Sch, instr, 1991; Bag Retrospective Exhib, cur, 1991; Univ Ill, Chicago, vis artist, 1999-; N Metro High Sch, coach; Dyett Acad Ctr; Sch Entreprenuership Chicago Pub Schs, coach; Ada S McKinley Develop Sch, art therapist; Kenwood Acad High Sch. **Orgs:** Founder, Black Arts Guild, 1971-76; USA rep, FESTAC, Second World Festival African Art & Cult, 1976; founder, Rhythmistic Sch Art, 1976; mem adv bd, Marwen Found. **Honors/Awds:** Certificate of Award, Nat Conference of Artists, 1972, 1974; Premiere Prix Auxfoyer, Int D'Accueil De Paris, 1978; Award of Excellence, Artist Guild Chicago, 1979; Lifetime Achievement/Pioneer's Award, Temple Univ, 2006; Pioneer Award, Glyph Comics Awards, 2006. **Special Achievements:** Publisher of NOG Protector of the Pyramides & Future Funk News, the only black-owned & published comic characters; publisher, Malcolm-10 Spawning The Black Age of Comics, 1992. Author of several comic books. **Home Addr:** 5100 S Ellis Ave, Chicago, IL 60615, **Home Phone:** (312)684-2280. **Business Addr:** Director, Onli Studios LLC, 1448 E 52nd St, Chicago, IL 60615, **Business Phone:** (773)536-0755.

### ONO, MUSASHI
Chief executive officer. **Personal:** married LaKeyshia Graves. **Educ:** Fla Metrop Univ; San Art Inst. **Career:** Black Child Films, chief exec officer, currently. **Business Addr:** Chief Executive Officer, Black Child Films, 100 Oceangate Blvd Suite 100, Long Beach, CA 90802, **Business Phone:** (562)628-5537.

### ONWUDIWE, EBERE C.
School administrator, editor. **Personal:** Born Oct 10, 1952, Isu-Njaba Imo; son of Nwamgbede Onyegbule Achigaonye and Onwudiwe Simon Achigaonye; married Mamle; children: Chinwe & Mbamemme. **Educ:** Am Col Switz, Univ Sci & Arts Okla, BA; Fla State Univ, Tallahassee, Fla, MA, int rel, 1981, MSc, econ, 1983, PhD, polit sci, 1986. **Career:** Professor (retired), executive; Cent State Univ, Wilberforce, OH, assoc prof, 1986, prof polit sci & dir, Nat Res Ctr African Studies; Antioch Col, Yellow Spring, OH, adj prof; Int J African Studies, ed, 1997-2007; Ken Nnamani Centre Leadership & Develop, exec dir, 2013-; Nigerian Tv Authority, host, 2013. **Orgs:** African Studies Asn; Acad Int Bus; Nat Asn Black Pol Scientists; World Acad Develop & Coop; vpres, Asn Nigerian Scholars Dialogue. **Honors/Awds:** Cong Citation, Publ Ed, US Senate, Cong Record, 1990. **Home Addr:** 1026 Trianon Dr, Xenia, OH 45385, **Home Phone:** (513)372-4596. **Business Addr:** Executive Director, Ken Nnamani Centre for Leadership and Development, 1 Lundi Close Off Miss, Abuja900001, **Business Phone:** (234)703293-3.

### ONYEJEKWE, DR. CHIKE ONYEKACHI
Physician. **Personal:** Born Jun 8, 1960, Okigwe; son of Engr E. **Educ:** Western Ky Univ, BS, biol, BS, chem, 1981; Howard Univ, MD, 1986. **Career:** DC Gen Hosp, internship, resident, fel, med officer, currently; pvt pract, currently. **Orgs:** Secy, Int Red Cross, 1976-78; Int Forum WKU, 1978-81; capt, WKU Soccer Club, 1980-81. **Honors/Awds:** Alpha Epsilon Delta Premed Hon Soc; Chief Resident, Howard Med Serv, DC Gen Hosp. **Home Addr:** 1930 E Orman Ave, Pueblo, CO 81004, **Home Phone:** (719)561-8574. **Business Addr:** Physician, Private Practitioner, 1925 E Orman Ave, Pueblo, CO 81004, **Business Phone:** (719)565-3320.

### OPEN, BARBARA LYNN. See LYNN, BARBARA.

### OPOKU, DR. EVELYN
Physician. **Personal:** Born Jun 14, 1946, Accra; daughter of Ebenezer and Barbara; children: James Boye-Doe. **Educ:** Univ Ghana Med Sch, W Africa, MD, 1971; Columbia Univ, MPH, 1990. **Career:** Korle Bu Teaching Hosp, house officer, 1971-72, med officer, 1972-75; Health & Hosp Corp, Harlem Hosp, pediat res, 1976-79; Southern Med Group, pediatrician, 1979-82; Hunts Pt Multi serv, pediatrician, 1982-85; City NY Dept Health, sr med specialist, 1986-91; Graham Windham, dir, health servs, beginning 1991; NYHHC & Cumberland Diag & Treat Ctr, Med Dir, 2001-02; Woodhull Med & Ment Health Ctr, pediatrician, 2005-08; pvt pract, currently. **Orgs:** Am Pub Health Asn, 1987-; fel Am Acad Pediat, 1990-; NY Task Force Immigrant Health, 1991-; Am Col Physician Execs. **Home Addr:** 408 Pondside Dr, White Plains, NY 10607. **Business Addr:** Pediatrician, 760 Broadway Ave, Brooklyn, NY 11206, **Business Phone:** (718)963-7956.

### ORDUNA, DR. KENNETH MAURICE
Educator. **Personal:** Born Dec 27, 1939, Omaha, NE; son of Alonzo and Florence; married Nancy Baker; children: Alon, Damian, Terry Lynn, Alisa & Kela. **Educ:** Calif State Univ, Dominquez-Hills, BA, human behav, 1978; Los Angeles City Univ, MA, bus mgt, 1987; Pac Theol Univ, PhD, theol, 1999. **Career:** US Cong, chief staff, 1980-92; Customer Serv Inc, vpres, 1992; PacTheoll Univ, dean, prof, 2001; Calif State Assembly, chief staff, 2002-08; Buckingham Univ, provost, 2009-. **Orgs:** Life mem, Nat Asn Advan Colored People, 1959-; pres, Coalition Better Govt, 1969-76; pres, Comt Peace & Democracy Mid E, 1971-80; fielddir, A Philip Randolph Inst, 1972-76; deacon, St Paul Bapt Church, 1989; dir educ, Western Bapt Conf USA, 1999; vpres, Cent Neighborhood Health Found, 2011-. **Home Addr:** 4436 W 58th Pl, Los Angeles, CA 90043, **Home Phone:** (323)296-5954. **Business Addr:** Provost, BUCKINGHAM UNIVERSITY, 6245 BRISTOL Pkwy 271, CULVER CITY, CA 90230.

### OREE, WILLIE ELDON
Hockey player, hockey executive. **Personal:** Born Oct 15, 1935, Fredericton, NB; son of Rosebud; married Deljeet M; children: Chandra M. **Career:** Professional ice hockey player (retired), executive; Boston Bruins, 1957-58, 1960-61; Nat Hockey League, USA Hockey Diversity Task Force, dir youth develop & ambassador, 1998-. **Orgs:** Nat Hockey League, Diversity Task Force. **Honors/Awds:** Los Angeles Blades Western Hockey League, goal scoring, 1964; three all star teams; San Diego Gulls, Western Hockey League, goal scoring, 1969; New Bruinswick Sports Hall of Fame, 1984; Lester Patrick Award, 2000; Order of New Brunswick, 2005; Outstanding Commitment to Diversity and Cross Cultural Understanding, San Diego State Univ, 2008; Order of Canada, Canadian Government, 2008; Breitbard Hall of Fame, 2008; Order of Canada, Highest Civilian Award Can Citizen, 2010; The Sports Museum, Hockey Legacy Award, 2011. **Special Achievements:** First Black player in the National Hockey League; Referred to as the "Jackie Robinson of ice hockey" due to breaking the colour barrier in the sport; played professional hockey for 21 years with only one eye; Author: The Willie O'Ree Story: Hockey's Black Pioneer. **Home Addr:** 7961 Anders Cir, La Mesa, CA 91942-2304, **Home Phone:** (619)463-9701. **Business Addr:** Director of Youth Development, National Hockey League, 1251 Avenue of the Americas Fl 47, New York, NY 10020, **Business Phone:** (212)789-2000.

### ORLANDERSMITH, DAEL (DONNA DAEL THERESA ORLANDER SMITH BROWN)
Playwright, poet, actor. **Personal:** Born Jan 1, 1959, New York, NY. **Educ:** Hunter Col. **Career:** Actress, 1970-; playwright, 1990-; Plays: Beauty's Daughter, 1995; Monster, 1996; Gimmick, 1998; Yellowman, 2002. Books: Beauty's Daughter, Monster, Gimmick: Three Plays, 2000; Yellowman, My Red Hand, My Black Hand: Two Plays, 2002. Film: Amateur, 1994; Get Well Soon, 2001; New Dramatists, playwright--residence, 2002-. **Honors/Awds:** Obie Award, Beauty's Daughter, Village Voice, 1995; Pulitzer Prize, 2002; Hellen Merrill Emerging Playwrights Award, 2003; Roger Stevens Playwrighting Award, 2003, Susan Smith Blackburn Award, Yellowman, 2003; PEN/Laura Pels Foundation Award for Drama, 2005. **Business Addr:** Playwright, c/o Judy Boals, 307 W 38th St Suite 812, New York, NY 10018, **Business Phone:** (212)500-1424.

### ORMSBY, WILLIAM M.
Judge. **Career:** Los Angeles Munic Ct, judge; State Calif Munic Ct, Inglewood Dist, judge, 1981-. **Home Addr:** 5251 Veronica St, Los Angeles, CA 90008, **Home Phone:** (213)292-4664. **Business Addr:** Judge, State of California Municipal Court Inglewood District, 1 Regent St Rm 205, Inglewood, CA 90301-1261, **Business Phone:** (213)419-5121.

### ORR, CLYDE HUGH
Executive. **Personal:** Born Mar 25, 1931, Whitewright, TX; son of Hugh and Melissa; married Maizie Helen Stell; children: 3. **Educ:** Prairie View Agr & Mech Col, BA, polit sci, 1953; Army Command Gen Staff Col, grad, 1965; Univ Okla, MPA, 1974. **Career:** Ft Ord, CA, mgr, 1968-70, mil adv, Ethiopia-Haile Salassie Body Guard Div, 1970-72; Lincoln Univ, adminr, ROTC, 1973-75; Metrop Sewer Dist St Louis, dir human resources. **Orgs:** St Louis Bi-state Red Cross; mem corp, YMCA Bd; Bd City Unit, Am Cancer Soc; Pkwy Sch Dist Affirmative Action Comt; vice chair, Hopewell Ctr; Sigma Pi Phi Fraternity; vpres, Ctr Acceleration African Am Bus inc. **Honors/Awds:** Lay Participant Award, St Louis Sch Syst; Boy Scouts of America Award, St Louis Chap, 1984; Lay Participant Award, Vounteer of the Year Award, Am Cancer Soc, 1992. **Home Addr:** 12866 Topping Manor Dr, St. Louis, MO 63131. **Business Addr:** Member, Center for the Acceleration of African American Business Inc, 1025 N Grand Blvd, St. Louis, MO 63106, **Business Phone:** (314)533-2411.

### ORR, DR. DOROTHY J. See Obituaries Section.

### ORR, LOUIS MCLAUGHLIN
Basketball player, basketball coach. **Personal:** Born May 7, 1958, Cincinnati, OH; married Amerine Lowry; married Yvette; children: Monica & Chauncey. **Educ:** Syracuse Univ, attended 1980. **Career:** Basketball player (retired), basketball coach; Syracuse, 1976-80; Ind Pacers, 1980-82, asst coach, 1996-2000; New York Knicks, 1982-88; Xavier, asst coach, 1991-94; Providence, asst coach, 1994-96; Siena, head coach, 2000-01; Seton Hall Univ, head coach, 2001-06; Bowling Green State Univ, head coach, 2007-14. **Home Addr:** 1333 Pine Valley Dr, Bowling Green, OH 43402-5207.

### ORR, MARLETT JENNIFER
Educator. **Personal:** Born Sep 30, 1970, Detroit, MI; daughter of Remal. **Educ:** Mich State Univ, BA, 1992; Univ Mich-Dearborn, MA, 1994. **Career:** Detroit bd Educ, educr, 1993-. **Orgs:** Coun, Except Stud, 1990-. **Home Addr:** 20213 Faust Ave, Detroit, MI 48219-1514, **Home Phone:** (313)794-7107. **Business Addr:** Educator, Detroit Public Schools, 28545 Thorn Apple Dr, Southfield, MI 48034, **Business Phone:** (313)873-0379.

### ORR, RAY
Executive, founder (originator), automotive executive. **Personal:** Born Feb 13, 1953, Marks, MS; son of Ella Kuykendall; married Patrice Ann Clayton; children: Jacqueline Denise, Ray Jr & Reuben Patrick. **Educ:** Memphis State Univ, BS, bus admin, 1978. **Career:** US Post Off Memphis, clerk, loader & sorter, 1975-77; Methodist Hosp, distrib agt, 1977-78; Fed Express Corp, cargo handler, sales trainee, sales rep sr sales rep, 1978-82; Big D Mailing Serv Inc, chmn, pres & chief exec officer, 1983-. **Orgs:** Founder, US Christian Chamber Com, 2005. **Honors/Awds:** Outstanding Sales Performance, Fed Express Corp, 1980; Businessman of the Day KKDA Radio Dallas, 1985; Entrepreneur of the Week, Dallas Morning News, 1986; Quest for Success Award, Dallas Black Chamber, 1987. **Special Achievements:** Author: "A Dream and A Dollar". **Business Addr:** President, Chief Executive Officer, Big D Mailing Services Inc, 1007 E Levee St, Dallas, TX 75207, **Business Phone:** (214)747-9400.

### ORTICKE, LESLIE ANN
Consultant, association executive. **Personal:** Born Dec 28, 1960, Los Angeles, CA; daughter of Lester Lionel and Gertrude Kathryn. **Educ:** Univ Calif, Los Angeles, BA, 1983. **Career:** Ariz State Univ, Southern Calif, Develop & Alumni Asn, coord, 1991-; United Negro Col Fund, asst to area dir, 1993-98; Unic Calif Los Angeles Alumni Asn, proj mgr, 1998-2005; YWCA Greater Los Angeles, event coordr, fund develop assoc, 2005-09; HIV educr & job trainer; Adolescent Pregnancy Childwatch, consult. **Orgs:** United Negro Col Fund; Delta Sigma Theta; Congregational Church Christian fel United Church Christ; YWCA; Jr League Los Angeles; nat gomt mem & chap pres, Delta Sigma Theta Sorority; Congregational Church Christian fel UCC; Jr League Los Angeles; Lullaby Guild Child's Home Soc; Nat Asn Female Execs; LA Bruin Club. **Honors/Awds:** Outstanding Young Woman, Delta Sigma Theta Sorority; Women's History Month Honoree, Los Angeles Black Employees Asn. **Business Addr:** Fund Development Associate, YWCA of Greater Los Angeles, 3345 Wilshire Blvd Suite 300, Los Angeles, CA 90010, **Business Phone:** (213)365-2991.

### ORTIZ, DELIA
School administrator. **Personal:** Born Nov 25, 1924; married Steve; children: Rosie, Vickie, Steven Jr, Clara, Sandra & Beinaldo. **Career:** Community Sch Bd, pres, 1973-75, secy, 1982-PS 43-PS125, pres; Fama Film Prod, pres; Knickerbocker Hosp Ambulatory Care, pres; Drug Referral, pres. **Honors/Awds:** Tenant of the year Grant, Housing Project, 1966; Community Award, Salinas Socia Club, 1970; School Service Award, Pres' coun Dist 5, 1972. **Home Addr:** 550 W 125th St Apt 13g, New York, NY 10027-3421, **Home Phone:** (646)692-4181. **Business Addr:** Secretary School Board, Community School District 5, 333 7th Ave, New York, NY 10001-5004, **Business Phone:** (917)339-1744.

### ORTIZ, VICTOR N.
Judge. **Personal:** Born Dec 12, 1946, New York, NY; son of Wendell and Manda Mays. **Educ:** BBA, mkt, 1970; JD, 1973. **Career:** Pvt pract civil & criminal law, 1977-78, 1981-85; Off Dist Atty, Dallas County, Tex, asst dist atty, 1978-81; Dallas County Ment Health Ctr, hearing officer, 1984-85; City Dallas, Tex, asst city atty, 1974-77, assoc munic judge, 1977-78, 1984-85, munic judge, admin judge, 1985-. **Orgs:** J L Turner Legal Asn, 1974-; Progressive Voters League, 1975-86; bd dir, Dallas Minority Repertory Theatre, 1976-81; vpres & mem dir, Comt 100, 1976-82; bd dir, Pk S YMCA, 1978-81; stewards bd, St Paul AME Church, 1978-; bd dir, Dallas Black Chamber Com, 1979-81; Nat Bar Asn, 1982-; Dallas Bar Asn; coun pres, Charles Rice Learning Ctr, 1999-. **Home Addr:** 711 W Redbird Lane, Dallas, TX 75232-3117,

**Home Phone:** (214)371-0408. **Business Addr:** Municipal Judge, City of Dallas Municipal Court, 2014 Main St Rm 210, Dallas, TX 75201, **Business Phone:** (214)670-5573.

### OSAKWE, PROF. CHRISTOPHER O.
Educator. **Personal:** Born May 8, 1942, Lagos; married Maria Elena Amador; children: Rebecca Eugenia. **Educ:** Univ Oxford, BA, jurisp; Moscow State Univ Sch Law, LLB, 1966, LLM, 1967, PhD, law, 1970; Univ Ill Col Law, JSD, 1974. **Career:** Univ Ill Col Law, res asst, 1970-71; Univ Notre Dame Law Sch, vis prof law, 1971-72; Russ Res Ctr Harvard Univ, res fel, 1972; Tulane Univ Sch Law, prof law, 1972-88, prof comparative law, 1981-; Univ PA Sch Law, vis prof law, 1978; St Anthony's Col, Oxford Univ, vis res prof law, 1980, 1988-89; Univ Mich Sch Law, vis prof law, 1981; Wash & Lee Univ Sch Law, visit prof law, 1985-86; Riddle & Brown, partner, 1989-91; Russ Fed Parliament, consult, 1990-93; Whittier Col Sch Law, Los Angeles, Calif, vis prof law, 1991-92; Eurolaw Group, managing partner, 1992-; World Bank & USAID, resident legal adv, 1994-97; Kazak State Law Acad, resident vis prof comparative pvt law & dir, 1997-99; Moscow State Univ, prog dir, vis prof, 1999-2007; Am Russ Law Inst, consult, currently; Nat Res Univ, prof civil law, currently. **Orgs:** Carnegie doctoral fel Hague Acad Int'l Law, 1969; ABA, 1970; Am Soc Int IL, 1970; res fel Russ Res Ctr, Harvard Univ, 1972; dir, Eason-Weinmann Ctr Comparative Law, 1978-86; dir & bd dir, Am Asn Comparative Study Law, 1978; vis fel Ctr Russ & E Europ Studies Univ Mich, 1981; Am Law Inst, 1982-; scholar, Sr US-Soviet Exchange Moscow State Univ Law Sch, 1982; dir, bd rev & devel, Am Soc Int Law, 1982-87; bd ed, Am J Legal Educ, 1983-85; bd ed, Am J Comparative Law, 1978-86; bd ed, Russ J Foreign Legis & Comparative Law, 2006-; bd ed, J Law & Pub Admin 21st Century, 2007-; bd ed, Russ J Comparative Law, 2009-. **Special Achievements:** Author, The Participation of the Soviet Union in Universal Intl Orgs, 1972; co-author, Comparative Legal Traditions in a Nutshell, 1982; co-author, Comparative Legal Traditions-Text, Materials, Cases, 1985. **Home Addr:** 339 Audubon Blvd, New Orleans, LA 70125-4124, **Home Phone:** (504)861-8421. **Business Addr:** Consultant, American Russian Law Institute, 250 W 57 St Suite 717, New York, NY 10107, **Business Phone:** (212)656-1810.

### OSBORNE, DR. ALFRED E., JR.
Educator, school administrator. **Personal:** Born Dec 7, 1944; son of Alfred and Ditta. **Educ:** Stanford Univ, BS, elec engineering, 1968, MA, econs, 1971, MBA, finance, 1971, PhD, bus econs, 1974. **Career:** Western Develop Labs, elec engr, 1968; Sec & Exchange CMS, econ fel, 1977-80; Univ Calif at Los Angeles, Grad Sch Mgt, asst prof, sr assoc dean, 1972-78; Anderson Schoolassoc prof, 1979-, asst dean, MBA Prog, dir, 1979-83, Anderson Sch, prof, assoc prof bus & global econs, 1972-, assoc dean, 2002-; assoc dean, 1984-87, Harold & Pauline Price Ctr Entrepreneurial Studies, sr assoc dean, founder & fac dir, currently. **Orgs:** Fel Brookings Inst Econ Policy, 1977-78; Dir, Times Mirror Co, 1980-; pres, Nat Econ Asn, 1980-81; dir, chair, Munic Financial Adv Comt City Los Angeles, 1981-; bd economists, Black Enterprise Mag, 1982-85; dir, Nordstrom Inc, 1987-; dir, Indust Bank, 1983-93; co-chair, Nat Conf Christians & Jews, 1985-94; dir, First Interstate bank CA, 1993-; dir, US Filter Corp, 1990-; dir, Greyhound Lines Inc, 1994-; gov, Nat Asn Securities Dealers Inc, 1994-; Coun Econ Advs CA, 1993-; dir, Equity Mkt Inc; dir, K2 Inc; dir, Kaiser Aluminum, currently; dir, Heckmann Corp, currently; dir, Wedbush Inc; dir, First Pac Advisors Family Mutual Funds; trustee, Fidelity Charitable Gift Fund; adv, InnoCal Venture; adv, RBC Capital Partners; Rustic Canyon Group; exec comt, Outdoor Sports Gear Inc; dir, EMAK Worldwide; Gov Pete Wilsons Coun Econ Advisors Calif. **Home Addr:** 3533 Beverly Ridge Dr, Sherman Oaks, CA 91423. **Business Addr:** Senior Associate Dean, Professor, University Calif Los Angeles Grad School Management, 405 Hilgard Ave, Los Angeles, CA 90024-1481, **Business Phone:** (310)825-3309.

### OSBORNE, CLAYTON HENRIQUEZ
Executive. **Personal:** Born Aug 16, 1945, Canal Zone; son of Clayton F and Hilda Rogers; married Dorelis Agnes; children: Clayton C & Sheldon R. **Educ:** Ohio Northern Univ, Ada, OH, 1965; State Univ NY, Albany, NY, BA, 1968, Sch Soc Welfare, MSW, 1972; Univ Mass Amherst, ABD. **Career:** Rochester Inst Technol, Rochester, NY, asst prof, 1974-75; NYS Div Youth, Rochester, NY, dist supvr, 1976-79, regional dir, 1976-88; Monroe Co, Rochester, NY, dep county exec opers, dir opers, 1987-92; Bausch & Lomb, talent mg, corp dir employee rel, workforce diversity, 1992-94, dir strategic staffing & diversity, 1994-99, vpres, staffing & diversity, 1999-2000, vpres, human resources, 2000, vpres, Global Diversity Orgn Effectiveness, chief privacy officer, 2010; True Insights Consult, pres, 2010-; St John Fisher Col, Exec Leadership Prog, adj prof, 2011-. **Orgs:** Bd mem, Urban League Rochester, 1986-; chmn, drug abuse, NYS Asn Counties, 1988-92; Monroe Co Bd thics, Monroe Co, 1988-92; bd mem, Monroe Co Employer Credit Union, 1988-92; bd mem, NYS Disabilities Counc, 1989-93; bd mem, Asn Battered Women, 1992-; bd mem, Rochester bus Opportunities Inc, 1992-93; chmn, Mayor Comn Against Violence, 1992-93; bd trustee, St Marys Hosp; Career Develop Serv Bd; United Way Rochester; Black Bus Asn; chair, Career Develop Servs, Nat Multi-cult inst; bd trustee, Equity Inc; founder, Greater Rochester Diversity Coun; Nat Asn Coop Educ; Rochester Rotary; Univ Rochester Eye Inst; bd chair, Ctr Govt Res; bd dir, ESL Fed Credit Union. **Home Addr:** 30 Stonebury Crossing, Pittsford, NY 14534-4211, **Home Phone:** (585)733-5258. **Business Addr:** President, True Insights Consulting LLC, 30 Stonebury Crossing, Pittsford, NY 14534, **Business Phone:** (585)733-5258.

### OSBORNE, GWENDOLYN EUNICE
Editor, activist, manager. **Personal:** Born May 19, 1949, Detroit, MI; daughter of George William and Ida Juanita Jackson; married Harry Kaye Rye; children: Kenneth Anthony Osborne Rye. **Educ:** Detroit Conserv Music, AA, 1966; Mich State Univ, BA, Eng educ, 1971; Medill Sch Jour, NW Univ, MSJ, 1976; Roosevelt Univ, litigation cert, 1986. **Career:** Detroit Free Press, reviewer; Penguin Inc Ed Serv, 1968-; Crisis Nat Asn Advan Colored People, contribed, 1973-78; Players Mag, bk ed, 1974-78; Unique Mag, arts bk & entertainment writer, 1976-78; Scott-Foresman & Co, asst ed permissions asst, 1978-79; Pioneer Press Newspapers Inc, lively arts ed, 1978-80; Rand McNally, prod ed, 1979; News Election Serv, Chicago regnl personnel mgr, 1980; Am Bar Asn, publ specialist, 1980-82; Southeastern Mich Transp Authority, publ specialist, 1982-84; Debbie's Sch Beauty Cult DebbieHowell Cosmetics, spec asst pres, 1985-86; Twenty first Century Woman, assoc ed, 1986; ABA Comn Opportunities Minorities Legal Prof, commun consult, 1988-89; Am Civil Liberties Union Ill, pub info dir, 1989-91; Univ Ill Chicago, arts & cult ed, 1991-95; Ill Inst Technol, Downtown Campus, pub affairs dir, 1995-; Romance Reader, contribr, 1997-; Mystery Reader, contribr, 1998-; Black Issues Bk Rev, regional ed, 1999, assoc ed, currently; Bk Mag, contribr, 2000; freelance writer. **Orgs:** Mich State Univ Black Alumni Asn; Second Baptist Church; Delta Sigma Theta; Nat Asn Black Journalists; Nat Black Publ Rel Soc; Nat Endowment Arts Off Partnership; Am Bar Asn; Am Civil Liberties Union; Nat Asn Advan Colored People. **Honors/Awds:** Editorial Award, Arts Category, Pioneer Press Newspaper, 1980; Certificate of Merit, Family Law Sect, Am Bar Asn, 1981-82; Proclamation, Off Mayor, City Detroit, 1983; Certificate of Appreciation, Off Gov, State Ill, 1983; Editorial Award, Arts Category, Pioneer Press Newspapers, 1980. **Special Achievements:** Author: Check it out; color of love. **Home Addr:** 635-5 Chicago Ave Suite 218, Evanston, IL 60202-2372. **Business Addr:** Associate Editor, Black Issues Book Review, 350 5th Ave Suite 1522, New York, NY 10118, **Business Phone:** (212)947-8515.

### OSBORNE, JEFFREY LINTON
Singer, drummer, songwriter. **Personal:** Born Mar 9, 1948, Providence, RI; son of Clarence Legs and Wanita; married Sheri; children: Tiffany, Dawn & Jeanine. **Career:** Love Men Ltd, singer, 1969; LTD, producer & singer; solo performer, currently. Singles: "On the Wings of Love", 1982; "I Really Don't Need No Light", 1982; "She's On the Left". Albums: Jeffrey Osborne, 1982; Stay With Me Tonight, 1983; Don't You Get So Mad, 1983; Plane Love, 1983; Don't Stop, 1984; Last Time I Made Love, 1984; The Borderlines, 1984; Let Me Know, 1985; You Should Be Mine, 1986; Emotional, 1986; Room with a View, 1986; In Your Eyes, 1986; Space balls, 1987; One Love, One Dream, 1988; Only Human, 1991; The Morning After I Made Love to You, 1991; If My Brother's in Trouble; Something Warm for Christmas, 1997; That's for Sure, 2000; Undercover Brother, 2002; Space balls Music Is Life, 2003; The Rest of Our Lives, 2003; Yes I'm Ready, 2005; From the Soul, 2005; A Time To Love, 2013. Film: The Young Messiah-Messiah XXI, 2006; The Office, 2006. TV series: "A Celebration of Life: A Tribute to Martin Luther King, Jr", 1984; "The Beach Boys: 25Years Together", 1987; "We Are the World", 1985; "The Parent 'Hood", 1995; "Christmas with the Stars", 2001; "Celebrity Duets", 2006. TV Movie: Ladykillers, 1988; Writer: Love & Mercy, 2014. **Honors/Awds:** New England Pell Award, Trinity Repertory Co, 2014. **Business Addr:** Singer, KOCH Entertainment, 22 Harbor Pk Dr, Port Washington, NY 11050, **Business Phone:** (516)484-1000.

### OSBORNE, OLIVER HILTON
Educator. **Personal:** Born Feb 17, 1931, Brooklyn, NY; son of Mildred Branch and Deighton Hamilton; married Mary P; children: Zarth Gazvoda; married Julianne Nason; children: Martin, Mary Ann, Michael, Michelle & Mathew. **Educ:** Hunter Col, NY, BS, nursing, 1958; NY Univ, MA, psychiatc ment health nursing, 1960; Mich State Univ, PhD, 1968. **Career:** Wayne State Univ, assoc prof nursing, adj prof anthrop, 1960; McGill Univ Montreal, ment health consult, 1969; Univ Wash, Dept Psychosocial Nursing, assoc prof & chmn, 1969-74, prof, 1974-96, Dept Psychosocial & Community Health, prof emer, 1996-, Dept Anthrop, adj prof, chief mkt & sales officer; Univ Botswana S Africa, assoc res fel, 1976-78; Yale Univ, Sch Nursing, vis prof, 1979; Sch Nursing Univ, Dept Afro-Am Studies, vis prof, 1979; E Carolina Univ, Sch Nursing, distinguished lectr, 1979. **Orgs:** Am Anthrop Asn; Am Nurses Asn; Soc Appl Anthrop; sec & treas, Soc Med Anthrop, 1970-73; Coun Nursing & Anthrop; Am Nurses Asn, 1976-80; Nat Adv CenterHealth Care & Res Sch Nursing Univ, TX, Austin, 1979-80; Psychiat Nursing Educ Rev Comn, NIMH, 1980-83; Nat Comn Develop Minority Curric Psychiat & Ment Health Disciplines, Howard Univ, NIMH, 1980-; Ogboni Soc Ibara Abeokuta Nigeria; Northwest Asn Clin Specialists Psychosocial Nursing; fel Am Acad Pract, 1985 Asn Adv Pract Psychiat Nurses, 2008. **Honors/Awds:** Chief Adila of Ibara, Ibara Abeokuta Nigeria, 1972; Frederick Douglass Scholar's Award, Nat Conf Black Scholars, 1988. **Special Achievements:** Numerous papers including, "Violence and the Human Condition, A Mental Health Perspective" Univ of WI Milwaukee, WI, 1979; "Psychosocial Nursing Research, The State of the Art" presented at the Conference, "Perspectivesin Psychiatric Care", 1980 Phila, PA; Research Approaches to the Social Ecology of Health Sch of Nursing Columbia Univ New York, NY 1982; Occasioning Factors of Urban Violence, African-American Studies Ctr Madison, WI; "Point Prevalence Study of Alcoholism and Mental Illness among Downtown Migrants" (with Whitley, Marilyn P and Godfrey, M) Social Science & Medicine, Int Journal, 1985. **Home Addr:** 102-18th Ave E, Seattle, WA 98112-5216, **Home Phone:** (206)328-2865. **Business Addr:** Professor Emeritus, University of Washington, Rm T-310 Health Sci Bldg 1959 NE Pacific St, Seattle, WA 98195, **Business Phone:** (206)543-8736.

### OSBORNE, DR. WILLIAM REGINALD, JR.
Health services administrator, educator. **Personal:** Born May 10, 1957, Worcester, MA; son of William Reginald Sr and Dolores Everett; married Cheryl Lowery; children: Justin, Blake & Maya. **Educ:** Morehouse Col, BS, 1979; Howard Univ Col Med, MD, 1983; Emory Hosp Atlanta, GA, internal med residency. **Career:** Morehouse Col, asst instr, anat & physiol, 1979-80, summer careers prog instr physics, 1980, Med Dept Internal Med, clin instr, 1986-; Health S, intern, 1986-89; Morehouse Sch Med, instr, 1986-90, assoc clin prof med, 1992-95; Southside Healthcare Inc, physician, vpres & med dir, 1989-91; Henry Med Ctr, chief staff, 1998-2000; Southeastern Primary Care Providers, physician, currently. **Orgs:** Omega Psi Phi Fratenity, 1976-; Southern Christian Leadership Conf, 1978-; Am Col Physicians, 1986; Nat Med Asn; Ga State Med Asn, 1989-; bd dir, Henry Med Ctr, 2000-; bd dir, Am Diabetes Asn; Acquired Immune Deficiency Syndrome Res Consortium. **Business Addr:** Physician, Southeastern Primary Care Providers, 105 Carnegie Pl Suite 103, Fayetteville, GA 30214, **Business Phone:** (770)716-7999.

### OSBOURNE, MAXWELL
Fashion designer. **Personal:** Born Jan 1, 1982, New York, NY. **Educ:** Sch Visual Arts, attended. **Career:** Pub Sch (Co), fashion designer (partners with Dao-Yi Chow), 2007-. **Honors/Awds:** Council of Fashion Designers of America, Young Menswear Designer of the Year, 2013; CFDA/Vogue Fashion Fund, Recipient, 2013. **Special Achievements:** Only menswear brand chosen by the Council of Fashion Designers (CFDA) in its inaugural business development program (2010).

### OSBY, GREGORY THOMAS
Saxophonist, composer. **Personal:** Born Aug 3, 1960, St. Louis, MO. **Educ:** Howard Univ, attended 1980; Berklee Col Music, MA, 1983. **Career:** Saxophonist, composer, producer & educator; Doris Duke Found Composer's, grant; Oztone Productions, chief exec officer, music producer & educr, 1987-; Blue Note Rec, rec artist, 1989-2005; Inner Circle Music, rec artist, 2005-, founder, chief exec officer, 2007-; Albums: Greg Osby & Sound Theater, 1987; Mind Games, 1989; Season of Renewal, 1990; Man-Talk for the Moderns V.X., 1991; 3-D Lifestyles, 1993; Black Book, 1995; Art Forum, 1996; Further Ado, 1997; Zero, 1998; Banned in New York, 1998; Friendly Fire, 1999; New Directions , 2000; Invisible Hand, 2000; Symbols of Light: A Solution, 2001; Inner Circle, 2002; St. Louis Shoes, 2003; Public, 2004; Channel Three, 2005, 9 Levels, 2008. **Orgs:** Daigoro Music; Urbanite Music. **Honors/Awds:** Jazz Musician of the Year, Playboy Mag, 2009; Best Alto Saxophonist, Jazz Journalists Asn; Chamber Music America Composer's Award. **Business Addr:** Saxophonist, Founder, Inner Circle Music Inc, c/o Kavon Artist Mgt, Wayne, PA 19087, **Business Phone:** (610)935-0108.

### OSBY, PARICO GREEN
Nutritionist, educator. **Personal:** Born Feb 7, 1945, Selma, AL; daughter of Marion L Sr and Rosetta Wilson; married Porter Jr; children: Patrick, Phyllis & Portia. **Educ:** Tuskegee Univ, BS, 1968; Baptist Hosp, ADA dipl, 1973; Cent Mich Univ, MA, 1977. **Career:** Univ Nev, Las Vegas, Nev, stud food serv mgr, 1968-70; Baptist Hosp, dietetic trainee, 1970-73; St Francis Xavier Hosp, clin dietician, 1973-75; St Elizabeth Hos, Dept of Nutrit, dir, 1976-87; Tuskegee Univ, instr, 1989-92, Hospitality Mgt Prog, actg cordr, instr, 1992-93; Ala Coop Exten Syst, regional exten agt III, 1993-. **Orgs:** Am Dietetic Asn, 1973-; NCP, 1975-; Ala Dietetic Asn, Scholar Comn, 1988-; Am Hotel & Motel Asn, 1991-; secy, Nat Exten Asn Family & Consumer Sci, 1999-2000; dir, Epsilon Sigma Phi, 2002. **Home Addr:** 318 Hollyridge Dr, Montgomery, AL 36109, **Home Phone:** (334)260-9340. **Business Addr:** Regional Extension Agent III, Alabama Cooperative Extension System, 306 S 3 Notch St, Troy, AL 36081, **Business Phone:** (334)566-0985.

### OSBY, PATRICIA ROBERTA
Social worker. **Personal:** Born Jul 6, 1958, Toledo, OH; daughter of Katherine L; children: Imari, Isaiah & Ileah. **Educ:** Univ Toledo, Assoc, 1983, BASW, 1994. **Career:** Ohio Youth Advocate Prog, treat coord, 1996-. **Orgs:** Pres, founder, chief exec officer, Miss Jr Toledo, 1995-; Gamma Phi Delta, 1999. **Special Achievements:** Musical work: Tell me, 2001. **Home Addr:** 2124 Calumet Ave, Toledo, OH 43607-1609, **Home Phone:** (419)536-0250. **Business Addr:** Founder, President & Chief Executive Officer, Miss Junior Toledo Pageant, 2124 Calumet Ave, Toledo, OH 43607, **Business Phone:** (419)536-0250.

**OSEYE, EBELE. See SOUTHERLAND, ELLEASE.**

### OSHIYOYE, DR. EMMANUEL ADEKUNLE, SR.
Physician, lawyer. **Personal:** Born Jan 1, 1951, Lagos; son of Alfred (deceased) and Grace; married Irene; children: Emmanuel Adekunle Jr & Justice. **Educ:** Univ State NY, BS, 1974; Columbia Univ, Sch Med, attended 1978; Am Univ Sch Med, MD, 1979; Thomas Cooley Law Sch, JD, 1997. **Career:** Chicago Bd Health, gynecologist, 1989-93; St Joseph Hosp, Obstet-Gynec, 1993-95; Wayne County Health Dept, family planning consult, 1995-96; Residential Home Care, dir care mgmt, staff physician, 1995-; Law Off Dr Emmanuel Oshiyoye, chief exec officer & atty, 1998-. **Orgs:** State Bar, MI, Health Comm, 1998-; Oakland County Bar Asn, Young Lawyers Comn, 1998-; MI Trial Lawyers Asn, 1998-; Mich State Med Soc, deleg, 1998-; Wayne County Med Soc, Med-Legal Comn, 1998-; Detroit Med Soc, Legis Comn, 1998-; Am Immigration Lawyers Asn, 1998; Mich State Bar. **Honors/Awds:** Scholar, Howard Univ, 1972-74; Scholar, Fed Govt Nigeria, 1972-79; Cerebral Palsy Medical Award, 1974; Beta Kappa Chi, Honor Society, 1974; Recognition Award, Alpha Phi Alpha, 1992. **Home Addr:** 29430 Marimoor Dr, Southfield, MI 48076, **Home Phone:** (248)357-7821. **Business Addr:** Chief Executive Officer, Attorney, Emmanuel Oshiyoye Law Offices, 23300 Greenfield Rd Suite 127, Oak Park, MI 48237-8408, **Business Phone:** (248)440-1006.

**OSSE, MCGHEE WILLIAMS. See WILLIAMS, MCGHEE.**

### OTHOW, HELEN CHAVIS
Educator. **Personal:** Born Apr 21, 1932, Oxford, NC; daughter of Benjamin F Sr and Elisabeth Ridley; married Paul Anade; children: Ajulonyodier Elisabeth. **Educ:** St Augustine Col, BA, 1952; NC Cent Univ, MA, 1958; Univ Wis-Madison, PhD, eng, 1971. **Career:** NCA Sec Sch, Eng, Fr teacher, 1952-63; St Augustines Col, Eng instr, 1963-66, eng assoc prof, 1971-74; Johnson C Smith Univ, assoc prof, Chair Div, 1974-79; Howard Univ, eng asst prof, 1980-81; Univ Juba, Juba, Sudan, eng assoc prof, 1981-82; NCA Cent Univ, eng assoc prof, 1982; Univ NCA, Chapel Hill, assoc prof, 1983; St Augustines Col, prof, eng, 1984-2001; NC Cent Univ, adj prof eng, 2001-; bk publ, John Chavis, 2001; Louisberg Col, part-time fac, 2007-. **Orgs:** Mem at large, Am Asn Univ Women, 1984-; Mod Lang Asn, 1984-; pres, John Chavis Hist Soc, 1986-; Col Lang Asn, 1989-; Nat Coun Teachers Eng, 1989-98; Asn Study Africa Am Life & Hist, 1990-; Nat Presenters Asn, 1990-; Zora Neale Hurston Soc, 1993-; chairperson, St Cyprians Episcopal Church. **Home Addr:** 1325 Raleigh St, PO Box 1737, Oxford, NC 27565-3750, **Home Phone:** (919)693-9133. **Business Addr:** Professor, Instructor, Louisburg College, 501 N Main St, Louisburg, NC 27549, **Business Phone:** (919)496-2521.

**OTIENO-AYIM, DR. LARBAN ALLAN**
Dentist. **Personal:** Born Sep 15, 1940; son of Jonathan and Dorcas; married Agness Auko; children: Peter, Paul, James & Anna A. **Educ:** Univ Wis, attended 1969; Meharry Med Col, Nashville, Tenn, DDS, 1973; Univ Minn Sch Pub Health, MPH, 1975. **Career:** Pilot City Health Ctr Minneapolis, clin dent, 1974-75; State Minn Dept Pub Welfare, staff dent, 1975-77; pvt pract dentist, 1977-. **Orgs:** Am Dent Asn; Minneapolis Dist Dent Soc; Minn Dent Asn; Am Pub Health Asn; Minn Pub Health Asn; Masons. **Home Addr:** 8400 Golden Valley Rd Apt 203, Minneapolis, MN 55427-4458, **Home Phone:** (763)544-4500. **Business Addr:** Dentist, Private Practice, Broadway Penn Dent Bldg 2126 W Broadway Ave, Minneapolis, MN 55411, **Business Phone:** (612)521-5443.

**OTIS, CLARENCE, JR.**
Chairperson, chief executive officer, executive director. **Personal:** Born Apr 11, 1956, Vicksburg, MS; son of Clarence Sr and Calanthus Hall; married Jacqueline Bradley; children: Calvin, Allison & Randall. **Educ:** Williams Col, BA, 1977; Stanford Law Sch, JD, 1980. **Career:** First Boston Corp, vpres, 1987-90; Giebert Munic Capital, managing dir, 1990-91; GMRI Inc, pres; Chem Securities Inc, mgr pub finance, vpres pub finance, 1991-92, managing dir, 1992-95; Darden Restaurants, vpres & treas, 1995-97, sr vpres investor relse, 1997-98, sr vpres finance, 1998-99, sr vpres, 1999-2002, chief financial officer, 2002, exec vpres, 2002, pres, chief exec officer, 2004-, chmn, 2005-; Red Lobster Seafood Co LLC, chief exec officer, 2004-14; Smokey Bones Restaurants div, pres, 2002-04; Verizon Commun Inc, independent dir, 2006. **Orgs:** Trustee, Williams Col; bd mem, Enterprise Fla Inc; bd mem, St. Paul Travelers; bd mem, VF Corp, 2004-; bd mem, Verizon Commun Inc, 2006-, dir; pres, Exec Leadership Coun. **Honors/Awds:** "Orlando Sentinel," 11th Most Powerful Person in Central Florida, 2010; "Black Enterprise," The 100 Most Powerful Executives in Corporate America, 2010. **Business Addr:** President, Chief Executive Officer, Darden Restaurants Inc, 1000 Darden Ctr Dr, Orlando, FL 32837, **Business Phone:** (407)245-4000.

**OTIS-LEWIS, ALEXIS D.**
Judge. **Personal:** Born Jul 9, 1951, St. Louis, MO. **Educ:** Southern Ill Univ, Carbondale, IL, BA, child develop, MA, Edwardsville, IL, coun; Wash Univ Sch Law, JD. **Career:** Judge (retired), assistant professor; St Clair Co, Ill, asst state's atty; E St Louis, Ill, pvt pract, 1989-92; St Clair County 20th Judicial Circuit, assoc judge, 1992, judge, 2008; Lindenwood Univ, asst prof criminal justice, currently. **Orgs:** Alpha Kappa Alpha Sorority; Jack & Jill Inc. **Business Addr:** Assistant Professor, Lindenwood University, 209 S Kings Hwy, St. Charles, MO 63301, **Business Phone:** (636)949-2000.

**OURLICHT, DAVID E.**
Investment banker. **Personal:** Born Oct 22, 1957, Detroit, MI; son of Borus and Myrtle; married Marybeth; children: David E II & Christine F. **Educ:** State Univ NY, Col Buffalo, BS, bus, 1979. **Career:** Nat Asn Securities Dealers, sr examr, 1981-84; Daniels & Bell, vpres, 1984-87; Marine Midland Bank, vpres, 1987-88; Drexel Burnham Lambert, vpres, 1988-90; Chase Manhattan, consult, 1990-91; State NY, exec dir, Coun Fiscal & Econ Priorities, 1991-93; Dillon Read & Co Inc, vpres, 1993-; Swarthmore Group, sr vpres; Javelin Holdings; Paradigm Asset Mgt; Blaylock Partners; Dillon Read & Co, Drexel, Burnham; Marine Midland; Daniels & Bell; Amalgamated Bank, sr vpres mkt & sales; GAMCO Investors Inc, advisor, GAMCO Asset Mgt, managing dir; investment banking, Dillon Read & Co; investment banking, Drexel; investment banking, Burnham; investment banking, Marine Midland; investment banking, Daniels & Bell. **Orgs:** Trustee, S St Seaport Mus, 1992-; bd mem, Univ Settlement Soc, 1992-; chair Investment Comt, comnr, NY Ins Fund; trustee, SUNY Construct Fund; sr vpres, Investment Policy Comt, mem Exec Comt, Swarthmore Group; sr mgt, Javelin Holdings; sr mgt, Paradigm Asset Mgt; sr mgt, Blaylock Partners; Adv Bd Emerging Mgr Consortium; LP Adv Coun Sponsors Educ Opportunities. **Honors/Awds:** Black Achiever Indust, YMCA Harlem, 1989. **Business Addr:** Managing Director, GAMCO Investors Inc, 1 Corp Ctr, Rye, NY 10580-1422.

**OUSLEY, HAROLD LOMAX**
Music publisher, music producer. **Personal:** Born Jan 23, 1929, Chicago, IL; son of Nellie Farabee; married Alice Inman; children: Sheronda Jordan, Saundra Hepburn & Renee Watson. **Career:** Broadcast Music Inc, composer, music publ, 1967-; Jazz Interactions, music cord, 1980-85; Jamaica Art Ctr, music dir & cord, 1982-; Queens Coun Arts, jazz mus cord, 1982-85; Jazz Circle Friends, OPTV, 1990; Manhattan Neighborhood Network, jazz cable show producer, 1992; Time, NY, 1998; Time Flushing, NY, "Harold Ousley Presents, " cable jazz producer; Leader Muse Records, Bethlehem Records, J's Why Records, rec artist; Albums: Tenor Sax, 1961; The Kid!, 1972; Sweet Double Hipness, 1972; The People's Groove, 1977; That's When We Thought of Love, 1992; Grit-Grittin' Feelin, 2000. Singles: The Grass Roots, 1972; Backlash That's Jazz 26, 1977; It's Uptown / The George Benson Cookbook, 1985; So Blue, So Funky - Heroes Of The Hammond, 1994; Funky Good Time The Freedom Jazz Dance Series, 1995; Full Cooperation, 1998; Giblet Gravy, 2000; Living In The Streets 2, 2001; The Grass Is Greener, 2005; Hot Grits Volume 1, 2006; Hammond's Delight, 2008; Return Of The Prodigal Son, 2008; Organist. **Orgs:** Therapeut music cord, Key Sch York Manor, Br Key Women Am, 1970-85; Nat Jazz Orgn, 1991-; Jazz Bur, 1991-. **Honors/Awds:** Jazz achievement, Jazz Home Club, 1972; wrote movie theme, "Not Just Another Woman", 1974; Key Women of America, Comn Serv, 1981; Jazz Pioneer Award, Broadcast Music Inc, 1984; Award, Greater Jamaica Develop Corp, 1997. **Home Addr:** 140-22 158th St, Jamaica, NY 11434-4322.

**OUTLAW, BO. See OUTLAW, CHARLES.**

**OUTLAW, CHARLES (BO OUTLAW)**
Basketball player. **Personal:** Born Apr 13, 1971, San Antonio, TX. **Educ:** S Plains Col, attended 1991; Houston Univ, attended 1993. **Career:** Basketball player (retired); Grand Rapids Hoops, 1993; Los Angeles Clippers, forward-ctr, 1993-97; Orlando Magic, forward, 1997-2002 & 2005-07; Phoenix Suns, forward, 2002-03 & 2004-05; Memphis Grizzlies, 2003-04. **Orgs:** Community Ambassador, Orlando Magic; Kerosene Lamp Found, 2009.

**OUTLAW, JOHN L.**
Basketball coach, basketball player, football player. **Personal:** Born Jan 8, 1945, Clarksdale, MS; married Linda; children: John Jerome. **Educ:** Jackson State Univ, BS, indust eng; Coppin State, MS, criminal justice. **Career:** Basketball player, football player (retired) basketball coach; New Eng Patriots, corner back, 1968-73; Boston Patriots, 1969; Philadelphia Eagles, 1973-79; Nc Cent Univ, asst football coach, 1979-90, defensive coordr; Denver Nuggets, scout, asst coach, 1990-97, dir community rels, dir col scouting; Wash Wizards, asst coach, 1997-99; St Louis Swarm, asst coach & dir player personnel; Nat Youth Sports Prog, dir; US Dept Educ, off safe & drug free schs, consult; Charlotte Bobcats, asst coach, 2003-07. **Business Addr:** Coaching staff, Charlotte Bobcats, 333 E Trade St, Sacramento, CA 95834.

**OUTLAW, LUCIUS T., JR.**
College teacher. **Personal:** Born Starkville, MS; married Freida D Hopkins; children: Lucius T III, Kofi & Chike. **Educ:** Fisk Univ, BA, philos, 1967; Boston Col, PhD, philos, 1972. **Career:** Fisk Univ, fac mem; Morgan State Univ, fac mem; Haverford Col, vis assoc prof, 1980-81, prof, 1985, dept chair, 1990-93, T. Wistar Brown Prof Philos, 1992-2000; Spelman Col, Distinguished Vis Assoc Prof, 1986-87; Howard Univ, vis prof philos, 1992-93; Hamilton Col, R. Hawley Truax Vis Prof, 1994; Boston Col, Hon David S. Nelson Prof Chair, 1997-98; Vanderbilt Univ, prof philos, 2000-. **Orgs:** Phi Beta Kappa, Am Philos Asn. **Special Achievements:** Author, "On Race and Philosophy" (Routledge, 1996), "Critical Social Theory in the Interests of Black Folks (Roman and Littlefield, 2005). Philosophy and Social Criticism, member editorial board; Speculative Philosophy, member editorial board. **Business Addr:** Vanderbilt University, 220 Furman Hall, Nashville, TN 37240, **Business Phone:** (615)343-8120.

**OUTLAW, DR. PATRICIA ANNE**
Preacher, educator. **Personal:** Born Baltimore, MD. **Educ:** Mt Providence Jr Col, AA, 1966; Towson State Univ, BA, 1968, MA, 1971; Univ Md, College Park; PhD, 1977; St Mary's Sem & Univ, MA, theol, 1985; Samford Univ Beeson Divinity Sch, DMin, 2002. **Career:** Baltimore City Sch, sch psychologist, 1970-71; Towson State Univ, dir study skills ctr, 1971-77, assoc dean students, 1977-79; Cheltenham Ctr, staff psychologist, 1979-83; St John African Methodist Episcopal Church, assoc minister, 1984-87; Walter P Carter Ctr, sr psychologist, 1985-94; Hemingway Temple African Methodist Episcopal Church, assoc minister, 1987-88; Mt Joy African Methodist Episcopal Church, pastor, 1988-92; Payne Memorial African Methodist Episcopal Church, assoc minister, 1992-; Spring Grove Hosp, staff psychologist, 1994-97; Outlaw & Assocs, pres, 1993-; Accessible Health Assocs Inc, vpres, 1995; Samford Univ, Beeson Divinity Sch, assoc prof divinity, currently; Bethel African Methodist Episcopal Church, pastor, currently. **Orgs:** Nat Coalition 100 Black Women. **Honors/Awds:** Strong Blacks in Health, 1995. **Special Achievements:** First woman to graduate from Beeson Divinity School's Doctor of Ministry Program, 2002; author: "Soul Food For Hungry Hearts", 2005; first African Methodist Episcopal clergy person to be appointed to the interdenominational faculty of Beeson Divinity School. **Home Addr:** 828 Castlemaine Dr, Birmingham, MD 35226. **Business Addr:** Senior Pastor, Bethel AME Church-Rising, 1300 First Ave W, Birmingham, AL 35208, **Business Phone:** (205)914-7220.

**OUTLAW, WARREN GREGORY**
Counselor. **Personal:** Born Mar 25, 1951, South Bend, IN; married Iris L Hardiman; children: Lauren & Gregory. **Educ:** Lincoln Univ, BS, health & phys educ, 1974; Ind Univ-S Bend, MS, educ, guid & coun, 1980. **Career:** S Bend Sch Corp, substitute teacher, 1974-75; YMCA Community Serv Br, asst dir, 1975-80; Univ Notre Dame, Educ Talent Search, assoc dir, 1980-83, dir, 1983-, assoc prof specialist, TRIO Prog, currently; Ind Univ, exec coun mem, currently. **Orgs:** Chmn scholar comn, Nat Asn Advan Colored People, 1984-; chmn, financial develop comn, Ind Mid-Am Asn Educ Opportunity Prog, 1985-; chmn, Black Comm Sch Comn, 1986-; Martin Luther King Jr Found St Joseph County, 1986-; Alpha Phi Alpha, Theta XI Lambda Chap, 1996-; Community Found St Joseph County, 1997-2002; bd trustee, Stanley Clark Sch, 1997-2001. **Honors/Awds:** Service Citation, YMCA, 1980; Ind Black Achievers Ind Black Expo, 1984; Youth Leadership & Service, John Adams High Sch, 1985; Groups Program Services Award, Ind Univ, 1994; Distinguished Consultant Award, Southern Asn Educ Opportunity Prog Personnel, 1995; Michiana Neal-Marshall Distinguished Alumnus Award, Ind Univ, 1998. **Home Addr:** 2902 Bonds Ave, South Bend, IN 46628-1957, **Home Phone:** (574)289-0245. **Business Addr:** Director, University of Notre Dame, PO Box 139, Notre Dame, IN 46556, **Business Phone:** (574)631-5670.

**OVERSTREET, DR. EVERETT LOUIS**
Civil engineer, manager. **Personal:** Born Oct 9, 1941, De Kalb, MS; son of Pervis and Myrtha Crawford; married JoAnn R Gregory; children: Lorie Danielle & Piper Sabrina. **Educ:** Ohio Univ, Athens, OH, BS, civil engineering, 1967; Carnegie Mellon Univ, Pittsburgh, Pa, MS, civil engineering, 1973; Calif Coast Univ, Santa Ana, Calif, PhD, engineering, 1988. **Career:** Alyeska Pipeline Serv Co, staff engr; Contra Tech Inc, Anchorage, AK, partner, 1978-85; Construct Control Serv Corp, staff; Anchorage Times, ed columnist, 1981-86; Tundra Times, ed columnist, 1986-88; Anchorage Sch Dist, Anchorage, AK, exec dir, 1986-92; All Alaskan Weekly, ed columnist, 1988-89; Trigen-Peoples Dist Energy Co, gen mgr, currently; Ralph Tyler Co, chief exec officer, currently. **Orgs:** Bd trustee, Alaska Pac Univ, 1985-92; bd dir, Alaska Black Caucus, 1980-92, pres; life mem, Golden Heritage; life mem, NAACP, 1994-; bd trustee, Ohio Univ Alumni Asn; trustee, First Christian Methodist Episcopal Church. **Honors/Awds:** Author, Black on a Background of White, 1988; Cited for Volunteer Serv, Alaska Legislature, 1988; Alumni Award, Ohio Univ, 2011. **Home Addr:** 3120 Blue Monanco St, Las Vegas, NV 89117-2510, **Home Phone:** (702)240-4396. **Business Addr:** Board of Trustee, Ohio University Alumni Association, Konneker Alumni Ctr, Athens, OH 45701, **Business Phone:** (740)593-4300.

**OVERSTREET, HARRY L.**
Architect. **Personal:** Born Jun 30, 1938, Conehatta, MS; son of Cleo Huddleston; children: Anthony, Harry II & Nile. **Educ:** Contra Costa Col, San Pablo, CA, 1956; Calif Col Arts, Oakland, CA, 1957. **Career:** Gerson Overstreet, San Francisco, CA, architect, vpres & prin, 1968-85, pres, 1985-; CA Poltechnic Univ, San Luis Obispo, adj fac mem. **Orgs:** Past pres & mem, Berkeley Planning Comt, 1967-73; bd mem, Hunter Pt Boys Club, 1975-; pres, Nat Org Minority Archits, 1988-90; co-founder, Northern CA Chap Nat Org Minority Architects, 1972; San Francisco Chap; bd mem, Calif Coun Am Inst Architects, 1992-93; co-chair, San Francisco Ho Chi Minh City Sister City comt, 1997-98. **Honors/Awds:** Award of Merit, Palace Fine Arts, 1975; Service for Engineering Career Day, U C Davis, 1979; Career Workshop, City Berkeley, 1979. **Home Addr:** 3224 Wisconsin, Oakland, CA 94602, **Home Phone:** (510)482-5214. **Business Addr:** President, Principal, Gerson Overstreet Architects, 5628 Martin Luther King Jr Way, Oakland, CA 94609-1618, **Business Phone:** (510)420-8467.

**OVERSTREET, MORRIS L.**
Educator, judge, association executive. **Personal:** married Brenda Kemp. **Educ:** Angelo State Univ, San Angelo, Tx, BA, sociol; Tex Southern Univ-Thurgood Marshall Sch Law, Houston, Tx, JD, 1975. **Career:** Dist Atty Off, Amarillo, first asst dist atty; Tex Ct Criminal Appeals, judge, 1991-99; Tex Southern Univ, Thurgood Marshall Sch Law, distinguished vis prof law, 1999-2000, prof law & dir clin legal studies prog, pvt pract atty, currently. **Orgs:** Life mem & nat legal coun, Phi Beta Sigma Fraternity Inc; life mem, Nat Asn Advan Colored People; gen coun, Tex State Baptist Conv; Mt Zion Baptist Church; Sigma Pi Phi Fraternity; Nat Bar Asn; cert contract adv, Nat Football League Players Asn; Steering Comt Mem, Am Bar Asn; auxillary, life mem, Nat Med Asn, 1999-2000; State Bar Tex Advan Criminal Law Sem. **Special Achievements:** First African-American to be elected to Statewide Off, TX. **Home Addr:** PO Box 817, Prairie View, TX 77446-0817, **Home Phone:** (936)857-5327. **Business Addr:** Attorney, 200 Williams, Prairie View, TX 77446.

**OVERTON, DOUGLAS M. (DOUG OVERTON)**
Basketball player, basketball coach. **Personal:** Born Aug 3, 1969, Philadelphia, PA; married Chanel; children: Miles Randall & Maya. **Educ:** La Salle Univ, attended 1991. **Career:** Basketball player (retired), basketball coach; Rockford Lighting, 1991-92; Illawarra Hawks (Australia), guard, 1992; Wash Bullets, guard, 1992-95; Denver Nuggets, 1995-96; Orlando Magic, 1999; Nj Nets, 1999, 2002; Philadelphia 76ers, 1999; Boston Celtics, 1999-2000; Charlotte Hornets, 2001; Kans City Knights (ABA), 2001-02; FC Barcelona (Spain), 2002; Sioux Falls Skyforce (CBA), 2003; Chicago Bulls, 2002-03; Los Angeles Clippers, 2003-04; Mich Mayhem (CBA), 2005; Philadelphia 76ers, 1996-98, dir players, 2005-06; St Joseph's Hawks, asst coach, 2006-08; Nj Nets, guard, 1999-2002, asst coach, 2008-13; Springfield Armor, head coach, 2013-14. **Business Addr:** Head Coach, Springfield Armor, 1 Monarch Pl Suite 220, Springfield, MA 01144, **Business Phone:** (413)746-3263.

**OVERTON, PROF. SPENCER A.**
College teacher. **Personal:** Born Aug 11, 1968, Detroit, MI; married Leslie C; children: Sterling & Langston. **Educ:** Hampton Univ, Hampton, VA, BA, mass media & jour, 1990; Harvard Law Sch, Cambridge, MA, JD, cum laude, 1993. **Career:** Harvard Law Sch, Cambridge, Mass, Charles Hamilton Houston fel, 1999-2000; Univ Calif, Davis, Calif, actg prof law, 2000-02; George Wash Univ, Wash, DC, assoc prof law, prof law, currently. **Orgs:** Md Bar; Mich Bar; Wash Bar; bd mem, Nat Voting Rights Inst, 1999-; bd mem, Fannie Lou Hamer Proj, 2000-; sr fel, Jamestown Proj at Yale; pres, chief exec officer, bd gov, Joint Ctr Polit & Econ Studies, 2013-. **Special Achievements:** Stealing Democracy: The New Politics of Voter Suppression. **Business Addr:** Professor of Law, George Washington Univ Law School, 2000 H St NW, Washington, DC 20052, **Business Phone:** (202)994-9794.

**OVERTON-ADKINS, DR. BETTY JEAN**
School administrator. **Personal:** Born Oct 10, 1949, Jacksonville, FL; daughter of Miriam Crawford and Henry Crawford; married Eugene; children: Joseph Alonzo III, Jermaine Lamar & Kevin. **Educ:** Tenn State Univ, BS, engineering, 1970, MA, eng, 1974; George Peabody Col, Vanderbilt Univ, PhD, higher educ leadership, 1980; Harvard Univ, Inst Educ Mgt, 1990. **Career:** Race Rels Reporter Mag, reporter, 1970-71; Metrop Nashville Sch Bd, teacher, 1970-72; Tenn State Univ, teacher, instr & assoc proj, 1973-76; Univ Tenn, instr, 1976-82; Nashville State Tech Inst, asst prof, 1976-78; Fisk Univ, asst prof, asst dean, 1978-83; Univ Ark, assoc dean, 1983-85, dean, 1985-91, dir res sponsored progs, 1986-88; W K Kellogg Found, coordr, higher educ, prog dir, asst dir, 1994-2001; Spring Arbor Univ, provost & chief acad officer, 2001-12; Univ Mich Sch Educ, Nat Forum Higher Educ Pub Good, dir, clin prof, 2012-. **Orgs:** Race Rels Info Ctr, reporter, 1970-71; bd mem, Nashville Panel Am Women, 1974-83; Nat Coun Teachers Eng, 1979-; admin fel, ACE, 1980; bd mem, Ark Womens Hist Inst, 1983-; bd mem, Teak Reportory Theatre, 1983-; bd dir, Ark Sci & Info Liaison Off, 1984-91; bd mem, Women Color United Against Domestic Violence, founding mem, 1985; chmn, bi-racial adv comt Little Rock Sch Dist, 1987-; fel, W K Kellogg Nat Leadership Develop, W K Kellogg Found, 1988-91; Ark Pub Policy Panel, 1988-91; Northern Bank Womens Adv Bd, 1988-91; Am Coun Educ, 1989-95; Cent Ark Libr Systs, 1990-92; Bread World, 1990-95; consult, Scarritt Col; bd dir, Ark Sci & Technol Authority, 1989-; consult, YMCA; Comn Higher Learning, N Cent Asn Col & Univ; Am Asn Higher Educ; ed bd, Lib Educ, Asn Am Col & Univ; bd mem, Coun Grad Schs; provost, Am Asn Univ Prof; Coun Int Exchange Scholars; Coun Independent Col; bd mem, Greater Jackson Chamber Com; Alpha Kappa Alpha. **Home Addr:** 910 Oak Grove Rd, Jackson, MI 49203, **Home Phone:** (517)789-103. **Business Addr:** Director, Clinical Professor, University of Michigan School of Education, 610 E Univ Ave, Ann Arbor, MI 48109-1259, **Business Phone:** (734)615-8882.

**OWAN, DR. RANSOME E.**
Executive. **Personal:** Born Aug 23, 1957, CR; son of Louis and Anna Etok; children: Lemmy & Lauren. **Educ:** City Univ, NYC Barach Col, BBA, orgn behav, 1980; Hofstra Univ, MBA, mgt, 1982; Univ Pa, MSc, energy mgt & policy, 1998, PhD, energy mgt & policy, 1998. **Career:**

NYC Housing Preserv, Community Energy & LILCO, tech energy analyst, 1981-86; Pace Global Energy Serv, sr analyst, 1986-2002; Wash Gas Energy Serv, dir, regulatory & external affairs, 2002-; Crane Infrastructure Co Ltd, sr energy specialist, 2011-; Nigerian Elec Regulatory Comn, chmn & chief exec officer; Race Global & NJ Transit, sr energy analyst. **Orgs:** Pres & founder, ETung Heritage Found, 2002; Int Asn Energy Econs; Energy Demand-Side Mgt Socs; sr mem, Asn Energy Engrs; independent dir, Port Harcourt Elec Distrib Co; charter mem, Energy Serv Mkt Soc. **Honors/Awds:** Energy Manager of the Year, Asn Energy Engrs, 1997. **Home Addr:** 7781 Black Horse Ct, Manassas, VA 20109-8207, **Home Phone:** (703)393-1911.

## OWENS, BISHOP ALFRED A., JR.
Clergy. **Personal:** Born Mar 18, 1946, Washington, DC; son of Alfred A Sr and Susie E; married Susie C; children: Alfred T & Kristel Moneek. **Educ:** Miner's DC Teachers Col, BS, eng; Howard Univ, MA, eng, 1985, MDIV, 1993, Sch Divinity, doctrate ministry, 1997. **Career:** Christ Answer Chapel, founder, 1966; Cardoza High Sch, eng instr; Howard Univ, eng instr; Joint Col African Am Pentecostal Bishops, dean, 2000-; Howard Univ Sch Divinity, adj prof; Greater Mt Calvary Holy Church, pastor, Archbishop, currently. **Orgs:** Bishop, 1988, vice bishop, 2001, 2nd vice bishop, sr bishop, presiding prelate, 2008-, Mt Calvary Holy Church Am Inc; Bishop Alfred A Owens, Jr Family Life Community Center. **Honors/Awds:** Hon doctorate, 1980. **Special Achievements:** Office of Sr Bishop, conferred upon by Caribbean Ministries Intl, 2002; Author, Sermons for a Victorious Life, Help Thou My Unbelief. **Home Addr:** 12603 Pleasant Prospect Rd, Bowie, MD 20721-2522, **Home Phone:** (301)430-7214. **Business Addr:** Pastor, Archbishop, Greater Mount Calvary Holy Church, 610 RI Ave NE, Washington, DC 20002, **Business Phone:** (202)529-4547.

## OWENS, ANDI
Educator, air force officer. **Personal:** Born Jul 21, 1934, Minneapolis, MN. **Educ:** Columbia Univ, BA, 1962; NY Sch Social Work, grad work, 1963. **Career:** Church St Edward Martyr, dir recreation, 1962-65; Indus Home Blind, asst dir recreation, 1965-72; Genesis II Gallery African Art, co-fdr, 1972; Met Mus Art, Rockefeller fel, 1973-74; Black Hist Mus Nassau Co, muscurator, 1974-75; Afro-Am Cult Found Westchester Co, coordr, 1976-77; Brooklyn Mus, mus prep 6 curatorial depts work proj, 1978-80; Genesis II Mus Int Black Cult, founder, dir, 1980-. **Orgs:** Fed exp drama group, Queens Revels Columbia Univ, 1958-62; Workshop Doc & Exhib Mus Educrs, 1974; Fedn Prot Welfare Agys, "Creative Comm Involvement", 1974; Met Mus Art, "Art Discovery WorkshopComm Grps", 1974; Met Mus rep designer YM-YWHA, 1974; chmn, Visual Arts Discipline Mid-W Regn; panelist, Blacks & Mus; Am Asn Mus, 1974; bd adv, Bronx Comm Bd 7 Cult Arts Ctr, 1974; NY State chmn exhib Nat Conf Artists, 1974; 2nd World Festival Black & African Arts & Cult, 1975; part NY State Coun Arts, 1975; Smithsonian Inst Mus Prog, 1975; panel chmn Mus & Visual Art Inst Regional, Nat Conf Artists, 1976. **Honors/Awds:** Grant recipient NY State Coun on Arts for Genesis II Traveling Exhib Prog, 1973. **Home Addr:** . **Business Addr:** Founder, Director, Genesis II International Museum of Black Culture, 2376 Adam Clayton Powell Jr Blvd, New York, NY 10030, **Business Phone:** (212)690-3800.

## OWENS, ARLEY E., JR.
State government official, administrator. **Personal:** Born Oct 14, 1948, Lima, OH; son of Arley E Sr and Loretta J; married Audrey M Bankston; children: Scott & Kevin. **Educ:** Ohio State Univ, BA, commun, 1977; Univ Phoenix, MBA, mkt, 2007; Columbus State Community Col, bus admin & mgt, gen. **Career:** Consoc, housing consult, 1976-78; Ball Realty, property mgr, 1978-79; Lane Realty, sales mgr, 1979-80; Ohio Dept Natural Resources, proj supvr, 1980-81, employee rels coordr, 1981-85, commun admin, 1984-2005, chief environ off, 2005-09; Earth Team Green, pres & chief exec officer, 2009-. **Orgs:** Commun comt chair person, vpres, Nat Orgn Minorities Recycling & Waste Mgt, 1991-; bd dir, Nat Recycling Coalition, 1991-; chair person, NRC Commun & Educ Comn, 1993-; chair person, NRC Minority Coun, 1993-; comt mem, Pub Rels Soc Am, 1994. **Home Addr:** 7954 Slate Ridge Blvd, Reynoldsburg, OH 43068, **Home Phone:** (614)868-8844. **Business Addr:** Administrator, Ohio Department of Natural Resources, Div Litter Recycling Prev, Columbus, OH 43224, **Business Phone:** (614)265-6363.

**OWENS, BILL.** See OWENS, SEN. WILLIAM.

## OWENS, BILLY EUGENE
Executive, basketball player, basketball coach. **Personal:** Born May 1, 1969, Carlisle, PA; married Nicole; children: 5. **Educ:** Syracuse Univ, attended 1991. **Career:** Basketball player (retired), basketball coach, executive; Golden State Warriors, power forward, 1991-94, small forward, 2000; BillyBall Inc, chief exec officer, 1991-2013; Miami Heat, shooting guard, 1994-95, small forward, 1995-96; Sacramento Kings, small forward, 1996-98; Seattle Supersonics, small forward, 1999; Philadelphia 76ers, power forward, 1999-2000; Detroit Pistons, power forward, 2000-01; FeFe Entertainment, owner, 2005-; Dallas Mavericks, asst coach, player develop coach, 2008; Rutgers Univ, Camden, asst coach, 2015-; PBI Sports & Entertainment, head basketball opers, 2013-. **Orgs:** US Nat Team. **Honors/Awds:** Most Valuable Player, McDonald's All-Am, 1988; Silver Medal, FIBA Americas Championship, 1989; Bronze Medal, World Championship, 1990; Silver Medal, Goodwill Games, 1990; Big East Conference Player of the Year, 1990-91. **Special Achievements:** NBA Draft, First round pick, No 3, 1991. **Business Addr:** Assistant Coach, Rutgers University, 303 Cooper St, Camden, TX 08102, **Business Phone:** (856)225-1766.

## OWENS, BRIGMAN (BRIG OWENS)
Executive, football player, president (organization). **Personal:** Born Feb 16, 1943, Linden, TX; son of Alfred L and Roxie Love; married Patricia Ann; children: Robin & Tracey Lynn. **Educ:** Univ Cincinnati, BA, 1965; Potomac Sch Law, JD, 1980. **Career:** Dallas Cowboys, prof athlete, 1965-66; Wash Redskins, prof athlete, 1966-78; Dir Black Econ Union, Wash, 1968-70; vpres Info Systs, 1970-72; Indian Acres Int, 1972-76; NFL Players Asn, asst exec dir, assoc coun, 1978-84; Brig Owens & Assocs, pres, currently. **Orgs:** Exec bd, Boy Scouts Am, 1974; vpres, Mondale's Task Force Youth Employ, 1978; Comn Caribbean Gov Fla, 1978; bd dir, USA Telecomm Inc 1985; bd dir Nat Bank Com, 1985; bd dir, Big Bros Am, 1985; vpres, Leukemia Soc 1985; press bd, Univ Cincinnati, 1990. **Home Addr:** 6902 Lupine Lane, Mc Lean, VA 22101. **Business Addr:** Board Director, Venture Philanthropy Partners, 1201 15th St NW Suite 420, Washington, DC 20005, **Business Phone:** (202)955-8085.

## OWENS, DR. CHARLES CLINTON
Consultant, vice president (government), dentist. **Personal:** Born Sep 3, 1942, Smithville, TX; son of E A; married Dianne Burdel Banks; children: Euau Cha & Chelsi Dion. **Educ:** A&M Univ, Prairie View, BS, 1965; Howard Univ Sch Dent, DDS, 1970. **Career:** Model Cities Lawton, dentist, 1971-72; Okla State Health Dept, dentist, 1972-79; Pub Investment Corp, vpres, 1978-, treas; pvt pract dentist, currently. **Orgs:** Consult, Okla State Health Dept, 1972-79; treas, Northside C C, 1979; OK Health Planning Com, 1973; Alpha Phi Alpha Fraternity; Selective Servs; United Way; Lawton Chap Red Cross. **Honors/Awds:** Outstanding Young Man of the Year, Lawton Jaycees, 1972; Appreciation Award Great Plains, Vo Tech, 1979; Appreciation Award, Eisenhower Sr High Sch, 1979. **Home Addr:** 6709 NW Oak Dale Dr, Lawton, OK 73505, **Home Phone:** (580)357-6519. **Business Addr:** Physician, Private Practice, 1316 NW Ferris Ave, Lawton, OK 73507, **Business Phone:** (580)248-6062.

## OWENS, DR. CHARLES EDWARD
Educator, teacher. **Personal:** Born Mar 7, 1938, Bogue Chitto, MS; married Otis Beatrice Holloway; children: Chris Edward, Charles Douglas & Bryant Holloway. **Educ:** WVa State Col, BA, 1961; WVa Univ, MA, 1965; Univ NM, EdD, 1971. **Career:** Wheeling, WVa, teacher, 1965-66; Charleston Job Corps Ctr Women, WVa, coordr testing & referals, 1966-67; Albuquerque Job Corps Ctr Women, NMex, counr, 1967-68; Univ Wis Madison, counr, 1969-71; Va Commonwealth Univ Richmond, counr, 1971-73; Univ Ala, Psychol Dept, assoc prof, 1973, Dept Sociol, Anthrop & Criminal Justice, prof; Univ N Fla, Dept Sociol, Criminal Justice & Anthrop, adj fac, prof emer, criminol & criminal justice, currently. **Orgs:** Plemarch Kappa Alpha Psi, WVa St Col, 1960-61; Phi Delta Kappa, WVa Univ, 1965; fel US Off Educ, Univ NMex, 1968-69; Am Psychol Asn; Nat Asn Black Psychol; Nat Asn Blacks Criminal Justice; Nat Asn Adv Colored People; Tuscaloosa Ment Health Asn. **Honors/Awds:** Books: Blacks & Criminal Justice, 1977; Mental Health & Black Offenders, 1980. **Home Addr:** 33 Parkside, Tuscaloosa, AL 35401. **Business Addr:** Professor Emeritus, University of North Florida, Rm 2304 Bldg 51 1 UNF Dr, Jacksonville, FL 32224-2659, **Business Phone:** (904)620-2850.

## OWENS, CURTIS (CURTIS DEREK OWENS)
Executive. **Personal:** Born Oct 18, 1938, Philadelphia, PA; married Edna Anderson; children: Curtis Derek. **Educ:** Cent State Univ Wilberforce, OH, BS, 1962; Temple Univ, MPA, 1970; Calif Coast Univ Santa Ana, CA, PhD. **Career:** Mercy Douglass Hosp, Pa, asst adminr, 1966; Gen Elect PA, oper & res analyst; Philco Ford Corp, sr instr; Neighborhood Health Svc, ctr admin; Temple Univ, Comprehensive Health Serv, prog adminr & dir; African Am Unity Ctr, pres; Rainbow PUSH Coalition, trade bur dir & chmn; Owens Develop Co, advisor, 2004-; entrepreneur; 2K9, Oxygen-Venue, owner. **Orgs:** Polit Sci Soc; Nat Health Consumer's Orgn; pres, Nat Asn Neighborhood Health Ctr Inc; Health Task Force Philadelphia Urban League; bd dir, Regional Comprehensive Health Planning Coun; pres, chief exec officer, Watts Health Found Inc; founder, Positive Partners. **Home Addr:** 4226 W Toluca Lake Lane, Burbank, CA 91505-4033, **Home Phone:** (818)846-0038. **Business Addr:** Advisor, Owens Development Co, 1425 K St NW Suite 350, Washington, DC 20005, **Business Phone:** (443)324-1030.

## OWENS, DR. CYNTHIA DEAN
Physician. **Personal:** Born Mar 14, 1952, Detroit, MI; daughter of Jimmie and Annie; children: Luke Stewart. **Educ:** Hughland Pk Jr Col, attended 1971; Wayne State Univ, BA, 1975; Mich Osteo Med Ctr, DO, 1979. **Career:** Gen med physician, 1981-82; Pvt Pract, internist, 1984-86, currently; Gulf Coast Primary Care, internist, 1986-95, 1997-; Biloxi VA Med Ctr, ER physician, 1995-97. **Orgs:** Bd mem, Slavation Army Soc Battered Women, 1991-94; prof ed chairperson & bd mem, Jackson County Am Cancer Soc, 1992-94; bd mem, Jackson County Sickle Cell Soc, 1996-. **Honors/Awds:** Citizen of the Year, Moss Point MS, 1998. **Home Addr:** 3820 Charmont Cir, Ocean Springs, MS 39564, **Home Phone:** (228)872-1445. **Business Addr:** Physician, Private Practitioner, Gulf Coast Primary Care, 4105 Hosp St Suite 105B, Pascagoula, MS 39581-5312, **Business Phone:** (228)549-2000.

**OWENS, DANA ELAINE.** See QUEEN LATIFAH.

## OWENS, DAVID KENNETH
Engineer, executive. **Personal:** Born Jun 14, 1948, Philadelphia, PA; son of Erwin D and Grace; married Karen P; children: Pharis, Phyllis & Kenneth. **Educ:** Howard Univ, BSEE, 1969, MSEE, 1977; George Washington Univ, MSEA, 1977. **Career:** US Securities & Exchange Comn, chief engr, 1974-80; Fed Power Comn, engr, div rates & corp regulation, 1970-74; Gen Elec Co, design & test engr, 1969-70; Pa Elec Co, 1968; Edison Elec Inst, dir rates & regulation, 1980-, sr vpres finance, regulation, vpres, power supply policy, exec vpres, bus opers, currently. **Orgs:** Inst Elec & Electronics Engrs; Kappa Alpha Psi Frat; Nativity BVM Ch; Blacks in Energy; Nat Black Engr's Asn; Am Asn Blacks Energy; Nat Acad Sci; chair, IDEA Pub Charter Sch Bd Trustees; chmn, Nat Inst Stand & Technol Smart Grid Adv Comt. **Honors/Awds:** Frat Schroller of Year Award, Kappa Alpha Psi, 1969; Superior Perf Award, 1972; Outstanding Award, 1974; Outstanding Employee of the Year Award, EEI, 1987; Most Distinguished Professional, EEI, 1988; Special Rec Award, EEI, 1990; James E. Stewart Award. **Special Achievements:** First African American to Hold an Officer Title at EEI. **Home Addr:** 307 Rittenhouse St NW, Washington, DC 20011. **Business Addr:** Executive Vice President of Business Operations, Edison Electric Institute, 701 Pa Ave NW 4 Fl, Washington, DC 20004-2696, **Business Phone:** (202)508-5000.

## OWENS, DR. DEBBIE A.
Journalist, college teacher. **Personal:** Born Jan 23, 1956, Brooklyn, NY. **Educ:** Brooklyn Col City Univ NY, BA, eng-humanities, 1977; Univ Ill, Urbana-Champaign, MS, jour, 1982; Univ Fla, PhD, commun, 1994; Univ Fla, cert geront, 1994. **Career:** Chicago Tribune Newspaper, reporter intern, 1976; NY Amsterdam Newspaper, reporter intern, 1977; NY City Bd Educ, eng teacher, 1978-79; JC Penney Co, NY, catalog copywriter, 1979-81; Freedom ways Mag, NY, bk reviewer, 1980; WPGU-FM, Black Notes, pub affairs reporter, 1981-82; Univ Ill, Urbana-Champaign, grad fel, 1981-82; Univ Ill, grad newsletter writer, 1981-82; WCIA-TV, news reporter & minority affairs prog prod, 1982-85; Edward Waters Col, radio & tv broadcast instr, 1985-86; E Carolina Univ, commun lect & instr, 1986-88; Bethune Cookman Col, pub speaking adj, 1991; Wash & Lee Univ, jour vis scholar, 1993-94; Fel Voice Am, reporter & writer, 1994; Bowling Green St Univ, jour asst prof, 1994-98; Fayetteville St Univ, commun assist prof, 1998-02; ASNE fel Charlotte Observer, reporter & ed, 2000; RTNDF Fel WRAL-TV5, Capitol Broadcasting Co, 2002; Univ Nebr-Lincoln, jour vis sum scholar, 2002; Oxford Round Table, res presenter, 2008; Educ Testing Serv, vis scholar, 2010; col bus writing across curric ambassador, Murray State Univ, 2010-12; fulbright specialists cand, Coun Int Exchange Scholars, 2011-; Murray State Univ, Dept Journ & Mass Commun, assoc prof, internship coordr, currently, grad prog dir, 2002-; assoc prof, Time Warner Col Professors Leadership Sem, 2013. **Orgs:** Mayor's Vol Action Ctr NY, 1980; NY Vol Urban Consult Group, 1980; Radio-TV News Dir Asn, 1982-; Ill News Broadcasters Asn, 1983-85; Nat Broadcasting Soc-Alpa Epsilon Rho; former Publ Bd & Gender Issues Div Pres, Broadcast Educ Asn, 2013, 1994-2013; JMC Nat Hon Soc-Kappa Tau Alpha; chair, Broadcast Educ Asn; Asn Am Univ; Col Press Ed Adv Bd; Cumberland-Fayett Arts Coun; fel, Inst Journalism Excellence, Am Soc Newspaper Ed, 2000; online journalism fel & online reporting sem partic, Poynter Inst, 2000; WTVD-TV Durham Adv Comn, 2001-02; excellence journalism educ proj, Radio-Tv News Dir Asn, 2002; Black Col Radio Adv Bd, 2002-03; Broadcast Educ Asn Publ Bd, 2003-; Women; chair, Gender Issues Div, 2006-07; vpres, Black Fac Staff Asn, 2007; tv programming sem, Int Radio-Tv Soc-ABC Disney, 2007; ed bd mem, J Mass Commun & Journalism, 2012-. **Honors/Awds:** Florida Governor's Award, 1986; Outstanding Young Women of America, 1988; Teacher of the Year Award, Fayett St Univ Perf/Fine Arts, 2001-02; FayettSt Univ, Col of Arts & Sci Conf, Res, & Pub Award, 2000-02; Key to theCity, Murray, Ky, 2004; Murray-Calloway NAACP Appreciation, 2004. **Business Addr:** Associate Professor, Internship Coordinator, Murray State University, 114 Wilson Hall, Murray, KY 42071-3311, **Business Phone:** (270)762-6318.

## OWENS, DONNA M.
Journalist. **Educ:** Hampton University, B.A. in Mass Media Arts; Columbia University Graduate School of Journalism (New York City), M.A. in Journalism with a concentration in science and health reporting, 2013. **Career:** Reporter for various CBS and NBC television affiliates and radio reporter/anchor; Freelance contributor for various publications such as: "Baltimore Sun," "NPR," "Chicago Tribune," "Miami Herald," "O, the Oprah Magazine," "Essence," AOL, NBC's TheGrio.com, and other trade publications. **Orgs:** Investigative Reporters and Editors (IRE), Member; Newswomen's Club of New York, Member. **Honors/Awds:** Society of Professional Journalists (SPJ Maryland chapter), Award Recipient; Public Radio News Directors Inc. (PRNDI), Award Recipient; National Association of Black Journalists (NABJ), Award Recipient; Anne O'Hare McCormick Scholarship, 2012-13; Columbia University's Robert Harron Award, 2013. **Special Achievements:** Co-author of three travel books for Fodor's (Random House).

## OWENS, EDWARD GLENN
Government official. **Personal:** Born Apr 23, 1958, Huntsville, TX; son of Edward and Hattie; married Rissie; children: Edward. **Educ:** Sam Houston State Univ, BS, crimino & corrections, 1980. **Career:** Government Official (retired); Tex Dept Criminal Justice, correctional officer, 1977-81; Tex bd Pardons & Parole, parole caseworker, 1981-83; Tex Dept Criminal Justice, line supvr, 1983-90, warden, 1990-95, regional dir, 1995-97, dep dir, 1997-2001, opers div dir, 2001-02, dep exec dir, 2002-07. **Orgs:** Alpha Phi Alpha fraternity, 1979; fel, Am Correctional Asn & Tex Corrections Asn; exec dir, Tex Youth Comn, 2007-. **Honors/Awds:** Service Award, Tex Dept of Criminal Justice, 2003. **Home Addr:** 180 Elkins Lake, Huntsville, TX 77340, **Home Phone:** (936)294-0262.

## OWENS, GEOFFREY
Actor, special education teacher. **Personal:** Born Mar 18, 1961, Brooklyn, NY; son of Major and Maria Cupril. **Educ:** Yale Univ, BA (cum laude), eng lit & theater studies, 1983. **Career:** TV series: "ABC After school Specials", 1990; "The Cosby Show", 1985-92; "Built To Last", 1997; "Law & Order", 1999; "Law & Order: Special Victims Unit", 2002; "That's So Raven", 2007; "The Wedding Bells", 2007; "It's Always Sunny in Philadelphia", 2007-11; "Boston Legal", 2007; "Las Vegas", 2007; "Journeyman", 2007; "Medium", 2008; "I Didn't Know I Was Pregnant", 2008; "Without a Trace", 2008. Films: The Paper, 1994; Stonebrook, 1999; Forgiven, 1999; The Cross, 2001; Play the Game, 2009; Sami's Cock, 2010; Dreams, 2013; Romeo and Juliet, 2014. Fla State Univ, teacher, assoc dean, prof; Yale Univ, actg teacher, coach, teacher; Brooklyn Shakespeare Co, founder & artistic dir, currently; Gene Frankel Studio, actg teacher, teacher; HB Studio, teacher, actg teacher; Circus Theatricals LLC, founder & artistic dir, currently. **Orgs:** New York Church Christ. **Home Addr:** 6231 Medici Ct Apt 205, Sarasota, FL 34243-5603. **Business Addr:** Actor.

## OWENS, ISAIAH HUDSON (IKE OWENS)
Educator, executive, football player. **Personal:** Born Jan 8, 1921, Columbus, GA; son of Isaiah H and Mary D; married Nell Craig; children: Whitlynn, Isaiah Jr, Bert & Barrington. **Educ:** Univ Ill, B FA, 1948; Ind Univ, BS, 1959. **Career:** Football player (retired); Roosevelt High Sch, Gary, teacher; Owens & Craig's Inc, pres; Wales, loose forward, 1945-49; Leeds, loose forward, 1946; Castleford, loose forward, 1946-49; Huddersfield, loose forward, 1946; Gt briT, loose forward, 1946; Stand Oil, indust distribr, 1950-58; Owens' Gift & Toy Shoppe, owner, 1949-65; Chicago Rockets, 1948. **Orgs:** Vpres, Midtown Busi-

nessmen Asn, 1970-73; Residence Com Model Cities; chmn, Econ Task Force; Gary Alumni Chap, Kappa Alpha Psi; Nat Asn Advan Colored People; Roosevelt High Sch Alumni Asn. **Home Addr:** 1901 Chase St, Gary, IN 46404. **Business Addr:** 1638 Broadway, Gary, IN 46404.

## OWENS, JAMES ROBERT

Trumpet player, composer, educator. **Personal:** Born Dec 9, 1943, New York, NY; son of James Robert and Eva Lois; married Lola Mae Brown; children: Milan & Ayan. **Educ:** Univ Mass, Amherst, MEd, 1975. **Career:** Assoc Musicians Greater New York, Local 802, AFM, 1958-; BMI, writer & publ, 1966-; MUSE, jazz workshop staff, 1968-73; Am Guild Authors & Composers, publ & composer, 1968-85; State Univ New York, Stony brook, lectr demonstration & concert, 1975; McLennan Community Col, Waco, TX, concerts & workshops, 1978; State Univ New York, Col Old W bury, adj prof, 1981-86; Jazzmobile Inc, workshop prog dir, New York, 1981-86; Queens bor Community Col, adj prof, 1984-85; Jazz mobile Inc, workshop prog dir, 1984-90; New Sch Social Res, Jazz Prog, part-time fac, 1990-; Oberlin Conserv Music, vis prof, 1992-93; Univ Pittsburgh, clin & trumpet master class, 1992, 1997; Thelonious Monk Inst, artistic dir, 1996; Youngstown State Univ, Col Fine Arts, workshop & master class, 1997; Greenwich High Sch, CT, workshop & adjudication, 1997; City Univ New York, vis prof, 1998. Compositions: Complicity; Dreaming My Life Away; Look Softly; Milan is Love; Never Subj to Chg; Jazz Fusions; Against Great Odds; TV doc sound tracks: "Conversations with Roy De Carava", 1983; "Hookers at the Pt 1 & 2", 1996-97; "Pimps up, Ho's Down", 1998; "Peaceful Walking", Jay-Oh Jazz Rec, A Div Jay-Oh Productions Inc, 2007. **Orgs:** Mech Copyright Protection Soc, 1967-76; bd gov, vpres, Nat Acad Rec Arts & Sci, New York, 1971-; jazz panelist, Nat Endowment Arts, 1972-76, 1990, 1998, 2009; Int Asn Jazz Educrs, 1974-2008; musical dir & bd dir, New York Jazz Repertory Co, New York, NY, 1974; Int Trumpet Guild, 1975-; exec comt & bd dir, Am Arts Alliance Inc, 1977-83; panelist, Mass Arts & Humanities Found, 1977; presenting Orgn panel, NY Coun Arts, 1978-81; bd dir, Jazz Found Am Inc, 1989-. **Honors/Awds:** America Achievement Award, Jazz Home Club Am, 1972; New Leaders for the'80s Award, Black Enterprise Mag, 1979; Survival of the Black Artist Award, Howard Univ, Washington, DC, 1980; International Success Award, Marabu Club, Italy, 1983; Manhattan Borough President's Award for Excellence in the Arts, 1986; Dr. Billy Taylor Humanitarian Award, Jazz Found Am, 2002; Lifetime Achievement Award, New York Brass Conf, 2007; Benny Golson Jazz Master Award, Howard Univ, 2008; A. B. Spellman NEA Jazz Masters Award, 2012. **Special Achievements:** Presidential Citation, Clark Col, Atlanta, GA, 1972; live performances of original orchestral works with Jimmy Owens Plus; Rochester Philharmonic Orchestra; Brooklyn Philharmonic Orchestra; Hannover Philharmonic; Metro pole Orchestra. Publication: "Jimmy Owens. How the Jazz Artist Practices, In Early 20th Century Brass Idioms", 2009; Jimmy Owens. Remembering Jamil Nasser, JazzTimes.com, 2010. **Home Addr:** 236 Park Ave S, New York, NY 10003-1401, **Home Phone:** (212)475-0358. **Business Addr:** Musician, Jay-Oh Productions Inc, 236 Park Ave S, New York, NY 10003, **Business Phone:** (212)475-0358.

## OWENS, DR. JAY R., JR.

Dentist. **Personal:** Born Feb 17, 1944, Pine Bluff, AR; married Staggie Darnelle Gordon; children: Kevin, Jay II & Latitia. **Educ:** Howard Univ, BS, 1967; Meharry Med Col, DDS, 1971. **Career:** Pvt pract, dentist, 1978-. **Orgs:** Pres, Ark Med Dent Pharmaceut Asn, 1982-83; vice speaker house, Nat Dent Asn, 1984-85; bd dir, Urban League Ark, 1984. **Home Addr:** 1117 Arthur Dr, Little Rock, AR 72204-1565, **Home Phone:** (501)666-7325. **Business Addr:** Dentist, Private Practice, 1123 S Univ Ave Suite 714, Little Rock, AR 72204, **Business Phone:** (501)666-5412.

## OWENS, DR. JERRY SUE (JERRY SUE OWENS THORNTON)

School administrator, educator. **Personal:** Born Jan 16, 1947, Earlington, KY; married Ronald L. **Educ:** Murray State Univ, BA, 1969, MA, 1970; Univ Tex, PhD, 1983. **Career:** President (retired); Earlington Elem Sch, 6th grade educ, 1970; Murray High Sch, Jr, Sr eng, 1970-71; Triton Col, instr, 1971-77, asst, assoc & dean arts & scis, 1978-85; Lakewood Community Col, pres, 1985; Cuyahoga Community Col, pres, 1991-2013. **Orgs:** Nat Coun Teachers Eng; Am Asn Comm & Jr Cols; Am Asn Higher Educ; Women Higher Educ; vpres bd, YWCA, St Paul, Minn; bd mem, United Way St Paul; Urban League, Nat Asn Advan Colored People. **Honors/Awds:** Chief Executive Officer Award, Asn Community Col Trustees, 1991. **Special Achievements:** Author: Cuyahoga Community College Alumni Directory, 1994. **Home Addr:** 1222 Birch Pond Trail, White Bear Lake, MN 55110.

**OWENS, DR. JOAN MURRELL.** **See Obituaries Section.**

## OWENS, DR. JUDITH MYOLI

Teacher, president (organization), educator. **Personal:** Born Jun 18, 1940, Carlisle, PA; daughter of Benjamin Myoli and Estella Pickens. **Educ:** Shippensburg Univ, BS, educ, 1962; Monmouth Univ, MS, educ, 1975; Nova Univ, EdD, 1990. **Career:** Educator (retired); NJ Educ Asn, pres, 1975-77; Asbury Pk Bd Educ, Bradley Sch, prin, 1987-91, elem teacher, math resource room teacher, chair person spec educ, affirmative action officer, supvr, vice prin; Col NJ, asst prof, 1991-95; Educ Testing Serv, consult. **Orgs:** Mensa Int, 1990-; exec comt, Nat Educ Asn.; NJ Educ Asn; Order Ky Colonels; Ctr Jersey Club NANB PWC Inc; pres, Nat Sch Boards Asn. **Home Addr:** 64 Kathy Ct, Brick, NJ 08724, **Home Phone:** (732)458-0820.

## OWENS, KEITH ALAN

Journalist. **Personal:** Born May 1, 1958, Denver, CO; son of Sebastian C and Geneva M; married Pamela Hilliard. **Educ:** Colo Col, BA, eng, 1980. **Career:** Freelance writer, columnist, ed & journalist; Littleton Independent, intern, 1984; Denver Post, intern, 1984-85; Los Angeles Times, Jour trainee, 1985-86; Ann Arbor News, reporter, 1986-89; Mich Chronicle; Ft Lauderdale Sun-Sentinel; Ft Lauderdale Sun-Sentinel, ed writer, reporter, 1989-93; Detroit Free Press, ed writer, columnist; Detroit Ink Publ, co-founder; Detroit Metro Times, columnist, journalist, ed & freelance writer, currently. **Orgs:** Nat Asn Broadcasters, 1984-; pres, Mid-Mich Asn Black Journalists, 1988-89; staff mem, Metro Times; chmn, Phillips Exeter Acad Com Excellence thru Diversity, 1988-89; Socs Prof Journalists; secy, 1991, parlimentarian, 1992, Palm Beach Asn Black Journalists, 1991. **Honors/Awds:** Presidents Award, Phillips-Exeter Acad, 1990; Service to PEA Award, Class 1976, 1991. **Home Addr:** 3430 E Jefferson Ave Suite 535, Detroit, MI 48207-4200. **Business Addr:** Freelance Writer, Editor, Detroit Metro Times, 733 St Antoine, Detroit, MI 48226, **Business Phone:** (313)961-4060.

## OWENS, KELLY D.

Association executive. **Personal:** Born Jan 1, 1966. **Educ:** Univ Calif, Los Angeles; La State Univ & Agr & Mech Col, BA, educ; Teachers Col Columbia Univ, MA, higher educ admin; Univ New Orleans, PhD, urban studies, 2012. **Career:** Howard Univ, residence hall dir, 1992-94; US House Representatives, dir residence life cong page prog, 1994-98; Cong Black Caucus Found Inc, dir, ann legis conf/educ progs, 1999-2006; Tulane Univ, Freeman Sch Bus, dir undergrad educ, 2006-07; Univ New Orleans, res asst, 2007-11; Dillard Univ, adj instr, 2010, vis asst prof & prog coordr, 2012-13; contract grant writer, 2011-14; IN-ROADS Inc, consult, 2011-13, dir res & sponsored progs, 2013-; Calif Lutheran Univ, dir sponsored res & proj, 2015-. **Orgs:** Grant writing & prog develop consult, Grants by Kelly, 2011-13. **Home Addr:** , DC. **Business Addr:** Director Research & Sponsored Programs, INROADS Inc, 10 S Broadway Suite 300, St. Louis, MO 63102, **Business Phone:** (314)241-7488.

## OWENS, LYNDA GAYLE

Consultant, educator. **Personal:** Born Jun 16, 1956, Elizabethtown, NC; daughter of David P and Eunice Bryant Houston; children: LaTisha, Larry, Solomon & Aljawanna. **Educ:** Rutledge Col, Richmond, Va, 1981; ICC Career Ctr, Richmond, Va, nurses aide, cert; Richmond Va Sem, J Sargeant Reynolds Col. **Career:** Richmond Pub Libr, Richmond, Va, pager, libr asst, 1979-81; Henrico Co Jail, Richmond, Va, supvr, 1982-85; City Richmond Recreation & Parks, Richmond, Va, vol, 1985-; Richmond Pub Sch, Richmond, Va, instr asst, 1985-; HEAL, Richmond, Va, AIDS health educr, 1991-; self-employed parental & family consult, 1989-; The Carver Promise, exec dir, 1992-96; Va Dept Juv Justice, coordr youth serv, currently. **Orgs:** Richmond Educ Asn, 1985-; vpres, Mosby PTA, 1989-; Speaker's Bur, 1989-; shared Decision Making Comt, 1990-91; exec secy, RAAC, 1991; assoc minister, Greater Mt Moriah Baptist Church; Nat Asn Advan Colored People; Eastern Star; Crusade Voters; Sistercare; N-Pac. **Honors/Awds:** Lynda G Owen Day, Dec 10, 1990, named in honor; America's Award, Positive Thinking Found, 1990; Proclamation, Mayor, City of Richmond, 1990; Resolution, Richmond City Coun, 1990; Outstanding Employee & Parent, Richmond Pub Sch Bd, 1990; Outstanding Citizen & Role Model, Bd Commissioners Richmond Redevelopment & Housing Authority; Community Service Award, Richmond Times Dispatch, 1992; Ascended Woman Award, 1992; Governor's Comn Citizen Empowerment Commonwealth Va, 1994; Person of the Week, ABC Nightly News; ABC-Family Values Special; ABC Special-Real Kids, Real Solution. **Special Achievements:** First woman ever recognized nationally as a National Unsung Hero who personified the American Dream for sacrificing and devoting her life to children in oppressed communities; numerous speeches, articles & documentaries. **Home Addr:** 517 Hunt Ave, Richmond, VA 23222, **Home Phone:** (804)714-0168. **Business Addr:** Consultant, Single Parenting & Empowerment, PO Box 7937, Richmond, VA 23223, **Business Phone:** (804)257-0407.

## OWENS, MERCY P.

Banker. **Personal:** Born Sep 30, 1947, Jenkinsville, SC; daughter of Fred Pearson Sr (deceased) and Unita; children: Tia & Trey. **Educ:** St Augustines Col; Cannon Trust Sch. **Career:** FNB/SCN, floater, customer serv opers officer; Resource Consult, pres; SCN/Wachovia Bank SC, C/D IRA coordr, trust officer, asset mgt acct officer; Wachovia Bank SC, corp compliance officer, CRA adminr, sr vpres; Citizens Bancshares Corp, Citizens Trust Bank, dir, 2004-. **Orgs:** Trumpeter gala, Richland Mem Hosp Ctr Cancer Treat; bd mem, Eboni Dance Theatre; compliance comm, SC Bankers Asn; adv bd, SC Low Income Housing Coalition; proj blueprint, United Way Midlands; Nat Asn Advan Colored People; exec comm, James R Clark Sickle Cell Found; SC Asn Urban Bankers; bd, St Augustine's Col Falcon Found; adv bd, Emory Hosp Winship Cancer Ctr; audit & compliance comt mem, Citizens Bancshares Corp. **Honors/Awds:** Eboni Keys Award, United Black Fund & Eboni Keys, Women Opening Doors, 1991; Minority Bankers of the Year, Minority Bus Develop Ctr, 1994; Positive Image Award, Pee Dee Times & Carolina Tribune, 1995. **Business Addr:** Director, Citizens Bancshares Corp, 75 Piedmont Ave NE, Atlanta, GA 30303, **Business Phone:** (404)659-5959.

## OWENS, NATHANIEL DAVIS

Judge. **Personal:** Born Feb 17, 1948, Hartsville, TN; married Barbara Catlin; children: Marsha. **Educ:** Univ S Sewanee, Tenn, BA, 1970; Emory Univ, Law Sch, JD, 1973; Northwestern Univ Sch Law, grad prosecutors course, 1976; Univ Nev, Reno, Grad Nat Judicial Col, 1979. **Career:** Atlanta, Ga, res, 1971-72; USMC Ast Defense Coun, spec prog, 1972; Atlanta Legal Aid Soc, 1972; Thelma Wyatt Atty, 1972-73; Kennedy Bussey Sampson Attys, 1973-74; Huie Brown & Ide Attys, 1974-; AUS AGO Basic Course AGOBC, 1974, Ft McClellan 1974-76; Jacksonville State Univ, adj prof, 1975-; 7th Judicial Circuit, asst dist atty, 1976-79; Dist Ct Cleburne & Calhoun Counties, dist ct judge, 1979-. **Orgs:** Mt Olive Baptist Church, 1975-; 32nd Degree Master Mason, 1976-; Royal Arch Mason Chap 47; Hartsville Commandry No 5 TN, 1976-; first vpres, Asn AUS, 1978-; bd dir, Anniston Area Chamber Com, 1978-79; pres, Club Ala State Demo Party, 1978-; Omega Psi Phi Theta Tau Chap, 1978-; chmn, State & Local Govt Com Chamber Com, 1978-80; co-chmn, Citizens Orgn Better Ed, 1979-82; Beta Kappa Boule Sigma Pi Phi, 1981-. **Honors/Awds:** Omega Man of the Year Award, Theta Tau Chap, 1979; Outstanding Service Award, Alpha Kappa Alpha Sorority Inc, 1980; Case Club Award, Appellate Arguments; Moot Court Competition Award, Emory Univ, Sch Law. **Special Achievements:** First African-American varsity athlete and the First African-American to graduate from the College; CAC wrestling champion in his weight class in 1968; First black judge in North East Alabama. **Home Addr:** 111 S Quintard Ave, PO Box 2641, Anniston, AL 36202, **Home Phone:** (256)391-1102. **Business Addr:** Judge, Calhoun County, 161 E Mich Ave, Battle Creek, MI 49014, **Business Phone:** (616)969-6504.

## OWENS, RICH DARRYL

Football player. **Personal:** Born May 22, 1972, Philadelphia, PA. **Educ:** Lehigh Univ. **Career:** Football player (retired); Wash Redskins, defensive end, 1995, right defensive end, 1996-97; Miami Dolphins, defensive end, left defensive tackle, 1999, defensive end, 2000; Kans City Chiefs, defensive end, 2001; Seattle Seahawks, defensive end, 2002. **Honors/Awds:** Rookie of the Year, 1995.

## OWENS, RISSIE LOUISE

Government official. **Personal:** Born Jun 9, 1959, TX; daughter of Oliver and Louise Anderson; married Edward G Jr; children: Edward G III. **Educ:** Sam Houston State Univ, BS, criminal justice, 1980; Univ Houston, MA, psychol, 1994. **Career:** Brajos County 272nd Dist Ct, ct coordr, 1981-82; Ment Health/Ment Health Retardom Brojos Valley, case mgr, 1982-84; Tex Dept Criminal Justice, coordr, 1984-90; Galveston County Adult Probation, probation officer, 1991-93; Amarillo ISD, drug prev coordr, 1993-95; Huntsville ISD, assoc sch psychol, 1995-97; Tex Bd Pardons & Paroles, chmn, 1997-, presiding officer, currently; Asn Paroling Authorities Int, vpres. **Orgs:** Leadership Tex, 1995-; Asn Paroling Authorities Int, 1997-; Tex Corrections Asn, 2000; Tex Bd Pardons & Paroles, 2009-.; Asn Paroling Int; bd trustee, Huntsville ISD; Cs Protective Serv Bd Walker Count. **Home Addr:** 180 Elkins Lk, Huntsville, TX 77340-7304, **Home Phone:** (936)294-0262. **Business Addr:** Chairman, Presiding Officer, Texas Board of Pardons & Paroles, 209 W 14th St Suite 500, Austin, TX 78711-3401, **Business Phone:** (936)291-2161.

## OWENS, DR. ROBERT LEON, III

Educator. **Personal:** Born Nov 3, 1925, Arcadia, FL; married Nancy Gray; children: Raymond, Ronald L & Nancy. **Educ:** Tuskegee Inst, BS, 1949; State Univ Iowa, MA, 1950, PhD, 1953. **Career:** State Univ La, instr psychol reading, 1953; Southern Univ, asst prof psychol to prof psychol, 1953-66, dean grad sch; Knoxville Col, pres & prof psychol, 1966-71; Univ Tenn, vis prof educ psychol, 1969-71; Howard Univ, Col Lib Arts, dean, 1971, prof emer, currently. **Orgs:** Exec comt, Land Grant Asn Deans Grad Schs, 1959-71; Exec Comt Deans Arts & Sci Land Grant Univs, 1963-65; LHD, N Pk Col, 1968; mem exec comt, Am Soc Curric Develop, 1970; symp leader, Ann Conf Inst Int Educ, 1971-76; discussant, Am Conf Acad Deans, 1973; exec comt, Coun Relig & Higher Educ Res Asn, 1974-77; chmn nominating comt, Am Conf Acad Deans, 1976; group leader, Am Conf Acad Deans, 1977; bd dir, Am Conf Acad Deans, 1977-80; life mem, Phi Delta Kappa. **Home Addr:** 212 Hermleigh Rd, Silver Spring, MD 20902-1629. **Business Addr:** Professor Emeritus, Howard University, 2400 6th St NW, Washington, DC 20059, **Business Phone:** (202)806-6100.

## OWENS, RONALD C.

Lawyer. **Personal:** Born May 1, 1936, Conway, AR; married Lois Adamson; children: Ronald, Alan David & Veronica. **Educ:** Morehouse Col, attended 1954; Univ Ark, Pine Bluff, BS, 1957; Univ Baltimore Law Sch, JD, 1973. **Career:** Johns Hopkins Univ, asst dir admis, 1969-73, pre-law adv, 1975-; pvt prac atty, 1974-; Ft Howard Am Bar Asn, corrective therapist; Baltimore City, asst states atty, asst city solicitor. **Orgs:** Monumental City Bar Asn; Phi Beta Gamma Legal Frat; Steward Douglas Memorial Church. **Honors/Awds:** Outstanding Advocate, 1972-73. **Business Addr:** Lawyer, 3904 Buncombe Dr, Greensboro, NC 27407, **Business Phone:** (336)323-6887.

## OWENS, TERRELL ELDORADO

Executive, actor, football player. **Personal:** Born Dec 7, 1973, Alexander City, AL; son of Tit Russell Sr and Marilyn Heard; married Melanie Paige Smith III; children: Mike Float, Atlin, Kylee & Dasha; married Rachel Snider. **Educ:** Univ Tenn, Chattanooga, attended 1996. **Career:** Football player, actor, producer, philanthropist, entrepreneur, fitness expert, model; San Francisco 49ers, wide receiver, 1996-2003; Philadelphia Eagles, wide receiver, 2004-05; Dallas Cowboys, wide receiver, 2006-08; Buffalo bills, wide receiver, 2009; Cincinnati Bengals, wide receiver, 2010; Allen Wranglers, Indoor Football League, 2011; free agt, currently. Films: Any Given Sunday, producer, 1999; Dysfunctional Friends, 2012; The Sub, producer, 2013; About Last Night, producer, 2014; Lap Dance, 2014. TV Series: "Elements of a Champion", 2004; "The Tracy Morgan Show", 2004; "It's the Shoes", 2005; "Under One Roof", 2008; "Keeping Up with the Kardashians", 2008; "The T.O. Show", writer, 2009, exec producer, 2009-11; "Tosh.0", 2009; "Kendra", 2009; "Cubed", fashion consult, 2010; "Necessary Roughness", 2011-12; "Single Ladies", 2011; "Go On", 2013; "90210", 2013. **Orgs:** Founder, Terrell Owens Found. **Honors/Awds:** All-Pro, 2000, 2001, 2002, 2004, 2007; Pro Bowl, 2000, 2001, 2002, 2003, 2004, 2007; Touchdowns Leader, Nat Football Conf, 2001, 2002, 2006; Excellence Sports Performance Yearly Award, 2003; Champion, Nat Football Conf, 2004. **Special Achievements:** TV skit, Desperate Housewives; Little T Learns to Share, writer, 2006.

## OWENS, TREKA ELAINE

Accountant, vice president (organization), chief financial officer. **Personal:** Born Dec 6, 1953, Chicago, IL; daughter of Alfred Berry and Pauline Berry; married Johnny C; children: Kellie. **Educ:** DePaul Univ, BSC, acct, 1975; DePaul Univ, Col Law, Chicago, IL, JD, 1990. **Career:** Arthur Young & Co, auditor, 1975-77; Avon Products, staff acct, 1977-78; Borg-Warner Corp, corp acct, 1978-80; Johnson Pub Co, chief acct, 1980-86, vpres & cheif financial officer, 1986-. **Orgs:** Am Inst Cert Pub Accountants, 1982-, IL Soc Cert Pub Accountants, 1982-; Am Bar Asn, 1991; vpres, pub rels, Ill Bar Asn, 1991; Chicago Bar Asn, 1991. **Business Addr:** Vice President, Chief Financial Officer, Johnson Publishing Co, 820 So Mich Ave, Chicago, IL 60605, **Business Phone:** (312)322-9200.

## OWENS, VICTOR ALLEN

Manager, executive. **Personal:** Born Sep 30, 1945, Bronx, NY; married Ruth Morrison; children: Malcolm. **Educ:** Wilberforce Univ, BA,

1967; Univ Dayton, MA, 1971. **Career:** Ohio Bell Tel, mgr, 1967-71; YWCA, bus mgr, 1971-76; Colonial Penn Group, mgr, 1976-79; Equitable Life Assurance Soc, asst vpres, vpres, 1979-. **Orgs:** Chmn, Minority Interchange; assoc mem, Big Bros; Int Commun Asn. **Home Addr:** 169 Rutland Rd, Brooklyn, NY 11225. **Business Addr:** Vice President, The Equitable Life Assurance Society, 787 7th Ave The Equitable, New York, NY 10019, **Business Phone:** (212)554-1234.

### OWENS, DR. WALLACE, JR.

Educator, painter (artist), executive. **Personal:** Born Dec 28, 1932, Muskogee, OK; son of Wallace Arthur and Sarah. **Educ:** Langston Univ, BA, art educ, 1959; Univ Cent Okla, MA, art educ, 1965; Inst Allende-Mexico, MFA Painting, 1966; Univ Rome, Italy, Fulbright Scholar, 1970; Northern Tex State Univ, attended 1971. **Career:** Educator (retired), exec; Langston Univ, prof art, 1966-80; Sterling HS Greenville SC, art instr, 1969-71; Lockheed Missile Co Sunnyvale, Ca, electronics tech, 1971-74; Cent State Univ, prof art, 1980-2005; Owens Arts Pl Mus Found Inc, owner & dir, 2005-. **Orgs:** Lions Int, 1976; Nat Conf Artists; Mem, Higher Educ Alumni Coun; Okla Educ Asn. **Honors/Awds:** Educators to Africans, African Am Inst Study Tour W Africa, 1973. **Special Achievements:** Executed Centennial Sculpture for Langston Univ, 1997. **Home Addr:** 3374 Sunny Acres Lane, Guthrie, OK 73044-7140, **Home Phone:** (405)282-1184. **Business Addr:** Owner, Director, Owens Arts Place Museum Foundation Inc, 1202 E Harrison Ave, Guthrie, OK 73044, **Business Phone:** (405)260-0204.

### OWENS, SEN. WILLIAM (BILL OWENS)

State government official. **Personal:** Born Jul 6, 1937, Demopolis, AL; son of Jonathan and Mary A Clemons; married Cindy Edwards; children: Laurel, Curtis, William Jr, Adam, Sharra & Brenda. **Educ:** Harvard Univ, MEd, 1971; Boston Univ, attended 1970; Univ Mass. **Career:** Senator (retired), administrator; Gibson Liberation Sch, chair; Sunrise Dry Cleaners, owner & mgr, 1960-68; Urban League Geater Boston, proj coord, 1968-70; St Dept Educ, dir career oppt prog, 1970; Proj Jesi-Jobs Univ Mass, local proj dir, 1971-72; Mass St, st rep, 1973-75, state sen, 1975-90. **Orgs:** Mass Leg Black Caucus; Mass Black Polit Assembly; Nat Black Polit Assembly; Dept Corrections Adv Task Force Voc Educ; bd dir, Roxbury Defenders; Resthaven Corp; Boston Black Repertory Co; S End Neighborhood Action Prog; Harvard Club Boston; Caribbean Am Carnival Day Asn; New Hope Baptist Church; Urban League Greater Boston; Boston Black United Front; Nat Asn Sch Adminr; Nat Asn Advan Colored People; Nat Educrs Asn; founder & dir, Health Educ & Learning Prog. **Honors/Awds:** Man of the Year Award; Black Big Bros Award of Excellence; Houston Urban League Plaque; Big Black Brother Alliance Award. **Home Addr:** 115 Hazelton St, Boston, MA 02126, **Home Phone:** (617)296-8568.

### OWENS, REV. ZELBA RENE

Executive, clergy. **Personal:** Born Feb 25, 1950, Rochester, NY; daughter of Robert Lee Carson and Shadie; children: Barbara Ann Spencer. **Educ:** Mich State Univ, BS, MA, 1971; Univ Mich Sch Med, attended 1973; Ashland Sem, cert, 1997. **Career:** Octagon House Inc, clin dir, 1973-79; Univ Mich Grad Sch Bus, res, 1980-81; Univ Mich Hosp, Allied Health Hosp, Mgt Assessment Ctr, role player res, 1980-81; Ann Arbor Community Ctr, substance abuse counr, 1986-87; Shelter Asn Ann Arbor, prog dir, 1987-91; Detroit Health Care Homeless, ment health prog dir, 1990-91; Harambee Inc, chief exec officer, 1992-; Univ Mich Sch Pub Health, res assoc, 1995-96; African Methodist Episcopal Zion Church, itinerate elder, 1997-; Huron Residential Servs Youth, asst treat supvr. **Orgs:** Delta Sigma Theta, 1969-; bd mem, Martin Chapel House Corp, 1980-; chair, Beyer Mem Hosp, Ethics Comm, 1994-99; bd dir, Metro Jail Ministries, 1995-; African Methodist Episcopal Zion Church, 1996-; Nat Coun Negro Women, 1996-; bd mem, Christine Therry Ministries, 1998-. **Home Addr:** 1508 Hanover, Chicago Heights, IL 60411. **Business Addr:** Chief Executive Officer, Harambee Inc, 3593 Oakwood St, Ann Arbor, MI 48104, **Business Phone:** (708)870-9333.

### OWENS-HICKS, SHIRLEY

State government official. **Personal:** Born Apr 22, 1942, Demopolis, AL; daughter of Johnathan and Mary; children: Dawn Deirdre & Stephanie Alicia. **Educ:** Chandler Sch Women, cert, 1961; Boston Univ Sch Educ, attended 1971; Harvard Univ Grad Sch Educ, EdM, 1972. **Career:** State government official (retired); Mass Sen, chief aide to sen, 1975-80; Urban League Eastern Mass Inc, dep dir, 1980-81, pres, exec dir, 1981-83; Boston Sch Comt, mem & vpres, 1984-88; Univ Mass Boston, advocacy counr, 1984-86; Commonwealth Mass, 1987; 6th Suffolk Dist, State Rep; Mass House Representatives, MA state rep, 1987-2007. **Orgs:** Delta Sigma Theta Sorority; Harvard Univ Alumni Asn; Urban League; Mass Black Legis Caucus; Nat Asn Advant Colored People; chair Joint, House & Senate Comn Educ, 1995-97; Nat Black Caucus State Legislators; bd mem, Brookview House Honary; Safe Futures, Mattapan goverance bd; Boston State Citizens Adv Comt; Phi Delta Kappa; chairwoman, House Comt on C & Families. **Honors/Awds:** Cert Appreciation Simmons Col, 1978; Achievement Plaque Urban League Guild Eastern Mass, 1983; Woman of the Year, Zeta Phi Beta Sorority, 1984; Cert Appreciation Boston Studs Adv Coun, 1985, 1987; Promoting Excellence in Educ Award Freedom House Inst on Schs & Educ, 1986; Educ Award Black Educrs Alliance MA, 1986; Bilingual Master Parents Adv Coun Award, 1986; Woman of the Year, Univ MA at Boston Black Studs Org, 1987; Cent Boston Elder Servs Distinguished Serv to Older Bostonians, 1989; Womans Ministry Outstanding Leadership Award, Berea 7th Day Adventist, 1993; City Boston, African Am Achievement Award in Pub Serv, 1995; Network for Women in Polit & Govt, 1996; Woman Yr Award; Distinguished Serv to Educ Award, Black Educrs Alliance MA, 1997. **Home Addr:** 15 Outlook Rd, Mattapan, MA 02126.

### OWSLEY, BETTY JOAN

Educator, librarian. **Personal:** Born Chicago, IL; daughter of Holsey C and Willa H. **Educ:** Fisk Univ, Nashville, TN, BA; Howard Univ, Wash, DC, MA, 1973; Ind Univ, Bloomington, IN, MLS. **Career:** Indianapolis Pub Sch, Indianapolis, Ind, teacher; Howard Univ, Allen MDaniel Law Lib, Wash, DC. **Orgs:** Bd mem, Indianapolis Coun Int Visitors, 1984-90; Am Libr Asn; ALA Int Rels Round Table; Black Caucus Am Libr Asn; Delta Sigma Theta Sorority, Indianapolis Alumnae Chap; librn, founder, Willa H Owsley Inst; adv comt & Host Family Comt; Coun Int Prog; Ind Univ; Int Ctr Indianapolis; Nat Asn Advan Colored People; Nat Coun Negro Women; Ind Int Coun Inc; Corinthian Baptist Church. **Home Addr:** 505 W 40th St, Indianapolis, IN 46208, **Home Phone:** (317)283-7883.

### OXENDINE, KENNETH QWARIOUS

Football coach, football player, executive. **Personal:** Born Oct 4, 1975, Richmond, VA; son of Carl Waller and Viola. **Educ:** Va Polytech Inst & State Univ, BS, psychol, 1998, MS, educ health promotions, 2004. **Career:** Football player (retired), football coach, executive; Atlanta Falcons, 1998, running back, 1999; Los Angeles Xtreme, XFL, 2001; Va Tech Univ, asst strength & conditioning coach, 2002-03; Duluth High Sch, running backs coach, 2003; Ga Southern Univ, asst coach, 2004-05; Nat Football League, Europe, asst coach, 2005-06; Notre Dame Acad, fac, dir player develop & phys educ teacher, 2006-; Brown & Oxendine Sports Group, co-founder & pres, 2012-. **Business Addr:** Director of Player Development & Physical Education Teacher, Faculty, Notre Dame Academy, 4635 River Green Pkwy, Duluth, GA 30096, **Business Phone:** (678)387-9385.

### OXLEY, DR. LEO LIONEL, JR.

Psychiatrist. **Personal:** Born Jul 9, 1934, Raleigh, NC; children: Keith Charles & Claire Elaine. **Educ:** St Augustine Col, Raleigh, NC, BS, 1955; Meharry Med Col, MD, 1959. **Career:** William Beaumont Gen Hosp, internship; Walter Reed Gen Hosp, chief resident, 1960-63; Brooklyn-Staten Island Ment Health Serv Health Ins Plan, Greater NY, dir, 1971-73; Natchaug Hosp, staff psychiatrist, 1973-74; Newington Veterans Admin Hosp, chief psychiat serv, 1974-78; Ga Ment Health Inst, supt, 1978-80; Inst Living, sr staff psychiatrist, 1980-82; Va Med Ctr, Chillicothe, Ohio, chief psychiat serv, 1982-83; Va Med Ctr, Leavenworth, KS, chief psychiat serv, 1983-84; Brecksville, Va Med Ctr, Nat Ctr Stress Recovery, assoc clin dir, 1984-85; Va MedCtr, chief ment hyg clin, 1985-86; Va Med Ctr, Cleveland, staff psychiatrist; Va Outpatient Clin, chief med officer, 1991-; Morehouse Sch Med, adj clin prof, psychiat, 1996-. **Orgs:** Alpha Phi Alpha Frat; Alpha Omega Alpha Hon Med Soc; Am Psychiat Asn, DAV, ROA, lic to pract med MO, GA; Am Bd Psychiat & Neurol; Am Bd Med Specialties. **Honors/Awds:** Publication, "Issues and Attitudes Concerning Combat Experienced Black Vietnam Veterans," Journal, Nat Med Asn. **Home Addr:** 2837 Lee Rd, Shaker Heights, OH 44120, **Home Phone:** (216)561-6479. **Business Addr:** Adjunct Clinical Professor, Psychiatry, Morehouse School of Medicine, 720 Wview Dr SW, Atlanta, GA 30310-1495, **Business Phone:** (404)756-1500.

### OYEKAN, DR. SONI OLUFEMI (DR. SONI OLUFEMI OLUBUNMI OYEKAN)

Engineer. **Personal:** Born Jun 1, 1946, Aba; son of Emilia Ikpe Inyang and Theophilous; married Priscilla Ann Parker; children: Ranti Valdez, Ima, Femi & Arit; married Emiliu Uduak. **Educ:** Yale Univ, BS, engineering & appl sci, 1970; Carnegie Mellon Univ, MS, chem engineering, 1972, PhD, chem engineering, 1977. **Career:** Univ Pittsburgh, lectr, instr, coordr, 1972-77; Exxon, res engr, 1977-78, sr engr, 1979-80; Engelhard Corp, res sect head, 1980-84, res mgr, 1985-86, sr engr & consult, 1986-90; Consult Ghaip, Tema, Ghana, 1986; Dupont, res assoc, 1991-93; Sun Co Inc, sr staff engr; Sun Oil Co, reforming process coordr, 1993-97; Sunoco, naphtha processing coordr, 1993-97; BP Amoco, sr process consult, 1997-99; Marathon Petrol Co, Marathon Ashland Petrol LLC, reforming & isomerization technologist, 1999-2012; Prafis Energy Solutions, pres, 2013-. **Orgs:** Chair, Pet Programming Comm, 1989-91, chair, Fuels & Petrol Div, AIChE, 1995, chair, Minority Affairs Comt, AIChE, 1998-99, dir, AIChE Exec Bd, fel AIChE, 1999, Am Inst Chem Engrs, 2000-02, CWRT/CCPS, 2000-02, founding mem, trustee, AIChE; Prog chair, fel Spring Mtg, 1994; Sigma Xi; Phi Kappa Phi Soc; Nat Asn Advan Colored People; Nat Orgn Prof Advan Black Chemists. **Honors/Awds:** Yale, Manuscript, 1969; Sigma Xi, Phi Kappa Phi, 1977; New Jersey YMCA, Black Achiever in Bus & Educ, 1984; Distinguished Senior Award, Minority Affairs Committee, Am Inst Chem Engrs, 2000; Distinguished Service Award, Fuels & Petrochemicals Div, Am Inst Chem Engrs, 2002; William W Grimes Award for Excellence in Chemical Engineering, Minority Affairs Committee, Am Inst Chem Engrs, 2008; Eminent Black Chemical Engineer, MAC, AIChE, 2008; Percy Lavon Julian Award, NOBCChE, 2009. **Special Achievements:** US patent 4, 539, 307, Novel Activation Procedure, 1985; US patent, Novel Catalyst System. **Home Addr:** 108 Parkview Dr, LaPlace, LA 70068, **Home Phone:** (985)651-5062. **Business Addr:** President, Prafis Energy Solutions, 5023 Crystal Bluff Ct, Richmond, TX 77407, **Business Phone:** (832)449-3289.

### OYESHIKU, DR. PATRICIA DELORES WORTHY

Educator. **Personal:** Born Nov 3, 1944, Miami, FL; daughter of Inez Brantley; married Anthony A; children: Kama Charmange Titilola & Chaundrissa Morenike. **Educ:** Knoxville Col, Knoxville, TN, BS, eng, 1964; San Diego State Univ, San Diego, CA, MA, curric, 1971; US Int, San Diego, CA, PhD, educ leadership, 1980. **Career:** Educator (retired); Peace Corp, Brazil, vol, 1964-66, San Francisco, Calif, recruiter, 1966-67, Boston, Mass, dep dir, recruiter, 1967-68; San Diego City Sch, San Diego Calif, eng teacher, 1970; Morse High Sch, eng teacher, 1971. **Orgs:** Vol, Homeless Shelter, San Diego Calif; Mult Sclerosis Soc. **Home Addr:** 7985 Hillandale Dr, San Diego, CA 92120, **Home Phone:** (619)286-3922.

### OYEWOLE, DR. SAUNDRA HERNDON

Educator. **Personal:** Born Apr 26, 1943, Washington, DC; daughter of Laurence Homer and Helen Kirkland; married Godwin G; children: Ayodeji Babatunde, Monisola Aramide & Kolade Olufayo. **Educ:** Howard Univ, BS, zool, 1965; Univ Chicago, MS, microbiol, 1967; Univ Mass, Amherst, PhD, microbiol, 1973. **Career:** Electron microscopist; Hampshire Col, asst prof microbiol, 1973-79, assoc prof microbiol, 1979-81; Trinity Col, Wash, DC, assoc prof bio, 1981-87, chair, health professions adv Comm, 1982-, prof bio, 1988, chair bio dept, 1990-98, dean fac, 1998-2002, Col Arts & Sci, dean, 2002-06, prof emerita biol, 2014-. **Orgs:** Pres, Epsilon Chap Phi Beta Kappa, 1983-85; Am Soc Microbiol Comm Status Minority Microbiologists Am Soc Microbiol, 1984-, treas, 1989-; exec comm, Northeast Asn Advs Health Professions, 1984-87; adv coun, Northeast Asn Advs Health Professions, 1987-; founder & dir, Post-Baccalaureate Premed Prog Trinity Col, 1993-; bd dir, Nat Asn Advs Health Professions, 1993-95, secy bd, 1994-96, pres, 1998-2000; prog dir, Div Undergrad Educ, Nat Sci Found, 1994-96; gov coun mem, Aspen Inst Wye Fac Sem, 1995-2004, vice chair, 1997-2004; vice chairperson, gov coun, Wye Fac Sem, 1997-; chairperson, MNY Educ Comm, Am Soc microbiol, 1997-; pres, Nat Asn Advisors Health Professions, 1996-2002, bd dir, 1998-2002, Comt Minority Affairs, chmn, 2000-02; Asn Am Med Cols; chairperson, Health Professions Adv Comm Trinity Col; coord, Pre-Nursing Prog Trinity Col; Beta Kappa Chi; Asn Women Sci. **Honors/Awds:** Danforth Associate, 1979; Clare Boothe Luce Professor of Biology, 1990-93. **Home Addr:** 8206 Riverside Rd, Alexandria, VA 22308-1538, **Home Phone:** (703)360-7510. **Business Addr:** Professor Emeritus of Biology, Trinity College, 125 Michigan Ave NE, Washington, DC 20017, **Business Phone:** (202)884-9000.

### OZANNE, DOMINIC L.

President (organization). **Personal:** Born Apr 10, 1953, Cleveland, OH; son of Leroy and Betty Peyton; married Gaile Cooper; children: Dominic & Monique. **Educ:** Boston Univ, Sch Mgt, Boston, MA, BS & BA, 1975; Harvard Law Sch, Cambridge, MA, JD, 1978. **Career:** Thompson, Hine, Flory, Cleveland, OH, assoc, 1978-80; Ozanne Construct Co, Cleveland, OH, pres & chief exec officer, 1990-. **Orgs:** Pres, Nat Asn Minority Contractors, 1989-90; bd dir, Notre Dame Col, 2005-; mem exec comt, Ohio Found Independent Col; 100 Black Men Greater Cleveland. **Honors/Awds:** Top Black Student, Black Enterprise Mag, 1975; 1990 Marksman, Engineering News Mag, 1990. **Special Achievements:** Company listed at no. 61 on Black Enterprise's list of the top 100 industrial/service companies, 1998. **Home Addr:** 18231 Sherrington Rd, Shaker Heights, OH 44122. **Business Addr:** President, Chief Executive Officer, Ozanne Construction Co, 1635 E 25th St, Cleveland, OH 44114-4214, **Business Phone:** (216)696-2876.

### OZANNE, LEROY

President (organization), president (organization), executive. **Personal:** children: Dominic. **Career:** Cleveland bldg inspector; Ozanne Construct Co Inc, founder, pres & chief exec officer, 1956-. **Business Addr:** Founder, Chief Executive Officer, Ozanne Construction Co, 1635 E 25th St, Cleveland, OH 44114-4214, **Business Phone:** (216)696-2876.

### OZIM, DR. FRANCIS TAINO

Surgeon. **Personal:** Born Oct 1, 1946, Lagos; married Margaret Fay Taylor; children: Brion Olufemi, Frances Adetola & Melissa Funmilayo. **Educ:** St Finbarrs Col, Lagos, Nigeria, WASC, 1965; St Gregorys Col, Lagos, Nigeria, HSC, 1967; Howard Univ Med Sch, MD, 1976; Univ Albuquerque, NM, 1972. **Career:** Georgetown Univ Med Ctr, intern, 1976-77; Howard Univ Hosp, resident surg, 1977-81; Dist Columbia Gen Hosp, attend surg, 1981-82; Charlotte Memorial Hosp & Med Ctr, active staff, 1982-86; Norfolk Community Hosp, active staff, 1987-; Louise Obici Memorial Hosp, Suffolk, 1987-; Norfolk Gen Hosp, 1987; Sufnor Surg Group, gen surgeon; Cass City, Mich, pvt pract, currently; Scheurer Hosp; Huron Med Ctr; Hills & Dales Gen Hosp. **Orgs:** Fel Southeastern Surg Cong, 1982-; Am Col Surgeons, 1986-. **Home Addr:** 632 Corapeake Dr, Chesapeake, VA 23322-7900. **Business Addr:** Physician, Private Practitioner, 4672 Hill St Suite 104, Cass City, MI 48726, **Business Phone:** (989)872-2121.

# P

### PACE, ORLANDO LAMAR

Football player, executive. **Personal:** Born Nov 4, 1975, Sandusky, OH; married Carla; children: Justin & Jalen. **Educ:** Ohio State Univ, BMT. **Career:** Football player (retired), executive; Saint Louis Rams, left tackle, 1997-2006, 2008, tackle, 2007; Chicago Bears, left tackle, 2009; Big O's Ltd Sports Bar, owner, currently. **Orgs:** Spokesperson, Our Little Haven "Safe & Warm" expansion project, 1998-; spokesman, Diversity Awareness Partnership, 2000. **Honors/Awds:** Lombardi Award, 1995, 1996; Outland Trophy, 1996; National Offensive Player of the Year, Football News, 1996; UPI Lineman of the Year, 1996; Jim Parker Award, 1996; Big Ten Football Most Valuable Player, 1996; Pro Bowl, 1999, 2000, 2001, 2002, 2003, 2004, 2005; Super Bowl Champion (XXXIV); Ed Block Courage Award, 2008; Rose Bowl Hall of Fame, 2013; Pro Football Hall of Fame, 2016. **Special Achievements:** First Overall Pick in National Football League Draft, 1997. **Home Addr:** , St Peters, MO. **Business Addr:** Professional Football Player, Chicago Bears, Halas Hall at Conway Pk, Lake Forest, IL 60045.

### PACK, ROBERT JOHN, JR.

Basketball player, basketball coach. **Personal:** Born Feb 3, 1969, New Orleans, LA; children: Robert III. **Educ:** Tyler Jr Col, attended 1989; Univ Southern Calif, BS, sociol, 1991. **Career:** Basketball player (retired), basketball coach; Portland Trail Blazers, point guard, 1991-92; Denver Nuggets, point guard, 1992-95, 2000-01; Wash Bullets, point guard, 1995-96; NJ Nets, point guard, 1996-97, 2003-04; Dallas Mavericks, point guard, 1997-2000; Minn Timberwolves, guard, 2001-02; New Orleans Hornets, point guard, 2003, asst coach, 2009-10; Pamesa Valencia, 2003-04; Zalgiris Kaunas, Lithuania, 2004-05; Toronto Raptors, pt guard, 2005; Los Angeles Clippers, asst coach, 2010-13; Okla City Thunder, asst coach, 2013-15; New Orleans Pelicans, asst coach, 2015-. **Orgs:** Founder, Robert Pack Found, 1997. **Business Addr:** Assistant Coach, Oklahoma City Thunder, 208 Thunder Dr, Oklahoma City, LA 73102, **Business Phone:** (405)208-4800.

### PACKER, DANIEL FREDRIC, JR.

Manager, president (organization), chief executive officer. **Personal:** Born Dec 8, 1947, Mobile, AL; son of Daniel F and Algie V Ervin; married Carlene; children: Timothy & Vanice; married Catherine

August; children: Randall Ross, Reginald Ross & Maria Ross. **Educ:** Tuskegee Univ, Tuskegee, Ala, attended 1968; Middlesex Community Col, Middletown, Conn, AS, 1978; Charter Oak Col, Hartford, Conn, BA, bus studies, 1980; Tulane Univ, MBA, bus admin, 1998. **Career:** US Nuclear Navy Prog, 1969-75; Conn Yankee Atomic Power, Haddam, Conn, training coordr, sr reactor operator, 1975-81; Gen Physics Corp, Columbia, Md, sr engr, 1981-82; Entergy Corp, Waterford 3 Nuclear Plant, training mgr, 1982; La Power & light, Tact, La, training mgr, 1982-90; Entergy New Orleans Inc, training mgr, plant mgr o&m, 1990, dir, 1996-, pres, 1996-2006, chief exec officer, 1998-2006, chmn, 1999; First Guaranty Bank, secy, dir, 2005-; US Nuclear Regulatory Comn, sr reactor operator; Urban Dimensions LLC, pres & chief exec officer, currently. **Orgs:** Chmn & presidnet emer, Am Asn Blacks Energy; Am Nuclear Soc, 1982-; dir, Syst Energy Resources Inc, 1996-; chmn, NFL Stadium Adv Comn, 2001; chmn, New Orleans Regional Chamber Com, 2001; chmn, New Orleans Aviation Bd, 2002; Bring New Orleans Back Comn, 2005-; Fore kids found; Adv Bd SAIL Capital Partners LLC, currently; Keystone Energy Bd, currently; Port New Orleans, bd mem, comnr, 2010-, treas & secy, currently; bd mem, New Orleans Jazz Orchestra; bd mem, La Community & Tech Col Syst; bd mem, Fore Kids Found; bd trustee, Loyola Univ New Orleans, currently; vice chmn, 2012, chmn, 2013-, Bd Port New Orleans; chmn, New Orleans Aviation Bd Louis Armstrong Int Airport. **Honors/Awds:** Black Achievement Award, YMCA, 1988; Sr Nuclear Plant Mgr Course, Inst Nuclear Power Opers, 1990; Weiss Award, Tulane Univ, 2001; Whitney Young Service Award, Boy Scouts Am, S E La Coun, 2004; Most Powerful African-American Executives, Black Enterprise's, 2005. **Special Achievements:** First African American to manage a nuclear power plant. **Home Addr:** 3630 Octavia St, New Orleans, LA 70125-4314, **Home Phone:** (504)652-7407. **Business Addr:** President, Chief Executive Officer, Urban Dimensions LLC, 729 Camp St, New Orleans, LA 70112.

### PACKER, ZUWENA

Educator, writer. **Personal:** Born Jan 12, 1973, Chicago, IL. **Educ:** Yale Univ, BA, 1994; Johns Hopkins Univ, MA, 1995; Univ Iowa, MFA, 1999. **Career:** Wallace Stegner & Truman Capote fels, Stanford Univ; Calif Col ofthe Arts, sr vis prof creative writing, writers residence, currently; Working first novel, adventures Buffalo Soldiers, currently; Bks: Once a galaxy, far, far away, johns hopkins univ, 1995; Drinking Coffee Elsewhere, riverhead bks, 2003. **Orgs:** San Francisco Writers Grotto. **Business Addr:** Writer-in-Residence, California College of the Arts, 1111 8th St, San Francisco, CA 94107, **Business Phone:** (415)703-9523.

### PADDIO, GERALD JAMES

Basketball player, basketball coach. **Personal:** Born Apr 21, 1965, Lafayette, LA. **Educ:** Kilgore Col, attended 1985; Seminole State Col Fla, attended 1986; Univ Nev, Las Vegas, attended 1988. **Career:** Basketball player (retired), basketball coach; Rockford Lightning, 1988, 1991-92; Rochester Flyers, 1988-89; BCM Gravelines, 1989-90; Cleveland Cavaliers, 1990-91; Grand Rapids Hoops, 1991; Zaragoza, Spain, 1992; Seattle Supersonics, 1992-93; Ind Pacers, forward & guard, 1993-94; Scavolini Pesaro, Italy, 1993-94; New York Knickerbockers, forward & guard, 1994; Wash Bullets, forward & guard, 1994; Rapid City Thrillers, 1994; Maccabi Rishon LeZion, Israel, 1994-95, 2000-01; Chicago Rockers, 1995-96; Ourense, Spain, 1996; Maccabi Giv'at Shmuel, Israel, 1996-97; Matsuhita Panasonic, Japan, 1997-99; Las Vegas Slam, 2001-02; Soles de Jalisco, Mex, Lebanon, 2002; Kahraba Beirut, 2002-03; Ferro Carril Oeste, Arg, 2003-04; Petroleros, Mex, asst coach, 2004.

### PADDIO-JOHNSON, DR. EUNICE ALICE

Clergy, college administrator, teacher. **Personal:** Born Jun 25, 1928, Crowley, LA; daughter of Henry Paddio and Ce; married John David Johnson Sr; children: Deidre Reed Dyson (deceased), Clarence III, Henry P, Bertrand J & Ce. **Educ:** Leland Col Baker; Grambling State Univ, BS, 1949; Univ Calif, Los Angeles, MA, 1960; La State Univ, attended 1966; Univ Minn, attended 1975; State Univ NY, attended 1980; Cornell Univ, MS, 1988; Progressive Univ, PhD, 1993. **Career:** St Helena Parish Sch, teacher, counr, 1949-72; St Helena Summer Head Start, assoc dir, 1965-69; St Helena Asst Resource Est, pres & dir, 1972-73; Cornell Univ, admin, 1973-85; St Helena Head Start, dir, 1986-87; Paddio-Johnson Enterprises Inc, pres, 1987-; Greater Rising Star AME Church, pastor, 1995-98; Gaines Chapel AME Church, pastor, 1998-99; Crystal Springs AME Chruch, pastor, 1999-2000. **Orgs:** Ed jour, exec comt mem La Educ Asn, 1964-69; sch bd mem, St Helena Parish Sch, 1972-74; Ithaca City Sch, 1975-82; Ithaca Neighborhood Housing Servs; P-R Found; Atlanta Child, 1975-; pres, Paddio-Johnson Human Rels Consult, 1980-; Am Asn Univ Women, 1980-; bd dir, Family & Childs Serv, Planned Parenthood, Tompkins Co; pres emer, Martin Luther King Jr Scholar Fund Ithaca Inc, 1982-86; Delta Sigma Theta Sorority; Nat Asn Advan Colored People; exec bd, African Methodist Episcopal Women Ministry, 1996-2000. **Honors/Awds:** Graduate Asniate, Matron La Esther Grand Chapter OES, 1963-74; Outstanding Citizen, New Orleans, 1973; Black Gold Award, Grambling State Univ, 1973; Citizen of the Year, 1974; Creat Career Express Program, 1975; Outstanding Humanitarian & Trailblazer Award, 1992. **Special Achievements:** Co-author: Wng Behavior Skills, 1976-77. **Home Addr:** PO Box 245, Greensburg, LA 70441, **Home Phone:** (225)222-4388. **Business Addr:** President, Paddio-Johnson Enterprises, 731 Hall Rd, Greensburg, LA 70441, **Business Phone:** (225)222-4388.

### PADGETT, PROF. JAMES A.

Painter (artist), educator, association executive. **Personal:** Born Nov 24, 1948, Washington, DC; son of James and Pauline C Flournoy; married Joan M Jemison; children: Anthony A. **Educ:** Corcoran Sch Art, WW; Howard Univ, BFA, 1972; Howard Univ Grad Sch, MFA, 1974. **Career:** Wilberforce Univ, Dept Art & Scis, prof, currently. **Orgs:** Howard Univ Mural Proj Comn, 1968-; DC Comn onArts Mural Proj Comn, 1968-72; murals erected & var sites, Howard Univ, Anacostia Mus, Smithsonian Inst, Sch Soc Work, Howard Univ; Shaw Com Comp Health Ctr Nat Med Asn, Found Howard Univ Hosp Col Med; co-dir, Martin Luther King Jr Arts Festival. **Honors/Awds:** Selected to participate in touring art exhib "Paintings from Am U"; Cert of Appreciation Univ Neighborhood Coun, 1964; Cert of Accom Summer Enrich Prog Art Dir, 1965; Wash Rel Arts Exhib Am Savings & Loan Asn DC; first prize Collage & Painting, 1966; Cert of Commen Upward Bound Col Prog Howard Univ, 1966; Corcoran Scholar Award, W W Corcoran Sch Art, 1967; Cert Art DC Rec Dept Art & Splst Instr, 1967-68; second prize The Town Sq Art Show Inc Collage & Painting, 1969; third prize Outdoor Art Exhib Painting, 1969; third prize Artists Unlmtd Painting, 1969; first & second prize Artists Unlmtd Painting, 1970; Monitor Asst Grant Howard Univ Col of Fine Arts, 1970; first prize Hon Mention Ch of the Brethren Arts Exhib Painting, 1971; Scholar Award, Howard Univ Col of Fine Arts, 1-72; Scholar Award, Howard Univ Grad Sch of Fine Arts, 1972-73; Scholar Award, Skowhegan Sch of Painting & Sculp summer, 1971; Afro-Am Artist a bio-bibliog dir; Images of Chg-1 Art Socs in Transition; Chmn 4th Inter Nat Conf on Art, in hon of hm Queen Elizabeth II, 1977; K Miller Galleries LTD, the Old Bank Gallery, 1979; Galerie Des Deux Mondes Gallery of Art, 1980. **Home Addr:** 2612 Coronette Ave, PO Box 208, Wilberforce, OH 45414-4812. **Business Addr:** Professor of Arts, Wilberforce University, PO Box 370, Wilberforce, OH 45384, **Business Phone:** (937)708-5676.

### PADILLA, ANTONIO FRANCESCO PENA. See PENA, TONY.

### PADULO, DR. LOUIS

Educator. **Personal:** Born Dec 14, 1936, Athens, AL; son of Louis and Helen Margaret Yarbrough; married Katharine Seamans; children: Robert Beauchanp & Joseph Ebenezer. **Educ:** Fairleigh Dickinson Univ, BS, elec & electronics engineering, 1959; Stanford Univ, MS, elec engineering, 1962; Ga Inst Tech, PhD, 1966. **Career:** RCA, systs analyst, 1959-60; San Jose State Col, asst prof, 1962-63; Ga State Col, asst prof, 1966-67; Ga Tech Eng Exp Sta, consult, 1966-69; Morehouse Col, assoc prof & chmn math dept, 1967-69; Stanford Univ, assoc prof, 1969-75; Columbia Univ, 1969; Harvard Univ, vis prof, 1970; Atlanta Univ & Ga Tech, founder & dir dual degree prog; Boston Univ, dean col engineering prof math & engineering, 1975-88, assoc vpres, 1986-87; Mass Inst Techno, Cambridge, Mass, vis prof, 1987-88, vis scientist, 1991-92; Univ Ala Huntsville, pres, 1988-90; Univ City Sci Ctr, pres & chief exec officer, 1991-97, pres emer, 1997-; Invictus, chmn, 1997-; GLOSAS & USA, vchmn; Cong Higher Educ, pres; Phila Univ Col Arch & Built Environ, founding exec dean (interim), 2011-, dir engineering, 2013, vis prof, 2014. **Orgs:** Chmn planning comn, Expanding Minority Opportunities Engineering, 1973-; Nat Acad Engineering Com Minorities Engineering; fel Am Soc Engineering Educ, 1988; fel Inst Elec & Electronic Engrs, 1991; pres, Cong Higher Educ, 1992-; trustee, Fairleigh Dickinson Univ, 1992-; bd mem, ZanAqua Technologies, 2009-12. **Honors/Awds:** Walter J Gores Award, Stanford Univ, 1971; W Elec Fund Award, 1973; Award for Excellence in Science & Engineering, Educ Nat Consortium Black Professional Develop, 1977; Reginald H Jones Award, Nat Action Coun Minorities Engineering, 1983; Vincent Bendix Award, 1984; Pinnacle Award, Fairleigh Dickinson Univ, 1989. **Special Achievements:** He also directed two National Science Foundation sponsored programs which he created: Computational Research in Mathematics (at Morehouse College), & the Late Entry Accelerated Program (LEAP, at Boston University). **Home Addr:** 2020 Walnut St Apt 32A, Philadelphia, PA 19103, **Home Phone:** (973)472-4221. **Business Addr:** President Emeritus, University City Science Center, 2020 Walnut St Suite 32A, Philadelphia, PA 19103, **Business Phone:** (215)564-6405.

### PAGE, HON. ALAN CEDRIC

Judge, football player. **Personal:** Born Aug 7, 1945, Canton, OH; son of Howard Felix and Georgianna Umbles; married Diane Sims; children: Nina, Georgianna, Justin & Kamie. **Educ:** Univ Notre Dame, BA, polit sci, 1967; Univ Minn Law Sch, JD, 1978. **Career:** Football player (retired), judge; Minn Vikings, prof football player, 1967-78; Chicago Bears, 1978-81; Nat Football League Players Asn, rep, 1970-74, 1976-77, exec comt, 1972-75; Lindquist & Vennum, assoc, atty, 1979-84; Turner Broadcasting Syst, color commentator, 1982; Nat Pub Radio, commentator, 1982-83; St Minn, spec asst atty gen, 1985-87, asst atty gen, 1987-93; Off Atty Gen Minn, atty, 1985-92; Minn Supreme Ct, assoc justice, 1993-2015. **Orgs:** Am Bar Asn, 1979-; Nat Bar Asn, 1979-; Minn St Bar Asn, 1979-85, 1990-; Minn Asn Black Lawyers, 1980-; Adv Bd, Mixed Blood Theater, 1984-; bd dir, Minneapolis Urban League, 1987-90; founder, Page Educ Found, 1988; bd regents, Univ Minn, 1989-93; Inst Bill Rights Law Task Force Drug Testing Workplace, 1990-91; Am Law Inst, 1993-. **Business Addr:** Associate Justice, Minnesota Judicial Center, 25 Rev Dr Martin Luther King Jr Blvd, St. Paul, MN 55155, **Business Phone:** (651)297-7650.

### PAGE, CLARENCE

Journalist. **Personal:** Born Jun 2, 1947, Dayton, OH; son of Clarence Hannibal and Maggie; married Leanita McClain; married Lisa Johnson; children: Grady. **Educ:** Ohio Univ, BS, jour, 1969. **Career:** NewsHour, essayist; Chicago Mag, writer; Chicago Reader, writer; Wash Monthly, writer; New Repub, writer; Wall St J, writer; New York Newsday, writer; Emerge, writer; reporter & free lance writer, 1969-; Middletown J, Middletown, OH, writer & photogr; Cincinnati Enquirer, Cincinnati, OH, writer & photogr, 1964; Dayton Herald, Dayton, OH, intern; Chicago Tribune, Chicago, IL, reporter & asst city ed, 1969-80; WBBM-TV, Chicago, dir community affairs, 1980-82, news dept reporter & planning ed, 1982-84; Chicago Tribune, mem ed bd & columnist, 1984-; Chicago Tribune, DC, mem ed bd & columnist, 1991-. **Honors/Awds:** Pulitzer Prize, Columbia Univ, 1972, 1989; Edward Scott Beck Award, 1976; Ill UPI Award, 1980; James P McGuire Award, Am Civil Liberties Union, 1987; Chicago Journalism Hall of Fame; Lifetime achievement awards, National Society of Newspaper Columnists, The Chicago Headline Club, The National Association of Black Journalists. **Special Achievements:** Author of The Jaws of Success and Showing My Color: Impolite Essays on Race & Identity. **Business Addr:** Columnist, Chicago Tribune, 1325 G St NW Suite 200, Washington, DC 20005, **Business Phone:** (202)824-8200.

### PAGE, DR. GREGORY OLIVER

Dentist. **Personal:** Born Feb 26, 1950, Philadelphia, PA; son of William and Bernice; children: Dylan Mikkel & Erin Leah. **Educ:** Howard Univ, BS, 1972; Univ Pennsylvania, DMD, 1976. **Career:** Hoston Community Col, CCNY, assoc adj prof; Harlem community; N Cent Bronx Hosp, attend dentist, 1978-80; Health Ins Prog NY, Bronx, dir dent, 1978-82; Am Dent Foreign Serv Inc; pvt pract dentist, 1982-. **Orgs:** Howard Univ Alumni Club NY City; Acad Gen Dent; Am Dent Asn; Am Dent Foreign Serv; Acad Gen Dent; St Phillip's Ch NY City; Am Cancer Soc, 1991. **Special Achievements:** Some Wisdom About Teeth, Ebony mag, author, 1987. **Business Addr:** Dentist, 10 W 135th St Suite 1-E, New York, NY 10037-2604, **Business Phone:** (212)281-5775.

### PAGE, HARRISON EUGENE (HARRY PAGE)

Television producer, writer, actor. **Personal:** Born Aug 27, 1941, Atlanta, GA; son of Roberta Fambro Hunter and Harry; married Christina Giles; children: Delisa Hutcheson & Terry Lynn. **Career:** NBC TV, Los Angeles, CA, actor, 1975-83; ABC TV, Los Angeles, CA, actor, 1984-85; New World TV, Los Angeles, CA, actor, 1985-87, actor, 1989; Universal Pictures & Imperials Pictures, Los Angeles, CA; actor, 1989; Orion Pictures, Los Angeles, CA, actor, 1991; Universal Pictures, Off Balance Producer, Los Angeles, CA, 1991; TV Episodes: "Ultraman: The Ultimate Hero"; "Columbo ", 1994; "Melrose Pl", 1995; "Quantum Leap"; "21 Jump Street"; "Murder She Wrote"; "Fame"; "Gimme a Break!"; "Benson"; "Hill Street Blues"; "Webster", "The Dukes of Hazzard"; "Kung Fu"; "Kojak"; "Mannix"; "Soap and Bonanza""The Wonder Years"; "Sister, Sister", 1995; "Profiler", 1996-97; "Goode Behav", 1996-97; "The Parent 'Hood", 1997; "Ally McBeal", 1997-01; "Boy Next Door", "Turning Thirty", 2000; "Queen Bee", "Raptor", "I'll Be Home for Christmas", "Dog Robber: Part 2", "Mixed Messages", 2001; "Chaos Theory", "Lockdown", "By gones", "Family Bus", "First Casualty", 2002; "Any Day Now ", 2002; "Back in the Saddle" "Blast from the Past", 2003; "Tremors ", 2003; "Cold Case", 2005; "JAG"; "The Kids in the Hall", 2007; "Standoff", 2007; Deadland, 2008; "Without a Trace ", 2008; Films: Vixen!, 1968; Beyond the Valley of the Dolls, 1970; Lionheart, 1990; Arly Hanks, 1993; Conflict of Interest, 1993; Carnosaur, 1993. **Orgs:** Buddhist, NSA, 1985-91; life mem, Lee Strasberg. **Honors/Awds:** Bronze Wrangler Award, 1970; Emmy Award, 1992. **Business Addr:** Actor, Ellis Talent Group, 4705 Laurel Canyon Blvd Suite 300, Valley Village, CA 91607, **Business Phone:** (818)980-8092.

### PAGE, JOHN SHERIDAN, JR.

Dean (education), librarian, administrator. **Personal:** Born Dec 29, 1942, Pace, MS; son of John Sheridan Sr and Mary Lee. **Educ:** Tougaloo Col, Tougaloo, BA, 1964, MS; Long Island Univ, Greenvale, NY, MS, 1967. **Career:** Oceanside Free Libr, Oceanside, NY, young adult librn, 1966-68; Stone-Brandel Ctr, Chicago, Ill, librn, 1968-69; Fed City Col, Washington, DC, sr media specialist, 1969-76; Univ Calif, Mellon ACRL Internship, 1974-75; Univ DC, Washington, DC, assoc dir, tech servs, 1976-84, asst dir, learning resources, 1984-99, Learning Resources Div, asst dean, 2000-. **Orgs:** Am Libr Asn; DC Libr Asn; Asn Col Res Libr, 1988-90; chair, stand & accreditation comt, 1990-92; Lit Award Comn, Choice Ed Bd, 1999-2003; Black Caucus Am Libr Asn, 2005-07. **Home Addr:** 3003 Van Ness St NW W522, Washington, DC 20008, **Home Phone:** (202)363-4990. **Business Addr:** Assistant Dean, University of the District of Columbia, 4200 Conn Ave NW, Washington, DC 20008, **Business Phone:** (202)274-5265.

### PAGE, LAMURRIEL. See PAGE, MURRIEL.

### PAGE, MURRIEL (LAMURRIEL PAGE)

Basketball player. **Personal:** Born Sep 18, 1975, Louin, MS. **Educ:** Fla Univ, BS, sports mgt, 1998. **Career:** Basketball player (retired), basketball player coach; Wash Mystics, forward, 1998-2005; Mangueira Brazil, 2000; Ros Casares Spain, 2001-02, 2004-05; Venezia Italy, 2002-03; Hondarrabia, Span Pro League, 2003-04, 2005-07; Valencia, Span Pro League, 2004-05; Los Angeles Sparks, forward, 2006-09; Baloncesto San Jose Spain, 2007-08; Soller Spain, 2008-10; Amanda Butler, head coach, 2010-11; Univ Fla, asst coach, 2010-. **Home Addr:** PO Box 1501, Bay Springs, MS 39422-1501. **Business Addr:** Assistant Coach, University of Florida, 100 Farrior Hall 100 Fletcher Dr, Gainesville, FL 32611-2015, **Business Phone:** (352)392-1521.

### PAGE, SOLOMON

Football player, football coach. **Personal:** Born Feb 27, 1976, Pittsburgh, PA. **Educ:** Univ Wva, grad. **Career:** Football player (retired), football coach; Dallas Cowboys, right tackle, 1999, 2001-02, left guard, 1999, right guard, 2002; San Diego Chargers, left tackle, left guard & right tackle, 2003; New York Giants, 2004; Detroit Lions, 2004; Carrollton Christian Acad, offensive line coach, 2008-. **Business Addr:** Offensive Line Coach, Carrollton Christian Academy, 2205 E Hebron Pkwy, Carrollton, TX 75010, **Business Phone:** (972)242-6688.

### PAGE, WILLIE F.

Executive director, educator, consultant. **Personal:** Born Jan 2, 1929, Dothan, AL; married Gracie Tucker. **Educ:** Wayne State Univ, BSME, 1961; Adelphi Univ, MBA, 1970; NY Univ, PhD, 1975. **Career:** Boeing Co, engr, 1961-63; Grumman Aerospace, asst dir, prod, 1967-70; Glen Cove Coop Col Ctr, State Univ NY, dir, lectr, 1971-72; Nassau-Suffolk CHES, exec dir, 1972-74; Brooklyn Col, Dept Africana Studies, chmn & assoc prof, 1974-79, emer prof African Am Studies; City Univ New York, assoc prof, 1979, prof emer, currently; New York Head Start Regional Training Off, consult, 1975-79; Nat Endowment Humanities, consult, 1977-78; New York Educ Dept, consult, 1977-79. **Orgs:** African Heritage Studies Asn, 1974-80; Am Educ Res Asn, 1974-80; bd mem, Weeksville Soc Brooklyn, 1979-80. **Honors/Awds:** EPDA Fellow, USOE, NYU, 1973; Dissertation Year Fellow, Nat Fel Fund Atlanta, 1975; Henry Meissner Res Award, Phi Delta Kappa, NYU, 1975; NEH Fellow of Seminary Slavery, Harvard Univ, 1978; PSC-CUNY Award, CUNY Brooklyn Col. **Special Achievements:** Author: "The Dutch Triangle: The Netherlands & the Atlantic Slave Trade, 1621-1664", "Encyclopedia of African History & Culture 5-Volume Set""The Encyclopedia of African History & Culture Set", " Encyclopedia of African Kingdoms"; "The Encyclopedia of Ancient Africa"; "The Encyclopedia of African Conquest and Colonization: 15th -19th Centuries". **Home Addr:** 497 Macon St, Brooklyn, NY 11233, **Home Phone:** (718)498-8600. **Business Addr:** Professor Emeritus, City University of New York, 2901 Bedford Ave, Brooklyn, NY 11210-2813, **Business Phone:** (718)951-5000.

## PAIGE, EMMETT, JR.
Military leader, president (organization). **Personal:** Born Feb 20, 1931, Jacksonville, FL; son of Emmet and Elizabeth Core; married Gloria Mc Clary; children: Michael, Sandra & Anthony. **Educ:** Univ Md, BA, 1972; Penn State, MA, 1974; Army War Col, attended 1974. **Career:** Military officer (retired); AUS, 1947; Un Command; US Forces Korea; 8th Army; 361st Signal Brigade AUS Vietnam, comdr, 1969; 11th Signal Brigade AUS, Ft Huachuca, Ariz, comdr, 1975; AUS Commun Electronics Eng Installation Agency's, comdr, 1976-79; AUS Info Syst Eng Command, comndg gen; AUS Commun Res & Develop Command, comdr, 1979-81; Armed Forces Commun & Electronics Asn, bd dir, 1980; AUS Electronics Res & Develop Command, 1981-84; AUS Info Systs Command, lt gen, 1984-88; OAO Corp, pres & chief oper officer, 1988-93 & 1997-; asst secy defense command, control, commun & intelligence, 1993-97; Link Plus Corp, dir, 1998; bd visitors, Univ Md Univ Col, currently; bd dir, Gtech Holdings, currently, 1997-2003. **Orgs:** Am Leg Post 224, 1976-; Am Radio Relay League; col's leadership circle, Univ Md Univ; bd dir, bd advisors, Nat Asn Corp dir; boards dir, bd advisors, Nat Sci Ctr; bd dir, boards advisors, Univ Syst Md Found. **Honors/Awds:** Alumni Award, Univ Md Univ Col, 1988; Lifetime Achievement Award, 1995; Communications Week magazine Visionary Award, 1996; Boy Scouts of America Silver Beaver Award, 1997. **Home Addr:** 122 Cross Foxes Dr, Fort Washington, MD 20744-5565, **Home Phone:** (301)567-8929. **Business Addr:** Board Visitor, University of Maryland, 3501 Univ Blvd E, Adelphi, MD 20783, **Business Phone:** (800)888-8682.

## PAIGE, DR. RODERICK RAYNOR (ROD PAIGE)
School administrator. **Personal:** Born Jun 17, 1933, Monticello, MS; son of Raynor C (deceased) and Sophie (deceased); married Gloria Crawford; children: Rod Jr; married Bettye Davis-Lewis; married Stephanie D Nellons. **Educ:** Jackson State Univ, BA, phys educ, 1955; Ind Univ, MS, phys educ, 1962, PhD, phys educ, 1970. **Career:** Utica Jr Col, head football coach, 1957-67; Hinds Agr High Sch, teacher health, phys educ & coached, 1957-63; Jackson State Univ, head football coach, 1964-68; Tex Southern Univ, asst football coach, asst prof, dean & athletic dir, 1971-80, head football coach, 1971-75; US secy educ, 2001-04; Chart well Education Group LLC, chmn, 2005-; Woodrow Wilson Ctr Wash, pub policy scholar. **Orgs:** Pres, Hirma Clarke Civic Club; secy, Houston Job Training Partnership Coun; adv bd mem, Prof United Leadership League; mem dir, Tri-Civic Assoc; comnr, Nat Comn Employ Policy, chair; coordr, Harris Co Explorer Olympics Boy Scouts Am; Nat Ctr Educ & Econ; Tex Educ Agency; State Bd Educ's Task Force; Nat Asn Advan Colored People; mem, Houston Job Training Partnership Coun; Community Adv Bd Tex Com Bank; Am Leadership Forum; bd dir, Tex Bus Educ Coalition; Phi Beta Sigma fraternity; Bd Educ, trustee, 1989-94, bd Educ, officer, 1990-94, supt, 1994-2000, Houston Independent Sch Dist; bd Broad Found; Nat Coun Econ Educ's Comn. **Business Addr:** Chairman, Chartwell Education Group LLC, 350 5th Ave Suite 7506, New York, NY 10118, **Business Phone:** (212)488-1596.

## PAIGE, STEPHONE
Football player. **Personal:** Born Oct 15, 1961, Long Beach, CA; married Paula; children: Stephone II, Elon & Brieon. **Educ:** Fresno State Univ, Saddleback Col. **Career:** Football player (retired); Kans City Chiefs, wide receiver, 1983-91, kick returner, 1984; Minn Vikings, 1993. **Home Addr:** 7415 Shelby St, Elk Grove, CA 95758.

## PAILEN, DONALD, SR.
Lawyer, executive. **Personal:** Born Mar 25, 1941, Washington, DC; son of William and Cora Johnson; married Wendy Boody; children: Donald Jr & William. **Educ:** Howard Univ, Wash, DC, BA, 1968, JD, law, 1971. **Career:** US Dept Justice, Civil Rights Div, Wash, DC, trial & supv atty, 1971-82; City Detroit, Detroit, Mich, corp coun, 1982-93; Pailen Law Off, founder, 1994-; Detroit Pub Schs, gen coun, 1998-2000; Ecumenical Theol Sem, vpres admin, 2007-08; New Mt. Zion Missionary Baptist Church, assoc minister, currently. **Orgs:** Nat Bar Asn, 1971-; Nebr State Bar Asn, 1972-; Mich State Bar Asn, 1982-; bd dir, Trinity Lutheran Sem, 2006-. **Honors/Awds:** Exceptional Performance Awards, US Justice Dept, 1975-82; Award Appreciation, Guardians Police Orgn, Chicago, 1977; Spec Commendation, US Justice Dept, 1981; Award of Appreciation, Ecumenical Theol Seminary. **Home Addr:** 17364 Muirland St, Detroit, MI 48221, **Home Phone:** (313)345-2032. **Business Addr:** Founder, Pailen Law Office PLC, 17620 W McNichols Rd, Detroit, MI 48235-3327, **Business Phone:** (313)355-9708.

## PAINTER, DR. NELL IRVIN
Artist. **Personal:** Born Aug 2, 1942, Houston, TX; daughter of Frank Edward and Dona Donato McGruder; married Glenn R Shafer. **Educ:** Univ Bordeaux, fr medieval hist, 1963; Univ Calif, Berkeley, BA, anthrop, 1964; Univ Ghana, Inst African Studies, attended 1966; Univ Calif, Los Angeles, MA, african hist, 1967; Harvard Univ, PhD, am hist, 1974; Mason Gross Sch Arts, BFA, 2009; RI Sch Design, MFA, 2011. **Career:** Ghana Inst Lang, lectr Fr, 1964-65; Harvard Univ, teaching fel, 1969-70, 1972-74; Ford Found fel, 1971-72; Univ Pa, asst prof, 1974-77, assoc prof, 1977-80; Am Coun Learned Soc fel, 1976-77; Charles Warren Ctr Studies Am Hist fel, Harvard Univ, 1976-77; Radcliffe Inst fel, 1976-77; Nat Humanities Ctr, fel Am Hist, 1978-79; Univ NC, prof hist, 1980-88; Princeton Univ, prof hist, 1988-91, Edwards prof, 1991-, dir, Prog African Am Studies Studies, 1997-2000, Edwards prof am hist emer, currently; Kate B & Hall J Peterson fel, Am Antiqn Soc, 1991. **Orgs:** Dir, Nat Asn Black Women Historians, 1982-84; Am Coun Learned Socs, 1982-; pres, Orgn Am Historians, 1984-87, 2007; Harvard & Radcliffe Alumni Against Apartheid; Ctr Adv Study Behav Sci fel 1988-89; Am Studies Asn, 1989-92; Nat Endowment Humanities fel 1992-93; Am Hist Asn, 1990-94; mem exec bd, Am Acad Polit & Social Sci, 2003-; Inst Southern Studies; pres, Southern Hist Asn, 2007; Asn Study Afro-Am Life & Hist; Berkshire Conf Women Historians; Asn Black Women Historians; Nat Bk Found; Schomburg Ctr Res Black Cult; Social Sci ResCoun; Southern Regional Coun; Phi Beta Kappa; counr, Soc Am Historians; Am Antiqn Soc; fel Am Acad Arts & Sci. **Honors/Awds:** Coretta Scott King Award, Am Asn Univ Women, 1969; John Simon Guggenheim Found, 1982-83; Graduate Society Medal, Radcliffe Col Alumnae, 1984; Candace Award, Nat Coalition 100 Black Women, 1986; Alumnus of the Year, Black Alumni Club, Univ Calif, Berkeley, 1989; DHL, Wesleyan Univ, 1996; DHL, Dartmouth Col, 1997; DHL, State Univ NY-New Paltz, 1998; Service Award, Asn Black Princeton Univ Alumni, 1998; Roelker Mentorship Award, Am Hist Asn, 2000; DHL, Yale Univ, 2003; Centennial Medal, Harvard Grad Sch Arts and Sci, 2011. **Special Achievements:** Published numerous books, articles, reviews and other essays. **Home Addr:** 577 Ridge St, Newark, NJ 07104, **Home Phone:** (973)483-1692. **Business Addr:** Edwards Professor of American History Emeritus, Princeton University, 129 Dickinson Hall, Princeton, NJ 08544-1017, **Business Phone:** (609)258-4159.

## PALCY, EUZHAN
Television director, movie director, writer. **Personal:** Born Jan 13, 1958, Martinique; daughter of Leon and Romauld. **Educ:** Sorbonne, Paris, France, BA, Fr lit; Vaugirard, Paris, France, filmmaking. **Career:** TV series: "The Messenger", producer & dir, 1975; "Sugar Cane Alley", 1984; "The Ruby Bridges Story", dir & co-producer, 1998; "Winds Against the Wind", 1998; "The Killing Yard", dir, 2001; "Parcours de dissidents", writer & dir, 2006; "Les Mariees de l'isle Bourbon", writer & dir, 2007. Films: Bourg-la-folie, 1982; Rue cases negres, 1983; Black Shack Alley, writer & dir, 1983; Dionysos, 1984; A Dry White Season, screenplay & dir, 1989; Simeon, producer, writer & dir, 1992; Comment vont lesenfants, 1993. **Honors/Awds:** Prestigious Cesar Award, 1984; Candace Award, Nat Coalition of 100 Black Women, 1990; Best Lead Actress Award, Venice Film Festival; Christopher Award, 1999; Sojourner Truth Award, Cannes Film Festival, 2001; Orson Welles Award; Unita Blackwell Award. **Special Achievements:** First African American woman to ever direct a hollywood studio movie with filmography, biography, photos, articles; First woman of African descentto ever direct a Hollywood Studio movie MGMs A Dry White Season. **Business Addr:** 9200 W Sunset Blvd , West Hollywood, CA 90069, **Business Phone:** (310)205-6999.

## PALMER, DR. ANNETTE
College teacher. **Personal:** Born Trinidad. **Educ:** Carleton Univ, Ottawa, Can, BA; Fordham Univ, MA, hist int rels, PhD, hist int rels. **Career:** Howard Univ, Wash, DC; Nat Endowment Humanities, prog officer; Morgan State Univ, hist dept, assoc prof, chairperson, currently. **Orgs:** Am Hist Asn; treas, Asn Study African Am Life Hist. **Business Addr:** Chairperson, Morgan State University, 1700 E Cold Spring Lane, Baltimore, MD 21215, **Business Phone:** (443)885-3190.

**PALMER, BENJAMIN AMBROSIO OGLIVIE.** See OGLIVIE, BENJAMIN AMBROSIO.

## PALMER, DARLENE TOLBERT
Administrator. **Personal:** Born Jul 4, 1946, Chicago, IL; married Mickey A; children: Terri, Jonathan & Tobi. **Educ:** State Univ NY, Albany, BA, 1973, MA, 1974; Harvard Grad Sch Bus Admin, cert broadcasting mgt, 1979. **Career:** Palmer Media Assoc Schenectady, partner, 1970-75; WTEN-TV Albany, prod, 1973-75; Little Enterprises Wash, DC div, pres, 1975-77; Nat Asn Broadcasters Wash, DC, asst dir broadcast mgt, 1977-79; Minority Telecomm Dev Nat Telecomm & Info Admin, prog mgr, 1979-. **Orgs:** Media rels dir Nat Hookup Black Women, 1976-78; co-chmn, Minority Ownership Cong Black Caucus Commun Brain Trust DC, 1977-78; Comt Media & Natural Disaster Nat Acad Sci DC, 1979; bd dir, Am Nat Metric Coun Wash DC, 1979; rec sec Am Women Radio & TV, 1980; chmn, Affirm Act Am Women Radio & TV, 1980. **Honors/Awds:** Prod "Black English" WTEN-TV Albany; Nat Med Asn. **Home Addr:** 10805 Hunt Club Rd, Reston, VA 20016, **Home Phone:** (703)464-7478.

## PALMER, DAVID LEE
Football player. **Personal:** Born Nov 19, 1972, Birmingham, AL; married Carmelita; children: David, Davin, Davida & Davia. **Educ:** Univ Ala. **Career:** Football player (retired); Minn Vikings, punt returner, 1994-98, kick returner, 1997-98, running back, 1998, 2000. **Honors/Awds:** Consensus national championship, 1992; Paul Warfield Award, 1993.

## PALMER, DR. DOREEN P.
Physician. **Personal:** Born Jun 1, 1949, Kingston; daughter of Granville and Icilola. **Educ:** Herbert H Lehman Col, Bronx, NY, BA, 1972; Down St Med Sch, Brooklyn, NY, MD, 1976. **Career:** NY Med Col, Valhalla, NY, asst prof, 1981-86; Johns Hopkins Univ, Baltimore City Hosp, fel gastroenterol, 1981; Metrop Hosp, NY City, asst chief, GI, 1981-88, chief GI, 1983-86; Lenox Hill Hosp, NY City, adj physician, 1986-; Cabrini Hosp, NY City, attend physician, 1986-; Doctors Hosp, NY City, attend physician, 1986-; pvt pract, currently. **Special Achievements:** First Black Women To Head A Department Of Gastreonterology; Author: Spelling Relief for Stomach Ailments. **Business Addr:** Physician, Private Practitioner, 50 Executive Blvd, Elmsford, NY 10523.

## PALMER, DOUGLAS HAROLD
Mayor. **Personal:** Born Oct 19, 1951, Trenton, NJ; son of George H and Dorothy P; married Christiana Foglio; children: Laila Rose. **Educ:** Bordentown Mil Inst; Hampton Inst, BS, bus mgt, 1973. **Career:** Trenton Bd Educ, sr acct, 1976-78, coordr comm educ, 1981-82, asst sec purchasing, 1982; Mercer Co Legislator, freeholder; City Trenton, NJ, mayor, 1990-2010; US Conf Mayors, Pres, currently. **Orgs:** Pres & mgr, W End Little League; treas, Trenton BrNat Asn Advan Colored People; bd dir, Am Red Cross; Forum Proj, Boy Scouts, WE Inc, Carver Ctr, Urban League Guild Metro Trenton, Proj Help; pres, Freeholder Bd; mem comn, Comn onStatus Women, TRADE Adv Bd, Disabled Adv Bd, Mercer Co Bd Social Serv, Cult & Heritage Comn; pres, NJ Conf Mayors; pres, Nat Conf Dem Mayors; Mayors Against Illegal Guns; pres, US Conf Mayors; Groove Phi Groove Social Fel Inc. **Honors/Awds:** Commission Service Awards: Fai-Ho-Cha Club, Twig Mothers, Hub City Distributors, Voice Publ, NJ Asn Black Social Workers; Outstanding Chmn, DE Valley United Way, 1977; Man of the Year, Omega Psi Phi Frat, 1984; Community Serv Awd, Lifeline Energy Shelter; Twenty Year Alumnus Award, Hampton Univ; Spirit of St. Francis Award, St Francis Hosp, Trenton; Peace Medal Award. **Special Achievements:** First African American mayor of the Trenton, NJ. **Home Addr:** 284 Spring St, Trenton, NJ 08618. **Business Addr:** Mayor, City of Trenton, 319 E State St, Trenton, NJ 08608, **Business Phone:** (609)989-3030.

## PALMER, EDGAR BERNARD
Counselor, educator. **Personal:** Born Aug 12, 1953, Hartford, CT; son of Clitus Vitelius and Emma Frances Ragins; married Carie Lyn Treske; children: Rachel Erin, Jordan Michael, Andrew & David. **Educ:** Gallaudet Univ, BA, hist, 1977, MS, 2003; Western Md Col, MEd, Deaf Educ, 1980; Gallaudet Univ, MS, spec educ admin, 2003. **Career:** Md Sch Deaf, Columbia Campus, instructional counr, 1980-81, Frederick Campus, instructional counr, 1981-82; Md State Dept Educ, voc rehab counr, 1982-88; Model Sec Sch Deaf, guidance counr, 1988-; Gallaudet Univ, guidance counr, 1988-93, adj prof hist, progs coordr, 1995-98, Gallaudet Univ, dir, Eng Lang Instutute, 1998-99, dir, Tutorial & Instrnl Progs, 1999-2000, dir, Off Stud with Disabilities, 2000-07, assoc dean, Ctr Acad Progs & Stud Serv, 2007-08, assoc dean, New Stud Orientation Progs, 2008-11, exec dir, Off Diversity & Equity Students, 2011-. **Orgs:** Nat Black Deaf Advocates, 1981; Co-chair, Nat Asn Deaf, 1983-85; adv bd mem, Tele Communs Exchange Deaf, 1985-87; bd mem & vpres, Am Deafness & Rehab Asn, Metro-Wash Chap, 1988-90; bd mem, Black Deaf Advocates, Inc, 1989-92; Black Deaf Advocates, Inc, 10th Anniversary Celebration, 1991; bd mem, People Encouraging People Inc, 1992-94; microcosm planning comt, Model Secondary Sch Deaf; bd dir, Penn Visions, 1994-; from mem to pres, Asn Late-Deafened Adults, 1999-2007; reg dir, Md Sch Deaf; vice-chair, Nat Deaf & Hard Hearing Consumer Advocacy Network. **Honors/Awds:** Certificate of Achievement, Md State Dept Educ, 1985; Counselor of the Year, Md State Dept Educ, 1986; Model Secondary School for the Deaf Coaching Award, Cross Country Girls Potomac Valley Athletic Conf Champions, 1990; Outstanding Achievement Award, Am Deafness & Rehab Asn, Metro Wash Chapter, 1991; National Academic Bowl Hall of Fame Inductee, Gallaudet Univ, 2016; Irving K. Jordan Distinguished Service Award, Asn Late-Deafened Adults Inc, 2016. **Special Achievements:** Preview Magazine, Pre-College Programs, Gallaudet University, Special Edition: Communication and Cultural Issues, fall 1990; Montgomery County Journal, write-up related to multi-cultural program sponsored by A G Bell, Associate & Gallaudet University, 1992. **Home Addr:** 4412 Stockbridge Ct, Bowie, MD 20720-3565, **Home Phone:** (301)717-6372. **Business Addr:** Executive Director, Associate Dean, Gallaudet University, 800 Fla Ave NE, Washington, DC 20002-3625, **Business Phone:** (202)651-5652.

## PALMER, DR. EDWARD, JR.
Physician. **Personal:** Born Jul 25, 1937, New York, NY; son of Edward Sr and Thelma Lester; married Maria; children: Neeco. **Educ:** Adelphi Univ, attended 1960; Meharry Med Col, MD, 1964. **Career:** Kings Co Hosp Ctr, internship, 1965; Bronx Ee Infirm, resident, 1970; Elmhurst Hosp Ctr, staff attend; Mt Sinai Sch Med, lectr, fel, 1972; Hosp Albert Einstein Col Med, staff attend; Montefiore Hosp & Med Ctr, staff attend; State Univ NY, assoc prof; Univ Hosp, dir eye serv; Palmer Eye Care & Laser Ctr, admin, currently. **Orgs:** Mem Cen NY State Ophthalmogic Soc; Am Acad Ophthal & Otolaryngol; fel Am Col Surgeons; NY Clin Soc; Int Eye Found Soc Surgeons; Am Asn Ophthal; assoc examr, Am Bd Ophthal. **Honors/Awds:** Founding editor Journal of Cataract; Numerous publications; Listed as one of Best Black Physicians in America, Black Enterprise Magazine, 1988. **Business Addr:** Founder, Palmer Eye Care & Laser Center, 100 Casals Pl, Bronx, NY 10475-3002, **Business Phone:** (718)671-8888.

## PALMER, DR. ELLIOTT B., SR.
Executive. **Personal:** Born Mar 7, 1933, Durham, NC; son of Ada Brown (deceased) and Clarence (deceased); married Juanita Brooks; children: Elliot, Douglas, Ruth & Tonya. **Educ:** NC Cent Univ, AB, 1955, MA, 1961; Duke Univ; Bemidji State Univ, MN; Univ NC, Chapel Hill, NC. **Career:** Executive (retired); Little River HS Durham Co, teacher, 1956-60; Lakeview Elem Sch Durham Co, prin, 1960-64; NC Teachers Asn Raleigh, exec dir, 1964-70; NC Aquarium Soc, bd dir; Raleigh Arts Comn; NC Asn Educr, asso exec dir, 1970-82; African Am Cult Complex Museum, founder, chief exec officer & cur, 1984; Col Community Chorale Soc, pres. **Orgs:** Nat Educ Asn; pres, Stand Gov, 1954; pres, Comn Urban Redev Durham, 1958; found Diversified Invest Spec Org, 1960; chmn, Nat Coun Off State Teachers Asn, 1969-71; Pi Gamma Mu Nat Soc Sci Honor Soc; Nat Asn Advan Colored People; Hunter Lodge FM & AM; gov comm Study NC Pub Schs, 1972; co-chmn, NEA Joint Comn Publ & Textbook Comn, 1972-73; Boy Scouts Raleigh, 1974; Mayor's Comn Plan & Dev, Raleigh, 1974; nat pres, Official Black Caucus Nat Ed Asn, 1985; exec dir, Hammocks Beach Corp. **Home Addr:** 119 Sunnybrook Rd, Raleigh, NC 27610, **Home Phone:** (919)231-0625.

## PALMER, BISHOP GREGORY VAUGHN
Religious leader, minister (clergy). **Personal:** Born Jan 1, 1954?, Philadelphia, PA; married Cynthia; children: Monica & Aaron. **Educ:** George Washington Univ, BA; Duke Univ Divinity Sch, MDiv. **Career:** Eastern Pennsylvania Conference of the United Methodist Church, ordained deacon and probationary member, 1977-81; East Ohio Conference of the United Methodist Church, elder, 1981, district supervisor of the Youngstown District; North Central Jurisdictional Conference, elected to the episcopacy Iowa Area, 2000-08, Illinois Area, 2008-12; Ohio West Area of the United Methodist Church, episcopal leader/resident bishop, 2012-. **Orgs:** United Methodist Gen Bd High Educ & Ministry, pres, 2004-08; United Methodist Coun Bishops, pres, 2008-10. **Honors/Awds:** Honorary degrees: Baldwin-Wallace College, Iowa Wesleyan College, Simpson College, Hood Theological Seminary, and Garrett-Evangelical Theological Seminary. **Special Achievements:** Author, "God's Renewed Creation: Call to Hope and Action", 2010. Contributor, "Finding Our Way: Love and Law in the United Methodist Church", 2014. **Business Addr:** West Ohio Conference, 32 Wesley Blvd, Worthington, OH 43085, **Business Phone:** (614)844-6200.

## PALMER, JAMES E.
Educator, clergy, teacher. **Personal:** Born Jul 6, 1938, Butler, AL; children: 2. **Educ:** Selma Univ, BTech; State Univ, Montgomery, BS; Appalachian State Boone, NC; NC State Univ; Birmingham Baptist

Col, DD. **Career:** Iredell County Pub Schs, Statesville, NC, teacher; Jones Chapel Baptist Church, Mooresville, NC; Catawba Col & Catawba County Pub Sch, teacher & counr; Univ Pk Baptist Church, Charlotte, pastor, 1972, sr pastor. **Orgs:** Moderator, Mt Catawba Asn; Jaycees; Mayor's Coun; bd mem, Gen State BdConv NC Inc; Nat Educ Asn; BSA; exec bd mem, YMCA; Black Pol Caucus; Nat Asn Adv Colored People. **Business Addr:** Senior Pastor, University Park Baptist Church, 6029 Beatties Ford Rd, Charlotte, NC 28216, **Business Phone:** (704)392-1681.

### PALMER, DR. ROBERT L., II

School administrator. **Personal:** Born Mar 1, 1943, Tuscaloosa, AL; son of Robert L and Arnetta Greene; married Beverly Spencer; children: Anthony, Tracie, Monifa, Reginald & Robert. **Educ:** Ind Univ, Bloomington, BS, educ, 1969, MS, col personnel admin, 1973; State Univ NY, Buffalo, NY, PhD, 1979. **Career:** State Univ Col Buffalo, Buffalo, New York, counr educ opportunity prog, 1972-74, asst dir educ opportunity prog, 1973-74; State Univ New York Buffalo, Buffalo, New York, asst vpres stud affairs, 1974-82, assoc provost, 1982-87, provost stud affairs, 1987-; CA State Univ, Fullerton, sr univ adminr, vpres, stud affairs, 1997-; Acad Affairs, assoc vpres; Assoc Provost, assoc vpres; Vice Provost, assoc vpres. **Orgs:** Bd dir, Buffalo Area Engineering Awareness, 1982-; Chmn, bd dir, Buffalo Urban League, 1987-90; Western New York Health Sci Consortium Minority Manpower Task Force Minorities, 1989-; co chair, United Negro Col Fund, Buffalo & Western New York Campaign, 1989-; bd dir, Coord Care, 1989-. **Home Addr:** 6 Troy View Lane, Williamsville, NY 14221, **Home Phone:** (716)633-3386. **Business Addr:** Vice President Student Affairs, California State University Fullerton, 800 N State College Blvd, Fullerton, CA 92831, **Business Phone:** (657)278-3946.

### PALMER, STEPHANIE

Association executive. **Personal:** Born Sep 23, 1952, Philadelphia, PA; daughter of Luther and Mae; children: Matthew Bowman. **Educ:** Middleburg Col, BA, Am studies, hist, 1974; Temple Univ, MA, educ admin, 1978. **Career:** New York Pvt Indust Coun, dir oper, 1985-93; Human Serv Coun New York, admin, 1992-96; New York Mission Soc, exec dir, 1996. **Orgs:** Vpres, Black Agency Execs, 1994-; Non Profit Coord Comt New York, 1998-; founding mem, Black Women Black Girls Giving Circle; Harlem Little League. **Honors/Awds:** Jack & Jill, Metropolitan Chap, Mother of The Year, 1999; Charls A Wolberg Multi Service Org Certificate of Honor, 2002; Isis Award, Leadership Insititute African Am Female Execs, 2004; Recognition Award, Baruch Col School of Public Affairs Alumni Asn, 2004; Charter Revision Commissioner, 2004. **Special Achievements:** Honored for being First African American woman to lead City's oldest social services organization. **Home Addr:** 301 Cathedral Pkwy Suite 1S, NEW YORK, NY 10026. **Business Addr:** Executive Director, New York City Mission Society, 646 Malcolm X Blvd, New York, NY 10010, **Business Phone:** (212)674-3500.

### PALMER, VIOLET (VIOLET RENICE PALMER)

Manager, basketball coach. **Personal:** Born Jul 20, 1964, Compton, CA; daughter of James and Gussie. **Educ:** Calif Poly Pomona Univ, BS, admin. **Career:** Cal Poly Pomona Col, pt guard, 1985; City Placentia Off High SchBasketball, recruting leader; City Los Angeles Nat Col Athletic AsnDiv I Col, recruiting supr & pt guard, 1986; Violet Palmer's Off Camp, founder, 2001-; Women Nat Basketball Asn & Nat Basketball Asn, referee, 2006-; W Coast Conf, co-ordr women's basketball officials, 2009, 2015. **Orgs:** Nat Col Athletic Asn; Women Nat Basketball Asn; Nat Basketball Asn; NCAA Div II. **Special Achievements:** First African American female to officiate games in the Nat Basketball Asn; First black female referee in the Nat Basketball Asn; First woman to referee an all-male professional sports league regular-season game from Ebony; One of two women officials to referee in any men's pro sports league; Guest speaker & clinician, Nat Basketball Asn Training - Pro Summer Leagues; Featured in mag including: Ebony & Sports Illustrated; The frequent target of sports critics, including ESPN; First female to officiate an All-Star Game. **Business Addr:** Referee, National Basketball Association, 645 5th Ave Fl 10, New York, NY 10022, **Business Phone:** (212)407-8000.

### PALMER, WENDY. See DANIEL, WENDY PALMER.

### PALMER-HILDRETH, BARBARA JEAN

Educator, social worker. **Personal:** Born Jan 10, 1941, Jackson, MS; daughter of John and Thelma; married Truman A. **Educ:** Jackson State Univ, BS, 1964; Nat Louis Univ, MS, 1986. **Career:** Social worker, teacher (retired); Canton Pub Sch, teacher, 1964-67; Rockford Bd Educ, from teacher to head-teacher 1967-92. **Orgs:** Big Sisters Inc, 1975-89; Second vpres & life mem, Nat Coun Negro Women, 1984; Legis Community, IEA 1986-87; Nat Asn Advan Colored People; Nat Alliance Black Sch Educr; Provident Baptist Church; Beta Pi Sigma; Delta Sigma Theta; Am Asn Univ Women; vol, Rockford Memorial Hosp; Winnebago County Health Bd; Little People Place Day Care Bd. **Home Addr:** 2228 Pierce Ave, Rockford, IL 61103, **Home Phone:** (815)877-1625.

### PALMORE, LYNNE A. JANIFER

Advertising executive, public relations executive. **Personal:** Born Oct 3, 1952, Newark, NJ; married Roderick; children: Jordan & Adam. **Educ:** Yale Univ, BA, hist, 1974. **Career:** J Walter Thompson, media trainee, 1975-76, media planner, 1976-78; Creamer Inc, media supvr, 1978-80; Needham Harper Worldwide Inc, vpres assoc media dir. **Orgs:** Northshore Chap Jack & Jill. **Home Addr:** 3745 Crain St, Skokie, IL 60076. **Business Addr:** Vice President, Associate Media Director, DDB Needham Harper Worldwide Inc, 303 E Wacker Dr, Chicago, IL 60601.

### PALMORE, RODERICK A.

Executive. **Personal:** Born Feb 14, 1952, Pittsburgh, PA; son of Jefferson and Sophie; married Lynne; children: Jordan & Adam. **Educ:** Yale Univ, BA, econs, 1974; Univ Chicago Law Sch, JD, 1977. **Career:** Berkman Ruslander, assoc, 1977-79; US Atty, asst US atty, 1979-82; Wildman Harrold Allen & Dixon, assoc, 1982, partner, 1986-93; Sonnenschein Nath & Rosenthal, partner, 1993-96; Nuveen Investments, dir; Sara Lee Corp, dep gen coun, 1996, sr vpres, gen coun & secy, 1999, exec vpres, gen coun & secy; Gen Mills, chief compliance & risk mgt officer, exec vpres, gen coun & secy, 2008-15; dir, currently; Dentons US LLP, sr coun, 2015-. **Orgs:** Bd mgrs, Chicago Bar Asn, 1992-94; bd dir, Chicago Bar Found, 1993-94; bd dir, Pub Interest Law Initiative, 1993-96; bd dir, Legal Assistance found Chicago, 1994-97; Ill Judicial Ethics Comn, 1996-; bd dir, Boys & Girls Clubs Chicago, 1997-; bd dir, Ctr New Horizons, 1997-; bd dir, Village Found, 1997-; bd dir, Chicago Bd Options Exchange, 1999-. United Way Metrop Chicago; dir, Asn Corp Coun; trustee, Chicago Symphony Orchestra; chmn, Publ Arts Adv Comn; exec comt, Asn Gen Coun; chair, Leadership Coun Legal Diversity; bd, Am Arbit Asn; fel MacPhail Sch Music; dir, CBOE Holdings Inc, 2000-; bd dir, Goodyear Tire & Rubber Co, 2012-; bd dir, Express scripts, 2014-. **Business Addr:** Executive Vice President, General Counsel, Sara Lee Corp, 3 First Nat Plz, Chicago, IL 60602, **Business Phone:** (312)726-2600.

### PALMS, SYLVIA J.

Executive, president (organization), chief executive officer. **Personal:** Born Jun 23, 1962, Honolulu, HI; daughter of Goldie Royal; children: Royal Christine Jones. **Educ:** Evergreen State Col, Tacoma, WA, BA, lib studies, 1991; City Univ, Leadership Inst Seattle, MA, appl behav scis, 1993. **Career:** US W, strategic acct mgr, 1988, Fed Servs, dir & lobbyist; Qwest Commun Int Inc, Supplier Diversity, dir, 1998-99, vpres, 1999; Greater Phoenix Black Chamber Com, pres & chief exec officer, 2001. **Orgs:** Bd mem, Urban League Metrop Denver, 1998-; chair, Rocky Mountain Minority Supplier Develop Coun, 1999; nat chair, Nat Minority Supplier Develop Coun, 2000. **Business Addr:** President, Chief Executive Officer, Greater Phoenix Black Chamber of Commerce, 201 E Wash St Suite 350, Phoenix, AZ 85004, **Business Phone:** (602)307-5200.

### PANNELL, BILL. See PANNELL, WILLIAM E.

### PANNELL, WILLIAM E. (BILL PANNELL)

College teacher, administrator. **Personal:** Born Jun 24, 1929, Sturgis, MI; son of William and Olive; married Hazel Lee Scott; children: Philip & Peter. **Educ:** Ft Wayne Bible Col, BA; Wayne State Univ, BA, black hist, 1951; Univ Southern Calif, MA, social ethics, 1980; Malone Col, DD; Geneva Col, DD. **Career:** Itinerant evangelist, 1951-78; Brethren Assemblies, asst pastor, youth dir, 1955-65; Christian youth groups, 1955-65; Youth Christ, asst dir leadership training, 1964-68; vice pres & assoc evangelist Tom Skinner Crusades, 1968-74; Christian Assemblies, pastor; Sch Theol, Fuller Theol Sem, dir black ministries, asst prof evangelism, 1974, assoc prof evangelism, Arthur DeKruyter/Christ Church Oak Brook prof Preaching, 1992, dean, 1992-98, spec asst pres & sr prof preaching, currently; Christianity Today, corresp ed; Author: My Friend, the Enemy, 1968; Evangelism from the Bottom Up, 1992; The Coming Race Wars? A Cry for Reconciliation, 1993. **Orgs:** Vpres, Tom Skinner Asn; Staley Found, lectr George Fox Col, Newburg, OR; speaker at many conferences incl consult onGospel & Cult Lausanne Comm, 1978; US Consult Simple Lifestyle, Ventnor, NJ, 1979; chmn, YouthChrist USA, 1980; speaker, Church & Peacemakinga Nuclear Age Conf, Pasadena, CA, 1983; pres, Acad Evangelism, 1983-84; Obsidian Soc; bd mem, Taylor Univ, Ind, currently; bd mem, Teen Ranch Ministries. **Home Addr:** 1760 Coolidge Ave, Altadena, CA 91001-3604. **Business Addr:** Special Assistant to President, Senior Professor Preaching, Fuller Theological Seminary, 135 N Oakland Ave, Pasadena, CA 91182, **Business Phone:** (626)584-5592.

### PAPPILLION, GLENDA M.

Government official. **Personal:** Born Nov 28, 1951, Lake Charles, LA; daughter of John and Viola. **Educ:** McNeese State Univ, BS, acct, 1973. **Career:** Revenue agt, New Orleans, spec agt, Philadelphia, 1975, Houston, 1977-81; Internal Revenue Serv, criminal investr, Houston, 1976-81, CI coord, 1981-82, criminal investr, Chicago, 1982-84, group supv, CI div, Chicago, 1984-86, br chief, CI div chief, Chicago, 1986-88, chief, criminal invest, Houston, 1988-91, asst dist dir, 1991-93, asst regional comnr criminal invest, 1993-, actg spec agt-in-charge, dir, dir cent area field opers. **Orgs:** AKA, 1971-; Big Sister/Big Bro, 1978-90; Nat Orgn Black Law Enforcement Execs, 1988-; Alpha Kappa Alpha Sorority; Asn improv minorities. **Home Addr:** 25 Lucas Dr, Palos Hills, WA 60465. **Business Addr:** Assistant Regional Commissioner, Director, Internal Revenue Service, 915 2nd Ave Rm 2498 M/S 600, Seattle, WA 98174, **Business Phone:** (206)220-6011.

### PARHAM, BRENDA JOYCE

Nurse, educator. **Personal:** Born Jun 3, 1944, Ft. Lauderdale, FL; daughter of Clarence Ray Sr; children: Grant III, Valorie, Stephanie & Deidra. **Educ:** Fla A&M Univ, BS, 1966; Memphis State Univ, MEd, 1972; Univ Tenn, Ctr Health Sci, MSN, 1981. **Career:** Holy Cross Hosp, staff nurse, 1966-67; Methodist Hosp, charge nurse, 1966-69, instr 1969-71; Plantation Gen Hosp, staff nurse, 1967; USAF, staff nurse, 1967-68; Shelby State Community Col, dept head nursing; Baptist Memorial Hosp, liaison nurse & supvr, 1971-72; Memphis State Univ, asst prof, 1972-80; Regioanl Med Ctr, staff nurse, supvr, asst dir, 1973-81; Methodist Hosp, staff develop coordr, 1982; Shelby State Community Col, assoc prof, instr, 1982-83, dept head nursing, 1984-87; asst prof nursing. **Orgs:** Tenn Nurses Asn, 1984-; Nat League Nurses, 1985. **Home Addr:** 5453 Bristol Meadow Cv, Memphis, TN 38125-4192, **Home Phone:** (901)758-8770.

### PARHAM, DASHTON DANIEL

Arts administrator. **Personal:** Born Jan 22, 1956, Brunswick County, VA; son of John and Sarah; children: Erin & Sarah. **Educ:** Va Commonwealth Univ, BFA, commun art & design, 1978. **Career:** Finnegan & Agee Advert, asst art dir, 1978; Cent Fidelity Bank, Pub Rels Dept, designer, 1979; Kell & Assoc, art dir, 1980; Designer's Folio, art dir & illusr, 1980-83; USA Today, illusr, 1983-85, design ed, 1983-, art dir, 1986-96, dir graphics, 1996-99; USA Weekend, art dir, 1985-86; Howard Univ Sch Jour, adj prof publ design, 1993-96. **Orgs:** Art dir Club Metrop Wash, 1980-86; Soc Newspaper Design, 1983-86; Nat Asn Black Journalist, 1994; mentor, J E B. Stuart High Sch Falls Church; Ariz Press Club, 2001; mem, Va Commonwealth Univ. **Home Addr:** 12439 Manchester Way, Woodbridge, VA 22192-5147, **Home Phone:** (571)659-0790. **Business Addr:** Design Editor, USA Today, 1000 Wilson Blvd I-19, Arlington, VA 22229, **Business Phone:** (703)276-5588.

### PARHAM, DR. JAMES B. (JIM PARHAM)

School administrator. **Personal:** Born Dec 6, 1942, Chattanooga, TN; son of James W and Pearl; married Loretta O Brien; children: Francia Greer, Scott, Trace, Quantrell, Perry O'Brien, Leah O'Brien & Aaron-Walton. **Educ:** Cent State Univ, BS, math, 1964; Eastern Ky Univ, MS, criminal justice, 1978; Univ Mich, Ann Arbor, PhD, bus admin, 1994; Nat Univ, MBA, 2010; . **Career:** Univ Pittsburgh, asst prof, 1972-96; Dept Army, proj mgr, comput assist edtraning, 1977-80; Readiness group, dir, sr consult, 1980-83; Dept Army Traning Prog, depy dir, 1983-85; Cent State Univ, dept chair, mil sci, 1985-88; Hampton Univ, dean, sch bus, 1996, prof mgt; Norfolk State Univ Bus Sch, actg dean. **Orgs:** Acad Mgt; Am Mgt Asn; Strategic Mgt Soc; Int Soc Strategic Mgt & Planning. **Home Addr:** 3808 Chesapeake Ave, Hampton, VA 23669, **Home Phone:** (757)727-0883.

### PARHAM, JOHNNY EUGENE, JR.

Association executive, executive director. **Personal:** Born Jan 22, 1937, Atlanta, GA; son of Johnny and Carolyn Anderson; married Ann Cox; children: Johnny Eugene III. **Educ:** Morehouse Col, Atlanta, GA, BA, 1958; Atlanta Univ, Atlanta, GA, MSW, 1960; Woodrow Wilson Col Law, Atlanta, GA, JD, 1978. **Career:** Association executive, executive director (retired); NY Urban League, Brooklyn, NY, br dir, 1962-65; Training Resources Youth, Brooklyn, NY, dept dir, 1965-66; Opportunities Industrialization Ctr, Brooklyn, NY, exec dir, 1966-67; Curber Assocs, New York, NY, exec vpres, 1967-70; Social Dimensional Assocs, New York, NY, pres, 1970-75; United Negro Col Fund, New York, NY, vpres, 1979-94; Thurgood Marshall Scholar Fund, exec dir, 1994-99. **Orgs:** Bd mem, Community League Retarded C, 1991; bd mem, Big Bros New York, 1970-75; bd mem, Nat Soc Fund Raising Execs, New York Chap, 1995-. **Home Addr:** 689 Columbus Ave, New York, NY 10025, **Home Phone:** (212)865-0637.

### PARHAM, LORETTA

Library administrator. **Educ:** Wittenberg University, General Studies-Medieval History; Southern Illinois University-Carbondale, B.S. in Communications, Broadcasting; University of Michigan, School of Information, MLS in Library Science-Administration, 1977. **Career:** Chicago Public Library, various administrative and public service positions, District Chief, 1977-91; Carnegie Library of Pittsburgh, Deputy Director, 1991-97; Hampton University, Director and University Librarian, 1998-05; Robert W. Woodruff Library, Atlanta University Center, CEO and Director, 2005-; EDUCAUSE Management Institute, Faculty Member. **Orgs:** American Library Association (ALA), Member; Association of College & Research Libraries (ACRL), Director-at-Large; The Society, Member; Georgia Humanities Council, Vice Chair of the Board; BRIDGES of Atlanta; OCLC, Trustee, 2005-12, Board Member, 2013-; HCBU Library Alliance, Co-Founder and Past Chair; Wayne State University School of Library & Information Science, Advisory Board Member; Heritage Preservation/Saving Special Collections, Advisory Committee Member; Atlanta Cyclorama, Member; Civil War Museum Task Force, Member.

### PARHAM, MARJORIE B.

Publisher, editor. **Personal:** Born Jan 1, 1918, Batavia, OH; married Hartwell; children: Bill M Spillers Jr; married Gerald Porter. **Educ:** Wilberforce Univ; Univ Cincinnati; Chase Sch Bus. **Career:** Fed Gov Cincinnati, staff, 1946-61; Turbine, bus mgr; Cincinnati Herald, pres, owner, ed, 1963-96, publ emer, currently. **Orgs:** Bd mem, Comn Chest & Coun United Appeal; chairwoman, Nat Afro-Am Mus & Cult Ctr; Hamilton County YMCA; treas, Nat Newspaper Publ Asn; trustee, Univ Cincinnati; bd mem, Cincinnati OIC; Hamilton County Am Red Cross; Greater Cincinnati Urban League; chmn bd, Cincinnati Tech Col; Women Commun Inc; Iota Phi Lambda Bus Women's Sor; St Andrew's Episcopal Church; Metrop YMCA; Dan Beard Coun, Boy Scouts Am; Great Rivers Coun Girl Scouts; Better Bus Bur; bd chair, Cincinnati Tech Col, Univ Cincinnati; Greater Cincinnati Community Chest Coun; Cincinnati Chap Nat Asn Advan Colored People. **Honors/Awds:** Iota Phi Lambda Business Woman of the Year, 1970; Outstanding Woman Communication, 1973; Outstanding Citizen Award, Omega Psi Phi, 1975; Community Serv Media Award, Nat Conf Christians & Jews, 1977; Hon DTL, Cincinnati Tech Col, 1977; Black Arts Festival Award, Univ Cincinnati, 1980; Cincinnati Jour Hall of Fame, 1980; YWCA Women of Achievement, 1988; AwardTop 100 Black Business Prof Am, Dollars & Sense Mag, 1988; Trailblazer Award, Nat Asn Black Journalists, 1993; Lifetime Achiever Award, Applause Mag, 1994; Ohio Women's Hall of Fame, 1994; Governor Outstanding Journalism Award, 1994; Glorifying the Lion Award, Urban League, 1994; Publisher, Pioneer & Mentor Awarded, 2007. **Special Achievements:** One of 12 Women Who Have Influenced The Queen City by The Cincinnati Post, 1974; Named one of Cincinnati's Most Influential Blacks over the past 50 years by WCIN, 2003. **Business Addr:** President, Publisher Emeritus, Cincinnati Herald, 354 Hearne Ave, Cincinnati, OH 45229, **Business Phone:** (513)961-3331.

### PARHAM, RICHELLE

Manager. **Educ:** Drexel Univ, LeBow Col Bus, BS, mkt, bus admin, design & merchandising, 1991. **Career:** Citibank, mgr, 1991-94; Digitas LLC, gen mgr & sr vpres, 1994-2007-; Lehman Bros Holdings Inc, acct exec; Citibank, acct exec, mgr, 2001-04; Rapp Collins Worldwide, sr vpres strategy & enablement, 2007-08; Visa, head global mkt serv, 2008-10, head global mkt innovation & initiatives, 2010; eBay Inc, eBay N Am, chief mkt officer, 2010-15; Girls Who Code, advisor, 2011-. **Orgs:** Steering comt, United Way Young Leaders Soc; Global Mkt Innovation & Initiatives Visa Inc, head; bd dir, Scripps Networks Interactive Inc, 2012-; bd trustees, Drexel Univ, 2014-; bd dir, LabCorp, 2016-. **Business Addr:** Chief Marketing Officer, eBay Inc, 2065 Hamilton Ave, San Jose, CA 95125, **Business Phone:** (408)376-7400.

### PARHAM, SANDRA

Library administrator, dean (education), librarian. **Educ:** Fisk Univ, BA, Eng lang & lit/lett, 1976; Univ Mich, MLIS, 1977. **Career:** Detroit Pub Libr, c's librn; Tenn State Univ, ref librn; Houston (Tex) Pub Libr

Syst, bus, sci, & technol librn; Tex Southern Univ, archivist & coordr spec collections, interim libr dean, 1984-99; Calif State Univ, dean libr, 1999-2014; David Lipscomb Univ (Nashville, TN), dir libr serv, 2014-. **Special Achievements:** First African American to hold the position of director of library services at David Lipscomb University.

### PARHAM HOPSON, REAR ADM. DEBORAH L. (REAR ADM. DEBORAH PARHAM HOPSON)

Nurse, government official. **Personal:** Born Apr 20, 1955, Glouster, OH; daughter of William M Parham Jr and Rose L Parham; married Kevin M; children: William. **Educ:** Univ Cincinnati, BSN, 1977; Univ NC, Chapel Hill, MSPH, 1979, PhD, 1990. **Career:** Dept Health & Human Servs, presidential mgt intern, 1979-81; Inst Med, res assoc, 1981-83; Nat Health Serv Corps, pub health analyst & chief nurse, 1983-86; Bur Health Care Delivery & asst, perinatal coordr, 1988-89, off surgeon gen, dep staff dir & spec asst, 1989-91, pub health analyst, 1990-91, br chief, 1991-97; HIV/AIDS Bur, DHHS, div dir, 1997-2000, dep bur dir, 2000-01, bur dir, 2002, assoc adminr, currently; US Pub Health Serv, rear adm & asst surgeon gen, 2003-. **Orgs:** Am Pub Health Asn, 1977-; Asn Nurses AIDS Care, 1997-; Nat Minority Health Asn, 1992-94; Acad Mgt, 1988-95; Am Nurses Asn, 1984-95, 1999-; Nat Black Nurses Asn, 1985-95; Coalition 100 Black Women, 1992-98; Urban League, 1992-94; life mem, NCNW; prin adv, assoc admin; Nat Acad Sci; Inst Med. **Honors/Awds:** Delta Omega Serv Award, Univ NC, 1979; PHS Meritorious Service Medal; Outstanding Service Medal; Commendation Medal; Achievement Medal; Administrator's Citation, HRSA, 1984; Director's Award, 1986; Chief Nurse Officer Award, 1991; Hildrus A Poindexter Award, Black Commissioned Officers Adv Group, 2003. **Special Achievements:** Elected as a Fellow in the American Academy of Nursing. **Home Addr:** 16119 Llewellyn Manor Way, Silver Spring, MD 20905, **Home Phone:** (240)342-2254. **Business Addr:** Associate Administrator for HIV/AIDS, Health Resources & Services Administration, 5600 Fishers Lane Suite 705 Parklawn Bldg Rm 7-90, Rockville, MD 20857, **Business Phone:** (301)443-0027.

**PARIS, BUBBA. See PARIS, WILLIAM H, JR.**

### PARIS, CALVIN RUDOLPH

Marketing executive, entrepreneur. **Personal:** Born Sep 5, 1932, New Haven, CT; son of Samuel Felix and Nellie Belle Baker; children: Calvin Jr, Priscilla Naomi, Theodore Thurgood & April Nell; married Claudette; children: Samuel Joshua. **Educ:** Howard Univ, BS, chem, 1956; Meharry Med Col Dent Sch, 1958. **Career:** Market executive (retired); Fla Enterprises Educ Corp, asst vp, gen mgr sls, 1958-81; Baskin Robbins 31 Flavors, Chicago IL, franchisee, 1980-90; Paris Health Systs Mgmt Inc, dba Nutri & Systs Weight Loss Centers, pres & treas, 1982-90; Estates Mango de Paris, developer, 1993; Fed Auto Plz & Shopping Ctr, owner, 1999; RPS, co-owner; Nutri, Syst Med Weight Loss Centers, Operator, Mich & Northern Ind. **Orgs:** Life mem, Nat Asn Advan Colored People. **Honors/Awds:** Thirty plus Honors & Awards, Field Enterprises Edl Corp, 1957-81; William H Douglass Citizen of the Yr Award, Dixwell Community House Alumni Asn, 1984; Pres & major stockholder in largest black owned chain of weight loss centers in world. **Home Addr:** 601 NW 12th St, Delray Beach, FL 33444, **Home Phone:** (561)243-0153.

### PARIS, WILLIAM H., JR. (BUBBA PARIS)

Football player, executive, broadcaster. **Personal:** Born Oct 6, 1960, Louisville, KY; married Lynne; children: Wayne, David, Austin, Brandon, Courtney & Ashley. **Educ:** Univ Mich, attended 1982. **Career:** Football player (retired), public speaker, executive; Paris Enterprises, founder, 1982-, pub speaker & head, currently; San Francisco 49ers, left tackle, 1983-90; Champions Christ Crusade Ministries, pres & founder, 1985-; Indianapolis Colts, left guard, 1991; Detroit Lions, 1991; CBS News, sideline reporter, anchor & show host, 1993-2003; KNBR Radio, sideline reporter, anchor & show host, 2000-01; Bubba Paris Friends Homeless, founder; Entertainment & Sports Programming Network, fooball analyst, 2004-05. **Honors/Awds:** Super Bowl champion, XIX, XXIII, XXIV; Len Eshmont Award, 1987; All-Big Ten; All-American; Academic All-American. **Special Achievements:** Publications: Born for this Moment. **Business Addr:** Professional Speaker, Head, Paris Enterprises, 374 W 6th St, Pittsburgh, CA 94565, **Business Phone:** (888)600-4937.

### PARISH, ROBERT LEE

Basketball coach, consultant, basketball player. **Personal:** Born Aug 30, 1953, Shreveport, LA; married Nancy Saad; children: 1. **Educ:** Centenary Col, attended 1976. **Career:** Basket player (retired), coach, consult; Golden State Warriors, ctr, 1976-80; Charlotte Hornets, ctr, 1994-96; Chicago Bulls, ctr, 1996-97; Maryland Mustangs, coach, 2000-01; Boston Celtics, ctr, 1980-94, consult, 2005-. **Orgs:** Nat Basketball Asn; Am Basketball Asn. **Business Addr:** Consultant, Boston Celtics, 226 Causeway St 4th Fl, Boston, MA 02114, **Business Phone:** (617)854-8000.

### PARKER, ANTHONY (WILL ANTHONY PARKER)

Football coach, executive, football player. **Personal:** Born Feb 11, 1966, Sylacauga, AL; son of Billy; married Mary; children: 2. **Educ:** Ariz State Univ, BS, phys educ. **Career:** Football player (retired), coach; Indianapolis Colts, defensive back, 1989; New York Knights, 1991; NJ Knights, 1991; Kans City Chiefs, 1991; Minn Vikings, punt returner, 1992, 1993, left cornerback, 1994; St Louis Rams, right cornerback, 1995-96; Tampa Bay Buccaneers, right cornerback, 1997-98; Hamilton High Sch, cornerbacks coach, 2006-; Fast-Twitch, owner, currently; Cambridge Acad, Queen Creek Campus, phys educ teacher, currently. **Business Addr:** Teacher, Cambridge Academy, 20365 E Ocotillo Rd, Queen Creek, AZ 85142, **Business Phone:** (480)987-3577.

### PARKER, ANTHONY E.

Football player. **Personal:** Born Dec 4, 1975, Denver, CO. **Educ:** Weber State Univ, BSc, tech sales bus mgt. **Career:** Football player (retired); San Francisco 49ers, defensive back, 1999-2002; Oakland Raiders, cornerback, 2002-03; Weber States Univ, coach; Ill Game Time Basketball, founder & head coach, 2016-. **Orgs:** Hall of Fame, Thornton High Sch. **Business Addr:** Founder, Head Coach, Illinois Game Time Basketball, Naperville, IL, **Business Phone:** (408)300-4798.

### PARKER, ANTHONY L.

Association executive, architect, manager. **Educ:** Howard Univ, Sch Archit & Urban Planning, Wash, DC, BArch, 1981. **Career:** Wayne County Sheriff's Dept, Dept Pub Serv, properties mgr, 1993-99; Farbman Group NAI, vpres develop, 1999-2002; Parkstone Develop LLC, pres & chief exec officer, 2002-06; Henry Ford Community Col, proj mgr, 2007-13; Wayne County Community Col Dist, Archit Engineering & Elec Serv, chief operating officer, 2013-. **Orgs:** Residential Builders & Maintenance & Alteration Contractors Bd, 2003-06. **Business Addr:** Chief Operating Officer, Wayne County Community College District, 8200 Outer Dr, Detroit, MI 48219, **Business Phone:** (313)943-4000.

### PARKER, ANTHONY MICHAEL

Basketball player. **Personal:** Born Jun 19, 1975, Naperville, IL; son of Larry and Sara; married Tamy; children: Alonso. **Educ:** Bradley Univ, attended 1997. **Career:** Basketball player (retired); Philadelphia 76ers, guard, 1997-99; Orlando Magic, 1999-2000; Quad City Thunder, 2000; Maccabi Tel Aviv, 2000-02; Lottomatica Roma, 2002-03; Maccabi Tel Aviv, guard, 2003-06; Toronto Raptors, 2006-09; Cleveland Cavaliers, 2009-12; LUXERO, founder, 2011.

**PARKER, APRIL D. See PARKER JONES, APRIL.**

### PARKER, AVERETTE MHOON

Physician, psychiatrist, chief executive officer. **Personal:** Born Jan 27, 1939, Memphis, TN; children: Rosalind. **Educ:** Hillsdale Col, BS, 1960; Howard Univ, MD, 1964. **Career:** C & Family Ment Health & Ment Retardation Unit, N Cent Philadelphia Comm, Ment Health & Ment Retardation Ctr, dir; Hillcrest C's Ctr to DC Headstart Prog, consult, 1968; Area B to DC Pub Sch, consult, 1969-70; Com Ment Health Ctr, dir adult outpatient dept, 1970-71; N County Ctr Fair fax Falls C Ment Health Ctr, dir, 1972-73; Corinthian Guid Ctr, assoc dir, 1973-74; Woodburn Ctr Comm Ment Health, dir, 1973; WNVT TV Nat Instrumental TV, consult, 1973-74; ARCH Inst Inc, pres & chief exec officer, currently. **Orgs:** Am Psychiat Asn, 1969-; prof adv com, Soc Ctr, 1973-75; adv coun N VA Hot Line, 1973; Pa Psychiat Soc, 1974-; appearanceWKBSTV DE Vly Today Ment Health Srvcs, 1975; SPVI TV Woman's Perspective & Perspective Yth "Black Family", 1975; panel mem, Blk Health Consumer Conf N Cent Philadelphia Comm Ment Health & Ment Retardation Ctr, 1975; panel mem, Pa Asn Ment Health Providers-Ann Meeting, 1975; panel mem Orthopsychiatry Ann Meeting Primary Prev & Early Intervention Progs, 1976; panel mem, Lectr "HostilityBlk Male-Fact or Fiction", N Cent Philadelphia Comm Ment Health & Ment Retardation Ctr, 1976; lects Blk Family Roles Swarthmore Col Upward Bound Parents, 1976; "HostilityBlack Male", 1976; "AggressionC & Adolescents", 1976; "Crisis Intervention-effects Women & their Family", 1976; bd dir, Royal Circle Found. **Honors/Awds:** Award for Achievement, Rec Neuro-Psychiatry Dept, 1964. **Business Addr:** President, Chief Executive Officer, ARCH Institute Inc, 3645 Veazey St NW, Washington, DC 20008-3136, **Business Phone:** (202)362-4550.

### PARKER, BARRINGTON DANIELS, JR.

Judge. **Personal:** Born Aug 21, 1944, Washington, WA; son of Barrington D Sr (deceased); married Toni Trent; children: 3. **Educ:** Yale Univ, BA, 1965, Law Sch, LLB, 1969. **Career:** Judge (retired); Hon Aubrey E Robinson Jr, law clerk, 1969-70; Sullivan & Cromwell, atty, 1970-77; Parker Auspitz Neesemann & Delehanty, partner, 1977-87; Morrison & Foerster, partner, 1987-94; US Dist Ct, Southern Dist NY, judge, 1994-2001; US Ct Appeals Second Circuit, chair, States Circuit Judge, 2001. **Orgs:** Trustee, Yale Corp; bd trustee, Gov Inst. **Business Addr:** States Circuit Judge, US Court of Appeals for the Second Circuit, 500 Pearl St, New York, NY 10007, **Business Phone:** (212)857-8500.

### PARKER, BERNARD F., JR.

Government official, county commissioner. **Personal:** Born Dec 16, 1949, Detroit, MI; married Sandra Bomar; children: Bernard III, Bukika, Bunia, Damon Bomar & Deric Bomar. **Educ:** Univ Mich, BA, 1973. **Career:** Oper Get Down, exec dir, 1971-, co-founder & chief exec officer, currently; Wayne Co, Detroit, Dist 2, comnr, 1990-; rep, Wayne County Airport Authority Bd. **Orgs:** Vpres, Universal Variable Staffing, 1979; bd dir, NAACP; bd dir, St John Hosp; bd mem, Southeast Mich Food Coalition, 1979; vpres, Midwest Grp Mgt, 1980; bd mem, Govrs Task Force Infant Mortality, 1985, Mich Bell Citizen Adv Grp, 1986; comn mem, Detroit Strategic Plng Comn, 1987; pres, CAD Cable, 1987-. **Honors/Awds:** Nat Community Serv Award, United Community Serv, 1979; Detroit City Coun Community Award, 1984; Michelob Comn Serv Award, 1985. **Home Addr:** 490 New Town St W, Detroit, MI 48215, **Home Phone:** (313)822-5505. **Business Addr:** Co-founder, Chief Executive Officer, Operation Get Down, 10100 Harper Ave, Detroit, MI 48213, **Business Phone:** (313)921-9422.

**PARKER, BILL. See PARKER, WILLIAM HAYES, JR.**

### PARKER, CANDACE

Basketball player. **Personal:** Born Apr 19, 1986, St. Louis, MO; daughter of Larry and Sara; married Shelden Williams, Nov 13, 2008; children: Lailaa Nicole Williams. **Educ:** Univ Tenn, BS, sports mgt & psychol, 2008. **Career:** U18 Team, player, 2004; Women's Nat Basketball Asn (WNBA), Los Angeles Sparks, 2008-; 2008 Olympics, team mem (Gold Medal); FIBA (Int Basketball Fedn) Europe, UMMC Ekaterinburg, 2010-; 2012 Olympics, team mem (Gold Medal). **Business Addr:** Basketball Player, Los Angeles Sparks, 5120 Goldleaf Cir Suite 130, Los Angeles, CA 90017, **Business Phone:** (213)929-1300.

### PARKER, CHARLES MCCRAE

Scientist. **Personal:** Born Aug 13, 1930, Farmville, NC. **Educ:** NC A&T State Univ, BS, 1951, BS, 1958; NIH. **Career:** Scientist (retired); Nat Inst Health, messenger clerk, 1961-65; USDA, biol sci tech, 1965-67, biol sci tech path, 1967-80, sr biol sci tech, 1980-87, FSIS, 1990; Armed Forces Inst Path, histotechnologist, 1990; Fed Am Socs Exp Biol. **Orgs:** Phi Beta Sigma. **Honors/Awds:** Qual Increase, APHIS USDA, 1975; Letter Achievement, FSIS USDA, 1983; Special Achievement, FSIS USDA, 1985; Honor Graduate, NCO Sch, 1956. **Home Addr:** 7131 8th St NW, Washington, DC 20012, **Home Phone:** (202)723-2254.

### PARKER, CHARLIE

Basketball coach. **Personal:** children: Sharmelle, Charles Jr, Cameron, Sharee & Lyndiemarried Lori; children: Christopher & Kendall. **Educ:** Univ Findlay, health & phys educ & sociol, 1972; Bowling Univ, MA, educ, 1974. **Career:** Univ Findlay, asst coach & head track; Bowling Green, asst coach; Wayne State, head coach, 1982-88; George Raveling, asst, 1989-94; USC, head coach, 1995-96; Dallas Mavericks, asst coach, 1995-2005; New Orleans Hornets, asst coach, 2006-07.

### PARKER, CLARENCE E.

Automotive executive. **Career:** Gresham Chrysler Plymouth Jeep Eagle, pres, chief exec officer, owner, 2009. **Business Addr:** Owner, President, Gresham Chrysler Jeep, 1990 E Powell Blvd, Gresham, OR 97080-8048, **Business Phone:** (503)665-7121.

### PARKER, CLAUDE A., JR.

Manager, executive, quality control inspector. **Personal:** Born Oct 24, 1938, Branchville, VA; son of Claude A Sr and Alma Virginia Wyche; married Constance Yvonne; children: Ryan. **Educ:** Community Col Baltimore, AA, 1960; Morgan State Univ, BS, 1964. **Career:** Joseph E Seagram & Sons Inc, chemist, 1965-66, supvr qual control, 1966, distiller, 1967-70, qual control mgr, 1970. **Orgs:** Am Mgt Asn, 1971; Appl Mgt Sci Inc, 1972; Wine Adv Bd Ca, 1972; Meritocrats Inc, YMCA. **Honors/Awds:** Ebony Success Libr, 1975. **Home Addr:** 15 Gondola View Ct, Woodstock, MD 21163-1136, **Home Phone:** (410)655-1096.

### PARKER, DAVID GENE (DAVE PARKER)

Baseball player, athletic coach, executive. **Personal:** Born Jun 9, 1951, Calhoun, MS; son of Dick and Dannie M; married Kellye Crockett; children: Danielle, David II & Dorian; married Stella Miller. **Career:** Baseball player (retired), baseball coach, executive; Pittsburgh Pirates, outfielder, 1973-83, spec hitting instr; Cincinnati Reds, outfielder, 1984-87; Oakland Athletics, outfielder, 1988-89; Milwaukee Brewers, outfielder, 1990-91; Calif Angels, outfielder, 1991; Toronto Blue Jays, 1991; Anaheim Angels, first base coach; St. Louis Cardinals, spec hitting instr, 1998; Popeye's Chicken & Biscuits, owner, currently. **Orgs:** Pirates AAA. **Home Addr:** 4036 Oak Tree Ct, Loveland, OH 45140-1090. **Business Addr:** Owner, Popeye's Chicken & Biscuits, 7131 Reading Rd, Cincinnati, OH 45237, **Business Phone:** (513)731-1997.

### PARKER, DE'MOND KEITH

Football player. **Personal:** Born Dec 24, 1976, Tulsa, OK. **Educ:** Okla State Univ. **Career:** Football player (retired); Green Bay Packers, running back, 1999-2000; Detroit Lions, 2001; Buffalo Bills, 2003.

**PARKER, DORIS S. See Obituaries Section.**

### PARKER, E. CHARMAINE ROBERTS

Editor, journalist. **Personal:** Born May 30, 1956, Salisbury, NC; daughter of James Deotis and Elizabeth Caldwell; married Ricardo; children: Jazmin Monet & Tangela. **Educ:** Howard Univ, BFA, 1977; Am Univ, grad studies, jour, 1978; Univ Southern Cal, MA, print jour, 1983. **Career:** The Wash Times, ed, copy ed, reporter, 1984; Strebor Bks Int, writer, sr ed & publ dir, currently; Author: The Next Phase of Life, The Trophy Wives. **Orgs:** Nat Asn Black Journalists, 1991. **Honors/Awds:** Soc Newspaper Design, Feature Section/Lifestyle, 1991-92; Design & Layout Awards, 1995-96. **Home Addr:** 9511 Gwynndale Dr, Clinton, MD 20735, **Home Phone:** (301)856-1423. **Business Addr:** Publishing Director, Strebor Books International, 9701 Apollo Dr, Largo, MD 20774, **Business Phone:** (301)583-0616.

### PARKER, G. JOHN, SR.

Firefighter. **Personal:** Born Dec 29, 1941, Drew, MS; son of Loys and Anna Mae Tyler (deceased); married Eva M Semien; children: Jannie Lynn, G John Jr, Dannette Shaton, Toni Michelle & Stephanie A. **Educ:** Ill Cent Col, E Peoria, IL, AA, 1975, AAS, 1979. **Career:** Caterpillar, Peoria, Ill, mach operator, 1964-65; Peoria Fire Dept, Peoria, Ill, 1965-91, fire chief, 1988; City Pomona, Pomona, Calif, fire chief, 1991; Los Angeles County, fire chief, 1994-98. **Orgs:** Int Asn Black Prof Firefighters, 1975-; Am Soc Pub Adminr, 1988-; Int Asn Fire Chiefs, 1988-; bd mem, Peoria Urban League, 1989-; bd mem, Aro Hall Fame, 1989-; bd mem, Pomona Valley Red Cross, 1991; Nat Forum Black Pub Adminr, 1991; Greater Pomona Kiwanis, 1992. **Honors/Awds:** Outstanding Service Arson Investr, Gov Ill, 1982; Outstanding Alumni Award, Ill Cent Col, Am Coun Educ, 1989; Dr Martin Luther King Leadership Award, South Side Pastors Asn, 1990; Sigma Image Award, Sigma Gamma Rho, 1990; Applaud Peoria-Outstanding Serv, Peoria Chamber Achievers, 1990. **Special Achievements:** First African American fire chief, sued the city in 1995 for $10 million. **Home Addr:** 13375 Cardinal Ridge, Chino Hills, CA 91709.

### PARKER, GEORGE ANTHONY

Executive. **Personal:** Born Jan 29, 1952, Norfolk, VA; son of Milton A and Lillian B Carr; married Michele Annette Fleuranges; children: Jenifer Ann. **Educ:** Wake Forest Univ, BS, math, 1974; Univ NC, Chapel Hill, MBA, 1976. **Career:** Continental Ill Nat Bank, banking assoc, 1976-78, second vpres, 1976-82, banking officer, 1979-80; DPF Comp Leasing Corp, vpres & treas, 1982-84; Atlantic Comp Funding Corp, chmn bd & pres, 1984; Conn Bancorp Inc, dir, 1986-88; Norwalk Bank, dir, 1986-88; Leasing Tech Int Inc, dir, vpres & chief financial officer, 1984-95, co-founder, exec vpres, chief mkt officer, 1996-; SCS Md Energy LLC, chief financial officer, 2014-; Ogos Renewable Energy Advisors LLC, chief operating officer, 2014-. **Orgs:** Vpres, Urban Bankers Forum Chicago, 1981-82; Glenwood Lake Comm Asn, 1983-, Nat Black MBA Asn, 1986-; YMCA, 1986; Wake Forest Univ Alumni Letterman Club, 1986-; dir & treas, St Bernard's Ctr Learning; bd dir, Eastern Asn Equip Lessors; Equip Leasing Asn. **Home Addr:** PO Box 7441, Wilton, CT 06897-7441. **Business Addr:** Co-Founder & Executive Vice President, Chief Financial Officer, Leasing Technologies International, 221 Danbury Rd, Wilton, CT 06897, **Business Phone:** (203)563-1100.

### PARKER, H. WALLACE

Lawyer, executive, association executive. **Personal:** Born Dec 8, 1941, NC; married Patricia W; children: Meriel S. **Educ:** Winston-Salem State Univ, BS, 1967; NCC Univ, JD, 1970. **Career:** Reg Herb Smith Lawyer fel Prog, 1970-72; Legal Dept, City Pontiac, DepCity atty, 1971-75; Bloomfield Law Ctr, pres, 1975-; Check Mate Transp Syst, pres, owner, 1974-; V-Tech Corp, vpres, atty, 1976-; Nat Asn Advan Colored People, gen coun, atty, chief coun; pres, Silver Stallion Develop Group LLC, currently; Parker, McGruder & Assocs P C, atty, pres, Currently. **Orgs:** Wolverine Bar Asn; chief legal counr, Nat Asn Advan Colored People, 1984-; atty, bd dir, OAR Prog, 1987-; Am Judicature Soc; chair, Criminal Law Div; Am Trial Lawyers Asn, Oakland County Corrections Adv Bd; Criminal Defense Attorneys Mich; Am Bar Asn; Nat Bar Asn; Oakland County Criminal Adv Bd; bd mem, N Oakland County Girl Scouts Inc; Pontiac Area Urban League; bd trustee, St John United Methodist Church; State Mich Econ Develop Comn; Mich Breeders Asn; chief coun, N Oakland County Chap Int Stafford. **Honors/Awds:** First black Deputy City Attorney, City Pontiac, 1971; Norcroff Award, Nat Asn Advan Colored People, 1986; Outstanding Service Award, 0AR, 1987; Theophilus Jefferson North cross Award, Nat Asn Advan Colored People; Lifetime Achievement Award, Dept Justice, Fed Bur Investn, Detroit Chap; Diversity Award, Waterford Sch Dist, 2004. **Home Addr:** 3332 Barlyn Lane, PO Box 99, Bloomfield Township, MI 48302, **Home Phone:** (248)332-8472. **Business Addr:** Attorney, President, Parker, McGruder & Associates P C, 44060 Woodward Ave, Bloomfield Hills, MI 48302, **Business Phone:** (248)332-0222.

### PARKER, HARRY

Vice president (organization), manager. **Personal:** Born Oct 20, 1954, Richlands, NC; children: 2. **Educ:** NC State Univ, BS, mech engineering, 1976. **Career:** Dupont Spruance site, engr, 1976; Dupont Nylon Supplex, brand mgr, 1991; Dupont Dacron filament, global mkt mgr, 1992, global bus dir, 1996; Dacron staple, dir, 1994; DuPont Dacron, vpres & gen mgr, 1998-2000; DuPont Surfaces, vpres & gen mgr, 2000-03; Gulf Shores Restaurant & Grill, owner; Du Pont Sales Effectiveness, vpres, 2003-. **Orgs:** Int Rotary; life mem, Alpha Phi Alpha; Nat Asn Advan Colored People. **Business Addr:** Vice President of DuPont Sales, General manager, DuPont Dacron, 1007 Market St, Wilmington, DE 19898, **Business Phone:** (302)774-1000.

### PARKER, HENRY ELLSWORTH

Government official, health services administrator, president (organization). **Personal:** Born Feb 14, 1928, Baltimore, MD; son of Henry and Daisy; married Janette; children: Curtis & Janet. **Educ:** Hampton Inst, BS, 1956; Southern Conn State Univ, MS, 1965; Sacred Heart Univ, JD, Hon, 1983. **Career:** State Conn Hartford, treas, 1975-86; Atlanta Sosnoff, sr vpres, pub fund sector, 1986-; Conn Health Found, treas, 1975-86. **Orgs:** Pres, Nat Assoc State Treas, 1985; pres, Kappa Alpha Psi Found, 1981-86 Fed Nat Mortgages Assoc Adv Comm, 1982-84; Past Grant Exalted Ruler Elks; 33 Degree Mason; trustee, Instnl Responsibility Res Corp; bd dir, Inst Living; bd mem, Conn Health Found; New Haven br, Nat Asn Advan Colored People; chmn, New Haven Black Coalition. **Honors/Awds:** Prince Hall Masons Bicentennial Award, 1975; Civil Rights Award, CT, NAACP, 1976; One of Ebony Mag 100 most influential Black Am, 1976-86; Lovejoy Award Elks, 1984; Lifetime Achievement Award, Nat Asn Advan Colored People. **Special Achievements:** First president of the National Association of State Treasurers. **Home Addr:** 315 Eastern St Apt D1512, New Haven, CT 06513-2513, **Home Phone:** (203)777-2888. **Business Addr:** Board Member, Connecticut Health Foundation, 74B Vine St, New Britain, CT 06052, **Business Phone:** (860)224-2200.

### PARKER, DR. HENRY H.

Educator. **Personal:** Born Sep 11, 1933, Memphis, TN; son of Ben. **Educ:** St Thomas Univ, BA, eng, 1956; Univ Minn, MA, eng, 1959; Univ Ill, PhD, Latin & Greek, 1975. **Career:** Univ Minn, asst prof, 1961-65; NDEA Rhet, lectr, 1965; Univ Northern Iowa, from asst prof to prof, 1965-84; Univ Ill, asst prof, 1968-71; Ford Found fel, 1969; Univ Tenn, Martin, Dept Psychol, prof psychol, cunningham distinguished prof, 1990-; Tenn State Supreme Ct task force; Gov's Sch, 1991; producer & star "the Hank Parker Show", Channel 7; Publication: "Minnesotas Golden Age: A Tribute to Saul Bellow". Books: Apollo vs. Dionysus: A Philosophy to Increase College Success by 85%, co-auth; Minnesotas Golden Age: A Tribute to Saul Bellow; Linnaeus on Intoxicants. **Orgs:** Pres, Off-Campus Univ consult firm; founder & prin, Waterloo-Pre-Sch Acad; Danforth Found; pres, Parker Reading Co; pub, Parker Reader Elem Sch Newspaper; co-dir, Marilyn Crist CP Collegians Gifted C's Prog; Nat Dir Curric, Jesse Jackson's PUSH-Excel; co-dir, People to People Citizen Ambassador Prog; People to People educ & humanitarian deleg to China, 2004; People to People deleg. **Special Achievements:** First black professor of University of Minnesota Morris. **Home Addr:** 139 Glenwood Dr, Martin, TN 38237. **Business Addr:** Professor of Philosophy, University of Tennessee Martin, 322 Humanities Bldg, Martin, TN 38238, **Business Phone:** (731)881-7545.

### PARKER, DR. HERBERT GERALD. See Obituaries Section.

### PARKER, HERBERT K.

Chief financial officer, vice president (organization). **Personal:** children: 2. **Educ:** Lee Univ, Cleveland, TN, BS, acct. **Career:** ABB Group, staff acct ABB C-E Systs, Chattanooga, Tenn, 1980-83, financial mgt trainee, Stamford, Conn, 1983-84, sr auditor & audit supvr C-E Systs, 1984-92, internal audit mgr ABB Australia & Nz, 1992-94, segment controller ABB China Ltd, Beijing, China, 1994-98, vpres & bus controller, Zurich, Switz, 1998-2001, Industs Div, Zurich, Switz, sr vpres & controller, 2001-02, Automation Technologies Div, Norwalk, Conn, chief financial officer, 2002-05, chief financial officer, N Am, Norwalk, Conn, 2006-08; Harman Int Industs Inc, exec vpres & chief financial officer, 2008-. **Orgs:** Bd dir, TMS International Corp; bd dir, TriMas Corp. **Home Addr:** , Weston, CT.

### PARKER, JACQUELYN HEATH

Association executive. **Personal:** Born Memphis, TN; daughter of Fred Heath and Nezzie Heath; married William A; children: Kimberly D & Shane E. **Educ:** Southern Ill Univ, BS, Eng, 1963, MS, histroy, 1967; Univ Ill. **Career:** Community High Sch Dist 218, content reading specialist, 1971-96; Top Ladies Distinction Inc, nat pres, 1987-91, prog coord, 1996-, dean, 1999-; Olive-Harvey COT Col, asst dean, 1996-; City Cols Chicago, Dean Instr, 1996-2004; Franchell Boswell Educ Found, pres, 2009-. **Orgs:** Scholar chmn, Build Inc, 1983-90; sponsor, NIA Club, 1985-95; pres, Theta Rho Omega Chap Alpha Kappa Alpha Sor, 1987-89; Jack & Jill Inc; exec bd, Links Inc, 1991-95; Ill state convener, Nat Coun Negro Women, currently. **Honors/Awds:** Soror of the Year, Theta Rho Omega Chap Ark Sorority; Lady of the Year, Top Ladies Distinction Chicago, 1985; Top 40 Finest Women COT, Women Together South Suburban Chicago, 1988; nominee, Top Women Chicago Midwest Ctr Chicago, 1989; Orchid Award, Top Ladies Distinction Inc, 1989; Ten Community Builders Award, South Suburban Chicago Ark, 1990; Jacquelyn Parker's Day, 1990; Mayor Cincinnati, OH, 1990; A Woman of Distinction Award Chicago, Top Ladies Distinction, 1991; winner, "Those Who Excel", Ill State Bd Educ, 1991; Outstanding Teacher Award, Univ Chicago, 1994. **Home Addr:** 254 E Denell Dr, Crete, IL 60417-1015, **Home Phone:** (708)672-9217. **Business Addr:** President, The Franchell Boswell Educational Foundation, PO Box 1714, Calumet City, IL 60409.

### PARKER, JAMES L. See Obituaries Section.

### PARKER, JERRY P.

Lawyer. **Personal:** Born Mar 1, 1943, West Blocton, AL; married Patricia Wall; children: Jerry & Jennifer. **Educ:** Bowling Green State Univ, BS & BA, 1965; Cleveland Marshall Sch Law, JD, 1970. **Career:** E Ohio Gas Co, syst analyst, 1965-68; c, tax supr, 1968-73; Sears Roebuck & Co, tax atty, 1973-; Gen Motors Corp, immediate past chmn, sr tax coun, currently. **Orgs:** Am Bar Asn; Nat Bar Asn; Cook Co Bar Asn; Chicago Bar Asn; Ill Bar Asn; Ill & Ohio St Bar Bd Trust Consult Prot Asn; bd trustee, Exec Comt Child Serv; bd trustee, Friendly Inn Settle House. **Home Addr:** 2910 Buttonwood Walk, Hazel Crest, IL 60429. **Business Addr:** Senior Tax Consultant, Immediate Past Chairman, General Motors Corp, 300 Renaissance Ctr, Detroit, MI 48243-1403, **Business Phone:** (313)556-5000.

### PARKER, JOSEPH CAIAPHAS, JR.

Clergy, lawyer. **Personal:** Born Sep 25, 1952, Birmingham, AL; son of Joseph C Sr (deceased) and Addie Ruth Fox; married J LaVerne Morris; children: Jessica, Janetta & Jennifer. **Educ:** Morehouse Col, BA, 1974; Univ Ga, MA, pub admin, 1976; Univ Tex, Austin, JD, 1982; Baylor Univ, George W Truett Theol Sem, Mdiv; Urban Ministry Gordon-Conwell Theol Sem, Boston, MA, PhD, ministry. **Career:** City Dallas, admin asst mgt serv, 1976-77, admin asst off city mgr, 1977-79, mgr summer youth employ prog, 1979; David Chapel Missionary Baptist Church, minister, 1982, assoc pastor 1984-92, pastor, 1992-94, sr pastor, 2006-; Travis Co Atty Off, trial atty, 1983-84, chief trial div, 1985-86; Long, Burner, Parks & Sealy PC, atty, dir & vpres, 1986-92; Univ Tex, Austin, instr trial advocacy, 1991. Books: Holy Change: A Systemic Approach to Transforming A Community, 2008. **Orgs:** Nat Conf Minority Pub Adminrs, 1974-80; Univ GA fel, 1974-76; Pi Sigma Alpha Hon Soc, 1976; Travis County Bar Asn, 1996-97; Am Soc Pub Admin; bd dir, Morehouse Col Nat Alumni Asn; bd dir, Austin Child Guid Eval Ctr; Conf Christians & Jews; Black Austin Dem; Urban League, Nat Asn Advan Colored People, Austin Jaycees; Travis County Pub Defender Task Force; State Bar Tex, Austin Young Lawyers Asn, Nat Bar Asn; Austin Black Lawyers Asn & Fed Bar Asn; Asn Trial Lawyers Am; Benjamin E Mays fel Ministry, Fund Theol Studies; bd mem, Safe Pl; Am Inns Ct; bd mem, Austin Area Urban League; fel, Tex Bar Found; bd mem, Baptist Stand newsmagazine bd, currently. **Special Achievements:** First African American president of the Travis County Bar Association, 1996-97. **Home Addr:** 12311 Wycliff Lane, Austin, TX 78727. **Business Addr:** Senior Pastor, David Chapel Missionary Baptist Church, 2211 E Martin Luther King Jr Blvd, Austin, TX 78702-1343, **Business Phone:** (512)472-9748.

### PARKER, KAI J.

Executive, government official. **Personal:** children: Darren & Darnel. **Educ:** Compton Col, AA, social welfare, 1965; Loyola Mary Mt Univ, grad studies psychol & guid coun, 1979, Human Construct Sexuality, 1980, Alcohol & Drug Studies, 1982; Univ Redlands, BA, mgt, 1981. **Career:** Am Tel & Tele, customer serv rep, 1966-68; Los Angeles County Dept Social Serv, eligibilty worker, 1968-70, eligibility supvr, 1970-79; Aide Sanit & Supply Co, mgt consult, 1979-80; Los Angeles County Assessment Appeals Bd, comnr, 1980-82; Group W Cable, pub affairs, govt rels coordr, 1982-91; Los Angeles County, Dept C Serv, spec progs coordr, 1991-. **Orgs:** Nat Asn Advan Colored People; Asian-Pac legal Defense & Educ Bd Dirs; United Negro Col Fund; Gardena Local Manpower Adv Bd; Gardena Interagency Health Comn; Gardena Martin Luther King Cult Comn; Asian Am Drug Abuse Prog; Calif Afro-Am Mus Art Coun; Mus African Am Art; vpres, S Bay Coalition Alcoholism; adv bd, Los Angeles County Child Health DisPrev; vpres, Gardenia Valley Lions; Serv Employees Int Union; pres, Santa Clara Valley Dem Laura Espinosa. **Honors/Awds:** Outstanding Service Award, Bd Supervisors, Dept Pub SocialServ, 1982; Nat Asn Counties Award, 1992-96; Women of the Year, US Cong House Representatives, 35th Dist, 1996; Outstanding Leadership Award, City Gardena; Recognition Award, Gardena Elks Leadership; Outstanding Service Award, AFL-CIO; Community Involvement Award, Sor optimist Int; Community Involvement Award, Gardena Sorptomist; Community Service Award, Calif Black Comn Alcoholism; Commendations, Los Angeles County; Political Award, Zeta Phi Beta; Founder, Gardenia African Centered Saturday Sch. **Home Addr:** 13123 Spinning Ave, Gardena, CA 90249-1720, **Home Phone:** (310)387-8880. **Business Addr:** Coordinator of Special Programs, Los Angeles County Department of Children Services, Rm 604 425 Shato Pl, Los Angeles, CA 90020.

### PARKER, KAREN LYNN

Journalist. **Personal:** Born Dec 21, 1943, Salisbury, NC; daughter of Fred and Clarice; married Christopher L Roe; married Peter A Kuttner; children: Jonah Evan Kuttner; married Barry Lambert. **Educ:** Univ NC, Greensboro; Univ NC, BA, jour & mass comn, 1965. **Career:** Winston-Salem J, 1962-65, copy ed, 1997-2010; Grand Rapids, MI, Press, 1965-67; Rochester Dem & Chronicle, 1967; Los Angeles Times, sunday news ed, 1978-93; Salt Lake Tribune, asst nat ed, 1994-95; Univ NC Press Club, vpres; Univ NC Journalist, ed. **Orgs:** Nat Asn Black Journalists, 1997-; Am Copy Eds Soc, 1997-; UNC Bd Visitors, 2005-; bd dir, UNC Gen Alumni Asn, 2005-08. **Honors/Awds:** Harvey E Beech Outstanding Alumni Award, Univ NC, 2004. **Special Achievements:** First African American woman to graduate from University of NC, Chapel Hill, 1965; Journal of 1963-64 placed in Southern Historical Collection, UNC Library, 2007; Novel, The Activist's Daughter, 1997. **Home Addr:** 2 Laurel Brook Ct, Greensboro, NC 27407, **Home Phone:** (336)855-6936. **Business Addr:** Copy Editor, Winston-Salem Journal, 416 N Marshall St, Winston-Salem, NC 27101, **Business Phone:** (336)727-7211.

### PARKER, DR. KEITH DWIGHT

Educator. **Personal:** Born Oct 15, 1954, Philadelphia, MS; married Emery D Woodruff; children: Narroyl & Malcolm. **Educ:** Delta State Univ, BA, psychol & sociol, 1978; Miss State Univ, MA, sociol, 1982, PhD, philos, sociol & criminol, 1986. **Career:** Delta State Univ, asst dean, 1979-82; Miss State Univ, resident asst, 1982-85, teaching asst, 1982-86; Auburn Univ, asst prof sociol, 1986-89; Univ Nebr-Lincoln, asst prof, assoc prof, 1989-203, African Am & African Studies Prog, dir, 1993-98, asst dean grad studies, assoc dean grad studies, 1999-2002; coordr undergrad res sociol dept, 2002-03; Univ Ga, assoc provost inst diversity, 2003-05, prof sociol, 2003-14; Nat Civil Rights Conf, founder & chmn, 2011-; Fla A&M Univ, prof, 2014-. **Orgs:** Adv, Black Stud Orgn, 1982; Minority Fels, Miss State, 1982; pres, Grad Black Stud Orgn, 1983; Alpha Kappa Delta, Miss State, 1983; adv, African People's Union, Univ Nebr, 1990-94; dir, African Am & African Studies, 1993-98; Inst Res Adv Bd, 2004-05; Am Soc Criminol; Am Sociol Asn; Mid-S Sociol Asn; Southern Sociol Soc; founder, PACE; Pres's sr staff; vpres, Nat Asn Advan Colored People; bd dir, Salvation Army; chair, MLK Freedom Breakfast Planning Comt; Nebr Partners, Prev Adv Comt; Mt Zion Baptist Church; Ebenezer Baptist Church-W Athens, GA. **Home Addr:** 121 Telfair Pl, Athens, GA 30606, **Home Phone:** (706)227-2671. **Business Addr:** Professor, Florida A&M University, 1601 Martin Luther King Jr Blvd Lee Hall Suite 100, Tallahassee, FL 32307.

### PARKER, LAWRENCE KRISNA

Rap musician. **Personal:** Born Aug 20, 1965, Brooklyn, NY; son of Sheffield Brown and Jacqueline Jones; married Ramona Scott; children: Randy Hubbard (deceased); married Simone. **Career:** Boogie Down Productions, DJ Scott LaRock, 1985; Edutainer Records & Human Educ Against Lies, founder, 1990; lectr; producer; A&R, Reprise, vpres, 1998-2000; Temple Hip-Hop, founder; Albums: Criminal Minded, 1987; By All Means Necessary, 1988; Ghetto Music: The Blueprint of Hip Hop, 1989; Edutainment, 1990; Live Hardcore Worldwide, 1991; Sex & Violence, 1992; Return of the Boom Bap, 1993; KRS-One, 1995; I Got Next, 1997; A Retrospective, 2000; The Sneak Attack, 2001; Best of B-Boy Records, 2001; Strictly for the Break dancers & Emceez, 2001; Spiritual Minded, 2002; The Mix Tape, 2002; Kristyles, 2003; D.I.G.I.T.A.L., 2003; Keep Right, 2004; Life, 2006; Hip-Hop Lives (with Marley Marl), 2007; Adventures In Emceeing (with Duck Down Records), 2008; Maximum Strength, 2008; Survival Skills, 2009; It's ALL Good, 2010; The Just-Ice and KRS-ONE EP Volume #1, 2010; Meta-Historical, 2010; Back to the L.A.B., 2010; Godsville, 2011; Royalty Check LP, 2011; The BDP Album, 2011; Return of the Boom Bip, 2011; Never Forget EP, 2013; Flims: I'm Gonna Git You Sucka, 1988; Who's the Man?, 1993; Subway Stories: Tales from the Underground, 1997; Rhyme & Reason, 1997; Boricua's Bond, 2000; Freestyle: The Art of Rhyme, 2000; The Freshest Kids, 2002; 2Pac 4 Ever, 2003; Beef, 2003; MuskaBeatz, 2003; War on Wax: Rivalries In Hip-Hop, 2004; Keep Right, 2004; Zoom Prout Prout, 2005; A Letter to the President, 2006; Bomb It, 2007; The Obama Deception, 2008; Good Hair, 2009; Rhyme and Punishment, 2011; GhettoPhysics, 2011; Something from Nothing: The Art of Rap, 2012. Singles: "The Bridge Is Over", 1987; "Sound of da Police", 1993; "I Can't Wake Up", 1993; "MC's Act Like They Don't Know", 1995; "Rappaz R. N.Dainja", 1995; "East Coast West Coast Killas", 1997; "Men of Steel", 1997; Step Into A World, 1997; "Clear 'Em Out", 2002; "Classic (Better Than I'veEver Been)", 2007; Books: Break the Chain KRS-ONE, 1994; The Science of Rap, 1996; Ruminations, 2003; The Gospel of Hip Hop: The First Instrument, 2009. **Honors/Awds:** Four gold records. **Special Achievements:** Receipient, Lifetime Acheivement Award, 2008. **Business Addr:** Singer, c/o Jive Records, 137 W 25th St Suite 139, New York, NY 10001, **Business Phone:** (212)727-0016.

### PARKER, LEE

Educator, consultant. **Personal:** Born May 31, 1949; children: 2. **Educ:** LeMoyne Owen Col, BS & BBA, 1979; Trevecca Nazarene Col, MEd, 1990. **Career:** US Treas, assoc nat bank examr, 1979-83; Nat Bank Com, Memphis, vpres, 1983-84; Gospel TV Network Inc, bus consult, 1984-; Memphis City Sch, teacher, BASIC prog & math, 1985- . **Orgs:** Co-chmn, Memphis Housing Comn; Securities & Exchange Comn; LeMoyne OwenCol Relig Life Comn; naval adv, NAUSUP-PACT forces. **Home Addr:** 301 Walker Ave, Memphis, TN 38126.

### PARKER, MARYLAND MIKE

Journalist. **Personal:** Born Feb 5, 1926, Oklahoma City, OK; married John Harrison; children: Norma Jean Brown, Janice Kay Shelby, Joyce Lynn, John H Jr, Cherie D Hite, Patrick Scott, Charles Roger & John H III. **Educ:** Univ Ariz, attended 1971; Mary Mt Col, attended 1977. **Career:** Md House Beauty, beautician, 1964-69; BACOS Newsletter, newspaper reporter, 1971-77; KINA BACOS, reporter, radio announcer, 1973-84; Kans State Globe, reporter & photogr, currently. **Orgs:** YWCA, 1958-, Saline County Dem Women, 1960-, VFW Aus, 1971-, Am Leg Aux, 1973-, Nat Fed Press Women, 1973-, Kans Press

Women, 1973-; Nat Asn Advan Colored People, youth adv, 1970-72, 1980; bd dir, Salina Child Care Asn, 1973; part time vol, Salvation Army, 1979-; Int Platform Asn, 1983-; bd dir, Gospel Mission, 1984; Am Bus Women Asn, 1991-; St. John Baptist Church. **Honors/Awds:** Good Citizenship Award, VFW 1432, 1982; Award of Merit, Salina Human Rels, 1986; Woman of the Year, Am Bus Asn, 1997. **Home Addr:** 920 Birch Dr, Salina, KS 67402. **Business Addr:** Reporter, Photographer, Kansas State Globe, PO Box 1309, Kansas City, KS 66104, **Business Phone:** (913)825-0468.

### PARKER, REV. MATTHEW

Clergy, executive. **Personal:** Born Nov 14, 1945, Cincinnati, OH; son of Matt (deceased) and Ruth Spann (deceased); married Karon Bethay; children: Matthew Lloyd Jr, Tiffany Barbara, Michael Jones, Kelly Betsy & Justin Gregory. **Educ:** Eastern High Sch, dipl, bus, 1963; Grand Rapids Sch Bible Music, dipl, gen bible, 1969; Wheaton Col, BA, sociol, 1977; Univ Detroit Mercy, MA, educ admin, 1987. **Career:** Chrysler Corp, assembly line worker, 1965-66; Black Campus Ministry Athletes Action Basketball Team Campus Crusade Christ, staff, 1971-72; Wheaton Col, minority stud adv, 1973-79; Great Comn Community Church, founder & pastor, 1978-83; Hamilton Missionary Baptist Church, founder & pastor, 1979-85; Detroit Afro Am Mission Inc, dir, 1979-80; J Allen Caldwell Schs, exec vpres, 1980-82; Urban Acad Affairs Dept, founder, 1981-88; William Tyndale Col, Instr cross cult studies, 1982-85, dir, Urban Ministry Prog, 1982-85, asst prof urban studies, 1985-88, assoc vpres urban acad affairs, 1985-88; Cong Evangelizing Black Am, chmn, 1986-88; Inst Black Family Develop, founder & pres, 1987-; Rosedale Pk Baptist Church, Pastors Team, 2002-. **Orgs:** Founder, Urban acad affairs Dept, 1981-88; exec comt, Relig Alliance Against Pornography, 1985-01, proj dir, Mich Neighbourhood Partnership, 1996-98; consult, Neighbourhood Serv Org, 1997-2001; co-dir, A Call to Serv, 2001-06; founder, Mich Faith Based Health Asn, 2005-06; consult, Christianity Today; consult, Zondervan Corp. **Honors/Awds:** Achievement Award, Wheaton Col, 1974; Outstanding Young Men of America, 1980-81; Whos Who Amongst Black America, 1986; Missions Leadership Award from Destiny, 1987; Men of Achievement, Cambridge England, 1988; Leadership Award, Nat Black Evangelical Assoc, 1988; Spiritual Care Award, Circle Family Care, 1991; Alumnus of the Year Award, Grand Rapids Sch Bible Music, 1998; Man of the Year Award, Rosedale Park Baptist Church, 2001. **Home Phone:** (313)835-4612. **Business Addr:** President, Founder, Institute for Black Family Development, 15151 Faust, Detroit, MI 48223, **Business Phone:** (313)493-9962.

### PARKER, MEL (MELVIN F PARKER)

Executive, businessperson. **Educ:** US Mil Acad, West Point, BS, 1989. **Career:** PepsiCo, team leader & regional gen mgr sales, 1994-2002; Staples Corp Express, corp vpres, US com sales, 2003-07; Newell Rubbermaid, vpres sales & channel mkt off prod NAm, 2007-09; Dell, exec dir-small & medium bus Am, 2009-10, vpres & gen mgr-consumer, small off & mem loyalty NAm, 2010-12; Brinks, pres NAm, 2012-14; Aggreko, managing dir NAm, 2016-. **Orgs:** Big Bro Big Sister Found Cent Tex exec adv bd, 2012; Nat Black MBA Asn bd dirs, 2012-; Vectrus bd dirs, 2014-. **Honors/Awds:** Named to the Top 100 Most Influential Blacks in Corporate America list, 2012, 2014. **Business Addr:** Aggreko, 15600 John F Kennedy Blvd Suite 900, Houston, TX 77032, **Business Phone:** (281)985-8200.

### PARKER, PAUL E. (PAUL E PARKER)

School administrator, engineer, association executive. **Personal:** Born Oct 23, 1935, Jenkins Bridge, VA; son of Edward L and E Alma Logan; married Ann Withers; children: Paul Jr & Kenneth. **Educ:** NC Agr & Tech State Univ, BSME, 1961; State Univ NY, Buffalo, MSME, 1969. **Career:** School administrator (retired); Bell Aerosystems, stress analyst, 1961-67; NC Agr & Tech State Univ, asst prof mech engineering, 1967-73, asst dean engineering, 1971-73; Nat GEM Consortium, asst dean & dir morrill engineering prog; Univ Ill, asst dean engineering & dir, minority engineering progs. **Orgs:** Engineering dir, NC A&T State Univ, 1970-73; pres, Nat Asn Minority Engineering Prog Adminr, 1985; Nat GEM Consortium; consult, Battelle Lab, 1984; selection comt mem, GEM Univs; bd dir, Urban League Champaign Co, 1983-90; bd trustee, Mt Olive Baptist Church, 1980-; chmn adv comm, Unit 4 Sch, 1975-78; bd dir, GEM, 1986-; ed, ASEE CIP newsletter, 1989-; Pi Tau Sigma Hon Soc; Tau Beta Pi Hon Soc. **Honors/Awds:** Vincent Bendix Minorities Engineering, Am Soc Engineering Educ, 1990; Black Engineer of the Year, U.S. Black Engr mag, 1991; outstanding faculty member, UIUC Dad's Asn, 1992; Minority Engineering Program Director of the Year, Nat Socs of Black Engrs, 2001; STAR Award for Educator of the Year, Univ Ill, 2007; Golden Torch Award, Nat Soc Black Engrs, 2001. **Home Addr:** 1203 Brighton Dr, Urbana, IL 61801, **Home Phone:** (217)328-2556.

### PARKER, PAULA JAI

Actor. **Personal:** Born Aug 19, 1969, Cleveland, OH; married Forrest Martin; children: 1. **Educ:** Howard Univ, BA. **Career:** TV series: "The Apollo Comedy Hour", 1992; "Townsend Television", 1993; Cosmic Slop, 1994; "Roc", 1994; "Pointman", 1995; "The Wayans Bros", 1995-96; "The Weird Al Show", 1997; "The Parent 'Hood", 1997; Riot, 1997; "Cosby", 1997; Always Outnumbered?, 1998; "NYPD Blue", 1998; "Snoops", 1999-2000; "Touched by an Angel", 2000; "The Proud Family", 2001-05; "Express Yourself", 2001; "I Love the '80s Strikes Back", 2003; "My Coolest Years", 2004; "The Shield", 2004; "Lilo & Stitch: The Series", 2005; "CSI: Miami", 2005; "CSI: Crime Scene Investigation", 2006; "Side Order of Life", 2007; "Baisden After Dark", 2007; Something with Bite, 2009; "Fear Itself", 2009; "The Mentalist", 2010; "Fish Hooks", 2010; "Funny or Die Presents", 2011; "Let's Stay Together", 2012; "Family Time", 2012; "The Exes", 2012; "The Soul Man", 2013; "Front Seat Chronicles", 2014; "True Blood", 2013-14. Films: Friday, 1995; Tales from the Hood, 1995; Don't Be a Menace to South Central While Drinking Your Juice in the Hood, 1996; Get on the Bus, 1996; Riot, 1997; Sprung, 1997; Always Outnumbered, 1998; Woo, 1998; Why Do Fools Fall In Love, 1998; The Breaks, 1999; 30Years to Life, 2001; High Crimes, 2002; Phone Booth, 2002; Love Chronicles, 2003; My Baby's Daddy, 2004; She Hate Me, 2004; Hustle & Flow, 2005; The Proud Family Movie, 2005; Animal, 2005; Idle wild, 2006; The Genius Club, 2006; Cover, 2007; Angels Can't Help But Laugh, 2007; So You Want Michael Madsen?, 2008; Jessica Sinclaire Presents: Confessions of A Lonely Wife, 2010; Jessica Sinclaire Presents: Confessions of A Lonely Wife, 2010; King of the Underground, 2011; When a Woman's Fed Up, 2013; Life of a King, 2013; Pastor Shirley, 2013; 4Play, 2014; Patterns of Attraction, 2014; Act of Faith, 2014. **Honors/Awds:** Cable ACE Award. **Business Addr:** Actress, c/o William Morris Agency, 1 William Morris Pl, Beverly Hills, CA 90212, **Business Phone:** (310)859-4000.

### PARKER, RAY, JR.

Television producer, songwriter, singer. **Personal:** Born May 1, 1954, Detroit, MI; son of Ray Sr (deceased) and Venolia (deceased); married Amanda; children: Zac, Taylor, & Julia; married Elaine Parker; children: Ray III, Redmen, Gibson & Jericho. **Career:** Singer, music producer, actor; Raydio, mem, 1977-; Albums: Ray dio, 1978; Rock On, 1979; Two Places at the Same Time, 1980; A Woman Needs Love, 1981; Greatest Hits, 1982; The Other Woman, 1982; Woman Out of Control, 1983; Chart busters, 1984; Sex & the Single Man, 1985; After Dark, 1987; The Best of Ray Parker Jr. & Raydio, 1990; I Love You Like You Are, 1991; Two Places at the Same Time, 1993; Greatest Hits, 1993; The Best of Ray Parker Jr., 1999; I'm Free, 2006; Ghost busters: The Encore Collection, 1999; The Heritage Collection, 2000; Featuring Ghost busters, 2004; The Best of Ray Parker Jr, 2004; I'm Free!, 2006; Singles: "Jack & Jill", 1978; "Is This A Love Thing", 1978; "You Can't Change That", 1979; "More Than One Way To Love A Woman", 1979; "Two Places At The Same Time", 1980; "For Those Who Like To Groove", 1980; "A Woman Needs Love (Just Like You Do)", 1981; "That Old Song", 1981; "It's Your Night", 1981; "The Other Woman", 1982; "Let Me Go", 1982; "It's Our Own Affair", 1982; "Bad Boy", 1983; "The People Next Door", 1983; "I Still Can't Get Over Loving You", 1983; "Woman Out Of Control", 1984; "Ghost busters", 1984; "Jamie", 1984; Girls Are More Fun", 1985; "One Sunny Day/Dueling Bikes From Quicksilver", 1986; I Don't Think That Man Should Sleep Alone", 1987; "Over You", 1988; "Than It", 1989; "The Past", 1990; "All I'm Missing Is You", 1990; "She Needs to Get Some", 1991; "Girl I Saw You", 1991. Films: Up town Saturday Night, 1974; Enemy Territory, 1987; Disorderlies, 1987; TV series:"Berrenger's", 1985; "The Kid Who Loved Christmas", 1990; Ray dio Music Corp, owner, currently; Ameraycan Rec Studios, founder & owner. **Honors/Awds:** BAFTA Film Award, 1985; Hollywood Walk of Fame, 2014. **Business Addr:** Singer, Owner, Raydio Music Corp, 23679 Calabasas Rd Suite 501, Calabasas, CA 91302, **Business Phone:** (818)225-2412.

### PARKER, RIDDICK THURSTON, JR.

Football player, executive. **Personal:** Born Nov 20, 1972, Emporia, VA. **Educ:** Univ NC, BA, hist, 1995; Walden Univ, MPA, non-profit, pub, orgn mgt, 2013, grad cert, curric, instr & assessment, sec educ, 2014. **Career:** Football player (retired), exec; San Diego Chargers, 1995; Seattle Seahawks, defensive tackle, 1997-98, left defensive tackle, 1999-2000; New Eng Patriots, 2001; Baltimore Ravens, 2002, defensive tackle, 2003; San Francisco 49ers, defensive tackle, 2004; Smith Barney, financial advisior, 2005-07; STARRS Group Home Inc, cofounder, cert prog adminr, 2005-12; Youth Ambassador Leadership Acad LLC, dir, 2007-. **Honors/Awds:** Super Bowl.

### PARKER, STAFFORD W.

Government official. **Personal:** Born Sep 12, 1935, Kansas City, MO; son of Cato and Erma Thurston Freeman; married Anita McBride; children: Monique V & Dana V. **Educ:** Univ Kans, Lawrence, KS, BA, polit sci, 1958, LLB, 1963. **Career:** Government official (retired); City Lawrence, KS, probation Offr, 1962; Travelers Ins Co Agency, Cleveland, OH & Oakland, Calif, claims examr, adjuster, 1963-66; San Francisco Redevelop Agency, San Francisco, Calif, admin asst to proj dir, 1966-67, asst bus relocation supvr, 1967-68, salvage sect coordr, 1967-68, community servs supvr, 1968; Fresno Redevelop Agency, Fresno, Calif, proj Mgr gen neighborhood renewal area, 1968-70, asst dir, 1970-77; City Fresno, asst dir Housing & Community Develop Dept, 1977-82, asst dir develop dept, 1982-88, Housing & Community Develop Dept, dir, 1988-91; Econ Develop Agency, City San Bernardino, dep dir, 1991-94; City Lancaster, redevelop dir & housing authority dir, 1995-2002. **Orgs:** Nat Asn Advan Colored People, 1968-; Nat Asn Housing & Redevelop Offs, 1975-; pres, Black Lawyers Asn Fresno, 1986-89; pres, Boys Club, W Fresno Chap, 1979-81. **Home Addr:** 1668 S Helm Ave, Fresno, CA 93727-5111, **Home Phone:** (209)251-9366.

### PARKER, DR. STEPHEN A.

Educator, consultant. **Personal:** Born Jan 1, 1945, Chicago, IL; son of Ilena; married Diana Louise; children: Stephen A II & Daniel Edmond. **Educ:** Chicago Teacher Col, BEd, 1965; Chicago State Col, MS, coun psychol, 1970; N Western Univ Evanston, PhD, clin & educ psychol, 1974; Ill State Brd Cert Coun; Nat Bd cert; Clin Cert Forensic Coun, Am Col Cert Coun, 2000. **Career:** Educator, consultant (retired); Chicago Bd Educ, teacher, 1965-70, recreational instr, 1966-70; Chicago State Univ, instr psychol, 1970-74, asst to dir financial aid, 1970-74, from asst to prof psychol, 1978-2003, dean admis & rec, 1983-86; consult. **Orgs:** Affil Henry Horner Chicago Boys Club, 1957-; Am Psychol Asn, 1974-; Phi Delta Kappa, 1975-; Nat Res Coun, Ford Found; panel mem, doctoral fel 1987; Int Coun Educ Teachers, 1987-; Ill Coun Asn. **Honors/Awds:** Black Studs Psychol Asn, 1975; Chicago Urban League Achievement Award, 1976; Spec Teaching Recognition Award, Chicago State Univ, 1977; Natl Asn Bahamian Cosmetologists, 1979; Appreciation Award, Bus Educ Stud Asn CSU, 1982; Distinguished Alumni Award Crane HS Hall of Fame, 1985; Special Guest Speaker Award, 1986; Distinguished Service Award, Henry Horner Boys & Girls Club, 1987; Distinguished West Sider Award, West side Org, 1988; Appreciation Award, Crane High Sch, 1990; Volunteer Award, Tougaloo Alumni Asn, Chicago Chapter, 1990; Alumni of the Year, Boys & Girls Clubs Am, 1991; Faculty Excellence Award, Chicago State Univ, 1992; Certificate of Apppreciation, Black Stud Psychol Asn, 1996; Recognition Award, Natl Coun Negro Women, 1997; Special Award, Sunshine Chapter 116, OES-PHA, 2000. **Home Addr:** 9729 S Bell Ave, Chicago, IL 60643-1641, **Home Phone:** (773)768-0273.

### PARKER, THOMAS EDWIN, III

Executive, government official. **Personal:** Born Dec 11, 1944. **Educ:** Howard Univ, BA, 1967; Princeton Univ, MPA, 1971; Woodrow Wilson Sch Pub & Int Affairs. **Career:** Wash Concentrated Employ Prog, prog coordr, 1967-69; City Coun DC, legis asst, 1971-74; Am Soc Pub Admin Wash, dir prog, 1974-76; Stand Oil Co, prog coordr, pub affairs rep, govt affairs, 1985; Amoco pub & Govt Affairs, pub affairs adv. **Orgs:** Nat Asn Advan Colored People; Int City Mgt Asn; Urban League; Opportunities Industrialization Ctr, NJ; admin prog develop consult, Ghana W Africa. **Honors/Awds:** Woodrow Wilson Fel; Pub Affairs Internship; Outstanding Young Men of America, 1972. **Business Addr:** Executive, Amoco Public & Government Affairs, 6 Executive Pk Dr NE, Atlanta, GA 30329.

### PARKER, VAUGHN ANTOINE

Football player. **Personal:** Born Jun 5, 1971, Buffalo, NY. **Educ:** Univ Calif, BA, sociol. **Career:** Football player (retired); San Diego Chargers, 1994, right tackle & tackle, 1995, 1998-2003, left tackle, 1996-97; Wash Redskins, offensive tackle, 2004.

### PARKER, VERNON B.

Lawyer, consultant. **Personal:** Born Nov 16, 1959, Houston, TX; son of Lillie Mae; married Lisa Farringer; children: Sonya Zepeda & Ian Bernard. **Educ:** Bilingual & Cult Inst, Cuernavaca, Mex, 1980; Calif State Univ, Long Beach, BS, finance, 1983; Georgetown Univ, JD, 1988. **Career:** Rockwell Int, financial analyst, 1983-85; US Off Personnel Mgt, counr dir policy, 1989-91, gen coun, 1992, dir; White House, spec asst pres, 1992-93; Kenny Rogers Roasters Chicago, vpres, 1993-94; Multinational Legal Serv, partner, 1994-; Parian Int, pres & chief exec officer; Parker, Farringer, Parker, atty, currently; Belsante Int LLC, pres & chief exec officer; Calvary Church, interim sr pastor; USDA, asst secy civil rights, 2003; Republican Party, mem; Paradise Valley, Ariz, mayor, 2008-10, pastor, councilman, currently; VBP Group LLC, pres & chief exec officer, currently. **Orgs:** Nat Bar Asn, 1991-; DC Bar, 1989-; Va Bar Asn, 1995; Stud Bar Asn; vpres, Georgetown Univ Law Ctr, 1986-87. **Honors/Awds:** Foreign Language Scholar recipient, 1980; Outstanding Leader, Georgetown Univ Law Ctr, 1988, Outstanding Tutor, 1988. **Special Achievements:** Editor-in-chief, Georgetown American Criminal Law Review; Author, "Annual Survey of White-Collar Crime Attorney Client Privilege", American Criminal Law Review, Winter 1986-87; Selected by President to represent US at swearing in of President of Ghana, 1993; First ever Assistant Secretary for Civil Rights at the United States Department of Agriculture; First African-American Mayor of Paradise Valley. **Home Addr:** , AZ. **Business Addr:** President, Chief Executive Officer, VBP Group LLC, 6619 N Scottsdale Rd Suite D, Scottsdale, AZ 85250-4421, **Business Phone:** (602)418-2350.

### PARKER, DR. WALTER GEE, JR.

Physician. **Personal:** Born Feb 11, 1933, Branchville, VA; son of Roosevelt and Theresa; married Henri Mae Smith; children: Jennifer L, Walter G Jr & Brian K. **Educ:** Hampton Inst, BS, 1955; Meharry Med Col, MD, 1962; Univ Mich, MPH, 1967. **Career:** Physician (retired), executive; G W Hubbard Hosp-Meharry Col, resident pediat; Univ Mich, Ann Arbor, Mich, instr pediat, 1966-69; Univ Mich, Sch Pub Health, res assoc, 1967-69; Wayne County Health Dept, pub health physician, 1969-75; Univ Mich, Ann Arbor, Mich, clin instr pediat, 1969-; Southwest Detroit Hosp, vpres med affairs, 1975-86; Wayne Correctional Facil, State Mich Dept Corrections, med dir, 1986-2000; Meharry Med Group, fiscal officer, currently. **Orgs:** Am Pub Health Asn, 1967-; Am Acad Pediat, 1973-; Detroit Med Soc, 1975-; Wayne Co Med Soc, 1975-. **Honors/Awds:** Delta Omega Pub Health Hon Soc, 1967-; Bd Certified Am Bd Pediat, 1971. **Special Achievements:** Article "Michigan Rheumatic Fever Study", in Michigan Med, 1969. **Home Addr:** 3626 Deerfield Pl, Ann Arbor, MI 48103-1711, **Home Phone:** (734)761-5758. **Business Addr:** Fiscal Officer, Meharry Medical Group, 1005 Dr DB Todd Jr Blvd, Nashville, TN 37208, **Business Phone:** (615)327-3176.

### PARKER, WILL ANTHONY. See PARKER, ANTHONY.

### PARKER, WILLIAM HAYES, JR. (BILL PARKER)

Movie director. **Personal:** Born May 2, 1947, Mt. Vernon, NY; married Yvonne Kelly; children: Eric Hayes, Steven Lee & Stella Cailan. **Educ:** Univ Cincinnati, attended 19666; Macomb Co Col, attended 1969; Los Angeles City Col, attended 1975. **Career:** EUE Screen Gems, prod mgr, 1977-78; New Genesis Prods, producer, 1978-79; BAV Inc, producer & ld, 1980-82; BPP, dir & producer, 1982; Renge Films Inc, dir & producer, currently. **Orgs:** C's Fund Defense. **Home Addr:** 1212 Lucerne Dr, Los Angeles, CA 90016-1609. **Business Addr:** Director, Producer, Renge Films Inc, 8400 DeLongpre Ave Suite 212 W, Los Angeles, CA 90069, **Business Phone:** (213)656-5941.

### PARKER JONES, APRIL (APRIL D PARKER)

Actor. **Personal:** Born Durham, NC; married Joseph J, Jun 30, 2007; children: Miana Marsh. **Educ:** NC Cent Univ, theater, attended. **Career:** Actress, stage theater, various productions at the Billie Holiday Theatre (New York City), Los Angeles productions of "A New Beginning" and "A Yankee Trader"; TV series "Jericho", 2006-08, "The Young and the Restless", 2007-08, "The Unit", 2008, "90210", 2009-10, "The Fosters", 2013-14, "If Loving You is Wrong", 2014-; theatrical release "Spider-Man 3", 2007, "Return to Zero", 2014; short film "Sleeping", 2008; TV movie "Have a Little Faith", 2011, "Heaven", 2012. **Honors/Awds:** Audelco Award Theatre, Best Actress, Nominee for "Plenty of Time".

### PARKER-ROBINSON, D. LAVERNE

Educator, executive. **Personal:** Born Jan 14, 1949, New York, NY; daughter of Tommie B (deceased) and Emma Smith; married Guy; children: Robinson Jr. **Educ:** Bernard M Baruch Col, City Univ NY, BA, 1974; Fordham Univ, MSW, social work admin, 1978; Univ Pa, cert fundamentals finanace & acct, acct & finance, 1979. **Career:** Harlem Dowling C's Servs, caseworker, 1974-77; Greater New York Fund Tri-State United Way, tech asst internal, 1977-78; Abraham & Straus Dept Stores, coordr pub affairs, 1978-79, asst mgr, comput operator, 1979-81, internal consult, spec proj mgrs, 1981-82, data processing financial controller, 1982-85; Strategic Intelligence Inc, vpres, chief financial officer, prod res, 1985-96; Mind-Builders Family Serv Ctr, dir family rehabilition prog, 1996-99; Robinson & Co Financial Serv, financial acct mgr, 1996-2000; Bor Manhattan Community Col, City Univ New York, adj prof, 2001-; New York Admin C's Servs, Agency Child Develop, dir social servs & info referral, 2000-02, cheif staff, 2002-05, exec dir, family support & parent serv, 2003-14, dir family support & client serv, 2005-09, qual assurance spec proj manger, 2014-. **Orgs:** Dinner Comt, Randolph Evans Scholar Awards, 1979-; bd mem, Strategic Intelligence Inc, 1985-; Mgt Assist Comt Greater New York Fund United Way, 1985-87; sch vol, New York Sch Vol Prog, 1986-87; pres, Brooklyn Mgt Club, 1986-87; bd mem, New York Ubran League, Manhattan Br, 1991-94; bd dir, Citizens Comt C New York, 2004-05; Nat Asn Social Workers. **Honors/Awds:** Distinguish Service Award, Salvation Army Brownsville Corps, 1979. **Home Addr:** 40 W 135th St Suite 12B, New York, NY 10037, **Home Phone:** (212)491-9140. **Business Addr:** Board of Director, Citizens Committee for Children of New York Inc, 105 E 22 St, New York, NY 10010, **Business Phone:** (212)673-1800.

## PARKER-SAWYERS, PAULA
Government official, administrator. **Personal:** Born Indianapolis, IN; daughter of Thomas and Dorthea Shelton; married James; children: Elizabeth, Parker & Patrick. **Educ:** Ball State Univ, Muncie, IN, attended 1971; George Washington Univ, Wash, DC, attended 1972; Purdue Univ, Indianapolis, IN, BA, polit sci, 1980. **Career:** LS Ayres & Co, Indianapolis, Ind, 1974-78; AT&T, Ind Bell, Indianapolis, Ind, 1978-85; Browning Investments, Indianapolis, Ind, 1985-86; Blue Cross/Blue Shield, 1986-89; City Indianapolis, Indianapolis, Ind, dep mayor, 1989-91; Ind Univ-Purdue Univ Indianapolis, assoc dir, 2001; Gov's Off Faith Based & Community Initiatives, exec dir, 2005-08; Nat Campaign to Prevent Teen & Unplanned Pregnancy, Wash, DC, dir outreach & partnerships, sr dir outreach & partnerships, currently. **Orgs:** Indianapolis Mus Art; Coalition 100 Black Women; Nat Coun Negro Women; sr dir, Indianapolis Campaign Healthy Babies; bd dir, Boys & Girls Clubs Indianapolis; bd dir, Christian Theol Sem; bd dir, Pacer's Found. **Home Addr:** 5211 Lancelot Dr, Indianapolis, IN 46208, **Home Phone:** (317)291-3210. **Business Addr:** Senior Director of Outreach & Partnerships, National Campaign to Prevent Teen & Unplanned Pregnancy, 1776 Mass Ave NW Suite 200, Washington, DC 20036, **Business Phone:** (202)478-8500.

## PARKINSON, NIGEL MORGAN, SR.
Executive, contractor. **Personal:** Born Aug 26, 1953, Freetown; children: Nigel Jr & Malcolm. **Educ:** Fla Agr & Mech Univ, BS, polit sci, 1974; Fla State Univ, MSPA, 1975; Leadership Wash, 1992; Mass Inst Technol, Ctr Real Estate, 1993; Harvard Bus Sch, attended 2005. **Career:** Davis Found, jr exec, 1975-78; Mgt Support Serv, 1978-83; Parkinson Construct co inc, Brentwood, Md, chief exec officer & pres, 1983-. **Orgs:** Bd mem & treas, DC Contractors Asn, 1988-93; treas, 1992-94, pres, 1994-; Nat Asn Minority Contractors; adv bd, US Gen Serv Adminr, 1991; US Chamber Com; Masonry Inst. **Home Addr:** 4437 Klingle St NW, Washington, DC 20016. **Business Addr:** President, Chief Executive Officer, Parkinson Construction Co Inc, 3905 Perry St, Brentwood, MD 20722, **Business Phone:** (301)985-6080.

## PARKS, DR. ARNOLD GRANT
School administrator. **Personal:** Born Nov 19, 1939, St. Louis, MO; son of Noble Grant and Estella Victoria Smith; married Lennette Bogee; children: LaShawn M Hampton, Anna L Holt & Alicia V. **Educ:** Harris Teachers Col, AA, 1959; Wash Univ, BS, 1962; St Louis Univ, MA, 1964, PhD, 1970. **Career:** St Louis Univ, instr, 1964-66; Delta Educ Corp, dep dir, 1966-69; Malone & Hyde Inc, training dir, 1969-71; Memphis State Univ, assoc prof, 1971-76; NSF, fac fel, 1976-79; Ethel Percy Andrus Geront Ctr, fel, 1979; Lincoln Univ, prof sociol, prof emer sociol; Parks Consult LLC, pres, currently, consult, currently. Books: Urban Education: An Annotated Bibliography, auth, 1981; Black Elderly in Rural America: A Comprehensive Study, auth, 1988. **Orgs:** Life mem Alpha Phi Alpha; United Methodist Church; Mo E Conf Congregational Develop Team; Am Diabetes Asn; bd trustee, Mo River Regional Libr; bd dir, treas, Mo Sch Relig & Ctr Rural Ministry; bd govs, Capital Region Med Ctr; deleg, Nat White House Conf Aging, 1995; St. Paul UMC; fel SW Soc Aging, 2002. **Home Addr:** 1817 Chelle Ct, Jefferson City, MO 65101, **Home Phone:** (573)635-0725. **Business Addr:** President, Consultant & Owner, Parks Consulting LLC, 1817 Chelle Ct, Jefferson City, MO 65101, **Business Phone:** (573)635-0725.

## PARKS, BERNARD, JR.
Lawyer, association executive. **Personal:** Born Jun 10, 1944, Atlanta, GA; married Joyce Williams; children: Bernard Jr. **Educ:** Morehouse Col, BA, 1966; Emory Univ, Sch Law, JD, 1969. **Career:** Jackson Patterson Parks & Franklin, ptr, 1970-73; Jackson & Handler Assoc, 1970; Patterson Parks Jackson & Howell, ptr, 1973-; Jud Elbert Parr Tuttle United Cir Ct Appeals, law clerk, 1969-70; Atlanta Legal Aid Soc Inc, law asst, 1968-69; Sen Horace Ward Atlanta, leg intern, 1968; Aldmn QV Williamson Atlanta City, gov intern, 1967; Ga Supreme Ct; Ga Ct Appeals; US Dist Ct; US Ct Appeals; US Supreme Ct. **Orgs:** Co-chmn, Men Health Comn Young Law Sect; Am Bar Asn; Atlanta Bar Asn; bd dir, Atlanta County Young Law; co-chmn, Ment Health Comn, Ga Bar Asn; vpres, Ga Legal Serv Prog Inc; Gate County Bar Asn; Nat Bar Asn; Law Com Civ Rights under Law; chmn, bd dir, Opp Ind Cent Atlanta; bd dir, Opp Ind Cent Am; chmn, bd mgr, E Cent Br Butler St Young Men's Christian Asn, bd dir; Gov Ment Health Community Task Force; Met Atlana County Crime & Juv Del; chmn Pri Alloc Com Uni Way Allo Com Comm Sec; Local Govt Task Force Com Atla C C; Atlanta Crim Just Coord Com; bd dir, Big Bros Asn; Atla Bus League; Atla Urban League; Nat Asn Advan Colored People; Am Civ Lib Un; SE Region Bd Young Men's Christian Asn; Atlanta Coal Curr Comm Aff; Omega Psi Phi Fraternity; Phi Alpha Delta Fraternity; Y Men Int. **Honors/Awds:** Outstanding Young Man of the Year, Omega Chap; Mr Psi of 1967, Omega Psi Phi Fraternity, Psi Chap, Morehouse Col; WSB Nesmaker Award, 1972; five Outstanding Young Men In 1974. **Home Addr:** 4640 Heatherwood Dr SW, Atlanta, GA 30331, **Home Phone:** (404)344-7104. **Business Addr:** 101 Marietta Towers, Atlanta, GA 30303.

## PARKS, BERNARD C.
Police chief, city council member. **Personal:** Born Dec 7, 1943, Beaumont, TX; married Bobbie; children: Felicia, Michelle, Trudy & Bernard Jr. **Educ:** Los Angeles City Col, Pepperdine Univ, BS, 1976; Univ Southern Calif, MA, pub admin, 1976; Loyola Univ, Interpersonal & Interracial Relationships, attended 1974; Fed Bur Invest Nat Acad, attended 1976; Univ Southern Calif, Mgt Policy Inst, cert grad, 1983; Peace Officers Stands & Training Exec Develop Course, cert grad, 1984; Nat Exec Inst, Fed Bur Invest, cert grad, 1993; New York Police Dept, Comp Stat Conf, cert completion, 1997. **Career:** Los Angeles Police Dept, from police officer to sgt, 1965-70, lt, 1973, capt, 1977, comdr, 1980, dep chief, 1988, asst chief, 1992, dep chief, 1994, chief police, 1997-2002; Bur Spec Invest, dep chief & comndg officer; Calif State Bar Asn, Judicial Eval Comn, Former Comnr; Los Angeles City Coun, 8th Dist, councilman, chmn budget & finance comt, vpres coliseum comn, 2003-. **Orgs:** Int Asn Chiefs Police; Nat Asn Black Law Enforcement Exec; Peace Officers Asn Los Angeles County; Fed Bur Invest Nat Acad Asn; founding mem, Oscar Joel Bryant Asn; pres, Drug Abuse Resistance Educ; bd mem, Challenger Boys & Girls Club; Police Exec Res Forum; Metrop Transp Bd Comnrs, 2005; life time mem, Nat Asn Advan Colored People; Los Angeles Urban League; Brotherhood Crusade. **Business Addr:** Councilman, City of Los Angeles Council District 8, 200 N Spring St Rm 460, Los Angeles, CA 90012, **Business Phone:** (213)473-7008.

## PARKS, DR. DONALD B.
Physician. **Personal:** Born Nov 2, 1950, Philadelphia, PA; son of Dewitt and Bertha; married Sharon; children: Laurie, Donald Drew & Sharon-Candace. **Educ:** Temple Univ, BS, 1968; Jefferson Med Col, Thomas Jefferson Univ, attended 1973. **Career:** Mercy Cath Med Ctr, Pa, resident, 1978. Smith Kline & Fr, group dir clin invest, 1981-85; Pk stone Med Asn, physician, med dir, 1985-; Temple Univ, assoc prof, prof, community med, currently, asst dean, currently, med dir, currently; SmithKline & Fr Labs, med dir. **Orgs:** Dept Health Educ & Welfare, consult, 1979-82; Health Policy & Manpower Comn, consult, 1980; Philadelphia Police & Fire Dept, consult, 1983; Exec Excellence Prog & Nat Urban League, bd mem, 1989-92; Am Found Negro Affairs, bd mem, 1988-; chmn, Develop Comn & Morehouse Sch Med, 1990-; PA Blue Shield, bd mem, 1994-97; Temple Univ Hosp Bd Gov. **Honors/Awds:** President James F Carter, Education & Community Involvement, 1980; Alpha Beta Alpha Sorority, Commun Involvement and Services to the Afro-American Historical & Cultural Museum, 1980; Practitioner of the Year, Philadelphia County Med Soc; NAACP Exemplar Award, 1997. **Business Addr:** President, Parkston Medical Associates, 2305 N Broad St, Philadelphia, PA 19132, **Business Phone:** (215)229-2022.

## PARKS, DR. EDWARD Y. A.
Lawyer. **Personal:** Born Feb 5, 1951, Thomson, GA; son of Roy L Sr; married Sequoyah; children: Akil-Dabe T & Alkebu S. **Educ:** Otterbein Col, BA, 1973; Howard Univ, JD, 1979. **Career:** Ohio Pub Interest campaign, assoc dir, 1979-81; Legal Aid Soc, atty, 1981-83; Pub Utilities Comn, atty examr, 1983-86; Ohio Dept Health, legal coun, 1986-89; Edward Y Parks Law Off, atty, pres & chief exec officer, 1989-; pvt pract lawyer, currently. **Orgs:** Nat Asn Advan Colored People, 1979-; Columbus Bar Asn, 1980-; Nat Conf Black Lawyers, 1980-; presiding officer, Asn Juv Atty, 1989-; Legal Aid Soc Lawyer Referral, 1989-; Urban League, 1991-; trustee, Shiloh Baptist Church, 1993; Nat Bar Asn, 1993-. **Honors/Awds:** Outstanding Legal Advocate, Welfare Rights, 1983; Community Service Award, Nat Asn Advan Colored People, 1985; Outstanding Service, Softball Prog, Shiloh Baptist Church, 1987-88. **Special Achievements:** Shiloh Baptist Church Plan, 1990; Book of Poems-In Progress. **Business Addr:** President, Chief Executive Officer, Edward Y Parks Law Office, 338 S High St, Columbus, OH 43215-4546, **Business Phone:** (614)255-2006.

## PARKS, DR. GILBERT R.
Psychiatrist. **Personal:** Born May 14, 1944, Arcadia, OK; married Jenice L; children: Garmez, Melanese & Ronee. **Educ:** Cent State Univ, BS, 1967; Thomas Jefferson Med Col, MD, 1973. **Career:** Topeka St Hosp, psychiatrist; Menninger Found, Topeka; Pvt Prac; Univ Okla hosp, psychiat asst, 1965-67; HEW, psychiat complete, 1976. **Orgs:** Rancher, 1960-69; Okla State Dept Pub Health, Environ Health Div Water Qual Control, 1967-69; dir, Health Career Progs, Philadelphia, 1970-72; chmn bd, Stud Nat Med Asn, 1972-73; admin consult & adv, Stud Nat Med Asn; Kans Dist Br, Am Psychiat Asn; consult, Health Resources Opp, Health Resources Admin Dept HEW; secy, Nat Asn Post Grad Physicians; bd dirs, Boys Club Topeka; Solomon Fuller fel 1975; chmn emer, Nat Med Asn. **Honors/Awds:** Outstanding Leadership Award, Nat Med Asn. **Home Addr:** 629 SE Quincy St Suite 205, PO Box 1321, Topeka, KS 66603, **Home Phone:** (785)233-1785. **Business Addr:** Chairman Emeritus, National Medical Association, 1012 10th St NW, Washington, DC 20001, **Business Phone:** (202)347-1895.

## PARKS, JAMES CLINTON, JR.
Marketing executive. **Personal:** Born May 12, 1944, Kannapolis, NC; married Corine Musgrave; children: Crystal Westray, James III & Shawnda M. **Educ:** Livingstone Col, BS, 1965. **Career:** EI Du Pont, employ supvr, 1965-77; Miller Brewing Co, mgr spec mkt prog, 1977-. **Orgs:** Mem Phi Beta Sigma, 1963-; bd dir, Milwaukee Min Chamber Com, 1983-86, Waukesha County WI Nat Asn Advan Colored People, 1984-86; Frontiers Int, 1987-; bd mem, Fayetteville State Univ Found; bd mem, Cal-Pac Corp Adv Bd. **Honors/Awds:** Order of Long Leaf Pine St NC, 1984; Distinguished Alumnus, Livingstone Col, l989. **Home Addr:** 225 Roger Dr, Salisbury, NC 28147, **Home Phone:** (202)863-2690. **Business Addr:** Manager-Special Marketing Programs, Miller Brewing Co, 3939 W Highland Blvd, Milwaukee, WI 53208, **Business Phone:** (414)931-2000.

## PARKS, JAMES EDWARD
Lawyer. **Personal:** Born Mar 22, 1946, Pine Bluff, AR; son of James and Cora; married Gwendolyn Jean Fane; children: James Jr, Latina & Lisa. **Educ:** Calif State Univ, BS, 1972; Harvard Law Sch, JD, 1975. **Career:** Dawson & Ninnis, atty, 1977-82; San Fernando Val Neighborhood Legal Serv Van Nuys CA, atty, 1975-77; Parks & Smith, 1982-89; pvt pract, atty, 1989-. **Orgs:** Fresno Co Bar Asn; Calif State Bar & Asn, 1976-; Asn Defense Coun; bd dir, Fresno Co Legal Servs Legan Adv, Black Polit Coun, Fresno, 1980; Fresno City Bar Asn; Fresno Trial Lawyer's Asn; United Black Men; Black Lawyers Asn Fresno; Nat Advan Asn Colroed People; bd mem, Fresno Tomorrow. **Home Addr:** 2166 E Omaha Ave, Fresno, CA 93720-0413, **Home Phone:** (559)299-4475. **Business Addr:** Attorney, 7750 N Fresno St Suite 101, Fresno, CA 93720, **Business Phone:** (559)436-6575.

## PARKS, KAREN ELAINE WEBSTER
Government official. **Personal:** Born Jan 6, 1960, Atlanta, GA; daughter of Donald and Isabell Gates. **Educ:** Univ Va, BA, hist, 1982; Ga State Univ, MA, pub admin, 1991. **Career:** Intern Us Mass Transp Authority, 1978; Us Dept Housing & Urban Develop, 1979; Atlanta City Coun, 1980-81; Admin intern Us Sen Mack Mattingly, 1982; Nat Republican Sen Comt, admin & res intern, 1982; Grocery Manufacturers Am, state legis aide, 1983; Fulton County Govt, law clerk, judge, 1984, law clerk, solicitor gen, 1984-98, partner retail sales consigment, 1984-97, dir, victim & witness prog, 1988-91, exec asst county mgr, 1991-92, exec dir, inter govt affairs, 1992-94, chief staff & chmn, 1994-95; Beers Construct Co, vpres, 1995-; Fulton County Dist 2, comnr, 1999-2001; Beers Skanska Inc, sr vpres, 1999-2002; Atlanta Downtown Improv Dist Bd, 2002-; Atlanta Bus Chronicle, highlights new exec dir; Fulton County Bd Commissioners, vchair; Atlanta Womens Found; Alt Life Paths Prog Inc, chief exec officer; Literacy Action Inc, pres & chief exec officer. **Orgs:** Bd mem, Regional Leadership Inst; chair, nominating comt, Young Women's Christian Asn, Greater Atlanta; southern area secy, Links Inc, 1993-; vpres, selection comt, Outstanding Atlantans, 1994; dist adv, Atlanta Jr League, 1994-; bd dir, Regional Leadership found, 1994; bd mem, Southern Inst, 1994-; Piedmont Pk Conservancy, 1994-97; adv bd mem, Alt Life Paths Prog Inc; bd mem, Polit Inst Women; bd mem, Literacy Action Inc; co-chair, Camp Best Friends, 1995, 1996 & 1998, chair, 1997; Atlanta C's Shelter, 1995-96; United Negro Col Fund, 1995-96; co-chair, Ga Conservancy Eco Benefits; Young Men's Christian Asn, 1996-97, pres, 1997; Fulton County Bd Commissioners, 1999-; United Way; Girl Scouts Us Am; bd mem, Hands Atlanta; mem league, Women Voters; Ga Chamber Com. **Home Addr:** 371 Fielding Lane SW, Atlanta, GA 30311, **Home Phone:** (404)691-7219. **Business Addr:** Board Director, Atlanta Downtown Improvement District Inc, 50 Hurt Plz Se Lbby, Atlanta, GA 30303-2914.

## PARKS, KENNETH D.
Executive. **Personal:** married Cynthia. **Educ:** Ga State Univ. **Career:** United Parcel Serv, vpres hr, proj mgr, hr mgr, currently; Jones World Design, cheif exec offcier & pres. **Orgs:** Bd mem, ACT-SO; BC Chamber Com; chmn, Black Exec Exchange Prog, Nat Urban League. **Business Addr:** Human Resources Manager, United Parcel Service, 55 Glenlake Pkwy NE, Atlanta, GA 30328-3474, **Business Phone:** (404)828-6000.

## PARKS, SONIA A.
Executive director. **Career:** Urban health Initiative, fel, 1999-2002; Blue Cross Blue Shield Mich, assoc med dir, Provider Rels Admin, sr assoc med dir.

## PARKS, SUZAN-LORI
Playwright, educator. **Personal:** Born Jan 1, 1964, Ft. Knox, KY; married Paul Oscher. **Educ:** Mt Holyoke Col, BA, eng & ger lit (Phi Beta Kappa), 1985, MA. **Career:** Playwright & educator; Drama studio, London, mem, 1986; Pratt Inst, NY, guest lectr, 1988; Univ Mich, Ann Arbor, guest lectr, 1990; Yale Univ, New Haven, Conn, guest lectr, 1990-91; NY Univ, guest lectr, 1990-91; Eugene Lang Col, NY, playwriting prof, 1990; New Sch Social Res, NY, writer-in-residence, 1991-92; Guggenheim fel, 2000; Calif Inst Arts, Valencia, dir, 2000; Yale Sch Drama, New Haven, assoc artist; Wilma Theater, Philadelphia, Pa, playwriting residency; Plays: The Sinner's Place, 1984; Imperceptible Mutabilities in the Third Kingdom, 1989; Betting on the Dust Commander, 1990; The Death of the Last Black Man in the Whole Entire World, 1990; Pickling, 1990; Third Kingdom, 1990; Locomotive, 1991; Girl 6, 1996; Devotees in the Garden of Love, 1992; TheAmerica Play, 1994; Venus, 1996; In The Blood, 1999; Fucking A, 2000; Topdog/Underdog, 2001; Their Eyes Were Watching God, 2005; 365 Days/365Plays, 2006; RAY CHARLES LIVE!-A New Musical, 2007; The Great Debaters, 2007; Father Comes Home from the Wars, 2009. **Business Addr:** Playwright, Steven Barclay Agency, 12 Wern Ave, Petaluma, CA 94952, **Business Phone:** (707)773-0654.

## PARKS, THELMA REECE
Government official, educator, association executive. **Personal:** Born Muskogee, OK; daughter of Thomas and Estella Reece; children: Dia Denise Parks Carter. **Educ:** Langston Univ, BS, elem educ, 1945; Univ Okla, MS, emphasis Guid, 1955; Cent State Univ, prof cert guid & coun, 1963. **Career:** Educator (retired); Bd mem; Dunbar & Truman Elem Schs, teacher, 1951-61; Douglass High Sch, eng teacher & dept head, 1961-70, counsr, 1970-71; US Grant High Sch, counsr & dept head, 1973; Okla City Housing Authority, comnr, 1977-84; Okla City Bd Educ, pres; Okla City Pub Schs, teacher; Okla City Pub Schs Bd Educ, bd mem, currently. **Orgs:** OEA COA; McFarland Br, YWCA, 1973-; adv, Capitol Improv Plan, Okla City, 1975-; Pres, Okla City Guid Asn, 1976-77; life mem, Nat Educ Asn; Adv Com Black Family; NE YMCA; life mem, Alpha Kappa Alpha Sorority; Nat Asn Advan Colored People; Urban League; bd dir, Urban League Guild; Womens Day speaker, Tabernacle Baptist Church, 1992, Wildwood Christian Ch, 1978; chmn, Blue Ribbon Comn Fund Raising, 1982-86; bd dir, YWCA, 1983-86; secy, Okla City Langston Alumni, 1986-88; panelist, Okla State Dept Ed Conf Educ, 1987; bd mem, Langston Univ Alumni Assoc, 1987-90; task force comn, OEA improving schs Okla, 1987-; Nat Sorority Phi Delta Kappa; Okla Sch Bd Asn, bd dir, 1992; bd dir, Black Caucus, 1992; panelist, Urban League Equal Opportunity Day, 1991; Okla City Educ Round Table, 1991-; pres, Nat Sorority Phi Delta Kappa, gamma Epsilon Chap, Ok, 1997; bd dir, Black Caucus, Nat Sch Bds Asn; life mem, Urban League; Nu Arts Asn; bd dir, Okla State Sch Boards Asn; bd dir, League Women Voters; chmn, Langston Univ Alumni Asn. **Honors/Awds:** Okla Achiever's Award, 1989; Soror of the Year, Alpha Kappa Alpha Sorority, 1990; Soror of the Year, Phi Delta Kappa, 1990; Volunteer of the Year Award, Urban League of Okla City, 1990; Distinguished Alumni, Langston Univ, 1990; Men of

Distinction, Outstanding Citizen, 1991; Nat Black Col Alumni, Hall of Fame, inductee, Atlanta, GA, 1991; Lady of Distinction, Nu Vista Club, 1991; Okla Black Pub Adminr Award, 1992; Top Ladies of Distinction, Outstanding Achievement Award, 1997; Oklahoma City NAACP Life Time Achievement Award. **Special Achievements:** First African-Am female mem, Kappa Delta Pi, Gamma Chap, Univ Okla, 1955; First African-Am female trustee, Faith Mem Bapt Ch, 1975; Elementary Sch named in her honor, Okla City, 1997; Langston University Distinguished Alumnus Award; Whos Who Among Black Americans; Whos Who Among Women in the World; Whos in America and Urban League Volunteer of the Year Award; Outstanding Public Service Award; First African American Counselor at US Grant School. **Home Addr:** 2804 NE 18, Oklahoma City, OK 73111-1938, **Home Phone:** (405)427-2053. **Business Addr:** Board Member, Oklahoma City Public Schools, 900 N Klein St, Oklahoma City, OK 73119, **Business Phone:** (405)587-0444.

## PARMALEE, BERNARD A.

Football coach, football player. **Personal:** Born Sep 16, 1967, Jersey City, NJ; married Angela; children: Nakia Marie, Torian & Tre Bernard. **Educ:** Ball State Univ, bus admin, 1991. **Career:** Football player (retired), football coach; Ball State Univ, running back, 1987-90; Miami Dolphins, running back, 1992-98, asst spec teams coach, 2002, asst spec teams coach & offensive asst coach, 2003, tight end coach, 2004; New York Jets, running back, 1999-2000; Univ Notre Dame, tight ends coach & spec teams coach, 2005-09; Kans City Chiefs, tight end coach, 2010-12; Oakland Raiders, running backs coach, 2015-. **Honors/Awds:** Freshman of the Year, Mid-Am Conf. **Business Addr:** Running Backs Coach, Oakland Raiders, 1220 Harbor Bay Pkwy, Alameda, CA 94502, **Business Phone:** (510)864-5000.

## PARMS, EDWIN L.

Lawyer, teacher. **Personal:** Born Jun 18, 1937; son of Johnson and Ophelia; married Margaret; children: Stephanie & Deborah. **Educ:** Univ Akron, BA, 1960, JD, 1965. **Career:** Parms, Purnell & Gilbert, atty, 1965; Akron Pub Schs, teacher, 1960-65; St Univ Akron, co-coun; Edwin L Parms Law Firm, owner; pvt prac atty, currently. **Orgs:** Pres, Nat Asn Advan Colored People, Akron. **Special Achievements:** First African American Chosen Young Man of Year, Akron Jr C. **Home Addr:** 209 S Main St Lowr, Akron, OH 44308-1307, **Home Phone:** (330)376-6136. **Business Addr:** Owner, Edwin L Parms Law Firm, 209 S Main St, Akron, OH 44308-1307, **Business Phone:** (330)376-6136.

## PARNELL, ARNOLD W.

Executive, president (organization). **Personal:** Born Jan 21, 1936, Philadelphia, PA; son of Jesie and Eva; married Thelma A; children: Steven, Paula & Michael. **Educ:** Villanova Univ, BSCE, 1957; Univ Southern Calif, MSCE, 1962; Univ Calif, Los Angeles. **Career:** N Am Aviation, sr res engr, 1957-62; Nellson Candies, owner & founder, 1962-68; TRW Syst Group, div staff mgr, 1962-82, dir indust res ctr, 1982-86; P&L Mgt Syst, dir, 1972-; ELI Mgt Corp, gen mgr, 1986; ADP & Assoc, pres; Forte Comput Easy Inc, dir, currently; 1st Source Commun Inc, pres, currently. **Orgs:** Am Inst Aeronaut & Astronaut, 1967-; fel Am Inst Aeronaut & Astronaut, 1970; Prof Lic Mech Engineering; Small Bus Develop Adv Bd. **Business Addr:** President, 1st Source Communications Inc, 2506 13th Ave, Los Angeles, CA 90018-1717.

## PARNELL, JOHN V., III

Executive, president (organization), manager. **Personal:** Born Oct 4, 1944, Boston, MA; married Patricia Meehan; children: Elizabeth, Monica & Andrea. **Educ:** Univ Mass, BS, 1966. **Career:** Gen Foods Corp, sr food tech, inventor, 1966-72, mgr lab & sr mgr lab, 1974-90; Latouraine Bickfords, mgr new prod develop, 1972; Miralin Co, mgr, prod develop, 1972-74; Kraft Gen Foods, group dir, 1990-95; Kraft Foods, group dir, 1995-99, res & develop, consult; Bates Group LLC, inventor. **Orgs:** Pres, AEPI Frat, 1965; vpres, Class 66; Inst Food Technologist; bd dir, 1970-80, pres, 1975-77, vpres, 1973-75, Univ Mass Alumni Asn; Univ Mass Found Inc, 1977-80; mem, Sportsmens Club Greater Boston. **Home Addr:** 5 Libra Lane, Mashpee, MA 02649. **Business Addr:** 5 Libra Lane, Mashpee, MA 02649, **Business Phone:** (508)477-7120.

## PARRIS, REV. ALVIN, III

Clergy. **Personal:** Born Sep 23, 1951, Washington, DC; son of Alvin Jr and L Edith Simmons; married Debra Bryant; children: Benjamin James, Christopher Alvin, Jonathan Gregory & Cherise Danielle. **Educ:** Eastman Sch Music, Rochester, NY, BMusEd, 1973. **Career:** Rochester City Sch Dist, John Marshall High Sch, Rochester, NY, orchestra dir, 1973-79; Parris Community Sch Performing Arts, Rochester, NY, dir, 1975; Univ Rochester, Rochester, NY, gospel choir dir, music instr, 1976-; Golden Heights Christian Ctr, Brockport, NY, music pastor, 1987-90; Syracuse Symphony Orchestra, Syracuse, NY, dir, Proj 2000 prog, composer, conductor, 1990-; New Life Fel, Rochester, NY, assoc pastor & music minister, 1990-; Joy Community Church, Worship Pastor; Int Worship Inst. **Orgs:** Music dir, Greater-Rochester Martin Luther King Festival Comn, 1986-; Rochester Rotary Club, 1987-89; New Life Ministries Inc; founder, Rochester Inst Technol, Nazareth Col, St John Fisher Col, Gospel Choirs; dir, Inter-High Brass Quintet; dir, Inter-High Jazz Ensemble. **Honors/Awds:** Community Service Award, St Monica Sch, 1986; Artistic Achievement Award, Colgate-Rochester Divinity Sch, 1987. **Home Addr:** 182 Winbourne Rd, Rochester, NY 14619, **Home Phone:** (716)328-4621. **Business Addr:** Music Director, New Life Ministries Inc, 330 Wellington Ave, Rochester, NY 14619-1210, **Business Phone:** (585)436-0085.

## PARRIS, TEYHONAH

Actor. **Educ:** SC Gov's Sch Arts & Humanities, attended 2005. **Career:** Actress, theatrical movie "How Do You Know", 2010, "Dear White People", 2014; TV Series "Mad Men", 2014, "Survivor's Remorse", 2014-; theatrical movie, "Five Nights in Maine", 2015, "Where Children Play", 2015. **Special Achievements:** Appeared in national McDonald's commercial, 2014.

## PARRISH, ALEX L.

Lawyer, college teacher. **Personal:** Born Jan 1, 1955?. **Educ:** Howard Univ, BA, 1977; Harvard Univ Law Sch, JD, 1980. **Career:** US Ct Appeals, Sixth Circuit, law clerk, 1980-81; Honingman Miller Schwartz & Cohn LLP, Wash, DC, atty, 1981-85, Mich, partner, 1985-; Mich Inst Continuing Legal Educ, fac, 1990-. **Orgs:** Pi Sigma Alpha; chmn, bd trustee, Music Hall Ctr Performing Arts; Am Bar Asn; State Bar Mich; trustee, Henry Ford Health Syst Found; trustee, Detroit Metrop Bar Asn Found; bd dir, Detroit Inst Arts. **Business Addr:** Attorney, Partner, Honingman Miller Schwartz & Cohn LLP, 2290 First Nat Bldg 660 Woodward Ave, Detroit, MI 48226-3506, **Business Phone:** (313)465-7000.

## PARRISH, ANTHONY W. See PARRISH, TONY.

## PARRISH, JAMES NATHANIEL

Insurance executive. **Personal:** Born Feb 3, 1939, Winter Park, FL; son of Amos L and Celeste Colston; married Carolyn Portia Payne; children: Bethany C & James N Jr; married Sammie Marge Campbell. **Educ:** Fisk Univ, BA, maths, 1958; Univ Wis, MS, actuarial sci, 1960. **Career:** Western & Southern Life Ins Co, asst actuary, 1960-67; Inter-Ocean Ins Co, vip, actuary, 1967-74; Sun Life Ins Co AME, second vpres, New Bus, 1974-75; Towers, Perrin, Foster & Crosby, consult, 1975-79; Fidelity Mutual Life Ins Co, vpres, actuary, 1979-86; NC Mutual Life Ins Co, sr vpres, actuary, 1986-90; NC Mutual Life Ins Co, exe vpres, bd dir, exe commitee, 1990-2001; Laurel Bluff Assocs Inc, pres, 2001-. **Orgs:** Mem, Am Acad Actuaries, 1969-; fel Soc Actuaries, 1971-; Asn NC Life Co; Int Asn Black Actuaries; bd dirs, N Carolina Mutual Life Ins Co. 1990; N Carolina Life Guaranty Asn. **Home Addr:** 405 Cottage Lane, Durham, NC 27713, **Home Phone:** (919)544-7866. **Business Addr:** President, Laurel Bluff Associates Inc, 6620 Chapel Crossing, Williamsburg, VA 23188-7288.

## PARRISH, MAURICE DRUE

Museum director, vice president (organization). **Personal:** Born Mar 5, 1950, Chicago, IL; son of Maurice and Ione Yvonne Culumns; married Gail Marie Sims; children: Theodore, Andrew, Brandon & Cara. **Educ:** Univ Pa, Philadelphia, PA, BA, 1972; Yale Univ, New Haven, CT, MA, archit, 1975. **Career:** Museum director (retired); H I Feldman fel, 1974-75; City Chicago, city planner, 1975-81; John D Hilts cher & Assoc Architects, vpres, 1981-83; Barnett, Jones, Smith Architects, Chicago, IL, prin, 1983-84; City Chicago, zoning adminr, 1984-87, bldg comnr, 1987-89; Detroit Inst Arts, dep dir, 1989-97, interim dir, 1997-99; exec vpres, 1999-2006; Compass Group Assocs, vpres, 2007-. **Orgs:** Chmn, St Philip Neri Sch Bd, 1982-85; pres, S Shore Comn, 1983-85; Co-chmn Mayor's, Affordable Housing Task Force, 1984-89; Lambda Alpha Land Use Soc, 1985; Chicago Econ Develop Comn, 1987-89; Chmn, Chicago Elec Comn, 1988-89; bd mem, Detroit Metro Conv & Visitors Bur; bd dir, Arts League Mich, 1994-97; Am Asn Mus; Int Coun Mus; Mosaic Youth Theatre Detroit, 2000, chmn, 2002. **Honors/Awds:** Nat Achievement Scholar, Nat Merit Scholar Corp, 1968-72; Franklin W Gregory Scholar, Yale Univ, 1973-74. **Home Addr:** 3330 Sherbourne, Detroit, MI 48221, **Home Phone:** (313)861-1103.

## PARRISH, TONY (ANTHONY W PARRISH)

Football player. **Personal:** Born Nov 23, 1975, Los Angeles, CA; married Lura Lynn Ryan. **Educ:** Univ Wash, BS, psychol. **Career:** Football player (retired); Chicago Bears, free safety, 1998, strong safety, 1999-2001; San Francisco 49ers, strong safety, 2002-06, free safety, 2002, safety, 2003; Dallas Cowboys, 2006; Las Vegas Locomotives, 2009. **Orgs:** Spokesperson, Ill State Liquor Control Comn; 49ers Reading Team; Courage House; athlete ambassador, Right to Play orgn. **Honors/Awds:** Brian Piccolo Award; Ed Block Courage Award; Len Eshmont Award; All-Pro, Assoc Press, 2003; Champion, United Football League, 2009. **Special Achievements:** First 49ers player to win the Len Eshmont Award.

## PARROTT-FONSECA, JOAN

Government official. **Educ:** Howard Univ, BA, 1973; George Washington Univ, MA, educ & human resource mgt, 1974; EEP Appeal Officer Training, cert, 1980; Georgetown Univ LawSch, JD, 1981; Harvard Univ, John F Kennedy Sch Govt, MS, pub admin, 1998; Tufts Univ, Fletcher Sch Law & Diplomacy, cert, int leadership & mgt, 1998; Univ Pa, Wharton Sch Bus, cert, fundamentals money mgt, 2002. **Career:** AM Herman & Assocs, sr assoc, 1986; US Gen Servs Admin, Off Enterprise Develop, assoc adminr, 1995; Minority Bus Develop Agency, Dept Com, dir, 1995-97; Jpf & Assoc, founder & pres, 1999-2005; Harvest Capitol Investments LLC, sr vpres bus develop; Dist Columbia's, Dept Consumer & Regulatory Affairs, actg dir & dep dir; Gov's Off Minority & Women, dir bus serv; Off Econ Develop Opportunity & Compliance, NY State Dept Transp, dir; Ann Spring Meeting Moderator; City Univ New York, Medgar Evers Col, Sch Bus, dean, 2006-07, prof, 2007-09, AARP, ny dir, currently. **Orgs:** Moderator, African Am Chamber Com Westchester & Rockland Counties, 2002; trustee, Dc Retirement Bd, 2001-06. **Special Achievements:** First woman named director of Minority Business Development Agency. **Business Addr:** New York State Director, AARP, 780 Third Ave 33rd Fl, New York, NY 10017, **Business Phone:** (866)227-7442.

## PARSON, RICHARD DEAN

Executive. **Personal:** Born Apr 4, 1948, Brooklyn, NY; son of Lorenzo Locklair and Isabelle; married Laura Ann Bush; children: Gregory, Leslie & Rebecca. **Educ:** Univ Hawaii, attended 1968; Union Univ, Albany Law Sch, JD, 1971. **Career:** NY Gov Nelson Rockefeller, asst coun, 1971-74; dep coun to US vpres, 1975; White House Domestic Coun, gen coun & assoc dir, 1975-77; Patterson, Belknap, Webb & Tyler, atty, 1977-78, partner, 1979-88; Dime Savings Bank, NY, chief operating officer, 1988-90, chmn & chief exec officer, 1990-95; Anchor Savings Bank, chmn & chief exec officer; Mayor Elect Transition Coun, head, 1993; NY Econ Develop Corp, chmn; Time Warner Inc, pres, 1995-99; AOL Time Warner, co-chief operating officer, 1999-2002, chief exec officer, 2002-07, chmn & coo, 2003-08; Hist TW Inc, chmn, chief exec officer & pres; Citigroup, chmn, 2009-12. **Orgs:** Presidential Drug Task Force; chair, Wildcat Serv Orgn; bd dir, Fed Nat Mortgage Asn; bd dir, Philip Morris Co; bd dir, New York Zool Soc; bd dir, Am TV & Commun Inc; adv bd, Rockefeller Bros Fund; trustee, Howard Univ; trustee, Metrop Mus Art; bd mem, Estee Lauder, 1999-; bd mem, Citigroup, 1996; co-chmn, Mayor's Comn Econ Opportunity, NY; chmn, Apollo Theatre Found; chmn bd, Jazz Found Am; trustee, Mus Mod Art; Am Mus Natural Hist.

## PARSONS, KARYN (KARYN ROCKWELL)

Actor. **Personal:** Born Aug 10, 1966, Hollywood, CA; daughter of Kenneth B and Louise; married Alexandre Rockwell; children: Lana & Nico; married Randy Brooks. **Career:** Films: Class Act, 1992; Major Payne, 1995; Death Spa, 1998; Mixing Nia, 1998; The Ladies Man, 2000; 13 Moons, 2002; 13 Moons, 2002; TV series: "The Bronx Zoo", 1987; "Hunter", 1988; "CBS Summer Playhouse", 1988; "The Fresh Prince of Bel Air", 1990-96; "Blossom", 1992; "Out All Night", 1992; "The John Larroquette Show", 1995; "Lush Life", 1996; "Gulliver's Travels", 1996; "Melrose Place", 1999; "Linc's", 1999; "The Job", 2001; "Static Shock", 2002; Nobody Wants Your Film, 2005; "Tavis Smiley", 2006; "E! True Hollywood Story", 2007; "Sweet Blackberry Presents", producer & writer, 2008. **Home Addr:** 8921 Sunset Blvd Suite B, Los Angeles, CA 90069. **Business Addr:** Actress, NBC-TV, 3000 W Alameda Blvd, Burbank, CA 91523-0001, **Business Phone:** (818)840-4444.

## PARSONS, RICHARD DEAN

Business owner, executive, chairperson. **Personal:** Born Apr 4, 1948, Brooklyn, NY; son of Lorenzo Locklair and Isabelle; married Laura Ann Bush; children: Gregory, Leslie & Rebecca. **Educ:** Univ Hawaii, Manoa, Hawaii, attended; Albany Law Sch, JD, 1971. **Career:** New York Govt Nelson Rockefeller, coun, 1971-74; Pres Gerald Ford, sr white house aide, 1975-77; Patterson, Belknap, Webb & Tyler, managing partner, 1977-88; Dime Bancorp Inc, chief operating officer, chmn & chief exec officer, 1988-91; Time Warner, pres, 1995, chief exec officer & chmn, 2002-09; Il Palazzone (an Ital vineyard), owner, 2000-; Citigroup, chmn, 2009-12; Los Angeles Clippers, interim chief exec officer, 2014-; Pres Barack Obama's U.S. Off Pres, coun jobs & competitiveness. **Orgs:** Co-chair, Social Security Comt, 2001; Transition Team New York Mayor-elect Michael Bloomberg, 2001; co-chair, Transition Team Gov-elect Eliot Spitzer, 2006; chmn bd dir, Jazz Found Am, 2007-; bd dir, Lazard Ltd, 2012-; sr advisor, Providence Equity Partners; bd dir, Estee Lauder Co, chair, Compensation Comt, Nominating & Bd Affairs Comt; bd dir, Madison Sq Garden Co, Audit Comt; chmn, Apollo Theatre Found; chmn, New York Educ Reform Comn; trustee, Mus Mod Art; trustee, Am Mus Natural Hist; Bd dir, Comn Presidential Debates; chmn emer, Partnership New York. **Honors/Awds:** Trustees Award, Nat Tv Acad, 2004; Sports Ball Leadership Recipient, Arthur Ashe Inst, 2008. **Special Achievements:** Top 100 Most Influential Blacks in Corporate America, Savoy, 2012. **Business Addr:** Interim Chief Executive Officer, Los Angeles Clippers, 1111 S Figueroa St Suite 1100, Los Angeles, CA 90015, **Business Phone:** (213)742-7500.

## PASCHAL, ELOISE RICHARDSON

City council member, educator, association executive. **Personal:** Born Feb 7, 1936, Hartsville, SC; married Willie Lee; children: William. **Educ:** Benedict Col, AB, 1958; Atlanta Univ, MSLS, 1967. **Career:** Educator, city councilor (retired); Tooms County Ga Pub Schs, teacher, 1958-60; Am Pub Sch, teacher, 1960-65; Staley Mid Sch, career media spec, 1965; City Americus, councilwoman, 1996. **Orgs:** Sumter County Ment Health Asn, 1971-; Flint River Girl Scout Coun, 1982-; chmn & bd dir, Sumter County Ment Health Ment Retardation, 1982-84; Am Libr Asn; Am Asn Sch Librns; Nat Ed Asn; Ga Asn Educ; Ga Libr Ans, Third Dist Dept; pres, GA Libr Media; GEO Southwestern State Univ Fund; adv coun, Rosalynn Carter Carenet; elected, Am City Coun; Delta Sigma Theta Sorority. **Honors/Awds:** Woman of the Year, Boy Scout Units No 226, 1980; Distinguished Service Award, Sumter County Ment Health Asn, 1982; First women ever elected to Americus City Council in its 139-year history. **Home Addr:** 310 Vista Dr, Americus, GA 31709. **Business Addr:** City Councilwoman, City of Americus, 101 W Lamar St, Americus, GA 31709-3595, **Business Phone:** (229)924-4411.

## PASCHAL, TIA

Basketball player, manager. **Personal:** Born Mar 22, 1969. **Educ:** Fla State Univ, criminal justice, 1993. **Career:** Basketball player (retired), proj mgr; AB Contern, Luxembourg, 1993-95; Visby Ladies, Sweden, 1997-98; Charlotte Sting, 1998; IBM Security, Atlanta, Ga, proj mgr, currently. **Business Addr:** Project Manager, IBM Corp, 4111 Northside Pkwy NW, Atlanta, GA 30327, **Business Phone:** (404)814-1806.

## PASCHAL, TRISA LONG

College administrator, association executive. **Personal:** Born May 13, 1958, Akron, OH; daughter of George W Long Jr and Pauline Long; married Nelson. **Educ:** Univ Akron, BS, 1981, MS, educ, 1987. **Career:** Univ Akron, asst dir asst dir alumni rels, 1983-85, assoc dir, 1985-88, assoc dir develop & dir ann giving, 1988; Spelman Col, Maj Gifts, campaign dir, 1993-96, Inst Advan, asn vpres inst advan, 1996-97, vpres, 1997-2003; Salvation Army USA Southern Territory, dir enduring gifts, 2004-08; MassMutual, financial serv prof, 2008-09; T. Paschal & Assocs, consult, 2011-; Clark Atlanta Univ, vpres instnl advan & univ rels, 2014-. **Orgs:** Leadership Atlanta; bd trustee, Hammonds House Gallery; Delta Sigma Theta Sorority; Cobb County Bd Dist 4; CASE; Antioch Baptist Ch N; Jr League Atlanta, 1995; dir enduring gifts, Salvation Army Evangeline Booth Col, 2004-08; dir develop & alumni rels, Golden Key Int Honour Soc, 2010-11; Asn Fundraising Professionals, 2015-. **Home Addr:** 1225 Heritage Lake Dr, Mableton, GA 30126. **Business Addr:** Vice President, Clark Atlanta University, 205 Harkness Hall, Atlanta, GA 30314, **Business Phone:** (404)880-6186.

## PASCHAL, WILLIE L.

School principal. **Personal:** Born May 9, 1926, Americus, GA; married Eloise Richardson; children: William Stanley. **Educ:** Morehouse Col, BA, bus admin, 1949; Atlanta Univ, MA, educ & admin, 1957; GA State Univ, Atlanta, GA, EdS EAS, 1978. **Career:** Webster City Bd Educ Preston, prin & teacher, 1949-52; Twiggs City Bd Educ, teacher,

1952-53; Sumter City Bd Educ, prin & teacher, 1953-72; Am Bd Pub Educ, prin; Eastview Elem Sch, prin. **Orgs:** Life mem, Alpha Phi Alpha Frat; asst secy, Am & Sumter City Payroll Develop; sr vice comn, Am Legion Dept Ga, 1984-85; Nat Asn Elem Sch Prin; Ga Asn Elem Sch, Prin 3rd Dist, 1984-85; Phi Delta Kappa, 1984-85; Ga Asn Educ Leaders, 1984-85; mem team chmn, Chamber Com, 1985; Americus Sumter County Chamber Com. **Honors/Awds:** Distinguished Citizen, Ment Health Asn Sumter City, 1982; Distinguish Service Ment Health Asn Sumter City, 1982. **Home Addr:** PO Box 461, Americus, GA 31709-0461, **Home Phone:** (229)924-2063.

## PASCHALL, EVITA ARNEDA
Lawyer, publisher, judge. **Personal:** Born May 18, 1951, Augusta, GA; daughter of Marion R and Lucille T; married Felix Bryan Andrews; children: Iman Andrews, Felix Bryan Andrews Jr & Evita Lucille Young. **Educ:** Howard Univ, BA, polit sci & govt, jour cum laude, 1973; Univ Ga, JD, 1976. **Career:** Augusta Ga, recorders ct judge, 1976-78; Richmond County, dist attys off, 1976-79; Augusta Judicial Circuit, asst dist atty, 1976-79; Self-employed, atty, 1976-; Brown & Paschall Attys Law, atty, 1979-81; Evita A Paschall PC, atty, 1981-; State Ct Ga, Augusta, asst solicitor, 1982-84; Magistrate Ct, Augusta, asst solicitor, 1984-86, solicitor, 1986-94; Munic Ct, judge, 1994-97; Augusta Asn African Am Attorneys, 2000-12; Magistrate Ct Richmond County, magistrate ct solicitor, 2012; Augusta Today Mag, ed, publ, currently. **Orgs:** Ga State Bar, 1976-; Leadership Augusta; NBA, 1983-; bd dir, Bethlehem Community Ctr, 1984-95; pres, Augusta CNF AFA Atty, 1992-93; Augusta Jaycees; Augusta Bar Asn; Howard Univ Stud Asn; Alpha Kappa Alpha. **Honors/Awds:** Woman of the Year, WHAM, 1973; Outstanding Young Women of America, 1979. **Home Addr:** 4352 Azalea Dr, Evans, GA 30809-8241, **Home Phone:** (706)722-0173. **Business Addr:** Attorney, Evita A Paschall PC, 137 Broad St, Augusta, GA 30901, **Business Phone:** (706)722-0173.

## PASCHALL, JIMMIE WALTON
Association executive, vice president (organization). **Personal:** married Matthew; children: 2. **Educ:** Howard Univ, BS, 1983. **Career:** XO Commun, vpres & chief human resources officer, 2000-03; Vols Am Inc, exec vpres external affairs, 2003-07; Marriott Int Inc, sr vpres external affairs, global diversity officer, 2008-11; Wells Fargo, exec vpres, head enterprise diversity & inclusion, 2012-; Vols Am Nat Bd Dir; Sodexho, staff; HMS Host Corp, staff. **Orgs:** Patton Boggs Diversity Adv Bd; Family & Child Serv; Consortium Chief Diversity Officers, Georgetown Univ; bd dir, Generations United, currently. **Home Addr:** , WA. **Business Addr:** Senior Vice President External Affairs, Global Diversity Officer, Marriott International Inc, 10400 Fernwood Rd, Bethesda, MD 20817, **Business Phone:** (301)380-3000.

**PASSMORE, JUANITA CARTER.** See Obituaries Section.

## PATE, ALEXS D.
Writer, college teacher. **Personal:** Born Jan 1, 1950, Philadelphia, PA; son of Alexander and Lois; children: Gyanni, Alexs & Chekesha. **Career:** Macalester, lectr, 1992-98; Univ Minn, lectr, African-Am & AfricanStudies, asst prof, assoc prof, 1993-; Poems: Losing Absalom, 1994, Finding Makeba, 1996, Contemporary African American Literature: AnywhereThe Wind Blows, 1996, Amistad, 1997, Innocent, 1998, West of Rehoboth, 2001. **Home Addr:** 1425 W 35th St, Minneapolis, MN 55408, **Home Phone:** (612)824-3208. **Business Addr:** Associate Professor, University of Minnesota, 808 Social Sci Twr 267 19th Ave S, Minneapolis, MN 55455, **Business Phone:** (612)626-7587.

## PATE, JOHN W., SR. (JOHNNY PATE)
Conductor (music), musician, composer. **Personal:** Born Dec 5, 1923, Chicago Heights, IL; son of Charles H Sr and Nora R; married Carolyn; children: John Jr, Yvonne, Donald & Brett. **Educ:** Midwestern Conservatory Music, Chicago, 1953; Univ Calif, Los Angeles, Elec Music, Script Writ, Act-Dir workshop. **Career:** Musician (retired); professional bass player, composer, producer, arranger, 1946-; Johnny Pate Trio, Chicago, founder & musician, 1957-62; ABC Rec, Chicago, midwest dir A&R, 1963-65; MGM-Verve Rec, NY, east coastdir artists & repetoire, 1966-68; UNLV, teacher film scoring, currently; Composer: Shaft in Africa, 1973; Satan's Triangle, Bucktown, 1975; Dr Black & Mr. Hyde, Sudden Death, 1976; "The Richard Pryor Show", 1977; Every Girl Must Have One, 1978; musical dir TV productions: "The Lou Rawls Special, "Future Stars", 1979. Albums: Johnny Pate Trio, 1956; Johnny Pate Trio, 1956; Johnnie Pate at the Blue Note, 1957; Jazz Goes Ivy League, 1958; Swingin Flute, 1958; A Date With Johnnie Pate, 1959; Outrageous, 1970; Superfly Conductor, 1972; Shaft In Africa, 1973; Bucktown, 1975. **Orgs:** Pres, Yvonne Publ & Nod-Jon Mus pub cons; BMI. **Honors/Awds:** Unsung Hero of Popular Music, 2003. **Special Achievements:** First African-American to become president of Local NARAS Recording Academy, Chicago Chapter. **Home Addr:** 7463 Trudy Lane, Las Vegas, NV 89123, **Home Phone:** (702)361-4308.

**PATERSON, HON. BASIL ALEXANDER.** See Obituaries Section.

## PATERSON, DR. DAVID ALEXANDER
Government official. **Personal:** Born May 20, 1954, Brooklyn, NY; son of Basil and Portia; married Michelle Paige; children: Ashley & Alexander Basil. **Educ:** Columbia Univ, BA, hist, 1977; Hofstra Law Sch, JD, 1982. **Career:** Queens Dist Attys Off; State NY, state sen, 1985-, dep minority leader, 1995-2002; Minority Leader, 2003-06, Lt gov, 2007-08; State New York, lt gov, 2006, gov, 2008-10; New York radio sta, 2010. **Orgs:** Am Found Blind; Achilles Track Club; Am Found Blind; Jewish Guild Blind; bd mem, Nat Asn Advan Colored People; chmn, Ny Dem Comt; bd mem, Dem Nat Comt, Dem Legis Campaign Comt; Achilles Track Club, 1999; senate minority leader, Dem caucus, 2002. **Special Achievements:** New York's First African-American governor. **Home Addr:** 45 W 132nd St, Newyork, NY 10037-3120. **Business Addr:** Governor, New York State, State Capitol, Albany, NY 12224, **Business Phone:** (518)474-8390.

## PATES, HAROLD
School administrator. **Personal:** Born Oct 31, 1931, Macon, MS; son of Squire and Amanda Beasley; children: 2. **Educ:** Wilson Junior Col, attended 1952; De Paul Univ, BA, eng, 1954, MA, 1956; Univ Chicago, PhD, 1976. **Career:** School administrator (retired); Loyola Univ; George Williams Col; Northeastern Ill Univ; DuSable Upper Grade Ctr, asst prin, 1964-68, counr; Loop Col, dir, admis dept, 1968; Concordia Col; Malcolm X Col, dean, 1981; Kennedy-King Col, Chicago Ill, dean, pres, 1983-97; Fuller Elem Sch; Forestville Elem Sch; Hyde Park Eve Sch, guid counr. **Orgs:** Founding mem, Kemetic Inst; Asn Black Psychologists; Nat Asn Black Sch Educr; Black United Front; Chicago Task Force Black Polit Empowerment; bd mem, Asn Study Class African Civilizations & Harold Wash Inst; bd dir, Black United Fund Ill, curently; founder, Chicago Communiversity & Asn African Educr; adv bd, Jacob H. Carruthers Ctr, Northeastern Ill Univ; founding dir, All African World Virtual Univ. **Business Addr:** Board Director, Black United Fund, 1809 E 71st St, Chicago, IL 60649, **Business Phone:** (773)324-0494.

## PATHON, JEROME
Football coach, football player. **Personal:** Born Dec 16, 1975, Cape Town. **Educ:** Acadia Univ, attended 1994; Univ Wash, BA, bus, mkt & advert, 1998. **Career:** Football player (retired), coach; Indianapolis Colts, wide receiver, 1998-2001; New Orleans Saints, wide receiver, 2002-05; Atlanta Falcons, wide receiver, 2005-06; Seattle Seahawks, 2005-06; Univ San Diego, asst coach, 2009-12; Univ S Fla, asst coach, 2012. **Honors/Awds:** AUS Football Rookie of the Year, 1993; CIAU Football Rookie of the Year, 1993.

## PATIN, DR. JOSEPH PATRICK
Physician, surgeon. **Personal:** Born Jan 10, 1937, Baton Rouge, LA; son of Henry W and Harriet D; married Rose; children: Joseph & Karla. **Educ:** Univ Mich, BS; Meharry Med Col, Md, 1964. **Career:** St Elizabeth Hosp, res, 1964-69; Raymond W Bliss Army Hosp, 1969; La State Univ, assoc prof; 85th Evac Hosp, chief surg, 1970-71; Patin & Mencer, pvt pract physician, currently. **Orgs:** Baton Rouge Parish Bd Health; Kappa Alpha Psi; Cancer Soc Greater Baton Rouge; Oper Upgrade Baton Rouge; Baton Rouge Med Soc; Soc Med Asn; Nat Med Asn Dipl Bd Surgeons, 1970; dir, Burn Unit; asst dir, Trauma Unit; Dipl, bd surg critical care, 1992; fel Am Col Surgeons. **Home Addr:** PO Box 14945, Baton Rouge, LA 70898. **Business Addr:** Physician, Patin & Mencer, 7777 Hennessy Blvd Suite 306, Salisbury, MD 21801, **Business Phone:** (225)769-1300.

## PATIN, JUDE W. P.
Military leader. **Personal:** Born Jan 25, 1940, Baton Rouge, LA; son of Henry Wilmot and Mary Harriett Domingue; married Rose Marie Darensbourg; children: Michelle & Steve. **Educ:** Southern Univ, Baton Rouge, LA, BS, archit eng, 1962; Ariz State Univ, Tempe, AZ, MA, indus eng, 1971; Harvard Univ, Cambridge, MA, John F Kennedy Sch Govt & Pub Mgt Sr Exec Course, 1990; AUS Engr Officer Advan Course; AUS Cmd & Gen Staff Col; Nat Security Mgt Course, Indust Col Armed Forces; AUs War Col. **Career:** Military leader (retired); Aus, brig gen, 1991; State La, secy transp & develop; Juro Co, pres, chief exec officer; Aus Corps Engrs N Cent Div, Comndg Gen, 1989-; La State Univ, dept construct mgt & indust engineering, prof residence; Univ Tex at San Antonio, Col Archit, sr lectr construct sci, currently. **Orgs:** Alpha Phi Mu Industrial Engineering Honor Soc; US co-chair Four intl joint comns dealing w & elem water resource mgt Great Lakes; vpres, Soc Am Military Engrs, 1991; Am Pub Works Asn; Asn US Army. **Honors/Awds:** Alpha Phi Mu Industrial Engineering Honor Society; Black Engineer of the Year, 1991; numerous public presentations involving engineering & military defense concerns, including speeches, briefings, articles & pub letters; registered prof engr Wisconsin. **Home Addr:** 501 Woodgate Blvd, Baton Rouge, LA 70808-5431, **Home Phone:** (225)766-0509. **Business Addr:** Senior Lecturer, The University of Texas at San Antonio, 1 UTSA Circle, San Antonio, TX 78249, **Business Phone:** (210)458-4011.

## PATNETT, JOHN HENRY
Executive, president (organization). **Personal:** Born Nov 21, 1948, New Orleans, LA; son of Melvin and Mary; married Lynn J. **Educ:** Southern Univ New Orleans, BA, 1971; Southern Univ, Baton Rouge, LA, cert furniture upholstery, 1980. **Career:** La Black Republican Coun, dir pub rels, 1983-85; Mel & Son Upholstery Inc, pres. **Orgs:** Bd mem, US Selective Serv, 1980. **Home Addr:** 7009 Queensway Dr, New Orleans, LA 70128-2626, **Home Phone:** (504)245-8123. **Business Addr:** President, Mel & Son Upholstery Inc, 2001 Touro St, New Orleans, LA 70116, **Business Phone:** (504)945-5187.

## PATRICK, PASTOR CHARLES NAMON, JR.
Executive, founder (originator), clergy. **Personal:** Born Feb 5, 1949, Birmingham, AL; son of Charles and Rutha Mae Robbins; married Gwendolyn Stephanie Batiste; children: Gentry Namon, Jessica Sherrie, Charles Stephan III, Hope Naomi & John Paul. **Educ:** Col Data Processing, Los Angeles, CA; Life Underwriters Training Coun, cert, 1979. **Career:** Pastor, entrepreneur; VIP Mfg, N Hollywood, Calif, sales dist, 1970-76; Prudential Ins Co, Los Angeles, Calif, sales agt/mgr, 1976-82; Pioneer Capital & Assoc, Dallas, Tex, western reg vpres; PPA Industs, 1982-83, owner, 1982-84; Patrick, Patrick & Assocs, Lawndale, Calif, pres, 1984; Austin Diversified Prod, Ingelwood, Calif, corp sales mgr, 1985-88; PPA Industs, Compton, Calif, owner, 1988-; Charter High Sch, supt; Titus 2 Women, founder; Sunago Christian Fel Church, founder, 1990; Fragment House Mission Int, founder; GEM Environ Serv LLC, prin partner, currently. **Orgs:** Admin/asst, Way Church Ingelwood, 1981; block club pres, Action Block Club, 1982-85; Greater La Visitors & Conv Bur, 1984, prog coord, Black Am Response African Community (BARAC), 1987-88; counr, Fel W Youth Ministries, 1987-88; NABSE (Nat Alliance Black Sch Educr), 2001; Foundations Future Generations. **Home Addr:** 636 W 170th St, PO Box 5365, Gardena, CA 90247, **Home Phone:** (310)344-3220. **Business Addr:** Founder, Sunago Christian Fellowship Church, PO BOX 5365, Compton, CA 90224-5365, **Business Phone:** (310)344-3220.

## PATRICK, DEVAL LAURDINE
Government official, attorney general (U.S. federal government). **Personal:** Born Jul 31, 1956, Chicago, IL; son of Laurdine Kenneth and Emily Mae Wintersmith; married Diane Louise Bemus; children: Sarah Baker & Katherine Wintersmith. **Educ:** Milton Acad, eng & am lit; Harvard Col, BA, 1978; Harvard Univ Law Sch, JD, 1982. **Career:** US Ct Appeals, law clerk; NAACP Legal Defense & Educ Fund, litigator & atty, 1983-86; Hill & Barlow, atty & partner, 1986-94; US Dept Justice, asst atty gen civil rights, 1994-97; Nat Church Arson Task Force, 1996-97; Day, Berry & Howard, pvt pract, 1997-99; Asst US Atty Gen; Global Legal Affairs, Texaco, chair, 1997-99, vpres & gen coun, 1999-2001; Coca-Cola Co, exec vpres, exec comt & gen coun, 1999-2005, corp secy, 2002-06; Commonwealth Mass, Mass Gov, 2006-15; Author: A Reason to Believe: Lessons From an Improbable Life; Faith in the Dream: A Call to the Nation to Reclaim American Values, 2012. **Orgs:** Mass Bar Asn; Black Lawyers Asn; vol chair, New Eng Comt; Nat Bd dir; Boston Bar Asn; Harvard Club Boston; dir, Harvard Alumni Asn, 1993-96; chair, Texaco Equality & Fairness Task Force, 1997; Fed Election Reform Comn; Nat Asn Advan Colored People Legal Defense Fund; vice chair, Mass Judicial Nominating Coun; asst atty gen civil right, Nation Top Civil Rights Post; Dem Party. **Special Achievements:** First African-American to have served as Governor of Massachusetts. **Home Phone:** (617)367-2006. **Business Addr:** Governor, Massachusetts State House, Rm 280, Boston, MA 02133, **Business Phone:** (617)725-4005.

## PATRICK, ESQ. DIANE
Labor relations manager. **Personal:** Born Jan 1, 1951, Brooklyn, NY; daughter of Lillian Bernus; married Deval; children: Sarah & Katherine. **Educ:** City Univ NY, Queens Col, BA, 1972; Loyola Law Sch, Los Angeles, CA, JD, 1980. **Career:** OMelveny & Myers, assoc, 1980-86; Harvard Univ, gen coun, atty, dir, assoc vpres, 1986-94; fel, Partnership, 1987-88; US Justice Dept Civil Rights div, head, 1994; Hogan & Hartson, Assoc, 1994-95; Ropes & Gray, partner, currently. **Orgs:** New York Bar Asn, 1984-; fel Partnership, 1987-88; trustee, Mass Maritime Acad, 1989-91; bd trustee, Cambridge Col, 1990-94; bd trustee, Epiphany Sch; overseer, C's Hosp, 1991-96; trustee, Brigham & Womens Hosp, 1992-98; trustee, dir, Arts Boston, 1995-97; bd dir, United Way Mass Bay, 2000-10, 2012-; bd dir, Jane Doe Inc, 2007-10; bd overseer, Boston Symphony Orchestra, 2008-10; bd dir, Posse Found. **Honors/Awds:** Chambers USA: Ams Leading Lawyers Bus, 2008-12; Massachusetts Super Lawyers, 2010-11; The Network Journal: 25 Influential Black Women in Business, Black Professionals & Small Business Magazine, 2010; Top Women of Law, Massachusetts Lawyers Weekly, 2012; Best Lawyers in Am, 2012. **Business Addr:** Partner, Ropes & Gray LLP, Prudential Twr, Boston, MA 02199-3600, **Business Phone:** (617)951-7451.

## PATRICK, HON. ISADORE W., JR.
Judge, computer executive. **Personal:** Born Mar 27, 1951, Jackson, MS; son of Isadore W Sr and Esterline; married Deborah Williams. **Educ:** Jackson State Univ, BS, 1973; Univ MS Law Sch, JD; Nat Judicial Col, judicial cert. **Career:** IBM, comput programmer, 1973-78; Hinds Co Pub Defender Off, pub defense atty; State Miss, Nineth Dist Circuit Ct, asst dist atty, 1981-89, Warren County Circuit Ct, trail judge, ruling judge, 1989-. **Orgs:** Nat Judges Asn; MS Conf Judges; MS State Bar; Magnolia State Bar; Warren Co Bar; bd dir, Salvation Army; Jackson State Alumni Asn; Am Bar Asn; Am Trial Lawyers Asn; Nat Bar Asn. **Honors/Awds:** Legal Award, Nat Asn Advan Colored People, 1989. **Special Achievements:** First African-American in Mississippi elected as a circuit court judge; First black judge of any Mississippi court. **Home Addr:** 112 Moonmist Dr, Vicksburg, MS 39180, **Home Phone:** (601)634-8042. **Business Addr:** Ruling Judge, State of Mississippi, 1 E Main St, Front Royal, VA 22630-3313, **Business Phone:** (540)635-2335.

## PATRICK, DR. JENNIE R.
Engineer. **Personal:** Born Jan 1, 1949, Gadsden, AL; daughter of James (deceased) and Elizabeth (deceased). **Educ:** Tuskegee Inst, 1970; Univ Calif, Berkeley, BS, chem engineering, 1973; Mass Inst Technol, ScD, chem engineering, 1979, PhD, chem engineering, 1979. **Career:** Engineer (retired); Dow Chem Co, asst engr, 1972; Stauffer Chem Co, asst engr, 1973; Mass Inst Technol, res assoc, 1973-79, gilliland fel, 1973; dupont fel, 1974; Chevron Res, engr, 1974; Arthur D Little Inc, engr, 1975; Am Asn Univ Women, fel, 1975; Gen Elect Co, res engr res & develop, 1979-83; Rensselaer Polytech Inst, adj prof chem engineering, 1982-85; Ga Inst Technol, adj prof chem engineering, 1983-87; Phillip Morris Inc, proj mgr res ctr, 1983-85; Rohm & Haas Co, mgr fundamental chem engineering res, 1985-90; Southern Co Servs Inc, asst exec vpres, 1990-93; Tuskegee Univ, Chem Engineering Dept, 3m eminent scholar & prof chem engineering, 1993-97; Raytheon Engrs & Constructors, sr consult, 1997-2000; Bus & Home Environ Rev, consult, 1999-; Environ Wellness Inst, founder, 2000-. **Orgs:** Chair, Tuskegee Univ, 1992-96; Sigma Xi, AIChE, NOBCChE. **Honors/Awds:** Outstanding Women in Science & Engineering Award, Nat Orgn Prof Advan Black Chemists & Chem Engrs, 1980; A subject in Exceptional Black Scientists Poster Prog, CIBA-GEIGY, 1983; Candace Award, Nat Coalition 100 Black Women, 1984; Tuskegee Inst, Hon Doctor Sci, 1984; Presidential Citation, Nat Asn Equal Opportunity Higher Educ, 1987; Teacher of the Year, Tuskegee Univ, 1994-95; Williams W. Grimes Award, Am Inst Chem Engrs, 2000; Black Achievers in Chemical Engineering Award, Am Inst Chem Engrs, 2008. **Special Achievements:** First African-American woman in U.S. to earn a doctorate in Traditional Chemical Engineering, 1979; First 3-M Scholar Eminent At Tuskegee University. **Business Addr:** Consultant, Business & Home Environmental Review, PO Box 51678, Amarillo, TX 79101, **Business Phone:** (806)353-1401.

## PATRICK, ESQ. LAWRENCE CLARENCE, JR.
Lawyer. **Personal:** Born Feb 8, 1945, Detroit, MI; son of Ada D and Bishop Lawrence C; married Raynona P Fuller; children: Lawrence C III, Joseph E, Ayana B & Goldie E. **Educ:** Wayne State Univ, Detroit, Mish, BA, 1972; Harvard Univ, JD, 1975. **Career:** Honigman Miller Schwartz & Cohn, Detroit, Mich, assoc, 1975-77; Patrick, Fields & Preston-Cooper, Detroit, Mich, partner, 1977-93; Detroit Bd Educ, pres, 1989-92, chair, Detroit 2000, vis fel, Hudson Inst, 1992-; Jaffe Raitt Heuer & Weiss PC, coun, partner & atty, currently. **Orgs:**

Mich Bar As, 1975-; bd dir, Wolverine Bar Asn, 1978-81; corp dir & bd chmn, Black United Fund, 1978-; Mich Transp Commn, 1979-84, vice chmn, 1981-84; chmn bd, Black United Fund, 1985-88; chmn bd, Wayne County Social Serv Bd, 1986-88; Detroit Bd Educ, 1989-95; pres, Cass Tech Alumni Asn, 1997-; chmn, N End Community Develop Corp; State Bar Mich; bd gov, Cranbrook Inst Sci; Nat Coun Sch Atty; Mich Coun Sch Atty; Asn Educr Pvt Pract; bd dir, Mich Future Inc; Wayne County Social Serv Bd, 1986-88. **Honors/Awds:** Michingan Senate, Mich Senate Resolution, 1981; Trio, Wayne State Univ, 1988; Founder's Award, Stud Motivational Prog, 1989, Outstanding Service, Church God Christ, 1989; David McKenzie Honor Award. **Home Addr:** 237 King St, Detroit, MI 48202-2128, **Home Phone:** (313)766-5956. **Business Addr:** Attorney, Partner, Jaffe Raitt Heuer & Weiss PC, 500 Griswold Suite 2400, Detroit, MI 48226, **Business Phone:** (313)961-1200.

### PATRICK, ODESSA R.

College teacher, laboratory technician. **Personal:** Born Oct 22, 1933, Mt. Gilead, NC; married Joe L; children: Krystal, Joseph & Jasmine. **Educ:** NC A&T State Univ, BS, 1956; Univ NC, Greensboro, MA, 1969. **Career:** Univ NC, Greensboro, lab technician, 1958-69, Biol Dept, biol instr, 1968, prof emer, 1996-. **Orgs:** Am Asn Univ Women; Delta Sigma Theta; Elisha Mitchell Sci Soc. **Special Achievements:** Scientific paper published in Journal of Elisha Mitchell Scientific Soc, 1969; Leader, Girl Scout. **Home Addr:** Rt 6 Box 100, Greensboro, NC 27405. **Business Addr:** Professor Emeritus, University of North Carolina, 1000 Spring Garden St, Greensboro, NC 27403, **Business Phone:** (336)334-5000.

### PATRICK, DR. OPAL LEE YOUNG

Educator, teacher. **Personal:** Born Jul 16, 1929, Tatums, OK; daughter of L P Young Jr and Connie V Mitchell; married Charles; children: Jacqueline R. **Educ:** Langston Univ, BA, 1951; Univ NMex, MA, 1963; Univ Utah, PhD, 1974. **Career:** Educator (retired); Pub Sch, Okla, teacher, 1951-56; Bur Ind Affairs, inst counr, 1956-63; Univ Md, Educ Ctr Independent Sch, 1963-66; USAFE W Ger, instr, lectr & teacher; Clear field Job Corp, inst counr & adminr, 1966-70; Univ Utah, from instr educ to asst prof educ, 1971-77; guest lectr, coordr, consult, tutor, 1979-91, 1994. **Orgs:** Presenter, Var Conf; partic & presenter, Nat Org; guest lectr & coord, var proj & res activ; State Ment Health Asn, 1973-; Nat Coun Teachers Eng, 1973-; vpres, Nat Coun Teachers Eng, 1973; Utah Acad Sci, 1974-; Asn Teach Educ, 1974-; Asn Sch & Curric Develop, 1975-; Nat Col Soc Studies, 1976-; pres, Davis Co, Nat Asn Advan Colored People, 1978. **Home Addr:** 920 Garnet St, Layton, UT 84041-2504, **Home Phone:** (801)544-9784.

### PATRICK, VINCENT JEROME

Marketing executive. **Personal:** Born Oct 21, 1959, Delray Beach, FL; son of Freddie W and Mattie Hough. **Educ:** Univ Fla, Gainesville, FL, BS, jour, concentration: pub rels & bus admin, 1981. **Career:** Jordan Marsh, Miami, Fla, pr assoc, sales promotions & spec events, 1981-82, sales mgr, 1982-83, retail buyer, 1983-85; Rouse Co, Miami, Fla, asst mkt mgr, 1985-88; Rouse Co, Atlanta, Ga, mgr, sales & mkt, 1988-92; VJP Mkt & Commun Inc, Hapeville, Ga, owner, pres & chief exec officer, 2011-. **Orgs:** Bd dir, Atlanta Downtown Partnership; bd dir, Travel Ga; Downtown Pub Rels Coun; Fernbank Mus Natural Hist Commun Adv Comt. **Honors/Awds:** Bayside Marketplace Grand Opening, MAXI/Mkt, 1989; Silver Anvil/Pub Relations, 1989; Phoenix Award, Pub Rels, 1989; Underground Atlanta Grand Opening, MAXI/Mkt, 1990; Paper Clip Award/Advertising, Underground Atlanta Advert Campaign, Atlanta Jour Const, 1990; Underground Atlanta; Int Coun Shopping Ctrs. **Home Addr:** 4955 Wynhurst Way, Stone Mountain, GA 30088-4238, **Home Phone:** (770)322-7141. **Business Addr:** Owner, Chief Executive Officer, Vincent J Patrick Marketing & Communications Inc, 981 Joseph E Lowery Blvd NW Suite 110, Atlanta, GA 30318, **Business Phone:** (404)817-9850.

### PATTEN, DAVID

Football coach, football player. **Personal:** Born Aug 19, 1974, Columbia, SC; son of David and Betty; married Galiena; children: Daquan, Quintin & David. **Educ:** Western Carolina Univ, BA, social work. **Career:** Football player (retired), football coach; Albany Firebirds, defensive back & wide receiver, 1996; New York Giants, wide receiver, 1997, kick returner, 1998, 1999; Cleveland Browns, wide receiver, 2000; New Eng Patriots, wide receiver, 2001-04, 2010; Wash Redskins, wide receiver, 2005, 2006; New Orleans Saints, wide receiver, 2007-08, tight end, 2008; Clevand Browns, 2009; Western Carolina Univ, asst coach, 2013-. **Orgs:** Wash Redskins; New Orleans Saints; Cleveland Browns; New Eng Patriots. **Honors/Awds:** Super Bowl Champion, XXXVI, XXXVII, XXXIX. **Special Achievements:** TV Special: "2001 AFC Championship Game", 2002; "Super Bowl XXXVI", 2002; "Super Bowl XXXIX", 2005. **Business Addr:** Assistant Coach, Western Carolina University, 201 HF Robinson Bldg, Cullowhee, NC 28723, **Business Phone:** (828)227-7124.

### PATTERSON, REV. ALONZO B., JR.

Clergy, administrator. **Personal:** Born Nov 5, 1937, New Orleans, LA; married Shirley May Smith; children: Edna, Mitchell, Norris, Janet & Kim. **Educ:** Am Bible Inst, ThD, 1977; Univ Alaska, AA 1973, BA, 1974; AA, 1974. **Career:** Shiloh Missionary Baptist Church, pastor, 1970-; Anchorage Sch Dist, person specialist, 1976; Shiloh Baptist Church, relig admin, 1970-75; MHE, supv, 1966-70; Alaska Ministries Am Baptist Nat Ministries, coordr, exec minister; Corinthian Baptist Church, pastor. **Orgs:** Chair, Alaska State Bd Parole, 1984-91; pres, Nat Asn Advan Colored People; Community Action; Human Rels Comn; Anchorage OIC; Ministerial Alliance; Civilian & Mil Coun; Anchorage Community Health Ctr; Minority Cult Asn; vpres, March Dimes; founder, chmn, Martin Luther King Jr Found, Alaska; Alaska Black Leadership Conf; Greatland State Baptist Conv; pres, Interdenominational Ministerial Alliance; Shiloh Community Develop Inc. **Home Addr:** 3727 Williams St, Anchorage, AK 99508-4537, **Home Phone:** (907)561-4262. **Business Addr:** Pastor, Shiloh Missionary Baptist Church, 855 E 20th Ave, Anchorage, AK 99510, **Business Phone:** (907)276-6673.

### PATTERSON, ANDRAE MALONE

Basketball player, basketball coach. **Personal:** Born Nov 12, 1975, Riverside, CA; married Kiana; children: Jayden & Kimora. **Educ:** Ind Univ, Bloomington, attended 1998. **Career:** Panellinios BC; KK Zadar; Ricoh Manresa; Adecco Estudiantes; Minn Timberwolves, forward, 1998-2000; Adecco Estudiantes, 2001-02, 2003-05; Ricoh Manresa, 2002-02, 2005-06; KK Zadar, 2006; Ironi Ashkelon, power forward, 2006; Panellinios BC, 2006-07; Egaleo AO, 2007-09; KK Igokea, 2008; Univ Tex Arlington, asst coach, 2012-14, dir opers; Idaho Stampede, asst coach, 2014-. **Business Addr:** Assistant Coach, Idaho Stampede, 233 S Capitol Blvd Suite 100, Boise, ID 83702, **Business Phone:** (208)388-4667.

### PATTERSON, BARBARA ANN

President (organization), association executive, educator. **Personal:** Born PA; married Billy W; children: Gwendolyn Patterson-Cobbs, Kimberly & Damali. **Educ:** Trinity Col, Wash, DC, BA, educ, 1984, MA, coun, 1993. **Career:** Independent & Pub Schs, teacher; pvt pract; Cross-Racial Communs & Personal Growth Coun prof; Black Stud Fund, IST Equity, Race & Educ, pres, dir. **Orgs:** Bd gov, Trinity Col; adv bd, Wash Nat Cathedral Scholars; Friends COT Future; bd trustee, Black Stud Fund; hon trustee, Pioneer Theatre Co. **Honors/Awds:** Washingtonians of the Year, Washingtonian mag, 1999. **Special Achievements:** Publisher: Chapter contributor "Promoting Independent School Enrollment", Visible Now Blacks in Private School by Slaughter & Johnson 1989; "Respecting the Strength of Black Youth," Black Issues in Higher Educ; researcher & resource for a History Deferred, A Guide for Teachers; "Pioneering Multiracial Education," Independent School, vol 53, 1993; In the January 2000 edition of the Washingtonian magazine along with 15 other distinguished community members Washingtonian has chosen her as "Local Heroes". **Home Addr:** 10320 Royal Rd, Silver Spring, MD 20903-1615. **Business Addr:** President, Black Student Fund, 3636 16th St NW 4th Fl, Washington, DC 20016, **Business Phone:** (202)387-1414.

### PATTERSON, HON. CECIL BOOKER, JR.

Judge. **Personal:** Born May 15, 1941, Newport News, VA; son of Cecil B Sr and Marie E; married Wilma M Hall; children: Angela D & Cecil M. **Educ:** Hampton Univ, Va, BA, 1963; Ariz State Univ, JD, 1971. **Career:** Judge (retired); Maricopa Co Legal Aid Soc, staff atty, 1971-72; Law fel, Reginald Heber Smith Prog, 1971; Bursh & Patterson, pvt law pract, 1972-73; Phoenix Urban League, house coun, 1973-75; Maricopa Tech Col, 1975-79; Ariz State Univ, fac assoc, 1973-80; Maricopa Co Pub Defend Off, trial atty, 1975-80; Maricopa Co Super Ct, judge, 1980-91; Atty Gen's Off, Human Serv Div, Ariz, chief coun, 1991-95; Ariz Ct Appeals, Div One, judge, 1995-2003; Glendale City Ct, Actg Presiding Judge, 2001-02. **Orgs:** Grant Martin L King Jr Woodrow Wilson Found, 1969; Nat Asn Atty Gen Civil Rights Comn; bd dir, Maricopa Co Br, Nat Asn Advan Colored People; Southminster Community Serv Forum; Minority Adv Comt, Ariz State Univ; bd dir, YMCA; Valley Sun United Way; Legal Aid Soc, 1971-75; Ariz Acad, 1975-78; bd gov, Ariz State Bar, 1977-79; rep, Am Bar Asn House Del, 1978-80; bd mem, Maricopa Co Red Cross, 1978; pres, Ariz Black Lawyers Asn, 1979-80; Nat Conf Christians & Jews, 1981-; bd mem, Valley Sun, Ariz United Way, 1984-; chair, Nat Bar Asn Judicial Coun, 2001-02; Permanent Judicial Comn. **Honors/Awds:** Law Scholarship Scholarship, Educ & Defense Fund, 1970; Distinguished Achievement Award, Arizona State University, 1985; Distinguished Service Award, National Bar Association Judicial Council, 1992; Arizona Black Lawyers Association Trailblazer Award, 1992; Marvin Award, Nat Asn Atty Gen, 1994-95; National Association of Attorneys General Marvin Award, 1995; Distinguished Citizen Award, Kappa Alpha Psi Fraternity, 1996; Martin Luther King Living the Dream Award, City Phoenix Ariz, 1998; Heman Marion Sweat Award, National Bar Association, 1998. **Home Addr:** 1955 E Bendix Dr, Tempe, AZ 85283, **Home Phone:** (480)730-8864.

### PATTERSON, CHERYL ANN

Accountant. **Personal:** Born Jul 5, 1957, Columbus, OH; daughter of John B and Geraldine; married Dale. **Educ:** Columbus State Community Col, AS, optom technol, 1979; Franklin Univ, BS, acct, 1984, MBA, 1998. **Career:** Ohio State Univ, Col Optom, optom technican; Ohio Dept Taxation, tax agt; Columbus Conv Ctr, jr acct, sr acct, vp treas, dir finance, currently. **Home Addr:** 6437 Hermitage Dr, Westerville, OH 43082-8910, **Home Phone:** (614)895-1352. **Business Addr:** Director of Finance, Greater Columbus Convention Center, 400 N High St, Columbus, OH 43215, **Business Phone:** (614)827-2500.

### PATTERSON, CHRISTINE ANN

School administrator. **Personal:** Born Sep 9, 1949, Wilkes-Barre, PA; daughter of James Samuel and Stella Bienwski; married Walter DeFrantz; children: Waltrina, Felicia & Amanda. **Educ:** Wilkes Univ, Wilkes-Barre, BA, commun, 1986, MS, educ, 1989; Pa State Univ, Univ Park, PhD, currently. **Career:** Penn State Univ, Media, coord minority advan placement prog, 1986, minority stud counsr, coordr, 1986-88, exten agt/4-H urban youth, 1988-89, dir, minority stud serv, 1989; Nat Mult Sclerosis Soc, bd coordr, 1987-88; Ind Univ-Purdue Univ Ft Wayne, Off Multicultural Serv, dir. **Orgs:** Martin Luther King Comt Social Justice, 1983-; coordr, Wilkes-Barre chap, Nat Asn Advan Colored People, 1986-88; pres coun, Undergrad Recruitment & Retention, Pa State Univ, 1989-; chair women, Color Winter Ball, 1990; chair, Forum Black Affairs, 1990; Ft Wayne Mayors Affirmative Action Coun; Wilkes Univ Adv Coun; Ind Univ-Purdue Univ Ft Wayne Diversity Coun; bd dir, Healthy Cities; bd dir, Homebound Meals; bd dir, United Way Race Dialogue; bd dir, YWCA; owner & mgr, CAP Diversity Consult & training. **Home Addr:** 1652 Oxford Cir, State College, PA 16803, **Home Phone:** (814)867-0396. **Business Addr:** PA.

### PATTERSON, REV. CLINTON DAVID

Clergy, manager. **Personal:** Born Nov 11, 1936, Uniontown, AL; son of David and Mattie Mason; married Lillie Young; children: Michael, Florencia, Donnetta A, Clintonia, Edshena & Bernita. **Educ:** Birmingham Bapt Col, attended 1963; Liamia, attended 1973; Elba Sys, attended 1970. **Career:** New Morning Star Baptist Church, pastor, 1965-72; Beulah Baptist Church, pastor, currently; Booker T Wash Inc Co, mgr; Demopolis Fed Credit Union, vpres; Fed Credit Union, loan off teller; asst term mgr. **Orgs:** Trustee bd, Peace Bapt Ch, 1957; Prof Bus Men's Asn, 1964-75; pres, Demopolis Ministerial Fel, 1966-72; pres, S Pratt City Civic Leag, 1967; bd dir, Together Demopolis; bd dir, BBM Fed Credit Union; bd dir, BBM Birmingham; Demopolis Fed Credit Union; Ala Cent Credit Union; Ala Bapt State Conv & Cong; Nat Bapt Sunday Sch & Training Union Cong; Nat Bapt Conv; Birmingham Bapt Min Conf; Jeff Co Dist Asn; NW Dist Conv; lectr, Jeff Co Dist Sun Sch & BTU Cong; hon mem, Ala Sheriff Asn, 1974; Ala Motorist Asn, 1974; Ala Fed Civic Leag; Geom Lodge 410; Nat Advan Asn Colored People; Ala Chris Movement Human Rights; Tuxedo Height Civic Leag; moderator, Jefferson County Asn; pres, NW Dist Conv; bd mem, A G boys & Girls Club; Jefferson County Dist Asn. **Honors/Awds:** C J Mc Near Award, 1963; Community Service Award, Pratt City, 1971; Community Service Award, Demopolis, 1972; Outstanding Salesmanship Award, NIA, 1974. **Home Addr:** 1101 Circle Trail, Birmingham, AL 35214-4413, **Home Phone:** (205)798-6010. **Business Addr:** Pastor, Beulah Baptist Church, 1022 2nd Ave N, Bessemer, AL 35020, **Business Phone:** (205)424-0861.

### PATTERSON, CURTIS RAY

Educator, college teacher. **Personal:** Born Nov 11, 1944, Shreveport, LA; married Gloria M Morris; children: Curtis R. **Educ:** Grambling State Univ, BA, arts educ, 1967; Ga State Univ, MVA, 1975. **Career:** Atlanta Pub Sch, art instr, chairperson, 1970-76; Caddo Parish Sch Bd, Shreveport, LA, art instr, 1968-70; Muscogee Co Sch, Columbus, GA, art instr, 1967-68; Gov Hon Prog, instr, 1973; Atlanta Col Art, GA, art instr, 1976-; Atlanta Life Ins Co, Adv Comt Art, 1979-80; Piedmont Arts Festival, juror, 1980; Atlanta Col Art, prof; Atlanta sculptor. **Orgs:** Black Artist Atlanta, 1974-80; 13 Minus One Sculpture Grp, 1975-80; adv bd mem, Atlanta Bur Cult Affairs, 1975-80; Sculpture Pk Comn, Atlanta Bur Cult Affairs, 1977; Sculpture Comn Metrop Atlanta Rapid Transit Authority, 1978; Atlanta Int Airport Sculpture Comn, Atlanta Bur Cult Affairs, 1980. **Home Addr:** 1536 Rogers Ave SW Suite A, Atlanta, GA 30310-2306, **Home Phone:** (404)758-5645. **Business Addr:** Professor, Atlanta College of Art, 1280 Peachtree St NE, Atlanta, GA 30309, **Business Phone:** (404)733-5020.

### PATTERSON, DEB. See LAWSON, DEBRA ANN.

### PATTERSON, DR. ELIZABETH ANN

Radiologist. **Personal:** Born Feb 2, 1936, Wilkes-Barre, PA; daughter of Benjamin A and Edythe E; children: Tonya L Henry. **Educ:** Univ MI, BS, 1957; Howard Univ Col Med, MD, 1961. **Career:** Radiologist (retired): Mercy Hosp, radiol, 1972-80; Univ Pgh/Magee Women's Hosp, asst prof radiol, 1981-85; Cent Med Ctr & Hosp, diag radiologist, 1985-88; Breast Imaging, Dept radiol, Hosp Univ Penn, radiologist, 1988-98. **Orgs:** Pres, Pittsburgh Roentgen Soc, 1982-83; pres, Gateway Med Soc, 1983-88; Counor, Am Col Radiol, 1985-91; Radiol Sect Nat Med Assoc, secy/prog chair, 1985-87, vice chmn, 1987-89, chair, 1989-91; bd dir, Am Cancer Soc, Pittsburgh Div, 1986-88, Philadelphia Div, 1992-; Am Asn Women Rad, Alpha Kappa Alpha; pres, Philadelphia Roentgen Ray Soc, 1994-95; Soc Breast Imaging; chmn, Nat Mammography Qual Assurance Adv Comm, 1994-97; pres, Pa Radiol Soc, 1996-97; adv coun, Susan G Komen Found; vpres, FSNW Ski Club Officers, 2001-02; fel Am Col Radiol; Intercultural Cancer Coun, 2004-. **Home Addr:** 14216 26th Ct SE, Mill Creek, WA 98012-5728, **Home Phone:** (425)337-4973.

### PATTERSON, ELIZABETH HAYES

Lawyer, school administrator. **Personal:** Born Jun 25, 1945, Boston, MA; daughter of Alan L Young and Lucille Young; married Jerome Alexander; children: Sala Elise & Malcolm Atiim. **Educ:** Sorbonne Univ Paris, dipl, 1966; Emmanuel Col, AB, fr, 1967; Stanford Univ, attended 1968; Columbus Sch Law Cath, Univ Am, JD, 1973. **Career:** Hon Ruggero Aldisert US Ct Appeals, law clerk, 1973-74; Hogan & Hartson Law Firm, assoc, 1974-77; Columbus Sch Law Cath Univ, adj prof, 1976; DC Pub Sev Comn, comnr, 1977-80, chmn, 1978-80; Georgetown Univ Law Ctr, assoc prof, 1980-, assoc dean JD & grad prog, 1993-97, prof emerita. **Orgs:** Trustee, secy, Nat Florence Crittenton Mission Found Bd; Am Law Inst; Trust Family & Child Sevr, Wash, DC, 1977-; Am Civil Liberties Union Litigation Screening Comn, 1977-80; DC Bar Div I Steering Comn, 1980-82, adv comt, DC Bar Screening Comn, 1985-86; adv comn, Procedures Judicial Coun DC Circuit, 1981-84; bd ed, Wash Lawyer, 1986-91; Secy State's Adv Comn, pvt Int Law; treas, Dist Columbia Bar, 1987-88; DC Law Rev Comn, 1990-93; bd dir, Frederick B Abramson Found, 1992-, bd trustees; trustee, Emmanuel Col, 1994-; bd dir, Child Welfare League Am, 1997; dep dir, Asn Am Law Schs, 2005-07, 2009-10. **Honors/Awds:** Center's Frank F. Flegal Teaching Award, 2001. **Home Addr:** 4420 18th St NW, Washington, DC 20011-4239, **Home Phone:** (202)291-8973. **Business Addr:** Associate Professor of Law, Georgetown University Law Center, 600 NJ Ave NW, Washington, DC 20001, **Business Phone:** (202)662-9384.

### PATTERSON, EVELYNNE R.

School administrator. **Personal:** Born Feb 28, 1930, Meadville, PA; married Herman; children: Alice & Patricia. **Educ:** NY Univ, BS, 1962; NY Univ, post grad. **Career:** NY Univ, exec asst to pres, dir off affirmative action, assoc dir, 1968-72, dir off community rel, assoc prof, 1972-, asst dep chancellor. **Orgs:** Adv bd, Harvard Univ, 1974-77; Comt Bd 2 Borough Manhattan, 1977-; bd dir, Wash Sq Asn, 1977-. **Home Addr:** 15 Lockwood Lane, Newburgh, NY 12550-1024, **Home Phone:** (845)236-2606.

### PATTERSON, GERALD WILLIAM

Executive. **Personal:** Born May 9, 1953, Cleveland, OH; son of William Robert Johnson and Willa Mae; married Diana Crump; children: Monique Camille. **Educ:** Mich State Univ, BA, 1975; Wayne State Univ, specialist, 1977; Cent Mich Univ, MA, 1978; Univ Wis, transp cert, 1987. **Career:** Ford Motor Co, sr transp agt, 1978-80; Amway Corp, traffic coordr, 1980-82, traffic supvr, 1982-83; Kellogg Co, truck pricing mgr, 1984-87, mgr logistics servs, 1988, mgr outside warehouses & dist centers, 1988-91, logistics mgr, 1992; BAX Global Logistics; Walker Int Trans LLC, vpres, currently; ADG Enterprises Inc, vpres opers; GRL Group LLC, chief exec officer, currently. **Orgs:**

Phi Beta Sigma, 1975-; Delta Nu Alpha, 1982-89; Southwest Mich Traffic Club, 1984-; Battle Creek Area Urban League, 1985-; adv, Jr Achievement, 1986-88; 60NR Comt, 1987-88; Global warehouse & food distrib centers; Nat Asn Advan Colored People, 1988-; adv, Upward Bound, 1989-; Coun Logistics Mgt, 1989. **Home Addr:** PO Box 923449, Norcross, GA 30092. **Business Addr:** Vice President, Walker International Transportation LLC, 70 E Sunrise Hwy Suite 604, Valley Stream, NY 11581-1260, **Business Phone:** (516)593-0905.

### PATTERSON, GRACE LIMERICK

Librarian. **Personal:** Born Nov 21, 1938, New York, NY; daughter of Robert and Frieda Sajac; married Joseph Nathaniel; children: Lorrayne & Joseph Jr. **Educ:** City Col NY, New York, NY, BA, 1971; Columbia Univ, New York, NY, MLS, 1975; Col New Rochelle, New Rochelle, NY, MS, 1989. **Career:** Paterson Pub Libr, Paterson, NJ, outreach coordr, 1975-79; Passaic County Col, Paterson, NJ, media specialist, 1979-81; Irvington Pub Libr, Irvington, NJ, br coordr, 1981-84; Rockland Community Col, Suffern, NY, assoc prof, 1984-89; Hudson County Community Col, head librn, libr dir, 1989-. **Orgs:** Am Libr Asn, 1978-; chair, Outreach Servs Comt, Nj Libr Asn, 1981-85; deleg, State Univ NY Libr Asn, 1984-89; chair, ALA Louise Giles Scholar Comt, 1985-87; Arts Coun Rockland County, 1987-89; chair, Pub Rels Comt, Black Caucus Am Libr Asn, 1988-90; chair, Instrnl Resources Comt, HCCC, 1995-98; secy & treas, INT FED Libr Asn, Kipert, 1996-97; Asn Col & Res Librs; rep, Am Libr Asn, Freedom Read Found; NJBLC. **Honors/Awds:** Title IIB Fel, Dept Educ, 1974-75; basic tutor, Literacy Vols Am, 1978; Pubic Relations Award, NJ Libr Asn, 1979 & 1996; Professional Librarian Certification, Educ Dept, NJ, 1981; Community Development Asniate, Mott Found, Flint, MI, 1983. **Business Addr:** Library Director, Head Librarian, Hudson County Community College, 70 Sip Ave 25 J Sq, Jersey City, NJ 07306, **Business Phone:** (201)714-2229.

### PATTERSON, JAMES C.

Executive. **Personal:** Born May 10, 1935, Augusta, GA; married Phyllis Black; children: Katy, Jacqueline & Jennifer M. **Educ:** St Col, MD, 1957. **Career:** Mutual NY, field underwriter, 1966; Supreme Life Philadelphia, debit & staff mgr, 1960-66; Business Unlimited Inc, pres, 1975. **Orgs:** Million Dollar Round Table; Mutual New York Hall Fame; Mutual NY Press Coun; Nat Assoc Life Underwriters; past mem, Philadelphia Jaycees; vpres, Philadelphia Chap Nat Bus League, 1972. **Honors/Awds:** Agency Man of The Year, 1967; Mutual of New York's highest honor Hall of Fame, 1974. **Home Addr:** 79 Overington Ave, Marlton, NJ 08053-1838, **Home Phone:** (856)596-1181. **Business Addr:** 146 Montgomery Ave, Bala Cynwyd, PA 19004.

### PATTERSON, JOAN DELORES

Military leader. **Personal:** Born Mar 17, 1944, Columbia, SC; daughter of David Creech; children: Torrey. **Educ:** City Col Chicago, AA, 1976; Chicago State Univ, BA, 1979; Univ N Fla, MEd, 1982. **Career:** USN, dir personal serv, 1982-83, educ tech, 1983-84, personnel clerk, 1984; USAF, guid counr, 1984-88, educ specialist, 1988-96, educ servs flight, chief, 1996-. **Orgs:** Am Soc Training & Develop, 1982-85; chief counr, Equal Employ Opportunity, 1984-85; mgr, Fed Women's Prog, 1984; Am Coun Asn, 1985-; Mil Educr & Counors Asn, 1985-, bd dir, 1989-94; Asn Multicultural Coun & Develop, 1985-; secy, Tuskegee Airman Inst, 1990-; Am Counors & Educr Gout, 1994-. **Honors/Awds:** Outstanding Performance Award, USF, 1992, US Navy, 1983; Letters of Commendation, USAF, 1986. **Home Addr:** 1271 White Oak Cir, Melbourne, FL 32934-7289, **Home Phone:** (321)255-5559. **Business Addr:** Chief of Education Services & Human Resources Flight, US Air Force, 1271 White Oak Cir, Melbourne, FL 32934, **Business Phone:** (321)494-4670.

### PATTERSON, KAY

State government official. **Personal:** Born Jan 11, 1931, Darlington, SC; son of James Hildred and Lelia; married Jean Millicent James; children: Eric Horace (deceased) & Pamela Maria. **Educ:** Allen Univ, AB, 1956; Temple Univ, attended 1959; SC State Col, MEd, 1971. **Career:** Educator (retired), senator; W A Perry Mid Sch, teacher, 1956-70; Benedict Col, instr, 1968; SC Educ Asn, uniserv rep, 1970-84; SC House Rep, rep, 1975-85; SC Legis, sen, 1985-2006; SC Sen, Richland County, Dist 19, mem, 1985-; SC Legis Black Caucus, chmn, 1990; Senate Transp Comn, comnr. **Orgs:** comnr, Richland County Recreation Comn, 1960-70; Nat Educ Asn; Nat Asn Advan Colored People; Educ Comm States, 1978-84; Southern Regional Educ Bd, 1985; trustee, Univ SC, 1983-85; Omega Psi Phi Fraternity; N Columbia Civic Club; life mem, Nat Asn Advan Colored People St. Lukes Episcopal Church; Prince Hall Mason; Omega Psi Phi Fraternity. **Special Achievements:** First Black to serve on the Board since Reconstruction. **Home Addr:** 6815 Gavilan Ave, Columbia, SC 29203-5156, **Home Phone:** (803)754-3746. **Business Addr:** Senator, South Carolina District 19, PO Box 142, Columbia, SC 29202.

### PATTERSON, KEVIN L.

Computer executive, technologist, association executive. **Personal:** married Charlene Price; children: Charise & Craig. **Career:** IBM, systs engr, 1977, adv systs engr, Wash, DC, customer ctr support mgr, 1985-87, systs engineering manger, 1987-90, acct develop mgr, 1990-91, sales mgr educ, Western NC, 1991-92, sales bus unit exec, 1992-93, sales specialist mgr, 1993-95, technol specialist mgr, 1995-98, mid range sales specialist mgr, 1998-2000, Bus Unit Exec, 2000-01, bus unit exec eserver Mid-Atlantic States, 2001, worldwide eServer iSeries sales exec, 2001, worldwide dir sales, POWER Syst Unit; Worldwide Sales eServer iSeries, dir, 2004. **Orgs:** Founder, Focus Leadership; founder, Charlottes African Am leadership orgn; Pres, 100 Black Men Am, greater charlotte chap; co-chair conv meetings, 100 Black Men Am; pres, United Way Bd Dir NC; chair, Friendship Missionary Baptist Church; Afro Am Cult Centers Bd; Arts & Sci Coun Bd Dirs; chair, Charlotte Mecklenburg Pub Arts Comn; grants panelist, ASC; chair, Mint's Celebrating Legacy; YMCA. **Honors/Awds:** Numerous recognition from various civic organisation inculding, JA; Inroads; YMCA; Focus Leadership, 100 Black Men Am; United Family Serv. **Special Achievements:** Charlotte Observer and Charlotte Post voted him one of the Top 10 Leaders in Charlotte.

### PATTERSON, LYDIA R.

Consultant, educator. **Personal:** Born Sep 3, 1936, Carrabelle, FL; daughter of Richard D Ross and Johnnie Mae Thomas Ross; married Edgar A Corley; children: Derek Kelley Corley; married Berman W. **Educ:** Hunter Col, BA, 1958. **Career:** US Energy Dept, NY, indus res specialist, 1966-68; NY State Div Human Rights, reg dir & mgr 1962-66, 1968-76; Columbia Univ, sem speaker; Wharton Sch Harvard Univ, sem speaker; Duke Univ, sem speaker; Cornell Sch IDL Rels, sem speaker, 1976-89; Bankers Trust Co, EEO Planning & Contract Rels, vpres & corp mgr, 1976-87; Extend Consult Serv, pres & chief exec officer, 1982-94; Lydia Patterson Commun, pres & chief exec officer, 1985-95, chief exec officer, 1996-; Merrill Lynch & Co, vpres, EEO Servs Dept, mgr corp & chief exec officer, 1987-90; Bor Manhattan Community Col, NY, adj lectr, 1991; DBA, Practical Resources, 2001-. **Orgs:** Govt affairs comn, Fin Women Asn & Nat Asn Bank Women, 1978-87; prof develop comn, Urban Bankers Coalition, 1978-86; Soc Human Resources Mgt, 1979-87, Nat Urban League, 1979-93; exec bd, NY Women Employ Ctr, 1985-87; exec bd & mem, EDGES, 1985-87; Women's Um, 1988-89; bd dir, Proj Discovery Columbia Univ, 1988; City Univ NY Voc & Tech Educ Adv Coun, 1990-91; bd dir & vp mktg, Wellington Edu Comm Found, 1992-94; chair, Palm W Chamber Com, Edu Comm, 1996-2000; Leadership Palm Beach Co, 1997-; Gulfstream Goodwill Industs, 1997; bd mem, Leadership Palm Beach Co, 1999-2001; bd mem, Palm W Chamber Com, Edu Comm, 2000-01; bd, Gulf Stream Goodwill Industs, 1997-; bd, Am Heart Asn; conf bd Cornell Univ; Bus Policy Rev Coun; Exec Leadership Coun. **Business Addr:** Founder, Consultant, Lydia Patterson Communications, 12689 Coral Breese Dr, Wellington, FL 33414-8070, **Business Phone:** (561)790-7380.

### PATTERSON, DR. ORLANDO HORACE

Historian, educator, writer. **Personal:** Born Jun 5, 1940, Jamaica; married Nerys; children: Rhiannon & Barbara; married Anita. **Educ:** London Univ, BS, econs, 1962; London Sch Econs, PhD, 1965; Harvard Univ, MA, 1971; Trinity Col, DHL, 1992; New Sch, NY, DHL, 2000; Northeastern Univ, DHL, 2001; Univ Chicago, DHL, 2002; La Trobe Univ, DHL, 2006. **Career:** London Sch Econs, asst lectr, 1965-67; Univ Wi, lectr, 1968-70; Harvard Univ, prof, dept Sociol, 1971-93, actg chmn, 1989-90, John Cowles prof sociol, 1993-; Allston Burr Sr, tutor, 1971-73; Univ Chicago, vis prof, 1994-95; Auth: The Sociology Slavery, 1967; The Children Sisyphys, 1964; An Absence Ruins, 1967; Die the Long Day, 1972; Slavery and Social Death, 1982; Freedom in the Making of Western Culture Vol 1, Basic Books, 1991, A Comparative Study; Ethnic Chauvinism: The Reactionary Impulse, Stein & Day, 1977; Slavery & Social Death, Harvard UNV Press, 1982; The Ordeal Integration, 1997: Progress & Resentment in AME's "Racial" Crisis, Civita sCounterpointBooks, 1997; Rituals Blood: Consequences of Slavery in Two AmericanCenturies, Civitas-Counterpoint, 1999; Freedom Freedom in the Modern World, 2006; The Cultural Matrix Understanding Black Youth, 2015. **Orgs:** AAAS; Am Acad Polit & Social Sci; Am Sociol Asn. **Honors/Awds:** Distinguished Contribution Scholarship Award, Am Sociol Asn, 1983; Ralph Bunche Award, Am Polit Sci Asn, 1983; Walter Channing Cabot Faculty Prize, Harvard Univ, 1983 & 1997; National Book Award, 1991; Medal Merit, Univ Calif, Los Angeles, 1992; Order Distinction Commander Class, 1999; Best Paper onCulture Award, Am Sociol Asn, 2006; Gold Musgrave Medal, 2015. **Business Addr:** Professor of Sociology, Harvard University, 520 William James Hall, Cambridge, MA 02138, **Business Phone:** (617)495-3707.

### PATTERSON, PICKENS ANDREW

Lawyer. **Personal:** Born Aug 1, 1944, Cotton Plant, AR; son of Rev Pickens A and Willie Mae; married Gloria P; children: Pickens A III & Staci E. **Educ:** Fisk Univ, BA, hist, 1965; Harvard Law Sch, JD, 1968. **Career:** Atlanta Legal Aid Soc, managing atty, 1969-70, pres; Jackson, Patterson & Parks, partner, 1970-77; N Cental Legal Asst, exec dir, 1977-78; Dept HUD, atty advisor, 1978-81; City Atlanta, asst city atty, 1981-82; Arrington Patterson Thomas, partner, 1982-85; Thomas, Kennedy, Sampson, Patterson, partner, sr partner, currently; Smith, Gambrell & Russell LLP, partner, currently; Clark Atlanta Univ, adj prof law. **Orgs:** Life mem, Alpha Phi Alpha Fraternity, 1962-; founding mem, Harvard Black Law Students Asn, 1967; Comt Specialization & Re cert, State Bar Ga, 1976; pres, Atlanta Guardsmen, 1993-; dir, pres, Sadie G Mays Nursing Home, 1994-; State Bd Bar Examiners, 1997-; State Bar GA, Adv Opinion Comt, 1998-; life mem, Alpha Phi Alpha Fraternity, Sigma Pi Phi Fraternity, 1998-; Formal Legal Adv Opinion Com, 1998-; Nat Asn Bond Lawyers, 1999; Nat Conf Bar Examrs, Comt Technol, 1999; Atlanta Charter Study Comn; chmn, Atlanta Judicial Comn; pres, Gate City Bar Asn; trustee, Louisville Presby Theol Sem, Louisville, Ky; chmn, State Bar Ga Bd Examiners, 2002; vice chairperson Bb trustee, Fisk Univ; bd dir, Atlanta Med Asn; life mem, Nat Asn Advan Colored People, Legal Redress Comt, chmn. dir; bd trustees, Gammon Theol Sem. **Honors/Awds:** Alumni Award for Scholarship, Fisk Univ Alumni, 1962; Valedictorian, AE Beach High Sch, 1961; Who's Who in American Law, 1985; Who's Who in the South and Southwest, 1986; Departmental Honors, Fisk Univ, 1965; Man of the Year, Cascade United Methodist Church, 1988; Man of the Year, Black Pages, 1998; Man of the Year, Women Looking Ahead Mag, 2008, 2016. **Special Achievements:** Publications: "Got Land Problems" pamphlet designed for landowners, 1972. **Home Addr:** 4044 Lyon Blvd SW, Atlanta, GA 30331-6421. **Business Addr:** Partner, Smith, Gambrell & Russell LLP, 1230 Peachtree St NE Promenade Suite 3100, Atlanta, GA 30309, **Business Phone:** (404)815-3708.

### PATTERSON, HON. ROBERT L.

Judge. **Personal:** Born Aug 2, 1945, Detroit, MI; son of Clarence (deceased) and Florence; married Joyce Hurst; children: Kevin & Robert II. **Educ:** Colo State Univ, Ft Colins, BS, sociol, 1968; Univ Colo, Boulder, JD, 1974. **Career:** Univ Colo, dir black educ prog, 1969; Colo State Univ, asst dir proj go, 1970-71; Legal Aid Soc, staff atty, 1974-76; Colo State Pub Defender, Dep Pub Defender, 1976-80; Western Dist Wash, asst fed defender, Fed Pub Defender, 1980-81; Colo Atty Gen, asst atty gen, 1981-85; Denver County Ct, judge, 1985, presiding judge, 1998-00; Colo Supreme Ct; US Dist Ct, Colo; US Dist Ct, Western Dist Wash; US Ct Appeals, Ninth Circuit; Best Best & Krieger LLP, atty, currently. **Orgs:** Nat Bar Asn, 1980-; pres, Delta Eta Boule, 1991-; Judicial Coun Nat Bar Asn; Colo Bar Asn; Denver Bar Asn; Sam Cary Bar Asn; Am Judges Asn; Am Judicature Soc; Colo Supreme Ct Comn Delay Reduction; Western Regional Officer, Sigma Pi Phi Fraternity, 1997-01; Nat Asn Ct Mgt, 1998-01; chair, Justice Ctr Planning Comn Denver Co Ct, currently. **Honors/Awds:** Man of Distinction, Lane Col Alumni Asn, 1990; Who's Who in American Law; Dynamic Duo Award, Am Asn Univ Women, 1999; Distinguished Service Award, Judicial Coun Nat Bar Asn, 2001; Living Sr Hall of Fame Award 4th Ann, Clyburn Sr Village, 2001; Living Legend Award, 2003; Outstanding Toastmaster, Toastmasters Int Downtown Speakeasy Club, 2002-03. **Special Achievements:** First African-American Presiding Judge in the history of the Denver Colorado Court, 1998-01. **Home Addr:** 400 S Steele St Suite 2, Denver, CO 80209, **Home Phone:** (303)744-6554. **Business Addr:** Attorney, Best Best & Krieger LLP, 74 760 Hwy 111 Suite 200, Indian Wells, CA 92210, **Business Phone:** (760)568-2611.

### PATTERSON, RONALD E.

Banker. **Educ:** Stephen F Austin State Univ, MBA, finance, 1977; Rutgers Univ, Stonier Grad Sch Banking, cert Graduation, com banking, 1986. **Career:** Repub Bank, Dallas, vpres com Loan Officer, 1977-86; First Bank & Trust, Lufkin, Tex; Commonwealth Nat Bank, Mobile, Ala, pres & chief exec officer, 1987-92; Chase Bank, vpres & com relationship mgr, 1994-2005; City Dallas, sr coordr econ develop, 2006-10; Fed Deposit Ins Corp, contract oversight mgr, 2010-. **Orgs:** Pres, Nat Asn Urban Bankers, Dallas Chap. **Business Addr:** Contract Oversight Manager, Federal Deposit Insurance Corp, 550 17th St NW, Washington, DC 20429, **Business Phone:** (877)275-3342.

### PATTERSON, RUBEN NATHANIEL

Basketball player. **Personal:** Born Jul 31, 1975, Cleveland, OH; son of Charlene (deceased); married Shannon; children: 3; married Dee. **Educ:** Univ Cincinnati, attended 1998. **Career:** Basketball player (retired), free agt; Independence CC, 1994-96; AEK Athens, Greece, 1998; Los Angeles Lakers, 1999; Seattle Sonics, 1999-2001; Portland Trail Blazers, 2001-06; Denver Nuggets, 2006; Milwaukee Bucks, small forward, 2006-07; LA Clippers, 2007; Champville, Lebanon, 2009; free agt, currently.

### PATTERSON, SALADIN K.

Writer, movie producer. **Career:** C/o 20th Century Fox, producer & writer, currently; Films: One Flight Stand, producer & writer, 2003; The Fighting Temptations, screenplay, 2003; TV series: Teen Angel, 1998; The PJs, story ed, 1999, writer, 2000; "Frasier", writer, 2000-03, producer, 2002-03; "The Bernie Mac Show", co-exec producer, 2003-06, writer, 2004-06; "Stacked", consult producer, 2005; Psych, writer, 2007-14, co-exec producer, 2007-11; "Two and a Half Men", 2013-15; "The Big Bang Theory ", consult producer, 2015. **Business Addr:** Writer, Producer, c/o The 20th Century Fox, 10201 Pico Blvd, Los Angeles, CA 90035, **Business Phone:** (310)369-1000.

### PATTERSON, WILLIAM BENJAMIN

Chief executive officer, administrator, vice president (government). **Personal:** Born May 19, 1931, Little Rock, AR; son of William Benjamin Sr and Perrish Childress; married Euradell Logan; children: William & David. **Educ:** Calif State Univ, San Francisco, BS, 1956, MS, 1963. **Career:** City Oakland, Off Parks & Recreation, recreation dir, 1952-56, head recreation dir, 1956-62, dist suprvr, 1962-74, admin supvr, 1964-74, visitor serv mgr, 1974-87, recreation serv mgr, 1987-89; City Oakland, Off Mayor Lionel J Wilson, spec consult, 1989; Webster Dent Care, orthodontist, cicero doctor; Growth Opportunities Inc, pres & chief exec officer; E Bay Munic Utility Dist Bd, bd dir, 1997, pres, 2004-06, vpres retirement bd, currently. **Orgs:** Foreman Alameda County Grand Jury, 1982-83; life mem, Kappa Alpha Psi Frat, 1982-; Oakland Baseball Athletics Adv Bd, 1982-; Nat Asn Advan Colored People, 1982-87; treas, bd dir, Joe Morgan Youth Found, 1983-; vpres & dir, Mitre Bus Org, 1983-88, pres & chief exec officer, 1988-; Sigma Pi Phi Frat, 1984-; pres, chair bd, New Oakland Comn, 1985; pres & bd chair, Greater Acorn Community Improv Asn, 1985-87; Calif Parks & Recreation Soc, E Bay Recreation Exec Asn; Am Asn Zool Parks & Aquariums; bd mem, pres, Oakland Nat Asn Advan Colored People; bd pres, Peralta Found; bd trustee mem, League Women Voters Oakland; Recreation Comn; Upper Mokelumne River Watershed Authority; Freeport Regional Water Authority; Oaklands Pub Ethics & Parks; Oakland Workforce Investment Bd, currently. **Home Addr:** 5861 Balmoral Dr, Oakland, CA 94619, **Home Phone:** (510)530-8431. **Business Addr:** Director, Vice President of Retirement Board, East Bay Municipality Utility District Board, 375 11th St, Oakland, CA 94607, **Business Phone:** (866)403-2683.

### PATTERSON, DR. WILLIS CHARLES

Entertainer, educator, founder (originator). **Personal:** Born Nov 27, 1930, Ann Arbor, MI; son of Ed Curtis; married Frankie Bouyer; children: Sharon, Kevin, Shelia & Jamal. **Educ:** Univ Mich, BMusEd, 1958, M Mus, 1959; Wayne State Univ, PhD, music. **Career:** Southern Univ, Baton Rouge, 1959-61; Va State Col, music fac, assoc prof, 1962-68; Our Own Thing Inc, founder, dir & conductor, currently; Univ Mich, Sch Music, Theatre & Dance, voice fac, 1968, Men's Glee Club, music dir, 1969-75, prof & assoc dean, prof emer, currently; Willis Patterson Our Own Thing Chorale, founder. **Orgs:** Nat Opera Asn; Nat Asn Teachers Singing; Alpha Phi Alpha; Nat Asn Advan Colored People; pres, Nat Asn Negro Musicians; exec secy, Nat Black Music Caucus; Fulbright fel. **Honors/Awds:** Marian Anderson Award. **Special Achievements:** He has appeared as King Balthazar on NBC-TV in its production of Menotti's opera Amal & the Night Visitors, has been seen professionally in such operas as Gershwin's Porgy and Bess, Beethoven's Fidelio & Puccini's La Boheme. **Business Addr:** Professor Emeritus, University of Michigan, EV Moore Bldg 1100 Baits Dr, Ann Arbor, MI 48109-2085, **Business Phone:** (734)764-0583.

### PATTERSON-TOWNSEND, MARGARET M.

Administrator, technologist. **Personal:** Born Jul 4, 1951, Flint, MI; daughter of Albert Patterson and Zelma V Stewart; children: Marc A & Sommer C Green. **Educ:** Bakers Bus Col, bus admin, 1987; Univ Mich, MS, health care admin, 1992; Univ Mich, Flint, BS, hosp & health care facil admin, 1993; Univ Mich Med Ctr, polysomnography, 1994. **Career:** Flint Gen Hosp, admin asst, 1978-86; Health Plus MI, from asst to dir spec accts, 1986-89; Manpower Inc, admin troubleshooter, 1990-91; Midwest APT, 1990-2012; Sleep Dis Inst MI, asst coordr, 1991-92; Genesee Co Substance Abuse, asst to dir develop, 1991-92; Mich Sleep Diagnostics & Res Ctr, dir, 1992-, pres, 1989-2006, chief exec officer, currently; Acute Alternative Sleep Ctr, sleep ctr dir, 2008-14; Townsend Consults, pres, 2012-; Welcome Med Serv, chief operating officer, 2015-. **Orgs:** Ambassador, Flint Chamber Com; dir, Nat Asn Female Execs; Am Bus Womens Asn; Flint Womens Forum, bus; dir, Mid Michs Coordr Nat Narcoleptic Found; Am Asn Sleep technologists (AAST), 2014. **Home Addr:** 1145 E Harvard Ave, Flint, MI 48505, **Home Phone:** (810)785-7153. **Business Addr:** Chief Executive Officer, Michigan Sleep Diagnostics & Research Center, 3237 Beecher Rd Suite M, Flint, MI 48532, **Business Phone:** (810)733-8338.

### PATTILLO, JOYCE M.
Executive, consultant. **Personal:** Born Apr 28, 1951, Little Rock, AR; daughter of Johnnie C and Mable Stubblefield; married Conrad; children: Conrad Peyton. **Educ:** Univ Ark Pine Bluff, BA, social & hist, 1972; Webster Univ, MA, human resources develop. **Career:** Social Security Admin, claims rep, 1973-80; US Dept Labor, investr, 1980-82; US Dept Army, chief tech serv, 1982-87; EEOC, investr, 1987-90; Alltel Info Serv, mgr affirmative action, diversity, 1990-; JPAT Consult, mgr, exec dir. **Orgs:** Alpha Kappa Alpha Sorority, 1970-; adv coun, Lions World Servs Blind, 1990-; bd mem, Ark ABIE, 1992-; Toastmasters, CTM, 1992-; Urban League, 1992; educ comm, Greater Little Rock Chamber Com, 1992-; Ark Human Resources Asn; Soc Human Resources Mgt; bd mem, Leadership Greater Little Rock, Class IX; Help Individuals Receive Employ; Lions World Serv adv coun Our town 1; bd mem, Ark C Mus; bd mem, United Way, allocations comn, 1993-. **Home Addr:** 20 Kings Arms Rd, Little Rock, AR 72227. **Business Addr:** Human Resources Executive, Rank Video Services America Inc, 9201 Faulkner Lake Rd, North Little Rock, AR 72117.

### PATTILLO, ROLAND A.
Physician, educator. **Personal:** Born Jun 12, 1933, DeQuincy, LA; son of James and Rhena; married Patricia; children: Catherine, Michael, Patrick, Sheri & Mary. **Educ:** Xavier Univ, BS, 1955; St Louis Univ, MD; Am Bd Obstet & Gynec, cert; WI State Med Lic, 1960-; GA State Med Lic, 1995-. **Career:** Med Col Wis, intern, 1959-60, resident obstet & gynec, 1960-67; Harvard Univ, fel, resident, 1960-64; Obstet & Gynecol J NIH, fel, 1965-67; Johns Hopkins Univ, fel, 1967; World Health Orgn, consult, 1977, prof, dir, cancerres & res sci; Med Col Wis, physician, 1968-; Marquette Univ; Morehouse Sch Med, interim chmn, 1996, HeLa Conf, founded, 1996, dir residency prog, Dept Obstet & Gynecol, prof, prof emer, currently. **Orgs:** Bd dir, Am Cancer Soc; Milwaukee Div Sci Jour Reviewer; J Nat Cancer Inst Sci; Cancer Res; Am J Obstetricians & Gynecologists; fel Am Cong Obstetricians & Gynecologists. **Honors/Awds:** Research Award, Am Col Obstetricians & Gynecologists, 1963, Found Thesis Award, 1975; Physician of the Year, Cream City Med Soc, 1990; Distinguished Service Award, Med Col Wis, 1994; Medallion, Trophoblast Soc, 2003; Atlanta Top Doctors, Atlanta Mag, 2002; Health Heroes, Atlanta Bus Chronicle, 2005. **Home Addr:** 2129 Roscoe Rd, Newnan, GA 30263-4004, **Home Phone:** (770)251-8046. **Business Addr:** Director, Professor Emeritus, Morehouse School of Medicine, 720 Westview Dr SW, Atlanta, GA 30310-1495, **Business Phone:** (404)616-6634.

### PATTON, ANTWAN ANDRE (BIG BOI)
Singer, actor, business owner. **Personal:** Born Feb 1, 1975, Savannah, GA; married Sherlita; children: Bamboo; children: Jordan, Cross & Bamboo. **Career:** Hip-hop duo Out Kast, currently; Pitfall Kennels, owner, currently; Albums: Southern playalist icadillacmuzik, 1994; ATLiens, 1996; Aquemini, 1998; Stankonia, 2000; Speaker boxxx/The Love Below, 2003; Sir Lucious Left Foot: The Son of Chico Dusty; Ghetto Musick; Got Purp? Vol 2, xXx: State of the Union, 2005; Idle wild, 2006; The Way You Move; Films/TV: "Benz or Beamer", 1995; "In Due Time", 1997; "High Schoolin'", 1999; "Speed ballin'", 2001; "B.O.B (Bombs Over Baghdad)", 2001; "B.O.B. (Bombs Over Baghdad)", 2002; "So Fresh, So Clean", 2002; "Land of a Million Drums", 2002; "Players Ball", 2002; "On & On & On", 2003; Films: Idle wild, co-producer, 2006; ATL, 2006; Idlewild, 2006; Who's Your Caddy, 2007; How 2 Build a Rapper, 2008; "Law & Order: Special Victims Unit", 2008; "BET News", 2008; Kiss and Tail: The Hollywood Jump off, 2009; Freaknik: The Musical, 2010. **Honors/Awds:** Player's Ball went gold, 1993; Southern playalist icadillacmuzik went platinum, 1993; Aquemini went double platinum, 1998; Two Grammy Awards for Stankonia, 2001; Three Grammy Awds for Speaker boxxx/The Love Below, 2004. **Business Addr:** Recording Artist, Singer, c/o Outkast, Atlanta, GA 30321.

### PATTON, DR. CURTIS LEVERNE
Scientist, educator. **Personal:** Born Jun 13, 1935, Birmingham, AL; married Barbara Beth Battle; children: Lynne Martine. **Educ:** Fisk Univ, BA, zool, 1956; Mich State Univ, MS, microbiol, 1961, PhD, microbiol, 1966. **Career:** Mich State Univ, asst microbiologist, 1960-63, from asst instr to instr, 1963-67; Rockefeller Univ, guest investr, 1967-70; Yale Univ, Sch Med, asst prof microbiol, 1970-74, dir grad studies, 1972-74, asst prof epidemiol, pub health & microbiol, 1974-76, assoc prof epidemiol, pub health & microbiol, 1976-2006, chair, Int Health, researcher, prof emer(retired), epidemiol, 2006. **Orgs:** Parasitol fel Rockefeller Univ, 1967-70; dir, Interdisciplinary Parasitol Training Prog; Minority Access Res Careers & Nat Ins Gen Med Sci, 1978-82; Nat Res Coun Community Human Res Eval Panel, 1979-81; consult, AUS Med Res & Develop Command, 1979-82; Am Asn Advan Sci; Am Soc Parasitologists; Soc Protozoologists; fel socs infectious dis. **Honors/Awds:** Biomedical Science Support Grant, 1966-67; Training Grant, USPHS, 1967-69, Research Grants, 1972-77, 1978-86; Edward A. Bouchet Leadership Award, 2004; Award for Excellence in Leadership Promoting Public Health, Social Justice & Human Rights, 2006. **Special Achievements:** First African-Am grad of Yale Col. **Home Addr:** 61 Whittier Rd, New Haven, CT 06515-2437, **Home Phone:** (203)397-2217. **Business Addr:** Professor Emeritus, Yale School of Public Health, 60 College St 319 EMD, New Haven, CT 06510, **Business Phone:** (203)785-6132.

### PATTON, JEAN E.
Executive, educator, consultant. **Personal:** Born Mar 14, 1947, Bronx, NY; daughter of John Henry and Estelle Witherspoon. **Educ:** City Univ NY, BA, psychol, 1971; Columbia Univ, advan cert, orgn develop & human resources mgt, 1999; Univ Mich, advan cert, orgn develop & human resources mgt, 1999; NY Univ Sch Continuing & Prof Studies, orgn & exec coaching, 2005. **Career:** Training Living Inst, group facilitator, 1971-73; Harlem Confrontation Drug Rehab Ctr, dir educ, 1973-75; Nat Westminster Bank, asst vpres, corp training & develop mgr, 1975-83; Second Skin Cosmetics, founder, pres, 1983-87; Color Educ Resources, founder, pres, 1986-; Securities Indust Automation Corp, sr training specialist, 1992-98, dir training & develop, 1998-2005; Credit Suisse, Shared Serv Inst, consult & contractor, vp learning partner, 2006-07, Leadership Inst, consult & contractor, dir, 2007; UBS, dir head home off educ, 2008-09, dir exec develop, 2009-10, dir managing dir serv, 2010-11. **Orgs:** Local & int bd, var community; Asn Image Consults Int; bd mem, Harlem Dowling-W Side Ctr C & Family Serv, 2009-. **Home Addr:** 321 W 29th St, New York, NY 10001, **Home Phone:** (212)564-3082. **Business Addr:** Board Member, Harlem Dowling-West Side Center for Children & Family Services, 2090 Adam Clayton Powell Jr Blvd, New York, NY 10027, **Business Phone:** (212)749-3656.

### PATTON, JOSEPH CEPHUS, IV
Football player. **Personal:** Born Jan 5, 1972, Birmingham, AL. **Educ:** Ala A&M Univ. **Career:** Football player (retired); Wash Redskins, guard, 1994, left tackle, 1995-97, left guard, 1997, right guard, 1998; Jacksonville Jaguars, 1999.

### PATTON, JOYCE BRADFORD
School administrator, educator. **Personal:** Born May 31, 1947, Shreveport, LA; married Jerry A; children: Blythe. **Educ:** Grambling State Univ, BA, 1969; State Univ NY, Teacher Col, Buffalo, MS, 1972; La State Univ, Shreveport, LA, 1983. **Career:** Caddo Mid Magnet, earth sci teacher, asst prin, curric & instr, currently. **Orgs:** Prog scholar comn, Alpha Kappa Alpha Inc, 1966-; Nat Educ Asn, 1972-; YWCA 1983-; Nat Sci Teachers Asn, 1984-; local sch chmn, Substance Abuse Prev Educ, 1984-; local bd 1st vpres, Parent Teacher Stud Asn, 1984-85; Nat Earth Sci Teachers Asn, 1986-; youth Sunday sch supt Mt Canaan Baptist Church, 1986-; Phi Delta Kappa, 1987-; exec bd mem, La Sci Teacher Asn, 1990-93; pres, Northwest La Sci Teachers Asn, 1991-92; chair, AKA Sorority Inc, Ebony Fashion Fair, 1993-94. **Home Addr:** 6306 Kenwood Dr, Shreveport, LA 71119-6211, **Home Phone:** (318)631-8359. **Business Addr:** Assistant Principal of Curriculum & Instruction, Caddo Middle Magnet, 7635 Cornelious Lane, Shreveport, LA 71106, **Business Phone:** (318)868-6588.

### PATTON, LEROY (LEROI PATTON)
Cinematographer. **Personal:** Born Apr 14, 1944, AL; son of Charles H and Neuria; married Jessie Maple; children: Mark A, Edward L & Audrey Maple. **Educ:** Ind Cent Col; Ind Univ, attended 1967; Calif Film Inst Filmmakers, attended 1971. **Career:** Cinematographer, camera operator; Films: Fame, asst camera, 1980; Fort Apache the Bronx, second camera operator, 1981; Brewsters Millions, collab dir photog, 1985; School Daze, second camera operator, 1988; Drop Squad, dir photog, 1994; The Walking Dead, camera operator, 1995; Love: In Brief; Rosewood, camera operator, 1997; Save the Children; fUp Against the Wall, cinematographer, 1991; Women Behind the Camera, cinematographer, 2007; Dear Willie, camera operator, 2011; TV series: "The Simple Life of Noah Dearborn", camera operator, 1999; "The Last Brickmaker in America", camera operator, 2001; "My Parents My Sister & Me", dir photog; LJ Film Productions Inc, founder & owner, 1974. **Orgs:** Pres, Concerned Black Filmmakers NYC; 100 Black Men Inc; Cameraman Union Iatse Local 644. **Honors/Awds:** First & Second prize, NY Black Film Festival, 1977; Freedoms Found Award, WCBS-TV spec "My Seeds Are Gone", 1979. **Special Achievements:** Published "How to Become a Union Camerawoman Film Videotape", 1977. **Home Addr:** 20 W 120th St, New York, NY 10027. **Business Addr:** Cinematographer, 20 W 120th St, New York, NY 10027.

### PATTON, MARVCUS RAYMOND
Football player, business owner. **Personal:** Born May 1, 1967, Los Angeles, CA; son of Raymond (deceased) and Barbara; married Ina; children: 2. **Educ:** Univ Calif, BS, polit sci, 1990. **Career:** Football player (retired), owner; Buffalo Bills, linebacker, 1990-94; Wash Redskins, 1995-98; Kans City Chiefs, 1999-2002; Girls Like Math LLC, owner, currently. **Business Addr:** Owner, Girls Like Math LLC, 14001 C St Germain Dr Suite 820, Centreville, VA 20121, **Business Phone:** (800)425-0119.

### PATTON, PRINCESS E.
Journalist, editor. **Personal:** Born Jan 1, 1954, Nashville, TN; daughter of Gill H Gordon Sr and Mary Frances Corder (deceased); married Alexander Jr; children: Keisha RaNese Simmons Clopton, Ayesha Patrice & H Eric Simmons. **Educ:** Fisk Univ, BA, 1978. **Career:** United Methodist Publ House, Abington Press, copy ed; Vanderbilt Univ, staff reporter, calendar ed, 1984-86; The Tennessean, forum ed, columnist, ed writer, 1986-92; Meharry Med Col, publ ed, 1994-. **Orgs:** Nat Asn Black Journalists, 1986-; Nashville Asn Minority Communicators, 1986-; Minority Journ Workshop, exe comt mem, 1991-92; Parents for Pub Edu, steering comt mem, 1990-91; Parents Against Paddling, adv comt mem, 1989-. **Honors/Awds:** Peace and Justice Award, Domestic Violence Prog, 1990. **Home Addr:** 765 Dover Glen Dr, PO Box 22698, Antioch, TN 37013-1863, **Home Phone:** (615)365-2292. **Business Addr:** Publications Editor, Meharry Medical College, 1005 D B Todd Blvd, Nashville, TN 37208, **Business Phone:** (615)327-6273.

### PATTON, RICARDO MAURICE
Basketball coach. **Personal:** Born Oct 23, 1958, Nashville, TN; son of Leroy Reed and Juanita; married Jennifer; children: Ricardo Jr & Michael. **Educ:** Belmont Col, BA, phys educ, 1980; Trevecca Nazarene Col, MA, admin & supv, 1989. **Career:** Two Rivers Mid Sch, head coach, 1985-86; Hillwood High Sch, head coach, 1986-87; Mid Tenn State Univ, Murfrees boro, asst coach, 1988-90; Ark-Little Rock Univ, asst coach, 1990-91; Tenn State Univ, asst coach, 1991-93; Univ Colo, Boulder, Colo, from asst coach to head coach, 1993-2007; Northern Ill Univ, head coach, 2007-11; Md Eastern Shore, asst coach, 2011-12; Cent High Sch, head coach, 2012-. **Orgs:** Nat Asn Basketball Coaches. **Business Addr:** Head Coach, Central High School, 306 S Bellevue Blvd, Memphis, TN 38104, **Business Phone:** (901)416-4500.

### PATTON, ROBERT
Mayor, government official, educator. **Personal:** Born Jun 29, 1947, Clarksdale, MS; married Dorothy J Johnson; children: Kamela, Darrell & Karen. **Educ:** Jackson State Univ, attended 1968; Delta State Univ, MA, 1976. **Career:** Shelby, Miss, vice mayor, 2001-05, mayor; Bolivar County Sch Dist 3, teacher; Bolivar County, city alderman. **Orgs:** Jackson State Alumni Asn; St Andrews Baptist Church; vpres, PTA Broad St Sch; trustee, St Andrews Baptist Church; Bolivar County Develop Bd. **Honors/Awds:** Outstanding Comm Leader, 1974-75. **Home Addr:** PO Box 766, Shelby, MS 38774-0766.

### PAUL, DR. ALVIN
Educator, school administrator. **Personal:** Born Feb 17, 1941, New Roads, LA; son of Alvin Jr and Pearl H; married Vera; children: Alvin Jerome, Calvin James & Douglas Fairbanks. **Educ:** Southern Univ, Baton Rouge, LA, BS, 1961; Northeastern Ill Univ, MEd, 1970; Nova Southeast Univ, Ft Lauderdale, EdD, 1979. **Career:** School administrator (retired); Pointe Coupee Parish Schs, New Roads, La, math & sci teacher, 1961-62; Gary Pub Schs, math teacher, 1962-71, team leader & asst prin, 1967-69; Marcy Newberry Ctr, Chicago, actg exec dir & dir, 1971; Prairie State Col, math & educ teacher, 1971-90, prof, math dept, 1990-2005, adj fac, prof emer, currently; Our Lady Solace Cath Sch Chicago, prin, 1974-75; Triton Col, River Grove Ill, math teacher, 1979-93. **Orgs:** Chair, St Dorothy Parish Coun, 1976-79, 1998-2003; pres & chmn, St Dorothy Sch Bd, 1976-79; adv bd, 1977-90, chmn, 1980-83, Prairie State Col, 1976-87; Archdiocese Chicago, Bd Educ, 1979-84; Keeper Rec, Chicago Height Alumni, 1982; Kappa Alpha Psi Chap Guide Right Comn, 1982, 1985, 1987, 1993-; chmn, Acad Prog Rev Comn, PSC, 1983-85; bd mem, Chicago Heights, BRCEDA, 1983-; dep grand knight, Knights Peter Claver Coun #158, 1987-89; treas, PSC Fed Teacher Union, 1995-98; Curric Comt & Fac Senate (PSC); bus mgr, Our Lady Peace Home Sch Asn; formermem, Our Lady Peace Parish Coun; pres, Asn Black Personnel, PSC; chair, Spiritual Life CMS; prayer group, promise keepers at St Dorothy Cath Church, 1996-2000; chair, N Cheektowaga Amateur Athletic Asn, Prairie State Col. **Home Addr:** 8505 S Philips Ave, Chicago, IL 60617. **Business Addr:** Professor Emeritus, Prairie State College, 202 S Halsted St, Chicago Heights, IL 60411, **Business Phone:** (708)709-3500.

### PAUL, TITO JERMAINE
Football player, insurance agent. **Personal:** Born May 24, 1972, Kissimmee, FL. **Educ:** Ohio State Univ, BA, econs, 1995. **Career:** Football player (retired), agent; Ariz Cardinals, defensive back, 1995-97; Cincinnati Bengals, right cornerback, 1997; Denver Broncos, 1998; Wash Redskins, 1999; State Farm Ins, ins agt, 2005-. **Orgs:** Bd dir, Red Cross; vol, Big Bros & Big Sisters. **Business Addr:** Insurance Agent, State Farm Insurance, 7 E Winter St, Delaware, OH 43015-1923, **Business Phone:** (740)369-4537.

### PAUL, VERA MAXINE
Educator. **Personal:** Born Dec 14, 1940, Mansfield, LA; daughter of Virginia Elzania Smith Hall and Clifton Hall; married Alvin James III; children: Alvin Jerome, Calvin James & Douglas Fairbanks. **Educ:** Southern Univ, Baton Rouge, BS, 1962; Chicago State Univ, Chicago, attended 1969; Roosevelt Univ, Chicago, MA, 1975. **Career:** Educator (retired); Union State High Sch, Shreveport, La, teacher, 1962-64; S Bend Community Sch Syst, S Bend, Ind, 1967-68; Chicago Bd Educ, Chicago, Ill, teacher, 1964-67; Chicago Bd Educ, Chicago, Ill, asst prin, 1968. **Orgs:** Chicago Teacher Union, 1964; Nat Asn Advan Colored People, 1965; Ill Teacher Union, 1968; Nat Math Asn, 1969-88; Ill Math Asn, 1975-88; Oper Push, 1975-88; Am Fedn Teachers, 1978; Urban League, 1980-88; Chicago Area Alliance Black Sch Educrs, 1982-87; life mem & Great Lakes regional dir, Zeta Phi Beta Sorority Inc, 1986-90; bd dir, elected dir, Retired Teachers Asn Chicago, 2002-04, 2006. **Home Addr:** 17439 Derwent Lane, Tinley Park, IL 60487-7685, **Home Phone:** (312)721-8439.

### PAUL, WANDA D.
Executive, vice president (organization). **Personal:** Born May 3, 1957, Philadelphia, PA; daughter of Henry and Maude Daniels; married Patrick. **Educ:** Temple Univ, BBA, bus admin & acct, 1979. **Career:** Deloitte Haskins & Sells, auditor, 1979; Goode Admin, dir commun fundraising, 1983-85; Philadelphia Convention Bur, vpres finance & admin, 1985, sr vpres finance & admin, currently. **Orgs:** Nat Asn Black Accountants, 1980-; chairperson-bd dir, 1980, chair, 1993-95, 1998-2000, Urban League Philadelphia; Int Asn Convention & Visitors Bur, 1989-; Am Inst Cert Pub Accountants, 1990-; Int Asn Hospitality Accountants, 1990-; Pa Inst Cert Pub Accountants, 1990-; vice chair, treas, bd dir, Steppingstone Scholars Inc, currently; bd dir, vice chair, Nat Adoption Ctr, currently; United Way Campaign Cabinet, 2008; Rhythm & Blues Found. **Home Addr:** 10 Heathrow Ct, Blackwood, NJ 08012-5249, **Home Phone:** (856)232-4705. **Business Addr:** Sr Vice President of Finance, Administration, Philadelphia Convention & Visitors Bureau, 1700 Market St Suite 3000, Philadelphia, PA 19103, **Business Phone:** (215)636-3300.

**PAWLEY, DR. THOMAS D, III.** **See Obituaries Section.**

### PAYDEN, REV. HENRY J., SR.
Clergy, chaplain. **Personal:** Born Apr 3, 1923, Columbus, OH; married Phyllis M Smith; children: Garnet, William B, Linda, Henry J Jr, Wendy M & Paula Y. **Educ:** Cert Clin Psychol & Pastoral Coun, Ashland Theol Sem, 1971; Capital Univ; Cleveland Bible Col, Westminster; Western Res Univ. **Career:** Holy Trinity Baptist Church, organizer & pastor, 1961, pastor emer, currently; St Paul Baptist Church, New Castle, pastor; Macedonia Baptist Church, Toledo; Gr Abyssinia Baptist Church, Cleveland; Black Shield Cleveland Police Unit, chap-

lain. **Orgs:** Cleveland Women's Sym Orch; Chaplain Amvets; Mt Pleasant Community Ctr; Pub Bd & Teacher Prog Nat Baptist Conv Inc. **Honors/Awds:** Awarded automobile as Soloist in Burts Hour Cleveland, 1947; Pastor of the Year, 1956. **Home Addr:** 3608 Rolliston Rd, Cleveland, OH 44120-5137. **Business Addr:** Pastor Emeritus, Holy Trinity Baptist Church, 3808 14 E 131 St, Cleveland, OH 44120, **Business Phone:** (216)561-4121.

## PAYNE, ALLEN

Actor. **Personal:** Born Jul 7, 1968, Harlem, NY. **Career:** Films: Rooftops, 1989; Cookie, 1989; New Jack City, 1991; CB4, 1993; Jason's Lyric, 1994; Vampire in Brooklyn, 1995; The Walking Dead, 1995; A Price Above Rubies, 1998; The Perfect Storm, 2000; 30 Years to Life, 2001; Blue Hill Avenue, 2001; From the Outside Looking In, 2003; Playas Ball, 2003; Crossover, 2006; TV series: "The Jeffersons", 1983; "The Cosby Show", 1990-92; "The Fresh Prince of Bel-Air", 1992; "A Different World", 1992; Roc, 1993; "The Tuskegee Airmen", 1995; "Malcolm & Eddie", 1996; Double Platinum, 1999; "Commitments", 2001; "All of Us", 2004; "CSI: NY", 2004; "Cross Over", 2006; "House of Payne", 2006-12. **Honors/Awds:** Black Reel, 2002. **Business Addr:** Actor, The Gersh Agency, 41 Madison Ave 33rd Fl, New York, NY 10010, **Business Phone:** (212)997-1818.

## PAYNE, ALLISON GRIFFIN

Television journalist. **Personal:** Born Feb 12, 1964, Richmond, VA; daughter of Dana and Kathryn. **Educ:** Univ Detroit, BA, lib arts, 1985; Bowling Green State, MA, radio, tv & film, 1992. **Career:** WNWO-TV, Toledo, Ohio, ABC News, 1987, intern, reporter, anchor, 1987-88; WNEM-TV, NBC News, Saginaw, Mich, anchor, 1988-90; WGN-TV, Chicago, Ill, reporter, tv journalist, 1990-2011, "People to People", co-anchor, 1993-; WVAZ-FM 102.7, "The Real Show", co-host, 2005-; Mark Perryman Polit Campaigns, press secy, 2011-12; Payne Productions, founder, 2011-. **Orgs:** Delta Sigma Theta. **Honors/Awds:** Numerous awards including Seven Emmy awards, Regional Award, Radio TV News Dirs, 1991; Mark of Excellence Award, Chicago Asn Black Journalists, 1992; Peter Lisage Award, Soc Prof Journalists, 1991; Silver Dome Award, Ill Broadcasters Asn, 1992. **Business Addr:** Founder, Payne Productions, 3501 N Southport Ave, Chicago, IL 60657-1435, **Business Phone:** (773)698-6779.

## PAYNE, CECILIA

Manager, executive director, marketing executive. **Personal:** Born Dec 5, 1962, Bronx, NY; daughter of Noah Blount and Patricia McKinney; married George T; children: George M. **Educ:** Sch Visual Arts, BFA, graphic design, 1984; Rensselaer Polytech Inst, MS, mgt & mkt, 2003. **Career:** Juv Diabetes Mag, assoc art dir & prod, 1987-88; Philip Morris Mag, assoc art dir & prod, 1987-88; Signs & Unique Designs, dir, co founder & cheif exec officer, 1991-99; St Joseph Col, creative design dir, 1999-; Hartford, asst dir mkt, 2006-07; Hartford Bd Educ, Sch Choice Specialist, dir mkt, 2007-; Hartford Pub Schs, dir mkt, 2007-. **Orgs:** Literacy Vols, CT; Dept Social Servs, Hartford, CT; Family Life Educ, Hartford, CT; Nat Conf Community & Justice, Windsor, CT. **Special Achievements:** Art Gallery Exhibitions : West Hartford Art League, Juried Art Show, West Hartford, CT, 1997; Art Space Gallery, Colors and Textures, Hartford, CT, 1998; Art Space Gallery, Women in Art, Hartford, CT, 2001; State Treasures' Office: Art in Public Spaces, Hartford, CT, 2001; The Pump House Gallery, CP2, Hartford, CT, 2003. **Home Addr:** 41 Claredon Ave, West Hartford, CT 06110-1208, **Home Phone:** (860)233-6694. **Business Addr:** Director of Marketing, Hartford Public Schools, 960 Main St 8th Fl, Hartford, CT 06103, **Business Phone:** (860)695-8000.

## PAYNE, DEBRA K.

Administrator, state government official. **Personal:** Born Aug 18, 1964, Memphis, TN; daughter of Robert and Dorothy. **Educ:** Capital Univ, BA, eng & prof writing; Ohio Dept Health Leadership Acad, grad, supvr training & develop prog, 2010. **Career:** Ohio Civil Rights Comn, civil rights rep, 1989-93; Ohio Dept Health, labor rels officer, 1993-98, affirmative action mgr, 1999-2012, Dept Admin Svcs, Equal Employ Opportunity officer & labor rels officer, 2012-. **Orgs:** Secy & exec comt, Columbus Asn Black Journalists, 1992-95; King Arts Complex, 1999-; YWCA, 2000-; Human Resources Asn Cent Ohio, 2000-; Nat Asn African Am Human Resources; Nat Asn Female Execs; OH Investors Asn; United Way Key Club; Jr League Columbus; United Way Cent Ohio; pub policy co-chair, Nat Coalition 100 Black Women; Lincoln Theatre; Southern Poverty Law Ctr; Nat Asn Human Rights Workers; Cent Ohio Diversity Consortium; Columbus Cult Arts Ctr. **Home Addr:** 5381-A6 Yorkshire Terr, Columbus, OH 43232, **Home Phone:** (614)575-9546. **Business Addr:** Equal Employment Opportunity Chief, Ohio Department of Health, 246 N High St 1st Fl, Columbus, OH 43215, **Business Phone:** (614)466-3543.

## PAYNE, FREDA CHARCELIA

Singer, actor, television actor. **Personal:** Born Sep 19, 1942, Detroit, MI; married Gregory Abbott; children: Gregory Jr. **Career:** Singer & actress; Albums: After the Lights Go Down Low and Much More!!!, 1964; Freda Payne in Stockholm, 1965; How Do You Say I Don't Love You Anymore, 1966; Band of Gold, 1970; Contact, 1971; Reaching Out, 1973; Payne & Pleasure, 1974; Out of Payne Comes Love, 1975; Stares and Whispers, 1977; Supernatural High, 1978; Hot, 1979; Freda Payne Sings the (Unauthorized) I Hate Barney Songbook: A Parody, 1995; An Evening with Freda Payne: Live in Concert, 1996; Christmas With Freda and Friends, 1996; Live in Concert, 1999; Come See About Me, 2001; On the Inside, 2007; Come Back to Me Love, 2014. Films: Book of Numbers, 1973; Private Obsession, 1995; Sprung, vocalist, 1997; Rag doll, 1999; Nutty Professor II: The Klumps, 2000; Deadly Rhapsody, 2001; Cordially Invited, 2007; TV Series: "The Tonight Show Starring Johnny Carson", 1973; Police Story, 1976; "Today's Black Woman", 1981; "Living Single", 1993; "Fire & Ice", 2001; "Love & Payne", 2003; "Saurian", 2006; Film: Book of Numbers, 1973; Private Obsession, 1995; Sprung, 1997; Ragdoll, 1999; Nutty Professor II: The Klumps, 2000; Deadly Rhapsody, 2001; Cordially Invited, 2007; Ella: First Lady of Song, 2014; The Divorce. Singles: "(Desafinado) Slightly Out of Tune", 1962; "Pretty Baby", 1963; "It's Time", 1963; "You've Lost That Lovin' Feelin'", 1966; "The Unhooked Generation", 1969; "Band of Gold", 1970; "Deeper & Deeper", 1970; "Cherish What Is Dear to You (While It's Near To You)", 1971; "Bring the Boys Home", 1971; "You Brought the Joy", 1971; "The Road We Didn't Take", 1972; "Through the Memory of My Mind", 1972; "Two Wrongs Don't Make a Right", 1973; "For No Reason", 1973; "It's Yours to Have", 1974; "I Get Carried Away", 1975; "You", 1975; "I Get High (On Your Memory)", 1976; "Bring Back the Joy", 1977; "Love Magnet", 1977; "Feed Me Your Love", 1978; "Happy Days Are Here Again/Happy Music (Dance the Night Away)", 1978; "I'll Do Anything for You", 1979; "Red Hot", 1979; "Can't Wait", 1979; "In Motion", 1982. **Honors/Awds:** Appeared on American Idol, 2009. **Home Addr:** 1505 Bluejay Way, Los Angeles, CA 90069. **Business Addr:** Actress, Fleischer Studios, 10160 Cielo Dr, Beverly Hills, CA 90210-2037, **Business Phone:** (310)276-7503.

## PAYNE, JACQUELINE LAVERNE

Lawyer. **Personal:** Born Dec 15, 1957, Atlanta, GA; daughter of Doris Hanson and Amos Jr; married Timothy Beckum; children: Alexis A, Brooke & Jordan T Beckum. **Educ:** Spelman Col, BA, sociol, cum laude, 1977; Univ Ga, JD, 1980. **Career:** Atlanta Legal Aid Soc Inc, staff atty, 1980-85, 88-90, managing atty, 1985-86, 1990-2005, sr atty, currently; Hyatt Legal Servs, managing atty, 1986-88. **Orgs:** Fel Reginald Heber Smith Community Lawyer, 1980-82; State Bar Ga, 1982-; troop leader, Northwest Ga Girl Scout Coun, 1991-99; exec comt, Atlanta Fulton Co Comn C & Youth, 1992; bd dir, Atlanta Bar Asn, 2004; Cobb Bar Assoc, 2005-; Ga Asn Black Women Attys; pres, Marietta Schs Found, founding mem, 10 Women Hope; Am Cancer Soc. **Honors/Awds:** Families First Award, Atlanta Bar Asn, Family Law Sect, 2001; Don Bradley Award, State Bar Ga, 2002; Families First Award, Atlanta Bar Asn, Family Law Sect, 2004; AVLF Special Guardian Award, 2004-05. **Home Addr:** 1582 Arden Dr SW, Marietta, GA 30008, **Home Phone:** (770)514-1257. **Business Addr:** Senior Attorney, Atlanta Legal Aid Society Inc, 30 S Pk Sq Suite 100, Marietta, GA 30060, **Business Phone:** (770)528-2568.

## PAYNE, JAMES E.

Lawyer, lecturer. **Educ:** Univ Houston, BS, polit sci, 1989; Univ Houston Law Ctr, JD, 1993; Nat Bd Trial Advocacy, civil trial advocate cert, 2001; Nat Bd Trial Advocacy, pretrial pract advocate cert, 2012. **Career:** Congressman William Lehman (Wash D.C.), staff; Vinson & Elkins LLP, atty, 1993-95; Provost & Umphrey (Houston, TX), personal injury atty, 1995-. Motivational speaker. **Orgs:** Life mem, Nat Asn Advan Colored People; State Bar Tex; Am Bd Trial Advocates (ABOTA); Am Asn Justice; Tex Trial Lawyers Asn; Jefferson County Black Lawyers Asn; Sigma Pi Phi Fraternity, Grand Sire/Nat pres; Alpha Phi Alpha Fraternity; fel Texas Bar Found; Multi-Million Dollar Advocates Forum; State Bar Tex; Col State Bar Tex. **Honors/Awds:** Thomson Reuters, Texas Super Lawyers List, Listee, 2003-14; "U.S. News," The Best Lawyers in America, Listee, 2006-15; Extraordinary Minorities in Texas Law, Texas Lawyer, 2015. **Special Achievements:** Author of "I Am Healed, But I am Still Sick?". **Business Addr:** Attorney, Provost Umphrey Law Firm LLP, 490 Park St, Beaumont, TX 77701, **Business Phone:** (409)203-5030.

## PAYNE, JERRY OSCAR

School administrator. **Personal:** Born Jul 31, 1953, Madera, CA; son of Oscar (deceased) and Sallie Ophelia Smiley; children: Deidre Avery & Jonathan & Keri. **Educ:** San Jose State Univ, San Jose, CA, BA, 1976; Ariz State Univ, Tempe, MA, 1978; Lewis & Clark Col, Portland, educ admin cert, 1984; Calif Sch Leadership Acad, attended 1990; Univ Calif, Davis/Calif State Univ, Fresno, Joint Doctoral Prog, EdD, 2002. **Career:** Fremont Unified Sch Dist, Sunnyvale, Calif, Title VII, instr, 1974-76; Phoenix Union High Sch, Phoenix, spec educ, Ariz hist instr, 1976-78; ElDorado High Sch, Las Vegas NV, spec educ instr, 1978-80; Clark County Classroom Teachers Asn, Las Vegas, negotiations chmn, 1978-80; Grant HighSch, Portland, spec educ instr, 1980-82; Benson Polytech High Sch, Portland, integration counsr, 1982-84, from admin asst to prin, 1984-87; Lincoln Summer High Sch Portland, prin, 1985-87; Martin Luther King, Jr, Jr High Sch, Sacramento Ca, prin, 1987-90; Univ Mich, Ann Arbor, Horace Rackham fel, 1990; Parker Elem Sch (K-6), Oakland, prin, 1990-96; Hayward Unified Dist, Hayward, dir stud serv, 1996-2002; St Helen Parish Sch, supt schs, prin, 2002-. **Orgs:** Asn Calif Adminrs; Asn Supv & Curric Develop; Am Asn Sch Adminrs; Comn Dist Adminrs; bd dir, treas, found Bd mem, & life mem, Nat Alliance Black Sch Educs; Am Voc Asn; Nat Coun Local Admin Voc, Tech & Practical Arts Educ; Hugh O'Brian Alumni Asn; Calif League Mid Sch; Nat Asn Elem Sch Prin; Ariz State Univ Alumni Asn; Kiwanis Int; Toastmasters Int; Harvard Prin's Ctr Alumni; Nat Asn Advan Colored People, life mem; Nat Asn Advan Colored People Legal Redress Comt; La Asn Sch Supts; La Asn Sch Bds; IEL Alumnus. **Business Addr:** Superintendent of Schools, Principal, St Helena Parish Schools, PO Box 4368, Baton Rouge, LA 70821, **Business Phone:** (225)222-6016.

## PAYNE, DR. JUNE P.

Psychologist. **Personal:** Born Jun 11, 1948, Charlottesville, VA; daughter of Walter A and Theola Reaves; married Charles R; children: Lauren R & Gregory A. **Educ:** Va State Univ, BA, 1970; Ball State Univ, MA, 1974, PhD, coun psychol, 1980. **Career:** Ball State Univ Coun Ctr, intern; Charlottesville Dept Pub Welfare, social worker, 1970-72; Cambridge House Inc, counr, 1974-75, dir treat, 1976-78; Comprehensive Ment Health Serv E Cent Ind, psych, 1980-83; Ball State Univ, Coun & Psychol Serv Ctr, coun psychol, 1983-, dir coun & health servs, currently. **Orgs:** Pres & secy, Ind Asn Black Psych, 1984-85; bd dir, Hospitality House; Nat Asn Advan Colored People; Delta Sigma Theta Sor; Coalition 100 Women; bd dir, Altrusa Club Muncie; vpres, Altrusa Internation, 2007-08, 2008-09; adv bd, community found; Am Psychol Asn; bd mem, Int Asn Coun Serv. **Honors/Awds:** Jack Beyerl Outstanding Professional, 2002; Indiana Women of Achievement, 2007. **Home Addr:** 7405 N Landings Trail, Muncie, IN 47303. **Business Addr:** Director, Counseling and Health Services, Ball State University, 2000 W Univ Ave, Muncie, IN 47306, **Business Phone:** (765)289-1264.

## PAYNE, KENNETH VICTOR

Basketball player, basketball coach. **Personal:** Born Nov 25, 1966, Laurel, MS; son of Cleveland; married Michelle; children: Alexander & Alexis. **Educ:** Univ Louisville, BS, sports admin, 2000. **Career:** Basketball player (retired), basketball coach; Philadelphia 76ers, forward-guard, 1989-93; Tri-City Chinook, 1993-94; Continental Basketball Asn; Taipans Cairns; Univ Ore, asst coach, 2004-10; Univ Ky, asst men's basketball coach, 2010-. **Orgs:** Louisville's NCAA championship squad, 1986. **Business Addr:** Assistant Coach, University of Kentucky, 100 WD Funkhouser Bldg, Lexington, KY 40506, **Business Phone:** (859)257-9000.

## PAYNE, LESLIE (LES PAYNE)

Journalist. **Personal:** Born Jul 12, 1941, Tuscaloosa, AL; married Violet S Cameron; children: Tamara Olympia, Jamal Kenyatta & Haile Kipchoge. **Educ:** Univ Conn, BA, eng, 1964. **Career:** Newsday, babylon town, ssociate mng ed, 1960, nat ed, investigative reporter, 1968-80, beat reporter, 1969, asst ed, 1970, ed, writer, 1971, minor affairs specialist, 1973-78, nat corresp & columnist, 1980-85, asst mng ed, assoc mng ed emer, currently; United Muslim Asn, Toledo, dep mng ed, currently; Papers New York, ed; Newsday, assoc ed; Bk: Malcolm X; Nat Asn Black Journalists, founder; Group's Fourth, pres; Columbia Univ, Grad Sch Jour, David Laventhol Chair; Tribune Media Serv, journalist; Columbia Univ, inaugural prof. **Orgs:** NY Asn Black Journalists, 1977-80; Int Press Inst; Nat Asn Black Journalists, 1978. **Honors/Awds:** Headliner Award, 1974; Sigma Delta Chi Award, 1974; Pulitzer Prize, 1974; Tobenkin Award, Columbia Univ, 1978; Man of the Yr Award, Nat Asn Black Bus & Prof Women, 1978; Frederick Douglass Prize, Nat Asn Black Journalists, 1978; Pulitzer Prize-winning American journalist; United Nations Hunger Award, 1983; AP & UPI Commentary Awards, 1983-84; Jour Prize, 100 Black Men; Unity Awards, Lincoln Univ; Hon Doctorate, Medgar Evers Col; Hon Doctorate, Long Island Univ; Pulitzer Prize Cable TV Ace Award, 1990. **Special Achievements:** Author: The Heroin Trail; Life and Death of the Symbionese Liberation Army. **Home Addr:** , Harlem, NY 10026. **Business Addr:** Assistant Managing Editor Emeritus, Newsday, 235 Pinelawn Rd, Melville, NY 11747-4250, **Business Phone:** (518)465-2311.

## PAYNE, MARGARET RALSTON

Educator, college administrator. **Personal:** Born Jan 31, 1946, Louisville, KY; daughter of Henry Morris and Rena Owens; married James Edward; children: Maya Renee. **Educ:** Kalamazoo Col, BA, 1968; Fourah Bay Col, Univ Sierra Leone, attended 1967; Kent State Univ, MA, 1972. **Career:** Executive, educator (retired); Kent State Univ, asst prof psychol, 1972-78, asst dean, prof develop serv, 1973-89, adj asst prof psychol, 1978, spec asst vice provost stud affairs, 1989-92, Corp & Found Rel, dir, 1992-96, bd trustees, exec asst pres & secy, 1996, proj coordr, 2009-10; Ralston Payne Enterprises, vpres, 2003-. **Orgs:** Ohio & Nat Asn Women Educ, 1979-2000; bd mem, Portage Co Comn Action Coun, 1979-85; pres, Kent Area Chap Links Inc, 1984-88; dist adv, Nat Alpha Lambda Delta, 1985-87; Nat Adv Comt, SAGE: bd mem, Akron Urban League, 1988-91; dir, Links Found Inc, 1992-94; pres, Kathryn Sisson Phillips Trust, 1994-96; dir, Summa Health Syst Found, 1995-; bd mem, Women's Endowment Fund, Akron Community Found, 1995-2000; chair, Grant, Awards & Scholar, Links Inc, 1998-2002; dir, Summa Health Syst, 1998-; bd mem, Western Res Girl Scout Coun; Nat Asn Black Journalists Nat Coun Colored Women Clubs; Athena Int. **Home Addr:** 797 Cliffside Dr, Akron, OH 44313-5609, **Home Phone:** (330)867-3538. **Business Addr:** Executive Assistant to President, Secretary, Kent State University, PO Box 5190, Kent, OH 44242-0001, **Business Phone:** (330)672-2210.

## PAYNE, MITCHELL HOWARD

School administrator. **Personal:** Born Feb 2, 1950, Shelbyville, KY; son of Llewellyn Rucker (deceased) and Hattie Cohrell; married Karen W Bearden; children: Janell Mitchet & William Mitchell. **Educ:** Western Ky Univ, BA, govt/hist, 1972, MPA, 1973; Univ Louisville, JD, 1978. **Career:** Univ Louisville, dir minority affairs; Commonwealth Ky, Frankfort KY, exec asst to sec finance comm admin; Ky State Univ, adj assoc prof Pub Affairs; Univ Louisville, dir minority affairs, 1973-85; assoc vpres, 1990-. **Orgs:** Nat Bar Asn; Am Soc Pub Admin; Nat Asn State Dir Admin & Gen Serv, 1987-; Kappa Alpha Psi Frat; bd mem, Prichard Comm Acad Excellence, 1987-; advcoun, Ky St Univ Sch Pub Affairs, 1987-; founding Pres, Ky Bluegrass Chap Nat Forum Black Pub Adminr, 1988-; steering comt, YMCA Black Achievers Prog, 1989-; Sigma Pi Phi Frat, 1989-; NACUBO, 1990; Ky Coc, Mny Bus, bus adv bd, 1992; Ky Heritage Coun, Afa heritage task force, 1992; 100 Black Men Louisville, founding mem; bd mem, Tri State Minority Supplier Develop Coun; bd mem, Kentuckiana Minority Supplier Develop Coun; comt, Univ Louisville; lifetime mem, Western Ky Univ; bd dir, Qual & Charity Care Trust Inc; Louisville Sports Comn; adv comt, Safe & Healthy Neighborhoods. **Home Addr:** 6400 Ocho Rios Ct, Louisville, KY 40228, **Home Phone:** (502)239-2903. **Business Addr:** Associate Vice President for Business Affairs, University Louisville, Off VPres Admin, Louisville, KY 40292, **Business Phone:** (502)852-5155.

## PAYNE, DR. NORMA JOYCE

School administrator. **Personal:** Born Jan 29, 1941, Washington, DC; daughter of Eunice Brown Johnson Tyson and Jesse Maryland Tyson; married Charles Harrington; children: April A & Wynton K. **Educ:** DC Teachers Col, Wash, DC, BS, 1971; Atlanta Univ, Atlanta, GA, MS, 1976, EdD, 1976. **Career:** Ford Fel, Ford Found, 1971; Presidential Coun Women's Educ Progs, DC specialist, 1977-79; Pres's Adv Coun Women, DC, educ specialist, 1979-81; Global Systs Inc, pres; Nat Asn State Univs & Land-Grant Cols, DC dir; Off Advan Pub Black Cols, dir, 1979-; Thurgood Marshall Scholar Fund, founder, 1984-, int consult, 2009-. **Orgs:** Foreign Serv Performance Eval bd, US State Dept; Zeta Phi Beta Sorority; founder, Coalition 100 Black Women Inc, Wash DC Chap; bd trustee, univ DC; exec dir, Nat Alliance Pub Trust; bd dir, AARP. **Home Addr:** 729 Decatur St NE, Washington, DC 20017, **Home Phone:** (202)832-7128. **Business Addr:** Founder, Thurgood Marshall College Fund, 80 Maiden Lane Suite 2204, New York, NY 10038, **Business Phone:** (212)573-8888.

## PAYNE, RONNIE E. (RON PAYNE)

Consultant, executive, founder (originator). **Personal:** Born Jun 12, 1940, Palmersville, TN; son of Noel and Thelma Williams; married Jerry; children: Angela, Sherri Williams, Anita & Antoinette Benford; married Norris. **Educ:** Tenn St Univ, BS, 1961; Ga St Univ, attended 1968. **Career:** Lockheed, Missiles & Space, subcontract crd, 1961-64, Ga, div purchasing supr, 1965-67; IBM, sr buyer, 1968-70, cent purchasing procurement mgr, 1971-76; Digital Equip corp, Springfield plant mgr, 1978-83, corp purchasing mgr, 1983-88, corp purchasing, vpres, strategic resources group staff mgr & vpres, 1988-93; Excel Partners Inc, gen partner, managing dir, 1993-95; Digital Equip Corp, vpres; Purchasing Serv Inc, founder & managing dir, 1995-; Gordon Col, adj prof. **Orgs:** Shawmut Middlesex Bank, 1986-; Nat Minority Supplier Develop, 1987-; steering comt co-chair, Digitals Nat Asn Advan Colored People & ACT-SO, 1987-92; boards & adv groups, Boston Univ, Sch Theol, 1990-; adv, Digital's african Heritage Alliance, 1990-; bd mem, ISM; founder, PSInPhilly Consult. **Honors/Awds:** A "Blueprint for Success" Leadership Ctr Study Black exec, subject of study. **Special Achievements:** First African ceo of the Greater Springfield Co, 1981-82. **Home Addr:** 15 Raymond Marchetti St, Ashland, MA 01721-1643. **Business Addr:** Founder, Managing Director, Purchasing Services Inc, 215 1/2 E Cliveden St, Philadelphia, PA 19119-2312, **Business Phone:** (215)438-8500.

### PAYNE, ULICE, JR.

Baseball executive, executive director, lawyer. **Personal:** Born Jan 1, 1955, Donora, PA; son of Ulice Sr and Mary; married Carmella; children: Amber & Ulice III. **Educ:** Marquette Univ, BA, bus admin, 1978, JD, 1982; Univ London, Eng, master law prog, 1988. **Career:** US Dist Co, E Dist WI, law clerk, 1972-83; Wis State Off, comnr securities, 1985-87; pvt pract attny, 1988-98; Foley & Lardner Law Firm, attny, 1998-2002; Milwaukee Brewers, pres & chief exec officer, 2002-03; Addison-Clifton LLC, pres, 2002-, managing mem, 2004-. **Orgs:** Bd dir, Milwaukee Brewers Baseball Club; WI chp, Nat MS Soc; nat bd dir, YMCA Metro Milwaukee; bd dir, Wis Energy Corp; bd dir, Badger Meter Inc; bd dir, Midwest Express Holdings; bd dir, State Financial Serv Corp; bd dir, Bradley Ctr Sports & Entertainment Corp; bd mem, Wis Energy Corp, 2003-; bd dir, C's Hosp WI; bd dir, Manpower Inc, 2007-; bd dir, Northwestern Mutual Life Ins Co; trustee, Northwestern Mutual Life Ins Co; trustee, Marquette Univ; trustee, Med Col Wis; bd mem, Midwest Air Group; Am Bar Asn; Bill Bradley Pres; Forward Together PAC; Jr Achievement; Metrop Milwaukee Asn Com; State Bar Wis. **Special Achievements:** First African American CEO of Milwaukee Brewers, 2002-03. **Business Addr:** President, Managing Member, Addison-Clifton LLC, 13255 W Bluemound Rd Suite 241, Brookfield, WI 53005, **Business Phone:** (262)784-0095.

### PAYNE, VERNON N.

School administrator, basketball coach. **Personal:** Born Apr 20, 1945, Michigan City, IN; married Dorphine; children: Linda, David & Arthur. **Educ:** Ind State Univ, BS, speech path & audiol, 1968, MS, guid & coun, 1972. **Career:** Int Bus Mach Corp, res intern, 1967; City Mich, Off Econ Opportunity, asst exec dir, 1968-70; Ind Univ, basketball coach; Univ Denver, basketball coach; Wayne State Univ, head basketball coach, 1977-82; Western Mich Univ, head basketball coach, 1982-89, off admis & orientation, asst dir, 1989-92, Univ recreation prog & facil, dir, 1992-98, asst vpres stud affairs, 1998-2001, assoc vpres stud affairs, 2001-. **Orgs:** Chair, Detroit Edison Sch County, Personnel Comn, 1977-79; mem scholar comn, Western Mich Univ, Fund Advan Minorities Educ, 1989-, diversity comn, 1989-; bd dir, Am Cancer Soc Kalamazoo County, 1990-91; brd dir, Lakeside Home, 1990-; adv bd, Kalamazoo County Walk Warmth, 1990-; chair, Resource Develop Comn, 1991; Mich Higher Educ Facil Authority, 1993-01; Info Tech Strategic Plan Comn, WMU, 1999-; Restricted Weapons Policy Comn, WMU, 1999-; Emergency Plan Comn, WMU, 1999-; Vertical Portal Develop Comn, 1999-; USAG, 2001-; SIS, 2001-. **Home Addr:** 1412 W Kilgore Rd, Kalamazoo, MI 49008-3578, **Home Phone:** (269)388-6043. **Business Addr:** Associate Vice President for Student Affairs, Western Michigan University, 2303 Faunce Stud Serv Bldg, Kalamazoo, MI 49008-5348, **Business Phone:** (269)387-2136.

### PAYNE, WILFORD ALEXANDER

Executive director. **Personal:** Born Jan 4, 1945, Youngstown, OH; son of Walter (deceased) and Mildred. **Educ:** Blufton Col, Blufton, OH, math, 1965; Youngstown State Univ, OH, BA, sociol, 1973; Ohio State Univ, MHA, 1975. **Career:** Health & Welfare Asn, scholar, 1973-75; St Joseph's Riverside Hosp, Warren OH, admin resident, 1974; OH State Univ Hosp, Columbus, admin asst, 1975; Monongahela Valley Asn Health Centers Inc, Fairmont, WVa, admin asst, health main coordr, 1976-77; Alma Illery Med Ctr, Primary Care Health Serv Inc, proj dir, 1977-, exec dir. **Orgs:** Bd dir, Eastern Allegheny Co Health Corp, 1977-; bd dir, Family Plng Coun Southwestern, Pa, 1977-; Nat Asn Comt Health Centers Inc, 1977-; instr, Tri Reg Cluster Trng Ctr, NY, 1979-; comt mem, United Way Rev Comt Plng & Allocations; alumni soc; Porter Prize, Univ Pittsburgh Grad Sch Pub Health, 1992. **Home Addr:** 109 Country Club Dr, Pittsburgh, PA 15235. **Business Addr:** Project Director, Chief Executive Officer, Alma Illery Medical Center, 7227 Hamilton Ave, Pittsburgh, PA 15208-1899, **Business Phone:** (412)244-4700.

### PAYNE, WILLIAM D.

Government official. **Personal:** Born Jul 8, 1932, Newark, NJ; children: Eric, Lisa, Gina & Kristi. **Educ:** Rutgers Univ, BA, polit sci, 1957. **Career:** Mkt Develop Consult, pub affairs; Urban Data Systs Inc, founder, pres & chief exec officer, 1969-88; Congressmen Donald M Payne, campaign mgr, 1988-; One to One/Nj Sch-Centered Mentoring Orgn, exec dir, 1992-94; Prudential Ins Co, mgr, 1993-98; Newark, cand mayor, 1994; Assemblyman Craig A Stanley, campaign mgr, 1995; Nj Cong Award Coun, 1995-; Assembly mem Craig Stanley, Irvington, NJ, chief staff, 1996-97; Nj State Assembly, assemblymember, 1998-2007, dep majority conf leader, 2002-07; Essex County Exec Off, dep chief staff, 2003-; William Payne & Assocs, Mkt Develop Consult, prin, currently. **Orgs:** Vice chair, Essex County Improv Authority, 1980-86; chair, Newark Housing Authority, 1986-89; NJ Coun Adult Literacy, 1992; Nj Coun on Adult Literacy, 1992; NJ Cong Award Coun, 1995; NJ Tourism Adv Coun, 1998-; Nj Tourism Adv Coun, 1998-; Nj Joint Comt on Mentoring, 1999-; pres & bd trustee, Chad Independent Sch, 2003-; pres & bd trustee, Chad Independent Sch, 2003-; comnr, NJ Criminal Disposition Comn, 2004-; comnr, Nj Amistad Comn; dist leader, Essex County Dem Comt; Small Bus Adv Coun; NY Fed Res Bank; golden heritage mem, Nat Asn Advan Colored People; chair, Assembly Regulatory Oversight Comt; vice chair, Budget Comt; Human Serv Comt. **Home Addr:** 111 Mulberry St Apt 5C, Newark, NJ 07102-4012, **Home Phone:** (973)242-2281. **Business Addr:** Deputy Chief of Staff, Essex County Executive Office, 465 Dr Martin Luther King Jr Blvd, Newark, NJ 07102, **Business Phone:** (973)621-4400.

### PAYNE-NABORS, COLLEEN J.

Executive, entrepreneur. **Personal:** Born Oklahoma City, OK. **Educ:** Okla Univ, petrol land mgt, 1980; Univ Tex Med Br, attended. **Career:** Nuclear med technologist; Frontier City Amusement Pk, staff; MCI Diag Ctr, pres, founder & chief exec officer, 1998-; CP Enterprises LLC, founder & chief exec officer, currently. **Orgs:** Am Col Radiol; Am Healthcare Radiol Adminrs; Am Registry Regist Technologists; Am Soc Regist Technologists; Internal Soc Accreditation Echocardiography; Internal Soc Accreditation Nuclear Med; Northeastern Okla Soc Nuclear Med; Soc Nuclear Med; Okla State Univ Women's Found; Planned Parenthood; Mothers Grp. **Honors/Awds:** Business Innovator of the Year, Black Enterprises Magazine, 2003; Community Service Award, Omega Psi Phi Fraternity Inc, 2003; Pinnacle Award, Tulsa Comn Status Women, 2004; Female Entrepreneur of the Year Award, AXA Advisors, 2004; Business Person of the Year, 2004; Business Innovator & Entrepreneur of the Year, 2004; Business Excellence Award, Tulsa People Mag, 2004; Woman of the Year, Jour Rec, 2006; Oklahoma Small Business Person of the Year, 2006 & 2007; One of Tulsa Most Influential People in 2008; Community Service Award, Alpha Kappa Alpha Sorority, 2010. **Special Achievements:** Oklahoma Venture of the Year finalist, Grace Franklin Bernsen Found, 2004; featured in several magazines & news publications & has received numerous media releases in the Tulsa World, Oklahoma Eagle, Tulsa People, Oklahoma Herald, Oklahoma Magazine, Tulsa Beacon & Ebony Tribune; featured in the Black Enterprise Report & featured in Fox News, ABC, NBC and other local TV & Radio shows; Americas fastest growing private companies, 2007 & 2008; One of Tulsas most influential people, 2008; Author: I Did it My Way....It Worked, 2008. **Business Addr:** Founder, Chief Executive Officer, CP Enterprises LLC, 7018 S Utica Ave, Tulsa, OK 74136, **Business Phone:** (918)493-2007.

### PAYTON, DR. BENJAMIN FRANKLIN

Educator. **Personal:** Born Dec 27, 1932, Orangeburg, SC; son of Leroy R (deceased) and Sarah M; married Thelma Plane; children: Mark Steven & Deborah Elizabeth. **Educ:** SC State Univ, BA, social studies, 1955; Harvard Univ, BD, philos theol, 1958; Columbia Univ, MA, philos relig, 1960; Yale Univ, PhD, social ethics, 1963. **Career:** Educator (retired); Danforth grad fel, 1955-63; Howard Univ, Wash, DC, asst prof sociol, relig & social ethics, 1963, Community Serv Proj, dir, 1963-65; Off Church & Race, Protestant Coun City NY, dir, 1965-66; Comn Relig & Race & Dept Social Justice Nat Coun Churches USA, exec dir, 1966-67; Benedict Col, pres, 1967-72; Ford Found Higher Educ & Res, prog officer, 1972-81; Tuskegee Univ, pres, 1981-; Seven Nation Tour Africa, educ adv to vpres George Bush, 1982; Presidential Task Force Agr Develop, Zaire, team leader, 1984. **Orgs:** Bd mem, ITT Corp, 1987-98; Tuskegee Syphilis Study Legacy Comt, 1996; Am S Bancorp; Bus-Higher Educ Forum; Am Soc Scholars; Alpha Phi Alpha Fraternity Inc; Nat Consortium Educ Access; Leadership Ala; bd, Ala Shakespeare Festival Royal Coun; Bd Visitors Air Univ; mem vis comt, Bd Overseers Harvard Univ; Am S Bank; bd mem, dir, Liberty Corp; bd mem, dir, PRAXAIR Inc; bd mem, dir, Ruby Tuesday Inc; bd mem, dir, Morrison Mgt Specialists Inc; chair, Bd Advisors Historically Black Cols & Univs, 2002; Am Higher Educ Asn; Phi Beta Kappa; Alpha Kappa Mu Hon Soc, SC State Univ; Sigma Pi Phi Boule; dir, ITT Corp; dir, SONAT Inc; bd, Am Socs Engineering Educ Study Nat Adv Coun; bd, Int Food & Agr Develop; Am Coun Educ; dir, AmSouth Bancorporation; dir, AmSouth Bank; bd, Nat Action Coun Minorities Engineering; bd gov, U.S. Air Force Civil Air Patrol; bd visitor, Maxwell Afb; dir, Asn Gov Boards, AmSouth Bancorporation. **Home Addr:** 399 W Montgomery Rd, Tuskegee, AL 36083-1519, **Home Phone:** (334)725-0041. **Business Addr:** President, Tuskegee University, 1200 W Montgomery Rd, Tuskegee, AL 36088, **Business Phone:** (334)727-8501.

### PAYTON, GARY DWAYNE

Basketball player. **Personal:** Born Jul 23, 1968, Oakland, CA; son of Al and Annie; married Monique James; children: Gary Jr, Julian & Raquel. **Educ:** Ore State Univ, attended 1990. **Career:** Basketball player (retired), actor; Seattle Supersonics, guard, 1990-2003; Milwaukee Bucks, guard, 2003; Los Angeles Lakers, guard, 2003-04; Boston Celtics, guard, 2004-05; Miami Heat, guard, 2005-07; NBA, free agt, currently; Films:White Men Can't Jump, 1992; Eddie, 1996, Like Mike. **Orgs:** Founder, Gary Payton Found, 1996. **Business Addr:** Free Agent, NBA, 477 Madison Ave, New York, NY 10022.

### PAYTON, JARRETT WALTER

Football player. **Personal:** Born Dec 26, 1980, Arlington, IL; son of Walter (deceased); married Trisha George, Mar 4, 2009. **Educ:** Miami Univ, Fla, BA, lib arts. **Career:** Football player (retired), host; Tenn Titans, running back, 2005; Nat Football League, Europe, Amsterdam Admirals, running back, 2005; Montreal Alouettes, 2007; Toronto Argonauts, 2009; Chicago Slaughter, 2010-12; Cy Fredrics Jewelers, 2014; ChicagolandSportsRadio.com, host; Game 87.7FM, co-host; Jarrett Payton's All-Am Wheat Ale, beer prod, prom & sales; WGN Radio, co-host, currently. **Orgs:** Founder, Jarrett Payton Found; Walter & Connie Payton Found. **Honors/Awds:** Hall of Fame, Nat Football League; MVP of the Orange Bowl, 2004; World Bowl champion (Amsterdam Admirals), 2005; Most Valuable Player, Orange Bowl, 2014. **Special Achievements:** Film: 2004 FedEx Orange Bowl, 2004. TV Series: "A Football Life", 2011. Host of The Jarrett Payton Show. **Home Addr:** 1701 Golf Rd Suite 3-700, Rolling Meadows, IL 60008, **Home Phone:** (312)505-0397. **Business Addr:** Co-Host, WGN Radio, 435 N Mich Ave Suite 720, Chicago, IL 60611, **Business Phone:** (312)981-7200.

### PAYTON, JEFF

Lawyer, judge. **Personal:** Born Sep 11, 1946, Canton, MS; married Carol E Rooks; children: Erin & Jeffrey. **Educ:** Ashland Col, BS, 1969; John Marshall Col Law-Cleveland State Univ, JD, 1975. **Career:** Cleveland HS OH, biol instr, 1969-71; US Dept Just, legal intern, 1972-73; Cleveland Legal Aid Soc, atty staff, 1975-77; Richland Co Legal Serv, dir, 1977-; Mansfield Munic Ct, judge, 1987; Ohio Judicial Col, fac; Ohio Supreme Ct, chief justice. **Orgs:** OH State Bar Asn; Richland Co Bar Asn; bd trustee, Ashland Alumni Asn; bd trustee, Planned Parenthood Asn, 1979-; bd trustee, Heritage Trials Girl Scouts Coun, 1979-; bd trustee, Richland Co Juv Just Comn, 1980; exec comt, Mansfield Chap, Nat Asn Advan Colored People, chmn, Legal Redress Comn; pres, Ohio Munic/Co Judges Asn, 2001; bd mem, Ohio Criminal Sentencing Comn; Ohio Jury Task Force; Ohio Futures Comn; Mt. Calvary Baptist Church; trustee & church treas. **Honors/Awds:** Special Achievement Award, Ashland Univ Alumni Asn. **Home Addr:** 743 Courtwright Blvd, Mansfield, OH 44907-2217, **Home Phone:** (419)756-7783. **Business Addr:** Judge, Mansfield Municipal Court, Munic Bldg 30 N Diamond St, Mansfield, OH 44902, **Business Phone:** (419)755-9615.

### PAYTON, NICHOLAS

Musician, trumpet player. **Personal:** Born Sep 26, 1973, New Orleans, LA; son of Walter and Maria. **Educ:** Univ New Orleans. **Career:** Trumpeteer, currently; Albums: Toured with Marcus Roberts, 1992; From This Moment, 1994; Jazz FuturesII, 1994; Elvin Jones, 1994; Gumbo Nouveau, 1995; Fingerpainting: The Music Of Herbie Hancock, 1997; Doc Cheatham & Nicholas Payton, 1997; Payton's Place, 1998; Nick****ht, 1999; Trumpet Legacy, 1999; Dear Louis, 2001; Sonic Trance, 2003; Live in New York 1.24.04, 2004; Mysterious Shorter, 2006; Into The Blue, 2008; Bitches, 2011; BAM: Live at Bohemian Caverns, 2013; Sketches of Spain, 2013. Tulane Univ, distinguished artist & vis lectr, 2011-13. **Honors/Awds:** Grammy Award, Best Solo Jazz Performance, Nat Acad Recording Arts & Sci, 1997. **Business Addr:** Musician, c/o Tree Lawn Artists Inc, 8331 Germantown Ave, Philadelphia, PA 19118, **Business Phone:** (215)248-5296.

### PAYTON, NOLAN H.

Lawyer. **Personal:** Born Dec 23, 1919; children: 1. **Educ:** Ariz State Univ, BA; Univ SC, MA, 1940; Am Col Life Underwriters, CLU, 1954, LLB, 1962. **Career:** Golden St Mut Life Ins, agt, 1938-42, mgt, 1942-49; pvt pract atty, 1969-; Payton Law Ctr, atty, currently. **Orgs:** Am Bar Asn; Beverly Hills Bar Asn; Langston Law Asn; Los Angeles County Bar Asn; Lawyers Club Los Angeles; SW Bar Asn; Am Arbit Asn; Nat Asn Advan Colored People; Sigma Lambda Sigma; Alpha Phi Alphi; Alpha Mu Gamma; Desert Bar Asn; life mem, Sigma Pi Phi Fraternity; Univ Southern Calif Alumni Asn; Legion Lex; Ariz State Alumni Asn. **Home Addr:** 4232 Monteith Dr, Los Angeles, CA 90043. **Business Addr:** Attorney, Payton Law Center, 4232 W Martin Luther King Jr Blvd, Los Angeles, CA 90043, **Business Phone:** (323)296-4971.

### PAYTON-NOBLE, JOMARIE (JO MARIE PAYTON-NOBLE FRANCE)

Actor. **Personal:** Born Aug 3, 1950, Albany, GA; daughter of Driscoll and Frankie Bell; married Leonard Downs, Dec 16, 2007; married Landrus Clark, Jan 1, 1998, (divorced 2004); married Rodney Noble, Apr 17, 1993, (divorced 1998). **Educ:** Albany State Univ. **Career:** ABC sitcom, 1987; Album: Southern Shadows, 1999; Films: The Hollywood Knights, 1980; Deal of the Century, 1983; Crossroads, 1986; Disorderlies, 1987; Colors, 1988; Troop Beverly Hills, 1989; Echoes of Enlightenment, 2001; In the Eyes of Kyana, 2002; Gas, 2004. TV series: "The New Odd Couple", 1982-83; "Silver Spoons", 1986; "Small Wonder", 1986-89; "Perfect Strangers", 1987-89; "Family Matters", 1989-98; "ABC TGIF", 1990; "Moesha", 1996-99; "Will & Grace", 1999-2000; "The Proud Family", 2001-05; "TV Moms", 2002; "In the Eyes of Kyana", 2002; Wanda at Large, 2003; "Reba", 2005; "The Rev", 2005, 2013-; "Desperate Housewives", 2006; "Meet the Browns", 2009; "The Glades", 2010; "From This Day Forward", 2012. **Orgs:** Alpha Kappa Alpha Sorority. **Honors/Awds:** Nominee for Image Award, 2003, 2005 & 2006. **Business Addr:** Actress, Jack Lippman Agency, 9151 W Sunset Blvd, West Hollywood, CA 90069, **Business Phone:** (310)276-5677.

### PEACE, EULA H.

Educator. **Personal:** Born Jul 22, 1920, Norfolk, VA; children: Wesley H III. **Educ:** Va Union Univ; Va St Col; NJ State Teacher Col. **Career:** City Playground, teacher; World Bk, mgr. **Orgs:** City-wide Girls' Week, 1948-68; Demo Comt woman, 1968-77; City Dem Comn, 1972-74; build rep, Educ Asn Norfolk, 1973-80; del, Va Educ Asn, 1974-80; bd mem, Hunterville Heighborhood Ctr, 1974; adv bd mem, Area III Model City Prog, 1974; Va Educ Asn Women Educ, 1977-78; del, Nat Educ Asn, 1978-80; secy & treas, Dist 19 Yr Child, 1978-80; part Gov Conf Educ; bd mem, Educ Asn Norfolk; chmn, Women Educ Asn Norfolk; Legislator & Polit Action Comn & Women Abuse Comn & Ment Retard Asn & C Need Comn & Les Gemmes Civic & Soc Club; city coordr, Gov's campaign; Norfolk Chap Asn Col Women; pres, former bd mem, League Women Voters & Demo Women's Club; Phi Delta Kappa; pres, Norfolk Club Asn Negro Bus & Prof Women. **Home Addr:** 2424 Armor Lane, Chesapeake, VA 23325, **Home Phone:** (804)420-5851.

### PEACE, METTA WORLD. See ARTEST, RONALD WILLIAM, JR.

### PEACOCK, NICOLE

Government official. **Career:** US Dept State, Bur African Affairs, dir & pub outreach, currently; Founder, State Dept. **Business Addr:** Public Affairs Coordinator, US Department of State, 2201 C St NW Rm 5242A, Washington, DC 20520, **Business Phone:** (202)647-3502.

### PEAGLER, OWEN FAIR. See Obituaries Section.

### PEAGLER, DR. RICHARD C.

Colonial administrator. **Personal:** Born Feb 14, 1946, Oak Grove, LA; son of Charles; married Vashti; children: Richard C II. **Educ:** Cent State Univ, OH, BS, 1968; Univ Conn, MA, 1971; Syracuse Univ, EdD, coun & human serv, 1993. **Career:** Wooster Prep Sch, dir, upward bound prog, 1968-70; Western Conn State Col, admis off, acad counr, 1972; State Univ New York, Cortland, counr, sr counr, 1972-96, sr counr, asst dir coun & dir stud support serv, 1996-98, dir coun & stud devel ctr, 1998-2010, interim vpres stud affairs, 2006-08, dir emer coun & stud develop, 2010-; Educ Prof Develop Act Fel Univ Conn; Financial Aid Off, intern; Admis Off, intern; Dean Men's Off, intern. **Orgs:** Asn Coun Ctr dir; Int Asn Coun Serv, 1980-2004; vpres, Seven Valleys Coun Alcoholism, 1993-95; vol, Red Cross, 1996-2004; Cortland High Sch Shared Decision Making Team, 1996-97; Cortland City Sch Bd, 1998-2004; Am Col Personnel Asn, 1998-2004; Cortland Chap Phi Kappa Phi; Comn VII Directorate, Am Col Personnel Asn, 1999; coordr, Cortland Urban Recruitment Educr prog; chmn, Phi Kappa Phi Grad Fel Comt; Vestry Bd Warden Grace Church. **Home Addr:** 3272 Coventry Lane, Cortland, NY 13045, **Home Phone:** (607)753-0710. **Business Addr:** Interim Vice President for Student Affairs, Director Emeritus Of Counseling & Student Development, State University of New York College Cortland, Corey Union Rm 407A, Cortland, NY 13045-0900, **Business Phone:** (607)753-2011.

## PEAL, DARRYL ALAN

Association executive, educator. **Personal:** Born Jun 15, 1963, Springfield, OH; son of Clinton Edward and Joann Marie; married Regina Randall. **Educ:** Ohio Weslyn Univ, BA, print & broadcast jour, 1986; Ohio Univ, MS, social sci, 1991. **Career:** Wilberforce Univ, dir residence life, 1989-90; Residence Hall Complex, dir, 1990-91; Ohio Univ, asst dir health educ & wellness, 1991-92; Health Edu & Wellness, asst dir, 1991-92; Wilberforce Univ, Coun Serv, dir, 1992-92, adj prof, currently; Otterbein Col, asst dean stud, coordror ethnic diversity, 1993-2000, adj prof black studies, 1996-2000; orgn mgt & behav, adj prof orgn mgt, 2000-04; Cent Ohio Transit Authority, mobility mgr, 2004; Diversity Initiatives United Way Cent OH, asst vpres & dir diversity, 2000-04; Ohio Wesleyan Univ, dir minority stud affairs, 2004-07; Ohio Dept Admin Serv, Equal Opportunity Div, dep dir, 2007-08; Cent State Univ, dean students, 2008-10; S Cent Ohio Minority Supplier Develop Coun, pres & ceo, 2010-12; Ohio Minority Supplier Develop Coun, pres & ceo, 2010-14; Univ Minn, exec dir off bus community & econ develop, 2014-. **Orgs:** Life mem, Ohio dist dir, Alpha Phi Alpha; Ohio Univ Alumni Asn; Columbus Black chap; Nat Asn Advan Colored People; Alliance Ethnic dir & Prof; pres & chief exec officer, S Cent Ohio Minority Supplier Develop Coun, 2010-12; New Salem Missionary Baptist Church. **Home Addr:** 600 Culpepper Dr, Reynoldsburg, OH 43068-7255, **Home Phone:** (614)755-9939. **Business Addr:** Executive Director, Business & Community Economic Development, University of Minnesota, 2221 Univ Ave SE Suite 136, Minneapolis, MN 55414, **Business Phone:** (612)624-0530.

## PEAL, DR. REGINA RANDALL (DR. REGINA LAVERNE RANDALL)

School administrator. **Personal:** Born Dec 26, 1964, Washington, DC; daughter of James Roland Randall and Marian Laverne Randall; married Darryl Alan. **Educ:** Ohio Univ, BSHEC, food serv mgt, 1988, MHSA, health admin, 1990, PhD, higher educ admin, 1998. **Career:** Columbus State Community Col, Coun & Adv Serv, counr, 1993-98, Off Stud Activities, coordr, 1998-99, Dept Stud Activ & Athletics, dir stud activ & athletics, 2000-02, registr, 2002-; Leadership Consult Co Regal Leadership Realm, founder, chief exec officer. **Orgs:** Regional coordr, Alpha Kappa Alpha Sorority Inc, Educ Advan Found; execasst great lakes regional dir, 1998-2002, pres, 2001-02, Alpha Sigma Omega chap; Top Ladies Distinction Inc; pres, Columbus Moles, 2002-04; Nat Asn Advan Colored People; mem campaign co-chair, Urban League, 2001-02; co-chair, United Way Young Leadership Group, 2002-03; Trinity Baptist Church; life mem, Ohio Col Personnel Asn; exec bd, Nat Asn Stud Personnel Admin, 2001-02; Am Col Personnel Asn; Am Asn Col Registrars & Admis Officers; Ohio Univ Black Alumni Columbus Chap; Links Inc. **Home Addr:** 660 Culpepper Dr, Reynoldsburg, OH 43068, **Home Phone:** (614)755-9939. **Business Addr:** Registrar, Columbus State Community College, 550 E Spring St, Columbus, OH 43215, **Business Phone:** (614)287-5353.

## PEARCE, OVETA W.

Educator. **Career:** Harrand Creek Elem Sch, Enterprise, AL, teacher & prog specialist, prin; Enterprise City Schs, dir fed prog, currently. **Orgs:** Delta Sigma Theta; pres, Ala State Dept Educ Fed Prog Div Bd Practr; secy, Enterprise City Chamber Com. **Home Addr:** 104 Oakview Cir, Enterprise, AL 36330-1588, **Home Phone:** (334)347-0383. **Business Addr:** Director of Federal Programs, Enterprise City Schools, 220 Hutchinson St, Enterprise, AL 36330, **Business Phone:** (334)347-9531.

## PEARCE, RICHARD ALLEN

Executive. **Personal:** Born Oct 4, 1951, New York, NY; son of Marvin and Edith Burwell; married Lois A Mayo; children: Alysia Daphine, Ryki Desiree & Zuri Damita. **Educ:** Hampton Inst, BS, buc mgt, 1973; Univ Bridgeport, MBA; Williams Col, Williams Sch Banking, 1978; Rutgers Univ, Stonier Grad Sch Banking, 1986. **Career:** Union Trust Co, Ct, staff; State Nat Bank, Ct, staff; Colonial Bank Ct, staff; Conn Savings Bank, govt serv; City W Haven, dir finance & comptroller, 1989-91; Fleet Bank, vpres; Rampart Financial Group, prin, 1994-2001; Evolution Enterprises LLC, founder, 2001-. **Orgs:** Carver Fed Savings & Loan Asn, New York, NY; Carteret Savings & Loan Asn, Newark, NJ; bd dir, Hampton Alumni Fed Credit Union, 1973-74; Alpha Phi Alpha; bd dir, New Haven Community Investment Corp; New Haven Neighborhood Housing Asn; C's Ctr Hamden, & Notre Dame High Sch; bd dir, Regional Growth Partnership Greater New Haven; bd dir, W Haven Community House; vpres, City Hamden's Econ Develop Corp; Turnaround Mgt Asn; Finance Comt; adv bd, Students Free Enterprise at Quinnipiac Univ Sch Bus; bd dir, Childrens Ctr Hamden CT; bd dir, Conn Afro-Am Hist Soc; bd dir, Greater New Haven Bus & Prof Asn; chair, Regional Workforce Develop Bd Greater New Haven; comnr, Econ Devlop Comn, Hamden, CT. **Home Addr:** 151 Promenade Dr, Hamden, CT 06514, **Home Phone:** (203)248-2661. **Business Addr:** Founder, Evolution Enterprises LLC, PO Box 185636, Hamden, CT 06518, **Business Phone:** (203)248-3677.

## PEARMAN, RAVEN-SYMONE CHRISTINA. See SYMONE, RAVEN.

## PEARSON, BISHOP CARLTON DEMETRIUS (CARLTON PEARSON)

Writer, public speaker, clergy. **Personal:** Born Mar 19, 1953, San Diego, CA; son of Adam and Lillie Ruth; married Gina Marie Gauthier; children: Julian DMetrius & Majeste Amour. **Educ:** Oral Roberts Univ, BA, bibl lit, 1975. **Career:** Oral Roberts Evangelistic Asn, traveling evangelist, 1975-77; Higher Dimensions Ministries, founder, pastor, 1978-05; Higher Dimensions Evangelistic Ctr, founder, pastor, 1981; AZUSA Fel Int Inc, 1991; Warner Bros Rec, rec artist, 1992-99; Atlantic Rec, 1999-; New Dimensions Worship Ctr, founder, sr minister, pastor 2006-; TV host. **Orgs:** AZUSA Fellowship Int; Higher Dimensions Family Church; Col Bishops Int Communion Charismatic Churches; New Dimensions Worship Center; Dimensions Life. **Honors/Awds:** National Academy of Recording Arts & Sciences, Grammy nomination, "Live at Azusa 3", 2000; Two-time Stellar Award-winning; Good Morning America, Dove & Stellar Award nomination, "Live at Azusa 3", 2000. **Special Achievements:** Books: Crisis At the Crossroads, Dmetrius Publishing, 1990; Everything Gonna Be All Right, Harrison House, 1992; Is There A Man in the House, Treasure House Books, 1999; Americas 10 Most Influential Black Ministers; The Gospel of Inclusion, 2006. **Business Addr:** Pastor, Founder, New Dimensions Worship Center, 15 E 5th St Suite 2950, Tulsa, OK 74103, **Business Phone:** (918)392-9982.

## PEARSON, DR. CLIFTON

School administrator, educator, consultant. **Personal:** Born Jun 24, 1948, Birmingham, AL; married Clementene Hodge; children: Monica Denise & Clifton Anderson. **Educ:** Ala A&M Univ, AL, BS, art educ & elem educ, 1970; Ill State Univ, MS, art educ & studio ceramics, 1971, EdD, studio ceramics, glass, art educ & educ admin, 1974; PhD, studio ceramics. **Career:** Ill State Univ, grad teaching asst, 1971-73; Ala A&M Univ, Dept Art & Art Educ, prof & chair, 1973-97, prof, 1997-98, artist residence, 1999-2000, Dept Fine Arts, prof & interim chmn, 2002-03; Lincoln Univ, Dept Fine Arts, asst prof, 1998-99; Stillman Col, Dept Fine Arts, prof & chmn, 2000-02; Univ Montevallo, Dept Art Glass & Art Educ, coordr art dept, prof art & visual art dept chair, 2008-; Ford Found fel, NY; Ill State Univ, acad fel; Ala A&M Univ, acad scholar; For Arts Sake, creator. **Orgs:** Southern Fel Fund. **Home Addr:** 333 Sunnyslope Trail, Madison, AL 35757-7657, **Home Phone:** (256)721-3950. **Business Addr:** Professor of Art, Chair, University of Montevallo, Rm 2 Bloch Hall Sta 6663, Montevallo, AL 35115-6000, **Business Phone:** (205)665-6407.

## PEARSON, DREW

Executive, football player, broadcaster. **Personal:** Born Jan 12, 1951, South River, NJ; married Marsha; children: Tori & Britni. **Educ:** Univ Tulsa, attended 1972. **Career:** Football player, coach (retired), executive; Dallas Cowboys, wide receiver & kick returner, 1973-83; CBS Sports, color commentator; Smokey's Express Barbecue Restaurant, partner; Dallas Texans, coach, 1991; Drew Pearson Mkt, founder, currently. **Orgs:** Chmn, March Dimes Crusade; Nat spokesman, Distilled Spirits Coun. **Honors/Awds:** Pro Bowl, 1974 & 1976-77; President's Award, Univ Tulsa; Inducted, Tulsa Athletics Hall of Fame, 1985; NFL Alumni Career Achievement Award, 2005. **Home Addr:** 3721 Mt Vernon Way, Plano, TX 75025-3729, **Home Phone:** (972)618-8806. **Business Addr:** Founder, Drew Pearson Marketing Inc, 15006 Beltway Dr, Addison, TX 75001, **Business Phone:** (972)702-8055.

## PEARSON, HERMAN B.

Government official, clergy. **Personal:** Born Mar 2, 1947, Omaha, NE; children: Nicole, Carmen, Selina & Quatica. **Educ:** Univ Nebr, BS, 1972. **Career:** Minister, 1973-; Mayor's Off, City Omaha, contract coordr; Wash Redskins, prof football player, 1972; Tabernacle Bapt Ch Coun Bluff, asst pastor. **Orgs:** Evaluator Ment Retardation Prog; Community Leader Among Young Adults; prof dj co-founder, First Black Owned Radio Sta Omaha Area, 1969; Recreational Activities Leader; NATRA. **Home Addr:** 4207 Wirt St, Omaha, NE 68111. **Business Addr:** 723 N 18 St, Omaha, NE 68111.

## PEARSON, MARILYN RUTH

Executive, consultant, vice president (organization). **Personal:** Born Nov 12, 1955, Saginaw, MI; daughter of Hollis Townsend and Bernice Richard; married Tommie L Sr; children: Tamara Bernice & Tommie L Jr. **Educ:** Saginaw Valley State Univ, Univ Ctr Mich, BA, Eng, 1978. **Career:** Ford Motor Credit Co, Saginaw MI, credit investr, 1977-80; Merrill Lynch, financial consult, 1980-84, sr training consult, 1984-87, asst vpres, 1987, vpres & retirement plan consult, 2003-07; Salomon Smith Barney, vpres, nat dir training corp retirement serv; TPB Legacy Group, pres, 2011-; First Citizens Bank, Instnl Philanthropic Serv, vpres & philanthropic consult, currently. **Orgs:** First vpres, Zeta Phi Beta Sorority Epsilon XI Zeta, 1980-; Exec Club Merrill Lynch, 1981-82; Pres Club, Merrill Lynch, 1983; Nat Asn Securities Prof, 1987-; bd mem, Jr Achievement Mercer County, 1987-; bd mem, Literacy Vols Am State NJ, 1988-; bd mem, YWCA, Trenton, 1989-; Nat Asn Advan Colored People; Shiloh Baptist Church; bd dir, Elizabeth City State Univ. **Honors/Awds:** Achievement Award, Nat Asn Negro Bus & Prof Women, 1982; CEBA Award, 1988; Zeta of the Year, Epsilon Xi Zeta Zeta Phi Beta Sorority, 1988; Faith, Hope & Charity Award, FAI HO CHA, Trenton NJ, 1988; featured in Merrill Lynch ad in Black Enterprise, Essence, Ebony, 1988-89; Black Achievers in the Industry Award, Harlem Branch YMCA, 1989; Int Bus & Prof Women Dollars & Sense, 1989. **Home Addr:** 11 E Darrah Lane, Lawrenceville, NJ 08648, **Home Phone:** (609)883-8423. **Business Addr:** Vice President, Philanthropic Consultant, 4300 Six Forks Rd, Raleigh, NC 27603, **Business Phone:** (919)716-4726.

## PEARSON, MICHAEL NOVEL

Banker, president (organization). **Personal:** Born Feb 12, 1956, Memphis, TN. **Educ:** Fisk Univ, BS, bus mgt & econs, 1978; Pepperdine Univ, George L Graziadio Sch Bus & Mgt, MBA, finance, 1980; Col Financial Planning, CFP, 1984. **Career:** Ford Motor Credit Co, cust acct rep, 1978-79; M-Bank Houston NA, energy loan officer, 1981-83; First City Nat Bank, vpres & relationship mgr, 1981-93; Pearson Assoc, financial planner, 1982-; First City Bank Corp, sr loan rev officer, 1984-89, Healthcare Group Wholesake Banking Div, vpres, 1989-92; Tex Com Bank, sr loan officer, 1992-99; JP Morgan Chase Bank, vpres & sr loan preview officer, 1993-01; Southwest Bank Tex, sr credit process officer, 2001-05; Amegy Bank Tex, sr vpres & relationship mgr, 2001-; Houston Arts Alliance, peer rev panelist, 2010-11. **Orgs:** Life Health Disability Ins lic State TX, 1986; Enrolled Agt-IRS; Alpha Phi Alpha Frat; Inst Cert Financial Planners, Int Asn Financial Planners; Ser 7 Regist Rep, HD Vest, 2001; bd dir, Risk Mgt Asn, 2004-; bd treas & finance comt chmn, Houston Area Urban League, 2009-; comt mem, Art Colony Asn Bayou City Art Festival, 2011-; adv bd mem, Houston Ctr Photog, 2011-; trustee, Battleship Tex Found, 2011-; bd dir, exec comt mem, Chinese Community Ctr, 2011-. **Home Addr:** 1522 Monarch Oaks St, Houston, TX 77055, **Home Phone:** (713)464-1113. **Business Addr:** Senior Vice President, Relationship Manager, Amegy Bank, 1100 La St, Houston, TX 77002.

## PEARSON, PRESTON JAMES

President (organization), football player. **Personal:** Born Jan 17, 1945, Freeport, IL; married Linda; children: Gregory & Matthew. **Educ:** Univ Ill, Urbana-Champaign, IL, attended 1967. **Career:** Football player (retired), executive; Baltimore Colts, running back, 1967, kick returner, 1968; Pittsburgh Steelers, running back, 1970-71, kick returner, 1972-73, fullback, 1973, 1974; Dallas Cowboys, running back, 1975-80, kick returner, 1975; Pro-Style Assos, pres, owner, 1981-; Time Inc & Am Tel Comun, mkt exec. **Orgs:** Founder, treas, Consult Mgt Enterprises; bd dir, Sickle Cell Anemia Found; YMCA; Paws City; N Tex Food Bank; NFL Alumni; Univ Ill Urbana-Champaign Alumni Group. **Honors/Awds:** NFL champion, 1968; Super Bowl Champion. **Special Achievements:** Broke his own record 47 Catches 1978; only player to appear in Super Bowl with three different teams Colts, Steelers, Cowboys; Led NFL in kickoff returns and kickoff returns for touchdowns; Set Cowboy record for running back with 46 receptions, 1977; Author of "Hearing the Noise", 1985. TV Movie: Super Bowl XIII, 1979; 1980 NFC Championship Game, 1981. **Home Addr:** 9104 Moss Farm Lane, Dallas, TX 75243-7429, **Home Phone:** (214)349-0026. **Business Addr:** President, Owner, Pro-Style Associates, 9104 Moss Farm Lane, Dallas, TX 75243, **Business Phone:** (214)349-0026.

## PEARSON, RAMONA HENDERSON (RAMONA ESTELLE HENDERSON)

Government official, president (organization). **Personal:** Born Oct 3, 1952, Baltimore, MD; daughter of Robert and Doris Green; married Edward; children: Leora. **Educ:** Morgan State Univ, BS, acct, 1975; Univ Detroit Mercy, MBA, finance, 1998. **Career:** Ernst & Ernst, staff auditor, 1975-76; Morgan Statue Univ, acct & auditing instr, 1976-77; Linwood Jennings Pa CPA's, assoc, 1977-79; Constant Care Comm Health Ctr Inc, controller, 1976-77; Arthur Young & Co, sr auditor, audit mgr, 1978-84; Wayne State Univ, dir internal audit, 1984-86; Ramona H Pearson CPA PC, pres, 1984-; Wayne County Govt, auditor gen, 1986-97; Herlong Cathedral Sch, chief exec officer, 1996-99; Highland Pk, financial mgr, 2001-; Pearson Group, pres & owner, 1999-; Walsh Col, acct rev instr, 2011-. **Orgs:** Nat pres, Nat Asn Black Accountants, 1973-2010; Am Inst CPA's, 1976-; Nat Asn Advan Colored People; Big Bros & Sisters Am; Mich Asn CPA's, 1981-, chair, 2011-13; Inst Internal Auditors, 1985-; Govt Accountants Asn, 1988-; Govt Finance Officers Asn, 1988-; Local Govt Auditors Asn, 1988-; Mich State Bd Accountancy; bd mem, Ecumenical Theol Sem, 2007-. **Honors/Awds:** Outstanding Member Award, Nat Asn Black Accts, 1983; Women of Excellence Award, Mich Chronicle, 2012; Women to Watch Award, Am Inst CPAs, 2012. **Special Achievements:** Article "How to Start a Small Business" Afro-American Newspaper, 1977. **Home Addr:** 19331 Canterbury Rd, Detroit, MI 48221-1807, **Home Phone:** (313)863-5606. **Business Addr:** President, The Pearson Group LLC, 26789 Woodward Ave Suite 107, Huntington Woods, MI 48070, **Business Phone:** (248)397-8501.

## PEARSON, DR. STANLEY E.

Physician. **Personal:** Born Oct 21, 1949, Quitman, GA; son of Rev Oliver and Jr Mattie A Bowles. **Educ:** Univ FL Gainesville, attended 1971; Meharry Med Col, MD, 1975; Am Bd Internal Med, dipl, 1978. **Career:** Providence Hosp, resident, 1975-78; Fitzsimons Army Med Ctr, fel, 1978-80; Landstahl Army Regional Med Ctr W Ger, chief cardiolo serv, 1981-83; AUs Europe 7th Med Command, cardiolo consult, 1982-83; Madigan Army Med Ctr, staff cardiologist, 1983-84; McDowell Health Care Ctr, chief staff; CIGNA Health Plan Ariz; dir, cardiac rehab, 1984-2007, staff cardiologist, chief staff, 1986-88; chmn, dept internal med, 1988, chief med off & sr med dir; Nat Imaging Assocs, physician, 2007-. **Orgs:** Mem Alpha Omega Alpha Hon Med Soc; fel Am Col Cardiolo; Colo Med Soc; Tau Epsilon Phi Frat; Asn Black Cardiologists; Am Col Physician Execs; chmn, Specialty Care CIGNA Health Care Ariz, 1998; adv bd mem, Wellness Community; founding mem, Community Health Asian Am. **Honors/Awds:** Am Bd Internal Med Cardiovasc Dis, 1981. **Home Addr:** 5530 N Camelback Canyon Dr, Phoenix, AZ 85018-1239, **Home Phone:** (602)522-9835. **Business Addr:** Physician, National Imaging Associates, 4801 E Wash St, Phoenix, AZ 85034, **Business Phone:** (602)572-2481.

## PEARSON-MCNEIL, CHERYL

Vice president (organization), marketing executive. **Educ:** Purdue Univ, BA, pub rels, 1984; Keller Grad Sch Mgt, MBA, mkt. **Career:** YWCA Metrop Chicago, dir mkt & commun, 1989-93; RJ Dale Advert, acct exec, 1994-96; Boys & Girls Clubs Chicago, vpres, 1996-2000; WMAQ TV, NBC5 Chicago, dir sta rels, 2000-04; Nielsen Co, vpres commun & community affairs, 2004-07, sr vpres commun, 2007-09, sr vpres pub affairs & govt rels, 2009-14, sr vpres US Strategic Community Alliances & Consumer Engagement, 2014-. **Orgs:** Bd dir, Girl Scouts Greater Chicago; bd dir, Northwest Ind & Better Govt Asn; co-chair, Execs Club Chicago's Civic Comt; Network Exec Women's Exec Leaders Forum's Steering Comt; advisor, Univ Chicago's Harris Sch Pub Policy mentor prog; bd mem, Mus Broadcast Commun; bd mem, Chicago Found Women. **Business Addr:** Senior Vice President, The Nielsen Company, 85 Broad St, New York, NY 10004, **Business Phone:** (800)864-1224.

## PEASE, DENISE LOUISE

State government official, banker. **Personal:** Born Mar 15, 1953, Bronx, NY; daughter of William Henry Jr and Louise Marion Caswell. **Educ:** Columbia Univ, NY, BA, Am hist & biol, 1980; Columbia Univ Grad Sch Bus, Spl Cert, 1982; Bernard Barauch Grad Sch Pub Admin, attended 1983; Europ Inst Bus Admin, Paris, exec mgt. **Career:** Elmcor Youth & Adult Activ, dir community servs, 1980-82; Essex County, Newark NJ, spl asst to co exec, 1982-83; NY State Dept Banks, urban anal III, 1983-86, exec asst to supt, 1986-87; dep supt, 1987, Com Banking Off NY Comptroller, found bd mem, asst comptroller & dir; New York Banking Comn, comptroller; regional adminr, US Gen Serv Admin's Northeast & Caribbean Region, currently. **Orgs:** Bd mem, Handier, 1974-; Govr's Econ Develop Sub-Cabinet, 1985-; bd mem, Cornell Univ Coop Ext Adv Comn, 1986-; bd mem, Elcor Youth & Adult Activ, 1986-87; Coalition 100 Black Women, 1988-; life mem, Nat Coun Negro Women, l988-; rep, Govr's, Housing Policy Cabinet, 1989; Fin Women's Asn, 1989; Soc Consumer Affairs Profs Bus; life mem, Nat Coun Negro Women; life mem, Nat Asn Advan Colored People; Coalition 100 Black Women; co-chmn, Fin Womens Asn NY; bd dir, Epilepsy Found Am; chairwoman, African Am Initiative. **Honors/Awds:** Professor Achievement Award, Nat Asn Negro Bus & Prof Women, 1980; Charles H Revson Fel on the Future of NY, Columbia Univ, 1981; Nat Urban Fel, Nat Urban Fellows Org, 1982; Cit Merit, NY State Assembly, 1989; Salute to Outstanding African Am Bus & Prof Women, Dollar & Sense Mag, 1990; Cit Merit, NY State Assembly, 1988; Gov Cit, 1993; Community Service Award, NY State Black & Puerto Rican Legislators Asn, 1993. **Home Addr:** 10321 35th Ave, Corona, NY 11368-1935, **Home Phone:** (718)898-6655. **Business Addr:** Regional Administrator, US General Services Administration, 1 Const Sq, Washington, DC 20417.

## PEAVY, HON. JOHN W., JR.

Judge. **Personal:** Born Apr 28, 1943, Houston, TX; married Diane Massey; children: 4. **Educ:** Howard Univ, BA, 1964; Howard Univ Sch Law, LLB, 1967. **Career:** Judge (retired); Nat Aero & Space Coun, White House, Wash, DC, acct, 1961-64, admin asst, 1964-67; Berry Lott Peavy & Williams, pract law, 1967-72; Harris Cty Comn Action Assoc, assoc field coord, 1967-68; Co Judge Bill Elliott, exec asst, 1968-70; Harris Co Ct Precinct 7, judge, justice peace position, 1973-77; 246th Dist Judicial Dist Ct Harris Co Houston, judge. **Orgs:** Assoc counr proj, Houston Bar Asn, 1970-71; app mem, Housing Asst Tech Adv Group, 1974; chmn, WL Davis Div Sam Houston Boy Scouts, 1976; Alpha Phi Alpha; Harris Cty Coun Orgs; life mem, NAACP; comn, Houston Bus & Prof Men's Club, YMCA Century Club; former dem precinct chmn, Precinct 292 Houston TX; mem adv bd, KYOK Radio Sta; legal adv, Riverside Lion's Club; bd dir, Mercy Hosp; steering comt, Phillip Randolph Inst; bd dir, Houston Citizens Chamber Com Proj Pull; Eliza Johnson Ctr Aged; Southern Ctr Br YMCA; United Negro Col Fund; Julia C Hester House, St Elizabeth Hosp; Houston Coun Human Rel; Vol Am; St Jr Bar Small Claims Ct Handbk Comn, 1977; hon co-chmn, Citizens Better Transit, 1978; Downtown Rotary Club Houston, Urban Policy Task Force City Houston, 1978; Pol Actg Comt Houston Lawyers Asn; bd dir, Nat Bar Found; Nat Bar Asn; Home Pilot Prog, Am Bar Asn; State Bar TX; Jr Bar Asn Houston; State Bar TX Ctr Reorg Comt, Judicial Coun. **Honors/Awds:** Outstanding Military Student Chicago Tribune Award; Eagle Scout & mem Order of the Arrow of Boy Scouts of Am, 1960; Distinguished Achievers Award, YMCA, 1973, 1977; YMCA Award for Outstanding Service to the Community, 1974; Outstanding Young Bus & Prof Man, Houston Young Adult Club, 1979; Appreciation Award, Exploring Div, Sam Houston Area BSA, 1979; Nat Judicial Int Achievement Award; Houston Lawyers Asn Achievement Award, 1980. **Special Achievements:** Certificate of Citation by the State of TX House of Reps, 1975. **Home Addr:** 5501 Blythewood St, Houston, TX 77021-1606, **Home Phone:** (713)747-3737.

## PEAY, HON. SAMUEL

Judge, lawyer. **Personal:** Born Jun 2, 1939, Ridgeway, SC; son of Geneva and English; married Lillian Bernice Chavis; children: Clifton Delmineo & Ira Aloysius. **Educ:** Basic Law Enforcement Training, cert; Univ Nev Nat Judicial Acad, 1985, 1986. **Career:** Judge (retired); Richland County Sheriff's Dept Columbia, SC, dep sheriff, 1964, sgt law enforcement, 1969, juv, arson, criminal invest, 1971-78; Richland County, judge, 1978-2011. **Orgs:** Pres, Richland Co Summary Ct Judges Asn, 1986-88; Nat Sheriff's Asn; SC Law Enforcement Asn; SC Summary Ct Judges Asn; Nat Judges Asn; Zion Canaan Baptist Church, Columbia, SC. **Honors/Awds:** Outstanding South Carolinian, Nat Coun Negro Women, 1980; Honored, Capital City Lodge No 47, Columbia, SC, 1985; "Respect for Law" Award, Optimist Club Columbia, 1986; Benedict Col Service Award, 1986; Honor, Columbia, SC Br Nat Asn Advan Colored People, 1991; Honor, Columbia Lawyers Asn, 1996; Honor, SC Black Lawyers Asn, 1996. **Special Achievements:** First black to serve as sergeant in Richland County Sheriff's Department. **Home Addr:** 954 E Campanella Dr, Columbia, SC 29203-5122, **Home Phone:** (803)754-1355.

## PECK, CAROLYN ARLENE

Broadcaster, basketball coach, basketball player. **Personal:** Born Jan 22, 1966, Jefferson City, TN; daughter of Stephen and Arlene Peck; married James Michael OBrien. **Educ:** Vanderbilt Univ, BA, commun, 1988. **Career:** Basketball player, basketball coach (retired), television sportscaster; Nashville TV sta, mkt consult; pharmaceut sales person; Nippondenso Corp, prof basketball player, 1991-93; Tenn Univ, asst coach, 1993-95; Univ Ky, asst coach, 1995-96; Purdue Univ, from asst coach to head basketball coach, 1996-99; USA Basketball, head coach, 1997-2004; Orlando Miracle, head coach, 1999-2001; WNBA franchise Orlando Miracle, head coach & gen mgr, 1999-2001; Fla Gator, head basketball coach, 2002-07; Univ Fla, head coach, 2003-04; ESPN, basketball analyst, currently. **Special Achievements:** First African American to win the Winged Foot Award. **Business Addr:** Basketball Analyst, ESPN Inc, ESPN Plz 935 Mid St, Bristol, CT 06010-1000, **Business Phone:** (860)766-2000.

## PECK, DR. DOROTHY ADAMS

Administrator. **Career:** Dreyfoos Sch Arts; Palm Beach County Sch Dist, area supt; AME Church, sr bishop, currently. **Orgs:** Bd mem, Bread World; Self Study Comn; Legacy Soc; pres, Women's Missionary Soc, currently. **Business Addr:** President, Women's Missionary Society, 1134 11th St NW, Washington, DC 20001, **Business Phone:** (202)371-8886.

## PECK, LEONTYNE CLAY

Chief executive officer, founder (originator), educator. **Personal:** Born Nov 14, 1958, Keyser, WV; daughter of Russell Clay Sr and Suellen Gaiter Clay; married Lyle; children: Whitney & Alexis. **Educ:** Am Univ, Wash, DC, BA, polit sci & pub admin, 1981; WVa Univ, Morgantown, WV, higher educ admin, 1992; Am Univ Rome, Rome, Italy, cert Ital studies. **Career:** US Dept Housing & Urban Dev, Wash, DC, consumer affairs specialist, 1978-81; Congressman Cleve Benedict, LB Johnson legis intern, 1981-82; US Conf Mayors, Wash, DC, pub affairs officer, 1984-88; Ctr Black Cult, Morgantown, WV, prog mgr, 1989-91; WV Univ, prog mgr, Potomac State Col WV; Gaye Clay Pottery, owner; Piedmont Housing Alliance, prog mgr, 2010-14; Afritique, founder & chief exec officer, currently; Queen Charlotte Tours LLC, tour guide, auth, speaker, 2015-. **Orgs:** Clay Family Socs; Charlottesville Albemarle Conv & Visitors Ctr; Alpha Kappa Alpha Sorority; Links Inc; life mem, Girl Scouts. **Business Addr:** Founder, Chief Executive Officer, Afritique, 1069 Somer Chase Ct, Charlottesville, VA 22911, **Business Phone:** (434)975-3943.

## PEEBLES, ALLIE MUSE

Educator. **Personal:** Born Apr 12, 1926, Danville, VA; daughter of Maude B Smith Muse and William Brown Muse Sr; married Millard R Sr; children: Martha Elaine Brown, Brenda LaVerne & Millard R Jr. **Educ:** Hampton Univ, VA, BS, 1947; St Augustine's Col, NC, cert renewal; NC Cent Univ, attended 1969. **Career:** Prince Edward Co Sch Syst, Va, eng teacher, 1947-48; Raleigh-Wake Co Sch Syst, NC, eng teacher, 1963-78; M R Peebles & Son Masonry Contractors, owner, pres, 1978-82; Telamon Corp, Smithfield NC, job counsr, 1983-86; Carolinian (newspaper), columnist, 1984-; St Augustine's Col, Raleigh, eng instr, 1987-. **Orgs:** Martin St Baptist Church, 1955-; pres, Raleigh Hampton Univ Alumni Asn, 1962-64, 1984-86, vpres, 1979-84, recruitment chmn; treas, Jack Jill Am, 1966-68; sec, Delta Sigma Theta-Raleigh Alumnae Chap, 1972-74, chmn publicity & pub rels, 1985-89, historian; chmn nat recruitment, Nat Hampton Alumni Asn, 1978-82, 2nd vpres NC reg, 1983-89, pres, currently; life mem, chmn, Raleigh-Apex Nat Asn Advan Colored People, 1978-; Wake Co Pvt Indust Coun, 1980-82; Raleigh Civil Serv Comn, 1980-82; bd mem, YWCA Wake Co, 1980-86; consult, Women Commun Workshop, 1987; Delta's Nat Comm Heritage & Arch; sec, Fin Comt, Martin Baptist Church, Raleigh, NC, 1989-93; chmn, Publicity Com, 1990-; pub rels dir, Delta Sigma Theta, Raleigh Chap, 1990-93, journalist, 2000-02; chmn publicity, Capital City Sertoma Club; Nat Coun Negro Women, Capital Area Sect; publicity chmn & adv, James P W, Raleigh Dist C City. **Home Addr:** 721 Calloway Dr, Raleigh, NC 27610-4011, **Home Phone:** (919)832-9042. **Business Addr:** Instructor, St Augustine College, 1315 Oakwood Ave, Raleigh, NC 27610, **Business Phone:** (919)516-4640.

**PEEBLES, DR. REV. CHARLOTTE REED. See REED, DR. CHARLOTTE.**

## PEEBLES, DANIEL PERCY, III (DANNY PEEBLES)

Football player, executive. **Personal:** Born May 30, 1966, Raleigh, NC; children: Damiya, Danny, Dylan & Jada. **Educ:** NC State Univ, acct & bus mgt, 1988. **Career:** Footplayer (retired), executive; NC State Football, wide receiver, 1985-88; Nc State Men's Track & Field, 1985-87; Tampa Bay Buccaneers, wide receiver, 1989-90; Cleveland Browns, 1991; Rise & Walk Ministries, owner & founder, currently . **Orgs:** Bd mem & pres, Rise & Walk Ministries; Nat Hon Soc. **Business Addr:** Founder, President, Rise & Walk Ministries, 12205 Fieldmist Dr, Raleigh, NC 27614, **Business Phone:** (919)990-3430.

## PEEBLES-WILKINS, DR. WILMA CECELIA

Educator. **Personal:** Born Apr 21, 1945, Raleigh, NC; daughter of Millard Peebles Sr and Mary Myatt Peebles; married James; children: Keith & Kenneth. **Educ:** NC State Univ, BA, 1967; Case Western Res Univ, MSSA, 1971; Univ NC, Chapel Hill, NC, PhD, 1984. **Career:** Cuyahoga Co Div Child Welfare, social worker, 1967-72; Ment Develop Ctr, dir intake, 1972-76; Eastern Ky Univ, asst prof, 1976-77; NC Memorial Hosp, chief pediat social worker, 1977-78; NC State Univ, assoc prof & dir social work, 1978-91; Boston Univ, assoc dean, 1991-93, dean & prof 1993-2006, prof, 2006-07, dean emer & prof emer, currently. **Orgs:** Nat Asn Black Social Workers, 1976-; consult, Wake Co Coun Aging, 1979; Raleigh Housing Authority, 1979; Swed Int Fel Youth Leaders & Social Workers, 1980; vice chmn, NC Cert Bd Social Work, 1984-; competence cert bd, Nat Asn Social Workers, 1984-; comn minority group concerns, Coun Social Work Educ, 1985-87; chmn, New Eng Asn Deans & Dir Sch Social Work, Nat Academies Pract. **Special Achievements:** Advanced the inclusion of African American social welfare leaders in the Encyclopedia of Social Work. **Home Addr:** 4801 Newham Ct, Raleigh, NC 27612, **Home Phone:** (919)571-4685. **Business Addr:** Dean Emerita, Professor Emerita, Boston University, 264 Bay State Rd, Boston, MA 02215.

## PEEK, BOOKER C.

Educator. **Personal:** Born May 22, 1940, Jacksonville, FL; son of Oscar and Estella; married Annette Jones; children: Cheryl, Joseph & Angela. **Educ:** Fla Agr & Mech Univ, BA, 1964; Oberlin Col, MA, 1966; Univ Fla, advan study. **Career:** Hampton Jr Col, teacher; Matthew W Gilbert High Sch, teacher; Ribault Sr High Sch, teacher; Albany St Col, fac; Oberlin Col, assoc prof emer, African Am studies, currently. **Orgs:** Pres, Toward Am Togetherness Common Orgn, 1968; Fla Star Teacher, 1968; coordr, Words Are Very Empowering; Am Asn Univ & Prof; Nat Asn Advan Colored People; Int Longshoremen's Asn. **Home Addr:** 589 Spruce Dr, Oberlin, OH 44074. **Business Addr:** Associate Professor Emeritus, Oberlin College, 323 Rice Hall 10 N Prof St, Oberlin, OH 44074, **Business Phone:** (440)775-8479.

## PEEK, GAIL LENORE

College teacher, vice president (organization), lawyer. **Personal:** Born Jan 18, 1950, Brooklyn, NY. **Educ:** City Col Univ NY, BA, polit sci, 1972; Princeton Univ, MA, polit, 1974, PhD, 1978; Univ Chicago, Law Sch, JD, 1984. **Career:** Williams Col, asst prof, 1976-80; Kirkland & Ellis, assoc, 1984-87; Premark Int Inc, sr atty, 1987-90, corp coun, 1990-91, gen coun, 1991-93; Ralph Wilson Plastics Co, vpres & gen coun, 1993-95; Wilsonart Int Inc, in-house coun, vpres & gen coun, 1993-2005; Beard Kultgen Brophy Bostwick Dickson & Squires LLP, atty, currently. **Orgs:** State Bar Tex; Am Bar Asn; Bell County Bar Asn; bd dir, Scott & White Health Plan; bd dir, United Way Cent Tex; pres, Ralph Wilson Youth Clubs Temple; comnr, Bd Cent Tex Housing Consortium; vis comt mem, Univ Mary Hardin Baylor; vis comt mem, Scott & White Hosps & Clins; Rotary Club Temple; bd dir, Tax Increment Financing Reinvestment Zone; McLennan County Bar Asn; chair, Citizen Adv Comt; Bell County Redistricting Adv Comt; Us Dist Ct Northern Dist Ill; Us Dist Ct Western Dist Tex. **Home Addr:** 3409 Whispering Oaks, Temple, TX 76504. **Business Addr:** Attorney, Beard Kultgen Brophy Bostwick Dickson & Squires LLP, 220 S 4th St, Waco, TX 76701, **Business Phone:** (254)776-5500.

## PEELER, ANTHONY EUGENE

Basketball player. **Personal:** Born Nov 25, 1969, Kansas City, MO; children: Marcus Anthony & Chynna. **Educ:** Univ Miss, attended 1992. **Career:** Basketball player (retired), basketball coach; Los Angeles Lakers, guard, shooting guard, 1992-96; Vancouver Grizzlies, shooting guard, 1996-98; Minn Timberwolves, shooting guard, 1998-2003; Sacramento Kings, guard, shooting guard, 2003-04; Wash Wizards, guard, shooting guard, 2004-05; Akasvayu Girona, guard, shooting guard, 2005; Panthers, asst coach, 2008-09; Div II Va Union Univ, asst coach, 2011-12; head coach, Luqman Jaaber; Shenyang Dongjin, asst. **Honors/Awds:** Big Eight Conference Player of the Year, 1992; Male Athlete of the Year. **Business Addr:** Assistant Coach, Virginia Union University, 1500 N Lombardy St, Richmond, VA 23220.

## PEELER, DIANE FAUSTINA

Educator. **Personal:** Born Mar 14, 1959, Greeneville, TN; daughter of Segeet and Marilyn. **Educ:** Univ Tenn, Knoxville, BS, 1982; Southern Univ New Orleans; Xavier Univ. **Career:** Orleans Parish Sch Bd, instr, 1982-; Orleans Parish Comn Schs, modern dance teacher, 1983-85; Off Employment Develop, summer youth counr, 1986. **Orgs:** Vpres, Delta Sigma Theta Sor Inc, 1980-81; phys therapy volunteer, Meadow creast Hosp, 1985-86.

## PEEPLES, AUDREY RONE

Association executive, president (organization). **Personal:** Born May 22, 1939, Chicago, IL; daughter of John Drayton and Thelma Shepherd; married Anthony; children: Jennifer Lynn & Michael Anthony. **Educ:** Univ Ill, BA, Eng, 1961; Northwestern Univ, Kellogg Sch Mgt, MBA, 1970. **Career:** Continental Bank, trust admin, 1961-73; Girls Scouts USA, assoc reg dir, 1973-77, GS Chicago, assoc exec dir, 1973-77, exec dir, 1977-87; YWCA Metrop Chicago, chief exec officer, 1987-2001; MAJA Inc, pres, 2002-. **Orgs:** Nat bd GS USA, 1971-73; Jack & Jill Chicago, 1973-; Chicago Network, 1988-; Econ Club Chicago, 1988; bd mem, United Way Chicago, 1988-92; bd mem, Chicago Network, 1991-95; trustee, First Non Profit Trust, 1992-97; bd mem, treas, Chicago Found Women, 1992-97; comnr, Gov Comn Women, 1997-; vpres & bd mem, Am Civil Liberties Union, 1999-; chair, YWCA USA Nat Coord Bd, 2002-; bd mem, Exec Serv Corp, 2002-; chief exec officer, Young Women's Christian Asn; bd mem, Adler Sch Prof Psychol, 2011-; bd mem, little Co Mary Hosp Found, 2012-; bd mem, Turnstone Develop Corp, 2012-; exec comt, Chicago Community Trust, 2012-. **Honors/Awds:** Kizzy Award; Outstanding Achievement Award, Girl Scouts Chicago; Merit Award, Nat Coun Negro Women, Cosmopolitan Sect; Thomas & Eleanor Wright Award, City Chicago Comn; Outstanding Women of Achievement, YWCA Metrop Chicago. **Home Addr:** 1240 N Paulina St Apt 3, Chicago, IL 60622-3852. **Business Addr:** President, MAJA Inc, 543 Abington Ave, Glenside, PA 19038-5005, **Business Phone:** (215)923-9999.

## PEER, WILBUR TYRONE

Educator, government official, administrator. **Personal:** Born Apr 28, 1951, Lee County, AR; married Patricia Nelson; children: Andre B, Yolanda & Wilbur T II. **Educ:** Univ Ark, Pine Bluff, BA, hist & govt; Univ Ark, Fayetteville, MA, voc educ. **Career:** Phillips Col, vet counr, 1974-76; Lee Co Coop clin, community develop specialist, 1976-82; Phillips Co Community Col, dean continuing educ, 1982-88, dir econ develop, 1992-93; Southern Develop Bank Corp, Arkadelphia, Ak, consult; Delta Improv Corp, Marianna, exec dir; Int Filter Mfg Corp, vpres sales, 1988-91; Ark Land & Farm Develop Corp, resource dir & proj developer, Fargo, mgt consult, 1991-92; Rural Develop Admin, actg adminr, 1992-93; Rural Bus-Coop Serv, assoc adminr, 1994. **Orgs:** Phi Beta Sigma, 1972; owner & oper, Wilbur Peer Farm, 1977-; justicepeace Lee Co quorum Ct, 1980-; owner & broker, Wilbur T Peer Realty Co, 1982-; exec dir, Delta Improv, 1982-; PIC E AR Pvt Indust Coun, 1983-. **Home Addr:** PO Box 34, La Grange, AR 72352.

## PEERMAN-PLEDGER, VERNESE DIANNE (V DIANNE PLEDGER)

Foundation executive, president (organization), chief executive officer. **Personal:** Born Jan 1, 1958, Pinehurst, NC; daughter of William Donald and Otelia Cooke; married Vincent Lewis. **Educ:** NC Cent Univ, BA, jour, 1979. **Career:** Eunice Advert, sr acct exec, bus mgr; Carrington & Carrington Advert, partner, bus mgr; Dudley Products Co Inc, nat advert mgr; Western Career Col, PR dir, high sch crd; Chapel Hill Carrboro Downtown Content Mgt Syst, dir spec projs; St Joseph's Historic Found Inc, coord, exec dir, pres & chief exec officer, currently; Hayti Heritage Ctr, exec producer, pres & chief exec officer, currently; Pledger Consult Group, pres, 1995-; NC Freedom Monument Proj, exec dir, 2011-. **Orgs:** Pres, NC Cultural Network, 1992-; bd dir, Scrap Exchange; Delta Sigma Theta Sorority Inc, Chapel Hill Carrboro Alumnae Chap; South Orange Black Caucus; vol, Am Cancer Soc; choir mem, St Paul Am Church, Steward Bd; bd, Chapel Hill Women's Ctr; Arts Advocates bd. **Home Addr:** 530 Piney Mtn Rd, Chapel Hill, NC 27514, **Home Phone:** (919)942-5870. **Business Addr:** Executive Director, North Carolina Freedom Monument Project, PO Box 33741, Raleigh, NC 27636, **Business Phone:** (919)224-0480.

**PEETE, CALVIN. See Obituaries Section.**

## PEETE, HOLLY ROBINSON (HOLLY ELIZABETH

**ROBINSON PEETE)**
Actor, singer, writer. **Personal:** Born Sep 18, 1964, Philadelphia, PA; daughter of Matt Robinson and Dolores; married Rodney; children: Rodney James, Ryan Elizabeth, Robinson James & Roman. **Educ:** Sarah Lawrence Col, grad, psychol & Fr. **Career:** CBS daytime talk show The Talk, co-host; Films: Howard the Duck, 1986; This Is the Life; Speed-Dating, 2010; 21 Jump Street, 2012. TV series: "Booker", 1989-90; "ABC TGIF", 1990; "21 Jump Street", 1987-91; "Hanging W/ Mr Cooper", 1992-97; "For Your Love", 1998; "One on One", 2001-02; "My Wonderful Life", 2002; "Like Family", 2003-04; "The Honeymooners", 2005; "Three's Co", 2005; "Hello Larry", 2006; "Anything But Love", 2006; "Fired Up", 2006; "Love Inc", 2005-06; "Football Wives", 2007; "Matters of Life & Dating", 2007; TV movies: "Dummy", 1979; "Howard the Duck", 1986; "The Jacksons: An American Dream", 1992; "Killers in the House", 1998; "After All", 1999; "My Wonderful Life", 2002; "Good Day Live", 2004; "Earthquake", 2004; "Love Inc", 2005; "Matters of Life and Dating", 2007; "The Bridget Show", 2009; "Mike & Molly", 2011-12; "RuPaul's Drag U", 2012; "Blue", 2013; "Instant Mom", 2014-. **Orgs:** Owner, HollyRod Found; Alpha Kappa Alpha Sorority, 2012. **Honors/Awds:** Image Award, Nat Asn Advan Colored People, 2011. **Special Achievements:** Proud Hands, 2008; Book: My Brother Charlie. **Home Addr:** , CA. **Business Addr:** Actress, William Morris Agency, 1 William Morris Pl, Beverly Hills, CA 90212, **Business Phone:** (310)859-4000.

## PEETE, NAN ARRINGTON
Clergy. **Personal:** Born Aug 19, 1938, Chicago, IL; daughter of Maurice Arrington and Phoebe Arrington; children: Richard & Valerie. **Educ:** Occidental Col, BA, econ, 1975; Univ Redlands, MA, human resources, 1978; Gen Theol Sem, Mdiv, 1984. **Career:** Interracial Coun Bus Opportunity, VISTA vol; Coopers & Lybrand, mgt consult, 1979-82; Episcopalian priest, 1984-; St. Mark's Church, Upland, CA, curate, 1984; All Saints Church, Indianapolis, IN, rec, 1985-89; Diocese Atlanta, Canon to Ordinary, 1989-94; Trinity Church Wall St, New York, assoc Pastoral & Outreach ministries, 1994-99; Diocese Southern Ohio, Canon Ministry, 1999-2003; Diocese Wash, Canon Deployment & Ordination, 2003. Gen Theol Sem, trustee, 2006; Holy Communion Episcopal Church, priest in-chg, 2009-11. **Orgs:** Diocesan Off Episcopal Church House, Wash, D.C., mem Black Ministries Adv Coun. **Special Achievements:** First ordained woman to address the Lambeth Conference, 1988; keynote speaker, Afro-Anglican conference, Cape Town, South Africa, 1995. **Business Phone:** (202)537-6531.

## PEETE, RODNEY
Talk show host, football player. **Personal:** Born Mar 16, 1966, Mesa, AZ; son of Willie and Edna; married Holly Robinson; children: Rodney Jackson, Ryan Elizabeth & Robinson James. **Educ:** Univ Southern Calif, BS, commun, 1989. **Career:** Football player (retired), talk show host; Detroit Lions, quarterback, 1989-93; Dallas Cowboys, 1994; Philadelphia Eagles, 1995-98; Wash Redskins, 1999; Oakland Raiders, 2000-01; Carolina Panthers, quarterback, 2002-04; Fox Sports Net, "The Best Damn Sports Show Period", co-host, currently. **Orgs:** Founder, HollyRod Found, 1996-; co-founder, HollyRod4Kids, 2004-. **Honors/Awds:** First team All-American, 1988; Johnny Unitas Golden Arm Award, 1989; Actor: The Fanatics, 1997; Why Did I Get Married Too, 2010; NCAA Silver Anniversary Award, 2014. **Special Achievements:** Appearance on ABCs Hangin With Mr. Cooper. **Home Addr:** , Los Angeles, CA. **Business Addr:** Host, Fox Sports Interactive Media LLC, 407 N Maple Dr, Beverly Hills, CA 90210, **Business Phone:** (310)969-7192.

## PEGRAM, ERRIC DEMONT
Football player, athletic trainer, manager. **Personal:** Born Jan 7, 1969, Dallas, TX; married Michelle; children: Taylor, Nadia, Natalia & Alex. **Educ:** Univ N Tex. **Career:** Football player (retired), athletic trainer, executive; Atlanta Falcons, running back, 1991-94; Pittsburgh Steelers, leading rusher, 1995-96; San Diego Chargers, 1997; New York Giants, running back, 1997; personal trainer; web engr; Match.com, configuration mgr, currently; N Tex Express, coach. **Home Addr:** , Naples, FL.

## PEGUES, FRANCINE (FRANCINE E PEGUES)
Insurance executive. **Personal:** Born Jun 18, 1947, Youngstown, OH; daughter of Charles and Edwina; children: Dwaylon, Jake, E'lida, Edwina & Tailor. **Educ:** Miami Univ, Ohio, BA, polit sci, 1969; Ohio State Univ, attended 1977. **Career:** State Ohio, var mgmt positions, 1970-77; City Detroit, census coordr, 1979-80; Mich Republican State Comn, urban dir, 1981-83; Health Care Network, regional dir, 1983-87; Igp Technologies Inc, Blue Cross Blue Shield Mich, Mkt & Regional Sales Dept, dir, 1983-2007; JustUs, sales & mkt advisor, prog dir, 2010-11; Dan Teak LLC, pres, 2008-; Belle Isle Golf Range, concessionnaire, 2015-. **Orgs:** Blue Cross Blue Shield Mgt Asn, 1987-; chair, Mich Metro Girl Scout Coun, develop comn, 1991-; bd mem, BluesPac, 1991-; Leadership Detroit XVI Grad, 1995; African Develop Found Adv Coun, 1992-94; chairperson, Civic Ctr Comn, City Detroit, 1997-; chmn, Dominican High Sch; bd dir, Oakland Com Bank, 1997-; trustee, 1998-2010, bd dir, 1998-2016, Parade Co; Greater Detroit Chamber Com; bd dir, Girl Scouts Metro Detroit, 1998-2010; bd dir, vpres, Arts & Scraps, 2008-10; adv bd mem, CORP Mag, 2008-11; bd dir, MWGA, 2009-10. **Honors/Awds:** Pioneer Award, Frederick Douglass Soc, 1966; Certificate of Honor, Sojourner Found, 1997; Crain's Detroit Business, Black Business Leadership 100, 1998; Barbara Wicking Knight Philanthropy Award. **Special Achievements:** Author: Wages Incentives: Good News or Bad, Hospital Topics, June 1976; LEAA Compliance Procedures, Cities and Villages, 1976; selected by the American Asn of Health Plans, Exec Leadership Prog, 1998-99. **Home Addr:** 961 Harcourt Rd, Grosse Pointe Park, MI 48230-1875, **Home Phone:** (313)822-9124. **Business Addr:** Concessionaire, The Belle Isle Golf Range, 175 Lakeside Dr, Detroit, MI 48207, **Business Phone:** (313)821-5218.

## PEGUES, DR. WENNETTE WEST
Administrator, educator, association executive. **Personal:** Born Nov 25, 1936, Pittsburgh, PA; married Julius; children: Mary Pamela, Michael David & Angela Suzette. **Educ:** Carlow Col Pittsburgh, BSN, 1958; Univ Tulsa, MS, 1975, EdD, 1978. **Career:** RN adminr, teacher & staff position, 1958-74; Univ Tulsa, grad asst, 1974-75, grad res fel, 1975-76, asst dean, 1976-78; Langston Univ Urban Ctr, assoc acad dean, 1979-80; Okla State Univ, Psychiat & Behav Sci, adj asst prof, asst dean students, registr & fin aid, emer, currently. **Orgs:** Osage Co Dept, Dist #55 Acad Cent Sch, 1979-80; comnr, Okla State, Dept Human Serv, 1979; Delta Sigm Theta, 1980; sch bd pres, Osage Co Dept, Dist#55 Acad Cent Sch, 1980-81; mem bd dir, Tulsa Sr Citizens, 1980; Am Asn Univ Women; Am Personnel & Guid Asn; Nat Conf Acad Advising; Pub Welfare Asn Sch Bd; Tulsa Alumni Asn; Okla State Univ Emer Asn. **Honors/Awds:** Educ Honor, Soc Kappa Delta; Outstanding Women, Community N Tulsa B&P Women; Distinguish Alumni Service Award, Educ Calow Col, 1979. **Home Addr:** 1814 W Newton St, Tulsa, OK 74127-3037, **Home Phone:** (918)585-2089. **Business Addr:** Emeritus, Oklahoma State University, 219 Student Union, Stillwater, OK 74078, **Business Phone:** (405)744-5000.

## PEGUESE, CHARLES R.
Librarian, school administrator, association executive. **Personal:** Born Aug 3, 1938, Philadelphia, PA. **Educ:** LaSalle Col, Philadelphia, Pa, BS, 1960; Drexel Univ, Philadelphia, Pa, MLS, 1965. **Career:** Librarian (retired); NE Area Young Adult Free Libr, Philadelphia, Pa, coordr, 1960-69; Action Libr Learning Ctr, Philadelphia Sch Dist, dir, 1970-74; State Libr PA, coordr networking & acad libr, 1974-88; Harrisburg Area Community Col, dir, McCormick Libr, librn, dean, instrnl resources, 1988; State Libr Pa; Harrisburg Redevelop Authority, chmn; HACC, bd trustee & dean. **Orgs:** OPP, 1957; pres, bd, N City Cong Philadelphia, Pa, 1966-74; comt mem, Penn Libr Asn, 1970; comt chmn, Am Libr Asn, 1971; adv bd, Philadelphia United Way, 1972-74; chair, Harrisburg Hist Archit Rev Bd, 1980-90; Hist Harrisburg Asn, 1980; City Harrisburg, Redevelopment Authority Bd, 1989; Leadership Harrisburg Area, 1993. **Honors/Awds:** Nat Leadership Award, Am Libr Asn & Asn Col & Res Libr, Leadership Award, 1990. **Special Achievements:** Writer, articles in PA Library Asn Bulletin, Libr Jour. **Home Addr:** 1108 Green St, Harrisburg, PA 17102, **Home Phone:** (717)232-7926. **Business Addr:** Dean, Harrisburg Area Community College, 1 HACC Dr, Harrisburg, PA 17110, **Business Phone:** (800)222-4222.

## PEGUESE, HERMAN A.
Executive. **Personal:** Born Nov 9, 1940, Philadelphia, PA; son of Herman R and Edmonia F; married Diana Lynn; children: Angela M, Kimberly Vicchiollo, Benjamin Myer, Christopher C, Nathaniel Myer & Cameron Myer. **Educ:** Howard Univ, BS, psychol, 1970; Univ Mo, MBA, mgt, 1974. **Career:** USAF, chief, radar technician, 1959-62, col, 1970-93; Atlantic Mgt Ctr Inc, prog mgr, 1994-99, sr prog dir, 1999-. **Orgs:** Vpres, Psi Chi, 1970; life mem Air Force Asn, 1970-; comdr, Quuantico Yacht Club, 1990; recorder, Knights Columbus, 1991; Refined Officers Asn, 1992-; prog chair, Nat Contract Mgt Asn, 1995; sr warden, St Clement Church, Vestry, 1999-2000; Phi Beta Kappa. **Home Addr:** 28676 Pienza Ct, Bonita Springs, FL 34119-8713, **Home Phone:** (239)591-3931. **Business Addr:** Senior Program Director, Atlantic Management Center Inc, 6066 Leesburg Pke Suite 700, Falls Church, VA 22041, **Business Phone:** (703)256-0509.

## PEGUS, CHERYL
Association executive. **Educ:** Brandeis, BS, biol; Cornell Univ Med Col, MD, 1988; Columbia Univ, Sch Pub Health, MPH. **Career:** New York Hosp Cornell Med Ctr, Memorial Sloan Kettering Hosp, fel, internship & resident; Pfizer Pharmaceut, Cardio vasc Risk Factors Group, med dir, 1996-2001; Lipo Sci, Prod Develop & Sci Alliances, vpres; Health Power Inc, vicechair; Aetna Inc, Blue Bell, Pa, nat med dir women health, Clin Prog Develop, nat med dir, 2004; SymCare Personalized Health Sols, gen mgr & chief med officer, 2007; Walgreen Co, chief med officer, 2010-; Vision-Sci Inc, dir, 2013-; Caluent LLC, pres; Pfizer Pharmaceut, Cardiovasc Risk Factors Group, med dir; Glytec, dir & strategic advisor; HealthFleet, dir & strategic advisor; New York Univ Sch Med, Div Gen Internal Med & Clin Innovation, dir, currently. **Orgs:** Bd dir, Heritage Affil Am Heart Asn; Dean Circle Cornell Univ Med Col; ed adv bd, DisMgt Advr; mem corp adv coun, Soc Women Health Res; Nat Med Asn Coun Concerns Women Physicians; Am Col Cardiol Inst; fel Am Asn Advan Sci, 1984; chair, Am Heart Asns health disparities task force, 2005-07; bd dir, US Acute Care Solutions; Weill Cornell Med Col, Dean's Circle; Nat Bus Group Health's. **Special Achievements:** First African-American woman to complete a fellowship in cardiology at Cornell University Medical College. **Business Addr:** Chief Medical Officer, Walgreen Co, 200 Wilmot Rd, Deerfield, IL 60015, **Business Phone:** (847)914-2500.

## PELOTE, DOROTHY BARNES
Government official. **Personal:** Born Dec 30, 1929, Lancaster, SC; daughter of Abraham Barnes and Ethel Green; married Maceo R; children: Deborah Allen & Miriam Heyward. **Educ:** Allen Univ, BS, 1953; Savannah State Col. **Career:** Government official (retired); Chatham Co Bd Educ, teacher, 1956-85; Chatham Co GA, co comnr. **Orgs:** Phi Delta Kappa Educ Frat, 1978; pres, Savannah Fedn Teachers, 1982-83; Legis Study Comm Memorial Med Ctr; pres, Carver Height Organ; Adv Comm Local Govt; Water & Sewer Auth Chatham Co; Chatham Asn Educ; Coastal Comm Food Bank bd dir, YMCA; bd mem, United Way; Bus & Prof Women's Club; bd mem, Phoenix Proj; Nat Coun Negro Women Inc; Chatham Co Employees Retirement Bd; Coastal Area Planning & Devel Commn Sem Agendas; Nat Asn Advan Colored People; Ga State House Representatives. **Honors/Awds:** Carver Heights Community Service Award, 1981-82; Rep Roy Allen Award, 1982; Minority Women the Year, Zeta Phi Beta, 1984; Dorothy Pelote Day City Savannah & Chatham Co, 1985; Martin Luther King Phenomenal Award, 1997; Hudson Hill Community Award, 1998; ILA Local 1414 Humanitarian Award, 1999; 50 Most Influential Black Women Georgia, 2000. **Special Achievements:** First Female elected Chatham County commissioner, 1985; First African American Black females to be elected to the Chatham County commission State Bd Post secondary Voc Educ by appointment of the Gov Ga elected vpres Black Caucus Asn Co Comnr Ga; Testimonial Banquet by Constituents of Eighth Comn Dist. **Home Addr:** 401 State Capitol, Atlanta, GA 30334, **Home Phone:** (404)657-8441.

## PELSHAK, TROY Z. (ZENRET TROY PELSHAK)
Administrator, football player. **Personal:** Born Mar 6, 1977; son of Smith and Janet Pyelshak. **Educ:** NC Agr & Tech State Univ, BA, mkt, 2003; Liberty Univ, MBA, bus admin & mgt, gen, 2015; Cent Piedmont Community Col, proj mgt plus cert prog, proj mgt, 2016. **Career:** Football player (retired), executive; St Louis Rams, linebacker, 1999 & 2000; Jacksonville Jaguars, linebacker, 2000; NFL Europe, Barcelona Dragons, 2001-02; Daspyel Global Enterprises Inc, dir, 2002-05; Amana Serv Inc, chief exec officer, 2002-06; Carolina Cobras, 2004; TroyPelshak.com, pub speaking & training, 2004-; Arena Football League, Columbus Destroyers, 2005; New York Dragons, offensive line & defensive line, 2006; Towergate Youth & Family Serv Inc, Qual Assurance & Qual Imporvemnt Supvr, 2007-08; Amana Global Serv Ltd, sr consult & proj mgr, 2008-; Charlotte Int Cabinet, vice chmn, 2013-. **Orgs:** Amana One World Orgn, 2003-; NFL Players Asn, 2005-. **Honors/Awds:** Rookie of the Year, 1999; Super Bowl XXXIV, 2000; Cobra Community Award, 2004; West Charlotte Community Appreciation Award, 2012; All-Conference honor; Defensive Most Valuable Player, NC Agr & Tech State Univ; First-team All-Mid-Eastern Athletic Conference. **Business Addr:** Senior Consultant, Project Manager, Amana Global Services Ltd, 7209-J E W T Harris Suite 255, Charlotte, NC 28227, **Business Phone:** (704)644-5580.

**PELSHAK, ZENRET TROY. See PELSHAK, TROY Z.**

## PEMBERTON, DAVID MELBERT
Insurance executive. **Personal:** Born Apr 24, 1926, Chicago, IL; son of David M Jr and Cleo Davis Ward; married Masseline Gibson; children: Dianna, Debra, Denise & Kim. **Career:** Midwest Nat Life Ins Co, reg mgr, 1965; Insurance Agent, currently. **Orgs:** Life Underwriters Asn Miami; elder Bethany SDA Church; Nat Asn Advan Colored People; treas, Locka Br; chmn, Commun Act Neighbourhood Coun; exec bd chair, bd mem, OPA Locka Comm Develop Corp. **Honors/Awds:** Civic Award, 1969; National Quality Award; Nat & Sales Achievement Award, 1974; 51st All-Star Hon Roll, 1973; Father of the Year, Urban League, 1993. **Home Phone:** (954)517-9884. **Business Addr:** Insurance Agent, 1200 SW 124th Ter, Pembroke Pines, FL 33027-4006, **Business Phone:** (954)432-6582.

## PEMBERTON, DR. GAYLE R.
Educator, writer. **Personal:** Born Jun 29, 1948, St. Paul, MN; daughter of Lounneer and Muriel E Wigington. **Educ:** Lake Forest Col, attended 1968; Univ Mich, BA, eng, 1969; Harvard Univ, MA, 1973, PhD, eng & Am lit & lang, 1981; Wesleyan Univ, MAA. **Career:** Educator (retired); Columbia Univ, lectr, 1974-77; WEB DuBois Found, fel, 1975-76; Middlebury Col, instr, 1977-80; Northwestern Univ, asst prof, 1980-83; Reed Col, vis assoc prof, 1983-84; Bowdoin Col, African-Am Studies, vis assoc prof, actg dir, 1986-88, Minority Affairs, dir, 1988-90; Princeton Univ, African-Am Studies, assoc dir, 1990-93; John Simon Guggenheim Fel, 1993-94; Wesleyan Univ, African-Am Studies, prof eng, 1994-2008, chair, William R. Kenan Prof Humanities, 1994, prof emer, currently; Mt Holyoke Col, vis prof, 2008-15; WW Norton, writer. Auth: "It's Thing That Counts", State Black Am, 1991; "A Sentimental Journey", Race-ing Justice En-Gendering Power, 1992; Hottest Water Chicago, 1992; Colored Girls Go; Black Women & Am Cinema. **Orgs:** Mod Lang Asn. **Home Addr:** 299 Harrison St, Princeton, NJ 08540, **Home Phone:** (609)497-7536. **Business Addr:** Visiting Professor of English, Mount Holyoke College, 50 Col St, South Hadley, MA 01075, **Business Phone:** (413)538-2000.

## PEMBERTON, HILDA RAMONA
Government official, social worker. **Personal:** Born Jun 29, 1940, Norman, NC; daughter of Archie C (deceased) and Judy Pearl; children: Eugenia & Charles. **Educ:** NC Cent Univ, BS, 1961; Southeastern Univ, masters, bus & pub admin, 1981. **Career:** Government official (retired); Prince Georges County govt: psychiat social worker, chief, employee rels div, off personnel, dep di personnel, coun mem, chair; Dimensions Healthcare Syst, vpres legis affairs. **Orgs:** Bd, Nat Asn Counties; pres, Nat Asn Black County Officials; bd mem, emer mem, Prince George's County Econ Develop Corp; chair bd, Coun Govts; bd, Wash Sanit Transit Authority; Nat Coun Negro Women; Alpha Kappa Alpha; First Baptist, Highland Pk. **Home Addr:** 11424 Abbottswood Ct, Upper Marlboro, MD 20774, **Home Phone:** (301)350-6091.

## PEMBERTON-HEARD, DR. DANIELLE MARIE
Lawyer. **Personal:** Born Nov 29, 1964, New York, NY; daughter of Dennis and Andrea; married Gregory McQuade. **Educ:** Tufts Univ, BA, 1986; Case Western Res Univ, Sch Law, JD, 1989; Columbia Univ. **Career:** Wiggin & Dana LLP, atty assoc, assoc, 1989-91; Cowan Liebowitz & Latman PC, assoc, 1990-93; Cowan Luiebowitz & Latman, atty assoc, 1991-93; Discovery Commun Inc, sr coun & dir legal & bus affairs, 1992-96; Time Warner Inc, vpres legal & bus affairs time life, 1996-2001; Thales Commun, group coun, 2001-03; Walker Mem Dinner Gala, Wash, DC, co-chair; Time Life Inc, vpres bus affairs; Pub Broadcasting Syst, Arlington, Va, group coun prog bus affairs, currently. **Orgs:** Delta Sigma Theta Sorority Inc, 1984-; vip prog, Prof Alliance, 1994-; Habitat Humanity, N Va, 1996-; Toy Indust Asn; group coun, busines affairs, Pub Broadcasting Serv; Time Warner Alumni; Entertainment Lawyers; Entertainment Law; trustee, Toy Indust Found, 2006-13. **Special Achievements:** Contributing Author, Journal of The Copyright Soc, 1992; 1991 Letter Updates, Trademark & Unfair Conpetion Law, Cases & Materials, The Michie Corp, 1990. **Home Addr:** 13528 Hunting Hill Way, Potomac, MD 20854, **Home Phone:** (301)208-8916. **Business Addr:** Group Counsel Program Business Affairs, Public Broadcasting System, 2100 Crystal Dr, Arlington, VA 22202, **Business Phone:** (703)739-5000.

**PENA, BUBBA. See PENA, ROBERT BUBBA.**

## PENA, ROBERT BUBBA (BUBBA PENA)
Actor, executive, football player. **Personal:** Born Aug 8, 1949, Wareham, MA. **Educ:** Dean Jr Col, AA; Univ Mass, attended 1972. **Career:** Offensive guard (retired), retired; Cleveland Browns, offensive guard, 1972; Film: Love Life; Dogs War; Ft Apache; Four Seasons;

TV pilot; bus ventures, Domingo's Chowder House Restaurant; W Falmouth Fish Mkt; Health Club Enterprises; Robert Pena & Assocs, pres; Mortgage Security Inc, pres, owner & chief exec officer, currently. **Orgs:** Founder & co-chmn, Roche Pires Scholar Fund; Cape Verdean Club, Falmouth; Lambda Chi Alpha Frat; vol work, Northampton Jail. **Honors/Awds:** Award from Falmouth MA Local Real Estate Beautification Comt for restoringa piece of historically zoned real estate. **Home Addr:** PO Box 870, West Falmouth, MA 02574-0870. **Business Addr:** President, Chief Executive Officer, Mortgage Security Inc, 31 Teaticket Hwy Suite 2-7, Teaticket, MA 02536-5644, **Business Phone:** (508)548-6618.

### PENA, TONY (ANTONIO FRANCESCO PENA PADILLA)
Baseball player. **Personal:** Born Jun 4, 1957, Montecristi; married Amaris; children: Tony Jr, Francisco Antonio & Jennifer. **Career:** Baseball player (retired), baseball coach, executive; Pittsburgh Pirates, infielder, 1980-86; St Louis Cardinals, infielder, 1987-89; Boston Red Sox, infielder, 1990-93; Cleveland Indians, 1994-96; Chicago White Sox, 1997; Houston Astros, 1997; New Orleans Zephyrs, mgr, 1999; Kans City Royals, mgr, 2002-05; New York Yankees, base coach, 2006-; bench coach, 2009-14; Boston Red Sox, mgr. **Business Addr:** Bench Coach, New York Yankees, Yankee Stadium 1 E 161st St, Bronx, NY 10451, **Business Phone:** (718)293-4300.

### PENCEAL, DR. BERNADETTE WHITLEY
Educator. **Personal:** Born Dec 16, 1944, Lenoir, NC; daughter of Walter Andrew Whitley and Thelma Simmons Whitley; married Sam. **Educ:** Syracuse Univ, NY, BS, 1966; City Col, NY, MA, 1973; Fordham Univ, NY, PhD, urban educ, 1989. **Career:** Fashion Inst Technol, NY, instr eng, 1973-74; Green Haven Maximum Security Prison, Stormville NY, instr eng, 1974-76, adj eng prof; Malcolm-King Col, NY, instr eng, 1974-78; Hunter Col, NY, instr reading, 1974-79; Col New Rochelle, NY, instr eng, 1977-89; New York Univ, NY, mentor eng, 1980-, instr, currently, prof eng compos & lit. **Orgs:** Asn Black Fac & Admin; Phi Delta Kappa, 1981-; pres & founder, Asn Black Women Higher Educ, 1985-87, J & B Whitley's Inc, 1985-; bd mem, Urban Women's Shelter, 1985-87; New York Urban League, 1987-; Am Asn Univ Women, 1989-. **Home Addr:** 129 W 147th St Apt 22J, New York, NY 10039-4356, **Home Phone:** (212)368-7046. **Business Addr:** Instructor, New York University, 239 Greene St Suite 811, New York, NY 10039, **Business Phone:** (212)998-5677.

### PENDER, MEL
Executive, athlete. **Personal:** Born Oct 31, 1937, Atlanta, GA. **Educ:** Adelphi Col, BS, social sci, 1976, PhD, humane lett, 1997. **Career:** Athlete (retired), executive; US Mens athletics Team, 1964, 1968; US Military Academy, head track coach; Nat Asn Homebuilders, southeast regional coordr; Atlanta Hawks, dir community affairs, 1990-96; Dekalb County Conventions & Visitors Bur, sports consult, 2000-04; Athletic Attic Sporting Goods Store, owner & operator; M&D Consult Firm, sr consult, chief exec officer & founder, 2007-; entrepreneur, philanthropist. **Orgs:** Pres & dir, Atlanta Hawks Found, 1990-96; Intl Track Asn; Georgia spec Olympics; 100 Black men Dekalb County; nat coordr, Nat Asn Home builders; athletic adminr, Nat Football League Players Asn; founder, Gathering Eagles Found. **Business Addr:** Senior Consultant, M&D Consulting Firm, 2330 Goodwood Blvd SE, Smyrna, GA 30080, **Business Phone:** (404)434-8514.

### PENDERGRAFT, MICHELE M.
Banker. **Personal:** Born Sep 6, 1954, Trenton, NJ; daughter of Leon Edward Meekins Sr and Lena Mae Kelly; married James William Sr; children: James William Jr. **Educ:** Mercer County Community Col, Trenton, NJ, 1977; Am Inst Banking, Anchorage, AK, 1983. **Career:** Mercer St Friends Ctr, Trenton, NJ, dance instr, 1970-78; Ginger Bread House, Anchorage, AK, asst mgr, 1978-79; First Nat Bank Anchorage, Anchorage, AK, customer serv rep, 1979-80, asst vpres, br mgr; First Nat Bank Alaska, br mgr, currently. **Orgs:** Bus Prof Women Club, 1990. **Home Addr:** 7041 Scalero Circle, Anchorage, AK 99507, **Home Phone:** (907)349-6952. **Business Addr:** Manager, First National Bank Alaska, 8725 Old Seward Hwy, Anchorage, AK 99520-0588, **Business Phone:** (907)777-4362.

### PENDERGRASS, EMMA H. (EMMA HATTIE PENDERGRASS)
Lawyer. **Personal:** Born Orangeburg, SC; daughter of W W Humphrey and Catherine; children: Bailey III & Gary W. **Educ:** Howard Univ, Wash, DC, BS; Westfield State Col, MEd, 1964; Armstrong Law Sch, JD, 1976; Calif Western Univ, Santa Ana, CA, PhD, educ emphasis coun, 1977. **Career:** US Govt, chemist, 1955-56; Chicopee High Sch, sci teacher, 1960-67; Hayward Unified Sch Dist, sci teacher, 1967-71; Hayward Unified Sch Dist, career educ coun, 1971-76; Law Off Emma H Pendergrass, atty law, 1976-. **Orgs:** Pres, Charles Houston Bar; bd dir, Young Men Chrisitan Asn Oakland; Nat Bar Asn; Delta Sigma Theta Sorority Inc; Alameda Co Bar Asn, 1977-; Pro Bono Serv Judicare Prog Charles Houston Bar Asn, 1977-80; pres, Calif Asn Black Lawyers Links Inc. **Home Addr:** 7677 Oakport St Suite 1050, Oakland, CA 94621-1929, **Home Phone:** (510)567-6100. **Business Addr:** Attorney at Law, Emma H Pendergrass Law Office, 7677 Oakport St Suite 1120, Oakland, CA 94621, **Business Phone:** (510)865-6300.

### PENDLETON, DR. BERTHA MAE OUSLEY
School administrator, school superintendent. **Personal:** Born Oct 15, 1933, Troy, AL; married Oscar; children: Gregory. **Educ:** Knoxville Col; US Int Univ; Univ San Diego, EdD, educ leadership, 1989. **Career:** Sch adminr, sch suprintendent (retired); Tenn Valley Authority, cartog eng aide, 1954-55; Chattanooga Pub Sch, 1956-57; Memorial Jr High Sch, teacher & counr, 1957-68; Morse High Sch, parent counr, 1968-70; Compensatory Educ Unit, coordr, 1970-72; Crawford High Sch, vice prin, 1972-74; Lincoln High Sch, prin, 1974-76; Prog Div, dir compensatory educ, 1976-83; Sch Opers Div, asst supt, 1983-85; Supt's Off, spec asst supt, 1985-86; Dep Supt's Off, dep supt, 1986-93; San Diego Unified Sch Dist, supt, 1993-98; Pt Loma Nazarene Col, adj prof. **Orgs:** United Way San Diego County; Natural Hist Mus; Nat Ctr Educ & Econ; Danforth Found Adv Comt; Asn Calif Sch Adminrs; Alpha Kappa Mu Hon Soc; Elem Inst Sci; YMCA; adv coun, US Dept Defense; pres, Alpha Kappa Alpha Sorority; Inst Educa Inquiry; bd dir, I Have Dream Fund; Acad Adv Bd, Beyond Bks; San Diego Asn Admin Women in Educ; Am Asn Sch Adminr-Urban Schs Comt; Asn Calif Sch Adminr; founder, Asn African Am Educr; exec bd, C's Initiative, exec bd, Coun Great City Schs. **Business Addr:** Director of the Board, I Have a Dream Foundation Inc, 3773 Howard Hughes Pkwy 3rd Fl S, Las Vegas, NV 89109, **Business Phone:** (702)734-2220.

### PENDLETON, FLORENCE HOWARD
School administrator. **Personal:** Born Jan 1, 1926?, Columbus, GA; daughter of John Milton and Elease Brooks; married Oscar Henry Sr; children: Oscar Henry Jr & Howard Thompson. **Educ:** Howard Univ, BS, 1949, MS, 1957; Am Univ, SScD, 1976; Cath Univ, SScD, 1970. **Career:** Senator (retired); DC Pub Sch, teacher, 1958-70, asst prin, 1970-80, prin, 1980-; Ward Five Dem Comt, chairperson, 1979-82, mem, 1979-; Ward Five CO7, Adv Neighborhood Comt, comnr; DC, shadow sen, 1991-2007. **Orgs:** Secy, Alpha Kappa Alpha; DC Asn Sec Sch Prin, 1980-; Nat Asn Sec Sch Prin. **Home Addr:** 4836 Roxbury Dr, Columbus, GA 31907.

### PENDLETON, TERRY LEE
Baseball player, athletic coach. **Personal:** Born Jul 16, 1960, Los Angeles, CA; son of Alfred and Ella; married Catherine; children: Stephanie, Terry & Trinity. **Educ:** Calif State Univ. **Career:** Baseball player (retired), baseball coach; St Louis Cardinals, third baseman, 1984-90; Atlanta Braves, 1991-94, 1996, hitting coach, 2002-; Fla Marlins, 1995-96; Cincinnati Reds, 1997; Kans City Royals, 1998. **Home Addr:** 332 Grass meade Way, Snell ville, GA 30078. **Business Addr:** Hitting Coach, Atlanta Braves, 755 Hank Aaron Dr, Atlanta, GA 30315, **Business Phone:** (404)522-7630.

### PENISTON, CECE (CECELIA PENISTON)
Singer. **Personal:** Born Sep 6, 1969, Dayton, OH. **Career:** A & M Rec, singer; Albums: Overweight Pooch's Female Preacher; I Like It, 1991; Finally, 1992; We Got A Love Thang, 1992; Keep On Walkin, 1992; Inside That I Cried, 1992; Crazy Love, 1992; Thought Ya Knew, 1994; I Know That He Loves Me Too; I'm In The Mood, 1994; Remix Collection, 1994; I'm Not Over You, 1994; Hit By Love, 1994; Keep Givin' Me Your Love, 1995; Sisters of Glory, 1995; Good News in HardTimes, 1995; Before I Lay, 1996; I'm Movin On, 1996; Somebody Else's Guy, 1998; Nobody Else, 1998; My Boo (The Things You Do), 1998; He Loves Me 2, 1999; Cancelled Album, 2000; Lifetime To Love, 2001; Reminiscin', 2001; For My Baby, 2003; Eternal Lover, 2004; Deeper Love, 2005; Shame Shame Shame, 2007, Still I; Above Horizons; CeCe, 2010; Divas of Disco: Live, 2010; Other Appearences: The Wendy Williams Show, 2009; Compilations: The Best of CeCe Peniston, 1998; Essential, 1999; Winning Combinations, 2000; 20th Century Masters: The Millennium Collection: The Best of CeCe Peniston. **Honors/Awds:** Miss Black Arizona, 1989; Miss Galaxy; Hall of Fame, Phoenix Col; Two Billboard Music Awards; Three ASCAP Awards; Twenty two Grammy Awards. **Special Achievements:** Album "Finally", topped Billboard magazine's dance chart, following the abolition of apartheid, she was the first female entertainer to visit and perform in South Africa. **Business Addr:** Singer, A&M Records, 2220 Colo Ave Suite 1, Santa Monica, CA 90404, **Business Phone:** (213)856-2755.

### PENN, ALGERNON H.
Executive. **Personal:** Born Oct 18, 1956, Chicago Heights, IL; son of Edward H and Vernell; married Suzanne Y; children: Jamula M McClinton, Drake E & Alexandra K. **Educ:** Thorton Community Col, AA, lib arts, 1978; Gov State Univ, BA, broadcast jour, 1986. **Career:** Nehemiaa Prog, regional dir, 2001-02; Nareb Housing Am Fund, nat prog dir, 2002-03; Residential Loan Centers Am, sr vpres, corp & indust rels, 2003-04; Home Gift USA Inc, vpres strategic partnerships, 2004-08; E4E Financial Serv, dir enterprise sales, currently; Expense Reduction Analysts, dir bus develop, 2008-10; Friends Abraham Lincoln Nat Airport Comn, chmn, 2005-14; Penn Consult Group, pres, 2010; Johnson, Penn & Shaw LTD, prin partner, 2013-. **Orgs:** Dearborn Realist Bd, vpres, 2001-04; Life mem, Pres's coun, Univ Ill, Chicago, 2002-; nat chair, down payment assistance progs, Nat Asn Real Estate Brokers, 2003-04; trustee, Village Univ Pk, Ill, 2003-05; Nat Sub Comt Chmn, Prod Develop Nat Asn Real Estate Brokers Inc, 2003-04; Rainbow-PUSH Coalition's Real Estate & Mortgage Trade Bur; chmn, Friends Abraham Lincoln Nat Airport Comn; vpres, Dearborn REALTIST. **Home Addr:** 2545 S Dearborn St Apt 504, Chicago, IL 60616-4986, **Home Phone:** (708)235-1302. **Business Addr:** President, Penn Consulting Group, 620 Sentry Pkwy Suite 110, Blue Bell, PA 19422-2315, **Business Phone:** (484)344-5601.

### PENN, CHRISTOPHER ANTHONY
Football player. **Personal:** Born Apr 20, 1971, Nowata, OK; son of James. **Educ:** Northeastern Okla A&M Col; Univ Tulsa, grad. **Career:** Football player (retired); Kans City Chiefs, 1994-95, wide receiver, 1996; Chicago Bears, wide receiver, 1997-98; San Diego Chargers, wide receiver, 1999.

### PENN, DEREK
Executive. **Personal:** Born Youngstown, OH. **Educ:** Duke Univ, BS, chem & engineering, 1979, Fuqua Sch Bus, MBA, 1984. **Career:** Morgan Stanley, equity trader, sr trading, 1984-92; Merrill Lynch, sr trading, head uk & europ equity trading, 1992-94; Lehman Bros Inc, sr vpres int equity trading, head int equity trading, 1994-98; Fidelity Capital Markets, sr vpres, head equity & fixed income trading, head equity trading, 1998-2005; Pershing LLC Bank New York Mellon, managing dir, 2006-; Bank New York Mellon Capital Markets, head equity sales & trading, pershing, 2006-14, head equity sales & trading, mellon, 2014-, managing dir, currently. **Orgs:** Bd mem, Duke Univ's Fuqua Sch Bus; bd mem, Duke Univ Athletic Adv; Duke's Cult Comt. **Honors/Awds:** "Black Enterprise," 75 Most Powerful Blacks on Wall Street, 2011. **Special Achievements:** Publications: Top 50 blacks on Wall Street. **Business Addr:** Managing Director, Head Equity Sales & Trading, Bank of New York Mellon Capital Markets LLC, 1 Wall St 18th Fl, New York, NY 10286, **Business Phone:** (212)635-1027.

### PENN, JAMES T., JR.
Funeral director. **Educ:** Cincinnati Col Mortuary Sci, grad, 1991. **Career:** Penn Funeral Home, owner & funeral dir, currently. **Business Addr:** Owner, Funeral Director, Penn Funeral Home, 3015 S Inkster Rd, Inkster, MI 48141, **Business Phone:** (313)278-6300.

### PENN, MINDELL LEWIS
Manager, government official. **Personal:** Born Mar 27, 1944, Detroit, MI; daughter of Artis Underwood and Mamie; married Leon; children: Michael Artis & Courtney. **Educ:** Wayne State Univ, Detroit, Mich, BS, bus admin, 1964. **Career:** Mich Consol Gas Co, Detroit, Mich, tele type operator, 1961-64; San Diego Gas & Elec Co, San Diego, Calif, credit rep, 1964-67; Pac Gas & Elec Co, Sacramento, Calif, community rels & finance exec, small bus affairs adminr, 1967-2002; City Richmond, coun mem, 1999-2005. **Orgs:** Chair, Sacramento Girl Scout Adv Bd; chairwomen, Sacramento Urban League, bd dir; bd mem, St Hope Acad; Sacramento Metrop Arts Comn's County Cult Awards Comt. **Home Addr:** 22849 Timberline Dr, Southfield, MI 48033, **Home Phone:** (248)352-9613.

### PENN, DR. NOLAN E.
Educator. **Personal:** Born Dec 1, 1928, Shreveport, LA; son of Henry and Bessie; married Barbara Pigford; children: Joyce & Carol. **Educ:** Calif State Univ, AB, 1949; Univ So Calif, MS, 1952; Univ Denver, PhD, clin & exp psychol, 1958; Harvard Med Sch, cert, comm ment health, 1969. **Career:** Metrop State Hosp, intern, 1954-55, psychol intern, 1955; Larue Carter Memorial Hosp, Indianpolis, staff psychologist, 1958-59; Univ Wis, Sch Med, postdoctoral fel, 1959-61, from asst prof to prof, 1963-70, founding chair, 1969; Mendota State Hosp, staff psychologist, 1961-63; Univ Calif, Sch Med, La Jolla, prof psychiat, 1970-97, reg dir, area health ed ctr off dean, 1982, prof emer psychiat, 1997-; Univ Calif-San Diego, assoc chancellor, 1988-, prof psychiat emer, 1997-, founding chair; Fielding Grad Univ, Santa Barbara, Calif, adj fac, Cross-Cult Personality Res Studies Team, founding dir, Sch Psychol, dir, 1999-, doctoral fac, currently; San Diego County Ment health Servs, San Diego, sr forensic psychologist, 2000-04. **Orgs:** Pres, Wis State Psychol Asn, 1967-68; Wis Leg Comt recodify Ment Health & Ment Retardation Codes, 1967-70; founder & chmn, Afro-Am Studies Dept, Univ Wis, Madison, 1969-70, Urban & Rural Studies, Univ Calif, San Diego, 1970-73; examr, Am Bd Prof Psychol, Am Psychol Asn, 1970-; dir, Comt & Forensic Psychol Trg UCSD, 1974-88; Am Psychol Asn, Inter-Am Soc Psychol, Sigma Xi; ed bd, J Consult & Clin Psychol, Am J Pub Health; fel Am Group Psychother Asn, 1994-; Nat Registry Cert Group Psychotherapists, 1994-; Acad Psychotherapists, 1997; Acad Experts Traumatic Stress, 1998; ethics comt, Calif Psychol Asn, 2002-05; fel Am Acad Experts Trauma; fel Am Asn Advan Sci; fel Am Forensics Soc; fel Am Orthopsychiatry Asn; fel Am Psychother Asn; Am Psychol Asn; fel Am Psychol Soc; Am Pub Health Asn; Asn Acad Minority Physicians; Asn Black Psychologists; Geront Soc Am; Inter Am Soc Psychologists; Int Cong Social Psychol; Int Coun Psychologists; Int Soc Study Hypertension Blacks; fel Soc Personality & Assessment; fel Western Psychol Asn; co-advisor, Psi Chi. **Honors/Awds:** Helen Margulies Mehr PhD Award, Div Pub Interest, Calif Psychol Assoc; Helen Margulies Mehr, Ph.D. Award, Calif Psychol Asn, 2002. **Business Addr:** Doctoral Faculty, Director, Fielding Graduate University, 2020 De la Vina St, Santa Barbara, CA 93105-3814, **Business Phone:** (800)340-1099.

### PENN, DR. SUZANNE Y.
Business owner. **Personal:** Born Chicago, IL; daughter of Willie B McDonald and Essie McDonald; married Algernon H; children: Jamila, Drake & Alexandria. **Educ:** Univ Ill-Chicago, BA, 1976; Univ Chicago, MBA, 1978; Kennedy-Western Univ, PhD, bus mgt, 2006. **Career:** First Nat Bank Chicago, portfolio mgr, 1977, security analyst, 1978-79; CEDCO Com Credit, co-mgr, 1979-81, mgr, 1981-82; McClinton Mgt Serv Inc, managing dir, chmn; McClinton Financial Serv Inc, founder & chief exec officer, 1981-; MTS Tax Solutions & MFS WealthCare, chmn & sr managing dir; Women N Power Int Ministries, ill n e regional dir, 2007. **Orgs:** Probe Inc, 1982; Chicago Reg Purchasing Coun, 1984-86; Cosmopolitan Chamber Com, treas, 1984-89; Chicage YWCA, dir, 1987; Christian Financial Ministries, pres, 2004-; Chicagos Cosmopolitan Chamber Com; Nat Black MBA Asn; Christian Vision Ctr; pres, Coun Univ Ill, 2003-; founder & pres, Christian Int Outreach Ministries, 2004-; Christian Vision Ctr. **Honors/Awds:** Kizzy Award Professional Achievement; Images-Leadership Award; Black Womens Hall Fame, 1985; Dollar & Sense, Chicago's Up & Coming Black Bus & Prof Women, 1985; Outstanding Professional Award, CCUP, 1986; Award, Nat Asn Negro Bus & Prof Womens Club Inc, 1986; Black Rose Award, League Black Women, 1988; Chicago Defender Women of Excellence Award, 2009; Mothers Informing Mothers Phenomenal Woman Award; Spirit of Greatness Award, New Orleans Ctr Successful Livings. **Special Achievements:** Author: "How to Finance Your Salon," 1984; co-author, "Family Networking Makes Good Business Sense," 1990; Interviewed, "Are You Living Beyond Your Means?" 1991; "The Pink Corner Office - Women Achieving Power In The Workplace," 2006; Featured in Newsweek, Today's Chicago Woman and Crain's Chicago Business Magazines. **Home Phone:** (708)359-1660. **Business Addr:** Managing Director, Chief Executive Officer, McClinton Financial Services Inc, 150 N Mich Suite 2800, Chicago, IL 60601, **Business Phone:** (800)374-5616.

### PENN, TENESIA SHARONE
Consultant. **Personal:** married Daniel Bernard Whitley. **Educ:** La State Univ. **Career:** Towers Perrin, benefits consult assoc, currently. **Home Addr:** , Arlington, VA. **Business Addr:** Benefits Consulting Associate, Towers Perrin, 2107 Wilson Blvd Suite 500, Arlington, VA 22201-3062, **Business Phone:** (703)351-4700.

### PENN-ATKINS, BARBARA A.
Executive. **Personal:** Born Nov 11, 1935, Gary, VA; married Will E; children: Lawrence Nichols, Cheryl Nichols Smith & Brian L Nichols. **Educ:** Mich State Univ, bus admin, 1955; Wayne State Univ, 1964; Oakland Community Col, 1979; Wayne Co Community Col, attended 1979. **Career:** Univ Detroit, admin asst; Wayne Co Community Col, accts rec supvr, 1968-72; BPA Enterprises Inc, vpres, 1980-88; Pica Systs Inc, founder, pres, chief exec officer, 1980-95; Penna Group LLC, coach, speaker, auth, 2007-. **Orgs:** Pres, Am Bus Women's Asn

& MCCC, 1981; gen co-chair, MI United Negro Col Fund, 1983-85; Allocations rev United Found, 1983-85; vpres & bd dir, Minority Tech Coun Mich, 1985; bd dir, Detroit C C. **Honors/Awds:** Woman of the Year, Motor City Charter Chap, Am Bus Women's Asn, 1979; Spirit Detroit Detroit Conv Bur, 1980; Founders Award, United Negro Col Fund, 1984; Minority Bus Award, Mich Dept Com, 1984; Pioneering Bus Award, Nat Asn Women Bus Owners, Mich Chap, 1985. **Special Achievements:** Publications: 70 is the New 40 -- Bonus Years Here We Come, 2009; We Need to Use Creative Energy to Weather Tough Times, 2009; Prepare for a Change, 2010; Life Coaches Can Help Retired Execs Find Purpose, 2011. **Home Addr:** 1119 Sleepy Hollow Lane, Beverly Hills, MI 48025-3619. **Business Addr:** Coach Speaker, Author, Penna Group LLC, PO Box 7166, Goodyear, AZ 85338, **Business Phone:** (623)466-2229.

### PENNICK, JANET
Law enforcement officer. **Personal:** Born Feb 6, 1946, Philadelphia, PA; daughter of Roosevelt and Ella; married Frank Nelson; children: Kelly Lynn. **Career:** Philadelphia Dep Sheriff's Off, lt, 1996-, dep sheriff capt. **Orgs:** Philadelphia Guardians Peace, pres, 1997-. **Home Addr:** 1315 N 57th St, Philadelphia, PA 19131, **Home Phone:** (215)877-7462. **Business Addr:** Lieutenant, Philadelphia Deputy Sheriff, 1600 Arch St 11th Fl, Philadelphia, PA 19103, **Business Phone:** (215)686-3530.

### PENNIMAN, RICHARD WAYNE
Entertainer, singer. **Personal:** Born Dec 5, 1932, Macon, GA; son of Charlie Sr (deceased) and Leva Mae Stewart; married Ernestine Campbell; children: Danny Jones. **Educ:** Oakwood Col, Huntsville, AL. **Career:** Performing & recording artist, 1948-57, 1960-76, 1986-; Albums: Here's Little Richard, 1958; The Fabulous Little Richard, 1959; Little Richard Sings Freedom Songs, 1964; King of Gospel Songs, 1965; Little Richard's Greatest Hits, 1972; Shut Up!: A Collection of Rare Tracks, 1951-64, 1988; Little Richard: Specialty Sessions, 1990; TV series: "Merv Griffin"; "The Tonight Show"; "Midnight Special, Rock 'n' Roll Revival", 1975; "Night Dreams", 1975; "Dinah", 1976; "Tomorrow", 1976; "Mother Goose Rock 'n' Rhyme", 1990; "Las Vegas", 2004; "The Simpsons", 2005; "Cold Case", 2006; "RBD: La familia", 2007; "Dancing with the Stars", 2008-09; "Rock-Suomi", 2010; "Willkommen Osterreich", 2010; Arsenio Hall Show; appeared at Radio City Music Hall, 1975; church soloist; Black Heritage Bible, salesman, 1977; Universal Remnant Church of God, minister; perin traveling medicine show; Films: Rock Around the Clock, 1956; The Girl Can't Help It, 1956; The London Rock and Roll Show, 1972; Jimi Hendrix, 1973; Mr Rock 'n' Roll, 1974; Catalina Caper; Down & Out in Beverly Hills, 1986; Last Action Hero, 1993; The Trumpet of the Swan, voice, 2001; Hit Singles include" Tutti-Frutti", 1955; "Long Tall Sally", 1956; "Slippin & Slidin", 1956; "Rip It Up", 1956; "The Girl Can't Help It", 1957; "Lucille", 1957; "Jenny, Jenny", 1957; "Keep a Knockin", 1957; "Good Golly, Miss Molly", 1958; Celebrity Duets, judge, 2007. **Orgs:** Charter mem, Rock & Roll Hall Fame. **Honors/Awds:** Rock and Roll Hall of Fame, 1986; received star Hollywood Walk of Fame, 1990; Little Richard Day recognition from Mayor Tom Bradley, Los Angeles, 1990; Grammy Lifetime Achievement Award, 1993; Rock & Roll Pioneer Award, Am Soc Young Musicians; inducted into the National Association for the Advancement of Colored People Hall of Fame, 2002; inducted into the Song writers Hall of Fame, 2003; Song writers Hall of Fame, 2003; inducted in to Apollo Theater Legends Hall of Fame, 2006, "Tutti Frutti" topped Mojo's The Top 100 Records, 2007; Apollo Theater Legends Hall of Fame, 2007; Louisiana Music Hall of Fame, 2009; Rhythm and Blues Music Hall of Fame, 2015. **Special Achievements:** Macon Convention & Visitors Bureau named goodwill abassador to hometown, 2000; 100 Greatest Artists of All Time, Rolling Stone Magazine, 2004. **Business Addr:** Entertainer, c/o William Morris Agency, 151 El Camino Dr, Beverly Hills, CA 90212, **Business Phone:** (310)859-4000.

### PENNINGTON, JESSE C.
Lawyer, real estate agent. **Personal:** Born Jul 1, 1938, Percy, MS; married Roberta; children: Bradford & Johnny. **Educ:** Howard Univ, BA, 1964, JD, 1969; Wright Jr Col, AA, 1969; Cent YMCA Real Estate Inst, cert; Nat Col Criminal Lawyers & Pub Defenders, attended 1974. **Career:** US Postal Serv, clerk, 1957-60; Seyfarth, Shaw, Fairweather & Geraldson Law Firm, off boy, 1957-60; Travis Realty Co, real estate broker, 1960-61; Sen Paul H Douglas, legis asst, 1964-67; Nat Labor Rels Bd, legal asst, 1967-68; Reginald Heber Smith fel, 1969-71; Northern Miss Rural Legal Serv, managing staff atty, 1969-72; Fed Home Loan Bank Bd, staff, 1968-69; Mary Holmes Col, instr, 1970-71; Pennington Walker & Turner, sr partner, 1973-; Micronesian Legal Serv Corp, directing atty; pvt pract atty, currently; Atty at Law, lawyer, currently. **Orgs:** Bd dir, Northern Miss Rural Legal Serv, 1973-, Trust Terr Pac Bar, 1976-; Miss Bar Asn; IA Bar Asn; Nat Bar Asn; Nat Conf Black Lawyers; pres, Miss Asn Attys; Nat Defense Lawyers Asn; Black Appalachian Comn; Clay County Community Develop Prog Inc; Miss Legal Serv Coalition. **Home Addr:** 453 Cedarwood Dr, Jackson, MS 39212-2203, **Home Phone:** (601)373-0902. **Business Addr:** Attorney, Private Practice, Rm 315 Moore Bldg 1400 Lynch St, Jackson, MS 39217-0001, **Business Phone:** (601)373-0902.

### PENNINGTON, DR. LEENETTE MORSE
Educator. **Personal:** Born May 10, 1936, Webster, FL; married Bernard; children: Bernadette & Brigette. **Educ:** Morgan State Col, BS, 1956; Univ Miami, EdM, 1970; Univ Fla, attended 1974. **Career:** Educator (retired); Fla State Welfare, case worker, 1958-63; educr, 1963-69; curric writer, 1969-70; Dade Co, admin asst, 1970-72; Inst Dade Co Div Staff Dev, coordr, 1971; Elem Basic Skills Proj Dade Co Pub Schs, Miami, proj mgr, 1973; Edward Waters Col, past interim pres. **Orgs:** Adv Coun, Elem Educ Fla Int Union; Asn Supv & Curric Develop; Int Reading Asn; pres, Nat Coun Negro Women; Sigma Gamma Rho; consult, Desegration Ctr, Univ Miami; Dade Co Comn Status Women; African Meth Epis Chap; New Bethel African Methodist Church. **Honors/Awds:** Outstanding Religious Service AME Chap, 1970; Outstanding Education Achievement Award, Sigma Gamma Rh, 1972; Outstanding Young AME Church woman 11 Epis Dist. **Home Addr:** 1222 Wentworth CIR, Rockledge, FL 32955, **Home Phone:** (321)636-3026.

### PENNINGTON, RICHARD J.
Police chief, government official, president (organization). **Personal:** Born Jan 1, 1947, Little Rock, AR; children: 2. **Educ:** Am Univ, BA, criminal justice; Univ DC, MA, coun; FBI Nat Acad George Wash Univ, exec develop prog; FBI Nat Exec Inst; Harvard Univ John F Kennedy, Sch Govt, sr exec prog. **Career:** Police officer (retired); Wash Metrop Police Dept, law enforcement, 1968, police officer, asst chief, 1994; New Orleans Police Dept, police chief, supt, 1994-2002; Atlanta Police Dept, polic chief, 2002-09. **Orgs:** Nat pres, Nat Orgn Black Law Enforcement Exec; Int Asn Chiefs Police; Maj Cities Chiefs Police Asn; Ga Asn Chiefs Police; 100 Black Men Atlanta; Kappa Alpha Psi Fraternity; Cascade United Methodist Church; Atlanta Police Found. **Honors/Awds:** Public Official of the Year. **Home Addr:** 669 Collier Rd NW, Atlanta, GA 30318-1714.

### PENNIX, JAMES A.
College administrator. **Personal:** Born Apr 10, 1966, Lynchburg, VA; son of Anna R; married Lisa B; children: Damian East, James II & Jordan. **Educ:** Roanoke Col, BS, math, 1988; Radford Univ, MSW, social work, 2001. **Career:** Herr Foods Inc, salesperson, 1988-93; UTZ Qual Foods, sales supvr, 1993-98; Roanoke Col, asst basketball coach, 1998-2001, asst dir admis, 2001-03, assoc dir admis, 2003-07; dir admis, 2007-10, Multicultural Recruitment coordr; Nat Res Ctr Col & Univ Admis, client, 2000-; InterVarsity Christian Fel, relationship with christ, 2001-10; Radford Univ, adj prof, 2006-07, dean admis, 2010-, enrollment mgt, 2011-. **Orgs:** Nat Asn Basketball Coaches, 1998-; Nat Asn Social Work, 1999-; deleg, Nat Asn Col Admis Counselors, 2001-; exec bd mem, Potomac & Chesapeake Asn Col Admis Coun; Va Asn Col Registr & Admis Officers; Western Va Basketball Officials Asn. **Home Addr:** 1539 Poplar Ave, Salem, VA 24153, **Home Phone:** (540)375-2679. **Business Addr:** Dean of Admissions, Radford University, 801 E Main St, Radford, VA 24142, **Business Phone:** (540)831-5000.

### PENNY, DR. ROBERT
Physician, educator. **Personal:** Born Jun 6, 1935, Cincinnati, OH; son of Ralph and Marie; married Joselyn E; children: Angeline E. **Educ:** Univ Cincinnati, BS, 1959; Ohio State Univ, MD, 1963. **Career:** C's Hosp, internship pediat, 1963-64, residency pediat, 1964-66; Loma Linda Univ, instr pediat, 1967-68; Johns Hopkins Hosp, Baltimore, fel ped endocrinol, 1968-71; Univ Southern Calif, from asst prof to assoc prof pediat, 1971-81, prof pediat, dir, Pediat Endocrine & Diabetic Clinics, 1985-91, pro, res med, 1991-93, dir, Core Molecular Biol Lab, prof emer, 1993-; Univ Calif, vis prof, 1985; Del State Univ, endocrinol lectr. **Orgs:** Ed bd, AJDC, 1988; assoc mem, Am Bd Pediat, 1989-91; vpres, Palos Verdes Monaco Homeowners Asn, 1993-96; adv bd, Univ Southern Calif Emer Col, 2003-05; Endocrine Soc; Lawson Wilkins Ped Endocrine Soc; Soc Pediat Res; Am J Dis Childhood; chair, Arch Pediat & Adolescent Med, Am Pediat Asn; Am Pediat Soc; pres, Rancho Palos Verdes Coun Homeowners Associations, pres, Rancho Palos Verdes Coun Homeowners Asn; Palos Verdes Peninsula Ctr Libr Neighborhood Planning Comt; Clin Res Ctr Adv Comt; chmn, Yr II Med Stud Endocrine Syst Comt; Yr II Med Stud Curric Comt. **Honors/Awds:** Rho Chi Soc Beta Nu Chap, Cincinnati, 1959; Chairperson, Endocrinology Sect Western Soc for Ped Res, 1983; question writer, Pediat Endocrinol Examination, 1984, 1989, 1991; reviewer, J Endo & Metabolism, AJDC & pediatres; Certificate of Recognition, AMA. **Special Achievements:** First Vice President of the Rancho Palos Verdes Council of Homeowners Associations. Published 53 articles in peer review journals; 9 chapters; 48 abstracts. **Business Addr:** Professor Emeritus Of Pediatrics, University of Southern California School of Medicine, 6311 Garners Ferry Rd, Columbia, SC 29208, **Business Phone:** (803)255-3400.

### PENNYWELL, PHILLIP, JR.
School administrator. **Personal:** Born Aug 1, 1941, Shreveport, LA; son of Phillip Sr and Rosa; married Shenya; children: 3. **Educ:** Southern Univ, BS, 1972, MEd, 1974; N Tex State Univ, PhD, 1980; La State Univ, PhD; Kans State Univ, PhD. **Career:** Professor (retired); Caddo Parish Sch Bd, teacher, 1972-74; Parish Govt, police juror, 1984-85; Singleton Law Firm, vpres opers, 2001-; La State Univ, adj prof; Southern Univ, chmn, Div Behav/Sci Educ, ful bright prog adv, Continuing Educ & Outreach Prog, dean, Acad Affairs, spec asst to vice chancellor; Bossier Parish Community Col, reviewer proposals; Wiley Col, reviewer proposals. **Orgs:** Phi Delta Kappa, 1976; Kappa Alpha Psi Frat, 1983; bd dir, Shreveport Leadership, Shreveport Chamber Comn; chmn bd dir, Socialization Serv Inc; exec dir, SSI Drug Alcohol Abuse Educ Prog; Dem State Cent Comt; City Shreveport River Front Develop; Citizens Adv Comt; Shreve Square; bd dir, Caddo-Bossier Port CMS Adv Bd; bd dir, La Asn Blind; Caddo Parish Police Jury; Am Psychol Asn; Charles F. Menninger Soc; Shreveport Alumni Chap; Delta Kappa Boule. **Home Addr:** 7412 McArthur Dr, Shreveport, LA 71106, **Home Phone:** (318)868-6849. **Business Addr:** Vice President Operation, Singleton Law Firm, 4050 Linwood Ave, Shreveport, LA 71108, **Business Phone:** (318)631-5200.

### PEOPLES, ALICE LEIGH
President (organization). **Career:** Jack & Jill Am Found Inc, nat pres, 2004-06. **Orgs:** Asst dir, Univ Mich Ross Sch Bus Exec Educ. **Home Addr:** 5445 Scott Ct, Ypsilanti, MI 48197, **Home Phone:** (734)487-5582. **Business Addr:** National President, Jack & Jill of Am Foundation Inc, 1930 17th St NW, Washington, DC 20009, **Business Phone:** (202)232-5290.

### PEOPLES, DR. DANITA L.
Dermatologist. **Educ:** Wayne State Univ Sch Med, MD, 1982. **Career:** Wayne State Univ, Detroit, Mich, med training, dermat residency, 1986; William Beaumont Hosp, Royal Oak, internal med internship, dermat residency, 1986; Henry Ford Health Syst, W Bloomfield, div head dermat; pvt pract dermatalogist, 1986-; Midmichigan Dermat, Midland, Mich, founder, pvt pract, 1994-; Bloomfield Hills, pvt pract, 1999-; Peroxsys Corp, founder, owner, 2006-. **Business Addr:** Founder, Owner, Midmichigan Dermatology, 5103 Eastman Ave Suite 255, Midland, MI 48640-6785, **Business Phone:** (989)832-2292.

### PEOPLES, DOTTIE
Singer. **Personal:** Born Aug 12, 1950, Dayton, OH; daughter of Robert Milton and Althea. **Career:** Gospel singer, currently; Church Door Rec, gen mgr, 1979-91; Albums: Church Door label, Surely God Able, 1984; it Worth All, 1987; Dottie Peoples Showcase, 1990; Live at Salem, 1993; On Time God, 1995; Christmas With Dottie, 1995; Count On God, 1996; Testify, 1997; Collection-songs Faith & Love, 1998; God Can & God Will, 1999; Show Up & Show Out, 2000; Greatest Hits, 2001; Churchin' With Dottie, 2002; Water I Give, 2003; Live in Memphis, 2005; Do It, 2008; I Got This, 2013; DP Muzik Group, founder. **Business Addr:** Gospel Singer, Dottie Peoples Ministries, PO Box 1705, Red Oak, GA 30272, **Business Phone:** (770)969-0747.

### PEOPLES, ERSKINE L.
Insurance agent, salesperson. **Personal:** Born Oct 16, 1931, Gadsden, AL; married Dorothy Thompson; children: E Ladell Jr & Tamatha M. **Educ:** Mus Educ TN A&I State Univ, BS, 1953; TN A&I State Univ, Addl Studies; Chattanooga Asn Life Underwriters. **Career:** Insurance agent (retired); Mutual Benefit Life Ins Co, salesman; BT Wash HS Chattanooga, band dir; Security Fed Savings & Loan Asn Chattanooga, vpres, dir. **Orgs:** Chmn, Hamilton Co Sch Bd Chattanooga, 1973-75; mem bd, Greater Chattanooga C C; Goodwill Industries Inc; Meth Neighbrohood Ctrs; deacon Mt Calvery Bapt Ch; Alpha Phi Alpha; Chattanooga Underwriters; pres, Club Mutual Benefit Life. **Honors/Awds:** Man of Year, Psi Lambda, 1968. **Home Addr:** 4812 Cordelia Lane, Chattanooga, TN 37416-2409, **Home Phone:** (423)894-4174.

### PEOPLES, FLORENCE W.
Health services administrator. **Personal:** Born Jul 21, 1940, Charleston, SC; married Earl Calvin; children: Patricia Lowe, Jonelle Elaine Washington, Deborah Simmons Jones, Sheyla Simmons, Pamela & Calvin. **Educ:** Northeastern Univ, BSN, 1977. **Career:** New Eng Reg Black Nurses, bd dir, 1982-85; H McCall Nurses Unit Grant Am Methodist Episcopal Church, pres, 1986-87; Am Cancer Soc, William Price Unit, bd dir, co-chairperson, 1987; Mass Ment Health Ctr, Boston, hosp supvr, currently. **Orgs:** Nat Black Nurses, 1978-; New Eng Regional Black Nurses Asn, 1978-; Am Nurses Asn, 1978-; Mass Nurses Asn, 1978-; Nat Asn Advan Colored People, 1982-; Eastern Mass Urban League, 1983-; Mass Ment health Ctr. **Home Addr:** 70 Nelson St, Dorchester Center, MA 02124. **Business Addr:** Supervisor, Massachusetts Mental Health Center, 74 Fenwood Rd, Boston, MA 02115, **Business Phone:** (617)734-1300.

### PEOPLES, DR. GERALD C.
Educator, chancellor (education). **Personal:** married Verjanis A. **Educ:** Grambling State Univ, BS, sociol, 1974, MS, guid & coun, 1975; Kans State Univ, PhD, higher edu admin, 1990. **Career:** Chancellor (retired); Grambling State Univ, freshman orientation instr, 1974-79, asst dir, 1974-79, coord alumni affairs, 1979-85, dean stud life, adj prof educ, asst dir high sch rels, 1990-92; State Supt La Dept Educ, spec asst to state supt, 1986-88; Kans State Univ, staff asst grad div, 1988-90; Southern Univ New Orleans, vice chancellor stud affairs, 1992-97, chancellor, 1997-2000, spec asst chancellor, 2000-04; Miss Valley State Univ, vpres, 2005-07, prof, 2007-08; Alcorn State Univ, Sch Coun & Clin Ment Health, prof, 2012-; Dean Stud Life, adj prof educ, coordr alumni affairs; City Grambling, city councilman; Southern Univ & A&M Col, Baton Rouge, vice chancellor stud affairs. **Orgs:** Pres & exec bd mem, Nat Asn Stud Affairs Professionals; Baker Sch Bd; chairperson, SME Found Boys Scouts Am; pres, Grambling Optimist Club; Phi Delta Kappa; Kappa Alpha Psi; Mt Pilgrim Baptist Church; Pi Gamma Mu Hon Soc; Nat Asn Stud Personnel Adminr; Am Coun Col Asn; Am Asn Higher Educ. **Honors/Awds:** Outstanding Leadership & Service Award, Nat Walnut Bus Asn, Stud Govt Asn, 2005; Ruben McCall Dedicated Service Award, McCall High Sch, 2005; Outstanding Leadership & Service Award, 2005; Professionals Appreciation Award, Nat Asn Stud Affairs, 2009. **Business Addr:** Professor, Alcorn State University, 1000 ASU Dr, Lorman, MS 39096-7500, **Business Phone:** (601)877-6202.

### PEOPLES, GREGORY ALLAN
Dean (education), school administrator. **Personal:** Born May 17, 1951, Ravenna, OH; married Alice Leigh; children: 4. **Educ:** Allegheny Col, BA, speech & commun, 1973; Kent State Univ, MEd, higher educ admin, 1977. **Career:** Allegheny Col, asst dir admis, 1973-75; Kent State Univ, resident hall dir, 1975-77; Ctr-Eastern MI Univ, coordr campus info, 1978-80; Eastern MI Univ, asst dir admis, 1980-82, assoc dir admiss, 1982-83; GMI Engrg & Mgt Inst, admis, corp spec, 1983-84, dir admis; Washtenaw Community Col, dir enrollment mgt, 1985-91; Eastern Mich Univ, sr adminr, 1991-2013, assoc dean stud, 1996-2004, ombudsman, 2004-13. **Orgs:** Delta Tau Delta, 1973-; treas, Black Fac & Staff Asn, 1978-82, 1991-95; Delta Sigma Pi, 1980; bd dir, Nat Orientation Dir Asn, 1981-; adv, Delta Sigma Pi, 1981-83, Delta Tau Delta, 1984-; trustee, Willow Run Bd Educ, 1986-94; pres, Lincoln Consol Sch Bd; bd mem, Washtenaw Intermediate Sch Dist; vpres, Hope Med Clin Bd dir; Alpha Kappa Alpha Sorority; Washtenaw United Way; comnr & bd mem, Ypsilanti Community Utilities Authority, 2007-; bd dir, Mich Asn Sch Boards, currently. **Home Addr:** 5445 Scott Ct, Ypsilanti, MI 48197, **Home Phone:** (734)487-5582. **Business Addr:** Director, Michigan Association of School Boards, 1001 Centennial Way Suite 400, Lansing, MI 48917-8249, **Business Phone:** (517)327-5900.

### PEOPLES, HARRISON PROMIS, JR.
Executive, consultant, business owner. **Educ:** Chapman Col, Orange, CA, BA, 1976; Pepperdine Univ, Malibu, CA, MS, 1986. **Career:** Motorola, Cupertino, Caluf, mgr, 1980-85; Transition Strategies, Los Altos, Calif, vpres, 1985-88; Nat Traffic Safety Ins, San Jose, Calif, instr, 1988-89, regional dir, 1990-96; US Census Bur, San Jose, Calif, mgr, 1989-90; Lighthouse Worldwide Solutions Inc, vpres, 1996-97; Peoples & Assocs, owner, consult, 1992-; Raychem Corp, Dir Human Resources, 1998; Valerie Frederickson & Co, exec coach, sr human resources, OD & outplacement counr, 2009-10; Modus Media Int, human resources mgr, 1999-2000. **Orgs:** Penninsula Assoc Black Personnel Admin, 1981-88; recorder, Human Resources Planning Soc, 1983; Orgn Develop Network, 1984-86; Nat Asn Advan Colored People, pres state, 1987-89, vpres, 1989; Generations Community Wellness, bd dir, 2009-12. **Home Addr:** 2762 Buena Pt Ct, San Jose,

CA 95121-2900. **Business Addr:** Owner, Consultant, Peoples & Associates, 1180 Coleman Ave, Milpitas, CA 95035, **Business Phone:** (408)946-6819.

## PEOPLES, DR. JOHN ARTHUR, JR.

School administrator, president (organization), vice president (organization). **Personal:** Born Aug 26, 1926, Starkville, MS; son of John A Sr and Maggie Rose; married Mary E Galloway; children: Kathleen Sedlak & Mark. **Educ:** Jackson State Univ, BS, 1950; Univ Chicago, MA, 1951, PhD, 1961. **Career:** President (retired), president emeritus; Froebel High Sch, teacher, prin, 1957-58; Lincoln Elem Sch, asst prin, 1958; Bannekar Elem Sch, prin, 1962-64; Jackson State Univ, assoc prof, asst to pres, 1964-65, vpres, 1966-67, pres, 1967-84, pres emer, currently; Am Coun Educ, fel, 1965-66; State Univ NY, Binghamton, asst to pres, 1965-66; Stud Govt Asn, pres. **Orgs:** Gov, Miss Crime Comn, 1967-68; chmn, 1972, Pres's Coun, 1967; Nat Asn Land-Grant Cols & Univs, 1968-71; chmn, 1969, Am Asn State Cols & Univs, 1969-72; Southeastern Regional Coun; Am Asn Higher Educ, 1970-71; chair, Am Coun Educ, 1970; Miss Comt Humanities, 1972; bd trustee, Am Col Test Corp, 1973-79; Nat Endowment Humanities, 1974; bd control, Southern Regional Educ Bd, 1974-86; consult, Killy Endowment Fund, 1976-77; bd dir, Miss Ballet Int Inc, 1980-; Noon Optimist Club Jackson, 1981-; consult, Kellogg Found, 1981-84; life mem, Nat Asn Advan Colored People; bd dir, Piney Woods City Life Sch; bd dir, Jackson Hinds Comprehensive Health Ctr; bd dir, Smith Robertson Mus & Cult Ctr; bd dir, Jackson State Nat Alumni Asn; Jackson Civil Serv Comn; deacon, Farish St Bapt Church; Omega Psi Phi Fraternity; Sigma Pi Phi; 33rd degree Mason; Alpha Kappa Mu Hon Soc. **Home Addr:** 386 Heritage Pl, Jackson, MS 39212, **Home Phone:** (601)371-2417. **Business Addr:** President Emeritus, Jackson State University, 1400 John R Lynch St, Jackson, MS 39217, **Business Phone:** (601)979-2121.

## PEOPLES, JOHN DERRICK, JR.

Journalist. **Personal:** Born Jul 23, 1951, Seattle, WA; son of J D Sr and Gertrude Johnson; married Julie Selman. **Educ:** Univ Mont, Missoula, MT, 1971; Tex Southern Univ, Houston, TX, 1979; Univ Wash, Seattle, WA, BA, commun, 1984. **Career:** The Times Seattle, Seattle, Wash, sports reporter, 1984-95; Microsoft Games studios, Web Producer, 1997-2009; Microsoft Games, site mgr, 2002-09. **Orgs:** NABJ, 1984. **Home Addr:** 4731 S Hudson St, Seattle, WA 98118, **Home Phone:** (206)723-5036.

## PEOPLES, DR. JOYCE P.

Educator. **Personal:** Born Aug 27, 1937, Huntsville, AL; children: Alycia Behling. **Educ:** Ala A & M Univ, BS, 1957, MS, 1965; Am Univ, PhD, 1977. **Career:** Ala A & M Univ, asst prof, 1967-76; Voorhees Col, dir, interdisciplinary studies, 1976-77; Univ MD-ES, asst vice chancellor, 1977-78; Inst Serv to Educ, spec asst to pres, 1978-83; Southern Univ, vice chancellor acad affairs, 1983; Atlanta Metropoliton Col, prof eng, emer, Currently. **Orgs:** Regional dir, Black Women Academicians, 1982-83; consult, Am Coun Educ, 1982-86; parliamentarian, NAUW, 1985-87; pres, Top Ladies Distinction Inc, 1985-87; bd mem, Nat Asn Univ Women, 1986-87; bd mem, historically black cols & univs. **Home Addr:** 5024 Asaff, Shreveport, LA 71107. **Business Addr:** Emeritius Faculty, Atlanta Metropolitian College, 1630 Metropolitian Pkwy SW, Atlanta, GA 30310, **Business Phone:** (404)756-4724.

## PEOPLES, DR. L. KIMBERLY

School administrator. **Educ:** Wayne State Univ, attended 1970, 1987. **Career:** Golightly Career & Tech Ctr, prin, 1985-92, dir, currently. **Orgs:** Asn Sec Sch Prin; Asn Supv & Curric Develop; Am Voc Asn; Alpha Kappa Alpha. **Business Addr:** Director, Golightly Career & Technical Center, 900 Dickerson Ave, Detroit, MI 48215-2900, **Business Phone:** (313)822-8820.

## PEOPLES, SESSER RANDALL

Educator, association executive. **Personal:** Born Dec 7, 1934, Newark, NJ; married Irma; children: 4. **Educ:** Jersey City State Col, BA, 1963; Kean Col, MA. **Career:** Jersey City State Col, black studies dir, 1969-73, affirmative action officer, 1973, presidential assts; Urban Processes Coord, coor, 1971; Ment Retarded Plainfield Pub Sch, teacher. **Orgs:** Third World Enterprises, 1968; African-Am Studies Asn, 1970-73; Urban Processes Coord Consult Firm, 1971; Nat Asn Black & Urban Ethnic Dirs, 1971-72; African Heritage Studies Asn; Phi Delta Kappa, 1972; mem bd dirs, Leaguers Inc. **Honors/Awds:** All Conference First Team honors, Jersey City State Col. **Home Addr:** 1410 Cornell Pl, Union, NJ 07083, **Home Phone:** (908)688-2289.

## PEOPLES, DR. VEO

Lawyer. **Personal:** Born Sep 13, 1947, St. Louis, MO; married Linda Sing; children: Nicole & Nissa. **Educ:** Univ Mo Rolla, BS, chem engr, 1970; St Louis Univ Sch Law, JD, 1975. **Career:** Monsanto Co, process design engr, patent agt, 1971-73; Ralston Purnia Co, patent agt, 1973-75, patent atty, 1973-78; Anheuser-Busch, assoc gen coun, 1978-84; Veo Peoples, pvt pract, 1984-88; Peoples & Hale Attorneys, partner, 1988-98; Haverstock, Garret & Roberts PC, partner, 1998-2009; Brown & James PC, prin, 2009-12; Peoples LLC, prin, 2012-; St Louis Regional Conv & Sports Complex Authority, co-gen coun. **Orgs:** Spec task force, Mo Bar Asn, 1976-77; entertainment chmn, Mound City Bar Asn, 1976-77; dist exec Mark Twain BSA, 1976-; Ralston Purina Corp Devel Bd, 1977; Optimist Club St Louis; circuite comn 22nd Judicial Bar, 1984-92; bd dir, Fed Res Bank St Louis, 1993-99; secy exec comn, bd dir, Legal Serv Eastern Mo Inc; dist comn Western Dist St LouisBoy Scouts Am; bd dir, W Co Am Cancer Soc; chmn, patent sect, BAMSL; pres & founder, CADRE 19 Inc; Bar Asn Metrop St Louis; Nat Bar Asn; Am Inst Chem Engrs; Alpha Phi Alpha Fraternity; Epsilon Psi Chap Alpha Chi Sigma; Phi Eta Sigma; Am Bar Asn; Mound City Bar Assoc. **Honors/Awds:** Rosalie Tilles Scholar 1966-70; Curators Scholar, Univ Mo, 1966; Stud Chap Award Excellence AIChE,1970; Univ Scholar Award Univ Mo, 1967; Undergrad Research Fel, 1970; Achievement Award Urban League, 1975; Acad Chem Engrs Univ Mo Rella, 1998; Theodore McMillian Award, St Louis Univ, 1998. **Home Addr:** 342 Jamboree Dr, Manchester, MO 63011, **Home Phone:** (314)242-5228. **Business Addr:** Principal, Brown & James PC, 1010 Mkt St 20th Fl, St. Louis, MO 63101-2000, **Business Phone:** (314)242-5228.

## PEOPLES, VERJANIS ANDREWS

Educator, college administrator. **Personal:** Born Aug 8, 1955, Monroe, LA; daughter of Willie and Vernita; married Gerald C; children: Takiyah & Nicholas. **Educ:** Grambling State Univ, BS, 1976, MS, 1978; Kans State Univ, PhD, 1990. **Career:** Bienville Parish Sch Syst, teacher, 1976-79; Grambling State Univ, lab sch, teacher, 1979-88, Col Educ, prof, 1989-90; Southern Univ, Col Educ, prof, 1991-92; Southern Univ & A&M Col, asst proj dir, asst dean acad & stud affairs & Dept Curric & Instr, assoc prof, dean, currently. **Orgs:** La Asn Teacher Educr, 1996; Asn Teacher Ed, 1996; Asn Supv & Curric Develop, 1996; La Alliance Educ Reform, 1996; La Coun Teacher Educ, 1996; Am Asn Col Teacher Educ, 1996. **Home Addr:** 4203 Daveco St, Baker, LA 70714, **Home Phone:** (504)774-9183. **Business Addr:** Dean of Academic & Student Affairs, Associate Professor, Southern University & A&M College, W W Stewart Hall Rm 234, Baton Rouge, LA 70813, **Business Phone:** (225)771-2291.

## PERARA, DR. MITCHELL MEBANE

Physician, surgeon. **Personal:** Born Feb 11, 1924, Tulsa, OK; married Jean Wolfe; children: Susan, Mark & Georgianna. **Educ:** Va Union Univ, BS, 1944; Howard Univ Col Med, Md, 1948. **Career:** Howard Univ Hosp, resident gen surg; Harlem Hosp Ctr, resident; Am Col Surgeons, dipl, 1955-85; pvt pract physician, 1955-85. **Orgs:** Fel Am Cancer Soc, 1955. **Home Addr:** 4234 Don Arellanes Dr, Los Angeles, CA 90008-4203, **Home Phone:** (323)295-9858.

## PERDREAU, CORNELIA WHITENER (CONNIE PERDREAU)

Educator, college administrator. **Personal:** Born Beacon, NY; daughter of Henry Whitener and Mazie Martin; married Michael; children: Maurice. **Educ:** Potsdam Col, Potsdam, NY, BA, fr lit & educ, 1969; Ohio Univ, Athens, OH, MA, fr lit, 1971, MA, ling/teaching eng, 1972. **Career:** Educator (retired); Ohio Univ, Athens, Ohio, lectr & study abroad coordr, 1976-98, dir off Educ Abroad, dir emer educ abroad; Haggerty Eng Lang Prog, dir, currently. **Orgs:** Pres, Ohio Teachers Eng Speakers Other Lang, 1987-88; trustee, Ohio Libr Asn, 1988-96; team mem, NAFSA: Asn Int Educr, 1988-90, 1991-93; Black Professionals Int Affairs, 1989-; Ohio Univ African-Am Fac, Adminr & Staff Caucus, 1990-91; Coop Grants Community, 1990-95; pres, Fulbright Enrichment Ctr Community, 1991-96; founder & chair, Black Prof Teachers Eng Speakers other Lang, 1992-; adv bd, USIA Eng Lang Prog, 1995-98; pres, 1996-97, Educ Testing Serv Policy Coun Test Eng Second Lang, 1998-2001; Chair, Adminr & Teachers Eng a Second Lang.Pres, Ohio Teachers Eng Speakers Other Lang, 1987-88; trustee, Ohio Libr Asn, 1988-96; team mem, NAFSA: Asn Int Educr, 1988-90, 1991-93; Black Professionals Int Affairs, 1989-; Ohio Univ African-Am Fac, Adminr & Staff Caucus, 1990-91; Coop Grants Community, 1990-95; pres, Fulbright Enrichment Ctr Community, 1991-96; founder & chair, Black Prof Teachers Eng Speakers other Lang, 1992-; adv bd, USIA Eng Lang Prog, 1995-98; pres, 1996-97, Educ Testing Serv Policy Coun Test Eng Second Lang, 1998-2001; Chair, Adminr & Teachers Eng a Second Lang. **Home Addr:** 92 Grosvenor St, Athens, OH 45701, **Home Phone:** (740)592-6022. **Business Addr:** Director, Haggerty English Language Program, New York City, NY 12561.

## PERDUE, REP. GEORGE, JR.

State government official. **Personal:** Born Mar 15, 1943, Birmingham, AL; married Delores; children: Cynthia & Joy (deceased). **Educ:** Morehouse Col, BS, math, 1964; Atlanta Univ, MS, math, 1968. **Career:** Ala House Reps, Dist 54, state rep, 1983-2007; Univ Ala, Human Resources Syst, proj coordr, asst vpres fin affairs & admin, 2007; UAB Off Women & Minority-Owned Bus Develop, founder & dir. **Orgs:** Nat Asn Advan Colored People; YMCA; bd dir, Birmingham Girls Club; Alpha Phi Alpha; SCLC; Fourth Ave YMCA Century Club; bd dir, Univ Credit Union Supvry Comn; alumni, Parker High Sch; chair, Ala Cong Black Caucus; vice chair, House Judiciary Comt; chair bd dir, S Region Minority Suppliers Develop Coun; bd mem, S Regions Minority Bus Coun; pres, S Region Minority Suppliers Develop Coun, 2010-11. **Home Addr:** 12th Ave N Suite 2, PO Box 2473, Birmingham, AL 35204, **Home Phone:** (205)252-7799.

## PERDUE, DR. WILEY A.

Vice president (organization), school administrator. **Educ:** Morehouse Col, grad, 1957; Atlanta Univ, MBA; Ind Univ-Bloomington, advan studies. **Career:** School administrator (retired); Savannah State Col, registr; Morehouse Col, bursar, bus mgr, vpres fiscal affairs, chief fiscal officer, actg pres, 1994-95.

## PEREZ, REV. ALTAGRACIA

Clergy. **Personal:** Born Sep 19, 1961, New York, NY; daughter of Ramon Eduardo and Esther Zoraida Maceira-Ortiz; married Carlos Rafael Alvarado. **Educ:** New York Univ, SEHNAP, BS, 1982; Union Theol Sem, MDiv, 1985, STM, 1986. **Career:** Astor Ment Health Ctr, spec educ teacher, 1982; Church Living Hope, day camp dir, 1984; Union Theol Sem, co-coordr, Women's Ctr, 1984-85; Mission San Juan Bautista, youth leader & minister, 1985-86; Pilsen Cath Youth Ctr, assoc dir, 1986-89; Diocese Chicago, coordr youth ministries, 1990; Episcopal Church Ctr, Nat prov youth coordr, 1991; Episcopal Church St Phillip, rector; Holy Faith Episcopal Church, Inglewood, Calif, rector, currently. **Orgs:** Founding bd mem, Hisp AIDS Network, 1986-, bd dir, 1992-; educ leadership coun, Hisp Designers Inc, 1990-; Comn End Racism, Episcopal Diocese Chicago, 1990-92; staff liaison, AIDS Task Force, Episcopal Diocese Chicago, 1990-; adv coun, Chicago Women's AIDS Proj, 1991-; co-chair, Chicago Area AIDS Care Givers Retreat, 1991-92; secy, Gen Conv Joint Comn AIDS, Episcopal, 1992-; bd dir, Urban Environ Policy Inst; Coalition LA; Clergy & Laity United Econ Justice; Coalition Better Inglewood; Campaign New Century; chair, Neighborhood Coun Rev Comn. **Honors/Awds:** Bertha Dixon Memorial Award, New York Higher Educ Opportunity Program, 1982. **Special Achievements:** First individuals from the church community to join the fight against Wal-Mart; A Faith of One's Own, "Este Es Mi Cuerpo," Crossing Press article in anthology, 1987; "The Spiritual Cost of Abuse," Prevention Resource Services: Journal on Abuse, 1992. **Home Addr:** 2801 S King Dr Suite 1504, Chicago, IL 60616, **Home Phone:** (312)326-5466. **Business Addr:** The Reverend, Rector, Holy Faith Episcopal Church, 260 N Locust St, Inglewood, CA 90301-1204, **Business Phone:** (310)674-7700.

## PEREZ, ANNA

Executive. **Personal:** Born Jan 1, 1951, New York, NY; married Ted Sims; children: 3. **Educ:** Hunter Col. **Career:** US Sen Slade Gorton, asst press secy & commun dir, 1981; US Congressman John R Miller, press secy, 1985; Barbara Bush, Wash, DC, press secy, 1989-93; Walt Disney Co, vpres Calif govt rels, 1995-98; Chevron Corp, 1998-2000, vpres Calif; Chevron Corp, gen mgr corp commun & progs, 1998-2001; Nat Sec Adv Condoleezza Rice, dep asst to pres & counr, 2001-04; NBC Universal, exec vpres commun, 2004; Universal Studios, head; Tacoma Facts, Tacoma, WA, publ; Sen Slade Gordon, press secy; Rep John Miller, press secy; Creative Artists Agency Inc, head media rels & external affairs, dep asst pres; Nat Security Coun, dir commun. **Orgs:** Calif Int Rels Found; Greek Theatre Los Angeles Found; Black Filmmakers Found; Int Womens Media Found Adv Comt; Ariel Capital Mgt; Gulf Found; fel Inst Polit John F Kennedy Sch Govt, Harvard Univ; Calif Film Comn; Joint Ctr Polit & Econ Studies; trustee, Save C USA. **Special Achievements:** First African American press secretary to First Lady Barbara Bush. **Home Addr:** , Santa Monica, CA. **Business Addr:** Executive Vice President Communications, NBC Universal, 100 Universal City Plz, Universal City, CA 91608, **Business Phone:** (818)777-1000.

## PERINE, JAMES L.

Educator. **Personal:** Born Jun 23, 1943, St. Louis, MO; married B Rosalie Hicks; children: Lori, Keith & Kelly. **Educ:** Mo State Univ, BA, philos & psychol, 1964; Univ Md, MA, 1968; Pa State Univ, PhD, 1979. **Career:** Off Econ Opportunity Wash, res psychol, 1964-68; Univ Md, oeo grad & teaching asst, 1965-67; Pa State Univ, instr community serv, Upward Bound Prog, dir, 1968, Black Studies Prog, coord, 1977-78, Col Human Develop, asst to dean, 1972. **Orgs:** Phi Delta Kappa; Nat Educ Hon Fraternity; Am Voc Asn; Am Personnel & Guid Asn; Am Psychol Asn; St Paul's United Methodist Church State Col; Nat Asn Adv Colored People; adv bd, Lewisburg Prison; bd dir, State Col Comn Theatre; Comn Vol Mountain view Unit Ctr Community Hosp; State Col Kiwanis Club.

## PERINE, MARTHA LEVINGSTON

Executive. **Personal:** Born Jun 27, 1948, Mobile, AL; married Savoyd Beard; children: David Sr, Alissa & Alison. **Educ:** Clark Atlanta Univ, Atlanta, GA, BA, bus & finance, 1969; Wash Univ, St Louis, MO, MA, econ, 1971. **Career:** Fed Res Bank St Louis, mgt trainee, sr br exec, asst vpres, vpres, regional exec, 1971-. **Orgs:** Nat Asn Bank Women, 1985; Am Inst Banking, 1985; fin sec, Holy Metro Missionary Bapt Chap, 1985; financial sec, Gamma Omega Chap, Alpha Kappa Alpha Sor Inc, 1989-90; bd mem, Memphis Tomorrow; bd mem, Memphis Regional Chamber; bd mem, United Way Mid S; bd mem, Mid S Minority Bus Coun; bd mem, Baptist Health Care Corp; bd mem, Better Bus Bur Mid S, bd mem, St. Jude Cs Res Hosp; Econ Club Memphis; Class Leadership Memphis, 1998; Class New Memphis Inst, 2000. **Home Addr:** 7624 Cornell Ave, St. Louis, MO 63130. **Business Addr:** Regional Executive, Vice President, Federal Reserve Bank of St Louis, 1 Fed Res Bank Plz Broadway & Locust St, St. Louis, MO 63101, **Business Phone:** (314)444-8444.

## PERKINS, BERNICE PERRY

Government official. **Personal:** Born Apr 5, 1931, West Point, MS; daughter of Willie B and Statie M. **Educ:** Univ Ill, Champaign-Urbana, IL, BS, 1954. **Career:** Government official (retired); Dept Veterans Affairs, Chicago, clinicdietician, 1964-66, dietetic servs asst chief, 1966-72, Salem, Va, dietetic servs chief, 1972-74, Cincinnati, dietetic servs chief, 1974-76, Boston, dietetic servs chief, 1976-82, Wash Dist, dietetic servs chief, 1982-87, dietetic servs dir, 1987-96; Deleg At-Large, House Delegates, Am Dietetic Asso, 2006. **Orgs:** Food admin sect co-chair, Ill Dietetic Asn, 1968-69; career guid chap, Dist Dietetic Asn, 1985-86; Am Soc Hosp Food Serv Admin, 1986-96; Qual mgmt, Am Dietetic Asn, dietetics educ task force, 1992-94; Dist Dietetic Asn, mgmt practices chair, 1992-93; treas, Nat Soc Health care Food Serv Mgmt, 1994; Nat Orgn Blacks Dietetics & Nutrit, currently. **Honors/Awds:** Certificate of Apppreciation, Dist Pub Sch, 1986; Certifictae of Pride in Public Serv, Veterans Admin, 1989; Honor Award, 1989; Presidential Rank Award, Dept Veterans Affairs, 1992; Am Heart Asn, Certificateof A; Am Asn Retired Persons. **Home Addr:** 10200 Rock Oak Ter, Cheltenham, MD 20623, **Home Phone:** (301)372-6119.

## PERKINS, CHARLES WINDELL

Executive, association executive. **Personal:** Born Mar 12, 1946, New Orleans, LA; married Marilyn M; children: Evany Joy. **Educ:** Univ Calif, Berkeley, BA, 1968; Southwestern Grad Sch Banking SMU, grad degree banking, 1978. **Career:** Security Pac Nat Bank, vpres; San Leandro, vpres & mgr, 1978. **Orgs:** Mgt trainee, Security Pac Bank, 1968; bd mem, Hunters Pt Boys' Club SF, 1972; asst vpres, San Mateo & SF; mgr, Foster City, 1974; asst mgr, Hayward, Fremont; asst cashier, SF; supvr, SF & Berkeley; treas, Foster City CC, 1974; co-founder, Black Officers Group Sec Pac Bank, 1980; Univ Calif Alumni Asn. **Honors/Awds:** All-conference basketball, Univ CA Berkeley, 1967; $1, 000, 000 trust Award, Security Pac Bank, 1979. **Home Addr:** 2287 Paloma St, Pasadena, CA 91104, **Home Phone:** (626)791-4340.

## PERKINS, DANIEL T.

Chief executive officer, foundation executive. **Personal:** Born Washington, DC. **Educ:** Univ Pittsburgh, Johnstown, PA, attended 1974; Pepperdine Univ, MA. **Career:** United States Marine Corps, Comn Officer, 1974-78; Booz Allen & Hamilton Inc, mgr staffing, 1978-89; Dual & Assocs, mem bd dir, vpres admin, 1989-91; MTS Technols Inc, pres, chmn, owner & chief exec officer, 1991-; Challenge Prog, chmn. **Orgs:** Founder, Challenge Prog, 2003-.bd dir, Challenge Prog. **Business Addr:** Chairman, Chief Executive Officer, MTS Technologies Inc, 2800 S Shirlington Rd Suite 1000, Arlington, VA 22206, **Business Phone:** (703)575-2900.

### PERKINS, EDWARD JOSEPH
Writer, college teacher, government official. **Personal:** Born Jun 8, 1928, Sterlington, LA; son of Edward Joseph Sr and Tiny Estella Noble Holmes; married Lucy Cheng mei Liu; children: Katherine Karla Shih-Tzu & Sarah Elizabeth Shih Yin. **Educ:** Univ Md, BA, 1967; Univ Southern Calif, MPA, 1972, DPA, 1978; St Augustine Col, DHL, Honis Causa, 1993. **Career:** AID Far E Bur Wash, asst gen serv officer; US Opers Mission to Thailand, Bangkok, asst gen serv officer 1967-69, mgt analyst 1969-70, dep asst dir mgt 1970-72; Off Dir Gen Foreign Serv Wash, staff asst, 1972, personnel officer, 1972-74; Bur Near Eastern & S Asian Affairs, admin officer, 1974-75; Off Mgt & Opers, mgt anal officer, 1975-78; Accra, counr polit affairs 1978-81; Monrovia, dep chief mission, 1981-83; Bur African Affairs Off W African Affairs, dir 1983-85; Dept State, ambassador to Liberia, 1985-86, ambassador to S Africa 1986-89, dir gen Foreign Serv 1989-92; Un & UN Security Coun, ambassador, 1992-93; US ambassador, Australia, 1993-96; Univ Okla, Int Progs Ctr, William J Crowe chair & exec dir, 1996-; Books: Mr. Ambassador: Warrior of peace; The Palestinian Refugees: Old Problems-New Solutions; The Middle East Peace Process: Vision Versus Reality; Palestinian Refugees: Traditional Positions and New Solutions; The seedlings of hope. **Orgs:** Epsilon Boule Sigma Pi Phi Fraternity; Kappa Alpha Psi Fraternity; Navy League; Hon Soc Phi Kappa Phi; Am Soc Pub Admin, 1971-; Veterans Foreign Wars, Chevy Chase Chap; Am Acad Diplomacy; Am Foreign Serv Asn; Am Polit Sci Asn; World Affairs Coun, Cent Okla & Wash, DC; Cranlana Prog, bd; Am Legion; Chester A Arthur Soc; Coun Foreign Rels; Foreign Policy Asn; Int Studies Asn; Pac Coun Int Policy; Pub Serv Comn; Am Consortium Int Pub Admin; bd dir, Ctr Study Presidency; Asn Diplomatic Studies & Trng; adv bd, Inst Int Pub Policy; bd trustee, Lewis & Clark Col; adv coun, Univ Off Int Progs, Pa State Univ; bd trustee, Woodrow Wilson Nat Fel Found; bd visitors, Nat Defense Univ; bd dir, Nat Acad Pub Admin; Am Acad Diplomacy; Am Foreign Serv Asn; Am Legion; Chevy Chase Chap; World Affairs Coun Okla; World Affairs Coun Wash, DC; Foreign Policy Asn; Inst Int Educ; Veterans Foreign Wars; life trustee, Lewis & Clark Col Portland. **Special Achievements:** First black United States ambassador to South Africa. **Home Addr:** 1025 Joe Keeley Dr, Norman, OK 73072. **Business Addr:** Executive Director, University of Oklahoma, 400 Whitehand Hall, Norman, OK 73019-5144, **Business Phone:** (405)325-1396.

### PERKINS, PROF. FRANCES J.
Educator, counselor. **Personal:** Born Dec 14, 1919, Boston, MA; married W Wentworth; children: Joseph W. **Educ:** Boston State, BSE, 1941; Tufts Univ, EdM, 1957; Boston Univ, EdM, coun, 1981. **Career:** St Mark Nursery Sch, Boston, Mass, founder & dir, 1941-53; Parent COOP, NSBelmont, Mass, dir, 1953-57; Red Barn Nursery Sch, dir, 1957-61; Tufts Univ, summer fac Eliot-Pearson Dept Child Study, 1960-65, lectr; Lemberg Lab Pre Sch, Brandeis Univ, dir, 1961-73; Garland Jr Col, instr, 1965-66; Head Start Training Prog Wheelock Col Sum, dir, 1966-67; Peace Corps, Tunisia, proj dir, 1966-67; EPDA Inst Garland Jr Col, asst dir, 1969; Head Start Progs, evaluator, 1970-85; Wheelock Col, instr psychol, 1970-73, assoc prof psychol, 1973-85, prof emer, Boston, Mass, 2000-; Jackson-Mann Early Childhood Prog, Horace Mann Sch Deaf, consult, 1974-75; Ctr Individual & Family Servs, consult; Family Mediation Prog, consult; Head Start progs, consult. **Orgs:** Nat Asn Educ Young C; Am Asn Univ Women; pres & bd dir, Freedom House Inc; Parents & C's Serv; MA Comn C & Youth; Prof Adv Comn Ft Hill Ment Health Asn; bd mem, Urban League Eastern MA; bd mem, NAUSET Workshop; pres, Ctr Individual & Family Servs, Cape Cod, MA; First Parish Unitarian Universal Church; bd mem, Eastham Coun Aging, Mass Appeal; Anti-Racism, First Parish Unitarian Universal Church. **Special Achievements:** One of the team of 3 to create Boston Head Start Program for Action for Boston Community Development, 1965. **Home Addr:** 25 Perkins Gln, Eastham, MA 02642, **Home Phone:** (508)240-2123. **Business Addr:** Professor Emerita, Wheelock College, 200 Riverway, Boston, MA 02215, **Business Phone:** (617)879-2000.

### PERKINS, DR. REV. JAMES CONNELLE
Clergy. **Personal:** Born Mar 14, 1951, Williamson, WV; son of Cecil (deceased) and Chaddy B (deceased); married Linda Carol Adkins; children: Tamaria Yvette & Lindsey Camille. **Educ:** Wiley Col, BA, 1972; Andover-Newton Theol Sch, Mdiv, 1974; United Theol Sem, DMin, 1990. **Career:** Gospel Ministry, 1974; St Paul Baptist Church, St Albans, WV, pastor, 1974-80; Greater Christ Baptist Church, pastor, 1981-. **Orgs:** Bd dir, Detroit Empowerment Zone; bd dir, Detroit One-Stop Capital Shop; bd dir, Detroit Design Collab; adv coun, St John Health Syst; bd dir, Detroit E COT Health Ctr; pres, Mich Progressive Baptist Conv; Detroit Baptist Pastors Coun; Nat Advan Asn Colored People, Detroit chap; Kappa Alpha Psi; Samuel Dewitt Proctor fel, United Theol Sem, 1990; founder, Fel Nonprofit Housing Corp, 1992; founder, Benjamin E Mays Male Acad, 1993; founder, Detroit Eastside Coalition Churches, 1993; vpres, Progressive Nat Baptist Conv Inc. **Home Addr:** 19575 Renfrew Rd, Detroit, MI 48221, **Home Phone:** (313)341-3098. **Business Addr:** Pastor, Greater Christ Baptist Church, 3544 Iroquois St, Detroit, MI 48214, **Business Phone:** (313)924-6900.

### PERKINS, JOHN M.
Executive. **Personal:** Born Jun 16, 1930, New Hebron, MS; son of Maggie; married Vera Mae; children: Spencer (deceased), Phillip, Joan, Derek, Debbie, DeWayne, Priscilla & Betty. **Career:** Voice Calvary Ministries, pres, 1960-81; Fed S Cooper, co-fed, 1967; S Cooper Devel Fund, co-fed; Voice Calvary Cooper Health Clin; People Develop Inc; Gen Session spkr Urbana, 1976; MS Billy Graham Crusade, steering com, 1975; Tom Skinner MS Mgt Sem, sponsor, 1975; Voice Calvary Bible Ins; Berean Bible Church; child care ctr; Pres Reagan Task Force, 1983-84; Reconicilers Fel, ed chief, 1992-98; John M. Perkins Found Reconciliation & Develop, pres, co founder; Mendenhall Ministries; Voice Calvary Ministries; Harambee Christian Family Ctr, 1984; Christian Community Develop Asn, 1989; Harambee Prep Sch; Int auth, speaker & lectr; Pres Emeritas, currently. **Orgs:** Bd mem, Bread world; founder, Christian Community Develop Asn; Nat Black Evangel Asn; Convenant Col; S Devel Found; Koinonio Partners; num lecuring posts travelled over US Ford Found, 1972-73; founder, Harambee Christian Family Ctr; founder, John M. Perkins Found Reconciliation & Develop Inc, 1982; founder, Harambee Prep Sch; founder, Spencer Perkins Ctr; bd dir, World Vision; bd dir, Prison Fel; bd dir, Nat Asn Evangelicals; bd dir, Spring Arbor Col; bd adv, Bible Literacy Proj. **Home Addr:** 1516 St Charles St, Jackson, MS 39209. **Business Addr:** President Emeritus, John M Perkins Foundation for Reconciliation and Development, 1831 Robinson St, Jackson, MS 39209, **Business Phone:** (601)354-1563.

### PERKINS, LOUVENIA BLACK (KITTY BLACK-PERKINS)
Fashion designer. **Personal:** Born Feb 13, 1948, Spartanburg, SC; daughter of Luther Black and Helen Goode Black; married Gary; children: Erika Nicole. **Educ:** Los Angeles Trade Tech Col, AA, fashion design, 1971. **Career:** Fashion designer: Miss Melinda Calif, Debbie Ross, A & O Couture; Mattel Inc, El Segundo, Calif, chief designer, 1976-. **Honors/Awds:** Chairmans Award, 1985; Employee of the Month, 1986; Chairmans Award, 1987; The Doty Award; Woman of the Year, Nat Coun Negro Women, 1994. **Special Achievements:** A special doll, designed & donated to the SC State Mus, 2001; Recognized, pursued by some of the industry's top mag & newspapers: Ebony Essence; LA Mag; Woman's Day; Sister to Sister; Los Angeles Mag; Fox TV's Personalities; The Tim & Daphne Show; I've Got a Secret, SC, 2002; African-American Hist Calendar; Guest speaker, Career Day events; Black Hall of Fame, 2001-. **Home Addr:** 924 Cara Pl, San Pedro, CA 90731. **Business Addr:** Chief Designer, Mattel Inc, 333 Continental Blvd, El Segundo, CA 90245-5012, **Business Phone:** (310)252-2000.

### PERKINS, MYLA LEVY
Educator, business owner. **Personal:** Born Feb 25, 1939, Pueblo, CO; daughter of Naomi and Addison; married Edgar L; children: Julie, Steven, Todd & Susan. **Educ:** Wayne State Univ, BS, 1960. **Career:** Detroit Pub Sch, teacher, 1960-66; Sugar N Spice Nursery Sch, co-owner, 1966-; Pyramid Elem Sch, co-owner, 1976-92. **Orgs:** Alpha Kappa Alpha Sor, 1957-; Tots & Teens Am, 1967. **Home Addr:** 19330 Parkside St, Detroit, MI 48221, **Home Phone:** (313)368-2899. **Business Addr:** Co-Owner, Sugar N Spice Nursery School, 16555 Wyo Ave, Detroit, MI 48221, **Business Phone:** (313)863-5600.

### PERKINS, DR. ROBERT E. L.
Oral surgeon, surgeon. **Personal:** Born May 17, 1925, Carthage, TX. **Educ:** Wiley Col, BS, 1945; Howard Univ, DDS, 1948; Tufts Univ, MSD, 1956. **Career:** Childrens Hosp Mich, courtesy staff, 1960-87; Metro Hosp Detroit, 1965-87; Hutzel Hosp, jr staff mem, 1983-87; oral & maxillofacial surgeon; Detroit Wiley Club, pres. **Orgs:** Am Dent Asn, 1949-87; Nat Dent Asn, 1963-87; pres & founder, DSACE, 1964-87; Mich & Am Asn Oral & Maxillofacial Surgeons, 1970-87; bd dir, treas, Your Heritage House, 1977-87; bd dir, Detroit Symphony Orchestra, 1980-87; life mem, Nat Asn Advan Colored People; Nat Urban League; United Negro Col Fund; Alpha Kappa Alpha; bd mem, Detroit Inst Arts; pres, Howard Univ Alumni Asn. **Honors/Awds:** Key to the City of Detroit; Patron of the Arts Award, Detroit Musicians Asn; Alumni Awards, College of Dentistry; Howard University Alumni Award1983. **Business Addr:** President, Detroit Wiley Club, 1760 Lincolnshire Dr, Detroit, MI 48203, **Business Phone:** (313)892-7002.

### PERKINS, SAM BRUCE (SAMUEL PERKINS)
Basketball player, businessperson, vice president (organization). **Personal:** Born Jun 14, 1961, Brooklyn, NY. **Educ:** NC State Univ, BA, commun, 1984. **Career:** Basketball player (retired), businessperson, executive; Dallas Mavericks, forward-ctr, 1984-90; Los Angeles Lakers, 1990-93; Seattle SuperSonics, 1993-98; Ind Pacers, 1998-2001, vpres player rels, 2008-; Neo Soul Cafe LLC, owner, currently. **Orgs:** United Negro Col Fund; Lupus Found; Big Bros & Big Sisters; founder, 848 prod. **Business Addr:** Owner, Neo Soul Cafe LLC, PO Box 2233, Addison, TX 75001, **Business Phone:** (972)923-1585.

### PERKINS, TONY
Meteorologist. **Personal:** Born Jan 1, 1960, New York, NY; son of Tommy and Constance Bellamy; married Rhonda; children: 1. **Educ:** Am Univ, Wash, DC, BA, commun. **Career:** WKYS-FM, "The Donnie Simpson Show", on-air contribr & radio producer, 1985-92; "stand-up comedian", 1985-92; WDCA-TV, "DC20 Breakaway", producer & host, 1986-88; WTTG-TV, "Comic Strip Live", 1989, "Fox 5 Morning News", co-anchor, 1998-99, tv weatherperson, 1993-99, weather forcaster, 2005-; ABC News, desk asst, 1980, "Good Morning America", weather forecaster, 1999-2005, "Less Than Perfect", cameo appearance, 2004, "Jimmy Kimmel Live, " guest appearance, "American Music Awards", presenter, VH1, "I Love the '90s Part Deux", comic commentator, "Stealing Scenes"; WKYS-FM, "The Morning Crew", radio show co-host, 1992-93. **Orgs:** Dean's Adv Coun, Am Univ Sch Commun. **Honors/Awds:** Emmy Award, 1988. **Business Addr:** Weather Forecaster, Fox Television Stations Inc, 5151 Wis Ave NW, Washington, DC 20016, **Business Phone:** (202)895-3000.

### PERKINS, WILLIAM O., JR.
Government official, educator. **Personal:** Born Jun 5, 1926, Gregory, NC; married Arthur; children: 4. **Educ:** Elizabeth City State Univ, BS, 1949; Atlanta Univ; Univ Ga. **Career:** Morgan Co Schs, teacher, 1949-51, 1953-56; Turner Co Schs, teacher, 1952-53; Atlanta Pub Schs, teacher, 1957-76; New Jersy St Bar Found, atty, currently. **Orgs:** YWCA, 1957-77; NEA, 1957-77; Gate City Teachers Asn, 1957-70; mem bd dir, Metro Atlanta Girls Club, 1972-75; bd dir, Atlanta Asn Educ, 1973-75; Ga Asn Educ, 1976-77; Nat Asn Advan Colored People; Secy, Atlanta Dist Baptist Missionary Soc, 1976-77; Beulah Baptist Church; Alpha Kappa Mu Nat Hon Soc; mem bd dir, Ga Asn Classroom Teachers; Metro Atlanta Coun Int Reading Asn. **Home Addr:** 37 Emory St, Jersey City, NJ 07304. **Business Addr:** Attorney, New Jersy State Bar Foundation, 1 Const Sq, New Brunswick, NJ 08901, **Business Phone:** (732)249-5000.

### PERRIN, BISHOP DAVID THOMAS PERRY
Clergy, bishop. **Personal:** Born May 16, 1951, Cleveland, OH; married Elizabeth Ann Jackson; children: Caleb Karamo, Quianne Shapearl & Mileah Niambi; married Allethia Yvonne Campbell. **Educ:** Carnegie Mellon Univ, BFA, 1975; Gordon-Conwell Theol Sem, MTS, 1978; Howard Univ, ABD; Andersonville Baptist Sem, PhD. **Career:** Corning Comm Col, instr, 1981-83; Friendship Baptist Church, pastor, 1981-83; Elmira Correctional Inst, vis lectr, 1982-83; TDX Systs Inc, sales analyst, 1984-85; Pkwy Baptist Church, pastor; Friendship Baptist Church, pastor; Cobb breeding Co, europ mgr tech serv; Carnegie Mellon Univ, bishop; Church Great Comn, sr pastor, 1986-99, bishop, currently; pres, Great Comn Global Ministries; Tom Skinner Assocs, Howard univ, chaplain, Christ Kingdom Church Dist Heights, Md, sr pastor. **Orgs:** Prince Georges County Baptist Asn; Collective Banking Group Inc; Prince Georges County Am Christian TV Inc; pres, Great Comn Global Ministrie; bd mem, CrossGlobal Link; vice chair person, bd dir, SIM USA. **Home Addr:** 13216 Glenmore Dr, West Palm Beach, FL 33349. **Business Addr:** Bishop, Church of the Great Commission, 5032 Forsyth Commerce Rd, Orlando, FL 32807, **Business Phone:** (321)206-4946.

### PERRINEAU, HAROLD, JR. (HAROLD WILLIAMS, JR.)
Actor. **Personal:** Born Aug 7, 1963, Brooklyn, NY; son of Harold Sr and Sylvia; married Brittany; children: Aurora Robinson, Wynter Aria & Holiday Grace. **Educ:** Shenandoah Conserv, music & theater. **Career:** Films: Fame, 1989; Flirt, 1995; Smoke, 1995; Romeo + Juliet, 1996; Blood and Wine, 1996; The Edge, 1997; Come To, 1998; Shakedown, 1988; King of New York, 1990; Lulu on the Bridge, 1998; The Best Man, 1999; Macbeth in Manhattan, 1999; A Day in Black & White, 1999; Woman on Top, 2000; Overnight Sensation, 2000; Someone Like You, 2001; Prison Song, 2001; On Line, 2002; The Matrix Reloaded, 2003; Enter the Matrix, 2003; The Matrix Revolutions, 2003; The Matrix Online, 2005; Random Acts of Kindness, 2005; 28 Weeks Later, 2007; Gardens of the Night, 2008; Ball Don't Lie, 2008; Felon, 2008; Your Name Here, 2008; The Killing Jar, 2010; Case 219, 2010; 30 Days of Night, 2010; Seeking Justice, 2011; The Hungry Rabbit Jumps, 2011; Transit, 2011; Cooler, 2011; Sunset Stories, 2012; Zero Dark Thirty, 2012; Snitch, 2013; Go for Sisters, 2013; The Best Man Holiday, 2013; Sabotage, 2014. TV series: "The Cosby Show", 1989; "Law & Order", 1990-93; I'll Fly Away", 1991-93; "ER", 1997; "Oz", 1997-2003; The Tempest, 1998; "Dead Like Me", 2003; "HBO First Look", 2003; "Players", 2003; "The Matrix Recalibrated", 2004; "The Burly Man Chronicles", 2004; "Lost", 2004-10; "The View", 2005; "Jimmy Kimmel Live", 2005; "Entertainment Tonight", 2005; "CSI", 2007; Demons, 2007; "Lost: Missing Pieces", 2007-08; "The Whole Truth", 2010; "Blade", 2011; "Phineas and Ferb", 2012; "Georgia", 2012; "Sons of Anarchy", 2012; "Wedding Band", 2012-13; "Law & Order: Special Victims Unit", 2013; "HitRECord on TV", 2014; "Growing Up Fisher", 2014; "Z Nation", 2014; "Newsreaders", 2014; "Constantine", 2014. Music: Yes We Can, 2008; "The Unusuals", 2009; "CSI", 2010; Video: Garfield Gets Real, 2007; Song: Stay Strong, co-writer, 2007; Moving On, 2011. **Orgs:** Screen Actors Guild. **Honors/Awds:** Independent Spirit Award, 1995; Image Award Nominee Outstanding Supporting Actor in a Motion Picture for: The Best Man (1999/I), 2000; Screen Actors Guild Award, 2006; Festival Award, World Music & Independent Film Festival, 2013; Hollywood Award, Acapulco Black Film Festival, 2014. **Business Addr:** Actor, c/o The Gersh Agency, 232 N Canon Dr, Beverly Hills, CA 90210, **Business Phone:** (310)274-6611.

### PERRY, DR. AUBREY M.
Psychologist, educator, executive director. **Personal:** Born Jan 14, 1937, Petersburg, VA; married Clarie S; children: Vanessa, Aubrey Jr & Kenneth. **Educ:** Va State Col, AB, 1958, MS, 1960; Ind Univ Med Ctr, dipl, 1972; Fla State Univ, PhD, 1972. **Career:** Crowns ville Hosp, psychologist intern, 1959; Cent State Hosp, staff psychologist, 1960; Fla Agr & Mech Univ, from asst prof psychol to assoc prof psychol, 1961-69, dean, 1972, prof psychol, 1997-2003, prof emer, 2003-, dir, currently; NSF, summer fel, 1964; Carnegie, fel, 1968; Ind Med Ctr, psychologist intern, 1971; Apalachee Comm Ment Health Serv, clin psychologist, 1972-. **Orgs:** Asn Black Psychologists; Psi Chi, Seastern Psychol Asn; Fla Psychol Asn; Asn Social & Behav Scientists; Phi Delta Kappa; Pi Gamma Mu; Leon Co Ment Health Asn; Omega Psi Phi. **Honors/Awds:** Teacher of the Year, Fla A&M Univ, 1961-62; Psychology Teacher of the Year, Fla A&M Univ, 1974-75; Famuan of the Century, 2000. **Home Addr:** 2616 Malin Dr, Tallahassee, FL 32308-2225, **Home Phone:** (850)893-1884. **Business Addr:** Professor Emeritus, Director, Florida Agricultural And Mechanical University, 501 Orr Dr GEC-C Suite 302, Tallahassee, FL 32307, **Business Phone:** (850)599-3014.

### PERRY, BETTY HANCOCK
Government official. **Educ:** Univ Calif Los Angeles Anderson Sch Mgt, cert, African Am Studies, 1993; Lincoln Univ, BBA, bus admin & mgt, 1972; Morgan State Univ, MCC, contract compliance, 2001. **Career:** Cook County, Bur Finance, Off Contract Compliance, head, dir, adminr, 1990-2010; Hancock Perry Consulting Inc, pres, 2011-. **Orgs:** Cook County Rep Cent Comn. **Business Addr:** President, Hancock Perry Consulting Inc, 8816 S Calumet Ave, Chicago, IL 60619.

### PERRY, BEVERLY L.
Vice president (organization), manager, lawyer. **Educ:** George Washington Univ, BS; Georgetown Univ, JD. **Career:** Frank, Bernstein, Conaway & Goldman, lawyer; Judge Marion Blank Horn US Claims Ct, law clerk; US Dept Interior, off solicitor, atty advisor; Potomac Elec Power Co, community & corp rels, mgr govt rels dc & fed affairs, gen mgr, 1997-99, vpres, 1999-2002, sr vpres, 2002-; Pepco Holdings Inc, vpres, 2002, sr vpres govt affairs & pub policy, 2002-, sr vpres external affairs, spec advisor, 2012-13. **Orgs:** Chair, Wash Conv Ctr Authority; bd dir, Greater Wash Urban League; Arena Stage; Eastgate Gardens Steering Comt; bd dir, African Am Civil War Memorial; Cong Black Caucus Polit Educ & Leadership Comt; Capital City Chap Links Inc; bd dir, Kiwanis Club Wash; Dept Interior Fed Credit Union Bd dir; bd dir, Family Life Ctr Found Shiloh Baptist Church; bd dir, Wash DC Alumnae Found; Delta Sigma Theta Inc; bd dir, Keep Wash DC Beautiful; Chesapeake Chap Soc Inc. **Business Addr:** Board Member, The Congressional Black Caucus Institute, 413 New Jersey Ave SE, Washington, DC 20003, **Business Phone:** (202)785-3634.

**PERRY, CLIFFORD R., III**
Banker, manager, vice president (organization). **Personal:** Born Feb 8, 1945, Chicago, IL; son of Clifford Jr and Gloria Dixon; married Mattie Pointer; children: Michele Walton, Renee Scott, Clifford R & Michael S. **Educ:** Gov State Univ, BA, mkt, 1991. **Career:** Harris Bank, dept vpres, 1971; Northwest Bank, pres; Wells Fargo Bank, mgr; Fifth Third Bank, community rels mgr, sr vpres community develop, 2005-, bus banking relationship mgr, 2009-. **Orgs:** Nat Bankers Asn, 1975-; investment comt bd, YMCA, 1992; bd mem, Boys Club, 1992; bd mem, Boy Scouts, 1992; bd mem, Omaha Small Bus Network, 1992; bd mem, N Omaha Bus Develop Corp, 1992; chmn, Greater Omaha Pvt Indust Coun, 1992-; adv chmn, SBA Region VII, Omaha Adv Coun, 1992-; Greater Omaha Chamber Com; Chicago Community Ventures. **Business Addr:** Senior Vice President Community Development, Manager of Community Relations, Fifth Third Bank, Bldg 4 810 Cres Ctr Dr Suite 160, Franklin, TN 37067, **Business Phone:** (615)771-5814.

**PERRY, DARREN**
Football player, football coach. **Personal:** Born Dec 29, 1968, Chesapeake, VA; married Errika; children: Danielle, Dominique, Dedriana & Devan. **Educ:** Pa State Univ, BA, bus admin & mgt, 1992. **Career:** Football player (retired), football coach; Pittsburgh Steelers, free safety, 1992-98, asst defensive backs coach, 2003, defensive backs coach, 2004-06; San Diego Chargers, 1999; Baltimore Ravens, 1999; New Orleans Saints, free safety & safety, 2000; Cincinnati Bengals, safeties coach, 2002; Oakland Raiders, defensive back coach, 2007-08; Green Bay Packers, sec safeties coach, 2009-; NFL, sec safeties coach, 2016, Currently. **Orgs:** Bd, Chesapeake Care Free Clinic. **Home Addr:** , Chesapeake, VA. **Business Addr:** Secondary Safeties Coach, Green Bay Packers, Lambeau Field Atrium, Green Bay, WI 54304, **Business Phone:** (510)864-5000.

**PERRY, EDWARD LEWIS, JR.**
Football player. **Personal:** Born Sep 1, 1974, Richmond, VA; married Sonja; children: Kamaya. **Educ:** James Madison Univ, BS, sociol. **Career:** Football player (retired); Miami Dolphins, tight end, 1997-2004; Kans City Chiefs, 2005, free agt. **Business Addr:** Free Agent, Kansas City Chiefs, 1 Arrowhead Dr, Kansas City, MO 64129, **Business Phone:** (816)920-9400.

**PERRY, ELLIOT LAMONTE**
Actor, basketball player. **Personal:** Born Mar 28, 1969, Memphis, TN. **Educ:** Univ Memphis, attended 1991. **Career:** Basketball player (retired); Los Angeles Clippers, guard, 1991; Charlotte Hornets, 1991-92; Portland Trail Blazers, 1992-93; La Crosse Catbirds, 1992; Rochester Renegade, 1992-93; Grand Rapids Hoops, 1993-94; Phoenix Suns, 1994-96; Milwaukee Bucks, 1996-99; NJ Nets, 1999-2000; Orlando Magic, 2000; Phoenix Suns, guard, 2000-01; Memphis Grizzlies, guard & minority share owner, 2002 & 2006-07; Radio Broadcast Team, color commentator, 2006-07; Actor: Eddie, 1996; I Am a Man: From Memphis, a Lesson in Life, 2009. **Home Addr:** , Germantown, TN.

**PERRY, EMMA BRADFORD**
Librarian. **Personal:** Born Hodge, LA; daughter of Ibe and Mattie Stringfellow; married Huey L; children: David Omari & Jeffrey Donovan (deceased). **Educ:** Grambling State Univ, Grambling, LA, BS, speech & drama, 1965; Atlanta Univ, Atlanta, GA, MLS, 1967; Western Mich Univ, Kalamazoo, MI, EdS, admin &, mgt, 1974. **Career:** Sevier Elem Sch, Ferriday, librn, 1965-66; Grambling State Univ, Libr Educ Prog, Instr and Coordr, 1967-70; Battle Creek Pub Sch, Battle Creek, MI, asst librn, 1971-72; Evanston Pub Libr, Evanston, br head, 1972-76; Tex A&M Univ, Col Sta, Tex, asst prof & head, 1977-83; State Libr La, Baton Rouge, LA, libr consult, 1985-87; Harvard Univ Bus Sch, Cambridge, MA, assoc lib dir & asst dir, 1987-89; Dillard Univ, New Orleans, LA, dir, univ libr, 1989-92; Southern Univ, John B Cade Libr, dean libr, 1992-. **Orgs:** Ill Libr Asn, 1972-76; Am Libr Asn, 1972-, ed bd, Col & Res Libr, accreditation team; Tex Libr Asn, 1977-87; Light Aircraft Manufacturers Asn, 1978-85; La Libr Asn, 1984-; People's Liberation Army, 1985-87; Asn Col & Res Libr, 1988-; Southern Asn Cols & Schs; Asn Col & Res Libr, 1988-; bd dirs & chair, Solinet, 1995-96; vpres, LLA. **Honors/Awds:** Personalities in the South, 1983; Finalist, CRL Academic Library Management Intern Program, 1983; Outstanding Young Women of America, 1970; Woman of the Year, Evanston, Ill. **Special Achievements:** First Dean of Libraries, 1992. **Home Addr:** 6145 Stratford Ave, Baton Rouge, LA 70808-3533, **Home Phone:** (225)928-4535. **Business Addr:** Dean of Libraries, Professor, Southern University, 167 Roosevelt Steptoe Ave, Baton Rouge, LA 70813, **Business Phone:** (225)771-4991.

**PERRY, EMMITT, JR.** See PERRY, TYLER.

**PERRY, EUGENE CALVIN, JR.**
Executive. **Personal:** Born Feb 8, 1953, Charlottesville, VA; son of Eugene C Sr and Elizabeth Blair; married Shelia Herndon; children: Shannon Janine Xavier & Eugene Calvin III. **Educ:** Wash Univ, BA, hist, 1975; Lee Univ, JD, 1978. **Career:** Justice Dept Fed Bur Invest, spec agt, 1978-86; Pop Warner Football, coach, currently; Wilkinson & Perry Ltd, pres, 1986-; Perry Group Int Inc, pres, 1987-89; Visions Video Ltd Inc, partner, currently. **Orgs:** Phi Alpha Delta Legal Fraternity, 1977-; parliamentarian, Jr Chamber Com, 1979-; Am Mgt Asn, 1983-; Wash & Lee Alumni Coun, 1985-; bd dir, Wash & Lee Univ Alumni, 1987-; Spec Olympics, Philadelphia Adopt-A-Sch Prog, Omega Psi Phi Inc; Nat Asn Advan Colored People, 1991-; First Baptist Church Lincoln Gardens; bd dir, First Baptist Community Develop Corp, 1994-; life mem, Omega Psi Phi Fraternity Inc. **Business Addr:** Partner, Visions Video Ltd Inc, PO Box 11361, New Brunswick, NJ 08906.

**PERRY, FELTON E.**
Actor, playwright. **Personal:** Born Sep 11, 1945, Chicago, IL. **Educ:** Roosevelt Univ, BA, Span/Fr; Univ Chicago, grad study; Univ Calif, Santa Barbara, MA, Span, 2003. **Career:** Films: Medium Cool, 1969; Night Call Nurses, 1972; Brute Corps, 1972; Trouble Man, 1972; Walking Tall, 1973; The Fuzz Brothers, 1973; Magnum Force, 1973; The Towering Inferno, 1974; Sudden Death, 1977; Mean Dog Blues, 1978; Down & Out in Beverly Hills, 1986; RoboCop, 1987; Weeds, 1987; Checking Out, 1989; RoboCop 2, 1990; Talent for the Game, 1991; Perfume, 1991; Let's Kill All the Lawyers, 1992; Relentless 3, 1993; RoboCop 3, 1993; Puppet Master 4, 1993; Dumb & Dumber, 1994; Dark Breed, 1996; The Sweeper, 1996; At Face Value, 1999; Buck & the Magic Bracelet, 1999; Hollywood Vampyr, 2002; TV series: Room 222, 1969; "Here Come the Brides", 1969-70; "Ironside", 1969-73; "Dragnet 1967", 1970; "Bracken's World", 1970; Dial Hot Line, 1970; "Nanny & the Professor", 1970; "Matt Lincoln", 1970; "The Partridge Family", 1970; "The Name of the Game", 1970; "Owen Marshall: Counselor at Law", 1971; "O'Hara, U.S. Treasury", 1971-72; "Adam-12", 1971-72; "Marcus Welby, M.D.", 1972; Jigsaw, 1972; Here Comes the Judge, 1972; "Mannix", 1972; "Cool Million", 1972; "The New Perry Mason", 1973; "Medical Center", 1974; "McMillan & Wife", 1974; "Police Story", 1975; The City, 1977; "Barnaby Jones, 1978; The Critical List, 1978; Hunters of the Reef, 1978; The Ordeal of Patty Hearst, 1979; Hill Street Blues, 1982-85; "Automan", 1984; "Legmen", 1984; "The Atlanta Child Murders", 1985; Seduced, 1985; Cagney & Lacey, 1985; "What's Happening Now!", 1986; "Stingray", 1987; "Harry", 1987; "Hooperman", 1987; "227", 1989; "Amen", 1989; "L.A. Law", 1986-90; Daughter of the Streets, 1990; "Murphy Brown", 1991; "The Fresh Prince of Bel-Air", 1991-92; Civil Wars, 1992; "Human Target", 1992; "Hangin' with Mr. Cooper", 1993; "The Adventures of Brisco County Jr.", 1993; Percy & Thunder, 1993; The American Clock, 1993; Menendez: A Killing in Beverly Hills, 1994; NYPD Blue", 1994; Derby, 1995; "Living Single", 1995; "The Pretender", 1996; "Sports Night", 1998; "Strong Medicine", 2001; "The West Wing", 2000-02; "Judging Amy", 2002; The Members, 2007; Theater appearances: Mac Bird, 1968; Chemin de Fer, 1969; The Meeting, 1987; Ritual, 1989-90; Killing Time, 1990; Hamlet, 1995; YAY Prod Co, founder; La Unified Sch Dist, teacher; TV: The Last Payment, writer, 1973. **Orgs:** Am Fedn TV & Radio Artists; Actors' Equity Asn; Screen Actors Guild. **Honors/Awds:** Image Award for Playwrighting, Nat Asn Advan Colored People. **Home Addr:** 540 S St Andrews Pl Suite 5, Los Angeles, CA 90020-4473, **Home Phone:** (213)383-6269. **Business Addr:** Actor, William Morris Agency, 1 William Morris Pl, Beverly Hills, CA 90212, **Business Phone:** (310)859-4000.

**PERRY, GARY W.**
Automotive executive. **Personal:** Born Jun 3, 1952, Roanoke, VA; son of Leroy Sr and Rosetta; married Carlleena Herring. **Educ:** Winston-Salem State Univ, BA, 1975; Northwood Inst, cert, 1979; Wharton Sch Bus, cert, 1990; Univ Mich, bus, cert, 1990; Univ Pittsburgh, Execs Sch Mgt, Katz Grad Sch Bus, grad, 1998. **Career:** Executive (retired); Gen Motors, Oldsmobile Div, asst off mgr, 1976-77, Oldsmobile Div, Boston Zone, dist t Zonemgr sales, 1977-80, Oldsmobile Div, Wash Zone, dist mgr sales, 1980-83, car distribr, 1983-86, Oldsmobile Div, Detroit, area fleet mgr, 1986-89, asst zone mgr sales, 1989, automakers northeast region, regional com mgr, 2007, fleet & com e region dir, 1976-2013. **Orgs:** Pres, Tau Phi Tau Frat, 1972; gen sales mgr bus process, Re-engineering Team-Oldsmobile. **Honors/Awds:** Distinguished Manager of the Year, Gen Motors, Oldsmobile Div, 1978, 1982-83; Robert Stempel, Highest Achievement, Gen Motors, 1991; Dale Carnegie, Highest Achievement Award, 1991; Highest Award, Human Rels, 1991; Highest Award, Reporting, 1991; John F Smith President's Coun Exceptional Performance Award, Gen Motors, 1992-95; Appointed vpres Gen Motors-Oldsmobile to Exec Leadership Team. **Home Addr:** 24 Saddle Ridge Rd, Southbury, CT 06488, **Home Phone:** (203)262-8748.

**PERRY, GERALD JUNE**
Baseball player. **Personal:** Born Oct 30, 1960, Savannah, GA; married Tara; children: Portia, Falon & Gerald Jr. **Career:** Baseball player (retired), hitting coach; Atlanta Braves, infielder & outfielder, 1983-89; Kans City Royals, infielder, 1990; St Louis Cardinals, infielder, 1991-95; Single-A Mich, hitting coach, 1997; Triple-A Pawtucket, hitting coach, 1998, hitting coordr, 1999; Seattle Mariners, hitting coach, 2000-02; Boston's Triple-A, hitting coach, 2000; Pittsburgh Pirates, hitting coach, 2003-05; Oakland Athletics, hitting coach, 2006; Chicago Cubs, hitting coach, 2007-09; AAA Pawtucket Red Sox, hitting coach, 2012; Erie SeaWolves, hitting coach, 2013; USA team, hitting coach, 2013. **Home Addr:** PO Box 1403, Hilton Head Island, SC 29928.

**PERRY, JEAN B.**
Educator, teacher. **Personal:** Born Aug 31, 1946, New York, NY. **Educ:** Fashion Inst Tech, AA, 1968; NY Univ, BS, 1970; NY Tech Col, AA, 1980; Columbia Univ, Teacher Col, MA, 1986. **Career:** Teacher (retired); New York Daily News "Good Living", sect, feature writer & reporter, 1970; Black Enterprise Mag, wrote "Black Bus in Profile", column on free lance basis, 1973-74; Daily News Conf HS Ed, speaker, 1974-75; Essence Mag, health & fitness ed, 1982-84; Ethical Cult Sch, asst teacher, 1985-87; Los Angeles Unified Sch Dist, teacher, 1986-11. **Orgs:** Kappa Tau Alpha; Kappa Delta Pi. **Home Addr:** 1038 S Meadowbrook Ave, Los Angeles, CA 90019, **Home Phone:** (213)934-6203. **Business Addr:** Educator, Los Angeles Unified School, 315 Holmby Ave, Los Angeles, CA 90024, **Business Phone:** (213)475-5893.

**PERRY, JEFFERY STEWART**
Consultant. **Personal:** Born Nov 15, 1965, Cleveland, OH; son of Elder and Rudolph Sr; married Dena Dodd; children: Jonathan Stewart & Donovan Rudolph. **Educ:** Babson Col, BS, mkt/quant methods, 1987; Harvard Univ, MBA, gen mgt, 1991. **Career:** BP Chem Inc, com assoc, 1987-89; Chicago C's Mus, co-chair; Booz-Allen Hamilton, assoc, 1991-93; CSC Index Inc, prin, 1994-97; AT Kearney Inc, vpres, 1997-2004; Ernst & Young LLP, integration pract leader, 2004-14, americas oper trans serv pract leader, 2004-14, global capital transformation oper leader, 2014-. **Orgs:** Bd dir, Nat INROADS Alumni Asn, 1987-89; bd dir, DuBois Group, 1991-93; Nat Black MBA Asn, 1991-; vpres, bd dir, Martin Luther King Jr Boys & Girls Club Chicago, 1999-; Chicago Coun Foreign Rel, Chicago comt, 2001-; vpres, Sigma Pi Phi Fraternity, 2002-; Bd mem, Chicago C's Mus, 2003-; nat bd dir, chmn emer, 2005-, Inroads Inc; corp bd mem, Boys. **Honors/Awds:** Roger W Babson Achievement Award, Babson Col, 1987; Meritorious Service Award, United Negro Col Fund, 1989; Chicago Alumni of the Year, INROADS, 1998. **Special Achievements:** Completed advanced intermediate study of French language, Sorbonne, Paris, 1991; Nominated/attended Harvard Exec Educ Prog, Leadership in Professional Service Firms, 1997; HBS Afr Amer Alumni Conf, Creating & Preserving Wealth, co-chair, 1999. **Home Addr:** 1505 Lanark St, Flossmoor, IL 60422-4382, **Home Phone:** (708)647-8360. **Business Addr:** Global Capital Transformation Operational Leader, Ernst & Young LLP, 5 Times Sq, New York, NY 10036-6530, **Business Phone:** (212)773-3000.

**PERRY, REV. JERALD ISAAC, SR.**
Administrator, consultant, clergy. **Personal:** Born Jun 3, 1950, Edenton, NC; son of John Isaac and Evelyn Jones; married Deborah Mayo; children: Jerald I Jr, Davin E & Felicia Shantique Mayo. **Educ:** Automation Mach Training Ctr, dipl, 1968; Roanoke Theol Sem, BA, divinity; Shaw Divinity Sch, MA, matriculating; Aviation Storekeeper A Sch Meridian MS. **Career:** Elizabeth City State Univ, comput oper, programmer, security adminr; WZBO-AM, gospel disc jockey/acct mgr, 1975; WBXB-Love 100 FM Sta, disc jockey/acct mgr; Whosoever Will Church God In Christ, pastor, currently. **Orgs:** NC Consortium Comn, 1972; Edenton Housing Authority, bd mem, 1979-86; bd mem, Am Heart Fund Asn, 1980-86; bd mem, Edenton Chowan Bd Educ, 1982-86; NC State Sch Bd Asn, 1982-; Nat Sch Bd Asn, 1982-; NC Humanities Comn, 1982-; bd mem, State Employees Asn NC, 1985; Black State Ministers Coalition; bd mem, Edonton Chowan Civic League; Sunday sch supt, Eastern NC Greater NC Diocese Church GodChrist; Meridian Lodge 18; JW Hood Consistory 155 United Supreme Coun; 33 degree AASR Freemasonry Prince Hall Affil; bd mem, Church GodChrist Trustee Bd. **Honors/Awds:** Outstanding Young Man of America, 1979, 1983; Kappa Delta Phi Honor Soc, Eliz City State Univ, 1982-83; Letter of Accomodation Commanding General for Expediting H1 Priority Documents; Letter of Accomodation for Serving as Wing NCO of Barracks when received Barracks of Quarter Selection; Bluejacket of the Month and Bluejacket of the Quarter MCAS Cherry Point, NC. **Home Addr:** 201 Dillard Ave, Edenton, NC 27932-9261, **Home Phone:** (252)482-7124. **Business Addr:** Pastor, Whosoever Will Church of God in Christ, 4109 Walker Dr, Edenton, NC 27932, **Business Phone:** (252)482-7124.

**PERRY, JOSEPH JAMES**
Clergy. **Personal:** Born Oct 8, 1936, Sprott, AL; son of Calloway Alphonso and Ola Mae Ford; married Dorothy M Cutts; children: Sherron, Joseph Jr, Kenneth, Keith & Andrea Davis. **Educ:** Union Baptist Sem, BTh, 1974; Southern Bible Sem, MTh, 1975; Univ Seattle, BA, 1976; New Era Baptist Sem, DTh, 1977. **Career:** Little Rock Missionary Baptist Church, pastor, 1957-62; Good Hope Missionary Baptist Church, pastor, 1960-62; Holly Grove Missionary Baptist Church, pastor, 1962-65; Exodus Missionary Baptist Church, pastor, 1971-; Wayne County Sheriff's Dept, chaplain, 1988; co-founder, PWR & W Inc, partner; Exodus Housing Develop Inc, pres. **Orgs:** Nat Asn Advan Colored People, 1957-; vpres, Nat Baptist Conv USA Inc, vpres, 1960-; treas, One Church One Child Mich, 1989-; exec dir, SCLC, Mich Chap, 1989-; pres, Baptist Missionary & Educ Conv Mich, 1991-96; Detroit Comm Fair Banking, 1992-; Plight Black Doctor, 1992-. **Home Addr:** 4120 W Outer Dr, Detroit, MI 48221, **Home Phone:** (313)861-2378. **Business Addr:** Pastor, Exodus Missionary Baptist Church, 8173 Kenney St, Detroit, MI 48234, **Business Phone:** (313)921-3690.

**PERRY, REV. JOSEPH NATHANIEL**
Clergy. **Personal:** Born Apr 18, 1948, Chicago, IL; son of Joseph N Sr and Mary Elizabeth Williams. **Educ:** St Mary Sem, Crown Pt, Ind, BA, theol, 1971; St Joseph Col, Rensselaer, Ind, BA, philos & Theol, 1971; St Francis Sem, MDiv, 1975; Cath Univ Am, JCL, canon law, 1981; St Joseph Col, E Chicago, Ind, span lang studies. **Career:** Archdiocese of Milwaukee, priest, 1975-98; St Nicholas Parish, Milwaukee, pastor, 1975-76; Milwaukee Archdiocese Tribunal, chief judicial officer, 1983-95; Canon Law Studies, Sacred Heart Sch Theol, Hales Corners, Wis, instr, 1983-98; All Saints Church, pastor, 1995-99; Titular Bishop Lead, 1998; Marquette Univ Law Sch, Milwaukee, instr, 1996-98; St Mary Lake Sem, Mundelein, Ill, instr, 1997-; Archdiocese Chicago, auxilary bishop, 1998-. **Orgs:** Fel Canon Law Soc Am, 1977-; bd mem, Archbishop Quigley Prep Sem, 1998-; Us Conf Cath Bishops Ad Hoc Comt Plenary Coun, 2002-; Us Conf Cath Bishops Comt Educ, 2003; US Conf Cath Bishops Ad Hoc Comt Catholics Use Holy Scripture, 2003-; episcopal liaison, catechetics, Archdiocese Chicago, 2003-; vpres, Nat Black Cath Cong, 2004-; Nat Chaplain Knights St Peter Claver & Ladies Auxiliary, 2004-; chmn, US Conf Cath Bishops Comt African Am Catholics, 2004-. **Home Addr:** 2132 E 72nd St, Chicago, IL 60649, **Home Phone:** (773)493-1513. **Business Addr:** Auxiliary Bishop, Archdiocese of Chicago, PO Box 733, South Holland, IL 60473, **Business Phone:** (708)339-2474.

**PERRY, JUNE CARTER**
Government official. **Personal:** Born Nov 13, 1943, Texarkana, AR; daughter of Bishop W and Louise E Pendleton; married Frederick M; children: Chad Douglass & Andre Frederick. **Educ:** Loyola Univ, BA, 1965; Univ Chicago, MA, 1967; Hamline Col, Middle East Inst, cert, 1968; Howard Univ. **Career:** Col instr & high sch teacher, 1967-70; Univ Md, instr; Nc A&T State Univ, instr; WGTS-FM & WTOP-AM, producer & commentator, 1973-74; WGMS-AM/FM, dir pub affairs, 1974-77; US Community Serv Admin, spec asst pub affairs, 1977-79; ACTION Peace Corps, dir pub affairs, 1979-83; Am Embassy, Lusaka, 1983-85, Harare, 1986-87; Dept State, polit officer, desk officer Botswana, 1987-89; Secy State, specasst, 1989-90; Am Embassy, Paris, first secy, polit affairs, 1990-93; Polit Mil Policy, state asst dir, 1993-95; Am Embassy Banguin, Cent Africa, dep chief mission, 1996-97, sr adv dep chief mission asst sec state, 1997-98, Antanarivo, dep chief missions; Int Orgn Bur, Off Social & Humanitarian Affairs, dir; Kingdom Lesotho, ambassador, 2004-07; Repub Sierra Leone, ambassador, 2004-10; Bur Int Orgn, actg dep asst secy; Off Policy & Planning Polit-Mil Affairs Bur, dir; Southern African Develop Community. **Orgs:** Am Asn Univ Women, 1973-76; AFTRA, 1974-78; vpres adv coun, Women's Inst, Wash, DC, 1975-; bd mem, Greater Wash Boys & Girls Club, 1975-79; Finance Comm Nat Capital YMCA, 1975-79; vpres, Friends Advan African Civilization, 1979; Am Foreign Serv Asn, 1985-; vpres, Thursday Luncheon Group; chmn, Fed City Pub Serv Found, currently; chmn, Africare, currently; bd dir, Asn Diplomatic Studies & Training; Woodrow Wilson Fel. **Honors/Awds:** Blacks in Industry Award, Harlem Y & Time Mag, 1975; Sup Achiever Award,

RKO Genl Broadcasting, 1976; Human Rights Award, UN Nat Capital Chap, 1977; Distinguished Alumna Award, Mundelein Col, 1980; Special Achievement Award, Action Agency, 1980; Outstanding Performance Award, Action Agency, 1982; Meritorious Service Award, 1985, 1987, Meritorious Honor Award, 1990; Superior Honor Award, Dept State, 1995, 1997; Diplomat-in-Residence of the Year Award, 2002; President's Meritorious Award, 2010. **Special Achievements:** Author of "Ancient African Heroines, " Washington Post, 1983. **Business Addr:** Chairman, The Federal City Public Service Foundation, PO Box 77144, Washington, DC 20013-8144.

### PERRY, JUNE MARTIN

Association executive, consultant. **Personal:** Born Jun 10, 1947, Columbia, SC; daughter of Mark Anthony (deceased) and Junie Alberta; children: Kevin & Krystle; married Bill Stevens. **Educ:** NC Cent Univ, BS, psychol, 1969; Univ Wis, MSW, social work, 1971; Univ Wis, PhD, urban studies. **Career:** Milwaukee Co DSS, social worker, 1971-73, purchase serv coord, 1973-75; New Concept Develop Ctr Inc, Milwaukee WI, co-founder, chief exec officer & exec dir, 1975-2006; Access to Success, prin, consult, founder, currently; fel Carnegie Mellon-Heinz Sch Bus; fel Stanford Sch Bus; AMTC, 2012-. **Orgs:** Delta Sigma Theta Sorority, 1969; NASW, 1971; Nat Black Child Develop Inst, 1986; bd dir, Girl Scouts Am, 1986-88; bd dir, Wis Coun Human Concerns, 1986; bd dir, Wis Advocacy Coalition, 1987; bd dir, Milwaukee Mgt Support Orgn, 1987; Nat Forum Black Pub Admin, 1988; founding mem, African Am Women's Fund; bd dir, Aurora Health Care Metro Region. **Honors/Awds:** Sojourner Truth Award, Eta Phi Beta, 1986; Trailblazer of the Year, Black Women's Network, 1986; Toast & Boast Award, Nat Women's Polit Caucus, 1986; Top Ladies of Distinction Community Service Award, 1987; Social Worker of the Year, Health Serv Profs Wis, 1988; Leadership America Alumnae, 1990; UWM School of Social Work, Alumni of the Year, 1993; Milwaukee NOW, Woman of the Year, 1994; Sacajawea Trailblazer Award; Woman of Influence Award; Mentor of the Year; Black Womens Network Lifetime Leader Award; Essence Award, Kraft Foods; Black Administrators in Child Welfare Long Term Leaders Award; Community Service Award, SET Ministries. **Special Achievements:** Author of Parents As Teachers of Human Sexuality, 1986; Wisconsin's Unsung Hero, Newsweek, 1988; Woman of the Year, Calvary Baptist Church, 1990. **Home Addr:** 6345 W Plz Cir, Milwaukee, WI 53223. **Business Addr:** Principal, Access to Success, 204 E Reservoir Ave, Milwaukee, WI 53212, **Business Phone:** (414)313-9762.

### PERRY, LAVAL

Automotive executive, president (organization). **Educ:** Univ Detroit, BE, mech engineering mfg, 1977, MBA, bus admin, 1982. **Career:** All Am Mgt Group, founder & pres; All Am Lincoln Mercury Inc, pres & owner, currently; DTP Trans Inc, founder, 1984; Ford Motor Minority Dealer Asn, vpres & prod design engr; All Am Ford, Saginaw, Mich, owner, pres & chief exec officer; PreBesto LLC, pres & chief exec officer, currently. **Orgs:** Vice chmn, Greater Mich Ford Dealer Advert Fund Asn, 1999; bd dir, Mich Ford Dealers Advertisers Fund; vpres, bd mem, Ford Lincoln-Mercury Minority Dealers Asn; bd mem, OIC Indust Coun; Univs Presidents Club; pres, Mich Automobile Dealer Asn, 2002; Saginaw Chamber Com; bd dir, Ferris Found; bd mem, Black Men; Ford Motor Minority Dealer Asn. **Business Addr:** President, Chief Executive Officer, PreBesto LLC, 1530 E Front St, Monroe, MI 48161, **Business Phone:** (734)242-9600.

### PERRY, LEE CHARLES, JR.

Manager, executive. **Personal:** Born Feb 22, 1955, St. Louis, MO; married Rena Armstrong; children: Raimon & Jonathan. **Educ:** Forest Park Comm Col, AS, elec eng tech, 1974; Comm Col Air Force, Electronics Honor Grad, 1975; Eastern KY Univ, BS, electronics & technol engineering, 1980; Indust Tech. **Career:** IBM St Louis, customer engr, 1980-83, prog support rep, 1983-85; IBM, exec proj mgr, 1980-, availability serv mgr, 1987-; IBM Reg Off Kans City, sr nsd specialist, 1985-87; Minister United Pentecostal Church, 1984-. **Honors/Awds:** IBM Means Service Award; Good Conduct Medal, USAF; Certificate of Recognition Outstanding Performance. **Home Addr:** 5171 Barkshire Dr, Memphis, TN 38141, **Home Phone:** (256)325-5978. **Business Addr:** Executive Project Manager, IBM Corp, 860 Ridge Lake Blvd Suite 200, Memphis, TN 38120, **Business Phone:** (901)762-5238.

### PERRY, LEONARD DOUGLAS, JR.

School administrator. **Personal:** Born Mar 14, 1952, Philadelphia, PA. **Educ:** Temple Univ, BS, MEd. **Career:** Temple Univ, resident coord, 1976-77, assoc dean stud, 1977-80; Purdue Univ, asst dean stud, 1980-85; Fla State Univ, assoc dean studs, 1985-92; Brown Univ, assoc dean stud life, 1992; Iowa State Univ, assoc dean & dir, 2007; Multicultural Stud Affairs, assoc dean, dir. **Orgs:** Nat Asn Advan Colored People; Urban League; Am Soc Training & Develop; Nat Asn Stud Personnel Adminr; Southern Asn Col Stud Affairs; Nat Soc Performance & Instr; bd dir, Black Families Am Inc; bd, CHOICES Inc; Ri Inc; 21 Century Youth Leadership Movement; Nat Stud Exchange; Acad Success Ctr. **Honors/Awds:** Martin Luther King Award, Florida State Univ, 1987; Advisor of the Year Award, Black Stud Union, Florida State Univ, 1987; Seminole Community Leadership Award, Fla State Univ, 1992; NAACP Chapter Award, 1992; Community Color Builders-Elders Award, Brown Univ. **Home Addr:** PO Box 1555, Ames, IA 50014-1555. **Business Addr:** Associate Dean, Director, Iowa State University, Memorial Union, Ames, IA 50011-2224, **Business Phone:** (515)294-6338.

### PERRY, LOWELL WESLEY, JR.

Executive, actor, manager. **Personal:** Born May 10, 1956, Ypsilanti, MI; son of Lowell Wesley Sr and Maxine Lewis; married Kathleen Tucker; children: Lowell Wesley III, Tucker Nichol & Trenton Lewis. **Educ:** Yale Univ, BA, admin sci, 1978; Seattle Univ, grad work mkt, 1987. **Career:** Nutone Div Scovill, sales rep, 1978-81; Seattle Seahawks, dir sales & mkt, 1981-88; Access Plus Commun, field sales mgr, 1988-89; Seattle Mariners, acct exec, 1989-90; Perry Mkt Group Inc, pres, 1990-94; Hiram Walker & Sons Inc, integrated mkt mgr, 1994-; Allied Domecq, integrated mkt mgr, 1994-96; Detroit Technologies Inc, pres & chief operating officer, 1996-99; LPJ Enterprises Inc, pres & chief exec officer, 1999-2007; Big Bros Big Sisters Mid Tenn, chief exec officer, 2005-12; Big Bros Big Sisters Am, chief diversity officer, svp corp & community engagement, 2012-14; Family Wellness Dallas: Safe Conversations, exec dir, 2014; Lowell Perry Enterprises, chief visionary leader, 2014-; Sisters Charity Found Cleveland, Cleveland Cent Promise Neighborhood, dir, 2015-. coms, indust training films, print ads, actor & model; Films: Deja Vu, 2006; Nothing But the Truth, 2008. **Orgs:** Chmn, Equal Opportunity Comm, 1975; corresp secy, Zeta Pi Lambda Chap Alpha Phi Alpha, 1983-84; pub relcomm, Eastside Ment Health Ctr, 1983-84; first vpres, Zeta Pi Lambda Alpha Phi Alpha, 1984-; bd mem, Kirkland C C, 1984-; bd, Kidsplace-Action Agenda Taskforce, 1985; Bd, E Madison YMCA, 1985-; bd advisor, Boys & Girls Clubs Southeastern Mich, 1996; bd, Coop Charities; bd mem, Wash Gens; Nat Asn Advan Colored People; SAG-AFTRA Rotary Int - Paul Harris Fel; life mem, Alpha Phi Alpha Fraternity Inc; Phelps Asn; Wolf's Head Soc; co-founder, Black Athletes Yale. **Honors/Awds:** Rookie of the Year, Nutone Div Scovill, 1978-79; Chmn, Sustaining Membership Drive East Madison YMCA, 1984-85; Project Developer & Coord of "Blow the Whistle on Drugs" a statewide family substance abuse prog; speaker of the house Seattle Marketing Executives. **Special Achievements:** Publications: Nonprofit CEOs Should Be Voting Board Members, Philanthropy News Dig, 2015; Nonprofit CEOs Should Be Voting Board Members, Philanthropy News Dig, 2015. **Home Addr:** 167 Gardenia Way, Franklin, TN 37064-4738, **Home Phone:** (615)794-8447. **Business Addr:** Director, Sisters of Charity Foundation of Cleveland, 2475 E 22nd St 4th Fl, Cleveland, OH 44103, **Business Phone:** (216)357-4470.

### PERRY, MARC AUBREY

Marketing executive, president (organization). **Personal:** Born MI; son of Lawrence C and Carrie O; married Pamela E; children: Aubrey Mariah. **Educ:** Eastern Mich Univ, BBA, mkt, 1978; Northwestern Univ Kellogg Sch Mgt, cert, orgn leadership. **Career:** Chevrolet, mkt spec 1978-90; Donald Coleman, acct supvn, 1990-94; Perry Mkt Group Inc, founder, pres & ceo, 1994-2000; Paper Plas, vpres, 2000-04; Infiniti Energy Inc, mkt mgr, 2001-; UniWorld Group, group acct dir, 2004-; Ford Motor Co, multicultural mkt mgr, currently. **Orgs:** Bd mem. Black United Fund; pres, Blacks In Advert, Radio & Tv; comm chair, Eastern Mich Alumni; Big Bros Big Sisters; Horizons Upward Bd; INROADS; Nat Black MBA Asn; Nat Newspaper Publishers Asn; Nat Black Pub Rels Soc Inc; Brightmoor Christian; Adcraft Club Detroit; VoiceOver City, 2014-. **Home Addr:** 33011 Tall Oaks St, Farmington, MI 48336-4551, **Home Phone:** (248)471-2422. **Business Addr:** Group Account Director, UniWorld Group, One MetroTech Ctr N 11th Fl, Brooklyn, NY 11201, **Business Phone:** (212)219-1600.

### PERRY, MARGARET

Librarian. **Personal:** Born Nov 15, 1933, Cincinnati, OH; daughter of Rufus Patterson and Elizabeth Munford Anthony. **Educ:** Western Mich Univ, BA, 1954; Univ de Paris, cert d'Etudes Sum, 1956; NY City Col, attended 1958; Cath Univ Am, MSLS, 1959. **Career:** NY Pub Libr, young adult & ref librn, 1954-55, 1957-58; AUS Europe, post librn, 1959-67; US Mil Acad W Pt, circulation librn, 1967-70; Univ Rochester, Libr Bull, assoc ed, 1970-73, head educ libr, 1970-75, assoc prof Afro-Am Lit, 1975-82, joint appt asst prof eng dept, 1973-75, head reader serv div actg dir libr, asst dir libr reader serv, 1975-82; Valparaiso Univ, dir libr & assoc prof, 1982-93, univ librn emer & assoc prof emer, currently; AUs, W Pt, librn. **Orgs:** Chair educ comt, 19th Ward Community Asn Rochester, 1972-73; second vpres, Urban League Rochester, 1978-80; pres, Northern Ind Area Libr, 1986-88; Am Libr Asn. **Honors/Awds:** Scholarship to Seminar of American Writing and Publishing, Schloss Leopoldskron Salzburg, Austria, 1956; First Prize, Armed Forces Writers League, Short Story Contest, Honorable Mention, 1965 & 1966; Second Prize, Frances Steloff Armed Forces League Short Story Contest, 1968; First Prize, Arts Alive, Short Story Contest, 1990; Second Prize, Willow Review, Short Story Contest, 1990. **Special Achievements:** Author, works include: A Bio-Bibliography of Countee P Cullen, Greenwood Press 1971; Silence to the Drums: A Survey of the Literature of the Harlem Renaissance, Greenwood Press 1976; Harlem Renaissance: An Annotated Bibliography and Commentary, Garland 1982; Short Fiction of Rudolph Fisher, Greenwood Press 1987; An Interview Margaret Perry, Cobblestone Magazine, 1991; Gwendolyn Brooks, Notable Black American Women, ed by Jessie Carney Smith, Gale Publishing, 1992; Contributor to Michigan Land Use Institute, 1994-2000; Carol Moseley Braun, Notable Black Am Women, ed by Jessie Carney Smith, Gale Pub, 1995; Margaret Perrys poetry and short stories have appeared in many journals, including Arts Alive, Forum, Obsidian II, Panache, Phylon, Short Story International, and Willow Review. **Home Addr:** 15050 Roaring Brook Dr, Thompsonville, MI 49683, **Home Phone:** (231)378-2514. **Business Addr:** University Librarian Emerita, Associate Professor Emerita, Valparaiso University, Kretzmann Hall, Valparaiso, IN 46383-6493, **Business Phone:** (219)464-5000.

### PERRY, MARLO (MALCOLM MARLO PERRY)

Football player. **Personal:** Born Aug 25, 1972, Forest, MS. **Educ:** Jackson State Univ. **Career:** Football player (retired); Buffalo Bills, 1994, 1996-97, 1999, left inside linebacker, 1995, linebacker, 1998. **Honors/Awds:** SWAC Freshman of the Year, 1993; Dick Butkus Award, 1993.

### PERRY, MICHAEL DEAN

Football player. **Personal:** Born Aug 27, 1965, Aiken, SC; son of Inez S (deceased) and Hollie Sr; married Trini; children: Taylor Denise, Amber & Tyrah. **Educ:** Clemson Univ. **Career:** Football player (retired); Cleveland Browns, defensive tackle, 1988, right defensive tackle, 1989-94; Denver Broncos, defensive tackle & right defensive tackle, 1995-97; Kans City Chiefs, defensivetackle, 1997; Subway sandwich store, owner, currently; Jughead's Downtown Clemson, currently. **Honors/Awds:** NFL All-Star Team, Sporting News, 1989; Asian Football Confederation Defensive Player of the Year, United Press Int, 1989; Defensive Player of the Year, 1989; Cleveland TouchdownClub, 1991; Pro Bowl, 1989-94, 1996. **Special Achievements:** McDonald's sandwich named in his honor.

### PERRY, PAM ELAINE

Publicist, writer. **Personal:** Born May 26, 1960, Detroit, MI; daughter of Ted and Connie Hunt; married Marc; children: Aubrey. **Educ:** Wayne State Univ, BA, jour, 1983. **Career:** Detroit Free Press, acct exec & freelance writer, 1983-90; Joy Jesus, develop dir, 1990-92; Salvation Army, dir pub rels, 1992-96; Ferry Mkt Group, vpres pub rels, 1996-01; Detroit Pub Schs, jour teacher, 2001; Herman off & Assoc, publicist, 2001-03; Ministry Mkt Solution, pres, currently. **Orgs:** Pub Rels Soc Am, 1983-85; founder & pres, Blacks Advert, Radio & TV, 1990-00; pres, Am Christian Writers Asn, 2000-; Christian African Am Booksellers Asn, 2003-; Life Changers Christian Ctr, Lansing; founder, Detroit Chap Am Christian Writers Asn. **Honors/Awds:** One to Watch, Am Women in TV & Radio, 1993; Emmy Award, Detroit Academy of TV Arts, 2002 Power Networker of the Year, George Fraser; Women of Excellence Award, The Michigan Chronicle. **Special Achievements:** Founder of non-profit group ACW/Det, 2000; columnist: Mich Chronicles, 2000-; author: Fruit Juice, 2002. **Business Addr:** President, Ministry Marketing Solutions, 33011 Tall Oaks, Farmington, MI 48336, **Business Phone:** (248)426-2300.

### PERRY, DR. PATSY BREWINGTON

Educator, administrator. **Personal:** Born Jul 17, 1933, Greensboro, NC; daughter of James C and Rosa Kirby; married Wade Wayne; children: Wade Wayne Jr. **Educ:** NC Col, Durham, NC, BA, 1954, MA, 1955; Univ NC, PhD, 1972. **Career:** Educator, administrator (retired); Georgetown High Sch, Jacksonville, NC, teacher, 1955-56; NC Cent Univ, Durham, NC, res librn, 1956-58, instr, 1959-63, asst prof, 1964-71, assoc prof, 1972-74, prof, 1974, Eng Dept chmn, 1979-90, Univ Hons Prog, spec asst to chancellor & dir, 1993-95, Acad Affairs, provost & vice chancellor, 1995-98; Univ NC, career teaching fel, 1968-69; NC Cent Univ, fac fel, 1964-71; Duke Univ, vis prof, 1975-76; Ford Found, writing fel, 1989. **Orgs:** Alpha Kappa Mu Honary Soc, 1953; bd mem, Links Inc, 1976-; Sigma Tau Delta Int Eng Hon Soc, 1983-; reader, Col Bd Eng Compos Test, 1985-; sen, Philol Asn Carolinas, 1986-; bd mem, Women Action Prev Violence, 1990-; bd gov & secy, Univ NC, 1999-2007; life mem, Col Lang Asn; S Atlantic Mod Lang Asn; Asn Dept Eng; Langston Hughes Soc. **Home Addr:** 2204 Chase St, Durham, NC 27707-2228, **Home Phone:** (919)493-8471.

### PERRY, RICHARD H.

Educator, novelist. **Personal:** Born Jan 13, 1944, New York, NY; son of Henry and Bessie Draines; married Jeanne Gallo; children: Malcolm David & Alison Wright. **Educ:** City Col, City Univ NY, BA, 1970; Columbia Univ, MFA, 1972. **Career:** Pratt Inst, Brooklyn NY, prof Eng, 1972, prof emer, currently, dean lib arts & sci, 1993-; Novels: Changes, Bobbs-Merrill, 1974; Montgomery's Children, Harcourt, 1984; No Other Tale to Tell, William Morrow, 1994; The Broken Land, St. Martin's Press, 1996. **Orgs:** PEN, Teachers & Writers Collab, Nat Coun Teachers Eng. **Home Addr:** 182B Central Ave, Englewood, NJ 07631. **Business Addr:** Professor Emeritus, Pratt Institute, 200 Willoughby Ave, Brooklyn, NY 11205, **Business Phone:** (718)636-3886.

### PERRY, RITA EGGLETON

Photographer, publisher, writer. **Personal:** Born Jul 24, 1943, Atlantic City, NJ; daughter of Christine Archer Luffborough and Jesse B Eggleton Jr; children: Sylvia Rosella Eggleton Carter. **Educ:** Univ Detroit; Norfolk State Univ. **Career:** Muziki Publ Co, adminr, 1965-68. Macon Times Newspaper, mng ed, 1968-71; Fla Star Newspaper, from asst to publ, 1971-73; Mel-Lin, Pres-Jas Broadcasting Co, vpres sls, 1973-85; Jacksonville Free Press, publ, owner, 1985-. **Orgs:** Pub rel officer, Bold City Chap Links Inc, 1993-; A L Lewis YWCA Bd; One Church/One Child Bd; former pres, Jacksonville Negro Bus & Prof Women; former secy, Southeast Black Publs Asn; former pres, Jacksonville Coalition Community Clubs; Nat Assault Illiteracy Prog Bd (AOIP); bd visitors, Edward Waters Col. **Honors/Awds:** Jacksonville Urban League Award, 1988; Award for Dedication to Black History Education, Florida Jr Col, 1990; Martin Luther King Found, Community Serv, 1990, 1996; Alpha Kappa Alpha Sorority, Community Service, 1992, 1994, Academy Award, 1995; Partner for Caring, Sickle Cell Found, 1991; Numerous Awards; State Onyx Award for Communication. **Special Achievements:** Edward Waters College, 1987; Visions of Jacksonville, 1990; One of 14 publishers called by Pres Bush for consultation, 1991; State of Florida Commendation for Voter Education Projects, 1993. **Home Addr:** PO Box 43580, Jacksonville, FL 32203-3580, **Home Phone:** (904)384-7667. **Business Addr:** Owner, Publisher & Writer, Jacksonville Free Press, 903 Edgewood Ave, Jacksonville, FL 32208, **Business Phone:** (904)634-1993.

### PERRY, DR. ROBERT LEE

School administrator, educator. **Personal:** Born Dec 6, 1932, Toledo, OH; son of Rudolph R and Katherine Bogan; married Dorothy Larouth Smith; children: Baye. **Educ:** Bowling Green St Univ, BA, sociol & psychol, 1959, MA, sociol, 1965; Wayne St Univ, PhD, sociol, 1978. **Career:** Lucas Co Juv Ct Toledo, Ohio, probation counr, 1960-64, juv ct ref, 1964-67; Detroit Inst Techn, asst prof, 1967-70; Bowling Green State Univ, Dept Ethnic Studies, chmn, 1970, dir, chair, 1979-96; Univ Calif, Los Angles, Am Soci Soc Inst Soc Res, post doctoral fel, 1980; lic prof counr, 1988; Ohio cert prev consult, 1989-; Eastern Mich Univ, Dept African Am Studies, prof & dept head, 1997-2003, African Am Ctr Appl Res & Serv, coordr grad studies, prof African Am studies & dir, currently. **Orgs:** Sigma Delta Pi Nat Span Hon Soc, 1958; Alpha Kappa Delta Nat Soc Hon Soc, 1976; consult, Nat Inst Law Enforcement & Criminal Just, 1978-82; bd mem, Citizens Rev Bd Lucas County Juv, Ct, Toledo, OH, 1979-91; consult, Div Soc Law & Econ Sci, NSF, 1980; consult, C Def Fund Task Force Adoption Asst, 1980; bd mem, Inst Child Advocacy Cleveland, OH, 1981-85; chair, Status Women & Minorities Comm N Cent Sociol Soc, 1983-85; chair, Search Comt. **Honors/Awds:** Charles C Irby Distinguished Service Award, Nat Asn Ethnic Studies, 1994. **Special Achievements:** Published hundreds of publications, refereed journal articles, book chapters. **Home Addr:** 1906 Potomac Dr, Toledo, OH 43607, **Home Phone:** (419)536-2503. **Business Addr:** Professor of African American Studies, Director, Eastern Michigan University, 620 Pray Harrold 487-3460, Ypsilanti, MI 48197, **Business Phone:** (734)487-0185.

### PERRY, STEVE

Writer, education reformer. **Educ:** University of Rhode Island, Bachelor's in Political Science; University of Pennsylvania, School of Social Work, Master's; University of Hartford, Ph.D. in Education. **Career:** ConnCAP (Connecticut Collegiate Awareness Program), Founder;

Capital Preparatory Magnet School (Hartford, CT), Founder and Principal, 2004-; CNN, Education Contributor; MSNBC, Education Contributor; "Essence" Magazine, Columnist; TVONE show "Save My Son," Host. **Honors/Awds:** "Hartford Courant," America's Best High Schools list; "U.S. News & World Reports," America's Best High Schools list. **Special Achievements:** Featured in CNN's "Black in America" series; author of "Man Up! Nobody is Coming to Save Us," Renegade Books (2006), "Raggedy Schools: The Untold Truth," Renegade Books (2009), and "Push Has Come to Shove: Getting Our Kids the Education They Deserve--Even If It Means Picking a Fight," Crown (2011).

### PERRY, TIMOTHY D. (TIM PERRY)
Basketball coach, basketball player. **Personal:** Born Jun 4, 1965, Freehold, NJ. **Educ:** Temple Univ, attended 1988; Neumann Univ, lib studies, 2011. **Career:** Basketball player (retired), basketball coach; Phoenix Suns, forward, 1988-92; Philadelphia 76ers, forward, 1992-95; NJ Nets, forward, 1995-96; Ourense, Spain, 1996-97; Pamesa Valencia, Spain, 1997-98; Leon, Spain, 1998-99; TDK Manresa, Spain, 1999-2000; Caceres, Spain, 2000-01; NJ Bullets, Eastern Basketball Alliance, ctr, currently; Holy Family Univ, asst coach, currently. **Business Addr:** Professional Basketball Player, New Jersey Bullets, 4751 Lindle Rd, Harrisburg, PA 17111, **Business Phone:** (717)986-0720.

### PERRY, TYLER (EMMITT PERRY, JR.)
Playwright, actor, theatrical producer. **Personal:** Born Sep 13, 1969, New Orleans, LA; son of Emmitt Sr and Willie Maxine (deceased); married Gelila Bekele; children: 1. **Career:** Plays: I Know Ive Been Changed, 1998; Woman Thou Art Loosed, 1999; I Can Do Bad All By Myself, 2000; Diary of a Mad Black Woman, 2001; Madeas Family Reunion, 2002; Madeas Class Reunion, 2003; Whats Done In the Dark; Film: Diary of a Mad Black Woman, 2005; Madea Goes to Jail, 2006; Why Did I Get Married?, 2007; Daddys Little Girls, 2007; Meet the Browns, 2008; The Family That Preys, 2008; Madea Goes to Jail, 2009; I Can Do Bad All by Myself, 2009; Star Trek, 2009; For Colored Girls Who Have Considered Suicide When the Rainbow Is Enuf, 2010; Madeas Big Happy Family, 2011; Good Deeds, 2011; Madea's Witness Protection, 2012; Alex Cross, 2012; Temptation: Confessions of a Marriage Counselor, 2013; Tyler Perry Presents Peeples, 2013; A Madea Christmas, 2013; The Single Moms Club, 2014; Gone Girl, 2014; Madea's Tough Love, 2015. **Orgs:** Founder, Tyler Perry Found. **Honors/Awds:** Helen Hayes Award for Excellence in Theater, 2001; Black Business Professionals Entrepreneur of the Year, 2004; BET Comedy Award, 2005; Black Reel Award, 2005, 2007, 2008; Quill Award: Best in Humor, 2006; Quill Award: Book of the Year, 2006; BET Tribute Award, 2007; Visionary Award; NAACP Image Award, 2007, 2008, 2009; NAACP Chairmans Award, NAACP Bd Chmn Julian Bond; Black Movie Award; Nickelodeon Kids Choice Award, 2010. **Special Achievements:** Ranked #7 on EW's The 50 Smartest People in Hollywood; Tyler Perry's first novel, Don't Make a Black Woman Take Off Her Earrings: Madea's Uninhibited Commentaries on Love and Life, 2006. **Business Addr:** Director, Actor, Atlanta, GA 30318, **Business Phone:** (800)498-9537.

### PERRY, VICTORIA
Counselor. **Educ:** Nova Southeastern Univ, EdD. **Career:** Bishop State Community Col, Div Stud Develop Serv, counr, 1996-. **Honors/Awds:** Paragon Award, Phi Theta Kappa, 2011; Distinguished Advisor Award, Phi Theta Kappa. **Business Addr:** Counselor, Bishop State Community College, 351 N Broad St, Mobile, AL 36603-5898, **Business Phone:** (251)405-7000.

### PERRY, PROF. WAYNE D., SR.
Association executive, educator. **Personal:** Born Oct 14, 1944, Denton, TX; son of Vada Woods and Vernon; married Linda Jackson; children: LaNitha, Chelese & Wayne Jr. **Educ:** Tuskegee Univ, BS, mech engineering; Univ NMex, MS, mech engineering; Carnegie Mellon Univ, PhD, quant econs & pub policy. **Career:** Ford Motor Co, Mfg Systs, indust engr; Sandia Nat Labs, mech eng, Thermal Sys Design & Anal, proj mgr; Carnegie Mellon Univ, Manpower Studies Proj, instr mgr, res coordr; Heinz Sch Pub Policy & Mgt, instr & res fel; Housing Studies, Defense Manpower & Energy Pol Studies; RAND Corp, sr econ & prog mgr; Pardee-RAND Sch Policy Studies, PhD supvr; Fla Agr & Mech Univ, prof & dir, div mgr sci & MBA prog; Tex Agr & Mech Univ Syst, dean & prof indust eng; Centreville Baptist Church, Ordained Deacon, prof engr; George Mason Univ, prof pub policy & opers res, dir Internships & prof develop, currently. **Orgs:** Am Statis Asn; Inst Opers Res & Mgt Sci; Economet Soc N Am; Am Soc Mech Engr; Omega Psi Phi; Nat Asn Advanc Colored People; UN Com Disarm, Peace & Security; co-founder, Concerned Black Employees Sandia Lab; La Youth Motivat Task Force; dir, Carnegie-Mellon Univ Alum Asn; dir Adminr & staff, Tau Beta Pi; Pi Tau Sigma; Nat Soc Prof Eng. **Honors/Awds:** Best Paper Award, Am Soc Mech Eng; Distinguished Alumni Award, Carnegie Mellon Univ; White House Award, Off Sci & Tech Policy, Model Univ Alliances with Fed Agencies, Nat Labs; Nuclear Weapons Service, US Atomic Energy Com; Best Paper Award Science & Technology Education, Int Acad Bus and Pub Adm Disciplines. **Special Achievements:** Licensed Professional Engineer. P.E. **Home Addr:** PO Box 631, Centreville, VA 20122-0631. **Business Addr:** Professor of Public Policy & Operations Research, George Mason University, Founders Hall 615 3351 Fairfax Dr, Arlington, VA 22201, **Business Phone:** (703)993-2276.

### PERRY, WILMONT DARNELL
Football player, football coach. **Personal:** Born Feb 24, 1975, Franklinton, NC. **Educ:** Livingstone Col, grad. **Career:** Football player (retired), football coach; Nat Football League, New Orleans Saints, running back, 1998-99; Carolina Panthers, running back, 2000; Arena Football League, Cape Fear Wildcats, running back & linebacker, 2002-03; Arena Football League, Columbus Destroyers, running back & linebacker, 2004-05; Louis burg Col, offensive line coach; Fayetteville Guard, 2007-09; Richmond Raiders, 2010; Cape Fear Heroes, 2011-. **Business Addr:** Staff, Cape Fear Heroes, 5701 Cloister Ct, Fayetteville, NC 28314, **Business Phone:** (910)263-8244.

### PERRY-HOLSTON, WALTINA D.
Economist. **Personal:** Born Jan 6, 1959, Augusta, GA; daughter of James W and Mabel Wingfield; married Kevin. **Educ:** Spelman Col, BA, econs, 1980; Ga State Univ, attended 1983. **Career:** Gen Servs Admin, technical support clerk, 1980-82; US Dept Edu, Litigation Unit, legal technician, legal asst, 1982-83; US Dept Labor, economist, 1983-. **Orgs:** Spelman Col Alumni Asn, 1980-; Nat Asn for Female Execs Inc, 1980-; Am Econ Asn. **Honors/Awds:** Savings Bond Canvasser, 1990; Combined Fed Campaign Council for Resource Development, 1991; Performance Management System Award, US Dept Labor, 1992; Women's Executive Leadership Prog 1994-95. **Home Addr:** 3768 Ozmer Ct, Decatur, GA 30034, **Home Phone:** (404)243-7252. **Business Addr:** Economist, US Department of Labor Bureau of Labor Statistics, 100 Ala St SW Suite 6B-90, Atlanta, GA 30303-8750, **Business Phone:** (404)347-7575.

### PERRY-MASON, GAIL F.
Banker. **Personal:** Born Dec 4, 1962, Detroit, MI; daughter of Clarence and Frankie; married Lance W; children: Brandon, Dexter & Scott. **Career:** Wayne County Commun Col, instr; Henry Ford Commun Col, instr; Marygrove Col, instr; Native Detroiter Mag, writer financial sect; Comcast Cablevision, host & exec producer, Womens Issues; Fahnestock & Co, Inc, vpres investments, currently; Oppenheimer & Co, vpres investments, sr dir investments. **Orgs:** Bd dir, Salvation Army; bd adv, Women-Detroit Entrepreneurs Inst; Nat Asn Securities Prof; finance comt, Women's Econ Club; Womens Exec Golf League; bd dir, That's What Friends Are For; Nat Asn Female Exec; Nat Asn Advan Colored People; founders soc, Detroit Inst Arts; Bus Womens Alliances; Blue Monday Network; adv bd, YWCA; Hope United Methodist Church; Blacks Advert Radio & TV; bd dir, Mariners Inn; African Am Women Tour; Spaulding C; dir, mentor, founder, First Money Camp; Wall St J Youth Investment Club; Nat Asn Securities Prof; Bus Women's Alliance; treas, Detroit Compact, bd dir; Detroit 300 Adv Bd; Catherine Ferguson Acad Mentorship Prog, Pershing HS; founder, Money Matters Youth; hon mem, Elliottorian Bus Prof Womens Club. **Honors/Awds:** Community Achievement Award, Gentlemen Wall St; Super Achievers Award, WJLB Radio; Women of Excellence, Oakland Cty Polit Action Comn; Who's Who Professional Bus Womens Award; Phenomenal Business Woman of the Year; Crains 40 Under 40, Gov Mich. **Special Achievements:** Author of articles published in Michigan Chronicle, Ebony, AAA, Black Enterprise, The Detroit News and Free Press, Research Magazine, Oakland Press and Tomorrow Magazine; author of Money Matters for Families, Pearson Publishing, 1999; author of "Girl Make Your Money Grow," Broadway Book, hosted the first Money Camp for Children in Detroit; hosted the first shareholders of Sara Lee Bus trip; Rosa and Raymond Parks Inst, Pathway to Freedom, 1996; Pershing High School, Catherine Ferguson Academy Mentorship Program; MFS Mutual Funds for Women and Investments, spokesperson; Keynote speaker for: Blacks in Govt Natl Conf, African American Women on Tour, Women of Excellence, Wall St Conf, County & Hosp Workers, Natl Assn of Securities Professionals, Natl Assn of Female Exec, Tavis Smiley Youth to Leaders Conf; Detroit's One of the Most Influential Women in the Financial Industry; Hosted the Detroit business exchange & building wealth of comcast cable vision; Hosted radio show building wealth. **Home Addr:** 1176 Buckingham, Grosse Pointe Park, MI 48230, **Home Phone:** (313)885-5786. **Business Addr:** Vice President of Investments, First of Michigan Corp, 131 Kercheval Suite 131, Grosse Pointe Farms, MI 48236, **Business Phone:** (313)259-2600.

### PERRYMAN, ANGELO R.
Executive, business owner. **Personal:** Born Jan 1, 1960; son of Jimmie Lee Sr. **Educ:** Auburn State Col, bus. **Career:** Brown & Root; Perryman Bldg & Construct Serv Inc, pres & chief exec officer, 1998-. **Orgs:** Founder, Bessie I Perryman Construct Educ Scholar; bd mem, Gen Bldg Contractors Asn Inc; dir, Greater Philadelphia Chamber Com. **Honors/Awds:** Ernst & Young Entrepreneur of the Year Award, 2009. **Business Addr:** President, Chief Executive Officer, Perryman Building & Construction Service Inc, 4548 Market St Suite M23, Philadelphia, PA 19139-3610, **Business Phone:** (215)243-4109.

### PERRYMAN, LAVONIA LAUREN
Executive, vice president (organization). **Personal:** Born Detroit, MI. **Educ:** Ferris State Univ, attended 1968; Wayne State Univ, BA, educ, 1971; Howard Univ, polit sci & commun, 1986; Cent Mich Univ, MA, educ, 2009. **Career:** Soc Res Applic Corp, comn dir; owner opr, first girls basketball clin; Pizazzz Corp, pres; Afbony Modeling & Talent Agency, prof model instr; Teai & Rec, pub rel dir; WRadio, report, 1973-76; WTVS-56, black jour reprt; Smith, Sanders & Perryman, vpres; Lavonia Perryman Communications Agency, Exec Dir, 1999-2012; Marygrove Col, Adj prof, 2010-; Lavonia & Friends TV prog, Host, 2010-; Henry Ford Community Col, Adj Prof, 2013-; PR Networks Inc, vpres, currently. **Orgs:** Vpres, Nat Asn Media Women; Nat Asn Advan Colored People; Negro Counc Women; Black Communicators; All Star Basketball Player; Congressman John Conyers Women Org; Stud Non-violents Org; Cong Black Women; cable comnr, DC; founding mem & pres, Nat Black Women's Polit Cong; pres & founding mem, Nat Coalition 100 Black Women DC Chap; co dir, Black Am Saves; cable comnr, DC; founding mem & pres, Nat Black Women's Polit Cong; charter mem, Future PAC. **Home Addr:** 3169 18th St NW, Washington, DC 20010. **Business Addr:** Vice President, PR Networks Inc, 555 Brush St Suite 1115, Detroit, MI 48226, **Business Phone:** (313)962-8822.

### PERRYMAN, ROBERT LEWIS, JR.
Football player, football executive, football coach. **Personal:** Born Oct 16, 1964, Raleigh, NC; married Sonya R; children: Krista & Robert Jr. **Educ:** Univ Mich, BS, sports mgt & commun, 1987. **Career:** Football player (retired), football executive; New Eng Patriots, running back, 1987, fullback, 1988-90; Denver Broncos, running back, 1991-92; United Way Merrimack Valley, Mkt & Labor Rels, vpres, regional coordr, currently; NFL, Jr Player Develop Prog, regional dir, 2005-; Merrimack Col, quaterback coach; Independent Women's Football League Boston Militia, asst coach, offensive coord, currently. **Orgs:** Nat Football League Alumni Asn; Pentuckey Bank Inc; Kiwanis club. **Home Addr:** 61 Mill Pond, North Andover, MA 01845-2902, **Home Phone:** (978)208-7063. **Business Addr:** Offensive Coordinator, Boston Militia, 95 Morse St, Norwood, MA 02062.

### PERSIP, CHARLES LAWRENCE (CHARLI PERSIP)
Educator, drummer. **Personal:** Born Jul 26, 1929, Morristown, NJ; son of Francis Roland and Doris Mary; married Sophia Miller; children: Jean Michelle & Erma Evangeline. **Educ:** Julliard Conserv, attended 1960. **Career:** Jazz Statesmen, co-founder, 1960; Jazzmobile Inc, instr, 1974-; New Sch Univ, jazz instr, 1993-; Queens bor Community Col, adj lectr, assoc prof, 2008-; New Sch Jazz & Contemp Music, instr, currently. **Orgs:** Local 802 Am Fedn Musician, 1954-; Int Asn Jazz Educr, 1993-. **Home Addr:** 1864 Adam C Powell Jr Blvd Suite 52, New York, NY 10026-2842, **Home Phone:** (212)864-1026. **Business Addr:** Instructor, The New School for Jazz & Contemporary Music, 55 W 13 St 5th Fl, New York, NY 10011, **Business Phone:** (212)229-5896.

### PERSON, CHUCK CONNORS
Basketball player, basketball coach. **Personal:** Born Jun 27, 1964, Brantley, AL; married Carmen; children: Millicent, Tiffany, Chuck Jr, Niketta, Raven & Jasmine. **Educ:** Auburn Univ, attended 1986. **Career:** Basketball player (retired), basketball coach; Ind Pacers, forward, 1986-92, spec asst; Minn Timberwolves, 1992-94; San Antonio Spurs, 1994-98; Charlotte Hornets, 1998-99; Seattle Supersonics, forward, 1999-2000; Cleveland Cavaliers, asst coach, 2000-01; Ind Pacers, asst coach, 2005-07; Sacramento Kings, asst coach, 2007-08; Los Angeles Lakers, asst coach, 2009-13; Jeonju KCC Egis, 2013-14; Auburn, asst coach, 2014-. **Business Addr:** Assistant Coach, Auburn University, 251 S Donahue Dr, Auburn, AL 36849, **Business Phone:** (334)844-4512.

### PERSON, DR. DAWN RENEE
College teacher. **Personal:** Born Dec 10, 1956, Sewickley, PA; daughter of Conrad Sr and Fannie Mae Thomas (deceased); married Harold Eugene Hampton; children: Bryson Thomas -Hampton & Amara Renee -Hampton. **Educ:** Slippery Rock Univ, BS, educ, 1977, MEd, 1979; Teachers Col, Columbia Univ, EdD, 1990. **Career:** Slippery Rock Univ, human rels counsr, 1978-79, minority affairs coord, 1979-80, advr black & int stud, 1980-81; Colo St Univ, dir, black stud serv, 1981-85; Lafayette Col, asst dean acad serv, 1985-90; Teachers Col, Columbia Univ, asst prof higher educ, 1990-97; Stud Develop Higher Educ, assoc prof; Calif St Univ, Long Beach, Calif, prof, co-dir, 1997-; Cerritos Col, internal evaluator; Howard Hughes Med Inst, internal evaluator; Calif State Univ, Fullerton, Calif, Educ Leadership Dept, prof, currently. **Orgs:** Workshop facilitator Male/Female Rel, 1978-; ACPA; Nat Asn Advan Colored People Easton PA Chap 1985-87; Black Conf-Higher Educ PA, 1986-87; NASPA; Leadership Lehigh Valley 1989-90; coordr, Community Col; dir, Ctr Res Educ Access & Leadership. **Home Addr:** 6718 El Salvador St, Long Beach, CA 90815, **Home Phone:** (562)598-6283. **Business Addr:** Professor, California State University, College Pk 520, Fullerton, CA 92834-6868, **Business Phone:** (657)278-4023.

### PERSON, LESLIE ROBIN
Executive. **Personal:** Born Nov 14, 1962, St. Louis, MO; married Kyro Jonathan Carter. **Educ:** Nichols State Univ, attended 1980; Kent State Univ, attended 1981; Univ Cincinnati, BA, 1982. **Career:** USAF, 2012 commun squadron atc officer trainee, 1984-85, 1903 commun squadron dep atc opers officer, 1985-86, 2146 commun group dep atc opers officer, 1986-. **Orgs:** Adv Coun 2012 CS Unit, 1984-85; assoc mem, Pima Country Spec Olympics Group, 1985; secy, Davis-Monthan Co Grade Officer GP, 1985-86; founding mem, Davis-Monthan Spec Olympics GP, 1985-86; Santas Blue, 1985-86; base chmn, Combined Fed Campaign, 1985. **Home Addr:** 11991 Hitchcock Dr, Cincinnati, OH 45240, **Home Phone:** (513)825-9151. **Business Addr:** Deputy ATC Operations Officer, United States Air Force, 2146 CG PSC, AE 96366.

### PERSON, ROBERT ALAN
Baseball player. **Personal:** Born Oct 6, 1969, Lowell, MA. **Educ:** Seminole Community Col, Sanford, Fla. **Career:** Baseball player (retired); Cleveland Indians, 1989-91; Chicago White Sox, 1992, 2004-05; Fla Marlins, 1992-94; New York Mets, pitcher, 1994-96; Toronto Blue Jays, 1997-99; Philadelphia Phillies, 1999-2002; Boston Red Sox, 2003.

### PERSON, DR. WAVERLY J.
Geophysicist, executive director. **Personal:** Born May 11, 1926, Blackridge, VA; son of Santee and Bessie Butts; married Sarah Walker. **Educ:** St Paul's Col, Lawrenceville, VA, BS, maths 1949; Am Univ, Wash, DC, 1960; George Washington Univ, Wash, DC, 1963. **Career:** Dept Agr, phys sci technician; Dept Com, seismic monitoring technician, Nat Oceanic & Atmospheric Admin, Boulder, Colo, geophysicist, 1958-73; U.S. Dept Com, technician, 1962-73; US Geol Surv, Denver & Golden, Colo, geophysicist, 1973-94, US Geol Surv, Nat Earthquake Info Ctr, Colo, staff, 1962, dir, 1977-, chief scientist, 2006. **Orgs:** Seismol Soc Am, 1965-, eastern sect treas, 1968-; pres, Flatirons Kiwanis, 1972-; Am Geophys Union, 1975-; bd dir, Boulder Co Crimestoppers, 1986-; mem retention chmn, Rocky Mountain Dist. **Honors/Awds:** Honorary Doctorate, St Paul's Col, 1988; Outstanding Government Communicator, Nat Asn Govt Communicators, 1988; Distinguished Alumni: Citation of the Year Award, Nat Asn Equal Opport Higher Educ, 1989; Meritorious Service Award, US Geol Survey, 1989; Annual Minority Award, Community Servs Dept, Boulder, Colo. **Special Achievements:** First African American chief scientist, 1977; First African American to serve as the director of the US Geological Survey; many publications on earthquakes in science journals & contributed a number of text books in the Earth Sciences. **Home Addr:** 5489 Seneca Pl, Boulder, CO 80303, **Home Phone:** (303)494-0904. **Business Addr:** Director, US Geological Survey National Earthquake Information Center, Mail Stop 967, Denver, CO 80225-0046, **Business Phone:** (303)273-8500.

**PERSON, WESLEY LAVON, SR.**
Basketball coach, basketball player. **Personal:** Born Mar 28, 1971, Crenshaw, AL; married Lillian; children: Wesley Jr, Wesley II, Nykeia & Aleyah. **Educ:** Auburn Univ, attended 1994. **Career:** Basketball player (retired), coach; Phoenix Suns, forward-guard & shooting guard, 1994-97; Cleveland Cavaliers, shooting guard, 1997-2002; Memphis Grizzlies, shooting guard, 2002-03; Portland Trail Blazers, shooting guard, 2003-04; Atlanta Hawks, 2004; Miami Heat, Small forward, 2004-05; Denver Nuggets, forward-guard, 2005; Enterprise-Ozark Community Col, asst women's basketball coach & head men's basketball coach. **Honors/Awds:** NBA All-Rookie Second Team, 1995. **Business Addr:** Enterprise State Community College, 600 Plaza Dr, Enterprise, AL 36330, **Business Phone:** (334)347-2623.

**PERSON, DR. WILLIAM ALFRED**
Educator, association executive. **Personal:** Born Aug 29, 1945, Henderson, NC; married Juanita Dunn; children: William Alfred II & Wilton Antoine. **Educ:** Johnson C Smith Univ, BA, 1967; Univ Ga, MEd, 1973, EdD, 1977. **Career:** Wilkes City Bd Educ, teacher, 1967-72; Univ Ga, grad asst & admin asst, 1973-77; Miss State Univ, asst prof, 1977-80, assoc prof, 1980, prof curric & instr, instr & dir grad studies, currently; Univ Southern Miss, interim dir, assoc dean, 1991-99, Alliance Grad Educ Miss, prin investr, 1999-. **Orgs:** Treas, Phi Delta Kappa, 1982-83; vpres, Phi Beta Sigma, 1982-83; pres, Phi Beta Sigma, 1983-; bd dir, Starkville Kiwanis Breakfast Club, 1984-. **Honors/Awds:** Two Acad Scholar, 1963-65; Sigma Man of the Year, Phi Beta Sigma, 1979. **Business Addr:** Director, Mississippi State University, Rm 116 Allen Hall, Mississippi State, MS 39762, **Business Phone:** (662)325-7400.

**PERSONS, W. RAY**
State government official, educator, lawyer. **Personal:** Born Jul 22, 1953, Talbotton, GA; son of William and Frances Crowell; married Wendy Joy Mottley; children: Conrad Ashley & April Maureen. **Educ:** Armstrong State Univ, BS, 1975; OH State Univ, Moritz Col Law, JD, 1978. **Career:** Armstrong State Col, col prof, 1979-80; Nat Lab Rel Bd, atty, 1980-82; Wells Braun Persons Law Firm, partner, 1982-; Cong Lindsay Thomas, legis coun; Arrington & Hollowell, PC, atty, 1986-95; Ga State Univ Col Law, adj prof litigation, 1989-98; State Ga, spec asst atty gen, 1989-99; Swift Currie McGhee & Hiers, partner, 1995-99; Hinton & Williams, partner, 1999-2001; King & Spalding, partner, 2001-; Publications: "Professionalism in the New Millennium", 2004; "Recent Developments in US Products Liability Law", 2004; "Preparing and Delivering the Defense Closing Argument", 2005; "A Threat to Judicial Independence", 2007; "The Rule of Law", The Atlanta Lawyer, 2008. **Orgs:** Pres, Atlanta Bar Asn, 2007-08; Am Col Trial Lawyers; Int Soc Barristers; Am Bd Trial Advocates; Fedn Defense & Corp Coun; Int Asn Defense & Corp Coun; Int Asn Defense Coun; Defense Res Inst & Trial Lawyers Asn; Am Health Lawyers Asn; State Bar Ga; Am Bar Asn; Ga Defense Lawyers Asn; bd dir, Tommy Nobis Found; Nat Coun, Moritz Col Law, Ohio State Univ; bd dir, Ohio State Univ Found; Litigation Coun Am; Trial Law Inst; Diversity Law Inst. **Honors/Awds:** Regents Scholar, Armstrong State Col, 1973-75; Distinguished Alumnus Award, Armstrong Atlantic State Univ, 2000; Distinguished Alumnus Award, Ohio State Univ, Moritz Col Law, 2005; Distinguished Service Award, Ohio State Univ, 2006; The Best Lawyers in America; America's Leading Lawyers for Business; "Legal Elite", Ga Trend mag; Ranked in Top 10 of Georgia Super Lawyers; State Bar of Georgia Tradition of Excellence Award; 2010 Leadership Award, Atlanta Bar Asn, 2010. **Special Achievements:** Publications includes: A Threat to Judicial Independence, The Atlanta Lawyer, 2007; The Rule of Law, The Atlanta Lawyer, 2008; Numerous Publications. **Home Addr:** 6330 Riverside Dr NW, Atlanta, GA 30328, **Home Phone:** (404)409-0434. **Business Addr:** Partner, Attorney, King & Spalding, 1180 Peachtree St NE Suite 3600, Atlanta, GA 30309-3521, **Business Phone:** (404)572-2494.

**PETERS, AULANA LOUISE**
Lawyer, executive. **Personal:** Born Nov 30, 1941, Shreveport, LA; daughter of Clyde A and Eula Mae; married Bruce Franklin. **Educ:** Notre Dame Sch Girls, dipl, 1959; Col New Rochelle, BA, philos, 1963; Univ Southern Calif, JD, 1973. **Career:** Publimondial Spa, secy & eng corresp, 1963; Fibramianto Spa, secy & eng corresp, 1963-64; Turkish Deleg Org Econ Coop & Develop, eng corresp, 1965; Org Econ Coop & Develop Sci Res Div, admin asst, 1965-67; Cabinet Braconnier AAA Transl Agency, translr & interpreter, 1966; Gibson Dunn & Crutcher, assoc & atty, 1973-80, partner, 1980-84, 1988-2000; US Securities & Exchange Comn, comnr, 1984-88; Minn Mining & Mfg Co, Northrop Grumman & Merrill Lynch & Co Inc, dir, 1992-; Mobil Corp, dir, 1992-; Minn Mining & Mfg Co Callaway Golf Co; Titan II Inc, dir. **Orgs:** Asn Bus Trial Lawyers, 1982; Dir, 3M Co, 1990-; pub oversight bd panel, Am Inst Cert Pub Accts, 2001-02; bd dir, Deere & Co, 2002-; Int Pub Interest Oversight Bd, 2005-; trustee, Mayo Clin Rochester, 2007-; bd dir, Community Tv Southern Calif; US Comptroller Gen's Accountability Adv Panel; Los Angeles Co Bar Asn; State CA Bar Asn; Langston Hughes Asn; Black Women Lawyers Asn; Am Bar Asn; Univ S Calif Law Sch Law Alumni Asn; Coun Foreign Rels Inc NY; bd mem, Pub Interest Oversight Bd. **Honors/Awds:** Washington Achiever Award, Nat Asn Bank Women Inc, 1986; Directors Choice Award, Nat Womens Econ Alliance Found, 1994; Women in Business Award, Hollywood Coc, 1995; One of the 50 Most Influential Women Attorneys in USA, Nat Law Jour. **Special Achievements:** First African American ever to serve as a commissioner of the SEC, and only the third woman ever to do so. **Business Addr:** Board of Director, Deere & Co, 1 John Deere Pl, Moline, IL 61265, **Business Phone:** (309)765-8000.

**PETERS, CHARLES L., JR.**
Executive, real estate developer, president (organization). **Personal:** Born Sep 20, 1935, New Orleans, LA; married Doris Jackson; children: Leslie Jean & Cheryl Lynne. **Educ:** So Univ, BS, 1955; Univ SC, MS, 1959, grad study. **Career:** Exec; Nat Housing Consult Inc, pres, chmn bd, 1973-; NHC Data Serv, pres & chief exec officer; Trinity COT Develop Corp, chief exec officer & exec dir. **Orgs:** Omega Psi Phi; La Urban League; YMCA; Nat Asn Housing & Redev Officials, Omega Life Mem Found. **Home Addr:** 5323 Stillwater Dr, Los Angeles, CA 90008. **Business Addr:** President, National Housing Consult Inc, 4640 Lankershim Blvd Suite 202, North Hollywood, CA 91602, **Business Phone:** (818)506-7976.

**PETERS, DR. FENTON. See Obituaries Section.**

**PETERS, KENNETH DARRYL, SR.**
Government official. **Personal:** Born Jan 27, 1949, Englewood, NJ; son of John C Jr and Lena Jones; married Katie M Coleman; children: Kenneth Jr & Kevin. **Educ:** Fisk Univ, BA, 1971; Univ Kans, MSW, 1973; Univ Calif, cert, 1973; Acad Health Sci Ft Sam Houston, cert, 1981. **Career:** Cath Social Serv, sch consult, 1973-78; State Calif Stockton, psychiat soc worker, 1978-80; Dept Develop Disabilities, Stockton, Calif, placement coordr, 1978-80; State Calif Sacramento, social serv consult, 1980-84, prog analyst, 1984, social serv admin; Calif Dept Transp, dist contracts officer, 1987-95; NIH, grant reviewer, 2002-; Calif Dept Health Serv, health trainer, currently; Ctr DisControl, Atlanta, Ga, part time consult, currently. **Orgs:** Bd dir, Fisk Stud Enterprises, 1968; vpres, Nat Asn Advan Colored People Colegiate Chap Nashville, 1968-69; minority recruitment comnr, Univ Kans, 1971-72; SanJoaquin Ment Health Adv Bd, 1978-88; bd dir, Maternal & Child Health Disability Prev Bd, 1979-86; secy, Alpha Phi Alpha Fraternity Inc, 1980; Nat Conf Social Welfare, 1982-88; Calif Respiratory Exam Bd, 1983-92. **Honors/Awds:** Eligible Bachelor, Ebony Mag, 1975; Commendations: Calif Assemblyman Pat Johnston, 1983; Calif Senator John Garamendi, 1983. **Home Addr:** 2911 Sleepy Hollow Dr, Stockton, CA 95209, **Home Phone:** (209)475-0199. **Business Addr:** Health Consultant, Trainer, California Department of Health Services, MS 7700, Sacramento, CA 95899-7413, **Business Phone:** (916)445-4171.

**PETERS, REV. DR. PAMELA JOAN**
Business owner, president (organization), founder (originator). **Personal:** Born Feb 3, 1947, York, PA; daughter of Maurice E and Ruth V. **Educ:** Tenn State Univ, Nashville, TN, BA, sociol & psychol, 1969; Southern Ill Univ, MS, coun educ, 1975; Walden Univ, PhD, human serv, 1991. **Career:** Pan Am World Airlines, airline stewardess, 1969-70; Del State Col, dir stud activ, 1970-74; Johnson & Johnson Corp, compensation admin, supvr traffic, 1974-76; Xerox Corp, personnel rep, 1976-78; ICI Americas Inc, recruiter, eeo analyst, 1979-84; Univ Del, dir coop educ, 1984-86; Ctr Stress Pain & Wellness Mgt Inc, pres, 1986-; Spirit Life Ministry, founder, 2002-. **Orgs:** Wilmington Women Bus, 1980; Founding mem, chair, prog nomination comts, Brandy wine Prof Assoc, 1981; chairperson, Forum Minority Engrs, 1981-83; bd dir, exec comt, chair personnel comm, YMCA, 1982-84; bd dir, Girl Scouts Am, 1984-86; Civil Rights Comn, 1985-86; Dela Guid Assoc, 1986-87; bd mem, Ment Health Asn, 1988; life mem, Delta Sigma Theta. **Special Achievements:** She is the author of books My Hands, Standing on My Feet, My Heart. **Home Addr:** 315 W 36th St, Wilmington, DE 19802, **Home Phone:** (302)764-4590. **Business Addr:** Founder, President, The Center for Stress, Pain, & Wellness Management Inc, 315 W 36th St, Wilmington, DE 19809, **Business Phone:** (302)654-1840.

**PETERS, ROBERT**
Executive. **Career:** Nextgen Mgt Group Inc, prin, 2000-. **Business Addr:** Principal, Nextgen Management Group Inc, 1887 Otoole Ave Suite C207, San Jose, CA 95131-2219, **Business Phone:** (408)922-2790.

**PETERS, SAMUEL A.**
Lawyer, educator. **Personal:** Born Oct 25, 1934, New York, NY; son of Clyde and Amy Matterson; married Ruby M Mitchell; children: Robert, Samuel Jr & Bernard. **Educ:** NY Univ, BA, 1955; Fordham Univ Sch Law, LLB, 1961. **Career:** Fed Commun Community, law clerk, 1961; US Dept Justice, trial atty, 1961-68; Lawyer's Community Civil Rights Under Law, staff atty, 1968-69; Atlantic Richfield Co, atty, 1970, litigation coun, 1970-73, employ rels coun, 1970-85, labor coun, 1972-79, sr coun pub affairs, 1980-85; Rio Hondo Col, prof law, 1987; mediator, currently. **Orgs:** Nat Bar Asn; Am Bar Asn; Fordham Law Rev Alumni Asn; Calif Musem Afro-Am Hist & Cult; Nat Advan Asn Colored People OC Chap; bd dir, Weingart Ctr Asn; Cent City E Task Force; Alpha Phi Alpha Fraternity, NuTau Lambda Chap; Toastmasters Int Club, 1391; bd dir, Women's Transitional Living Ctr; Langston Bar Asn; Los Angeles County Bar Asn; Toastmasters Int; Alpha Phi Alpha; sec, Nu Tau Lambda. **Home Addr:** 11471 Kensington Rd, Los Alamitos, CA 90720, **Home Phone:** (562)431-3900. **Business Addr:** B100j 3600 Workman Mill Rd, Whittier, CA 90601.

**PETERS, DR. SHEILA RENEE**
Psychologist. **Personal:** Born Jun 27, 1959, Columbus, MS; daughter of Dr James Calvin Sr and Anne Glover. **Educ:** Univ NC Chapel Hill, BA, psychol, 1981; Vanderbilt Univ, MA, clin psychol, 1985, PhD, clin psychol, 1989. **Career:** Luton Community Ment Health Ctr, dept psychol, human develop doctoral cand clin psychol prog, clin therapist; Meharry Med Col, "I Have A Future" teenage pregnancy prev prog, partner, coordr community servs; Greene, Peters & Assoc, clin & consult psychol prog, partner; Fisk Univ, asst prof psychol, 1997, sr prog mgr, Gender-specific Prog Training & Tech asst, Off Juv Justice & Delinq Prev, interim assoc provost, currently, Regist Reinvention Work group, chair, currently, Race Rel Inst, interim dir, currently, Coun Ctr, dir, currently. **Orgs:** Pres, Org Black Grad & Prof Studs, 1982-85, steering comn, 1983; Eco-Psychol Conf, 1982-83; dir, youth ministries Key-Stewart UM Church, 1983-87; treas, Asn Black Psychologists, 1984-85; Div Psychol Women, 1984-87, Div Comn Psychol, 1984-87, Southeastern Psychol Asn, 1986-87, Nashville Alum Chap Delta Sigma Theta, 1986-87; dir, Youth Ministries Ernest Newman UM Church, 1988-91; treas, Nashville Asn Black Psychologist, 1989-; nominations chairperson, Tenn Conf United Methodist Women, 1989; bd mem, Wesley Found, dist trustee, UM Church; pres, Nat Asn Advan Colored People Nashville; chair, Metrop Nashville/Davidson County Human Rels Comn; comnr, Tenn Comn C Youth; bd mem, Tenn affil Am Civil Liberties Union. **Honors/Awds:** Outstanding Young Woman of America, 1981; Peabody Minority Fel Vanderbilt, 1981-84; Crusade Scholar Bd Global Ministries, 1982-85; NIMH Traineeship, 1984-85. **Home Addr:** 4811 Fairmeade Ct, Nashville, TN 37218-1601, **Home Phone:** (615)299-9568. **Business Addr:** Interim Director, Interim Associate Provost, Fisk University, 1000 17th Ave N, Nashville, TN 37208, **Business Phone:** (615)329-8617.

**PETERS, WILLIAM ALFRED**
Executive, manager. **Personal:** Born Mar 1, 1940, Atlantic City, NJ; married Warren Davidson. **Educ:** Temple Univ, BS, 1963; Pace Univ, MBA, 1978. **Career:** Time Inc, dir educ; Emerson Hall Pub, vpres mkt, 1970-72; Harper & Row Pub, ed, 1968-70, mkt & rep, 1976-80; Fortune Mag Time Inc, asst circulation dir, 1978-79, mkt dir; Ft Lauderdale's Gay & Lesbian Community Ctr, exec dir; Rainbow Endowment, co-chair bd dir, currently; Equality Fla, bd dir, currently; Lambda Legal Defense & Educ Fund, develop dir; Greater New York Campaign United Negro Col Fund, mgr, dir; Fortune Circulation Time Inc, nat sales dir; New York's Gay Men African Descent, head; Gay Men African Descent, exec dir, 2000-02. **Honors/Awds:** Black Achievers in Industry Award, Harlem Br YMCA, 1978. **Home Addr:** 6520 NE 21st Ave, Ft. Lauderdale, FL 33308-1034, **Home Phone:** (954)267-8973. **Business Addr:** Co-Chair, Rainbow Endowment, 1501 Cherry St, Philadelphia, PA 19102, **Business Phone:** (215)241-7280.

**PETERSEN, ARTHUR EVERETT, JR.**
Consultant. **Personal:** Born Feb 5, 1949, Baltimore, MD; son of Arthur E Sr and Marguerite. **Educ:** Baltimore City community Col, AA, urban develop, 1971; Morgan State Univ, BS, urban studies, 1973; Clark Atlanta Univ, MBA, transp, 1975. **Career:** Transp Inst NC Agr & Tech State Univ, res assoc, 1975-77; Exec Off Transp & Construct, sr planner, 1977-79; Simpson & Curtin Inc, consult, 1979-80; Lawrence Johnson & Assoc, res assoc, 1980-82; Ctr Transp Studies, Morgan St Univ, proj dir, 1982-83; Pub Tech, proj mgr, 1983-88; Baltimore Minority Bus Develop Ctr, procurement specialist, 1986, Mgt Serv, from dir to exec dir, 1989-93; Assoc Enterprises Inc, consult, 1988-89; David j Burgos & Assoc, Wash, DC, Minority Bus Develop Ctr, sr bus develop specialist, 1994-96; Coun Econ & Bus Opportunity Inc, vpres, bus consult group, 1996-2001; AEP advisors, prin consult, 2001-09; Ezcertify.com LLC, vpres, 2006-07; Capital Region Small bus Develop Ctr, bus counr, 2007-08; BrooAlexa LLC, bus develop officer, 2009-10; Md Dept Pub Safety & Correctional Serv, contract compliance officer & agency procurement specialist, 2010-; Boone, Young & Assoc Inc; John Milligan & Assoc, PC. **Orgs:** Conf Minority Transp Officials Transp Res Bd; Nat Forum Black Pub Admin; Baltimore Mkt Asn. **Home Addr:** 624 E 36th St, Baltimore, MD 21218, **Home Phone:** (410)243-2885. **Business Addr:** Contract Compliance Officer, Agency Procurement Specialist, Maryland Department of Public Safety & Correctional Services, 300 E Joppa Rd Hampton Plz Suite 1000, Towson, MD 21286-3020, **Business Phone:** (410)339-5929.

**PETERSEN, HON. EILEEN RAMONA**
Judge, educator, government official. **Personal:** Born Apr 18, 1937, St. Croix; daughter of Hugo R and Anna Leevy. **Educ:** Hampton Inst, BA, speech ther & eng, 1958, MA, 1959; Howard Univ, JD, 1966; George Washington Univ, MA, advan studies, 1970. **Career:** Judge (retired), educator; Christiansted High Sch, teacher Eng; Cath Univ PR, Exten Prog, instr; US VI, asst atty gen, actg atty gen; Territorial Ct VI, judge. **Orgs:** Am Bar Asn, 1967-; Nat Asn Women Judges; Am Judges Asn; World Assoc Judges World Through Peace Law Ctr; League Womens Voters & Bus & Prof Women's Club; coun mem, VI Coun Boy Scouts Am; bd mem, VI Girl Scouts Am, 1982-85; chmn, VI Casino Control Comn; Int Gaming Regulators; VI Bar Asn; Nat Bar Asn; DC Bar Asn; Am Bar Asn; Nat Asn Women Lawyers; Am Judges Asn & Nat Coun Juv Ct Judges; Oper Sisters United Bd. **Honors/Awds:** Outstanding Woman of the Year, Howard Univ, 1970; Women of the Year, Bus & Prof Women's Club, 1976; William Hastie Award, Nat Bar Asn, 1982; Image Award, Nat Asn US VI Affairs; Thurgood Marshall Award, Nat Bar Asn. **Special Achievements:** First Woman to serve as a Judge in the United States Virgin Islands; First female to be selected to the Virgin Islands Council of Boy Scouts of America. **Business Addr:** Member, Virgin Islands Casino Control Commission, 3005 Orange Grove, Christiansted, VI 00820-3005, **Business Phone:** (340)773-3616.

**PETERSON, REV. DR. ALAN HERBERT**
Association executive, writer. **Personal:** Born Jul 9, 1948, East Orange, NJ; son of William Willis (deceased) and Evelyn Lucretia Hughes (deceased); married Michelle Monica Morrison. **Educ:** Cent Tex Col, criminal invest cert, 1970; La Salle Law Sch, cert, 1971; Essex Co Police Acad, 1972; Bergen Co Police Acad, cert, 1978; Law Enforcement Officers Training Sch, cert, 1979; DDiv, 1985; Nat Inst Study Satanology, Las Vegas, NV, cert, 1990. **Career:** Rutgers Univ Police Dept, police officer, 1971-72; Bewildering array co, found, pres, chief exec officer, 1971; E Orange NJ Aux Police, patrolman, 1972-; Essex Co Sheriffs Dept NJ, spec dep, 1972-75; Mod Carpet Serv NJ, vpres, 1972-75; Conrail Police Dept, police officer & investr, 1975-85; Survival Asn, pres & chief exec officer, 1975-; Masters Philanthropy, chief exec officer, 1982; Suicide Prev Group PA, exec dir, suicidologist, 1985-; ordained minister, 1985; Law Enforcement Spec Agt, Law Enforcement Div, NJ Soc Prev Cruelty Animals, 1988; US Citizens Comn Crime & Narcotics, founder, pres & chief exec officer, 1988; Montgomery Co Constables Off, Precinct 2, ritual crime investr, 1990; US Citizens Comn Crime & Narcotics, nat exec dir, currently. **Orgs:** NJ Narcotic Enforcement Officers Asn NJ, 1976-; Am Criminal Justice Asn, 1979-, Police Benev Asn NJ 304, 1982-; Nat Disabled Law Officers Asn NJ, 1983-; Candle lighters Fnd DC, 1984-; first black sec, 1984, first black pres, 1985; NJ Law Enf Lions Club; Nat Asn Black Achievers, 1990-; Tex Narcotic Officers Asn, 1991-; Tex Ritualistic Crime Info Network, 1991-; nat pres, Nat Police Officers Asn Am, 1991-; Int Narcotic Enforcement Officers Asn; Nat Org Black Law Enforcement Execs. **Home Addr:** 4535 W Sahara Ave Suite 105 126M, Las Vegas, NV 89102. **Business Addr:** National Executive Director, US Citizen's Commission on Crime & Narcotics, PO Box 1092, South Orange, NJ 07079.

**PETERSON, ALPHONSE**
Dentist, educator. **Personal:** Born Sep 9, 1926, St. Louis, MO; son of Alphonse H and Pearl; married Jessie Clark; children: Alphonse Jr, Alan & Alex. **Educ:** Howard Univ, Wash DC, BS, 1948; Meharry Med Col, Sch Dent, Nashville, TN, DDS, 1954; Royal Soc Health, Engl, DDS, 1954; Northwestern Univ Dent Sch, attended 1961; State

Univ Iowa, attended 1963; St Louis Univ, attended 1965; Wash Univ Sch Dent, attended 1969; Univ Nebr Med Ctr, attended 1971; Harvard Univ, attended 1971; Armed Forces Inst Path, attended 1972. **Career:** Dentist (retired); Gen pract dentist, 1957-; Wash Univ Sch Dent Med, St Louis MO, assoc clin prof oral diag & radiol, 1972-84; Homer G Phillips Hosp & Ambulatory Ctr, St Louis MO, asst chief, dept oral surg, dir, cardiopulmonary resuscitation educ, 1973-85; Meharry Med Col, Sch Dent, Nashville TN, assoc prof, adj prof, 1981-; Mo House Representatives, chief clerk; Peterson Dent SVC, dentist, currently. **Orgs:** Sec treas, Guam Dent Soc, 1956-57; pres, fel Am Acad Dent Electrosurgery, 1977; pres, Downtown St Louis Lions Club, 1983; Kappa Alpha Psi Frat; Pleasant Green Missionary Baptist Church; Chi Delta Mu Med-Dent Fraternity; Thirty third Degree Prince Hall Free Masons; Medinah Temple; bd dir, Ferrier Harris Home Aged; bd dir, St Louis Br Opportunities Industrialization Ctr; Kappa Sigma Phi Scholastic Hon Frat; Gamma Chap; Omicron Kappa Upsilon Nat Dent Hon Soc; chairperson, Bloss Memorial Healthcare Dist; fel Royal Socs Health Eng & Am Col Dentist. **Honors/Awds:** Sixty sixth Ann World Dent Cong Fedn Dentaire Internationale, Madrid Spain, 1978; Hall of Fame, Charles Summer High Sch, 1995; Lifetime Achievement, St. Louis Am Found, 2010. **Special Achievements:** Published: "Diagnostic Electrosurgery, To Rule In or Out Malignancy of Oral Tissues," Quintessence International Dental Digest, 1977, & "The Use of Electrosurgery in Reconstructive & Cosmetic Maxillofacial Surgery," Dent Clin North Am, 1982; Author, "Electrosurgical Correction of Maxillary Double Lip", Dent Digest, 1972; Elected Fel, Am Acad Dent Electrosurgery, 1989; Elected Fel, Am CLG Dentists, 1991; Selected to represent the US at the Third Kenyan-Am Dent Seminar, Nairobi, Kenya, 1973; elected Fel, Royal Soc Health, Eng, 1972; lect, The Use of Electrosurgery in Reconstructive Surgery of the Tongue, Lip, Ear & Nose. **Home Addr:** 3001 Norwood Dr W, St Louis, MO 63115-1062, **Home Phone:** (314)383-5872.

**PETERSON, ANTHONY WAYNE.** **See PETERSON, TONY.**

**PETERSON, COLEMAN HOLLIS**
Executive, president (organization). **Personal:** Born Apr 6, 1948, Birmingham, AL; son of George and Doris; married Shirley; children: Rana & Collin. **Educ:** Loyola Univ, BA, 1972, MS, 1977. **Career:** Venture Stores, dist personnel mgr, 1978-79, regional personnel mgr, 1979-82, vpres, Orgn Devel, 1982-84, sr vpres, Human Resources, 1984-94; Wal-Mart Stores Inc, exec vpres, people div, 1994-2004; Hollis Enterprises LLC, pres & chief exec officer, 2004-. **Orgs:** Life mem, Kappa Alpha Psi Fraternity; Sigma Pi Phi Fraternity; Nat Asn Advan Colored People; mem adv Bds, Univ Fl, Fla A&M Univ; fel, Nat Acad Human Resources; bd mem, Northwest Ark Community Col; bd dir, J.B. Hunt Transp Lowell; bd dir, Build-A-Bear Workshop St. Louis, Mo; bd dir, Cracker Barrel Restaurants; bd dir, Nat Acad Human Resources. **Home Addr:** 42 Pinnacle Dr, Rogers, AR 72758. **Business Addr:** President, Chief Executive Officer, Hollis Enterprises LLC, 44 Gull Pt, Hilton Head Island, SC 29928, **Business Phone:** (843)671-7442.

**PETERSON, GERARD M.**
Manager, government official, executive director. **Personal:** Born Sep 10, 1932, Hartford, CT; son of Edythe and Rufus; children: Brian & Bradford. **Educ:** Univ Conn, BA, econs, 1957; cert data processing, 1965. **Career:** Aetna Life & Casualty, Ins Div, admin roles, 1957-69, asst secy, Pub Health Mgt's, dir mkg, 1973, mkg mgr, 1975-83; US Great Soc progs, mgr plans progress, 1965-66; OUR Corp, pres, 1969-72; Nat Alliance Businessmen, exec vpres, 1969-70; Stanford Univ, asst dean grad sch bus, 1970-73; Star Lite Indust, dir, 1970-71; Hartford Civic Ctr, exec dir & chief exec officer, 1983-93; Johnson Controls Inc, proj mgr, 1995-96; GMP Enterprises, gen mgr, currently. **Orgs:** Alpha Phi Alpha; Nat Asn Advan Colored People; Urban League; Int Asn Auditorium Mgrs; chmn, Greater Hartford Red Cross; dir & trustee, Hartford Club; Hartford Hosp; St Francis Hosp; Kaisen Permanente; St Joseph Col; Bay Bank Conn; comm, US Golf Asn; coun mem, Hartford Chamber Com. **Honors/Awds:** Arena & Manager of the Year, Performance Mag Readers Poll, 1986; Facility Manager of the Year. **Home Addr:** 22 Debettencourt Cir, PO Box 1047, Oak Bluffs, MA 02557.

**PETERSON, JUANITA SHELL.** **See SHELL, DR. JUANITA.**

**PETERSON, LLOYD, JR.**
School administrator. **Personal:** Born Jul 20, 1958, San Antonio, TX; son of Lloyd Sr and Dorothy Garrett Phifer; married Debra Gay Culbertson; children: Jaela Culbertson Grayson. **Educ:** Colo State Univ, BA, eng lit, 1980, MS, educ, 1982. **Career:** Colo State Univ, admis counr, 1982-83; Colo Col, admis officer, 1982-88; Yale Univ, sr admis officer, 1988-95; Vassar Col, dir admis, 1995-99; Col Coach LLC, vpres educ, 1999-. **Orgs:** Bd dir, Jolly Jills Civic & Social Club, 1983-; bd dir, Urban League Colo Springs, 1984-; bd dir, Asn Black Admis & Financial Aid Officers, Ivy League & Sister Schs. **Home Addr:** 3843 Glenmeadow Dr, Colorado Springs, CO 80906-5056, **Home Phone:** (719)527-9212. **Business Addr:** Vice President of Education, College Coach LLC, 233 Needham St Suite 200, Newton, MA 02464, **Business Phone:** (617)527-4441.

**PETERSON, PROF. LORNA INGRID**
Librarian. **Personal:** Born Jul 22, 1956, Buffalo, NY; daughter of Raymond George and Sybil Odette Lythcott. **Educ:** Dickinson Col, Carlisle, PA, BA, 1977; Case Western Res Univ, Cleveland, OH, MS libr sci, 1980; Iowa State Univ, PhD, prof studies educ, 1992. **Career:** Wright State Univ, Dayton, OH, humanities ref libr & spec col cataloger, 1980-81; Ohio Univ, Athens, OH, spec col cataloger, 1982-82; Iowa State Univ, Ames, IA, cataloger, 1983-85, bibliog instr, 1985-91; State Univ NY Buffalo, Buffalo, NY, asst prof, 1990, assoc prof, Sch Libr & Info Studies, currently. **Orgs:** Black Caucus Am Libr Asn, 1980, 1988-; bd mem, Ames, ISU YWCA, 1984-89; chair communs comt, Iowa Libr Asn; Asn Col Res Librs, 1984-86; rep Am Libr Asn; RTSD Org & Bylaws, Am Libr Asn, 1984-86; chair mem comt, Iowa Libr Asn; Asn Col Res Librs, 1987-88; African Am Librn Asn Western NY, 1990-; Am Libr Asn; RASD & MOPSS, Catalog comt, 1992-96; Am Libr Asn-Lirt Res comt, 1994-96; Am Libr Asn; Asn Col Res Librs; BIS, Educ Biblio Instr, 1994-96; comt Accreditation, 1997-2001. **Honors/Awds:** OCLC/ALISE Research Award, 2001; Diversity Grant, 2002; Gender Grant, 2002-04. **Home Addr:** 1088 Del Ave Apt 7C, Buffalo, NY 14209-1628, **Home Phone:** (716)886-1973. **Business Addr:** Associate Professor, The State University of New York, 534 Baldy Hall, Buffalo, NY 14260, **Business Phone:** (716)645-1479.

**PETERSON, ROCKY LEE**
Lawyer. **Personal:** Born Apr 29, 1952, New York, NY; son of Natalia Lee; married Paulette Sapp; children: Malik, Danita & Corrie. **Educ:** Cornell Univ, BA, 1974, JD, 1977. **Career:** Cornell Legal Aid Clin, Criminal Div, dir; Admin Off Courts, clerk-civil pract, 1977-78; NJ Div Criminal Justice, dep atty gen, 1978-83; Hill Wallack, partner, sr coun, 1983-; City Trenton, city atty, 1990-98; Mercer County Community Col, coun; Twp Ewing, coun; Trenton Sch Bd, solicitor; Trenton Housing Authority, atty; Trenton Head Start, atty; Lorman Inst, lectr. **Orgs:** Bd trustee, Nat Asn Advan Colored People, 1988-89; trustee, Garden State Bar Asn; YMCA, 1988-89; Granville Acad, 1988-89; NJ Bar Asn Minorities Profession, 1988-; Mercer Cty Bar Asn, 1989-; Disciplinary Rev Bd NJ Supreme Ct, 1991-; US Supreme Ct, 1992; Kappa Alpha Psi, 1993-; State Ct Nj, 1997; chmn, Disciplinary Rev Bd Supreme Ct, Nj, 2001-04; US Ct Appeals Third Circuit. **Honors/Awds:** Service Award, NJ Bar Minorities Profession, 1995; Service Award, Crossroads Theatre Co, 1994. **Home Addr:** 8 Grace Hill Ct, Titusville, NJ 08560-1446, **Home Phone:** (609)818-0662. **Business Addr:** Attorney, Partner, Hill Wallack, 202 Carnegie Ctr, Princeton, NJ 08540, **Business Phone:** (609)734-6311.

**PETERSON, THERESA H.**
Manager. **Personal:** daughter of Vivian and Joe; married Terence; children: Terence Joseph & Taylor Grace. **Educ:** Simmons Col Boston, BA, finance & mgt, 1985; Univ Va Sch Archit, MA, urban & regional planning, 1989. **Career:** Fairfax County Govt, planner, 1989-95; US Sen Wyche Fowler Jr. (D-Ga), sr legis asst, 1991-92; Congressman Don Johnson, Gas 10th Dist, legis dir, 1992; 3M Corp, mgr res & develop funding prog, 1995-2004, sr exec external affairs & technol progs, 2004-; Gen Elec Co., GE Global Res, mgr, dir govt rels, sr exec external affairs & technol prog, 2004-. **Orgs:** Womans Leadership Forum, Partic; Cong Black Caucus Found, Corp Adv Coun; Alpha Kappa Alpha Sorority Inc; NOVA Chap Jack & Jill. **Honors/Awds:** Indiana Expo Women of Vision Award, 2009; The Network Journal: Black Professionals and Small Business Magazine, 25 Influential Black Women in Business, 2010. **Business Addr:** Manager, 3M Corp, 3M Ctr, St Paul, MN 55144-1000, **Business Phone:** (888)364-3577.

**PETERSON, TONY (ANTHONY WAYNE PETERSON)**
Football player, chairperson. **Personal:** Born Jan 23, 1972, Cleveland, OH; married Anita; children: Anthony. **Educ:** Univ Notre Dame, BA, finance & econs, 1994. **Career:** Football player (retired), administrator; San Francisco 49ers, linebacker, 1994-96, 1998-2000; Chicago Bears, 1997; Wash Redskins, 2000; Merrill Lynch, investment advisor, 2000-04; CarMax, purchasing mgr, 2004-, Regional Giving Comt, chairperson, 2011-13. **Business Addr:** Purchasing Manager, CarMax, 12800 Tuckahoe Creek Pkwy, Richmond, VA 23238, **Business Phone:** (804)747-0422.

**PETETT, DR. FREDDYE J. WEBB**
Association executive. **Personal:** Born Dec 27, 1943, Monroe, LA; daughter of Barbara Mansfield; children: Andre. **Educ:** Portland State Univ, BS, bus admin, 1973; Union Inst, Cincinnati, PhD, sociol. **Career:** Portland Community Col, programmer analyst, 1969-70; Portland Model Cities, syst coordr, 1970-71; Nero & Assocs, proj dir, 1971-73; Off Emergency Servs, coordr, 1973-74; Crime & Prev Bur, dir, 1974-76; Mayors Off City Portland, asst to mayor, 1976-79; Portland Urban League, exec dir, 1979-86; State Ore, pub welfare admin, 1987-90; W K Kellogg Found, Battle Creek, assoc prog dir, 1990-92, Kellogg Int Leadership Prog, dir, 1993-98, Found's Mid S Delta Initiative, coordr, 1998-2005; Univ Ark, Clinton Sch Pub Serv, asst prof leadership & philanthropy, Ctr Community Philanthropy, founding dir, emer asst prof, 2007-. **Orgs:** bd dir, bd chair, Housing Auth Portland; Delta Sigma Theta Sorority; World Affairs Coun; bd mem, dir, Fed Home Loan Bank Seattle; Battle Creek Urban League; dir, Kellogg Int Leadership Prog, W K Kellogg Found, coordr; Nat Community Develop Inst. **Honors/Awds:** Woman of Excellence, Delta Sigma Theta Sorority, 1985; Southern Rural Develop Initiative Award. **Special Achievements:** Author: My Life's Journey in Voices of Women Moving Forward with Dignity & Wholeness, 1995. **Home Addr:** 603 W 37th Ave, Pine Bluff, AR 71603-6723, **Home Phone:** (870)536-4138. **Business Addr:** Emeritus Assistant Professor, University of Arkansas, Sturgis Hall 1200 President Clinton Ave, Little Rock, AR 72201, **Business Phone:** (501)683-5200.

**PETRICK, DR. JANE ALLEN**
Psychologist, journalist. **Personal:** Born Apr 12, 1945, Bridgeport, CT; daughter of William A Allen and Jane Briscoe; married John Andrew Banyat; married Jonathan Schiesel; children: Seth Briscoe Schiesel. **Educ:** Barnard Col, BA, econs, 1967; Teacher's Col, Columbia Univ, NY, MA, higher educ & stud personnel admin, 1970; State Univ NY, Albany, NY, MS, educ psychol, 1980; Saybrook Inst, San Francisco, CA, PhD, orgn psychol, 1985. **Career:** Univ Calif, Berkeley, fac; Herbert H Lehman Col, fac; State Univ New York, Albany, fac; Ulster County Community Col, fac; JEA Assocs, Woodstock, NY, pres, 1977-89; Knight-Ridder Inc, Miami, Fla, internal consult, 1989-; Knight-Ridder News Serv, Wash, DC, columnist, 1989-; Miami Herald Publ Co, Miami, Fla, columnist, 1989-; AT&T Wireless Serv, vpres people develop; Capella Univ, Grad Sch Bus, adj prof; Good Catch Publ, proj mgr/ed, currently; Informed Decisions Int, vpres, currently. **Orgs:** Am Psychol Asn, 1978-; Soc Indust Orgn Psychologists, 1980-; bd mem, Villagers flagship S Fla cult & hist preserv socs. **Special Achievements:** Author: Beyond Time Management: Organizing the Organization, Addison-Wesley, 1985; Making the Connection: Getting Work to Work, Informed Decisions Publishing, 1995; One of 100 Best Business Women in America, Ebony Mag. **Business Addr:** Vice President, Organizational Psychologist, Informed Decisions International, 1117 Castile Ave, Coral Gables, FL 33134, **Business Phone:** (800)632-7246.

**PETTAWAY, CHARLES**
Educator, pianist. **Personal:** Born Jun 7, 1949, Philadelphia, PA; son of Charles Henry and Lorraine Thornton; children: Ashley. **Educ:** Philadelphia Mus Acad, BM, 1971; Fontainbleau Acad France, attended 1973; Ravel Acad France, cert, 1974; Temple Univ, MM, 1976. **Career:** Debose artist, 1976; Lincoln Univ, Lincoln, tenured prof music, assoc prof music, interim dept chair, assoc prof piano, visual & performing arts, currently; Musical performances: Tour Switz summer, 1981; Great Hall Moscow Conserv, Russia; Carnegie Hall, NY; Acad Music Philadelphia; Philharmonic Hall, NY; Yacht Club Chicago; Boston Univ; Music Hall Ciboure; Palais de Fontainebleau France; Ctr Col, KY; Windsor Sch, NC; Tanglewood Music Fest Recanti Auditorium TelAviv, Israel; Kennedy Ctr, Wash, DC; Orchestra Hall, Chicago; Settlement Sch Music, concert pianist & teacher; Pa Humanities Coun, commonwealth speaker, 2010-; Walter Damorsch Memorial Music Fel; Baranke Fel; Edward Gerrugus Fel. **Orgs:** Bd mem, Manyunk Coun Arts, 1990-; bd mem, Philadelphia Gospel Sem, 1996; founding mem, Bonalis Piano Trio, 2001. **Honors/Awds:** First Place Winner, Robert Casadesus Int Int Piano Competition, France, 1974; De Bose Artist, Southern Univ, Baton Rouge, LA, 1997; First Prize, Bartok-Kabalevsky Int Piano Competition, Radford, VA, 1998; Douglas Humes and Victor Marianne Music Award. **Special Achievements:** Article published in Society Newsletter (musical publication) "The American Audience" 1984, first commercial recording released "Charles Pettaway Performs Music by Russian Composers" 1985. **Home Addr:** 1531 Coolidge Ave, Abington, PA 19001, **Home Phone:** (215)706-0617. **Business Addr:** Associate Professor, Interim Department Chair, Lincoln University, 111 Ware Ctr 1570 Baltimore Pke, Lincoln, PA 19352, **Business Phone:** (484)365-7419.

**PETTIES, CAROLYN D.**
Executive director, manager. **Educ:** Univ Memphis, BBA, bus admin; HR Cert Inst, cert, sr prof human resources. **Career:** 3 Re.com, dir human resources, 1998-2001; Memphis Area Transit Authority, human resources mgr, 2001-04; Serv Master TruGreen Co, regional human resources mgr, 2004-05; AutoZone, human resources mgr, 2005-07; Regions Financial Corp, vpres, area human resources mgr, 2008-09; Express Scripts, human resources mgr, 2010-13; Petties & Assocs Orthotics-Prosthetics LLC, exec dir, opers & human resources, 2013-; HCA, human resources bus partner, 2015-. **Orgs:** Dir, Mid-S Transp Mgt. **Business Addr:** Executive Director, Petties & Associates Orthotics-Prosthetics LLC, 1089 Eastmoreland Ave, Memphis, TN 38104, **Business Phone:** (901)590-0785.

**PETTIGREW, HON. GRADY L., JR.**
Judge. **Personal:** Born Jun 21, 1943, Forrest City, AR; married Carolyn Landers; children: Dawn Karima & Grady Landers. **Educ:** Ohio State Univ, BA, 1965; Howard Univ Sch Law, attended 1969; Ohio State Univ, JD, 1971. **Career:** Columbus State Hosp, activ therapist, 1965; Huntington Nat Bank Columbus, mgr trainee, 1968; Legal Aid Agency DC, investr law clerk, 1969; Vorys Sater Seymour & Pease, assoc atty, 1971-77; US Bankruptcy Ct, judge, 1977-86; Arter & Hadden, partner; Law Sch Capital Univ & Ohio State Univ Col Law, adj prof law, 1979-85; Pettigrew & Assoc, Partner, 2000-. **Orgs:** Nat Conf Bankruptcy Judges; Law Capital Univ; Ohio State Univ; chmn, Community Develop Comt Ctrl Community House, 1972-75; bd trustee, Ecco Manor, 1973; United Way Franklin City, 1974-75; solicitor, Village Urbancrest OH, 1975-76; Fed Judicial Ctr, Wash, DC; Columbus & Ohio State Bar Asn; Am Bar Asn; corr sec, Robert B Elliott Law Club, 1977-. **Honors/Awds:** Nat Moot Ct Championship Young Lawyers Comt, NY Bar Asn, 1971; Outstanding Young Men Am Chicago, 1972. **Special Achievements:** Author of two books; Speaker to National Conference of Bankruptcy Judges, the National Association of Chapter 13 Trustee's, the Credit Union Executive Society, the Ohio CLE Institute, the Columbus Bar Association CLE Institute. **Business Addr:** Partner, Pettigrew And Associate LLC, 115 W Main St Suite 400, Columbus, OH 43215-5099, **Business Phone:** (614)224-1113.

**PETTIGREW, DR. L. EUDORA**
President (organization), school administrator, educator. **Personal:** Born Mar 1, 1928, Hopkinsville, KY; daughter of Warren C and Corrye L Newell; children: Peter W Woodard. **Educ:** WVa State Col, BMus, 1950; Southern Ill Univ, MA, couns, 1964, PhD, educ psychol, 1966. **Career:** Educator (retired); Southern Ill Univ, instr, 1964-66; Univ Bridgeport, assoc prof, 1966-70; Mich State Univ, prof, chair, 1970-80; Univ Del, assoc provost, 1981-86; State Univ NY Col, Old Westbury, pres, 1986-98. pres emeritus, 1998-. **Orgs:** Long Island Reg Adv Coun Higher Educ, 1986-, chair, 1988-91; Long Island Forum Technol, 1987-; Am Asn State Col & Univs, 1991-94; N Am Coun IAUP, exec bd, 1992-; adv com, Economists Allied Arms Reduction, 1996; Int Asn Univ Pres (IAUP/UN), chair, Comm Disarmament Educ, Conflict Resolution & Peace, 1996-; Comm Univ Peace, Costa Rica, 1997; bd, Univ Pretoria Fund, S Africa, 1997; vice chair, Comt Int Educ; UNESCO's Peace Programme; chair, State Univ New York at Old Westbury. **Business Addr:** President Emeritus, State University of New York, 223 Store Hill Rd, Old Westbury, NY 11568, **Business Phone:** (516)876-3000.

**PETTIS, BRIDGET (BRIDGE PETTIS)**
Basketball player. **Personal:** Born Jan 1, 1971, East Chicago, IN. **Educ:** Cent Ariz Col, attended 1991; Univ Fla, BS, 1993. **Career:** Basketball player (retired, basketball coach; Fenerbache, guard, 1993-95; Anatalya Koleji, Turkey, 1995-96; Faenza, Italy, 1996-97; Phoenix Mercury, 1997-2001; Ind Fever, guard, 2002-03; Phoenix Mercury, asst coach, 2006-09; Women's Nat Basketball Asn, coach, 2007-09; Phoenix dir 2010-11; Los Angeles Sparks, asst coach, 2013-; Tulsa Shock, asst coach, 2014-. **Business Addr:** Assistant Coach, Phoenix Mercury, 201 E Jefferson St, Phoenix, AZ 85004, **Business Phone:** (602)379-7900.

### PETTIS, GARY GEORGE
Baseball player, athletic coach. **Personal:** Born Apr 3, 1958, Oakland, CA; married Peggy; children: Paige, Shaye, Kyler & Dante. **Educ:** Laney Jr Col. **Career:** Baseball player (retired), baseball coach; Calif Angels, 1982-87, Detroit Tigers, 1988-89, 1992; Tex Rangers, 1990-91, coach, 2006-; San Diego Padres, 1992; Oakland Athletics, 1993; Chicago White Sox, coach, 2001-02; New York Mets, coach, 2003-04; Nashville Sounds, hitting coach, 2005-06. **Home Addr:** 1802 Vista Marea, San Clemente, CA 92673-3658. **Business Addr:** Baseball Coach, Texas Rangers, Globe Life Pk Arlington 1000 Ballpark Way Suite 400, Arlington, TX 76011, **Business Phone:** (817)273-5222.

### PETTIS, DR. JOYCE OWENS
Educator. **Personal:** Born Mar 14, 1946, Columbia, NC; daughter of Howard and Victoria Hill; married Bobby Dennis; children: Darryl; married Enoch Charles Temple. **Educ:** Winston Salem State Univ, BA, 1968; E Carolina Univ, MA, 1974; Univ NC Chapel Hill, PhD, 1983. **Career:** NC Pub Schs, teacher, 1968-71; Pitt Tech Inst, teacher, 1972-74; Carolina Univ, asst prof Eng, 1974-85; NC State Univ, asst prof eng, prof eng, prof emer, 2006-. **Orgs:** Alpha Kappa Alpha; Popular Cult Asn; Col Lang Asn; NC Hist Summer Inst, 1984; minority presence fel Univ NC, 1978-80; Summer Inst Inc New Scholar Women, 1984; ed bd, NC Lit Rev. **Honors/Awds:** UNC Board of Gov Doctoral Award, Univ NC, 1981; National Humanities Faculty Member Award, 1984; Scholar Award, Col Lang Asn. **Special Achievements:** Author: Toward Wholeness in Paule Marshall's Fiction, 1995; Publications: Reading Ann Petry's The Narrows into Black Literary Tradition, Univ Tenn Press, 1997; The Marrow of Tradition: Charles Chesnutt's Novel of the South, She Sung Back in Return; Editor: Obsidian II: Black Literature in Review. **Home Addr:** 2104 Pendleton St, Greenville, NC 27834, **Home Phone:** (919)872-5224. **Business Addr:** Professor Emeritus, North Carolina State University, Rm 221 246 Tompkins Hall, Raleigh, NC 27695-8105, **Business Phone:** (919)515-3866.

### PETTWAY, JO CELESTE
Judge. **Personal:** Born Mar 18, 1952, Consul, AL; daughter of Joseph and Menda G. **Educ:** Auburn Univ, BA, 1973; Univ Ala, BSW, 1976, MSW, 1978, JD, 1982. **Career:** C's Aid Soc, social worker, 1975-77; Jefferson Co Dept Pensions & Security, social worker, 1977; Miles Col, instr social work, 1978-79; Legal Serv Corp Ala, clerk, 1980; Eng & Bivens PC, assoc, 1982-84; Jo Celeste Pettway Atty Law, solo practr, 1984; Wilcox County, dist judge, 1984-, chair currently. **Orgs:** Nat Bar Asn; Am Bar Asn; Nat Asn Women Judges; Nat Asn Juv & Family Ct Judges; Ala Lawyers Asn; pres, Zeta Eta Omega Chap Alpha Kappa Alpha Sor Inc; bd dir, Health Improv Proj; Nat Coun Negro Women; Basileus Zeta Eta Omega Chap Alpha Kappa Alpha Sor Inc. **Honors/Awds:** Outstanding Achievement Award, BLSA Univ Ala; Outstanding Alumni, Black Law Students Asn, Univ Ala, 1987; Humanitarian Award Concordia Col, 1988; Soror of the Year, South Eastern Region, 1989. **Home Addr:** PO Box 87, Alberta, AL 36720, **Home Phone:** (205)573-2728. **Business Addr:** District Judge, State of Alabama District Court Wilcox County, 12 Water St Rm 302, Camden, AL 36726-0549, **Business Phone:** (334)682-4619.

### PETTY, BOB
Journalist, television news anchorperson. **Personal:** Born Nov 26, 1940, Memphis, TN; married Cora; children: Bobby & Cory. **Educ:** Ariz State Univ, BS, 1970; Gov State Univ, MS, commun, 1979. **Career:** KAET TV, Tempe, Ariz, news cameraman, soundman, film ed & lighting dir, 1968; KPHO TV News, 1969; KOOL TV News, writer, reporter & producer, 1969-71; Univ Chicago, urban jour fel prog, 1970, William Benton fel prog, 1986; ABC 7 Chicago, weekend anchor, gen assignment reporter & host, 1971-02, Action 7, reporter, 1975-77, "Weekend Edition", producer & host, 1978-83. **Orgs:** Mem fundraising comn, Hyde Park YMCA; Provident St Mel Cath HS only black cath HS Chicagos Westside. **Honors/Awds:** William Benton Fellow in broadcast journalism, 1987. **Special Achievements:** One of several black broadcasters honors by Club Date Magazine of Chicago, 1974.

### PETTY, JERVIE SCOTT, SR.
Educator. **Personal:** Born Jan 28, 1947, Andrews, SC; daughter of Leroy Scott and Carrie Scott; married John Anthony; children: Donoval Anthony, William Scott & Lynnette Maria. **Educ:** NC A&T State Univ, BS, social studies, 1970; Bowie State Univ, MA, admin & supv, 1981. **Career:** Henry E Lackey High Sch, fac, 1971-87, admin, 1998, prin, currently; Thomas Stone High Sch, Waldorf, Md, vice prin, 1987-94; Somers Mid Sch, LaPlata, Md, prin, 1994-98. **Orgs:** Charter pres, Delta Sigma Theta Sorority, Ft Wash Alumnae Chap, 1990-94; pres, Metrop Prince George's Chap, Nat Polit Cong Black Women; Nat Asn Sec Sch Prin; Md Asn Sec Sch Prin. **Home Addr:** 114 Cross Foxes Dr, Ft. Washington, MD 20744-5565, **Home Phone:** (301)686-0148. **Business Addr:** Principal, Henry E Lackey High Sch, 3000 Chicamuxen Rd, Indian Head, MD 20646, **Business Phone:** (301)743-5431.

### PETTY, OSCAR, JR.
Educator, musician. **Personal:** Born Apr 5, 1960, Newark, NJ; son of Oscar Sr and Bessie. **Educ:** Montclair State Univ, BA, music, 1984; Rutgers Univ, MA, music, oboe, 1993. **Career:** Orange Pub Schs, music educr, woodwinds, 1985-89; Orchestra St. Peter by Sea, prin oboe, 1986-92; Roselle Pub Schs, music educr, band, 1990-94; Arts High Sch, Newark, fac, 1994-; Rome Festival Orchestra, prin solo oboe; Virtuosi de Camera, prin solo oboe; Harlem Festival Orchestra, prin solo oboe; Bergen Philharmonic, prin solo oboe. **Orgs:** Amer Fed Musicians, 1987-; Int Double Reed Soc, 1997-; Day Nursery Mountclair NJ Bd, 1999; Arts High Sch, Whole Sch Reform Comt, 1996-99; mem coaching staff young artist, Star Ledger Scholar prog at NJ Performing Arts Ctr Newark NJ. **Home Addr:** PO Box 175, Montclair, NJ 07042, **Home Phone:** (201)349-3176. **Business Addr:** Teacher of Woodwinds/Music Theory, Arts High School, 550 Dr Martin Luther King Blvd, Newark, NJ 07102, **Business Phone:** (973)733-7102.

### PETTY, DR. RACHEL MONTEITH
Psychologist, educator. **Personal:** Born Jun 21, 1943, Columbia, SC; daughter of Frank H Sr (deceased) and Susie E; married LaSalle Petty Jr; children: Adrienne & Erin. **Educ:** Howard Univ, BS, psychol, 1964, MS, psychol, 1968; Univ Md, PhD, human develop & psychol, 1980. **Career:** Howard Univ, lectr, 1968-71; Prince Geo Pub Sch, sch psychol, 1968-72; DC Pub Sch, sch psychol, 1967-68; St Ann's Infant Home Hyattsville, Md, consult psychiat, 1974-; Univ DC, campus rep, chairperson & asst prof psychol, dean, Col Arts & Sci, 1998-2012, asst dean & actg provost & vpres acad affairs, currently, chief operating officer, 2012-13. **Orgs:** Asn Black Psychol; AAAS; Md Asn Sch Psychol; Black Child; consult, DC Dept Human Serv, 1987-88; bd mem, Lutheran Soc Serv Nat Capital Area, 1989-. **Honors/Awds:** Paul Phillips Cooke Lifetime Achievement Award. **Home Addr:** 2124 Sudbury Pl NW, Washington, DC 20012-2225, **Home Phone:** (202)545-1785. **Business Addr:** Acting Provost & Vice President for Academic Affairs, Chief Operating Officer, University of the District of Columbia, Rm 405 Bldg 41, Washington, DC 20008, **Business Phone:** (202)274-5707.

### PETTY-EDWARDS, LULA EVELYN
School administrator. **Personal:** Born Mar 10, 1945, Cedar Bluff, MS; daughter of William Jr and Omy A Deans; married Ozzie L; children: Brett Tirrell, Daryl Westfield & Omy Lela. **Educ:** Mary Holmes Col, assoc degree, 1965; Knoxville Col, BD, 1968; Ill State Univ, MD, 1973; Northeastern Univ, EdD, 2014. **Career:** Univ Mich, lectr, 1974-78; Mary Holmes Col, fac, Dir Reading Ctr, dir, Alumni, 1980-81; Univ Louisville, part-time fac, 1982-85; Imani Inst, pvt elem sch Roxbury, Mass, co-found; N eastern Univ, coord, reading, writing, study skills, 1985-93, asst dir, acad & cult prog, 1989-93, assoc dean, dir, spec asst to dean, adminr, currently. **Orgs:** Nat Coun Teachers Eng; Nat Asn Stud Personnel Adminrs; Black Educator's Alliance MA; Nat Polit Congress Black Women Inc. **Business Addr:** Associate Dean, Director & Administrator, Northeastern University, 360 Huntington Ave, Boston, MA 02115, **Business Phone:** (617)373-3143.

### PEYTON, REV. JASPER E.
Administrator, clergy. **Personal:** Born Dec 30, 1926, Richmond, VA; children: Rose La Verne Abernathy. **Educ:** Univ Philippines, bus admin, attended 1946; City Col NY, 1952; Wagner Col, Staten Island, New York, labor studies; Rutgers Univ, jour. **Career:** Retired; Local 66 Int Ladies Garment Workers, trade unionists, shop steward, 1952-64; ILGWU, coordr, educ dept, 1963-82; Civil Rights Comm Dir Educ, exec bd mem dir, 1965-69, asst dir educ; Fordham Univ, Black Studies Dept, adj prof. **Orgs:** Coun Chs Brooklyn Div; assoc minister Bethany Bapt Ch; bd dir, CLICK-COM Labor Indust Corp Kings Brooklyn Navy Yard; bd mem, founder, Fulton Art Fair; interim pastor, Bethany Bapt Ch; pres, Cong Christian Educ Ny Progressive Nat Baptist Conv; chaplain, Ny Supreme Ct Officers Asn; pres sr choir, Pres Presidents Coun; Pres Va Club; chmn bd, Deacons; pastor, Hist Bethany Baptist Church. **Honors/Awds:** Award, Pub Rel Dir Bethany Bapt Ch; DHL, Eastern Theol Sem. **Home Addr:** 76 Kingston Ave, Brooklyn, NY 11213, **Home Phone:** (518)256-0237. **Business Addr:** Interim Pastor, Bethany Baptist Church, 460 Marcus Garvey Blvd, Brooklyn, NY 11216, **Business Phone:** (718)455-8400.

### PHARRIS, CHRYSTEE
Actor, singer. **Personal:** Born Mar 7, 1976, Middletown, OH; married Tron Larkins. **Educ:** Emerson Col, Boston, BFA, 1998, MA, theater. **Career:** Films: Understanding Me; Guilty or Not, 1999; Let's Be Real, 2000; Leprechaun in the Hood, 2000; Buds for Life, 2004; Why; Faded; Paved with Good Intentions, 2006; Steppin; Only in Your Dreams, 2006; Lord Help Us, 2007; My girl friend's back; Steppin: The Movie, 2009.Theater: In Search of O; George Washingtons boy; Jitney; Body Language; Whatever happened; If you Don't Believe; Uncle Herbert; Last man out; Oasis; Fame; Our Countrys Good; For Colored Girls; Dream Girls; TV Series: WB, "The Steve Harvey Show", 1998; WB, "Sister Sister", 1998; UPN, "Moesha", 1998; NPN, "Grown Ups", 2000; WB, "7th Heaven", 2000; ABC, "General Hosp", 2000; Internet Romance.Net; Passions; Spyder Web; "Eve", 2004; "Scrubs", 2005; Haley's Comet; "Cuts", 2005; "Teachers", 2006; "Passions", 2006; "All of Us", 2006; "Lincoln Heights", 2007. **Orgs:** Faithful Cent Bible Church; Save Our Youth. **Business Addr:** Actress, Coast to Coast Talent Group, 3350 Barham Blvd, Los Angeles, CA 90068, **Business Phone:** (323)845-9200.

### PHELPS, CONSTANCE KAY
School administrator, educator. **Personal:** Born Sep 16, 1940, Topeka, KS; daughter of Lucille Mallory and C Kermit. **Educ:** St Mary's Col, BA, 1962; Wash Univ, St Louis, AM, 1970, PhD, 1977; Ctr Concern, Wash, DC, 1986; Bryn Mawr, 1991. **Career:** Denver Parochial Sch Syst, teacher, 1962-68; St Mary Col, prof sociol, 1970-; Long Range Planning proj, proj mgr, 1977-78, dean students, 1986-95, vpres stud life, 1995, interim pres, 1997; Harvard MIT, res asst, 1970; Comn Crisis Intervention Ctr, res asst, 1974-75; HEW, grant reviewer, 1979. **Orgs:** Dir, Sisters Charity Leavenworth, 1959-; Am Soc Assoc, 1969-; campus coordr, small col consortium, Washington, DC, 1977-80; consult, Nat Consult Network, 1977-; assoc mem, Danforth Asn, 1980; asst doc, Ghana Mission UN, 1981; coordr, Social Justice Network Sisters Charity Leavenworth, 1985; bd dir, Leavenworth City-County Alcohol & Drug Abuse Coun, 1985; Civilian Based Defense, 1986; bd dir, St Vincent Clin, 1988-94; Cath Social Serv, 1988-93; consult & evaluator, N Cent Asn Cols & Schs, 1988-; Nat Asn Stud Personnel Admin; chair, Leavenworth County Human Rels Comn, 1990-; bd dir, Providence & St John Hosp, 1997-; bd dir, Leavenworth Cath Schs, 1997-; bd trustees, Carroll Col, currently; bd mem, St Francis Health Ctr, currently. **Honors/Awds:** Nat Delta Epsilon Sigma Acad Honor Soc, 1970-; fel, Hamline Univ, 1973; fel, Wash Univ, 1973-75; Fulbright Hays fel, Ghana, W Africa, 1975-76. **Home Addr:** 4200 4th St, Leavenworth, KS 66048-5054, **Home Phone:** (913)682-7500. **Business Addr:** Vice Chairman of the Board, Carroll College, 1601 N Benton Ave, Helena, MT 59625, **Business Phone:** (406)447-4300.

### PHIFER, B. JANELLE BUTLER (B JANELLE BUTLER)
Lawyer, association executive. **Personal:** Born Jul 26, 1949, Springfield, MA; daughter of Hampton J and Beatrice A Williams; married Jesse III; children: 2. **Educ:** Howard Univ Sch Bus, BA, 1971; Howard Univ Sch Law, JD, 1975. **Career:** State Ohio, asst atty gen, 1975-78; Toledo Legal Aid Soc, exec dir, 1978-; Toledo Legal Aid Soc, staff atty, 1990-2000; Legal Aid Western Ohio Inc, staff atty, 2001-. **Orgs:** Ohio State Bar, 1975; Toledo Bar Asn; pres, Thurgood Marshall Law Asn; Toledo Chap, Links Inc; Delta Sigma Theta Sorority, Toledo Alumnae Chap; pres, Jack & Jill Inc, Toledo Chap; co-leader, troop, 1077, Maumee Valley Girl Scout Coun; St Paul Baptist Church; vol, Ohio Legal Assist Found. **Honors/Awds:** Outstanding Young Women of America; Delta Sigma Theta Sor Toledo Alumnal Chap; Outstanding Professional Development, Toledo Legal Aid, 1982, 1992; Woman of the Year in Law, Model Neighborhood Develop Asn, 1983; Certificate of Appreciation, Supreme Court Ohio Continuing Legal Educ Comn, 1989, 1990; ProBono Pub-Toledo Bar Asn, 1990; LSNO Appeciation Award; LAWO 25 and 30 year service awards; graduating mother certitification, Jack & Jill of America, Inc. **Special Achievements:** State v. Dorf, Court of Appeals of Ohio, Sixth District, Wood County, June 30, 1993 Not Reported in N.E.2d 1993 WL 241732 92-WD-059; Poskarbiewicz v. Poskarbiewicz, 152 Ohio App.3d 307, 2003-Ohio-1626. **Home Addr:** 1323 Upton Ave, Toledo, OH 43607, **Home Phone:** (419)724-0030. **Business Addr:** Staff Attorney, Legal Aid of Western Ohio Inc, 525 Jefferson Ave Suite 400, Toledo, OH 43604-1094, **Business Phone:** (419)724-0030.

### PHIFER, MEKHI THIRA
Actor, rap musician, movie director. **Personal:** Born Dec 29, 1974, Harlem, NY; son of Rhoda; married Malinda Williams, Jan 1, 1999?, (divorced 2003); children: Omikaye; married Onanong Souratha, May 9, 2007; children: Mekhi Thira Jr; married Reshelet Barnes, Mar 30, 2013. **Career:** Films: Clockers, 1995; Sureshot, 1996; Girl 6, 1996; High School High, 1996; Hav Plenty, 1997; Soul Food, 1997; Hell's Kitchen, 1998; I Still Know What You Did Last Summer, 1998; Lover Man, 1998; An Invited Guest, 2000; Shaft, 2000; Head Games, 2001; O, 2001; The Other Brother, 2002; Imposter, 2001; Paid in Full, 2002; 8 Mile, 2002; Honey, 2003; Dawn of the Dead, 2004; Slow Burn, 2005; Easier, Softer Way, 2006; Puff, Puff, Pass, producer & dir, 2006; A day in the Life, 2007; This Christmas, exec producer, 2007; A Talent for Trouble, 2008; Nora's Hair Salon II, actor & producer, 2008; Flypaper, 2011; The Love Section, 2013; The Suspect, actor & exec producer, 2013; Divergent, 2014. TV series: "Homicide", 1993; "New York Undercover", 1995-96; "Models Inc", 1995; "The Tuskegee Airmen", 1995; "Homicide: Life on the Street", 1996-98; SUBWAY Stories: Tales from the Underground, 1997; "A Lesson Before Dying", 1999; "Uninvited Guest", 1999; "Carmen: A Hip Hopera", 2001; "Brian's Song", 2001; "ER", 2002-08; "Curb Your Enthusiasm", 2005; "Lie to Me", 2009-10; "Torchwood", 2011; "Psych", 2012; "White Collar", 2012; "Husbands", 2012; "House of Lies", 2014; "A Day Late and a Dollar Short", 2014. Album: New York Related: The HF Project, 1999. **Orgs:** Screen Actors Guild, 1995-. **Honors/Awds:** Black Reel Award, 2000; Rising Star Award, 2002; Image Award, Nat Asn Advan Colored People, 2004 & 2005; Icon Award, 2009. **Business Addr:** Actor, William Morris Agency, 1 William Morris Pl, Beverly Hills, CA 90212, **Business Phone:** (310)859-4000.

### PHIFER, ROMAN ZUBINSKY
Football player, football coach. **Personal:** Born Mar 5, 1968, Plattsburgh, NY; married Alexis Eggleston; children: Jordan; married Linda; children: Michael Jordan, Angelo & Milan. **Educ:** Univ Calif, Los Angeles, grad, 1991. **Career:** Football player (retired), football coach; Los Angeles Rams, right linebacker, 1991-94; St Louis Rams, right linebacker, 1995-98; New York Jets, right outside linebacker, 1999-2000, linebacker, 2000; New Eng Patriots, linebacker, 2001-03, defensive end, 2001, right inside linebacker, 2004; New York Giants, 2005; Denver Broncos, asst linebackers coach, 2009-11; Nat Amateur Sports, partner & dir bus develop, 2011-. **Honors/Awds:** Rookie of the Year, 1991; Ed Block Courage Award, 1994; Super Bowl Champion (XXXVI, XXXVIII, XXXIX); Pro Bowl Alternate, 1995, 1996, 2002, 2003. **Special Achievements:** Produced his first documentary film entitled Blood Equity, 2009. TV Series: "Super Bowl XXXIX", 2005; "Sporting Grace", 2006. **Business Addr:** Partner, Director of Business Development, National Amateur Sports, 7421 Carmel Exec Pk Suite 330, Charlotte, NC 28226, **Business Phone:** (704)341-4645.

### PHILANDER, DR. S. GEORGE H
Scientist, educator, association executive. **Personal:** Born Jul 25, 1942, Calendon; son of Peter J and Alice E; married Hilda Storari; children: Rodrigo. **Educ:** Univ Cape Town, BS, 1962; Harvard Univ, PhD, 1970. **Career:** Mass Inst Tech, res assoc, 1970-71; Princeton Univ, res assoc, 1971-78; NOAA, Dept Com, sr res oceanogr, 1978-89; Mus Nat d'Histoire Naturelle, vis prof, 1982; Princeton Univ, full prof, Dept Geol & Geophys Scis, 1990-, Atmospheric & Oceanic Scis Prog dir, 1990-2006, Dept Geol & Geophys Scis, chmn, 1994-2001; Calif Inst Technol, Gordon Moore Scholar, 2002; Knox Taylor prof geo sci, 2005-; ACCESS, res dir, 2007; Univ Cape Town, res prof, 2007-. **Orgs:** Consult, World Meteorol Org, 1973-; Nat Acad Scis Gate Comn, 1977-79; chmn, EPOCS Steering Comn, 1978-85; lectr with rank prof, geol & geophys scis, Princeton Univ, 1980-; SEQUAL Steering Comn, 1981-87; chmn, CCCO Atlantic Panel, 1981-; Mass Inst Tech Vis Comt; Nat Acad Scis TOGA Panel, 1985-; Dynamics Atmospheres & Oceans; Geofisica Int; Oceanographie Tropicale; Univ Consortium Atmospheric Res, bd mem, 1991-; elected mem, Am Acad Arts & Scis, 2003; fel Am Acad, 2003; coucil Int Ctr Theoret Physics; Sci & Arts Franklin Inst Comt, Philadelphia; Massachusetts Inst Technol Vis Comt; trustee, Univ Corp Atmospheric Res; Dept Geosciences, Tulane univ, Copenhagen univ, Columbia univ, Tex A&M univ. **Honors/Awds:** NOAA Environ Res Labs, 1979; Distinguished Authorship Award, 1979; NOAA Environ Res Labs, 1983; Distinguished Authorship Award, 1983; Awarded Sverdrup Gold Medal by Am Meteorol Soc, 1985; Dept Com, 'Gold Medal', 1985; Elected 'Fel Am Meteorol Soc', 1985. **Special Achievements:** Numerous articles in oceanographic research journal; contributor, "The Sea", 1977; El Nino, La Nina & The Southern Oscillations, Acad Press, 1989; Author, Is The Temperature Rising? The Uncertain Science of Global Warming, Princeton Univ Press, 1998; Sextant to Satellite; the Education of a Land-based Oceanographer Chapter in History of Physical Oceanography Developments since 1960, Springer/New York, 2006. **Home Addr:** 81 Woodside Lane, Princeton, NJ 08540-5417. **Business Addr:** Knox Taylor Professor, Director, Atmospheric & Oceanic Science Program, Princeton University, M46 Guyot Hall, Princeton, NJ 08544, **Business Phone:** (609)258-5683.

**PHILLIP, DR. MICHAEL JOHN**
Educator. **Personal:** Born May 27, 1929, Port-of-Spain; married Germaine J; children: Roger & Brian. **Educ:** Univ Toronto, BS, 1960, MS, 1962; Mich State Univ, PhD, 1964. **Career:** John Carroll Univ, Cleveland, assoc prof biol, 1969-72; Univ Detroit, prof microbiol, 1977-, dir genetics, 1982; Univ Fla, dean grad minority prog; Univ Northern Colo, minority affairs, vpres. **Orgs:** Vice chmn & bd dirs, Alexandrine House Detroit, 1979-; bd trustees, St Mary's Hosp, 1983-. **Honors/Awds:** Outstanding Foreign Student, Mich State Univ, 1963; Distinguished Faculty Award, Univ Detroit Black Alumni, 1983. **Home Addr:** 4401 NW 19th Ave, Gainesville, FL 32605-3474, **Home Phone:** (352)378-3113.

**PHILLIPS, REV. ACEN L.**
Clergy, executive, chief executive officer. **Personal:** Born May 10, 1935, Hillhouse, MS; married E La Quilla Gaiter; children: Acen Jr, Gregory, Delford, Vicky Lynn, Aaron La Bracc & Carole Knight. **Educ:** Denver Univ, BA, MA; Conservative Baptist Theol Sem, BD; Iliff Sch Theol, MRC; Am Baptist Theol Sem, DD. **Career:** Denver Pub Schs, educr; Ace Enterprises, pres; Mt Gilead Baptist Church, minister, sr pastor; Am Church United, pres & chief exec officer, currently. **Orgs:** Pres, WSBC; state vpres, NBC USA Inc; pres, E Denver Ministers Alliance; organizer, Denver OIC; organizer, founder, first chmn bd & pres, Productions Inc; organizer, founder, pres & bd chmn, Ace Enterprises Inc; pres, Nat Am Church Union Inc; chmn, Int InterdenomiNatMinisters Alliance; bd chmn, DTP Ministers Inc; 4th vpres, Nat Baptist Conv USA Inc; pres, Ala Phillips Ministry. **Honors/Awds:** Brought opening prayer for US Congress, 1976; Listed in Congressional Record; Man of the Year; Gave opening prayer for US Senate, 1981. **Home Addr:** 12351 E Cedar Cir, Aurora, CO 80012. **Business Addr:** Chief Executive Officer, President, American Church United, 195 S Monaco, Denver, CO 80224.

**PHILLIPS, ANTHONY DWAYNE**
Executive, football player. **Personal:** Born Oct 5, 1970, Galveston, TX; children: 2. **Educ:** Trinity Valley Community Col; Tex A&M Univ, Kingsville, BS, health care. **Career:** Football player (retired), exec; Atlanta Falcons, defensive back & right corner back, 1994-96; Minn Vikings, 1998; Progressive Alternatives, currently. **Honors/Awds:** Dream Award, 2011. **Business Addr:** Progressive Alternatives, PO Box 20054, Kalamazoo, MI 49019-1054, **Business Phone:** (269)207-0091.

**PHILLIPS, CHARLES E., JR.**
President (organization). **Personal:** Born Jun 1, 1959?, Little Rock, AR; married YaVaughnie Wilkins; married Karen; children: Chas. **Educ:** AUS Acad, BS, comput sci, 1981; Hampton Univ, MBA, 1986; NY Law Sch, JD, 1993. **Career:** Bank New York Mellon Corp, vpres software, 1986; SoundView Technol Group, sr vpres, 1990-93; Kidder Peabody, sr vpres, 1990-94; Morgan Stanley & Co, prin, 1994-95, managing dir, 1995-2003; Oracle Corp, exec vpres, 2003-04, pres & bd dirs, 2004-10; Infor, chief exec officer, currently. **Orgs:** Bd mem, Viacom Corp, 2004-; bd mem, Jazz at Lincoln Ctr New York; bd mem, New York Law Sch; bd mem, Viacom Inc; bd mem, Morgan Stanley, 2006-; Pres's Econ Recovery Adv Bd; Phillips Charitable Orgn; bd dir, Infor; bd dir, Oracle Corp, 2004-10; bd mem, Am Mus Natural Hist. **Business Addr:** Chief Executive Officer, Infor, 641 Avenue of the Americas, New York, NY 10011, **Business Phone:** (678)319-8000.

**PHILLIPS, DELORES**
Writer. **Personal:** Born Jan 1, 1950, Bartow County, GA. **Educ:** Cleveland State Univ, BA, eng. **Career:** State psychiat hosp, nurse, currently; freelance writer, currently; Author: The Darkest Child, soho press, 2005; Beloved or The Color Purple. **Home Addr:** 242 Armstead Circle, Griffin, GA 30223, **Home Phone:** (770)229-9612. **Business Addr:** Nurse, State Psychiatric Hospital.

**PHILLIPS, EDWARD ALEXANDER (ED PHILLIPS)**
Manager. **Personal:** Born Jul 27, 1942, Cordele, GA; son of Sylvester and Eloise Moore; married Maxine Broussard; children: Kimberly L. **Educ:** Tuskegee Univ, Tuskegee, AL, BSME, 1965; Univ Idaho, Moscow, ID, 1981. **Career:** Pac Gas Transmission Co, Bend, Ore, eng, 1966-73; Pac Gas & Elec Co, Oakland, Calif, sr engr, 1973-74, dist gas supt, 1979-81, San Rafael, Calif, supt ops/engr, 1974-79, San Francisco, Calif, gas engr, 1981-82, Salinas, Calif, div gas supt, 1982-85, Sacramento, Calif, region gas mgr, 1982-90, region gen serv mgr, 1990; Pac Gas & Elec Co, regional gas mgr, 1990-94; M&M Power Prods, pres & gen mgr, 1994-; Phillips Enterprises Inc, prin, pres & owner, 1995-. **Orgs:** Awards comt, Pac Coast Gas Asn, 1970-; Pac Coast Elec Asn, 1970-; bd mem, Sacramento Black Employees Asn, 1986-; Sacramento Urban League, 1989-; pres, chmn, Sacramento Black Chamber Com, 1989-; bd mem, Nat Asn Advan Colored People, 1990-; Calif Expos & State Fair bd; Sacramento Metro Chamber; Los Rios Community Col Found; 100 Black Men Sacramento. **Honors/Awds:** Community Service Award, Pacific Gas & Elec Co, 1989 & 1990. **Home Addr:** 430 Deer River Way, Sacramento, CA 95831, **Home Phone:** (916)421-6850. **Business Addr:** President, Owner, Phillips Enterprises Inc, 3600 Sunset Ave, Ocean, NJ 07712, **Business Phone:** (732)493-3191.

**PHILLIPS, ERIC MCLAREN**
Manager. **Personal:** Born Oct 19, 1952, Mahaicony; married Angela; children: Takeisha Sherrill, Eric McLaran & Ashley Nicole. **Educ:** McMaster Univ, BS, chem engineering, 1976; NY Univ, MBA, mkt & int bus, 1983; Stevens Inst Tech & Bell Labs, cert telecom engineering, 1985. **Career:** Apollo Technologies, test engr, 1977-78, proj engr, 1978-79, sr proj engr, 1979-80, r&d prod develop leader, 1980-82; AT&T Commun, staff mgr local area networks, 1983-85, staff mgr network plng, 1985-86; AT&T Bell Labs, supvr mem tech staff, 1986-, proj mgr; White House, fel, 1990-91; AT&T Cent Europe Ltd (Belg), mng dir, 1993; AT&T Africa & Mid E, mng dir, 1994; AT&T Subsaharan Africa, sls vpres, 1994; African Continental Telecom Ltd, chief operating officer, dir, 1995; Matrix Cellular Inc, pres, 1995; Guyana Goldfields Inc, consult; Reform Group, co-founder; ASC Inc, dir; Africa Union Holdings, dir; Combination Ther Med Solutions, dir; NZINGHA Dance Group, founder; Safika Holdings Pty, chief operating officer; African Cult & Develop Asn, exec dir; COLLACO, dir; Guyana Found, exec dir, trustee; esseQuibo Group, chairperson, founder; Univ Guyana, Dept Bus & Mgt, lectr, currently. **Orgs:** Pres, Phillips Smith & Assocs Inc, 1982; exec dir, Caribbean Theatre Performing Arts New York, 1983; pres, prog dir, 1986, NY Univ Black Alumni Asn, 1985. **Honors/Awds:** R&D Scientific Achievement of the Year Award, Apollo Technologies Inc, 1981; Merit Award, Grad Sch Bus Admin New York Univ, 1983; Bell Labs Outstanding Serv Award, 1990; AT & T Bell Labs; Senior Vice President Award, AT&T, 1993. **Special Achievements:** Top Engineer 6 consecutive Quarters, Apollo Technologies Inc, 1979-80. **Home Addr:** 16 Wetmore Ave, Maplewood, NJ 07040, **Home Phone:** (201)763-0654. **Business Addr:** President, Matrix Cellular Inc, 544 Irvington Ave, Maplewood, NJ 07040, **Business Phone:** (201)761-7373.

**PHILLIPS, REV. DR. F. ALLISON**
Clergy. **Personal:** Born Jan 5, 1937, Brooklyn, NY; married Velma Carr; children: Denise Mitchell & Alyson. **Educ:** Va Union Univ, BA, 1958; Colgate Rochester Divinity Sch, BD, 1967; NY Theol Sem, STM, 1975, DMin, 1981. **Career:** YMCA, assoc dir, 1958-64; Garrison Blvd Community Ctr, dir, 1967-71; N Congregational Church, pastor, 1971-82; Mt Zion Congregational Church, pastor, 1982; Div Am Missionary Asn, gen secy, 1994-. **Orgs:** Alpha Phi Alpha. 1955-; bd mem. Am Red Cross. 1983-87; pres. Inner City Renewal Soc, 1984-; moderator, African Am Family Congress, 1986-; bd mem, Greater Cleveland Roundtable, 1986-; Leadership Cleveland 1986-; bd dir, Amistad Res Ctr, currently. **Home Addr:** 3183 Ludlow Rd, Shaker Heights, OH 44120. **Business Addr:** Board of Director, Amistad Research Center, Tilton Memorial Hall 6823 St Charles Ave, New Orleans, LA 70118, **Business Phone:** (504)862-3222.

**PHILLIPS, FRANK EDWARD**
Executive, government official. **Personal:** Born Mar 3, 1930, Pittsburgh, PA; son of Emanuel and Annie Evans; married Mary E Britt, Jun 19, 1953; children: Nancy Phillips-Perry, Judith Lynne & Yvette Jacobs Davis; married Thelma Harrison, Jun 10, 1989; children: Jay Clark; married Saundra Thompson-Kuy Kendall, Nov 29, 1997; children: Michael & Michelle. **Educ:** Shaw Univ, AB, 1952; Howard Univ, LLB, 1955. **Career:** Government official (retired); IRS, Wash DC, rev officer, 1955-62; IRS Los Angeles, CA, off chief coun tax atty, 1962-66, sr tax atty, 1966-69, staff asst to regional coun, gen litigation, 1969-72, asst dist coun, tax ct litigation, 1972-86. **Orgs:** Nat Bar Asn; Fed Bar Asn; VA St Bar; bd dir, Crenshaw YMCA; Christian Dcsn Dept Episcopal Church; bd dir, Crenshaw Neighbors; Alpha Kappa Mu Hon Soc; Omega Psi Phi; bd dirs, African Am Unity Ctr; bd dir, African Am Unity Ctr. **Honors/Awds:** First Chief Counsel, EEO Award, IRS, 1980; 3 Outstanding Award, IRS, 1980; Gallatin Award, 1986; Outstanding Award, Treasury Dept; Shaw Univ, Athletic Hall of Fame, 1996; Hall of Fame, Nat Bar Asn, 1997. **Home Addr:** 4194 S Cloverdale Ave, Los Angeles, CA 90008, **Home Phone:** (323)294-7043.

**PHILLIPS, DR. FREDERICK BRIAN**
Psychologist. **Personal:** Born Sep 2, 1946, Philadelphia, PA; married Vicki Altemus; children: Jamali & Jasmine. **Educ:** Penn State Univ, BA, social welfare, 1968; Univ Penn, MSW, 1970; Fielding Grad Univ, PhD, psychol, 1978. **Career:** DC Govt, psychologist, 1978-81; Inst Life Enrichment, assoc dir, 1981-83; Progressive Life Ctr, pres, chief exec officer, founder & sr advisor, 1983-; Progressive Life Inst, clin psychologist & cert master coach, 1983-; Psychol Group Wash, staff, currently. **Orgs:** Kappa Alpha Psi, 1965-85; past pres, Nat Asn Black Psychologists, 1978-85; vice chmn, Fielding Grad Univ; bd dir, Philadelphia African-Am Chamber Com; past pres, Wash DC Consortium Child Welfare; bd mem, Wash DC Comn Ment Health. **Home Addr:** 1206 Fairmont St NW, Washington, DC 20009. **Business Addr:** Founder, Senior Advisor, Progressive Life Center, 1704 17th St NE, Washington, DC 20002, **Business Phone:** (202)842-4570.

**PHILLIPS, DR. GLENN OWEN**
Educator, school administrator. **Personal:** Born Sep 26, 1945, Bridgetown; son of Ernest Owen and Dorothy Esther; married Ingrid Denise Tom; children: Mariette. **Educ:** Univ Southern Caribbean, AA, theol; Atlantic Union Col, BA, relig & hist, 1967; Andrews Univ, MA, hist, 1969; Howard Univ, PhD, hist, 1976. **Career:** Atlantic Union Col, 1967; Andrews Univ, 1969; Caribbean Union Col, lectr, 1969-71; Howard Univ, res assoc, 1976-1978, asst prof hist, 1981-82; Morgan State Univ, asst prof hist, 1978-79, asst dir Univ Hons Prog, actg dir, 1984-88, res assoc, 1982-92, actg dir, Inst Urban Res, 1984-88, assoc prof hist, 1988-89, actg chair, Dept Hist, 1989-90 & 1995-96, assoc prof, prof hist, currently. Author: Making of Christian College, 1977; The Caribbean Basin Initiative, 1989; Adventism in Barbados, 1991. **Orgs:** MSU Liaison Officer NAFEO, DC, 1985-94; pres, Barbados Nat Asn Wash Dist Columbia, 1985-87; vice chair, Community Coun Caribbean Orgn, DC, 1987-88; bd trustee, Caribbean Union Col, 1989-93; Sch Bd Chair, 1991-94; G E Peters Elem Sch, 1991-94; Asn Am Univ Professors, 1995-97; Nat Hist Hons Soc; Am Asn Univ Professors; Asn Caribbean Historians. **Special Achievements:** Author of several books. **Home Addr:** 16234 Whitehaven Rd, Silver Spring, MD 20906-1128, **Home Phone:** (301)570-6020. **Business Addr:** Professor, Morgan State University, 325 Holmes Hall, Baltimore, MD 21239, **Business Phone:** (443)885-1792.

**PHILLIPS, DR. JAMES LAWRENCE**
Physician, school administrator, educator. **Personal:** Born Mar 1, 1932, Sharon, PA; son of Daniel S and Roxie B; married Barbara A Eiserman; children: James Jr, Jeffrey & Steven. **Educ:** Wash & Jefferson Col, BA, 1954; Case Western Res Univ Sch Med, MD, 1958; Am Bd Pediat, cert, 1963; Harvard Univ, advan mgt prog, 1979. **Career:** W Ohio Permanente Med Group Inc, physician chief, 1968-86; Kaiser Found Hosp Parma, 1970-; Case Western Res Univ Sch Med, asst clin prof pediat, 1972-87, assoc dean stud affairs & minority prog; Cleveland Cavaliers Basketball Team, asst team physician, 1973-79; Rocky River Med Off, physician incharge, 1986-87; Baylor Col Med, Dept Pediat, clin prof & prof, Sect Acad Gen Pediat, sr assoc dean & prof, 1993-; Saturday Morning Sci Prog, founder; Brandt's Candies Inc, owner. **Orgs:** Bd trustee, Mt Pleasant Church God, 1976-82; pres, Case Western Res Univ Sch Med Alumni Asn, 1980-81; bd trustee, Wash & Jefferson Col, 1982-; chmn, United Way Serv New Progs Comt, 1985; pres, Northern Ohio Pediat Soc, 1988-89; bd trustee, Wash & Jefferson Col, 1988-94; Cleveland Med Asn, 1988-; Acad Med Cleveland; Ohio State Med Asn; N Ohio Pediat Soc; Am Acad Pediat; Ambulatory Pediat Asn; bd mem, InterCult Cancer Coun; bd mem, Geriat Ctr Excellence; adv bd mem, Col Union Health Related Educ; chair bd, Bay Ridge Christian Col; chair, Mid Am Christian Univ. **Honors/Awds:** Birch Scholar Award, Wash & Jefferson Col, 1954; Jessie Smith Noyes Found Med Sch Scholar, 1954-55; Leadership Award, Cleveland, 1989-90; Hon Doctorate of Science, Washington & Jefferson Col; Physician of the Year Award, Baylor Col Med, 2013; First Educational Leader of the Year Award, Baylor Col Med, 2013; Health Advocate Award, Nat Med Asn; HAMAH Civic Award, Hisp Am Med Asn Houston. **Home Addr:** 2177 S Overlook Rd, Cleveland Heights, OH 44106, **Home Phone:** (216)229-9726. **Business Addr:** Owner, Brandt's Candies Inc, 1238 Lost Nation Rd, Willoughby, OH 44094, **Business Phone:** (440)942-1016.

**PHILLIPS, JERRY P.**
Executive. **Personal:** Born Jul 24, 1939, Lyons, GA; son of P T and Ase Lue; married Maxine Glass; children: Damon J & Dyelan J. **Educ:** Savannah State Col, 1959; Rollins Col, BS, 1985. **Career:** Harris Corp, receiving & shipping supvr, sr mat adv, 1980-89; Alphatech Systs Inc, pres, 1989-. **Orgs:** NCP, 1975-; Hist Underutilized Bus Coun; Palm Bay Chamber Com, 1990-; Nat Minority Supplier Develop Coun, 1990-; trustee, bd mem, bldg Comt, chair, Macedonia Baptist Church, 1991-; hon chair, United Negro Col Fund, Men Who Cook, 1991-; Palm Bay Fla, Citizen Assistance Comt, 1994-96; Palm Bay Fla, Citizen Saturday Comt, 1994-; treas, Melbourne/Palm Bay Area, 1996-; mgr, Brevard County Workforce Develop Bd, 1996-. **Home Addr:** 1069 Pineapple Ave NE, Palm Bay, FL 32905, **Home Phone:** (407)724-8824. **Business Addr:** President, Alphatech Systems Inc, 1216 Prospect Ave, Melbourne, FL 32905, **Business Phone:** (321)729-0419.

**PHILLIPS, JULIAN MARTIN**
Television journalist. **Personal:** Born Dec 5, 1955, New York, NY; son of Cecil and Enola; married Barbara King. **Educ:** Purdue Univ, BA, radio-tv-film, 1977. **Career:** ABC-TV, desk asst, 1977; Black Enterprise Mag, staff, 1980; WNEW-TV, Channel 5, prod asst, 1981; WNBC-TV, Channel 4, mgr community rels, 1984, anchor & journalist; WPIX-TV, on-air corresp; Fox News Channel, anchor & gen assignment reporter, 2002-07; Phillips Media Strategies, chief exec officer, 2007-. **Orgs:** Adv bd mem, Nat Puerto Rican Forum, 1984-90; sr employ adv bd, New York Dept Aging, 1985-89; region vpres, Nat Broadcast Asn Community Affairs, 1985-89; adv bd mem, Crohns & Colitis Found Am, 1989-92; bd dir, NY Coalition Adoptable C, 1992-; Nat Asn Black Law Enforcement Execs, 1994-; bd dir, Boys Town, New York; Purdue Univ's Col Lib Arts Adv Bd & Discovery Pk External Adv Bd. **Home Addr:** 3 St Johns Pl, Port Washington, NY 11050-3311, **Home Phone:** (516)944-6547. **Business Addr:** General assignment reporter, Anchor, Fox News Channel, 1211 Ave of the Americas, New York, NY 10036, **Business Phone:** (212)301-3000.

**PHILLIPS, JUNE M. J.**
Educator, association executive. **Personal:** Born May 31, 1941, Ashdown, AR; married A W; children: Roderick & Calandra Camille. **Educ:** Philander Smith Col, BA, Eng, 1963; La State Univ, MA, Eng, 1971; NW State Univ, doctoral cand; Bakers Prof Real Estate Col, lic, 1977. **Career:** Port Arthur Tex Schs, teacher, 1963-65; Caddo Parish Schs, teacher, 1965-68; Southern Univ, Shreveport, assoc prof, eng, 1968-, Div Humanities, chair, coordr hons prog, currently; Bd Los Angeles Cols & Univs, trustee, 1983-; const educ minorities; orator & poet. **Orgs:** Caddo Parish Sch Bd, 1976-77; sales assoc, Century 21, 1977-79; Lester Realty, sales assoc, 1979-83; United Way NW, 1979-; Caddo Parish Charter Study Com, 1981-82; Ferdinand Realty, sales assoc, 1984-; Lynell's Cosmetics, consult, 1984-; Dem Nat Conv, 1984; NAUW; OEO #175; Shreveport Chap Links; Zeta Phi Beta Sor; La Philos Educ Soc; CODAC; La Cols & Univs, gubernatorial apptmt; chairs acad affairs comm9 La cols; NDEA, Tex So & So Univ; ed & critic, Holbrook Press, NY & Roxbury Press, Calif. **Honors/Awds:** Woman of the Year, Zeta Phi Beta Sor Inc, 1975; City Shreveport, Woman Who Has Made a Difference. **Special Achievements:** First African-American female to serve on state board. **Home Addr:** 3761 Bobbitt Pl, Shreveport, LA 71107=3801, **Home Phone:** (318)221-5957. **Business Addr:** Associate Professor of English, Chairperson, Southern University, Rm A-217 LC Barnes Admin Bldg, Shreveport, LA 71107-4795, **Business Phone:** (318)670-6365.

**PHILLIPS, LIONEL GARY**
Media executive. **Personal:** Born May 1, 1950, New York, NY; son of Oscar and Johnetta. **Educ:** City Col New York, BA, Eng & sociol, 1973. **Career:** WCBS TV News, desk asst, assignment ed & writer, 1972-80, segment producer, 1987-96, news mgr, 1987-96; CBS News, producer, 1980-86, field producer, 1985, CBS Morning News, producer, 1986-87; NJ Network News, exec prod, 1986-87; Phillips Media, owner, 1997-, exec producer, 1986-87, news mgr, 1999-2001; WNBC, freelance assignment ed, 1997-98; Mag Rack, producer, 2001-03; MSNBC, segment producer, 2003-04; IDT, mgr media rels, 2005-06; CBS2 News, freelance writer, 2006; CNN, freelance writer, 2006-07; NJ Dept Labor Prof Serv Group, trainer, 2006; ABC News, freelance producer, 2007-13; News 12 NJ, freelance writer, 2015; Al Jazeera Am, freelance writer & producer, 2016. **Orgs:** Nat Asn Black Journalists; Writers Guild Am; instr, NABJ Jour Short Course, Temple Univ, 1995; Cathedral Int; Khalfani Big Bros Ministry. **Honors/Awds:** Ny Regents Scholar, 1968; Nat Merit Scholar, 1968; Black Achievers Indust, Harlem YMCA, 1976; Emmy Award, Nat Acad TV Arts & Sci, 1978, 1989; Writers Guild Am Award, 1987; Alfred I Dupont Gold Baton Award, 1987. **Home Addr:** 4 Astor Pl, Avenel, NJ 07001, **Home Phone:** (732)634-6558. **Business Addr:** Owner, Phillips Media Group LLC, 212 N Main, Harrison, AR 72601, **Business Phone:** (870)743-0602.

**PHILLIPS, MILDRED EVALYN**
Physician. **Personal:** Born Jan 1, 1928, New York, NY; daughter of Fitzgerald and Kathleen; children: Tippi Brooke. **Educ:** Hunter Col, NY, BA, 1946; Howard Univ Col Med, MD, 1950. **Career:** King's Co Hosp, Brooklyn, NY, intern, 1950-52; Mt Sinai Hosp, NY, resident path, 1952-54; Presby Hosp, fel surg path, 1954-55, resident asst surg path, 1954-55; State Univ NY, Downstate Med Ctr, instr path, 1955-

56, asst prof, 1957-68, prof, 1980, prof emer, currently; New York State University, Medical Center, assoc prof, pathology; Univ London & London Hosp, fel, 1956-57. **Orgs:** Am Soc Exp Pathol, 1960-95; Int Acad Pathol, 1960-95; Am Asn Cancer Res, 1960-67; Am Soc Dermatopathology, 1982-; Int Acad Dermatopathology, 1982-; Asn Academic Minority Physicians, 1990-; Howard Univ Med Alumni Asn Inc. **Honors/Awds:** Hall of Fame, Hunter Col, 1983; hon med soc, Alpha Omega Alpha, 2000. **Special Achievements:** First black to intern at King's County Hoapital, Brooklyn, NY. **Home Addr:** 511 E 20th St, New York, NY 10010, **Home Phone:** (212)228-1056. **Business Addr:** Professor Emeritus, State University of New York, Stony Brook, NY 11794.

## PHILLIPS, RALPH LEONARD

Manager, planner. **Personal:** Born May 11, 1925, Sacramento, CA; son of Harry Wendall Jr and Bessie Wundus; married Jeanne. **Educ:** Univ Calif, Berkeley, AB, 1949, MA; Inst African Studies Northwestern Univ, spec studies. **Career:** Manager (retired); Bur Int Rels Univ Calif Berkeley, res assoc, 1950, teaching fel polit sci, 1952-55; USIA, info officer, cult attache, 1956-68; Arabic lang training, Beirut, 1959-61; spec asst to dir, E & Southeast Asia, serv Mid E, Wash Hq, 1963-64; Mobil Oil corp, corp advisor, 1969-93; Community & Pub Affairs Tripoli Libya, 1969-71; sr planning analyst, Int Div, 1971-93. **Orgs:** Sir, Planning, Educ Task Force, Coun Econ Develop NY, 1971-72; bd dir, DPF Inc (NYSE), 1972-74; Mayor's Adv Coun Housing, Princeton, 1973-75; bd dir, Coun Int Prog, 1975; Zoning Bd Princeton, 1977-79; vpres, Princeton Republican Asn, 1978-80; Princeton Regional Planning Bd, 1981-86; bd trustee, St Paul's Col Lawrence Va, 1983-84; Prince Hall F&A Masons Aaron No 9 Princeton NJ; 32nd Degree Ophir Consistory, Trenton NJ; Shriner Prince Hall Masons Kufu, Princeton NJ; Am Legion Post No 218 Princeton NJ. **Honors/Awds:** Merit Award, Hon Stud Soc, Univ Calif; Dept St, 1956; Pi Sigma Alpha Nat Polit Sci Hon Soc; Delta Sigma Rho, Nat Forensic Hon Soc. **Home Addr:** 156 13th St SE, Washington, DC 20003, **Home Phone:** (202)546-5619.

## PHILLIPS, DR. ROBERT HANSBURY

Labor relations manager. **Personal:** Born Nov 19, 1924, Detroit, MI; son of William and Bertha Hansbury; married Rose Mary Franklin; children: Hilanius Hansbury; married Consuelo Q; children: Eric Quintong. **Educ:** Wayne State Univ, Detroit, Mich, BS, 1952, MPA, 1967, PhD, 1987. **Career:** Labor relations manager (retired); City Detroit Personnel Dept, Detroit, Mich, personnel mgr, 1953-88. **Orgs:** Int Personnel Mgt Asn, 1953-; past dir, Personnel Mgt Asn, Mich Chap, 1953-; Pub Personnel Admin; Am Polit Sci Asn, 1983-88; Detroit Personnel Coun, 1953-88. **Honors/Awds:** Equal Employment Opportunity, Affirmative Action, Mayoral Initiatives & Bureaucratic Responses; The Case Detroit, Dissertation, 1987. **Special Achievements:** Author: A Peek Through the Curtain: A Trilogy; Men Are Like A Puff of Wind; Lives of Tears; Up Jumped the Canaille, 1991; Coping With osteoarthritis, 2001; Coping with lupus, 2001; Guy gets girl, girl gets guy, 2004; Coping with Lupus, 4th Edition, 2012. **Home Addr:** 2900 Cove Cay Dr Apt 7G, Clearwater, FL 33760, **Home Phone:** (727)539-0009.

## PHILLIPS, DR. ROMEO ELDRIDGE

Educator. **Personal:** Born Mar 11, 1928, Chicago, IL; son of James M Sr and Sissieretta Lewis; married Deloris R Jordan; children: Pamela Marlene & Arthur JH. **Educ:** Roosevelt Univ, BB, 1949, MM, 1951; Eastern Mich Univ, MA, 1963; Wayne State Univ, PhD, 1966. **Career:** Chicago IL Pub Schs, teacher, 1949-55; Detroit MI Pub Schs, teacher, 1955-57; Inkster MI Pub Schs, teacher, 1957-66; Kalamazoo Col, asst prof educ, tenured african am prof educ & music, 1968-93, chmn dept educ, 1974-86, prof emer educ & music, 1993-; Mich Col, Comt Scholars Accreditation, mem, 1982-84; Portage MI, city coun man, 1991-. **Orgs:** Am Asn Col Teacher Educ; Music Educrs Nat Conf; Mich Sch Vocal Asn; Asn Supervison & Curric Develop; Mich Asn Supv & Curric Develop; Mich Asn Improv Sch Legis; Nat Alliance Black Sch Educr; Nat Asn Negro Musicians; Phi Delta Kappa; Kappa Alpha Psi; conductor, African-Am Chorale; past chair, Southwest Mich Black Heritage Soc; chairperson, OMIK Amateur Radio Asn Inc; pres, Kalamazoo Chap Nat Asn Advan Colored People. **Honors/Awds:** Leadership Award, Omega Psi Phi, 1982; Kalamazoo Nat Asn Advan Colored People Appreciation Award, 1982; Fulbright Scholar, Liberia W Africa, 1984, 1985. **Special Achievements:** First tenured African American professor at Kalamazoo College; 13 jour publs; 1 mag article; 2 book reviews; chapters contributed to or credit given in 6 books; Invited by the govt of the Republic of Nigeria West Africa to be a guest to the World Festival of Black & African Art, 1977. **Home Addr:** 6841 Welbury St, Portage, MI 49024, **Home Phone:** (616)327-1736. **Business Addr:** Professor Emeritus of Education & Music, Kalamazoo College, 1200 Acad St, Kalamazoo, MI 49006-3295, **Business Phone:** (616)337-7033.

## PHILLIPS, TARI LYNN

Basketball player. **Personal:** Born Mar 6, 1969, Orlando, FL; daughter of John and Doris. **Educ:** Univ Cent Fla, BS, commun, 1991; Univ Ga. **Career:** Seattle Reign, forward, 1996-97; Colo Xplosion, forward, 1997-98; Orlando Miracle, 1998-99; New York Liberty, 2000-04; Houston Comets, free agt, 2005-06; Acer ERG Priolo, forward, 2008.

## PHILLIPS, TERESA LAWRENCE

Basketball coach, athletic director. **Personal:** Born Jun 15, 1958, Chattanooga, TN; married Michael; children: Micah & Kyle. **Educ:** Vanderbilt Univ, BA, econs, 1980; Tenn State Univ, MA, educ, 1999. **Career:** Vanderbilt Univ, asst basketball coach, 1981-84; Fisk Univ, head women's basketball coach, 1986-89; Tenn State Univ, Lady Tigers basketball prog, head coach, 1989-2000, assoc athletics dir, 1995-2001, interim athletics dir, 2001-02, athletics dir, 2002-, head men's basketball coach, 2003. **Orgs:** Fel Christian Athletes Bd; Vanderbilt Alumni Adv Bd; NCAA Basketball Rules; chair, Ohio Valley Conf Athletic dir Comt; bd dir, Boys' & Girls' Club, 1995-; Black Coaches Asn; Women's Basketball Coaches Asn; NCAA HBCU Adv Bd; exec bd, Nashville Sports Coun; NCAA Admin Cabinet; NCAA Championship Cabinet; Alpha Kappa Alpha Sorority Inc; Nashville Final Four Exec Bd; Kroger Dinner Champions Comt; Girls Prep Sch Alumni Bd; inaugural mem, Girls Prep Sch Sports Hall Fame; Athletic Hall Fame, GPS, currently. **Special Achievements:** First woman to coach an NCAA Division 1 men's basketball team. **Home Addr:** 825 W Nocturne Dr, Nashville, TN 37207-4211, **Home Phone:** (615)650-1920. **Business Addr:** Athletics Director, Tennessee State University, 3500 John A Merritt Blvd Keen Hall Rm 131, Nashville, TN 37209, **Business Phone:** (615)963-5034.

## PHILLIPS, W. THOMAS

Executive, vice president (organization). **Personal:** Born Aug 2, 1943, Charleston, MS; son of Jessie and Walter; married Carline Bradford; children: Craig, Lee & Ernest. **Educ:** Univ Northern Iowa, BA, bus, 1966; Northeastern Univ, Boston, MA, mgt develop, 1978; Harvard Univ, Grad Sch Bus, advan mgt prog, 1988. **Career:** Executive, Vice president (retired); Gen Foods, sales rep dist mgr, 1966-72; Quaker oats, sales planning zone mgr, 1973-77, mgr sales develop, 1978-79, mgr dir corp prog, 1980-84, vpres corp progs, 1984-94; Pioneer Hi-Bred Int Inc, consult, dir community investments, 1994-2007. **Orgs:** Loaned Exec Assoc, United Way Chicago, 1979-; bd mem, Chicago Hearing Soc, 1979-82; Donors Forum Chicago, Nat Charities Info Bur, 1984-; Asn Black Found Execs; United Negro Col Found; Inst Character Develop; Univ Northern Iowa; Iowa Comn Vol Serv; Dr. Carline Bradford Phillips Fund; Dr. Carline Phillips Delta Legacy Scholar Fund, Delta Sigma Theta Sorority Inc, 2007. **Home Addr:** 2415 N Douglas Ave, Arlington Heights, IL 60004.

## PHILLIPS, WILBURN R.

Banker. **Career:** Home Fed Savings Bank, Detroit, Mich, pres, chief exec officer, dir emer & bd dir; Cape Code Realty, St Clair Shores, mgr, broker & owner, currently. **Orgs:** Chmn trustee bd, Plymouth United Church Christ, 1949-, secy, Deacon Bd, secy, chmn, trustee, 1957; Credit Union Nat Asn, Am's Community Bankers. **Business Addr:** Owner, Broker, Cape Code Realty, 1254 Woodbridge St, Saint Clair Shores, MI 48080, **Business Phone:** (586)777-3327.

## PHILPOTT, ETHEL

Vice president (organization). **Career:** Executive (retired); Teachers Asn Chicago, vpres, pres. **Orgs:** Retired Teachers Asn Chicago; Rural Transp Advocacy Coun. **Home Addr:** 7400 S Oglesby Ave, Chicago, IL 60649.

## PHILYAW, DINO (DELVIC DYVON PHILYAW)

Executive, football player. **Personal:** Born Oct 30, 1970, Dudley, NC; married Angela; children: Antonio, Ava, Mia & Kiara. **Educ:** Univ Ore, BA, sociol, sr, 1995. **Career:** Football player (retired), exec; N Carolina Panthers, running back, 1995-97; New Orleans Saints, kick returner, 1999; NJ Hitmen, 2001; SSD LLC, owner & mgr, 2005-11; Philyaws Cookout & Catering, owner, 2008-; orthopedic sales, rep; construct co owner. **Business Addr:** Owner, Philyaws Cookout & Catering, 1050 Bethel Dr, Eugene, OR 97402, **Business Phone:** (541)357-2377.

## PICHON, RISE JONES

Judge. **Personal:** Born Oct 3, 1951, Tacoma, WA; daughter of LaVerta and Fairbanks; married Ulysses; children: Evann. **Educ:** Xavier Univ; Santa Clara Univ, BS, mathematics, 1973; Santa Clara Univ Sch Law, JD, 1976. **Career:** County Santa Clara, dep pub defender, 1976-79, dep county coun, 1979-83, ct comnr, 1983-84, Munic ct judge, 1984-98; Calif Judicial Col, instr, 1989, 1990; Nat Judicial Col, instr, 1991, 1992; State Calif, super ct judge, 1998-, Munic ct judge, 1984-98; Calif Judicial Col, instr, 1989, 1990; Nat Judicial Col, instr, 1991, 1992; State Calif, super ct judge, 1998-; Judicial Performance, Calif Comn, 1999-2007; Palo Alto Ct Facil, supv judge, 2006-09; Santa Clara County Super Ct, Exec Comt, 2008-09. **Orgs:** Calif Judges Asn, 1984-; Nat Bar Asn, 1985-; Links Inc; San Jose Chap; Am Bar Asn; Am Leadership Forum; bd dir, Santa Clara Univ Sch Law Alumni, 1988-93, pres, 1990-91; bd visitor, Santa Clara Univ Sch Law, 1989-97; Calif Judicial Coun, 1994-97; Joint Venture Silicon Valley, Vision Leadership Team, 1998; co-chair, Civic Action Network Planning Comn, 1998-99; Comn Judicial Performance, State Calif, 1999-2003; Trial Ct Budget Comn, Calif Judicial Coun, 1999-2003; bd mem, vpres, St Thomas More Socs Inc. **Honors/Awds:** Women of Distinction, Santa Clara Univ Women Studs, Challenges Conf, 1991; Thurgood Marshall Achievement Award, Santa Clara Univ Black Law Studs Asn, 1992; Owens Lawyer of the Year, Santa Clara Univ Sch Law, 1994. **Home Addr:** 10128 Mello Pl, Cupertino, CA 95014, **Home Phone:** (408)255-3808. **Business Addr:** Superior Court Judge, Santa Clara County Superior Court, 191 N First St, San Jose, CA 95113, **Business Phone:** (408)808-7170.

## PICKARD, VIVIAN R.

Executive. **Educ:** Ferris State Univ, BS, human serv admin; Cent Mich Univ, MS, bus admin. **Career:** Gen Motors Corp, admin & mgt positions, 1978, vice chair, dir community rels, pres, dir corp rels, 2009-15; Detroit Econ Club, officer. **Orgs:** Bd dir, Gleaners Community Food Bank Livingston; bd mem, Nat Coun Negro Women; pres, Renaissance Chap Links Inc; nat chair corp rels, Corp Rels Comt, Links Inc; life mem, Nat Black MBA Asn; life mem, Nat Asn Advan Colored People; Inforum; Nat Asn Accredited Cosmetology Schs; Detroit Inst Arts; Fleet Air Arm Asn Australia; ConnectMichigan Alliance; bd mem, Memorial Found Inc; bd mem, Habitat Humanity Int; bd mem, Friends African & African Am Art; bd mem, Detroit Regional Chamber Found; bd mem, Parade Co; bd mem, Fifth Third Bank-Eastern Mich; bd mem, Coun Mich Foundations; bd mem, CultureSource; bd mem, Trumpet Awards Found; bd mem, St. John Providence Health Syst; bd mem, Sphinx Orgn; Nat Urban League's Nat Employer Adv Coun; Exec Leadership Coun; Links Inc, exec comt; pres, Black Women's Agenda Inc; pres, GM Found; trustee, Hartford Memorial Baptist Church. **Honors/Awds:** Chairman's Award, 100 Black Men Am Inc, 2004; President's Award, Links Inc, 2006; Central Area Director's Award, Links Inc, 2007; Women of Excellence Award, Mich Chronicle, 2009; Inforum Inner Circle Honoree, 2010; Rainbow PUSH Bridge Builder Award, 2011; Alpha Award of Honor, Alpha Phi Alpha Fraternity Inc, 2011; Top Influential Women in Corporate America Award, Savoy Magazine, 2012; Community Leadership Award, Arab Am & Chaldean Coun's, 2013; Corporate Community Service Award, 100 Black Men New York Inc, 2013; Women of Achievement Award, Mich Women's Found, 2013; Ferris State University Alumni of the Year, Ferris State Univ, 2014; Global Community Award, NAIAS Multicultural Media Luncheon, 2014; Distinguished Service Award for Education, Gamma Lambda, 2014; Diversity Business Leader Award, Corp! Magazine, 2014; Door Opener Award, Payne-Pulliam Sch Trade & Com, 2014; Heritage Hall of Fame Gallery, Int Heritage Found, 2014; Role Model Award, Alternatives Girls, 2015; 25 Influential Black Women In Business, Network J, 2015; Charles H. Moore Award for Leadership in Corporate Community Engagement,Comt Encouraging Corp Philanthropy, 2015; Multicultural Media Award for Global Community Leadership, 2016; Driven's Philanthropic Pioneer Award, 2016; Spirit of the Dream Award, United Negro Col Fund, 2016; Eagle Scout Award, Detroit Area Coun, Boy Scouts Am. **Business Addr:** Director of Corporate Relations, President, General Motors Corp, 300 Renaissance Ctr, Detroit, MI 48265-3000, **Business Phone:** (313)556-5000.

## PICKARD, WILLIAM F.

Business owner, businessperson, entrepreneur. **Personal:** Born Jan 28, 1941, La Grange, GA; son of William H and Victoria Woodyard; married Vivian; children: 1. **Educ:** Flint Mott Col, AS, 1962; Western Mich Univ, BS, 1964; Univ Mich, MSW, 1965; Ohio State Univ, PhD, 1971. **Career:** Cleveland Urban League, dir educ, 1965-67; Nat Asn Advan Colored People, exec dir, 1967-69; Cleveland State Univ, assoc dir urban studies, 1971-72; Wayne State Univ, prof, 1971-74; McDonald's, franchise owner, 1971-; Global Automotive Alliance, chmn & chief exec officer, 1985-; Regal Plastics Co, owner & operator; VITEC LLC, chief exec officer & chmn bd; GrupoAntolin-Wayne, chief exec officer & chmn bd; ARD Logistics, LLC, chief exec officer & chmn bd; Commonwealth Regal Industs, chief exec officer & chmn bd; MGM Grand Detroit, co-managing partner; Univ Mich, Ann Arbor, adj prof. **Orgs:** Bus Leaders Mich; chmn, African Develop Found, 1983-87; Mich Nat Corp., 1989-; Malan Realty Investors, Inc., 1994-; Asset Acceptance Capital Corp., 2004-11; Flagstar BanCorp. Inc., 2008-09; WTVS; Nat Asn Black Automotive Suppliers; Detroit Econ Develop Corp; Mich Cancer Found; Detroit Sci Ctr; Nat Asn Advan Colored People; Nat Urban League; Stand Fed Bank. Mem U.S. Adv Comt Trade Policy & Negotiations. Trustee: Community Found Southeast Mich; trustee, Western Mich Univ, 2016; Grand Valley State Univ. **Honors/Awds:** National Institute of Mental Health Fellowship, 1964; Haynes Fellowship, National Urban League, 1965; Honorary Doctorate in Business Administration, Cleary College, 1980; Western Michigan University Distinguished Alumnus, 1980; Michiganain of the Year, Detroit News, 2002; Detroiter of the Year, Hour Detroit Magazine, 2010. **Special Achievements:** Author, Seven Principles of Entrepreneurship; established the Dr. William F. Pickard Business Scholarship at Grand Valley State University. **Business Addr:** 2627 Clark St, Detroit, MI 48210, **Business Phone:** (313)297-6676.

## PICKARD, DR. WILLIAM FRANK

Executive, chief executive officer. **Personal:** Born Jan 28, 1941, LaGrange, GA; son of Willie H and Victoria Woodyard (deceased); married Vivian; children: 1. **Educ:** Flint Mott Col, Flint, MI, AS, 1962; Western Mich Univ, Kalamazoo, MI, BS, 1964; Univ Mich, Ann Arbor, MI, MSW, 1965; Ohio State Univ, Columbus, OH, PhD, 1971. **Career:** Ment Health NIMH fel, 1964; Nat Inst Ment Health Fel, 1964; Cleveland Urban League, dir educ, 1965-67; Nat Urban League, Haynes fel, 1965; Wayne State Univ, prof, 1971-74; Mc Donalds Res, owner, 1971-; Cleveland State Univ, Cleveland, Ohio, assoc dir urban studies, 1971-72; Wayne State Univ, Detroit, Mich, assoc prof, 1972-74; McDonald's restaurant franchises, owner/operator, 1985; VITEC LLC, chief exec officer & chmn bd; GrupoAntolin-Wayne, chief exec officer & chmn bd; ARD Logistics LLC, chief exec officer & chmn bd; Global Automotive Alliance, chmn & chief exec officer, 1985-; Regal Plastics Co, Roseville, Mich, chmn & chief exec officer, 1985-. **Orgs:** Exec dir, Nat Asn Advan Colored People, 1967-69; bd dir, Nat Asn Black Automotive Suppliers, 1986-; bd dir, Stand Fed Bank, 1989-; dir, Mich Nat Corp, 1989; bd dir, Fed Home Loan Bank, Indianapolis, Ind, 1990-; trustee, Community Found Southeastern Mich; dir, WTVS; dir, Nat Asn Black Automotive Suppliers; dir, Detroit Econ Develop Corp; dir, Mich Cancer Found; dir, Malan Realty Investors Inc, 1994; mem, US Adv Comt Trade Policy & Negotiations; exec Bd, Nat Asn Advan Colored People; independent dir, Flagstar BanCorp; Flagstar Bank, 2008-2009; chmn, African Develop Found; Metrop Affairs Corp; Detroit Renaissance; Hartford Memorial Baptist Church; dir, Asset Acceptance Capital Corp, 2004-11. **Special Achievements:** First chairman of the African Development Foundation (ADF), 1982. **Home Addr:** 335 Pine Ridge Dr, Bloomfield Hills, MI 48304, **Home Phone:** (313)258-6520. **Business Addr:** Chairman, Chief Executive Officer, Regal Plastics Company, 9200 N Royal Lane, Irving, TX 75063, **Business Phone:** (800)441-1553.

## PICKENS, CARL MCNALLY

Football player. **Personal:** Born Mar 23, 1970, Murphy, NC. **Educ:** Univ Tenn, grad. **Career:** Football player (retired); Cincinnati Bengals, punt returner & wide receiver, 1992-99; Tenn Titans, wide receiver, 2000. **Honors/Awds:** American Football Conference Rookie of the Year, Assoc Press, 1992; Offensive Rookie of the Year, Nat Football League, Offensive Rookie of the Year, 1992; Pro Bowl, 1995, 1996.

## PICKENS, JAMES, JR.

Actor, television actor. **Personal:** Born Oct 26, 1954, Cleveland, OH; married Gina; children: Carl Tharps & Gavyn. **Educ:** Bowling Green State Univ, BFA, 1976. **Career:** Films: F/X, 1986; Hotshot, 1987; Trespass, 1992; Boiling Point, 1993; Menace II Society, 1993; Hostile Intentions, Jimmy Hollywood, 1994; Dead Presidents, Nixon, 1995; Power 98, Sleepers, Ghosts of Mississippi, 1996; Gridlock'd, Rocket Man, 1997; Sphere, Bulworth, How Stella Got Her Groove Back, 1998; Liberty Heights, 1999; Traffic, 2000; Home Room, 2002; White Rush, 2003; Venom, 2005; Ball Don't Lie, 2008; Just Wright, 2010; The Realest Audition Ever, exec producer, 2012; 42, 2013. TV series: "Another World", 1986-90; "Roseanne", 1990-96; Blossom, 1992; "Beverly Hills, 90210", 1991-92; Exclusive, 1992; "NYPD Blue", 1993-2000; Sodbusters, A Child's Cry for Help, Lily in Winter, 1994; Sharon's Secret, Trial by Fire, 1995; Bloodhounds, 1996; The Uninvited, 1996; "Something So Right", 1996-97; "The Practice", 1997-2000; "Brooklyn South", 1997-98; "Any Day Now", 1998-2000; "The X Files", 1998-2002; "A Slight Case of Murder", "Vengeance Unlimited", 1999; "City of Angels",

"Family Law", 2000; Philly, 2001-02; "SemperFi", 2001; "Crossing Jordan", 2002; "Six Feet Under", 2002-03; Becker, 2002-03; "CSI: Miami", "The Lyon's Den", 2003; "Line of Fire", 2004; "Curb Your Enthusiasm", 2005; "Grey's Anatomy", 2005-14; "Private Practice", 2007-09; "Seattle Grace: Message of Hope", 2010. **Honors/Awds:** Nate Love Lifetime Achievement Award, Western States Black Res Educ Ctr, 2005; Satellite Award, 2006; Outstanding Performance by an Ensemble in a Drama Series (shared), Screen Actors Guild, 2007; Image Award, 2012. **Business Addr:** Actor, William Morris Agency, 1 William Morris Pl, Beverly Hills, CA 90212, **Business Phone:** (310)859-4000.

### PICKERING, ROBERT PERRY
Government official, educator, executive director. **Personal:** Born Oct 23, 1950, Charleston, SC; married Deborah DeLaine; children: Robert, Richard, Russell & Randall. **Educ:** Voorhees Col, BS, 1972. **Career:** Chas Co Health Dept, environ teacher, 1976; DHEC SC State, epidemiol asst, 1978-80; SC Swine Flu Prog Col, state coordr, 1979; Health Dept ChasCo, SC, prog dir, 1980-81; Congressman T H Harnett, spec asst; Garrett Acad Community Educ Prog, dir, currently. **Orgs:** Treas, Mitchell Elem Sch PTA, 1978-85; pres, St Patrick Parish Coun, 1979-82; chmn, Mitchell Elem Sch Adv Coun, 1979-83; bd mem, Charleston OIC, 1980-83; bd mem, Morris Col Indus Bd, 1983-86; adv, SC Nat Black Republican Coun, 1984-. **Home Addr:** 179 Line St, Charleston, SC 29403, **Home Phone:** (843)722-4588. **Business Addr:** Director, Garrett Academy, 2731 Gordon St, North Charleston, SC 29405, **Business Phone:** (843)529-3926.

### PICKETT, CECIL BRUCE
Biologist. **Personal:** Born Oct 5, 1945, Canton, IL; son of Charles and Florence; married Shirley; children: 2. **Educ:** Calif State Univ, Hayward, CA, BS, biol, 1971; Univ Calif, Los Angeles, CA, PhD, cell biol, 1976. **Career:** Univ Calif, Los Angles, fel cellular biol, 1976-78; Merck Res Labs, Montreal, Can, sr res chemist, 1978-93, sr vpres, 1993; Howard Univ, Col Med, vis asst prof, 1978-83; NJ Sch Med & Dent, adj assoc prof, 1985-88; Univ Montreal, assoc prof, 1990; McGill U; Schering Plough Corp, corp sr vpres, 2002-06; Schering-Plough Res Inst, pres; Biogen Idec Inc, pres, res & develop & a mem bd dirs, 2006-09; Zimmer Holdings Inc, dir, 2008-. **Orgs:** US Food & Drug Admin Sci Bd; Am Soc Cellular Biol; Am Soc Biochem & Molecular Biol; Am Asn Cancer Res; Am Asn Advan Sci; adv comt, Dir Nat Insts Health; adv comt, Nat Cancer Policy Bd Inst Med; Nat Acad Sci; Am Asn Cancer Res. **Honors/Awds:** Alumni Association Award for Scholarly Achievement and Academic Distinction, UCLA, 1976; Macy Scholar, Marine Biol Labs, Woods Hole, Mass, 1978; 'first Robert A. Scala Award and Lectureship in Toxicology', Rutgers Univ; Univ Med & Dent, New Jersey, 1993; Disting Lecturer, Jonsson Comprehensive Cancer Ctr, UCLA, 1995; Founders Award, Chem Ind Inst Technol Ctrs Health Res, 2001. **Special Achievements:** Published extensively in leading research journals & has been a frequent speaker at scientific symposia & conferences. **Business Addr:** Director, Zimmer Holdings Inc, 345 E Main St, Warsaw, IN 46580, **Business Phone:** (574)267-6131.

### PICKETT, DONNA A.
Executive. **Personal:** Born Jun 11, 1949, Lexington, VA; daughter of Mallory Wayne Harris and Gladys Jones Harris; married Edward E; children: Monica & Aaron. **Educ:** Va Commonwealth Univ, Richmond, VA, BA, eng. **Career:** Va Power, Richmond, Va, off supvr, supvr personnel servs, supvr rec mgt, Minority Affairs & Pub Affairs Dept, dir currently, 1969-. **Orgs:** Bd mem, Va Black Hist Mus & Cult Ctr, 1989-; chairperson, Va Coun Status Women, 1991-94; chmn, bus adv coun, Orgn Chinese Am; vpres, external rels, Am Asn Blacks Energy. **Home Addr:** 7805 Kahlua Dr, Richmond, VA 23227, **Home Phone:** (804)262-4670. **Business Addr:** Chairperson, Virginia Council on the Status of Women, PO Box 26666, Richmond, VA 23261, **Business Phone:** (804)771-4797.

### PICKETT, REV. HENRY B., JR.
Educator, clergy. **Personal:** Born Mar 21, 1938, Morehead City, NC; married Mary Louise Hoffler; children: Marquis DeLafayette & Sherry Louise. **Educ:** Elizabeth City State Univ, BS, elem educ, 1961; NC Cent Univ, MA, guid & coun, 1973, cet admin, 1994; Shaw Divinity Sch, Shaw Divinity Sch, MDiv, 1977. **Career:** Guidance counselor, educator, clergy (retired); Raleigh City, elem teacher, 1963-72; St Augustine's Col, counr foreign stud adv, 1972-73; Fuguay Varina, counr, 1973-76; E Millbrook Mid Sch, coun, 1976-91; Oberlin Baptist Church, pastor, 1977-80; Wendell First Baptist Church, pastor, 1982-85; Wake County Pub Sch, staff, 1991(retired); Pine Grove Missionary Baptist Church, interim pastor; Cosmopolitan Baptist Church, assoc pastor, currently; Mid Schs Raleigh, NC, substitute teacher. **Orgs:** Pres, Black Dem Caucus; chmn, Wake Co, 1974; Baptist Minister Wake Co Bd Edn; Am Personnel & Guid Asn; Am Sch Counr Asn; NEA; NCPGA; NC Asn Educr; Phi Delta Kappa; Nat Asn Advan Colored People; Kingwood Forest Comn Asn Inc; Omega Psi Phi Frat Inc; bd trustee, Elizabeth City State Univ, 2001; secy, Bd Native Morehead City, NC; trustee emer, Elizabeth City State Teachers Col. **Honors/Awds:** Man of the Year, Oberlin Baptist Church, 1968; Boy Scout District Award Merit, 1971; Omega Achievement Award; Citizen of the Year, Phi Delta Kappa, 1974; Outstanding Alumni Service Award, Elizabeth City State Univ, 1995; Downtown Housing Improvement Award, 1995; Sertoma Club Service to Mankind Award, 1997; NC Conference of Branches, NAACP; President Award, 1997; State NC The Order of the long Leaf Pine, 2000; Presidential Citation recognition of exemplary experiences honor Elizabeth City State Univ, NAFEO, 2003. **Home Addr:** 1604 E Davie St, Raleigh, NC 27610-3316, **Home Phone:** (919)833-4007. **Business Addr:** Associate Pastor, Cosmopolitan Baptist Church, 988 85th Ave, Oakland, CA 94621, **Business Phone:** (510)569-6441.

### PICKETT, ROBERT E. See Obituaries Section.

### PICKLES, DR. PATRICIA L.
School administrator, executive. **Personal:** Born Waukegan, IL; children: 2. **Educ:** Col Lake County, Grayslake, IL, AA, educ; Barat Col, Lake Forest, IL, BA, eng lit, 1975; E Tex State Univ, Com, TX, MS, educ admin, 1983; Tex Woman's Univ, PhD, reading & educ admin, 1990; Nat Louis Univ, PhD, 1999; Stanford Univ, CA, post-doctoral, 2003; Fordham Univ, NY, post-doctoral, 2006; Univ Tex, Austin, post-doctoral, 2009; Oxford Univ, Eng, post-doctoral; Harvard Univ, Boston, post-doctoral. **Career:** Educator (retired), executive; Dallas Pub Schs, prin, asst prin & teacher, 1976-91; Dallas Co Community Col, Dallas, TX, adj prof, 1983-85; Arlington Independent Sch Dist, Arlington, TX, prin, 1991-92; Tex Womans Univ, Denton, TX, adj prof, 1991-92; Tex Educ Agency, sr dir, 1992-95; Region XIII Educ Serv Ctr, Austin, TX, coordr statewide initiatives, 1995-97; N Chicago Sch Dist 187, supt, 1997-2002; Portland Pub Schs, chief acad officer, 2002-05; Pflugerville Independent Sch Dist, pflugerville, TX, Sup, 2005-06; A+ Stand Excellence & Equity Educ, Austin, TX, pres & chief exec officer, 2007-; Author: Are You In a Pickle?Lessons Learned Along The Way: Student's Performance And Achievement Gaps. **Orgs:** Young Women Christian Asn; Boy Scouts Am; Girl Scouts Am; United Way; Clara Abbot Found; Girlstart; Tex Asn Partners Educ; Adv Coun, Col Lake Co; Task Force, Teacher Educ & Prof Develop; Congressman Porters Screening comt; Ore Literacy Steering Comt; Vice Chair, Nat Sch Demonstration Sites; Congressman Kirks Kitchen Cabinet Educ Policy; HEB Excellence Educ Awards Comt; Fed Impact Aid Legis & Senate Bill 1, Tex; Am Asn Sch Adminr; Nat Asn Sch Boards; Asn Bilingual Educ; McDougall Littel Leadership Conf. **Business Addr:** President, Chief Executive officer, A+Standards of Excellence & Equity, Austin, TX 73301.

### PICKRUM, LISA M.
Businessperson. **Personal:** Born Jan 1, 1970. **Educ:** Vassar Col, BA, polit sci; Univ Pa, MBA; Stanford Law Sch, JD. **Career:** Fed Commun Comn, atty, 1994-96; Accenture, sr consult, 1998-99; Katalyst Venture Partners, prin, 1999-2003; RLJ Co, exec vpres & chief operating officer, 2004-; RLJ Acquisition Inc, chief financial officer, 2010-12; Christopher & Banks Corp, dir, 2011-. **Orgs:** Bd dir, Rollover Systs & CW Wellspring Entertainment; secy, UTB Educ Finance LLC; mem adv bd, McLarty Capital Partners LLC; dir, DeVry Inc, 2008-; dir, Urban Trust Bank. **Special Achievements:** Named one of the "50 Most Powerful Black Women in Business" by Black Enterprise, Feb, 2006. **Business Addr:** Executive Vice President, Chief Operating Officer, The RLJ Companies, 3 Bethesda Metro Center, Bethesda, MD 20814, **Business Phone:** (301)280-7700.

### PICKRUM, MICHAEL
Executive, chief financial officer. **Educ:** Stanford Univ, BS, elec engineering, 1992, ME, engineering-econ systs, 1994; Wharton Sch Bus, Univ Pa, MBA, finance & entrepreneurial mgt, 1998. **Career:** Black Entertainment Tv Interactive, vpres bus develop, 1999, exec vpres & chief operating officer, 2003-07, chief financial officer, 2007; Black Entertainment Tv Networks, exec vpres & chief financial officer, 2003-; BET Interactive, vpres bus develop, sr vpres, exec vpres, 2000-, chief operating officer, 2000-07, chief financial officer, bus develop & strategy, 2007-; Quad Learning Inc, chief financial officer, currently; Mercer Mgt Consult, strategy consult. **Orgs:** Meridian Bd Trustees; treas, US Capital Chap YPO; bd mem, ATA Charter Sch; bd mem, Charter Bd Partner. **Business Addr:** Chief Financial Officer, Quad Learning Inc, 509 7th St NW 4th Fl, Washington, DC 20004, **Business Phone:** (202)654-7068.

### PIERCE, AARON
Football player. **Personal:** Born Sep 6, 1969, Seattle, WA; son of Samuel. **Educ:** Univ Wash, grad. **Career:** Football player (retired); New York Giants, 1992, tight end, 1993-97, free agt, currently; Baltimore Ravens, tight end, 1999. **Business Addr:** Free Agent, New York Gaints, Giants Stadium, East Rutherford, NJ 07073, **Business Phone:** (201)935-8111.

### PIERCE, AARONETTA HAMILTON
Association executive. **Personal:** Born Jan 8, 1943, Somerville, TN; daughter of David A and Clementine Lofties; married Joseph A Jr; children: Joseph Aaron & Michael Arthur. **Educ:** Tenn St Univ, Nashville, TN, 1961; St Univ Iowa, Iowa City, IA, BA, 1963. **Career:** San Antonio Independent Sch Dist, San Antonio, Tex, teacher, 1964-67; Tex Comn Arts, 1985; Camino Real Bank, dir, 1994-2001; Premier Artworks Inc, pres, owner, currently. **Orgs:** Bd trustee, Fisk Univ, 1992-; Comnr, Tex Comn Arts, 1985-91; chairperson, Mayor's Blue Ribbon Comt Arts San Antonio, 1988-89; chairperson, first Martin Luther King Jr. Comn & Celebration San Antonio, Nat Arts dir, Links Inc, 1994-98, 1986-87; chairperson, Tex Arts Award, Tex Arts Alliance, 1988; exec comt, United Way San Antonio, 1988-94; reg arts comt chairperson, Alpha Kappa Alpha Sorority, 1991; founding mem, Southwest Ethnic Arts Soc; Educ Fund Educ Partnership; bd trustee, San Antonio Mus Asn; Univ Tex San Antonio Develop Bd; Tex Cult Trust; San Antonio Spurs Found; adv bd, Sterling Bank; Witte Mus; San Antonio Libr Found; area dir, Arts Links Inc; chair, Arts Subcomt Alpha Kappa Alpha Sorority S Cent Region; Rockefeller Found to fight poverty; bd trustee, San Antonio Mus Asn; Tex Cult Trust; San Antonio Libr Found; Nat civic orgn African-Am women. **Honors/Awds:** San Antonio Women's Hall of Fame, City of San Antonio, 1984; JC Penney Golden Rule Award, Cultural Category, 1984; Texas Black Women's Hall of Fame, 1986; Headliner Award, Women in Communications, 1989; Nominee, Inductee into Texas Women's Hall of Fame, 1993; Texas Women's Hall of Fame, 1993; barge named for her, carriers tourists along San Antonio River. **Special Achievements:** First African-American woman appointed to the Texas Commission on Arts. **Home Addr:** 19114 Boca Del Mar, San Antonio, TX 78258, **Home Phone:** (210)494-7838. **Business Addr:** President, Owner, Premier Artworks Inc, 209 Canada Verde St, San Antonio, TX 78232, **Business Phone:** (210)490-4084.

### PIERCE, ABE E., III
Mayor, educator. **Personal:** Born Oct 28, 1934, Monroe, LA; married Dorothy Richard; children: Abe E IV & Ava E. **Educ:** Southern Univ, BA, biol, chem, 1956; Univ Southwestern La; Univ Calif; Northeast La Univ. **Career:** Terzia High Sch, sci teacher, 1956-66, prin, 1969-72; Robinson Elem Sch, prin, 1966-69; Ouachita Parish sch syst, supvr sec educ, 1972-78, asst supt, 1978; Mayor, Monroe (LA), pres, 1996; Richwood High Sch, teacher, supvr & asst supt. **Orgs:** Ouachita Parish Police Jury; Nat Asn Advan Colored People. **Business Addr:** Member, National Association for the Advancement of Colored People, 4805 Mt Hope Dr, Baltimore, MD 21215, **Business Phone:** (410)580-5777.

### PIERCE, DR. CHESTER MIDDLEBROOK
Educator. **Personal:** Born Mar 4, 1927, Glen Cove, NY; son of Samuel Riley and Hettie Elenor Armstrong; married Jocelyn Patricia Blanchet; children: Diane Blanchet Williams & Deirdre Anona. **Educ:** Harvard Col, AB, 1948; Harvard Med Sch, MD, 1952. **Career:** Univ Cincinnati, instr psychiat, 1957-60; Univ Okla, from asst prof to prof, 1960-69; Am Bd Psychiat & Neurol, pres, 1977-78; Polar Rsch; Mass Inst Technol, Psychiat; Harvard Grad Sch Educ, prof, prof emer educ & psychiat, currently; Mass Gen Hosp, sr psychiatrist, currently. **Orgs:** Sr consult, Peace Corps, 1965-69; advisor, C's TV Workshop (Sesame St), 1969-; founding nat chmn, founding pres, Black Psychiatrists Am Asn, 1969; nat consult, sr consult, USAF, 1976-82; pres, Am Bd Psychiat & Neurol, 1978; pres, Am Orthopsychiatric Asn, 1983; chair, NASA's Life Sci & Microgravity Sci Res Adv Comn, 1996; fel Am Acad Arts & Sci, 1997; Carter Ctr Ment Health Task Force, 2001-04; chmn, Behav & Performance Working Group; nat chairperson, Child Develop Assoc Consortium; advisor, US Arctic Res Comn; Nat Res Coun; Nimh; Nsf; Nat Aeronaut & Space Admin; Nat Acad Sci; C's Tv Network; US Arctic Res Comn; chair comts, Nat Inst Ment Health; Nat Res Coun; Nat Sci Found; World Asn Social Psychiat. **Honors/Awds:** Pierce Peak (in Antartica for biomedical res), 1968; Special Recognition Award, Nat Med Asn, 1974; hon fel, Brit Royal Col Psychiatrists; hon fel, Royal Australian & New Zealand Col Psychiat, 1978; Solomon Carter Fuller Award, Am Psychiat Asn, 1986; Chester M Pierce Annual Res Sem, Nat Med Asn, 1988-; Masserman Award, World Psychiat Assoc, 1989; hon fel, Royal Col Psychiat, 1995; Division of Global Psychiatry, Mass gen Hosp, named in honor, 2009. **Special Achievements:** Published over 180 bks, articles & reviews, chiefly on extreme environ, racism, media, and sports med; First African-American full professor at Massachusetts General Hospital. **Home Addr:** 50 S Huntington Ave Apt 12, Jamaica Plain, MA 02130-4753. **Business Addr:** Professor Emeritus Psychiatry, Harvard Graduate School of Education, 13 Appian Way, Cambridge, MA 02138, **Business Phone:** (617)495-3414.

### PIERCE, CHINYERE NNENNA. See FREELON, NNENNA.

### PIERCE, DR. GREGORY W.
Physician. **Personal:** Born Sep 25, 1957, Vallejo, CA; son of Raymond O Jr and Geraldine Brunridge; married Eurica Hill. **Educ:** Wabash Col, BA, 1979; Meharry Med Col, MD, 1983. **Career:** Univ Tenn Jackson-Madison Co Gen Hosp, intern & resident, 1983-86; Family Health Assocs, staff physician, 1986-; Bd Cert, Am Bd Family Pract, 1986-99; Patient First, med dir, Continuing Med Educ, dir & staff physician, 1992-; pvt pract, currently. **Orgs:** Chmn, J Comm Malcolm X Inst Black Studies Wabash Col; jr class pres, sr class pres, Meharry Med Col; term trustee, Meharry Med Col Bd Trustees; cert instr, Advan Cardiac Life Support; Am & Tenn Med Asns; Am & Tenn Acad Family Physicians; Southern Med Asn; NMA; chmn, Dept Med, Mid Tenn Med Ctr, 1990-91; Alpha Omega Alpha Hon Med Soc. **Honors/Awds:** Honor Scholarship & Dean's List Wabash Col; Alvin P Hall Scholarship; Mosby Scholarship Book Award; Upjohn Award for Excellence, Clin & Academic Obstet & Gynecol; Pre-Alumni Asn Annual Senior Recognition Award. **Home Addr:** 231 Loch Cir, Hampton, VA 23669. **Business Addr:** Director, Staff Physician, Patient First, 5486 Indian River Rd, Virginia Beach, VA 23464, **Business Phone:** (804)968-5700.

### PIERCE, ESQ. JOSEPH
Lawyer. **Personal:** married Kama; children: Marco, Julian & Jasmine. **Educ:** Georgetown Univ, BA, bus admin, 1991; Univ Pa Law Sch, JD, 1998; Wharton Sch Bus, MBA, 1998. **Career:** Jacksonville Jaguars, assoc gen coun, 2002-05; Hornets Sports & Entertainment, vpres & gen coun, 2013-; Comcast Sports Group, vpres bus & legal affairs; Bank Am, sr vpres & assoc gen coun global mkt & corp affairs; Wilson Sonsini Goodrich & Rosati Palo Alto, Calif, corp lawyer. **Business Addr:** Vice President, General Counsel, Hornets Sports & Entertainment, Time Warner Cable Arena 333 E Trade St, Charlotte, NC 28202, **Business Phone:** (704)688-8600.

### PIERCE, DR. KAMA B.
Educator. **Educ:** Georgetown Univ, BA, eng, 1991; Northwestern Univ Sch Law, JD, 1994. **Career:** US Ct Appeals, Third Circuit Philadelphia, staff atty, 1994-96, Hon Theodore McKee, judicial clerk, 1998-99; Theatreworks Inc, atty; Off Pub Defender, Doylestown, asst pub defender, 1996-98; Fla Coastal Sch Law, adj prof; St Mark's Sch, dir mkt, 2003-05; Episcopal Acad, Lower Sch, Merion, assoc dir admis, 2006-09; Charlotte Sch Law, asst prof, 2009-, asst dean acad affairs, 2013-14; Charlotte School of Law, assoc dean pract ready educ & assoc prof law, 2014-. **Business Addr:** Assistant Professor, Charlotte School of Law, 1211 E Morehead St, Charlotte, NC 28204, **Business Phone:** (704)971-8594.

### PIERCE, HON. LAWRENCE WARREN
Judge. **Personal:** Born Dec 31, 1924, Philadelphia, PA; son of Harold and Leora Bellinger; married Wilma Lorina Taylor; children: Warren Wood, Michael Lawrence & Mark Taylor; married Cynthia Straker. **Educ:** St Joseph Univ, Philadelphia, Pa, BS, 1948; Fordham Univ Sch Law, LLB, 1951. **Career:** Judge (retired); Gen law pract, New York, 1951-61; Legal Aid Soc, NY, staff atty, 1951-53; Kings Co, NY, asst dist atty, 1954-61; New York Police Dept, dep police comnr, 1961-63; NY State Div Youth, Albany, dir, 1963-66; NY State Narc Addiction Cont Comn, chmn, 1966-70; State Univ NY, Albany, Grad Sch Crim Justice, vis prof, 1970-71; S Dist New York, US dist judge, 1971-81; US Foreign Intelligence Surveillance Ct, judge, 1979-81; US Ct Appeals, Second Circuit, judge, 1981-90; sr judge, 1990-95; Cambodian Ct Training Proj Int Human Rights Law Group, 1995. **Orgs:** Pres, Cath Inter Coun, 1957-63; NBA; Am Bar Asn; bd mem, Lincoln Hall Boys, 1972-92; trustee, Fordham Univ, 1985-91; bd mgrs, Havens Relief Fund Soc; Am Law Inst, CARE USA; bd mem, St Joseph's Univ, Philadelphia, Pa; bd trustee, Practising Law Inst; Am Law Inst; deleg, Africa, Sweden, England, Japan, Vietnam, Korea, W Ger & People's Rep China study

legal, judicial & correctional systems; Coun Foreign Rels. **Honors/Awds:** BALSA's Ruth Whitehead Whaley Award for Distinguished Legal Achievement, Fordham Univ Sch Law; Judicial Friends' Judge Jane Bolin Award; DHL, St Joseph Univ, 1967; LLD, Fairfield Univ, 1972; LLD, Fordham Univ, 1982; LLD, Hamilton Col, 1987; LLD, St John's Univ, 1990. **Special Achievements:** Third African-American to serve on the second circuit.

### PIERCE, PAUL ANTHONY
Basketball player. **Personal:** Born Oct 13, 1977, Oakland, CA; son of Lorraine Hosey; married Julie Landrum; children: Prianna, Adrian & Prince. **Educ:** Univ KS, BA, crime & delinq studies. **Career:** Boston Celtics, small forward & capt, 1998-2013; Brooklyn Nets, small forward, 2013-14; Wash Wizards, 2014-15; Los Angeles Clippers, small forward, 2015-. **Orgs:** mem, FIBA World Championship, US Nat Team, 2002; FIBA World Championship, US Nat Team, 2006. **Honors/Awds:** Freshman of the Year, 1995-96; Most Valuable Player, Big 12 Conf Tournament, 1996-97; 1997-98; All-Rookie First Team, Nat Basketball Asn, 1999; Rookie of the Month, 1999; Player of the Month Award, Nat Basketball Asn, 2001; Player of the Week Award, Nat Basketball Asn; Champion, Nat Basketball Asn, 2008; Finals Most Valuable Player, Nat Basketball Asn, 2008. **Home Addr:** 25201 Prado Del Misterio, Calabasas, CA 91302-3600. **Business Addr:** Professional Basketball Player, Los Angeles Clippers, 1111 S Figueroa St Suite 1100, Los Angeles, CA 90015, **Business Phone:** (213)742-7500.

### PIERCE, PONCHITTA A.
Television show host, journalist, editor. **Personal:** Born Aug 5, 1942, Chicago, IL; daughter of Alfred Leonard and Nora Vincent. **Educ:** Cambridge Univ, eng, 1962; Univ Southern Calif, BA, jour, 1964. **Career:** Ebony Mag, asst ed, 1964-65, assoc ed, 1965-67; Johnson Publ Co, New York ed bur chief, 1967-68; CBS News, spec corresp, 1968-71; McCall's Mag, contrib ed, 1973-76; Reader's Dig, staff writer, 1975-77, roving ed, 1977-80; PBS, WNET Channel 13, host; WNBC-TV, mag writer & TV host; Parade Mag, contrib ed, 1994. **Orgs:** Bd dir, Foreign Policy Asn; Thirteen/WNET; Inner-City Scholar Fund Cath Archdiocese NY; Housing Enterprise Less Privileged; Josephson Inst Ethics; Women's Foreign Policy Group; Cuban Artists Fund; External affairs comt mem, Hirshhorn Mus; external affairs comt mem, Sculpture Garden; Econ Club New York; Lotos Club; Columbia Presby Health Sci Adv Coun; exec comt mem, Coun Adv, Nat Ctr C Poverty; Theta Sigma Phi New York Chap; Am Fedn TV & Radio Artists; Am Women Radio & TV; Nat Acad TV Arts & Sci, New York Chap; Womens Forum; adv bd mem, Univ Southern Calif, Ctr Pub Diplomacy, currently; Coun Foreign Rels. **Honors/Awds:** Penney-Mo Magazine Award, 1967; Headliner Award, Nat Theta Sigma Phi, 1970. **Home Addr:** 780 Madison Ave, New York, NY 10021. **Business Addr:** Advisory Board Member, University of South California, 3502 Watt Way Suite G4, Los Angeles, CA 90089-0281, **Business Phone:** (213)821-2078.

**PIERCE, DR. RAYMOND O, JR. See Obituaries Section.**

### PIERCE, RICKY CHARLES
Basketball player, basketball coach, executive. **Personal:** Born Aug 19, 1959, Dallas, TX; children: Aron. **Educ:** Rice Univ, BS, kinesiology, 2012. **Career:** Basketball player (retired), executive; Detroit Pistons, 1982-83; San Diego Clippers, 1983-84; Milwaukee Bucks, 1984-91, 1997-98; Seattle Super Sonics, 1991-94; Golden State Warriors, 1994-95; Ind Pacers, 1995-96; Denver Nuggets, 1996-97; Charlotte Hornets, 1997; AEK Athens, 1997; Accushot22, chief exec officer, 2004-.

### PIERCE, ESQ. RUDOLPH F.
Lawyer. **Personal:** Born Aug 12, 1942, Boston, MA; married Carneice; children: Kristen & Khari. **Educ:** Hampton Inst, BA, 1967; Harvard Law Sch, JD, 1970. **Career:** Crane Inker & Oteri, asso, 1972-74; Keating Perretta & Pierce, partner, 1975-76; U.S. Dist Ct, Mass, us magistrate, 1976-79; Mass Super Ct, judge, 1979-85; US Dist Ct Mass, Fed Magistrate; Harvard Law Sch, lectr, 1981-2008; Boston Col Law Sch, 1982-85; Nat Judicial Col, Instr Sentencing, 1983-85; Goulston & Storrs, atty, 1991-. **Orgs:** Pres, Boston Bar Asn, 1989-90; fel Am Col Trial Lawyers, 1995-; Int Acad Trial Lawyers; New Eng Aquarium; trustee, C's Hosp; chmn, Nat Inst Trial Advocacy, trustee; trustee, Inst Health care Improv. **Honors/Awds:** American Leading Business Lawyers, Chambers & Partners, 2003-10; Best Lawyers in Am, 2006 & 2008; Martindale Hubbell Peer Review Rated AV Preeminent Tm, "America's Leading Business Lawyers" Chambers USA, 2003-10; Best Lawyers in America, 2006-13. **Special Achievements:** First African American president of the Boston Bar Association; co-author, The "Other" Costs of Securities Class Action Settlements, Find Law, 2004. **Home Addr:** 150 Staniford St Suite 718, Boston, MA 02114. **Business Addr:** Attorney, Goulston & Storrs, 1999 K St SW Suite 500, Washington, DC 20006-1121, **Business Phone:** (202)721-0011.

### PIERCE, WALTER J., SR.
Educator. **Personal:** Born Jan 16, 1941, Minden, LA; married Iopha Douglas; children: Gay, Gwenevera & Iopha Anita. **Educ:** BS, 1964. **Career:** Educator (retired); Atascadero State Hosp, recreation therapist, 1964-69; Kiwanis Club, counr, 1968-70; Tulare View, dir rehab, 1969-70; Northside Hosp, dir activ, 1970-71; Calif State Univ, affirmative action coordr, 1972-74, asst coord advising & testing serv, 1974, Advising Serv, asst dir. **Orgs:** Kiwanis Club, 1968-70; Nat Asn Advan Colored People; Black Educr, Fresno, CA; Fresno Housing Affirmative Comt; Baptist Sunday Sch Supt; Plan Variation; chmn, Man Power & Econ Area 6. **Honors/Awds:** Outstanding Young Men America, 1970; Certificate of Merit, Nat Acad Adv Asn, 1986. **Home Addr:** 6040 W Birch Ave, Fresno, CA 93722-2874, **Home Phone:** (559)276-1160.

### PIERCE, DR. WILLIAM DALLAS
Psychologist. **Personal:** Born Nov 16, 1940, Sunbury, NC. **Educ:** Univ Pittsburg, BS, 1962; Ohio State Univ, MA, 1965, PhD, 1967. **Career:** Pvt pract, clin psychologist, 1969-; Univ Calif Berkeley, Dept Psychol, lectr, 1970-; Dept Ment Health Comn Mass, regional serv admin, 1979-80. **Orgs:** Founding mem, Asn Black Psychologists, 1968; chmn comn ment health, Asn Black Psychologists, 1971-73; dir clin serv, 1971-73, exec dir, 1973-77, Westside Community Ment Health Ctr; pres, Bay Area Asn Black Psychologists, 1978-79. **Honors/Awds:** Appreciation Award, Asn Black Psychologists, 1970; Blacks in the West Hall of Fame, San Francisco African Hist Cult Soc, 1976; Annual Award for leadership, Serv Asn Black Psychologisgts, 1980. **Business Addr:** President, William D Pierce PhD, 361 Upper Terr, San Francisco, CA 94117-4517, **Business Phone:** (415)771-3938.

### PIERRE, DR. DALLAS
Dentist. **Personal:** Born Jun 9, 1933, Charenton, LA; son of Russell Sr; married Carol Ann Yates; children: James Darian. **Educ:** Prairie View A&M Univ, BS, 1955; Tex State Univ, MS, 1963; Univ Tex, Dental Br, DDS, 1968; Trinity Univ, adv study. **Career:** Pvt pract dentist, currently. **Orgs:** E Tex Area BSA; Nat Platform Asn; Phi Beta Sigma; Univ Tex Alumni Asn; Citizens C C Angelina Co; Baptist Church; pres, Gulf State Dent Asn; secy, E Tex Med Dent Phar Asn; Golden Heritage mem, Nat Asn Advan Colored People; E Tex Minority Bus Develop Found Inc, 1974-; Lufkin Daily News Ed Roundtable; Am Dent Asn; deleg, Nat Dent Asn; emer, Acad Gen Dent; golden heritage mem, NAACP; Tex Dent Asn; E Tex Dent Soc; Lufkin ISD Sch Bd; Int Platform Asn; Acad Gen Dent; pres, Adm's Club. **Honors/Awds:** Honoree, Colgate Dental Health Educ Adv Bd; Top Ladies of Distinction; Citizen of the Year, Prof Activ Club Nacogdoches & Angelina Counties; NAACP, Golden Heritage Mem; honoree, Notable Am Bicentennial Era; honoree, Community Leaders & Noteworthy Americans; Who's Who in the South and Southwest, 1973-74; Who's Who Among Black Americans, 1975-76; Who's Who Among American Dentists, 1995-96; Eagle Award, Angelina Citizens Chamber Com, 2008. **Home Addr:** 106 McMullen St, Lufkin, TX 75901. **Business Addr:** Dentist, 809 Kurth Dr, Lufkin, TX 75904-2037, **Business Phone:** (936)632-5255.

### PIERRE, JENNIFER CASEY
Executive. **Personal:** Born Aug 25, 1953, Baltimore, MD; daughter of Johnny Casey and Mary L Murreld; married Clifford Marston; children: Marianne Alicia & Marissa Janelle. **Educ:** Carnegie Mellon Univ, Pittsburgh, PA, BS, math, 1975; Columbia Bus Sch, New York, NY, MBA, 1977. **Career:** Gen Foods Corp, White Plains, New York, asst brand mgr, 1977-79; Am Can Co, Greenwich, Conn, assoc brand mgr, 1979-81; RJ Reynolds Tobacco Co, Winston Salem, NC, mgr fulfillment, mgr tracking & eval, 1981-97; vis prof, Nat Urban League BEEP, 1986-. **Orgs:** Vol, Forsyth Ct Vols, 1981-84; bd mem, Baldwin Sch, 1985; United Way. **Home Addr:** 5412 Kingsbridge Rd, Winston Salem, NC 27103-5994. **Business Addr:** Manager, RJ Reynolds Tobacco Co, 401 N Main St, Winston Salem, NC 27101, **Business Phone:** (919)741-7548.

### PIERRE, DR. PERCY ANTHONY
Research administrator, educator, executive. **Personal:** Born Jan 3, 1939, St. James, LA; son of Percy and Rosa Villavaso; married Olga A Markham; children: Kristin Clare & Allison Celeste. **Educ:** Univ Notre Dame, BSEE, 1961, MSEE, 1963; Johns Hopkins Univ, PhD, elec engineering, 1967. **Career:** Johns Hopkins Univ, instr elec eng, 1963-64; Morgan State Col, instr physics, 1964-66; Univ MI, instr info & control eng, 1967-68; Univ Calif, Los Angeles, instr systs eng, 1968-69; RAND Corp, res engr commun, 1968-71; Off Pres, White House, fel spl asst, 1969-70; Howard Univ, dean sch eng, 1971-77; Alfred P Sloan Found, prog officer eng educ, 1973-75; Percy A. Pierre & Assoc, eng mgt consult, 1981-83; Prairie View A&M Univ, pres, 1983-89, Hitachi, bd dir, 1988-; Honeywell, prof elec eng, 1989-90; CMS Energy Corp, bd mem, 1990-; Mich State Univ, vpres, 1990-95, dir sloan scholar prog, prof elec & comput eng, 1995-2005, vpres & prof emer, 2005-; Aerospace Corp, bd mem, 1991-; Dual Inc, bd mem, 1992; Old Kent Financial Corp, dir, 1992-; IDL Technol IST, bd dir, 1992-94; White House FelsFound & Asn, dir; TracLabs Inc, dir. **Orgs:** Ctr Naval Anal, 1987-94; trustee emer, Univ Notre Dame, 1973-; Inst Elec & Electronis Eng; Sigma Xi; Tau Beta Pi; Sci Res Soc Am; trustee, Hampshire Col, 1996-; bd mem, Nat Action Coun Minorities Engineering, 1983-89. **Honors/Awds:** AAAS Lifetime Mentor Award, Mem Nat Acad Engineering; Hon Doctoral Degree, The Univ Notre Dame, 1977; Award of Merit, Sen Proxmire, 1979; Distinguished Civilian Service Award, AUS, 1981; Reginald Jones Award, Nat Action Coun Minorities Engineering, 1984; Hon Doctoral Degree, Rensselaer Poly tech Inst, 1984; Super Public Service Award, USN, 1993; Frazier Thompson Pioneer Award, Black Alumni Univ Notre Dame, 1997; The Golden Torch Award, Nat Soc Black Eng, 2003; Frederick Scott Award, Soc Black Alumni Johns Hopkins Univ, 2003; Founder's Award, Nat Action Coun Minorities Engineering, 2004; Diversity Award, Mich State Univ, 2004; Lifetime Mentors Award, AAAS, 2008. **Special Achievements:** Author of over thirty articles on engineering research, engineering educ, systs anal & military research & develop; the first African Am to earn a doctorate in electrical engineering, 1967; First African-American appointed assistant secretary, USArmy Res & Develop; First African-American appointed acting Secretary of the Army. **Home Addr:** 2445 Emerald Lake Dr, East Lansing, MI 48823, **Home Phone:** (517)351-4544. **Business Addr:** Professor Emeritus, Vice President Emeritus, Michigan State University, 3224 Engineering Bldg, East Lansing, MI 48824, **Business Phone:** (517)432-5148.

### PIERRE-LOUIS, DR. CONSTANT
Educator, physician, association executive. **Personal:** Born Feb 11, 1939; married Jeany; children: Marilyn, Pascale & Carolyn. **Educ:** State Univ Port-au-Prince Med Sch, MD, 1963. **Career:** Physician (retired); Columbia Univ, 1971-75; Downstate Univ, clin asst prof urol; Brookdale Hosp; St John's Epis Hosp; Unity Hosp, staff; pvt pract urologist. **Orgs:** Am bd urol; fel Am Col Surg; NY State Med Soc, Nat Med Asn; founder, bd mem & pres, Asn Haitian Physicians Abroad, 1975-76; founding partner, Adelphi Med Art Asn. **Honors/Awds:** Essay Contest Third prize, 1969. **Special Achievements:** Publisher: "Lymphoma of the Urethra Masquerading as a Caruncle" 1972; "Morphologic Appearance of Leydig Cells in Patients with Prostatic Cancer & Benign Prostatic Hypertrophy", NY Acad Med Urol Resd; "Delayed Subcapsular Renal Hematoma" Urol, 1977. **Home Addr:** 1141 Eastern Pkwy, Brooklyn, NY 11213, **Home Phone:** (718)523-3680.

### PIERSON, DERRON
Executive, vice president (organization). **Career:** Solo Construct Corp, vpres & sales exec, 1978-. **Business Addr:** Vice President, Sales Executive, Solo Construction Corp, 15251 NE 18th Ave Suite 12, North Miami Beach, FL 33162, **Business Phone:** (305)944-3922.

### PIERSON, KATHRYN A.
Chief executive officer, lawyer. **Personal:** Born May 27, 1956, Chicago, IL; daughter of Edward and Myrtle; married Cedric Hendricks; children: Malcolm, Marcus & Nikki Henricks. **Educ:** George Washington Univ, BA, jour, polit sci, 1979; Howard Univ, JD, 1985. **Career:** Pierson & Archibald, lawyer & partner, 1987-93; Minority Asset Recovery Contractors Asn, exec dir, 1993-95; Trade winds Int, dir bus develop, 1995, bus develop consult, 1996; Malnikus Real Estate Enterprises Inc, chief exec officer; ING Financial Partners, gen agt; DC Bus Incubator, consult, currently; Regal Finance & Consult, chief exec officer, currently. **Orgs:** Chair, bd dir, WPFW-FM, 1982-84; secy, chair, develop comt, Pacifica Found Corp, 1984-90; bd mem, Marshall Heights Community Develop Orgn, 1989-91; bd trustee, Rhythm & Blues Found, 1990; chair, bd dir, Dist Curators, 1991-. **Business Addr:** Chief Executive Officer, Regal Finance & Consulting Llc, 5726 6th St NW, Washington, DC 20011-0000.

### PIERSON, RANDY
Executive, founder (originator), chief executive officer. **Career:** Solo Construct Corp, co-founder, 1978-, pres, chief exec officer, dir, currently. **Business Addr:** Co-Founder, Chief Executive Officer, Solo Construction Corp, 3855 Com Pkwy, Miramar, FL 33025-3940, **Business Phone:** (954)447-2800.

### PIGGEE, JAMES M.
School administrator. **Career:** Educator (retired); Horace Mann High Sch, dean stud; Lew Wallace High Sch, high sch asst or vprin, 2005-06; Gary Community Sch Corp, asst prin. **Business Addr:** Assistant Principal, Coach & Administrator, Gary Community School Corp, 415 W 45th Ave, Gary, IN 46408-3998, **Business Phone:** (219)980-6305.

### PILE, MICHAEL DAVID MCKENZIE
Administrator. **Personal:** Born Jan 28, 1954, New York, NY; son of Ernest S and Ulalie. **Educ:** Colgate Univ, Hamilton, NY, BA, 1976; NY Univ, New York, NY, MPA, 1983. **Career:** Queens Hosp Ctr, Queens, NY, asst dir, 1978-86; Long Island Jewish Hillside Med Ctr, Queens, NY, 1984-86; Syracuse Univ, Syracuse, NY, health serv adminr, 1983-89; Calif State Univ, Sacramento, Calif, dir univ health Ctr, 1989. **Orgs:** Am Pub Health Asn, 1981; Am Col Health Asn, 1984-; chair, Constitution & Bylaws, Pacific Coast Col Health Asn, 1990-92. **Home Addr:** PO Box 191206, Sacramento, CA 95819-1206, **Home Phone:** (916)361-8529. **Business Addr:** CA.

### PILGRIM, DR. DAVID
Educator. **Personal:** Born Jan 3, 1959, Manhattan, NY; son of Eustace and Jean Shears; married Margaret Ryan; children: Haley Grace, Gabrielle Lynn & Eustace Jamison. **Educ:** Jarvis Christian Col, Hawkins, Tex, BA, 1980; Ohio State Univ, MA, 1982, PhD, applied sociol, 1984. **Career:** St Mary's Col, asst prof, 1984-89; Ferris State Univ, prof sociol, 1990-, chief diversity officer, Diversity & Inclusion, vpres; Jim Crow Mus, founder & cur, 1998-; Documentary Jim Crow's Museum, produced, 2004; UPN TV show, "All Of Us", consult to Will Smith, 2006. **Orgs:** Bd dir, Mich Mus Asn, 2003; dir, Am Black Studies Libr; Ferris State Univ Diversity Counts Comt. **Home Addr:** 189 Cahill Dr, Rockford, MI 49341, **Home Phone:** (616)866-3086. **Business Addr:** vice president, Ferris State University, 1201 S State St CSS 312, Big Rapids, MI 49307-2225, **Business Phone:** (231)591-3946.

### PILLOW, VANITA J.
Salesperson. **Personal:** Born Dec 16, 1949, Nashville, TN. **Career:** Des Moines Main PO Supply & Procurement Asst; TN State Univ, part time instr, 1971; Exp Theatre sponsor; Elec Dance Workshop Sponser, 1972; Fayette Co Bd Educ, sec instr & Beta Hon Soc sponsor, 1973; speech dramatics arts grad asst; S Cent Bell Bus Off, sales rep teller. **Orgs:** Theta Alpha Phi, 1969; USO Tour Ger, Holland, Belg, 1970; Women's Bowling League, 1971; Univ Couns; pres, TN State Players Guild; Nat Asn Advan Colored People; Minority Consumer Commun Theatre Nashville, 1974. **Honors/Awds:** Best female actress, 1971; C Theatre Chicago Grad top 10 percent class. **Home Addr:** 1010 N 7 St, Nashville, TN 37207.

### PILOT, ANN HOBSON
Musician. **Personal:** Born Nov 6, 1943, Philadelphia, PA; daughter of Harrison and Grace Stevens Smith; married R Prentice; children: Lynn & Prentice. **Educ:** Cleveland Inst, BM, 1966; Bridgewater State Col, PhD, fine arts. **Career:** Prin Harpist (retired); Pittsburgh Sym Orchestra, second harpist, 1965-66; Wash Nat Sym, prin harpist, 1966-69; Ambler Music Festival, fac, 1968-69; New Eng Conserv Music, Boston, MA, harp teacher, 1971-; Boston Sym Orchestra, asst prin harpist, prin harpist, 1980-09; Tanglewood Music Ctr, Lenox, MA, harp fac, 1989-; Pa Musical Acad, fac; Philadelphia Musical Acad, former fac; Boston Univ, fac. **Orgs:** Partic, Marlboro Music Festival; fac, New Eng Conserv Music, Berkshire Music Ctr; soloist, Boston Sym Orchestra; founder mem, New Eng Harp Trio, 1971-; Contemp Music Ensemble, Col performances Europe, Japan, ChinaHaiti; bd dir, Holy Trinity Sch Haiti; bd trustees, Longy Sch Music, 1993-96; bd dir, Boston Music Educ Collab; Boston Symphony Chamber Players; Ritz Chamber Players; founder, New Eng Harp Trio. **Honors/Awds:** Hon Professional, Arts Soc Philadelphia, 1987; Honorary Doctorate of Fine Arts, Bridgewater State Col, 1988; Distinguished Woman of the Year, 1991; Sch Music Alumni Achievement Award, 1992; Distinguished Alumni Award, Cleveland Inst Music, 1993 & 2010; Col Club Career Award, 1997. **Special Achievements:** Recordings for Boston Records, Ann Hobson Pilot, solo harp. Contrasts, music for flute and harp with Leone Buyse. for Koch Intl, Ginastera and Mathias Concerti with the English Chamber Orchestra. Dello-Joie harpconcerto with the New Zealand Symphony; Chamber Music of William Mathias and Arnold Bax, performed the Mozart Concerto again at Tanglewood in

2005. **Home Addr:** 319 Osprey Pt Dr, Osprey, FL 34229-9252, **Home Phone:** (617)232-4769.

**PINADO, ALAN E., SR.**
Educator, real estate agent. **Personal:** Born Dec 15, 1931, New York, NY; son of Herman E and Agnes Steber; married Patricia LaCour; children: Alan E Jr, Jeanne M Pinado-Getter, Anthony M & Steven L. **Educ:** Fordham Univ, Col Bus Admin, BS, mktg, 1953; Univ Notre Dame, MBA, 1958. **Career:** Educator, real estate agent (retired); Wm R Morris Agency, S Bend, IN, real estate sales, devel, 1960-61; Allied Fed Savings & Loan, Jamaica, NY, exec vpres & mortgage loan officer, 1961-67; IBM Corp, NY, mktg rep, 1967-68; NY LIfe Ins Co, NY, asst vpres, vpres real estate finance, 1968-84, vpres, mgt coordr & training, 1984-85; Real Estate Inst Clark Atlanta Univ Morehouse Col, dir, 1986-2002; Ernst & Young, managing partner. **Orgs:** Dir emer, Minority Interchange, 1975-; dir, Oppty Funding Corp, 1979-90; dir, Urban Home Ownership Corp, 1980-92; NY Life Pac, 1983-85; Wilton Conn United Way, 1983-85; dir, United Mutual Ins Co, 1985-87; dir, Nat Housing Coun, 1994-98; adv comt, Prudential bank, 1995-97; dir, Univ Comt Devel Corp, 1996; Archdiocesan Planning & Devel Coun; chmn, Urban Education Coalition Inc. **Honors/Awds:** James J & Jane Hoey Award, Catholic Interracial Coun NY, 1972; DLL, Mary Holmes Col, 1976; Horace Sudduth Award, Nat Bus League, 1978. **Home Addr:** 650 Phipps Blvd NE Apt 1809, Atlanta, GA 30326-3297.

**PINCKNEY, ANDREW MORGAN, JR.**
Administrator. **Personal:** Born Jul 2, 1933, Georgetown, SC; married Brenda Cox; children: Meika & Margo. **Educ:** Morris Brown Col, Atlanta, BS, 1960; Lasalle Col Phila, bus admin, 1968; Univ Pa, Phila, wharton mgt, 1976. **Career:** Franklin Inst Lab Phila, res chemist, 1961-62; Skin & Cancer Hosp Phila, res assoc, 1962-63; Merck Sharp & Dohme W Pt PA, adminr; Merck Sharp & Dohme, res Biol, 1963-73. **Orgs:** Am Mgt Asn; Black Univ Liasion Comt Merck & Co; steering comt United Way; pres, Philadelphia Alumni Chap Morris Brown; pres, Club Noble Gents; financial sec Black Polit Forum, 1975; bd mem, Merck Sharp & Dohme Fed Credit Union; Campaign Merck Sharp & Co, 1976-79. **Honors/Awds:** Morris Brown Col Athletic Hall of Fame, TAY Club Atlanta, 1975; Purple & Black Service Award, Morris Brown Col Nat Alumni Atlanta, 1979. **Home Addr:** 1610 E Mt Pleasant Ave, Philadelphia, PA 19150-1209, **Home Phone:** (215)924-9354.

**PINCKNEY, CLEMENTA C.**
Government official. **Personal:** Born Jul 30, 1973, Beaufort, SC; son of John and Theopia (deceased); married Jennifer Benjamin; children: Eliana Yvette & Malana. **Educ:** Allen Univ, BA, 1995; Univ SC, MPA, 1999; Lutheran Southern Sem, grad, 1999. **Career:** Princeton Univ, res fel summer, 1994; Mt Horr AME Church Yonges Island, pastor; State Rep, SC, serv house, 1997-2000, sen, Dist 45, 2001-. **Orgs:** Fel Princeton Univ Res, 1995; bd mem, STOP Tax; bd dir, Southern Mutual Ins Co. **Home Addr:** PO Box 507, Ridgeland, SC 29936, **Home Phone:** (843)726-6019. **Business Addr:** Senator, State South Carolina, 512 Gressette Bldg, Columbia, SC 29201, **Business Phone:** (803)212-6148.

**PINCKNEY, EDWARD LEWIS**
Basketball coach, basketball player. **Personal:** Born Mar 27, 1963, Bronx, NY; married Rose Marie; children: Shea, Spencer, Austin & Andrea. **Educ:** Villanova Univ, Villanova, PA, 1985. **Career:** Basketball (retired), coach; Phoenix Suns, 1985-87; Sacramento Kings, 1987-89; Boston Celtics, 1989-94; Milwaukee Bucks, 1994-95; Toronto Raptors, 1995-96; Philadelphia 76ers, 1996, color analyst, 2009-10; Miami Heat, 1996-97; Miami Heat orgn, radio & TV analyst, 1997-2002, dir mentoring progs, 2002-03; Villanova Wildcats, asst coach, 2003-07; Minn Timberwolves, asst coach, 2007-10; Chicago Bulls, asst coach, 2010-15; Denver Nuggets, asst coach, 2015-16. **Honors/Awds:** Tournaments Most Outstanding Player; Champions, Nat Col Athletic Asn, 1985; Most Outstanding Player, Nat Col Athletic Asn, 1985; Robert V Geasey Trophy, Herb Good Basketball Club, 1985. **Special Achievements:** NBA Draft, First round pick, 10, 1985; Selected 10th overall by the Phoenix Suns in the 1985 NBA Draft. **Business Addr:** Assistant Coach, Chicago Bulls, 1901 W Madison St, Chicago, IL 60612-2459, **Business Phone:** (312)455-4000.

**PINCKNEY, JAMES L., SR.**
Government official. **Personal:** Born Jun 24, 1942, Fairfax, SC; married Gladys M Simmons; children: Janet, Jerome, Zachary & Lorraine. **Educ:** Allen Univ, BS, phys educ, 1964. **Career:** Lower Saunnal Coun Govts, bd mem, 1984-; Govt Allendale County, Dist 3, coun mem & legis deleg, 1985-, coun chmn, 2005, coun vice chmn, currently. **Orgs:** Bd mem, Allendale-Fairfax HS Advy Coun, 1982-84. **Home Addr:** PO Box 425, Fairfax, SC 29827. **Business Addr:** County Council Member, Vice-Chairman, Government of Allendale County, 526 Memorial Ave, Allendale, SC 29810, **Business Phone:** (803)584-3438.

**PINCKNEY, LEWIS, JR.**
Executive, hospital administrator. **Personal:** Born Dec 25, 1932, Columbia, SC; son of Louis Sr and Channie Hopkins; married Johnnye Caver; children: Lewis III & Johnette V. **Educ:** Benedict Col, attended 1953; Cook Co Grad Sch Med, ARRT, 1957; DePaul Univ, attended 1975. **Career:** Cook County Hosp, staff tech, 1957-64, qual control supv, 1964-68, chief x-ray tech educ dir, 1968-69, admin asst to chmn, 1969-73, admin; St Bernard Hosp, dir radiol serv. **Orgs:** John Jones Lodge No 7 F & AM Ill, 1963-; Ill State Soc Radiologic Tech, 1971-74; Lions Asn, 1971-73; Am Soc Radiologic Tech, 1973; Am Hosp Radiol Admin, 1973-76; WA Pk YMCA, 1974; conf leader, Inst Graphic Commun, 1974; evaluating qual control, Cook Co Grad Schl Med, 1977. **Home Addr:** 9209 S Luella Ave, Chicago, IL 60617. **Business Addr:** Director, St Bernard Hospital, 64th & Dan Ryan Expressway, Chicago, IL 60612, **Business Phone:** (773)962-3900.

**PINCKNEY, STANLEY**
Teacher, artist, educator. **Personal:** Born Sep 30, 1940, Boston, MA. **Educ:** Famous Artist Sch, W port, CT, com art, 1960; Sch Boston Mus Fine Arts, Boston, MA, dipl, 1967, cert, Grad Prog, 1969. **Career:** Teacher (retired); artist; Boston Univ Prog Artisanry, guest artist, 1967; Sch Boston Mus Fine Arts, teacher, 1972-2006; Blanche E Colman fel, Blanche E Colman Found, Boston, Mass, 1978; Northeastern Univ, African-Am Artists-in-Residency, 1978; Albert H Whitin fel, Sch Boston Mus Fine Arts, 1978; Col Art, guest artist, 1979. **Honors/Awds:** Ford Found Grant, Music Sch Fine Arts, Boston, MA, 1978.

**PINDELL, HOWARDENA D.**
Curator, artist, educator. **Personal:** Born Apr 14, 1943, Philadelphia, PA; daughter of Howard Douglas and Mildred Lewis. **Educ:** Boston Univ, Sch Fine & Appl Arts, BFA, painting, 1965; Yale Univ, Sch Art & Archit, MFA, 1967. **Career:** Mus Mod Art, exhib asst, curatorial asst & assoc cur, 1967-79; Pratt Inst, guest lectr, 1972; Hunter Col, fac, 1972; Morivian Col, fac, 1973; Queens Col, fac, 1973; Sch Visual Arts, fac, 1973, 1975; Montclair State Col, fac, 1974; Brooklyn Mus, staff, 1976; State Univ NY, Stony Brook, prof, 1979-; Yale Univ, vis prof, 1995-99. **Orgs:** Afro-Am Artists, 1973; Guggeneheim fel 1987-88; Joan Mitchell fel 1994; Int Art Critics Asn; Int House Japan; Col Art Asn; ACASA. **Honors/Awds:** Honorary Doctorate, Massachusetts Col Art, Boston, MA; Honorary Doctorate, Parson Sch Design & New Sch Univ, New York; Two National Endowment for the Arts Grants; A Joan Mitchell Grant; Alumni Award Distinguished Service to Professor, Boston Univ, 1983; Guggenheim Fellowship, 1987; Most Distinguished Body of Work or Performance Award, Col Art Asn, 1990; Studio Museum Harlem Artist Award, 1994; Women Caucus Art Distinguished Contribution to the Professor Award, 1996; Honorary Doctorate of Fine Arts, Mass Col Art, 1997; Community Service Award, NY State United Teachers, 1998. **Special Achievements:** Author: The Heart of the Question, 1997. **Business Addr:** Professor, State University of New York at Stony Brook, Rm 4211 2224 Staller Ctr Arts, Stony Brook, NY 11794-5400, **Business Phone:** (631)632-7250.

**PINDER, REV. NELSON W.**
Executive, clergy. **Personal:** Born Jul 27, 1932, Miami, FL; son of George and Coleen Saunders; married Marian Grant; children: Gail (deceased) & Squire. **Educ:** Bethune Cookman Col, BA, 1956; Nashotah House Sem, BD, 1959; Inst IN Univ, Adult Educ, 1959; Urban Training Ctr, 1964; FL A & M, MEd, 1974; Bethune Cookman Col Daytona Beach FL, DD, 1979. **Career:** Clergy (retired), executive; St John Baptist Episcopal Church, vicar, 1959-69; Awareness Ctr Orlando, dir, 1969-71; Diocese Ctr FL, staff mem, 1971; St John Baptist Episcopal Church Orlando, priest, 1974, interim rector; Union Black Episcopalians, vpres, currently; Episcopal Relief & Develop Fund, coord. **Orgs:** Joint Comn Church Small Comt, 1970-; Chmn, Recruitment & Equal Employ Oppor Comn, Prov VI Episcopal Church, 1972-; mem bd dir, Union Black Episcopalians, 1973-74; assoc trustee, Bethune Cookman Col; bd trustees Bethune Cookman Col; Dept Urban Affairs; Phi Delta Kappa; Walt Disney World Awards Comt, 1973; past Pres, Delta Ix Lambda; trustee, Univ S, Sewanee, TN, 1983-; Nat Comn Social & Specialized Ministry, 1989-; chair, Anti-Racism Training Comt Diocese Cent Fla, currently; 100 Black Men Orlando Inc. **Honors/Awds:** United Negro College Fund Award, 1971; 1st Annual Disney World Community Service Award, 1972; Black community Award, 1972; Alpha Kappa Alpha Community Award, 1972; US Congress Chaplains Award, 1973; Knights Columbus Citizenship Award, 1974; Bethune Cookman medallion, 1975; Lifetime Achievement Award, 100 Black Men Orlando Inc, 2013. **Home Addr:** 2632 Marquise Ct, Orlando, FL 32805, **Home Phone:** (407)295-5937. **Business Addr:** President, Union of Black Episcopalians, 1550 Magnolia Dr, Cincinnati, OH 45215, **Business Phone:** (513)281-5200.

**PINES, DARRYLL J.**
College teacher, college administrator, engineer. **Personal:** Born Aug 28, 1964, Oakland, CA. **Educ:** Univ Calif, Berkeley, BS, mech engineering, 1986; Mass Inst Technol, MS, mech engineering, 1988, PhD, mech engineering, 1991. **Career:** Chevron Corp; Space Tethers Inc; Lawrence Livermore Nat Lab, tech staff mem, 1992-95; Univ Md, asst prof, 1995, dir Sloan Scholars Prog, 1996, dir GEM Prog, 1999, prof, 2003-15, aerospace engineering dept chair, 2006-09, A. James Clark Sch Engineering, Nariman Farvardin Prof Engineering & dean, 2009-; DARPA (Defense Advan Res Proj Agency), Defense Sci Off & Tactical Technol Off, prog mgr, 2003-06. **Orgs:** Inst Physics, Am Soc Mech Engrs, Am Soc Engineering Educ, Am Helicopter Soc, Am Inst Aeronaut & Astronaut. **Business Addr:** University of Maryland, College Park, MD 20742, **Business Phone:** (301)405-8335.

**PINKARD, BEDFORD L.**
Government official, commissioner. **Personal:** Born Oct 9, 1931, Jacksonville, TX; son of Adela and Dee; married Irene Stephens; children: Derek Louis & Keven D. **Educ:** La State Col, attended 1958, Calif Polytech Col, 1951; Ventural Col, AA, 1953; Calif State Univ, Northridge, BS, 1973. **Career:** Oxnard City, Community Youth Pro, dir, 1979-80, recreation supvr, 1959-91, councilman, Parks & Recreation Comn, comnr; Venutura County, Harbor Comn, comnr, currently. **Orgs:** Oxnard Noontimers Lions Club 1964-; pres, Bd Educ Oxnard Union High Sch Dist, 1972-92; Ventura County Grand Jury; Oxnard Sch Dist Personnel Comn; Multi-Cult Festival; Citizen Adv Comt Calif Youth Authority; Calif State Univ Ventura Campus Adv Bd; Ventura County Martin Luther King, Jr. Comt; Oxnard Ambassadors; Bethel AME Church; founder, Oxnard Youth Employ Serv; Black Am Polit Asn Calif; founder, World Renown La Colonia Youth Boxing Prog. **Home Addr:** 2047 Spyglass Trl E, Oxnard, CA 93036-2771, **Home Phone:** (805)485-9566. **Business Addr:** Commissioner, Ventura County, 800 S Victoria Ave 300 W 3rd St, Ventura, CA 93009.

**PINKARD, DR. DELORIS ELAINE**
Educator, college administrator. **Personal:** Born Oct 22, 1944, Kansas City, KS; daughter of Andrew D Jackson and Ella Mae Williams Jackson; children: Karisse Grigsby Whyte & Robert C Edwards. **Educ:** Emporia State Univ, BS, elem educ, 1966, MS, educ admin, 1984; Univ Kans, MS, educ psychol & res, 1980; Univ Kans, EdD, 1995. **Career:** Educator, college administrator (retired); Wash Dist Schs, Kans City, Kans, teacher, 1966-69; Kans Cath Diocese, Kans City, Kans, teacher, 1970-72; Kans City Kans Pub Schs, Kans City Kans, teacher, 1972-82, admininern, 1982-83, prin, 1983-86, personnel dir, 1986-92, vpres exec serv, dean human resources; Kans Kans Comm Col, dean human resources, 1992-94, vpres exec serv, 1994-2000; DEP2 Consult, chief exec officer; Ctr Sch Dist, prin & dist coordr. **Orgs:** Kappa Delta Pi, 1966; bd mem, Yates Br YWCA, 1969; bd dir, Wyandotte Co Ment Health Comn, 1971; Phi Delta Kappa, Emporia State Univ; conf presenter, Networking Women Educ Admin, 1984; induction speaker, Lyons Co Phi Delta Kappa, Fighting Teacher Burnout, 1985; keynote speaker, Sorority Founders Recognition, Equity With Excellence, 1986; Mo Valley Sch Personnel Admin Asn, 1986-; Asn Sch, Col & Univ Staffing, 1986-; Am Asn Sch Personnel Admin, 1986-; evangelism chairperson, Mason Mem UM Church; pres & bd dir, Kans City KS Womens Chamber Com, 1987-; conf presenter, Direction Educ Minority Stud & Legis Alternatives, Kans Black Legis Conf, 1987; secy, Kans-Nat Alliance Black Sch Educ, 1988-; bd dir, Martin Luther King Urban Ctr, 1988-; interim secy, Nat Asn Advan Colored People, 1989; coordr, United Negro Col Fund Dr, 1989; community adv bd, Jr Gordens CsProj, 1995-; bd dir, Univ Kans Alumni Asn, 1998-. **Home Addr:** 7823 Walker Ave, Kansas City, KS 66112, **Home Phone:** (913)334-6476.

**PINKETT, ALLEN JEROME**
Salesperson, football player. **Personal:** Born Jan 25, 1964, Washington, DC. **Educ:** Univ Notre Dame, BBA, 1986. **Career:** Football player (retired), salesperson; Houston Oilers, running back & kick returner, 1986-91; New Orleans Saints; Notre Dame Football, Westwood One, color commentator, 2001-; ESPN 1000, host, currently; Hartford Financial Serv Group Inc, sales rep, currently. **Business Addr:** Sales Representative, Hartford Financial Services Group Inc, 1 Hartford Plz, Hartford, CT 06155, **Business Phone:** (860)547-5000.

**PINKETT, JADA KOREN.** See SMITH, JADA PINKETT.

**PINKETT, DR. RANDAL D.**
Entrepreneur, executive. **Personal:** Born Apr 9, 1971, Philadelphia, PA; son of Leslie and Elizabeth; married Zahara Wadud; children: Amira Leslie. **Educ:** Rutgers Univ, BS, elec engineering, 1994; Univ Oxford, Eng, MS, 1996; Mass Inst Technol, MBA, bus admin, 1998, MS, elec engineering, 1998, PhD, media arts & sci, 2001. **Career:** MBS Enterprises, co-founded, pres & chief exec oficer, 1993-2001; Gen Elec, analog & digital design engr, 1994; AT&T Bell Labs, tech staff, 1995; Lucent Technologies, tech staff, 1997-98; Partners Inc, Bus & Cot Technol, dir, 2000-; BCT Partners LLC, co-founder, chmn, pres & chief exec officer, 2000-; Verizon Commun, brand ambassador; Outback Steakhouse, brand ambassador; Miller Urban Entreprenuers Ser, brand ambassador; State Dem Comt, chair, 2009. **Orgs:** Alpha Phi Alpha fraternity; Nat exec bd, Nat Soc Black Engrs, 1993-94; Cap & Skull orgn; Asn Am Rhodes Scholars, 1996-; Black Grad Stud Asn, 1996-; Nat Black MBA Asn, 2000-; Trump Orgn, 2005-06. **Honors/Awds:** Col All-Academic First Team, USA Today, 1993; Nat Soc Black Engineers, Nat Member of the Year, 1994; Rhodes Scholarship, The Rhodes Trust, 1994; NCAA, Acad All-Am, 1994; NSF Graduate Fellowship, Nat Sci Found, 1996; Rockefeller Next Generation Leadership Program Fellowship, 2002; Paul Robeson Leadership Award, Concerned Black Men Mass, 2006. **Special Achievements:** Mass Inst Technol (MIT) "Product Development Process Modeling and Analysis of Digital Wireless Telephones" masters thesis, 1998; Univ Oxford, England, "Hardware/Software Co-Design and Digital Speech Processing" masters thesis, 1996; 30 Leaders for the Future, Black Enterprise Magazine, 2000; 30 Leaders for the Future, Ebony Magazine, 2001; MIT, "Creating Cot Connections; Sociocultural Constructionism & An Asset-Based Approach to Comm Tech & Comm Building In Low-Income Comm," doctoral dissertation, 2001; Men's Track and Field Team as a high jumper, long jumper & sprinter winning NCAA Academic All-American honors; Season 4 Winner NBC's hit reality tv. Author: The Student Entrepreneur's Guide to Launching a Multimillion-Dollar Business, 2007. **Home Addr:** 343 Smithwold Rd, Somerset, NJ 08873, **Home Phone:** (732)356-5536. **Business Addr:** President, Chief Executive Officer, BCT Partners LLC, 105 Lock St Suite 207, Newark, NJ 07103, **Business Phone:** (973)622-0900.

**PINKINS, TONYA**
Singer, actor. **Personal:** Born May 30, 1962, Chicago, IL; daughter of Thomas Swoope and Anita; married Hubert Kelly, Jan 1, 1984?, (divorced 1987); married Ron Brawer, Feb 12, 1987, (divorced 1993); children: Maxx Brawer & Myles Brawer; married Eric Winters, Jan 1, 2009. **Educ:** Carnegie Mellon Univ, music theatre prog, 1981; Columbia Col, BA, 1995. **Career:** Films: Beat Street, 1984; See No Evil, Hear No Evil, 1989; Above the Rim, 1994; Romance & Cigarettes, 2005; Premium, 2006; Enchanted, 2007; Noah's Arc: Jumping the Broom, 2008; Newlyweeds, 2013; Home, 2013; Aardvark, forthcoming; TV: "American Dream", 1981; "Law & Order", 1990-2006; "All My Children", 1991, 2004-09; "Love Hurts", 2002; "Sleeper Cell", 2005; "Criminal Minds", 2006; "Cold Case", 2006; "The River", 2006; "Unfabulous", 2007; "Working in the Theatre", 2007; "The Closer", 2008; "Army Wives", 2009; "24", 2009; "Hostages", 2013; "Nurse Jackie", 2015; "Gotham", 2015; "For Justice", 2015; "11.22.63", forthcoming, 2016; Theatre appearances: Death & the Kings Horseman, 1979-80; Merrily We Roll Along, 1981-82; Five Points, 1982; Just Say No, 1988; Joe Turner's Come & Gone, 1989-90; Jelly's Last Jam, Broadway, 1992; Children And Art, 2005; Caroline or Change, 2006; Radio Golf, 2007; Milk Like Sugar, 2011; Hurt Village, 2012; Storefront Church, 2012; A Time To Kill, 2013; The Fabulous Miss Marie, 2014; Holler If Ya Hear Me, 2014; Rasheeda Speaking, 2015; TV appearances: "The Guardian", 2001-04; "In Loco Parentis", 2002; "Dennis Miller", 2004; "Happy Birthday Oscar Wilde", 2004; "Bid Whist Party Throwdown", 2005; "Black Theater Today: 2005", 2005; "Black in the 80s", 2005; "Soap-Talk", 2004-06; "ShowBusiness: The Road to Broadway", 2007. **Orgs:** Bd dir, Nontraditional Casting Proj; bd dir, Carousel Theatre; Actors Equity Asn; Am Fed TV & Radio Artists; Org Black Screen Writers. **Home Addr:** , NY. **Business Addr:** Actress, The Gersh Agency, 41 Madison Ave Suite 33, New York, NY 10010-2210, **Business Phone:** (212)997-1818.

**PINKNEY, ANDREA DAVIS**
Vice president (organization), editor. **Personal:** Born Sep 25, 1963, Washington, DC; married Brian; children: 2. **Educ:** Syracuse Univ, BA, jour, 1985. **Career:** Essence Mag, ed; Hyperion Bks C; Houghton Mifflin; Scholastic Trade, vpres & ed-at-large; author of children's fiction & nonfiction books. Books: Illustrated books Sit-In: His Words,

Her Songs; Alvin Ailey, 1993; Seven Candles For Kwanzaa, 1993; Dear Benjamin Banneker, 1994; Bill Pickett: Rodeo-ridin' Cowboy, 1996; Duke Ellington, 1997; Shake Shake Shake, 1997; I Smell Honey, 1997; Pretty Brown Face, 1997; Watch Me Dance, 1997; Mim's Christmas Jam, 2001; Ella Fitzgerald, 2002; Fishing Day, 2003; Boycott Blues, 2008; Sojourner Truth's Step-Stomp Stride, 2009; How Rosa Parks Inspired a Nation; How Four Friends Stood Up by Sitting Down, 2010; Martin & Mahalia, 2013. Novels: Hold Fast To Dreams, 1995; Solo Girl, 1997; Raven In A Dove House, 1998; Silent Thunder: A Civil War Story, 2001; Abraham Lincoln: Letters From A Slave Girl, 2001; Dear America: With The Might Of Angels, 2011; Bird In A Box And The Forthcoming With The Might Of Angels, 2011; The Red Pencil, 2014. Narrative Nonfiction: Let It Shine: Stories Of Black Women Freedom Fighters, 2001; Meet The Obamas: America's First Family, 2009; Ten Nine Eight: Teen Business Blasts Off, 2010; Hand In Hand: Ten Black Men Who Changed America, 2012; Peace Warriors, 2013; Rhythm Ride, 2015. Anthologies: Stay True: Short Stories For Strong Girls, 1998; Be Careful What You Wish For: Ten Stories About Wishes, 2007.

## PINKNEY, DR. BETTY KATHRYN

Government official, lawyer, school administrator. **Personal:** Born Cleveland, OH; daughter of Naomi Inez Yates Butts and Emmett Maceo; married Charles E; children: Jacqueline Royster, Pamela & Merle. **Educ:** Cent State Univ, BA, 1956; Case Western Res Univ, MA, 1961; Cleveland State Univ Marshall Law Sch, JD, 1976; Levin Col Urban Affairs, PhD. **Career:** Cleveland Pub Sch, teacher, adminr, 1961-77; Carl J Character Law Firm, assoc, 1977-79; EEOC, Cleveland, trial atty, 1979-81; E Ohio Gas Co, sr atty, 1981-96; Const Commun Sys, dist dir, currently; Stephanie Tubbs Jones, Shaker Heights Off, dist dir. **Orgs:** Bd trustee, supt, Judge Lloyd O Brown Scholar Fund, 1984-; vol, Cleveland Bar Assn, 1984-; adv comt, supt, Cleveland Pub Sch Syst, 1987-; ABA; Ohio St Bar Assn; Nat Bar Assn; Delta Sigma Theta; chmn bd, Cent State Univ Bd Trustees, 1987; bd mem, Cleveland C's Mus; Ohio Bar; bd, Judson Retirement Community; bd, Cleveland Natural Hist Mus; Levin col vis comm mem, currently; Ward 4 community. **Honors/Awds:** Dr Martin Luther King Jr, Orchestra Community Rels Comts Community Serv Award, 2013. **Home Addr:** , OH.

## PINKNEY, DOVE SAVAGE

Government official. **Personal:** Born Macon, GA; daughter of Edward Warren Savage Sr (deceased) and Mildred G; children: Rhonda Michelle Pinkney Washington & Roderick Stephen. **Educ:** Talladega Col, attended 1954; Inst Path Case-Western Res Univ, cert med tech, 1955; Univ Denver; Univ Calif Los Angeles. **Career:** Univ Hosp Cleveland, technologist & supvr, 1955-59; C's Hosp Los Angeles, technologist in-charge out-patient clin lab, 1960-73, hematologyclin lab mgr, 1973-94, gov affairs coor dr, 1994-95; Los Angeles Chap, pres, currently. **Orgs:** Delta Sigma Theta Head Start Bd, 1970-76; chairperson & supvr, C's Hosp Los Angeles Employee Recog Comm, 1973-89; campaign chairperson C's Hosp Los Angeles United Way Campaign, 1975; treas, 1978-80, 1981-, chair, 1988-90, bd mgr, Crenshaw/28th St YMCA; del 20 nat conventions; chairperson, ASMT Forum Concerns Minorities By-Laws Com, 1979-86; pres, Calif Asn Med Lab Technol, Los Angeles Chap, 1982-83, treas, 1978-80; trustee & exec bd, 1978-95; treas, New Frontier Dem Club, 1989-90, pres, 1992-93, bd, 1989-; dir, Calif SocMed Technol, 1981-83, 1983-85; coord CSMT Stud Bowl, 1983; del 15 state conventions; nat pres, Talladega Col Alumni Asn, 1984-87; reg pres, 1997-2001, bd, fund raiser, United Negro Col Fund, 1981-, life mem, Nat Coun Negro Women; life mem, Delta Sigma Theta Sorority; Urban League, NOW; PUSH; Nat Asn Advan Colored People; Comm Rels Coun Southern CA; Black Women's Forum, African-Am Mus, Mus Afro-Am Hist & Cult, Trinity Baptist Church; bd dir, Delta Sigma Theta Life Develop (sr citizens prog), 1982-92; fin secy, 1989-93, 1998-, mem, Nat Coalition 100 Black Women, 2007-; LA County Comnr, 1994-; Los Angeles Delta Minerva Found, 1998-; Los Angeles Care Community Adv Bd; vice chair, Base Hosp Adv Comm. **Honors/Awds:** Awards received from Delta Sigma Theta Los Angeles Chap, Talladega Col Local Alumni Asn, Talladega Col Nat Alumni Asn, Crenshaw YMCA, UNCF, Am Soc Med Technol, New Frontier Democratic Club, Children's Hosp Los Angeles Employees, Fed Credit Union. **Special Achievements:** Co-author of two professional (scientific) papers; CA Assembly; CA State Senate; LA Care. **Home Addr:** 5601 Coliseum St, Los Angeles, CA 90016-5005, **Home Phone:** (310)295-3437. **Business Addr:** President, Los Angeles Chapter, PO Box 56337, Los Angeles, CA 90056-0337, **Business Phone:** (310)837-5495.

## PINKNEY, DR. ENID C.

Educator, social historian, association executive. **Personal:** Born Oct 15, 1931, Miami, FL; daughter of Henry Curtis and Lenora Curtis; married Frank; married Frank. **Educ:** Talladega Col, BA, 1953; Barry Univ, MS, 1967. **Career:** Educator (retired), social worker; YWCA, Miami, adult prog dir; Chicago, group worker; social worker, 1953-55; Dade County Pub Sch Syst, teacher, 1955, counsr, 1967, asst prin, 1971, asst prin guid, 1985; S Miami MidSch, asst prin, 1991; African Am Comt, founder; Brownsville & N CentDade community, historian; Lemon City Cemetery Community Corp, chair; Hist Hampton House Community Trust Inc, founder& pres. **Orgs:** NEA; FEA; Dade Co Adm Asn & Guid Asn; S Fla Guid Asn; Am & Sch Coun Asn; Am Guid & Personal Asn; AAUW; Hi Delta-Kappa; bd dir, Miami YWCA; bd dir, Fla Conf United Church Christ; charter mem, Chair Open Door; UCC Fruits States; Miami Inter Alumni Coun, UNCF; Sigma Gamma Rho Sor; pres, Dade Heritage Trust Hist Preserv Orgn, 1998; Hist Hampton House Community Trust Inc, 2002. **Honors/Awds:** Cert of Appreciation, Sigma Gamma Rho Sorority; Enid C. Pinkney Humanitarian Award, The Miami Talladega Col Alumni Asn, Named in Honor. **Special Achievements:** First African American President of Dade Heritage Trust, 1998; Produced numerous videos on history. **Business Addr:** Chair, Lemon City Cemetery Community Corp, 4990 NW 31st Ave, Miami, FL 33142.

## PINKNEY, JERRY

Educator, illustrator. **Personal:** Born Dec 22, 1939, Philadelphia, PA; son of James H and Willie Mae Landers; married Gloria Jean Maultsby; children: Troy Bernardette, Jerry Brian, Scott Cannon & Myles Carter. **Educ:** Univ Arts, Philadelphia, PA, attended 1959. **Career:** Rustcraft Publ Co, Dedham, Mass, designer, 1960-62; Barker-Black Studio, Boston, Mass, designer-illusr, 1962-64; Kaleiodoscope Studio, Boston, Mass, designer-illusr, 1964-66; Jerry Pinkney Studio, Boston, Mass, designer-illusr, 1966-70; Ri Sch Design, vis critic, 1969-70; Jerry Pinkney Inc, Croton-on-Hudson NY, pres, 1970-; Pratt Inst, Brooklyn NY, assoc prof, 1986-87; Univ Del, distinguished vis prof, 1986-88, assoc prof art, 1988-92; US Mil Acad, W Pt, NY, lectr; Univ Buffalo, Buffalo, NY, vis prof art. **Orgs:** Soc Illusrs; US Postal Serv Citizens Stamp Adv Comn, 1982; Artist Team NASA, Space Shuttle Columbia, 1982; US Postal Serv Qual Assurance Comn, 1986-92. **Home Addr:** 41 Furnace Dock Rd, Croton On Hudson, NY 10520, **Home Phone:** (914)271-5659.

## PINKNEY, JOHN EDWARD

Manager, chief executive officer, business owner. **Personal:** Born May 6, 1948, Landover, MD; married Gloristine Wilkins; children: Nikole, John & April. **Educ:** Prince George Community Col, AA, 1973; Bowie State Col, BS, 1976. **Career:** Dept Agr, comput oper, 1970-71; Shady side Barber & Beauty Salon, hairstylist & co-owner, 1971-77; Philip Morris USA, sales rep, 1977-79, miliary mgr, 1979-80, div mgr, 1980-88; An Answer 4 U Telecommunications Co, owner & chief exec officer, 1991-. **Orgs:** Youth task force partic Nat Alliance Bus, 1981-83; pres, Nat Bus League, Southern Md, 1981-83, bd dir, 1984-. **Honors/Awds:** Community Service Award, Dist of Columbia; Presidential Citation, Natl Asn Equal Opportunity Higher Educ. **Home Addr:** 6110 Joyce Dr, Camp Springs, MD 20748. **Business Addr:** Owner, Chief Executive Officer, An Answer 4 U.

## PINKNEY, ROSE CATHERINE

Executive, vice president (organization). **Personal:** Born Oct 6, 1964, Prince George's County, MD; daughter of Joseph and Maud. **Educ:** Princeton Univ, BA, sociol, 1986; Univ Calif Los Angeles Anderson Sch mgt, MBA, entertainment mgt & mkt, 1988. **Career:** Twentieth Century Fox TV, dir programming; Uptown Entertainment, vpres & head; Paramount Pictures TV, sr vice pres comedy develop, 1995-2002, sr vpres dept head, 2002; TV One, exec vpres programming & prod, 2005; Cinema Gypsy, Laurence Fishburne's prod co, head TV arm, 2008-; TV Movie: How to Be a Player, co-producer, 1997; "State of the Black Union: Jamestown-The First 400 Years", exec producer, 2007; "State of the Black Union: Jamestown-Memorable Moments", exec producer, 2007. TV Series: "Who's Got Jokes?", exec producer, 2006; "Can You Hear Me Now: The Evolution of Gospel Music", exec producer, 2008; "Family Reunion", exec producer, 2008; "Murder in Black & White", network exec producer, 2008; "Mean Streets: Cities Under Fire", exec producer, 2009; "No Justice, No Peace: A Sharp Talk Special", exec producer, 2010; "Wedding Planner Mystery", assoc producer, 2014. **Orgs:** Bd mem, Women in Film; treas, New Leaders; lifetime mem, Asn Black Princeton Alumni. **Business Addr:** Head of the Television Arm, Programming & Production, Cinema Gypsy Productions Inc, 5750 Wilshire Blvd Suite 580, Los Angeles, CA 90036.

## PINKNEY, WILLIAM D.

Executive, vice president (organization). **Personal:** Born Sep 15, 1935, Chicago, IL; son of William Sr and Marion Henderson; married Yvonne Glover, Jan 1, 1957?, (divorced 1962); children: Angela Walton; married Ina, Jan 1, 1964?, (divorced 2001); married Migdalia Vachier, Jan 1, 2003?; children: Angela Walton & Pinkney. **Educ:** NY Community Col; Adelphi Univ. **Career:** Executive (retired); Astarte, nat sales mgr, 1971-72; Cleopatra Creations, vpres, 1972-73; Revlon, mkt mgr, 1973-77; Johnson Prod Co, dir mkt, 1977-80; Dept Human Serv City Chicago, dir family serv, pub info officer, 1980-83; Combined Construct Co, vpres; Dessert Kitchen Ltd, dir; Am Sail Training Asn, dir. **Orgs:** Nat Assoc Broadcast Engineering & Technol, 1970-; Lake Mich Yacht Racing Asn, 1974-; commodore, Belmont Yacht Club; life mem, Lake Mich Singlehanded Soc; Royal Yacht Club Tasmania, Australia; Chicago Yacht Club; New York Yacht Club; capt, Mystic Seaport Mus, Freedom Schooner Amistad Proj, 2000-03; trustee, Mystic Seaport. **Special Achievements:** The first African American to solo-circumnavigate the world via Cape Horn. **Home Addr:** 348 Swain Ave, Meriden, CT 06450-7283.

## PINN, DR. MELVIN T., JR.

Physician. **Personal:** Born Oct 6, 1947, Lynchburg, VA; son of Vera Ferguson and Melvin Pinn; married Evora; children: Tanika, Melva & Melvin III. **Educ:** Johnson C Smith Univ, BS, chem, 1970; Univ Va, MD, 1976; Univ NC-Chapel Hill, MPH, 1991. **Career:** Univ Ma mem Healthcare, family med resident; Worcester City hosp, family med resident; Neighborhood Health Ctr, med dir, 1979-96; Wellness Plan NC (Va Premier Health Plan Inc), med dir, 1996, sr med dir, 2003-. **Orgs:** Am Acad Family Physicians; NC Acad Family Physicians; Nat Med Asn; Montgomery County Med Soc; Omega Psi Phi, 1967-. **Honors/Awds:** Am Acad Family Physicians, fel, 1980, Nat Family Physician of the Year, 1998; Omega Man of the Year, Omega Psi Phi, 1989, Citizen of the Year, 1998; Citizen of the Year, Community Pride, 1998. **Home Addr:** 5611 Ruth Dr, Charlotte, NC 28215, **Home Phone:** (704)536-4968. **Business Addr:** Senior Medical Director, Virginia Premier Health Plan Inc, 600 E Broad St, Richmond, VA 23220-0307, **Business Phone:** (804)819-5151.

## PINN, DR. SAMUEL J., JR.

Educator, association executive. **Personal:** Born May 25, 1935, Brooklyn, NY; married Cynthia; children: Samuel II, Gregory & Charles (deceased). **Educ:** Morgan State Univ, BA, 1959; Rutgers Univ, MSW, 1970; Mary Holmes Col, LLD. **Career:** SJP Consult, pres, 1968-; Mayors Action Task Force, dir, 1968-71; Wiltwick Sch, exec dir, 1971-73; Ramapo Col, assoc prof social sci, prof, prof emer, currently; Ft Greene Coun Inc, co-founder & chmn, 1973-; Jazz 966, co-founder & exec producer. **Orgs:** Col Human Serv, 1973-75; Nat Conf Penal Reform, 1975-76; consult, Nassau & Co Equal Opptunity Comn, 1976; chmn, Comm Sch Bd Dist, 1996; pres, Bedford Study Inst Afro-Am Studies & Continuing Educ; chmn & founder, Ft Greene Sr Citzen Ctr; chmn, Brooklyn Core; sr citizen columnist, NY Amsterdam News; Human Resource Dist 11; Omega Psi Phi; Asn Black Social Workers; Youth Leadership Recreation Teacher Asn. **Honors/Awds:** Community Service Award, John Jay Col; Civic Leadership, Brooklyn Civic Asn; Sam Pinn Educator-Activist Award. **Special Achievements:** Book: "Committee Organizing for Small Groups", 1970. **Home Addr:** 283 McDonough St, Brooklyn, NY 11233-1006. **Business Addr:** Professor Emeritus, Ramapo College of New Jersey, Rm G226 505 Ramapo Valley Rd, Mahwah, NJ 07430-1623, **Business Phone:** (201)684-7500.

## PINN, DR. VIVIAN

Executive director, college president, association executive. **Personal:** Born Apr 21, 1941, Halifax, VA. **Educ:** Wellesley Col, BA, 1963; Univ Va Sch Med, MD, 1967. **Career:** Tufts Univ, Sch Med, asst prof path & asst dean stud affairs, 1970-82; Howard Univ Col Med, Dept Path, prof & chair; Nat Insts Health, assoc dir res women's health, Off Res Women's Health, dir, 1991-2011. **Orgs:** Elected Pres Nat Med Asn, 1989; elected a fel Am Acad Arts & Sci, 1994; elected to Inst Med, 1995; fel Am Acad Arts & Sci, 1994. **Honors/Awds:** American Medical Women's Association, Elizabeth Blackwell Award, 1995; Tufts University School of Medicine, Dean's Medal, 2011; National Medical Fellowships Founder Award, 2013; Athena Award; New York Academy of Medicine, Honorary Fellow; The Academy Medal for Distinguished Contributions in Health Policy and Special Recognition Award, Association of American Medical Colleges. **Special Achievements:** Was the only woman and only minority in her class at the University of Virginia School of Medicine; first African-American woman appointed to chair the pathology department at Howard University School of Medicine in 1982; first full-time director for the Office of Research on Women's Health; The University of Virginia established the Vivian W. Pinn Distinguished Lecture in Health Disparities and named an advisory college for medical students the Vivian Pinn College in 2010.

## PINO, REV. JEROME KING DEL

Clergy, educator. **Personal:** Born Sep 12, 1946, Savannah, GA; son of Jerome Frank and Flossie Mae Childs; married Kathleen Joy Peterson; children: Jerome Curtis & Emily Kathleen. **Educ:** Gustavus Adolphus Col, BA, 1969; Boston Univ, Sch Theol, ThM, 1972; Boston Univ Grad Sch Arts & Sci, PhD, 1976. **Career:** Union United Methodist Church, Boston, stud pastor, 1968-69; Emerson Col, Boston, lectr, 1971-72, instr; St Andrew's United Methodist Church, Worcester, co-pastor, 1971-72; Greenwood Memorial United Methodist Church, Dorchester, pastor, 1973-76; Wesley United Methodist Church, Springfield, pastor, 1978-89; Wesley United Methodist Church, Springfield, pastor, 1978; Boston Univ Sch Theol, vis lectr, 1980-82; Luther & Northwestern Theol Sem, St Paul, vis lectr, 1984-85; Crawford Memorial United Methodist Church, Winchester, pastor, 1989-; United Methodist Church, pastor, 1993-98; Metropolitian Boston S Dist, supt, 1997-2001; Metropolitian United Methodist Church, sr pastor, 1998; United Methodist Church, Nashville, Gen Bd Higher Educ & Ministry, dir, 1981-88, gen bd discipleship, 1998-96, gen secy, 2001-10; Africa Univ, bd dir, currently. **Orgs:** Am Soc Church Hist, 1971; Rockefeller Fel Fund Theol Educ Princeton, 1971-73; fel Inst Reformation Res, St Louis, Mo, 1973; N Am Black Doctorate Fel Fund Theol Educ, 1976-77; deleg, Gen Conf UMC, 1976, 1980, 1984, 1988; NE Jurisdictional Conf, UMC, 1976, 1980, 1984; dir gen, bd Higher Educ & Ministry, UMC, 1980-88; Div Ordained Ministry, UMC, 1980-88; pres, Black Ecumenical Comn MA, 1983-85; adv coun, Word & World Journ, 1985; gov, Gen Bd Discipleship, United Methodist Church, 1988; gov, Gen Coun Ministries, United Methodist Church, 1988-; United Methodist Bd Higher Educ & Ministry. **Honors/Awds:** First Decade Alumni Achievement Award, Gustavus Adolphus Col, St Peter MN, 1978. **Home Addr:** 53 Birchwood Dr, Holden, MA 01520-1937. **Business Addr:** Board of Director, Africa University, Fairview Rd, Mutare1320, **Business Phone:** (600)756-0026.

## PINSON, HERMINE DOLOREZ

College teacher, writer. **Personal:** Born Jul 20, 1953, Beaumont, TX; daughter of Robert B and Enid Davis Harris; married Donald E; children: Leah Courtney. **Educ:** Fisk Univ, BA, eng, 1975; Southern Methodist Univ, MA, eng, 1979; Rice Univ, PhD, am lit, 1991. **Career:** Community Col, Houston, 1977-79; Tex Southern Univ, asst prof, 1979-92; Col William & Mary, assoc prof eng, 1992-; Univ Mich, Ann Arbor, King Chavez-Parks vis prof; Editor: Critical Voicings of Black Liberation; Author: Ashe, 1991; Mama Yetta & Other Poems, 1999. **Orgs:** Nat Endowment Humanities, 1988; Acad Am Poets; ASCAP; Southern Conf African-Am Studies; Am Lit Asn; Southern Mod Lang Asn; Collegium African Am Res; Arbor Asn; fel, Ford Postdoctoral, 1991; Macdowell Colony, 1996; Yaddo Colony, 1996; Vt Studio Ctr, 1997; Va Found Humanities; Callaloo Fel. **Home Addr:** 120 Magruder Lane, Williamsburg, VA 23185-5317. **Business Addr:** Associate Professor, College of William & Mary, Tyler Hall 320, Williamsburg, VA 23187-8795, **Business Phone:** (757)221-2437.

## PINSON, MARGO DEAN

Administrator, president (organization). **Personal:** Born Oct 29, 1937, Washington, DC; daughter of Millard R and Irene F C; married Thomas J; children: Wendie F Barbee. **Educ:** Howard Univ, cert, dent hyg, 1959, BS, 1977; Cath Univ, summer session, 1973, 1974. **Career:** Adminr (retired); Michael Reece Hosp, clin dent hygienist, 1959-61; Jewish Memorial Hosp, clin dent hygienist, 1961-62; DC Gov, clin dent hygienist, 1966-68, dent hyg counr, 1968-77; Howard Univ, spec events officer, 1977; Southeastern Univ, exec asst pres; Book: Highland Beach on the Chesapeake Bay: Maryland's First African American Incorporated Town. **Orgs:** Pres, Sigma Phi Alpha Dent Hyg Hon Soc, 1963-64; Howard Univ Alumni Asn, 1977-; Howard Univ Dent Hyg Alumni Asn, 1960-; Nat Asn Adv Colored People Montgomery Co Br, 1991-, fund raising dinner comt, 1992, 1993; bd gov, Westover Sch, 1986-92, bd govs, chair ann fund, 1990-92; pres, N Easterners, Wash Chap, 1988-90, nat vip, 1990-92, nat pres, 1992-; bd comnrs, town treas, Town Highland Beach, 1984-99, app comnr finance, 1992-99; Nat Coalition 100 Black Women, 1990-93; South west Neighborhood Assembly, currently. **Home Addr:** 3316 Brooklawn Terr, Chevy Chase, MD 20815, **Home Phone:** (301)656-3284.

## PIPER, ADRIAN MARGARET SMITH

Educator, artist. **Personal:** Born Sep 20, 1948, New York, NY; daughter of Daniel Robert and Olive Xavier Smith. **Educ:** Sch Visual Arts, NY, NY, AA, fine arts, 1969; City Col NY, NY, BA, philos, 1974; Harvard Univ, Cambridge, MA, philos, 1977, PhD, philos, 1981. **Career:** Harvard Univ, grad teaching asst, 1976-77; Visual Artists fel, Nat Educ Asn, 1979-82; Univ Mich, asst prof, 1979-86; Stanford Univ, mellon res fel, 1982-84; Georgetown Univ, assoc prof, 1986-88; Guggenheim fel, 1988-89; Univ Calif, San Diego, assoc prof, 1988-90; Woodrow Wilson Int Scholars fel, 1989-90; Wellesley Col, prof philos, 1990-2005; Nat Endowment Humanities Col Teacher's res fel, 1998; Internationales Forschungszentrum Kulturwissenschaften, fel, 2004; Royal Danish Acad Art, Vis Guest Prof, 2005-07. **Orgs:** N Am Kant Soc, 1979-; Am Philos Asn, 1979-; Am Asn Univ Prof, 1979-; Asn Polit & Legal Philos, 1979-; Col Art Asn, 1983-; Soc Philos & Pub Affairs; Phi Beta Kappa; Fel New York Inst Humanities, 1994; founder, Adrian Piper Res Archive Found, 2002-; founder, Berlin J Philos, 2011. **Home Phone:** (617)431-9918. **Business Addr:** Professor of Philosophy, Wellesley College, 106 Central St, Wellesley, MA 02481, **Business Phone:** (781)283-1000.

### PIPER, ELWOOD ARTHUR
Educator, business owner. **Personal:** Born Apr 13, 1934, Bastrop, TX; son of John H and Ruby; married Ora Lean Williams; children: Malcom, Karen, Adrian & Kenneth. **Educ:** Wiley Col, BA, 1956; Tex Southern Univ, MA, 1965. **Career:** Educator (retired), business owner; Houston Independent Sch Dist, teacher & coach, 1958-65, from asst prin to prin, 1965-85; Piper's Automotive Serv Ctr, owner, currently. **Orgs:** Pleasantville Civil Club; Rotary Houston; Phi Delta Kappa; Nat Asn Sect Prin; Boy Scouts Am; Big Broth Am; Tex J Prin Asn. **Home Addr:** 8755 Cowart st, Houston, TX 77029-3320, **Home Phone:** (713)675-5076. **Business Addr:** Owner, Piper's Automotive Service Center, 2004 N Main St, Baytown, TX 77520-2747, **Business Phone:** (281)420-2374.

### PIPER, DR. PAUL J.
Physician. **Personal:** Born Jun 19, 1935, Detroit, MI; married Mary K Harris; children: Paul & Michael. **Educ:** Univ Mich, BS, 1962, MS, 1967; Wayne State Univ, MD, 1973. **Career:** Wayne St Univ Affil Hosp, resident gen surg; Vet Affairs Med Ctr, resident gen surg; Detroit Rec Hsp-U Hlth C, resident gen surg; Mich Dept Corrections, physician; pvt pract physician. **Orgs:** Detroit Med Soc; Sigma Phi Pi; Detroit Surg Soc; Nat Med Asn. **Home Addr:** 19120 Kingston Rd, Detroit, MI 48221-1813, **Home Phone:** (313)863-0434. **Business Addr:** Physician, 3496 E Lake Lansing Rd, East Lansing, MI 48823.

### PIPER, DR. W. ARCHIBALD
Physician, surgeon. **Personal:** Born Apr 13, 1935. **Educ:** Mt Allison Univ, BSc, 1961; Dalhousie Univ, Md, 1966; McGill Univ Can, MSc, 1969; FRCS 1972; FACS, 1976. **Career:** Physician, surgeon (retired); W Archibald Piper PC, plastic surgeon; Mich St Univ, asst prof surg. **Orgs:** AMA; Mich St Med Soc; Am Col Surgeons; Am Soc Plastic Recons Surgeons; Flint Acad Surgeons; Mich Acad Plastics Surgeons; Rotary Club; pvt pilot; Int Col Surgeons; bd dir, Motts C health Ctr, chmn; bd dir, US Sugar. **Honors/Awds:** Bd cert Am Bd Plastic Surg; MSc thesis "The Fibroblast in Wound Healing"; Dr Clement A Alfred Humanitarian Award, 2008, 2009. **Home Addr:** 2313 Stone Bridge Dr, Flint, MI 48504.

### PIPKINS, ROBERT ERIK
Athlete. **Personal:** Born Feb 23, 1973, Buffalo, NY; son of Robert E and Joan E. **Educ:** Drexel Univ, BS, archit engineering & civil engineering, 1995. **Career:** Athlete (retired); luger Olympics, Mens Singles, US, jr develop team, mem, 1987-88; jr cand team, mem, 1988-89; jr nat team mem, 1989-92; Jr World Champion, 1992; sr nat team mem, 1992-94; US luger Olympics team, mem, 1994. **Special Achievements:** Pipkins was also the first African-American luge racer at the international level participant. **Home Addr:** 13 Bailey Pl, Staten Island, NY 10303, **Home Phone:** (718)720-1957.

### PIPPEN, SCOTTIE MAURICE
Actor, basketball player, basketball coach. **Personal:** Born Sep 25, 1965, Hamburg, AR; son of Preston and Ethel; married Larsa Younan; children: Sophia, Justin, Preston & Scotty Pippen Jr; married Karen McCollum; children: Antron. **Educ:** Univ Cent Ark, attended 1987. **Career:** Basketball player (retired), basketball coach; Nat Basketball Asn, player; Chicago Bulls, forward-guard, 1987-98, 2003-04; Houston Rockets, 1998-99; Portland Trail Blazers, 1999-2003; Los Angeles Lakers, spec asst coach, 2005; ESPN, part-time analyst; ABC, studio analyst, 2005-06; Torpan Pojat, 2008; Sundsvall Dragons, 2008; speaker, currently.TV Series: "Slam City with Scottie Pippen", 1994; "ER ", 1996; "He Got Game", 1998; "Midgets Vs. Mascots", 2009; "Fresh Off the Boat"; "Chicago Fire", 2015. **Business Addr:** Speaker, Playing Field Promotions, 277 S Forest St, Denver, CO 80246-1148, **Business Phone:** (303)377-1109.

### PITCHER, JUDGE FREDDIE, JR.
Educator, judge. **Personal:** Born Apr 28, 1945, Baton Rouge, LA. **Educ:** Southern Univ A&M Col, BA, polit sci, 1966; Southern Univ Sch Law, JD, 1973; Nat Judicial Col, Reno, NE, attended 1984, 1987 & 1994; NY Univ Sch Law, Appellate Judges Inst, attended 1993. **Career:** Judge (retired), educr; Baton Rouge City Ct, judge; La Supreme Ct, assoc justice ad hoc; State La, off atty gen, spec coun; E Baton Rouge Parish, asst dist atty; Pitcher Tyson Avery & Cunningham, prin partner; Phelps Dunbar LLP, Baton Rouge off, partner; Southern Univ Law Ctr, adj prof, 1983-, chancellor & prof law, 2002-; La State Univ Law Ctr, adj prof, 1996-. **Orgs:** Am Bar Asn; Nat Bar Asn; La State Bar Asn; Baton Rouge Bar Asn; pres, Stud Bar Asn; mediator, Mediation Arbit Prof Systs Inc; Bd dir, Baton Rouge Area Found; bd dir, Southern Univ Systs Found; bd dir, Indigent Defender Assistance Compensation Bd; bd dir, Cath Community Serv Inc; bd dir, Young Leaders Acad Baton Rouge; bd dir, Founders & Friends Endowment Womans Hosp Baton Rouge; secy, Greater Baton Rouge Area Chamber Com; Baton Rouge Recreation Comn Found; Omega Psi Phi; Sigma Pi Phi fraternity; Firm's appellate pract group. **Special Achievements:** First African American elected to a judgeship in Baton Rouge with his election to the City Court in a city-wide election in April 1983; First African American elected to the 19th Judicial District in a parish-wide election in 1987; In 1992, he achieved another first with his election to the Louisiana First Circuit Court of Appeal, without opposition. **Business Addr:** Chancellor, Professor of Law, Southern University Law Center, 2 Roosevelt Steptoe Dr Suite 261, Baton Rouge, LA 70813, **Business Phone:** (225)771-2552.

### PITCHER, CAPT. FREDERICK M. A. (FRED PITCHER)
Pilot, airplane pilot. **Personal:** Born Mar 9, 1932, Washington, DC; son of Hardy and Sylvia Saunders; children: Frederick II, Riccardo, Tia Clarke, Mikela, Ericka & Elliott. **Educ:** DeVry Tech Inst, Dipl, 1953; Northrop Univ, cert, Lic A&P, 1965; Fowler Aeronaut, Dipl, 1966; LA Trade Tech Col, Dean's List, 1969; Univ Calif, Los Angeles, Teaching Credential, 1977; Nat Radio Inst, Dipl, 1977; KIIS Radio Broadcasting, Dipl, 1979. **Career:** US Naval Model Basin, engrg aide, 1955; Burroughs Corp Comput, electronic tech, 1955-59, electronics engr, 1959-64; Tech Enterprises, owner, oper, 1961-; Electronic Memories Inc, qual control, 1964; Western Airlines, airline pilot, 1966-87; Rose Aviation, flight instr, 1975-85; Delta Airlines, airline pilot, 1987-. **Orgs:** Pilot & instr, Civil Air Patrol, 1948-; cert flight instr Worldwide, 1961-85; sta engr, KFAR-TV, 1962-63; builder, Exp Aircraft Asn, 1965-; chief exec officer, Tech Enterprises, 1966-; guestlectr, LA Sch Dist, 1968-85; Educare USC Alumni, 1977; dir mem, Northrop Univ Alumni, 1979-; chief fin Officer, DW Ford Corp Inc, 1982-85; pres, Mkt Int Ltd, 1983-; dir, DW Ford Sem Asn, 1983-85; exec vpres, Worldwide Tax & Bus Consult Inc, 1984-85; reading tutor, CA Literacy Prog, 1984-87; LA Urban Bankers Asn, 1984-85; w reg vpres, Orgn Black Airline Pilots, 1984-86; indust resource person, Los Angeles Sch Dist, 1986-; advisor, Black Flight Attendants Am Inc; restorer, March Afb Mus, Calif, 1988-89; founder, Socr Preserv Antique Tech Equip, 1989; comm rel Offr AirlinePilots Assoc, 1983-85. **Honors/Awds:** Scholarship Science, Bosch & Lomb, 1950; People & Choices Harcourt BraceJovonovich Publ Co, 1971; Community Service, LA Sch Dist, 1971; Distinguished Alumni Award, Northrop Univ, 1976; Good Samaritan Award, Church Jesus Christ of Latter Day Saints, 1976; Commendation Calif State Senator Green Comm Asst, 1980; Professional Recognition, Edges Group Inc Fortune 500 1984; Certificate of Recognition, State Senator Bill Greene, California, 1989. **Special Achievements:** First black pilot for Western Airlines. **Home Addr:** Broadway-Manchester Sta, PO Box 73CN, Los Angeles, CA 90003, **Home Phone:** (213)750-7275. **Business Addr:** Airline Pilot, Delta Airlines, 6060 Avion Dr Dept 030, Los Angeles, CA 90009, **Business Phone:** (310)342-9909.

### PITCHFORD, GERARD SPENCER
Executive. **Personal:** Born Dec 8, 1953, Jersey City, NJ; son of Gordon and Gloria Oliver; married Janet F Hardy; children: Uonisha & Paris. **Educ:** Rutgers Univ, attended 1970. **Career:** Dynamic Serv Unlimited, sales mgr, 1976; Commun Equip Repair Inc, pres, 1977; Time to Order Corp, pres, 1984-86; Corp Promotions Int, pres & founder; GC Capital Inc, prin; Trendsetters, pres, 1990-2007; Brazils Fav Franchise Co, pres, 1991-2001; ARFI Corp, pres, 2007-. **Orgs:** Bd mem, treas, Chicago Regional Purchasing Coun, 1980-; bd mem, Chicago State Univ Found, 1982-; bd mem, Pvt Indust Coun, 1984-; deacon, Chicago United, 1987; bd mem, Push Int Trade Bur; comnr, City Chicago Dept Human Rights; chmn, Chicago Reg Purchasing Coun Comt. **Honors/Awds:** Vendor of the Month, State Ill, 1986. **Home Addr:** 75 West End Ave Suite P19D, New York, NY 10023, **Home Phone:** (212)245-8845. **Business Addr:** President, AFRI Corp, 121 St Nicholas Ave Suite 5C, New York, NY 10026-2106, **Business Phone:** (212)866-6532.

### PITRE, PROF. MERLINE
School administrator, educator. **Personal:** Born Apr 10, 1943, Opelousas, LA; daughter of Robert and Florence. **Educ:** Southern Univ, BS, 1966; Atlanta Univ, MA, 1967; Temple Univ, MA, 1972, PhD, 1976. **Career:** St Augustine's Col, prof, 1967-70; Tex Southern Univ, prof hist, Col Lib Arts & Behav Sci, dean, 1976-. **Orgs:** Coordr, Southern Conf Afro-Am Studies; Southern Hist Asn; Black Women Historian; Tex State Hist Asn; Org Am Historian; Speakers Bur Tex Coun, currently; Tex Coun Humanities; managing ed, African Am Handbk Tex. **Special Achievements:** First African American President of the Texas State Historical Association. **Home Addr:** 7626 Glenvista St, Houston, TX 77061-2129, **Home Phone:** (713)644-0006. **Business Addr:** Professor, Dean, Texas Southern University, BJ/ML Pub Affairs COLABS Suite 315, Houston, TX 77004, **Business Phone:** (713)313-4287.

### PITT, DR. CLIFFORD SINCLAIR
School administrator. **Personal:** Born Georgetown, WA; son of Alphonso and Carmen; children: Amanda & Carolyn. **Educ:** Newbold Col, BA, theol, 1971; Andrews Univ, MA, relig, 1972; Univ London, PhD, theol, 1976; Miles Law Sch, JD. **Career:** British Union Seventh-Day Adventists, minister; Oakwood Col, assoc prof; Miles Col, prof, dean acad affairs; Int Bus Co, gen mgr. **Orgs:** Valedictorian & pres, Newbold Col Sor Class, 1971. **Home Addr:** PO Box 7802, Birmingham, AL 35228.

### PITTMAN, DR. AUDREY BULLOCK
Educator. **Personal:** Born Dec 16, 1916, Philadelphia, PA; daughter of Oscar Wyle and Annie Beaden; married James; children: Joyce Ann. **Educ:** Morgan State Univ, BA, 1948; Univ Pa, MSW; Waldon Univ, PhD, 1984. **Career:** Philadelphia Dept Welfare, supvr, 1951-57; C's Aid Soc, adoption supvr & consult, 1957-64; Penn State Dept Welfare, day care dir, 1964-69; Temple Univ, assoc prof 1969-84, prof emer, 1984-. **Orgs:** Founding mem, Philadelphia Asn Black Social Workers, 1969-; bd pres; Christian Educ AME Church, 1971-; trustee, Cheyney Univ, 1977-; adv bd, Philadelphia Dept Welfare 1981-88; bd mem & vpres, Black Family Serv, 1984-; bd mem, Women's Christian Alliance, 1986-89; Philadelphia County Bd Assistance, 1990-; trustee, Valentine Found, 1990; bd mem & vpres, Phila Child Guid Clin, 1994-. **Home Addr:** 1227 S 61st St, Philadelphia, PA 19143-2925. **Business Addr:** Professor Emeritus, Temple University, 1801 N Broad St, Philadelphia, PA 19107, **Business Phone:** (215)204-7000.

### PITTMAN, DARRYL E.
Government official. **Personal:** Born Jul 11, 1948, Pittsburgh, PA; son of J Ronald and Eunice W; married Deborah Durham; children: Darryl M, Sholah, Jordan, Cassi & Nolan. **Educ:** Columbia Col, New York, NY, BA, 1970; Columbia Univ Sch Law, New York, NY, JD, law, 1973. **Career:** Hahn Loeser, Freedheim, Dean & Wellman, Cleveland, OH, assoc; City E Cleveland Oh, mayor, 1984-89; Pittman, Alexander, Cook & Assocs, Cleveland, OH, atty, pres & managing partner, 1994-. **Orgs:** Pres, Software Specialist; Norman Minor Bar Asn; former pres, Ohio Chap Black Mayors; 21st Dist Cong Caucus; bd mem, Cleveland Br Nat Asn Advan Colored People. **Special Achievements:** First mayor to lead the City. **Home Addr:** 16119 Oakhill Rd, East Cleveland, OH 44112-3538, **Home Phone:** (216)541-8964. **Business Addr:** Managing Partner, President, Pittman, Alexander, Cook & Associates, 2940 Noble Rd Suite 202, Cleveland, OH 44121-2254, **Business Phone:** (216)291-1005.

### PITTMAN, KAVIKA CHARLES
Football player. **Personal:** Born Oct 9, 1974, Frankfurt. **Educ:** McNeese State Univ. **Career:** Football player (retired); Dallas Cowboys, defensive end & left defensive end, 1996-99; Denver Broncos, defensive end, 2000-02; Carolina Panthers, defensive end, 2003-04. **Honors/Awds:** Southland Conference Defensive Player of the Year, 1995; Louisiana Defensive Player of the Year, 1995; Division I-AA All-American, 1995; Rookie of the Year, 1996.

### PITTMAN, KEITH B.
Government official, vice president (government). **Personal:** Born Jan 1, 1971. **Career:** New Orleans, legislative aide, Metrop Conv & Visitors Bur, dir govt affairs, 1997; vpres govt affairs, currently. **Business Addr:** Vice President Governmental Affairs, New Orleans Metropolitan Convention & Visitors Bureau, 1520 Sugar Bowl Dr, New Orleans, LA 70112, **Business Phone:** (504)566-5055.

### PITTMAN, DR. MARVIN B.
Dentist. **Personal:** Born May 31, 1931, Blakely, GA; son of Johnnie Will and Lucile Brewster; married Amanda B Nelson; children: Marvin B Jr. **Educ:** Savannah State Col, BS, 1953; Univ Mich, MS, 1957; Howard Univ, DDS, 1966. **Career:** VA Ctr Los Angeles, res biochemist, 1957-62; Los Angeles, pvt pract dentist, 1970-. **Orgs:** Am Dent Asn; Calif Dent Asn; Angel City Cent Soc; Century Club Univ SC; Holman Meth Church; Urban League, Nat Asn Advan Colored People; Alpha Phi Alpha; Young Men's Christian Asn; Res Officers Asn; bd dir, pres, JW Ross Med Ctr; bd dir, Omicron Kappa Upsilon; bd dir, Beta Kappa Chi; bd dir, Los Angeles Free Clin. **Home Addr:** PO Box 8207, Los Angeles, CA 90008-0207. **Business Addr:** Dentist, Private Practice, 1818 S Western Ave Suite 402, Los Angeles, CA 90006, **Business Phone:** (323)731-8586.

### PITTMAN, MICHAEL
Football player, football executive. **Personal:** Born Aug 14, 1975, New Orleans, LA; son of Henry and Mae; married Melissa; children: Jordanne, Michael Jr, Mycah & Mykava Kaelyn. **Educ:** Fresno State Univ. **Career:** Ariz Cardinals, running back, 1998-2001; Tampa Bay Buccaneers, running back, 2002-07; Denver Broncos, 2008; Fla Tuskers, running back, 2009; Va Destroyers, 2011-; free agt, currently. **Orgs:** Alpha Phi Alpha. **Home Addr:** , San Diego, CA 92101. **Business Addr:** Professional Football Player, Florida Tuskers, 501 Riverside Ave Suite 904, Jacksonville, FL 32202.

### PITTMAN, WINSTON R., SR.
Automotive executive. **Personal:** Born Aug 31, 1950, Grenada, MS; married Alma Jean Dent. **Educ:** Jackson State Univ Jackson, MS, acct, 1971. **Career:** Pittman Enterprises, chief exec officer, pres, 1987; Cardinal Chrysler Jeep Dodge Inc, owner & pres, 1988-; Chatham Pkwy Toyota, owner; Cardinal Auto Group, dealer prin. **Orgs:** Bd mem, Fifth Third bd; pres, Nat Asn Minority Automobile Dealers, 1997-98, chmn, 1998-99; Daimler Chrysler Minority Dealer Asn; Dodge Advert Asn; Lexus Dealer Coun; bd mem, Greater Louisville Inc. **Business Addr:** President, Owner, Cardinal Chrysler Jeep Dodge Inc, 5311 Dixie Hwy, Louisville, KY 40216-1557, **Business Phone:** (502)449-1900.

### PITTS, BRENDA S.
Vice president (organization), executive. **Personal:** Born Aug 29, 1950, Madison, IN; daughter of Kenneth W and Theola I; married Joseph David; children: Nichole & Christopher. **Educ:** Ind Univ, Bloomington, IN, BS, engineering educ, 1972. **Career:** Vice president (retired); Knox Co News, writer, 1972-73; Cummins Engine Co Inc, commun spec, 1973, couns, 1975, personnel admin, 1975-78, mgr EEO, 1978-82, mgr personnel, 1982-83, dir personnel, 1983-88, exd personnel, 1988-92, vpres, human resources, 1995-97, vpres, diversity & corp responsibility, 1997-2000. **Orgs:** Alpha Kappa Alpha Sorority, 1970-72; scholar chmn, Laws Found, 1975-79; comnr, Columbus Human Rights Comn, 1978-79; vpres, Columbus Nat Asn Advan Colored People. **Home Addr:** 382 S Sussex Pl, Columbus, IN 47201-9649, **Home Phone:** (812)372-9146. **Business Addr:** Vice President, Cummins Engine Co, PO Box 3005, Columbus, IN 47202-3005, **Business Phone:** (812)377-3127.

### PITTS, CORNELIUS
Lawyer. **Personal:** Born Aug 3, 1933, Detroit, MI; son of Percy Jame and Zenolia O; married Mildred D Johnson; children: Byron Horace. **Educ:** Wayne State Univ, BS, polit sci, LLB, 1964. **Career:** Pvt pract atty, 1965-. **Orgs:** Wolverine Bar Asn, 1965-; Nat Bar Asn, 1965-; Detroit Bar Asn, 1965-; Mich Bar Asn, 1965-. **Home Addr:** 3850 Sawgrass Way Suite 2715, Naples, FL 48207, **Home Phone:** (239)352-0535. **Business Addr:** Attorney, 535 Griswold St Suite 1630, Detroit, MI 48226, **Business Phone:** (313)964-0066.

### PITTS, DONALD FRANKLIN
Judge. **Personal:** Born Aug 30, 1933, Pontiac, MI; married Patricia Florence Washington; children: Gregory Leroy, Gail Lynn, Kimberly Marie Thomas, Mark Robert Brown, Donald F Jr & Maureen Alyce. **Educ:** E Los Angeles Col, AA, 1952; Calif State Univ, BA, 1954; Southwestern Univ, JD, 1962. **Career:** Judge (retired); La Calif, probation officer, 1955-63, atty law, 1963-71; Super Ct, ref, 1969-71, comnr 1971-84, judge, 1984-2000; Calif State Univ Long Beach, assoc prof, 1972-75. **Orgs:** State Bar Calif; Nat Bar Asn; John M Langston Bar Asn; La Cty Bar Asn; Long Beach Bar Asn; YMCA; Nat Asn Advan Colored People; bd dir, Comm Develop Inc. **Home Addr:** 6724

Wooster Ave, Los Angeles, CA 90056-2136, **Home Phone:** (310)670-4862.

**PITTS, GEORGE EDWARD**
Writer, photojournalist. **Personal:** Born Sep 10, 1951, PA; son of George Sr and Phyllis; married Janis. **Educ:** Howard Univ, 1970; Skowhegan Sch Painting & Sculpture, 1971; Bennington Col, BA, Painting, Lit, 1973. **Career:** Phillips Exeter Acad, art teacher, Summer, 1972; Time Inc Picture Collection, picture researcher, 1979-90; Sports Illusr Picture Collection, picture reseacher, 1982; Entertainment Weekly Mag, asst picture ed, 1990-93; Spin Ventures, Photog Dir, 1993-04; Vibe Mag, dir photog & Photog Dir, 1993-07; Parsons New Sch Design, facult, 1998-, Dir, 1998-; New York Times, Fine Art Photogr, 1995-; Sch Visual Art, teacher, 2001; LIFE Mag, dir Photog, 2004-07; Time Inc, Photog Dir, 2004-07; Latina Mag, consult Dir, 2007-10; Supplementaire, contrib photogr, 2009-; SEEN Documentaries, assoc producer, 2010-. **Orgs:** Soc Publ Design, 1994-. **Honors/Awds:** Winner, Skowhegan Sch Painting & Sculpture, 1971; Photography Award, Commun Arts, 1991-93; Exhibition of Vibe Fashion Photography, Festival De La Mode, Louvre Museum, Paris, 1994; SPD GOLD Award, 1994, 2001; Best Photography, Vibe Magazine, 1994, 1995, 2000; Certificate of Merit, Am Photog, 1995; Lucie Award, 2006. **Special Achievements:** Group Art Exhibition: Social Studies: Truth, Justice, and the Afro-American Way, Illinois State University, 1989; Men, Myth, and Masculinities, Ledisflam Gallery, NYC, 1993; The Return of the Cadavre Exquis, The Drawing Center, NYC, 1993; Go Back and Fetch It, Gallery Annex I & II, 1994, 1995; 3 ASME Nominations for "Best Editorial Photography" for VIBE Magazine : 1994, 1995, 2001; 2 ASME Nominations for "Best Magazine Cover" for LIFE magazine: 2006, 2007. **Home Addr:** 256 Wyckoff St Apt 1, Brooklyn, NY 11217-2250, **Home Phone:** (718)834-9395. **Business Addr:** Director, The New School For Design, 66 5th Ave, New York, NY 10011, **Business Phone:** (212)229-8900.

**PITTS, LEE H.**
Athletic coach, swimmer. **Personal:** Born Jul 7, 1960, Birmingham, AL; son of Johnnie. **Educ:** Talladega Col, BBA, 1982; Clark Atlanta Univ, MA, econs, 1985. **Career:** A G Gaston Boys Club, swim instr, 1979; Colville Pool, head swim instr, 1981; Norwood Pool, head swim team, coach, 1982; City Birmingham, swim instr; Atlanta Parks & Recreation, swim instr; Adams Pk Pool, heads wim instr, 1984; Qual Life Ctr, aquatics dir, head swim team coach, lead swim instr; Star Swimming Complex, Ft Myers, Fla, head swim instr; Lee Pitts Swim Sch, Ft Myers, Fl, founder, 1990-; Dr Martin Luther King Pool, head swim team, coach, 1992; WEVU-TV Talk Show, Lee Pitts Live, exec producer & host, currently; Qual Life Ctr, lead swim instr; Carver Ranches Boys & Girls Club, aquatics dir, 2005-. **Orgs:** Nat Assn Urban Bankers, 1988; bd dir, Am Red Cross, 1990; Nat Assn Black Scuba Divers, 1992; Nat Assn Swim Instr, 1993; Phi Beta sigma fraternity; US swim; bd dir, Am Red Cross. **Honors/Awds:** Outstanding Community Involvement Award, Nat Assn Advan Colored People, 1984; Image Award, Nat Assn Advan Colored People; Alumni Spotlight Award, Talladega Col, 1991; Outstanding Youth Devt Award, Edison Community Col, 1991; Outstanding Contribution to Swimming, Am Red Cross, 1991; Distinguished Service Award, Nat Assn Advan Colored People, 1993; Crime Prevention Among Black Youths, Fl, 1994; Alumni Hall of Fame, Boys & Girls Clubs Am, 1998; Intl Swim Hall of Fame. **Special Achievements:** First and only African American swim instructor in the role; First African American to produce, direct, write, and star in a swim lesson video, 1993; First African American to be a spokesman on swim instruction commercials for NBC-TV, 1992; Author of 25 published swimming-related articles; Keynote speaker at numerous elementary, high schools & colleges around the country; Inducted into the SW Florida Black History Museum, 1995; spokesman for WFLA, Channel 8, NBC, pool safety commercials in Tampa Bay; Author of article, "Black Splash: The History of African-American Swimmer"; Jet Magazine recognized Pitts as a role model for swimmers. **Home Addr:** 8765 Azalea Ct Suite 103, PO Box 2662, Tamarac, FL 33321-2027. **Business Addr:** Founder, Lee Pitts Swim School, 8765 Azalea Ct Suite 103, Tamarac, FL 33321, **Business Phone:** (877)830-0391.

**PITTS, LEONARD, JR.**
Columnist, journalist. **Personal:** Born Oct 11, 1957, Orange, CA; son of Leonard Garvey and Agnes Rowan; married Marilyn Vernice Pickens; children: 5. **Educ:** Univ Southern Calif, BA, Eng, 1977. **Career:** Soul Mag, writer, ed, 1976-80; KFWB radio Los Angeles, writer, 1980-89; Westwood One Inc, writer, 1989-91; Miami Herald, music critic, 1991-95, My Opinion, syndicated columnist, 1995-. **Orgs:** Am Asn Sunday & Feature Ed; Atlantic City Press Club; Fla Soc Newspaper Ed; Nat Asn Black Journalists. **Honors/Awds:** American Society of Newspaper Editors, ASNE Award for Commentary Writing, 2001; National Society of Newspaper Columnists, Columnist of the Year, 2002; GLAAD Media, Outstanding Newspaper Columnist, 2002, 2009; Pulitzer Prize for Commentary, 2004; National Association of Black Journalists, Journalist of the Year, 2008; honorary doctorate degrees in humane letters from Old Dominion University and Utica College. **Special Achievements:** Author: "Becoming Dad: Black Men and the Journey to Fatherhood" (Longstreet Press, 1999); "Before I Forget" (Agate Bolden, 2009); Forward from "This Moment: Selected Columns, 1994-2008" (Agate Bolden, 2009); Freeman (Agate Bolden, 2012).

**PITTS, MEAGAN R.**
Executive. **Educ:** Univ Mich, BA, Eng lang & lit, gen, 2003; Mich State Univ, Eli Broad Grad Sch Mgt, MBA, integrative mgt, 2015. **Career:** City Detroit, Off Mayor, exec asst & team leader, 2003-10; Dave Bing Mayor Polit Campaign, dep press secy, 2008-09; Henry Ford Health Syst, dir, community outreach & partnerships, 2011-; Career Ctr. **Orgs:** 13th Cong Dist Future Leaders; Detroit Chap; Nat Asn Advan Colored People; Young Adult Comt; Young Dem Am. **Business Addr:** Director, Henry Ford Health System, 1 Ford Pl, Detroit, MI 48202, **Business Phone:** (800)436-7936.

**PITTS, RONALD JAMES, SR.**
Lawyer. **Personal:** Born Nov 2, 1942, Wheeling, WV; married Nellie M Price; children: Ronnelle J, Rhonda & Ronald J II. **Educ:** BS, 1966; LLB, 1969; JD, 1970. **Career:** Atty, pvt prac; IRS Estate & Gift Tax Reg Analyst Cincinnati, estate tax group mgr; IRS, atty; Greensboro Dist, Greensboro NC, qual & productivity coord, currently; tech revr, 1997-. **Orgs:** Vpres, Nat Asn Advan Colored People Huntington WVa; Huntington URA Comnr; Legal Coun Bluefield St Alumni; secy, Nat Asn Advan Colored People, 1973-74; chmn, C-H Human Rights Coun, 1970-73; WVa Black Caucus; supvr, UNIDN, chmn; pres, Chap 64 Nat Treas Employ Union; secy, Mtn St Bar Asn, 1972-73, histrn; WVa St Bar Asn; Am Bar Asn, 1969; pres, Coun Wheeling Col; EEO Consult RJP Consult Fed Fed Basketball Leag, 1970; comnr, 1970-75; bd mem, Tri-St Tax Inst, 1975; St Legist Interim Com; qual instr Reg, 1987; nat exec bd, AIM-IRS, 1986-87, nat parliamentarian, 1986-; OD, consult. **Honors/Awds:** Distingushed Performer, 1986, 1987. **Home Addr:** 4412 Indian Wells Dr, Greensboro, NC 27406, **Home Phone:** (336)674-3468. **Business Addr:** Greensboro Local Off, 2303 W Meadowview Rd Suite 201, Greensboro, NC 27407, **Business Phone:** (800)669-4000.

**PITTS, DR. VERA L.**
Educator, school administrator. **Personal:** Born Jan 23, 1931, Wichita, KS; daughter of Wade Johnson and Maggie; married Leonard. **Educ:** Mills Col, AA, 1950; Univ Calif, Berkeley, BA, 1953; Sacramento State Univ, MS, 1962; Mich State Univ, PhD, 1967. **Career:** Stockton Unified Sch Dist, teacher, counr & admin, 1954-65; City Col NY, asst prof, 1967-69; Palmer Handwriting Co, consult, 1975-; Rockefeller Postdoctoral Fel, 1978-80; Calif St Univ, Hayward, prof sch admin & supv, dept chair & ed admin, Dept Educ, prog mgr, 1986-87; Oakland Unified Sch Dist, assoc supt, l987-88; Oakland Pub Schs, Oakland, Calif, interim supt, 1989; Nat Hisp Univ, San Jose, Calif, provost, 1990-91; IHSD, secy currently. **Orgs:** League Women Voters, 1975-; Western Assoc Accrediting Teams, 1975-; SanMateo Br Am Assoc Univ Women, 1976-77; Calif St Div Am Asn Univ Women, 1978-80; Foster City Ed Facil Comm, 1983; Univ Calif Alumni Assoc, 1979-83; Nat Urban League Ed Adv Community, 1979; Nat Coun Admin Women Educ, 1982; Phi Delta Kappa, 1982-85; bd trustee, Pac Sch Religon, 1989; Rotary Int, 1988-; Family Serv Agency, 1999-; Sr FocusMills Peninsula Hosp, 1999; Am Social Health Asn, 1999-; Arthritis Found Advocacy Com, 1999-; Congregational Church San Mateo United Church Christ; pres & founding mem, Childcare Coord Coun, UC Berkeley Alumni Asn. **Home Addr:** 1557 Beach Pk Blvd, Foster City, CA 94404-1437, **Home Phone:** (650)573-9459. **Business Addr:** Secretary, IHSD, 155 Bovet Rd Suite 300, San Mateo, CA 94402, **Business Phone:** (650)578-3440.

**PLATT, RICHARD A.**
Executive. **Career:** Platt Construct Inc, Franklin, owner, pres, 1972-, treas. **Orgs:** Am Col Cardiol; Wis Underground Contractors Asn, 1987-; MWCA; Turkish Cypriot Community Asn; bd mem, Nat Asn Minority Contractors; bd mem, Wheaton Franciscan Healthcare. **Home Addr:** 7270 S 92nd St, Franklin, WI 53132-1909, **Home Phone:** (414)525-4777. **Business Addr:** Owner, President, Platt Construction Inc, 7407 S 27th St, Franklin, WI 53132-6021, **Business Phone:** (414)761-3868.

**PLEAS, DR. JOHN ROLAND**
Psychologist, educator. **Personal:** Born Nov 11, 1938, East St. Louis, IL; son of Henry and Daisy Walton; married Katherine; children: Chandra. **Educ:** McKendree Col, BS, 1960; Univ Ill, Urbana-Champaign, MEd, 1967; Vanderbilt Univ, Nashville, Tenn, PhD, 1980. **Career:** Univ Chicago, Billings Hosp, res tech, 1963-67; St Leonards House, dir com develop, 1967-71; Competence Inc, pres, 1975-; Vanderbilt Univ, weight Mgt prog, co-dir, 1977-84; Columbia Col, asst prof, 1984-85; Mid Tenn State Univ, assoc prof, 1985-2004, prof emer, 2004-. **Orgs:** Danforth fel Vanderbilt Univ, 1971-73. **Honors/Awds:** Recognition Award, Nat Med Asn Northwest Ind, 1988; Certicate of Recognition Award, Naval Health Res Ctr, San Diego, CA, 1990; Fac Award named in hon, Mid Tenn State Univ, 1996; Outstanding Teaching Award, 1999. **Special Achievements:** Author: "Walking", W W Norton & Co, 1981. **Business Addr:** Professor Emeritus, Middle Tennessee State University, 1301 E Main St, Murfreesboro, TN 37132-0001, **Business Phone:** (615)898-2706.

**PLEASANT, ALBERT E., III**
Administrator, accountant. **Personal:** Born May 22, 1944, Cincinnati, OH; son of Albert E Jr and Margaret Nesbitt; married Barbara Greene; children: Dennis R Green Sr; married Byrdean; children: Albert E IV. **Educ:** Univ Cincinnati, BS, 1973. **Career:** Univ Cincinnati, Col Med, Deans Off, fiscal asst, 1969-74; Cs Hosp Med Ctr, Div Neonatology, bus mgr, 1974-89; Univ Cincinnati, Dept Peds, bus affairs asst, 1974-79, sr bus admin, 1979-89; Howard Univ, dir off res adminr, 1989-90; Univ Cincinnati Med Ctr, Dept Environ Health, assoc dir admin & bus serv, exec dir, 1990-93; Pharm Sources Int Inc, bus mgt consult, 1995-96; Sears Indust Sales, acct mgr, 1996. **Orgs:** Nat Coun Univ Res Adminr, 1974-; Soc Res Adminr, 1974-; lay deleg fifty first Reg Conv Lutheran Church Mo Synod, 1975; Asn Am Med Cols Group Bus Affairs, 1982-; assoc mem, Nat Health Lawyers Asn, 1984-; bus mgt consult, Nat Inst Child Health & Human Develop, Pub Health Serv, Dept Health & Human Serv, 1985-; Ohio Dist Bd Parish Serv, 1985-87. **Home Addr:** 3401 York W, Cincinnati, OH 45215.

**PLEASANT, ANTHONY DEVON**
Football coach, football player. **Personal:** Born Jan 27, 1968, Century, FL; married Renita; children: Hannah Denette. **Educ:** Tenn State Univ, BA, criminal justice. **Career:** Football player (retired); Cleveland Browns, defensive end & right defensive end, 1990-95; Baltimore Ravens, right defensive end, 1996; Atlanta Falcons, 1997; New York Jets, right defensive end, 1998-99; San Francisco 49ers, defensive end, 2000; New Eng Patriots, defensive end & defensive tackle, 2001-03; Kans City Chiefs, defensive line coach, 2010-12; Houston Texans, Asst strength & conditioning coach & Asst defensive coach, 2014-15. **Business Addr:** Assistant Defensive coach, The Houston Texans, 2 NRG Pk, Houston, TX 77054, **Business Phone:** (832)667-2002.

**PLEASANT, MAE BARBEE BOONE.** **See Obituaries Section.**

**PLEDGER, V DIANNE.** **See PEERMAN-PLEDGER, VERNESE DIANNE.**

**PLEDGER, VERLINE SANDERS**
Educator, teacher. **Personal:** Born May 11, 1927, Macon, GA; married Charles L; children: Charles III & Bever Lyne. **Educ:** Morris Brown Col, BS, 1957. **Career:** Atlanta Girls Club, teacher, 1946-48; Pilgrim Health & Life Ins Co, bookkeeper, 1950-51; Atlanta Bd Educ, teacher except c (EMR), 1957-. **Orgs:** Exec bd, Nat Asn Advan Colored People; chmn voter regist, Atlanta Br; AAE; NEA; CEC; Altanta C Theatre Guild, 1969-; pres, Atlanta Chap, Las Amigas, 1969-71; Wheat St Baptist Church; secy, Deacon's Wives' Circle; treas, Adams ville Garden Club, 1972-74; parliamentarian & founding mem, Atlanta Chap Cont Socs Inc, 1972-; vpres, Loyal Friends Birthday Club, 1972-; Breast Cancer Screening Proj. **Honors/Awds:** Award Merit Civic Work, Gov GA, 1971; Most Dist Exhib Award, Conclave Las Amigas, 1970; Merit Outstation Work, CF Harper, 1965; Yearly Cert, Voter Reg Fulton Co, 1968; asst chmn procedure book, CF Harper; chmn, Girl Scout Prog. **Home Addr:** 150 Clement Way, Atlanta, GA 30331, **Home Phone:** (404)472-9515.

**PLESS, WILLIE**
Executive, football player. **Personal:** Born Feb 21, 1964, Anniston, AL; married Rhonda; children: Shamelle, Mariette & Sierra. **Educ:** Univ Kans. **Career:** Football player (retired), exec; Can Football League, Toronto Argonauts, linebacker, 1986-89; BC Lions, quarterback, 1990; Edmonton Eskimos, linebacker, 1991-98, 2000; eskimo community ambassador, 2011-; Sask Roughriders, 1999; personal trainer, currently. **Honors/Awds:** All-Star, Can Football League, 1986, 1988, 1990, 1991, 1992, 1993, 1994, 1995, 1996, 1997, 1998; All-Star East, Can Football League, 1986, 1988; Outstanding Defensive Player, Toronto Argonauts, 1986, 1988; Outstanding Rookie, Toronto Argonauts, 1986; All-Star West, Can Football League, 1990, 1991, 1992, 1993, 1994, 1996, 1997, 1998; Outstanding Player, BC Lions, 1990; Outstanding Defensive Player, Edmonton Eskimos, 1991, 1992, 1993, 1994, 1995, 1996, 1997; Norm Fieldgate Trophy, 1992, 1994, 1995, 1996, 1997; Outstanding Defensive Player, Can Football League, 1992, 1994, 1995, 1996, 1997; Champion, Grey Cup, 1993; Outstanding Defensive Player, Sask Roughriders, 1999; Wall of Honour, Edmonton Eskimos, 2004; Canadian Football Hall of Fame, 2005. **Business Addr:** Eskimo Community Ambassador, Edmonton Eskimos, Commonwealth Stadium 11000 Stadium Rd, Edmonton, AB T5H 4E2, **Business Phone:** (780)448-1525.

**PLUMMER, DR. DIANE LORETTA**
Educator. **Personal:** Born Feb 11, 1956, Montgomery, AL; daughter of Edward and Grace; children: Jonathan Wise. **Educ:** Morris Brown Col, BA, 1978; Univ Ga, MS, 1982, PhD, 1985. **Career:** Univ Md, S Korea, prof, 1985-86; Morris Brown Col, Learning Res, dir, 1985-; Four County Comprehensive Ment Health Ctr, coordr res, 1986-87; Clark Atlanta Univ, assoc prof, social psychol & interim chair, 1987-, fac adv, currently; Line berger Consult Serv, res assoc, 1998-. **Orgs:** Am Psychol Asn; Southeastern Psychol Asn; Ga Psychol Asn, Acad Affairs Comn; exec bd, Continental Colony Elem Sch PTA; bd trustee, Univ Senate, 1993-96, Clark Atlanta Univ; den leader, Boys Scout Am; adv bd, Ctr Acad Comput. **Home Addr:** 3936 Kenner Dr SW, Atlanta, GA 30331-3728, **Home Phone:** (404)505-8814. **Business Addr:** Faculty Advisor, Associate Professor, Clark-Atlanta University, Knowles Hall Rm 210, Atlanta, GA 30314-4381, **Business Phone:** (404)880-8238.

**PLUMMER, GLENN E.**
Actor. **Personal:** Born Aug 18, 1961, Richmond, CA; married DeMonica Santiago; children: 2. **Career:** Films: Who's That Girl, 1987; Hearts Of Stone, 1988; Colors, 1988; Funny Farm, 1988; Downtown, 1990; Past Time, 1991; Wedlock, 1991; Frankie & Johnny, 1991; South Central, 1992; Trespass, 1992; Menace Ii Society, 1993; Speed, 1994; Showgirls, 1995; Strange Days, 1995; Things To Do In Denver When You're Dead, 1995; Beyond The Edge, 1995; Small Time, 1996; The Destiny Of Marty Fine, 1996; The Substitute, 1996; Psalms From The Underground, 1996; Up Close & Personal, 1996; Speed Ii, 1997; Tear It Down, 1997; One Night Stand, 1997; A House Divided, 1998; Thursday, 1998; Heist, 1998; Interceptors, 1999; History Is Made At Night, 1999; Love Beat the Hell Outa Me, actor & exec producer, 2000; Road Dogs, 2000; Macarthur Park, 2001; Knight Club, 2001; Deadly Rhapsody, 2001; The Salton Sea, 2002; Go For Broke, 2002; Pool Hall Junkies, 2002; How To Get The Man's Foot Outta Your Ass, 2003; Road Dogs, 2003; Shade, 2003; Vegas Vampires, 2003; Gang Of Roses, 2003; Last Night With Angel, 2003; The Day After Tomorrow, 2004; Lexie, 2004; Sugar Valentine, 2004; Constellation, 2005; Brothers In Arms, 2005; Saw Ii, 2005; Voodoo Curse: The Giddeh, actor, dir, writer & producer, 2006; El Cortez, actor & assoc producer, 2006; The Long Shots, 2008; The Joshua's Soul Film Short, 2009; Janky Promoters, 2009; Cash, 2010; Showgirls 2: Penny's From Heaven, 2011; Monsters In The Woods, 2012; Scandalous, 2012; Winnerz, 2013; Imperial Dreams, 2014; The Other Side, 2014; Teeth And Blood, actor, writer & producer, 2014. TV Series: Hands Of A Stranger, 1987; The Father Clements Story, 1987; Terrorist On Trial: The United States Vs. Salim Ajami, 1988; "tour Of Duty", 1988; "l.a. Law", 1988-89; The Women Of Brewster Place, 1989; Heat Wave, 1990; "murderous Vision", 1991; "wedlock", 1991; "er", 1994-2007; "convict Cowboy", 1995; "pronto", 1997; "lawless", 1997; Bad Cop, 1998; "the Hunger", 1999; "the Corner", 2000; "ruby's Bucket Of Blood", 2001; "three Blind Mice", 2001; "reversible Errors", 2004; "go For Broke 2", 2005; "bones", 2006; Dexter, 2007; "sons Of Anarchy", 2008-09; "raising The Bar", 2009; "cold Case", 2010; "southland", 2012; "scorpion", 2014. **Honors/Awds:** Black Reel Award, 2001. **Business Addr:** Actor, c/o Innovative Artists Young Talent Division, 3000 Olympic Blvd, Santa Monica, CA 90404, **Business Phone:** (310)553-5200.

**PLUMMER, MICHAEL JUSTIN**
Sociologist, educator. **Personal:** Born Apr 15, 1947, Cambridge, MA; son of Justin and Kathleen. **Educ:** Trinity Col, BA, relig, 1970; Harvard Univ, Grad Sch Educ, MEd, 1972; Brandeis Univ, Florence Heller Sch, MMHS, 1986; Boston Col, MA, 1993, ABD, sociol, 1994, PhD, sociol, 2002. **Career:** Integrated Systs Info Serv Co, founder, prin, 1986-; Northeastern Univ, Boston, Mass, vis lectr sociol, 1989-

90; Boston Col, Chestnut Hill, Mass, teaching fel, adj prof, Sociol, 1990-2001; Univ Mass, Boston & Lesley Col, Cambridge, Mass, adj prof, sociol, 1994-; Bunsai Gakuen Intercultural Sch, Lincoln, Mass, esl instr, 1994-95; Boston Univ, lectr, social, currently. **Orgs:** Chmn, Proposal Rev Comt, 1983 & bd mem, Cambridge, Somerville, MA, Coun C, 1983-84; Human Servs Comn, 1995-96. **Home Addr:** 154 Fayerweather St, Cambridge, MA 02138, **Home Phone:** (617)547-0684. **Business Addr:** Staff, Boston College, 140 Commonwealth Ave, Chestnut Hill, MA 02467-3407.

### PLUMMER, MILTON
Banker. **Career:** City Nat Bank NJ, Newark, NJ, chief exec. **Business Addr:** Chief Executive, City National Bank of New Jersey, 900 Brood St, Newark, NJ 07102, **Business Phone:** (973)624-0865.

### PLUMMER, ORA BEATRICE
Educator, nurse. **Personal:** Born May 25, 1940, Mexia, TX; daughter of Macie I Echols; children: Kimberly, Kevin & Cheryl. **Educ:** Univ NMex Sch Nursing, BSN, 1961; Univ Calif, Los Angeles, MSN, 1966; Fac Pract Nursing Course, 1973; Univ Colo, postgrad. **Career:** Nurse (retired); staff nurse, 1961-64 & 1967-68; staff nurse & relief super, 1962-64; USPHS, nurse traineeship, 1964-66; NM Col Nursing, Albuquerque, instr, 1968-69; Univ CO Sch Nursing, sr instr, 1971-74, asst prof, 1974-76; W Interstate Comn Higher Educ, staff assoc III, 1976-78; Garden Manor, dir nursing serv, 1978-79; Colo Dept Pub Health & Environ, nursing consult, 1979-87, long term care process trainer, 1986, training coordr, 1987-96, regulatory nurse, survr. **Orgs:** Black Educ Day Boulder, 1971; coordr, Comm Bacc Prog; Minority Affairs Comm, 1971-74; Navy Orientation tripeducrs & admins, 1971; Air Force Orientation Trip, 1971; fWICHE Proj Fac Develop Meet Minority Group Needs, 1971-73; coordr & implementation pre-nursing prog, Univ Colo Sch Nursing, 1972; ac devel comn, Sch Nursing, 1974-; Inter disciplinary AMSA Proj, 1975-76; res, Effects Nursing Reassurance Patients Vocal Stress Levels, 1976; Nat Black Nurses Asn, 1976-; adv bd, Sickle Cell Anemia, 1976-; St Instnl Child Abuse & Neglect, 1983-92; adv comm, Metrop St Col, 1989-94, bd trustees, Colo Acad, 1990-96; Am Soc Training & Develop, 1990-; Nat Asn Female Execs, 1990-; bd dir, Domestic Violence Initiative, 2001; Am & Co Nurses Asn; Alpha Tau Delta; Phi Delta Kappa; Colo Black Nurses Coun. **Honors/Awds:** Certificate of Appreciation, 1994; Certificate of Appreciation, Dept Pub Health & Environ, 1999; Nightingale Nominee, 2003. **Special Achievements:** Scholar, Am Bus Women's Asn, 1958-60; scholar, Confederated Art Club, 1958-59; scholar, NM Med Soc Women's Aux, 1960; Author: Long Term Care, Implications of Med Practice, 1988; co-author: "Nursing Reassurance, Patient Denial & Vocal Distress, Nursing Res," 1976; "A Demonstration Model for Patient Educ, A Final Report", Western Interstate Commission Higher Education, 1978; "Improvement of Rehabilitative Nursing Serv to the Elderly in Long Term Care Facilities in Colo, A Final Report," 1989. **Home Addr:** 17144 E Amherst Dr, Aurora, CO 80013-2132, **Home Phone:** (303)690-7884.

### PLUMMER, WILLIAM B.
Vice president (organization), chief financial officer. **Educ:** Mass Inst Technol, BS, aeronaut & astronaut, 1980, MS, aeronaut & astronaut, 1982; Stanford Univ, Grad Sch Bus, MBA, 1986. **Career:** Gen Elec Capital Corp, exec, 1990-97; Mead Corp, treas, 1997-98, vpres corp strategy & planning, 1998-2000, pres, 2000; Alcoa Inc, vpres & treas, 2000-06; Dow Jones & Co, chief financial officer, 2006-07; United Rentals Inc, exec vpres & chief financial officer, 2008-. **Orgs:** Dir, John Wiley & Sons Inc, 2003-; dir, Integris Metals Corp; Financial Execs Int; New York Soc Security Analysts; dir, UIL Holdings Corp, 2013-. **Business Addr:** Executive Vice President and Chief Financial Officer, United Rentals, Inc, 100 First Stamford Pl Suite 700, Stamford, CT 06902, **Business Phone:** (203)622-3131.

### PLUMPP, PROF. STERLING DOMINIC
Educator. **Personal:** Born Jan 30, 1940, Clinton, MS; son of Cyrus Hampton and Mary Emmanuel; married Falvia Delgrazia Jackson; children: Harriet Nzinga. **Educ:** St Benedict's Col, Atchison, KS, 1962; Roosevelt Univ, Chicago, IL, BA, 1968, attended 1971. **Career:** US Postal Serv, Chicago, Ill, distrib clerk, 1962-64, 1966-69; N Park Col, Chicago, Ill, counr, 1969-71; Univ Ill, Chicago, Ill, instr, 1971-84, African Am Studies & Eng Dept, assoc prof, 1984, African Am Studies & Eng Dept, prof, African Am Studies & Eng Dept, prof emer, 2001; Evanston Sch, Ill, poet residence; Chicago State Univ, vis prof; Youth Black Heritage Theater Ensemble Studio, dir young writer's workshop urban gateways. Books: Portable Soul, writer, 1969; Half Black, Half Blacker, writer, 1970; Muslim Men, writer, 1972; Black Rituals, writer, 1972; Steps to Break the Circle, writer, 1974; Clinton, writer, 1976; Somehow We Survive: An Anthology of South African Writing, ed, 1981; The Mojo Hands Call, I Must Go, writer, 1982; Blues: The Story Always Untold, writer, 1989; Johannesburg & other poems, writer, 1993; Hornman, writer, 1995; Harriet Tubman, writer, 1996; Ornate With Smoke, writer, 1997; Paul Robeson, writer, 1998. **Orgs:** Black Am Lit Forum, 1980-89. **Home Addr:** 645 N Central Ave Suite 2, Chicago, IL 60644-1507, **Home Phone:** (773)378-8716. **Business Addr:** Visiting Professor, Chicago State University, 5801 S Ellis Ave, Chicago, IL 60637, **Business Phone:** (773)702-1234.

### PLUNKETT, RAPHAEL HILDAN
Manager, editor. **Personal:** Born Feb 11, 1966, Chicago, IL; daughter of Ralph B Marrs Sr and Hettie Perry Mahan; children: Tabitha Talai Marrs. **Educ:** De Paul Col, lib arts. **Career:** Helene Curtis, Chicago, Ill, customer support specialist, 1987-. **Orgs:** Ed, Helene Curtis Newsletter, 1989-92; United Way/Crusade of Mercy Vol, 1987-93. **Honors/Awds:** Crusade of Mercy Rep, 1992-93. **Home Addr:** 23840 Country View Dr, Diamond Bar, CA 91765-2617, **Home Phone:** (909)861-5636.

### POCKNETT, LAWRENCE WENDELL
Insurance executive. **Personal:** Born Sep 23, 1934, Boston, MA; married Mary Seiter; children: Lawrence Jr & Lorraine. **Educ:** Boston Univ Sch Lib Arts, BA, 1962. **Career:** Insurance executive (retired); Liberty Mutual, chief underwriter, 1971-73; Aetna Ins, underwriting mgr, 1973-76; Hartford Ins Grp, vpres. **Honors/Awds:** Black Achiever's Award, ITT, 1979. **Home Addr:** 58 Stagecoach Rd, Avon, CT 06001, **Home Phone:** (860)675-5121.

### POE, ALFRED
Executive, executive director. **Personal:** married Carol; children: 2. **Educ:** Polytech Inst Brooklyn, BS, 1971; Harvard Univ, MBA, 1975. **Career:** Mars Inc, vpres, brands dir, com dir, 1982-91; Campbell's Soup Co, corp vpres, 1991-96; Meal Enhancement Group, pres, 1993-96; State St Corp, bd dir, 1994; B&G Foods Inc, dir, 1997-; Super Nutrit Corp, chief exec officer, chmn, 1997-2002; Aja Restaurant Corp, chmn & chief exec officer, 1999-; B&G Foods, dir, 1997-; MenuDirect Corp, chmn, dir, 1997-99, pres, chief exec officer, 2001; Primary PDC Inc, dir, 2000-; Ctr pl Inc, bd dir, 2004-; Gen Foods Corp, group proj mgr; Testamints Inc, chief exec officer & pres. **Orgs:** Trustee, Am Bar Asn; Exec Leadership Coun. **Business Addr:** Director, B&G Foods Inc, 4 Gatehall Dr Suite 110, Parsippany, NJ 07054, **Business Phone:** (973)401-6500.

### POE, DR. BOOKER
Physician, pediatrician. **Personal:** Born Jul 9, 1936, Eustis, FL; son of Rev William (deceased) and Janie Jackson (deceased); married Gloria Reeves; children: Janita L & Brian D. **Educ:** Tenn State Univ, BS, 1957; Meharry Med Col, MD, 1963. **Career:** Childrens Hosp, training Pediat, Hurley Med Ctr, training Pediat; Pvt pract, pediatrician, currently. **Orgs:** Breakfast prog chmn, Atlanta Med Asn, 1970-76; chmn bd dir, GA Med Asn, 1973; chmn, med legs GA State Med Asn, 1976; chmn, GA State Med Asn, 1977; bd dir, treasr, Health lst HMO, 1979-89; comm advisor, Min Dent & Physicians, GA, 1980; pub rels, Atlanta Med Asn; bd dir prec, Morehouse Sch Med; exe bd, Atlanta Br Nat Asn Advan Colored People; assoc clin prof pediat, GA Univ; leglt, GA Am Acad Pediat; Morehouse Sch Med. **Honors/Awds:** Young Physician of the Year, Atlanta Med Asn, 1974; Physician of the Year, Atlanta Med Asn, 1980; Doctor of the Year, GA House Rep, 1980; Pres Award GA Med Asn, 1982; President's Award, GA State Med Asn, 1982, 1986; 25years of Service Award, Atlanta Med Asn, 1989; President's Award, 25 years of service McHarry Med Col, 1989; Distinguished Service Medallion, G State Med Asn, 1990; Nash Carter Honoree, Atlanta Med Asn, 1992; Father of the Year Award, Concerned Black Clergy of Atlanta, 2000; Cot Service Award, Southwest Hosp & Med Ctr, 2001; honoree, field med, Eustis Afr-Am Heritage Comm, 2002; Distinguished Alumni Medallion, Tenn State Univ, 2002. **Special Achievements:** Publisher: "EPSDT and the Black Medical Community in Georgia", Nat Med Assoc J, 1979, "Why Attend a Legislative Breakfast?", The Microscope Newsletter, 1980. **Home Addr:** 3518 Lynfield Dr SW, Atlanta, GA 30311, **Home Phone:** (404)696-5970. **Business Addr:** Physician, 2600 Martin Luther King Jr Dr SW Suite 202, Atlanta, GA 30311, **Business Phone:** (404)691-4354.

### POE, FRED J.
Chief executive officer. **Career:** Southgate Automotive Group, chief exec officer, 1994-. **Business Addr:** Chief Executive Officer, Southgate Automotive Group, 15800 Eureka Rd, Southgate, MI 48195, **Business Phone:** (734)282-1010.

### POE, KIRSTEN NOELLE
Consultant, president (organization), chief executive officer. **Personal:** Born Mar 30, 1965, New York, NY; daughter of Robert L Jr and Dolores; married Lawrence Vincent Hill Jr. **Educ:** Syracuse Univ, BS, tv, radio & film mgt, 1985; NY Univ, MA, media ecol, 1988. **Career:** Time Warner Cable, sls coordr, 1986; WNBC, sr sls admin, 1987-91; CNBC, media rel mgr, 1991-94; Noelle-Elaine Media, co-pres & chief exec officer, 1993-; Pocket PR Shop, owner & pres, 2010-; Mid-Life Mommy, blogger, 2011-. **Orgs:** Syracuse Univ, Pub Rel Coun; Newhouse Prof Gallery Syracuse Univ; sch vol, Learning Leaders; former vol, Literacy Vols; lectr, Am Womens Econ Develop; lectr, Learning Annex; peer tutor, Syracuse Univ, Nat Asn Clack Female Exec, 2001; Nat Asn Black Journalists, Nat Asn Black Female Exec Music & Entertainment. **Honors/Awds:** Natl Academy of TV Arts & Science, finalist, 1987; CEBA Award, produc team, 1988; Walter Raitz Foundation, Fellow, 1991; Newhouse Professional Gallery, 2001; Awarded the Chancellor Citation Award, Excellence in Public Relations. **Special Achievements:** Beginning Spanish; Basic Sign Language (ASL); One of her college's top honors by being inducted into the Professional Gallery at the communications school, 2000. **Business Addr:** Co-president, Noelle-Elaine Media Inc, 118 E 28th St Suite 207, New York, NY 10016, **Business Phone:** (646)424-9750.

### POELLNITZ, FRED DOUGLAS
Administrator, educator. **Personal:** Born Aug 3, 1944, Philadelphia, PA; married Stephanie Snead; children: Andrew & Michelle. **Educ:** Univ Pittsburg, BSEE, 1966; NY Univ, MSEE, elec engineering, 1970; Harvard Univ, MBA, finance & acct, 1972; Wilmington Univ, EdD. **Career:** Bendix Corp, proj engr, 1967-70; Touche Ross & Co, consult, 1972-76; Sor bus Inc, dir acct, 1976-80; Smith Kline Beckman, asst mgr, 1980-81; Meharry Med Col, vpres, finance; Peirce Col, prof bus admin, 1999-; ACBSP, co-facilitator, currently. **Orgs:** Bd dir, Electronic Typesetting Corp, 1972-76; Alpha Phi Alpha Fraternity; Nat Asn Accountants; Nat Asn Black Accountants, Fin Exec Inst; Founding Charter Mem Philadelphia Chap; bd adv, Tenn State Univ Bus Sch; bd dir, Turning Points C; bd dir, Urban League. **Home Addr:** 1530 Locust St Suite 70, Philadelphia, PA 19102-4401. **Business Addr:** Professor, Peirce College, 1420 Pine St, Philadelphia, PA 19102, **Business Phone:** (215)545-6400.

### POGUE, BRENT DARYL
Executive. **Personal:** Born Sep 3, 1954, Sumter, SC; son of Clarence W and Arnetta McCain Ellison. **Educ:** Cornell Univ, Ithaca, NY, BS, mech engineering, 1976, ME, mech engineering, 1977; Univ St Thomas, IT/IS, 2000. **Career:** Polaroid Corp, Cambridge, MA, tech supvr, 1977-80; Bechtel Power Corp, San Francisco, Calif, sr engr, 1980-85, 2007-08; Pac Gas & Elec Co, syst engr; Impell Corp, Walnut Creek, Calif, lead sr engr, 1985-88; Pac Gas & Elec, San Francisco, Calif, nuclear generation engr, 1988-95; NextEra Energy Resources, sr engr, 2008-09; Trivis Inc, sr proj engr, 2010-11; Enercon Serv, 2011-12; SHINE Med Technologies Inc, sr licensing engr, 2012-13; HukariAscendent, sr engr, 2012-14; Duke Energy Corp, sr licensing engr, 2013-14; Xcel Energy Corp, consult; Am Elec Power Co, consult; Beckman & Assoc, sr engr; Exelon Corp, consult, currently. **Orgs:** Cornell Univ Soc Engrs, 1980-; Am Soc Mech Engrs, 1980-; Am Asn Blacks Energy, 1989-; Am Nuclear Soc, 1984; Urban Serv Proj San Francisco, 1995; San Francisco Proj Inform, 1996-; Commonwealth Club Calif, 1997-; fel ASI. **Home Addr:** 1958 Greenwich St, San Francisco, CA 94102, **Home Phone:** (415)775-2309. **Business Addr:** Consultant, Exelon Corp, 10 S Dearborn St 48th Fl, Chicago, IL 60680-5398, **Business Phone:** (800)483-3220.

### POGUE, D. ERIC RICK
Labor relations manager, executive, executive director. **Personal:** Born Feb 12, 1949, Southampton, NY; son of Isaiah P (deceased) and Virginia Mines; married J Marie; children: Eric Spencer. **Educ:** Heidelberg Col, BS, psychol, 1970; Bowling Green State Univ, MA, 1971. **Career:** Case Western Res Univ, asst dir acad support, 1971-72; Cleveland State Univ, staff devel trainer, 1972-76; Diamond Shamrock Corp, mgr human resources, 1976-82; Cuyahoga Community Col, adj prof, 1978-79; Reichhold Chem Inc, White Plains NY, vpres human resources, 1982-87, sr vpres, 1987-88; Philip Morris Co Inc, vpres employee rels, 1988-92; Marvel Entertainment, vpres human resources, 1994-97; Revlon Inc, sr vpres, human resources, 1997-2000; Campbell Soup Co, sr vpres global human resources, 2001-02; Am Red Cross, sr vpres, human resources & chief diversity officer, 2003-07; Kaleida Health, exec vpres & chief human resources officer, 2008-11; Continuum Health Partners Inc, sr vpres & chief human resources officer, 2011-13; Inst Family Health, vpres & chief human resources officer, 2014; DEP Consult Partners, Independent Healthcare HR Prof & Exec Coach, 2014-; City Mt Vernon, Comnr Human Resources, 2016; Altria Group Inc, corp vpres human resources, vpres employee rels. **Orgs:** Mem Soc Human Resource Mgt, 1980-; coord-ann dir, United Way Greater Cleveland, 1982; Westchester/Ct Personnel Round Table, 1983-88; Human Resources Coun; Am Mgt Asn, 1987-; bd adv, Cornell Univ Sch Indust & Labor Rels, 1990-; bd dir, Nat Alliance End Homelessness. **Business Addr:** Senior Vice President of Human Resources, Chief Diversity Officer, American Red Cross, 2025 E St NW, Washington, DC 20006, **Business Phone:** (202)303-4498.

### POGUE, FRANK G., JR.
Educator, school administrator. **Personal:** Born Nov 3, 1938, Mobile, AL; son of Annie B; married Dorothy Dexter; children: Constance L. **Educ:** Bishop Jr Col, attended 1959; Ala State Univ, BA, sociol, 1961; Atlanta Univ, MA, sociol, 1966; Univ Pittsburgh, PhD, sociol, 1973. **Career:** Educator, school administrator (retired); Philander Smith Col, Little Rock, asst prof, 1962-66, dean; Chatham Col, Pittsburgh, founder & dir afro-am studies, instr, 1969-71; Meharry Med Col, Nashville, asst prof, 1971-73, sr med res assoc; State Univ New York, Albany, chair, dept African & Afro-Am Studies, 1973-83, assoc vpres res educ develop, 1982-83, vpres stud affairs, 1983-96, vice chancellor stud affairs & spec progs, 1986-96; State Univ New York, Cobleskill, Interim Pres, 1992-93; Edinboro Univ Pa, pres emer, 1996-2007, pres emer; Chicago State Univ, interim pres, 2008-09; Grambling State Univ, pres, 2010-; Acad Search Professionals Inc, adv consult, currently. **Orgs:** Nat Asn Stud Personnel Adminrs; Nat Asn Study Afro-Am Life Hist; Col Stud Personnel Asn NY State; Chief Stud Affairs Adminrs State Univ NY; Sigma Pi Phi Fraternity; Nat Coun Black Studies; Delta Sigma Pi Prof Bus Fraternity; Alpha Phi Alpha fraternity. **Home Addr:** 509 Isadore Dr, New Castle, DE 19720-5631, **Home Phone:** (302)836-8880. **Business Addr:** President, Grambling State University, 403 Main St, Grambling, LA 71245.

### POGUE, REV. RICHARD JAMES (RICK POGUE)
Government official, baptist clergy. **Personal:** Born May 25, 1943?, Cortelyou, AL; married Birdie Raine; children: Tiffany Denise & Karen Lanise. **Educ:** Ala State Univ, BS, 1971; Pepperdine Univ, attended 1977; Int Sem, Plymouth, FL, PhD, theol studies. **Career:** Robins AFB, personnel mgt specialist, 1971-73; Air Force Reserves, personnel mgr, 1973-75; Air Training Command, San Antonio, Tex, personnel mgt specialist; Keesler AFB, chief recruitment & staffing, 1975-76; Randolph AFB, personnel mgt specialist, 1976-79; HQ USAF Pentagon WA DC, dep eeo, 1979-80; Robins AFB, GA, equal oppor/affirmative action officer, 1980-86, chief employee devt & training sect, 1986-91, chief, Employ & Staffing, Classifications, 1992-; Oakridge Baptist Church, pastor; Friendship Memorial Baptist Church, pastor, currently. **Orgs:** Nat Asn Advan Colored People, 1980-; pres, Chief exec officer, K&R Shoes Inc, 1983-85; pres, Int Personnel Mgt Asn, 1984-85; Better Mgt Asn, 1985-; Blacks Govt, 1985-; bd career advs, Atlanta Univ, 1986; historian, Alpha Phi Alpha Frat Inc, 1986-87; bd dir, Mid Ga Educ Talent Search, 1986-; bd dir, Air Force Asn, 1986-; bd dir, Combined Fed Campaign; pres, Stud Govt Asn. **Home Addr:** 110 River Valley Ct, Kathleen, GA 31047-2154, **Home Phone:** (478)987-8010. **Business Addr:** Pastor, Friendship Memorial Baptist Church, 2832 Ledo Rd, Albany, GA 31707, **Business Phone:** (229)436-5700.

### POINDEXTER, REV. CHARLES L. L.
Clergy. **Personal:** Born Apr 11, 1932, Richmond, VA; son of Walter E and Pearl Maria Robinson; married Judith L Owens; children: Maria, Byroh & Evangeline. **Educ:** WVa State Col, BA, 1954; Philadelphia Divinity Sch, MDiv, 1958. **Career:** Clergy (retired); St Ausgustine's Church, vicar, 1958-65; St Monica's Church, rector, 1963-65; St Barnabas Church, rector, 1965-68; St Luke's Church, rector, rector emer, 1968. **Orgs:** Nat jr vpres, Phi Beta Sigma, 1953-54; The Brahaman Soc, 1955-; bd, Springside Sch, 1974-80; bd, All Saints Hosp, 1975-81; Sigma Pi Phi Boule, 1980-; pres, Home Homeless Fund, 1985-; nat vpres, Union Black Episcopalians, 1986-92; pres, Aids Task Force, 1987-92. **Honors/Awds:** DHL, St Augustine's Col, 1988; Achievement, Col Four Chaplins, 1988; Achievement Award, St Barnaba's Founders, 1989; Achievement Award, Union Black Episcopalians, 1991. **Special Achievements:** St Barnabas Episcopal Sch, headmaster, 1969-75, founder, Wissahickon Deanery, dean, 1975-81; Pamphlet, Aids in the Black Church, 1990; Book, History St Luke's Church, 1991. **Home Addr:** 5421 Germantown Ave, Philadelphia, PA 19144, **Home Phone:** (215)844-8544.

### POINDEXTER, HON. GAMMIEL GRAY
Lawyer. **Personal:** Born Sep 22, 1944, Baton Rouge, LA; daughter of James and Lee Ethel; married Gerald G; children: John L R &

Christopher R. **Educ:** Univ Ind, AB, 1965; La State Univ, JD, 1969. **Career:** Judge (retired); Off Solicitor, US Dept Labor, staff atty, 1968-70; Richmond Legal Aid Soc, dept dir, 1971-73; Poindexter & Poindexter, partner, 1973-; Surry Co, Va, commonwealth's atty, 1976-95, commonwealth judge, 1995-2001; Sussex Co Gen Dist Ct, chief judge, 1999-2002, Sixth Judicial Dist Gen Dist Ct, judge, 2002-07; Prince George County Schs, judge. **Orgs:** Pres, Old Dom Bar Asn, 1980-82; bd vis, Old Dom Univ, 1982-; chmn, Surry Co Dem Party, 1983-95; bd dir, Va Asn Black Elected Off; Am Bar Asn; bd mem, Va State Ct Col Syst, 1990-95; Va State Bar Coun, 1991-95. **Honors/Awds:** Martin Luther King Jr. Memorial Award, Old Dom Univ, 1989; Lifetime Achievement Award. **Special Achievements:** First African American woman commonwealth attorney in Surry county. **Home Addr:** 6601 Courts Dr, PO Box 187, Prince George, VA 23875-0187, **Home Phone:** (804)733-2631.

### POINTER, DR. RICHARD H.

Scientist, educator. **Personal:** Born Jun 4, 1944, Covington, GA; son of Hugh Brooks (deceased) and Sarah Eunice Weaver; married Rosie Lee Davis; children: Richard Hamilton Jr, Rawlinson Lee & Robert Lewis. **Educ:** Morehouse Col, BS, biol chem, 1968; Brown Univ, ScM, 1973, PhD, biochem, 1975. **Career:** Vanderbilt Univ, res assoc, 1975-77; Mass Gen Hosp, res biochemist, 1977-78; Harvard Univ, instr, 1977-80; Howard Hughes Med Inst, res fel, 1978-80; Howard Univ, Dept Biochem & Molecular Biol, asst prof, 1980-87, prof, 1980-2014, Preliminary Acad Reinforcement Prog, course dir, asst prof, prof; Membrane Regulataty Sect, Lab Cellular & Develop Biol, Nat Inst Diabetes & Digestive & Kidney Dis, NIH, vis scientist, 1992; African Sci Inst, fel, 2006. **Orgs:** AAAS, 1972-; Sigma Xi, 1973; secy exec bd, PACE, 1973-74; Am Physiol Soc, 1975-; Am Diabetes Asn, 1979-; Adult Leader Boy Scouts Am, 1979-; sci fair judge, Southern Md Sch Area, 1988-; bd dir, PG County Chap, Am Diabetes Asn, 1988-89; vpres, PG Co Chap, Am Diabetes Asn, 1989-90; pres, PG County Chap, Am Diabetes Asn, 1990-92; Am Soc Biochem & Molecular Biol, 1995-; Nat Acad Critical Thinking, 1999-; Omicron Kappa Upsilon, Pi Pi Chap, 2006; secy, African Methodist Episcopal Church. **Honors/Awds:** Commissioners Award, Boy Scouts Am, 1988; Meritorious Service Award, Am Diabetes Asn, 1992; Sharp Hands Award, NASA Goddard Space Flight Ctr, 1995, 1996; Johnetta Davis Mentorship Award, Grad Sch Arts & Scis, 1996; Outstanding Teacher Award, Col Dent, Howard Univ, 2002; Science Spectrum Trailblazer Award, 2006. **Special Achievements:** Publications in Biochemistry, Physiology & Pharmacology Journals. **Home Addr:** 7501 Epping Ave, Ft Washington, MD 20744-2121, **Home Phone:** (301)248-9230. **Business Addr:** Professor, Howard University College of Medicine, 520 West St NW, Washington, DC 20059, **Business Phone:** (202)806-6270.

### POITIER, SIDNEY L.

Administrator, television producer, actor. **Personal:** Born Feb 20, 1927, Miami, FL; son of Reginald and Evelyn Outten; married Juanita Hardy; children: Beverly, Pamela, Sherri & Gina; married Joanna Shimkus; children: Anika & Sydney. **Career:** Actor; Films: Sepia Cinderella, 1947; No Way Out, 1950; Cry the Beloved Co, 1951; Red Ball Express, 1952; Go Man Go, 1954; Blackboard Jungle, 1955; Good-bye, My Lady, 1956; Edge of the City, 1957; Something of Value, 1957; Band of Angels, 1957; The Mark of the Hawk, 1957; Virgin Island, 1958; The Defiant Ones, 1958; Porgy & Bess, 1959; All the Young Men, 1960; A Raisin in the Sun, 1961; Paris Blues, 1961; Pressure Point, 1962; The Long Ships, 1963; Lillies of the Field, 1963; The Bedford Incident, 1965; The Greatest Story Ever Told, 1965; A Patch of Blue, 1965; The Slender Thread, 1965; Duel at Diablo, 1966; To Sir, with Love, 1967; In the Heat of the Night, 1967; Guess Who's Coming to Dinner, 1967; For Love of Ivy, 1968; The Lost Man, 1969; They Call Me Mister Tibbs, 1970; Brother John, 1971; The Organization, 1971; Buck & the Preacher, dir, 1972; A Warm December, dir, 1973; Uptown Saturday Night, dir, 1974; The Wilby Conspiracy, 1975; Let's Do it Again, dir, 1975; A Piece of the Action, dir, 1977; Stir Crazy, dir, 1980; Hanky Panky, dir, 1982; Fast Forward, dir, 1985; Little Nikita, 1987; In the Hall of the Mountain King, 1987; Hard Knox, 1987; Shoot to Kill, 1988; Little Nikita, 1988; Deadly Pursuits, 1988; Ghost Dad, dir, 1990; Sneakers, 1992; A Century of Cinema, 1994; Wild Bill: Hollywood Maverick, 1996; The Jackal, 1997; Simple Life of Noah Dearborn, 1999; Ralph Bunche: An American Odyssey, 2001; MacKenzie, 2004; Mr. Warmth: The Don Rickles Project, 2008; "Free of Eden", actor & exec producer; TV Films: "Separate but Equal", 1991; "Children of the Dust", 1995; "To Sir, with Love II", 1996; "Mandela and de Klerk", 1997; "David & Lisa", 1998; "Free of Eden", 1999; "The Simple Life of Noah Dearborn", 1999; "The Last Brickmaker in America", 2001; "Tell Them Who You Are", 2004; "The Oprah Winfrey Show", 2005; Books: This Life, 1980; The Measure of a Man: A Spiritual Autobiography, 2000; Life Beyond Measure-letters to my Great-Granddaughter, 2008; UNESCO, bahamas ambassador, 1997-2007; Verdon Cedric Productions, pres & chief exec officer, currently. **Orgs:** Bd dir, Walt Disney Co, 1994-. **Special Achievements:** First Bahamian and first African-American to win an Academy Award for Best Actor for his role in Lilies of the Field, 1964. **Business Addr:** President, Chief Executive Officer, Verdon Cedric Productions Inc, PO Box 2639, Beverly Hills, CA 90213, **Business Phone:** (310)274-7253.

### POITIER, SYDNEY TAMIIA

Actor. **Personal:** Born Nov 15, 1973, Los Angeles, CA; daughter of Joanna Shimkus and Sidney; married Dorian Heartsong; children: A'Zalia Delancey Coffey. **Educ:** NY Univ. **Career:** Films: True Crime, 1999; Happy Birthday, 2000; MacArthur Park, 2001; The Devil Cats, producer, 2004; I'm Perfect, 2005; Nine Lives, 2005, Hood of Horror, 2006; Grey's Anatomy, 2006; The List, 2007; Death Proof, 2007; Grindhouse, 2007; Blues, 2008; Page 36, 2010; Yard Sale, 2010; Big Tweet, 2011; Night of the Living Dead: Origins 3D, 2014. TV Series: "Free of Eden", 1998; "Noah's Ark", 1999; "First Years", 2001; "Abby", 2003; "Veronica Mars", 2004; "Knight Rider", 2008-09; "Private Practice", 2011; "Supah Ninjas", 2011; "Hawaii Five-0", 2012; "Kendra", 2012; "Chicago P.D.", 2014. **Honors/Awds:** The 50 Most Beautiful People, People Mag's, 2001; Scream Awards, 2007; 21st Annual Soul Train Music Awards, 2007. **Business Addr:** Actress, Thruline Entertainment Inc, 9250 Wilshire Blvd, Beverly Hills, CA 90212-3343, **Business Phone:** (310)595-1500.

### POLK, ANTHONY JOSEPH

Military leader. **Personal:** Born Mar 8, 1941, New Orleans, LA; son of Middleton Brooks (deceased) and Edolia Stephens (deceased); married Maxine; children: Patricia, Michael & Stephen. **Educ:** McNeese State Univ, Lake Charles, BS, 1966; Bowling Green State Univ, MS, 1974. **Career:** Clin Lab Serv, Ft Hood Tex, dir, 1967; US Europ Command Tri-Serv Blood Prog, dir, 1974-78; Shape, dir, 1974-78; NATO Blood Prog, officer, 1982-84; Dept Defense Tri-Serv Blood Prog, dir, 1984-92; ANRC, chief staff, 1992-96; ARC Southeast Reg Blood Testing Ctr, chief exec officer, 1996-98, diversity officer, 2000-. **Orgs:** Clin lab mgr, Ft Rucker, 1967-68; joint blood prog officer, CP Zama, Japan, 1968-72; lab mgr blood bank manage, Ft Hood, 1974-78; comdr blood bank, Landstuhl, Ger, 1978-81; joint blood prog officer, Stuttgart, Ger, 1981-83; NATO blood prog officer, Shapie BE, 1983-84; dir, DVD Armed Serv blood prog, Pentagon, 1984-91. **Honors/Awds:** Numerous military awards; Defense Meritorous Medal, 1, Meritorious Sevice Medals, 3. **Special Achievements:** Publication in military journal. **Home Addr:** 12047 Bridle Post Pl, Manassas, VA 20112-5515, **Home Phone:** (703)750-2502. **Business Addr:** Chief Diversity Officer, American Red Cross, 2025 E St NW, Washington, DC 20006, **Business Phone:** (202)303-4498.

### POLK, DON

Chief executive officer, president (organization). **Educ:** Boston Univ, BS, psychol, BA, pub rel. **Career:** Romar Group Inc, mkt specialist, pres & chief exec officer; Romar Studios Inc, chmn, currently; Romar Studios Inc, mgt, 2000-05; Rainbow/PUSH Coalition, Nat Bd Mem, 2002-; Fashion & Film Studios Inc, consult, 2008-. **Orgs:** Nat bd mem bd trustee, Nat Asn Advan Colored People; Nat Black Cauccus State Legislatures; nat bd mem, Rainbow/PUSH Coalition; bd mem, Urban Educ Partnership; nat bd mem, Romar Studios Inc. **Business Addr:** Chairman, Romar Studios Inc, 837 Traction Ave Suite 406, Los Angeles, CA 90013, **Business Phone:** (213)621-4409.

### POLK, EUGENE STEVEN S., SR.

Consultant. **Personal:** Born Oct 24, 1939, Detroit, MI; son of Wardell and Josephine; married Barbara Jean Edwards; children: Camille, Kent, Eugene Jr & Chris. **Educ:** Shaw Col, Detroit, MI, BA, 1971. **Career:** Ford Motor Co, employ coord, 1966-69; Pontiac Gen Hosp, asst dir personnel, 1970-74; Comprehensive Health Serv, Detroit, personnel dir, 1975-79; Kelly Serv Inc, mgr hq personnel, 1980-87; Mazda Mfg, Prof, personnel adminr, 1987-93, employee rels, leader; Madison Madison Int Inc, HR dir, 1993-98; Edwards Polk & Assoc Inc, sr hr consult, sr acct rep, 1998-. **Orgs:** Bd mem, pres, Arc Detroit; bd mem, S.T.E.P; bd mem, Metro Detroit Youth Found, 1983-87; polemarch Detroit Alumni Chap Kappa Alpha Psi Frat, 1984-88; bd mem, N side Family YMCA, 1985-88; pres, Indust Rel Assoc Detroit, 1985-86; chmn bd dir, S Oakland Family YMCA, 1986-87; bd mem, DonBosco Hall, 1986-89; Nat Asn Advan Colored People, Detroit Urban League. **Honors/Awds:** Minority Achiever, Kelly Service Inc Metro, Detroit YMCA, 1987. **Home Addr:** 1700 Balmoral Dr, Detroit, MI 48203-1447, **Home Phone:** (313)892-9210. **Business Addr:** Senior Account Representative, Edwards Polk & Associates Inc, 220 Bagley Ave Suite 408, Detroit, MI 48226-1412, **Business Phone:** (313)964-3106.

**POLK, DR. GENE-ANN.** **See Obituaries Section.**

### POLK, RICHARD A.

Athletic coach, association executive. **Personal:** Born Jun 4, 1936, Moss Point, MS; married Mary Dennis; children: Clay, Phyllis, Beverly & Richard. **Educ:** Alcorn St Univ, Lorman, MS, BS, 1957; TN A&I Univ, Nashville, MS, 1965. **Career:** Newton & Carthage MS, tchr, athletic coach, 1957-66; STAR Inc, 1966-70, bd dir; Mound Bayou Community Hosp, dir, 1970; Hosp & Health Ctr, dir, 1972; Fed Equal Empl Opport Comm, invstgtn supr. **Orgs:** Jackson Urban League, 1968-70; STAR Inc, 1971-; Delta Ministry, 1975-; S Legal Rights Corp, 1975-; Leake Co Voters League, 1975-; Delta Found Greenville, MS, 1975-; MS Cncl Hum Rels, 1970; MS ACLU, 1974; MS Cath Found, 1975; pres, Parish Cnsl St Anne Cath Ch Carthage MS; bd dir, Epilepsy Found, Mich; Alcorn State Hall Fame; Nat Asn Advan Colored People. **Honors/Awds:** Alcorn State Hall of Fame, 1966; Applicant, oper rights, Jackson MS TV station OEO Award, 1969; MS Inst of Polit Fel, 1971. **Home Addr:** Rt 3 PO Box 302, Carthage, MS 39051. **Business Addr:** 203 W Capitol St, Jackson, MS 39201.

### POLK, REV. DR. ROBERT L.

Clergy, school administrator. **Personal:** Born May 8, 1928, Chicago, IL; son of Tillman and Lillie Bell; children: George R. **Educ:** Doane Col, BA, 1952; Hartford Theol Sem, Mdiv, 1955; Huston-Tillotson, DDiv, 1984. **Career:** Congregational Church Berthold ND, pastor, 1955-57; Riverside Church, minister youth, 1960-66, minister urban affairs, 1969-76; Dillard Univ New Orleans, La, dean chapel & dean stud, 1966-68; Edwin Gould Serv C, exec dir, 1976-80; Coun Churches City NY, exec dir, 1980-88; City Col New York, City Univ New York, actg vpres external rels & pub info, 1988-. **Orgs:** Youth prog secy, YMCA Minot ND, 1957-60; chmn, bd trustee, City Univ New York Constr Fund; Mayors Comm Relig Leaders; Assoc Black Charities; Hole-in-the-Wall-Gang Camp Inc; New York Bd Educ, Capital Task Force Construct Renovation Pub Sch; Ny Dept Educ Interfaith Educ Adv Coun Commr Educ; Govs Comm Scholastic Achievement; Health Watch Adv Bd. **Home Addr:** Candlewood Isle, PO Box 356, New Fairfield, CT 06812, **Home Phone:** (203)746-1464. **Business Addr:** Acting Vice President, City College NY, 138th St Convent Ave A 2050, New York, NY 10031, **Business Phone:** (212)690-5361.

### POLK, DR. WILLIAM C.

Educator, association executive. **Personal:** Born Aug 2, 1935, Philadelphia, PA; son of William Sr and Ruby; married Aundria Willis; children: Catherine Collette & William David. **Educ:** W Chester State Col, BS, 1958; Columbia Univ, MA, 1961; Pa State Univ, DEd, 1970. **Career:** Neshaminy Sch Dist, teacher, 1958-68; PA St Univ, grad asst, 1968-70, asso prof; Slippery Rock Univ, prof educ, prof emer, elem educ/early childhood, currently. **Orgs:** Bd dirs, EL Cunningham Comm Ctr, 1963-70; Phi Delta Kappa, 1968-; fac sponsor, Black Action Soc, Slippery Rock St Col, 1972 & 1975-77; Nat CounSoc Studies; comnr, Teacher Cert & Rural Educ; secy, Md wstrn Pa Coun Soc Studies, 1973-; guest lectr, Int Studies Inst, Westminster Col, 1974-75; consult, Commodore Perry Sch, 1976; Nat Geog Soc; Alpha Tau Chpt; Rho Chap Alpha Phi Alpha. **Honors/Awds:** Outstanding Educator, 1972. **Home Addr:** 240 Kelly Blvd, Slippery Rock, PA 16057-1128, **Home Phone:** (724)794-8173. **Business Addr:** Professor Emeritus, Slippery Rock University, 1 Morrow Way, Slippery Rock, PA 16057, **Business Phone:** (724)738-2015.

### POLLARD, ALFONSO MCINHAM

Musician, government official. **Personal:** Born Jun 13, 1952, Washington, DC; son of Alfonso and June Reynolds; married Lynda Lea Harrod; children: Prentice Odell & Lauren Jamille. **Educ:** Boston Univ, attended 1972; Juilliard Sch, BS, 1975; Cath Univ, MS, 1978. **Career:** Wash DC Youth Orchestra, 1970-92; USF Band, bandsman, tech sgt, 1975-79; Howard Univ, assoc prof music, 1979-91; Metrop Cult Productions, pres, 1986-; Orchestra Found Metro Wash DC, chief exec officer, 1989-92; Am Fedn Musicians, Local 161-710 AFL-CIO, Local 40-543, dir; Am Univ, Residence Conductor, 1994-96; Commun Workers Am, legis rep, polit dir, currently. **Orgs:** Performance fel, Young Artist Prog, Tanglewood, 1968; Acad fel, Music Assistance Fund, 1972-75; Prin timpanist, Annapolis Symphony Orchestra, 1976-87; prin timpanist, Filene Ctr Orchestra, Wolf Trap, 1986-; Am Symphony Orchestra League, 1988-; prin timpanist, Baltimore Opera Orchestra, 1989-99; nat legis dir, Am Fedn Musicians, 1995; Coalition Black Trade Unionists, 1999-. **Honors/Awds:** Individual Fellowship Performance Award, DC Comm Arts & Humanities, 1986; Travel Award to Brazil, Am Partner, 1990; teaching & conducting grant, US Info Agency, 1990; Maestro Alfonso Pollard Day, Wash DC, City Coun, 1991; Outstanding Service to Education, Wash DC Bd Educ, 1992. **Home Addr:** 3013 Memory Lane, Silver Spring, MD 20904, **Home Phone:** (301)890-1941. **Business Addr:** Political Director, Legislative Representative, Communications Workers of America, 501 3rd St NW, Washington, DC 20001, **Business Phone:** (202)434-1334.

### POLLARD, DR. ALTON BROOKS, III

Educator. **Personal:** Born May 5, 1956, St. Paul, MN; son of Alton Brooks Jr and Lena Laverne Evans; married Jessica Bryant; children: Alton Brooks IV & Asha Elise. **Educ:** Fisk Univ, BA, relig & philos & bus mgt, 1978; Harvard Univ, Divinity Sch, Mdiv, 1981; Duke Univ, PhD, 1987. **Career:** Thomas J Watson Fel, Fisk Univ, 1978; Fund Theological Educ Fel, Princeton, NJ, 1978-81, 1983-86; John St Baptist Church, pastor, 1979-82; Clark Univ, dir, 1981-82; New Red Mountain Baptist Church, pastor, 1984-86; Andrew Mellon Fel, Duke Univ, 1986-87; St Olaf Col, asst prof, 1987-88; Wake Forest Univ, from asst prof to assoc prof, 1988-98; Emory Univ, Candler Sch Theol, Black Church Studies, dir & assoc prof relig & cult; Howard Univ Sch Divinity, dean, 2007-. **Orgs:** Soc Sci Study Relig, 1984-, Assoc Sociol Relig, 1985-; Am Baptist Conv; Nat Asn Advan Colored People; Am Acad Relig, 1987; Relig Res Asn, 1988-; Soc Study Black Relig, 1989-; bd trustee, Wash Theol Consortium, 2012-; bd mem, Comm Accred/ATS, 2010-. **Home Addr:** , Stone Mountain, GA. **Business Addr:** Dean, Howard University School of Divinity, 2900 Van Ness St NW, Washington, DC 20008, **Business Phone:** (202)806-0500.

**POLLARD, DR. DIANE MAE STEWART.** **See Obituaries Section.**

### POLLARD, MARCUS LAJUAN

Football executive, football coach, football player. **Personal:** Born Feb 8, 1972, Lanett, AL; married Amani; children: Myles Ashton, Micah Jayden, Aja Amani & Ayris Mae. **Educ:** Bradley Univ, BA, criminal justice. **Career:** Football player (retired); football coach; Indianapolis Colts, 1995, tight end, 1996-2004, fullback, 1999, wide receiver, 2000, running back, 2001; Detroit Loins, tight end, 2005-06, fullback, 2006; Seattle Seahawks, tight end, 2007; New Eng Patriots, 2008; Atlanta Falcons, tight end, 2008-09; Lanett High Sch, coach, 2008-12; Jacksonville Jaguars, dir player develop, 2013-. **Business Addr:** Director of Player Development, Jacksonville Jaguars, 1 EverBank Field Dr, Jacksonville, FL 32202, **Business Phone:** (904)633-6000.

### POLLARD, MURIEL RANSOM

Engineer, executive director. **Personal:** Born Nov 5, 1953, Isola, MS; daughter of Arthur; children: Kendra, Eyphra & Elverna. **Educ:** Meharry Med Col, biomed sci, summer prog, 1974; Dillard Univ, New Orleans, BA, chem, 1975. **Career:** S Cent Bell Tel Co, engr supvr, 1977-; Basics Community Outreach Inc, dir. **Orgs:** Delta Sigma Theta Sorority, 1973-; Tel Pioneers Am, 1981-; consult relig speech writing & delivery, 1984-; admin comn, S Polit Action Community S Cent Bell, 1986-. **Honors/Awds:** President's Award, Miss Head Start Parents Asn, 1989; Recognition Serv, Miss Delta Community Col, 1989; BellSouth Area Operations Counc Recognition Award, 1990; BellSouth Dept Head Award, 1996; BellSouth PRIDE Award, 1996; BellSouth, VIP's GALAXY Award, 1997. **Business Addr:** Director, Basics Community Outreach Inc, 106 Roberts Rd, Indianola, MS 38751, **Business Phone:** (662)887-4490.

### POLLARD, PERCY EDWARD, SR.

Consultant, executive, manager. **Personal:** Born Jun 3, 1943, King and Queen County, VA; son of George T (deceased) and Hattie Bell Taylor (deceased); married Annie Randolph; children: Tracie Anita & Percy Jr. **Educ:** Va State Univ, BS, indust educ & electronics, 1966, MS, 1997; Emory Univ, cert mgt develop prog, 1985. **Career:** Manager (retired), career coach; IBM Corp, jr instr, 1966, sr educ specialist, 1969, equal oppor admin, 1970, mgr equal opportunities, 1972, mgr equal opportunites & comm progs, Gaithersburg, 1973, dist personnel prog mgr Off Prods Div, 1976, regional personnel mgr Wash & Baltimore Metro area, 1977, personnel planning mgr Off Prods Div Franklin Lakes, NJ, 1979, corp mgr equal opportunities prog, 1981, admin asst to vpres personnel, 1982, personnel mgr Res Div Yorktown, NY, 1984, mgr staff servs White Plains, NY, 1986-, Spec Asst Employee Charitable Contrib, 1988, IBM Corp HQ, personnel mgr, 1989, dir, Cult & Human Servs Prog, 1991-93, IBM Fac Loan, 1993-95; Pollard Consult Serv, 1997; Rappahannock Community Col, career coach, 2008-. **Orgs:** Bergen Co Urban League; trustee, Franklin

Lakes United Methodist Church; Press Exec Exchange Assoc; steering comt, Orgn Resource Counselors; Va State Univ Alumni Asn, NJ Chapt; Kappa Theta Lambda Chap Alpha Phi Alpha Frat; founder & chmn, Va State Univ Spec Action Team; deacon, First Mt Olive Baptist Church; chmn bd, Environ Careers Org; chm, adv coun, Richmond Tech Ctr; Southside Baptist Asn, 1999; pres, Richmond Rotary Club, 2001-; chair, First Mt Alive Baptist Church; secy, treas & bd mem, Bay Consortium Workforce Investment Bd Inc. **Honors/Awds:** Certificate of Merit, Broome Co New York, Nat Asn Advan Colored People, 1972; Family & Childrens Soc Special Recognition Certificate, 1973; Kiwanis Club Presidents Award, 1975; Alpha Phi Alpha Outstanding Tenure Award, 1976; Sustained Serv Award, 1977; President's Impact Award, 1978; IBM Office Products Div People Management Award, 1979; Division Excellence Award, IBM, 1988; Lead IBMs Charitable Contribution, 1988; Presidential Exec Exchange, 1980-81; Sr Management Citation Dept of Health & Human Serv, 1981; Outstanding National Achievement Award, 1981; Alpha Phi Alpha Iota Theta Lambda Chap Award, 1983; SES Candidates Certificates of Recognition Dept of Health & Human Service, 1983; Alpha Phi Alpha New York/New Jersey Archives Award, 1983; NAFEO Presidential Citation Award, 1986; Alumnus of the Year, Va State, 1989; President's Special Recognition Award, Alpha Phi Alpha, 1990; ed, Sphinx Magazine, Alpha Phi Alpha; Award of Merit, Am Vocational Asn, 1998. **Home Addr:** PO Box 280, St. Stephens Church, VA 23148, **Home Phone:** (804)769-2222. **Business Addr:** Secretary, Treasurer, Bay Consortium Workforce Investment Board Inc, 479 Main St, Warsaw, VA 22572, **Business Phone:** (804)333-4048.

**POLLARD, RAYMOND J.**
School administrator. **Personal:** Born Mar 31, 1932, Lamar, SC; son of Gussie and Ethel; married Eloise Wilson. **Educ:** Fla State Univ, EdB, 1953; Univ Pa, MEd, 1957; Antioch Col, MS, 1977. **Career:** School administrator (retired); Internal Revenue, mail clerk, 1953-54; Kenderton Sch, spec educ teacher, 1957-58; McIntyre Sch, teacher, 1958-61; CPA, caseworker male clerk, 1961-62; LP Hill Sch, 1962-64 & 1967-71; Levering Sch, 1966-67; Turner Mid Sch, phys educ teacher, 1971-73; Penn Fed Teachers, staff rep, 1973, gen vpres. **Orgs:** Vpres, Negro Trade Union Leadership Coun, 1971; vice-chmn, Phillip Randolph Inst, 1972; finance sec mem, Usher Bd C Sch Scholar Comt; co-dir, Met Bapist Church; pres, Fayetteville State Univ Alumni, bus mgr, chmn, hospitality comt; exec bd, Progressive Philadelphia Fed Teachers, co-chmn; bldg rep, LP Hill Sch & JP Turner Sch; Nat Asn Advan Colored People; PUSH; CORE; SCLC; APHI; treas, BSA. **Home Addr:** 802 Felton Ave, Sharon Hill, PA 19079, **Home Phone:** (610)583-3340.

**POLLARD, DR. WILLIAM LAWRENCE**
Educator. **Personal:** Born Nov 27, 1944, Raleigh, NC; son of Linwood and Bettie; married Merriette Maude Chance; children: William L II & Frederick Touissaint. **Educ:** Shaw Univ, AB, sociol, 1967; Univ NC Chapel Hill, MSW, community orgn & advocacy, 1969; Univ Chicago, Sch Social Admin, PhD, policy & planning, 1976. **Career:** Livingstone Col, instr, 1969-71, asst prof & dir social welfare prog, 1973-76; Univ Pittsburgh, assoc prof & chmn comn orgn skill set sch social work, 1976-82, Community Orgn Skills Set, coordr; Grambling State Univ, assoc prof & dir undergrad social work, 1982-89, Sch Social Work, dean & founder, 1984-89; Syracuse Univ, Syracuse, NY, dean, 1989-2000, Col Human Serv & Health Professions, founding dean, 2000-02; Univ DC, Wash, pres, 2002-07; Nat Asn State Univ & Land-Grant Col, vpres, 2007-08; City Univ New York, Medgar Evers Col, pres, 2009-13. **Orgs:** House dels Coun Social Work Educ, 1974-77, 1979-82; bd dir, Friendship House Salisbury, NC, 1974-76; sec bd dir, Dial Help Salisbury, 1974-76; bd dir, YMCA Salisbury, 1975-76; fel Grant Met Appl Res Corp, 1974; A Study Black Self Help R&E Res Assocs, 1978; "Black Child" proc New Concepts Human Serv Develop Child, 1978; bd dir, Nat Asn Deans & Dirs Schs Social Work, 1991-; bd trustee, City Univ New York, 2009-13; bd dir, Coun Social Work Educ; adv comn Citizen Educ Action Group Criminal Justice; bd dir, Salvation Army; bd dir, Elmcrest C's Ctr; chmn, Brooklyn Col; adv bd, Fed City Coun; adv bd, DC Bd Trade; trustee, John Wesley A.M.E. Zion Church; bd dir, Am Humanics Kans City; trustee, Livingstone Col; Am Asn State Cols & Univs; Nat Asn Equal Opportunity Higher Educ; co chair, New York Haitian Community Hope & Healing Fund; Kappa Alpha Psi; Chorale Soc; Sociol Club; pres, Social Work Stud Orgn; founding mem, Black Stud Movement; Univs Nat Asn; Advan Pub Black Cols; Dc community; bd dir, DC Chamber Com; Leadership Greater Wash Class, 2006. **Honors/Awds:** Distinguished Grad, Shaw Univ, 1991; Awardee, First Ann NY Gov Award, African-Am of Distinction; Social Worker of the Year, Nat Asn Social Workers; Citizen of the Year Award, Temple Adath Yeshurun; Social Worker of the Year Award, Nat Asn Social Workers. **Special Achievements:** Co-Author, "How Do We Get There: Strategic Planning for Schs of Social Work", Journal Social Work Education, 1992; Dissertation entitled "Black Welfare Developments in the Southeast, 1890-1915". First African-American Department Chair at a Brooklyn College's History Department. **Home Addr:** 516 Scott Ave, Syracuse, NY 13224-1910, **Home Phone:** (315)449-0414. **Business Addr:** President, The City University of New York, 1650 Bedford Ave, Brooklyn, NY 11225, **Business Phone:** (718)270-5000.

**POLLARD-BUCKINGHAM, ALICE F.**
Police officer. **Educ:** Lincoln Univ. **Career:** City St Louis, from exec asst to dir pub safety, comnr corrections, dep supt corrections, currently. **Orgs:** MCA Legis Comt; Am Jail Asn; Am Correctional Asn; Sigma Gamma Rho Sorority; Lincoln Univ Alumni. **Special Achievements:** First female to hold the position of commissioner of corrections in St Louis. **Home Addr:** 4403 Arco Fl 2, St Louis, MO 63110, **Home Phone:** (314)531-0986. **Business Addr:** Deputy Superintendent of Corrections, City of St Louis, 200 S Tucker Blvd, St Louis, MO 63102, **Business Phone:** (314)621-5848.

**POLYNICE, OLDEN**
Basketball player, basketball coach. **Personal:** Born Nov 21, 1964, Port-au-Prince; son of Jean-Lester and Suzanne; children: Tiara & Armani; married Raechel; children: Nikolas, Chayce, Alexis & Gabriella. **Educ:** Univ Va, attended 1986. **Career:** Basketball player (retired), basketball coach; Hamby Rimini, 1986-87; Seattle Supersonics, ctr, 1987-91, 1998-99; Los Angeles Clippers, ctr, 1991-92, 2003-04; Detroit Pistons, ctr, 1992-94; Sacramento Kings, ctr, 1994-98; WNBA's Sacramento Monarchs, color commentator, 1997-; Utah Jazz, ctr, 1999-2001; Las Vegas Slam, 2001-02; Grand Rapids Hoops, 2002-03; Pennsylvania ValleyDawgs, 2003; Gary Steelheads, 2003; Long Beach Jam, 2004; Michigan Mayhem, 2004-05; Los Angeles Aftershock, ctr, 2005-06; Am Basketball Asn, play coach; Long Beach Breakers, head coach, currently. Films: Eddie, 1996. TV Series: "The Brian McKnight Show", 2010. **Orgs:** Founder, Helping Out Our People Found. **Home Addr:** PO Box 220339, Newhall, CA 91322-0339. **Business Addr:** Head Coach, Long Beach Breakers, 4700 E 10th St, Long Beach, CA 90804, **Business Phone:** (562)987-4487.

**PONDER, EUNICE WILSON**
Educator, association executive. **Personal:** Born Sep 4, 1929, Kansas City, MO; daughter of Kate and Austin; married Henry; children: Cheryl & Anna. **Educ:** Langston Univ, BS, 1951; Okla State Univ, MS, 1958; Univ SC, EdD, 1977. **Career:** Educator (retired); Okla teacher pub schs, 1951-58; Planning Res & Mgt Benedict Col, inst researcher, 1977-84; Benedict Col, teacher, 1977-84; Millie Lewis Agency, Columbia, SC. **Orgs:** Nat Delta Pi Epsilon Bus Frat, 1958-; Nat Asn Instnl vol worker Red Cross; NCATE Self-Study Team HEW, 1978-80; reader tite IV HEW, 1979-80; life mem, Delta Sigma Theta Sor. **Honors/Awds:** Dissertation: A Study of Selected Characteristics Affecting the Survival Rate of Black & White Students at the Univ of SC", 1977. **Home Addr:** 101 County Rd 312, Cullman, AL 35057, **Home Phone:** (256)734-6966.

**PONDER, DR. HENRY**
School administrator, consultant, educator. **Personal:** Born Mar 28, 1928, Wewoka, OK; son of Frank and Lillie Mae; married Eunice Wilson; children: Cheryl & Anna. **Educ:** Langston Univ, BS, 1951; Okla State Univ, MS, 1958; Ohio State Univ, PhD, 1963. **Career:** Okla State Univ, res asst, 1956-58; Va State Col, asst prof, 1958-61, Dept Agr & Bus, chmn, 1963-64; Ohio State Univ, res asst, 1961-63; Ft Valley State Col, chmn dept bus & econ, 1964-66; Irving Trust Co, econ consult, 1968; Fed Res Bank, consult; Philadelphia Nat Bank, consult; Chase Manhattan Bank, consult; Irving Trust Co, consult; Omaha Nat Bank, consult; Ala A&M Univ, dean, 1966-69, vpres acad affairs, 1969-73; Tenn Univ, pres; Benedict Col, pres, 1973-84; Fisk Univ, pres, 1984-96; Fisk Univ, Nat Asn Equal Opportunity Higher Educ, chief exec officer & pres, 1996-2001; Talladega Col, pres, 2002-. **Orgs:** Am Econ Asn; Am Farm Econ Asn; Mason 32nd Deg C C; gen pres, Alpha Phi Alpha, 1989-92; Nat Asn Equal Opportunity Higher Educ; chmn bd dir, Fed Res Bank Richmond; bd dir, JP Stevens & Co Inc; Bd ETV Endowment; bd dir, Sun trust Bank Nashville; bd dir, SCANA Corp SC; bd dir, Comm Col Air Force. **Honors/Awds:** Distinguished Alumnus Award, Okla State Univ, 1986; Distinguished Alumnus Award, Ohio State Univ; Bennett Distinguished Service Award, 1997; Honored as 100 Most Effective College Presidents in the United States. **Special Achievements:** Hundred Most Effective College Presidents in US, 1986. **Home Addr:** , Hilton Head Island, SC. **Business Addr:** President, Talladega College, 627 W Battle St, Talladega, AL 35160, **Business Phone:** (256)761-0206.

**PONDER-NELSON, DEBRA**
Association executive, chief executive officer, president (organization). **Personal:** Born Jun 8, 1957, Midwest City, OK; daughter of Bishop Alonzo L Ponder and Beulah Jacobs Ponder; children: Kristen & Karmen. **Educ:** Okla State Univ, BS, 1979. **Career:** Okla City Limousine Serv, owner, 1979-81; B & P Maintenance, owner, gen mgr, 1979-83; Gen Mills Inc, territory mgr, 1983-89; Okla Minority Supplier Develop Coun, exec dir, 1990, pres & chief exec officer, currently. **Orgs:** Okla State Alumni Asn; Soc Women Bus; vol, Delta Sigma Theta Sorority; Jack & Jill Am; Okla Consortium Minority Bus Develop; Okla Pvt Indust Coun; adv bd, Dept Ment Health & Substance Abuse Serv; vol, Habitat For Humanity. **Home Addr:** PO Box 18228, Oklahoma City, OK 73154-0228, **Home Phone:** (405)767-9900. **Business Addr:** President, Chief Executive Officer, Oklahoma Minority Supplier Development Council, 6701 W Broadway Exten Suite 216, Oklahoma City, OK 73116, **Business Phone:** (405)767-9900.

**POOL, VERA C.**
Police officer, president (organization). **Personal:** Born Jul 27, 1946, Greenwood, MS; daughter of Alberta Lofton Corbin and Rayfield Corbin; married John; children: Sheina Karia. **Educ:** Portland Community Col, Portland, OR, AA, 1969; Univ Portland, Portland, OR, BA, psychol, 1972, MA, educ, 1974, MS, criminal justice, 1978. **Career:** Veterans Admin, Portland, Ore, food serv, 1965-70; Multnomah Co Sheriff's Dept, Portland, Ore, lt & comdr, 1970; NOBLE Northwest Chap, pres, currently. **Orgs:** App nat bd, NABCJ, 1979-86, 1989-; nat assist secy, Bd Police Stand & Trng, 1981-89; founder, former chap pres, Nat Asn Black Correctional Justice, 1984-91; sgt at arms, Delta Sigma Theta Sorority, 1989; Gov Steering Comt Sex Offenders, 1990. **Honors/Awds:** Woman of the Year, Am Bus Women's Asn Chap, 1979; Service to the Community, 1987, The Chairman Emeritus Award, 1989, Nat Asn Black Correctional Justice; Professional Achievement, Delta Sigma Theta Sorority, 1988; Award for Dedicated Services in Corrections Prison, Albina Ministrial Alliance, 1990; NOBLE National Fundraiser Winner. **Home Addr:** 3113 NE 140th Ave, Portland, OR 97230, **Home Phone:** (503)257-7842. **Business Addr:** President, NOBLE Northwest Chapter, 1120 SW 3rd Ave, Portland, OR 97204, **Business Phone:** (503)988-3397.

**POOL-ECKERT, MARQUITA JONES**
Journalist. **Personal:** Born Feb 19, 1945, Aurora, IL; daughter of Jeanne Boger and Mark E; married Stephen C Pool; married Knut Eckert. **Educ:** Boston Univ, BS, 1966; Columbia Univ, MA, Jour, 1969. **Career:** WABC-TV NY, producer, 1970-74; WNET/13 Pub TV, producer, 1974-75; CBS News, assoc producer, 1975-84, producer, 1984-90, sr producer & journalist, Sunday Morning, 1990-. **Orgs:** New York Asn Black Journalists, 1985-; pres, 1976-85, bd dir, 1976-89, pres, 1976-85, Nzingha Soc Inc; NY Assoc Black Journalists, 1985-; Womens Media Grp, 1986-; bd dir, NY Women Film, 1994-; bd dir, Frederick Douglas Creative Arts Ctr, 1994-98; Coun Foreign Rels; Friends Mus Mod Art, NY, 1995-; Links Inc; Metro-Manhattan chap. **Honors/Awds:** Emmy Award for "The Bombing of Beirut", 1983, "The Black Family A Dream Deferred", 1983, "Racism", 1986, "Pan Am 103 Crash", 1988, "Diana, Princess of Wales", CBS Sunday Morning, 1998; National Monitor Award, 1988; InterNational Monitor Award, "80's Remembered", 1990; Career Achievement Award, Norfolk State Univ, 1996; Black Career Women Lifetime Achievement Award, 1997; Muse Award, NY Women In Film & Television, 1999; Alumni of the Year Award, Columbia Univ, 2002. **Special Achievements:** Top 100 Professional Black Women, Dollars & Sense Magazine Award, 1986. **Home Addr:** 7 Glenwood Rd, Upper Saddle River, NJ 07458, **Home Phone:** (201)825-2532. **Business Addr:** Senior Producer, Journalist, CBS News, 524 W 57th St, New York, NY 10019, **Business Phone:** (212)975-6708.

**POOLE, DILLARD M.**
Educator. **Personal:** Born Sep 15, 1939, Birmingham, AL. **Educ:** Cleveland State Univ, BA, history, 1971; MA, history, 1977; Ind Univ, PhD, Latin Am hist. **Career:** State OH, clerk; Warner & Swasey Mach Tool Co, tool supply worker; Cleveland State Univ, asst to dean stud life, 1971-72, acad advisor, currently, Transfer Advising Off, asst dean, Afro-Am Cult Ctr, dir. **Orgs:** Nat Conf Artists, 1973-74; trustee, Parkwood CME Ch, 1974-. **Honors/Awds:** Dean's list Cleveland State Univ, 1970. **Home Addr:** 3531 Bainbridge Rd, Cleveland, OH 44118-2239. **Business Addr:** Academic Advisor, Cleveland State University, 1899 E 22nd St Main Classroom 110, Cleveland, OH 44115, **Business Phone:** (216)687-2018.

**POOLE, DR. RACHEL IRENE**
Nurse, consultant. **Personal:** Born Dec 2, 1924, Uniontown, PA; married Marion L; children: Andrea Lynell & Adriene Charisse Dilworth. **Educ:** Univ Pittsburgh PA, BSN, 1947, M Litt, nursing educ, 1952, PhD, 1977. **Career:** Nurse, consultant (retired); Univ Pittsburgh, Dept Psychiat Ment Health Nursing Sch Nursing, assoc prof & assoc chmn, 1967-72, assoc prof, 1972-73; health integrator, 1972; Inst Higher Educ Sch Educ Univ Pittsburgh, lectr, admin asst, 1974-77; Community Col Allegheny Co, adminsr intern, admin asst to pres, 1977-79; Allegheny Campus Community Col Allegheny Co Pittsburgh PA, asst dean life sci & dir nursing prog, 1979-84; Home wood-Brushton Br Allegheny Comm Col, part-time adv, counsr, 1984; Western Psychiat Inst & Clin, dir nursing, assoc prof. **Orgs:** Bd dir, Ille Elegba, 1968-74; org, treas, Black Women's Forum, 1969-71; Am Nurses Asn; Am Asn Higher Educ, 1975-76; adv bd mem, Visions: Women's Art Collective, 1989-; Univ Pittsburgh African Am Alumni Scholar Comt, 1989-. **Honors/Awds:** Black Achiever of the Year, NIP Magazine, 1986; Special Recognition Award, Community Col Alleg County, 1986; Outstanding Dedicated Services Award, Student Advisory Bd, Community Col Allegheny County Allegheny Campus, 1990; Distinguished Alumnus Award, Univ Pittsburgh Sch Nursing, 1990; Outstanding Black Nurse Citation, City Coun, Pittsburgh. **Special Achievements:** Author of many writings; Sigma Theta Tau, 1953; Selected PA Nurses Asn "Brain Trust", 1965-67; Interviewee "Racism" WIIC's TV Prog Face to Face, 1968; "Proposal for a Plan of Action" Com on Recruitment of Minorities into Nursing Dept of Health Common wealth, 1973; Penn Bar Asn, legal assistants, paralegals, single mothers, sec, nurses, ex-convicts, fed women employees, & women in military on the subject of "Assertiveness", 1979-88, 1988-90; Panelist Minorities and Nursing WQED's TV Prog Black Horizons, 1981; Panelist Nursing Programs WTAE's TV Prog Pgh Today 1982; First African American Associate Professor & Director of Department of Mental Health at Western Psychiatric Institute and Clinic; Author: The Girl With Green Bean Hair, 2010. **Home Addr:** 137 Kilmer St, Pittsburgh, PA 15221-1041, **Home Phone:** (412)731-8118.

**POOLE, TYRONE**
Football player. **Personal:** Born Feb 3, 1972, LaGrange, GA; married Jennifer; children: Nakai & Tyra; married Jennifer. **Educ:** Fort Valley State Univ, bus. **Career:** Football player (retired); Carolina Panthers, left corner back & right corner back & Punt returner, 1995-98; Indianapolis Colts, right corner back & defensive back, 1998-2000; Denver Broncos, 2001-02; New Eng Patriots, corner back & right corner back, 2003-05; Oakland Raiders, corner back, 2006; Houston Texans, 2007; Denver Broncos, corner back, 2008. Tennessee Titans, corner back, 2008. **Special Achievements:** Selected in the first round/22nd overall pick in the 1995 NFL Draft. Films: 1995 NFL Draft, 1995; 1996 NFC Championship Game, 1997; Super Bowl XXXVIII, 2004; Author: "Ultimate Success In The Game Of Life", 2011. **Business Addr:** PO Box 680130, Marietta, GA 30068, **Business Phone:** (770)906-6976.

**POOLER, SHIRLEY.** **See KINSEY, SHIRLEY.**

**POPE, BISHOP COURTNEY A.**
Clergy, president (organization). **Personal:** Born Mar 29, 1964, Philadelphia, PA; son of Cromwell and Gloria J; married Audrey D; children: Anthony, Jazmine & Chaz. **Educ:** Temple Univ, BA, commun, 1988; Int Christian Univ, DDiv. **Career:** Eastern Atlantic Diocese Youth Cong, pres, 1984-97; Church Living God, Nat HYPBC, vpres, 1985-87; Holy Temple Church, pastor, 1995, bishop, currently; Eastern Atlantic Diocese, dist elder, 1996-99. **Orgs:** Philadelphia Music Alliance, 1992; Pennsgrove Carneys Pt Ministerium, 1995-; Salem County Men Christ, 1995; pres, Jhazzi Music Publ, 1997-; exec dir & bd dir, Bishop Williams Community Ctr, 1998-; founder & bd dir, Fresh Harvest Ministries, 1998-; US Chaplains Asn, 1999-; adv bd, LIFELINES, 1999-; World Heritage Coun. **Home Addr:** 1044 Serrill Ave, Yeadon, PA 19050, **Home Phone:** (610)394-9194. **Business Addr:** Bishop, Holy Temple Church of the Fresh Harvest, Willis & Cumberland Sts, Penns Grove, NJ 08069, **Business Phone:** (856)299-2737.

**POPE, DERRICK ALEXANDER**
Educator, lawyer. **Personal:** Born Dec 7, 1964, Atlanta, GA; son of Howard and Sallie. **Educ:** Morris Brown Col, BA, polit sci, 1987; NC Cent Univ Sch Law, law, 1990; Loyola Univ Sch Law, JD, 1992. **Career:** Morris Brown Col, adj prof law, beginning 1992; Spec Judiciary Comt, legal coun, 1992-93; Ga Gen Assembly, lawyer & asst legis coun, 1993-94; Med Asn Ga, lawyer, leg coun, 1994-96; Law Off Derrick Alexander Pope P.C, prin, 2001-08; Col Law, Ga State Univ, adj prof, 2007-08; Lawpartners, prin exec, 2009-; Fulton County Bd Commissioners, exec coun, 2015-; spec proj dir, Asn Black Cardiologists;

pvt pract, currently. **Orgs:** Alpha Phi Alpha Fraternity, 1984-; State Bar Ga, 1993-; Atlanta Inner Circle, 1993-; Am Bar Asn, 1993-; Phi Alpha Delta Law Fraternity; US Supreme Ct Hist Soc. **Home Addr:** 3419 Leyanne Ct, Decatur, GA 30034-6757, **Home Phone:** (404)390-3341. **Business Addr:** Lawyer, The Law Office of Derrick Alexander Pope PC, 127 Peachtree St NE Suite 923 Candler Bldg, Atlanta, GA 30303-1800, **Business Phone:** (404)588-1066.

## POPE, HAROLD D.

Lawyer. **Personal:** Born Aug 29, 1955, Newton, NJ; son of Harold and Getrude Taylor; married Renay Q; children: Daman M & Ebony A. **Educ:** Concordia Col, BA, 1976; Duke Univ Sch Law, JD, 1980. **Career:** Lamb, Chappell, Hartung, Gallipoli & Coughlin, law clerk, 1979, assoc, 1980-84; Lewis, White & Clay, PC, assoc, 1984-88, shareholder, 1989-94; Segue, Adams & Pope, PLC, partner, 1994-99; Jaffe Raitt Heuer & Weiss, PC, partner, 1999-2016; Dykema Gossett Pllc, sr coun, 2016-. **Orgs:** Garden State Bar Asn, 1982-84; Renaissance Optimist Club, 1987-89; treas, Detroit Pub Schs Stud Motivational Prog, 1988-89, exec bd, 1988-90; secy, Pontiac Area Transitional Housing, bd dir, 1990-91; bd dir, Nat Bar Inst, 1992-94, exec comt, 1992-94, vpres, 1994-98, pres, 1999-2000, chair, 2002-; chair, Detroit Metrop Bar Asn, 1992-95; bd dir, Am Diabetes Asn, 1997-98; pres, Nat Bar Asn, 1999-2000; bd trustee, Detroit Metrop Bar Asn Found, 2004-; Am Bar Asn, 2000-04, chair, 2004-, bd gov, 2009-14; State Bar Mich Judicial Qualifications Comt, 2008-13; Alpha Phi Alpha; Nat Asn Advan Colored People; NJ Bar Asn; D. Augustus Straker Bar Asn; life mem, Nat Asn Advan Colored People; trustee, Lawyers Comt Civil Rights Under Law; Wolverine Bar Asn; State Bar Mich; chmn, Am Bar Asn Coun Racial & Ethnic Justice; Am Bar Asn Audit Comt; Am Bar Found Bd Dirs. **Honors/Awds:** Michigan State Bar Champion of Justice, 2000; C. Francis Stratford Award, Nat Bar Asn, 2006; Damon J. Keith Community Service Award, Wolverine Bar Asn, 2008; Cora T. Walker Legacy Award, Nat Bar Asn Com Law Sect, 2011; Michigan Super Lawyer, 2011-13; Trailblazer Award, D. Augustus Straker Bar Asn, 2015. **Home Addr:** 18292 Fairfield, Detroit, MI 48221. **Business Addr:** Senior Counsel, Dykema Gossett PLLC, 400 Renaissance Ctr, Detroit, MI 48243, **Business Phone:** (313)568-6842.

## POPE, DR. HENRY

Psychiatrist, army officer. **Personal:** Born May 1, 1922, Athens, GA; children: 4. **Educ:** Howard Univ, BS, 1949; Meharry Med Col, MD, 1958. **Career:** Provident Hosp, intern, 1958; St Elizabeths Hosp, staff physician, 1960-65; self employed, psychiatrist, 1960-; Crownsville Hosp Ctr, resident psychiat & staff psychiat, 1970-. **Orgs:** Nat Med Asn, 1960-; DC Med Soc, 1970. **Home Addr:** 11005 Willowbottom Dr, Columbia, MD 21044. **Business Addr:** Psychiatrist, Private Practice, 1509 Penn Ave SE, Washington, DC 20003, **Business Phone:** (212)427-4256.

## POPE, DR. ISAAC S.

Physician, pediatrician. **Personal:** Born Mar 6, 1939, South Pittsburg, TN; married Joan Darby; children: David, Stephen & Theresa. **Educ:** Gonzaga Univ, Spokane, WA, BS, 1965; Univ WA Seattle, MPA, 1970; Univ WA, Seattle, MD, 1974. **Career:** State Univ NY Upstate Med Univ Hosp, internship; Albert Einstein Col Med, resident; Peace Corps, Sierra Leone, vol, 1965-67; Peace Corps Training Prog Gambia, dir, 1969, model cities prog Seattle, asst dir employee econ develop, 1969-70; Madigan Healthcare Syst, resident, 1974-77; AUS Ft Leonard Wood, Mo, staff pediatrician, 1977-79; pvt pract pediatrician, 1979-; Popes Kids Pl, vol pediatrician, currently. **Orgs:** Reg dir Stud, Nat Med Asn, 1972-73; WA State Med Asn Lewis Co Med Soc; WA State Soc Pediat; Kiwanis, 1979-92, pres, 1985; bd mem, Lewis County Work Opportunity, 1981-86; bd mem, Lewis County Spec Olympic, 1983-86; pres, Twin Cities, 1987; Chehalis City Coun; bd mem, founder, popes kids pl. **Honors/Awds:** Conc patient care Ft Leonard Wood Army Hosp, 1978; Army Commendation Medal, AVS, 1979; Businessmen of the Year, Daily Chronicle, 1988; Service to Mankind Award, Sertoma Club, 1989; Distinguished Alumni Merit Award, Gonzaga Univ, 1990; Distinguished Citizenship Award, Elks, 1991; Service to Mankind Award, Sertoma Club, 1994; Duncan Award, 1994; Award for Excellence, Nat Asn Counties, 1995; Best of Lewis County Med Doctor, 1997, 1998, 1999; Real Heroes Award, AMR Red Cross, 1998; Citizen of the Year, WA State Elks, 1999; Jefferson Award Washington State, 2002; Physician Excellence Award, Providence Centralia Hosp, 2005. **Home Addr:** 1631 SW Gails Ave, Chehalis, WA 98532, **Home Phone:** (360)748-3202. **Business Addr:** Pediatrician, Pope's Kids Place, 230 Wash Way, Centralia, WA 98531, **Business Phone:** (360)736-9178.

## POPE, MCCOY S.

Federal government official. **Personal:** Born Oct 5, 1937, New York, NY; son of Travis M and Rose Murphy; married Geraldine Cooper; children: David C & Jason McCoy. **Educ:** Thomas Edison Col, AA, 1977; Southern Ill Univ, BS, 1980. **Career:** Police officer (retired); USAF, military police supvr, investr, 1959-80; US Defense Invest Serv, Groton, CT field off, spec agent charge, 1981-94; East CT & RI New London Alternative Incarceration Ctr, counselor & substance abuse specialist, 1994; bd chmn, Alderhouse Inc, 1995-. **Orgs:** Air Force Asn; pres, Kiwanis Club, 1994-; Nat Asn Advan Colored People New London, Conn; vpres, New london, Conn Hist Soc, 1996-. **Honors/Awds:** Hixson Medallion Award, Kiwanis Int, 1999. **Special Achievements:** USAF Certification for Fluency in Spanish, Italian & French Languages; Initiated New London Amistad league & began progs to promote the then unknown event, 1996; First African American field office chief of fed investigative agency in New England history. **Home Addr:** 1860 Ala Moana Blvd, Waikiki, HI 96815, **Home Phone:** (808)943-6449. **Business Addr:** Consultant, New London, CT 06320.

## POPE, MIRIAN ARTIS

Manager, executive. **Personal:** Born Nov 3, 1952, Franklin, VA; married Johnnie Lee Jr; children: Ebonee Johndrea & Courtney LaVerne. **Educ:** Norfolk State Univ, BS, 1975; Old Dom Univ. **Career:** United Va Bank, br mgr, 1975-81; Community Fed Savings & Loan Asn, chief exec, managing officer, 1981-. **Orgs:** Adv bd, Jr Achievement Tidewater, 1976; Adv bd banking & fin comt, Norfolk State Univ, 1977-81; Nat Asn Bank Women, 1977-81; dir, Am Red Cross Tidewater Chap, 1979-81; Order Eastern Star Va, 1979-; dir, Norfolk C C, 1980; dir, United Way, 1981-82; Norfolk Conv & Visitors Bur. **Home Addr:** 387 Brock Cir, Norfolk, VA 23502. **Business Addr:** Member, Norfolk Convention and Visitors Bureau, 232 E Main St, Norfolk, VA 23510, **Business Phone:** (757)664-6620.

## POPE, RUBEN EDWARD, III

Labor relations manager, lawyer. **Personal:** Born Jun 28, 1948, Cleveland, OH; son of Ruben Jr and Marie Danzy (deceased); married Cheryl Ann Jones; children: Walter, Yolanda & Yvonne. **Educ:** Kenyon Col, BA, 1970; Boston Col Law Sch, JD, 1973. **Career:** Arthur Andersen & Co, auditor, 1973-75; Wyman-Gordon Co, develop benefits mgr; Cleveland Munic Housing Ct, magistrate, 1995-. **Orgs:** Ohio Bar, 1978; Am Bar Asn, 1978; bd dir, United Way Cent Mass; treas, Youth Guide Asn Inc; bd dir, Prospect House Inc, 1980; fin secy, Quinsigamond Lodge, IBPOE W Elks; sec, Belmont St AME Zion Church; Alpha Delta Phi Fraternity. **Home Addr:** 1200 Ontario St, Cleveland, OH 44113-1610, **Home Phone:** (216)664-2464.

## PORCHE-BURKE, LISA

Psychologist, educator. **Personal:** Born Nov 9, 1954, Los Angeles, CA; daughter of Ralph and June; married Peter Alston; children: Mallory, Dominique & Lauren. **Educ:** Univ Southern Calif, BA, 1976; Univ Notre Dame, MA, 1981, PhD, 1983. **Career:** Calif Sch Prof Psychol, asst prof, prof training fac, 1985-87, asst prof, 1987-90; Ethnic MNY Ment HTH Proficiency, coordr, 1987-90, assoc prof, 1990-91; Multicultural COT Clin Proficiency, coordr, 1990-92, actg provost, 1991-92, chancellor; Phillips Grad Inst, pres & chief exec officer, 1999-2009; Touro Univ Worldwide, dir psychol progs, currently. **Orgs:** Asn Black Psychologists, 1980-; exec comt, AMR Psychol Asn, DIV 45, SOC Study Ethnic MNY Issues, 1985-; exec comt, NAT Coun Schs Prof Psychol, 1990-92; sr exec, AMR Psychol Asn, DIV 45, SOC Study Ethnic MNY Issues, 1991-; exe bd, DIV Psychother, 1991-; chair, NAT Coun Schs Prof Psychol, 1992-; bd mem, CAL Psychol Asn found, 1992-; AM Asn Higher EDUC, 1993-; bd mem, Holy Family Serv; bd mem, exec bd mem, Millennium Momentum Found Inc. **Special Achievements:** First African American woman to earned doctorate in counseling psychology from Notre Dame University; First African American woman chancellor of a CSPP campus. **Business Addr:** Director of Psychology Programs, Touro University Worldwide, 10601 Calle Lee Suite 179, Los Alamitos, CA 90720, **Business Phone:** (818)575-6800.

## PORCHER, ROBERT, III

Football player, executive. **Personal:** Born Jul 30, 1969, Wando, SC; married Kimberly; children: Morgan Latreese. **Educ:** SC State Univ, BA, criminal justice. **Career:** Football player (retired), owner; Detroit Lions, defensive tackle, left defensive end, right defensive tackle, 1992-2004; Detroit Breakfast House & Grill, owner, currently; Sweet Ga Brown, owner, currently; Seldom Blues, bus partner, currently. **Orgs:** Omega Psi Phi Fraternity; Chairperson, Metro Detroit Am Heart Asn Heart Walk, 1997. **Honors/Awds:** First-round draft pick, 1992; Pro Bowl, 1997, 1999, 2001; Extra Effort Award, Nat Football League, 2003; Robert Porcher Man of the Year, named in honor. **Business Addr:** Business Partner, Seldom Blues, 400 Renaissance Ctr, Detroit, MI 48243, **Business Phone:** (313)567-7301.

## PORTEE, REV. DR. FRANK, III

Clergy. **Personal:** Born Jun 16, 1955, York, SC; son of Frank Jr and Alvon Pendergrass; married Yvonne Fersner; children: Alyssa Shanee & Akela. **Educ:** Carson-Newman Col, BA, 1977; Interdenominational Theol Sem, Mdiv, 1980; Univ Calif, Los Angeles, CA, BA, alcohol & drug coun. **Career:** New Light United Methodist Church, pastor, 1980-83; United Methodist Church SC, coordr youth ministry, 1980-83; Charleston Col, campus minister, 1983-; Old Bethel United Methodist Church, pastor, 1983; Redeemer Church, pastor, 1991, sr pastor, 1999; Interfaith Impact, dir empowerment & organizing; Union Inst, Fuller Theol Sem, adj prof; Southern Calif Sch Ministry, adj fel; Emory Univ, Candler Sch Theol, res fel; Amandla Group, prin, currently; Pac Inst Word & Witness, conf dean & founder; Church Good Shepherd, United Methodist Church, pastor/chief spiritual officer, currently. **Orgs:** Vpres, Nat Kidney Found, 1984-; bd mem, Action Coun Community Ment Health, 1984-; columnist, Charleston Chronicle, 1985-; bd mem, Community Rels Coun, 1985-; Florence Crittenton Homes, 1986; consult, Gen Bd Global Ministries, 1987; chmn, First Cong Dist Rainbow Coalition, 1988; pres, Greater Charleston Community Develop Inc, 1988-; chmn, Avery Res Bd, 1988-; founder, Pac Inst Word & Witness; exec bd, Los Angeles Metrop Churches; exec secy, African Am Ministries; nat shalom coordr, gen bd Global Ministries, United Methodist Church; Lincoln Memorial United Church Christ; commun adv bd mem, Homeless agency. **Home Addr:** 513 Huger St, Charleston, SC 29403, **Home Phone:** (803)577-5269. **Business Addr:** Pastor, Chief Spiritual Officer, Church of the Good Shepherd, 110 Buckingham Dr, Willingboro, NJ 08046, **Business Phone:** (609)877-6088.

## PORTER, BILLY

Singer, actor. **Personal:** Born Sep 21, 1969, Pittsburgh, PA. **Educ:** Pittsburgh Creative and Performing Arts School, Musical Theatre Program, B.F.A. in Drama; University of California, Los Angeles, The Professional Program in Screenwriting, Certification. **Career:** Actor, Broadway musicals, "Miss Saigon" (1991), "Grease" (1994), "Songs for a New World" (1995), "Radiant Baby" (1998), "Five Guys Named Moe," "Smokey Joe's Cafe," "Topdog/Underdog" (2002), "Jesus Christ Superstar," "Dreamgirls," "Ghetto Superstar (The Man That I Am)," "Angels in America" (2010), "Kinky Boots" (2013); Actor, TV, "Another World" (soap opera), "Shake, Rattle and Roll: An American Love Story" (movie, 1999), "Law & Order," "So You Think You Can Dance"; Actor, feature film, "The Broken Hearts Club: A Romantic Comedy" (2000); Singer, Albums: "Billy Porter" (A&M Records, 1997), "At the Corner of Broadway + Soul" (Sh-K-Boom Records, 2005), "Kinky Boots Cast Recording" (2013). **Honors/Awds:** Star Search, Best Male Vocalist, 1992; Tony Award, Best Actor in a Musical (for "Kinky Boots"), 2013; Drama Desk Award (for "Kinky Boots"), Outstanding Actor in a Musical, 2013; Outer Critics Circle Award, Outstanding Actor in a Musical (for "Kinky Boots"), 2013. **Special Achievements:** Performed in The 67th Annual Tony Awards, 2013.

## PORTER, DR. CHARLES WILLIAM

Publisher, educator, editor. **Personal:** Born Oct 6, 1939, Mobile, AL; son of Quillie and Rosie; married Joyce A Wallace; children: Nikki, Terri, Michael & Stanley. **Educ:** Bishop State Jr Col, AS, 1960; Ala State Univ, BS, 1962; Univ Ala, MA, 1970; Ala Interdenominational Sem, Mdiv, 1972; Chicago City Col, attended 1973. **Career:** Pub sch teacher, 1962-68; Mobile Press Regist, news reporter, 1968-69; Univ Ala, Tuscaloosa Inst, 1969-70; Tougaloo Col, Tougaloo, MS, dir pub rels, 1970-71; Northwestern Univ, sr publ ed, 1971-74; Mobile Beacon, ed, 1974-76; Inner City News, ed & publ, 1976-; Inner City Printers, owner, 1977-; Bishop State Jr Col, dir pub rels, 1982-86, instr jour, 1984-87; Inner City Pub Rels, pres, consul, 1986-; Bishop State Community Col, Minority Tech & Entrepreneural Ctr, exec dir, currently. **Orgs:** Founder & pres, Media Coalition, 1976-; chmn bd, OIC Mobile Area, 1980-81; Sigma Delta Chi; Nat Asn Black Journalist; Am Col Pub Rels Asn; Educ Writers Asn; Nat Coun Col Pub Adv; Nat Asn Advan Colored People; Sickle Cell Res Found; Omega Psi Phi Fraternity; Concerned Citizens Police Reform, Chicago; Southern Christian Leadership Conf: hon mem, YWCA; YMCA; Urban League; exec dir, Human Rels Comn. **Honors/Awds:** Nat, regional & local hons establishing Southern Ala Task Force Illiteracy; hon doctorate, Ala Interdenomi Nat Sem, 1991; numerous hons community serv. **Home Addr:** 1318 Poleris Dr, Mobile, AL 36693-4644, **Home Phone:** (251)666-0088. **Business Addr:** Executive Director, Bishop State Community College, 351 N Broad St, Mobile, AL 36603-5898, **Business Phone:** (334)690-6880.

## PORTER, DR. CLARENCE A.

Educator, president (organization), executive director. **Personal:** Born Mar 19, 1939, McAlester, OK; son of Myrtle E Johnson and Lloyd C; children: Richard Alan & Cory Steven. **Educ:** Portland State Univ, BS, 1962; OR State Univ, MS, 1964, PhD, invert zool & parasitol, 1966. **Career:** Educator (retired); OR St Univ, grad asst, 1961-64, asst vet med, 1964-66; Portland St Univ, asst prof, 1966-70, exec asst to pres & assoc prof, 1970-72; Univ NH, asst vice provost acad affairs, 1972-76; St Univ MN, assoc vice chancellor acad affairs, 1976-78; Phyllis Wheatley Comm Ctr, exec dir, 1979-83; Cheyney Univ Penn, vpres acad affairs, 1983-84; Montgomery Col, Takoma Park, MD, instrnl dean, 1985-2000, vpres & provost, 2000-04. **Orgs:** Sigma Xi; Helminthological Soc Wash; Nat Coun Instrnl Adminrs; pres, Nat Coun Black African Am Affairs; Col Mgt Prog, Carnegie Mellon, 1988; League Innovation Community Col, Exec Leadership Inst, 1997; Am Red Cross Life Bd; Helminthological socs Helminthological socs. **Honors/Awds:** Summer Fel, LA State Univ, 1968. **Special Achievements:** First convener of the deans collegewide in Montgomery Col. **Home Addr:** 7186 Lasting Light Way, Columbia, MD 21045, **Home Phone:** (410)290-8079. **Business Addr:** Academic Dean, Montgomery College, 7600 Takoma Ave Suite 310, Takoma Park, MD 20912-4141, **Business Phone:** (301)650-1312.

## PORTER, EDWARD MELVIN

Politician, businessperson, lawyer. **Personal:** Born May 22, 1930, Okmulgee, OK; son of Victor E and Mary Cole; married Jewel; children: E Melvin II & Joel Anthony. **Educ:** Tenn State Univ, BS, 1956; Vanderbilt Univ, Vanderbilt Sch Law, LLB, 1959; Shorter Col, LLD. **Career:** Okla House Representatives, republican, 1962; Okla State Senate, sen, 1964-86; Okla County Commissioners, assessor, 1992-94; Okla City, atty, currently. **Orgs:** Pres, Okla Nat Asn Advan Colored People, 1961-; Okla County Bar Asn; Okla Bar Asn; Am Bar Asn; Am Judicature Soc; Young Mens Christian Asn; Okla City Chamber Com; Sigma Rho Sigma; Kappa Alpha Psi; Okla Hist Soc. **Home Addr:** 800 N Anita Dr, Oklahoma City, OK 73127-5128. **Business Addr:** Attorney, 2116 NE 23 St, Oklahoma City, OK 73111.

## PORTER, REV. DR. GLEN EUGENE, SR.

Minister (clergy). **Personal:** Born Elizabeth, NJ; married Lisa Parker; children: Glenn Eugene Jr, Luke Proctor & Adam DeWitt. **Educ:** Va Union Univ, Sam Va Union Univ, Samuel D Proctor Sch Theol, DMin, 1989, Mdiv, 2001; Rowan Univ, BA, mass commun & jour, 2000. **Career:** Div Clergy Baptist Gen Conv Va, pres; Mt Zion Baptist Church, pastor; Gillfield Baptist Church, Petersburg, Va, pastor; Am Baptist Churches NJ, assoc regional pastor & area minister; Queen St Baptist Church, sr pastor, 2008-; Tidewater Community Col, adj assoc prof, 2013-. **Orgs:** Gen Bd Baptist Gen Conv Va. **Business Addr:** Pastor, Queen Street Baptist Church, 413 E Brambleton Ave, Norfolk, VA 23510, **Business Phone:** (757)622-4458.

## PORTER, GLORIA JEAN

Administrator. **Personal:** Born Apr 15, 1951, Baltimore, MD; daughter of Percy and Lillian. **Educ:** Adelphi Univ, BS (summa cum laude), 1973; Univ Ill, MSW (summa cum laude), 1974. **Career:** Univ Mass Ment Health Serv, therapist, 1975-78; Univ Southern Calif Coun Serv, psychotherapist, asst dir, dir, 1978-84; Univ Southern Calif; Data products Corp, employee asst mgr, 1984-90; Los Angeles County, Employee Assistance Prog, dir, 1991; Greene Co, CASA Coordr, currently. **Orgs:** Bd dir, Ebonics; Alcohol Info Ctr San Fernando Valley Coun Alcoholism; Nat Asn Advan Colored People; Black Women's Forum; Black Women's Network; black Agenda; Urban League; Women Mgmt, Am Personnel & Guidance Asn; NASW Reg Clin Soc Workers; Nat Asn Soc Workers; Asn Black Soc Workers; Nat Health Attitudes Res Proj; Am Personnel & Guidance Asn; NASW Regist Clin Social Workers. **Home Addr:** 5250 Village Green, Los Angeles, CA 90016. **Business Addr:** CASA Coordinator, Greene Co, 2100 Greene Way Blvd, Xenia, OH 45385, **Business Phone:** (937)562-4000.

## PORTER, BISHOP HENRY LEE

Bishop. **Personal:** Born Jan 2, 1948, Sarasota, FL; son of Lee Ernest and Hazel Elkins; married Cynthia E Johnson; children: Henry, Etienne Jaberly, Zacchur Chalome & Tsadok Hazel. **Educ:** Fla Agr & Mech Univ, BS, math, 1969; Yale Univ, CT, doctoral studies, PhD, math, 1971. **Career:** Westcoast Gospel Chorus Fla, founder, 1969; Westcoast Ctr Human Develop, founder, 1971; Fla Agr & Mech Univ, prof, math, 1973-75; Westcoast Sch Human Develop, prin, founder, 1981-2000; Trinity Col Ministerial Arts, vis prof, 1985-; Westcoast Mag, Publ, 2003-; Black Action Mag, publ, 1986-; Henry L Porter Nursery Primary Sch, Takum, Nigeria, W Africa, 1990-; Westcoast Theol Sem, pres, 1989-; HL Porter Sch music, pres, currently. **Orgs:**

Ivy League Club Sarasota; life mem, Grand Chap Kappa Alpha Psi Fraternity, 1967-, pres, 1968-69; pres, Alpha Kappa Mu Nat Hon Soc, 1968-69; pres & founder, Henry L Porter Evangelistic Asn, 1971-; Am Asn Univ Profs, 1973-; Math Asn Am, 1973-; Yale Club Sun Coast, 1989-; Yale Club Sarasota; bd mem, Bobby Jones Gospel, 1989; silver life mem, Nat Asn Advan Colored People; Nat Acad Rec Arts & Sci Grammy; Gospel Music Asn; bd mem, Adv Bd Educ Nigeria, 1993. **Honors/Awds:** Harvard Prize Book, Harvard Univ, 1964; Scholar of the Year, Alpha Kappa Mu, 1968; Doctoral Fellowship in Mathematics, Ford Found, 1969; one of The 100 Most Influential People in Sarasota, Sarasota Magazine, 1993, 2002; Men Give Back to the Community, Ebony Man Magazine, 1993; Nat Asn for Advancement of Colored People Freedom Award, 1999; Commendation from Governor Jeb Bush of Florida, 1999; White House performance, Wash, DC, 2000; Governor's Point of Light Award, 2002; Henry Porter & The Love Campaign; Florida Gospel Music Hall of Fame, 2003; The Gospel Awards; Henry L Porter Award, 2003; Broadcasters Hall of Fame, Akron, OH, 2004; Sarasota Hall of Fame, 2004; The Golden Gavel Award, Sarasota Herald Tribune; Honorary Degrees, United Bible Col, 1986; Honarary Degreees, Trinity Col Ministerial Arts, 1989. **Special Achievements:** Cover Story, The Master's Touch, Charisma Magazine, May, 1981; Manuals: "How to Start a Prayer Group" 1991; "Africa Alive" video 1993, "Forgiveness Manual" 1990, "Duties of an Assistant" 1991; Featured: Westcoast School for Human Development, "Street Stories with Ed Bradley," CBS-TV 1993; Poetry Books: Therapy 1990, Faces of Love 1990; Books: Child of the Thought 1989, Healing, A Gift from God1988, Seasons of the Rains 1999; Higher Thoughts and Peaceful Ways 1990; Composed over 2000 songs; Recorded 17 Albums/DVDs; Senate Advisory Board on Education, Federal Republic of Nigeria, 1992; Visiting Professor, Trinity College of Ministerial Arts 1992-; Television Broadcast, "Henry Porter and the Love Campaign"; Intl Lusanne Conference of Upcoming Christian Leaders, US Delegate to Singapore, 1988. **Business Addr:** Founder, President, Henry L Porter Evangelistic Association, 403 N Wash Blvd, Sarasota, FL 34236-4237, **Business Phone:** (941)366-4539.

## PORTER, JOHN T.

Executive, vice president (organization). **Personal:** Born Feb 21, 1941, Brady, TX; children: John Jr & Christian (deceased). **Educ:** Ill Col, BA, 1968; Sangamon State Univ, MA, 1971. **Career:** Executive, vice president (retired); Ill Bell Telephone Co, dist mgr training, 1979-80, dist mgr, 1980-90, dir, human resources, 1990-91; Power Process Engineering, vpres, gen mgr. **Orgs:** Mem Disabled Am Veterans, 1963-; pres, Hope Sch, 1975-81; chairperson, Ill Planning Coun on Developmental Disabilities, 1984-; bd mem, Ill State Asn Retd Citizens, 1984-; bd mem, Ill Self Sufficiency Trust, 1989-; bd mem, Hope Sch Trust, 1989-; Nat Asn Developmental Disability Couns, 1994; Ray Graham Asn; Nat Conf State Legislatures; Pub Aid Adv Comt. **Home Addr:** 250 S Cedar Ave, Wood Dale, IL 60191-2293, **Home Phone:** (630)595-0959.

## PORTER, KARL HAMPTON

Musician, conductor (music), educator. **Personal:** Born Apr 25, 1939, Pittsburgh, PA; son of Reginald and Naomi Arzetta; children: Marc, Turin, Nadia, Kenneth, Michael, Kelly, Kevin & Elizabeth. **Educ:** Carnegie-Mellon, 1960; Peabody Conserv, 1962; Juilliard Sch Music, 1963; Domaine Sch Conductors, 1963; Fordham Univ, 1978; State Univ NY, attended 1986; John Hopkins Univ, 1987. **Career:** Univ Denver, instr, 1963-64; Denver Symphony Orchestra, 1963-64; Gil EvansBand, 1967-69; Harlem Youth Symphony, 1968; Harlem Philharmonic Orchestra, founder, dir, 1969-; Pittsburgh Youth Symphony Orchestra; Am Wind Symphony Orchestra; Newark Community Arts Ctr, teacher, 1969-71; Woodwind LI Inst Music, instr, 1969-75; New Breed Brass Ensemble, Harlem String Quartet, Harlem Woodwind Quintet, 1970; BMI Composers Competition, judge, 1970-74; Baltimore Sym, conductor, 1971-72; New York Tech Col, instr, 1972-90; Josephine Baker, music dir & conductor, 1974; Finale Productions, pres; Massapequa Sym, conductor, 1975-78; Park W Sym, conductor; Harlem Philharmonic, conductor; NYCTC/City Univ New York, instr; Harlem Music Soc, dir, 1980-91; Col New Rochelle, instr, 1980; St Thomas Apostle, choir dir, 1988-99; NY Coun Arts, consult, 1990-99; Elmcor Youth Ctr, Dir counr, 1991-93 free-lance bassoonist & guest conductor, currently. **Orgs:** Sickle Cell, 1970-; Dance Theatre Harlem, 1971-78; Arts & Lett, 1974-; pres, Finale Prods, 1978-87; coach, NY Asn Jr Cols, Am Symphony Orchestra League, Performing Arts Asn New York; Soc Black Composers; Nat Soc Symphony Conductors Clubs: Bohemians; Bd dirs Empire Trust; Hon bd dirs Sickle Cell; Baton Rouge; La; Nat Asn Advan Colored People, Act-So, 1988-2001. **Honors/Awds:** Martha Baird Rockefeller Grant, 1969; Nat Endowment Grant, 1970. **Special Achievements:** First African-American bassoonist to perform with a major orchestra. **Business Addr:** Bassoonist, Conductor, 425 Cent Pk W, New York, NY 10025, **Business Phone:** (212)865-5280.

## PORTER, REV. DR. KWAME JOHN R.

Clergy. **Personal:** Born Apr 2, 1932, Mineral Springs, AR; son of Steve and Retha Hendricks; married June Carol McIntosh; children: John Thomas, Joseph Dubois, Julia Magdilene, Jessica Retha, Jorja Angela & Jerrianne Carol. **Educ:** IO Wesleyan Col, BA, sociol, 1959; Garrett Evan Theol Sem, MDiv, 1962; Union Grad Sch, PhD, 1975. **Career:** Clergy (retired); Christ United Meth Ch, pastor, 1962-71, 1979-95; Sch Human Dignity, dir, 1967-70; Northeastern Ill Univ's Ctr, adj prof, 1968-70; Chicago Ctr Black Relig Studies, grad dean, 1971-74; Urban Young Life, vpres, 1974-79; Fel United Methodist Church, part-time pastor, 1996-2001; Nat Urban Black Church Growth Inst, dean; George Williams Col, teacher. **Orgs:** Stud Asn Garrett Theol Sem, 1961; founding mem, Oper Breadbasket PUSH, 1966; Garrett Theol Sem, adj prof; Int Black Writers, 1980; founder, PEACE, 1990-; pres, community trainer, JCPT CAPS, Chicago Alliance Neighborhood Safety, 1995-96. **Honors/Awds:** The First African American elected as President of the Dempster League, 1961; Pub articles best black sermons Vol II Judson Press, 1979; pub articles Metro Ministry David C Cook Pub, 1979; Three awards for work in 7th Dist's CAPS proj; Alumnus of the Year, 1996 Iowa Wesleyan Col, 1994-95; Received numerous honors for his commitment to social and racial justice. **Special Achievements:** Auth, The Dating Habits of Young Black Americas, 1979; Res writer, proposal develr, chair, Engle wood's New Village, EZEC proj, 1994-95; Pending publ Black Male Violence, 1997; "How Black folk and Others Die", 1997; "Basic Training Manual for 21st Century Christians". **Home Addr:** 5403 S Greenwood Ave, Chicago, IL 60615, **Home Phone:** (773)324-7875.

## PORTER, LINSEY

Mayor. **Personal:** Born Jan 1, 1954; married Patricia. **Career:** Colonial Life & Accident Ins Co, sales dir; City Highland Pk, councilman, 1983-87, coun pres, 1987-91, mayor, 1992-2004.

## PORTER, LIONEL

Executive, educator. **Personal:** Born Jan 26, 1943, Canton, MS. **Educ:** State Univ, BA, 1966; Univ CT, MA, ABD, 1975, JD, 1985. **Career:** Arsenal Tech HS, eng teacher, 1966-68; Aetna Life Casualty, mgt trainee, 1968-69; Hartford Pub High Sch, eng teacher, 1969-70; Univ Hartford, instr & amlit, 1975-78; Univ Conn Health Ctr, title XX cons, trng dir, 1978-. **Orgs:** Vpres, Blue Hills Civic Assoc, 1978-80; partic, Leadership Greater Hartford, 1980-81; bd mem, Community Coun Capitol Reg, 1981-82; Am Heart Assoc, 1984-. **Honors/Awds:** Outstanding Young Men in America Award; EPDA Fellowship, Univ CT, 1970-75. **Business Addr:** Training Director, University of Connecticut Health Center, 263 Farmington Ave, Farmington, CT 06030, **Business Phone:** (860)679-2000.

## PORTER, MIA LACHONE

Computer scientist. **Personal:** Born Jan 21, 1965, Birmingham, AL; daughter of John T (deceased) and Dorothy Rogers (deceased). **Educ:** Univ Ala, Birmingham, attended 1985; Ala State Univ, BS, 1988; Samford Univ, attended 1991. **Career:** Southern Co Servs, client comput analyst I, currently. **Orgs:** Alpha Kappa Alpha Sorority Inc, 1987-; Alpha Kappa Psi Prof bus Fraternity, 1988; Nat Mgt Asn, 1989-; fin secy, Am Asn Blacks Energy, 1990-91. **Home Addr:** 707 Tree Corners Pkwy, Norcross, GA 30092, **Home Phone:** (404)447-1952. **Business Addr:** Client Computing Analyst, Southern Company Services, 64 Perimeter Ctr E, Atlanta, GA 30346, **Business Phone:** (770)821-4800.

## PORTER, MICHAEL ANTHONY

Engineer. **Personal:** Born Sep 4, 1968, Bronx, NY; son of Ryland and Delrose; married Tanya. **Educ:** Howard Univ, BS, mech engineering, 1993; State Univ NY, Binghamton, MS, mech engineering, 1996. **Career:** Ford Motor Co, prod engr, 1987-91; Environ Protection Agency, envr engr, 1992-93; Martin Marietta Control Systs, prod design engr, 1993-; Northrop Grumman Shipbuilding, mech engr, 1998-2010; Amtrak, High Speed Rail Systs Engineering, mech engr, 2012-. **Orgs:** Prof advisor, Nat Soc Black Engrs, 1992-; chmn, Engineering Explorer Post, 1993-; Alpha Phi Alpha. **Home Addr:** 921 Lehigh Dr, Vestal, NY 13850, **Home Phone:** (607)797-3247. **Business Addr:** Product Design Engineer, Martin Marietta Control Systems, 600 Main St MD R29, Johnson City, NY 13790-1888, **Business Phone:** (607)770-2100.

## PORTER, MICHAEL C.

Vice president (organization). **Educ:** Univ Detroit Jesuit High Sch, attended 1971; Kettering Univ, indust admin, 1972; Univ Mich, Dearborn, MI, BBA, mkt, 1975; Univ Detroit, MBA, finance, 1982. **Career:** Am Motors Corp, mkt staff, 1976-83; Stroh Brewery Co, staff, 1983-94; vpres mkt, 1990-94; McCann-Erickson, Detroit, sr vpres, 1994-97; DTE Energy Co, vpres corp commun, 1997-11; Think Detroit PAL, chief exec officer, 2011. **Orgs:** Bd trustee, DTE Energy Found; Children's Hosp Mich; vice chair, Detroit Pub TV; dir, Univ Detroit, Jesuit High Sch; Dean's Adv Coun, Univ Mich, Dearborn Sch Mgt; Citizen's Adv Coun, Univ Mich, Dearborn; Commun Adv Coun, Nuclear Energy Inst; bd dir, Metrop Affairs Coalition; bd dir, Univ Detroit Jesuit High Sch. **Business Addr:** Board Director, University of Detroit, 8400 S Cambridge Ave, Detroit, MI 48221, **Business Phone:** (313)862-5400.

## PORTER, DR. MICHAEL LEROY

Administrator, founder (originator), writer. **Personal:** Born Nov 23, 1947, Newport News, VA; son of Doretha Bradley and Leroy. **Educ:** Va State Univ, BA, sociol, 1969; Atlanta Univ, MA, hist 1972; Leonardo DaVinci Acad, Rome, Italy, MCP, contem 1984; Emory Univ, PhD, hist/Am studies, 1974; Sorbonne Univ, post doctorate, hist, Paris, France, 1979; Thomas Nelson Community Col, cert crim justice, 1981; US Armed Forces Staff Col, Norfolk, Va, US Pres Appt, 1987. **Career:** WA State Univ, asst prof hist, black studies prog, 1974-75; Mohegan Comm Col, Dept Hist lectr, 1975-76; Newport News VA, asst educ coordr, educ comp, target proj prog, 1977; Hampton Univ, asst prof hist, 1977-80; NC Mutual Ins Co, life ins underwriter, 1980-81; Mullins Prot Serv VA Bch, pvt investr, 1981-83; Am Biog Inst Raleigh, media free-lancer, 1984-85, publ dir, dep gov, 1985-; Old Dom Univ, Norfolk VA, consult, 1985; Michael Porter Enterprises INT, pres & founder, 1985-88; Int Biog Ctr, Cambridge Eng, dep dir gen, 1986; Tv Progs: Journey African Am Athlete, 1995; Eve's Bayou, 1997; 4 Little Girls; Kennedy Ctr Hons, 1998; Miss World Pagent, 2002; People News, 2003; Soul Train, 2003; Cited World News Tonight; Hard Copy; 60 Minutes; Current Affairs; Entertainment Tonight; 27th Am Music Awards; CBS Eve News; Remarkable Journey; NBC Nightly News. **Orgs:** Life patron, World Inst Achievement, 1985; curator "Michael L Porter Historical & Literary Collection"; World Literary Acad, 1984-85; World Biographical Hall Fame, 1985; bd governors, Am Biog Inst, 1986; chair, US Selective Serv Bd 32, 1986-92; Republican Ntl Convention, 1988; Int Advisory CNL, 1989-99; FDL Braintrust, 1990; chief delegate, Int Congress on Arts & Commun, Nairobi, Kenya, 1990; Elite INT, 1992; Int Acad Intellectuals, 1993; African American Hall Fame, 1994; Phi Beta Kappa; Famous Poet's Soc, 1996; Outstanding People20th Century, 1999; Speaker's Circle, 2000; Schomburg SOC, 2000; Int Honor Soc, 2002; Honors, Supria Omnia, 2002; Arte & Labore, 2002; Int Biographical Ctr, vice-counsel, United Cultural Convention, secy gen, 2002-05; World Peace & Diplomacy Forum, 2003; Colonial Williamsburg Burgesses, 2003. **Honors/Awds:** First Black Concert Pianist to play Carnegie Hall, 1963; Lyon Dissertation Prize, 1974; Selected Works: Black Atlanta, 1974; Eligible Bachelor, Ebony Magazine, 1975; Jet Magazine SOC World, 1978; Read Between the Lines, 1985; One of 500 Leaders of Influence in the 20th Century; International Hall of Leaders, Am Biographical Inst, 1988; US Presidential Inauguration, Guest of Honor, 1989; Great American, 1991; Golden Academy Award, 1991; Outstanding Black, 1992; Hero, 1992; International Honors Cup, 1992; Abira Genius Grant, 1992; World Greetings, 1992; Pioneer Award, 1992; World Intellectual, 1993; porter streets: Chicago, New York, Richmond, Hong Kong China, SAO Paulo, Brazil; San Juan, Pureto Rico; participant (exhibit), DuSable Museum of Black History, 1988; honoree, Int Exhibit, Singapore, Malaysia, 1988; Outstanding Man of the World, Ormiston Palace, Tasmania, Australia, 1989; Exhibit, Int Music Museum, London, Eng, 1989; Poetry Reading, Royal Palace, Lisbon, Portugal, 1998; Michael Porter Poetry Exhibit, Int Poetry Hall of Fame, 1997-2002; honoree, poetry recognition, Pope PaulVI, Krakow, Poland, 2002; Lecture, Oxford Univ, Oxford, ENG, 1997; Famous Quote, Leningrad, Russia, 1998; 20th Century Award for Achievement, 1990; 21st Century Gallery of Achievement, Black History Maker, 1992; Man of the Year, 1992; Most Admired Person of the Decade, 1990-99; Recipient, Grant For Exceptionally Gifted Poets, 1998; Loner of Appreciation, Nat Sci Fed, 2003; US Congress, Certificate of Appreciation, 1991; Atlanta African American Festival, Honoree, 1992; Appearances before US President's Council of Economic Advisors & Senate Finance Committee, 1992; Historical Marker, Hampton History Ctr, 1992; Honorary US Congressman, 1993; US Presidential Medal of Freedom, 1993; PrizeWinner, International Golf Classic, Bermuda UPA Masters, 1995; US Presidential Legion of Merit, 1996; Honorary Knighthood, 1997; Great Thinker, 1999; Outstanding Speaker/Golden Gavel, 2000; honoree, Millenium Celebration Giza, Egypt, 2000; honoree, Va General Assembly, 2000; Int Ambassador of Goodwill, 2003; Living Legends Award, 2003; ABI World Laureate, 2003; Great honoree, 40th Anniversary March on Wash, DC, 2003; Int Peace Prize, 2002; 100 MostIntriguing People, 2003; Minds of The 21st Century. **Special Achievements:** Film: The Making of Black Atlanta, 1974; First African American Elected to Intl Academy of Intellectuals, Paris, France, 1993; Publications: Ebony, Jet, Intl, Digest, Talent; Contemporary Authors; Directory of American Scholars; Radio: Empire State Bldg Broadcasting Ctr, WRIN, 1997; Radio FM 95.7, Black Man Legacy of Achievement, 2003. **Home Addr:** 3 Adrian Cir, Hampton, VA 23669-3814, **Home Phone:** (757)723-8781. **Business Addr:** Archives Administrator, 3 Adrian Cir, Hampton, VA 23669-3814, **Business Phone:** (757)722-6815.

## PORTER, RUFUS

Football player. **Personal:** Born May 18, 1965, Amite, LA; married Anita; children: Atina & Rufus Jr. **Educ:** Southern Univ, attended 1988. **Career:** Football player (retired); Seattle Seahawks, 1988, linebacker, 1989, right linebacker, 1989-94; New Orleans Saints, left linebacker, 1995-96; Tampa Bay Buccaneers, left linebacker, 1997. **Orgs:** 8 to 80. **Honors/Awds:** Pro Bowl, 1988 & 1989; All-Pro, 1989. **Home Addr:** 211 Nottaway Dr, Destrehan, LA 70047-3145.

## PORTER, DR. TEMILLE

Psychologist. **Personal:** Born Jul 4, 1958, Muskogee, OK. **Educ:** San Diego State Univ, BA; Conn Valley Hosp, Middletown, CT, APA; Calif Sch Prof Psychol, San Diego, PhD, MA. **Career:** Lic Clin Psychologist; St John's Child & Family Develop Ctr's Am Psychol Asn; Accredited Psychol Training Prog, Calif, dir; Calif State Univ, Stanislaus, dir coun servs; Univ Southern Calif, dir disability servs & progs, USC Stud Coun Ctr, staff psychologist, sr staff psychologist; San Diego State Univ, Depts African Studies, Women's Studies, lectr; Whittier Col Stud Coun Servs, dir, currently; Positive Action Coun Serv, staff; King Abdullah Univ Sci & Technol, clin psychologist & mgr, 2009-. **Orgs:** Am Psychol Asn; Asn Black Psychologists; CPA; Orgn Coun Ctr Dirs Higher Educ; Asn Univ & Col Coun Ctr Dirs. **Business Addr:** Manager, Clinical Psychologist, King Abdullah University of Science & Technology, Student Ctr Bldg 18 Rm 4213, Thuwal23955-6900, **Business Phone:** (966)02808-31.

## PORTER, TERRY

Ambassador, basketball player, basketball coach. **Personal:** Born Apr 8, 1963, Milwaukee, WI. **Educ:** Univ Wis, Stevens Point, BS, commun & media studies, 1985. **Career:** Basketball player (retired), basketball coach; Portland Trail Blazers, guard, 1985-95; Minn Timberwolves, 1995-98; Miami Heat, 1998-99; San Antonio Spurs, guard (retired), 1999-2002; Sacramento Kings, asst coach, 2002-03; Milwaukee Bucks, head coach, 2003-05; Detroit Pistons, asst coach, head coach, 2006-08; Phoenix suns, head coach, 2008-09; Minn Timberwolves, asst coach, 2011-2014; Portland Trail Blazers, alumni ambassador, currently. **Orgs:** Proj Grad; Smart Moves; Sixth Man Found; Boys & Girls Club. **Business Addr:** Assistant Coach, Minnesota Timberwolves, 600 1st Ave N, Minneapolis, MN 55403, **Business Phone:** (612)673-1600.

## PORTER-ESMAILPOUR, CAROL D.

Graphic artist. **Personal:** Born Mar 4, 1948, Washington, DC; daughter of Wiley Waverly and Alma Dodson; married Assad Esmailpour. **Educ:** Howard Univ, attended 1967; Independent Study Tour Europ Capitals, 1970; Moore Col Art, BFA, 1971; Sterling Inst, 1975; Hartford Grad Ctr, 1976; Poynter Inst Media Studies, 1986; Sch Visual Arts; Corcoran Sch Art; Torpedo Factory Art Ctr. **Career:** WJLA-TV7 Wash, graphic artist, 1971-73; WBBM-TV2 Chicago, graphic artist, 1973-75; WFSB-TV3 Hartford, art dir, 1975-77; WDVM-TV9, asst art dir, graphic designer, 1977-79; Needham Harper & Steers Advert Falls Church, art dir & graphic designer, 1979-80; Wash Post, graphic designer, 1980-84, 1985-; Ketchum Advert, art dir, 1984-85; Moore Col Art & Design, bd mgr, 1990-96. **Orgs:** Alpha Kappa Alpha Sor; sec, Nat Acad TV Arts & Scis; Capital Press Club; vol, Family Pl; art dir, Freelance Design; Speakers Bur Wash Post; Broadcast Designers Assoc; Soc Newspaper Design; second vpres, Capital Press Club, 1987-89; moderator, partic, Howard Univ Community Conf: workshop careers newspaper commun, 1988. **Honors/Awds:** Emmy Award Outstanding Individual Achievement in Scenic Design, 1972; Wash Art Dirs Club Awds Merit, 1973, 1979, 1981, 1983; Awards Excellence Chicago '75 Communs Collaborative Show for TV Spots, 1975; bd gov, Wash Chap, Nat Acad TV Arts & Scis, 1979; Award Merit Soc Newspaper Design, 1986; Award Excellence Page Design, Print Magazine, 1988; Award Excellence Portfolio of 6 Page Designs, Soc Newspaper Design, 1989; Award of Excellence Page Design, Wash Art Dirs Club, 1989; Award of Excellence Portfolio Page Design, Soc Newspaper Design, 1990; Award of Excellence Page Design, Wash Metro Art Dirs Club, 1990; Bronze Award, Soc Newspaper Design; Print Magazine Award, Soc Newspaper Design; distinguished Alumna of the Year, Moore Col Art & Design, 2002; John Albano Memorial

Grand Prize for Design, 2003. **Home Addr:** 8708 1st Ave Apt 409, Silver Spring, MD 20910-3521, **Home Phone:** (301)565-2599. **Business Addr:** Graphic Designer, The Washington Post, 1150 15th St NW, Washington, DC 20071, **Business Phone:** (202)334-4551.

### PORTIS, KATTIE HARMON (JESSIE KATE HARMON)

Executive director, association executive. **Personal:** Born Oct 28, 1942, Kinterbish, AL; married Jesse; children: Dawn, Luther, Torris, James, Faye & Raymond. **Educ:** Franconia Col, BA, 1976; Antioch Col, MA, human serv mgt. **Career:** Women Inc, Dorchester, Mass, founder & exec dir; Stamford Outreach Proj Turnabout, 1973; First Residental Drug-Free Prog Women & C Abusing Alcohol Drugs, founder, 1973; Concilio Drug Prog, counr, 1974; Nat Women AIDS Risk Network (WARN) Proj, community coordr & founder, 1987-; New Eng Med Ctr, community coordr, 1992-97; Mass Sober Housing Corp, dir, currently. **Orgs:** Third World Womens Caucus, 1974; consult, Women & Health, 1975; Res & Demonstration Proj, 1975; Treatmnt Conf Women, 1976; chmn, Boston Univ Screening Bd; Mayor Coord Coun Drug Abuse; Mass Comn C & Youth Adv Bd. **Honors/Awds:** Certificate, Yale Univ, 1973; Hero Award, Boston Parents Paper; Abigal Adams Award; Metro Boston Alive Leadership Award; Leadership Award, Dept Pub Health; Outstanding Service for Children, Off C. **Home Addr:** 31 Radcliff Rd, Hyde Park, MA 02136, **Home Phone:** (617)364-4354. **Business Addr:** Director, Massachusetts Sober Housing Corp, PO Box 2230, Worcester, MA 02345-2230, **Business Phone:** (508)987-3388.

### PORTLOCK, DR. CARVER A. See Obituaries Section.

### POSEY, ADA LOUISE

Government official. **Educ:** Carleton Col, BA, polit sci, film arts, 1998. **Career:** Prudential Ins Co, expense mgt & pension oper staff, 1978-85, internal auditing staff, 1985-89; Minn Mut, corp budgeting staff, 1989-93; White House, Wash, assoc dir gen svcs, off admin, 1993-96, dep dir off admin, 1996-97, dir off admin, 1997-99; Off Nat Drug Control Policy, Wash, spl adv, 1999; US Dept Energy, Wash, sr policy advisor & chief, diversity & civil rights & prin consult, 1999-2001; Posey Cons Group, pres & prin consult, 2001-03, chief exec officer, 2013-15; Raytheon Tech Svcs, dir diversity & compliance, 2003-10; Raytheon Intelligence Info & Serv, dir, diversity & inclusion, 2010-13; Wash Metrop Area Transit Authority, mgr, workforce diversity & policy compliance, 2015-. **Orgs:** Trustee, Carleton Col, 1994-98; Capital City Links Chap. **Business Addr:** Director, Raytheon Co, 870 Winter St, Waltham, MA 02451-1449, **Business Phone:** (781)522-3000.

### POSEY, BRUCE KEITH

Lawyer, executive director. **Personal:** Born Mar 22, 1952, Baton Rouge, LA. **Educ:** Univ Ore, BS, polit sci, 1974; Univ Mich Law Sch, JD, 1977. **Career:** Stoel Rives Boley Fraser & Wyse, atty, 1977-; Urban League Portland, dir, 1979-; MediaOne Inc, vpres pub policy & external affairs, 1994-97; US W Commun telecommunications co, sr vpres, 1997-2000; AuraServ Comm, gen coun & corp secy, 2000-01; iPass Inc, gen coun, sr vpres, secy, 2002-09; Openwave Systs Inc, sr vpres, gen coun, corp secy, 2009-11; Intelepeer, sr vpres, gen coun, corp secy, 2011-12; Qualys Inc, vpres & gen coun, corp secy, 2012-; Martin Luther King Jr Scholar Fund Ore, pres; US W Commun; Pac NW Bell. **Orgs:** Am Civil Liberties Union; secy, Ore State Bar Affirmative Action Steering Comn; Asn Ore Black Lawyers; Phi Beta Kappa. **Business Addr:** Vice President, General Counsel, Qualys Inc, 1600 Bridge Pkwy, Redwood City, CA 94065, **Business Phone:** (650)801-6100.

### POSEY, DEBORAH

Executive. **Personal:** Born Dec 16, 1949, Detroit, MI; daughter of James and Kathleen Parker; children: Kelly M McGee & Raymond Jr. **Educ:** Wayne State Univ, BA, 1975. **Career:** Bus Communications, sales mgr, 1982-83; Frontier Communications, supvr customer serv, 1984-90, supvr credit collection, 1990-94, sr mgr credit collections, 1994-96, vpres credit & collections, rev protection, 1996-. **Orgs:** NACM, 1990-; WTDE; Nat Asn Toll Fraud mgrs. **Home Addr:** 7712 Summerdale Cir, Ypsilanti, MI 48197.

### POSEY, JEFFERY LAVELL

Football player. **Personal:** Born Aug 14, 1975, Bassfield, MS. **Educ:** Univ Southern Miss. **Career:** Football player (retired); San Francisco 49ers, defensive end & left defensive end & left linebacker, 1998-2000; Carolina Panthers, linebacker, 2001; Jacksonville Jaguars, defensive end & linebacker, 2001; Houston Texans, defensive end, 2002; Buffalo Bills, linebacker & left linebacker, 2003-05; Wash Redskins, linebacker, 2006.

### POSEY, JOHN R., JR.

Entrepreneur, educator, chief executive officer. **Personal:** Born Nov 17, 1953, Evanston, IL; son of John R Sr and Lois; married Margo K; children: Mercedes A. **Educ:** Dartmouth, BA, hist, 1975. **Career:** Ft Worth Mayor's Off Spec Events, dir mkt, 1984-87; Events Mkt & Mgt, pres, 1987-89; N HTH Corp, dir mkt, 1989-90; Ft Worth Black Chamber, exec dir, 1990-92; writer, consult, 1991-; AALR, founder, 1992-94; BSPIN Media Group, owner, chief exec officer & founder, 1998-; Urban Sports News, publ & chief exec officer, 2003-. **Orgs:** Founding mem, Freelance Writer's Network; Nat Press Photogr's Asn; Am Mgt Asn; Nat Asn Black Journalists; Fuji Prof Servs; Rotary Int; Am Mkt Asn; Tex Black Sports Hall Fame; Tex Photog Soc; Dallas & Ft Worth Asn Black Communicators; Austin Writer's League; TCU Creative Writing Workshop. **Home Addr:** 5509 Vicksburg Dr, Arlington, TX 76017-5988. **Business Addr:** Chief Executive Officer, Publisher, Urban Sports News, 14902 Preston Rd, Dallas, TX 75254, **Business Phone:** (214)929-8573.

### POSTELL-BOYD, GLORIA

Social worker. **Personal:** Born May 1, 1954, Detroit, MI; daughter of Charles and Jeanette; children: Charlene Lynette. **Educ:** Western Mich Univ, BA, 1975; MSW, 1977. **Career:** State Mich, social worker, 1977-. **Orgs:** Delta Sigma Theta, 1972. **Home Addr:** 17534 Edinborough, Detroit, MI 48219, **Home Phone:** (313)794-7699. **Business Addr:** Social Worker, State of Michigan, 2929 Russell, Detroit, MI 48207, **Business Phone:** (313)396-0414.

### POSTEN, HON. WILLIAM S., SR.

Judge. **Personal:** Born Mar 10, 1931, E Moline, IL; son of Aquilla Teague and Vernie Teague; married Pauline Ann; children: Karen, Scott, David, Elaine & Melissa. **Educ:** Minneapolis Col Law, BSL, 1953; William Mitchell Col Law, JD, 1959; Augustana Col, BSL. **Career:** US Govt SS Admin, 1960-61, asst city atty, 1961-73; Hennepin Co, munic ct judge, 1973-76; Minneapolis Dist Ct, judge; pvt atty, currently. **Orgs:** Adv Bd, Turning Pt; adv bd, Genesis II; adv bd, Salvation Army; Minn & Hennepin Co Bar Asn; Am Asn Black Lawyers; Am Legis, Nat Asn Advan Colored People; Health & Welfare City; Metrop Minneapolis March Dimes. **Business Addr:** Attorney, 1225 LaSalle Ave Apt 503, Minneapolis, MN 55403, **Business Phone:** (612)338-1553.

### POSTON, CARL, III

Executive, sports agent, lawyer. **Personal:** Born Detroit, MI; married Sherea McKenzie; children: Carl IV, Kirkland & Madison. **Educ:** Fisk Univ, BS, math & bus, 1977; Wayne State Univ, JD, 1981; Saginaw Valley Univ, MBA, 1981; NY Univ, LLM, 1983. **Career:** O'Melveny & Myers, atty, 1980-85; Howeter Corp, exec dir, Oshobori Division, pres, 1985-89; McKenzie & Poston, managing partner; Prof Sports Planning Inc, co-owner & chmn, 1989-. **Orgs:** Sports Lawyer Asn; Nat Bar Asn; Am Bar Asn; Omega Psi Phi Fraternity Inc. **Honors/Awds:** All-America Tennis Player, Nat Col Athletic Asn; American Jurisprudence Record in Contracts; Z Alexander Looby Award. **Home Addr:** 5625 Dolores St Apt A, Houston, TX 77057-5709. **Business Addr:** Chairman, Co-owner, Professional Sports Planning Inc, 777 Post Oak Blvd Suite 320, Houston, TX 77056, **Business Phone:** (713)659-2255.

### POSTON, KEVIN D.

Sports manager, sports agent. **Personal:** Born Saginaw, MI; married Kathy L; children: Garrison L, Myles & Alexx L. **Educ:** Fisk Univ, BBA, bus admin, 1981; Tex Southern Univ, Thurgood Marshall Sch Law, JD. **Career:** Saginaw Bd Realtors, assoc realtor; real estate broker; Miller Canfield, atty; Miro, Miro & Weiner, partner & shareholder; Prof Sports Planning Inc, owner, pres & chief exec officer, 1987-2012; Deal LLC, pres & chief exec officer, 2012-. **Honors/Awds:** Lifetime Achievement Award, Fisk Univ, 2007; Alumni Achievement Award, Fisk Univ, 2011; Professional Achievement Award, Fisk Univ. **Special Achievements:** Negotiated an unprecedented thirteen-year, $68 million dollar contract for Orlando Magic star Anfernee Hardaway; first and only Lifetime Achievement Award form Fisk University.Books: A Mustard Seed of Faith and The Grace of God: My Family from American Slavery into the Early 21st Century; Making Life Your Best Sport: Lessons in Effective Self- Leadership, 2014. **Business Addr:** President, Chief Executive Officer, Deal LLC, 28025 S Harwich, Farmington Hills, MI 48334, **Business Phone:** (248)932-1007.

### POTTER, JAMIE

President (organization), association executive. **Career:** Cut Core Demolition Inc, founder & pres, currently. **Business Addr:** Founder, President, Cut Core Demolition Inc, 1575 N Lake Ave Suite 201, Pasadena, CA 91104-2340, **Business Phone:** (626)794-2120.

### POTTER, JUDITH DIGGS

Educator. **Personal:** Born Jul 23, 1941, Norwood, MA; children: Wende Beth & Kimberly Ann. **Educ:** Lesley Col, BS, educ, 1964; Wheelock Col, MS, educ, 1977; Trinity Univ. **Career:** Boston Pub Schs, teacher, 1964-65, 1968-; Medway Pub Sch, teacher, 1965-66; Brookline Head start, teacher, 1968. **Orgs:** Found secy & treas, Black Caucus Boston Teachers Union, 1966, 1978-83; deleg, MA Fed Teachers, Am Fed Teachers, 1977-85; deleg, Boston Labor Coun, Bldg Rep-Boston T Union, 1977-87; coordr, Try Arts & Chap 188 Boston Pub Sch, 1978-86; grad adv, Delta Sigma Theta Inc Boston Alumnae, 1980-81; dcps, substiitute teacher, 2005-. **Home Addr:** 41 Bowker St Apt 1, Brookline, MA 02445-6912, **Home Phone:** (617)277-5612.

### POTTER, MYRTLE STEPHENS

Executive. **Personal:** Born Sep 28, 1958, Las Cruces, NM; daughter of Albert Stephens and Allene Baker; married James; children: Jamison & Lauren Elizabeth. **Educ:** Univ Chicago, Chicago, BA, polit sci, 1980. **Career:** Executive (retired); Int Bus Mach, mkt intern, 1979-80; Merck, 1980-96; Procter & Gamble, sales rep, 1980-81, dist sales training mgr, 1981-82; Merck Sharp & Dohme, sales rep, 1982-84, mkt analyst, 1984-85, training & planning mgr, 1985-86, field meeting serv mgr, 1986-87, dist sales mgr, 1987-89, prod mgr, 1989-90; Astra/Merck affairs, dir, 1990-92, sr dir sales planning, sr dir mkt planning, 1992-93, vpres, Nebr region bus group, Human Health Div, 1993-96; Northeast Region Bus Group, vpres, 1993-96; Bristol-Myers Squibb, vpres strategy & econs, 1996-2000, Worldwide Mkt & Sales Force Effectiveness, vpres, 1997, vpres worldwide meds group, 1997-98, US Cardiovascular Metabolics, sr vpres sales, 1998, pres, 1998-2000; Genentech Inc, chief operating officer, exec vpres comm operations & exec comt mem, 2000-, pres com opers, 2004-05; Myrtle Potter & Co LLC, chief exec officer, 2005-; Myrtle Potter Media Inc, chief exec officer, 2009-. **Orgs:** Philadelphia Urban League, 1988-96; bd trustee, Del Valley Boys & Girls Club, 1996-00; indust fac assoc, Univ Mich Bus Sch, 1996-2000; bd dir, Calif Healthcare Inst, 2002-; adv bd, Healthcare Bus Women's Asn, 2003-; Citizens Fin Accountability Oversight Comt, currently; bd dir, Amazon.com; bd dir, FoxHollow Technologies eV3; bd dir, adv coun dean Stanford Bus Sch; bd dir, Medco Health Solutions Inc; bd dir, Everyday Health Inc; bd dir, Eleuthera Properties LTD; bd, Medco Health Solutions Inc, 2007-12; bd, Express Scripts, 2012; bd trustee, Univ Chicago, currently; bd dir, Rite Aid Corp, 2013-. **Home Addr:** 128 Encinal Ave, Atherton, CA 94027-2103, **Home Phone:** (650)473-6566. **Business Addr:** Chief Executive Officer, Myrtle Potter & Co LLC, 1346 The Alameda Suite 7-290, San Jose, CA 95126, **Business Phone:** (408)993-1614.

### POTTS, ROOSEVELT BERNARD

Football coach, football player. **Personal:** Born Jan 8, 1971, Rayville, LA; married Tenisha; children: Taylor, Ragan & Roosevelt Jr. **Educ:** Northeast La Univ. **Career:** Football player (retired); Indianapolis Colts, running back & fullback, 1993-97; Miami Dolphins, fullback, 1997; Baltimore Ravens, fullback, 1998; Memphis Maniax, 2001; Taylor Univ, asst coach, currently. **Honors/Awds:** Offensive Player of the Year, Thundering Herd Fan Club. **Home Addr:** 10421 Bicknell Cir, Fishers, IN 46038-5792.

### POTTS, SAMMIE

School administrator. **Educ:** Univ Mass, MS, PhD. **Career:** Vpres, Barber-Scotia Col, 1979-88; Pres, Barber-Scotia Col, 1996-2004; Mary Holmes Col, West Point MS, pres. **Business Addr:** President, Mary Holmes College, PO Box 1257, West Point, MS 39773, **Business Phone:** (662)495-5100.

### POUNDER, C. C. H. (CAROL CHRISTINE HILARIA POUNDER)

Actor. **Personal:** Born Dec 25, 1952, Georgetown; daughter of Ronald Urlington (deceased) and Betsy Enid Arnella James; married Boubacar Kone; children: Nicole, Libya & Matthew. **Educ:** Ithaca Col, BFA, 1975. **Career:** Films: All That Jazz, 1979; Union City, 1980; I'm Dancing as Fast as ICan, 1982; Prizzi's Honor, 1985; Out of Rosenheim, 1987; Postcards From the Edge, 1990; The Importance of Being Earnest, 1992; Benny & Joon, 1993; Sliver, 1993; Robocop 3, 1993; Tales from the Crypt: Demon Knight, 1995; Face/Off, 1997; Blossoms & Veils, 1998; Melting Pot, 1998; End of Days, 1999; Things Behind the Sun, 2001; The Big Day, 2001; Tet Grenne, 2002; Baby of the Family, 2002; Rain, 2008; Orphan, 2009; Avatar, 2009; My Girlfriend's Back, 2010; Home Again, 2012; The Mortal Instruments: City of Bones, 2013. TV series: "Hill Street Blues", 1981-86; "Booker", 1984; "Go Tell It on the Mountain", 1985; "The Atlanta Child Murders", 1985; "Cagney & Lacey", 1986; "Valerie", 1986; "As Summers Die", 1986; "Resting Place", 1986; "If Tomorrow Comes", 1986; "Women in Prison", 1987; "Run Till You Fall", 1988; "No Place Like Home", 1989; "Third Degree Burn", 1989; "Common Ground", 1990; "Murder in Mississippi", 1990; "Cop Rock", 1990; "Psycho IV: The Beginning", 1990; "Return to Lonesome Dove", 1993; "The Disappearance of Christina", 1993; "For Their Own Good", 1993; "The Ernest Green Story", 1993; "Biker Mice from Mars", 1993; "ER", 1994-97; "Jack Reed: One of Our Own", 1995; "Living Single", 1995; "White Dwarf", 1995; "Zooman", 1995; "Millennium", 1996-98; "If These Walls Could Talk", 1996; "AllShe Ever Wanted", 1996; "Things That Go Bump", 1997; "House of Frankenstein", 1997; "Final Justice", 1998; "Little Girl Fly Away", 1998; "A Touch of Hope", 1999; "Detention", 1999; "Funny Valentines", 1999; "To Serve & Protect", 1999; "Net Force", 1999; "Batman Beyond", 1999; "Disappearing Acts", 2000; "CoraUnashamed", 2000; "The Outer Limits", 2000; "Rude Awakening", 2000; "The West Wing", 2000; "Static Shock", 2000-01; "Law & Order: Special Victims Unit", 2001-10; "Strong Medicine", 2001; "Boycott", 2001; "The Practice", 2001; "The District", 2001; "For the People", 2002; "The Shield", 2002-08; "Girlfriends", 2004; "Redemption: The Stan Tookie Williams Story", 2004; "Justice League", 2004-06; "Numb3rs", 2005; "W.I.T.C.H.", 2006; "American Masters", 2007; "The Tower", 2008; "Law & Order: Special Victims Unit" (4 episodes), 2001-08; "The No. 1 Ladies' Detective Agency", 2009; "The Boy with an African Heart", 2009; "Warehouse 13", 2009-14; "11-04-08: The Day of Change", 2009; "Brothers", 2009; "Revenge", 2011; "Perception", 2013; "Sons of Anarchy", 2013-14; "NCIS", 2014; "Beware the Batman", 2014. **Orgs:** Artistsa New South Africa, 1989. **Honors/Awds:** Golden Satellite Award, 2003 & 2004; Black Reel Award, 2005. **Business Addr:** Actress, c/o Susan Smith & Associates, 121 N San Vicente Blvd, Beverly Hills, CA 90211, **Business Phone:** (213)852-4777.

### POUNDS, DR. AUGUSTINE WRIGHT

College administrator. **Personal:** Born Jul 20, 1936, Wadley, AL; daughter of Cortelyou Busbee and Flossie Wilkes; married Russell G; children: Karen Williams & Georgina Young. **Educ:** Pontiac Bus Inst, attended 1960; Oakland Community Col, attended 1965; Oakland Univ, BA, 1973, MA, 1975; Iowa State Univ, PhD, 1980. **Career:** Oakland Univ, consult black cult ctr, 1966-68, admin asst to vpres urban affairs, 1968-71, asst dir community serv, 1971-73, asst dir stud ctr, 1973-75; Iowa State Univ, asst dir minority stud affairs, 1975-76, adminr, from asst dean stud life to dean stud life, 1976-84; Univ Zambia, vis prof, 1984; Murray State Univ, vpres stud develop, 1988-90; Anne Arundel Community Col, col develop & intercollegiate athletics, vpres & dean stud servs, 1990-95, vpres emer, currently; Am Coun Educ, sr assoc. **Orgs:** White House Conf Families, Des Moines, IA, 1980; consult evaluator, N Cent Asn Col & Schs, 1987; bd mem, Iowa Stud Personnel Jour, 1987-; chair exec comt, ACPA/CMA, 1988-89; vpres Asn rels, pres, Nat Asn Women Deans, Adminr & Counselors, 1993-94; vpres, Women's Action Coalition, 2000-02; chair, Am Asn Univ Women, Women Color Caucus, 2001-; Am Human Rels Comn; bd mem, United Way Ames, Am Col Personnel Asn; adv bd, Fine Arts Inst Region V US Off Educ; staff adv, Asn Black Studies; City Human Rel Comn; bd mem, Family Serv Oakland Co; vpres, Oakland Co Nat Asn Advan Colored People; bd mem, New Horizons Oakland Co; Am Coun Educ, Nat Identification Prog; Stud Personnel Asn; Nat Asn Stud Personnel Adminr; admin bd, All Univ Community Coun; founding co-chair, Iowa State Univ birthday celebration comn, Martin Luther King Jr; Nat Asn Women Deans Admin & Counrs; Alumni Bd Govs, Iowa State Univ; pres, AAUW Legal Advocacy Comn; pres, Womans Action Coalition, Prince Georges County. **Home Addr:** 8210 Woburn Abbey Rd, Glenn Dale, MD 20769-2023, **Home Phone:** (301)262-3410. **Business Addr:** Vice President Emeritus, Anne Arundel Community College, 101 Col Pkwy, Arnold, MD 21012-1895, **Business Phone:** (410)777-2222.

### POUNDS, DARRYL LAMONT

Football player. **Personal:** Born Jul 21, 1972, Ft. Worth, TX. **Educ:** Nicholls State Univ, grad. **Career:** Football player (retired); Wash Redskins, defensive back & corner back & safety, 1995-99; Denver Broncos, defensive back & corner back, 2000. **Honors/Awds:** Rookie of the Year, 1995.

**POUNDS, ELAINE**
Public relations executive. **Personal:** Born Dec 31, 1946, Detroit, MI; daughter of George and Ethel Loyd; children: Adrian Molett & Allen Parks. **Educ:** Los Angeles Southwest Col, attended 1971; Calif State Univ, Los Angeles, BA, 1978; Los Angeles City Col & Santa Monica City Col, attended 1980. **Career:** KNBC Tv, prod asst; KACE Radio, producer, corp mktg asst; Theta Cable Tv, programming asst; Grp W Cable & Westinghouse Broadcasting Co, promos coordr & traffic mgr; KTTV & Metromedia Tv, asst traffic mgr; KCET channel28, corp mkt asst; Los Angeles Black Media Coalition, exec dir, currently. **Orgs:** Nat Asn Media Women; Alliance Black Entertainment Technicians; Women Show Bus; Nat Asn Advan Colored People; REEL Black Women; Southern Christian Leadership Conf; comnr, Los Angeles City Cult Affairs. **Business Addr:** Executive Director, Los Angeles Black Media Coalition, 1114 W 99th St, Los Angeles, CA 90044, **Business Phone:** (213)564-2383.

**POUNDS, DR. MOSES B.**
Health services administrator. **Personal:** Born Feb 18, 1947, Baltimore, MD; son of Moses B Sr and Katherine McCutcheon; married Ann P McCauley; children: M Andrew. **Educ:** Univ Calif, Santa Cruz, AB, anthrop, 1974; Univ Calif, Berkeley, MA, anthrop, 1975; Univ Calif, Berkeley & San Francisco, PhD, med anthrop, 1982. **Career:** Johns Hopkins Univ, Sch Hyg & Pub Health, Dept Behav Scis & Health Educ, asst prof, 1982-88; Univ Md, Baltimore, asst to pres, Mid-Atlantic AIDS Regional Educ & Training Ctr, proj dir, princ investr, 1988-91; US Pub Health Serv, Health Resources Servs Admin, Bur Health Resources Develop, Off Sci & Epidemiol, sr staff fel, 1991-94, med anthropologist, 1994-. **Orgs:** Am Anthrop Asn; Soc Med Anthrop; Kroeber Anthrop Soc; Am Pub Health Asn; AIDS & Anthrop Res Group, 2001. **Home Addr:** 5224 Even Star Pl, Columbia, MD 21044-1832, **Home Phone:** (410)997-5125. **Business Addr:** Medical Anthropologist, HAB Health Resources Services Administration, 5600 Fishers Lane Rm 7C-07, Rockville, MD 20857, **Business Phone:** (301)443-2894.

**POUSSAINT, DR. ALVIN FRANCIS**
Educator. **Personal:** Born May 15, 1934, East Harlem, NY; son of Christopher and Harriet Johnston; married Tina Inez Young; children: Alison; married Ann Ashmore; children: Alan. **Educ:** Columbia Col, BA, 1956; Cornell Univ Med Col, MD, 1960; Neuro Psychiat Inst; Univ Calif, Los Angeles, MS, 1964. **Career:** Tufts Univ Med Sch, sr clin instr, 1965-66, asst prof, 1967-69; Med Comn Human Rights, Jackson, Miss, southern field dir, 1965-67; Columbia Pt Health Ctr, dir psychiat, 1968-69; Mass Ment Health, assoc psychiatrist, 1969-78; Harvard Med Sch, assoc dean students, dean students, 1975-78, Judge Baker C's Ctr, Boston, sr assoc psychiat, 1978-2010, prof psychiat & fac assoc dean stud affairs, dir off recruitment & multicultural affairs, currently. **Orgs:** Mem bd trustee, Wesleyan Col, 1968-69; treas, Nat Med Comn Human Rights, 1968-69; mem bd trustee, Nat Afro Am Artists, 1968; Nat Med Asn, 1968-; mem bd dir, Oper PUSH, 1971-85; life fel Am Psychiat Asn, 1972-; chmn bd, Solomon Fuller Inst, 1975-81; fel AAAS, 1981-; Am Acad Child Psychiat, 1985-; fel Am Ortho psychiat Asn, 1987-; Med Alumni Asn, Univ Calif Los Angeles; Nat Asn Advan Colored People; Urban League; Am Acad Child & Adolescent Psychiat; Am Acad Arts & Sci, 2014. **Home Addr:** 28 Bellingham Rd, Chestnut Hill, MA 02467. **Business Addr:** Professor of Psychiatry, Faculty Associate Dean for Student Affairs, Harvard Medical School, 260 Longwood Ave, Boston, MA 02115-5750, **Business Phone:** (617)432-2159.

**POUSSAINT, RENEE FRANCINE**
Journalist, educator, chief executive officer. **Personal:** Born Aug 12, 1944, New York, NY; married Henry J Richardson III. **Educ:** Sorbonne Paris France & Yale Law Sch, attended 1967; Sarah Lawrence Col, Bronxville, NY, BA, Eng lit, 1964; Univ Calif, Los Angeles, MA, African studies, 1970; Ind Univ, PhD, 1972; Columbia Univ Sch Jour, attended 1973. **Career:** African Arts Mag Los Angeles, ed, 1969-73; Ind Univ Bloomington, lectr & doctoral cand, 1972-73; WBBM-TV Chicago, reporter, anchor & show host, 1973-77; CBS Network News Chicago, Wash, DC, anchor, reporter, 1977-79; WJLA-TV, anchor & reporter, 1978-; Nat Visionary Leadership Proj, co-founder, producer & educr, 2001. **Orgs:** Prog dir, AIESEC NY, 1967-69; dancer, Jean Leon Destine Haitian Daznce, 1967; translr UC Press, 1970; peaker, var pvt & govt orgn, 1977-; Sigma Delta Chi; lifetime mem, Nat Asn Advan Colored People; Women Commun Awards TV Reporting Nat Asn Media Women, 1975; Ill Ment Health Asn, 1975; Young Achiever YMCA Chicago, 1976; Am Fire fighters Asn, 1977; Am Asn Univ Women, 1979; Sr Fel Univ Md's Acad Leadership; Wisdom Works, Inc, pres, founder & chief exec officer, 2008-. **Honors/Awds:** Outstanding serv US Dept of Labor Ed Women, 1979; Emmy National Acadamy of TV Arts & Scis, 1980; religiton in Media, 1980, 2004; hon doctorate, George town Univ & Mt Vernon Col. **Special Achievements:** Co-edited a book: "A Wealth of Wisdom: Legendary African American Elders Speak". **Business Addr:** President, Chief Executive Officer, Wisdom Works Inc, 4620 Delmar Blvd, St. Louis, MT 63108, **Business Phone:** (314)361-9473.

**POUSSAINT-HUDSON, DR. ANN ASHMORE (ANNE ASHMORE HUDSON)**
Psychologist. **Personal:** Born Jun 23, 1942, Atlanta, GA; daughter of Clifford and Willie Mae; married James L; children: Alan Poussaint, Ayanna & Julia. **Educ:** Spelman Col, Atlanta, GA, BA, Eng & psychol, 1963; Simmons Col Sch Soc Work, MS, 1965; Univ Calif, Berkeley, MA, clin psychol, 1976, PhD, clin psychol, 1979. **Career:** State Univ Calif, San Francisco, lectr, 1968-70; Pac Psychother Asn, consult clinician, 1970-73; US Pub Health Scholar, fel, 1971-73; pvt pract, 1974-81; Urban Psychol Assocs, founder & pres, 1980-95; State Dept, Sr Foreign Svc Selection Bd, 1996; US Info Agency, Selection Bd, 1998; Howard Univ, E. Franklin Frazier Inst, vis scholar, 2000; DC Comn Arts & Humanities, chair. **Orgs:** Mem pub rel com, Am Psychol Asn; vis fel Harvard Univ, W.E.B. Du Bois Inst, 1985-87; former bd dir, United Way Mass, 1992-94; bd dir, Sasha Bruce Youth Works, 1994-; bd dir, Mass Sch Prof Psychol; bd dir, Roxbury Community Col Found; pres, Links Inc; vpres progs, Potomac Chap Links, 1999-; bd dir, WashBallet, 1999-; community adv bd, WHUT. **Honors/Awds:** Precedent Setting in Jury Selection, Asn Black Psychologists, 1974; Civil Rights Award, Clark-Atlanta Univ; Volunteer of the Year, Young Women Christian Asn, Cambridge. **Special Achievements:** Lectr & Contribr of articles in field to mags/newspapers. **Home Addr:** 2200 20th St NW, Washington, DC 20009-5004, **Home Phone:** (202)234-0431.

**POWE, JOSEPH S.**
Engineer, scientist. **Personal:** Born Jul 26, 1946, Bremerton, WA. **Educ:** Univ WVa, BS, 1968; MS, physics, 1971; MS, aeronaut & astronaut engineering, 1972. **Career:** Hughes Aircraft Co, sr scientist. **Orgs:** Mensa. **Home Addr:** 5335 Village Green, Los Angeles, CA 90016, **Home Phone:** (323)295-0550.

**POWELL, ADAM CLAYTON, III**
Foundation executive. **Personal:** Born Jul 17, 1946, New York, NY; son of Adam Clayton Jr and Hazel Dorothy Scott; children: Adam Clayton IV & Sherman Scott. **Career:** CBS News, New York, mgr & producer, 1976-81; Columbia Univ, lectr, 1985-94; Gannett Ctr Media Studies, Columbia Univ, New York, fel lectr & consult, 1985-94, ctr fel, 1990 & 1993; Nat Pub Radio, Wash, DC, news vpres, 1987-90; Quincy Jones Entertainment, exec producer, 1990-91; Freedom Forum Media Studies Ctr, dir technol studies & progs, 1994-96; Freedom Forum, vpres technol & progs, 1986-2001; Newseum Radio, creator & exec producer, 1997-2001; Howard Univs WHUT-TV, gen mgr; Univ Calif, USC Ctr Pub Diplomacy Annenberg Sch, vice provost, 2007-; Univ Southern Calif, dir wash policy. **Orgs:** Acad Polit Sci; Am Asn Polit & Social Sci; AAAS; Nat Asn Black Journalists; Soc Prof Journalists; Songwriters Guild Am; bd adv, Black Col Commun Asn; bd dir, Int Webcasting Asn; bd dir, Internet Policy Inst; Internet Soc Nominations Comt; ed bd, Jour Studies Quart; Mass Inst Technol, Tech Comt; Nat Soc Black Engrs; Tech Adv Comt, Nat Urban League; bd visitors, Syracuse Univ, Info Studies; bd counr, USC, Integrated Media Systs Ctr; adv fund, Web Develop Fund; Nsfs Res Ctr; fel USC Ctr Pub Diplomacy; Univ Fel USC Ctr Pub Diplomacy. **Honors/Awds:** World Technol Award, 1999; Overseas Press Club Award; Peabody Columbia-duPont Armstrong & Ohio State awards. **Special Achievements:** Co-author of Lethargy '96: How the Media Covered a Listless Campaign; Online News; contributed to: Next Media; The Internet for the Broadcasters; Demystifying Media Technology; Death by Cheeseburger: High School Journalism in the 1990s and Beyond; Written articles: Media Ethics Quarterly; Reason; RTNDA Communicator; Wired Magazine; Co=producer of the movie, Keep the Faith, Baby. **Home Addr:** 1350 Beverly Rd Suite 115, PO Box 251, McLean, VA 22101-3917, **Home Phone:** (703)748-0577. **Business Addr:** Vice President of Technology and Programs, The Freedom Forum, 1101 Wilson Blvd, Arlington, VA 22209, **Business Phone:** (703)528-0800.

**POWELL, ALMA VIVIAN JOHNSON**
Activist. **Personal:** Born Oct 27, 1937, Birmingham, AL; daughter of Robert Johnson and Mildred; married Colin L; children: Michael Kevin, Linda Margaret & Annemarie. **Educ:** Fisk Univ, BA, 1957, Emerson Col, PhD. **Career:** Boston Guild Hard Hearing, audiologist, 1959-62; Kennedy Ctr, vice chmn, bd trustee, currently. **Orgs:** Chmn, 1989-00, bd dir, 1989-, Nat Coun Best Friends Found; Kennedy Ctr, Community & Friend Bd, 1991-; bd trustee, vice chair, John F Kennedy Ctr Performing Arts, 1993-; bd chmn, Am's Promise Alliance; adv bd, Pew Ctr Civic Chg; hon pres, Assoc Am Foreign Serv Worldwide; adv bd, Hospitality & Info Serv; hon mem, Dept State Fine Arts Comt; adv bd, Our Mil Kids; adv, Red Cross Mil Dist Wash; pres bd advisor, Historically Black Cols & Univs; adv bd, Civic Chg Inc; chmn, Nat Coun Best Friends Found; co-chair, Am's Promise, currently. **Honors/Awds:** Hon DHL, Emerson Coll, 1996; Civic Change Award, Pew Partnership for Civic Change, 1997; Nat Polit Congress Black Women, 1998; Washingtonian of the Year, 2000; Leadership Award, Women's Ctr, VA. **Special Achievements:** Author: My Little Wagon; America's Promise, 2003. **Business Addr:** Vice Chairman, Board of Trustee, John F Kennedy Center for the Performing Arts, 2700 F St NW, Washington, DC 20566, **Business Phone:** (202)467-4600.

**POWELL, DR. ARCHIE JAMES**
Educator. **Personal:** Born Jun 1, 1950, Lakeland, FL; son of Archie Lee (deceased) and Audrey Daniels; married Shirley (deceased); children: Kevin J. **Educ:** Univ Nantes, France, cert, 1971; Morehouse Col, BA, 1972; Brown Univ, MA, 1974, PhD, 1984. **Career:** More house Col, grant, 1970-71; Ford Found fel, 1972-75; RI Dept Educ, planning specialist, 1978-81; Brown Univ, minority affairs officer, 1981-85; Albany Med Col, asst prof, 1985-, asst dean minority affairs, 1985; world-renowned Morehouse College Glee Club, singer. **Orgs:** New Eng Asn Black Educr; Org Am Historians; Am Hist Soc; Asn Study Afro-Am Life & Hist; Ri Black Heritage Soc; Nat Asn Med Minority Educr; conf co-chair, NE regional coord, 1987; bd dir, Albany Symphony Orchestra, 1986-; bd dir, Albany Boys Club, 1986-; bd dir, Black Dimensions Art, 1986-; trustee, Israel African Methodist Episcopal Church, 1986-. **Home Addr:** 285 Hudson Ave, Albany, NY 12210. **Business Addr:** NY.

**POWELL, ARTHUR F.**
Executive, banker. **Personal:** Born Atlanta, GA. **Educ:** Purdue Univ, BS, math. **Career:** AGH Financial Corp, pres & founder; Grigsby Brandford Powell Inc, prin; Powell Capital Markets Inc, founder, chief exec officer & pres, 1990-. **Orgs:** Bd trustee, St James Prep Sch; bd trustee, Newark Mus; bd trustee, NJ Inst Technol; Omega Psi Phi; Nat Asn Guardsmen; Sundowners Inc; bd trustee, Hosp Ctr Orange; NJ Develop Authority Small, Women, Minority Owned Bus; Newark Progressive Develop Corp; NJ Tennis & Sports Found; Seton Hall Leadership Coun; bd visitor, SC State Univ; Secy, Autism Educ Found MUJC; Nat Inst Drug Abuse. **Business Addr:** Chief Executive Officer & President, Founder, Powell Capital Markets Inc, 280 Corp Ctr 3 Becker Farm Rd, Roseland, NJ 07068, **Business Phone:** (973)740-1230.

**POWELL, BETTYE BOONE**
Banker. **Personal:** Born Apr 10, 1947, Garysburg, NC; daughter of James W Boone Jr; married Carlie W; children: Carlton G. **Educ:** NC Cent Univ, BA, 1969. **Career:** Capital One Bank, employee rels coord, 1981-84; asst personnel off, benefits coord, 1984-88; AVP, sr compensation analyst, 1988-90; EEO/AA officer & vpres, 1990-. **Orgs:** New Orleans Chap Links Inc, 1975-; found bd, Southern Univ New Orleans, 1990-; bd dir, C's Bur, 1992-; bd dir, YMCA Greater New Orleans, 1992-; Human Rels, adv comt, 1994-. **Honors/Awds:** Black Achiever In Business, Dryades YMCA, 1989; Business Coordinator of the Year, Inroads/New Orleans Inc, 1990-91. **Home Addr:** 7031 W Renaissance Ct, New Orleans, LA 70128. **Business Addr:** Vice President, EEO Affirmative Action Officer, HR/Diversity, Capital One Investment Services LLC, PO Box 61540, New Orleans, LA 70161, **Business Phone:** (504)533-3262.

**POWELL, BILL.** See POWELL, DR. WILLIAM O, JR.

**POWELL, DR. C. CLAYTON**
Executive, association executive, optometrist. **Personal:** Born Apr 11, 1927, Dothan, AL; son of Willie and Evelyn; married Romae Turner; children: C Clayton Jr & Rometta E; married Deborah S Goodlett. **Educ:** Morehouse Col, AB; Ill Col Optom, BS; Col Optom, OD; Univ Mich, MPH, grad study prog; Atlanta Univ, MEd. **Career:** Executive (retired); Pvt pract, 1953-; Metro-Atlanta Child Develop Ctr & Health & Vision Clin, develop vision specialist, exec dir; Atlanta S side Comprehensive Health Ctr, chief optom, 1968-73, exec dir, 1973-76; jr high sch teacher, asst prin; Pa Col Optom; Sou Col Optom; Develop Authority Fulton Co, chmn, exec dir. **Orgs:** Nat Eye Inst, NH; adv comt, State Univ, NY; Nat Asn Neighborhood Health Ctr; Am Pub Health Asn; legis comt, NANHC; pres, Am Nat Optom Asn, 1969-74, co-founder; Ga Vision Serv; organizer, chmn, Metro Atlanta OEP Study Group; Beta Kappa Chi; Nat Sci Hon Soc; Tomb & Key Nat Hon Optom Soc; Beta Sigma Kappa Int Hon Optom Soc; Mu Sigma Pi Prof Fraternity; Omega Psi Phi Fraternity. **Honors/Awds:** Outstanding Man of the Year, Clark Col; Outstanding Man of the Year, More house Col; Outstanding Man of the Year, Morris Brown Col; Outstanding Achievement Award, Fulton Co Rep Club; Outstanding Achievement Award, Atlanta Postal Acad; Outstanding Achievement Award, Pine Acres Town & Country Club; Optometrist of the Year, Nat Optom Asn, 1984; Hon Degree, Doctor of Ocular Sci, Ill Col, 1987; Hon DOS, Ill Col Optom, 1987; Founders Award, Nat Optom Asn; The Kaufman Award, Nat Asn Advan Colored People; Outstanding Leadership Award, St Peter Missionary Baptist Church. **Special Achievements:** Inducted into National Optometry Hall of Fame; First African American to Join the Georgia Optometric Association and American Optometric Association. **Home Addr:** 1347 Cascade Falls Dr SW, Atlanta, GA 30311-3637, **Home Phone:** (877)394-2020. **Business Addr:** Executive Director, Development Authority of Fulton County, 141 Pryor St SW Suite 5001, Atlanta, GA 30303, **Business Phone:** (404)730-8101.

**POWELL, CARL DEMETRIS**
Football player. **Personal:** Born Jan 4, 1974, Detroit, MI. **Educ:** Univ Louisville. **Career:** Football player (retired); Indianapolis Colts, 1997; Rhein Fire, defensive end, 1999; Baltimore Ravens, 2000; Chicago Bears, 2001; Wash Redskins, left defensive tackle, right defensive tackle, 2002; Cincinnati Bengals, defensive end, 2003-04, left defensive tackle, 2005. **Orgs:** Life Athletes mems. **Business Addr:** Member, Life Athletes Members, 400 Pl Bldg 210 S Michigan St, South Bend, IN 46601, **Business Phone:** (574)237-9000.

**POWELL, CHARLES ARTHUR**
Publisher. **Personal:** Born May 22, 1933, Atlantic City, NJ; son of John and Colleen; children: Charles A II & Martin Kennedy. **Educ:** Lincoln Univ, BS, hist, 1962; Univ PA, MSW, 1966. **Career:** Child Guid Clin, Media, Pa, psych social worker; Headstart Progs, Deleware County, Pa, dir; Chester, Pa, Anti-Poverty Prog, dir; Bell Atlantic Corp, dir econ devel prog Philadelphia; Quantum Leap Publ, owner, founder, 1990-; Auth: Servants Power, 1990. **Business Addr:** Publisher, Quantum Leap Publisher Inc, 2604 Christy St, Tracy, CA 95376, **Business Phone:** (209)839-1643.

**POWELL, CHRISTOPHER R.**
Media executive, vice president (organization). **Educ:** Northwestern Univ, BS; Harvard Univ, CTAM's Exec Educ Prog, attended 2008. **Career:** Ford Motor Co, field sales mgr, 1990-93; Northwestern Univ, asst dir admis, 1993-95; Deloitte & Touche (Chicago), recruiting mgr, 1994-95; Marriott Int, Wash, D.C., 1996-2001; ING, vpres, human resources; E.W. Scripps Co, div head human resources, 2007-08; Scripps Networks Interactive, exec vpres human resources, 2007-13; BlackbookHR, ceo, 2014-. **Orgs:** Knoxville Area Urban League; Leadership Knoxville Prog, 2012; Univ Tenn, Chancellor's Assoc Coun; bd dir, Women Cable & Telecommunications (WICT); bd dir, Cable & Telecommunications Human Resources Asn (CTHRA). **Business Addr:** Chief Executive Officer, BlackbookHR, 538 Reading Rd Garden Level, Cincinnati, OH 45202, **Business Phone:** (513)399-6301.

**POWELL, CLARENCE DEAN, JR.**
Airplane pilot. **Personal:** Born Aug 26, 1939, Kansas City, MO; son of Clarence Sr and Capitola; children: Pamela Diane. **Educ:** Univ Kans City, 1960; Troy State Univ, Montgomery, AL, 1966. **Career:** TWA Inc, first officer, 1966, capt; Darben Clifton & Gordon Construct Co, proj engr, 1968-69; Hadden Invest & Develop Co, proj engr & cons, 1971-72; Afro Air Inc, pres & chief exec officer, 1974-77; Prof Photogr. **Orgs:** Negro Airmen Int, 1967; Nat Asn Advan Colored People, 1967-; consult, Nat Urban League, 1967-77; eastern relig vpres, Org Black Airline Pilots, 1979; Tuskegee Airman Inc, 1990-. **Honors/Awds:** Honor grad, AUS Basic Training & Warrant Officer Training, 1962-63; Award of Excellence, TWA Airlines, 1979. **Special Achievements:** First Officer on the Popes charter flights, 1979. **Home Addr:** 2986 Balearic Dr, Marietta, GA 30067.

**POWELL, GEN. COLIN LUTHER**
Military leader, executive, businessperson. **Personal:** Born Apr 5, 1937, New York, NY; son of Luther Theophilus and Maud Arial; married Alma Vivian Johnson; children: Michael, Linda & Anne Marie. **Educ:** City Col NY, BS, geol, 1958; George Washington Univ, MBA, 1971; Nat War Col, attended 1976. **Career:** AUS, second lt, 1958, career army inf officer, 1958, first lt, 1959, capt, 1962, maj, 1966, lt col,

1970, 101st Airborne Div, col, 1976, brig comdr, 1976-77, brig gen, 1979, fourth Inf Div, Ft Carson, CO, asst div comdr, 1981-82, Dep Sec Def, mil asst, 1982-86; maj gen, 1983, lt gen, 1986, nat security adv, 1987-89, gen, 1989; Joint Chiefs Staff, chmn, 1989-93; US George W Bush Admin, secy state, 2001-05; Kleiner Perkins Caufield & Byers, strategic ltd partner, 2005-; Nat Mentoring Month, spokesperson, 2008; Salesforce.com, bd dir, 2014. **Orgs:** Founding chmn, Am Promise; Alliance Youth; bd trustee, Howard Univ; bd dir, United Negro Col Fund; bd gov, Boys & Girls Club Am; adv bd, C Health Fund; chm, Eisenhower Fel Prog, 2006. **Honors/Awds:** Inducted Horatio Alger, Asn Distinguished Americans, 1991; Sylvanus Thayer Award, US Mil Acad, 1998; Living Legend Award; Liberty Medal, 2002; Bishop John T Walker Distinguished Humanitarian Service Award, 2005; Andrus Award, AARP, 2006; Presidential Medals of Freedom; President's Citizens Medal; Congressional Gold Medal; Secretary of State Distinguished Service Medal; Secretary of Energy Distinguished Service Medal; Silver Buffalo Award, Boy Scouts Am; received numerous awards and medals including: Purple Heart, 1963; Bronze Star, 1963; Legion of Merit Awards, 1969 & 1971; District Service Medal; Defense Distinguished Service Medal, Defense Superior Service Medal; Soldier's Medal; Air Medal; Presidential Citizens Medal; Nat Bd Advisors, High Pt Univ, 2014. **Special Achievements:** First African American Secretary of State; first African American to serve on the Joint Chiefs of Staff; Author, biography, My American Journey; First of two consecutive African American office-holders to hold the key administration position. **Business Addr:** Strategic Limited Partner, Kleiner Perkins Caufield & Byers, 2750 Sand Hill Rd, Menlo Park, CA 94025, **Business Phone:** (650)233-2750.

### POWELL, COUNCIL, SR.

Public utility executive. **Personal:** children: Council Jr. **Career:** Northside Check Exchange Inc, owner & mgr, currently. **Business Addr:** Owner, Manager, Northside Check Exchange Inc, 2102 St Stephens Rd, Mobile, AL 36617-3727, **Business Phone:** (251)471-5280.

### POWELL, CRAIG STEVEN

Football player. **Personal:** Born Nov 13, 1971, Youngstown, OH. **Educ:** Ohio State Univ, econ, 1994. **Career:** Football player (retired); Cleveland Browns, linebacker, 1995; Baltimore Ravens, linebacker, 1996; New York Jets, linebacker, 1998; San Francisco Demons, linebacker, 2001.

### POWELL, DANTE (LEJON DANTE POWELL)

Baseball player. **Personal:** Born Aug 25, 1973, Long Beach, CA. **Educ:** Calif State Univ. **Career:** Baseball player (retired); San Francisco Giants, outfielder, 1997-98, 2001, free agt, 2002; Ariz Diamondbacks, 1999; Tampa Bay Devil Rays, free agt, 2002; Anaheim Angels, ctr fielder, 2005. **Business Addr:** Professional Baseball Player, Anaheim Angels, Los Angeles Angels Anaheim, Anaheim, CA 92806.

### POWELL, ESQ. DARLENE WRIGHT

Lawyer. **Personal:** Born Dec 1, 1960, Brooklyn, NY; daughter of Franklin P Wright III and Elaine; married Clayton J Jr; children: Jessica Marie. **Educ:** Cornell Univ, Sch Indust & Labor Rels, Ithaca, NY, BS, 1981; Univ Md, Sch Law, Baltimore, MD, JD, 1985; Harvard Law Sch Cambridge, Mass, cert, 1987. **Career:** Frank, Berstein, Conaway & Goldman, law clerk, 1983-84; Daily Rec, staff writer, 1983-84; Burke, Gerber, Wilen, Francomano & Radding, law clerk, summer, 1984; Fidelity & Deposit Co Md, claims atty, 1986; Md-Nat Capital Pk & Planning Comn, assoc gen coun, 1986-87; Kaiser Permanent, assoc regional coun, 1987-88; Md Off Pub Defender, contract atty, 1989-90; Powell & Powell PC, prin atty, 1990-92; Law Off Darlene Wright Powell PA, managing atty, prin atty, 1992-; Mission Love Inc, chairperson, 1997-98, advisor, dir, 1998-2002, exec bd mem. **Orgs:** Bd trustee, State Md Pub Defender Syst, 1990-92; bd mem, Univ Md Prince George's County Alumni Club, 1990-91; chairperson, bd dir, Mission Love Inc, 1997-98, adv, 1998-2002; exec bd mem; chairperson, Charles Co, Cornell Alumni Admis Ambassador Network Comt, 2002-14; Prince George's County, 2002-; Prince George's County Mgt Oversight Panel, 2002; local bd, Citizen's Rev Bd C, 2003-06; bd dir, Community Crisis Serv Inc, 2014-; comt mem, Prince George's County Bar Asn Comt, Continuing Legal Educ Comt; Bar Asn Baltimore City; Pub Serv Comt Md State Bar Asn's Young Lawyers' Sect; Am Asn Justice; Dist Bar Asn. **Honors/Awds:** Participant, Harvard Law School's Prog Instr Lawyers, June, 1987; Young Careerist, Bus & Prof Women's Clubs, Bowie-Crofton Chap, 1987-88; Finalist Award, Young Career Woman Competition, Md Fed Bus & Prof Women's Clubs, 1987-88. **Home Addr:** 2116 Bermondsey Dr, Mitchellville, MD 20721, **Home Phone:** (301)249-3024. **Business Addr:** Principal Attorney, Law Offices of Darlene Wright Powell PA, 16701 Melford Blvd Suite 400, Bowie, MD 20715, **Business Phone:** (301)464-6260.

### POWELL, DARRELL LEE

Television journalist. **Personal:** Born Mar 20, 1959, Cumberland, MD; son of Gloria Louise; married Jacqueline Lavern Barnes. **Educ:** Frostburg State Univ, Frostburg, MD, BS, sociol, 1983. **Career:** Frostburg State Univ, Frostburg, Md, librn aid, 1978-83; Western Md Consortium, Cumberland, Md, counr, 1983; Allegany County Sch Bd, Cumberland, Md, teacher, 1985-87; TCI Cable Vision, Cumberland, Md, photogr & writer, 1984-87; WTBO/WKGO Radio, Cumberland, Md, disc jockey, 1987; WHAG-TV 25, Hagerstown, Md, rep, 1987-; City Cumberland, Dept Community Develop, fair housing specialist. **Orgs:** Treas, Nat Asn Advan Colored People, 1980-; Human Resource Develop Comn Bd, 1990-; Voc Educ Adv Coun, 1990-; Cumberland Theatre bd, 1993-. **Home Addr:** 223 Montgomery Ave Suite 2, Cumberland, MD 21502-3622. **Business Addr:** Fair Housing Specialist, City of Cumberland, 57 N Liberty St, Cumberland, MD 21502, **Business Phone:** (301)722-2000.

### POWELL, DEBRA A.

Mayor. **Personal:** Born Apr 30, 1964, East St. Louis, IL; daughter of James and Barbara; married Anthony Tarvin; children: Anthony Tarvin Jr & Karmeen Childress. **Educ:** Univ Nebr, BA, communs, 1985. **Career:** City E St Louis, pub rel asst, 1986, city coun person, 1993-98, mayor, 1999-2003; Pasadena, Calif, munic pub rels prof, 1986-90; Gateway E Metrop Ministries, news anchor & news dir, 1990-98. **Orgs:** Batari Inst Youth; Youth-A-Flame.

### POWELL, DOC (WILLIAM POWELL)

Guitarist, composer. **Personal:** Born Spring Valley, NY. **Educ:** Univ Charleston. **Career:** Luther Vandross & Group, B B & Q Band, musical dir; Five Heartbeats, musical dir; Down & Out Beverly Hills, musical dir; Turner & Hooch; Goonies, Hero; Albums: Love Where It's At, 1987; Doctor, 1992; Inner City Blues, 1996; Laid Back, 1996; Don't Let Smooth Jazz Fool Ya, 1997; I Claim Victory, 1999; Life Changes, 2001; 97th & Columbus, 2003; Cool Like That, 2004; Doc Powell, 2006; For Old Times Sake, 2010; DPR Music Group Inc, owner, guitarist; Headsup Int; jazz label, owner. **Honors/Awds:** Grammy nominated, Best R & B Instrumental. **Business Addr:** Recording Artist, c/o Headsup Intl, 23309 Commerce Pk Rd, Cleveland, OH 44122, **Business Phone:** (216)765-7381.

### POWELL, DOROTHY A.

Educator. **Personal:** Born Temple, TX; daughter of Norman and Josephine Armstrong; married Allison B. **Educ:** Prairie View A & M Univ, BS, 1954, MA, 1963. **Career:** Educator (retired); Temple Independent Sch Dist, teacher, 1959-71, prin, 1971-95. **Orgs:** Tex State Teachers Asn; Nat Educ Asn, 1959-95; Phi Beta Kappa Sorority; Zeta Phi Beta Sorority; Rotary Int; Campfire Boys & Girls; Top Ladies Distinction; vpres, Tex Retired Teachers Asn. **Home Addr:** 901 S 38th St, Temple, TX 76501, **Home Phone:** (254)773-4950.

### POWELL, ELAINE

Basketball player. **Personal:** Born Aug 9, 1975, Monroe, LA; daughter of James and Merlene. **Educ:** Pearl River Community Col, attended 1995; La State Univ, attended 1997. **Career:** Basketball player (retired), basketball coach; Portland Power, guard, 1997-98; Orlando Miracle, 1999-2002; Women's Nat Basketball Asn, pt guard, 1999-2008; Detroit Shock, guard, 2002-05, 2006-08, free agt, 2008; Chicago Sky, 2006; Grambling State Univ, asst coach, 2008-12; Ohio Womens Basketball Prog, asst coach, 2012-. **Orgs:** Women's Basketball Coaches Asn. **Business Addr:** Assistant Coach, CBS Interactive Inc, 235 2nd St, San Francisco, CA 94105, **Business Phone:** (415)344-2000.

### POWELL, GAYLE LETT

Executive, teacher, business owner. **Personal:** Born Dec 18, 1943, Manhattan, NY; daughter of Robert A and Claire G. **Educ:** Cent Univ, BSE, 1966. **Career:** Newark Bd Educ, teacher, 1966-72; She Creations Inc, corp pres, 1969-80; Essex Col Bus, teacher, 1980-81; Fur Vault, fur sales, 1981-82; Antonovich Furs Inc, fur sales, 1982-84; Fur You Inc, Outside Fur Sales, corp off, 1984-; Fur Mart Inc, retail furs & serv mfr, chief exec officer, 1985-; Fur Mart Fur Store, E orange, owner. **Orgs:** Alpha Kappa Alpha Sorority; Master Furriers Guild; Am Bridge Asn; Nat Asn Female Exec; Fur Info Coun Am. **Home Addr:** 24 Tuers Pl, Upper Montclair, NJ 07043-2520, **Home Phone:** (973)744-1844. **Business Addr:** Chief Executive Officer, Fur Mart Inc, PO Box 43153, Upper Montclair, NJ 07043, **Business Phone:** (973)744-1844.

### POWELL, REV. DR. GRADY WILSON, SR.

Clergy. **Personal:** Born Aug 6, 1932, Brunswick County, VA; son of Herbert V and Lillie T; married Bertie M; children: Sandra Z, Dorthula H, Grady W Jr, Herbert C & Eric C. **Educ:** St Paul's Col, BS, 1954; Va Union Univ Sch Theol, MDiv, 1959. **Career:** Clergy (retired); Amity Baptist Church, pastor, 1953-58; Greensville Co Pub Schs, Emporia, Va, teacher, 1954-56; Quioccasin Baptist Church, pastor, 1958-61; Richmond Pub Schs, teacher, 1959-60; Gillfield Baptist Church, pastor, 1961-97, minister; Diversity Food's Processing, indust chaplain. **Orgs:** Treas & bd mem, C's Home Va Bapist Inc, 1959-70; secy, Va Coun Churches, gov bd, 1960-66; Petersburg Biracial Comn, 1961-62; bd mem, secy, State Bd Corrections, 1974-78; gov bd, Nat Coun Church Christ, 1979-; adv bd, Nations Bank, 1988-; adv bd, Energy Share, Va Power, 1989-; adv bd, United Way, 1989-; corp bd, WCVE-TV, 1990-; hosp authority, Southside Regional Med Ctr, 1991-; regional vice chmn, bd trustee, Va Hist Soc. **Honors/Awds:** Distinguished Service, Nat Asn Advan Colored People, 1961; Man of the Year, Omega Psi Phi Frat, 1963; Hon Degree, St Paul's Col, 1976; Presidential Citation, Nat Asn Equal Opportunity Higher Educ, 1979. **Home Addr:** 1824 W Princeton Rd, Petersburg, VA 23805-1115, **Home Phone:** (804)732-0875.

### POWELL, JUAN HERSCHEL (JUAN POWELL)

Manager, chief executive officer. **Personal:** Born Aug 11, 1960, Roanoke, VA; son of John Henry and Shirley Oliver; married Eugenia Toliver; children: Jamaal Khari. **Educ:** Howard Univ, BS, civil engineering, 1982; Univ Md, MBA, finance, 1988. **Career:** CECO Corp, construct engr, 1983-85; George Hyman Construct Co, proj engr, 1985-89, proj mgr, 1990-; Carr Am Develop Inc, vpres, sr proj mgr, 1994-2004; Neighborhood Develop Co, chief operating officer, prin, 2004-; Buildtech Construct Co, prin. **Orgs:** Am Soc Civil Engrs, 1979-; Alpha Phi Alpha Frat Inc, 1980-; Tau Beta Pi Nat Engineering Hon Soc, 1982-; Nat Black MBA Asn, 1986-; pres, George Hyman Chap, Toastmasters Inc, 1988; DC Contractors Asn, 1989; pres, Howard Univ Engineering Alumni Asn, 1989-92. **Honors/Awds:** Leadership Award, Am Soc Continuing Educ Howard Univ, 1982; Certificate of Appreciation, Alpha Phi Alpha Beta Chap, 1983. **Home Addr:** 515 Ingraham St NW, Washington, DC 20011, **Home Phone:** (202)291-7852. **Business Addr:** Chief Operating Officer, Principal, Neighborhood Development Co, 3232 Ga Ave Suite 100, Washington, DC 20010, **Business Phone:** (202)722-6002.

### POWELL, KEMPER O.

Banker. **Personal:** Born Chicago, IL. **Educ:** Univ Chicago, BS, econs, 1994. **Career:** Northern Trust Corp, securities custody adminr, internal vpres, 1993-. **Orgs:** Pres, Urban Financial Serv Coalition, Chicago Chap, 2000-; Alpha Phi Alpha Frat. **Home Addr:** 457 E 89th Pl, Chicago, IL 60619-6721, **Home Phone:** (773)487-0435. **Business Addr:** Internal Vice President, Northern Trust Corp, 50 S LaSalle St B2, Chicago, IL 60603, **Business Phone:** (312)630-6000.

### POWELL, KENNETH ALASANDRO

Management consultant. **Personal:** Born Nov 26, 1945, Mobile, AL; son of William O Sr and Myrtle E. **Educ:** Howard Univ, BS, math, 1967; Harvard Bus Sch, MBA, finance, 1974. **Career:** McKinsey & Co, assoc mgmt consult, 1974-77; Chase Manhattan Bank, second vpres, strategic mgmt, 1977-83; HSBC, Marine Midland Bank, vpres & mgr, mgt info sys, 1983-90; Powell Consult Corp, pres, strategy, mkt, real estate, fin, 1990-; Key Exec Servs, Right Mgt Consults, sr vpres, 2002-10, Career Mgt consult, currently; Hogan Assessment Systs Inc, hogan advan cert, 2012-; Harvard Univ, vpres bd mgr & chair nominating comt; G Burns & Assocs LLC, exec coach. **Orgs:** COGME Fel Coun Grad Mgmt Educ, Boston, 1972-74; Martin Luther King Fel Woodrow Wilson Found, 1972-74; pres, E 87 Tenants Corp, 1983-90; pres, Harvard Bus Sch Club NY, 1983-86, life bd mem, 1986-; bd mem, African-Am Alumni Asn, Harvard Bus Sch, 1983-88, pres, 1986; bd mem, Found Dance Prom, 1987-90; bd mem, Safe Horizon Victim Serv & Travelers Aid, 1989-03; Am Soc Training & Develop, 1988-90; trustee, New York Am Inst Banking, 1990; bd mem, Found Leadership Qual & Ethics Pract, 1991-94; bd chmn, Jobs Youth, 1995-2004, vice chmn, treas, 1991-95 & bd mem, 1991-2004; vpres, Inwood House, bd mem, chair investment comt, 1993-2004; adv bd, Harvard Bus Sch African Am Stud Union, 1995-97; pres, 245 Harvard Bus Sch African Am Alumni Asn, 1995-; life mem, bd mem & pres, Harvard Club NY, 2005, vpres bd mgr; past pres, Beta Chap, Alpha Phi Alpha Distinguished Mil Grad Campus Pals Sr Class Officer; past pres, Harvard Bus Sch Alumni Bd; dir, Harvard Bus Sch Club Greater New York Inc. **Honors/Awds:** Howard Univ Distinguished Alumnus, Nat Asn Educ Oppor, 1984; Bert King Service Award for Alumni Distinction, Harvard Bus Sch, 1997. **Home Addr:** 245 E 87th St Apt 11E, New York, NY 10128-3249, **Home Phone:** (212)289-3525. **Business Addr:** Career Management Consultant, Right Management, 1818 Market St 33rd Fl, Philadelphia, PA 19103.

**POWELL, LEJON DANTE. See POWELL, DANTE.**

### POWELL, MARVIN, JR.

**Personal:** Born Aug 30, 1955, Ft. Bragg, NC; married Kristen; children: Amerique & Beronique. **Educ:** Univ Southern Calif, BA, speech & polit sci, 1977. **Career:** Football player (retired); New York Jets, right tackle, 1977-85; Tampa Bay Buccaneers, tackle, 1986-87; New Orleans Saints, 1999. **Orgs:** Vpres, Nat Football League Players Asn; player rep, New York Jets, 1977-85, Tampa Bay Buccaneers, 1986-87. **Honors/Awds:** Most Valuable Player, 1979; Forrest Gregg Offensive Lineman of the Year, 1982. **Special Achievements:** Elected president of the players' union.

### POWELL, MICHAEL K.

Government official. **Personal:** Born Mar 23, 1963, Birmingham, AL; son of Colin and Alma; married Jane Knott; children: Jeffrey & Bryan. **Educ:** Col William & Mary, BA, 1985; Georgetown Univ Law Ctr, JD, 1993. **Career:** AUS, cav off, 1985-88; Dept Defense, asst to secy, policy advisor, 1988-90; US Ct Appeals, judicial clerk chief judge, 1993-94; O'Melveny & Myers LLP, assoc, 1994-96; Dept Justice, Antitrust Div, chief staff, 1996-97; Fed Communs Comn, comnr, 1997-, chmn, 2001-05; Nat Cable & Telecommunications Asn, pres & chief exec officer, 2011-. **Orgs:** Bd visitors, Col William & Mary & Georgetown Univ Law Ctr, 2002-09; Henry crown fel, Aspen Inst, 2005; bd visitors, rector, 2006. **Home Addr:** 7921 Bracksford Ct, Fairfax Station, VA 22039-3164. **Business Addr:** President, Chief Executive Officer, National Cable & Telecommunications Association, 25 Massachusetts Ave NW Suite 100, Washington, DC 20001-1413, **Business Phone:** (202)222-2300.

### POWELL, MIKE (MICHAEL ANTHONY POWELL)

Athlete, television sportscaster. **Personal:** Born Nov 10, 1963, Philadelphia, PA; son of Preston and Carolyn Carroll. **Educ:** Univ Calif, Irvine, BA, sociol, 1986. **Career:** Athlete (retired), television sportscaster; US Olympics, long jumper, Silver, 1988, 1992; World Championships Athletics, gold, 1991, 1993, Bronze, 1995; Olympics, competitor, 1996; Goodwill Games, competitor, 1998; Univ Calif, Los Angeles, coach; Yahoo Sports Olympic Track & Field coverage, analyst, currently; Acad Speed Rancho, long jump coach, currently-. **Orgs:** Alpha Phi Alpha. **Business Addr:** coach, Academy of Speed, 10339 Dorset St, Rancho Cucamonga, CA 91730, **Business Phone:** (855)267-7733.

### POWELL, DR. MYRTIS HALL

Educator. **Personal:** Born Feb 6, 1939, Evergreen, AL; daughter of Arthur Lee and Lula B Jones; married Lavatus; children: Kimberly Holmes, Robin, Judy Powell Olson & Lavatus III. **Educ:** Univ Cincinnati, AS, 1968, BS, 1969, MA, sociol, 1974, PhD, sociol & higher educ admin, 1978; Harvard Univ, cert higher educ mgt, 1975; Salzburg Sem Am Studies Salzburg Austria, cert, 1980. **Career:** Univ Cincinnati, adj asst prof, 1968-78, teacher asst, 1969-71, asst dean & lectr, 1971-73, assoc dean, adj & asst prof, 1973-78, United Black fac; Edna McConnell Clark Found, prog dir, 1979-81; Miami Univ Oxford Campus, exec asst to pres, adj & asst prof, vpres stud affairs, 1989-2002; Pub Welfare Found, vice chair, dir, 2002-13; Seven Hills Neighborhood Houses Inc; Col Nursing at Gen Hosp, UC Grad Nursing Prog, asst; Nat Network Runaway & Youth Servs Inc, Wash, UNIFI Mutual Holding Co, dir, currently; Ameritas Mutual Holding Co, dir, currently; Union Cent Mutual Holding Co, dir, currently; Greater Cincinnati Found, dir, currently; Union Cent Life Ins Co, dir, currently. **Orgs:** Bd mem, Leadership Cincinnati Alumni Asn; Mayerson Acad Human Resource Develop; Clin Ctr Women's Health Initiative; Nat Child Labor Comm, New York; Hamilton County Alcohol & Drug Addiction Serv; Univ Cincinnati, CLG Med, COT Geront Prog; dir, Pub Welfare Found; trustee, Bethesda Inc; pres & chief exec officer, Cincinnati Youth Collab, 2003. **Honors/Awds:** Alumni Achievement Award by Class, Univ Cincinnati, 1966, African American Alumni Asn, Sankofa Award for Excellence in Higher Educ, 1997; Asn Black Excellence Award, 1973, 1978; Leadership Education & Service Award, 1976, 1978; Cincinnati Urban League Guild Leadership Award, 1977; Nat Coun Urban League Guilds Leadership Award, 1978; Salute Outstanding Volunteer, 1978; COT Service Award, 1978; Cincinnati COT Chest & CNL Outstanding Leadership Award Allocations Div, 1979; Carver COT Ctr Leadership Award, Peoria Ill, 1981; New Hope Baptist Church Outstanding Black American Recognition Award, 1983;

Career Woman Achievement, YWCA, 1984, Black Achiever Award, 1991; Leadership Cincinnati Graduate Class VIII, 1984-85; Brotherhood Award, Nat CNF Christians & Jews, 1988; Woman Year Award, Cincinnati Enquirer, 1991; Beacon Light Award, Lighthouse Youth Services, 1996; Joseph A Hall Award, United Way & Community Chest, 1996; New Voices Award, Mallory Hist Asn, 1998; Woman Distinction Award, Great Rivers Girl Scout Coun, 1998; A.K.Morris Award, Miami Univ, 1999; Talbot House Community Service Award, 2005; Glorying the Lions Award, Urban League, 2005. **Special Achievements:** First African American to be an associate dean at the University of Cincinnati; First African American to hold an upper management position at Miami University; First African American to serve as a program officer at the Edna McConnell Clark Foundation in New York City. **Home Addr:** 8315 Crestdale Ct, Cincinnati, OH 45236, **Home Phone:** (513)793-9320. **Business Addr:** Director, Public Welfare Foundation, 1200 U St NW, Washington, DC 20009-4443, **Business Phone:** (202)965-1800.

### POWELL, PATRICIA
Educator, writer. **Personal:** Born May 4, 1966, Spanish Town; daughter of Philip and Winifred. **Educ:** Wellesley Col, BA, eng, 1988; Brown Univ, MFA, creative writing, 1991. **Career:** S Boston High Sch, lectr, 1987-88; Brown Univ, teaching asst, 1990-91; Univ Mass, Boston, lectr, 1990-91, creative writing asst prof, 1991-, eng dept, 1991; Harvard Univ, Briggs-Copeland Lectr Fiction, 1991; Mass Inst Technol, Martin Luther King Jr vis prof writing, 2003-; Hvv Univ, lectr fiction, 2001-; Novel: Me dying trial, 1993; Pagoda, 1998; A Small Gathering Bones, 2003; Fullness Everything, 2009. **Orgs:** Acad adv, Wellesley Col Acad Adv, 1987-88; peer adv, 1987-88, Carib beanlit course consult, 1991, Boston Pub Sch; African Writers Conf, 1991; Independent Black Filmmakers Ser, 1991; chmn Black Studies, Search Comn, 1992; MacDowell Fel, MacDowell Writers Colony, 1992. **Business Addr:** Martin Luther King Jr Visiting Professor of Writing, Massachusetts Institute of Technology, 77 massachusetts ave Rm 11-400, Cambridge, MA 02139-4307, **Business Phone:** (617)253-1000.

### POWELL, PAULA LIVERS
Historian, educator, administrator. **Personal:** Born Jul 3, 1955, Indianapolis, IN; daughter of Bellwood Livers and Mary Evans; children: Carmin & Camira. **Educ:** Fisk Univ, BA, hist minor educ, 1977; Butler Univ, Indianapolis, IN, MEd, 1987; Univ Calif-Santa Cruz, MA, African-Am hist, women's hist, Europ hist, 1989, PhD, 1991. **Career:** Ind Christian Leadership Conf, planning dir, 1977-80; Martin Luther King Ctr Social Chg, asst dir protocol, 1980-81; All state Ins Co, sales agt, 1981-83; Indianapolis Pub Schs, Grad Sch, teacher, 1983-87; UCSC-Graudate Div, GOP fel, 1987; Univ Calif, Santa Cruz, African-Am Resource & Cult Ctr, founding dean dir, 1988-2010; Black By Bay Inc, educ & cult Consults, founder & chief exec officer, 1997-; Cabrillo Col, adj prof African-Am hist, 2001-09; Solano Community Col, adj prof hist, 2001-; Generation "A" Educ Consult, pres/founder, 2005-; Grooming Greatness, pres & founder, 2011-. **Orgs:** Pres, Nat Asn Advan Colored People-Santa Cruz County Br, 1994-; grad advr, Alpha Kappa Alpha Sorority Inc, 1994; Links, Montery Bay Chap, Int Trends & Servs, 1995-; Jack & Jill Am Inc; Nat Forum Black Pub Admin, 1996-; Am Asn Univ Women, 1999-; Nat Alliance Black Sch Educrs, 1999-; Community Missionary Baptist Church; Progressive Missionary Baptist Church; SCLC Women, Inc, Nat Adv Bd, Asn Black Cult Ctrs; Nat Asn Stud Affairs Professionals; Asn Am Historians; Am Fedn Teachers; Stanford Parent Asn; Fisk Alumni Asn; Nat Trust Hist Preserv; Nat Crispus Attucks High Sch Alumni Asn; founder/publ, Indianapolis Soc Black Hist & Cult, 2010-. **Honors/Awds:** Student Affairs, Incentive Award, Thumbs Up Award, UCSC, 1995, 1996, 1997; Community Service Award, Alpha Kappa Alpha Sorority Inc, 1996; Vision Award, Univ Calif Berkeley Black Leadership Conf, 1997; Appreciation, The Links Inc, Monterey Bay, 1998; Living Historymakers Award, Turning Point Mag; NAACP Outstanding Leadership Award, 2009; Service Award, Martin Luther King, Jr. Convocation Comt, 2009; Outstanding Service Award, Delta Sigma Theta Sorority, Inc, 2010; Twenty Years of Dedicated Service Award, Univ Calif Off Pres. **Home Addr:** 4908 Bonnie Brae St, Indianapolis, IN 46228-3032, **Home Phone:** (317)251-1056. **Business Addr:** Founder, Publisher, The Indianapolis Society of Black History & Culture, PO Box 88412, Indianapolis, IN 46208, **Business Phone:** (317)432-4226.

### POWELL, RENEE
Golfer. **Personal:** Born May 4, 1946, East Canton, OH; daughter of William J and Marcella(deceased). **Educ:** Ohio Univ; Ohio State Univ; Univ St Andrews, LLD, 2008. **Career:** Ladies Prof Golf Asn Tour, prof golfer, 1967-80; golf instr Africa & Europe, 1980-88; Renee Powell Youth Golf Camp Cadre Prog, founder, 1996; First Tee Prog, develop & programming consult; LPGA Girls Golf Club, E Canton, OH, founder, 2000; Clearview Golf Club, E Canton, OH, head prof, 2010-, operator. **Orgs:** Hon mem, Exec Comn LPGA & Club Pro Div; Designated Pro Class A mem LPGA & PGA of Am; hon mem, Exec Comn of the LPGA. **Honors/Awds:** Budget Serv Award, 1999; First Lady of Golf Award, Prof Golfers' Asn, 2003; Rolex For the Love of the Game Award, 2007; Futures Tour Trainor Award, 2009; Ohio Golf Hall of Fame. **Special Achievements:** Second African American to play on the Ladies Professional Golf Association Tour, 1967; first African-American female Class A member of The PGA of America and the LPGA, 1995; appeared in 257 tournaments as a professional; part of first group of women given honorary membership to the Royal and Ancient Golf Club; One of only three African American women to ever play on the Ladies Professional Golf Association's Tour; First black golfer to play in the US Girls Junior Championship; One of the first professional golfers to travel to Vietnam during the war and staged five clinics per day for three weeks in war zones across Vietnam. **Business Addr:** Head Professional, Clearview Golf Club, 8410 Lincoln St SE, East Canton, OH 44730, **Business Phone:** (330)488-0404.

### POWELL, RICHARD MAURICE
Banker. **Personal:** Born Jan 8, 1951, Baltimore, MD; son of John J and Peggy A; married Debra S; children: Richard Jr, Hakim & Qiana. **Educ:** Temple Univ, Philadelphia, PA, BS, 1974. **Career:** First PA Bank, Philadelphia, PA, com loan officer, 1974-79; Crocker Nat Bank, San Diego, Calif, asst vpres, 1979-81; San Diego Trust & Savings Bank, San Diego, Calif, vpres & mgr, 1981-89; First Interstate Bank, San Diego, Calif, vpres, 1989-. **Orgs:** Treas, Southeast San Diego Rotary Club, 1981-87; Door Hope Salvation Army, 1981-83; Health care Fin Mgmt Asn, 1982-85; Lay Adv Comt, Mercy Hosp & Med Ctr, 1988-89. **Home Addr:** 6565 Farm Rd 1699, Avery, TX 75554-7270. **Business Addr:** Vice President, Corporate Banking, First Interstate Bank of California, 401 B St Suite 2201, San Diego, CA 92101, **Business Phone:** (619)699-3127.

### POWELL, ROBERT JOHN
Vice president (organization), executive. **Personal:** Born May 20, 1961, New York, NY; married Carlotta; children: Selene, Jonathan & Courtney. **Educ:** Fla State Univ, attended 1981; Univ Cent Fla, BA, orgn commun, 1990; Ill State Univ, MBA, bus admin, 2006. **Career:** Walt Disney World, prof musician, personnel rep, sr personnel rep, HRD rep, 1983-94; Carlson Companies, mgr employee rel, dir employee rel, vpres, human resources, 1994-99; Porex Corp, corp vpres, human resources, 1999-2000; AT&T Broadband, vpres, human resources, 2000-01; Archer Daniels Midland, vpres, HR Oper & Workforce Planning, 2001-07, vpres, HR, 2007-; Wesco Distrib Int, sr vpres human resources, vpres, human resources, 2007-10; RDP Mgt LLC, chief exec officer, currently; Ann & Robert H Lurie C's Hosp Chicago, chief human resources officer, 2011-12; Invictus Leadership Group, chief exec officer, 2012-; Vistage Int, leader chief exec officer, 2013-; C's Memorial Hosp, chief human resources officer; Sparks-Childrens Med Res Charity, vpres, pres. **Orgs:** Human resources adv bd, Am Heart Asn, 1997-; regional mem large, vpres, Kappa Kappa Psi; bd dir, Cochran Mill Nature Ctr; Corpsvets Sr Drum & Bugle corps, 2000-01; bd dir, Human Resources Wesco Distrib Int; bd dir, Human Resources Mgt Asn Chicago, 2011-14. **Honors/Awds:** Outstanding Young Man of America, 1984. **Home Addr:** 1401 Waterford Pl, Champaign, IL 61821. **Business Addr:** Chief Executive Officer, RDP Management LLC, 1597 Wash Pke, Bridgeville, PA 15017-2894, **Business Phone:** (412)200-2264.

### POWELL, WAYNE HUGH
Sales manager, financial manager. **Personal:** Born Jul 29, 1946, Petersburg, VA; son of Willie and Lena; married Leslie J; children: Farrah, Brandi & Kristin. **Educ:** Lincoln Univ, BS, bus admin, 1970; Rockhurst Col, MBA, fin, 1979. **Career:** Administrator (retired); Gen Mills, reg off mgr, 1975-79, reg credit mgr, 1980-81, financial analyst, mgr groupanal, 1981-82, Northern Calif Regional Sales Off, mgr admin, 1982-85; sales territory mgr. **Home Addr:** 8780 Banner Ridge Dr, Anaheim, CA 92808-1665, **Home Phone:** (714)281-2325.

### POWELL, WILLIAM. See POWELL, DOC.

### POWELL, DR. WILLIAM O., JR. (BILL POWELL)
Dentist, educator. **Personal:** Born Sep 19, 1934, Andalusia, AL; son of William O Sr and Myrtle Estelle; married Anna D Thompson; children: Rosalyn F & Michelle R. **Educ:** Talladega Col, AB, 1955; Howard Univ, Col Dent, DDS, 1967. **Career:** Ft Detrick, Dept Defense, histopath tech, 1958-61; Walter Reed Army, Med Ctr, res biologist, 1961-63; Mt Sinai Hosp, internship, 1968; Howard Univ, Col Dent, asst prof, 1968-69, dir, dent therapist training, 1969-75; pvt pract dentist, 1968-. **Orgs:** Omega Psi Phi Frat; Am Dent Asn; Nat Dent Asn; Md State Dent Asn; Southern Md Dent Soc; Robert T Freeman Dent Soc; Kiwanis Int; Montgomery County Md Drug Abuse Adv Coun; NNGA; Nomads Golf Asn; Pro Duffers Golf Club; Sigma-Pi Phi Frat; Rotary Int; Guardsmen DC; fel Am Col Dentists, 1989. **Home Addr:** 14803 Waterway Dr, Rockville, MD 20853-3616, **Home Phone:** (301)460-7880. **Business Addr:** Dentist, Private Practice, 809 Veirs Mill Rd Suite 213, Rockville, MD 20851-1632, **Business Phone:** (301)762-5575.

### POWELL, WILLIAM S., SR.
Dentist, air force officer. **Personal:** Born Mar 6, 1935, Greenville, MS; married Carolyn M. **Educ:** Xavier Univ, New Orleans, attended 1957; Meharry Med Col Sch Dent, attended 1963. **Career:** DDS Inc, Bakersfield, CA, pvt prac dent, 1965-. **Orgs:** Am Dent Asn; Calif Dent Asn; Kern Co Dent Soc; Am Endodontic Soc; Aca Gen Dent; Pierre Favehard Acad; Asn Mil Surg; Nat Dent Asn; Kern Co Dent Soc, treas, 1971, secy, 1972, pres, 1974; health & wellness adv, Kappa Alpha Psi Frat; Nat Asn Advan Colored People. **Home Addr:** 7212 Mesa Verde Way, Bakersfield, CA 93309-2334, **Home Phone:** (661)832-9155.

### POWELL, WILMA D.
Executive. **Personal:** married LeVon. **Educ:** Univ Redlands, BA, bus mgt, 1985. **Career:** Executive (retired); Long Beach Harbor Inc, Marine Exchange Los Angeles, pres, opers secy, pub rels specialist, asst dir pub rels, Chief Wharfinger, dir trade & maritime serv, 1967-2004; Port Long Beach, dir trade & maritime serv, 1967-2004. **Orgs:** City Long Beach Black Managers Asn; hon bd gov, Leadership Long Beach, currently; Long Beach YMCA; adv bd mem, Conserv Corps Long Beach, currently; bd dir, Long Beach Chamber Com. **Business Addr:** Honorary Board of Governor, Leadership Long Beach, 743 Atlantic Ave, Long Beach, CA 90813, **Business Phone:** (562)997-9194.

### POWELL-JACKSON, REV. DR. BERNICE
Administrator, president (organization), teacher. **Personal:** Born Mar 9, 1949, Washington, DC; daughter of Otis Fletcher and Bernice Fletcher; married Robert C S; married Franklin. **Educ:** Wilson Col, BA, 1971; Columbia Univ Grad Sch Jour, MS, 1975; Union Theol Sem, MDiv, 1991. **Career:** Administrator (retired); Wash, DC Sch Syst, teacher, 1971-72; Nat Coun Ch, Africa dept asst, 1972-74; Renewal Mag, asst managing ed, 1974-75; Nat Urban League, commun specialist, 1975-77; Equitable Life Assur Soc, assoc mgr pub rel, 1977-79; Women's Div Gov Off NY, spec asst pub info, 1979-; United Church Christ, exec assoc pres, 1989-93, exec dir, CMS Racial Justice, 1993-2000, exec minister, Justice & Witness Ministries, head; nat staff UCC; World Coun Churches, interim pastor, pres, N Am, 2004; United Church Christ Comn, exec dir; New Orleans UCC congregation, pastoral ministry, exec, currently. **Orgs:** Bd mem, Manhattan Br NY Urban League, 1978-80; chmn, Riverside Ch Video Proj, 1979-80; vpres, Coalition 100 Black Women, 1980-81; dir, Bishop Tutu Scholar Fund; pres, NY Coalition 100 Black Women, 1981-85; dir, Bishop Tutu Southern African Refugee Scholar Fund. **Honors/Awds:** Hon Doctorate Humane Letters, Defiance Col, 1994. **Business Addr:** Executive, New Orleans UCC Congregation, 700 Prospect Ave, Cleveland, OH 44115, **Business Phone:** (216)736-2100.

### POWERS, CLYDE JOSEPH
Football player, sports manager, football coach. **Personal:** Born Aug 19, 1951, Pascagoula, MS. **Educ:** Okla Univ. **Career:** Football player (retired), coach, director; New York Giants, strong safety, 1974-77; Kans City Chiefs, defensive back, 1978; Indianapolis Colts, asst coach, 1980-82, col scout, 1982-85, 1988-91, dir pro player personnel, 1985-87, 1992. **Orgs:** Bd dir, Kids Voice Ind, 2006-08. **Honors/Awds:** Coaches All Am "Ernie Davis" Award Winner. **Special Achievements:** Earned All-Big Eight Hons at cornerback as a Sr at Okla Univ. **Business Addr:** Director of Pro Player Personnel, Indianapolis Colts, 7001 W 56th St, Indianapolis, IN 46254, **Business Phone:** (317)297-2658.

### POWERS, GEORGIA M.
Government official. **Personal:** Born Oct 19, 1923, Springfield, KY; daughter of Frances Walker Montgomery and Ben Montgomery; married James L; children: Cheryl Campbell & Deborah Rattle; married Norman F Davis; children: William F Davis (deceased). **Educ:** Lou Munic Col, attended 1942. **Career:** Senator (retired); airplane fuselages, riveter; civil rights movement leader; KY State Senate, sen, 1967-88. **Orgs:** Jeff Co Dem Exec Comm, 1964-66; Cities Comm; YWCA; Nat Asn Advan Colored People; Urban League; Bd overseas Univ Louisville; bd dir, Fund Women Inc; Chmn, Senate Health & Welfare comm, 1970-76, Rules Comt, 1976-78, Labor & Indust comm, 1978-88; hon mem, Sigma Gamma Rho sorority, 1993. **Special Achievements:** First woman and First African American elected to the Kentucky Senate. **Home Addr:** 800 S 4th St Apt 2705, Louisville, KY 40203-2135, **Home Phone:** (502)568-2270.

### POWERS, LAURA WEIDMAN
Executive director, vice president (organization), entrepreneur. **Personal:** Born Jan 1, 1983?; daughter of Lila A Coleburn and John W Weidman; married Michael Powers, Sep 1, 2011?. **Educ:** Harvard Univ, AB, psychol & Span, 2004; Bucerius Law Sch, attended 2009; Stanford Univ Law Sch, JD, 2010; Stanford Univ Grad Sch Bus, MBA, 2010. **Career:** CityStep, dir, 2004-05; ARTiculate, web producer, 2005-06; Garden Transit, Portraits Hope, dir opers, 2006-07; Paul Hastings, summer assoc, 2008; Ogilvy & Mather, corp summer intern, 2008; Border Stylo, vpres prod develop, 2009-11; CODE2040, co-founder & chief exec officer, 2012-. **Orgs:** Yr Up Bay City, Leadership Coun; CityStep, Bd Co-chair, 2005-07; Fel, StartingBloc, 2006; Silicon Valley Launch Comt, Yr Up Bay Area, 2012-13; Exec Dir, CODE2040, 2012-. **Business Addr:** chief executive officer, executive director, CODE2040, 901 Mission St, San Francisco, CA 94103.

### POWERS, RAY (RAYMOND L POWERS)
Business owner, manager, executive. **Personal:** Born Mar 6, 1946, Topeka, KS; son of Margaret Clark; married Rheugena; children: Rachelle Spears & Brian C. **Educ:** Johnson County Community Col, AA, bus admin, 1980; Cent Mont State, BS, graphic arts tech mgmt, 1982; Baker Univ, MS, mgmt, 1996. **Career:** Hallmark Cards, sect mgr, 1967-77, litho engr, 1977-79, dept mgr, GA tech develop, 1979-87, corp safety, environ dir, 1987-89, prod mgr, 1989-92, plant mgr, KC Mfg Prod Facil, 1992-95, Graphic Arts/N Am Prod, vpres, creative officer, 1995-2000, opers vpres mfg, currently; Com Arts Enterprise Inc, owner, 1971-73. **Orgs:** Bd mem, Minority Supplier Coun; graphic arts adv bd, Cent Mont State Univ; bd chair, Minority Suppiler Coun, 2001. **Home Addr:** 10650 S Glenview Lane, Olathe, KS 66061-7452, **Home Phone:** (913)768-7574. **Business Addr:** Operations Vice President Graphics Arts/Directory Product Quality Execution, Hallmark Cards, 2501 McGee St, Kansas City, MO 64108, **Business Phone:** (816)274-5111.

### POWERS, DR. RUNAS, JR.
Physician. **Personal:** Born Dec 11, 1938, Jackson, AL; son of Runas Sr and Geneva; married Mary Alice; children: Tiffany, Trina & Runas III. **Educ:** Tenn State Univ, BS, 1961; Meharry Med Col, MD, 1966. **Career:** Mich State Univ, Hurley Med Ctr, Internship, 1966-67, resident, 1969-72; Stanford Univ, fel, 1972-74; Russell Med Ctr, pvt pract physician, currently. **Orgs:** Arthritis Found; Am Rheumatism Asn; Nat Med Asn; Am Fed Clin Res; Am Col Rheumat; AMA. **Honors/Awds:** Man of the Year, Alexander City, 1991. **Home Addr:** 2266 Hillabee Rd, PO Box 475, Alexander City, AL 35010, **Home Phone:** (256)329-8936. **Business Addr:** Physician, 3368 Hwy 280 Suite 108, Alexander City, AL 35010, **Business Phone:** (256)329-8417.

### PRATER, DR. OSCAR L.
School administrator, college president. **Personal:** Born Sylacauga, AL; married Jacqueline P; children: Lamar & Marcus. **Educ:** Talladega Col, BA, 1961; Hampton Univ, MA, 1967; Col William & Mary, MS, 1968, EdD, 1977. **Career:** Educator, college administrator (retired); Middlesex Co Pub Schs, math teacher, 1961-62; Wmsbg-James City Pub Schs, math teacher, 1962-72; Rappahanock Community Col, chmn div math, 1972-79, adminr & instr; Hampton Univ, vpres admin serv, 1979-90, prof mathematics; Ft Valley State Col, coun 1890 pres, chancellors chair & pres, 1990-2001; Talladega Col, pres, 2005-07. **Orgs:** Human Serv Bd; Hampton Roads Cult Action Comn; trustee & chmn, First Baptist Church, 1980-84; instnl rep, Am Coun Teacher Educ, 1980-; mgt consult, Human Admin Leadership Team, 1982-84; bd visitors, Va State Univ, 1982-. **Home Addr:** PO Box 2160 Rte 4, Ft Valley, GA 31030.

### PRATHER, SUSAN LOUISE
Educator, hospital administrator. **Personal:** Born Nov 15, 1959, Norfolk, VA; daughter of William L and Rebecca J. **Educ:** Norfolk State Univ, AS, 1982; Hampton Inst, BS, 1984; Hampton Univ, MS, advan adult nursing & educ, 1987; Grambling State Univ, EdD, attended 2015. **Career:** Eighteenth Field Hosp, USAR, Norfolk, Va, coordr code blue team, 1985-92, asst weight control officer, 1985-92, security clearance officer, 1986-92, head nurse, ICU, 1986-92, CV Mos-

by Co, item writer, 1989-92; Norfolk State Univ, asst prof, 1987-89, 1995; Nursing Educ Servs, dir, pres, 1990-10; Grambling State Univ, asst prof, 1992-94; Univ Fla, vis asst prof, 1997-98; Univ Guam, instr, 1998-2000; Publicity Club Chicago, co-pres, currently, Long Range Planning chair, pres, 2007-09. **Orgs:** Asn Black Nursing Fac Higher Educ, 1987; Sigma Theta Tau Soc, 1987; Am Med Detachment Regt, 1987; Tidewater Heart Asn, 1988; Va Cot Cols Asn, 1990; Nat Asn Female Execs; bd dir, Chicago Athletic Asn; Delta Iota Chap, Sigma Theta Tau Hon Nursing Soc. **Home Addr:** 824 W 27th St, Norfolk, VA 23517-1122, **Home Phone:** (757)616-0698. **Business Addr:** Long Range Planning Chair, Publicity Club of Chicago, 155 N Harbor Dr Suite 2212, Chicago, IL 60601, **Business Phone:** (312)861-0980.

## PRATT, A. MICHAEL

Lawyer. **Personal:** Born Apr 1, 1959, Grindstone, PA; son of Joan A Richardson and Brady; married Carla Denise; children: Jeanine, Payton & Christopher. **Educ:** Wash & Jefferson Col, BA, econs & eng, 1981; Univ Stockholm, Int Grad Sch, attended 1984; Harvard Law Sch, JD, 1985. **Career:** Hon Nathaniel R Jones, Sixth Circuit Ct Appeals, law clerk, 1985-86; City Philadelphia Law Dept, chief dep city solicitor, 1992-94; Pepper Hamilton LLP, atty & partner, 1986-92, 1994-; Honeywell Int Inc, chief litigation coun, 2002-03; Pa Turnpike Comnrs, comnr, currently. **Orgs:** Pres, Barrister Asn Phila, 1991-92; Philadelphia Bar Asn, Young Lawyers Sect, 1991; bd govs, Nat Bar Asn, 1992-; house deleg, Pa Bar Asn, 1993-, chancellor, 2008; Omega Psi Phi Fraternity; bd dir, City Philadelphia Activ Fund, 1995; Standing Comt Pro Bono & Pub Serv, Am Bar Asn, 1998-; Found Educ Excellence; Community Legal Serv Philadelphia; vchair, Pa Turnpike Comn; bd mem, trustee, Wash & Jefferson Col; Defender Asn Philadelphia; past mem, bd dir, Pa Legal Aid Network Inc; past chmn, bd trustee, Community Legal Serv Inc; Philadelphia; big bro Philadelphias local Big Bro Big Sister Asn; bd dir, African Am Mus Philadelphia; pres, Barristers Asn Philadelphia. **Honors/Awds:** Ten Fresh Faces for the 90's, Del Valley Counr, 1989; 40 Under 40 Business Award, Philadelphia Bus Jour, 1991; Nelson Mandela Service Award, Nat Black Law Students Asn, 1992; Equal Justice Award, Community Legal Serv Inc, 1993; Presidential Award, Nat Bar Asn, 1994; Recipient of a numerous honors and awards. **Special Achievements:** Co-authored numerous articles & publications. **Home Addr:** 6400 Woodbine Ave, Philadelphia, PA 19151-2405, **Home Phone:** (215)879-9587. **Business Addr:** Attorney, Partner, Pepper Hamilton LLP, 3000 Two Logan Sq 18th & Arch St, Philadelphia, PA 19103-2799, **Business Phone:** (215)981-4386.

## PRATT, ALEXANDER THOMAS

School administrator, educator. **Personal:** Born Sep 18, 1938, St. Martinville, LA; son of Louise Thompson and Oliver Thompson; married Mable Agnes Lee; children: Thomas & Thaddeus. **Educ:** Prairie View A&M Univ, BA, 1961, MA, 1963. **Career:** Prairie View A&M, asst circulation libr, 1962-63; La Marque Ind Sch, teacher & head hist dept, 1963-70; Col Mainland, instr, 1970-76, soc sci div, chmn, assoc acad dean, Dept Soc & Behavioral Sci, assoc prof, prof emer, currently. **Orgs:** Mayor, pro tem City La Marque, 1974-; Galveston Co Hist Comn, 1975-; Galveston Co Mayors Asn, 1979-80; Tex State Comt Urban Needs, 1980-; Phi Alpha Theta; Galveston Hist Found. **Honors/Awds:** HK "Griz" Eckert Award, Col Mainland, 1975; Jaycee of the Year, The La Marque Jaycee, 1975-76; Distinguished Service Award, La Marque Jaycee, 1978; Outstanding Community Service, Delta Sigma Theta, 1980. **Home Addr:** 2616 Lake Pk Dr, La Marque, TX 77568, **Home Phone:** (409)935-9569. **Business Addr:** Professor Emeritus, College Mainland, 1200 Amburn Rd, Texas City, TX 77591, **Business Phone:** (409)938-1211.

## PRATT, AWADAGIN

Pianist, educator, founder (originator). **Personal:** Born Mar 6, 1966, Pittsburgh, PA; son of Theodore and Mildred. **Educ:** Univ Ill, Urbana-Champaign, violin scholar; Peabody Conserv Music, piano & violin, conducting; Banff Ctr Arts, Can. **Career:** Albums incl: A Long Way From Norm, 1994; Beethoven Piano Sonatas, 1996; Live From SafricA, 1997; Transformations, 1999; Caveman's Valentine, 2002; Univ Cincinnati, Col-Conserv Music, chair piano, asst prof piano & artist-in-residence, 2004-; Cramer/Marder Artists, pianist, currently; Next Generation Festival, artistic dir, currently. **Orgs:** Founder, Pratt Music Found; Am Symphony Orchestra League. **Honors/Awds:** Performer's Certificate, Peabody Conserv Music; First prize, Naumburg Competition, NY, 1992; Prestigious Avery Fisher Career Grant, 1994; numerous others; 50 Leaders of Tomorrow, Ebony Mag. **Special Achievements:** Published numerous articles; First student in the school's history to receive diplomas in three performance areas, piano, violin and conducting; First African-American pianist to win the Naumburg International Piano Competition. **Home Addr:** 3610 Stardust Dr NE, Albuquerque, NM 87110, **Home Phone:** (505)766-9689. **Business Addr:** Professor of Piano, Artist-in-Residence, University of Cincinnati, Rm 442 Mary Emery Hall, Cincinnati, OH 45221-0003, **Business Phone:** (513)556-2063.

## PRATT, HON. JOAN M.

Government official. **Educ:** Hampton Univ, BS, acct, 1976; Univ Baltimore, MS, taxation, 1978. **Career:** City Baltimore, comptroller, 1995-, Bd Estimates, secy, currently; Coopers & Ly brand; Baltimore Legal Aid Bur, comptroller, 13 yrs; Joan M Pratt CPA & Assoc, pres, currently. **Orgs:** Trustee, Bethel AME Church; bd mem, Pk Reist Corridor Coalition; Walters Art Gallery, African Am Steering Comt; Baltimore Mus Art; AKA, Rho Xi Omega Chap; ex-officio bd trustee, City Baltimore. **Home Addr:** 112 E Northern Pkwy, Baltimore, MD 21212, **Home Phone:** (410)433-4421. **Business Addr:** Comptroller, City of Baltimore, Rm 204 City Hall 100 N Holliday St, Baltimore, MD 21202, **Business Phone:** (410)396-4755.

## PRATT, KYLA ALISSA

Actor. **Personal:** Born Sep 16, 1986, Los Angeles, CA; daughter of Johnny McCullar and Kecia Pratt-Mccullar; married Danny Kirkpatrick; children: Lyric Kai, Liyah & Kirkpatrick. **Educ:** Hamilton Acad Music. **Career:** Actor, 1995-; Films include: The Baby-Sitter's Club, 1995; Mad City, 1997; Riot, 1997; Barney's Great Adventure, 1998; Doctor Dolittle, 1998; Love & Basketball, 2000; One on One, 2000; Dr Dolittle 2, 2001; The Seat Filler, 2004; Fat Albert, 2004; The Proud Family Movie, 2005; Dr. Dolittle 3, 2006; Dr. Dolittle: Tail to the Chief, 2008; Hotel for Dogs, 2009; Dr Dolittle Million Dollar Mutts, 2009; I Can Do Bad All By Myself, 2009. TV series: "Barney & Friends", 1995; "The Parent' Hood", 1995-99; "In the House", 1996; "Sisters", 1996; "Smart Guy", 1997-98; "A Walton Easter", 1997; "Monday After the Miracle", 1998; Jackie's Back!, 1999; Moesha, 1999-2000; "Smart Guy", 1998; "Jackie's Back", 1999; "Strong Med", 2000; "The Proud Family", 2001-05; "Lizzie McGuire", 2001; "One on One", 2001-06; "Maniac Magee", 2003; The Picnic, 2005; The Beach, 2005; Hell on Earth, 2007; ER, 2009; "Let's Stay Together", 2012-; "Big Time Movie", 2012. Album: It's All About Me; A Dream Is A Wish Your Heart Makes. **Honors/Awds:** Nickelodeon Kids Choice Award, Favorite Rising Star, 1999. **Special Achievements:** Best Nominee for NAACP Image Awards, Young Artist Award & Blockbuster Entertainment Awards. **Business Addr:** Actress, ACME Talent & Literary, 4727 Wilshire Blvd Suite 333, Los Angeles, CA 90010, **Business Phone:** (323)954-2263.

## PRATT, MABLE

Government official, educator, teacher. **Personal:** Born May 27, 1943, Houston, TX; married Alexander T; children: Thomas & Thaddeus. **Educ:** Prairie View A&M Univ, BS, home econ educ, 1967; Univ Houston, MS, educ mgt, 1978; doctoral prog, 1985. **Career:** Galveston, second-grade teacher; Queen Peace Sch Lamarque, second teacher, 1969-70; Sacred Heart Sch Galveston, third grade teacher, 1970-71; Rosenberg Elem Galveston, fifth grade teacher, 1971-77; Rosenberg Elem Galveston, title I reading/math teacher, 1977-82; Alamo Elem Galveston, fifth grade teacher, 1982-; LaMarque Sch Dist, bd mem; McMasters Elem Sch, prin. **Orgs:** Asn Childhood Educ; Tex Classroom Assoc; Tex Prof Educ; Alpha Kappa Alpha Sorority; Am Bus Women's Asn; Am Sch Bd Assoc; Gulf Coast Area Asn Sch Bds; Lamarque Gifted & Talented, Sch Home Adv Panel Educ; dir, LaMarque Youth Aid Proj, United Way Mainland; LaMarque Sch Bd; Queen Peace Instr, Interior Decorating COM; LaMarque Parent Teachers Asn; Helped to organize Non-Graded Reading Prog, GISD; Teacher Adv Coun; Policy Rev Comn, Pres & several other offs ACE, state vpres, Asn Childhood Educ; hospitality chmn, Rosenberg; served Admin, Designee, ARD Meetings. **Honors/Awds:** Jaycee-ette of the Year, 1974 & 1975; Tex Hon Life Mem, Jaycee-ettes, 1978; Texas Hon Life Mem, PTA, 1980; Service Above Self-Rotary International Award, 1978; Outstanding Young Woman of America, 1979. **Special Achievements:** Attended many seminars on HB 246, HB 72, Chap 75. **Home Addr:** 2616 Lake Park Dr, LaMarque, TX 77568-3725, **Home Phone:** (409)935-9569. **Business Addr:** Principal, McMasters Elementary School, 1011 Bennett Dr, Pasadena, TX 77503, **Business Phone:** (713)740-0640.

## PRATT, MARVIN E.

Politician, mayor. **Personal:** Born May 26, 1944, TX; son of Joyce; married Dianne Sherrill; children: Michael & Andrea Ellzey. **Educ:** Marquette Univ, attended 1972. **Career:** Milwaukee Common Coun, 1968-87, chmn, 1996-2000, pres, 2000, 2004, actg mayor, 2004, interim, 2011. **Special Achievements:** First person to serve as both Milwaukee Mayor and Milwaukee County Executive. **Home Addr:** 4045 N 16th St, Milwaukee, WI 53209-6912, **Home Phone:** (414)264-0644.

## PRATT, DR. RUTH JONES K.

Educator. **Personal:** Born Aug 2, 1923, Baltimore, MD; married James; children: Karl & Noreen. **Educ:** Frederick Douglass High Sch, Baltimore, MD, dipl, 1939; Coppin State Teachers Col, BS, 1943; Howard Univ, Wash, DC, MA, 1948; Univ Md, DEd, 1985. **Career:** Educator (retired); teacher, 1943; demo teacher, 1945-49; supr teacher, 1952-55; sr teacher master teacher, 1959-61; curric specialist elem sch, 1961-63; asst prin elem sch, 1963-68; elem prin, 1968-75; Towson State Univ, consult, 1968-70; cosmetics consult, wig stylist, 1968-77; Reading Workshops, consult, 1968-71; Morgan State Univ, asst prof reading develop & educ psychol, 1969-73, admin asst community rels off supt, assoc prof; Catonsville Community Col, instr; Youth Summer Human Rels Workshop Nat Conf Christians & Jews, 1969-70; Baltimore City Pub Sch, chief educ officer, Off Supt; admin asst community rels; Coppin State Univ, adj prof; Community Col Baltimore County, Instr. **Orgs:** Exec, com dir search talent, 1969-76; chmn, 85th Anniv Sharon, 1970; pres, Prof United Serv Cherry Hill Comn, 1970-75; Comn, Leaders Am, 1971; chmn, Miss United Negro Col Fund Contest, 1972-76; vpres, Provident Hosp Aux, 1974-75; pres, Baltimore Aluminae Chap Delta Sigma Theta Sor, 1974-76; chmn, United Fund CICHA Campaign Baltimore City Pub Schs, 1975-77; allocation panel United Fund, 1976-77; bd dir, United Way, 1976-79; chmn, Baltimore Employ Adv Com, 1976-77; long range planning comn, Girl Scouts Cent, Md, 1976-79; Mayor's Bicent Ball Comn, 1976; Afro Am Expo Steering Com, 1976-77; bd dir, YWCA Cent Md, 1977; comn, Preserv Orchard St Ch, 1977; Sharon Bapt Ch; organ dir, Sunday Sch Choir; chmn, Ann Mus Scholar Benefit; Nat Coun Negro Women Inc. **Special Achievements:** First African-American assistant administrator, as well as the first African-American principal, of a predominantly-white elementary school. **Home Addr:** 4208 Oakford Ave, Baltimore, MD 21215-4834, **Home Phone:** (410)542-8793.

## PRELOW, ARLEIGH

Movie director, writer, graphic artist. **Personal:** Born Feb 1, 1953, Los Angeles, CA; daughter of Leona Kern and Clifford Nathaniel; children: Alison Guillory & Kara Guillory. **Educ:** Univ Calif, Berkeley, BA, 1974; Laney Col, Oakland, CA, 1986; Univ Calif, Los Angeles, 1989. **Career:** Black Thoughts Newspaper, feature ed & writer, 1973-74; Portland Observer, writer, 1975; KQIV-Radio, Portland, OR, prog producer, host, writer, & spot announcer, 1975; KPIX-TV, San Francisco, CA, segment producer & writer, researcher, prod asst & secy, 1975-77; WTBS-TV, Atlanta, GA, producer, writer, researcher & on-air dir, 1977-78; WSB-TV, Atlanta, segment writer & researcher, 1977; Inspirit Commun, founder; WETA-TV, Wash, DC, assoc producer, 1978-80; Scott Hall Prod, San Anselmo, CA, adminr, 1980-81; Moti-Vision, Richmond, CA, exec dir & producer, 1981-84; Arleigh Prelow Design, Los Angeles, owner & graphic designer, 1984-90; ROJA Prod, Boston, MA, filmmaker & adminr, 1990-93; Inspirits Commun, founder, dir, writer, producer, 1993-; Howard Thurman Family; freelance writer, Boston, MA; DoubleTake Summer Doc Inst, teaching fel. **Orgs:** Writer, Soul Newsmagazine, 1978; secy & mem, Nat Asn Negro Bus & Prof Women's Clubs, 1986-89; Worship 89 Conf Planning Comm, Synod Southern Calif & Hawaii Presby Church USA, 1988-89; treas & mem, Presby Women, Redeemer Presby Church, Los Angeles, 1988-. **Honors/Awds:** Acad TV Arts & Sci, Atlanta, 1978; Cappy Awards, Calif Pub Info Officers Asn, 1988; Howard Thurman Award; regional Emmy award winner; Mercury Awards, Gold Winner Mag Design Int, 1988; City Hall Digest Awards, Ggrand Prize, Best Publ, US & Canada, 1988. **Special Achievements:** We're Power Together, a video documentary exploring the Committee for Boston Public Housing's impact on the lives of Boston's public housing residents, Men of Vision for the Boston Museum of Afro American History, and two segments of Simon and Schuster's interactive videodisc on Harriet Tubman for eighth grade classrooms; author: Howard Thurman: Spirit of the Movement for the Museum of the African Diaspora. **Home Addr:** 65 Dartmouth St, Belmont, MA 02478, **Home Phone:** (617)489-9956. **Business Addr:** Founder, Director, Inspirit Communications, 2342 Shattuck Ave Suite 203, Berkeley, CA 94704, **Business Phone:** (510)305-1148.

## PRESLEY, DR. OSCAR GLEN

Veterinarian. **Personal:** Born Dec 19, 1942, Kosciusko, MS; married Ethel Rita Scott; children: Wanda, Glen Jr & Corey. **Educ:** Rust Col, BS, 1966; Tex Southern Univ, MS, 1971; Tuskegee Inst, DVM, 1974. **Career:** Meridian Pub Sch, teacher, 1967-69, dir independent study, 1968-69; Tuskegee Sch Vet Med Freshman Class, pres, 1969-70; Lexington Animal Clin, pres; Hanging Moss vet Clin, vet, currently. **Orgs:** Bd mem, Jackson Chap Nat Bus League, 1977-; bd mem, K & S Chem, 1979-; bd mem, New Hope Church, 1980-84; vpres, Miss Vet Med Asn, 1983; Nat chmn Fund Raising Rust Col, 1983; Phi Beta Sigma, 1985. **Honors/Awds:** Outstanding Young Man of America, 1972; Outstanding Service Award, Jackson State Univ Minority Stud, 1985, 1986. **Home Addr:** 571 Woodson Dr, Jackson, MS 39206. **Business Addr:** Veterinarian, Hanging Moss Veterinary Clinic, 1250 Forest Ave, Jackson, MS 39206-3219, **Business Phone:** (601)362-1147.

## PRESSEY, REV. DR. JUNIUS BATTEN, JR.

Real estate agent, executive. **Personal:** Born Apr 6, 1947, Hampton, VA; son of Junius Sr (deceased); married Elaine F Jenkins. **Educ:** Cent State Univ, bus admin, 1972; Ind Univ, BS, bus, 1975; Col Financial Planning; Lake Charles Bible Col, doctor ministry, 2004. **Career:** Magnavox Corp, acct, 1972-73; City Utility Ft Wayne, Ind, acct trainee, 1974; Nat Life & Acct Ins Co, life ins agt, 1975-76; Metrop Life Ins Co, sales rep, 1976-79; Lincoln Nat Sales Corp, tax deferred prog mgr, 1979-; Lincoln Nat Life Employee Benefits Div, pensions mkt, 1984-86; Pressey Financial Planning Group Inc, pres, chmn, Commun consult, currently; BreadFromHeaven Int Ministries, Sch Trust, lect, teacher, writer & pres, currently; RealtyFlex, realtors, currently; Ft Wayne Community Schs, admin assistance. **Orgs:** Bd mem, Ft Wayne Opportunity Indust Ctr Inc, 1975-; Ft Wayne Nat Life Underwriters Asn, 1976-, Ind Life Ins Leaders Club; bus consult, Proj Bus Jr Achievement, 1978; bd mem, Ft Wayne Sickle Cell Found, 1978-; pres, Nat Asn Advan Colored People, Ft Wayne, 1978-; chmn, Econ Task Force Ft Wayne Future Inc C C, 1978-79; chmn, Ft Wayne Affirmative Action Adv Coun, 1980-86; Harvest Food Bank, 1983-87; chmn, Ft Wayne NBE & WBE Coun, 1984-86; Ft Wayne Anti-Apartheid Action Comn, 1985; pres, Ft Wayne & Allen City Martin Luther King Jr Mem Inc, 1985-87; bd mem, Ft Wayne Bus Coun, 1986; Int Fin Planners Asn, 1986; Ind Healthy Marriage & Family Coalition; treas, Bd dir, Healthy Marriages Allen County. **Home Addr:** 6005 Sawmill Woods Dr, Ft Wayne, IN 46835, **Home Phone:** (260)918-3411. **Business Addr:** Realtor, RealtyFlex Of NE Indiana LLC, 6315-C Mutual Dr, Ft Wayne, IN 46825, **Business Phone:** (260)471-3539.

## PRESSEY, PAUL MATTHEW

Basketball coach, basketball player. **Personal:** Born Dec 24, 1958, Richmond, VA; married Elizabeth; children: Angela, Phillip, Ashley & Matthew. **Educ:** Univ Tulsa, BS, phys educ, 1982. **Career:** Basketball player (retired), basketball coach; Milwaukee Bucks, 1982-90; San Antonio Spurs, player, 1990-92, coach, 1994-2000; Golden State Warriors, player, 1992-93, asst coach, 1992-94; Orlando Magic, asst coach, 2000-04; Boston Celtics, asst coach, 2004-06; New Orleans Hornets, asst coach, 2007-10; Cleveland Cavaliers, asst coach, 2010-13; Los Angeles Lakers, asst coach, 2014-. **Business Addr:** Assistant Coach, Los Angeles Lakers, 555 N Nash St, El Segundo, CA 90245, **Business Phone:** (310)426-6000.

## PRESSLEY, CONDACE L.

Journalist. **Personal:** Born Jan 1, 1964, Marietta, GA. **Educ:** Univ Ga, ABJ, broadcast jour, 1986. **Career:** Clarke Broadcasting WGAU-WNGC, news anchor, 1983-85; Univ Ga, resident asst, 1983-85; WRFC-AM, news reporter & news anchor, 1985-86; Lockheed Martin, intern & pub rels, 1986; Meredith Corp & Ga Radio News Serv, bd operator & news anchor, 1986; WSB Radio, anchor & reporter, 1986-87, news assignment ed, 1987-92, managing ed, 1992-94; asst news dir, 1994-99, asst prog dir, 1999-. **Orgs:** Atlanta Asn Black Journalists, 1986-, pres, 1992-95; Nat Asn Black Journalists, 1987-, Region IV, regional dir, 1995-99, vpres broadcast, 1999-01, pres, currently; UNITY: Journalists Color, treas, 2003-; bd dirs & regional dir, RTNDA, 2003. **Honors/Awds:** One of Ten Outstanding People in Atlanta, Outstanding Atlanta, 1994; Murrow Award, RTNDA; Outstanding Young Alumnus, Univ Ga; Radio News Woman of the Year, Am Women Radio & Television. **Business Addr:** Assistant Program Director, WSB Radio, 1601 W Peachtree St, Atlanta, GA 30309, **Business Phone:** (404)897-6297.

## PRESSLEY, DELORES

Manager, consultant, founder (originator). **Educ:** Univ Akron, BA, educ, 1978. **Career:** Motivational speaker, trainer, consult; B Successful, pres, currently; Dimensions Plus Model Agency, founder & dir, currently; WHBC, Mid Radio Show, co-host; Plus USA, pres, 1980-2006; B Successful Inst, confidence expert & keynote speaker, 1998; Procter & Gamble, consult & speaker, 2006; Walsh Univ, supvr, 2007-09; DeLores Pressley Worldwide, founder, chief exec officer, pres & motivational speaker, 2008-; BizTV Shows, Talk Show, host, 2015-. **Orgs:** Pres Ohio, Nat Speakers Asn; vpres, Asn Better Community Develop, currently; founder, Plus USA Woman Beauty Pageant & Conv; spokesperson, Humanitarian Hands Charities, 2010; founder, UP Woman Nation, 2012-; Nat Educ Asn; vpres, ABCD Inc; O'Jays Entertainers Scholar Comt. **Honors/Awds:** Outstanding Community

Service Award, Univ Akron; Successful Business Women & Leadership Award, Women's Leadership Caucus; Successful Entrepreneur, Madelyne Blunt Found; Hall of Fame, YWCA's Stark County Women's; Hall of Fame, Women Color Found's. **Special Achievements:** Top Ten Ohio Women Business Owners by the National Association of Women Business Owners (NAWBO) & Key Bank Corporation; ATHENA Finalist sponsored by Inside Business Magazine. Author, Clean Out the Closets of Your Life, Advanced Revelations to Modeling and Believe in the Power of You, 2002; co-author, Oh Yes You Can!, 2010. host of the "DeLores Pressley Show", a success and inspirational show, heard on Joy 1520 am radio and a television host of The BornSuccessful Show. **Business Addr:** Director, Founder, Dimensions Plus, 551 36th St NW, Canton, OH 44711, **Business Phone:** (330)649-9809.

**PRESSON, RONALD TYSON. See TYSON, RON.**

**PRESTAGE, DR. JAMES JORDAN**
Educator. **Personal:** Born Apr 29, 1926, Deweyville, TX; son of James and Mona Wilkins; married Jewel Limar; children: Terri White, James Grady, Eric Warren, Karen Washington & Jay Wilkins. **Educ:** Southern Univ, Baton Rouge, BS, biol, 1950; Univ Iowa, MS, zool, 1955, PhD, zool, 1959. **Career:** Educator (retired); Prairie View A&M Univ, Prairie View, instr, biol, 1955-56; Southern Univ, Baton Rouge, from asst prof to assoc prof, biol, 1959-68, dir comput ctr, chair, comput sci, 1968-73; La Coord Coun Higher Educ, asst dir, 1972-73; Southern Univ, Baton Rouge, LA, dean acad affairs, 1973, vpres, 1973-82, chancellor, 1982-85; Dillard Univ, distinguished prof biol, 1987-97, chair, div Nat Sci, 1991-97. **Orgs:** Vpres, Conf LA Cols & Univ, 1974-75; comn scholars, State Ill Bd Higher Educ; pres, Beta Iota Lambda Chap, Alpha Phi Alpha Fraternity, 1975; exec bd, Istrouma Coun, Boy Scouts Am; bd trustee, Am Col Testing, 1983-88. **Home Addr:** 2145 77th Ave, Baton Rouge, LA 70807, **Home Phone:** (225)355-4035.

**PRESTON, EDWARD MICHAEL**
Columnist, journalist. **Personal:** Born Mar 7, 1959, Baltimore, MD; son of James Sr and Grace; married Patricia Ann Mack; children: Eboni & Marcellus. **Educ:** Towson Univ, BA, mass commun, 1981. **Career:** News Am, agate clerk, 1978-79; Baltimore Sun, agate clerk, 1982-87, soccer writer, 1987-88, Col football writer, 1988-93, feature writer, 1993-96, Ravens beat writer, 1996-2000, sports columnist, 2000-; Boys Varsity Lacrosse, coach. **Orgs:** Asst dir, Sports Ministy, Westminster, MD, 2000-; bd selector, Nat Football League Hall Fame, 2001-; Md Youth Lacrosse Asn. **Home Addr:** 1131 Western Chapel Rd, New Windsor, MD 21776-8817, **Home Phone:** (410)876-3055. **Business Addr:** Sports Columnist, Baltimore Sun, 501 N Calvert St, Baltimore, MD 21278, **Business Phone:** (410)332-6000.

**PRESTON, EUGENE T.**
Executive. **Personal:** Born Jan 10, 1952, Zanesville, OH; married Karen Y Booker. **Educ:** Cent State Univ, attended 1971; Franklin Univ, BS, bus mgt; Eastern Union Bible Col; Ashland Theol Sem, MA. **Career:** Perry Community Drug Abuse Coun, pres, 1973-80; Rendville, mayor, 1975-80; Rendville Housing Auth, vpres, 1976-80; Perry Community Planning Comn, chmn, 1976-80; Arvin Systs Inc, asst serv mgr; Am Elec Power, contract dir, currently. **Orgs:** Committeeman, Dem Cent, 1971-79; Rendville Village Coun, 1973-75; exec dir, Perry Community Planning Comn, 1976-78; deacon, New Salem Baptist Church; past pres, Ohio Bapt Gen Conf Laymens Aux, 1978-82; pres, Lancaster-Fairfield Co Nat Asn Advan Colored People, 1980-84; former vpres, Providence Baptist Asn, BTU; former treas, Providence Baptist Asn Laymen's Aux; fel N Am Baptist Men; spec proj comn, Nat Baptist Conv USA Laymens Aux; Omega Psi Phi Fraternity. **Special Achievements:** Listed in Nat Jaycee's Outstanding Young Men of America, 1983. **Home Addr:** 348 Kendall Pl, Columbus, OH 43205-2017, **Home Phone:** (614)253-7773.

**PRESTON, FRANKLIN DEJUANETTE**
Automotive executive. **Personal:** Born Nov 28, 1947, Kansas City, KS; son of Vivian A Wilson and Beryl L Sr; married Alpha Theresa Johnson; children: Kameron DeJon, Ashley Terese & Christopher Franklin. **Educ:** Gen Motors Inst, BS, mech engineering, 1970; Univ Mo, indust eng prog, 1977; Univ Mo, MS, indust engineering, 1980; Gen Motors Inst Engineering & Mgt Inst, MS, mfg mgt, 1991; Kettering Univ, MS, opers mgt, 2000, MS, mfg mgt, 2001. **Career:** Exective (retired); Gen Motors, Assembly Div, Fairfax, engr & supvr, 1970-76, hq sr proj engr, 1977-79, Doraville, qual control supt, 1979, Fisher Body Div, div & plant engr, 1982-85, BOC, FAD, facil engr & dir, 1985-92, CLCD, mfg tech staff & mgr, 1992-94, N Am Opers Metal Fabricating Div, Pontiac Site Oper, mgr, dir, 2003-07; DJ Franklin Consult, pres & chief managing officer, currently; Univ Phoenix, Instr/facilitator, 2010-. **Orgs:** Chair & men's fel, Trinity Baptist Church, 1977-; Oakland County Chap, Jack & Jill Am, 1978-; sunday sch teacher, Trinity Baptist Church, 1983-; bd deacons & secy, Trinity Baptist Church, 1985-89; Adv Bd, ASPIRE, 1986-88; vice chmn, Trinity Baptist Church, 1989-; bd dir, Metro Housing Partnership Flint & Genesse Co, 1992-95; bd dir, Kettering Univ, currently. **Home Addr:** 1647 Caliper Dr, Troy, MI 48084-1407, **Home Phone:** (248)649-3129. **Business Addr:** President, Chief Managing Officer, DJ Franklin Consulting, PO Box 985, Troy, MI 48099-0985, **Business Phone:** (866)406-6057.

**PRESTON, GEORGE NELSON (OSAFUHIN KWAKU NKONYANSA)**
Educator. **Personal:** Born Dec 14, 1938, New York, NY; married Adele Regina; children: Matthew, Afua-Magdalena & John. **Educ:** City Col NY, BA, 1962; Columbia Univ, MA, 1967, PhD, art hist & archeology, 1973. **Career:** Rutgers Univ, asst prof art & art hist, 1970-73; Livingston Col, Dept Art, fac; City Univ, City Col, Dept Art & Hist, from asst prof art to prof, 1973-2006, prof emer; Mus Art & Origins / Moaao, co-founding dir & chief cur, 2005-. **Orgs:** Spec consult, Ny Community Arts, 1967-68; spec consult, New World Cultures, Brooklyn Mus, 1968; foreign area fel, Joint Comt Am Coun Learned Soc & Soc Sci Res Coun, 1968-70, 1972; assoc, Columbia Univ Sem Primitive & Precolumbian Art, 1973-80; bd dir, Bd Adult Educ, Mus African Art, Wash, DC, 1972-80; Roger Morris-Jumel Hist Soc, 1973-80; bd dir, Cinque Gallery, New York, NY, 1977-79. **Home Addr:** 7 Sylvan Terr, New York, NY 10032. **Business Addr:** Co-Founding Director, Chief Curator, Museum of Art and Origins, 430 W 162nd St, New York, NY 10032, **Business Phone:** (212)740-2001.

**PRESTON, JOSEPH, JR.**
State government official. **Personal:** Born May 28, 1947, New Kensington, PA; son of Joseph and Therese Mae Buckner; married Odelfa Smith; children: Joseph III & Diana. **Educ:** Univ Pittsburgh, BA, polit sci & psychol, 1979. **Career:** Pa House Rep, 24th Legis Dist, rep, 1983-2013. **Orgs:** Bd mem, Homewood Revit Develop Corp; bd mem, Allegheny Acad; Pittsburgh Water & Sewer Authority; Nat Orgn Women; Nat Conf Black State Legis; Nat Asn Advan Colored People; Pittsburgh River Life Task Force; trustee, Temple Baptist Church; E Liberty Chamber Com. **Home Addr:** 208 N Highland Ave, Pittsburgh, PA 15206, **Home Phone:** (412)361-3692. **Business Addr:** Legislator, Pennsylvania House of Representatives, 332A Irvis Off Bldg, Harrisburg, PA 17120-2024, **Business Phone:** (717)783-1017.

**PRESTON, RODENA MARIE. See PRESTON-WILLIAMS, DR. RODENA.**

**PRESTON, ROELL**
Football player. **Personal:** Born Jun 23, 1972, Miami, FL. **Educ:** Univ Miss, grad. **Career:** Football player(retired); Atlanta Falcons, kick returner, 1995, wide receiver, 1996; Wash Redskins, 1997; Green Bay Packers, 1997, kick returner, punt returner, 1998; Tenn Titans, 1999; Miami Dolphins, 1999; San Francisco 49ers, wide receiver, 1999; Chicago Enforcers, Sask Roughriders, 2001; Xtreme Football League, wide receiver, 2001. **Honors/Awds:** Pro Bowl (x1), 1998; All-Pro, 1998. **Home Addr:** 2001 NW 67th St Apt 105, Miami, FL 33147.

**PRESTON, DR. SWANEE H. T., JR.**
Physician. **Personal:** Born Mar 10, 1924, Dallas, TX; son of Swanee and Beulah M Williams; married Hazel Elizabeth Bjorge; children: Dorrlyn Jean, Tyrone Hudson & Wayne Raynard. **Educ:** Wiley Col Marshall, Tx, BS, 1943; Great Lakes Col, OH, MM, 1948, DM, 1952; Am T Univ Arcade Mo, NDak, 1953; Univ Cincinnati, Conn. **Career:** Physician (retired); pvt pract, 1952; Hair Weev Inc, adv, 1957-72; City Cleveland, EMT para medic, 1973-79; Oper Newstart, soc worker, drug coun spt, 1976-80; Salvation Army, supvr stores, 1980-83; Dept Intimate Serv, actg unit dir soc serv, 1982-92. **Orgs:** Vpres, NY Naturapathic Soc; founder, Phys Med Soc; Am Technol Asn; First Aid & Emergency Care; Am Red Cross; CPR, Am Heart Asn; bd, YMCA; Nat Hole One Asn; USGA; PGA; ordained elder, Presbyteria USA; N Lake Presbyterian Church; leader, Extended Holy Communion Table Ministry; asst teacher, Bible group; choir mem, small group leader. **Honors/Awds:** Aus Man of the Year, Hair Inc, 1964; Busn Man Day Radio Sta WDOK; Myr Coun City Cleve Carl Stokes Mayor; La soc Int Who's Who; International Man of the Year, Twentieth Century Award for Achievement, IBC, 1999-2000. **Home Addr:** 9378 SE 174 Loop, Summerfield, FL 34491, **Home Phone:** (352)347-1370.

**PRESTON-WILLIAMS, DR. RODENA (RODENA MARIE PRESTON)**
Musician, business owner. **Personal:** Born Apr 7, 1938, Houston, TX; daughter of George and Robbie; children: Deborah Del Cambre, Henry Sloan Jr, Renee Hence & Regina McDuel. **Career:** La Unified Sch Dist, admin asst, 1980-00; Preston Music Group, owner & musician, currently; Gospel Music Workshop Am, music dir, min music, 1999-. Album: Look Where God Has Brought Us, 1977. **Orgs:** Choir coordr, McDonald's Gospel fest, 1996-00; dir music/pianist, Brookins AME Ch, 1999-; bd mem, performance div chair, Gospel Music Workshop; chap rep, Los Angeles Chap, bd dir, vice chair, mass choir, Gospel Music Workshop Am; Conv's Minister Music. **Home Addr:** PO Box 56167, Los Angeles, CA 90056, **Home Phone:** (323)937-7102. **Business Addr:** Board of Director, Gospel Music Workshop of America Inc, 3908 W Warren, Detroit, MI 48208, **Business Phone:** (313)898-6900.

**PRESTWIDGE-BELLINGER, BARBARA ELIZABETH**
Banker, vice president (organization). **Personal:** Born Dec 5, 1945, Baltimore, MD; daughter of Algernon A and Gladys Thompson (deceased); married George M; children: Monique A Jackson & Melanie K Jackson. **Educ:** Howard Univ, BA, 1967; Southern Conn State Univ, MS, educ, 1972; Conn Sch Broadcasting, grad, 1979. **Career:** Essex Co Col, adj instr, 1972-77; S End Community Day Care Ctr, exec dir, 1972-74; Kean Col, adj instr, 1974-77; Farleigh Dickinson Univ, adj instr, 1975-77; Messiah Luthern Day Care Ctr, dir, 1976-77; Child Care Gtr Bpt, exec dir 1977-78; Sacred Heart Univ, adj instr, 1980; Peoples Bank Bridgeport, br mgr, 1984, asst treas, 1984-86, asst vpres, mgr, boston ave off, 1986, vpres, 1987-94, vpres, mgr, sales serv & tech training, 1994-96, vpres, mgr, recruiting, 1996-98, vpres, mgr, employee rel, 1998, vpres human resources; Conn State Dept Educ, pres, currently. **Orgs:** Moderator Todays Woman radio talk show WICC Radio Bridgeport, 1979; United Way Fairfield Co, allocation comm, 1980-, loaned exec, 1983; Action Bridgeport Comm Dev Inc, vice chmn, 1982, chmn, 1982-87; Coalition 100 Black Women, 1986-; adv bd mem, Bridgeport Pub Educ Fund, 1984-; bd mem, Greater Bridgeport Symphony, 1989-; bd mem, Am Festival Theater Stratford; bd mem, Mus Art, Sci & Indust Bridgeport. **Home Addr:** 135 Brooklawn Ave, Bridgeport, CT 06604, **Home Phone:** (203)384-9228. **Business Addr:** President of Education, Connecticut State Department of Education, 165 Capitol Ave, Hartford, CT 06106, **Business Phone:** (860)713-6543.

**PRETTYMAN, PROF. QUANDRA**
Educator. **Personal:** Born Jan 19, 1933, Baltimore, MD. **Educ:** Antioch Col, BA, 1954; Univ Mich, grad study, 1957. **Career:** New Sch Social Res, lectr, 1959-62; Col Ins, instr, 1962-67; Scholastic Bk Serv, NY, Open Boat & other short stories by Stephen Crane, ed, 1968; Barnard Col, sr assoc eng prof, currently. **Special Achievements:** Out Of Our Lives: A Selection of Contemporary Black Fiction, Howard UnivPress, ed, 1975, poems in many anthologies Most Notable Arnold Adoff, The Poetry of Black America, Black World Barnard Publication'; Her poem "When Mahalia Sings? was included in the landmark book I Am the Darker Brother published in 1968. First African American Professor at the Barnard's College. **Home Addr:** 300 W 107th St, New York, NY 10025-2710, **Home Phone:** (212)864-0131. **Business Addr:** Senior Associate Professor of English, Barnard College, 3009 Broadway, New York, NY 10027-6598, **Business Phone:** (212)854-2116.

**PREWITT, J. EVERETT**
Writer, real estate agent. **Personal:** children: Eric & Lia. **Educ:** Lincoln Univ, Pa, BA, bus admin; Cleveland State Univ, MS, urban studies. **Career:** White Motors, int div, mgr admin; Housing Info Serv, Cuyahoga Plan Ohio, Inc, dir; Northland Res Corp, pres, 1982-; Books & non-fiction: Urban Residential Real Estate Mkt Analyst; Snake Walkers. **Orgs:** Pres, Cleveland Asn Real Estate Brokers; pres, Cleveland Area Bd Realtors; chmn, bd E End Neighborhood House; vice-chmn, Bd Greater Shaker Sq Develop Corp; Glenville Community Cleveland; trustee emer, Myers Univ. **Honors/Awds:** Distinguished alumni, Lincoln Univ, Pa; Distinguished alumni, Cleveland State Univ; Realtor of the Year award, Cleveland Area Bd Realtors; Award for Civic Service, Citizen's League Greater Cleveland; Bronze Award, 2005; Best Books Awards, 2005, USABookNews.com; Book Award for Best Fiction-Cheryls Choice, 2005; Fresh Voices Book Award, Writers Mkt Asn, 2006; Fiction Honor Award, Black Caucus Am Library Asn, 2006. **Special Achievements:** Novel placed first for fiction in the 2nd Ann Los Angeles Black Book Expo; Semi Finalist in Independent Publication Book Awards, 2005; Finalist in Cushcity's Best New Author Award, 2006. **Business Addr:** President, Northland Publishing Co, 11811 Shaker Blvd Suite 414, Cleveland, OH 44120, **Business Phone:** (216)707-1300.

**PREWITT, DR. LENA VONCILLE BURRELL**
Consultant, educator, vice president (organization). **Personal:** Born Feb 17, 1932, Wilcox, AL; daughter of Cornelia Burrell and Leo Burrell; children: Kenneth Burrell. **Educ:** Stillman Col, BS, bus educ, 1954; Ind Univ, MA, bus educ, 1955, EdD, bus educ, 1961, postdoctoral study, 1965; Tex Southern Univ, postdoctoral study, 1969; Univ Calif, Los Angeles, attended 1978; Ga Inst Technol, attended 1980; Harvard Univ, attended 1987; Univ Scand, attended 1987; Univ Bocconi, Milan Italy, attended 1988. **Career:** Stillman Col, from asst prof to prof, 1955-67; Marshall Space Flight Ctr, Huntsville, AL, employee develop officer, 1964; Tex Southern Univ, assoc prof, dept chmn, 1967-69; Pac Tel & Tel, Los Angeles, Calif, spec mgt consult, 1968; Florence State Univ, assoc prof, 1969-70; Univ Ala, assoc prof, 1970-74, prof mgt, 1974-94; interim vpres fiscal affairs, 1998-99; distinguished prof mgt, 1999-2000; Int Bus Mach, consult; USAF, consult; US Fire Col, Charles pfizer, consult; US Cong, adv; Union Inst & Univ, core prof, prof emer, currently. **Orgs:** Fel Presby Church US, 1958-60; fel Ford Found, 1965; fel Urban League, 1966; Acad Mgt; Europ Found Mgt Develop, 1968-; Spec res consult, TTT Proj, Tex Southern Univ, 1969; Southern Mgt Asn; Am Asn Univ Women; Nat Bus Educ Asn; Delta Pi Epsilon; gen exec bd, Presby Church US, 1973-; vpres, FOCUS Sr Citizens; Century Club YMCA; chmn, US Selective Serv Appeals Bd, 1980-; bd dir, AMI-W Ala Hosp, 1986-; adv comt, Church Wide Compensation, 2003. **Honors/Awds:** Named one of Top 5 Faculty Women, Univ Ala, 1978; Outstanding Educator of the Year Award, Lucy Sheppard Art Federated Club, 1976; High Profile Professor of the Year Award, Univ Ala Crimson White, 1991. **Special Achievements:** First female African American faculty member at the University of Alabama; First female African american faculty in the College of Commerce and Business Administration; published numerous articles. **Home Addr:** 412 Woodbridge Dr, Tuscaloosa, AL 35401, **Home Phone:** (205)345-3615. **Business Addr:** Professor Emeritus, Union Institute & University, 440 E McMillan, Cincinnati, OH 45206, **Business Phone:** (513)861-6400.

**PREZEAU, LOUIS E.**
Banker. **Personal:** Born Mar 4, 1943, Port-au-Prince; son of Yia Roy and Emile; married Ramona A; children: Jasmine, Louis Jr & Rodney. **Educ:** Baruch Col, pub acct, 1968; Bernard M Baruch, New York, NY, BBA, 1970. **Career:** Freedom Nat Bank NY, chief operating officer, 1975-, act pres, 1987-88, sr exec offcier, controller; Fonkoze Financial Servs, inventor; City Nat Bank NJ, Newark, NJ, pres & chief exec officer, 1989-2011. **Orgs:** New york Soc Cert Pub Acct, 1973-; treas, trustee, Community Serv Soc, 1985-; investment comn, Nat Coun Churches, 1988-; trustee, Newark Chamber Com, 1991; NJ Bankers Asn, exec comn. **Honors/Awds:** Golden Door Award, Intl Inst NJ, 1999. **Special Achievements:** Only African-American owned and operated commercial bank in the state of New Jersey. **Home Addr:** 85-27 Edgerton Blvd, Jamaica, NY 11432.

**PREZEAU, DR. MARYSE P.**
Educator, college teacher. **Personal:** Born Feb 20, 1942, Port-au-Prince. **Educ:** City Univ NY, Hunter Col, BA, 1970, MA, 1971; City Univ NY, PhD, 1975. **Career:** Hunter Col, adj lectr, 1970-76; York Col, adj asst prof, 1973-77; Barnard Col, lectr, 1977-78; NY Inst Tech, asst provost, 1978-87; La Guardia Community Col, CUNY, dean inst advan, 1987-90; New York Inst Technol, vpres stud affairs, 1990-2001, prof eng, 2001-, prof humanities, currently. **Orgs:** Bd mem, Nassau Community Med Ctr, 1978-88; NYIT Corp rep, Am Asn Univ Women, 1982-87; Coun Grad Sch, 1990. **Home Addr:** 38 Hillside Ave, Woodbury, NY 11797-1326, **Home Phone:** (516)367-4175. **Business Addr:** Professor of English, Vice President Student Affairs, New York Institute of Technology, Northern Blvd 268 Wheatly Rd, Old Westbury, NY 11568, **Business Phone:** (516)686-1000.

**PRICE, PROF. ALFRED DOUGLAS**
Educator. **Personal:** Born Jul 6, 1947, Buffalo, NY; son of Alfred D and Virginia M Allen; children: A Douglas V. **Educ:** Princeton Univ, AB, sociol, 1969, MArch, urban planning, 1975. **Career:** Harvard Univ, co dir, AAEO, 1969-71; Sch Arch-NJ, Inst Tech, asst dean, 1975-77; Sch Archit & Planning, State Univ NY, Buffalo, assoc dean, 1977-82; UB Sch Archit & Planning, assoc prof planning, currently; Univ Buffalo, State Univ New York, Dept Urban & Regional Planning, Assoc Prof, currently; US Environ Protection Agency, consult, 1997-2005. **Orgs:** Bd dir, Seventy-Eight Restoration Corp, 1979-84; chmn, City

Buffalo Urban Design Task Group, 1980-; US Assn Club Rome, 1980-; chair, selection Buffalo City Arts Comn, 1980-97; chmn, archit comn Episcopal Diocese Western NY, 1980-; bd dir, Buffalo Conventional Ctr, 1981-84; exec coun, Episcopal Ch USA, 1997-2003; chair, comm state church (Episcopal). **Home Addr:** 77 Huntington Ave, Buffalo, NY 14214, **Home Phone:** (716)832-1110. **Business Addr:** Associate Professor of Planning, UB School of architecture & planning, Hayes C 05N, Buffalo, NY 14214, **Business Phone:** (716)829-5471.

## PRICE, ANDREA R.

Hospital administrator, association executive. **Personal:** Born Jun 16, 1959, Flint, MI; daughter of Jones and Clara; married Edward Johnson; children: 4. **Educ:** Univ Mich, Ann Arbor, Mich, BA, psychol, 1981; Tulane Univ, Sch Pub Health, New Orleans, La, MHA, 1983. **Career:** DC hosp Asn, ambulatory resident, 1983-84; DataCom Systs Corp, mgr, ambulatory care servs, 1984-85; C's Nat Med Ctr, fel, 1985-86, asst vpres ambulatory servs, 1988-89, vpres prof servs, 1989-99; Howard Univ, Grad Sch Bus, adj asst Prof, 2000; Hurley Med Ctr, Flint, Mich, exec vpres & chief operating officer, 2000-06, interim pres & chief exec officer, 2001-02; Sparrow Health Syst, Lansing, exec vpres & chief operating officer, 2006-09; Mercy health partners, chief operating officer, Regional pres & chief exec officer, sr vpres, 2009-14; Am Col Healthcare Execs, bd gov, 2003-06, fel, 2013-. **Orgs:** Pres, Am Col Health Care Exec Women's Forum, 1988-89; pres, Asn Health Care Admins DC, 1991-92; nat bd mem, mem chmn, Nat Asn Health Servs Execs, 1986-91; vpres, secy, DC chap; bd dir, Toledo Chamber Com, 2010; Rotary Club Toledo, 2010; bd dir, Toledo Regional Growth Partnership, 2010-; Toledo-Lucas County Port Authority, 2011; bd dir, Hosp Coun Northwest Ohio, Lucas County Healthy Communities Found, 2011-; div chair, Am Heart Asn, 2011; nat pres, Nat Asn Health Servs Execs, 2011-13; bd dir, Inst Diversity Health Mgt, 2011-13; prog coun, adv bd, Midwest Healthcare Execs Group & Assocs, 2011-13; AHRQ Med Liability Commun & Resolution Tech Expert Panel, 2013-14; mem regional policy bd, Am Hosp Asn, 2014-. **Honors/Awds:** Excellence in Health Care Industry, Int Bus Network, 1987; Young Health Services Excellence Award, NAHSE, 1992; Early Career Award, Am Col Health Care Execs, 1992; Senior Health Services Executive of the Year, Nat Asn Health Serv Execs, 2003; Senior Healthcare Executive of the Year Award, Am Col Healthcare Execs, 2003; Distinguished Service Award, Am Col Healthcare Execs, 2008; Regents Senior Level Healthcare Executive Award, 2008, Midwest Healthcare Executives Group & Associates, 2010; Michigan Regent Senior Level Executive Award, Am Col Healthcare Execs, 2010; Exemplary Service Award, Am Col Healthcare Execs, 2012. **Business Addr:** President, Chief Executive Officer, Mercy, 3131 Queen City Ave, Cincinnati, OH 45238, **Business Phone:** (513)389-5000.

## PRICE, BRENDA G.

Executive, administrator. **Educ:** Oakland Univ, BA, polit sci, 1979; Wayne State Univ, MEd, educ & instrnl technol, 1993. **Career:** Daimler Chrysler Corp, assembly line worker; Detroit pub sch, substitute teacher; Blue Cross & Blue Shield Mich, local govt liaison; Community Found Southeastern Mich, prog consult, sr prog officer & prog dir; John S James L knight Found, community liaison prog officer, 2004-, prog dir, currently; Knight Found, prog dir. **Orgs:** Dir, African Am Legacy Prog; SW Detroit Bus Asn; bd mem, City Connect Detroit. **Home Addr:** , MI. **Business Addr:** Program Director, John S & James L Knight Found, Wachovia Financial Ctr Suite 3300, Miami, FL 33131-2349, **Business Phone:** (305)908-2600.

## PRICE, JUDGE CHARLES

Judge. **Personal:** Born May 9, 1940, Montgomery, AL; married Bernice B; children: Susan Y & Charles II. **Educ:** VA Union Univ, BS, 1969; Nat Law Ctr; George Wash Univ, JD, 1972. **Career:** US Dept Justice, Wash, DC, intern, 1972-73; St Ala, asst atty gen, 1973-75, circuit ct judge, 1983-; Escambia County, AL, actg dist atty, 1974; Montgomery County, AL, dep dist atty, 1975-78, asst munic judge, 1982-83; pvt law pract, 1978-83; Ala State Univ, adj instr polit sci & criminal justice; Jones Law Sch, adj prof law, currently; Ala Univ, adj prof law, currently. **Orgs:** Nat Bar Asn; pres, Montgomery City Trial Lawyers Asn, 1982-83. **Honors/Awds:** John F Kennedy Profile in Courage Award, 1997; Dr. Martin Luther King Humanitarian Award, Nat Educ Asn, 1998. **Special Achievements:** First African-American district attorney in Alabama; First African-American to hold this position in Montgomery County; First African-American to receive the John F. Kennedy Profile in Courage Award. **Home Addr:** 501 Wiltshire Dr, Montgomery, AL 36117-0006, **Home Phone:** (334)215-0006. **Business Addr:** Circuit Court Judge, State of Alabama, 251 S Lawrence St, Montgomery, AL 36104, **Business Phone:** (334)832-1331.

## PRICE, SR. FRED L.

Executive. **Personal:** Born Pittsburgh, PA. **Educ:** Reed Col, Portland, OR, BA, 1971; Univ Calif, Berkeley, CA, MS Amer Studies, journ, 2008. **Career:** Medgar Evers Col, spokesperson, dean, exec dir, sr develop officer & spec projs, dir alumni rels, currently; City Univ New York, dir alumni rels & develop, 1998-. **Orgs:** Life mem, Nat Asn Advan Colored People; 100 Black Men, NY. **Honors/Awds:** Tom Boyland Award, Black & Puerto Rican Legislators; 100 Black Women Citation. **Special Achievements:** Produced and Directed "Home" a film documentary on Ghana; published article on "Samana" the African American Community in the Dominican Republic. **Business Addr:** Director of Alumni Relations, City University of New York, 217 E 42nd St, New York, NY 10017, **Business Phone:** (212)997-2869.

## PRICE, GEN. GEORGE BAKER

Manager, military leader. **Personal:** Born Aug 28, 1929, Laurel, MS; son of James A and Kate Baker; married Georgianna Hunter; children: Katherine, James, William & Robert. **Educ:** SC State Col, BS, 1951; AUS Command & Gen Staff Col, cert, 1965; AUS War Col, cert, 1971; Shippensburg State Col, MS, 1971. **Career:** Military leader (retired), manger; AUS, platoon leader 3rd Bn, 30 Inf Rgt, 1951, platoon leader L Co, 179 Inf Rgt, 1952, co comdr specialist training regt, 1953-57, opers officer, 1957-61, personnel mgr, 1961-62, adv 1st Vietnamese inf div, 1964-65, dept army staff, 1965-68, battalion comdr, 1968-70, brigade comdr, 1971-73, Am city, Nurnberg, Ger, city mgr, 1971-76, chief staff, 1973-74, asst div comdr, 1974-76, chief staff, 1976-78; Tech dyn Syst Corp, dir govt oper, 1978-81; Unified Indust, spl asst to pres, 1981-82; Southern Brand Snack Inc, exec vpres, 1978-81; Price Enterprises, personal mgr Leontyne Price, currently. **Orgs:** Kappa Alpha Psi Fraternity; Mil & Veterans Adv Comm Nat Urban League; Vietnam Vet Mem Fund, 1980-85; bd visitors, US Mil Acad, W Pt; bd advr, Womans Vietnam Vet Mem. **Honors/Awds:** Distinguished Patriot Award, Nat Womens Republican Club; Distinguished Service Award, SC State Col, 1975; Distinguished Vietnam Vet Nat Asn Paramedics, 1989-. **Home Addr:** 5542 Phelps Luck Dr, Columbia, MD 21045, **Home Phone:** (301)596-0185. **Business Addr:** Personal Manager, Leontyne Price Enterprises, 1133 Broadway, New York, NY 10036.

## PRICE, GLENDA DELORES

School administrator, educator. **Personal:** Born Oct 10, 1939, York, PA; daughter of William B and Zelma E McGeary. **Educ:** Temple Univ, BS, med technol, 1961, MEd, educ media, 1969, PhD, educ pyshol, 1979. **Career:** Temple Univ, Clin Lab Sci, prof, 1969-79, Col Allied Health, asst dean, 1979-86; Univ Conn, Sch Allied Health Prof, asst dean, 1986-92; Spelman Col, provost, 1992-98; Temple Univ, Alumni fel, 1992; Marygrove Col, Detroit, pres, 1998-2006; Mich Cols Found, interim pres, 2008-12; Detroit Pub Schs Found, pres, 2012-. **Orgs:** Pres, Am Soc Med Technol; Alpha Kappa Alpha Sorority Inc, 1959-; Am Asn Higher Educ; bd mem, Asn Sch Allied Health Professions, 1988; Comn Accreditation Phys Ther Educ; chief deleg, Int Asn Med Lab Technologists; pres, Nat Certifying Agency Med Lab Personnel; financial adv bd, City Detroit; chmn, bd dir Focus HOPE;vice chmn, Detroit Symphony Orchestra; mem bd, Community Found Southeast Mich; Coun Mich Foundations; Detroit Receiving Hosp; YES Found; Detroit 90/90; Mich Sci Ctr; Jewish Fund; active mem Links Inc; Alpha Kappa Alpha Sorority Inc. **Special Achievements:** First African American female to be the President of Marygrove College. Only African American to held American Society for Medical Technology. **Home Addr:** 19460 Burlington Dr, Detroit, MI 48203-1454, **Home Phone:** (313)893-4069.

## PRICE, HUBERT P., JR.

State government official, president (organization). **Personal:** Born Sep 28, 1946, Pontiac, MI. **Educ:** Mich State Univ, BS. **Career:** Oakland County Bd Comnrs, comnr; Mich House Rep, state rep; Synergistics Consult, pres, currently. **Orgs:** Nat Asn Advan Colored People; Pontiac Area Urban League; Oakland Ice Ctr Oakland County; Coalition Black Trade Unionists; Nat Asn County Officials; Nat Asn Black County Officials; Trinity Missionary Baptist Church; bd mem, United Way; bd advisor, Partnership Learning; Great Start Collab-Oakland. **Home Addr:** 583 Pearsall, Pontiac, MI 48341. **Business Addr:** President, Synergistics Consulting, 50 Wayne St Suite B, Pontiac, MI 48342, **Business Phone:** (248)334-1800.

## PRICE, HUGH BERNARD

Educator, association executive. **Personal:** Born Nov 22, 1941, Washington, DC; son of Kline Armond Sr and Charlotte Schuster; married Marilyn Lloyd; children: Traer, Janeen & Lauren. **Educ:** Amherst Col, BA, 1963; Yale Law Sch, LLB, 1966. **Career:** New Haven Legal Assistance Asn, atty, 1966-68; Black Coalition New Haven, exec dir, 1968-70; Cogen Holt & Assoc, partner, 1970-76; City New Haven, dir human resources admin, 1977-78; Urban Renewal Agency New Haven Redevel Agency, asst couns; New Haven Legal Asst Asn, neighborhood atty; City New Haven, Human Resources Admin, dir, 1977-78; NY Times, ed writer, 1978-82; WNET & Thirteen, NY, sr vpres, 1982-88, dir; Nat Urban League, pres, chief exec officer, 1994-2003; Metrop Life Inc, dir; Sears, Roebuck & Co, dir; Nynex Corp, Corp Gov Comt, mem; DLA Piper Rudnick Gray Cary US LLP, sr adv & co-chair, 2003-05; Brookings Inst, sr fel, Econ Studies Prog, 2006-08, non-resident sr fel, Econ Studies Prog, 2008-; Princeton Univ, Woodrow Wilson Sch Pub & Int Affairs, vis prof, 2008-. **Orgs:** Bd dir, Ctr Comt Chg Wash DC; bd dir exec comt & real estate comt, New Haven Water Co; Distrib Comt New Haven Found; bd dir & vpres, United Way Greater New Haven; Nat Bus League; Nat Asn Advan Colored People; Alpha Phi Alpha Frat; Proj Planning Comt, Greater New Haven Black Soc Civic Orgn Higher Educ Fund; Metrop Life Ins Co; Verizon; bd dir, New Haven Legal Asst Asn Day top Inc; Polly T McCabe Ctr; Greater New Haven UMCA; Lewis Latimer Found; trustee, Rochefeller Bros Fund, 1987-88; vpres, Rockefeller Found, NY, 1988-94; trustee, Nat Asn Advan Colored People, Legal Defense & Educ Fund, 1988; trustee, Munic Art Soc, 1990-; trustee, Pub Develop Corp, 1991-; Am Philos Soc; Mayo Clin Found; co-chair, Asn Supv Curric Develop, 2006-07; Alpha Phi Alpha Frater; Coun Foreign Rels; Century Asn; Bretton Woods Committee; Adv Bd, Future Am Democracy Found; Jacob Burns Film Ctr; Acad Polit Sci; Westchester Clubmen; Boule. **Home Addr:** 21 Trenor Dr, New Rochelle, NY 10804-3731, **Home Phone:** (914)636-3413. **Business Addr:** Non-resident Senior Fellow, Brookings Institution, 1775 Massachusetts Ave NW, Washington, DC 20036, **Business Phone:** (202)797-6058.

## PRICE, JOANN H.

Founder (originator), executive. **Educ:** Howard Univ. **Career:** Nat Asn Investment Co, pres; Fairview Capital Partners Inc, co-founder & managing partner, 1994-, meminvest comt, currently. **Orgs:** Adv bd, Black Enterprise/Greenwich St Corp Growth Partners; New Vista Capital; Pacesetter Growth Fund; dir, Initiative a Competitive Inner City; vice chair, Apollo Theater Found; chairperson, Amistad Ctr Art & Cult; bd visitor, Howard Univ; bd dir, YMCA Greater Hartford; independent dir, Vantagepoint Funds - Vantagepoint 500 Stock Index Fund, 2013-; bd dir, Regents CT, 2013-; bd dir, YMCA Metrop Hartford Inc; bd dir, Conn Bd Regents Higher Educ; adv bd, Pacesetter Growth Fund I, LP; bd dir, Hartford Found Pub Giving; Union Baptist Church Hartford. **Honors/Awds:** "Black Enterprise", 75 Most Powerful Blacks on Wall Street, 2011; Trailblazer Award, Sixth Ann Womens Pvt Equity Summit, 2013; Woman of the Year Award, The Villages, 2014. **Business Addr:** Co-founder, Managing Partner, Fairview Capital Partners Inc, 75 Isham Rd Suite 200, West Hartford, CT 06107, **Business Phone:** (860)674-8066.

## PRICE, JOHN WILEY

County commissioner. **Personal:** children: John Jr, John Nicholas & Angelina Monique. **Career:** KKDA radio, host, regular guest host, currently; KNON, host; Dallas County Comnr Ct, Dist 3, county comnr, 1985-. **Orgs:** Chmn, Dallas County Civil Serv Comn; vpres, Dallas County Juv Bd; chmn, Comnrs Ct Sheriff Liaison Comt; chmn, Delinq Tax Collection Selection Comt; Loop 9 Policy Adv Group; vpres, Dallas County Housing Finance Corp; chmn, Pub Health Adv Comt; Adult & Juv Health Adv Comt; Tex Juv Crime Comn; Dallas Housing Acquisition & Develop Corp Bd; pres, Tex Orgn Black County Comnrs; founder & pres, KwanzaaFest Inc, 1991; St Luke Community United Methodist Church. **Honors/Awds:** Juanita Craft Award in Politics, NAACP; NAACP Medgar Evers Award; Lifetime Achievement Award, Dallas & Fort Worth Asn Black Communicators; Community Leadership Award, Malcolm X Day Organizing Comt; Newsome Award, Black United Fund Tex. **Special Achievements:** KKDA-AM, "Talk Back", talk show host; first black elected to the Commissioners Court in Dallas. **Business Addr:** Dallas County Commissioner, Dallas County Commissioner, 411 Elm St 2nd Fl, Dallas, TX 75216, **Business Phone:** (214)653-6670.

## PRICE, DR. JOSEPH L.

Clergy, business owner, real estate agent. **Personal:** Born Dec 25, 1931, Gary, IN; married Edria Faye; children: 6. **Educ:** E Los Angeles Jr Col; Moody Bible Inst; Chicago Baptist Bible Inst; Ind Christian Theol Sem, attended 1969. **Career:** Church God Christ, bishop dist supt & pastor, 1963-71; St Jude Deliverance Centers Am, pastor, evangelist minister organ & founder, 1971-; photo, welder, owner, furniture & appliance store; real estate & ins broker; Whittier Col, assoc prof relig. **Home Addr:** 5028 Terrace Ave, Indianapolis, IN 46203. **Business Addr:** 975 N Delaware, Indianapolis, IN 46202.

## PRICE, JUDITH

Executive. **Personal:** Born Feb 10, 1937, New York, NY; children: Toni & Marc. **Educ:** City Col NY; Bernard Baruch Sch, bus admin. **Career:** James B Beam Import Corp, vpres & dir, 1972-, admin dir & asst secy; Beam distilling co. **Orgs:** Traffic Asn, Liquor Indust. **Home Addr:** 5800 Arlington Ave Apt 3j, Bronx, NY 10471-1405, **Home Phone:** (718)543-6604. **Business Addr:** Vice President, Director, James B Beam Import Corp, 245 Pk Av, New York, NY 10017.

## PRICE, KELLY CHERELLE

Singer, songwriter, actor. **Personal:** Born Apr 3, 1973, Queens, NY; daughter of Joseph and Evangelist Claudia; married Jeffrey Rolle; children: Jeffrey Jr & Jonia. **Career:** Singer, songwriter, author, actress; R&B vocalist, composer, arranger, producer, currently; Albums: Soul of a Woman, 1998; Mirror Mirror, 2000; One Family: A Christmas Album, 2001; Priceless, 2003; This Is Who I Am, 2006; Kelly, 2011; Sing Pray Love, Vol. 1: Sing, 2014; Singles: "Friend of Mine", 1998; "Secret Love", 1999; "It's Gonna Rain", 1999; "Love Sets You Free", 2000; "As We Lay", 2000; "You Should Have Told Me", 2000; "Mirror or Mirror", 2001; "Take It To The Head", 2002; "In Love at Christmas", 2002; "Someday", 2002; "How Does It Feel?", 2002; "He Proposed", 2003; "God's Gift", 2006; "Healing", 2006; "Tired", 2010; "Not My Daddy", 2011; "Himaholic", 2011; "It's My Time", 2014; Island Black Music Recs, 1994-96; Def Soul Recs, 1996-2005; Ecclecti Sounds Recs, owner, 2006-; Sang Girl, My Block, 2010-. **Orgs:** Sigma Gamma Rho Sorority Inc, 2006-. **Business Addr:** Singer, Universal Music Group, 1755 Bdwy, New York, NY 10019, **Business Phone:** (212)333-8000.

## PRICE, LEONTYNE (MARY VIOLET LEONTYNE PRICE)

Soprano. **Personal:** Born Feb 10, 1927, Laurel, MS; daughter of James A and Kate Baker; married William C Warfield. **Educ:** Cent State Col, BA, 1948; Juilliard Sch Music, 1952; Florence Page Kimball, pvt study. **Career:** Opera singer (retired); Porgy & Bess, Europe, 1952-54; recitalist, soloist with symphonies in US, Canada, Australia, Europe, 1954; performed in Tosca, NBC Opera Theater, 1954; soloist, Hollywood Bowl, 1955-59, 1966; appeared in concert, India, 1956-64; San Francisco Opera, 1957-59, 1960-61, 1963, 1965, 1967, 1968, 1971; RCA recording artist, 1958; Vienna Staatsopera, 1958-59, 1960-61; Berlin Festival, 1960; Metrop Opera House Lincoln Ctr, artist, 1961; six performances at the White House; performed Live from Lincoln Ctr; performed at 2 retiredial inaugrations & for the Pope; Films: Romeo Juliet, voice, 1996. **Orgs:** Bd mem, Campfire Girls; co-chair, Rust Col Upward Thrust Campaign; trustee, Int House; hon vice chmn, US Comt UNESCO; Am Fedn TV & Radio Artists; Am Guild Mus Artists; Actors Equity Asn; Sigma Alpha Iota; Delta Sigma Theta; Nat Inst Music Theater; Nat Asn Advan Colored People; Whitney Young Found; bd trustees, NY Univ. **Honors/Awds:** Twenty Grammy Awards; Spirit of Achievement Award, Albert Einstein Col Med, 1962; Silver Medal of San Francisco Oper Italy's Order of Merit; Presidential Medal of Freedom, 1965; Spingarn Medal, Nat Asn Advan Colored People, 1965; Schwann Catalog Award, 1968; Kennedy Center Honors, 1980; Kennedy Center Honarary, 1985; Nat Medal of Arts, 1985; Lifetime Achievement Award, 1989; Handel Medallion New York; Grammy Life time Achievement Award, Asn Black Charities, 1989; Nat Endowment Arts, 2008; 26 hon doctorates. **Special Achievements:** First African Americans to become a leading artist at the Metrop Opera; First African Americans to gain prominence in major performance halls in that musical genre. **Home Addr:** 1133 Broadway, New York, NY 10010, **Home Phone:** (212)243-0476.

## PRICE, MARCUS RAYMOND

Football coach, administrator, football player. **Personal:** Born Mar 3, 1972, Port Arthur, TX. **Educ:** La State Univ, finance, 1995. **Career:** Football player (retired), football coach; Jacksonville Jaguars, 1995-96; San Diego Chargers, tackle, 1997-98; New Orleans Saints, 2000-01; Buffalo Bills, 2002-04; Dallas Cowboys, guard, 2005; W view High Sch, coach; summer youth clinics, keynote speaker; high sch football camps, keynote speaker; Lincoln High Sch, Port Arthur, recruiting expert; NCSA, educ speaker, currently. **Business Addr:** Recruiting Expert, NCSA Athletic Recruiting, 1415 N Dayton St 4th Fl, Chicago, IL 60642-2643, **Business Phone:** (312)624-7400.

**PRICE, MARY VIOLET LEONTYNE. See PRICE, LEONTYNE.**

**PRICE, PAMELA ANITA**
Librarian. **Personal:** Born Nov 30, 1952, Washington, DC; daughter of John Robert and Gwendolyn Elizabeth Moses. **Educ:** NC Agr & Tech State Univ, Greensboro, BS, 1974; Univ Wis-Madison, MS, 1975. **Career:** Univ Md, Col Pk, MD, serials cataloger, 1975-76; Del State Col, Dover, coordr eve reader serv, 1976-81; Mercer County Community Col, Trenton, NJ, libr supvr, 1981, dir, currently. **Orgs:** Am Libr Asn, 1974-; Kappa Delta Pi, 1974-; Delta Sigma Theta Sorority, 1977-; YWCA, Trenton, NJ, 1987-; United Way Princeton Area Community, 1987-; Cent Jersey Regional Libr Coop. **Home Addr:** 2501 Annina Lane, Bensalem, PA 19020-2994, **Home Phone:** (609)586-4800. **Business Addr:** Director, Mercer County Community College, 1200 Old Trenton Rd, Trenton, NJ 08550, **Business Phone:** (609)570-3562.

**PRICE, DR. PAUL SANFORD**
Librarian. **Personal:** Born Mar 30, 1942, Coffeyville, KS; son of Ovie and Anna Belle. **Educ:** Univ Conn, Storrs, CT, BA, hist, 1971, MA, hist, 1974, PhD, higher educ admin, 1982; Univ Denver, Denver, CO, MA, librarianship & info mgt, 1985. **Career:** Librarian, director (retired); Univ Conn Libr, Storrs, CT, dept mgr, 1972-84; The Quinoco Cos, Denver, Colo, rec adminr, 1985-87; Three Rivers Community Tech Col, dir, learning resources, 1987-2002. **Orgs:** Southeastern CT Libr Asn, 1987-; Conn Libr Asn, 1987-; New Eng Libr Asn, 1987-; Am libr Asn, 1987-; Mountain & Plains Libr Asn, 1984-87. **Home Addr:** 3772 Cr 1675, Coffeyville, KS 67337, **Home Phone:** (620)948-3272. **Business Addr:** KS.

**PRICE, PHILLIP G.**
Automotive executive. **Career:** Red Bluff Ford Lincoln Mercury Inc, owner & chief exec, 1989-. **Business Addr:** Owner, Chief Executive, Red Bluff Ford Lincoln Mercury, 2950 Main St, Red Bluff, CA 96080, **Business Phone:** (530)527-2816.

**PRICE, RAY ANTHONY**
Television producer, educator. **Personal:** Born Jun 21, 1957, High Point, NC; son of Johnny and Carrie; married Gayle Lynnette; children: Samuel Ray, Rajeana Lynn & Michael Terrell. **Educ:** Yuba Col, AS, 1984; Calif State Univ, BA, 1986; Regent Univ, MA, 1993. **Career:** Continental Cablevision, Channel 5, producer, 1984-91; KVIE, Channel 6PBS, prod asst, 1990-91; Yuba Community Col, TV instr, 1990-91; Portmouth Pub Sch, Channel 28, assoc producer, 1992-; Portmouth City Channel 29, video technician, 1992-; Newport News Pub Sch, educ supvr telecommunications, prog adminr, 1992-; Hampton Univ, adj prof, 1998. **Orgs:** Bd mem, Marysville Chamber Com, 1987-91; bd mem, Big Bro Big Sister, 1988-91; bd mem, Yuba-Sutter Regional Arts Coun, 1990-91; vpres, Marysville Kiwanis Club, 1990-91; Hampton Roads Black Media Professionals, 1994-; bd mem, Youth Entertainment Studios. **Home Addr:** 210 Graham Dr, Newport News, VA 23606, **Home Phone:** (757)930-1448. **Business Addr:** Education Supervisor Telecommunications Education, Program Administrator, Newport News Public Schools Telecommunications Center, 4 Minton Dr, Newport News, VA 23606, **Business Phone:** (757)591-4687.

**PRIDE, CHARLEY FRANK**
Singer, baseball player. **Personal:** Born Mar 18, 1938, Sledge, MS; son of Mack; married Rozene; children: Kraig, Dion & Angela. **Career:** Baseball player (retired), singer: Negro Baseball League, Detroit, Birmingham Black Barons, Memphis Red Sox, Los Angeles Angels, baseball player; Anaconda Mining; solo rec artist; Albums: Very Best of Charley Pride, 1987-89 & 2003; RCA Country Legends, 2000; A Tribute to Jim Reeves, 2001; Comfort of Her Wings, 2003; Country Legend, 2003; Anthology, 2003; 20 Classics, 2004; Greatest Songs, 2005; The Pride of Country Music [American Legends], 2005; Country Music Superstars: Charley Pride & Conway Twitty, 2005; 16 Biggest Hits, 2005; Sings His Best, 2006; The Essential Charley Pride, 2006; Pride & Joy: A Gospel Music Collection, 2006; The Snakes Crawl at Night, Before I Met You, Just Between You & Me; The Lawrence Welk Show; Billboard Hot 100: All I Have to Offer You (Is Me), (I'm So) Afraid of Losing You Again, I Can't Believe That You've Stopped Loving Me, I'd Rather Love You, Is Anybody Goin' to San Antone, Wonder Could I Live There Anymore?, I'm Just Me & Kiss an Angel Good Mornin; Mississippi Cotton Picking Delta Town, Someone Loves You, Honey, When I Stop Leavin' (I'll Be Gone), Burgers & Fries, I Don't Think She's in Love Anymore, Roll On Mississippi, Never Been So Loved (In All My Life) & You're So Good When You're Bad; Kaw-Liga, Honky Tonk Blues & You Win Again; Tex Rangers Maj League Baseball club, spec investor & minority owner, 2010-. **Business Addr:** Singer, Cecca Productions, 3198 Royal Lane Suite 200, Dallas, TX 75229, **Business Phone:** (214)350-8477.

**PRIDE, CURTIS JOHN**
Baseball player. **Personal:** Born Dec 17, 1968, Washington, DC; son of John and Sallie; married Lisa. **Educ:** Col William & Mary. **Career:** Baseball player (retired), baseball coach; Montreal Expos, outfielder, 1993, 1995, 2001; Detroit Tigers, outfielder, 1996-97; Boston Red Sox, outfielder, 1997, 2000; Atlanta Braves, outfielder, 1998; NY Yankees, outfielder, 2003; Anaheim Angels, outfielder, 2004-06; Los Angeles Angels of Anaheim, outfielder, 2005-06; Atlantic League, Southern Maryland Blue Crabs, outfielder, 2008; Gallaudet Univ, head baseball coach, 2008-. **Orgs:** Together With Pride Found. **Home Addr:** 1288 Lake Breeze Dr, West Palm Beach, FL 33414-7953, **Home Phone:** (561)753-9833. **Business Addr:** Head Baseball Coach, Gallaudet University, 800 Fla Ave, Washington, DC 20002-3695, **Business Phone:** (202)651-5000.

**PRIDE, HEMPHILL P., II**
Lawyer. **Personal:** Born May 19, 1936, Columbia, SC; son of Maud Pendergrass and Hemphill P (deceased); married Nathalie Helene Dingalt; children: Pride Hemphill III, Elliott, Ki-Ga, Touami & Linous. **Educ:** Fla A&M Univ, BL, 1963, JD. **Career:** JenkinsPerry & Pride, partner, 1963-76; SC Housing Authority, vice chmn, 1972-77; Nat Bar Asn, adv bd, 1972-76; SC Taxpayers Asn, atty, 1973; Co Columbia, asst pros, 1973-75; Gov's Bi-Centennial Comn, 1976; Law Off Hemphill P. Pride II LLC, Pvt pract, atty, 1983-; Richland Co Sch Dist 1, atty, 1999-2003; Self Employed, atty. **Orgs:** SC Bar, 1963; pres, Nat Asn Advan Colored People, cola br, 1964-, life mem, 1965-; Nat Bar Asn, 1964; State Dem Comn 100, 1970; gen coun, Allen Univ, 1977; legal coun, Nat Asn Advan Colored People, 1977. **Honors/Awds:** Patriotic Service Award, SC's Observance of Our Nation's Bicentennial, 1976; South Carolina Black Family Summit Award, 1987; Award of Appreciation, St. John Baptist Church, 1993; National Urban League Inc. Quarter Century Club, 1997; Matthew J. Perry Award, Columbia Black Lawyers Asn, 2002; Award of Appreciation, Youth Advocate Prog, Inc, 2005; The Whitney M Young Jr Award, Columbia Urban League Inc, 2008; Key to the City of Columbia, South Carolina, Mayor Stephen K. Benjamin, 2013. **Special Achievements:** First African-American to hold office in the South Carolina, 1968; First Black to construct 55 unit high-rise 236 housing project in 1970; First African-American to serve as a prosecutor and was appointed Assistant Prosecutor for the City of Columbia, 1973; First African-American to serve as attorney for Richland County School District 1, 1999. **Business Addr:** Attorney at Law, Law Firm of Hemphill P Pride Ii, 1401 Gregg St, Columbia, SC 29201, **Business Phone:** (803)256-8015.

**PRIDE, J. THOMAS**
Executive. **Personal:** Born Jan 18, 1940, Highland Park, MI; married Vernester Green; children: Leslie Faye, Thomas A & Alesia. **Educ:** Highland Park Jr Col, attended 1962; Wayne State Univ, attended 1964. **Career:** J Walter Thompson Co, Detroit, pres, media buyer, 1964-69; Campbell Ewald Co, acct exec, 1969-72; Ross Roy Inc, vpres; Am Asn Advert Agency, teacher; Chrysler Corp, advert exec, advert prog mgr; Health Alliance Plan, dir commun, advert & pub rels, assoc vpres, currently. **Orgs:** Blacks Against Racism, 1969; spkr Black Appl Res Ctr, 1972; trustee, Kirkwood Gen Hosp Club; Adcraft Club Detroit Nat Asn Mkt Devel; Black Appl Res Ctr; Detroit Boat Club. **Home Addr:** 8333 Sorrento, Detroit, MI 48228. **Business Addr:** Associate Vice President, Health Alliance Plan, 2850 W Grand Blvd, Detroit, MI 48202, **Business Phone:** (313)872-8100.

**PRIDE, JOHN L.**
Association executive. **Personal:** Born Nov 4, 1940, Youngstown, OH; married Sallie Curtis; children: Jacqueline & Curtis. **Educ:** Capital Univ Columbus, BA, 1963; Howard Univ, psychol. **Career:** US Off Educ, chief SE oper bran, 1970-72, dep asst dir oper, 1972-74; US Dept HEW, spec asst dep, asst sec human dev & dep exec dir, 1974-. **Orgs:** Consult, White House Conf Food Health & Nutrit, 1969; US Senate Select Comn Human Needs, 1968; Nat Adv Comn Civil Dis, 1968; Adv Comn Spec Educ Montgomery Co, Md Pub Schls; Adv Comm Family Life & Human Dev Mont Co, Md Pub Schs; pres, Mont Co Asn Lang Handicapped C; Big Bros Nat Capital Area. **Business Addr:** Deputy Executive Director, The US Department of Health & Human Services, 200 Independence Ave SW, Washington, DC 20201, **Business Phone:** (202)619-0257.

**PRIDE, RITA MCKINLEY**
Soprano, educator. **Personal:** married Joseph J; children: Ashley & Ashton. **Educ:** Temple Univ, BA, mus; State Univ NY, Binghamton, MA, mus, opera. **Career:** Lincoln Univ, vis instr music & voice, 2005-; Opera Everyone Inc, founder & artistic dir, currently; Opera N, artistic dir; Mainline Performing Arts Center, founder & artistic dir; Tri-Cities Opera Co, artist-in-residence, founder & dir. **Home Addr:** 213 Magnolia Ter, Upper Darby, PA 19082-1014, **Home Phone:** (484)365-4303. **Business Addr:** Visiting Instructor of Music & Voice, Lincoln University of the Commonwealth of Pennsylvania, 1570 Old Baltimore Pke, Lincoln University, PA 19352, **Business Phone:** (484)365-8000.

**PRIDE, WILLIAM L., JR.**
Automotive executive. **Personal:** Born Apr 25, 1948, Crenshaw, MS; son of William L and Savannah; married Sarah B; children: Cynthia P & William L III. **Educ:** Northwest Community Col, BA, electronics, 1982; Ford Training, cert, 1996. **Career:** Pride Auto Sales Inc, owner & gen mgr, 1985-96; Pride Ford Lincoln Mercury Inc, gen mgr & chief exec officer, pres, dir, 1996-. **Orgs:** Bd mem, Boy Girl Club; bd mem, Chamber Com; bd mem, Coahoma Co Arts Craft. **Home Addr:** Curtis Rd, Batesville, MS 38606, **Home Phone:** (662)563-5260. **Business Addr:** Chief Executive Officer, President, Prideford Lincoln Mercury Inc, 730 S State St, Clarksdale, MS 38614-4802, **Business Phone:** (662)627-2800.

**PRIDGEN, ROSIE.** See THOMPSON, ROSIE L.

**PRIEST, DR. MARLON L.**
Physician, educator, school administrator. **Personal:** Born Moulton, AL; son of Charlie W Sr and Odra McKelvy. **Educ:** Univ N Ala, Florence, AL, BS, chem, 1974; Univ Ala, Birmingham Sch Med, Birmingham, AL, 1977. **Career:** Baptist Med Ctr, Birmingham, AL, resident, dir outpatient Med, 1980-81; Univ Ala Birmingham, resident, dep Med dir, Emerg Dept, 1982-85, dept Critical Care Transp, med dir, Univ Hosp emerg dept, chief qual officer, 1985-89, asst prof surg, 1985-86, assoc prof surg, 1986-94, prof, 1994, asst vpres health affairs, 1988-92, div dir & emergency servs, 1989-90, dir, emergency Med residency prog, 1989-90; Univ Ala Med Ctr, assoc vpres; Univ Ala, Sch Med, assoc dean, 1992-98, prof emergency med, currently; Lister Hill Ctr Health Policy, scholar, currently; Bon Secours Health Syst, exec vpres, chief med officer & mkt lead sr serv, currently. **Orgs:** Nat counr, 1990-93, Ala Chap, pres, 1988-90, bd dir, 1982-, Am Col Emergency Physicians; pres, Mineral Dist Med Soc, 1988-90; bd dir, Am Heart Asn Jefferson & Shelby, 1984-; Ala Affil Am Heart, pres, 1994-95; underGrad curric comt, Soc Acad Emerg Med, 1984-86; pres, Beta Beta Beta, 1973; admiss comt, Univ Ala Sch Med, 1983-86; bd dir, Univ Ala Birmingham Nat Alumni Asn, 1989-93; pres adv coun, Univ Ala Birmingham, 1982-; Cath Health Asn, bd trustee, 2000-; bd dir, Sisters Mercy Health Syst; fel, RWJF Health Policy; bd dir, Sister Charity Leavenworth Healthcare Syst; Premier Healthcare Alliance Qual Improv Comt; Alpha Omega Alpha. **Home Addr:** 912 Conroy Rd, Birmingham, AL 35222, **Home Phone:** (205)595-6653. **Business Addr:** Executive Vice President, Chief Medical Officer, Bon Secours Health System Inc, 1505 Marriottsville Rd, Marriottsville, MD 21104, **Business Phone:** (410)442-5511.

**PRIESTER, JULIAN ANTHONY**
Jazz musician, composer, educator. **Personal:** Born Jun 29, 1935, Chicago, IL; son of Lucius Harper and Colelia Smith; married Jaymi; children: Julia Antoinette, Claudette Ann Campbell, Adebayo & Atuanya. **Educ:** Sherwood Sch Music, Chicago, Ill; Cornish Col Arts, DFA. **Career:** ECM Recs, Riverside Recs, trombonist & band leader, 1954-91; Sun Ra Archestra, trombonist & soloist, 1954-56, 1990; Max Roach Quintette, trombonist & soloist, 1959-61, 1964-65; Art Blakey's Jazz Messingers, trombonist & soloist, 1968; Duke Ellington Orchestra, lead trombonist, 1970; Herbie Hancock Sextet, trombonist & soloist, 1971-73; John Coltrane, soloist; Lone Mountain Col, fac, 1976-77; Dave Holland Quintet, trombonist & soloist, 1984-87; Cornish Col Arts, Music Dept, admin fac, 1979-2011, prof emer, currently; Albums: Keep Swinging, 1960; Spiritsville, 1960; Love Love, 1973; Polarization, 1977; Hints on Light & Shadow, 1997; In Deep End Dance, 2002; Monoliths & Dimensions Album, 2009; Blue Stride, 2012. **Orgs:** Prog dir & fac, Cazadero Music Camp, 1978-80; Music Adv Coun, 1979-80; fac, Naropa Inst, 1981-83; fac, Banff Ctr Arts, 1984-87; bd dir, Pac Jazz Inst, 1987; comnr, Seattle Arts Comn, 1988-91. **Honors/Awds:** Commemorative Plaque Msingi Workshop, 1972; Grant, NEA, 1975; Best Horn Player Award, Bay Area Music Mag, 1978; Commemorative Plaque San Francisco Jazz Comt, 1979; King County Arts Comn Grant, 1987; Seafirst Faculty Award, 1990; Record of the Year, In Deep End Dance, Earshot Jazz, 2002; Honor, Pac NW Chap Rec Acad, 2005. **Home Addr:** 9908 Beacon Ave S, Seattle, WA 98118-5624, **Home Phone:** (206)725-4469. **Business Addr:** Professor Emeritus, Cornish College of the Arts, 1000 Lenora St, Seattle, WA 98121, **Business Phone:** (800)726-2787.

**PRIESTLEY, MARILYN**
Association executive, vice president (organization). **Educ:** Rider Univ, BS, labor rels. **Career:** Novartis Pharaceuticals Corp, vpres human resources & vpres diversity & Inclusion; InQUEST Consult LLC, sr partner, currently. **Business Addr:** Senior Partner, InQUEST Consulting LLC, 30 S Wacker Dr Suite 2200, Chicago, IL 60606, **Business Phone:** (312)466-5717.

**PRIGMORE, KATHRYN TYLER (KATHRYN BRADFORD TYLER)**
Architect. **Personal:** Born Nov 21, 1956, St. Albans, NY; daughter of Richard and Shirley Tyler; married James Craig; children: Crystal Andrea & Amber Sheriesse. **Educ:** TCWilliams, dipl, 1974; Rensselaer Polytech Inst, BS, bldg Sci, 1977, BA, 1978; Cath Univ Am, MS, Engineering admin, 1982. **Career:** VVKR Inc, architect, 1975-81; Robert A hawthorne Architects PC, architect, 1981; Robert Traynham Cols, architect, PC, architect, 1982-83; Segreti Tepper Architects, assoc, 1983-90; Howard Univ, Sch Archit & Planning, assoc prof, assoc dean, 1989-2003; Col Engineering, Archit & Comp Sci, asst dir, 1997-98; Einhorn Yaffee Prescott Archit & Engineering, sr assoc, 1998-2003; HDR Archit Inc, vpres, 2003-. **Orgs:** Northern Va Urban League, 1980-81; fel Am Inst Architects, 1981-10; Nat Orgn Minority Architects, 1985-10; archivist, Black Women Archit, 1990-; et al, 1993-, chmn, 1996-97, 1999-2000, 2001-02, Va Bd Architects, Prof Engrs, Land Surveryors; adv coun, exam comnr, 1993-2001, chmn, 2000, comt mem, Nat Coun Archit Regist Bds, 1993-2005; AIA Nat Ethics Coun, currently. **Honors/Awds:** Oustanding Young Women in America, 1983. **Special Achievements:** One of the first African Am women licensed to practice architect in US. **Home Addr:** 8911 Union Farm Rd, Alexandria, VA 22309-3936, **Home Phone:** (703)360-8015. **Business Addr:** Vice President, HDR Architecture Inc, 8404 Indian Hills Dr, Omaha, NJ 68114-4098, **Business Phone:** (402)399-1000.

**PRIMM, ANNELLE BENEE**
Psychiatrist. **Personal:** Born Jan 26, 1956, Geneva; married Herbert; children: India. **Educ:** Harvard Univ, BA, pre-med/biol, 1980; Howard Univ Col Med, MD, 1980; Johns Hopkins Sch Pub Health, MPH, 1985. **Career:** Johns Hopkins Hosp, resident training gen psychiat, 1980-84, staff psychiatrist & other positions, 1984-93; COSTAR (Community Support Treat & Rehab), co-founder, 1985; Provident Hosp, Baltimore, MD, psychiatrist, 1985-86; Johns Hopkins Sch Med, assoc prof psychiat; Johns Hopkins Hosp Community Psychiat Prog, med dir, 1993-2003; Springfield State Hosp, dir City Div; Our Own, psychiat consult; Am Psychiat Asn, dir Minority Fel Prog & Div Diversity & Health Equality, 2004-15, Dep Med Dir, 2009-15; Urban Behav Assocs, sr psychiatrist advisor, 2015-. **Orgs:** Am Psychiat Asn, Am Col Psychiatrists. **Special Achievements:** Video producer, "Black and Blue" (1999), "Gray and Blue" (2001); coeditor, "Women in Psychiatry: Personal Perspectives" (2012). **Business Addr:** 2317 Sulgrave Ave, Baltimore, MD 21209, **Business Phone:** (410)262-4552.

**PRIMO, QUINTIN, III**
Executive. **Personal:** Born Mar 14, 1955, Rochester, NY; son of Quintin E Jr (deceased) and Winnifred; married Diane; children: Francesca & Quintin IV. **Educ:** Ind Univ, BS, finance, 1977; Harvard Bus Sch, MBA, 1979. **Career:** Q Primo & Co, managing dir, co-founder, 1988-92; Capri Capital Partners LLC, chief exec officer & chmn, 1992-; Citicorps Real Estate, vpres. **Orgs:** Chicago Sinfonetta; bd mem, Chicago Community Trust; Fed Res Bank Chicago Adv Bd; bd mem, Univ Chicago Hosps; Real Estate Coun; bd chmn, Primo Women & C Ctr; trustee, Church Pension Group Serv Corp; dir, Real Estate Roundtable; chmn, Capri Real Estate Securities, 2013-; non exec chmn, Capri Global Capital Ltd, 2013-; chmn, Trilogy Capital Advisors, LLC; AMLI Residential Properties Trust; bd mem, Chicago Coun Global Affairs; civic & charitable orgn. **Home Addr:** 2400 N Lakeview Ave Apt 701, Chicago, IL 60614-2734, **Home Phone:** (312)291-9150. **Business Addr:** Chairman, Chief Executive Officer, Capri Capital Partners, 875 N Mich Ave Suite 3430, Chicago, IL 60611, **Business Phone:** (312)573-5300.

**PRIMOUS, EMMA MOORE**
Educator, secretary general. **Personal:** Born Oct 5, 1942, Olive Branch, MS; daughter of Loyal Sr; married Commodore Cantrell; children: Commodore & Christopher. **Educ:** Memphis State Univ, BS, 1964, MEd, 1971. **Career:** Memphis Pub Schs, teacher; MSU Reading Workshop Elem Sch Teachers, cons; WKNO-TV County Schs Prog, panel mem; Open-Space Schs Benoit, cons; MSU TN State Univ

LeMoyne-Owen Col, supr teacher & stud teachers; Prog Prob-solving Skills Memphis City Bd Educ, staff teacher; night adminr, Adult High Sch; Memphis City Schs, instrnl facilitator; Delta fine arts, secy, currently. **Orgs:** Ant Educ Asn; TN Educ Asn; Memphis Educ Asn; vip Rubaiyats Inc; LesCasuale Bridge Club; Cherokee Civic Club; Nat Asn Advan Colored People; Delta Sigma Theta Sorority; Kappa Delta Pi; Int Reading Asn. **Honors/Awds:** Outstanding Young Educator of the Year, Parkway Village Jaycees, 1974; Outstanding Teacher Award, Phi Delta Kappa, 1990. **Home Addr:** 896 Surrey Oaks Cove E, Collierville, TN 38017-7360, **Home Phone:** (901)861-4052. **Business Addr:** Secretary, Delta Fine Arts, PO Box 41022, Memphis, TN 38174-1022.

**PRIMUS-COTTON, DR. BOBBIE J.**
Educator, research scientist. **Personal:** Born Jul 20, 1934, Daytona Beach, FL; daughter of William (deceased) and Lillie Rose (deceased); married Jesse; children: Robyn & Jonathan R. **Educ:** Fla A&M Univ, Tallahassee, FL, BS, 1952; Univ NC, Chapel Hill, NC, MPH, 1972; Va Polytech Inst & State Univ, Blacksburg, VA, EdD, cert pub policy, 1984; Univ Calif Los Angeles, Berkeley, CA, post-doctorate, 1986. **Career:** B-CC's nursing dept, 1976-81; Am Asn State Cols & Univs, Wash, DC, Allied Health Proj, assoc coordr, 1980-82; Howard Univ, Col Allied Health, Wash, DC, assoc coordr allied health proj, 1982-84; Cancer Prev Awareness, assoc coordr, 1984-86; Nat Insts Health, Bethesda, Md, Am Red Cross, Wash, DC, Black Elderly Proj, assoc coordr, 1984-86; Nat Cancer Inst, Cancer Prev Awareness Prog Black Am, Co-Authored with J Hatch, L Monroe, 1985; Morris Brown Col, Atlanta, Ga, Dept Nursing, chair, 1986-88; Univ Cent Fla, Orlando, Fla, assoc prof nursing, coordr spec proj, 1988-93; Bethune Cookman Col, Daytona Beach, Fla, assoc prof, coordr, dir, currently. **Orgs:** Pres, Prof Images Int, 1984-; Dir, Proj SUCCEDS, 1987-; minority grantsmanship chmn, Nat Insts Health, 1988-90; trustee, Daytona Beach Community Col, 1988-93; vpres & chmn, Nat Black Nurses Asn, 1992-. **Home Addr:** 528 Fred Gamble Way, Ormond Beach, FL 32174, **Home Phone:** (904)672-7148. **Business Addr:** Associate Professor of Nursing, Bethune-Cookman College, 640 Dr Mary McLeod Bethune Blvd, Daytona Beach, FL 32114, **Business Phone:** (386)481-2000.

**PRINCE, ANDREW LEE**
Basketball coach, football executive, basketball player. **Personal:** Born Dec 14, 1952, Victoria, TX; son of Hazel Lewis and Andrew. **Educ:** Abilene Christian Univ, BS, 1975, MS, sch admin, 1980. **Career:** Basketball player (retired), basketball coach, football executive; Barcelona, Spain, pro basketball, 1975; Graz, Austria, pro basketball, 1979; Gottingen, Ger, pro basketball, 1981; Abilene Christian Univ, asst coach, 1983, Kinesiology Dept, instr, Multi-Cult Ctr, dir; Stephen F Austin State Univ, asst basketball coach; TX Tech, acad couns specialist; Univ Ill, Fighting Illin football squad, lead acad counr, 2001-. **Orgs:** Black Coaches Assn; Nat Assn Basketball Coaches. **Home Addr:** 4203 NE Stallings Apt 407, Nacogdoches, TX 75961. **Business Addr:** Academic Counselor, University of Illinois Football, Memorial Stadium 1402 S 1st St, Champaign, IL 61820, **Business Phone:** (217)333-1400.

**PRINCE, EDGAR OLIVER**
Government official. **Personal:** Born Sep 13, 1947, Brooklyn, NY. **Educ:** City Univ NY, NY, Christian Coun Ctr, AA, Lib Arts, 1968; State Univ NY, Stony Brook, BA, sociol, 1971, MA, sociol, 1974; CW Post Ctr Long Island Univ, MPA, pub admin, 1980; New York Univ, PhD, pub admin. **Career:** Mission Immaculate Va, 1968; St Agatha's Home C, 1969; St Vincent Hall, 1970-71; sr residential child care counr; State Univ NY, Stony Brook, sociol grad teaching asst ship, 1971-73; Suffolk Co Summer Intern Prog Youth Bd, res analyst, 1972; CW Post Ctr Long Island Univ, dept Criminal Justice, adj asst prof, 1974-79; Suffolk Co Criminal Just Coordr Coun, coexec off sr res analyst, 1974-75; Suffolk Co Dept Health Serv, sr res analyst, 1975-. **Orgs:** Am Pub Health Asn, 1975-; Am Soc Pub Admin, 1976-; Int Soc Syst Sci Health Care, 1980-; Nat Forum Black Pub Admins, 1983-; charter mem, Statue Liberty Ellis Island Found Inc, 1984-; Cong Black Caucus Health Brain Trust, 1984-; charter mem & trustee, Repub Presidential Task Force, 1984-. **Honors/Awds:** Presidential Medal Merit, 1985; Presidential Honor Roll, 1985; Certificate of Merit, Presidential Comn Repub Presidential Task Force, 1986; Certificate of Recognition, Nat Repub Cong Comn. **Special Achievements:** Numerous publ. **Home Addr:** 22 E 29th St Apt 214, New York, NY 10016.

**PRINCE, GINA MARIA.** **See PRINCE-BYTHEWOOD, GINA.**

**PRINCE, DR. JOAN MARIE**
Hematologist. **Personal:** Born Jan 14, 1954, Milwaukee, WI. **Educ:** Univ Wis-Milwaukee, BA, 1977, BS, 1981, MS, 1992, PhD, urban educ, 1999. **Career:** St Joseph's Hosp, hematologist, 1981-; Covenant Health Care Systs, clin lab supvr; Med Sci Labs, supvr & hemat, 1988; Univ Wis Med Sch, Milwaukee, Wis, clin lectr, 1993-, mgr health professions partnership initiative, asst chancellor, vice chancellor, 2000-; Prince Group, pres & chief exec officer; Health Professions Partnership Initiative, dir; CG Schmidt Inc dir; Froedtert Memorial Lutheran Hosp Inc, dir. **Orgs:** Delta Sigma Theta Sor, 1974-; assoc mem, Am Soc Clin Pathologists, 1981-; pres, Black Women's Network; Group Cancer & Black Am Community, 1982-; task force mem, Black Women's Health Proj, 1983-; speakers bur, Ronald McDonald House, 1984-86; bd dir, Am Cancer Soc, 1985-; assoc mem, Am Soc Med Technologists; bd dir, UW Milwaukee Alumni Asn, 1985-86; Citizens Rev Bd, 1987; Future Milwaukee, 1988-; bd mem, Greater Milwaukee Found; vice chmn, Nat Kidney Found Wis; bd mem, Wis Women's Coun; dir, Coun Foundations Inc; bd dir, Milwaukee Pub Libr; Community Brainstorming Conf Exec Comt; Wis African Am Women; bd dir, Ko-Thi Dance Co; Managed Health Serv Wis. **Honors/Awds:** Future Milwaukee Community Service Award, 1992; Women of Color Recognition Award, 1991; Future Milwaukee Community Service Award, 1993; WITI-TV 6 & The Milwaukee Times, Black Excellence Award for Community Service, 1994; First Annual Executive Committee Award for Volunteerism-Community Brain Storming Conference, 1996; Distinguished Professional Award, N Cent Serv Club; TEMPO Mentor of the Year Award; UWM Alumni Citizenship Award; Sciences-Omicron Sigma Award, Am Soc Clin Lab. **Special Achievements:** Ffirst African American graduate of the bachelor's program in Medical Technology, as well as the Masters Program in Clinical Laboratory Sciences at University Wisconsin Milwaukee. Published article "Black Women & Health", 1984; 1989 Black Role Model Milwaukee Public Library 1989; 12 articles in The Business Journal magazine, topic: "Instilling Entrepreneurial Spirit In Youth" 1989. **Home Addr:** 8712 W Spokane St, Milwaukee, WI 53224-4826, **Home Phone:** (414)353-4414. **Business Addr:** Vice Chancellor, University of Wisconsin-Milwaukee, Chapman Hall 118 2200 E Kenwood Blvd, Milwaukee, WI 53201-0413, **Business Phone:** (414)229-1122.

**PRINCE, RICHARD EVERETT**
Journalist. **Personal:** Born Jul 26, 1947, New York, NY; son of Jonathan Joseph and Audrey Elaine. **Educ:** New York Univ, BS, 1969. **Career:** Newark Star-Ledger, reporter, 1967-68; Wash Post, reporter 1968-77; Dem & Chronicle, asst metro ed, 1979-81, asst news ed, 1981-85, ed writer, columnist, 1985-93, op-ed ed, 1993-94; Communities Sch Inc, publ ed, 1994-98; Nat Asn Black Journalists Wash Post, 1999-2008 p/t copy ed; ed, Black Col Wire, 2002-2007; columnist, Maynard Inst Journalism Educ, 2002-. **Orgs:** Nat Assoc Black Journalists, 1984-; pres, Rochester Assoc Black Communicators, 1986-87; Writers & Bks, 1988-94; Nat Conf Ed Writers, Assoc Opinion Journalists, 1993-; Nat Soc Newspaper Columnists, 1989-90; NABJ Jour, co-ed, 1990-93, assoc ed, 1994-97. **Honors/Awds:** Third place writing competition, commentary, Nat Asn Black Journalists, 1987, 1988, 1989; Second place writing competition, Nat Soc Newspaper Columnists, 1989; President's Award, Nat Asn Black Journalists, 2003; Let's Do It Better, Columbia U Grad School of Journalism, 2007; Robert G McGruder Award for media diversity, Kent State U, 2010; Ida B Wells Award, Nat Asn of Black Journalists & Medill School, Northwestern U, 2013. **Home Addr:** 11 E Oxford Ave, Alexandria, VA 22301. **Business Addr:** Columnist, Maynard Institute for Journalism Education, 11 E Oxford Ave, Alexandria, DC 22301, **Business Phone:** (703)362-8197.

**PRINCE-BYTHEWOOD, GINA (GINA MARIA PRINCE)**
Administrator, writer, movie producer. **Personal:** Born Jun 10, 1969; married Reggie Rock; children: Cassius & Toussaint. **Educ:** Univ Calif Los Angeles, Sch Theatre, attended 1991. **Career:** TV Series: "CBS Schoolbreak Special"; "A Different World", 1992-93; "Courthouse", 1995; "Felicity", 1998; "Disappearing Acts", dir, 2000; Biker Boyz, producer, 2003; Daddy's Girl, producer, 2007; TV Series: "The Bernie Mac Show", 2000; "Everybody Hates Chris", 2005; "Everybody Hates the Laundromat", 2005; "Girlfriends", 2005; "Odds & Ends", 2005; "Fits & Starts", 2005; "Reflections", co-producer, 2007; Editor: South Central; "Sweet Justice", 1994-95; Director & Writer: Stitches, 1991; What About Your Friends?, 1995; Love & Basketball, 2000; Secret Life of Bees The, 2008; Beyond the Lights, 2014; Writer: "Damn Whitey", 1997. **Home Addr:** , SC. **Business Addr:** Actor, International Creative Management, 8942 Wilshire Blvd, Beverly Hills, CA 90211, **Business Phone:** (310)550-4000.

**PRINGLE, MIKE (MICHAEL A PRINGLE)**
Football player. **Personal:** Born Oct 1, 1967, Los Angeles, CA. **Educ:** Wash State Univ, grad; Calif State Univ, Fullerton, criminal justice. **Career:** Football player (retired); Nat Football League, Atlanta Falcons, 1990-91; Can Football League, Edmonton Eskimos, running back, 1992, 2003-04; World League Am Football, Sacramento Surge, running back, 1992; Can Football League, Sacramento Gold Miners, running back, 1993; Can Football League, Baltimore Stallions, 1994-95; Nat football league, Denver Broncos, 1996; Can Football League, Montreal Alouettes, running back, 1996-2002, 2005. **Honors/Awds:** All-Star, Can Football League, 1994-95, 1997-2000, 2003; East All-Star, Can Football League, 1994, 1996-2001; Most Outstanding Player, Can Football League, 1995; Most Outstanding Player, Can Football League, 1995, 1998; Grey Cup champion, 1995, 2002-03; West All-Star, Can Football League, 2003; Canadian Football Hall of Fame, 2008. **Special Achievements:** Most Rushing Touchdowns Game, 2004; One of the CFL's Top 50 players of the league's modern era by Canadian sports network, 2006. **Home Addr:** 344 Tanner Dr, Oxford, MS 38655.

**PRINGLE, DR. NELL RENE**
Counselor, educator. **Personal:** Born Jun 21, 1952, Baytown, TX; daughter of Earlest Fontenot Sr and Elsie M Fontenot; married Danny C Sr; children: Danny Jr, Courtney Tenille & Jaime Reshaude. **Educ:** Lee Col, AA, 1971; Lamar Univ, BS, 1973; Tex Southern Univ, MEd, 1976, EdD, 1991. **Career:** Crosby Independent Sch Dist, educr, 1975-89; San Jacinto Col, dir couns, 1989; Kellogg fel, 1997; San Jacinto Col, assoc dean instr technol, currently; Lic Specialist Sch Psychol (LSSP), diagnostician; Tex Southern Univ, counr. **Orgs:** Tex Jr Col Teachers Asn. **Honors/Awds:** Scholar, Ford Found, 1971; Most Representative Student Award, Lee Col, 1971; Fellows Award, Tex A&M Univ, 1990. **Home Addr:** PO Box 197, Highlands, TX 77562, **Home Phone:** (713)451-6233. **Business Addr:** Associate Dean of Instructional Technology, San Jacinto College North Campus, Brightwell Techl Bldg 5800 Uvalde, Houston, TX 77049, **Business Phone:** (281)998-6150.

**PRIOLEAU, OSCAR EUGENE, JR.**
Lawyer. **Personal:** Born Oct 11, 1963, Columbia, SC; son of Oscar Sr and Lillian; married Edilinda E; children: Monica, Oscar III & Antonio. **Educ:** Univ SC, BS, bus, 1985; Tex Southern Univ, JD, 1988; Georgetown Univ Law Ctr, LLM, labor law, 1989. **Career:** Ogletree Deakins, assoc atty, 1993-95; Jackson Lewis PC, assoc atty, 1995-96; Johnson Prioleau Kenison & Lynch LLC, managing partner, 1996-99; Prioleau & Assocs, managing partner, 1999-2011, owner, atty, founding partner, currently, sr partner, 2011-; Prioleau & Milfort LLC, atty, currently. **Orgs:** Omega Psi Phi, 1982-; Phi Delta Phi, 1985; Fulfur County Off Workforce Develop Bd, 2001-; Nat Employ Lawyers Asn. **Home Addr:** 800 Peachtree St NE Apt 2102, Atlanta, GA 30308-6019. **Business Addr:** Founding Partner, Senior Partner, Prioleau & Associates, 505 Pryor St SW, Atlanta, GA 30312, **Business Phone:** (404)526-9400.

**PRIOLEAU, PETER SYLVESTER**
Banker. **Personal:** Born Dec 10, 1949, Hopkins, SC; son of Jessie and Ruth Byrd; married Brenda Mickens. **Educ:** Midland Tech Col, AA, retail mgt, 1974; Benedict Col, BS, bus, 1975. **Career:** Davision-Macys Dept Store, assoc mgr, 1972-75; Bank Am, vpres, 1975-01; NationsBank, vpres & community investment coordr, currently. **Orgs:** SC Bankers Asn, 1975-01; Greater Columbia Chamber Com, 1975-01; NCP, 1978-; Comt, 100 Black Men. **Home Addr:** PO Box 1823, Columbia, SC 29202. **Business Addr:** Vice President, NationsBank, PO Box 727, Columbia, SC 29222, **Business Phone:** (803)343-7930.

**PRIOLEAU, PIERSON OLIN**
Football player. **Personal:** Born Aug 6, 1977, Charleston, SC; married Alicia; children: Pierson Jalen, Pace Jordan & Parker Jayden. **Educ:** Va Tech Univ, interdisciplinary studies. **Career:** Virginia Tech, Defensive Back, 1995-98; San Francisco 49ers, defensive back, 1999-2000; Buffalo Bills, 2001-04; Wash Redskins, defensive back, 2005-07; Jacksonville Jaguars, 2008-09; New Orleans Saints, defensive back, 2009-10. **Home Addr:** PO Box 447, Radford, VA 24143-0447.

**PRIOLEAU, DR. SARA NELLIENE (SARA MCKEEVER)**
Administrator, dentist. **Personal:** Born Apr 10, 1940, Hopkins, SC; daughter of Willie Oree and Wilhelmina; married William R Montgomery; children: Sharon, Myra & John; married William F McKeever; children: Kara I & William P. **Educ:** SC State Col, BS, 1960, MS, 1965; Univ Pa, DMD, 1970. **Career:** Philadelphia Gen Hosp, gen dentist intern, 1970-71; Comph Group Health Serv, pub health dent, 1971-72; Hamilton Health Ctr, dir dent serv, 1972-97; Community Dent Assoc PC, pres, 1976-; Seltnsgrace Ctr, 1999-2002. **Orgs:** Nat Dent Asn, 1970-; Am Dent Asn, 1970-; Harrisburg Dent Soc, Links Inc, 1976-, pres, 2002; Exec Women Int Harrisburg Chap, 1984-90; vchmn, Status Women, 1986-87; bd dir, Ment Health Asn Tri County Inc, 1986-88; pres, Soroptimist Int Harrisburg, 1987-89; chmn health, Soroptomist Int N Atlantic Region, 1988-89; Dent dir, Healthmate health maintenance orgn, Hamilton Health Ctr, 1988-96; pres, Soroptomist Int Harrisburg, 1989-90; med assistance, Dent Sub Comt State Pa; bd trustee, 1990-99, vpres, 1997-99, Harrisburg Area Community Col; vpres, 2000-01, pres, 2001-02, Harrisburg Area Dent Soc. **Honors/Awds:** Working Woman of the Year, Health Service Pomoys, 1982; Woman of the Year, Black Women's Caucus; Cumberland Co Ment Retardation Award, 1987 & 1995; Koser Award, Athena Recipient, 1995; fel, Int Col Dent, 1996; Pa Best 50Women Bus, 1997. **Home Addr:** 117 Trenton Ave, Lavallette, NJ 08735, **Home Phone:** (717)545-5501. **Business Addr:** President, Community Dental Associates PC, 2451 N 3rd St, Harrisburg, PA 17101, **Business Phone:** (717)238-8163.

**PRIOR, ANTHONY EUGENE**
Football player, writer. **Personal:** Born Mar 27, 1970, Lowell, MA; children: Anthony Jordan. **Educ:** Wash State Univ, philos. **Career:** Football player (retired), author, owner; NY Jets, defensive back, 1992-95; Minn Vikings, 1996-97; Oakland Raiders, 1998; Calgary Stampeders, defensive back, 2000-01, 2003; BC Lions, defensive back, 2002; auth & pub speaker, currently; Stone Hold Bks Corp, owner, author, currently; Ocean Speed Camp, owner, chief exec officer & coach, 2004-. **Orgs:** Nat Football League Players Asn. **Business Addr:** Owner & Coach, Chief Executive Officer, Ocean Speed Camp, 3861 Lofton Pl, Riverside, CA 92501, **Business Phone:** (951)816-8400.

**PRITCHARD, DARON**
Government official. **Personal:** Born Aug 26, 1954, Vicksburg, MS; married Juanita Hill; children: LaTonzia, LaToya, LaKeita & Daron Jamaal. **Educ:** Utica Jr Col; Alcorn State Univ, Lormaums, BA, 1977. **Career:** Eastern Foods Inc, br mgr; Town Edwards, mayor, currently. **Orgs:** Deacon Friendship MB Church. **Home Addr:** 1805 Meadowbrook Rd, Jackson, MS 39211-6526. **Business Addr:** Mayor, Town of Edwards, PO Box 215, Edwards, MS 39066-0215, **Business Phone:** (601)852-5461.

**PRITCHARD, MICHAEL ROBERT**
Football player, radio host. **Personal:** Born Oct 26, 1969, Shaw AFB, SC. **Educ:** Univ Colo. **Career:** Football player (retired), caller, host; Atlanta Falcons, wide receiver, 1991-93; Denver Broncos, wide receiver, 1994-95; Seattle Seahawks, wide receiver, 1996-99; ESPN 1100 Radio Sta, Mitch & Pritch Show, host, caller, currently. **Honors/Awds:** Colo Most Valuable Person. **Business Addr:** Caller, ESPN 1100 Radio Station, 8755 W Flamingo Rd, Las Vegas, NV 89147, **Business Phone:** (702)876-1460.

**PRITCHARD, ROBERT STARLING, II**
Composer, pianist, founder (originator). **Personal:** Born Jun 13, 1927, Winston-Salem, NC; son of R Starling Sr and Lucille Pickard. **Educ:** Syracuse Univ, Syracuse NY, BS, 1948, MM, 1950; pvt piano study with Edwin Fischer, Arturo Benedetti Michelangeli, Carl Fried berg, Hans Neumann, & Robert Golds band. **Career:** Touring concert pianist, 1951-; Conservatoire Nationale D'Haiti, Port-au-Prince, Haiti, artist-in-residence, 1958; Univ Liberia, Monrovia, artist-in-residence, 1959; New Sch Social Res, New York, NY, fac mem, 1962; Black Hist Month, founder, 1965; Panamerican & Panafrican Asn, Baldwinsville, NY, co-founder & chmn, 1968-; Kahre-Richardes Family Found, Baldwinsville, cofounder & chmn, 1972-; Impartial Citizen Newspaper, Syracuse, NY, publi, 1980-; Lincoln Univ Pa, artist-in-residence, 1988-. **Honors/Awds:** Doctorate honoris causa, Nat Univ Haiti, 1968; citation, Orgn Am States, 1969; founder & organizer, Louis Moreau Gotts chalk Int Pianists & Composers Competition, Dillard Univ, 1970; artistic dir, Gala Concert Peace & Reconsiliation DAR Constitution Hall, Wash DC, 1970; artistic dir, UN Gen Assembly Concert Gala US, Bicentennial & 13th Anniversary Orgn African Unity, 1976; artistic dir, Martin Luther King Concerts, Riverside Church & Cathedral St. John Divine, 1978; Black Hist Month Founder's Citation, Gov New York, 1987; Bayard Rustin Human Rights Award, A Philip Randolph Inst, 1988; President's Centennial Medal, Lincoln Univ, 1988; artistic dir, Black Hist Month Concert Gala, Lincoln Univ, 1989. **Special Achievements:** First African American concert pianist to tour Europe, the Middle East, and North Africa as a solo performer.

**Business Addr:** Chairman, Co-Founder, Panamerican/Panafrican Association Inc, PO Box 143, Baldwinsville, NY 13027, **Business Phone:** (315)638-7379.

### PRITCHETT, KELVIN BRATODD
Football player. **Personal:** Born Oct 24, 1969, Atlanta, GA. **Educ:** Univ Miss, grad. **Career:** Football player (retired); Detroit Lions, 1991, 2000, 2003-04, right defensive end, 1992-94, defensive tackle, 1999, 2001, defensive tackle, left defensive end & right defensive end, 2002; Jacksonville Jaguars, left defensive end, 1995, 1997-98, defensive tackle, 1996. **Special Achievements:** TV show: "Super Bowl Fever"; "1991 NFL Draft", 1991; "Home Improvement", 1994-95. **Home Addr:** 4765 Guilford Forest Dr SW, Atlanta, GA 30331.

### PRITCHETT, STANLEY JEROME, JR.
Football player, football coach, teacher. **Personal:** Born Dec 22, 1973, Atlanta, GA; son of Stanley and Sharon; children: 4. **Educ:** Univ SC, BA, hist, 1995; Grand Canyon Univ, MEd, sec educ & teaching, 2012. **Career:** Football player (retired), football coach, teacher; Miami Dolphins, fullback, 1996-99, running back, wide receiver, 1999; Philadelphia Eagles, running back, 2000-01; Chicago Bears, 2001, fullback, 2002-03, tight end, 2002; Atlanta Falcons, fullback, 2004-05; Booker T. Wash High Sch, teacher & football coach, 2008-11; N Atlanta High Sch, head coach, 2011-12; Westlake High Sch, head coach, 2012; Arabia Mountain High Sch, teacher & head coach, 2013-. **Orgs:** Kappa Alpha Psi Fraternity Inc; Stanley Pritchett, Jr. Found. **Business Addr:** Teacher, Head Coach, Arabia Mountain High School, 6610 Browns Mill Rd, Lithonia, GA 30038, **Business Phone:** (678)875-3602.

### PROCOPE, ERNESTA G
Insurance executive, association executive. **Personal:** Born Jan 1, 1931?, Brooklyn, NY; married John L; married Albin Bowman. **Educ:** Howard Univ, Adelphi Univ, Marymount Manhattan Col, JD; Morgan State Univ, Doctor, humane lett, Brooklyn Col; Pohs Inst Ins. **Career:** E G Bowman Inc, founder, pres, chief exec officer, 1953-; Procope Capital Mgt, chairperson, part-owner, 1990; Bowman-Procope Assoc, 1970; Brinkerhoff Homes, Jamaica, NY, developer. **Orgs:** Chubb Corp; Columbia Gas Syst Inc; trustee, Cornell Univ; Avon Products; S St Seaport Mus; New York Zoological Soc; Boys & Girls Clubs Am; trustee, Adelphi Univ. **Honors/Awds:** Woman of the Year, Tuesday mag, White House Ceremony, First Lady Patricia Nixon, 1972; Entrepreneurial Excellence, Dow Jones / Wall St Jour, 1992; Crain's New York Business All-Star Award, 1993; Entrepreneur of the year, 1993; Small Business Person of the Year, US Small Bus Admin, 1993; Helen Garvin Outstanding Achiever Award, Nat Asn Ins Women, 1995; Woman of the Year, Police Athletic League, 1995; Minority Business Enterprise Legal Defense & Reeducation Fund, Parren J. Mitchell Award; Heritage Award, Exec Leadership Council & Foundation, 1997; hon degrees from Howard Univ, Adelphi Univ, Marymount Manhattan Col, Morgan State Univ; Gambia, Spec Ambassador; Minority Business Hall of Fame and Museum, 2006. **Special Achievements:** E.G. Bowne is now America's largest minority-owned and woman-owned insurance brokerage firm; First Women of Power Summit; First Negro Woman to Build Homes in New York State; trustee, Cornell Univ; trustee, Adelphi Univ; First African American-owned business to be located on Wall Street, 1979. **Business Addr:** Chief Executive Officer, President, E G Bowman Inc, 97 Wall St, New York, NY 10005-3518, **Business Phone:** (212)425-8150.

### PROCOPE, JONELLE
Lawyer, foundation executive. **Personal:** Born Mar 20, 1951; daughter of John L Sr and Corinne; married Frederick O Terrell; children: Matthew & Evan. **Educ:** Howard Univ, BA, econs; St. John's Univ, JD. **Career:** Skadden, Arps, Slate, Meagher & Flom, assoc atty, 1977; Viacom Int Inc, 1980; Bristol-Meyers Squibb Co, dir bus affairs, 1988-94; Blackground Rec, vpres bus & Legal Affairs, 1998-2003; Apollo Theater Found, pres & chief exec officer, 2003-; Pvt pract atty, specializing entertainment law; Advert & Media departments co's Consumer Prod Group, legal coun. **Orgs:** bd trustee, Apollo Theater Found, 1999-2003; Mus Mod Art, Friends Educ Comt. **Honors/Awds:** Matrix Award, New York Women Commun; Named in Portfolio magazine's 73 Biggest Brains in Business, Ebony magazine; One of 100 Women Who Shape Our City, The New York Daily News. **Business Addr:** President, Chief Executive Officer, Apollo Theater Foundation, 253 W 125th St, New York, NY 10027, **Business Phone:** (212)531-5300.

### PROCTER, HARVEY THORNTON, JR.
Automotive executive, association executive, lawyer. **Personal:** Born Dec 29, 1945, Monongahela, PA; son of Harvey T Sr (deceased) and Charlene McPherson (deceased); children: Karyn Michele. **Educ:** Southern Ill Univ, BA, 1967; Roosevelt Univ, MA, 1970; Wayne State Univ, JD, 1976. **Career:** Univ Ill Law, fel; Ill Gen Assembly, scholar; Chicago Comn Youth Welfare, asst zone dir, 1966, dir spec events, 1967; Ford Motor Co, union rels mgr, 1968-; Univ Mich, Sch Bus, LEAD Prog, lectr, 1986-; Nat Urban League, Black Exec Exchange Prog, vis prof, 1988-. **Orgs:** Detroit Bar Asn, MI; Asn Trial Lawyers Am; Am Mgt Asn; Soc Human Resource Mgt; Midwest Co op Educ Asn; Employ Mgt Asn; life mem, Alpha Phi Alpha; life mem, Nat Asn Advan Colored People; parish coun, St Thomas Apostle Church; chmn, Midwest Col Placement Asn, 1983-; pres, bd dir, Earhart Village Homes; Bus Adv Coun Mgt Inst, 1987-90; pres, exec bd, Midwest Col Placement Asn, 1988-; Bus Adv Coun Clark Atlanta Univ Ctr, 1988-89; Bus Adv Coun Univ Mich Comprehensive Studies Prog, 1989-; task force mem, Nat Gov Asn, 1990-; pres, Midwest Asn Col & Employ, 1990-91; State Bar Mich; vpres, employ rels, bd gov, Col Placement Coun, 1991-; pres, Nat Asn Cols & Employers, 1997-98. **Honors/Awds:** Vice Presidents Award Youth Motivation, vpres US, 1970; Citation of Merit, City Detroit Police Dept, 1990, 1991; Award of Merit, Jarvis Christian Col, 1990, 1992. **Home Addr:** 3678 Wellington Cross Rd, Ann Arbor, MI 48105-3044, **Home Phone:** (734)995-2372. **Business Addr:** Union Relations Manager, Ford Motor Co, The Am Rd Suite 367, Dearborn, MI 48121, **Business Phone:** (313)322-4540.

### PROCTOR, BARBARA GARDNER
Executive, chief executive officer. **Personal:** Born Nov 30, 1932, Black Mountain, NC; daughter of Bernice Gardner; married Carl; children: Morgan. **Educ:** Talledega Col, BA, psych sociol, BA, eng educ, 1954. **Career:** Downbeat mag, contrib ed; Vee Jay Rec Int, int dir, 1961-64; Post-Keyes-Gardner Advt, 1964-68; Gene Taylor Asn, 1969; N Advert Agency, copy suprv, 1969-70; Proctor & Gardner Advert Inc, pres. **Orgs:** Contg ed Down Beat Mag, 1958; Chicago Econ Devel Corp; Chicago Media Women; Nat Radio Arts & Sci; Chicago Advertising Club; Chicago Womens Advertising Club; Female Exec Assoc; Better Bus Bur, Cosmopolitan C C; chmn, WTTW TV Auction; Chicago Econ Devel Corp, Chicago Urban League, Nat Asn Advan Colored People; Seaway Nat Bank, Mt Sinai Hosp, Ill State C C, Coun Univ Ill. **Business Addr:** President, Proctor & Gardner Advertising Inc, 111 E Wacker Dr Suite 931, Chicago, IL 60601-3713, **Business Phone:** (312)565-5400.

### PROCTOR, SONYA T.
Police chief, government official. **Educ:** FBI Nat Acad. **Career:** Police officer (retired); DC Metrop Police Dept, police cadet, 1973, police officer fifth dist, 1974-79, sgt second dist, 1979-84, patrol sgt, detective sgt, admin sgt, lt, 1984-88, Internal Affairs Div, asst br comdr, 1984-88, admin lt, 1988-91, Med Serv Div, admin lt, 1990, Spec Opers Div, capt, 1991-93, Off Internal Affairs, dir, Planning & Develop Div, Spec Opers Div, comdr spec events br, 1991-93, inspector, 1993-95, 3rd dist comndg officer, 1995-97, asst chief police, 1997-98, interim police chief, 1997-98. **Special Achievements:** First female to head the Washington, DC police force; First African American woman to head the 3700-member department. **Home Addr:** 9610 Covenant Ct, Owings, MD 20736-3336.

### PROCTOR, WILLIAM H.
Consultant, educator. **Personal:** Born Jan 15, 1945, Baltimore, MD. **Educ:** Pa State Univ, BS, 1967; NC Cent Univ Law Sch, JD, 1970; Univ Pa, MBA, 1973. **Career:** Fed Trade Comn, examr mgt mkt, 1970-71; Pagan & Morgan, consult, 1973; Morgan State Univ, Earl G Graves Sch Bus & Mgt, Bus Admin Dept, asst prof bus & mgt, assoc prof, currently. **Orgs:** Kappa Alpha Psi Frat, 1963; pres, CBH Invest Corp, 1966-; Phi Alpha Delta Law Frat, 1971; Rapid Transit Coal Balt, 1973-; bd mem, Harris & Proctor, 1973-; bd mem, Proctor Enterprises, 1974-; US Supreme Ct, 1976; Phi Alpha Delta; Kappa Alpha Psi; Am Bar Asn; Pa Bar Asn; York Co Bar. **Home Addr:** 1535 Northgate Rd, Baltimore, MD 21218. **Business Addr:** Associate Professor, Morgan State University, Rm 213D McMechen Com Bldg, Baltimore, MD 21251, **Business Phone:** (443)885-1689.

### PROFIT, EUGENE A.
Founder (originator), executive, chief executive officer. **Personal:** Born Nov 11, 1964, Baton Rouge, LA; son of Shirley; married Michelle Quash; children: 5. **Educ:** Yale Univ, BA, econs. **Career:** Football player (retired); Nat Football League, New Eng Patriots & Wash Redskins, cornerback, player, 1986-91; Legg Mason, financial consult, broker, 1994-96; Profit Investment Mgt LLC, founder, pres & chief exec officer & portfolio mgr, 1996-. **Orgs:** Bd mem, Montgomery County Community Found; bd mem, Nat Asn Securities Professionals; Profit Charitable Found. **Honors/Awds:** Reginald F. Lewis Foundation, Award Recipient, 2011; "Black Enterprise", 75 Most Powerful Blacks on Wall Street, 2011. **Special Achievements:** Profiled in various financial media including "Business Week", "Smart Money", "Black Enterprise", "Pensions & Investments", "Investors Business Daily" and a news program guest on "Wall Street Week", "Money Line", CNBC, and CNN. **Business Addr:** Founder, President & Chief Executive Officer, Profit Investment Management LLC, 7500 Old Georgetown Rd Suite 700, Bethesda, MD 20814, **Business Phone:** (301)650-0059.

**PROFIT-MCLEAN, RENE.** See MCLEAN, RENE.

### PROPHET, TONY
Vice president (organization). **Educ:** Kettering Univ, BS, indust engineering, 1982; Stanford Grad Sch Bus, MBA, 1986. **Career:** Booz Allen Hamilton, partner, 1986-94; Honeywell, pres power systs, 1994-2001; United Technologies Corp, sr vpres opers, carrier corp, 2001-05; Hewlett-Packard, sr vpres opers, 2006-14; Microsoft, corp vice pres windows & search mkt, 2014-15, corp vice pres educ mkt, 2015-. **Orgs:** Nat Academies Sci Bd Energy & Environ; Stanford Grad Bus Sch, Adv Coun; Gannett, bd dir mem & transformation comt chmn, 2013-. **Business Addr:** Corporate Vice President Education Marketing, Microsoft.

### PROTHRO, GERALD DENNIS
Executive director, computer executive. **Personal:** Born Sep 27, 1942, Atlanta, GA; son of Charles Emery and Esther Jones; married Brenda Jean Bell; children: Gerald Dennis. **Educ:** Howard Univ, BS, physics, 1966, MS, physics, 1969; Harvard Bus Sch, exec MBA, 1975. **Career:** Goddard Space Flight Ctr, physicist, 1965-69; NDEA Fel, 1967-69; Int Bus Mach, Burlington, VT, assoc syst analyst, 1969, sr syst anaylst, 1969-71, mgr process linecent eng syst, 1971, mgr process line cent anaylsis syst, 1971-73, proj mgr syst facil & support, 1973-74, Syst Prod Div, mgr info syst strategy, 1974-75, dir syst assurance & data processing prod group, 1975-78, Poughkeepsie Develop Lab, Data Syst Div, mgr processors syst, 1978-79, mgr site resources & bus planning, 1979-81, qual assurance mgr, 1981, vpres & site gen mgr, 1989, secy mgt bd, 1989-98, vpres corp strategy, 1992, chief info officer, 1994, dir & secy corp mgt comt; Nationwide Financial Serv Inc, dir, 1997-2009; IKT Inc, managing dir, 1998-99; Broad Stream Commun Inc, sr vpres & chief technol officer, 1999-2000; Broad Stream Commun Corp, sr vpres & chief technol officer, 1999-2000; IKT Investments Ltd, managing dir, 2000-; Nationwide Life Ins Co, dir, 2002-; Epik Commun Inc, advisor, currently; IBM Worldwide Internet Protocol Network, architect, vpres, exec & sr mgt. **Orgs:** Nat Asn Advan Colored People; Urban League; Am Inst Phys; AAAS; Automatic Comput Mach Asn; adv bd, Saturn Venture Capital Partners; bd trustee, Howard Univ, 1991-; Ralph Lauren Ctr Cancer Care. **Honors/Awds:** Black Achievers Award, YMCA, 1976; received numerous awards. **Special Achievements:** Author of numerous articles on computer science. **Business Addr:** Board of Trustee, Howard University, 2400 6th St NW Suite 440, Washington, DC 20059, **Business Phone:** (202)806-2250.

### PROTHROW-STITH, DR. DEBORAH BOUTIN
Physician, educator. **Personal:** Born Feb 6, 1954, Marshall, TX; daughter of Mildred Prothrow and Percy Prothrow Jr; married Charles; children: Percy, Mary & Mildred. **Educ:** Spelman Col, BA, math, 1975; Harvard Univ, Med Sch, MD, 1979; Wheelok Col, EdD, 1992. **Career:** Boston City Hosp, sr resident charge Med & Surg unit, 1982, staff physician, 1982-87; co-prin investr, 1984-87; City Boston, Dept Health & Hosps, Health Prog Ctr Urban Youth, co-dir, 1985-87; Harvard St Neighborhood Health Ctr, clin chief, 1986-87; Commonwealth Mass, comnr pub health, 1987-89; Community Care Systs Inc, vpres, med dir, 1989-90; Harvard Univ, Sch Pub Health, asst dean gov & comunity progs, 1990-97, assoc dean fac develop, 1997-, prof pub health pract, 1994-97, dir, Div Pub Health Pract, 1997-, Henry Pickering Walcott prof pract pub Health, 1997-2008, prof pract, 1990-2008, adj prof pract pub health, currently; Spencer Stuart, consult, 2008-16; Charles R. Drew Univ, Col Med, dean, 2016-. **Orgs:** Trustee, Spelman Col, 1989-; trustee, Hyams Found, 1990; Am Pub Health Asn. **Honors/Awds:** Honorary Degrees, N Adams State Col, 1988; PSD, N Adams State Col, 1988; Exceptional Achievement in Public Service, SCY Louis Sullivan, 1989; Secretary of Health & Human Service Award, 1989; Rebecca Lee Award, Mass Dept Pub Health, 1990; Hildrus A Poindexter Distinguished Service Award, Black Caucus Health Workers, 1992; World Health Day Award, Am Asn World Health, 1993; inducted, IST Medicine, 2003. **Special Achievements:** First woman Commissioner of Public Health for the Commonwealth of Massachusetts; Author of numerous works including: Violence Prevention Curriculum for Adolescents, 1987; Deadly Consequences: How Violence is Destroying Our Teenage Population, 1991; Health Skills for Wellness, Prentice Hall, 1994; Murder Is No Accident: Understanding and Preventing Youth Violence In America, 2003. **Home Addr:** 53 Parsons, Brighton, MA 02135, **Home Phone:** (617)782-4844. **Business Addr:** Dean, Charles R Drew University of Medicine and Science, 1731 E 120th St, Los Angeles, CA 90059, **Business Phone:** (323)563-4800.

### PROUT, PATRICK M.
Banker. **Personal:** Born Jul 8, 1941, Port-of-Spain; son of Iris Smith and Rupert; married Faye Whitfield; children: Nicole, Danielle & Dominique. **Educ:** US Naval Acad, Annapolis, MD, BS, eng, 1964; Harvard Univ, Grad Sch Bus, Cambridge, MBA, gen mgt, 1973. **Career:** IBM, Wash, mkt rep, 1968-71; Miller Brewing Co, Milwaukee, prod mgr, 1973-75; Am Petrol; Chase Manhattan Bank, New York, NY, vpres, 1975-82; Ranier Bank, Seattle, vpres, 1982-84; Seafirst Bank, Seattle, sr vpres, 1984-90; Bank Am, San Francisco, exec vpres, 1990; Bank One Cleveland, pres, chief operating officer & vice chmn; Rainier Bank, Seattle; Heidrick & Struggles, partner; Prout Group, pres & chief exec officer, currently. **Orgs:** Exec Leadership Coun; Harvard Bus Sch Alumni Asn, Cleveland Chap; US Naval Acad Alumni Asn; NAUB. **Home Addr:** 26600 George Zeiger Dr No 410, Beachwood, OH 44122, **Home Phone:** (216)342-4215. **Business Addr:** President, Chief Executive Officer, The Prout Group Inc, 1111 Super Ave Suite 1120, Cleveland, OH 44114, **Business Phone:** (212)593-8240.

### PROVOST, MARSHA PARKS
Counselor. **Personal:** Born Feb 6, 1947, Lynchburg, VA; married George H; children: Geoffrey. **Educ:** Hampton Inst, BA, 1969; Univ TN Chattanooga, MEd, 1976; Univ TN Knoxville, EdD, 1982; Univ Mich, C3 Experience, counr comput & creative chg, 1984; Univ Tenn, Inst Leadership Effectiveness, 1984. **Career:** Guil Ford Co, Dept Social Servs, counr-intern, 1968, social worker II, 1971-75; City Hampton, juv probation officer, 1969-71; Coun & Career Planning Ctr UTC, counr, 1977-81, asst dir. **Orgs:** Am Asn Coun & Develop; Am Col Personnel Assoc; Chattanooga Area Psychol Asn; vpres Women Higher Educ Tenn, 1981-82; pres mem, Chattanooga Alumnae Chap Delta Sigma Theta Inc; New Dimensions Club Toastmistress Inc; Chattanooga Bus & Prof Women's Club, 1982-83; Chattanooga Chap Am Soc Training & Develop, 1982-84; Leadership Chattanooga, 1984-85. **Honors/Awds:** Outstanding Young Woman Am, Outstanding Young Women Am Inc, 1981; Woman of the Year, Chattanooga Bus & Prof Women's Clubs, 1981-82; Nat Cert Counr, Nat Bd Cert Counrs, 1984. **Home Addr:** 2441 Leann Circle, Chattanooga, TN 37406. **Business Addr:** Assistant Director of Counseling, Univ Tenn Chattanooga, 615 McCallie Ave, Chattanooga, TN 37403, **Business Phone:** (423)425-4111.

### PRUDHOMME, DR. NELLIE ROSE
Educator. **Personal:** Born Aug 28, 1948, Lafayette, LA; daughter of Richard and Mary; married Hilton James; children: Eunisha & Shannon. **Educ:** Univ Southwestern, BS, nursing, 1970; Tulane Univ Sch Pub Health, MPH, 1974; Univ Southern, MS, 1977; Univ Southwestern, attended 1984. **Career:** Lafayette Charity Hosp, staff nurse, 1970; Vermilion Parish Sch Bd, health nurse, 1971-72; Touro Infirmary City Health Dept, staff nurse, 1972-73; Univ Sch Pub Health, traineeship, 1972-73; Tulane Univ Sch Pub Health, aaron fel, 1972-73; Univ Southern MS Nursing Sch, asst prof, 1973-78; Family Health Found, staff nurse, 1973; Univ Southwestern, Nursing Sch, asst prof, 1978-81; Univ Med Ctr, staff nurse II, 1981-82; TH Harris Vo-Tech Sch, instr, 1983-84; Univ Med Ctr Lafayette, RN IV nurse consult, 1986-; LA State Univ, asst prof; Pennigton Biomed Res, fac scholar, 1997-98; Southern Univ A&M Col, assoc prof & dir, nursing res, 2000-. **Orgs:** Sigma Theta Tau, 1978-; USL Nursing Hon Soc, 1981-; Zeta Phi Beta Sorority Inc, 1988; March Dimes Birth Defects Found, 1989-; Mayor's Human Servs Comn, 1989-; Ethnic Minority fel Am Nurses Asn, 1994-97; bd pres, SW LA Health Educ Coun, 1997; Phi Kappa Phi Hon Soc, 1999-; Southern Nursing Res Soc; Am Nurses Asn; corresp secy, Acadiana Black Nurses Asn. **Honors/Awds:** Four Years Achievement, 1983; Outstanding District RN, 1989; Army Commendation & Meritorious Service, 1990; Career Achievement Award, 1994; DNS, LA State Univ Med Ctr, 1997. **Home Addr:** 157 S Richter Dr, Lafayette, LA 70501, **Home Phone:** (337)237-2017. **Business Addr:** Director, Southern University & A&M College, 801 Harding Blvd, Baton Rouge, LA 70807, **Business Phone:** (225)771-4500.

**PRUITT, FR. ALONZO CLEMONS**
Clergy. **Personal:** Born Feb 20, 1951, Chicago, IL; son of Alonzo (deceased) and Louise Clemons Hodges; married Linda Celeste Powell; children: Alexander & Nicholas. **Educ:** Roosevelt Univ, Chicago, IL, BA, pub admin, 1975; Univ Ill, Chicago, IL, MSW, 1978; Seabury-Western Theol Sem, Evanston, IL, MDiv, 1984; Grad Theol Found, DMin. **Career:** Lake Bluff Homes C, Pk Ridge, Ill, 1973-79; Mary Bartelme Homes, Chicago, Ill, dir, social worker, 1979-84; St George & St Matthias Church, Chicago, Ill, pastor, 1984; Seabury-Western Theol Sem, Evanston, Ill, adj prof, 1989-; Episcopal Church Ctr, New York, NY, interim nat staff officer black ministries, 1990; St Philips Episcopal Church, rector, currently; Richmond Sheriff's Chaplains, exec dir, 2006-08; Richmond Sheriff's Chaplains, Chief Chaplains, 2008. **Orgs:** Community organizer, Chicago Urban League, 1971-73; pres, Chicago Chap, Union Black Episcopalians, 1979-; Mayor Wash Ministers, 1982-87; convenor, Soc St Francis, 1982-; bd vpres, Chicago Work Ethic Corp, 1987; diocesan coun mem, Episcopal Diocese Chicago, 1987-; dean, Chicago S Episcopal Deanery, 1989-. **Honors/Awds:** Community Service Award, Oak Village, Community Rels Comn, 1974; Field Prize for Preaching, Cotton Award, Seabury-Western Theol Sem, 1984. **Home Addr:** 10616 S Leavitt, Chicago, IL 60643, **Home Phone:** (312)881-1138. **Business Addr:** Executive Director of Chaplains, Richmond City Sheriff's Office, 1701 Fairfield Way, Richmond, VA 23223, **Business Phone:** (804)321-1266.

**PRUITT, REV. EDDIE JAY DELANO**
Clergy. **Personal:** Born Apr 17, 1946, Detroit, MI; son of Samuel and Norma; married Bonita Joyce Phillips; married AlAnne Izzard; children: Eddie J D Jr. **Educ:** Lawrence Univ, attended 1984; Ashland Univ Sem, MDiv, 1994. **Career:** Christian Methodist Episcopal Church, pastor, currently. **Orgs:** Detroit Police Chaplan Corps. **Honors/Awds:** Spirit Detroit Award, City Coun Detroit, MI; Certificate Honorable Community Service, Detroit Police Dept; Certificate of Completion, HIV & Substance Abuse prevention for African American Communities of Faith, 2002. **Home Addr:** 10046 Minock St, Detroit, MI 48228-1344, **Home Phone:** (313)836-2809. **Business Addr:** Pastor, Christian Methodist Episcopal Church, 35757 Vinewood St, Romulus, MI 48174-4036, **Business Phone:** (734)326-0210.

**PRUITT, FRED RODERIC**
President (organization), physician. **Personal:** Born Dec 17, 1938, Birmingham, AL; married Joan Simmons; children: Christopher & Lisa. **Educ:** Tenn State Univ, BS, 1961; Howard Univ, MS, 1963; Meharry Med Col, MD, 1967. **Career:** St Elizabeth Hosp, intern, 1967-68, resident gen pract, 1971-73; phys specialist internal med, 1973-. **Orgs:** Med dir, Mahoning Co Drug Prog Inc; Lions Int; pres & bd men, Lions Club; Nat Med Asn; Boh State Med Asn; Alpha Phi Alpha Frat; Mahoning Co Med Soc. **Home Addr:** 550 Parmalee Ave Suite 310, Youngstown, OH 44510, **Home Phone:** (330)746-5576. **Business Addr:** Physician, 333 Pk Ave, Youngstown, OH 44504-1564, **Business Phone:** (330)746-5576.

**PRUITT, DR. GEORGE ALBERT**
School administrator, educator. **Personal:** Born Jul 9, 1946, Canton, MS; married Pamela Young; children: Shayla Nicole. **Educ:** Ill State Univ, BS, 1968, MS, 1970; Union Grad Sch, PhD, 1974. **Career:** Ill State Univ, asst to vpres acad affairs, 1968-70; Towson State Univ, dean stud, 1970-72; Morgan State Univ, vpres, exec asst to pres, 1972-75; Tenn State Univ, vpres, 1975-81; Coun Adult & Experiential Learning, exec vpres, 1981-82, chmn bd trustees; Seedco Financial Serv Inc, dir; Peoples Bancorp Inc, Trenton Savings Bank FSB, 1991, dir; Sun Bancorp Inc, dir, 2003-10; Thomas Edison State Col, pres, 1982-. **Orgs:** Comn Higher Educ & Adult Learner, ACE, 1982-88; bd trustee, CAEL, 1983-87; chair, Comt Alternatives & Innovation Higher Educ, Am Asn State Col & Univ, 1985-87; bd trustee, Union Inst, 1988-; bd dir, Mercer Co Chamber C, 1988-; bd dir, Mercer Med Ctr, 1989-97; bd dir, NJ Asn Cols & Univs, 1989-93; US Educ Dept, Nat Adv Comt Accreditation & Instnl Eligibility, 1989-92; adv, Kellogg Nat Fel Prog, Group XII, 1990-93; bd dir, SEEDCO, 1990-; bd mgrs, Trenton Savings Bank, 1991-99; bd dir, Am Cancer Soc, NJ, 1992-97; bd mem, dir, MIDJersey Chamber Com; nat adv comt mem, Inst Qual & Integrity, 1993-; adv, Kellogg Nat Fel Prog, Group XV, 1994-97; bd dir, Sun Bancorp, 2001-; Robert Wood Johnson Found Nurses; bd dir, Capital City Partnership Inc; bd trustee, Rider Univ, 2001-; bd dir, SEEDCO; Am Coun Educ; US Dept Educ; bd, Sun Nat Bank; chmn, Nj Presidents Coun; Nj State Planning Comn; vice chair, Nat Comn Higher Educ Attainment. **Honors/Awds:** Governor's Citation for Outstanding Service Gov Alexander, Tenn, 1981; Outstanding Service to Education Award, Tenn State Univ, 1981; Outstanding Alumni Achievement Award, Illinois State Univ, 1984; Achievement in Education Award, Nat Asn Negro Bus & Prof Clubs Inc, NJ, 1987; Doctor of Public Service, Bridgewater State Col, MA, 1990; Good Guy Award, George Washington Coun, Boy Scouts Am, 1991; Humanitarian Award, Nat Conf Christians & Jews, 1992; Elder of the Year, Black NJ Mag, 1993; Col of Education Hall of Fame, Ill State Univ, 1995; DHL, Empire State Col, 1996; DHL, Ill State Univ, 1994; Distinguished Alumni Award, Ill State Univ, 1996; Citizen of the Year, Mercer Co Chamber Com, 1997. **Special Achievements:** Named one of the most effective college presidents in the United States, EXXon Education Foundation Study, 1986. **Home Addr:** 33 Woodmont Dr, Lawrenceville, NJ 08648. **Business Addr:** President, Thomas Edison State College, 111 W State St, Trenton, NJ 08608-1176, **Business Phone:** (609)984-1105.

**PRUITT, GREGORY DONALD, JR.**
Football player, executive. **Personal:** Born Aug 18, 1951, Houston, TX. **Educ:** Univ Okla, BA, jour. **Career:** Football player (retired); Cleveland Browns, running back, punt returner, kick returner, 1973-81; Los Angeles Raiders, running back, punt returner, kick returner, 1982-84; Pruitt-Vaughn Inc, Sports Mgt, pres & chief exec officer. **Orgs:** OPP Fraternity. **Honors/Awds:** All-American, 1972-73; Heisman Trophy, 1973; Pro Bowl, 1973, 1974, 1976, 1977, 1983; Offensive Player of the Year, Cleveland Browns, 1974; Led Browns Rushing, 1974-79; ABC's Superstars, 1979; Okla Football Hall of Fame, 1998. **Special Achievements:** One of only two Players that has 2, 000 yards in four categories: Rushing, Receiving, Punt & Kickoff returns; Greater Cleveland Sports Hall of Fame, 2003; Cleveland Browns Legends, Class 2000; 4th All Time Rushes, Cleveland Browns, 5,672 yards. **Home Addr:** 13851 Larchmere Blvd, Cleveland, OH 44120.

**PRUITT, JAMES BOUVIAS**
Football player. **Personal:** Born Jan 29, 1964, Los Angeles, CA. **Educ:** Calif State Univ. **Career:** Football player (retired); Miami Dolphins, wide receiver, 1986-88, 1990-91; Indianapolis Colts, wide receiver, 1988-89; Cleveland Browns, 1993. **Business Addr:** Wide Receiver, Indianapolis Colts, 7001 W 56th St, Indianapolis, IN 46254, **Business Phone:** (317)297-2658.

**PRUITT, MICHAEL**
Business owner, football player. **Personal:** Born Apr 3, 1954, Chicago, IL; married Karen Boulware; children: Aaron. **Educ:** Purdue Univ, BA, bus admin. **Career:** Football player (retired), business owner; Nat Football League, Cleveland Browns, full back, running back, 1976-84; Buffalo Bills, running back, 1985; Kans City Chiefs, full back, 1985-86; Pruitt & Grace Develop Corp, pres; Mike Pruitt's Honda, owner, currently. **Honors/Awds:** Second-team All-Big Ten, 1975; Best Offensive Player, TD Club Cleveland, 1980; Miller Man of the Year, 1980; Cleveland's Most Valuable Player of the Year, 1980; Akron Booster Club, 1981; Pro Bowler, 1979 & 1980; Cleveland Sports Hall of Fame, 2003. **Home Addr:** , Strongsville, OH. **Business Addr:** Owner, Mike Pruitt Honda, 43 Pruitt Blvd, Akron, OH 44310, **Business Phone:** (330)633-6060.

**PRUITT-LOGAN, DR. ANNE SMITH**
School administrator, consultant. **Personal:** Born Bainbridge, GA; daughter of Loring Smith and Anne Ward Smith; married Harold G; children: Harold J, Minda & Andrew; married Ralph L; children: Leslie, Diane, Sharon, Ralph Jr & Pamela Green. **Educ:** Howard Univ, BS, psychol, 1949; Teachers Col, Columbia Univ, MA, 1950, EdD, 1964; postdoctoral training admin. **Career:** Howard Univ, counr, 1950-52; Hutto HS, dir guid, 1952-55; Albany State Col, dean students, 1955-59; Fisk Univ, dean students & dean women, 1959-61; Case Western Res Univ, prof educ, 1963-79; Ohio State Univ, Grad Sch, assoc dean, 1979-85, prof Educ Policy & Leadership, 1979-95, assoc provost, 1985-86, Ctr Teaching Excellence, dir, 1986-94, prof emer, 1995-; Coun Grad Sch, dean residence, 1994-96, scholar residence, 1996-2002, assoc provost; consult, currently. **Orgs:** Alpha Kappa Alpha Sorority; Links Inc; Cosmos Club; Deacon, Peoples Congregational United Chap Christ; consult, Women's Job Corps creation; pres, Lyndon Johnson's War Poverty, 1964; bd trustee, Cleveland Urban League, 1965-71; consult, Southern Regional Educ Bd, 1968-81; bd trustee, Cent State Univ, 1973-82; moderator, Mt Zion Congregational Church, 1975-78; secy, J bd mem, pres, Am Col Personnel Asn, 1976-77; Res Task Force Southern Educ Found, 1978-87; consult, Southern Regional Educ Bd; Adv Comm USCG Acad, 1980-83; Am Asn Coun & Develop; Am Educ Res Asn; Am Asn Higher Educ; Am Asn Univ Prof; Mayor's Task Force Pvt Sect Initiatives, Columbus, OH, 1986-88, bd trustee, Case Western Res Univ, 1987-2002; bd dir, Columbus Area Leadership Prog, 1988-92; Columbus Educ Comn, 1988-92; coordr, CIC Alliance Success Planning Comn, 1989-90; Nat Sci Found, Comn Equal Opportunities Sci & Eng, 1989-95; co-chairperson, Ohio State Univ United Way Campaign, 1990-91; ETS Vis Panel Res, 1996-2002; pres, Black Women's Agenda, 1998-2002; NSF GK-12 External Experts Panel mem, 2001-; BEST Expert Panel, 2002-; fel Am Coun Educ. **Home Addr:** 8340 Greensboro Dr Suite 1023, McLean, VA 22102, **Home Phone:** (703)356-7496. **Business Addr:** Professor Emeritus, Ohio State University, Enarson Hall 154 W 12th Ave, Columbus, OH 43210, **Business Phone:** (614)292-1868.

**PRYCE, TREVOR WESLEY, II**
Football player. **Personal:** Born Aug 3, 1975, Brooklyn, NY; married Sonya; children: Khary, Kamryn & Trevor III. **Educ:** Clemson Univ. **Career:** Football player (retired), free agt; Denver Broncos, defensive end & defensive tackle & right defensive tackle, 1997-2005; Baltimore Ravens, defensive end & right defensive tackle, left defensive tackle, 2006-10; New York Jets, 2010; free agt, currently. **Honors/Awds:** Pro-Bowl Player, 1999-2002; All Pro, 1999-2001; Super Bowl champion, XXXII, XXXIII. **Special Achievements:** NFL Draft, First round pick, #28, 1997; Author Children Book: Army of Frogs: A Kulipari Novel. **Home Addr:** , Ellicott City, MD.

**PRYDE, ARTHUR EDWARD**
Engineer, business owner, manager. **Personal:** Born Jul 8, 1946, Providence, RI; married Lydia. **Educ:** RI Sch Design, BFA, indust design, 1970. **Career:** AVID Corp E Prov RI, designer, 1971-74; Gen Motors Corp, interior design mgr & perceived qual auditor, 1973-2008, design mgr, 2008-; LPA Design, owner, 1983-85. **Orgs:** Design consult to Different Drummer; crew tech C Little Racing, 1983-85; racing 2 liter Can-Am Championship Car, 1984. **Home Addr:** 17249 Melrose, Arthur Pryde, MI 48075.

**PRYOR, CALVIN CAFFEY.** **See Obituaries Section.**

**PRYOR, DR. CHESTER CORNELIUS, II**
Ophthalmologist, educator, association executive. **Personal:** Born Jan 2, 1930, Cincinnati, OH; married Audrey; children: Marcus. **Educ:** Cent State Univ, BS, 1951; Howard Univ Col Med, MD, 1955. **Career:** Boston City Hosp, resident, 1957-58; MA Eye & Ear Infirmary, heed fel, 1959; Univ Cincinnati Col Med, asst prof; Deaconess & Christ Good Samaritan Hosp, assoc; Jewish Bethesda & C's Clermont County Hosp, staff; pvt practr ophthal, 1961-; Univ Cincinnati Col Med, vol clin fac, emer prof opthalmology. **Orgs:** Beta Kappa Chi, 1950; Alpha Kappa Mu, 1950; Am Chem Soc, 1951; dipl, Am Bd Ophthal, 1960; Coun Aging, 1962-68; FA&M, 1962; King Solomon Consis, 1962; treas, Delta Gamma Lambda Chap, 1963-77; bd dir, Cincinnati Asn Blind, 1968-; treas, Cincinnati Acad Med, 1969; chmn sec opthal, Nat Med Asn, 1970-71; dir, Unity State Bank, 1970-76; fel Am Col Surgeons, 1971-; Worshipful Master, 1972; com dr chief, King Solomon Consis 20, 1972-73; GIG, 1975; pres, Cincinnati Ophthal Soc, 1976; Eye & Ear Infirmary; charter mem, Delta Xi; Nat Asn Advan Colored People; Argus Club; True Am Lodge 2; Noble Sinai Temple 59; Alpha Phi Alpha Fraternity. **Home Addr:** 2401 Ingleside Ave Unit 3d, Cincinnati, OH 45206, **Home Phone:** (513)751-1100. **Business Addr:** Professor Emeritus, University of Cincinnati, 231 Albert Sabin Way, Cincinnati, OH 45267, **Business Phone:** (513)558-5151.

**PRYOR, LILLIAN W.**
Educator. **Personal:** Born Dec 13, 1917, New Orleans, LA; children: Mignon M Schooler. **Educ:** Univ Calif, Berkeley, CA, BA, 1942; Roosevelt Univ, MA, 1966; Loyola Univ Sch Soc Work. **Career:** Dept Pub Asst, social worker, 1943-48; Chicago Bd Educ, elem teacher, 1948-53; Cook Co Hosp, med social worker, 1948-53; teacher physically handicapped c, 1963. **Orgs:** Co-chmn, Ill State Educ; women's bd, Am Cancer Soc; Mus Contemp Art; Art Inst; bd mem, Chicago S Side Nat Asn Advan Colored People; bd mem, Coun Except C; bd mem, S Side Comn Art Ctr; Women's Benefit Bd Oper PUSH; Bravo Chap, Lyric Opera; comt mem, Harris "Y"; Nat Asn Adv Colored People; Urban League Women's Coun Proj 75. **Home Addr:** 4850 S Lake Pk Ave Suite 207B, Chicago, IL 60615.

**PRYOR, MALCOLM D.**
Banker, chairperson. **Educ:** Howard Univ, BA, mkt & econs, 1968; Univ Pa Wharton Sch, MBA, finance, 1980. **Career:** Goldman Sachs & Co, instnl fixed income salesman; formed investment partnership, 1979; Pryor, Govan, Counts & Co, founder, 1981; Pryor, Mc Clendon, Counts & Co, chmn; Pep Boys Inc, bd mem; Fox Chase Cancer Ctr, sustaining mem, bd mem; Poliwogg LLC, managing dir; Goldman, Sachs & Co, instnl fixed income salesman, instnl sales rep; Pryor, Counts & Co, chmn & founding partner, currently; S African Econ Develop Fund, pres & chief exec officer, currently; CAL Bank Ltd, bd dir, currently, African Export Import Bank, founding shareholder, investment banker; Pryor Counts Co Inc, chief exec officer; Ghana Home Loans, founding shareholder; Pvt Equity Fund investing southern Africa region, chief exec. **Orgs:** Mem, Risk Mgt comt Bank; New York Cocoa & Coffee Exchange; Philadelphia Stock Exchange. **Special Achievements:** Co is largest African-Am-owned investment bank in the US; Black Co is ranked No 2 on Black Enterprise's list of top 12 Black-owned investment banks. **Business Addr:** Chairman, Pryor, Counts & Company Inc, 1515 Mkt St Suite 819, Philadelphia, PA 19102, **Business Phone:** (215)569-4544.

**PRYOR, VIKKI L.**
President (organization), chief executive officer. **Personal:** children: Daniel. **Educ:** State Univ NY, Buffalo, BA, 1975, JD, 1978; Univ Ill, Chicago, MBA. **Career:** SBLI USA Mutual Life Ins Co Inc, pres & chief exec officer, 1999; Oxford Health Plan Conn, sr vpres opers; Chg Create Transform LLC & Found, founder & managing prin, currently. **Orgs:** Independent dir, Columbia Funds Variable Ser Trust II, 2006-; dir, New York Independent Syst Operator Inc, 2014-; dir, Sagicor Life Ins Co, 2015-; bd mem, Partnership New York; bd mem, Am Coun Life Insurers' Forum 500; Citi Adv Bd Citigroup's Security & Fund Serv; Small Bus & Agr Adv Coun Fed Res Bank New York; Chg Create Found; Dean's Adv Coun Univ at Buffalo Law Sch; Nat Bd Girl Scouts USA; Blue Cross Blue Shield Mass; Am Red Cross; dean's adv coun, Univ at Buffalo Law Sch. **Honors/Awds:** DHL, Sacred Heart Univ, 2004; Presidential Medallion, Bronx Community Col, 2008; "Black Enterprise", 75 Most Powerful Women in Business, 2010. **Business Addr:** Managing Principal, Founder, Change Create Transform LLC, 3 Int Dr Suite 140, Rye Brook, NY 10573, **Business Phone:** (914)481-5914.

**PUALANI, GLORIA**
Executive director, manager. **Personal:** Born Nov 30, 1950, San Augustine, TX; daughter of R C Phelps and Mary Lee Phelps; married Jeffrey Ortiz; children: Ronald Bree. **Educ:** Calif State Univ, BA, 1979; Univ Calif, Los Angeles, purchasing cert, 1981; Nat Univ, MBA, 1989. **Career:** ABC TV, script supvr, prod asst, 1976-80; Pac Aircraft, buyer, 1980-81; Northrop Grumman Corp, adminr, socio-Econ Bus Prog & Govt Rels, Integrated Syst, corp dir, 1981-. **Orgs:** Dept Com Minority Enterprise Develop, 1988; Black Bus Asn Adv Bd, 1988-; vpres, External Affairs, Southern Calif Regional Purchasing Coun, 1989-; Nat Asn Women Bus Owners, 1989-; dir, Northrop Grumman Corp; Asn Black Women Entrepreneurs Adv Bd, 1990-; Orange Co Regional Purchasing Coun, 1991-; Nat Veteran Owned Bus Asn. **Home Addr:** PO Box 781322, Los Angeles, CA 90016, **Home Phone:** (310)331-4784. **Business Addr:** Corporate Director, Socio-Economic Business Program, Northrop Grumman Corp, 2980 Fairview Pk Dr, Falls Church, VA 22042, **Business Phone:** (703)280-2900.

**PUGH, DR. CLEMENTINE A.**
Educator. **Personal:** Born Raleigh, NC; daughter of Alberta Harris High and Otho; married George Douglas Pugh; children: Douglas & Janet. **Educ:** Shaw Univ, BA, 1945; Columbia Univ, MSW, 1948; Univ Mass, Amherst, EdD, 1982. **Career:** Hunter Col, soc worker, res assoc educ clin; Comm Serv Soc Family, psych soc; Herbert H Lehman Col, prof educ, 1970-90, prof emer, 1991. **Orgs:** Fel Am Orthopsychiatric Asn, 1975-, prog fac, 1980-; Nat Asn Black Social Workers, 1980-; bd dir, Homes Homeless; C; life mem, Nat Asn Advan Colored People; bd trustee, Bank Street Col, 1990-94. **Home Addr:** 4555 Henry Hudson Pkwy Apt 1010, Bronx, NY 10471-3840, **Home Phone:** (631)726-1934.

**PUGH, MARY E.**
Executive, vice president (organization), chief executive officer. **Personal:** Born Sep 16, 1959; married Michael Scoggins; children: Angela & Alex. **Educ:** Yale Univ, BA, econs, 1981. **Career:** Pugh Capital Mgt Inc, founder, chief investment officer & pres, 1991-; Wash Mutual Bank, bd mem, 1999-2008, Portfolio Mgt Div, sr vpres; Fed Res Bank San Francisco, Seattle, dir; Wash Mutual Corp, chmn Finance Comt, Portfolio Mgt Div, sr vpres; San Francisco Fed Res Bank, Seattle Br, dir, currently. **Orgs:** Bd mem, Wash Mutual Inc, 1999-2008; trustee, Seattle Found; Investment Comt, YWCA Greater Seattle; Investment Comt, Univ Wash; Cascade Natural Gas Corp, 2001; bd mem, Cascade Natural Gas Corp, 2004-; Americans Republican Majority; Obama Am. **Business Addr:** President, Chief Investment Officer, Pugh Capital Management Inc, 1414 31st Ave S Suite 302, Seattle, WA 98144, **Business Phone:** (206)322-4985.

**PUGH, ROBERT WILLIAM, SR.**
Executive. **Personal:** Born May 10, 1926, New York, NY; son of William R and Vennette I; married Barbara Johnson; children: Robert Jr & Lori. **Educ:** Mus Mod Art, attended 1946; NY Univ, attended 1948;

Newark Sch Fine Indust Art, attended 1949. **Career:** Wynson Inc, designer, 1945-46; Desagnet Housing Corp, 1946; Nowland & Schladermundt, designer, 1949-51; Asn Granite Craftsman's Guild Inc, pres, 1975; Keystone Monument Co Inc, founder, pres; Edward M Bleser Monument Co, pres, currently. **Orgs:** Indust Designer's Inst; Design Guild NJ; bd mgrs, Harlem YMCA; bd trustee, Youth Consult Serv; pres, Asn Granite Craftmen's Guild Inc, 1976-77 & 1979-80; bd mem, NY State Monument Builders Asn Inc; Monument Builders N Am; bd dir, NY State Monument Builders Asn Inc; Frank Silvera Workshop. **Home Addr:** 633 Olmstead Ave, Bronx, NY 10473. **Business Addr:** President, Edward M Bleser Monument Co, 37 Conway St, Brooklyn, NY 11207, **Business Phone:** (718)455-5153.

### PULLEN-BROWN, STEPHANIE D.

Lawyer, teacher. **Personal:** Born Dec 11, 1949, Baltimore, MD; married Gerald O; children: Margot. **Educ:** Md Inst Art, BFA, 1970; Coppin St Col, MEd, 1973; Loyola Col, MEd, 1979; Univ Md, JD, 1991. **Career:** Baltimore City Pub Sch, teacher, 1970-74, admin specialist, 1974-80; Univ Md, coop extn serv city dir, 1980-86, asst & vpres & dean, 1986-91; atty, currently. **Orgs:** Comnr Baltimore City Comn Women, 1984-86; Johnson Found Bd Baltimore MusArt, 1985-; bd mem, YMCA, 1985-; chair, Environ Commitee, Cercla Update. **Honors/Awds:** Search for Professional Excellence, Nat Asn Co Agr Agts, 1983; Woman Manager of the Year, Conf Women MD State Serv, 1984. **Home Addr:** 30 S Charles St, Baltimore, MD 21201-3018, **Home Phone:** (410)669-7263.

### PULLIAM, REV. BETTY E.

Clergy, executive, president (organization). **Personal:** Born Jun 4, 1941, Woodruff, SC; daughter of Shewerl Douglas Ferguson and Gertrude Greene Ferguson; married Herman K; children: Trudy, Vanessa & Herman Jr. **Educ:** Wayne State Univ; Nat Judicial Col, Reno, Nev, attended 1989; Univ Nev, cert, hearings & appeals/admin law judge, 1991. **Career:** St Mark's Community Church, secy, 1958-64; Mayor's Youth Employ Prog Comn Human Resources Develop, 1965-69; Robert Johnson Assoc Training Inst, off mgt, 1971-73; Payne-Pulliam Sch Trade & Com, dir, pres & co-owner, 1973-; Mich State Liquor Control Comn, comnr, 1989; ordained minister. **Orgs:** Assoc minister, Greater New Mt Moriah Baptist Church; pres & chair, Evangelistic comm, Inter Prayer Group; pres & chairwoman, Booker T Wash Bus Asn; Greater Detroit Chamber Com; secy & bd mem, Mt. Moriah Community Develop Corp. **Honors/Awds:** Business Woman of the Month; Pinch Certificate of Achievement, 1978; Spirit of Detroit Award, 1983; Detroit City Council Community Award, 1983; Proclamation from the Mayor Detroit, 1983; Golden Heritage Award for Education Excellence, 1984; Black History Month Recognition Award, 1985; Certificate of Appreciation, Nat Bus Week, 1985; Achievement Award, Wayne County Exec Off, 1986; Certificate of Recognition, Highland Park city, 1987; Certificate of Recognition from the Mayor, 1987; Outstanding Achievement, Hist Accomplishment, 1987; Community Service Award, Councilwoman Barbara R Collins, 1988; Lifetime Achievement Award, Nat Asn Advan Colored People; Women of Excellence, Women Excellence, 2013. **Special Achievements:** First Woman licensed to preach at Gtr New Mt Moriah Missionary Bapt Church; First Female pres & chairwoman of the board Booker T Washington Buisness Associates. **Home Addr:** 18945 Woodingham Dr, Detroit, MI 48221-2159, **Home Phone:** (313)861-1984. **Business Addr:** President & Co-owner, Director, Payne-Pulliam School of Trade & Commerce, 2345 Cass Ave, Detroit, MI 48201-3305, **Business Phone:** (313)963-4710.

### PURCE, DR. THOMAS LES

Engineer, dean (education). **Personal:** Born Nov 13, 1946, Pocatello, ID; married Jane Sherman; children: Deborah, Sarah & Miriam. **Educ:** Idaho State Univ, BA, psychol, 1969, MEd, 1970, EdD, 1975; Harvard Univ, Inst Educ Mgt; Univ NC, hon doctor humane lett, 2009; State Univ NY, Geneseo, hon degree doctor laws, 2014. **Career:** Wash State Univ, counr psychologist, 1970-72; Idaho State Univ, Res Pk & Econ Develop, spec asst, dir co op educ, 1974-75, asst prof counr educ, 1975-77; Pocatello, Idah, coun, 1973, mayor, 1976-77; State Idaho, Dept Admin, adminstr, div gen serv, 1977-79, dir, 1979-81; State Idaho, Dept Health & Welfare, dir, 1981-83; Power Engineering Inc, chief operating officer, 1983; Evergreen State Col, vpres col advan, 1989, interim pres, exec vpres, 1992-95, pres, 2000-; Wash State Univ, Extended Univ Affairs, vpres, Extended Acad Progs, dean, 1995-. **Orgs:** Asn Univ Prof; Asn Counr Educ & Supr; Asn Idaho Cities; Asn Black Psychologists; vchmn, City Coun; Idaho Water & Sewage Cert Bd; Nat Asn Advan Colored People; pres, Counc Pub Lib Arts Cols, 2001-02; bd dir, Asn Am Cols & Univs; Urban League Task Force; SE Idaho Counc Govt; Idaho Housing Agency; Kappa Alpha Psi; City Coun man; bd mem, Community Found S Puget Sound; bd mem, Northwest African Am Mus; bd mem, Wash Campus Compact; pres, Nat Asn Intercollegiate Athletics. **Honors/Awds:** Hon DHL, Univ NC, Asheville, 2009; Outstanding Young Men of Amer; State Exec Com Dem Party; Governor's Award. **Special Achievements:** First African American elected as official in the state of Idaho as councilman and then mayor of Pocatello. **Home Addr:** PO Box 2187, Hailey, ID 83333. **Business Addr:** President, The Evergreen State College, Rm 3200 2700 Evergreen Pkwy NW Libr Bldg, Olympia, WA 98505, **Business Phone:** (360)867-6100.

### PURCHASE-OWENS, FRANCENA

Consultant. **Personal:** Born Nov 14, 1960, Milwaukee, WI; daughter of Johnny Purchase Senior and Arlene Pleas Brown. **Educ:** Bryant & Stratton Col, AA, admin assisting & secretarial sci, 1982; Western Mich Univ, BS, appl lib studies, 1997, MA, educ leadership, 2004; Grand Rapids Community Col; Milwaukee Area Tech Col; Grand Valley State Univ; Univ Phoenix & Capella Univ. **Career:** Manpower Int, exec secy, 1982-85; M&I Bank, Investment mgt secy, 1984-85; Patricia Stevens Col, Human resource asst, comput programmer & secy, 1985-86; United Develop Corp, 1986-88; Weathermasters Industs, 1989; Francena Purchase Consult Serv, consult, chief exec officer, 1998-; Directions Res, res specialist, 2004-05. **Orgs:** Pres, Francena Purchase Int Hons & Awards Soc, 1999-; bd dir, Touchstone Innovare Ment Health Agency, 1999-2007; personnel, finance, prog comt, Touchstone Innovare Ment Health Agency Ad Hoc, 1999-2007; secy elect, Southeast End Neighborhood Asn, 2005-08; comt, Cherry St Health Serv, 2005; Dwelling Pl Grand Rapids, Task Force, 2005; co-chair, Community Investment Coun, United Way, 2006-; Agency Impact Comt, United Way, 2006-; bus prog adv comt, ITT Tech Inst, 2010-; Princeton Global Network, 2011; W Mich Postal Customer Coun; Western Mich Univ Alumni Asn; Community Media Ctr; Phi Lambda Theta; Alzheimers Asn; Parkinson's Asn. **Honors/Awds:** Outstanding College Student of America; Marquis Who's Who of Medicine & Healthcare; International Who's Who of Professionals; Student Speaker for Graduation, Nat Hon Soc; Int Pen Pal Stud Rep; Shorthand Award; Century Award; Leadership Award, Bus Off Educ Club; Creative Writing Award; Journalism Award; Presidential Physical Fitness Award; Certificate of Award, N Shore Animal League. **Home Addr:** 4150 Norman, Grand Rapids, MI 49508, **Home Phone:** (414)461-5111. **Business Addr:** Chief Executive Officer, Consultant, Francena Purchase Consulting Services, PO Box 88304, Kentwood, MI 49518, **Business Phone:** (616)285-5568.

### PURDEE, NATHAN

Artist, actor, photographer. **Personal:** Born Aug 6, 1950, Tampa, FL; son of Emmanuel Johnson and Anna Beatrice Alston; married Roberta Morris; children: Taylor Armstrong. **Educ:** Metro State, AA, ment health; Linfield Col, theatre arts, criminol. **Career:** TV Series: "Ebony Jet Showcase"; "Dynasty", 1983; "St Elsewhere", 1984; "Santa Barbara", 1984; "Knots Landing", 1985; "The Young & the Restless", 1986-91; "You Again", 1986; "Cheers", 1988; "One Life to Live", 1995-09; "Law & Order"; Karmic Release Ltd, pres; Wallowitch & Ross This Moment, exec producer, 1999; Films: Living in Captivity; The Return of Superfly, 1990; Daytime's Greatest Weddings, 2004; Living in Captivity, 2008; Law & Order, 2008; NYC 22, 2012; House of Cards, 2013; Nathan Purdee Studios, owner & photogr, currently. **Orgs:** NATAS ATAS, 1985-93; Installations Art Gallery, charter mem, 1988-93; Art Studios League, artist, 1993. **Honors/Awds:** National Association of Travel Agents Singapore, Emmy Honors, Best Drama, 1985, 1986; Hollywood Tribute to Soaps, Favorite Newcomer, 1985; Soap Opera Digest, Top Ten TVQ, 1990, 1991, 1992. **Special Achievements:** Featured artist, Am Dream Art Festival, 1988; "I Will Not Be Denied, "performance art, 1990; "The Other Side of Daytime", variety show, 1990, 1991; "Stars Behind Bars", self-motivational seminar, 1987-88. **Home Addr:** 227 Riverside Dr Suite 7N, New York, NY 10025-6811, **Home Phone:** (212)222-5840. **Business Addr:** Owner, Photographer, Nathan Purdee Studios, PO Box 3561, Easton, PA 18043, **Business Phone:** (610)9239-684.

### PURNELL, CAROLYN J.

Lawyer. **Personal:** Born Aug 16, 1939, Memphis, TN; daughter of James Clarence and Mardine (Taylor); children: Monica & Mardine. **Educ:** Univ WA, BA, 1961; Univ Wash Sch Law, JD, 1971. **Career:** Pros Atty Off, sr legal internship, 1971, civil dep, 1972-74; King County, dep pros atty, 1972-74, metro exec dir & dep county exec, 1994; City Seattle, legal couns mayor, 1974-77; Weyerhaeuser Co, atty, 1977, corp atty, dir corpmatls; Wash Round Table, Metro Legal Serv Div, chief coun, 1990, dep dir, 1993, exec dir, 1993-95, mgt consult, 1996-; pvt consult, currently. **Orgs:** Vpres, Housing Corp Devel Wash, 1977; Panelist Human Rights Comn Tribunal; exec bd secy, March Dimes; bd trustee, Epiphany Sch; Phi Alpha Delta Legal Frat; sec, Delta Sigma Theta Sor; Providence Hosp Found; Wash State Bd Bar Examrs, City Seattle Bd Adjustments, Scholastic Hon Soc; Pac Med Ctr Bd, Mayors Centennial Parks Comn, Mayors Zoo Comn; King County Bar Asn. **Honors/Awds:** Outstanding Young Women Director US, 1976; 1 of 100 Lawyers in US to attend Amer Assembly on Law. **Home Addr:** 3415 Denny Way, Seattle, WA 98122, **Home Phone:** (206)325-7741. **Business Addr:** Consultant, 1304 Bigelow Ave N, Seattle, WA 98109-3255, **Business Phone:** (206)285-0883.

### PURNELL, LOVETT SHAIZER

Football player. **Personal:** Born Apr 7, 1972, Seaford, DE; son of Ronald Harmon and Betty. **Educ:** WVa Univ, grad. **Career:** Football player (retired); New Eng Patriots, 1996, tight end, 1997-98; Baltimore Ravens, 1999; Tampa Bay Buccaneers, tight end, 2000; Chicago Enforcers, 2001. **Honors/Awds:** Delaware Sports Museum & Hall of Fame, 2007.

### PURNELL, MARK W.

Consultant. **Personal:** Born Oct 23, 1957, Wilmington, DE; son of Ernest W Sr and Yolanda V; married Brenda Dillard; children: Devon, Faith & Brandon. **Educ:** Del State Col, BS, acct, 1979; Univ Wis, Madison, MBA, finance & invests, 1982. **Career:** Del State Univ, alumni, 1975-79; Andersen Consult, consult, 1982-84; Milwaukee, cert invest mgt analyst, 1989-; Peat Marwick & Mitchell & Co, sr acct; Arthur Andersen & Co, consult; Offerman & Co Inc, div mgr; Kemper Securities Inc, sr vpres, invest; Wells Fargo, managing partner, 1989-2016; Purnell Wealth Mgt LLC, managing partner & portfolio mgr, 1989-; Sullivan & Assocs Wealth Mgt, LLC, Portfolio & Planning Assoc, first vpres, 2016-. **Orgs:** Nat Asn Black Acct, 1995; chair, Nat Conv; Univ Wis Alumni Asn; Milwaukee Athletic Club; bd dir, Found Bd mem, Univ Wis, Milwaukee, 2003-12; bd mem, Nat Winter Sports Educ Found, 2011-16. **Honors/Awds:** Distinguished Service Award, Consortium Grad Study Mgt, 1991; CIMA Designation, Invest Mgt Consult Asn. **Special Achievements:** Managed Money: The Dynamics of Personalized Investing, Research Magazine, June 1992. **Home Addr:** 2877 N 117th St, Wauwatosa, WI 53222, **Home Phone:** (414)778-0916. **Business Addr:** Managing Partner, Portfolio Manager, Purnell Wealth Management LLC, 1300 N Prospect Ave Suite 401, Milwaukee, WI 53202-3048, **Business Phone:** (414)271-0444.

### PURNELL, MARSHALL E.

Architect. **Personal:** Born Jun 8, 1950, Toledo, OH; son of Curtis (deceased) and Lelia Givens; married Tawana Cook; children: Justin, Tara & Austin. **Educ:** Univ Mich, Ann Arbor, Mich, BS, archit & urban planning, 1973, MA, archit, 1973. **Career:** Univ Md, Wash, DC, lectr teaching 2nd yr studio, 1973-74; Fry & Welch Architects, Wash, DC, architect, 1973-74; The Am Inst Architects, Wash, DC, adminr, 1974-78, pres, 2008-; Devrouax & Purnell Architects, Wash, DC, prin, 1978-. **Orgs:** Pres, Nat Org Minority Architects, 1975, coun mem; chmn, United Way, 1999; Bd Advocacy & Diversity comt; Hist Resources & Housing comts; Wash Urban League; DC Comn Arts; fel Am Inst Architects, pres. **Honors/Awds:** Univ Mich Alumni Scholar, Univ Mich. **Special Achievements:** First African American President in AIA History, 2007. **Home Addr:** 98 Hodges Lane, Takoma Park, MD 20912, **Home Phone:** (301)587-6747. **Business Addr:** Principal, Devrouax & Purnell Architects, 717 D St Northwest 5th Fl, Washington, DC 20004, **Business Phone:** (202)483-2878.

### PURVIS, ANDRE LAMONT

Football player. **Personal:** Born Jul 14, 1973, Jacksonville, NC. **Educ:** Univ NC, grad. **Career:** Football player (retired); Cincinnati Bengals, defensivetackle, 1997-99, 2000; Arena Football League, Carolina Cobras, offensive line & defensive line, 2002.

### PURVIS, ARCHIE C.

Consultant, executive. **Personal:** Born May 24, 1939, New York, NY; son of Archibald Sr and Millicent; married Candace H Caldwell; children: Christian. **Educ:** Univ Munich, attended 1960; City Col NY Sch Bus, BS, bus & polit sci, 1960; Stanford Univ Grad Sch Bus, exec prog, 1989. **Career:** Gen Foods Corp, acct mgr, dist mgr, 1963-69; Polaroid Corp, nat sales mgr, 1969-76; Lear Purvis Walker & Co, exec vpres, 1977-79; MCA Inc Univ Studios, vpres ind mkt, 1977-79; Am Broadcasting Co, pres, vpres & gen mgr video sales div; ABC Distrib Co, pres, 1989, sr vpres; Capital ABC Inc, Ambroco Media Group, pres, 1980-95; Purvis Enterprises Inc, pres, 1996-; Los Angeles Conv Ctr Comn, pres, 2009-13; Orphalese Global Strategies Inc, media consult, currently. **Orgs:** Dir, San Fernand Fair Housing, 1979; dir, Corp Pub Broadcasting, 1987-91; bd dir, GTE Calif, 1988-; bd dir, Gen Tel W, 1989-93; bd, Rebuild LA, 1992-97; dir, GTE W; bd dir, YMCA Metrop, 1993-2010; adv bd, REZN8 Inc, 2001; comnr, Off Pub Safety Oversight Comt City Los Angeles, 2010; bd dir, Los Angeles Visitors & Conv Bur, 2010; secy, Keep Calif Beautiful; adv, Los Angeles Community Col; Yosemite Nat Inst; dir, Resn 8Technol & Communs; Am Mkt Asn; Am Mgt Asn; Sales Exec NY; dir, Int C Sch; Acad Motion Picture Arts & Sci, Hollywood Radio & TV Soc; bd dir, GTE Calif; UCLA Bd Counors; advisor, Los Angeles Community Col Dists LA Prosper prog; trustee, US Dept Justice; trustee, Cent Dist Calif. **Honors/Awds:** Los Angeles County Outstanding Adopt-A-Highway Volunteer of the Year, 1997. **Home Addr:** 16541 Goldenrod Pl, Encino, CA 91436. **Business Addr:** Media Consultant, Orphalese Global Strategies Inc, 5304 Ballona Lane, Los Angeles, CA 90230, **Business Phone:** (310)390-9270.

### PURYEAR, DR. ALVIN NELSON

Educator. **Personal:** Born Apr 6, 1937, Fayetteville, NC; son of Byron and Gladys; married Catherine; children: Pamela, Susan & Karen. **Educ:** Yale Univ, BA, 1960; Columbia Univ, MBA, 1962, PhD, 1966. **Career:** Mobil Oil Corp, employee rels adv, 1965-66, financial analyst, 1966-67; Allied Chem Corp, comput systs specialist, 1967-68; Rutgers Univ, assoc prof, 1968-69; Baruch Col City Univ New York, assoc prof, 1970-72, dean, 1972-75, prof mgt, 1972-, Lawrence N. Field prof entrepreneurship & prof mgt, dean, 1972-75, co-dir, master sci indust rels prog & dir small bus lab, 1977-81, chmn dept mgt, 1978-79, Prof Emer Mgt & Entrepreneurship, currently; City NY, first dep controller, 1983-85; N Fork Bank, dir, 2004; Samuel Bronfman fel; John Hay Whitney fel. **Orgs:** Vpres org & mgt, Dep Comptroller City New York, Ford Found, 1980-82; Smithsonian Nat Bd, 1989-95; trustee, Green Pt Savings Bank, 1992-; dir, Greenpoint Financial Corp, 1992-2004; chmn, Broadcast Capital Fund Inc, 1993-95; trustee, Yale Univ, 1994-96; dir, Green Pt Fin Corp, 1994-; dir, Bank Tokyo-Mitsubishi Trust Co, 1997; dir, Am Capital, 1998-2006, lead dir, 2006-; trustee, Comm Serv Soc New York, 1997-; dir, N Fork Bancorporation Inc, 2004; dir, Am Capital Agency Corp, 2008-; trustee, Union Theol Sem & Presby Sch Christian Educ; dir, Am Capital Mortgage Investment Corp, 2011; dir, CIBT Inc; dir, Travel Logistics Ltd; dir, Presby Church (U.S.A.) Investment & Loan Corp; dir, Interracial Coun Bus Opportunity; bd dir, Am Passport Express, LLC. **Home Addr:** 4580 Delafield Ave, Bronx, NY 10471. **Business Addr:** Professor Emeritus of Management and Entrepreneurship, Professor of Management, Baruch College of the City University of New York, 1 Bernard Baruch Way, New York, NY 10010, **Business Phone:** (646)312-1000.

### PURYEAR, MARTIN

Artist, sculptor. **Personal:** Born May 23, 1941, Washington, DC; married Jean Gordon; children: 1. **Educ:** Cath Univ Am, Wash, DC, BA, 1963; Swed Royal Acad Art, Stockholm, Sweden, attended 1968; Yale Univ, Sch Art & Archit, MFA, sculpture, 1971. **Career:** MacArthur Found fel, 1989; Fisk Univ, asst prof art, 1971-73; sculptor, currently; McKee Gallery, artist, currently. **Orgs:** Vol, Peace Corps, 1964-66; Am Acad & Inst Arts & Lett, 1992. **Honors/Awds:** NEA, fellowship, 1978; Guggenheim Memorial Found grant, 1984; The Francis J. Greenburger Foundation Award, 1988; Grand prize, Sao Paulo Bienal, 1989; Creative Arts Awards, Brandeis Univ, 1989; John D. and Catherine T. MacArthur Found Award, 1989; Louis Comfort Tiffany grant; Skowhegan Medal for Sculpture, 1991; College Art Association Award, 1993; honorary doctorate, Yale Univ, 1994; Institute Honors for Collaborative Acheivement, Am Inst Architects, 2003; Jury, World Trade Ctr Site Memorial Competition, 2004; Gold Medal, Am Acad Arts & Lett, 2007; LongHouse Medal, LongHouse Reserve, 2008; National Medal of Arts and Humanities, Wash, DC. **Business Addr:** Artist, c/o McKee Gallery, 745 5th Ave, New York, NY 10151, **Business Phone:** (212)688-5951.

**PUTNAM, GLENDORA M. See Obituaries Section.**

### PYLES, J. A.

School administrator, vice president (organization). **Personal:** Born Feb 23, 1949, Sanford, FL. **Educ:** Bethune-Cookman Col, BA, 1971; Roosevelt Univ, MA, 1975. **Career:** United Negro Col Fund, asst area dir; Alpha Kappa Alpha Sorority Inc, prog specialist; Social Security Admin St Petersburg, 1970; Bethune Cookman Col, vpres develop, vpres, 1990-. **Orgs:** Soc Fund-Raising Execs; Nat Soc Fund-Raising Execs; Bethune-Cookman Col Alumni Asn; Roosevelt Univ Alumni Asn; consult, AGAPE Ministries; MtCarmel Baptist Church. **Home Addr:** 2 Lakewood Pk Dr, Ormond Beach, FL 32174. **Business Addr:** Vice President, Bethune-Cookman College, 640 Dr Mary McLeod Bethune Blvd, Daytona Beach, FL 32114, **Business Phone:** (386)481-2000.

# Q

### QAMAR, NADI ABU

Composer, musician. **Personal:** Born Jul 6, 1917, Cincinnati, OH; son of William Givens and Alberta Bennett Givens; married Rose Ann Dolski; children: Fabian Billie & Alberta Edith. **Educ:** Int Univ Found Independence MO. **Career:** Jazz pianist, composer & arranger, 1934-65; Inaugural Hist Jazz ser, composer & musician, 1965-77; Bedford Study Youth Action, oratorio composer & mus dir; Countee Cullen, concerts, 1965-68; New Lafayette Theatre, artist residence, 1970-72; Nina Simone World Tours, 1972-74; "WyMbony Sita", ballet, New York, 1973; Mus Natural Hist NY, perf ser, 1976; Leader Workshops Var Univs & Study Ctrs, lectr, 1977-89; Bennington Col, prof voice, piano & orchestra, 1978-85; Nuru Taa African Idiom & Nuru Taa Music, afro musicologist, dir & composer, currently. Albums: The Mama-Likembi Instruction Record, 1975; The Nuru Taa African Musical Idiom, 1975; Likembi Song Book, 1979. **Orgs:** Broadcast Music, 1958-; Am Fedn Musicians; Nat Music Publs Asn Inc. **Home Addr:** Rte 1, Kewaunee, WI 54216, **Home Phone:** (920)388-2941. **Business Addr:** Composer, Nuru Taa Arts, Rte 1, Kewaunee, WI 54216, **Business Phone:** (920)388-2941.

### QUANDER, ESQ. ROHULAMIN

Administrative court judge. **Personal:** Born Dec 4, 1943, Washington, DC; son of James W and Joheora Rohualamin; married Carmen Torruella; children: Iliana Amparo, Rohulamin Darius & Fatima de los Santos. **Educ:** Howard Univ, Wash, DC, BA 1966, JD, 1969. **Career:** Neighborhood Legal Serv, staff, 1969-71; Geo Wash Univ, fac, 1970-72; Int Investors Inc, mkt consult, atty, state dir, 1973-; pvt pract, 1975-; DC govt, admin judge; Off Adjudication DC Govt, staff, 1986-2002; Off Employee Appeals DC Govt, staff, 2002-; DC Dept Consumer & Regulatory Affairs, admin law judge, sr admin judge & mayors agt Hist Preserv, 1998-2010. **Orgs:** Omega Psi Phi Frat, 1964-; Phi Alpha Delta Law Fraternity, 1967; founder, Howard Univ, Chap Black Am Law Studs Asn, 1968; pres, Stud Bar Asn, 1968-69, vpres, 1967-68; bd dir, Wash Urban League, 1969-70; pres, Howard Univ Alumni Club, Wash, DC, 1970-71; bd mem, Super Ct, DC, 1975; US Dist Ct, DC, 1976; bd dir, Wash DC Parent & Child Ctr, 1977-81; chief archivist, Quander Family Hist, 1977-; reg chmn, Howard Univ Alumni, 1979-87; chmn, Educ Inst Licensure Comn, DC, 1979-; Quanders United, Inc, 1983-; Columbia Hist Soc, Int Platform Speakers Asn, 1985-; pres, founder, Quanders Hist Soc Inc, 1985-; MLK Holiday Comn, DC, 1987-89; bd dir, Pigskin Club, 1986-; dir & vpres, Torruella-Quander Gallery Ltd, 1988-; co-chair, founder, Benjamin Banneker Orial Community Inc, 1991; founder & pres, IliRoFa Int Inc, 1991-; Ct Appeals DC; Phi Alpha Theta His Soc; Am Bar Asn; Nat Bar Asn; DC Bar Asn; Bar Supreme Ct, PA; US Dist Ct Eastern PA; founder & pres, Quander Hist Soc Inc. **Honors/Awds:** Man of Year Award, Omega Psi Phi Fraternity, 1965, 1968; Special Award, Howard Univ, 1969; Outstanding Service Award, Quanders United Inc, 1991. **Special Achievements:** Author: The History of the Quander Family, 1984; have published numerous articles for Howard Univ Alumni newspaper. **Home Addr:** 1703 Lawrence St NE, Washington, DC 20018. **Business Addr:** Senior Administrative Judge, Mayors Agent for Historic Preservation, District of Columbia Government, 717 14th St NW 3rd Fl, Washington, DC 20005, **Business Phone:** (202)727-0004.

### QUANSAH-DANKWA, DR. JULIANA ABA

Dentist. **Personal:** Born Aug 11, 1955, Apam; daughter of S T and Elizabeth; married Joseph Ofori. **Educ:** Univ Mich Dent Sch, BS, zool, 1976, DDS, 1980. **Career:** Lawrence D Crawford, DDS, PC, assoc dentist, 1980-81; Com Action Comn, dent dir, 1981-85; Riverfront Dent Ctr, dentist, 1982-83; pvt pact, dentist, 1984-. **Orgs:** Nat Asn Advan Colored People, 1984; chmn, Int Trends & Serv Tri City Links Inc, 1984-; African Greater Flint Inc, 1984-; Saginaw Chamber Com, 1985; bd mem, Headstart Saginaw, 1985-. **Honors/Awds:** Commendation Award, Ross Med Educ Ctr, 1986; Appreciation Award, Averill Career Opportunities, 1986. **Business Addr:** Dentist, Private Practice, 1928 E Genesee Ave, Saginaw, MI 48601, **Business Phone:** (989)753-1993.

### QUARLES, ALICIA

Journalist, 001172, television journalist. **Personal:** Born Fontana, CA. **Educ:** Univ Southern Calif, BA, broadcast jour, 2003. **Career:** Associated Press, Los Angeles, producer, 2003-05, producer and reporter/text and television, 2005-07, North America Entertainment Editor, 2007-09, Global Entertainment Editor, 2009-12; FUSE Television, New York City, 2011-12; E! News/NBC News, correspondent and reporter, 2012-15. **Special Achievements:** Appearances on The Today Show, MSNBC, and the Weather Channel for E! News; author, fashion blog on E! Online; Miss Universe, judge, 2013.

### QUARLES, GEORGE R.

School administrator. **Personal:** Born Jul 14, 1927, Morgantown, WV; son of George and Mabel; married Barbara Louise; children: Nia Caron Martin & Niama Burnley. **Educ:** Hampton Inst, BS, 1951; NY Univ, MA, 1956. **Career:** School administrator (retired); US Dept Educ, Wash, DC, Off Voc & Adult Educ, dep asst secy, 1980-81; Sewanhaka Cent High Sch Dist, Floral Pk, NY, dir occup educ, 1985-90; Southern Westchester Bd Coop Educ Serv, Richard Lerer Ctr Tech & Occup Educ, asst dir, 1991-95; Ctr Career & Occup Educ, chief admin; NY City, bd educ; City Univ NY, dir regional opportunity ctr; Sam Harris Assoc Ltd, Wash, DC, exec vpres; NJ State Educ Dept, dir voc educ; Newark Manpower Training Skill Ctr, assoc dir, dir; New Rochelle High Sch, teacher. **Orgs:** US Aid African Bur, 1983-84; Acad Educ Devel, 1984-91; consult, Mitshita Educ Found, 1988-89; New Rochelle Civil Serv Comn, 1998; NY St Adv Coun Voc Educ; New Sch Soc Res; Voc Educ, Omega Psi Phi Fraternity; tech revpanel, Nat Inst Educ Study Voc Educ; Nat Fac Nat Ctr Res Voc Educ, Ohio St Univ; consult, US Dept Educ Regarding Grant Awards, Nat Proj; co-founder, chair, bd dir, Community Ctr Employ & Trainning; Am Voc Asn; St Catherine AME Zion Church. **Honors/Awds:** Community Service Award, Interreligious Coun New Rochelle, 2000; NY State Sidney Platt Award; Winged Trophy, Newark Anti-Poverty Agency; Omega Man of the Year, Omicron Iota Chap; Educ Secy Spec Achievement Pin. **Special Achievements:** Numerous radio & TV appearances articles for various newspapers on vocational education; major paper on Equity in Vocational Education, National Center for Research in Vocational Education; numerous articles & studies on vocational education & youth employment. **Home Addr:** 22 Vaughn Ave, New Rochelle, NY 10801, **Home Phone:** (718)465-7168.

### QUARLES, DR. NANCY L.

**Personal:** Born Jun 6, 1954; married Larry. **Educ:** Univ Detroit, BS, bus admin; Cent Mich Univ, MA, mgt; Western Mich Univ, PhD, pub affairs & pub admin. **Career:** IBM, sr mkt consult, 1976-92; Mich House Reps, house rep, 1996-2002; Western Mich Univ, adj prof; Cent Mich Univ, adj prof, fac, 2002-; Oakland Univ, staff; Advantage Consult Group, founder & pres, owner, currently; Oakland County, comnr. **Orgs:** Chair, pres, Southern Oakland County Nat Asn Advan Colored People, currently; exec adv bd mem, Women Impacting Pub Policy; Nat Parliamentary Asn; Nat Found Women Legislators; chair, Mich House Women's Leadership Caucus; Mich Munic Bond Authority; Elizabeth Copeland Glass Educ Found; Thurgood Marshall fel; chief whip, Dem Caucus; dem vice chair, House Tax Policy & Regulatory Affairs & Local Govt Comts; Fin & Ins Comt; Gen Govt & Planning & Bldg Comts; Mich Capitol Comt; adv, Mich Dem Party; Southfield-Lathrup Village Dem Club. **Business Addr:** President, Owner, Advantage Consulting Group, 5000 Merrick Rd, Massapequa, NY 11758, **Business Phone:** (516)795-7300.

### QUARLES, NORMA R.

Journalist. **Personal:** Born Nov 11, 1936, New York, NY; children: Lawrence & Susan. **Educ:** Hunter Col; City Col NY. **Career:** Katherine King Assocs, real estate broker, 1957-65; WSDM-FM, Chicago, IL, news reporter, 1965-66; NBC News Training Prog, 1966-67; KYC-TV, Cleveland, OH, news reporter & anchorwoman, 1967-70; NBC-TV, news reporter, 1970; WNBC, reporter; NBC, New York corresp; WMAQ TV, producing & reporting; Cable News Network's New York, day time anchor, 1988-90, corresp, 1990-98; freelance journalist, 1998-. **Orgs:** Bd gov, Nat Acad TV Arts & Sci; Sigma Delta Chi; Nat Asn Black Journalists. **Honors/Awds:** Front Page Award, WNBC-TV, 1973; Deadline Club Award, Sigma Delta Chi, 1973; The League of Women Voters Vice Presidential Debate, 1984; National Association of Black JournalistsJ Hall of Fame, 1990; CINE Golden Eagle, 1993; Emmy Award, New York Association of Black Journalists Awards. **Special Achievements:** Selected as a panelist, The League of Women Voters Vice Presidential Debate. **Home Addr:** 1 Hillside Ave, Pelham, NY 10803.

### QUARLES, SHELTON EUGENE, SR.

Football player, executive. **Personal:** Born Sep 11, 1971, Nashville, TN; married Damaris; children: Gabriela Nicole, Shelton Jr & Carlos Antonio. **Educ:** Vanderbilt Univ, human & orgn develop. **Career:** Football player (retired), exec; Miami Dolphins, 1994; BC Lions, 1995-96; Tampa Bay Buccaneers, 1997-98, linebacker, 1999-2001, mid linebacker, 2002-05, mid linebacker, linebacker, 2006, pro scout, 2007-11, coordr pro scout, 2011-13, dir pro scouting, 2013-14, dir football opers, 2014-. **Orgs:** Founder, Shelton Quarles IMPACT Found; Nat Hon Soc; bd, Tampa Bay Area Regional Transp Authority, 2009. **Honors/Awds:** Pro Bowl, 2002; Champion, Super Bowl, XXXVII; JB Award, Nflpa Players Inc. **Special Achievements:** Hosted the All Pro Dad seminar. **Home Addr:** 17019 Candeleda De Avila, Tampa, FL 33613-5213. **Business Addr:** Director of Football Operations, Tampa Bay Buccaneers, 1 Buccaneer Pl, Tampa, FL 33607, **Business Phone:** (813)870-2700.

### QUEEN, EVELYN E. CRAWFORD

Judge, educator. **Personal:** Born Apr 6, 1971, Albany, NY; daughter of Richard Carter and Iris Crawford; married Charles A; children: Angelia Y & George Y. **Educ:** Howard Univ, BS, 1968, JD, 1975. **Career:** Judge, educator (retired); NIH, support staff, 1968-75; Metrop Life Ins Co, atty, 1975-77; US Dept Com, Maritime Admin, atty-adv, 1977-79; US Atty Off, asst US atty, 1979-81; DC Super Ct, comnr, 1981-86, judge, 1986-01; Howard Univ Law Sch, adj prof, 1990; Univ DC Sch Law, adj prof, 1991-92. **Orgs:** Sigma Delta Tau; ABA, 1975-; NBA, 1975-. **Home Addr:** 1727 Kalmia Rd NW, Washington, DC 20012, **Home Phone:** (202)361-3244.

### QUEEN LATIFAH (DANA ELAINE OWENS)

Actor, singer. **Personal:** Born Mar 18, 1970, Newark, NJ; daughter of Lance Owens Sr and Rita Owens. **Educ:** Bor Manhattan Community Col, broadcasting. **Career:** Films: Jungle Fever, House Party 2, 1991; Juice, 1992; My Life, 1993; Set It Off, 1996; Hoodlum, 1997; Sphere, Living Out Loud, 1998; Bone Collector, 1999; Bringing Out Dead, 1999; The Country Bears, Brown Sugar, Chicago, 2002; Bringing Down the House, exec producer, Scary Movie 3, 2003; Barbershop 2: Back in Business, The Cookout, producer, Taxi, 2004; Beauty Shop, producer, 2005; Last Holiday, Stranger Than Fiction, 2006; Hairspray, 2007; The Perfect Holiday, 2007; Mad Money, What Happens in Vegas, The Secret Life of Bees, 2008; Ice Age: Dawn of the Dinosaurs, 2009; Valentine's Day, Just Wright, 2010; The Dilemma, 2011; Ice Age: Continental Drift, 2012; Joyful Noise, 2012; House of Bodies, exec producer, 2013; 22 Jump Street, 2014. TV Series: "Sisters in the Name of Rap", 1992; "Living Single", 1993-98; "Mama Flora's Family", 1998; "Queen Latifah Show", host & exec producer, 1999-2001, 2013-; "Spin City", 2001; "Living with the Dead", 2002; "Kung Faux", 2003; "The Muppets' Wizard of Oz", 2005; "Life Support", exec producer, 2007; "Who's Your Caddy?", 2007; "Wifey", 2007; "Steel Magnolias", 2012; Albums: All Hail Queen, 1990; Nature a Sista, 1991; X-tra Naked, 1992; Black Reign, 1994; Order in Court, 1998; She's a Queen: A Collection of Hits, 2002; The Dana Owens Album, 2004; Trav'lin' Light, 2007; Flavor Unit Management, chief exec officer, currently; Flavor Unit Records, owner, currently. **Honors/Awds:** Numerous honors & awards including Best New Artist, New Music Seminar, 1990; Best Female Rapper, Rolling Stone Readers' Poll, 1990; Grammy Award nominee, 1990; Soul Train Music Awards, Sammy Davis Jr Award, Entertainer of the Year, 1995; Black Film Award, Acapulco Black Film Festival, 1997; Artist of the Year, Harvard Found, 2003; Nominated for Oscar Award, 2003; BET Award, 2003; Teen Choice Award, 2003; Screen Actors Guild Award, 2003 & 2008; Black Reel Award, 2003 & 2008; Critics Choice Award, Broadcast Film Critics Asn, 2003 & 2008; Icon Award, Elle Women Hollywood Awards, 2004; BET Comedy Award, 2004; Image Award, Nat Asn Advan Colored People, 2004 & 2008; Wannabe Award, 2005; Star on the Walk of Fame, 2006; Hollywood Film Award, 2007 & 2008; Blimp Award, 2007; Golden Globe Award, 2008; Satellite Award, 2008; Gracie Allen Award, 2008; Ensemble Cast Award, Palm Springs Int Film Festival, 2008; People's Choice Award, 2014. **Special Achievements:** First female rapper to be nominated for an Academy Award. **Business Addr:** Chief Executive Officer, Flavor Unit Management, 155 Morgan St, Jersey City, NJ 07302, **Business Phone:** (201)333-4883.

### QUESTLOVE (AHMIR KHALIB THOMPSON)

Music director, music producer, musician. **Personal:** Born Jan 20, 1971, Philadelphia, PA; son of Lee Andrews and Jacqui Thompson. **Educ:** Philadelphia High Sch Creative & Performing Arts. **Career:** Professional drummer, 1983-; The Roots, co-founder and drummer, 1993-; album producer, 1993-; actor, 2000-; Chappelle's Show, original sketch music writer, Comedy Central, 2004; Late Night with Jimmy Fallon, musical dir and musician, 2009-13; The Tonight Show Starring Jimmy Fallon, musician, 2014-; Top Five, film score composer, 2014; Inside Amy Schumer, composer, 2015; Vincent N Roxxy, film score composer, 2016. Television: Chapelle's Show, Comedy Central, 2006; Yo Gabba Gabba!, Nickelodeon, 209; iCarly, Nickelodeon, 2012; The Cleveland Show, Fox, 2012; Parks and Recreation, 2015; The Jim Gaffigan Show, 2015; Empire, Fox, 2015; Inside Amy Schumer, Comedy Central, 2016; Night Train with Wyatt Cenac, 2016. Film: Bamboozled, 2000; Brooklyn Babylon, 2001; The Being Experience, 2013; Popstar: Never Stop Never Stopping, 2016. **Honors/Awds:** Grammy Award, 2011. **Special Achievements:** Albums with the Roots: Organix, 1993, Thinss Fall Apart, 1999, Game Theory, 2006, Rising Down, 2008, How I Got Over, 2010. Mixtapes: Babies Makin' Babies, Urban Theory, 2002; Babies Makin' Babies 2: Misery Strikes Back, 2006. Author, Mo' Meta Blues: The World According to Questlove, 2013; Something to Food About, 2016. **Business Addr:** The Tonight Show Starring Jimmy Fallon, 30 Rockefeller Plz, New York, NY 10112-0015.

### QUICK, GEORGE KENNETH

Banker. **Personal:** Born Apr 14, 1947, Orangeburg, SC; son of Oscar and Geneva Shokes; married Gloria Grainger; children: Jeffrey George & Erica Camille. **Educ:** SC State Univ, Orangeburg, SC, BS, 1968; Atlanta Univ, Atlanta, GA, MBA, 1975; S La State Univ, Sch Banking, Baton Rouge, LA, cert, 1986. **Career:** First Union Nat Bank, Charlotte, NC, asst vpres, 1975-86; Community Affordable Housing Equity Corp, finance dir; Mutual Savings & Loan Asn, Durham, NC, exec vpres & Chief operating officer, 1986-; Mutual Community Saving Bank Inc, pres & chief exec officer, 1994-2001; Durham County Gov, finance dir, 2001-. **Orgs:** Chmn bd, UDI/CDC, 1987-; chmn, Pvt Ind Coun, 1989-; bd dir, NC Mus Life & Sci, 1989-; bd trustee & mem, St Joseph AME Church, 1990-; bd dir, Chamber Com, 1991-; bd trustee, Durham County Hosp Corp; chmn bd dir, SC State Univ Found; bd mem, Community Affordable Housing Equity Corp. **Honors/Awds:** Distinguished Alumnus of the Year, NAFEO, 1990; Distinguished Business Alumnus, SC State Univ, 1992. **Home Addr:** 1326 Elmira Ave, Durham, NC 27707, **Home Phone:** (919)688-7497. **Business Addr:** Director, Durham County Government, 200 E Main St 4th Fl Mezzanine Old Courthouse, Durham, NC 27701, **Business Phone:** (919)560-0035.

### QUICK, MIKE ANTHONY

Football player, radio host. **Personal:** Born May 14, 1959, Hamlet, NC; son of James and Mary; children: Ronson & Stephen. **Educ:** NC State Col, grad. **Career:** Football player (retired), host, executive; Philadelphia Eagles, wide receiver, 1982-90; Assoc Press First-Team All-Pro, 1983, 1985; Eagles Honor Roll; All Pro Fitness and Racquet Club, Maple Shade NJ, co-owner; Philadelphia Eagles Radio Broadcasts 94.1 WYSP, announcer, Philadelphia Eagles radio, color commentator. **Orgs:** Big Brothers/Big Sisters; KYW-TV's Project Homeless Fund; WCAU-TV's School Vote Program; 7-Eleven/Coca Cola Freedom RunSickle Cell. **Honors/Awds:** Five time Pro-Bowler, 1983-87; The Pride of Hamlet-The Fantastic Four, 1985; Eagles Ed Block Courage Award, 1989. **Special Achievements:** First Eagle in history to surpass 1, 000 yards receiving in 3 straight seasons; Honor Roll inductee, 1995; Films: 1982 NFL Draft, 1982; The Complete History of the Philadelphia Eagles, 2004; Invincible, 2006; New Jersey's Last Patriot, 2012. **Business Addr:** Announcer, Philadelphia Eagles, 1 NovaCare Way, Philadelphia, PA 19145, **Business Phone:** (215)463-2500.

### QUIGLESS, DR. MILTON DOUGLAS, JR.

Surgeon, educator. **Personal:** Born Oct 15, 1945, Durham, NC; son of Milton Douglas Sr (deceased) and Helen Gordon (deceased); children: Leslie, Matthew, Christine, Ashley & Maryanna. **Educ:** Morehouse Col, BS, 1970; Meharry Med Col, MD, 1971. **Career:** George W Hubbard Hosp, Meharry Med Col, internship, Gen Surg, residency; Meharry Med Col, instr surg, 1976-77; Univ NC, Chapel Hill, clin assoc prof surg, 1986-; Wake County Med Ctr, pres/med staff, 1986-87; pvt pract, currently; Blue Ridge Hernia Ctr, pres. **Orgs:** St Augustine Col Bd, 1985-88; fel Am Col Surgeons. **Home Addr:** 3410 Six Forks Rd, Raleigh, NC 27609-7234, **Home Phone:** (919)571-1170. **Business Addr:** Surgeon, Keller Army Community Hospital, Credentials Off 900 Wash Rd, West Point, NY 10996, **Business Phone:** (845)938-3470.

### QUINCE, KEVIN

Government official, president (organization), business owner. **Personal:** Born Jul 4, 1950, Atlantic City, NJ; son of Remer and Doris Pratt Griffith; married Regina Gumby; children: Gyasi & Khary. **Educ:** Hampton Univ, BA, sociol, 1972; Rutgers Univ, city & regional planning, 1974; Univ Pa, Wharton Sch, attended 1980. **Career:** NJ Housing & Mortgage Finance Agency, sr develop officer, 1974-80, syndication officer, 1980-84, asst dir res & develop, 1984-86, dir res & develop, 1986-88, asst exec dir, 1988-90, exec dir, 1990-; Kevin Quince Assoc Inc, Real Estate Develop Consult, owner & pres, currently. **Orgs:** Vpres, E Windsor Planning Bd, 1982-83; chmn, Mercer County Housing Adv Bd, 1987-89; vpres & secy, Housing Assistance

Corp, 1988-; bd dir, Police Athletic League, 1989; bd mem, Coun Affordable Housing, 1990-; Harvard Univ, Prog Sr Execs, 1990. **Honors/Awds:** Achievements in Affordable Housing, NJ Chap Housing & Redevelop Off, 1989; Achievements in Affordable Housing, NJ Black Housing Adminr, 1990. **Home Addr:** 975 Old York Rd, Hightstown, NJ 08520, **Home Phone:** (609)443-1344. **Business Addr:** President, Owner, Kevin QuInce Associates Inc, 975 Old York Rd, Hightstown, NJ 08520-4708, **Business Phone:** (609)371-2321.

## QUINCE, PEGGY A.

Judge. **Personal:** Born Jan 3, 1948, Norfolk, VA; daughter of Solomon; married Fred L Buckine; children: Peggy LaVerne Buckine & Laura LaVerne Buckine. **Educ:** Howard Univ, BS, zool, 1970; Cath Univ Am, JD, 1975. **Career:** Rental Accommodations Off, Wash, DC, hearing officer; pvt pract, 1977-80; Fla Atty Gen's Off, Criminal div, asst atty gen, Tampa bur chief, 1980-93; Fla Second Dist Ct Appeals, judge, 1993-98; Fla State Supreme Ct, judge, 1998-; justice, 1999; chief justice, 2008-10; Supreme Ct Fla, justice, currently. **Orgs:** Fla Bar Asn; Va State Bar; Nat Bar Asn; Tallahassee Asn Women Lawyers; William H Stafford Inn Ct; Govt Lawyers Sect, Criminal Law Sect; Alpha Kappa Alpha; Urban League; Jack & Jill Am; Nat Asn Advan Coloured People; Tampa Orgn Black Affairs; Links Inc, currently; New Hope Missionary Baptist Church; Phi Alpha Delta Law Fraternity; Black Am Law Students Asn. **Honors/Awds:** Jurist Award, Nat Bar Asn, Women Virgil Hawkins Bar Asn Award; Appreciation Award Lawyers Div; Virgil Hawkins Bar Asn Award; Appreciation Award, Broward County Sch Bd; Appreciation Award, Hillsborough County Sheriff's Black Adv Coun; Lakeland NAACP Award; African-American Production Company Personal Achievement Award; Paul C Perkins Bar Association Appreciation Award; Award of Distinguished Service & Continuing Commitment, Fort Lauderdale Bnai Brith; Florida State University College of Law, Appreciation Cert; Off of the Atty Gen, Fla Crime Prev Training Inst for Exemplary Contrib to Crime Prev in the State of Fla, cert; Honorary Doctor of Law, Stetson Univ Col Law, 1999; Woman of Distinction Award, Girl Scouts, 2001; William H Hastie Award, Judicial Coun, Nat Bar Asn, 2002; Florida Girls State Award, 2002, 2003; Florida Bar Equal Opportunities in the Profession Award, 2002; Helping Hand Award, 2003; Southern Women in Public Service Pacesetter Award, 2003; Pioneering the Future in our Community Award, 2003; Outstanding Jurist & Howard University Alumna Award, 2003; Honorary doctor of laws degree, St Thomas Univ Sch Law, 2004; Black Law Student Association Alumni Achievement Award, Cath Univ of Am, Columbus Sch of Law, 2004; Key to the City of Panama City, 2004; Lee County Association for Women Lawyers & the Lee County Bar Association Award, Fla judiciary, 2004; Key to the City of Winter Haven, 2005; Richard W Ervin Equal Justice Award, 2005; Margaret Brent Women Lawyers of Achievement Award, 2006; Rickards High School Outstanding School Volunteer Award, 2006; Florida Women's Hall of Fame award, 2007; Lifetime Achievement Award, The Fla Bar's Govt Lawyer Sect, 2008. **Special Achievements:** First African American female appointed to a FL district court of appeal, 1993; Second African American and third woman to hold to serve as Chief Justice; First African-American woman to head any branch of Florida government; First African-American woman to sit on the state's highest Court and the third female Justice. **Home Addr:** 2909 Whittington Dr, Tallahassee, FL 32309-8219, **Home Phone:** (850)668-9020. **Business Addr:** Justice, Supreme Court Florida, 500 S Duval St, Tallahassee, FL 32399-1925, **Business Phone:** (850)922-5624.

## QUINN, DIANE C.

Government official. **Personal:** Born May 9, 1942, Chicago, IL; children: Caren Clift. **Educ:** Am Univ, MS, human resources, orgn develop & human resources mgt, 1988. **Career:** Nat Alliance Bus, lectr, 1972-74; Ill Bell Tel Co, sales mgr, 1974-79; C&P Tel Co, indust mgr, 1978-79; Wilberforce Univ, consult, 1979; AT&T, mkt mgr, 1979-83, mgr mgt employ, 1983-84, mgr univ rels, 1984-87; Col Bd Conf Indust Partnerships, lectr, 1986; R Burton & Co Inc, consult, 1986; Dept Pub & Assisted Housing, regional mgr, 1989-94; DC Dept Recreation & Parks, exec asst dir, 1994, admin res, policy & planning, currently; DC Dept of Transp, adminstrator & human capital mgt, 2000-03; Sunrise Sr Living, human resources mgr, 2005-15. **Orgs:** AT&T Rep Nat Urban League, 1972-. **Home Addr:** 1708 15th St NW, Washington, DC 20009, **Home Phone:** (202)234-7565. **Business Addr:** Administrator of Research, Policy & Planning, DC Department of Recreation & Parks, 1800 Anacostia Dr SE, Washington, DC 20009, **Business Phone:** (202)698-2250.

## QUINTON, DR. BARBARA ANN

Educator. **Personal:** Born Jul 1, 1941, Sharptown, MD; children: Keith F Nichols & Kyle B Nichols. **Educ:** Morgan State Univ, BS, 1963; Meharry Med Col, MD, 1967. **Career:** Hubbard Hosp, internship, 1967-68; St Louis C's Hosp, resident, 1968-69, fel, 1969-71; Howard Univ fel, 1971-74, asst prof, 1974-76, assoc prof, Col Med, Med Genetics Clin, dir; Howard Univ Hosp, practices Pediat, currently. **Orgs:** Hon mem, Intern/Resident Asn, Howard Univ, 1983; church rep, Nat Asn Advan Colored People, 1985-; Am Zion Methodist Church Lay Coun. **Home Addr:** 4701 Red Fox Rd, Rockville, MD 20852-2315, **Home Phone:** (301)984-3964. **Business Addr:** Pediatrics Practioner, Howard University Hospital, 2041 Georgia Ave NW, Washington, DC 20060, **Business Phone:** (202)865-3022.

## QUIVERS, DR. ERIC STANLEY

Physician. **Personal:** Born Oct 27, 1955, Winston-Salem, NC; son of William Wyatt and Evelyn Cecelia; married Mara Williams; children: Micah Stanley & Lucas Sorrell. **Educ:** Morehouse Col, BS, magna cum laude, 1979; Howard Univ Col Med, MD, 1983; Pediat Cardiol, pediat, Bd Cert. **Career:** Howard Univ Hosp Dist Columbia, resident pediat, 1983-86; Pk W Med Ctr, staff pediatrician, 1986; Sinai Hosp, provisional med staff, 1986-88; Mayo Clin, pediat cardiol fel, 1988-91; Healthcare Forum's Cardiovasc Health, fel, 1998-99; C's Nat Med Ctr, Dept Cardiol, staff cardiologist, prevent cardiol & Exercise Labo, dir, 1991-2004; C's Hosp Pittsburgh, Prev Cardiol Clin, dir, 2004-10; Dean Health Syst, med dir, 2010-; Univ Pittsburgh Sch Med, asst prof pediat, currently; pvt pract, currently. **Orgs:** Phi Beta Kappa, 1977; Beta Kappa Chi, 1977; AMA; Nat Med Asn, 1983-; fel Am Acad Pediat; Dis Hunger Proj, 1992; Mayor's CMS Food, Health & Nutrit, 1993-; Asn Black Cardiologists, 1990-; Take AIM, chair, int adv comt; Int Soc Heart & Lung Transplantation; Am Col Sports Med. **Honors/Awds:** Certificate of Appreciation, Howard Univ Col Med SGA, 1983; Roland B Scott Departmental Award in Pediatrics, 1983; listed, Who's Who in Black America, 1987; Co-Teacher of the Year Award, 2000; Outstanding Resident Faculty Teaching Award, 2000. **Special Achievements:** Co-author: "Hepatic Cyst Associated with Ventricular Peritoneal Shunt in a Child with Brain Tumor", Child's Nervous System, 1985; "Variability in Response to a Low-fat, Low-cholesterol Diet in Children with Elevated Low-density Lipoprotein Cholesterol Levels", Pediatrics, 1992; Echocardiographic Evidence for Ductal Tissue Sling Causing Discrete Coarctation of the Aorta in the Neonate: Case Report, 1997; "Pediatric Preventive Cardiology: Healthy Habits Now, Healthy Hearts Later". **Home Addr:** 14 Foxlair Ct, Gaithersburg, MD 20882, **Home Phone:** (301)212-9748. **Business Addr:** Medical Director, Dean Health System, 1800 W Beltline Hwy, Madison, WI 53713, **Business Phone:** (800)576-8773.

# R

## RABB, MADELINE MURPHY

Art consultant, art patron. **Personal:** Born Jan 27, 1945, Wilmington, DE; daughter of Madeline Wheeler Murphy and Willian H Murphy Sr; married Maurice F Jr; children: Maurice F III & Christopher. **Educ:** Univ Md, attended 1963; Md Inst Col Art, BFA, 1966; Ill Inst Tech, MS, 1975. **Career:** Tuesday Publ, asst dir art & prod, 1966-68; Myra Everett Design, vpres & bus mgr, 1977-78; Corp Concierge, acct exec, 1978-79; Rabb Studio & Gallery, artist, 1978-83; Chicago Off Fine Arts, exec dir, 1983-91; Nat Assembly Local Arts Agencies Ann Conv, Portland, OR, panelist, 1987; Local Progs Nat Endowment Arts, 1987-88; Murphy Rabb Inc, pres, 1992-; Ariel Capital Mgt, cur African Am art collections; Brown Capital Mgt, cur African Am art collections; Chicago Dept Cult Affairs Pub Art Comt, panelist; Ill Arts Coun Grants Maj Cult Insts, panelist; Columbia Col, Chicago, bd mem, currently; Md Inst Col Art, adv bd, mem, currently. **Orgs:** Univ Chicago Women's Bd, 1980-85; bd mem, Hyde Pk Arts Ctr, 1981-83; Afro-Amer Newspaper Co, Baltimore, MD, 1981-84; adv, Folk Art Exhib Field Mus Nat Hist, 1984; treas, US Urban Arts Fed, 1984-86; adv, Black Creativity Celebration Mus Sci & Indust, 1985-86; Chicago World's Fair, 1985; bd mem, Channel 20 WYCC TV, 1985-86, Ill Arts Alliance, 1986-88; co-chair, Spec Interest Areas Nat Assembly Local Arts Agencies, 1986-88; panelist, Nat Assembly Local Arts Agencies Conv, WA DC, 1986; moderator, Ill Arts Alliance Ann Conf, 1986; Arts Cult & Entertainment Comn, 1992; Woman's Bd Mus Contemp Art. **Honors/Awds:** The HistoryMakers. **Special Achievements:** First African American and professionally trained artist to head the city's fine arts office. **Business Addr:** President, Murphy Rabb Inc, 161 E Chicago Ave Suite 34A, Chicago, IL 60611, **Business Phone:** (312)664-0018.

## RABOUIN, ESQ. E. MICHELLE

Lawyer, educator. **Personal:** Born Nov 7, 1956, Denver, CO; daughter of John V and Eva M Thomas; children: Dion Malik. **Educ:** Univ Colo, BS, 1977; Univ Denver, MBA, 1984, JD, 1984. **Career:** Coal Employ Proj, asst dir, 1983-85; Colo Off Atty Gen, asst atty gen, 1986-89; Colo Educ ASn, legal coun, 1989-90; Comm Colo Denver, mgt chairperson & fac, 1991-94; Tex Southern Univ, vis prof law, 1994-95; Washburn Univ Sch Law, assoc prof law, 1994; Tex Wesleyan Univ Sch Law, vis prof, 1999-2000; Rabouin Zeman Law Group LLC, managing officer, currently. **Orgs:** Bd mem & ed, Colo Black Women Polit Action, 1979-; bd mem, Northeast Womens Ctr, 1980-82; fel Colo Energy Res, 1983; Colo Bar Asn, 1984-; founding mem, Colo Chap, Nat Asn Black Women Atty, 1987-; Colo Womens Bar Asn, 1988-; Jr League Denver, 1988-91; Colo Coalition Mediators & Mediation Orgn, 1990-; bd mem, Am Civil Liberties Union, 1991-92. **Home Addr:** 4986 Worchester St, Denver, CO 80239, **Home Phone:** (303)373-4156. **Business Addr:** Managing Officer, Rabouin Zeman Law Group LLC, Crossroads Durango Bldg 1099 Main Ave Suite 324, Durango, CO 81301, **Business Phone:** (970)769-0039.

## RABY, CLYDE T.

Government official. **Personal:** Born Sep 14, 1934, Baton Rouge, LA; married Elaine Miller; children: Dwight Tillman, Iris R Locure, Wayne A, Eric C & Trudi E. **Educ:** Southern Univ, BS, 1960; Tuskegee Inst, DVM, 1964; La State Univ, MS, 1992. **Career:** Professor (retired), veterinarian; Southern Univ, asst prof, 1964-70; Plank Rd & Port Allen Animal Hosps, owner, 1970-; La Dept Agr, asst comnr, 1980-96; Plank Rd Animal Hosp, vet, currently. **Orgs:** Beta Kappa Chi, 1962; Am Vet Med Asn 1963-; Beta Beta Beta Biol Soc, 1970-; chmn, LaVet Med Asn, 1982; bd dir, Reddy Cult Ctr, 1985; bd dir, Arts Coun Baton Rouge, 1988-98; African Sci Inst; Hon Biol Soc. **Home Addr:** 5835 Brown Rd, Ethel, LA 70730-4027, **Home Phone:** (225)683-8266. **Business Addr:** Veterinarian, Plank Road Animal Hospital, 7660 Plank Rd, Baton Rouge, LA 70811, **Business Phone:** (225)355-5676.

## RACINE, KARL A.

Lawyer. **Personal:** Born Dec 14, 1962, Port-au-Prince. **Educ:** Univ Pa, BA, 1985; Univ Va Sch Law, JD, 1989. **Career:** Venable LLP, litigation assoc, 1989-92, dep managing partner, partner, currently; DC Pub Defender Serv, staff atty; White House, assoc coun; Cacheris & Treanor, atty, 1994-97. **Orgs:** DC Bar Asn; Md Bar Asn. **Honors/Awds:** Spoon Award, 1985; 50 Most Influential Minority Leaders in America, Nat Law J, 2008; Selected in District of Columbia Super Lawyers, 2009; Washington Business Leaders Award, 2010; Outstanding Acheivement Award, Wash Lawyers Comt, 2011; National Haitian Elected Officials Humanitarian Award, 2011; Maya Way Award, Maya Angelou Pub Charter Sch, 2011; 100 Most Influential Black Lawyers in America, Black Lawyer, 2012. **Special Achievements:** First African-American managing partner of a top-100 law firm. **Business Addr:** Partner, Venable LLP, 575 7th St NW, Washington, DC 20004, **Business Phone:** (202)344-8322.

## RACKLEY, LURMA M.

Writer. **Personal:** Born Apr 24, 1949, Orangeburg, SC; daughter of L G (deceased) and Gloria Blackwell; children: Rumal Blackwell. **Educ:** Clark Atlanta Univ, BA, eng, 1970; Columbia Univ, Grad Sch jour, spec masters, 1970. **Career:** Wash Star, reporter, ed, 1970-79, freelance writer, 1970-; Dist Columbia Govt, press secy & dept comms dir, 1979-90; Hill & Knowlton Pub Affairs Worldwide, vpres, media rel, 1993-95; Amnesty Int USA, dep exec dir commun, 1995-98;Eddie Bauer, dir pub affairs & social responsibility, 1998-02; Care, pub rel officer, 2002-09; Habitat Humanity Int, writer, ed, resource develop commun mgr, 2009-; Lurma Rackley & Assocs, pub rel consult, 2009-10; Sister 2 Sister Mag, writer, currently. **Orgs:** Dep exec dir commun, Amnesty Int USA, 1995-98; Alpha Kappa Alpha; DC Clark Atlanta Univ Club; bd, Seattle Urban Enterprise Ctr; Capital Press Club; Black Pub rel Soc; DC Hampton Univ Parents Club; Stud Govt Asn; bd mem, Unitarian Universalist Serv Comt; Habitat Humanity Int, resource develop commun mgr, 2009-. **Honors/Awds:** Commitment to Excellence Award Dep Mayor for Economic Devel, 1985; Outstanding Women DC Govt, 1989-90; Corp Leadership Award, Ncp Youth, Col & Young Adult Div, 2001. **Home Addr:** 28519 Ne 151st St, Duvall, WA 98019, **Home Phone:** (404)979-9450. **Business Addr:** Writer, Sister 2 Sister Magazine, 6930 Carroll Ave Suite 200, Takoma Park, MD 20912, **Business Phone:** (301)270-5999.

## RAE, ISSA

Television director, television writer, television producer. **Educ:** Stanford University, B.A.; New York Film Academy, Attended. **Career:** Actress TV series shorts: "Dorm Diaries"; "Fly Guys present the F Word"; "Mis-Adventures of Awkward Black Girl," 2011-13; Producer TV series shorts: "How Men Become Dogs," 2013; "Little Horribles," 2013; "The Choir," 2013. **Honors/Awds:** L.A. Web Series Festival, Outstanding Directing in a Web Series and Outstanding Writing in a Web Series for "Fly Guys present the F Word," 2011; MMTC Digital Media Pioneer Award, 2011; Shorty Award for Best Web Show, 2012; "Forbes," 30 Under 30; "The Root" Magazine, The Root 100 Honorees, 2013.

## RAGLAND, SHERMAN LEON, II

Real estate developer, president (organization), chief executive officer. **Personal:** Born Jul 4, 1962, Stuttgart; son of Sherman L and G Anita Atkinson. **Educ:** Towson Univ, Towson, MD, BS, mass commun, 1984; Wharton Sch Univ Pa, Philadelphia, PA, MBA, fin & real estate, 1986; Univ Va, Sch Archit, MA, urban & environ planning, 2000; Concord Univ Sch Law, JD. **Career:** Lic Real Estate Broker, DC; Xerox Realty Corp, Stamford, Conn, 1986-87, Lansdowne, assoc develop dir & chief financial officer, 1987-88; Oliver Carr Co, develop proj mgr, 1988-89; Bd Zoning Appeals City Alexandria Va, planning comnr & vice chmn; Govt DC, chief architect Pub Facil Plan; Tradewinds Realty Partners LLC, managing dir, 1989-, fin adv, proj mgr, 1990-; GSA, Consult, 1993-2001; Signature DCA, Partner, 1993-2012; Realinvestors Acad Greater Wash, chief visionary realinvestors, com real estate investing & com real estate broker, 2001-; Tradewinds Int, founder, pres & chief exec officer, 2001-; Glazer-Kennedy Insider's Circle, titanium mem, 2004-11; PDA Mkt, client, 2004-13. **Orgs:** Chmn, Bowie Econ Develop Comn; Net Am Found; bd dir, pres, Nat Asn Black Real Estate Prof, 1988; bd dir, Christmas April USA, 1988; Christmas April Alexandria, 1988; bd advs (alumni), Wharton Real Estate Ctr, 1988; bd dir, Towson State Univ Alumni Asn, 1989; comnr, Alexandria Human Rights Comn, 1989, Alexandria Equal Opportunities Comn, 1989; pres, Wharton Alumni Club Wash, 1989-; Alexandria Bd Zoning Appeals, 1990-93; vice chmn, Alexandria bd Zoning Appeals, 1990-93; Alexandria Planning comn, 1993; Urban Land Inst; bd mem, Md Chamber Com; bd mem, Prince George's Community Col; Md Higher Educ Comn; founder, Real Estate Investor's Asn, Greater Wash, DC. **Honors/Awds:** Johnson & Johnson Leadership Award, Johnson & Johnson, 1984; Wharton Public Policy Fellowship, The Wharton Sch, 1985; Alumni of the Year Award, Towson State Univ, 1999; Blue Vase Award, 2002; Investor of the Year, National Real Estate Investors Conference in Atlanta, Ga, 2002; Joseph D. Wharton Award, Wharton Club Wash, 2013. **Special Achievements:** Author of numerous publications like Motivation, 1985, Lease vs Purchase Real Estate, 1989; "50 Future Leaders", Ebony Mag, Nov, 1992; "Dead Men Walking" ASAE Mag; Co-Author with New York Times best-selling author, Robert G. Allen, of New Rules of the Game. **Home Addr:** 15901 Pinecroft Lane, Bowie, MD 20716-1740, **Home Phone:** (301)390-3771. **Business Addr:** Founder & President, Chief Executive Officer, Tradewinds International, 400 E Pratt St Suite 800, Baltimore, MD 21202, **Business Phone:** (410)225-2181.

## RAGLAND, DR. WYLHEME HAROLD

Clergy. **Personal:** Born Dec 19, 1946, Anniston, AL; son of Howard and Viola Pearson; children: Seth H III & Frederick D. **Educ:** Jacksonville State Univ, BA, 1972; grad sch, 1973; Emory Univ, Mdiv (cum laude), 1975; Vanderbilt Univ, DMin, 1978. **Career:** Ctr Grove United Methodist Church, pastor, 1975-77; King's Memorial United Methodist Church, sr pastor, 1977-; N Ala Regional Hosp, Decatur, AL, dir relig serv, coordr employee assistance prog, 1984-, patient rights implementer, 1989-; staff develop officer, chaplain, currently. **Orgs:** Charter mem, Employee Assistance Soc N Am, 1985; chairperson, Rights Protection Advocacy Comt, 1987-89; Morgan County Hist Comn, Decatur, 1988; adv comt, Albany Clin, 1989; Mem adv bd Albany Clin, Decatur, 1989; Ministerial Alliance Decatur, 1989; Community Unity Decatur, 1989; Quest Adv Bd, 1990-; Northwest Coun Ctr, Decatur, 1990; N W Coun Ctr Bd, 1991; mgt info, 1992; admin exec comt, 1992; mem Nat Asn Advan Colored People, 1993; process action team, 1993-1994; Ala Dem Conf, 1994; Mayor's Task Force, 1994; QUEST Recovery Adv Comt, 1994, vol Meals Wheels Christmas April, 1995; Habitat Humanity, 1997; human resources comt, 1997; Bd Ordained Ministry, 1997; Staff Develop Asn, 1997; Human Resources Comt, 1997; Connect Decatur, 1998; AARP, 1998; mgr info comt N Ala Regional Hosp, admin exec comt, process action comt, patient care comt, mem City Decatur Ecumenical Task Force, 1998; mem adv comt City Decatur Adult Educ, 1999; patient care comt, 1992; Mem Ala Chaplains Asn; Decatur Dist Ministers Asn; Employee Assistance Soc; Northern Ala Staff Develop Asn; Sigma Tau Delta; Pi Gamma Mu; Phi Alpha Theta. key vommunicator, Decatur Educ Bd; Phi Alpha Theta; Pi Gamma Mu; Sigma Tau Delta; N Ala Study Club; Morgan County Hist Soc; Ment Health Asn Morgan

County; Needs Assessment Comt; Decatur City Bd Educ; Lift Every Voice & Sing Video Comt; N Ala Conf, United Methodist Ctr; Bd Ordained Ministry, bd dir, Birmingham, Ala, Ethnic Minority Ministries, Comn Church & Safety, Birmingham. **Home Addr:** 511 Walnut St NE, Decatur, AL 35601, **Home Phone:** (205)351-6257. **Business Addr:** Chaplain, North Ala Regional Hosp, 4218 Hwy 31 S, Decatur, AL 35609, **Business Phone:** (256)353-9433.

### RAINES, FRANKLIN D.

Government official. **Personal:** Born Jan 14, 1949, Seattle, WA; son of Janitor; married Wendy; children: Sarah. **Educ:** Harvard Law Sch, BA, 1971; Oxford Univ, Rhodes Scholar, polit, 1973; Magdalen Col; Harvard Law Sch, JD, law, 1976. **Career:** Lazard Freres & Co, gen partner, 1979-90; Fed Nat Mortgage Asn (Fannie Mae), vice chmn, 1991-96; Off Mgt & Budget, dir, 1996-98; Fannie Mae, vice chmn, 1991-96, chmn, 1997, chief exec officer & chmn, 1999-2004, retired chmn & chief exec officer, 2004-; Revolution LLC, dir, 2005-08; dir, 2006-10; Exclusive Resorts, dir, 2005-; XappMedia Inc, 2013-; Serve Virtual Enterprises Inc, dir; GenNext Media Corp, dir. **Orgs:** Horatio Alger Asn Distinguished Ams. **Business Addr:** Director, Revolution Health Group LLC, 1250 Connecticut Ave NW, Washington, DC 20036, **Business Phone:** (202)223-8671.

### RAINES, TIMOTHY (TIM RAINES)

Baseball manager, baseball player. **Personal:** Born Sep 16, 1959, Sanford, FL; son of Ned Sr and Florence; married Virginia Hilton; children: Tim Jr & Andre; married Shannon Watson; children: 2. **Career:** Baseball outfielder (retired), baseball coach, executive; Maj League Baseball, left fielder, 1979-2002; Montreal Expos, outfielder, 1979-90, 2001; Chicago White Sox, outfielder, 1991-95, coach, 2004-06; New York Yankees, outfielder, 1996-98; Oakland Athletics, outfielder, 1999; Baltimore Orioles, outfielder, 2001; Fla Marlins, outfielder, 2002; Brevard County Manatees, mgr, 2003; Maj League Team, 2004; World Ser Championship, base coach, 2005, bench coach; Newark Bears, mgr, asst coach, dir player develop; Atlantic League, mgr; Can Am Asn Prof Baseball, mgr; Harrisburg Senators, hitting coach, currently; Toronto Blue Jays, outfield coach, 2013-. TV Series: "MLB All-Star Game", 1983-84, 1986. **Special Achievements:** Little Big League, 1994. **Home Addr:** 2316 Airport Blvd, Sanford, CA 32771. **Business Addr:** Outfield Coach, Toronto Blue Jays, Rogers Ctr 1 Blue Jays Way Suite 3200, Toronto, ON M5V 1J1, **Business Phone:** (416)341-1000.

### RAINEY, TIMOTHY MARK

Editor, clergy. **Personal:** Born Jul 27, 1956, Mobile, AL; son of Rev W D (deceased) and E S; married Gloria Johnson; children: Tiria Janiece & Mark II. **Educ:** Troy State Univ, BS, jour, 1977; Huntsville Bapt Inst, BA, Theol, 1994; Faith Evangel Sem, MA, theol , 2008. **Career:** Mobile Press Regist, reporter, 1977-78; Ala A&M Univ, publ & news specialist, 1978-82; Huntsville Times, ed, 1982-; Mt Lebman Presby Church, pastor, 1991-96; Indian Creek PB Church, pastor, 1996-98, full time pastor, 1998-09, full time asst pastor, 2009-. **Orgs:** Huntsville Ministerial Alliance; Sch Relig; dean relig, Tri-State PB Conv; bd trustees & sch registr, Huntsville Baptist Inst; Fel Mallard Creek P.B. Asn's Evangelistic Bd. **Honors/Awds:** Excellence in Journalism, Sigma Delta Chi, 1974; Associated Press Newswriting Award, Second Place, 1984; Alabama Press Asn Award, Honorable Mention, 1987; Douglas L Cannon, Med Jour Award, 1990; Journalism Alumnus of the Year, Troy State Univ, 1997. **Special Achievements:** Elder Rainey became the church's first full-time pastor, 1998. **Home Addr:** 100 Nobleton Lane NW, Huntsville, AL 35806-4014, **Home Phone:** (256)837-0664. **Business Addr:** Pastor, Indian Creek PB Church, 884 Indian Creek Rd, Huntsville, AL 35810, **Business Phone:** (256)837-2890.

### RAINFORD, VALERIE I.

Executive director. **Educ:** Fordham Univ, BA, econs. **Career:** Fed Res Bank New York, sr vpres; JPMorgan Chase, managing dir, home lending bus support exec, bus mgr, 2007; Firms Head Global Compliance & Regulatory Mgt, chief staff, 2011; Consent Order Remediation Team, chief operating officer, chief exec officer & head mortgage controls; Corp Sectors Banking Opers, Technol & Serv Team, managing dir; Wash Mutual Inc, prog mgr; Bear Stearns Co Inc, prog mgr. **Orgs:** Co-founder, Women Color Mentoring Group; Mortgage Bank leadership team; Consent Order Remediation Team; co-founder & pres, Black Women Influence; bd trustee, Grand St Settlement; comt mem, Black Women Black Girls giving circle; Exec Leadership Coun. **Business Addr:** Managing Director, JPMorgan Chase & Co, 245 Pk Ave, New York, NY 03360.

### RAINSFORD, DR. GRETA M.

Pediatrician. **Personal:** Born Dec 28, 1936, New York, NY; daughter of George Maurice and Gertrude Eleanor Edwards; married Samuel K Anderson. **Educ:** AB, 1958; Howard Univ Col Med, MD, 1962. **Career:** Meadowbrook Hosp, fel, internship, 1962-63, resident; Nassau Co Med Ctr, Internship, 1962-63, resident pediat, 1963-65; Mercy Hosp, assoc attend pediatrician, 1965-; NCMC, asst attend pediatrician, 1965-; pvt pract physician & pediatrician, 1965-; Sickle Cell Clin, dir, 1971-85; Planned Parenthood Nassau County, med adv bd, 1971-; Roosevelt Sch Dist, sch physician, 1975-; Hempstead Sch Dist, sch pediatrician, 1975-77; Old Westbury Campus State Univ, NY, clin physician, 1976-; Winthrop Univ Hosp, 1979-84; Hofstra Univ, Saltzman Community Serv Ctr, exec dir, 1990-2000; Ctr Developmentally Disabled, staff pediatrician, 1991-; Nassau Health Care Corp, dir, 1998-. **Orgs:** Dipl, Bd Pediat, 1967; Community Health & Educ, 1971-; dir large, Am Cancer Soc, 1973-76; Mercy Hosp, Emergency Room Comt, 1975-89, Transfusion Comt, 1990-; bd mem, Nassau Pediatrician Soc; bd dir, Roosevelt Ment Health Ctr, 1976-81; fel Am Acad Pediat, 1977; bd trustee, Hofstra Univ, 1978-92, Human Subjects Comt, 1994-2000; pres bd dir, Long Island Gate, 1979-81; State Univ New York Stony Brook Coun, 1981-95; Nassau Co Med Soc; NY Med Soc; bd mem, Planned Parenthood, Nassau County, 1986-91; Nassau Chap Am Red Cross, 1991-96, vice chmn, 1995-96, bd, 1995-98, chair, 1997-2000; bd, Nassau Health Care Corp, 1996-; Comn to End Racial Disparity Healthcare; Nat Med Asn; Am Med Women's Asn; Stony Brook Col Medicin, 1999-; vpres, HWC, 1999-; Am Bd Pediat; AMA; Nassau Pediat Soc; chairwoman, Church Vestry, 2008-13, treas, 2014-; chairperson, Mercy Med Ctr, 2009-11; secy, bd trustee, Acad Med, 2012-13, vpres, 2013-14, pres. **Honors/Awds:** Nassau Div Am Cancer Soc, 1971-74; Plaque Serv Sickle Cell Anemia, 1972; Plaque Serv Youth & Mankind, 1974; Commendation Serv Youth Hempstead C of C, 1974; Distinguish Service Award, HCTA, 1974; Community Service Award, Nat Asn Norwood Bus & Prof Women's Club, 1974; Community Service Award, Black Hist Mus, 1977; Med Service Award, LI Sickle Cell Proj, 1977; MLK, JR Birth Celebration Award, 1988; Equal Award, Nass NOW, 1991; FSA Community Lead Award, 1991; Women of Dist, March Dimes, 1992; Community Serv, Am Med Writers Asn, 1994; Community Service Award, NOW Alliance, 1995; Health Award, Women Job, 1995; Woman Achievers Against the Odds Award, LI Fund Women & Girls, 1996; Sojourner Truth Award, Cent Nassau Club NAofNBPWC Inc, 1997; Trail Blazer Award, 1999; Pathfinder Award, 1999; Mr. & Mrs. Henry P. Davison Memorial Award, Am Red Cross, Nassau Chap, 2000; Certificate of Honor, Women's Hist Luncheon, League Women Voters, 2001; Jr League of LI Volunteer Merit Award, Am Red Cross, 2001; Woman of Distinction, State Sen Kemp Hannon, 2002; The Riland Medal, NY Col Osteop Med, 2006; Volunteer of the Year, NC Med Res Corp LI, 2008; St. John's Episcopal Church Rosa Parks Award, 2009; Appreciation for Service, Sickle Cell Anemia, 2012. **Home Addr:** 60 Long Dr, Hempstead, NY 11550-4626, **Home Phone:** (516)481-6633. **Business Addr:** Pediatrician, Private Practice, 756 Front St, Hempstead, NY 11550-4626, **Business Phone:** (516)481-6633.

### RAKESTRAW, KYLE DAMON

Engineer, executive. **Personal:** Born Apr 9, 1961, Dayton, OH; son of Delores Robinson. **Educ:** Univ Cin, BS, indust mgt, 1984; Xavier Univ, Cincinnati, OH, MBA, 1988. **Career:** Gen Motors Corp, prof pract, 1982-84, Delco Moraine Div, Dayton, purchasing agt, 1986-89, sr proj engr, 1990-92; Pepsi Cola Co, Indianapolis, ware house opers mgr, 1989-90; ITT Automotive Elec Syst, N Am, bus planner, pricing adminr, 1994-96; Allied Signal Inc, pricing mgr, 1996; Honeywell, pricing mgr, 1996-2002, prog mgr, 2003-07, leader strategic mkt world air transp & regional mkt segments, 2007-09; Honeywell Aerospace, sr prog mgr pricing, 2009-. **Orgs:** Nat Black MBA Asn, 1987; Literacy Vols Maricopa County; Black Bd Dirs Proj. **Honors/Awds:** Voorheis Col Scholarship, Univ Cin, 1979, Dorothy Gradison Memorial Scholarship, 1983. **Home Addr:** 1140 S Country Club Dr Suite 108-41, Meas, WA 85210-4617. **Business Addr:** Senior Program Manager Pricing, Honeywell Aerospace, 101 Columbia Rd, Morristown, NJ 07962, **Business Phone:** (973)455-2000.

### RALPH, SHERYL LEE

Singer, entrepreneur, actor. **Personal:** Born Dec 30, 1956, Waterbury, CT; daughter of Stanley and Ivy; married Vincent Hughes; married Eric George Maurice; children: Etienne & Ivy Victoria. **Educ:** Rutgers Univ, BA, theater arts & eng lit. **Career:** TV Series: "It's a Living", 1986-89; "New Attitude"; "Designing Women"; "George"; "Moesha"; Films: A Piece Action, 1977; Oliver & Co, voice, 1988; Mighty Quinn, 1989; Skin Deep, 1989; To Sleep With Anger, 1990; Distinguished Gentlemen, 1992; Sister Act 2, 1993; White Man's Burden, 1995; Bogus, 1996; Mistress; Personals, 1999; Deterrence, 1999; Unconditional Love, 1999; Lost Pershing Pt Hotel, 2000; Baby Family, 2002; Whoopi, 2003; Kink My Hair, 2004; Barbershop, 2005; "7th Heaven", 2005; "ER", 2006; Odicie, 2007; "Exes & Ohs", 2007; Frankie D, 2007; "Hannah Mont", 2008; "Zevo-3", 2010; "Young Justice", 2011; "One Love", 2014; "Instant Mom", 2013-15; C-wear designer; Broadway: Dreamgirls, 1992; Secrets; Island Girls Productions, owner; Ann Int Jamaican Film Festival, creator & dir; actress, singer, writer, dir & producer, currently. **Orgs:** Screen Actors Guild; Actor's Equity; Am Fed TV & Radio Artists; Diva, AIDS fundraiser. **Home Addr:** c/o Lorimar Home Video, 10202 W Wash Blvd, Culver City, CA 90232. **Business Addr:** Actress, MKS & Associates, 8695 W Washington Blvd Suite 204, Culver City, CA 90232.

### RAMBISON, DR. AMAR B.

Clergy. **Personal:** Born Nov 22, 1950, El Dorado; son of Ram Bisoon and Chando; married Eutrice; children: Candis. **Educ:** Luther Rice Sem, BDiv, 1979; Andersonville Baptist Sem, DTh, 1994, PhD, 1995; Lake Charles Bible Col, DMin, 1996; Southwest Bible Col, PhD, christian educ, 1997. **Career:** Deeper Life Assembly, sr pastor, 1990-; Metro Orlando Dist, supvr, 2002-; New York Metro Dist, supvr, 2003-; Southwestern Bible Col, adj prof. **Orgs:** Pres, Independent Ministers Asn, 1997-; div supt, Church Foursquare Gospel, 2000-. **Special Achievements:** Written: The Unfinished Man; Jumping Jehoshaphat: The Ups and Downs of Leadership; Prospering Through Good Leadership; The Biblical Art of Personal Evangelism; 18 Missing Years of Christ Found. **Home Addr:** 13137 Plum Lake Circle, Clermont, FL 34711, **Home Phone:** (352)394-1862. **Business Addr:** Supervisor, New York City Metro District, 8825 A D Mims Rd, Orlando, FL 32818-8604, **Business Phone:** (407)290-8510.

### RAMBO, BETTYE R.

Educator. **Personal:** Born Sep 2, 1936, Jasper, CO; married Leon Taylor; children: Valencia A & Sherryle B. **Educ:** Stillman Col, BA, 1959; Ind Univ, MA, 1968; Univ Ill, post grad study; Laverne Col; Moray House Col, Edinburgh, Scotland, attended 1974; Ill State Univ. **Career:** Educator (retired); Springfield Bd Educ, educr, 1968-2000. **Orgs:** Jasper Co Teachers Asn, 1959-68; life mem, Nat Educ Asn, 1959-74; Miss Teachers Asn, 1959-68; Ill Educ Asn, 1968-74; human rels coordr Region 32, Human Rels Comn, Ill Educ Asn, 1974-75; secy, PDK, 1985-87; educ chair, ABWA, 1986; life mem, Springfield Civic Garden Club, 1988; Order Eastern Star, 1989; secy, St Patrick's Sch Bd, 1992-94; chair, Zion bapitst; Trustee Bd, Springfield Educ Asn; vice chmn, Zion Missionary Baptist Church; bd dir, Stillman Col Alumni Asn; NDEA Inst Culturally Disadvantaged Youth; deleg, NEA Conv; Nat Asn Advan Colored People, Smithsonian Asn, NRTA; St Missions Bd; Airline Passengers Asn. **Home Addr:** 2025 Gregory Ct, Springfield, IL 62703, **Home Phone:** (217)544-7583.

### RAMEY, ADELE MARIE

Lawyer, government official. **Personal:** Born Jun 30, 1954, New York, NY; daughter of Wilburn Taylor Sr and Delphenia A Taylor; married Martin G. **Educ:** Ohio Wesleyan Univ, BA, 1976; Ind Univ, paralegal cert, 1985, JD, 1989. **Career:** Sears, Roebuck & Co, mgr trainee, 1976-77; Churches Chicken, mgr, 1977-79; Red Lobster, asst mgr, 1979-81; Lucky Steer Restaurant, exec asst mgr, 1981-82; McDonalds, asst mgr, 1982-84; Marion Co Pub Defender's Off, paralegal, 1984-89; State Ind Pub Defenders Off, dep pub defender, 1989. **Orgs:** Am Bar Asn; Ind Bar Asn; Nat Bar Asn. **Home Addr:** 7313 E 49th St, Indianpolis, IN 46226-2711, **Home Phone:** (317)542-8708.

### RAMEY, DR. FELICENNE H.

School administrator, educator. **Personal:** Born Philadelphia, PA; married Melvin R; children: 2. **Educ:** Pa State Univ, PA, BS; Duquesne Univ, MS; Univ Calif, JD; Calif State Univ, MA. **Career:** Self-employed atty, Davis, Calif, 1975-84; City & County Sacramento, dir litigation, 1975-76; Calif State Univ, Sacramento, Col Bus Admin, Calif, prof bus law, 1975-03, asst pres, 1984-86, dept chair, 1984-86, assoc dean, 1988-94; dean, 1997-2000, dean emer, 2000-, prof emer bus law, 2003-; Ebon Art, owner. **Orgs:** Bd dir, chair, Educ Comt, Sacramento Black Chamber Com, Sacramento, Calif, 1990-; bd dir, Cal Aggie Alumni Asn, 1989-; pres, Western Bus Law Asn, 1975-; Nat Asn Women Deans, Adminr's, & Counrs, 1990-; Calif Bar Asn, 1973-; Nat Asn Women Edu, 1989-; fel, Univ Calif, Am Coun Edu, 1992-93; bd trustee mem, Sutter Davis Hosp; Am Coun Educ Nat Identification Prog; Women Educ; Am Leadership Forum, Mountain Valley Chap; Comstock Club; Discovery Mus Hist; Greater Sacramento Urban League; Sacramento Entrepreneurship Acad; Sacramento Valley Forum. **Home Addr:** 612 Cleveland St, Davis, CA 95616-3128. **Business Addr:** Professor Emeritus of Business Law, California State University, Psychol Serv CtrAmador Hall Rm 241, Sacramento, CA 95819-6088, **Business Phone:** (916)278-7030.

### RAMEY, DR. MELVIN R.

Educator. **Personal:** Born Sep 13, 1938, Pittsburgh, PA; son of Ethrem and Eleanor; married Felicenne; children: David & Daina. **Educ:** Pa State Univ, BS, civil engineering, 1960; Carnegie Mellon Univ, MS, civil engineering, 1965, PhD, civil engineering, 1967. **Career:** Professor (retired), emeritus professor; Pa Dept Highways, bridge design engr, 1960-63; Univ Calif, Davis, prof, 1967, asst track coach, 1967-92, assoc dean, fac asst to vice chancellor, 1989-90, chairperson, 1991-97, Vice Chairperson, dept exercise sci, 1999; prof emer, currently; Ga Inst Technol, vis prof, 1980; Mass Inst Technol, vis prof, 1988; Ctr Advan Health & Human Performance, 1997-99, Dept Exercise Sci, vice chairperson, 1998-99. **Orgs:** Hon mem, Golden Key Nat Hon Soc, 1992; Am Soc Biomechanics; Am Soc Civil Engrs; Am Concrete Inst; Am Asn Higher Educ. **Home Addr:** 44791 N El Macero Dr, El Macero, CA 95616, **Home Phone:** (530)756-6765. **Business Addr:** Professor Emeritus, University of California, 1 Shields Ave 2001 Engineering III, Davis, CA 95616, **Business Phone:** (530)752-0896.

### RAMIREZ, RICHARD M.

Executive. **Educ:** Trinity Univ, BS, bus admin, 1975. **Career:** Apex Securities Inc, partner, pres & chief exec officer, 1987; Hilltop Securities Inc, managing dir, 2008-; Goldman Sachs; JP Morgan; AG Edwards & Sons Inc, staff; Chase Securities Tex Inc, staff, currently; Team Tex, vpres, currently; Bond Buyer's Tex Pub Finance Conf, speaker, currently. **Orgs:** First hisp chmn, Memorial Hermann Hosp Syst Found, 1999-2000; trustee, City Houston Munic Employees Pension Fund; Greater Houston Partnership; Grand Pkwy; Houston Mus Natural Sci; San Jacinto River Authority; chmn, Tex Munic Adv Coun Tex; Williamson County CASA Bd. **Business Addr:** Staff, Chase Securities of Texas Inc, 3725 Forest Lane, Dallas, TX 75244, **Business Phone:** (972)243-7091.

**RAMISTELLA, JOHN HENRY. See RIVERS, JOHNNY.**

### RAMPERSAD, ARNOLD

Educator, college teacher, writer. **Personal:** Born Nov 13, 1941, Port-of-Spain. **Educ:** Bowling Green State Univ, Bowling Green, OH, BA, 1967, MA, 1968; Harvard Univ, MA, 1969, PhD, 1973. **Career:** Univ VA, asst prof, 1973-74; Stanford Univ, prof, 1974-83, Sara Hart Kimball prof humanities, sr assoc dean humanities, 2003-06, prof emer, currently; Rutgers Univ, NB, NJ, prof, 1983-88; Columbia Univ, NY, prof, 1988-90; Princeton Univ, Woodrow Wilson prof Lit, 1990-98, Prog Am Studies, 1990-95; MacArthur fel, 1991; Books: The Art & Imagination of W.E.B DuBois, 1976; The Life of Langston Hughes, 2 vols, 1986 & 1988; Days of Grace: A Memoir, 1993; Jackie Robinson: A Biography, 1997; Ralph Ellison: A Biography, 2007; Editor: Collected Poems of Langston Hughes; Selected Letters of Langston Hughes, co-ed; Richard Wright, Library of America edition, ed; Slavery & the Literary Imagination, co-ed; Race & American Culture book series, co-ed. **Orgs:** Am Acad Arts & Sci; Am Philos Soc. **Home Addr:** 840 Lathrop Dr, Stanford, CA 94305-1053, **Home Phone:** (650)213-9139. **Business Addr:** Professor Emeritus, Stanford University, 840 Lathrop Dr, Stanford, CA 94305-1053.

### RAMSEUR, ANDRE WILLIAM

Poet, human services worker. **Personal:** Born Jan 15, 1949, Manhattan, NY; son of Otho William Jr and Creola Howard. **Educ:** St Augustines Col Raleigh, BA, eng, 1971; Miami Univ, Oxford, OH, attended 1972; George Washington Univ, DC, attended 1980; VA Polytech Inst & State Univ, MS, educ; Emphasis Adult educ, 1992. **Career:** Miami Univ Oxford OH, grad asst, 1971-72; St Augustines Col, instr eng, 1972-74; Equitable Life Assurance Soc US, agency secy & asst suprv; New Bus Indianapolis, Wash, DC, admin trainee, 1974-77; Eton Towers Tenants Assoc, legal coordr, 1975; Pres Comn White House Fel, staff asst, 1977-79; Off Personnel Mgt, Wash, DC, ed specialist, 1979-86; Defense Info Syst Agency, supervr employee develop specialist, 1986-92; Strayer Univ, adj prof, 1996-; Dept Com, human resources specialist, 2002; Northern Va Interdenominational Mass Choir, bus mgr. **Orgs:** Co-founder, Sta to Sta Performance Poets & Writers Collective, 1980; Fed Educations & Technol Assoc. **Honors/Awds:** Outstanding Young Man Dees & Fuller Org, 1975; Notable Am Award Notable Historian Soc Raleigh, 1976-77; Spec Achievement Award, Pres Comn White House Fel, 1979; Special Achievement OPM Director's Award, 1984; Spec Act Serv Info Systs Agency, 1986; Spec Achievement, DISA, 1987-88; Outstanding Act or service, Def Info Systems Agency, 1990; Letter Appreciation, DISA Inspector Gen Participation & Performance, org Assessment Audit Team, 1996; DISA Award, HRM Team Proj, 2000; Great Performer Award, DISA, 2002; The Journey, 2003. **Special Achievements:** Author, poetry: "You

Never Tried" Clover Publ 1976, "After the Fact" Young Publ, 1978, "Greenhouse Poetry" Collection of Love Poems Triton Press, 1977-78, "Greenhouse Poetry" Vol 2, 1979-80; Vintage Poetry, 2002; Finalist Clover Int Poetry Contest Wash DC, 1975; Group performances Sta 2 Sta, 1980-85; Ann 1 man poetry performance, 1982; Poetry collection progress Its About Time, 1989. **Home Addr:** 5745 Independence Cir, Alexandria, VA 22312-2628, **Home Phone:** (703)256-5379.

### RAMSEUR, ISABELLE R.

Government official. **Personal:** Born Feb 21, 1906, NC; married Charles; children: Harold D & Albertine. **Career:** Philadelphia Gen Hosp, nursing vol work; Mercy Douglas Hosp; Nursery Sch Fernwood, teachers asst; Boro Darby, council woman. **Orgs:** Needlework Guild Am, 1933; Ladies Aux, WMCA, Philadelphia; Blessed Virgin Mary Church; Nat Asn Advan Colored People; matron, Order E Star; chartered mem, Rose Sharon Chap. **Home Addr:** 228 N 10 St, Darby, PA 19023.

### RAMSEY, DAVID P.

Actor. **Personal:** Born Nov 17, 1971, Detroit, MI; son of Nathaniel and Jeraldine. **Educ:** Wayne State Univ, fine arts. **Career:** Films: The Line, 1980; Scared Stiff, 1987; The Nutty Professor, 1996; AVery Brady Sequel, 1996; Con Air, 1997; A Short Wait Between Trains, 1998; Three to Tango, 1999; Pay It Forward, 2000; Mr Bones, 2001; Big Fish, 2003; Runaway Jury, 2003; Hair Show, 2004; Central Booking, 2005; Resurrection: The J.R. Richard Story, 2005; Bathsheba, 2005; Jane Doe: The Wrong Face, 2005; Hello Sister, Goodbye Life, 2006; The Death & Life of Bobby Z, 2007; The Coverup, 2008; The Rub, 2009; Mother and Child, 2009; Draft Day, 2014. TV series: "Lovers & Friends/For Richer, For Poorer", 1977; "Sanctuary of Fear", 1979; "Deutschland lied", 1996; Her Costly Affair, 1996; "The Good News", 1997; "Mama Flora's Family", 1998; CHiPs'99, 1998; "Mutiny", 1999; "For Your Love", 2000-01; "Ali: An American Hero", 2000; "Thieves", 2001; The Long Con, 2001; "Girl friends", 2001; "Romeo Fire", 2002; "One on One", 2002-03; "It's a Miserable Life", 2003; "Navy NCIS: Naval Criminal Investigative Service", 2003; The Flannerys, 2003; "Wannabe", 2004; "Crossing Jordan", 2004; "Ghost Whisperer", 2005-08; "Cold Pizza", 2005; "All of Us", 2005; "Huff", 2005; "CSI: Crime Scene Investigation", 2006; "Love Still Won't Die", 2006; "The West Wing", 2006; "Fatal Contact: Bird Flu in America", 2006; "Criminal Minds", 2007; "Journeyman", 2007; "Wildfire", 2008; "Hollywood Residential", 2008; "Dexter", 2008-09; "Castle", 2009; "Grey's Anatomy", 2010; "Outlaw", 2010; "The Defenders", 2010-11; "Blue Bloods", 2011-14; "Arrow", 2012-15; "Rectify", 2014; "The Flash", 2014. **Business Addr:** Actor, c/o Nils Larsen, 1635 N Caheunga Blvd 5th Fl, Los Angeles, CA 90028, **Business Phone:** (323)461-2000.

### RAMSEY, DONNA ELAINE

Librarian. **Personal:** Born Oct 10, 1941, Charlotte, NC; daughter of William A Epps (deceased) and Mabel Brown Tatum (deceased); married Reginald E; children: Gina M Clark (deceased), Ona B Paskadi & Reginald E II. **Educ:** Johnson C Smith Univ, BA, 1969; Atlanta Univ, MSLS, 1971; Univ NC, attended 1973 & 1977; Kent State Univ, attended 1976. **Career:** Barber-Scotia Col, Concord, NC, ref/circulation librn, 1971-73; Friendship Jr Col, Rock Hill, SC, chief librn, 1973-77; Nmex State Univ, Las Cruces, NM, asst serials librn, 1977-81; Cochise Col, Ft Bliss, Tex, librn, 1984-85; AUS Air Defense Artil Sch Libr, Ft Bliss, Tex, supvry librn, 1985-89, librn, 1989-92; AUS Sergeants Maj Acad, Ft Bliss, Tex, librn, 1992-97; AUS Air Def Art Sch, Mickelsen Libr, librn, 1997-01; Van Noy Libr, Ft Belvoir, Va, librn, 2001-. **Orgs:** Am Libr Asn, 1976-; Black Caucus Am Libr Asn, 1978-; Staff Orgn Roundtable, ALA, 1979-; Nat Asn Advan Colored People, 1989-; golden life mem, Delta Sigma Theta Sorority Inc, 1989-; chair, prog planning, Ft Bliss Black Employ Prog Comt, 1989-90; chair-elect, 1990-91; chair, 1991-93; Ann Prog Chair, 1991-93; Const & Bylaws Chair, 1993; Am Biog Inst, 1994-2000; Am Platform asn, 1995-; Tex Libr Asn Leadership Develop Comt, 1998-2001; Tex Libr Asn Leadership Develop Comm, chair, 1999-2000; Am Libr Assoc Comt Accreditation, External Rev Panel, 2001-06; Armed Forces Libr Roundtable, 1985-, pub rels chair, Mem Comt Chair, 2003-07, prog chair, 2004-05, prog convenor, 2005; Libr Cong, Fed Libr & Info Comt Human Resources Working Group, 2005-, Educ Working Group, 2006-. **Honors/Awds:** Civic Achievement Award, United Way, Las Cruces, 1981; Certificate of Achievement, Dept Army, 1990 & 1991; Certificate of Achievement Award, 1992; Certificate of Achievement, Am Libr Asn, 1992; Certificate of Appreciation, Am Biographical Inst, 1995; Kent State Univ Grad Assistanceship; Asn Col & Res Libr, Certificate of Recognition; Certificate of Achievement, US Army, 1997. **Special Achievements:** Who's Who of American Women, 2006-; Who's Who in America 2002-. **Home Addr:** PO Box 1045, Fort Belvoir, VA 22060, **Home Phone:** (703)209-0260. **Business Addr:** Librarian, US Army Van Noy Library, 5966 12th St Bldg 1024, Fort Belvoir, VA 22060, **Business Phone:** (703)806-0096.

### RAMSEY, FREEMAN, JR.

Photographer. **Personal:** Born Oct 8, 1943, Nashville, TN; son of Freeman (deceased) and Rosetta Scott (deceased); married Doretha Pipkin; children: Freeman III, Ronald & Christine Renee. **Educ:** Tenn State Univ, BS, 1970; Nashville Tech Inst, Nashville, TN, dipl commun & photog, 1983. **Career:** CBS Rec, Nashville, Tenn, rec engr, 1969-82; Ramsey's Photog, Nashville, Tenn, self employed, photogr, 1982-85; Metro Bd Educ, Nashville, Tenn, transp, 1984-90; The Tennessean, Nashville, Tenn, staff photogr, 1989-. **Orgs:** Nat Press Photogr Asn, 1989-; Tenn Press Asn, 1989-; Nat Asn Black Journalists, 1989-. **Honors/Awds:** Photographic Achievement, The Tennessean, 1965 &1966; Feature Picture Award, AP, 1991; Third Place, Feature Picture, NPPA, 1991; Third Place, Sports Feature Photo, AP, 1991; First Place, News NPPA Awards, 1991 & 1993; Gannett Well Done Awards, 1991 & 1994; Second Place & Third Place, News Picture, AP, 1992; Second Place, Southern Short Course in News Photography, 1992; Honorable Mention, 1993; Outstanding Achievement Award, Tennessean, 1993; Honorable Mention, Atlanta Seminar in Photojournalism, 1993; Best of Gannett, Second Place, Color Photography, 1994; First Place, Feature Picture, AP, 1994; Best News Picture, Tenn Press Asn, 1994; Second Place, Gordon Parks Photography Competition, 1994; Third Place, NABJ Photog Competition, 1994; First & Second Place, AP Awards, 1994; First Place, News Picture, Penn Press Asn, 1995; Best News Picture Story, AP, 1995. **Home Addr:** 4312 Shady Dale Rd, Nashville, TN 37218, **Home Phone:** (615)876-6200. **Business Addr:** Staff Photographer, The Tennessean, 1100 Broadway, Nashville, TN 37203, **Business Phone:** (615)259-8300.

### RAMSEY, DR. JEROME CAPISTRANO

Lawyer, executive, association executive. **Personal:** Born Mar 28, 1953, San Bernardino, CA. **Educ:** Univ Calif, Berkeley, Calif, BA (hons) 1975, Sch Law, JD, 1978. **Career:** Holland & Hart, atty, 1978-80; US Dept Justice, asst US atty, 1980-82; cable exec, 1982-; Am Tv & Commun, Denver, vpres & gen coun, 1982; Mile Hi Cable vision, vpres/gen coun, 1982-86; Paragon Commun, regional vpres, 1986-90; Am Telecommunications, New Eng Div, pres, chief exec officer, 1990-95; Time Warner Entertainment, Time Warner Cable, vpres, pres sports investments, 2000-03; WUSA New York & Orlando, pres team mkts, currently; 12Dot5, owner & managing mem, 2003-; Time Warner Cable's Western Pa Div, pres; Paragon Commun, vpres div affairs. **Orgs:** Am Bar Asn, 1978-; Colo & Denver Bar Asn, 1978-; bd mem, chmn, New Eng Cable TV Asn, 1990; chmn, Maine Exec Comt, 1991; bd, New Eng Cable Tv Asn; Maine State Chamber Com; Univ Maine Sch Law; U.S. Small Bus Adv Comt. **Honors/Awds:** Distinguished Service, US Dept Justice, 1982; Executive Excel the Minority Professional Directory, 1984. **Home Addr:** 4901 Oakmoor Ct, Raleigh, NC, NC 27614, **Home Phone:** (919)841-0802. **Business Addr:** Attorney, 1511 Cravens Ave, Torrance, CA 90501.

### RAMSEY, PATRICIA PIERCE

College teacher, college administrator. **Personal:** married Roscoe W Ramsey Jr; children: 3. **Educ:** Norfolk State Univ, BS; Harvard Univ, MA; Howard Univ, MS; Georgetown Univ, PhD. **Career:** Shaw Univ, vpres acad affairs, 2000-04; Bowie State Univ, prof & chair dept natural sci, 2005-16, provost & vpres, 2004, interim pres, 2006; Lincoln Univ, provost & vpres acad affairs, 2016-. **Orgs:** Harvard Club Wash; Sigma Xi Res Soc, 1991-; Southern Christian Leadership Conf (Va Unit), 1996-2000; chmn bd, Ripen MeriSTEM, 2014-; co-founder, Community Partnership Excellence Educ; C's Rights Coun Md, Md Adv Coun Nat C's Mus, Banneker Inst Sci adv bd. **Honors/Awds:** Named a National Role Model by Minority Access, 2012. **Special Achievements:** Appointed to the Governor's Task Force on Clean Energy, 2013. **Business Addr:** Lincoln University, 1570 Baltimore Pke, Lincoln University, PA 19532, **Business Phone:** (484)365-7437.

### RAMSEY, WALTER S.

Executive. **Personal:** married Grace E Walker; children: Walter S Jr. **Educ:** City Col NY, BS. **Career:** US Signal Corps, physicist, 1942-43; Standard Eletronics, physicist, 1943-45; Raytheon Mfg Co, proj engr, 1945-46; Sylvania Electric, proj engr, 1946-53; Ramsey Electronics, owner, mgr, consult, 1953. **Orgs:** Adv comt mem, August Martin HS Jamaica NY; bd Queens Child Guid; bd chmn, Nat Asn Advan Colored People Jamaica; Montauk Day Care Ctr; educ chmn, Queens boro Fed Parents Clubs; pres, Jamaica Br Nat Asn Advan Colored People.

### RAND, A. BARRY

Executive, chief executive officer, vice president (organization). **Personal:** Born Nov 5, 1944, Washington, DC; son of Addison Penrod and Helen Matthews; married Donna; children: 2. **Educ:** Rutgers Univ, Camden, NJ; Am Univ, BA, mkt, 1968; Stanford Univ, MBA, 1972, MA, mgt sci, 1973. **Career:** Xerox Corp, Rochester, NY, from sales rep to regional sales rep, 1968-80, corp dir mkt, 1980-84, vpres eastern opers, 1984-86; Xerox Corp, Stamford, Conn, corp vpres, pres US opers, 1986-92; pres US mkt group, 1987-92, exec vpres worldwide opers, 1992-98, exec vice pres bus opers, 1992-96; Abbott Labs, bd dir, 1992-2006; Avis Group Holdings Inc, chmn, bd dir & chief exec officer, 1999-2001, chmn emer, 2003-; Agilent Technologies, bd dir, 2000-15; Howard Univ, trustee, 2001, chmn, 2006-14; AT&T Wireless, bd dir, 2001-; Equitant Inc, co-chmn, 2001-, dir, chmn & chief exec officer, 2003-05; Aspect Commun, interim chmn bd dir, 2003-; Campbell Soup Co, bd dir, 2005-; Avis Rent A Car Inc, chief exec officer, chmn; Ameritech, bd dir; Am Asn Retired Persons, chief exec officer, 2009-14; Honeywell Corp, bd dir. **Orgs:** Bd dir, Urban Family Inst; bd dir, Teachers Ins Annuity Asn; bd dir, Cong Black Caucus Found; Sloan Exec Fel; bd dir, Garth Fagan Dance Theatre. **Business Addr:** Member of the Board of Directors, Campbell Soup Co, 1 Campbell Pl, Camden, NJ 08103, **Business Phone:** (856)342-4800.

### RAND, CYNTHIA

Government official. **Educ:** Hampton Univ, BS, math; Fairleigh Dickinson Univ, MS, comput sci. **Career:** Govt off (retired); Transp Dept, Info Resources Mgt, dir, 1991; US Dept Defense, prin dir info mgt. **Business Addr:** Principal Director for Information Managemen, US Department of Defense, 1400 Defense Pentagon, Washington, DC 20301-1400, **Business Phone:** (703)571-3343.

### RANDALL, ALICE

Writer, songwriter. **Personal:** Born May 4, 1959, Detroit, MI; daughter of George S and Bettie Branham; married David Ewing; married Avon Williams II; children: Caroline Ewing. **Educ:** Harvard Univ, eng & am lit, 1981. **Career:** Wolf Trap Performing Arts Ctr, Wash DC, writer, 1980; Author: The Wind Done Gone, 2001; Pshkin & the Queen of Spades, 2004; Rebel Yell, 2009; Co-author, TV Movie Screenplay: "XXX's & OOO's", 1994, "Their Eyes Were Watching God", "Brer Rabbit", "Parting the Waters"; songwriter, 1983-; Film & TV companies: Black & White Pictures, She Writes Movies Inc; Houghton Mifflin Co, country songwriter, auth, currently. **Orgs:** Harvard-Radcliffe Club; ASCAP; African-Am Hist & Geneal Asn; Belle Meade Plantation; Carnton; Hermitage; Traveler's Rest; Metro Hist Comn Nashville; Andrew Jackson Slave Descendent Proj; African-Am Hist; Geneal Asn; Family Cemetary Proj; Andrew Jackson's Slave Descendent Proj; Fisk Univ. **Honors/Awds:** Outstanding Fiction Award; ASCAP Number One Club, 1994; Al Nueharth Free Spirit Award, 2001; Finalist NAACP Image Award, 2002; Literature Award of Excellence, Memphis Black Writers Conf, 2002; BWC 2002 Literary Award, Memphis Black Writers Conf & Southern Film Festival, 2002; Myers Outstanding Book Award, Gustavus Myers Ctr Study Bigotry & Human Rights, 2004; Inducted into ASCAP's Silver Circle Ryman Auditorium, 2008. **Special Achievements:** Only African-American woman in history to write a Number 1 country song. **Business Addr:** Author, Songwriter, Houghton Mifflin Co, 215 Pk Ave S, New York, NY 10003, **Business Phone:** (212)420-5830.

### RANDALL, ANN KNIGHT

Educator, librarian. **Personal:** Born Oct 19, 1942, New York, NY; daughter of Ruth (Bayton) and Robert; married Julius Thomas; children: Christine Renee. **Educ:** Barnard Col, BA, 1963; Columbia Univ, MLS, 1967, Columbia Univ, DLS, 1977. **Career:** US Social Security Admin NYC, claims adjuster, 1963-64; AUS Bamberg Ger, lib asst, 1964-65; Brooklyn Pub Libr, libr adult trainee, 1965-67; City Univ NY Queens Col, instr, 1967-69; Univ S Educ Resources Info Ctr ERIC, indexer, 1967-68; Columbia Univ, pratt Inst, teacher part-time, lectr, 1970-73; Rutgers Univ, Queens Col, teacher part-time, 1970-73; Urban Ctr Columbia Univ, libr consult, 1970-; Urban Resources Syst Univ MI, 1973; RR Booker, pub consult, 1973; Brooklyn Col Libr, asst prof, 1973-76; Ready Reckoner Bowker, bk consult, 1973-75; Brooklyn Col, adj lectr, 1976-; Brown Univ, asst univ librn, 1977-82; New Eng Regional Med Libr Serv, consult, 1979-80; Nat Endowment Humanities, rev panelist, 1980; Dept State Libr Serv, 1980; Brown Univ, asst librn, 1982; City Col Libr, prof & chief librn, 1982-; Regent Nat Libr Med, 1985-. **Orgs:** YWCA Brooklyn; Acad Pol Sci; Am Libr Asn, 1966-; Asn Study African Am Life Hist, 1968-; exec bd, Spec Libr Asn NY Group, 1969-71; pres, NU chap Columbia Univ, Beta Phi Mu, 1971-72; comt chmn, Young Women's Christian Asn, 1976; Advisor Concord Baptist Church Day Care, 1977; N Atlantic Health Sci Libr, 1979; rep, Res Libr Group, 1980-82; regional chmn, N Atlantic Health Sci Libr, 1980-81; counr, 1980-94, coun comt, 1985-87, Am Libr Asn, 1985-; advisor gov, Task Force Libr, 1981; chmn educ & behav sci sect, Asn Col & Res Libr, 1981-82; mgt consult, Asn Res Libr, 1982; advisor Mass, Coun Arts & Humanities, 1985-; chap pres, Greater New York Asn Col & Res Librarians, 1985-86; Archons Colophon. **Home Addr:** 114 Linden Blvd, Brooklyn, NY 11226, **Home Phone:** (718)636-3429.

### RANDALL, MARLENE WEST

Educator, city council member. **Personal:** Born Oct 18, 1934, Portsmouth, VA; daughter of James E West and Gladys M Pretlow; married Vernon W; children: Ricardo C, Veronica L Williams & Michelle D Bryant. **Educ:** Va State Univ, BS, 1954, admin, cert; Columbia Univ, MA, 1960; Univ Va, Sch Law; Old Dom Univ, admin & supv cert; NOVA Univ, EdD. **Career:** Educator (retired); Portsmouth Pub Schs, teacher, 1955-66, reading specialist, 1966-70, asst prin, 1970-76, prin, 1976-89, admin asst, 1989-93; Va First City, chmn; City Portsmouth, Va, vice mayor, currently. **Orgs:** Sister City Comn; Cent Civic Forum; bd dir, Her Shelter, Portsmouth Sch Found, YMCA S Hampton Roads Bd, bd dir, bd chair, Effingham St YMCA; Chamber Com; bd dir, Am Red Cross; Sch Bd Oversight; Clean Community Comn; bd dir, Portsmouth Empowerment 2010 Bd; Election Precinct Officer; Urban League; Girl Scout Coun Colonial Coast; nat treas, Jack & Jill Am Inc; Coalition 100 Black Women; Links Inc; Drifters Inc; Portsmouth Moles Inc; Sigma Gamma Rho Sorority; Saturday Eve Bridge Club; Pinochle Bugs Inc; Am Asn Univ Women; New Bethel Baptist Church; Criminal Justice Serv Bd. **Home Addr:** 206 Wynn St, Portsmouth, VA 23701-3148, **Home Phone:** (757)465-3578. **Business Addr:** Vice Mayor, Portsmouth City Hall, 801 Crawford St, Portsmouth, VA 23704, **Business Phone:** (757)393-8639.

### RANDALL, DR. QUEEN FRANKLIN

School administrator, educator. **Personal:** Born Jan 28, 1935, Pine Bluff, AR; son of Samuel and Ollie (Boykins); children: Barbara J. **Educ:** Lincoln Univ, BS, educ, 1956; Ind Univ, AM, 1961; Nova Univ, EdD, 1975. **Career:** School administrator, educator (retired); Lincoln Univ, math instr, 1956-58; Am River Col, math instr, 1962-70, math & engineering dept chmn, 1970-72, assoc dean instr, 1972-76; Pioneer Community Col, dean, instrnl syst & stud develop, 1976-78, pres, 1978-80; Metrop Comm Col, asst chancellor, 1980-81; El Centro Col, pres, 1981-84; Am River Col, pres, 1984-93; Los Rios Community Col Dist, chancellor, 1993; Lincoln Univ, adj prof. **Orgs:** Alpha Kappa Alpha, 1953; fel John Hay Whitney Found, 1961; pres, Soroptimist Club Kans City MO, 1981; bd dir, Indust Develop Corp, 1982-85; pres, Delta Kappa Gamma; adv bd, Contact Dallas Advert Bd; Treescape Dallas Adv Bd; bd dir, Crocker Art Mus; bd dir, Mercy Healthcare Sacramento; bd dir, Methodist Hosp Sacramento; bd dir, Sacramento Theatre, Co; Asn Calif Community Col Adminr; Am Asn Women Community & Jr Cols; Soroptimists. **Honors/Awds:** Outstanding Educr, YWCA, 1985; Outstanding Alumni, Nova Univ, 1985; Women of Distinction Award, Soroptimist Int Sacramento N, 1986; Dollars & SenseMag's Second Annual Salute to Am Top 100 Bus & Prof Women, 1986. **Home Addr:** 7123 Murdock Way, Carmichael, CA 95608, **Home Phone:** (916)944-3121.

### RANDALL, DR. REGINA LAVERNE. See PEAL, DR. REGINA RANDALL.

### RANDLE, CARVER A.

Lawyer, teacher. **Personal:** Born Jan 12, 1942, Indianola, MS; married Rosie Knox; children: Regina, Carver Jr & Rosalyn. **Educ:** Miss Valley State Univ, BS, 1965; Univ Miss, JD, 1973. **Career:** Pattonlane High Sch, teacher coach, 1965-67; Carver Elem Sch, teacher, 1965-66; Wash Co Schs, teacher, 1967-68; Quitman Co, spec proj dir, 1968-69; Indianola Schs, teacher, 1970-71; N Miss Rural Legal Serv, staff atty; Sacred Heart Sch, staff; Randle & McDaniel, partner & prin, currently. **Orgs:** ACSC, 1967-70; cand mayor, City Indianola, 1968; cand state rep, Miss, 1971, Miss Bar Asn, 1973; Miss Coun Human Rels, 1977-; Nat Conf Black Lawyers; Miss Nat Bar Asn; bd dir, Indianola Fed Credit Unoin; pres, Sunflower Co, Miss Br Nat Asn Advan Colored People. **Honors/Awds:** Coach of the Year, N Cent Athletic Conf, 1965-66; Award for Outstanding Achievements & Leadership, Indianola, 1973. **Home Addr:** 1507 BB King Rd, Indianola, MS 38751-3700, **Home Phone:** (662)887-1874. **Business Addr:** Partner, Principal, Randle & McDaniel, 130 2nd St, Indianola, MS 38751-0546, **Business Phone:** (662)887-5436.

### RANDLE, JOHN ANTHONY

Football player. **Personal:** Born Dec 12, 1967, Hearne, TX; married Rosie; married Candace; children: Jonathan & Ryann. **Educ:** Tex

A&M Univ, grad. **Career:** Football player (retired); Minnesota Vikings, 1990, left defensive end, 1991, right defensive tackle, 1992-97, right defensive end, 1998, defensive end & defensive tackle, 1999-2000; Seattle Seahawks, right defensive tackle, 2001-03. **Honors/Awds:** Hall of Fame, Div II Football; NFL Sacks leader, 1997; All Tackle Machine, Tackle Mag, 1999; College Football Hall of Fame, 2008; Pro Football Hall of Fame, 2010; Texas Sports Hall of Fame, 2010; Minnesota Vikings Ring of Honor. **Special Achievements:** Film: 1998 NFC Championship Game, 1999. TV-Series: "NFL Monday Night Football" 1990-2000; "ESPN's Sunday Night Football" 1991-2003; "TNT Sunday Night Football", 1991-94; "Arli$$", 1997; "WCW Monday Nitro" 1998; "NFL on FOX", 1998-2000; "Pros vs. Joes", 2008. **Home Addr:** , Medina, MN.

**RANDLE, LUCIOUS A, SR. See Obituaries Section.**

### RANDLE, THERESA ELLEN
Actor. **Personal:** Born Dec 27, 1964, Los Angeles, CA. **Educ:** Beverly Hills Col. **Career:** Films: Maid to Order, 1987; Near Dark, 1987; Easy Wheels, 1989; The King of New York, 1990; The Guardian, 1990; Heart Condition, 1990; The Five Heartbeats, 1990; Jungle Fever, 1991; Malcolm X, 1992; CB4, 1993; Sugar Hill, 1993; Beverly Hills Cop III, 1994; Bad Boys, 1995; Girl 6, 1996; Space Jam, 1996; Spawn, 1997; Bad Boys II, 2003; The Hunt for Eagle One, voice, 2006; The Hunt for Eagle One: Crash Point, voice, 2006; Ink, 2010; Shit Year, 2010; TV series:"A Different World", 1989; "Seinfeld", 1991; "Duckman: Private Dick/Family Man", 1997; "Livin' for Love: The Natalie Cole Story", 2000; "Partners & Crime", 2003; "Law & Order: Criminal Intent", 2006; "State of Mind", 2007; "Lost & Found", 2007; "Passion Fishing", 2007; "Helpy Helperpants", 2007; "O Rose, Thou A Different Worldk", 2007. **Business Addr:** Actress, c/o William Morris Agency, 151 El Camino Dr, Beverly Hills, CA 90212, **Business Phone:** (310)859-4000.

### RANDLE, WILMA JEAN-ELIZABETH EMANUEL
Journalist. **Personal:** Born Apr 20, 1955, Chicago, IL; daughter of Emanuel and Ruth Helen. **Educ:** Rosary Col, River Forest, IL, BA, hist, commun arts, 1977; Univ Southern Calif, MA, int journ, 1991. **Career:** Chicago Independent Bulletin, news ed, 1977-78; The Maynard Inst Journ Educ, fac, summer prog, 1978, 1986; Muskegon Chronicle, reporter; St Paul Pioneer Press Dispatch, reporter, columnist, 1984-88; Chicago Tribune, bus writer & gen assignment reporter, 1988; Int Women's Media Found, bus reporter. **Orgs:** Nat Asn Black Journalists; Int Woman's Media Found; bd mem, African Women's Media Ctr, Dakar, Senegal. **Honors/Awds:** Int Women's Media Found Int CNF, delegate, 1990; Univ Southern Calif, Ctr for Int Journalism Fel, 1990; Davenport Bus & Econs Reporting Fel, 1984. **Home Addr:** 1434 W Thome Ave, Chicago, IL 60660.

### RANDOLPH, DR. BERNARD CLYDE, SR.
Physician. **Personal:** Born May 22, 1922, New York, NY; son of William F and Jessie K Briggs; married Bille Jean Coleman; children: Dana Grace, Bernard C Jr & Paul Allen. **Educ:** City Col NY, BS, 1943; Howard Univ Col Med, MD, 1947. **Career:** Peoples Hosp, resident Internal Med; Homer G Phillips Hosp, resident; Mound City Med Forum, pres, 1963-65; Mo Pan-Med Asn, pres, 1966-67; Talent Rec Coun, Nat Med Asn, chmn, 1972-81; SSM St Joseph Health Ctr, physician; St Louis Orthop Inst, physician; pvt pract physician, currently. **Orgs:** Founder & pres, St Louis Coun Env Health & Safety; past pres, Gamma Chap Chi Delta Mu Frat; Phi Beta Sigma Frat; life mem, golden herita gemem, Nat Asn Advan Colored People; Nat Health Comn; chair, St. Louis Br, NCP, Health & Hosp Comn; chair, Health & Hosp Comn; chmn, Health Comn, 5th Sen Dist Corp &Prof Round Table; selection comm, Dorothy I Height Lifetime Achievement Award, 5th Biennial Symp Minorities, Med Under served & Cancer, 1995. **Honors/Awds:** Mission to W Africa Nat Med Asn, 1961; NMA delegate Conference on Hosp Discrimination Pres John F Kennedy, 1963; Practitioner of the Year, Nat Med Asn, 1988; Community Service Award, Legal Serv Eastern Mo, 1989; Awards for fifty years of med practice, Howard Univ Med Alumni Asn & Mo State Med Asn. **Home Addr:** 1209 Castle Gate Villas Dr, St Louis, MO 63132-3183. **Business Addr:** Physician, 3737 N Kingshighway Blvd Suite 201, St Louis, MO 63115, **Business Phone:** (314)383-1746.

### RANDOLPH, LAURA B.
Publishing executive, writer, editor. **Personal:** Born Aug 1, 1957, Washington, DC; daughter of Horace and Anna; married Ronny Lancaster. **Educ:** George Washington Univ, BA, 1979; Georgetown Univ Law Ctr, JD, 1987. **Career:** US Dept Health & Human Serv, regulations analyst, 1980-82, health policy specialist, 1982-84, prog analyst, 1984-85, legal assistance specialist, 1985-87; Ebony, journalist & writer, 1987-96, managing ed, 1996-99, sr staff ed; Johnson Publ Co Inc, ed, 1987-. **Orgs:** US Senate/House Press Gallery, 1987; White House Correspondents Asn, 1992-. **Honors/Awds:** Superior Achievement Award, US Dept Health & Human Serv, Secy HHS, 1982; NAACP Image Award, 1996. **Home Addr:** 76 Sheridan St NE, Washington, DC 20011, **Home Phone:** (202)291-7616. **Business Addr:** Editor, Johnson Publishing Co Inc, 1750 Pennsylvania Ave NW Suite 1201, Washington, DC 20006, **Business Phone:** (202)393-5860.

### RANDOLPH, LEONARD WASHINGTON
Police officer. **Personal:** Born Oct 15, 1954, Newark, NJ; son of Leonard Sr and LaVera Conover. **Educ:** Correction Officers Training Acad, Trenton, NJ, 1981; NJ State Police Acad, Sea Girt, NJ, drug enforcement, 1981; FBI Training Acad, Gloucester Co Col, Gloucester, NJ, 1993; Middlesex Co Police Acad, Interviewing & Interrogation Tech, Union, NJ, 1994; Bergen Co Police Acad, NJ Narcotica Task Force, Top Gun St Survival Training, Mahwah, NJ, 1996; NY State Police Acad, Interviewing & Interrogation Tech, Albany, NY, 1997. **Career:** NJ Dept Corrections, E Jersey State Prison, correctional officer, 1979-90, Internal Affairs Inc, 1990-, sgt-at-arms, currently; Correction Offrs Training Acad, Trenton, NJ, hostage negotiations hostage trainer, 1985; Div Criminal Justice, Lawrenceville, NJ, co & state investr, 1991. **Orgs:** Chap deleg, Men & Women Justice NJ Coun Charter Mem Nat Black Police Asn, 1988-; chap deleg, Men & Women Justice, Nat Black Police Asn, 1988-; first vpres, Nat Bd Men & Women Justice, 1989-; pres, Men & Women Justice, NJ Chap, 1989-; Social Fel Inc, NJ Grand chap, 1997; Grove Phi Grove; Nat Asn Advan Colored People. **Home Addr:** 1152 Grove St, Irvington, NJ 07111, **Home Phone:** (201)372-8970. **Business Addr:** Senior Investigator, Information Officer and Sergeant-at-Arms, New Jersey Department of Corrections, PO Box 863, Trenton, NJ 08625, **Business Phone:** (609)292-4036.

### RANDOLPH, LONNIE MARCUS
Lawyer, state government official, judge. **Personal:** Born Aug 7, 1949, Auburn, AL; son of Charles Boyd and Gertha Mae; married Linda Diane; children: Lakesha & Lonnie Marcus II. **Educ:** Northern Ill Univ, BS, 1973; John Marshall Law Sch, JD, 1978. **Career:** State Ill, asst state's atty, 1978-79; State Ind, dep prosecutor, 1979-81; self employed, atty, 1981-; State Ind, state sen, 1993-98, 2008-; E Chicago City Ct, judge, 1998-2008; Lonnie Randolph & Assocs, atty. **Orgs:** Bd mem, Nat Asn Advan Colored People, 1983-; Lions Club, 1983-; Exchange Club, 1983-; adv bd mem, Boys Club; Cook County Bar; bd mem, E Chicago Boys Club; Fed Bar; James C Kimbrough Bar; Lake County Bar. **Home Addr:** 4437 Alder St, East Chicago, IN 46312, **Home Phone:** (219)397-5540. **Business Addr:** Senator, Indiana State Senate, 200 W Wash St, Indianapolis, IN 46204, **Business Phone:** (800)382-9467.

### RANDOLPH, DR. ROBERT LEE
Educator, economist. **Personal:** Born Jan 2, 1926, East St. Louis, IL; children: Heather. **Educ:** DePauw Univ, BA, 1948; Univ Ill Urbana, MS, 1954, PhD, 1958; Case Western Reserve Univ, attended 1960; Univ Mich, PhD, 1962. **Career:** Springfield Col, Westfield, MA, from instr to assoc prof, 1958-65, chmn dept, 1960-63, dir evening & summer schs, 1960-64; Job Corps, dep assoc dir, 1965-67; Equal Employment Oppor Commn Wash, dep exec dir, 1967-68; Chicago State Univ, exec vpres, 1969-73; Westfield Col MA, pres, 1973-79; MA State Col Syst, vice chancellor, 1979-81; Ala State Univ, pres, 1981-83; Univ Montevallo, Montevallo, AL, prof economics, 1983-. **Orgs:** Vpres Springfield Urban League, 1962-66; pres, Randolph Asn Birmingham AL, Boston 1983-; Am Asn State Colls & Univs; Am Asn Polit & Social Scis; Am Econ Asn; Phi Delta Kappa; Alpha Phi Omega; Kappa Alpha Psi. **Business Addr:** Professor of Economics, University of Montevallo, Sta 6230, Montevallo, AL 35115, **Business Phone:** (205)665-6230.

### RANDOLPH, WILLIE LARRY, JR.
Baseball player, athletic coach, manager. **Personal:** Born Jul 6, 1954, Holly Hill, SC; married Gretchen Foster; children: Taniesha, Chantre, Andre & Ciara. **Career:** Baseball player (retired), baseball coach, manager; Pittsburgh Pirates, infielder, 1975; New Yorker Yankees, infielder, 1976-88, asst gen mgr, 1993, coach, 1994-2004; Los Angeles Dodgers, infielder, 1989-90; Oakland Athletics, infielder, 1990; Milwaukee Brewers, infielder, 1991, coach, 2009-10; New York Mets, infielder, 1992, mgr, 2005-08; Baltimore Orioles, coach, 2011; World Baseball Classic, base coach, 2012-. **Home Addr:** 648 Juniper Pl, Franklin Lakes, NJ 07417. **Business Addr:** Coach, Baltimore Orioles, 333 W Camden St, Baltimore, MD 21201, **Business Phone:** (410)685-9800.

### RANDOLPH, ZACH (ZACHARY MCKENLEY RANDOLPH)
Basketball player. **Personal:** Born Jul 16, 1981, Marion, IN; son of Mae; married Faune; children: MacKenley,Maziya & Zachary Jr. **Educ:** Mich State Univ, attended 2001. **Career:** Portland Trail Blazers, forward, 2001-07; New York Knicks, 2007-08; Los Angeles Clippers, 2008-09; Memphis Grizzlies, 2009-. **Business Addr:** Basketball Player, Memphis Grizzlies, 175 Toyota Plz Suite 150, Memphis, TN 38103, **Business Phone:** (901)205-1234.

### RANDOLPH-JASMINE, CAROL DAVIS
Lawyer, journalist, community activist, talk show host, columnist. **Personal:** Born St. Louis, MO; daughter of John and Clarice; married Frank; children: Jen Randolph. **Educ:** Fisk Univ, BA, biol; Wash Univ, MA, sci educ; Cath Univ Columbus Sch Law, JD. **Career:** WDVM TV, talk show host; Court TV, anchor, host, moderator, 1986; Goldfarb, Kaufman & OToole, 1988-91; Wash Times, columnist, 1988-91; Walls Commun Inc, sr vpres; Akin & Randolph Agency LLC, co-founder; Miller & Long Concrete Construct, vpres strategic commun, currently. **Orgs:** Pa Bar Asn; Dc Bar Asn; Women's Mus; AFTRA, 1970-; chair, Links Inc, 1984-; comnr, DC Comn Arts, 1987-; ACLU, nomination comt, 1988-93; Zonta, 1992-; bd dir, Progressive Life Ctr; bd dir, Ctr Dispute Resolution; gen coun, New African Visions Inc. **Business Addr:** Co-Founder, Akin & Randolph Agency LLC, 1 Gateway Ctr Suite 2600, Newark, NJ 07102, **Business Phone:** (973)623-6834.

### RANGEL, CHARLES BERNARD
Government official. **Personal:** Born Jun 11, 1930, New York, NY; son of Ralph and Blanche Mary Wharton; married Alma Carter; children: Steven & Alicia. **Educ:** NY Univ, BS, bus admin, 1957; St Johns Univ Law Sch, LLB, 1960, JD, 1968. **Career:** Weaver Evans Wingate & Wright, atty, 1961-62; pvt law pract, 1960-61; Southern Dist New York, asst atty, 1961-62; New York State Assembly, 72nd Legis Dist Cent Harlem, mem, 1967-70; US House Rep, 18th Dist, rep, 1971-73, 19th Dist, rep, 1973-83, 2013-, 16th Dist, rep, 1983-93, 15th Cong Dist, rep, 1993-2013. **Orgs:** House Judiciary Comt, 1973-74; co-founder & chmn, Cong Black Caucus, 1974-75; House Comt Ways & Means, 1975-; chmn, House Select Comt Narcotics Abuse & Control, 1976-93; dean, NY State Cong Deleg, 1993-; Joint Comt Taxation, 1995-; Cong Adv US Trade Rep, 1995-; Pres Export Coun, 1995-; New York Bar Asn; 369th Vet Asn; chmn, House Ways & Means Comt, 2007-10; Community Educ Prog. **Honors/Awds:** Lifetime Achievement Award, Jackie Robinson Found's, 2005; Distinguished Service Award, Wash Int Trade Asn, 2006; Presidential Medal, Baruch Col, 2006. **Special Achievements:** First African American Chair of the House Ways and Means Committee. **Home Addr:** 40 W 135th St, New York, NY 10037, **Home Phone:** (212)225-4365. **Business Addr:** Representative, US House of Representatives, 163 W 125th St Suite 737, New York, NY 10027, **Business Phone:** (212)663-3900.

### RANKIN, DR. EDWARD ANTHONY
Surgeon, orthopedist. **Personal:** Born Jul 6, 1940, Holly Springs, MS; son of Robbie Lee and Edgar Everett Jr; married Frances Espy; children: Tony Jr (deceased) & Marc Espy. **Educ:** Lincoln Univ, BS, biol, 1961; Meharry Med Col, MD, 1965. **Career:** Walter Reed Gen Hosp, rotating internship, 1965-66, orthop surg resident, 1967-70; Dewitt Army Community Hosp, resident, 1966-67; Epps Gladden Rankin, pvt prac, 1973-87; Howard Univ Sch Med, from asst prof to assoc prof, 1973-89, prof, 1989-; Providence Hosp, chief orthop surg, 1977-; Georgetown Univ Sch Med, assoc prof, 1982-; Rankin Orthopaedic Ctr, partner, 1988; Howard Univ, prof, 1988; DC Gen Hosp, actg chief c's orthop, 2000; Sports Med Today, ed bd; ed bd orthop, currently. **Orgs:** Eastern Ortho Asn, 1973; Am Col Surgeons, 1975; deleg bd coun, Am Acad Ortho Surg, 1975, 1982-; Am Orthop Foot & Ankle Soc, 1977; Am Soc Surg Hand, 1979; comt mem, Regional Advisors Am Col Surgeons, 1980-; oral examr, Am Bd Ortho Surg, 1980-84, 1993-; Wash Soc Surg Hand, 1983-; comt mem, Regional Advisors Am Acad Ortho Surg, 1984-; bd dir, Blue Cross Blue Shield, 1985-88; Am Ortho Asn, 1988; pres, Metro Wash Soc Surg Hand, 1989; sec tres, pres, Wash Ortho Soc, 1989-; vpres & pres, Metro Wash Chap, Am Col Surg, 1989-91; prog chmn, Liberia Proj, Ortho Overseas, 1989; bd dir, Meharry Med. Col, 1990-2000; pres, Wash Acad Surg, 1998; bd dir, Am Acad Orthopaedic Surgeons, 1996-98, 2001-04, secy, 2001-04, vpres, 2006-, fel; pres, Ea Orthop Soc, 2002-03; Lincoln Univ Nat Alumni Asn; Sigma Phi Phi; fel ACS; AMA; Am Optom Asn. **Honors/Awds:** Association's Distinguished Alumni Award, Lincoln Univ Nat Alumni Asn, 1992; Pub Works 2 Chap Award, DC Med Soc Comt Serv, 2002; Hall of Fame, Lincoln Univ; Distinguish Service Award, 2002; Community Service Award, DC Med Soc, 2004; received number of awards. **Home Addr:** 7731 Rocton Ct, Chevy Chase, MD 20815. **Business Addr:** Chief Orthopaedic Surgeon, Providence Hospital, 1160 Varnum St NE Suite 312, Washington, DC 20017-2110, **Business Phone:** (202)526-7031.

### RANKIN, DR. MARC E.
Orthopedic surgeon. **Personal:** son of E Anthony and Frances Espy. **Educ:** Hampton Univ, BA, biol, 1992; Howard Univ Col Med, MD, med, 1997. **Career:** Howard Univ Col Med, resident, 2002; Cincinnati Sportsmedicine & Orthopaedic Ctr, fel, 2003; Howard Univ Hosp, Dept Orthopaedic Surg, asst clin prof; Veterans Admin Consult, physician; Providence Hosp, Rankin Orthop & Sports Med Ctr, orthop surgeon, currently. **Orgs:** Fel Am Acad Orthopaedic Surgeons. **Business Addr:** Orthopedic Surgeon, Rankin Orthopaedic & Sports Medicine Center, 1160 Varnum St NE Suite 312, Washington, DC 20017, **Business Phone:** (202)526-7031.

### RANKIN, MARLENE OWENS
Foundation executive, executive director, association executive. **Personal:** Born Apr 19, 1939, Cleveland, OH; daughter of James Cleveland (Jesse) and Minnie Ruth Solomon; married Stuart McLean; children: Stuart Owen. **Educ:** Ohio State Univ, Columbus, OH, BSW, 1961; Univ Chicago, IL, MSW, 1978. **Career:** Cook County Dept Pub Aid, Cs Div, Chicago, Ill, social worker, 1961-66; Chicago Youth Ctrs & Proj Learn, Chicago, Ill, social worker, 1968-69; Chicago Comt Urban Opportunity & Model Cities, Chicago, Ill, planning unit coord, sr planner, 1969-74; Govs Off Human Resources, social serv planner, 1974-75; United Charities Chicago, Ill, clin social worker, personnel assoc, dir human resources, 1978-88; Mus Sci & Indust, Chicago, Ill, dir human resource mgt, 1988-90; Jesse Owens Found, Chicago, Ill, exec dir, 1990-. **Orgs:** Acad Cert Social Workers, 1980-; bd dir, Jesse Owens Found, 1980-, mng dir, 1990-; bd mem, OSU Alumni Asn, 1985-90; sustaining mem, bd dir, Hyde Pk Neighborhood Club, 1985-; bd dir, City Chicago Bd Ethics, 1987-92; bd dir, Univ Chicago Sch Social Serv Adminr, 1990-93; chairperson, Ohio State Univ Ann Fund; 1991-95; chmn, OSU Ann Fund, 1991-95; bd, Sporting Chance Found, 1995-; Hyde Pk Neighborhood Club; Sporting Chance Found. **Honors/Awds:** Annual Orchid Award, Top Ladies of Distinction, 1992; Distinguished Service Award, OSU, 1993. **Special Achievements:** Hundred Women Making A Difference, Today's Chicago Woman, 1992. **Home Addr:** 4800 Chicago Beach Dr, Chicago, IL 60615. **Business Addr:** Managing Director, The Jesse Owens Foundation, 4800 Chicago Beach Dr Suite 2203 N, Chicago, IL 60615, **Business Phone:** (773)538-4560.

### RANKIN, HON. MICHAEL LEE
Judge. **Personal:** Born Holly Springs, MS; married Zinora M Mitchell; children: Lee, John-Michael, Michael Joseph & Everette. **Educ:** Lincoln Univ, BA, 1967; Howard Univ Sch Law, JD, 1970. **Career:** US Dept Justice, staff atty; Us Dept Justice, staff atty; Off Gen Coun, Off Econ Opportunity, atty advisor; DC, pub defender, 1972-76; Dist VI, pub defender, asst fed pub defender, 1976-78; Wesley Williams Assocs, pvt pract, 1978-80; US Atty DC, asst, 1980-84, spec asst, 1981; US Attys off, US Attys off Felony Trial Div, dep chief, 1984-86; Super Ct DC, assoc judge, 1986-, Criminal & Spec Opers Divisions, presiding judge, 1998-2001, Criminal Div, dep presiding judge, currently; George Washington Univ Law Sch, lectr law, currently. **Orgs:** Co-chair, Ct's Qual Serv Coun; Criminal Justice Coord Coun; chair, Pretrial Systs Subcomt; Ct's Rules Comt; voting mem, Dist Columbia Police Officer Training Stand Bd; Master, Charlotte E Ray Am Inn Ct. **Business Addr:** Lecturer, The George Washington University Law School, Washington, DC 20052, **Business Phone:** (202)994-1010.

### RANKIN, SHEILA
Manager, executive, businessperson. **Educ:** Ohio State Univ, BBA, acct; Xavier Univ, MBA, finance; Inst Mgt Accountants, cert mgt acct; State Ohio, cert pub acct. **Career:** NCR Corp, Consult Serv Proj Cost Acct & Support, mgr, 1998-2000, Financial Reporting & Asset Mgt, dir, 2002, dir bus opers, dir external reporting & policies, 2002-03; Procter & Gamble, Employee Serv Governance, global acct mgr, 2004-07, Financial Shared Serv, group mgr, 2007-09, Retail Mkt Serv, NA MDO, stewardship mgr, 2009-12, NA Food Channel, customer team finance mgr, 2012-13. **Business Addr:** Director of External Reporting Policies, NCR Corp, 1700 S Patterson Blvd, Dayton, OH 45479, **Business Phone:** (937)445-5000.

**RANN, DR. EMERY LOUVELLE, JR.**
Physician. **Personal:** Born Mar 9, 1914, Keyestone, WV; son of Emery Sr and Vicie Froe; married Flossie Aurelia Fox; children: Judith Thompson, Emery L III, J D, Lara Diane, Jonathan Cheshire & Flossie Aurelia. **Educ:** Johnson C Smith Univ, BS, 1934; Univ Mich, MS, 1936; Meharry Med Col, MD, 1948. **Career:** Kate Bitting Reynolds Memorial Hosp, internship; Charlotte Memorial Hosp, staff; Charlotte Community Hosp, staff; Charlotte Rehab Hosp, staff; NC Acad Fmly Pract, dist dir, 1981; Good Samaritan Hosp, chief staff. **Orgs:** Mecklenburg County Med Soc, 1954; vpres, Mecklenburg Co Med Soc, 1958; pres, Charlotte Jr Chamber Com; pres, Pan-Hellenic Coun Charlotte; pres, Old N State Med Soc, 1959; chmn, Imhotep Conf Hosp Integ, 1961-63; bd trustee, Sigma Pi Phi Fraternity, 1968; Nat Med Asn, 1969, chmn, 1971-72; fel Am Acad Family Pract, 1975; past chmn, bd trustee, Johnson C Smith Univ, pres; life mem, Alpha Phi Alpha fraternity; exec dir, Mediation Servs Forsyth County; former pres, Charlotte Med Soc; bd trustee, Charlotte Tuberc Asn; former pres, Old N State Med Soc; Med Soc NC; AMA; Am Acad Gen Pract; chmn, Third Imhotep Nat Conf; bd trustee, Jubilee Hosp. **Honors/Awds:** Award of Merit, Johnson C Smith Univ, 1954, 1968; Doctor of the Year, Old N State, 1961; Charlotte Med Soc, 1972; ZOB merit ZOB Sor, 1981; hon Scd, Johnson C Smith Univ, 1981; Merit Scs Award, Family Practice Div NMA, 1984; Southeast Regional Sire Arc hon, Sigma Pi Phi, 1989-91; Alpha Omega Alpha Meharry Chap, 1991. **Special Achievements:** First African-American physician to be accepted, Mecklenburg County Med Soc. **Home Addr:** 203 Todd St, Belmont, NC 28012-3048.

**RANSBURG, FRANK S.**
Educator. **Personal:** Born Jan 29, 1943, Keatchie, LA; married Ivory Bowie; children: Ursula. **Educ:** Southern Univ, BA, 1965; La State Univ, MA, 1970; Inst Polit Loyola Univ, New Orleans, grad, inst polit, 1994. **Career:** Southern Univ, counr, 1965-69, asst dean, 1969, instr, 1969; Jr Div La State Univ, counr, 1969-73; Southern Univ, A&M Col, Baton Rouge, dean stud act, 1969-81, dir, int stud affairs, 1981-87, dir planning, 1987-91, asst to chancellor, 1991-97, vice chancellor stud affairs, 1997-99, prof polit sci, currently; Cleo Fields Gov, state campaign mgr; polit consult, 1999; Lt Gov's Off, admin asst, 1973, 1974; HS Rel La State Univ, asst dir, 1975; Appl Literacy & Learning Inc, Adv Bd, mem, currently. **Orgs:** Admin asst, Lt Gov's Off, 1973, 1974; La Comn Campaign Pract, 1974; hon mem, La State Sen, 1974; Am Polit Sci Asn; Southern Polit Sci Asn; Am Asn Univ Profs; Nat Asn Advan Colored People; Am Personnel & Guid Asn; Nat Asn Personnel Workers; Old State Capitol Bd; pres, Common Cause La; bd chair, La Leadership Inst; FOCUS; Baton Rouge Comn Fear & Violence; Lyndon Baines Johnson Found; Polit Historian, Southern Univ. **Home Addr:** 23294 Gen Gardner Lane, Zachary, LA 70791, **Home Phone:** (225)658-9642. **Business Addr:** Professor, Southern University, Baton Rouge, LA 70813, **Business Phone:** (225)771-4500.

**RANSBY, BARBARA**
College teacher, community activist, writer. **Personal:** Born May 12, 1957, Detroit, MI. **Educ:** Columbia Univ, BA, hist, 1984; Univ Mich, MA, hist, 1987, PhD, hist, 1996. **Career:** Columbia Univ, Inst African Affairs & Dept Hist, res asst, 1982-84; Woodrow Wilson Fel Found, Nat Mellon fel, 1984-86; Univ Mich Rackham Grad Sch Fel, Mich Minority Merit fel, 1986-90; Univ Mich, Women's Studies & Women's Studies Prog, instr, 1986-88, Ctr Afro-Am & African Studies, teaching asst, 1987, res asst, 1988, instr, 1989-90; Mus African Am Hist, cur Nineteenth & Twentieth Century spec proj, 1989-90; Chicago Clergy & Laity Concerned, grp trainer, 1992; Crossroads Found, grouptrainer, 1992; DePaul Univ, Dept Hist, instr, 1992-95, dir ctr african am res & asst prof hist, 1995-96; Progressive Media Proj, contrib writer, 1993-; Ancona Sch, consult & grp facilitator, 1993; Chicago Hist Soc, consult & panelist, 1993; Mac Arthur Found, consult, 1994; Am Col Testing, consult, 1996; Univ Ill, Dept Hist & Dept African-Am Studies, asst prof, 1996-2002, assoc prof, 2002-09, Gender & Women's Studies, dir, 2008-, prof, 2009, Planning & Progs, interim vice provost, 2011-12; NW Univ, manuscript reviewer, 1997; Roja Productions, consult, 2003; Pub Radio Int, consult, 2004. Books: Ella Baker & The Black Freedom Movement: A Radical Democratic Vision, 2003; Eslanda: The Large and Unconventional Life of Mrs. Paul Robeson, 2012. **Orgs:** Bd mem, Anti-Racism Inst, Clergy & Laity Concerned; fel, Nat Mellon Humanities & Woodrow Wilson Fels Found, 1984-86; founder, African Am Women Defense Ourselves Orgn, 1991; founder, Ella Baker-Nelson Mandela Ctr Anti-Racist Educ, 1998; fel, Mich Minority Merit, Univ Mich & Rackham Grad Sch, 1986-90; bd mem, Chicago Coalition Solidarity Southern Africa, 1990-94; stud mem, Univ Mich, Hist Dept Search Comm; Ed Bd, Jour Race & Class, London, Eng; bd mem, Ella Baker-Nelson Mandela Ctr Anti-Racist Educ, Univ Mich, 1988-91; Asn study Afro-Am Life & Hist; Asn Black Women Historians; Coord Comm Women Hist Prof; comt mem, Orgn Am Historians; co-founder, United Coalition Against Racism; co-founder & co-chairperson, Free S Africa Coord ComM; Fel, bd mem, Chicago Reporter Mag; Fel, bd mem, Crossroads Fund; comt mem, 1998-2000, Fel, Inst Res Race & Pub Policy, Univ Ill Chicago, 1998-99; fel, Post-doctoral Ford Found, 1999-2000; fel, Nat Ford Found Minority Fel Prog, 2000-01; co founder, Black Radical Cong, 2002; bd dir, Cross-Roads Fund, Chicago Reporter Mag, Anti-Racism Inst & Chicago Coalition Solidarity Southern Africa; Asn Black Women Historians; Coord Comt, Women in Hist Profession & Orgn Am Historians; ed adv comt, Univ Nc Press, 2011-. **Home Addr:** 719 S Ridgeland Ave, Oak Park, IL 60304-1432, **Home Phone:** (708)524-0683. **Business Addr:** Professor, Department of History, University of Illinois, 913 Univ Hall, Chicago, IL 60607-7109, **Business Phone:** (312)996-2961.

**RANSIER, FREDERICK L., III**
Lawyer. **Personal:** Born Dec 3, 1949, Brooklyn, NY; son of Frederick L Jr and Doris A; married Kathleen Hayes; children: Bradley, Charles & Frederick IV. **Educ:** Cent State Univ, BA, polit sci, 1971; Ohio State Univ Col Law, JD, 1974. **Career:** Ohio Atty Gen, ast atty gen, 1974-76; Ransier & Ransier, partner, 1976-; Southern Dist Ohio, bankruptcy trustee, 1988-; Cent State Univ, chair, 1996-2000, bd trustee, 1996-2005; Vorys, Sater, Seymour & Pease LLP, Columbus off, partner & atty, currently. **Orgs:** Columbus Bar Asn, 1974-; law dir, Village Urbancrest, Ohio, 1978-97; chair, Legal Aid Soc Columbus, 1986-87, mem, 1981-87; comnr, Columbus Munic Civil Serv Comn, 1987-99, pres, 1994-99; US Bankruptcy Ct, Southern Dist Ohio, Eastern Div, Judicial Liaison Comt, 1992-94, Trustee Adv Comt, 1992-97; chair, Columbus Works, 1994-97; chair, Supreme Ct Ohio, Bd Comnrs Unauthorized Pract Law, 1995-2000, chair, 1998-2000; Columbus Bar Found, 1999-; Columbus City, Coun, 2000; bd trustee, chair, finance comt & exec comt, Columbus Col Art & Design, 2000-09; bd trustee & founding mem, KidsOhio.org, 2002-; chair, exec comt & finance comt, Franklin Pk Conserv Joint Recreation Dist Bd Dir, 2002-; chair & exec comt, Experience Columbus, 2004-; vice chair, Ohio State Univ Med Ctr Univ Hosp E bd trustee, 2006-; spec master, US Dist Ct, 2007; chair, Ohio State Univ, City Columbus, Columbus Metrop Housing Authority Partnership Oversight Comt, 2011-; chair, City Columbus, Ohio State Univ, Columbus Metrop Housing Authority Partnership Oversight Comt, 2011-; bd trustee, pub policy comt & chair, United Way Cent Ohio, 2014-; chair, Cent State Univ Bd Trustees; Nat Asn Bankruptcy Trustees; Am Bankruptcy Inst; Nat Bar Asn; Ohio State Bar Asn; Am Bar Asn; Columbus Bar Asn. **Honors/Awds:** Community Service Award, Columbus Bar Asn, 1990; Minority Business Advocate Award, Soc Nat Bank, 1993; Urban Columbus Urban League Equal Opportunity Day Award of Excellence, 1998; Alumnus of the Year Award, Alumni Asn, Cent State Univ, 1999; Presidential Citation, Nat Asn Equal Opportunity Higher Educ, 1999; Col of Law Alumni Community Service Award, Ohio State Univ, 2002. **Home Addr:** 1801 E Long St, Columbus, OH 43203, **Home Phone:** (614)258-7743. **Business Addr:** Attorney, Partner, Vorys Sater Seymour & Pease LLP, 52 E Gay St, Columbus, OH 43215, **Business Phone:** (614)464-8226.

**RANSOM, DERRICK WAYNE, JR.**
Football player, consultant. **Personal:** Born Sep 13, 1976, Indianapolis, IN; married Karen; children: 3. **Educ:** Univ Cincinnati, BBA, finance & int bus, 1998. **Career:** Football player (retired), executive; Kans City Chiefs, defensive tackle, 1998-2000, defensive tackle, nose tackle & right defensive tackle, 2001, nose tackle, 2002; Ariz Cardinals, def tackle, 2003; Jacksonville Jaguars, defensive tackle, 2005; UBS, financial advisor, 2006-07; AXA Advisors, fin consult, 2007-10; 212 Capital Group, financial adv, 2010-14; Copley-Fairlawn Youth Football, dir; FirstMerit Bank, vpres, client advisor, 2014-. **Orgs:** Coun mem, BGC Connect; Leadership Akron Alumni Asn; Fairlawn Community Found, 2010-; bd mem, Boys & Girls Clubs Western Res, 2012-; bd mem, 2013-, bd chair, 2016-, InfoLine Summit County. **Business Addr:** Vice President, Client Advisor, First Merit Trust Department, 106 S Main St Suite 5, Akron, OH 44308, **Business Phone:** (330)384-7300.

**RANSOM, GARY ELLIOTT**
Judge. **Personal:** Born Dec 23, 1941, New Brunswick, NJ; married Gloria P. **Educ:** Rutgers Univ, BA, econ, 1965; Univ Pac-McGeorge Sch Law, JD, 1974. **Career:** Judge (retired); NJ Div Civil Rights, field rep, 1965-66; Sacramento Cty Pub Defenders Off, asst pub defender, 1974-81; Sacramento Munic Cty Dist, judge, 1981-88; Ct Appeals-Third Appellate Dist, justice pro tem, 1983; Calif Super Ct, judge. **Orgs:** Bd dir, Planned Parenthood Asn Sacramento, 1978-81; life mem, Kappa Alpha Psi; bd dir, Easter Seals Soc Gr Sacramento, 1978-; pres, Wiley Manuel Bar Asn, 1981; bd dir, Family Serv Agency Greater Sacramento, 1981-; Calif Judges Asn, 1981-; Sigma Pi Phi, Gamma Epsilon Boule, Prince Hall F&AM thirty third Deg; life mem, No Calif Peace Officers Asn; vpres, Calif Asn Black Lawyers, 1981; Int Platform Asn; pres, bd dir, chmn, Greater Sacramento Easter Seals Soc, 1988-. **Honors/Awds:** Phi Nu Pi Award, Kappa Alpha Psi Frat, 1981; Sacramento Wardens & Masters Achievement Award, 1982; Earnest E Robinson Jr Award, Black Law Stud Asn Univ Pac, 1982; Bernard S Jefferson Jurist Award, Calif Asn Black Lawyers, 1989; McKusick Award, Friends Outside, 1994. **Special Achievements:** First African American attorney. **Home Addr:** 1406 Commons Dr, Sacramento, CA 95825.

**RANSOM, LETICIA BUFORD**
Consultant. **Personal:** Born Dec 25, 1964, Chicago, IL; daughter of Harold G and Mary F West. **Educ:** Dillard Univ, BA, bus admin & mgt, gen, 1987; Roosevelt Univ, Chicago, IL, MBA, mkt & finance, 1995. **Career:** Allied Educ Corp, financial aid dir, 1988-90; Motorola Inc, credit analyst, 1990-91, field inventory analyst, 1991-92, COF syst support, group analyst, 1992-93, customer oper adminr, 1993-99, price bk mgr, 2000-04; Bryn Mawr Community Church, acct, 1995-2001; Chicago Urban League, Anheuser-Busch Scholar & Coors Excellence Prog, educ specialist, instr, 2004-06; interim educ dir, 2005-07; Family Focus Inc, assoc human resources dir, 2007-13; Taproot Found, pro bono HR prof, 2013-15; Fay Servicing LLC, human resources mgr, 2013-16; DuSable Mus African Am Hist, human resources & payroll dir, 2016-. **Orgs:** UNCF Inter Alumni Coun, 1987-; Motorola Finance Club, 1991-97; Dist bd dir, Boy Scouts Am, 1994-; life mem, Nat Black MBA Asn, Chicago, 1995-; chair, Ebony Fashion Fair, 1995-2001; chair, UNCF Scholar Pageant, 2000; pres, treas, Dillard Univ Alumni, Chicago Chap, 1995-; pres, Better Investors Through Educ, 1997-2001; Dillard Univ Nat Alumni Asn, 2004; Greater Chicagoland Non Profit Human Resources Dirs Group, 2009; Chicago Soc Human Resource Mgt, 2010; Roosevelt Univ S Side Alumni Asn, Pres S Side Alumni Asn, 2012. **Honors/Awds:** Service Award, Dillard Univ, Steering Comt, Dillard Alumni Campaigns, 1993-95; Motorola Worldwide Employee Recognition Award, 1995, 1997; Outstanding Alumni, 1996; President's Outstanding Service Award, 2000. **Special Achievements:** Author: LinkAge, 2000; AgeLess Pain, 2006. **Home Addr:** 7333 S Chappel Ave, Chicago, IL 60649-3117, **Home Phone:** (773)288-5729. **Business Addr:** Human Resources, Payroll Director, DuSable Museum of African American History, 740 E 56th Pl, Chicago, IL 60637.

**RANSOM, LILLIE SHARON**
College administrator, teacher. **Personal:** daughter of Frank L and Martha Louise; children: Christopher Leslie & Michael Arthur. **Educ:** Oberlin Col, Oberlin, OH, BA, commun studies, 1976; Gallaudet Univ, Wash, DC, MA, deaf educ, 1979; Univ Md, College Park, MD, PhD, mass commun, 1996. **Career:** Univ Md, Col Pk Scholars Prog, teacher, 1998-2004; Univ Md, Col Pk Scholars & Am Cultures, fac codir & lectr, 1998-2004, interim exec dir & asst dean, 2003; Gallaudet Univ, assoc prof commun studies, 2002, 2004-; Md Sch Deaf, pres, 2004-. **Orgs:** Bd trustee & vice chair, Md Sch Deaf; asn educr, Jour & Mass Commun; Eastern Commun Asn; Nat Commun Asn; Potomac Chap Registry Interpreters Deaf; Registry Interpreters Deaf. **Home Addr:** 1225 Edgevale Rd, Silver Spring, MD 20910-1612. **Business Addr:** Associate Professor, Gallaudet University, Rm 201C Kendall Hall 800 Florida Ave NE, Washington, DC 20002-3695, **Business Phone:** (202)651-5420.

**RANSOM, DR. PRESTON L.**
Dean (education), educator, school administrator. **Personal:** Born Jan 2, 1936, Peoria, IL; son of James and Spezzie; married Mildred D Murphy; children: Patricia Lynn & Michael Murphy. **Educ:** Univ Ill, Urbana-Champaign, BS, 1962, MS, 1965, PhD, 1969. **Career:** Raytheon Co, Bedford, Mass, elec engr, 1962-63; Univ Ill Urbana-Champaign, grad res asst, 1963-67, instr, 1967-70, asst prof, 1970-72, assoc prof, 1972-88, prof elec & comput engineering, asst dean engineering & dir off continuing engineering educ, cont engr educ, prof emer, surge dir, currently; Univ Ill, Paul V Golvin teaching fel, 1967-68; Univ Col London, hon res fel, 1976. **Orgs:** Sr mem, Inst Elec & Electronic Engrs, 1970-; Am Soc Engr Educ, 1972; Optical Soc Am, 1972-; Ete Kappa Nu Hon Soc; Minority Engineering Grad Recruitment Prog, 1997. **Home Addr:** 2609 Lakeview Dr, Champaign, IL 61821-7543. **Business Addr:** Surge Director, Assistant Dean, University of Illinois Urbana-Champaign, 422 Engineering Hall MC266, Urbana, IL 61801-2936, **Business Phone:** (217)333-6634.

**RASBERRY, REV. ROBERT EUGENE**
Clergy, educator. **Personal:** Born Philadelphia, PA; married Gloria E Hooper; children: Roslyn, Robert Jr, John & Denise. **Educ:** Morgan State Col, AB, 1955; Howard Univ, Sch Soc Work, 1956; NY Univ, MA, 1958; Andover Newton Theol Sch, BD, 1966. **Career:** Clergy, educator, pastor (retired); Big Bros Baltimore, social case worker, 1954-56; Bur Child Welfare NYC, social investr, 1956-57; First Baptist, pastor, 1957-59; Friendship Baptist, pastor, 1959-62; Bethany Baptist Church, Syracuse, NY, pastor; Messiah Baptist, pastor, 1962-65; Mt Calvary Baptist Church, Springfield, MA, pastor, 1965-73; Springfield Tech Community Col, asst prof, 1969-73; Episcopal Church Atonement, Westfield, MA, from asst to rector, 1970-72; State Dept Correctional Servs, chaplain; WSYR Words & Music Sunday Morning Syracuse, host producer. **Orgs:** Exec comt, Am Asn Univ Prof; Urban League; Human Righst Comn; Protestant Comn Ministries; bd dir, Syracuse Univ Hill Corp Syracuse Chap OIC's Am; coun rep, NY State Coun Churchs; past exec comt, Am Baptist Churches Mass; asn moderator, Pioneer Valley Am Baptist Churchs, MA. **Special Achievements:** Ten most watchable men Post Standard Newspaper Syracuse, 1977. **Home Addr:** PO Box 6461, Syracuse, NY 13217.

**RASBY, WALTER HERBERT, III**
Football player, executive, broker. **Personal:** Born Sep 7, 1972, Washington, NC; married Cortney. **Educ:** Wake Forest Univ, BS, commun, 1994. **Career:** Football player (retired), real estate broker, executive; Pittsburgh Steelers, tight end, 1994; Carolina Panthers, 1995-97; Detroit Lions, 1998-2000, wide receiver, 1999; Wash Redskins, tight end, 2001-02 & 2004, fullback, 2002; New Orleans Saints, tight end, 2003; Pittsburgh Steelers, tight end, 2004-05; Charlotte Chamber Com, Funds Dr Team-Diversity, 2005-07; New Eng Patriots, 2006; New York Jets, 2006; Legacy Real Estate Advisiors LLC, broker, 2006-; Clear Sight Funding LLC, bus develop mgr, 2010-12; SMS-Advisors LLC, capital proj lead, proj mgr, prof athlete & entertainer liaison, 2012-. **Business Addr:** Broker, Legacy Real Estate Advisors LLC, 1001 Elizabeth Ave Suite 1-D, Charlotte, NC 28204, **Business Phone:** (704)373-1800.

**RASHAD, DR. AHMAD (ROBERT EARL MOORE)**
Broadcaster, football player. **Personal:** Born Nov 19, 1949, Portland, OR; married Phylicia Ayers Allen, Jan 1, 1985, (divorced 2001); children: Condola Phylea; married Sale Johnson, Jan 1, 2007, (divorced 2013); married Ana Luz Rodriguez-Paz, Jan 1, 2016. **Educ:** Univ Ore, BA, 1972; Univ Puget Sound, PhD, jour. **Career:** Football player (retired), broadcaster; St Louis Cardinals, kickoff returner & wide receiver, 1972, wide receiver, 1973; Buffalo Bills, wide receiver, 1974-76, Seattle Sea hawks, wide receiver, 1976, Minn Vikings, wide receiver, 1976-82; KMSP-TV, Minneapolis, MN, host monday night football preview show; WCCO-TV, Minneapolis, MN, sports reporter; Real TV, host; NBC Sports, host, studio anchor, game reporter, sportscaster, 1982; NBA Entertainment, managing ed, exec producer, currently. **Orgs:** Bd trustee, Univ Ore; Omega Psi Phi Fraternity Inc. **Honors/Awds:** MVP Award, Pro Bowl, 1979; Emmy Award; University's Pioneer Award; Col Football Hall of Fame, 2007; Honorary Degree of Doctor of Journalism, Univ Puget Sound. **Special Achievements:** Author, Rashad: Vikes, Mikes and Something on the Backside. **Business Addr:** Executive Producer, NBA Entertainment, 450 Harmon Meadow Blvd Suite 200, Secaucus, NJ 07094-3618, **Business Phone:** (201)865-7700.

**RASHAD, JOHARI MAHASIN**
Government official. **Personal:** Born Mar 13, 1951, Washington, DC; daughter of Henry Jones and Millie Lucerita Adams; children: Chekesha Wajeehah. **Educ:** Howard Univ, BA, 1976, PhD, orgn commun, 1997; Univ DC, MBA, adult educ & human resource develop, 1981. **Career:** US Customs Serv, GS-4, clerk typist, 1976, GS-5, 1977; US Civil Serv Comn, stand specialist, 1976; Off Personal Mgt, instr, 1980; UScG, employee develop specialist, 1986; Bur Land Mgt, personnel mgt specialist, 1990-93; Howard Univ, IPA assignment, 1993-94, sr training specialist BLM, 1994-95, actg asst dir human resources mgt, 1997; Off Merit Systs Oversight & Effectiveness, human resource workforce effectiveness advocate, 2000; US Environ Protection Agency, Off Personnel Mgt, human resources specialist, 2004, Human Resources Policy Div, policy writer & telework coordr, 2006, actg dir, 2007, sr human resources specialist, currently; Lutheran Col Wash Semester, instr; Fed Emergency Mgt Agency, Dept Homeland Security, dir, workforce progs div, 2010; Coast Guard, mem. **Orgs:** Am Asn Univ Women; Phi Beta Kappa, 1976; Kappa Delta Pi Educ Hon Socs, 1976; Delta Sigma Theta Sorority Inc; Am Soc Training & Develop; Int Commun Asn; Nat Career Develop Asn; Int Asn Career Mgt Professionals; Capitol Hill Seventh Day Adventist Church, Wash, DC; Am Socs Training & Develop; Socs Human Resource Mgt; Annenberg speaker, Partnership Pub Serv, 2008-10; moderator, Telework Exchange; Off Telework Adv Group, Personnel Mgt. **Honors/Awds:** Exceptional Service Award, Downtown Jaycees, 1984; Out-

standing Service Award, Downtown Jaycees, 1985; Directors Service Award, 1986; President's Distinguished Service Award, 1987; Special Achievement Award, Bur Land Mgt, 1992; Board of Directors Award, Metro-DC Chap, ASTD, 1998; Volunteer Partnership Award, 1998; Superior Service Award, Dept Interior, 2000; Sustained Superior Performance Award, US Off Personnel Mgt, 2000, 2001; Special Act Awards, US Off Personnel Mgt, 2001, 2002; Performance Award, US Off Personnel Mgt, 2002; Thanks a Million Award, US Dept Transp, 2002; Time Off award, US Off Personnel Mgt, 2002-04; Special Act Award, US Environ Protection Agency, 2006, 2007; performance Award, US Environ Protection Agency, 2007-10; Meritorious Service Award-Bronze medal & plaque, US Environ Protection Agency, 2008; Time off Award, US Environ Protection Agency, 2010. **Home Addr:** 430 M St SW Suite 706, Washington, DC 20024-2650, **Home Phone:** (202)484-2171. **Business Addr:** Senior Human Resources Specialist, US Office of Personnel Management, 1900 E St NW, Washington, DC 20415-1000, **Business Phone:** (202)606-1800.

### RASHAD, PHYLICIA

Actor. **Personal:** Born Jun 19, 1948, Houston, TX; daughter of Andrew A (deceased) and Vivian Elizabeth Ayers; married William Lancelot Bowles Jr, May 13, 1972, (divorced 1975); children: William Lancelot Bowles III; married Victor Willis, Apr 28, 1978, (divorced 1982); married Ahmad, Dec 14, 1985, (divorced 2001); children: Condola Phyleia. **Educ:** Howard Univ, BFA, 1970. **Career:** Off-Broadway & Broadway actress: Into the Woods; Dream girls; The Whiz; Ain't Supposed to Die a Natural Death; Great Women of Television & Comedy, 2003; A Raisin in the Sun, 2008. TV series: soap opera, One Life to Live; The Cosby Show, 1984-92, 2005, 2007; Cosby, 1996-2000. TV specials: "Uncle Tom's Cabin", 1987; "A Different World", 1988-90; "False Witness", 1989; "Polly", 1989; "Polly Once Again", 1990; "Jailbirds", 1990; "Blossom", 1991; "American Playhouse", 1993; "Tough Love", 1994; "Cosby Mysteries", 1994; "Touched by an Angel", 1994-2002; "Little Bill", 1994-2004; "In the House", 1995; "The Old Settler", actress & exec producer, 2001; "Bull"; "Murder, She Wrote: The Last Free Man", 2001; "PBS Hollywood Presents", 2001; The Last Chapter, 2002; Character Studies, host, 2005; "Everybody Hates Chris", 2007; "Psych", 2007-14; "The Life & Times of Tim", 2008; "The Cleveland Show", 2012; "Gods Behaving Badly", 2013; "Do No Harm", 2013. Films: Once Upon a Time...When We Were Colored, 1995; Loving Jezebel, 2000; The Visit, 2000; Just Wright, 2010; Frankie & Alice, 2010; For Colored Girls, 2010; Good Deeds, 2012; Steel Magnolias, 2012; Gods Behaving Badly, 2013; Creed, 2015. **Orgs:** Spokesperson, Save C, 1989-91; spokesperson, Cancer Info Serv, 1990-91; bd dir, Recruiting New Teachers, 1990-; Alpha Kappa Alpha sorority. **Honors/Awds:** People's Choice Awards, 1985 & 1989; Image Award, Nat Asn Advan Colored People, 1988, 1997 & 2009; Honorary Doctorate of Humanities, Barber-Scotia Col, Concord, NC, 1989; Outstanding Achievement Award, Women Film, 1991; Honoree of the Year, Harvard Found, 1991; Honorary Doctorate, Providence Col, Providence, RI, 1991; Emmy Award; Muse Award, 2001; Woman of the Year, 2003; Tony Award, 2004; DFA, Brown Univ, 2005; Emmy Award, 2008; Black Reel Award, 2011; Impact Award, 2011; The BET Honors, 2015. **Special Achievements:** Two Emmy nominations for The Cosby Show; Ace Award nomination for best supporting actress in tv film, Uncle Tom's Cabin. **Home Addr:** 25 Magnolia Ave, Mount Vernon, NY 10036. **Business Addr:** Actress, c/o Kaufman Astoria Studios, 34-12 36th St, Astoria, NY 11106, **Business Phone:** (718)392-5600.

### RASHEED, FRED H.

Executive, association executive, president (organization). **Educ:** Rutgers Univ, BA, econ & bus admin, JD; Rockhurst Col, bus law courses. **Career:** Nat Asn Advan Colored People, co-interim exec dir, Econ Develop Prog, dir, nat dir econ develop, 1982-95; Quaker Oats, Hardee's Food Systs, Food Lion, Coors Brewing Co, Brown-Forman Corp, Mazda N Am Opers & Global Crossing, clients. Pantheon Bus Consult. Rasheed Assocs, owner, founder & pres, currently; Articles: "The Discordant Sound of Music (A Report on the Status of Blacks in the Record Industry" & "Out of Focus-Out of Sync (a Report on the status of Blacks in the Film Industry)". **Orgs:** Gov's Adv Coun Minority Bus Develop State; Bell Atlantic Nj Exec Consumer Adv Panel; Nj Transit Consumer Adv Coun; Bd Alliance Pub Technol. **Home Addr:** 3429 Dijon Ave, Ocean Springs, MS 39564, **Home Phone:** (228)875-0876. **Business Addr:** Founder, President, Rasheed Associates, 614 Cent Ave Suite 3, East Orange, NJ 07018-1942, **Business Phone:** (973)414-8518.

### RASHFORD, DR. JOHN HARVEY

Educator. **Personal:** Born May 10, 1947, Port Antonio; son of Winifred Jacobs and Hector G; married Grace Maynard. **Educ:** Friends World Col NY, BA, 1969; City Univ NY, Grad Ctr, MA, PhD, 1982. **Career:** Crossroads Africa, group leader, 1971; City Univ NY, adj lectr; BrooklynCol, fac, 1974-75; Queens Col, fac, 1977-80; Lehman Col, fac, 1977-82; Rutgers Univ, vis lectr, 1980-82; Col Charleston, prof anthrop, 1982-. **Orgs:** Soc Econ Bot, 1979-; ed bd, SC Hist Soc, 1989-; Phi Kappa Phi, Col Charleston, 1989; Omicron Delta Kappa; Charleston Friends Quaker Meeting; bd dir, Gaylord & Dorothy Donnelley Found. **Home Addr:** 8546 Sentry Cir, North Charleston, SC 29420-8349, **Home Phone:** (843)552-0422. **Business Addr:** Professor of Anthropology, College of Charleston, Rm 203 19 St Philip St, Charleston, SC 29424, **Business Phone:** (843)953-8188.

### RATCLIFF, WESLEY D.

Computer executive. **Personal:** Born Jan 1, 1944?, Crockett, TX; married Marie. **Educ:** Prairie View Univ, BS; Univ Houston, MS, math. **Career:** IBM, mgr, 1976, Brooklyn, mgr, 1990; Advan Technol Solutions S Inc, pres, chief exec officer & founder, 1993-; Independence Community Bank Corp, dir, 1994-2004, dir emer, 2004-; Nat Aeronaut & Space Admin, engr. **Orgs:** Freestone County Exten Serv Beef; Landowners Asn Tex; chairperson, Tex Black Chamber Com; bd mem, Bus Coun NY Inc. **Honors/Awds:** Recipient Year, Tex Chapter Orgn & Agr Comt, 2005; Special Achievement Business Award. **Business Addr:** Director Emeritus, Independence Community Bank Corp, 195 Montague St, Brooklyn, NY 11201, **Business Phone:** (718)722-5400.

### RATCLIFFE, DR. ALFONSO F. (RICK RATCLIFFE)

School administrator. **Personal:** Born Oct 21, 1928, St. Louis, MO; son of William Morgan and Alice Elizabeth Carter; married Dolores Corita Potter. **Educ:** Univ Calif, LA, BA, physics, 1951, MS, engineering, 1963, PhD, engineering, 1970. **Career:** Ogden Technol, Monterey Pk, Calif, dir spec proj, 1955-69; Mattel Inc, Hawthorne, Calif, staff engr, 1969-75; Audio Magnetics Corp, Gardena, Calif, mgr spec proj, 1973-74; Calif State Univ, Northridge, Calif, prof eng, 1975-80, actg chmn & assoc dean eng, 1980-81, dean eng, 1981-92, dean emer, 1992-, prof emer engineering, currently; Inst Advan Engineering, fel, 1983. **Orgs:** Sr mem, Inst Elec & Electronics Engrs, 1978; fel Inst Advan Eng, 1983; bd mem, Pac Southwest Sect, Am Soc Eng Educ, 1984-86, chmn, 1986-87; chmn, 1988-90; bd mem, San Fernando Valley Engrs Coun, 1990-91; Am Soc Eng Educ; Nat Soc Prof Engrs; La Coun Black Engrs. **Special Achievements:** First Black engineering dean in the California State University system. **Home Addr:** 1301 N Kenter Ave, Los Angeles, CA 90049-1319, **Home Phone:** (213)472-4927. **Business Addr:** Professor Emeritus, California State University, 18111 Nordhoff St EN IOI, Northridge, CA 91330-8295, **Business Phone:** (818)677-1200.

### RATCLIFFE, RICK. See RATCLIFFE, DR. ALFONSO F.

### RATES, REV. DR. NORMAN M. See Obituaries Section.

### RATHMAN, THOMAS DEAN

Football coach, football player. **Personal:** Born Oct 7, 1962, Grand Island, NE; married Holly R; children: Nicole, Ali & Samantha. **Educ:** Univ NE, attended 1985. **Career:** Football player (retired), football coach; San Francisco 49ers, running backs, 1986, 1993, fullback, 1987-92, running backs coach, 1997-2002, 2009-; Los Angeles Raiders, fullback, 1994; Oakland Raiders, fullback, 1994, running backs coach, 2006-08; Menlo Coll, offensive coordr, 1996; Detroit Lions, running backs coach, 2003-05. **Honors/Awds:** Post-season play, 1988, 1989: NFC Championship Game, NFL ChampionshipGame; Super Bowl champion, 1989, 1990. **Home Addr:** 6 Cadiz Cir, Redwood City, CA 94065-1333. **Business Addr:** Running Back Coach, San Francisco 49ers, 4949 Centennial Blvd, Santa Clara, CA 95054, **Business Phone:** (408)562-4949.

### RATLIFF, DR. JOE SAMUEL

Clergy, college teacher. **Personal:** Born Jul 24, 1950, Lumberton, NC; married Doris Gardner. **Educ:** Morehouse Col, BA, hist, 1972; Interdenominational Thel Ctr, Atlanta, MDiv, 1975, DMin, 1976. **Career:** Cobb Mem Church, Atlanta, pastor, 1971-78; Morehouse Col, prof, 1974-77; Brentwood Baptist Church, Atlanta, pastor, 1980-; Charles Merrill fel, 1985; Interdenominational Thel Ctr, chmn, bd trustee; Morehouse Sch Relig, chmn, bd trustee; Nat African-Am Fel Southern Baptist Conv, founding pres; Howard Univ, Andrew Rankin Mem Chapel, Preacher. **Orgs:** Chmn & bd trustee, Interdenominational Theol Ctr, Atlanta, 1986-; Cong Black Caucus Found, 2002; Alpha Phi Alpha Fraternity Inc; chmn & bd trustee, Morehouse Sch Relig; exec bd trustee, Joe Samuel Ratliff Lifelong Learning Ctr; Doris Gardner Ratliff Ctr Child Develop; Union Baptist Asn; founder, Brentwood Community Found, 1993; founder, Brentwood Fed Credit Union, 1993; founder, Brentwood Econ Community Develop Corp, 1993; bd dir, Houston Grad Sch Theol; bd dir, Martin Luther King, Jr Mem Proj Found, 2006-; founding mem, Truett Theol Sem, Baylor Univ; Tex Comn Alcohol & Drug Abuse. **Honors/Awds:** Minister of the Year, Nat Conf Christians & Jews, 1985; Hon Doctor Divinity, Interdenominational Theol Ctr, 1988; Spiritual Enlightenment Award, Turner Broadcasting Systs, 2003; Preacher Andrew Rankin Memorial Chapel, Howard Univ; Spiritual Enlightenment Award. **Special Achievements:** Featured in several nat media outlets including: CNN; Assoc Press; Wall St Jour; NY Times; USA Today; Black Enterprise; TIME & Houston Chronicle; First African-Am pastor to lead the Union Baptist Assn; Co-auth, Church Planting in the African-Am Community, Southern Baptist Preaching Today; Portrait was hung in the Martin Luther King Jr Int Chapel Hall of Fame at Morehouse; African American Pulpit; Power in the Pulpit. **Home Addr:** 8202 Frontenac Dr, Houston, TX 77071-3658, **Home Phone:** (713)270-7743. **Business Addr:** Pastor, Brentwood Baptist Church, 13033 Landmark, Houston, TX 77045, **Business Phone:** (713)852-1400.

### RATLIFF, THEO (THEOPHILUS CURTIS RATLIFF)

Executive, basketball player. **Personal:** Born Apr 17, 1973, Demopolis, AL; son of Camilla; married Kristina; children: 6. **Educ:** Univ Wyo, commun, 1995. **Career:** Basketball player (retired), executive; Detroit Pistons, forward-ctr, 1995-97, 2008; Portland Trail Blazers, 2004-06; Philadelphia 76ers, 1997-2001, 2008-09; Atlanta Hawks, 2001-04; Portland Trailblazers, forward-ctr, 2004-06; Boston Celtics, 2006-07; Minn Timberwolves, 2007-08; San Antonio Spurs, 2009-10; Charlotte Bobcats, 2010; Los Angeles Lakers, 2010-11; Rome Gladiators, owner. **Orgs:** Exec vpres, Nat Basketball Player's Asn, 1998-2011; Founder, Theo Ratliff Activity Center, 2004-; Founder, Theo Ratliff Found, 2013-. **Business Addr:** Founder, Theo Ratliff Foundation, 303 Peachtree St Suite 1660, Atlanta, GA 30308, **Business Phone:** (888)994-4866.

### RAUCH, ESQ. DOREEN E.

Lawyer, college administrator, educator. **Personal:** Born Jul 17, 1947, Port-of-Spain; daughter of Joseph Fernandes (deceased) and Stella M B Estrada (deceased); married Terry M; children: Camille M Welch, J Roxanne, Jeanne M & Terry Michael. **Educ:** Univ Cincinnati, BA, anthrop & psychol, 1976; Howard Univ Sch Law, JD, 1984. **Career:** Emerson Law Sch, fac, 1984-89; Univ Mass, instr, 1985-86; Mass Bay Community Col, instr, 1985-86; Murray State Univ, dir equal opportunity & affirm action, 1991-93; Northern Mich Univ, affirmative action officer; Rauch Group, founder & pres, 2008-; Rauch Found, pres, 2009. **Orgs:** Nat Orgn Women, 1990-; Am Asn Univ Women, 1990-; Am Asn Affirmative Action, 1990-; Am Asn Univ Adminrs, 1995. **Honors/Awds:** Am Jurisprudence Award Criminal Law, 1982; Am Jurisprudence Award Contracts, 1983; Am Jurisprudence Award, Howard Univ, Commercial Paper, 1983. **Business Addr:** President, Founder, The Rauch Group, 40702 Lenah Run Circle, Aldie, VA 20105, **Business Phone:** (703)327-3052.

### RAVELING, GEORGE HENRY

Basketball coach, executive, association executive. **Personal:** Born Jun 27, 1937, Washington, DC; married Vivian James; children: Mark. **Educ:** Villanova Univ, BS, econ, 1960. **Career:** Wash State Univ, head basketball coach, 1972-83; Univ Iowa, head basketball coach, 1983-86; Villanova Univ, asst basketball coach; Univ Md, asst basketball coach; Sun Oil Co, mkt anal & sls rep; Converse Rubber Co, promos rep; syndicated newspaper Pac NW, columnist; Univ Southern Calif, head basketball coach, 1987-94; CBS Sports & FOX Sports Net, color commentator; Nike Worldwide Camps, global basketball sports mkt dir, 2000, dir int basketball, currently; Coaching success, owner, currently. **Orgs:** Nat Speakers Asn; Sports Illus Speakers Bur; Nat Asn Basketball Coaches; bd trustee mem, Naismith Memorial Basketball Hall Fame; Am Humor Studies Asn; adv bd, Uniroyal Corp, Spaulding Corp, Joseph P Kennedy Found Ment Retarded, Letterman Coach & Athletic Mags. **Honors/Awds:** Black Hall of Fame, Nat Black Sports Found; Hon Cert Citizenship, Kans City & New Orleans; Pac-8 Coach of Year, 1975; UPI West Coast Coach of the Year, 1975; Coach of the Year, Nat Col, 1977; Pac-10 Coach of the Year, 1983; Distinguished Alumnus & Humanitarian Awards, Villanova Univ; Cert Merit Outstanding Sales, Pub Rels, & Mkt, Philadelphia Tribune Newspaper. **Special Achievements:** Book: "War on the Boards; A Rebounders Workshop". **Home Addr:** 5521 W 62nd St, Los Angeles, CA 90056-2007, **Home Phone:** (310)337-1634. **Business Addr:** Director of International Basketball, Nike Inc, 1 Bowerman Dr, Beaverton, OR 97005, **Business Phone:** (503)671-6453.

### RAVEN, RICKY A.

Lawyer. **Educ:** Univ Houston, BS, polit sci, 1983; Univ Houston Sch Law, JD, 1986. **Career:** Harris Co Dist Atty Off, 1994-2000; Woodard, Hall & Primm, prin, 1994-2001; Porter & Hedges LLP, partner, 2000-02; Thompson & Knight LLP, partner, 2004-; ReedSmith LLP, partner, 2015-. **Orgs:** Julia C Hesten House Inc; bd mem, Ronald McDonald House; bd mem, Houston Symphony Orchestra; Houston Golf Asn; bd mem, Univ Tex Health Sci Ctr Develop Bd; Am Bar Asn; bd dir, Houston Zoo; bd dir, Yellowstone Acad; bd dir, Zina Garrison Acad; bd dir, S Cent YMCA; bd dir, CSTEM; bd dir, Univ Houston Alumni Asn; bd dir, Ronald McDonald House Houston; exec coun, Houston Forum; comnr, Police Officers' Civil Serv Comn; Col State Bar Tex; Tex Asn Defense Coun; DRI-Voice Defense Bar; Int Asn Defense Coun; New York Bar Asn, Ark Bar Asn, Supreme Ct Bar; comnr, State Comn Judicial Conduct State Tex; Houston Bar Found; Univ Tex Sch Pub Health Adv Coun; Am Bd Trial Advocates; US Supreme Ct Bar. **Honors/Awds:** African American Achiever, 1997; The Best Lawyers in America, Woodward White Inc, 2008-14; Dr. Marguerite Ross Barnett Alumni Achievement Award, Univ Houston African Am Studies Prog, 2012. **Special Achievements:** First African American partner in the history of the firm; Publications: Skills and Strategies for Defending White Collar Criminal Cases, 2008; A Conversation With Our New NASA Administrator, 2009; Archon Hall Named Chairman of the Board, 2010; The Achievement Gap and Why it is Our Greatest Civil-Rights Issue, 2010; Mass Torts Breakout - Warning: Mass Tort Settlement Ethics Ahead, 2013; US EPA Study May Soon Impact Fracking Litigation, 2014; The EPA, H20, and Fracking, 2014; This Scientific Development Could Impact Fracking Litigation, Tex Lawyer, 2015. **Home Addr:** 3322 Larkwood Lane, Sugar Land, TX 77479-2273. **Business Addr:** Partner, Thompson & Knight LLP, 1722 Routh St Suite 1500, Dallas, TX 75201, **Business Phone:** (214)969-1700.

### RAVENELL, REV. JOSEPH PHILLIP

Clergy. **Personal:** Born Jan 20, 1940, Pinesville, SC; married Mary Jane Frazier; children: Joseph, Phillip & Byron. **Educ:** St Peters Col, BS, hist, 1973; Princeton Theol Sem, MDiv, 1976. **Career:** NJ St Prison, instnl chaplain; US Postal Serv, lett carrier, 1966-75; Trenton St Col, col chaplain, 1975-78; Samaritan Baptist Church, spiritual leader & advisor, pastor, 1979-; Community Network, founder & pres, currently. **Orgs:** Pres, NJ Chap St Chaplain Orgn, 1978-; AUS Nat Guard Asn, 1978-; Mil Chaplains Asn, 1978-; Am Correctional Chaplains Asn, 1978-; dir, Com Network Proj, 1979-; bd dir, Community Network; bd dir, Trenton Ecumenical Area Ministry, currently. **Home Addr:** 223 Rosemont Ave, Trenton, NJ 08618-4425, **Home Phone:** (609)656-2871. **Business Addr:** Pastor, Samaritan Baptist Church, 531 Martin Luther King Jr Blvd, Trenton, NJ 08618, **Business Phone:** (609)393-0016.

### RAVENELL, MILDRED

Executive, educator. **Personal:** Born Dec 1, 1944, Charleston, SC; married Armstead Louis Robinson; children: William Samuel & Teressa Emlynne. **Educ:** Fisk Univ, BA, 1965; Howard Univ, JD, 1968; Harvard Univ, LLM, 1971. **Career:** IBM, systs engr, 1968-70; mkt rep, 1970; Boston Univ, asst dean admis & financial aid, 1971-72; FL State Univ, assoc prof law, 1976-84; Univ VA, vis assoc prof law, 1984-85. **Orgs:** Phi Beta Kappa; Am Bar Asn; MA Bar Asn; Bethel AME Church; Delta Sigma Theta Sor; Jack & Jill Am Inc; bd dirs, Terrell House Tallahassee; bd trustees, Law Sch Admis coun; Bd Bus Regulation Fla. **Special Achievements:** The only Black Member of the Florida State University Law School. **Home Addr:** 1600 Laguna Dr, Tallahassee, FL 32308-0922, **Home Phone:** (850)385-8078.

### RAVENELL, WILLIAM HUDSON

Lawyer, educator. **Personal:** Born May 31, 1942, Boston, MA; son of William S and Isabella T; children: William Samuel & Teressa Emlynne. **Educ:** Lincoln Univ, BA, hist, 1963; St Col, Boston, MEd, bus educ, 1965; Howard Univ, Sch Law, JD, 1968. **Career:** John Hancock Ins Co, analyst, 1968-71; Housing Inspection Dept, admin, 1971-72; St Dept Comm Affairs, dep secy, 1972-75; Fla Dept Comm Affairs, secy, 1975-79; Fla A&M Univ, prof, 1979, atty, tenured prof, Bus Law, prof, 1985-; Fla Off Atty Gen, spec asst, 1979-80; US Dept Transp Fed Hwy Admin, chief coun, 1980-81; St Fla, asst atty gen, 1982-85. **Orgs:** Chmn, Fla Comn Human Rels, 1975-77; chmn, Fla Manpower Serv Coun, 1975-80; bd dir, First Union Bank, 1990-; Fla Nat Am Bar Asn; Phi Alpha Delta, Omega Psi Phi, Fla Coun 100; life mem, Nat Asn Advan Colored People; bd mem, Am Mock Trial Asn; Bethel Baptist

Church; Fla Bar Asn. **Honors/Awds:** Most Outstanding Professor. **Home Addr:** 1600 Laguna Dr, Tallahassee, FL 32312, **Home Phone:** (850)385-8078. **Business Addr:** Professor, Lawyer, Administrator, Florida A&M University, Rm 112 Tucker Hall 1800 Wahnish Way, Tallahassee, FL 32307-5200, **Business Phone:** (850)412-7761.

## RAWLINGS-BLAKE, STEPHANIE

Lawyer, mayor. **Personal:** Born Mar 17, 1970, Baltimore, MD; daughter of Pete Rawlings and Nina; married Kent; children: Sophia. **Educ:** Oberlin Col, BA, polit sci, 1992; Univ Md Sch Law, JD, 1995. **Career:** Baltimore Off Pub Defender, atty, 1998-2006; City Baltimore, city coun, 1995-2007, city coun pres, 2007-10, 49th mayor, 2010-; Dem Nat Comt, secy, 2013-. **Orgs:** Bd trustees, pres, US Conf Mayors, 2015; Mayor's Water Coun; Criminal & Social Justice, Standing Comt; Alpha Kappa Alpha Sorority Inc; at-large mem, Alliance Black Women Attorneys; Epsilon Omega chapter; Links Inc; Baltimore Conv & Tourism Bd; Baltimore Mus Art; Nat Aquarium Baltimore; Baltimore Substance Abuse Systs Inc.; Living Classrooms Found; Waterfront Partnership Baltimore; & Parks & People Found. **Honors/Awds:** "The Daily Record," Maryland's Top 100 Women, 2007 and 2011; Shirley Chisholm Memorial Award Trailblazer, Nat Cong Black Women; National Association of Negro Business, Young Women on the Move; Professional Women's Clubs, Women on the Move; "The Root" Magazine, The Root 100 Honorees, 2013; First Citizen Award, Md State Senate. **Special Achievements:** Youngest person ever elected to Baltimore's City Council; second woman to serve as mayor of Baltimore. **Business Addr:** Mayor, City of Baltimore, Rm 250 City Hall, Baltimore, MD 21202, **Business Phone:** (410)396-3835.

## RAWLINS, DR. SEDRICK JOHN

Dentist. **Personal:** Born May 29, 1927, New York, NY; married Alyce Taliaferro; children: Wayne & Mark T. **Educ:** Lincoln Univ, AB, 1950; Meharry Med Col, DDS, 1954. **Career:** E Hartford Conn, pvt pract dentist, 1956-; Conn Savs & Loan, incorporator, 1969-70; Manchester Memorial Hosp, 1969-72; Univ Conn, asst clin prof. **Orgs:** Manchester Human Rels Comn, 1959-; Conn State Bd Parole, 1959-; pres, Nat Asn Advan Colored People, 1959-60; chmn, Conn State Bd, 1966-68; chmn, correction comt, 1967-69; sr vpres, Nat Dent Asn, 1968-70; Conn House Del, 1970; Conn Govt Planning Comt Criminal Admin; Am & Conn Dent Asn; Conn Coun Nat Paroling Authorities; Phi Beta Sigma; Bapt; High Noon Club. **Honors/Awds:** Service Award, Nat Asn Advan Colored People, 1960; Recipient Human Relation Award, 1970. **Home Addr:** 66 Waranoke Rd, Manchester, CT 06040-4527. **Business Addr:** Dentist, Private Practice, 183 Burnside Ave E, Hartford, CT 06103, **Business Phone:** (860)289-4141.

## RAWLINSON, DAVID L., II

Vice president (organization), lawyer, counselor. **Personal:** married Nadia Nicole Johnson. **Educ:** Citadel, BA, polit sci; Harvard Bus Sch, MBA, 2008; Univ SC, JD. **Career:** White House Conf Youth, Drugs & Violence, appointee, 1997; Locke Lord LLP, assoc atty, 2001-04; K&L Gates, assoc atty, 2004-06; White House Chief Staff, White House fel & spec asst, 2008-09; ITT Corp, dir of corp responsibility, gen coun & vpres, 2009-12; MonotaRO Co., Ltd, mem of the bd of dirs & chmn of the nominating comt, 2014-; Grainger, vpres, dep Gen coun & corp secy, 2012-. **Orgs:** Bd dir, Bryan's House; bd mem, YMCA Community Serv Dallas; bd mem, Young Orpheus Orchestra Leadership Coun NY; Econ Club Chicago. **Business Addr:** Vice President, Deputy General Counsel & Corporate Secretary, W.W. Grainger , Inc., 100 Grainger Pkwy, Lake Forest, IL 60045.

## RAWLS, DR. GEORGE H.

Surgeon. **Personal:** Born Jun 2, 1928, Gainesville, FL; son of Nicholas and Lona; married Lula M; children: Yvonne, Bettye Jo & Sherree. **Educ:** Fla A&M Univ, attended 1948; Howard Univ Sch Med, Md, 1952; Am Bd Surg, dipl, 1961. **Career:** Assistant dean (retired), educator; Va Hosp Dayton, surg res, 1955-59; OH State Univ, clin instr surgeon, 1957-59; pvt surg pract, 1959-93; Ind Sch Med, asst dean & clin prof surg, prof emer surg, clin prof emer surg. **Orgs:** Life mem bd, Nat Nat Asn Advan Colored People, 1961-91; fel Am Col Surgeons, 1963; guest examr, Am Bd Surg, 1977; pres, Ind State Med Asn, 1979; co-chmn & life mem, Nat Asn Advan Colored People; pres, Marion Co Med Soc; life mem, Alpha Phi Alpha Fraternity; bd dir, Urban League; C's Mus; bd dir, Flanner House; Sigma Pi Phi Fraternity; One Hundred Black Men; pres, Ind State Med Socs; pres, Indianapolis State Med Socs; Ind State Med Licensure; pres, Aesculapian Med Soc. **Honors/Awds:** Alpha Phi Alpha Man of the Year, Alpha Phi Alpha, Indianapolis, 1970; Citizen of the Year, Omega Psi Phi, 1971; Citizen of the Year, Federated Clubs, 1976; Sagamore of Wabash, Gov Or, 1988; Sagamore of Wabash, Governor Bayh, 1990; Scholarship Fund named in honor, Wishard Found, 2000. **Special Achievements:** Co-author: The History of the Black Physician in Indianapolis; The Surgeons Turn; Papa; I want to be a Surgeon; Managing Cancer, The African Americans Guide to Prevention, Diagnosis and Treatment; So you Want to be a Doctor. **Home Addr:** 4000 N Merridan St Condo 12D/E, Indianapolis, IN 46208-4023, **Home Phone:** (317)283-4065. **Business Addr:** Clinical Professor Emeritus of Surgery, Indiana University, 340 W 10th St Suite 6200, Indianapolis, IN 46202-3082, **Business Phone:** (317)278-3048.

## RAWLS, MARK ANTHONY

Insurance executive, printer, journalist. **Personal:** Born May 6, 1967, Brownsville, TN; son of Oliver Lee and Mary. **Educ:** Lane Col, Jackson, Tenn, BS, 1989. **Career:** Dayton-Hudson Inc, sls consult, 1989-90; Golden Circle Life Ins Co, asst vpres & dir ins serv, 1993-; Rawls Funeral Home, printer, 1995-. **Orgs:** Nat Ins Asn, undersec, 1995-; HCL Talk Show, co-host, 1997-; Nat Asn Advan Colored People, 1997-, vpres, Hagwood Co br, 2000-. **Honors/Awds:** Honor Award, Nat Asn Advan Colored People, 1998, 1999; Junior Achievement Certificate, 1999; United Way, 1998. **Special Achievements:** Lane College Poetry Magazine, 1988; Jerusalem Center for Biblical Studies, 1989; NAACP, publisher, 1997-; Brownsville-States Graphic Newspaper, 1997-; Nashville Pride, 2000; Metro Forum Newspaper, 2000. **Home Addr:** 902 N Grand Ave, Brownsville, TN 38012, **Home Phone:** (731)772-5154. **Business Addr:** Assistant Vice President, Director of Insurance Services, Golden Circle Life Insurance Co, 39 S Jackson Ave, Brownsville, TN 38012, **Business Phone:** (901)772-9932.

## RAWLS, RALEIGH RICHARD

Lawyer. **Personal:** Born Jun 12, 1925, Gainesville, FL; married Annie R Robinson; children: Regina D, Rene N, Renard A & Rodney P. **Educ:** Howard Univ, BA, 1950, JD, 1956. **Career:** Veterans Admin; Atty, pvt prac, 1957-; City Ft Lauderdale, pub defender, 1973-. **Orgs:** Braward Co Bar Asn; Nat Bar Asn; life mem, Alpha Phi Alpha; Nat Advan Asn Colored People; St John's United Methodist Church. **Home Addr:** 1241 NW 30 Terr, Ft. Lauderdale, FL 33311-5025, **Home Phone:** (954)583-7998. **Business Addr:** 1024 NW 6th St, Ft. Lauderdale, FL 33311-8006, **Business Phone:** (954)467-7908.

## RAY, DR. ANDREW A.

Educator. **Personal:** Born Feb 4, 1948, Centerville, MS; son of Perry and Ruby. **Educ:** Southern Univ, BS, econ, 1969; State Univ NY, MS, educ, 1970; Univ Buffalo, MS, admin, 1982, PhD, admin & policy, 1994. **Career:** Dept St, intern, 1968; US Cong, intern, 1974; Urban League, career educr, 1983; Adolescent Voc Explor Prog NY, dir; CSD, Rochester Childrens Zone, instr, dean, 1985-, admin, vprin, 1988-96, prin, 1997-2005, admin prin, 2005-; United States Congress, presidential fellow. **Orgs:** Chmn, Baden Fed Credit Union, 1978-; comt mem, YMCA, 1979-; first vice dist rep, Omega Psi Phi, 1984, dist rep, 1986; bd dir, Omega Scholar Found, 1991; founder, Black Educrs Asn; co-chair, Centennial Celebration Comt. **Home Addr:** , Rochester, NY. **Business Addr:** Administrative Principal, CSD Rochester Childrens Zone, 131 W Broad St, Rochester, NY 14614, **Business Phone:** (585)262-8456.

## RAY, FRANCIS

Nurse, writer. **Personal:** Born Jul 20, 1944, Richland, TX; daughter of McRadford Sr and Venora; married William H; children: Carolyn Michelle. **Educ:** Tex Woman's Univ, BS, nursing, 1967; Am Nursing Asn, Sch Nurse Practr, 1992. **Career:** Parkland Memorial Hosp, staff nurse, 1967-68; Chester Clin & Hosp, LVN Prog, teacher, 1968-71; Dallas City Health Dept, nursing supvr, 1971-82; Dallas Publ Schs, sch nurse pract, 1982; The Turning Point Legal Fund, owner, 2001-; Books: Dellas House of Style; Rosies Curl & Weave; Welcome to Leos; Going to the Chapel; I Know Who Holds Tomorrow, 2002; Someone To Love Me; Somebodys Knocking at My Door; A Whole Lotta Love; Rocking Around That Christmas Tree; Trouble Dont Last Always; How Sweet the Sound; Like the First Time, 2004; The Turning Point; Any Rich Man Will Do; Chocolate Kisses; You and No Other; Dreaming of You; Fallen Angel, 1992; Forever Yours, 1994; Spirit of the Season, anthology, 1994; Undeniable, 1995; The Bargain, translated Taiwan/Italian, 1995; Only Hers, 1996; Romantic Times Magazine, p 53, April, 1996; Incognito, 1997; Todays Black Woman, excerpt of Incognito, 1997; Silken Betrayal, 1997; Heart of the Falcon, 1998; Heart of the Falcon, 1998; Forever Yours, 1998; Living Large, 2003; Getting Merry: A Christmas Anthology, 2002; The Falcon Saga, 2004; First Touch, 2004; Love at Leo, 2004; In Another Mans Bed, 2007; Irresistible You, 2007; Only You, 2007; Not Even If You Begged, 2008; The Way You Love Me, 2008; Until There Was You, 2008; Nobody But You, 2009; And Mistress Makes Three, 2009; It Had To Be You, 2011; Only Hers, 2011; Heart Of The Falcon, 2011; Break Every Rule, 2011; Undeniable, 2011; Twice The Temptation, 2011; Trouble Dont Last Always, 2011; All Of My Love, 2013; After The Dawn, 2013; All That I Need, 2013; All That I Desire, 2013. **Orgs:** Romance Writers Am, 1984-; Women Writers Color, 1992-; Am Nurses Asn, 1992-. **Honors/Awds:** Yellow Rose Award, North Texas Romance Writers, for Service, 1990; Multicultural Career Achievement Award, Romantic Times Magazine, 1995-96; Outstanding Achievement, Dallas Pub Libr, Polk Wisdom Branch, 1996; Appreciation Award, Texas Black Women's Writers, 1996; Emma Award; The Golden Pen Award; The Atlantic Choice. **Special Achievements:** New York Times and USA Today bestselling Author. **Home Addr:** 5935 Fox Hill Lane, Dallas, TX 75232, **Home Phone:** (214)375-5418. **Business Addr:** Owner, The Turning Point Legal Fund, PO Box 764651, Dallas, TX 75376, **Business Phone:** (214)559-2170.

## RAY, JACQUELINE WALKER

Social worker, educator. **Personal:** Born May 14, 1944, Buffalo, NY; married Lacy Jr. **Educ:** State Univ NY, Buffalo, BA, 1965, MSW, 1967; NY Univ, PhD, 1975. **Career:** Columbia Univ Coler Proj, social worker, 1967-68; New York Housing Authority Model Cities Prog, field supvr, 1968-70; Jersey City State Col, asst prof psychol, 1970-71; urban educ res trainee, City Univ New York, 1982-83; fac fel, City Univ New York, 1989-90; City Univ New York, York Col, assoc prof psychol, Dept Psychol, chair, prof emer, behav sci, currently. **Orgs:** Fel City Univ New York, 1982-83; Am Psychol Assoc; Community Mediation Servs; Queens City Ment Health Soc; Alpha Kappa Alpha; League Women Voters Region II; Ment Health Consult; Job Corps. **Honors/Awds:** Ford Found Study Grant, 1980; CUNY DRC Award. **Special Achievements:** Articles: Journal Gen Educ, 1979, Journal Intergroup Tensions, 1983, Journal Col Stud Personnel. **Home Addr:** PO Box 22, Old Westbury, NY 11568. **Business Addr:** Professor Emeritus Of Behavioral Sciences, York College, 94 20 Guy R Brewer Blvd, Jamaica, NY 11451, **Business Phone:** (718)262-2682.

## RAY, JAMES R., III

Educator, lawyer, consultant. **Personal:** Born Feb 10, 1963, Brooklyn, NY. **Educ:** John Jay Col, BA, 1988; Long Island Univ, MBA, 1996; Univ NH Law Sch, JD. **Career:** BEST Adv Group, chief exec officer; prof; Da Bag Productions, founder, currently. **Orgs:** Am Trial Lawyers Asn; Am Bar Asn; Ny Bar Asn; New York County Lawyers Asn; chair small bus comt, Metrop Bar; Omega Psi Phi Fraternity, 1986-. **Honors/Awds:** Black Achievers in Industry Award, Harlem YMCA, 1991; National Sales Quality Award; Excellence in International Business, 1996. **Home Addr:** PO Box 400769, Brooklyn, NY 11240.

## RAY, JOHNNY (JOHN CORNELIUS RAY)

Baseball player. **Personal:** Born Mar 1, 1957, Chouteau, OK; son of Ray Charles and Dorothy; married Tammy McNack; children: Jasmine & Johnny Jr. **Educ:** Northeast Okla A&M Col, Miami, Okla; Univ Ark, Fayetteville, Ark. **Career:** Baseball player (retired); Pittsburgh Pirates, infielder, 1981-87; Calif Angels, infielder, 1987-90; Japan's Cent League, Yakult Swallows, 1991 & 1992. **Home Addr:** Rt 2, PO Box 545, Chouteau, OK 74337.

## RAY, DR. JUDITH DIANA

Educator, association executive, writer. **Personal:** Born Sep 14, 1946, St. Louis, MO; daughter of Arthur Charles Sr and Pauline (Malloyd) R. **Educ:** Harris Stowe Teachers Col, St Louis, MO, BEd, 1968; Wash Univ, St Louis, MO, MEd, 1972; Wash State Univ, Pullman, WA, MS, 1979; Univ Minn, PhD, 1996. **Career:** St Louis Bd Ed, teacher, 1968-72; Wash Univ, St Louis, Mo, grad teaching, res asst, 1970-79; ARC Milwaukee Pierre Marquette Div, nat field rep, 1972-73; City Univ New York York Col, Jamaica Queens, lectr, 1973-75; Wash State Univ, Sch Vet Med, equine researcher; W Chester Univ, asst prof kinesiology, 1977. **Orgs:** Vol teacher, ARC, 1960-80; Am Alliance Health PE & Rec & Dance, 1968-80; vol & mem, Am Soc Testing & Mat, 1978-89; Int & Am Soc Bio mech, 1978-89; Gamma Sigma Sigma, Nat Serv Sor, 1978-80; Phi Delta Kappa W Chester, 1978; Int Soc Bio mech Sport; Alpha Kappa Alpha; US Fencing Coaches Asn; US Tennis Asn; US Prof Tennis Asn; USPTR, Registry; fac adv, Phi Beta Sigma; Adv Coun mem, W Chester Area Sr Ctr; founding mem, Am Soc Bio Mech. **Special Achievements:** Co-author: EEG Analysis of Equine Joint Lameness, 1977; The Effects ofDifferent Ground Surfaces of Equine Joint, 1980; Motion As Analyzed byEEG, Journal of Biomechanics, vol 13, p 191-200, 1980; An Instrument Designed to Quantify Spinal Motion in Athletic Performance, Book of Abstracts Pre-Olympic Congress Intl Congress on Sport Science, Sports Medicine & Phys Educ, 2000-; Sport As a Medium for Upward Social Mobilityfor African Americans in the USA, German Olympic Institute Yearbook, 2001; Sport: An Oppressive or Liberating Force - A Feminist Perspective, International Council of Sports Science & Physical Education, 2002. **Home Addr:** 316 Sturzebecker Bldg, West Chester, PA 19380. **Business Addr:** Assistant Professor of Kinesiology, West Chester University, 206 Sturzebecker Health Sci Ctr, West Chester, PA 19383, **Business Phone:** (610)436-2260.

## RAY, MICHAEL

Vice president (organization). **Educ:** Towson State Univ, BA, bus admin & mgt, gen, 1986. **Career:** Legg Mason Trade Control, purchase & sales clerk, 1987-88; Legg MasonTrade Support, trader asst, 1988-89; Legg Mason, Capital Mgt, jr trader, 1989-90, head trader, 1990-96, vpres & head equity trader, 1996-2006, dir trading, 2006-13. **Orgs:** Bd mem & community trustee, Baltimore Educational Scholarship Trust. **Honors/Awds:** "Baltimore Business Journal," Power 20, 2011; "Black Enterprise," 75 Most Powerful Blacks on Wall Street, 2011.

## RAY, REV. PATRICIA ANN

Executive, association executive. **Personal:** Born Jan 30, 1950, Bremond, TX; daughter of Leon and Leola Jewel Moody; married Billy Clark; children: Selwin Carroll & Krissa Leola. **Educ:** Anchorage Community Col, AA, sociol, 1976; Univ AK, Anchorage, AK, BS, sociol, 1980; AK Bible Col, Bible cert, theol, 1993, AA, theol, 1996; Am Baptist Theol Sem, ThB, 1998. **Career:** Eaton County Libr, librn aide, 1969-70; Montgomery Wards, salesperson, 1970-71; Dr RH Lewis, chair side dent asst, 1969-70; Dr BobB Bliss, chair side dent asst, 1971-72; Chugach Elec Assoc Inc, serv rep, 1972; shiloh assoc minister, currently; 6th Ave Women's Jail, chaplain, 1996-; AK Regional Hosp, chaplain, 1997-; Eagle River Meadow Creek, chaplain, 1998-; Anchorage Police Dept, chaplain, 1998-. **Orgs:** Statistician, NW Regional Colored Womens Club, 1973; big sister, Big Bro Big Sister, 1980-82; pres, Tom Thumb Montosorn Parents Teachers asn, 1983; AK State Asn Colored Women'sClub, pres, 1986-91; pres, Mothers Christian Fel Club, 1987; Delta Sigma Theta Sorority, life mem, 1989-; youth coord, Nat Asn Colored Womens Club; Nat Asn Advan Colored People, life mem; bd dir, Janet Helen Tolan Gamble & Tony Gamble, Educ Trust Fund, 1998. **Honors/Awds:** AK Black Caucus, Recognition of Excellence, 1988; American Baptist Churches, scholarship, 1998-99; Business Professional Woman, 1997; NW Regional CWC, Outstanding Dedicated Service, 1987; AK State Asn CWC, Woman of the Year, 1986-89; Mother's Christian Fellowship CWC, Mother of the Year. **Home Addr:** 12561 Beachcomber Dr, Anchorage, AK 99515-3627, **Home Phone:** (907)345-8680. **Business Addr:** Shiloh Associate Minister, Shiloh Missionary Baptist Church, 855 E 20th Ave, Anchorage, AK 99518, **Business Phone:** (907)276-6673.

## RAY, ROSALIND ROSEMARY

Lawyer, executive. **Personal:** Born Jun 29, 1956, Washington, DC; daughter of Walter I Jr and Rosemary W. **Educ:** Georgetown Univ; Harvard Univ, attended 1976; Boston Univ, BA, 1978; Howard Univ, Sch Law, JD, 1990. **Career:** Law Offices Jack Olender & Howard Univ, Earl B Davis Trial Advocacy, 1988; DC Super Ct, law clerk, 1990-91; Law Off Indus J Daniel Jr, atty, 1991-; Law Off Leonard L Long Jr, atty, 1991-93; Entertainment Resources, asst gen coun, 1992; DC Housing, hearing officer, 1994-; Law Offices Rosalind R Ray PLLC, atty, currently. **Orgs:** Nat Bar Asn, asst ed, 1987-; Am Bar Asn, 1987-; Alpha Kappa Alpha Sorority, 1977-; Phi Delta Phi Legal Frat, 1987-; Howard Univ Law Alumni Asn, 1990-. **Honors/Awds:** Merit Scholarship for High Academic Achievement, Howard Univ, 1988-90. **Home Addr:** 1205 Morningside Dr, Silver Spring, MD 20904, **Home Phone:** (301)384-9155. **Business Addr:** Lawyer, Law Offices Rosalind R Ray PLLC, 6856 E Ave NW Suite 308, Washington, DC 20012-2112, **Business Phone:** (202)722-7282.

## RAY, WALTER I., JR.

Executive, writer, vice president (organization). **Personal:** Born Sep 2, 1923, Newburgh, NY; son of Walter I Sr and Mary Bingham R Robinson; married Rosemary White; children: Rosalind R & Walter I III. **Educ:** WVa State Col, attended 1943; Howard Univ, BS, 1949. **Career:** Anheuser Busch Inc, sales/sales supvr, 1958-70, br mgr, 1971-81; Game Prod Inc, vpres, 1982-83; Esoray Publ Co, Bus & Mkt, consult, 1983-85, pres, 1983-; John N Miller Assoc, assoc vpres, 1983-; Broadcast Music Inc, writer; DC Gov, consult; Books: De Colored Section, Esoray Publ Co, 2005; Ben's Chili Bowl. **Orgs:** Life mem, Nat Asn Advan Colored People; Masons Shriners Const; Omega Psi Phi; Nat Capital Parks, 1973; United Black Fund, 1979; Leadership mem, BSA, 1979. **Home Addr:** 9039 Sligo Creek Pkwy Apt 705, Silver Spring, MD 20901-3350, **Home Phone:** (301)588-7101. **Business**

Addr: President, Esoray Publishing Co, 1205 Morningside Dr, Silver Spring, MD 20904, **Business Phone:** (301)384-9155.

## RAY, PROF. WILLIAM BENJAMIN, SR.

Educator, opera singer, advocate. **Personal:** Born Jan 1, 1925?, Lexington, KY; son of Mason and Beatric Clifton Smith; married Carrie Walls Kellogg; children: Alexander Pierre & William Jr. **Educ:** Acad Music, Vienna, Austria; Ky State Col, attended 1947; Oberlin Col, BA, 1952; Western Res Univ, attended 1953; Univ Heidelberg, Ger, attended 1981; Boston Univ, MEd, 1982. **Career:** Educator (retired); De Paur's Inf Chorus, featured soloist, 1953-54; Karamu Theater, opera singer, 1954-56; Cleveland Playhouse, opera singer, 1954-56; Frankfurt Opera Frankfurt, Ger, opera singer, 1957; Decca, Intercord, Marcato, BBC, CBS, rec artist, 1960-78; John Hopkins Univ, Peabody Conserv Music, prof voice, 1982-92; Concert Tour Europ, concert/opera singer, 1983; Howard Univ, prof voice, head voice dept, 2000-02; Int Music Inst, Austria, voice fac. **Orgs:** Asst prin, Alpha Phi Alpha Fraternity, 1947-; founder/pres, Black Theater Prods, 1974-82; Nat Asn Negro Musicians; Gamma Boule Sigma Pi Phi Fraternity, 1993; bd mem, Annapolis Opera Inc; life mem, NCP. **Honors/Awds:** Recipient of Gold Medal, Lions Club Italy, 1978; inducted into Howard Univ, Pi Kappa Lamda Music Soc, 1993; Merit Award for Professional Achievement & Outstanding Service to students, Howard Univ; Lift Every Voice Legacy Award, Nat Opera Asn, 2007; Annie Award, Arts Coun Anne Arundel County, 2009. **Special Achievements:** Actor/singer appeared in 14 different roles in Germany and Austrian Filmand Television, in the German language; appointed as an exclusive American representative to select operatic talent for the Kaleidoscope Production Company, Munich, Germany; listed in Blacks in Opera by Eileen Southern, Berlin Opera Yearbook by Walter Felsenstein, Black Americans in Cleveland by Russell Davis. **Home Addr:** 539 Higgins Dr, Odenton, MD 21113-2001, **Home Phone:** (410)551-2869. **Business Addr:** Assistant Principal, Oxford Area School District, 125 Bell Tower Lane, Oxford, PA 19363, **Business Phone:** (610)932-6600.

## RAYBURN, DR. WENDELL GILBERT, SR.

School administrator. **Personal:** Born May 20, 1929, Detroit, MI; son of Charles Jefferson and Grace Victoria Winston; married Gloria Ann Myers; children: Rhonda Reneen & Wendell Gilbert. **Educ:** Eastern Mich Univ, BA, 1951; Univ Mich, MA, 1952; Wayne State Univ Detroit, EdD, 1972. **Career:** Detroit Pub Sch, teacher, admin, 1954-68; Univ Detroit, asst dir to dirspec proj, 1968-72, assoc dean acad support prog, 1972-74; Univ Louisville, dean, 1974-80; Savannah State Col, pres, 1980-88; Lincoln Univ, pres, 1988-90; Penson Assocs Inc, vpres, secy, treas, sr assoc, consult, sr assoc, currently. **Orgs:** Am Asn Higher Educ; Nat Asn Equal Opportunity Higher Educ; Kappa Alpha Psi; Sigma Pi Phi; dir, Jefferson City Area Chamber Com; Jefferson City Rotary Club; bd dir, Am Asn State Col & Univs; bd trustee, Stephens Col; bd dir, Capital Region Med Ctr; bd dir, United Way; exec bd, Boy Scouts Am, Great Rivers Coun; dir, Mo Capital Punishment Resource Ctr; bd, Int Food & Agr Develop, 1988-; mem, Univ Detroit. **Home Addr:** 601 Jackson St, Jefferson City, MO 65101, **Home Phone:** (314)635-9727. **Business Addr:** Senior Associate, Penson Associates Inc, 110 S Marion Suite 402, Oak Park, IL 20815, **Business Phone:** (708)267-4224.

**RAYE, JOHN. See SMITH, DR. JOHN RAYE.**

## RAYE, VANCE WALLACE

Lawyer, state government official, judge. **Personal:** Born Sep 6, 1946, Hugo, OK; son of Edgar Allen and Lexie Marie; married Sandra Kay Wilson; children: Vanessa. **Educ:** Univ Okla, BA, polit sci & econs, 1967, JD, 1970. **Career:** Bulla & Horning, atty, 1970-72; USF, asst staff judge advocate, Beale AFB chief mil justice, chief civil law, judge advocate, 1972-74; Calif Atty Gens Off, civil div, from dep atty gen to sr asst atty gen, 1974-82, dep legis secy, 1982-83; Gov Cali, legal affairs secy, adv, legal coun, 1983-89; Sacramento County Super Ct, judge, 1989-91; Calif Ct Appeal, Third Dist, assoc justice, 1991-10, presiding justice, 2010-; Lincoln Law Sch, instr; Calif Pub Contract Law, contribr. **Orgs:** State Bar Calif, 1972-89; Calif Asn Black Lawyers; Nat Asn Advan Colored People; Urban League; chmn, Staff Adv Coun Nat Gov Asn Comn Criminal Justice & Pub Safety; vice chair, Gov Emergency Opers Exec Coun; peer reviewer, Nat Inst Justice; Sacramento Health Decisions; 100 Black Men Sacramento; Nat Bar Asn; Wiley Manuel Bar Asn; Calif Judges Asn; chmn, Judicial Coun Comt Family Law; criminal justice stand comn, Am Bar Asn; Calif Comn Future Courts; chair, Family Rels Comn; chair legis subcomt, Judicial Coun Appellate Stand Comt; Calif Comn Status African Am Male; Davis Med Sch Leadership Coun, Univ Calif; Calif Coun Judicial Performance. **Home Addr:** 3005 Nikol St, Sacramento, CA 95826, **Home Phone:** (916)362-7773. **Business Addr:** Presiding Justice, California Court of Appeal, 10th Fl 621 Capitol Mall, Sacramento, CA 95814-4869, **Business Phone:** (916)654-0209.

## RAYFIELD, DENISE E.

Executive, labor relations manager. **Personal:** Born Jan 13, 1955, New York, NY; daughter of Thomas and Laura Chandler. **Educ:** Temple Univ, BA, 1976; Fordham Univ, MBA, 1981. **Career:** WR Grace & Co, benefits admin asst, 1977-81; Ziff-Davis Publ Co, benefits mgr, 1981-83; Hearst Corp, asst mgr, employee benefits, 1983-90, mgr, employee benefits, 1990-94, sr mgr, employee benefits, 1994-, dep dir. **Home Addr:** 6535 Kendale Ct, Charlotte, NC 28270-1737. **Business Addr:** Deputy Director, Senior Manager, The Hearst Corp, 227 W Trade St, Charlotte, NC 28202, **Business Phone:** (704)348-8000.

## RAYFORD, BRENDA L.

Administrator, social worker, association executive. **Personal:** Born Apr 3, 1940, Dayton, OH; married Kent A; children: Blake Nyette & Valdez Kamau. **Educ:** Cent State Univ, BA, sociol, 1962; Wayne State Univ, MSW, 1971. **Career:** Comp Health Serv, soc worker, 1969; Highland Pk Pub Sch Spl Proj, soc work supr, 1967-69; Travelers Aid Soc, soc worker, 1966-67; Montgomery Co Wlf Dept, soc worker-intake, 1962-66; Detroit Black United Fund Inc, vice chair, 2005-06; Black United Fund Inc, exec dir. **Orgs:** Consult Creative Strategies Inc; vice chmn, Nat Black United Fund Inc, 2005-07, treas, currently; field work supr Wayne St Univ Sch Soc Work; chmn, Fund Raising Comn Bus & Prof Wmn Inc New Metro Chap; adv comn, Detroit Pub Sch. **Honors/Awds:** Community Service Award, World Islam W Community, 1978; Who's Who in Black America; WSU Citizen of the Year; The Spirit of Detroit Award. **Special Achievements:** Co-author, The Guy Who Controls Your Future, 1970. **Home Addr:** 16535 Marlowe, Detroit, MI 48235, **Home Phone:** (313)836-0526. **Business Addr:** Treasurer, National Black United Fund, 40 Clinton St, Newark, NJ 07102, **Business Phone:** (973)643-5122.

## RAYFORD, FLOYD KINNARD

Baseball player. **Personal:** Born Jul 27, 1957, Memphis, TN; married Mary Luvenia Hawkins. **Career:** Baseball player (retired), coach; Baltimore Orioles, infielder, 1980 & 1982, 1984-87; St Louis Cardinals, infielder, 1983; Triple-A Scranton/Wilkes-Barre Red Barons, 1989-91; New Brit Rock Cats, coach, 2005-. **Business Addr:** Coach, New Britain Rock Cats, New Brit Stadium, New Britain, CT 06051, **Business Phone:** (860)224-8383.

## RAYFORD, LEE EDWARD

Government official, educator, association executive. **Personal:** Born Nov 17, 1935, Fordyce, AR; married Billie Knight; married La Neal Lucas; children: Vickie & Celese. **Educ:** Agr Mech & Norm Col, Pine Bluff, AR, BS, 1961; Univ Ar, MS, 1963; E Tex State Univ, EdD, 1979. **Career:** Clark County Sch Dist, adult educ teacher, 1969-74, res teacher, 1973, asst prin; CCSA Las Vegas, site admin, 1970-72; Econ Opportunity Bd, Las Vegas, ESAA prog dir, 1974; State Nev Equal Rights Comn, Las Vegas, exec dir, 1979-80; Redeemer Lutheran Elem Sch, prin, 1998-, advisor. **Orgs:** Bd dir, Westside Community Develop; treas bd dir, OIC/A; Nat Asn Advan Colored People, Las Vegas; SW Equal Employ Opportunity Officers; IntAsn Human Rights Agency; Personnel Adv Comn State Nev; Kappa Alpha Psi, Las Vegas; Phi Delta Kappa, Las Vegas; Kappa Delta Psi, Las Vegas; Clark County Asn Sch Adminr; bd dir, Sheppard Hills Develop. **Honors/Awds:** Publ "Criteria for the Selection of Pub Elementary Sch Principal of the State NV", 1979. **Home Addr:** 7096 Spring Beauty Ave, Las Vegas, NV 89131-0136, **Home Phone:** (702)645-1105. **Business Addr:** Principal, 1730 N Pecos, Las Vegas, NV 89115.

**RAYMOND, MICHAEL. See KELLY, MIKE.**

**RAYMOND, USHER TERRY, IV. See USHER.**

**RAYMOND, VAL. See WHITING, VAL.**

## RAYNOR, ROBERT G., JR.

Lawyer, government official. **Personal:** Born Jul 18, 1954, New Bern, NC; son of Robert G Sr and Cora P. **Educ:** NC Cent Univ, BA, 1977, Sch Law, JD, 1981. **Career:** Harmon & Raynor, Atty Law, lawyer, 1984-87; pvt pract lawyer, 1987-; Mayor Pro-Tem, City New Bern, NC, 1987-89, 2004; City New Bern, NC, Second Ward, 1989-2001, currently, First ward, bd alderman. **Orgs:** Kappa Alpha Psi Fraternity Inc, 1973-; bd dir, Big Bros-Big Sisters Lower Neuse, 1984-86; NC Asn Black Lawyers, 1984-; Nat Asn Advan Colored People, 1985-; Craven County Voters League, 1985-; secy, Neuse River Develop Authority Inc, 1986-; NC Asn Black Elected Munic Officials, 1986-; trustee, New Bern-Craven County Libr, 1987-; Nat Black Caucus Local Elected Officials, 1988-, parliamentarian, 1999-2001; bd dir, Wachovia Bank NC; adv bd, Neuse River Community Penalties; New Bern Craven County Libr Found; N Carolina Acad Trial Lawyers; NC State Bar; bd dir, New Bern Chamber Com; life long mem, St Pauls Cath Church. **Home Addr:** 1511 Spencer Ave, New Bern, NC 28560-5417, **Home Phone:** (252)637-5276. **Business Addr:** Alderman, City of New Bern, 950 Hwy 55 W, New Bern, NC 28563, **Business Phone:** (252)514-6387.

## READY, STEPHANIE

Television broadcaster, basketball coach. **Personal:** Born Jan 1, 1972?, Takoma Park, MD; married Perry. **Educ:** Coppin State Univ, BS, psychol, 1998. **Career:** Coppin State Univ, women's volleyball coach, 1998-2000, men's basketball asst coach, 2000-01; Greenville Groove, asst coach, 2001-03; Wash Mystics, asst coach; ESPN, reporter, 2006; ABC, reporter, 2006; Charlotte Bobcats, Nat Basketball Asn, tv sideline reporter, currently. **Business Addr:** Television Sideline Reporter, Charlotte Bobcats, 333 E Trade St, Charlotte, NC 28202, **Business Phone:** (704)688-8600.

## REAGON, DR. BERNICE JOHNSON

Composer, museum curator, singer. **Personal:** Born Oct 4, 1942, Dougherty, GA; daughter of Jesse Sr and Beatrice; married Cordell Hull; children: Toshi & Kwan Tuana; married Cordell Reagon; children: Toshi & Kwan. **Educ:** Albany State Col, Albany, Ga, BA, 1962; Spelman Col, Atlanta, Ga, BA, hist, 1970; Howard Univ, Wash, DC, PhD, USA hist, 1975. **Career:** Singer, composer, music producer, educator, curator; Albany Movement, mem exec comt, 1961-62; Student Non Violent Coord Comt Freedom Singers, field secy & mem, 1962-63; singer, composer & music producer, 1961-; pub lectr/songtalker, 1962-; Harambee Singers, Atlanta, Ga, founder, 1968, dir, 1968-70; DC Black Repertory Theater, Wash, DC, vocal dir, 1972-77; Ithaca Col, vis lectr African-Am music, 1972; Howard Univ Sch Music, teaching fel, 1973-74; Sweet Honey in the Rock, Wash, DC, founder & artistic dir, 1973-2004; Smithsonian Inst, Wash, DC, folklorist, 1974-76; Skidmore Col, vis scholar African-Am cult hist, 1976; Univ Calif, vis fel African-Am cult, 1977; Smithsonian Inst Mus Am Hist, dir & cult historian program Black Am cult, 1976-88, cur, 1988-93, cur emer, 1993-; Portland State Univ, vis fel women's studies prog, 1980; Am Univ, Wash, DC, distinguished prof hist, 1993-2002, prof emer, 2002-; Spelman Col, Atlanta Ga, William & Camille Cosby Endowed prof fine arts, 2002-04; Sound recordings: We Shall Overcome, 1963; Songs of the South, 1964; Give Your Hands to Struggle, producer & performer, 1975; Sweet Honey In The Rock, 1977; B?lieve I?ll Run On, See What The End?s Gonna Be, 1978; For Somebody to Start Singing, music composer & performer, 1979; Good News, 1981; We All. Everyone of Us, exec producer & performer, 1983; The Other Side & Feel Something Drawing Me On, producer & performer, 1985; River of Life, producer & performer, 1987; Live At Carnegie Hall, co-producer, 1987; All For Freedom, co-producer & performer, 1989; In This Land, co-producer, 1992; Still On The Journey, co-producer, 1993; I Got Shoes, exec producer & performer, 1994; Sacred Ground, co-producer, 1995; Wade in the Water: African American Sacred Music Traditions, producer, compiler & author, 1996; Selections, 1976-88, producer, compiler & performer, 1997; Africans in America, producer, composer & performer, 1998; Still the Same Me, producer & performer, 2001; Alive In Australia, co-producer, 2002; Rutha Harris: I am On the Battlefied, producer, 2004; Temptations of St Anthony, exec producer, composer & librettist, 2006; Books: The African Diaspora: World Family of Black Culture, 1980; Compositions One: The Original Compositions of Bernice Johnson Reagon, 1986; Black American Culture & Scholarship, Contemporary Issues, 1986; We Who Believe in Freedom: Sweet Honey in the Rock Still on the Journey, ed & contrib, 1993; We'll Understand It Better By & By Pioneering African American Gospel Composers, ed & contrib, 1993. **Honors/Awds:** The Martin Luther King Jr Center for Nonviolent Social Change Trumpet of Conscience Award, 1986; Charles E Frankel Prize, 1995; George F. Peabody Award, 1995, 1999; Isadora Duncan Dance Award, 1996; Leeway Laurel Award, 2000; Heinz Foundation Award, 2003; Hon doctorates: Bates Col, 1991; Old Dominion Univ, 1991; Princeton Univ, 1992; Swarthmore Col, 1993; Williams Col, 1995, Spelman Col, 1997; Boston Col, 1997; St Mary's Col, 2000; Univ Mich, Ann Arbor, 2000; Wesleyan Univ, 2001; Haverford Col, 2001; Colby Col, 2004; Rockford Col, 2005; Gallaudet Univ, 2006, Berklee Col Music, 2009. **Special Achievements:** Her "Temptation" completed a run at the Paris Opera House de Garnier (the first African American cast to play in the house since the 19th century). **Home Addr:** 1315 Kennedy St NW, Washington, DC 20011. **Business Addr:** Professor Emerita of History, American University, 4400 Massachusetts Ave NW, Washington, DC 20016-8033, **Business Phone:** (202)885-2700.

## REARDEN, SARA B.

Lawyer. **Personal:** Born Edgefield, SC; daughter of Oacy and Mamie Lewis; married Nigel Lauriston; children: Kai Nicole. **Educ:** Howard Law Sch, JD, 1969; NC Agr & Tech State Univ, BS, bus admin with hons. **Career:** Fel NLS, prog staff, 1969-71; Reginald H Smith Comn Law Fel Prog; Neighborhood Legal Serv, managing Comt, atty, 1971-73; Equal Employement Opportunity Comn, atty adv, 1973-74; Equal Employement Opport Comt, supr atty, 1974-79; George Washington Law Ctr, part-time asst prof, 1978-82; US Merit Systs Protection Bd, sr appellate atty, 1979-; Equal Employ Div, act assoc gen coun, actg dir, currently. **Orgs:** Howard Law Jour, 1968-69; Admin Bars Supreme Ct SC, 1971, DC, 1973; USDist Ct DC, 1973, US Ct Appeals DC, 1973; secy, Bd Wash DC, NeighborhoodLegal Serv, 1980-; co-chmn bd dir, Neighborhood Legal Serv Prog, Wash DC; Am Bar Asn; Nat Conf Black Lawyers; Nat Asn Black Women Attys; vpres, Howard Law Alumni Asn; Nat Couns Negro Women; pres, first & second yr lawclass; Coun Legal Educ Opportunity, 1990; Bar US Supreme Ct, 1983; US CtAppeals Fed Circuit; bd dir, Fed Circuit Bar Asn. **Honors/Awds:** Winner Constance Baker Motley Scholar, 1968; MSPB Merit Awards, 1986-91; Chairmans Award for Extraordinary Performance, 1992; MSPB, Chairmans Award for Legal Excellence, 1999. **Home Addr:** 15308 Lions Den Rd, Burtonsville, MD 20866. **Business Addr:** Lawyer, Acting Director Equal Employment Division, US Merit Systems Protection Board, Rm 818 1120 Vt Ave NW, Washington, DC 20419, **Business Phone:** (202)653-7171.

## REASON, J. PAUL

President (organization), executive, naval officer. **Personal:** Born Mar 22, 1941, Washington, DC; son of Joseph and Bernice; married Dianne Lillian Fowler; children: Rebecca L & Joseph P Jr. **Educ:** US Naval Acad, Annapolis, attended 1965; US Naval Post Grad Sch, attended 1970. **Career:** Exec, Naval officer (retired); USN, USS J D Blackwood, 1967; USS Truxtun, 1968-70; USS Enterprise, 1971-75; USS Truxtun, Bur Naval Personnel, assignment officer, naval aide to Pres US, 1976-79; USS Miss, exec officer, 1979-81; USS Coontz, USS Bainbridge, comndg officer; Naval Base Seattle, comdr, 1986-88; Cruiser-Destroyer Group One, comdr, 1988-91; US Atlantic Fleet, Naval Surface Force, comdr, 1991-94, comdr chief, 1996-99; Syntek Technol Inc, vpres ship systs, 1999-2000; US Defense Dept, Dep Chief Naval Opers, 1994-96; Metro Mach Corp, Ship Repair Yards, Norfolk, Va, pres, coo, 2000-05, vice chmn & dir, 2005-06; Norfolk Southern Corp dir; Todd Shipyards Corp, dir. **Orgs:** Bd mem, AMGN Inc; bd mem, Amgen, 2001-; bd mem, Norfolk Southern, 2002-; bd mem, Wal-Mart, 2001-06; bd, Metro Machine Corp, 2005-. **Business Addr:** Board of Director, Amgen Inc, 1 Amgen Ctr Dr, Thousand Oaks, CA 91320-1799, **Business Phone:** (805)447-1000.

## REASON, REBECCA R.

Vice president (organization). **Career:** Worldspace Found Inc, mgr; Worldspace Inc, vpres human resources. **Business Addr:** Vice President of Human Resources, Worldspace Inc, 2400 N St NW, Washington, DC 20037, **Business Phone:** (202)969-6000.

## REAVES, REV. DR. BENJAMIN FRANKLIN

Vice president (organization), minister (clergy), executive director. **Personal:** Born Nov 22, 1932, New York, NY; son of Ernest McKinley and Lella Brinson; married Jean Manual; children: Terrilyn Jackson, Pamela & Benjamin. **Educ:** Oakwood Col, Huntsville, AL, BA, 1955; Andrews Univ, MA, MDiv; Chicago Theol Sem. **Career:** Mich Conf Seventh-Day Adventist, pastor, 1956-68, minister, Ctr Global Leadership, dir, secy; Westside Hosp, counr, 1968-72; Andrews Univ, youth pastor, 1972-73, assoc prof, 1973-77; AUS, instr homeletics, 1977-85; Oakwood Col, pres, 1985-96; Adventist Health Syst, vpres mission & ministries, currently. **Orgs:** Vision, 2000; adv bd, Andrews Univ; adv bd, Loma Linda Univ; United Negro Col Fund; Nat Asn Equal Opportunity Higher Educ; Coun Advan Pvt Cols; Huntsville Chamber Com Bd; Rotary Club; Urban Ministries Prog; bd dir, United Negro Col Fund; Chicago Sunday Eve Club. **Honors/Awds:** Distinguished Alumnus Award, Oakwood Col, 1973; Teacher of the Year, Oakwood Col, 1983; Music Humanitarian Award, Oakwood Col, 1984; Outstanding Leadership Award, Oakwood Col, 1986; The Medallion of Distinction. **Special Achievements:** Author of articles in numerous journals such as: Message, Review & Herald, Ministry, Adventist Laymen, Colgiate Quarterly, South African Signs Times. **Business Addr:** Vice President of Mission and Ministries, Adventist Health System, 111 N Orlando Ave, Winter Park, FL 32789, **Business Phone:** (407)647-4400.

### REAVES, DARRYL
Accountant. **Home Addr:** 3315 NW 49th, Miami, FL 33142, **Home Phone:** (305)635-9018.

### REAVES, E. FREDERICKA M
Educator, association executive. **Personal:** Born Nov 7, 1938, Washington, DC; married Robert Reeves IV; children: Reginald & Ricardo. **Educ:** Morgan St Univ, BS, 1960. **Career:** Jr High Sch, math teacher, 1961; Guam Pub Schs, math teacher, 1964; SanDiego City Sch, math teacher, 1966; Alameda Unified Sch, math teacher, 1967-83; Oakland Unified Sch Dist, 1984-86. **Orgs:** Nat Ed Asn, 1967-; secy, Alameda Nat Asn Advan Colored People, 1967-; bd mem, Alamedans HOPE, 1967-70; adv, Youth Nat Asn Advan Colored People, 1968-75; bd mem, Am Red Cross, 1970; chair, Multicult Inst Impl Article 3.3 Calif Ed Code Training Group, 1970-74; Nat Coun Teacher Math, 1970-82; Phi Delta Kapna, 1973-. **Honors/Awds:** PTA Scholar, Fairmont Heights High, 1956; Merit Scholar, Morgan St Univ, 1957. **Home Addr:** 762 Santa Clara Ave, Alameda, CA 94501, **Home Phone:** (510)865-0839. **Business Addr:** Insurance Adjuster, US Perishables, 7700 Edgewater Dr, Oakland, CA 94621, **Business Phone:** (866)294-1189.

### REAVES, REV. FRANKLIN CARLWELL
Clergy, social worker, association executive. **Personal:** Born Aug 7, 1942, Mullins, SC; son of Fred and Vestena; married Algenia; children: Ron, Randy, Dexter & Brandon; married Willie Dean White; children: Kathy Juanita, Jacquelyn C, Frankie Diana & Anthony. **Educ:** Fayetteville State Univ, BS, 1968; NC Agr & Tech State Univ, MS, hist, 1974, MS, admin & supv, 1982; LaSalle Ext Univ, LLB, 1978; Univ Santa Barbara, PhD; Lutheran Theol Sem. **Career:** Columbus Co Bd Educ, teacher, 1968-; Oper HELP, pres & founder, 1968-; African Methodist Episcopal Church, pastor, currently. **Orgs:** Pres, Marion Co Chap Nat Asn Advan Colored People, 1973-76; Am Friends Serv Comn, 1978-84; pres, SC Affil ACLU, 1979-82; Nat Bd Dirs Am Civil Liberties Union, 1982-; pres, Black Educr Leadership Coun, 1984; pres, Columbus Co Unit NC Asn Educr; pres, NC Region V Leadership Prevocational Planning Coun; Southern Regional Coun; founder, Rev Dr & Mrs Franklin C & Algenia Reaves Found Legal Ministry; Maj & Ruth Davis Humanitarian Found; founder & pres, Oper Help Econ Linkage Poor; SC Affil Southern Christian Leadership Conf; Nat Platform Asn. **Honors/Awds:** Honorary Doctorate Humanity, Allen Univ, 1984. **Special Achievements:** Book: "An Analysis of Legislative Segregation in Black & White Schools, Public & Private, During the Periods of 1948-54 & 1985-1990", 2007. **Home Addr:** 906 N Smith St, Mullins, SC 29574-1722, **Home Phone:** (843)464-6286. **Business Addr:** President, Operation HELP, PO Box 534, Mullins, ND 29574-0534.

### REAVES, GINEVERA N.
Educator, teacher. **Personal:** Born Jan 21, 1925, Greenwood, MS; married Henry Eugene Sr; children: Henry Eugene Jr & Naomi Normene (deceased). **Educ:** Rust Col, BA, 1951; Univ Chicago, MA, 1954; Univ Tenn; Va State Col; Tex State Col; Tenn State Univ; Southern Univ New Orleans; Ball State Inst. **Career:** Miss Pub Sch, teacher, 1942-64; Rust Col, asst prof, 1964, dir teacher educ. **Orgs:** Chair person, First Cong Dist Dem Party MS, 1972; alt del, Dem Nat Mid-Term Conf, 1974; st exec bd, Dem Party MS; MS Affirmative Action Com, 1975; Phi Delta Kappa; Am Asn Univ Wy; Miss Teacher Asn; Historian Phi Delta Kappa, 1976-77; US Comn Civil Rghts, 1976-77; vpres, Miss Asn Higher Educ; Delta Sigma Theta Sor; Benton Co; Nat Asn Advan Colored People. **Honors/Awds:** Runner-up Teacher of the Year, Rust Col, 1966; Sargent Shriver Award, alleviating poverty in rural Am, 1966; Miss Finer Wmnhd Award, Zeta Phi Beta, 1968; Teacher of the Year, Rust Col, Zeta Phi Beta, 1972; ginevera Reaves Day, Benton Co Nat Asn Advan Colored People, 1975. **Home Addr:** RR 2, PO Box 126, Holly Springs, MS 38635.

### REAVIS, JOHN WILLIAM
Educator, association executive, teacher. **Personal:** Born Oct 30, 1935, Nyack, NY; son of John and Frances; married Doris S Bailey; children: Dawn, John III & Timothy; married Catherine Smith. **Educ:** Fayetteville State NC Univ, BS, 1959; NY Univ, MA, 1965; Univ Rochester, NDEA, inst guid, 1965; State Univ NY, Albany, higher educ. **Career:** Continental Can Co, mach tender, packer, 1953-55, part-time, 1956-59; Grand St Sch, teacher, 1959-61, asst prin, 1967-68; Elem Eng Negro Hist, adult educ teacher, 1961-62; Montgomery St Sch, elem guid counr, 1962-67, prin, 1968-69; Cent Admin State Univ NY, coordr spec progs, 1969-72, asst dean, 1972-80; EDPA Grant Garnett Patterson Jr High Sch, consult, 1972-73; State Univ NY, Farmingdale, Educ Opportunity Ctr, asst pres affirmative action, 1980-81, dean, 1981-86, prof, 1986-90; Minority Youth Groups Sports, consult; Col Dormitory, asst; Port Chester Carver Ctr, Port Chester, NY, exec dir; sports statistician; newspaper pub rels writer; athletic teams, mgr. **Orgs:** Nat Asn Supv & Curric Develop, 1969-; pres bd, dir, Schenectady Carver Community Ctr, 1973-78; adv coun Suffolk Co, BOCES Dist III, 1978-89; Grumman Ski Club, 1980-; vice chmn, Suffolk County Human Rights Comn, 1981-89; educ comn, life mem, Nat Asn Advan Colored People, 1981-; chmn draft bd, US Selective Serv Suffolk Co, 1983-89; eastern regional racing coordr, Nat Brotherhood Skiers, 1994-98, nat youth racing dir, 1996-98; pres, Metrop New York Ski Coun Inc; life mem, Omega Psi Phi Fraternity Inc; Phi Delta Kappa; Nat Alliance Black Sch Educ; comt mem, Nat Legis Comn; NY State Teachers Asn; NY State Guid Asn; Fayetteville St Col Alumni Asn; New York Univ Alumni Asn; life mem, PTA; pres, Grand-Montgomery St Schs; pres, Port Chester Town Rye Coun COT Serv; Port Chester Midget Football League; St Francis' AME Zion Church, Stewart; steering comn, Campaign Kids Estchester Co; bd dir, Sno-Burners Ski & Sports Asn, adult tracing comt chairperson, currently. **Honors/Awds:** Notable American, 1976-77; Omega Man of the Year, 1977-78; Dedicated Service, State Univ NY Col, Farmingdale, 1986; Presidential Citation to Distinguished Alumni NAFEO, 1987. **Home Addr:** 325 King St, Port Chester, NY 10573, **Home Phone:** (914)937-6613. **Business Addr:** Adult Racing Committee Chairperson, Board of Director, Sno-Burners Ski & Sports Association Inc, State Off Bldg 263 W 125 St, New York, NY 10027, **Business Phone:** (914)937-6613.

### RECASNER, ELDRIDGE DAVID
Basketball player, executive. **Personal:** Born Dec 14, 1967, New Orleans, LA; son of Joyce; married Karen R; children: Sydney, Erin, Lauren & Eldridge III. **Educ:** Univ Wash, BA, archit, 1990. **Career:** Basketball player (retired), coach, executive; TTL Bamberg, 1990-91; Louisville Shooters, Continental Basketball Asn, guard, 1991-92; Yakima Sun Kings, Continental Basketball Asn, 1992-93; Galatasaray, 1993-94; Denver Nuggets, shooting guard, 1994-95; Houston Rockets, shooting guard, 1995-96; Atlanta Hawks, shooting guard, 1996-98; Charlotte Hornets, pt guard, 1999-2001, shooting guard, 2001-02; Los Angeles Clippers, pt guard, 2001-02; Bellevue Blackhawks, asst coach, 2004; real estate bus, currently. **Orgs:** Nat Basketball Retired Players Asn. **Honors/Awds:** All-Pac-10, 1990; Most Valuable Person, Continental Basketball Asn, 1995; CBA, All-League First Team, 1995. **Home Addr:** 6159 164th Ave SE, Bellevue, WA 98006-5613.

### REDD, ORIAL ANNE
Government official, journalist. **Personal:** Born Apr 19, 1924, Rye, NY; daughter of William A and Ethel Griffin; married M Paul Sr; children: Paula Zeman & M Paul Jr. **Educ:** Bennett Col, BA, 1946. **Career:** Urban League Westchester, housing specialist, 1970-72, prog dir, 1972-74; Co Human Servs Dept, asst to county, exec Human Servs, 1974-83, Rec & Arch, dep co clerk, 1983-91; Westchester Co Press, vpres, pres & exec ed, 1986-. **Orgs:** Black Dem Westchester; Zeta Phi Beta; Nat Asn Advan Colored People; bd adv, Equal Justice Am, currently. **Honors/Awds:** Hon DHL, Mercy Col; Community Service Award, NY State Black & Puerto Rican Caucus; Government Achievement Award, Nat Asn Minority Bankers; Community Service Award, NY State Conference, Nat Asn Advan Colored People Brs; Government Achievement Award, Westchester Co Bd Legislators; Community Service Award, United Hosp Med Ctr; Woman of the Year, Daughters Isis; Ernest G Lindsay Award, Black Dem Westchester; Community Service Award, Westchester Community Opportunity Prog; Community Service Award, Oper PUSH Westchester. **Home Addr:** 100 Nyack Pl, Nyack, NY 10960, **Home Phone:** (845)353-1197. **Business Addr:** Board of Advisor, Equal Justice America, Bldg II 13540 E Boundary Rd Suite 204, Midlothian, VA 23112, **Business Phone:** (804)744-4200.

### REDD, WILLIAM L.
Lawyer, educator. **Personal:** Born Sep 3, 1950, Wilcoe, WV; married Marie E; children: Le Marquis & D'Ann. **Educ:** Marshall Univ, BA, 1972; NC Cent Univ Law Sch, JD, 1976. **Career:** Marshall Univ, instr, 1976, prof legal asst technol, currently; Henderson & Redd, atty, 1976-82; Law Off, pvt atty, 1982-. **Orgs:** Grad Chap Omega Psi, 1971; WVa State Bar, 1976-; legal redress officer, Huntington Br, Nat Asn Advan Colored People, 1976-; Legal Redress Comt WVa Conf, 1976-; pres, Black Alumni Inc, 1978-81; pres, Mountain State Bar Asn, 1980-82; pres Cabell Co Dep Sheriff's Civil Serv Comt, 1981-; secy, Cabell Co Comn Crime & Delinq, 1982-83; chmn bd dir, Green Acres Found, 1982-84; Marshall Univ Orial Tournament Comt, 1984; vpres, Green Acres Ment Retardation Ctr, 1981-; trustee, First Baptist Church Huntington, 1981-; chmn, Scottie Reese Scholar Bd First Baptist Church, 1982-; Big Green Scholar Fund Marshall Univ, 1982-; adv coun, Lic Practical Nurses Cabell Co, 1982-; chmn, Minority Recruitment Comt Fac & Staff Marshall, Nat Asn Advan Colored People, 1984-; panelist, Nat Bar Asn. **Home Addr:** 530 5th Ave, Huntington, WV 25701-1908, **Home Phone:** (304)529-3222. **Business Addr:** Professor of Legal Assisting Technology, Marshall University, 324 Corbly Hall, Huntington, WV 25755-2725, **Business Phone:** (304)696-3009.

### REDDICK, ALZO JACKSON, SR.
Government official, educator. **Personal:** Born Nov 15, 1937, Alturas, FL; married Elouise Williams; children: Nesper, Tausha, Alzo J Jr & Jason. **Educ:** Paul Quinn Col, BS, 1960; Fla A&M Univ, ME, 1971; Nova Univ, EdD, 1977. **Career:** High Sch, teacher; Valencia Comn, asst vpres planning; Rollins Col, asst dean, 1970-; State Fla, 39 dist, state rep, 1982; Univ Cent Fla, Orlando, Fla, Soldiers To Scholars, dir spec prog, dir defense transition servs, currently. **Orgs:** Pres elect, SABAP; chmn, Fla Caucus Black Dems; consult, Fla Drug Abuse Trust; adv, Criminal Justice Task Force; bd dir, Youth Prog Inc; bd dir, Addn Orange Co Inc; bd dir, Mid-FL Ctr Alcoholism; bd dir, Channel No 24 Pub TV; Fla Bur Hist Mus; Fla Humanities Coun; Initiative Better Living; Youth Comn, chmn dep majority leader, Dem Nat Comn, 1984-86; bd dir, Better Bus Bur; Fla Comn Tourism; Fla Citrus Sports Asn; chmn, Affirmative Action Comn, Fla Dem Party, Orlando Single Mem Dist Task Force; Orlando Mus Art; Am Asn Higher Educ, Southern Col Placement Asn; Enterprise Fla Bd dir; bd dir, Orange Co Addn; bd dir, Better Bus Bur, Brookwood Comn Hosp, Guardian Care Nursing Home; Alpha Phi Alpha, Phi Delta Kappa; chmn, Mercy Dr Neighbors Action; exec comm, 1976-82, chmn, 1980-81, Orange Co Dem; Fla Police Stand Comn, 1980-81;Fla House Rep, 1982-2000; chmn, United Negro Col Fund; Mt. Pleasant Missionary Baptist Church; bd mem, Holocaust Memorial Resource & Educ Ctr; bd mem, Black Bus Capital Finance Corp. **Home Addr:** 2116 Monte Carlo Trl, Orlando, FL 32805, **Home Phone:** (407)293-7437. **Business Addr:** Director of Defense Transition Services, University Central Florida, 907 S Kirkman Rd, Orlando, FL 32811, **Business Phone:** (407)445-5500.

### REDDICK, LANCE S.
Actor, musician. **Personal:** Born Dec 31, 1969, Baltimore, MD; married Stephanie D. **Educ:** Eastman Sch Music, Rochester, compos; Yale Drama Sch, actg. **Career:** Actor, musician, business owner; Wall St Jour, paperboy; Films: The Siege, 1998; Godzilla, 1998; Great Expectations, 1998; I Dreamed of Africa, 2000; Don't Say a Word, 2001; Bridget, 2002; Brother to Brother, 2004; Dirty Work, 2006; Tennessee, 2008; The Way of War, 2009; Jonah Hex, 2010; Seige; Remains, 2011; Won't Back Down, 2012. White House Down, 2013; Oldboy, 2013; The Guest, 2014; Faults, 2014; John Wick, 2014. TV series: New York Undercover, 1996; Swift Justice, 1996; What the Deaf Man Heard, 1997; Witness to the Mob, 1998; The Fixer, 1998; The West Wing, 1999; Falcone, 2000; "The Corner", 2000; "Oz", 2000-01; "Law & Order", 2001-04; "Law & Order: Special Victims Unit", 2000-01; "100 Centre Street", 2002; "The Wire", 2002-08; "Keep the Faith, Baby", 2002; "Probability", 2003; "Law & Order: Criminal Intent", 2003; "City Hall", 2004; "Independent Lens", 2005; "CSI: Miami", 2005-06; "Vengeance", 2005; "Alliances", 2006; "Numb3rs", 2007; "Lost", 2008-09; "Fringe", 2008-13; "Behind the Real Science of 'Fringe Season 1'", 2009; "Evolution", 2009; "Svetlana", 2010; "It's Always Sunny in Philadelphia", 2011; "TRON: Uprising", 2012; "The Avengers: Earth's Mightiest Heroes", 2012; "DrOne", 2012; "Comedy Bang! Bang!", 2013; "Wanda Sykes Presents Herlarious", 2013; "Wilfred", 2013; "NTSF: SD: SUV", 2013; "Bosch", 2014; "American Horror Story", 2014; "Beware the Batman", 2014; "The Blacklist", 2014; "Intelligence", 2014; "Key and Peele", 2014. YNC Films, owner, 2006-; Album: Contemplations & Remembrances, 2008; Songs: Contemplationa & Remembrances, 2008. **Home Addr:** 12024 Sarah St, Valley Village, CA 91607-4131, **Home Phone:** (818)821-8238. **Business Addr:** Actor, c/o Thomas Cushing, 1505 10th St, Santa Monica, CA 90401, **Business Phone:** (310)656-5100.

### REDDING, GLORIA ANN
School administrator, educator, consultant. **Personal:** Born Apr 4, 1952, Courtland, AL; daughter of W D Watkins Sr and Mary Ella Mitchell; children: Clifford Cannon. **Educ:** Ohio State Univ, MLS, family rels & human develop, 1971, BS, home econ, MA. **Career:** Kroger Co, asst mgr, 1975-76; Grocery Prod Grp, sls rep, 1976-77; Borden Inc, food serv unit mgr, 1977-79; Advan Bus Commun, commun consult, 1979-80; WIC Prog, proj asst & nutritionist, 1980-83, pub health educr, 1982-85; Ohio State Univ Young Scholars Prog, reg prog dir, 1988; Ohio Dept Educ, asst dir, 2005-11, Ohio Schs Watch prog, co dir, ODE GEAR UP coordr & consult, currently; High Schs That Work Making Mid Grades Work, consult, 2011-12; Vineyard Church Columbus, marriage & family life intern, 2011-12; Generating Learning Opportunities LLC, founder, chief exec officer, family life educr, 2011-. **Orgs:** Golden life mem, vpres, Delta Sigma Theta Sorority Inc, 1982; vpres, Ohio State Univ Black Alumni Asn; Ohio State Univ Mentor Prog; bd trustee, Neighborhood House Inc; adv coun, Women Infants & C; Nat Alliance Black Sch Educr; Olde Orchard Alternative Sch Parents Asn; A Gathering Sisters; women's day chairperson & womens breakfast fel comt, New Salem Missionary Baptist Church, Missionary Soc; Nat Forum Accelerate Mid grade Reforms; Nat Coun Family Rels Emer Mem; United Way Cent Ohio. **Honors/Awds:** Professional Mentor Achievement Award, Ohio State Univ Mentoring Prog, 1989-91; Outstanding Service Award, Ohio State Univ Young Scholars Prog, 1990. **Home Addr:** 300 Caro Lane, Gahanna, OH 43209, **Home Phone:** (614)428-7777. **Business Addr:** Founder, Chief Executive Officer, Generating Learning Opportunities LLC, PO Box 43004, Blacklick, OH 43004, **Business Phone:** (614)859-0007.

### REDDRICK, MARK A.
Executive, chief executive officer. **Career:** Phoenix Oil Co, chief exec officer, pres, 1987-. **Business Addr:** Chief Executive Officer, President, Phoenix Oil Co, 1434 W 76th St, Chicago, IL 60620, **Business Phone:** (312)224-8809.

### REDMAN, JOSHUA (JOSHUA SHEDROFF)
Saxophonist, composer. **Personal:** Born Feb 1, 1969, Berkeley, CA; son of Dewey and Renee Shedroff. **Educ:** Harvard Univ, BA, social studies, 1991. **Career:** Saxophonist, Recording Artist, Composer; Berkeley High Jazz Ensemble, 1982-86; Joshua Redman, 1993; Wish, 1993; Mood Swing, 1994; Spirit of the Moment: Live at the Village Vanguard, 1995; Freedom in the Groove, 1996; Timeless Tales, 1998; Beyond, 2000; Passage of Time, 2001; Elastic, 2002; Momentum, 2005; Back East, 2007; Compass, 2009; Walking Shadows, 2013; Trios Live, 2014; SFJAZZ Collective, artistic dir, 2000-07; Wilkins Mgt, rec artist & composer, currently. **Orgs:** Phi Beta Kappa Soc. **Honors/Awds:** First Place, Thelonius Monk Int Jazz Saxophonist Comp, 1991; Jazz Times Best New Artist, 1992; Down Beat Readers Poll, Jazz Artist of the Year, 1994; Album of the Year, Down Beat Readers Poll, 1994; Best Jazz Artist, Rolling Stone Critics Poll, 1994 & 1995. **Special Achievements:** Appeared in the Robert Altman film Kansas City; wrote the original soundtrack to Louis Malle's last film, Vanya on 42nd Street, & played on the soundtrack to the Clint Eastwood films Midnight in the Garden of Good & Evil & Space Cowboys. **Business Addr:** Recording Artist, Composer, Wilkins Management Inc, 323 Broadway, Cambridge, MA 02139, **Business Phone:** (617)354-2736.

### REDMAN, R. (REGINALD (REGGIE) NOBLE)
Actor, rap musician. **Personal:** Born Apr 17, 1970, Newark, NJ. **Career:** Albums: Whut? Thee Album, 1992; Dare Iz a Darkside, 1994; Muddy Waters, 1996; Doc's Da Name 2000, 1998; Blackout!, 1999; Malpractice, 2001; Red Gone Wild, 2006; Blackout! 2, 2009; Reggie, 2010; Muddy Waters II: Even Muddier, 2012, Blackout! 3, 2012; Film: Rhyme & Reason, 1997; Ride, 1998; PIGS, 1999; Boricua's Bond, 2000; Backstage, 2000; How High, 2001; Statistic: The Movie, 2001; Rock the Bells, 2006; How High 2, 2012; TV guest appearances: "The Jamie Foxx Show", 2000; "Method & Red", producer, 2004; "Wild 'N Out ", 2007; "Celebrity Rap Superstar", 2007. **Business Addr:** Recording Artist, Def Jam Records, 825 8th Ave, New York, NY 10019, **Business Phone:** (212)333-8000.

### REDMON, KENDRICK ANTHONY
Executive, manager, football player. **Personal:** Born Apr 9, 1971, Brewton, AL; married Stephanie; children: Haleigh & Kelseigh. **Educ:** Auburn Univ, BS, adult & continuing educ & teaching, 1994. **Career:** Football player (retired), coordinator, manager; Ariz Cardinals, right guard, 1994-97; Carolina Panthers, guard, 1998, right guard, 1999; Atlanta Falcons, right guard, 2000; K. A. Redmon LLC, pres, 2004-; Michelin N Am, mfg coordr, 2005-09, area sales mgr, 2009-13, regional sales mgr, 2013-. **Business Addr:** Regional Sales Manager, Michelin North America Inc, PO Box 19001, Greenville, SC 29602-9001.

### REDMOND, DEVERA YVONNE
Executive, advocate. **Personal:** Born Dec 6, 1948, Baltimore, MD. **Educ:** Morgan State Univ, BS, bus admin, 1970; Univ Baltimore, MPA, pub admin, 1980. **Career:** US Small Bus Admin, bus spec, 1978-86; DR & Assocs, pres & owner, 1986-; Agr Mkt Serv Agency; US Dept Transp, Off Small Disadvantaged Bus Utilization, Small Bus Specialis, Procurement Assistance Div, supvr, currently; URS Group Inc, SB liaison officer, currently; Serv Disabled Veteran-Owned Small

Businesses, advocate; Women-Owned Small Businesses, advocate. **Orgs:** Bd mem, Salvation Army, Wash, DC; Nineteenth St Baptist Church; Alpha Kappa Alpha Sorority; trustee, Mus Afr Art; Asn Univ Women; comnr, Com Nat Community Serv, Wash, DC; AT&T Small Bus adv coun, 1996; chair, Comt Employer Support Guard & Res, 1998-2004; Secy Defense; Chair Columbia. **Business Addr:** Supervisor, US Department of Transportation, 1200 NJ Ave SE W56-485, Washington, DC 20590, **Business Phone:** (202)366-1930.

## REDMOND, DR. EUGENE B.

Poet, educator, writer. **Personal:** Born Dec 1, 1937, East St. Louis, IL; son of John Henry and Emma Hutchinson; children: Treasure & Ira. **Educ:** Southern Ill Univ, BA, 1964; Wash Univ, St Louis, MO, MA, 1966. **Career:** E St Louis Beacon, E St Louis, IL, assoc ed, 1961-62; E St Louis Eve Voice, asst ed, 1962-63; Monitor, E St Louis, IL, contributed, 1963-65, exec ed, 1965-67, ed page & contrib ed, 1967-; Southern Ill Univ, Edwardsville, E St Louis IL br, Exp Higher Educ, teacher & counr, 1967-68, poet residence & dir lang workshops, 1968-69; Oberlin Col, Oberlin, OH, writer residence & lectr Afro-Am studies, 1969-70; Calif State Univ, Sacramento, CA, prof eng & poet residence ethnic studies, 1970-85; Eugene B. Redmond Writers Club, E St Louis, IL, co-founder & bd dir, 1986-; E St Louis Pub Schs, E St Louis, IL, spec asst supt cult & lang arts, 1985; Wayne State Univ, Detroit, MI, Martin Luther King Jr-Cesar Chavez-Rosa Parks, distinguished vis prof, 1989-90; Black River Writers Press, founder & publ; Ann Third World Writers & Thinkers Symp, coordr, 1972-; fel, NEA Creative Writing; Henry Dumas Creative Writing Workshop, coordr, 1974-; Literati Int & Original Chicago Blues Ann, assoc publ; Southern Ill Univ, prof eng, 1990; prof emer eng currently; Univ Wis, vis writer residence; Univ MSR-St Louis, vis writer residence; Southern Univ Baton Rouge, vis writer residence; Bks: Sides River, 1969; Sentry Four Golden Pillars, 1970; River Bones & Flesh & Blood, 1971; Songs from an Afro/Phone, 1972; a Time Rain & Desire, 1973; Drumvoices, 1976; Eye Ceiling, 1991; Echo Tree: Collected Short Fiction Henry Dumas, 2003; Consider Loneliness These Things; Lookingback, Jazzstained Jayne; A Kwansaba Mother Richie. **Orgs:** Cong Racial Equality; Am Newspaper Guild; Nat Newspaper Publishers Asn; Nat Asn African Am Educrs; African Asn Black Studies; Calif Asn Teachers Eng; Calif Writers Club; Nat Asn Third World Writers; Northern Calif Black Eng Teachers Asn; founder, Eugene B Redmond Writers Club, 1986. **Honors/Awds:** First prize, Wash Univ Ann Festival of the Arts, 1965; First prize, Free Lance mag, 1966; Literature Achievement Award, Sacramento Regional Arts Coun, 1974; Best of the Small Press Award, Pushcart Press, 1976; Poet Laureate, E St Louis, Ill, 1976; Faculty research Award, Calif State Univ, Sacramento, 1976; Calif Arts Coun grant, 1977; Ill Arts Coun grant, 1977-78; Nat Endowment for the Arts fellowship, 1978; Pyramid Award, Pan African Movement USA, 1993; American Book Award, for collection of poems The Eye in the Ceiling, 1993; Illinois Author of the Year, Ill Asn Teachers Eng, 1989; Pushcart Prize; Lifetime Achievement Award, Pan-African Movement USA; Inductee, National Hall of Fame Writers African Descent; Sterling Brown Award, ALAs African Am Lit & Cult Asn; Staying the Course Award, ETA Chicago; St Louis American Foundations Lifetime Achievement Award. **Special Achievements:** Has authored six volumes of poetry and has edited many more; Author: Sentry of the Four Golden Pillars, Black River Writers, 1971; Songs from an Afro/Phone, Black River Writers, 1972; In a Time of Rain and Desire: Love Poems, Black River Writers, 1973; Drum voices: The Mission of Afro-American Poetry, A Critical History, Anchor, 1976; Visible Glory: The Million Man March, Southern Ill Univ, 1998; First African American student editor of the university newspaper. **Home Addr:** PO Box 6165, East St. Louis, IL 62202. **Business Addr:** Emeritus Professor, Southern Illinois University, Il State Rte 157, Edwardsville, IL 62026-1431, **Business Phone:** (618)650-2000.

## REDMOND, DR. JANE SMITH

College administrator. **Personal:** Born Jul 20, 1948, Cleveland, TN; daughter of V Campbell and Earnestine; children: Gyasi R. **Educ:** Knoxville Col, BS, 1971; Univ Tenn, MS, 1974; Ohio State Univ, PhD, 1991. **Career:** Educator (retired); Univ Tenn, Knoxville, Prog Off, youth counr, 1974-76, counr coordianator, 1976-78, prog advr, 1978-80, Women's Ctr dir, 1980-82, Off Minority Stud Affairs Univ Tenn, 1982-87, dir, Minority Stud Affairs, asst vice chancellor, 1982-08; Ohio state univ, Columbus, grad admin assoc, 1987-91. **Orgs:** Bd dir, United Way Knoxville, 1984-; bd dir, Knoxville Inst Arts, 1985-; Alpha Kappa Alpha Sorority; Martin Luther King Commemorative Comn; Boys & Girls Club Corp Bd; Knoxville Area Urban League; Greater Warner African Methodist Episcopal Church Zion. **Home Addr:** 8650 Eagle Pointe Dr, Knoxville, TN 37931. **Business Addr:** TN.

## REDON, LEONARD EUGENE

Executive. **Personal:** Born Nov 4, 1951, St. Louis, MO; son of Leonard and Joyce Woodfox (deceased); married Denise Socquet; children: Jason & Jennifer. **Educ:** Worchester Polytech Inst, Worchester, MA, BS, chem engineering, 1973. **Career:** Eastman Kodak Co, Rochester, New York, dist serv mgr, 1984-86, prod serv mgr, 1986-87, mkt mgr copy prod, 1987, corp acct exec, 1987-88, asst chmn & pres, 1988-89, dir serv parts mgt, 1989, vpres & dir rochester area opers, currently; Paychex Inc, vpres western opers, 2001-11; Harnischfeger Industs Inc, dir rochester area opers; City Rochester, dep mayor, 2011-; Univera Healthcare Inc, vice chmn. **Orgs:** Asn Field Serv Managers, 1984-; bd chmn, Network N Star Inc, 1989-; bd dir, Ctr Youth Serv, 1989-; Urban League Rochester, 1989-; mem bd trustee, CGR; mem bd trustee, Eastman House; mem bd, Finger Lakes Health Systs Agency, 2011-13; bd mem, Wilson Commencement Pk; trustee, Worcester Polytech Inst; bd dir, Lifetime Healthcare Inc. **Home Addr:** 48 Pine Brook Cir, Rochester, NY 14616, **Home Phone:** (716)377-4344. **Business Addr:** Vice President, Western Operations, Paychex Inc, 911 Panorama Trail S, Rochester, NY 14625-0397, **Business Phone:** (585)385-6666.

## REDUS, GARY EUGENE

Baseball player. **Personal:** Born Nov 1, 1956, Athens, AL; married Minnie Diggs; children: Lakesha, Manesha, Nakosha & Gary II. **Educ:** Athens State Univ. **Career:** Baseball player (retired), Baseball coach (retired); Cincinnati Reds, outfielder, 1982-85; Philadelphia Phillies, outfielder, 1986; Chicago White Sox, outfielder, 1987-88; Pittsburgh Pirates, infielder & outfielder, 1988-92; Tex Rangers, outfielder, 1993-94; Calhoun Community Col, coach. **Home Addr:** PO Box 202, Tanner, AL 35671.

## REECE, GUY L., II

Judge. **Personal:** Born St. Louis, MO. **Educ:** Univ Nebr, BGS, bus, 1972; Ohio State Univ Law Sch, Moritz Col, JD, 1981. **Career:** Colonel (retired), judge; City Columbus, chief labor atty & asst city atty, 1981-89; Franklin Co Munic Ct, judge, 1990-91; Common Pleas Ct, Judge, 1992-95; City Jakarta, Indonesia, legal adv, 1995-96, consult, 1996-97; vis judge, 1998; Franklin Co, Bd Elections, dir, 1998-2003; Franklin Co Ct Common Pleas, judge, 2003-; Franklin Co, dir bd Elections, currently. **Orgs:** Nat Asn Advan Colored People; Vietnam Veterans Am; bd trustee, Maryhaven; Metrop Bd YMCA Cent OH; bd trustee, Direction Youth; deacon, Second Baptist Church; John Mercer Langston Bar Asn; Columbus Bar Asn, Ohio Bar Asn; Am Bar Asn, & Nat Bar Asn. **Home Addr:** 5266 Heathmoor St, Columbus, OH 43235, **Home Phone:** (614)462-5888. **Business Addr:** Judge, Franklin Co Ct Common Pleas, 345 S High St 3rd Fl Ct Rm 6A, Columbus, OH 43215, **Business Phone:** (614)462-7200.

## REECE, STEVEN, SR.

Executive. **Personal:** Born Sep 12, 1947, Cincinnati, OH; son of Edward and Claudia; married Barbara Howard; children: Alicia Michelle, Steven Jr & Tiffany Janelle. **Educ:** Xavier Univ, BS, commun, 1970; Ohio Bus Col, BA, 1985; Amos Tuck, Dartmouth Col, MBA, 1987; Temple Bible Col, DHL. **Career:** Univ Cincinnati's Eve Col, prof; WCPO-TV, TV dir; Motown Rec, rd mgr Supremes, Temptations, Stevie Wonder; Cincinnati's 1st Black Mayor Theodore M Berry, exec asst; Kool Jazz festival, assoc producer; Communiplex Serv Inc, pres & founder, currently; Reece & Reece Enterprise, Cincinnati OH, owner & founder, currently; State Comn African Am Males, 2007-; Cincinnati Advertising Club, vpres. **Orgs:** Pres & life mem, Oper PUSH; co-chmn, Rev Jesse Jackson's Presidential Campaign, Hamilton Co; local chmn, Oper PUSH Int Trade Bur; vpres, Greater Cincinnati Conv & Visitors Bur; mkt chmn, Greater Cincinnati Chamber Com; jr grand warden, Prince Hall Masons; prom dir, Prince Hall Shriner's Free & Accepted; trustee bd & deacon bd, New Friendship Baptist Church; chairperson, Withrow High Sch Adv Comt;founder, Oper Step-Up; Integrity Hall Child Care Ctr; Communiplex Nat Woman's Sports Hall Fame; state chairperson, AAU Jr Olympic Girls Basketball; lif mem, Nat Asn Advan Colored People; lif mem, Rainbow Coalition; founder, Communiplex & Martin Luther King & Educ & Sports Classic; founder, producer, Cincinnati Pub Sch Nat Teleconf. **Home Addr:** 5479 Sprucewood Dr, Cincinnati, OH 45239, **Home Phone:** (513)481-4972. **Business Addr:** President, Founder, Communiplex Services Inc, 2081 Seymour Ave, Cincinnati, OH 45222, **Business Phone:** (513)731-6300.

## REED, ANDRE DARNELL

Football player, president (organization). **Personal:** Born Jan 29, 1964, Allentown, PA; married Cyndi; children: Auburn & Andre Jr. **Educ:** Kutztown State Col. **Career:** Football player (retired), executive; Buffalo Bills, wide receiver, 1985-99; Jerry Maguire, 1996; Wash Redskins, wide receiver, 2000; Denver Broncos, 2000; Fitness Powerhouse Gym, owner; ESPN2, Cold Pizza, NFL Europe & NCAA football commentator, currently; Andre Reed Enterprises, owner, currently; TV: "Football: Who's Got Game", 2006. **Orgs:** Celebrity spokesperson, Big Bros Big Sisters Western NY; chmn, Andre Reed Found, currently. **Business Addr:** Owner, Andre Reed Enterprises, 1806 Watermere Lane, Windermere, FL 34786, **Business Phone:** (888)550-6672.

**REED, BOBBY.** See REED, KWAME OSEI.

## REED, BRANDY CARMINA

Basketball player. **Personal:** Born Feb 17, 1977, San Francisco, CA. **Educ:** Univ Southern Miss, attended 1998. **Career:** Southern Miss Women's Basketball, 1994-96; Phoenix Mercury, forward, 1998, 2000-02; Minn Lynx, forward, 1999.

## REED, CAROLIESE INGRID FRINK

Educator, librarian. **Personal:** Born Dec 24, 1949, Jacksonville, FL; daughter of Neal and Catherine Danberg; married Dwight D Sr (deceased); children: Kasimu Clark & Kali. **Educ:** Temple Univ, BS, 1976; Drexel Univ, MS, 1980; Univ Ghana, attended 1993. **Career:** Free Libr Philadelphia, c librn, 1980-81; Prince William County Libr, Woodbridge, Va, librn, 1982-84; Nassau County Sch Bd, Fernandina Beach, Fla, librn, 1985-87; Sch Dist Philadelphia, librn, 1987-; Fitzsimons Mid Sch, librn, 1996-. **Orgs:** Media selection & rev comt mem, Pa Sch Librns Asn, 1990-91; pres, admin assist, Nat Asn Black Storytellers, 1994-96, 1986-92; Black Caucus Am Libr Asn; Chairperson, Nat Festival Black Storytelling; Nat Asn Preserv & Perpetuation Storytelling. **Home Addr:** 859 N 29th St, Philadelphia, PA 19130-1145, **Home Phone:** (215)236-1118. **Business Addr:** Librarian, The School District of Philadelphia, 440 N Broad St, Philadelphia, PA 19130, **Business Phone:** (215)400-4000.

## REED, DR. CHARLOTTE (DR. REV. CHARLOTTE REED PEEBLES)

Educator, college administrator, congregational clergy. **Personal:** Born Apr 27, 1948, New York, NY; daughter of Thomas L and Lillian M; married Twain M Peebles; children: Mark D Peebles. **Educ:** City Univ NY, Richmond Col, BA, eng, 1972; Univ Va, MEd, 1977, EdD, 1980. **Career:** New York Pub Schs, eng teacher, 1972-76; Charlottesville Pub Schs, behav modification teacher, 1976-77; Univ Va, proj dir, 1977-81; Univ Louisville, asst prof, 1981-87; Alverno Col, asst prof & assoc prof, 1987-90; Purdue Univ, Calument, assoc prof, 1990-92; Ind Univ Northwest, dir & assoc prof, 1992-2004, exec dir & prof, prof emer, 2005-11; Lynwood Educ Serv Ctr, chief exec officer & founder, 2011-. **Orgs:** Am Educ Res Asn; exec bd mem, Chap, 1029, Phi Delta Kappa, 1978-, pres, 1993-96, 2000-01; adv coun & bd mem, Int Alliance Invitational Educ, 1982-; Nat Asn Multicultural Educ; Nat Coun Black Studies; comn mem, Asn Teacher Educrs, pres, 1992, chmn, ATE Resolutions Comt, 2002-05; sch bd, Sunnybrook Sch Dist, 1999-2009, vpres, 2000, pres, 2001-; Ill Sch Bd Asn, 1999-2009; co-chmn, Comn Urban Educ, 2008-; founder, Northwest Ind Consortium Community Partnerships; founder, Nat Soc Leadership & Success; Outcome 6 Comt, Ind Univ Northwest, currently. **Home Addr:** 19725 Orchard Ct, Lynwood, IL 60411-1442, **Home Phone:** (708)418-3539. **Business Addr:** Chief Executive Officer, Founder, Lynwood Educational Services Center, 2551 Glenwood Lansing Rd, Lynwood, IL 60411, **Business Phone:** (708)418-8378.

## REED, CLARA TAYLOR

Health services administrator. **Personal:** Born Isola, MS; daughter of N C and Ethel Lee; married Henry Jr; children: Pamela & Henry III. **Educ:** Miss Valley State Univ, pract nurse prog, 1963, MVSU's Regist Nurses Prog, nursing, 1970, BA, geront, 1990. **Career:** Mid-Delta Home Health Inc, owner, chief exec officer & chief financial officer, 1978-; Miss Valley State Univ, vice Chmn, develop comt, co-chair. **Orgs:** Bd dir, Miss Valley State Univ. **Business Addr:** Chief Executive Officer, Chief Financial Officer, Mid-Delta Home Health Inc, 441 Hwy 6 E Suite 1, Batesville, MS 38606, **Business Phone:** (662)624-4910.

## REED, CLARENCE HAMMIT, III

Executive, sales manager, salesperson. **Personal:** Born Oct 25, 1957, Amite, LA; son of Clarence II (deceased) and Eunice Paddio Johnson; married Sandra A; children: Doreal Hayes & Matthew David. **Educ:** Cornell Univ, Ithaca, NY, BS, 1979. **Career:** Eli Lilly & Co, Indianapolis, Ind, sales, 1979-81; Solar Resources Am, Columbus, OH, sales mgr, 1982-83; Xerox Corp, Columbus, OH, sales, 1983-86; Reed Enterprises & Develop, Columbus, OH, owner, 1986-; Animed Comput Syst, Oshkosh, Wis, sales, 1986-88; CMHC Systs, Dublin, OH, sales rep, 1988-02, sr sales rep, regional acct mgr, currently. **Home Addr:** 2332 Vendome Dr, Columbus, OH 43219-1437, **Home Phone:** (614)258-7292. **Business Addr:** Senior Sales Representative, CMHC Systems Inc, 570 Metro Pl N, Dublin, OH 43017, **Business Phone:** (614)764-0143.

## REED, DR. CLIFFORD

Educator. **Educ:** Western Mich Univ, BS, 1973; Wayne State, MFA, 1983, PhD, 1987. **Career:** Loyola Marymount Univ, Theatre Dept, asst prof. **Business Addr:** Assistant Professor, Loyola Marymount University, 1 Loyola Marymount University Dr, Los Angeles, CA 90045, **Business Phone:** (310)338-2700.

## REED, CORDELL

Executive. **Personal:** Born Mar 26, 1938, Chicago, IL; son of Clevon and Carrie Bell; married Bernice; children: Derrick, Brian, Barry, Steven & Michael. **Educ:** Univ Ill, BS, mech engineering, 1960. **Career:** Executive (retired); Commonwealth Edison, engr, 1960, nuclear eng dept, mgr, 1975; vpres nuclear oper, sr vpres, ethics officer & chief diversity officer, 1994-97; Nat Home Centers Inc, Corp Secy, Corp Controller. **Orgs:** Am Nuclear Soc; W Soc Engrs; Nat Tech Asn; trustee, Metrop Comn Church; trustee, Abraham Lincoln Ctr; dir, Independent Bank Chicago; bd dir, LaSalle Bank; bd dir, Walgreen Co; Inst Elec & Electronics Engrs; Nat Acad Eng, 1992; Dir, Underwriters Labs Inc, Walgreen Co., 1994-2010, LaSalle Bank Corp, LaSalle Bank NA, Stand Fed Bank NA.Tau Beta Pi Eng Hon Soc; Urban Fin Serv Asn; Ill Acad Decathlon Asn; Cal-Met Village Sr Citizen Housing; bd dir, John G Shedd Aquarium; Develop Fund Black Stud; adv bd, Metrop Family Serv; Underwriters Labs; Wash Group Int, 2002-; Independent Dir, URS Energy & Construct Inc, 2002-; Nat Tech Asn. **Home Addr:** 8446 S Kimbark Ave, Chicago, IL 60619.

## REED, DR. DAISY FRYE

Educator. **Personal:** Born Washington, DC; daughter of James Edward and Alberta Ruth Edwards; children: James S Jr & Kristel M. **Educ:** DC Teachers Col, BS, 1956; George Washington Univ, MA, 1961; Teachers Col, Columbia Univ, EdD, 1975; Loyola Univ, MRE, 1994. **Career:** Wash DC Publ Schs, teacher, 1956-73; Teachers Col Columbia Univ, asst prof, dir teacher corps proj, 1975-76; Publ Sch Syst Va, consult; State Dept Educ, consult; Va Commonwealth Univ, Sch Ed, prof, 1976-2000, emer prof teaching & learning, 2000-. **Orgs:** Zeta Phi Beta Sorority, 1955-; ATE, 1978-; Asn Teacher Educators Va, 1988-91; Phi Delta Kappa. **Honors/Awds:** Reise-Melton Award for Promoting Cross-Cultural Understanding, Va Commonwealth Univ, 1990-91; Outstanding Service Award, 1991-92; Outstanding Teacher Award, 1994-95; Phi Kappa Phi; Bd Visitors, teaching fellow, 1998-2000; Distinguished Faculty Award in Teaching, Va Commonwealth Univ, 2000; Innovation Award, DC Publ Schs Washington; Minority Stud Scholar, Teachers Col Columbia Univ. **Special Achievements:** Co-Author: Classroom Management for the Realities of Today's Schools; Author of book chapter in J Wood's Mainstreaming; articles published in Action in Teacher Education; NASSP Journal; Middle School Journal; Research Studs: Resilient At-Risk Children; Teaching in Culturally Diverse Classrooms; Overage & Disruptive Students in the Middle School; Social Reconstructionism for Urban Students, 1999. **Home Addr:** 5100 Monument Ave Suite 502, Richmond, VA 23230-3646, **Home Phone:** (804)673-9159. **Business Addr:** Professor Emeritus, Virginia Commonwealth University, School of Education, 1015 W Main St, Richmond, VA 23284-2020, **Business Phone:** (804)827-2670.

## REED, DERRYL L.

Marketing executive, chief executive officer, executive. **Personal:** Born Chicago, IL; son of Jesse A Jr. **Educ:** Southern Ill Univ, BS, math & chem minor, 1970; Univ Chicago, MBA, mkt & fin, 1976. **Career:** Chicago Bd Educ, substitute teacher, 1970-77; Am Can Co, sales rep, 1970-73, acct mgr, 1973-75, area mgr, 1975-77, assoc prod mgr, napkins, 1977-78, asst prod mgr, Aurora Bathroom Tissue, staff, 1978-80; Tetley Inc, prod mgr soluble tea prod, 1980-83, prod mgr tea bags, 1983-85, sr prod mgr tea bags, 1985-86, sr prod mgr tea prod, 1986-87; Heublein Inc, dir mkt prepared drinks, 1987-89; Teachers Ins & Annuity Asn Am, asst vpres ins servs, 1989-94; Clear Channel Commun, dir multicultural mkt & event sponsorship, 2004-05; SBC; Ameritech, dir brand mgmt, dir mkt planning & develop, 1994-95, dir mkt, 1995-97, dir multicultural mkt, advert, 1998-2000, dir muticul mkt, SCBDO, 2000-; Smokin' Joe Prod, LLC, pres & chief exec officer, 2008-; Derryl L. Reed & Assocs, LLC, Chicago Gospel Showcase &

Awards, pres & founder, currently. **Orgs:** Bd dir, Chicago, Nat Am Advan Colored People, 1975; consult partner, Reed & Reed Assocs; bd dir, Nat Black MBA Asn, 1986-; assoc bd dir, Tea Asn USA Inc; chmn, NY Corp Matching Gift Fund Lou Rawls Parade Stars Telethon United Negro Col Fund; Kappa Alpha Psi Frat; Consumer Prom Comn, Asn Nat Advertisers; nat pres, Nat Black MBA Asn; adv bd mem, Southern Ill Univ Sch Bus, 1992-; bd overseers, Univ Conn, Sch Bus Admin, 1993-95; founding mem, multicultrual mkt comt, radio advert & sports & events mkt comt, Asn Nat Advertisers; celebrity entertainment comt & prog consult, Spec Olympics World Games, 1995. **Honors/Awds:** A Black Achiever in Industry Award, Am Can Co; Outstanding Service & Achievement Award, Kappa Alpha Psi Frat; MBA of the Year, 1988. **Special Achievements:** Featured in Oct 1985 issue of Black Enterprise Magazine, Fortune, Ebony, New York Time, LA Times, Chicago Sun Times, the Michigan Chronicle, Black Issue in Higher Education; participant in 2 TV progs, hosted by Phil Donahue; guest speaker, Connecticut Public TV; guest lectr, Univ Conn & Atlanta Univ; honored for outstanding leadership & contrib to bus community, Leonard N Stern Sch Bus, NY Univ; selected An Achiever in History, Am Can Co. **Home Addr:** 3297 Woodview Lake Dr, West Bloomfield, MI 48323-3572, **Home Phone:** (248)851-5586. **Business Addr:** President, Founder, Derryl L Reed & Associates LLC, 3297 Woodview Lake Rd Suite 100, West Bloomfield, MI 48323, **Business Phone:** (586)214-5557.

### REED, ESQ. GREGORY J.

Lawyer, executive. **Personal:** Born May 21, 1948, MI; son of James and Bertha Mae; children: Arian Simone & Ashley Sierra. **Educ:** Mich State Univ, BS, 1970, MS, 1971; Wayne State Univ, JD, 1974, LLM, 1978. **Career:** Price Waterhouse, Tax Specialist, 1976; AHR Packaging Consult Corp, Mich, pres, developer, 1987-; Wayne State Univ, Detroit Mich, prof, 1988-89; Mich Bar Continuing Legal Educ, teacher, 1992; Detroit Entertainment Comn, chmn, founder; Keeper Word Found, chief exec officer, founder; Gregory J Reed & Assocs PC, owner, atty, currently. **Orgs:** Founder, Advan Amateur Athletics Inc, 1986; Gregory J. Reed Scholar Found, 1986-; chmn, US State Bar Mich Arts Commun Sports & Entertainment Sect, 1987-88; vpres, Black Entertainment & Sports Lawyers Asn, 1992-93; Mich State Univ Found, vice chairperson, 1996-97; vice chmn, Detroit Inst Arts Auxiliary FAAAA; fel BUF Mich, 1996-; chmn, founder, Keeper Word Found, 1996-; chairperson, Martin Luther King Statue Comt; bd dir, Mich Asn Community Arts Agencies; Nat Bar Asn; bd, Mich State Univ Found; Omega Psi Phi; comt mem, Am Bar Asn; Am Bar Asn; Acct Aide Soc Metro Detroit; bd comt, New Detroit Inc; tax & corp advisor BUF; Mich State Bar Taxation & Corp Div; Am Arbit Asn; bd dir, BESLA Entertainment Law Asn; bd dir, Mich Asn Community Arts Agencies; State Bar Law Media Comn; adv bd mem, US Internal Revenue Serv; co-founder, Black Entertainment & Sports Lawyers Asn; co-founder, Rosa Parks Libr & Mus; adv bd mem, Rhythm & Blues Found Inc; founder, Hip Hop Entertainment Clin; co-founder, Parks Legacy; bd mem, Benjamin Mays Acad; advisor, City Coun. **Honors/Awds:** Distinguished Alumni of the Year Award, Mich State Univ, 1980; Implemented Gregory J Reed Scholarship Foundation, 1986; Award for Contributions to the arts Black Music Month, State Mich House of Rep, 1987; Ggovt appointment Martin Luther King Comn Mich, 1989-; Hall of Fame inductee by BESLA, 1992 ; Nat Book Award, 1994; Keeper of the Word Found, 1994; John Hensel Award, State Bar Mich, 2003; American Book Award; Resolution for Achievement State of Mich Senate, City of Detroit; John Hensel Award for Significant Contribution to the Art, State Bar Mich; NAACP Image Award; Chicago's Teacher Award. **Special Achievements:** Author: Tax Planning and Contract Negotiating Techniques for Creative Persons, New National Pub Co, 1983; This Bus of Boxing & Its Secrets, 1981; This Bus of Entertainment and Its Secrets, 1985; Negotiations Behind Closed Doors, 1987; Economic Empowerment through the church, Am Book Award, 1994; Obama Talks Back: Global Lessons-A Dialogue with America's Young Leaders, 2012; Professional Athletes and Entertainers; "Quiet Strength," co-author with Rosa Parks; "Dear Mrs Parks," co-author with Rosa Parks; Economic Empowerment Supplement book guide; NCP Image, for outstanding literature; Author of sixteen books. **Business Addr:** Chairman, Detroit Entertainment Commission, 1201 Bagley, Detroit, MI 48226, **Business Phone:** (313)961-3580.

### REED, ISHMAEL SCOTT

Educator, writer. **Personal:** Born Feb 22, 1938, Chattanooga, TN; son of Henry Lenoir and Thelma Coleman; married Priscilla Rose; children: Timothy & Brett; married Carla Blank; children: Tennessee Maria & Timothy Brett. **Educ:** St Univ NY, Buffalo, attended 1960; Univ Buffalo, DSc, 1995. **Career:** Educator (retired), writer; E Village Other, co-founder, 1962; Yardbird Pub Co Inc, Berkeley, CA, co-founder, 1971, ed dir, 1971-75; Reed Cannon & Johnson Commns Co, Berkeley, co-founder, 1973; Columbus Fdn, Berkeley, co-founder, 1976; Y'Bird mag, ed-in-chief, 1978-80; Ishmael Reed & Al Young's Quilt, Berkeley, co-founder, 1980; US cols & Univs, guest lectr num; judge lit competitions, 1980-81; Berkeley Art Comn, chairperson; Univ CA, Berkeley, lectr; am poet, essayist & novelist, currently; Quilt mag, co-ed, 1981; Terrible Twos, 1982; God Made Alaska Indians, 1982; Reckless Eyeballing, 1986; Thirty-Seven Yrs Boxing Paper, 1988; Univ CA, Santa Barbara, regents lectr, 1988; Terrible Threes, 1989; Airing Dirty Laundry, 1993; Japanese by Spring, 1993; Conversations with Ishmael Reed, 1995; A Walk Oakland, 2003; Bks: Free-Lance Pallbearers, 1967; Yellow Back Radio Broke-Down, 1969; Mumbo Jumbo, 1972; Last Days La Red, 1974; Flight to Can, 1976; Secy to Spirits, 1978; Shrovetide Old New Orleans, 1978; Terrible Twos, 1982; Reckless Eyeballing, 1986; Terrible Threes, 1989; Japanese By Spring, 1993; Juice!, 2011; Ishmael Reed Publ Co, owner; Univ Calif, Berkeley, fac, vis scholar, currently. **Orgs:** Chmn bd dirs, Coordinating Coun Lit Mags, 1975-79, adv bd chmn, Coordinating Coun Lit Mags, 1977-79; Authors Guild Am; PEN; Celtic Found; Umbra Writers Workshop; founder, Before Columbus Found, 1980. **Honors/Awds:** National Endowment for Arts, Writing Fel, 1974; Guggenheim Fellow, 1975; Rosenthal Foundation Award, 1975; American Academy Award, 1975; Michaux Award, 1978; Award, ACLU, 1978; Langston Hughes Medal, City College of New York, 1997; John D. and Catherine T. MacArthur Foundation Fellowship Award, 1998; Fred Cody Award, Bay Area Book Reviewers Association, 1999; Rene Castillo OTTO Award, 2002; Phillis Wheatley Award, Harlem Book Fair, 2003; Robert Kirsch Award, 2004; Commonwealth Club of California's Gold Medal; Lila Wallace Reader's Digest Award; Hall of Fame of Writers of African Descent, Chicago State Univ's Nat Lit; DC Area Writing Project's 2nd Annual Exemplary Writer's Award; Barbary Coast Award, San Francisco lit festival, 2011; Literary Legacy Award, Just Buffalo Lit Ctr, 2014. **Special Achievements:** First SF Jazz Poet Laureate. Published numerous novels, poetry and plays. **Home Addr:** 870 53 St, Emeryville, CA 94608, **Home Phone:** (510)450-0219. **Business Addr:** Poet, Essayist, Novelist, Ishmael Reed Publishing Co, PO Box 3288, Berkeley, CA 94703.

### REED, DR. JAMES W.

Physician, endocrinologist, writer. **Personal:** Born Nov 1, 1935, Pahokee, FL; son of Thomas and Chineater Gray Whitfield; married Edna; children: David M, Robert A, Mary I & Katherine E. **Educ:** WVa State Col, BS, summa cum laude, 1954; Howard Univ Col Med Wash, DC, MD, 1963. **Career:** Madigan Army Med Ctr, resident & internal, 1966-69; Univ Calif, San Francisco, res fel, 1971; AUS Med Dept, chief med, 1978-81; Univ Tex, Dallas, dir internal med educ, 1982-84; State WA Med Asst Prog, int med consult, 1984-85; Morehouse Sch Med, prof & assoc chmn dept med, 1985-, Grady Hosp, chief endocrinol & chief med serv; Co-auth: Black Man's Guide to Good Health, Perigee Bks, 1994; updated ed, Hilton Publ, 2000; Hypertension: What Every African Man & Woman should Know About Living with High Blood Pressure, Hilton Publ, 2002; Living With Diabetes: A Guide Patients & Parents, Hilton Publ Co, 2005; Metab Res Unit Univ Calif Med Ctr, San Francisco, fel endocrinol & metab. **Orgs:** Consult med, Tuskegee, Va Hosp, 1982-; med dir, MMA, 1982-; Am Med Asn; Am Diabetic Asn; Am Endocrine Soc; bd dir Int, Indisciplinary Soc Hypertension Blacks; pres, Int Soc Hypertension Blacks, 1987-; pres, Int Soc Hypertension Blacks; course dir, seventh Int Conf Hypertension Blacks, 1992; lifetime hon trustee, Morehouse Sch Med; fel Am Col Endocrinol; adv bd mem, Novo Nordisk & AstraZeneca. **Home Addr:** 380 McGill Pl NE, Atlanta, GA 30312, **Home Phone:** (404)525-1803. **Business Addr:** Professor of Medicine, Associate Chair for Research, Morehouse School of Medicine, 720 Westview Dr SW, Atlanta, GA 30310, **Business Phone:** (404)756-5788.

### REED, JASPER PERCELL

Educator. **Personal:** Born Mar 2, 1929, Centenary, SC; married Sandra Lee; children: Rosalyn Jackson, Rene Jackson & Valerie Linette. **Educ:** SC State Col, BS, biol, 1957; Pa State Univ, MEd, bio sci, 1968, DEd, bio sci, 1977. **Career:** Educator (retired); Community Col Philadelphia, prof bio, 1965; Temple Univ Med, asst instr, 1957-65; City Univ Syst, NY, evaluator, 1970; Educ Testing Serv, Col Level Educ Prog, test prod, 1970-73. **Orgs:** Kappa Alpha Psi, 1956-; Beta Kappa Chi, 1957; bd deac, White Rock Bapist Church, 1962-; Am Soc Allied Health Prof, 1979; Allied Health Admin, Am Asn State Col & Univ, 1979; Am Soc Pharmacol & Exp Therapeut.

### REED, ESQ. JERRILDINE

Politician. **Personal:** Born Jersey City, NJ; daughter of Jesse Henry and Della Mae Anderson; children: Steven M Adams. **Educ:** Temple Univ, BS, 1961; Temple Law Sch, JD, 1981. **Career:** Daniel Preminger PC & Hugh Clark Esq, law clerk, 1981-83; Cong Staff Robert A Borski MC, 1983-86; Greater Pa Chamber Com, 1986-90; Rohm & Haas Co, in-house coun, Polit Action Comm, treas, 1990-97; US House Representatives, constituent serv, 1995; Congressman Chaka Fattah, atty, 1998, spec asst, 2000-02; Ct Common Pleas Philadelphia, civil case mgr, 2000-05; Retired and loving it, 2009-12; Clark County Bar Asn, seeking receptionist position, 2012; libetty tax, tax preparer, 2011-12. **Orgs:** Delta Sigma Theta, 1961-00; trustee, Community Col Philadelphia, 1980-92; NJ Bar Asn, 1990-00; Am Bar Asn, 1990-00; Nat Bar Asn, 1990-00; Barristers Asn Philadelphia, 1990-00; homeless advocacy, Proj Bar Asn, 1990-96; mentor, Phildelphia Futures, 1990-96. **Home Addr:** 6760 Emlen St, Philadelphia, PA 19119, **Home Phone:** (215)843-4360.

### REED, JOE LOUIS

Teacher, executive, secretary (office). **Personal:** Born Sep 13, 1938, Evergreen, AL; son of Louis (deceased) and Eula Morgan; married Mollie Perry; children: Irva, Joe & Steven. **Educ:** Ala State Univ, BS, 1962; Case W Resv Univ, MA, polit sci, 1966. **Career:** Trenholm HS, teacher, 1962; Ala State Univ, stud act, 1963; Ala State Teachers Asn, exec secy, 1964-69; Ala Educ Asn Inc, assoc secy, 1969-; Ala Dem Conf (ADC), chmn, currently; Dem Party Minority Affairs, vice chmn, currently. **Orgs:** Nat co-chmn Com EducrHumphrey-muskie pres tkt, 1968; del Dem Nat Conv, 1968; chmn, Nat Asn Advan Colored People Comn Econ, 1969-; Loc State & Nat Prof Asn; life mem, NEA; mem exec bd, NCSEA, 1969-75; consult, AL Educ Asn Prof Rts & Resp Comn; staff adv, Unit Teaching Prof; delg, NEA Conv & Rep Assembly; pres, Ala League Advan Educ Chmn Ala Dem Conf, 1970-; chmn, DuShane Com Teachers Rights NEA, 1971-; Ala Adv Comn Civil Rights; vchmn, Minorty Affairs Ala Dem Party, 1974-; city cnclmn City Montgomery, 1975-; coord vpres, NCSEA, 1975; pres NCSEA, 1976-; Masons; Omega Psi Phi Frat; past chmn bd trustees, Ala State Univ; chmn, Ala Deleg, 2000; chmn, Ala Dem Conf; vice chair, Dem Party Minority Affairs; bd trustees, Ala State Univ. **Honors/Awds:** Abraham Lincoln Award, Nat Educ Asn; initial report, Ala League Advan Educ, "The Slow Death of the Black Educator in Alabama"; pres, jr class, Ala State Univ, 1960-61; pres, student body, Ala State Univ, 1961-62; Addressed Democratic Nat Conv, 1972; Rated as one of the ten most influential citizens in the State of Alabama; Honorary Doctor of Law Degree, Ala State Univ, 1980. **Home Addr:** 874 John Brown Ave, Montgomery, AL 36106. **Business Addr:** Associate Secretary, Alabama Education Association, 422 Dexter Ave, Montgomery, AL 36104, **Business Phone:** (334)834-9790.

### REED, HON. KASIM

State government official, lawyer, mayor. **Personal:** Born Jun 10, 1969, Plainfield, NJ; son of Rev Arthur E Langford Jr (deceased); married Sarah-Elizabeth; children: Maria Kristan. **Educ:** Howard Univ, Washington, BA, polit sci, 1991; Howard Univ Sch Law, JD, 1995. **Career:** Ga House Representatives, state rep, 1998-2002; Ga State Senate, vice chmn senate dem caucus, 2002-09; City Atlanta (GA), Mayor, 2010-; Paul, Hastings, Janofsky & Walker LLP, atty; Atlanta Mayor Shirley Franklin, campaign mgr; Holland & Knight LLP, partner. **Orgs:** Bd trustee, Howard Univs Bd Trustees, 2002-; Aspen Inst-Rodel Fel Class1998, 2000, 2007; former bd mem, Nat Black Arts Festival; former bd mem, Metrop Arts Fund; chmn, U.S. Conf Mayors, Transp & Commun Comt; chmn, Atlanta Regional Comn, Regional Transit Comt; Ga Gen Assembly; Cascade United Methodist Church. **Honors/Awds:** "Georgia Trend" Magazine, 40 Under 40 Rising Stars, 2001; "Outstanding Atlanta," 10 Outstanding Atlantans list; "The Root" Magazine, The Root 100 Honorees, 2013; LLD, Howard Univ; Distinguished Leadership Award, Nat Forum Black Pub Adminr; Louis E. Martin Great American Award. **Special Achievements:** Youngest general trustee to serve on Howard's Board of Trustee. **Business Addr:** Mayor, City of Atlanta GA, 55 Trinity Ave Suite 2500, Atlanta, GA 30303, **Business Phone:** (404)330-6004.

### REED, KATHLEEN RAND

Sociologist. **Personal:** Born Feb 6, 1947, Chicago, IL; daughter of Johnie Viola Rand Cathey and Kirkland James. **Educ:** Columbia Col Chicago, radio tv prod, multimedia & graphic arts, 1972; San Francisco State Univ, BA, biol, 1996; Univ Md, Col Pk, MAA, biol, cult, med & corp anthrop, 1999; Georgetown Univ, cert, bioethics, 2001. **Career:** Ill Supreme Ct Comm Character & Fitness, Chicago, Ill, investr & res consult, 1970; ETA Pub Rels Chicago, Ill, acct exec, 1970-72; WTVS TV 56, Detroit, MI, pub rels & prom dir, 1972-73; WJLB Radio Detroit, Mich, pub affairs dir, 1972-74; KH Arnold San Francisco, Calif, bus resource & resource consult, 1974-80; Hq Co Subsid United Tech, spec proj dir, 1980-81; Nat Alliance Bus San Francisco, Calif, admin mgr, 1981-83; Michael St Michael & Corp Leather (self-employed), chief exec officer, mfg exec & pres, 1982-96; Necronomics & Ethnographics, Palo Alto, Calif, pres, 1989; Geog Genetic Systs, pres, 2001; Rand Reed Group, chief exec officer, pres & appl biocultural anthropologist & ethnomarketer, 1991-; Dept Health & Human Serv, grant proposal reviewer; About Time Mag, assoc ed & white house corresp, 2004-; Lincoln Univ, spec curric consult provost & sr vpres acad affairs, 2006-; Breakthrough Mkt Technol, coun appl cult anthropologist, 2009-; Hon Lew Frederick, Ore House Representatives Dist 43- Portland, OR, sociopolitical strategist, 2010-. **Orgs:** Pres, Am Futurists Educ Women; World Future Soc; Nat Orgn Women; Womens Inst Freedom Press; World Affairs Coun; Bay Area Urban League; League Women Voters; Nat Women Studies Asn; Nat Coun Negro Women; Commonwealth Club Calif, 1977; Int Aff Com; Women Comn; Media & Pub Info Comn; consult & contrib, Black Esthetics, 1972; bd dir, San Francisco Conv & Vis Bur, 1987-90, Urban Coalition W, Phoenix, Ariz, 1987-93; chmn, African Am Donor Task Force, 1990-; NIH; inst rev bd, Nat Heart, Lung, Blood Inst; panelist, Nat Res Coun Workshop Race & Ethnic Classification; Am Anthrop Asn; Soc Appl Anthrop; Am Asn Geographers; Afro-Am Hist & Geol Soc; Kennedy Inst Ethics, Georgetown Univ; Am Anthrop Asn; Am Women Radio & Tv; Nat Asn Black Journalists; Nat Insts Health. **Honors/Awds:** Nat Asn Negro Bus & Prof Women, Western Region Vol Award, 1977; San Mateo Co Women's Hall of Fame, 1993. **Special Achievements:** Publications/productions: "San Francisco Government, The City, The Citizen & Technetronics", 1978; Univ San Francisco Lecturer "Women and the Working World", 1978; "Femininity" Book Review Women's Review of Books, 1984; Lectures/Speeches, Univ Calif Davis "The Black Female in Contemporary Society" Afro-American Studies & Women's Studies Combined Session, 1984. **Home Addr:** , Menlo Park, CA 94025. **Business Addr:** Chief Executive Officer, President, The Rand Reed Group, 133 Thomas St NW, Washington, DC 20001, **Business Phone:** (202)234-2506.

### REED, ESQ. KIMBERLEY DEL RIO

Lawyer. **Personal:** Born Jan 7, 1957, Detroit, MI; daughter of William F II and Charlie Johnson; children: William Mandela Matthews. **Educ:** Ky State Univ, BS, 1978; Howard Univ Sch Law, JD, 1981; Wayne State Univ Sch Law, LLM, 1995. **Career:** US Dept Labor, law clerk, 1980-81; UAW Legal Dept, law clerk, 1981-82; Legal Aid & Defender Assoc, dep defender, 1982-92; Am Inst Paralegal Studies, law instr, 1986-87; Mich Paralegal Inst, law instr, 1988-89; Oak Grove Am Church, sun day sch teacher, 1992-; Detroit Recorders Ct, State Judicial Coun, chief legal coun, judicial asst, 1992-. **Orgs:** Life mem, Delta Sigma Theta Sorority Inc, 1975-; Oak Grove Am Church, chancel choir, 1982-; treas, Detroit chap, Ky State Unive Alum Asn, 1987-90; vpres, Detroit chap, Howard Univ Alum Asn, 1987-88; Detroit Alumnae Chap, 1990-; African Am Enrichment Asn, 1990-; consult, Jr Achievement, 1992-. **Honors/Awds:** Outstanding Alumnus, Outstanding Alumnus Mumford High Sch, 1984; Service Award, Ky State Univ Alum Asn, 1991; Service Award Teen lift, Delta Sigma Theta Sorority Inc, 1993; Service Award, Mumford Class of 1974, 1994. **Special Achievements:** Publications: The Exclusionary Rule is There Life After Lean? Vol I Criminal Practice Law Rev 137, 1980; The Economic Impact of Colonialism on the Legal Systems of Cameroon, Cote D'Ivorie and Senegal; Wayne State Law Lib, Masters Essay, 1994; Admitted to the State Bar of MI, 1992. **Home Addr:** 19215 San Juan Dr, Detroit, MI 48221, **Home Phone:** (313)864-7510. **Business Addr:** Chief Legal Counsel, Judicial Assistant, Detroit Recorder's Court, 1441 St Antoine St Suite 104, Detroit, MI 48226, **Business Phone:** (313)224-2501.

### REED, KWAME OSEI (BOBBY REED)

Lawyer, clergy. **Personal:** Born Apr 28, 1948, McComb, MS; son of Charles James and Helen Marie Garner; married Rita Wallace; children: Nene & Kojo. **Educ:** Howard Univ, BA, polit sci, 1972, Sch Law, JD, 1975; Yale Univ Divinity Sch, MDiv, 1979. **Career:** Oberlin Col, Black Studies Dept, instr, 1976-77; Comt Reconciliation, 1979-81; Univ Pittsburgh, 1980-81; N MSP Legal Servs, 1982-83; United Church Christ, Heritage Fel, 1983-87; Legal Servs Northern Va, 1992-93; Potomac Asn Cent Atlantic Conf, United Church Christ, clergy, 1987, assoc conf minister, 1987-; Nat Capital Area, exec officer; Oberlin Col, fac; Univ Pittsburgh, Legal Studies Dept, fac; Kwame O. Reed Assocs, atty law, 1993-, atty, 2015-. **Orgs:** Founder, Heritage Fel United Church Christ; co-founder, Hope Med Clin, Accra, Ghana, 1993-98; founding mem, United Church Christ Atty Network, 1996-98; Andrew Rankin Memorial Chap Howard Univ; chmn, Potomac Asn. **Honors/Awds:** Outstanding Contribution to Reston, Va in its First 20 Years, 1985; Calvin Coolidge High School Alumni Award, 1995; Visiting scholar, Yale Law Sch. **Special Achievements:** Yale Law Sch Vis Scholar Res Law & Religion, 1981-82. **Home Addr:** 11651 N Shore Dr Apt 12, Reston, VA 20190-4615. **Business Addr:** Associate Conference Minister, Potomac Association of the United Church of Christ, 916 S Rolling Rd, Baltimore, MD 21228-5318, **Business Phone:** (410)788-4190.

**REED, ESQ. MICHAEL H., JR.**
Lawyer, teacher, administrator. **Personal:** Born Jan 17, 1949, Philadelphia, PA; married Yalta Gilmore; children: Alexandra & Michael Jr. **Educ:** Temple Univ, BA, polit sci, 1969; Yale Univ, Law sch, JD, 1972. **Career:** Pepper Hamilton LLP, Philadelphia, Pa, partner, 1972-; Rutgers Univ, Camden Law Sch, adj prof, 1983; Temple Univ, Sch Law, adj prof, 1989; Us Ct Appeals, Third Circuit, 1992-93, chmn, 2000 & 2014; Pa Supreme Ct, lawyer, 2004-07; pvt pract Pa, currently. **Orgs:** Trustee, Episcopal Hosp, 1986-; chmn, Prof Guid Comt, Philadelphia Bar Asn, 1986; trustee & corp secy, Acad Natural Sci, 1988-; chmn, Pa Bar Asn, Minority Bar Comt, 1988-90; Pa Judicial Inquiry & Rev Bd, 1990-93; chmn, bd gov & pres, Pa Bar Asn, 1993-; fel Am Col Bankruptcy; bd dir & bd adv, Pub Interest Law Ctr Philadelphia; exec bd, Comt Seventy; Chambers USA; bd gov, Am Bar Asn; Corp Restructuring & Bankruptcy Pract Group; Am Law Inst; mem exec, Young Lawyers Sect; vpres, Barristers Asn Philadelphia; Bus Law Sect Publ Bd; chmn, Prof Guid Comt; Interest Lawyers Trust Acct Bd; Lawyers Local Bankruptcy Rules Adv Comt, US Dist Ct Eastern Dist Pa, 1998-99; chmn, Eastern Dist Pa Bankruptcy Conf, 1999. **Home Addr:** 225 N 23rd St, Philadelphia, PA 19103-1005, **Home Phone:** (215)557-9934. **Business Addr:** Partner, Pepper Hamilton LLP, 3000 2 Logan Sq 18th Arch St, Philadelphia, PA 19103-2799, **Business Phone:** (215)981-4416.

**REED, ROBIN LYNN. See REED-HUMES, ROBI.**

**REED, DR. RODNEY J.**
School administrator, educator. **Personal:** Born May 16, 1932, New Orleans, LA; son of Ursul C Desvignes and Edgar J; married Vernell M Auzenne; children: Karen & Ursula. **Educ:** Clark Col, BA, 1951; Univ Mich, MA, music educ, 1956; Univ Calif, Berkeley, PhD, educ policy, planning & admin, 1971. **Career:** Southern Univ, Baton Rouge, asst prof, assoc conductor, 1956-61; Oakland Calif Unified Sch Dist, high sch teacher & vice prin, 1961-68; Univ Calif, Berkeley, Urban fel, 1968-70, from asst prof to prof, 1970-90, asst res educr, 1973, co-dir, 1979, fac asst chancellor affirmative action, 1980-82, prof emer, 1991-; Pa State Univ, Col Educ, prof & dean, 1990-97, dean emer & prof emer, 1999-. **Orgs:** Am Ed Res Asn, 1970-; ed bd mem, Educ & Urban Soc, 1972-86; pres, Fornax Inc, 1975-88; life mem, Nat Asn Advan Colored People, 1975-; Asn Calif Sch Admin, 1976-90; ed bd, Policy Studies Rev Ann, 1976-86; Nat Conf Prof Ed Admin, 1977-94; chair, Ed Comt Bay Area Black United Fund, 1979-82; vice chair & mem bd, Bay Area Urban League, 1980-89; ed bd, Educ Researcher, 1982-90; ed bd, Nat Forum Educ Admin & Supervisors, 1983-; Omega Psi Phi Fraternity; Sigma Pi Phi Frat, 1983-; Am Asn Sch Admin, 1986-94; Phi Delta Kappa, 1971-; Am Educ Res Asn, 1974-; Omicron TauTheta, Nat Hon Soc, 1990-; ed adv bd, J African Am Male Studies, 1990-94; Cleveland Nat Forest, 1991-2002; treas, Exec Comt, Asn Cols & Schs Educ State Univs & Land Grant Cols & Affiliated Pvt Univs, 1992-95; ed bd, Educ ADM Quart, 1993-96; mem-at-large & bd dir, Holmes Partnership, 1994-96; mem-at-large & bd dir, Am Asn Cols Teacher Educ, 1994-97; bd dir, Pa Goals, 1994-96 & 2000; pres, Asn Cols & Schs Educ State Univs & Land Grant Cols & Affiliated Pvt Univs, 1995-98; bd dir, Am Asn Cols Teachers Educ, 1996-98; life mem, Pa State Univ Alumni Asn; life mem, Univ Calif, Berkley, Alumni Asn; Asn Col Educ & Schs Educ State Univs & Land Grant Cols & Affiliated Pvt Univs; co-founder, Univ's Prof Develop Prog; bd dir, Young Musicians Prog; co-dir, Univ Calif/Oakland Unified Sch Dist Teacher Corps Proj; founder, Univ's Ann Inst Sch Adminr; bd dir, San Francisco-Bay Area Urban League; bd dir, Nat Asn Sec Sch Principals. **Honors/Awds:** Outstanding Man of the Year, Omega Psi Phi Frat Sigma Iota, 1966; Bronze Award, Bay Area Black United Fund, 1982; Order of the Golden Bear, Univ Calif, Berkeley, 1985-; California State Legislatue Assembly & Senate Resolutions, 1989; California Assembly Speakers Plaque, 1989; Alumnus of the Year Award, Black Alumni Club & Univ Calif Berkeley Alumni Club, 1992; Golden Key, Nat Honor Soc; Pa Gov's Pa 2000. **Special Achievements:** Author, Expectation & Student Achievement; co-author, (James W Gutherie) Edtl Admin Policy Ldshp Am Ed, Second Edition, 1991; co-author, The Politics of Urban Educ in the US, 1992; co-author, Restructuring Public Schooling: Europe, Canada, America, 1997; First African American dean at the University of California. **Home Addr:** 6623 Glen Oaks Way, Oakland, CA 94611. **Business Addr:** Dean Emeritus, Professor Emeritus, Pennsylvania State University College of Education, 274 Chambers Bldg, University Park, PA 16802, **Business Phone:** (814)865-1542.

**REED, SHEILA A.**
Editor, journalist. **Educ:** Univ Fla, Gainesville, FL, BSJ, 1981. **Career:** Sarasota Herald Tribune, Sarasota, FL, 1982-83; Gainesville Sun, Gainesville, FL, 1984-86; Fla Times-Union, Jacksonville, FL, 1986-87; St Petersburg Times, St Petersburg, FL, 1987-91, seniority ed, currently; Gannett Suburban Newspaper, White Plains, NY, 1991-94; Lexington Herald-Leader, Lexington, KY, 1994-98; Atlanta J-Const. **Orgs:** Nat Asn Black Journalists, 1990-. **Home Addr:** 1074 Peachtree Walk NE Apt B418, Atlanta, GA 30309. **Business Addr:** Seniority Editor, St Petersburg Times, PO Box 1121, St Petersburg, FL 33731, **Business Phone:** (727)893-8452.

**REED, DR. THERESA GREENE**
Physician, educator. **Personal:** Born Dec 9, 1923, Baltimore, MD; daughter of William James Greene and Theresa Greene Evans; married Hermas. **Educ:** Va State Col, BS, chem, 1945; Meharry Med Col, MD, 1949; Johns Hopkins Univ, MPH, 1967; DC State Med Lic, cert, 2014. **Career:** Homer G Phillips Hosp, internship, 1949-50, staff physician, pub health physician, 1950-58, asst clin dir, 1958-66; pvt pract physician, 1950-65, currently; Johns Hopkins Univ & Sinai Hosp, prev med fel, 1966-68, lectr clin pharma col; Johns Hopkins Univ, resident, 1967-68, fel; US Food Drug Admin, med officer, 1968-92, supvry med officer, 1977-80, 1988-92; Howard Univ, assoc prof community med; Nat Med Asn, historian. **Orgs:** founder & chmn, Black female med soc, 1963; Chmn, Comt Admin & Financial Affairs, Nat Med Asn, 1987-89; pres, Medico-Chirurgical Soc DC, 2001-; Am Col Epidemiol; fel Am Col Prev Med; Soc Epidemiol Res; Am Soc Micro biol; Am Med Womens Asn; Am Pub Health Asn; Asn Teachers Prev Med; Am VD Asn; fel City Med Soc; Int Epidemiol Asn; life mem, Alpha Kappa Alpha; secy & treas, Daniel Hale Williams Med Reading Club; Chi Delta Mu Fraternity; Delta Omega; Homer G Phillips Alumni Asn; Xi Zeta Omega Ch; Nat Asn Advan Colored People; Trinity Episcopal Church; pres, African Am Hist & Gen Soc; ROOTS Users Group; Uncrowned Queens Inst Res & Educ Women Inc; St. Louis Med Soc; Saints Episcopal Church. **Honors/Awds:** Public Health Serv Special Recognition Award, 1985; Commendable Service Award, Food & Drug Admin, 1985; Outstanding Service Award, Nat Med Asn, 1986-87; Pub Health Serv Supvr Service Award, 1991; Community Service Award, Am Med Women's Asn, 1992; Equal Opportunity Achievement Award; Distinguished Service Award, Nat Med Asn Region II. **Special Achievements:** The founder and first president of the first African female medical society in 1963; One of the first members of the St Louis Medical Society; First Black Female Med Epidemiologist; Author of numerous papers in medical journals. **Home Addr:** 11516 Patapsco Dr, Rockville, MD 20852-2454, **Home Phone:** (301)468-6830. **Business Addr:** Physician, Private Practitioner, 2041 Georgia Ave NW, Washington, DC 20060, **Business Phone:** (301)468-6830.

**REED, DR. VINCENT EMORY**
Government official, educator. **Personal:** Born Mar 1, 1928, St. Louis, MO; son of Artie David and Velma Veander; married Frances Bullitt. **Educ:** WVa State Col Inst, BS, educ, 1952; Howard Univ, MA, educ, 1965; Univ PA, Wharton Sch Finance & Comn, completed inst Collective negotiations, 1969; VA St Col, Guid NDEA Scholar; Iowa Univ. **Career:** Educator (retired); WV St Col, football coach & physiology instr, 1955; Jefferson Jr HS, teacher, 1956; Anacostia HS, Cardozo HS, Jefferson Jr HS, counr, 1963; Manpower Develop Training Prog DC Pub Schs, asst dir, 1964; Dunbar HS, Wilson HS, asst prin; Woodrow Wilson Sr HS; DC Pub Sch, asst supt personnel, 1969-70; DC Pub Sch, asst supt safety & security, 1970, exec asst, 1970-71, asst supt, 1971-74, assoc supt off state admin, 1974-75, supt, 1975-80; pres US, asst secy elem & sec educ, 1981-82; Wash Post, vpres communs, 1982-98. **Orgs:** Nat Asn Advan Colored People, mem Jr Achievement Wash, DC; bd dir, Stonewall Athletic Club; bd dir YMCA; bd dir, Nat Conf Christians & Jews; bd trustees, Univ DC; bdtrustees, Southeastern Univ; bd trustees, Gallaudet Col; bd trustees, Am Univ; found trustee, WV St Col; exec comt Conv & Visitors Ctr; Howard Univ Charter Day Comt; bd dir, Big Bros Inc; chmn, Sch & Summer Jobs Bd Trade Wash, DC; bd dir, Girl Scouts; bd dir, Boy Scouts; bd dir, Boys' & Girls' Club DC Police Dept; Merit Select Panel US Magistrates; DC chmn, United Way; past mem, Am Asn Sch Personnel Admin; Am Personnel & Guid Asn; past chmn Area Supts Study Sem; past bd dir, Goodwill Indust. **Honors/Awds:** Community Service Award, SE Citizens Asn, 1970; Superior Service Award, DC Bicentennial Assembly, 1976; Outstanding Achievement Award, WV State Col, 1976; Outstanding Community Service Award, NAACP, 1977; Distinguished Service Award, Phi Delta Kappa Intl George Washington Univ, 1979; Keynote Speaker, NY State Urban League Convention; Keynote Speaker, Nat Head Start Conf; Keynote Speaker, Seven-State Conf PTA; comn eval qualifications pvt sch admin vocational training DC pub schs; Principal Speaker, Commencement Exercises Univ DC, Southeastern Univ, etc; Honorary degrees, WV State Col, HHD; Southeastern Univ, Doctor Pub Admin; Georgetown Univ, Doct Humane Letters; Univ DC, Doctor Laws; Strayer Col, Doctor Humane Letters; Harris-Stowe Univ, Doctor Humane Letters, 1990; Doctor of Humane Letters, Slippery Rock Univ, 1990. **Special Achievements:** Award is given in the name of Dr. Vincent Reed, the distinguished educator. **Home Addr:** 7115 16th St NW, Washington, DC 20012, **Home Phone:** (202)291-3926. **Business Addr:** Federal Education Official, Washington Post Co, 1150 15 St NW, Washington, DC 20071-0002, **Business Phone:** (202)664-6000.

**REED, WILLIS, JR.**
Basketball executive, basketball player, vice president (organization). **Personal:** Born Jun 25, 1942, Lincoln Parish, LA; married Gale Kennedy; children: Carl & Veronica; children: 2. **Educ:** Grambling State Univ, LA, attended 1964. **Career:** Basketball player, basketball coach (retired), basketball executive; New York Knicks, ctr, forward, 1964-74, head coach, 1977-79; St John's Univ, vol asst basketball coach, 1980-81; Creighton Univ, head basketball coach, 1981-82, 1984-85; Atlanta Hawks, asst coach, 1985-87; Sacramento Kings, asst basketball coach, 1987-88; New Jersy Nets, head coach, 1987-88, basketball & bus develop, vpres, 1989-90, basketball opers, sr vpres, 1990, exec vpres & gen mgr, 1993, sr vpres, 1994-96; New Orleans Hornets, vpres basketball oper, 2004-07. **Orgs:** Phi Beta Sigma fraternity. **Business Addr:** Vice President of Basketball Operations, New Orleans Hornets, Okla Tower 210 Pk Ave Suite 1850, Oklahoma City, OK 73102, **Business Phone:** (405)208-4600.

**REED-CLARK, LARITA DIANE**
Financial manager, government official, association executive. **Personal:** Born Sep 26, 1960, Chicago, IL; daughter of Henry and Joyce Hinton. **Educ:** Loyola Univ, Chicago, Ill, BBA, 1982, CPA, Ill, 1983; Kellogg Sch Bus, Northwestern Univ, MS, mgt, 1993. **Career:** KPMG, Chicago, Ill, auditor, 1982-84; McCormick Pl, Chicago, Ill, asst controller, 1982-84, controller, fiscal opers dir, 1984-97, dir finance & admin, 1997-; Metrop Pier & Expos Authority, dir finance & admin, controller, 2010-. **Orgs:** Nat Asn Black Acct, 1980-; Am Inst CPAs, 1983-; Ill CPA Soc, 1983-; Family Christian Ctr Ch, 1992-; Govt Fin Officers Asn, 1984-; fel Leadership Greater Chicago, currently; Strive Community Serv Orgn, 1997-2000. **Honors/Awds:** Named among top black business & professional women, Dollars & Sense Magazine, 1988. **Home Addr:** 1928 Spruce Cir, Munster, IN 46321-3859, **Home Phone:** (219)922-1370. **Business Addr:** Controller, Metropolitan Pier & Exposition Authority, McCormick Pl 301 E Cermak Rd, Chicago, IL 60616, **Business Phone:** (312)791-7500.

**REED-HUMES, ROBI (ROBIN LYNN REED)**
Casting director. **Personal:** Born Mt. Vernon, NY; children: Noah & Summer. **Educ:** Hampton Univ, BS, speech commun & theatre, 1980. **Career:** Films: The Falcon & the Snowman, production asst; Best Seller, casting asst; She's Gotta Have It, 1984; Sch Daze, 1988; I'm Gonna Git You Sucka, 1988; Harlem Nights, actor, 1989; Do the Right Thing, 1989; Harlem Nights, 1989; Mo' Better Blues, 1990; Jungle Fever, 1991; Poetic Justice, 1993; Malcolm X, 1993; Soul Food, 1997; Never Die Alone, 2004; The Gospel, 2005; House of Grimm, 2005; Waist Deep, 2006; Crossover, 2006; Somebody Help Me, 2007; Next Day Air, 2009; For Colored Girls, 2010; Mama I Want to Sing, 2011. TV: "Roc, The Robert Guillaume Show, A Different World, In Living Color & Good News; Michael Jackson's Music Video, "Remember the Time", casting dir, 1993; "Woo", casting dir, 1998; Wifey, 2007; "8 Days a Week", casting dir, 2011; Mali Music: Beautiful, actor, 2014. Others: McClean & DiMeo, casting asst; To The Glory of God, founder & pres; Robin Reed-Humes & Assocs, pres, currently. **Orgs:** Delta Sigma Theta Sorority Inc; Gamma Iota Chap, Hampton Univ; Pres & founder, Reed Hope Found, 2012-14. **Home Addr:** 8306 Wilshire Blvd Suite 429, Beverly Hills, CA 90211. **Business Addr:** Casting Director, Raleigh Studios, 5300 Melrose Ave, Los Angeles, CA 90038, **Business Phone:** (213)871-4440.

**REED-MILLER, ROSEMARY E.**
Manager, businessperson, educator. **Personal:** Born Jun 22, 1939, Yeadon, PA; married Paul E; children: Sabrina E & Paul D. **Educ:** Temple Univ, BA, hist & anthrop, 1962. **Career:** US Dept Agr, info specialist, 1966-67; jewelry design, crafts develop, journalist, Jamaica, WI & Wash, DC; Toast & Strawberries Inc, Boutique, owner, 1966-; Hist Soc Wash, DC, DC pograms, 1969-2011, progs & mgr, 2011-; Econ Develop Bd Mayor's Off, 1983; Howard Univ, Sch Fine Arts & Ecol Awards, adj teacher; TV Shows, 1993; Work Post Home Mag, 1995; radio show, Fashion Bus, Capital Ed WUSA, News WJLA, Inaugural Dressup, Wash Post; independent contractor, 2011-. **Orgs:** Pres, Task Force Educ & Train Minority Bus Ctr, 1973-74; Interracial Coun Bus, 1973; pres, Howard Univ Fac Wives Asn, 1973; founding group Asn Women Bus Owners, 1974; Dupont Cir N Bus Asn; DC Barristers Wives Asn; DC Govt Econ Develop Comn, 1983-86; TV Shows, Eye Wash, Maternity Fashions, 1985; Woodley House, 1986; Wash Ethical Soc Sch, 1997. **Honors/Awds:** Bus Award Century Club Nat Asn Negro Bus & Prof Women's Clubs, 1973; Business Service Award, Wash Black Econ Develop Corp, 1973; Delegate White House Conference Small Business Award; delegate, White House Comn Entrepreneural Educ, 1973; Business woman of the Year, Nat Coun Small Bus Develop Eastern Reg, 1974; Black Acad Develop Alpha Kappa Alpha Sor, 1975; Appreciation Plaque Award, Bus & Prof Women's League, 1980; Black Women Sisterhood Calendar Honoree, 1982; Business Service Award, Century Club Club, 1983; Business Service Award, Howard Univ, Inst Urban Affairs, 1984; Business Service Award, Blacks With-in Govt, 1984; Committe Service Award, RSVP Club, 1984; Minority Women's Enterprise Fund, bus Accomplishment, 1995; DC Private Industry Corriel Award, 1996; National Theatre Supporter Award, 1996; The Path Toward Enpowerment Award, Am Soc Study African Am History, 1998; Phenomenal Business Women Award, Wash Bus Guide Mag, 2002. **Special Achievements:** Author, The Threads of Time, The Fabric of History: Profiles of African Am Designers & Dressmakers, 2002. **Home Addr:** 1300 Geranium St NW, Washington, DC 20012-1706, **Home Phone:** (202)829-5588. **Business Addr:** Owner, Toast & Strawberries, 1532 Upshur St NW, Washington, DC 20011, **Business Phone:** (202)723-9007.

**REESE, ALBERT A., JR.**
Football player. **Personal:** Born Apr 29, 1973, Mobile, AL. **Educ:** Grambling State Univ, grad. **Career:** Football player (retired); San Francisco 49ers, defensive tackle, 1997; Grand Rapids Rampage, 2003; Dallas Desperados, 2005.

**REESE, CALVIN, JR. See REESE, POKEY.**

**REESE, DELLA (DELLAREESE PATRICIA EARLY)**
Actor, composer, singer. **Personal:** Born Jul 6, 1931, Detroit, MI; daughter of Richard Early and Nellie Early; married Vermont Taliaferro, Jul 1, 1951?; married Franklin T Lett Jr, Jan 12, 1983; children: Deloreese, James, Franklin & Dominique; married Leroy Gray, Dec 28, 1959. **Educ:** Wayne State Univ. **Career:** Albums: Melancholy Baby, 1957; And That Reminds Me/ I Cried for You, 1957; Amen!, 1958; Sermonette/My Dreams End at Dawn, 1958; A Date with Della Reese (At Mr. Kelly's in Chicago), 1958; Don't You Know?/Soldier, Won't You Marry Me?, 1959; And That Reminds Me, 1959; The Story of the Blues, 1959; What Do You Know About Love?, 1959; Della (Album), 1960; And Now/There's Nothin' Like a Boy, 1960; Not One Minute More, 1960; Someday (You'll Want Me to Want You), 1960; Della By Starlight, 1960; Special Delivery, 1961; The Most Beautiful Words, 1961; Won'cha Come Home, Bill Bailey?, 1961; A Far Far Better Thing, 1961; Della Della Cha-Cha-Cha, 1961; The Best of Della Reese, 1962; Della Reese On Stage; 1962; The Classic Della, 1962; Waltz With Me, 1963; Della Reese At Basin Street East, 1964; C'mon & Hear, 1964; I Like It Like Dat!, 1965; After Loving You, 1965; It Was a Very Good Year [Live], 1966; Della Reese Live, 1966; One More Time, 1967; On Strings of Blue, 1967; I Gotta Be Me... This Trip Out, 1968; Black Is Beautiful, 1970; Games People Play, 1970; Compared To What, 1970; The Best of Della Reese, 1972; Let Me In Your Life, 1975; The ABC Collection, 1976; One of a Kind, 1978; Sure Like Loving You, 1985; And Brilliance, 1990; Some of My Best Friends Are the Blues, 1995; Voice of an Angel, 1996; My Soul Feels Better Right Now, 1998; The Della Reese Collection, 1998; Sure Like Lovin' You, 2000; Legendary Della Reese, 2001; Della, 2002; Give It to God, 2006. Films: The Mod Squad, 1968; The Bold Ones: The New Doctors Grace Dayton, 1970; Getting Together, 1971; Voyage of the Yes, 1973; Daddy's Girl, 1973; Twice in a Lifetime, 1974; Police Woman, 1974; McCloud, 1974; Petrocelli, 1975; Joe Forrester, 1975; Police Story, 1975; Cop on the Beat, 1975; The Rookies, 1975; Psychic Killer, 1975; Chico & the Man, 1975; McCloud, 1976; Medical Center, 1976; Flo's Place, 1976; Nightmare in Badham County, 1976; Vega$, 1978; Welcome Back, Kotter, 1979; Insight, 1980; The Love Boat, 1982; It Takes Two, 1983; The A-Team, 1985; Crazy Like a Fox, 1986; Charlie & Co., 1986; ABC Afterschool Specials, 1986; 227, 1987; A Pup Named Scooby-Doo, 1988; Night Court, 1989; Harlem Nights, 1989; 227, 1990; The Kid Who Loved Christmas, 1990; The Young Riders, 1990; MacGvver, 1991; Married People, 1991; The Royal Family, 1991; Dream On, 1992; The Distinguished Gentleman, 1992; Designing Women, 1993; L.A. Law, 1993; Picket Fences, 1993; Touched by an Angel, 1994; Promised Land, 1996; A Thin Line Between Love & Hate, 1996; Happily Ever After: Fairy Tales for Every Child, 1997; A Match Made in Heaven, 1997;

Miracle in the Woods, 1997; Emma's Wish, 1998; Mama Flora's Family, 1998; Chasing Secrets, 1999; Having Our Say: Anya's Bell, 1999; Dinosaur, 2000; Expecting Mary, 2010; actress; Jubilee, RCA, Victor Records, ABC Paramount, rec artist; Della Variety Show, hostess, 1969-70; Sahara-Tahoe, Caesar's Palace, Coconut Grove, MrKelly's, Caribe Hilton, Flamingo, performer. TV series: "Beauty Shop", 2005; "If I Had Known I Was a Genius", 2007; minister, currently; tv movie roles: Anya's Bell, 1999; Having Our Say: The Delany Sisters' First 100 Yrs, 1999; The Secret Path, 1999; The Moving of Sophia Myles, 2000; "That's So Raven", 2006; "The Young & the Restless", 2009. TV Appearance: The Tonight Show; Merv Griffin Show; Ed Sullivan; McCloud; Police Woman; Twice in a Lifetime; Chico & the Man; Petro celli; Mike Douglas Show; Mahalia Jackson Troupe, performed, 1945-49; solo rec artist, 1957-; Let's Rock, 1958; The Last Minstrel Show, 1978. **Business Addr:** Actress, William Morris Agency, 151 El Camino Dr, Beverly Hills, CA 90212, **Business Phone:** (310)786-4700.

### REESE, REV. DR. FREDERICK DOUGLAS
Clergy, educator, activist. **Personal:** Born Nov 28, 1929, Dallas County, AL; married Alline Toulas Crossing; children: Frederick Jr, Valerie, Marvin, Christa & Alan. **Educ:** Ala State Univ, BS; Atlanta Bible Inst Clark Col, adv study; Southern Univ; Selma Univ, DD; Univ Ala; Livingston Univ, MEd, AA, Eds; Wartburg Col, DDiv. **Career:** Ebenezer Bapt Church, Selma AL, sr pastor, 1965-; AL State Univ, Pan Hellenic Coun, Campus Socs Musicians, pres; Citizens Adv Coun, chmn, 1998; E side Jr High & Selma High Sch, prin; Supt educ, admin asst; Wilcox County Training Sch, asst prin; city councilman; Wilcox County Teacher Planning Comt, chmn; Selma Educ Asn, pres. **Orgs:** Nat Educ Asn; Ala Educ Asn; Dist VI Educ Asn; Phi Beta Sigma; bd dir, YMCA; pres, Dallas County Voters League, 1960; chmn, Wilcox County Teachers Planning Comt; Nat Baptist Conv USA; Ala Baptist State Conv; Southwest Dist State Conv Econ Opportunity Bd; bd dir, Good Samaritan Hosp Selma City Coun; bd dir, Carver Br YMCA; state dir, Bigger & Better Bus. **Honors/Awds:** Abraham Lincoln Award; Outstanding Leadership Educr, NEA, Detroit, 1971; Dr Frederick D Reese Parkway, 2000; Teacher of the Year Award, Selma City Teachers Asn; Good Guy Award, Unit Appeal; Numerous plaques & Certificates for Outstanding Leadership in Education and Civil Rights; National Black College Alumni Hall of Fame Inc, 2007. **Special Achievements:** First African American President of Selma Education Association Local leader in 1965 Voters Rights Movement, Selma, organized black teachers for the right to vote, led demonstrations against local newspaper, resp for black clerks and cashiers in stores and banks, organized black citizens for position on Dallas County Dem Executive Committee. **Home Addr:** 1566 Marie Foster St, Selma, AL 36703-3422, **Home Phone:** (334)874-4385. **Business Addr:** Senior Pastor, Ebenezer Baptist Church, 1548 Legrande St, Selma, AL 36703, **Business Phone:** (334)875-6526.

### REESE, GREGORY LAMARR
Librarian. **Personal:** Born Jul 30, 1949, Cleveland, OH; son of Jasper and Margaret Smith; married Evangeline Bynum; children: Michael. **Educ:** Morehouse Col, BA, hist, 1975; Case Western Res Univ, MLS, 1977. **Career:** Cuyahoga County Pub Libr, librn, 1975-80, br mgr, 1980-85; E Cleveland Pub Libr E, asst dir, 1985-88, exec dir, 1988-. **Orgs:** Past pres, E Cleveland Kiwanis; Cleveland, Area Metrop Libr Serv, 1980-; Alpha Phi Alpha Fraternity, 1986-; Cleveland Opera Multicult Awareness Prog, 1988-. **Honors/Awds:** Alumni Fund Chairman, Case Western Reserve, 1981; Jazz Volunteer, Northeast Ohio, 1989; Friend of Literacy Award, Project Learn, 1990; Ohio Librarian of the Year, 1991; Martin Luther King Jr, Altruism Award, East Cleveland Citizens for Sound Government; Librarian of the Year, Ohio, 1992; Robert P. Bergman Prize, Cleveland Arts Prize, 2006. **Special Achievements:** First African-American to walk through their doors. **Home Addr:** 1935 Janette Ave, Cleveland Heights, OH 44118-2251, **Home Phone:** (216)932-7073. **Business Addr:** Executive Director, East Cleveland Public Library, 14101 Euclid Ave, East Cleveland, OH 44112, **Business Phone:** (216)541-4128.

### REESE, IKE (ISAIAH REESE)
Football player, radio host. **Personal:** Born Oct 16, 1973, Jacksonville, NC. **Educ:** Mich State Univ, commun. **Career:** Football player (retired), radio host; Philadelphia Eagles, linebacker, 1998-2004; Atlanta Falcons, linebacker, 2005-07; 610 WIP Sportsradio, host, 2008-; KYW-TV & WPSG-TV Philadelphia, sports anchor, currently; 94 WIP, host, currently. **Honors/Awds:** Jack Edelstein Memorial Award, 2002; Pro Bowler Selection, 2004. **Business Addr:** Radio Host, Sports Radio 94WIP, 400 Mkt St 9th Fl, Philadelphia, PA 19106, **Business Phone:** (215)625-9460.

### REESE, IZELL
Football player, executive. **Personal:** Born May 7, 1974, Dothan, AL. **Educ:** Univ Ala, Birmingham. **Career:** Football player (retired), executive; Dallas Cowboys, 1998, 2005, linebacker, free safety, safety, strong safety, 1999, free safety, 2000, corner back, left corner back, 2001; Denver Broncos, free safety, 2002; Buffalo Bills, free safety, 2003-04; Carolina Panthers, 2001; Miami Dolphins, 2001-02; Nat Col Scouting Asn Athletic Recruiting, exec vpres, 2008-; Nat Football League Players Asn, vpres atlanta chap, 2009-12. **Orgs:** Co-founder, RisingSeniors.com & Rising Seniors Found, 2010-. **Business Addr:** Executive Vice President, NCSA Athletic Recruiting, 1415 N Dayton St 4th Fl, Chicago, IL 60642, **Business Phone:** (866)495-5172.

### REESE, MAMIE BYNES
Educator. **Personal:** Born Gibson, GA; married William J. **Educ:** Spelman Col, BS, 1933; Drake Univ, MS, 1948; Ohio State Univ, adv study; Univ So Calif; Simmons Col; Boston Univ. **Career:** Dean women (retired); Ctr HS, teacher; Des Moines Tech HS; Baker & Burke Counties, home demon agent; Albany State Col, assoc prof dean women; Albany State Col, Southwest Ga Inst, dean women. **Orgs:** Ga State Bd Pardons & Pardons; pres, Nat Asn Colored Wom Club Inc; Ga Asn Educat; NEA; Sigma Rho Sigma Honor Sor; aux Ga Osteop Med Asn; Nat Health Asn, Delta Sigma Theta Sor Inc; Asn Parol Author; Am Correct Asn; World Fed Meth Wom; Hines Mem Butler St Meth Episco Chs; Albany Urban League & Guide; Albnay C C; Govs Spec Coun Fam Plan; Semper Fidel Club; Ga Div Am Cancer Soc; comt mem, Girl Scouts Am; num offNat Asn Advan Colored People. **Home Addr:** PO Box 43134, Albany, NY 31704-3134.

### REESE, POKEY (CALVIN REESE, JR.)
Baseball player. **Personal:** Born Jun 10, 1973, Columbia, SC; children: Naquwan & LaBresha. **Career:** Baseball player (retired); Princeton Reds, 1991; Cincinnati Reds, infielder, 1997-2001; Pittsburgh Pirates, infielder, 2002-03; Boston Red Sox, infielder, 2004; Seattle Mariners, infielder, 2005; Fla Marlins, 2006; Red Sox, free agt, 2003-06.

### REESE, VIOLA KATHRYN
Social worker. **Personal:** Born Aug 23, 1953, Lexington, TN; daughter of Rev Billy Frank and Willie Mae Smith; married J Monroe Jr; children: Idesha & James III. **Educ:** Tenn State Univ, BS, 1975; Wash Univ, MSW, 1977. **Career:** C's Ctr Behav Develop, therapist, 1977-80, satellite coordr, 1980-82, interim clin dir, 1982-83, family therapist, coordr, 1983-84; RDS Found Inc, exec dir, 1986-; Jackson State Univ, Off vpres acad affairs & stud life, exec asst to vpres. **Orgs:** Nat Asn Social Workers, 1972-, Nat Asn Black Social Workers, 1972-, Ill Asn Sch Social Workers, 1976-; St Clair Co Comn Difficult C, 1980-84; bd dir, Coun House, 1981-84; Big Bros & Big Sisters; pvt consult, 1981-; bd mem, Lexington Charter, Optimist Int, 1989-; secy, Caywood PTO, 1988-90; bd mem, E-911, 1989-91; TENA, 1989-90; bd mem, LHCCN, 1990-; PADA, 1991-; SEC, 1992-95; Jonah, 1995; Nat Org Women, 1975-84; Friends LHS, 1997; Delta Sigma Theta Sorority; Comprehensive Emergency Servs; bd, United Assistance, 1999-. **Honors/Awds:** Outstanding Black Col Female, Essence Mag, 1975; University Scholar, Tenn State Univ, 1975; Outstanding Achievement, Big Brothers & Big Sisters, 1982, 1984; Certificate Achievement, CCBD, 1984; Outstanding Parent Volunteer, Caywood PTO, 1989; Outstanding Parent Volunteer, Caywood PTO, 1990; Outstanding Parent Volunteer, 1991, 1992-95; Outstanding Volunteer, 1992; FKIX County Award, 1991; Volunteer Award, Caywood Sch, 1992-93; Outstanding Parent Volunteer, 1993-98; School of Bell Award, 1994-95; Community Service Award, Jackson Girl Scout Coun; Community Service Award, Big Brothers Big Sisters. **Home Addr:** 221 Eastern Shore Dr, Lexington, TN 38351-1203, **Home Phone:** (731)968-6736. **Business Addr:** Executive Assistant to the Vice President, Jackson State University, 7th Fl Admin Twr 1400 Lynch St, Jackson, MS 39217, **Business Phone:** (601)979-2246.

### REESE-RANDLE, BERDINE CARONELL
Executive, educator. **Personal:** Born Mar 18, 1929, Lufkin, TX; married Lucious C; children: Lydia L. **Educ:** Prairie View A&M Univ, BA, 1949, MS, 1955; Univ Houston, post grad. **Career:** Phys educ teacher, 1946, 1948, 1949, 1951; YMCA Waco, dance instr; teacher elem sch, 1951-55; Marlin ISD, phys educ teacher, 1951-57; HI SD Houston, 1957-72; Miss Lucy's Acad & Early Childhood Educ Ctr, exec dir, 1969; Friendship Realty Co, owner, 1970-. **Orgs:** AAHPER, 1955-; golden life mem, Delta Sigma ta Sorority, 1972; SACUS, 1973-; NAESP, 1973-; HALBPWC, 1973-; NALBPWC, 1973-; adv bd consult, Clan House Bees Halfway House, 1973-77; AUCW, 1974-77; vpres, N Forest Sch Bd, 1974-76; ACEI, 1974-77; life mem, YWCA, 1975; vpres, Fontaine Scenic Woods Civic Club, 1976-; Nat State & Houston Area Asn Educ Young C, 1976-; chairperson, NFTFO, 1976-; chairperson, F SWCC, 1976; Alpha Tau Chap, ta Nu Sigma Nat Sor; charter mem, Diamond Jubilee; Nat Coun Negro Women; Nat Asn Advan Colored People; bd dir, Habitat Humanity & Delta's Educ Found; financial secy, Houston Metrop Alumnae Chap. **Home Addr:** 5203 Long Creek Lane, Houston, TX 77088-4402, **Home Phone:** (281)445-5585. **Business Addr:** Miss Lucy's Academy And Early Childhood Education, 10620 Homestead Rd, Houston, TX 77016.

### REEVES, ALAN M.
Automotive executive. **Career:** Ford motor, salesman, 1970; Qual Ford Sales Inc, Columbus, Ga, chief exec officer; Spalding Ford, owner, 1982-; Spalding Ford Lincoln-Mercury Inc, Griffin, Ga, chief exec officer, 1982-; Albany Ford Inc, Albany, Ga, chief exec officer, currently. **Business Addr:** Chief Executive Officer, Spalding Ford-Lincoln-Mercury Inc, 1710 N Expressway, Griffin, GA 30223, **Business Phone:** (770)229-1600.

### REEVES, BRENDA
Founder (originator), president (organization). **Career:** Reeves Automated Off Servs, founder & pres, 2003-. **Orgs:** Exec Women Int. **Business Addr:** President, Founder, Reeves Automated Office Services, Marquette Bldg 243 W Cong St Suite 350, Detroit, MI 48226-3262, **Business Phone:** (313)961-6657.

### REEVES, CARL DONMARK, JR.
Executive, football player. **Personal:** Born Dec 17, 1971, Durham, NC; married Iris; children: Deja. **Educ:** NC State Univ. **Career:** Football player (retired), exec; Chicago Bears, 1995-96, 1998, right defensive end, 1997; Barcelona Dragons, 1997; Carolina Cobras, Arena Football League, offensive line & defensive line, 2000-01; Protect Am, sales mgr, currently. **Home Addr:** 5613 Old Forest Cir, Knightdale, NC 27545-8116, **Home Phone:** (919)217-4830. **Business Addr:** Sales Manager, Protect America, 2530 Meridian Pkwy, Durham, NC 27713, **Business Phone:** (888)936-3385.

### REEVES, DIANNE
Singer. **Personal:** Born Oct 23, 1956, Detroit, MI; daughter of Vada Swanson. **Educ:** Univ Colo. **Career:** Clark Terry Band, singer; Co Symphony Orchestra; Monterey Jazz Festival; worked with: Sergio Mendez, Harry Belafonte, George Duke, Herbie Hancock, numerous others; Albums: Welcome To My Love, 1977; For Every Heart, 1984; Jazzvisions: Echoes of Ellington, 1986; Better Days, 1987; I Remember, 1988; Never Too Far, 1990; Dianne Reeves, 1991; Art & Survival, 1993; Quiet After Storm, 1994; Quiet After the Storm, 1994; The Grand Encounter, 1996; Palo Alto Sessions, 1996; That Day, 1997; New Morning, 1997; Bridges, 1999; The Calling: Celebrating Sarah Vaughan, 2001; A Little Moonlight, 2003; Christmas Time is Here, 2004; Good Night & Good Luck, 2005; Lush Life, featured, 2007; Music Lovers, 2007; When You Know, 2008; Beautiful Life, 2013. **Honors/Awds:** Grammy Award, 2001, 2002-03 & 2006. **Special Achievements:** Only singer to have won this Grammy three consecutive albums. **Business Addr:** Singer, c/o EMI Records, 8730 Sunset Blvd 5th Fl, Los Angeles, CA 90069, **Business Phone:** (310)659-1700.

### REEVES, JOHN E.
Government official, commissioner. **Career:** Southfield City Coun, councilman, 1996; Mich Veterans' Memorial Pk Comn, comnr, currently. **Orgs:** Kappa Alpha Psi Frat; chmn, bd dir, Cypriaw Ctr. **Home Addr:** 24530 Santa Barbara, Southfield, MI 48075, **Home Phone:** (248)569-9062. **Business Addr:** Commissioner, Michigan Veterans Memorial Park Commission, 234 W Baraga Ave, Marquette, MI 49855, **Business Phone:** (906)225-8182.

### REEVES, JULIUS LEE
Engineer, manager. **Personal:** Born Nov 10, 1961, Detroit, MI; son of Troy Sr and Delores. **Educ:** Wayne State Univ, Detroit, Mi, BSIE, 1986; Univ Chicago, Booth Sch Bus, MBA, finance & bus econs, 1991; Univ Mich, Dearborn, MI, MS, indust & systs engineering, 2002. **Career:** Midwest Aluminum Corp, eng asst, 1983; Kelsey-Hayes, mfg engr, 1984-85; Electronic Data Syst, syst engr, 1985-86; Gen Motors, Warren, engr, 1986-89, bus planner, 1989-92, fel, 1989, sr engr, 1992-97, strategic bus planner, 1997-98, prog mgr, 1998-2000, eng group mgr, mgr strategic initiatives, 2003-06, mgr prod develop, 2012-; TFE LLC, owner, 2004-. **Orgs:** Phi Delta Psi, 1979-; Inst Indust Eng, 1983-; Eng Soc Detroit, 1984-; chap pres, Phi Delta Psi Fraternity, 1984-85; nat pres, Phi Delta Psi Fraternity, 1990-92; vpres, African-Am MBA Asn, 1990-91. **Honors/Awds:** Col of Engineering Deans List, Wayne State Univ, 1984-85; Nat Deans List, 1984-85. **Home Addr:** 3294 Woodview Lake Rd, West Bloomfield, MI 48323-3570, **Home Phone:** (248)865-1178. **Business Addr:** Manager, General Motors, 777 Joslyn Rd MC 483-720-410, Pontiac, MI 48340-2920, **Business Phone:** (313)667-7175.

### REEVES, KHALID
Basketball player. **Personal:** Born Jul 15, 1972, Queens, NY; children: Justice & Justin. **Educ:** Univ Ariz, attended 1994. **Career:** Basketball player, basketball coach; Miami Heat, pt guard, 1994-95; Charlotte Hornets, pt guard, 1995-96; NJ Nets, pt guard, 1996-97; Dallas Mavericks, pt guard, 1997-99; Detroit Pistons, pt guard, 1999; Aris, Greece, pt guard, 1999; Pau-Orthez, France, pt guard, 1999; Chicago Bulls, pt guard, 1999-2000; Grand Rapids Hoops, Continental Basketball Asn, 2000-01; Phoenix Eclipse, Am Basketball Asn, 2001-02; Fla Sea Dragons, Us Basketball League, 2002; Cafe Najjar, Lebanon, 2003-04; Panteras de Miranda, Venezuela, 2005-05; Christ King Regional High Sch, asst coach, 2006-07; Deportivo Saprissa, Costa Rican League, 2007. **Orgs:** YMCA; Spec Olympics. **Honors/Awds:** East Team Most Valuable Player, McDonalds All-America Game, 1990; NCAA Champions, Ariz Wildcats, 1994. **Special Achievements:** First round pick, No 12, NBA Draft, 1994. **Business Addr:** Basketball Player, Costa Rican League, San Jose524-1000, **Business Phone:** (224)0-4034.

### REEVES, LOUISE
Government official. **Personal:** Born Aug 13, 1944, St. Louis, MO; married Charles B Mitchell. **Educ:** St Louis Univ, BA, polit sci, 1976; Webster Col, MA, pub admin, 1980. **Career:** SIU Edwardsville IL, fel, 1974; St Louis Agency Training & Employ, dep dir, 1977-; St Louis Met YWCA, dir housing & coun, 1976-77; Consult Neighborhood Serv Inc, assoc dir, 1965-76; Mo State Housing Develop Comn, comnr, 1978-; Freedom Res Inc, pres, 1978-79; Women Comm Serv, dir, 1983-95; Grace Hill Neighborhood Serv, assoc exec dir, 1995-; Jobs & Employ Support Serv, exec dir, 2007-; L Reeves & Assocs, prin. **Orgs:** Chmn, Monsignour John Schocklee Scholar Comm, 1979-; YMCA & YWCA; St Louis Wom Polit Caucas, 1975-; Coun Negro Women, 1976; Family Support Coun Mem. **Honors/Awds:** YWCA Service (vol) Award, St Louis Met YWCA; 70001 Support Award, St Louis Chap 70001 Youth Orgn, 1979. **Special Achievements:** First African-American woman in St. Louis to attain this international certification. **Home Addr:** 1342 Union Blvd, St Louis, MO 63113.

### REEVES, MARTHA ROSE (MARTHA LAVAILLE)
Entertainer, city council member. **Personal:** Born Jul 18, 1941, Eufaula, AL; daughter of Elijah Joshua and Ruby Lee Gilmore; children: Eric. **Career:** The Vandellas, lead singer, 1963-71; Martha Motown Records, leader. Albums: Willie Dynamite Soundtrack, 1973; Martha Reeves, 1974; The Rest of My Life, 1977; We Meet Again, 1978; Home to You, 2004. Films: Fairy Tales, 1979; Definitely Dusty, 1999; Standing in the Shadows of Motown, 2002. TV: "Thank Your Lucky Stars", 1964; "Shindig!", 1965; "Ready, Steady, Go!", 1964-66; "Where the Action Is", 1966; "Get It Together", 1970; "Soul Train", 1971-74; "Rock Concert", 1974; Rainbow, 1975; "Saturday Night Live", 1975; "Musikladen", 1976; "The Midnight Special", 1976; For the Rest of My Life, 1977; "Good Old Days", 1977; Gotta Keep Moving, 1980; Motown 25: "Yesterday, Today, Forever", 1983; "Super Night of Rock 'n' Roll", 1984; "Motown Returns to the Apollo", 1985; "Brown Sugar", 1986; "Ebony & Jet Showcase", 1986; "Dancin' in the Street", 1987; "Legendary Ladies of Rock & Roll", 1988; "The Original Leads of the Temptations", 1992; "Motorworld", 1995; "Rock & Roll", 1995; "The Temptations", 1998; "E! True Hollywood Story", 1998-2003; "Hollywood Squares", 2002; "Never Mind the Buzzcocks", 2004; "Jimmy Kimmel Live!", 2006; "Queens of British Pop", 2009; "Loose Women", 2009. Singles: "Power of Love", 1974; "Wild Night", 1974; "Love Blind", 1977; "Nowhere to Run", 1999; "(Love Is Like A) Heatwave", 2000; "(Love Is Like A) Heat Wave", 2002; "It's Easy to Fall in Love (With a Guy Like You)", 2005; "Dancing in the Street", 2006; "I'm Not Leaving with Crystal Method", 2012; Detroit City Coun, coun mem, 2005-09. **Orgs:** AFTRA; AGUA; SAG; Negro Women's Asn; Mt Zion Bapt Ch; Detroit's Metrop Church. **Honors/Awds:** Inducted into Rock & Roll Hall of Fame, 1995; Ranked No 56 on VH1's 100 Greatest Women of Rock N Roll; Recipient 7 Gold Singles; numerous Grammy nominations; 12 albums; Alabama Music Hall of Fame; MOJO Merit Award, 2011. **Home Addr:** 1300 E Lafayette St Apt 1211, Detroit, MI 48207. **Business Addr:** Council Member, Detroit City Council, 1340 Coleman A Young Municipal Ctr, Detroit, MI 48226, **Business Phone:** (313)224-4510.

**REEVES, MICHAEL STANLEY**
Executive. **Personal:** Born Oct 2, 1935, Memphis, TN; son of William (deceased) and Grace Stanley (deceased); married Patricia; children: Michael & Michelle. **Educ:** Roosevelt Univ, BA, 1964; Northwestern Univ, MBA, 1972. **Career:** Peoples Gas, mkt mgr, 1972-73, customer rel supt, 1973-74, off pres admin asst, 1974-75, customer rels dept gen supt, 1975-77, vpres 1977-87, exec vpres, 1987-; St Bernard Hosp, chmn; Peoples Gas Light & Coke Co, vpres; N Shore Gas. **Orgs:** Dir, Better Bus Bur, 1978-; chmn, Better Bus Bur Chicago & Northern Ill, 1994; exec, Leadership Coun; dir, Shedd Aquarium; adv comt, Local Initiatives Support Corp Chicago; bd mem, Abraham Lincoln Ctr; bd mem, C's Memorial Hosp; bd mem, Am Heart Asn Metrop Chicago; Am Asn Blacks Energy; Am Gas Asn. **Home Addr:** 8054 So Clyde Ave, Chicago, IL 60617, **Home Phone:** (773)734-8066. **Business Addr:** Executive Vice President, The Peoples Gas Light & Coke Co, 130 E Randolph Dr 24th Fl, Chicago, IL 60601-6207, **Business Phone:** (312)240-4000.

**REGISTER, DR. JASPER C.**
Educator, association executive, army officer. **Personal:** Born Jan 15, 1937, Valdosta, GA; son of Audra Mae Hall and Perry. **Educ:** Morehouse Col, AB, 1959; Univ KY, MA, 1969, PhD, 1974. **Career:** Stillman Col, instr, 1966-67; Baldwin-Wallace Col, asst prof, 1971-73; E Carolina Univ, assoc prof emer sociol, currently. **Orgs:** Am Sociol Assoc, 1974-; Southern Sociol Soc, 1974-; Human Rels Coun, 1980-83; bd dir, Ment Health Assoc, 1984-87, 1989-92. **Honors/Awds:** Research Award, Social Sci Rsch Coun, 1968; Assoc Dan forth Found, 1981-86; Department of Sociology Teaching Excellence Award, 1998. **Home Addr:** 5074 Greyfield Pl, Valdosta, GA 31605-7087, **Home Phone:** (229)671-1056. **Business Addr:** Associate Professor Emeritus, East Carolina University, A-416 Brewster Bldg E Tenth St, Greenville, NC 27858-4353, **Business Phone:** (252)328-6883.

**REID, ANTONIO (ANTONIO M LA REID)**
Songwriter, television producer, executive. **Personal:** Born Jun 7, 1956, Cincinnati, OH; son of Emma; married Perri McKissick; children: Antonio Jr & Aaron; married Erica; children: Addison Kennedy & Ariana Manuelle. **Career:** Deele, R&B group, singer, 1981-88; Arista Rec, pres & chief exec, 2000-04; Island Def Jam Music Group, chmn & chief exec officer, 2004-11; Epic Label Group, chief exec officer, 2011-; LaFace, founder & co-pres; Hitco Music Publ, pres & chief exec officer, currently; Albums: St Beat; Mat Thanz; Eyes Of A Stranger; Producer, songwriter with Kenny Edmonds (Babyface) albums: Bobby Brown; Karyn White; Sheena Easton; Pebbles; Paula Abdul; MAC Band. **Honors/Awds:** Producer of the Year Non-Classical, 1992; BMI Urban Awards, 2006; Grammy Award, 2013; Business of Entertainment Award, BET Hons; President's Merit Award, Nat Acad Rec Arts & Sci, 2013. **Special Achievements:** Grammy award nomination for song "Every Little Step", 1989; Accomplished songwriters producing music which sold a double-platinum album for Bobby Brown, a Grammy nomination for Karyn White, and a Top-10 single for Paula Abdul. **Business Addr:** President, Chief Executive Officer, Hitco Music Publishing, 500 Bishop St NW Suite A-5, Atlanta, GA 30318, **Business Phone:** (404)352-5911.

**REID, CHRISTOPHER (CHRISTOPHER KID)**
Actor. **Personal:** Born Apr 5, 1964, Bronx, NY; married Kimberly Turner; children: Cameron, Christina & Cailin. **Educ:** Lehman Col Bronx. **Career:** Librarian; filing clerk; theatrical stage worker; freelance journalist; nanny & tutor; actor, currently. TV Series: "Kid 'n' Play", 1990; "Minor Adjustments", 1996; "Sister, Sister", 1996-97; "Smart Guy", 1997; "The Temptations", 1998; "Border Line", 1999; "VIP", 2000; "That's Life", 2001; "Barbershop", 2005. Videos: Sword of Honor, producer, 1994. Films: House Party, 1990; House Party 2, 1991; Class Act, 1992; House Party 3, 1994; Pauly Shore Is Dead, 2003; War of the Worlds 2: The Next Wave, 2008; Straight out of L.A., 2010; Supah Ninjas, 2011; MAD, 2013; House Party 5, 2013. TV shows: "Your Big Break"; "It's Show time at the Apollo"; Song: "Why Don't You Stay?", 2008. **Honors/Awds:** Eric Gregory Award, 1978; Prudence Farmer Award, 1978 & 1980; Somerset Maugham Award, 1980; Hawthornden Prize, 1980. **Business Addr:** Actor, Endeavor Talent Agency, 9601 Wilshire Blvd Fl 3, Beverly Hills, CA 90210, **Business Phone:** (310)248-2000.

**REID, DR. CLARICE D.**
Physician, government official. **Personal:** Born Nov 21, 1931, Birmingham, AL; daughter of Noah Edgar Sr and Willie Mae Brown; married Arthur Joseph Reid Jr; children: Kevin, Sheila, Jill & Clarice. **Educ:** Talladega Col, BS, biol, 1952; Meharry Med Col, med tech, 1954; Univ Cincinnati Sch Med, MD, 1959. **Career:** Physician, government official (retired); Pediatrician pvt prac, Cincinnati, 1962-68; Ohio Dept Health, pediat consult, 1964-70; Univ Cinncinati Sch Med, asst clin prof pediat, 1965-70; Pediat Jewish Hosp, Dept Health, Educ & Welfare, dir pediat, 1969-70, Pediat Dept, chmn, 1970; Nat Heart, Lung & Blood Inst, dir, 1973; Nat Ctr Family Planning, Health Servs & Ment Health Admin, med consult, 1972-73, dep dir, 1973-76; Howard Univ Col Med, asst clin prof pediat, 1979-94; US Nat Insts Health, Sickle Cell Prog, Div Blood Dis & Resources, actg dir, 1988-89, dir, 1994-98. **Orgs:** Nat Med Asn; Am Asn Advan Sci; Am Acad Pediat; NY Acad Sci; Am Soc Hemat; chair, vpres, Am Bridge Asn Found; dir pediat educ, Jewish Hosp, 1969, chmn, Pediatricks Dept. **Honors/Awds:** Outstanding Student Faculty Award, Meharry Med Col, 1954; Director Award, Merit Award, NIH; Special Recognition Award, Pub Health Serv, 1989; Superior Service Award, Pub Health Serv, 1989; Presential Meritoroius Executive Award, Pub Health Serv, 1991. **Special Achievements:** First African-American pediatrician in private practice in Cincinnati, 1962-68; Book of Black Heroes, Volume II: Great Women in the Struggle; The Third African American to Graduate With An M.d. From Ohio's University Of Cincinnati College Of Medicine. **Home Addr:** 9715 Fernwood Rd, Bethesda, MD 20817-1554, **Home Phone:** (301)530-8851.

**REID, DAPHNE ETTA MAXWELL**
Founder (originator), actor, executive. **Personal:** Born Jul 13, 1948, New York, NY; daughter of Green and Rosalee; married Timothy L; children: Christopher Tubbs, Tim Jr & Tori. **Educ:** Northwestern Univ, BA, interior design & archit, 1970. **Career:** Screen Actors Guild, bd mem, 1974-76; Screen Actors Guild, co-chmn, conserv comt, 1977; Daphne Maxwell Inc, pres; Timalove Enterprises Inc, vpres, currently; New Millennium Studios, co-founder, currently; ForReal, exec producer, 2003; TV series: "The Duke", 1979; "A Man Called Sloane", 1979; "Coach of the Year ", 1980; "WKRP in Cincinnati", 1980-82; "Hill Street Blues", 1981-85; "The Love Boat", 1982; "Hardcastle and McCormick", 1982; "Simon & Simon", 1983-87; "The Duck Factory", 1984; "Matt Houston", 1984; "Protocol", 1984; "Paper Dolls", 1984; "The A-Team", 1983-85; "Cagney & Lacey", 1985; "The Long Journey Home", 1987; "Frank's Place", 1987; "Murder, She Wrote", 1988; "ABC Afterschool Specials", 1989; "Snoops", 1989; "You Must Remember This", 1992; "The Cosby Show", 1992; "The Fresh Prince of Bel-Air", 1993-96; "Sister, Sister", 1996; "In the House", 1998; "Linc's", 1999; "Alley Cats Strike", 2000; "Crossing Jordan", 2004; "Slavery and the Making of America", 2004; "Eve", 2003-06; "Polly and Marie", 2007. Films: Once Upon a Time... When We Were Colored, 1995; Asunder, 1999; For Real, exec producer, 2003; Troop 491: the Adventures of the Muddy Lions, 2013; Movie: Shooting the Prodigal, 2016. **Orgs:** Bd visitor, Va State Univ, 2008-; hon mem, Delta Sigma Theta sorority, 2010. **Honors/Awds:** First Commercials, 1967; Ladies Home Jour as 1 of 14 Most Beautiful Women, 1970; Starred in Frank's Place, Snoops, The Tim & Daphne Show, Exposed; Fresh Prince Bel Air; Best New Product Award, Linc's Home Sewing & Crafts Asn, 1993; Norfolk State Univ Hon Degree, 1996; outstanding supporting actress a comedy ser & Nat Asn Advan Colored People, 1996; Hon Doctorate Degree, Va Common wealth Univ, 1999; honorary member, Delta Sigma Theta. **Special Achievements:** Created and produced videotape package with the McCall Pattern Company, "Suddenly You're Sewing"; created pattern line at the McCall Pattern Company; "The Daphne Maxwell Reid Collection"; First African American Homecoming Queen, Northwestern Univ, 1967; First African Am on the cover, Glamour Mag, 1969. **Business Addr:** Co-Founder, New Millennium Studios, 1 Millenium Dr, Petersburg, VA 23805, **Business Phone:** (804)957-4200.

**REID, DESIREE CHARESE**
Executive. **Personal:** Born Jan 13, 1964, Bronx, NY; daughter of John Jr and Elsie McDaniels. **Educ:** Seton Hall Univ, BA, 1984; Paralegal Inst, 1988; Adelphi Univ, MBA, 1993; NY Restaurant Sch, prof mgt develop prog, 1998. **Career:** Jordache Enterprises, charge back supvr, 1985-86; H Cotler Co, exec acct mgr, 1986-92; John Kaldor, acct rec supvr, 1992; Farber ware, corp credit mgr, 1994-96; M Kamenstein, accounts receivable mgr, 1998-99; Millionaire Acad Network, acct dir, 1999-2002; New York State Assembly, campaign mgr & speech writer, 2002-; Katharine Gibbs Sch, stud accounts mgr, 2002-04; Paper Enterprises Inc & Consol Paper, credit & a/r supvr, 2005-06; Sanford Brown Inst White Plains, bursar, stud accounts mgr & bus off mgr, 2006-08; Billionaire Mastermind Forum, finance mgr & admin dir, 2008-; Community Activist; 2009-; New York Inst Spec Educ, Community Activist, 2011-; Reid Enterprises, currently. **Orgs:** Co-chmn, Black Stud Union, 1982-83; Delta Sigma Theta Sorority, 1983-; Nat Asn Advan Colored People, 1992-; vol, Mayor Dinkins Re-Election Camp, 1993; Black Filmmaker Asn; Thruway Homeowners Asn; Nat Asn Female Exec; Drama Soc; Nat Asn Credit Mgt; New York Credit & Financial Mgt Asn. **Home Addr:** 3118 Mickle Ave, Bronx, NY 10469-3104, **Home Phone:** (718)379-5261. **Business Addr:** President, Ms Reid Enterprises, PO Box 1061, Bronx, NY 10469, **Business Phone:** (718)379-5347.

**REID, DON**
Basketball player. **Personal:** Born Dec 30, 1973, Washington, DC. **Educ:** Georgetown Univ, BA, 1995. **Career:** Basketball player (retired); Detroit Pistons, power forward, 1995-2000, 2002-03; Wash Wizards, power forward, 1999-2000; Orlando Magic, power forward, 2000-02.

**REID, DUANE L.**
Automotive executive, chief executive officer, president (organization). **Personal:** married Wanda; children: Katie, Alex & Evan. **Educ:** Western Carolina Univ, BS, bus admin, 1982. **Career:** Reid Automotive Grp, chief exec officer; Peachtree Ford-Mercury, pres & owner, 1992-2001; Rome Ford Lincoln Mercury Inc, pres, 2000-07; Rome City Comn, 2006, comnr, ward 2, 2007-, pub safety & fire overview comts, mayor & chair, 2008-, Northwestern Mutual, financial rep, 2008-09; Duane Reid & Assocs, prin & broker, 2009-12; JM Family Enterprises, autosales2 consult, 2011-13; APCO EasyCare, Sr Regional Mkt Consult, 2013-. **Orgs:** Vice-chmn, Greater Rome Chamber Com; bd gov, Rome Area Hist Mus; Rome-Floyd County Plng Comn; bd dir, Rome Rotary Club; bd chmn, Am Red Cross, Coosa Valley Chap; Ford Lincoln Mercury Dealer Develop Alumni Asn. **Business Addr:** President, Rome Ford Lincoln Mercury Inc, 101 Hwy 411 SE, Rome, GA 30161-7270, **Business Phone:** (706)235-4453.

**REID, HERMAN, JR. (J R REID)**
Basketball player, basketball coach. **Personal:** Born Mar 31, 1968, Virginia Beach, VA; son of Herman Reid Sr and Jean; married Pansy King; children: Kaylah, Jaylen & Zoe. **Educ:** Univ NC, Chapel Hill, NC, commun, 1989. **Career:** Basketball player (retired), basketball coach; Charlotte Hornets, power forward, 1989-93 & 1997-99; San Antonio Spurs, power forward, 1992-96; New York Knicks, power forward, 1995-96; Paris Basket Racing, France, 1996-97; Los Angeles Lakers, power forward, 1998-99; Milwaukee Bucks, power forward, 1999-2000; Cleveland Cavaliers, power forward, 2000-01; Strasbourg, 2001-02; Baloncesto Leon, 2002-03; Patrick Henry Community Col, asst coach, currently. **Home Addr:** 121 Cemetary St, Chester, SC 29706-1620. **Business Addr:** Assistant Coach, Patrick Henry Community College, 645 Patriot Ave, Martinsville, VA 24112, **Business Phone:** (276)638-8777.

**REID, HON. INEZ SMITH**

**REID, DR. IRVIN D.**
School administrator, educator. **Personal:** Born Feb 21, 1941, Pawleys Island, SC; son of Joseph and Etta Louise; married Pamela Trotman; children: Nicole Reid Gore & Dexter. **Educ:** Howard Univ, BS, psychol, 1963, MS, psychol, 1966; Univ Pa, Wharton Sch, MBA, 1970, PhD, appl econs, 1975; Harvard Univ, cert, educ admin. **Career:** Drexel Univ, prof, mkt; Howard Univ, prof, 1978-79; Wayne State Univ, prof, 1978-79, pres, 1997-2008; pres emer, 2008-; Univ Tenn Chattanooga, prof, 1979-97, dean, admin, 1983-97; Montclair State Univ, pres, admin, 1989-97; Community Engagement, Eugene Applebaum Chair, 2008-. **Orgs:** Nat Conf Christians & Jews; Pres Comn Nat Col Athletic Asn; Detroit 300 Comt; bd trustee, Detroit Med Ctr; Econ Club Detroit; bd mem, chair trust comt, Fleet Bank; bd mem, Mack-Cali Real Estate Investment Trust, 1994-; chair, Mack-Cali Real Estate Trust, 1994-; Alpha Soc; Beta Gamma Sigma; Omicron Delta Epsilon; Phi Kappa Phi; Alpha Kappa Psi; Mich Econ Develop Corp; Fed Res Bank Chicago, 2002-; First Tenn Bank Chattanooga; NatWest Bank Nj; chair trust comt, NatWest Bank USA; bd mem, Handleman Co, 2003-; bd mem, Pep Boys, 2005-. **Home Addr:** , MI. **Business Addr:** President Emeritus, Eugene Applebaum Chair, Wayne State University, Detroit, MI 48202.

**REID, J R. See REID, HERMAN, JR.**

**REID, JANIE ELLEN**
Administrator. **Personal:** Born Feb 15, 1950, Pelzer, SC. **Educ:** SC State Col, BS, bus admin, 1972. **Career:** SC Assoc Stud Finan Aid Admin, mem, 1973-87, secy, treas, 1975-77; JESirrine Scholar Adv Bd, mem, 1974-75, chmn, 1980-82; SC Comm Higher Ed, adv bd mem, 1975-78; US Dept Ed Bur Stud Financial Aid, inst appl revpanel mem, 1976; Greenville Tech Col, fin aid dean, currently. **Orgs:** Instr, New Financial Aid Officer Workshop Southern Asn Stud Fin Aid Admin, 1978-79; charter mem, Greenville Urban League's Early Leadership & Confidence Training, 1978-79; adv bd, SC Stud Loan Corp, 1981-83; chmn, adv bd Greenville Urban League's Ed Talent Search Prog, 1982-84; minister, ed Shady Grove Baptist Ch, 1983-85; ed, adv comm SC Appalachian Coun Gov, 1983-89; chmn, Greenville Community Human Rels Comm, 1985. **Honors/Awds:** Citizenship Award, Greenville Civitan Club, 1968; Iota Phi Lambda, Delta Eta Chap 1971-; Annual Pastor's Award, Shady Grove Baptist Ch, 1981, 1982, 1983. **Home Addr:** 405 Old Hundred Rd, Pelzer, SC 29669. **Business Addr:** Director, Dean of Financial Aid, Greenville Technical College, 225 S Pleasantburg Dr, Greenville, SC 29607-5616, **Business Phone:** (864)250-8128.

**REID, JOEL OTTO**
Educator, association executive, writer. **Personal:** Born May 17, 1936, Newark, NJ; children: Joel II & Nicol. **Educ:** NY Univ Sch Educ, BS, 1959; Montclair State Col, MA, 1965; Claremont Grad Sch, Claremont, CA, PhD, 1973. **Career:** Elizabeth Pub Sch Syst, Elizabeth, NJ, teacher; White Plaines High Sch, counr, teacher, 1962-65; White Plaines Bd Educ, prof recruiter, 1965-67; Nat Teachers Corps, Migrant Univ, Southern Calif, teacher, leader, 1967-68; Claremont Grad Sch, staff mem, 1971-72, Social Sci Dept, prof, 1978; Pasadena City Col, dean continuing educ, 1968-78, prof social sci, 1978, prof emer social sci, currently. **Orgs:** Chmn, Eval Com Western Asn Sch & Col, 1969, 1970 & 1974; Pasadena Educ Asn; Pasadena City Col Fac Asn; NEA; Los Angeles Co Adult Educ Adminr Asn; chmn, bd dir, Urban League Com Educ Fund Dr; Fair Hsg Comt Westchester Co, New York; Am Friends Serv Comt Hsg, Pasadena; coun Neighborhod Youth Ctr. **Honors/Awds:** Two Year Scholar Col; Kiwanis Rotary Club Scholar; Valley Settlement House Scholar, West Orange, NJ; Womens Aux Scholar, West Orange, NJ. **Special Achievements:** Author: "Existentialism in Black American Literature", 1973. **Business Addr:** Professor Emeritus of Social Science, Pasadena City College, 1570 E Colorado Blvd, Pasadena, CA 91106, **Business Phone:** (626)585-7123.

**REID, JOY-ANN**
Journalist, television journalist. **Personal:** married Patrick Abner. **Educ:** Harvard University, B.F.A. in Visual Arts with a concentration in Documentary Film, 1991; Knight Center for Specialized Journalism, Fellow, 2003. **Career:** WTVJ, Internet News Editor, 2000-04; America Coming Together, State Deputy Communications Director; IMAGELAB Films, Managing Partner, 2005; "Wake Up South Florida," Co-host, 2006-07; Barack Obama presidential campaign, Florida's urban media outreach, 2008; WSVN; "Miami Herald," Columnist, 2010-; TheGrio.com, Managing Editor, 2011-; MSNBC, On-air Contributor; Political Blog, "The Reid Report," Writer. **Orgs:** South Florida Black Journalists Association, Member; Miami NAACP, Member. **Honors/Awds:** Tamika Award for Best TV Program, 1993; Knight Center for Advanced Journalism Fellow, 2003. **Special Achievements:** Has interviewed Bill Cosby, O.J. Simpson, Russell Simmons, and then-Senator Barack Obama.

**REID, DR. LESLIE BANCROFT**
Educator. **Personal:** Born Nov 7, 1934, Clarendon; son of Walter Bancroft and Brenda May Whyne; married Norma A Morris; children: Donovan & Deanne. **Educ:** Howard Univ, BS, 1968, DDS, 1972. **Career:** Govt Bact Lab Jamaica, med tech, 1953-59; Tia Maria Ltd, Jamaica, chemist, 1959-64; Cafritz Hosp, Wash, DC, med tech, 1966-72; Howard Univ Dent Sch, fac mem, 1972-; Reid & Asn, pres. **Orgs:** Bd trustee, Charles County Community Col, 1969-76; dir, Reid-& Yip Young DDS PA, 1973-; consult, Ministry Health, Jamaica, 1974; consult, Ministry Health, Guyana, 1976; partner, E over Dent Serv, 1979-; consult, Ministry Health Belize Cent Am, 1984; bd trustee, Hospice Charles County, 1985-; staff, Greater Southeast Comn Hosp, 1986-; bd trustee, Warner Pac Col, 1989-; clinician, Numerous Dent Conv; Omicron Kappa Upsilon Inducted, Howard Univ Col Dent. **Home Addr:** 11865 Federal Sq Suite 102, Waldorf, MD 20601, **Home Phone:** (301)645-2211. **Business Addr:** Member, Howard University

College of Dentistry, 600 W St NW, Washington, DC 20059, **Business Phone:** (202)806-0440.

**REID, MALISSIE LAVERNE**
Interior designer, real estate agent, manager. **Personal:** Born Aug 23, 1953, Orange, NJ; daughter of Joseph Wilbur Sr and Malissie Elizabeth. **Educ:** Rider Univ, BA, polit sci, 1975; Prof Sch Bus, ins broker, 1978; NYK Sch Interior Design, 1982; Kovats Sch Real Estate, 1987. **Career:** Union Camp Corp, Tax Dept, ade asst, 1975-76; Aetna Life & Casualty, com lines underwriter, 1976-78; Chubb Custom Mkt, specialty lines underwriter, 1978-81; Cigna Ins Co, underwriting mgr, 1981-86; Home Ins Co, underwriting mgr, 1986-87; Reid's Interior Decorators & Upholstery, exec vpres, 1987-; Weichert Realtors, sales rep, 1987-2010, broker, currently. **Orgs:** Bd adjustments, Town Nutley, 1991-; bd dir, Community Ment HTH, 1991-. **Home Addr:** 35 Hopper Ave, Nutley, NJ 07110-2522, **Home Phone:** (973)667-4689. **Business Addr:** Executive Vice President, Reid's Interior Decorators & Upholstery, 573 Bloomfield Ave, Montclair, NJ 07042, **Business Phone:** (973)667-1778.

**REID, N. NEVILLE**
Lawyer. **Personal:** married Adonna Davis; children: Julian, Winston, Everett, Emmanuel & Rebecca. **Educ:** Harvard Univ, BA, 1984; Harvard Law Sch, JD, 1987. **Career:** Mayer, Brown, Rowe & Maw LLP, assoc, 1987-96, partner, 1991-2010; Fox Hefter Swibel Levin & Carroll LLP, atty & partner, 2010-; Bankruptcy, Restructuring & Creditors Rights Group, co-chair; St Mark United Methodist Church Sch, supt. 2005-. **Orgs:** Panel pvt trustee, Northern Dist Ill, 1994-; Am Bankruptcy Inst, 1994-; bd dirs, Good Shepherd Community Servs Org, 1995-99; Am Bar Asn Conf Minority Partners Majority/Corp Law Firms, 1996-99; chmn, Beverly Area Local Dev Corp, 1996; fel Leadership Greater Chicago, 1997-98; Bankruptcy Focus Group; adv mem, Cabrini Green Legal Aid Clin; bd mem, LINK Unlimited, 2005-06; Kairos Prison Ministries, 2011-; bd mem, Chicago Scholars, 2009-10; bd dir, Nat Asn Bankruptcy Trustees, 2014-. **Honors/Awds:** Harvard Col Scholar, Harvard Univ, 1981; John Harvard Col Scholar, 1982-84; Rhodes Scholar Finalist, 1983; Illinois Super Lawyer, 2005-06, 2012-15. **Business Addr:** Partner, Attorney, Fox Hefter Swibel Levin & Carroll LLP, 200 W Madison St Suite 3000, Chicago, IL 60606, **Business Phone:** (312)224-1245.

**REID, NATALIE DESSELLE. See DESSELLE, NATALIE.**

**REID, DR. PAMELA TROTMAN**
Educator, college administrator. **Personal:** Born Jun 1, 1946, Bronx, NY; daughter of Louis Hilary and Gloria Legare Trotman; married Irvin D; children: Nicole Legare & Irvin Dexter. **Educ:** Howard Univ, BS; Temple Univ, MA; Univ Pa, PhD. **Career:** Prof develop psychol; assoc provost & dean acad affairs; interim provost, City Univ New York Grad Ctr; Univ Mich, dir women's studies prog; Univ Mich, prof educ & psychol; Univ Mich, Inst Res Women & Gender, res scientist; Roosevelt Univ, provost & exec vpres, 2004-08, prof; St Joseph Col, Pres, currently. **Orgs:** Am Psychol Asn. **Business Addr:** President, Saint Joseph College, 1678 Asylum Ave, West Hartford, CT 06117, **Business Phone:** (860)231-5399.

**REID, RALPH D.**
Vice president (organization). **Educ:** Oakwood Univ, BS, bus admin & acct; Univ Mo, Kans City, MO, JD, 1987. **Career:** Sprint, vpres corp social responsibility, 2005-. **Orgs:** Pres, Sprint Found; pres bd dir, Kans City Downtown Minority Develop Corp; vice chmn, Greater Kans City Urban League; bd mem, Shawnee Mission Med Ctr; bd mem, Boys & Girls Club Greater Kans City; bd mem, Kans City Repertory Theater; bd mem, Heart Am United Way; bd mem, Salvation Army; bd mem, Greater KC Chamber Com; bd mem, Oakwood Univ; bd mem, Pk Univ; bd mem, Univ Mo; vpres, Kans City United Community Action Agency. **Business Addr:** Vice President, Sprint Communications Inc, 6200 Sprint Pkwy, Overland Park, KS 66251, **Business Phone:** (703)433-4000.

**REID, ROBERT KEITH**
Basketball player. **Personal:** Born Aug 30, 1955, Atlanta, GA; married Diana; children: Robert & Keva Rachel. **Educ:** St Mary's Univ, attended 1977. **Career:** Basketball player (retired), basketball coach; Houston Rockets, 1977-82, 1983-88; Charlotte Hornets, 1988-90; Portland Trail Blazers, 1989; Tulsa Fast Breakers, 1990-91; Philadelphia 76ers, coach, 1991; Tri-City Chinook, 1991-92; YakimaSun Kings, coach, 1992-93; Tex Rim Rockers, 2003; Brevard Blue Ducks, head coach, 2004; Lakeland Blue Ducks, 2004; Debreceni Vadkakasok, 2004-05; Robert Reid Basketball Clinics, coach, 2006-; Ranger Col, basketball coach, 2011-13, 2014-15; ABA's S Fla Gold, assoc head coach, currently. **Orgs:** Spec Olympics, Big Brothers, hosp groups. **Home Addr:** 1727 Chesapeake Bay Ct Suite A, Houston, TX 77084, **Home Phone:** (281)599-1693. **Business Addr:** Head Coach, ABA South Florida Gold, 4975 Pk Ridge Blvd, Boynton Beach, FL 33426, **Business Phone:** (954)850-4045.

**REID, DR. ROBERTO ELLIOTT (ROBERTO BOBBY REID)**
Educator, physician. **Personal:** Born Nov 12, 1930, Panama City; son of Exley Neilson and Esther McDonald; married Joyce. **Educ:** NY Univ, AB, 1954; Case Western Res Univ Sch Med, MD, 1958. **Career:** Philadelphia Gen Hosp, 1959, asst prof urol to assoc prof urol, 1965-73; Albert Einstein Col Med, assoc prof urol, 1963-85, prof urol; Bronx Munic Hosp, dir urol, 1973; Cleveland VA Hosp, resident; Philadelphia Gen Hosp, resident; Albert Einstein Col, resident; Weiler Hosp, chief urol; pvt practr, currently. **Orgs:** Coun, Fel Am Col Surgeons, 1975-77; New York sec rep, AVAA, 1976; Sigma Pi Phi; Am Urol Asn Inc. **Home Addr:** 10 Greens Way, New Rochelle, NY 10805-1222, **Home Phone:** (914)563-2416. **Business Addr:** Surgeon, Eastchester Professional Center, 1695 Eastchester Rd Suite 306, Bronx, NY 10461, **Business Phone:** (718)904-0222.

**REID, RONDA A.**
Security guard, air force officer. **Personal:** Born May 1, 1955, Dayton, OH; married Washington Jr; children: Darnell & Byron. **Educ:** Sinclair Community Col, Dayton, AS, law enforcement, 1974; Univ Dayton, Dayton, BS, crim justice, 1976; Cent Mich Univ, Mount Pleasant, MS, pub adm, 1992. **Career:** USF, civilian, Wright Patterson AFB, Dayton, res & develop, admin support, 1977-84, Nasa's Johnson Space Ctr, defense security specialist, 1984-86; Gen Elec Co, Cin, security specialist, 1986-88, Jnson Space Ctr, Houston, security specialist, 1988; USAF Int Affairs Officer, Pentagon, security specialist, 1989-. **Orgs:** Nat Classification Mgt Soc, 1985-; vpres, 1984-85, pres, 1985-86, Am Bus Women's Asn, Gem City Chap; holds one six seats, USAF Security Career Prog Training & Develop Panel; Blacks Gov Pentagon Chap. **Honors/Awds:** Outstanding Performance Rating, 1979; Sustained Superior Performance Award, 1984; Superior Performance Award, 1985; Notable Achievement Award, 1986; Quality Step Increase, 1986; Performance Award, 1987, 1990-92, USF. **Home Addr:** 6132 Surrey Sq Lane Suite 202, Forestville, MD 20747, **Home Phone:** (301)516-0964. **Business Addr:** Security Specialist, US Air Force International Affairs Office, Rm 4C1074, Washington, DC 20330-1010, **Business Phone:** (202)695-6057.

**REID, RUBIN J.**
Real estate agent. **Personal:** children: 2. **Educ:** Va, Grad Col, Bus, 1963; BS, bus admin. **Career:** Glenarden, mayor, vice mayor; Gitelson Neff Assoc Inc, real estate agt; Coldwell Banker Residential Brokerage, sales assoc, currently. **Orgs:** Chmn, Town Coun. **Home Addr:** 7904 Cawker Ave, Glenarden, MD 20706, **Home Phone:** (301)773-0890. **Business Addr:** Sales Associate, Coldwell Banker Residential Brokerage, 9410 Annapolis Rd Suite 100, Lanham, MD 20715, **Business Phone:** (301)474-5700.

**REID, SHIRLEY WOODSON. See WOODSON, SHIRLEY A.**

**REID, TIMOTHY L.**
Writer, actor, television producer. **Personal:** Born Dec 19, 1944, Norfolk, VA; son of William Lee and Augustine Wilkins; married Daphne Maxwell; children: Christopher Tubbs; married Rita; children: Tim II & Tori LeAnn. **Educ:** Norfolk State Col, BBA, 1968. **Career:** Dupont Corp, mkt rep, 1968-71; Tim & Tom Comedy Team, 1971-75; stand-up comedian; Timalove Enterprises, founder, 1979; United Image Entertainment Enterprises, co-founder, 1990, co-chmn; New Millennium Studios, Co-founder, 2009-; TV Series: "Easy Does It. Starring Frankie Avalon", 1976; "The Marilyn McCoo & Billy Davis, Jr. Show", 1977; "The Richard Pryor Show", 1977; "WKRP In Cincinnati", 1978-82; "You Can't Take It With You", 1979; "Teachers Only", 1983; "Simon & Simon", 1983-87; "Frank's Place", actor, writer & co-exec producer, 1987-88; "Snoops", actor & co-creator, exec producer, 1989-90; "Perry Mason: The Case of the Silenced Singer", 1990; "Stephen King's It", 1991; "The Family Business", 1991; "You Must Remember This", 1992; "Race to Freedom: The Underground Rail road", 1994; "Sister, Sister", actor, creator & producer, 1994-99; "Simon & Simon: In Trouble Again", 1995; "Linc's", dir & exec producer, 1998; "About Sarah", exec producer, 1999; "Blue Moon", exec producer, 1999; "Alley Cats Strike", 2000; "The Contender", dir & producer, 2000; "You Wish!", 2003; "The Reading Room", 2005; "That 70's Show", actor, 2004-06; "That's So Raven", 2005; "Treme", 2010-12. "The Soul Man", 2012; "For Colored Boys, Redemption", 2013; "Blues in the Night", dir & writer, 2013. Films: Dead Bang, 1989; The Fourth War, 1990; Once Upon a Time; When We Were Colored, actor, producer & dir, 1995; Out-of-Sync, producer, 1995; Spirit Lost, producer, 1997; Asunder", producer & dir, 1999; Others: For Real, actor, writer & dir, 2003; On the One, 2005; Trade, 2007; "Roommates", 2009; Troop 491: the Adventures of the Muddy Lions, actor & producer, 2013. **Orgs:** Writers Guild Am; Screen Actors Guild; bd dirs, Phoenix House Calif; Norfolk St Univ, Commonwealth Va; bd dirs, Nat Acad Cable Programming; AFTRA; Doctor Humane Lett, Cent State Univ, 2000; life mem, Nat Asn Advan Colored People; Alpha Phi Alpha, 2010; bd dir, Am Civil War Ctr, 2011. **Honors/Awds:** Emmy Award; Critics Choice Award, 1988; Q Award, Viewers Qual Tv Awards, 1988; Image Award, Nat Asn Advan Colored People, 1990; Best Actor in a Comedy Award, Viewers for Quality Television, 1988; Nat Black Col Alumni Hall Fame, 1991; Audience Choice Award, 1995, St. Louis Int Film Festival; Directional Award, Ft. Lauderdale Int Film Festival; Best Producer, Houston Int Film Festival; Image Award Nominee for Producer, Nat Asn Advan Colored People; Oscar Micheaux Award, Producer's Guild of America, 1999; Christopher Award, 1999. **Special Achievements:** Involved in efforts to provide scholarship funds for Minority students; organizer, sponsor: Annual Tim Reid Celebrity Tennis Tournament, Norfolk St University Campus; actively involved in anti-drug movement since 1969; testified many times before House and Senate Sub-committees. **Home Addr:** 16030 Ventura Blvd Suite 380, Encino, CA 91436. **Business Addr:** Co-Founder, New Millennium Studios, 1 New Millennium Dr, Petersburg, VA 23805, **Business Phone:** (804)957-4200.

**REID, TRACY LASHAWN**
Basketball player. **Personal:** Born Nov 1, 1976; daughter of Clarence. **Educ:** Univ NC, BS, commun, 1998. **Career:** Charlotte Sting, forward, 1998-2000; Miami Heat, 2001; Phoenix Mercury, 2002-03; Universitat FC Barcelona, 2003-04; Maccabi Ramat Hen, 2005; Acis Incosa Leon 2005-06; Acis-Incosa Leon, 2005-07; Halcon Avenida 2007-08; CB Olesa Espanyol, guard, 2008-09.

**REID, VERNON ALPHONSUS**
Rock musician, guitarist, composer. **Personal:** Born Aug 22, 1958, London; married Gabri Christa; children: 1. **Educ:** Brooklyn Tech. **Career:** Living Colour, founder & singer, 1985-; Black Rock Coalition 1, co founder, singer; Albums: Vivid, 1988; Time's Up, 1990; Biscuits, 1991; Stain, 1993; Films: Fresh Kill, 1994; Vintage - Families of Value, 1995; Dr. Hugo, 1998; Ghosts of Attica, 2001; That's My Face, 2001; Paid in Full, 2002; Mr. 3000, 2004; Twelve Disciples of Nelson Mandela, 2005; Shadow: Dead Riot, 2006; Guitar Hero III: Legends of Rock, 2007; TV series: "Almost Home", 2006. Discography: Smash & Scatteration, 1984; Mistaken Identity, 1996; GTR OBLQ, 1998; This little room, 2000; Front End Lifter, 2002; Right Back, 2002; Known Unknown, 2004; The Tao Of Yo, 2004; Other True Self, 2006; Urban Mythology Volume 1 - Free Form Funky Freqs, 2007. Album: No Escape From the Blues, producer, 2003; Other True Self, 2006. **Honors/Awds:** With Living Colour: two Grammy Awards, two MTV Music Awds, two Int Rock Awards, 1988-93; Grammy nomination for Best Rock Instrumental, 1996. **Special Achievements:** Named No 66 on Rolling Stone's 100 Greatest Guitarists of All Time. **Business Addr:** Singer, The Black Rock Coalition, Cooper Sta, New York, NY 10276, **Business Phone:** (212)713-5097.

**REID-MERRITT, DR. PATRICIA ANN**
Educator. **Personal:** Born Oct 31, 1950, Philadelphia, PA; daughter of Curtis and Etrulia; married William Thomas Merritt; children: Christina, Brahim, Jeffrey & Gregory. **Educ:** Cabrini Col, BA, 1973; Temple Univ, MA, social work, 1975; Univ Pa, advan cert, social work educ, 1979, PhD, social work, 1984, DSW. **Career:** Auth, Educr, choreographer, performing artist, adminr, costume designer, costume maker, grant writer, booking agt, promotional dir; Distinguished Prof Social Work & Africana Studies; Prog Coordr; Pa Gen Hosp, psychiat social worker, 1975-76; Lawnside Pub Schs, sch social work consult, 1980-; Nat Asn Black Social Workers, nat interim exec, 1984-85; Stockton Univ, Distinguished Prof & Prog Coordr, currently. **Orgs:** Founder & artistic dir, Afro-one Dance, Drama & Drum Theatre Inc, 1973-93; NJ Black Issues Conv, 1984-; Willingboro Black Bus & Prof Asn, 1985-89; co-founder & chair, founding pres, Burlington County Inter Orgn Black Leadership Coun, 1986; bd dir, founder & pres, Asn Black Women Higher Educ, 1986-88; Black United Fund NJ, Burlington County, 1986-; founder & pres, Nat Asn Black Social Workers, SJ; pres, Asn Black Women Higher Educ, Greater Pa, 1986-88; bd dir, Nat Coun Black Studies, 1994-2010. **Special Achievements:** Chairman, National Fannie Lou Hamer Statue Committee. **Home Addr:** 2 Rosewood Terr, Hamilton Township, NJ 08620. **Business Addr:** Distinguished Professor of Social Work & Africana Studies, Coordinator, Stockton University, Jimmy Leeds Rd, Pomona, NJ 08240-0195, **Business Phone:** (609)652-4542.

**REIDE, ATTY. JEROME L.**
Lawyer, educator. **Personal:** Born Apr 23, 1954, New York, NY; son of Leonora E and St Clair E Sr. **Educ:** State Univ NY, New Paltz, BA, sociol, 1977; Hofstra Univ Law Sch, JD, law, 1981; Columbia Univ, Grad Jour Sch, MS, jour, 1983; Mich State Univ, MA, polit sci, 1989, PhD, polit sci urban studies, 1991. **Career:** Am Civil Liberties Union, Access to Justice, 1986-87; State Univ NY, Ctr Labor Studies, polit sci lectr, 1986-87; Eastern Mich Univ, African Am studies lectr, 1987-88, adj lectr, 2010; Detroit City Coun, spec proj asst, 1987-88; Mich State Univ, dean, Urban Studies, res asst, 1988-90; Nat Asn Advan Colored People, Spec Contrib Fund Midwest, develop dir, 1990-93, regional dir, 1999-2001, Nat Field Opers, dep dir, 2001-03, regional field organizer, 2009-10, regional field dir, 2011-; Wayne State Univ, Sch Educ, lectr, 1992-93; Wayne County Comn, Chair Ways & Means, legis aide, 1993-94; Wayne State Univ, Interdisciplinary Studies, asst prof, 1994-95; Law Off Jerome L Reide PC, atty, 1996-2009; Raheem, Eickemeyer & Reide PLLC, 1997-99; Baltimore City Community Col, adj fac, 2004-05; Bowie State Univ, adj fac, 2004-05; Mckinney & Assocs, 2004; State Bar Mich, dir justice initiatives, 2005-07. **Orgs:** Nat Asn Advan Colored People, 1975-; press aide, Sutton Mayor, 1977; nat press secy, Black Law Students Asn, 1980-81; press secy, Nat Conf Black Lawyers, 1986-87; Urban League, Mich, 1988-; Urban Affairs Grad Studies Asn, 1989-90; Dispute Resolution Coord Coun, 1991-95; Boniface CtAction, 1991-95; pres, Global Econ Develop Conf, 1993; exec comt, Wayne State Univ, Ctr Peace & Conflict Studies, 1994; atty & counr, State Bar Mich, 1996; Am Bar Asn, 1997-; Wolverine Bar Asn, 1997-; Team Justice, 1997; chmn, Civil Rights Comt, IRR Sect, Am Bar Asn, 2006-, coun mem, 2008-09; bd mem, Sugar Law Ctr; Nat Adv Bd; Lansing Asn Black Lawyers; Nat Bar Asn. **Honors/Awds:** Governor Ky, Order Ky Colonels, 1991; Fair Housing Award, Jackson Fair Housing CMS, 1992; Special Tribute, State Legis Mich, 1994; CLL Teaching Excellence Award, Wayne State Univ, ISP, 1997; Freedom Fighter Award, Detroit Branch, Nat Board, Nat Asn Advan Colored People, 1999; Foot Soldier's in the Sands Award, Nat Bd, Nat Asn Advan Colored People, 2007. **Special Achievements:** Author, Justice Evicted, Am Civil Liberties Union, 1987; exec producer & moderator, "The State of Black Mich," 1989-; ed, Mulitcultural Edu Resource Guide, Mich State edu, 1990; exec producer, "Human Rights and Civil Wrongs," Museum of African American History, 1991; Writer, "NAACP Ct Economic Development," The Crisis Magazine, 1992; "Human Rights and Natural Disaster, Human Rights Magazine, IRR, ABA, co-editor, 2006; Foot Soldiers in the Sands Award, Nat Asn Advan Colored People, 2007. **Home Addr:** 3401 Ramsgate Dr, Lansing, MI 48906. **Business Addr:** Regional Field Director, National Association for the Advancement of Colored People, 4805 Mt Hope Dr, Baltimore, MD 21215, **Business Phone:** (410)580-5777.

**REIDE, SAINT CLAIR EUGENE, JR.**
Nurse. **Personal:** Born Aug 24, 1950, Brooklyn, NY; son of Saint Clair E Sr and Leonara E; married Portia Gayle; children: Saint Clair E, III & Nicole A. **Educ:** Morris High Sch, LPN, 1968; Boro Manhattan Community Col, AAS, 1971; Hunter Col, Bellevue Sch Nursing, BSN, 1974. **Career:** NY Univ Med Ctr, LPN, 1968-71, staff nurse sr, 1971-74; Dept Health, Prison Health Nursing, psy staff nurse, 1974; Dept Vet Affairs, nursing supvr, 1974-. **Orgs:** Pastoral asst, Trinity Luthern Church, 1970, sunday sch supdt, 1993; life mem, Reserve Officers Asn, 1975. **Honors/Awds:** Manhattan Community Col, Dean List, 1971; Dept Vet Affairs, St Albans, Employee of the Month, 1987. **Special Achievements:** Portrait Photographer, Owner Creative Photography by Saint studio; American Nurses Assn, certification in Nursing Admin, 1989-93, Gerontological Nurse, 1989-93; USA Goju, karate, Brown Belt, 1972; Radio License Novice, KB2CQA. **Home Addr:** 115-02 223rd St, Cambria Heights, NY 11411, **Home Phone:** (718)527-7838. **Business Addr:** Nursing Supervisor, St Albans VA - Extended Care Center - Department of Vet Affairs, 179 St & Linden Blvd Nursing Off 1182, Jamaica, NY 11425, **Business Phone:** (718)526-1000.

**REINHARDT, JOHN EDWARD. See Obituaries Section.**

### RELAFORD, DESI (DESMOND LAMONT RELAFORD)

Nutritionist, baseball player. **Personal:** Born Sep 16, 1973, Valdosta, GA; married Cassandra Sapphire Daley; children: Jevin & Casmond. **Educ:** Integrative Inst Nutrit, AADP, 2012; Univ N Fla, nutrit & dietetics, 2013. **Career:** Baseball player (retired), baseball coach, executive, nutrition Coach; Philadelphia Phillies, shortstop, 1996-2000; San Diego Padres, 2000; New York Mets, infielder, 2001; Seattle Mariners, 2002; Kans City Royals, infielder, 2003-04; Colo Rockies, infielder, 2004-05; Baltimore Orioles, 2006; Tex Rangers, 2007; free agt, currently; 6 Hole Rec, founder, chief exec officer, 2001-10; Desi Relaford Health Alternative, Holistic Nutrit Counr, 2011-; Relaford & Brown Nutrit & Meditation Solutions Athletes, nutrit coach, 2013-. **Home Addr:** 12483 Highview Dr, Jacksonville, FL 32225-5725, **Home Phone:** (904)683-0803. **Business Addr:** Nutrition Coach, Relaford & Brown Nutrition and Meditation Solutions For Athletes, 12483 Highview Dr, Jacksonville, FL 32225, **Business Phone:** (781)708-2099.

### REMBERT, DR. EMMA WHITE

Educator. **Personal:** Born Brookfield, WI; daughter of Zinerva and Jessie. **Educ:** Fla Agr & Med Col, AB, Med; Syracuse Univ, EdD. **Career:** Pinellas Co, supvr & teacher; Mobilization Youth New York, supvr clinician; Charles E Merrill Pub, educ consul; Fla Int Univ, prof, asst & dean; Bethune-Cookman Col, prof, chairperson educ, Educ Div, head, dir; Bowie State Univ, assoc prof. **Orgs:** State organizer, Nat Coun Negro Women; Phi Delta Kappa; Kappa Delta Pi; Pi Lambda Theta; consult & lectr, Ministry Educ-Commonwealth Bahamas; dir, adult educ, Okeechobee Schs Ed & prof consult, Textbk Ser C E Merrill Co; pub com Int Reading Asn; manuscript reviewer McGraw Hill & Allyn & Bacon Co; dir, Hemispheric Women's Cong; chairperson, Delta Sigma Theta Fla Coun; Delta Sigma Theta Leadership Acad. **Honors/Awds:** Competence Award, State Florida; International Scholarship-Leadership Award, Delta Sigma Theta; EPDA Fel, Syracuse Univ; Florida Outstanding Teacher & Educator; CRA Service Award. **Special Achievements:** Book: "Alternative Strategies". **Home Addr:** PO Box 3382, Ft Pierce, FL 34948, **Home Phone:** (504)241-5788. **Business Addr:** Director of Education Division, Bethune-Cookman College, 640 Dr Mary McLeod Bethune Blvd, Daytona Beach, FL 32114, **Business Phone:** (386)481-2000.

### REMY, ESQ. DONALD M.

Executive, lawyer. **Personal:** Born Feb 8, 1967, Petersburg, VA; son of Donald and Ann; married Monitra C; children: J Alexander & Jason A. **Educ:** La State Univ, BA, polit sci, 1988; Howard Univ Sch Law, JD, 1991. **Career:** Judge Nathaniel Jones, judicial clerk, 1995-96; O'Melveny & Myers LLP, assoc, 1996-97; US Dept Justice, sr coun policy, dep asst Atty Gen, 1997-2000; Fannie Mae, vpres & dep gen coun, 2000-02, sr vpres, dep gen coun & chief compliance officer, 2002, sr lawyer & bus exec, 2002-06; Housing & Community Develop, sr vpres & chief compliance officer; Latham & Watkins LLP, partner; Nat Col Athletic Asn, gen coun & vpres legal affairs, currently. **Orgs:** Kappa Alpha Psi, 1987-; Am Bar Asn, 1991-; Nat Bar Asn, 1991-; Blacks Govt, 1991-2000; Wash Bar Asn, 1993-; fel Global Training & Career Enhancement Comt. **Home Addr:** 8135 Haddington Ct, Fairfax Station, VA 22039, **Home Phone:** (703)495-0103. **Business Addr:** General Counsel, Vice President, National Collegiate Athletic Association, 700 W Wash St, Indianapolis, IN 46206-6222, **Business Phone:** (317)917-6222.

### RENDER, AMBASSADOR ARLENE

Government official, ambassador. **Personal:** Born Aug 16, 1943, Cleveland, OH; children: Jonathan Blake & Kiara Isabella. **Educ:** WVa State Col, BS, 1965; Univ Mich, MPH, 1967. **Career:** US Diplomat, 1970-; Bur African Affairs, int rels officer, 1979-81; Kingston & Cayman Islands, consul gen, 1984-86; US Embassy Accra, dep chief mission, 1986-89; US Ambassador Gambia, 1990-93; Rwandan Genocide, 1994-95; US Ambassador Repub Zambia, 1996-99; US Ambassador Repub Cote d'Ivoire, 2001-04; Spelman Col, Int Affairs Ctr, dipl-in-residence, 2004-. **Orgs:** Dir, Cent African Affairs. **Business Addr:** Diplomat-in-Residence, Spelman College, 350 Spelman Lane SW, Atlanta, GA 30314, **Business Phone:** (404)270-5526.

### RENDER, DR. WILLIAM H., SR.

Executive, government official, physician. **Personal:** Born Feb 9, 1950, LaGrange, GA; son of Elizabeth; married Barbara Jean; children: Eric C & Keyiana. **Educ:** Emory Univ, A Med, 1974; GA State Univ, Pre-med; Meharry Med Col, Sch Med, MD, 1984. **Career:** Dr James B Palmer Atlanta GA, physician asst, 1975-80; Emory Univ Affil Hosp, med resident, 1984-87, internship; pvt pract internal med, 1987-; Fulton County Jail, physician, 1987-92, Med dir; Piedmont Hosp, physician, currently; Render's Primary Care Ctr PC, physician, currently. **Orgs:** Atlanta Med Asn; Ga State Med Asn; Southern Med Asn; Am Col Physician; Hon Med Soc; Alpha Omega Alpha, 1984. **Honors/Awds:** Bd Certified, Internal Med. **Home Addr:** 5025 Jackson Brook Pl NW, Lilburn, GA 30047-4968. **Business Addr:** Physician, Owner, Render Primary Care Center PC, 970 Martin Luther King Jr Dr Suite 305 SW, Atlanta, GA 30314, **Business Phone:** (404)524-1721.

### RENE, ALTHEA (ALTHEA MCCULLERS JOHNSON)

Flutist. **Personal:** Born Dec 25, 1958, Detroit, MI; daughter of Dezie and Barbara McCullers; children: Brandon & Stephen. **Educ:** Howard Univ, attended 1981; Wayne County Sheriffs Dept Police Acad, attended 1998. **Career:** Police Academy, police officer & flutist; Althea Rene & Co, band leader, 1984; Wayne County Sheriffs Dept, police officer, 1992; County Court House, jailer; Straight Ahead Female Jazz Group, band mem, 1997; Althea Rene Productions LLC, flutist, currently; Albums: Flute Talk, 2000; Chocolate Rush, 2003; Chocolate Caramel Music; In the Moment, 2006; Koch Entertainment; No Restrictions, 2008; In the Flow, 2013. **Special Achievements:** Opened for Tony Bennett in Puerto Rico, 1998; performed in Jamaica, 1997. **Home Addr:** 3259 Oakman Blvd, Detroit, MI 48238, **Home Phone:** (313)958-4461. **Business Addr:** Flutist, Althea Rene Productions LLC, PO Box 3073, Spring, TX 77383, **Business Phone:** (281)214-4270.

### RENFORD, EDWARD J.

Executive. **Career:** Executive (retired); Grady Health Syst, pres, chief exec officer; Grady Mem Hosp, pres. **Home Addr:** 1309 Cascade Falls Dr SW, Atlanta, GA 30311-3656, **Home Phone:** (404)699-9938.

### RENFRO, MELVIN LACY (MEL RENFRO)

Football coach, football player, actor. **Personal:** Born Dec 30, 1941, Houston, TX; children: 4. **Educ:** Univ Ore. **Career:** Football player, football coach (retired); Dallas Cowboys, defensive back, scout, 1964-77; Miller Beer Dallas, acct mgr; Los Angeles Express, defensive sec coach; St Louis Cardinals, defensive back coach; motivational speaker, currently. Film: "Super Bowl X", 1976; "Super Bowl VI", 1972; "Super Bowl V", 1971. **Orgs:** Melvin Renfro Found; Pigskin Club Wash; Involvedvarious charitable activ. **Honors/Awds:** Most Valuable Player, E & W Game, 1960; Most Valuable Player, Nat Golden WTrack Meet HS, 1960; Pro Bowl, 1964-1973; Most Valuable Player, Pro-Bowl Nat Football League, 1970; Dallas Cowboys Ring of Honor; Texas Stadium Ring of Honor, 1981; Col Football Hall of Fame, 1986; Inducted to University of Oregon Athletic Hall of Fame, 1992; Pro Football Hall of Fame, 1996. **Special Achievements:** Listed in famous people raised in Houston.

### RENICK, DR. JAMES CARMICHAEL

School administrator, chancellor (education). **Personal:** Born Dec 8, 1948, Rockford, IL; son of James and Constance Carmachael; married Peggy O Gadsden; children: Karinda. **Educ:** Cent State Univ, Wilberforce, OH, BA, 1970; Kans Univ, MSW, 1972; Fla State Univ, PhD, pub admin, 1980. **Career:** Univ W Fla, prof, 1975-81; Univ S Fla, prof, 1981-83, from asst to pres, 1983-85, asst dean & educ chmn, 1985-88, depart chair, 1988-89; George Mason Univ, Fairfax, Va, assoc provost, 1989-91, vice provost, 1991-93; Univ Mich-Dearborn, prof & chancellor, 1993-99; Nc Agr & Tech State Univ, chancellor, 1993, pres, 1999-2006; Polit Sci NC Agr & Tech State Univ, chancellor & prof, 1999-2006; Am Coun Educ, Wash, DC, sr vpres prog & res, 2006-08; sr assoc, Penson Assocs Inc, currently; Jackson State Univ, vpres acad affairs, sr advisor to pres, 2015. **Orgs:** Trustee, Univ Pshycol Ctr, 1984-; fel Am Coun Educ; chmn, Am Asn Higher Educ Black Caucus, 1985-; Fla Leadership Network, Community C, 1985-; Fla Inst Govt Policy Coun, 1986-89; exec, comn Coun Fel Am Coun Educ, 1987-89; founder, Millennium Leadership Initiative, Am Asn State Cols & Univs. **Home Addr:** 551 Golfcrest Dr, Dearborn, MI 48124. **Business Addr:** Senior Associate, Penson Associates Inc, PO Box 12802, Palm Desert, CA 92255, **Business Phone:** (760)565-3088.

### RESPERT, SHAWN CHRISTOPHER

Basketball player, athletic director, basketball coach. **Personal:** Born Feb 6, 1972, Detroit, MI; married Lenae; children: Cheyenne & Aaron. **Educ:** Mich State Univ, BA, commun, 1995. **Career:** Basketball player (retired), basketball coach, director; Milwaukee Bucks, guard, 1995-97; Toronto Raptors, 1997-98; Dallas Mavericks, 1998; Phoenix Suns, guard, 1999; Adecco Milano, 1999-2000; Near E, Greece, 2000-01; Fillattice Imola, 2001-02; Spojnia Stargard Szczecinski, 2002-03; Prairie View A&M Univ, asst vol basketball coach, 2003-04, vol coach, 2004; Imola Basketball Club, Ital League, asst coach; Komfort Kronopolus Basketball Club, Polish League, asst coach; Rice Univ, dir basketball opers, 2005; NBA Develop League, dir basketball opers; Houston Rockets, dir player prog, 2008; Minn Timberwolves, player develop coach, 2011-13; Memphis Grizzlies, asst coach, 2013-. **Orgs:** Goodwill Games, USA Basketball Team. **Home Addr:** 11122 Desert Springs Cir, Houston, TX 77095, **Home Phone:** (281)304-6016. **Business Addr:** Assistant Coach, Memphis Grizzlies, 175 Toyota Plz Suite 150, Memphis, TN 38103, **Business Phone:** (901)205-1234.

### REUBEN, GLORIA

Actor. **Personal:** Born Jun 9, 1964, Toronto, ON; married Wayne Isaak. **Career:** Films: Immediate Family, 1989; Wild Orchid II: Two Shades of Blue, 1992; The Waiter, 1993; Timecop, 1994; Nick of Time, 1995; MacBeth in Manhattan, Pilgrim, David & Lola, 1999; Shaft, Pilgrim, Bad Faith, 2000; Happy Here & Now, Salem Witch Trials, 2002; The Sentinel, Kettle of Fish, 2006; Padre Nuestro, exec producer, 2007; Sangre de mi sangre, exec producer, 2007; The Understudy, 2008; Ice Grill, U.S.A., exec producer, 2009; Lincoln, 2012; Admission, 2013; Reasonable Doubt, 2014. TV series: "Polka Dot Door", 1971; "CBS Schoolbreak Special", 1987; "Alfred Hitchcock Presents", 1987; "21 Jump Street", 1988; China Beach, 1990; The Flash, 1990-91; "The Young Riders", 1991; "The Round Table", 1992; Shadow hunter, 1993; Percy & Thunder, 1993; "Silk Stalkings", 1993; Dead Air, 1994; Confessions: Two Faces of Evil, 1994; "McKenna", 1994; "ER", 1995-2008; Johnny's Girl, 1995; "Homicide: Life on the Street", 1995; "Indiscreet", 1998; "Deep In My Heart", 1999; Sara, 1999; "Sole Survivor", 2000; "The Agency", 2001-02; "Feast of All Saints", 2001; Little John, 2002; The District, 2002; "Law & Order: Special Victims Unit", 2002-11; Salem Witch Trials, 2002; "Little John", 2002; "1-800-Missing", assoc producer, 2003; "Numb3rs", 2005; Life Support, 2007; Positive Voices: Women & HIV, producer, 2007; "Raising the Bar", 2008-09; "Jesse Stone: Innocents Lost", 2011; "Untitled Bounty Hunter Project", 2013; "Betty and Coretta", 2013; "Falling Skies", 2013; "Happy Face Killer", 2014. **Honors/Awds:** Numerous honors & awards including "Miss Black Ontario", 1986; Screen Actors Guild Award, 1997, 1998 & 1999; OFTA Television Award, 1997; Q Award, Viewers for Quality Television Awards, 1997, 1998. **Special Achievements:** In 1996 she was chosen by People as one of the 50 most Beautiful People in the World; She sang back up for Tina Turner on her Twenty Four Seven Tour, 2000. **Business Addr:** Actress, c/o Untitiled Entertainment, 322 Eighth Ave Suite 601, New York, NY 10001, **Business Phone:** (212)777-1214.

### REUBEN, DR. LUCY J.

Educator. **Personal:** Born Sumter, SC. **Educ:** Oberlin Col, BA, econ; Univ Mich, MBA, 1974, PhD, bus admin, 1981; Stonier Grad sch banking, post doctoral studies; Inter-Univ Consortium, post doctoral studies, polit & social res. **Career:** Earhart Found, fel; Ford Motor, finance staff coordr, 1974-75; Financial Res AssociatesInc, pres & co founder, 1884-92; George Mason Univ, vis assoc prof, finance, scl bus admin, 1986-88; Fla A&M Univ, assoc prof, 1989-95; Banc Boston Mortgage Corp, fac consult, 1992; SC State Univ Sch Bus & Marshall B Williams, prof & dean, bus, 1995-2002; NC Cent Univ, provost & vice chancellor, acadamic affairs, 2002-04, prof, finance, 2002-06; Univ Mich Ctr Educ Women, vis scholar, 2006-07; Duke Univ, John hope franklin ctr, vis scholor, 2005-06, Fuqua Sch Bus, vis prof, 2006-08, prof pract bus admin, 2008-, LEAD summer bus inst, curriculam dir, 2008-, DukeEngage, Trinidad & Tobago, 2008-10, Phd pipeline opportunity prog, dir, 2010-; witwatersrand univ, guest lectr, 2010. **Orgs:** Ayres fel Stonier grad sch banking; leadership fel Kellogg found MSI & NAFEO; Teaching fel & res asst, Gradute sch bus adminstration, Univ Mich; bd dir, Int Educ Resource Ctr; exec comt, Metrop Wash Planning & Housing Asn, 1987-90, pres & bd dir, 1989-90; bd gov, Univ Mich Bus Sch Alumni Soc, 1990-99; Fla Black Bus Investment Bd, 1993-95; Orangeburg County United Way, 1995-99; Sc small bus develop ctr consortium, 1995-2002, chair, 1997-98; Black Enterprise Bd Economists, 1995-2001; bd dir, SC World Affairs Coun, 1996-98, adv bd, 1998-2002; Mgt educ alliance, 1996-2002, chair, 2000-02; N am Econs & finance Asn adv bd, 1998-2002; Asn Advan Col Sch Bus, 1998-2001; Sc sci & technol adv coun, 1998-2002; bd dir, Charlotte Off Fed Res Bank, Richmond, 1999-2005; vis comt, Univ Mich Ross Bus Sch, 1999-2009, womens leadership coun, 2002-; Urban League columbia, SC, 2001-02; bd dir, Providence Hosp, 2001-02; Orangeburg County Chamber Com; palmetto inst, 2001-02; SC Technol Transition Team, 2001-02; Early Col High Sch Adv bd, NCCU & Durham Pub Schs, 2002-04; SC Export Consortium, 2002; Greater Res Triangle Coun, 2003-04; minority bus consult prog, 2005-; bd dir, chair, Achievement Acadamy durham, 2006-07, adv bd, 2008-; Nat urban league's coun Econ Advisors, 2007-; Nat Asn Urban Bankers, Wash, DC, 2007-11; Womens leadership initiative, 2010-; Durham nativity sch, 2011-; N carolina support ctr, 2011-; YWCA; Hayti Develop Corp, Durham, NC; life mem, Nat Asn Black MBAs; life mem, Nat Coun Negro Women; life mem, Nat Asn Advan Colored People; Pan African Enterprise Res Coun, 2012-; pres's adv bd, Oberlin col, 2012-. **Home Addr:** 4400 Thetford Rd, Durham, NC 27707, **Home Phone:** (919)403-3471. **Business Addr:** Professor, Duke University, 100 Fuqua Dr, Durham, NC 27708-0120, **Business Phone:** (919)660-7661.

### REUBEN, DR. LUCY JEANETTE

Educator. **Personal:** Born Dec 15, 1949, Sumter, SC; daughter of Odell Richardson and Anna Mays; married John A Cole; children: John Akayomi Cole; children: Kwame Odell Oliver. **Educ:** Oberlin Col, BA, econs, 1971; Univ Mich, MBA, 1974, PhD, finance, 1981. **Career:** Ford Motor Co, financial analyst, 1974-75; Earhart Found, fel, 1978; Ayres fel, Stonier Grad Sch Banking, 1982; NC Cent Univ, prof, dean, provost & vice chancellor; SC State Univ, Sch Bus, prof, dean; Fla Agri & Mech Univ, assoc prof finance; George Mason Univ, vis assoc prof finance; Univ Chicago, Nissan fel; Fed Res Syst, vis scholar; Duke Univ, Fuqua Sch Bus, vis prof, Prof Pract Bus Admin, 2006-. **Orgs:** Adv bd, Hayti Develop Corp, 1982-84; adv bd, Wash DC Urban Bankers Asn, 1984-; adv bd, Wash DC Women Economists, 1984-; consult, Nat Bankers Asn, 1984-; consult, US Dept Com, 1984-; bd dir, Metrop Wash Planning & Housing Asn, 1986-; bd dir, Fed Res Bank Richmond, 1999-2005; Am Fin Asn; Eastern Fin Asn; life mem, Nat Black MBA Asn; Nat Econ Asn; Nat Asn Female Exec; Nat Asn Black MBAs; Nat Coun Negro Women; Nat Asn Advan Colored People; Alpha Kappa Alpha; adv bd, Links Inc; Nat Urban League, 2007-11; bd dir, Int Educ Resource Ctr. **Home Addr:** 2943 Landing Way NE, Orangeburg, SC 29118. **Business Addr:** Visiting Professor, Duke University, 100 Fuqua Dr, Durham, NC 27708, **Business Phone:** (919)660-7700.

### REVELLE, ROBERT, SR.

Clergy. **Personal:** Born Jan 6, 1947, Harrellsville, NC; son of Hugh L (deceased) and Carrie L; married Annie M Adams; children: Sharon Marie & Robert Jr. **Educ:** Goldey Beacom Bus Col, AA, mgt, 1971; Nat Grad Univ, cert, 1973; Wilmington Col, BBA, 1978; Eastern Theol Sem, cert, 1989. **Career:** CDA, Wilmington, planner, consult, 1971-73, admin chief, 1973-74; Community Affairs, dept dir, 1974-75; Community Ctr, supt, 1975-84; Wilmington City, dir, minority bus prog, 1984-87, dep personnel dir, 1987, Del State, personnel recruitment specialist, 1994-98; Holy Christian Church Am Inc, pastor, presiding bishop; Robert Revelle Sr. Ministries, pastor, 2000-. **Orgs:** AUS Personnel Sch Personnel Mgt, 1967; pres, Am Cancer Soc, 1973-75, vpres; pres, vpres, Price Run Child Ctr, 1976-84; YMCA Resource Ctr, 1983-84; mem chmn, orgn community Police, Community Coun, Wilmington, 1983-85; Del Minority Bus Med Week, Trade Fair Comn, 1984-87; Del Pvt Indust Coun, 1988-90; ambassador, YMCA Black Achievers Prog, 1989-; pres, Del chap, Nat Forum Black Pub Adminr, 1990-; pres, World Import Visions Inc 1999-; pres, Robert Revelle Sr. Ministries 1999-; Nat Asn Advan Colored People; Wilmington Small Bus Develop Ctr. **Home Addr:** 4109 Kennett Pke, Wilmington, DE 19807-2020, **Home Phone:** (302)575-9155. **Business Addr:** Pastor, Robert Revelle SR Ministries, 110 W 37th St, Wilmington, DE 19802, **Business Phone:** (302)764-7656.

### REVELY, REV. DR. WILLIAM, JR.

Clergy, social worker. **Personal:** Born Jan 20, 1941, Charlottesville, VA; son of William Sr (deceased) and Reaver E Carter (deceased); children: Christana Re & Christopher. **Educ:** Howard Univ, BA, 1960, Mdiv, 1967, MSW, 1971, DMin, 1982; Am Univ. **Career:** Home-Rule mayor wash, spec asst; Mt Gilead Baptist Church, pastor, 1979; Union Baptist Church, pastor, 1965-79; Nara II Aftercare Unit BureauRehab, chf, 1973-76; Shaw Residence III (Hlfway House) Bur Rehab, dir, 1976-77; Howard Univ, Sch Social Work, 1977-79; Messiah Baptist Church, pastor, 1989-99; Holy Hope Heritage Church, pastor, 2001-. **Orgs:** Nat Asn Advan Colored People; SCLC; ACA; NABSW; Nat Progressive Baptist Conv; Nat Baptist Conv USA Inc; bd trustee, Shaw Divinity Sch; bd chmn, GOIC, Detroit, 1991; bd dir, mortuary sci, Univ DC, 1989; Lott Carey Foreign Missions Conv, clergy support comt; Int FoundEduc & Self Help; dir, Opportunities Industrialization Ctr; chmn, Unify Detriot Coalition. **Honors/Awds:** Vernon Johns Preaching Award, Sch Religion, Howard Univ, 1967; NIMH Fel, 1967-71; Listed in "Who's Who Among Black Americans"; African American Humanitarian Award, City Detroit, 1996. **Special Achievements:** Author of Poetry, 'From the Heart', Foster Publ, 1988. **Home Addr:** 3430 Sherbourne Rd, Detroit, MI 48221-1877. **Business Addr:** Pastor, Holy Hope Heritage Church, 18641 Wyoming St, Detroit, MI 48221-2009, **Business Phone:** (313)397-9350.

**REVIS, DR. NATHANIEL W.**
President (organization), scientist. **Personal:** Born Jul 27, 1939, Glen Ridge, NJ; children: Natalie & Jarrett. **Educ:** Fairleigh Dickinson Univ, NJ, BS, chem, 1962; Univ Louvain, Belg, Med Sch, 1968; Univ Glasgow, Scotland, PhD, biochem, 1972. **Career:** Talladega Col, Nsf, lectr, 1979-81; Oak Ridge Realty Holdings Inc, scientist & pres, 1981-; Oak Ridge Nat Lab & Univ, Tenn, scientist, asst prof, 1975-81; Univ Glasgow, Dept Cardiol, asst prof, 1972-75; Sci & Techn Resources Inc, dir & sr scientist, 1994-; Nominating Comt, Oak Ridge Res Inst, chairperson, currently. **Orgs:** Int Soc Biochem, 1972; Am & Int Soc Cardiol, 1975; adv, Cong Black, 1978; Health Brain Trust, Black Cong Caucus, 1978-85; adv, Nat Cancer Inst, 1979; Oak Ridge Rotary Club, 1986-; bd mem, Methodist Med Ctr, 1987-94; bd mem, E Tenn Econ Coun, 1997-; bd & exec mem, Community Reuse Orgn E Tenn, 1998-; bd mem, Knoxville Chamber Com, 2000-03; bd mem, Nine Counties-One Vision, 2000-03; bd mem, Oak Ridge Chamber Com, 2001-04; Gov Bredesen's Bus Round Table, 2003-; chmn, E Tenn Econ Develop Coun, 2005-06; comt mem, Oak Ridge Breakfast Rotary Club, 2008-. **Honors/Awds:** Carnegie Research Fellow Award, 1969; Fogarty Award, NIH, 1980; Administration Award of Excellence, 1985, 1992, 1995 & 2001. **Home Addr:** 1060 W Outer Dr, Oak Ridge, TN 37830-8638, **Home Phone:** (865)482-2065. **Business Addr:** President, Illinois, Oak Ridge Realty Holdings Inc, 702 S Illinois Ave B103, Oak Ridge, TN 37830, **Business Phone:** (865)481-6088.

**REVISH, DANIELLE A.**
Executive director. **Personal:** married Elder Jerry; children: Nicole & Jerome. **Career:** Fashion Group Int Columbus Inc, regional dir & event founder, currently; Unity Temple Church God Christ Inc, co-pastor; "Columbus Bride Magazine Show", producer. **Orgs:** Pres, Young Women's Christian Coun; choir mem, Unity Temple Church God Christ Inc; pres, Women's Ministries Unity Temple Church God Christ. **Business Addr:** Regional Director, Event Founder, Fashion Group International of Columbus Inc, 4413 Beech Wood Loop, Dublin, OH 43016, **Business Phone:** (614)659-9722.

**REVISH, JERRY**
Television journalist. **Personal:** Born Mar 15, 1949, Youngstown, OH; son of Dewey and Estelle; married Danielle; children: Nicole & Jerome II. **Educ:** Youngstown State Univ, attended 1969; Chapman Col, attended 1970. **Career:** WBBW Radio, bd operator, 1972-74; WBNS Radio, assignment ed & reporter, 1974-80; WBNS-10 TV, anchor & reporter, 1980-. **Orgs:** Nat Asn Black Journalists, 1985-; National Association for the Advancement of Colored People, 1990-; pres, Columbus Asn Black Journalists, 1991-92; founder, High Sch Journalism Workshop Minority Students Columbus; bd mem, United Way, Proj Diversity, 1991-. **Honors/Awds:** Best Series, Sigma Delta Chi, 1979; Best Spot, news, feature & doc, Asn Press, 1980-90; Best Spot, news, feature & doc, UPI, 1980-90; 16 Emmy Nominations, 1980-90, 5 Emmy Awards, Nat Acad TV Arts & Sci; NABJ Best International Reporting Award, 1996; Achievement in Journalism Award, Cent Ohio Chap Prof Journalists; Hall of Fame, Ohio Broadcasters, 2005; Blue Chip Award in Communications; Carl Day Award for Outstanding Achievement. **Special Achievements:** Two tours Persian Gulf Operation Desert Shield Desert Storm, 1991. **Business Addr:** TV News Anchor, Reporter, WBNS-10TV, 770 Twin Rivers Dr, Columbus, OH 43216, **Business Phone:** (614)460-3950.

**REYES, RICARDO A.**
Executive. **Career:** Int Transp Solutions Express Inc, founder, sales mgr, 2001-03, pres & chief exec officer, 2003-; Choice Courier, area mgr. **Honors/Awds:** Achievement Award "40-Under-Forty", Black Bus Mag, 2003. **Business Addr:** President, Chief Executive Officer, International Transport Solutions Express Inc, 43 49 10th St Suite 302, Long Island City, NY 11101, **Business Phone:** (718)752-0757.

**REYNOLDS, ANDREW BUCHANAN**
Consultant, vice president (organization), educator. **Personal:** Born Jun 29, 1939, Winston-Salem, NC; son of Andrew Buchanan and Florence Terry. **Educ:** Lincoln Univ, BA, 1960; NC Agr & Tech State Univ, BS, 1962; Columbia Univ Grad Sch Jour, cert journ, 1970. **Career:** Bowman Gray Sch Med, Dept Pharmacol, res asst, 1962-63; CORE, dir, 1963; Madigan Gen Hosp, Ft Lewis, WA, radioisotope tech, 1964-65; NC Advan Sch, counr & teacher, 1966-67; PA Advan Sch, curric & develop specialist, 1967-70; WCAU-TV, reporter & producer, 1970-71; September & Assoc, prod dir, 1973-75; New Day Inc, prod dir, 1975; City Seattle, Seattle Dept Parks & Recreation, mgr, mkt & pub rels, 1987-93; Exec Diversity Serv Inc, owner, sr assoc, 1987-2010, vpres, 1993-2006; consult, 2004-10; Intercultural Commun Inst, instr, 1997-; Wash State Lottery Comn, chair; King Broadcasting Co, TV news reporter; SIETAR USA, pres & bd mem, 2006-10; Andy Reynolds & Assocs, owner & pres, 2007-; Exec Diversity Serv (EDS), sr vpres, 1993-2007, vpres, 2009; Mt Baker Community Club, pres, chmn & bd mem, 2011-14. **Orgs:** Nat Asn Advan Colored People, 1978; pres, bd trustees, Educ Opportunity Prog Univ Wash; chmn & ed, Leadership Tomorrow; chmn, WA State Lottery Comn; prog chmn, UNCF Telethon Comn; Pub Defender Asn; Northwest Aids Found; Seattle/King Co Red Cross; bd mem, Greater Seattle Chamber Com, 1998-2000. **Honors/Awds:** Hon, Sigma Delta Chi Features, 1973; First Place, Sigma Delta Chi Spot News, 1975; Third Place, Sigma Delta Chi Doc, 1977; Humbolt Award, 1978; Hon, Puget Sound Pub Rels Soc America, 1983; Outstanding Alumni Award, Leadership Tomorrow, 1992. **Home Addr:** 3315 37th Ave S, Seattle, WA 98144, **Home Phone:** (206)722-4757. **Business Addr:** Owner, President, Andy Reynolds & Assocs, 16 Georges Quay, Dublin97225.

**REYNOLDS, REV. DR. BARBARA A.**
Columnist, editor. **Personal:** Born Aug 17, 1942, Columbus, OH; daughter of Harvey and Elizabeth Taylor; children: John Eric. **Educ:** Ohio State Univ, BA, jour, 1967; Howard Univ, Sch Divinity, MA, relig studies, 1992; United Theol Sem, Dayton, DMin, 1998. **Career:** Cleveland, social worker; Ebony Mag, Chicago, IL, ed, 1968-69; Chicago Today, 1969; Chicago Tribune, Chicago, IL, reporter, 1969-81; Harvard Univ, Nieman fel, 1976-77; USA Today, Arlington, VA, founfding ed, ed & columinist, 1982-96-; NBC-TV, consult; Reynolds News Serv, pres, owner, currently; Mt Calvary Baptist Church, Wash, DC, minister, 1995-; Barbaras Bk & Life Chg Coach, pres, 2009-; Shenandoah Univ, Winchester, VA, Jessie Ball Dupont, chair jour & prof, currently; Summer Grove Church, minister; Howard Univ Sch Divinity, ordained minister, adj prof, ministry teacher; JFJ Publishing, pres. **Orgs:** Chmn, Women's Task Force; Nat Asn Black Journalists, 1991-; pres, Womens Christian Action Network; Calvary Bible Inst. **Special Achievements:** First African American female ministers asked to serve as Chaplain of the Week at Chautauqua Institution. **Home Addr:** 13901 New Acadia Lane, Upper Marlboro, MD 20774-8647, **Home Phone:** (301)899-1341. **Business Addr:** Owner, President, Reynolds News Service, 7124 Temple Hills Rd Suite 176, Camp Springs, MD 20748, **Business Phone:** (301)899-1341.

**REYNOLDS, CHARLES MCKINLEY, JR.**
Executive. **Personal:** Born Jan 11, 1937, Albany, GA; son of Johnnie Hadley and Charles McKinley; married Estella Henry; children: Eric Charles & Gregory Preston. **Educ:** Morehouse Col, BA, 1954; Wayne State Univ, mortuary sci cert, 1962; Albany State Col, mid grades cert, 1964. **Career:** Southside Jr High Sch, Dept Social Studies, teacher & chmn, 1962-65; US Treas Dept, asst examr, 1965-69, nat bank examr, 1969-71; Citizen Trust Bank, vpres, 1971, pres, 1971; Atlantic Nat Bank, pres & chief exec officer, 1975-88; Reynolds & Assocs, pres, 1988-. **Orgs:** Bd dir, Atlantic Nat Bank; bd dir, Norfolk C C; Jr Achievement Tidewater Inc; Tidewater Area Minority Contractors; exec comt, Greater Norfolk Develop Corp; treas, Norfolk Investment Co Inc; bd visitors, James Madison Univ; treas, bd dir, Norfolk State Univ Found; corp bd mem & chmn, Audit Comt, SCI Systs Inc; adv bd mem, Norfolk State Univ Bus & Social Work; gerontol adv coun, Hampton Inst; life mem, Alpha Phi Alpha Frat; Sigma Pi Phi Fraternity; Guardsman Inc; Rotary Club; Old Dom Univ Exec Adv Coun; treas, Bank St Mem Baptist Church; treas, William A Hunton YMCA; Sire Acron, SPP; Cong Racial Equality, 1975; Nat Assoc Minority Contractors, 1984; bd mem, Nat Caucus & Ctr Black Aged Inc. **Home Addr:** 4504 Kelley Ct, Virginia Beach, VA 23462, **Home Phone:** (757)490-7191. **Business Addr:** President, Chief Executive Officer, Reynolds & Associates, 1430 G St NE, Washington, DC 20002, **Business Phone:** (202)396-8982.

**REYNOLDS, DERRICK SCOTT.** See REYNOLDS, RICKY SCOTT.

**REYNOLDS, DR. EDWARD**
Educator. **Personal:** Born Jan 23, 1942; son of Elizabeth; children: Joel. **Educ:** Wake Forest Univ, BA, 1964; Ohio Univ, MA, 1965; Yale Univ, Mdiv, 1968; Univ London Sch Orient & African Studies, PhD, hist, 1972; Univ Calif San Diego, int studies progs. **Career:** Christ United Presby, assoc pastor, 1982-; City San Diego, planning comnr, 1989-93; Univ Calif, San Diego, asst prof, 1971-74, assoc prof, 1974-83, assoc dir acad affairs, prof hist, w african econ hist & missionary hist, prof emer hist, currently. **Orgs:** Vice moderator, Presbytery San Diego, 1993, moderator, 1994; dir, Univ Calif Study Ctr, 1994-96. **Home Addr:** 4275 Federman Lane, San Diego, CA 92103. **Business Addr:** Professor Emeritus of History, University of California-San Diego, H&SS Rm 5045, La Jolla, CA 92093-0104, **Business Phone:** (858)534-1996.

**REYNOLDS, IDA MANNING**
Government official, executive director. **Personal:** Born Sep 8, 1946, Hines, FL; daughter of James Westley and Catherine Mosley; married Wilfred Jr; children: Ronald Jr, Katrina, Joseph Hayes Rawls, Tina & Wilfred III. **Educ:** Lincoln Tech Inst, comput sci, 1966. **Career:** Alachua City, FL, benefit & payroll supv, 1963-73, personnel specialist, 1973-79, personnel mgt analyst, 1979-81, dir equal opportunity div, 1981-. **Orgs:** Secy, Local Chap, Am Soc Personnel Admin, 1979; vpres, Cent Fla Conf, Women Missionary, 1980-; state coordr, Am Asn Affirmative Action, 1982; adv bd, Santa Fe Community Col, Human Serv, 1982-; bd dir, Fla Asn Community Prof, 1983-; chmn, Area XIV Fla Church Women United, 1984-; bd dir, United Gainesville Community Develop Corp, 1984-; reg pres, Fla Asn Community Rels, 1984-; bd dir, One Church One Child Black Adoption, 1986-; Gov Comn Martin Luther King Commemorative Celebration, 1986; Alachua County Black Adoption Bd; producer/host, Forum Black Social & Econ Issues, 1989-; vpres, Nat Forum Black Pub Admin, 1990-; chap chair, Nat Asn Human Rights Workers, 1990-; vpres, N Cent Fla Nat Forum Black Pub Admin, 1990-; Am Asn Pub Admin & Conf Minority Pub Admin; bd dir, Gainesville/Alachua County Martin Luther King Fund Inc; Develop, implemented & coord pvt & pub participation Countywide Ann Conf Human Rights & Equal Opportunity Law. **Home Addr:** 2203 NE 7th Pl, Gainesville, FL 32641, **Home Phone:** (904)374-6930. **Business Addr:** Director, Alachua County Equal Opportunity Office, 105 SE 1st Ave Suite 1, Gainesville, FL 32602, **Business Phone:** (352)374-5275.

**REYNOLDS, JAMES**
Actor, artistic director, business owner. **Personal:** Born Aug 10, 1946, Oskaloosa, KS; son of Leonard and Dorothy J Cotton; married Lissa Layng; children: Jed. **Educ:** Washburn Univ, Topeka KS, BFA, prelaw & jour, 1970. **Career:** Windward Marine, reporter; Topeka Daily Capital, writer; Los Angeles Repertory Theater, managing artistic dir, 1975-82; La Famille Enterprises, pres, 1987-; S Pasadena Repertory Theater, managing artistic dir, 1989-; La Famile Films, S Pasadena, Calif, pres, 1990-; Generations, Burbank, Calif, lead actor, 1990-91; Classics Unlimited, S Pasadena, vpres; Free St Productions, chief exec officer & partner, 1996-; Fremont Ctr Theater, exec bd vpres, artistic dir, currently; Films: Mr. Majestyk, 1974; Fun with Dick & Jane, 1977; The Magic of Lassie, 1978; CHOMPS, 1979; TV series: "Keeper of the Wild", 1977; Devil Dog: The Hound of Hell, 1978; Jennifer: A Woman's Story, 1979; "The Incredible Hulk", 1979; "Time Express", 1979; "Diff'rent Strokes", 1979-80; M Station: Hawaii, 1980; "Days of Our Lives", 1981-2009; "Hotline", 1982; "Generations", 1991; Days of Our Lives' 35th Anniversary, 2000. **Orgs:** Mem adv bd, Topeka Performing Arts Ctr, 1989-; bd dir, Kans State Hist Soc; Nat Asthma Ctr. **Honors/Awds:** Man of the Year, Nat Jewish Hosp, Nat Asthma Ctr, 1985, 1986, 1987; Volunteer of the Year, Dir Vols Am, 1987; Honorary Citizen, Wichita, Kans, 1988; Business Person of the Year, 1994; Artistic Dir Award, Outstanding Comedy-Actor; Nominated for Emmy for Outstanding Actor Drama Series, 1991; Heroes & Legends Award, 2003; Soap Chat, Best Supporting Actor, 2003; Nominated for Image Awards, 2002, 2004, 2007; Nominated for Day Time Emmy Award, 1991, 2004. **Special Achievements:** Only actor to play the role of Abe Carver. **Home Addr:** 1925 Hanscom Dr, South Pasadena, CA 91030-4009, **Home Phone:** (323)259-0159. **Business Addr:** Executive Board Vice President, Fremont Centre Theatre, 1000 Fremont Ave, South Pasadena, CA 91030, **Business Phone:** (626)441-5977.

**REYNOLDS, JAMES, JR.**
Founder (originator), chief executive officer, chairperson. **Educ:** Univ Wis, La Crosse, BA, polit sci; Northwestern Univ, Kellogg Grad Sch Mgt, MBA, mgt & finance, 1982; AIMR, chartered financial analyst, 1991. **Career:** PaineWebber, head Midwest Munic Bond Sales Desk; Merrill Lynch, mgr; Loop Capital Markets LLC, co-founder, chmn, chief exec officer, 1997-. **Orgs:** Bd mem, Chicago Alliance to End Homelessness; bd mem, Chicago United; bd mem, Lyric Opera Chicago; bd mem, Univ Chicago Hosps; vice chair, Chicago Urban League; adv bd mem, Levy Inst/Kellogg Sch Mgt, Northwestern Univ; bd mem (appointee), World Bus Chicago; bd mem (appointee), Ill Sports Facil Authority, 2011; appointee, Econ Recovery Comn; Chicago Community Trust; co-chair, Get Chicago, 2013; Ill Bus & Econ Develop Corp; Univ Chicago Med Ctr; CFA Inst. **Honors/Awds:** "Black Enterprise", 75 Most Powerful Blacks on Wall Street, 2011. **Business Addr:** Chairman, Chief Executive Officer, 111 W Jackson Blvd Suite 1901, Chicago, IL 60604, **Business Phone:** (312)913-4900.

**REYNOLDS, JAMES W.**
Government official. **Personal:** Born Jun 25, 1944, Florence, AL; son of Welton and Evelyn M; married Dianne Daniels; children: Rodney James. **Educ:** Talladega Col, AB, mathematics, 1966; Ala A&M Univ, MBA, 1975; Fla Inst Technol, MS, acquistion mgt, 1980; Grad, AUS Logamp Prog, 1992. **Career:** Government Official (retired); Florence City Sch, math teacher, 1966; AUS Missile Command, procurement intern, 1966-67, procurement agt, 1970-71; AUS Corps Engrs, contract specialist, 1971-80, br chief, acquisition mgt, 1980-86, dep dir contracting, 1986-91, dir contracting, 1991-2002; FPMI Solutions, asst dir contracts & contracts adminr, 2004-07; Defense Acquisition Inc, sr acquisition analyst, 2009-11. **Orgs:** Nat Contract Mgt Asn, chap prog chmn, 1982-83, chap vpres, 1983-84, chappres, 1984-85, chap dir, 1987-89; treasr, Huntsville High Sch PTA, 1986-87; chmn southern region meeting, Talladega Col Alumni, 1989, chap secy, 1991-98; deacon bd secy, Church St Cumberland Presby Church, 1991-96; deacon bd chmn, 1997-98; elder, Church Christ, 2003-; MBR Huntsvile Rehab Bd, 2003-. **Honors/Awds:** Chapter Man of the Year, Omega Psi Phi Fraternity, 1986; Meriterious Civilian Service Award, 2002. **Home Addr:** 128 Heritage Lane, Madison, AL 35758, **Home Phone:** (205)461-4220.

**REYNOLDS, JERRY ICE**
Basketball coach, basketball player. **Personal:** Born Dec 23, 1962, Brooklyn, NY. **Educ:** Madison Area Tech Col, attended 1982; La State Univ, attended 1985. **Career:** Basketball player (retired), basketball coach; Milwaukee Bucks, guard, 1985-88; Seattle Super sonics, guard, 1988-89; Orlando Magic, guard, 1989-93; Atlanta Trojans, 1995; Milwaukee Bucks, guard, 1995-96; Polti Cantu, 1996-97; Connecticut Pride, 1995, 1997; Gigantes de Carolina, 1997; Fontanafredda Siena, 1997-98; Indios de Mayaguez, 1999; Brooklyn Kings, 2000; Achilleas, 2000; Florida Sea Dragons, 2001; Webber Int Warriors, Webber Int Univ, assoc head coach, 2005; Jersey Express, head coach, 2008-09.

**REYNOLDS, MELVIN JAY, SR.**
Politician, consultant. **Personal:** Born Jan 8, 1952, Mound Bayou, MS; son of J J and Essie Mae Prather; married Marisol; children: Corean, Marisol Elizabeth & Melvin J Jr. **Educ:** Chicago City Col, AA, 1972; Univ Ill, Champaign-Urbana, BA, philos, 1974; Oxford Univ, LLB, 1979, MPA, 1981; Harvard Univ. **Career:** Roosevelt Univ, asst prof polit sci, prof; US House Rep, dem congressman, Ill, 1993-95; House Ways & Means Comt, mem; Rainbow Coalition, consult, 2001-; Salem Baptist Church, community develop dir, 2001-; Int Bus Mach. **Orgs:** Halfway house resident, Salvation Army, 2001. **Business Addr:** Consultant, Rainbow PUSH Coalitions, 930 E 50th St, Chicago, IL 60615, **Business Phone:** (773)373-3366.

**REYNOLDS, DR. NANETTE LEE**
Founder (originator). **Personal:** Born Feb 22, 1946, Oberlin, OH; married Murphy L; children: Malika & Michon Imani. **Educ:** Howard Univ, BS, 1967; Southern Ill Univ, Carbondale, MEd, 1969; Harvard Univ, EdD, 1978. **Career:** Director (retired); Mass Inst Technol, asst dean stud affairs, 1970-72; Brown Univ, asst dean acad affairs, 1972-74; RI Consortium Continuing Educ Human Serv & Community Welfare, exec dir, 1977-78; Reynolds Grp Human Res Consult, mng dir, 1980-81; Fed Coun Domestic Violence Progs, exec dir, 1982-83; Off Mich's Govt, prog specialist educ & civil rights, 1983-85; Mich Dept Civil Rights, exec asst dir, 1985-87, community serv bur, dir, 1987-93, dir & mem gov's cabinet, 1993-03; Reynovations, LLC, founder, 2003-; Grand Valley State Univ, sr adv pres, 2004-. **Orgs:** Trinity AME Church; Nat Asn Advan Colored People; Delta Sigma Theta Sorority Inc; The Links Inc; bd mem, Eles Pl grieving c; cochair, 1997-98, Greater Lansing UNCF Campaign; adv bd, J Inter-grp Rels, 1996-; Mich Psychol Asn Found bd; gov bd Coun, Educ Pub Health, 2013. **Honors/Awds:** Ford Fel Black Am, 1975-78; Directors Award, Mich Dept Civil Rights, 1987; Harvard Graduate School of Education Alumni Council Award for Outstanding Contribution to Education, 2012; Numerous awards & recognition for civil rights work. **Special Achievements:** First African-American female to head Michigan's Civil Rights Department; Nat Asn for Equal Opportunity Hon, Distinguished Alumna Historically & Predominately Black Col & Univ, 1994; Hon "Delta Legacy: Women Making a Difference", 1994; Listings in "Outstanding Young Women of America" and "Outstanding Black Americans". **Home Addr:** 1126 Sunset Lane, East Lansing, MI 48823. **Business Addr:** Senior Advisor, 1 Campus Dr, Allendale, MI 49401-9403, **Business Phone:** (616)331-5000.

**REYNOLDS, PAMELA TERESE**
Journalist. **Personal:** Born Dec 10, 1963, Los Angeles, CA; daughter of Theodore; married Philip G Roth. **Educ:** Univ Mo, Columbia Sch Jour, BJ, 1985. **Career:** Boston Globe, feature writer, reporter & nat

reporter, 1987-89, asst arts ed, 1990-91, asst living ed, 1991-97; Univ Va, res assoc & writer, 2002-07; MondoBoston, prin, 2008-. **Orgs:** Sigma Delta Chi, 1984; Young Black Journalists Under 30, 1985; Boston Assoc Black Journalists, 1986; tutor, Literacy Vol Mass, 1987. **Honors/Awds:** Nat Achievement Scholar, 1981; Reynolds Scholar Donald W Reynolds Found, 1983; Kappa Tau Alpha Hon Jour Soc, 1985; Best Stud Journalist, New Eng Women's Press Assoc, 1985; Best Fashion Writer of the Year. **Special Achievements:** Won first place in Feature Writing category for two of her articles. **Home Addr:** 51 Pettee St Suite 21, Newton, MA 02464, **Home Phone:** (617)244-1233. **Business Addr:** principal, mondoboston.com.

### REYNOLDS, RICKY SCOTT (DERRICK SCOTT REYNOLDS)

Founder (originator), football player. **Personal:** Born Jan 19, 1965, Sacramento, CA. **Educ:** Wash State Univ, attended 1987. **Career:** Football player (retired), owner; Tampa Bay Buccaneers, left cornerback, 1987-92, right cornerback, 1993; New Eng Patriots, left cornerback, 1994-95, right cornerback, 1996; Reynolds Child Develop Ctr, owner, currently; Fox 13, sports analyst, 2004-08; Mo Media Group Inc, exec vpres athlete rels, 2010-12; Ricky Reynolds Found Inc, pres, 2008-12. **Orgs:** Pres, NFLPA Former Players Chap Tampa, 2009-12; 2nd vpres, NFLPA Former Players Tampa Chap, 2012-14. **Business Addr:** Owner, Reynolds Child Development Center, 8474 W Hillsborough Ave, Tampa, FL 33615, **Business Phone:** (813)885-6262.

### REYNOLDS, ROBERT JAMES

Baseball player. **Personal:** Born Apr 19, 1959, Sacramento, CA; children: Fawn Rashelle & Robert IV. **Educ:** Sacramento City Col; Cosumnes River Col. **Career:** Baseball player (retired); Los Angeles Dodgers, outfielder, 1983-85; Pittsburgh Pirates, outfielder, 1985-90; Yokohama Taiyo Whales, outfielder, 1991-92; Kintetsu Buffaloes, outfielder, 1993; Japanese Baseball League, outfielder, 1991-94; Mex League, Yucatan Lions, outfielder, 1994. **Home Addr:** 7076 El Soreno Cir, Sacramento, CA 95831.

### REYNOLDS, SANDRA MICHELE

Financial manager, founder (originator), investment banker. **Personal:** Born Apr 9, 1964, Chicago, IL; daughter of Odessa O and Mitchell; married James Jr; children: James III, Kendall Marie & Miles Joseph. **Educ:** Stanford Univ, Sch Mgt, AB, 1984; Northwestern Univ, MM, 1987. **Career:** First Chicago Capital Markets, bond broker, vpres, 1985-95; Loop Capital Markets LLC, investment banker, partner, co-founder & managing dir, 1997-; IntraLink Global, partner & svpres, 2013-. **Orgs:** AKA Sorority, 1982-; Nat Black MBA Asn, 1985; Asn Investment Mgt & Res, chartered fin analyst, 1994-; bd mem & audit comt chmn, Choose Chicago, 2013-. **Home Addr:** 200 Inwood Dr, Wheeling, IL 60090-6711. **Business Addr:** Managing Director, Loop Capital Markets, LLC, 200 W Jackson Blvd Suite 1600, Chicago, IL 60606, **Business Phone:** (312)356-5890.

### REYNOLDS-BROWN, BLONDELL

Government official. **Personal:** Born Oct 16, 1952, Sumter, SC; daughter of Whittmore and Sadie Reynolds; married Howard; children: Andrew & Brielle. **Educ:** Pa State Univ, BS, elem edu, 1974 MS, edu, 1975; Univ Pa Community Leadership Prog, grad. **Career:** Sch Dist Philadelphia, elem sch teacher; prof dancer; Pa State Univ-Philadelphia Recruitment Ctr, assoc dir admin; Philadelphia Urban League, youth proj dir; Philadelphia Opportunities & Industrialization Ctr, dir community affairs & fund develop; State Sen Chaka Fattah, legis dir; State Sen Vincent Hughes, community affairs dir; 24th Ward, committeeperson, 1982-86;City Coun Philadelphia, city coun woman, 2000-. **Orgs:** Bd mem, Philadelphia Conv & Visitor's Bur; bd mem, Pa Ballet; bd mem, Wellness Community Philadelphia; bd mem, Greater Philadelphia Cult Alliance; bd mem, Fairmont Pk Hist Preserv Trust; Delta Sigma Theta Sorority; charter class mem, Philadelphia Urban League Leadership Inst; dir Community Affairs & Fund Develop, Opportunities Industrialization Ctr; dir, Youth Proj, Philadelphia Urban League; dir, Philadelphia Recruitment Ctr, Pa State Univ; deleg, Dem Nat Conv, 1984, 1988, 1996 & 2000; chair woman, City Coun Comt Parks, Recreation & Cult Affairs, 2000-; bd mem, Philadelphia Cult Fund, 2000-; fel Urban Health Initiative Prog, Robert Wood Johnson Found, 2002-05; Charter Class, Philadelphia Urban League Leadership Inst; Philadelphia Young Playwrights; Greater Philadelphia Cult Alliance; Pinn Memorial Baptist Church, W Philadelphia. **Honors/Awds:** Marian Anderson Award, African Am Mus Philadelphia; Woman of Distinction, Philadelphia Bus J; Women's History Month Award, Pa Comn Women, 2008; One of 50 of Pa's most influential women in the bk, VOICES; Woman of the Year Award, Nat Coalition 100 Black Women; Philadelphia Young Playwrights Advocate Award; Strong, Smart & Bold Award, Girls Inc; Leadership Award, Women's Way Powerful Voice. **Special Achievements:** Only woman to win a Philadelphia At-Large Council seat since 1999. **Business Addr:** Councilwoman-At-Large, City Council of Philadelphia, City Hall Rm 581, Philadelphia, PA 19107, **Business Phone:** (215)686-3438.

### RHAMES, VING (IRVING RAMESES RHAMES)

Actor. **Personal:** Born May 12, 1959, New York, NY; son of Ernest and Rather; married Valerie Scott; married Deborah Reed; children: Rainbow, Freedom & Tiffany. **Educ:** State Univ NY, Purchase; Juilliard Sch Drama, BFA, 1983. **Career:** Stage: The Boys of Winter, 1985; TV Series: Go Tell It on the Mountain, 1985; "Miami Vice", 1985-87; Men, 1989; Rising Son, 1990; The Long Walk Home, 1990; When You Remember Me, 1990; Terror on Track 9, 1992; "Philly Heat", 1994; "Suicide Squad"; "ER", 1994-96; Deadly Whispers, 1995; "Don King: Only in Am", 1997; "Holiday Heart", 2000; Am Tragedy, 2000; "UC: Undercover", 2001; Sins of the Father, 2002; "RFK", 2002; "Lilo& Stitch", 2002; "Little John", 2002; The Dist:, 2002-03; "Freedom: A Hist of Us", 2003; Kojak, co-exec producer, 2005; "Mercy Reef", 2006; "Leroy & Stitch", 2006; Aqua man, 2006; Football Wives, 2007; Frank Lucas, 2007, "Am Gangster", 2007; "Gravity", 2010; "Cubed", 2011; "Zombie Apocalypse", 2011; "Black Jack", 2011; "Monday Mornings", 2013; "A Day Late and a Dollar Short", 2014. Films: Go Tell It on the Mountain, 1984; Native Son, 1986; Patty Hearst, 1988; Casualties of War, 1989; Jacob's Ladder, 1990; Flight of the Intruder, 1991; The People Under the Stairs, 1991; Homicide, 1991; Stop! Or My Mom Will Shoot, 1992; Dave, 1993; Bound by Hon, 1993; The St of Ft Wash, 1993; Drop Squad, 1994; Pulp Fiction, 1994; Kiss of Death, 1995, Striptease, 1996; Mission: Impossible, 1996; Dangerous Ground, 1997; Rosewood, 1997; Con Air, 1997; Body Count, 1998; Out of Sight, 1998; Entrapment, 1999; Bringing Out the Dead, 1999; Mission Impossible II, 2000; Baby Boy, 2001; Final Fantasy: The Spirits Within, 2001; Undisputed, 2002; Lilo & Stitch, 2002; Dark Blue, 2002; Sin, 2003; Envy, 2004; Dawn of the Dead, 2004; Back in the Day, co-exec producer, 2005; Mission: Impossible III, 2006; Idle wild, 2006; A Broken Life, 2007; Ascension Day, producer, 2007; I Now Pronounce You Chuck & Larry, 2007; Day of the Dead, 2008; Animal 2, 2008; Saving God, 2008; Phantom Punch, 2009; The Bridge to Nowhere, 2009; Evil Angel, 2009; Echelon Conspiracy, 2009; Give 'em Hell, Malone, 2009; The Tournament, 2009; The Goods: Live Hard, Sell Hard, 2009; Surrogates, 2009; 'Master Harold' ... And the Boys, 2010; Operation: Endgame, 2010; Piranha 3D, 2010; King of the Avenue, 2010; Caged Animal, 2010; The River Murders, 2011; Pimp Bullies, 2011; Julia X, 2011; Mission: Impossible - Ghost Protocol, 2011; 7 Below, 2012; Piranha 3DD, 2012; Soldiers of Fortune, 2012; Money Fight, 2012; Won't Back Down, 2012; Mafia, 2012; Percentage, 2013; Armed Response, 2013; Force of Execution, 2013; Jamesy Boy, 2014. **Honors/Awds:** Golden Globe Award, 1998; OFTA Television Award, Online Film & Tv Asn, 1998; ShoWest Award, ShoWest Convention, 2000; Locarno International Film Festival Award, 2001. **Business Addr:** Actor, William Morris Agency, 1 William Morris Pl, Beverly Hills, CA 90212, **Business Phone:** (310)859-4000.

### RHEA, MICHAEL

Manager, association executive. **Personal:** Born Oct 3, 1946. **Educ:** Univ Calif, Los Angeles, MBA; Memphis State Univ; Tokyo Univ; Los Angeles Writers Workshop, post grad. **Career:** Met Manpower Comn, Indianapolis, dept adminr, 1973; WLWI TV "Here & Now", host, 1970-74; Econ Develop Corp, mgr, 1970-73; Thomas Ryan Inc Mgt Consult, reg mgr, 1969-70. **Orgs:** Govs Commn Status & Women, 1973; chmn bd dir, Youth Market Pl, 1973; pres & chmn bd, People Better Broadcasting, 1973; Jaycees; adv, Black Student Union; adv, Black Arts Workshop; Mayor's Task Force Improve City Govt; Indianapolis Cable Steering Com; Adult Educ Coun Central Ind; bd City & State Black Caucus; CORE; Young Rep; Nat Asn Execs & Mgr; Prof Mgrs Club; Artist Am; Midwst Poet's Org; adv Boys Club Am. **Home Addr:** 612 Berkley Rd, Indianapolis, IN 46208. **Business Addr:** 2101 N Col Ave, Indianapolis, IN 46202.

### RHEAMS, LEONTA DEMARKEL

Football player. **Personal:** Born Aug 1, 1976, Tyler, TX. **Educ:** Univ Houston, grad. **Career:** New Eng Patriots, defensive tackle, 1998; Xtreme Football League, Memphis Maniax, defensive tackle, 2001-. **Business Addr:** Defensive Tackle, Memphis Maniax, 315 S Hollywood St, Memphis, TN 38104, **Business Phone:** (901)515-2000.

### RHETT, ERRICT UNDRA

Football player, football coach. **Personal:** Born Dec 11, 1970, Pembroke Pines, FL; married Sandy; children: Errict Jr, Morgan & Amaurri. **Educ:** Univ Fla, BS, 1995. **Career:** Football player (retired), coach; Tampa Bay Buccaneers, running back, 1994-96, 1997; Baltimore Ravens, running back, 1998-99; Cleveland Browns, running back, 2000; Piper High Sch, Sunrise, Fla, running back coach, currently. **Orgs:** Omega Psi Phi Fraternity Inc; chief exec officer, Errict Rhett Found, currently; chief exec officer, Errict Rhett Custom Homes, currently. **Honors/Awds:** Offensive Rookie of the Year, Nat Football League Players Asn, 1994; Most Valuable Player, Pro Bowl, 1994; Florida-Georgia Hall of Fame; Athletic Hall of Fame, Univ Fla, 2005. **Business Addr:** Running Back Coach, Piper High School, 8000 NW 44 St, Sunrise, FL 33351, **Business Phone:** (754)322-1700.

### RHETT, MICHAEL L.

Law enforcement officer. **Personal:** Born Dec 1, 1954, Charlottesville, VA; son of Walter P Sr and Bernice N; married Susan G; children: Cole. **Educ:** Newberry Col, attended 1974; Ohio State Univ, attended 1978. **Career:** Police officer (retired); State Ohio, Nat Resources, pk ranger, 1978-80; Stand Oil Ohio, mgr, 1980-82; City Columbus, Div Police, police officer, 1982-2004. **Orgs:** Newsletter ed, Fraternal Order Police Conductor, 1982-92; bd mem, Crittenton Family Serv, 1983-, bd chair, 1986-87, bd chair, 1993-94; bd mem, Cent Community House, 1992-, bd chair, 1994-95; vpres, Fraternal Order Police, 1992-; bd chair, Cent Community House, 1997-. **Home Addr:** 3592 Aaron Dr, Columbus, OH 43228, **Home Phone:** (614)351-0707. **Business Addr:** Police Officer, City of Columbus, 120 Marconi Blvd, Columbus, OH 43215, **Business Phone:** (614)645-4805.

### RHETTA, HELEN LOWE

Physician. **Personal:** daughter of B M. **Educ:** Univ Mich, AB; Univ Mich Med Sch, MD, 1937; Univ Mich Sch Pub Health, US Dept HEW, MPH, 1976. **Career:** Provident Hosp, intern & resident, 1938-39, physician, 1939. **Orgs:** IL State, Chicago, Med Soc; Am Mgt Asn; Am Pub Health Soc; Delta Sigma Theta; Am Physicians Art Asn; fel US Pub Health, 1966-67. **Honors/Awds:** Superior Service Award, US Dept HEW, 1972; Nat Asn Col Women Award; Am Physicians Recognition Award; Zeta Phi Beta Woman of the Year. **Home Addr:** 9404 S Martin Luther King Dr, Chicago, IL 60619.

### RHIMES, SHONDA

Television writer, television producer. **Personal:** Born Jan 13, 1970, Chicago, IL; children: Harper Rhimes (b.2002), Emerson Pearl Rhimes (b. 2012), and Beckett Rhimes (b.2013). **Educ:** Dartmouth College, Bachelor's, 1991; University of Southern California, School of Cinema-Television, M.F.A. **Career:** Documentary "Hank Aaron: Chasing the Dream," Research Director, 1995; Short film "Blossoms and Veils," Director, 1998; HBO movie "Introducing Dorothy Dandridge," Writer, 1999; feature film "Crossroads," Writer, 2002; feature film "The Princess Diaries 2: Royal Engagement," 2004; ABC television show "Grey's Anatomy," Creator, Writer, and Executive Producer, 2005-; ABC television show "Private Practice," 2007-13, Creator, Writer, and Executive Producer; ABC television show "Scandal," Creator, Writer, and Executive Producer, 2012-. **Orgs:** John F. Kennedy Center for the Performing Arts, Trustee (appointed by President Barack Obama). **Honors/Awds:** Gary Rosenberg Writing Fellowship Award, Recipient; Writers Guild of America, Best New Series ("Grey's Anatomy"), 2006; Women in Film Lucy Awards, Lucy Award, 2007; PGA Awards, Outstanding Producer of Episodic Television, Drama ("Grey's Anatomy"), 2007; Image Awards, Outstanding Writing in a Dramatic Series, "Grey's Anatomy" 2007, 2008, 2009, 2010, Outstanding Writing in a Dramatic Series, "Private Practice" 2011; GLAAD Media Awards, Golden Gate Award, 2012; TV Guide Awards, Fan Favorite Award ("Scandal"), 2013; "Time" Magazine, 100 Most Influential People in the World, 2013; "Fortune" Magazine, 50 Most Powerful Women in Business, 2013; "Hollywood Reporter," Women in Entertainment Power 100, 2013; Director's Guild of America, Diversity Award, 2014.

### RHINEHART, JUNE ACIE

Publishing executive. **Personal:** Born Jul 1, 1934, McKeesport, PA; daughter of William Elmer Acie (deceased) and Gladys Cornelia Allen Acie (deceased); married Vernon Morel. **Educ:** Wilson Jr Col, AB, 1962; Roosevelt Univ, Chicago, BA, 1968; Northwestern Univ; Loyola Univ, Chicago, Grad Sch Bus, 1972; Loyola Univ, Chicago Sch Law, JD, 1980. **Career:** Johnson Publ Co Inc, secy, 1955-60, admin asst, 1960-71, vpres, asst to publ, 1971-80, sr vpres & gen coun, 1980, vice chmn & gen coun, 2005. **Orgs:** Adv bd exec prog, Stanford Univ, 1976-78; Roosevelt Univ Alumni Bd; bd trustee, Chic St Univ Found; Alpha Kappa Alpha Sor; Chicago Network; Women's Div Oper PUSH; Chicago Focus. **Honors/Awds:** Achievement Award, Nat Coun Negro Women, 1973; 1000 Successful Blacks. **Home Addr:** 1335 Prairie, Chicago, IL 60605. **Business Addr:** Vice Chair, Johnson Publishing Company Inc, 820 S Mich Ave, Chicago, IL 60605, **Business Phone:** (312)322-9200.

### RHINEHART, N. PETE, JR.

Executive, chairperson, chief financial officer. **Career:** AT&T, vpres & chief financial officer, currently. **Orgs:** Chmn audit comt, USATF. **Business Addr:** Chairman, USATF, 1 RCA Dome Suite 140, Indianapolis, IN 46225, **Business Phone:** (317)261-0500.

### RHINES, JESSE ALGERON

Educator. **Personal:** Born Jul 30, 1948, Washington, DC; son of Jacinto and Julia Marie Watson Barbour. **Educ:** Antioch Col, BA, polit commun, 1974; NY Univ, film prod cert, 1983; Yale Univ, MA, Afro-Am studies, 1983; Univ Calif, Los Angeles, MA, polit sci, 1986; Univ Calif, Berkeley, PhD, ethnic studies, 1993. **Career:** YMCA World Ambassador Hong Kong, Japan, S Korea, 1975; Congressman RDellums, leg intern, admin aide, 1975-76; Mayor, New Haven, leg affairs officer, 1978-89; U-Skate Rollerskates, founder, 1979-81; Opers Crossroads Africa Inc, Mali group leader, 1980; Int Bus Machs Corp, systs eng, 1981-83; State NY Mortgage Agency, comput systs analyst, 1989-90; Cineaste Mag, asst ed, co-ed, Race Contemp Cinema Sect, 1992-2000; Eugene Lange Col, instr, 1993; Rutgers Univ, African Am & African Studies Dept, asst prof, 1993-; "BLACK FILM/WHITE MONEY", 1996; "BLACK HARVARD/BLACK YALE", 1999; tutor, 2006-08; Rotary Club, prof, 2011-12; Augmented Reality Bootcamp, stud, 2013; "BLUE SKY FOR BLACK AM", nortia publishers, 2014. **Orgs:** Black Filmmaker Found; Independent Feature Project; Nat Asn Advan Colored Peope; Soc Cinema Studies; fel, Nat Coun Black Polit Scientists, 1976; fel, Am Polit Sci Asn, 1976. **Home Addr:** 219 W 16th St Suite 1A, New York, NY 10011-6028. **Business Addr:** Assistant Professor, Rutgers University, 249 University Ave, Newark, NJ 07102-1896, **Business Phone:** (973)353-5205.

### RHOADES, DR. SAMUEL THOMAS, III

School administrator. **Personal:** Born Aug 11, 1946, Raleigh, NC; children: Audria Michelle Humes. **Educ:** NC Cent Univ, BA, psychol, 1967, JD, 1973. **Career:** Durham Col, coun & coop ed, 1973-77; St Pauls Col, spec asst & fed progs, 1977-; Nat Asn Title III Admin, Va Union Univ, parliamentarian, 1978, pres, pres emer & spec asst pres, univ adminr, currently; NC Cent Univ, pres emer. **Orgs:** Treas, Phi Alpha Delta Law Fraternity, 1975; Am Legion, Omega Psi Phi Fraternity, Beauty Dunn Lodge F&A Masons; life mem, NC Cent Univ Alumni Asn; Nat Asn Advan Colored People; pres, Nat Asn HBCU Title III Adminr, 2003-07; exec dir & pres, Nat Asn Historically Black Cols & Univs Title III Adminr Found, 2003-07. **Business Addr:** Special Assistant to President, President Emeritus, Virginia Union University, 1500 N Lombardy St, Richmond, VA 23220, **Business Phone:** (804)257-5600.

### RHODEMAN, CLARE M.

Educator. **Personal:** Born Jul 21, 1932, Biloxi, MS; married Thomas Johan; children: Rennee Maria, Thomas Johan & Nichole Irene. **Educ:** Xavier Univ, New Orleans, BA, 1953, MA, 1957. **Career:** Elem, Jr High & Sr High teacher & Sr High coun; Nicholas Jr HS Biloxi Municipal Separate Sch Syst, Jr HS coun; MTA BEA, coordr, 1973-74. **Orgs:** MS Personel & Guide Asn; prof Stand Com; chmn guide Com 6th dist MS Teacher Asn; Nat Educ Asn; Cath 67, sec 67-71, vpres, 1971-72 Biloxi Interparochial Sch Bd; Our Mother Sorrows Cath Ch; Parish Coun; pres, MS Gulf Coast Alumnae Chap Delta Sigma Theta Sorority, 1983-84; Biloxi Nat Asn Advan Colored People; bd dir, Harrison Co Devl Comn; Harrison Co Community Action Prog; Harrison Co United Found; Dem Party; vol worker, Mothers March Birth Defects, Heart Fnd & PTA. **Home Addr:** 392 Fayard St, Biloxi, MS 39530, **Home Phone:** (228)435-8171. **Business Addr:** 950 Bellman St, Biloxi, MS 39530-3906.

### RHODEN, DWIGHT

Choreographer, artistic director. **Personal:** Born Jan 1, 1962, Dayton, OH. **Educ:** Boston Conserv, PhD. **Career:** Dayton Contemp Dance Co, dancer, 1976-82; Les Ballets Jazz de Montreal, dancer, 1982-86; Alvin Ailey Am Dance Theatre, dancer, 1987-94; Complexions Contemp Ballet, co-founder, artistic dir & resident choreographer, 1994-; NC Dance Theatre, resident choreographer; Arizon Ballet; Aspen Santa Fe Ballet Co; BalletMet; Dance Theater Harle; Colo Ballet; Joffrey Ballet; Miami City Ballet; New York Ballet & Diamond Proj; Pa Ballet; Phildanco; Marinsky Ballet; Minneapolis Dance Theater; Phoenix Dance Co; Sacramento Ballet; Oakland Ballet; Pittsburg Ballet Theater; Wash Ballet; Zenon Dance Co; "You Think You Can

Dance", dir & choreographer; E!Entertainment's "Tribute to Style", dir & choreographer; Amci & Cirque Du Soleil's Zumanity, dir & choreographer; One Last Dance, choreographer. **Business Addr:** Artistic Director, Resident Choreographer, Complexions Contemporary Ballet, 37 W 39th St Suite 401, New York, NY 10018, **Business Phone:** (212)777-7771.

**RHODEN, DR. RICHARD ALLAN, SR.**
Scientist. **Personal:** Born May 8, 1930, Coatesville, PA; son of Dorothy; married Stephanie Auroa Thompson; children: Richard Jr. **Educ:** Lincoln Univ, BA, chem, 1951; Drexel Univ, MS, 1967, PhD, environ toxicol, 1971. **Career:** Scientist (retired); Naval Air Develop Ctr, res chemist, 1972; Environ Protection Agency, environ scientist, 1972-75; Nat Inst Occup Safety & Health, res pharmacologist, 1975-82; Nat Inst Health, health scientist adminr, 1982-89; Am Petrol Inst, health scientist, 1989-97. **Orgs:** Exec secy, subcomt toxicol, exec comt, Sci adv bd, US Environ Protection Agency, 1979; Environ Studies Inst Adv Comm, Drexel Univ, 1980-84; Alpha Omega Chap, Omega Psi Phi Frat Inc, 1992-97; Am Chem Soc; Soc Toxicol; Am Indust Hyg Asn; Fel AAAS; Fel Am Inst Chemists. **Home Addr:** 430 Oglethorpe St NW, Washington, DC 20011-2149, **Home Phone:** (202)545-1967.

**RHODES, ARTHUR LEE, JR.**
Baseball player. **Personal:** Born Oct 24, 1969, Waco, TX; children: Jade & Jordan (deceased). **Career:** Baseball player (retired); Baltimore Orioles, pitcher, 1991-99; Seattle Mariners, pitcher, 2000-03; Oakland Athletics, pitcher, 2004; Cleveland Indians, pitcher, 2005; Philadelphia Phillies, 2006; Seattle Mariners, pitcher, 2008; Fla Marlins, pitcher, 2008; Cincinnati Reds, pitcher, 2009-10; Tex Rangers, pitcher, 2011; St Louis Cardinals, relief pitcher, 2011-. **Business Addr:** Relief Pitcher, St Louis Cardinals, Busch Stadium, St. Louis, MO 63102, **Business Phone:** (314)345-9600.

**RHODES, C. ADRIENNE**
Consultant, journalist. **Personal:** Born Jul 16, 1961, Camden, NJ; daughter of Lawrence Wilmer and Adele Clark Polk. **Educ:** Pratt Inst, Sch Art & Design, BFA, 1980; Fashion Inst Technol, AAS, 1984, BS, 1989; NY Univ, attended 1995. **Career:** New York Times Mag Group, circulation & prom serv asst, 1980-82; Diane Von Furstenberg Inc, pub rels mgr, 1982-84; United Negro Col Fund, mgr media rels, 1984-86, asst dir commun, 1986-89, dir commun, 1989-93; Daily News LP, dir commun & media rels, 1993-98, vpres & dir commun, consult, 1993-2000; Columbia Univ, instr, 1994-; Ny Consumer Protection Bd, chmn & exec dir, 2000-02; Chisholm-Mingo Group, vpres & managing dir pub rels, 2002-05; Ny, Dept Youth & Community Develop, proj dir, 2005-08; Independent consult, 2008-. **Orgs:** Sen, Stud Govt Asn, Pratt Inst, 1979-80; PRSA Young Professionals Comn, NY Chap, 1983-84; assoc mem, New York Asn Black Journalists, 1986; Pub Rels Soc Am, Nat Chap, 1987-89; mkt chmn, Nat Asn Black Journalists, 1989; co-founder, Black Pub Rels Soc Greater New York, 1990; US Comn Minority Bus Develop, Media & Perception Task Force, 1991; Nat Black Women's Po lit Caucus, media & entertainment comn, 1993-; chair, 1989-99, adv bd, 1993-, New York Urban League; Publ's Liasion, Harlem Y Steering Comt, 1994; fund raiser, Manhattan Adv Bd, chair, World Women Leaders Conf, 1999; chair, exec dir, New York Consumer Protection Bd, 2001. **Special Achievements:** Highest-ranking African-American woman in the print news business in the media capital of the world. **Home Addr:** 310 E 44th St Apt 621, New York, NY 10017, **Home Phone:** (212)949-9805. **Business Addr:** Consultant, Daily News LP, 450 W 33rd St, New York, NY 10001, **Business Phone:** (212)210-2100.

**RHODES, EDWARD THOMAS, SR.**
Executive. **Personal:** Born Mar 20, 1933, Cumberland, MD; son of John Henry and Ella Harrison Burgee; married Ovetta Lyles Williams; children: Shari & Edward Jr. **Educ:** Kenyon Col, BA, polit sci, 1955. **Career:** WPAFB, contract negotiator, 1958-61; GSFC, sr procurement analyst, 1961-64; FWPCA, dept int, dir div gen serv, 1964-71; EPA, dir contract mgt div, 1971-75, dept asst adv, 1975-78; HEW dept asst sec grants & procurement mgt, 1975, dept asst sec grants & procurement, 1978-80, dep assoc dir, admin off of personnel mgt, 1980-86; Wash metro Area Transist Authority, dir, 1986-92; Sectek Inc, pres, 1992-. **Orgs:** Past mem, Nat Bd Adv; Nat Contract Mgt Asn; mem bd, Regents Inst Cost Anal; pres, Nat Asn Black Procurement Prof; dir, Procurement Roundtable. **Home Addr:** 3251 S Leisure World Blvd, Silver Spring, MD 20906-1759, **Home Phone:** (301)438-9640. **Business Addr:** President, Sectek Inc, 11413 Isaac Newton Sq S, Reston, VA 20190, **Business Phone:** (703)435-0970.

**RHODES, GERALD N. (JERRY RHODES)**
Executive. **Personal:** Born Linden, NJ; married Sharon. **Educ:** Stevens Inst Technol, Hoboken, NJ, BS, eng; Columbia Univ, NY, MBA, bus admin. **Career:** Gen Foods Corp, White Plains, NY, mkt mgr; Citibank, NY, pvt banking group, vpres, Citiphone Sales Ctr, vpres, bus mgr, vpres mkt; Sprint, Kans, Mo, vpres emerging markets & vpres mkt; Aerial Comun, Chicago, vpres mkt, sales & chief mkt officer, 1996-99; Peco Energy Co, vpres, 1999, pres; Exelon Energy, pres, 1999-. **Business Addr:** President, Exelon Energy, Monroe Serv Bldg, Norristown, PA 19403, **Business Phone:** (215)841-4000.

**RHODES, JACOB ALEXANDER**
Association executive. **Personal:** Born Nov 30, 1949, Brownsville, TN; son of Franklin A and Mary J; married Phyleata Harris; children: Jalena, Alex & Franklin. **Educ:** Tenn State Univ, Nashville, Tenn, BS, health & phys educ, 1970; Univ Wis, Milwaukee, WI, MS, urban affairs, 1980; Union Inst & Univ, Cincinnati, Ohio, PhD, bus admin & mgmt, 1990. **Career:** YMCA Greater Houston, Vpres Urban Serv, 1978-91; YMCA Greater Rochester, pres & chief exec officer, 1992-98, dir; Butler St YMCA, pres & chief exec officer, 2000-06; Jacob Rhodes Inc, pres & chief exec officer, 2006-; Coldwell Banker-Bullard Realty Co, realtor assoc, 2008-. **Orgs:** Bd dir, Ga Partnership Excellence Educ; chair, CRA Comt, M & T Bank Adv Bd; Finger Lakes Blue Cross & Blue Shield Adv Bd; Chamber Com CEO Roundtable; United Way Steering Comt; Planning Priorities Comt; Sigma Pi Phi Fraternity; Auburn Ave Bus Asn; Omega Psi Phi Fraternity. **Honors/Awds:** Youth Services Award, Ny Asn Black & Puerto Rican Legislators; Heritage Award, YMCA East Field; Distinguished Service Award, Police Rosewood Club & Rochester Police Dept; Executive of the Year Award, United Way; Outstanding Achievement Award, HELP Inc. **Special Achievements:** Author: Managing in a Changing Environment, 1982; "Management Styles of 30 CEOs", Jun 1990. **Home Addr:** 270 Acton Dr, Fayetteville, GA 30215-7402, **Home Phone:** (678)817-0568. **Business Addr:** Realtor Associate, Coldwell Banker Bullard Realty Co, 201 Prime Point, Peachtree City, GA 30269-3306, **Business Phone:** (770)487-1917.

**RHODES, JEANNE SIMMONS.** **See Obituaries Section.**

**RHODES, JERRY.** **See RHODES, GERALD N.**

**RHODES, JOHN K.**
Government official, consultant, president (organization). **Personal:** Born Mar 18, 1965, San Francisco, CA; son of Gus and Lillian. **Educ:** Univ Nev, Las Vegas, NV, BS, 1987, post grad, 1989; Univ Nebr-Lincoln, attended 1984. **Career:** Univ Med Ctr, personnel, 1989; Clark County, agt, 1989-94; John K Rhodes Consult, pres, 1991-; N Las Vegas County, councilman. **Orgs:** Life mem, Omega Psi Phi Fraternity, 1988-; founding mem, Committed 100 Men Helping Boys, 1991-; City Las Vegas, Task C, 1992; bd mem, Lied Discovery Mus, 1992-93; bd mem, DARE Inc, 1992-93; Bd Equalization, 1995-. **Home Addr:** 1316 Walstone Rd, North Las Vegas, NV 89031, **Home Phone:** (702)649-0860. **Business Addr:** President, John K Rhodes Consulting Inc, 3028 Diana Dr, North Las Vegas, NV 89030, **Business Phone:** (702)649-0860.

**RHODES, KARL DERRICK (TUFFY RHODES)**
Baseball player. **Personal:** Born Aug 21, 1968, Cincinnati, OH. **Career:** Baseball player (retired); Gulf Coast League, 1986; Fla State League, batting, 1988; Houston Astros, 1990-93; Chicago Cubs, 1993-95; Boston Red Sox, 1995; Kintetsu Buffaloes Osaka Kintetsu Buffaloes, 1996-2003; Yomiuri Giants, Japanese Cent League, 2004-05; Orix Buffaloes, 2007-09. **Honors/Awds:** Best Nine Award, 1997, 1999, 2001-04, 2008; Nippon Professional Baseball All-Star, 1997-2004, 2007, 2008; Most Valuable Player Award, Pacific League, 2001. **Business Addr:** Player, Orix Buffaloes, Green Stadium Kobe, Suma-Ku654-1234.

**RHODES, LISA D.**
Counselor, college administrator, minister (clergy). **Educ:** Wheeling Jesuit Univ, BA; Univ Md, Baltimore, MSW; Emory Univ, Mdiv; Union Theol Sem, doctorate ministry. **Career:** Centers DisControl & Prev, coordr Women & Minority Health Progs, 1993-96; Hist Ebenezer Baptist Ctr, assoc pastor, 1995-2001; Payne Theol Sem, prog mgr; Interdenominational Theol Ctr, prog mgr; Spelman Col, dean Sisters Chapel & Dir WISDOM (Women Spiritual Discernment Ministry) Ctr, 2001-; Care & Coun Ctr Ga, advan resident counr. **Orgs:** Trustee, Interfaith C Movement Ga. **Special Achievements:** Designer and host of global conference, Sisters of African Descent: Connecting Spirituality, Religion, and Vocation. **Business Addr:** Sisters Chapel and WISDOM Center, PO Box 357, Atlanta, GA 30314, **Business Phone:** (404)270-5728.

**RHODES, DR. PAULA R.**
Educator, lawyer. **Personal:** Born Jul 18, 1949, New Orleans, LA; daughter of Leroy and Marie Richard. **Educ:** Am Univ, BA, 1971; Harvard Univ, JD, 1974. **Career:** Legal Serv Corp, atty, demonstration proj mgr, 1977-79; Howard Univ Sch Law, assoc prof, 1979-90; Mid Atlantic Legal Educ, prof, 1980; Univ San Diego Law Sch, vis prof, 1983-84; Univ Bridgeport, vis prof, 1985; Univ Denver Col Law, Denver, Colo, vis prof, 1989-90, prof & dir, LLM Am & Comp Law Prog, 1990-, assoc prof, currently. **Orgs:** Dist Columbia Bar Asn; US Supreme Ct Bars; Am Bar Asn; Am Soc Int Law; vice chair & assoc clerk, Am Friends Serv Comt; African Am UN Comt; Transafrica; Fin Comt, Mountainview Friends Meetings; Soc Am Law Teachers; chair, Sam Carey Bar Asn; Am Soc Int Law; Consortium Human Rights Develop; Supreme Ct CO Gender Fairness Judicial Educ Ads Comt; bd, DC Chap Fed Bar Asn, 1980-87; Nat Coun, 1980-81; chmn, Sturm Col Admis & Fin Aid Comt; Co-chmn, Univ Denver Fac Color Asn; chairwoman, Stiles African Am Heritage Ctr. **Home Addr:** 4255 S Olive St Apt 11, Denver, CO 80237, **Home Phone:** (303)758-0541. **Business Addr:** Professor, University of Denver, 2199 S Univ Blvd 435B, Denver, CO 80208, **Business Phone:** (303)871-6258.

**RHODES, RAYMOND EARL**
Football player, football coach, football executive. **Personal:** Born Oct 20, 1950, Mexia, TX; married Carmen; children: Detra, Candra, Tynesha & Raven. **Educ:** Tex Christian Univ; Univ Tulsa. **Career:** Football player, football coach (retired), football exec; New York Giants, wide receiver & defensive back, 1974-79; San Francisco 49ers, defensive back, 1980, asst sec coach, 1981-82, defensive backfield coach, 1983-88, defensive coordr, 1989-91; Green Bay Packers, defensive coordr, 1992-93, headcoach, 1999; Philadelphia Eagles, head coach, 1995-98; Wash Redskins, defensive coordr, 2000; Denver Broncos, defensive coordr, 2001-02; Seattle Seahawks, defensive coordr, 2003-05, defensive asst, 2005-07, spec projs, defense, 2005; Houston Texans, asst defensive backs coach, 2008-10; Cleveland Browns, defensive asst, 2011-12. **Honors/Awds:** Assistant Coach of the Year Award, Nat Football League, 1993; Super Bowl XXIX, 1995; Coach of the Year Award, Nat Football League, 1995. **Special Achievements:** One of only a few African Am NFL coaches, third in NFL history. **Business Addr:** Assistant Defensive Backs Coach, Houston Texans, 2 Reliant Pk, Houston, TX 77054, **Business Phone:** (832)667-2000.

**RHODES, DR. ROBERT SHAW**
Physician. **Personal:** Born Mar 3, 1936, Orangeburg, SC; son of John D and Emma W; married Gwendolyn M; children: Robin, Robert Jr, Nekole Smith & Candace Smith. **Educ:** Meharry Med Col, MD, 1962; Univ Mich Sch Pub Health, MPH, 1983. **Career:** Meharry Med Col, resident, 1963-67; U Cincinnati Kettering Lab, resident; Vanderbilt Univ Sch Med, fel, 1967-70; Meharry Med Col, head div hemat, 1972-78; Multiphasic Screening Lab, dir, 1973-78; Hubbard Hosp, med dir, 1975-78; Hydra-matic Div GMC, assoc med dir, 1978-80, med dir, 1980-82; Health Serv & Safety, div dir, 1982-87; Univ Mich Hosp, fel; Gen Motors Corp, Detroit W Med Region, regional med dir; pvt pract, currently. **Orgs:** Chairperson, Sickle Cell Adv Comn, 1977-81; Mich Occup Med Asn; chmn, Med Audit Comn Beyer Hosp, 1980-83; vpres ed comn, Nat Sickle Cell Found, 1983-84; pres, house deleg exec bd, Wolverine County BSA, 1988-90, bd dir, 1990; Am Col Occup Med; pres, ACOEM, 1997-98. **Home Addr:** 2350 Londonderry, Ann Arbor, MI 48104. **Business Addr:** Physician, 7393 Whittingham Way, West Bloomfield, MI 48322-3288, **Business Phone:** (248)788-1290.

**RHODES, RODRICK**
Basketball coach, basketball player. **Personal:** Born Sep 24, 1973, Jersey City, NJ; children: Ro. **Educ:** Univ Ky, 1995; Univ Southern Calif, BA, 1997. **Career:** Basketball player (retired), basketball coach; Houston Rockets, guard-forward, 1997-98; Vancouver Grizzlies, guard, 1998-99; Dallas Maverick, 1999-2000; Dafni Athens (Greece), 2000-01; Air21 Express (Philippines), 2002; Brooklyn Kings (USBL), 2003; prof leagues, player, Cyprus, Greece, Philippines, France & Pr; Univ Tex-Pan Am, mens basketball prog, asst coach; St Edward's Univ, asst coach; Idaho St Univ, asst coach, 2006-07; Univ Mass, asst to head coach & dir player personnel; Seton Hall Univ, admin asst coach; Cordia Lions, head coach, currently. **Business Addr:** head coach, Cordia Lions, 6050 Lotts Creek Rd, Hazard, KY 41701, **Business Phone:** (606)785-4457.

**RHODES, TUFFY.** **See RHODES, KARL DERRICK.**

**RHONE, SYLVIA M.**
Executive. **Personal:** Born Mar 11, 1952, Philadelphia, PA; daughter of James and Marie Christmas. **Educ:** Univ Pa, Wharton Sch Bus & Com, MA, 1974. **Career:** Bankers Trust, 1974; ABC Rec, regional promotional mgr, 1978; Atlantic Recs, Nat Black Music Prom, dir, 1985, Black Music Opers, vpres & gen mgr, sr vpres, 1988; E W Rec Am, chairperson, chief exec officer, 1991; Atco-EastWest label, chief exec officer, 1991-94, chairperson; Elektra & EW Co, chair, 1994; Universal Rec, exec vpres, 2004-11; Motown Rec, pres, 2004-11; Vested Cult, chief exec officer & founder, 2012-; Elektra Entertainment Group, chmn, chief exec officer; Ariola Rec; Buddah Recs, admin asst, promotions coordr. **Orgs:** Alumni Trustee, Univ PA; mem bd dir, Alvin Ailey Am Dance Theater; Rock & Roll Hall Fame. **Honors/Awds:** Honoree, Jack the Rapper, convention, Atlanta, 1991; Trumpet Award, Turner Broadcasting, 2004; Life Member Award, Nat Coun Negro Women; Black Girls Rock Corporate Award, 2007; Lexus Pursuit Of Perfection Award, African Am Women, 2010; Lifetime Achievement Award, Black Alumni Pratt; DHL; Herbert H Wright Award, Nat Asn Mkt Developers; American Music Excellence Award, Sonys Soul; Whitney M Young Service Award, Boy Scouts Am; Executive Of The Year Award, Urban Network; Hon DHL, Univ Adelphi. **Special Achievements:** First African American woman to head a major record company when she wasnamed Chief Executive Officer & President of Atlantic's new East WestRecords America division. Ms. Magazine named Rhone Woman Of The Year. **Home Addr:** 21 S End Ave, New York, NY 10280, **Home Phone:** (212)786-1020. **Business Addr:** Chief Executive Officer, Founder, Vested in Culture, 550 Madison Ave, New York, NY 10022.

**RHYMES, BUSTA (TREVOR TAHIEM SMITH, JR.)**
Actor, rap musician, songwriter. **Personal:** Born May 20, 1972, Brooklyn, NY; son of Trevor Smith Sr and Geraldine Green; married Joanne Wood; children: T'Ziah, T'Khi & Trillian; children: Tahiem Jones (deceased) & Mariah. **Career:** The Leaders of The New Sch, mem; Group Albums: Future Without A Past, 1990; T.I.M.E The Inner Mind's Eye: The Endless Dispute With Reality, 1993; Solo Albums: The Coming, 1996; When Disaster Strikes, 1997; Extinction Level Event (The Final World Front), 1998; Anarchy, 2000; Genesis, 2001; It Ain't Safe No More, 2003; The Big Bang, 2006; Back on My B.S, 2009; Year of the Dragon, 2012; Extinction Level Event 2, 2012; TV series appearances: Cosby, 1997; TV movies: The Oz, 2002; Film appearances:Higher Learning, 1994; Extinction Level Event (The Final World), 1998; Shaft, 2000; Finding Forrester, 2000; Halloween: Resurrection, 2002; The Punisher, 2003; Waiting, 2003; The Neptunes Present: Dude We're Going to Rio!, 2003; Death of a Dynasty, 2003; Full Clip, 2004; Strong Arm Steady, 2004; Busta Rhymes: Everything Remains Raw, 2004; Def Jam Fight for NY, 2004, The Game: Documentary, 2005; The Boondocks, 2007; Breaking Point, 2009; The Unforgiven, 2011; J records, rapper, 2001-. **Business Addr:** Rapper, J Records, 745 5th Ave Fl 6, New York, NY 10151, **Business Phone:** (646)840-5600.

**RIBBS, WILLIAM THEODORE, JR. (WILLY T RIBBS)**
Race car driver. **Personal:** Born Jan 3, 1956, San Jose, CA; son of William T Sr and Geraldine Henderson; married Suzanne; children: Sasha Wanjiku & William Theodore III. **Educ:** San Jose City Col, San Jose, CA, 1975. **Career:** Car racing (retired); formula ford circuit, driver, 1977; formula atlantic events; sports 2000 events; neil deatley trans-Am team, driver, 1984; ford motors sports, 1984-85; digard & brooks racing, 1986; racing driver dan gurneys all Am racers, Santa Ana, Calif, 1987; NASCAR Craftsman Truck Ser, 2001. **Orgs:** Nat Sporting Clays Asn. **Honors/Awds:** Dunlop Star Tomorrow Champion Europe, 1977; International Driver of the Year Europe, 1977; British Sports Writers Award, 1977; Trans-Am Rookie of the Year, 1983; Winner of Trans-Am series opener in Phoenix (10 victory in 25 Trans-Am starts), 1985; Norelco Driver Cupt Award winner; Proclamation Willy T Ribbs Day City of Miami, 1984, City of Atlanta, 1984; City of St Petersburg, 1987; Interamerican Western Hemisphere Driving Champion, 1984; All American Drivers Award, Motorsports Press Assoc, 1984-85; Norelco GTO Driver of the Year, Phillips Business systems, l988; Norelco GTO Driver of the Year; SCCA; Trans American All Time Money Earner, l988; First bl to compete in Indianapolis 500, 1991; Johnson Triple Crown Award. **Special Achievements:** First African American to qualify and compete in the Indianapolis 500; First African American to compete in NASCAR's Winston Cup series; First African American to compete in CART/Indy Car Championship in partnership with entertainer, Bill Cosby; First and only African American to test for Formula 1 Grand Prix team in Estroil, Portugal; One of

the only African American NASCAR racers. **Home Addr:** 2343 Ribbs Lane, San Jose, CA 95116, **Home Phone:** (408)272-3479.

### RIBEAU, DR. SIDNEY A.

College president, educator. **Personal:** married Paula Whetsel; children: 3. **Educ:** Wayne State Univ, BS, 1971; Univ Ill, MS, 1973, PhD, interpersonal & group commun, 1979. **Career:** Educator, administrator (retired); Calif State Univ, prof commun studies, 1976-87, dean, undergrad studies univs San Bernardino campus, 1987-90; Calif State Polytech Univ, Col Lib Arts, dean, 1990-92; Calif State Polytech Univ Pomona, vpres acad affairs, 1992-95; Bowling Green State Univ, pres, 1995-2008; Howard Univ, pres, 2008-13. **Orgs:** Trustee, Teachers Ins & Annuity Asn; bd dir, pres coun, Nat Col Athletic Asn; chair, Inter Univ, Coun Pres, 2005-06; Toledo Urban League; Toledo Symphony; Andersons Inc; Convergys Corp; Worthington Indust; chair, Univs Pan African Studies Dept; bd dir, Teachers Ins & Annuity Asn Col Retirement Equities Fund; bd dir, Coun Int Exchange Scholars; bd dir, Asn Gov Boards; bd dir, Asn Am Cols & Univs; bd dir, Consortium Univ Presidents; Regional Growth Partnership. **Honors/Awds:** Distinguished Alumnus Award, Wayne State Univ; Distinguished Alumnus Award, Univ Ill; Scholarly recognition, Natl Commun Asn; Presidents Award, Nat Asn Stud Personnel Adminr, 2003; campus plaza and a student development program named in honor, Bowling Green State Univ, 2009; Educator of the Year, World Affairs Coun, 2012. **Business Addr:** President, Howard University, 2400 6th St NW Suite 402, Washington, DC 20059, **Business Phone:** (202)806-2500.

### RIBEIRO, ALFONSO

Actor, television director. **Personal:** Born Sep 21, 1971, New York, NY; son of Michael and Joy; married Robin Stapler; children: Sienna; married Angela Unkrich; children: Alfonso Lincoln Jr. **Educ:** Univ Calif & Valley Prof Sch Los Angeles. **Career:** Films: Seek & Hide, 2004; Love wrecked, 2005. TV series: "Oye Willie", 1980; "Silver Spoons", 1984-87; "Magnum, P.I.", Christmas, 1986; Mighty Pawns, 1987; "CBS School break Special", 1988; Out on the Edge, 1989; "A Different World", 1990; "The Fresh Prince of Bel-Air", 1990-96; "Bill Nye, the Science Guy", 1994; Happily Ever After: Fairy Tales for Every Child, 1995; Kidz in the Wood, 1996; "In the House", 1995-99; "Spider-Man", 1996-97; "Extreme Ghostbusters", 1997; "One on One", "The Rerun Show", 2002; "The Brothers Garcia", 2002-03; "Cedricthe Entertainer Presents", 2003; "All of Us", dir, 2004-07, writer, 2007; "One on One", dir, 2005-06; "Cuts", dir, 2006; "Eve", dir, 2006; "Meet the Browns", dir, 2009-10; Game Show Network, "Catch 21", host, 2008-; Are We There Yet?, dir, 2011-12; Things We Do for Love, dir, 2011; "Big Time Rush", 2012; "Shake It Up!", dir, 2012-13; "Let's Stay Together", dir, 2013-14. **Orgs:** Say No to Drugs: Hands Across Am. **Honors/Awds:** Hollywood Press Club's Rising Star Award, 1985; Image Award, Nat Asn Advan Colored People, 1996 & 1998. **Special Achievements:** Two-time winner of the Toyota Pro/Celebrity Race in 1994 & 1995. **Business Addr:** Actor, c/o United Paramount Network, 11800 Wilshire Blvd, Los Angeles, CA 90025, **Business Phone:** (310)575-7000.

### RICARD, REV. JOHN HUSTON

Bishop. **Personal:** Born Feb 29, 1940, Baton Rouge, LA; son of Maceo and Albanie St Amant. **Educ:** St Joseph Sem, Wash, DC, 1968; Tulane Univ, New Orlenas, LA, MA, 1970; Cath Univ, Wash, DC, PhD, 1983; Josephite Col Sem, Newburgh, NY. **Career:** Holy Redeemer, pastor, 1972-75; Holy Comforter-St. Cyprian Church, 1975-79; Cath Univ Am, instr, 1976-78; Perpetual Help Church, pastor; Archdiocese Baltimore, auxiliary bishop, 1984-96; Cath Relief Serv, chair, 1995-2002; Diocese Pensacola-Tallahassee, bishop, 1997, bishop emer; St Joseph Sem, rector, 2011. **Orgs:** Chmn, Domestic Policy Comt, US Conf Cath Bishop, 2002-05; Int Policy Comt; chair, Church Africa, Ad Hoc Comt; bd trustee, Nat Black Cath Cong Inc; rector, St Josephs Soc Sacred Heart. **Home Addr:** 1231 Durnford Pl, Pensacola, FL 32503, **Home Phone:** (850)433-1191. **Business Addr:** Bishop Emeritus, Diocese of Pensacola-Tallahassee, 11 N B St, Pensacola, FL 32502, **Business Phone:** (850)435-3500.

### RICARDO, JAIME. See NIX, RICK.

### RICE, BISHOP ALLEN TROY, SR.

Football player, clergy. **Personal:** Born Apr 5, 1962, Houston, TX; married Cheryl; children: 4. **Educ:** Wharton Co Jr Col; Ranger Jr Col; Baylor Univ. **Career:** Football player (retired), clergy; Minn Vikings, running back, 1984-90, spiritual leader; Green Bay Packers, running back, 1991; Joy Temple Apostolic Church, fel; Together We Stand Christian Church, founder, 1996-, sr pastor, currently. **Home Addr:** , Eden Prarie, MN 55344. **Business Addr:** Founder, Senior Pastor, Together We Stand Christian Church, 1432 Tex Pkwy, Missouri City, TX 77489, **Business Phone:** (281)403-0373.

### RICE, DR. CONDOLEEZZA

Politician, government official. **Personal:** Born Nov 14, 1954, Birmingham, AL; daughter of John Wesley (deceased) and Angelena Ray (deceased). **Educ:** Univ Denver, BA, cum laude & phi beta kappa, 1974, Grad Sch Int Studies, PhD, polit sci, 1981; Univ Notre Dame, MA, polit sci, 1975. **Career:** US Dept State, intern, 1977, Joint Chiefs Staff, spec asst, 1996, nat security adv, 2001-05, secy state, 2005-09; Rand Corp, intern, 1980; Polit sci consult, 1980; Univ Stanford, asst dir ctr int security & arms control, 1981-86, from asst prof to assoc prof, 1981-93, provost, 1993-99, prof, 1993-, denning prof, 2010-, Global Ctr Bus & Econ, dir; Nat Security Coun, dir, sr dir Soviet, 1989-91, spec asst to pres, 1990-91, Soviet & E Europ Affairs, advisor, George W Bush presidential campaign, nat security consult, 2000, natl security adv, 2001-05; Millennium Challenge Corp, chair; RiceHadleyGates LLC, founding partner. **Orgs:** Phi Beta Kappa, 1974; arms control fel Stanford Univ, 1980-81; nat fel 1985-86, sr fel Thomas & Barbara Stephenson Sr Fel Pub Policy, 1999-, Freeman Spogli Inst Int Studies, Hoover Inst, sr fel 2009-; life mem, Coun Foreign Rels, 1986-87; Trans Am Corp; bd dir, Chevron Corp, 1991-2000; bd dir, Transamerica Corp, 1991-99; bd dir, Hewlett Packard, 1991-93; bd dir, Charles Schwab Corp, 1999-2000; bd dir, C3, LLC, 2009-; trustee, bd trustee, Aspen Inst, 2010-; adv bd, Stanford Inst Econ Policy Res, 2013-; dir, bd dir, dropbox inc, 2014-; bd dir, Carnegie Corp; Carnegie Endowment Int Peace; Nat Coun Soviet & E Europ Studies; Mid-Peninsula Urban Coalition; William & Flora Hewlett Found; bd trustee, Univ Notre Dame; Int Adv Coun, JP Morgan; San Francisco Symphony Bd Gov; founding bd mem, Ctr New Generation; vpres, Boys & Girls Club Peninsula; fel Am Acad Arts & Sci. **Honors/Awds:** Walter J Gores Award, 1984; Honorary doctorates: DLL, Morehouse Col, 1991; School of Humanities and Sciences Dean's Award, 1993; DHL, Univ Ala, 1994; Honorary Doctorate, Univ Notre Dame, 1995; John P McGovern Medal, 1996; Doctor of National Security Affairs, hon degree, Nat Defense Univ, 2002; President's Award, Nat Am Advan Colored People Image Awards, 2002; DLL, Miss Col Sch Law, 2003; Doctor of Public Service, hon degree, Univ Louisville, 2004; DHL, Mich State Univ, 2004; DLL, Boston Col, 2006; DHL, Air Univ, 2008; DLL, Southern Methodist Univ, 2012; DHL, Clark Atlanta Univ, 2015; Award for Excellence in Teaching, Stanford Univ. **Special Achievements:** First African-American Secretary of State; First African-American chief acad & budget officer & second-ranking off behind the pres, Stanford Univ, 1993-99; author: "The Gorbachev Era"; co-author: "Germany Unified & Europe Transformed"; ranked as the most powerful woman in the world by Forbes magazine in 2005 & number two in 2006; ranked among the world's 100 most influential people by Time magazine in 2006; Books: "Uncertain Allegiance: The Soviet Union and the Czechoslovak Army, Princeton Univ Press", 1984; "The Gorbachev Era, edited with Alexander Dallin", Stanford Alumni Press Serv, 1986; "Germany Unified and Europe Transformed: A Study in Statecraft", Harvard Univ Press, 1995; "The Strategy of Campaigning, with Kiron Skinner, Univ Mich Press", 2007; "Extraordinary, Ordinary People: A Memoir of Family, Crown Archetype", 2010; "No Higher Honor: A Memoir of My Years in Washington, Crown Archetype", 2011. **Business Addr:** Political Science Professor, Stanford University, 450 Serra Mall, Stanford, CA 94305, **Business Phone:** (650)723-2300.

### RICE, DR. CONSTANCE WILLIAMS

Social worker, school administrator, business owner. **Personal:** Born Jun 23, 1945, Brooklyn, NY; daughter of Beulah Marshall and Elliott; married Norman Blann; children: Mian A. **Educ:** Queens Col, BA, 1966; Univ Wash, MA, pub admin, 1970, PhD, higher educ admin, 1974; Carnegie Mellon Univ, Sr Exec Mgt, 1983. **Career:** State Bd, prog asst; Shoreline Community Col, chairperson; Corp Comn METRO, mgr; US W, Seattle, Wash, adv bd, 1981-; Pub Rels/Mgt Firm, pres, 1984-89; Seattle Chap, Links Inc, pres, 1985-86, nat western vice area dir; Sec Pac Bank, Seattle, Wash, bd dir, 1985-; Community Col Dist VI, vice chancellor; N Seattle Community Col, interim pres, 1995-97; Seattle Community Cols, vice chancellor, sr vpres, currently, sr chancellor; Univ Wash's Ctr, affil prof Human Design Engineering, currently; CWR Inc, pres, currently; NW News Coun, founder; Shoreline Community Col, Ethnic Studies Dept, chair; Western Wash Univ, Ctr Urban Studies, dir; Univ Wash, Ctr Workforce Develop, scientist. **Orgs:** Vpres, Seattle King Co United Way, 1983-84; pres-elect, Seattle Chap 101 Black Women, 1984-85; trustee, Seattle Found, 1984-92; bd mem, Am Soc Pub Admin, 1984; asst exec dir, Wash Educ Asn, 1987-88; bd gov, Shoreline Community Col Found; bd mem, Fred Hutchinson Cancer Res Found; vice chair, King Co Open Space Commn, 1989; bd mem, King Co Chamber Com, 1989-96; rotary, Evergreen State Col; bd dir, Seafirst, 1992-96; bd dir, Bonneville Broadcast GRP, 1993-96; founding exec dir, Seattle Desmond Tutu Peace Found USA, 2000-; managing dir, Prev & Family Support Casey Family Found, Seattle, 2002; managing dir prev & family support, Casey Family Progs, 2004-; Nat Sci Found Traineeship; past pres & founder, Strategic Educ Centers; founder, Seattle Health & Nutrit Proj; Technol Access Found; Swed Hosp; Seattle Art Mus; vice chair, Wash Stud Achievement Coun; Seattle Downtown Rotary; Inst Pub Serv; Rainier Club; Swed Hosp; chair, Seattle Community Cols, Bd trustee, trustee, 2008-. **Honors/Awds:** Professional Director Award; Kellogg Grant; NW Outstanding Young Woman, 1983-86; Women Entrepreneur of The Year runner-up, 1985; White House Small Bus deleg, 1986; Top 25 Influential Women, (Seattle), The Seattle Weekly, 1986; Dorothy Bullitt Award, Women's Funding Alliance, 1991; Matrix Table, 1993; Seattle's First Citizen of the Year, Seattle-King County Bd Realtors, 1993; Odessa Brown C's Clin, 1998; Woman of Distinction Award, Nat Coun Jewish Women's; Torch of Liberty & Distinguished Community Service Award, B'Nai B'rith; Special Individual Award, Njeri Temple; hon doctorate, Seattle Univ, 2002; Outstanding Advocate for Equity Award, Trustees Asn Community and Tech Cols, 2011; Community Hero, Dollars Scholars, 2011; City Year Ripple of Hope Award, 2011; Numerous civic & humanitarian orgn have honored Dr. Rice her industrious, unflagging community serv. **Special Achievements:** First African American woman to receive a doctorate in higher educ admin from the Univ Wash, Sch Educ; One of the 25 most powerful women in Seattle, Puget Sound Bus J. **Home Addr:** 1711 Lake Wash Blvd S, Seattle, WA 98144-4960, **Home Phone:** (206)322-3877. **Business Addr:** Trustee, Seattle Community College, 1500 Harvard Ave, Seattle, WA 98122, **Business Phone:** (206)587-4100.

### RICE, DERICA W.

Chief financial officer, vice president (organization). **Personal:** Born Decatur, AL; married Robin; children: Solomon, Isaiah & Malachi. **Educ:** Kettering Univ, BS, elec engineering, 1988; Ind Univ, MBA, 1990. **Career:** Eli Lilly & Co, int treas assoc, 1990-, finance dir & chief financial officer Lilly Can, 1995-97, exec dir & chief financial officer London, 1997-2000, gen mgr Lilly UK & Repub Ireland, 2000-03, vpres & controller, 2003-06, sr vpres, 2006-10, chief financial officer, 2006-, vpres global serv, 2010-. **Orgs:** Bd dir, Target Corp, 2007-; bd dir, ImClone, 2008-; bd dir, Clarian Health N; bd dir, Ctr Leadership Develop; bd trustee, Ind Univ, 2010-13; bd gov, Indianapolis Mus Art; IU Health N. **Business Addr:** Senior Vice President, Chief Financial Officer, Eli Lilly and Co, DC 1201, Indianapolis, IN 46285, **Business Phone:** (317)433-3221.

### RICE, DON. See RICE, J. DONALD, JR.

### RICE, FLORENCE M.

Consumer advocate. **Personal:** Born Mar 22, 1919, Buffalo, NY; daughter of Hubert and Amy; children: Joyce Garrett. **Career:** ILGW, 1948-62; Consumers Edu Coun, founder & dir, 1963-; League Autonomous Bronx Orgs Renewal, consumer educ consult, 1966; Malcolm King Col, instr consumer educ; 30 Minutes with Florence M Rice, Channel 34, host, currently. **Orgs:** Founder & nat pres, Nat Black Consumers, 1973-; trustee, Harlem Community Law Off; bd dir, Community Nutrit Inst; adv comn, Ny Pub Utility Law Proj; New York Senate Consumer Adv Community; adv comm, NewYork Urban League, Manhattan Chap; secy, New York Black Republicans; nat stand comn, Am Bankers Asn; vpres, New York Independent Black Women's Polit Caucus; New York Mayor's Adv Coun Consumer Affairs; founder & pres, Harlem Consumer Educ Coun, currently; Int Ladies Garment Workers Union. **Honors/Awds:** Sojourner Truth Award; Ophelia DeVore Award for Community Service; Consolidated Edison Better Business Award; Frederick Douglas Award, Urban League; Josephine Shaw Lowell Award; Woman of the Year, New York Republican Club, 1997; Certificate of Congressional Recognition, 2005. **Special Achievements:** US Delegation to World Congress of Int Women's Year, Berlin, official mem; UN Cong Non-Govt Orgs, rep; initiated Son-in-Law Day. **Home Addr:** 540 W 158 St, Manhattan, NY 10032-7252, **Home Phone:** (212)795-0234. **Business Addr:** Founder, President, Harlem Consumer Education Council Inc, Triboro Sta 550 W 155th St, New York, NY 10032, **Business Phone:** (212)283-7011.

### RICE, FREDRICK LEROY

Lawyer. **Personal:** Born Feb 26, 1950, Indianapolis, IN; son of Willie B and Marion I; married Ellen M; children: John F & Edward C. **Educ:** Beloit Col, BA, sociol, 1972; Ind Univ Sch Law, JD, 1977. **Career:** Landman & Beatty, assoc atty, 1977-82; UAW Legal Serv Plan, staff atty, 1982-83; Indianapolis Pub Sch, gen coun, 1983-95; State Ind, gen coun, 1990; Ind Supreme Ct, Disciplinary Comn, staff atty, 1996-, exec secy, 2007-08. **Orgs:** Bd, ITC; pres, Waycross; bd mem, Ment Health Asn Marion County; bd gov, Indianapolis Bar Asn; atty, bd mem, Nat Sch Bds Asn Coun Sch; Ind State Bar Asn; Marion County Bar Asn. **Home Addr:** 4451 N Pk Ave, Indianapolis, IN 46205-1834, **Home Phone:** (317)283-2165. **Business Addr:** Staff Attorney, Indianapolis Supreme Court Disciplinary Commission, 115 W Washington St Suite 1165 S Twr, Indianapolis, IN 46204, **Business Phone:** (317)232-1807.

### RICE, GLEN ANTHONY, SR.

Basketball player. **Personal:** Born May 28, 1967, Flint, MI; married Cristina Fernandez; children: Brianna & Giancarlo; married Tracey Starwood; children: Glen Anthony Jr & G'Mitri. **Educ:** Univ Mich, attended 1989. **Career:** Basketball player (retired); Miami Heat, guard, 1989-95; Charlotte Hornets, 1995-98; Los Angeles Lakers, 1998-2000; New York Knicks, 2000-01; Houston Rockets, 2001-03; Los Angeles Clippers, 2003-04.

### RICE, DR. HORACE WARREN

Manager, lawyer, college teacher. **Personal:** Born Feb 14, 1944, Huntsville, AL; son of John W and Lucy E; children: Tasha M. **Educ:** Chicago City Col, AA, 1964; Ala A&M Univ, BS, 1966; Univ Toledo, JD, 1973. **Career:** Chicago Legal Asst C Found, atty, 1972-75; Univ Ala-Huntsville, prof, 1976-82; Ala A&M Univ, prof, 1976-2011, Dept Mgt & Mkt, prof bus law & ethics, prof emer, 2011-; self-employed, player rep, sports agt, 1977-84; self-employed, arbitrator & mediator, 1977-. **Orgs:** Am Arbit Asn; Acad Legal Studies Bus; Am Mgt Asn; Soc Profs Dispute Resolution; Nat Football League; Ohio State Impasse Plan. **Honors/Awds:** Am Arbit Asn, Nat Panel, 1980; Fed Mediation & Conciliation Serv, Nat Panel, 1982; US Postal Serv, Nat Panel, 1983; Appointed to Arbitration Panel, Ohio State Impass Panel, 1985; Citizens Ambassador Prog, US State Dept, educr, Europe, Russia, Africa, 1988-89; Hall of Fame, Ala A&M Athletics, 2002. **Special Achievements:** Zoning: A Substantive Analysis, AAMU Fac Res Jour, 1978; "What Consumers Should Know About Installment Buying," Bus Newsletter, 1980; "Labor Arbitration: A Viable Method of Dispute Resolution," Am Bus Law Asn Jour, 1983; "Class Actions Under the 1964 Civil Rights Act," AAMU Fac Res Jour, 1989; Published 23 arbitration cases in Bureau of Natl Affairs, Commerce Clearinghouse, Labor Relations Reporter, Labor Arbitration In Govt. listed in Who's Who International, 1998. **Home Addr:** 3100 Dyas Dr NW, Huntsville, AL 35810, **Home Phone:** (205)852-8406. **Business Addr:** Professor, Alabama A&M University, Rm 315 C 4900 Meridian St N, Normal, AL 35762, **Business Phone:** (256)372-5000.

### RICE, J. DONALD, JR. (DON RICE)

President (organization), chief executive officer. **Personal:** son of J Donald Sr. **Educ:** Kettering Univ, BS, eng; Harvard Bus Sch, MBA. **Career:** Gen Motors, automotive engr; Merrill Lynch & Co, founding mem, munic derivatives dept; Rice Financial Prod Co, pres, chmn & chief exec officer, 1993-, Apex Pryor Securities, chmn & chief exec officer, currently. **Orgs:** Bd dir, Ny Thruway Authority, 2010-; bd dir, NY United Neighborhood Houses; NYC Admin C's Serv; bd trustee, Kettering Univ. **Business Addr:** Founder, Chief Execuitve Officer & President, Rice Financial Products Co, 17 State St 40th Fl, New York, NY 10004, **Business Phone:** (212)908-9200.

### RICE, J. DONALD, JR.

Founder (originator), chief executive officer. **Educ:** Kettering Univ, BS, engineering, 1981; Harvard Bus Sch, MBA. **Career:** Rice Financial Prod Co, chief exec officer, 1993-; Kettering Univ, bd trustee, chair investment comt, currently; Goldman Sachs, sr munic, retired; Merrill Lynch, sr munic, retired; Citi, sr munic, retired; UBS, sr munic, retired; Morgan Stanley, sr munic, retired. **Orgs:** Harvard Bus Sch, bd trustee; Ny Thruway Authority, bd dir; United Neighborhood Houses (New York), bd dir; C's Serv Off Head Start (New York), gov bd; bd dir, Kettering Univ. **Honors/Awds:** "Black Enterprise", 30 for the Next 30, 2000; National Association of Securities Professionals (NASP), Entrepreneur of the Year, 2002; "Black Enterprise", 75 Most Powerful Blacks on Wall Street, 2011. **Special Achievements:** Named among 2011's "Top Blacks on Wall Street" by Black Enterprise magazine; The New Black Power on Wall Street; selected as the Entrepreneur of the Year by the National Association of Securities Professionals, 2002. **Business Addr:** Chief Executive Officer, Rice Financial Products Co, 17 State St 40th Fl, New York, NY 10004, **Business Phone:** (212)908-9200.

**RICE, JERRY LEE**
Football player. **Personal:** Born Oct 13, 1962, Crawford, MS; son of Brick Mason and Eddie; married Jackie Mitchell; children: Jaqui Bonet, Jerry Jr & Jada Symone. **Educ:** Miss Valley State Univ, attended 1985. **Career:** Football player (retired); San Francisco 49ers, wide receiver, 1985-2000, 2006; Oakland Raiders, wide receiver, 2001-04; Seattle Seahawks, wide receiver, 2004; Denver Broncos, 2005. **Orgs:** Phi Beta Sigma Fraternity Inc. **Honors/Awds:** Champion, Super Bowl, XXIII, XXIV, XXIX; NFC Rookie of the Year, UPI, 1985; NFC Offensive Rookie of the Year, Nat Football League Players Asn, 1985; Offensive Player of the Year, Nat Football League, 1986, 1987; Pro Bowl, 1986, 1987, 1988, 1989, 1990, 1991, 1992, 1993, 1994, 1995, 1996, 1998, 2002; Bert Bell Award (Player of the Year), Nat Football League, 1987; NFC Player of the Year, UPI, 1988; Most Valuable Player, Pro Football Writers Asn, 1988; Champion, Nat Football Conf, 1988, 1989, 1994; Most Valuable Player, Super Bowl XXIII, 1989; NFL Player of the Year, Sports Illustrated, 1986, 1987, 1990, 1993; NFL Player of the Year, Sporting News, 1987, 1990; Len Eshmont Award, 1993; Offensive Player of the Year, Nat Football League, 1987, 1993; Most Valuable Player, 1996; All-Pro selection, 1986-96, 2002; College Football Hall of Fame, 2006; Bay Area Sports Hall of Fame, 2007; Pro Football Hall of Fame, 2010. **Special Achievements:** First non-kicker in NFL hist to score 1000 points in his career; Career touch downs rec holder; most 100-yard games a receiver; co-hosts radio talkshow "Afternoon Blitz"; co-host on NBC 11's Sports Sunday; One Tree Hill; Co-authored two bks about his life: Rice, 1996; Go Long: My Journey Beyond Game and Fame, 2007; Without a Paddle: Nature's Calling, 2009. **Business Addr:** Sasha Marin Taylor Management, PO Box 1026, Campbell, CA 95009, **Business Phone:** (408)230-3000.

**RICE, JIM (JAMES EDWARD RICE)**
Baseball player, athletic coach. **Personal:** Born Mar 8, 1953, Anderson, SC; married Corine Gilliard; children: Chauncy Brandon & Carissa Jacinda. **Career:** Baseball player (retired), athletic coach, commentator; Boston Red Sox, outfielder, 1974-89, Roving, batting coach, 1992-94, hitting Instr, 1995-2000, instrnl batting coach, 2001-, analyst; New Eng Sports Network, commentator, 2003-; So Bank & Trust Co, Greenville, SC, pub rels rep. **Orgs:** Hon chmn, Jimmy Fund, Fund raising Arm Dana-Farber Cancer Inst, Boston, 1979; Red Sox Orgn. **Home Addr:** 135 Wooden Way, Winter Haven, MA 33880. **Business Addr:** Instructional Batting Coach, Boston Red Sox Organization, 4 Yawkey Way, Boston, MA 02215, **Business Phone:** (617)226-6000.

**RICE, JUDITH CAROL**
Government official. **Personal:** Born Jul 30, 1957, Chicago, IL; daughter of Fred Rice and Thelma Dean Martin. **Educ:** Loyola Univ, BA, cum laude, 1981; John Marshall Law Sch, JD, 1988. **Career:** Cook County, staff asst, 1982-88, asst state's atty, 1988-89; City Chicago, dir ade adjudication, 1990-92, parking adr, 1992-93, revenue dir, 1993-95, exec asst Mayor, 1995-96; comnr, Chicago Dept Water, 1996-99; head, Chicago Dept Transp, 1999-2000; city treas, 2000-06; Mayor's staff, 2006-07; BMO Harris Bank, Head Community Affairs & Econ Develop, vpres, 2007-10; sr vpres, 2010-14; Cook County 7th Subcircuit, judge, 2014-. **Orgs:** Assoc bd mem, Chicago Bar Asn; March Dimes; bd mem, STEP Sch, Sch Treat C Emotional Prob, 1996-; Better Boys Found; chmn gov bd, UCAN; Phi Delta Phi International Legal Fraternity; bd mem, Uhlich C's Advantage Network; bd mem, United Negro Col Fund. **Business Addr:** Mayor's Staff, Mayors Office, City Chicago, 121 N LaSalle St Rm 106, Chicago, IL 60602, **Business Phone:** (312)744-3356.

**RICE, LEWIS, JR.**
Police officer. **Personal:** married Karen; children: 4. **Educ:** St John's Univ, Queens, NY, BS, criminal justice, 1974. **Career:** Drug Enforcement Admin, 1974-84, Miami, Fla, supvry spec agt, 1984-97, Detroit, Mich, spec agt-in-charge, New York, NY, head, 2001; Estee Lauder Co, vpres global security & trademark protection, 2003-. **Orgs:** Nat Asn Black Law Enforcement; Drug Enforcement Admin, Career Bd; NY Law Enforcement Exploring Prog; chair, Boy Scouts Am; chmn emer, Law Enforcement Explorer's; Hale House New York; vpres global security, Fed Law Enforcement Found, currently. **Honors/Awds:** Achievement Award, Nat Asn Black Law Enforcement, 1997; Senior Executive Service Award, Drug Enforcement Admin, 1997; Alumni of the Year Award, St John's Univ, 1997; Nat Demand Reduction Award, 1998; Meritorious Executive Award, Drug Enforcement Admin, 1998; honoree, New York's Finest Found, Ann Chiefs' Night Gala, 1999. **Special Achievements:** One of two African Americans heading DEA field offices. **Business Addr:** Vice President of Global Security, Federal Law Enforcement Foundation, 335 Madison Ave 14th Fl, New York, NY 10017, **Business Phone:** (212)527-8650.

**RICE, LINDA JOHNSON**
Publishing executive. **Personal:** Born Mar 22, 1958, Chicago, IL; daughter of John H Johnson and Eunice W Johnson; married S Andre; children: Alexa Christina; married Mel Farr Sr. **Educ:** Univ Southern Calif, Annenberg Sch Commun & Jour, BA, jour, 1980; Northwestern Univ, J L Kellogg Grad Sch, MBA, 1987. **Career:** Johnson Publ Co Inc, Ebony Mag, publ, fashion ed, 1980-85, vpres, 1985-87, pres & chief operating officer, 1987-2002, chief exec officer, 2002-, chmn, 2006-, JET Mag, publ; spec asst publ, fashion coordr, Ebony Fashion Fair, fashion coordr. **Orgs:** Nat Asn Black Journalists; bd dir, Kimberly-Clarke Corp; Omnicom; bd dir, Viad Corp; bd dir Mag Publishers Asn; bd dir, Bausch & Lomb; bd trustees, Univ Southern Calif; adv bd, Nat Underground Rr Freedom Ctr; adv bd, Women's Bd Art Inst Chicago; Nat Asn Advan Colored People; Exec Club Chicago; Nat Mus African Am Hist & Cult; MoneyGram Int Inc; United Negro Col Fund; Northwestern Memorial Corp; Econ Club Chicago; Com Club Chicago; bd dir, Continental Bank Corp; bd dir, Princess Grace Found. **Honors/Awds:** Women Power Award, Nat Urban League; Tower Power Award, Trumpet Awards; Crain's Chicago Bus 40 Under 40 Award; From Whence We Came Award, All State Insurance Co, 1999; Alumni Year Award, Kellogg Grad Sch; Phenomenal Woman Award, 2000; Alumni Merit Award, Univ Southern Calif. **Special Achievements:** Named one of Chicago's 100 Most Powerful Women & one of the Top 10 Women in Media by the Chicago Sun-Times; first African American woman to be named chief exec officer of a company listed among the top five of the Black Enterprise. **Business Addr:** Chairman, Chief Executive Officer, Johnson Publishing Company LLC, 820 S Mich Ave, Chicago, IL 60605, **Business Phone:** (312)322-9200.

**RICE, LOIS DICKSON**
Executive, educator, association executive. **Personal:** Born Feb 28, 1933, Portland, ME; daughter of David A and Mary D; married Alfred B Fitt; children: Susan E & Emmett John Jr. **Educ:** Radcliffe Col, AB, 1954; Columbia Univ, attended 1955; Brown Univ, LLD, 1981; Bowdoin Col, LLD, 1984; Radcliffe Col, Phi Beta Kappa, grad. **Career:** Nat Scholar Serv Fund Negro Students, dir, 1955-59; Col Entrance Exam Bd, dir, 1959-62, 1973-74, vpres, 1974-81; Ford Found, educ specialist, 1963-64; HSB Group; Control Data Corp, sr vpres govt affairs, 1981-91; McGraw Hill, bd dir, 1987-2003; Int Multi foods, 1991-2003; Brookings Inst, guest scholar, 1991-; George Washington Univ, trustee, 1992-98. **Orgs:** Bd dir, Beauvoir Sch, 1970-76; bd dir, C TV Workshop, 1970-73; bd dir, Fund Improv Post Sec Educ, 1972-75; bd trustee, Urban Inst PotomacInst; Carnegie Coun Policy Studies Higher Educ; Community Acad Affairs, Am Coun Educ, 1974-76; DC Community Post Sec Educ, 1974-76; nat adv bd, Inst Study Educ Policy, 1974; chmn, Afro-Am Studies, Harvard Univ, 1974-77; Govt Temp State Comn Future Post sec Educ, NY, 1976-77; trustee, Stephens Col, 1976-78; Pres's Foreign Intelligence Bd, 1993-95; trustee, Ctr Naval Anal, Mgt Leadership Tomorrow, Pub Agenda. **Honors/Awds:** Distinguished Service Award, HEW, 1977. **Special Achievements:** Numerous publications. Co-Author: Subsidizing Higher Education Through Tax and Spending Programs. **Home Addr:** 2332 Mass Ave NW, Washington, DC 20008-2801, **Home Phone:** (202)667-2332. **Business Addr:** Guest Scholar, Brookings Institute, 1775 Mass Ave NW, Washington, DC 20036, **Business Phone:** (202)797-6000.

**RICE, DR. LOUISE ALLEN**
Educator. **Personal:** Born Jan 1, 1941, Augusta, GA; daughter of Elnora and Willie; married Wilson L Sr; children: Wilson L Jr & Robert Christopher. **Educ:** Tuskegee Univ, BS, Eng, 1963; Columbia Univ, Teachers Col, MA, remedial reading & psychol sch subjects, 1969; Univ Ga, PhD, reading edu, 1979. **Career:** Washington High Sch, eng teacher, 1963-66; Lucy Laney High Sch, eng teacher, 1966-68; Paine Col, instr & reading specialist, 1968-71; Lansing Sch Dist, instr & reading specialist, 1971-72; Paine Col, assoc prof, 1972-77; Paine Col, asst acad dean, 1979-81; Lamar Elem Sch, instr leadteacher, 1981-84; Augusta St Univ, assoc dir admis, 1984-88, asst prof educ & reading, 1988-2003, assoc prof learning support, 1989-2003, assoc prof reading, assoc prof reading emer, currently; Minority Adv Prog, coordr, 1998-2003; Nat Serv Orgn, chief exec officer. **Orgs:** Adv comt, Richmond County Bd Educ, 1982-; bd dir, CSRA Econ Opportunity Authority Inc, 1984-; golden life Mem, Diamond life mem, dir southern region, Delta Sigma Theta Sorority, 1986-91, chair, 1996-2000, 23rd nat pres, 2004-, nat secy, chief exec officer; Educ Comn, Augusta Human Rels Comn, 1989-90; bd dir, Richmond County Dept Family & C Serv, chair; CSRA Coun Girl Scouts Am; bd mem, Cent Savannah River Area Econ Opportunity authority Inc, treas; pres & vice pres, charter mem, Augusta Alumnae Chap; pres, Augusta Chap Links Inc; life mem, Nat Coun Negro Women; Leadership Augusta; Tabernacle Baptist Church. **Honors/Awds:** Black Womanhood Speaker's Award, Paine Col, 1983; Distinguished Service Award, Augusta Pan-Hellenic Coun, 1984; Urban Builders Award, Augusta Black History Comn, 1985; Outstanding Commission Services, Leadership and Achievement Certificate, Am Asn Univ Women, 1986; Educator of the Year, Lincoln League, Augusta, 1988; Distinguished Leadership Award, United Negro College Fund, 1990; Woman of the Year, Augusta Alumnae Chap, Delta Sigma Theta Sorority, 1991; Nat Soc Delta Sigma Theta Sorority Inc, 1992-96; Citizen of the Year, Augusta Chap, Nat Social Workers, 1999; Omega Psi Phi Fraternity Inc. **Home Addr:** 3340 Wheeler Rd, Augusta, GA 30909, **Home Phone:** (706)733-8078. **Business Addr:** Associate Professor Emeritus of Reading, Augusta State University, 2500 Walton Way, Augusta, GA 30910, **Business Phone:** (706)737-1685.

**RICE, DR. MITCHELL F.**
Educator. **Personal:** Born Sep 11, 1948, Columbus, GA; son of Joseph M and Clarice Mitchell; married Donna Artis; married Cecelia Hawkins; children: Colin C, Melissa E, Van Artis & Michael Overton. **Educ:** Los Angeles City Col, AA, 1969; Calif State Univ, Los Angeles, CA, BA, polit sci, 1970, MS, pub admin, 1973; Claremont Grad Sch, PhD, govt, 1976. **Career:** Bonita Unified Sch Dist, pub sch teacher, 1971-76; Prairie View A&M Univ, asst prof, 1976-77; Tex State Univ, assoc prof, polit sci, 1977-85; Mgt Develop & Training Consult Serv, pres & owner, 1980-; La State Univ, prof, pub admin & pol sci, 1985-97; Tex A&M Univ, prof polit sci, currently. **Orgs:** Fel Am Coun Educ, 1982-83; Postdoctoral fel Nat Res Coun Ford Found, 1984-85; Postdoctoral fel Rockefeller Found, 1985-86; Lifetime fel Nat Acad, Pub Admin, 1999-; pres & nat chair, Conf Minority Pub Admin; Am Polit Sci Asn; Nat Conf Black Polit Scientists; Am Soc Pub Admin; pres, Southeastern Conf, Pub Admin. **Special Achievements:** Appointed to Governor Edwin W. Edwards Administration and Fiscal Transition Team, March 1992; Appointed by Governor Edwin W. Edwards to the State of Louisiana, Rural Health Care Authority, 1994-96; Appointed by Deputy Director- Texas Department of Health, Texas Department of Health to the Models for Community Health Practices Ad Hoc Committee, 1999-2000; Appointed by the Executive Director of the Texas Department of Economic Development to the State of Texas Mexico NAFTA Office Advisory Committee in May 2000, Elected Chair in August 2000, Re-elected Chair in 2003-04; Appointed member of Texas Higher Education Opportunity Project by the Office of Population Research, Princeton University, 2000-04. **Home Addr:** 5000 Crystal Downs Ct, College Station, TX 77845-8953. **Business Addr:** Professor of Political Science, Texas A&M University, 2010 Allen Bldg Rm 2082, College Station, TX 77843-4348, **Business Phone:** (979)845-6785.

**RICE, HON. NORMAN BLANN**
Executive, mayor. **Personal:** Born May 4, 1943, Denver, CO; son of Otha Patrick (deceased) and Irene Johnson Powell (deceased); married Constance Williams; children: Mian A. **Educ:** Highline Community Col, AA, 1970; Univ Wash, BA, commun, 1972, MPA, 1974. **Career:** KOMO TV News, reporter, news asst & ed, 1971-72; KIXI Radio, asst dir; Seattle Urban League, asst dir, media action proj monitor, 1972-74; Puget Sound Coun Govts, exec asst & dir govt serv, 1974-75; Rainer Nat Bank, mgr corp contrib & social policy, 1976-78; City Seattle, coun mem, 1978-83, pres, 1983-90, mayor, 1989-97; U.S. Conf Mayors, pres, 1995-96; Fed Home Loan Bank Seattle, pres & chief exec officer, 1998-2004; Seattle Fed Home Loan Bank, pres & chief exec officer, 1999-2005; Univ Wash, Daniel J Evans Sch Pub Affairs, distinguished practr-in-residence, 2007-; Seattle Found, chief exec officer & pres, 2009-14; Capital Access LLC, vice chmn. **Orgs:** Am Soc Pub Admin; life mem, Nat Asn Advan Colored People; Pi Alpha Alpha; adv bd mem, Evans Sch Alum. **Honors/Awds:** Outstanding Pub Citizen, Nat Asn Social Workers, 1991; Nat Award Leadership on Behalf of Neighborhoods, Nat Neighborhood Coalition; Isabel Coleman Pierce Award, Youth Women's Christian Asn, King Co chairperson; Mark F Cooper Leadership Award, Wash Coun Crime & Delinquency; Distinguished Community Serve Award, Alpha Kappa Alpha; Faces of Courage Award, NW Coalition Against Malicious Harassment; Civic Leadership in the Arts Award, Corp Coun for the Arts; James. R. Ellis Regional Leadership Award, Munic League King County; The American Jewish Federation's Human Relations Award; National Award for Leadership on Behalf of Neighborhoods, Nat Neighborhood Coalition's; YWCA's Isabel Coleman Pierce Award; Outstanding Alumni Award, Am Asn Community Col Students. **Special Achievements:** Seattle's First and only African-American mayor. **Home Addr:** 1711 Lake Wash Blvd S, Seattle, WA 98144. **Business Addr:** Distinguished Practitioner-In-Residence, University of Washington, Rm 105 Parrington Hall, Seattle, WA 98195-3055, **Business Phone:** (206)221-3893.

**RICE, DR. PAMELA ANN**
Psychotherapist, counselor, educator. **Personal:** Born Jun 27, 1956, Baltimore, MD; daughter of Shirley Carrington and Edward Rice. **Educ:** Va State Univ, BS, psychol, 1977; Coppin State Col, MEd, voc rehab coun, 1980; Johns Hopkins Univ, advan degree, coun & guid, 1982; Am Univ, Wash, DC, EdD, coun & develop, 1982, 1988. **Career:** Baltimore City Pub Sch Syst, substitute teacher, 1977-78; Md Dept Juvenile Serv, Juvenile Counr, 1978-91; Essex Community Col, Criminal Justice Dept, adj instr, 1983-94; Psychol Dept, Prince George's Community Col, instr, 1989-90; Coppin State Univ, res asst, adj prof, 1989-90; Howard Univ, Sch Educ, res fel, 1989-89; Anne Arundel Community Col, Psychol Dept, adj instr, 1994; Youth Incentive Entitlement Prog, Comprehensive Employment & Training Act, worksite supvr; Rice Coun Serv, psychotherapist, currently; US probation & pretrial serv, US probation officer, currently. **Orgs:** VA State Alumni Asn, Baltimore Metro Chapter, 1980-, Am Asn Coun & Develop, 1980-, Alpha Kappa Alpha Sorority, 1982-; Am Asn Play Ther; Am Asn Christian Counselors; Am Coun Asn; Am Ment Health Counselors Asn. **Home Addr:** 4223 Red Haven Rd, Pikesville, MD 21208-5857, **Home Phone:** (410)484-2241. **Business Addr:** Psychotherapist, The Rice Counseling Service, 40 S Caroline St, Baltimore, MD 21231, **Business Phone:** (410)522-1830.

**RICE, RONALD**
Executive, football player. **Personal:** Born Nov 9, 1972, Detroit, MI. **Educ:** Eastern Mich Univ, BS, criminal justice, 1995; Wayne State Univ, MA, sports admin, 2011. **Career:** Football player (retired), exec, coach; Detroit Lions, defensive back & safety & free safety & strong safety, 1995-2001; pvt equity investor, 2002-; Nat Football League Players Asn, pres, 2009-11; Farmington Hills (MI) Harrison, defensive coach, currently. **Orgs:** Founder, Ron Rice Found, 1999; Detroit Chap pres & found dir, Nat Football League Alumni Asn, 2011-. **Honors/Awds:** Walter Payton Man of the Year Award, Nat Football League, 2000. **Business Addr:** Detroit Chapter President, Defensive Coach, Harrison High School - Farmington Public Schools, 29995 West Twelve Mile Rd, Farmington Hills, MI 48334, **Business Phone:** (248)489-3499.

**RICE, SANDRA DORSEY**
Association executive. **Personal:** children: Kellee. **Educ:** San Jose State Univ, BA, jour, radio & tv; New Sch, New York, NY, MA, media studies. **Career:** ABC TV, coordr awards & spec proj, 1980-84, distrib mgr, 1984-92, mkt mgr, 1992-97; Am Women Radio & TV, pres; MAP Int, dir int med resources; Found Minority Interests Media, W Coast Regional Off, dir, currently, Eastern Region, vpres, currently; Emma Bowen Found Minority Interests Media, regional dir western region, 1997-2000, eastern region, vpres, 2000-12, Eastern Region & Nat Recruitment, sr vpres, 2012-. **Orgs:** Pres, Am Women Radio & TV (AWRT), 1997; bd mem, Calif Girls State, bd mem, MAP Int; bd dir, Ctr Great Expectations, Somerville, NJ; ad bd, Embrace Kids Found, Nb, NJ; vpres, Friends Plainfield Pub Libr; chair, Nat Coalition 100 Black Women; assoc mem, Jack & Jill Am Inc. **Honors/Awds:** Everett C Parker Award, Minority Media & Telecommunications Ctr, 2002; Achievement Award, Am Women Radio & Tv, 2002; Distinguished Mother Award Eastern Region, Jack & Jill Inc, 2005 & 2012; Multicultural Leadership Award, Diversity & Leadership Conf, 2012; Black Media Legends Trailblazer Award, McDonalds, 2013. **Home Addr:** , NY. **Business Addr:** Senior Vice President, Emma Bowen Foundation For Minority Interests In Media, 524 W 57th St, New York, NY 10019, **Business Phone:** (212)975-2545.

**RICE, SIMEON JAMES**
Football player, executive. **Personal:** Born Feb 24, 1974, Chicago, IL; son of Henry and Evelyn. **Educ:** Univ Ill, BA, speech communs, 1996; NY Film Acad, attended 2009. **Career:** Football player (retired), executive; Ariz Cardinals, right defensive end, defensive end, 1996-98, defensive end, 1999-2000; Tampa Bay Buccaneers, defensive end, 2001-06; T3K-Thermal 3000, 2004; Nat Football League Network, media day corres, 2005; Indianapolis Colts, 2007; Denver Broncos, 2007-08; New York Sentinels, 2009; Lucid Dream Entertainment, co-founder & chief exec officer, currently. Films: When I Was King, dir. **Honors/Awds:** Defensive Rookie of the Year, Nat Football League, 1996; Pro Football Writers Asn, 1996; Defensive Rookie of the Year, All-Pro, 1996, 1999, 2002, 2003; Pro Bowl, 1999, 2002, 2003; Alumni Defensive Lineman of the Year, Nat Football League, 2002; Champion, Super Bowl, XXXVII; Sacks leader, Nat Football League, 2002. **Special Achievements:** Featured on the cover of The Sporting News, 2003; Named to The Sporting News 2003 NFLocos 100 Best Players List; Hosted Simeon Rice Back-2-Sch Workout prog with Fair Play Found, The Univ Area Community Develop Corp Inc & Buchanan Mid Sch,

2004; Hosted The Simeon Rice Back-2-School Workout program for 50 at-risk youth at the University Center Complex in Tampa in 2004; Appeared in Slum Village video "Climax; Director: When I Was King, 2011, Unsullied, 2014, The Gold Rush Boogie. **Business Addr:** Co-Founder, Chief Executive Officer, Lucid Dream Entertainment Group, 3816 W Linebaugh Suite 210, Tampa, FL 33618, **Business Phone:** (813)374-3825.

### RICE, AMBASSADOR SUSAN ELIZABETH

Government official. **Personal:** Born Nov 17, 1964, Washington, DC; daughter of Lois Dickson Fitt and Emmett J Rice; married Ian Cameron; children: 2. **Educ:** Stanford Univ, BA, hist, 1986; New Col, Oxford, MPhil, 1988, Dphil, 1990. **Career:** Foreign policy aide; McKinsey & Co, mgt consult; Natl Security Coun, staff, 1993-97, sr adv, 2007-08; Intl Orgn Peacekeeping, dir, 1993-95; spec asst to pres & sr dir African Affairs, 1995-97; State African Affairs, asst secy, 1997-2001; Intellibridge, managing dir & prin, 2001-02; foreign policy adv to John Kerry, 2004; Us Ambassador to Un, 2009-13; asst to pres nat security affairs, 2013-. **Orgs:** Nat Dem Inst; US Fund Un C's Fund; bd dir, Atlantic Coun, Bur Nat Affairs; Partnership Pub Serv; eauvoir Nat Cathedral Elem Sch; adv bd, Freeman Spogli Inst Int Studies; Stanford Univ Foreign Rels; Aspen Strategy Group; fel Brookings Inst, 2002-09. **Honors/Awds:** Awarded a Rhodes Scholarship; recipient, Walter Frewen Lord prize, Royal Commonwealth Society, 1990; Association prize, Chatham House British Intl Studies, 1992; Samuel Nelson Drew Memorial Award (co-recipient), NSC, 2002; Stanford's Black Alumni Hall of Fame, 2002. **Special Achievements:** Third woman ambassador to the UN; youngest assistant secretaries of state ever. **Business Addr:** Ambassador, Press & Public Diplomacy Section, 140 East 45th St, New York, NY 10017, **Business Phone:** (212)415-4062.

### RICE, SUSIE LEON

Government official. **Personal:** Born Dec 28, 1922, Corona, AL; married Robert Calvin; children: Brenda Sue Wright. **Educ:** Ohio State Univ, BS, educ, 1948; Western Res Univ, MA, educ, 1953; John Carroll Univ, cert, elem admin & guid, 1968; Cleveland State Univ, continued studies, 1975. **Career:** Government officical (retired); Cleveland Bd Educ, elem teacher, 1948-69, jr/sr high guid counr, 1969-78; Woodmere Ohio, city coun woman, 1978-83. **Orgs:** Bd mgt, Glenville YWCA, 1962-68; bd dir, Valley YMCA-YWCA, 1969-75; pres, Lambda Phi Omega Chap, Alpha Kappa Alpha Sorority Inc, 1980-81. **Honors/Awds:** Outstanding Volunteer Service Award, Valley YM-YWCA Bd Dirs, 1975; Professional Honors Achievements Pi Lambda Theta Cleveland State Univ, 1977. **Home Addr:** 3707 Avondale Rd, Beachwood, OH 44122.

### RICE, VALERIE MONTGOMERY

Founder (originator), college president. **Educ:** Georgia Institute of Technology, Bachelor's in Chemistry; Harvard Medical School, M.D.; Emory University School of Medicine, Residency in Obstetrics and Gynecology; Hutzel Hospital (Detroit), Fellowship in Reproductive Endocrinology and Infertility; Drexel University College of Medicine (Philadelphia), completed Executive Leadership in Academic Medicine program. **Career:** Univ Kans Sch Med, var admin & fac positions; Meharry Med Col, Nashville, TN, Sch Med, sr vpres health affairs, Ctr Women's Health Res, founder & dir; Morehouse Sch Med, Dean & exec vpres, 2011-14, pres, 2014-. **Orgs:** Wal-Mart, External Advisory Board, 2006-08; American Board of Obstetrics and Gynecology, Board Examiner, 2007-; Wal-Mart Healthcare Insights Panel, Chair, 2007-10; National Aids Fund Board of Trustees, 2007-11; National Center on Minority Health and Health Disparities Special Emphasis Panel, 2009; National AIDS Fund Board of Trustees, 2009-10; Every Life Matters, Every Dollar Counts Campaign, Chair; Strategic Planning Committee, Office of Women's Health Research, NIH, 2010; President's Commission on White House Fellowships Regional Panelist Selection Committee, 2010; Scientific Committee, American College of Obstetricians and Gynecologists, 2007-11; FDA Advisory Committee for Reproductive Health Drugs, 2011-; March of Dimes Board Member, 2012-, National Institute of Minority Health and Disparities and Office of Women's Health/NIH, Board Member, 2013-; Society for Women's Health Research Board Member, 2012-13, executive committee, 2013. **Honors/Awds:** The Links, Inc. Portia Searcy Award, 2007; Maternal Infant Health Outreach Program Award, 2009-10; Vanderbilt University, Maternal Infant Health Outreach Worker (MIHOW) Mentorship Award, 2009; American Medical Women's Association, Elizabeth Blackwell Award, 2011; Working Mother Media Multicultural Women's Legacy Award, 2011; National Medical Association's President's Citation Award, 2013. **Special Achievements:** First African American woman to lead a freestanding medical school.

### RICE, DR. WILLIAM ARNOLD

Radiologist. **Educ:** Howard Univ Col, MD, 1967. **Career:** Sinai Hosp, Baltimore, resident; Edward J Meyer Meml, intern; Army med corps, cap; Wyman pk hosp, chief radiologist; Am Radiol Servs Northpointe, radiologist; pvt prac, Howard. **Orgs:** Am Bd Radiol. **Business Addr:** Radiologist, 7350 Van Dusen Rd Suite B10, Laurel, MD 20707.

### RICE, WILLIAM E.

Government official, commissioner. **Personal:** Born Dec 18, 1933, Huntsville, AL; married Delores; children: Duane, Donald & Marvin. **Educ:** Ala Univ, BS, 1955; De Paul Univ, grad stud, 1971. **Career:** Mich Employee Secy Comn, prog coordr, 1955-62; Bur Labor Statist, regional employee anal, 1962-65, asst regional dir, 1967-70, dep regional adminr, 1970-71, regional comnr, 1971; OEO Chicago, asst regional mgr admin, 1965-67. **Orgs:** Am Statist Asn; Am Soc Pub Admin; Chicago Guid Asn; Indust Rels Res Asn; Exec Club Chicago; chmn, Adv Comt, Roosevelt Univ, Sch Pub Admin; chmn, Econ & Manpower Develop Adv Comt, Chicago Urban League; chmn, Res Comt Chicago Construct Coordr Comt; Adv Comt Current Develop; Young Men's Christian Asn Col. **Honors/Awds:** Recipient Outstanding Vc Award, Chicago US Dept Lib, 1964. **Special Achievements:** Authored number of articles on regional library market and analysis. **Home Addr:** 4103 Juniper Dr NW, Huntsville, AL 35810, **Home Phone:** (256)851-9851. **Business Addr:** 230 S Dearborn, Chicago, IL 60604.

### RICH, BETTY

Ballet director, television show host. **Personal:** Born May 30, 1938, Philadelphia, PA; daughter of Samuel and Bertha Richburg; children: Larry Williams. **Career:** WOAV TV, "Children Hour Show", Philadelphia, Pa; "Paul Whiteman Teen Club", WFIL TV; "Ted Mack Amateur Hour"; "The Liborio"; "The Copacabana"; "San Juan's Condado Beach Hotel"; "The Jungle Room"; toured SE US for Dept Labor, vocalist, Job Corps Ctrs; "Step Toledo tv show", host & assoc producer, 6 years; Betty Rich House Ballet, ballet teacher, dir, currently. **Honors/Awds:** Step Toledo Salutes Betty Rich, 1991; Ghanian Foundation Award, 1997; Award for Dedicated Service to Children, Redeemer Lutheran Church, 1998; Award to Betty Rich House of Ballet, Dr King's 17th Annual Oratorical Contest, 2001; Numerous other awards. **Home Addr:** 1805 Oakwood Ave, Toledo, OH 43607-1625, **Home Phone:** (419)537-1284. **Business Addr:** Ballet Teacher, Betty Rich House of Ballet, 1805 Oakwood Ave, Toledo, OH 43607-1625, **Business Phone:** (419)537-1284.

### RICH, ISADORE A.

Counselor, school administrator. **Personal:** Born Montgomery, AL; son of Lydia. **Educ:** Ala State Univ, BS, Eng, 1967, MEd, coun & guid, 1970. **Career:** Ala State Univ, counr; Stillman Col, counr; Ky State Univ, Ctr Coun & Career Placement, Early Admis students, counr, basketball team, acad advisor, coordr athletics, Upward Bound Prog, tutorial coordr, currently. **Orgs:** Am Personnel & Guid Asn; Nat Asn Acad Advisors Athletics; Southern Asn Col & Employers; Nat Asn Col & Employers; Alpha Phi Omega Serv Frat; Phi Delta Kappa Educ Fraternity. **Honors/Awds:** Outstanding Young Man of America; Man of Achievement Award; Teacher of the Year, State Ga; Distinguished Service Award, Ky State Univ; Staff Employer of the Month, Ky State Univ; Athletes Service Award; Outstanding Advisor Award, APA, Beta Nu Chap; Gov Brereton C Jones, Ky Colonels, 1994. **Special Achievements:** Professional Consultant; Kentucky State University Marching Band, halftime announcer, special events coordinator; Articles: "The Urge to Conform," Off to College Journal, Feb 1979; "Coaching and Academic Counseling: A Case of Role Strain," Black Excellence, Nov/Dec 1991; "Hasty Conclusion: The Freshman College Athlete," Black College Today, 1999; Advisors, "Athletes Team up to Close the Educational Gap," Blacks Issues in Education, 2001; "Faculty Adopt Coach Role in Classroom," Black Issues in Higher Education, 2003; NCAA News. **Home Addr:** 333 Brighton Pk Blvd, Frankfort, KY 40601-3713, **Home Phone:** (502)848-9936. **Business Addr:** Career Counselor/Academic Advisor for Athletics, Kentucky State University, Rm 241 400 E Main St, Frankfort, KY 40601, **Business Phone:** (502)597-6063.

### RICH, MATTY (MATTHEW STATISFIELD RICHARDSON)

Movie director, video producer, writer. **Personal:** Born Nov 26, 1971, Brooklyn, NY; son of Beatrice; married Leah Johnson. **Educ:** Tisch Sch Arts, NY Univ, film; John Jay Col Criminal Justice. **Career:** Films: Straight Out of Brooklyn, writer, producer, dir & actor, 1991; Inkwell, dir, 1994; 187 Ride or Die, dir & writer, 2005. BNP Productions, film producer & dir & writer, 1990-96; Short-term& Long-term Thinking, auth, 1991; William Morris Agency, film maker, 1991; Blacks N Progress Prod co, film prod, co-founder & owner, currently; Disney/Touchstone Pictures, dir, 1994-95; Ubisoft, Creative Dir & Artistic Dir, 2004-05; Matty Rich Games/MRG Headphones, chief exec officer & exec producer, 2005-. **Business Addr:** Filmmaker, William Morris Agency, 151 S El Camino Dr, Beverly Hills, CA 32767, **Business Phone:** (310)859-4000.

### RICH, STANLEY C.

Police officer, commissioner, accountant. **Personal:** Born Feb 25, 1920; married Coralie. **Educ:** Morris Brown Col, BA; Wayne State Univ, MA. **Career:** Mich Police Dept, Detroit, sec dep comnr; Detroit Health Dept, jr acct, 1947-50; Mayor's Com Human Resources Develop, sr acct, 1964-65, 1967; Small Bus Develop Ctr, adminr, 1965-67; equal employ officer small & minor bus. **Orgs:** Kappa Alpha Psi Fraternity; United Community Serv Met Detroit; bd dir, St Peter Claver Community Ctr. **Special Achievements:** First African American to be named deputy commissioner of Detroit Police Dept. **Home Addr:** 20170 Carol, Detroit, MI 48235.

### RICH, WILBUR C.

Educator. **Personal:** Born Sep 28, 1939, Montgomery, AL; son of Savage and Lydia; married Jean; children: Rachel & Alexandra. **Educ:** Tuskegee Inst, BS, social sci, 1960; Univ Ill, EdM, 1964, PhD, polit sci & govt, 1972. **Career:** Univ Wis, Dept Ment Health, Ill, counr asst admin, 1965-67; Ment Health CT, Ill Dept Ment Health, asst unit supvr, 1968-70, asst dir, 1969-72; Wesleyan Univ, vis lectr, 1971; Univ Ill, vis asst prof, 1972-73; Columbia Univ, asst prof polit sci, 1973-80; Wayne State Univ, Master Pub Admin Prog, dir, 1980-86, Dept Polit Sci, assoc prof & prof, 1980-91; Univ Mich, vis assoc prof polit sci, 1986; Univ Wis-Madison, vis La Follette distinguished prof, 1990; Harvard Univ, John F. Kennedy Sch Govt, vis Scholar, 1993-94; Wellesley Col, prof polit sci, 2007-10, prof emer, 2010-. **Orgs:** Ed bd mem, Pub Mgt & Productivity Rev, 1977-; NASPAA Comt Diversity, 1985-89; ed bd mem, Am Rev Pub Admin, 1988-; Harold D Lasswell Award Comt, Am Polit Sci Asn, 1989; Educ comt, Am Polit Sci Asn, 1990-93; Ralph Bunche Bk Award Comt, Am Polit Sci Asn, 1994;exec comt, Urban Polit Sect, Am Polit Sci Asn, 1994-95; chmn, Urban Polit Bk Award Comt, Am Polit Sci Asn, 1993; Exec coun mem, Policy Studies Orgn, 1998-2000; prog chair, Northeastern Polit Sci Asn, 1998-99, pres, 1999-2000; vis scholar, Russell Sage Found, 2001; mem coun, Urban Sect, Am Polit Sci Asn, 2002-04, pres, 2006-08; Comt Status Blacks Profession, Am Polit Sci Asn, 2003; vpres, New Eng Polit Sci Asn, 2006-07, pres, 2008-09; pres, Am Pol Sci Asn, 2007; ed bd mem, Commun Quart, 2008-; ed bd mem, Polit Sci Quart, 2010-; Am Soc Pub Admin; Nat Conf Black Polit Sci; Alpha Phi Alpha; Chi Gamma Iota; Phi Delta Kappa; Am Soc Pub Admin; Urban Affairs Asn; Am Educ Res Asn; Eastern Educ Res Asn; Eastern Commun Asn; Nat Conf Black Polit Scientists. **Honors/Awds:** Career Development Chair Award, Wayne State Univ, 1989-90; NYASPA Award; Listed in Who's Who Among Black Americans; Norton Long Career Achievement Award, Am Polit Sci Asn, 2009; Listed in Whos Who Among Black Americans; Received Numerous Awards. **Special Achievements:** Author: The Pol its Urban Personnel Policy, 1982; Coleman Young & Detroit Polits, 1989; Black Mayors & Sch Pol its, 1996; The Politics of Minority Coalitions, 1996; David Dinkins and New York Politic: Race, Images and the Media, 2006; African American Perspectives on the Political Science Discipline, 2007; The Post-Racial Society Is Here: Recognition, Criticss and the Nation-State; Author of Numerous Books. **Home Addr:** 26 Leighton Rd, Wellesley, MA 02482-6951, **Home Phone:** (781)237-6156. **Business Addr:** Emeritus Professor, Wellesley College, 106 Cent St, Wellesley, MA 02481, **Business Phone:** (781)283-1000.

### RICHARD, ALVIN J.

Dean (education), teacher, educator. **Personal:** Born Oct 14, 1932, New Orleans, LA; married Arlene Lecesne; children: Terrence, Kent & Wendy. **Educ:** Xavier Univ La, BS, 1955, MA, 1967; Univ Ill, EdD, 1972. **Career:** Orleans Pre Sch Bd, teacher, 1957-65; Xavier Univ, asst dean men, 1965-66, dean men, 1966-70, dir univ admin, 1972-75, dir recruitment, 1972-, dean admins & financial aid, 1975-, dean grad sch & dir grad admis grad sch, currently; Univ Ill, staff asst, 1970-72; Ford Found, fel, 1972; S Univ New Orleans, assoc prof, 1973. **Orgs:** Consult, Consortium Admin & Financial Admin, 1974-; Am Asn Col Reg & Admis Officers; Southern Asn Col Regs & Admin Officers; La Asn Col Regs & Admin Officers; Nat Asn Col Deans Regs & Admin Officers; Am Soc Allied Health Profs; bd mem, Young Adults Sports Asn; Met Area Com; Strng Com Am Found Negro Affairs. **Home Addr:** 5100 Chamberlain Dr, New Orleans, LA 70122. **Business Addr:** Dean Graduate School, Xavier University, 1 Drexel Dr, New Orleans, LA 70125, **Business Phone:** (504)483-7487.

### RICHARD, DR. ARLENE CASTAIN

Physician. **Personal:** Born Mar 1, 1955, St. Martinville, LA; daughter of Joseph Soban and Mary Luna Louis; married Donald Ray; children: Dawnia, Donald Jr, Sterlyn, Arlen & Orlando. **Educ:** Univ Southwestern La, BS, BA, acct, (Cum Laude), 1977; Howard Univ Col Med, MD, 1983. **Career:** Earl K Long Memorial Hosp, internship, 1983-84; LA State Univ Affiliated Hosps, internship, 1983-84; Univ Med Ctr, LSU staff physician, 1985; Howard Univ Hosp, family pract resident, 1985-87; pvt pract, currently. **Orgs:** Alpha Kappa Alpha Sor, 1974-, Am Med Asn. **Home Addr:** 2725 Ducharme Rd, Opelousas, LA 70570, **Home Phone:** (337)948-8000. **Business Addr:** Physician, Richard Medical Clinic, 507 N Market St, Opelousas, LA 70570, **Business Phone:** (337)948-1212.

### RICHARD, DR. FLOYD ANTHONY

Orientalist, gynecologist, physician. **Personal:** Born May 5, 1952, Opelousas, LA; married Robin; children: Keiana, Floyd II & Jonathan. **Educ:** Southern Univ, BS, 1973; Meharry Med Col, MD, 1981. **Career:** Conoco Oil, process control chemist, 1973-74; Upjohn Co, asst res chemist, 1976-77; Meharry Med Col, asst prof dept Obstets & Gynec, 1985; Cent N Ala Health Servs, chief dept Obstets & Gynec; pvt practr, Nashville, TN, currently; Meharry Med Col, adj fac, currently. **Orgs:** Chmn, youth div Second Ward Voters League, 1976. **Business Addr:** Adjunct Faculty, Meharry Medical College, 1005 Dr DB Todd Jr Blvd, Nashville, TN 37208, **Business Phone:** (615)327-5572.

### RICHARD, DR. HENRI-CLAUDE

Physician. **Personal:** Born Feb 12, 1944, Port-au-Prince; son of Theophile and Christiane; children: Maurice. **Educ:** Howard Univ Col Lib Arts, BS, 1968; Howard Univ Col Med, MD, 1972. **Career:** Radiol Mercy Hosp & Med Ctr, Internship, 1972-73, resident, 1973-74; Bridgeport Hosp, resident diag radiol, 1975-77; Ireland Army Hosp, radiologist, 1977-87; Breckenridge Memorial Hosp, radiologist, 1980-94; Pk duValle Health Ctr, radiologist, 1992; Radcliff Radiol Serv, radiologist, currently. **Orgs:** Am Med Asn; Ky Med Asn; Hardin Co Med Asn; Radiol Soc N Am; Am Col Radiol; Am Inst Ultrasound Med; Falls City Med Soc; Inter-Am Col Physicians & Surgeons. **Home Addr:** 1548 Redbud Cir, Radcliff, KY 40160-2830. **Business Addr:** Physician, Radcliff Radiology Services, 650 W Lincoln Trl Blvd Suite 101, Radcliff, KY 40160-2602, **Business Phone:** (270)351-4342.

### RICHARD, STANLEY PALMER

Football player. **Personal:** Born Oct 21, 1967, Miniola, TX. **Educ:** Univ Tex. **Career:** Football player (retired); San Diego Chargers, defensive back, free safety, 1991-94; Wash Redskins, defensive back, free safety, 1995-98. **Home Addr:** , Hawkins, TX.

### RICHARDS, DELEON MARIE

Actor, singer. **Personal:** Born Sep 18, 1976, Lake Forest, IL; daughter of Robert Leon Jr and Deborah Y Wallace; married Gary Sheffield; children: Jaden Amir & Christian Emari. **Educ:** Steve Scott, Goodman Theatre; Northwestern Univ, Music Dept; Sherwood Conservatory. **Career:** TV Series: Brewster Place, 1990; Legends from the Land of Lincoln; Patti LaBelle Gospel Special; Ebony/Jet Showcase; March of Dimes Telethon; McDonald Gospel Fest; Kelly & Co. Theatre Appearances: Polly & the Dinosaurs, World Book Encyclopedia Musical. Albums: DeLeon, 1985; Don't Follow the Crowd, 1987; Christmas, 1988; We Need to Hear from You, 1989; New Direction, 1992; Straight From the Heart, 2001; Here In Me, 2007; My Life; Videos: DeLeon in Concert; "When", 1993; The Mighty Clouds of Joy; Contributed musical input for Nancy Reagan's anti-drug film, "I Believe in Me", 1986; The Women of Brewster Place, 1990. DeMari Publishing and Entertainment Inc, pres & owner. **Honors/Awds:** Participated in the Chicago Gospel Fest at the age of 5, 1982; Grammy Nomination (youngest artist ever to be nominated), 1986; GMWA Award, 1988; Stellar Nomination, 1991; GMWA Award. **Special Achievements:** Youngest artist ever signed to a major Gospel label; Youngest person ever to be nominated for a Grammy; One of the Most Outstanding Role Models in America. **Home Addr:** PO Box 303, North Chicago, IL 60064, **Home Phone:** (708)689-0662. **Business Addr:** Gospel Singer, Word Records, 4800 W Waco Dr, Nashville, TN 37219.

### RICHARDS, GEORGE, JR.

Vice president (organization). **Educ:** Fisk Univ, BA. **Career:** Sr vpres & retail mkt mgr (retired); Comerica's Southeast Mich Banking ctr, Mich Exec Leader; Comerica Bank, banking ctr mgr, personal banker;

Southeast Mich banking ctr, Comerica Bank, sr vpres. **Orgs:** Trustee, Art League Mich; Mich Mgt Coun, Comerica Bank; Urban League; Arts League Mich; Real Life 101; bd visitors, Wayne State Univ Sch Med, 2014-. **Business Addr:** Board of Visitor, School of Medicine Wayne State University, 540 E Canfield Suite 1320, Detroit, MI 48201, **Business Phone:** (313)577-1429.

### RICHARDS, DR. GERMAINE GAIL BRANCH

Counselor, educator. **Personal:** Born Philadelphia, PA; daughter of Earl Joseph Branch and Germaine Lopez Jackson Branch; children: Kwadjo. **Educ:** Interamerican Univ PR; Bennett Col, BA, 1969; Montclair State Col, MA, 1971; Ohio State Univ, PhD, 1984. **Career:** NJ Bd Educ, Orange, teacher, 1969-71; Guilford Co NC Neighborhood Youth Corps, ed specialist, 1971-73; Ohio Dominican Col Upward Bound, assoc dir, 1973-77; Ohio State Univ, grad admin assoc, 1978-82; Ohio Bd Regents, res assoc, 1980; Ohio State Univ, Minority Assistance Prog, dir, 1982-89; Ohio State Univ, Med path Col Med, dir, 1989-91; Palm Beach Community Col, adj prof; Lynn Univ, adj prof; Nova Southeastern Univ, adj prof, 1991-94; Palm Beach County Sch, Royal Palm Beach High Sch, counr, 1994-. **Orgs:** Am Personnel & Guid Asn, 1978-; Nat Asn Women Deans & Counr, 1978-; adv bd, Upward Bound Prog, Ohio State Univ, 1979-91; team sec, Mifflin Youth Asn, 1985-89; personnel admin, Nat Asn Stud, 1985-; consult, State Ohio, 1986; NW Col Placement Asn, 1986; Asn Study Class African Civilizations, 1986-; vpres, Asn Black Psychologists, 1988-89; Palm Beach County Coun Asn. **Home Addr:** 177 Bobwhite Rd, Royal Palm Beach, FL 33411-1734, **Home Phone:** (561)753-3665. **Business Addr:** Counselor, Royal Palm Beach High School, 10600 Okeechobee Blvd, Royal Palm Beach, FL 33411, **Business Phone:** (561)753-4000.

### RICHARDS, DR. HILDA

School administrator, association executive, writer. **Personal:** Born Feb 7, 1936, St. Joseph, MO; daughter of Togar Young-Ballard and Rose Avalynne Williams Young-Ballard; married Alfredo. **Educ:** St John's Sch Nursing, St Louis, grad, nursing, 1956; City Univ NY, BS, 1961; Columbia Univ, Teachers Col, MEd, 1965, EdD, 1976; NY Univ, MPA, 1971; Inst Educ Mgt Harvard Univ, cert, 1981. **Career:** Payne Whitney Clin, nurse, 1956-58; City Hosp, Adolescent Psychiat Unit, head nurse, 1958-63; Harlem Rehab Ctr, Dept Psychol, Div Rehab Serv, coordr clin serv, 1965-69; Harlem Hosp Ctr, dept chief, 1965-71; Medgar Evers Col, dir nursing prog, 1971-76, from assoc prof to prof, 1971-76; Acad Admin Am Coun Educ, fel, 1976-77; City Univ NY, assoc dean acad affairs, 1976-79; Ohio Univ Col Health & Human Serv, dean, 1979-86; Ind Univ, Pa, provost & vpres acad affairs, 1986-93; Ind Univ NW, chancellor & pres, 1993-2001, chancellor emer & prof emer, 2001-. **Orgs:** Bd mem, 1974-77, 1983-84, 1988-91, first vpres, 1984-88, immediate past pres, Nat Black Nurses Asn; exec comm, Am Coun Educ, 1982-85; bd mem, AVANTA Network, 1984-; bd mem, Ind Co Comm Action, 1986-91; Pa Nurses Asn, 1986-; Econ Develop Comn, 1986-; bd mem, Citizen's Ambulance Serv, Ind Co, 1987-; Asn Black Women Fac, 1988-; Asn Black Women Higher Educ, 1988-; exec comm, Pa Black Conf Higher Educ, 1988; Nat Asn Advan Colored People, life mem, exec comm, Ind Chap, 1988-; Am Nurses Asn; Am Asn Higher Educ; Am Pub Health Asn; Nat Asn Allied Health Prof; Nat Women's Studies Asn; bd mem, Big Bros/Big Sisters, 1989-; Pa Acad Prof Teaching, bd mem, 1990-; Am Asn Univ Adminr; Am Asn Univ Women; Asn Black Nursing Fac Higher Educ; Asn Black Women Fac; Pa Nurses Asn; Phi Delta Kappa; Sigma Theta Tau; ACE Comn Minorities Higher Educ, Diversity & Social Chg; Zonta Club Ind County; bd dir, Sta 56-TV; Active NW Satir Inst, Execs Coun, NW, Ind; Urban League, 1993; NW Ind Forum, 1993; Bank One Regional bd, Merrillville, Ind, 1994; Meth Hosp Inc, Gary, 1994; Lake Area United Way, 1994; Boys & Girls Clubs, NW, Ind; NW Kiwanis; Gary Educ Develop Found, AIDS Found, Chicago. **Honors/Awds:** Martin Luther King Grantee, NYU, NYC, 1969-70; Recipient, Rockefellow Found Award, Am Coun Educ, Wash, 1976-77; Grant Found Grantee, Harvard Inst Educ Mgt, Cambridge, MA, 1981; Black Achiever Award, Black Opinion Mag, 1989; Outstanding Woman of Color, 1990, Special Recognition Award, 1991, Am Nurses Asn Inc; Distinguished African/American Nurse Educator, Queens County Black Nurses Asn, Queens borough Comm Col, 1991; Athena Award, Bus & Prof Women's Club Ind, 1991; Lifetime Achievement Award, Asn Black Nursing Fac, 1996; Dr, Medgar Evers College, City University of New York; 100 Most Influential Black Americans, Ebony magazine, 1999-03. **Special Achievements:** Co-author of "Curriculum Development and People of Color: Strategies and Change," 1983, editor of "Black Conf on Higher Education Jour, 1989-93, Journal of the National Black Nurses Association; First female and first African American academic dean at Ohio University; First black graduate of St. Johns School of Nursing in St. Louis. **Home Addr:** 7807 Hemlock Ave, Gary, IN 46403-2164. **Business Addr:** Chancellor Emeritus, Professor Emeritus, Indiana University Northwest, 3400 Broadway, Gary, IN 46408-1101, **Business Phone:** (219)980-6500.

### RICHARDS, JAIME AUGUSTO, III

Actor. **Personal:** Born Aug 28, 1973, Washington, DC. **Educ:** Univ Southern Calif, Sch Dramatic Arts. **Career:** Films: Why Do Fools Fall in Love, 1998; Good Burger, 1997; Any Day Now, 2000; Paved with Good Intentions, 2006; TV Series: "The Cosby Show", 1988; "Family Matters", 1993; "Undressed", 1999; "Moesha", 2000; "Running Mates", 2000; "Critical Assembly", 2003; "CSI Miami", 2004; "Angel", 2004; "Conviction", 2006; "The 4400", 2006; "Raising the Bar", 2008; "The Practice"; "Chicago Hope"; "Any Day Now"; "Nash Bridges"; "Any Day Now"; "The Temptations", 1998, singer; "Mutiny"; "The West Wing"; "The Mentalist"; "The Time Warp"; "Sliders" "Syfy's Warehouse 13"; ""The Bridge"; "Arrow", 2013; "Agents of S.H.I.E.L.D.", 2013; "Lobby Hero". **Orgs:** Make-A-Wish Found. **Honors/Awds:** Won numerous scholarships & grants. **Special Achievements:** Named No 10 of the Top Ten Sexiest Men of the Buffy. **Business Addr:** Actor, c/o Rising Stars, PO Box 99, China Spring, TX 76633, **Business Phone:** (254)836-0273.

### RICHARDS, DR. JOHNETTA GLADYS

Educator, association executive. **Personal:** Born Jul 18, 1950, Brooklyn, NY; daughter of Leo and Nettie James. **Educ:** Va State Col, BA, Am hist, 1972; Univ Cincinnati, MA, Am hist & ethnic lit, 1974, PhD, Am hist & social movements, 1987. **Career:** Northeastern Univ, adj instr Afro-Am hist, 1971; Univ Cincinnati, danforth fel, 1972-73, lectr Am hist, 1976-77; Univ Calif, Santa Barbara, lectr Afro-Am hist, 1977-78, Ctr Black Studies, Dissertation fel, 1977-78; Nat Fel Fund, Atlanta, Ga, Doctoral fel, 1978-79; Trinity Col, asst prof hist, 1979-84; State Univ Fresno, Women's Studies Calif, assoc prof, 1984-88; San Francisco State Univ, assoc prof black studies, prof africana studies, currently. **Orgs:** Phi Alpha Theta Nat Hon Fraternity Historians, 1974-; Asn Study Afro-Am Life & Hist, 1978; Nat Asn Advan Colored People, Hartford, CT, 1979-80; life mem, Asn Black Women Historians, 1983-; chair, Far Western Region Asn Black Women Historians, 1986-88; nat dir, Asn Black Women Historians, 1990-92; Am Hist Asn, Pac Coast Br; life mem, African Am Mus Libr, Oakland. **Home Addr:** 27 Gladys Ave, Brisbane, CA 94005-1768, **Home Phone:** (415)203-9361. **Business Addr:** Professor of Africana Studies, San Francisco State University, Rm 123 Ethnic Studies & Psychol Bldg 1600 Holloway Ave, San Francisco, CA 94132, **Business Phone:** (415)338-7589.

### RICHARDS, LAVERNE W.

School administrator. **Personal:** Born Jun 19, 1947, Gaffney, SC; married Walter; children: Brant & Jerrel. **Educ:** San Jose State Col, BA, 1969; Univ Calif, Berkeley, CA, teach cert, 1970; Univ Houston, Houston, TX, MEd, 1974, mid mgt adminr, 1981. **Career:** Educator (retired); Oakland Unified Sch Dist, teacher, 1969-72; Delta Sigma Theta Inc, prog asst, 1972; El Paso ISD, teacher, 1974-76; Houston ISD, teacher, 1972-74, 1977-85, asst prin; T M Fairchild Elem, prin. **Orgs:** Fine arts chmn, Delta Sigma Theta Ft Bend, 1984; coordr, United Way Clifton Middle Sch, 1985-87; coordr, United Negro Col Fund, 1985-87; finance comt Houston Assoc Sch Adminrs, 1985-; TX Assoc Sec Sch Prins, 1985-; phi Delta Kappa, Assoc Supervision & Curriculum, 1985-; Urban League Guild, 1986-; scholarship chmn, Human Enrichment Life Prog, 1987; Human Enrichment Life Prog, 1986-; Exec bd mem, Windsor Village Elem Vanguard Parents Asn, 1983-85; HISD Instructional Adv Comn Houston, 1984; Bd mem, MEAD GROUP. **Home Addr:** 12211 Preakness Way, Houston, TX 77071, **Home Phone:** (713)729-5537. **Business Addr:** TX.

### RICHARDS, LEON

School administrator, educator. **Personal:** Born Jun 7, 1945, Montgomery, AL; son of Carrie Mae Smith and John; married Pauline Sakai; children: Kayin Takao & Kalera Toyoko. **Educ:** Ala State Univ, BS, hist & polit sci, 1968; Univ Hawaii-Manoa, MA, polit sci, 1970, PhD, polit sci, 1974; MA, ESL, 2000. **Career:** Univ Hawaii, EW Ctr, Honolulu, HI, res asst, 1970-71, 1974-75; Leeward Community Col, Pearl City, HI, staff develop specialist, 1975-77; Kapiolani Community Col, Honolulu, HI, asst dean instr, 1977-81, actg provost, 1983-84, 2002, dean instr, 1983-, interim chancellor, 2005-07, chancellor, 2007-; Honda Int Ctr, exec dir, sr acad dean, currently. **Orgs:** Vpres, Hawaii Asn Staff, Prog & Orgn Develop, 1978-90; Summer in-residence fel Nat Ctr Res Voc Educ, 1979; Nat Comn Black Polit Scientist, 1979-; Am Coun Educ Fel Acad Admin, 1981-82; Field Study fel, Peking Univ; Fulbright-Hayes Study Abroad to China, Thailand, Loas, Cambodia, Vietnam Scholarships; Nat Coun Resource Develop, 1980-; EWt Ctr fel 1993-97. **Home Addr:** 98-363 Puaalii St, Aiea, HI 96701, **Home Phone:** (808)487-2087. **Business Addr:** Executive Director, Senior Academic Dean, University of Hawaii-Kapiolani Community College, 4303 Diamond Head Rd Ilima Bldg Rm 213, Honolulu, HI 96816-4421, **Business Phone:** (808)734-9565.

### RICHARDS, SR. LORETTA THERESA

Religious educator, teacher, religious leader. **Personal:** Born Apr 8, 1929, New York, NY; daughter of David A and Mary Cornelius Edwards. **Educ:** Col Mt St Vincent, New York, NY, BA, 1954; Cath Univ, Wash, DC, MA, 1960; Catechetical Inst, Yonkers NY, MRS, 1984. **Career:** St Aloysius Sch, New York NY, teacher, 1954-55, 1957-61; St Thomas Sch, Wilmington NC, teacher, 1955-57; Cathedral High Sch, New York NY, teacher, 1961-64; FHM, New York NY, sch supvr, 1964-74, congregation pres, 1974-82; St Aloysius Parish, New York NY, pastoral assoc, 1982-90, congregation pres, 1990-98, vpres, 1998-2006; vice minister, currently. **Orgs:** Pres, Nat Black Sisters Conf, 1985-89; vpres & congregation minister, Nat Black Cath Cong, 1989-91; Nat Forum Catechumenate, 1990-; Vicariate Coun Cent Harlem; congregation minister, Franciscan Fed. **Honors/Awds:** Doctor of Pedagogy, New York Col Podiatric Med, 1981; Doctor of Humane Letters, Col New Rochelle, 1997; Distinguished Alumni Award. **Home Addr:** Handmaids Mary Convent, 15 W 124th St, New York, NY 10027, **Home Phone:** (212)289-5655. **Business Addr:** Vice Minister, Head Sister, Franciscan Handmaids of Mary, 15 W 124th St, New York, NY 10027-5634, **Business Phone:** (212)289-6179.

### RICHARDS, WILLIAM EARL

Executive, secretary of the navy. **Personal:** Born Oct 16, 1921, New York, NY; son of John Earl Jr and Camily Pauline Deravaine; married Ollun Elizabeth Sadler; children: William Jr. **Educ:** Washburn Univ, BA, econs, 1971; NY Univ, addn study; Officer Cand Sch, AF Spec Weapons Sch. **Career:** Lipsett Steel Co, gen supt, 1946-49; Progressive Life Ins, agt, 1949-51; NAACP, staff dir, legis agt, 1972; Kans Comn Alcoholism, 1972-73; Kans Dept Soc & Rehab Serv, comn income maintenance & med asst, 1973-83; Richards Et Cie, pres; Myers & Stauffer CPA's, sr consult; Cottonwood Technol Corp, Kans City, Kans, pres, 1988-93; Topeka Human Rels Comn, comnr, vice chmn. **Orgs:** Washburn Alumni Asn; Retired Officers Asn; Assn AUS; Mil Order World Wars; Alpha Phi Alpha; SPP; life mem, Nat Asn Advan Colored People; Euclid Lodge; Kaw Valley Consistory; 33 Degree Mason; pres, Topeka Br Nat Asn Advan Colored People; Topeka Knife & Fork Club. **Home Addr:** 4722 SW Brentwood Rd, Topeka, KS 66606-2204, **Home Phone:** (785)234-4555.

### RICHARDS, DR. WINSTON ASHTON

Educator. **Personal:** Born Mar 7, 1935, Chaguanas; son of Edward Ivan and Leanora Nimblett; married Kathleen Marie Hoolihan; children: Ashton, Winston, Marie, Michael, Bridgette, Mary, Patricia & Edward. **Educ:** Marquette Univ, Milwaukee, WI, BS, 1959, MS, 1961; Univ Western Ont, London, Ont, MA, 1966, PhD, 1970. **Career:** Aquinas Col, Grand Rapids, Mich, instr, 1961-62; Wayne State Univ, Detroit, Mich, lectr, 1962-64; Univ Western Ont, grad asst, 1964-69; Penn State Univ, Penn State Harrisburg, Middletown, Pa, assoc prof emer math sci, 1969-; Univ Wi, Trinidad, from vis sr lectr to sr lectr, 1980-82; Stanford Univ, Dept Statist, vis prof, 1995-97. **Orgs:** Fel IST Statisticians, 1985; treas, 1987, pres, 1989-90, 1992-93, Harrisburg Chap, Am Statist Asn; Math Asn Am; Inter Am Statist Inst; Inst Statisticians; Int Statist Inst; Pa Black Conf Higher Educ; fel Am Statist Asn, FASA, 1997. **Home Addr:** 2100 Chestnut St, Harrisburg, PA 17104-1333, **Home Phone:** (717)236-8939. **Business Addr:** Associate Professor Emeritus of Mathematical Sciences, Pennsylvania State University, W255 Olmsted Bldg, Middletown, PA 17057, **Business Phone:** (717)948-6090.

### RICHARDS-ALEXANDER, BILLIE J.

Consultant, executive. **Personal:** Born Austin, TX; daughter of Johnnie M Barber Bacon and Roy A Bacon; married Castomal S Sr; children: Roy, Dianne E & Reginald A Richards. **Educ:** Huston Tillotson Col, Austin, Tex, BS, 1962; Univ Tex, Austin, Tex, attended 1963; Scarritt Col, Nashville, Tenn, attended 1966; Univ Tex, Arlington, Tenn, attended 1974; London Sch Bus, London, Eng, attended 1986. **Career:** Ebenezer Baptist Church, Austin. Tex, dir educ, 1960-61; Dunbar High Sch, Temple, Tex, teacher, 1961-64; Bethlehem Community Ctr, asst dir to dir, 1965-73; Fed Home Loan Bank Bd Ctr Exec Develop, urban prog coordr, 1972-73; Neighborhood Housing Serv Dallas Inc, exec dir, 1973-78; Dallas Fed Savings & Loan Asn, Urban Lending Dept, vpres & dir, 1978-80, sr vpres, 1980-87; Int Bus fel, 1986; Billie Richards & Assocs Inc, pres. **Orgs:** Alpha XI Omega Chap. **Honors/Awds:** Woman of the Year, United Action Women's Affil Dallas Black Chamber Com, 1978; Community Affairs Award, Com 100, 1978; Trailblazer Award, S Dallas Bus & Prof, Women's Orgn, 1979. **Special Achievements:** First Black female vice president of a major financial institution in the Southwest, 1978; First African American female senior vice president, 1980. **Business Addr:** President, Billie Richards & Associates Inc, 1517 Bar Harbor Dr, Dallas, TX 75232-3015, **Business Phone:** (214)375-5565.

### RICHARDS-ROSS, SANYA

Entrepreneur, athlete. **Personal:** Born Feb 26, 1985, Trelawny; daughter of Archie Richards and Sharon Richards; married Aaron, Jan 1, 2010?. **Educ:** Univ Tex, Austin, attended 2006. **Career:** Track athlete, 2002-16; Sanya's Glam & Gold, subj & exec producer, 2013; SRR Inc, chief exec officer; motivational speaker. **Orgs:** Sanya Richards Fast Track Program, founder, 2007. **Honors/Awds:** IAAF Gatorade National High School Girls Track & Field Athlete of the Year, 2002; World Junior Championships, silver medal 400m and bronze medal, 200m, 2002; NCAA 400m champion, 2003; USATF Youth Athlete of the Year, 2003; World Outdoor Championships, gold medals, 4x400 gold, 2003, 2007, 2009, 2011; Summer Olympics, gold medals 4x400 gold, 2004, 2008, 2012; World Outdoor Championships, silver medal 400m, 2005; Visa Humanitarian of the Year, 2005; World Cup, gold medals 200m and 400m, 2006; World Athlete of the Year, 2006, 2009; Jesse Owens Award, 2006, 2009; Summer Olympics, bronze medal 400m, 2008; World Indoor Championship, silver medal 4x400m, 2012; World Indoor Championship, gold medal 400m, 2012; Summer Olympics, gold medal 400m, 2012. **Special Achievements:** Considered the best female 400m runner in the world and one of the world's fastest women; American record holder in the 400m; NCAA Indoor 400m record holder. **Business Addr:** USA Track & Field, 132 East Washington St Suite 800, Indianapolis, IN 46204, **Business Phone:** (317)261-0500.

### RICHARDSON, ALBERT DION

Executive, president (organization). **Personal:** Born Dec 14, 1946, New York, NY; son of Robert L McKinney and Onolda Jacquelyn McKinney; married Beverly V A; children: Dara & Erika. **Educ:** Mercer County Community Col, Trenton, NJ, attended 1973. **Career:** Richardson Environ Contracting, pres, 1986-. **Orgs:** Nat Asn Minority Contractors, 1986-. **Home Addr:** 26 Timber Lane, Willingboro, NJ 08046-3826, **Home Phone:** (609)877-3992. **Business Addr:** President, Richardson Environ Contracting Inc, 253 W Fed, Burlington, NJ 08016, **Business Phone:** (609)386-8884.

### RICHARDSON, ANDRA VIRGINIA

Magistrate. **Personal:** Born Apr 16, 1954, Detroit, MI; daughter of James Law and Odessa Law; married William Lee; children: Brittney Leigh & Chelsea Anne. **Educ:** Wayne State Univ, BS, 1984; Wayne State Univ Law Sch, JD, 1987. **Career:** Delta Airlines, reservation sales agt, 1977-86; Oakland County, prosecutor, asst prosecuting atty, 1988-90; 52nd Dist Ct-1st Div, magistrate, 1990-; Eastern Mich Univ, adj prof, 1998-; part-time law pract, currently. **Orgs:** Exec bd & chair, Oakland County Chap Child Abuse & Neglect Coun, 1990-94; bd dir, Girl Scouts Am, 1991-94; exec bd, rec secy, Top Ladies Distinction Inc, 1993-95; exec bd, parlimentarian, Jack & Jill Am Inc, 1993-95; pres, Top Ladies, 1995-97; Doll League, 1998-; Legis Liaison, 1998-; Wolverine Bar Asn; Asn Black Judges Mich. **Honors/Awds:** Outstanding Business & Prof Award, Dollars & Sense Mag, 1993; Prof Woman of the Year, Nat Asn Negro Bus & Prof Women Club Inc, 1993. **Home Addr:** 6296 Charles Dr, West Bloomfield, MI 48322-2296, **Home Phone:** (248)865-7575. **Business Addr:** Magistrate, 52nd District Court -1st Division, 48150 Grand River Ave, Novi, MI 48374-1222, **Business Phone:** (248)305-6511.

### RICHARDSON, DR. ANTHONY W.

Dentist. **Personal:** Born Mar 15, 1957, New York, NY; son of Archie and Harriet Boyd Brooks; children: Solunda Yvette, Sherie Odetta & Toni Charisse. **Educ:** Bucknell Univ, BS, 1979; Fairleigh Dickinson Univ Sch Dent Med, DMD, 1983. **Career:** Montefiore Hosp & Med Ctr, gen pract resident, 1983-84; Fairleigh Dickinson Univ Sch Dent Med, asst dir minority affairs, 1984-86, asst prof, 1984-87, asst dir admis, 1986-87, asst dir prog grads non approved dent sch, 1986-87, dir minority affairs, 1986-87; Con-Ct Dent Assocs, Bronx, NY, owner, 1989-. **Orgs:** Charter mem, Phi Beta Sigma Fraternity Iota Gamma Chap, 1977; Am Assoc Dent Sch; Acad Gen Dent; Nat Dent Asn; NJ Commonwealth Dent Soc; adv bd, Health Careers Prog Montclair State Col, 1983-90; chap adv, Phi Beta Sigma Fraternity Xi Omicron Chap, 1984-85; Phi Beta Sigma Fraternity; Greater Metrop NY Dent Soc; USCG Auxillary; bd dir, Fordham Hill Owners Corp, 1998-2001. **Honors/Awds:** NY State Govs Citation, 1975; Outstanding Serv Cert, Nat Dent Asn, 1982 & 1983; NJ Soc Dentistry C Award, 1983; NJ Commonwealth Dent Soc Award, 1983; Outstanding Young Men Am,

1986. **Home Addr:** 3 Fordham Hill Oval Suite 5F, Bronx, NY 10468. **Business Addr:** Owner, Con-Court Dent Assocs, 840 Grand Concourse Suite 1BB, Bronx, NY 10451, **Business Phone:** (917)294-4880.

### RICHARDSON, ANTONIO. See RICHARDSON, TONY.

### RICHARDSON, CLINT DEWITT, JR.
Basketball player. **Personal:** Born Aug 7, 1956, Seattle, WA; son of Clint Sr; married Vicki; children: Tiffany Jade. **Educ:** Seattle Univ, attended 1979. **Career:** Basketball player (retired); Philadelphia 76ers, guard, 1979-85, Ind Pacers, guard, 1985-87; CYO athletics, dir & coach, currently.

### RICHARDSON, DAMIEN A.
Physician, football player. **Personal:** Born Apr 3, 1976, Los Angeles, CA. **Educ:** Ariz State Univ, grad; Harvard Univ, MA, pub health. **Career:** Football player (retired); Carolina Panthers, 1999, 2002, strong safety, 1998, defensive back, safety, 2000, strong safety, 2001; Az state Sun Devils, currently; Univ Med Ctr, orthop physician. **Honors/Awds:** All-conference honor, 1997. **Business Addr:** Orthop Physician, Univ Med Ctr, 1111 E McDowell Rd, Phoenix, AZ 85006, **Business Phone:** (602)839-2000.

### RICHARDSON, DERUTHA GARDNER (DERUTHA DEE RICHARDSON)
Educator, administrator. **Personal:** Born May 3, 1941, Muskogee, OK; married Alfred; children: Allyn Christopher & Adrian Charles. **Educ:** Muskogee Jr Col, OK, AA, 1960; NE State Col, Tahlequah, OK, BS, 1962, MS, 1964. **Career:** School adminstrator, educator (retired), owner; L'Ouverature High Sch, teacher sec, 1962-63; Mountain High Sch, sec bus teacher, 1963-65; Cent High Sch, first black sec bus teacher, 1965-66; Taft St C Home Matriculation Sch, exec sec & teacher, 1966-67; Muskogee County Head Start, sec bk keeper, 1966-68; Muskogee High Sch, first black bus dept head & teacher coord, chief exec officer; YWCA Connells St Col, adult bus teacher, 1975-77; W Jr High Sch, asst, prin; Antique Store, owner, currently. **Orgs:** Zeta Phi Beta Sorority Inc, WA, 1973-74; treas, Alpha Lambda Zeta Sorority, 1975-80; pres, Eastern Dist Okla Educ Asn, 1977-78. **Honors/Awds:** First Black Teacher of the Year, Muskogee Educ Asn, 1977; Teacher Year finalist, Oklahoma Educ Asn, 1977; Black Heritage hon, Mt Calvary Baptist Church, Muskogee, 1977; first black fourth place & second runner-up plaques, Oklahoma Teachers, 1978-80; outstanding teachers plaque, Du Bois School Reunion, 1980; author Dear Teacher, Carlton Press, NY, 1980; Recipient of over 35 Awards, state, regional and national. **Special Achievements:** First African American teacher in Muskogee Public Schools; Published author of three books; Books: "Dear Teacher", "Spread Your Wings & Fly", "Projecting Professional Images". **Home Addr:** 105 S Crabtree Rd, Muskogee, OK 74403-6106, **Home Phone:** (918)687-6576. **Business Addr:** Assistant Principal, West Junior High School, 6400 Mathew Dr, Muskogee, OK 74401.

### RICHARDSON, DESMOND
Dancer. **Personal:** Born Jan 1, 1969, Sumter, SC. **Educ:** Alvin Ailey Am Dance Ctr, attended 1986. **Career:** Ailey Repertory Ensemble, 1986; Alvin Ailey Am Dance Theater, prin dancer, 1987-94; Frankfurt Ballet, 1994-96; Am Ballet Theatre, prin dancer, 1997-99; Broadway Musical Fosse, 1998; Dance Conv Pulse, fac mem; Swed Opera Ballet; Wash Ballet; Teatro at La Scala; San Francisco Ballet; Complexions Contemp Ballet, co-artistic dir & co founder, currently; NY City Dance Alliance, guest fac, currently; Broadway dancer, 1998-; actor, 2001-. **Honors/Awds:** Merit scholarship, Alvin Ailey Am Dance Ctr, 1983-86; summer academy scholarship, ternational Academie des Tanz, Cologne, 1984-85; Presidential Scholar Award for the Arts, 1986; NFAA Alumni Award; Bessie Award, 1992; New York Times Critics Choice Award, 1995; Tony Award Nomination for Fosse, 1999; Dance Magazine Award, 2007; Capezio Dance Award, 2011. **Special Achievements:** First African-American principal dancer at Amer Ballet Theatre. **Business Addr:** Co-Artistic Director, Co-Founder, Complexions Contemporary Ballet, 37 W 39th St Suite 401, New York, NY 10018, **Business Phone:** (212)777-7771.

### RICHARDSON, DR. EARL STANFORD
College administrator, president (government). **Personal:** Born Sep 25, 1943, Westover, MD; son of Phillip; married Sheila Bunting; children: Eric. **Educ:** Univ Md, Eastern Shore, BA, social sci, 1965; Univ Pa, MS, educ admin, 1973, EdD, educ admin, 1976. **Career:** Univ Md, Eastern Shore, exec asst to chancellor, dir career planning & placement, 1970-75, actg dir admis & reg, 1970-71, exec asst to chancellor, 1975-82; Univ Penn, grad asst sch study coun, 1973-74; Univ Md Syst, asst to pres, 1982-84; Morgan State Univ, interim pres, 1984-85, pres, 1984-2010. **Orgs:** Alpha Kappa Mu Hon Soc Int, 1964-65; pres, bd dir, mem, Somerset City Head Start Prog, 1974-; chap pres, Alpha Phi Alpha Fraternity Inc, 1976-79; pres, Panhellenic Coun Eastern Shore, 1977-79; consult, Col Placement Serv, 1979; Phi Kappa Phi Hon Soc Int, 1979-; Sigma Pi Phi Fraternity Gamma Boule; Md State Bd Higher Educ, 1984-; Goldseker Found, 1985-; Life Bridge; NIH; Baltimore Vision 2030 Comt; State Bd Higher Educ, 1986-88; Md Higher Educ Comn; 1988-10; Segmental Adv Coun; Am Coun Educations Comn Int Educ; Goldseker Found; adv bd, Md Educ Coalition; Educ Testing Serv; bd dir, Nat Black Col Alumni Hall Fame Found, 1994; Nat Asn Equal Opportunity Higher Educ; bd mem, Baltimore Symphony Orchestra; bd mem, Greater Baltimore Comt; Alvin Ailey Dance Theater Found Md; Md Bus Round table Educ; bd dir, Baltimore Coun Boy Scouts Am; fel Task Force Study Col Readiness Disadvantaged Capable Students, 2000-01; Baltimore Region Rail Syst Plan Adv Comt, 2001-02; State Planning Comt Higher Educ, 2004; Comn Develop Md Model Funding Higher Educ, 2006-08; Joint Legis & Exec Comn Oversight Pub Pvt Partnerships, 2010; chair, Nat Asn Equal Oppurtunity Higher Educ; Assoc Black Charities Md, 2010. **Home Addr:** 2412 Coll Ave, Baltimore, MD 21214. **Business Addr:** President, Morgan State University, 1700 E Cold Spring Lane 409 Truth Hall, Baltimore, MD 21251, **Business Phone:** (443)885-3220.

### RICHARDSON, ELAINE CYNTHIA POTTER. See KINCAID, PROF. JAMAICA.

### RICHARDSON, DR. ELISHA ROSCOE
Educator, dentist, scientist. **Personal:** Born Aug 15, 1931, Monroe, LA; daughter of Warren Carter and Hannah Mariah; married Pattye Whyte; children: Scott, Jonathan & Mark. **Educ:** Southern Univ, BS, 1951; Meharry Med Col, DDS, 1955; Univ Ill Med Ctr, MS, 1963; Univ Mich & Harvard Univ, attended 1973; Univ Mich, PhD, 1988. **Career:** Meharry Med Col, Sch Dent, Regional Res Ctr, from asst prof to prof, 1967-85, dean, 1977-85, dir, 1992-; Meharry Med Col, Sch Dent, dir res, 1969-78, dent dean, 1988-92, prof & chmn orthod; Hbrd Hosp, pres med & dent staff, 1971-72; Univ Colo, Div Orthodont, prof & chmn, 1985-88Sch Dentist, Dept Orthdont, assoc dean & chmn. **Orgs:** Chmn, Orthodont Am Asn Dent Sch, 1972-73; pres, Craniofacial Biol, 1978-79; pres & chmn bd, Nat Dent Asn, 1980-81; chmn, Coun Educ Am Asn Orthodontists, 1987; Am Asn Orthdnontist; Am Soc Dent C; Int Asn Dent Res; Am Asn Dent Schs; AAAS; Craniofacial Biol Group; Meharry Alumni Asn; Univ Ill Orthdont Alumni Asn; Am Pub Health Asn; Am Col Dentists, Alpha Phi Alpha; Nat Asn Advan Colored People; Nashville Urban League; YMCA; Nashville Symphony Asn; Civitan Int. **Honors/Awds:** One of the 100 Most Influential Black Americans by Ebony Magazine, 1981. **Home Addr:** 5325 Forest Acres Dr, Nashville, TN 37220-2103, **Home Phone:** (615)370-4873. **Business Addr:** Physician, Private Practice, 390 Hardind Pl Suite 106, Nashville, TN 37211-3998, **Business Phone:** (615)832-8989.

### RICHARDSON, ERNEST A.
Manager, consultant. **Personal:** Born Aug 2, 1925, New York, NY; married Olive; children: Brenda. **Educ:** Columbia Univ, New York, BA, 1952; NY Univ, MBA, 1958. **Career:** Schnly Indust, acct, 1952-60; Int Pearl Corp, controller, 1960-66; St Regis Paper Co, minority affairs mgr; consult. **Orgs:** Bd chmn, New York Task Force Youth Motivation; nat chmn, pres, Nat Urban Affairs Coun; indust chmn, Fisk Univ Cluster; bd adv, Tenn State Univ Cluster; adv com, Nat Task Force Youth Motivation; Black Corp Caucus; adv com, Nat Urban League Skills Bank. **Honors/Awds:** Executive of the Year, Asn Meeting Planners, 1983; Crusade Award, Am Cancer Soc, 1985; Merit Award, St Regis, 1985; Certificate of Appreciation, Nat Urban Affairs Coun, 1987. **Home Addr:** 18630 Mangin Ave, Jamaica, NY 11412, **Home Phone:** (718)454-3069.

### RICHARDSON, FRANK
Politician, artist. **Personal:** Born Jan 14, 1950, Baltimore, MD. **Educ:** Md Inst Col Art, AA; Towson St Col, Baltimore, BFA. **Career:** Third World Prep Sch Art, headmaster, 1975; News Am, 1976-; Baltimore's Black Art's Mus, dir, 1976; Enoch Pratt Free Libr Br 17, painter; Phase's Gallery, 1977; Ebony Collective, 1977; Dem Party, City Coun Baltimore, coun mem, currently; Univ Ife Bookshop Ltd, Nigeria, Art show. **Orgs:** Black Cult Endowment, 1974; artist fel prog, Md Arts Coun, 1977; Nat Soc Pub Poets. **Home Addr:** 552 Baker St, Baltimore, MD 21217-3306, **Home Phone:** (410)889-8058. **Business Addr:** Council Member, Baltimore City Council, Baltimore City Hall 100 Holliday St, Baltimore, MD 21202, **Business Phone:** (410)396-3100.

### RICHARDSON, FREDERICK D., JR.
Government official. **Personal:** Born Sep 4, 1939, Nymph, AL; son of Frederick (deceased) and Helen; married Ruby; children: Lawanda Lawson, Lisa & Frederick III. **Educ:** Carver State Voc Col, attended 1969; Bishop State Community Col, attended 1971; Univ S Ala, BA, polit sci & hist, 1974, MA, hist. **Career:** Mobile Infirmary Hosp, housekeeper; US Postal Serv, substitute lett carrier, mgr sta & br opers, 1992-; City Mobile, city coun mem dist 1, vpres, currently. **Orgs:** Treas, Neighborhood Organized Workers, 1968; Nat League Cities, 1997-; Ala League Cities, 1997-; World Conf Mayors; bd chair, Hist Mus Mobile; Bd Zoning Adjust; exec bd mem, Mobile Tricentennial Inc; nat coord, Nat Coalition Justice & Equality; Exploreum; bd deacon, Stone St Baptist Church; Gulf Coast Emporium Mus Sci Bd; chmn, Pub Safety Comt. **Home Addr:** 1803 S Indian Creek Dr, Mobile, AL 36607, **Home Phone:** (334)473-3268. **Business Addr:** Council Member, Vice President, City of Mobile, 205 Govt St 9th Fl S Twr, Mobile, AL 36633-1827, **Business Phone:** (334)208-7441.

### RICHARDSON, GEORGE C.
Legislator. **Personal:** Born Jan 5, 1929, Newark, NJ. **Educ:** USAF Admin Sch; Jersey City Tech. **Career:** NJ Gen Assembly, asst minority leader, 1961-. **Orgs:** Chmn, NJ Black Legis Caucus; NJ State Narcotics Div Comn, Inst & Agency; Com Transp & Pub Utilities Sub-Comn Hwy & Com Taxation; pres, Periscope Asn; pres & founder, Nat Comt Declare War Drugs. **Home Addr:** 435 S 12th St, Newark, NJ 07103. **Business Addr:** Assistant Minority Leader, New Jersey General Assembly, 21 N Main St, Cape May Court House, NJ 08210, **Business Phone:** (609)465-0700.

### RICHARDSON, GLOSTER VAN
Teacher, football player, football coach. **Personal:** Born Jul 18, 1942, Greenville, MS; son of Willie Sr and Mary Alice Tompkins; married Bettye Neal; children: Glasetta & Maury. **Educ:** Jackson State Col, attended 1965. **Career:** Football player (retired), football coach; Kans City Chiefs, 1967-70; Dallas Cowboys, wide receiver, 1971; Chicago pub Sch, phys educ teacher, 1971-2003, coach & safe sch assessment specialist, dir & organizer, touch football, 1990; Cleveland Browns, 1972-74, 1976. **Orgs:** Better Boys Found; NFL Retired Players Asn; Mt Carmel high sch Fathers Asn; vpres, Rainbow Bench, 1991-92. **Honors/Awds:** AFL Champion, 1969; Played in 3 Super Bowl Championships; Football Hall of Fame, Jackson State Univ; NFL Alumni Award, NFL Alumni Asn, 1990-91. **Home Addr:** 9143 S Euclid, Chicago, IL 60617-3749, **Home Phone:** (773)933-7357.

### RICHARDSON, HENRY J., III
Educator. **Personal:** Born Mar 24, 1941, Indianapolis, IN; married Renee Poussaint. **Educ:** Univ Besancon, France, cert hist, 1962; Antioch Col, AB, hist, 1963; Yale Law Sch, LLB, 1966; Univ Calif, Sch Law, Los Angeles, LLM, 1971. **Career:** Govt Malawi, Cent Africa, int legal adv, 1966-68; Maxwell Afro-Asian, fel, 1966-69; Univ Calif, Los Angeles, African Studies Ctr, fac africanist law, fel, 1969-71; Ind Univ, Sch Law, from asst prof to assoc prof, 1971-75, fac res fel, 1973; Northwestern Univ Sch Law, vis assoc prof law, 1975-76; White House, Nat Security Coun, staff, 1977-79; Congressman Charles Diggs, sr foreign policy advisor, 1979; Howard Univ, dept polit sci, vis adj prof, 1979-80; Temple University Law School, vis scholar, 1979, assoc prof, 1981, co-dir & prof, prof law, currently; Off Gen Coun, Intelligence Int, Investigative Policy, Dept Defense, atty advisor, 1979-81; Joint Center for Political & Economic Studies; Temple's Int and Comparative Law J, co-founder. Book: Reverend Leon Sullivan's Principles, Race and International Law, 2001; Patrolling the Resource Transfer Frontier, 2007; Dr. Martin Luther King, Jr. as an International Human Rights Leader, 2007; The Origin of African-American Interests, 2008. **Orgs:** AID Res Team Law & Social Chg, 1971; chmn, Int Legal Educ Africa, 1973; exec coun, pres, 1975-, vpres, 1990-92, chair & creator, 1993-98, Am Soc Int Law; co-dir, ASIL, PAIL, Ford study Women & Minorities Int Law, 1986-87; adv comt, ITT Inter Nat Fel Prog; founding mem, chmn, Nat Conf Black Lawyers; chmn, Task Force Int Affairs; rep, UNNGO; Ind Bar; World Peace Through Law Ctr, Sect Int Legal Ed; Int Affairs Comt, Nat Bar Asn; Overseas Develop Coun; Lawyers Comt Civil Rights Under Law; founding mem, Proj Advan African-Ams Int Law, 1996; Coun Foreign Rels; advisor, Const Comn Rwanda Drafting new Rwandan Const, 2002; Int Human Rights; Const Law & Foreign Policy. **Business Addr:** Professor of Law, Temple University, Klein Hall Rm 706 1719 N Broad St, Philadelphia, PA 19122-2585, **Business Phone:** (215)204-8987.

### RICHARDSON, JEROME, JR. (POOH RICHARDSON)
Basketball coach, basketball player. **Personal:** Born May 14, 1966, Philadelphia, PA. **Educ:** Univ Calif, attended 1989. **Career:** Basketball player (retired), head coach, business owner; Minn Timberwolves, guard, 1989-92; Ind Pacers, guard, 1992-94; Los Angeles Clippers, guard, 1994-99; Adecco Milano, 1999-2000; Maywood Laguneros, Am Basketball Asn, head coach, 2005-. **Business Addr:** Head Coach, Maywood Laguneros, 4801 E 58th St, Maywood, CA 90270, **Business Phone:** (323)562-5722.

### RICHARDSON, JOHNNY L.
Executive, consultant. **Personal:** Born Jul 14, 1952, Cleveland, MS; married Mary Goins; children: Teria D & Rapahelle K. **Educ:** Ripon Col, BA, econ, 1974. **Career:** Miller Brewing Co, pricing analyst, 1974-75, merchandising rep, 1975-77, area mgr, 1977-82, reg mkt mgr, 1985-96; CBS Radio, acct exec, 1997-2007; Mkt Connections, consult, currently. **Orgs:** Vpres, Nat Urban League, 1981-82; Chicago Merchandiser Exec Club, 1982; grad instr, Dale Carnegie Inst, 1984; dir, Pk Ridge Jaycees, 1984-85; Ripon Col Alumni Bd, 1984-87. **Honors/Awds:** Director of the Year, Chicago S End Jaycees, 1980; Pres Award, Merit Chicago South-End Jaycees, 1982. **Home Addr:** 1539 Potter Rd, Park Ridge, IL 60068-1405, **Home Phone:** (847)698-3033. **Business Addr:** Consultant, Marketing Connections, 712 N Wells St Suite 200, Chicago, IL 60610, **Business Phone:** (312)587-1465.

### RICHARDSON, JOSEPH
Business owner, executive. **Personal:** Born Apr 23, 1940, Kansas City, MO; son of Joseph and Genevieve; married Jacqueline; children: Jolawn Ollita. **Educ:** Lincoln Univ, BA, sociol & psychol, 1964; Augsburg Col, Minneapolis, MN, MA, leadership, 1989. **Career:** FJR & Assocs Inc, pres, 1980; The Toro Co, dir employees rels mgr, 1979-80, corp mgr manpower planning, 1978-79, corp training mgr, 1977-78, corp employ mgr, 1976-77; Mgt Recruiters, acct exec, 1973-76; John Tschohl & Assocs, vpres, 1972-73; Butler Mfg Co, div employee rels mgr, 1970-72; Butler Mfg Co, copr employ rep, 1968-70; Pan HellenicCoun, pres, 1978-; Minneapolis Coun Ex-offender Employ, pres, 1979-; Honeywell Inc, sr human resources rep, 1984, Orgn Develop Specialist, 1983-99; Metro Transit, human resource dir, 2000-06; Metrop State Univ, community fac mem, instr, 2006-; Richardson Properties, owner. **Orgs:** Twin City Personnel Asn, Vietnam Serv; vpres, Gamma Xi Lambda Alpha Phi Alpha Frat, 1977. **Honors/Awds:** Medal-AUS Commedation Medal; Pres Citation Oak Leaf Cluster AUS. **Home Addr:** 4230 Oakview Lane N, Minneapolis, MN 55442-2773, **Home Phone:** (763)559-1910. **Business Addr:** Community Faculty Member, Metropolitan State University, 1501 Hennepin Ave, Minneapolis, MN 55403, **Business Phone:** (651)793-1342.

### RICHARDSON, JULIEANNA
Executive director, founder (originator), lawyer. **Personal:** Born Jun 10, 1954, Pittsburgh, PA; daughter of Julius and Margaret. **Educ:** Brandeis Univ, BA, theater arts & Am studies, 1976; Harvard Law Sch, JD, 1980. **Career:** Jenner & Block, atty; City Chicago, Off Cable Commun, asst & chief cable adminr; Cable Shopping Channel, founder, 1985-; SCTN Teleproductions, chief exec officer, founder; HistoryMakers, founder, exec dir, 1999-. **Orgs:** Hons Coun Lawyers Creative Arts; Comcast NBC Universal African Am Diversity Coun, 2011. **Honors/Awds:** Howard University, Honorary Doctorate of Humanities, 2012. **Home Addr:** , Chicago, IL. **Business Addr:** Founder, Executive Director, The HistoryMakers, 1900 S Michigan Ave, Chicago, IL 60616, **Business Phone:** (312)674-1900.

### RICHARDSON, REV. DR. LACY FRANKLIN
Clergy, consultant, executive. **Personal:** Born Apr 8, 1937, Lyndhurst, VA; son of Roxie E Burgess and Lacy; married Regina L Crick; children: Darnel, Tina, Dori & Alexander. **Educ:** Ohio Christian Col, BTh, summa cum laude, 1972; Univ Pittsburgh, BA, cum laude, 1976, MSW, 1977; Bible Philos Int Sem, PhD, summa cum laude, 1984. **Career:** US Steel, laborer, 1955-64; Westinghouse Air Brake, tester, 1964; Auburn & Assocs, design draftsman, 1964-68; Kaiser Engs, design draftsman, 1968-72; Mt Zion Baptist Church, W Newton, PA, pastor, 1971-74; Mon Yough Community Servs Inc, dir consult & educ, 1972-85, human resources dir, 1985-; First Baptist Church, Donora, PA, pastor, 1974-78; St John Baptist Church, Wilmerding, PA, pastor, 1979-81; Metrop Baptist Church, Northside, Pittsburgh PA, pastor, 1981-; Dept State Bur Prof & Occup Affairs, pastor. **Orgs:** Bd dir, Govs Justice Comn; bd dir, Auberle Home Boys; bd dir, Coun & Tutoring Serv; McKeesport Area Sch Dist, Parents Adv Coun; Baptist Ministers Conf Pittsburgh & vicinity; vpres, Northside Pastor's Alliances; Nat Asn Advan Colored People; bd dir, Res & Planning Comt, Mon Valley Health Ctr; Boy Scouts Am. **Honors/Awds:** Humanitarian Award for

Outstanding Achievement, Mon-Yough Community Serv Inc, 1985; Humanitarian Award, Parents Adult Ment Ill, 1986; Outstanding Employee Award, Mon-Yough Community Serv Inc, 1986; Outstanding Service Award, Auberle Homes Boys, 1987. **Home Addr:** 1501 Libr St, McKeesport, PA 15132-4716, **Home Phone:** (412)673-1750. **Business Addr:** Pastor, Metropolitan Baptist Church, 22 Sampsonia Way, Pittsburgh, PA 15212-4475, **Business Phone:** (412)231-2554.

### RICHARDSON, LATANYA
Actor. **Personal:** Born Jan 1, 1949, Atlanta, GA; married Samuel L Jackson; children: Zoe. **Educ:** Spelman Col, BA, theater, 1974; NY Univ, MA, drama. **Career:** Film appearances: Hangin' with the Homeboys, 1991; The Super, 1991; Fried Green Tomatoes, 1991; Lorenzo's Oil, 1992; Juice, 1992; Malcolm X, 1992; Sleepless in Seattle, 1993; The Last Laugh, 1994; When a Man Loves a Woman, 1994; Losing Isaiah, 1995; Lone Star, 1996; Julian Po, 1997; Secrets, 1998; Loved, 1998; US Marshalls, 1998; The Fighting Temptations, 2003; Freedom land, 2006; Blackout, 2007; All About Us, 2007; Blackout, 2007; Mother and Child, 2009; TV series: "One Life to Live", 1968; "Life Choice", 1991; "Frannie's Turn", 1992; "Sisters of Mercy", 1992; "Midnight Run for Your Life", 1994; "Private Lives", 1994; "A Memory Play", 1994; "Cutting Edges", 1995; "Heavin' Can Wait", 1995; "Betrayal", 1997; "Call Him Johnny", 1998; "Judging Amy", 1999; "100 Centre Street", 2001; "Chapter Sixty-Two", 2003; TV movies: The Nightman, 1992; Shameful Secrets, 1993; Losing Isaiah, 1995; The Deliverance of Elaine, 1996; Introducing Dorothy Dandridge, 1999; Within These Walls, 2001; "100 Centre Street", 2002; "Boston Public", 2003; "Harry's Law", 2011; Hairstory, director, 2000; "The Watsons Go to Birmingham", 2013. **Honors/Awds:** Frederick D. Patterson Award, United Negro Col Fund. **Business Addr:** Actress, Framework Entertainment, 9057 Nemo St Suite C, West Hollywood, CA 90069, **Business Phone:** (310)281-4868.

### RICHARDSON, LAURA
**Personal:** Born Apr 14, 1962, Los Angeles, CA; married Anthony Batts. **Educ:** Univ Calif, BA, 1984; Univ Southern Calif, MA, 1996. **Career:** Xerox Corp, 1987; Govt off; Long Beach City, Councilwoman, 2000-06; Calif State Assembly, Assemblymember, 2006-07; State Govt Off; congressperson; Us House Representatives, rep, 2007-. **Orgs:** Comt Sci & Technol; New Dem Coalition; Cong Asian Pac Am Caucus. **Business Addr:** Representative, Capitol Office, 1725 Longworth House Off Bldg, Washington, DC 20515, **Business Phone:** (202)225-7924.

### RICHARDSON, DR. LEO O.
Government official, executive director. **Personal:** Born Dec 19, 1931, Marion, SC; son of Ethel and Isiah; married Mary Jane Frierson; children: Sandra Jane, Alfred Leo & Beverley Lynette. **Educ:** Morris Col, BS, 1954; Tuskegee Univ, MA, 1961; State Univ NY, Buffalo, PhD, 1985. **Career:** Athletics, dir, 1961; Dept Health & Phys Educ, 1961; Morris Col, head football & basketball coach, 1961-64; Savannah State Col, head football coach, 1964-68, basketball coach, 1964-71, asst prof biol, 1964; State Univ New York, Buffalo, head basketball coach & adminr, 1972-84; SC Dept Social Servs, asst to comnr 1984-86, dep comnr, 1986; Sc Inst Poverty & Deprivation, exec dir, currently. **Orgs:** Nat Asn Basketball Coaches, 1971-78; Nat Asn Basketball Coaches Clin Comt, 1974-76; Buffalo Urban Caucus, 1974-78; Black Educr Assoc Buffalo, 1975-76; PUSH Inc, 1976; Nat Assoc Basketball Coaches Res Comn, 1976-78; Comt Action Orgn, educal task force comt, 1977-84; Buffalo Pub Schs, task force discipline chmn, 1979; sports adv comt chmn, 1979-80; bd dir, Nat Asn Advan Colored People, 1979-82; pres, Housing Assistance Ctr Niagara Frontier Inc, 1979-82; chmn, Dept Educ, adv comm single parents/homemakers & sex equity pgms 1985; bd trustee, Francis Burns United Methodist Church, 1985; Leadership Columbia, 1986; Alpha Phi Alpha Frat; Morris Col Bd trustee; Leadership SC Bd Regents; St. Mark's Wood Neighborhood Asn; City Columbia Com Revolving Loan Fund Rev Bd; City Columbia Strategic Planning Bldg Strength Group; Columbia Rotary Club; bd trustee, Morris Col; bd dir, Cities Schs, Columbia, Sc; pres, Morris Col Nat Alumni Asn. **Home Addr:** 241 King Charles Rd, Columbia, SC 29209, **Home Phone:** (803)783-0989. **Business Addr:** Executive Director, South Carolina Institute on Poverty & Deprivation, 2219 2 Notch Rd, Columbia, SC 29202, **Business Phone:** (803)256-7219.

### RICHARDSON, LEON T.
Manager, executive. **Personal:** Born Dec 1, 1964, Nashville, GA; son of Joe Lee King; married Alfreda; children: Demetrius Leon. **Educ:** Stillman Col, BA, commun & human resources, 1987. **Career:** Shaw Industs, prod supvr, 1987, training mgr, 1990, human resources supv, 1993, regional human resources mgr, 1997, corp employee resources mgr, currently; COI, human resources mgr, 2001-05; Mediacom Commun, sr human resource mgr, 2005-. **Orgs:** Kappa Alpha Psi, dean pledges, 1985; Big Bro Big Sister, 1997; Dr MLK Comt Serv, 1997. **Honors/Awds:** Stillmam CLG, Dean's List, 1984-86. **Home Addr:** 506 Mack Dr, Valdosta, GA 31602-1600. **Business Addr:** Manager, Shaw Industries Inc, 616 E Walnut Ave, Dalton, GA 30722-2128, **Business Phone:** (800)441-7429.

### RICHARDSON, LEROY
Basketball executive, manager. **Personal:** Born Aug 21, 1964, Brooklyn, NY. **Career:** Va High Schs, off; Calif Basketball Asn, off; NBA, referee, currently. **Orgs:** Mentor, speaker, Tidewater Detention Ctr, Chesapeake, VA; Youth Ministries New First Baptist Church, Portsmouth, VA; Nat Basketball Referees Asn. **Honors/Awds:** Sailor of the Year, Training Group Atlantic, 1991-92; United States Navy Sailor of the Year, Damneck, VA, 1991-92; Navy Achievement Medal-Surface warfare qualification, 1992-93; Officiated 2003 NBA All-Star Saturday Game and 2003 Japan Games; Officiated the 2000 Schick Rookie Game. **Home Addr:** PO Box 61993, Virginia Beach, VA 23466. **Business Addr:** Member, NBA Referee, National Basketball Referees Association, 1455 Pennsylvania Ave NW Suite 225, Washington, DC 20004, **Business Phone:** (202)638-5090.

### RICHARDSON, LINDA WATERS
Executive. **Personal:** Born Nov 21, 1946, Philadelphia, PA; daughter of Lester Waters and Bertha Stovall; married Albert J Pitts; children: Aissia, Tarik, Monifa & Mariama. **Educ:** Over brook HS, Bus, 1964; Southern Nh Univ, MS, community econ develop, 1990. **Career:** BEDC Inc, asst dir, 1971-73; Peoples Fund, coord, 1973-74; Philadelphia Clearing House, dir, 1974-81; Black United Fund, exec dir, 1982-89, pres, chief exec officer; Uptown Entertainment & Develop Corp, pres, 1995-; Richard & Assoc, owner, 2000-. **Orgs:** Nat Black United Fund, 1983-89; Willingboro Home & Sch, 1986; African Am Mus Philadelphia, 2012; adv comt, Episcopal Community Serv; Interfaith Revolving Loan Fund; Women Philanthropy; Asn Black Found Execs; African Am United Fund; gov's adv, African Am Affairs. **Honors/Awds:** Merit Chapel 4 Chaplains, 1985; Community Leadership Award, Comm Leadership Seminars, 1985; Minority Mental Health Advocacy Task Force Award, 1989. **Home Addr:** 181 Northampton, Willingboro, NJ 08046. **Business Addr:** President, Uptown Entertainment & Development Corp Inc, 2227 N Broad St Suite 2F, Philadelphia, PA 19132, **Business Phone:** (215)236-1878.

### RICHARDSON, LITA RENEE (LITA SPENCER)
Manager, lawyer. **Personal:** Born Nov 24, 1964, San Diego, CA; daughter of Victor and Barbara Nason; married Leonard; children: Abi Olajuwon & Lauren. **Educ:** Rice Univ, Jesse H. Jones Grad Sch Bus, BBA, 1986; Univ Houston, Bates Sch Law, JD, 1988. **Career:** NASA Space Ctr, stud intern, 1981; Judge Michael O'Brien, law clerk, 1986-88; Brown, Collett & Pryce, atty, 1990-91; Reed & Assoc, atty, 1992-97; Magic Johnson Mgt Group, personal mgr & ent vpres, 1997-; supermodel Beverly Johnson; Doctors Tv Show, producer & atty. **Orgs:** Alpha Kappa Alpha Sorority, 1983-; La County Bar Assoc, 1990-; State Bar Calif, 1990-; Black Women Lawyers Assoc, 1990-; Black Child Develop Inst, 1992-; Women Film, 1998-; vpres, Magic Johnson Mgt Groups; former entertainment atty, John Singleton; entertainment atty, Regina King, Miguel Nunez; entertainment atty, Vanessa Bell Calloway. **Special Achievements:** Manage the careers of over 20 television & film personalities. **Home Addr:** 4570 Van Nuys Blvd Suite 432, Sherman Oaks, CA 91403, **Home Phone:** (323)956-8932. **Business Addr:** Entertainment Vice President, Magic Johnson Management Group, 9100 Wilshire Blvd St 700 E Twr, Beverly Hills, CA 90212, **Business Phone:** (310)247-2033.

### RICHARDSON, MAJ. LONNEAL
Administrator. **Career:** Salvation Army Midland Div, St Louis, Mo, div comdr, currently. **Business Addr:** Commander, Salvation Army Midland Division, 1130 Hampton Ave, St. Louis, MO 63139, **Business Phone:** (314)646-3000.

### RICHARDSON, REV. LOUIS M., JR.
Executive, government official, clergy. **Personal:** Born Nov 7, 1927, Johnstown, PA; son of Lewis and Leatha Elizabeth Hemphill; married Allie; children: April, Louis III, Emmett, Alan T, Hope C, Peter & Holly A. **Educ:** Livingstone Col, BA, 1955; Hood Theol Sem NC, BD, 1958. **Career:** First AME Church, minister, 1964-; NJ State Employ Serv, counr, 1967-70; Paterson Bd Educ, vpres, 1969-74; OIC, pres, 1970-71; Martin Luther King Comm Ctr, dir, 1970-73; Paterson CETA Prog, dir, 1973-76; Varick Memorial AME Zion Church, pastor, 2005-08, relig leader; City Paterson City Hall, affirmative action coordr. **Orgs:** Paterson Rotary Club No 70, 1970-74; pres, Alpha Phi Alpha Frat; presiding elder, Jersey City Dist. **Honors/Awds:** Citizenship Award, Paterson Teachers Asn, 1971. **Home Addr:** 347 E 38th St, Paterson, NJ 07504-1327, **Home Phone:** (973)278-1145. **Business Addr:** NJ.

### RICHARDSON, DR. LUNS C.
Educator, association executive. **Personal:** Born Apr 29, 1928, Hartsville, SC. **Educ:** Bendict Col, AB, 1949; Columbia Univ Teachers Col, MA, 1958. **Career:** Denmark Tech Educ Ctr, dean, 1949-64; pastor, 1958; St Helena HS, prin, 1964-66; Wilson HS, prin, 1967-68; Benedict Col, staff & actg pres, 1967-73, Col Educ Achievement Proj, coordr, dir Basic Studies, assoc dean, Instnl Self-study Reaffirmation Accreditation, dir, dean admis; Voorhees Col, vpres, 1973-74; Morris Col, pres, 1974-. **Orgs:** Chmn, Com Res & Spec Proj, Southern Asn Cols & Schs; bd dir, SC State CC; bd dir Sumter C C; Wateree Comt Actions Bd; adv bd, Citizens & Southern Bank Sumter; Omega Psi Phi Frat; NEA; Am AsnHealth Educ; Am Acad Polit & Social Sci; SC Educ Asn; Sumter Co Econ Develop Admin Com; Sumter Human Rels Coun; Nat AsnAdvan Colored People; Alpha Kappa Mu Hon Soc; Phi Delta Kappa; SC Higher Educ Tuition Grants Comn; bd dir, United Negro Col Fund. **Honors/Awds:** Hon Ped D Benedict Col; Hon LHD Morris Col; Citation Links, 1973; Citation Voorheez Col BD Trustees, 1974; Outstanding Alumnus Award, Benedict Col; Outstanding Alumnus Award, Columbia Univ; Order of the Palmetto, conferred Gov Beasley, 1996; SC Black Hall of Fame, 1997; named one of 60 "20th Century Press Who Have Influenced Higher Edu Landscape", Black Issues Higher Educ, 1999. **Home Addr:** PO Box 471, Hartsville, SC 29550. **Business Addr:** President, Morris College, 100 W College St, Sumter, SC 29150-3599, **Business Phone:** (803)934-3225.

### RICHARDSON, DR. MADISON FRANKLIN
Otolaryngologist, surgeon. **Personal:** Born Dec 26, 1943, Prairie View, TX; son of William; married Constance; children: Kelly, Kimberly & Karen. **Educ:** Howard Univ, BS, 1965, MD, 1969. **Career:** Walter Reed Med Ctr, residency otolaryngol, dir, dir head, chief, head & neck surg, 1974-76; Johns Hopkins Hosp; Martin Luther King Hosp, chief head & neck surg, 1977-; Voice Inst Beverly Hills, dir; Unic Calif Los Angeles, fac; USC, Dept Surg, fac; Cedars Sinai Med Ctr, clin chief otolaryngol, currently; Otolaryngol Specialist, pvt practr, currently; Calif Med Bd. **Orgs:** Bd chair, Los Angeles Urban League, 1984-87; pres, Charles Drew Med Soc, 1984-85; chief surg serv, Daniel Freeman Hosp, 1986-87; pres, bd chair, Nat Urban League, 1986; Calif Med Bd, 1987-; bd dir, Charles Drew Med Sch, 1988; bd dir, Salerni Collegium; Alpha Omega; pres, Med Soc; bd mem, KCET; bd mem, Los Angeles Opera; bd mem, Los Angeles Philharmonic; gov, US Polo Asn; Ctr Study Serv; fel Am Col Surgeons; Socs Head Neck Surgeon. **Honors/Awds:** Member of Distinction, Los Angeles AME Church, 1982; Meritorious Award, La NAACP, 1983; Distinguished Alumnus, Howard Univ, 1987; Appointee of Governor to California Medical Board, 1988; America's Top Doctors, Center for the Study of Services; Charter Day Alumni Award, Howard Univ, 2003. **Home Addr:** 814 S Hudson Ave, Los Angeles, CA 90048, **Home Phone:** (323)935-8255. **Business Addr:** Clinical Chief of Otolaryngology, Cedars-Sinai Medical Center, 8700 Beverly Blvd, Los Angeles, CA 90048, **Business Phone:** (310)423-3277.

### RICHARDSON, DR. MARY MARGARET
School administrator. **Personal:** Born Feb 19, 1932, Christian County, KY. **Educ:** Ky Community Col, AA, 1970; Valdosta State Col, BSN, 1973; Med Col Ga, MSN, ment health & psychol nursing, 1974; Univ Southern Miss, EdD, 1994. **Career:** Educator (retired); Brooks Hosp, officer nurse, 1952-72; Western Ky State Ment Hosp, clin nurse, 1956-71; Jennie Stuart Memorial Hosp, pvt duty nurse, 1970-71; Col Manor Hosp, part time head nurse, 1974-75; Univ N Ala Florence, Sch Nursing, asst prof, 1974-75; Med Col, Grad Sch Nursing, asst prof, 1975; Valdosta State Col, asst prof nursing, 1975-78, assoc prof nursing, 1978-80, prof, asst dir nursing, dept head, 1981, undergrad studies, asst dean stud develop. **Orgs:** Nat League Nursing; Am Nursing Asn; Ga League Nursing; Ga Nurses Asn; Ky Fed LPN; Am Asn Univ Prof; Am Asn Univ Women; task force leader, Fac Develop Proj, SREB Valdosta State; Sigma Theta Tau, Epsilon Pi Chap; Hosp Authority Valdosta-Lowndes County; bd mem, Lowndes Co Partnership Health; VSU Found; VSU Col Nursing Adv Bd. **Honors/Awds:** Fed Traineeship Scholar, 1973; Nursing Endowment Dinner, Valdosta State Col; Honored Richardson with Profiles in Caring Award, Valdosta State Univ Col Nursing, 2012; Distinguished Alumna of the Year, Valdosta State Univ, 2015. **Home Addr:** 415 Northside Dr, Valdosta, GA 31601. **Business Addr:** Assistant Dean for Student Development, Valdosta State University, 1500 N Patterson St, Valdosta, GA 31698, **Business Phone:** (229)333-5800.

### RICHARDSON, MATTHEW STATISFIELD. See RICH, MATTY.

### RICHARDSON, MUNRO CARMEL
Consultant, executive. **Personal:** Born Jul 24, 1971, Pittsburgh, PA; son of Frederick and Dianna; married Teresa Hu; children: Melina, Kara & Neela. **Educ:** Lincoln Col Prep Acad, 1989; Univ Kans, BA, E Asian lang & cultures, 1993; Harvard Univ, MA, E Asia regional studies, 1995; Oxford Univ, MPhil, int rels, 1996; Univ Ill, Urbana-Champaign, PhD, polit sci, 2010. **Career:** Us Dept State, intern, 1995; Us Senate, Comt Foreign Rels, legis asst, 1996, prof staff mem, 1997-98; Greater Kans City Community Found, mgr community leadership, 1998-2000; Inner City Consul Group, managing dir, 2000-01; BCT Partners Inc, co-founder, 2000-02; Kauffman Found, dir, 2002-10, vpres, 2010-12; myEDmatch, co-founder, chief operating officer, 2012-13; LigoSphere, co-founder, chief exec officer, 2014-15; Read Charlotte, exec dir, 2015-. **Orgs:** Nat Asn Advan Colored People; bd dir, United Inner City Serv, 2000-; City Plan Comn, City Kans City, MO, 2000-01; bd secy, Hisp Econ Develop Corp, 2000-; bd, Int Rels Coun, 2000-; adv bd mem, Confucius Inst Univ Kans, 2006-15; bd mem, Ewing Marion Kauffman Sch, 2010-; bd mem, Kauffman Scholars Inc, 2012-; bd mem, Turn Page KC, 2013-15; Phi Beta Kappa; staff mem, comt foreign Rels US Senate. **Honors/Awds:** National Achievement Scholar, Nat Merit Corp, 1989; Golden Key, Golden Key Nat Hon Soc, 1992; Rhodes Scholar, Rhodes Trust, 1994; Up and Comers Award, Junior Achievement of Greater Kansas City, 2000. **Business Addr:** Executive Director, Read Charlotte, 220 N Tryon St, Charlotte, NC 28202, **Business Phone:** (704)666-5717.

### RICHARDSON, NOLAN, JR.
Basketball coach, basketball player. **Personal:** Born Dec 27, 1941, El Paso, TX; son of Nolan Sr and Clareast (deceased); children: Madalyn, Bradley & Nolan III; married Rose Davila; children: Yvonne (deceased) & Sylvia. **Educ:** Tex Western Col, El Paso, BA, 1964. **Career:** Basketball player (retired), basketball coach; UTEP Miners basketball, forward, 1961-64; Bowie High Sch El Paso, Tex, coach, 1968-78; Western Tex Jr Col, coach, 1978-81; Univ Tulsa, head coach, 1981-85; Univ Ark, head basketball coach, 1985-2002; Panamanian Nat Team, head coach, 2005-07; Mex Nat Team, head coach, 2007-; Tulsa Shock, head coach & gen mgr, 2009-11. Films: The Sixth Man, 1997; He Got Game, 1998. **Orgs:** Bd dir, Am Red Cross; chmn, Easter Seal. **Home Addr:** 2539 E Joyce St, Fayetteville, AR 72703.

### RICHARDSON, ODIS GENE
Writer, educator. **Personal:** Born Nov 29, 1940, Lake Charles, LA; son of Lucky Sip and Estella Scott; children: Ron Pressley & Odis G II. **Educ:** Univ Tampa, BS, 1965; Chicago State Univ, MA, 1971; Roosevelt Univ, MS, 1983; Northwestern Univ, post grad studies. **Career:** Educator (retired), writer; Boy Scouts Am, exec, 1965-66; Dept Pub Assistance, social caseworker, 1966-67; Chicago Pub Sch, teacher, 1967-, free lance writer, currently. **Orgs:** Chicago Debate Comn(CRS), 1998, Small Schs Movement, Du Sable Urban Ecol Sanctuary Bd; pub rels chmn, Ill Speech & Theatre Asn, 1985-86; pres bd dir, Maranatha Youth Ministries, 1985-87; fel, Northwestern Univ, 1986; IL Coun Except C; dir, Richardson Spec Educ Consults; Phi Beta Sigma, Phi Delta Kappa, Chicago Urban League, Nat Asn Advan Colored People; deacon S Shore Bible Baptist Church; Emergency Land Fund; bd dir, Chicago Citizens Schs Comt, 1987-89; fel, Golden Apple Found, life mem, 1986-89; res linker, Chicago Teacher's Union, Educ Res & Develop; vol proj Image, Man-BoyConf, 1988-89; precinct capt, Fourth Ward Reg Dem, 1981-; teacher sponsor, PAPPA Club, Pan African Pen Pal Asn, 1988-89; writer & diarist, Catalyst Mag-Chicago Sch Reform, 1990-91; bd dir, Don Nash Community Ctr; bd dir, Marantha Youth Ministries Head Start; pres, Gary pub libr, 2014-. **Home Addr:** 8108 S Eberhart, Chicago, IL 60619, **Home Phone:** (773)846-9473. **Business Addr:** President, Gary Public Library, 1835 Broadway, Gary, IN 46407, **Business Phone:** (219)886-9120.

### RICHARDSON, OTIS ALEXANDER, SR.
Executive. **Personal:** Born Jan 16, 1943, Newport News, VA; son of Mildred C and Carey D; married Corrine Foots; children: Otis Alexander II & Shamagne Nicole. **Educ:** Hampton Univ, BS, acct & finance, 1965; Pace Univ, MBA, exec mgt, 1978; Kennedy-Western Univ, PhD, bus admin, 1999. **Career:** Johnson & Johnson, nat sales mgr, 1979-80, dir sales planning & develop, 1980-82, dir prof markets, 1982-83, dir new prod develop, 1983-85, group prod dir, 1985-86; Oral Health USA Inc, pres, chief exec officer, 1986-. **Orgs:** Nat

Asn Accts, 1965-72; Am Acad Dent Group Practices, 1981-89; steering comt, Nat Asn Dent Labs, 1985-86; corp sponsor, Nat Dent Asn, 1986-92; Dent Group Mgt Asn, 1987-90. **Honors/Awds:** Clinician Commerative Award, Nat Dent Asn, 1983; Clinician Commerative Award, MAC Dent Technol, 1985. **Special Achievements:** Numerous articles and seminars including Clinical Marketing Techniques for Dental Labs, 1984-86; Practice Building for Dental Groups, 1980-84; "Make That Dental Center Your New Account", Dental Lab Review, 1986; State of Art-Dental Restoratives, 1990; Presentation & Seminar, Use of Color in Dentistry, 1991. **Home Addr:** 32 Coventry Cir, Piscataway, NJ 08854-5251, **Home Phone:** (732)572-4308. **Business Addr:** President, Chief Executive Officer, Oral Health USA Inc, 44 Stelton Rd Suite 200, Piscataway, NJ 08854-2663, **Business Phone:** (732)424-3435.

**RICHARDSON, POOH. See RICHARDSON, JEROME, JR.**

**RICHARDSON, RALPH H.**
Lawyer. **Personal:** Born Oct 12, 1935, Detroit, MI; son of Ralph Onazime and Lucinda Fluence; married Arvie Yvonne; children: Traci, Theron (deceased), Cassandra Jo Williams, Arvie Lyn Williams & Tanya Elaine Hunter. **Educ:** Wayne St Univ, BA, 1964; Wayne St Law Sch, JD, 1970. **Career:** City Detroit, clerk, pub aid worker, 1956-65; Ford Motor Co, sr labor rel rep, 1965-70, wage admin, 1966, labor rel rep, 1967; Citizens Urban Opportunity Fund, dir, 1970; Brown Grier & Richardson PC, sr partner, 1970-71; Richardson & Grier PC, sr partner, 1971-73; Stone & Richardson PC, labor arbitrator & sr partner, 1973-. **Orgs:** App by Gov to serve bd appealsHosp Bed ReductionSE Mich, 1982; app spec asst atty Gen by Frank J Kelley, Atty GenState Mich, 1984; master, Hiram Lodge #1, 1986; comdr-in-chief, Wolverine Consistory #6 1988; Marracci Temple #13, potenate, imp potentate, imp legal adv, Shriners, 1988; David Leary Lodge #6, GEM, knight templar, 1989; Optomist Club, 1990-; Mich State Bar Fel, 1990-; eminent comdr, Eureka Comdry #1 Knights Templars, 1995; most eminent grand comdr, Grand Comdry Knights TemplarsState Mich, 1997; grand sr deacon most worthy Grand Lodge Stat Mich, Prince Hall Affil (PHA); Wolverine Bar Asn; Am Arbit Asn; Mich Trial Lawyers Asn; Am Judicial Soc; Mich Criminal Defense Lawyers; Phi Alpha Delta, Kappa Alpha Psi; Smithsonian Inst; Nat Geog Soc; Recorder's Ct Bar Asn; Labor Arbitrators; Am Arbit Asn; Thirty-Third degree Mason; Greater Detroit Chamber Com; Palmer Woods Asn; Econ Club Detroit; Renaissance Club; Detroit Bar Asn; Nat Bar Asn; State Bar Mich; Am Bar Asn; Am Trial Lawyers Asn; Mich Asn Prof; Boy Scouts Am; exec bd, Detroit Golden Gloves Inc; bd dir, Legal Aid & Defenders Asn 5; Jr Vice Polemarch Northern Reg. **Honors/Awds:** Cert of Appreciation Native Am Strategic Serv, 1976; MI State Bar Young Lawyers Sect Prison Project Service Award, 1977; Award of Merit Mother Waddles Perpetual Mission, 1979; Distinguished Recognition Award, Detroit City Coun, 1981; Spirit of Detroit Award, 1981, Honored Citizen Award, Mayor Coleman Young, Distinguished Detroit Citizen Award, 1981; Office of the City Clerk James Bradley, 1981; life membership, NAACP, 1983; contributing supporter Golden Heritage (NAACP), 1989; Appointed to committee on Child Care Homes by City Council member Mehaffey, 1988-89; hon special agent, office of Inspector General, US Printing Office, 1997; Featured in Michigan Super Lawyers, 2006. **Home Addr:** 2910 E Jefferson Ave, Detroit, MI 48207, **Home Phone:** (313)393-6700. **Business Addr:** Labor Arbitrator, Senior Partner, Stone & Richardson PC, 11000 W McNichols Suite 103, Detroit, MI 48221, **Business Phone:** (313)340-7771.

**RICHARDSON, RHONDA KAREN**
Government official. **Personal:** Born Dec 8, 1956, Louisville, KY; daughter of Charles Robert and Dorothy Bryant. **Educ:** Fisk Univ, Nashville, TN, BA, psychol; Univ Louisville, JD, 1987. **Career:** Crawford Law Centre, PC, owner, 1983-; City Louisville, 10th Ward, bd aldermen, 1990-; pvt pract atty, 2014-. **Home Addr:** 9719 Grandin Woods Rd, Louisville, KY 40299, **Home Phone:** (502)582-1942. **Business Addr:** Attorney, Private Practitioner, 934 S 6th St, Louisville, KY 40203-3318, **Business Phone:** (502)584-8861.

**RICHARDSON, ROBERT EUGENE**
Lawyer. **Personal:** Born Jul 16, 1941, Kansas City, MO; son of Joseph and Genevieve; married Shirley Ann Durham; children: Kerri L & Patrick G. **Educ:** Georgetown Univ, Wash, DC, BA, polit sci & govt, 1972; Georgetown Univ Law Sch, JD, 1975. **Career:** Georgetown Univ, asst exec vpres, 1970-74, Dir Affirmative Action Progs, 1972-75; Mediator, atty law, 1976-; US Gen Serv, asst legal policy coordr, 1975-76; US Dept Justice Civil Div, trial atty, 1976-78, spec asst asst atty gen, 1977-79, sr trial atty, 1979-85; Howard Univ, exec asst vpres legal affairs & gen coun, 1986-87, pvt pract atty, agency owner, 1986-95; US Dept Veterans Affairs, admin atty, 1995-2012; mediator, Fed courts, 1995-; vol atty, AARP Legal Coun, 2012. **Orgs:** Alpha Phi Alpha Fraternity. **Honors/Awds:** Academic Fellow Whitney M Young, 1973-75. **Home Addr:** 1371 Underwood St NW, Washington, DC 20012, **Home Phone:** (202)726-3131. **Business Addr:** Attorney, US Department of Veterans Affairs, 810 Vt Ave NW, Washington, DC 20420, **Business Phone:** (202)461-0905.

**RICHARDSON, DR. ROGER GERALD**
School administrator, educator, vice president (organization). **Personal:** Born Dec 23, 1953, Chicago, IL; son of Eddie and Ella Brown. **Educ:** Univ Wis-Stout, BA, psychol, 1976, coun & guid, 1979; NY Univ, PhD, higher educ admin & planning, 2001. **Career:** Univ Wis-Stout, Educ & Culturals Enrichment Ctr, coordr, 1976-79, dir black stud servs, 1979-80; Col Human Ecol, Cornell Univ, admin mgr, counr, 1980-84, actg dir, coun servs, assoc dir minority educ affairs & state progs 1984-85; Dartmouth Col, asst dean residential life, 1986-88; NY Univ, dir, African-Am Stud Serv, 1988-99; Ithaca Col, dir off multicultural affairs, 2000-02, asst vpres, stud affairs & campus life, 2002-06, assoc vpres acad & stud affair, dean, 2006-15, assoc provost, 2015-; Inst Higher Educ Leadership, Wash, DC, educ policy fel. **Orgs:** Am Asn Higher Educ; Col Stud Personnel Asn; Nat Asn Stud Personnel Adminr; One Hundred Black Men Inc; chmn, Affirmative Action Task Force; Educ Opprtunity Adv Bd, Cornell; Chancellors Task force Diversity Conflict Stud Life Comt, New york Univ; Ithaca City Sch Dist Bd Educ, 2003-06; trustee, New Roots Charter Sch; adv bd, Ithaca New York. **Home Addr:** 1 Washington Sq Village, New York, NY 10012, **Home Phone:** (212)979-1615. **Business Addr:** Associate Vice President, Dean, Ithaca College, 341 Egbert Hall, Ithaca, NY 14850-7181, **Business Phone:** (607)274-1623.

**RICHARDSON, SALLI (SALLI ELISE RICHARDSON-WHITFIELD)**
Actor. **Personal:** Born Nov 23, 1967, Chicago, IL; daughter of Duel and Marcia Harris; married Dondre T; children: Parker W & Dre Terrell W. **Educ:** Univ Chicago Lab Schs, grad, 1985. **Career:** Kuumba Workshop, actor; Films: Mo' Money, 1992; Prelude to a Kiss, 1992; How U Like Me Now, 1993; Sioux City, 1994; Posse; A Low Down Dirty Shame, 1994; Once Upon a Time When We Were Colored, 1996; The Great White Hype, 1996; Rude Awakening, 1998; Butter, 1998; Lillie, 1999; Book of Love, 2002; The Antwone Fisher Story, 2002; Baby of the Family, 2002; Biker Boyz, 2003; Anacondas: The Hunt for the Blood Orchid, 2004; I Am Legend, 2007; Black Dynamite, 2009; Pastor Brown, actor & co-producer, 2009; I Will Follow, 2010; We the Party, 2012; Playin' for Love, 2013; TV series: "Roc", 1991; "Star Trek: Deep Space Nine", 1993; "New York Undercover", 1994; "I Spy Returns", 1994; "Lily in Winter", 1994; "Soul of the Game", 1996; "True Women", 1997; "Stargate SG-1", 1997; "The Pretender", 1998; "The Jamie Foxx Show", 1999; "True Women", 1997; "Gargoyles", 1994-96; "Rude Awakening", 1998; "Family Law", 1999-2002; "Antwone Fisher", 2002; "CSI: Miami", 2003; "Line of Fire", 2004; "Second Time Around", 2004; "NYPD Blue", 2004; "1-800-Missing", 2005; "The War at Home", 2005; "House M.D.", 2005; "Eureka", actress, 2006-12, dir, 2011-12; "Bones", 2006; "I Am Legend, 2007; "Sports Medicine"; "Criminal Minds", 2009; Co Host: "Midnight Soul", 2007; "The Secret Lives of Wives, 2012; "The Finder", 2012; "The Newsroom", 2012-13; "Teachers", actress & exec producer, 2013; "NCIS", 2013-14; "House of Lies", 2014; "Castle", 2014. **Business Addr:** Actress, Craig Dorfman & Associates, 6100 Wilshire Blvd Suite 310, Los Angeles, CA 90048, **Business Phone:** (323)937-8600.

**RICHARDSON, TIMOTHY LEE**
Consultant, association executive, president (organization). **Personal:** Born Jul 28, 1958, Los Angeles, CA; son of Irving and Christeale Dandridge; married Ayoka Chenzira; children: Camille & Bradley. **Educ:** W Los Angeles Col, AA, 1980; Chapman Univ, George L Argyros Sch Bus & Econs, Orange, CA, BS, bus admin & mkt, 1986. **Career:** Boys & Girls Club Tustin, Calif, prog dir, 1980-85; Boys & Girls Clubs Am, Hollywood, Calif, Olympic Sport Prog, coord, 1985-89, sr dir sports, fitness & recreation, vpres mil serv & int proj & sr dir prog serv, 1987-2009; New York, NY, Atlanta, Ga, Nat Prog Servs, asst dir, 1989-94, dir, 1994-96, sr dir, 1997-; Sports Spirit Newspaper, founding ed, 1987-90; Legacy Int LLC, pres & chief exec officer, 2009-; MLK Ctr Nonviolent Social Chg, consult prog & resource develop, 2011; Kognito, mil & govt outreach, 2013-14. **Orgs:** Exec comt, US Table Tennis Asn, 1986-91; deleg, US Olympic Acad XI, 1987; bd mem, US Olympic Comt, 1989-, dir; Athlete Identification & Develop Comn, 1990-93, bd dirs, Women's Sports Found, 1990-95; head US deleg, Int Olympic Acad, Olympia Greece, 1992; panelist, Nat Strategic Planning Forum, 1993; Educ Comt, 1993-; consult, Asn Better Zambian Youth Proj, 1993; asst envoy, Centennial Olympic Games, 1996; assoc, Cult Enrichment Found; Pres Coun Phys Fitness & Sports; consult, Jackie Joyner Kersee Youth Found; consult, Southern Christian Leadership Conf; consult, Inkanta Freedom Party Youth Brigade; bd mem, Nat Recreation Found; bd mem, Nat Guard Youth Found; bd mem, Maynard Jackson Youth Found. **Honors/Awds:** Coach of the Year, Nat Youth Sports Coaches Asn, 1983; Womens Sports Found President Award, 1995; US Olympic Committee Rings of Gold Award; RJ McElroy Award, Univ Northern Iowa; US Coast Guard Guiding Principles Award; National Guard Bureau Minuteman Award. **Special Achievements:** NIKE Kids Movement Summit, organizer, 1993; Secured a $3 million congressional grant to serve children of Desert Storm war; author, Boys & Girls Club Guide to Military Outreach; negotiated with US Air Force, Marine Corps & Navy to convert on-base youth centers into Boys and Girls Clubs, 1995-96; Nike Youth Sports Summit, organizer, 1996; NIKE PLAY Daily, Nat Youth Fitness Prog, co-creator & proj mgr; US Information Agency. **Home Addr:** 4155 Sheppard Crossing Way, Stone Mountain, GA 30083-4598. **Business Addr:** President, Chief Executive Officer, Legacy International LLC, 14 Jackson St SE, Atlanta, GA 30312, **Business Phone:** (404)295-5637.

**RICHARDSON, TONY (ANTONIO RICHARDSON)**
Football player. **Personal:** Born Dec 17, 1971, Frankfurt; son of Ben. **Educ:** Auburn Univ, BEd, 2000; Webster Univ, MBA, 2004. **Career:** Football player (retired); Dallas Cowboys, 1994; Kansas City Chiefs, full back, 1995-2005; Minn Vikings, full back, 2006-07; New York Jets, full back, 2008-09, full back, running back, 2010. **Orgs:** Derrick Thomas Acad; founder, Rich Spirit Found, 2000; chmn, Buck Buchanan Spec Olympics Sports Festival, 2000; Good Guys Sports, Sporting News, 2002, 2003, 2004; exec comt, Nat Football League Players Asn. **Honors/Awds:** Ed Block Courage Award, 2000, 2001; Arthur S Arkush Humanitarian of the Year, Pro Football Weekly, 2003; Distinguished Citizen Award, Nat Conf Community & Justice, 2005; Four times Pro Bowl, 2003, 2004, 2005, 2007; Whizzer White Man of the Year, Nat Football League, 2010; Walter Payton Award, 2010. **Special Achievements:** Spokesperson for Various Program. **Home Addr:** , Long Island City, NY.

**RICHARDSON, VALERIE K.**
Financial manager, manager, consultant. **Personal:** Born Aug 5, 1955, Oakland, CA; daughter of Clyde Sr and Clarice; married Victor E Richardson II; children: Whitney K & Victor E III. **Educ:** San Jose State Univ, BA, 1981; St. Mary's Col Calif, MBA, 2004. **Career:** Ketchum Communs, res asst, 1978-81; Mc Kesson CRP, proj mgr, 1982-86; Mervyn's CRP, media/mkt planner, 1986-87; Pac Gas & Elec Co, CPN mkt analyst, 1988-, eval/qual control specialist, 1991-2007, supvr measurement & eval, 1997-2008, mgr outreach & eval, 2006-07; KEMA Inc, sr prin consult, 2007-; DNV GL, prin consult, 2008-. **Orgs:** Am Asn BlacksEnergy; Am Mkt Asn; chair, Vermont Pub Serv Bd. **Home Addr:** 173 Highland Ave Apt A, San Francisco, CA 94110-5846, **Home Phone:** (415)441-7803. **Business Addr:** Senior Principal Consultant, KEMA Inc, 67 S Bedford St Suite 201E, Burlington, MA 01803-5177, **Business Phone:** (781)273-5700.

**RICHARDSON, DR. WALTER T.**
Clergy. **Personal:** Born Jul 2, 1948; son of Walter H and Poseline M; married Dolores; children: Walter L & LaKisha. **Educ:** Miami-Dade Community Col, music, 1968; St Thomas Univ, BA & MA, relig, 1989; Trinity Col & Theol Sem, PhD, coun, 1995; Harvard Divinity Sch, cert, relig, 2004. **Career:** Omega Psi Phi Fraternity, chaplain, 1967-2011; St Thomas Univ, adj prof, 1989-; Miami-Dade Police Dept, sr chaplain, 1989-; Sweet Home Missionary Baptist Church, Perrine, FL, sr pastor emer, 1983-2010; Dr Walter T Richardson Ministries, pastor, currently. **Business Addr:** Pastor, Dr Walter T Richardson Ministries, PO Box 570248, Miami, FL 33257.

**RICHARDSON, WAYNE MICHAEL**
Lawyer. **Personal:** Born Sep 22, 1948, Philadelphia, PA. **Educ:** Cheyney State Col, BA, 1970; Temple Univ Law Sch, JD, 1976. **Career:** Pa Dept Educ, regional legal coun, 1976-83; Pa State Syst Higher Educ, first chief legal coun, 1983-95; Rutgers Univ, Dept Gen Servs, asst coun, 1995-96, employ & labor coun, 1996-2002; Fairleigh Dickinson Univ, gen coun & secy, 2002-11, consult atty, currently. **Orgs:** Alpha Phi Alpha Fraternity Inc, 1968-; bd dir, Nat Asn Col & Univ Attys, 1977-; bd trustees, Pa Fac Health & Welfare Trust Fund, 1995; bd dir, Nat Asn Col & Univ Attorneys, 1999-2001; trustee & treas, Syst's Fac Health & Welfare Trust Fund; secy bd dir, Fairleigh Dickinson Univ Brit Columbia Found. **Honors/Awds:** Distinguished Service Award, Comn Univs, Pa State System Higher Educ, 1995; Distinguished Service Award, United Cerebral Palsy Asn Capital Area, 1996; Citation, Nat Asn Col & Univ Attys, 2002; Distinguished Service Award, Nat Asn Col & Univ Attorneys, 2012. **Home Addr:** 688 Cranbury Cross Rd, Bryn Mawr, PA 19010-4205, **Home Phone:** (732)342-8448. **Business Addr:** Consulting Attorney, Secretary, Fairleigh Dickinson University, 1000 River Rd H-DH3-03, Teaneck, NJ 07666, **Business Phone:** (201)692-7003.

**RICHARDSON-WHITFIELD, SALLI ELISE. See RICHARDSON, SALLI.**

**RICHIE, DR. BETH E.**
College teacher. **Educ:** Cornell Univ, Ithaca, NY, BSW, 1979; Wash Univ, St Louis, MO, MSW, 1980; City Univ NY, Grad Sch & Univ Ctr, New York, NY, PhD, sociol, 1992. **Career:** Inter Am Univ, San Juan, Dept Sociol, adj instr, 1983-84; City Univ New York, Hunter Col, Prog Community Health Educ, from adj instr to instr, 1984-91, Prog Community Health Educ, from asst prof to assoc prof, 1992-98, Undergrad Prog Community Health Educ, prog dir, 1993-94; Winston Churchill fel, 1987; New Sch Social Res, Grad Fac Polit & Social Sci, NY, vis fac, 1993; Univ Ill, Chicago, IL, Womens Health Policy fel, 1994, Ctr Res Women & Gender, fel, 1994-95, Depts Criminal Justice & Gender & Women Studies, assoc prof, 1998-2002, Great Cities Inst, fac scholar, 2001-02, Dept African-Am Studies, head & assoc prof, 2002-03, chairperson & prof, 2003-; Inst Res Race & Pub Policy, dir; Books: Black Women, Male Violence and the Build-up of a Prison Nation; Compelled to Crime: The Gender Entrapment Of Battered Black Women, 1996; Articles: "Battered Black Women: A Challenge for the Black Community", 1985; "Gender Violence Incarceration and Women's Health: The Prevalence of Abuse History Among Newly Incarcerated Women in a New York City Jail", 1986; "Linking Women In Jail To Community Services: Factors Associated With Rearrest and retention of Drug-Using Women Following Release From Jail", 1998; "Coming Up In the Boogie Down: The Role of Violence in the Lives of Adolescents in The South Bronx", 1999; "Exploring the Link between Violence Against Women and Women's Involvement in Illegal Activity", 2000; "A Black Feminist Reflection on the Antiviolence Movement", 2000; "Reintegrating Women Leaving Jail Into Urban Communities: A Description of A Model Program", 2001; "Challenges Incarcerated women Face as They Return to Their Communities: Findings From Life History Interviews", 2001; "From Over the Wall: Writing About Women In Prison", 2004; "Coming Home From Jail: The Social and Health Consequences of Reentry from Jail for Incarcerated Women and Male Adolescents, their Families and Communities", 2005. **Orgs:** Ctr Fathers, Families & Pub Policy; Chicago Found Women; Chicago Black Feminist Network; mentor, Women Community Serv, US Dept Health & Human Servs, Violence Against Women Grants Rev Panel; Mortar Bd Hon Soc, 1979; consult, Social Sci Res Coun; consult, Nat Inst Corrections; Incite Women Color Against Violence; Steering Comt Inst Domestic Violence African Am Community. **Home Addr:** 4616 S Woodlawn, Chicago, IL 60653, **Home Phone:** (773)624-4505. **Business Addr:** Professor, Head, University of Illinois, BSB 4044 1007 W Harrison St, Chicago, IL 60607, **Business Phone:** (312)355-2468.

**RICHIE, LEROY C.**
Lawyer, executive. **Personal:** Born Sep 27, 1941, Buffalo, NY; son of Leroy C and Mattie Allen; married Julia C Thomas; children: Leroy, Lamont, Loren, Brooke & Darcy. **Educ:** City Col NY, BA, philos, 1970; NY Univ Sch Law, JD, 1973. **Career:** White & Case NY, atty, 1973-78; Fed Trade Comns NY Off, dir, 1978-83; Chrysler Corp, asst gen coun, 1983-84, assoc gen coun, 1984-86, vpres & gen coun, 1990-97; Intrepid World Commun, pres, 1998-99; Capitol Coating Technol Inc, chmn & chief exec officer, 1999-2000; Kerr-McGee Corp, dir, 1998-, chmn audit comt, 2003-; Q Stand World Wide Inc, chmn & chief exec officer, 2000-; bd dir, J.W. Seligman & Co, 2000-; Digital Ally, lead outside dir & chmn, 2005-. **Orgs:** Bd dir, Infinity Energy Inc, 1999-; independent dir, Tri-Continental Corp, 2000-; coun, Lewis & Munday PC, 2005-; independent dir, OGE Energy, 2007-14; dir, Columbia Seligman Commun & Info Fund Inc, 2008-; trustee, Columbia Seligman Premium Technol Growth Fund Inc, 2009-; Columbia Funds Ser Trust II - Columbia Seligman Commun & Info Fund,2011-; chmn, Vis Nurse Asn; chmn, Highland Pk Develop Corp; bd mem, Marygrove Col; bd mem, St Josephs Hosp, Pontiac; bd mem, Detroit Bar Found; gen coun, US Golf Asn; secy, Detroit's Mus African Am Hist; officer, Detroit Black Chamber Com; mem bd dir, RiverSource Funds; mem bd dir, J.&W. Seligman & Co; mem bd dir, Vibration Control Technologies; mem bd dir, Great Lakes Assemblies; Am Bar Asn; chmn, HP Devco; chmn & co-founder, Detroit Pub Schs

Found; chmn, Brazeal Dennard Chorale; chmn, Plowshares Theater Co; cvice chmn, Detroit Med Ctr & Detroit Econ Growth Corp; independent trustee, Columbia Funds Trust II - Columbia Mid Cap Value Fund; bd dir, Ameriprise Financial Inc; dir, Okla Gas & Elec Co & Infinity Inc; trustee, New York Univ Law Ctr Found. **Honors/Awds:** Arthur Garfield Hays Civil Liberties Fellowship Award, NY Univ Law Sch, 1972; Lifetime Achievement Award, Crain's Detroit Bus. **Special Achievements:** Only African American in the top ranks of the giant Detroit automaker, Chrysler Corp; First African American to serve as general counsel to the Executive Committee of the US Golf Asn, 1992; First African American accepted into the extremely exclusive Bloomfield Hills Country Club, 1992. **Home Addr:** 585 Shirley Rd, Birmingham, MI 48009-1642, **Home Phone:** (248)644-3562. **Business Addr:** Lead Outside Director, Digital Ally, 9705 Loiret Blvd, Lenexa, KS 66219, **Business Phone:** (913)814-7774.

### RICHIE, LIONEL BROCKMAN, JR.

Songwriter, actor, singer. **Personal:** Born Jun 20, 1949, Tuskegee, AL; son of Lionel Brockman Sr (deceased) and Alberta R Foster; married Diane Alexander; children: Miles Brockman & Sofia; married Brenda Harvey; children: Nicole Camille Escovedo & Nicole. **Educ:** Tuskegee Univ, attended 1974. **Career:** The Mystics; The Commodores; Brockman Music, Los Angeles, CA, pres; Songs: "Truly", writer & producer, 1982; "All Night Long", 1983; "Hello", 1984; "Say You, Say Me", writer & producer, 1985, "Are We Done Yet?", 2007; "Lady", writer & producer; "All Night Long", writer & producer; "Can't Slow Down"; writer & producer; "Dancing on the Ceiling", writer & producer; "Easy", writer & producer; "Three Times a Lady", writer & producer; "Still", writer & producer; "Sail On", writer & producer; "Am the Beautiful", composer, 2001; "Undercover Brother", composer, 2002; "House of 1000 Corpses", composer, 2003; "Grattis Victoria", composer, 2004; "80s", composer, 2005. Films: Endless Love, songwriter & composer; Scott Joplin, actor, 1977; Thank God It's Friday, actor, 1978; Live Aid, actor, 1985; We Are the World, 1985; The Preacher's Wife, actor, 1996; Pariah, actor, 1998; The Simpsons, 2007; Who Do You Think You Are?, 2011; Lionel Richie: Dancing On the Ceiling, 2011; Oprah Winfrey's Master Class, 2014. Albums: Time, 1998; Renaissance, 2000; Encore, 2002; Just for You, 2004; Coming Home, 2006; Are We Done Yet?, 2007; Baby Mama, 2008; Tropic Thunder, 2008; Duplicity, 2009; Tuskegee, 2012. Transformers: Revenge of the Fallen, 2009; Just Go, 2009; Tuskegee, 2012. **Orgs:** United Negro Col Fund; Am Soc Composers, Authors & Publishers; Nat Acad Rec Arts & Sci; Am Acad Motion Picture Arts & Sci; Nat Asn Song writers. **Honors/Awds:** Three Platinum Albums; 4 Gold Albums; American Award, 1979, 1982, 1983, 1984, 1985 & 1987; People's Choice Award for Best Song, 1979, 1980, 1982, 1983 & 1986; Best Young Artist in Film, 1980; Nat Music Publications Award, 1980, 1981 & 1984; People's Choice Award for Best Composer, 1981; Grammy Award, 1982, 1985 & 1986; American Movie Award, 1982; Image Award, Nat Asn Advan Colored People, 1983; Black Gold Award, 1984; Man of the Year, Children's Diabetes Foundation, 1984; Alumnus of the Year, United Negro Col Fund, 1984; Writer of the Year, Am Soc Composers, Authors & Publishers, 1984, 1985 & 1986; Publisher of the Year, Am Soc Composers, Authors & Publishers, 1985; ABAA Music Award, 1985; Honorary Degree in Music, Tusee Univ, 1986; Academy Award, 1986; Golden Globe Award, 1986; Entertainer of the Year Award, NAACP, 1987; Pop Award, Am Soc Composers, Authors & Publishers, 1987; American Music Academy Award, 1987; Favorite Male Vocalist, Soul/R&B Award, Am Music Acad, 1987; Star, Hollywood Walk of Fame, 2003; Golden Note Award, Am Soc Composers, Authors & Publishers, 2008; George & Ira Gershwin Lifetime Achievement Award, Univ Calif, Los Angeles, 2008. **Special Achievements:** Grammy nominee 18 times; Grammy Award, Producer of the Year, 1982, Producer of the Year, 1984, Album of the Year, 1984, Song of the Year, 1985; Golden Globe Award, 1986. **Business Addr:** Composer, 5750 Wilshire Blvd, Los Angeles, CA 90036.

**RICHIE, DR. WINSTON HENRY.** **See Obituaries Section.**

### RICHMOND, DELORES RUTH

Real estate agent. **Personal:** Born May 28, 1951, Chicago, IL; daughter of Arthur Lee and Mamie Elizabeth McBride; married Larson; children: Tesha Elizabeth, Dwayne L & Nicole L. **Educ:** Real Estate Educ Sch, S Holland, Ill, cert, 1985; Ramah Consortium Bibl Inst Theol, BA, pastoral coun, MA, pastoral coun, PhD, ministry, 2007. **Career:** Ill Dept Ins, agt & producer; US Fed Govt, Chicago, Ill, adminr, 1970-79; Continental Bank, Matteson, Ill, asst supr, 1981-84; TV 38 Christian Sta & Radio, Chicago, Ill, studio audience coordr, 1984-87, Christian Tribune article, columnist-writer; Mt Olive Theol Bible Col, Flossmoor, IL, vpres; Century twenty one Dabbs & Assoc, Homewood, Ill, broker, asso relocation dir, 1985; Richmond GMAC Real Estate, owner & pres, 1999-. **Orgs:** Homewood Full Gospel Church, 1981-; Nat Asn Advan Colored People, 1982-; pres, Today Your Day, 1985-, bd dir, Century Twenty One Dabbs & Assoc, 1986-; Jack & Jill, 1988-; publicity dir & pres, Women's Coun Realtors, 1988-; UNCF, 1989-; pres, Rich Star, 1990; Asn W-S Suburban Chicago; bd dir, Prof Stand & Grievance Comt; Ill Asn Realtors; Greater Northwest Ind Asn Realtors; Ind Asn Realtors; founder & chief exec officer, Mothers Informing Mothers Int Ministry, 1997; Nat Asn Realtors; Notary Pub-State Ill; Grad Real Estate Inst GRI; vpres, Women's Coun Realtors, 2004, pres, 2005-07; chairperson, St James Hosp & Health Care Ctr, 2005; chairperson, Chicago Community Health Ctr, 2006; state pres, Ill State Chap Women N Power, 2006-. **Honors/Awds:** Bronze, Silver, & Gold medals, Ill Asn Realtors, 1985-94; Centurian Award, Nat Century 21, 1985-91; Appreciation Award, Ford Motor Co, 1987, 1988, 1989; Kizzy Award, Kizzy Scholar Fund Found, 1989; Abbey Foundation Award, 2003; has received hundreds of other real estate awards. **Special Achievements:** Stockbroker Series 6 & 22, Lic, 1992. **Home Addr:** 20223 St Andrews Dr, Olympia Fields, IL 60461, **Home Phone:** (708)503-0797. **Business Addr:** Owner, President, Richmond GMAC Real Estate, 3309 Vollmer Rd, Flossmoor, IL 60422, **Business Phone:** (708)647-9200.

### RICHMOND, JACQUELINE

Executive. **Career:** Acad Educ Develop, sr health mkt & commun specialist. **Business Addr:** Senior Health Marketing, Communications Specialist, Academy for Educational Development, 1825 Connecticut Ave NW, Washington, DC 20009.

### RICHMOND, MITCH (MITCHELL JAMES RICHMOND, III)

Basketball player, basketball executive. **Personal:** Born Jun 30, 1965, Ft. Lauderdale, FL; son of Ernell O; married Juli; children: Phillip, Jerin & Shane. **Educ:** Moberly Area Jr Col; Kans State Univ, BA, soc sci, 1988. **Career:** Basketball player (retired), basketball executive; Golden State Warriors, guard, 1988-91, spec asst, scout, currently; Sacramento Kings, guard, 1991-98; Wash Wizards, guard, 1998-2001; Los Angeles Lakers, guard, 2001-02. **Orgs:** Founder, Solid As a Rock Found, 1992; bd mem, Nat Comm Prevent Child Abuse; Nat Basketball Asn. **Business Addr:** Scout, Golden State Warriors, 1011 Broadway, Oakland, CA 94607, **Business Phone:** (510)986-2200.

### RICHMOND, MYRIAN PATRICIA

Government official. **Personal:** Born Sep 28, 1942, Birmingham, AL; children: Brian & Kevin. **Educ:** Lane Col, BA, 1965; Atlanta Univ, attended 1972. **Career:** Beau ford City Sch, teacher, 1967-69; Onyx Corp, consult, 1973-75; WAOK Radio, writer/reporter, 1973-76, news dir, 1976-78; Fulton City Govt, info officer, beginning 1978, dep dir, dept info & pub affairs; MPR Creative Works, pres. **Orgs:** Alumna Leadership, Atlanta 1980-; TV show host, GA Pub TV, 1981-84; consult, Martin L King Ctr, 1982-84; Atlanta Asn Black Journalists, 1984-85; bd mem, Neighborhood Arts Ctr, 1984-85. **Home Addr:** 2649 The Fontainebleau SW, Atlanta, GA 30331-2719, **Home Phone:** (404)344-3827.

### RICHMOND, RODNEY WELCH

Labor activist, vice president (organization). **Personal:** Born Jul 25, 1940, Washington, DC; son of Vernon and Ella Welch; married Joyce Reeves; children: Inga, Anthony & Ronda. **Educ:** Howard Univ, Wash, DC, BA, 1977; Am Univ, Wash, DC, attended 1985; Univ DC, Wash, DC, attended 1986. **Career:** Wash Metrop Transit Authority, Wash, DC, bus operator, 1962-86; Amalgamated Transit Union, Wash, DC, int vpres, 1986-. **Orgs:** Res Civil Sheriff, Civil Sheriff's Off, 1989-. **Home Addr:** 5573 Stillwater Dr, New Orleans, LA 70128, **Home Phone:** (504)245-1377. **Business Addr:** International Vice President, Amalgamated Transit Union, 2701 Whitney Pl, Forestville, MD 20747, **Business Phone:** (301)568-6899.

### RICHO, ANNA

Vice president (organization). **Educ:** Cornell Univ, BS, indust & labor rels; DePaul Univ Col Law, JD. **Career:** Baxter Healthcare Corp, chief litigation coun, 1991-97; Baxter-Bioscience, vpres Law, 1997-2003; Amgen Inc, vpres, law, 2003-08, sr vpres & chief compliance officer, 2008-12; Univ Calif, Berkeley, exec vpres & gen coun, 2012-. **Orgs:** Co-chair, Straus Inst Coun Distinguished Advisors, Pepperdine Univ's Sch Law; bd dir, Cytyc Corp, 1998-03. **Honors/Awds:** "Black Enterprise", 75 Most Powerful Women in Business, 2010.

### RICKMAN, RAY

State government official, business owner, association executive. **Personal:** Born Nov 25, 1948, Galatin, TN; son of James Bailey and Betty (Richards) Rickett. **Educ:** Eastern Mich Univ, Ypsilanti, attended 1968; Wayne State Univ, Detroit, BA, 1971. **Career:** US Congressman John Conyers, Detroit, chief asst, 1971-74; Jeff Chalmers Non-Profit Corp, exec dir, 1974-77; Harmony Village Non-Profit Corp, exec dir, 1977-79; Mass Medicaid Handicapped Prog, dir, 1979; Police Abuse Housing Issues, lectr; Providence Human Rels Comn, exec dir, 1979-, providence equal opportunity officer; Affirmative Action, consult; Mass Housing Finance Agency, assoc dir compliance off, 1982-85, assoc dir; Cornerstone Bks, owner, 1985-; Gen Assembly RI, state rep, 1986-96; Shades-Talk Show, host, producer, 1986-; RI Secy State, dep secy, 2000-02; Lifespan Diversity Off, asst dir, 2004-06; Adopt A Doctor, founder & pres, 2003-; Shape Up RI, pres, chief advisor, currently. **Orgs:** Pres, Friends Belle Isle, Detroit, 1974-78; bd mem, ACLU RI, 1979-80; bd mem, Nat Asn Advan Colored Perople, RI Chap, 1980-82; bd mem, Langston Hughes Ctr, 1986-89; comnr, Providence Hist Dist Comn, 1986-; bd mem, RI Hist Soc, 1989-, secy; Affirmative Action & Equal Opportunity Dir, City Providence, 2003-; pres, RI Black Heritage Soc; treas, Heritage Harbor Mus; secy, Ri Hist Socs; RI Coun; sr policy dir, Shape Up RI. **Home Addr:** 11 Barnes St, PO Box 2591, Providence, RI 02906-0591, **Home Phone:** (401)861-7244. **Business Addr:** Founder, President, Adopt A Doctor, 101 Dyer St, Providence, RI 02903, **Business Phone:** (401)421-0606.

### RICKS, MIKHAEL ROY

Football coach, executive, football player. **Personal:** Born Nov 14, 1974, Galveston, TX; married Kristi; children: Kiera. **Educ:** Stephen F Austin State Univ, grad. **Career:** Football player (retired), coach, executive; San Diego Chargers, wide receiver, 1998-2000; Kans City Chiefs, 2000-01; Detroit Lions, tight end, 2002-03; Velocity, San Diego, sports performance dir; Dallas Cowboys, 2004; Mr. Sports Performance Fitness, sports performance & fitness coach, currently. **Honors/Awds:** Most Valuable Player of Blue-Gray Game, 1998. **Special Achievements:** Street named in honor Anahuac, Texas; FCS record for yards per reception (29.8 yards per catch). **Home Addr:** 3840 Amalfi Dr, Hollywood, FL 33021-3026. **Business Addr:** 2170 NE 123rd St, N Miami, FL 33181, **Business Phone:** (305)892-1200.

### RICKSON, GARY AMES

Executive, artist, poet. **Personal:** Born Aug 12, 1942, Boston, MA; children: Mary Pendeton, Kianga Akua, Tianee Rayna & Alea Sekua. **Career:** Boston African Am Artist, pres, 1964-68; Monographs & Solo Exibs: Boston Negro Artists Asn, 1967; Reflections Within & Without: Black Artist, 1968; Rose Art Mus, 1969; Contemp Crafts Inc, 1969, 1976; Mus Nat Ctr Afro-Am Artists, 1969 & 1971; Afro-Am Artist: A Search Identity, 1973; Harvard Radio Boardcast Corp, artist-poet, 1974-84; Persistence & Discontinuity Traditional Perception Afro-Am Art, 1975; Art & Ethnics: Background Teaching Youth Pluralistic Soc, 1977; Kalamazoo Pub Libr, 1980; Nat Endowment Arts, 1981; Community Murals: People's Art, 1984; Twentieth-Century Am Art, 1985 & 2002; Boston Pub Libr, 1991; Scarecrow Press, 1991; Toward People's Art: Contemp Mural Movement, 1998; Walls Heritage, Walls Pride: African Am Murals, 2003; artist, currently. **Orgs:** Cult adv, Roxbury YMCA, 1984-85; Boston Urban Gardeners, 1984-; pub rels, founder, Boston African Am Artists, 1985-; Roxbury Boys Club, 1970. **Honors/Awds:** Outstanding Roxbury Citizen Award, Black Bros Assoc, 1970; Nat Endowment Grant, 1970; Champ of Black Youth Award, Roxbury Boys Club, 1970. **Special Achievements:** Began Mural Movement in Boston in 1968; Author of the Black Artist Bible 21st Century Artist, 1998. **Home Addr:** 107 Dewitt Dr, Roxbury, MA 02119. **Business Addr:** Artist, Gary A Rickson Studio, 107 DeWitt Dr, Roxbury, MA 02120, **Business Phone:** (617)445-2823.

### RICO, DR. TRACEY

Physician, artist. **Educ:** Bd cert emergency & pediat emergency med; Howard Univ, MD, 1992. **Career:** Physician, artist; Quilts: Aunt Jemima's Debut; Our Glory; A Talisman Coffled; Mammy's Cakewalk, 2002; Bamboozled, 2002; Beth Israel Hosp, emergency care physician; Maimonides Med Ctr, pediat emergencies physician; Brooklyn Hosp, emergency residency; pvt pract, currently; Jade Rico Designs, owner & artist, currently. **Special Achievements:** One of a handful of residency & fellowship-trained physicians in the United States who has Board Certification in both Emergency and Pediatric Emergency Medicine. **Home Addr:** 2234 Rogers Ave, Los Angeles, CA 90023-1223. **Business Addr:** Artist, Owner, Jade Rico Designs, 5482 Wilshire blvd suit 1630, Los Angeles, CA 90036.

### RIDDICK, EUGENE E.

Engineer, manager. **Personal:** Born Jan 23, 1938, Lee Hall, VA; son of James Wesley and Gertrude Burks Reid; married Evelyn G McNeese; children: Eric. **Educ:** Howard Univ, BSME, 1961; State NJ, Prof Engrs lic, 1970; State Ky, PE lic, 1989; State Wyo, PE lic, 2003; Can PE, Ont, 2003. **Career:** Gibbs & Cox Inc, asst engr, 1963-64; MW Kellogg, sr engr, 1964-70; Badger Engrs Inc, mgr, fired heaters, 1970-74, mgr, piping eng, 1974-79, mgr, eng aux, 1979-82, mgr, heat transfer, 1982-95; Kinetics Technol Intl Corp, mgr, heat transfer group, 1995-99; Technip USA, mgr mech group & task force chmn, 1999-. **Orgs:** Am Soc Mech Engrs, 1972-; chmn, Am Petrol Inst Mfg & Contractors S/C Fired Heaters, 1984-94; treas, First Parish Unitarian Church, 1980-82, chmn, Art Comt, 1980-87. **Honors/Awds:** Black Achiever of 1989, Boston YMCA, 1989; Raytheon Black Achievers Alumni, 1990-95; Certificate of Appreciation, Am Petrol Inst, 1994, 1999. **Home Addr:** 14161 Heathervale Dr, Chino Hills, CA 91709-5902. **Business Addr:** Manager Mechanical Group, Technip USA Corp, 555 W Arrow Hwy, Claremont, CA 91711-4805, **Business Phone:** (909)447-3600.

### RIDDLE, R. LUCIA

Vice president (organization). **Educ:** Drake Univ, MBA. **Career:** Executive (retired); Prin Financial Group, vpres fed govt rels, 1997-2012; Sister Strength LLC, owner, 2012-. **Orgs:** Am's Health Ins Plans (AHIP); Am Benefits Coun (ABC); Am Coun Life Insurers (ACLI); Bus Roundtable (BRT); Financial Serv Roundtable (FSR); Securities Indust & Financial Mkt Asn (SIFMA); bd mem, Smithsonian Nat Mus African Art; bd mem, Exec Leadership Coun; bd mem, Des Moines Art Ctr; bd mem, African-Am Experience Fund Nat Parks Serv (AAEF); bd mem, Nat Coalition & Caucus Black Aged; bd mem, Americans UNFPA; fel Fel Life Mgt Inst (FLMI); Wash Govt Rels Group; Alpha Kappa Alpha Sorority; Sigma Iota Epsilon; Links Inc; exec comt, Planned Parenthood Action Fund; Guttmacher Inst, exec comt.

### RIDEAU, IRIS

Business owner. **Personal:** Born New Orleans, LA; married Jimmy; children: Renee & gentleman. **Career:** Rideau Ins Agency, owner, 1967-99; Rideau Retirement Planning Consults Inc, owner; Rideau Securities Firm, owner, 1982; Rideau Vineyards, vintner & owner, 1997-. **Orgs:** Chmn, Mayor's Affirmative Action Comt, 1973-76. **Honors/Awds:** Business Innovator of the Year, Black Enterprise, 2004. **Special Achievements:** Part time model for Victoria's Secret; featured in numerous magazines; only African-American female winery owner in the United States; first woman appointed to two national insurance companies. **Business Addr:** Owner, Rideau Vineyard, 1562 Alamo Pintado Rd, Solvang, CA 93463, **Business Phone:** (805)688-0717.

### RIDEAU, WIBERT

Journalist, editor, photographer. **Personal:** Born Feb 13, 1942, Lawtell, LA. **Career:** Angolite mag, ed, 1976-.ABC-TV, DayOne corresp, 1993-94; Fresh Air, WHYY-FM, corresp, 1994-95; Soros Justice Media, fel, 2007; consult, currently. **Orgs:** Pres, Angola Human Rels Club, 1997-. **Honors/Awds:** Charles C Clayton Award, Southern Ill Univ Sch Jour, 1977; Robert F Kennedy Jour Award, RFK Found, 1979; Silver Gavel Award, Am Bar Asn, 1979; The George Polk Award, Long Island Univ, 1980; The Sidney Hillman Award, Sidney Hillman Found, 1982; The Most Rehabilitated Prisoner in America, Life magazine, 1993; Golden Eagle Award, Coun on Int Non-Theatrical Events, 1995; Acad Award, Doc Feature, Sundance Film Fest, 1998; Champion of Justice Award, Nat Asn Criminal Defense Lawyers, 2005; Human Rights Award, Southern Ctr Human Rights, 2005. **Special Achievements:** Auth: "The Wall Is Strong: Corrections In Louisiana", USL, 1989, Second Edition, 1991, Third Editon, 1996; "Life Sentences: Rage & Survival Behind Bars", Times Books, 1992; "Unforgiven", Amy Bach, 2002. **Home Addr:** 75546 Ash 1 La State Prison, Angola, LA 70712. **Business Addr:** Editor, The Angolite Magazine, La State Penitentary, Angola, LA 70712, **Business Phone:** (504)655-4411.

### RIDENHOUR, CARLTON DOUGLAS (CHUCK D RIDENHOUR)

Rap musician, writer, journalist. **Personal:** Born Aug 1, 1960, Roosevelt, NY; son of Lorenzo; married Gaye Theresa. **Educ:** Adelphi Col, NY, Graphic Design. **Career:** New York, bike messenger; Pub Enemy, rapper, 1987-; Fox News Channel, commentator & corresp, 1998-; MP3 & file sharing technol, pub supporter, 2000; Albums: Lies, 1984; Shifting Gears; Check Out the Radio, 1984; Greatest Misses, 1986-92, 1992; Yo! Bum Rush The Show, 1987; It Takes A Nation of Millions to Hold Us Back, 1988; The Cinderella Theory, 1989; Fear Of A Black Planet, 1990; Apocalypse, 1991: The Enemy Strikes Black, 1991; Muse Sick n Hour Mess Age, 1994; Autobiography of Mistachuck, 1996; Revolverlution, 2002; How You Sell Soul To A Soulless People Who Sold Their Soul?, 2007; Songs: "Don't Believe The Hype", 1988; "Fight The Power", 1989; "911 Is A Joke"; "Kool Thing", 1990; "Causa E Efeito

", 2010, Rise Above: 24 Black Flag Songs to Benefit the West Memphis Three; Film appearances: Rhyme & Reason, 1997; Anthem, 1997; Voices of the Voiceless, 2001; Underground Poets Rr, 2003; Grand Theft Auto, 2004; Wake Up, 2004; Beyond Beats & Rhymes, 2006; The Black Candle, 2008; Anchorman: The Legend of Ron Burgundy; The Dillinger Escape Plan, 2011; TV Ser: "In Living Color", 1991; "Johnny Bravo", 1997; "Dark Angel", 2000; "Harlem Globetrotters", 2005; "Independent Lens"; "The Henry Rollins Show"; "Space Ghost Coast to Coast "; "Johnny Bravo"; Movie compositions: Less Than Zero, 1987; Do the Right Thing, 1989; Mo' Money, 1992; CB4, 1993; Shadow Boxing, 1993; Film: An Alan Smithee, 1997; Burn Hollywood Burn, 1997; He Got Game, 1998; Bulworth, 1998; Bamboozled, 2000; Paid in Full, 2002. **Special Achievements:** MTV "Enough Is Enough" antidrugs/antiviolence program, spokesperson, 1993; MTV News, reporter for Republican Convention, video music awards, 1998; co-author of Fight The Power: Rap, Race, Reality, 1997; Top 50 Hip-Hop Lyricists of All Time; Unfiltered, Air America Radio. **Business Addr:** Commentator, Correspondent, Fox News Channel, 1211 Avenue of the Americas, New York, NY 10036, **Business Phone:** (212)301-3000.

## RIDENOUR, LIONEL
Executive. **Career:** Arista Recs, exec vpres, sr national dir prom; La Face Recs, co-founder; Virgin Recs, exec vpres urban music, 2003-; MusicWerks Online, co-owner, 2008. **Business Addr:** Executive Vice President, Virgin Records, 304 Pk Ave S, New York, NY 10010, **Business Phone:** (212)253-3100.

## RIDER, ISAIAH, JR. (J R RIDER)
Basketball player. **Personal:** Born Mar 12, 1971, Oakland, CA. **Educ:** Allen County Community Col, attended 1990; Antelope Valley JC, attended 1991; Univ Nev, Las Vegas, NV, attended 1993. **Career:** Basketball player (retired); Minn Timberwolves, shooting guard, 1993-96; Portland Trail Blazers, shooting guard, 1996-99; Atlanta Hawks, shooting guard, 1999-2000; Los Angeles Lakers, shooting guard, 2000-01; Denver Nuggets, shooting guard, 2001-02. **Orgs:** Sky Rider Found. **Honors/Awds:** NCAA All-American Second Team, 1993; Big West Conference Player of the Year, 1993; All-Rookie First Team, Nat Basketball Asn, 1994; Slam Dunk Champion, Nat Basketball Asn, 1994; Espy Award, ESPN, 1995; Champion, Nat Basketball Asn, 2001. **Special Achievements:** Album: Funk in the Trunk, 1994.

**RIDER, J R. See RIDER, ISAIAH, JR.**

## RIDGEL, DR. GUS TOLVER
Vice president (organization), school administrator. **Personal:** Born Jul 1, 1926, Poplar Bluff, MO; son of Herford S and Lue Emma Davis; married Gertrude Cain; children: Betty Bolden. **Educ:** Lincoln Univ, BS, 1950; Univ Mo, Columbia, MO, MA, 1951; Univ Wis & Cath Univ Am, Madison, PhD, 1956. **Career:** Ft Valley State Col, Ft Valley, Ga, head dept bus, 1952-58; Wiley Col, Marshall, Tex, dean acad affairs, 1958-60; Ky State Univ, Frankfort, KY, dean, Sch Bus, 1960-84; Cent State Univ, Wilberforce, Ohio, vpres, acad affairs, 1972-74; Barber Scotia Col, Bus Affairs, vpres; Ky State Univ, pres, vpres; Southern Univ, Baton Rouge, vpres acad affairs, 1985; Ky State Col, vpres admin affairs, currently. **Orgs:** Adv bd, Repub Savings Bank, 1983-86; LA Univ, Marine Consortium Coun, 1986-; Dean, Sch Bus; Ford Found Study & Res Fel; Gen Elec Found Fel & Fulbright Fel. **Home Addr:** 312 Cold Harbor Dr, Frankfort, KY 40601-3082, **Home Phone:** (502)875-8368. **Business Addr:** Vice President, Ky State College, 400 E Main St, Frankfort, KY 40601, **Business Phone:** (502)597-6000.

## RIDGEWAY, DR. BILL TOM
Educator, zoologist. **Personal:** Born Aug 26, 1927, Columbia, MO; married Leta M Baker; children: Mark B, Myra Chesser & Beth A. **Educ:** Freidns Univ, Wichita, AB, 1951; Wichita Univ, MS, 1958; Univ Mo, Columbia, PhD, biol & biomed sci, 1966. **Career:** Wichita St Univ, grad res asst, 1956-58; SW Col, Winfield, KS, asst prof zool, 1958-66; Univ Mo, Columbia, asst prof zool, 1966; Eastern Ill Univ, Dept Zool, prof zool, 1966-95, Afro-Am Studies, dir, 1971-73, prof emer, 1995-; Ill Dept Conserv, contract res sci, 1970-; Univ Md, Natural Resources Inst, res assoc, 1974, vis prof, 1976. **Orgs:** Regional dir, Alpha Phi Alpha, 1969-77; treas, Concerned Citizens Charleston Assoc, Nat Asn Advan Colored People, 1975-; prog officer, 1981, presiding officer, 1985, Midwest Conf Parasitologists; Spec Ministries Comn, 1982, Soc Concerns Comn Episcopal Diocese Springfield; pres, Rotary Club Charleston, 1986. **Honors/Awds:** Graduate Fellowship in Zoology, Wichita State Univ, 1957; NSF Fellowship, Univ Wash Marine Sta, 1960; NSF Fellowship, Univ Mich Biol Sta, 1961-62; Research Fellowship in Zoology, Univ Mo, Columbia, 1963-66. **Home Addr:** 2614 S 5 St, Charleston, IL 61920-4109, **Home Phone:** (217)345-7418. **Business Addr:** Professor Emeritus, Eastern Illinois University, 600 Lincoln Ave, Charleston, IL 61920-3099, **Business Phone:** (217)581-5000.

## RIDGEWAY, WILLIAM C.
Executive. **Personal:** Born Sep 24, 1942, Selma, AL; married Charlotte A Nicholson; children: Traci L & Kristina L. **Educ:** Tenn State Univ, BSEE, 1965. **Career:** Chevy Motor Div, auto engr, 1965-67; IBM Corp, jr component engr, 1967-68, assoc component engr, 1968-69, sr assoc component engr, 1969-72, staff component engr, 1972-73, proj engr, 1973-76, proj mgr. **Orgs:** IBM Golf Club; IEEE; vpres, Sr Class Tenn St Univ. **Home Addr:** 4524 Royale Pk Ct, San Jose, CA 95136-2027, **Home Phone:** (408)629-8185.

## RIDLEY, DR. ALFRED DENNIS
Educator. **Personal:** Born Jun 23, 1948, Kingston; married Pamela; children: Andrew & Jon. **Educ:** Middlesex Univ, BSc, dipl elec & electronic engineering, 1969; Univ Wis, St Augustine, Trinidad, MSc, elec engineering, 1977; Clemson Univ, Clemson, SC, PhD, engineering mgt, 1982. **Career:** Jamaica Pub Serv Comn, mgr syst plng, 1970-79; Int Atomic Energy Agency, fel, 1977; Clemson Univ, lectr, 1979-82; George Mason Univ, asst prof decision sci, 1982-84; Howard Univ, asst prof info systs & anal, 1984-87; Fla A&M Univ, Sch Bus & Indust, assoc dir, assoc prof mgt scioper res & statist, prof prod & oper res mgt & global logistics, currently; Entrepreneurs Club, fac advisor. **Orgs:** Fel OAS, 1980; Eng Mgt Consult, 1983-. **Home Addr:** 9004 Glen Eagle Way, Tallahassee, FL 32312-4013, **Home Phone:** (850)668-0635. **Business Addr:** Professor Of Production & Operations Research Management, Global Logistics, Florida A&M University, Rm 410W 1 SBI Plz, Tallahassee, FL 32307-5200, **Business Phone:** (850)412-7730.

## RIDLEY, DR. CHARLES ROBERT
Educator. **Personal:** Born Aug 6, 1948, Philadelphia, PA; married Iris Rochelle Smith; children: Charles & Charliss. **Educ:** Taylor Univ, BA, bibl lit, 1970; Ball State Univ, MA, stud personnel admin, 1971; Univ Minn, PhD, coun psychol, 1978. **Career:** Veterans Admin Hosp, psychol intern, 1974-76; Ind Univ, Dept Coun & Guid, asst prof, 1977-79, dir training, 1993-99, 2006-07, Dept Coun & Educ Psychol, from assoc prof to prof, 1990-2007; Res & Univ Grad Sch, assoc dean, 1999-2005; Univ Md Col Pk, Dept Coun & Personnel Serv, asst prof, 1979-80; Personnel Decisions Inc, consult psych, 1980-83; Fuller Theol Sem Grad Sch Psych, from asst prof to assoc prof, 1983-90; Tex A & M Univ, prof & co-dir res core, 2007-. **Orgs:** Bd mem, Urban League Marion, Ind, 1971-73; Am Psych Asn, 1979-82, 1990-93,1995-98, 2002-04-; Consortium Instnl Coop, Acad Leadership Prog, 1992-93; chair, fel Am Psychol Asn, 2004-05; Soc Consult Psychol; Soc Coun Psychol; fel Consortium nstitutional Coop. **Honors/Awds:** Rsch Grant Spencer Found, 1978; "Clinical Treatment of the Nondis closing Black Client, A Therapeutic Paradox" Amer Psych, 1984; Division 17 of the American Psychological Association; Distinguished Alumni for Professional Achievement, Taylor Univ, 2001; Gus Meyers Center Award. **Special Achievements:** Published numerous books and articles between 1984-95. **Home Addr:** 1923 Jefferson Dr, Pasadena, CA 91104. **Business Addr:** Professor, Texas A & M University, 4225 TAMU 606 Harrington Off Bldg, College Station, TX 77843-4225, **Business Phone:** (979)862-6584.

## RIDLEY, JOHN
Television writer, television producer. **Personal:** Born Oct 1, 1965, Milwaukee, WI; son of John Ridley III and Terri; married Gayle Yoshida; children: 2. **Educ:** NY Univ, east asian lang & cult. **Career:** Stand-up comedian; Writer, producer & dir; Films: U Turn, screenplay & producer, 1997; Cold Around Heart, writer & dir, 1997; Three Kings, writer, 1999; Undercover Bro, screenplay & exec producer, 2002; Undercover Bro: Animated Ser, writer & exec producer, 2004; Justice League, writer, 2004; Bobby, co-producer, 2006; St Kings, producer, 2008; Red Tails, 2008; L.A. Riots, producer, 2010; TV ser: "John Larroquette Show", writer, 1993; Martin, writer, 1993-94; "Fresh Prince Bel-Air", writer, 1994; "Team Knight Rider", writer, 1997; Trinity, writer, 1998; "Static Shock", writer, 2000; "Third Watch", writer, 1999-2001; Chang Family Saves World, producer, 2002; I Got You, exec producer, 2002; "Platinum", dir, writer & exec producer, 2003; "Barbershop", exec producer, 2005; Wanda Sykes Show, head writer & co-exec producer, 2009; Novels: Stray Dogs, 1997; Love a Racket, 1998; Everybody Smokes Hell, 1999; A Conversation with Mann, 2002; Those Who Walk Darkness, 2003; What Fire Cannot Burn, 2006; Authority: Human Inside; MSNBC, "Morning Joe", contibr, 2007. **Business Addr:** Author, Alfred A Knopf Inc, 1745 Broadway, New York, NY 10020, **Business Phone:** (212)782-9000.

## RIDLEY, DR. MAY ALICE
School administrator. **Personal:** Born Nashville, TN; children: Donald G Jr & Yvonda P. **Educ:** Tenn State Univ, BS, 1959, MS, 1967; Univ Pittsburgh, PhD, US hist, 1982. **Career:** Metro Pub Sch, teacher, 1962-84; Univ Pittsburgh, asst prof, 1975-76; Tenn State Univ, adj prof, 1982-; Tenn State Dept Educ, Off Civil Rights, dir civil rights, 1984, exec dir off civil rights, currently. **Orgs:** Tenn State Bd Educ, 1981-; chair, Spec Schs Community, Tenn State Bd Educ, 1982-83; Metro Nashville Human Rels Comt; St Vincent de Paul Church; Alpha Kappa Alpha Sorority; Phi Delta Kappa Ed Frat; bd mem, Links Inc; Jr League Nashville; second vpres, Societas Docta Inc; Phi Alpha Theta Hon Soc. **Honors/Awds:** Alumnus of the Year, Tenn State Univ, 1978-79; Award of Appreciation from Nashville Mayor, 1979; Humanitarian Award, Tenn State Univ, 1985; Tenn Colonel State Honor. **Home Addr:** 2024 Jordan Dr, Nashville, TN 37218-2119, **Home Phone:** (615)244-4090. **Business Addr:** Executive Director, Tennessee State Department of Education, 26th Fl William Snodgrass Tower 312 8th Ave N, Nashville, TN 37243, **Business Phone:** (615)532-4982.

**RIDLOFF, LAUREN TERUEL. See TERUEL, LAUREN.**

## RIGGINS, JEAN
Executive. **Career:** Capitol Rec, vpres & gen mgr, 1983-93; Arista Rec, Black Music, sr vpres, 1993-96; Universal Rec, exec vpres & gen mgr, pres, head mkt, currently; Label, Black Music, pres. **Orgs:** YWCA, New York, 1999; exec bd mem, Nat Asn Black Female Execs Media & Entertainment. **Business Addr:** President, Universal Records, 1755 Broadway 7th Fl, New York, NY 10019, **Business Phone:** (212)373-0600.

## RIGGS, HON. ELIZABETH A.
Judge. **Personal:** Born Jan 2, 1942, Camden, NJ; children: Luke, Michael & Adam. **Educ:** Bennett Col, BA, 1963; Rutgers Univ Sch Law, JD, 1973. **Career:** San Diego Co Dist Atty, dep dist atty, 1974-77; State Calif, dep atty gen, 1977-79; Munic Ct, Gov, 1979; El Cajon Judicial Dist, judge munic ct, 1979-84, presiding judge, 1984-86, judge, 1985; Calif Judicial Col, inr, felony sentencing, 1986; Hastings Trial Advocacy Summer Sch, 1983-86; El Cajon, asst presiding judge, 1997; State Calif Munic Ct El Cajon Dist, judge, 1998-2002. **Orgs:** Dir, YWCA Greensboro NC, 1964-65; Camden City OEO; crd, Neighborhood Youth Corp; dir, Head Start, 1966-68; Rutgers Univ Proj, Talent Search, 1968-70; citizens adv bd, Rutgers Univ, 1970-73; Calif State Bar, 1974-; San Diego Co Black Atty's Asn, 1974-; Calif Asn Black Lawyers, 1976-; Dimensions, 1977-; Legal Aid Soc Lawyers Club, 1977-79; chmn, MNY Affairs Comn San Diego City Bar, 1978-79; bd dir, Black Atty Asn; Speakers Bur San Diego Co Nat Conf Negro Women; Mayors Comn Status Women; dimensions & charter 100 Prof Womens Asn; Nat Asn Women Judges; Calif Judges Asn; Co Women's Network; Soroptimist Int; Nat Bar Asn; founder, Black Attorneys Asn; San Diego Legal Aid Soc; bd mem, Urban League San Diego; bd mem, African-Am Mus Fine Art; Earl B Gilliam Bar Asn; bd dir, Urban League, 1989-91; founding chair, Earl B Gillman Bar Asn. **Honors/Awds:** Woman of the Year, San Diego Tribune, 1974; Black Achievement Award In Law, 1980; Delta Epsilon Chap Kappa Alpha Psi Award in Law, 1980; Distinguished Service Award, Black Student Union Grossmont College, 1981; Distinguished Service Award, 1982; Womens Criminal Defense Appreciation Award, 1983; Valuable Service Award, 1983; California Women Government Law & Justice Award; Commission Appreciation Award, Earl B Gillian Bar Asn, 1984; NAWJ, Moderator; Alice Paul Award, Nat Womens Polit Caucus, 1986; 39th Senate Districts Woman of the Year, Senator Christine Kehoe, 2007; Women's Hall of Fame, San Diego County, 2008. **Special Achievements:** Only African American woman judge ever appointed or confirmed in the history of San Diego County. **Home Addr:** 4346 Caminito De La Escena, San Diego, CA 92108. **Business Addr:** Judge, State of California Municipal Court El Cajon District, 250 E Main St, El Cajon, CA 92020-3941, **Business Phone:** (619)441-4336.

## RIGGS, GERALD ANTONIO
Football player. **Personal:** Born Nov 6, 1960, Tullos, LA; children: Gerald Jr. **Educ:** Ariz State Univ, grad. **Career:** Football player (retired); Atlanta Falcons, running back, 1982-88, Wash Redskins, running back, 1989-91. **Honors/Awds:** Post-season play: Pro Bowl, 1985-87; Two Times All-Pro, 1984-85. **Special Achievements:** Pro Bowl selection, 1985, 1986, & 1987; All-Pro selection, 1984 & 1985. Films: 1982 NFL Draft, 1982; 1991 NFC Championship Game, 1992; Super Bowl XXVI, 1992.

## RIGSBY, ESTHER CATHERINE MARTIN
School administrator. **Personal:** Born Port Gibson, MS; daughter of Alex L Martin (deceased) and Annie M Wilson Martin (deceased); married John D; children: Reginald, Atty Delbert, Mark & Kenneth. **Educ:** Alcorn State Univ, BS, 1954; Ind Univ, MS, 1959; Univ Mass, addn study, 1980; Mass State Univ, doctoral study, 1983; Univ Southern Mass, doctoral study, 1985. **Career:** Jackson Pub Sch, teacher, 1960-, chmn, eng & j teacher, 1960-; Alcorn State Univ, adj instr, 1965; Alpha Kappa Alpha Sor Inc, regional dir, currently. **Orgs:** MS Ed Asn, 1960-; Nat Educ Asn, 1975-; Nat Asn Advan Colored People, 1975-; Nat Coun Negro Women, 1977-; liaison coord Jackson Coun & Nat Coun Eng Teachers, 1979; Jackson Urban League, 1980-; admin bd, New Hope Baptist Church, 1982-85; nat bd mem, Alpha Kappa Alpha Sor Inc, 1982-86; supt adv coun, Jackson Pub Sch, 1984-85; YWCA, 1985; Opera S Guild, 1985; Links Inc, 1987; co-ordr, Africare Fundraising health Care Proj- Gambia Village; founder, Harriet Terry Scholar-Ala A&M Univ; exec bd, jackson Nat Asn Advan Colored People (NAACP) Br; chmn, Deaconess, choir dir & musician, New Hope Baptist Church; charter mem, Historian & financial & corresp Secy, Links Inc, Lefleurs Bluff Chap; chmn, Pub Rels Womens Missionary Baptist State Conv; chmn, Essay & Dissertation Reader students; pres, Beta Delta Omega; Regional Dir, 17th S Eastern; coordr, Area Cluster IV; reader, Centennial Travelling Exhib; evaluator, Nat Heritage Comt Alpha Kappa Alpha Sorority Inc; Resolution, Jackson City Coun; presentation, Hinds County Supervisors; exemplary leadership, UNCF Andrew Mellon Found. **Honors/Awds:** Service Award, Alpha Kappa Alpha Sor Inc, 1975-85; Award Loyal Alumnae, Alcorn State Univ, 1977; Service Award, Nat Coun Negro Women, 1981; Service Award, Women Prog, 1981; Women of the Year, 2012; Hall of Honor, Alcorn State Univ; Community Service, National Council of Negro Women. **Special Achievements:** Author: History of the South Eastern Region 1921-86; co-author of Capturing A Vision: The History of Alpha Kappa Alpha Sorority Inc; she Established the Collaboration Award; guest speaker; Established the Connection Award; Originated the Basilei Council Award; Established the Newsletter Award; Martin Luther King Heritage Awards Banquet, from Jackson State Univ, 2012. **Home Addr:** 5952 Hanging Moss Rd, Jackson, MS 39206-2147. **Business Addr:** Southeastern Regional Director, Alpha Kappa Alpha Sorority Inc, PO Box 788, Normal, AL 35762, **Business Phone:** (256)851-7799.

## RIHANNA (ROBYN RIHANNA FENTY)
Singer, actor, fashion designer. **Personal:** Born Feb 20, 1988, St. Michael; daughter of Ronald Fenty and Monica Braithwaite. **Career:** Singer, Albums "Music of the Sun", 2005; "A Girl Like Me", 2006; "Good Girl Gone Bad", 2007; "Rated R", 2009; "Loud", 2010; "Talk That Talk", 2011; "Unapologetic", 2012; actress, theatrical release, "Bring it On: All or Nothing", 2006; "Battleship", 2012; "Katy Perry: Part of Me", 2012; "This is the End", 2013; "Annie", 2013; "Home", 2015; Armani, fashion designer, 2011-. **Orgs:** Founder, Believe Found, 2006-; Cartier Love Charity Bracelet Ambassador. **Honors/Awds:** Maxim Magazine, Hot 100, 2007; "Billboard" Magazine, Digital Songs Artist of the 2000s; "Q" Magazine, Top 100 Acts of the Last Century; "Esquire" Magazine, Sexiest Woman, 2011; "Time" Magazine, 100 Most Influential People in the World, 2012; "Maxim" Magazine, Hot 100 (#14), 2014. **Special Achievements:** As of 2014, she has had nine number one Hot 100 singles; only female in U.S. history to follow-up a number one single with another; American Music Awards: 8 awards from 15 nominations; BET Awards: 4 awards from 16 nominations; Billboard Music Awards: 22 awards from 60 nominations; Grammy Awards: 7 awards from 24 nominations; MTV Music Awards: 4 awards from 23 nominations; NAACP Image Awards: 6 nominations; People's Choice Awards: 7 awards from 12 nominations; Soul Train Music Awards: 2 awards from 6 nominations; Teen Choice Awards: 6 awards from 38 nominations; World Music Awards: 4 awards from 27 nominations.

**RIJO, ABREU. See RIJO, JOSE ANTONIO.**

## RIJO, JOSE ANTONIO (ABREU RIJO)
Baseball player, baseball executive. **Personal:** Born May 13, 1965, San Cristobal; son of Gladys; married Josefina Araujo; married Rosie Marichal; children: Jose Jr; married Teddy; children: 1. **Career:** Baseball player (retired), baseball executive; New York Yankees, pitcher, 1984; Oakland Athletics, pitcher, 1985-87; Cincinnati Reds, pitcher, 1988-95, 2001-02; Wash Nationals, spec asst to gen mgr, 2009. **Special Achievements:** Supporting role in the baseball film Sugar, 2008. **Home Addr:** Cent Cabral Suite 66, San Cristobal10700.

**RILEY, AMBER**
Singer, actor. **Personal:** Born Feb 15, 1986, Los Angeles, CA; daughter of Elwin Riley and Tiny Hightower Riley. **Career:** Fox television show, "Glee," (character Mercedes Jones), 2009-; "Glee: The 3D Concert Movie," (character Mercedes Jones), 2011. **Orgs:** Do Something, Campaign Spokesperson; VH1 Save the Music Foundation, Campaign Spokesperson; State Farm's "Celebrate My Drive," Spokesperson. **Honors/Awds:** Screen Actors Guild Award, Outstanding Performance by an Ensemble in a Comedy Series, 2010. **Special Achievements:** First African American woman to win TV dancing contest "Dancing with the Stars," 2013; Democratic National Convention, sang National Anthem, 2012.

**RILEY, ANTONIO**
State government official. **Personal:** Born Aug 22, 1963, Chicago, IL. **Educ:** Carroll Col, BA. **Career:** Milwaukee Mayor's Off, staff asst; Wisc State Assemblyman, Dist 18; Wisc State Capital, state rep, 1992-2002; Wis Housing & Econ Develop Authority, exec dir, 2003-. **Orgs:** YMCA; Transcenter for Youth; Greater Milwaukee Am Red Cross; Ctr Policy Alternatives; chmn, Milwaukee Westside Health Care Asn; comn chmn, Milwaukee Metrop Sewerage Dist; chmn, Dem Leadership Coun; Midtown Neighborhood Asn; adv bd, Dem Leadership Coun. **Business Addr:** Executive Director, Wisconsin Housing & Economic Development Authority, 201 W Wash Ave Suite 700, Madison, WI 53703-1728, **Business Phone:** (608)266-7884.

**RILEY, BARBARA P.**
Librarian. **Personal:** Born Nov 21, 1928, Roselle, NJ; daughter of Charles Carrington Polk and Olive Bond Polk; married George Emerson; children: George Jr, Glenn & Karen; married William F Scott. **Educ:** Howard Univ, AB, 1950; NJ Col Women, BS, 1951; Columbia Univ, MS, 1955; Cath Univ; Jersey City State Col; Rutgers Univ; Kean Col. **Career:** Librarian (retired): FL A&M Univ, asst librn, 1951-53; Morgan, asst librn, 1955; US Dept Defense, lib, 1955-57; SC State Col, asst librn, 1957-59, 1960; Univ WI, asst lib, 1958-59; Atlanta Univ, circulation acq librn, 1960-68; Union Co Tech Inst, lib, 1968-82; Union Co Col, librn, Scotch Plains campus, 1982-92, Plainfield Campus, librn, 1992-95. **Orgs:** Asst dir, Union Co Anti-Poverty Agency, 1968; Just-A-Mere Lit Club; ALA Black Lib Caucus; Alpha Kappa Alpha Sor; Bd Educ, Roselle, NJ, 1976-78; bd dir, Union Co Psychiat Clin, 1980-83; bd dir, Pinewood Sr Citizens Housing, 1982-85; NJ Coalition 100 Black Women, 1983-90; NJ Black Librns Network, 1983-, bd dir, 1986; bd dir, Black Womens Hist Conf, 1986-89; Links Inc; Urban League Eastern Union Co; bd dir, Roselle, NAACP, 1984-88. **Home Addr:** 420 E 1st Ave, Roselle, NJ 07203, **Home Phone:** (908)241-5036.

**RILEY, EDWARD THEODORE.** **See RILEY, TEDDY.**

**RILEY, ERIC KENDALL**
Basketball player. **Personal:** Born Jun 2, 1970, Cleveland, OH. **Educ:** Univ Mich, attended 1993. **Career:** Basketball player (retired); Houston Rockets, ctr, 1993-94; Los Angeles Clippers, 1994-95; Minn Timberwolves, 1995-96; Apollon Patras, Greece, 1996-97; Dallas Mavericks, 1997-98; Boston Celtics, 1998-99; Ind Legends, 2000-01; Cocodrilos de Caracas, 2001; Euro Roseto, 2001-02; San Antonio Spurs, ctr, 2002; Liaoning Dinosaurs, 2002-03; Proteas EKA AEL, 2003-04. **Orgs:** Founder, High Rise Found, 2009.

**RILEY, HON. EVE MONTGOMERY**
Judge. **Personal:** Born Oct 8, 1955, Sedalia, MO; daughter of Ralph and Neppie Elizabeth Gerhardt; married Joel Younge; children: Max Sebastian & Cruz Dylan. **Educ:** Fisk Univ, Nashville, TN, attended 1974; Carthage Col, Kenosha, attended 1975; Roosevelt Univ, Chicago, IL, BA, 1976; Valparaiso Univ Sch Law, Valparaiso, IN, JD, 1978; Fontbonne Col, Clayton, MO, MBA, 1995. **Career:** US Off Spec Coun, Wash, DC, law clerk, 1979-80, staff atty, 1980-82; US Merit Systs Protection Bd, Philadelphia, Pa, admin judge, 1982-87; Support Ctr Child Advocates, Philadelphia, Pa, exec dir, 1987; St Louis Univ Sch Law, St Louis, Mo, instr, 1988-89; St Louis, Mo, atty law, 1988-94; Social Security Admin, admin law judge, 1994-, hearing off chief admin law judge, currently. **Orgs:** Nat Asn Women Bus Owners, 1987-89; pres, Fed Bar Asn, St Louis Chap, 1988-90; leader, Girl Scout Coun Greater, St Louis, 1989-; dir, Lawyer Referral Serv, St Louis Br, Nat Asn Advan Colored People, 1993-94; Delta Mu Delta Hon Soc, EOR Bus Admin, 1994; Mission Coun, 1999-; C Work Comn, 1997-; ed, Greater St Louis Suzuki Asn Newsletter, 1999-; Color Justice, Nat Asn Women Judges, 2001; Ladue Chapel Presby Church; Lyon Soc. **Home Addr:** 5577 Lindell Blvd, St Louis, MO 63112, **Home Phone:** (314)432-5156. **Business Addr:** Hearing Office Chief Administrative Law Judge, Social Security Adminstration, 200 N Broadway Suite 900, St Louis, MO 63102, **Business Phone:** (314)588-7534.

**RILEY, GLENN PLEASANTS**
Television producer. **Personal:** Born Jan 17, 1960, Milwaukee, WI; son of Robert and Annie; married Felice Ligon. **Educ:** Milwaukee Area Tech Col, Milwaukee, WI, AAS, 1980; Univ Wis, Milwaukee, WI, attended 1986. **Career:** WITI TV6 Inc, Milwaukee, WI, traffic log keeper, 1980-81; WMVS/WMVT TV, Milwaukee, WI, prod specialist, 1982-; MPTV, studio supvr, dir & producer; Milwaukee Area Tech Col, first yr instr, dir, currently. **Orgs:** Nat Asn Black Journalists, 1987-; Wis Black Media Asn, 1988-; Wis Broadcasters Asn. **Home Addr:** 4164 N 40th St, Milwaukee, WI 53216, **Home Phone:** (414)449-8542. **Business Addr:** First Year Instructor, Director, Milwaukee Area Technical College, 1200 S 71st St, Milwaukee, WI 53233, **Business Phone:** (414)271-1036.

**RILEY, KENNETH JEROME, II**
Football coach, football player. **Personal:** Born Aug 6, 1947, Bartow, FL; married Barbara Moore; children: Kimberly, Ken II & Kenisha. **Educ:** Fla A&M Univ, BS, health & phys educ, 1969; Univ N Fla, MS, admin, 1974. **Career:** Football player, football coach (retired); Cincinnati Bengals, right corner back, 1969-83; Green Bay Packers, asst coach, 1984-86; Fla A&M Univ, football coach, 1986-93, head coach; athletic dir, 1994-2003. **Orgs:** Bd dir, Big Bros Polk County; Alpha Phi Alpha Frat; Mt Gilboa Bapt Church; consult Fla A&M Nat Alumni; adv bd, Nat Football League; adv comt, NCAA. **Honors/Awds:** All-Pro selection, 1975, 1976, 1983; Distinguish Alumni Award, Fla A&M Univ, 1988; Polk County Hall Fame, 1992, 2000; MEAC coach of the year, Mid-Eastern Athletic conf. **Home Addr:** 1865 E Gibbons St, Bartow, FL 33830-6712.

**RILEY, ROSETTA MARGUERITTE**
Automotive executive. **Personal:** Born Oct 25, 1940, Kansas City, MO; children: Courtney Elizabeth. **Educ:** Calif State Univ, Los Angeles, BS, 1968; Univ Calif, Los Angeles, MA, 1969. **Career:** Bendix Corp, Detroit, Mich, mgr bus planning & mkt mgr; Gen Motors, Detroit, Mich, prod team, mgr qual, Rochester NY Prods Div, qual improv mgr, Buick Oldsmobile Cadillac Group, Detroit, Mich, mgr opers planning, Cadillac Motor Car Div, Detroit, Mich, dir, currently. **Orgs:** Zeta Phi Sorority, 1964-; life mem, Nat Asn Advan Colored People, 1984-89; United Found, 1984-; Detroit Inst Arts, 1987-; Am Soc Qual Control; Gen Motors Key Exec Tenn State Univ. **Home Addr:** 5928 Naneva Ct, West Bloomfield, MI 48322, **Home Phone:** (248)626-1842. **Business Addr:** Director, General Motors Corp, PO Box 33170, Detroit, MI 48232-5170, **Business Phone:** (800)222-1020.

**RILEY, SHAUNCE R.**
Counselor, educator, association executive. **Personal:** Born Mar 23, 1970, Savannah, GA; son of William Jr and Mary; married Karla Patrice Wright. **Educ:** Savannah State Univ, BBA, CIS & MAN with Teacher's cert, 1996; Cent Mich Univ, MA, educ, 2002. **Career:** Savannah State Univ, Off Human Resources, rec coordr, 1996-99, Ctr Stud Develop, staff asst, 1999-2001, Stud Support Servs, prog spec, 2001-, freshman experience instr, 2001-, coordr career serv, currently. **Orgs:** Southeastern Asn Educ Opport Prog; Ga Col Personnel Asn; Phi Beta Lambda; Savannah State Univ, 2002 Homecoming Comt, chairperson, 2002-03. **Home Addr:** RR 1, PO Box 149-2LA7, Hardeeville, SC 29927, **Home Phone:** (843)748-5074. **Business Addr:** Program Specialist/ Student Advisor, Savannah State University, Rm 238 Whiting Hall 3219 Col St, Savannah, GA 31404, **Business Phone:** (912)358-3128.

**RILEY, TEDDY (EDWARD THEODORE RILEY)**
Television producer, songwriter, musician. **Personal:** Born Oct 8, 1967, Harlem, NY; children: 3. **Career:** Jazz Singer: Guy, 1988; High Hat, 1989; The Future, 1990; Juice, 1992; Dangerous, 1992; Bobby, 1993; Eleven, 1993; recording appears on Heavy Ds album Peaceful Journey; Solo: "D-O-G Me Out"; "Let's Chill"; "Long Gone"; "No Diggity"; has produced, written & played for: Bobby Brown, Stevie Wonder, Boy George, Kool Moe Dee, Michael Jackson; BLACKSTREET, 1994-; Little Man Rec, owner, currently; Teddy Riley Music Group, currently; writer: New Jack City, 1991; Madonna: Truth or Dare, 1991; House Party 2, 1991; Strictly Business, 1991; CB4, 1993; The Meteor Man, 1993; Ghost in the Machine, 1993; Blankman, 1994; Get on the Bus, 1996; The Rugrats Movie, 1998; Music of the Heart, 1999; Love & Basketball, 2000; The 40 Year Old Virgin, 2005; My Brother, 2006; Wild Hogs, 2007; This Is It, 2009. **Business Addr:** Owner, Teddy Riley Music Group, 1317 N San Fernado Blvd, Burbank, CA 91504, **Business Phone:** (470)444-9879.

**RILEY, VICTOR ALLAN**
Football coach, football player. **Personal:** Born Nov 4, 1974, Swansea, SC; children: 1. **Educ:** Auburn Univ. **Career:** Football player (retired), coach; Kans City Chiefs, right tackle, 1998-2001, flanker, 1999; New Orleans Saints, right tackle, 2002-04, right guard, 2002; Houston Texans, left tackle & right guard, 2005; Auburn Univ, offensive line coach. **Honors/Awds:** Rookie of the Year, 1998; Mack Lee Hill Award winner, 1998.

**RILEY, DR. WAYNE JOSEPH**
Physician, health services administrator, president (organization). **Personal:** Born May 3, 1959, New Orleans, LA; son of Emile Edward Jr (deceased) and Jacqueline Cerf; married Charlene M Dewey; children: Erin Elizabeth & Alexis Camille; married Charlene M Dewey. **Educ:** Yale Univ, BA, anthrop, 1981; Tulane Univ, New Orleans, LA, MPH, health systs mgt, 1988; Morehouse Sch Med, MD, 1993; Baylor Col Med, Am Bd Internal Med, dipl, 1996; Rice Univ, Jesse H Jones Grad Sch Mgt, MBA, execs prog, 2002. **Career:** Off Mayor, New Orleans, from admin asst to mayor, 1981-86, from exec asst to mayor, 1986; Off Pub Health, LA, health serv planner, 1987-88; Lectr, Adolescent Health Concerns Proj, Emory Univ, 1989; Alpha Omega Alpha Stud res fel, 1991; Morehouse Sch Med, Minority AIDS Educ Proj, proj asst, consult; Baylor Col Med, asst prof med, 1996-, asst dean, 2001-, Health Affairs Govt Rels, vpres, vice dean; Ben Taub Gen Hosp, asst chief med; Rice Univ, Jesse H Jones Grad Sch Mgt, adj prof; Tex Med Ctr, vpres, vice dean health affairs & govt rels, assoc prof med; Baylor Col Med, Dept Med, staff, asst dean, 2000-04, vpres & vice dean, 2004-06; Meharry Med Col, pres & chief exec officer, 2007-13; Michael E DeBakey Veteran Affairs Med Ctr, attend physician & staff; Tex Acad Internal Med; Tex Chap Am Col Physicians; Vertex Pharmaceut Inc, independent dir, 2010-15; Robert Wood Johnson Found Health Policy Ctr, Meharry, sr health policy assoc, currently; Vanderbilt Univ, Nashville, Healthcare Mgt, adj prof, Vanderbilt Univ Sch Med, Clin Prof, currently. **Orgs:** Am Col Physicians, Nat Med Asn; Kingsley Trust Asn Yale Univ, 1981-, Yale Alumni Asn LA, 1981-88; bd dir, LA Youth Sem, 1984-86; Nat Asn Advan Colored People, Am Med Stud Asn, Am Med Asn, Stud Nat Med Asn; exec dir, LA Independent Fedn Electors, 1985-88; pres, Tulane Univ Black Prof Stud Asn, 1987-88; sec, treas, Yale Alumni Asn LA, 1988; fel NMF/ Prudential Found AIDS Educ & Pub Policy, 1990; EtaLambda Chap, Alpha Phi Alpha Fraternity Inc; Nat coordr, Standing Comm Minority Affairs, AMSA, 1990-91; Stud Govt Asn, Morehouse Sch Med, vpres, 1990-91, pres, 1992-93; class pres, Class 1993, Morehouse Sch Med; adv, Boy Scouts Am Health Explorer's Post, 1990-93; AUC Stud Leadership Forum, 1992-93; bd dir, Cath Charities, Diocese Galveston-Houston, 2002-; co-chair, Baylor Col Med Educ Mission Strategic Planning Task Force, 2003; Nat Black MBA Asn, 2003-; chmn, Harris County Hosp Dist Med Bd, 2003-06; bd dir, Nashville Symphony Asn; Pinnacle Financial Partners; Cheekwood Bot Mus; Rotary Club Nashville; dir, Pinnacle Financial Partners Inc, 2007-13; Loews Vanderbilt Hotel Adv Coun; chmn bd trustee, Milton H Jones Jr; Inst Meds Planning Comt; asst dir, Methodist Hosp; dir, Baylor Travel Med Serv; Dean's Comt, Michael E. DeBakey Veteran Affairs Med Ctr; dir, Hosp Corp Am Holdings Inc, 2012-; adv coun, Nat Insts Health; Soc Med Adminr; Nat Acad Sci. **Home Addr:** , TN. **Business Addr:** Adjunct Professor, Clinical Professor, Vanderbilt University Owen Graduate School of Management, 401 21st Ave S Ctr Bldg, Nashville, TN 37203, **Business Phone:** (615)322-2534.

**RILEY, WILLIAM SCOTT**
Police officer, mayor. **Personal:** Born Sep 24, 1940, Chester, PA; son of Benjamin and Leanna; married Deloris L; children: Kimberly, Kelly & William S Jr. **Educ:** Eastern Carolina Col, attended 1961; Lincoln Univ, MS, human servs, attended. **Career:** Police officer (retired); City Chester, Police Dept, police officer, liaison, mayor. **Orgs:** Bd mem, Del Co Selective Serv Bd, 1987; bd mem, Del Co Dem Exec Bd, 1987; polit chmn, Cult Develop Coun Del Co, 1990-; bd mem, Chester Community Prev Coalition, 1990-; pres, Chester Police Athletic League; chair, bd trustees, Providence Bapt Church, 1990-98; comdr, Charles Horsey Post 300, Am Legion, 1995-98; fed adv bd, Chester-Upland Schl Dist, 1998, treas. **Honors/Awds:** Outstanding Community Service Award, Chester Scholarship Comn, 1983; Eva Lou Winters Johnson Freedom Awards, Chester Br, Nat Asn Advan Colored People, 1985; Citizen of the Year, Omega Psi Phi Fraternity Inc, Epsilon Pi Chap, 1993; Westend Ministerial Fellowship's Presidential Award for Youth Service, 1993; The American Legion's Past Commander's Award, 1996. **Home Addr:** 918 Lloyd St, Chester, PA 19013-3513, **Home Phone:** (610)874-6804.

**RIMMER, JUNE COLLINS**
Manager. **Educ:** Ball State Univ, BS; Butler Univ, MS; Ind Univ, PhD. **Career:** Seattle Pub Schs, chief acad officer; Indianapolis Pub Schs, asst supt; Univ Wash, Ctr Educ Leadership, assoc dir, 2011. **Orgs:** Prog dir & mgr, Stupski Found, 2004-; Marion County Health Dept; Bd trustee, Breakthrough Collab. **Business Addr:** Program Director, Program Manager, Stupski Foundation, 90 New Montgomery St Suite 315, San Francisco, CA 94105, **Business Phone:** (415)536-4202.

**RINGGOLD, FAITH**
Educator, writer, painter (artist). **Personal:** Born Oct 8, 1930, Harlem, NY; daughter of Andrew Jones and Willi Jones; married Robert Earl Wallace; children: Michelle Wallace & Barbara Wallace; married Burdette. **Educ:** City Col NY, BS, 1955, Grad Sch, MA, 1961. **Career:** Teacher; Am Asn Univ Women, Sculpture fel, 1976; Nat Endowment Arts, sculpture fel, 1978; artist & writer; Univ Calif, prof art, 1987-2002, prof emer, currently; Wilson Col, artist-in-resident. Written and illustrated books which includes: Tar Beach, Aunt Harriet's Underground Railroad in the Sky, Dinner at Aunt Connie's House, 7 Passages To A Flight, O Holy Night, Bronzeville Boys and Girls, What Will You Do for Peace?, Cassie's Colorful Day, If a Bus Could Talk, The Invisible Princess; Faith Ringgold Inc, chief exec officer. **Orgs:** Nat Black Feminist Orgn, 1974; Women Students & Artists Black Art Liberation; founding mem, Where We At Black Women Artists. **Honors/Awds:** The Creative Artists Public Service Award, 1971; National Endowment for the Arts Award, 1978 & 1989; Wonder Woman Foundation Award, 1983; Warner Communications Candace Award, 100 Black Women, 1984; honorary doctor of fine art, Moore Col Fine Art, 1986; doctor of fine art, Wooster Col, 1987; John Simon Guggenheim Foundation Award, 1987; The New York Foundation For the Arts Award, 1988; La Napoule Foundation Award, 1990; Honorary Doctor of Fine Art, Massachusetts Col Art, 1991; Honorary Doctor of Fine Art, City Col New York, 1991; Gold Award for Illustration, Parent's Choice, 1991; ALA Notable Children's Book, Tar Beach, 1991; Honorary Doctor of Fine Arts, Brockport State Col, 1992; Best Children's Book Award, The NY Times, 1992; Coretta Scott King Award; Booklist Editor's Choice, Aunt Harriet's Underground Railroad Sky, 1993; Reading Magazine Award, Parenting Mag, 1993; Picture Book Award, Jane Addams Peace Asn, 1993; Honorary Doctorate, Calif Col Arts & Crafts, 1993; Honorary Doctorate, Brockport State Univ, 1993; Nat Endowment for the Arts Travel Award, 1993; Woman's Caucus for the Arts Honors Award, Outstanding Achievement in the Visual Art, NY, 1994; Honorary Doctor of Fine Arts, Rhode Island Sch Design, 1994; Honors Award for Outstanding Achievement in the Visual Arts, Women's Caucus Arts, 1994; Art Start for Children Award, Guggenheim Museum C's Prog, 1994; Recognition Award, New York State Fibers Asn, 1994; Townsend Harris Medal, City Col, Alumni Asn, 1995; Key to the City, Lake Charles, LA, 1995; Parent's Choice Award, 1996; Honorary Doctor of Fine Arts, Parsons Sch Design, 1996; Honorary Doctor of Fine Arts, Russell Sage Col, 1996; Honorary Degrees: Russel Sage, Troy, NY, 1996; Parsons Sch Design, NYC, 1996; Wheelock Col, Boston, 1997; Molloy Col, NYC, 1997; New Jersey Artist of the Year Award, NJ Ctr Visual Arts, 1997; City arts Award, 1999; Image Award, Nat Asn for the Advan of Colored People, 1999; Hon Art Degree, Mary Grove Col, 2000; Dedicators Award, 2001; California Art Educators Association Living Artists Award, 2002; Moore College of Art and Design's Visionary Women Award, 2005; James A. Porter Colloquium African Am Art Honoree; Amistad Center for Art & Culture Presidents Award, 2005; Golden Legacy Visual Arts Award, Harlem Arts alliance, 2006; Peace Corps Award, 2009; First Annual Cultural Arts Award, City Col New York, 2011; received more than 75 awards, fellowships, citations and honors, including the Solomon R. Guggenheim Fellowship for painting, two National Endowment for the Arts Awards and seventeen honorary doctorates. **Home Addr:** 127 Jones Rd, Englewood, NJ 07631-3730, **Home Phone:** (201)816-1374. **Business Addr:** Professor Emeritus, University of California, 9500 Gilman Dr, La Jolla, CA 92093-0327, **Business Phone:** (858)534-2230.

**RIPPY, RODNEY ALLEN**
Actor. **Personal:** Born Jul 29, 1968, Long Beach, CA; son of Fred and Flossie Hubbard. **Educ:** Cerritos Col, AA, bus admin, 1991; Calif State Univ. **Career:** Actor; cameraman; Films: Blazing Saddles, 1974; Oh, God! Book II, 1980; Checking the Gate, 2003, Dickie Roberts: Child Star, 2003. TV series: "The Light at the Threshold", 1973; "Marcus Welby, M.D.", 1973-74; "The Harlem Globetrotters Popcorn Machine", 1974; "Medical Center", 1974; "The Odd Couple", 1975; "The Six Million Dollar Man", 1975; "Police Story", 1976; "Laugh-In", 1977; "The Hunter Hunted", 1980; "Vega$", 1980; "Parker Lewis Can't Lose", 1990-92; "Misplaced", 2012. The Rodney Allen Rippy Show, host; Bow Tie Productions, partner, currently; RAR Entertainment, founder, ac-

tor, writer, producer, 2000-; Ripped Mkt Group, owner. TV projects: "Baby Youre A Star"; "BACKUP"; Feature Flim projects: "HT"; "Holding an Angel". **Home Addr:** 1900 Avenue of the Stars, Los Angeles, CA 90067, **Home Phone:** (818)591-1700. **Business Addr:** Founder, RAR Entertainment, PO Box 251402, Glendale, CA 91225-1402, **Business Phone:** (323)665-9006.

## RISON, ANDRE PREVIN

Football player. **Personal:** Born Mar 18, 1967, Flint, MI; married Tonja; children: 2. **Educ:** Mich State Univ. **Career:** Football player (retired), coach, executive; Indianapolis Colts, wide receiver, 1989; Atlanta Falcons, wide receiver, 1990-94; Cleveland Browns, wide receiver, 1995; Green Bay Packers, 1996; Jacksonville Jaguars, 1996; Kans City Chiefs, wide receiver, 1997-98, split end & wide receiver, 1999; Oakland Raiders, wide receiver, 2000; Toronto Argonauts, CFL, wide receiver, 2004-05; Beecher High Sch, asst coach, 2006-08; Flint Northwestern High Sch, head coach, 2010; Rincon High Sch, head coach, 2014; Best Wide Receiver Sch, owner, chief exec officer, currently. **Honors/Awds:** Pro Bowl, 1990, 1991, 1992, 1993 & 1997; Won Super Bowl XXXI, 1996; Kans City Chiefs, Most Valuable Player, 1997; Won 92nd Grey Cup, 2004. **Business Addr:** Chief Executive Officer, Owner, The Best Wide Receiver School, PO Box 33513, North Royalton, OH 44133.

## RISON, DR. FAYE

Educator. **Personal:** Born Feb 25, 1942, Nacogdoches, TX; daughter of Rebecca and Archie Lee; married Levy Sallie Scott; children: Sondra Roshona. **Educ:** Prairie View A&M Univ, BS, regist nursing & regist nurse, 1964; Univ Colo, MA, 1970, PhD, nursing & commun, 1984. **Career:** Denver Health & Hosp, psychiat nurse, 1960-70; Univ Colo Med Ctr, psychiat nurse, 1965-67; NW Team Dept Health Hosp, Denver, CO, psychiat nurse, 1967-71; Metro State Col, 1970-2000, from asst prof to assoc prof, 1971-98, prof human serv; Rison's Consult, pres & chief exec officer, 1970-2001; Rison Group, owner, 1980-92; Colo Tech Univ, adj prof, currently; Christmas Proj Toys Kids, founder; Breast Cancer Awareness Proj, founder; Egyptian Adventures with Dr Faye & Friends LLC, travel coordr, 2010-; Rison & Co, chief exec officer, 2013-. **Orgs:** Bd mem, Nat Orgn Human Serv, 1980-84; Am Civil Liberties Union; Delta Sigma Theta; Black Womens Network; Denver Sister Cities; Black Women with Advan Degrees; chairperson, Rd Called STRATE. **Honors/Awds:** Doct Fellowship, Univ Colo, 1980-82; Outstanding Faculty Award Human Service, 1979-82; Sertoman of the Year, 2000; Sertoma International Tribune Award, Presidents Award, 2001; In the Black Smart Women, 2001. **Special Achievements:** Publications: Group Dynamics and Leaderless Groups, 1984. **Business Addr:** Travel Coordinator, Egyptian Adventures With Dr Faye & Friends LLC, 8792 E Kent Pl, Denver, CO 80237-1603, **Business Phone:** (303)773-6852.

## RIST, SUSAN E.

Lawyer. **Personal:** Born Chicago, IL; daughter of Seward Sr (deceased) and Irma Tatum (deceased); married Steve F Sbraccia. **Educ:** Principia Col, BA; Boston Univ, MS; Suffolk Univ, JD, 1995. **Career:** KAAY Radio, news anchor, reporter, 1978-80; WHDH Radio, news anchor, reporter, 1980-82; WLVI-TV, news anchor, reporter, 1982-85; WBOS Radio, news anchor, 1985-87; WHBQ-TV, news reporter, 1987; WBZ Radio, news anchor, reporter, 1987-95; Emerson Col, broadcast jour instr, 1987-92; Suffolk Co Dist atty Off, asst dist atty, 1995-. **Orgs:** Nat Asn Black Journalists, 1989-95; Soc Prof Journalists, 1990-95; Black Law Students Asn, 1992-95; Am Trial Lawyers Asn, 1994-; Mass Bar Asn, 1995-. **Honors/Awds:** Harold Goodwin Best Trial Advocate Award, 1994. **Home Addr:** 29 Irving St, Newton, MA 02459-1611, **Home Phone:** (617)243-0205. **Business Addr:** Assistant District Attorney, Suffolk County District Attorney, 1 Bulfinch Pl, Boston, MA 02114, **Business Phone:** (617)619-4000.

## RITCHIE, JOE (JOSEPH EDWARD RITCHIE, II)

Journalist, educator. **Personal:** Born Jul 10, 1949, Oak Hill, WV; son of Joseph E Sr and Dorothy; married Louise Reid; children: Jabari Russell & Akin Zachary. **Educ:** Tilden Tech High Sch, dipl, 1966; Calvin Col, Grand Rapids, MI, AB, ger, 1970; Ruprecht Karl Univ, Heidelberg, W Ger, 1972; Ohio State Univ, Columbus, OH, MA, ger, 1973, MA, jour, 1975. **Career:** Woodrow Wilson fel, 1970; Ohio State Univ, Columbus, OH, teaching asst, 1972-75; Kicker-sportmagazin, praktikant, 1974, intern, 1974; Wash Post, Wash, DC, asst foreign ed, 1975-86, vacation relief ed, 1977-86; Duke Univ, Wash, postdoctoral fel, 1981; Hampton Univ, vis prof journalist, 1982-84; Detroit Free Press, nat & foreign ed, 1986-92; Int Herald Tribune, copy ed, 2001-09; Fla A&M Univ, prof & knight chair jour, 1992-2013; New York Times, copy ed, 2005-06, staff editor, 2013-; The Univ Hong Kong, vis prof, 2009-16. **Orgs:** Advisor, Nat Asn Black Journalists; Soc Prof Journalists; bd dir, Am Coun Ger, 1984-; adv bd mem, Pew Ctr Civic J, Jim Batten Prize Excellence Civic Jour, 1995-2002; mem rules & referees comn, US Team Handball Fedn; treas, Black Col Commun Asn: bd dir, Am Coun Ger; bd mem, Calvin Col Alumni Asn; Dow Jones Newspaper Fund; Nat Hon Socs. **Honors/Awds:** French-Am Found Young Leader. **Home Addr:** 1001 Lasswade Dr, Tallahassee, FL 32312-2862, **Home Phone:** (850)385-4955. **Business Addr:** Professor, Knight Chair in Journalism, Florida A&M University, Rm 3016 Tucker Hall Suite 305 3rd Fl, Tallahassee, FL 32307, **Business Phone:** (850)599-3880.

## RITCHIE, DR. LOUISE REID

Newspaper executive, educator. **Personal:** Born Jul 10, 1951, Niskayuna, NY; daughter of Antoinette Lyles and Lester Frank Reid Sr; married Joseph E II; children: Jabari Russell & Akin Zachary. **Educ:** Harvard Univ, Radcliffe Col, Cambridge, MA, AB, govt, 1973; George Washington Univ, MPhil, psychol, 1982, PhD, 1986. **Career:** Assoc Press, Atlanta, Ga, Nashville, TN, reporter, 1974-76; Wash Post, Wash, DC, reporter, 1976-77; Detroit Urban League, Detroit, Mich, dir, substance abuse prev, 1987-88; Detroit Free Press, columnist, 1987-92, exec asst to publ, 1990-92; self-employed prof pub speaker, 1987-; Wayne State Univ, instr, 1988-92; Knight-Ridder Inc, human resources consult, 1992-93; Fla Agri & Mech Univ, assoc prof, 1993-99; Fla Inst Leadership Excellence, Fla Agri & Mech Univ, founding dir, 1998-99, Coordr Info/Publ, 2013-15; Media & Graphic Arts, Fla A&M Univ, Tallahassee, Fla, assoc prof jour, currently. **Orgs:** Delta Sigma Theta Sorority, 1984-; Hartford Memorial Baptist Church; Mich Prof Speakers Asn; Sorosis Arts & Literacy Club; Nat Speakers Asn; mem bd dir, Radcliffe Col Club, Wash, DC, 1985-86; Samaritan Hosp Substance Abuse Comt, 1987; Wayne County Juv Ct Substance Abuse Comt, 1988; Childrens Ctr Perinatal Health Comt, 1988; mem admis comt, Harvard Univ, 1989-92; vice chmn, community adv bd, WTVS-TV, Detroit, MI, 1989-90; Newspaper Asn Am Diversity, sub comt cochair, 1992-95; Class secy, Radcliffe Col; bd mem, Big Bend March Dimes; bd mem, Waverly Hills Neighborhood Asn; bd mem, Coun Arts & Cult. **Home Addr:** 1001 Lasswade, Tallahassee, FL 32312-2862, **Home Phone:** (850)385-4955. **Business Addr:** Associate Professor, Florida A&M University, 1601 S Martin Luther King Blvd Suite 100, Tallahassee, FL 32307, **Business Phone:** (850)599-3413.

## RIVERA, EDDY

Lawyer. **Personal:** Born Jul 23, 1938, St. Croix; son of Margot M and Adelo; married Gloria Maria Rojas; children: Lisette M, Julia I, Eddy Jr & Vanessa M. **Educ:** Interam Univ San Ger, attended 1960; Univ PR, San Juan, BBA, 1963, JD, 1972. **Career:** VI Properties Inc, chief acct, 1966-69; Govt VI, asst atty gen, 1973-76, sen, 1979-80; pvt pract atty; CRC Law List Co Inc, atty, currently. **Orgs:** PR Bar Asn, 1973; bd mem, Camp Arawak Youth Serv Orgn, 1974-76; pres, Hispanos Unidos VI Inc, 1974-78, 1992-; bd educ, Govt VI, 1976-78; VI Bar Asn, 1976; pres, Full Gospel Bus Men's Fel Int, 1981-86; Am Bar Asn, 1981-96; Asn Trial Lawyers, 1982-94. **Home Addr:** 231 Judiths Fancy Christiansted, St Croix00823, **Home Phone:** (809)773-7097. **Business Addr:** Attorney, CRC Law List Co Inc, 1168 King St Sunny Isle Christiansted Suite 2, St. Croix00823, **Business Phone:** (340)773-5756.

## RIVERA, GERALD MAXWELL

Singer. **Personal:** Born May 23, 1973, Brooklyn, NY. **Career:** The Coffee Shop, waiter; Albums: Maxwell's Urban Hang Suite, 1996; MTV Unplugged, 1997; Embrya, 1998; Now, 2001; BLACK summers' night, 2009; Maxwell & Jill Scott: The Tour, 2010; Singles: "Til the Cops Come Knockin", 1996; "Ascension (Don't Ever Wonder)", 1996; "Sumthin', Sumthin'", 1996; "Whenever, Wherever, Whatever", 1997; "Luxury: Cococure", 1998; "Matrimony: May be You", 1998; "Each Hour Each Minute Each Second Each Day: Of My Life", 1998; "Let's Not Play the Game", 1999; "Fortunate", 1999; "Get to Know Ya", 2000; "Lifetime", 2001; "This Woman's Work", 2001. **Honors/Awds:** Soul Train Awards, 1996, 2000 & 2009; Grammy Award, 1997-2000, 2002 & 2010; Billboard Music Award, 1999; BET Awards, 2001-02 & 2010; American Music Award, 2009; Alma Awards, 2009; Image Award, Nat Asn Advan Colored People, 2002 & 2010. **Business Addr:** Singer, Columbia Records, 550 Madison Ave, New York, NY 10022-3211, **Business Phone:** (212)833-8000.

**RIVERA, GERALD MAXWELL.** **See MAXWELL.**

## RIVERA, LANCE

Executive, writer. **Career:** Untertainment Rec, chief exec officer & label co-founder, currently; Writer: Perfect Holiday, 2007; Dir: Cookout, 2004, Perfect Holiday, 2007, Charlie Murphy: I Will Not Apologize, 2010, Cookout 2, 2011; Producer: Perfect Holiday, 2007; Life Support, 2007, Angie Martinez Show, 2008, Broke & Famous, 2009, Percentage, 2013; Exec Producer: Katt Williams: Kattpacalypse, 2012. **Business Addr:** Chief Executive Officer, Label Co-founder, Untertainment Records, 3 E 28th St 9th Fl, New York, NY 10016, **Business Phone:** (718)390-3928.

## RIVERO, MARITA

Librarian. **Personal:** Born Nov 25, 1943, West Grove, PA; daughter of Manuel and Grace; children: Raafi Muhammad. **Educ:** Tufts Univ, BS, 1964; Wharton Sch Bus, exec mgt prog, 1981; Stanford Bus Sch, exec mgt prog, 1994. **Career:** WGBH, producer, 1970-76, vpres, mgr, 1988, gen mgr, radio & TV, 2005-, producer, currently; WPFW, vpres & gen mgr 1981-88. **Orgs:** Nat Fed Community Broadcasters, 1982-86; NPR, Distrib Interconnection Bd, 1985-88; Pub Radio Int, 1990-2002; Kolcrobiley Inst, Ghana, 1992-; Partnership, 1996-; chair, Mus African Am Hist, 1996-; Inst Contemp Art; Urban League Eastern Mass, 1999-; chair, Nat Black Programming Consortium Bd; bd dir, NPR. **Honors/Awds:** Vision Award, Women Film, 2000; Peabody Award, Univ Ga, 2000; Acad Women Achievers, YWCA, 2001; Honarary Doctor of Arts, Pine Manor Col, 2002; Pinnacle Award, Greater Boston Chamber of Commerce, 2007; Image Award; other community & professional awards. **Special Achievements:** Helped build an educational institution in Ghana. **Business Addr:** General Manager for Radio & Television, Producer, WGBH, 125 Western Ave, Boston, MA 02134-1008, **Business Phone:** (617)300-2000.

## RIVERS, ALFRED J.

Executive. **Personal:** Born Sep 18, 1925, Crisp, GA; married Vera Stripling; children: Gwendolyn Thrower, Gregory & Glenda. **Educ:** LUTC, 1976; Tenn State Univ. **Career:** NC Mutual Ins Co; Gillespie Selden Comn Devel Ctr, dir, vpres, 1972-77; Cordele City Comn, vchmn, 1972-77; Mid Flint Planning APDC, dir, 1973-77; Crisp Cordele & C C, dir, 1973-77. **Orgs:** Nat Asn Advan Colored People; Local Am Legion; Cancer Soc. **Home Addr:** 504 W 15th Ave, Cordele, GA 31015-2433.

**RIVERS, DOC.** **See RIVERS, GLENN ANTON.**

## RIVERS, DOROTHY

Administrator, executive director. **Personal:** Born Aug 14, 1933, Chicago, IL. **Educ:** John Marshall Law Sch, 1951; Northwestern Univ, BA, 1959. **Career:** Michael Reese Hosp & Med Ctr, exec adminstr, dept psychtry; Pritzker Grinker Sch, exec adminr; Campus Chicken, officer & mgr; Nelson Prods Inc, vpres. **Orgs:** Founder, chwmn, Women's Div Chicago Ec Develop Corp; founder, XXI Michael Reese Hosp; chwmn, 1st, 2nd & 3rd Midwest Regional Conf on BusOpportWomen; vp, bd dir Chicago Ec Develop Corp; bd dir, Chicago Fin Dev Corp; chairperson, Vanguard Chicago Urban Leag; chairperson, exec adv bd Big Buddies Yth Serv, 1964-; Bravo Chap Lyric Opera; bd dir, Oper PUSH Found; womens bd United Negro Col Found; Chicago Chap Links; found & exec dir, Chicago Ment Health Found, 1983; Rainbow PUSH Coalition. **Honors/Awds:** Vol Service Award, Gov of Ill, 1967; Recip Vol Service Award, Chicago Ec Develop Corp, 1973; Lady of the Day Award, Radio Sta WAAF & WAIT; Cert of ldrshp Met YMCA, 1975; Cert merit, Chicago Heart Asn, 1975; M F Bynun Community Service Award, 1975. **Business Addr:** Founder, Chicago Mental Health Foundation.

## RIVERS, GLENN ANTON (DOC RIVERS)

Basketball player, basketball coach, vice president (organization). **Personal:** Born Oct 13, 1961, Chicago, IL; son of Grady and Betty; married Kristen Campi; children: Jeremiah, Callie, Austin & Spencer. **Educ:** Marquette Univ, attended 1983. **Career:** Basketball player (retired), basketball coach, executive; Atlanta Hawks, guard, 1983-91, Los Angeles Clippers, 1991-92, New York Knicks, 1992-94; San Antonio Spurs, 1994-96; Orlando Magic, head coach, 1999-2003; NBA ABC, commentator; Boston Celtics, head coach, 2004-13; Los Angeles Clippers, head coach & sr vpres, 2013-. **Orgs:** All-Star Adv Coun; mem nat adv bd, Positive Coaching Alliance, currently. **Special Achievements:** Book: Those Who Love the Game, 1993; Film: Eddie, 1996. **Business Addr:** Head Coach, Senior Vice President, Los Angeles Clippers, Staples Ctr 111 S Figueroa St Suite 1100, Los Angeles, CA 90012, **Business Phone:** (213)742-7500.

## RIVERS, JESSIE

Administrator. **Educ:** Wayne State Univ. **Career:** Camp Gilman, supvr; Mich Reformatory, dep warden; Mich Parole Bd, staff; Egeler Correctional Facil, warden, 1993-94; Ryan Regional Correctional Facil, warden, 1995.

**RIVERS, JOHN MILTON.** **See RIVERS, MICKEY.**

## RIVERS, JOHNNY (JOHN HENRY RAMISTELLA)

Singer. **Personal:** Born Nov 7, 1942, New York, NY. **Career:** Rivers Music, pres; Imperial Records, rcrdng artst, 1963-; Albums: At The Whisky A Go-Go, 1964; Meanwhile, 1965; "..and i know you want to dance", 1966; Rewind, 1967; Realization, 1968; Touch Of Gold, 1969; Homegrown, 1971; L.A. Reggae, 1972; Blue Suede Shoes, 1973; Last Boogie In Paris, 1974; Road, 1974; The Very Best Of, 1975; New Lovers And Old Friends, 1975; Wild Night, 1976; Outside Help, 1979; Borrowed Time, 1980; Not A Through Street, 1983; Memphis Sun, 1991; Last Train To Memphis, 1998; Back at the Whisky, 2000; Reinvention Highway, 2004; Last Boogie in Paris: The Complete Concert, 2007; Shadows of the Moon, 2009; Compilations: Johnny Rivers' Golden Hits, 1966; Touch of Gold, 1969; Johnny Rivers, 1972; The Very Best of Johnny Rivers, 1975; The Best of Johnny Rivers, 1987; Anthology, 1964-77, 1991; Summer Rain: The Essential Rivers, 1964-75, 2006; Secret Agent Man: The Ultimate Johnny Rivers Anthology 1964-2006, 2006; Soul City Records, LA, owner, 1967-; Soul City Prods, Johnny Rivers Mus. **Orgs:** First hit Record Memphis. **Honors/Awds:** Louisiana Music Hall of Fame, 2009. **Business Addr:** Singer, Soul City Records, 3141 Coldwater Canyon Lane, Beverly Hills, CA 90210.

## RIVERS, JOHNNY

Chef. **Personal:** Born Oct 5, 1949, Orlando, FL; son of Johnnie Mae; married Shirley Capers; children: Johnny Jr, Djuan, Dwain, Tanya & Zina. **Educ:** Johnson & Wales Univ, Doctor Culinary Arts (hon). **Career:** Cherry Plz Hotel, cook; Mission Inn Country Club, chef, 1963-64; Flountainbleu Miami FL, chef, 1968; Palmer House, chef, 1969; Walt Disney World Co, exec chef, beginning 1970, corp exec chef, 1989-95; JR Intl Enterprises Inc, chef & restaurateur, 1995-; Johnny Rivers' Smokehouse Express, owner, currently; Darden Restaurants, consult; Smokehouse & BBQ Co, Chef & Owner, currently; McArthur Dairy, chef, currently. **Orgs:** Pres, Cent Fla Chef Asn, 1974-75; host & chairperson World Chef Cong, 1984; pub rels, Am Culinary Fed, 1984-85; Orange City Sch Bd, 1985; Cent Fla Community. **Honors/Awds:** Acad Chefs Am Culinary Fed, 1976-77; Award of Gratitude, Brown Col, 1979; Chef of the Year, Cent Fla Chef Asn, 1980; Chef Professionalism Award, Am Culinary Fedn, 1992; Orlando Mag Golden Palm Awards; Fla Trend's Golden Spoon Awards; Orlando Sentinel Foodie Awards; Cornell Culinarian Hospitality Artists Award. **Special Achievements:** TV appearance: "Good Morning Am"; "Today Show"; "Oprah Winfrey Show"; "Live! With Regis & Kathie Lee"; publ including: Time mag; Natl Restaurant News; Redbook; Southern Living; Bon Appetit; Chef mag; Food Arts; Better Homes & Gardens; Ebony mag; Cooked for U.S. Presidents Nixon, Ford, Carter, Reagan and Clinton, and for South African President Nelson Mandela. **Home Addr:** 7133 Tallow Tree Lane, Orlando, FL 32810. **Business Addr:** Chef, Owner, Smokehouse & Bbq Co, 5370 W Colonial Dr, Orlando, FL 32808, **Business Phone:** (407)293-5803.

## RIVERS, LEN C.

Athletic coach. **Educ:** Springfield Col, attended 1957. **Career:** Athletic coach (retired); Franklin Twp High Sch, head football coach; NJ Nets, dir community affairs; Univ Conn, coach; Univ Princeton, coach; Univ Montclair, coach; Lakewood High Sch, athletic dir & chairperson; Ocean County All Stars, coaching staff. **Orgs:** Chmn, football comt, NJ State Interscholastic Athletic Asn; chmn, Football Comt. **Home Addr:** 80 Fairway Ct, Lakewood, NJ 08701-7220, **Home Phone:** (732)370-3932.

## RIVERS, DR. LOUIS

Educator. **Personal:** Born Sep 18, 1922, Savannah, GA; married Ligia Sanchez; children: Luisa, Liana, Loria & Leigh. **Educ:** Savannah State Col, BS, 1946; NY Univ, MA, 1951; Fordham Univ, PhD, 1975. **Career:** WV State Col, instr, 1951-52; Southern Univ, instr, 1952-53; Tougaloo Col, asst prof, 1953-58; New York Tech Col, prof; Andrew Mellon creative writing fel, 1984; City Univ New York, emer, currently. **Orgs:** Natl Writers Club; Dramatist Guild; Speech Commun Asn; Col Lang Asn; Phi Delta Kappa; Kappa Delta Pi. **Home Addr:** 333 Lafayette Ave Apt 5A, Brooklyn, NY 11238-1338, **Home Phone:** (718)857-1567. **Business Addr:** NY.

**RIVERS, MICKEY (JOHN MILTON RIVERS)**
Baseball player. **Personal:** Born Oct 31, 1948, Miami, FL; children: Mickey Rivers Jr. **Educ:** Miami-Dade Community Col, attended 1969. **Career:** Baseball player (retired); Calif Angels, outfielder, 1970-75; New York Yankees, outfielder, 1976-79; Tex Rangers, outfielder, 1979-84. **Home Addr:** 350 NW 48th St, Miami, FL 33127-2459.

**RIVERS, DR. ROBERT JOSEPH, JR.**
Physician, educator, surgeon. **Personal:** Born Nov 14, 1931, Princeton, NJ; married Ruth J Lewis; children: Michael, Scott, Wendy & Robert Jr. **Educ:** Princeton Univ, AB, biol, 1953; Harvard Med Sch, MD, 1957. **Career:** Educator, physician (retired); Pvt pract, vascular surg, 1965-86; Univ Rochester Sch Med & Dent, dept med & surg, prof clin surg, 1984-89, assoc dean minority affairs, 1984-89. **Orgs:** Trustee, Princeton Univ, 1969-77; bd trustee, Rochester Savings Bank, 1972-83; chief, Div Vascular Surg, Genesee Hosp, 1978-85. **Honors/Awds:** President's Citation Medical Society of the State of NY, 1971; Distinguished Alumni Service Award, Asn Black Princeton Alumni, 1982; Outstanding Service Award, Nat Asn Med Minority Educr Inc, 1989. **Special Achievements:** First African American students admitted to Princeton, 1949; The first African American elected by the Board to serve as a Trustee, 1969. **Home Addr:** 164 Highland, Williamsburg, VA 23188-7467, **Home Phone:** (508)255-7184.

**RIVERS, RONALD LEROY**
**Personal:** Born Nov 13, 1971, Elizabeth, NJ; married Myla; children: Malia. **Educ:** Fresno State Univ, bus admin & mgt, 1994. **Career:** Football player (retired), coach, motivational speaker; Detroit Lions, running back, 1995-99; Atlanta Falcons, running back, 2000; motivational speaker, 2002-; Freedom High Sch, asst varsity football coach, 2002-; Heritage High Sch, head softball coach, 2006-. **Honors/Awds:** Special Teams Most Valuable Player, Detroit Lions, 1995. **Business Addr:** Head Softball Coach, Heritage High School, 101 American Ave, Brentwood, CA 94513.

**RIVERS, TOM. See WAGONER, J. ROBERT.**

**RIVERS, VALERIE L.**
Lawyer, government official. **Personal:** Born Nov 25, 1952, Birmingham, AL; daughter of Eddie. **Educ:** Tuskegee Inst, BS, 1975; Southern Univ Sch Law, JD, 1980. **Career:** Wayne County Community Col, asst dir human resources, 1976; Gov Off Consumer Protection State La, investr 1979-80; B'ham Area Legal Serv, staff atty cand, 1981; Birmingham City Coun. **Orgs:** Phi Alpha Delta Law Frat Int, 1978-; adv comn, minor recruiter, Big-sister, 1983-; bd dir Big Bros/Big Sisters Gr Birmingham, 1985-88; Am Soc Pub Admin, 1981-; Nat Forum Black Admin, 1983-; exec dir, Downtown Redevelop Authority. **Home Addr:** 1908 Huntington Cir, Birmingham, AL 35214.

**RIVERS, VERNON FREDERICK, JR.**
School principal, teacher. **Personal:** Born Jul 25, 1933, Peekskill, NY; married Audrey Cherry; children: Gregory, Pamela & Karen. **Educ:** State Univ NY, Plattsburgh, NY, BS, educ, 1955; Teachers Col, Columbia Univ, grad work, 1960; City Col, grad work, 1963; State Univ NY, New Paltz, NY, MS, educ, 1971. **Career:** School administrator (retired); Peekskill New York Sch Syst, teacher, 1957-61; Irvington New York Sch Syst, teacher, 1961-68; Elmsford New York Sch Syst, prin, 1968-72, fed funds coordr, 1971-72; Ossining New York Sch Syst, teacher adult educ, 1975; Brewster Sch Syst, prin, 1972-88, dir prof serv, 1988-91. **Orgs:** Kappa Alpha Psi Fraternity, Inc; Am Asn Retired Persons; bd dir, Salisbury Wicomico Arts Coun; Deer's Head Hosp; Ward Mus Wild fowl Art; bd dir, Mid-Delmarva Family YMCA; bd dir, Inst Retired Persons/SSU; vice chmn, Diocese Easton, Md; Sigma Pi Phi; Westchester County Football Officials & Coaches Asn; chmn, Salisbury MidShore Family YMCA Bd; bd mem, Fairview Found; founder, Yorktown Community Rels Comt; vice chmn, Diocesan Coun Easton; recreation comnr & treas, Yorktown Touchdown Club; Tri-County Asn Black Admin. **Honors/Awds:** Vanguard Award, Peekskill Nat Asn Advan Colored People, 1959; Certificate of Appreciation, Elmsford Comt, 1972; Certificate of Appreciation, Lions Club Yorktown & Rotary Club Brewster, 1974; Certificate of Appreciation, Yorktown Area Jaycees, 1978; Cert Safety & Good Medal. **Special Achievements:** First African American teacher & principal in each school system employed. **Home Addr:** 1001 E Schumaker Manor Dr, Salisbury, MD 21804-6065, **Home Phone:** (410)860-4645.

**ROACH, DELORIS**
Public relations executive, president (organization), business owner. **Personal:** Born Apr 15, 1944, Pine Bluff, AR; children: Yvette Guyton, Frank, Anthony & Monica. **Educ:** Univ Calif, Berkeley, Calif, jour & polit, 1975; San Francisco State Univ, MA, radio & tv, 1979. **Career:** KQED-TV Educ TV, admin asst, 1979-81; KQED-TV Educ Films, researcher, 1981-82; New Images Prod Inc, prod coordr, 1982-84; Fleming Co Inc, advert coordr; Emery Unified Sch Dist, mem, bd trustee; TLW Pub Rels Inc, pres, owner & principle consult, 2004-. **Orgs:** Consult, Calif Schs Bd Assoc, 1979; Calif Sch Bds Assoc; Alameda Co Sch Bds Assoc, 1979; Calif Black Sch Bd Mem Assoc, 1981; Pub Rels Soc Am; FFSC-Chamber Com; Nat Notary Asn; Solano County Dem Cent Comt. **Honors/Awds:** Outstanding Citizen Award, Emery ville Neighborhood Assoc, 1981; Disting Service Award, Alameda Co Sch Bds Assoc, 1984; Hermes Creative Award, 2007, 2008. **Home Addr:** 140 Olympic Cir, Vacaville, CA 95687-3306. **Business Addr:** President, Owner, TLW Public Relations Inc, 340 2 Travis Blvd Suite 167, Fairfield, CA 94533, **Business Phone:** (707)208-9479.

**ROACH, PROF. HILDRED ELIZABETH**
Educator. **Personal:** Born Mar 14, 1937, Charlotte, NC; daughter of Howard and Pearl Caldwell. **Educ:** Fisk Univ, Nashville, TN, BA, 1957; Juilliard Sch Music, NY, attended 1959; Yale Univ, New Haven, CT, MM, 1962; Univ Ghana, attended 1969. **Career:** Tuskegee Inst, Tuskegee, Ala, fac, 1957-60; Fayetteville State Col, Fayetteville, NC, fac, 1962-66; Howard Univ, Wash, DC, fac, 1966-67; Va State Col, Petersburg, Va, fac, 1967-68; Univ DC, prof music, dept visual & performing arts, 1968-. Published: Black American Music: & Present, 2nd ed, 1994. **Orgs:** Alpha Kappa Alpha; Nat Black Music Caucus; Nat Asn Advan Colored People; NANM; Phi Beta Kappa. **Home Addr:** 12909 Fox Bow Dr, Upper Marlboro, MD 20774. **Business Addr:** Professor of Music, University of the District of Columbia, 4200 Conn Ave NW Bldg 46W Rm A05A, Washington, DC 20008, **Business Phone:** (202)274-5810.

**ROACH, LEE**
Association executive, teacher, business owner. **Personal:** Born Jan 3, 1937, Rock Hill, SC. **Educ:** Lincoln Univ, BA, 1960; Bryn Mawr Col, MSW, 1969; Cornell Univ. **Career:** Restaurant, owner, mgr, 1955-74; teacher, 1960-66; Health & Welfare Coun, asst dir, 1966-67; Grad Sch Soc Work, Bryn Mawr, comn orgn instr, 1970-71; Health Adminr Prog, 1972; Regional Comprehensive Health Planning Coun Inc, sep assoc dir; Equestrian Acad; US Dept Agr; Roach Labs Inc. **Home Addr:** 2231 Norwood Ave, Pennsauken, NJ 08110, **Home Phone:** (856)486-0332.

**ROAF, WILLIAM LAYTON**
Football player. **Personal:** Born Apr 18, 1970, Pine Bluff, AR; son of Clifton and Andree; married Angela Hernandez. **Educ:** La Tech Univ. **Career:** Football player (retired); New Orleans Saints, tackle, 1993-2001; Kans City Chiefs, offensive tackle, 2002-05; Santa Monica Col, offensive line coach, 2009. **Honors/Awds:** NFC Offensive Lineman of the Year, Nat Football League Players Asn, 1994; Offensive Lineman of the Year, Nat Football League Alumni Asn, 1995; Louisiana Tech Athletic Hall of Fame, 2003; Arkansas Sports Hall of Fame, 2007; New Orleans Saints Hall of Fame, 2008; Louisiana Sports Hall of Fame, 2009; Pro Football Hall of Fame, 2012; College Football Hall of Fame, 2014. **Special Achievements:** TV Series: NFL on FOX , 1994; NFL Monday Night Football, 1970; ESPN's Sunday Night Football, 1987.

**ROANE, DR. PHILIP RANSOM, JR.**
Educator, virologist, microbiologist. **Personal:** Born Nov 20, 1927, Baltimore, ME; son of Philip Ransom and Mattie Brown; married Vernice Haynes; children: Crystal Reed & Donald H Reed. **Educ:** Morgan State Col, BS, 1952; Johns Hopkins Univ, ScM, 1960; Univ MD, PhD, virol, 1970. **Career:** Johns Hopkins Univ, Dept Microbiol, asst prof, 1960-64; Microbiol Assocs Inc, virologist, 1964-72, dir qual control, 1967-72; Howard Univ, asst prof microbial, 1972-79, asst prof col, 1977-, assoc prof microbiol, 1979-. **Orgs:** Am Asn Immunologists; Virol Study Sect Nat Insts Health; Am Soc Microbiol; Nat Insts Health Virol Study Sect, 1976-80; Dept Army Viral & Rickett seal Dis Rev Group, 1979-81; Sigma Xi; res publs field virol; HU-IBC Comt, Howard Univ. **Honors/Awds:** Kaiser Permanente Award for Distinguished Teaching, 1979; Inspirational Leadership Award, Pre-Clinical Prof, 1982; Merit Award at the Outstanding Instructor in Microbiology, Howard Univ Grad Student Coun, 1982; Certificate of Appreciation, Med Col Class, 1987; Kaiser Permanent Award for Excellence in Teaching, 2004. **Home Addr:** 14248 Bradshaw Dr, Silver Spring, MD 20905-6503, **Home Phone:** (301)236-0279. **Business Addr:** Associate Professor, Howard University, 520 W St NW, Washington, DC 20059, **Business Phone:** (202)806-6270.

**ROBBINS, AUSTIN DION**
Football coach, executive, football player. **Personal:** Born Mar 1, 1971, Washington, DC. **Educ:** Univ NC, Chapel Hill, speech commun, 1994. **Career:** Football player (retired); Los Angeles Raiders, 1994; Oakland Raiders, defensive tackle, 1995, 2000; New Orleans Saints, 1997, right defensive tackle, 1996, defensive tackle, 1998-99, left defensive tackle, 1999; Green Bay Packers, defensive tackle, 2000-01; Chattahoochee Tech Col, coach, 2010-11; Prudential Ga Realty, realtor, 2005-13; Berkshire Hathaway Home Serv, realtor, 2013-. **Orgs:** NFL Alumni; NFL Players Asn; Champions Club Prudential; founder & pres, Rumor Foundation, 1998-. **Business Addr:** Realtor, Berkshire Hathaway Home Services, 3775 Roswell Rd, Marietta, GA 30064, **Business Phone:** (678)525-1886.

**ROBBINS, CARL GREGORY CUYJET**
Executive, manager. **Personal:** Born Feb 2, 1948, Philadelphia, PA; son of Leon Wallace Sr and Agnes; married Sydney; children: 5. **Educ:** Univ Pa, BA, Am hist, 1970; Univ Pa, Wharton Sch, MBA, labor rels mgt, 1980. **Career:** Ivy League Champion Penn team, capt, 1970; FMC Corp; Towers Perrin; Univ Pa; Vanguard Group Inc, inst mkt, sr mgr consult rels & instnl sales, currently; Harvest Fund Advisors LLC, consult rels dir, 2010-. **Honors/Awds:** NAT Achievement Scholar, 1966-70. **Home Addr:** 5 Hathaway Cir, Wynnewood, PA 19096-1901, **Home Phone:** (610)658-0807. **Business Addr:** Consultant Relations Director, Harvest Fund Advisors LLC, 100 W Lancaster Ave Suite 200, Wayne, PA 19087, **Business Phone:** (610)341-9700.

**ROBBINS, JESSICA DOWE**
Physician. **Personal:** Born Sep 19, 1956, Birmingham, AL; daughter of Jesse and Janie; married Gilbert; children: Janaya Alyce. **Educ:** Dillard Univ, BA, 1978; Howard Univ, PhD, 1983; Univ Louisville, MD, 1996, MD, 1999. **Career:** Procter & Gamble Labs, toxicologist, 1986-87; Hoescht Roussel Pharmaceut, mgr sci affairs, 1987-89; Marion Merrell Dow Pharmaceut, mgr clin pharma cokinetics, 1989-92; Correctional Med Serv, chief med officer, 1999-; Full Circle Family Pract Psc, pres & chief exec officer, 2000-; pvt pract, currently. **Orgs:** Full Circle Med Soc, 1999-; indigent comt, Jefferson County Med Soc, 1999-; double degree mem, New Zion Baptist Church, 1999; teacher Sunday Sch, Green Castle Baptist Church, 2001; Humana Qual Improv Comt, 2001-02; Health Care Excel QA Comt, 2002. **Home Addr:** 3108 Ridgemoor Ct, Prospect, KY 40059, **Home Phone:** (502)228-5348. **Business Addr:** Physician, 1009 N Dixie Hwy, Elizabethtown, KY 42701, **Business Phone:** (270)765-4361.

**ROBBINS, KEVIN F.**
Lawyer, district court judge. **Personal:** Born Nov 17, 1958, Detroit, MI; son of Robert J and Beryl E Claytor; married Juanita; children: Landon, Aubrie & Averie. **Educ:** Univ Mich, Ann Arbor, BA, hist, 1980; Thomas M Cooley Law Sch, Lansing, JD, 1984. **Career:** City Detroit, Detroit, Mich, Law Dept, asst corp coun, 1985-89; Kmart Corp, Troy, Mich, pub liability atty, 1989; Detroit Pub Schs, asst gen coun, 2001; Davenport Univ, lectr; 36th Dist Ct, judge, 2002-; Third Judicial Circuit Ct Drug Treat Ct, judge, 2006-; Davenport Univ, City Detroit Law Dept, adj instr; Anointed Men God Mentoring Prog, mentor. **Orgs:** Nat Minority Coun Demonstration Prog; Asn Defense Trial Coun; Am Corp Coun Asn; Detroit Bar Asn; Wolverine Bar Asn; mediator, 36th Dist Detroit; mediator, Mich Mediation Asn Wayne Co; Greater Christ Baptist Church; life mem, Nat Asn Advan Colored People; United Way Community. **Honors/Awds:** Faculty Commendation Award, Am Inst Paralegal Studies, 1990; Operation Reach Back Inc, Orby Award for Distinguished Community Service, 2002; Detroit City Council Spirit of Detroit Award, 2003; Jackets for Jobs Inc, Community Service Award, 2004. **Home Addr:** 541 S Pk, Detroit, MI 48215. **Business Addr:** Chief Judge, Court Administrator, Michigan's 36th District Court, Rm 438 421 Madison Ave Ct, Detroit, MI 48226, **Business Phone:** (313)965-2406.

**ROBBINS, LEONARD**
Housing developer, architect, executive director. **Personal:** Born Nov 3, 1955, Okaloosa County, FL; son of Bonzie and Elizabeth Eady; married Celia King. **Educ:** Syracuse Univ, archit, 1979; NY Univ, Dipl, construct mgt, 1987; Upsala Col, small bus mgt, 1989. **Career:** City Syracuse, Dept Bldgs, architect, 1979-81; Syracuse NHS, rehab specialist, 1981-82; NHS E Flatbush, Brooklyn, NY, construct specialist, 1982-85; Creative Restoration Consult Inc, vpres & owner, 1984-91; NHS NY City Inc, neighborhood dir, 1985-87; LR construct Mgt, Maplewood, NJ, sole owner, 1990-; Housing & Community Develop Network NJ, dir, housing develop, 1998-. **Orgs:** Bldg Trades Asn, 1988; Nat Asn Home Builders, 1989-90; Builders Asn Metrop NJ, 1989-90; Newark Community Develop Network; Unified Vailsburg Serv, Newark, NJ, dir housing develop, 1991-98; bd mem, Essex County Land Trust. **Honors/Awds:** Certificate, NY State, Construct Code, 1981; Certificate, HUD Default Coun HUD, 1984; Safety Certificate, OSHA, New York Bldg & Construct Indust Coun, 1986; Recognition, McCreary Report, WNEW-TV Channel 5, NY, 1988; Recognition, Entrepreneur Ser, WWOR-TV Channel 9, NY, 1989. **Home Addr:** 90 Plymouth Ave, Maplewood, NJ 07040-2320, **Home Phone:** (973)763-3677. **Business Addr:** Director, Housing & Community Development Network of New Jersey, 145 W Hanover St, Trenton, NJ 08618, **Business Phone:** (609)393-3752.

**ROBERSON, HON. DALTON ANTHONY, SR.**
Judge. **Personal:** Born May 11, 1937, Mt. Vernon, AL; son of Drue and Sarah Ann Williams; married Pearl Janet Stephens; children: Portia & Dalton Jr. **Educ:** Mich State Univ, BA, JD; Detroit Col Law, BA, JSD. **Career:** State Mich, social worker, 1964-68; Wayne City, asst prosecutor, 1969-70; US Dist, atty, 1970-71; Harrison Friedman Roberson, criminal defense lawyer, 1970-74; Recorders Ct City Detroit, from judge to exec chief judge, 1974-99. **Orgs:** Mich State Bar Asn, 1969; Wolverine Bar Asn, 1969; Criminal Defense Lawyers Asn, 1970-74; Mich Civil Rts Comn, 1972-73; chmn, Mich Civil Rts Comn, 1973-74; Mich Judges Asn, 1974-; bd mem, State Mich, 1989-; chmn, Asn Black Judges Mich; bd mem, Detroit Br, Nat Asn Advan Colored People; exec comn, Combines Wayne Circuit/Recorders Ct; mem exec comt, Mich Judges Asn. **Honors/Awds:** Judge of the Year Award, Nat Conf Black Lawyers, 1991. **Home Addr:** 3297 Sherbourne Rd Dr, Detroit, MI 48221. **Business Addr:** Executive Chief Judge, Recorder's Court for the City of Detroit, 1441 St Antoine St Rm 801, Detroit, MI 48226-2384, **Business Phone:** (313)224-2444.

**ROBERSON, F. ALEXIS H.**
President (organization), chief executive officer, administrator. **Personal:** Born Sep 20, 1942, Aiken, SC; daughter of F M Gomillion Hammond and T A Hammond; children: Alan. **Educ:** Howard Univ, Wash, DC, BA, 1963, MA, educ, 1974; Univ DC, Wash, DC, postgrad. **Career:** Opportunities Industralization Ctr, dir remedial educ, 1967-70, curric specialist, 1970-73, dep dir, 1973-80; Bus Develop, consult; Dept Recreation, Dept Employ Serv, Wash, DC, dir, 1987-, pres & chief exec officer, currently; DC Water & Sewer Authority, prin, currently. **Orgs:** Comnr, Wash DC Bd Appeals & Rev, Comn Post-Sec Educ; chairperson, bd dir, US Youth Games; Links; Girl Friends; Wash Chap, Nat Asn Advan Colored People; Zion Baptist Church; Govt Rep, Wash DC Wage-Hour Bd; Pvt Indust Coun; pres, Wash Metrop Area Chap; Nat Forum Black Pub Admin, 1987-; bd dir, DC Water & Sewer Authority; bd dir, Employee Compensation Appeals; bd dir, DC Chap, Wash, DC; bd dir, DC Urban League; bd dir, Dc Bd Appeals; bd dir, Rev & Univ Dc Intercollegiate Athletic Adv Bd, Nat Asn Advan Colored People; bd dir, Us Youth Games & Kennedy Ctr Performing Arts; dir, DC Dept parks & Recreation; bd, Dc Wage-Hour bd; Links Inc; DC Occup Info Coord Coun. **Home Addr:** 6230 9th St NW, Washington, DC 20011. **Business Addr:** President, Chief Executive Officer, Opportunities Industrialization Center, 3031-B Martin L King Jr Ave SE, Washington, DC 20032, **Business Phone:** (202)561-2004.

**ROBERSON, PROF. GLORIA GRANT**
Educator, librarian. **Personal:** Born Feb 6, 1945, East Meadow, NY; daughter of William Grant and Lillie Cofield Grant; married Clifford; children: Gloriane, Cynthia & Clifford. **Educ:** Adelphi Univ, Garden City, NY, BS, 1980, MS, educ, 1988, legal res course, 1989; Long Island Univ, Brookville, NY, MLS, 1985. **Career:** Adelphi Univ, Garden City, NY, asst prof, 1975, prof & librn, prof emer; Hofstra Univ, Hemp, NY, adj asst prof, ref librn, 1980; Books: World of Toni Morrison: Guide to characters and places in her novels, 2003; Guide to publishing opportunities for librarians, NY, 1994. **Orgs:** Corresp secy, Acad & Spec Libr Nassau County Libr Asn, 1989-90; Am Asn Univ Professors; Black Caucus Am Libr Associatiom; charter mem & newsletter bibliogr, Toni Morrison Auth Soc; Mem Black Caucus, Am Libr Associatiom; site evaluator, Comn Higher Educ Domestic; Nat Coun Women/UN, 2002-05. **Business Addr:** Professor Emeritus, Adelphi University, 1 S Ave Rm 205, Garden City, NY 11530, **Business Phone:** (516)877-3578.

**ROBERSON, LAWRENCE R.**
Consultant, executive. **Personal:** Born Aug 26, 1946, Birmingham, AL; son of Mack and Aressa. **Educ:** Ala A&M Univ, BS, 1967; Ind Univ, Bloomington, IN, MBA, finance & mgt, 1970; Col Financial Planning, CFP, 1986. **Career:** Int Bus Mach, systs engr, 1967-68, financial analyst, 1969; Ford Motor Co, supvr financial anal, 1973-83;

Dearborn Fed Credit Union, Consult, 1979-80; Wealth Mgt Group Inc, pres, owner, founder & sr portfolio mgr, 1985-. **Orgs:** Inst Cert Financial Planners, 1983-; Int Asn Financial Planning, 1984-; dir, Int Exchange Coun, 1986-; pres, Nat Black Master Bus Admin Asn, 1978-79. **Honors/Awds:** White House Fel Prog Regional finalist, 1983-84. **Home Addr:** 30350 Old Stream St, Southfield, MI 48076-5341, **Home Phone:** (248)723-5678. **Business Addr:** President, Owner, Wealth Management Group Inc, 220 W Cong 2nd Fl, Detroit, MI 48226, **Business Phone:** (313)223-2500.

### ROBERSON, SANDRA SHORT. See SHAKOOR, DR. WAHEEDAH AQUEELAH.

### ROBERSON, DR. VALERIE R.
Chancellor (education), dean (education), president (organization). **Educ:** Bradley Univ, BS, psychol, 1982; Roosevelt Univ, master degree, adult educ, 1985; Ill State Univ, PhD, higher educ admin, 2002. **Career:** Heartland Community Col, vpres, dean acad support, dir, 1992-99; City Cols Chicago Dist Off, assoc vice chancellor acad affairs & adult educ, 1994-2004, Olive-Harvey Col, interim pres, interim vpres, 2004-06, pres, 2006-10; Joliet Jr Col, vpres acad affairs, 2010-13; Roxbury Community Col, pres, 2013-. **Orgs:** Bd mem, S Chicago Chamber Com; S Chicago YMCA; Int Stevenson Found; Ill Coun Community Col Adminr. **Business Addr:** President, Roxbury Community College, 1234 Columbus Ave, Roxbury Crossing, MA 02120, **Business Phone:** (617)427-0060.

### ROBERTS, DR. ALFRED LLOYD, SR. (ALFRED L ROBERTS)
School administrator. **Personal:** Born Dec 18, 1942, Austin, TX; son of James and Ellen Woodfork Arnold; married Billie Kerl; children: Alfrelynn, Latasha & Alfred Jr. **Educ:** Prairie View Agr & Mech Univ, BS, animal sci, 1963; Tex Agr & Mech Univ, Med, curric & admin, 1966, PhD, curric & admin, 1973. **Career:** Dallas Independent Sch Dist, teacher, 1965-69, elem prin, 1969-71, dir community rels, 1971-75; E Oak Cliff Sub Dist, Dallas Pub Sch, dep asst supt, adminr sub-dist III, exec dir, 1975-89, asst supt personnel, 1989-93, exec dir alternative cert, exec dir crisis prev, 2003; Paul Quuinn Col, prof emer, adj instr, 2010-. **Orgs:** Nat Educ Asn; Phi Delta Kappa; Dallas Sch Adminr Asn; pres, Nat Asn Black Sch Educr; Alpha Phi Alpha; St Luke Comn United Methodological Church; Hist Preserv League; YMCA; Tex Alliance Black Sch Educr; nat pres, Nat Alliance Black Sch Educr; Dallas Regional Alliance Black Sch Educr. **Home Addr:** 3305 Wendelkin St, Dallas, TX 75215, **Home Phone:** (214)421-4296. **Business Addr:** Executive Director of Crisis Prevention, Dallas Public Schools, 3700 Ross Ave, Dallas, TX 75204-5491, **Business Phone:** (972)925-3700.

### ROBERTS, ANGELA DORREAN
Administrator, vice president (organization). **Personal:** Born Nov 21, 1960, Chicago, IL; daughter of Betty Williams and Morris Peoples; married Marvin James; children: Anjai G Shields. **Educ:** Calif State Univ, BA, commun, 1983. **Career:** Weiss, Jones & Co, data processing mgr, 1979-85; Assoc Students Univ Calif Los Angeles, mgr, comput opers, 1984-90; Acad Students, Univ Calif, Los Angeles, sr mgt, comput opers mgr, 1985-89; Housing Authority City Los Angeles, MIS dir, 1990-97; AltaMed Health Serv Corp, vpres admin serv, chief info officer & vpres facil develop & mgt, 1997-. **Orgs:** Advisor, State Calif e-Health Tech Adv Comt, currently. **Business Addr:** Vice President of Facility Development, Chief Information Officer, AltaMed Health Services Corp, 2040 Camfield Ave, Los Angeles, CA 90040, **Business Phone:** (323)725-8751.

### ROBERTS, BIP (LEON JOSEPH ROBERTS)
Baseball player, media executive. **Personal:** Born Oct 27, 1963, Berkeley, CA; married Janina; children: Lantavio. **Educ:** Chabot Col. **Career:** Baseball player (retired), baseball coach, media executive; San Diego Padres, infielder, 1986, 1988-91, 1994-95; Cincinnati Reds, 1992-93; Kans City Royals, 1996-97; Cleveland Indians, 1997; Detroit Tigers, 1998; Oaklands Atheltics, 1998; Skyline High Sch, baseball coach, 2008-; Acad Arts Univ, Urban Knights DII-PacWest Baseball prog, asst coach, 2010-2012; Comcast Sports Net, co-host, currently. **Home Addr:** 3569 Rosincress Dr, San Ramon, CA 94582-5078, **Home Phone:** (925)208-2013. **Business Addr:** Co-host, Comcast SportsNet, 1 Union Ctr 3601 S Broad St, Philadelphia, PA 19148, **Business Phone:** (215)336-3500.

### ROBERTS, BRETT JOSEPH
Baseball player. **Personal:** Born Mar 24, 1970, Portsmouth, OH. **Educ:** Morehead State Univ, attended 1992. **Career:** Baseball player (retired); Elizabethton Twins, 1991; Kenosha Twins, 1992; Fort Myers Miracle, 1993-94; Nashville Xpress, 1994; Hardware City Rock Cats, 1995; Salt Lake Buzz, 1996-97; Fargo-Moorhead Redhawks, 1997; old high sch, asst prin. **Honors/Awds:** Player of the Year, Ohio Valley Conference, 1992; Scoring Champion, Nat Col Athletic Asn, 1992. **Home Addr:** , OH, **Home Phone:** (614)778-3102.

### ROBERTS, BRYNDIS WYNETTE
School administrator, lawyer. **Personal:** Born Sep 4, 1957, Sylvania, GA; daughter of Roy Heyward and Josie Spencer Walls; children: Jennifer Yvonne & Jessica Kathleen. **Educ:** Wesleyan Col, Macon, GA, BA, 1978; Univ Ga, Athens, GA, JD, 1981. **Career:** State Law Dept, Atlanta, Ga, asst atty gen, 1981-87; Univ Ga, Athens, Ga, spec asst, vpres legal affairs, 1987-98; Jenkins & Roberts LLC, partner, 1998-; pvt pract atty, currently. **Orgs:** Exec ed, Ga Law Rev Mag; chmn, Rev Panel; State Bar GA; Jenkins & Roberts LLC, 1981; Nat Asn Col & Univ Atty's, 1986-92; chmn, GA State Bd Accountancy, 1988-; secy, Sch & Col Law Sect, State Bar, 1988-89; Classic City Pilot Club, 1991-92; vice chmn, mem, Wesleyan Bd Trustee, 1991-; African Am Hist Geneal Soc. **Home Addr:** 415 Sandstone Dr, Athens, GA 30605, **Home Phone:** (706)369-9660. **Business Addr:** Partner, Jenkins & Roberts LLC, 3427 Main St, College Park, GA 30303, **Business Phone:** (404)522-6386.

### ROBERTS, CECILIA
Executive director, insurance executive. **Career:** Majestic Life Ins Co, chief exec officer, pres, currently. **Honors/Awds:** Black Enterprises list of top insurance companies, 1994. **Business Addr:** Chief Executive Officer, President, Majestic Life Insurance Co, 1125 N Cleybon St, New Orleans, LA 70116, **Business Phone:** (504)827-0705.

### ROBERTS, CHARLES L.
Government official. **Personal:** Born May 25, 1943, Farmerville, LA; married Charlesetta Shoulders; children: Traci Smith & Channa. **Educ:** Ky State Univ, BS; Univ Louisville, MS; Univ Ga. **Career:** City Louisville, dir sanitation; Louisville Sch Dist, teacher, 1964-70; Met Parks & Recreation Bd, asst dir, 1970-74. **Orgs:** Am Pub Works Asn; Mgmt Planning Coun; State Reg Crime Coun; Nat Asn Advan Colored People; Omega Psi Phi. **Home Addr:** 207 N 36 St, Louisville, KY 40212. **Business Addr:** 400 S 6 St, Louisville, KY 40202.

### ROBERTS, CHERYL DORNITA LYNN
Educator, basketball coach, physician. **Personal:** Born Jul 31, 1958, Martinsburg, WV; daughter of Dorothy J Davenport and Shelby L Sr. **Educ:** Shepherd Col, BS, 1980; Univ DC, MA, 1984. **Career:** Edgemeade Md, recreation specialist, 1980-81; Univ DC, asst coach, ens basketball, 1981-85; Vet Affairs Med Ctr, recreation therapist, 1985-87, voc rehab specialist, 1987-88, asst chief, Domiciliary Care Prog, 1988-94, educ specialist, 1994-, Twelveth Nat Vet Golden Age Games, coord, 1997-98; Jefferson High Sch, head coach girls basketball, 1995; Wva Sec Sch, coach, currently. **Orgs:** Bd dir, Focus, 1991-96, treas, 1992; Delta Sigma Theta Sorority Inc; Golden Life; Shepherd Col Alumni Asn; life mem, Nat Asn Advan Colored People; adv, Employees Asn, Va Med Ctr; Mandela Chap Blacks Govt; Asbury United Methodist Church. **Home Addr:** 329 W German St, PO Box 217, Shepherdstown, WV 25443, **Home Phone:** (304)876-2277. **Business Addr:** Basketball Coach, West Virginia Secondary School, 2875 Staunton Tpke, Parkersburg, WV 26104-7219, **Business Phone:** (304)485-5494.

### ROBERTS, DEBORAH
Television journalist. **Personal:** Born Sep 20, 1960, Perry, GA; daughter of Benjamin and Ruth; married Al Roker; children: Leila Roker & Nicholas Albert Roker. **Educ:** Univ Ga, Henry W Grady Col Jour & Mass Commun, BA, jour, 1982. **Career:** WTVM-TV, Columbus, reporter, 1982-84; WBIR-TV, Knoxville, gen assignment reporter, 1984-87; WFTV-TV, Orlando, bur chief, NASA field anchor & weekend news co-anchor, 1987-90; NBC News, Atlanta, gen assignment reporter, 1990-92; Dateline NBC, corresp, 1992-95; ABC, 20/20, news corresp, 1995-; The View, guest host, 2006; Lifetime TV, Lifetime Live, host, currently. **Orgs:** Manhattan Soc. **Special Achievements:** Sports Emmy nomination for coverage of the 1992 Olympics. **Home Addr:** 325 W End Ave Apt 11D, Manhattan, NY 10023-8144, **Home Phone:** (212)362-2323. **Business Addr:** News Correspondent, 20/20 ABC, 77 W 66th St, New York, NY 10023, **Business Phone:** (212)456-7777.

### ROBERTS, EDWARD A.
School administrator, lawyer. **Personal:** Born Jun 17, 1950, Brooklyn, CA; married Yuklin B John. **Educ:** City Col NY, BA, econ, 1979; St John's Univ Law Sch, JD, 1984. **Career:** City Col NY, Off Dean Studies, asst higher educ officer, 1975-76; City Univ NY, bd trustees, 1976-80; Univ Stud Senate City, Univ NY, chmn, 1976-80; 902 Auto Inc, asst dir, 1980; NY State Div Housing & Community Renewal, supv assoc atty, 1984-89; Bedford Stuyvesant Community Legal Serv, dep dir & housing dir, 1989-91; pvt law pract, atty, 1991-. **Orgs:** City Col Pres Policy Adv Comt, 1976-77; pres, Carter's Action Review Comn, 1977; exec mem, Comn Pub Higher Educ, 1977-79; NY State Higher Educ Serv Corp, 1978; Gov's Task Force Higher Educ, 1979; NY State Bar Asn; Brooklyn Chapter Nat Asn Advan Colored People; Asn Strategic Progress Trinidad & Tobago; pres, Carter's Comn Volunteerism. **Honors/Awds:** Outstanding Enlisted Man Award, AUS, 1972; Award of Merit, Bronx Community Col, 1979. **Special Achievements:** First student-voting member of the CUNY Board of Trustees. **Home Addr:** 270 E 32nd St, Brooklyn, NY 11226. **Business Addr:** Attorney, 3009 Glenwood Rd, Brooklyn, NY 11210-2641, **Business Phone:** (718)421-4300.

### ROBERTS, DR. ESTHER PEARL
Psychiatrist, physician. **Personal:** Born Nov 9, 1942, Little Rock, AR; daughter of S O and Marion T; children: Ashley & Marion. **Educ:** Fisk Univ, BA, 1964; Meharry Med Col, MD, 1968; Columbia Univ, MPH, 1972. **Career:** US Dept State, sr consult, physician & psychiatrist, 1980-. **Orgs:** Am Psychiat Asn, 1978-; Nat Med Asn, 1980-; Am Col Psychiatrists, 1986-; Am Occup Med Asn; Royal Soc Med, London, 1997-; fel American Psychiatrist Assoc, 1998. **Home Addr:** 4201 Wilson Blvd Suite 103, Arlington, VA 22203-4182, **Home Phone:** (202)663-1905. **Business Addr:** Physician, Regional Psychiatrist, US Department of State, 2401 S St SE, Washington, DC 20020, **Business Phone:** (202)663-2517.

### ROBERTS, DR. GRADY H., JR.
College teacher, administrator. **Personal:** Born Feb 8, 1940, Pittsburgh, PA. **Educ:** Cent State Univ, Xenia, OH, BS, 1963; Univ Pittsburgh, MSW, 1965, MS, pub health, 1971, PhD, 1974. **Career:** College teacher (retired), professor emeritus; Madigan Gen Hosp, Tacoma, Wash, clin soc work officer, social work serv, 1965-67; Western Psychiat Inst & Clin, psychiat social worker, 1967-69; Univ Pittsburgh Sch Social Work, assoc dean, dean admis & stud affairs, assoc prof, prof, 1969-2003, assoc dean & assoc prof emer social work, 2003-. **Orgs:** Asn Black Soc Workers; Coun Soc Work Ed; Nat Asn Soc Workers; Alpha Phi Alpha; Nat Asn Advan Colored People; pres emer, Pa Col Personnel Asn; pres, Bloomfield-Garfield Corp; Pittsburgh Jazz Preserv Soc; bd dir, United Cerebral Palsy; bd dir, Univ Pittsburgh Sch Social Work. **Home Addr:** 5321 Broad St, Pittsburgh, PA 15224-2446, **Home Phone:** (412)661-7318. **Business Addr:** Associate Professor Emeritus, Associate Dean Emeritus, School of Social Work, 2117 Cathedral of Learning, Pittsburgh, PA 15260, **Business Phone:** (412)624-6304.

### ROBERTS, GREGORY G.
Government official. **Personal:** children: 4. **Educ:** Cent Mich Univ, sociol. **Career:** Metrop Detroit Youth Found's Learning Ctrs Achievement, dir; Wayne County's Dept Community Justice, dep dir; Congresswoman Carolyn CheeksKil patrick, dist dir; State Mich, Off Faith Based Community Initiatives, co-chair, 2003, assoc dir, dir, 2005-. **Business Addr:** Director of Community-Based Initiatives, Office of Faith Based Community Initiatives, Cadillac Pl, Detroit, MI 48202, **Business Phone:** (313)456-0020.

### ROBERTS, J. EDGAR
President (organization), executive, county government official. **Personal:** Born Aug 8, 1946, Valdosta, GA; son of John and Fannie Mae Davis; married Mary Catherine Gardner; children: Tia Charlotte, Sherri Latrell & Carla Maria. **Educ:** Temple Bus Sch, Wash, DC, attended 1966; Cent Bus Sch, Valdosta, GA, attended 1970; Ga Military Col, Valdosta, GA, attended 1972. **Career:** Elcona Mobile Homes, Valdosta, Ga, receiving clerk, 1969-71, 1972-73, purchasing mgr, 1973-76; self employed, Valdosta, Ga, minit mkt mgr, 1971-72; A-1 Construct Co Inc, Valdosta, Ga, pres/treasr, founder, 1976-; TCR Inc, A-1 Southeast Inc & J. Edgar Roberts Construct Co Inc, pres, 1986; Lowndes County, Ga, dist I comnr, 2004; VSU Minority Found, Chmn; Thomas Chapel Baptist Church, Valdosta, Ga, pastor & visionary, currently. **Orgs:** Trustee, Valdosta State Col Found, 1988-; chmn, Valdosta State Col Minority Found, 1988-; vpres, Minority Bus Group Valdosta, 1989-; bd dir, First State Bank & Trust, 1989-; adv bd, Supt Lowndes Co Schs, 1989-; bd dir, Leadership Lowndes, 1989-; pres & owner, James Scott & Son FuneralHome Inc, 1989-; exec bd, Valdosta-Lowndes Co Chamber Com, 1990-; bd dir, Art Comn, 1990-; VSC Sch Bus, 1990-; mem bd, Govs Comn Econ &Efficiency State Govt, 1990-; bd dir, Ga Asn Minority Entrepreneurs, 1991-; Home Builders Asn Ga. **Home Addr:** PO Box 56, Valdosta, GA 31603-0056, **Home Phone:** (912)244-8232. **Business Addr:** Pastor, Principal, Thomas Chapel Baptist Church, 2235 Smith St, Valdosta, GA 31601, **Business Phone:** (229)241-0790.

### ROBERTS, HON. JACQUELINE JOHNSON
Consultant, state government official. **Personal:** Born Apr 30, 1944, Dermott, AR; daughter of Gertrude Colen Johnson and Ocie; married Curley; children: Lisa LaVon, Curlee LaFayette & Dwyane Keith. **Educ:** Ark AM&N Col, BS, instnl dietetics, 1967, elem educ teaching cert, 1968, libr sci, 1970. **Career:** Bradley Elem, Warren, AR, teacher, 1967-68; Ark AM & N Col Libr, shipping & receiving, 1969-74; B&W Tobacco Co, sales rep, 1979-83; Dancy Oil Co, off mgr, 1983-85; St John Apt, mgr, 1986-89; State Ark, state rep, 1991-98; Jefferson County, justice peace, 1999-2006; Camden-El Dorado, dist consult, currently. **Orgs:** Bd mem, Asn Community Orgs Reform Now, 1986-; secy, Jefferson Co Black Caucus, 1987-; Ark Dem Party, Filing Fee Comn, 1988-90; Nat Comn Preserve Social Security, 1988-90; Pine Bluff Downtown Develop, Spec Events Comn, 1990-; Pine Bluff Chamber Comm, Mem Comm, 1990-; Urban League Ark, 1991-; chair & vice chair, State Agencies & Govt'l Affairs- House Elections Subcommittee; vice chair, Energy; vice chair, Pub Health, Welfare & Labor Comt-House; vice chair, Pub Health-House Labor & Environ Subcomt; vice chair, Legis Audit-State Agencies; Delta Sigma Theta. **Honors/Awds:** Certificate of Honor for Community Service, Top Ladies Distinction, 1990; Recognition of Outstanding Achievement, Ark State Press & Cent Ark Asn Black Journalist, 1991; Certificate of Recognition, Female Black Action Inc, 1991. **Home Phone:** (870)535-0771. **Business Addr:** Consultant, PO Box 2075, Pine Bluff, AR 71613-2075, **Business Phone:** (870)536-5703.

### ROBERTS, JANICE L.
Government official, executive director. **Personal:** Born Dec 31, 1959, Pine Bluff, AR; daughter of James C and Deloris Diane Strivers. **Educ:** Univ Ark Pine Bluff, Pine Bluff, AR, BA, econ, 1981; Univ Southern Calif, Los Angeles, CA, MPA, 1989; NY Univ, Baruch Col, New York, NY, MPA, 1991. **Career:** US Dept Agr, Soil Conserv Serv, economist, 1979-85; AUS Corps Engr, Los Angeles, Calif, economist, 1985-90; World Port Los Angeles, Port Los Angeles, Los Angeles, Calif, exec dir spec assist, 1990-; Nat Urban fel urban studies, 1991; Ark State Electoral Coalition, legis analyst & head lobbyist; contestant, Ark Pine Bluff, Jefferson County Univ; City Pine Bluff Coun, ward four, rep, currently; J Connection, owner currently. **Orgs:** Nat Asn Female Exec, 1982-; treas, Delta Sigma Theta Sorority, 1987-; asst chairperson, stud adv, Los Angeles Chap, Nat Forum Black Pub Adminrs, 1987-; Am Asn Port Authorities, 1990-; SRI Int Asn, 1990-; Pine Bluff city coun, aldermen. **Home Addr:** 4903 W 13th Ave, Pine Bluff, AR 71603, **Home Phone:** (870)879-1509. **Business Addr:** Representative Ward 4, City of Pine Bluff, 4903 W 13th Ave, Pine Bluff, AR 71603, **Business Phone:** (870)879-1846.

### ROBERTS, JOHN CHRISTOPHER
Automotive executive. **Personal:** Born Sep 12, 1944, Boston, MA; son of John Warren and Lillian G; married Joan Clarke; children: John Michael, Jason Martin & Kristen Renee. **Educ:** GMI Eng & Mgt Inst, BSME, 1967; Xavier Univ, MBA, 1970. **Career:** Gen Motors, Inland Div, eng mrg, 1962-79, hydramatic div, mgr exp, 1981-89, dealer develop trainee, 1989-91; Ford Motor Co, sr prod planner, 1979-81; Roberts Buick Saab GMC Truck Inc, pres, 1991-; Best Buick Saab Gmc Truck, dealer, currently. **Orgs:** Pres, Miami Valley sect, 1972-76; treas, Mich Alumni Asn, 1976-86; dir, Wolverine Coun, Boy Scouts, 1981-89; treas, GMI Alumni fed, 1982; Soc Automotive Engrs; Geo Tech Develop Adv Comt, 1986-89; Gen Motor Dealer Asn, 1991-; Haverhill Coun, 1992-; dir, Bethany Home bd, 1992-; Soc Plastics Engrs; Rotary Int; Nat Asn Minority Automobile Dealers; bd dir, Merrimac Valley Red Cross; Northern Essex Community Occup Adv Coun; bd dir, ESRA Inc; nat adv bd, Gen Motors Youth Educ Syst. **Home Addr:** 261 River Rd, Andover, MA 01810, **Home Phone:** (978)689-7958. **Business Addr:** Dealer, Best Buick Saab Gmc Truck, 901 S Main St, Haverhill, MA 01835, **Business Phone:** (508)373-3882.

### ROBERTS, DR. JONATHAN
Hospital administrator. **Educ:** Tulane Univ, PhD, pub health. **Career:** Dept Veterans Affairs Adv Comt, employee; LSU Hosp Syst, chief acad officer; Earl K Long Med Ctr, chief exec officer; Nat Hansen Dis Ctr, dep dir; Charity Hosp Syst, asst secy health & hosps, dir; La State Univ,

Health Scis Ctr, Healthcare Servs Div, chief analytics officer, currently. **Business Addr:** Chief Academic Officer, Louisiana State University Health Sciences Center Healthcare Services Division, 8550 United Plz Blvd, Baton Rouge, LA 70809-2256, **Business Phone:** (225)922-0798.

## ROBERTS, PROF. KAY GEORGE

Musician, educator. **Personal:** Born Sep 16, 1950, Nashville, TN. **Educ:** Fisk Univ, Nashville, TN, BA, music; Yale Univ, New Haven, CT, MM, violin performance, MMA, violin performance & orchestral conducting, DMA, orchestral conducting. **Career:** Ensemble Americana, Stuttgart, Ger, music dir & founder, 1989-; Artemis Ensemble, Stuttgart, Ger, conductor, 1990-; Ger Acad Exchange Serv, res grant, 1990, 1992 & 1998; String Currents, music dir & founder, 1994-; Harvard Univ, res fel, 1997-2003; W E B Du Bois Inst Afro-Am res fel, 1997-2003; Univ Mass, Lowell, conductor-univ orchestra, dir string proj, prof music, currently; New Eng Orchestra, founder, currently; Boston Symphony Orchestra, cover conductor; Opera N Inc, prin conductor; UMass Lowell String Proj, founder & dir. **Home Addr:** 7 Arlington St Apt 42, Cambridge, MA 02140-2763, **Home Phone:** (617)864-8532. **Business Addr:** Professor, University of Massachusetts Lowell, 35 Wilder St Suite 3 Durgin Hall 219, Lowell, MA 01854, **Business Phone:** (978)934-3867.

## ROBERTS, KIM (KIM ROBERTS HEDGPETH)

Executive. **Personal:** Born May 28, 1957, New York, NY; daughter of Howard A and Doris Marie Galiber (deceased). **Educ:** Harvard Univ, BA, 1978; Georgetown Univ Law Ctr, JD, 1981. **Career:** Am Fedn Tv & Radio Artists New York Local, contract adminr, asst exec dir/House coun, Co-Exec Dir, 1981-86, Am Fedn Tv & Radio Artists San Francisco Local, exec dir, 1987-92, from asst nat exec dir to assoc nat exec dir, 1992-2005, nat exec dir, 2005-; Harvard Univ, dir labor & employee rels; 1998-2000; Safe Horizon, vpres human resources, 2000-01; Am Youth Soccer Orgn, nat exec dir, 2013-. **Orgs:** New Eng Human Resources Asn; Mayors Film Adv Coun, San Francisco, 1990; San Francisco Labor Coun, deleg, 1989-92; NY Cent Labor Coun, deleg, 1986-87; NAB, 1992-98; Gov African-Am Adv, CMS, 1999-; exec secy, Assoc Actors & Artistes Am; bd dir, AFM-AFTRA Intellectual Property Rights Distrib Fund, 2005-12; mem bd dir, SoundExchange, 2005-12; trustee, AFTRA Health & Retirement Funds, 2005-12; Nat Asn Black Journalists, 2013. **Special Achievements:** First African American to be named chief executive of a major US media industry labor organization. **Home Addr:** 332 Franklin St Suite 401, Cambridge, MA 02139. **Business Addr:** National Executive Director, American Federation of Television & Radio Artists (AFTRA), 260 Madison Ave, New York, NY 10016-2401, **Business Phone:** (212)532-0800.

**ROBERTS, LEON JOSEPH. See ROBERTS, BIP.**

## ROBERTS, LILLIAN DAVIS

Executive, social worker. **Personal:** Born Jan 2, 1928, Chicago, IL; daughter of Henry Davis and Lillian Henry. **Educ:** Univ Ill, attended 1945; Roosevelt Univ, Labor Sch, attended 1960. **Career:** Lyng-in-Hosp, nurse aide, operating room technician, 1945-58; Chicago AFSCME, Dist Coun 19, 34, labor organizer, ment health employees, 1958-65; Dist Ct 37, AFSCME Div dir, Hosp Div, New York, 1965-67, assoc dir, AFSCME, AFL-CIO, New York, 1967-81, int vpres am fedn state, 2012-; NY Comnr Labor, app, 1981-86; Total Health Systs, sr vpres, 1987-92; Cigna, consult, 1991-; Dist Coun 37, Polit Action Comt, chairperson, exec dir, 2002-14; Univ Chicago Hosp, secy; New York Cent Labor Coun, vpres. **Orgs:** Nat Med Fel; nat exec bd, Jewish Labor Community, Am Jewish Congr; adv bd, Resources C Spec Needs Inc, Philip Randolph Inst; bd dir, Col New Rochelle; Am Dem Action; Nat Asn Advan Colored People New York Br; hon mem, Delta Sigma Theta Sorority; hon mem, AFSCME, New York, Clerical Employees Union, Local 1549. **Honors/Awds:** hon degree, Col New Rochelle, 1973; Adam Clayton Powell Govt Award, Opportunity Indust Ctr, 1982; Friends of Education Award, Asn Black Educr New York, 1983; Roy Wilkins Award, Nat Asn Advan Colored People; Benjamin Potoker Award, New York State Employees Brotherhood Comt; Achievement Award, Westchester Minority Contr Asn; Histadrut Humanitarian Award, Am Trade Coun Histadrut; Good Govt Award, New York State Careerists; Honorary Award, Hispanic Women's Ctr; Frederick Douglass Award, New York Urban League; Labor Award, Episcopal Churchwomen; Distinguished Leadership Award, United Negro Col Fund; Freedom Fighter Award, Coalition Black Trade Unionists; Probably the most powerful black person in American labor, Essence Mag. **Special Achievements:** A Salute to America's Top 100 Black Business and Professional Women, 1985; 30 Most Influential Black New Yorkers by the New York Post in, 2007; First black woman to New York State industrial commissioner. **Home Addr:** 115-02 221st St, Cambria Heights, NY 11411, **Home Phone:** (718)723-4146.

**ROBERTS, LORRAINE MARIE PETTIE. See Obituaries Section.**

## ROBERTS, LYNNETTE DAURICE

City planner. **Personal:** Born Oct 8, 1971, East Orange, NJ; daughter of Gale Bennett and Gus. **Educ:** Trenton State Col, BA, polit sci, 1994; GA Inst Tech, masters, city planning, 1996; GA State Univ, real estate cert, 1996. **Career:** City E Orange Dept Planning Col Assoc, 1993-94; GA Inst Tech Community Serv Grad Intern, 1995-96; Buckhead Coalition/BellSouth Mobility Intern Planner, 1996-98; Fulton County, sr land use planner, Dept Environ & Community Develop Planner, 1998-; His Will - Destiny Praise, asst dir & prod mgr. **Orgs:** Am Planning Asn, 1995-96, 2000-; Ga Planning Asn, 1995-96, 2000-; Toastmasters Int, 1999-2000; Am Inst Cert Planners, 2001-; lead serv programmer & producer, Destiny Metrop Worship Church. **Special Achievements:** Worked with Buckhead Coalition to install 911 Call boxes, 1999; American Inst Certified Planners Exam, certified, becoming only African-Am female in Fulton Co Dept Environment & Community Develop with this certification, 2001. **Home Addr:** 1036 Pepper Circle NW, Acworth, GA 30101-7374, **Home Phone:** (770)529-3261. **Business Addr:** Senior Planner III, Fulton County, 141 Pryor St Suite 5001, Atlanta, GA 30303, **Business Phone:** (404)730-8023.

## ROBERTS, MARCUS

Pianist, educator. **Personal:** Born Aug 7, 1963, Jacksonville, FL. **Educ:** Fla State Univ, BA, 1985. **Career:** Jazz pianist, composer, arranger, educator; Albums: J Mood, 1986; Standard Time, Vol. I, 1987; Live at Blues Alley, 1988; The Majesty of the Blues, 1989; Crescent City Christmas Card, 1989; Standard Time, Vol II, 1991; Thick in the South: Soul Gestures in Southern Blue, 1991; Uptown Ruler:Soul Gestures in Southern Blue, 1991; Levee Low Moan: Soul Gestures in-Southern Blue, 1991; Blue Interlude, 1992; Tribute to John Coltrane "ALove Supreme", 1994; Live at the Village Vanguard, 1999; Higher Ground, 2006; Deep in the Shed: A Blues Suite, 2010; 2002 Winter Olympic Games, artist-in-residence, 2002; Fla State Univ, Housewright Scholar, 2003-04, asst prof jazz studies, currently; Jazz Education, assoc artistic dir, 2008. **Business Addr:** Pianist, Marcus Roberts Enterprises Inc, PO Box 320159, Boston, MA 02132, **Business Phone:** (617)323-2658.

## ROBERTS, MARGARET MILLS

Pathologist, educator. **Personal:** Born Dec 5, 1936, Pittsburgh, PA; daughter of Everett and Isabelle; married Vernard T Sr; children: Vernard Jr & Sharon Renee. **Educ:** Fisk Univ, attended 1957; Ohio State Univ, BA, 1962, MA, 1964, PhD, 1966. **Career:** Professor (retired); C's Hosp, founder & dir speech path & audiol, 1966-95; Ohio State Univ, adj asst prof, 1972-94; MMR Consults, 1995. **Orgs:** Fel Am Speech-Lang-Hearing Asn, 1980-96; Elected legis counr, vpres var comts, Crittenton Family Servs Bd, 1976-85, 1987-; bd mem, Develop Disabilities, 1982-89; chair, Ohio Bd Speech Path & Audiol, 1984-91; Ohio State Univ Alumni Adv Coun, 1985-93; pres, Ohio Speech & Hearing Asn, 1993. **Honors/Awds:** Community Service Award, Alpha Kappa Alpha, 1972; Community Service Award, Delta Sigma Theta, 1986; Outstanding Alumni Award, Ohio State Univ Alumni Asn, 1991. **Home Addr:** 2365 Bellevue Ave, Columbus, OH 43207-2819, **Home Phone:** (614)445-6398.

## ROBERTS, MARGARET WARD

Educator. **Personal:** Born Jul 18, 1934, Chapel Hill, NC; daughter of James S and Margaret S Skinner. **Educ:** Va State Col, BS, 1960; Old Dom Univ, spec educ, 1975; reading cert, 1988. **Career:** Educator (retired); Portsmouth Sch Syst, state remedial teacher. **Orgs:** Prog develop, Work Incentive Prog; Chesapeake Chap Pinochle Bugs Inc; vpres, Norfolk Chap, Delicados Inc; chairperson, literacy proj, teacher yr comt, Portsmouth Reading Coun; Va Reading Asn; Portsmouth Educ Asn; Nat Educ Asn; Dem Women; Asn Supv & Curric Develop; Delta Sigma Theta; Grace Episcopal Church; Jack & Jill Mother, Chesapeake Chap; Coalition Black Women, Tidewater Chap; Urban League Hampton Rd; bd mem, Boys & Girls Club Hampton Roads; coor dr, Safety & Crime Prev, Level Green Civic League; Proj (AIMS), Activ Intergrate Math & Sci. **Home Addr:** 986 Level Green Blvd, Virginia Beach, VA 23464, **Home Phone:** (804)424-3613.

## ROBERTS, MICHAEL V., SR.

Business owner, executive, businessperson. **Personal:** Born Oct 24, 1948, St. Louis, MO; son of Victor and Delores Talley. **Educ:** Linden wood Col, BS; Hague Acad Int Law, Hague Holland, cert, 1972; Int Inst Human Rights, cert, 1973; St Louis Univ, Law Sch, JD, 1974. **Career:** Roberts Roberts & Assoc, pres, chmn & chief exec officer, 1974-; Jimmy Carter, campaign mgr, 1976; St Louis Brd Aldermen, officer, 1977-85; Alamosa PCS Holding, brd dir; ACME Commn, brd dir; Roberts Bros Properties, 1982; Roberts Tower Co; Roberts Broadcasting Co, owner, 1989-; Roberts Isle & Resort, founder, 1998; Roberts Wireless Commun, founder, 1998; Roberts Plaza, owner, 1999; guest speaker; Roberts Crowne Plaza Hotel, owner; Roberts Comfort Inn-Busch, owner; Roberts Best Western Hotel, owner; Roberts Clarion Jackson Hotel, owner; Roberts Courtyard by Marriott Hotel, owner; Roberts Mayfair Hotel, owner; Roberts Indigo Hotel, owner; Roberts Holiday Inn Hotel, owner; Roberts Radisson Hotel, owner; Roberts Clarion Hotel, owner; Roberts Bros Properties, owner; Roberts Orpheum Theater, owner; Roberts Custom Cabinetry & Woodworking, 2005. **Orgs:** Kappa Alpha Psi Fraternity; Phi Delta Phi Legal Frat; MO Athletic Club; St Louis Coun World Affairs; St Louis Arts & Educ Coun; Cert PADI Scuba Diver's Asn; bd mem, Better Family Life; bd mem, Home Shopping Network; All Saints Episcopal Church; leader, Am Youth Found; alt comnr, St Louis Land Reutilization Authority; trustee, Int Counc Shoppin Centres; chmn, Nat Asn Black hotel Owners, Operators & Developers; bd dir, Nat Asn Black Owned Broadcasters; Fed Commun Comn Diversity Adv Comt, 2009. **Honors/Awds:** JCCA tennis champion; Danforth Found Fellowship; Morehouse Col Dist Leader; Ernst 7 Young Enterpreneur of the Year Award, 2007; Trumpet Award for Business, 2009. **Special Achievements:** Black Enterprise's Top 100 Industrial & Service companies list, ranked 94, 2000; Author of the book, "Action Has No Season: Strategies And Secrets To Gaining Wealth And Authority"; He Has been the feature story for many magazines; Has been a guest speaker at various renowned stages. **Home Addr:** 5025 Lindell Blvd, St Louis, MO 63108. **Business Addr:** President, Chief Executive Officer, The Roberts Companies, 1408 N Kings Hwy Suite 300, St Louis, MO 63113, **Business Phone:** (314)367-4600.

## ROBERTS, MICHELE A.

Executive director, association executive, lawyer. **Personal:** Born South Bronx, NY. **Educ:** Wesleyan Univ, BA, 1977; Univ Calif, Boalt Hall Sch Law, JD, 1980. **Career:** DC, pub defender serv, 1980-88, Trial Div, chief; Akin Gump, 2004-11; Skadden, Arps, Slte, Meagher & Flom LLP, atty, partner, 2011-; NBA Players Asn, exec dir, 2014-; Harvard Law Sch, adj fac. **Orgs:** Fel Am Col Trial Lawyers. **Honors/Awds:** ESPNW, Impact 25. **Special Achievements:** First female union chief in major North American sports. **Business Addr:** Executive Director, National Basketball Players Association, 1133 Avenue of the Americas, New York, NY 10036, **Business Phone:** (212)655-0880.

## ROBERTS, NYREE KHADIJAH

Basketball player. **Personal:** Born Mar 10, 1976, Jersey City, NJ. **Educ:** Old Dom Univ, elem educ, 1998. **Career:** Basket player (retired), consult; Houston Comets, ctr, 1998-99; Wash Mystics, ctr, 1999-2000; Cleveland Rockers, ctr, 2002; Tenn Titans; Los Angeles Sparks; Lady Monarchs; Paghiakos Greece; IBM Southeast Employees Fed Credit Union, Auto Advisor, 2010-11; Fluor Corp, MWR Technician, 2012-. **Business Addr:** Technician, Fluor Corp, 6700 Las Colinas Blvd, Irving, TX 75039, **Business Phone:** (469)398-7000.

## ROBERTS, PAQUITA HUDSON

Educator. **Personal:** Born Mar 2, 1938, Andrews, SC; children: Craig, Tali & Paquita. **Educ:** SC State Col, BA, 1961; Newark State Col, MA, 1967. **Career:** Educator (retired); Hosp Ctr Orange, speech pathologist, 1964-67; Newark Bd Educ, 1968-69; Mt Carmel Guild, prog dir, 1969-75; NJ Dept Educ, educ prog specialist; Learning Resource Ctrs N, presch consult. **Orgs:** Consult, Orange Head Start, Inter coastal Bus Assocs; Barnett Hosp Speech & Hearing Div, CH Aston Assocs; adv bd, RAP NY Univ Coun Except C, 1979-; vpres, chairperson bd educ, Christian St Marks AME Church. **Home Addr:** 29 Burchard Ave, East Orange, NJ 07017-1604, **Home Phone:** (973)676-1180. **Business Addr:** NJ.

**ROBERTS, PATRICIA. See ROBERTS, TRISH.**

## ROBERTS, RICHARD RAY, JR.

Football player, football coach, executive. **Personal:** Born Jun 3, 1969, Asheville, NC; married Beth Garvey; children: Reagan, Slade & Pryce. **Educ:** Univ Va, BS, communs, 1992; Univ Wash, MS, athletic leadership, 2007. **Career:** Football player (retired), football coach, executive; Seattle Seahawks, tackle, 1992-95; Detroit Lions, 1996-2000; Interlake High Sch, Bellevue, Wash, coach; Microsoft, diversity specialist; Simplicity Lifestyle Mgt, founder & pres; Lake Wash High, Kirkland, Wash, head coach, 2008-10; Va Cavaliers football prog, dir life skills, 2011-. **Orgs:** Founder & pres, TheRayRoberts.com. **Business Addr:** Founder, President, TheRayRoberts.com, **Business Phone:** (206)601-9272.

## ROBERTS, ROBIN RENE

Television journalist. **Personal:** Born Nov 23, 1960, Tuskegee, AL; daughter of Lawrence and Lucimarian. **Educ:** Southeastern La Univ, BA (cum laude), commun, 1983. **Career:** WDAM-TV, Hattiesburg, Miss, sports anchor & reporter, 1983-84; WLOX-TV, Biloxi, Miss, 1984-86; WSMV-TV, Nashville, Tenn, sports anchor & reporter, 1986-88; WAGA-TV, Atlanta, Ga, sports anchor & reporter, 1988-90; V103, radio host, 1988-90; ESPN, sportscaster, 1990, contribr, 1990-2005; ABC News, Good Morning Am, reporter & news anchor, 1995-2005, co-anchor, 2005-. **Orgs:** Arthur Ashe Athletic Asn; Women's Sports Found. **Business Addr:** Co-Anchor, ABC TV Network, 190 N State St Suite 1100, Chicago, IL 60607, **Business Phone:** (312)899-4250.

## ROBERTS, DR. RONA DOMINIQUE

Educator. **Personal:** Born Dec 18, 1969, Christiansted, VI; daughter of Robert D and Constance E. **Educ:** Duquesne Univ, BA, 1992, MS, 1994; Univ Southern Miss, PhD, 2004. **Career:** Duquesne Univ, asst dir, 1992-94; Marietta City Schs, Woods-Wilkins Ctr, teacher, 1995-2000, syst administrator, 1995-, testing dir, 2006-08; high school teacher, 2010-; Hickory Hills Elem Sch, asst prin to admin asst curric & opers, currently. **Orgs:** Ga Asn Educrs, 2003-; Cobb Educ Consortium. **Home Addr:** 1642 Ashmar Lane, Marietta, GA 30064, **Home Phone:** (770)499-8088. **Business Addr:** Administrative Assistant for Curriculum & Operations, Hickory Hills Elementary School, 500 Redwood Dr, Marietta, GA 30064, **Business Phone:** (770)429-3125.

## ROBERTS, ROY J.

Educator, executive director. **Personal:** Born Jul 1, 1940, Carthage, TX; son of Baker and Thelma Hicks; married Barbara Brown; children: William & Ronan. **Educ:** Willey Col, BS, 1964; Yeshiva Univ, attended 1969; State Univ NY, Stony Brook, attended 1970; Adel phi, attended 1974. **Career:** John Marshall High Sch, physics instr, 1964-66; E Islip, New York, math teacher, 1966-67; Bellport New York, math teacher, 1967-70; Long Island Asn Black Counrs, treas, 1969; Dowling Col, upward bound proj dir, affirmative action community, chairperson, 1973-77. **Orgs:** Bayshore Control Islip, Nat Asn Advan Colored People, 1966-; Cits United Betterment Educ, 1967-; NEA, 1968-; Bellport fel 1968-; Vol Bellport Ambulance Co, 1968-; Minority Educr Asn Long Island, 1974-; treas, Asn Equality & Excellence Educ, 1979-. **Home Addr:** 180 Baiting Pl Rd, Farmingdale, NY 11735-6245, **Home Phone:** (516)551-6301.

## ROBERTS, ROY S.

Vice president (organization), automotive executive. **Personal:** Born Magnolia, TX. **Educ:** Western Mich Univ, BBA; Harvard Bus Sch, Exec Develop Prog; Wayne State Univ. **Career:** Navistar Int, vpres & gen mgr, 1988-90; Gen Motors Corp, staff, 1977-92; GM Flint Automotive Div, MI, vpres personnel, 1988; Cadillac Motor Car, gen mfg mgr, 1990-92; Pontiac Gen Motors Corp Div, vpres & gen mgr, 1992-98; Gen Motors Corp, N Am Vehicle Sales, Serv & Mkt, group vpres, 2000; M-Xchange.com, staff, 2000-; Detroit Pub Schs, emergency mgr, emergency financial mgr, 2011; Gen Motors Assembly Plant, N Tarrytown, NY, mgr; Reliant Equity Investors LLC, managing dir. **Orgs:** Exec Comt, Nat Urban League; pres, Nat Boy Scout; bd Trustees, Western Mich Univ; bd Trustees, Morehouse Sch Med; Volvo Heavy Truck; bd dirs, Air Rd Express; United Negro Col Fund; bd dirs, Saginaw Power Train Inc; Bloomfield Hills Country Club controversy; bd dir, Abbott Labs; bd dir, Burlington Northern Sante Fe Pac; officer, Nat Asn Advan Colored People; bd dirs, Aspen Inst; bd chmn, Educ Achievement Authority Mich; Nat Exec Bd Boy Scouts Am. **Honors/Awds:** Hon Doctorate, Fla A&M Univ, Grand Valley State Col, Paine Col; American Success Award; Executive of the Year; Received Numerous Honorary Degrees. **Business Addr:** Emergency Manager, Detroit Public Schools, 3011 West Grand Blvd, Detroit, MI 48202, **Business Phone:** (313)870-3772.

**ROBERTS, REV. DR. SAMUEL KELTON. See Obituaries Section.**

**ROBERTS, TARA LYNETTE**
Publisher. **Personal:** Born Feb 5, 1970, Atlanta, GA; daughter of Melvin Murphy and Lula. **Educ:** Mt Holyoke Col, BA, commun studies, 1991; NY Univ, MA, pub studies, 1994. **Career:** New York Univ, publ fel, 1991-93; Scholastic Bks, asst ed, 1992-93; Essence Mag, ed asst, 1993-94, lifestyle ed, 1994-97, online ed, 1997, contrib writer, 1993-2007; Heart & Soul, lifestyle ed, 1998; Syracuse Univ, instr, 1999-2000; Fierce Mag, publ, 2001-05; Am Online, ed programming mgr, 2006-07; Essence Ebony, Heart & Soul, ed; CosmoGirl mag, sr ed, 2007-08; Freelance, ed & blogger, 2007-15; Girltank, chief exec officer & founder, 2011-; AOL Living, staff; Ed: Am I the Last Virgin? Ten African Reflections On Sex & Love. **Orgs:** Alpha Kappa Alpha Sorority Inc, 1989-; Black Filmmaker Found, 1991-94; comt mem, Mt Holyoke Col Alumnae Quart, 1995-; Nat Asn Female Execs, 1996-; fel Start-Up Chile, 2011-12. **Business Addr:** Senior Editor, CosmoGirl magazines, 300 W 57th St Fl 20, New York, NY 10019, **Business Phone:** (212)649-3851.

**ROBERTS, DR. TERRENCE JAMES**
Executive, executive, executive, psychologist, educator. **Personal:** Born Dec 3, 1941, Little Rock, AR; son of William L and Margaret G; married Rita Anderson; children: Angela Rayschel & Rebecca Darlene. **Educ:** Calif State Univ Los Angeles, Los Angeles, CA, BS, sociol, 1967, MA, social welfare, 1970; Southern Ill Univ, Carbondale, IL, PhD, psychol, 1976. **Career:** Southern Ill Univ, Carbondale, Ill, asst prof, 1972-75; Pac Union Col, Angwin, Calif, asst prof, 1975-77; St Helena Hosp, Deer Park, Calif, dir, ment health, 1977-85; Univ Calif Los Angeles, Los Angeles, Calif, asst dean, 1985-93; Antioch Univ, core fac & co-chair, Masters Psychol Prog, 1993-2008; Little Rock Sch Dist, off desegregation consult; Terrence J Roberts & Assoc, chief exec officer, currently; Terrence Roberts Consult, prin, currently. **Orgs:** Am Psychol Asn, 1980-; Asn Black Psychologists, 1985-88; bd mem, African Am Cult Inst, 1988-; bd mem, Eisenhower Inst World Affairs, 1991-; bd mem, Econ Resources Corp, 1995-; bd mem, Winthrop Rockefeller Found, 1998-; bd mem, Econ Resources Ctr, S Ca; bd mem, Western Justice Ctr Found; bd mem, Little Rock Nine Found; bd mem, Facing Hist & Ourselves. **Home Addr:** 932 S Oakland Ave, Pasadena, CA 91106-3727, **Home Phone:** (626)296-8441. **Business Addr:** Principal, Terrence Roberts Consulting, PO Box 96, Pasadena, CA 91102, **Business Phone:** (626)644-4956.

**ROBERTS, TOURE**
Entrepreneur, writer, clergy. **Personal:** Born Jan 1, 1972?; children: Three children. **Educ:** Trinity College, B.S. in Business Administration; Pastoral Theology and Urban Ministry (Van Nuys, CA). **Career:** One Church International, Senior Pastor, 2002-; Toure Roberts Ministries, Owner, 2011-; Artist Resource Center (ARC) Entertainment, Founder and CEO, 2012-. **Orgs:** San Fernando Valley Faith Coalition, Council Member. **Honors/Awds:** "The Root" Magazine, The Root 100 Honorees, 2013.

**ROBERTS, TRISH (PATRICIA ROBERTS)**
Basketball player, basketball coach. **Personal:** Born Jun 14, 1955, Monroe, GA. **Educ:** N Ga Col; Emporia State Col; Cent Mich Univ, MA; Univ Tenn, attended 1979. **Career:** Basketball player (retired), coach; Women's Basketball League, 1978-82; Cent Mich Univ, women's basketball asst coach, 1982-84; Univ Ill, asst coach, 1984-85; Univ Wis, asst coach, 1985-86; Univ NC, 1986-88; US Jr Nat Team, asst coach, 1992; Univ Mich, women's basketball head coach, 1995-96; Atlanta Glory, head coach, 1996-97; Stony Brook Univ, head coach, 1999-2004; Agnes Scott Col, head coach, 2011-13; Univ ME, Women's Basketball, coach. **Orgs:** US Basketball Selection Comt, 1988-96; Emporia State Col Hall Fame, 1994; Women Sports & Educ Hall Fame, 1996; Black Caucus Asn; Women's Basketball Coaches Asn; Women's Basketball Hall Fame. **Honors/Awds:** World Univ Team, 1979; Hall of Fame, Emporia State Col, 1994; Women In Sports & Educ Hall of Fame, 1996; Inductee, Women's Basketball Hall of Fame, 2000; Coach of the Year, State NY Div I, 2000; Olympic silver Medalist; Tennessee Lady Volunteer Hall of Fame, 2003; Female Coach of the Year Award; Georgia Sports Hall of Fame. **Special Achievements:** First African-American player to compete at the University of Tennessee. **Home Addr:** 39 Hurtin St, Port Jeff Station, NY 11776. **Business Addr:** Head Coach, Agnes Scott College, 141 E College Ave, Decatur, GA 30030, **Business Phone:** (404)471-6359.

**ROBERTS, TROY**
Journalist. **Personal:** Born Sep 9, 1962, Philadelphia, PA; son of Robert and Ellen. **Educ:** Univ Calif, Berkeley, BA, polit Sci, 1984. **Career:** KPIX-TV, mag show host, anchor & producer, 1985-87; KATV-TV, reporter, 1987-90; WCBS-TV, anchor, corresp, 1990-93; CBS News, anchor "Up to the Minute" 1993-94, anchor Morning News, 1995-96, corresp Evening News, 1996-98; 48 Hours, corresp, 1998-. **Orgs:** Nat Asn Black Journalists; Harlem YMCA; Big Brothers Am. **Honors/Awds:** Nat Emmy Award, Olympic Park Bombing, 1997. **Business Addr:** Correspondent, 48 Hours CBS-TV, 524 W 57th St, New York, NY 10019, **Business Phone:** (212)975-4290.

**ROBERTS, VICTORIA A.**
Judge. **Personal:** Born Nov 25, 1951, Detroit, MI; daughter of Grace and Manuel; married John Conyers. **Educ:** Mich Univ, BA, 1973; Northeastern Univ Sch Law, JD, 1977. **Career:** Mich Ct Appeals, res Atty, 1976-77; Detroit Col Law, Mich State Univ, legal res & writing teaching fel, 1977-78; Lewis, White, Clay & Graves, assoc, 1977-85; Am Motors Corp, sr litigation atty, 1983-85; Eastern Dist Mich, US atty, 1985-98, US dist dt judge, 1998-; Pvt pract, Detroit, MI, 1988-98; Goodman, Eden, Millender & Bedrosian, 1988-93, partner, 1992-95, managing partner, 1995-98; Mayor-Elect Dennis Archer Transition Team, Gen coun, 1993-94. **Orgs:** Am Bar Asn, 1989-, House Delegs, 1990-97; State Bar MI, 1976-; Wolverine Bar Asn, 1976-; Women Lawyers Asn MI, Wayne Region, 1976-; Nat Bar Asn; Am Arbit Asn; Mich Trial Lawyers Asn; Am Trial Lawyers Asn; bd dir, Fair Housing Ctr Metro Detroit, 1985-91, chairperson, 1986-89; State Bar Mich, 1976-97; bd dir, State Bar Mich Found, 2002-; N Rosedale Pk Civic Asn; Detroit Inst Arts Founders Soc. **Business Addr:** Judge, United States District Court, 231 W Lafayette Rm 123, Detroit, MI 48226, **Business Phone:** (313)234-5230.

**ROBERTS, REV. WESLEY A.**
Clergy, educator. **Personal:** Born Jan 3, 1938, Jamaica, WI; son of Ignatius and Rayness Wong; married Sylvia Y Forbes; children: Paul, Carolyn, Suzanne & Michael. **Educ:** Waterloo Lutheran Univ, BA, 1965; Toronto Baptist Sem, Mdiv, 1965; Westminster Theol Sem, ThM, 1967, DDiv, 2002; Univ Guelph, MA, 1968, PhD, 1972. **Career:** Gordon-Conwell Theol Sem, asst prof black studies, 1972-73, asst prof Christian Thought, 1974-75, assoc prof Church Hist, 1977-84, asst dean, acad prog, 1980-84, prof Church Hist, 1984-85; Gordon Col, Wenham, MA, adj prof hist, 1974; Peoples Baptist Church, Boston, MA, interim pastor, 1980-82, sr pastor, 1980-. **Orgs:** Soc Study Black Relig; Am Soc Church Hist; Conf Faith & Hist; Assoc Theol Schs, US & Can, 1980-84; pres, Black Ministerial Alliance Greater Boston, 1994-04, pres emer. **Home Addr:** 1 Enon Rd, Wenham, MA 01984, **Home Phone:** (978)468-6685. **Business Addr:** Senior Pastor, Peoples Baptist Church of Boston, 134 Camden St, Boston, MA 02118, **Business Phone:** (617)427-0424.

**ROBERTS, WILLIAM HAROLD**
Football player, football coach. **Personal:** Born Aug 5, 1962, Miami, FL. **Educ:** Ohio State Univ. **Career:** Football player (retired), football coach; New York Giants, guard & left guard & right tackle & left tackle, 1984-94 & 1997; New England Patriots, left tackle, 1995-96; New York Jets, asst coach, 1999-2001. **Honors/Awds:** Pro Bowl, 1990. **Home Addr:** 27 Bath St, Long Beach, NY 11561.

**ROBERTS-SMITH, DEBRA**
Executive. **Personal:** married Carlos F. **Career:** Centers Foot & Ankle Care, off mgr. **Business Addr:** Office Manager, Centers for Foot and Ankle Care, 711 W N Ave Suite 210, Chicago, IL 60610, **Business Phone:** (312)642-3440.

**ROBERTSON, ANDRE LEVETT**
Baseball player. **Personal:** Born Oct 2, 1957, Orange, TX; married Lanier Hebert; children: Ryan Andre, Chrystina Ulyssa & Jace Christian. **Educ:** Univ Tex, Austin, TX, BBA, mgt. **Career:** Baseball player (retired), executive; Dunedin Blue Jays & Syracuse Chiefs, 1979; New York Yankees, shortstop, 1981-85; Tex Rangers & Okla City 89ers, 1989; Dupont De Nemours El & Co, staff, currently. **Honors/Awds:** Athlete of the Century in Baseball; American League Championship Series, 1981; World Series, 1981. **Home Addr:** 3190 Chasse Ridge Dr, Orange, TX 77632-1511, **Home Phone:** (409)882-0012. **Business Addr:** Staff, Dupont DeNemours El & Co, Orange, TX 77630, **Business Phone:** (409)886-6359.

**ROBERTSON, CHARLES E., JR.**
Administrator, consultant, manager. **Personal:** married Angela; children: Kendall. **Educ:** Southern Univ, BS, bus mgt, 1986; Mountain State, mgt develop, 1987; Dale Carnegie Mgt Sem, 1990; Am Hotel & Motel Asn, Cert Security & Loss Prev Mgt, 1990. **Career:** Harmony Ctr, Baton Rouge, La, counr, 1982; Capitol House Hotel, Baton Rouge, La, mgt trainee prog, 1984-86; Copper Mountain Resort, Copper Mountain Co, mgr, 1986-94; Denver Parks Recreation Dept, dep mgr parks, mayor, 1994; CER Assocs, pres, currently; Univ Colo, off pres, comn mem, currently; Colo Concessions Unlimited, entrepreneur, owner, currently. **Orgs:** Utility Consumers Bd; Summit County Chamber Com Statesmen Comt; Nat Coalition Black Meeting Planners; Relig Conf Mgt Asn; Soc Govt Meeting Planners; Phi Beta Sigma Frat; Nat Brotherhood Skiers; founder, Young Adults Positive Action; comn mem, Univ Colo Syst. **Home Addr:** 4944 Ursula St, Denver, CO 80239-4346, **Home Phone:** (303)576-9305. **Business Addr:** Founder, Young Adults for Positive Action, 4800 Telluride St Bldg 5, Denver, CO 80249, **Business Phone:** (720)541-6522.

**ROBERTSON, DELORES W.**
Educator. **Personal:** Born Jul 11, 1934, Richmond, VA; married Benjamin W; children: Benjamin W Jr (deceased). **Educ:** Va Union Univ, BA, 1957; Va Commonwealth Univ; Univ Va. **Career:** Educator (retired); Robertson's Kiddie Col, founder, pres, 1958-80; BW Mem-Choir, mentor, 1980; Bellevue Elem Sch, teacher; Whitcomb Elem Sch, teacher, 1989. **Orgs:** Richmond Educ Asn; Eastern Star 79 E End; Minister Wives Richmond &Vicinity; Int Ministers' Wives & Widows; Nat Asn Advan Colored People; Southern Christian Leadership Conf; Progressive Nat Baptist Conv Inc; chairperson, Deaconess Bd; secy, Educ Tutorial Prog; bd dir, BWR Ministries & Sem; co-founder, admin dir Nat Christian Educ Conv; hon mem, execbd, Richmond Va Sem; pres, Va Theol. **Home Addr:** 8901 Strath Rd, Richmond, VA 23231, **Home Phone:** (804)795-1111.

**ROBERTSON, DEWAYNE JAMAR**
Football player. **Personal:** Born Oct 16, 1981, Memphis, TN. **Educ:** Univ Ky, grad. **Career:** Football player (retired); New York Jets, defensive tackle, 2003, 2006, left defensive tackle, defensive tackle, 2004-05, nose tackle, 2007; Denver Broncos, defensive tackle, left defensive tackle, nose tackle, 2008. **Honors/Awds:** Freshman All-SEC, 2000. **Business Addr:** Defensive Tackle, Denver Broncos, 7505 S Potomac St, Englewood, CO 80112, **Business Phone:** (303)649-9777.

**ROBERTSON, EVELYN CRAWFORD, JR.**
School administrator. **Personal:** Born Nov 19, 1941, Winchester, TN; son of Evelyn and Pearl; married Hugholene Ellison; children: Jeffrey Bernard & Sheila Yvette. **Educ:** Tenn State Univ, BS, 1962, MA, 1969; Southwest Mo State Univ, NDEA cert, 1970. **Career:** School Administrator(retired); Allen White High Sch, teacher coach, 1962-68; Allen White Elem Sch, prin, 1969; Cent High Sch, asst prin, 1970-74; Western Ment Health Inst, asst supt, 1974-79, supt, 1983-91; Nat T Winston Develop Ctr, supt, 1979-83; Tenn Univ, Dept Ment Health & Ment Retardation, comnr, 1991-95; Bank Bolivar, dir, 1991-; SW Tenn Develop Dist, exec dir, currently. **Orgs:** Pres, Hardeman Co Teachers Asn, 1973; chmn, Whiteville Civic League, 1976-79; chmn bd, Hardeman Co Develop Serv Ctr, 1977-78; bd mem, Am Heart Asn affil, 1980-; pres, Bolivar Civitan Club, 1981; vpres, Whiteville Bus Enterprise Inc, 1982; chmn, admin div, SEAAMD, 1983; consult, Hardeman Ment Health Asn, 1983; bd dir, Quinco Ment Health Ctr; bd dir, Nat Asn Develop Orgn; Univ Tenn at Martin, WestStar Alumni Coun, 2011-. **Home Addr:** 2665 Newsom Rd, Whiteville, TN 38075-5803, **Home Phone:** (731)254-8508.

**ROBERTSON, FRANKIE GEORGE**
Association executive. **Educ:** La State Univ & Agr & Mech Col; Southern Univ & Agr & Mech Col, Baton Rouge, MS, pub admin, 2009. **Career:** Sears, Roebuck & Co, nat exec develop trainee mgr, 2000-01; La State Senate, Opers Specialist, 2001-02; Gardere Lane Kids Activ Group, bd pres; La Leadership Inst, Baton Rouge, LA, exec dir, 2002-04; Southern Univ & Agr & Mech Col, coordr training, community progs sr mgr, 2004-08; March Dimes, state dir, 2008-, regional dir advocacy & govt affairs, 2016-. **Honors/Awds:** Where Service Matters Award, WAFB-TV, 2001; Listed in Young Leaders of the Future, Ebony Mag, 2003; LA Chapter-Chapter of the Year- Diversity, 2008-11, LA Chapter-Chapter of the Year- Revenue, 2009, LA Chapter-President's Team Award, 2009, 2012, LA Chapter-Basic Program Excellence, 2013, LA Chapter-Program Impact Award, 2014, March Dimes Nat Off. **Business Addr:** State Director, Regional Director of Advocacy and Government Affairs, March of Dimes, 12015 Justice Ave, Baton Rouge, LA 70816, **Business Phone:** (225)295-0655.

**ROBERTSON, KAREN A.**
Librarian. **Personal:** Born Montclair, NJ; daughter of Joesph C and H June Hawkins. **Educ:** Morgan State Univ, Baltimore, Md, BA, 1966; Atlanta Univ, Atlanta, Ga, MSLS, 1967; Univ Baltimore, MBA, 1983. **Career:** Prince George's County, Hyattsville, Md, ref librn, 1967-68; Morgan State Univ, Baltimore, Md, Br Mgr, chief ref librn, 1968-80, dir libr serv, 1980-; Seymour Chambers, secy. **Orgs:** Alpha Kappa Alpha Inc, 1964-; Md Libr Asn, 1974-; Am Libr Asn, 1975-. **Home Addr:** 42 Palmer Green, Baltimore, MD 21210-1502, **Home Phone:** (443)885-3488. **Business Addr:** Director of Library Services, Morgan State University, 1700 E Cold Spring Lane, Baltimore, MD 21239-4098, **Business Phone:** (443)885-3488.

**ROBERTSON, MARCUS AARON**
Football player, football coach. **Personal:** Born Oct 2, 1969, Pasadena, CA; married Holly; children: Morgan, Milan & Marcus Andrew. **Educ:** Iowa State Univ. **Career:** Football player (retired), coach; Houston Oilers, 1991, free safety, 1992-94, 1996, defensive back, 1995; Tenn Oilers, free safety, 1997-98; Tenn Titans, free safety & safety, 1999-2000, dir player develop, 2003-06, asst sec coach, 2007-08, sec coach, 2009-11; Seattle Seahawks, free safety, 2001-02; Detroit Lions, asst sec coach, 2012-13, sec coach, 2013-14, defensive backs; Oakland Raiders, asst defensive backs coach, 2014, defensive backs coach, 2015-. **Honors/Awds:** Ed Block Courage Award, 1994. **Business Addr:** Defensive Backs Coach, Oakland Raiders, 1220 Harbor Bay Pkwy, Alameda, TN 94502, **Business Phone:** (510)864-5000.

**ROBERTSON, DR. MARILYN ANITA**
Physician. **Personal:** Born Dec 19, 1959, Curacao; daughter of David and Nina; married Curtis E Fisher; children: Michael, Christopher, Matthew & Christian. **Educ:** Hofstra Univ, MA, 1984; Med Col PA, MD, 1989. **Career:** Nassau County Med Ctr, bd mem, resident obstet & gynec, 1989-93; staff physician, 1990-93, part time staff physician, 1993-97; staff physician, 1990-93; KMLT Gynec Assoc, assoc physician, 1993-96; Hempstead Gynec & Obstet Assoc, physician, 1995-96; pvt pract, 1996-; Franklin Hosp Med Ctr, physician, actg dir obstet, dir womens health ctr, 2000-, chief gynec, currently. **Orgs:** Philadelphia Med Soc, 1985-89; Am Med Asn, 1993-; vpres, Coalition Comm Develop, 1995-97; Am Col Obstetricians & Gynecologists, 1995-; Franklin Hosp Med Ctr, 1998-. **Honors/Awds:** Distinguished Service Award, Hofstra Univ Alumni Asn, 1997; Annual Award for Excellence, NY State Governor George Pataki, 2001; Woman of the Year, Town of Hempstead, 2001. **Home Addr:** 3379 Courtney Pl, Baldwin, NY 11510, **Home Phone:** (516)868-3935. **Business Addr:** Chief Gynecology, Franklin Hospital Medical Center, 900 Franklin Ave, Valley Stream, NY 11580, **Business Phone:** (516)256-6000.

**ROBERTSON, OSCAR PALMER**
Executive, basketball player, businessperson. **Personal:** Born Nov 24, 1938, Charlotte, TN; son of Bailey and Mazell Bell; married Yvonne Crittenden; children: Shana Shaw, Tia & Mari. **Educ:** Cincinnati Univ, BS, bus, 1960. **Career:** Basketball player, guard (retired), president, chief executive officer; Cincinnati Royals NBA, guard, 1960-70; Milwaukee Bucks NBA, 1970-74; Oscar Robertson Construct, pres & chief exec officer, 1975-; Avondale Town Ctr, Cincinnati, developer, 1981; Orchem Corp, pres, chief exec officer & owner, 1981-; TV sports announcer; OR Group, pres & chief exec officer; Oscar Robertson & Assocs, pres, 1983-; Oscar Terr (affordable housing units), Indianapolis, Ind, developer/owner, 1989; Orpack-Stone Corp, pres & chief exec officer, 1990-; Oscar Robertson Media Ventures, 1998-; Oscar Robertson Doc Mgt Servs, 2000-; Oscar Robertson Foods, pres, currently; OR Solutions, pres, currently. **Orgs:** Pres, Nat Basketball Players Asn, 1964-74; St Dept Tour Africa, 1971; World Championship Team, 1971; trustee, Ind High Sch Hall Fame, 1984-89; Nat Asn Advan Colored Poeple Sports Bd, 1987; trustee, Basketball Hall Fame, 1987-89; nat dir, Pepsi Cola Hot Shot Prog; pres, NBA Retired Players Asn, 1993-99; bd mem, Countrywide Savings & Loan, 2000-; Nat Basketball Hall Fame; Ind Basketball Hall Fame; spokesperson, Nat Kidney Found; Salvation Army; trustee, Lupus Found Am. **Home Addr:** 1125 Elm Pk Dr, Cincinnati, OH 45216-2209, **Home Phone:** (513)242-2330. **Business Addr:** Owner, Orchem Corp, 4293 Mulhauser Rd, Fairfield, OH 45014, **Business Phone:** (513)874-9700.

**ROBERTSON, QUINCY L.**
School administrator, association executive, army officer. **Personal:** Born Jul 30, 1934, Wedowee, AL; son of Jessie and Viola Wilkes; married Dollie Williams; children: Lee Stephanie. **Educ:** Tenn State Univ, BA, 1955, MA, 1957. **Career:** School administrator (retired); Richmond County Bd Educ, guid counr, 1959-68; Paine Col, dir upward bound, 1968-69, bus mgr, 1970-83, Admin & Fiscal Affairs, vpres, 1983-99, chief financial officer. **Orgs:** Bd dir, USO, 1964-68; comn, Richmond Cty Personnel Bd, 1973-78; chmn, Thankful Baptist Church Trustee Bd, 1977-85; vpres, Frontiersman, 1984-85; bd dir, EIIA, 1985-; bd dir, Univ Hosp; bd mem, Richmond County Hosp Authority; bd mem & treas, Gertrude Herbert Art Inst; bd mem, Sun

Trust Nat Bank; bd mem, Augusta Rescue Mission; Am Asn Affirmative Action, 1982-; Nat Asn Black Pub Admin, 1983-; Nat Asn Human Rights Workers, 1986-; DeKalb Co Nat Asn Advan Colored People; den leader, Boy Scouts Am, 1992-. **Honors/Awds:** Man of the Year, Thankful Baptist Church, 1969; Admin of the Year, Paine Col, 1973-74; Citizen of the Year, Alpha Phi Alpha Frat, 1984; Outstanding Young Men of America, 1984; Distinguished Service Award, Univ Ga, 1985; Community Service Award, Black Pages Magazine, 1990; Minority Business Advocate of the Year, 1991. **Home Addr:** 3219 Tate Rd, Augusta, GA 30906, **Home Phone:** (706)796-8143.

### ROBERTSON, QUINDONELL STINSON
Educator, association executive, executive. **Personal:** Born Dallas, TX; married J William. **Educ:** BA, 1954, MA, 1970. **Career:** Educator (retired); Dallas Independent Sch Dist & Sch Sec, educ, 1957-58, educ cluster coord, 1984; Tex Col. **Orgs:** Am Asn Univ Women, 1986; master educr, Am Bd Master Educr, 1987; NEA; Tex St Teacher Asn; Classroom Teachers Dallas; Tex Classroom Teacher; Tex Asn Teacher Educ; Amigos; Phi Delta Kappa; Tex St Univ Alumni Asn; life mem, YWCA; charter mem, Dallas Urban League Guild; pres, Top Ladies Distinction Inc; bd dir, Dallas Pan Hellenic Coun; charter mem, Sigma Gamma Rho Sorority Inc. **Honors/Awds:** Cup for chartering Arlington Tex, Sigma Gamma Rho, 1983; Gold Charm for serving 3 yrs as pres of Sigma Gamma Rho, 1985-88; Gold Teacher of The Year, 1990-91; Yellow Tea Rose Award, SW Region Sigma Gamma Rho, 1992; Region Sigma Gamma Rho Service Award, 1992; 9 plaques for leadership & service; 1 silver tray for leadership & service; Gavel for leadership; 2 trophies for leadership & service; Medallion for YWCA Quota Buster. **Home Addr:** 1588 N Atoll Dr, Dallas, TX 75216-3215.

### ROBICHAUX, JOLYN H.
Executive, chief executive officer. **Personal:** Born May 21, 1928, Cairo, IL; daughter of Edward Howard and Margaret Love; married Joseph J; children: Sheila & Joseph Jr. **Educ:** Fisk Univ, Nashville, TN; Chicago Teachers Col, BA, educ, 1960; Pa State Univ, Ice Cream Tech, cert, 1975. **Career:** Med asst; State Dept Tour Africa, spec nutritions consult, 1956; Betty Crocker Home Serv, Dept Gen Mills, secy & fund raiser, 1960-65; Cook Cty, jury comm, 1971-72; Baldwin Ice Cream Co, secy, pres & chief exec officer, 1971-92; Univ Tex, Dallas, Tex, heart dis proj, 1999-2001. **Orgs:** Bd dir, Chicago United Way, 1984. **Special Achievements:** First African American employee of Betty Crocker. **Home Addr:** 8455 S Mich Ave, Chicago, IL 60619.

### ROBIE, CLARENCE W.
Business owner. **Educ:** Ga Inst Technol, attended 1974. **Career:** B & S Elec Supply Co Inc, owner & pres, 1980-. **Orgs:** Greater Atlanta Elec League. **Home Addr:** 1340 Niskey Lake Trail SW, Atlanta, GA 30331-6314, **Home Phone:** (404)349-3527. **Business Addr:** Owner, President, B & S Electrical Supply Co Inc, 4505 Mills Pl SW, Atlanta, GA 30336, **Business Phone:** (404)696-8284.

### ROBINET, HARRIETTE GILLEM
Writer. **Personal:** Born Jul 14, 1931, Washington, DC; daughter of Richard Avitus and Martha Gray; married McLouis Joseph; children: Stephen, Philip, Rita, Jonathan, Marsha & Linda. **Educ:** Col New Rochelle, NY, BS, 1953; Cath Univ Am, Wash, DC, MS, 1957, PhD, 1962. **Career:** C's Hosp, Wash, DC, bacteriologist, 1953-54; Walter Reed Army Med Ctr, Wash, DC, med serologist, 1954-57, res bacteriologist, 1958-60; Xavier Univ, New Orleans, La, instr biol, 1957-58; Aus, Qm Corps, civilian food bacteriologist, 1960-62; free-lance writer, 1962-; Bks: Jay & the Marigold, 1976; Ride the Red Cycle, 1980; C of the Fire, 1991; Miss Chariot, 1994; If You Please, pres Lincoln, 1995; Wash City is Burning, 1996; The Twins, The Pirates & The Battle of New Orleans, 1997; Forty Acres & Maybe a Mule, 1998; Walking to the Bus Rider Blues, 2000; Missing From Haymarket Sq, 2001; Twelve Travelers, Twenty Horses, 2002. **Orgs:** Soc Childrens Bk Writers & Illustrators; Nat Writers; Soc Midland Authors; Sisters Crime; Mystery Writers Am; Nat Writers Union. **Honors/Awds:** Carl Sandburg Award, Wash City Burning, 1997; Children's Literature Award, Friends Am Writers, Children Fire, 1991; Notable Children's Trade Books Social Studies: Miss Chariot, 1994; Children of the Fire, 1991; Books for the Teen Age, NYC Librarians: Mississippi Chariot; Children's Literature Award, "The Twins, the Pirates & the Battle of New Orleans", Society of Midland Authors, 1998; Scott O'Dell Award, children's historical fiction, 1999; Walking to Bus Rider Blues nominated for an Edgar, Mystery Writers, Jane Addams Peace Award Honor Book. **Home Addr:** 214 S Elmwood Ave, Oak Park, IL 60302-3222, **Home Phone:** (708)848-3141.

### ROBINSON, ALBERT ARNOLD
Salesperson. **Personal:** Born May 2, 1937, Lawrenceville, VA; married Mary Elizabeth Wright; children: Terence, Todd, Trent, Tevis & Lisa. **Educ:** Va State Univ, BS, 1958; Cent State Univ, BS, 1968; E Calif Univ, attended 1977. **Career:** Salesperson (retired); US Army, commissioned officer, 1958-78; Ford Motor Co, manufacturing supvr, 1978-80; Bechtel Power Corp, supvr reprographics, 1980-84; Nat Reproductions Corp, sales rep, 1984-85; Eastern Mich Univ, mgr serv opers, special asst vpres bus & finance, 1985-2002. **Orgs:** Trustee, chmn, Second Baptist Ch; Ypsilanti& Willow Run Br Nat Asn Advan Colored People; councilman, Ypsilanti City Coun; Ann Arbor & Ypsilanti Bus & Prof League; Emanon Club; Beta Kappa Chi Honorary Scientific Frat, 1958; Kappa Phi Kappa Hon Educ Frat, 1958. **Honors/Awds:** Meritorious Serv Medal. **Home Addr:** 918 Pleasant Dr, Ypsilanti, MI 48197, **Home Phone:** (734)482-5861.

### ROBINSON, ALBERT M.
Association executive. **Personal:** Born Oct 1, 1958; married Jane B Carter; children: Albert Jr & Kimberly. **Educ:** VA State Col, BS; Rutgers Univ; Rider Col. **Career:** United Progress Inc, exec dir; Dept Comm Affairs NJ, relocation officer; councilmember N wd; Trenton House Auth, mgr; Lockerman High Sch Denton, teacher; Home Depot Usa Inc, asst mgr. **Orgs:** Pres, Nat Asn Advan Colored People, Trenton Br. **Honors/Awds:** Brotherhood Award, Jewish Fed; Pol Action Council Award, 1967; Trenton Public Service Award, 1968; Outstanding & Community Service Award, 1970; Outstanding Achievement Community Affairs, Nat Asn Advan Colored People, 1971. **Home Addr:** 178 Brunswick Ave, Trenton, NJ 08618, **Home Phone:** (609)695-5801.

### ROBINSON, ALCURTIS
Insurance executive. **Personal:** son of Eris Sr and Corean Skinner. **Educ:** Harris Teachers Col, AA, 1960; Purdue Univ, Prof Mgt Inst, 1976. **Career:** Mutual Omaha-United Omaha, St Louis, Mo, salesman, 1967-69, sls trng instr, 1969-70, dist mgr, 1970-73; Mutual Omaha-United Omaha, Omaha, Nebr, assoc dir mgt trng, 1973-75, asst vpres career develop & mgt trng, 1975-77, second vpres, 1977-82, vpres career develop & pub affairs, 1982-85, vpres pub serv & minority affairs, 1985-, vpres minority & community affairs, 1988-; Ins Indust Designation, regist health underwriter, currently. **Orgs:** pres, Omaha Sch Found, 1990-91; NAACP, Baltimore, Md; bd mem, Nat Assoc Sickle Cell DisInc; Black Exec Exchange Prog, Nat Urban League Inc, NY; Nat Alliance Bus; Career develop adv comm, Nat Urban League; develop dir, United Negro Col Fund Dr; chmn, pub employees retirement bd, State of Nebr; chmn, bd dir, Christian Urban Educ Serv; Urban League of Nebr; bd dir, YMCA of Omaha. **Honors/Awds:** Distinguished Alumni Award, Harris-Stowe State Col, 1992; Distinguished Eagle Award, Nat Eagle Leadership Inst, 1997; African-American Award, Western Heritage Museum, Omaha, 1998; Otto Swanson Spirit of Service Award, Nat Conference for Comm & Justice, 2000. **Home Addr:** 1411 N 128th Cir, Omaha, NE 68154, **Home Phone:** (402)493-5824. **Business Addr:** Vice President Minority & Community Affairs, Mutual of Omaha Insurance Co, 3300 Mutual Omaha Plz, Omaha, NE 68175, **Business Phone:** (402)342-7600.

### ROBINSON, ALFREDA P.
School administrator, dean (education). **Personal:** Born May 7, 1932, Charlotte, NC. **Educ:** Upsala Col, BA, 1954; Rutgers Sch Social Work, attended 1957; Union Grad Sch, doctoral cand. **Career:** School administrator, dean (retired); Financial Aid Douglass & Cook Col, Rugers Univ, dir; Essex Co Probation Dept, sr probation officer; NJ Bur C Serv Nat, case worker; Rutgers Univ Grad Sch Bus & Admin, asst dean in-chg stud serv; Rutgers Grad Sch Mgt, dean in-chg stud serv; Trial Advocacy, assoc dean. **Orgs:** Proj comt mem, Delta Sigma Theta; Nat Scholar & Stand Comn, NJ Alumnae Chap; corr secy, ed, Eastern Asn Stud Financial Aid Admin; counman, Nat Coun Stud Financial Aid; NJ Asn Stud Financial Aid Admin; Counman, Col Entrance Exam Bd; Mid States Regional Counman Pub & Guid Comn; Upper Div Scholar Rev; NJ Alumnae Chap; vpres, bd trustee, St Timothy House; chair, Standing Comt Judicial Selection, currently. **Honors/Awds:** Community Service Award, Sigma Gamma Rho, 1979; Service Award, Rutgers Black MBA Asn, 1979; Alfreda P Robinson Award; Heman Marion Sweatt Award, Nat Bar Asn. **Home Addr:** 298 S Clinton St, East Orange, NJ 07018.

### ROBINSON, DR. ANDREW A., JR.
Administrator, educator. **Personal:** Born Feb 16, 1939, Chicago, IL. **Educ:** Chicago State Univ, BA, 1966; Roosevelt Univ, MA, 1970; Northwestern Univ, PhD, 1973. **Career:** Chicago Pub Schs, teacher, 1966-69; Chicago Urban League, educ dir, 1970-73; Univ IL, vis instr, 1972-73; Urban & Ethnic Educ, Asst dir; Pub Inst Chicago, supt, 1973-74; Chicago City Cols, adminr, 1974-75; Univ KY, asst prof, assoc dir Ctr urban educ; Univ N Fla, first interim pres, 1980-82. **Orgs:** Phi Delta Kappa; Am Asn Sch Admins; Am Asn Teacher Educ; Nat Alliance Black Sch Educators; Prog Planning Comt Am Assoc Col Teacher Educ. **Special Achievements:** First principal of William Raines Senior High School.

### ROBINSON, ANGELA YVONNE
Television journalist. **Personal:** Born Jul 14, 1956, Atlanta, GA; daughter of Johnny (deceased) and Ann Roberts. **Educ:** Syracuse Univ, Syracuse, NY, BS, jour, pub commun, tv & radio broadcasting, 1978. **Career:** WAGA TV, Atlanta, Ga, prod asst, 1978-84; WTTG Fox news, reporter & anchor, 1984-94; WXIA, reporter & anchor, 1994-97; ARC Media LLC, Atlanta, Ga, pres & chief exec officer, 1998-. **Orgs:** Nat Assn Black Journalists; Wash Chap, Nat Coun Negro Women, 1989-; Atlanta Assn Black Journalists; Natl Assn Black Journalists Region 4 Hall of Fame; Atlanta Press Club; United Negro Coll Fund; Adv bd, SI Newhouse Sch Commun, Syracuse Univ; 100 Black Men of Atlanta Inc; Success Circle; Natl Acad Tv Arts & Sci; Outstanding Young Women of AME; bd mem, Fund Southern com. **Honors/Awds:** Emmy Awards, Natl Acad Tv Arts & Sci, 1980; United Press International Award, 1980, Editing Award, 1981; Emmy Award Nominee, Natl Acad Tv Arts & Sci, 1986, 1989, 1990; Outstanding Enterprise Reporting, Associated Press International; Award of Distinction, George Aman, 1989; National Association of Black Journalists Award, 1990; Associated Press Award, Sports Feature, 1990, Feature/Humor Interest, 1991; National Association of Black Journalists Award, 1991-92; Omega Psi Phi Fraternity Inc, Public Service Award, 1992; Atlanta Assn of Media Women; Chancellor's Citation, Syracuse Univ, Distinguished Achievement in Journalism; Angela Y Robinson, Student Scholarship, Syracuse Univ; Atlanta Business League: 100 Women of Vision; Several Awards of Excellence, Nat Assn Black Journalists; Southern Regional Emmy Awards, News Anchor, 1995, Best Newscast & Olympic Special, 1996, Special Series, 1997; Atlanta Association of Black Journalists Pioneer Award, Special Reports, 1995, 1997; Southern Regional Emmy Award; Absolute Africa Award, Absolute Inc & Women Looking Ahead magazine. **Special Achievements:** News Anchor, Southern Regional Emmy Awards, 1995; is noted in Who's Who Among African Americans and Outstanding Young Women of America. **Business Addr:** President, Chief Executive Officer, ARC Media LLC, 3141 Gold Dr SW, Atlanta, GA 30311, **Business Phone:** (678)595-7096.

### ROBINSON, ANN GARRETT
Educator, psychologist. **Personal:** Born Jun 8, 1934, Greenville, NC; married Charles; children: Angela Carol & George Carl. **Educ:** NC Cent Univ, BA, 1954; Wayne State Univ, MA, 1957; Nova Univ, EdD, 1975; Yale Univ, res fel, 1986. **Career:** NC Bd Corrections, 1956-57; Cent State Hosp, clin psychol, 1958-64; LaRue Carter Hosp, clin psychol, 1958-64; Augusta State Hosp, clin psychol, 1958-64; Yale Univ Child Study Ctr, res asst, 1968-70; Trinity Col, Hartford, asst prof psychol, 1970-72; Gateway Community Col, prof psychol, 1972-99, prof emer, psychol, 2000-; freelance writer, 1983-; New Haven Regist, newspaper columnist, 1985-; Robinson Behav Sci Consult, New Haven, co-owner. **Orgs:** Bd dir, S Cent Conn Ment Health Planning Reg, 1974-77; NEA, Am Psychol Asn; bd deaconnesses, Immanuel Baptist Church; Alpha Kappa Alpha; Black Educrs Asn; Afro-Am Hist Bd; Jack & Jill Am Inc; regional vpres, N EPsi Beta Inc; Nat Hon Soc Psychol; pres-elect, Nat Coun, Psi Beta Inc; chairlady, Immanuel Baptist Church, bd deaconesses, 1985. **Honors/Awds:** Nannie H Burroughs Award Outstanding Black Educator of New Haven, 1974; Presidential Citation Award, SCCC, 1977; Community Service Award, New Haven; Church of Christ National Youth Conference Award, 1986; Most Scholarly Award, SCCC, 1987; Most Influential Professor, SCCC Student Government Award, 1987; Professional Woman of the Year, Elm City Business & Prof Women. **Special Achievements:** Author: "Clouds & Clowns of Destiny", "Behind Krome Detention Center Walls", "Are the Doors to Higher Education Starting to Close", "Heroic Women of the Past, The Three Wives of Booker T Washington"; contributed articles to the New Haven Register, as well as to other newspapers. **Home Addr:** 406 Dixwell Ave, New Haven, CT 06511-1702, **Home Phone:** (203)785-1605. **Business Addr:** Professor Emerita, Gateway Community College, 60 Sargent Dr, New Haven, CT 06511, **Business Phone:** (203)285-2000.

### ROBINSON, ANTHONY W.
Executive, president (organization), chief executive officer. **Personal:** Born Dec 11, 1948, Clarksville, TN; son of Charles C and Eva Mae Childs; married Yvonne Davis; children: Charles Anthony & Camille A. **Educ:** Morgan State Col, BS, polit sci, 1970; Wash Col Law, Am Univ, JD, 1973. **Career:** US Equal Employ Opportunity Comn, legal coun, 1972-75; Law Firm Singleton, Dashiell & Robinson, Baltimore, Md, co-founder, 1975; Spec Coun US Congressman Parren J Mitchell, 1976-86; Minority Bus Enterprise Legal Defense Educ Fund, pres, chief exec officer, 1984-; Md State Inmate Grievance Comnr, chmn. **Orgs:** Legal coun, Us Equal Employ Opportunity Comn, 1972-75; Md Bar; Us Supreme Ct; Us Ct Appeals Fourth Judicial Ct; Us Dist Ct Dist Md; advisor, Const & Civil Rights Comt U.S. House Representatives. **Home Addr:** 8134 Scotts Level Rd, Pikesville, MD 21208. **Business Addr:** President, Minority Business Enterprise Legal Defense & Education Fund, 1100 Mercantile Lane Suite 115A, Largo, MD 20774, **Business Phone:** (301)583-4648.

### ROBINSON, BEVERLY JEAN (BEV ROBINSON)
Publishing executive. **Personal:** Born Dec 15, 1957, Bath, NY; daughter of George Wesley and Alice Jackson; married Christopher K Chaplin; children: Christopher & Khalif. **Educ:** Dowling Col, Oakdale, NY, BA, Eng & creative writing, 1979; New Sch Social Res, New York, NY, MA, media & commun, 1988. **Career:** Random House Inc, New York, NY, advert asst, 1979-82; Ballantine Publ Group, New York, NY, publicity coord, 1982-87, publicity mgr, 1987-90, asst publicity dir, 1990-93, assoc, dir press rels, 1993-99, dir publicity, currently, free lance publicist & consult writer; Hempstead Pub Schs, spec educ teacher, 2010-11; Hempstead Pub Schs, teacher, 2010-; Hempstead High Sch, secy. **Orgs:** Women Communs, 1983-85. **Honors/Awds:** Excellence in Publicity Award, Lit Mkt Pl, 1991. **Special Achievements:** Member of the team that founded One World, the first multicultural imprint at a major publishing house, 1992. **Home Addr:** 135 Clinton St Apt 4V, Hempstead, NY 11550-3209, **Home Phone:** (516)564-6064. **Business Addr:** Director of Publicity, Random House Inc, 1745 Broadway, New York, NY 10019, **Business Phone:** (212)572-2717.

### ROBINSON, CARL CORNELL
Engineer, executive director, lawyer. **Personal:** Born Sep 21, 1946, Washington, DC; son of Louis W and Florence A. **Educ:** Univ Mich, BSE, aeronaut engineering, 1969; Golden Gate Univ, MBA, 1974; Univ Calif, Los Angeles, JD, 1977. **Career:** O'Melveny & Myers, atty, 1977-84; Robinson & Pearman LLP, atty & partner, 1984-; Robert C Pearman, Atty & Arbitrator, partner, currently. **Orgs:** Dir, Univ Calif Los Angeles Law Alumni Asn, 1977, 1997; dir, San Fernando Valley Neighborhood Legal Serv, 1981-91, chair, 1982-86; dir, Univ Calif Los Angeles Pub Interest Law Found, 1982-89, chair, 1982-84; vpres, Nat Black MBA Asn, Los Angeles, 1985; Legal Serv Trust Fund Comn CA, 1985, Judicial Eval Comn Los Angeles Co Bar Asn, 1986, 1988, 1990, 1994, 1998, 2000; dir, Nat Asn Securities Prof, 1986-94; dir, John M Langston Bar Asn, 1987-94; dir, Western Ctr Law & Poverty Inc, 1988-94; Calif State Bar Asn, 1977-. **Home Addr:** 3924 S Sycamore Ave, Los Angeles, CA 90008-1121, **Home Phone:** (323)290-2926. **Business Addr:** Partner, Attorney, Robert C Pearman Attorney & Arbitrator, 3699 Wilshire Blvd Suite 890, Los Angeles, CA 90017, **Business Phone:** (213)487-1400.

### ROBINSON, DR. CARL DAYTON
Pediatrician. **Personal:** Born Jun 14, 1942, Tallulah, LA; son of Bernie Dayton and Emily Parker; married Sandra Lawson; children: Michael & Carla. **Educ:** Howard Univ, BS, 1964, MD, 1968; Tulane Univ Sch Pub Health, MPH, 1977. **Career:** Childrens hosp, intern, 1969, resident, 1970, fel, 1971; Letterman Army Med Ctr, cheif prenatal, infant serv, 1971-73; Flint Goodridge Hosp, dir sickle cell prog, 1973-78; Tulane Univ Med Sch, clin asst prof pediat, 1973-; Genetic DisCtr, med dir, 1978-81; Robinson Med Grp, pres, 1978-; APTECH Inc, pres, 1978-; LA Health Corp, pres, 1984-; C Hosp, New Orleans, pres med staff, 1986-88; Develop Ctr Am, New Orleans, pres, 1990-; Key Mgt, vpres, med dir, 1990-; Kids First Prytania, pediatrician, currently. **Orgs:** Nat Sickle Cell Adv Comn, 1976-78; Reg Med Prog, LA, 1976-78; LA Comn Prenatal Care, 1977-81; vpres, SE LA Med Qual Rev Found, 1979-81; secy, Dept Health & Human Resources, LA, 1984; life mem, Alpha Phi Alpha Am Publ Health Asn; pres, Orleans Parish Sch Bd, 1990; fel Am Acad Pediat; fel Int Col Pediat. **Special Achievements:** Book : "Dr. Carl Robinson's Basic Baby Care", 1998. **Home Addr:** 5841 Wright Rd, New Orleans, LA 70128, **Home Phone:** (504)244-0313. **Business Addr:** Pediatrician, Kids First Prytania, 3600 Prytania St Suite 100, New Orleans, LA 70115, **Business Phone:** (504)899-5437.

### ROBINSON, CAROL EVONNE
Journalist. **Personal:** Born Sep 15, 1959, Sacramento, CA; daughter of Herbert Allen and Claudia Cleatus Buford. **Educ:** Univ Calif, Davis, CA, BA, mass commun, 1983; Cosumnes River Col, Sacramento, CA,

1986; Maynard Inst Journalism Educ, Berkeley, CA, Summer Prog Minority Journalists, 1988. **Career:** Meracor Mortgage, Sacramento, Calif, asst loan closer, 1986-87; Calif Personnel Serv, Sacramento, Calif, word processor, 1988; Bellingham Herald, Bellingham, Wash, educ writer, 1988-89; Daily Repub, Fairfield, Calif, reporter, 1989-92; Contra Costa Times, staff writer, 1992-97; ANG Newspapers, staff writer, 1998-2001; Calif Pub Utilities Comn, San Francisco, Calif, asst info officer, 2001-05; Calif Energy Comn, info officer & ed, 2005-; Mission Clarity, owner, 2011-. **Orgs:** Nat Asn Black Journalists, 1989-; Sacramento Black Journalists Asn, 1990-; Soc Prof Journalists, 1989-; writer/ed, Calif Sch Boards Asn, 1997-98. **Honors/Awds:** First Place, Government Reporting, Society of Professional Journalists, Northwest Chapter, 1989. **Home Addr:** 2118 60th Ave, Sacramento, CA 95822, **Home Phone:** (916)427-0399. **Business Addr:** Information Officer, Editor, California Energy Commission, PO Box 188372, Sacramento, CA 95818-8372, **Business Phone:** (916)654-5015.

### ROBINSON, CAROL W.
Librarian. **Personal:** Born Dec 4, 1953, New Rochelle, NY; daughter of Richard Word and Dorothy Clark; married Curtis; children: Ujima, Zakiyyah & Saliym. **Educ:** Atlanta Univ, Ga, attended 1973; Northeastern Univ, Boston, Ma, BA, 1976; Pratt Inst, Brooklyn, NY, attended 1982; Queens Col, Flushing, NY, MLS, 1984. **Career:** Libr Cong, Wash, DC, libr intern, 1973; MIT Hist Collections, Cambridge, MA, mus intern, 1974-76; Coopers & Lybrand, Wash, DC, libr asst, 1976-78; Wash DC Pub Schs, Wash, DC, teacher, 1978-80; Mt Vernon Pub Libr, Mt Vernon, NY, librn, 1981, asst dir, actg dir, 1997; Montclair Pub Libr, dep libr dir, asst dir, currently. **Orgs:** Westchester Libr Asn, 1981-; Am Libr Asn, 1982-; NY Black Librarians Caucus, 1984-; Black Caucus Am Libr Asn, 1990-; vpres, Sons & Daughters African Unity Inc; NY Libr Asn, 1994-; chair, African Am Librarians Westchester, 1994-; adv bd, Jr League Montclair, 1999-; Women's Hist Proj, 1999-. **Honors/Awds:** Phi Alpha Theta, Zeta-Tau Chapter, 1975-; Beta Phi Mu, Beta Alpha Chapter, 1985-. **Home Addr:** 19 Beechwood Cir, Wappingers Falls, NY 12590-4956, **Home Phone:** (845)298-2034. **Business Addr:** Assistant Director, Montclair Public Library, 50 S Fullerton Ave, Montclair, NJ 07042, **Business Phone:** (973)744-0500.

### ROBINSON, CATHERINE
Executive, educator. **Personal:** Born Sep 11, 1904, Petersburg, VA; children: Lynne, McDonald II & Valarie. **Educ:** RI Col, Univ RI. **Career:** Family & Bus Rel Serv, field interviewer, 1959-63; So Prov Proj Univ RI, Coop Exten Serv, asst dir, asst home econ leader, 1963-75; TV Ser Home Econ & Other Areas, hostess; Univ Ri, asst dir. **Orgs:** Founder, Scitamard Players, 1937; Bd dir, Opportunity Ind Ctr; Women's Coun United Way; Civil Rights Comn RI Adv Comn US Comn Civil Rights; bd dir Black Heritage Soc. **Honors/Awds:** Community leader Award, United S Providence Block Club, 1971; Community Service Award, 1973; Citation Distinguished Service, Univ RI Coop Exten Serv, 1974; RI Heritage Hall Fame, 1975.

### ROBINSON, DR. CECELIA ANN
Educator. **Personal:** Born May 28, 1948, Dallas, TX; married Kenneth E. **Educ:** Prairie View A&M Univ, BA, Eng, 1969; Univ Mo, MEd, 1971, Eng educ, 1971; Univ Oxford, advan grad studies, 1976; Univ Kans, EdD, Eng edu, 1986. **Career:** Univ Mo, epda fel, 1970-71; Prairie View A&M Univ, Eng Inst, 1971-72; Oak Pk HS, instr Eng, 1972-79; Penn Valley Community Col, Eng instr, 1974-79; Univ Oxford Eng, Eng Speaking Union fel, 1976; Maple Woods Community Col, Eng instr, 1979-2008; Writing Ctr, dir; William Jewell Col, Dept Eng, fac, 1979, prof eng, prof emer, 1979-2013. **Orgs:** Ed bd, Col Eng Handbk, 1999-2000; Delta Kappa Gamma; Delta Sigma Theta Inc; Sigma Tau Delta; Pi Lambda Theta; MO Asn Teachers Eng; founder, Pens Across Metroplex; Rebuilding Together Liberty Bd; Clay County African Am Legacy Inc; Nat Coun Teachers Eng; Clay County Hist Millennium Bd. **Honors/Awds:** Community Service Award, Mo Martin Luther King Comt, 1992; Council Award Human Relations work, 1993-94; Liberty Outstanding Citizen Award, 1995; Pkwy Baptist Church Distinguished Prof Award, William Jewell, 1996; Excellence in Teaching Award, Northland Chamber Com, 1996; Anne Robb Townsend Women Excellence Award, 1996; AT&T Leadership Liberty Sertoma Outstanding Serv, Mankind Award, 2000; Joe Wally Award for Community Serv, Liberty Fel Concerned, 2003; Outstanding Missourian Award, Mo House Representatives, 2004; Look North Award, Clay County Econ Develop Coun, 2004; Evelyn Wasserstrom Social Justice & Community Service Award, Kans City Southern Christian Leadership Conf, 2004; Parkway Baptist Church Distinguished Professor Award, William Jewell Col; DeVerne Lee Calloway Award, Community Serv & Social Justice, Mo State House Representatives & Senate, 2015. **Special Achievements:** First African American educator at Oak Park High School in Kansas City. **Home Addr:** 1108 N Ridge Rd, Liberty, MO 64068-1357, **Home Phone:** (816)781-1885. **Business Addr:** Emeritus Professor, William Jewell College, 500 College Hill, Liberty, MO 64068, **Business Phone:** (816)781-7700.

### ROBINSON, CHARLES
School administrator. **Personal:** Born Mar 19, 1940, Philadelphia, PA; married Bernice Ann Baker; children: Deborah Ann & Lesly Denise. **Educ:** Cheyney State Univ, BS, 1966. **Career:** Philadelphia Dept Recreation, dec leader, 1962-66; Philadelphia Pub Schs, teacher, 1966-75, admin asst, 1975-84, teacher, 1984-85; Friends & Family Serv, supvr, 1997-2005. **Orgs:** Scout master, Troop 713, 1968-74; chmn, Edgewater Pk Twp Juv Conf Comt, 1970-85; bd educ, Edgewater Pk Twp, 1977-87; adv bd, Burlington Co Voc Tech, 1978-85; pres & bd trustee, Edgewater Pk Football Asn, 1981-83; vpres, Burlington Co Sch Bds Asn, 1982-86; NJ Sch Bd Asn, vpres, 1984-85, bd dir, 1988-91; vpres, NJ Sch Bd Asn. **Home Addr:** 104 Powder Mill Lane, Edgewater Park, NJ 08010, **Home Phone:** (609)387-9032.

### ROBINSON, CHARLES S. (CHARLIE ROBINSON)
Actor. **Personal:** Born Nov 9, 1945, Houston, TX; married Dolorita Noonan; children: 3; married Venus Duran; children: 3. **Career:** Television Credits: "Night Court"; "Love & War"; "Home Improvement Ink"; "Buddy Faro", 1998; Film Credits: Together Brothers; Sugarhill, 1974; Black Gestapo, 1975; Uncle Joe Shannon; Apocalypse Now; The River; Set It Off, 1996; Land of Fire, 1997; Scam, 2001; Antwone Fisher, 2002; Jackson, 2002; Break A Leg, 2005; Triple Cross, 2005; Even Money, 2006; Steam, 2008; Natural Disasters, 2008; The House Bunny, 2008; Jackson, 2008; Krews, 2010; Falling Away, 2012; Swerve, 2012; plays include: My Sweet Charlie; Spoon River Anthology; The Night Thoreau Spentin Jail; Othello; Television Film credits: Set This Town on Fire, 1973; A Killing Affair, 1977; The Trial of Lee Harvey Oswald, 1977; Rehearsal for Murder, 1982; Haywire, 1980; Crash Course, 1988; Murder C.O.D, 1990; Project: ALF, 1996; Land of the Free, 1997; The Last Dance, 2000; Miss Lettie & Me, 2002; Santa Jr, 2002; Secret Santa, 2003; Mercy Street, 2006; River's End, 2005; McBride: Requiem, 2006; TV episodes: "Cold Case", 2005; "McBride: Requiem", 2006; "Still Standing", 2004-06; "How I Met Your Mother", 2006; "McBride: Dogged", 2007; "The Riches", 2007; "The Game", 2007-14; "Big Love", 2009; "Hank", 2009; "Sweet Kandy", 2009; "Alligator Point", 2009; "The Secret Life of the American Teenager", 2010; "$#*! My Dad Says", 2010; "Harry's Law", 2011; "The Soul Man", 2012; "Hart of Dixie", 2012-14; "Key and Peele", 2013; "Underwater Upside Down", 2016; "Grey's Anatomy", 2016; "The Adventures of Ronald and Edgar", 2016; NEXTEL, "agitating my dots", currently; Ore Shakespeare Festival, currently. **Orgs:** Actors Studio, 1960-. **Honors/Awds:** Image Award, Outstanding Actor, Nat Asn Advan Colored People. **Business Addr:** Actor, The Artists Agency, 1180 S Beverly Dr Suite 301, Los Angeles, CA 90035, **Business Phone:** (310)277-7779.

### ROBINSON, CHARLOTTE L. See Obituaries Section.

### ROBINSON, CHRISTOPHER SEAN
Basketball player. **Personal:** Born Apr 2, 1974, Columbus, GA. **Educ:** Western Ky Univ, attended 1996. **Career:** Basketball player (retired); Vancouver Grizzlies, guard & shooting guard, 1996-98; Sacramento Kings, guard, 1998; Sioux Falls Skyforce, 1999; La Crosse Bobcats, 1999-2000; Gaiteros del Zulia, 2001; N Charleston Lowgators, 2001; Huntsville Flight, 2002; SLUC Nancy, 2002; Verviers-Pepinster, 2002-03; Carolina Thunder, 2004-05. **Honors/Awds:** Conference Player of the Year, Sun Belt, 1995; All-Conf Hons, 1995.

### ROBINSON, CLEO PARKER
Dancer, business owner. **Personal:** Born Jan 1, 1948?, Denver, CO; daughter of Jonathan and Martha Parker; married Tom. **Educ:** Colo Women's Col, BS, psycho & dance. **Career:** Univ Colo, instr; Cleo Parker Robinson Dance Ensemble, founder, 1970-; Int Asn Blacks Dance, vpres, currently; Flim: Run Sister Run; Margie Soo Hoo Lee. **Orgs:** Vpres, Int Asn Blacks Dance; bd dir, Denver Ctr Performing Arts; Nat Coun Arts; Nat Endowment Arts; Lila Wallace Found; Pew Charitable Trust Fund; vpres, Int Asn Blacks Dance; bd trustee, DCPA. **Honors/Awds:** Govenor's Award, 1974; Mayors award, 1979; Performing Arts Award, 1986; Honorary doctorate, Univ Denver, 1991; Blacks in Colo Hall of Fame, 1994; Coming Up Taller Award, Pres's Comt Arts & Humanites, 2000; Choreography fellowships, Colorado Council on the Arts; Lifetime achievement award, Business & Professional Women Aurora Chapter; Oni Award, International Black Woman's Congress; Oni Award, International Black Womans Congress. **Special Achievements:** Chosed as one of the Colorado 100, 1992. **Business Addr:** Founder, Cleo Parker Robinson Dance, 119 Pk Ave W, Denver, CO 80205, **Business Phone:** (303)295-1759.

### ROBINSON, CLIFFORD RALPH (CLIFF ROBINSON)
Basketball player. **Personal:** Born Dec 16, 1966, Buffalo, NY; married Heather Lufkins; children: Isaiah. **Educ:** Univ Conn, attended 1989. **Career:** Basketball player (retired); Portland Trail Blazers, forward, 1989-97; Phoenix Suns, 1997-2001; Detroit Pistons, 2001-03; Golden State Warriors, 2003-05; New Jersey Nets, 2005-07. **Home Addr:** 98 S Bardsbrook Cir, Spring, TX 77382-2858.

### ROBINSON, CRYSTAL LATRESA
Basketball player, basketball coach. **Personal:** Born Jan 22, 1974, Atoka, OK; daughter of Billy and Nancy Washington. **Educ:** Southeastern Okla State Univ, health & phys educ, 1996. **Career:** Basketball player (retired), basketball coach; Colo Xplosion, forward, 1996-98; New York Liberty, forward, 1999-2005; Wash Mystics, asst coach, 2006-07; McAlester High Sch, head coach, 2009-10; Murray State Col, head coach, 2009-13; Utah State Univ, asst coach, 2013; Tex Christian Univ, Horned Frogs, asst coach, 2014-. **Orgs:** Big Bros Big Sisters. **Business Addr:** Assistant coach, Texas Christian University, 2800 S Univ Dr, Ft. Worth, TX 76129, **Business Phone:** (817)257-7000.

### ROBINSON, CURTIS. See Obituaries Section.

### ROBINSON, DAMIEN DION
Football player. **Personal:** Born Dec 22, 1973, Dallas, TX; married Michele; children: Zoya & Zariah. **Educ:** Univ Iowa, grad. **Career:** Football player (retired); Tampa Bay Buccaneers, 1997, safety, 1998, free safety, 1999-2000; New York Jets, free safety, 2001-02; Seattle Seahawks, free safety & strong safety, 2003-04.

### ROBINSON, DAVID MAURICE
Clergy, basketball player. **Personal:** Born Aug 6, 1965, Key West, FL; son of Ambrose and Freda; married Valerie Hoggatt; children: David Maurice Jr, Corey & Justin. **Educ:** US Naval Acad, math, 1987. **Career:** Basketball player (retired), clergy; Naval Acad, 1983-84, 1986-87; San Antonio Spurs, ctr, 1989-2003; US Olympic Basketball Team, 1988, 1992, 1996; Oak Hills Church, staff, 2004-. **Orgs:** Funder, David Robinson Found, 1992-. **Business Addr:** Staff, Oak Hills Church, 6929 Camp Bullis Rd, San Antonio, TX 78256, **Business Phone:** (210)698-6868.

### ROBINSON, DAWN SHERRESE (DAWN TSHOMBE)
Songwriter, singer, actor. **Personal:** Born Nov 28, 1968, New London, CT; married Dre Allen. **Career:** Films: Another 48 Hrs, 1990; Conceiving Ada, 1997; Batman Forever, 1995; Tank Girl, 1995; I Got the Hook Up, 1998; Life, performer, 1999; Shaft, 2000; The Last Request, 2006; Queen of Media, 2011; TV series: "Saturday Night Live", 1992; "A Different World", 1993; Roc, 1993; "SeaQuest DSV", 1995; Albums: Born to Sing, 1990; Remix to Sing, 1991; Funky Divas, 1992; Runaway Love EP, 1993; EV3, 1997; Best of En Vogue, 1998; The Very Best of En Vogue, 2001; Hold On & Other Hits, 2005; Solo career: Dawn, 2002; Sound Tracks: In Living Color, 1993; Love & Basketball, 2000. **Honors/Awds:** Platinum, Born to Sing, 1990; Grammy nominations, Nat Acad Rec Arts & Sci, best short video, "Free Your Mind", rock duo or group; Funky Divas, r&b duo or group. **Business Addr:** Singer, c/o David Lombard, 4859 W Slauson Ave, Los Angeles, CA 90056, **Business Phone:** (213)962-8016.

### ROBINSON, DEANNA ADELL
Manager. **Personal:** Born Jul 31, 1945, Chicago, IL; married Willie. **Educ:** MI State Univ, BS, 1967. **Career:** Palmer House Hilton Hotel, conv serv mgr. **Orgs:** Nat Coalition Black Meeting Planners, 1986. **Home Addr:** 9842 S Bensley Ave, Chicago, IL 60617, **Home Phone:** (773)978-3147. **Business Addr:** Assistant Director Convention Service, Palmer House-Hilton Hotel, 17 E Monroe St, Chicago, IL 60603, **Business Phone:** (312)726-7500.

### ROBINSON, DENAUVO M.
Manager. **Personal:** Born Apr 10, 1949, Quincy, IL. **Educ:** Northeast Mo St Univ, BS, 1971; MA, 1971; Northern IL Univ, EdD, 1977. **Career:** Western Ill Univ, Macomb, counr, 1971-72; Drexel Univ, dir Spec Serv; Northern Ill Univ, CHANCE Dekalb, Ill, counr, 1972-74, assoc dir, 1974, Spec Proj Off, head, actg dir. **Orgs:** Am Pub Gas Asn; Northern Ill Univ; Am News Women's Club; Inst Govt & Pub Affairs; Civil Liberties Union; Nat Asn Adv Col People.

### ROBINSON, EDDIE JOSEPH, JR.
Football player. **Personal:** Born Apr 13, 1970, New Orleans, LA; married Tonja. **Educ:** Ala State Univ, BS, chem, 1993. **Career:** Football player (retired); Houston Oilers, right linebacker, 1992, left linebacker, 1993-95; Jacksonville Jaguars, left linebacker, 1996, right linebacker, 1997; Tenn Oilers, left linebacker, 1998; Tenn Titans, left linebacker, 1999, right linebacker, 2000-01; Buffalo Bills, right linebacker, 2002. **Orgs:** Omega Psi Phi Fraternity. **Honors/Awds:** Second round draft pick, 1992; Southwestern Athletic Conference Defensive Player of the Year.

### ROBINSON, EDITH B.
Executive. **Personal:** Born Dec 31, 1924, Buffalo, NY; married James C; children: Wesley. **Educ:** Wilberforce Univ, Wilberforce, OH, BS, 1946; State Univ NY, MSW. **Career:** Erie Co Dept Social Servs, caseworker, unit supvr, dist supvr, asst dep comnr, dep Comnr, 1947-81; Pub Welfare, caseworker, sr caseworker, unit supvr, dist supvr, 1947-77; State Univ Col SEEK Prgm, adj prof, 1969-70. **Orgs:** Past pres, Nat asn Social Workers ACSW; exec bd, NY State Welfare Conf, 1970-72; chmn, Nat Field Adv Coun Alexandria Am Red Cross, 1977-78; vice chmn, Greater Buffalo Chap ARC; pres, Am Lung Asn NY, 1977; vpres, pres elect, Zonta Club Buffalo, 1970; YWCA, 1972; Links Inc; Commun Adv Coun, State Univ NY Buffalo; vice chmn, secy, Nat Am Res Cross; Buffalo Philharmonic Soc; Samaritan Coun ctr; pres, Bry Lin Hosp; Interima Home Health Care; Admis Comt United Way Buffalo; Golden Soror, Alpha Kappa Alpha Sorority Inc; Xi Epsilon Omega Chap, pres, currently. **Home Addr:** 90 Meyer Rd Apt 204, Amherst, NY 14226-1007. **Business Addr:** President, Xi Epsilon Omega Chapter, PO Box 1861, Amherst, NY 14226-7861.

### ROBINSON, EDWARD A.
Educator. **Personal:** Born Jun 13, 1935, Gary, IN; married Lavada Hill; children: Edward Allen & Arlen Yohance. **Educ:** Howard Univ, BA, 1959; Univ Chicago, MAT, 1970; Northwestern Univ, PhD, 1974. **Career:** Carver High Sch, Chicago, instr, 1959-60; Harlan High Sch, Eng Dept, instr & chmn, 1960-69; Wendell Phillips & Summer High Sch, Chicago, instr, 1961-64; NDEA Inst, Univ Chicago, summer partic, 1965; Univ Chicago, experienced teacher fel, 1969-70; Lake Forest Col, IL, eng instr, 1970-72; Chicago Bd Educ High Sch, eng consul, 1970-72; Ford Found, Black Americans, fel, 1973-74; Northeastern Ill Univ, Chicago, asst prof, prof, prof emer. **Orgs:** Nat Urban League, 1968-74; S Shore Valley Community Orgn, 1969-74; Oper PUSH, 1972; Faulkner Sch Asn, 1974-75; Faulkner Sch Father's Club, 1974-75. **Special Achievements:** Author of numerous publication; TV ser: "The Giants", "The Common Men", narrator, 1967; "Like It Was the black man in America", teacher & host, 1969. **Home Addr:** 10011 S Hoxie Ave, Chicago, IL 60617-5326, **Home Phone:** (773)699-1245. **Business Addr:** Professor Emeritus, Northeastern Illinois University, 550 N St Louis Ave, Chicago, IL 60625-4699, **Business Phone:** (773)583-4050.

### ROBINSON, DR. EDWARD ASHTON, III
Lawyer, executive. **Personal:** Born Jan 1, 1949, Hammond, LA. **Educ:** Grambling Univ; State Univ, NY; Rutgers Univ. **Career:** Pvt pract, atty, 1979-; Baton Rouge La, chief adminr, state atty gen; Robinson Edward Ashton III Dr, owner. **Orgs:** La State Bar, currently. **Honors/Awds:** Outstanding Young Man, La Jaycees, 1977; Alumni Hall of Fame, Grambling State Univ, 1987. **Business Addr:** Attorney, 600 N Foster Dr, Baton Rouge, LA 70806-1801, **Business Phone:** (225)928-7876.

### ROBINSON, PROF. ELLA S.
Educator, school administrator. **Personal:** Born Apr 16, 1943, Wedowee, AL; daughter of Less Scales and Mary Ella MacPherson Scales; married John William; children: John William Jr. **Educ:** Ala State Univ, BS, 1965; Univ Nebr, MA, 1970, PhD, 1976. **Career:** Univ Ill, asst prof, 1975-77; Atlanta Univ, asst prof, 1977-79; Univ Nebr-Lincoln, prof eng, 1979; Tuskegee Univ, assoc prof; Concordia Col, Selma, AL, Humanities & Fine Arts Dept, head, currently. **Orgs:** MLA, 1974-87; chmn, afro-lite session SMLA, 1985-86; life time mem, Nat Asn Advan Colored People, 1986-; Ala African Am Poet Heritage Room, Bennet Martin Libr, 1989; CLA; NCTE; pres, Ala Media Prof, 2006-. **Home Addr:** 6607 Luxembourg Cir, Montgomery, AL 36117-3447, **Home Phone:** (334)270-8785. **Business Addr:** Head of Humanities, Concordia College, 1804 Green St, Selma, AL 36703, **Business Phone:** (334)874-5700.

**ROBINSON, EUGENE HAROLD**
Editor, writer. **Personal:** Born Mar 12, 1954, Orangeburg, SC; son of Harold I and Louisa S; married Avis Collins; children: Aaron E & Lowell E. **Educ:** Univ Mich, BA, 1974. **Career:** Harvard Univ, Nieman fel, 1988; San Francisco Chronicle, reporter, 1975-80; Wash Post, city hall reporter, 1980-82, asst city ed, 1982-84, city ed, 1984-87, S Am corresp, 1988-92, London corresp, 1992-94, foreign ed, 1994, assoc ed, asst managing ed. Books: Coal to Cream: A Black Man?s Journey Beyond Color to an Affirmation of Race, auth, 1999; Last Dance in Havana: The Final Days of Fidel & the Start of the New Cuban Revolution, auth, 2004; Disintegration: The Splintering of Black America. New York, auth, 2010. **Orgs:** Nat Asn Black Journalist, 1987-; Coun Foreign Rels, 1995-; chmn & bd dir, Wash Metrop Scholars; bd dir, Int Women's Media Found, currently. **Special Achievements:** Film: Rosenwald, 2015. **Home Addr:** 5302 N 18th St, Arlington, VA 22205, **Home Phone:** (703)534-9471. **Business Addr:** Board of Director, International Women's Media Foundation, 1625 K St NW Suite 1275, Washington, DC 20006, **Business Phone:** (202)496-1992.

**ROBINSON, EUGENE KEEFE**
Football player, football coach, radio host. **Personal:** Born May 28, 1963, Hartford, CT; married Gia; children: Brittany & Brandon. **Educ:** Colgate Univ, BS, comput sci. **Career:** Football player (retired), coach, radio broadcaster; Seattle Seahawks, defensive back, 1985, free safety, 1986-95; Green Bay Packers, free safety, 1996-97; Atlanta Falcons, free safety, 1998-99, safety, 1999; Carolina Panthers, free safety & safety, 2000, Radio Network, color analyst, 2006-; WCNC, co-host, 2015-; Inter Mix Rec, co-owner; Charlotte Christian Sch, varsity football & wrestling coach, currently. **Honors/Awds:** Champion, Nat Football Conf, 1996, 1997, 1998; Champion, Super Bowl, XXXI. **Special Achievements:** Film: "Super Bowl XXXII", 1998. **Business Addr:** Color Analyst, Carolina Panthers, 800 S Mint St, Charlotte, NC 28202, **Business Phone:** (704)358-7000.

**ROBINSON, EUNICE PRIMUS**
Counselor, teacher. **Personal:** Born Oct 17, 1935, Hardeeville, SC; married DeWitt T Jr; children: Janice, De Witt III & Glenn. **Educ:** Savannah State Col, BS, elem educ, 1953; Univ SC, MEd, 1972. **Career:** Hardeeville Elem Sch, teacher, 1953-55; SC State Col, counr, 1955-59; Allen Univ, counr, dir stud activ, 1959-63; Rosenwald Elem Sch, teacher, 1965-67; Benedict Col, dean women & counr, 1968-71; Aiken County Pub Schs, transp supvr; Midlands Tech Col, counr. **Orgs:** Nat Dirs Orientation Asn; founder & adv, Afro Am Club Midlands Tech Col, 1972-; team mother, Pony League, Dixie Youth League Baseball Prog, 1972-75; secy, Fairwald Elem Sch Parent Teacher Asn, 1974-; treas, Fairwald Mid Sch Parent Teacher Asn; secy, Altar Guild, St Lukes Epis Church, 1974-; secy, Omega Psi Phi Frat Wives, 1974-75; Columbia Pan Hellenic Coun; Scholar Found Booker T Wash, 1975; Zeta Phi Beta Sorority; SC Pers & Guid Asn, 1975; chairperson, Episcopal Diocese Upper SC, Bena Dial Scholar, 2004. **Honors/Awds:** Mother Of The Year, Zeta Phi Beta Sorority, 1959; Counselor Most Seen by Students, Midlands Tech Col, 1973; Mother of The Year, Afro-Am Club, Midlands Tech Col, 1975. **Home Addr:** 4039 Pine Cone Dr, Columbia, SC 29204, **Home Phone:** (803)754-2489. **Business Addr:** Counselor, Midlands Technical College, PO Box Q, Columbia, SC 29250.

**ROBINSON, FRANK, JR.**
Baseball player, baseball manager, baseball executive. **Personal:** Born Aug 31, 1935, Beaumont, TX; son of Frank and Ruth; married Barbara Ann Cole; children: Frank Kevin & Nichelle. **Educ:** Xavier Univ, Cincinnati, OH. **Career:** Baseball player (retired), baseball coach, baseball manager, baseball executive; Cincinnati Reds, farm syst teams, 1953-56, player, 1956-65; Santurce Crabbers, mgr; Baltimore Orioles, outfielder, 1966-71, coach, 1978-80, 1985-87, mgr, 1988-91; Los Angeles Dodgers, player, 1972; California Angels, player, 1973-74, coach, 1977; Cleveland Indians, player, 1974-76, mgr, 1975-77; Rochester Red Wings, mgr, 1978; San Francisco Giants, mgr, 1981-84; Milwaukee Brewers, coach, 1984; Ariz Fall League, dir baseball opers; Montreal Expos, mgr, 2002-06; Washington Nationals, mgr, 2005-06; ESPN, analyst, 2007; Bud Selig, spec asst, 2009-10, sr vpres maj league opers, 2010-11, exec vpres baseball develop, 2012-15; Maj League Baseball, vpres on-field opers, 1999-2002, spec advisor baseball opers, 2007-09, sr advisor & hon am league pres, 2015-. **Home Addr:** 15557 Aqua Verde Dr, Los Angeles, CA 90077. **Business Addr:** Honorary American League President, Senior Advisor, Major League Baseball, 245 Pk Ave 31st Fl, New York, NY 10167, **Business Phone:** (212)931-7800.

**ROBINSON, DR. REV. FRANK JAMES, JR.**
Educator, clergy. **Personal:** Born Nov 18, 1939, Montgomery, TX; married Reecie; children: Lady Robinson Nelson, Portia Elaine, Frank J Jr & Gusta Jovon. **Educ:** Tex Southern Univ, BS, 1964. **Career:** Bowid Dance Studio, Houston, instr dramatics; Houston Community Col, instr; Urban Theatre, tech dir; Assured Blessing Ministry Church 39, tech dir; Cent Conv Tex Brotherhood, treas; Greater St Matthews Baptist Church, clergyman; Greater Second Baptist Church, asst pastor; Great Faith Missionary Baptist Church, founder, pastor. **Orgs:** Chmn, Tex State Conf Br, Nat Asn Advan Colored People; vpres, Alpha Mu Omega; W End Civic Club. **Home Addr:** 4007 Wuthering Heights Dr, Houston, TX 77045, **Home Phone:** (713)721-7786. **Business Addr:** Pastor, Greater Faith Missionary Baptist Church, 4438 Rosa Parks Blvd, Detroit, MI 48208-2738, **Business Phone:** (313)831-6162.

**ROBINSON, DR. GENEVIEVE**
Archivist. **Personal:** Born Apr 20, 1940, Kansas City, MO; daughter of James L and Helen Williams. **Educ:** Mt St Scholastica Col, BA, hist, 1968; N Mex Highlands Univ, MA, hist, 1974; Cath Univ Am, attended 1979; Boston Col, PhD, hist, 1986. **Career:** Lillis High Sch, hist teacher, 1969-73 & 1974-75, hist dept chairperson, 1970-73, admin & curric dir, 1974-75; Donnelly Community Col, instr, 1976-78; Boston Col, instr, 1983, Gasson fel, 1984-85; Rockhurst Univ, instr, 1985-86, asst prof, 1986-91, assoc prof, 1991-2002, dir hon prog, 1990-2001, chair dept hist, 1994-2001 & 2003-09, prof, 2002-2007; Fontbonne University, Dean of Undergraduate Students, 2007-12; St. Mary's University of Minnesota, Dean of School of Arts and Humanities, 2012-14; Mount St. Scholastica, Archivist, 2014-. **Orgs:** Phi Alpha Theta; Kappa Mu Epsilon; Orgn Am Historians; Immigration Hist Soc; Pi Gamma Mu; Ethical Rev Bd, 1988-; Rockhurst Col, presidential grant, 1988; bd dir, Notre Dame de Sion Schs, 1990-95; regional rep, Nat Asn Women Cath Higher Educ; St Monica Sch Bd, 1999-2002; hon mem, Sigma Delta Pi. **Home Addr:** 801 S 8th St, Atchison, KS 66002, **Home Phone:** (913)360-6200. **Business Addr:** Archivist, Mount St. Scholastica, 801 S 8th St, Atchison, KS 66002, **Business Phone:** (913)360-6200.

**ROBINSON, GLENN ALANN**
Basketball player, basketball coach. **Personal:** Born Jan 10, 1973, Gary, IN; son of Jesse Mack and Christine Bridgeman; children: Gelen III. **Educ:** Purdue Univ, attended 1994. **Career:** Basketball player (retired), basketball coach; Milwaukee Bucks, small forward, 1994-2002; Atlanta Hawks, small forward, 2002-03; Philadelphia 76ers, small forward, 2003-05; San Antonio Spurs, small forward, 2005; Franklin & Marshall Col, head coach, currently. **Honors/Awds:** Indiana Mr. Basketball Award, 1991; Player of the Year, Naismith College, 1994; John Wooden Award, 1994; Adolph Rupp Trophy, 1994; Oscar McDonald's All American, 1991; Player of the Year, US Basketball Writers Asn, 1994; Robertson Trophy, US Basketball Writers Asn, 1994; Player of the Year, Nat Asn Basketball Coaches, 1994; AP College Player of the Year, 1994; UPI College Player of the Year, 1994; Sporting News College Player of the Year, 1994; Big Ten Conference Player of the Year, 1994; Big Ten Conference Athlete of the Year, 1994; NBA All-Rookie Team, 1995; National College Basketball Player of the Year; 1995, NBA All-Rookie Team; 1996, NBA All-Star Team, 2000, 2001; Champion, Nat Basketball Asn, 2005; Glenn Robinson Award, 2014. **Special Achievements:** Selected in first round, first pick of NBA draft, 1994. **Business Addr:** Head Coach, Franklin & Marshall College, 415 Harrisburg Ave, Lancaster, PA 17603, **Business Phone:** (717)291-3911.

**ROBINSON, GLORIA W.**
Government official. **Educ:** Univ Mich, BA; Mich State Univ, MA. **Career:** City's Planning & Develop Dept, dir, 1994-97; Head-up display, asst secy, 1997-98; City Detroit, Planning, Community & Econ Develop dept, dir; Bill Clinton admin, appointee; Heritage Vision Plans, chief operating officer, 2006-; US Dept Housing & Urban Develop Wash, asst to secy. **Orgs:** Mortarboard Sr Women's Hon Soc; Am Inst Cert Planners & a regist community planner; fel Am Inst Cert Planners, 2004. **Business Addr:** Chief Operating Officer, Heritage Vision Plans Inc, 19010 Livernois Ave, Detroit, MI 48221-2259.

**ROBINSON, REV. HAROLD OSCAR**
Educator, clergy. **Personal:** Born Apr 21, 1943, Trenton, NJ; son of Oscar Alexander and Emma; married Alice Louise Steele; children: Kheesa & Harold Jr. **Educ:** Rutgers Univ, BA, 1973, MEd, 1974, EdD cand, 1978; Hood Theol Sem, Mdiv, 1998. **Career:** African Methodist Episcopal Zion Church, pastor, 1989-90, first resident missionary, 1994-1996, assoc minister, 1996-2000; Brown Hill African Methodist Episcopal Zion Church, 1990-94; Cabarrus County Schs, chmn dir diversity task force, 1997-99; Shaw Univ, adj prof humanities, 1997-2001; Livingstone Col, dir career coun, 1998-99; Ala Brown HS, teacher, 1999-2001; First Cong United Church Christ, pastor, 2000-; Carolinas Med Ctr, chaplain resident, 2002-03. **Orgs:** Deleg, Dem Nat Conv, New York, 1980; pres, Cabarrus County br, Nat Asn Advan Colored People, 1991-93; bd visitors, Barbara Scotia Col, 1993-2000; Nat Boy Scout dir African Methodist Episcopal Zion Church, Charlotte, 1994-2000; Leadership Cabarrus, 1994; Community Bldg Task Force Community, 1997-98; bd dir, Hist Cabarrus, 1998-2001; pres, Charlotte Br, Asn Study African Am Life & Hist; Phi Beta Sigma. **Home Addr:** 3735 Rock Hill Church Rd, Concord, NC 28027, **Home Phone:** (704)786-9550. **Business Addr:** President, Association for the Study of African American Life and History, Suite C 142 525 Bryant St NW, Washington, DC 20059.

**ROBINSON, DR. HARRY, JR.**
Museum director, chief executive officer. **Personal:** Born Sep 16, 1941, New Orleans, LA; son of Harry Sr and Ruth. **Educ:** Southern Univ, BA, lib sci, 1964; Atlanta Univ, MSLS, lib sci, 1965; Univ Ill, EdD, 1969; Getty Mus Mgt Inst, attended 1984. **Career:** Bishop Col, libr dir, assoc dean acad affairs, music dir spec asst pres & vpres develop, 1974; African Am Mus, pres & chief exec officer, 1974-; Good St Baptist Churc, librn, currently. **Orgs:** Soc SW Activ; Am Libr Asn; pres, African Am Mus Asn; Dallas Theater Ctr; Dallas Arboretum & Bot Soc; Booker T Wash High Sch Visual & Performing Arts; SW Black Arts Festival; bd trustee, Dallas Mus Art; bd dir, Friends Dallas Pub Libr; bd mem, S fair Comm Devp Corp; bd mem, Natl Mus & Lib Brd; Dallas Arboretum & Bot Socs Inc; bd mem, Inst Mus & Libr Serv; pres, Asn African Am Mus; African Am Libr As; Inst Mus & Libr Sci. **Special Achievements:** Editor of The Lives and Times of Black Dallas Women, 2002. **Business Addr:** President, Chief Executive Officer, African American Museum, 3536 Grand Ave, Dallas, TX 75210, **Business Phone:** (214)565-9026.

**ROBINSON, HARRY G., III**
City planner, educator, architect. **Personal:** Born Jan 18, 1942, Washington, DC; son of Harry G Jr and Gwendolyn Herriford; married Dianne O Davis; children: Erin K, Leigh H & Kia L. **Educ:** Howard Univ, BA, 1966, MCP, 1970; Grad Sch Design, MCP, urban design, 1972. **Career:** DC Redevelop Land Agency, archit planner, 1968-72; Woodrow Wilson Found, Martin Luther King Jr fel, 1969-70; US DOT, urban transp res fel, 1969-70; Univ Wash, prof, 1969-70, 1971-74; Morgan State Univ, chmn & prof, 1971-79; TRG Consult, managing prin, 1993-; Howard Univ, dean arch & planning, 1979-95, vpres, 1995-2000, prof, prof & dean emer, currently; Am Battle Monument Comn, exec architect, 2010-. **Orgs:** Am Inst Cert Planners, 1974-; Am Inst Arch, 1976-; pres, DC Bd Exam & Reg Arch, 1983-89; pres, Nat Coun Archit Regist, 1992-93; chmn, US Comn Fine Arts, 1995-; prof adv, Goree Mem & Mus, Dakar, Senegal, 1995-97; pres, Nat Archit Accrediting Bd, 1996-97; prof adv, Nat Underground RR Freedom Ctr, Cincinnati, OH, 1996-99; trustee & secy, Nat Bldg Mus; trustee, Cooper-Hewitt Nat Mus Design; founder & dir, African-Am Archit Initiative; dir; Arch Adventure/City Pl; chmn, UNESCO Int Comn GOREE Mem & Mus; trustee, Idea Pub Charter Sch; trustee, Booker T Wash Charter Sch; Int Adv Bd, IIBC, Tokyo, Japan; dir, Vietnam Veterans Mem Fund; master mason, Prince Hall Free & Accepted Masons; Comt Preserv White House; White House Hist Asn; trustee, John F Kennedy Ctr Performing Arts; chmn, Pa Ave White House Pres Comt; Comt 100 Fed City; dir, Chauncey Group Int; hon mem, Trinidad & Tobago Inst Archit; hon mem, Mex Soc Architects; pres, Robinson Group. **Honors/Awds:** Faculty Gold Medal in Design, Howard Univ, 1965; Silver Medal, Tau Sigma Delta, Hon Soc, 1988; Whitney M Young Jr Citation, 1990; Richard T Ely Distinguished Educator, Lambda Alpha Int Land Econ Soc, 1991; NOMA Honor Award, 1991; Special Award, 1992; The Centennial Medal, Wash Chap AIA, 2003; Architect of the Year, DC Coun Eng & Archit Soc, 2004; D C Hall of Fame, 2006; Tau Sigma Delta Silver Medal. **Special Achievements:** Author of the award winning third history of Howard University, The Long walk: The Placemaking Legacy of Howard University and producer of the Telly recognized documentary by the same name; First African American to be elected president of the National Architectural Accrediting Board; First African American elected president of the National Council of Architectural Registration Board. **Home Addr:** 7412 14 St NW, Washington, DC 20012-1502, **Home Phone:** (202)506-3757. **Business Addr:** Professor, Dean Emeritus, Howard University, Rm 218 2366 6th St NW, Washington, DC 20059, **Business Phone:** (202)806-5585.

**ROBINSON, HENRY**
Government official, mayor. **Personal:** Born Oct 2, 1936, Port Royal, SC; son of William and Elizabeth; married Jannie Middleton; children: Elizabeth, Tracy & Stephanie. **Career:** John Demosthenes Co Marines Corps Recruit Depot Parris Island; Lowcountry Coun Govt; Town Port Royal, coun mem & mayor pro-tempore, 1999-. **Orgs:** Pres, Community Ctr Port Royal; second vpres, Dem Party Port Royal Prec; Wardle Family YMCA; Hist Port Royal Found; Beaufort-Jasper Equal Opportunity Comn; Union Baptist Church; bd dir, SC Munic Asn; SC Conf Black Mayors Robert Smalls Alumni Asn; Beaufort County Foster Parents Asn. **Honors/Awds:** Outstanding Community Service. **Home Addr:** 632 Fort Fredrick Ct, Port Royal, SC 29935, **Home Phone:** (843)521-4490. **Business Addr:** Council Member & Mayor Pro Tempore, Town of Port Royal, 632 Ft Frederick Circle St, Port Royal, SC 29935, **Business Phone:** (843)525-2973.

**ROBINSON, JACK A, JR.**
Lawyer. **Personal:** Born Mar 20, 1942, Chicago, IL; son of Jack Sr and Clara L Jones; married Flora G; children: Jacqueline, Craig & Christopher. **Educ:** Chicago Teachers Col, BE, 1963; Chicago Kent Col Law, JD, 1970. **Career:** Lawyer (retired); Miller & Pomper, atty, 1970-71; Argonne Nat Lab, atty, 1971-97. **Orgs:** Nat Bar Asn; Cook County Bar Asn; Omega Psi Phi Fraternity. **Home Addr:** 8624 S Wolcott Ave, Chicago, IL 60620-4730, **Home Phone:** (773)779-1812.

**ROBINSON, JACK E.**
Publisher, editor, president (organization). **Personal:** Born Indianapolis, IN; son of Jack and Billie; children: Jacqueline, Errol & Sarah. **Educ:** Boston Univ, AA, BS, 1955; Boston Col, educ & bus, 1957. **Career:** Wash Globe, ed, publ; Pk Dale Nursing Home; Burton Nursing Home; Compact Advt; Burton Realty Trust; Am Bus Mgt; Consol Liquors; Am Beverages Corp; Robinson Construct Corp, pres; Universal Distributing; Compact Corp; Apex Construct Co, Boston, Mass, chief exec officer; Alpha Construct Co, pres; Converse Construct Co, pres; Trans Am Commodity Corp, pres; Nat Asn African Americans, pres & chief exec officer, 1975-; Robinson & Robinson Advert Agency, pres. **Orgs:** Pres, Commonwealth Rep Club; pres, Nat Asn Advan Colored People, 1975-95; Sportsmen Tennis Club; pres, State Enterprises; Nat Asn Minority Contractors, 1985-; Real Estate Owners Asn; bd dir, Vol Action Ctr; ABCD; Circle Asn; pres, Am Motorist Asn; Omega Psi Phi Frat; Phi Epsilon Kappa Frat; Bay State Golf Club; pres, Oak Bluffs Tennis Club; Alliance Safer Greater Boston; sr mem, US Dept Com, Domestic & Int Bus Admin; pres, NAAA, 1975-. **Honors/Awds:** Civil Liberties Union Adv Com Man of Year, Construct Engineering News Mag, 1971; Man of Year, Boston Bldg Dept; Save energy Award, Dir US Dept Com; Builder Of The Year, City Boston, 1972; Excellence Award, US Dept Com, 1972. **Home Addr:** PO Box 255, Boston, MA 02130, **Home Phone:** (617)524-7300. **Business Addr:** President, Chief Executive Officer, National Association of African Americans, 1231 N Broad St, Philadelphia, PA 19122, **Business Phone:** (215)235-6488.

**ROBINSON, JAMES EDWARD**
Executive, radio director, air force officer. **Personal:** Born Aug 31, 1943, Asheville, NC; married Shirley Byrd; children: Geno Nigel, Tajuana Yvette, Tanya & Aisha Monique. **Educ:** Taylor Sch Broadcast Tech, AA, 1969; Elkins Inst Broadcasting, cert, 1971. **Career:** Model Cities Agency, pub info asst, 1971-74; City Asheville, pub info officer, 1974-76; Radio Sta WBMU-FM, founder, pres, gen mgr, 1974-. **Orgs:** Nat Asn Black Owned Broadcasters; NC Soc Pub Rel Dir. **Business Addr:** Founder, President, WNMU-FM, 1401 Presque Isle Ave, Marquette, MI 49855, **Business Phone:** (906)227-2600.

**ROBINSON, JAMES L.**
Architect, entrepreneur, city planner. **Personal:** Born Jul 12, 1940, Longview, TX; son of W L and Ruby Newhouse; children: Kerstin G, Maria T, Jasmin Marisol, Ruby Nell, Kenneth & James L Jr. **Educ:** Southern Univ, BArch, 1964; Pratt Inst, MCP, 1974. **Career:** The Port New York Authority, 1964; WT Grant Co, 1964-65; Herbst & Rusciano AIA, architect, 1965; Carson Lundin & Shaw, architect, 1965-67; Carl J Petrilli, architect, 1967-68; Kennerly Slomanson & Smith, architect, 1968-70; Beyer Blinder Belle AIA, 1970-71; James L Robinson PC, architect, 1970-84; City Col New York, 174-76; Pratt Inst, 1976-80; Robinson Architect PC, architect, 1984, chief exec officer, 1989-, chief Honcho-; J & K Construct, 1998-; 55C Construct Corp, owner, currently. **Orgs:** Independent Platform Asn; former bd dir, Boys Clubs Am; arbitrator, Am Arbitration Asn, 1979. **Honors/Awds:** National Housing Award, Design & Environ, 1976; Bard Award, Fulton Ct Complex, 1976, 1977. **Special Achievements:** Two Thousand Notable Americans. **Home Addr:** 608 S Ctr St, Orange, NJ 07050, **Home Phone:** (973)674-2678. **Business Addr:** Owner, 55C Construction Corp, 55C Delancey St, New York, NY 10002, **Business Phone:** (212)966-7828.

**ROBINSON, JAMES WAYMOND**
Physician. **Personal:** Born Nov 6, 1926, Wilmington, NC; son of Sam and Addie Best; married Carol Blackmar. **Educ:** NC Col, Durham, BS, 1950; Meharry Med Col, MD, 1960. **Career:** Physician (retired); internship, 1960-61; resident, 1961-65; Joint Dis N Gen Hosp, asst attend physician; Beth Israel's Methadone Maintenance Treat Prog, assoc chief; Beth Israel's Methadone Maintenance Treat Prog Harlem Unit, unit dir, 1965-75; Arthur C Logan Memorial Hosp, assoc attend physician, 1965-79; Harlem Hosp, asst attend physician, 1965-92, chief activ therapist. **Orgs:** Med Soc State & Co NY; Omega Psi Phi Fraternity; ASIM; NY Soc Indust Med; NYCSIM. **Special Achievements:** Author: "Methadone Poisoning, Diagnosis & Treatment"; "Methadone Treatment of Randomly Selected Criminal Addicts". **Home Addr:** 4000 Poinsett St, North Myrtle Beach, SC 29582-5067, **Home Phone:** (843)272-4688.

**ROBINSON, DR. JAMUIR MICHELLE**
Association executive. **Personal:** married Jason Lawrence. **Educ:** Clark Atlanta Univ, BA, psychol, 1997, MSW, health/ment health, 2000; Cornell Univ, PhD, policy anal & mgt, 2003; George Washington Univ, MPH, epidemiol/biostatistics, 2004. **Career:** Oncol Data Serv, oncol data specialist, 1999-2003; Nat Cancer Inst, Cancer Prev, post doctoral fel, 2003-08, Off Educ & Spec Initiatives, currently; Walden Univ, Sch Health Sci, fac, 2008-; Innovative Eval Solutions, sr evaluator & co-founder, 2008-; Christ United Methodist Church, website coordr. **Orgs:** Delta Sigma Theta Sorority Inc. **Business Addr:** Faculty, Walden University, 100 Washington Ave S Suite 900, Minneapolis, MN 55401, **Business Phone:** (888)502-6865.

**ROBINSON, DR. JANE ALEXANDER**
Clinical psychologist. **Personal:** Born Jan 17, 1931, Chicago, IL; daughter of Cornelius and Janie Burruss-Goodwin; children: David, Amorie & Richard. **Educ:** BS, 1952, MS, 1963; Univ Detroit, PhD, 1977. **Career:** Detroit Pub Schs, elem teacher, 1957-63; Southfield Bd Educ, sch psychol, 1964-68; Detroit Bd Educ, sch psychol, 1968-97; pvt pract, clin psychologist, currently. **Orgs:** Founder & secy, Mich Asn Black Psychol, 1968-70, pres, 1975-76; Psi Chi nat Hon Soc Psychol, Univ Detroit Chap. **Honors/Awds:** Award for Organisation Leadership, Nat Asn Black Psychol, 1976. **Special Achievements:** Books:"Self-Esteem, Racial Consciousness & Perception of Difference Between the Values of Black & White Americans", 1977. **Home Addr:** 79 Rhode Island St, Highland Park, MI 48203-3356, **Home Phone:** (313)865-4129. **Business Addr:** Clinical Psychologist, Private Practice, 3011 W Grand Blvd Suite 418, Detroit, MI 48202, **Business Phone:** (313)875-4433.

**ROBINSON, JEANNETTE**
School administrator. **Personal:** Born Atlanta, GA; daughter of Reginald and Mary; children: Yolanda C Wade. **Educ:** Essex Co Col, Newark, NJ, AS, 1975; Rutgers Univ, BS, 1977; Fairleigh Dickinson Univ, MBA, 1980. **Career:** Newark Educ Inst, adminr, 1973-80; Dept Planning & Econ Develop Div Employ Training, contract mgt supvr, 1980-83; Essex County Col, Newark, dir human resources, 1983-. **Orgs:** Arbitrator Better Bus Bur, NJ, 1982-; NJ Educ Asn, NJ Asn Equality & Excellence Educ; Asn Black Women Higher Educ; Delta Sigma Phi Frat; Nat Asn Col & Univ Personnel Admin; sub comt mem, Leadership, Governance & Adminr, essex county col; trustee, Offender Aid & Restoration Essex County Inc. **Home Addr:** 317 Lilac Dr, Union, NJ 07083-7825. **Business Addr:** Trustee, Offender Aid & Restoration of Essex County Inc, 303 Wash St 3rd Fl, Newark, NJ 07102, **Business Phone:** (973)373-0100.

**ROBINSON, JEFFREY A.**
Executive, educator, consultant. **Personal:** Born Sep 13, 1971, East Orange, NJ; son of Ronald (deceased) and Doreen; married Valerie Mason; children: 3. **Educ:** Rutgers Univ, Rutgers Col, BA, urban studies, 1995, Col Eng, BS, civil engineering, 1995; Ga Inst Technol, MS, civil engineering mgt, 1996; Columbia Univ, Grad Bus, MPhil, mgt & orgn, 2002, PhD, mgt & entrepreneurship, 2005. **Career:** Prof, int speaker & entrepreneur; Ga Inst Technol, GEM Fel; MBS Enterprises LLC, founder & bd mem, 1993-2001; Law Engineering, staff engr, 1995; Merck & Co Inc, proj engr, 1996-98; BCT Partners, founding mem & partner, 2001-; Loyola Col Md, Sellinger Sch Bus, teaching fel & adj prof, 2001-03; Leonard N Stern Sch Bus, NY, asst prof mgt, 2003-08, Berkley Ctr Entrepreneurial Studies, fac advisor, 2004-, interim res dir, 2007-; LagosBusiness Sch, vis prof, exec educ, 2007-; Eden Organix, vpres strategy, 2007-; Ctr Urban Entrepreneurship Econ Dev, asst dir; Rutgers Univ, Rutgers Bus Sch, asst prof mgt & entrepreneurship, asst dir, 2008-, acad dir, assoc prof, 2014-. **Orgs:** Nat vice chair, Nat Soc Black Engrs, 1995-96, nat conv chair, 1996-97; Nat Black MBA Asn, 1998-; PhD Proj Doctoral Studs Asn, 1998-; mem bd, Nat Inst Urban Entrepreneurship, 2004-; mem bd, NJ Pub Policy Res Inst, 2005-; life mem, Nat Black MBA Asn; Alpha Phi Alpha Fraternity; bd mem, Abundant Life Community Dev Corp, 2007-;; Nj Social Innovation Inst; Nat Black MBA Asn; Alpha Phi Alpha Fraternity Inc;bd mem, Nj Pub Policy Res Inst & Abundant Life Community Develop Ctr; sr fel, Ctr Urban Entrepreneurship & Econ Develop, 2014-. **Home Addr:** 1939 Eutaw Pl, Baltimore, MD 21217, **Home Phone:** (410)225-2773. **Business Addr:** Assistant Professor, Rutgers, The State University of New Jersey, 111 Washington St, Newark, NJ 07102, **Business Phone:** (973)353-1621.

**ROBINSON, DR. JIM C.**
College teacher. **Personal:** Born Feb 9, 1943, Ackerman, MS. **Educ:** Calif State Univ, BA, 1966, MA, 1968; Stanford Univ, MA, 1972, PhD, 1973. **Career:** San Jose St Col, teacher; Calif State Univ, Long Beach, assoc prof black studies, spec asst vpres acad affairs, dean fac & staff affairs, prof; Calif State Univ, Long Beach, emer prof, 2003-. **Orgs:** Nat Alliance Black Sch Educrs; Am Asn Univ & Prof; dir regents, Progs W Am Asn Higher Educ; chmn, Asn Black Fac & Staff Calif; Mayor's Task Force Fiscal Mgt & Control, Compton. **Business Addr:** Professor Emeritus, California State University, 1250 Bellflower Blvd, Long Beach, CA 90840, **Business Phone:** (562)985-5561.

**ROBINSON, JOHN E.**
Executive, president (organization). **Personal:** Born Jul 12, 1942, Hollywood, AL; son of John Karie and Anna Naomi Ellison Edwards; children: Dana L. **Educ:** Clark Col, BA, 1979; Atlanta Univ, MBA, 1979. **Career:** Soc Savings Bank, asst br mgr, 1964-69; Wesleyan Univ, asst personnel dir, 1969-73; WSC Corp, admin vpres, 1973-77; Aetna Life & Casualty, adminr, 1981-01; producer, host talk show, WVIT Channel 30, 1983-; Aetna Inc, mkt consult, currently. **Orgs:** Pres, Beta Sigma Lambda Chap Alpha Phi Alpha, 1981-; Sigma Pi Phi, 1983-; Univ Club Hartford, 1983-95; bd mem, Greater Hartford Bus Develop Ctr, 1984-; bd mem, Trinity Col, Comm Child Ctr, 1986-94; bd mem, Univ Club Scholar Fund; chmn, Youth Prog Serv Comt, YMCA, 1992-95; life mem, Alpha Phi Alpha; Craftery Art Gallery, 1994-99; bd mem, Cath Charities, Cath Family Serv, 2001-02. **Home Addr:** 485 High St Suite E, New Britain, CT 06053, **Home Phone:** (860)224-9492. **Business Addr:** President, Chief Executive Officer, RJ Enterprises LLC, 485 High St, New Britain, CT 06053, **Business Phone:** (800)224-9492.

**ROBINSON, JOHN F.**
Executive, chief executive officer. **Personal:** Born May 3, 1944, Brooklyn, NY; children: Timothy. **Educ:** AAS; BBA; NY Community Col; Baruch Col Off Serv. **Career:** F Chusid & Co, off serv dir, 1966-68; Cancer Care Inc, dir, 1968-76; New York Educ & Training Consortium Inc, pres, exec dir; Nat Minority Bus Coun, pres & chief exec officer, 1972-. **Orgs:** Am Mgt Asn; Soc Advan Mgt; chmn, Alliance Minority Bus Orgn Inc; bd Harlem YMCA; pres, bd dir, Serv Underserved, 1989-92; pres, Minority Bus Exec Prog Alumni Asn; Small Bus Admin Adv Coun; pres, First Church Community Urban Develop Corp; Wildlife Conserv Soc, int progs; bd advisors, St John's Univ & Peter J Tobin Sch Bus; pres bd, Gatewave Inc, 2015-. **Home Addr:** 8043 Utopia Pkwy, Jamaica, NY 11432, **Home Phone:** (718)591-8223. **Business Addr:** President, Chief Executive Officer, National Minority Business Council Inc, 120 Broadway Fl 19, New York, NY 10271, **Business Phone:** (212)693-5050.

**ROBINSON, JOHN G.**
Executive. **Personal:** Born Feb 22, 1942, Birmingham, AL; son of Johnny G Sr and Addie B; married Yvonne R Young; children: Brittany Ann. **Educ:** Miles Col, BA, 1963; Univ Minn, attended 1968. **Career:** Executive (retired); Control Data Corp, compen consult, 1971-75, human resources mgr, 1986-86; Magnetic Peripherals Inc, staff, employee rels & training mgr, 1975-79, remote site personnel mgr, 1979-80, div personnel mgr, 1980-82; ETA Systs Inc, human resources mgr, 1986-89; John Robinson & Assocs, pres, 1989-93; Co Anoka, diversity coordr, housing opers mgr, 1993-2005. **Orgs:** Life mem, Alpha Pi Alpha Fraternity, 1961-; Minneapolis Vikings Pub Rel Game Staff, 1968-93; Twin City Personnel Asn, 1986-89; fund distrib comt, United Way Minneapolis, 1992-98; Minneapolis Asn Human Rights Workers, 1993-; bd dir, Law Enforcement Opportunities, 1995-; Nat Asn Pub Sector Equal Opportunity Officers, 1996-. **Home Addr:** 14620 Carriage Lane, Burnsville, MN 55306, **Home Phone:** (952)892-7837.

**ROBINSON, JOHN MOSES**
Executive, president (organization), chief executive officer. **Personal:** Born May 22, 1949, Philadelphia, PA; son of Marvin and Janie Hines; married Alisa Ramsey; children: Faith Caryn. **Educ:** Edward Waters Col, attended 1971; Dartmouth Univ, Amos Tuck, 1991. **Career:** SI Handling Syst, sales engr, 1971-76; Black Diamond Enterprises Ltd, founder & pres, 1978-; Edward Waters Col, vis prof, 1989. **Orgs:** Nat Asn Advan Colored People; Soc Mfg Engrs; Omega Psi Phi; Int Mat Mgt Soc; Opers Crossroads African Inc; Minorority Bus Educ Legal Defense Fund; prison adv bd; pres, Easton Br Nat Asn Advan Colored People. **Home Addr:** 100 Pa Ave, Easton, PA 18042. **Business Addr:** Founder, President, Black Diamond Enterprises Ltd, 430 W Lincoln St, Easton, PA 18042-0019, **Business Phone:** (610)559-7370.

**ROBINSON, JOHNATHAN PRATHER**
Executive, vice president (organization). **Personal:** Born Apr 7, 1953, Cleveland, OH; son of Verdix and Robbie Luster; married Deborah Lynn Turner; children: Rikki Lauren & Jorie Patrice. **Educ:** Northwestern Univ, Evanston, IL, BS, radio tv film, 1975. **Career:** Nat Talent Assocs, Chicago, Ill, asst mgr, 1975-77; Wash Nat Ins Co, Evanston, Ill, mkt asst, 1977-80; WorldBook Childcraft Int, Chicago, Ill, proj supvr, 1980-81; Kemper Financial Servs, Chicago, Ill, sales prom specialist, 1981-82; ShopTalk Publ Inc, Chicago, Ill, vpres, 1982-90; Burrell Consumer Promotions, exec vpres, managing dir, 1989-92; Interactive Video Enterprises, nat dir, 1993-95; Petry Interactive, vp sales, 1995-97; NetChannel, vpres, 1997-98; Smartage.com, exec vpres, 1998-2000; Everyone.net, vpres advert sales & Bus Develop, 2000-01; Topica Inc, sr vpres sales & mkt, 2001-06; PhotoActive.com, vp mkt & sales, 2007-08; The Paquin Group, vpres, 2007-09; Zuberance Inc, consult, 2009; Leadtail Inc, vp mkt & sales, 2009-12; Blaze Mobile, vpres advert, 2012; RedAwning.com Inc, vpres, mkt, 2012-; Career Tv Network Inc, vpres mkt, sales. **Orgs:** Omega Psi Phi Fraternity Inc, 1972-; servs comn, bd dir, Howard/Paulina Develop Corp, 1989-; steering comt, Promotional Mkt Asn Am, 1990-. **Home Addr:** 1440 W Birchwood, Chicago, IL 60626, **Home Phone:** (312)764-7243. **Business Addr:** Senior Vice President of Sales & Marketing, Topica Inc, 1 Post St Suite 875, San Francisco, CA 94104, **Business Phone:** (415)344-3854.

**ROBINSON, JONTYLE THERESA**
Writer, educator, curator. **Personal:** Born Jul 22, 1947, Atlanta, GA. **Educ:** Clark Col, BA, span, 1968; Univ GA, MA, art hist, 1971; Univ Md, PhD, contemp caribbean & Latin Am art hist, 1983. **Career:** Univ GA, Study Abroad Prog fel, res asst, 1970; Philander Smith Col, chairperson, 1971-72; Univ MD, Eastern Shore, instr, 1972-75; Emory Univ, instr, 1978-83, asst prof, joint appointment AFA & AFR Studies Prog/art hist, 1983-86, designer, AFA & AFR studies/art hist, Summer Study Abroad Prog, Haiti, Jamaica, 1984, 1986, Haiti, Dominican Repub, Pr, 1985; WVA State Col, assoc prof, 1986-87; Smithsonian Inst & Arch Am Art, res retrospective exhib, catalogue raisonne, Am painter Archibald John Motley Jr, 1986-88; Kenkeleba Gallery, res fel, co-cur, 1987-88; Winthrop Col, assoc prof, 1989; Spelman Col, Depart Art, assoc prof, cur & prof, currently. **Orgs:** Nat exec secy, Nat CNF Artists, 1971-72; DST; Phi Kappa Phi Nat Hon Soc; Atlanta Spelman Col art hist fac. **Honors/Awds:** Amoco Faculty Award, 1992. **Special Achievements:** Author: "Archibald John Motley Jr", Chicago Historical Society, 1991; "Archibald John Motley Jr: Painting Jazz and Blues," paper, College Art Association, Chicago, Feb 13-15, 1992; "Archibald John Motley Jr: The Artist in Paris, 1929-30," paper, AFAs and Europe INT CNF, Paris, Feb 5-9, 1992; "Bearing Witness: Contemporary Works by African American Women Artists", Spelman College & Rizzoli International Publications Inc, 1996; Review: "Black Art-Ancestral Legacy: The AFR Impulse in AFA Art," AFR Arts Magazine, Jan 1991; Judge: Contemporary Art Exhibition, Nat Black Arts Festival, Atlanta, 1988; consult: Archibald John Motley Jr Exhibition, Your Heritage House, Detroit, 1988; curator: "VH-4 Decades: The Art of Varnette P Honeywood," Spelman Col, 1992; numerous other television/public lectures, tours, panels, publications. **Home Addr:** PO Box 4613, Atlanta, GA 30302. **Business Addr:** Professor, Curator, Spelman College, 350 Spelman Lane SW, Atlanta, GA 30314, **Business Phone:** (404)223-7672.

**ROBINSON, REV. JOSEPH, JR.**
Clergy. **Personal:** Born Jul 28, 1940, Orangeburg, SC; married Lizzie Miller; children: Jonathan, Joseph C & Jason. **Educ:** Claflin Col, BA, 1964; Interdenominational Theol Ctr, BD, 1967, MDiv, 1973. **Career:** Morris Brown Col, chaplain, 1965-66; Turner Theo Sem, teacher, 1966-67; Woodbury, NJ, Campbell AME, chmn, 1967-68; St NJ, social worker, 1967-68; St Johns AME Church, minister, 1968-72; Grant AME Church Boston, minister, 1972-78; Bethel AME Church, Freeport, NY, minister, 1978-86; Bethel AME Church, New Haven, CT, minister, 1986; Trinity AME Church, pastor, currently. **Orgs:** Phi Beta Sigma; bd dir, Mass Coun Churches; Family Serv Div Prof Couns Staff Boston; pres & bd dir, Brightmoor Terr Inc; Minstl All Greater Boston; vice chmn & trustee bd, New Eng Ann Conf AME Ch; deleg, Gen Conf AME Ch Atlanta, 1976; trustee, NY Ann Conf, AME Church, 1976-; pres, Nat Asn Advan Colored People Freeport & Roosevelt Br, 1978-79; comnr, Human Rels Coun Freeport; trustee, NY Ann Conf; bd examiners, New York Ann Conf; coordr, First Dist Episcopal Hq; bd dir, Liberty Pk Housing; chmn bd, Paul Quinn Fed Credit Union; Self Help, First Episcopal Dist, 1989; NF Housing Authority, hearing officer; bd dir, Christians & Jews Am. **Honors/Awds:** School Award, Phi Beta Sigma, 1964; Jackson Fisher Award, 1964; Turner Memorial Award, 1967; 19 Years Ahead of Time Leadership Award, Macedonia AME Church, 1986; Scholar Award, Interdominal Theol Ctr, 1966-67; Mortgage Reduction Citation; speaker, Religious Emphasis Week, Morehouse Col, Martin Luther King Col of Ministers. **Home Addr:** , Philadelphia, PA 19115, **Home Phone:** (215)289-8444. **Business Addr:** Pastor, Trinity African Methodist Episcopal Church, 2502 N 27th St, Philadelphia, PA 19132, **Business Phone:** (215)229-5619.

**ROBINSON, DR. JOYCE RUSSELL**
Educator. **Personal:** Born Jul 15, 1950, Palmer Springs, VA; children: William Russell. **Educ:** Bennett Col, BA, 1971; NC Cent Univ, MA, 1982; Emory Univ, PhD, 1991; Univ Tenn. **Career:** NC Pub Sch Syst, instr, 1972-84; Univ Tenn, Knoxville, teaching assoc, 1984-87; St Augustines Col, assoc prof, assoc dir, Bush-Hewlett Writing Across the Curric, 1987-96; NC State Univ, Meredith Col, adj prof, 1994-95; Fayetteville State Univ, proj dir, assoc prof, African Am & womens lit, 1996-; Haverhill MA Pub Schs, dir mgt & finance. **Orgs:** Asn Dept Eng, 1992; Col Lang Asn, 1993-; Nat Coun Teachers Eng, 1993-95; asst secy, John Chavis Soc, 1997; Sankore Charter Sch, 1999. **Home Addr:** 1027 Buckhorn Rd, Garner, NC 27529-3752, **Home Phone:** (919)661-2996. **Business Addr:** Associate Professor, Fayetteville State University, Rm 132 Butler Bldg 1200 Murchison Rd, Fayetteville, NC 28301-4298, **Business Phone:** (910)672-1111.

**ROBINSON, KENNETH**
Government official, business owner, executive. **Personal:** Born Dec 10, 1947, Chicago, IL; son of Seayray Govan and Henry Lee; married Etta D Clement. **Educ:** Ill State Univ, BA, bus admin, 1974. **Career:** Am Hosp Supply Corp, tax acct; Abbott Labs, staff tax admin; Ill Dept Revenue, revenue auditor; Lake County Community Action, econ develop coordr, admin dir; Baskin Robbins, owner, 1996-2015; City N Chicago, city treas, 2005-13. **Orgs:** Pres, Five Points Econ Develop Corp, 1981-; bd mem, Lake County Urban League, 1981-; bd mem, N Chicago Plan Comt, 1982-; sch bd mem, pres, Dist 64 No Chicago, 1984-; bd mem, Lake City Pvt Indust Coun, 1994; treas, 911 Bd; treas, Police Pension Fund; pres, Ill Municipals Treasurers Asn; treas & bd mem, Fire Pension Fund; cert munic treas, Cert Prof Finance Investment Mgr. **Home Addr:** PO Box 1181, North Chicago, IL 60064-8181. **Business Addr:** City Treasurer, City of North Chicago, 1850 Lewis Ave, North Chicago, IL 60064, **Business Phone:** (847)596-8628.

**ROBINSON, KENNETH EUGENE.** **See Obituaries Section.**

**ROBINSON, DR. KITTY KIDD (WILLIE MAE KIDD)**
Educator. **Personal:** Born Jan 7, 1921, West Point, MS. **Educ:** Tenn State Univ, BS, 1949; De Paul Univ, MEd, supv & admin, 1960; Northwestern Univ, PhD, 1974. **Career:** Chicago Pub Sch, pr teacher, 1956-66; Univ Chicago, Recipient Independent Workshop fel, 1967; Chicago State Univ, grad admis counr, supvr, 1968-76, Dept early child educ, prof, asst dean, grad div & counr, grad admis, currently. **Orgs:** Chmn, Asn Child Educ, 1974; pan mem, Coop Urban Teacher Educ Work shp; Am Asn Univ Prof; Nat Educ Asn Int; Asn Child Educ Int; Ill Asn Supv & Current Devel; Nat Coun Teaching Eng Res Asn; bd mem, Asn Mammequins; Nat Reading Conf; Chicago Urban League; S Shore Community Serv; Women Mobil Chg; PUSH; Asn Mannequins; Trophy Sch Fund Bd Jeffery-Yates Neighbour base oper, Shore Patrol; pres, 79th St Block Club; Widows Club; Peace Corps Adv Coun. **Home Addr:** R5, PO Box 532, West Point, MS 39773. **Business Addr:** Professor, Assistant Dean, Chicago State University, 9501 S King Dr, Chicago, IL 60628, **Business Phone:** (773)995-2000.

**ROBINSON, LARRY**
Basketball player. **Personal:** Born Jan 11, 1968, Bossier City, LA; married Katrina Thomas; children: Jasmine, Felicity, Larry III & Giorgio. **Educ:** Eastern Okla State Univ, 1988; Centenary Col La, 1990. **Career:** Basketball player (retired), basketball executive; Wash Bullets, 1990-91, 1992-93; Golden State Warriors, 1991; Boston Celtics, 1991-92; Rapid City Thrillers, 1991-92; Houston Rockets, 1993-94; Vancouver Grizzlies, 1997-98; Cleveland Cavaliers, 2001; Atlanta Hawks, 2000-01; NY Knickerbockers, forward-guard, 2001-02; Horseshoe Casino & Hotel, casino host, 2004, dir player develop, 2006-. **Business Addr:** Director of Player, Horseshoe Casino and Hotel, 711 Horseshoe Blvd, Bossier City, LA 71111-4417, **Business Phone:** (318)742-0711.

**ROBINSON, DR. LAWRENCE DANIEL, JR.**
Physician. **Personal:** Born Sep 20, 1942, Baltimore, MD; children: 1. **Educ:** Univ Pittsburgh, BS, 1964; Howard Univ, MD, 1968. **Career:** Martin L King Jr Hosp; Johns Hopkins Hosp, intern, 1968-69; res, 1969-70; Cedars Sinai Med Ctr, chief res, 1970-71; Aus Ped Dir Sicle Cell Dis Prog, 1971-73; Charles R Drew Post grad Med Sch Unic Calif Los Angeles Immunol, Fel; Allergys & Immunol, asst prof pediat, dir; John Muir Med Ctr. **Orgs:** Nat Med Asn; Sci Adv Com, Nat Asn Sickle Cell Dis; bd, Cert by Am Bd Ped; Bd Allery & Immunol, 1975; Am Thoracic Soc; Am Acad Ped; mem bd, Am Lung Asn LA; Immunization Action Comn, 1978-80; co-chmn, Nat Immunization Prog, LA. **Special Achievements:** Has written & present many publications at meet of Am Ped Soc Atlantic City, Am Ped Soc Wash; Contributing Editor Essence Mag; presented papers to American Academy of Allergy. **Home Addr:** 6517 Whitworth Dr, Los Angeles, CA 90035. **Business Addr:** Physician, 1523 W Ave J Suite 7, Lancaster, CA 93534, **Business Phone:** (661)945-2221.

**ROBINSON, DR. LUTHER DABNEY**
Physician, educator. **Personal:** Born Dec 22, 1922, Tappahannock, VA; son of William H and Fannie E; married Betty Boyd; children: Jan, Barry & Vance. **Educ:** VA State Col, BS, 1943; Meharry Med Col, MD, 1946; Gallaudet Col, DSc, 1971. **Career:** Mercy Hosp Phila, intern, 1946-47; Lakin State Hosp Lakin WV, staff, 1947-49; Freedmen's Hosp Wash, psychiat residency, 1953-54; St Elizabeths Hosp, residency, 1954-55, staff, 1955-; Howard Univ Col Med, clin instr, 1956-68, vis lectr, assoc prof emer psychiat, currently; Gallaudet Col, lectr, 1968-; Geo Wash Univ, clin assoc prof, 1969-; Georgetown Univ Sch Med, fac mem, 1974-; St Elizabeths Hosp Wash, supt, 1975; Howard Univ Hosp, psychiat, currently. **Orgs:** World Fedn Deaf Originated Ment Health Prog Deaf St Elizabeths Hosp, 1963; Medico Chirurgical Soc; Med Soc DC; Wash Psychiat Soc; AMA; nat chmn, Commn Med & Audiol 7th World Cong; co-founder, AA Prog St Elizabeths Hosp; life mem, Am Psychiat Asn; Am Bd Psychiat & Neurol. **Honors/Awds:** Edw Miner Gallaudet Award, 1974; Meritorious Achievement Award, Nat Med Asn. **Special Achievements:** First African-American director of the prestigious St Elizabeth's Hosp in Washington. **Home Addr:** 2017 Spruce Dr NW, Washington, DC 20012-1026, **Home Phone:** (202)882-7215. **Business Addr:** Psychiatrist, Howard University Hospital, 2041 Ga Ave NW Suite 5B02, Washington, DC 20060, **Business Phone:** (202)865-6100.

**ROBINSON, DR. MALCOLM KENNETH**
Physician, surgeon. **Personal:** Born Nov 22, 1961, Philadelphia, PA; son of James H and Soiesette Furlonge; married Alyssa Shari Hayworde; children: James H III. **Educ:** Harvard Med Sch, AB, 1983, MD, 1987. **Career:** Brigham & Women'S Hosp, fel, 1992-2000, resident, 1994-2000; Harvard Med Sch, instr, 1994-2000, asst prof, 2001-; Dana Farber Cancer Inst, consult surgeon & physician, 1995-; Mass Gen Hosp, asst surgeon, 1997-; Nutrit Restart Ctr, sr res consult, 1998-2000; Faulkner Hosp, attend surgeon, 1998-; W Roxbury Veterans Admin Hosp, attend surgeon, 1999-; Brigham & Women's Hosp, dir, Metab Support Serv, 2000; pvt pract, currently; Ed: JPEN J Parenteral & Enteral Nutrit, New Eng J Med, Arch Surg, J Am Col Surgeons, J Women's Health & Topics Clin Nutrit. **Orgs:** Amer Med Asn, 1984-; MA Med Soc, 1984-; Am Asn Acad Surg, 1995-; Soc Black Acad Surgeons, 1995-; Soc Surg Alimentary Tract, 1996-; Boston Surg Soc, 1998-; Am Obesity Asn, 1999-; Boston Obesity Nutrit Res Ctr, 2000-; Am Soc Metab & Bariatric Surg; Am Col Surgeons. **Honors/Awds:** Nat Insts Health, Nat Res Service Award, 1990-92; Maurice Shils Research Award, Am Society for Parenteral & Enteral Nutrition, 1996, 1997. **Special Achievements:** Published numerous articles. **Home Addr:** 183 Mt Vernon St, West Newton, MA 02465, **Home Phone:** (617)965-5636. **Business Addr:** Physician, Brigham & Womens Hospital, 75 Francis St Carrie Hall 103, Boston, MA 02115, **Business Phone:** (617)732-8272.

**ROBINSON, MALCOLM S.**
Lawyer, executive, association executive. **Personal:** Born Jan 1, 1948, Chicago, IL; children: Brian M. **Educ:** Ottawa Univ, Ottawa, KS, BS, speech communs, 1970; Univ Kans Sch Law, Lawrence, Kans, JD, 1975. **Career:** Alliance Am Insurers, Chicago, Ill, corp coun, 1975-79; Scor Reinsurance Co, Dallas, Tex, gen coun, corp coun & vpres, 1979-84; Robinson W & Gooden, PC, FKA Robinson & W, Dallas, Tex, sr managing partner & co-founder, 1984-2002; Robinson & Hoskins LLP, atty, co-founder & managing partner, 2002-. **Orgs:** Dallas Bar Asn Found; Dallas Bar Asn; State Bar Tex; pres, Dallas Black Chamber Com, 1990-92, gen coun; vpres, Nat Bar Asn, 1998-2001, pres, 2002; chmn, 2000, bd dir, Dallas Conv & Visitors Bur; Am Bar Asn; dir, J L Turner Legal Asn; chmn, Greater Dallas Crime Comn; dir, N Tex Comn; chmn, bd trustees, State Bar Tex Ins Trust; former mem, Dallas Citizens Coun. **Honors/Awds:** Awarded, Quest for Success, 1984; Dallas Black Chamber of Commerce, Chairman's Award, 1999-00; President's Award, J.L. Turner Legal Asn, 1999; C.B. Bunkley Award, J.L. Turner Legal Asn, 2000; Presidential Award, National Bar Asn, 2001; Martin L. King, Jr. Justice Award, Dallas Bar Asn, 2003; Distinguished Alumni Award, Univ KS Sch Law, 2003. **Special Achievements:** First African American named chairman of the Dallas Conv and Visitors Bureau. **Home Addr:** 6203 Parkstone Way, Dallas, TX 75208, **Home Phone:** (972)709-6537. **Business Addr:** Co-Founder, Managing Partner, Robinson & Hoskins LLP, 400 S Zang Blvd Suite 600, Dallas, TX 75208, **Business Phone:** (214)941-0717.

**ROBINSON, MARCUS (MARCUS ANTONIO ROBINSON)**
Football player. **Personal:** Born Feb 27, 1975, Ft. Valley, GA. **Educ:** Univ SC, BS, elem educ. **Career:** Football player (retired); Chicago Bears, 1998, wide receiver, 1999-2002; Baltimore Ravens, wide receiver, 2003; Minn Vikings, wide receiver, 2004-06; Detroit Lions, 2007-08; St Viator, wide receiver coach, currently; Marian Hurricanes, sprint coach, currently; physical trainer, currently. **Orgs:** Founder, Marcus Robinson Found.

**ROBINSON, MAURICE C.**
Lawyer. **Personal:** Born Mar 4, 1932, St. Andrew; son of Herbert Ulysses and Mildred Anastasia Magnus; married Hazel Thelma Chang; children: Mark Wayne, Janet Marie & Wade Patrick. **Educ:** Univ Col Wi, BA, 1954; LLB. **Career:** Manton & Hart, assoc, 1959-64, partner, 1964-77; secy, Air Jamaica Ltd, 1968-69; Air Jamaica Ltd, legal officer, 1970-80; Eric Fong-Yee Eng CoLtd, chmn; Pub Utility Comn, 1972-76; Jamaica Pub Utility Comn, chmn, 1972-77; Myers, Fletcher & Gordon, consult, 1977-; Ericsscon Jamaica Ltd, staff; Jamaican Bar, distinguished & sr mem. **Orgs:** Bd dir, Victoria Mutual Property Servs Ltd, 1972-; bd dir, Victoria Mutual Investments Ltd, 1972-; chair, Victoria Mutual Bldg Soc; dir Travel Planners Ltd; Dyoll/ Wataru Coffee Co Ltd; dir, Security Adv & Mgt Servs Ltd; Inst Trade Mark Agts; bd dir, Victoria Mutual Ins Co Ltd; bd dir, Restaurant Asn Ltd, Burger King Franchise; assoc mem, Int Trademark Asn. **Honors/Awds:** Full University Colours for Field Hockey, 1953. **Home Addr:** 8 Benson Terr, Kingston78397. **Business Addr:** Consultant, Myers Fletcher & Gordon, Pk Pl 21 E St, Kingston78397, **Business Phone:** (876)922-5860.

**ROBINSON, DR. MILTON J.**
Executive director, educator, state government official. **Personal:** Born Aug 16, 1935, Asbury Park, NJ; married Sadie Pinkston; children: Valerie & Patricia. **Educ:** Univ Mich, BS, 1958, MSW, 1966, PhD, 1980; Columbia Univ, MA, 1962. **Career:** Battle Creek Urban League, exec dir, 1966-69; Flint Urban League, exec dir, 1969-70; Dept Civil Rights State Mich, exec dir, 1970-72; State Mich, parole bd mem, 1972-, exec sec parole & rev bd, currently; Wayne State Univ, Sch Social Work, adj prof, 1975-, GMI Engineering & Mgt Inst, admin & corp rels consult; Kettering Univ, Off Multicultural Stud Initiatives, int co-op advocate, consult to pres, 1990-2011. **Orgs:** Kappa Alpha Psi Frat; bd mem, United Neighborhood Ctrs Am, 1972-; pres, Cath Youth Orgn, 1978-; Lions Int, 1979-; bd mem, Detroit Metro Youth Prog, 1985-; rep, SECME. **Honors/Awds:** Community Service Award, City Battle Creek, 1969; Outstanding Professional Service Award, Flint Urban League, 1978; Outstanding Contributor to Continuing Judicial Education, Mich Judicial Inst, 1979; Meritorious Service Award, Catholic Youth Orgn, 1984; Certificate of Achievement, Nat Coun Juvenile & Family Court Judges, 1986; Inducted to Co-op Hall of Fame, Kettering Univ, 2011. **Home Addr:** 7023 Stanhope Pl, University Park, FL 34201, **Home Phone:** (941)780-0570. **Business Addr:** Consultant to the President, Kettering University, 1700 University Ave, Flint, MI 48504-4898, **Business Phone:** (810)762-9500.

**ROBINSON, DR. MURIEL F. COX**
Physician. **Personal:** Born Nov 6, 1927, Columbus, OH; daughter of Henry W and Veola. **Educ:** Ohio State Univ, attended 1948; Meharry Med Col, MD, 1952. **Career:** Homer G Phillips Hosp, affiliated w & Wash Univ Sch Med, psychiat resident, 1953-56; St Louis Munic Child Guid Clin, staff psychiatrist, 1956-57; Napa State Hosp, staff psychiatrist, 1958; Richmond Ment Health Ctr, staff psychiatrist, 1959-75; E Oakland Ment Health Ctr, staff psychiatrist, 1976-79; pvt psychiat pract, psychiatrist, 1960-79; Calif Youth Authority, staff, 1979-92; Locum Tenens Group, 1992-94. **Orgs:** N Richmond Neighborhood House; Am Psychiat Asn, 1957-; Black Psychiatrists Am; Nat Asn Advan Colored People Sacramento, 1987-; life mem, Am Psychiat Asn, 1991-; AMA, 1957-; AAAS, 1989-; Nat Med Asn, 1960-. **Business Addr:** Physician, 7310 Mandy Dr, Sacramento, CA 95829-2148, **Business Phone:** (916)427-8070.

**ROBINSON, MYRON FREDERICK**
Association executive, chief executive officer. **Personal:** Born Dec 15, 1943, Youngstown, OH; son of Romeo and Virginia L; married Brenda King; children: Myron Rodney & Myra Michele. **Educ:** Ohio State Univ, Youngstown, OH, BA; Univ Pittsburgh, Pittsburgh, PA; Univ Wis; Nat Urban League Exec Develop Training. **Career:** Association executive (retired); Urban League New Haven Ct, pres, 1991; Urban League, Madison, Wi, pres & chief exec officer; Urban League Greater Cleveland, pres & chief exec officer, 1972-2008, trustee, 2015-16. **Orgs:** Bd dir, Am Fed Bank; bd dir, YMCA; Greenville SC, Rotary Club; Govs Task Force Reducing Health Cost; bd dir, Christ Episcopal Church; State Ohio Gov's Workforce Policy Bd; John Carroll Univ; KeyBank Adv Bd; Univ Hosp Health Syst; Greater Cleveland Workforce Investment Bd; Fannie Mae Northeast Ohio Adv Coun. **Home Addr:** 12113 Whistling Way, Lakewood Ranch, FL 34202.

**ROBINSON, NINA**
Public relations executive. **Personal:** Born Jul 17, 1943, Stamford, CT; daughter of Henry Scott (deceased) and Olga Larionova Scott (deceased); married Lawrence Donniva; children: Lawrence Damian & Lauren Danielle. **Educ:** NY Univ, attended 1962. **Career:** New York Urban League, New York, NY, adminr, Brownstone Prep, 1968-72; Newark Bd Educ, Newark, NJ, staff trainer, researcher, 1972-74; Chad Sch, Newark, NJ, adminr, 1974-82; New York Times Co, New York, NY, coordr pub rels & media, 1983-. **Orgs:** A Better Chance, 1980-83; bd mem, Newark Bd Educ, 1982-83; New York Black Journalists, 1992-93; exec bd, Fund Raising chairwoman, 1992-; Newark Citizen Educ Comt; bd mem, Newark Beth Israel Hosp, CDC, 1998-. **Honors/Awds:** Miss Manhattan, 1961. **Special Achievements:** Contributing writer, New York Times, New Jersey Edition. **Home Addr:** 19 Lyons Ave Suite 409, Newark, NJ 07112, **Home Phone:** (201)923-2952. **Business Addr:** Coordinator of Public Relations Media, The New York Times Co, 229 W 43rd St, New York, NY 10036-3959, **Business Phone:** (212)556-1234.

**ROBINSON, PATRICIA WILSON**
Executive. **Personal:** Born Apr 18, 1951, Miami, FL; children: Lennard & Patrice. **Educ:** Miami-Dade Community Col, AA, 1981; Barry Univ, BS, 1983. **Career:** Dade City Circuit Ct, ct calendar clerk, 1974-77; Dade County Dept Human Resources, admin officer, 1977-83, newsletter asst ed, 1983-87, adminr, 1987-89; Thomas & Doyle Real Estate Inc, assoc realtor, 1979-85; ERA Empress Realty Inc, assoc realtor, 1985-86; Coldwell Bankers, referral agt, 1986-87; MetLife Fin Serv, Fin Adv, currently. **Orgs:** Nat Forum Black Pub Admin; Iota Phi Lambda Sor; Nat Asn Advan Colored People; trustee, bd chair, Valley Grove MB Church; Nat Assoc Life Underwriters; Barry Univ, Alumni Asn; Fla Real Estate Coun; Nat Asn Female Exec. **Honors/Awds:** Employee of the Year, Dept Human Resources Off Admin, 1985; Honored for Outstanding Business Achievement, 1989; National Quality Award; National Sales Achievement Award; Million Dollar Round Table Qualifier. **Home Addr:** 2400 W Lake Miramar Cir, Miramar, FL 33025, **Home Phone:** (754)816-5324. **Business Addr:** Financial Advisor Representative, MetLife Financial Services, 806 S Douglas Rd Suite 800, Coral Gables, FL 33134, **Business Phone:** (305)446-3268.

**ROBINSON, PETER LEE, JR.**
Artist, graphic artist, consultant. **Personal:** Born Jan 16, 1922, Washington, DC; married Romaine Frances Scott. **Educ:** Howard Univ, AB, 1949. **Career:** USN, supr illusr, 1957-62; NASA, Graphics & Mgt Presentations Div, dir, visual info officer, 1962-77; fine artist, graphics designer, consult. **Orgs:** Dir, founder, HEM Res Past; pres, treas DC Art Asn; vpres, Soc Fed Artists & Designers, Fed Design Coun; US State Dept "Arts Embassies Prog"; speaker, Rice Univ, 16th Int Tech Comn Conf, 1969; Morgan State Col, 1969; 19th Int Tech Comn Conf, 1970; NAIA, 1971; 19th Int Tech Comn Conf, 1972; 1st Indust Graphics Int Conf, 1974; 4th Tech Writing Inst, 1974, Nat Conf Artists, 1980. **Honors/Awds:** Award of Excellence in Visiting Comm Soc of Fed Artists & Designers, 1961; Meritorious Civilian Service Award, 1960; Apollo Achievement Award, 1969; NASA Exceptional Service Medal, 1973; NASA Outstanding Performance Award, 1975; NASA Spaceship Earth Award, 1975.

**ROBINSON, DR. PREZELL RUSSELL**
President (organization), school administrator, government official. **Personal:** Born Aug 25, 1922, Batesburg, SC; son of Clarence and Annie; married LuLu Harris; children: JesSanne. **Educ:** St Augustine's Col, Raleigh, NC, AB, 1946; Bishop Col, LLD, 1951; Cornell Univ, NY, MA, 1951, EdD, 1956. **Career:** Acad adminr; Alt Rep, Us Am; Voorhees Sch & Jr Col Denmark SC, instr Fr/math/sci, 1948-54; Cornell Univ Ithaca NY, fel, 1954-56; St Augustine's Col, prof sociol, 1956, dean, 1956-64, exec dean, 1964-66, actg pres, 1966-67, pres, 1967-95, pres emer & instr anthrop, 1995-, Charles A Mott Endowed Distinguished Prof Social Sci; Univ Nairobi Kenya, vis prof, 1973; Univ Dar es Salaam Tanzania, vis prof, 1973; Haile Selassie Univ Addis Ababa Ethiopia, vis prof, 1973; Univ Guyana, vis prof, 1974; alt rep gen assembly UN, 1996; Episcopal Church, lay reader; NC Inst Minority Econ Develop, dir emer, currently. **Orgs:** Asn Advan Sci; Study Negro Life & Hist, Am Acad Pol & Soc Sci; bd dir, Wachovia Bank & Trust Co; state bd ed, NC; exec comt, NC Asn Col & Univ; bd dir, pres, Nat Asn Equal Oppty Higher Ed; bd dir, Tech Asst Consortium Improve Col Serv; pres, United Negro Col Fund, 1978-80; bd dir, Occoneechee Cty BSA; pres, Nat Assoc Equal Opportunity Higher Educ, 1981-84; bd dir, C C; pres, Coop Raleigh Cols, 1981, 1986-88; exec comt, Asn Episcopal Col, Omega Psi Phi; 47th Gen Assembly, UN, pub mem ambassador, 1992; Alternative Rep US UN, 1992; vice chmn, NC State Bd Educ; African Am Cult Complex; Pres's Comt Race Rels; advan chmn, Occonneechee Coun Boy Scouts Am; vice chmn, Nc Bd Educ; Raleigh Chamber Com; Int Asn Univ Presidents; bd trustee, Voorhees Col; active mem, Episcopal church & Episcopal Church Pension Fund; bd trustee, St Augustine's Col. **Home Addr:** 821 Glascock St, Raleigh, NC 27604, **Home Phone:** (919)829-0546. **Business Addr:** President Emeritus, St Augustine's College, 1315 Oakwood Ave, Raleigh, NC 27610-2298, **Business Phone:** (800)948-1126.

**ROBINSON, DR. RANDALL M.**
Association executive, lawyer, educator. **Personal:** Born Jul 6, 1941, Richmond, VA; son of Doris Jones and Maxie Cleveland; children: Anike & Jabari; married Hazel; children: Khalea Ross. **Educ:** Va Union Univ, BA, sociol, 1967; Harvard Law Sch, JD, 1970; Georgetown Univ Law Ctr, PhD, 2003. **Career:** Civil rights atty, Boston, 1971-75; US rep William Clay, 1975; US Rep Diggs, admin asst, 1976; Ford fel; Trans Africa, founder & exec dir, 1977-06, pres, 2001; writer, 2001-; lawyer; activist; nationalist & adminr; Pa State Univ, Dickinson Sch Law, distinguished scholar residence, currently; Books: Defending the Spirit: A Black Life in America, author, 1998; The Debt: What America Owes to Blacks, author, 2000; The Reckoning: What Blacks Owe To Each Other, author, 2002; Quitting America: The Departure of a Black Man from His Native Land, author, 2004; An Unbroken Agony: Haiti from Revolution to the Kidnapping of a pres, author, 2007; MAKEDA, author; The Emancipation of Wakefield Clay. **Orgs:** Community organizer, Roxbury Multi-Serv Ctr, 1972-74; founder, TransAfrica, 1977-. **Special Achievements:** ABC World News Tonight Person of the Week. **Business Addr:** Distinguished Scholar in Residence, Penn State University, Lewis Katz Bldg, University Park, PA 16802, **Business Phone:** (814)867-2792.

**ROBINSON, DR. RANDALL S.**
Teacher, educator. **Personal:** Born Nov 26, 1939, Philadelphia, PA; married Janice Whitley; children: Randall & Ginger. **Educ:** Ohio State Univ, BS, 1961; Univ Pa, MS, 1965; Temple Univ, EdD, 1972. **Career:** Philadelphia Bd Educ, teacher, 1961-65; Summer Sch Improv Proj, 1967; Educ Mat Co, proj coordr, res & develop, 1968-69; Temple Univ, adj prof, 1968-69, consult & group leader ann summer workshop lang arts; Tioga Community Youth Coun, educ consul disruptive youth, 1971; Rowan Univ, Dept Elem & Early Childhood Educ, assoc prof, Teacher Educ, prof, 2007, prof emer, 2007-; Egg Harbor Sch Syst, NJ, consult. **Orgs:** Wash Twp Bd Educ, 1973-76; Curric Rev Comt; early childhood educ & curric develop comt mem, Glassboro State Col; Dept Tenure & Recontracting Comt; Urban Educ Curric Develop Comt; fac adv, Black Cult Leg; counr, Adv Upward Bound Stud; counr & adv, Martin Luther King Scholars Fac; Glassboro State Fedn Col Teachers; Nat Coun Social Studies; Negotiations Comt; Wash Twp

Educ; Curric Comt; Balanced Group Wash Twp; Teachers Pension & Annuity Fund. **Honors/Awds:** Plaque, Tioga Community Youth Coun, 1973. **Business Addr:** Professor Emeritus, Rowan University, 201 Mullica Hill Rd, Glassboro, NJ 08028-1700, **Business Phone:** (856)256-4000.

### ROBINSON, RASHAD

Civil rights activist, writer, executive director. **Personal:** Born Oct 13, 1978. **Educ:** Marymount University (Arlington, VA), Bachelor's in Politics with a minor in History and Communications. **Career:** Claim Democracy Conference, Lead Organizer, 2003; Center for Voting and Democracy, National Field Director; Right to Vote Campaign, Communications Director; FairVote, Advisory Committee; freelance writer, articles have appeared in "The Huffington Post," "The Los Angeles Times," and "Newsday"; Gay and Lesbian Alliance Against Defamation (GLAAD), Senior Director of Media Programs; ColorofChange.org, Executive Director, 2011. **Orgs:** Race Forward (formerly Applied Research Center), Board of Directors; ALLOUT, Board of Directors; The Global Campaign for LGBT Equality, Board of Directors; State Voices, Board of Directors; FairVote, Board of Directors; Democracy Action Project; Board of Directors. **Honors/Awds:** "The Root" Magazine, The Root 100 Honorees, 2010, 2011, 2012, 2013. **Special Achievements:** Has made television appearances on CNN, MSNBC, ABC, BET, OWN, NPR, and Current TV.

### ROBINSON, RENAULT ALVIN

Police officer, government official, consultant. **Personal:** Born Sep 8, 1942, Chicago, IL; son of Robert S and Mabel; married Annette Richardson; children: Renault Jr, Brian, Kivu & Kobie. **Educ:** Roosevelt Univ, BS, 1970, MS, urban studies, 1971; Northwestern Univ, urban fel, 1973. **Career:** Chicago Post Off, 1960-62; Printer Union Tank Car Co, 1962-64; Chicago Police Dept, patrolman, police officer & vice detective, 1964-83; Afro-Am Patrolmen's League, pres, 1968-70, exec dir, 1970-; Chicago Housing Authority, chmn brd dirs, 1979-87, chmn brd commissioners, 1983-87; ASI Personnel Serv Inc, sr mgt assoc, vpres, 1989-; Renault Robinson Staffing Assocs, pres, currently. **Orgs:** Exec dir, Afro Am Police League, 1968-83; secy & treas, Improve Community, 1978-; co found, chmn bd dir, Afro-Am Police League, 1983-; Nat Asn Advan Colored People; Chicago Urban League; Natl Forum Black Pub Admin; natl inform officer, exec officer, Nat Black Police Asn. **Honors/Awds:** Subject of "The Man Who Beat Clout City", 1977; Renault A Robinson Award, named in honor, Nat Black Police Assn, 1979; Youth Award, John D Rockefeller III Found, 1979; over 50 awards from government, business & community organizations. **Home Addr:** 1755 E 55th St Apt 1103, Chicago, IL 60615-5977. **Business Addr:** President, Renault Robinson Staffing Associates, 111 W Wash St Suite 1815, Chicago, IL 60602, **Business Phone:** (312)236-6169.

### ROBINSON, RICHARD DAVID, SR.

Football player, executive. **Personal:** Born May 3, 1941, Mt. Holly, NJ; son of Leslie H and Mary E Gaines; married Elaine Burns; children: Richard (deceased), David & Robert (deceased). **Educ:** Pa State Univ, BS, civil engineering, 1962. **Career:** Football player (retired), business executive; Green Bay Packers, linebacker & placekicker, 1963-72; Wash Redskins, linebacker & placekicker, 1973-74; Campbell's Soup, Camden, NJ, engr; Schlitz Brewing Co, Youngstown Ohio, dist sales mgr; Mars Dist Co, exec vpres, 1984; Super Beverage Akron, MARS Div, vpres, 1984-2001; Pro Football Hall Fame, secy & trustee, currently. **Orgs:** Nat Football League Players Asn; Nat Football League Player rep, 1967-70; vpres, Players Asn, 1968-70; YMCA; Big Bros; bd dir, Pro Football Hall Fame, 2013. **Home Addr:** 406 S Rose Blvd, Akron, OH 44320, **Home Phone:** (216)867-6685. **Business Addr:** Secretary, Trustee, Pro Football Hall of Fame, 2121 George Halas Dr NW, Canton, OH 44708, **Business Phone:** (330)456-8207.

### ROBINSON, ROBERT G.

Health services administrator, educator. **Personal:** Born Aug 11, 1943, New York, NY; son of Robert Garl and Dorothy May Wilson. **Educ:** City Col NY, BA, 1967; Adelphi Univ, MSW, 1969; Univ Calif, Berkeley, CA, MPH, 1977, PhD, 1983. **Career:** Health service administrator (retired), educator; Adelphi Univ, chap, asst prof, 1969-76; Reach Inc, psychotherapist, 1973-75; Univ Cal, Berkeley, staff, 1977-84; Am Cancer Soc, prin investr, 1983-85; Nat Cancer Inst fel, Cancer Control Sci Asn, 1985-88; Fox Chase Cancer Ctr, assoc mem, 1988-90, dir cot planning & develop, 1990-92; Ctrs Dis Control, assoc dir prog develop; Emory Univ, Rollins Sch Pub Health, adj assoc prof, 1997-. **Orgs:** Nat Black Leadership Initiative Cancer Philadelphia, 1988-93; bd, Up town Coalition Tobacco Control & Pub HTH, 1989-93; bd, Stop Teenage Addiction Tobacco, 1990-; nat ed bd, Jour Health Care Poor & Under served, 1990-; Am Pub Health Asn; Nat Med Asn; Aaas; ed adv bd, An Int Jour, 1992-; Nat African Am Tobacco Prev & Control Network, 1999-. **Home Addr:** 3495 Hidden Acres Dr, Doraville, GA 30340, **Home Phone:** (770)934-4329. **Business Addr:** Adjunct Associate Professor, Emory University, 1518 Clifton Rd NE, Atlanta, GA 30322.

### ROBINSON, ROBERT LOVE, JR.

Accountant. **Personal:** Born Apr 21, 1961, Madera, CA; son of Robert L Sr and Evelyn Barnes. **Educ:** Univ Pac, BS, acct, 1982. **Career:** PriceWaterhouseCoopers, staff auditor, 1982-85; Sun Diamond Growers Calif, internal auditor, 1985-86; Grupe Co, Stockton, Calif, sr acct, 1986-89, acct mgr, 1989-92; Delta Syst Assoc, staff consult, 1992-94; Nat Health Plans, assist controller, 1994-97; E & J Gallo Winery, internal auditor, 1997-2000; Quest Northern Calif RUG, vpres, 1999-2000; Durr Systs Inc, bus systs supvr, 2000-06; Health Care REIT Inc, systs mgr, 2006-. **Orgs:** Calif State Soc CPAs, 1985-; adv, Sacramento Valley Chap Nat Asn Black Acct, 1985-; pres, Sacramento Valley Chap Nat Asn Black Acct, 1989; Univ Phoenix Alumni Asn, 1986-; Quest Int Users Group, 1997-; bd dir, Big Ten Users Group, 2001-09; Mich Oracle Users Group, 2007-09; bd mem, Quest Real Estate SIG, 2008-; bd mem, Quest BI SIG, 2008-; bd pres, Aurora Proj Inc, 2009-; Mich Oracle Users Group; SewHope, 2010-11; bd pres, Aurora Proj Inc; Quest JD Edwards Adv Bd, 2011-. **Honors/Awds:** Award of Excellence, Grupe Co, 1990. **Home Addr:** 7023 Germanna Ct, Stockton, CA 95219-3117, **Home Phone:** (209)477-1525. **Business Addr:** Systems Manager, Health Care REIT Inc, 4500 Dorr St, Toledo, OH 43615-4040, **Business Phone:** (419)247-2800.

### ROBINSON, ROBIN (ROBIN CAROLLE ROBINSON)

Journalist, television news anchorperson. **Personal:** Born Aug 4, 1957, Chicago, IL; daughter of Louie and Mati; married Steve Williams, Jan 1, 1980?; children: Jade; married Terrence Brantley, Jan 1, 1986, (divorced 1990); children: Cameron; married Dennis Allen, Jan 1, 1991, (divorced 1994). **Educ:** San Diego State Univ, BA, jour, 1981. **Career:** Anchor (retired); KGTV, McGraw Hill, reporter & news reader, 1979-82, anchor, 1987-93; KMGH-TV, McGraw Hill, consumer reporter, 1982-84; WBBM-TV, CBS, consumer reporter, anchor, 1984-87; WFLD-TV, Fox News, anchor, co-anchor, 1987-2013. **Orgs:** Chicago Asn Black Journalists, 1985-; bd mem, S Cent comm Serv, 1993-; Child Abuse Prev Serv, spokeswoman, 1995. **Honors/Awds:** Emmy Awards on Art Achievement, San Diego Chap, 1980; Emmy Awards on Art Achievement, Nat Acad TV Arts & Sci, Chicago Chap, 1985-87, 1993, 1997. **Business Addr:** Anchor, WFLD-TV, 205 N Mich Ave, Chicago, IL 60601-5911, **Business Phone:** (312)565-5532.

### ROBINSON, RONNIE W.

Executive, vice president (organization). **Personal:** Born Dec 26, 1942, Louisville, KY; son of Lawrence and Donetta L Smith; married Veronices Gray; children: Kelli & Ronnie Jr. **Educ:** Ky State Univ, Frankfort, KY, BS, 1964. **Career:** ICI Am Inc, Charlestown, Ind, mgr ballistics lab, 1965-71, mgr EEO, 1971-73, mgr employ, 1973-77; Johnson & Johnson, Chicago, Ill, mgr, personel admin, 1977-82; Hartmarx Corp, sr vice pres human resources & admin; Hart Schaffner & Marx, Chicago, Ill, dir human resources admin, 1982-88, vpres human resources & admin, sr vpres human resources & admin, currently. **Orgs:** Bd mem, Soc Human Resources Profs, 1982-83; bd mem, Cosmopolitan Chamber Com, 1983-; Chicago Urban Affairs Coun, 1983-; chmn, Human Resources Comt, Ill State Chamber Com, 1986-87; personnel comt, Chicago Youth Ctr, 1986-; bd mem, Duncan YMCA, 1987-. **Home Addr:** 10315 S Prospect Ave, Chicago, IL 60643, **Home Phone:** (312)881-4961. **Business Addr:** Senior Vice President of Human Resources & Administration, Hart Schaffner & Marx, 101 N Wacker Dr, Chicago, IL 60606-7389, **Business Phone:** (312)372-6300.

### ROBINSON, HON. ROSALYN KAREN

Judge, lawyer. **Personal:** Born Dec 5, 1946, Norristown, PA; daughter of James H (deceased) and Patricia; married Warren B. **Educ:** Dickinson Col, BA, 1968; Boston Col, Law Sch, JD, 1973. **Career:** Chem Bank NY, NY, mgt trainee, officer's asst, 1968-70; Hon Doris M Harris, Ctr Common Pleas, law clerk, 1973-74; Philadelphia Dist Atty's Off, asst dist atty, 1974-79; Pa Dept Aging, chief coun, 1979-83, Gen Coun, dep gen coun, 1983; Commonwealth Pa, Ct Common Pleas, First Judicial Dist Pa, judge, 1997-. **Orgs:** Emer trustee, Dickinson Col, 1968-; treas, Barrister's Asn, 1973-; Philadelphia Bar Asn, 1973-; vpres, Dickinson Col Alumni Coun, 1974-80; Am Bar Asn, 1979-83; Pa Bar Asn, 1982-; cls chmn, Dickinson Col Ann Giving, 1984; Pa Coalition 10 Black Women, 1984-; Harrisburg Chap Links Inc, 1984-; bd trustee, Dickinson Col, 1985-; Alpha Kappa Alpha Sorority Inc, Rho Theta Omega Chap, 1990-. **Special Achievements:** One of 79 to watch in 1979, Philadelphia Mag, 1979. **Home Addr:** 529 Glen Echo Rd, Philadelphia, PA 19119. **Business Addr:** Judge, Commonwealth of Pennsylvania Court of Common Pleas, Rm 284 City Hall, Philadelphia, PA 19107, **Business Phone:** (215)686-6652.

### ROBINSON, DR. RUFUS E.

Dean (education), educator. **Personal:** Born Feb 9, 1941, Baton Rouge, LA; son of Beatrice Jackson. **Educ:** Southern Univ, BA, hist; Webster Univ, MA, pub admin, pub policy & int develop; Howard Univ, PhD, orgn commun. **Career:** Howard Univ, assoc dir off career serv; Strayer Univ, Columbia Campus, campus dean, 2005-; Johnson C Smith Univ, Charlotte, NC, asst vpres instnl advan, currently; La Dept Educ. **Home Addr:** 10647 Hill Point Ct, Charlotte, NC 28262, **Home Phone:** (704)688-5480. **Business Addr:** Assistant Vice President, Johnson C. Smith University, 100 Beatties Ford Rd, Charlotte, NC 28216, **Business Phone:** (704)378-1000.

### ROBINSON, RUMEAL JAMES

Basketball player. **Personal:** Born Nov 13, 1966, Mandeville. **Educ:** Univ Mich, attended 1990. **Career:** Basketball player (retired); Atlanta Hawks, guard, 1990-92; NJ Nets, 1992-93; Charlotte Hornets, 1993-94; Rapid City Thrillers, CBA, 1994-95; Shreveport Crawdads, CBA, 1995; Shreveport Storm, 1955; Conn Pride, CBA, 1995-96; Portland Trail Blazers, 1997; Los Angeles Lakers, 1996-97; Phoenix Suns, 1997; Grand Rapids Hoops, 1997-98; Detroit Pistons, guard, 1997; La Crosse Bobcats, 1998; Europ League, KK Zadar, Croatia, 2001-02; Skipper Bologna, Italy, 2002; Fortitudo Pallacanestro Bologna, Italy, 2002; Marinos de Oriente, Venezuela, 2002.

### ROBINSON, S. YOLANDA

School administrator, educator. **Personal:** Born Oct 1, 1946, Gilliam, WV; daughter of Rudolph V and Lucy M; children: Chad Heath. **Educ:** Franklin Univ, attended 1965; Univ Mass, MEd, 1981. **Career:** Actg mgr (retired); Midwest Inst Equal Educ, admin assist, 1971; Inst Black Community Res & Develop, res coordr, 1980-81; Ohio State Univ, admin secy, 1980-81, prog coordr, 1998; Ohio State Univ Dept Black Studies Community Exten, actg prog mgr, 1988-98; 2 B Natural By Design, City Adminr, 2008-10; Corp Nat & Communtiy Serv, peer reviewer, 2010-; Educ Serv Franklin County, instrnl coach, 2010-11; All Our Family, owner, 2011-; Ohio State Univ, Dept Black Studies Exten Ctr, nat conf chmn, currently; Cmacao Head Start, mgr; Ohio Youth Advocate Prog, instr; Head Start, family wellness mgr; All Women One Cause, lay health advoc; Columbus Col & Post, writer; Columbus Metrop Area Community Action Orgn, mgr. **Orgs:** Conf chair, Nat Coun Black Studies, 1978-; vpres, Ohio Black Polit Assembly, 1978-81; pres, founder, Cardinal 9 to 5, 1985-86; Ohio State Univ Affirmative Action Comt, 1985; bd mem, Call VAC, 1990; pres, African-Am Triumphs Consortium, 1992-; Columbus Black Women's Health Proj; Trinity Baptist Church; organizer, Family & Med Leave Act; secy, Ohio Black Studies Consortium. **Honors/Awds:** President's Award, Nat Coun Black Studies, 1988; Distinguished Affirmative Action Award, Ohio State Univ, 1988; Coalition of 100 Black Women, Mwanawake, 1992; OSU Women Coming Together Advocate Year Award; Avery International Award; Carter G. Woodsen Award; John Glenn Best Practice Award. **Special Achievements:** Editor: "Research Profiles," OSU Dept of Black Studies, 1982; International Business and Professional Women, 1990; Blue Chip Profile, 1992. **Home Addr:** 2960 E 11th Ave, Columbus, OH 43219.

### ROBINSON, DR. SAMUEL

School administrator, association executive, executive director. **Personal:** Born Dec 18, 1935, Memphis, TN; son of Omar R Sr (deceased) and Sarah; married Hugh Ella Walker; children: Debra Meadows & Charlotte Marchall. **Educ:** Tenn State Univ, BS, 1956, MS, 1958; Ind Univ, EdD, 1974. **Career:** Lincoln Inst, dean ed, 1964-66; Lincoln Sch, prin, 1967-70; Shawnee High Sch, prin, 1970-73; Lincoln Found, exec dir, 1974-; pres; Bellarmine Univ, exec-in-residence. **Orgs:** Asn Black Found Exec, 1974-; nat exec dir, Phi Beta Sigma Ed Found, 1980-; Black Achievers Asn, 1980-; bd mem, Presby Health Ed & Welfare Asn, 1982-; Louisville Presby; Sigma Phi Phi, 1983-; chmn, Ky Humanities Coun, 1984-; Ky Ctr Arts, 1988-; bd trustee, Bellarimme Col, 1990; Ky State Bd Educ, 1991; Outstanding Community Serv, Nat Conf Christians & Jews, 1993; KY Bd Educ; Ky Civilian Aide Sec Army. **Honors/Awds:** Recipient Outstanding Young Man Award, Louisville C C, 1963; Outstanding Young Educator Award, Shelbyville Jr C C, 1966; Disting Service Award, Zeta Phi Beta, 1974; Outstanding Citizen Award, Louisville Defender, 1975; Comt Service Award, Alpha Kappa Alpha, 1976; Social Action Award, Phi Beta Sigma; Outstanding Black Achiever Award, Louisville, 1980; Distinguish Citizen Award, Alpha Kappa Alpha, 1980; Man of the Year, Sigma Pi Phi, 1986; Berea Col Community Service Award, 1986; Achiever of the Year, Black Achievers Asn, 1987. **Home Addr:** 711 Waterford Rd, Louisville, KY 40207-1756, **Home Phone:** (502)893-7282. **Business Addr:** Executive in Residence, Bellarmine University, 2001 Newburg Rd, Louisville, KY 40205, **Business Phone:** (502)272-8000.

### ROBINSON, ESQ. SANDRA HAWKINS

Lawyer. **Personal:** Born Jul 17, 1951, Lynchburg, VA; daughter of William Sterlon and Mary Alice Baker; children: Mary Alysia. **Educ:** Oberlin Col, BA, 1973; Howard Univ Grad Sch, attended 1975; Cath Univ Sch Law, JD, 1982. **Career:** Robinson & Robinson, partner, atty, 1985-87; FDL Election CMS, sr atty, 1987-90; Jack H Olender & Assoc PC, sr trial atty, 1990-; Robinson Law Firm, atty, currently. **Orgs:** Md Bar, 1983; Prog coord, Nat Asn Black Women Attys, 1985-; DC Bar, 1985; master, Charlotte E Ray Am Inn Ct, 1994-; co-chair, Nat Bar Asn; Am Bar Asn; pres, Trial Lawyers Asn, Metropolitan Wash, 1997-98; Mar Trial Lawyers Asn; Wash Bar Asn; bd gov, Asn Trial Lawyers Am; pres, vpres, Civil Justice Found; treas, pres, 1997-2001, Women's Bar Asn Found; fac, Nat Inst Trial Advocacy; pres, Pub Justice Found; bd gov, Am Asn Justice. **Honors/Awds:** Distinguished Black Woman in the Twenty Third Annual Scholarship Calendar, Black Women Sisterhood Action; The Pursuit of Justice Award, Am Bar Asn; Alumna of the Year, Black Law Students Asn, Catholic Univ Columbus Sch Law; Presidential Award, Wash Bar Asn; Presidential Award, Nat Bar Asn, 1996; Charlotte E Ray Award, Greater Wash Area Chap, Women's Div, Nat Bar Asn, 1998; Trial Lawyer of the Year, Trial Lawyers Asn, 2000-01; Star of the Bar, Women's Bar Asn, 2003; Marie Lambert Award, Am Asn Justice Women's Caucus, 2007; Ollie May Cooper Award, 2014; One Top 50 Women Wash, DC Super Lawyers, Law & Polit Mag; Wash Bar Asn Hall Fame, 2016. **Special Achievements:** First African-American president of the Public Justice Foundation. **Home Addr:** 1359 Kalmia Rd NW, Washington, DC 20012, **Home Phone:** (202)291-7057. **Business Addr:** Senior Trial Attorney, Jack H Olender & Associates PC, 888 17th St NW Fl 4, Washington, DC 20006, **Business Phone:** (202)879-7777.

### ROBINSON, DR. SANDRA LAWSON

Physician, health services administrator. **Personal:** Born Mar 22, 1944, New Orleans, LA; daughter of Alvin J Lawson and Elvera Martin; married Carl Dayton; children: Michael David & Carla Marie. **Educ:** Howard Univ Col, Lib Arts, Wash, DC, BS, 1965; Howard Univ Col Med, MD, 1969; Health Care Admin, Tulane Univ Sch Pub Health & Trop Med New Orleans, LA, MPH, 1977. **Career:** Nat Med Ctr Dist Columbia, C's Hosp, intern, 1969-70, resident pediat, 1970-71; Univ Calif, Gen Hosp, pediat residency fel ambulatory care, 1971-72; Neighborhood Health Clin New Orleans, med dir, 1973-77; Ambulatory Care/Outpatient Serv Charity Hosp, dir, 1977-81; Minority Afrs LA State Med Ctr, coordr, 1979; Ambulatory Care Serv Childrens Hosp, dir, 1981-84; LA State Univ & Tulane Univ Sch Med, clin asst prof pediat; LA State, state health officer; Tulane Univ Sch Pub Health & Trop Med, adj asst prof; Dept Health & Human Resources, secy/comnr, 1984-88; Robinson Med Group, vpres, 1988-96; C's Med Care, pres affil off; C Hosp Med Pract Corp, physician, 1996-; New Orleans Health Dept, dep dir. **Orgs:** Proposal Dev Comprehensive Health Serv New Orleans Parish Prison Inmates, 1974; Common Health Prob Manual Neighborhood Health Clin, 1974; Coord Prev Med Prog Nat Med Asn Conv, 1974; Ross Roundtable Upper Resp Dis, 1974; Proj Anal Paper, New Orleans Neighborhood Health Clinics, 1975; bd mem, Kingsley House, 1976-79; bd mem, Family Serv Soc, 1976-79; consult, Westington Corp Headstart Prog, 1976-80; bd mem, New Orleans Area Bayou River Systms Agency, 1977-82; Plan Dev Com Health Systms Agency, 1978-82; Comn Use Human Subjects Tulane Univ; bd mem, Urban League Greater New Orleans, 1967-82; bd mem, Isidore Newman Sch, 1978-88; bd admin, Tulane Univ; Robert Wood Johnson "Coverny Kid", nat adv bd, 1998- Tulane Bd Adminr Healthcare Syst LC Bd; dean's adv coun, Tulane Lib Arts & Sci. **Honors/Awds:** Howard Univ Alumni Region V Award; Black Org for Leadership Develop Outstanding Community Service Award; Woman of the Year, Nat Asn Black Social Workers, 1987; The Scroll of Merit, Nat Med Asn Award, 1988; Cited, Who's Who in Black America; Who's Who in America Women; Distinguished Speaker, Tulane Med Alumni Asn; National Health Service Corps Directors Award; Scroll of Merit, National Medical Association; Role Model Award, YWCA. **Home Addr:** 5841 Wright Rd, New Orleans, LA 70128. **Business Addr:** Pediatrician, Deputy Director, New Orleans Health Department, 1300 Perdido St Suite 8E18, New Orleans, LA 70112, **Business Phone:** (504)658-2500.

**ROBINSON, SHARON**
Writer, baseball executive, musician. **Personal:** Born Jan 1, 1958, CT; daughter of Jackie and Rachel. **Educ:** Howard Univ, attended 1973; Columbia Univ, attended 1976; Univ Pa, Sch Nursing, post-master's cert. **Career:** Nurse midwife; PUSH, dir, 1985-90; Yale Univ Sch Nursing, asst prof; Maj League Baseball, vpres educ programming, currently. Books: Stealing Home: An Intimate Family Portrait by the Daughter of Jackie Robinson, 1996; Jackie's Nine: Jackie Robinson's Value to Live, 2002; Promises to Keep: How Jackie Robinson Changed Am, 2004; Safe at Home, 2006; Slam Dunk, 2007; Testing the Ice: A True Story About Jackie Robinson, 2009. **Orgs:** Vice chmn, Jackie Robinson Found, 1976-; bd trustess, Am Col Nurse-Mid wives Found; nat adv comm, Robert Wood Johnson Found, 1998-; United Negro Col Fund & A Better Chance. **Home Addr:** , New York, NY 10001. **Business Addr:** Vice President, Educational Programming, Major League Baseball, 245 Pk Ave 31st Fl, New York, NY 10167, **Business Phone:** (212)931-7800.

**ROBINSON, DR. SHARON PORTER**
Association executive, chief executive officer, president (organization). **Personal:** Born Louisville, KY; children: 1. **Educ:** Univ Ky, Lexington, BA, eng, psychol, educ, 1966, MA, curric & instr, 1976, EdD, admin & supv, 1979. **Career:** Classroom teacher; Nat Educ Assoc, dir instr & prof develop, 1980-89, dir res & develop; Jefferson County Educ Consortium, assoc dir; Ky Desegregation Training Inst, grad asst; Nat Bd Prof Teaching Stands, consult; US Dept Educ, Educ Res & Improv, asst secy educ; Educ Testing Serv, vpres st & fed rels, sr vpres & chief oper officer; Am Asn Col Teacher Educ, pres & chief exec officer, currently. **Orgs:** Bd mem, Alfred Harcourt Found; bd mem, Jobs Americas Graduates; bd mem, Suppl Educ Task Force Columbia Univ; bd mem, Diversity Issues Measurement Comt Nat Coun Measurement Educ. **Business Addr:** President, Chief Executive Officer, American Association of Colleges for Teacher Education, 1307 New York Ave NW Suite 300, Washington, DC 20005-4701, **Business Phone:** (202)293-2450.

**ROBINSON, SHAUN**
Television news anchorperson, actor. **Personal:** Born Jul 12, 1962, Detroit, MI; daughter of Joanne Oglesby and Wylie. **Educ:** Spelman Col, Eng & Mass Communs. **Career:** WGPR-TV62, reporter; WISN-TV, Milwaukee, Wisc, anchor & reporter; KEYE-TV, Austin Tex, anchor, reporter, 1989; WSVN-TV, Miami, Fla, anchor, reporter; TV One Access, host; Xtra, entertainment news reporting Access Hollywood, weekendanchor, currently; TV: "Bruce Almighty", "America's Sweethearts" "Dr.Dolittle 2", "Everybody Hates Chris", "Studio 60 on the Sunset Strip", "DIRT", "Charmed", "She Spies", "The Parkers", "The Proud Family", "Half & Half", "Days of our Lives" & "Any Day Now"; "The View", 1997; Oper Shock and Awe... Some, 2008; "The Morning Show with Mike & Juliet", 2009; " Okla City bombing"; Actress: Any Day Now, 2000; Am's Sweethearts, 2001; Dr. Dolittle 2, 2001; Blue Crush, 2002; The Parkers, 2002; "Share Your Heart, Share Your Home"; "Tournament of Roses Parade", 2004; "ShoWest Awards", 2005; "Miss Teen USA Pageant", 2006; "Studio 60 on The Sunset Strip", 2006; "Operation Shock and Awe... some", 2008; "Monk", 2009; "Last Man Standing", 2012; "Real Husbands of Hollywood", 2013. **Orgs:** Nat Asn Black Journalists; Am Fed TV & Radio Artists; Screen Actors Guild. **Honors/Awds:** Associated Press Award; Media Award, Am Heart Assn; Commendation Award, Am Women in Radio & TV; Austin Bus Journal, Profiles in Power; EMMY, A Grand Night in Harlem, WNBC. **Special Achievements:** Presenter, 15th Annual Soul Train Awards, 2001; Presenter, 16th Annual Soul Train Awards, 2002; Host, Pre-Show, 59th Golden Globe Awards, 2002; Host, Pre-Show, 75th Annual Academy Awards, 2003. **Home Addr:** 18460 Cherrylawn, Detroit, MI 48221, **Home Phone:** (313)862-8356. **Business Addr:** Weekend Anchor/Weekday Correspondent, Access Hollywood, 3000 W Alameda Ave, Burbank, CA 91523, **Business Phone:** (818)526-7000.

**ROBINSON, SHERMAN**
Executive, consultant, business owner. **Personal:** Born Sep 16, 1932, Piqua, OH; son of Sherman and Anna Lou; married Beverly J Clark; children: Tod, Tina & Tracy. **Educ:** Cent St Col, attended 1953; Ohio Univ, archit design, 1956, attended 1959. **Career:** Western Fixture Co, equip dealer, draftsman, 1959-60; JG Richards & Assocs, draftsman, designer, vpres, 1961-69; Saylor Rhoads Equip Co, proj supt, designer, draftsman, 1969-70; Sherman Robinson Inc, food facil consult, pres & owner, 1970-. **Orgs:** Pres, Keystone Optimist Club, 1972-73; bd dirs, Foodservice Consults Soc Int, 1992-95; consult, Food Facil Soc; assoc mem, AIA Rippledale Optimist Club; Multi-Cult Foodservice & Hospitality Alliance. **Honors/Awds:** Optimist International Award, Keystone, Indianapolis, Ind Chap, 1972-73; Volume Feeding Award, Insts Mag, 1975; Client of the Year Award, Indianapolis Bus Develop Found, 1979; Honorable Mention Award, Constructions Specif Inst, 1982; Outstanding Achievement Award, Ct Leadership Develop, 1983; Governor's Reception Award, Outstanding Bus Develop African Am Community, Indiana Black Expo, 1992-95; Black Businessman Entrepenuer Award, The Links, 1997. **Special Achievements:** Numerous Certificates of Appreciation for speaking engagements and other donated services. **Home Addr:** 5211 Blvd Pl, Indianapolis, IN 46208. **Business Addr:** President, Owner, Sherman Robinson Inc, 708 Bungalow Ct, Indianapolis, IN 46220, **Business Phone:** (317)257-4485.

**ROBINSON, SMOKEY (WILLIAM ROBINSON, JR.)**
Executive, musician, business owner. **Personal:** Born Feb 19, 1940, Detroit, MI; son of William Sr and Flossie; married Claudette Rogers; children: Berry William, Tamla, Claudette & Trey; married Frances Glandney. **Educ:** Jr Col, BS, elec engineering, 1959. **Career:** Detroit Nightclub, performer; Motown Rec Corp, singer, 1959-60, vpres, 1961-88; Smokey Robinson & The Miracles, rec artist, 1957-72; solo rec artist, 1972-; Big Time, exec producer, 1977; "An Eve With Smokey Robinson", 1985. Albums: The Miracles: Hi; We're the Miracles, 1961; Shop Around, 1962; Doin' Mickey's Monkey, 1963; The Fabulous Miracles, 1964; Going to a Go Go, 1964; Away We Go, 1965; Make It Happen, 1968; Spec Occasion, 1969; Time Out, 1970; Four in Blue, 1970; Smokey & the Miracles, 1971; The Miracles, 1977. Solo Albums: Renaissance, 1973; Smokey, 1973; Pure Smokey, 1974; A Quiet Storm, 1974; City of Angels, 1974; Love Mach, 1975; Smokey's Family Robinson, 1975; Power of the Music, 1977; Deep in My Soul, 1977; Love Breeze, 1978; Warm Thoughts, 1980; Being with You, 1981; Yes It's You, 1981; Touch the Sky, 1983; Essar, 1984; Our Very Best Christmas, 1999; Intimate, 2000; Food for the Spirit, 2004; The Live Collection, 2004; Motown Legends: Shop Around, Being With You, 2004. My World: The Definitive Collection, 2005; Legends, 2006; Timeless Love, 2006; Soul Legends, 2006; Gold, 2006; 50th Anniversary Collection, 2006; Time Flies When You're Having Fun, 2009; "Am Idol", guest judge, 2003; SFGL Foods Inc, owner & dir, 2004-. Songs: "Tracks of My Tears", 1965; "Baby Come Close", 1973; "Quiet Storm", "Baby That's Backatcha", "The Agony & the Ecstasy", 1975; "You really got a hold on me", "Tears of a Clown", 1978; "pops, we love you", "Cruisin", 1979; "Being With You", 1981; Just to See Her", 1987; "One Heartbeat", 1987; "Baby Come Close"; "It's a Good Feeling", 2004; "Going to a Go Go"; "If You Can Want"; "Really Gonna Miss You", 2005; "I Love Your Face", 2006; "Love Bath", 2009; "The Way You Do", 2014. **Orgs:** Great Am Smokeout. **Home Addr:** 631 N Oakhurst Dr, Beverly Hills, CA 90210-3530. **Business Addr:** Owner, Director, SFGL Foods Inc, 100 N Brand Ave Suite 200, Glendale, CA 91203, **Business Phone:** (818)500-0420.

**ROBINSON, STEVE**
Basketball coach. **Personal:** Born Oct 29, 1957, Roanoke, VA; married Lisa; children: Shauna, Kiaya, Tarron & Denzel. **Educ:** Ferrum Col, assoc, arts, 1979; Radford Univ, BS, health & phys educ, 1981, MS, coun, 1985. **Career:** Radford Univ, asst coach, 1983-86; Cornell Univ, asst coach, 1986-88; Univ Kans, asst coach, 1988-95, 2002-03; Univ Tulsa, head men's basketball coach, 1995-97; Florida State Univ, head men's basketball coach, 1997-2002; Univ NC, asst coach, 2003-. **Orgs:** Nat Asn Basketball Coaches; bd visitor, Radford. **Business Addr:** Assistant Coach, University of North Carolina, 440 W Franklin St, Chapel Hill, FL 27516, **Business Phone:** (919)962-2211.

**ROBINSON, DR. THELMA MANIECE**
Educator, association executive. **Personal:** Born May 1, 1938, Tuscaloosa, AL. **Educ:** Ala State Univ, BS, 1960; Univ Ala Tuscaloosa, MA, 1970, Ed D. **Career:** TVA, personnel clerk, exam officer; Florence Bd Educ, guid counr; Coffee High Sch, sr guid counr. **Orgs:** Am Personnel & Guid Asn; Am Sch Counr Asn; AL PGA & AL SCA; St secALPGA; Nat Educ Asn; AEA; Florence Educ Asn; pres, Delta Sigma Theta Sororoty; Ala Asn Univ Women; Florence League Women Voters; Lauderdale Co Chap, ARC, treas; vpres, Muscle Shoals Asn Ment Health; Ala Coun Asn; Bd Metrop YMCA; Bd advisors Univ N Ala Sch Bus; trustee, Bethel col; Am Red Cross, Lauderdale county; Ala Comt Humanities; Ala Adv Coun Am Col Testing Prog; chmn, State Bd Ment Health Asn, 1979-80. **Honors/Awds:** Chosen Outstanding Sec educr, 1974. **Special Achievements:** Shoals Citizen of Year, 1981. **Home Addr:** 2402 Chisholm Rd, Florence, AL 35630-1307, **Home Phone:** (256)572-2501.

**ROBINSON, THOMAS DONALD**
Health services administrator, chief executive officer, vice president (organization). **Educ:** Marshall Univ, BBA, 1964; Ga State Univ, MHA, 1977. **Career:** Welch Emergency Hosp, adminr, 1977-80; Pkwy Reg Med Ctr, asst adminr, 1980-84; Newport News Gen Hosp, adminr, 1984-85; Tyrone Hosp, chief exec officer, 1985-92; Penn St Univ, Continuing Educ Fac, 1988-; Quoram Health Resources, Robinson Grp, Pittsburgh Off grp, vpres. **Orgs:** Bd Tyrone Salvation Army, 1986; pres, Tyrone Rotary Club, 1986; pres, Tyrone Area Chamber Com, 1987; bd, Blair County United Way, 1987; pub affairs comm Hosp Assoc Western Pa, 1987; reg adv bd, Mellon Bank; Blair County Human Servs bd; adv bd, Mc Dowell Co Bus; adv bd, Marshall Univ Found. **Honors/Awds:** Fel Am Col Healthcare Execs, 1981. **Home Addr:** 10492 Olde Villa Dr, Gibsonia, PA 15044.

**ROBINSON, TRACY CAMILLE JACKSON**
Marketing executive. **Personal:** Born Jun 4, 1966, Detroit, MI. **Educ:** Univ Mich, Dearborn, BSE, indust engineering, 1987, Ann Arbor, MBA, mkt, 1990; Roosevelt Univ, cert, non-profit mgt. **Career:** 3M Corp, mfg engr, 1987-88; Kraft Foods, brand asst, 1990-91, assoc brand mgr, 1991-92, proj mgr, 1993-94, geog mkt mgr, 1994, brand mgr, equity, 1994-97; Amtrak, cent region mktg dir, 1997-. **Orgs:** Comt mem, Alpha Kappa Alpha Sorority, 1984-; troup leader, Girl Scouts Am, 1991-95; Nat Black MBA Asn, 1993-; bd mem, Uhlich C's Home, 1994-; treas, Transp Mkt & Community Asn; Midwest Travel Suppliers Asn. **Home Addr:** 1169 S Plymouth Ct Apt 119, Chicago, IL 60605-2055. **Business Addr:** Central Region Marketing Director, Amtrak, 60 Mass Ave, Washington, DC 20002, **Business Phone:** (800)872-7245.

**ROBINSON, VERNEDA BACHUS**
Chief executive officer, manager, association executive. **Personal:** Born Dec 17, 1960, Memphis, TN; daughter of C L Bachus and Wilma; married Curtis; children: Bria & Bryan. **Educ:** Washburn Univ, BBA, acct, 1984; Webster Univ, MA, mgt, 1992, MBA, 1995. **Career:** Western Resources Inc, vp customer serv, 1990-94; Miss Gas Energy, vp customer serv & acct, 1994; V Robinson & Co Inc, founder, pres & chief exec officer, 1995-2001; Swope Community Enterprise, chief operating officer & chief human resource officer, 2001-; Bachus Consult Group, consult, 2013-; Friend Family Health Ctr, chief exec officer, 2013-. **Orgs:** Bd mem, Jr Achievement Mid Am; bd mem, Gem Theater; bd mem, Kans City Pub TV; bd mem, Negro Leagues Baseball Mus; Nat Asn Women Bus Owners; Kans City friends Alvin Riley; Greater Kans city Coun; Minority Supplier Coun; bd dir, YouthNet. **Honors/Awds:** New Business of the Year, Minority Enterprize Develop, 1997. **Special Achievements:** Featured by Fox 4 News, Women On the Move Segment, 1997. **Business Addr:** Chief Operating Officer, President, Swope Health Service, 3801 Blue Pkwy, Kansas City, MO 64130, **Business Phone:** (816)923-5800.

**ROBINSON, VIRGIL, JR.**
Football player, chief executive officer. **Personal:** Born Nov 2, 1947, Inverness, MS. **Educ:** Grambling State Univ; Univ Okla-Norman; Am Inst Banking. **Career:** Football Player, pres, vpres, chief exec officer; Green Bay Packers; New Orleans Saints; Shreveport Steamers; Liberty Bank & Trust, exec vpres; Jefferson Guaranty Bank Metairie, sr vpres; Dryades Savings Bank, pres & chief exec officer, 1994-2007; Robinson Investments Inc, pres, currently; La Health Serv & Indemnity Co, dir, currently; Friends NORD, bd dir. **Orgs:** Bd dir, La Recovery Authority; La Bd Regents; Am Inst Banking; Bur Govt Res; New Orleans & River Region Chamber Com; New Orleans Found; Urban League Greater New Orleans; bd dir, New Orleans Police Found; bd dir, Chamber New Orleans; bd dir, Downtown Develop Dist; bd dir, Blus Cross/Blue Shield La; bd dir, Jefferson Bus Coun; bd dir, New Orleans Bus Coun. **Business Addr:** Director, Louisiana Health Service & Indemnity Co, 5525 Reitz Ave, Baton Rouge, LA 70809-9029, **Business Phone:** (225)295-3307.

**ROBINSON, DR. WALKER LEE**
Educator, neurosurgeon. **Personal:** Born Oct 13, 1941, Baltimore, MD; son of Edward F and Wilma L Walker; married Mae Meads; children: Kimberly Yvette & Walker Lee Jr. **Educ:** Morgan State Col, BS, chem engineering, 1962; Univ Md, MD, 1970; Univ London, attended 1975; Univ Rochester, attended. **Career:** AUS, capt, 1962-64; C & P Tel Co, mgr, 1964-66; Intern surg, Strong Memorial Hosp, 1970-71; Resident neurosurg Univ Md, 1971-76; fel neurol Univ, 1974-75; Head pediat neurosurg Univ Md, 1978-97; assoc prof neurosurg & pediat, 1989-97; Neurotrauma Univ Md, shock trauma ctr & dir, 1989-91, 1994-95; Neurosurg Univ Md Med Sch, actg chmn 1989-92; Pediat neurosurg, dir; Inst Edison, 1997; Seton Hall Univ Sch Grad Med Educ, prof, dept neuroscience, 1997; Nat Cancer Inst, consult, 1985-91; NINCDS, 1983-91; Centers DisControl & Prev, 1997; Am Asn Neurosurg, chmn, 1991-95. **Orgs:** Pres, Clarence S Green, Md neurosurg Soc, 1984-87; Nat Med Asn, Wash, 1985-1987; bd dir, Urban Cardiol Res Ctr, 1986-91; pres, Baltimore Urban Serv Found, 1986-87; bd dir, Variety Club Baltimore, 1988; pres, Black Fac & Staff Asn, Univ Md, 1989-90; Am Soc Pediat Neurosurg, Univ Md Med Systs, Cancer Comt, 1989-94; Int Soc Pediat Neurosurg; fel, Am Col Surgeons; fel, Am Acad Pediat; Am Soc Pediat Neurol; Am Med Asn; Am Asn Neurosurgeons; Cong Neurol Surgeons. **Home Addr:** 719 Cinder Rd, Edison, NJ 08820. **Business Addr:** Neurosurgeon, Carle Spine Institute, 610 N Lincoln Ave, Urbana, IL 61801, **Business Phone:** (217)383-6555.

**ROBINSON, WENDY RAQUEL**
Actor, movie producer. **Personal:** Born Jul 25, 1967, Los Angeles, CA; married Marco Perkins. **Educ:** Howard Univ, BA. **Career:** TV series: "Martin", 1993; "The Sinbad Show", 1993; "Thea", 1993; "Dream On", 1994; "MANTIS", 1994; "Sisters", 1994; "Me & the Boys", 1994; "The Watcher", 1995; "Vanishing Son", 1995; "Minor Adjustments", 1995; "NYPD Blue", 1996; "The Steve Harvey Show", 1996-2002; "Getting Personal", 1998; "Baby Blues", 2000-02; "A Baby Blues Christmas Special", voice, 2002; "Cedric the Entertainer Presents", 2002; "Heroes of Black Comedy", 2002; "Yes, Dear", 2002; "The Parkers", 2003; "All of Us", 2004-05; "Girlfriends", 2006; "The New Adventures of Old Christine", 2006; "Family Guy", 2007; "The Game", 2006-14; "Grey's Anatomy", 2010; "Glenn Martin DDS", 2010-11; "Malibu Country", 2012; "My Dad's a Soccer Mom", 2014. Films: The Walking Dead, 1995; A Thin Line Between Love & Hate, 1996; Ringmaster, 1998; Miss Congeniality, 2000; Two Can Play That Game, 2001; Mind Games, 2003; With or Without You, 2003; Reflections: A Story of Redemption, 2004; Squirrel Man, 2005; Rebound, 2005; Something New, 2006; Angels Can't Help But Laugh, 2007; Keys, producer, 2007; Contradictions of the Heart, 2009; He's Mine Not Yours, 2011; 35 and Ticking, 2011; Amazing Grace Conserv, founder & artistic dir, currently. **Honors/Awds:** Nominee for Image Award 6 times; Image Award, Nat Asn Advan Colored People, 2014. **Business Addr:** Founder, Artistic Director, Amazing Grace Conservatory, 2401 W Washington Blvd, Los Angeles, CA 90018, **Business Phone:** (323)732-4283.

**ROBINSON, WILLIAM, JR. See ROBINSON, SMOKEY.**

**ROBINSON, WILLIAM A.**
Educator, government official, real estate agent. **Personal:** Born Jun 30, 1920, Harrisburg, PA; son of Earnest and Saddie; married Beatrice S; children: Paula, Evelyn & Nancy. **Educ:** Lincoln Univ, BA, 1942; Pa State Exten Courses, acct; Air Force & Army, mgt courses. **Career:** Lincoln Univ, trustee, emer trustee, currently; real estate sales, currently. **Orgs:** Lay dep, Gen Nat Conv Episcopal Church, 1985, 1988; Harrisburg City Coun; Vestry St Stephens; Cathedral Dioces Cent Pa; Bd Realtors Pa; Nat Asn Realtors; bd dir, Harristown; Comn Ministry Episcopal Dioces Cent Pa; life mem, Nat Asn Advan Colored People; life mem, Omega Psi Phi; bd mem, Pa Coun Churches. **Home Addr:** 2309 Edgewood Rd, PO Box 10466, Harrisburg, PA 17104-1413, **Home Phone:** (717)236-6759. **Business Addr:** Emeritus Trustee, Lincoln University of the Commonwealth of Pennsylvania, 1570 Baltimore Pke, Philadelphia, PA 19352, **Business Phone:** (484)365-8000.

**ROBINSON, DR. WILLIAM ANDREW**
Administrator, physician. **Personal:** Born Jan 31, 1943, Philadelphia, PA; son of Colonial and Lillian; married Jacqueline E Knight; children: William Jr & David. **Educ:** Hampton Inst, BA, 1964; Meharry Med Col, MD, 1971; Johns Hopkins Sch Hyg & Pub Health, MPH, 1973; Nat Bd Med Examiners, dipl. **Career:** George W Hubbard Hosp, Nashville, emergency rm physician, 1972; US Food & Drug Admin, reviewing med officer, 1973-75; Health Resources & Servs Admin, med officer, 1975-80, dep bur dir, 1980-87, chief med officer, 1987-89; Pub Health Serv, Off Minority Health, dir, 1989-91; Health Resources & Serv Admin, chief med officer, 1991-, actg adminr, 1993-94, Ctr Qual, dir, 1997-. **Orgs:** Delta Omega Hon Pub Health Soc, 1993; Am Pub Health Asn; chair, Sc Rural Health Res Ctr; Sr Execs Asn; Fed Physicians Asn; Am Acad Family Physicians, Nat Med Asn; AMA. **Home Addr:** 16608 Frontenac Ter, Rockville, MD 20855-2048, **Home Phone:** (301)869-1165. **Business Addr:** Chief Medical Officer, Center for Quality Director, Health Resources & Services Administration, Rm 7-100 5600 Fishers Lane, Rockville, MD 20857, **Business Phone:** (301)443-0458.

**ROBINSON, WILLIAM EARL**
Mayor, government official. **Personal:** Born Nov 18, 1940, Morton, MS; son of P B and Gladys; children: Jacqueline & William E II. **Educ:** Miss Valley State Univ, soc sci & pol sci, 1962.

**Career:** Consultant (retired), government official; N Las Vegas City, councilman, 1983-; N Las Vegas, mayor pro tempore, currently; Sch Success Monitor; Clark County Sch Dist, outreach consult. **Orgs:** N Las Vegas Redevelop Adv Comm; hon dir, N Las Vegas Chamber Com, 1973-80; Founding mem, N Las Vegas Pop Warner Football, 1973-80; Gaming policy comn, State Nev, 1973-81, 1975-81; pres, N Las Vegas Jaycees, 1974; chmn, N Las Vegas Fair Show Family Yr, 1975-76; dir, Nev Jaycees Chaplin, Nev Nat, 1976-78; US & Int Jaycees; chmn, Libr, Pks & Recreation Adv Bd, 1977-80; life mem, US & Int Jaycees JCI Sen, 1977; S Nev Comn Gov Job Training Bd; Nat League Cities Community & Econ Develop, 1983-88; Nev Develop Authority Alt Bd, 1983-97; Chmn, Real Property Adv Bd; Econ Opportunity bd, 1983-97, exec mem, 1997-04; chmn, Clark Co Health Dist, 1983-97; chmn, Crime Prev Task Force, 1984-97; chmn, N Las Vegas Housin Authority, 1985-; secy pres, vpres, Nev League Cities, 1987-88; bd mem, N Las Vegas Lib, 1995-; Nev Develop Authority exec bd, 1997-; exec mem, econ Opportunity bd, 1997-04; Las Vegas conv & Visitor's Authority bd, 2001-; chmn, bd dir, N Las Vegas Dem Club; chmn, Crime Prev Task Force; Clark co Health Dist; Environ Qual Policy Rev bd; Job Training bd; N Las Vegas Lib Dist; bd dir, Southern Nev Dist bd Health & Southern Nev Comn; bd mem, bd dir, N Las Vegas Redevelop Agency; pres, Nev League Cities & Munic; Community & Econ Develop Comt Small Cities Nat League Cities; bd mem, Las Vegas Conv & Visitor's Authority, 2001-; Work Force Investment Bd; Criminal Justice Adv Comn. **Honors/Awds:** Jaycee of the Year, N Las Vegas Jaycees, 1972, 1974, 1975; Man of the Year, N Las Vegas Jaycees, 1974, 1976; Who's Who Outstanding Young Men of Am, 1976; Public Official of the Year, NV League Cities, 1989. **Home Addr:** 2417 Mango Bay Ave, North Las Vegas, NV 89031-0973, **Home Phone:** (702)639-6401. **Business Addr:** Mayor Pro Tempore, Councilman, City of North Las Vegas, 2200 Civic Center Dr, North Las Vegas, NV 89030, **Business Phone:** (702)633-1484.

## ROBINSON-IVY, JACQUELINE (JACKI ROBINSON-IVY)

Banker, vice president (organization). **Educ:** Western Ill Univ, BS, speech path & audiol, 1987. **Career:** Northern Trust Bank, securities opers mgr, 1992-98, relationship mgr, 1998-2005 vpres, 2005-. **Business Addr:** Vice President, Northern Trust Bank, 50 S LaSalle B-7, Chicago, IL 60675, **Business Phone:** (312)630-6000.

## ROBINSON-JACOBS, KAREN DENISE

Journalist. **Personal:** Born Aug 21, 1956, Chicago, IL; daughter of Dymple Orita McIntyre and S Benton; married Ralph M. **Educ:** Univ Ill, Champaign, IL, BS, jour, 1978; Univ Wis, Milwaukee, Milwaukee, WI, 1985. **Career:** Champaign News-Gazette, Champaign, Ill, reporter, 1977-80; Milwaukee Jour, Milwaukee, Wis, asst metro ed, asst state ed, n suburban ed & reporter, 1980-89; Los Angeles Times, Los Angeles, Calif, asst metro ed & reporter, 1989-2004; Times New Media Unit, assoc ed; Dallas Morning News, contribr & food indust reporter, 2004-, hospitality indust reporter, 2004-13. **Orgs:** Delta Sigma Theta Sorority, 1976-; vpres, Wis Black Media Asn, 1982-89; bd dir, Hansberry Sands Theatre Co, 1986-89; vol, United Negro Col Fund, 1988-; chairperson, Minority Ed Caucus: Los Angeles Times, 1990-; bd dir, Black Journalists Asn Southern Calif, 1991-. **Honors/Awds:** Black Achiever Award, YMCA, 1986. **Home Addr:** 11225 Peachgrove Suite 305, North Hollywood, CA 91601, **Home Phone:** (818)769-1970. **Business Addr:** Contributor, Dallas Morning News, PO Box 655237, Dallas, TX 75265, **Business Phone:** (214)977-8222.

## ROBINSON-WALKER, MARY P.

Dancer. **Personal:** Born Pittsburgh, PA; daughter of William and Eula. **Educ:** Iron City Col; Rose Demars Legal Sec Sch; Fr Inst; Henry George Sch Social Socs; Hunter Col. **Career:** Executive, dancer (retired); Am Comn Africa, secy, 1960-64; Artist CivilRights Asst Fund, spec proj dir, 1965-66; Savings Bank Asn NY, sec, 1967-68; Metro Appl Res Ctr, secy, 1968-70; Black Econ Res Ctr, admin secy, 1970-76; Pearl Bailey Rev, Phillip-Ft Dancers, prof dancer, dance instr; Ctrs Reading & Writing, NY Pub Libr. **Orgs:** Emcee Comn Discrimination Housing; bd dir, Harlem Philharmonic Soc, 1969-; co-chmn, Am Red Cross, Harlem Div, 1974-; admin asst, 21st Century Found; Cent Baptist Church, 1993-. **Home Addr:** 53 W 89 St Suite 1B, New York, NY 10024.

## ROBISON, LOUIS

Consultant, educator. **Personal:** Born Sep 9, 1950, Miami, FL; son of Rudolph and Joanne Miller; married Yvette McIntosh; children: Louis Audra, Shoneji, Carta & Maureik. **Educ:** Fla A & M Univ, BS, 1972; Fisk Univ, MA, 1974; Univ S Fla, EdD, 1997. **Career:** Sch Bd Sarasota Co, prin, 1976-96, 2000-01; Correctional Serv Corp, vpres, 1996-99; LAYR Group, pres & chief exec officer, 2000-. **Orgs:** Phi Delta Kappa, 1986-; Fla A & M Alumni Assoc, life mem, 1995-; Omega Psi Phi Fraternity Inc, 1986-; Sigma Pi Phi Fraternity Inc, mem chair. **Home Addr:** 3935 Trentwood Pl, Sarasota, FL 34243, **Home Phone:** (914)351-4428. **Business Addr:** President, The LAYR Group, 3935 Trentwood Pl, Sarasota, FL 34243, **Business Phone:** (941)538-2279.

## ROBY, KIMBERLA LAWSON

Writer. **Personal:** Born May 3, 1965, Rockford, IL; daughter of LB Lawson and Arletha Stapleton; married Will M Roby Jr. **Educ:** Rock Valley Col, Bus Assoc, 1988; Cardinal Stritch Univ, BBA, 1993. **Career:** Sundstrand Corp, asst repair admin, 1985-89; State IL, welfare caseworker, 1989-91; Greenlee Textron, hr admin, 1991-93; First Fin Bank, customer serv rep for loans, 1993-94; City Rockford, fin analyst housing, 1994-96; auth/novelist, 1996-; Lenox Press, pres, currently; Author: Behind Closed Doors, 1997; Here & Now, 1999; Casting the First Stone, 2000; It's A Thin Line, 2001; Sin No More, 2008; Love & Lies; Changing Faces; The Best-Kept Secret; Too Much of a Good Thing; A Taste of Reality; Books: A House Divided; Perfect Marriage; Reverend's Wife; Secret Obsession; Love; Hon, & Betray; Be Careful What You Pray For; A Deep Dark Secret; Best Everything; One A Million; Sin No More; Love & Lies; Changing Faces; Best-kept Secret; Too Much A Good Thing; A Taste Reality; It's A Thin Line; Casting First Stone; Here & Now; & Her Debut Title; Behind Closed Doors. **Orgs:** Adv bd, Womanspace, 1997-. **Honors/Awds:** Author Award, Chicago Book Fair, 1997; Blackboard Book of the Year, Nominee, 1998; Blackboard Fiction Book of the Year Award, 2001; Author of the Year Female award, African American Literary Award Show, 2006, 2007 &2009; NAACP Image Award Winner for Outstanding Literary Work, 2013. **Home Addr:** 10615 Wentworth Pl, Belvidere, IL 61008, **Home Phone:** (815)885-4053. **Business Addr:** President, Lenox Press, PO Box 17016, Rockford, IL 61110-7016, **Business Phone:** (815)885-4053.

## ROCHE, JOYCE M.

Marketing executive. **Personal:** Born Jan 1, 1948, New Orleans, LA. **Educ:** Dillard Univ, BS, math educ, 1970; Columbia Univ, MBA, 1972; Stanford Univ, sr exec prog grad, 1991. **Career:** Avon Prod Inc, vpres global mkt, 1993-94; Carson Inc, exec vpres global mkt, 1995-96, pres & chief operating officer, 1996-98; Southern New Eng Telecommunications Corp, dir, 1997-98; mkt consult, 1998-2000; AT&T Inc, dir, 1998-2000; Anheuser-Busch Co Inc, dir, 1998-; Federated Dept Stores Inc, dir; Dillard Univ, Bd Trustees, chmn; Tupperware Corp, dir, 1998-; May Dept Stores Co, dir, 2003-06; Macy's Inc, dir, 2006-; Dr Pepper Snapple Group Inc, dir, 2011-. **Orgs:** Corp Governance & Nominating Comt & Pub Policy & Environ Affairs Comt; Dillard Univ, hon degree; N Adams State Col, hon degree; Girls Inc, pres & chief exec officer, 2000-2010; chair bd trustees, Dillard Univ. **Honors/Awds:** The 21 Women of Power & Influence in Corp Am, 1991; 40 Most Powerful Black Executives, Black Enterprise, 1994; Business Week, Top Managers to Watch, 1998; Legacy Award, Black Enterprise, 2006; Distinguished Alumna Award, Columbia Univ Women in Bus, 2007; hon doctorate, Dillard Univ; doctorate, Mass Col Lib Arts. **Special Achievements:** Featured on the cover of Fortune, 1997. **Business Addr:** Chief Executive Officer, President, Girls Inc, 120 Wall St, New York, NY 10005-3902, **Business Phone:** (212)509-2000.

## ROCHESTER, GEOF

Manager, vice president (organization), executive. **Personal:** Born Sep 20, 1959, St. Michael; son of Edric G and Elma I. **Educ:** Georgetown Univ, BS, 1981; Univ Pa, Wharton Sch, MBA, mkt, 1985. **Career:** Procter & Gamble, sales, Folgers Coffee, 1981-83, prod mgr, Bain de Soleil, Oil Olay, Clearasil, 1985-89, mkt assoc, 1985-88, assoc mkt mgr, Richardson-Vicks Div, 1988-89; Marriott Hotels, dir bus transient mkt, 1989-90; Radisson Hotels, sr vpres mktg, 1990-95; Comcast Commun, sr mkt positions; Showtime Networks, sr vpres mkt, 2002-05; World Wrestling Entertainment, exec vpres mkt, 2006-09; GRC Consult, founder, 2009-10; Nature Conservancy, chief mkt officer, 2010-, managing dir, chief visibility officer, spokesperson, 2014-. **Orgs:** Bd gov, Georgetown Univ Alumni Senate, adv coun, 1990-92; bd dir, Hoya Hoop Club, 1990-92; ecoAmerica; Whartons Initiative Global Environ Leadership. **Business Addr:** Chief Marketing Officer, Managing Director, The Nature Conservancy, 4245 N Fairfax Dr Suite 100, Arlington, VA 22203-1606, **Business Phone:** (800)628-6860.

## ROCHESTER, DR. MATTILYN T.

School administrator, teacher. **Personal:** Born May 14, 1941, Chester, SC; married Enoch B; children: Enoch B II & Mattilyn C. **Educ:** Bennett Col, BS, 1962; Glassboro State, MA, 1966; Temple Univ, PhD, 1985. **Career:** School administrator (retired); John T Williams Jr High Sch, math teacher, 1962-63; Burlington Samuel Smith Sch, fifth grade teacher, 1964-76; Perry L Drew Sch, vice prin, 1976-77; Wilbur Watts Mid Sch, vice prin, 1977-79; Robert Stacy Sch, prin, 1979-82; Capt James Lawrence Sch, prin, 1982-86; Burlington City Sch Dist, prin, 1986-90; Pine Hill Sch Dist, supt. **Orgs:** Am Asn Sch Admin; NJ Asn Sch Admin; Camden County Asn Sch Admin; Asn Supv & Curric Develop; Nat Cong Parents & Teachers Asn; Phi Delta Kappa; gen bd, Nat Coun Churches Christ; Burlington Kiwanis Club; Acad Advan Teaching Mgt; Nat Supt Acad; Am Asn Sch Admin; exec secy, Woman's Home & Overseas Missionary Soc, African Methodist Episcopal Zion Church. **Special Achievements:** High school's first black principal. **Home Addr:** 129 Sagebrush Dr, Belleville, IL 62221, **Home Phone:** (618)257-8481.

## ROCHON, LELA (LELA ROCHON STAPLES)

Actor. **Personal:** Born Apr 17, 1964, Los Angeles, CA; daughter of Samuel and Zelma; married Antoine Fuqua; children: Asia Fuqua & Brando; married Adolfo Quinones. **Educ:** Calif State Univ, BA, broadcast jour, 1986. **Career:** Fred Amsel & Assocs Inc, modeling: Spudette Bud Lite TV com; dancer: music videos for Lionel Richie, Luther Vandross & Levert; TV series: "A Bunny's Tale", 1985; "The Facts of Life", 1987; "The Cosby Show", 1987; "Into the Homeland", 1987; "What's Happening Now!", 1987; "Amen", 1988; "Facts of Life", "21 Jump street", 1990; "The Fresh Prince of Bel-Air", 1991; "Extralarge: Black and White", 1991; "Homefront", 1992; "Roc", 1992;"Tales from the Crypt", 1992; "Hangin' with Mr. Cooper", 1992-94; "Out All Night", 1993; "The Sinbad Show", 1993; "The Wayans Bros.", 1995; "Mr. and Mrs. Loving", 1996; "The Outer Limits", 1997; "Ruby Bridges", 1998; "The Charlotte Austin Story", actress & exec producer, 2009; "The Division", 2001; "Reed Between the Lines", 2011; "Let the Church Say Amen", 2013. Films: Harlem Nights, 1989; Boomerang, 1992; Waiting to Exhale, 1995; The Chamber, 1996; Gang Related, 1997; The Big Hit, 1998; Knock Off, 1998; Why Do Fools Fall in Love, 1998; Any Given Sunday, 1999; Labor Pains, 2000; First Daughter, 2004; Running Out of Timein Hollywood, 2006; Balancing the Books, 2008; Brooklyns Finest, 2009; Fatal Secrets, assoc producer, 2009; Blood Done Sign My Name, 2010; Supremacy, 2014; Reversion, 2015. **Honors/Awds:** One of the 50 most beautiful people in the world, People (USA) magazine, 1996; one of the "The 10 Sexiest Women of the Year", Black Men Magazine, 2000. **Business Addr:** Actress, International Creative Management, 8942 Wilshire Blvd, Beverly Hills, CA 90211, **Business Phone:** (310)550-4000.

## ROCK, CHRIS (CHRISTOPHER JULIUS ROCK, III)

Actor, comedian, singer. **Personal:** Born Feb 7, 1965, Andrews, SC; son of Julius (deceased) and Rosalie; married Malaak Compton; children: Lola Simone & Zahra Savannah. **Career:** Film: Beverly Hills Cop II, 1987; Comedy's Dirtiest Dozen, 1988; I'm Gonna Git You Sucka, 1988; Who Is Chris Rock, 1989; New Jack City, 1991; Boomerang, 1992; CB4, 1993; The Immortals, 1995; Panther, 1995; Sgt Bilko, 1996; Beverly Hills Ninja, 1997; Dr. Dolittle, 1998; Lethal Weapon 4, 1998; Torrance Rises, 1999; Dogma, 1999; Nurse Betty, 2000; Down to Earth, 2001; AI: Artificial Intelligence, 2001; Pootie Tang, 2001; Osmosis Jones, 2001; Jay and Silent Bob Strike Back, 2001; Bad Company, 2002; Comedian, 2002; Pauly Shore Is Dead, 2003; Head of State, 2003; The N-Word, 2004; Paparazzi, 2004; The Aristocrats, 2005; Madagascar, 2005; The Longest Yard, 2005; I Think I Love My Wife, 2007; Bee Movie, 2007; You Don't Mess with the Zohan, 2008; Madagascar: Escape 2 Africa, 2008; Good Hair, 2009; Death at a Funeral, 2010; Grown Ups, 2010; What to Expect When You're Expecting, 2012; Madagascar 3 2012; Grown Ups 2, 2013; Madly Madagascar, 2013; Top Five, 2014. Album: Born Suspect, 1991; Roll with the New, 1997; Bigger & Blacker, 1999, Never Scared, 2004; Kill the Messenger, 2008. TV series: "Uptown Comedy Express", 1987; "Miami Vice", 1987; "Saturday Night Live", 1990-94; "In Living Color", 1993-94; "Big Ass Jokes", 1994; "The Fresh Prince of Bel-Air", 1995; "The Moxy Show", 1996-98; "Martin", 1996; "Homicide: Life on the Street", 1996; "Bring the Pain", 1996; "Politically Incorrect", 1996; " MTV Music Video Awards", 1997; "The Chris Rock Show", 1997-2000; " King of the Hill", 1998; " MTV Music Video Awards", 1999; " Bigger & Blacker", 1999; "MTV Music Video Awards", 2003; "ChalkZone", 2004; " Never Scared", 2005; "77th Academy Awards", 2005; "Everybody Hates Chris", 2005-09, "Kill the Messenger", 2008; " Louie", 2011-12; "Totally Biased with W. Kamau Bell", 2012. **Honors/Awds:** CableAce Award, 1995 & 1997; Primetime Emmy Award, 1997, 1999 & 2009; Grammy Awards for best spoken album, 1998 & 2000, forbest comedy album, 2006; Blockbuster Entertainment Award, 1999; American Comedy Award, 2000; Special Award, ShoWest Convention, 2001; Star on the Walk of Fame, 2003; BET Comedy Award, Black Entertainment Tv, 2005; Kid's Choice Awards, USA, 2006; Blimp Award, Kids' Choice Awards, 2006; Wannabe Award, Kids' Choice Awards, 2006; Hollywood Film Award, 2014. **Special Achievements:** Author of Rock This!, 1998. **Home Addr:** Fort Greene, Brooklyn, NY 10036. **Business Addr:** Actor, Writer, Director, c/o Home Box Office Inc, 1100 Ave of the Americas, New York, NY 10036, **Business Phone:** (212)512-1000.

## ROCKETT, DAMON EMERSON

Manager, executive. **Personal:** Born Nov 13, 1938, Chicago, IL; married Darlene Sykes; children: Deborah & Sean Damon. **Educ:** Drake Univ, BS & BA, 1960. **Career:** Allstate Ins Co, claims super, 1964-69; City Harvey, comn pub health & safety; Ill Bell Tel Co, bus off mgr, 1969-80, phone ctr mgr, 1980-81, staff-assessment ctr, 1981-82, regional dir community rels; US Second Cong Off; S Suburban Col, mgr retention serv, acad skills adv, transition adv, currently. **Orgs:** Pres, Harvey Rotary Club, 1971-80; S Suburban Human Rels Comt, 1973; bd mem & policy comn chmn, Thornton Commiunity Col, 1975-79; bd mem, CEDA, 1980; YMCA Task Force, 1984; Rotary Club Pk Forest, 1984; S Suburban Asn Com & Indust, 1984; S Suburban Mayors & Managers Asn, 1984; bd mem, chmn, Red Cross African Relief Campaign, 1985; Nat Asn Advan Colored People; adv bd mem, W Haywood Burns Inst; bd mem, Sch Dist 152 Found; pres, S Suburban YMCA; Jones Community Ctr; Bethel Community Facil; pres, S Suburban Housing Ctr; pres, S Suburban Focus Coun. **Special Achievements:** First African-American to be elected a commissioner in the city of Harvey. **Home Addr:** 731 W Sunset Dr, Glenwood, IL 60425, **Home Phone:** (708)798-4205. **Business Addr:** Academic Skills Advisor, Manager of Retention Services, South Suburban College, 15800 S State St, South Holland, IL 60473-1200, **Business Phone:** (708)596-2000.

## ROCKS, MUSTAFA. See ABDULLAH, MUSTAFA.

## ROCKWELL, KARYN. See PARSONS, KARYN.

## RODDY, HOWARD W.

Health services administrator, administrator, vice president (organization). **Personal:** Born Feb 28, 1950, Nashville, TN; son of Howard Walden and Marie Bright; married Donna Norwood; children: Howard Carthie & John Travis. **Educ:** Austin Peay State Univ, Clarksville, TN, BS, chem, 1971; E Tenn State Univ, MS, environ health admin, 1974. **Career:** Chattanooga-Hamilton Co Health Dept, environmentalist, dir vector control proj, 1971-76; Alton Pk/Dodson Ave Comm Health Ctrs, asst admin planning/eval, 1976-81; Chattanooga Hamilton Co Health Dept, adminr/dir, 1981-98; Memorial Health Care Syst, vpres, Healthy Comm Initiative, 1998. **Orgs:** Am Pub Health Asn, 1977-98; Ten Pub Health Asn, 1981-, pres, 1991-92; bd, Chattanooga-Hamilton County Air Pollution Control Bur, 1983-96; treas, Leadership Chattanooga Alumni Asn, 1985-89; bd exec comm, Chattanooga Area Urban League, 1986-93; bd, United Way Greater Chattanooga, 1987-92, 1995-97; pres, Friends Festival, 1991-92; Chancellor's round table Univ Tenn Chattanooga, 1991-94; bd ber, Chattanooga Venture, 1991-96; bd, E TN Area Health Educ Ctr, 1991-97, pres, 1993-95; bd ber, Vol Community Sch, 1993-96; 100 Black Men Am Inc-Chattanooga Chap, 1992-; First vpres, Southern Health Asn, 1995, 1998; pres, Develop Corp, Orchard Knob, 1995-99; bd, Univ Chattanooga Found, 1997-; bd, Community Found Greater Chattanooga; bd chair, Alexian Bros Community Serv Adv Bd, 1998-2002; bd, Chattanooga Trust Pub Land, 1998-, bd, First Things First, 1999-; bd, Friends Chickamauga & Chattanooga Nat Mil Pk, 2000-; bd, YMCA Metro Chattanooga, 2000-; adv bd, Salvation Army Chattanooga, 2000-; bd, Tenn Valley Fed Credit Union, 2000-; bd, Allied Arts Greater Chattanooga, 2001; bd, E Tenn State Univ Found, 2002-; bd, Alexian Bros Southeast, 2003-; bd, Regional Health Coun, 2003-. **Home Addr:** 7133 Saratoga Lane, Chattanooga, TN 37421, **Home Phone:** (423)855-2153. **Business Addr:** Vice President, Memorial Health Care System, 2525 deSales Ave, Chattanooga, TN 37404, **Business Phone:** (423)495-8686.

## RODEZ, ANDREW LAMARR

Police chief. **Personal:** Born Oct 9, 1931, Chicago, IL; married Patricia Lander; children: Angelina, Andy & Rita. **Educ:** Va Union Univ, AB; Nebr Ill State Univ, MA; Mich State Univ, PhD; FBI Nat Acad NW Traffic Inst, dipl. **Career:** Off-The-St-Boys Club, group worker, 1956-57; Cook County Welfare Dept, case worker, 1957-58; Evanston Police Dept, police officer, 1958; Chessmen Evanston, co founder, 1958; Chicago Bd Educ, teacher, 1958-64; Benton Harbor, chief police, 1973-79;

Benton Harbor Area Sch Dist, asst prin, 1979-82; Maywood Police Dept, chief police, 1982-. **Orgs:** Pres, Task Force Youth Motivation, 1970; charter mem, vpres, Nat Org Black Law Enforcement Reg IV, 1984; Kappa Alpha Psi; NW Univ Traffic Inst Alumni; FBI Nat Acad Alumni Asn; Phi Delta Kappa Ed; Ill Asn Chiefs Police; W Suburban Chiefs Police; Nat Asn Advan Colored People; founding mem, Nat Orgn Black Law Enforcement Execs. **Honors/Awds:** All CIAA Football & Track, 1951-52; Negro Col All-Am, 1952; Outstanding Alumni Award, Kappa Alpha Psi, 1968; Outstanding Citizen Award, Nat Asn Advan Colored People, 1970; Model Cities Award, 1974; Bicent Award Lake Mich Col, 1976. **Special Achievements:** First African American Police Chief in Benton Harbor, Michigan. **Home Addr:** 518 S 6th Ave, Maywood, IL 60153. **Business Addr:** Chief of Police, Maywood Police Department, 125 S 6th Ave, Maywood, IL 60153.

### RODGERS, ANTHONY RECARIDO, SR.

Law enforcement officer. **Personal:** Born Apr 2, 1951, Jacksonville, FL; son of Clarence and Clara Lee Maddox Washington; children: Anthony Jr, Martisha, Edward & Eric. **Educ:** Fla Jr Col, Jacksonville, FL, attended 1972; Northeastern Fla Criminal Justice Educ & Training Ctr, 1973. **Career:** Deputy sheriff (retired); Duval Co Sheriffs Off, Jacksonville, Fla, sch attendance officer, abandoned property officer, cert radar operator, Dep Sheriff, field training officer, 1973, hon guard, 1973, sch resource officer, 1990; PAL officer, 1996. **Orgs:** Jacksonville Urban League, 1973; pres, Jacksonville Brotherhood Police Officers Inc, 1978; pres, Bliss Sertoma Club, 1979; treas, Viking Athletic Booster Club Raines High Sch, 1980; pres, Jacksonville Brotherhood PoliceOfficers Inc, 1981-91 Jacksonville Job Corps Community Rels Coun, 1983; Moncrief Improv Asn, 1984; Just US Comn Community Prob, 1986; Fla Community Col Jacksonville Adv Bd New Direction, 1987; charter mem, 100 Black Men Jacksonville, 1992; bd dir, NE Fla Community Action Agency Inc, 1992; pres, Edward Waters Col, Tiger Athletic Booster Club, 1994; pres, Jacksonville Br, Nat Asn Advan Colored People, 1995-96, vpres; vpres, Southern Region Nat Black Police Asn, 1996. **Home Addr:** 5720 Oprey St, Jacksonville, FL 32208.

### RODGERS, DR. AUGUSTUS

Educator. **Personal:** Born Jan 27, 1945, Columbia, SC; son of William Augustus and Susanne Gaymond; married Claudia Taylor; children: Christopher, Mark Adejolah & Shaundra Ave. **Educ:** Benedict Col, Columbia, SC, BA, 1965; NY Univ, New York, NY, MSW, 1969; Univ SC, Columbia, SC, PhD, 1977; Luthern Theol Southern Sem, Columbia, SC, Mdiv, 1988. **Career:** SC Dept Ment Health, psychiat worker, 1965-71; Univ SC, Columbia, SC, assoc prof, prof, prof emer, 2002-. **Orgs:** Dir, Nat Black Family Summit, 1986-; vice basileus, Omega Psi Phi Fraternity, Omicron Phi Chap; Phi Delta Kappa; Nat Asn Social Work; Coun Social Work Educ; dir, Nat Black child develop Inst. **Home Addr:** PO Box 11446, Columbia, SC 29211. **Business Addr:** Professor Emeritus, University South Carolina, 1731 Col St R 205, Columbia, SC 29208, **Business Phone:** (803)777-0555.

### RODGERS, BARBARA LORRAINE (BARBARA RODGERS DENNIS)

Television journalist. **Personal:** Born Sep 27, 1946, Knoxville, TN; daughter of Jackson and Anna Connor; married James Dennis. **Educ:** Knoxville Col, Knoxville, TN, BS, bus educ, 1968; State Univ NY, Buffalo, NY, 1976; Univ Chicago, Chicago, IL, 1986. **Career:** Tv Journalist (retired); Eastman Kodak Co, Rochester, NY, urban affairs researcher, computer programmer, 1968-71; Educational Opportunity Center, Rochester, NY, dept head/instructor, 1971-76; WOKR-TV, Rochester, NY, anchor/reporter/show host, 1972-79; KPIX-TV, San Francisco, Calif, anchor & reporter, 1979. **Orgs:** Co-founder, pres, bd mem, treas, Bay Area Black Journalists Asn, 1981-; bd mem, World Affairs Coun N CA, 1990-; bd mem, Regional Cancer Found, 1989-; bd mem, Western Ctr Drug Free Schs & Communities, 1987-90; quart chair, Commonwealth Club Calif, 1990; Alpha Kappa Alpha Sorority, 1966-. **Honors/Awds:** Emmy, North California Chapter/Nat'l Academy of Televison Arts & Sciences, 1980-88; William Benton Fellowship in Broadcast Journalism, University of Chicago, 1985-86; Eugene Block Journalism Award, 1990; Miss Knoxville College, 1968. **Home Addr:** c/o Jim Dennis, PO Box 193094, San Francisco, CA 94119-3094. **Business Addr:** Anchor, Reporter, CBS 5 & KPIX-TV, 855 Battery St, San Francisco, CA 94111, **Business Phone:** (415)765-8640.

### RODGERS, CAROLYN MARIE

Writer, teacher. **Personal:** Born Dec 14, 1945, Chicago, IL; daughter of Bazella Colding and Clarence. **Educ:** Roosevelt Univ, Chicago, IL, BA, 1965; Univ Chicago, MA, eng, 1984. **Career:** Educator, writer; Columbia Col, Chicago, Ill, Afro-Am lit instr, 1968-69; Univ Wash, 1970; Malcolm X Community Col, Chicago, Ill, writer-in-residence, 1971-72; Albany State Col, 1972; Ind Univ, Bloomington, Univ Ind, vis prof Afro Am lit, 1973; Roosevelt Univ, Chicago, Ill, writer-in-residence, 1983; Chicago State Univ, Chicago, Ill, lectr, 1985; Eden Press, Chicago, Ill, ed & publ, currently; Columbia Col, Eng & poetry workshop instr; Poets & Writers Inc, poet, currently; Poems: Paper Soul, 1968; Songs of a Blackbird, 1969; How I Got Ovah, 1975; The Heart as Evergreen, 1978; The Heart As Ever Green, 1978; Echoes, From a Circle Called Earth, 1988; A Little Lower Than The Angels, 1988; Morning Glory, 1989; Eden & Other Poems, 1987; We're Only Human, 1994; A Train Called Judah, 1996; The Girl with Blue Hair, 1996; The Salt of The Earth: The Book of Salt, 1999; The Chosen. Short Stories: Blackbird in a Cage, 1967; A Statistic, Trying to Make It Home, 1969; One Time, 1975. **Orgs:** Black Am Culture; Delta Sigma Theta; YMCA, 1963-66. **Home Addr:** 12750 S Sangamon, Chicago, IL 60643. **Business Addr:** Poet, Writer, Poets & Writers, Inc, PO Box 422460, Palm Coast, FL 32142, **Business Phone:** (386)246-0106.

### RODGERS, BISHOP CHARLES

Clergy. **Personal:** Born Jul 28, 1941, Memphis, TN; son of E W and Ruth; married Gloria Jean Dickerson; children: Adrian R, Victor Byron, Allison Faithe & Carlos. **Educ:** Int Col Bible Theol, BDiv, bibl studies; Mid-West Theol Sem, MBS, Mdiv, pastoral studies; Fuller Theol Sem, CEU; Ark Baptist Col; LeMoyne-Owen Col; Dallas Theol Sem, CEU. **Career:** Emanuel Church God Christ, assoc pastor, 1966-74; Memphis Press-Scimitar, staff writer, 1969-74; Covington Church God Christ, pastor, 1969-96; Memphis Pub Co, dir recruiting & job coun, 1973-74; Covington Dist Church God Christ, dist supt, 1978-84; Cent Tenn Jurisdiction Church God Christ, from second asst to bishop, 1982-89, admin asst bishop, 1984-88; Cent Tenn Jurisdiction Church God Christ, admin asst bishop, 1984-88; New Dimensions Ministries, founder, pastor, 1985-2008; Fifth Jurisdiction Tenn Church God Christ, from admin asst to bishop, 1989-97; bishop, 2003-. **Orgs:** Pres, Eastern Pa Church God Christ, 1967; bd dir & sec vpres, Teen Challenge, 1972-80; Church God Christ, 1972-84, dir, 1972-86, chmn; pres, Tipton County Ministers Asn, 1972-75; Shelby United Neighbors, 1973-74; dir, News Serv Church God Christ Int Conv, 1981-87; founder & chmn, Impact Fel Int, 1996-; pres, Raleigh Ministers, 1995-98; Exec bd mem, Give Me A Chance Ministry, 1995-2000. **Honors/Awds:** Man of the Year, Congressman H Ford, 1976; Certificate for Outstanding & Meritorious Service, 1976; Civil & Religious Award; Whos Who in American Religion; Who's Who in American Journalism; Dr. Charles Rodgers Road, named in honor. **Home Addr:** 7593 Thorn Tree Lane, Cordova, TN 38016, **Home Phone:** (901)754-8084. **Business Addr:** Founder, Chairman, Impact Fellowship International, 3607 Frayser Raleigh Rd, Memphis, TN 38168-1085, **Business Phone:** (901)377-1195.

### RODGERS, DERRICK ANDRE

Football player. **Personal:** Born Oct 14, 1971, Memphis, TN; married Kareff, Jun 1, 2001; children: Elasia. **Educ:** Ariz State Univ. **Career:** Football player (retired); Miami Dolphins, right linebacker, 1997, left linebacker, 1998, linebacker, 1999-2002, left outside linebacker, 2002; New Orleans Saints, linebacker, 2003-04. **Honors/Awds:** NFL Defensive Rookie of the Year, Sports Illustrated, 1997. **Special Achievements:** Film: 1997 Rose Bowl, 1997. TV Series: "Burn Notice", 2010; "Fractured Lies", 2011. **Home Addr:** 15222 SW 52nd St, Miramar, FL 33027.

### RODGERS, EDWARD

Judge. **Personal:** Born Aug 12, 1927, Pittsburgh, PA; married Gwendolyn Baker; children: 3. **Educ:** Howard Univ, BA, polit sci, 1949; Fla A&M Univ Law Sch, LLB, 1963. **Career:** Judge (retired); Palm Beach Co Sch Sys, teacher; asst co Solicitor; Cities W Palm Beach & Riviera Beach Fla, prosecutor ad litem; City W Palm Beach, judge ad litem; Pvt Atty; Palm Beach Co Bd, circuit ct judge, 1995; Riviera Beach City, city councilman & mayor. **Orgs:** Bd dir, Cancer & Soc; Masons; Vis Nurses Asn; Ment Health Asn; PB Community Found; Urban League; Palm Beach County Bar Asn; Nat Bar Asn. **Honors/Awds:** Jefferson Award, US Supreme Ct. **Special Achievements:** First Black county prosecutor in Palm Beach County, 1964; First black assistant state attorney and First African American judge. **Home Addr:** 1170 Bimini Lane, West Palm Beach, FL 33404, **Home Phone:** (561)842-2088.

### RODGERS, HORACE J.

Executive, vice president (organization), lawyer. **Personal:** Born Dec 10, 1925, Detroit, MI; married Yvonne Payne; children: Kimberly & Pamela. **Educ:** Univ Mich, BA, 1948; Univ Mich, Sch Law, JD, 1951. **Career:** Asst US Atty; Fedn Housing Admin, reg atty; Stand Mortgage Corp, vpres; BertL Smokler & Co, vpres; Premier Mortgage Corp, founder & chmn bd; Rodgers & Morgenstein, partner, currently. **Orgs:** Adv bd, Govt Nat Mortgage Asn; Com Visitors, Univ Mich, Law Sch; adv bd mem, Fedn Nat Mortgage Asn; Nat Corp Housing Partnerships; chmn, Nat Urban Affairs Comt, MBA; dir, Nat Bank Southfield; life mem, Nat Asn Advan Colored People; Alpha Phi Alpha; Sigma Pi Phi; chmn, Class Officers & Leaders Coun, Univ Mich Alumni Asn, dir; trustee & vice chancellor, Episcopal Diocese, Mich; pres, St Luke's Episcopal Health Ministries; vpres, Canterbury Health Care Inc; dir & vpres, Cranbrook Acad Arts. **Honors/Awds:** Distinguished Service Award, Univ Mich Alumni Asn. **Home Addr:** 245 Orange Lake Dr, Bloomfield Hills, MI 48302, **Home Phone:** (248)335-2369. **Business Addr:** Partner, Rodgers & Morgenstein, 24445 NW Hwy Suite 209, Southfield, MI 48075-2437, **Business Phone:** (248)351-0550.

### RODGERS, JOHNATHAN ARLIN

Executive, president (organization), chief executive officer. **Personal:** Born Jan 18, 1946, San Antonio, TX; son of M A and Barbara; married Royal Kennedy; children: David & Jamie. **Educ:** Univ Calif, Berkeley, BA, jour, 1967; Stanford Univ, MA, commun, 1973. **Career:** TV network exec; Sports Illus, reporter, 1960; Newsweek Mag, assoc ed, 1972-73; WNBC-TV, writer-producer, 1973-74; WKYC-TV, Cleveland, OH, reporter, 1974-75; WBBM-TV, Chicago, Ill, asst news dir, 1976-78; KCBS-TV, Los Angeles, Calif news dir, exec producer & sta mgr, 1978-83, sta mgr, 1982-83; CBS News, exec producer, 1983-86; WBBM-TV, chicago, gen mgr & vpres, 1986-90; CBS TV Stas Div, pres, 1990-96; Discovery Networks, pres, 1996-2002; NIKE Inc, bd dir, 2006-; Procter & Gamble Co, bd dir, 2001; TV One LLC, pres & chief exec officer, 2003-11; TV One pres, ceo; Discovery Networks, US Pres, 1996-2003; CBS Tv Stas; Sports Illus, writer, reporter; Mem Bd, Nike, 2006-; Procter & Gamble, 2001-. **Orgs:** Alpha Phi Alpha; bd dir, Nat Cable & Telecommunications Asn; trustee, Univ Calif Found. **Home Addr:** , Washington, DC 20544. **Business Addr:** President, Chief Executive Officer, TV One LLC, 1010 Wayne Ave 10th Fl, Silver Spring, MD 20910, **Business Phone:** (301)755-0400.

### RODGERS, NAPOLEON B.

Banker. **Educ:** Univ Akron, BS, finance; Univ Detroit, MBA, finance. **Career:** Comerica Bank, Detroit, MI, first vpres, pres; Woodbridge Capital Mgt, vpres, dir; Cash Mgt & Tax Exempt Securities at Munder Capital Mgt, vpres, dir. **Orgs:** Investment Policy Comt; Bond Club Detroit; Urban Financial Serv Coalition; Nat Asn Securities Professionals. **Business Addr:** President, Comerica Bank, PO Box 75000, Detroit, MI 48275, **Business Phone:** (313)222-3435.

### RODGERS, NILE GREGORY

Music producer, musician. **Personal:** Born Sep 19, 1952, NY. **Career:** Musician & music producer; Sesame Street Band, session guitarist; Boys, group mem; Chic, group mem; Ear Candy Rec, co-pres; Let's Dance, producer, 1983; Nile Rodgers Prodn Inc, pres, currently; Albums with Chic: Chic, 1977, C'est Chic, 1978; Risque, 1979; Real People, 1980; Take It Off, 1981; Soup for One, 1982; Tongue in Chic, 1982; Believer, 1983; Chic-Ism, 1992; Dance, Dance, Dance: The Best of Chic, 1992; Live at the Budokan, 1999; Up All Night, 2013. Solo albums: Adventures in the Land of the Good Groove, 1983; B Movie Matinee, 1985; (with Out loud) Out Loud, 1987; Chic Freak & More Treats, 1996; Productions: Norma Jean, 1978; We Are Family, 1979; King of theWorld, 1980; Love Somebody Today, 1980; diana, 1980; I Love My Lady, 1981; Koo Koo, 1981; Let's Dance, 1983; Situation X, 1983; "Invitation ToDance", 1983; Trash It Up, 1983; "Original Sin", 1984; Like a Virgin, 1984; "The Reflex", 1984; "The Wild Boys", 1984; Flash, 1985; She's TheBoss, 1985; Here's to Future Days, 1985; Do You, 1985; When The Boys MeetThe Girls, 1985; Home of the Brave, 1986; Notorious, 1986; Inside Story, 1986; Inside Out, 1986; L Is For Lover, 1986; "Moonlighting Theme", 1987; "Route 66", 1987; Cosmic Thing, 1989; Slam, 1989; Decade: Greatest Hits, 1989; So Happy, 1989; Workin' Overtime, 1989; Family Style, 1990; Move ToThis, 1990; The Heat, 1991; "Real Cool World", 1992; Good Stuff, 1992; Black Tie White Noise, 1993; Your Filthy Little Mouth, 1994; Azabache, 1997; Us, 1997; Samantha Cole, 1997; On & On, 1998; Everything is Cool, 1998; Su Theme Song, 1998; Just Me, 2001; Dellali, 2001; "We Are Family", 2001; Only A Woman Like You, 2002; Shady Satin Drug, 2004; Astronaut, 2004; Evolution, 2007. **Honors/Awds:** Numerous honors including Named top singles producer, Music Week, 1985; Named number one pop singles producer, Billboard, 1985; Grammy Award, 1986; Dance Music Hall of Fame, 2005; Lifetime Achievement Award; Heroes Award, Nat Acad Rec Arts & Sci; Humanitarian Award, We Are Family Found, 2011; Lifetime Achievement Award, Winter Music Conf, 2012. **Business Addr:** Musician, Warner Brothers Records, 75 Rockefeller Plz Suite 1, New York, NY 10019, **Business Phone:** (212)275-4600.

### RODGERS, PAMELA E.

President (organization), automotive executive, association executive. **Personal:** Born May 8, 1958, Detroit, MI; daughter of Horace J and Yvonne S. **Educ:** Univ Mich, BA, econ, 1980; Duke Univ, MBA, finance, 1983. **Career:** Ford Motor Co, Car Prod Develop, financial analyst, 1984-86, dealer cand, 1988-90; Heritage Ford Flint Inc, pres, 1990-92; Harrell Chevrolet, gen mgr, 1992-93; Ford Motor Co, All Am Ford, dealer cand, 1992; Flat Rock Chevrolet Oldsmobile Inc, pres & gen mgr, 1993-96; Internet Corp, dir, 1999; Gen Motors Fixed Opers Adv Bd, bd mem; Rodgers Chevrolet Inc, pres & owner, 1996-. **Orgs:** Secy, Nat Asn Minority Automobile Dealers; bd, Gen Motors Minority Dealer Asn; bd, Family Serv Wayne City; pres, Flat Rock Rotary Club; Big Bros Big Sisters; Detroit Metro Chevrolet Dealer Asn; Links; Nat Women Auto Asn; Girlfriends; New Detroit Coalition; Southeastern Mich Community Found; Detroit Med Ctr Harper Hosp; Downtown Develop Authority; Merrill Palmer Inst, Wayne State Univ; Univ Mich Dean's Adv Coun. **Honors/Awds:** Special Tribute, State Mich, 1992; Kizzy Award, 1997; Dealer of the Year, Gen Motors; Professional Achievement Award, 2006. **Home Addr:** 100 Riverfront Suite 1902, Detroit, MI 48226, **Home Phone:** (313)393-6733. **Business Addr:** President, Owner, Rodgers Chevrolet Inc, 23755 Allen Rd, Trenton, MI 48183, **Business Phone:** (734)676-9600.

### RODGERS, SHIRLEY MARIE

Manager. **Personal:** Born Dec 29, 1948, Saginaw, MI. **Educ:** Mich State Univ, 1970, BA, 1984. **Career:** Manager, administrator (retired); Blue Cross Mich, serv rep, 1970-71; Mich State Univ, tutor for athletic dept, 1970-71; Lansing Sch Dist, comm relations liaison, 1972, tutor, 1972; Mich State Univ, prog coordr Teach-a-Brother, 1972-73, prog coordr National Jr Tennis League, 1973; Meridian 4 Theaters, cashier, 1973; Lansing Sch Dist, Personnel Dept, clerk, 1975-76, payroll clerk IV, 1976-81, acad secy to dir of adult & continuing educ, 1981-82, acad secy to dep supt, 1982-94, payroll supervisor. **Orgs:** Zeta Phi Beta Sor Inc Mich State Univ, 1970; Lansing Asn Educ Secretaries, 1976-82; Mich Democratic Party, 1980-; vice chair, Ingham Co Democratic Party, 1980-; bd dir, Mich State Univ Black Alumni Inc, 1980-; Ingham Co Sch Officers Asn, 1981-; bd trustee, Lansing Comm Col, 1981-93; State Adv Coun for Voc Educ, 1983-84; Gr Lansing Mich State Univ Black Alumni Chap, 1983-; Mich State Univ Alumni Asn, 1984; Nat Asn Advan Colored People, 1985; State Coun Voc Educ, 1985; Treas, Lansing Bd Educ, 2007-; Ingham County Rd Comn; Tri-county Regional Planning Comn; City Lansing Pub Serv Adv Bd. **Honors/Awds:** Citizen of the Year in Education, Phi Beta Sigma Frat Inc, 1985; Black Distinguished Alumni, Mich State Univ, 1989; Governors Award, Outstanding Local Elected Official, 1989; Certificate of Recognition, Am Citizens for Justice, Detroit Chapter.

### RODGERS, VINCENT G. J.

Educator. **Personal:** Born Feb 17, 1958, St. Louis, MO; son of Bennie and Frances; married Padmini Srinivasan. **Educ:** Univ Dayton, BS, physics, 1980; Syracuse Univ, MS, theoretical particle physics, 1982, PhD, theoretical particle physics, 1985. **Career:** Univ Dayton, Res Inst & Wright Paterson Air Force Base, res asst & numerical analyst, 1979-80; Univ Fla, Gainesville, Fla, Inst Fundamental Theory, postdoctoral res assoc, 1985-87; State Univ New York, Stony Brook, NY, Yang Inst Theoretical Physics, postdoctoral res assoc, 1987-89; Univ Iowa, asst prof, 1989-95, assoc prof, 1995-2004, prof, 2004-. **Orgs:** Nat Soc Black Physicists, 1990-; NSBP Electronic Network Monitor, 1993-2002; NSBP Newsletter Editor, 1996-98; Am Physical Soc, 1985-; Am Asn Physics Teachers, 2004-. **Home Addr:** 1310 Teg Dr, Iowa City, IA 52246-4743, **Home Phone:** (319)354-7553. **Business Addr:** Professor of Physics & Astronomy, University of Iowa, 513 Van Allen Hall, Iowa City, IA 52242-1479, **Business Phone:** (319)335-1219.

### RODGERS, WILLIAM M., JR.

Engineer. **Personal:** Born Dec 22, 1941, Friars Point, MS; son of William M Sr and Leanna Felix (deceased); married Venora Ann Faulkerson; children: William III, Melita Elizabeth & Steven Eric. **Educ:** Tenn State Univ, BS, 1963; Dartmouth Col, MS, 1970. **Career:** Nat Inst Health, mathematician, 1963-64; Honeywell Inc, Electronic Data Processing Div, systs analyst, 1964-66; Data Anal Ctr Itek Corp, sr sci programmer, 1966-67; Bell Tel Labs, tech staff, 1968; Exxon Refinery Tex, systs analyst, 1970-75; Lockheed Elect Co Inc, staff engr, 1975-77; Xerox Corp, mgr comput graphics req & appl, 1977-82, proj mgr, CAD/CAM acquisition, 1982-83, mgr, 1983-87, CAD/CAM strategy & planning, 1987-88, prin engr, 1988-. **Orgs:** Asn Comput Mach; Soc Prof Engrs; Dartmouth Soc Engrs; Dartmouth Alumni Org; Dartmouth Soc Engrs Stud Exec Comt, 1969-70. **Honors/Awds:** Sears Roebuck Scholar, 1959; Univ Counr Tenn State Univ, 1961-62; Conducted presentation on CAD/CAM system acquisition, related topics, Univ Wis, 1985, Rochester Inst Tech, 1987; University Scholar Award; Conducted presentation on large scale CAD/CAM Acquisitions, Nat Coop Grocers Asn, 1989. **Home Addr:** 14 Coach Side Lane, Pittsford, NY 14534-9413, **Home Phone:** (585)381-9125. **Business Addr:** Principal Engineer, Xerox Corp, Advanced Systems Tools for Product Development, 800 Phillips Rd, Pittsford, NY 14534, **Business Phone:** (716)422-3253.

## RODGERS-ROSE, DR. LAFRANCES AUDREY
Educator, association executive. **Personal:** Born Jul 19, 1936, Norfolk, VA; daughter of Carroll M and Beulah Smith; married Vattel T; children: Henry D & Valija C. **Educ:** Morgan State Univ, BA, 1958; Fisk Univ, MA, sociol & anthrop, 1960; Univ Iowa, PhD, sociol, social psychol & anthrop, 1964. **Career:** State Olaf Col, asst prof sociol, 1964-69; Case Western Res Univ, asst prof sociol, 1970-72; Educ Testing Serv, res sociologist, 1972-73; Princeton Univ, African Am studies, lectr, 1973-88; Int Black Womens Cong, pres, 1983-99, founder & chief exec officer, 2000-; Drew Univ, 1988-94. **Orgs:** Delta Sigma Theta Sorority, 1963-; founding mem, pres, Asn Black Sociologists, 1970-2012; Am Sociol Asn, 1971-; chap pres, Black Child Develop Inst, 1979-81; Nat Black United Fund, 1994-; pres, Asn Social & Behavorial Scientists, 1995-96; Asn Study Class African Civilizations, 1998-; Univ Louisville, Plight Black Men African Diaspora, 2007; Asn Social & Behav Scientists. **Honors/Awds:** Mayor Proclamation, City Newark, NJ, 1985; Fannie Lou Hamer Award, US Organization, 1995; Noble/Women International Leadership Award, Nat Orgn Black Elected Legis Women, 2000; WEB DuBois Award, Asn Social & Behav Scientists, 2001; James E Blackwell Founders Award, Asn Black Sociologists, 2003. **Special Achievements:** Author: Black Woman, 1980, co-author: Black Male and Female Relationships, 1985, River of Tears, 1993, Every Black Woman Should Wear a Red Dress, 2003; Healing Black from Violence, Traces Publication, 2011. **Business Addr:** Founder, Chief Executive Officer, International Black Women's Congress, 645 Church St Suite 200, Norfolk, VA 23510, **Business Phone:** (757)625-0500.

## RODMAN, DENNIS KEITH
Basketball player, business owner, actor. **Personal:** Born May 13, 1961, Trenton, NJ; son of Philander Jr and Shirley; married Michelle Moyer, May 13, 2003; children: D J & Trinity; married Carmen Electra, Nov 14, 1998; married Annie Bakes, Sep 28, 1992, (divorced 1993); children: Alexis. **Educ:** Cooke Co Jr Col, attended 1983; S Eastern Okla State Univ, attended 1986. **Career:** Basketball player (retired), business owner; Dallas-Ft Worth Airport, janitor, 1978; Detroit Pistons, forward, 1986-93; San Antonio Spurs, 1993-95; Chicago Bulls, 1995-98; Los Angeles Lakers, 1998-99; Dallas Mavericks, forward, 1999-2000; Long Beach Jam, 2003-04; Rodman Underground Inc, owner, currently; Orange County Crush, 2004-05; Tijuana Dragons, 2005-06; Lingerie Football League, comnr, 2005; Torpan Pojat, 2005; Brighton Bears, 2006; Dennis K Rodman Inc, owner, currently. Films: Double Team, actor, 1997; Simon Sez, actor, 1999; Coming Attractions, actor, 2006, The Minis, 2008. TV Series: "Soldier of Fortune Inc", 1997; "Cutaway", 2000; "Stripper's Ball", 2003; "Lingerie Bowl", 2006. **Business Addr:** Owner, Rodman Underground Inc, 6811 Ash St, Frisco, TX 75034, **Business Phone:** (972)335-7114.

## RODMAN, JOHN A.
Computer executive, president (organization). **Career:** Fed Info Exchange Inc, pres, currently. **Business Addr:** President, Federal Information Exchange Inc, 555 Quince Orchard Rd Suite 200, Gaithersburg, MD 20878, **Business Phone:** (301)975-0103.

## RODMAN, MICHAEL WORTHINGTON
Banker. **Personal:** Born Sep 29, 1941, Indianapolis, IN; son of Hubert E Dabner and Faye R Dabner; married Kaaren; children: Michael H & Heather L. **Educ:** Ind Univ, BS, edu, MBA, 1990. **Career:** Midwest Nat Bank, asst cashier, 1972-74; INB Nat Bank, br mgr & asst vpres, 1974-81, AVP, CRA officer, 1981-86, vip, sr compliance officer, 1986-; NBD Neighborhood Revitalization Corp, pres, 1986-. **Orgs:** Ind Housing Policy Study Comn, 1989-; 100 Black Men, 1991-; Frontiers, 1991-; edu com chair, Indianapolis Urban League, 1992-; secy, Ind Sch Bd, 1994, pres, 1996; Ardyth Burkhart Ser; Vol Action Ctr; county treas, Marion. **Honors/Awds:** HOURS Award for COT Service, INB Nat Bank, 1979; CLD, Outstanding Achievement in Business, 1983; Outstanding Service Award, United Way, 1984; Presidential Citation, ABA, 1986. **Home Addr:** 5444 N Capitol, Indianapolis, IN 46208.

## RODNEY, KARL BASIL
Founder (originator), publisher, chief executive officer. **Personal:** Born Nov 29, 1940, Kingston; married Faye A; children: Michele, Denine & Karlisa. **Educ:** City Univ NY, Hunter Col, BA, econ, 1966, MA, 1970. **Career:** Equitable Life Assurance Soc US, analyst, proj mgr, div mgr, 1967-82; New York Carib News, publ, chief exec officer, co-founder, currently. **Orgs:** Chmn, Caribbean Educ & Cult Inst, 1976-; dir, Martin Luther King Jr Living Dream Inc NY, 1985-; bd mem, mem exec comt, New York United Way; bd mem, mem exec comt, United Way Int; chmn, Am Found Univ Wi; bd mem, New York Partnership; bd mem, New York Sport Found; bd mem, New York Urban League; founding mem, Caribbean Am Chamber Com & Indust; founding mem, Black Equity Alliance; bd mem, New York Police Found; regional pres, Nat Asn Black Publishers; chief exec officer, Carib News Found; bd mem, exec comt, Greater Harlem Chamber Com; Sigma Pi Phi Fraternity; chmn, Caribbean Tourism Orgn Found. **Honors/Awds:** Community Service Award, 1980; WA Domingo Award, 1980; Excellence in Ethic Journ Harlem Week, 1985; Black Journalist Award, Pepsi-Cola NY, 1986; Award of Excellence, Caribbean Tourism Orgn, 2005. **Home Addr:** 525 Baldwin Pl, Mamaroneck, NY 10543, **Home Phone:** (914)698-5582. **Business Addr:** Publisher, Chief Executive Officer, New York Carib News, 28 W 39th St, New York, NY 10018, **Business Phone:** (212)944-1991.

## RODRIGUEZ, ARGELIA VELEZ
Educator. **Personal:** Born Nov 23, 1936, Havana; daughter of Pedro Velez; married Raul; children: Raul P & Argelia M. **Educ:** Marianao Inst, BS & BA, 1955; Univ Havana, Sch Sci, PhD, math & astron, 1960. **Career:** Marianao Inst, Havana, Cuba, instr, asst prof, math & physics, 1957-61; Tex Col, asst prof math & physics, 1962, chmn dept, 1962-64; Bishop Col, dir, Summer Prog Advan High Sch Students Math, 1964, Mod Math NSF-Serv Inst Sec Sch Teachers, 1964-68, Educ Prof Develop Act-Teachers Training Develop, coord, 1970-73, prof math, 1972-77, dept head math & sci, 1978-79, dir, Coop Col Sch Sci-Nat Sci Found, coordr, Math Proj Jr High Sch Teachers, coordr, 1972-74, Coop Doc Prog Math Educ Houston, assoc dir, 1973-74, Dept Math Sci, chairwoman, 1975-78; Minority Insts Sci Improv Prog, Wash, DC, prog mgr, 1979-80; US Dept Educ, prog dir, 1980-, Robert C. Byrd Hons Scholar prog, head, sr prog officer, DC Col Access Prog, exec dir, Minority Sci Improv Prog, dir. **Orgs:** AAAS; DC Am Math Soc Providence; Nat Coun Teachers Math; DC Tex Acad Sci, Austin; Math Asn Am, DC; mem comn, Affirmative Acton Conf Bd Math Sci; Am Asn Univ Prof, DC; Asn Univ Women, DC; Young Women Christ Asn, Dallas; Cuban Cath Asn, Dallas; speaker, Ann Conv Nat Coun Teacher Math, NC Sec, Nov, 1972; bd dir, Dallas Br, Am Asn Univ Women, 1973-; chmn, Int Rel Com Am Asn Univ Women, 1973-; dir, NSF Minority Inst Sci Improv Proj, 1976-78; dir, NSF Pre-Col Teacher Develop Math Proj, 1977-78; Nat Sci Found, Math Educ Progs. **Special Achievements:** First Black woman to earn a doctorate in mathematics in Cuba. **Home Addr:** 838 Foxboro Lane, Dallas, TX 75241. **Business Addr:** Director, US Department of Education, 400 Maryland Ave SW, Washington, DC 20024, **Business Phone:** (800)872-5327.

## RODRIGUEZ, DORIS L.
Association executive, executive director. **Personal:** Born Mar 8, 1927, New York, NY; married Jules S; children: Anna, Julio & Louis. **Educ:** Queens Col. **Career:** Litman Dept Store NY, comparison shopper, interpretor, 1946-48; Pvt Nurse, 1948-51; Manhattan Gen Hosp, obstet nurse, 1951-58; Bilingual Adv Dists 27 & 28; Originals Jamaica Inc, Urban Ctr, exec dir. **Orgs:** Assoc, St Marys Sch Girls & Convent, 1950; Musical Art Group, 1950; 103rd Precinct Comm Coun, 1969; Concerned Parents Day Care Ctr, 1969; Queensboro Coun Soc Welfare, 1971; bd dir, Youth Consult Serv, 1972-; exec bd mem, PTA Manlius Mil Acad; Adv Coun Reimbursable Funds, Dist 27 & 28 City wide; Queens Child Guid Comn; founding mem, Ida B Wills Sch; Christ Ch Sag Harbor, NY. **Home Addr:** 3 Pk Lane, Westport, CT 06880-4413, **Home Phone:** (631)525-7153.

## RODRIGUEZ, RUBEN
Executive. **Career:** Motown Rec, Nebr regional mkt & promotions mgr; Casablanca Rec, staff; Columbia Rec, sr vpres, 1985-90; Pendulum Rec, pres, chief exec officer, 1990-, Joint Venture with Elektra Entertainment, founder, pres & chief exec officer, sr vpres, 1991-95, Elektra Rec, sr vpres, 1991-95; Ruben Rodriguez Entertainment Inc, founder, chief exec officer, owner, 1998-; RAM Talent Group, founder, chief exec officer, 2009-. **Orgs:** Nat Acad Rec Arts & Sci; Gospel Music Asn. **Business Addr:** President, Founder, Ruben Rodriguez Entertainment Inc, 96 Linwood Plz Suite 354, Fort Lee, NJ 07024, **Business Phone:** (201)363-1461.

## ROEBUCK, GERARD FRANCIS
Entrepreneur. **Personal:** Born Sep 26, 1953, New York, NY; son of Gladys Johnson and Waldamar; married Sharon Jeffrey; children: Jared & Jashaun. **Educ:** City Col New York, New York, NY, BA, 1978; Pratt Inst, Brooklyn, NY, MLS, 1980. **Career:** New York Pub Libr, New York, NY, supv librn, 1980-89; Black Expo USA, New York, NY, founder & chmn, 1987-; New York City Bd Educ, New York, NY, media dir, 1989-90. **Orgs:** Nat Asn Adv Coloured People; bd dir, OL-MEC Toy Corp; Atlanta Chamber Com; Black Librn Caucus; Nat Asn Mkt Developers, 1989-. **Honors/Awds:** Class Leader, Xavier Summer Prog Higher Achievement Prog; Promoter of the Year, New York City Promoters Orgn, 1981. **Special Achievements:** Concert & rap group promoter. **Business Addr:** Founder, Chairman, Black Expo USA, 600 W Peachtree St NW, Atlanta, GA 30308, **Business Phone:** (404)892-2815.

## ROEBUCK, REP. JAMES RANDOLPH, JR.
State government official. **Personal:** Born Feb 12, 1945, Philadelphia, PA; son of James Randolph Sr and Cynthia Compton; married Cheryl Arrington. **Educ:** VA Union Univ, BA, 1966; Univ VA, MA, 1969, PhD, 1977. **Career:** Drexel Univ, lectr hist, 1970-77, asst prof hist, 1977-84; City Philadelphia, Off Mayor, legal asst, 1984-85; PA House Reps, rep gen assembly, 188th Dis, 1985-. **Orgs:** Philadelphia Coun Boy Scouts Am; Child Crisis Treat Ctr; Nat Asn Advan Colored People; Univ VA Alumni Asn; bd deacons, Mt Olivet Tabernacle Baptist Church; bd dir, Pa Higher Educ Assistance Agency; Philadelphia Community Col; Pa Hist & Mus Comn; Pa Legis Black Caucus; Pa Hist & Mus Comn, 1990-96; People Philadelphia Chap, 1990-; bd dir, Hist Socs Pa, 1993-; bd, Pa Higher Educ Assistance Agency, 1995-; bd dir, Christian St Br Ymca, 1997-; bd trustee, Int House. **Honors/Awds:** Recognition Award, United Negro Col Alumni, 1978; Chapel of the Four Chaplians Legion of Honor Award, 1980; Conestoga District Award of Merit, Boy Scouts Am, 1983; Silver Beaver Award, 1986; Achievement Award, VA Union Univ Alumni, 1986; Citation, Nat Asn Equal Opportunity Higher Educ, 1987; fel grant, Foreign Affairs Scholars Prog; Southern Fel Fund; Mutual Educ Exchange Grant, US Off Educ & Fulbright Prog; Nat Endowment for the Humanities Grant; German Federal Republic Grant. **Special Achievements:** First African American Student Council president at UVA. **Home Addr:** 435 S 46th St, Philadelphia, PA 19143-2142, **Home Phone:** (215)382-1268. **Business Addr:** Representative, Pennsylvania House of Representatives, 208 K Leroy Irvis Office Bldg, Harrisburg, PA 17120-2188, **Business Phone:** (717)783-1000.

## ROEBUCK-HAYDEN, MARCIA
Publishing executive. **Educ:** Nat Louis Univ, Nat Col educ, BS, educ, MS, educ ther. **Career:** Ebony Jr, managing ed, 1980; Scott Foresman & Co, ed asst, 1986-, adult basic educ, vpres eng; Vaughn Mkt Group, vpres opers; DC Heath & Co, sr ed; Harcourt Brace Jovanovich, exec Ed; Houghton Mifflin, educ consult, currently; Scott Foresman Publ, Res & Curric, ed dir, Eng Second Lang, Adult Basic Educ, ed vpres, currently. **Orgs:** Chair, Am Civil Liberties Union Fla; Wellington High Sch Adv Coun; Village Wellington Educ Comt; Int Reading Assoc; Nat Black Child Developments Inst; Chicago Asn Black Journalists; Everychild; Edpress; Tesol; C Reading Roundtable; DuSable Mus. **Business Addr:** Editorial Vice President, English as a Second Language Basic Adult Education, 1900 E Lake Ave, Glenview, IL 60025, **Business Phone:** (708)729-3000.

## ROGERS, ALFRED R.
Public utility executive. **Personal:** Born Apr 7, 1931, Hartford, CT; son of John and Oretta; married Alice. **Educ:** Univ Conn, BA, 1953, JD, 1963; Am Inst Real Estate Appraisal; Rensselar Polytech Inst Conn; Univ Mich, Pub Utilities Exec Prog, attended 1982; Edison Elec Inst, Pub Utilities Exec Prog. **Career:** Bur Rights Ways Conn Dept Transp, chief pub utilities sect, 1957-64; Hartford Elec Light Co Legal & Real Estate Dept, sr land agt, 1964-69; Hartford Elec Light Co, mgr, 1970-85; Northeast Utilities Cent Region, vpres, 1985-94. **Orgs:** Pres & sec, Bd Educ, Hartford, 1965-73; state treas, Conn Asn Bds Educ, 1966-69; Govt Adv Coun Voc Educ, 1967-71; Govt Clean Air Task Force, 1967-69; exec bd, Long River Coun BSA, 1973-; adv bd, Salvation Army, 1973-; corporator, Newington Childrens Hosp, 1975-; dir, Hartford Hosp, 1982-; trustee, Young Men Christian Asn, 1990-; trustee, Boys Club Hartford; dir, Mech Savings Bank Hartford; trustee, St Joseph Col, W Hartford; pres & chief exec officer, Urban League Greater Hartford. **Home Addr:** 200 Cold Spring Rd Apt 513B, Rocky Hill, CT 06067-5315, **Home Phone:** (860)257-3025.

## ROGERS, DR. BERNARD ROUSSEAU
Physician. **Personal:** Born Jan 17, 1944, Winston-Salem, NC; married Linda Hargreaves. **Educ:** NC Cent Univ, BS, 1966; Meharry Med Col, Sch Med, MD, 1971. **Career:** Youngstown Hosp, intern & resident pathol, 1971-72; Univ Minn, MN, residency, radiation oncol, 1973-76; pvt pract physician, currently; Oncol Servs, dir, brachy ther, 1991-; Chesapeake Regional Cancer Ctr, Charlotte Hall, Md, med dir; Community Cancer Treat Ctr, physician; Regional Cancer Ctr, Bon Secours-Holy Family Hosp, currently. **Orgs:** Am Med Asn, 1976-; Am Col Radiol, 1977-; Am Endocurie ther Soc, 1985-; Am Soc Therapeut Radiologists & Oncologists, 1976-; Am Brachy ther Soc. **Home Addr:** 50 Dana Ave, Auburn, ME 04210, **Home Phone:** (207)784-3731. **Business Addr:** Physician, Community Cancer Treatment Center, 400 Highland Ave, Lewistown, PA 17044, **Business Phone:** (717)242-7297.

## ROGERS, CARLOS DEON
Basketball player. **Personal:** Born Feb 6, 1971, Detroit, MI. **Educ:** Univ Ark-Little Rock, attended 1991; Tenn State Univ, attended 1994. **Career:** Basketball player (retired); Golden State Warriors, forward & ctr, 1994-95; Toronto Raptors, power forward, 1995-98; Portland TrailBlazers, Power forward, 1998-99; Houston Rockets, ctr, 1999-2001; Ind Pacers, forward & ctr, 2001-02. **Honors/Awds:** Ohio Valley Conference Player of the Year, 1993, 1994; NBA Draft, 1994.

## ROGERS, CHARLES
Football player. **Personal:** Born May 23, 1981, Saginaw, MI; son of Charles Brown and Cathy; married Naija Washington; children: 7. **Educ:** Mich State Univ, BA, sociol. **Career:** Detroit Lions, wide receiver, 2003-05; free agt, currently. **Honors/Awds:** All State Honoree Thrice; Fred Biletnikoff Award, 2002; Unanimous All American, 2002; Paul Warfield Trophy, 2002.

## ROGERS, CHARLES D.
Designer, artist, educator. **Personal:** Born Jan 5, 1935, Cherokee County, OK; son of Henry and Alberta Lay; children: Warren Donald. **Educ:** Calif State Col, BA, 1964; Ohio State Univ, MA, 1971; Univ Nc, Greensboro, NC, MFA, painting, 1977. **Career:** Artcraft Studios, Los Angeles, com designer, 1964-69; Watts Summer Festival, Watts, Calif, co-dir, 1967-69; Vanguard Studios, Van Nuys, Calif, com designer, 1970; Bennett Col, Greens boro, NC, produced Harlem Renaissance, 1972; Johnson C Smith Univ, Charlotte, NC, assoc prof arts, 1972-, art prog dir, currently; Cd Rogers Art, chief operating officer, prin. **Orgs:** Charlotte Guild Artists, 1980-; Nat Conf Artists, 1986-; Black Arts Coun, Los Angeles, CA. **Honors/Awds:** Teaching Fellow Award, Ohio State Univ, Columbus, 1970; Teaching Fellow Award, African Am Inst, 1974; Scholar in Residence, New York Univ, 1993-95. **Special Achievements:** Author of Prints by Am Negro Artists & Black Artists On Art. **Home Addr:** 3322 Anson St, Charlotte, NC 28209-1902, **Home Phone:** (704)523-0122. **Business Addr:** Associate Professor, Johnson C Smith University, 100 Beatties Ford Rd, Charlotte, NC 28216, **Business Phone:** (704)378-1000.

## ROGERS, CHARLES LEONARD
Aerospace engineer. **Personal:** Born Jul 27, 1951, Decatur, AL; son of Felix M E and Estelle Holmes; married Ramona. **Educ:** Northern Ill Univ, BS, 1976; W Coast Univ, MS, 1986. **Career:** Common Wealth Edison, tech staff engr, 1976-80; Lockheed Martin Astronaut, chief launch opers, 1988-97; Athens/MSLS Launch Opers, pres, mgr, 1997-. **Orgs:** Nat Mgt Asn. **Honors/Awds:** Martin Marietta, Jefferson Cup, 1992; Certificate of Recognition, Black Engr Mag, 1992; Dollars & Sense Mag, Ams Best & Brightest, 1993. **Home Addr:** 161 Galaxy Way, Lompoc, CA 93436, **Home Phone:** (805)733-3228. **Business Addr:** Manager Launch Operations, Lockheed Martin, Bldg 8500, Vandenberg Air Force Base, CA 93437-1681, **Business Phone:** (805)734-8232.

## ROGERS, CHRIS
Football player. **Personal:** Born Jan 3, 1977, Washington, DC. **Educ:** Howard Univ, grad. **Career:** Football player (retired); Minn Vikings, cornerback, defensive back, 1999; Seattle Seahawks, corner back, 2001-03.

## ROGERS, DAVID WILLIAM
Television journalist, meteorologist. **Personal:** Born Feb 2, 1959, Cleveland, OH; son of David Louis and Thelma Elizabeth Grahma; children: David & Chloe. **Educ:** Temple Univ, Philadelphia, PA, jour, 1983. **Career:** WCAU-TV, Philadelphia, Pa, news producer, 1979-85; WBBJ-TV, Jackson, Tenn, news anchor, 1985-86; WTVR-TV, Richmond, Va, 1986-87; WJBK-TV, Detroit, Mich, weather anchor, 1987-;

KYW-TV, seasoned weatherman; WKYC-TV3, chief meteorologist; CBS-2, meteorologist; WVIR-TV NBC29, morning weekend & part-time noon show meteorologist, currently. **Orgs:** YMCA, 1979; Nat Asn Advan Colored People, 1989; bd dir, C Aid Soc; Nat Asn Black Journalists, 1985; proj coord, United Negro Col Fund, 1986; Westland Cult Soc, 1987; Muscular Dystrophy Asn, 1987; bd dir, C Aid Soc. **Honors/Awds:** Award of Outstanding Achievement, United Negro Col Fund, 1986; Barrier Awareness Award, Am Asn Handicapped Persons, 1987; Award of Appreciation, Am Cancer Soc, 1988; numerous Emmy Awards in the Anchor Weathercaster category. **Special Achievements:** Various articles published in the Philadelphia Inquirer, l979-8l. **Home Addr:** 24788 Verdant Suite 75201, Farmington Hills, MI 48331, **Home Phone:** (313)474-9574. **Business Addr:** Meteorologist, WVIR-TV NBC29, 503 E Mkt St, Charlottesville, VA 22902, **Business Phone:** (434)220-2900.

## ROGERS, DR. DECATUR BRAXTON (DECATUR B ROGERS)

School administrator. **Educ:** Tenn State Univ, BS, mech engineering, 1967; Vanderbilt Univ, MS, eng mgt, MS, mech engineering, 1969, MS, mech engineering, 1971, PhD, mech engineering, 1975. **Career:** Grumman Aero-Space Corp, tool designer, 1963; NASA Goddard Space Flight Ctr, thermal engr, ASEE-NASA Fac Fels Prog, 1981-82; Fla State Univ, prof mech engineering, 1988, dean; Tenn St Univ, Col Eng, Technol & Comput Sci, Nashville, Tenn, asst prof, dean & prof mech eng, 1988-; Fed City Col, fac; Prairie View A&M Univ, fac & dean; LEM, thermal control engr; Univ Planning, asst prof & dir. **Orgs:** Am Soc Eng Educ; Am Sos Mech Engrs; NAMEPA; Nat Soc Prof Engs; Nat Asn Advan Colored People; Phi Delta Kappa; Pi Tau Sigma; Mech Eng Hon Soc; Tau Beta Pi; Nat Eng Hon Soc; Phi Kappa Phi; SECME Univ Coun Insts; Return Flight Task Group; Tenn State Univ Engineering Alumni Asn; bd dir, Metrop Govt Nashville Thermal Transfer Corp; State Tenn Bd Boiler Rules; Appl Engineering Technol Div Adv Comt Y-12; bd dir, Pa State Univ; bd dir, Appl Res Lab; NASA Return-To-Flight Task Force Tech Group. **Honors/Awds:** NASA Service Award, NASA Return-To-Flight Task Force Tech Group. **Special Achievements:** Publications: Thermodynamics of Fiber-Power Insulation; The Engineering Pipeline: A Long-Term Talent Development Strategy for Minorities on the Recruitment and Retention of Minorities and Women in Engineering and Preparing Black Children to Become Engineers. First Associate Dean in the FAMU-FSU College of Engineering. **Business Addr:** Dean, Professor of Mechanical Engineering, Tennessee State University, 3500 John A Merritt Blvd, Nashville, TN 37209-1561, **Business Phone:** (615)963-5000.

## ROGERS, DESIREE GLAPION

Vice president (organization), chief executive officer, federal government official. **Personal:** Born Jun 16, 1959, New Orleans, LA; daughter of Roy Glapion (deceased) and Joyce Glapion; married John W Jr; children: Victoria. **Educ:** Wellesley Col, BA, polit sci, 1981; Harvard Bus Sch, MBA, 1985. **Career:** AT&T, custom serv mkt mgr; Levy Orgn Lobby Shop Div, dir develop; Mus Opers Consult Asn, pres; Ill State Lottery, dir, 1990-97; People's Energy, vpres corp commun, 1997-2000, chief mkt officer, sr vpres customer serv, 2000-04; Corp Commun, vpres, 2000, sr vpres, 2001; Peoples Gas & N Shore Gas, pres, 2004-07; Allstate Financial, pres social networking, 2008-10; Obama Am, White House social secy, 2008-10; Johnson Publ Co, chief exec officer, 2010-; Choose Chicago, chmn, 2013-; Integrys Energy Group, sr vpres. **Orgs:** Vpres, Peoples Energy, 1997, sr vpres, 2001; Ravina; WTTW Channel 11, Mus Sci & Indust; sr vpres, Customer Serv; pres, Peoples Gas & N Shore Gas, 2004; bd dir, Allstate Life Ins Co; bd mem, Equity Residential, 2003-; bd mem, Blue Cross Blue Shield Ill; vice chmn, Lincoln Pk Zoo & Mus Sci Indust; chmn, Chicago C's Mus; Young Presidents Orgn; Com Club Chicago; Chicago Network; 2016 Chicago Olympic Cult Comt; bd mem, Northwestern Memorial Found; bd mem, Polk Found; exec comt mem, Chicago's Mus Sci & Indust; co-chair, Chicago Mayor Rahm Emanuel's, 2011 Inaugural Comt. **Special Achievements:** First person of African-American, Barack Obama's office, White House Social Secretary. **Home Addr:** 1301 N Astor St, Chicago, IL 60610-2113, **Home Phone:** (312)787-4632. **Business Addr:** Chief Executive Officer, Johnson Publishing Co LLC, 820 S Mich Ave, Chicago, IL 60605, **Business Phone:** (312)322-9200.

## ROGERS, EARLINE S.

Educator, consultant. **Personal:** Born Dec 20, 1934, Gary, IN; daughter of Earl Smith and Robbie Hicks Smith; married Louis C Rogers Jr; children: Keith C & Dara Dawn. **Educ:** Ind Univ, Bloomington, IN, BS, 1957, MS, 1971. **Career:** Educator (retired), senator; Gary Community Sch Corp, teacher, 1957-95; Gary City Coun, pres & coun mem, 1980-82; Ind House Representatives, rep, 1982-90; Ind State Senate, Dist 3, asst minority leader, asst minority whip, sen, 1991-, Indiana Black Legislative Caucus; educ consult, currently. **Orgs:** Am Fedn Teachers; Black Prof Women; Bus Prof Women; Campagne Acad; Drug Free Ind, Lake County; Hoosier Boys Town; Ind State Teachers Asn; Nat Asn Advan Colored People; Nat Coun Negro Women; Urban League; Young Women's Christian Asn; Ind Lakes Mgt Work Group; Northwest Ind Transp Study Comt; Ind Black Legis Caucus. **Special Achievements:** First woman elected president of Gary Common Council. **Home Addr:** 3636 W 15th Ave, Gary, IN 46404-1828, **Home Phone:** (219)949-7578. **Business Addr:** Senator, Indiana State Senate, 200 W Wash St, Indianapolis, IN 46204-2785, **Business Phone:** (800)382-9467.

## ROGERS, ELIJAH BABY

Executive, president (organization), chief executive officer. **Personal:** Born Nov 2, 1939, Orlando, FL; married Jean Doctor. **Educ:** SC State Col, BA, 1962; Univ SC, attended 1965; Howard Univ, MSW, 1967, MA, 1972. **Career:** SC Dept Corrections, supvr soc work serv, 1967-69; Wash Bur Nat UrbanLeague, asst dir, 1968-70; Nat Urban League, sr field rep, 1969; Bowie Md, asst mgr, chief staff, 1970-71; Richmond, Va, asst city mgr, 1972-74; Berkeley, Calif, asst city mgr, mgr, 1974-76; City Berkeley, city mgr, 1976-79; DC, Wash, DC, city adminr, 1979-83; Grant Thornton, asst managing partner, 1983-88; Delon Hampton & Assoc, chief operating officer, pres & chief exec officer, 2001-05, bd dir & sr advisor, 2005-. **Orgs:** Young Prof Task Force, 1971-72; mem adv comt, Sch Soc Work, 1972-73; Spec Task Force Minorities, 1973-74; bd dir, Great Richmond Transit Co, 1973-74; adj prof, Urban Studies, 1973-74; chairperson, Minority Exec Placement Bd, 1975-; Comn Mgt Labor Rel, 1976; adv comt, Econ Develop Nat Inst Advan Studies, 1977; transp steering comt, Nat League Cities, 1977; bd dir, Met Wash Coun Govs, 1980; vice chmn, Wash Metrop Airports Authority, 1986-88; bd trustee, Found Nat Capital Region, 1993; chmn, Wm Bd Fitzgerald Scholar Fund, 1994-; chmn, Mayor's Blue Ribbon Panel Health Care Reform, 1994; Mayor-Elect Marion Barry's Fin Transition Team, 1994; secy, Fed City Coun Bd Wash trustee, 1998; Nat Asn Soc Workers; Acad Cert Soc Workers Inc; City Mgt Assoc; fel Int City Mgt. **Home Addr:** 7129 16th St NW, Washington, DC 20012-1537. **Business Addr:** Senior Advisor, Board of Director, Delon Hampton & Associates, 800 K St NW Suite 720 N Lobby, Washington, DC 20001-8000, **Business Phone:** (202)898-1999.

## ROGERS, GEORGE

School administrator. **Personal:** Born Jan 8, 1947, Chicago, IL; son of George II and Gertrude Ellington; married Rita F Guhr; children: Tara M & Bret Z. **Educ:** Wilson City Col, AA, 1967; Bethel Col, BS, 1969; Wichita State Univ, MEd, 1972; Univ AR, PhD. **Career:** Bethel Col, track coach, 1969, dir athletics, asst to coach, defensive coordr, assoc prof phys ed, 1997; Whitewing Construct Inc, secy & treas & estimator, 2003-, chief financial officer, currently. **Orgs:** Newton Jaycee's, 1970; bd dir, FARM House, 1975; pres, USD No 373 Sch Bd, 1987-88, 1994-95; pres, Harvey Co Rural Water Dist 3, 1987-88; bd dir, Meadowlark Homestead Inc, 1996; bd dir, Mirror Inc, 1996; Kappa Alpha Psi Fraternity; First Step Indust; Nat Asn Stud Personnel Adminr. **Honors/Awds:** Coach of the Year, NAIA Area 3 Track Coach, 1975; Athletic Administrator of the Year, Kansas, NAIA, 1989-90. **Home Addr:** 3219 Royer W Dr, Newton, KS 67114-9639, **Home Phone:** (316)283-5272. **Business Addr:** Chief Executive Officer, Treasurer, Whitewing Construction Inc, 1410 E 12th St, Newton, KS 67114, **Business Phone:** (316)283-8180.

## ROGERS, DR. GEORGE

Educator. **Personal:** Born Sep 23, 1935, McKeesport, PA; married Emalyn Martin; children: Cheryl Jeanne Mincey, Rhea Avonne & Emalyn Cherea. **Educ:** Langston Univ, BS, educ, 1961; Cent State Univ, MS, educ, 1968; Univ Kans, EdD, 1971. **Career:** Ala A&M Univ, asst prof, 1968-71; Wichita State Univ, assoc prof, 1971-83; Langston Univ, vpres acad, 1983-86, from prof spec asst to pres, 1986-. **Orgs:** Phi Delta Kappa 1969; Alpha Phi Alpha Frat, 1970; pres, George Rogers & Asns, 1972-; Sigma Pi Phi Frat, 1986. **Home Addr:** 10201 C N Finely Rd, Oklahoma City, OK 73120. **Business Addr:** Professor, Special Assistant to President, Langston University, Langston, OK 73050.

## ROGERS, GWENDOLYN H.

Executive director. **Career:** Equal Bus Opportunity Comn, exec dir; Columbus City Coun, Columbus, Ohio, legis analyst. **Special Achievements:** First black woman executive director of the Equal Business Opportunity Commission. **Business Addr:** Executive Director, Equal Business Opportunity Commission, 1393 E Broad St 2nd Fl, Columbus, OH 43205, **Business Phone:** (614)645-4764.

## ROGERS, JOHN W., JR.

Executive, chairperson, chief executive officer. **Personal:** Born Mar 31, 1958, Chicago, IL; son of John Sr and Jewel Lafontant (deceased); married Desiree Glapion; children: Victoria; married Sharon Fairley. **Educ:** Princeton Univ, AB, econs, 1980. **Career:** Basketball player; Ivy League, capt, 1979-80; William Blair & Co, stockbroker, 1980-83; Ariel Investments LLC, founder, chmn & chief exec officer, 1983-, Aon dir, 1993, chmn audit comt, chief investment officer, currently; Ariel Fund & Ariel Appreciation Fund, lead portfolio mgr, currently; Robert F. Kennedy Ctr, dir justice & human rights. **Orgs:** Bd dir, chmn, Chicago Urban League; Family Focus; bd dir, Chicago Symphony Orchestra; bd dir, Lake Forest Col; bd dir, Am Nat Bank; bd dir, Aon Corp; bd dir, Burrell Communs Group; bd pres, Chicago Pk Dist; bd dir, First Chicago NBD Corp; bd dir, First Nat Bank Chicago; bd dir, Invest Comt; dir, John S & James L Knight Found; trustee, Rush-Presby-St Lukes Med Ctr; invest adv, Ariel Invest Trust; chmn, Econ Club Chicago; bd dir, Bally Total Fitness; dir Exelon Corp; dir, McDonalds Corp; trustee, Univ Chicago; Rainbow/PUSH Coalition; Oprah Winfrey Found; trustee, Princeton Univ, 1990-94; Black Princeton Alumni; bd dir, Princeton Varsity Club; Alumni Schs Comt; co-chmn, Obama's Ill finance comt; chmn, Univ Chicago Lab Schs bd; bd dir, chmn, Chicago Urban League; Family Focus; bd dir, Chicago Symphony Orchestra; bd dir, Lake Forest Col; bd dir, Am Nat Bank; bd dir, Aon Corp; bd dir, Burrell Communs Group; pres, Chicago Pk Dist; bd dir, First Chicago NBD Corp; bd dir, First Nat Bank Chicago; bd dir, Invest Comt; dir, John S & James L Knight Found; trustee, Rush-Presby-St Lukes Med Ctr; invest adv, Ariel Invest Trust; chmn, Econ Club Chicago; bd dir, Bally Total Fitness; dir, Exelon Corp; dir, McDonalds Corp, currently; trustee, Univ Chicago; Rainbow/PUSH Coalition; Oprah Winfrey Found; trustee, Princeton Univ, 1990-94; Black Princeton Alumni; bd dir, Princeton Varsity Club; Alumni Schs Comt; co-chmn, Obama's Ill finance comt; chmn, Univ Chicago Lab Schs bd; dir, Robert F Kennedy Ctr Justice & Human Rights; co-chmn, Presidential Inaugural Comt, 2009; Pres Adv Coun Financial Capability, 2010-; Am Acad Arts & Sci. **Business Addr:** Chairman, Chief Executive Officer, Ariel Investments LLC, 200 E Randolph Dr Suite 2900, Chicago, IL 60601, **Business Phone:** (312)726-0140.

## ROGERS, ESQ. JOYCE Q.

Executive, chief executive officer. **Personal:** Born Indianapolis, IN. **Educ:** Ind State Univ, BS, psychol, 1979; Ind Univ Sch Law, Indianapolis, JD, 1996. **Career:** Caseworker & family counr; Family & Social Servs Admin, dir contract mgt; Ind Black Expo Inc, chief operating officer, 2001-04, pres & chief exec officer, 2004-07; Ivy Tech Community Col, vpres develop; Diversity, Equity & Multicultural Affairs, IU Found, vpres develop & external rels. **Orgs:** Indianapolis Bar Asn; Am Bar Asn; Ind Bar Asn; Marion County Bar Asn; Stanley K Lacey Leadership Asn; United Way; Ind Fever Adv Bd; Women's Collab Cent Ind; Circle City Classic Exec Comt; Black Coaches Asn Adv Bd; Pvt Indust Coun Bd.; Bowen Found Bd; Mind Trust Bd; Dress Success Bd. **Business Addr:** Vice President for DEMA, Indiana University Foundation, 1500 N State Rd 46 Bypass, Bloomington, IN 47408, **Business Phone:** (812)855-8311.

## ROGERS, JUDITH W. (JUDITH ANN WILSON ROGERS)

District attorney, judge. **Personal:** Born Jul 27, 1939?, New York, NY; daughter of John Louis (deceased). **Educ:** Radcliffe Col, AB, cum laude, 1961; Harvard Law Sch, LLB, 1964; Univ Va Law Sch, LLM, 1988; DC Sch Law, hon doctorate. **Career:** Juv Ct DC, law clerk, 1964-65; DC, asst US atty, 1965-68; US Dept Justice, Criminal Div, trial atty, 1967-71; San Francisco Neighborhood Legal Assistance Found, staff atty, 1968-69; Cong Comn Orgn, gen coun, 1971-72; DC Govt, off asst mayor, legis prog coordr, 1972-74; DC Govt, Legis Mayor, spec asst, 1974-79; DC Govt, Intergovernmental Rels, asst city adminr, 1979; DC, corp coun, 1979-83; DC Ct Appeals, assoc judge, 1983-88, chief judge, 1988-93; US Ct Appeals, DC Circuit, judge, 1994-. **Orgs:** Phi Beta Kappa. **Business Addr:** Judge, United States Court of Appeals, 333 Constitution Ave NW, Washington, DC 20004, **Business Phone:** (202)216-7260.

## ROGERS, ORMER, JR.

Government official, postmaster general. **Personal:** Born Jul 23, 1945, Mt. Vernon, TX; son of Ormer Sr and Susie; married Helen Pettis. **Educ:** Dallas Baptist Univ, BCA, 1977; Abilene Christian Univ, MS, 1978; Mass Inst Technol, attended 1990. **Career:** Postmaster (retired); USS Postal Serv, dir, customer serv, 1983-86, opers prog analyst, 1986-87, field dir, mkt, 1987-88, drr, city opers, 1988-91, field dir, opers support, 1991, dist mgr, postmaster, 1991-92, area mgr, Great Lakes, 1992, dist mgr, Kansas City; Mid Am Dist, dist mgr. **Orgs:** Fed Exec Bd, 1991-93; Rotary Chicago, 1992-93; Univ Ill, Chicago, Dept Med, develop coun, 1992-93; Combined Fed Campaign, chair, 1993; Life Source, bone marrow donor com, 1992-93; United Way, Crusade Mercy, minority outreach com, 1992-93; deacon, Baptist church; life mem, Nat Asn Advan Colored People; bd sec, MCEDC; Theta Boules Sigma Pi Phi Fraternity; life mem, VFW; Nat Adv Bd Negro Leagues Nat Mus. **Home Addr:** 14900 Alhambra St, Overland Park, KS 66224-3905. **Business Addr:** IL.

## ROGERS, RODNEY RAY, JR.

Basketball player, entrepreneur. **Personal:** Born Jun 20, 1971, Durham, NC; son of Willie Wadsworth (deceased) and Estella; married Tisa White; children: Roddreka, Rydeiah & Rodney Rogers II; married Faye Suggs; children: Denvonte Knox. **Educ:** Wake Forest Univ. **Career:** Basketball player (retired), entrepreneur; Denver Nuggets, forward, 1993-95; Los Angeles Clippers, forward, 1995-99; Phoenix Suns, forward, 1999-2002; Boston Celtics, forward, 2002; NJ Nets, forward, 2002-04; New Orleans Hornets, forward, 2004-05; Philadelphia 76ers, 2005; RRR Trucking Inc, owner, currently. **Home Addr:** , Durham, NC 27713. **Business Addr:** Owner, RRR Trucking Inc, 2900 E Pettigrew St, Durham, NC 27703.

## ROGERS, ROY LEE, JR.

Basketball player, basketball coach. **Personal:** Born Aug 19, 1973, Linden, AL; married Trish; children: Jasmine & Jordan. **Educ:** Univ Al, BS, mkt mgt, 1996. **Career:** Basketball player (retired), basketball coach; Vancouver Grizzlies, forward & power forward, 1996-97; Boston Celtics, 1997-98; Toronto Raptors, power forward, 1998; Denver Nuggets, power forward, 1999-2000; CSKA Moscow, 2000-01; Aurora Basket Jesi, Italy, 2002; Poland, 2003-04; Notec Inowroclaw, 2003-04; Huntsville Flight, asst coach, 2005; NJ Nets, asst coach; Tulsa 66ers, asst coach, 2006-07; Okla Storm, head coach, 2007; Boston Celtics, 2010-11; Detroit Pistons, 2011-13; Brooklyn Nets, asst coach, 2013; Wash Wizards, asst coach, 2014-16; Houston Rockets, assn coach, 2016-. **Business Addr:** Assistant Coach, Houston Rockets, 1510 Polk St, Houston, TX 77002, **Business Phone:** (202)661-5050.

## ROGERS, SAMMY LEE, SR.

Football player. **Personal:** Born May 30, 1970, Pontiac, MI; married Leslie S; children: Sam Jr, Aaron, Ariel & Armani Lee. **Educ:** Univ Colo. **Career:** Football player (retired); Buffalo Bills, 1994, right outside linebacker, 1995-97, left outside linebacker, 1998-99, linebacker, 1999-2000; San Diego Chargers, 2001; Atlanta Falcons, linebacker, 2002-03, free agt, 2002. **Home Addr:** 6340 Green Valley Cir Apt 110, Culver City, CA 90230-7093, **Home Phone:** (310)258-9558. **Business Addr:** Free Agent, Atlanta Falcons, 4400 Falcon Pkwy, Georgia, GA 30542, **Business Phone:** (770)965-3115.

## ROGERS, SHAUN CHRISTOPHER ORLANDO

Executive, football player. **Personal:** Born Mar 12, 1979, Houston, TX; son of Ernie. **Educ:** Univ Tex, grad. **Career:** Football player; Detroit Lions, defensive tackle & nose tackle & right defensive tackle, 2001-07; Cleveland Browns, defensive tackle & defensive end, 2008-10; New Orleans Saints, defensive tackle & nose tackle, 2011; New York Giants, defensive tackle & left defensive tackle & right defensive tackle, 2012-13; free agt, currently. **Honors/Awds:** Mel Farr Rookie of the Year; Pro Bowl sel, 2005-06 & 2008; Pro Bowl, 2004, 2005 & 2008. **Special Achievements:** Appeared in com advert, The Lion King, 2003. TV Series: "2001 NFL Draft", 2001; "ESPN's Sunday Night Football", 2005; "NFL Monday Night Football", 2008; "Rome Is Burning", 2010. **Business Addr:** MS World LLC, 1270 Crabb River Rd, Richmond, TX 77469, **Business Phone:** (847)864-8052.

## ROGERS, REV. DR. VICTOR ALVIN

Clergy, educator, association executive. **Personal:** Born Oct 2, 1944, St. Peter; son of Grafton Simmons and Violet; married Gloria Fay Buck; children: Nicholas, Paul & Matthew. **Educ:** Univ W Indies, LTH, 1971; Laurentian Univ, BA, 1973; Jackson State Univ, MA, sociol, 1977; Miss State Univ, PhD, sociol, 1987. **Career:** Diocese Barbados, St Paul's Church, cur, 1969-70, St Philip's Parish Church, cur, 1970-71; Diocese Long Island, St Philip's Episcopal Church, 1973-74; Diocese MSP, St Mark's, rector, 1974-83; St Luke's Episcopal Church, rector, 1983-; Southern Con State Univ, asst prof, 1992, adj prof, currently. **Orgs:** Bd mem, Downtown Coop Ministry, 1986; bd mem, Habitat Humanity, 1988; bd mem, Soc Increase Ministry, 1992. **Honors/Awds:** Outstanding Community Serv, Aldermanic Cit. **Special**

**Achievements:** Co-author with VV Prakassa Rao, Sex, Socio-Economic Status and Secular Achievement Among High School Students, The Researcher, Vol 9 winter, p 25-36. **Home Addr:** 1375 Paradise Ave, Hamden, CT 06514-1016, **Home Phone:** (203)281-1551. **Business Addr:** Rector, St Luke's Episcopal Church, 111 Whalley Ave, New Haven, CT 06511, **Business Phone:** (203)865-0141.

## ROGERS-GRUNDY, ETHEL W.

Educator, insurance executive. **Personal:** Born Dec 3, 1938, Macclesfield, NC; daughter of Russell Wooten and Martha Pitt Wooten; married Sherman; children: Duane A Rogers & Angela S. **Educ:** St Augustine Col, BA, 1960; Temple Univ, MEd, 1970; Cath Univ Am; Univ Md. **Career:** Educator, ins exec (retired); St Augustines Col, NC, asst dean stud, 1965-66; Johnston Co Sch, Smithfield, NC, asst dir headstart, 1966-67; Woodson St High Sch, chmn bus dept, 1972-74; Fed City Col Wash, adj prof, 1975; Franklin Life Ins Co, agency mgr; DC Bd Educ, coordr off. **Orgs:** Delta Phi Epsilon, 1969; Eastern Bus Teacher Asn; Nat Bus Educ Asn; DC Bus Educ Asn; charter pres, Prince Georges Co Alumnae Chap Delta Sigma Theta Inc; pres, Md Coun Deltas; secy, St Augustines Col Nat Alumni Asn; mem bd dir, Lung Asn Southern Minn Inc; Alpha Zeta Chap Delta Phi Epsilon; managing dir, Prince Georges Co; Nat Asn Advan Colored People; managing dir, Womens Polit Caucas Prince Georges Co; managing dir, Pan Hellenic Coun Prince Georges Co. **Home Addr:** 145 Leonard Lane, Harrisburg, PA 17111-4777, **Home Phone:** (717)545-3174.

## ROGERS-JONE, KELIS

Singer, songwriter. **Personal:** Born Aug 21, 1979, New York, NY; daughter of Kenneth and Eveliss; married Nasir Jones; children: Knight. **Career:** Singer & songwriter; R&B trio Black Ladies United, 1994-96; backup singerfor Gravediggaz' recording Fairytalz, 1997; Virgin Records, 1998-; Albums: Kaleidoscope, 1999; Wanderland, 2001; Tasty, exec producer, 2003; Kelis Was Here, 2006; The Hits, 2008; After Ten So Good, 2009; Flesh Tone, 2010; Food, 2014. TV series: "WaSanGo", 2001; "Me and Mr. Jones", exec producer, 2007; "Freaknik: The Musical", 2010. **Honors/Awds:** Kelis, 2001; NME Award, Best R&B Singer, 2001; Q magazine Award, Best Video ("Caughtout There"), 2003; Winner, Brit Award, Nominee, Grammy Awards, Twice. **Business Addr:** Singer, Songwriter, c/o Virgin Records, 338 N Foothill Rd, Beverly Hills, CA 90210, **Business Phone:** (310)278-1181.

## ROGERS-LOMAX, DR. ALICE FAYE

Physician, educator. **Personal:** Born Jan 20, 1950, Darlington, SC; daughter of James Rogers and Alice McCall Rogers; married Michael W; children: Lauren & Whitney. **Educ:** Holy Family Col, BA, 1972; Philadelphia Col Osteop Med, DO, 1976. **Career:** Philadelphia Col Osteop Med, asst prof pediat, 1979-80, chmn, divambulatory pediat, 1981, prof emer; NY Col Osteop Med, vis lectr, 1980; Sch Nursing Univ Pa, adj clin preceptor, 1981-; Osteop Med Ctr Philadelphia, chmn, div ambulatory pediat, 1981-89; Lomax Med Assoc, Philadelphia, Pa, pvt pediat pract, 1989-. **Orgs:** Am Osteop Asn, 1976-; Am Col Osteop Ped, 1977-; Pa Osteop Med Soc, 1979-; Stud Admis Comn, 1982-, Philadelphia Pediat Soc, 1983-; Ambulatory Pediat Asn, 1983-; Osteop Med Ctr, 1982-86; Med Soc Eastern Pa, 1987-; Am Acad Pediat. **Honors/Awds:** Beta Beta Beta Nat Biol Hon Soc, 1972; Legion Honor, mem, Chapel Four Chaplains, Philadelphia, 1983. **Home Addr:** 2041 Stone Ridge Lane Suite L, Villanova, PA 19085, **Home Phone:** (215)338-3652. **Business Addr:** 300 N 52nd St, Philadelphia, PA 19139-1518, **Business Phone:** (215)472-1500.

## ROGERS-REECE, SHIRLEY

Executive, school administrator, vice president (organization). **Personal:** Born Carson, CA; married Guy; children: 3. **Career:** McDonalds Corp, Opers Trainee, restaurant mgr, 1981, area supvr, 1982-83, opers consult, 1983-85; McDonalds Hamburger Univ, prof, 1986-87, training mgr, 1987-88, opers mgr, 1988-90, field serv mgr, 1990-91, dean, 1991-94, Indonesia, dir opers, 1995-97, gen mgr, 1997; Worldwide Training, Learning & Develop, vpres, 2004-06; McDonalds Corp, Ohio region, vpres & gen mgr, 2006-. **Orgs:** Bd mem, YWCA; Columbus Acad; First Tee; Hon Chair UNCF Celebrity Golf Tournament; bd trustee, Ronald McDonald Childrens Charities, currently. **Business Addr:** Vice President, General Manager, McDonalds Corp, 2 Easton Oval Suite 200, Columbus, OH 43219-6013, **Business Phone:** (614)418-3300.

## ROHADFOX, DR. RONALD OTTO

Executive director, executive. **Personal:** Born Mar 12, 1935, Syracuse, NY; son of Otto and Rita; children: Renwick, Roderick, Reginald & Rebekah. **Educ:** Ind Inst Technol, BSCE, 1961; Woodbury Univ, MBA, 1980; Century Univ, PhD, 1984. **Career:** Anal Construct Co, pres; Rohadfox Construct Control Servs Corp, chief exec officer, pres, currently. **Orgs:** Kappa Alpha Psi, 1960; fel Am Soc Civil Engrs, 1996; Am Pub Works Asn, 1977, Soc Mkt Prof Serv, 1982; Nat Asn Minority Contractors, 1985. **Honors/Awds:** Republican Inner Circle, 1985; NC Transp Board, Appointment, 1991-92. **Special Achievements:** One of the Top 100 Black Successful Businessmen, Black Enterprise Magazine, 1974. **Home Addr:** 2498 Brucewood Rd, Graham, NC 27253. **Business Addr:** President, Chief Executive Officer, Rohadfox Construction Control Services Corp, 1410 W Chapel Hill St, Durham, NC 27701, **Business Phone:** (919)682-5741.

## ROHE, BERNIE (BERNIE GODDARD)

Designer, executive. **Personal:** married Uli. **Educ:** Barbizon Sch Modeling. **Career:** Liz Claiborne, fashion model, 1975-91; Roberto Cavalli, fashion model, 1977-90; Bernie New York Inc, pres & chief designer, 1991-. **Special Achievements:** Featured in Essence Mag, Black Enterprise Mag; TV Show, "B. Smith with Style". **Business Addr:** President, Chief Designer, Bernie of New York Inc, 241 W 37th St Suite 801, New York, NY 10018-6764, **Business Phone:** (212)764-3320.

## ROJAS, DON

Entrepreneur, journalist. **Personal:** Born Jan 1, 1949?; married Karen Codrington; children: 3. **Educ:** Univ Wis Madison, jour & commun. **Career:** Afro Am newspaper, asst ed; Grenadian Prime Minister Maurice Bishop, press secy, 1979-83; Nat Granadian newspaper, ed chief, 1979-83; NY Amsterdam News, exec ed & asst publ, 1990; Pacifica sta WBAI, gen mgr; New York Amsterdam News, exec ed; Oxfam Am, media mgr; Black World Radio Network, founder, 1996-; Communs New Tomorrow LLC, founder, pres & chief exec officer, 1996-; Black World Today, chief exec officer, founder, publ, currently. **Orgs:** Exec bd, Int Orgn Journlists, 1980; asst dir commun, Nat Urban League; communs dir, Nat Asn Advan Colored People, 1993. **Honors/Awds:** Webby Award, The Black World Today, 1998; Silicon Alley Dozen, 1999; influential voice of the Citys African American communities for over 100 years; Outstanding Contribution for Journalism, Inst Caribbean Studies. **Special Achievements:** First Communications Director of the National Association for the Advancement of Colored People. **Business Addr:** Founder, President, Chief Executive Officer, The Black World Today, 729 E Pratt St Suite 500, Baltimore, MD 21202, **Business Phone:** (410)521-4678.

## ROKER, ALBERT LINCOLN

Television broadcaster, writer. **Personal:** Born Aug 20, 1954, Queens, NY; son of Albert Lincoln Sr and Isabel; married Deborah Roberts; children: 3. **Educ:** State Univ NY, Oswego, BA, commun, 1976. **Career:** WTVH-TV, Syracuse, NY, weekend weatherman, 1974; WTTG; CNBC, meteorologist & talk show host, 1978; NBC News, regular substitute for forecaster, 1983-96, Today Show, host, 1990-95, The Al Roker Show, host, 1995, MSNBC game show, 1996-97; WNBC, New York, weekend meteorologist & weekend weathercaster, 1983; Al Roker Prod Inc, founder & owner, 1994-; CNBC Today Show, weatherman, 1996-; The Weather Channel, co-host, 2009; The Morning Show Murders, 2009; Author: Don't Make Me Stop This Car: Adventures in Fatherhood, 2001; Big Bad Book of Barbecue, 2002; Hassle-Free Holiday Cookbook, 2003; parenthood; two cookbooks; The Morning Show Murders; In Celebration of Dads & Fatherhood, 2005. **Orgs:** Fel Ronald McDonald House Charities, 2007-. **Honors/Awds:** Emmy Awards; 1997 Daytime Emmy Award nominee, Outstanding Game Show Host; hon doctorate, State Univ New York, Oswego. **Special Achievements:** Television show : "Family Guy"; Films: Undercover Brother; Madagascar; The Simpsons; Drawn Together; Unaccompanied Minors; Men in Black. **Business Addr:** Owner, Al Roker Productions Inc, 250 W 57th St Suite 1525, New York, NY 10107, **Business Phone:** (212)757-8500.

## ROLAND, BENAUTRICE, JR.

Manager. **Personal:** Born Dec 11, 1945, Detroit, MI; married Brenda Thornton; children: Michele S & Michael L. **Educ:** Univ Detroit, BS, finance, 1972; Wharton Grad Sch Univ PA, MBA, finance, 1974. **Career:** Morgan Guaranty Trust NY, euro-currency trader, 1974-75; Ford Motor Co, financial analyst, 1975-79; MI Bell Tele Co, staff supr, 1979-; BRS Industries Ltd, agent. **Orgs:** Bd dirs, Univ Pa Alumni Club; co-chmn, Secondary Sch Com. **Home Addr:** 3171 Lindenwood Dr, Dearborn, MI 48120, **Home Phone:** (313)336-9549.

## ROLISON, NATE (NATHAM MARDIS ROLISON)

Baseball player. **Personal:** Born Mar 27, 1977, Petal, MS. **Career:** Baseball player (retired); Minor League: Gulf Coast Marlins, 1995, 2001; Kane County, 1996; Brevard County, 1997, 2001; Portland Sea Dogs, 1998-99, 2001; Calgary Cannons, 2000-02; Maj League: Fla Marlins, infielder, 2000; Tacoma Rainiers, 2002; Seattle Mariners, 2002; Colombus Clippers, 2003; Chicago White Sox, infielder, 2004.

## ROLLE, JANET

Vice president (organization), executive, manager. **Personal:** Born Dec 25, 1961, Mt. Vernon, NY; daughter of William Sr and Barbara; married Mark Keye; children: Jason. **Educ:** State Univ NY, Purchase, BFA, dance, 1984; Columbia Univ Bus Sch, MBA, mkt & film, 1991; Stanford Univ Law Sch, dir col, 2015. **Career:** HBO, spec asst chmn, 1991-92, mgr, multiplex mkt, 1992-93, dir mkt & sales prom; MTV Networks, Programming enterprises & bus develop, vpres, 2000-05; Am Online Inc, Am Online Black Voices serv, vpres & gen mgr, 2005-07; BET Networks, exec vprs & chief mktg officer, 2007-11; CNN Worldwide, exec vprs & chief mktg officer, 2011-13; Independent Consult, prin, 2014-; Carver Bancorp, dir. **Orgs:** Black filmmaker found, 1990-; NY women film & TV, 1991-; NY Coalition 100 Black Women, 1992-; mentor, Harlem YMCA Mentoring Prog, 1993-; chairperson, Multicultural Participation Comn; bd dir, US Tennis Asn; bd adv, City At Peace NY; bd dir, Coun Urban Professionals; chair, 2003-08, nominating comt, 2009-12, presidential appointee, 2014, Us Tennis Asn; dir, Carver Bancorp Inc, 2010; dir, Am Found Univ W Indies, 2011; WOMEN Am, 2013. **Home Addr:** 420 Highland Ave, Mount Vernon, NY 10553. **Business Addr:** Executive Vice President, Chief Marketing Officer, BET Networks, 1235 W St NE, Washington, DC 20018-1211, **Business Phone:** (202)608-2000.

## ROLLINS, AVON WILLIAM, SR.

Government official, executive director. **Personal:** Born Sep 16, 1941, Knoxville, TN; son of Ralph Kershaw and Josephine Rollins Lee; married Sheryl Clark; children: Avon Jr & Avondria F. **Educ:** Knoxville Col; Univ Tenn. **Career:** Stud Nonviolent Coord Comn, nat exec; Southern Christian Leadership Conf, spec asst; Tenn Valley Authority, mgr; Rollins & Assocs Inc, pres & chief exec officer; Beck Cult Exchange Ctr Inc, exec dir & chief exec officer, currently; Knoxville-based Rollins & Assocs Inc, pres & chief exec officer; Nat Urban League, adj prof. **Orgs:** Co-founder, nat exec, Stud Non-violent Coord Comt Raleigh NC, 1960; asst late Rev Dr Martin Luther King Jr; bd dir, Mgt Comn Knoxville Int Energy Expos, 1982; chmn & founder, Magnolia Fed Savings & Loan Asn; adv, chmn & founder, TVA Employees Minority Invest Forum; Chancellors Asn; alumnus mem, Univ Tenn; pres, Round Table Knoxville Col; chmn emer, chmn bd & founder, Greater Knoxville Minority Bus Bur Inc; chmn & pres, Knoxville Comm Coop; mem, Nat Rural Cable TV Task Force; co-founder, Greater Knoxville Urban League; co-founder & bd dir, Knoxville Opportunity Indust Ctr Inc; US Cong Black Caucus Braintrust; E Tenn Cancer Socs. **Home Addr:** 3321 Andover Dr, Knoxville, TN 37914-5703, **Home Phone:** (865)544-2808. **Business Addr:** Chief Executive Officer, Director, Beck Cultural Exchange Center Inc, 1927 Dandridge Ave, Knoxville, TN 37915-1909, **Business Phone:** (865)524-8461.

## ROLLINS, ETHEL EUGENIA

Social worker. **Personal:** Born Feb 16, 1932, Paris, TX; daughter of Elisha and Julia; married Edward C; children: Vyla LeJeune & Rojeune Bali. **Educ:** Jarvis Christian Col, BA, 1954; Univ Pittsburgh, MSW, 1958. **Career:** Social worker (retired); Dayton C Psychol Hosp & Child Guid Clin, psychol soc worker, 1958-62; Family & Childrens Serv Asn Dayton, psychol soc worker, 1964-65; Denver County Pub Sch Psychol Serv, sch social worker, 1965-68; Ft Logan Ment Health Ctr, Denver, psychol soc worker, 1972-95; Denver Univ, assoc prof soc work, 1975. **Orgs:** Colo Christian Home Bd, Colo Christian Home C, Denver, 1970-75; human servs, adv bd, Metro State Col, Denver, 1979-84, chap, 1984-; week compassion comn, Christian Ch Disciples Christ Indianapolis, 1975-80; adv bd, Mother to Mother Ministry, 1978-80; bd & comn mem, Habitat Humanity, 1979-80; leg & social concerns, Colo Coun Church, 1980-82; sec, Colo coun Churches, 1981-82; chmn, Outreach Christian Church Disciples Christ Colo, WY Reg Outreach Reg Needs, 1982-83; activist, Peace/Justice Movement/Nuclear Freeze Movement, 1982-84; evaluator, Ann Ethnic Youth Leadership Conf, United Methodist Church, 1986-91; vol/lay-ministry /vice chair person, Info & Servs, Christian Church Disciples Christ Gen Assembly, 1997; team mem, Anti-racism ProreCouniation Initative, Cent Rocky Mountain region Christian Church, 2001-02. **Honors/Awds:** Hon Award for Leadership State Fair, TX 4-H Club, 1949; "Student Contributing Most to the Religious Life of Campus" Award, Jarvis Christian Col, 1952; Outstanding Leadership Award, Col Christian Home, 1971-75; Rojeune, Edward & Ethel appeared as family on KCNC NBC Affil Denver CO, 1983; discussing film "The Day After"; Outstanding Member, Chair, Human Services Dept/Human Serv Educ Org, 1988. **Special Achievements:** Author, "Changing Trends in Adoption", Nat Conf Social Welfare, 1971. **Home Addr:** 2439 S Dahlia Lane, Denver, CO 80222-6119.

## ROLLINS, DR. JUDITH ANN

Sociologist, educator, writer. **Personal:** Born Boston, MA; daughter of Edward B and Edith F. **Educ:** Howard Univ, BA, 1970, MA, 1972; Brandeis Univ, PhD, 1983. **Career:** Fed City Col, instr sociol, 1972-77; Boston Col, instr sociol, 1977-83; Northeastern Univ, asst prof sociol, 1983-84; Simmons Col, from asst prof to assoc prof, 1984-92; Wellesley Col, assoc prof Africana studies & sociol, 1992-95, prof, 1995-2009; prof emer, 2009-; Books: Between Women: Domestics and Their Employers, 1985; All is Never Said: The Narrative of Odette Harper Hines, 1995; Voices of Concern: Nevisian Women's Issues, 2010. **Orgs:** Am Sociol Asn; Asn Black Sociologists; Soc Study Soc Probs; Delta Sigma Theta Sorority; Asn Soc & Behav Scientists; Caribbean Studies Asn; pres, Asn Black Sociologists, 2007-2009; Int Sociol Asn. **Business Addr:** Professor emerita, Wellesley College, 106 Cent St, Wellesley, MA 02481.

## ROLLINS, LEE OWEN

Executive. **Personal:** Born Dec 22, 1938, Kansas City, KS; married Rosalie D; children: Lori, Linda, Larry, Lonny & Lyle. **Educ:** Univ Nebr, psychol, 1963. **Career:** Flintkote Co, Los Angeles, Calif, mkt rep, 1963-66; San Diego Gas & Elec, lic negotiator, 1966-68, employ rep, 1968-78, mgr employ, 1979. **Orgs:** Outstanding Kappa Man ETA Chap Univ Nebr, 1960; vpres, transp SD Jr C C, 1970-74; dir, Southeast Rotary, 1974-79; chmn, Affirmative Action Com WCPA, 1975-78; bd mem, Western Col Placement Asn, 1975-80; vpres, campus rels Soc Advan Mgt, 1979-; dir, Amigos del Serv, 1979-80. **Home Addr:** 10594 Ponder Way, San Diego, CA 92126. **Business Addr:** Manager, San Diego Gas & Electric Co, 101 Ash St, San Diego, CA 92101.

**ROLLINS, SONNY.** **See ROLLINS, WALTER THEODORE.**

## ROLLINS, TREE (WAYNE MONTE ROLLINS)

Basketball player, basketball coach. **Personal:** Born Jun 16, 1955, Winter Haven, FL; married Michelle; children: Nicolas, Undria, Kendall & Katreesa. **Educ:** Clemson Univ, attended 1977. **Career:** Basketball player (retired), basketball coach; Atlanta Hawks, ctr, 1977-88; Cleveland Cavaliers, 1988-90; Detroit Pistons, 1990-91; Houston Rockets, 1991-93; Orlando Magic, backup ctr, 1993-95, asst coach, 1996-99; Ky Colonels, pres & gen mgr, 1994-; Greenville Groove, coach; NBA Pre-Draft Camp, head coach; Wash Wizards, asst coach, 1999-2000; Ind Pacers, asst coach, 2000-02; Greenville Groove, head coach, 2002-03, 2006; Wash Mystics, asst coach, 2006-07, interim head coach, 2007-08; WNBA Chicago Sky, asst coach, 2013-. **Business Addr:** Assistant Coach, WNBA Chicago Sky, 5500 W Howard, Skokie, IL 60077, **Business Phone:** (312)828-9550.

## ROLLINS, WALTER THEODORE (SONNY ROLLINS)

Composer, musician. **Personal:** Born Sep 7, 1930, New York, NY; son of Valborg and Walter; married Lucille Pearson; married Dawn Finney. **Career:** Pianist, saxophonist, tenor; Rec, 1949, Recorded with Bud Powell, Dizzy Gillespie, Max Roach, Clifford Brown & Thelonious Monk; discography contains 71 recordings, 1997; Albums: Sonny Rollins Quartet, 1951; Sonny & the Stars, 1951; Sonny Rollins with the Modern Jazz Quartet, 1951; Mambo Jazz, 1951; Moving Out, 1954; Sonny Rollins Plays Jazz Classics, 1954; Sonny Rollins Quintet, 1954; Taking Care of Business, 1955; Work Time, 1955; Saxophone Colossus, 1956; Sonny Rollins Plus Four, 1956; Three Giants, 1956; Tenor Madness, 1956; Rollins Plays for Bird, 1956; Sonny Boy, 1956; Tour de Force, 1956; Sonny Rollins, Vol. 1, 1956; Alternate Takes, 1957; Way Out West, 1957; Sonny Rollins, Vol. 2, 1957; Wail March, 1957; Sonny's Time, 1957; Newk's Time, 1957; Night at the Village Vanguard, 1957; Sonny Rollins Plays/Jimmy Cleveland Plays, 1957; European Concerts, 1957; Sonny Side Up, 1957; Sonny Rollins On Impulse, 1966; East Broadway Run Down, 1966; Don't Stop the Carnival, 1978; This Is What I Do, 2000; Without a Song: The 9/11 Concert, 2001; Sonny Please, 2006; Road Shows, Vol. 1, 2008; Road Shows, Vol. 2, 2011; Road Shows, Vol. 3, 2014. **Honors/Awds:** Numerous honors & awards including Guggenheim Fellow, 1972; Hall of Fame, Downbeat Mag; hon Doctorate, Music Bard Col, 1992; hon doctorate fine arts, Wesleyan Univ, 1998; hon doctorate music, Long Island Univ, 1998; hon doctorate, fine arts, Duke Univ, 1999; Lifetime Achievement Award, Tufts Univ, 1996, hon doctorate music, Grammy Award, 2001

& 2006; Grammy Award for lifetime achievement, 2004; New England Conserv, 2002; hon doctorate Music Berklee Col Music, 2003 & Polar Music Prize, 2007; National Medal of Arts, 2010; Kennedy Center Honors, 2011. **Special Achievements:** The city of Minneapolis, Minnesota officially named 31 October 2006 after Rollins in honor of his achievements and contributions to the world of jazz. **Home Addr:** Rte 9G, Germantown, NY 12526, **Home Phone:** (518)537-6112. **Business Addr:** Composer, Rte 9G, Germantown, NY 12526, **Business Phone:** (518)537-6112.

**ROLLINS, WAYNE MONTE. See ROLLINS, TREE.**

## ROMAIN, PIERRE R.
Executive. **Personal:** Born Sep 24, 1967, Nyack, NY. **Career:** Jack La Lanne fitness ctr, prog dir & mgr, 1986; JP & Assocs Advert, pres; Harolds Evergreen Restaurant, partner & dir mkt, 1990-91; Giraldi Entertainment, vpres, 1991-93; Pierre Romain Inc, chmn, chief exec officer & producer, 1994-; Workout Partners Fitness Inc, chmn & chief exec officer, 1994. **Orgs:** Dir tv & film prod, St. Jude's Champions Charity Found, 1996; Chief Financial Officer Serv Network Group. **Business Addr:** Chairman, Chief Executive Officer, Workout Partners Fitness Inc, 208 W 29th St Suite 203, New York, NY 10001, **Business Phone:** (212)564-0177.

**ROMEO, LIL. See MILLER, PERCY ROMEO, JR.**

## ROMES, CHARLES MICHAEL
Football player. **Personal:** Born Dec 16, 1954, Verdun; married Redalia; children: Twila Redalia. **Educ:** NC Cent Univ. **Career:** Football player (retired); Buffalo Bills, right cornerback, 1977-86; San Diego Chargers, 1987; Seattle Seahawks, 1988.

## ROMNEY, EDGAR O.
Executive director, labor activist. **Personal:** Born Feb 9, 1943, New York, NY; son of Edward Sr and Ida Johnstone; married Gladys Talbot; children: Juliette, Monique, Nicola & Edgar Jr. **Educ:** Hunter Col, attended 1975; Empire State Labor Col, attended 1982. **Career:** Local 99, Int Ladies' Garment Workers' Union, New York, NY, organizer & bus agt, 1966-75; Local 23-25, Int Ladies' Garment Workers' Union, dir orgn, 1976-78, asst mgr, 1978-83, mgr & secy, 1983; Int Ladies' Garment Workers' Union, New York, NY, exec vpres, 1989-; UNITE!, exec vpres, 1995; UNITE HERE, vpres, secy-treas; Workers United, secy-treas, pres, 2009; Amalgamated Bank, bd mem. **Orgs:** Bd dir, Am Labor ORT Fedn, 1986-; bd dir, Garment Indust Develop Corp, 1987-; nat secy, A Philip Randolph Inst, 1987-; bd dir, NY Urban League, 1987-; bd dir, NY State Dept Labor Garment Adv Coun, 1988-; bd dir, Bayard Rustin Fund, 1989-; co-chair, New York Labor Comt Against Apartheid, 1989-94; Brain trust Labor Issues, 1991-; second vpres, NY Labor Coun AFL-CIO, 1992-; co-chmn, New York Comt African Labor Solidarity, 1994-; Cong Black Caucus. **Honors/Awds:** Recognition Award, Negro Labor Comt, 1984; Nelson Mandela Award, Coalition Black Trade Unionists, 1984, 1989; Achievement Award, NAACP, NY Br, 1987; Roberto Clemente Appreciation Award & Hispanic Labor Comt, 1987; NAACP Man of the Year Award, NAACP, 1987; Recognition Award, China town, YMCA, 1988; Outstanding Leadership in Labor & Community Service, Borough of Manhattan Community Col, 1989; Leadership Award, Am ORT Fedn, 1989; Outstanding Service & Commitment & Hispanic Labor Comt, 1989; Distinguished Service Award, AFL-CIO, 1990. **Special Achievements:** First African-American to head an American labor federation. **Home Addr:** 20618 47th Ave, Bayside, NY 11361, **Home Phone:** (718)428-1096. **Business Addr:** President, Workers United, 31 W 15th St 3rd Fl, New York, NY 10011, **Business Phone:** (917)832-1558.

## RONEY, RAYMOND GEORGE
Educator, publisher. **Personal:** Born Jul 26, 1941, Philadelphia, PA; son of Wallace and Rosezell Harris; married Ruth A Westgaph; children: Andre. **Educ:** Cent State Univ, BA, polit sci, 1963; Pratt Inst, MS, libr sci, 1965; Cath Univ, post grad, 1985. **Career:** Howard Univ Libr, supr ref dept, 1965-66; Nat League Cities & US Conf Mayors, dir libr serv, 1966-70; Wash Tech Inst, dir libr serv, 1970-78, chmn med tech dept, 1971-78; Univ DC, dep dir learning resources, 1978-83; El Camino Col, assoc dean learning resources, 1984, dean instrnl serv, 1988-, retired; Libr Mosaics Mag, publ & founder, 1989-; Yenor Inc, pres & publ, 1989-. **Orgs:** Pres, Shepherd Pk Citizens Asn, DC, 1972-74; exec bd, Paul Community Sch, 1974-83; bd mem, COLT, 1978; Phi Delta Kappa, 1980; pres, Coun Lib & Media Tech, 1983; United Way Adv Bd, 1988-; dir, Calif Libr Employees Asn, 1988; libr adv bd, Afro-Am Mus, CA, 1989-; long range planning comt mem, Calif Libr Asn, 1988-91, mem comt, 1989-91; prog planning comt mem, CARL, 1989-91; bd mem, Learning Resources Asn Calif Community Col, 1994-; pres, Cent State Univ S Calif Alumni Chap, 1999-; Am Libr Asn. **Honors/Awds:** Outstanding Achievement, Bright Hope Baptist Church, 1963; Grass Roots Award, DC Fed Civic & Citizens Asn, 1975; Outstanding Achievement, Shepherd Park Citizens Asn, 1975; Administrative Excellence Award, INTELECOM, 1993; ADR of the Year Award, Calif Asn Post Secondary Educ & Disabilities, 1997; Special Friend Award, El Camino Alumni Asn, 2000. **Home Addr:** 5640 W 63rd St, Los Angeles, CA 90056-2013, **Home Phone:** (310)410-1573. **Business Addr:** President, Publisher, Yenor Inc, PO Box 5171, Culver City, CA 90231, **Business Phone:** (310)645-4998.

**ROOKS, SEAN LESTER. See Obituaries Section.**

## ROPER, BOBBY L.
School administrator, school principal, educator. **Personal:** Born Jan 1, 1930, Chicago, IL; son of William and Irvia Carter; children: Reginald. **Educ:** Chicago Teachers Col, BEd, 1959; Chicago State Univ, MS, 1966. **Career:** Principal (retired); Chicago Pub Sch, master teacher, 1962-64, adjust teacher, 1965-68, asst prin, 1968-71; Lawndale Comm Acad, prin. **Orgs:** Bd dir, Lawndale Homemakers, 1970-75; bd dir, Chicago Youth, 1975-; bd dir, Marcy New berry, 1982-83. **Home Addr:** 9206 S Bennett, Chicago, IL 60617, **Home Phone:** (773)221-9150.

## ROPER, DEIDRE MURIEL (DJ SPINDERELLA)
Rap musician, business owner. **Personal:** Born Aug 3, 1971, New York, NY; children: Christenese. **Career:** Films: Stay Tuned, 1992; Kazaam, 1996; TV includes: Sinatra:"The 6th Annual Soul Train Music Awards", 1992; "Saturday Night Live", 1994; "80 Years My Way", 1995; "Wrestle mania XI", 1995; KKBT fm, 2003-06; The Surreal Life, 2005; Behind the Music, 2005; Comedy Central Roast of Flavor Flav, 2007; The Salt-N-Pepa Show, 2007; Singer:"Juice", 1992; "Space Jam", 1996; beauty salon, owner, 1997; She Things Salon & Day Spa, owner, currently; . **Orgs:** Hip hop group; Salt N Pepa. **Business Addr:** Owner, Rapper, She Things Salon & Day Spa, 230-08 S Conduit Ave, Jamaica, NY 11413, **Business Phone:** (718)276-5212.

## ROPER, RICHARD WALTER
Executive. **Personal:** Born Sep 20, 1945, DeLand, FL; son of Henry and Dorothe; married Marlene Peacock; children: Jelani Y & Akil S. **Educ:** WVa State Univ, econs, 1965; Rutgers Univ, BA, econs, 1968; Princeton Univ, MA, pub policy, 1971. **Career:** NJ Dept Higher Educ, Trenton, NJ, asst vice chancellor, 1968-69; Dept Transp & Plng Greater London Coun, London, res asst, 1971; Mayors Educ Task Force, Off Newark Studies, Newark, NJ, staff coordr, 1971-72; NJ Dept Insts & Agencies, Div Youth & Family Servs, Trenton, NJ, 1972-73; Greater Newark Urban Coaltion, NJ Educ Reform Proj, Newark, NJ, dir, 1973-74; Mayor Kenneth A Gibson, Newark, NJ, legis aide, 1974-76; Off Newark Metrop Studies, Newark, NJ, dir, 1976-78; Carter Admin, asst, 1978-80; US Dept Com, Off Secy, Wash, DC, dir, 1979-80, spec asst intergovernmental rels; Woodrow Princeton Univ, Wilson Sch Pub & Int Affairs, lectr pub & int affairs, dir, 1980-88, asst dean grad career servs & govt rels, 1988-92; Port Authoritys Off Econ Policy Anal, dir, 1992; Off State & Local Govt Assistance, dir; Roper Groups, founder & pres, 1996-2007; Grad Career Serv & Govt Rels, asst dean; Port Authority New York & New Jersey, Dept Plng, dir, currently; Nelson A Rockefeller Inst Govt, sr fel, Nj Field Res Analyst, 2013-; Pub Policy Consult, 2010-. **Orgs:** Bd trustee, Newark Pub Radio; Gov Taskforce Child Abuse & Neglect, 1984-; NJ Child Life Protection Comn; bd dir, NJ Pub Policy Res Inst; bd trustee, exec comt mem, Boys' & Girls' Clubs Newark, NJ; bd dir, Asn Black Princeton Alumni; bd dir, Greater Jamaica Develop Corp, NY; bd overseers, Rutgers Univ Found; adv comt, Ctr Govt Servs, Rutgers Univ; adv bd, Nj Nat Ctr Pub Productivity; dir, Prog NJ Affairs; exec dir, Coun NJ Affairs; trustee, Newark Emergency Serv Families; bd, Newarks Econ Develop Corp; Brick City Develop Corp; fel Nj Supreme Courts Adv Committe. **Home Addr:** 12 Rutgers St, Maplewood, NJ 07040, **Home Phone:** (973)763-2201. **Business Addr:** Founder & President, The Roper Group, 550 Broad St Suite 601, Newark, NJ 07102, **Business Phone:** (973)286-2780.

## ROSCOE, DR. WILMA J.
Association executive, administrator. **Personal:** Born Aug 24, 1938, Kershaw, SC; daughter of Chalmers Harris and Estelle Harris; married Alfred D Roscoe Jr; children: Alfred D III, Jenae V & Jeneen B. **Educ:** Livingstone Col, Salisbury, NC, BS, 1960. **Career:** Howard Univ, Wash, DC, admis asst, 1963-69; Fayetteville State Univ, Fayetteville, NC, dir tutorial prog, 1969-74; Nat Asn Equal Opportunity Higher Educ, Wash, DC, vpres, sr vpres & chief operating officer, 1975-96; interim pres & chief exec officer, 1996-97. **Orgs:** Am Personnel & Guid Asn; Nat Coalition Black Meeting Planners; Delta Sigma Theta; Boys and Girls Club, 1980-86; Alfred St. Baptist Church, 1981; Nat Coun Negro Women; Nat Polit Cong Black Women, mem, Inc Nat Urban League. **Honors/Awds:** Distinguished Service Award, Nat Asn Equal Opportunity Higher Educ, 1986; Hon degrees: Miles Col, AR Baptist Col, Livingstone Col, Shaw Univ; Nat Bus League Award; Outstanding Service Award, Langston Univ; Outstanding Service Award, Denmark Tech Col; Inducted Livingstone College Leaders Hall of Fame; Inducted National Black College Hall of Fame Atlanta. **Home Addr:** 6001 Joyce Dr, Temple Hills, MD 20748, **Home Phone:** (301)899-6690. **Business Addr:** MD.

## ROSE, ANIKA NONI
Actor. **Personal:** Born Sep 6, 1972, Bloomfield, CT. **Educ:** Am Conserv Theater. **Career:** Films: King of the Bingo Game, 1999; From Justin to Kelly, 2003; Temptation, 2004; Surviving Christmas, 2004; Dream girls, 2006; One Part Sugar, 2007; Razor, 2007; Just Add Water, 2007; The Princess and the Frog, 2009; For Colored Girls, 2010; Company, 2011; Skyler, 2012; As Cool As I Am, 2013; Half of a Yellow Sun, 2013; Imperial Dreams, 2014. TV series: "100 Centre Street, "2001; "Third Watch", 2002; "Caroline, or Change", 2004; "The Startet Wife", 2007; "The No 1 Ladies' Detective Agency", 2008-09; "Tavis Smiley", 2009; "The Good Wife", 2010-11; "The Watsons Go to Birmingham", 2013; "A Day Late and a Dollar Short", 2014. Stage: Valley Song, 1998; Threepenny Opera, 1999; Tartuffe, 1999; Footloose (musical), 2000; Carmen Jones, 2001; Caroline, or Change, 2003-04; Cat on a Hot Tin Roof, 2008; Company, 2011. **Honors/Awds:** Tony Award for Best Performance by a Featured Actress in a Musical, 2004; Lucille Lortell Award; Theatre World Award; Clarence Derwent Award; Los Angeles Critic's Circle Award; Ovation Award; Obie Award; Drama-Logue Ensemble Award; Black Reel Award, 2010, 2014. **Business Addr:** Actress, c/o Don Buchwald & Associates, 10 E 44th St, New York, NY 10017, **Business Phone:** (212)867-1070.

## ROSE, BESSIE L.
Electrical engineer. **Personal:** Born Mar 2, 1958, Lafayette, LA; daughter of Andrew and Iritha Stevens. **Educ:** Southern Univ, Baton Rouge, BSEE, 1980. **Career:** Naval Air Rework Faci, Pensacola, coop stud, 1976-78; Xerox, Rochester, summer intern, 1979; Commonwealth Edison, Chicago, elec engr, 1980-. **Orgs:** Alpha Kappa Alpha, 1977-; Nat Black MBA Asn, 1990-; League of Black Women, 1990-. **Special Achievements:** Section Engr (responsible for defining, developing and implementing an entirely new dept on quality control). **Home Addr:** 5137 S Ellis Ave Suite 2, Chicago, IL 60615, **Home Phone:** (773)955-0384. **Business Addr:** Section Engineer, Commonwealth Edison Co, 1319 S 1st Ave, Maywood, IL 60153, **Business Phone:** (708)450-5267.

## ROSE, JALEN ANTHONY
Basketball player, broadcaster, executive. **Personal:** Born Jan 30, 1973, Detroit, MI; son of Jimmy Walker (deceased). **Educ:** Univ Mich, attended 1994; Univ Md, Univ Col, BS, mgt studies, 2005. **Career:** Basketball player (retired), broadcaster, executive; Denver Nuggets, guard, 1994-96; Ind Pacers, 1996-2002; Chicago Bulls, 2002-04; Toronto Raptors, 2004-06; New York Knicks, guard-forward, 2006; Phoenix Suns, 2006-07; ESPN, studio analyst & broadcaster, 2007-; Three Tier Entertainment, chief exec officer & founder, 2007-. **Orgs:** Founder, Jalen Rose Found; Make-a-Wish Found; Fab Five. **Honors/Awds:** All-Rookie Second Team, Nat Basketball Asn, 1995; Most Improved Player Award, Nat Basketball Asn, 2000; Fox Sports Net Bull of the Year, 2002-03; CDW Chicago Bulls Player of the Year, 2002-03; Chicago Bulls Lubin Award, 2003; Community Assist Award, Nat Basketball Asn, 2003, 2005; Magic Johnson Award, Prof Basketball Writers Asn, 2003; Eastern Conference Player of the Week, Nat Basketball Asn, 2005; One of America's Leading Individual Donor Black Philanthropists, Black Enterprise Magazine. **Business Addr:** Chief Executive Officer, Founder, Three Tier Entertainment, 8981 Sunset Blvd Suite 103, West Hollywood, CA 90069, **Business Phone:** (310)888-7774.

## ROSE, LINDA D.
College administrator, college teacher, college president. **Personal:** children: 2. **Educ:** W Los Angeles Col, AA; Calif State Univ, Dominguez Hills, BA, MA, 1993; Univ Calif, Los Angeles, EdD, 2007. **Career:** TRW, employee; Cerritos Col, fac mem, 1994-2005, instrnl dean, 2005-11; Santa Ana Col, vpres acad affairs, 2011-14, pres, 2016-; Los Angeles Southwest Col, 2014-16. **Orgs:** Mem bd dirs, Los Angeles Southwest Col Found; Taller San Jose; Calif Community Col Chancellors Off, Workforce & Econ Develop Prog Action Comt. **Honors/Awds:** Cerritos College Outstanding Administrator Award; Cerritos College Outstanding Faculty Award for the Liberal Arts Division; National Institute for Staff and Organizational Development Teaching Excellence Award. **Business Addr:** Santa Ana College, 1530 West 17th St, Santa Ana, CA 92706, **Business Phone:** (714)564-6975.

## ROSE, MALIK JABARI
Basketball player. **Personal:** Born Nov 23, 1974, Philadelphia, PA. **Educ:** Drexel Univ, BS, educ & comput info systs, 1996, MS, sports mgt, 2011. **Career:** Basketball player (retired), executive; Charlotte Hornets, forward & power forward, 1996-97; San Antonio Spurs, power forward, 1997-2005; Malik Philly Phamous, owner, 2003; New York Knicks, forward & power forward, 2005-09; Okla City Thunder, 2009; Madison Sq Garden Co, color analyst, 2009-11; Fox Sports Southwest, color analyst, 2010-11; Comcast Sports, color analyst, 2012-; New York Knicks, studio analyst, currently; Austin Toros, lead color analyst, currently; Philadelphia 76ers, broadcaster, 2011-15; Atlanta Hawks, mgr, currently. **Honors/Awds:** America East Conference Player of the Year, 1995, 1996; NBA champion, 1999, 2003; NBA Community Assist Award, 2003; Tommy Award. **Special Achievements:** He was the First player of an Opposing Team of the Boston Celtics to win the Tommy Award. **Business Addr:** Manager, Atlanta Hawks, Centennial Tower, Atlanta, GA 30303, **Business Phone:** (866)715-1500.

## ROSE, RACHELLE SYLVIA
Social worker. **Personal:** Born Aug 19, 1946, Chicago, IL. **Educ:** DC Teachers Col, BS, 1974; Howard Univ Grad Sch Social Work, MSW, 1976. **Career:** Lic clin social worker, currently. **Orgs:** Kappa Delta Pi; Nat Teachers Hon Soc, Howard Univ; Nat Asn Social Workers; Calif Soc Clin Social Workers; Alpha Kappa Alpha Sorority, Mu Lambda Omega Chapt, Culver City, Calif. **Home Addr:** 5145 Shenandoah Ave, Los Angeles, CA 90056. **Business Addr:** Clinical Social Worker, 5725 Canterbury Dr, Culver City, CA 90230-6546, **Business Phone:** (323)783-7553.

## ROSE, SHELVIE, SR.
Educator, government official, association executive. **Personal:** Born Jan 5, 1936, Covington, TN; married Odessa White; children: Delores, Shelvie Jr, Saundra, Kelda La Trece & Kenny. **Educ:** Tenn State Univ, BS; Memphis State Univ. **Career:** Aquatics, pro boy scout instr, 1959-63; Tipton County Pub Sch Syst, instr, 1959, Covington alderman, Dist 1, bd mem, currently; Tipton County Bd Educ, health & driver educ instr; Tipton County, Dist 1, comnr; Memphis Area Legal Serv, client representatives. **Orgs:** Finance & admin, Alderman Community; Gen Welfare-Pub Rel; bd control, Tipton County Pub Works; Tipton County Voters Coun; bd mem, Tenn Voters Coun. **Home Addr:** 415 Long Ave, Covington, TN 38019, **Home Phone:** (901)476-8791. **Business Addr:** Alderman District, City Covington, 200 W Wash, Covington, TN 38019, **Business Phone:** (901)476-8791.

## ROSE, TRICIA
Educator. **Personal:** Born Jan 1, 1962?, New York, NY. **Educ:** Yale Univ, BA, sociol, 1984; Brown Univ, MA, PhD, Am civilization, 1993. **Career:** Williams Col, Charles G. Bolin Fel, 1990, 1991; Princeton Univ, Afro-Am Rockefeller Found fel, 1993-94; Am Asn of Univ Women Fel, 1996-97; NY Univ, Goddard fel, 1996; Ford Found fel, 1996-97; Univ Calif Santa Cruz, prof am studies; NPR, expert commentator; Brown Univ, prof, africana studies, Ctr for the Study of Race and Ethnicity, dir, currently; TV contribr; MSNBC; Cable News Network. Book: Black Noise: Rap Music and Black Culture in Contemporary America, 1994; Longing To Tell: Black Women Talk About Sexuality and Intimacy, 2003. **Orgs:** Nathan Cummings Found; Black Girls Rock Inc; chair, Dominican Univ, 2014; Nat Pub Radio. **Home Addr:** , RI. **Business Addr:** Professor of Africana Studies, Brown University, 155 Angell St, Providence, RI 02912, **Business Phone:** (401)863-3137.

## ROSEMAN, JENNIFER EILEEN
Manager. **Personal:** Born Sep 6, 1952, Spokane, WA; daughter of Jerrelene Hill Williamson and Sam Williamson; married Larry Sr; children: Larry Jr & Maya. **Educ:** NY Univ, BA, jour, 1974; Gonzaga Univ, Spokane, Wash, MA, orgn leadership, 1989. **Career:** New York Daily News, NY, intern, 1973-74; San Diego Union, San Diego, Calif, reporter, 1974-78; Spokesman-Rev, Spokane, Wash, ed/ed writer, 1978-92; Ct Col Spokane, dir commun & develop, vice chancellor, instl advan, 1992-2000; Sisters Providence, Mother Joseph Prov, dir Commun & Develop, 2001-. **Orgs:** Trustee, Spokane Pub Libr;

Wash Comn Humanities; Casey Family Partners-Spokane; bd dir, Nat Commun Network Women Relig; Philanthropy Comn Coun Advan & Support Educ; Wash State African Am Affairs Comn; Wash Comn Humanities; Nat Asn Black Journalists. **Honors/Awds:** Distinguished Journalism Award, Ncp, San Diego br, 1977; African-Am Pioneer Award, Links Inc, Spokane chp, 1995; Woman of the Year, Spokane Falls Ct Col, Asn Women Students, 1998; Trailblazer Diversity, Comm Col Spokane, 2000; Woman of the Year, Soroptimist Club, 2001; Ct Activist Award, Ncp, Spokane br, 2002. **Home Addr:** 4312 E 39th Ave, Spokane, WA 99223, **Home Phone:** (509)443-0701. **Business Addr:** Director of Communications & Development, Sisters of Providence, 9 E 9th Ave, Spokane, WA 99202, **Business Phone:** (509)474-2395.

## ROSENTHAL, ROBERT E.

President (organization). **Personal:** Born Apr 9, 1945, Phillips, WI; son of Inez and J R; children: Robert E Jr. **Educ:** Univ Fla, attended 1967; Jackson State Univ, BS, chem grad studies finance, 1971, sci-shem, bus, 1973. **Career:** Whitten Jr High Sch, Jackson, teacher, 1972; PO Jackson, EEO coun, 1974; PO Dist Jackson, staff mgr, 1976; PO US Postmaster, 1978; Mid-S Rec Inc, vpres, co-owner, 1978-94; mgt & mkt consult artists & rec cos; Who's Who Black Music, ed, 1986; Who's Who Music, ed, 1987; Programming Radio, ed, 1987; Rosenthal & Maultsby Music Res Int, nat pub rels mgr young Black Programmer Coalition & Black Music Asn; Philadelphia Int Rec, mkt & nat pub rels mgr; Corps Engrs, staff mgr & equal employ oppurtunity officer; From A Whisper To A Scream, consult, 1989-; Int Trade Inc, vpres, pres, int developer african countries, 1995-2008; Richboy Entertainment Inc, oper mgr; Rosenthall Group, real estate developer, investor & chief operating officer, pres, chief exec officer, 2005-; Brilliant Minds Pub Rels, consult, 2005-. **Orgs:** Miss Teachers Asn; Nat Bus League; Nat Asn Postmasters; Nat Asn Advan Colored People; NAREB Realist; Urban League; Jackson State Univ Alumni; Nat Coun Affirm Action; Minority Bus Brain Trust Cong Black Caucus, 1982-83, 1984, 1986, 1987-; Rock Music Asn; Young Black Programmers Coalition; adv bd, Presidential bus. **Honors/Awds:** Best All Around Student Award, Rosa Scott High Sch, Madison, Miss, 1963; Music Scholar, Jackson State Univ, 1964. **Home Addr:** PO Box 1051, Vicksburg, MS 39180, **Home Phone:** (601)918-9035. **Business Addr:** President, International Trade Inc, PO Box 1051, Vicksburg, MS 39181, **Business Phone:** (601)918-9035.

## ROSHELL, PAMELA P. (PAMELA JOHNSON)

Association executive, founder (originator), government official. **Educ:** Columbia Col, BA, pub affairs, 1989; Univ SC, MA, social work macro pract, 1994; Columbia Clark Atlanta Univ, PhD, social policy, planning & admin, 2002. **Career:** AARP SC, state dir, 2000-04; Family Care Solutions Homecare & Companion Serv, pres & founder, 2005-11; AARP Ga, state dir, 2011-12; US Dept Health & Human Serv, Region IV, regional dir, 2012-. **Special Achievements:** First black female to hold the position of Regional Director of the Department of Health and Human Services. **Business Addr:** Regional Director, US Department of Health & Human Services, Rm 5B95 61 Forsyth St, Atlanta, GA 30303-8909, **Business Phone:** (404)562-7888.

## ROSHELL, WIN C.

President (organization), chief executive officer. **Personal:** Born Chattanooga, TN. **Educ:** Morehouse Col, BA, mkt, 1992; Wesleyan Col, MBA, int bus, 2008. **Career:** Walt Disney World, sr diversity recruiter, opers mgr, 1992-98; After Five Prof Networking Assn, founder, pres & chief exec officer, 2000-08; Merck, sales rep, sr sales consult, 1998-2009; Family Care Solutions Inc, pres, chief exec officer, vpres, bus develop, 2006-11, owner, 2009-11; Comcast, sales consult, 2012-14; AARP, proj dir-SCSEP, 2014-. **Special Achievements:** First African American Professional Networking Association, Middle Georgia. **Business Addr:** Project Director, AARP, 309 N Wash Sq Suite 110, Lansing, MI 48933.

## ROSS, ADRIAN

Football player, football coach, president (organization). **Personal:** Born Feb 19, 1975, Santa Clara, CA. **Educ:** Colo State Univ, BS, animal sci, 1998. **Career:** Football player (retired), football coach, exec; Cincinnati Bengals, linebacker, 1998-2003; Sacramento State Univ, asst defensive line, 2006; free agt, currently; Athlete Mgt Professionals LLC, football opers, 2009-12; Signature Sports Reps, player develop, 2012-13; Top Crop Sports Agency, Partner, Football Opers, 2013-. **Orgs:** Pres, Maddbacker Found, 2001-10; Make A Wish Found Sacramento & Northern Calif. **Business Addr:** Football Operations, Athlete Management Professionals LLC, 400 E Van Buren St, Phoenix, AZ 85004-2202, **Business Phone:** (916)844-6244.

## ROSS, DR. ANTHONY ROGER (TONY ROSS)

School administrator, basketball coach. **Personal:** Born Jan 28, 1953, Jamaica, NY; son of Esther and Abram; children: Jamal & Shama. **Educ:** St Lawrence Univ, BA, sociol, 1975, MA, coun, 1978; Northern Ariz Univ, EdD, educ leadership & admin, gen, 1984. **Career:** Utica Col Syracuse Univ, counr higher educ opportunity prog, 1975-76; St Lawrence Univ, Higher Educ Opportunity Prog, dir, 1976-81, asst basket ball coach, 1977-80, bd trustee; Northern Ariz Univ, asst assoc dean, 1983-84, dean students, 1985, adj prof, 1986-, asst vpres stud serv, 1989, fac mem, 1991-92, 2002; Wichita State Univ, assoc to pres, interim vpres stud affairs, 1994-99; Weber State Univ, fac mem, 1993; Edison Sch Inc, vpres develop; Calif State Univ, vpres, stud affairs, 2000-15, Charter Col Educ, assoc prof, 2000-; dir strategic initiatives, 2015-; N Cent Asn Schs & Cols, consult evaluator. **Orgs:** Pres, Higher Educ Opportunity Prog Prof Org, 1976-81; Am Asn Coun& Develop, 1978-; Am Col Personnel Asn, 1978-; pres, Higher Educ Opportunity Prog, 1979-80; bd, 1992-94, Nat Asn Stud Personnel Admin, 1980-, fac mem & mentor, 2002-; Nat Asn Advan Colored People, 1982-; coach, Youth League Basketball & Soccer, 1982-; coach, Big Bros Flagstaff, 1983-; coach, Buffalo Soldiers Flagstaff, 1984-; Blacks Prog Higher Edu, 1985-; bd dir, Coconino Community Guid Ctr, 1986; comnr, Flagstaff City Parks & Recreational Comn, 1986-92; pres, Ariz Asn Stud Personnel Adminr, 1990-91; Nat Asn Presidential Assts Higher Educ, 1995-99, chair, 1997; James E. Scott Acad Adv Bd, 2001-04. **Honors/Awds:** Athlete of the Year, St Lawrence Univ, 1975; Hall of Fame, St Lawrence Univ, 1986; Distinguished Alumni Award, Northern Ariz Univ, 1989; Americas Best & Brightest Young Business & Professional Men, Dollars & Sense Magazine, 1992; Distinguished Service Award, Ariz Alliance Black School Educr, 1992; NAACP Image Award, Wichita branch, 1997; Pillar of the Profession, Nat Asn Student Personnel Adminr, 2006; Outstanding Commitment to Leadership and Service Award, Am Knowledge Community, Nat Asn Student Personnel Adminr, 2006; Professional Achievement Award, Nat Asn Presidential Assts Higher Educ, 2006. **Home Addr:** 4100 Spring Meadow Cir, Flagstaff, AZ 86004. **Business Addr:** Vice President, Associate Professor, California State University, 5151 State Univ Dr SA 108, Los Angeles, CA 90032, **Business Phone:** (323)343-3100.

## ROSS, BILL. See ROSS, WILLIAM R.

## ROSS, DR. CATHERINE LAVERNE

Executive director, educator. **Personal:** Born Nov 1, 1948, Cleveland, OH; married Thomas Daniel; children: 2. **Educ:** Kent State Univ, BA, hist, sociol & educ cert, 1971; Cornell Univ, MA, reg planning, 1973; Cornell Univ, PhD, city & reg planning, 1979; Univ Calif, Berkeley, post-doctorate work. **Career:** Am Soc Planning Officials, Ford Found fel, 1971-73; Reg Planning Comn, Cleveland, grad asst, 1972; Daton Dalton Little Newport Shaker Hights, OH, transp planner, 1973-74; Cornell Univ, res asst officer transp, 1975-76; Cornell Univ, Rockefeller Found fel, 1975; Ga Inst Tech, asst prof, 1976-83, assoc prof, 1984-89, prof, 1990, vice provost acad affairs, assoc vpres acad affairs, Transp Res & Educ Ctr, co-dir & Col Archit's PhD Prog, dir, Ctr Qual Growth & Regional Develop, dir Harry W chair, currently; Atlanta Univ, asst prof, 1977-79; Ga Tech Eng Exp Sta, consult, 1979; Comn Serv Admin Atlanta, consult res, 1979; Ga Regional Transp Authority, exec dir; Sch City, Advan Prof. **Orgs:** AAAS, 1978; Black Women Academicians, 1979; policy analyst, Am Planning Asn, Wash, DC, 1979; mem, Nat Acad Pub Admin; pres, Nat Asn Col Schs Planning; bd exec comt, policy advisor, Transp Res; bd dir, ENO Transp Found; adv commitee, Obama Admin first-ever White House Off Urban Affairs, 2009; pres, Nat Asn Col Schs Planning. **Business Addr:** Director, Harry West Chair, Georgia Institute of Technology, 760 Spring St Suite 213, Atlanta, GA 30332, **Business Phone:** (404)385-5130.

## ROSS, CATHY D.

Vice president (organization), chief financial officer. **Personal:** Born Henderson, TN. **Educ:** Christian Bros Univ, BS, acct; Univ Memphis, MBA, finance, 1982. **Career:** Buckeye Cellulose Corp, acct supvr & staff acct, 1978-82; Kimberly-Clark Corp, cost analyst & cost anal supvr, 1982-84; Fed Express Corp, sr financial analyst, 1984-98, vpres-Express Financial Planning, 1998-2004, exec vpres & chief financial officer, 2004-. **Orgs:** Bd dir, Steelcase Inc, 2006-; bd mem, Women's Found Greater Memphis; bd mem, Nat Civil Rights Mus; bd dir, Univ Memphis Nat Alumni Asn; Univ Memphis Res Found Team; Univ Memphis Tiger Athletics Adv Bd; Delta Sigma ta Sorority; Tenn Women's Forum; Delta Sigma Pi Prof Fraternity & Links Inc; Links Inc. **Business Addr:** Chief Financial Officer, Executive Vice President, Federal Express Corp, 3610 Hacks Cross Rd, Memphis, TN 38125, **Business Phone:** (901)369-3600.

## ROSS, CATHYE P. (CATHYE ROSS AMOS)

Executive, president (organization), vice president (organization). **Educ:** Univ Southern Miss, BBA, personnel mgt, 1983; Millsaps Col, MBA; Univ Okla, Econ Develop Inst. **Career:** Trustmark Nat Bank, mgr, 1988-90; Hinds Co Econ Develop Dist, asst dir opers, 1990-93; Grand Casino Biloxi, vpres guest servs, vpres mkt opers, 1994-2005, bd dir; Isle Capri Casinos Inc, sr dir mktg, 2005-07; Ross Bus Partnerships LLC, pres & chief mgt consult, 2008-. **Orgs:** Co-comt chair, Hartley Educ Fundraiser, Tabernacle Baptist Church; comt mem, Silver Cloud Dist, Pine Burr Area Coun, Boy Scouts Am; bd trustee, Walter Anderson Mus Art; Leadership Gulf Coast; leadership bd, Coast Community Bank; bd dir, Lynn Meadows Discovery Ctr; bd mem, Chamber Com; leadership bd mem, Coast Community Bank; comnr, Gulfport Civil Serv Comn; bd mem, Miss Arts Comn; bd mem, Miss Coast Coliseum & Conv Ctr. **Business Addr:** President, Chief Management Consultant, Ross Business Partnerships LLC, 12477 Preservation Dr, Gulfport, MS 39530, **Business Phone:** (228)326-2677.

## ROSS, DR. DENISE ELIZABETH

Educator. **Personal:** Born Jan 1, 1971, OH. **Educ:** Spelman Col, BA, eng, 1993; Columbia Univ, Teachers Col, MA, spec educ stud behavior disorders, 1995, PhD, appl behav anal & spec educ, 1998. **Career:** Fla Atlantic Univ, fac, 2002; Columbia Univ, Teacher's Col, visiting asst prof psychol & educ, asst prof, psychol & educ; Western Mich Univ, assoc prof, psychol; Verbal Behavior Analysis: Inducing and Expanding Verbal Capabilities in Children with Language Delays, co-auth, 2008. **Business Addr:** Assistant Professor of Psychology, Western Michigan University, 1903 W Michigan Ave, Kalamazoo, MS 49008-5439, **Business Phone:** (269)387-2000.

## ROSS, DIANA (DIANE ERNESTINE EARLE ROSS)

Actor, singer. **Personal:** Born Mar 26, 1944, Detroit, MI; daughter of Fred and Ernestine; married Arne Naess Jr; children: Ross Arne Naess & Evan; married Robert Ellis Silberstein; children: Tracee Joy & Chudney; married Berry Gordy; children: Rhonda Ross Kendrick. **Career:** The Primettes, mem; The Supremes, mem; Diana Ross & The Supremes, lead singer, 1960-68; Hit Singles: "Where Did Our Love Go, "; "Baby Love, "; "Come See About Me, "; "Stop! In the Name of Love, "; "Back in My Arms Again, "; "I Hear A Symphony, "; "Reflections, "; "Love Child, "; "Someday We'll Be Together"; solo performer, 1970-; Albums: Diana Ross; Everything is Everything; Ross; Why Do Fools Fall in Love; Silk; Take Me Higher; Voice of Love, 2000; Take Me Higher, 2000; Gift of Love, 2000; Sing Motown, 2000; Stop! In the Name of Love, 2000; 20th Century Masters-The Millennium, 2000; Love From Diana Ross, 2000; Chain Reaction, 2000; Classic: The Universal Master Collection, 2000; The Motown Anthology, 2001; Life & Love: The Very Best of Diana Ross, 2001; Best of Diana Ross[Import], 2001; Best of Diana Ross, Vol 1, 2001; Stolen Moments: The Lady Sings Jazz & Blues, 2002; Stolen Moments: The Lady Sings Jazz & Blues, 2002; Diana Ross (1970), 2002; Reach Out & Touch: The Very Best of Diana, 2002; No 1's, 2003; To Love Again, 2003; Diana, 2003; Too Cool for Christmas, 2004; Ultimate Collection, 2004; Legends, 2006; The Definitive Collection, 2006; Blue, 2006; I Love Yoy, 2006; Films: Lady Sings the Blues, 1972; Mahogany, 1975; The Wiz, 1978; Out of Darkness, 1994; The Making and Meaning of We Are Family, 2002; ATL, 2006; TV series: "Tarzan", 1968; "An Evening with Diana Ross", 1977; "Standing Room Only", 1981; "Diana", 1981; "For One And For All", 1983; "Daria", 2000; "VH1 Divas 2000: A Tribute to Diana Ross", 2000; "The Wire", 2003; "Tsunami Aid", 2005; "Shminiya, Ha-", 2006; "Everybody Hates Chris", 2006; "Nobel Peace Prize Concert", 2006; "BET Awards 2007", 2007; "Kennedy Center Honors:, 2007; "The Sopranos", 2007; Met With Sandra Ellison and Tamia Holmes, 2010; Muppet Show; TV movie: Double Platinum, 1999; Diana Ross Enterprises Inc, pres; Anaid Film Prods; RTC Mgt Corp; Chondee Inc; Ross town; Rossville Music Publ Co; Soundtrack: Maid in Manhattan, 2002; Juwanna Mann, 2002; Bridget Jones's Diary, 2001; Chicken Little, 2005; Talk to Me, 2007; Books: Secrets of a Sparrow, 1993; ed, Diana Ross: Going Back, 2002. **Orgs:** Rhythm & Blues Found, 2003-. **Honors/Awds:** Grammy Award for Best Female Vocalist, 1970; Billboard, Cash Box, & Rec World Awards for Best Female Vocalist, 1970; Female Entertainer of the Year, Nat Asn Advan Colored People, 1970; Cue Award, 1972; Tony Award, 1977; Rock 'n' Roll Hall of Fame, 1988; Lifetime Achievement Award, MIDEM, 1994; Walk of Fame Award, Black Entertainment TV, 1999; Heroes Award, Nat Acad Rec Arts & Sci, 2000; Legendary Female Award from the Capitol Gold Legends Award, 2003; Kennedy Center Honors, 2007; Ella Fitzgerald Award, 2014; Dick Clark Award for Excellence, 2014. **Special Achievements:** Nominated for 12 Grammy awards; nominated for Best Actress for Lady Sings the Blues, Academy Award, 1972; honoured by the Guinness Book of World Records in 1993 as the most successful female singer of all time; Female Entertainer of The Century, Billboard Mag; two stars on the Hollywood walk of fame, one for her work with The Supremes and one for her solo career; one of only 7 African-American actresses to receive the Best Actress Oscar nomination; Golden Globe Award; John F. Kennedy Center for the Performing Arts Honors Award, 2007. **Business Addr:** Singer, Actress, Grabow & Associates Inc, 4219 Creekmeadow Dr, Dallas, TX 75287-6806, **Business Phone:** (972)250-1162.

## ROSS, DR. EDWARD

Cardiologist. **Personal:** Born Oct 10, 1937, Fairfield, AL; son of Carrie Griggs and Horace Ross; married Catherine I Webster; children: Edward, Ronald, Cheryl & Anthony. **Educ:** Clark Col Atlanta, BS, 1959; Ind Univ Sch Med, MD, 1963; Am Bd Internal Med, dipl, 1970; Am Soc Hypertension, cert, clin specialist hypertension, 1999. **Career:** William N Wishard Memorial Hosp, intern, 1963-64; Ind Univ Sch Med, residency, internal med, 1964-66, chief residency, 1968; Edward Ross Inc, pres & chief exec officer, 1970-; Med Cardiovasc Data Inc, pres & chief exec officer, 1982; Pvt pract, cardiologist; Methodist Hosp Ind, dir cardiovasc patient care progs, chief cardiovasc med, 1989-95, 2001, dir cardiovasc serv, 1990-, physician, currently; Winona Hosp, chief, Cardiovasc Dis, 2000, dir, Interventinal Cardiol, 2000-; Clarian Health, Cardiologist, currently. **Orgs:** Fel Woodrow Wilson, 1959; Cent Ind Comprehensive Health Plannning Coun; res fel Dept Cardiol, Cardiol Dept Med, 1968-70; med dir, Martindale Health Ctr, 1968-71; chief fel int med Ind Univ, 1969-70; clin asst prof, Ind Univ Schl Med, 1970-75; apt Nat Cent Health Serv Res & Develop, 1970; fel Int Col Angiol, 1971-; bd dir, Cent Ind TB & Resp Dis Asn, 1971-74; Comprehensive Health Plannning Coun Marion County, 1972-73; Secy, Div Nat Med Asn, 1972-73; fel Royal Soc Prom Health, 1974; NMA pres Hoosier State Med Asn, 1980-86; bd dir, Asn Black Cardiologists, 1990-92, fel; Am Soc Angiol, 2003-; Sire Archorn alpha eta Boule, Indianapolis Ind Sigma Pi Phi Fraternity, 2006-; Marion County Med Soc; Ind State Med Asn; Royal Soc Prom Health; Am Col Physicians; Aesculapean Med Soc; Nat Med Asn; fel Am Col Cardiol; fel Am Col Angiol; Ind State Med Asn; Coun Sci Assembly; bd dir, Int Col Angiol Inc, fel; fel Am Col Angiol; fel Am Col Cardiol. **Honors/Awds:** Nat Federation Health Scholarship, 1955; Certificate of Merit Scientific Achievements in Biology, 1959; Lifetime Achievement Award in Cardiology, Center for Leadership Development Of Indianapolis, IN, 2003. **Home Addr:** 8358 Hidden Pt Dr, Indianapolis, IN 46256, **Home Phone:** (317)966-4848. **Business Addr:** Methodist Cardiology Physician, Methodist Hospital, 1801 N Senate MPC 1 Suite 310, Indianapolis, IN 46202, **Business Phone:** (317)962-2500.

## ROSS, EMMA JEAN

School principal. **Personal:** Born Sep 6, 1945, Independence, LA; daughter of Isaac E Sr and Lillie Leola Brown. **Educ:** Southern Univ, BS, 1970; Southeastern La Univ, MA, guid & coun, 1974, MA, admin, supv, 1979. **Career:** Wash Parish Sch, librn, 1970-84, guid counr, 1984-, Lic Prof Counr, 1990-; Varnado High Sch, prin, 1993-. **Orgs:** Theta Theta Zeta, 1974-; La Sch Counr's Asn, 1989-; La Coun Asn, 1989-; La Asn Multi-Cult Develop, 1989-. **Home Addr:** 27344 Hwy 21, Angie, LA 70426, **Home Phone:** (985)986-2491. **Business Addr:** Principal, Varnado High School, 25543 Wash St, Angie, LA 70467, **Business Phone:** (985)732-2025.

## ROSS, FRANK KENNETH

Certified public accountant. **Personal:** Born Jul 9, 1943; son of Reginald (deceased) and Ruby; married Cecelia M Mann; children: Michelle & Michael. **Educ:** Long Island Univ, BS, 1966, MBA, 1968. **Career:** Peat, Marwick, Mitchell & Co CPA, partner, 1966-73, 1977-87; Ross, Stewart & Benjamin, PC, CPA, pres & owner, 1973-76; KPMG LLP, partner, 1976-2003, Mid-Atlantic Audit & Risk, managing partner, 1996-2003; Howard Univ, instr, vis prof, 1982-, Ctr Acct Educ, dir, 2004-. Mid Sch Math & Sci, treas, currently. **Orgs:** Nat pres & founder, Nat Asn Black Acct, 1969-70; Am Inst CPA's, 1969-; treas, Ellington Fund, 1982-; Bd Counr, Col Bus & Pub Mgt, Univ Dist Columbia, 1983-; treas, Wash Urban League, 1986-; bd adv, Howard Univ Sch Bus, 1990-; pres, bd mem, Iona Sr Serv; vpres, Corcoran Mus & Sch Art, 1994-, treas; bd adv, George Wash Univ Sch Bus & Pub Admin, 1996-; trustee, Hoop Dreams Scholar Fund; trustee, Corcoran Gallery Art; Gore, 2000; mem bd, Pepco Holdings, 2004-; United Negro Col Fund Wash & Baltimore Bd; chmn, Bd KPMG Found; chair audit comt, Cohen & Steers Mutual Funds Group. **Honors/Awds:** Black Achievers in Industry, YMCA Greater NY, 1980; Outstanding Achievement Award, Wash DC Chap NABA, 1984; Distinguished Service Award, NABA, 1985; Accountant of the Year, Beta Alpha Psi, 1994; Alumni of the Year, Long Island Univ, 1998; DHL, Long Island Univ, 2001; DHL, Univ Wash, DC, 2004; Selected as 100 Most

Influential People in Accounting by Accounting Today, 2008. **Special Achievements:** One of the nine co-founders and the first President of the National Association of Black Accountants; author of Quiet Guys Can Do Great Things, Too: A Black Accountant's Success Story, 2006. **Home Addr:** 10130 Darmuid Green Dr, Potomac, MD 20854. **Business Addr:** Treasurer, Visiting Professor & Director, Howard University, 405 Howard Pl NW, Washington, DC 20059, **Business Phone:** (202)806-1637.

### ROSS, KEVIN ARNOLD
Lawyer, educator. **Personal:** Born Apr 22, 1955; married Gornata Lynn Cole; children: Kelly Alexis & April Whitney. **Educ:** Dartmouth Col, BS, econs, 1977; Emory Univ Sch Law, JD, 1980. **Career:** Emory Univ Sch Law, adj prof; Kilpatrick & Cody, summer legal clin, 1979; Donald L. Hollowell prof law; Long & Aldridge, assoc atty, 1980; Hunton & Williams, managing partner, 1992-2002; Kaj Pub Affairs Group, pres; Attache Pub Affairs, staff; Kevin Ross Group, founder, owner & pres, 2002-. **Orgs:** State Bar Ga, 1980-; Vol Lawyer Arts, 1981-84; secy, vpres & pres, Gate City Bar Asn, 1982-85; vpres, Atlanta Chap Am Diabetes Asn, 1982-84; State Licensing Bd Used Car Dealers, 1984-89; Sci & Technol Mus Atlanta; Metrop Atlanta Arts Fund; Bd Pub Broadcasting Atlanta; YMCA; chair, Fulton County Dist Attys transition comt; Sci & Technol Mus Atlanta. **Honors/Awds:** Donald L. Hollowell Professor of Law Chair; Leader Under 30, Ebony Mag, 1985; Distinguished Alumni Award, Emory Univ Sch Law, 1999; Dr. Louis Sullivan Award, Pub Broadcasting Atlanta, 2010. **Home Addr:** 2163 Golden Dawn Dr SW, Atlanta, GA 30311. **Business Addr:** Owner, President, Kevin Ross Group, The Forum 3290 Northside Pkwy Suite 775, Atlanta, GA 30327, **Business Phone:** (404)841-7811.

### ROSS, LEE ELBERT
Educator, college administrator. **Personal:** Born Mar 16, 1958, Tuskegee, AL; son of Geneva Trimble and Silas Bates Sr; married Leslie Ann; children: Christopher Daniel & Alexander Nelson. **Educ:** Niagara Univ, BA, criminal justice, 1981; Rutgers Univ, Grad Sch Criminal Justice, MA, 1983, PhD, criminol & criminal justice admin, 1991. **Career:** NY Sentencing Guidelines Comn, res asst, 1982; NY State Sentencing Guidelines Comn, 1984; NJ Admin Off Cts, res intern, 1984; Kean Col, Polit Sci Dept, lectr, 1984; US Treas Dept, customs officer, 1984-91; Bloomfield Col, Dept Sociol, lectr, 1991; WIS Teaching fel, 1996; Univ Wis-Milwaukee, asst prof, assoc prof, criminal justice, 1991-97, field placement coordr, 1994-97, Col Arts & Sci, internship coordr & supvr, 1999-2003, Criminal Justice Dept, assoc prof & dept chmn, 1999-2003; Nat Institue Justice, techincal reviewer grant applications; Domesttic Abuse Intervention Prog, group facilitator; Univ Cent Fla, Dept Criminal Justice & Legal Studies, grad coordr, 2004-05, hon maj coordr, 2003-07, asso prof criminal justice, 2003-, provost fel & assoc prof, 2005-06, pub affairs doctoral prog coordr, 2010-12; UFF-UCF Union Chap, vpres, 2015-. **Orgs:** Am Soc Criminol, 1984-; exec bd mem liaison, regional trustee, Acad Criminal Justice Sci, 1991-; Nat Orgn Black Law Enforcement Exes, 1991-; Am Civil Liberties Union, bd mem, 1992-; ed & bd mem, J Crime & Justice, 1996-98; bd mem, Southern Criminal Justice Asn; Provost Fel Univ Cent Fla; group facilitator, Task Force Family Violence, 1999-2003; facilitator, Milwaukee Domestic Abuse Intervention Prog; regional trustee & exec bd mem, Acad Criminal Justice Sci, 2008-11. **Home Addr:** 7045 N Braeburn Lane, Milwaukee, WI 53209-2609. **Business Addr:** Provost Fellow, Associate Professor, University of Central Florida, 4000 Cent Fla Blvd, Orland, FL 32816-1600, **Business Phone:** (407)823-2000.

**ROSS, LINDA TRACEY. See ROSS, TRACEY.**

### ROSS, MARTHA ERWIN
Entrepreneur. **Personal:** Born Jun 4, 1944, Tyler, TX; daughter of Carvie Earnest Sr and Miner Mae Jackson; married Lamont W; children: Stetron Proncell & Trelitha Rochelle Bryant. **Educ:** Bus degree secretarial sci, 1967; Bellevue Univ, mgt degree, hons, 1994. **Career:** AT&T, secy, 1964-66, pub rels, 1966-80, network sales support info rep, 1980-85; Qual Nutri & Painting Contractors, pres, 1985; United Way Midlands Western/Central, region mkt mgr, loaned exec, 1986-88, customer serv training tech, 1988-91; OSHA safety inspector, 1991-94, materials auditor, 1994-; Youth Motivation Task Force, mkt mgr, 1991; Midwest Market Place, owner, currently. **Orgs:** Urban League Nebr, 1970-; Urban League Guild, 1970-; ambassador, United Way the Midlands, 1978-86; auctioneer, 1985, ambassador, 1985-86, Nebr Pub TV; COC, 1985-; YMCA Youth Camp Campaign, 1985-86; Church Christ, numerous auxiliaries. **Honors/Awds:** Top 10 in Jefferson Award, KETV Channel 7, 1988; United Way, Loaned Exec Honor, Commercial Div, 1988; Top ambassador, NPTV, 1987, 1988; Top Honors, Annual Campaign, Chamber of Commerce, 1988-89; Urban League of Nebraska, Top Honors, Membership Drive, 1987-89; Omaha Opportunities Industrialization Ctr Honors, 1992, 1993. **Home Addr:** 5741 Tucker Circle, Omaha, NE 68152, **Home Phone:** (402)572-0357. **Business Addr:** Owner, Midwest Marketplace, 5741 Tucker Circle, Omaha, NE 68152, **Business Phone:** (402)572-5773.

### ROSS, N. RODNEY
Graphic artist, photographer. **Personal:** Born Jun 28, 1957, Indianapolis, IN; son of Virginia Cottee and Norman. **Educ:** Ind Univ, Herron Sch Art, BFA, visual commun, 1982. **Career:** Noble Industries, Indianapolis, Ind, art dir, 1984-87; Poster Display Co, Beach Grove, Ind, graphic artist, 1987-91; Ross Concepts, Art Dept, Indianapolis, Ind, pres, 1982-90; Career Com, Advertising Design, prof, 1990-92; Ivy Tech State Col, graphic arts instr; Clark Col, fac mem; Turner, Potts & Ross, Indianapolis, Ind, vpres, currently. **Orgs:** Youth leader, counr, Community Outreach Ctr, 1985-; Cent IN Bicycling Assn, 1988-; African Based Cultures Study Group Indianapolis, 1989-; Indy Rennaissance, AFA Artists Network, 1990-. **Honors/Awds:** Addy Award, 1992. **Home Addr:** 2208 Riviera St, Indianapolis, IN 46260-4349, **Home Phone:** (317)466-1800. **Business Addr:** Vice President, Turner Potts & Ross, 2825 Thornton Lane, Indianapolis, IN 46268-1257, **Business Phone:** (317)848-2825.

### ROSS, OLIVER CALVIN, III
Football player. **Personal:** Born Sep 27, 1974, Culver City, CA; married Billie. **Educ:** Iowa State Univ. **Career:** Football player (retired); Dallas Cowboys, tackle, 1998; Philadelphia Eagles, 1999; Pittsburgh Steelers, left tackle & right guard & right tackle, 2000-04; Ariz Cardinals, left tackle & right tackle, 2005-07; New Eng Patriots, guard, 2008; Ariz Cardinals, offensive lineman, 2009. **Orgs:** Rookie of the Year, 1998.

### ROSS, OLIVER CALVIN
Football player. **Personal:** Born Sep 27, 1974, Culver City, CA; married Billie. **Educ:** Iowa State Univ. **Career:** Football player (retired); Dallas Cowboys, 1998; Philadelphia Eagles, tackle, 1999; Pittsburgh Steelers, left tackle, right guard, 2001, right guard, 2002, left tackle, right tackle, 2003, right tackle, 2004; Ariz Cardinals, tackle, 2005, 2007, right tackle, 2006; New Eng Patriots, 2008; Ariz Cardinals, 2009. **Business Addr:** Member, Arizona Cardinals, PO Box 888, Phoenix, AZ 85001-0888, **Business Phone:** (800)999-1402.

### ROSS, PHYLLIS HARRISON
Broadcaster, educator, psychiatrist. **Personal:** Born Aug 14, 1936, Detroit, MI; married Edgar. **Educ:** Albion Col, Albion, MI, BA, 1956; Wayne State Univ, Detroit, MD, 1959; Kings Co Hosp, Brooklyn, internship, 1960. **Career:** Physician pediat, adult & child psychiat, 1959-; NY Hosp, Cornell Med Col, residency-pediat, 1960-62; Cornell Med Sch, instr; Jacoby Hosp Albert Einstein Col Med, residency-adult & child psychiat, 1962-66; Albert Einstein Col Med, fel, 1964-66; instr, pediat & psychol, 1966-68; Metrop Hosp, Community Ment Health Ctr, dir, emer attend psychiatrist, chief psychiat, Med Bd, pres, 1973-99; State Univ NY, Empire State Col, bd dir, 1972-79; Bank St Col, bd dir, 1972-79; C's TV Workshop, bd dir, 1976-; Phyllis Harrison-Ross Assocs, behav med & telepsychiatry, 1998-; Black Psychiatrists Greater New York & Assoc, founder, managing dir & pres emer, 2000-; NY Med Col, prof psychiat, emer prof psychiat & behav health sci, currently; WBAI FM, Ethics Air, co-host, currently. **Orgs:** Pres, Black Psychiatrists Am, 1976-78; Med Rev Bd, NY State Comn Corrections, 1976-2008, chair, 2008-; Minority Adv Comt, ADAMHA, 1978-; trustee, secy, NY Soc, Ethical Cult, 2001-; chair, Social Servs Bd, United Social Serv Inc, 2001-; pres, All Healers ment health Alliance, 2005-; tustee, Ethical Cult Fieldston Sch; trustee, Northside Ctr Child Develop; trustee, Pub Health Solutions Inc; ed bd, NY Amsterdam News; Int Adv Bd Auschwitz Inst Peace & Reconciliation. **Honors/Awds:** Achievement Award, Greater NY Links, 1973; Distinguished Alumnus Award, Albion Col, 1976; Leadership in Medicine Award, Susan Smith McKinney Steward Med Soc, 1978; Award of Merit, Public Health Asn New York City, 1980; Lifetime Achievement Award, Am Psychiat Asn; Solomon Carter Fuller Award, Am Psychiat Asn, 2004. **Special Achievements:** Author of "Getting It Together A Psychology Textbook", 1972; Author of "The Black Child A Parents Guide" 1973. **Home Addr:** 41 Cent Pk W Suite 10C, New York, NY 10023, **Home Phone:** (212)799-8055. **Business Addr:** Professor Emeritus of Psychiatry & Behavioral. Sciences, New York Medical College, Behavioral Health Ctr, Valhalla, NY 10595, **Business Phone:** (914)493-7120.

### ROSS, REV. DR. RALPH M.
Clergy, educator. **Personal:** Born Dec 23, 1936, Miami, FL; son of Leroy and Effie Mae; married Gertrude Jean Thomson; children: Sharlene, Lydia, Ralph, Ray, Simona & Randall. **Educ:** BA, 1961; BD, 1965; MDiv, 1970; DMin, 1988. **Career:** Beth Salem United Pres b Church, Columbus, Ga, minister, 1965-66; Eastern Airlines Atlanta, ramp agt, 1965-66; Mt Zion Baptist Church, Miami, assoc minister, 1966-68, pastor, teacher, 1990-; Urban League Miami, field rep, 1967-68; Knoxville Col, campus minister, 1968-70, dean stud; UTK noxville, lectr relig dept, 1969-; NC Agr & Tech State Univ, dir, relig activ, 1978-86, asst dean stud devel, 1986-90. **Orgs:** Theta Phi Hon Soc, 1965; bd dir, Blacks Higher Educ, Knoxville; Knoxville Interdenominational Christian Ministeral Alliance; life mem, Alpha Phi Alpha; Nat Asn Advan Colored People; Baptist Ministers Coun & FaithCity; ROA; chmn, Mt Zion Baptist Church; chmn, Hist Mt Zion Missionary Baptist Church; African-Am Coun Christian Clergy. **Honors/Awds:** YMCA Best Blocker Award, Knoxville Col, 1959; Rockefeller Fellowship Award, 1964. **Special Achievements:** Named first African-Am capt in the USNR Chaplains Corps. **Home Addr:** 501 NE 96th St, Miami, FL 33138-2735, **Home Phone:** (305)751-5291. **Business Addr:** Pastor, Teacher, Historic Mount Zion Missionary Baptist Church, 301 NW 9th St, Miami, FL 33136, **Business Phone:** (305)379-4147.

**ROSS, TONY. See ROSS, DR. ANTHONY ROGER.**

### ROSS, TRACEE ELLIS (TRACEE JOY SILBERSTEIN)
Actor. **Personal:** Born Oct 29, 1972, Los Angeles, CA; daughter of Robert Ellis Silberstein and Diana. **Educ:** Brown Univ, attended 1994; William Esper Actg Studio. **Career:** Mirabella Mag, fashion ed; New York Mag, fashion ed; Films: Far Harbor, 1996; Sue, 1997; A Fare to Remember, 1998; Hanging Up, 2000; In the Weeds, 2000; I-See-You. Com, 2006; Daddy's Little Girls, 2007; Labor Pains, 2009; TV series: "The Dish", 1997; "Race Against Fear", 1998; "Lyricist Lounge Show", 2000; "Girlfriends", actor & dir, 2000-08; "Second Time Around", 2004; "Trial & Errors", 2005; "In Too Deep", 2006; "Life Support", 2007; "Private Practice", 2010; "CSI: Crime Scene Investigation", 2011; "Reed Between the Lines", 2011; "Five", 2011; "Bad Girls", 2012; "Black-ish", 2014-. **Honors/Awds:** BET Comedy Award, 2005; Image Award, Nat Asn Advan Colored People, 2007, 2009 & 2012. **Business Addr:** Actress, c/o International Creative Management, 10250 Constellation Blvd, Los Angeles, CA 90067, **Business Phone:** (310)550-4000.

### ROSS, TRACEY (LINDA TRACEY ROSS)
Actor. **Personal:** Born Feb 27, 1959, Brooklyn, NY; married Kashif; children: Bryce. **Educ:** Rutgers Univ. **Career:** Films: Best Defense, 1984; The Cotton Club, 1984; Solar Eclipse, 1995; Mr.Payback: An Interactive Movie, 1995; Small Time, 1996; Cold Around the Heart, 1997; Unconditional Love, 1999; Steps of Faith, 2014. TV series: "Jacqueline Susann's Valley of the Dolls", 1981; "Miss Black America Pageant", 1985; "Braker", 1985; "Ryan's Hope", 1985-87; "Mayflower Madam", 1987; "The Cosby Show", 1989; "Doctor Doctor", 1991; "Roc", 1991; "Lies of the Twins", 1991; "On Our Own", 1994; "Bay watch Nights", 1996; "Passions", 1999-2008; "Providence", 2002; "House of Payne", 2008; "Brothers", 2009. **Honors/Awds:** Miss New Jersey Pageant, 1975; Spokes model category in the television series "Star Search"; Image Award, Nat Asn Advan Colored People, 2007. **Special Achievements:** First $100, 000 Star Search spokes model in 1980s; Nominated consecutively from 2000 to 2007 for an NAACP Image Award's. **Business Addr:** Actress, c/o NBC Viewer Relations, 30 Rockefeller Plz, New York, NY 10112.

### ROSS, WILLIAM R. (BILL ROSS)
Association executive. **Career:** Off Neighborhood Com Revitalization, vice chair; Booker T Wash Bus Asn, exec dir, pres & chief exec officer, currently. **Orgs:** Adv bd mem, Coun Asian Pac Americans; bd dir, Detroit Alliance Fair Banking. **Business Addr:** President, Chief Executive Officer, Booker T Washington Business Association, 2885 E Grand Blvd, Detroit, MI 48202, **Business Phone:** (313)875-4250.

### ROSS, WINSTON A.
Social worker. **Personal:** Born Dec 2, 1941; son of Reginald and Ruby Swanston; married Rosalind Golden. **Educ:** NY City Community Col, AAS, 1961; NY Univ, BS, 1963; Columbia Univ Sch Social Work, MS, 1971; Adelphi Univ Sch Social Work, doctoral cand. **Career:** New York Dept Social Serv/Prev Serv/Bur Child Welfare, caseworker, supv, 1966-73; St Dominic's Home, Blauvelt NY, exec supv, 1973-74; Graham Home & Sch, Hastings NY, social work supv, 1975-76; Wiltwyck Sch, Yorktown NY, unit dir, 1976-78; Westchester Community Opportunity Prog Inc, exec dir & chief exec officer. **Orgs:** Chmn trustee bd, Metrop AME Zion Ch, 1969-; pres, Yonkers, NY Br Nat Asn Advan Colored People, 1971-78; dir, Westchester Regional NY Conf Nat Asn Advan Colored People, 1977-; co-chmn, 5th Ann Whitney M Young Conf Racism & Del Human Serv, NASW, 1978-83; chmn, Westchester Div, NY Chap NASW, 1979-80, secy, 1981-83; chmn, Minority Affairs Comn, NY NASW, 1979-84; chmn, Career Guid Adv Coun, Educ Oppor Ctr Westchester, 1979-85; chairperson, Nat Nominations & Leadership Comn, NASW, 1984-; Statewide Adv Coun, NYS Div Human Rights, 1984-; NY Bd Social Work, 1987-. **Honors/Awds:** Freedom Fighter Award, Yonkers NAACP, 1978; Eugene T Reed Medalist, NY Conf NAACP, 1983; Social Worker of The Year, West Div NASW, 1982; Citizen of The Year, Omega Psi Phi Frat, Beta Alpha Alpha Chap, 1983. **Home Addr:** 5 Rte 202, Yorktown Heights, NY 10598-6628. **Business Addr:** Executive Director, Chief Executive Officer, Westchester Community Opportunity Program Inc, 2269 Saw Mill River Rd Bldg 3, Elmsford, NY 10523, **Business Phone:** (914)592-5600.

**ROSS-JONES, DONNA. See JONES, DONNA L.**

### ROSS-LEE, DR. BARBARA
School administrator. **Personal:** Born Jun 1, 1942, Detroit, MI; daughter of Ernestine (Deceased); married James; married Edmond Beverly; children: 5. **Educ:** Wayne State Univ, BA, chem & biol, 1960, MA; Mich State Univ, Col Osteop Med, DO, 1973. **Career:** Mich State Univ, assoc dean, 1983-93; prof, Mich State Univ Dept Family Pract, 1983; Us Dept Health & Human Serv, educ consult, 1984; off Sen Bill Bradley, legis asst, 1991; Ohio Univ Col Osteop Med, dean, 1993-2001; NY Inst Technol, dean sch life sci & allied health & vpres, health sci & med affairs, 2001-, NY Col Osteop Med, vpres, health sci & med affairs, 2001-, dean, 2002-06. Sch Allied Health & Life Sci, dean, 2001-02. **Orgs:** Chair, Am Osteop Asn, 1974-; Am Col Osteop Gen Practrs, 1982-; Ingham County Osteop Soc, 1984-; Nat Asn Med Minority Educrs, 1985-; Osteop Gen Practrs Mich, 1985-; Am Asn Family Practrs, 1986-; Mich Asn Family Practrs, 1986-; Nat Acad Pract, 1986-; Acad Osteop dir Med Educ, 1988-91; AMA, 1989-; community rep, Gov Mich Minority Health Adv Comt, 1990; chair, Dept Family Med at Mich State Univ; Robert Wood Johnson Health Policy Fel, 1991; pres, Nat Osteop Med Asn, 1992-; Ohio Osteop Asn, 1993-; fac mem, Phi Kappa Phi Hon Soc, 1994; bd dir, Nat Fund Med Educ; Nat Coun Minority Health Disparities; bd trustee, Nassau County Health Care Corp; Med Educ Futures Studies; Nat Coun Physician & Nurse Supply; pres & bd dir, Asn Acad Health Centers; chair, Am Asn Cols Osteop Med Bd Gov; mem, Nat Teacher Corps. **Business Addr:** Vice President, New York Institute of Technology, Rockefeller Bldg Rm 107, Old Westbury, NY 11568-8000, **Business Phone:** (516)686-1000.

### ROSSER, DR. JAMES M.
School administrator, educator. **Personal:** Born Apr 16, 1939, East St. Louis, IL; son of William M and Mary E Bass; children: Terrence. **Educ:** Southern Ill Univ, Carbondale, BA, 1962, MA, 1963, PhD, 1969. **Career:** Holden Hosp, diag bacteriologist, 1961-63; Health Educ & Coordr Black Am Studies, instr, 1968-69; Eli Lily & Co, res bacteriologist, 1963-66; Southern Ill Univ, mem grad fac, 1966-70; Univ Kans, ten assoc prof & assoc vice chancellor, 1970-74; State Univ NJ, Dept Higher Ed, vice chancellor, 1974-79, actg chancellor, 1977; Sanwa Bank Calif, dir; Calif State Univ, pres, 1979-2013, pres emer, 2013, prof health care mgt, currently; Edison Int, dir, 1988-; NIH, consult. **Orgs:** Bd dir, Hisp Urban Ctr, Los Angeles, CA, 1979-; bd dir, Am Coun Educ, 1979-; bd dir, LA Area Coun, Boy Scouts Am, 1979-; bd dir, Community TV Southern Calif KCET, 1980-89, 1998-; bd dir, Los Angeles Urban League, 1982-95; bd dir, Southern Calif Edison, 1985-; bd dir, AmArts, 1985; bd gov, Am Red Cross, 1986-91; bd dir, Los Angeles Philharmonic Asn, 1986-99; bd dir, FEDCO Inc, 1987-2001; LA's Best Avd Comn, 1988-; adv bd mem, Blue Cross Calif, 1989-; Nat adv coun mem, Nat Sci Found Directorate Educ & Human Resources, 1989-96; bd dir, Nat Health Found, 1990-98; bd dir, Calif Chamber Comn, 1993-; bd dir, United Calif Bank, 1993-2002; bd trustee, Woodrow Wilson Nat Fel Found, 1993-; vice chair, Am Asn State Cols & Univs-Steering Comn or Coun Urban & Metrop Cols & Univs, 1993-96; Calif Coun Sci & Technol, 1998-; hon mem, Rotary Club LA, 1998-; TEXACO & CHEVRON Task Force Equality & Fairness, 1999-2002; Los Angeles Adv Alliance, Pasadena Tournament Roses, 2000-; bd dir, LA AllianceStud Achievement, 2001-; Audubon Ctr Campaign Adv Comn, 2001-; CA Community Found, 2003-; Calif Dept Educ; Pac Coun Int Policy; fac mem, Pharamacol & Toxicol & Higher Educ; Los Angeles Econ & Jobs Comt; Rebuild Los Angeles Task Force; Los Angeles Unified Sch Dist's Blue Ribbon Panel Bud-

get Reform; Cong Caucus Sci & Technol; Am Coun Educ's Comt Sci & Technol; Nat Acad Engineering Panels & Forums; Nat Academies Govt-Univ-Indust Res Roundtable Coun; CSUPERB-Calif State Univ Prog Educ & Res Biotechnology.

### ROSSER, DR. SAMUEL BLANTON

Physician. **Personal:** Born Jul 13, 1934, Tallapoosa, GA; married Pearl L; children: Charles B. **Educ:** Clark Col, BS, 1954; Wayne St Univ, MS, 1956; Howard Univ Col Med, MD, 1960. **Career:** Physician (retired); Freedmen's Hosp, resident gen surgeon, 1961-66; C's Hosp Nat Med Ctr, resident, 1970-72; Howard Univ, Col Med, pediat surg assoc prof, 1972-2002. **Orgs:** Asn Former Interns & Residents Howard Univ Hosp; fel Am Col Surgeons; Am Acad Pediat; Am Pediat Surg Asn. **Special Achievements:** First African American certified in pediatric surgery, 1975. **Home Addr:** 2222 Westview Dr, Silver Spring, MD 20910-1328, **Home Phone:** (301)589-2456.

### ROSSUM, ALLEN BONSHACA LAMONT

Football player. **Personal:** Born Oct 22, 1975, Dallas, TX; married Angela; children: Trinity Amaia, Talia Alyse, Alexa & Avian. **Educ:** Univ Notre Dame, BS, admin, mkt finance & comput application, 1998; Wharton Sch Bus, bus educ & bus develop, 2006; Kellogg Sch Mgt, exec prog entrepreneurship & high growth entrepreneurship, 2009. **Career:** Football player (retired); Philadelphia Eagles, punt returner & kick returner, 1998, 1999; Green Bay Packers, 2000-01; Atlanta Falcons, 2002-03, 2005, cornerback, 2004, right cornerback, 2006; Pittsburgh Steelers, 2007; San Francisco 49ers, wide receiver, 2008, 2009; Dallas Cowboys, 2009; Straight A's Home Preserv LLC, pres & owner, 2009-13; Masada Resource Group, vice-pres proj develop, latin am; 2009-13; Cocke & Finkelstein inc, prin, 2012-; CF Cares Inc, exec dir, 2013-; Capital Contracting Serv Llc, chief exec officer, 2013-; Allen Rossum Golf Tournament, host. **Orgs:** Founder, Rosum's Healthy Kids Klub, 2003-11; bd mem, Sunshine a Ranney Day, 2014; managing bd mem, CF Cares Inc, 2012; bd & finance comt mem, Warrick Dunn Charities Inc, 2014. **Honors/Awds:** NFC Spec Teams Player Week, 1999-2000; Nat Fatherhood Award, 2005; Pro Bowler Alt, 2000; Pro Bowler Selection, 2004; Pro Bowl, 2000, 2004; Falcons' all time career kick off return yards; National Fatherhood Award, 2005; Impact Player Award for Community service; Falcons' All Time Career Return yards Leader. **Special Achievements:** TV Series: "Quite Frankly with Stephen A. Smith", 2006. Film: Onward Notre Dame: Mutual Respect, 2015. **Business Addr:** Chief Executive Officer, Capital Contracting Services LLC, 303 Perimeter Ctr N Suite 201, Atlanta, GA 30346, **Business Phone:** (404)410-7427.

### ROTAN, DR. CONSTANCE S.

Educator, administrator, association executive. **Personal:** Born Apr 19, 1935, Baton Rouge, LA; married James Rotan Jr; children: Kevin & Michael. **Educ:** Southern Univ, BA, 1956; Howard Univ Sch Law, JD, 1967; Howard Univ Grad Sch, MA, 1968. **Career:** Educator (retired), administrator; US Dept Justice, gen trial atty, 1968-70; United Planning Orgn, ast gen coun, 1970-72; Howard Univ Sch Law, ast dean, asst prof, 1972-75; Howard Univ, exec ast vpres admin, 1975-87, univ secy, bd trustee secy, 1987-92, vpres admin, 1989-92. **Orgs:** Nat Bar Assoc; Kappa Beta Pi Int Legal Sor; Alpha Kappa Alpha; Assoc Am Law Sch; Nat Assoc Col & Univ Atty; US Dist Ct DC; US Ct Appeals DC; dean, Howard Univ Chap Kappa Beta Pi Int Legal Sor, 1963-64; co-chmn, Comn Age Majority DC; DC Bar; Phi Sigma Alpha; founding mem, officer Waring & Mitchell Law Soc; Pub Assoc Foreign Serv; treas, Horizon Found, 2003-. **Home Addr:** 9216 Creekbed Ct, Columbia, MD 21045-1804, **Home Phone:** (301)596-6713. **Business Addr:** Treasurer, The Horizon Foundation, 10480 Little Patuxent Pkwy Suite 900, Columbia, MD 21044, **Business Phone:** (410)715-0311.

### ROULHAC, DR. EDGAR EDWIN

Dean (education), school administrator. **Personal:** Born Sep 28, 1946, Chicago, IL; son of Portia Goodloe and Edgar Elijah; married Patricia Gayle Johnson. **Educ:** Southern Ill Univ, Carbondale, BS, health educ, 1969, MS, community health educ, 1971, PhD, higher educ admin, 1974; Johns Hopkins Univ Sch Pub Health, MPH, pub health, 1975; Harvard Univ, attended 1987. **Career:** Southern Ill Univ Sch Med, prof health care planning, 1972-74; Towson State Univ, prof health sci, 1975-78; Johns Hopkins Univ, dean studs, 1978-85, asst provost, 1986-93, provost's off, vice provost, 1985-2011, interim vpres human resources, 1994-95; Mid States Comn Higher Educ, comnr & mem, 2009-11; Johns Hopkins Montgomery County Campus, founding dir. **Orgs:** Life mem, Kappa Alpha Psi Fraternity, 1965-; Hon Educ Phi Delta Kappa, 1972-; Hon Educ Kappa Delta Pi, 1972-; vpres, MD Soc Med Res, 1981-84; Hon Pub Health Delta Omega, 1982-; Sigma Pi Phi, 1986-; Henry M. Minton fel Sigma Pi Phi Fraternity, 1986-, AAHE, APHA, BCHW, SOPHE; adv bd, Drew-Meharry-More house Med Sch Cancer Prev Consortium, 1987-99; trustee, Provident Hosp Baltimore, 1978-82; gov bd, Cent MD Health Systs Agency, 1976-80; Dunbar-Hopkins Health Partnership; Elijah Cummings & Jerold C Hoff berger Youth Prog Israel; Md Asn of Higher Educ; Am Pub Health Asn; fel Soc Pub Health Educ; Phi Delta Kappa; Kappa Delta Pi; life mem, SIU Alumni Asn; Dunbar High Sch/Johns Hopkins Health Partnership; Jerold C Hoffberger Youth Prog Israel; Md 7th Cong Dist US Mil Serv Acad Rev Bd; Delta Omega Hon Pub Health Soc; Henry M Minton Fel Sigma Pi Phi Fraternity; James P Brawley Fel Sigma Pi Phi Fraternity; Md Asn Higher Educ; Leadership Alliance; Md Independent Col & Univ Asn; Md Higher Educ Comn; DC Educ Licensure Comn; Minority Recruitment Comt. **Honors/Awds:** Acad PubHealth Recognition Award, Asn Schs Pub Health, 1985; Meritorious Service Award, Johns Hopkins Minority Med Fac Asn, 1986; Meritorious Service Award, Johns Hopkins Alumni Asn Exec Comt, 1983. **Home Addr:** 24 Dinaden Cir, Pikesville, MD 21208. **Business Addr:** Vice Provost for Academic Services, Johns Hopkins University, 265 Garland Hall 3400 N Charles St, Baltimore, MD 21218, **Business Phone:** (410)516-6087.

### ROUNDTREE, DOVEY JOHNSON

Lawyer, clergy, army officer. **Personal:** Born Apr 17, 1914, Charlotte, NC; daughter of James Eliot Johnson and Lela Bryant Johnson; married Bill. **Educ:** Spelman Col; Howard Law Sch, attended 1950. **Career:** Lawyer, clergy, army officer, ordained minister (retired); Mil officer, civil rights activist, lawyer, ordained minister; lawyer, criminal & civil; co-coun, 1955; African Methodist Episcopal Church, ordained minister, 1964-96. **Orgs:** Gen Coun, Nat Coun Negro Women.

### ROUNDTREE, RALEIGH CITO

Athlete, football player. **Personal:** Born Aug 31, 1975, Augusta, GA; son of Richard and Angela; married Sondra Way. **Educ:** SC State Univ, indust educ. **Career:** Football player (retired); Nat Football League, Offensive Guard, 1997-2003; San Diego Chargers, guard, 1997-2001; Ariz Cardinals, 2002-03; Edmonton Eskimos, offensive line, 2006-07. **Home Addr:** 4558 Logans Way, Augusta, GA 30909-9141.

### ROUNDTREE, RICHARD

Actor. **Personal:** Born Jul 9, 1942, New Rochelle, NY; son of John and Katheryn; married Karen; children: Kelly, Nicole & Morgan Elizabeth; married Mary Jane Grant; children: 2. **Educ:** Southern Ill Univ, attended. **Career:** Barney's, suit salesman; model; Stage Appearances: Negro Ensemble Co; Kongi's Harvest Man; Better Man; Mau-Mau Rm; The Great White Hope; Shaftin Africa; Recorded Song: St Brother; Films: What Do You Say To A NakedLady?, 1970; Shaft, 1971; Shaft's Big Score, 1972; Parachute to Paradies, Embassy, 1972; Shaft in Africa, 1973; Charley One-Eye, Earthquake, 1974; Man Friday, 1975; Diamonds, 1975; Escape to Athena, 1979; An Eye for an Eye, 1981; The Winged Serpent, 1982; The Big Score, 1983; City Heat, 1984; Killpoint, 1984; Portrait of a Hitman, 1984; A Time to Die, 1991; Amityville: A New Gen, 1993; Ballistic, 1995; Once Upon a Time When We Were Colored, 1996; George of the Jungle, 1997; Shaft, 2000; Antitrust, 2001; Shoot, 2001; Corky Romano, 2001; Al's Lads, 2001; Boat Trip, 2002; Wild Seven, 2006; Ladies of the House, 2008; Speed Racer, 2008; Set Apart, 2009; What Do You Say to a Naked Lady?, 2009; The Confidant, 2010; Go Beyond the Lens, 2011; Collar, 2011; Retreat!, 2012; This Bitter Earth, 2012; Duke, 2013. TV series: "The Merv Griffin Show"; "Search for Tomorrow"; "The New Yorkers"; "Inside Bedford-Stuyvesant"; "The Dean Martin Show, Shaft", 1973-74; "Outlaws", 1987; "413 Hope St", 1997; "Having Our Say: The Delany Sisters' First 100 Years", 1999; "Joe & Max", 2002; "The Rise & Fall of Jim Crow", 2002; "As the World Turns", 2002-03; "The Closer", 2005; "Painkiller Jane, Painkiller Jane", 2005; "Blade: The Series", 2006; "Grey's Anatomy", 2006; "Heroes", 2006; "Close to Home", 2006; "Heroes", 2006; "Final Approach", 2007; "Lincoln Heights", 2007-09; "Point of Entry", 2007; "Knight Rider", 2009; "Diary of a Single Mom", 2009-11; "The Mentalist", 2011; "Private Practice", 2012; "Being Mary Jane", 2013-; advocate, currently. **Orgs:** Negro Ensemble Co. **Honors/Awds:** Golden Globe Nominee for Most Promising Newcomer-Male, 1972; MTV Movie Award for Life time Achievement, 1994; AAFCA Award, African-Am Film Critics Asn, 2011, 2012. **Special Achievements:** Ranked No 62 on Premiere Magazine's 100 Greatest Movie Characters of All Time in 1971. **Business Addr:** Actor, Agency for Performing Arts, 9200 W Sunset Blvd Suite 900, Los Angeles, CA 90028, **Business Phone:** (310)273-0744.

### ROUNTREE, ELLA JACKSON

Educator, elementary school teacher. **Personal:** Born Feb 27, 1936, Griffin, GA. **Educ:** Ft Valley State Col, BS, 1957; Western Conn State Col, MS, 1973. **Career:** Ala State Elem Sch, 1957-60; Moore Elem Sch, 1960-63; Grassy Plain Sch, teacher, 1963-. **Orgs:** Danbury City Coun, 1973-77; 6th Ward, 1973-; Bethel Educ Asn; Conn Educ Asn; Nat Educ Asn; Phi Lambda Theta; Nat Hon & Prof Asn Educ; Nat Asn Advan Colored People; Alpha Kappa Alpha Sorority; Waterbury Chap, LINKS; Mt Pleasant, AMEZ Church. **Home Addr:** 279 Whitworth Dr SW, Atlanta, GA 30331-3815. **Business Addr:** 241 Greenwood Ave, Danbury, CT 06810.

### ROUSE, JACQUELINE ANNE

Educator. **Personal:** Born Feb 1, 1950, Roseland, VA; daughter of Fannie Thompson. **Educ:** Howard Univ, BA, African-Am black studies & hist, 1972; Atlanta Univ, Atlanta, MA, African Am hist, 1973; Emory Univ, Atlanta, PhD, African Am women hist, 1983. **Career:** Pal. Beach Jr Col, Lake Worth, sr instr, 1973-80; Ga Inst Teachers, Atlanta, guest lectr, 1983; Morehouse Col, Atlanta, assoc prof, 1983; Am Univ Smithsonian Inst, Landmarks, prof African Am hist, 1989-91, consult; Ga State Univ, Dept African Am Studies, assoc fac, 1992, assoc prof hist, currently; Lincoln Col; Oxford Univ, Oxford, Eng, 2003; Univ Pretoria, S Africa, Hist & Hist Preserv Dept, guest lectr, 2004; Author: Lugenia Burns Hope, Black Southern Reformer; Women in the Civil Rights Movement; Trailblazers & Torchbearers, 1941-65; Nurturing Seeds of Discontent: Septima P. Clark and Participatory Democracy. **Orgs:** Asst ed, Jour Negro Hist, 1983-89; adv, ref Harriet Tubman Historial & Cult Mus, Macon, 1985; panelist, Am Asn Univ Women, 1985-; prin scholar, Steering Comt, Nat Conf Women Civil Rights Movement, 1988; panelist, Jacob Javits Fel, Dept Educ, 1989; pres, nat vice dir, Asn Black Women Historians Inc, 1989-; vpres, Asn Social & Behav Scientists, 1989-; consult, adv, Atlanta Hist Soc, 1989; historian consult, Apex Collection Life & Heritage, 1989; pres, Southern Asn Women Historians, 2001; Presidential Comn Status Women; White House Comn Status Women. **Home Addr:** 887F Gatehouse Dr, Decatur, GA 30032, **Home Phone:** (404)292-8164. **Business Addr:** Associate Professor, Georgia State University, 25 Park Pl Suite 2000, Atlanta, GA 30303, **Business Phone:** (404)413-6385.

### ROUTTE-GOMEZ, ENEID G.

Journalist. **Personal:** Born May 16, 1944, Long Island, NY; daughter of Jesse Wayman and Maud Gomez. **Educ:** Univ Mo, Sch Journ, multicultural mgmt prog, 1984; Univ PR. **Career:** San Juan Star, San Juan, PR, reporter, ed & columnist, 1964-94; Univ Puerto Rico, prof jour, currently. **Orgs:** Pres, Caribbean Women's Network, 1984-; dir, Displaced Homemakers Coun Region II, 1990-; dir & ex-pres, Overseas Press Clubs Pr, 1975-; Nat Asn Black Journalists, 1984; Pr Endowment for the Humanities, 1990. **Honors/Awds:** Numerous civic and press awards. **Business Addr:** Editor, Special Writer, San Juan Star, PO Box 9020058, Old San Juan00902.

### ROUX, DR. VINCENT J., SR.

Physician. **Personal:** Born Apr 27, 1937, New Orleans, LA; son of John (deceased) and Beatrice Grammer; married Lois Milton; children: Bridgette, Vincent Jr & Denise. **Educ:** Xavier Univ, BS, 1961; Howard Univ Col Med, MD, 1965; Nat Bd Med, Bd Examiners, dipl, 1965; Am Bd Surg, cert, 1971. **Career:** Montreal Neurol Inst, extern, 1964; Freedmen's Hosp, intern, 1966; Howard Univ Col Med, resident gen surgeon, 1966-70, Dept Surg, asst prof, chief resident, 1969-70, assoc dean & clin affairs, 1972-75, Dept Comn Health Practices, clin instr, 1972, med dir, assoc dean alumni & pub affairs, currently; Am Col Surgeons, fel, 1975. **Orgs:** AMA; Nat Med Asn; Am Col Surgeons; Med Chirurgical Soc DC; chmn & bd dir, DC Chap United Way, 1974-76; mem & bd dir, Nat Cap Med Found DC Chamber Com. **Honors/Awds:** Daniel Hale Williams Award, 1966; Physician's Recognition Award, AMA, 1969; Charles R Drew Memorial Award, 1965; 1st Annual Clarence Sumner Green Award, 1965. **Special Achievements:** Publication: "The Stimulation of Adenosine 3', 5' Monophosphal Prodn by Antidiuretic Factors", "The CV Catheter, An Invasive Therapeut Adj" 1977. **Home Addr:** 9506 Clement Rd, Silver Spring, MD 20910-1643, **Home Phone:** (301)587-7342. **Business Addr:** Associate Dean, Howard University College Of Medicine, 520 W St NW, Washington, DC 20059, **Business Phone:** (202)806-6270.

### ROWAN, MICHAEL TERRANCE

Vice president (organization), physician. **Personal:** Born Indianapolis, IN; son of Charles and Odessa. **Educ:** Miami Univ, OH, BA, bus admin, 1980; Univ Mich, MHSA, hosp admin, 1982. **Career:** Dist Columbia Gen Hosp, admin extern, 1981; Univ Penn Hosp, admin resident, 1982-83, Transp Serv Dept, dir, 1982-83; St Vincent's Hosp, outpatient admin, Dept Psychiat, 1983-84; St Vincent Med Ctr, asst vpres, 1985-87; Memorial Med Ctr, vpres, admin, 1987-92; Sarasota Memorial Hosp, exec vpres & chief operating officer, 1993-99; Humility Mary Health Care Corp, Youngstown, Ohio, pres & chief exec officer, 1999-2003; St John Health, exec vpres & chief operating officer, 2002-04; Cath Health Initiatives, exec vpres & chief operating officer, 2004-14, pres Health Serv Delivery & chief operating officer, 2014-; St Vincent Med Ctr, Toledo; St Vincent's Hosp, NY; Consorta, vchmn; Wash Univ Sch Med, adj instr. **Orgs:** Fel, Am Col Healthcare Execs, 1981-; health div chmn, United Way, Coastal, GA, 1991; bd mem, Am Heart Asn, Southwest FL, 1994-; bd mem, Savannah Area Chamber Com, Southside, 1989-92; bd mem, Sarasota Family Coun Ctr, 1994-; bd mem, JH Floyd Sunshine Manor Nursing Home, 1994-; bd mem, Nat Asn Health Serv Execs, 2004-10; bd mem, Centura Health Colo; bd nominating comt, Cath Health Asn Am; Nat Healthcare Exec Coun Am Red Cross; dir, Cath Health Initiatives Health; dir, KentuckyOne Health. **Home Addr:** 4501 Quail Run Lane, Sarasota, FL 34232, **Home Phone:** (813)379-0429. **Business Addr:** Executive Vice President, Chief Operating Officer, Catholic Health Initiatives, 198 Inverness Dr W, Englewood, CO 80112, **Business Phone:** (303)298-9100.

### ROWE, REV. DR. ALBERT P.

Clergy, athlete. **Personal:** Born Sep 22, 1934, Columbia, SC; son of John and Esther; married Dorothy Collins. **Educ:** Morgan St Col, BA, 1958; Crozer Theol Sem, attended 1962; Princeton Theol Sem, attended 1969; Eastern Bapt Theol Sem, DMin, 1982. **Career:** Cent Baptist Church, pastor, 1962-68; Calvary Baptist Church, pastor, 1968-; Paterson Bd Educ, comnr, 1977-82; Paterson City Coun, councilman-at-large, 1982-90, pres, 1989-90; Morgan State Univ Football, capt; Calvary Baptist Comn Ctr, founder, pres; Cavalry Baptist Housing Develop Corp; Calvary Baptist Comn Health Ctr. **Orgs:** Vpres, Nat Asn Advan Colored People, 1966-68; vpres, Passiac Valley United Way, 1974-82, 1978-82; bd trustee, Barnett Mem Hops, 1980-84; vpres, chmn. Allocation comt Passaic Valley United Way.; bd trustee, Passaic-Bergen County Urban League, 1990-96; bd trustee, Nat Coun Churches; chmn, PNBC Home Mission Bd; bd trustee, Colgate Rochester Crozer Divinity Sch; Paterson Boys Club; Paterson YMCA; Alpha Phi Alpha Fraternity Inc; bd dir, Barnert Hosp; gov bd, Nat Coun Churches Christ. **Honors/Awds:** Nominated Young Man of the Year, Wilmington JC'S, 1967; Distinguish Service Award, Calvary Baptist Church, 1973; Community Service Award, Paterson Nat Asn Advan Colored People, 1974; CIAA Wrestling Champion; Avenue named in honor, 2009. **Special Achievements:** Official observer, first free election, South African, Nelson Mandella elected president; Named African chief Nii Addo Ayee, Accrea Ghana Council of Chiefs; preaching missions to Russia, Cuba, Ghana, Puerto Rico, Haiti & Kenya; The First African American preacher to preach for the Kenya Baptist Convention in Nairobi Kenya, West Africa. **Home Addr:** 415 19th Ave, Paterson, NJ 07504-1228, **Home Phone:** (973)345-0852. **Business Addr:** Pastor, Calvary Baptist Church, 575 E 18th St, Paterson, NJ 07514, **Business Phone:** (973)278-1849.

### ROWE, AUDREY

Educator. **Personal:** Born Nov 4, 1946, New York, NY. **Educ:** Univ DC, Fed City Col, BA, edu, 1971; George Washington Univ, bus pub admin. **Career:** Nat Asn Advan Colored People, asst dir, 1967-68; SASA House Sum Prog, consult, 1969; CPB dir Womens Activ; Nat Yough Alternative Proj, consult; Fed City Col Exten Prog, prog asst, 1970-72; Nat Welfare Rights Orgn, spec asst to exec dir, 1972-73; Proj New Hope, ed dir, 1972-72; C's Defense Fund, educ specialist/child advocate, policy analyst, 1973-75; Nat Comn Observance Int Womens Yr, commr; Womans Adv Com Sec Lbr, 1973; Nat Womens Pol Caucus, nat vice chairperson, 1973-75, nat chairperson, 1975-77; Nat Youth Alternatives Proj, consult, 1975; Media Productions, consult, 1976; Corp Pub Broadcasting, dir women's activ, 1976-79; Off Youth Affairs, Wash, DC, spec asst to mayor, 1979-80; DC Govt, Dept Human Serv, comnr social serv, 1980-88; Rockefeller Found, Equal Opportunity Div, consult, 1988-91; USDA, food & nutrit serv, adminr; City New Haven, Conn, human resources adminr, 1990-91; State Conn Dept Social Serv, comnr social serv & comnr income maintenance, 1991-95; Dept Social Servs CT, comnr; Nat Urban League Inc, exec vpres & chief operating officer, 1995-96; Lockheed Martin IMS, C & Family Serv, sr vpres & managing dir, 1996-2002; ACS Inc, sr vpres pub affairs & managing dir, 2002-05; Affiliated Comput Serv Inc, sr vpres pub affairs, 2005-; Accenture LLP, consult, 2005-06; Alt & Assocs Consult Serv Inc, pres, 2007-. **Orgs:** Nat Coun Negro Women, 1967; chairperson, Juv Justice Adv Group DC; founder, DC Womens Pol Caucus, 1972; pres bd, Movement Econ Justice, 1974; bd mem rep, Womens Task Force; bd mem, Womens Campaign Fund; DC Comm Mgt; chair, Nat Comn Family Foster Care; bd mem, Joint Ctr Polit & Econ Studies; bd mem, Am Pub Welfare Asn; bd mem, Child Welfare League Am; fel John F Kennedy Sch Govt, Harvard Univ, Inst Polits;

bd trustee, Coun Dc, currently. **Honors/Awds:** Organic Award DC Black Economic Union Commission; Sojourner Truth Award, 1974. **Special Achievements:** Publication: The Feminization of Poverty: An Issue for the 90's, Yale Univ J of Law and Feminism, Fall 1991; Ed: The State of Black Am, 1991, To Be Equal, Nat Urban League. **Home Addr:** 300 Cent Pk Suite 29G, New York, NY 10024, **Home Phone:** (508)548-3492. **Business Addr:** Board of Trustee, The Council of the District of Columbia, 1832 Taylor St NW, Washington, DC 20011.

### ROWE, CHRISTA F.

Nun, educator. **Personal:** Born Jun 10, 1959, Clearwater, FL; daughter of Peter John Sr and Theresia Roberson. **Educ:** Hillsborough Community Col, Tampa, FL, AA, 1986; St Leo Col, St Leo, FL, BSW, 1988; Boston Col, MEd, 1998; Hawkstone Ctr Spirituality & Renewal, Shrewsbury, Eng, 2000. **Career:** Holy Family Cath Church, San Diego, Calif, sec, 1980-82; St Lawrence Cath Church, Tampa, Fla, pastoral minister, 1983-87; Diocese St Petersburg, Off Black Cath Ministries, St Petersburg, Fla, assoc dir, 1988-90; Diocese St Petersburg, St Petersburg, Fla, columnist, 1988-90; Diocese St Petersburg, Tampa, Fla, productions coordr, inner vision radio prog, 1988-90; Our Lady Queen Peace Church, New Port Richey, Fla, dir relig educ, 1990-96; Sisters St Clare, New Port Richey, Fla, formation dir, 1996-98; St Vincent de Paul Parish, adult educ coordr, 1997-98; St Josephs Parish, St Petersburg, Fla, pastoral assoc & dir relig educ, 1998-99; Sacred Heart Oratory, Wilmington, DE, dir outreach, mgr, 2000-2006; Sacred Heart Village, mgr, 2006-10; House Joseph II, dir, 2012-. **Orgs:** Fools Jesus Mime & Pantomine Clown Troup, 1976-79; vocations promoter, Sisters St Clare, 1986-91; Nat Asn Social Workers, 1987-89; Campaign Human Devt, 1988-91; Nat Asn Black Cath Adminrs, 1988-89; Liturgical CMS Diocese, St Petersburg, 1991-94; Vocations Team, Sisters St Clare, 1992-96, Regional Team, 1992-95; Regional Counr, 2003-. **Home Addr:** 1105 W 8th St, Wilmington, DE 19806.

### ROWE, JIMMY L.

Association executive. **Personal:** Born Dec 6, 1932, Haskell, OK; children: Dianna, Leonardo, James, Kimberly & Michael. **Educ:** SC State Col, BA, industrial educ, 1956. **Career:** Trans Oppor Prog Pico Rivera, CA, training coordr, 1967-68, asst dir, 1968-71, actg dir, 1971-72; Sons Watts Own Recog Proj, dir, 1971-74. **Orgs:** Tulsa Personnel Asn; Nat Asn Pretrial Release Asn; Com Rel Comn Employ Com; dir, coalition LA Model Ctys; employ dir, Tulsa Urban League; asst pastor & minister christian ed St Luke Bapt Ch; youth minister, Doublerock BCCompton, CA; Truevine BC Hawthorne, CA; Nat Asn Advan Colored People; Black Econ Union LA; Mex Am Polit Asn. **Honors/Awds:** Received Resolution Los Angeles City Coun Outstand Leadership.

### ROWE, MARILYN JOHNSON

Consultant. **Personal:** Born Nov 9, 1954, Batesburg, SC; married Thaddeus E Jr; children: Brandolyn & Alesia. **Educ:** Univ SC, BA, Educ, 1977. **Career:** SC Human Affairs Comn, sr equal employ opportunity consult; Olive Branch Baptist Church, dir music. **Orgs:** Am Asn Affirmation Action, 1979-; Nat Asn Human Rights Worker, 1979-; Tau Beta Sigma USC, 1976; vol, Metro Community Rels Coun, 1989-90. **Honors/Awds:** Employee of the Year, SC Human Affairs Comn, 1990. **Home Addr:** 105 Tawny Br Rd, Columbia, SC 29212. **Business Addr:** SC.

### ROWE, DR. NANSI IRENE

Executive, lawyer. **Personal:** Born May 6, 1940, Detroit, MI; children: Leslie Anika-Ayoka. **Educ:** Detroit Inst Tech, BBA, 1965; Wayne State Univ, JD, 1973; Payne Sem, Mdiv. **Career:** City Detroit Corp, corp coun, dep corp coun, 1974-78; City Detroit, corp coun & dep corp coun, 1975-78; Detroit Econ Growth Corp, vpres, gen coun, secy to bd dir, 1979-82; EO Constructors Inc, pres, chmn bd, 1980-; Nansi Rowe & Assoc PC, pres, chief coun, partner, atty, 1982-. **Orgs:** Secy, treas, Wayne Cnty Com Col Found; secy, gen coun, Detroit Eco Growth Corp; bd mem, Homes Black C; bd mem, United Community Serv, 1978-81; State Bar Mich; Am Arbit Asn; Nat Asn Advan Colored People; Inner-City Bus Improv Forum, Southeastern Mich Bus Develop Ctr; Am Bar Asn; Detroit Bar Asn; life mem, Nat Bar Asn; bd mem, Southeastern Mich Transit Auth; bd mem, Brent Gen Hosp; bd mem, Southeastern Mich Transit Authority. **Home Addr:** 5470 Wessex Ct Apt 107, Dearborn, MI 48126-2680, **Home Phone:** (313)908-2014. **Business Addr:** Attorney, Nansi Rowe & Associates PC, 333 W Ft St Suite 1410, Detroit, MI 48226, **Business Phone:** (313)861-5733.

### ROWELL, VICTORIA LYNN

Actor. **Personal:** Born May 10, 1959, Portland, ME; married Radcliffe Bailey; married Tom Fahey; children: Maya; married Wynton Marsalis; children: Jasper. **Educ:** Cambridge Sch Ballet, Cambridge, MA. **Career:** Actor, ballet dance & author; Films: Leonard Part 6, 1987; As the World Turns, 1988; Distinguished Gentleman, 1992; Dumb & Dumber, 1994; One Red Rose, 1995; Barb Wire, 1996; Eve's Bayou, 1997; Secrets, 1997; Dr Hugo, 1998; A Wake in Providence, 1999; Fraternity Boys, 1999; Black Listed, 2003; Motive, 2004; Midnight Clear, 2005; A Perfect Fit, 2005; Home of the Brave, 2006; Polly & Marie, 2007; Of Boys & Men, 2008; Ghost Whisperer, 2010; Grand Theft Auto V, 2012; TV Series: "The Cosby Show", 1989-90; "The Fresh Prince of Bel-Air", 1990; "The Young & The Restless", 1990-98, 2000, 2002-07; "Hermans Head", 1991-93; "Diagnosis Murder", 1993-01; "Deadly Games", 1995; "Late Show with David Letterman", 1998; "Hollywood Squares", 1999; "Feast of All Saints", 2001; "Family Law", 2001; "The Wayne Brady Show", 2003-04; "The Tyra Banks Show", 2006; "The View", 2007; "The Morning Show with Mike & Juliet", 2007; "Tavis Smiley", 2008; "The Wendy Williams Show", 2010; "The Mo'Nique Show", 2010; TV Movies: "Full Eclipse", 1993; "Secret Sins of the Father", 1994; "A Town Without Pity", 2002; "Without Warning", 2003; "Without Warning", 2003; "Noah's Arc", 2006; "Polly and Marie", 2007; "All of Us", 2007; "Law & Order: Special Victims Unit", 2013; Plays: Drucilla Winters, 1990. **Orgs:** Founder & pres, Rowell Foster C's Postive Plan, 1990-; spokesperson, Child Welfare League Am, 1992; ambassador, St Lucian Bd Tourism, 1995; spokesperson, Annie E Casey Found; Sigma Gamma Rho Sorority. **Honors/Awds:** Best Actress in a Daytime Drama, Nat Asn Advan Colored People, 1993; Soap Opera Awards, Scene Stealer, 1994; Image Award for Outstanding Actress in aDaytime Drama Series, 1994, 1996, 1997, 1998, 1999, 2001, 2003, 2004, 2005, 2006; DHL, Univ Southern Maine, 2006. **Special Achievements:** Full Scholarship Recipient of the American Ballet Theatre School of NYC; American Ballet Theater II, NYC; Guest Teacher, resident of the Elma Lewis School of Fine Arts/Mass; Guest resident teacher of the Roxbury Ctr of the Performing Arts, Roxbury, Mass. **Home Addr:** c/o CBS Television City, 7800 Beverly Blvd, Los Angeles, CA 90036. **Business Addr:** Founder, President, The Rowell Foster Children Positive Plan, Rm 651 425 Shatto Pl, Los Angeles, CA 90020, **Business Phone:** (323)857-1717.

### ROWLAND, KELLY TRENE (KELENDRIA TRENE ROWLAND)

Singer, actor. **Personal:** Born Feb 11, 1981, Atlanta, GA; married Tim Witherspoon; children: 1. **Career:** Albums: Destiny's Child, 1998; The Writing's On the Wall, 1999; Survivor, 2001; Eight Days of Christmas, 2001; Dilemma; Stole, 2002; Train On a Track, 2003; Here We Go, 2005; Ms Kelly, 2007; Here I Am, 2011; TV series: "The Hughleys", 2002; "Born to Diva", 2003; "American Dreams", 2003; "Eve", 2003; "Wild n Out", 2003; "Girlfriends", 2006; Girlfriends3, 2006; The 20th Annual Soul Train Music Awards, 2006; "Clash of the Choirs", 2007; The British Soap Awards, 2008; The Party, 2008; Episode dated 26 May 2008, 2008; "TRL Italy", 2008; "So You Think You Can Dance", 2009; "The Fashion Show", 2009; Ode to la Mode, 2009; It's in the Cards, 2009; Blood, Sweat and Sparkle, 2009; "Single Ladies", 2011; "Bag of Bones", 2011; "The X Factor", 2011; "What Would Dylan Do?", 2013; "Real Husbands of Hollywood", 2013. TV guest appearance: "Smart Guy", 1997; "Brandy and Ray J: A Family Business", 2010; "The Spin Crowd", 2010; "X Factor Germany", 2010; "X Factor Australia", 2010; "La Las Full Court Wedding", 2010; "The A-List: New York", 2010. Films: Freddy vs Jason, 2003; The seat Filler, 2004; Asterix at the Olympic Games, 2008; The Goree Girls, 2011; Think Like a Man, 2012. Soundtrack appearance: Down to earth, 2001; monaLisa Smile, 2004; Album appearances: Seperated (Remix), 1999; Oh Why, 2003; How I Feel, 2005; Solo Albums: Simply Deep, 2002; R&B group, ling: A Planet Rock, 2007, "This Morning", 2009; Two of 12 Voted Off, 2009; "So You Think You Can Dance", 2009; Tours: Simply Deeper Tour, 2003; Ms Kelly Tour, 2007; Supafest, 2010; Kelly On Tour, 2011; FAME Tour, 2011. **Honors/Awds:** Grammy Awards, 2001-03, 2010; Survivor, 2002; Ebel Award, 2003; Capital FM Awards, 2003; TMF Awards, 2003; Billboard R&B/Hip-Hop Awards, 2003; Soul Train Lady of Soul Awards; Image Award, Nat Asn Advan Colored People; Artist Direct (ADOMA) Awards; ASCAP Women Behind the Music Awards, 2010; International Dance Music Awards, 2010. **Business Addr:** Recording Artist, Singer, Sony BMG Music Entertainment Inc, 550 Madison Ave, New York, NY 10022-3211, **Business Phone:** (212)833-8000.

### ROXBOROUGH, MILDRED BOND

Secretary (organization), association executive, consultant. **Personal:** Born Jun 30, 1926, Brownsville, TN; daughter of Ollie S and Mattye Tollette; married John W II. **Educ:** Howard Univ, Wash Square Col, BA, 1947; Columbia Univ, MA, 1953; Univ Paris; Univ Mexico. **Career:** Executive (retired), consult; Nat Asn Advan Colored People, nat field secy, 1954-58, dir, Life Mem Prog, 1958-63, admin asst to exec dir, 1963-67, exec ast to exec dir, 1967-75, asst dir, 1975-78, dir opers, 1978-84, dep dir progs, 1984-86, dir develop, 1986-97, consult, 1997-; Inter Group Corp, dir, 1987-2006. **Orgs:** Nat Asn Advan Colored People, 1958-; bd dir, vice chair, Inter group Corp; former vice chair, bd dirs, chair, Personnel Comm, Am's Charities; former chair, Personnel Comm Morning side Retirement & Health Inc; bd mem, Morningside Retirement & Health; Nat Mus African Am Hist & Cult. **Honors/Awds:** James Weldon Johnson Medal; Medgar Wiley Evers Award; Ams Charities Distinguished Service Award. **Special Achievements:** She was the first woman to serve the organization in the role of Director of programs in Nat Asn Advan Colored People. **Home Addr:** 100 LaSalle St Apt 12G, New York, NY 10027. **Business Addr:** Development Consultant, National Association for the Advancement of Colored People, 39 Broadway Suite 2201 22nd Fl, New York, NY 10060-3060, **Business Phone:** (212)344-7474.

### ROY, JAN S.

Executive. **Personal:** Born Jan 19, 1954, Evanston, IL; daughter of Bedford McCowan; married Anthony E; children: Harrison & Erica. **Educ:** Harold Wash Col, AS, hospitality mgt, 1991; Roosevelt Univ, BS, hospitality mgt, 1997; Capella Univ, PhD. **Career:** Cent State Univ, Wilberforce, OH, asst prof Hospitality Mgt; Grand Valley State Univ, Allendale, Mich, asst prof Hospitality Mgt; St Xavier Univ, adj instr; Roosevelt Univ, adj instr; APUS group, prog dir Hospitality Mgt Prog; Ramada Hotel, conv sales mgr, 1987-89; Navy Pier; Hotel Sofitel Chicago; Sheraton Int Hotel, conv sales mgr, 1989-91; Am Med Asn, sr rep, 1991-94; Hospitality Mgt, prog dir; McCormick Pl Conv Ctr, mgr sales prom, 1994-96; Chicago Conv & Tourism Bur, dir corp sales, 1996-. **Orgs:** Bd mem, Network Exec Women Hospitality, 1995-96; Am Hotel Lodging Asn; Prof Conv Mgt Asn; Nat Coalition Black Meeting Planners; adv bd mem, Harold Wash Coll, 1996-; bd mem, Meeting Prof Int, 1997-. **Home Addr:** 1911 Warren St, Evanston, IL 60202, **Home Phone:** (847)491-9124. **Business Addr:** Director, Chicago Convention and Tourism Bureau, 2301 S Lake Shore Dr, Chicago, IL 60616, **Business Phone:** (312)567-8500.

### ROY, JOHN WILLIE

Automotive executive. **Career:** Southland Chrysler Plymouth, pres & dir, currently. **Business Addr:** President, Director, Southland Chrysler Plymouth Inc, 118 N Cong St, Jackson, MS 39205, **Business Phone:** (662)349-3700.

### ROYAL, ANDRE TIERRE

Football player. **Personal:** Born Dec 1, 1972, Northport, AL; children: Tierra Andrena. **Educ:** Univ Ala, criminal justice. **Career:** Football player (retired); Carolina Panthers, linebacker, 1995-98, right inside linebacker, 1997; Indianapolis Colts, right linebacker, 1998-2000.

### ROYAL, DONALD ADAM

Basketball player, basketball coach. **Personal:** Born May 22, 1966, New Orleans, LA; married Robin; children: Shauntel. **Educ:** Notre Dame Univ, attended 1987. **Career:** Basketball player (retired), basketball coach; Pensacola Tornados, 1987-88; Cedar Rapids Silver Bullets, 1988-89; Minn Timberwolves, 1989-90; Maccabi Tel Aviv, Israel, 1990-91; Tri-City Chinook, 1991; San Antonio Spurs, 1991-92; Orlando Magic, 1992-96, 1997-98; Golden State Warriors, 1996-97; Charlotte Hornets, 1997-98; Idaho Stampede, 1997; Brevard Blue Ducks, asst head coach, 2002. **Business Addr:** Assistant Head Coach, Brevard Blue Ducks, 100 Hive Dr, Melbourne, FL 32941-0064, **Business Phone:** (321)751-2583.

### ROYAL, KING. See HOOKS, KEVIN.

### ROYE, MONICA R HARGROVE

Lawyer. **Personal:** Born Feb 7, 1955, Atlanta, GA; daughter of Ernest Crawford and Bettye Forston; children: Stephen Paul. **Educ:** Dartmouth Col, Hanover, BA, govt/urban studies, 1976; Univ Mich Law Sch, Ann Arbor, JD, 1979; Wesley Theol Sem, MDiv, 2003. **Career:** Kutak Rock & Huie, Atlanta, paralegal, 1976; IBM Legal Dept, Armonk, summer law clerk, 1978; US Dept Justice, Antitrust Div, trial atty, 1979-83; US Air Inc, Arlington, Va, from atty to asst gen coun, assoc gen coun, 1983-2003; Airports Coun Int-N Am, gen coun, 2008-13; Metrop Wash Airports Authority, dep gen coun, 2013-16, vpres & secy, 2016-. **Orgs:** Henry & Mayme Sink Scholar Fund, 1986-91; Celestial Echoes, 1986-91; Celestial Echoes, assoc pastor, 1993-96; Lomax Am Zion Church; secy, USAM Corp, 1988-96; judicial coun, Am Zion church; Bicentennial Revival COM, 1996; Dartmouth Lawyers Asn; chair, Am Bar Asn, 2013-; chair, Fed Bar Asn, 2013-. **Honors/Awds:** Outstanding Performance Award, US Dept Justice, 1980. **Home Addr:** 11220 Devereux Manor Lane Suite L, Fairfax Sta, Fairfax, VA 22039, **Home Phone:** (703)764-9499. **Business Addr:** Deputy General Counsel, The Metropolitan Washington Airports Authority, 1 Aviation Cir, Washington, DC 20001.

### ROYE, ORPHEUS MICHAEL

Football player. **Personal:** Born Jan 21, 1973, Miami, FL. **Educ:** Fla State Univ, criminal justice. **Career:** Football player (retired); Pittsburgh Steelers, defensive end & left defensive end, 1996-99, 2008; Cleveland Browns, defensive end & right defensive tackle & right defensive tackle, 2000-07. **Honors/Awds:** Champion, Super Bowl, XLIII. **Business Addr:** Defensive End, Pittsburgh Steelers, 100 Art Rooney Ave, Pittsburgh, PA 15212-5721, **Business Phone:** (412)323-1200.

### ROYSTER, DON M., SR. (DONALD M ROYSTER, SR.)

Executive, banker. **Personal:** Born Mar 12, 1944, Baltimore, MD; married Vertie M Bagby; children: Don M Jr & Denise C. **Educ:** Morgan State Univ, attended 1963; Agr Tech Univ NC, attended 1964; Nat Col, BA, 1970; Am Col, CLU, 1976; Life Off Mgt Assoc, FLMI, 1977. **Career:** Wash Nat Ins Co, asst vpres, 1967-85, vpres Individual Health Div, 1967-92 adminr, 1985-89, mkt serv officer, 1989-92, vpres opers; Atlanta Life Ins Co, pres, chief operating officer, 1992-95, pres/chief exec officer, 1993; ING, Life Ins Co of Ga, Exec vPres, 1995-98; United Ins Co Am, sr vpres, 1998-2000, Career Agency Div, pres, 1998-2010; Starphire Technologies LLC, bd mem; Reliable Life Ins Co, pres, 2001-; Mercer & Assocs LLC, prin, 2009-. **Orgs:** Chicago Chap Chartered Life Underwriters, 1976-92; Chicago Chap FLMI, 1977-92; Chicago Asn Health Underwriters, 1979-92; vpres, dir, Ment Helath Asn Evanston, 1981-83; chair, counr, Evanston Human Rels Comn, 1981-84; secy, bd dir, Sweet Auburn Area Improv Asn Atlanta, 1992-; dir, bd adv, Martin Luther King Jr, Ctr Nonviolent Social Chg, 1992-; bd dir, Atlanta Bus League, 1993-; bd dir, Cent Atlanta Progress, 1993-; dir, bd visitors, Clark Atlanta Univ, 1993-; bd visitors, Emory Univ, 1994-; dir, Ga Inst Technol; exec adv bd, Ivan Allen Col, 1994-; bd dir, Life Insurers Conf, 1994-. **Home Addr:** 210 Redding Rdg, Peachtree City, GA 30269-3317. **Business Addr:** President, United Insurance Company of America, 1 E Wacker Dr Fl 6, Chicago, IL 60601, **Business Phone:** (312)661-4500.

### ROYSTER, PHILIP M.

Educator, writer. **Personal:** Born Jul 31, 1943; married Phyliss M; children: Rebecca Suzanne, Francesca Therese, Barbara Kaye Hammond & Tara LynnHammond. **Educ:** Univ Ill, attended 1962; DePaul Univ, BA, 1965, MA, 1967; Roosevelt Univ, Black Cultures Sem, 1969; Loyola Univ, PhD, Am & brit lit, 1974. **Career:** St. Mel's High Sch, instr, 1966-67; Loyola Univ, asstship, 1967-68, fel, 1968-69, temp instr, 1969-70; Fisk Univ, Eng Dept, instr, 1970-74, asst prof, 1974-75; State Univ NY Albany, Dept African & Afro-Am Studies, asst prof, 1975-78; Syracuse Univ, Dept ARO Studies, assoc prof, 1978-81, instr, Develop Writing, Higher Educ Opportunity Prog; Le Moyne Col, adj assoc prof, 1979-81; State Univ of New York Cortland, lectr, eng, 1979-81; Kans State Univ, Dept Eng, assoc prof, 1981-85, Am Ethnic Studies Prog, coordr, 1984-88, prof, 1985-87; Bowling Green State Univ, Dept Ethnic Studies, prof, 1987-92, asst chmn, 1990-91; Univ Ill, Chicago, Dept African Am Studies, dir, 1991-2011, African Am Cult Ctr, prof, 1991-2011, interim dir, 1998-99, coord, 2009-11, prof emer eng African Am Studies, 2011-. **Orgs:** Popular Cult Asn, 1976-; bd mem, Soc New Music, 1979-81; Mellon Found, Mellon Proj, 1980; African-Am Drum Ensemble, 1987-; Asn Black Cult Ctrs, 1991-; Nat Steering Comn, 1991-; Const laws Subcomn, 1991-; Hon Soc Phi Kappa Phi, 1992-; Ill Comn Black Concerns Higher Educ, 1992-; Univ Ill Chicago Black Alumni Asn, 1992-; Mod Lang Asn; Col Lang Asn; Nat Coun Black Studies; Nat Asn Church God Summit Meeting Task Force; chairperson, Emerald Ave Church God, Hist Comn. **Home Addr:** 1547 Tina Lane, Flossmoor, IL 60422, **Home Phone:** (708)922-0779. **Business Addr:** Director African American Cultural Center, Professor of African American Studies, University of Illinois, 209 Addams Hall MC 20 830 S Halsted St, Chicago, IL 60607-7030, **Business Phone:** (312)413-2705.

### ROYSTER, SCOTT ROBERT

Executive. **Personal:** Born Jul 17, 1964, New Haven, CT; son of Robert and Jean. **Educ:** Duke Univ, BA, econs & psychol, 1987; Harvard Univ, MBA, 1992. **Career:** Chem Venture Partners, analyst, 1987-90; Capital Resource Partners, prin, 1992-94; TSG Capital Group, prin, 1995-96; Radio One Inc, exec vpres & chief financial officer, 1996-2007; Maarifa Educ, chief exec officer; Latimer Educ, co-founder, chief exec officer, 2009. **Orgs:** Bd mem, Telemedia, 1999-; bd mem, Netscan iPublishing, 1999-; bd visitors, Duke Univ, 2000-. **Home Addr:** 1425 Ri Ave NW Penthouse 1, Washington, DC 20005, **Home Phone:** (202)215-3520. **Business Addr:** Chief Executive Officer, Maarifa Education.

## ROYSTER, DR. VIVIAN HALL

College administrator, educator, dean (education). **Personal:** Born Feb 21, 1951, Monticello, FL; daughter of Emma L and Henry; married Charles; children: Renee Gwendolyn-Juanita. **Educ:** Fla A&M Univ, Tallahassee, FL, BS (magna cum laude), 1973; Atlanta Univ, Atlanta, GA, MSLS (summa cum laude), 1974; Fla State Univ, Tallahassee, FL, PhD, 1986. **Career:** Atlanta Univ GSLIS, educ fel, 1973-74; Fla State Univ, Tallahassee, Fla, assoc univ librn, 1974-80; Univ Md, E Shore Princess Anne, Md, admin librn, 1980-83; Fla A & M Univ, Tallahassee, Fla, assoc dir, TitleIII prog, 1982-84, assoc prof foreign lang, 1984-86; Fla A & M Univ Libr, Tallahassee, Fla, univ librn & head acquisitions dept, 1986-03; Del State Univ, dean libr, exec dir, 2003-; Fla A&M Univ, dept head & univ librn. **Orgs:** Am Libr Asn, 1976-; Am Libr Asn Black Caucus, 1978-; financial secy, Fla A & M Univ Friends Black Arch, 1988-; secy & bd dir, Asn Col & Res Libr, Fla Chap, 1989-; libr adv bd, Bond Comm Br Libr-Leon County Pub Libr Syst, 1989-; steering comm mem, E A Copel & Scholar Dr, Fla A & M Univ Found, 1989-; dir, Talaaka Serv Found Inc. **Home Addr:** 935 Br St, Montecello, FL 32344-2910, **Home Phone:** (850)997-4309. **Business Addr:** Dean of Libraries, Executive Director, Delaware State University, 1200 N Dupont Hwy, Dover, DE 19901, **Business Phone:** (302)857-7108.

## ROYSTON, EVELYN ROSS

Business owner, consultant, executive. **Personal:** Born Dec 14, 1959, Victoria, MS; daughter of Ethel M Brown; children: Gariel Brownlee & Natasha Brownlee. **Educ:** Tenn State Univ, attended 1981; State Tech Inst, Memphis, TN, attended 1999. **Career:** Construct Code Enforcement, plans & permit reviewer, 1984-94; Royston Construct Consults, pres, 1994-, chief exec officer, currently. **Orgs:** Asn Construct Inspectors, 1996-; Better Bus Bur, 1999-; rep mem, Memphis & Shelby County Land Use Control Bd. **Honors/Awds:** Iris Award, HER Bus News, 1999; Business Award, Small Minority Bus, 2000. **Home Addr:** 1605 N Germantown Pkwy Suite 111, Cordova, TN 38016, **Home Phone:** (901)757-3725. **Business Addr:** President, Chief Executive Officer, Royston Construction Consultants Inc, 1605 N Germantown Pkwy, Cordova, TN 38016, **Business Phone:** (901)340-1878.

## ROZIER, CLIFFORD GLEN, II

Basketball player. **Personal:** Born Oct 31, 1972, Bradenton, FL; son of Diane; married Trina. **Educ:** Univ NC, attended 1991; Univ Louisville, attended 1994. **Career:** Basketball player (retired); Golden State Warriors, ctr-forward, 1994-96; Pamesa Valencia, Spain, 1997; Toronto Raptors, 1996-97; Minn Timberwolves, ctr, forward, 1997-98; Continental Basketball Asn, Quad City Thunder, 1998; US Basketball League, Brevard Blue Ducks, 2000. **Honors/Awds:** Metro Conference Player of the Year, 1993, 1994; NCAA All-American First Team, 1994; First round pick, NBA Draft, 1994.

## ROZIER, GILBERT DONALD

Executive, association executive, business owner. **Personal:** Born Oct 19, 1940, West Palm Beach, FL; married Juanella Miller; children: Ricardo & Rellisa. **Educ:** Benedict Col, BA, 1963; Southern Conn State Col, MA, urban studies, 1973. **Career:** W Side YMCA NYC, youth worker, 1963-66; W Main St Comm Ctr, prog dir, 1966-67; Stamford Neighborhood Youth Corp, dir, 1967-74; Urban League S Weston Fair field, asso dir, 1970-74; Urban League Union CO, pres, 1974; Urban League S Weston, exec dir; Ky Fried Chicken Restaurants, franchise owner & pres, currently. **Orgs:** Secy, Conn State Fedn Demo Clubs, 1974; pres, AFLO Am Dem Club, 1979; life mem, Kappa Alpha Psi; bd trustees, Benedict Col; trustee, Stamford Bethel Am Methodist Episcopal Church; bd mem, Stanford Planning. **Honors/Awds:** Outstanding Young Man of the Year; Outstanding Young Men of America, 1973; Outstanding Citizen Union Co New Jersey Human Resources, 1979; Outstanding Citizen St John Lodge 14, Stamford, CT, 1980. **Special Achievements:** First black to own and operate a Kentucky Fried Chicken in Stanford. **Home Addr:** 285 W Main St, Stamford, CT 06902. **Business Addr:** President, Kentucky Fried Chicken, 356 Strawberry Hill Ave, Stamford, CT 06902, **Business Phone:** (203)348-6048.

## RUBIN, CHANDA

Tennis player. **Personal:** Born Feb 18, 1976, Lafayette, LA; daughter of Edward D and Bernadette Fontenot. **Educ:** Harvard Exten Sch, BA, econs. **Career:** Pro tennis player, 1991-. **Orgs:** Dir, US Tennis Asn Bd Dirs, 2013; Am Heart Asn. **Honors/Awds:** Orange Bowl, 1988; National Championship, 1988-89; ITF Winner, Int Tennis Fedn, 1991, 1995-96; Wimbleton Junier Singles, 1992; WTA Winner, Womens Tennis Asn Winner, 1993-96, 1997, 1999, 2000, 2002-03; ATA Athlete of the Year, 1995; USTA Female Athlete of the Year, 1995; Silver Medal, Bronze Medal, Pan Am Games, 1995; Australian Open Womens Double Winner, 1996; Most Caring Ahtlete, USA Weekend Mag, 1997; Arthur Ashe Leadership Award, 1997; Player Who Makes A Difference Award, Family Circle & Hormel Foods, 2002; Winner, Eastbourne, 2002; Winner, 2003; USTA Service Bowl Award, 2003; Madrid, 2003; Louisiana Sports Hall of Fame, 2013. **Home Addr:** , Lafayette, LA. **Business Addr:** Professional Tennis Player, United States Tennis Association, 70 W Red Oak Lane, White Plains, NY 10604-3602, **Business Phone:** (914)696-7000.

## RUBIO, JACQUELINE

Army officer. **Personal:** Born Nov 25, 1961, Hempstead, NY; children: Joseph, Justin & Jessica. **Educ:** Morgan State Univ, attended 1981; Fayetteville Community Col, attended 1986; Miller Motte Bus Col, attended 1991; Forsyth Tech Community Col, attended 1993. **Career:** AUS, instr, 2000-. **Orgs:** Greeter & usher, City Refuge Christian Church, 1997-. **Business Addr:** Staff, US Army, Staff Sgt Rubio 88M30, Fort Drum, NY 13603, **Business Phone:** (315)772-5996.

## RUCKER, ALSTON LOUIS

Banker. **Personal:** Born Aug 29, 1949, Greenwood, SC; son of Thomas L (deceased) and Annie (deceased); married Shirley Gordon; children: Montrice Ginelle & Aaron Louis. **Educ:** SCA State Col, BA, bus admin, 1971. **Career:** LaSalle Bank FSB, savings rep, 1973-81, retirement acct specialist, 1981-84, human resources mgr, 1984-85, asst secy, 1985-86, br mgr, 1986-87, br officer, 1987-91, asst vpres, 1992. **Orgs:** SCA State Col, Chicago Chap, 1975-; prog speaker, Chicago Asn Com & Ind, Youth Motivation Prog, 1981-; Lillydale Progressive Missionary Baptist Church, 1985-; Dolton Sch Dist 149, PTA, 1990-; Thornton High Sch, Dist 205, PTA, 1992; bd mem, Teen Living Progs Inc, 1993-; bd mem & treas, The Harvey 100 Club Inc, 1995-. **Honors/Awds:** Black & Hispanic Achievers, Chicago South Side YMCA, 1991; Americas Best & Brightest Young Business & Professional Men, 1992; Branch Administration Certificate Achievement, LaSalle Bank, FSB, 1994. **Home Addr:** 15305 Grant St, Dolton, IL 60419.

## RUCKER, CLYDE

Vice president (organization). **Educ:** Univ Colo, Boulder, BA; Cent Mich Univ, MS. **Career:** Arby's, staff; KFC, staff; Burger King Holdings Inc, staff, 1994-2000; vpres US franchise oper, 2000-03, sr vpres diversity capability & bus develop, 2003-04, sr vpres global commun & external affairs, 2005-07; Burger King Brands Inc, sr vpres global commun & external affairs; Quiznos, chief admin officer, 2007-08, exec vpres, 2007-10, chief operating officer & pres latin am opers, 2008-10. **Orgs:** Bd trustee, Fla Memorial Univ; 100 Black Men Am Inc. **Business Addr:** Executive Vice President, Chief Administrative Officer, Quiznos, 7595 Technology Way Suite 200, Denver, CO 80237, **Business Phone:** (720)359-3300.

## RUCKER, DARIUS

Guitarist, singer. **Personal:** Born May 13, 1966, Charleston, SC; married Beth Leonard; children: 2. **Educ:** Univ SC. **Career:** Lead vocalist/guitarist, Hootie & the Blowfish, formed, 1986; released self-financed EP, Kootchypop, 1991; platinum album Cracked Rear View, 1994, features hit single "Hold My Hand"; released Fairweather Johnson, 1996; Musical Chairs, 1998; Take 2, 2000; Albums: The Return of Mongo Slade, 2001; Back to Then, 2002; Learn to Live, 2008; Singles: Message in a Bottle, 1999; "God's Reasons", 2007; Don't Think I Don't Think About It, 2008; Films: Shallow Hal, 2001; TV series: "The Daily Buzz", 2005; "I Married", 2004; Learn to Live, 2008-09; History in the Making, 2009; True Believers, 2012-. **Honors/Awds:** Two Grammy Awards, including best new group, for Cracked Rear View. **Special Achievements:** Ranked in Golf Digest's "Top 100 in Music", 2006. **Business Addr:** Recording Artist, c/o Sony BMG Music Entertainment Inc, New York, NY 10022-3211, **Business Phone:** (212)833-8000.

## RUCKER, REV. RALEIGH

Clergy. **Career:** Ga State Patrol, chaplain; Ga State Nat Orgn Black Law Enforcement, Chaplain, currently; Ga chapter, chaplain; Ga Bur Invest, chaplain; Raleigh Rucker Funeral Home, proprietor, currently; chief adv, Monticello Police Dept, currently. **Orgs:** Chaplain, Edward-Miller Found. **Special Achievements:** First African American chaplain for the GA Bureau of Investment. **Home Addr:** 341 Candler Rd SE, Atlanta, GA 30317, **Home Phone:** (404)288-7015. **Business Addr:** Proprietor, Raleigh Rucker Funeral Home, 2199 Candler Rd, Decatur, GA 30032, **Business Phone:** (404)288-7016.

## RUCKER, DR. ROBERT D.

Judge, lawyer. **Personal:** Born Jan 1, 1952, Canton, GA; married Jacqueline Pace; children: James, Dawn & Fanon. **Educ:** Ind Univ, BA, 1974; Valparaiso Univ Sch Law, JD, 1976; Univ Va Law Sch, ML, judicial process, 1998. **Career:** Judge; Lake County, Ind, dep prosecutor, 1979-85; pvt prac, 1985-90; City Gary, dep city atty, 1987-88; Ind Ct Appeals, judge, 1991-99; Ind Supreme Ct, judge, 1999-. **Orgs:** Bd dir, Ind Trial Lawyers Asn; bd dir, Northwest Ind Legal Serv Orgn Nat Bar Asn, Judicial Coun, chair, 2009-10; Marion County Bar Asn; fel Indianapolis Bar Asn; Ind State Bar Asn; vice chair, Ind Comn Continuing Legal Educ; Am Bar Asn; Ind Judges Asn; fel Indianapolis Bar Found; chm, Lake County Judicial Nominating Comn. **Business Addr:** Judge, Indiana Supreme Court, 315 Ind State House, Indianapolis, IN 46204, **Business Phone:** (317)232-1930.

## RUCKS, ALFRED J.

Engineer, association executive. **Personal:** Born Oct 20, 1935, Bellwood, TN; son of Alfred and Horty. **Educ:** Tenn A&I State Univ, BSEE, 1958. **Career:** Engineer (retired); Defense Atomic Support Agency, 1958-62; White Sands Missile Range, electronics engr, 1962-85, EEO counr, 1973-85, chief safety engrg br, 1985-93. **Orgs:** IEEE, 1959-; assoc mem, NSPE; trustee, N Mesquite St Church Christ, 1962-; chmn, Minority Housing Bd City Las Cruces NM, 1968-80; pres, NM State NAACP, 1970-86; chmn, Reg VI NAACP, 1974-84; nat bd dir, NAACP, 1981-87; pres, Dona Ana County NAACP, 1990-; State NM, Martin Luther King Comn, 1985-86; Las Cruces Community Develop Bd, 1990-; NM Pvt Ind Counc, 1994-. **Honors/Awds:** Commanders Award White Sands Missile Range, 1975, 1982, 1993; NMex NAACP Award, 1972, 1979, 1986, 1992; Nat Merit Acad Award, 1973; Region VI Award, 1990; City Las Cruces, NMex Award, 1980; NMex Gov, 1975, 1985, 1993; Omega Psi Phi, NMSU chap, Citizen of the Year Award, 1992; Hispanic Leadership & Development Program Award, 1993; NMSU 'African-American Citizen of the Year', 1993; Tennessee NAACP, 1994. **Home Addr:** 733 Hellenic Dr, Las Cruces, NM 88011, **Home Phone:** (575)522-5152.

## RUDD, CHARLOTTE JOHNSON

Teacher, educator, administrator. **Personal:** Born Jul 4, 1948, Columbus, OH; daughter of James W and Helen; children: Toyia Lynn. **Educ:** Ohio State Univ, BS, 1970, MS, 1985. **Career:** Columbus Pub Schs, high eng teacher, 1970-73, Drop Out Prev Proj Move Ahead, coordr, 1973-79, mid sch reading/lang arts teacher, 1980-83, Human Rels, staff develop supt, 1983-85, mid sch asst prin, 1985-91, Effective Schs Process, dist adminr, 1991-; Broadleigh Elem Sch, ohio, prin; Ohio Ave Elem Sch, prin, 2009-. **Orgs:** Mortar bd, Ohio State Univ, 1970; co-founder, Doris L Allen Minority Caucus-OEA, 1974; PRIDE Inc group develop stud self-esteem & leadership, 1974; treas, Minority Caucus, 1974-76; exec comm, Ohio Educ Asn, 1978-83; dept & team leader, Franklin Alternative Mid Sch, 1979-83; Phi Delta Kappa, 1979; bd mem, Prof Develop Comm, 1979-83; Nat Educ Asn, 1981-83; Ohio House Rep, 1983-90; designer, Staff Develop Model Sch Improv, 1984; Nat Alliance Black Sch Educrs, 1989-93; child abuse & neglect adv bd, Comn Inter prof Educ & Pract, Ohio State Univ; comm clothes dr, House Rep Miller's, 1992-93. **Home Addr:** 1282 Pk Plz Dr, Columbus, OH 43213-2606. **Business Addr:** Principal, Ohio Avenue Elementary School, 505 S Ohio Ave, Columbus, OH 43205-2794, **Business Phone:** (614)365-6130.

## RUDD, DWAYNE DUPREE

Football player. **Personal:** Born Feb 3, 1976, Batesville, MS; children: 1. **Educ:** Univ Ala. **Career:** Football player (retired), free agt; Minn Vikings, linebacker, 1997, 1999-2000, right linebacker, 1998; Cleveland Browns, linebacker, 2001-02; Tampa Bay Buccaneers, line backer, 2003; free agt, currently. **Honors/Awds:** Second Team All-Pro Selection, 1998. **Home Addr:** 2292 Leicester Way SE, Atlanta, GA 30316.

## RUDOLPH, DAVID ERICSON

Public relations executive. **Personal:** Born Oct 7, 1966, Detroit, MI; son of Grover and Thelma. **Educ:** Mich State Univ, BS, criminal justice, 1989; Univ Cambridge, comparative law, 1989; Univ Nsw, comparative law, 1991; Fla State Univ, MS, int rels, bus & trade, 1994. **Career:** Detroit Pistons, Player Progr, coordr, 1994-95; Palace Sports & Entertainment, Pub Rels & Community Rels, 1994-96; D Ericson & Assocs Pub Rels, consult, pres & chief exec officer, sr managing partner, founder, 1996-; Caponigro Pub Rels Inc, sr acct exec, 1999-2001. **Orgs:** Bd dir, Detroit Club, 1994; fel Nat Socs Fundraising Execs, 1996; bd dir, Non Profit PR Network, 1998-99; vol, Detroit Grand Prix Asn, 1998-99; off vol, Ford Montreux Jazz Festival; Corp Commun & Community Rels Dept, Piston-Palace Found; bd dir, Nat Asn Fundraising Execs; BravoBravo!-Creator Leadership Detroit XXIV Detroit Emerging Leaders; Sphinx Orgn; bd dir, Detroit Enterprise Acad Charter Sch; bd dir, Habitat Humanity Detroit; bd dir, Neighborhood Serv Orgn; bd dir, Encore! Mich Opera Theater; Nat Asn Black Journalist Non-Profit Pub Rels Network; bd dir, Sphnix Org, currently. **Home Addr:** 5027 Greenway St, Detroit, MI 48204, **Home Phone:** (313)834-7117. **Business Addr:** Board of Director, Sphinx Organization, 400 Renaissance Ctr Suite 2550, Detroit, MI 48243, **Business Phone:** (313)877-9100.

## RUDOLPH, MAYA KHABIRA

Actor, television actor. **Personal:** Born Jul 27, 1972, Gainesville, FL; daughter of Dick and Minnie Riperton (deceased); married Paul Thomas Anderson; children: Pearl Bailey, Lucille Minnie Ida & Jackson Wright. **Educ:** Univ Calif, Santa Cruz, BA, photog, 1994. **Career:** The Rentals (music group), keyboard player & backup singer, 1994-96; The Groundlings (comedy troupe), Los Angeles, Calif, cast member, 1996-99; actress & comedienne, 1999-; TV series: "Liver Let Die", 1996; "Chicago Hope", 1996-97; "Action"; "City of Angels", 2000; "TV Funhouse", 2001; "Saturday Night Live", 2000-14; "Campus Ladies", 2006; The Simpsons, 2007; "Kath & Kim", 2008-09; "Up All Night", 2011-12; "We Need Help", 2013; "Portlandia", 2014; "The Awesomes", 2014; "Family Guy", 2014; "The Maya Rudolph Show", producer, 2014. Films: Gattaca, 1997; The Devil's Child, 1997; A Glance Away, 1999; Chuck & Buck, 2000; Duets, music supvr, 2000; Duplex, 2003; 50 First Dates, 2004; Wake Up, Ron Burgundy: The Lost Movie, 2004; A Prairie Home Companion, 2006; Idiocracy, 2006; Shrek The Third, Voice, 2007; Prop 8: The Musical, 2008; Away We Go, 2009; Grown Ups, 2010; MacGruber, 2010; Zookeeper, 2011; Bridesmaids, 2011; Zookeeper, 2011; Friends with Kids, 2011; The Way Way Back, 2013; Grown Ups 2, 2013; Turbo, 2013; The Nut Job, 2014; Inherent Vice, 2014. **Honors/Awds:** Vogue Fashion Awards, 2002; Nominee, Golden Satellite Award, 2005, Image Awards, 2007, Best Ensemble Cast, 2006; MTV Movie Award, 2012. **Special Achievements:** Voted No 20 on Entertainment Weekly's list of Funniest People in America in April 2004. **Business Addr:** Actor, c/o Saturday Night Live, 30 Reockefeller Plz, New York, NY 10012, **Business Phone:** (212)315-9016.

## RUFFIN, DR. JANICE E.

Psychologist, nurse, consultant. **Personal:** Born Dec 6, 1942, Cleveland, OH. **Educ:** Ohio State Univ Sch Nursing, BS, 1964; Rutgers State Univ Col Nursing, MS, psychiat nurs, 1967; City Univ NY Grad Ctr, MPhil, 1984, PhD, clin psychol, 1985. **Career:** Conn Ment Health Ctr, New Haven, Conn, dir nursing, 1974-77; Yale Univ Sch Nursing, asst prof grad prog psychiat nursing, assoc prof, 1975-77; City Col City Univ NY, lectr dept psychol, 1978-80; Bronx Psychiat Ctr, psychologist Highbridge out-patient clin, 1980-85; Baruch Col Off Coun & Psychol Serv, psychologist, 1985-, dir, 1986-94, dir, stud health serv, 1990-. **Orgs:** Sigma Theta Tau, 1968-; bd dir, NY Black Nurses Asn, 1971-74; chmn, Comn Nursing Soc Crisis, 1969-72; Affir Action Task Force, 1972-76; ed bd, Perspectives Psychiat Care, 1973-83; Historian Nat Black Nurses Asn, 1972-82; bd dir, Nat Black Nurses Asn, 1972-74; chmn, 1971-72 & vpres, 1972-73, Oper Success Nursing Educ; bd dir, Inst Comm Organ & Personal Effectiveness, 1974-77; Nurse Trng Rev Comn, NIMH, 1974-78; AK Rice Inst, 1979. **Honors/Awds:** Certificate & Gold Medal Ohio State Univ Sch Nursing, 1970; Certificate of Excellence, Am Nurses Asn, 1975; Certificate in Psychiatric Mental Health Nursing, Am Nurses Asn, 1975; Award Nat Asn Negro Bus & Prof Women's Clubs, 1977; Dedicated Professional Service Award, Nat Asn Negro Bus & Prof Womens Clubs, 1977; Excellence in psychology, City Col, City Univ NY, 1987. **Special Achievements:** Author: Affirmative action programming for the nursing profession through the American Nurses' Association, 1975; A Strategy for change : papers presented at the conference held June 9-10, Albuquerque, New Mexico, 1979; An exploratory study of adult development in black, professional women, 1985. **Home Addr:** 278 Atlantic Ave Suite 4, Brooklyn, NY 11201.

## RUFFIN, JOHN

Executive director, educator. **Personal:** Born Jun 29, 1943, New Orleans, LA; son of Wesley and Olivia; married Angela Beverly; children: John Wesley, Meeka & Beverly. **Educ:** Dillard Univ, BS, biol, 1965; Atlanta Univ, MS, biol, 1967; Kans State Univ, PhD, syst & develop biol, 1971; Harvard Univ, PhD, biol, 1977. **Career:** Southern Univ Baton Rouge, biol instr, 1967-68; Atlanta Univ, asst prof, 1971-74; AL

Agri & Mech Univ, assoc prof biol, 1974-75; NC Cent Univ, prof biol, 1978-86, chmn biol, Col Arts & Sci, dean, 1986-90; NIH Off Res Minority Health, dir; Nat Ctr Minority Health & Health Disparities, dir, 1990; Harvard Univ, cabot teaching fel. **Orgs:** Consult, NIH, 1978-; consult, Bd Sci & Tech, 1983-; consult, ADAMHA, NIMH, 1984; Asn Environ & Exp Botany; Asn Southeastern Biologists; N Carolina Acad Sci, Bot Soc Am. **Honors/Awds:** Samuel L. Kountz Award; NIH Directors Award; National Hispanic Leadership Award; Beta Beta Beta Biological Honor Society Award; Department of Healthand Human Services Special Recognition Award; US Presidential Merit Award; Martin Luther King Legacy Award, 2007; Cura Personalis Award, Georgetown Univ Med Ctr; honorary doctor of science, Spelman Col, Tuskegee Univ, Univ Mass Boston, Nc State Univ, Morehouse Sch Med, Meharry Med Col, Tulane Univ, Dillard Univ & Medgar Evers Col. **Home Addr:** 2612 McDowell St, Durham, NC 27705. **Business Addr:** Director, National Center on Minority Health & Health Disparities, 6707 Democracy Blvd Suite 800, Bethesda, MD 20892-5465, **Business Phone:** (301)402-1366.

### RUFFIN, JOHN WALTER, JR.

Executive, president (organization), chief executive officer. **Personal:** Born Jun 15, 1941, Moncure, NC; son of John Sr and Theima Harris; married Dorothy L Walton; children: Jonathan & Jehan. **Educ:** Morgan State Univ, AB, 1963; Cornell Univ, MS, 1970. **Career:** Pantry Pride Inc, vpres, 1980-85; Paradies Airport Shops, partner, consult; JD Ruffin Assoc Inc, consult, pres & chief exec officer, currently. **Orgs:** Chmn bd, Urban League Broward, 1984-87; adv bd, Barnett Bank, 1985-87; chmn, Broward Employ & Training, 1986; chmn, Coral Springs Econ Develop Found, 1995-97, chmn, CRA Bd, 2015; vice chair, Fla Memorial Univ, trustee; vice chair, Broward Ed, financial adv bd; 33rd Degree Mason, 1996; pres, Sigma Pi Phi Fraternity, Alpha Rho Boule, 1997; chmn, Broward Alliance, 2006-07; exec comt, bd dir, Broward County, S Fl; coun mem, InternetCoast Econ Develop Adv. **Home Addr:** PO Box 8589, Coral Springs, FL 33075. **Business Addr:** President, Chief Executive Officer, J D Ruffin Associates Inc, PO Box 8589, Coral Springs, FL 33075, **Business Phone:** (954)931-1172.

### RUFFIN, PAULETTE FRANCINE

Military leader, educator. **Personal:** Born Dec 13, 1956, Alexandria, VA; daughter of Paul and Rosetta Payton; children: M Joshua & D Christopher. **Educ:** Lehigh Univ, Bethlehem, PA, BS, mkt, 1978; Univ NC, Chapel Hill, NC, MA, social psychol, 1987. **Career:** AUS, Ord Sch, Aberdeen Provin Ground, Md, stud basic course, 1978; Stud Officer Co, Aberdeen Provin Ground, Md, exec officer, 1978-79; Mil Acad, W Pt, NY, admis officer, 1979-80; 9th INF Div, Ft Lewis, WA, asst secy to gen staff, 1980-85; Mil Acad, W Pt NY, assoc prof, 1987-90; 41st Area SptGroup, Panama, Log Oper, mat off, exec off, 1990-93; Army Mat Command HQ, spec asst comndg gen, speech writer, 1994-96, Georgetown Univ, dir Army ROTC, 1996-99; Army Times Publ Co, media rels & prog mgr; Gannett Govt Media, conferences & events mgr, currently. **Home Addr:** 8126 Clifforest Dr, Springfield, VA 22153, **Home Phone:** (703)913-1997. **Business Addr:** Events Manager, Gannett Government Media, 6883 Commercial Dr, Springfield, VA 22159-0500, **Business Phone:** (703)750-7400.

### RUFFIN, RONALD R.

Government official. **Personal:** Born Jul 23, 1947, Saginaw, MI; son of William and Catherine; married Verlie M; children: Tulani M & Omari A. **Educ:** Mich State Univ, BS, bus, 1970; Atlanta Univ, MA, criminal justice admin, 1990. **Career:** Lakeside Labs, pharmaceut rep, 1970-73; Ayerst Labs, pharmaceut rep, 1973-77; CYSP (Ceta), exec admin, 1977-78; City Detroit, mgr, Neighborhood City Halls, 1978-81, exec admin, Municipal Parking Dept, 1981-94; Wayne Co Comm Col, part-time instr, 1990-; City Detroit, dir munic parking dept, 1994-2007. **Orgs:** Nat Asn Advan Colored People, 1965-; Kappa Alpha Psi Fraternity, 1967-; Motown Athletic Club, 1982-; Municipal Parking Asn, 1983-; Prince Hall F &A Masons, 1993-; Detroit Zoological Soc, 1993-; Inst & Municipal ParkingCong, 1994-; Mus African Am Hist, 1995; exec ct adminr, Third Judicial Circuit Mich; Mich Asn Circuit Ct Adminr. **Business Addr:** Executive Court Administrator, Third Judicial Circuit Of Michigan, 711 Coleman A Young Munic Ctr, Detroit, MI 48226, **Business Phone:** (313)224-5261.

### RUFFIN-BARNES, WENDY YVETTE

Insurance agent. **Personal:** Born Jan 10, 1961, Ahoskie, NC; daughter of Audrey H and Linzy M; married Roy T Jr; children: Mia. **Educ:** Univ NC, Chapel Hill, BA, 1982; Old Dom Univ, attended 1988. **Career:** Brown's & Williamson Tob Corp, sales rep, 1982-91; State Farm Ins, agt, 1991-. **Orgs:** Kappa Alpha Sorority Inc; exec comt, Rotary, 1994-; chmn, Hertford Econ Develop Comt, 1994-; treas, Roanoke Chowan Assoc Life Underwriters, 1995-, alpha vice chmn; vice chmn, Hertford Co Schs Job Ready, 1997-; chmn, Hertford Co Wellness Ctr, 1997-; bd mem, Wachovia Bank NC, 1998-. **Honors/Awds:** Serv Above Self, Alpha Kappa Alpha Sorority Inc, 1997. **Home Addr:** 417 Colony Ave N, Ahoskie, NC 27910-2511, **Home Phone:** (252)332-5684. **Business Addr:** Insurance Agent, State Farm Insurance, 101 S Acad St, Ahoskie, NC 27910, **Business Phone:** (252)332-4458.

### RUFFINS, REYNOLD

Illustrator, designer. **Personal:** Born Aug 5, 1930, New York, NY. **Educ:** Cooper Union Univ, attended 1951. **Career:** Cooper Union, 1951; Sch Visual Arts, instr, 1967-70; Dept Visual Commun Col Visual & Performing Arts Syracuse Univ, vis adj prof, 1973; Queens Col, vis distinguished prof, 1989-90, prof, currently. **Orgs:** Push Pin Studio; New York Art Dirs Club; Am Libr Asn; Soc Publ Designers; Soc Illus. **Honors/Awds:** Best Illustration Award, NY Times Book Rev, 1973; Bologna (Italy) Children's Book Fair, 1976; Am Inst Graphic Arts Art Dir Club; Calif mag Award; Soc Illus Award; Professional Achievement Award, Cooper Union, 1972; 200 Years Am Illus NY Hist Soc; outstanding achievements, integrity, & commitment excellence educ, NYC, 1991; The Youth Friends Award, 1991; Augustus St Gaudens Award, 1993; Coretta Scott King Award, Am Libr Asn, 1997. **Special Achievements:** His designs and illustrations have been internationally recognized in group show exhibitions at the Louvre, Paris, Milan, Tokyo and at the Society of Illustrators Annual Shows, AIGA shows, Art Directors Club of New York and many other corporate shows. **Home Addr:** 51 Hampton St, Sag Harbor, NY 11963-4236, **Home Phone:** (631)725-3480. **Business Addr:** Dept of Fine Arts, Parsons School of Design, 66 5th Ave, New York, NY 10011, **Business Phone:** (212)229-8900.

### RUFFNER, RAYMOND P.

Business owner, insurance executive, real estate appraiser. **Personal:** Born Aug 11, 1946, Washington, DC; married Patricia Smith; children: Damien Earl. **Educ:** Wash Lee HS, grad, 1964; Acct Corresp Course, 1967. **Career:** Larry Buick Ar & VA, body & fender mech, 1969-71; United Co Life Ins Co, ins sls, 1971, ins sale & mgmt, 1971-77; Ruffner & Assocs Inc, ins sls & mgt, sole proprietor, pres, 1977-. **Orgs:** Investor, Real Estate, 1973-. **Honors/Awds:** Public Service to High Sch & Col, 1984. **Home Addr:** 1233 Old Elliott Rd Suite A, PO Box 8, Cassatt, SC 29032-9287, **Home Phone:** (803)713-0841. **Business Addr:** President, Sole Proprietor, Ruffner Associates Inc, 87 W Lee Hwy Suite 27, Warrenton, VA 20186, **Business Phone:** (540)349-1320.

### RUSH, BOBBY LEE

Mayor. **Personal:** Born Nov 23, 1946, Albany, GA; married Carolyn Thomas; children: 6. **Educ:** Roosevelt Univ, BA, 1974; Univ Ill, MA, polit sci, 1994; McCormick Theol Sem, MA, theol studies, 1998. **Career:** Ins salesman; Beloved Community Christian Church, pastor; Chicago City Coun, mayor, 1983-92; US House Rep, 1st dist, rep, congressman, 1992-. **Orgs:** Stud Nonviolent Coord Comt, 1966; Cong Black Caucus; Iota Phi Theta Fraternity Inc; Chicago City Coun; Dem Whip Orgn, 1993; co founder, Ill Black Panther Party; Beloved Community Christian Church; Coordr, Free Med Clin; assoc, Cong Hisp Caucus; Cong Human Rights Caucus; Cong Hunger Caucus; Cong Postal Caucus; Cong Travel & Tourism Caucus; Cong Urban Caucus; Cong Vietnam-Era Veterans Caucus. **Business Addr:** Congressman, Representative, US House of representatives, 2268 Rayburn House Off Bldg, Washington, DC 20515-1301, **Business Phone:** (202)225-4372.

### RUSH, EDDIE F.

Basketball executive. **Personal:** Born Sep 19, 1961, Columbus, GA. **Educ:** Ga State Univ, attended 1983. **Career:** Continental Basketball Asn, referee; Nat Basketball Asn, referee, currently. **Home Addr:** PO Box 490838, Atlanta, GA 30349. **Business Addr:** NBA Referee, National Basketball Association, Olympic Twr 645 5th Ave, New York, NY 10022-5986, **Business Phone:** (212)407-8000.

### RUSH, OTIS

Guitarist, singer. **Personal:** Born Apr 29, 1935, Philadelphia, PA; son of O C and Julia Boyd; children: Lena & Sophia; children: 4. **Career:** Guitarist, singer; Albums: I Can't Quit You Baby, 1958; Chicago: The Blues Today!, 1966; Door To Door, 1969; Mourning in the Morning, 1969; Screamin' & Cryin', 1974; Cold Day In Hell, 1975; So Many Roads, 1976; Right Place, Wrong Time, 1976; Troubles Troubles, 1978; Groaning the Blues, 1980; Tops, 1989; Blues Interaction-Live In Japan 1986, 1989; His Cobra Recordings, 1989; Lost in Blues, 1991; Live In Europe, 1994; Ain't Enough Comin' In, 1994; Any Place I'm Going, 1998; The Essential Otis Rush, 2000; All Your Love I Miss Loving, 2005; Live & From San Francisco, 2006; Chicago Blues Festival 2001, 2009; Compilations: Door To Door, 1969; I Can't Quit You Baby, 1989; Good Uns, 2000; The Essential Otis Rush, 2000; Blue on Blues, 2002; All Your Love I Miss Loving, 2005; Live At Montreux 1986, 2006; Singles: I Can't Quit You Baby, 1956; My Love Will Never Die, 1956; Groaning The Blues, 1957; Jump Sister Bessie, 1957; She's A Good 'Un, 1957; Checking On My Baby, 1958; Double Trouble, 1958; All Your Love, 1958; So Many Roads So Many Trains, 1960; You Know My Love, 1960; Homework, 1962; Gambler's Blues, 1969; Otis Rush Music Inc, 2004-; Bates Mayer Inc. **Business Addr:** Musician, Bates Mayer Inc, 714 Brookside Lane, Sierra Madre, CA 91024, **Business Phone:** (626)355-9201.

### RUSH, SONYA C.

Educator, manager, association executive. **Personal:** Born Aug 23, 1959, Columbia, LA; daughter of Walter C and Shirley Cross. **Educ:** Ga Inst Tech, BChE, 1981; Univ Mich, MBA, 1983. **Career:** Black Exec Exchange Prog, vis prof; Philip Morris USA Inc, opers analyst, 1983-88, supt-mfg, 1988-90, MBA assoc, 1990-92, sr planning analyst, 1992, asst brand mgr, 1992-93, assoc brand mgr, 1993-97, sr brand mgr, consult, dir mkt, currently. **Orgs:** Allocations mem, United Way; adv Jr Achievement; Nat Coalition 100 Black Women; charter mem, Alpha Kappa Alpha Sor; Friends Art; Leadership Metro Richmond; bd mem, Greenwich House; exec comt mem, trustee, Ga Tech Alumni Asn; Pan Hellenic Coun; Nat Soc Black Engrs; Harlem Small Bus Initiative Pilot; Black Exec Exchange Prog; Leadership Metro Richmond. **Honors/Awds:** President's Award, Philip Morris USA, 1989. **Home Addr:** 1005 Abercorn Dr SW, Atlanta, GA 30331-7514, **Home Phone:** (404)629-9832. **Business Addr:** Director of Marketing, Philip Morris USA Inc, 120 Pk Ave, New York, NY 10017, **Business Phone:** (917)663-2000.

### RUSHEN, PATRICE LOUISE

Musician, composer, singer. **Personal:** Born Sep 30, 1954, Los Angeles, CA; daughter of Allen Roy and Ruth L; married Marc St Louis. **Educ:** Univ Southern Calif, Los Angeles, music educ, piano performance, 1976. **Career:** Albums: Prelusion, 1974; Before the Dawn, 1975; Shout It Out, 1976; Let There Be Funk: The Best Of Patrice Rushen, 1976; Patrice, 1978; Pizzazz, 1979; Posh, 1980; Straight from the Heart, 1982; Now, 1984; Anthology of Patrice Rushen, 1985; Watch Out, 1986; The Meeting, 1990; Anything But Ordinary, 1994; Haven't You Heard-The Best of Patrice Rushen, 1996; Signature, 1997; The Essentials: Patrice Rushen, 2002. Singles: "Haven't You Heard", 1980; "Forget Me Nots", 1981; "Never Gonna Give You Up", 1981; "Don't Blame Me"; "Remind Me"; "You Remind Me"; "Feels So Real", 1984; "Watch Out", 1987; "Anything Can Happen", 1987; "Come Back to Me", 1988; "Watch Out", 1988. TV Series: "The Women Brewster Place"; "The Midnight Hour", 1990; The "Steve Harvey Show", 1996; "Cora Unashamed", 2000; "Fire & Ice", 2001; "The Killing Yard", 2001; "Our America ", 2002; "Just a Dream", 2002; "For One Night", 2006; "Burning Sands", 2006. CBS-TV, musical dir, conductor & arranger, 1990; John Lithgow's Kid-Size Concert Video, musical dir & arranger; For One Night, 2006. Films: Without You I'm Nothing, Hollywood Shuffle, 1987; Baby of the Family, 2002; Just a Dream, 2002. Composer: for Robert Townsend & His Partners in Crime Part I, II, III, IV, HBO; Pacific Bell radio campaign, 1988; Kid's Talk; musical dir of's highest honor, Emmy Awards, 1991, 1992; musical dir for "Comic Relief V", 1992; Berklee Col Music, prof, 2008; rec artist, composer, currently. **Honors/Awds:** Nat Acad Recording Arts & Scis, Best R&B Vocal Performance, "Forget Me Nots, " 1982, Best R&B Instrument, "Number One, " 1982; Songwriter's Award, Am Soc Composers, Auth & Publ, 1988; Image Awards TV Spec, Nat Asn Advan Colored People, 1989-90; Legacy of Excellence Award, USC Black Student Assembly, 1992; Crystal Award, American Women in Film, 1994; American Society of Composers, Authors and Publishers Award, 1998; 48th Annual Grammy Awards, 2004-06; Honorary Doctorate of Music, Berklee Col Music, 2005. **Special Achievements:** First woman to serve as Musical Director for the 46th, 47th & 48th Annual Grammy Awards; first woman in 43 years to serve as Head Composer/Musical Director for televisions highest honor, the Emmy Awards. **Business Addr:** Recording Artist, Composer, Shelley, Jeffrey & Associates, 433 N Camden Dr 6th Fl, Beverly Hills, CA 90210.

### RUSHING, BYRON D.

State government official, educator. **Personal:** Born Jul 29, 1942, New York, NY; son of William and Linda Turpin; children: Osula Evadne. **Educ:** Roxbury Community Col, AA, 1989; Episcopal Divinity Sch, attended 1994; Harvard Col; Mass Inst Technol. **Career:** Northern Stud Movement, community organizer, 1964-65; Community Voter Regist Proj, dir, 1964-66; Comn Church & Race MA Coun Churches, field dirm, 1966-67; Ctr Inner-City Chg, adminr, 1969-70; Mus Afro-Am Hist, pres, 1972-85; Commonwealth Mass, House Rep, state rep, 1983-; Episcopal Divinity Sch, adj fac, 1991-; House Deputies, pres, 2012; Episcopal Urban Caucus, founding member, currently. **Orgs:** Pres, Roxbury Hist Soc, 1968; lay dep, Gen Conv Episcopal Church, 1974; chaplain, Gen Conv Episcopal Church, 1994; treas, St John's & St James Episcopal Church, 1975-; co-chair citizens adv comn, Roxbury Heritage Pk, 1985-; Roxbury Hist Soc; Episcopal Network Econ Justice; Shirley Eustis House Asn; Unitarian Universalist Urban Ministry; Episcopal Church Arch Bostonian Socs; Calvert Social Investment Fund; Civil Liberties Union Mass; Environ Diversity Forum; Grassroots int; St James Educ Ctr; Southend & Lower Roxbury Healthy Boston Coalition. **Honors/Awds:** Human Rights Campaign Fund Award, 1985; Bay State Banner 20th Anniversary Celebration, 1985; Public Official of the Year, Boston Teachers Union, 1987; hon degree, Roxbury Community Col, 1989; Action for Boston Community Development Award, 1992; hon degree, Episcopal Divinity Sch, 1994. **Home Addr:** 25 Concord Sq, Boston, MA 02118-3101, **Home Phone:** (617)262-5023. **Business Addr:** State Representative, The Commonwealth of Massachusetts, Rm 121 State House, Boston, MA 02133, **Business Phone:** (617)722-2006.

### RUSHING, CORETHA M.

Executive. **Personal:** married Howard Smith; children: Cameron. **Educ:** E Carolina Univ, BS, indust psychol, 1978; George Washington Univ, MS, human resources & coun, 1981; Soc Human Resource Mgt, cert sr prof human resources. **Career:** Int Bus Mach Corp, human resources mgt, 1983-94; Pizza Hut, dir human resource Midwest div, 1994-96; Coca-Cola Co, 1996-2000, sr vpres human resources, 2000-05; Cameron Wesley LLC, Atlanta, Ga, exec coach & human resource consult, 2004-06; Equifax Inc, sr vpres, chief people officer, chief human resources officer, 2006-; E River Savings & Loan, training dir; R.H. Macy's & Co, recruiter & corp training specialist. **Orgs:** Bd dir, Big Bros & Big Sisters Atlanta; bd dir, Soc Human Resource Mgt, 2011-; dir & mem nominating & corp governance comt, 2U Inc, 2016-. **Special Achievements:** The 100 Most Powerful Executives in Corporate America, Black Enterprise, 2012. **Business Addr:** Chief Human Resource Officer, Equifax Inc, 1550 Peachtree St NW, Atlanta, GA 30309, **Business Phone:** (404)885-8000.

### RUSK, REGGIE (REGINALD LEON RUSK)

Football player, executive. **Personal:** Born Oct 19, 1972, Galveston, TX. **Educ:** Tex A&M Univ; City Col San Francisco, AA, telecommunication, 1994; Univ Ky, telecommunication, 1996. **Career:** Football player (retired), exec; Tampa Bay Buccaneers, corner back, 1996-97; Seattle Seahawks, corner back, 1997-98; San Diego Chargers, corner back, 1999-2001; Platinum Limousines Inc, pres & owner, 2001-07; Next Level Sports Performance, owner & trainer, 2007-. **Business Addr:** Owner, Trainer, Next Level Sports Performance, 2351 Main St, League City, TX 77056, **Business Phone:** (281)914-2351.

### RUSS, BERNARD DION

Football player. **Personal:** Born Nov 4, 1973, Utica, NY. **Educ:** Wva Col, grad. **Career:** New Eng Patriots, linebacker, 1997-99; Scottish Claymores, 1999; New York/NJ Hitmen, 2001; Sask Roughriders, free agent, 2002. **Honors/Awds:** Rookie of the Year, 1997. **Business Addr:** Free Agent, Saskatchewan Roughrider, Mosaic Stadium, Regina, SK S4P 3E1, **Business Phone:** (306)569-2323.

### RUSS, TIMOTHY DARRELL

Actor. **Personal:** Born Jun 22, 1956, Washington, DC; son of Walter H and Josephine D; children: Madison Camille. **Educ:** Ill State Univ, Bloomington, Ill, post grad theater; St Edwards Univ, BS, theater, psych, 1978. **Career:** Films: Crossroads, 1986; Fire with Fire, 1986; Death Wish 4: The Crackdown, 1987; Spaceballs, 1987; Pulse, 1988; Bird, 1988; Eve of Destruction, 1991; Night Eyes II, 1992; Mr Saturday Night, actor & dir, 1992; Dead Connection, 1994; Star Trek: Generations, 1994; East of Hope Street, actor, executive producer & writer, 1998; The Cabinet of Dr. Caligari, 2005; Unbeatable Harold, 2006; The Oh in Ohio, 2006; Live Free or Die Hard, 2007; Mistaken Identity, writer, 2008; Rampart, 2011; Play by Play, dir & writer, 2011; A Night at the Silent Movie Theater, dir, 2012; Greyscale, 2014; Asteroid vs. Earth, 2014; Alongside Night, 2014; Vitals, 2014. TV series: "The Twilight Zone, 1985-87; "Amazing Stories", 1986; Samaritan: The Mitch Snyder Story, 1986; Casebusters, 1986; The Highwayman, 1987; Timestalkers, 1987; "The Highwayman", 1988; Roots: The Gift, 1988; Police Story: Cop Killer, 1988; Who Gets the Friends?, 1988; "The People Next Door", 1989; "The Fresh Prince of Bel-Air", 1990-92; "Freddy's Nightmares", 1990; "CopRock", 1990; The Bakery, 1990;

Dead Silence, 1991; The Heroes of Desert Storm, 1991; "Tequila & Bonetti", 1992; Journey to the Center of the Earth, 1993; "Sea Quest DSV", 1993; "Star Trek: Deep Space Nine", 1993-95; "Hangin' with Mr. Cooper", 1993-94; "Living Single", 1993; "Murphy Brown", 1993; "Dark Justice", 1993; "Star Trek: The Next Generation", 1993; "Melrose Place", 1994; Bitter Vengeance, 1994; "Monty", 1994; "Star Trek-Voyager", 1995-2001; "Psychic Investigators", 2002; "Any Day Now", 2002; "ER", 2005; "Unfabulous", 2005; "General Hospital", 2006; "Navy NCIS: Naval Criminal Investigative Service", 2006; "Twenty Good Years", 2006; "General Hospital", 2006-07; "Hannah Montana", 2007; "Without a Trace", 2007; "Samantha Who?", 2007-09; "iCarly", 2007-12; "Divas of Novella", dir & co-producer, 2008; "Lincoln Heights", 2009; "The Later Show", dir, 2010; "Life of the American Teenager", 2010; "CSI: Miami", 2010; "Reformed Tramp", 2010; "Sym-Bionic Titan", 2010-11; "Suits", 2011; "The Young and the Restless", 2011; "Bloomers", actor & dir, 2011-13; "The Soul Man", 2012; "Shmagreggie Saves the World", 2012; "Guys with Kids", 2013; "Arrested Development", 2013; "Lab Rats", 2013; "Social Nightmare", 2013; "Castle", 2013; "Regular Show", 2014. Stage appearances: Romeo & Juliet; Barrabas; Dream Girls; As You Like It; Twelfth Night; Cave Dwellers. **Orgs:** Nat Asn Advan Colores People Hollywood Br, 1986. **Honors/Awds:** Sony Innovator Award, 1991; Image Award, theater, Nat Asn Advan Colored People, 1987; New York International Independent Film & Video Festival Feature Film Award for Best Urban Drama, 1998; Indie Series Award, 2012; Emmy Award, Pac Southwest Emmy Awards, 2014. **Home Addr:** PO Box 36A24, Los Angeles, CA 90036, **Home Phone:** (213)938-9662. **Business Addr:** Actor, Stone Manners Agency, 8091 Selma Ave, Los Angeles, CA 90046, **Business Phone:** (323)655-1313.

## RUSSELL, BEVERLY ANN

Writer, librarian, manager. **Personal:** Born Jan 15, 1947, Riverside, CA; daughter of James H (deceased) and Hazel M Hawkins. **Educ:** Calif State Col, BA, polit sci, 1971; Calif State Univ, MS, libr sci, 1973. **Career:** Riverside Pub Libr, libr asst, 1974-75; Univ Calif, asst libr, 1975-76; CA State Dept Rehab, off asst, 1976-77, librn, 1978; Magnavox Res Labs, libr tech, 1976-83; Burbank Unified Sch Dist, libr asst, 1985-86, bookroom librn, 1986-90; Roots & Wings, co-auth, 1986; Three Women Black, co-auth, 1988; Social Serv Dept, off technician, 1988-92; Social Voc Servs, cot supvr, 1990-94; Pleasant Valley State Prison, libr tech asst, 1994-. **Orgs:** Alpha Kappa Alpha 1973-; Intl Black Writers & Artists 1983-; Black Advocates State Serv Calif, 1995-; Calif Asn Black Correctional Workers, 1995-. **Home Addr:** 250 Truman St Suite 250, Coalinga, CA 93210, **Home Phone:** (559)935-5749. **Business Addr:** Library Technical Assistant, Pleasant Valley State Prison, 24863 W Jayne Ave, Coalinga, CA 93210-1135, **Business Phone:** (559)935-4900.

## RUSSELL, BILL (WILLIAM FELTON RUSSELL)

Broadcaster, basketball player. **Personal:** Born Feb 12, 1934, West Monroe, LA; son of Charles and Katie (deceased); married Rose Swisher; children: William Jr, Karen & Jacob; married Dorothy Anstett; married Marilyn. **Educ:** Univ San Francisco, BA, 1956. **Career:** Basketball player (retired), broadcaster; Boston Celtics, ctr, 1956-69, coach, 1966-69, consult, 1999-; NBC-TV, sportscaster, 1969-8, CBS, 1980-83; Seattle SuperSonics, head coach, 1973-77; Superstars, co-host, 1978-79; Sacramento Kings, head coach, 1987-88, dir player personnel, 1988-89; IMG Speakers Bur, speaker. **Orgs:** Bd mem, Nat Mentoring Partnership; Naismith Memorial Basketball Hall Fame; Nat Col Basketball Hall Fame; Gamma Alpha chap Kappa Alpha Psi fraternity. **Special Achievements:** First African American player to achieve superstar status in the NBA.

## RUSSELL, BRYON DEMETRISE

Basketball player, television broadcaster. **Personal:** Born Dec 31, 1970, San Bernardino, CA; married Kimberli; children: 3. **Educ:** Calif State Univ, criminal justice, 1993. **Career:** Basketball player (retired); Utah Jazz, forward, 1993-2002; Wash Wizards, guard-forward, 2002-03; Los Angeles Lakers, forward, 2003-04; Denver Nuggets, forward, 2004-06; Hollywood Fame, 2006-07; Santa Barbara Breakers, 2007; Long Beach Breakers, 2007-09; Los Angeles Lightning, forward, 2007-09; TV Series: "The 1997 NBA Finals", 1997; The Jamie Foxx Show, 2000; "ESPN SportsCentury ", 2002; "The 2004 NBA Finals", 2004. **Business Addr:** Player, Los Angels Lightening, **Business Phone:** (310)770-3960.

## RUSSELL, CAMPY (MICHAEL CAMPANELLA RUSSELL)

Executive director, basketball coach. **Personal:** Born Jan 12, 1952, Jackson, TN; married Robyn; children: Allex, Mandisa, Oyin, Saki & Michael II. **Educ:** Univ Mich, BS, sports mgt, 1974. **Career:** Basketball player (retired), dir; Cleveland Cavaliers, forward, 1974-80 & 1984, outer mkt event specialist, currently, dir alumni rels, currently, Youth Prog, trainer, currently; Cavaliers pregame & postgame show, co-host; NY Knicks, forward, 1980-82, 1985; Detroit Spirits, forward, 1984-85; WOIO & WUAB TV, Cleveland, basketball analyst, currently. **Orgs:** Sr advisor, Nat Asn Black Sports Professionals. **Home Addr:** 88 Clayton Rd, Ecru, MS 38841-9705, **Home Phone:** (662)489-2127. **Business Addr:** Director of Alumni Relations, Cleveland Cavaliers, 1 Ctr Ct, Cleveland, OH 44115-4001, **Business Phone:** (216)420-2165.

## RUSSELL, CLIFFORD

President (organization), executive. **Educ:** Univ Md, College Park. **Career:** NASA Goddard Space Flight Ctr, syst adminr, 1996-99; Univ Md--Col Pk, syst analyst, 1999-2007; Russellvisual, LLC, photogr, 2006-09; Bridge Dataworks, photogr, pres & chief exec officer, 2007-; HeiTech Serv Inc, chief info officer, 2010-12; Morehouse Col, chief info officer, 2013-. **Orgs:** Adv bd mem Dell Enterprise Technol; bd mem, Univ Md, Small Bus & Technol Develop Ctr. **Honors/Awds:** Smart CXO Award, Executive Management Team Winner, 2011. **Special Achievements:** His photography has been published internationally. **Business Addr:** Chief Information Officer, Morehouse College, 830 Westview Dr SW, Atlanta, GA 30314, **Business Phone:** (404)681-2800.

## RUSSELL, DEREK DWAYNE

Football player. **Personal:** Born Jun 22, 1969, Little Rock, AR; children: Nicolis. **Educ:** Univ Ark, grad. **Career:** Football player (retired); Denver Broncos, wide receiver, 1991-94, kick returner, 1993; Houston Oilers, wide receiver, 1995-96; Tenn Oilers, wide receiver, 1997. **Special Achievements:** Film: 1991 AFC Championship Game, 1992. **Business Addr:** Wide Receiver, Tennessee Titans, 460 Great Circle Rd, Nashville, TN 37228, **Business Phone:** (615)565-4000.

## RUSSELL, DIAN BISHOP

Media executive, association executive, teacher. **Personal:** Born Sep 24, 1952, Rich Square, NC; daughter of Paul A Jr and Genora Tann; married Larry; children: Tammy, Paula & Letitia. **Educ:** Fayetteville State Univ, Fayetteville, NC, BS, 1976; NC Cent Univ, Durham, NC, MLS, 1980, cert, educ admin, 1985; Durham City Sch, Durham, NC, cert, mentor, 1988. **Career:** T S Cooper Elem, Sunbury, NC, librn, 1974-77; Durham County Sch, NC Testing Consortium, Durham, NC, testing clerk, 1978; Durham County Libr, Proj LIFT, Durham, NC, spec asst to the dir, educ brokering, 1979; Durham City Sch, Durham, NC, lead teacher, summer comput progs, 1986-89, media coordr, 1980-, site coordr summer enrichment, 1990; Baskerville Elem Sch, Media Specialist, currently. **Orgs:** Assoc rep, 1985-, past treas, 1987, past secy, 1988, Durham City Educ; spec regist comnr, Durham County Bd Elections, 1988-; past vice, 1985, treas, 1990-, Eta Beta Zeta Chap, Zeta Phi Beta Sorority, 1990-; directress, Union Baptist Youth Choir, 1985-. **Honors/Awds:** Durham City Schools Superintendent's Creative Teaching Award, 1985; Gold Star Awards, Final Four Teacher of Year, 1987; Women in Achievement, Durham City Sch, 1989. **Home Addr:** 2114 Bridgewood Rd, Rocky Mount, NC 27804-9204. **Business Addr:** Media Specialist, Baskerville Elementary School, 1100 Stokes Ave, Rocky Mount, NC 27801, **Business Phone:** (252)451-2880.

## RUSSELL, DOROTHY DELORES

Publishing executive. **Personal:** Born Sep 11, 1950, Hayti, MO; daughter of Carrie Vianna Lewis and Jimmie Sr. **Educ:** Southeast Mo State Univ; Three Rivers Comm Col; Lincoln Univ. **Career:** Univ Ark CES, clerk steno I, 1973-76; Dept Natural Resources, clerk steno II, 1976-78; Mo Exec Off, secy receptionist, 1978-79; Mo Patrol State Water, admin secy, 1979-80; Community Rev Newspaper, ed, writer & photogr, 1983-84; Pemiscot Publ Co, corresp, copy setter, circulation & classified mgr, 1989-. **Orgs:** Former bd mem, vpres, Community Rev Paper expired, 1983-84; organizer, Southeast Mo Black Writers Club, 1989; former asst, 4-H Leader; missionary, Church Jesus Christ Congregation. **Honors/Awds:** Certificate of Apppreciation, Univ Mo Extension Prog, Pemiscot County, 1983; Certificate of Apppreciation, Hayti Junior High Sch, 1985; Certificate of Apppreciation, Educ & Pub Serv, Cent Star Chap 114, Order Eastern Star, 1988; Certificate of Apppreciation, St James Word Faith, 1988. **Home Addr:** PO Box 725, Caruthersville, MO 63830, **Home Phone:** (314)359-1452. **Business Addr:** Circulation Manager, Pemiscot Publishing Co, PO Box 1059, Caruthersville, MO 63830-1059, **Business Phone:** (573)333-4336.

## RUSSELL, GEORGE ALTON, JR.

Chief executive officer, president (organization), banker. **Personal:** Born Boston, MA; married Faye Sampson; children: Martin Bakari. **Educ:** Clark Univ, BA, 1972; NY Univ, MBA, finance, 1974. **Career:** Urban Bus Assistance Corp, pres 1972-74; State St Bank & Trust Co, vpres, 1979-84; City Boston, treas, chief financial officer; Freedom Nat Bank NY, chief exec, pres & chief exec officer; State St Corp, credit analyst/loan officer trainee, 1974, vpres, corp banking div. 1984-88, dir community affairs, exec vpres, currently, treas & chief financial officer, city boston; State St Found, chmn & ceo. **Orgs:** Dir, Dimock Comn Health Ctr, 1983-; bd mem, Boston Indus Develop Finance Auth, 1984-; treas-custodian, State Boston Retirement Syst, 1984-; Boston Arson Comn, 1984-; custodian, Boston Pub Sch Teachers Retirement Fund, 1984-; Bus Asn Club, 1984-; Govt Finance Officers Asn, 1984-; MA Collector-Treas Asn, 1984-; trustee, Boston Concert Opera; corp, Boston Sci Mus dir Orgn New Equality, 1985-; trustee, United Methodist Church, 1985-; chmn, Urban League Eastern Mass; Fin Serv Acad; bd advisor, African Presidential Arch & Res Ctr, Boston Univ; bd dir, OneUnited Bank; mem bd visitors, Univ Massachusetts; bd dir, Massachusetts Taxpayers Found; Greater Boston Chamber Com; Orgn a New Equality; Conf Bd's Community & Pub Issues Coun; Exec Comt Boston Munic Res Bur's Bd dir; Tufts Health Plan Found; trustee, Massachusetts Math & Sci Initiative. **Home Addr:** 116 Skyline Dr, Westwood, MA 02090-1072, **Home Phone:** (781)461-8144. **Business Addr:** Executive Vice President, State Street Corp, State St Financial Ctr 1 Lincoln St, Boston, MA 02111, **Business Phone:** (617)786-3000.

**RUSSELL, HERMAN JEROME.** **See Obituaries Section.**

## RUSSELL, JEROME

Executive, president (organization). **Personal:** Born Jan 1, 1962; son of Herman J; married Stephanie Marie Beasley; children: Herman III, Sydney, Mori & Kelsey. **Educ:** Ga State Univ, BS, bus admin & mgt, 1985. **Career:** City Beverage Co, mgr, pres, 1988-95; Gibraltar Land Inc, proj mgr, 1988-92; HJ Russell & Co, exec vpres, 1992-94, chief operating officer, 1995, pres russell new urban, 1994-. **Orgs:** Zoo Atlanta; Citizens Trust Bank; Ga Affordable Housing Coalition; Atlanta Urban League; Concessions Int; Metro Atlanta YMCA; Cent Atlanta Progress; Urban Land Inst; Atlanta Rotary; Atlanta Chamber Com; 100 Black Men Atlanta; Young Pres Orgn. **Business Addr:** President of Russell New Urban, HJ Russell & Co, 504 Fair St SW, Atlanta, GA 30313, **Business Phone:** (404)330-1000.

## RUSSELL, JOHN PETERSON, JR.

College administrator, executive director. **Personal:** Born Aug 26, 1947, Cora, WV; son of Johnnie P Sr and Mary Louise Thompson; married Gail P Davis; children: Kim & Janelle. **Educ:** Bluefield State Col, BS, 1970; WVa Col Grad Studies, MA, 1975; VPI & SU, CAGS, 1978. **Career:** Nathaniel Macon Jr High Sch, sec teacher, 1970-71; Omar Jr & Logan HighSch, sec teacher, 1971-74; Southern WVa Community Col, counr, 1974-76, dean students, 1979-81, asst dean students, dir fin aid, 1986-87; Walters St Community Col, Morristown, TN, exec dir, coordr trng, 1987-, Coun & Testing Ctr, exec dir, currently. **Orgs:** Chmn, bd dir, New Employ Women, 1981-; appt Amer Friends Serv Comm Rel Comm, 1982-; Amer Friends Serv Exec Comm 1983-; polemarch, Knoxville Chap, 1989-, field dep, Eastern Region, 1990-, Kappa Alpha Psi Fraternity; chmn, community rels comt, Am Friends Serv, 1985-86; Kappa Alpha Psi, Polemarch S Cent Prov, 1994; chmn, Kappa Alpha Psi Social Actions Comt. **Home Addr:** 1608 Blackwood Dr, Knoxville, TN 37923, **Home Phone:** (615)691-4136. **Business Addr:** Executive Director, Walters State Community College, Rm 207 500 S Davy Crockett Pkwy Col Ctr, Morristown, TN 37813-6899, **Business Phone:** (423)585-6806.

## RUSSELL, JOSEPH J.

Executive, association executive, educator. **Personal:** Born Apr 11, 1934. **Educ:** VA State Col, BS, 1960; Ind Univ, MS, 1968, EdD, 1971. **Career:** Richmond Soc Serv Bur, soc worker, 1960-64; Richmond Pub Sch, vis teacher, 1964-67; Ind Univ, chmn, 1972, Afro-Am Studies, dean; Ohio State Univ, dir, 1970-72, vice provost, 1989-94; Global Team Am Inc, 1995-. **Orgs:** Adv comt, Urban Affairs, 1973-; adv comt, Univ Div, 1974-; standing comt, Bloomington Campus, 1974-; fac hearing officer, 1974-; chmn, Afro-Am Conf Group, IHETS, 1974-; Ind State Adv Bd, 1974-; Stud Life Study Comn, 1977; chmn, Dept Afro-Am Studies; exec dir, Nat Coun Black Studies. **Honors/Awds:** Commission Service Award, Second Baptist Church, 1976; Outstanding Educr Award, Phi Beta Sigma, 1976; Serv Appreciation Plaque, NM Black Studies Consortium, 1977; Nat Develop & Leadership Award, Nat Coun Black Studies, 1977; Distinguished Alumni Service Award, 2008. **Special Achievements:** Num Presentation & Papers; OSU African American Student Affairs Council of Honor, 1995; 100 Most Influential Friends for 1977. **Home Addr:** 2858 Hollow Cove Ct, Columbus, OH 43231, **Home Phone:** (614)901-0602.

## RUSSELL, KEITH BRADLEY

Ornithologist. **Personal:** Born Aug 13, 1956, Augusta, GA; son of John Raphael and Barbara Elaine Jefferson. **Educ:** Cornell Univ, Ithaca, NY, BS, biol, 1977; Clemson Univ, Clemson, SC, MS, zool, 1981. **Career:** Acad Natural Sci, Philadelphia, PA, collection mgr, 1982-92; Birds N Am Inc, asst ed; Audubon Pa, Fairmount Pk Outreach, coordr, 2006-. **Orgs:** Del Valley Ornith Club, 1973-; Nat Audubon Soc, 2003-. **Home Addr:** 6222 McCallum St, Philadelphia, PA 19144-2606, **Home Phone:** (215)844-2810. **Business Addr:** Fairmount Park Outreach Coordinator, Audubon Pennsylvania, 100 Wildwood Way, Harrisburg, PA 17110, **Business Phone:** (215)844-2810.

## RUSSELL, LEON W.

Government official, president (organization). **Personal:** Born Nov 3, 1949, Pulaski, VA. **Educ:** E Tenn State Univ, BS, 1972; E Tenn State Univ, Sch Grad Studies, attended 1974. **Career:** Tenn State House Reps, legis intern & asst, 1973; E Tenn State Univ Dept Polit Sci, grad teaching asst, 1972-73; Tenn Munic League, mgt intern& res asst, 1974; Ky Comn Human Rights, field rep, 1975-77; Pinellas County Govt Off Human Rights, affirmative action, equal employ opportunity officer, 1977-85, human rights equal employ opportunity officer, 1985-. **Orgs:** Charter mem, Beta Zeta Alumni Chap, Alpha Kappa Lambda Frat; nat bd dir & pres, Nat Asn Human Rights Workers; Int City Mgt Asn; bd dir, OIC Suncoast; Clear water Br, Nat Asn Advan Colored People; pres, Fla State Nat Asn Advan Colored People Conf Br; E Tenn State Univ Alumni Asn; Allocations Comm bd dir, United Way Pinellas County; bd dir, Fla Asn Comn Rels Prof; bd dir, Fla Asn Equal Opportunity Prof Inc; Am Soc Pub Admin; nat bd dir, Nat Asn Advan Colored People, 1990-98; pres, Fla State Conf, Nat Asn Advan Colored People, 1996-2000; pres, Int Asn Off Human Rights Agencies, 2007-; vice chmn, Nat Bd, currently; Nat Forum Black Pub Adminr; bd dir, Cs Campaign Fla; bd mem, Pinellas Opportunity Coun; pres & bd mem, Nat Asn Human Rights Workers; Blueprint Comn Juv Justice; chmn, Floridians Representing Equity & Equality. **Business Addr:** President, International Association of Official Human Rights Agencies, 400 S Ft Harrison Ave 5th Fl, Clearwater, FL 33756, **Business Phone:** (727)464-4880.

## RUSSELL, DR. LEONARD ALONZO

Dentist. **Personal:** Born Dec 27, 1949, Paris, KY; son of Joseph Bailey and Celia; children: 2. **Educ:** Eastern Ky Univ, BS, engineering, 1971; Cent State, BS, biol, 1978; Case Western Res Univ Sch Dent Med, DDS, 1983. **Career:** High Sch, Dayton, Ohio, teacher; Med Univ Ohio, resident; Leonard A Russell DDS Inc, pres & dentist, 1983-; pvt pract, dentist, 1984-. **Orgs:** Nat parliamentarian Stud Nat Dent Assoc, 1981-82; Am Acad Gen Dent, 1981-; Ohio Dent Assoc, 1982-; pres, Forest City Dent Soc, 1986-87; Am Den Asn; Nat Dent Asn; Cleveland Dent Soc; Ohio Acad Gen Dent; DocShop. **Honors/Awds:** Leonard A Russell Award, Kappa Alpha Psi Frat, 1971; Kenneth W Clement Award, Cleveland City Coun, 1981; Outstanding Young Man America, US Jaycees, 1984. **Business Addr:** Dentist, President, Leonard A Russell DDS Inc, 2204 S Taylor Rd, Cleveland Heights, OH 44118, **Business Phone:** (216)321-3462.

## RUSSELL, MARK

Newspaper executive, newspaper editor. **Personal:** Born St. Louis, MO; married Christina; children: 2. **Educ:** BJ, jour, 1984. **Career:** Wall St J Cleveland & Pittsburgh bureaus, staff reporter; Plain Dealer, metro news, bus ed, asst managing ed; Wall St J, reporter; Boston Globe, asst metro ed, 1993-95, ed; Orlando Sentinel, managing ed, 2004-. **Orgs:** Bd mem, Columbia Missourian; bd mem, Fla Soc News Ed; chmn bd dir, Missourian Publ Asn; Inst Advan Journalism Studies NC A&T Univ. **Business Addr:** Managing Editor, Orlando Sentinel, 633 N Orange Ave, Orlando, FL 32801-1349, **Business Phone:** (407)420-5467.

## RUSSELL, MICHAEL (MIKE RUSSELL)

Vice president (organization), chief executive officer. **Personal:** Born Atlanta, GA; son of Herman; married Lovette Twyman; children: 2. **Educ:** Univ Va, BS, civil engineering, 1987; Ga State Univ, MBA, 1990. **Career:** Herman J Russell & Co, field engr, proj mgr & head bus develop, exec vpres, chief exec officer, 2003-; Citizens Trust Bank, bd mem; John Portman, construct mgr architect; Ga Power Co, bd mem; Wachovia Bank, bd mem. **Orgs:** Kennesaw Univ Found; Nat Asn Minority Contractors; Va Eng Found; Ga State Athletic Asn Bd;

pres, Asn Builders & Contractors Ga; Metro Chamber Exec Comt; bd dir, Com Club; bd trustee, Univ Va Eng Sch; C's Health care Found bd; 100 Black Men Atlanta; bd mem, Atlanta Chamber Com. **Business Addr:** Chief Executive Officer, H J Russell & Co, 504 Fair St SW, Atlanta, GA 30313, **Business Phone:** (404)330-1000.

**RUSSELL, MICHAEL CAMPANELLA. See RUSSELL, CAMPY.**

## RUSSELL, SANDRA ANITA (SANDI RUSSELL)

Jazz singer, teacher, writer. **Personal:** Born Jan 16, 1946, New York, NY; daughter of James Oliver and Gazetta. **Educ:** Syracuse Univ, AB, music, 1968; NY Univ, grad studies, 1969; Hunter Col, grad studies, 1971. **Career:** Writer & jazz vocalist; NY Bd Educ, teacher, 1968-76; jazz vocalist, 1977-81; San Francisco Clothing Co, mgr, 1981-84; writer & jazz vocalist, 1984-; Durham Univ, Eng, vocal instr, 2005-. Albums: Sweet Thunder; Incandescent; Noval: Color. **Honors/Awds:** CP Memorial Award, CP Memorial Fund, 1990; Author's Foundation Award, Soc Authors, 1991; Northern Arts Award, 1993; Guest of Honor, Univ Angers, France, Int Conf Orality in Short Fiction, 2005. **Special Achievements:** Co-authored several books; Drama. Essay: "Minor Chords/Major Changes," in Glancing Fires, ed Lesley Saunders, Women's Press, London, 1987; author, Render Me My Song: African-American Women Writers, Pandora Press St Martins, NY, 1990, updated ed, 2001; theatrical performance, "Render Me My Song' One-Woman Show in Words and Song," 1990; contrib ed, The Virago Book of Love Poetry, London/NY, 1990; Sister, short story in Daughters of Africa, ed, Busby, London, Cape Pantheon, NY, 1992; recorded album, 'Incandescent, ' 2001, (Freedom Song); recorded album, 'Sweet Thunder', 2007. Lyricist: 'Feet on the Ground', 'Given Time', 2007; Mark Rowles Music; 'ELLA!' - one woman theatrical show: conceived, researched, written and performed, 2009-. **Home Addr:** 11 Tenter Ter, Durham CityDH1 4RD, **Home Phone:** (191)386-0092.

## RUSSELL, WESLEY L., SR.

Executive. **Personal:** Born Nov 6, 1938, Camp Hill, AL; son of Cordie Mae Mennifield and Pearlie L; married Geraldine K; children: Derek, Dante, Deirdre & Derwin. **Educ:** Tuskegee Inst, BS, 1963; San Diego State Univ. **Career:** General Dynamics Electronics Systems Inc, assoc engr, 1963, elec engr, 1964, sr elec engr, 1968, mgr, tactical syst sect head, 1984-, prog mgr, 1990-. **Orgs:** Nat Mgt Asn. **Honors/Awds:** Letter of Commendation in support of initial operational evaluation of P5604 Secure Telecommunication Terminals, Tinker AFB Okla, 1974; Numerous extraordinary achievement awards. **Business Addr:** Program Manager, General Dynamics Electronics Systems Inc, MZ 6164-P, San Diego, CA 92150-9008.

**RUSSELL, WILLIAM FELTON. See RUSSELL, BILL.**

## RUSSELL-MCCLOUD, PATRICIA

Orator, writer. **Personal:** Born Sep 14, 1946, Indianapolis, IN; daughter of Willie and Janniel; married E Earl McCloud. **Educ:** Ky State Univ, BA, 1968; Harvard Univ, MA; Howard Univ Sch Law, JD, 1973. **Career:** Fed Commun Comn, atty, 1973-83; Broadcast Bur Fed Commun Comn, chief complaints br, 1975-83; Russell-McCloud & Assoc, pres & owner, 1983-; Auth: A is For Attitude: An Alphabet for Living, 2006. **Orgs:** Nat parliamentarian, Alpha Kappa Alpha Sorority Inc; pres, Links Found Inc; pres, Links Inc; Am Entertainment Int Speakers Bur Inc; Coun Legal Educ Opportunity. **Business Addr:** President, Professional Orator, Russell-McCloud & Associates, PO Box 310043, Atlanta, GA 31131, **Business Phone:** (404)691-5073.

## RUTH, JAMES A.

Judge. **Personal:** Born Jan 1, 1956, Palatka, FL. **Educ:** Fla State Univ, BS, criminol, 1979, MS, pub admin, 1980; Fla State Univ Col Law, JD, 1984. **Career:** Off Pub Defender, invest intern; Fla Dept Corrections, Dade Correctional Inst, counr & instr, 1980-81; Broward Co Juv Restitution Prog, criminal justice coun, 1981-82; Off State Atty, Fourth Judicial Circuit, Jacksonville, Fla, div chief, 1985-91; Duval Co Courthouse, judge, 1991-2009; St Francis Barracks, lt col, currently. **Orgs:** Vol & sponsor, Tots-N-Teens Theater Inc; bd mgt, YMCA; Fla Coun Co Ct Judges; Jacksonville Bar Asn; DW Perkins Bar Asn; Fla Bar Found; Mod Soc Free & Accepted Masonry; Fla Army Nat Guard Offrs Asn; Northside Busmens Club. **Home Addr:** 10115 NW 23rd Ct, Coral Springs, FL 33065, **Home Phone:** (954)796-9229. **Business Addr:** Lieutenant Colonel, St Francis Barracks, 82 Marine St, St. Augustine, FL 32084, **Business Phone:** (904)823-0384.

## RUTLEDGE, DR. ESSIE MANUEL

Educator, sociologist, association executive. **Personal:** Born Midway, AL; daughter of Ollie M Jordan Jones and Algie L Manuel Sr (deceased); married Albert C; children: Jeffrey A. **Educ:** Fla A&M Univ, BA, 1958; Univ Wis, Madison, MA, 1965; Univ Mich, PhD, social sci, 1974. **Career:** Sixteenth St Jr High Sch, St Petersburg, social studies teacher, 1958-61; Gibbs & St Petersburg Jr Col, instr, 1961-67; Macomb County Community Col, asst prof sociol, 1968-71; Univ Mich, Flint, asst prof sociol, 1974-76; Western Ill Univ, Afro-Am Studies, chairperson, 1976-84, from asst prof sociol to prof sociol, 1976-2006, chair dept african am studies, prof emer, 2006-; Geront Soc AME, Prog Appl Gerontlogy, post doctoral fel, 1989; Lions Club, pres. **Orgs:** Pi Gamma Mu Nat Social Sci Hon Soc, Fla A&M Univ, 1965; Am Sociol Asn, 1967-, memship chmn, 1970-84, pres, 1985-86, exec officer, 1996-99; Asn Black Sociologists, pres; Comt Status Women Am Sociol Asn, 1978-80; Ill Counc Black Studies, 1979-; adv bd, McDonough Co Health Dept, 1979-81; Ch Women United, 1980; Equal Opportunity & Fair Housing CMS City Macomb, Ill, 1986-; exec bd, Univ Professionals Ill, local 4100, 1990-97; Southern Sociol Soc, 1992, hons comt, 1995-98; publ comt, Sociologists Women Soc, 1993-96; ed bd mem, J African Am Studies. **Honors/Awds:** Rackham Fel, Univ Mich, 1971-74; Award for Service to Enhance Position of Women Western Orgn for Women, Western Ill Univ, 1979; Inducted into Gamma Lambda Chapter, Honorary Order of Omega, 1990; Faculty Excellence Award, Western Ill Univ, 1991; Blue Key Fraternity, Hon Fac, Western Ill Univ, 1993; Affirmative Action Directors Award, Western Ill Univ, 2006. **Special Achievements:** Published numerous articles on Black Women, Role Knowledge, Black Husbands & Wives, Separatism, Black Families, racism, socialization, and suicide in the following bks, doc & journals: The Black Woman, ERIC Doc, Reflector, Genetic Psychol Monogr, J of Negro Hist, Marriage and Family Ther, Contemp Sociol, J of Comparative Family Studies, Minority Voices, Ethnic Issues in Adolescent Ment Health. **Home Addr:** 7 Indian Trail Rd, Macomb, IL 61455-1021, **Home Phone:** (309)833-2062. **Business Addr:** Professor Emeritus, Western Illinois University, Morgan Hall 404 1 Univ Cir, Macomb, IL 61455, **Business Phone:** (309)298-1056.

## RUTLEDGE, GEORGE

Executive director, automotive executive. **Career:** Rutledge Chevrolet Oldsmobile, chief exec officer, currently. **Honors/Awds:** Company is listed No 11 on list of top 100 autodealers, Black Enterprise, 1994. **Business Addr:** Chief Executive Officer, Rutledge Chevrolet Oldsmobile Cadillac & Geo Inc, 107 E Jackson St, Sullivan, IL 61951, **Business Phone:** (217)728-4338.

## RUTLEDGE, JENNIFER M.

Management consultant. **Personal:** Born Sep 12, 1951, White Plains, NY; daughter of James and Elizabeth. **Educ:** Mich State Univ, BS, indust psychol, 1973; Pace Univ, Lubin Sch Bus, MBA, 1982. **Career:** Allstate Ins, personnel, 1973-76; Nat Asn Advan Colored People Legal Defense & Educ fund, dir personnel, 1976-79; Nat Coun Negro Women, nat coord work exp prog, 1979-80; Girls Clubs Am Inc, NE Serv Ctr, dir, 1983-86; Delphi Consult Group Inc, partner, 1984-, partner & vpres, currently; Univ Va, adj fac; Fordham Univ, adj fac; Adelphi Univ, lead consult. **Orgs:** Bd mem, Westchester Urban League, 1976; bd mem, Afro-Am Cult Asn, 1976; bd mem, vpres Afro-Am Civic Asn, 1978; bd mem, Support Network Inc, 1988; bd mem, Greenwich Girls Club, 1989-; bd mem, Westchester Community Found, 1996; bd mem, Alzheimer's Asn, 1999-; Nat Asn Female Exec; assoc fel Am Mgt Asn; Nat Asn MBA's; guest lectr, Bus & Prof Women's Clubs; Meeting Planners Int; bd mem, Lubin Grad Sch Bus Alumni Asn, Pace Univ; Delta Sigma Theta; bd mem, Yonkers Pvt Indust Coun Affiliated Nat Ctr Non-Profit Bds Mem-Res Bd Adv-ABI; Meeting Planners Int; Charter Sr Assocs Bd Source. **Honors/Awds:** Business Woman of the Year, Afro-Am Civic Asn, 1987; Professional of the Year, Westchester Chap Negro Bus & Prof Women's Club Inc, 1993; Honoree of the Year, Nat Conf Community & Justice, 1997. **Special Achievements:** Contributing writer to numerous publications and has been cited in numerous articles. **Home Addr:** 35 Roundtop Rd, Yonkers, NY 10710-2327. **Business Addr:** Partner, Vice President, Delphi Consulting Group Inc, 445 Hamilton Ave Suite 1102, White Plains, NY 10603, **Business Phone:** (914)684-2400.

## RUTLEDGE, ROD (RODRICK ALMAR RUTLEDGE)

Football player. **Personal:** Born Aug 12, 1975, Birmingham, AL; son of Wallace and Rose. **Educ:** Ala Univ. **Career:** Football player (retired); New Eng Patriots, tight end, 1998-2001; Houston Texans, tight end, 2002. **Honors/Awds:** Rookie of the Year, 1998; Lifter of the Year.

## RUTLEDGE, DR. WILLIAM LYMAN

Surgeon. **Personal:** Born Jun 27, 1952, Little Rock, AR; children: Rodney B, Estelle A & Jessica M. **Educ:** Tex Southern Univ, BA, 1975; Meharry Med Col, MD, 1979. **Career:** G W Hubbard Hosp Meharry Col, resident gen surg, 1979-84; Ark Surg Assocs, pres, 1984; Cancer Control Outreach Ctr, Little Rock, gen pract, currently; gen surgeon, ark, currently. **Orgs:** Alpha Omega Alpha Hon Med Soc, 1978; Nat Med Asn, 1979; dist comnr, Boy Scouts Am, 1986; secy, Scott Hamilton Dr Med Clin Inc, 1986; exec bd, Urban League; minority adv bd, Univ Ark Med Sci Campus. **Home Addr:** 264 River Ridge Pt, Little Rock, AR 72207, **Home Phone:** (501)224-3808. **Business Addr:** General Surgeon, Private Practitioner, 1119 S Van Buren St, Little Rock, AR 72204, **Business Phone:** (501)661-1303.

## RYAN, AGNES C.

Lawyer. **Personal:** Born Sep 17, 1928, Houston, TX; children: 3. **Educ:** Howard Univ, BA, 1947; Fordham Univ, JD, 1950. **Career:** Legal Aid Bureau, lawyer, 1951-52; pvt pract, lawyer, 1952-53; supvry lawyer. **Orgs:** Chicago Bar Asn; Am Bar Asn; bd mem, Bartelme Homes. **Honors/Awds:** Educational Award, Elks, 1971. **Business Addr:** Supervisory Lawyer, Legal Aid Bureau, 14 E Jackson Blvd, Chicago, IL 60604, **Business Phone:** (312)922-5625.

## RYAN, MARSHA ANN

Executive. **Personal:** Born Mar 12, 1947, New Orleans, LA; married Cecil James; children: Michelle & Marisa. **Educ:** Fisk Univ, BA, 1968; Tenn State Univ, teacher cert, 1970. **Career:** Neely's Bend Jr High Sch, teacher, 1970-71; Gen Elec Co, data processing instr, 1971; Xerox Ed Prod Div, area sales rep, 1973; Singer, area sales mgr, 1974; Ore Dept Transp, career develop anal, 1975, affirmative action & officer, 1977-78; Ore Motor Vechicles Div, prog develop, 1978-79; Ore Dept Human Resources, dir prog anal, 1979-80; Ore Adult & Family Serv Dir Multnomah Reg Off, prog exec bd, supvr pre-admis screening & resource unit, 1980; Ore Dept Transp Serv Employ Prog, mgr, 1984. **Orgs:** Am Asn Affirmative Action; Gov Tri-Co Affirmative Action Asn; Affirmative Action Officers Asn; adv coun, Wash Co Dept Aging Servs; adv coun, Wash Co Retired Sr Vol Prog; adv bd, Portland Community Col Prof Skills Prog. **Home Addr:** 8300 W Stark St, Portland, OR 97229, **Home Phone:** (503)297-5772.

## RYAN-CORNELIUS, STACEY

Auditor, manager, controller. **Educ:** City Univ NY, Baruch Col, BBA, acct, 1992. **Career:** Price Waterhouse Coopers, audit staff & sr, 1992-95, audit mgr, 1995-99; Ogilvy & Mather, sr partner dir financial planning N Am, 1999-2004, N Am controller, 2004-08, worldwide controller, 2008-, regional controller corp finance. **Orgs:** Am Inst CPAs (AICPA); Nat Asn Black Accountants (NABA). **Honors/Awds:** Black Enterprise, 75 Most Powerful Women in Business, 2010. **Business Addr:** Worldwide Controller, Ogilvy & Mather, 636 11th Ave, New York, NY 10036, **Business Phone:** (212)237-4000.

## RYAN-WHITE, JEWELL

Television producer, executive, president (organization). **Personal:** Born May 24, 1943, Columbus, MS; daughter of Larry A Sr and Martha; children: Donald Andre. **Educ:** Alcorn A&M Col; Joliet Jr Col; Olive Harvey Col; IL State Univ; Rueben Cannon Master Ser, screenwriting. **Career:** Ill Bell Tel Co, opr investr dial serv admin, 1967-76; Community Workers Am Local 5011, pres, 1972-86; Am Cable systs Midwest, comm TV, 1985-88, pub rel, promotions coord, 1987; Am Film Inst, admin campus oprs, 1989-91; NCP Image Awards, tv comm, 1990-92; Nat Asn Advan Colored People Image Awards, TV Comm, 1990-92; Marla Gibbs Crossroads Arts Acad, adminr, 1991-; Turner Broadcast Syst, Trumpet Awards, script supvr, 1993-98; Clark Atlanta Univ, sr assignment mgr, CAU-TV News 3, adj fac, 1994-97; Olympic Games Atlanta Comm, internship placement coord, mgr prof comm outreach, 1996; US Dept Community, Bur Census, partnership specialist, 1999-; Off Labor-Mgt Progs, ed, 2003-; Calif Sch Employees Asn, CBS prog analyst; independent producer, currently; Robert Brilliant Inc, Columbia Broadcasting Syst-tv City, producer, host, cable tv mkt researcher. **Orgs:** Nat pres, Nat Black Commun Coalition, 1975-85; pres Joliet chap Ladies Columbus, 1976-87; chmn bd dir, Joliet Will County Community Action Bd, 1982; chmn, bd dir, United Way Will County, Joliet Cath High Sch, 1983-85; bd dir, Big Bros, 1984; personnel & pub policy comts Nat Campaign Human Dev, 1985-87; Comt Elect Mayor John Bourg, Joliet, 1985-86; bd dir, Joliet Jr Col MNY, Intercult Affairs, 1985-87; campaign mgr, Comt to Elect Andy Hinch, Joliet, 1985-87; vice pres, bd dir, chmn, Nat Fedn Local Cable Programmers, Equal Employ Opportunity Comn & Assoc Arts comts, Wash, 1985-90; Women Cable, 1986-87; comnr, 1986, cbd, 1987, Housing Authority Joliet; Nat Asn Housing & Redevelop Officials, 1986-87; chmn bd, Housing Authority Joliet, 1987; bd dir, Sr Serv Ctr, 1987; bd dir, Sr Companion Prog, 1987; chmn, EEO/AA Comm, Nat Fedn Local Cable Progrs, 1988-90; Nat Asn Advan Colored People, Beverly Hill/Hollywood Chap, 1989-90; Los Angeles Urban League, 1989-92; Los Angeles Black Educ Comn, 1989-93; vpres bd dir, arbitrator, Nat Bd Arbitrators, 1989; State Ill Lit Coun, Govrs Grievance panel; Coalition Black Trade Unionists; Oper PUSH; Vol Parent Guardian Angel Home; St John Vianney Cath Church; SCLC; Cath Educ Asn; Smithsonian Asn; master plan comt, City Los Angeles Cult Arts; Active Urban League; Oper People United Save Humanity; Guardian Angel Home; Southern Christian Leadership Conf; Lit Resource Task Force. **Honors/Awds:** Scholarship in Clothing, 1961; Award Salesclerking RE Hunt HS, 1961; Award Newly Elected Officers Training Sch CWA, 1973; Certificate Merit IL Bell Tele Co, 1974; Award of Appreciation CWA, 1976; United Way Will Co, 1977; City of Hope COPE, 1977; Pace Setter Award, City of Hope, 1979; Crusade Award, Am Cancer Soc, 1980; Citizen of the Month, City of Joliet, 1982; Certificate of Achievement, Pro-Skills, 1986, Achievement Award, 1986, American Ambassador Award, 1986; Award of Appreciation Campaign Human Develop Joliet Catholic Diocese, 1986; Award of Appreciation, Nat Campaign Human Dev Wash DC, 1987; Award for Cable Excellence, Cable Television Admin & Mkt Soc, 1987; 3 Awards for overall contribution to field of adult educ/illiteracy, Joliet Jr Col, 1987; Public Speaking American Cable Systems Midwest, 1987; named to Nat Bd Consumer Arbitrators, 1989; NFLCP, Jewell Ryan-White Cultural Annual Diversity Award. **Home Addr:** 8575 Pineview Lane, Jonesboro, GA 30238-4326, **Home Phone:** (678)846-5297. **Business Addr:** Editor, Office of Labor-Management Programs, 1350 Pa Ave NW Suite 324, Washington, DC 20004, **Business Phone:** (202)727-4999.

## RYCE, SUNDRA L.

President (organization). **Personal:** Born Buffalo, NY. **Educ:** State Univ NY Col, Buffalo, NY, BS, bus studies, 1996; Medaille Col, Buffalo, MS, educ. **Career:** SLR Contracting Serv Co Inc, chmn, pres & chief exec officer, 1996-; Sundra Ryce Inc, pres & chief exec officer, 2012-. **Orgs:** Bd trustee, Western NY Pub Broadcasting Asn; bd trustee, Buffalo Urban Develop Corp; bd dir, Buffalo St Col Found Bd; bd dir, Western NY Health Syst; trustee, bd mem, Buffalo Niagara Partnership; bd trustee, Buffalo State Col; Alpha Kappa Alpha Sorority; trustee, Amherst Chamber Com; trustee, Great Lakes Health; trustee, Buffalo Soc Natural Sci. **Business Addr:** President, Chief Executive Officer, SLR Contracting & Service Co Inc, 1487 Main St, Buffalo, NY 14209, **Business Phone:** (716)896-8148.

## RYCRAW, EUGENIA (EUGENIA MILLER-RYCRAW)

Basketball player, basketball coach. **Personal:** Born Dec 6, 1968; married Richard; children: Robert, Mia, Richard & Janelle. **Educ:** Calif State-Fullerton, Col Humanities & Social Sci, BA, psychol, 1994. **Career:** Basketball player (retired), basketball coach; Titan Athletics, 1987-91; Japan Airlines, basketball player, 1991-93; Calif State-Fullerton, asst coach, 1993-94, 2003-06; Los Angeles Sparks, ctr, 1998-99. **Home Addr:** 20700 San Jose Hills Rd Apt 41, Walnut, CA 91789-1327.

# S

## SAADIQ, RAPHAEL (CHARLIE RAY WIGGINS)

Musician, singer, business owner. **Personal:** Born May 14, 1966, Oakland, CA. **Career:** Tony Toni Tone, vocalist, co-founder; D'Angelo albums, co-producer. Albums: "Lucy Pearl & first string solo", 1999-2004; Instant Vintage, 2002; All Hits at the House of Blues, 2003; RayRay, 2004. Songs: "Ask of You", 1995; "Get Involved", 1999; "Be Here", 2002; "Rifle Love", 2004; "Expanded output & second string", 2004-; "I Want You Back", 2005; "Never Give You Up", 2009; "Stone Rollin", 2011. Pookie Entertainment, founder, currently. **Business Addr:** Founder, Pookie Entertainment, 4850 Vineland Ave, North Hollywood, CA 91601.

### SAAR, BETYE IRENE

Artist, designer, educator. **Personal:** Born Jul 30, 1926, Los Angeles, CA; daughter of Jefferson Maze Brown (deceased) and Beatrice Lillian Brown; children: Lesley & Alison. **Educ:** Univ Calif, BA, 1949; Pasedena City Col, Calif State Univ, Long Beach, grad, printmaking, 1962. **Career:** Whitney Mus Mod Art, solo exhib, 1975; Studio Mus Harlen, solo exhib, 1980; Monique Knowlton Gallery, NY, solo exhib, 1981; Jan Baum Gallery, LA, solo exhib, 1981; Quay Gallery, San Francisco, 1982; WAM & Canberra Sch Art, Australia, solo exhib, 1984; Ga State Univ Gallery, 1984; Mus Contemp Art, LA, solo exhib context, 1984; MIT Ctr Gallery, 1987; Site Installations, 1989; Sanctified Visions, 1990; J PaulGetty Fund Visual Arts fel, 22nd Ann Artist Award, 1990; Art Betye & Alison Saar, 1990-91; Savannah Col Art & Design, distinguished lectr, 2000; Solo exhibs: Connections: Sentimental Souvenirs, 1991; With Breath Our Ancestors, 1992; Signs Times, 1992; Out Cold, 1993; Betye Saar: Secret Heart, 1993; Limbo, 1994; Generation Mentors, 1994; US Deleg Fifth Biennial Havana, 1994; Art Betye Saar & John Otterbridge, 1994, 1995; Personal Icons, 1996; Bearing Witness, 1996; The Three Outdoor Installations, 1996; Tangled Roots, 1996; Ritual & Remembrance, 1997; Workers & Warriors: Return Aunt Jemima, 1998; Crossings, 1998; A Women's Boat: Voyages, 1998; Art & Cult, 1900-2000, 1999; Betye Saar: Time Goes By, 2000; Serv: A Version Survival, 2000; Betye Saar: Personal Icons, 2002; Betye Saar: Colored-Consider Rainbow, 2002; Crocker Art Mus, Sacramento, Calif, 2006, Scottsdale Mus Contemp Art, 2016; group exhibs: Secrets, Dialogues, Revelations: 500 Yrs: Am Century: Uncommon Threads: Contemp Artists & Clothing, 2001; Contemp Romanticism, 2001; Some Assemblage Required, 2002; Layers Meaning, 2003; Univ Calif; Otis Col Art & Design. **Honors/Awds:** Award, Nat Endowment Arts, 1974, 1984; honorary doctorates: Calif Col Arts & Crafts, 1991, Otis/Parson, 1992, San Francisco Art Inst, 1992, 1995, Mass Col Art, 1992, 1995, Calif Inst Arts, 1995; James Van Der Zee Award, Brandywine Workshop, 1992; Distinguished Artist Award, Fresno Art Mus, 1993; Visual Arts Award, Flintridge Found, 1997; National Artist Award, Anderson Ranch Art Ctr, 1999; Living Artists Award, Calif Art Educ Asn, 1999; Pioneer Award, IAM, 2000; Hon Doctorate Degrees, Calif Col Arts & Crafts; Hon Doctorate Degrees, Mass Col Art; Edward MacDowell Medal, 2014. **Business Addr:** Artist, Michael Rosenfeld Gallery, 24 W 57th St, New York, NY 10019, **Business Phone:** (212)247-0082.

### SABREE, CLARICE SYLLA

Administrator, jazz singer, educator. **Personal:** Born Oct 25, 1949, Camden, NJ; daughter of Roy McClendon and Clara Ingram; children: Zahir, Anwar, Ameen & Hassan. **Educ:** Rutgers Univ Camden, BA, 1978. **Career:** Lawn side Bd Educ, teacher, 1978-80; Camden Bd Educ, elem teacher, 1980-82; DMC Energy Inc, energy conserv specialist, 1983-87; CAPEDA, energy analyst, 1987-88; Energy Conserv, supvr monitors, 1988-; NJ Dept Community Affairs, Div Housing & Community Resources, Off Low-Income Energy Conserv, adminr, prog supvr, 1993-; jazz vocalist, poet, african dance performances. **Orgs:** Res Intl Black Dolls, 1979; bd mem, S African Freedom Comt; owner, Cult Concepts Trenton, African Art, Wearing Apparel; bd mem, Nat State & Community Serv Prog. **Home Addr:** 1406 S Broad St, Trenton, NJ 08610-6236, **Home Phone:** (609)989-7298. **Business Addr:** Supervisor, New Jersey Department of Community Affairs, 101 S Broad St, Trenton, NJ 08625, **Business Phone:** (609)292-6055.

### SADDLER, DR. ELBERT M., II

Psychologist. **Personal:** Born Aug 17, 1948, Philadelphia, PA; son of Elbert and Jeannette; married Joyce B; children: Elbert III, Bradley & Amanda J. **Educ:** Rutgers Univ, BA, 1975; Temple Univ, MEd, 1980, PhD, 1985. **Career:** City Philadelphia, Voc coun; Eastern Col, adj asst prof; St Joseph's Col, adj asst prof; Temple Univ, adj asst prof; W Chester Univ, assoc prof psychol, 1985, Coun Ctr, psychologist, 1985; Chi Alpha Epsilon Nat Hon Soc, founder, 1990-. **Orgs:** Am Psychol Asn; PA Psychol Asn; Omega Psi Phi; Nat Asn Develop Edu; founder, Chi Alpha Epsilon Nat Hon Soc, 1990-. **Honors/Awds:** Outstanding Service, Nat Asn Develop Educ, 2000; Education Equity Award, Pa Human Rels Comn. **Home Addr:** 1119 Donna Dr, Ft. Washington, PA 19034-1615, **Home Phone:** (215)643-1442. **Business Addr:** Associate Professor, West Chester University, 700 S High St, West Chester, PA 19383-4120, **Business Phone:** (610)436-2301.

### SADDLER, JOSEPH

Rap musician. **Personal:** Born Jan 1, 1958, Barbados. **Career:** Albums: Grandmaster Flash & the Furious Five, mem; The Chris Rock Show, HBO, musical dir; Solo Albums: They Said It Couldn't Be Done, 1985; The Source, 1986; Ba Dap Boom Bang, 1987; On the Strength, 1988; Greatest M Wildessages, 1983; Grandmaster Flash vs the Sugar hill Gang, 1997; Greatest Mixes, 1998; Adventures on teh Wheels of Steel, 1999; On the strength, 2000; Official Adventures of Grandmaster Flash, 2002; Essential Mix: Classic Edition, 2002; Mixing Bullets & Firing Joints, 2005; The bridge concept of culture, 2009. Film: Wild Style, actor, 1982; Grandmaster Flash Enterprises, founder, currently. **Business Addr:** Founder, Grandmaster Flash Enterprises, 600 Johnson Ave Suite E7, Bohemia, NY 11716, **Business Phone:** (631)218-2942.

### SADLER, DONNIE LAMONT

Baseball player. **Personal:** Born Jun 17, 1975, Clifton, TX. **Career:** Baseball player (retired), baseball coach; Boston Red Sox, second baseman-shortstop, 1998-2000; Cincinnati Reds, 2001; Kans City Royals, 2001-02; Tex Rangers, 2002-03; Ariz Diamondbacks, 2004, 2007; Chicago White Sox, shortstop, 2004; Milwaukee Brewers, 2008; Pac League: Triple-A Tucson, 2007; Philadelphia Phillies, hitting coach, currently. **Business Addr:** Hitting Coach, Philadelphia Phillies, Veterans Stadium 3501 S Broad St, Philadelphia, PA 19148, **Business Phone:** (215)463-6000.

### SADLER, DR. KENNETH MARVIN

Dentist. **Personal:** Born Gastonia, NC; son of Edward Dewitt Sr and Mildred Jackson; married Brenda Arlene Latham; children: Jackson Lewis Ezekiel & Raleigh DeWitt Samuel. **Educ:** Lincoln Univ, BA, 1971; Howard Univ Col Dent, DDS, 1975; Golden Gate Univ, MPA, 1978. **Career:** Howard Univ Col Dent, instr & coordr, 1972-76; AUs Dent Corps, capt & dentist, 1975-78; Kenneth M Sadler DDS & Assocs PA, pres, admin dir, 1978-. **Orgs:** Life Mem, Omega Psi Phi, 1969; Am Dent asn, 1975-; Acad Gen Dent, 1976-; chmn, bd trustees, Lincoln Univ, 1983-; Old N State Dent Soc, chmnpeer rev comt, 1986; bd dir, Old Hickory Coun Boy Scouts Am, 1988-; vpres, BSA, Old Hickory Coun, 1990; Lewisville Town Coun, mayor pro tempore, 1991-; Am Asn Dent Sch, consult, 1991; bd trustee, Forsyth Tech Cmnty Clg; Winston-Salem Forsyth County Appearance Comn, 1992-98; Winston-Salem Forsyth County Indust Financing Pollution Control Authority; fel Am Col Dentists, 1995; fel Acad Dent Int; Fel Int Col Dentists; lewisville-clemmons chamber com; secy, treas, Am Acad Dent Group Pract, 2011-. **Honors/Awds:** Int Col Dent Award, 1975; The Am Asn Endodontics Award, 1975; US Army, dental diploma-gen pract, 1976; Acad Gen Dent, Master, 1996; Recognition Cert, Chicago Dental Soc, 1989; Plaque-Appreciation, Fifth Dist Dental Soc, 1989; Lecture & Table Clinic, Chicago Mid-winter Meeting, 1989; TableClinic, Thomas P Hinman Dental Meeting, 1989, 1996; United Way Forsyth County, chmn budget review panel, 1991; Forsyth County Dental Hygiene Soc, lecturer, 1991; NAFEO, Distinguished Alumni of the Year, 1986; Citizenship Award, 1996, NCDS; Mastership Acad Gen Dent; Silver Beaver Award, OHC BSA; Distinguished Alumni Award, Howard Univ Col Dentistry, 2000. **Special Achievements:** Presentations include: DC Dental Soc; Howard Univ, Post-grad Seminar; Pellican State Dental Soc; Nat Dental Soc; Forsyth County Dental Assistant Soc; Lincoln Univ, Chemistry Dept; Am Acad Dental Group Practice; Palmetto State Dental Med Pharmaceutical Assn; author: "Resin Bonded Retainers, "Journal of Nat Dental Assn, 1984; Acad Gen Dentistry, 2003. **Home Addr:** 8519 Brook Meadow Lane, Lewisville, NC 27023-9736, **Home Phone:** (336)945-4439. **Business Addr:** President, Administrative Director, Kenneth M Sadler DDS & Associates PA, 201 Charlois Blvd, Winston Salem, NC 27103, **Business Phone:** (336)331-3500.

### SADLER, DR. WILBERT L., JR.

Educator. **Personal:** Born Atlanta, GA; son of Willie Mae Sanford and Wilbert Sr; married Carolyn Johnson; children: Anthony Lee, Wilbert Bryant & Crystal Yolanda. **Educ:** Paine Col, BS, 1970; Morgan State Univ, MS, 1972; Boston Univ, EdD, 1981; Univ Pa, post doctorate study, 1981; Columbia Univ, post doctorate study, 1988. **Career:** Morgan State Col, instr, 1970-74; Boston Univ, grad asst, 1974-76; Livingstone Col, asst prof, 1976-82, adj prof, 2001-; Winston-Salem State Univ, assoc prof, 1982-92, prof, 1992-2001, prof emer, 2001-. **Orgs:** Pinehurst Comm Club, 1976-; Asn Col & Univ Profs; Nat Asn Advan Colored People; life mem, Alpha Upsilon Alpha, NC Col Read; life mem, Col Reading Asn; Int Reading Asn; Alpha Kappa Mu Hon Soc; Beta Mu Lambda; life mem, Alpha Phi Alpha Frat Inc; coordr, ELE; bd trustee, Rowan Pub Libr; Alpha Upsilon Alpha, Nat Reading Hon Soc, 1989-90; Phi Delta Kappa, Nat Educ Hon Soc, 1989-90. **Home Addr:** 708 Pinehurst St, Salisbury, NC 28144-6339, **Home Phone:** (704)642-0066. **Business Addr:** Professor Emeritus, Winston-Salem State University, 601 S Martin Luther King Jr Dr, Winston Salem, NC 27101, **Business Phone:** (919)750-2694.

### SAFFOLD, DR. OSCAR E.

Dermatologist, physician, educator. **Personal:** Born Feb 20, 1941, Cleveland, OH. **Educ:** Fisk Univ, BA, 1963; Meharry Med Col, MD, 1967. **Career:** George W Hubbard Hosp, intern, 1967-68; Boston Univ Med Ctr, resident, 1968-69, 1971-73; Tufts Univ Sch Med, asst resident dermatologist, 1968-72; Boston City Hosp, chief resident dermatologist, 1972-73; Case Western Res Med Sch, Dept Dermat, asst clin prof, assoc clin prof; Mid-Fla Dermat Assocs, physician, currently. **Orgs:** Univ Hosp Cleveland, 1973-; Mass St Bd; Ohio St Bd; Am Bd Dermat, 1974; secy, Dermat Sect, Nat Med Asn, 1975-; fel Am Acad Dermat; Am Soc Dermat Surg; AMA; Cleveland Acad Med; Cleveland Dermat Asn; Nat Med Asn; Ohio St Med Asn. **Business Addr:** Physician, Mid-Florida Dermatology Associates, 7652 Ashley Pk Ct Suite 305, Orlando, FL 32835, **Business Phone:** (407)299-7333.

### SAFFOLD, SHIRLEY STRICKLAND

Judge. **Personal:** Born Jan 1, 1951?; married Oscar E; children: Sydney. **Educ:** Cent State Univ, BA; Cleveland-Marshall Col Law, JD. **Career:** Cleveland Munic Ct, judge, 1987-94; Legal Aid Soc, Criminal Div, staff atty; Cuyahoga County Common Pleas, Ct, judge, 1995-. **Orgs:** Nat Bar Asn; Nat Asn Women Judges; past pres, resolutions comt, pres, Am Judges Asn. **Honors/Awds:** Judge of the Year, Dew Ward Club. **Special Achievements:** First African American woman to serve in an executive position in the American Judges Association. **Home Addr:** 8 W Mather Lane, Bratenahl, OH 44108-1158. **Business Addr:** Judge, Cuyahoga County Commons Pleas Court, Rm 21B 1220 Ont St Ct, Cleveland, OH 44114, **Business Phone:** (216)443-8560.

### SAFFORE, LATEEF

Oncologist, research scientist. **Personal:** married Yetunde Aranmolate. **Educ:** W Va State Univ, BS, biol gen, 1996; Marshall Univ, MS, biol res environ microbiol, 1999; Univ Akron, PhD, pub admin urban studies, 2011. **Career:** Ridgeway Biosystems, Assoc Res Biologist, 2000-01; Dept Cancer Biol, Lerner Res Inst, lead res technologist, sr res biologist, 2001-; Cleveland Clin Found, res oncologist scientist, 2003. **Business Addr:** Research Technologist, Senior Research Biologist, Cleveland Clinical Foundation, 9500 Euclid Ave NA20, Cleveland, OH 44195, **Business Phone:** (216)444-9977.

### SAGERS, RUDOLPH, JR.

Marketing executive. **Personal:** Born Feb 14, 1955, Chicago, IL; married Carol Hillsman; children: Ryan Christopher & Randall. **Educ:** Univ Ill Urbana-Champaign, BS, psychol, 1978; Univ Cincinnati, MS, health admin, 1980; Moraine Valley Community Col, cert, workflow & health info mgt redesign specialist, 2012. **Career:** Alpha Phi Alpha Fraternity Inc, fraternity mem, 1975-; Veterans Admin, mgt analyst trainee, 1979-80, chief staff to med ctr dir, 1979-84, mgmt analyst, 1980-81, health systs specialist, 1981-84; Int Bus Mach, adv mkt rep & team leader, 1984-92; Unisys, sr acct exec, 1992-96; AT&T, sr acct mgr, 1996-99; FileNet Corp, sr acct exec, 1999-2002; Edge Technol Resources Inc, dir bus develop, 2002-04, bus develop mgr, 2003-05; Technol Consortium Group LLC, sr sales exec, 2004-07; CIBER Inc, sr sales exec & bus develop, 2007-10; Advan Concepts Chicago Inc, info mgt redesign consult, 2010-12; Empyrion Solutions, bus develop exec, 2012-. **Orgs:** Amer Col Hosp Adminrs, 1982; MI Health Coun, 1982; Am Health Plng Assoc, 1983; Soc Hosp Plng, 1983; Black Data Prof Assoc, 1986-; Asn Info & Image Mgt, 1999; Bus Process Mgt Inst, 2007-; Int Soc Six Sigma Professionals, 2010-; Proj Mgt Inst, 2013-; Univ Ill Freshman Acad Hon Soc; Martial Arts; Alpha Kappa Alpha Sorority Inc. **Honors/Awds:** Outstanding Young Man of America Award, 1983; Veterans Admin Achievement of Service Award, 1983; Veterans Admin Superior Performance Award, 1983; Veterans Admin Special Contribution Award 1984; Branch Manager Award, Int Bus Mach, 1985-86; National 100% Sales Club Award, Int Bus Mach, 1985-86; Medical Ctr Director's Commendation of Excellence Award. **Home Addr:** 2737 Tarpon Ct, Homewood, IL 60430. **Business Addr:** Business Develop Manager, Edge Technological Resources Inc, 230 W Cermak Rd Suite 2A, Chicago, IL 60616, **Business Phone:** (312)842-4617.

### SAILOR, ELROY

Executive, government official, secretary (office). **Personal:** Born Oct 26, 1969, Detroit, MI; son of Rev DeAnna and Clarence; married Angela; children: Alamni Deje & E Claybyrne Prescot. **Educ:** Morehouse Col, BA, polit sci, 1990; Mich State Univ, mich polit leadership prog, pub policy, 1994; Wayne St Univ, master, urban planning, 1998. **Career:** Gov John Engler, ast to gov, 1991-93, dir urban affairs, re-election campaign, dep polit dir, 1993-94; US Senate Spencer Abraham, spec ast, 1995-, advisor; House Republican Conf, dir; JC Watts Co, founder, 2003, chief exec officer, managing partner, currently. **Orgs:** Exec bd mem, US Senate Black Legis Staff Caucus, 1995-96, founder; co-host, Youngbloods NAT Empowerment TV, 1995-96; pres & owner, Sailor CPN Vending Mach, 1996-; Fel Chapel, 1990-; vol, COTS-Homeless Shelter, 1991-92; Black Farmers & Agriculturalists asn; bd mem, Red Br Technologies Inc. **Honors/Awds:** Detroit News, Detroits Five Future Leaders, 1995; MPLP Mic St Univ, Fellowship, Pub Policy Prog, 1994. **Special Achievements:** Entered Morehouse COL at age 16, 1986. **Home Addr:** 809 Helen St, Inkster, MI 48141-1289, **Home Phone:** (313)865-9166. **Business Addr:** Chief Executive Officer, Managing Partner, JC Watts Companies, 600 13th St NW, Washington, DC 20005, **Business Phone:** (202)207-2854.

### SAINT-JEAN, OLIVIER. See ABDUL-WAHAD, TARIQ.

### SAINT-LOUIS, RUDOLPH ANTHONY

Lawyer. **Personal:** Born Dec 28, 1951, Port-au-Prince; son of Libner and Georgette; married Elizabeth H Saint; children: Shaundri, Melissa & Yolanda. **Educ:** St Joseph's Col, BA, psychol & fr, 1973; Univ Wis Law Sch, Madison, JD, law, 1976. **Career:** Attorney (retired); Wis Dept Ind, Unemploy Div, hearing examr, 1976-77; ICC, atty, adv, 1977-81, SBA, staff atty, 1981-83, OPA, actg dir, 1983, staff atty, 1983; US Atty Off spec, asst US atty, 1980-81; United Airlines, reservations, 1995-2007; US Dept Transp, staff atty, 1996-2011, assisted cong & pub consistencies field transp, beginning 2011. **Orgs:** Chair employee bd educ, ICC; agency rep, Fed Bar Asn, 1980; pres, ICCToastmasters, 1988, 1990; pres, Com Co Club, 1991-95; pres, LowFrequency Radio Astron, 1993-95. **Honors/Awds:** Cot Service Award, 1990 & 1991; EEO Award, ICC, 1991. **Home Addr:** 6500 Killarney St, Clinton, MD 20735-3823, **Home Phone:** (301)856-7174.

### SAINTE-JOHNN, DON

Radio broadcaster, executive. **Personal:** Born Jul 9, 1949, Monroeville, AL; son of Walter Johnson and Nell B Henderson; married Brenda L Hodge; children: W Marcus & J'Michael Kristopher. **Educ:** La City Col, attended 1968; San Francisco State Univ, MS, instrnl technol, MA, BA; Am River Col, cert, 2009. **Career:** Air talent & basketball coach; XEGM Radio, San Diego, Calif, prog dir, 1968-69; KYUM Yuma Ariz, sports dir, 1968; KWK, St Louis, prog dir, 1969-71; Aradcom Prod, St Louis, pres, 1970-71; WJPC Radio, Chicago, am air personality, 1971-74; KFRC RKO Broadcasting Inc, air personality, 1974-94; KSFM-FM, Sacramento, air talent, 1983; KWIN, Stockton, Calif, 1984; KYA, San Francisco, 1994; KFRC, San Francisco, 1994; KSOL, San Francisco, 1995; KBGG, San Francisco, air personality, 1994-99; KIOI, San Francisco, 1997; KHYL, Sacramento, air personality, 1999-2013; KQLL-FM, air talent; St Davids Schs, El Sobrante Boys Club, Richmond Police Activ League, basketball coach; St Davids Sch, athletic dir; Am River Col, prof journalism, air personality, pub speaker, 1999-; Cosumnes River Col, prof journalism, air personality, pub speaker, 1999-; Don Ste-Johnn Consult, pres, 2012-. **Orgs:** Nat Asn Radio-TV Ammoun; Calif Real Estate; bd mem, E Bay Zool Soc; Bay Area March Dimes Superwalk, Nat Acad TV Arts & Sci, Am Fed TV & Radio Art; Alpha Epsilon Rho; SC Broadcaster Asn; bd dir, Paul J Hall Boys Club; bd mem, Diocesan Boys Athletic Coun Oakland; Soc Prof Journalists; Nat Asn Broadcasters; bd mem, Oakland Zool Soc; Journalism Asn Community Cols, 2008; Broadcast Educ Asn, 2008. **Honors/Awds:** Most Outstanding Radio Student, La City Col, 1967; Billboard Air Personalities of the Year, 1973, 1974; Honored as Concerned Spon for Chicago Pin-Killers Bowl Club, 1974; Air Personality of the Year, Billboard Mag, 1974, 1975; Air Personality on Pop Radio Award, Black Radio Exclusive Mag, 1980. **Home Addr:** 40 Bellam Rd Suite 10101, San Rafael, CA 94912-0101, **Home Phone:** (510)543-6248. **Business Addr:** Air Talent, KQLL-FM, 2625 S Mem, Tulsa, OK 74129, **Business Phone:** (918)664-2810.

### SALAAM, ABDEL R.

Executive, choreographer, association executive. **Personal:** Born Jan 1, 1950, Harlem, NY. **Educ:** Herbert H Lehman Col, BFA prog, 1973; Univ Ife, Nigeria, cert, yoruba arts & cult, 1979. **Career:** Ailey Dance Co, dancer; Joan Miller Chamber Arts/Dance Players, prin dancer & soloist; Fred Benjamin Dance Co; Ron Pratt's Alpha Omega 1-7 Theatrical Dance Co; Otis Salid's New Art Ensemble; Chuck Davis Dance Co, assoc artistic dir; Am Contemp Ballet Co, guest artist; Contemp Chamber Dance Theater, guest artist; Forces Nature Dance Theatre Co, co founder, exec artistic dir & choreographer, 1981-; Nat Endowment Arts, choreographers fel, 1991-93, 1994-96; Apollo Theatre's Ann Kwanzaa Regeneration Night, artistic dir, currently; Am Dance Festival Durham, NC, fac; Am Dance Festival at Sejeung Performing Arts Ctr Seoul, Korea, fac; Lehman Col City Univ New York, fac; Ailey Am Dance Theatre, guest instr choreography. **Orgs:** Lehman Black Stud Orgn. **Honors/Awds:** Dance Africa Award, Brooklyn Acad Music, 1987; Carla Sayrce Alumni Award, Lehman Col City Univ NY, 1989; Morani Shujaa Award, Lehman Col City Univ NY, 1990; Monarch Merit Award, Nat Coun Arts & Cult, 1993; Silver Anniversary Award, Lehman Col City Univ NY, 1994; Better Family Life Lifetime Achievement Award, 2000; Entertainment Award, Best Musical Show in the World Within a Theme Park, 2004; Dance Company of the Year, Excellence Black Theater Award, 2013. **Special Achievements:** First African Episcopal Mass for the Church using African dance and music as a liturgical voice; First artist in residence, 2002-07. **Home Addr:** 14 Mt Morris Pk W Apt 6, New York, NY 10027-6380, **Home Phone:** (212)289-2057. **Business Addr:** Executive Artistic Director & Choreographer, Co-Founder, Forces of Nature Dance Theater Co, 230 Malcolm X Blvd 2nd Fl, New York, NY 10027, **Business Phone:** (212)722-3320.

**SALAAM, DR. ABDUL (LEO MCCALLUM)**
Dentist. **Personal:** Born Aug 18, 1929, Newark, NJ; son of Roosevelt and Katie Allen; married Khadijah; children: Sharonda Khan, Valerie Best, Robert, Darwin & Abdul II. **Educ:** Wash Sq Col, NY Univ, BS, 1952; Columbia Univ Sch Oral Dent Surg, DDS, 1956; Acad Gen Dent, FAGD, 1973. **Career:** Specialty Promotions Co Inc, founder, 1959; Inst Grad Dent, postgrad instr, 1966-72; Bks & Things, owner, 1969; Lincoln Dent Soc Bull, ed, 1972; Guaranty Bank, Chicago, Ill, bd dir, 1976; Muhammad Ali Investment Corp, treas, 1988-90; Inst Gen Semantics, guest lectr, 1988-; Am Muslim Jour, newspaper columnist; Construct Systs Inc, chmn; First Africa Capital Investment Corp, Chicago, Ill, treas, 1988-; pvt pract dent, currently. **Orgs:** Am Dent Asn, 1956-; pres, Specialty Promo Co Import Export, 1959-; Am Equilibration Soc, 1963-; pres, Commonwealth Dent Soc, NJ, 1964; Pierre Fauchard Soc; orgn pres, Nation Islam, 1976; bd dir mem, Am Muslim Jour, 1982-84; pres, bd dir, New Earth Child Care Community Network, 1984-88; rep, Chicago Dent Soc Dialogue Dent, 1987-89; pres, Kenwood Hyde Park Br Chicago Dent Soc, 1987-88; bd dir, Masjid Al' Fatir, 1987-; bd dir, Chicago Dent Soc, 1993-96. **Honors/Awds:** Man of the Year, Commonwealth Dental Soc, NJ, 1966; Dentist of the Year Award, Lincoln Dent Soc, Chicago, IL, 1989; Named in Honor, Dr Abdul Salaam Day, Mayor's Office, City Newark, NJ, 1989. **Special Achievements:** First African American in the Columbia University School of Oral & Dental Surgery school; First African American to import & distribute an English translation of the Holy Quran; Contributor of Archival Film & Consultant to "Malcolm X, An American Experience", TV Documentary. **Business Addr:** Dentist, Abdul Salaam DDS, 1502 E 63rd St, Chicago, IL 60637, **Business Phone:** (773)496-5138.

**SALAAM, EPHRAIM MATEEN**
Broadcaster, football player. **Personal:** Born Jun 19, 1976, Chicago, IL; son of Malikah. **Educ:** San Diego State Univ, child develop, 1998. **Career:** Football player (retired), analyst; Atlanta Falcons, right tackle, 1998-2001, tackle, 1999; Denver Broncos, left tackle, 2002-03, right tackle, 2002; Jacksonville Jaguars, left tackle, 2004-05; Houston Texans, left tackle, 2006-08, 2009-10; Detroit Lions, 2009; Fox Sports 1, analyst, 2013-. **Orgs:** EMS Found. **Honors/Awds:** Bronze Panther Academic Award; Super Bowl. **Special Achievements:** TV series: The Game, 2007; Dead Tone, executive producer, 2007; The Girls Next Door, 2008; The 2010 VH1 Do Something Awards, producer, 2010; Food Wars, 2010; The Amazing Race, 2013; Supremacy, associate producer, 2014. **Business Addr:** Analyst, Fox Sports 1, 500 E Broward Blvd Suite 1300, Fort Lauderdale, FL 33394, **Business Phone:** (954)375-3634.

**SALAAM, RASHAAN IMAN**
Football player. **Personal:** Born Oct 8, 1974, San Diego, CA; son of Sultan and Khalada. **Educ:** Univ Colo, Boulder. **Career:** Football player (retired); Chicago Bears, running back, 1995-97; Oakland Raiders; Cleveland Browns, 1999; Green Bay Packers, 1999; Memphis Maniax, 2001; San Francisco 49ers, 2003; Toronto Argonauts, 2004. **Honors/Awds:** Heisman Trophy, 1994; Doak Walker Award, 1994; Walter Camp Award, 1994; Jim Brown Award, 1994; Unanimous All-American, 1994.

**SALLEY, JOHN THOMAS**
Basketball player, television show host, actor. **Personal:** Born May 16, 1964, Brooklyn, NY; son of Quillie (deceased) and Mazie Carter; married Natasha Duffy; children: 3. **Educ:** Ga Tech Col Mgt, 1988. **Career:** Basketball player (retired), TV show host; Detroit Pistons, power forward, 1986-92; Miami Heat, power forward, 1992-95; Toronto Raptors, power forward, 1995-96; Chicago Bulls, power forward, 1996; Panathinaikos, Greece, 1996; Los Angeles Lakers, 1999-2000; Funkee's Enterprises, pres, 100.3 The Beat, host, 2005-06. Others: "The John Salley Block Party", 2005-06; Fox Sports Network, "The Best Damn Sports Show Period", currently; "One on One", 2005; "HE's a lady", 2005; "Stranded with a star, who would you choose?", 2005; "Fast cars & superstars: Th Young guns celebrity Race", 2007; "Shaken not Stirred", 2008-09; "Comedy Central Roast Of Larry The Cable Guy", 2009; Hollywood Fame, co-owner, 2006-. Films: Bad Boys, 1995; A Fare to Remember, producer, 1998; A Fare to Remember, exec producer, 1999; The Ultimate Christmas Present, 2000; Bad Boys II, 2003; The Ultimate Christmas Present; Eddie, 2003; Coast to Coast, 2003; Mr.3000, 2004; Naughty or Nice, 2004; Hair Show, 2004; Rebound, 2005; Ladies Night, 2005; Confessions of a Shopaholic, 2009; Black Dynamite, 2009; Something Like a Business, 2010. TV Series: "Malcolm & Eddie", 1997; "I Can't Believe You Said That", 1998; "Sin City Spectacular", 1998; "Getting Personal", 1998; "Sabrina, the Teenage Witch", 2000; "Son of the Beach", 2001; "DAG", 2001; "Girlfriends", 2002; "Baby Bob", 2003; "Come to Papa", 2004; "Noah's Arc", 2005; "Rescue Me", 2006; "Cook Her Pants Off", 2012; "Love That Girl", 2012; "Mike & Mike", 2012-15; "A Healthy You & Carol Alt", 2014; "Sin City Saints", 2015; "Exhale", 2015; "Dads Doin' Dishes", 2015; "Q N' A with Mikki and Shay", 2015. **Orgs:** BeBest You Can Be; Metro Youth Found; Cancer Asn; Omega Phi Psi; NBA Stay Sch, Hepatitis B Campaign; comnr, Am Basketball Asn, 2006-; Omega Psi Phi. **Home Addr:** 14027 Aubrey Rd, Beverly Hills, CA 90210. **Business Addr:** Host, Fox Sports Net, 10201 W Pico Blvd Bldg 101 Suite 5420, Los Angeles, CA 90035, **Business Phone:** (310)369-1000.

**SALLEY, LAWRENCE C.**
Commissioner. **Career:** Commissioner (retired); Westchester County Dept Transp, transp comnr.

**SALMON, DR. JASLIN URIAH**
Executive, educator, consultant. **Personal:** Born Jan 4, 1942, Darliston; son of Leaford and Jane Sylent; married Anita Hawkins; children: Janet Felice & Jennifer Renee. **Educ:** Olivet Nazarene Univ, BA, sociol, 1969; Ball State Univ, MA, sociol, 1970; Univ Ill, Chicago, PhD, sociol, 1977. **Career:** Ball State Univ, teaching asst, 1969-70; George Williams Col, asst prof sociol, 1970-76; Triton Col, prof sociol, 1976-77, 1977-79, dir ctr parenting, 1985-88; Human Resource Develop Govt Jamaica, dir, 1977-79; Off Prime Minister Jamaica, dir adv, 1997-; Jamaica Red Cross, chmn, vpres, 2002, Poverty Eradication Prog, nat coordr, pres, 2006-; Int Inst Social, Polit & Econ Chg, founder, pres & cheif exec officer, currently. **Orgs:** Social worker, Dept Ment Health IL, 1968-69; dir, HOPE, 1973-75; dir & mem, Chicago Forum, 1971-72; chmn, Acad Senate George Williams Col, 1974; consult, Parenting Women & Minorities; pres, Nat Asn Advan Colored People Oak Pk, Ill Br, 1989-94; vpres, Int Fedn Red Cross & Red Crescent Socs, 2009-. **Honors/Awds:** Teacher of the Year, George Williams Col, 1973; listed in the "International Who Is Who Among Intellectuals", "Men of Achievement" and "Who Is Who Among African Americans"; Augusto Pinaud Honor, Venezuela Red Cross, 2008. **Special Achievements:** Author: Black Executives in White Business, 1979; Parenting, A Child's Perspective 2007. **Home Addr:** Lot 3 Woodlands Red Hills, PO Box 1, St Andrews60303-0586. **Business Addr:** President, Chief Executive Officer, International Institute for Social, Political & Economic Change, 19 Norwood Ave, Kingston, NY 12401, **Business Phone:** (918)906-8189.

**SALMOND, DR. JASPER**
Consultant. **Personal:** Born Jul 5, 1930, Camden, SC; son of James and Dora James; married Thelma Brooks; children: Jeryl Stanley Salmond & Jenita LaZelda Salmond Belton. **Educ:** Benedict Col, BA, educ, 1954; Columbia Univ, Teachers Col, MA, educ admin, 1960; Atlanta Univ, Sch Systs Admin, cert, 1963; Univ SC, exten course; Xerox Oper Mgt Training Sch, Lynchburg. **Career:** Board Chair/Commissioner (retired) Richland Co Sch Dist One(1990-2010); Corporate Executive, 1972-2009; sch teacher & prin, 1954-72; Benedict Col Nat Alumni, pres, parliamentarian, 1960-98; SC Elem Sch Prins, pres, 1971-72; Wilbur Smith Assocs Inc, prin assoc & VP, UN contact, proj develop, community involvement planning, sr mktg coordr, vpres, 1972; Terrific Kids Prog, chmn, 1975-99; Midlands Tech Col, bd comm, 1975-91; Richland Memorial Hosp, bd trustees; Midlands Tech Col, comn secy, 1989-90; Richland Co Sch Dist One, bd comnrs, 1990-, chmn, 1993-94, chmn finance & facil comm, 1995-97, parliamentarian, 1998; Rep Nat Bank, bd dir, 1992-94; Benedict Col Nat Alumni Assn, vp, parliamentarian, 2008-10; Richland County SC, Voter Registration and Election Commission Exec. Dir. 2012. **Orgs:** Secy, 1990-2003, SC Sch Bds Asn, vpres, 1995-96, pre-elect, 1997, pres, 1998, bd dir, 1992-2000; regional rep, Afro-Am Coalition Comm, Asn Community Col trustee, 1990-91; Alpha Kappa Mu Hon Soc; regional officer, completing distinguished toastmasters req, Toastmasters Int, 1993-; bd dir, 1993-2000, chmn, 1996-97, Guardian Ad Litem; bd dir, technol comm, 1994-98, Mortgage bd, 1998-, Carolina First Bank; chmn, Exec Coun & Exec Comm, Greater Columbia Chamber Com, 1996-98; bd dir, 1996-2005, treas, Palmetto Health Systs; Alpha Phi Alpha Fraternity; Alpha Psi Lambda Chap; chap chmn, Am Red Cross; chmn, Conv Plenary Presenter; pres & exec comm mem, Columbia Kiwanis Club; NEA, Nat Prin Asn; life mem, Nat Asn Advan Colored People; Richland County Sch; bd dir, Pledged Alpha; chmn, First Calvary Baptist Church Deacon Bd; TRIO, Univ SC. **Special Achievements:** ORDER OF THE PALMETTO, STATE OF SOUTH CAROLINA. **Home Addr:** 4035 Coronado Dr, Columbia, SC 29203-5409, **Home Phone:** (803)765-2795. **Business Addr:** 4035 Coronado Dr, Columbia, SC 29203.

**SALMONS, JOHN RASHALL**
Basketball player. **Personal:** Born Dec 12, 1979, Philadelphia, PA. **Educ:** Miami Univ, attended 2002. **Career:** Philadelphia 76ers, forward, 2002-06; Toronto Raptors, 2006, 2013-14; Sacramento Kings, 2006-09, guard, 2007-09, 2011-13; Chicago Bulls, 2009-10; Milwaukee Bucks, 2010-11. **Business Addr:** Professional Basketball Player, Sacramento Kings, 1901 W Madison St, Sacramento, CA 95834, **Business Phone:** (916)928-0000.

**SALONE, MARCUS R.**
Judge. **Personal:** Born Apr 28, 1949, Chicago, IL; son of Herbert Spencer and Anna Rae; married Valee Glover; children: Lisa Michelle & Andrea Valee. **Educ:** Univ Ill, Chicago Circle Campus, BA, 1974; John Marshall Law Sch, JD, 1981. **Career:** Cook Co State's Atty's Off, asst, 1981-83; Chicago, police officer; Salone, Salone, Simmons, Murray & Assocs, 1983-91; Circuit Ct Cook Co, assoc judge, 1991-95; State Ill, First Dist, 3rd Div, appellate judge;Ill Supreme Ct, judge, 2011-12; Law Offices Marcus R. Salone, pres, 2012-. **Orgs:** Life mem, Kappa Alpha Psi Fraternity, 1987-; bd dir, Cook Co Bar Asn, 1988-; bd dir, Ancona Montessori Sch, 1988-90; bd dir, John Howard Asn, 1994-. **Home Addr:** 6830 S Bennett, Chicago, IL 60649, **Home Phone:** (312)684-2656. **Business Addr:** Appellate Judge, Illinois Courts, 3101 Old Jacksonville Rd, Springfield, IL 62704, **Business Phone:** (217)558-4490.

**SALTER, KWAME S.**
Executive, vice president (organization). **Personal:** Born Jan 31, 1946, Delhi, LA; son of Samuel Leon (deceased) and Reva Daniels; married Phyllis V Harris; children: Kevin-Jamal, Keri-JaMelda & Matthew-Harrison. **Educ:** Wis State Univ, Whitewater, EdB, 1968; Univ Wis, Madison, MA, educ admin & policy studies, 1971. **Career:** Milwaukee Pub Sch Bd Educ, teacher, 1968-69; Wis State Univ, Whitewater, acad counr, 1968-70; Univ Wis, Madison, proj asst, 1969-70; Univ Wis, Madison, Afro-Am Cult Ctr, exec dir, 1970-73, Ford Found, fel educ, 1970; Dane Co Parent Coun Inc, exec dir, 1976-86; Bd Educ Madison Metrop Sch Dist, pres, 1982-86; Oscar Mayer Foods Corp, dir employ pub rels; Kraft/Oscar Mayer Foods Corp, vpres human resources, sales & customer serv, 1986-, HR Sales & Customer Serv, 1999-2004, HR Global Functions, 2004-05, HR Global Supply Chain, sr vpres, 2005-08; Salter Group LLC, pres, 2008-, Concordia Univ, Chicago, Col Bus, Adj Prof, 2009-. **Orgs:** Pres, Exec Coun Cult Interaction & Awareness Inc, 1973; vpres, Nat Asn Advan Colored People, Madison Chap, 1974-75; Madison Downtown Optimist Serv Club, 1977; pres, Common Touch Inc, 1977-; Admin Mgt Soc, 1978-; vpres, Madison Metrop Sch Dist Bd Educ, 1980; Phi Delta Kappa, 1980-; chmn, Wis State Adv Comn US Civil Rights Comn, 1985-87; chmn, Stud Readiness Comt, Gov's Comn 21st Century; African-Am Alumni Asn; Nat Career Develop Asn. **Home Addr:** 510 Nova Way, Madison, WI 53704. **Business Addr:** Vice President for Human Resources, Sales & Customer Service, Kraft/Oscar Mayer Foods Corp, 910 Mayer Ave, Madison, WI 53704, **Business Phone:** (608)241-3311.

**SALTER, ROGER FRANKLIN, SR.**
Executive, president (organization). **Personal:** Born Jul 15, 1940, Chicago, IL; married Jacqueline M Floyd; children: Dawn, Roger J, Marc Cpres & Sanmar Fin. **Educ:** Chicago Teachers Col, BE, 1962; DePaul Univ, BS. **Career:** Chicago MetAsrnc Co, second ldng agt, 1962-63; Ins Sales, asst mgr, 1964; Mutual Benifit Life, agt, 1965-70; Blkbrn Agency Mutual Benifit Life, asst gen agt, 1970-74; World-Renowned Sanmar Financial Network, founder & chief exec officer, 1974; Sanmar Financial Planning Corp, pres & chief exec officer, currently. **Orgs:** Dir, sec second vpres, first vpres, S Side Br Chicago Assn Life Underwriters; exec dir, Fin S Shore Comm; pres, Ekrsll Nghrs Comm Grp; bd dir, Mile Sqr Health Ctr; Nat Asn Advan Colored People; Chicago Urban League; Natl Bus League; Chicago Area Coun Boy Scouts Am; Omega Psi Phi Frat; life mem, Mlln Dllr Rnd Tbl, 1972-; fourth Blk US. **Home Addr:** 5512 S Harper Ave, Chicago, IL 60637-1830, **Home Phone:** (773)363-2215. **Business Addr:** President, Sanmar Financial Planning Group, 1327 W Wash Blvd Suite 102, Chicago, IL 60607, **Business Phone:** (708)422-6600.

**SALTER, SAM**
Singer. **Personal:** Born Feb 16, 1978, Los Angeles, CA. **Career:** Albums: It's On Tonight, 1997; The Little Black Book, 2000; Strictly For Da Bedroom, 2008, Sinking In Quicksand, 2011; Singles: "After 12, Before 6", 1997; "There You Are/It's on Tonight", 1998; "Tell Me", 1996; "Never Make a Promise", 1997; "In My Bed", 1997; "We're Not Making Love No More", 1997; "Once My Shit (Always My Shit)", 2000; "Straight 2 Heaven", 2010; "Got Me", 2010; "To Be Loved", 2011; "Mayday", 2013. **Business Addr:** Vocalist, c/o Red Zone Entertainment, 400 Galleria Pkwy SE Suite 1500, Atlanta, GA 30339, **Business Phone:** (678)244-1100.

**SALTERS, DR. CHARLES ROBERT. See Obituaries Section.**

**SAM, SHERI LYNETTE**
Basketball player. **Personal:** Born May 5, 1974, Lafayette, LA; daughter of Wilton and Rose. **Educ:** Vanderbilt Univ, BS, 1996. **Career:** San Jose Lasers, guard, 1996; Orlando Miracle, 1999; Miami Sol, free agt, 2000-03; Seattle Storm, forward-guard, 2004; Charlotte Sting, guard, 2005-06; Ind Fever, forward, guard, 2007; Ashdod, 2007-08; Detroit shock, 2008; Panionios, 2008-09. **Business Addr:** Professional Basketball Player, Indiana Pacers, Conseco Fieldhouse, Indianapolis, IN 46204, **Business Phone:** (317)917-2500.

**SAMARA, NOAH AZMI**
Attorney general (U.S. federal government), executive. **Personal:** Born Aug 8, 1956, Addis Ababa; son of Ibrahim Azmi and Yeshiemebet Zerfou; married Martha Debebe; children: Leila & Gideon. **Educ:** E Stroudsburg Univ, E Stroudsburg, PA, BA, eng, 1978; Univ Calif, Los Angeles, hist; Georgetown Univ, WA, MBA, int bus diplomacy, 1985, Sch Law, JD, 1985, MS, int bus dipl. **Career:** Law Offices Rothblatt & Millstein, Wash, DC, law clerk, 1981-84; Geostar Corp, Wash, DC, staff atty, 1984-86, dir internal affairs, 1986-88; Robbins & Laramie, Wash, DC, coun, 1988-89; Venable, Baetjer & Howard, Wash, DC, coun, 1989-90; WorldSpace Inc, Wash, DC, founder, chmn & chief exec officer, 1990-, dir; Yenura Pte Ltd, chief exec officer, chmn. **Orgs:** Bd dir, United Therapeut, 1997-. **Home Addr:** 8903 Ellsworth Ct, Silver Spring, MD 20910, **Home Phone:** (301)585-1452. **Business Addr:** Founder, Chairman, Chief Executive Officer, WorldSpace Inc, 1 Worldspace 8515 Georgia Ave 8th Fl, Silver Spring, MD 20910, **Business Phone:** (301)960-1200.

**SAMKANGE, DR. TOMMIE MARIE (TOMMIE MARIE ANDERSON SAMKANGE)**
Psychologist, educator, association executive. **Personal:** Born Aug 1, 1932, Jackson, MS; daughter of Harry and Marie Hughes; married Stanlake John Thompson; children: Stanlake Mudavanhu & Harry Mushore. **Educ:** Tougaloo Col, BS, 1953; Ind Univ, MS, 1955, PhD, 1958. **Career:** Tougaloo Col, asst prof, 1955-56; African Pub Rels, Harare, psychologist, mkt researcher, 1959-64; Tuskegee Inst, assoc prof, 1964-67; Tenn St Univ, assoc prof, 1967-71; Harvard Univ, Cambridge, Mass, sr tutor, 1971-74; Harvard Univ, Afro-Am Studies Dept, lect headtutor, 1971-74; Tufts Univ, asst prof, 1974-76; Northeastern Univ, lect, 1979; Ministry Educ & Cul, Zimbabwe, chief educ officer, psychol, spec educ, early childhood educ, 1981-94, dir, 1994-; Govt Zimbabwe, chief educ psychologist, 1981-94; Chinyaradzo C's Home, Zimbabwe, bd dir, 1982; Moleli Sec Sch, Selous, Zimbabwe, bd govt, 1988; Stnlk Smkng, prof; Salem St Col, asst dir minority affairs; Ranche House Col, chairperson, 1992-96; Nyatsime Col, Chitungwiza, fac, 1995; Proposed S African Method Univ, fac, 1997. **Orgs:** Am Psychol Asn; League Women Vtrs; Health Prof Coun Zimbabwe; Zimbabwe Psychol Asn; Ranche House Col Citizenship; bd dir, C's Protection Soc, 1980; St John Ambulance, 1982; bd dir, Rusike C's Home, 1984; fel Am Asn Advan Sci; consult, Zimbabwe Nat Asn Ment Health, 1985; Pi Lambda Theta. **Honors/Awds:** Outstanding Young Woman of America, Tougaloo Col, 1965; Mellon Found Grant, 1977; Mellon scholar, Tufts Univ, 1977-78; Consortium of Doctors, Women of Color in the Struggle, 1993. **Special Achievements:** Co-author, Hunhuism or Ubuntuism, 1980. **Home Addr:** The Castle Chiremba Rd PO Hatfield, Harare00000.

**SAMPLE, BILL. See SAMPLE, WILLIAM AMOS.**

**SAMPLE, HERBERT ALLAN**
Journalist. **Personal:** Born Mar 19, 1961, Los Angeles, CA; son of Herbert Warner and Ramona Adams. **Educ:** Pepperdine Univ, Malibu, CA, 1981; Calif State Univ, Sacramento, CA, BA, govt, journ, 1983. **Career:** Los Angeles Times, reporter, 1983-85; Sacramento Bee, reporte, capitol bur, 1986-91, 1992-93, Bay Area Corresp, 2001, writer, currently; Dallas Times Herald, chief capitol bur, 1991; Mc-Clatchy Newspapers, Wash Bur, reporter, 1993-2000; Red Herring magSacramento, 2007; Assoc Press, 2008-11; Bee, Bay; freelance writer & ed, currently. **Orgs:** Vpres, Black Journalists Asn Southern Calif, 1985; Nat Asn Black Journalists, 1986-2000; pres & founder, Sacramento Black Journalists Asn, 1988-; Wash Asn Black Journalists, 1993-2000, pres, 1999; Bay Area Black Journalists Asn, 2001-. **Business Addr:** Reporter, Associated Press, 500 Ala Moana Blvd Suite 7-590, Honolulu, HI 96813, **Business Phone:** (808)536-5510.

**SAMPLE, WILLIAM AMOS (BILL SAMPLE)**
Writer, baseball player, broadcaster. **Personal:** Born Apr 2, 1955, Roanoke, VA; son of William T and Nora; married Debra Evans; children: Nikki, Ian & Travis. **Educ:** James Madison Univ, BS, psychol, 1978. **Career:** Baseball player (retired), broadcaster, writer, actor, dir; Tex Rangers, outfielder 1978-84; Topps All Rookie Team, 1979; NY Yankees, 1985; Atlanta Braves, 1986; AtlantaBraves, TV & radio broadcaster, 1988-89; Universal 9 WWOR-TV, broadcaster, 1990; ESPN, broadcaster, studio analyst, color analyst, 1991-93; Baseball Weekly, USA Today, writer; Seattle Mariners, TV broadcaster, 1992; Calif Angels, radio anal, play by play broadcaster, 1993-94; Pennant Chase-Baseball Inside Out, Phoenix Comn, 1996; Maj League Baseball Radio, talk show host, reporter, writer, 2001-; MLB TV, corresp; Seattle Mariners & Calif Angels, broadcaster; NPR, CBS Radio & MLB.com, broad caster. Films: The Meat Puppet, 2012; Gravedigger, 2013; Reunion 108, 2013; Clean Cut, 2016. **Orgs:** Maj League Baseball Players Asns Licensing Comt, 1986-87; consult, Maj League Baseball-Umpire Rev Bd, 1995. **Home Addr:** 10 Pascack Rd, Township of Washington, NJ 07676, **Home Phone:** (201)664-4347. **Business Addr:** Writer, Reporter, MLB Advanced Media, 75 9th Ave 5th Fl, New York, NY 10011, **Business Phone:** (512)434-1542.

**SAMPLES, JARED LANIER**
Government official, association executive. **Personal:** Born Jan 22, 1965, Atlanta, GA; son of Cadmus Allen and Dorothy Burns. **Educ:** Ga State Univ, BS, 1989. **Career:** Atlanta Housing Authority, Atlanta, GA, weatherization specialist, 1982; NW Perry Recreation Ctr, Atlanta, GA, youth counr, 1985; Ga State Univ, handicapped serv counr, 1988; Metrop Atlanta, Rapid Transit Authority, Atlanta, GA, intern, 1989; Atlanta City Coun, coun mem, Dist 9, 1996; campaign mgr, 2003. **Orgs:** Bd mem, bd comnr, Atlanta Housing Authority; bd dir, Econ Opportunity Atlanta; bd mem, Atlanta Police Citizen Rev Bd; vpres, Perry Homes Tenant Asn; Ga State Univ, Affirmative Action Adv Commitee. **Honors/Awds:** Martin Luther King Tribute Speaker Award, J C Harris Elem Sch; 50 Most Young Promising Black Am, Ebony Mag; Lt Colonel, Aide De Camp, Former Gov Joe Frank Harris; Proclamation Outstanding Community Serv, State Ga. **Home Addr:** 712 Hightower Rd, Atlanta, GA 30318, **Home Phone:** (404)799-9128. **Business Addr:** Council Member, Atlanta City Council, 55 Trinity Ave SW, Atlanta, GA 30303, **Business Phone:** (404)330-6044.

**SAMPSON, REV. DR. ALBERT RICHARD**
Clergy. **Personal:** Born Nov 27, 1938, Boston, MA; son of Paul and Mildred Howell. **Educ:** Shaw Univ, BA, relig & social sci, 1963; Governors State Univ, MA, cult studies, 1973; McCormick Theol Sem, Mdiv, 1977; Union Baptist Theol Sem, DDiv, 2000. **Career:** Newark New Jersy Poor People's Campaign, proj dir; Zion Baptist Church Everett MA, pastor; Fernwood United Methodist Church, sr pastor, 1975-. **Orgs:** Spokesman Ministers Action Comn Jobs, 1985-92; pres, Nat Black Farmers Harvest & Bus Corp, 1989; speaker, Million Man March, 1995; consult, Poverty prog, Syracuse NY, Wilmington DE, Indianapolis IN, Boston MA; founder, Black Churches Coun; int vpres, training Allied Workers Int Union; vice chmn, Mayor Harold Wash's First Source Task Force; vpres, Roseland Clergy Asn; bibl scholar, Original African Heritage Bible; chmn, Million Man March MAPCO, Metro Area, planning corp, Chicago; nat field secy, Nat African Leadership Summit; bd mem, Univ Ill Col Urban Bus; chaplain, World Conf Mayors; United Methodist S End Coop Parish Chicago; Southern Christian Leadership Conf; Nat Asn Real Estate Brokers; chaplain, World Conf Mayors; bd mem, largest Black-Owned banks Am; pres, Farmers Agribusiness Resource Mgt; pres, Metrop Coun Black Churches Chicago; pres, Neighborhood Social Entrepreneurs Soc; pres, Metro Area African Am Seniors Resource Network; pres, Youth & Col Chapters Nat Asn Advan Colored People; pres, Metrop Coun Black Church. **Home Addr:** 10056 S Parnell, Chicago, IL 60628, **Home Phone:** (773)445-7125. **Business Addr:** Senior Pastor, Fernwood United Methodist Church, 10057 S Wallace St, Chicago, IL 60628, **Business Phone:** (773)445-7125.

**SAMPSON, CHARLES**
Entertainer. **Personal:** Born Jul 2, 1957, Los Angeles, CA; married Marilyn; children: Laurence Charles & Daniel. **Educ:** Cent Ariz Col, attended. **Career:** Bull rider (retired); Rodeo Cowboys Asn circuit, prof, 1977; Presidential Command Performance Rodeo, 1983; bull rider, 1994; Berkshire Farm Ctr & Serv Youth, mentor, Therap Riding Prog, asst dir, currently. **Honors/Awds:** World Champion Bull Rider, 1982; Championships: Sierra Circuit, 1984; Turquoise Circuit, 1985-86, 93; Copenhagen & Skoal, 1992; Calgary Stampede, Pendleton (OR) Round-Up; Grand Nat Rodeo; Calif Rodeo; Del Rio bull-riding buckle; Rodeo Superstars; Prof Rodeo Hall of Fame, 1996; Ellensburg Rodeo Hall of Fame, 2009; 2-time bull riding champion, Pendleton Round-Up. **Special Achievements:** First African-American to win a PRCA world championship, 1983; hired by Timex to promote the durability of their watches; appeared 10 times in Nat Finals Rodeo. **Home Addr:** 924 Stonemill Manor Ave, Lithonia, GA 30058, **Home Phone:** (770)484-1526. **Business Addr:** Assistant Director, Berkshire Farm Center & Services for Youth, 13640 Rte 22, Canaan, NY 12029, **Business Phone:** (518)781-4567.

**SAMPSON, DR. HENRY THOMAS, JR.**
Engineer, executive director. **Personal:** Born Apr 22, 1934, Jackson, MS; son of Henry T and Esther; children: Henry III & Martin; married Laura Howzell Young. **Educ:** Morehouse Col; Purdue Univ, BS, chem engineering, 1956; Univ Calif, Los Angeles, MS, chem engineering, 1961; Univ Ill, Urbana-Champaign, MS, nuclear engineering, 1965, PhD, nuclear physics, 1967. **Career:** US Naval Weapons Ctr, China Lake, Calif, res chem engr, 1956-61; res consult several doc films; Pioneer Black Filmmakers, lectr; Aerospace Corp, El Segundo, Calif, proj engr, 1967-81, dir Planning & Opers, dirate Space Test Prog, 1981-87. **Orgs:** AAAS; Am Nuclear Soc; Omega Psi Phi; bd dir, Southwest Col Found, fac adv comn, Nuclear Eng, 1976-. **Honors/Awds:** Several patents engineering devices, 1957-65; US Naval Educ Fel, 1962-64; Atomic Energy Comn (AEC), Fel, 1964-67; Scarecrow Press, 1977; Black Image Award, Aerospace Corp, 1982; 'Blacks in Engineering, Applied Science, & Education Award', Los Angeles Counc Black Prof Engrs, 1983. **Special Achievements:** Swinging on the Ether Waves: A Chronological History of African Americans in Radio & Television Programming, 1925-55; Co-invented the Gamma-Electric cell, 1971; Author: "Blacks in Black & White-A Source Book on Black Films 1910-50", "Blacks in Blackface, A Source Book on Early Black Musical Shows", Scarecrow Press, 1980; "The Ghost Walks, A Chronological History of Blacks in Show Business 1863-10", Scarecrow Press, 1987; "Blacks in Black and White", Scarecrow Press, 1995; That's Enough Folks: Black Images in Animated Cartoons, Scarecrow Press, 1998. First African American in the United States to earn a Ph.D. in nuclear engineering. **Home Addr:** PO Box 648, El Segundo, CA 90245. **Business Addr:** Director of Planning and Operations, Aerospace Corp, 2350 E El Segundo Blvd, El Segundo, CA 90245-4691, **Business Phone:** (310)336-5000.

**SAMPSON, JAMES S.**
Executive. **Career:** Sampson Assocs, managing dir, pres, currently. **Business Addr:** Managing Director, President, Sampson Associates, 4100 Redwood Rd Suite 359, Oakland, CA 94619, **Business Phone:** (510)531-4237.

**SAMPSON, KELVIN**
Basketball coach. **Personal:** Born Oct 5, 1955, Laurinburg, NC. **Educ:** Pembroke State Univ, BA, phys educ & polit sci, 1978; Mich State, MS, coaching admin, 1980. **Career:** Basketball player (retired), basketball coach; Pembroke State, guard, 1974-78; Mich State Univ, asst coach, 1979-80; Mont Tech, from asst coach to coach, 1980-85; Wash State Univ, from asst coach to head coach, 1985-94; UnivOkla, head coach, 1994-2006; Ind Univ, coach, 2006-08; Milwaukee Bucks, asst coach, 2008-11; Houston Rockets, asst coach, 2011-14, coach, 2014-. **Orgs:** USA Basketball Men's Col Comt, 1997-2000. **Business Addr:** Coach, Houston Rockets, 1510 Polk St, Houston, TX 77002, **Business Phone:** (713)758-7200.

**SAMPSON, MARVA W.**
Government official, executive, association executive. **Personal:** Born Sep 4, 1936, Hamilton, OH; daughter of Willie Ray Sudbury (deceased) and Isiah Wells (deceased); married Norman C; children: Raymond & Anthony. **Educ:** Miami Univ; Univ Dayton, MPA, 1976. **Career:** Executive (retired); Hamilton Ohio City Sch Syst, pvt secy, 1954-58, off mgr, 1958-59; Citizens Coun Human Rels, coord secy, 1966-70; City Middletown, dept community develop, relocations officer, 1964-66, dir dept human resources, 1971; Middletown Job Opportunity Inc, secy & coordr. **Orgs:** Bd dir, Youth Men's Christian Asn, 1971; Ohio Munic League, 1978; bd trustee, ASPA, 1978; pres, Pi Alpha Alpha, 1979; pres, Ctr Forensic Psychiat, 1979-80; choir dir, Pianist 2nd Baptist Church; exec bd mem, Arts Middletown; bd trustee, Cent Ohio River Valley Asn; exec comt mem, Butler County C Serv Bd; pres, Middletown Area Safety Coun; exec comm mem, Middletown Area United Way; Nat Asn Social Workers; Ohio Pub Health Asn; Human Serv Coun; Friends Sorg; Ohio Parks & Recreation Asn; Nat Parks & Recreation Asn; Am Soc Pub Admin; Human Resources Comt; Int Personnel Mgt Asn; ecec mem, Alcohol & Drug Addiction Serv Bd; criminal justice bd, City Hamilton. **Honors/Awds:** Cert Merit, Serv C C, 1968; Lady of the Week, Woman of the Year, WPFB Radio Sta, 1970; Red Triangle Award, Youth Men's Christian Asn, 1971-76; Outstanding Citizens Award, Knights Social Club, 1972; Community Center Selective Award; Leisure Professional Cert, Ohio Parks & Recreation Asn, 1992-95; Nat Asn Advan Colored People & South side Community Image Award, Nat Asn Advan Colored People, 1994; Volunteer of the Year, Middletown United Way, 1996; JC Penney Golden Rule Award, 1997; Woman of the Year, Butler County, 1997. **Home Addr:** 6366 W Alexandria Rd, Middletown, OH 45042-8907, **Home Phone:** (513)422-4968.

**SAMPSON, RALPH LEE, JR.**
Basketball coach, basketball player. **Personal:** Born Jul 7, 1960, Harrisonburg, VA; married Aleize Rena Dial; children: 4; children: 1. **Educ:** Univ Va, BA, speech commun, 1983. **Career:** Basketball player (retired), basketball coach; Univ Va, ctr basketball player; Houston Rockets, 1983-87; Golden State Warriors, 1987-89; Sacramento Kings, 1989-90; Wash Bullets, 1991; Unicaja Ronda, 1992; James Madison Univ, asst coach, 1992-93; Rockford Lightning, 1994-95; Richmond Rhythm, coach, 1999-2000; Minor league, Richmond, Va, coach.

**SAMPSON, ROBERT R.**
Pharmacist. **Personal:** Born Oct 17, 1924, Clinton, NC; son of Frank J and Annie Curry; married Myrtle B; children: Frank R. **Educ:** Fayetteville State Univ, attended 1943; Howard Univ, BS, 1950. **Career:** Sampson's Pharm, owner, 2002-. **Orgs:** Pres, NC Old N St Pharm Soc; mem-at-large, Nat Pharmaceut Asn; Incorp Chap Stock holder Gateway Bank; Am Pharm Asn; Nat Asn Retail Druggists; Greensboro Med Soc; Greensboro Soc Pharm; Omega Psi Phi Frat; Nat Pharm Asn; UMLA; Greensboro C C. **Home Addr:** 4608 Splitrail Ct, Greensboro, NC 27406, **Home Phone:** (336)697-1220. **Business Addr:** Owner, Sampson Pharmacy, 1502 E Mkt St, Greensboro, NC 27401, **Business Phone:** (336)272-3131.

**SAMPSON, RONALD ALVIN (RONALD A SAMPSON)**
Advertising executive. **Personal:** Born Nov 13, 1933, Charlottesville, VA; son of Percy and Lucile Mills Martin; married Norvelle Johnson; children: David Alan & Cheryl Annual. **Educ:** DePaul Univ, BS, com, 1956. **Career:** Advertising executive (retired); Ebony Mag, advert sales rep, 1958-63; Foote Cone & Belding Advert, merchandising supvr, 1963-66; Tatham Laird Kudner Advert, acct mgr, partner & mgt supvr, 1966-78, contact dept mgr; Am Asn Advert Agencies, advisor, 1972; Burrell Advert, exec vpres, 1978-81, sr vpres, exec vp develop; DArcy MacManus Masius Advert, advert agency acct mgr & sr vpres, 1981-88; Chicago United, deacon; Burrell Commun Group, dir develop. **Orgs:** Vpres, bd dir, Community Renewal Soc, 1969-94; bd dir, Deacon Chicago United, 1992-94; co-chair, Protestants Common Good, 1996-; Am Advert FED Diversity Comn; Chicago Forum, bd mem, MidAmerica Leadership Found; bd mem, Am Advert Fedn. **Home Addr:** 6715 S Oglesby Ave, Chicago, IL 60649-1493, **Home Phone:** (773)667-4638.

**SAMPSON, THOMAS GATEWOOD**
Lawyer. **Personal:** Born Oct 4, 1946, Durham, NC; son of Daniel (deceased) and Claretta; married Jacquelyn; children: Thomas G II & Alia J. **Educ:** Morehouse Col, BA, polit sci, 1968; Univ NC, Sch Law, JD, 1971. **Career:** Thomas Kennedy Sampson & Tompkins LLP, managing partner & atty, 1971-, sr prtner, currently; Int Bus fel, 1983; Ga State Law Sch, adj prof law, 1985-93; Ga State Univ Col Law, adj prof law, 1986-93; Atlanta Col Trial Advocacy, instr; Nat Inst Trial Advocacy, instr; Logan E Bleckley Inn Ct, master; Logan Inn Am Inns Ct, master; Atty Gen State Ga, spec asst. **Orgs:** NC & Ga Bar Asn; regional dir, Nat Bar Asn, 1974-75, mem, curently; vpres, Atlanta Coun Younger Lawyers, 1974-75; pres, Gate City Bar Asn, 1977; vpres, Atlanta Legal Aid Soc, 1979; fel Int Bus, 1983; vice-chmn, State Bar Disciplinary Bd, 1984; Ga Supreme Ct Comn Racial & Ethnic Bias; Chief Justice's Comn Professionalism, 1990-94; chmn, State Bar Ga Client's Security Fund, 1991; bd dir, Atlanta Bar Asn, 1992-93; bd dir, Atlanta Urban League & Sr Citizens Serv; Am Bd Trial Advocates, 1993; bd gov, State Bar Ga, 1994-; Ga Supreme Ct Comn Racial & Ethnic Bias, 1994-96; vice-chair, Judicial Nominating Comn State Ga, 1999-; charter fel Litigation Coun Am. **Honors/Awds:** Inductee, Georgia Chapter of the American Board of Trial Advocates; Man of the Year, Omega Psi Phi, Psi Chap, 1991; Best Lawyers in America, 1991-; Listed in Best Lawyers, Atlanta Mag, 2000 & 2002. **Special Achievements:** First African American to have been inducted into the Georgia Chapter of the American Board of Trial Advocates. **Home Addr:** 4220 Greentree Lane, College Park, GA 30349, **Home Phone:** (404)344-7039. **Business Addr:** Attorney & Managing Partner, Senior Partner, Thomas Kennedy Sampson & Tompkins LLP, 3355 Main St, Atlanta, GA 30337, **Business Phone:** (404)688-4503.

**SAMUEL, ANTOINETTE ALLISON (TONI SAMUEL)**
Chief executive officer. **Educ:** Chatham Col, BA, anthrop & sociol, 1975; Tex Southern Univ, Houston, TX, MPA. **Career:** Nat League Cities, ctr dir, 1994-98, dep exec dir, 2013-; Employee Asst Prof Asn, chief exec officer, 2000-04; Am Soc Pub Admin, exec dir, 2004-13. **Orgs:** UN Asn; exec mgmt, Am Soc Asn Execs, 2005-06; bd adv, US Pub Serv Acad; fel Nat Acad Pub Admin; fel Am Soc Asn Execs, 2012. **Business Addr:** Executive Director, American Society for Public Administration, 1301 Pennsylvania Ave NW Suite 700, Washington, DC 20004, **Business Phone:** (202)393-7878.

**SAMUEL, DAVID**
Executive. **Educ:** State Univ NY, BS, econs, 1973; Harvard Bus Sch, PMD, bus, 1995. **Career:** GTE Corp, indust mkt mgr, dir mkt opers, commodity & supply mgr, 1975-86; Informix Software, nat acct mgr, 1986-88; Digital Equip Corp, prog dir, healthcare mkt mgr, channels mkt mgr, 1988-94; AT Kearney, dir, 1994-96; AT&T Solutions, mgr & pract leader, 1996-98; Boston Edison Co, vpres, customer care, 1997-98; NSTAR Elec & Gas Corp, vpres info serv & cio, 1999-2001; IBM Corp, Global Energy & Utilities, gen mgr, 2001-05; David Samuel Seminars, managing dir, 2005-08; Big Bros Big Sisters Metro Atlanta, exec vpres, chief prog officer, 2008-11; CIO Serv Group, managing partner, 2011; BlueWave Comput, client strategy exec, 2011-. **Orgs:** Edison Elec Inst; Am Gas Asn; bd dir, Whittier State Health Ctr, Roxbury, Mass; New Vision Found, Framingham, Mass. **Business Addr:** Client Strategy Executive, BlueWave Computing, 2251 Corp Plaza Pkwy, Smyrna, GA 30080, **Business Phone:** (770)980-9283.

**SAMUEL, JASPER H.**
Executive, lithographer. **Personal:** Born Dec 13, 1944, Brooklyn, NY; son of Frederick and Ruby. **Career:** Jasper Samuel Printing Co, pres, currently. **Orgs:** NCP. **Home Addr:** 17 Fairview Ave, South Orange, NJ 07079. **Business Addr:** President, Jasper Samuel Printing Co, 46 Alder St, Jersey City, NJ 07305-4836, **Business Phone:** (201)433-3123.

**SAMUEL, LOIS S.**
Educator, social worker. **Personal:** Born May 26, 1925, Boston, MA; children: David & Judith. **Educ:** Simmons Col, BS; Columbia Univ Sch, SSW. **Career:** Educator (retired); Leake & Watts Childrens Home, soc worker, 1947-49; Youth Consult Serv, soc worker, 1949-51; New York Bd Educ Bur, child guid, 1955-73, supvr, 1973-79; Dist 29 Drug Abuse Prev & Educ Prog, dir, 1971-79; Queens High Sch Unit, clin supvr, 1979-85. **Orgs:** Acad Cert Social Workers; Nat Asn Social Workers; Nat Asn Black Social Workers; br pres, Nat Asn Advan Colored People, 1972-76; Community Adv Coun; Hemp stead Sch Bd; bd mem, Wndhm C Serv; trustee, Congreg Ch S Hempstead; Delta Sigma Theta Sorority; pres, Nassau Alumni Chap. **Home Addr:** 243 Carolina Ave, Hempstead, NY 11550.

**SAMUEL, SEAL HENRY OLUSEGUN OLUMIDE ADEOLA**
Singer. **Personal:** Born Feb 19, 1963, London; son of Francis and Adebisi; married Heidi Klum; children: Henry Guenther Ademola Dashtu, Johan Riley Fyodor Taiwo & Lou Sulola. **Career:** Albums: Seal, 1991; The Acoustic Session, 1991; Violet: Acoustic EP, 1991; Seal

II, 1994; Human Being, 1998; Seal IV, 2003; Seal: Best 1991-2004, 2004; Live in Paris, 2005; One Night to Remember, 2006; System, 2007; Livein Hattiesburg, 2008; Soul, 2008; Hits, 2009; The Platinum Collection - Seal, Seal II, Soul, 2010; 6: Commitment, 2010; Soul 2, 2012. **Honors/Awds:** Grammy Awards for Record, 3; Song, Pop Male Vocal, 1995. **Business Addr:** Vocalist, Warner Brothers Records, 75 Rockefeller Plz, New York, NY 10020-1604, **Business Phone:** (212)275-4600.

**SAMUEL, TONI. See SAMUEL, ANTOINETTE ALLISON.**

**SAMUELA, LEORA. See JONES, LEORA SAM.**

**SAMUELS, BRYAN**
Executive director, commissioner. **Educ:** Univ Notre Dame, BA, econs; Univ Chicago, Harris Sch Pub Policy Studies, MA, pub policy. **Career:** Ill Dept C & Family Serv, dir, 2003-07; Chicago Pub Schs, chief staff, 2007-09; US Dept Health & Human Serv, Admin C & Families, Admin C, Youth & Families, comnr, currently; Chapin Hall at Univ Chicago, exec dir. **Business Addr:** Executive Director, Chapin Hall, 1313 E 60th St, Chicago, IL 60637, **Business Phone:** (773)256-5116.

**SAMUELS, CHARLOTTE**
Educator. **Personal:** Born May 27, 1948, Philadelphia, PA. **Educ:** Cent State Univ, BS, 1969; Temple Univ, MS, educ, 1973; Supervisory cert; prin certif. **Career:** Educator (retired), executive; Sch District Philadelphia, mathematics chairperson, 1969-99, cluster Facilitator; Foundations Inc, consultant, 1999-; Prentice-Hall, math consult, 2000-08; Pa High Sch Coaching Initiative, math mentor, 2005-09; Acad Consult, Proj GRAD, 2009-11; Mathematics Academic Consult, Proj GRAD USA, currently; Voyager Learning, contractor, 2013-. **Orgs:** Assoc Supv & Curric Develop, Nat Coun Teachers Math; Assoc Teachers Math Philadelphia & Vicinity, Black Women's Educ Alliance; Assoc Prof & Exec Women, Joint Ctr Polit Studies, COBBE; Nat Asn Advan Colored People; Big Sisters Am, Campaign Comm State Rep Dwight Evans; vol Victim Crime Prog mem, Nat Forum Black Pub Adminr Philadelphia Chapt; Nat Asn Univ Women; Mathematics, Sci Leadership Cong. **Home Addr:** 9 Plum Ct, Lafayette Hill, PA 19444-2503, **Home Phone:** (610)834-9894. **Business Addr:** Mathematics Academic Consultant, Project GRAD USA.

**SAMUELS, EVERETT PAUL, SR.**
Executive. **Personal:** Born Aug 27, 1958, Tulsa, OK; son of Chester R and Gwendolyn Verone Busby; married Patricia Ann Harris; children: Everett Paul II & Paige Noelle. **Educ:** Cent State Univ, BS, 1980. **Career:** Westin Hotel, Tulsa, OK, hotel mgt, 1980-82; Xerox Corp, sr mgt rep, 1983-84, mkt exec, 1984-85, acct exec, 1985-86; Progressive Mgt Assocs, exec vpres, 1985-; EPS Mgt Servs, Tulsa, OK, pres & owner, 1989-; Dean Witter Reynolds Inc, vpres, 1991-2007; Morgan Stanley & Co Inc, financial advisor, 2007-; Morgan Stanley Smith Barney, financial advisor, 2009-. **Orgs:** Tulsa Pub Sch, 1982-; bd dir, Tulsa Econ Develop Corp, 1984-, pres, 1987-90; asst treas, bd trustee, Friendship Baptist Church, 1985-, asst secy, Deacon Bd, 1986-; bd mem, Sickle Cell Anemia Found, 1987-; bd mem, Gilcrease Hills Homeowners Asn, 1989-; bd mem, N Tulsa Heritage Found, 1990-; Phi Mu Alpha Fraternity; Nat Asn Advan Colored People; vol, United Negro Col Fund. **Honors/Awds:** Outstanding American Award; Outstanding Young Americans. **Home Addr:** 11420 S Col Ave, Tulsa, OK 74137, **Home Phone:** (918)296-7740. **Business Addr:** Financial Advisor, Morgan Stanley Smith Barney, 2200 S Utica Pl Suite 300, Tulsa, OK 74114, **Business Phone:** (918)744-4600.

**SAMUELS, RONALD S. See Obituaries Section.**

**SAMUELS, DR. WILFRED D.**
Educator. **Personal:** Born Feb 7, 1947, Puerto Limon; son of Noel L Sr and Lena Jones; married Barbara Fikes; children: Michael Alain & Detavio Ricardo. **Educ:** Univ Calif, Riverside, CA, BA, eng & black studies, 1971; Univ Iowa, MA, Am studies & African Am studies, 1974, PhD, Am studies & African Am studies, 1977. **Career:** Univ Colo, Boulder, Colo, asst prof, 1978-85; Col Arts & Sci, Univ Calif, Los Angeles, fel, 1982 & 1983; Ford Found, fel, 1984 & 1985; Benjamin Banneker Hon Col, Prairie View AM, Tex, assoc prof, 1985-87; Univ Utah, Salt Lake City, UT, assoc prof eng & ethnic studies, 1987-, African Am Studies Prog, dir, currently, Ethnic Studies Prog, actg coordr, currently. **Orgs:** Popular Cult; Modern Lang Asn; exec bd, Am Lit Asn; founding pres, African Am Lit & Cult Soc. **Home Addr:** 9537 S 1335 E, Sandy, UT 84092, **Home Phone:** (801)849-1666. **Business Addr:** Professor of English & Ethnic Studies, University of Utah, 3407 LNCO Lang & Commun Bldg, Salt Lake City, UT 84112, **Business Phone:** (801)581-3288.

**SAMUELSSON, MARCUS**
Chef. **Personal:** Born Jan 25, 1970, Addis Ababa; married Maya Haile. **Educ:** Culinary Inst, Goteborg. **Career:** Michelin restaurant; Georges Blanc Lyon, asst chef, 1992-94; Aquavit Restaurant, exec chef & co-owner; Riingo; Umea Univ Sch Restaurant & Culinary Arts, vis prof int culinary sci; Marc Burger; St Food; Norda; Ginnys Supper Club; Red Rooster, 2010; C-House. **Honors/Awds:** Best "Rising Star Chef", James Beard Found, 1999; Best Chef: New York City, James Beard Found, 2003; World Econ Forum, "Global Leaders for Tomorrow"; "The Great Chefs of America"; James Beard Foundation award, 2013. **Special Achievements:** Books: New American Table, The Soul of a New Cuisine & Marcus Off Duty. **Business Addr:** Executive Chef, Co-Owner, Red Rooster Harlem, 310 lenox ave, New York, NY 10027, **Business Phone:** (212)792-9001.

**SANCHEZ, DR. SONIA BENITA (WILSONIA BENITA DRIVER)**
Columnist, educator, poet. **Personal:** Born Sep 9, 1934, Birmingham, AL; daughter of Wilson L and Lena Driver (deceased); married Albert; children: Morani, Mungu & Anita; married Etheridge Knight. **Educ:** Hunter Col, BA, political science, 1955; NY Univ, attended 1957; Wilberforce Univ, PhD, 1972. **Career:** Author, poet, educator (retired); Downtown Sch, New York, instr, 1965-67; San Francisco State Col, instr, 1966-67; Univ Pittsburgh, instr, 1968-69; Rutgers Univ, asst prof, 1969-70; Manhattan Community Col, asst prof, 1970-72; Amherst Col, assoc prof, 1973-75; Temple Univ, resident poet, prof eng & womens studies, Laura Carnell chair, 1975-99; Pew Fels Arts, 1993; Philadelphia's Poet Laureate, 2012-14. Poetry: Homecoming, 1969; We a Badd DDD People, 1970; Liberation Poem, 1970; Love Poem, 1973; A Blues Book for Blue Black Magical Women, 1973; Ive Been a Woman: New and Selected Poems, 1978; Homegirls & handgrenades, 1984; Under a Soprano Sky, 1987; Does your house have lions?, 1995; House of a Friend, 1995; Like the Singing Coming Off the Drums: Love Poems, 1998; Shake Loose My Skin: New and Selected Poems, 1999; Ash, 2001; Bum Rush the Page: A Def Poetry Jam, 2001; Morning Haiku, 2001. PLAYS: Sister Son/ji, 1969; The Bronx Is Next, 1970; Dirty Hearts, 1973; Uh Huh: But How Do It Free Us?, 1974; Malcolm Man/Dont Live Here No Mo, 1979; Im Black When Im Singing, Im Blue When I Aint, 1982; Black Cats Back and Uneasy Landings, 1995. AUTHOR: Its a New Day: Poems for Young Brothas and Sistuhs, 1971; The Adventures of Fat Head, Small Head and Square Head, 1973; A Sound Investment and Other Stories, 1979. EDITOR: Three Hundred Sixty Degrees of Blackness Comin, 1971; We Be Word Sorcerers: Twenty-five Stories by Black Americans, 1973. Anthologies: We Be Word Sorcerers: 25 Stories by Black Americans; 360 of Blackness Coming at You. **Orgs:** Pa Coun Arts; contrib ed, Black Scholar & J African Studies; adv bd, SISA, MADRE & WILPF; Plowshares; Brandywine Peace Community; Cong Racial Equality; Poetry Soc Am; Am Studies Asn; Acad Am Poets; Nat Asn Advan Colored People. **Honors/Awds:** PEN Writing Award, New York City, 1969; NEA Recipient, Wash, DC, 1978-79; Fellowship Award, Nat Endowment Arts, 1978-79; Lucretia Mott Award, Nat Endowment Arts, 1984; American Book Award, 1985; Honorary Doctorate, Trinity Col, 1987; Governor's Award for Excellence in the Humanities, 1988; Freedom, Peace & Freedom Award, Women Int League Peace, 1989; Honorary Doctorate, Baruch Col, 1993; Freedom Award, 2000; Robert Frost medal. 2001; National Visionary Leadership Award, 2006; Lindback Award; American Book Award, Homegirls & Hand grenades; Outstanding Arts Award, Pa Coalition 100 Black Women; Community Service Award, Nat Black Caucus State Legis; National Academy & Arts Award. **Special Achievements:** Discography: "A Sun Lady for All Seasons Reads Her Poetry", Folkways Records, 1971; "Every Tone a Testimony", Smithsonian Folkways, 2001. First Presidential Fellow at Temple University. **Home Addr:** , Philadelphia, PA.

**SANDERS, ANUCHA BROWNE (ANUCHA CHIOGU BROWNE)**
Vice president (organization). **Personal:** children: 3. **Educ:** Northwestern Univ, BS, commun, 1985; Fla State Univ, MBA, mkt commun. **Career:** Executive, basketball player (retired); IBM Corp, prog mgr, 1996-2000; NY Knicks, Madison Sq Garden, mkt exec, 2000, sr vpres mkt & bus opers, 2002-06; Univ Bufflalo, sr assoc athletics dir, mkt & sr woman adminr, Mkt, 2007-. **Orgs:** Vice pres, Nat Col Athletic Asn. **Business Addr:** Associate Athletics Director, marketing & senior woman administrator, University at Buffalo, 102 Alumni Arena, Buffalo, NY 14260, **Business Phone:** (716)645-6129.

**SANDERS, BARBARA A.**
Automotive executive. **Personal:** Born New Orleans, LA; daughter of Arma L Atkins Miles and Otis Miles; married Joe Jr; children: 1. **Educ:** Southern Univ, Agr & Mech Col Baton Rouge, BS, physics, 1969; Rutgers State Univ Nj-Nb, MS, physics, 1972; Ind Univ Bloomington, Kelley Sch Bus, exec develop prog, 1983; Thunderbird Sch Global Mgt, Int Exec Develop Prog, 1997; Harvard Univ, cert exec educ prog, 1985. **Career:** Fiber-reinforced plastics, designing mat; exp physicist, 1972; Gen Motors Corp, composites mat dept head, 1979-81, composites processing mgr, 1981-83, CAD/CAM dir, 1983-85, Electronic Data Systs, CAM Tools dir, 1984-86, artificial intelligence dir, 1985-87, advan mfg engineering dir, 1987-89, prog mgr, 1989-90; Truck & Bus Baltimore Assembly Plant, Paint Syst; Gen Motors Tech Ctr, Advan Engineering Staff, dir, 1991-; Delphi Corp, dir eng, 1992-, dir, 2004-09; Delphi Thermal & Interior, R&D/core prod engineering, 2004-; Delphi Automotive Systs, engineering dir, 2004-. **Orgs:** Engineering Soc Detroit, 1981-86; Soc Mfg Engrs, 1983-86; key exec, GM/Southern Univ Key Inst Prog, 1984-86; chairperson entrepreneurs comt, Minority Tech Coun Mich, 1985-89; class sec, Harvard Univ PMD-49, 1985-87; Women Econ Club; bd, Trinity Missionary Baptist Church Sch, 2010-; Alpha Kappa Alpha Sorority Inc; engineering adv bd mem, Univ Del; engineering adv bd mem, Rensselaer Polytech Inst Sch Engineering. **Honors/Awds:** Outstanding Alumni, Southern Univ Alumni Detroit Chap, 1982-86; Distinguished Alumni, Nat Asn Equal Opportunity, 1986; US Black Engr of the Year, 1988; Hon Doctorate, Southern Univ, 1989; Automotive Product Design Award, 1995; PRW Europe Award of Excellence in Transportation, 1996; SPE International Plastics Industry Product Design Award, 1996; IBEC Design Award, 1996; Modern Plastics International Process Award, 1997; SPE Automotive Innovation Award; Recycler of the Year Award, 1999; Lifetime Achievement Award, Societies Plastics Engineers Automotive Divsion, 2006. **Special Achievements:** Dollars & Sense mag as an honoree at the Tribute to African-Am Bus & Prof Men & Women, as well as being selected by Prof Engr's mag's Top 20 Minority Engrs of the 1980s; numerous articles/presentations in Tech Area, Lasers, CAD/CAM, AI, Composite Mat, 1979-86. **Home Addr:** 5865 Clearview Dr, Troy, MI 48098. **Business Addr:** Director, Delphi Corp, 5725 Delphi Dr, Troy, MI 48098-2815, **Business Phone:** (248)813-2000.

**SANDERS, BARRY DAVID**
Football player. **Personal:** Born Jul 16, 1968, Wichita, KS; son of William and Shirley; married Lauren Campbell; children: 4; children: Barry James. **Educ:** Okla State Univ, attended 1989. **Career:** Football player (retired); Detroit Lions, running back, 1989-98. **Honors/Awds:** Kick returner, 1987, running back, 1988, Sporting News Col All-Am Team; Heisman Trophy winner, 1988; Maxwell Award, 1988; Col Football Player ofthe Year, 1988, Sporting News NFL Rookie of the Year, 1989, Sporting News; Unanimous All-American, 1988; Chic Harley Award, 1988; NFL All-Star Team, Sporting News, 1989; NFC Most Valuable Player, Nat Football League Players Asn, 1991; Bert Bell Award, 1991, 1997; Pro Bowl, 1989, 1990, 1991, 1992, 1993, 1994, 1995, 1996, 1997, 1998; Most Valuable Player, Nat Football League, 1992, 1998; Offensive Player of the Year, Asn Press, 1994; Most Valuable Player of the Year, Asn Press, 1997; Alumni Running Back of the Year, Nat Football League, 1997; Most Valuable Player, NFL Newspaper Ent. Assoc, 1997; Player of the Year, Nat Football League, 1998; Pro Football Hall Fame, 2004. **Special Achievements:** Ranked 2 in ESPN's list of the Top 25 Greatest College Football Players Ever. **Home Addr:** 7412 Carlyle Xing, West Bloomfield, MI 48322-3283, **Home Phone:** (248)592-1239.

**SANDERS, BRANDON CHRISTOPHER**
Football coach, football player, executive. **Personal:** Born Jun 10, 1973, San Diego, CA. **Educ:** Univ Ariz. **Career:** Football player (retired), coach; Kans City Chiefs, 1996; New York Giants, defensive back, 1997-99, free safety, 1999; Cleveland Browns, 1999; Las Vegas Outlaws, 2000-01; Amsterdam Admirals, 2001; Montreal Allouttes, 2002; Pueblo Magnet High Sch, athletic dir, head coach, currently. **Business Addr:** Head Football Coach, Athletic Director, Pueblo Magnet High School, 3500 S 12th Ave, Tucson, AZ 85713, **Business Phone:** (520)225-4300.

**SANDERS, REV. DR. CHERYL JEANNE**
Religious educator, clergy. **Personal:** married Alan Carswell; children: Allison & Garrett. **Educ:** Swarthmore Col, BA, math; Harvard Univ Divinity Sch, Mdiv, ThD, appl theol. **Career:** Church God, Anderson, IN, clergy; Howard Univ Sch Divinity, prof christian ethics, 1984-; Third St Church God, Wash, DC, sr pastor, 1997-. Books: Saints in Exile: Empowerment Ethics for a Liberated People, 1995; Living the Intersection, 1995; The Holiness-Pentecostal Experience in African American Religion and Culture, 1996; Ministry at the Margins, 1997. **Home Addr:** 7704 Morningside Dr NW, Washington, DC 20012-1447, **Home Phone:** (202)829-7638. **Business Addr:** Professor, Howard University School of Divinity, 2900 Van Ness St NW, Washington, DC 20008, **Business Phone:** (202)806-0500.

**SANDERS, CHRISTOPHER DWAYNE**
Football player, football coach. **Personal:** Born May 8, 1972, Denver, CO; married Stacie; children: Chris Jr. **Educ:** Ohio State Univ, grad. **Career:** Football player (retired), football coach; Ohio State track & field team, 1992-94; Houston Oilers, wide receiver, 1995-96; Tenn Oilers, wide receiver, 1997-98; Tenn Titans, wide receiver, 1999-2001; Cleveland Browns, 2002; Christ Presbyterian Aca, coach, 2005-08, asst coach; Montgomery Bell Acad, wide receiver, athletics counr, 2008-; Ohio State Univ, multi-sport athlete. **Honors/Awds:** Named the Ohio State Athlete of the Year, 1994. **Business Addr:** Athletics Councilor, Montgomery Bell Academy, 4001 Harding Rd, Nashville, TN 37205, **Business Phone:** (615)298-5514.

**SANDERS, DEION LUWYNN (NEON DEION)**
Athlete. **Personal:** Born Aug 9, 1967, Ft. Myers, FL; son of Mims and Connie Knight; married Pilar Biggers; children: Shilo, Shedeur & Shelomi; married Carolyn Chambers; children: Diondra & Deion Luwynn Jr. **Educ:** Fla State Univ, attended 1988. **Career:** Baseball player (retired), football player (retired), TV host; MLB NY Yankees, outfielder, 1989-90; NFL Atlanta Falcons, defensive back, 1989-93; Atlanta Braves, outfielder, 1991-94; San Francisco 49ers, 1994; Cincinnati Reds, 1994-95, 1997, 2001; San Francisco Giants, 1995; Dallas Cowboys, 1995-99; Wash Redskins, 2000; CBS Sports, The NFL Today, feature reporter, contribr, commentator, 2001-04, studio analyst, currently; Baltimore Ravens, 2004-05; Nat Women's Basketball League, Dallas Fury, asst coach, 2004; ESPN Radio, host; NFL Network, NFL Game Day, host, currently; AFL, Austin Wranglers, owner, 2006-; Films: Celtic Pride, 1996; David Blaine: Street Magic, 1996; Albums: Prime Time, 1994; The Encore Remix, 2005. **Orgs:** Potters House Church. **Home Addr:** 1036 Liberty Pk Dr, Austin, TX 78746, **Home Phone:** (512)732-8939. **Business Addr:** Owner, Austin Wranglers, 2209 W Braker Lane, Austin, TX 78758, **Business Phone:** (512)491-6600.

**SANDERS, DORI**
Farmer, writer. **Personal:** Born Jan 1, 1934, York, SC. **Career:** Peach farmer, Author & Novelist; Novels: Clover, auth, 1990; Her Own Place, auth, 1993; Dori Sanders Country Cooking: Recipes & Stories from the family farm stand, 1995; Promise Land: a Farmer Remembers, 2004. **Home Addr:** 2275 Filbert Hwy, Filbert, SC 29745. **Business Addr:** Farmer, Sander, 2101 Filbert Hwy, Filbert, SC 29745-9777, **Business Phone:** (803)684-9156.

**SANDERS, FRANK VONDEL**
Football player, radio host. **Personal:** Born Feb 17, 1973, Ft. Lauderdale, FL; married Tracy. **Educ:** Auburn Univ. **Career:** Football player (retired), host; Ariz Cardinals, wide receiver, 1995-2002; Baltimore Ravens, 2003; WJOX 94.5 FM, host.

**SANDERS, DR. GEORGE L.**
Physician, cardiologist. **Personal:** Born Jul 4, 1942, Vidalia, GA; son of Felton (deceased) and Eva Mae Sanders (deceased); married Frances; children: G Eldridge & Cleaver. **Educ:** Morehouse Col, attended 1965; Univ Miami Sch Med, MD, 1969; Air War Col, grad, 1992. **Career:** Jackson Memorial Hosp, intern, 1970, resident, 1974, fel cardiol, 1976; Pvt pract, phy internal med & cardiol; USF, Eglin AFB, Cardiopulmonary Lab, dir; Lenard W Swain Memorial Trust Fund Inc, pres, dir. **Orgs:** Life mem, Phi Beta Sigma Frat; Phi Delta Epsilon; bd dir, Spectrum Prog Inc, 1977; Univ Miami Sch Med, assoc clin prof, vpres, Greater Miami Heart Asn; Am Col Physicians; med dir, N Shore Med Ctr Cardiol, 1985-90; life mem, NCP. **Honors/Awds:** Am Col Cardiol, fel, 1992; Am Bd Internal Med, Dipl; Student of the Year, Phi Beta Sigma, 1966; Student Award, Nat Med Asn, 1976; Nat Med Found, fel, 1965-69. **Home Addr:** 8503 Hollow Bluff Dr, PO Box 19594, Haughton, LA 71037, **Home Phone:** (505)870-7464.

### SANDERS, GLADYS N.
Consultant, educator. **Personal:** Born Jun 27, 1937, Martinez, GA; daughter of Rile Nealous and Rebecca; married Robert B; children: Sylvia Lynne & William Nealous. **Educ:** Ottawa Univ; Univ Kans; Atlanta Univ; Paine Col, Augusta, GA, BA, 1959. **Career:** Educator (retired); Columbia County Ga Pub Schs, math teacher, 1959-61; Richmond County Ga Pub Schs, math teacher, 1961-62; Lawrence KS Pub Schs, math coordr, teacher, 1973-98; Macmillan Pub Co Inc, nat math consult, 1991; Univ Kans, 1999. **Orgs:** Vice chair, Nat Bd Prof Teaching Stand, 1992-99; coun chief state sch officers, Interstate New Teacher Assessment Consortium, 1993; Kans State Dept Educ, Writing Team Qual Performance Accreditation, 1994; Rev Team Kans Math Assessment, 1996; Kans Curric Stand Comt, 1997-9; Kans Math Stand Comn, 1997-99; NCTM-NCATE, 1996-99; reviewer, Technol Challenge Grants, 1997; team leader, US Dept Educ. **Home Addr:** 4500 Bob Billings Pkwy Unit 139, Lawrence, KS 66049-7871, **Home Phone:** (785)842-6169.

### SANDERS, GLENN CARLOS
Consultant, computer engineer. **Personal:** Born May 24, 1949, Bastrop, TX; son of Charles Sr and Marjorie; married Catherine McCarty; children: Chandra & Brian. **Educ:** Tex Southern Univ, attended 1969; Calif Baptist Col, BS, 1987; cert netware engr, 1995. **Career:** Zales Jewelers Inc, asst mgr, 1973-76; TRW Info Serv, programmer analyst, 1976-80; Riverside Co Data Processing, data base analyst, 1980-83; Transamerica Life Co, sr systs programmer, 1983-95; Sandcastle Enterprises, consult, 1995-. **Orgs:** Phi Beta Sigma, 1968-; Planetary Soc, 1985-; vpres, Southwestern Info Mgt Users Group, 1986-88; bd mem, Parents Against Gangs, 1989-92. **Honors/Awds:** Nat Student Merit Qualifying Test Commended Candidate; First Place State Extemporaneous Speaking Competition, 1967; Second Place State Debate Competition, 1967; Deans List Freshmen Year, TX Southern Univ, 1968; Top DivSales Zales Jewelers, 1973. **Home Addr:** 22750 Shadowridge Lane, PO Box 8528, Moreno Valley, CA 92557-2632, **Home Phone:** (951)242-4745.

### SANDERS, DR. GWENDOLYN W.
School administrator. **Personal:** Born Dec 17, 1937, St. Louis, MO; daughter of Adolph Fisher and Burnette B Harris Fletcher; married Gordon B; children: Darrell F, Romona R Fullman & Jocelyn M. **Educ:** St Louis Univ, BS, 1956; Harris Teachers Col, BA, 1962; St Louis Univ, MEd, educ syst urban educ & admin, 1967; Nova Univ, EdD, higher educ admin & stud develop; Univ Del, Col Urban Affairs, PhD, prog; Harvard Grad Sch Educ, psychol & pluralism; George Washington Univ, educ outcomes. **Career:** Pvt Phy St Louis, med tech, 1956-59; Harris Teachers Col, St Louis, lab asst, 1959-62; St Louis Pub Sch, master teacher, 1962-68; Lincoln Pub Sch, teacher, 1966-68; St Peters Cathedral-Wilmington Pub Sch, teacher dir, 1968-70; Opportunity Indust Ctr, teacher, 1969-70; City Demonstration Agency, educ consult & planner, 1969-72; Del Tech & Comm Coll, planning coordr, 1972-73, dean stud serv, 1974-2000, dean develop, 1989-92; Univ Del, instr, 1973-75; Springfield Col, Sch Human Serv, adj prof, prof develop specialist, 2000-; Wilmington Col, MEd, coun & clin supvr; Family & Workplace Connection, Childcare Provider, educr & trainer; Wesley Col, Nat Training Inst Child Care Health, consult; Univ NC, Chapel Hill, consult. **Orgs:** Delta Sigma Theta; Nat Women's Polit Caucus; United Way Critical Issues Taskforce; adv bd, Headstart; vpres, Educ Comt, Nat Asn Advan Colored People; consult, US Dept Justice; pres, Northeast Coun Black Am Affairs; bd mem, vpres pub rels & pres, Nat Coun Black Am Affairs, 1974-; Am Asn Community & Jr Col; consult, NJ Dept Higher Educ, Middle States Comn Higher Educ; reader & evaluator, US Dept Higher Educ; vpres, Brandy wine Prof Asn, Am Acad Cosmetic Dent, 1980-; Denver Ctr Performing Arts; NAFSA; Am Asn Health Educ; NCRD; People People Int; exec bd, Del Acad Youth; field reader, Okla Bd Regents; rep, Nat Coun Early Childhood Develop; bd dir, Col Resource Ctr; bd mem, Metro Urban League. **Honors/Awds:** Outstanding Community Service Award, Alliance Ministers Bus & Agencies, 1988; Outstanding Community Service Award, Delaware Head Start, 1988; Outstanding Achievers Award-Education, BPA, 1989. **Special Achievements:** Developed bi-lingual bi-cultural day care center, 1970, developed and initiated ESL Prog, Delaware Tech, 1976, developed freshman orientation course, human potential and career & life planning courses, developed and initiated career centers Stanton and Wilmington campuses, developed, implemented & coordinated Springfield College Academic Support Center, Wilmington Campus. **Home Addr:** 507 Wyndham Rd, Wilmington, DE 19809-2844, **Home Phone:** (302)762-0422. **Business Addr:** Owner, G & G Enterprise, 507 Wyndham Rd N Hills, Wilmington, DE 19809-2844, **Business Phone:** (302)762-0422.

### SANDERS, HANK (HENRY SANDERS)
State government official, lawyer. **Personal:** Born Oct 28, 1942, Baldwin County, AL; son of Sam and Ola Mae Norman; married Rose M Gaines; children: Malika A, Kindaka J & Ainka M; children: Charles, Maurice, Rosie & Jennifer. **Educ:** Talladega Col, BA, 1967; Harvard Law Sch, JD, 1970. **Career:** Stucky Lumber Co, saw mill worker, 1960-61; Honeywell, elec tech, 1962-63; Reginald Heber Smith fel, 1971; Chestnut Sen, Sanders Sanders & Pettway, atty, 1972-; Ala State Senate, sen, 1982-. **Orgs:** Co founder & pres, Ala Lawyers Asn, 1972; co founder & pres, Campaign News, 1982; co founder & bd mem, 21st Century Youth Leadership Monument, 1985-95; co founder & pres, Ala New S Coalition, 1988-90, 1997-2000; co founder & chmn, Nat Voting Rights Mus & Inst, 1992-95; co founder & chmn, Coalitions Alabamians Rebuilding Educ, 1992-98; Nat Conf Black Lawyers; pres, Harvard Black Law Studs Asn; Am Bar Asn; Campaign New S; Coop Assistance & Relief Everywhere; Nat Bar Asn; chair, Senate Finance & Taxation, Educ Comt, currenlty. **Home Addr:** 1 Imani Way, PO Box 1290, Selma, AL 36702-8326, **Home Phone:** (334)875-1395. **Business Addr:** Senator, Alabama State Senate District 23, 11 S Union St, Montgomery, AL 36130-4600, **Business Phone:** (334)242-7860.

### SANDERS, DR. ISAAC WARREN
School administrator. **Personal:** Born Aug 9, 1948, Montgomery, AL; son of Hurley W Sr and Bertha Lee McKenize; married Cora Allen; children: W Machion, Christin Michael & Bryant Allen. **Educ:** Tuskegee Inst, BS, educ, 1971; Cornell Univ, MS, rural sociol & econ, 1973; Kans State Univ, PhD, higher educ admin & bus mgt, 1984; Columbia Univ, Sch Bus, NY, post grad cert, 1988. **Career:** Grad Fel, Cornell Univ, 1971-73; Ft Valley State Col, instr res assoc, 1973-75; Claflin Col, fed rels officer, 1975-76; Troy State Univ, Montgomery, AL, adj prof; Ala State Univ, Montgomery, dir fed rels, 1976-82, exec asst to pres, staff asst bd trustees, 1996-97; Kellogg Nat fel, Kellogg Found, 1990-93; Tuskegee Univ, Tuskegee, AL, assoc prof & vpres, enrollment mgt stud serv, 1991-96; Stillman Col, Tuscaloosa, AL, vpres, assoc prof; E Stroudsburg Univ Pa, vpres advan, 2000-08, exec dir. **Orgs:** Nat Soc Fund raising Execs 1980-; bd mem, Greater Trenton NJ Ment Health, 1984-; vpres, Woodrow Wilson Nat Fel Found, 1984-86; vpres & bd mem, Optimist Club Lower Bucks, PA, 1985-; pres, Tuskegee Univ Philadelphia Area Alumni Asn, 1986-; assoc dir, NE Region Tuskegee Alumni Assoc 1986-; Kappa Alpha Psi; dir, Nat Action Coun Minorities Eng, 1986-90, vpres, 1990-91; bd dir, Nat Asn Advan Colored People Bucks Co, PA, 1989; Tuscaloosa Rotary Club 1998-; pres, Tuscaloosa Exchange Club, 1998-; Phi Delta Kappa; Golden Key Int Hon Soc; E Stroudsburg Univ Found, secy; W K Kellogg Found; vol chmn & consult, United Negro Col Fund/Lilly Endowment, Fairfax, VA; consult, Asn Gov Boards; consult, US Dept Educ, Wash DC; Rotary Club; Exchange Club; United Way; bd dir, Pocono Mountain Chamber Com. **Home Addr:** PO Box 1195, Tuscaloosa, AL 35403. **Business Addr:** Vice President, Executive Director, East Stroudsburg University, 200 Prospect St, East Stroudsburg, PA 18301-2999, **Business Phone:** (570)422-3211.

### SANDERS, JASMINE
Media executive, radio broadcaster, executive. **Personal:** Born Oct 21, 1967, Chattanooga, TN; daughter of Joseph and Joyce; children: Joey. **Educ:** Mid Tenn State Univ, BS, mass commun, 1990. **Career:** Phoenix Commun, midday on-air personality, 1990-92; Brewer Broadcasting, morning show host, 1992-94; Gaylord Entertainment, talent, 1995-97; Dickey Bros Broadcasting, midday on-air personality, 1998-2001; Cumulus Broadcasting, mkt & promotions dir, 1997-2004, WNPL, morning show co host, 2002-04; Cannon Group, actor & talent, 2000-06; ARPR Mkt, E Coast div, head, 2004-; Virgin Capitol Recods, radio promotions, 2005-07; EMI Music, radio promotions, 2005-07; Capitol Rec, radio promotions, 2005-07; WBLS, midday on-air personality, 2007-09; WNPL-Nashville, morning show host; WWFS Fresh 102.7, night show host, 2010-13; BET Centric TV, host & corresp, 2012-13; Just My Talents Inc, chief exec officer, 2005-; Reach Media, radio show host, 2013-; DL Hughley Radio Show, co host, 2013-; CNN, Index Panel Corresp, 2015. **Orgs:** Delta Sigma Theta Sorority, 1986-. **Honors/Awds:** One of 10 Most Influential Black Women, Girls Inc, 1994; YMCA Black Achievers, 1997. **Home Addr:** 1411 Cranapple Cove, Nashville, TN 37217. **Business Addr:** Co-Host, The Nationally Syndicated Radio Show, 1900 Pineview Rd, Columbia, SC 29209, **Business Phone:** (803)695-8600.

### SANDERS, JOSEPH STANLEY
Lawyer, association executive, executive director. **Personal:** Born Aug 9, 1942, Los Angeles, CA; son of Hays and Eva (Cook) S; children: Edward Moore & Justin Hays; married Melba Binion; children: Alexandria Thedarin & Chelsea Winifred. **Educ:** Whittier Col, BA, 1963; Magdalen Col Oxford Univ, BA & MA, 1965; Yale Law Sch, LLB 1968. **Career:** Yale Univ Transitional Yr, dir pro tem & instr, 1967-68; Western Ctr Law & Poverty Los Angeles, staff atty, 1968-69; Lawyer's Com Civil Rights Under Law La, exec dir, 1969-70; Wyman Bautzer Finell Rothman & Kuchel Beverly Hills, assoc, 1969-71; Rosenfeld Lederer Jacobs & Sanders Beverly Hills, partner, 1971-72; Sanders, Tisdale, Eng, Tooks & Williams, founding partner; Sanders & Tisdale La, partner, 1972-77; Sanders & Dickerson Los Angeles, atty partner, 1978-92; Barnes, McGhee & Pryce, Law Off J Stanley Sander, assoc & sr partner, 1992-. **Orgs:** Co-founder, Watts Summer Festival, 1966; Am Bar Asn, 1969-; bd dir, W LA United Way, 1970; LA World Affairs Coun, 1971-; trustee, Ctr LawPub Interest, 1973-80; bd trustee, Whittier Col, 1974-; bd dir, Econ Resources Corp, 1974-; Mayor's Com Cult Affairs, 1975-; bd dir, Am Red Cross LA, 1975-; bd dir, Arthritis Found So, Calif Chap, 1976-; co-chmn, Calif Dem Party Rules Comm, 1976-; pres, LA Recreation & Parks Comt, 1986-93; chair, LA orial Coliseum Comm, 1980-; dir, Black Arts Coun; Langston Law Club LA Co Bar Asn; chmn, United Way Task Force Minority Youth Employ, 1985-; NCAA Found, bd trustee; Mus Contemp Art, Los Angeles; legal practr, Health Maintenance Orgn; mem bd dir, Metrop Transp Authority. **Honors/Awds:** Rhodes Scholar; 1st Team NAIA All-Am Football, 1961; Small Col NAIA Discus Champion, 1963; Ten Outstanding Young Men American Award, 1971; Fifty Distinguished Alumni Award Los Angeles City Sch Bicentennial, 1976. **Special Achievements:** Pub: "I'll Never Escape the Ghetto", Ebony Mag, 1967, "Rhodes Scholar Looks at South Africa", Ebony Mag, 1970. **Business Addr:** Senior Partner, Law Office J Stanley Sanders, 2015 Wellington Rd, Los Angeles, CA 90016-1824, **Business Phone:** (323)737-6334.

### SANDERS, DR. KAREN ELEY
School administrator. **Personal:** Born Sep 8, 1962, Newport News, VA; daughter of Alvin Eley and Margaret; married Reliford Jr; children: Theo III & Micaela Karynne Eley. **Educ:** Va State Univ, BS, psychol, 1985, MS, clin psychol, 1992; Univ Ark, Fayetteville, EdD, adult & develop educ, 2000; Appalachian State Univ, develop educ specialist, 2003. **Career:** Univ Ark, Boyer Ctr Stud Serv, dir, 1992-97, Minority Edu Serv, dir, 1997-2001; Va Tech, Ctr Acad Enrichment & Excellence, dir, 2001-; Va Tech, asst provost, 2004-08, assoc vice provost acad affairs & dir stud success, 2008-, interim vpres diversity & inclusion, 2010; Va Tech Carilion Sch Med, chief diversity officer, 2014-. **Orgs:** Brownie Troop Leader; Montgomery County Br Nat Asn Advan Colored People; Nat Acad Advising Asn, 1993-; Phi Beta Kappa, 1995-; life mem, Delta Sigma Theta Sorority Inc, 1997-; Va Asn Develop Educ, 2001-; Nat Asn Develop Educ, 2001-; Nat Col Learning Ctr Asn, 2002-, Am Asn Blacks Higher Educ, 2000-; supt, Sunday sch, Asbury United Methodist Church. **Home Addr:** 1679 St Andrews Cir, Blacksburg, VA 24060, **Home Phone:** (540)961-3847. **Business Addr:** Assistant Provost for Academic Support, Virginia Tech, 110 Femoyer Hall (0276), Blacksburg, VA 24061, **Business Phone:** (540)231-5499.

### SANDERS, LARRY KYLE
Educator. **Personal:** Born Oct 16, 1970, Hammond, LA; son of Frank and Shirley. **Educ:** Southern Univ, BA, jour, 1993, MA, mass commun, 1994. **Career:** Wiley Col, instr, 1997, dir mass commun, 1999; Alcorn State Univ, instr Mass Commun, news dir, WPRL 91.7 FM, currently; E Tex Baptist Univ. **Orgs:** Am Asn Univ Profs, 1997-; Nat Asn Advan Colored People, 1997-; Int Commun Asn, 1997-; Asn Educ Jour & Mass Commun, 1997-; Nat Asn Black Journalists, 1997-; life mem, Southern Univ Alumni Fedn; Alpha Phi Alpha, 1998. **Home Addr:** 144 N Shields Lane Apt E 8, Natchez, MS 39120, **Home Phone:** (985)514-0421. **Business Addr:** Instructor of Mass Communication, News Director, Alcorn State University, 1000 Alcorn State Univ Dr, Alcorn State, MS 39096-7500, **Business Phone:** (601)877-6632.

### SANDERS, LAURA GREEN
Executive director, executive. **Personal:** Born Nov 14, 1942, Victoria, TX; daughter of Althea McNary Green and Cluster Green; married Willie; children: Laresee Harris. **Educ:** Victoria Jr Col, attended 1968; Tex State Mgt Develop Ctr, managers prog, 1986. **Career:** Tex Workforce Solutions Golden Crescent, exec dir, currently. **Orgs:** African Am Chamber Com, Victoria; Victoria Hispanic Chamber Com; Victoria Area Chamber Com; DeWitt County Chamber; Calhoun County Chamber; Victoria Financial Educ Coalition; Golden Crescent Pvt Indust Coun; asst prof, Commun Sci & Dis; FW Gross Alumni; Victoria Prof Women's Group; bd dir, Victoria County Sr Citizens; Univ Houston-Victoria Presidents Adv Coun; Women In Partnership Progress; Int Asn Personnel Employment Serv; Tex Pub Employee Asn; Mt Nebo Baptist Church; exec dir, Golden Crescent Workforce Develop Bd; trustee, Victoria Tex. **Home Addr:** PO Box 175, Nursery, TX 77976. **Business Addr:** Executive Director, Texas Workforce Solutions of the Golden Crescent, 120 S Main Suite 501, Victoria, TX 77902, **Business Phone:** (361)576-5872.

### SANDERS, DR. LAWRENCE, JR.
Physician, association executive, college teacher. **Educ:** Clemson Univ, BS, chem; Vanderbilt Univ, Nashville, Tenn, cert; Univ Pa, MBA. **Career:** Centers DisControl, epidemic intelligence serv; Philadelphia Dept Pub Health, Neighborhood Health Ctr, med dir; Kaiser Permanete, Ga Region, physician mgr; DeKalb County Bd Health, dep dir; Managed Care at Grady, med dir; Southwest Hosp (Atlanta), med dir; Morehouse Sch Med, prof; Grady Health Syst, physician advisor clin doc improv, care mgt & hosp throughput. **Orgs:** Pres, Atlanta Med Asn; pres, Ga State Med Asn; Am Asn Med Cols (AAMC), Mem Steering Comt Group Fac Pract; bd dirs, W Montague NMA Health Cobb Inst; immediate past pres, Nat Med Asn, Bd Trustees & Officers, Speaker House Delegates, 2014-. **Business Addr:** Physician, Morehouse Health Care, 1800 Howell Mill Rd NW Suite 275, Atlanta, GA 30318, **Business Phone:** (404)756-1480.

### SANDERS, DR. LOU HELEN
Librarian, college teacher. **Personal:** Born Mar 2, 1951, Bolton, MS; daughter of Eddie and Irene Singleton; children: Nicol. **Educ:** Jackson State Univ, BA, 1973, EdS, 1981; Univ Mich, Ann Arbor, MI, AMLS, 1974; Univ Pittsburgh, Pittsburgh, PA, PhD, 1989. **Career:** Jackson State Univ, Jackson, Miss, res & asst dir libr, 1974-76, sci technol div lib, 1976-77, instr libr sci, 1977-87, asst prof lib sci, 1983-87, dean libr, prof, dept educ leadership, currently; Atlanta Univ FIPSE Internship, 1985-88. **Orgs:** MSP Libr Asn, 1974-; educ bibliog instr, Am Libr Asn, 1974-, 1990-90; Phi Kappa Phi, 1976; Univ Mich Alumni Asn, 1977-; life mem, Jackson State Univ Alumni Asn; Southeastern Libr Asn, 1979-; Alpha Kappa Alpha, 1983-; Am Soc Info Sci, 1988-; Beta Phi Mu, 1989-; chair, State Miss Libr Dir Coun, 1990-; vice chair, Info Anal & Eval, 1990; chair, Am Socs for Indust Security, 1991. **Home Addr:** 135 Presidential Pl, Jackson, MS 39213, **Home Phone:** (601)982-7012. **Business Addr:** Professor of Education, Jackson State University, 1400 Lynch St, Jackson, MS 39217, **Business Phone:** (601)979-2121.

### SANDERS, MELBA T.
Vice president (organization), executive. **Personal:** married Stan. **Educ:** Calif State Univ, Dominguez Hills, BS, polit sci & psychol, 1986; Fashion Inst Design & Merchandising, merchandising & mkt. **Career:** Bill Cosby's financial & entertainment serv co; Berkhemer Clayton Inc, atty, vpres bus develop & co founder, currently. **Orgs:** Bd mem, Planned Parenthood Los Angeles; bd mem, Pop Educ; bd mem, Big Sisters Los Angeles; bd mem, Santa Monica Col Found; Women Bus; dir, GLAZA & Women Mgt. **Business Addr:** Co Founder, Vice President of Business Development, Berkhemer Clayton Inc, 241 S Figueroa St Suite 300, Los Angeles, CA 90012, **Business Phone:** (213)621-2300.

### SANDERS, MICHAEL ANTHONY (MIKE SANDERS)
Basketball coach, basketball player. **Personal:** Born May 7, 1960, Vidalia, LA; married Crystal Tate; children: Lamar & Kendra. **Educ:** Univ Calif, Los Angeles, CA, BA, hist, 1982. **Career:** Basketball player (retired), basketball coach; Mont Golden Nuggets, 1982-83; San Antonio Spurs, 1983; Sarasota Stingers, 1983; Phoenix Suns, 1983-88; Philadelphia 76ers, 1984-88; Cleveland Cavaliers, 1988-89, 1992-93; Ind Pacers, 1989-91; Wis Blast, head coach, 1998-99; Black Hills Gold, head coach, 1999-2000; Wash Congressionals, coach, 2000; Detroit Pistons, asst coach, 2000-01; Asheville Altitude, asst coach & dir player personnel, 2001-05; Adirondack Wildcats, head coach, 2002-04; Milwaukee Bucks, asst coach, 2005-07; Charlotte Bobcats, asst coach, 2007-08; Minot SkyRockets, 2008-09; Ft Wayne Mad Ants, asst coach, 2009-11; Utah Jazz, mgr player develop, asst coach, 2012-14. **Business Addr:** Assistant Coach, Utah Jazz, Delta Ctr 301 W S Temple, Salt Lake City, UT 84101, **Business Phone:** (801)325-2500.

### SANDERS, PATRICIA ROPER
Executive director, management consultant. **Personal:** Born Dec 23, 1945, Tulsa, OK; daughter of Rev Anderson and Harold M; married C Edward; married Thomas Roper; children: Lark Godwin Leet & Thomas Bradford Roper. **Educ:** Lincoln Univ, BA, 1966; PRSA, accreditation, 1977. **Career:** US Senate Cand, dir res & policy info, 1970-71; Blue Cross Hosp Serv St Louis, sr vpres PR community rels pub affairs & spec events, 1971-73; Blue Cross, AT&T, sr vpres; PR community Opers Philip Morris Indust, rels pub affairs & spec events; Western Elect Co, managing com affairs spec, 1973-77; Philip Morris Indust Milwaukee, mgr commun, 1977-78, vpres int PR opers; Rho-

par Report & RHOPAR, pres & publ, 1978-85; PR Assocs, 1979-86; TRB Speakers Agency, pub rels consult, 1986-90; Int Black Network Exchange, dir, 1990; Int Bus Consult, dir, 1990-; Transatlantic Link, founder; P&E Assoc, sr consult, 1990-; 50 Hoops Tournaments & Health Fairs, co-founder, 1998-. **Orgs:** Dir pub rels & adv bd mem, UNCF OIC Sherwood Forest St Louis, 1974-77; bd adv, Lincoln Univ, 1975-77; Panel Judges Coro Found, 1976; chmn, Steering Comt Comn Pride Expo Milwaukee, 1977; Pub Rel Soc Am, 1977-80; bd dir, Chicago Forum, 1979; bd mem, Winnie Mandella Women's Ministries, 1987; Links Inc; exec dir & co-founder, RMBD, 1990-92; principle fundraiser & solicitor, VIP & Celebrity Support Orgn; Alpha Kappa Alpha Sorority; pres, NPFR; Black Bus Women's Forum. **Honors/Awds:** Distinguished Service Awards, 1974-77; Golden Phoenix Award, 1983; CA Government Honored Woman of the Year, 1985. **Special Achievements:** Author: Pub Relations for Small Bus; producer, moderator & host: "A Woman's Place", WYMS; "Focus on Black Bus Woman", KJLH; "Ask Me", KACD, 1977-80; "Living Positively"; Black Wallstreet, producer, 1990; African Heritage World Celebration, spec events coordr, 1995. She's been an International Speaker, TV & Radio personality in South Africa, Canada, Caribbean & London. With her husband, they developed the 50 Hoops & NPFR program models for National African American outreach initiatives. **Business Addr:** Senior Consultant, P&E Associates, 14902 Preston Rd Suite 404-744, Dallas, TX 75254, **Business Phone:** (972)517-1254.

### SANDERS, PRENTICE EARL
Police chief, writer. **Personal:** Born Oct 12, 1937, Nacogdoches, TX; married Espanola. **Educ:** Golden Gate Univ, BS, criminal justice; MS, pub admin. **Career:** Arcade Publishing (retired), auth; San Francisco Police Dept, staff, 1964, investr, homicide investr, 1971, inspector, asst police chief, police chief, 2002-03. **Orgs:** Officers Justice. **Business Addr:** Author, Arcade Publishing, 116 John St Suite 2810, New York, NY 10038, **Business Phone:** (212)475-2633.

### SANDERS, REGINALD LAVERNE (REGGIE SANDERS)
Baseball player. **Personal:** Born Dec 1, 1967, Florence, SC; married Wyndee; children: Cody, Carigon, Cooper & Carson. **Career:** Baseball player (retired); Cincinnati Reds, outfielder, 1991-98; San Diego Padres, 1999; AtlantaBraves, 2000; Ariz Diamondbacks, 2001; San Francisco Giants, 2002; Pittsburgh Pirates, 2003; St Louis Cardinals, 2004-05; Kans City Royals, 2006-07; free agent-. **Orgs:** Reggie Sanders Found; Maj League Baseball Players Alumni Asn. **Honors/Awds:** AL MVP Voting, 1992; Most Valuable Player, Midwest League, 1990; NL All-Star Team, 1995; World Series champion, 2001.

### SANDERS, DR. RELIFORD THEOPOLIS, JR.
Psychologist. **Personal:** Born Sep 30, 1961, Kansas City, MO; son of Reliford Sr and Elizabeth Barber; married Karen Eley; children: Reliford T III & Micaela K E. **Educ:** Benedictine Col, BA, psychol & sociol, 1983; Univ ILL, MA, clin psychol, 1987, PhD, 1997. **Career:** Univ Ark, lic clin psychologist, 1991-2001; Va Tech, lic clin psychologist, 2001-. **Orgs:** Am Psychol asn; Us Tennis asn; Alph Phi Alpha Fraternity Inc, Nat Asn Advan Colored People. **Home Addr:** 1679 St Andrews Cir, Blacksburg, VA 24060, **Home Phone:** (540)961-3847. **Business Addr:** Licensed Clinical Psychologist, Thomas E Cook Counseling Center, 240 McComas Hall 0108, Blacksburg, VA 24060, **Business Phone:** (540)231-6557.

### SANDERS, RHONDA SHEREE
Journalist, writer. **Personal:** Born Jun 25, 1956, Montgomery, AL; daughter of Isaac and Marie Williams Hamilton. **Educ:** Univ Mich, Ann Arbor, MI, BA, 1978, MA, jour, 1979; Wayne State Univ, Detroit, MI, 1990-. **Career:** Flint Jour, Flint, Mich, reporter, 1980-07, j staff writer, currently; View Newspapers, staff writer, 2011-; Author: Bronze Pillars: An Oral Hist of African Am in Flint, 1996; Univ of Mich, adj instr, 2010-. **Orgs:** Mid-Mich Asn Black Journalists, 1982-92; Nat Asn Black Journalists, 1987-. **Honors/Awds:** Media Award, Nat Asn Media Women, 1983, 1990; Wade McCree Memorial Award, Justice Award Media, 1989; Press Award, Mich Press Asn, 1989. **Home Addr:** 3108 Wagon Trail, Flint, MI 48507-1214, **Home Phone:** (810)733-8481. **Business Addr:** Journal Staff Writer, Flint Journal, 200 E 1st St, Flint, MI 48502, **Business Phone:** (810)766-6374.

### SANDERS, RICKY WAYNE
Football player. **Personal:** Born Sep 30, 1962, Temple, TX; married Michelle; children: Ashlynn & Richard Wayne. **Educ:** SW Tex State Univ. **Career:** Football player (retired); US Football League, Houston Gamblers, 1984-85; Wash Redskins, wide receiver, 1986-93; Atlanta Falcons, wide receiver, 1994-95; Miami Dolphins, wide receiver, 1995; Southwest Tex State; US Football League. **Honors/Awds:** Most Valuable Player, Palm Bowl, 1982; Most Valuable Player, Wash Redskins, 1988; Super Bowl champion (XXII, XXVI). **Special Achievements:** Film: New York Chinatown, 1982.

### SANDERS, ROBER LAFAYETTE
Engineer, scientist. **Personal:** Born Feb 14, 1952, Raleigh, NC. **Educ:** NC State Univ, BSEE, 1973; MIT, MSEE, 1976; Univ Ariz, Phoenix, MBA, 1983. **Career:** IBM, prog mgr, currently. **Orgs:** Vpres, IEEE, 1973, 1986; ACME, 1973-; Am Physicists, 1973-; basileus Omega Psi Phi Frat, 1982-90; pres, Scholastic Aptitude, 1983-; State Nat Asn Advan Colored People, pres, 1983-90; Br Nat Asn Advan Colored People, pres, 1983-90; treas, Tucson Black Forum, 1985-87; Optimist Club, vpres, 1985-91; treas, Tucson Dem Party, 1986-87; Black Engrs Am, pres, 1989-. **Honors/Awds:** Outstanding Young Man, Jaycees, 1985, 1986; 'Engineer of the Year', BEA, 1986; Man of the Year, Omega Psi Phi, 1986; Citizen of the Year; Omega Psi Phi, Asst KF, 1994. **Home Addr:** 429 N St SW Suite 702, Washington, DC 20024, **Home Phone:** (202)640-4294. **Business Addr:** Program Manager, IBM Corp, 9221 Corp Blvd, Rockville, MD 20850, **Business Phone:** (301)640-4294.

### SANDERS, DR. ROBERT B.
Biochemist, consultant, educator. **Personal:** Born Dec 9, 1938, Augusta, KS; son of Robert and Lois Jones; married Gladys Nealous; children: Sylvia Schneider & William. **Educ:** Paine Col, Augusta, GA, BS, chem, biol, mathematics, 1959; Univ Mich, Ann Arbor, MI, MS, 1961, PhD, 1964; Univ Wis, Madison, attended 1966. **Career:** Battelle Memorial Inst, vis scientist, 1970-71; US Dept Educ, consult & panel mem, 1972-2012; Univ Tex Med Sch, Houston, vis assoc prof, 1974-75; Nat Insts Health, consult & panel mem, 1972-84; Nat Sci Found, prog dir, 1978-79; Univ Kans, Lawrence, from asst prof to prof, 1966, assoc dean, Grad Sch, 1987-96, assoc vice chancellor, Res Grad Studies & Pub Serv, 1989-96, coordr minority Grad Stud Support, 1996-99, prof biochem, 1996-2004, consult & panel mem, 2010, prof emer, 2004-. **Orgs:** Bd dir, United Child Develop Ctr, 1968-93; consult, Interx Res Corp, 1972-80; Nat Res Coun, 1973-77; NIH, 1982; NSF, 1983-94, Dept Educ, 1993-97, 2003-10; bd Higher Educ, United Meth Church, 1976-80; Am Lung Asn Cent States, 2006-12; chmn bd dirs, Am Lung Asn USA Nationwide Assembly, 2008-09; Am Lung Asn Plains Gulf, 2010-; Am Soc Biochem & Molecular Biol; Am Soc Pharmacol & Exp Therapeut; Am Asn Univ Professors; Sigma XI. **Honors/Awds:** Postdoctoral fel, Am Cancer Soc, 1964-66; fel, Battelle Mem Inst, 1970-71; postdoctoral fel, Nat Inst Health, 1974-75; more than 57 research grants. **Special Achievements:** Published more than 60 scientific articles. **Home Addr:** 4500 Bob Billings Pkwy, Lawrence, KS 66049-3812, **Home Phone:** (785)842-6169. **Business Addr:** Professor Emeritus Biochemistry, University of Kansas, 2045 Haworth Hall, Lawrence, KS 66045-7534, **Business Phone:** (785)864-4301.

### SANDERS, ROBIN RENEE
Government official, chief executive officer. **Personal:** Born Hampton, VA. **Educ:** Hampton Univ, BA, communs; Ohio Univ, MA, int rels & African studies, MS, communs & jour; Robert Morris Univ, DSc, info systs & commun, 2010. **Career:** Nat Security Coun, dir, African Affairs, 1986-88, 1997-99; Under Secy State Polit Affairs, spec asst latin am, africa, 199697; US Dept State, Off Pub Diplomacy, dir, 2000-02, Repub Congo, US ambassador, 2002-05, US ambassador, Nigeria, 2007-; FEEEEDS Advocacy Initiative, chief exec officer ambassador. **Orgs:** Alpha Kappa Alpha Sorority; Coun Foreign Rels; Women Int Security; DC Chamber Com; Oper Hope; dir, Nat Security Coun; bd mem, Oper Hope; U.S. permanent rep, W African Regional Orgn ECOWAS; Nat Security Coun, White House; int affairs advisor & dep comdr, U.S. mil's premier Nat Defense Univ; advisor, Robert Morris Univ; U.S. trade rep, Africa Adv Comt; chairwoman, U.S. EXIM Africa Comt; prestigious Acad Diplomacy; trustee, RMU & Smithsonian African Art Mus; advisor, Oper HOPE Africa;U.S. Nat Scholar Socs. **Business Addr:** Ambassador, Republic of the Congo, 4891 Colo Ave NW, Washington, DC 20011, **Business Phone:** (202)726-5500.

### SANDERS, SALLY RUTH
Registered nurse, social worker. **Personal:** Born Jun 1, 1952, Tyler, TX; married Donald Ray; children: Carla, Candace & Christopher. **Educ:** Tex Eastern Sch Nursing, Tyler Jr Col, dipl nursing asst, 1975, 1974; Univ Tex Tyler, BSN, 1984. **Career:** Relief Health Care Servs, dir, 1985-86; Triage, head nurse; Progressive Health Care, asst admin, 1986-. **Orgs:** Historian Diabetes Asn, 1984-85; asst dir, Marche Inc, 1986-; Negro Bus & Prof Women's Org; Rose Bud Civitan Club, Civitan; dir, chief exec officer, Sanders Community Health Servs. **Honors/Awds:** Woman of the Year, UTHCT, 1985. **Home Addr:** 3002 King St, Tyler, TX 75701, **Home Phone:** (903)533-8867. **Business Addr:** Nurse Clinician, 737 Grant St, De Pere, WI 54115, **Business Phone:** (920)676-5241.

### SANDERS, STEVEN LEROY
Financial manager. **Personal:** Born Oct 26, 1959, Philadelphia, PA; son of Willie E and Elouise Tooten; married Kelly DeSouza; children: 1. **Educ:** Howard Univ, Wash, DC, BBA, risk mgt, 1982. **Career:** Aetna Life & Casualty, Pittsburgh, Pa, employee benefit rep, 1982-85; Mellon Bank, Philadelphia, Pa, credit analyst, 1985-86; Hunt & Sanders Financial Adv, Philadelphia, Pa, partner & founder, 1986-; MDL Capital Mgt, pres & chief exec officer; Your Money Matters Prog, New York, NY, Citibank Master Card & Visa lectr, 1989-; Beltraith Capital, LLC, chmn; United Bancshares, vice chmn, 2006, retired, dir, 2002-06; First Genesis Financial Group, chmn & chief exec officer, 2005, Chief Investment Strategist, 2006-09; Stone Ridge Investment Partners LLC, chief investment strategist & portfolio mgr, chmn & chief exec officer, 2009-; Zonzia Media Inc, dir, 2015-; WURD Radio, co-host. **Orgs:** Bd dir, Help Line, 1984-85; pres, Howard Univ Alumni, Pittsburgh Chap, 1984-85; Scout Master Troop 629, Boy Scouts Am, 1986-88; Bus Educ Adv Comt, 1987-89; African Am Chamber Com; bd dir, Freedom Theatre, 1990-; Greater Philadelphia Chamber Com; Howard Univ EliInst Bd Entrepreneurship; vice chmn, 2006, dir, 2002-06, United Bank Philadelphia, To Our C's Future With Health; bd trustee, Pa Acad Fine Arts; Philadelphia Found. **Honors/Awds:** Chairperson of the Month, Vectors Pittsburgh, 1985; Nat Speaker-Citibank Master Card & Visa Money Matters for Young Adults, 1989-; Leaders Club, The New England, 1990. **Special Achievements:** Black Enterprise Top 100 Asset Managers List, 2000; author of "Money Matters for Young Adults. **Home Addr:** 13 Stockton Dr, Voorhees, NJ 08043, **Home Phone:** (609)753-1128. **Business Addr:** Chief Investment Strategist, Chief Executive Officer, StoneRidge Investment Partners LLC, 301 Lindenwood Dr Suite 310, Malvern, PA 19355, **Business Phone:** (610)647-5287.

### SANDERS, WILLIAM E.
Clergy, executive, military leader. **Personal:** son of George and Veala M. **Educ:** Morehouse Col, Atlanta, GA, BA, 1971; Union Theol Sem NY, assoc degree, Mdiv, 1976; Walter Reed Army Med Ctr. **Career:** Military leader(retired), clergy; NY Army Nat Guard, chaplain; Ohio Army Nat Guard, chaplain; 37th Armor Brigade, brigade chaplain; Third Baptist Church, Toledo, Oh, assoc Minister; Calvary Baptist Church, Jamaica, NY, asst pastor; Bethany Baptist Church, Brooklyn, NY, asst pastor; William E Sanders Family Life Ctr, staff; Lee Road Baptist Church, Cleveland, OH, pastor & bd dir, 1977-2013. **Orgs:** Mem exec bd, Nat Asn Advan Colored People; chair, Cleveland Baptist Asn. **Special Achievements:** First Black chaplain to serve in the Ohio Army National Guard. First pastor to retire.

### SANDERS, DR. WOODROW MAC
Educator, manager. **Personal:** Born Aug 4, 1943, Luling, TX; son of Alburnice Stewart and Revern; children: Rodrigo R, Justin W & Jennifer M. **Educ:** Univ Alaska; Univ ND, attended 1966; Tex A&I Univ Kings ville, BA, hist, 1971; TX A&I Univ, Corpus Christi, MS, guid & coun, 1977; Univ N Tex, Denton, PhD, 1992; Social Work Licenses, 1993. **Career:** Bee Co Col, Bee ville, TX, counr & instr, 1978-81; Nueces Co Ment Health/Ment Retardation Ctr, dir outpatient serv, 1972-78; Gateway Wholesale Sporting Goods, asst mgr, 1971-72; USN Coun & Asst Cntgr Corpus Christi, TX, consult assn psychologist, 1973-78; Univ TX Austin, Inst Alcohol Studies, 1977; S TX Housing Corp, bd pres, 1978; S western Bell Tel Co, Laredo, TX, mgr engineering, 1981-89; Bee County Col, Beeville, TX, counr & instr, 1989-91; TX Dept Health-Social Work Servs, part time instr Bee County Col, med case mgr. **Orgs:** Sdv bd mem, Nueces House Tex Youth Coun, 1977-78; bd mem, Coastal Bend Bus & Indsl Devel Inc, 1977-; Nat Asn Advan Colored People; US Rifle Marksmanship Team USAF, 1962-64; vpres & bd dir, C's Heart Inst Tex, 1985-; Tex Asn Telecommunication Engrs, 1981-89; Southwest Asn Stud Spec Servs Prog, 1989-; Tex Asn Coun & Develop, 1989-91. **Honors/Awds:** Presidential Unit Citation USAF, 1965; Republic of Vietnam Medal of Valor USAF, 1966; Youth Service Award Corpus Christi Police Dept, 1967; Award for Ser in Drug Abuse - Prevention, Coastal Bend Council of Govts Drug Abuse Adv Com Corpus Christi, 1976-77; fellowship TX Research Inst of Mental Sci Houston, 1978. **Home Addr:** 341 Merrill Dr, Corpus Christi, TX 78408-3344, **Home Phone:** (361)888-6272. **Business Addr:** Instructor, Texas Department of Health-Social Work Services, 1322 Agnes St, Corpus Christi, TX 78401, **Business Phone:** (512)888-7762.

### SANDERS-JOHNSON, LINA
Educator. **Personal:** Born Apr 9, 1937, Johnston County, NC; children: Gary & Gretchen. **Educ:** BS, 1964. **Career:** Educator (retired); Johnson Co Bd Educ, teacher; Smithfield Jr High Sch, teacher; John Tech Inst Sec, part-time instr. **Orgs:** Secy, Nat Asn Univ Women; pres, NC Asn Educ; NEA; Asn Classroom Teachers; chairperson, Polit Act Comt Educ; parliamentarian, Dist 2 ACT; NCAE Comn Foreign Benefits & Spec Serv; NCAE Prof Negoti Comn; Nat Asn Advan Colored People; NC All City Times-NC Asn Educrs; secy, Johnston Co Bd Elections; secy & treas, Johnston Co Industs, 1995; NC Retired Sch Person. **Honors/Awds:** Outstanding Elementary Teacher of America, 1973; Teacher of the Year, Smithfield Jr High Sch, 1975-76; Human Relation Nominee, NC Asn Educrs, 1977. **Home Addr:** 405 Ash St, Smithfield, NC 27577-5050, **Home Phone:** (919)934-2376.

### SANDERSON, RANDY CHRIS
Executive, consultant, association executive. **Personal:** Born Dec 23, 1954, St. Louis, MO; married Toni M Harper. **Educ:** Univ Mo, St Louis, BS, bus admin, 1977, cert pub acct. **Career:** May Dept Stores, mgr, dir, 1979-81; May Dept Stores, Calif, advert controller, 1981-84; Caldor Inc, asst controller, 1987-89; Lord & Taylor, div controller, 1989-91; May D&F, vpres, controller, 1991-93; Famous Barr Dept Store, vpres, controller, 1993-96; Dollar Gen Corp, vpres, controller, 1996-2001; Millennium Digital Media, vpres, contoller, 2003-06; Inroads, vpres consumer prods, health & retail industs, 2006-08; Retail Servs Indust, vpres; consult, currently; Perpetua, chief financial officer, 2008-14; 100 Black Men Greater St. Louis, chief financial officer, currently; SB 360 Group, co managing partner, 2014-; Mathews Dickey Boys & Girls Club, interim chief financial officer, 2014-. **Orgs:** Chmn, Nat Alumni Assoc Inroads, 1985-87; bd dir, Mathews Dickey Boys & Girls Club, currently; chmn, Fin Comt; Inroads Inc; Nat Bd Dir; bd mem, Nat Baptist Publ Bd; trustee, First Baptist Church Chesterfield, 2007-13. **Honors/Awds:** John C Willis Award, Nat Asn Black Accountants, 1976; Inductee for the NIAA Hall of Fame, 1993. **Home Addr:** 117 Highrock Rd, Sandy Hook, CT 06482. **Business Addr:** Chief Financial Officer, Mathews Dickey Boys and Girls Club, 4245 North Kingshighway Blvd, St. Louis, MO 63115, **Business Phone:** (314)382-5952.

### SANDIDGE, KANITA DURICE
Executive, chairperson. **Personal:** Born Dec 2, 1947, Cleveland, OH; daughter of John Robert Jr and Virginia Louise Caldwell. **Educ:** Cornell Univ, BA, 1970; Case Western Res Univ, MBA, 1979. **Career:** AT&T Network Systs, actg sect chief, 1970-72, sect chief cost control, 1972-78, dept chief data processing & acct, 1978-79, dept chief acct anal, 1979-80, admin mgr, 1980-83, sales forecasting & anal mgr, 1983-86, planning & develop mgr, 1986-87, admin serv dir, 1987-91, div staff dir, 1991-94, supplier diversity dir, 1994-98; Sandidge Consult Group, prin consult, 1999-2005; Nat Minority Supplier Develop Coun, chairperson, dir new bus develop, 2005-11; New Bus Develop, interim dir, 2007-14, vpres progs, 2011-. **Orgs:** Beta Alpha Psi Acct Hon, Am Mgt Asn, Alliance AT&T Black Mgrs, Nat Black MBAs, Nat Asn Female Exec; life mem, Nat Asn Advan Colored People; black execs exchange prog NUL, 1986-; bd dir, E-W Corp Corridor Asn, Ill, 1987-90, Quad County Urban League, Ill, 1988-90; dir, Nat Minority Supplier Develop Coun; NJ Minority Supplier Develop Coun, Chairperson Bd, 1997, bd dir, 1996-98; adv coun mem, Thunderbirds Nat Minority, 1994-98; bd dir, Diversity Info Resources, 1994-98; bd mem, TRY US Resources; bd mem, Minority Bus Develop Group; bd dir, Inst Supply Mgt Supplier Diversity Group, 1995-99, 2008-15. **Honors/Awds:** Harlem YMCA Black Achiever in Industry, 1981; Tribute to Women & Industry Achievement Award YWCA, 1985. **Home Addr:** 10 Trade Winds Dr, Randolph, NJ 07869-1238, **Home Phone:** (201)366-1187. **Business Addr:** Vice President, National Minority Supplier Development Council, 1359 Broadway 10th Fl Suite 1000, New York, NY 10018, **Business Phone:** (212)944-2430.

### SANDIDGE, DR. ONEAL C.
Clergy. **Personal:** Born Lynchburg, VA; son of Hattie and Wardie; married Janice Oliver; children: Jermaine Oneal & Ieke Monique. **Educ:** Lynchburg Col, BA, 1977; Howard Univ Divinity Sch, MA, christian educ, 1986; Columbia Univ, MA, 1988; Drew Univ, DMin, 1992; Capella Univ, PhD ,cand higher educ, currently. **Career:** Pastor, 1979-86; Madison County Public Sch, teacher; Campbell County Pub Sch, teacher; Petersburg Pub Sch, teacher, 1982-90; Piedmont Va Community Col, teacher, 1989-90; author; workshop leader; preacher; Beulah Heights Bible Col, assoc prof, 1994-96; Luther Rice Sem, teacher, 1995-96; Conv Ave Baptist Church, minister christian educ, 1997-98; Alexandria Pub Sch, teacher, 1999-; Defiance Col, prof, 1999-; Trinity Episcopal Sch Ministry Sem, adj prof; Md Pub Sch, Eng teacher, 2000-06; Liberty Univ, Lynchburg, Va, prof relig, 2006;

Nat Bible Col & Seminary, fac, currently. **Orgs:** Member numerous prof orgns. **Honors/Awds:** Merrill Fellowship, Harvard Univ, 1992-93; Achievement Award for Outstanding Leadership, Lynchburg Col Alumni, 1993; Memphis Writer's Award; Award for Christian education of the the year, 2004; LABBE Award, Los Angeles Book Expo. **Special Achievements:** Books published by National Baptist USA, Inc: Beyond the Classroom; Strategies for the Director of Christian Edu in the African Church; Teacher Training in the African American Church, I'm Stuck! Help Me Start a Youth Ministry in the African American Church; Articles Published: book review, "Black Religious Leaders-Conflict in Unity," The Journal of Black Scholar, Sept 1991; "Tracing Gospel Roots with Professor Thomas Dorsey," Score Gospel Magazine, Jan/Feb 1992; "Black History," Virginia Education Association Journal, Feb 1992; "The Uniqueness of Black Preaching," The Journal of Religious Thought, Howard University, 1992; "Glancing at Curriculum," June 1995, "Whosoever Will Come," Dec/Jan 1995-96, Journal of Church School Today; Informer Journal, four articles, 1999; "Twelve Teaching Tips for Church Educators," 2000; "Back to the Basics: Teaching Teenagers at Home and at School," 2000; "Assessing Your Students," 2001; "Can Your Students Read Scripture Without Knowing the Vocabulary," 2001. **Home Addr:** PO Box 9473, Richmond, VA 23228. **Business Addr:** Undergraduate College Dean, National Bible College & Seminary, 6700 Bock Rd, Fort Washington, MD 20744, **Business Phone:** (301)567-9500.

### SANDIFORD, ORPHIA
Administrator, scout. **Educ:** Bay State Col, AA, criminal justice, 1986. **Career:** Mass State Police, dir recruitment, recruitment coordr, 2003. **Business Addr:** Director, Massachusetts State Police, 470 Worcester Rd, Framingham, MA 01702, **Business Phone:** (508)820-2300.

### SANDLER, DEBRA A.
Marketing executive. **Educ:** Hofstra Univ, BBA, int trade, 1982; NY Univ, Stern Sch Bus, MBA, mkt, 1989; Long Island Univ, CW Post Campus, PhD, pharm, 2007. **Career:** PepsiAmericas, mkt dir, 1985-95; PepsiCo Inc, mkt vpres, 1995-98; McNeil Nutritionals LLC, gen mgr, worldwide pres, 1999-2009, Worldwide Group vpres mkt, 2002; Johnson & Johnsons McNeil Specialty Prod Co, vpres worldwide mkt, 1999-; Johnson & Johnson Personal Prod Co, vpres worldwide mkt; Johnson & Johnson, worldwide vpres womens health, 2002-03; Mars Inc, chief consumer officer, 2010-12, Chocolate N Am, pres, 2012-14; Gannett, bd dir, 2015-; chief health & wellbeing officer, 2014-; La Grenade Group LLC, pres, chief exec officer, 2015-; Archer Daniels Midland Co, bd dir, 2016-. **Orgs:** Trustee, Hofstra Univ, 2008-; dir, Philadelphia Orchestra Asn. **Honors/Awds:** Power 50 Marketers Award for Excellence in Marketing, Advertising Age, 2004; Distinguished Alumna Award, Association of Hispanic and Black Business Students, 2005; hon PhD, pharm, Long Island Univ, 2007; Corporate Executive of the Year, Black Enterprise, 2008; 100 Most Powerful Executives in Corporate America, Black Enterprise, 2009; 75 Most Powerful Women in Business, Black Enterprise, 2010. **Business Addr:** President, Mars Inc, 1600 Broadway, New York, NY 10019, **Business Phone:** (212)295-3850.

### SANDLER, JOAN DELORES
Activist, association executive, executive director. **Personal:** Born Oct 2, 1934, Harlem, NY; children: Eve & Kathe. **Educ:** City Col NY; Univ Mexico. **Career:** Ins Co, clerk; Bloomingdale Family Serv, teacher dir, 1963-66; Metro Appl Res Ctr, res, 1966-68; Dept Cult Affairs, prog specialist, 1968-72; Black Theatre Alliance, exec dir, 1972-77; Dept Cult Affairs, prog specialist, 1975; Senghor Found, staff, 1977-80; Metro Mus Art, assoc mus educ charge comn educ, 1983-87; Nat Endowment Arts, regional dir; Mus Am Folk Art, dir; Romau Bearden Found, exec dir, 2001; New York Univ, fac; Marymount Col, fac; Princeton Col, fac; Hunter Col, lectr & fac mem; consult arts educ, currently. **Orgs:** Panelist & consult, Nat Endowment Arts, 1971-74; consult, NY State Coun Arts, 1972-; adv, VISIONS KCET & TV Pub Broadcasting Corp, 1974; theater panel, Theater Develop Fund; bd dir, Nat Coun Women; bd dir, C Arts Carnival; Opportunity Resources; adv, Gov's Task Force; bd dir, First Am Cong Theatre, NSINGHA; Nat Coalition 100 Black Women; Am Mus Asn; Mus Educr Roundtable. **Honors/Awds:** Audelco Award, 1973; has received a number of awards and honors for contributions to arts education. **Home Addr:** 392 Cent Pk W, New York, NY 10025, **Home Phone:** (212)222-8561.

### SANDOVAL, DOLORES S.
Educator, founder (originator), association executive. **Personal:** Born Sep 30, 1937, Montreal, QC. **Educ:** Univ Mich, Sch Archit & Design, BSD, 1960; Ind Univ, BA, interior design & S asian studies, MS, 1968, PhD, curric & fine arts, 1970; Harvard Univ, Educ Mgt Iem, 1975. **Career:** State Univ Col, Buffalo, assoc prof, 1970-71; Univ Vt, assoc prof, educ, 1971, chair, 1981-82, prof emer, currently; Mid E studies, asst to pres, human resources, 1972-77, co-chair, 1994-; Ri Sch Design, 1981; US House, representatives Vt, 1988, 1990; Univ Senate; Challenges to Unity: Europ COT, Maastricht, fel, 1995; DaCosta-Angelique Inst, pres & founder, 2006-; Musee-Observatoire de L Immigration, vpres, 2007-. **Orgs:** Gov's Comn Status Women, 1972; Gov's Task Women, 1974; fel NAT Endowment Humanities Summer African Cult, 1987; bd mem, Pub Access Govt TV Channel 17 (VT), 1991-95; fel Univ Nmex Col Fine Arts, Nat Arts Proj, Daring To Do It, 1993-94; bd mem, Sister Cities, Burlington, VT Arad (Israel & Bethlehem), 1995-96; pres, Vt & Honduras, 1997-; pres, Partners AMEs; St. James Literary Society, 2002-04; mem bd dir, Musee-Observatoire de l'immigration, 2009-11. **Honors/Awds:** Fel mem bd trustees, 1976-82; Rhode Island Sch Design, 1981, Univ Senate, Univ Vt, chair, 1981-82; Primary candidate, 1988; Contributions to Duke Ellington Concert & Speech Series Award, Black Am Heritage Fund NY, 1989-92. Malone Fel Arab and Islamic Studies in Tunisia, summer, 1989; Elected Democratic candidate for Congress from VT, 1990; Malone Alumni Fel Jordan, Israel, Palestine and Syria, summer, 1991. **Special Achievements:** Be Patient Abdul, Simon & Shuster, 1996; Coloured Pictures in Family Frames, 2002. **Home Addr:** 1058 Williston Rd, Williston, VT 05495. **Business Addr:** Professor Emeritus, University of Vermont, 16 Colchester Ave, Burlington, VT 05405-0001, **Business Phone:** (802)656-3131.

### SANDOZ, JOHN HENRY
Judge. **Personal:** Born Houston, TX. **Educ:** Univ Calif, Los Angeles, AB, math, 1955; Univ SC, JD, 1970. **Career:** Judge (retired); fed govt, 1958-60; Ford Motor Co aerospace div, 1960-67; Univ SC, dir legal serv, 1975-80, comnr, 1981-92; Los Angeles County, judge, 1995; Los Angeles Super Ct, judge, 2002-06. **Home Addr:** 111 N Hill St Dept 60, Los Angeles, CA 90071.

### SANDRIDGE, DR. JOHN SOLOMON
Artist, physician. **Personal:** Born Gadsden, AL; son of Edward (deceased) and Lucille; married Frances; children: Peter, Priscilla & David. **Educ:** Fesperman Sch Naturopathic Med, ND, 1983. **Career:** Artist, auth & physician; Creative Displays, supvr; Gadsden City Bd Educ, teacher; Luv life Collectibles Inc, chief exec officer, founder & pres; Dr. John's Natural Health Prods, formulator, currently; Self-Healing Ministries Inc, founder & pres, currently; Trees Wealth Inc, founder & pres, currently; SYST, designer & formulator; Simply Results Inc, consult & physician, currently. **Orgs:** Pres, Carver Theatre; Sandridge Mus Living Hist. **Honors/Awds:** Numerous honors and awards including Key to Birmingham, Gadsen, Rainbow City, Fairfield, Ala; Certificate of Appreciation, Gov Ala, 1982; Certificate of Appreciation, Black Bus Asn, 1983; National Vendors Award, JC Penney's, 1993; Outstanding Citizen's Award, Roberta Watts Med, 1993; City Gadsden Award; Black Business Association Award. **Special Achievements:** First African-American to be licensed by The Coca-Cola Company to create a series of paintings incorporating an African-American theme. **Home Addr:** PO Box 1628, Gadsden, AL 35902-1628. **Business Addr:** Consultant, Physician, Simply Results Inc, 3100 Lorna Rd Barbizon Bldg Suite 301, Birmingham, AL 35216, **Business Phone:** (205)979-3933.

### SANDS, GEORGE M.
College teacher, consultant. **Personal:** Born Jan 15, 1942, Port Chester, NY; married Mary Alice Moxley; children: Jeffrey & Kenneth. **Educ:** Western Mich Univ, BS, 1964; Hunter Col Sch Social Work, MSW, 1970. **Career:** Cage Teen Ctr Inc, exec dir, 1972-78; Empire State Col, lectr, 1981-; Westchester Comm Col, adj prof, 1973, assoc prof, 1988-2001; Sands Assocs, owner, dir, 1978-. **Orgs:** Educ chmn, Middletown Nat Asn Advan Colored People; Am Soc Personnel Admin; bd dirs, Michael Schwerner Found, 1970-72; personnel chmn, Middletown Bd Educ, 1976-82; consult, trainer, Stony Brook Univ, 1977-; bd mem, Orange Co Pvt Indus Coun, 1983-; trainer, Cornell Univ Sch Indust Labor Rels. **Honors/Awds:** Teacher of the Year, Westchester Comm Col, 1982; Service Award, Middletown Bd Educ, 1982. **Home Addr:** 16 Ross Lane, Middletown, NY 10940, **Home Phone:** (914)692-5033. **Business Addr:** Director, Sands Associates, 1204 Spinnaker Dr, North Myrtle Beach, SC 29582-6810, **Business Phone:** (914)692-6296.

### SANDS, JERRY LEIGH
Athletic coach. **Personal:** married Torrie Lynn Gant. **Career:** Univ Ark Pine Bluff, linebacker coach & spec teams coordr, currently. **Business Addr:** Linebacker Coach, University of Arkansas Pine Bluff, 1200 N Univ Dr, Pine Bluff, AR 71611, **Business Phone:** (870)575-8000.

### SANDS, PROF. MARY ALICE
School administrator. **Personal:** Born Oct 20, 1941, Indianapolis, IN; daughter of Frank O Moxley and Velma Goodnight Moxley; married George M; children: Jeffrey & Kenneth. **Educ:** State Univ Iowa, attended 1960; Western Mich Univ, BS, occup ther, 1964; Bank St Col Ed, MS, educ, occup ther & coun & guid serv, 1982. **Career:** School administrator (retired); Bronx Munic Hosp Ctr, asst chief, 1965-70; Harlem Hosp OT Dept, supvr clin ed, 1971; Rockland Community Col, chmn OTA Prog, 1973-77; Orange Cty Community Col, Occupational Ther Asst Dept, chmn, full prof, OTA Prog, 1977-2001, prof emer, currently; Occup Ther Plus, founder, owner, partner, 1986-2001. **Orgs:** Nat Asn Advan Colored People; Alpha Kappa Alpha; Am OT Asn; AOTA Prog Adv Comm, 1983-86; bd dir, Orange Cty Cerebral Palsy Asn, 1984-87; chair, NY Bd Occup Ther, 1986-89; bd dir, Horton Med Ctr, 1998-2000; chair, Am Occup Ther Asn Comn Educ, 1989-92; fel chair, Am Occup Ther Asn, 1994. **Honors/Awds:** Award of Merit, Pract NY State OT Asn, 1985; Service Award, Am Occup Therapy Assoc, 1992; Certificate of Appreciation, Hudson-Taconic District NYSOTA, 1992. **Special Achievements:** Contributing author, Willard & Spackman's Occupational Therapy, 1997, 2003. **Home Addr:** 27186 Sora Blvd, Wesley Chapel, FL 33544. **Business Addr:** Professor Emeritus, Orange County Community College, 115 S St, Middletown, NY 10940, **Business Phone:** (845)344-6222.

### SANDS, DR. ROSETTA F.
School administrator. **Personal:** Born Homestead, FL; daughter of John H and Annie Pickett Harriel; married Charles H; children: Michael H. **Educ:** Harlem Hosp Sch Nursing, NY, dipl, 1954; Univ Md, Sch Nursing, Baltimore, MD, BSN, 1966; Univ Md, College Park, MS, 1970; Johns Hopkins Univ, Baltimore, MD, postgrad study, 1977; Union Grad Sch, Cincinnati Ohio, PhD, 1980. **Career:** Univ Md Sch Nursing, Baltimore, Md, instr med & surg, nursing, 1970-71, asst prof, regist nursing prog, 1971-83, team coordr, 1971-74, asst dean, 1974-79; Tuskegee Univ, Tuskegee Inst Ala, dean & assoc, 1983-87; William Patterson Univ, Sch Nursing, Wayne, NJ, dean & prof, 1987-93; Stud Retention In Acad Nursing, nurse consult, 1993-. **Orgs:** Trustee Nat Sorority House, 1976-79; Chi Eta Phi Sorority Nurses; Sigma Theta Tau Intl Hon Soc Nursing, 1969; Peer Rev Panel, Spec Proj Grants, Dept Health & Human Servs, 1976-85; Task Force on Teaching Culturally Diverse Studs, 1977-82; Phi Kappa Phi Hon Soc, 1977; pres, bd trustee, Provident Hosp, 1978-81; bd dir, Md Blue Cross, 1980-83; Md Adv Comt, US Civil Rights Comt, 1981-83; pres, Md Nurse Asn, 1981-82; bd dir, Am Asn Cols Nursing, 1986-88; Zeta Phi Beta Sorority Inc; bd trustee, United Hosps Med Ctr, 1993-96. **Home Addr:** 4406 Norfolk Ave, Baltimore, MD 21216, **Home Phone:** (410)448-3563. **Business Addr:** Consultant, 4406 Norfolk Ave, Baltimore, MD 21216, **Business Phone:** (410)448-3563.

### SANFORD, MARK
Executive. **Personal:** Born Nov 24, 1953, St. Louis, MO; son of Levi; children: Tifani Iris & Marcus L Alexander. **Educ:** Wash Univ, BA, biol, 1975; St Louis Univ, MHA, hosp admin, 1981; St Louis Community Col, AND, nursing, 1991. **Career:** St Louis Univ Med Ctr, staff assoc, 1981-82; St Mary's Hosp, vpres, 1981-89; People's Community Action Corp, exec adminr; People's Health Ctrs, outreach coordr, planning & develop officer, exec vpres, 1989-. **Orgs:** Exec, Am Col Healthcare, 1981-; bd mem, Black Music Soc; St Louis Chap Black MBA's, 1985-; youth chmn, UNCF Telethon; bd mem, African-Am Chamber Com; 100 Black Men; pres, Nat Black MBA Asn St Louis Chap; exec, Nat Soc Fund Raising, 1992; nat conf chmn, Nat Conf NBMBAA; bd mem, Nat Black MBA; bd mem, Am Heart Asn; bd mem, BABAA; bd mem, People's Community Action Corp; Promise Ctr Developmentally Disabled. **Home Addr:** 5103 Wash Pl, St. Louis, MO 63108, **Home Phone:** (314)367-1242. **Business Addr:** Executive Vice President, People's Health Centers, 5701 Delmar blvd, St. Louis, MO 63112, **Business Phone:** (314)367-7848.

### SANKOFA, MIKA'IL. See LOFTON, MICHAEL.

### SANTIAGO, O. J. (OTIS JASON SANTIAGO)
Football player. **Personal:** Born Apr 4, 1974, Whitby, ON. **Educ:** Kent State Univ, attended 1996. **Career:** Football player (retired); Atlanta Falcons, tight end, 1997-99; Dallas Cowboys, tight end, 2000; Cleveland Browns, 2000, tight end, 2001; Minn Vikings, 2002; Oakland Raiders, tight end, 2003, 2006-07; Denver Broncos, 2004; New Eng Patriots, tight end, 2006; Edmonton Eskimos; Montreal Alouettes, 2010, free agt, currently. **Orgs:** Crockett Found, currently. **Honors/Awds:** Arthur Ashe National Award; Academic All-MAC. **Special Achievements:** Film: 1998 NFC Championship Game, 1999. **Business Addr:** Member, The Crockett Foundation, PO Box 3774, Hallandale Beach, FL 33008, **Business Phone:** (954)200-1924.

### SANTIAGO, ROBERTO
Journalist, writer. **Personal:** Born Jun 30, 1963, New York, NY; son of Francisca Castro and Fundador. **Educ:** Oberlin Col, BA, hist & creative writing, 1985. **Career:** McGraw Hill Inc, NY, corp writer, 1985-87; Times Mirror Inc, NY, sports writer, 1987-88; Emerge Mag, NY, staff writer, 1989-92; Plain Dealer, columnist, 1992; New York Daily News; Miami Herald, sr staff writer, auth & reporter, 2003-; Bks: Our Times 2, Bedford Bks, 1991; Contemp Reader, Harper Collins, 1992. **Orgs:** Mystery Writers Am; The Newspaper Guild. **Honors/Awds:** Int Am Press Assn, Award Commentary, 1991; Guest Lectr: Rutgers Univ; Princeton Univ; Vassar Clg; Oberlin Col; CBS-TV; Columbia Univ; Trenton State Co. **Special Achievements:** Publications: Boricuas: Influential Puerto Rican Writings, 1995. **Home Addr:** PO Box 6617, New York, NY 10128. **Business Addr:** Senior Staff Writer, Miami Herald, 1 Herald Plz, Miami, FL 33132, **Business Phone:** (305)350-2111.

### SANTISIMA, LANGSTON FAIZON. See LOVE, FAIZON.

### SANTOS, EDWIN JOSEPH, JR.
Executive. **Personal:** married Paula; children: Erica, Steven & Michael. **Educ:** Bryant Univ, BS, 1981. **Career:** FleetBoston Financial Corp, chief auditor; Citizens Financial Group Inc, group exec vpres, gen auditor, 2004-. **Orgs:** Bd trustee, Roger Williams Med Ctr, 2009; vice chmn bd trustee, Bryant Univ; bd dir, Crossroads RI; Bd, Delta Dent; bd trustee, co-vpres, Rock Hill Sch, 2007-; chmn, CharterCARE Health Partners; co-vpres, Rocky Hill Sch; bd dir, Delta Dent; Pyramis Global Advisors, 2010-; bd dir, Wash Trust Co, 2012-; bd dir, Ri community. **Honors/Awds:** Rhode Island Black Heritage Society Award, Labor & Enterprise, 2008. **Home Addr:** 234 Mourning Dove Dr, Saunderstown, RI 02874-2214, **Home Phone:** (401)667-7618. **Business Addr:** Executive Vice President, General Auditor, Citizens Financial Group Inc, 1 Citizens Plz, Providence, RI 02903, **Business Phone:** (401)456-7000.

### SANTOS, HENRY JOSEPH
Educator, pianist. **Personal:** Born Aug 29, 1927, Lewistown, ME; son of Beulah Benjamin and Henry; married Leola Waters; children: Nancy Gainer (Curtis). **Educ:** Boston Univ, Sch Fine & Appl Arts, BA, music, 1952; Harvard Univ, Grad Study, 1968; Boston Univ, pvt study piano Alfredo Fondacaro, 1960, MA, music, 1980. **Career:** Perkins Sch Blind, instr, 1956-70; Bridgewater State Col, asst prof music to prof music, 1971-99, prof emer, currently; Henry Santos Piano Summer Piano Inst High Sch Stud, founder. **Orgs:** Ethnic Heritage Task Force Mass, 1974; chmn, Mass Coun Arts & Humanities, 1986; Support panel mem, Ri Arts Coun, 1987, 1989; vis mem, Blue Ribbon Comn, Ri Arts Coun, 1991; Music Ed Nat Conf; Nat Entertainment Conf Am; Asn Instr Blind; adv bd, Fuller Art Mus. **Honors/Awds:** Chosen instr perf Albert Schweitzer Fest, 1950; Citizens Achievement Award, Cape Verdean Benef Soc, 1968; semi-fin 1st Louis Moreau Gottschalk Int Competition Pianists & Comp, Dillard Univ, 1970; TV prog Say Bro, 1971; prog WGBH Performance European & Afro-Am Composers for Piano, 1972; lectr recital, St Eastern Reg Conf, Music Educ Nat Conf, 1973; Ethnic Herit Task Force of Commonwealth of MA by Gov Francis Sargent, 1974; grant, MA Council on Arts & Humanities for Trade Europe & Afro-Am music progs for elem & sec sch child Bridgewater St Col, 1974; compositions: Androscoggin Pines, 1983, Sonata for Piano, 1985, Massin G Major, 1987, Two Dances for Piano, 1988, Healing Song, 1988, Movement for Piano Brass Quintet, 1990, Songs of Innocence, 1990; Henry Santos Scholar, Bridgewater State Col, named in honor; performance of classical music for piano by Afro-Am Composers; Piano recitals chamber music prog in major cities of NE US & Europe. **Home Addr:** 225 Everett St, PO Box 1391, Middleboro, MA 02346-1224, **Home Phone:** (508)947-9909. **Business Addr:** Professor Emeritus, Bridgewater State College, 131 Summer St, Bridgewater, MA 02346-1224, **Business Phone:** (508)531-1000.

**SANTOS, MATHIES JOSEPH**
Educator. **Personal:** Born Jan 10, 1948, Providence, RI; son of Matthew J and Rosemarie Lopes; married Michelina Doretto; children: Chiara & Mathies-Kareem. **Educ:** Brown Univ, Providence, RI, BA, sec educ & Ital studies, 1977; RI Col, Providence, RI, BA, managerial econs, 1982. **Career:** Educator (retired); Ri Col, Providence, RI, fin aid officer, 1978-80, dorm dir; State Ri, Dept Educ, consult, 1980-82, proj dir, 1983-85, Gov's Off, sr policy analyst, 1985, Dept Admin, exec asst, 1985-90, spec asst to comnr educ; Lippitt Mayor, Providence, RI, campaign mgr, 1982. **Orgs:** CRP mem, Delta Dent Ri; Brown Univ Third World Alumni Activ Comn; bd mem, Ri Col Alumni Asn; Ri Black Heritage Soc; Nat Asn Advan Colored People; Gov's Adv Comt Refugee Resettlement Mgt; trustee, Wheeler Sch; Providence Boys & Girls Club. **Home Addr:** 666 Hope St, Providence, RI 02906-2657, **Home Phone:** (401)421-9802.

**SAPP, LAUREN B.**
Librarian. **Personal:** Born Jul 13, 1937, Smithfield, NC; daughter of Lee and Senoria Burnette; children: Corey, Christopher & Cheston Williams. **Educ:** NC Cent Univ, Durham, NC, BA, 1967; Univ Mich, Ann Arbor, Mich, AMLS, 1971; Fla State Univ, Tallahassee, FL, Adv MS, 1979, PhD, 1984. **Career:** Voorhees Col, Denmark, NC, instr librn, 1971-74; Fla State Univ, Tallahassee, FL, librn, 1974-84; NC Cent Univ, Durham, NC, vis prof, 1985-96; Duke Univ, Durham, NC, librn, 1984-96; Univ NC Chapel Hill, adj prof, 1993-95; Fla A&M Univ, Samuel H Coleman Memorial Libr, Tallahassee, Fl, dir libr, 1996-. **Orgs:** Am Libr Asn; Black Caucus, LAMA, ACRL; chair, docs caucus, Fla Libr Asn, 1982; chair, docs Secy, NC Libr Asn, 1988-89; secy, State & Local docs Task Force GODORT, 1987-88; ACRL Int Rels Comn, 1994-98; Beta Phi Mu Hon Soc, 1980-; Lama Cult Diversity Comn, 1997-2001; Lama Publs Comn Fund Raising & Fin Develop Sec, 1997-; treas, Libr Dir Asn, 1998-. **Honors/Awds:** EEO Fell, bd Regents, State Fl, 1978-79, 1982; Title II Fell, Univ Mich, 1970-71; Women Achievement Award, YWCA, Durham, NC, 1988; Star Award, Perkins Libr, Duke Univ, 1989, 1991. **Home Addr:** PO Box 6326, Tallahassee, FL 32314, **Home Phone:** (850)514-1817. **Business Addr:** Director of Libraries, University Librarian, Florida A & M University, 1500 S Martin Luther King Blvd 525 Orr Dr, Tallahassee, FL 32307-4100, **Business Phone:** (850)599-3370.

**SAPP, PATRICK**
Football player, executive. **Personal:** Born May 11, 1973, Jacksonville, FL. **Educ:** Clemson Univ, grad. **Career:** Football player (retired), owner; San Diego Chargers, left linebacker, 1996-97; Coast-2Coast Men's Clothing, owner, 1997-2002; Ariz Cardinals, linebacker, 1998-99; Indianapolis Colts, 2000; Memphis Maniax, 2001; Xceleron Sports, vpres, 2002-06; Clemson Univ, dir maj gifts, 2006-15, dir maj gifts & dir alumni engagement, 2015-. **Honors/Awds:** Rookie of the Year, 1996. **Business Addr:** Director of Major Gifts, Director of Alumni Engagement, Clemson University, Clemson, SC 29634, **Business Phone:** (864)656-3311.

**SAPP, WARREN CARLOS**
Football player, executive. **Personal:** Born Dec 19, 1972, Orlando, FL; son of Annie Roberts; married JaMiko Vaughn; children: Mercedes & Warren Carlos; married Chantel Adkins; children: Autumn Jade Adkins. **Educ:** Univ Miami, attended 1994. **Career:** Football player (retired), executive; Tampa Bay Buccaneers, defensive tackle, 1995-2003; Oakland Raiders, defensive tackle, 2004-07; Showtime Networks Inc, studio analyst & commentator, 2008-; Dancing With the Stars, currently. TV series: "Judge Sapp", 2012; "Funny or Die Presents", 2011; Film: "Our Family Wedding ", 2010; "NFL GameDay Morning ", 2006. **Orgs:** Nat Football League Network. **Business Addr:** Studio Analyst, Showtime Networks Inc, 1633 Broadway, New York, NY 10019, **Business Phone:** (212)708-1600.

**SARDIN, JAMES E.**
School administrator. **Educ:** Southeast Mo State Univ, BA; Alcorn State Univ, BA & MA, agr educ; Miss State Univ, doctorate; Univ Mo, MA. **Career:** Miss Dept Educ, Vocational Education & Workforce Development (OVE&WD), assoc state supt, currently, assoc dir, interim dep dir, dep supt; JMG, prog mgr, consult. **Orgs:** Bd mem, Nat Tech Hon Socs; bd trustee, Am Tech Educ Asn. **Business Addr:** Associate Superintendent, Interim Deputy Director, Director of Vocational Education & Workforce Development, Mississippi Department of Education, 359 N W St Suite 249, Jackson, MS 39205-0771, **Business Phone:** (601)359-3764.

**SARGEANT, LARRY (LAWRENCE E SARJEANT)**
Executive. **Educ:** Rutgers Univ, attended 1976; Brown Univ, AB, philos. **Career:** Seattle-King County Legal Aid, staff atty, 1976; State Wash, asst atty; Pac NW Bell Tel Co, Seattle, Wash, atty, 1983; US W, vpres Fed Regulatory; US Telecom Asn, vpres, Law & Gen Coun, currently. **Orgs:** DC Bar Asn; Wash State Bar Asn; Fed Commun Bar Asn; Nat Bar Asn. **Business Addr:** Vice President Law, General Counsel, United States Telecom Association, 607 14th St NW Suite 400, Washington, DC 20005, **Business Phone:** (202)326-7300.

**SARGENT, DR. VIRGINIA HIGHTOWER**
Executive, business owner, management consultant. **Personal:** Born Jun 24, 1963, South Boston, VA; daughter of Virginia Maude Dixon Hightower and Obey Hightower; children: Ashley. **Educ:** Pace Univ, BA, com, 1993; Baruch Col, MPA, 2000; George Washington Univ, CPM, 2002; Univ Phoenix, Doctorate, bus admin, 2006. **Career:** ABC-TV & Disney Inc, ed, 1993-99; DC govt, commun, dir, 2000-03, health care, dir mkt & pr, 2003-05; Univ Md Univ Col, adj bus prof; Daily Bus Blessing.com, Publ, leadership & mgmt bus consult, currently; Sargent Bus Consult, chief exec officer. **Orgs:** Pres & founder, Young Readers Network, 1995-; bd dir, Proj Ctrl NYC. **Honors/Awds:** Pres's Service Award, 1997; Volunteerism in Children Award, 1997; NYC Principal for a Day, 1998, 1999 & 2000; Silver Inkwell Award, Int Asn Bus Communicators, 2002; Aegis Award, 2002. **Special Achievements:** Author: With Vision People Profit, 2007, Ed, Spiritual Expressions, 2005; creator, Reeedy Readercize; 9-time marathon runner. **Business Addr:** Chief Executive Officer, Business Coach, Sargent Business Consulting, 549 Brummel Ct NW, Washington, DC 20012-1854, **Business Phone:** (202)722-2788.

**SARJEANT, LAWRENCE E. See SARGEANT, LARRY.**

**SARKODIE-MENSAH, DR. KWASI**
Librarian. **Personal:** Born Jun 13, 1955, Ejisu Ashanti; son of Thomas Kwaku Mensah and Margaret Akua Barnieh; children: Kofi, Kwame & Nana Akua. **Educ:** Univ Complutense, dipl, 1978; Univ Ghana, BA, 1979; Clarion Univ, MSLS, 1983; Univ Ill, PhD, 1988. **Career:** Ahmadiyya Sec Sch, teacher, 1979-80; Origbo County High Sch, teacher, 1980-82; Clarion Univ, grad asst, 1982-83; Univ Ill, grad asst, 1984-86; Xavier Univ La, head pub serv, 1986-89; Northeastern Univ, libr instr coordr, 1989-92; Boston Col, chief ref librn, 1992-95; Commonwealth Mass, ct interpreter, 1992-; Boston Col Libr, mgr instr servs, 1995-; US Atty Gen's Off, Boston, consult, African lang; Col Advancing Studies, adj prof; Boston Col, fac, 1996-, O'Neill Libr, instr servs mgr, currently. **Orgs:** Am Libr Asn, 1984-; Northeastern Univ Comn to Improve Col Teaching, 1989-92; adv bd mem, Mass Fac Develop Consortium, 1992-; Multicultural Network, 1992-; chair, ACRL/IS Diverse Comn, 1993-95; Boston Col, Martin Luther King Com, 1993-; ACRL/IS Com Educ Libr Instrs; bd mem, African Pastoral Ctr, Archdiocese Boston; Benjamin E Mays Mentor, 1995-, fac adv, Ignacio Volunteers, 1997-, Boston Col; liaison comt, Libr Instr Roundtable, 1999-2001; lectr, St Malachy's Parish, 1999-; Archdiocese Boston, Cardinal's Advisory Bd Member; ed bd, Reference Librarian. **Honors/Awds:** Univ Ghana, Scholar, 1975-79; Scholar to study abroad, Span Govt, 1978; Best Teacher, Origbo County High Sch, 1981, 1982; Top 20 Articles in Libr Instruction, Res Strategies, 1986; Fel, Univ Ill, 1986-87; Certificate for Outstanding Achievement in Multicultural Education in Boston County, 1993; Bill Day Award, 1995, Annual Teaching, Advising & Mentoring Grant, 1999-00, County Service Award, 2001, Boston Col; Rev John R Trzaska Award, 2001; Leadership Award, Boston Col AHANA Community, 2007; Massachusetts State Lottery Community Champion Award, 2008; Article-Plagiarism & the International Student, 2010. **Special Achievements:** Auth works include: Making Term Paper Counseling More Meaningful, 1989; Writing in a Language You Don't Know, 1990; The Int Ta: A Beat from a Foreign Drummer, 1991; Dealing with International Students in a Multicultural Era, 1992; Paraprofessionals in Reference Services: An Untapped Mine, 1993; ed: Library Instruction Roundtable Newsletter, 1991-92; consul: Northeastern Univ Project Hist Black Writing, 1990-; The Int Student in the US Acad Libr: Building Bridges to Better Bibliographic Instruction; Nigerian Americans, 1995; Human Aspect of Reference in the Era of Technology, 1997; Using Humor for Effective Library Instruction, 1998; International Students US Trends, Cult Adjustments, 1998; Reference Services for the Adult Learner, 1999; Research In The Electronic Age; How To Distinguish Between Good & Bad Data, 1999; "The Difficult Patron Situation: A Window of Opp to Improve Library Service", Catholic Literary World, 2000; "The International Student on Campus: History, Trends, Visa Classification & Adjustment", Teaching the New Libr to Today's Users, 2000; Helping the Difficult Library Patron: New Approaches to Examining & Resolving a Long-Standing & Ongoing Problem, 2002; Managing the twenty first Century Reference Department, 2003. **Home Addr:** 26 Marjorie Rd, Wilmington, MA 01887. **Business Addr:** Manager Instructional Services, Boston College Libraries, 312 O, Chestnut Hill, MA 02467-3810, **Business Phone:** (617)552-4465.

**SARMIENTO, SHIRLEY JEAN**
Arts administrator, educator, playwright. **Personal:** Born Nov 28, 1946, Buffalo, NY; daughter of John C and Claudia Hall; children: Tolley Reeves & William Jr. **Educ:** Medaille Col, BS, 1980; Canisius Col, attended 1983; NY Univ, Buffalo, Am studies & women's studies, 1988; State Univ NY, Buffalo, NY, MA, 2000. **Career:** Offender Aide & Restoration, coord family support mgr, 1982-83; Night People homeless, worker, 1985-86; Buffalo Bd Educ, sub teacher; Jesse Nash Health Ctr, family life prog; Gowanda Psychiat Ctr, Western NewYork Peace Ctr, rep & peace educr; Ny Univ, Buffalo, lectr, 1989; St Ann's Community Ctr, Learning Club, dir, 1990; Langston Hughes Inst, ct advocate; Buffalo Urban Arts Inc, co-founder & producer, 1994-; Colored Girl, chief exec officer, 2010-11; Color Girl, auth/poet, currently; Screenplay: Tolley's Pl, Meeting, Black n Blue Theatre, Yolley's Pl. Books: Celebrating Self, 2013; Alley, 2015. **Orgs:** Family advocate, Western New York Peace Ctr Learning Disabled Asn; founder, An African Am Artist Agenda, 1994. **Home Addr:** 205 Marine Dr Suite 4D, Buffalo, NY 14202-4215, **Home Phone:** (716)854-0119. **Business Addr:** Founder, Producer, Buffalo Urban Arts, 2495 Main St Suite 500, Buffalo, NY 14214, **Business Phone:** (716)833-4450.

**SARREALS, E. DON**
Scientist, businessperson. **Personal:** Born Sep 22, 1931, Winston-Salem, NC; son of Espriela and Sadie Scales; married Florence B Coleman; children: Cheryl Lynn & Esquire. **Educ:** New York Univ, BS, meteorol, 1955, MS, meteorol, 1958. **Career:** Nat Weather Serv Forecast Off, NYC, supr & radar meteorologist, 1961-69; WRCTV Nat Broadcasting Co, TV meteorologist, 1969-75; Storm Finders Inc, pres & cons meteorologist, 1969-75; Nat Weather Serv Hq, dissemination meteorologist, 1976-80; MD Ctr Pub Broadcasting, TV meteorologist, 1976-81; NEXRAD Proj, NOAA/NWS, chief, oper, 1981-92; Fed Coordr Meteorol, asst fed coordr, NOAA/NWS, 1992-97; E Don Sarreals Inc, pres, 1988; bus currently. **Orgs:** Prof mem, Am Meteorol Soc, 1955-; lectr & meterol, City Col NY, 1957-69; chmn bd dir, 157th St & Riverside Dr Housing Co Inc, 1966-68; lectr, Smithsonian Inst Wash DC, 1972; Montgomery Ctr Sch Community Sec Sch, 1976-78; Nat Acad Sci Comt Common Disasters & Media, 1977-75; Nat Tele Communs Info Agency's Teletext Comn, 1978-80; Nat Weather Asn, 1980-; bd mem, D Rumaldry Homes Asn, 1984-; subcomt, Natural Disaster Reduction, 1994-; Nat Sci & Technol Coun & Comt Environ & Natural Resources. **Honors/Awds:** Ward Medal, Meteorol City Col, NY, 1957; Teaching Fellowship, CCNY, 1957; Community Service Award, River Terr Mens Club New York, 1969; Service Awards, NWS, 1964-65, 1980, 1984. **Special Achievements:** Published NWS Forecasting Handbook 2NWS, 1978; Next Generation Weather Radar Operators Concept, 1983, Prod Description Doc, 1984, second ed 1987; "NEXRAD Prod" 23rd Amer Meteorol Society Con on Radar Meteorology, 1986; "NEXRAD Operation Capability" proc 1987 ann meeting of the Nat Weather Asn; "NEXRAD Prod & Operation Capability" proc of 25th Aerospace Science meeting Amer Institute of Aeronaut & Astronaut, 1987. **Home Addr:** 6300 Contention Ct, Bethesda, MD 20817. **Business Addr:** Owner, E Don Sarreals Private Co, 3685 S Leisure World Blvd 14f, Silver Spring, MD 20906-1717, **Business Phone:** (301)598-7910.

**SARTIN, JOHNNY NELSON, JR.**
Television journalist. **Personal:** Born Nov 29, 1960, Hattiesburg, MS; son of Johnny N Sr and Corean Anderson; married Natalie Renee Bell. **Educ:** Univ Southern Miss, Hattiesburg, MS, BS, 1982. **Career:** WLOX-TV, Biloxi, Miss, TV news photojournalist, 1982-86; WKRG-TV, Mobile, Ala, TV news photojournalist, 1986-88; KFOR-TV, Oklahoma City, Okla, TV news photojournalist, 1988-. **Orgs:** Alpha Phi Alpha Fraternity; Nat Press Photographers Asn; Nat Asn Black Journalists; Okla City Black Media Assocs. **Honors/Awds:** Award of Excellence & Photojournalism, Nat Asn Black Journalists, 1989, 1990. **Home Addr:** 2112 NW 115th Ter, Oklahoma City, OK 73120, **Home Phone:** (405)751-2434. **Business Addr:** Television Photojournalist, KFOR-TV, 444 E Britton Rd, Oklahoma City, OK 73120, **Business Phone:** (405)478-6333.

**SATCHELL, ELIZABETH (LIZ SATCHELL)**
Educator, radio broadcaster, television writer. **Personal:** Born Eastville, VA; daughter of Abe Peed and Alice Watson; children: Troi Eric. **Educ:** Drake Col Bus, attended 1969; Radio Sales Univ, Radio Advert Bur, dipl, 1988; NJ Realty Inst, dipl, 1989; Kean Univ, BS, mgt sci, MPA, pub admin, 1997. **Career:** CBS/WCAU-TV Channel 10, sales asst, 1970-75, prod asst, news prod asst, 1975-77, newswriter & reporter, 1977-79; WNJR Radio, dir pub rel & news editorials, 1979-80, prog dir, 1980-81, vpres & prog dir, 1981-82, vpres & sta mgr, 1982-92; Realty World Prof Assoc, Scotch Plains, NJ, realtor assoc, 1989; Kean Univ, Ctr Integration Math & Sci, Reform Teacher Educ Proj, adminr, New Vistas Prog, prog recruiter, instr, 1997-, managing asst dir, 2014-. **Orgs:** Bd dir, Future Devel Group, 1986; bd dir, New York Mkt Radio Braodcasters Asn, 1989; Nat Asn Broadcasters; Nat Asn Black Owned Broadcasters; Radio Advert Bur; Greater Newark Chamber Com; pres, Pi Alpha Alpha Hon Soc; Am Soc Pub Admin; Nat Women's Polit Caucus; Am Acad Broadcasting; advisor, Omega Phi Chi Multicultural Sorority; ct app spec advocate, CASA Union County, 2015. **Home Addr:** 948 W 8th St, Plainfield, NJ 07060, **Home Phone:** (908)561-4577. **Business Addr:** Managing Assistant Director, Instructor, Kean University, 1000 Morris Ave, Union, NJ 07083, **Business Phone:** (908)737-3823.

**SATCHELL, ERNEST R.**
Chairperson, educator. **Personal:** Born Jul 29, 1941, Exmore, VA; married Elsa Martin; children: Kwame & Keita. **Educ:** Md State Col, BS, art educ, 1959; Towson State Col, MEd, art educ, 1971, MFA, 1988; St Josephs Col, Philadelphia. **Career:** Chairman (retired); Boeing Aircraft Co, tech illusr; Boeing Vertol Corp, Philadelphia, com art dir; Va Hosp, Philadelphia, art rapist; Univ MD, Eastern Shore, chair, 1974-88, art coordr, 1988-99, chair, fine arts dept, 1999-2010, prof, chmn & instr ceramics, 1971-2010. **Orgs:** Nat Conf Artists; Ant Art Educ Assoc; Md State Teachers asn; NEA; Alpha Phi Alpha; bd dir, Somerset Co Art asn; Union Baptist Church, Comm Higher Educ; chmn, State Art Credit Count Comt, 1985-87. **Honors/Awds:** Pennsylvania State Univ, 1971; One man Show, Academy of the Arts, Easton, Md, 1974; Exhibits Towson State Col, 1974. **Home Addr:** 31268 Williams Rd, PO Box 1022 UMES, Princess Anne, MD 21853-3664, **Home Phone:** (410)651-3094.

**SATCHELL, LIZ. See SATCHELL, ELIZABETH.**

**SATCHER, BOBBY. See SATCHER, DR. ROBERT LEE, JR.**

**SATCHER, DR. DAVID**
Government official, health services administrator. **Personal:** Born Mar 2, 1941, Anniston, AL; son of Wilmer and Anna; married Nola; children: Gretchen, David, Daraka & Daryl. **Educ:** Morehouse Col, BS, 1963; Case Western Res Univ, MD & PhD, cytogenetics, 1970; Strong Memorial Hosp, residential & fel training; Univ Rochester, residential & fel training; Univ Calif Los Angeles Sch Med, residential & fel training; Martin Luther King Jr-Harbor Hosp, residential & fel training. **Career:** Strong Mem Hosp, Univ Rochester, resident, 1971-72; King-Drew Med Ctr, dir, 1972-75; Charles Drew Post grad Med Sch, Macy fac fel, 1972-75; King-Drew Sickle Cell Ctr, assoc dir, 1973-75, asst prof, interim chmn, 1974-75; Univ Calif Los Angeles, Sch Med & Health, asst prof, 1974-76, resident, 1975-76; Charles R. Drew Postgrad Med Sch, interin dean, 1977-79; King-Drew Med Ctr, Morehouse Col, Sch Med, Dept Family Med, prof, chmn, 1979-82; Meharry Med Col, pres, 1982-93; Agency Toxic Substances & DisRegistry, adminr, dir, 1993-98; Ctr Dis Control, head, dir, 1993-98; US Asst Secy Health, 1998-2001; US Health & Human Serv Dept, asst secy Health, Surgeon Gen, PHS, 1998-2002; Nat Ctr Primary Care Morehouse Sch Med, dir, 2002-04; Morehouse Sch Med, Nat Health Ctr, head, 2004-06, interim pres, 2004-06; Nat Cancer Inst, Ctr Reduce Cancer Health Disparities, proj invest; King-Drew Sickle Cell Res Ctr, dir. **Orgs:** Med dir, Second Baptist Free Clin; Am Acad Family Physicians, Am Soc Human Genetics; bd dir, Soc Teachers Fam Med, Joint Bd Family Pract Ga, Phi Beta Kappa chap Delta, 1977; Alpha Omega Alpha Hon Med Soc; AAAS; Am Cancer Soc; AMA; Am Health Asn; Nat Med Asn; Nat Asn Advan Colored People; Urban League; bd dir, First Am Bank Nashville; vis comn mem, Univ Ala, Sch Med; bd dir trustee, Carnegie Found Advan Teaching; Inst Med; Nat Acad Sci; Alpha Omega Alpha; surgeon gen & asst secy, US Dept Health & Human Serv, 1998-2001; 4 star adm, US Pub Health Serv Comn Corps; bd mem, Johnson & Johnson, 2002-13; bd dir, Metrop Life Ins Co, 2007-; trustee, Starbright Found; bd dir, Henry J Kaiser Family Found; bd dir, Am Found Suicide Prev; dir, MetLife Inc, 2007-13; dir, Ctr Excellence Health Disparities; dir, Satcher Health Leadership Inst; co-chair, Adv Comt Pub Issues Ad Coun; sr vis fel, Kaiser Family Found. **Home Addr:** 12 N Dr, Bethesda, MD 20814. **Business Addr:** Board of Director, Metropolitan Life Insurance Co, 1 Madison Ave, New York, NY 10010.

**SATCHER, DR. ROBERT LEE, SR.**
Administrator, educator, college president. **Personal:** Born Sep 18, 1937, Anniston, AL; son of Wilmer and Anna Curry; married Marian Hanna; children: Serena, Robert Jr, Rodney & Robin. **Educ:** Ala State Univ, BS, 1959; Ariz State Univ, MS, 1963; Ore State Univ, PhD, 1971; Univ Mo; Okla Univ; Tufts Univ; Tex A&M Univ; Mass Inst Technol. **Career:** Educator, administrator (retired); Booker T Wash HS, sci & math inst, 1959-62; Ala State Univ, inst, chem, phys sci, 1963-65; Hampton Inst, chief planning officer, instr to assoc prof, chem, 1965-79; Tororo Women Col, Uganda, E Africa, prof chem, sci adv, 1973; Voorhees Col, exec vp, acad dean, prof chem, 1979-82; Fisk Univ, interim pres, 1984, acad dean & provost, prof chem, 1982-88; St Paul's Col, actg pres & provost, 1988-89, vpres, acad affairs & provost, 1988-92, prof chem, 1988, interim pres, exec adv, pres, 2007-12; Frances Emily Hunt Trust Summer Sci & MathInstitute, dir; Johnson-Johnson Found Saturday Sci Acad, dir; Nat Asn Advan Colored People, advisor; St Paul's Memorial Chapel Sunday Sch Prog, advisor & Supt. **Orgs:** Fel Ford Found, 1969-71; fel acad admin Am Coun Educ, 1975-76; consult, USOE/AIDP, Univ Asn, Wash, DC, 1975-78; Moton Inst Capahosic Va, 1977; external eval, Tenn State Univ, 1977-81; Comn Cols SACS, Atla GA, 1978-86; Norfolk State Univ, 1980-83; eval Title III, US Dept Educ WA, 1980-; Pres, Conf Acad Deans Southern States, SACS, 1990; Oper Push; Nat Asn Advan Colored People; SCLC; Am Nuclear Soc; AKM Nat Hon Soc; BKX Nat Hon Sci Soc; Nat Inst Sci; AAAS; Soc Col & Univ Planning; AIR; Beta Kappa Chi Nat Hon Sci Soc; Alpha Kappa Mu Hon Soc; Omega Psi Phi Fraternity; bd trustee, Community Memorial Health Ctr; Indust Develop Authority Brunswick County; bd dir, Brunswick County Fed Teachers Credit Union. **Honors/Awds:** Fel grants, US Atomic Energy Comn, Ford Found, 1968-71; Rockfeller Found, 1975-76; NIH grantee, 1972-77; Citizen of the Year, Zeta Omicron Chap, Omega Psi Phi, 1977; Change Mag, 1978; Silver Beaver, BSA, 1988; Outstanding Service Award, Epsilon Gamma Chapter; Omega Man of the Year, Omicron Omega Chapter, Omega Psi Phi, 1990; Outstanding Service Award, Omega Psi Phi, 1992; Outstanding Service Award, CIC, Wash, DC, 1992; NSF. **Special Achievements:** Author of many books & articles. **Home Addr:** PO Box 806, Lawrenceville, VA 23868-0806, **Home Phone:** (804)848-2259. **Business Addr:** President, Saint Paul's College, 115 College Dr, Lawrenceville, VA 23868, **Business Phone:** (434)848-3111.

**SATCHER, DR. ROBERT LEE, JR. (BOBBY SATCHER)**
Medical scientist, surgeon, astronaut. **Personal:** Born Sep 22, 1965, Hampton, VA; son of Robert and Marian; married DJuanna O White; children: Daija & Robert III. **Educ:** Mass Inst Technol, BS, chem engineering, 1986; Mass Inst Technol, PhD, chem engineering, 1993; Harvard Med Sch, MD, health scis & technol div, 1994. **Career:** Mass Inst Technol, Cambridge, MA, postdoctoral res, 1993-94; Univ Calif, San Francisco, CA, internship gen surg, 1994-95, postdoctoral res fel, 1997-98; Univ Calif, San Francisco, CA, resident orthop surg, 1995-2000; Univ Calif, Berkeley, CA, postdoctoral res fel, 1997-98; Univ Fla, Gainesville, orthop oncol fel, 2000-01; Robert H Lurie Comprehensive Cancer Ctr, Inst Bioengineering & Nanotechnology Advan Med, Northwestern Univ, asst prof, orthopaedic surg, currently; Feinberg Sch Med, Dept Orthopaedic surg, asst prof, 2001-08; C Memorial Hosp Chicago, Ill, orthopaedic oncol, prof, 2001-08; Univ Fla, Musculoskeletal Oncol, fel, 2001; Northwestern Univ, biomed engineering, asst prof, 2002-08; El DuPont de Nemours & Co Inc, Wilmington, Del, internships; NASA, Lyndon B Johnson Space Ctr, astronaut, 2004-11; Univ Tex MD Anderson Cancer Ctr, clin asst prof, currently. **Orgs:** Founder & dir Sarcoma Conf, Robert H Lurie Comprehensive Cancer Ctr, Feinberg Sch Med, Northwestern Univ; Black Alumni MIT; Harvard Alumni Asn; vice chmn, Orthop Res Soc; Hinton-Wright Biomed Soc Steering Comt, Harvard Med Sch; Tau Beta Pi Eng Hon Soc; fel Albert Schweitzer Hosp; leadership fel Am Acad Orthopaedic Surgeons; ABC fel Am Orthopaedic Asn; fel UNCF/Merck Res; fel Robert Wood Johnson Found; bloomberg leadership fel Johns Hopkins Univ; Musculoskeletal Tumor Soc; Am Acad Cancer Res; Connective Tissue Oncol Soc; Nat Med Asn; Soc Black Acad Surgeons; Doctors United Med Missions; Nat Comprehensive Cancer Network; bd, CSTEM; Nat Soc Black Engrs; Am Inst Chem Engineering. **Home Addr:** 539 Wisteria St, Bellaire, TX 77401. **Business Addr:** Clinical Assistant Professor, The University of Texas MD Anderson Cancer Center, 1515 Holcombe Blvd, Houston, TX 77030, **Business Phone:** (713)792-2121.

**SATTERFIELD, HON. PATRICIA POLSON**
Supreme court justice. **Personal:** Born Jul 10, 1942, Christchurch, VA; daughter of Thea A Polson and Grady H Polson (deceased); married Preston T; children: Danielle Nicole. **Educ:** Howard Univ, BME, 1964; Ind Univ, MM, 1967; St Johns Univ Sch Law, JD, 1977. **Career:** Sewanhaka High Sch Dist, vocal music teacher, 1968-77; UCS Coun Off Ct Admin, asst dep coun, sr coun, 1978-90; Unified Ct Syst State New York, queens county, judge, 1991-94; New York Supreme Ct, actg supreme ct justice, 1994-98, supreme ct justice, 1998-2011. **Orgs:** St John's Univ, Cult Diversity Comm, Sch Law, 1991-; bd dir, law alumni, 1991-; co-chair, bd dir, Queens Women's Network, 1983-90; bd dir, Human Resources Ctr St Albans, 1990-; Asn Women Judges, 1991-; Metrop Black Lawyers Asn, 1988-; Queens Co Bar Asn, 1989-; pres, Jack & Jill Am Inc Queens Co, 1978-87; St Albans Congregational Ch, United Ch Christ, 1996-; pres, Greater Queens Chapt Links Inc, 1998-; Nat Asn Advan Colored People; Calvary Baptist Church. **Honors/Awds:** Alva T Starforth, Outstanding Teacher of the Year, 1976; Outstanding Community Leader of the Year, Alpha Kappa Alpha, Epsilon Omega Chap, 1991; Ascension to Bench, Queens Co Women's Bar Asn, 1991. **Special Achievements:** First African-American woman judge elected in Queens County, NY, 1990. **Home Addr:** 13157 230th St, Laurelton, NY 11413-1831, **Home Phone:** (718)712-4110.

**SATTERWHITE, DR. FRANK JOSEPH OMOWALE**
President (organization), executive, founder (originator). **Personal:** Born Oct 3, 1942, Akron, OH; son of Arthur and Ethel Gindraw; children: Frank Jr, Kuntu, Onira & Kai. **Educ:** Howard Univ, BA, educ, 1965; Southern Ill Univ, MS, col admin, 1967; Stanford Univ, PhD, col admin, 1975. **Career:** Western Regional Off, col entrance exam bd, assoc dir, 1968-71; Oberlin Col, african am studies, assoc dean & chmn, 1971-72; Ravenswood City Sch Dist, asst to supt & actg supt, 1972-76; Community Develop Inst, pres, 1978-; W.K.Kellogg Found, kellogg nat fel, 1986-89; Community Develop Inst, bd dir; Nat Community Develop Inst, founder & sr advisor, 2000-10; Appl Mgt & Orgn Serv, founder & pres, 2010-; Leadership Inc, founder & pres, 2012-. **Orgs:** Councilman, EPA Munic Coun, 1974-78; Narobi Secretarat, 1979-85; planning comn, SMC Planning Comn, 1980-83; BAPAC, 1981-85; Mid-Peninsula Urban Coalition, 1982-85; councilman, EPA City Coun, 1983-85; chair, Alliance Nonprofit Mgt. **Home Addr:** 2275 Euclid Ave, East Palo Alto, CA 94303, **Home Phone:** (650)322-7072. **Business Addr:** Founder & Senior Advisor, National Community Development Institute, 321 Bell St, East Palo Alto, CA 94303, **Business Phone:** (650)327-5846.

**SAULNY, CYRIL B.**
Association executive. **Personal:** married LaVerne. **Educ:** Xavier Univ, La, attended 1983. **Career:** Nat Asn Advan Colored People, New Orleans chap, pres, 1997-2002; Cadre Bus Solutions LLC, owner, currently. **Home Addr:** 3611 Franklin Ave, New Orleans, LA 70122, **Home Phone:** (318)238-2054. **Business Addr:** Owner, Cadre Business Solutions LLC, 1827 St Philip St, New Orleans, LA 70116, **Business Phone:** (504)822-4874.

**SAULSBERRY, CHARLES R.**
Lawyer. **Personal:** Born Sep 4, 1957, Goshen, AL; son of Asia William and Ruby Lee; married Dana Scott; children: Kara E & Kalyn S. **Educ:** Harvard Univ, AB, 1979; Northwestern Univ, Sch Law, JD, 1982. **Career:** Winston & Strawn, summer assoc, 1980-81, assoc, partner, 1982-92; Parker, Chapin, Flattau & Klimpl, summer assoc, 1981; Thompson & Mitchell, partner, 1992-2000; Stinson Morrison Hecker LLP, partner, 2000-02; Husch Blackwell Sanders Peper Martin, partner, 2002-05; Leadership Roundtable, St. Louis, 2005-09; Saulsberry & Assocs LLC, managing partner, 2005-; Stud Funded Pub Interest Fels Inc, pres. **Orgs:** Chicago Comt Minorities Large Law Firms, 1990-92; Bar Asn Metrop, St Louis; bd mem, St.Louis Black Leadership Roundtable, 1995-2013; Chicago Coun Lawyers, secy, bd, 1985-86; Cabrini Green Legal Assistance Found, bd, 1985-86; Minority Legal Educ Resources Inc, secy, bd, 1986-87; Am Bar Asn; Ill State Bar Asn; Nat Basketball Asn; Chicago Bar Asn; Cook County Bar Asn; Nat Asn Securities Prof; interim chief exec officer, vice chair, bd mem, St Louis Black Leadership Round table, 2005-09. **Honors/Awds:** Outstanding Student, Coun Legal Opportunities Comn, 1979; Earl Warren Scholar, Earl Warren Found, 1979; Visionary Award, St Louis Leadership Round table, 2001; Regional Small Business Advocate of the Year, SBA, 2002; Outstanding Volunteer Award, Hopewell Ctr Inc, 2005. **Special Achievements:** Bond counsel to city of Chicago on $489, 735, 000, O'Hare International Terminal special revenue bonds, 1990; underwriters' counsel on over $1.9 billion housing bonds for Illinois Housing Development Authority, 1984-91.Outstanding Young St. Louisans Award, 1995. **Home Addr:** 11100 Apache Trl, St. Louis, MO 63146, **Home Phone:** (314)872-8807. **Business Addr:** Managing Partner, Saulsberry & Associates LLC, 11469 Olive Blvd Suite 252, St. Louis, MO 63141, **Business Phone:** (314)560-6123.

**SAULSBY, LINDA E.** See GASTON, LINDA SAULSBY.

**SAULTER, GILBERT JOHN**
Executive. **Personal:** Born Apr 20, 1936, Seattle, WA; son of Bernice and Gerald; married Mae Frances; children: Bradford, Melonie & Daryl. **Educ:** Univ Wash, BSEE, 1962; Univ Calif Los Angeles; Univ Wash. **Career:** Executive (retired); Boeing Co, engr aid, 1958-62; Northrop, 1962-65; Itek, 1965-67; Sundstrand Data Control, 1967-71; Harvard Univ, regist prof engr, 1969, sr mgt prog, 1988; US dept Labor, saf engr, 1971-74, area dir, 1974-76, reg admin Nebr Region, 1976-78, reg admin, SW Region, 1978-95, eng consul; Desoto City Planning & Zoning Comn, comnr, 1996-98, councilman, 1998-2001. **Orgs:** Chmn, YMCA Youth Comn; Indian Guide prog, 1970; vice chmn, adv comm Boy Scouts Am, 1970-74;Nat Asn Advan Colored People; Kappa Alphi Psi; pres, Nw Counc Black Prof Engrs; Opportunity Industrialization Ctr, 1985-88; US deleg Petrol Conf, Lagos, Nigeria, 1985; chief, US deleg Int Labor Orgn Geneva, Switz, 1986; Class Guitar Soc, 1986-87; Family Pl, 1987-90; chmn, Dallas & Ft Worth Combined Fed Campaign, 1989-91; chmn, DFW Fed Exec Bd, 1993-94; head, US deleg NAFTA Joint Tech Conf Safety Health Petrochemical Indust, Edmonds, Can, 1994. **Home Addr:** 9804 Clocktower Ct, Plano, TX 75025-6583, **Home Phone:** (972)396-1343.

**SAUNDERS, BARBARA ANN**
Tour guide, administrator. **Personal:** Born Jun 5, 1950, Roanoke, VA; married Byron Creighton. **Educ:** Hampton Univ, VA, BA, fine arts, 1972. **Career:** Amer Security Bank, Wash, DC, cust serv rep, 1973-75; freelance writer; Ga Dept Ind, Trade & Tourism, acct asst, 1975-76, pr prog coord, 1980-90; Ga Film & Videotape Off, pr specialist, 1976-80; freelance com voice-over talent, 1985-; tour & travel develop asst dir, 1990-94; tourism mktg consult, 1994; Southern int Press ctr, 1996; Arthur M Blank Family Found, prog assoc, 2002, prog officer, 2002-08; Atlanta Symphony Orchestra Talent Develop Prog, dir found rels, 2008-12; Abraham J. & Phyllis Katz Found, grants & prog mgr, 2012-. **Orgs:** Pres, Sigma Gamma Nu Social Club, Hampton Univ, 1971; bd mem, WomenFilm-Atlanta, 1977-79. **Home Addr:** 430 Lindbergh Dr NE A3, Atlanta, GA 30305. **Business Addr:** Grants & Program Manager, Abraham J & Phyllis Katz Foundation, 25001 Emery Rd Suite 150, Cleveland, OH 44128-5632, **Business Phone:** (216)896-0360.

**SAUNDERS, DAVID J.**
Executive, chief executive officer. **Personal:** Born Jun 28, 1951, Washington, DC; married Sharon; children: David Jr, Santosha & Michael. **Educ:** Univ Toledo, BA, bus; Carnegie Mellon Univ, Grad Sch Indus Admin. **Career:** Burroughs Corp, 1971; Sara Lee, vpres & gen mgr, serv oper, 2000-06; Venue Int Professionals Inc, co-founder & chief exec officer, currently. **Orgs:** Bd dir, Dist Columbia Chamber Com; vice chairperson, Int Trade Comt; vice chairperson, Int Travel Tourism Comt; Black Pres Round table Asn; nat bd dir, Blacks Govt; spec advisor, Howard Univ's Small Bus Develop Ctr; Small Bus Admin; Africa Travel Asn; pres, ATA's Mid-Atlantic Chap, 1997-2000; assoc mem, ATA Int Bd Dir; Const Adv Comt, Strategic Planning Comt, Educ & Training Comt; dir, Mgt & Admin Serv Constituency Africa. **Business Addr:** Chief Executive Officer, Co-Founder, Venue International Professionals Inc, PO Box 1872, Clinton, MD 20735, **Business Phone:** (301)856-9188.

**SAUNDERS, DR. ELIJAH**
Physician, educator. **Personal:** Born Dec 9, 1934, Baltimore, MD; married Sharon; children: Kevin, Donna, Monzella, Veronica & Kyle. **Educ:** Morgan State Col, BS, 1956; Univ Md, Sch Med, MD, 1960. **Career:** Univ Md Hosp, intern, 1960-61, asst res, 1961-63, fel, 1960-65; Md Gen Hosp, asso cardiol, 1965-84; Univ Md, Sch Hosp, instr, 1965-84, prof, Hypertension div, 1984-, clin dir hypertension & vascular biol ctr; pvt pract, 1965-; Provident Hosp, chief cardiol, 1966-84, dir, 1968, chief, 1969-71, actg chief, 1973-75; Meharry Med Col, Nashville, Tenn, clin assoc prof med; Univ Md, grad med educ & affiliations, vpres. **Orgs:** Num pos; Am Heart Asn; Cent MD Chap, MD Affil, Nat Dallas; chmn, Nat Scholar Fund; Unit Ch Jesus Christ Apost; Med & Chirurgi Fac MD; AMA; Pres Med Staff, Provident Hosp, 1966-74; admsns com Univ MD, 1970-75; Ed Bd, Spirit; trste bd, 1st Un Ch Jesus Christ Apost; chmn, steer com Hyperten Contr Prog; chmn, Adv Coun MD Related end right factors; Hyperten Contr Prog; MD Soc Cardiol; Am Col Physician; fel Am Col Cardiol; fel Am Col Angiol; chmn, lifetime hon trustee, Int Socs Hypertension Blacks; adv coun, Nat Heart Lung & Blood Inst, Nat Insts Health; founding mem, chmn bd, pres Asn Black Cardiologists; Urban Cardiol Res Ctr Inc; co-founder, Heart House Am Col Cardiol; pres, Md High Blood Pressure Coord Coun; charter mem, Am Socs Hypertension; num other asns & com; fel Am Heart Asn; Asn Acad Minority Physicians; Ama; Nat Med Asn; Baltimore City Med Soc; Med Alumni Asn Univ Md; cofounded, Univ Players Orchestra. **Honors/Awds:** Bronze Service Medal; Presidential Award, Maryland Affiliates, 1975; Pres Plaque Cent MD Heart Asn, 1975; Silver Distinguished Service Medal, 1976, Am Heart Asn; House Resol 15 Del Webs, 1976; fel, Am Col Cardiol, 1976; Distinguished Leadership Plaque, MD High Blood Pressure Coordinating Coun, 1982; Outstanding Achievement in Health Care Award, Black Nurses Asn Baltimore, 1985; Marcus Garve Memorial Found Plaque, 1987; Louis B Russell Award, Award of Merit, Am Heart Asn, MD Affiliate, 1991; Honoree of the Year, Am Heart Asn, 1991; Doctor of the Year, Jentry McDonald Sr Group Home, 1991; Honoree, Nat Kidney Found MD, 1994; Keynote Speaker, Egyptian Hypertension League & Israel Hypertension Comt Prog, 1994; People Who Make Things Happen, Baltimore Times, 1995; Top Doctors, Baltimore Mag, 1995; Community Service Award, Baltimore City Med Soc, 1996; Louis B Russell Award, Am Heart Asn, 1998; Lifetime Achievement Award, Consortium Southeastern Hypertension Control, 1998; Morgan State University Hall Fame, 1998; Community Service Award, NCP, 1999; hon doctorate, Med Univ SC, 1999; Alumni Hall of Fame Award, Morgan State Univ, 2000; Plaque featuring special report The Doctor Are In, Black Enterprise, 2001; received many honorary awards; Herbert W. Nickens Award, Asn Am Med Cols, 2011. **Special Achievements:** Author & Producer of Numerous film strips; Numerous appearances on TV & radio; First African American Resident In Internal Medicine, Univ Md Sch Med, 1960; First African American Cardiologist, State Md, 1965. **Home Addr:** 2310 Cavesdale Rd, Owings Mills, MD 21117, **Home Phone:** (410)363-0482. **Business Addr:** Professor of Medicine & Cardiology, Head of the Division of Hypertension, University of Maryland, 419 W Redwood St Suite 620, Baltimore, MD 21201, **Business Phone:** (410)328-4366.

**SAUNDERS, DR. ELIZABETH ANN**
Teacher, educator, executive director. **Personal:** Born Apr 12, 1948, Centralia, IL; daughter of George (deceased) and Nyla. **Educ:** Freed Hardeman Univ, AA, bus admin, 1967; Memphis State Univ, BS, bus educ, 1970, MS, reading, 1975; E Tenn State Univ, EdD, supv & admin, 1983. **Career:** Haywood High Jr Div, Brownsville, instr eng & reading lab, teacher, 1970-76; Anderson Grammar Sch, Brownsville, instr reading, 1976-77; Haywood High Sch, teacher, 1976-78; Haywood High Sch, Brownsville, Tenn, instr eng & reading, 1977-78; E Tenn State Univ, doctoral fel, 1981-83; Freed Hardman Univ, Henderson, Tenn, acad advr & prof interdisciplinary studies & educ, 1983-2001, instr, teacher, 1978-81; Freed-Hardeman Univ, prog dir, prof educ, 2001-02 & 2014-, dir grad studies, 2002-14. **Orgs:** Alpha Kappa, 1969-; HEA/WTEA/TEA/NEA, 1970-78; Tenn Asn Super & Curric Develop, 1978-; Int Reading Asn, 1979-; Nat Asn Advan Colored People; comn chmn, FHC Women's Club & Stud Rels Comn, Fac Self-Study Comn, 1979-; teacher, Lucyville Church Christ; Am Pers & Guid Asn, 1980; bible sch teacher, Educ Comt, N Henderson Church Christ; speaker, Ladies Day Prog; speaker, Christian Singles Conf; chester county adv bd, Carl Perkins Ctr; henderson bd, Aldermen, 1989-2002; adv bd mem, Chester County Mid Sch; mem bd dir, African Christian Schs; Am Asn Cols Teacher Educ; Int Reading Asn; Tenn Asn Cols Teacher Educ; Tenn Conf Grad Schs. **Home Addr:** 154 N Carolina Ave, Henderson, TN 38340. **Business Addr:** Director of Graduate Studies, Professor of Education, Freed-Hardeman University, 158 E Main St Rm Gardner Ctr 02A, Henderson, TN 38340, **Business Phone:** (731)989-6087.

**SAUNDERS, JERRY, SR.**
Association executive, executive. **Personal:** Born Apr 23, 1953, Columbus, OH; son of Earl and Rosalie; married Gayle; children: Jerry Jr. **Educ:** Ohio Wesleyan Univ Upward Bound, cert, 1971; Oberlin Col, BA, 1975; Ohio State Univ, attended 1976. **Career:** Futon Corp, draftsman, 1976-77; Las Vegas Dealers Basketball Team, player, 1977-79; Ohio Wesleyan Univ, assoc dir Upward Bound, 1979-80; JC Penney Ins, ins adjuster, 1980-87; Eldon W Ward YMCA, exec dir, 1987-97; UCAN Networks, owner, 1997; Africentric Personal Develop Shop Inc, Columbus, Ohio, pres & chief exec officer, 1997-; Saunders Co, managing partner, 2014-. **Orgs:** Unique Community & Neighborhood Networks, 1989-; Columbus Urban League, 1991-95; chmn trustee bd, Flintridge Baptist Church, 1979-; adv bd, Columbus Pub Schs, 1991-; prog dir, MVP Basketball Camps, 1989-; prog coordr, Make Right Choice, 1992-; chmn, Blue Chip Mag Awards Gala, 1992-; chmn, 100 Black Men, Cent Ohio; chmn, Compassionate Commun Cent Ohio; bd trustee, Columbus City Schs Educ Found; Ohio State Univ Youth Violence Prev Adv Bd; Pickerington Schs 21st Century Adv Bd; Community Properties Ohio 'Bridges Out Poverty' Steering Comt; bd trustee, Mid Ohio Stranger Abduction Alert; chmn, After-Sch All-Stars Columbus Bd trustee; bd trustee, Franklin County C Serv; Franklin County Bd Ment Retardation & Develop Disabilities. **Home Addr:** 1681 Bryden Rd, Columbus, OH 43205.

**Business Addr:** Chief Executive Director, President, Africentric Personal Development Shop, 1409 E Livingston Ave, Columbus, OH 43205, **Business Phone:** (614)253-4448.

### SAUNDERS, JOHN EDWARD, III
State government official, executive director, chief executive officer. **Personal:** Born Jan 17, 1945, Bryn Mawr, PA; son of John Edward and Eleanor Smith; married Vivian E Williams; children: John Edward IV, Jason Elliott & Shanna Marie. **Educ:** Cent State Univ, BS, bus admin, 1968; LaSalle Col & Univ Pa, Social Serv Agency Mgt Educ & Develop Prog, cert, 1982; IBM Comm Exec Sem, cert, 1982; Lincoln Univ, MA, human serv admin, 1983; Duke Univ, Sanford Inst Pub Policy, Strategic Leadership Sem, 1993. **Career:** Dun & Bradstreet Inc, credit analyst, 1972-76; Urban League Philadelphia, prog dir, 1976-78, sr vpres, 1978-83; Urban League Greater Hartford Inc, pres & chief exec officer, 1983-88; Hartford Health Network Inc, chmn, 1984-88; Almada Lodge Times Farm Camp Corp, bd mem, 1985-; Oper Fuel Inc, chmn, 1986-97; State Conn, dep labor comnr, 1988-97; Nat Forum Black Pub Adminr, Washington, DC, exec dir, 1997-. **Orgs:** Fel Am Leadership Forum Hartford, 1985; corporator, St Francis Hosp, 1986-96; bd mem, Conn Prison Asn, 1986-92; bd mem, World Affairs Coun, 1986-90; bd mem, Conn Law Enforcement Found, 1987-90; trustee, Watkinson Sch, 1987-; bd mem, Sci Mus Conn, 1988-96; trustee, Watkinson Sch, 1988-96; bd mem, Salvation Army, 1990-; trustee, IST Living, 1992; vice chmn, Am Lendership Forum, 1992; Hartford Rotary Club; Asn Black Social Workers; Conn Civil Rights Coord Community; Tuscan Lodge 17; F&AM; Pulmonary Hypertension Asn; bd dir, Nat Urban Fellows; bd dir, Nat Forum Black Pub Adminr; fel Nat Acad Pub Admin. **Home Addr:** 2505 James Monroe Cir, Herndon, VA 20171. **Business Addr:** Executive Director, Board of Director, National Forum Black Public Administrators, 777 N Capitol St NE Suite 807, Washington, DC 20002-4239, **Business Phone:** (202)408-9300.

### SAUNDERS, JOHN P.
Television show host, broadcaster. **Personal:** Born Feb 2, 1955, Toronto, ON; married Wanda R; children: 2. **Educ:** Western Mich Univ, attended 1976; Ryerson Univ, attended 1977. **Career:** CKNS Radio, news dir, 1978; CKNY-TV, sports anchor, 1978-79; ATV News, anchor, 1979-80; ESPN, host basketball & hockey, 1986-, sportscenter, journalist, currently; Toronto Raptors, Play-by-play announcer, 1995-2001; ABC Sports, host football & baseball, 1990-. **Orgs:** Bd mem & tireless advocate, Jimmy V Found. **Home Addr:** 150 Pinecrest Dr, Hastings On Hudson, NY 10706-3702. **Business Addr:** Journalist, ESPN, 935 Middle St ESPN Plz, Bristol, CT 06010, **Business Phone:** (860)766-2000.

### SAUNDERS, KIM D.
President (organization), chief executive officer. **Educ:** Univ Pa, BS, finance & econs, 1982. **Career:** Enterprise Fed Savings Bank, exec vpres & chief lending officer, 1995-98; City First Bank, Wash, DC, exec vpres & chief lending officer, 1998-2003; Greater Richmond Chamber Com, bd mem; Abigail Adams Nat BanCorp Inc; Consol Bank & Trust Co, pres & chief exec officer, 2003-07; Mech & Farmers Bank, chief exec officer & pres, 2007-14; M&F Bancorp Inc, chief exec officer & pres, 2007-; Eads Group Inc, pres & chief exec officer, 2014-. **Orgs:** Va Fair Housing Bd; bd mem, St Catherine's Sch; bd mem, World Affairs Coun; bd mem, Bon Secours Richmond Health Syst; vice chair, Richmond Renaissance; bd mem, Va Biotech Res Pk Corp; St Catherines Sch; World Affairs Coun; bd mem, Mech & Farmers Bank, 2008-; bd mem, M&F Bancorp Inc, 2009-; bd dir, Va Housing Develop Authority; bd dir, Va Port Authority; adv coun, Fed Res Bank Richmond; Fed Deposit Ins Corp; bd dir, Nc Chamber Com; bd dir, Nat Bankers Asn; found treas, Nc Mus Art; bd visitor, Wake Forest Baptist Health; Consumer Financial Protection Bur. **Business Addr:** President, Chief Executive Officer, Mechanics & Farmers Bank, 2634 Durham Chapel Hill Blvd, Durham, NC 27707, **Business Phone:** (919)687-7800.

### SAUNDERS, PROF. RAYMOND JENNINGS
Educator, artist. **Personal:** Born Oct 28, 1934, Pittsburgh, PA. **Educ:** Carnegie Inst Technol, BFA, 1960; Calif Col Arts & Crafts, MFA, 1961. **Career:** Calif State Univ, prof emer, 1962-89; Guggenheim fel, 1976; Calif Col Arts & Crafts, prof, 1989-; Solo exhibs: "New Works", Stephen Wirtz Gallery, 1999; Cooley Memorial Art Gallery, Reed Col, Portland, 2000; "Paintings & Works Paper", Stephen Wirtz Gallery, 2001; "Raymond Saunders", Centre Jerome Cuzin a AUCH, France, 2002; Gallery Resche, Paris, France, 2004. **Home Addr:** , Oakland, CA. **Business Addr:** Professor of Painting, Drawing, California College of Arts & Crafts, 1111 8th St, San Francisco, CA 94107-2247, **Business Phone:** (415)703-9500.

### SAUNDERS, VINCENT E., III
Financial manager, vice president (organization). **Personal:** Born Jan 28, 1954, Chicago, IL; son of Vincent E Jr and Doris Elaine; married Lynette M Smith; children: Vincent IV, Asia Imani & Evan Paul. **Educ:** Howard Univ, Wash, DC, BA, AA, studies, econ, pol sci, 1976; Inst Financial Educ, Chicago, IL, cert, 1980; Dept Defense, Equal Opportunity Mgt Inst Grad, 1988; Univ Ill, Chicago, pub admin, 1989; Keller Grad Sch Mgt, Chicago, IL, MBA, finance, 1997. **Career:** Citibank, FSB, sr financial serv Rep, asst br mgr, 1978-86; 126th Air Refueling Wing IL Air Nat Guard, exec officer, 1983-99; Drexel Nat Bank, Retail Banking, dept mgr & vpres, 1986-89; Midway Airport Concessionaires, off admin & info syst, mgr, 1989-97; Environ Protection Agency, fin specialist, 1997-2001, admin officer, 2001-02, budget analyst, 2002-05, div budget coordr, 2005-12, Info & Technol Sect, Superfund Div, chief, 2012-; Tuskegee Airmen Inc, nat treas, 2010-11. **Orgs:** Fin secy, Alpha Phi Alpha Fraternity, 1986-88; bd mem, Elliot Donnelley Chicago Youth Ctr, 1986-89; asst scout master, Boy Scouts Am, 1998-2001; vpres, Chicago Chap Tuskegee Airmen, 1998-2010; Toastmasters Int, CTM, 1999-2003; Chicago chap, Nat Black MBA Asn; chap treas, New Kemet Harambe Chap, Blacks Govt; chap treas, Chicago Chap Tuskegee Airman Inc; life mem, Nat Guard Asn US. **Honors/Awds:** Outstanding Young Men of America, US Jaycees, 1981; Up Coming Bus & Professionals, Dollars & Sense Magazine, 1989; Bronze Medal Superior Fin Serv, EPA, 2000. **Home Addr:** 9718 S Indiana Ave, Chicago, IL 60628-1442, **Home Phone:** (773)821-7696. **Business Addr:** Chief, Environmental Protection Agency, 77 W Jackson Blvd, Chicago, IL 60606, **Business Phone:** (312)353-9077.

### SAUNDERS, WILLIAM BILL
Commissioner, broadcaster. **Personal:** Born Feb 14, 1935, Johns Island, SC; married Henrietta J; children: William Jr, Sharon, Loretta, Kathleen, Byron, Gary, Alphea, Myra, Clinton & Tamara. **Educ:** Southern Bus Col, bus mgt, 1974; Southern Ill Univ, voc educ, 1978. **Career:** AM radio sta WPAL, co-owner, operator, 1972-98; Pub Serv Comn SC, First Dist, comnr, 1994-2004, chmn, 2000-02. **Orgs:** Pres, SC Broadcasters Asn, 1988; Nat Asn Broadcasters; Nat Asn Regulatory Utility Comt; Nat Water Comt; founding mem, Trident Urban League; Wesley United Methodist Church; founder & chief exec officer, Comt Better Racial Assurance; bd gov, Col Chas Bus Sch; Rotary Intl Breakfast Club; pres, YMCA, 1991; bd visitors, Charleston Southern Univ; Black Hall Fame; Admin Law-Fair Hearing, Univ NV. **Honors/Awds:** Broadcasters Hall of Fame; Malcolm D Haven Community Service Award; Harvey Gantt Award; Outstanding Service Award, Nat Asn Advan Colored People; Public Service Award, Arabian Temple No 139; Outstanding Service in the Arts Award, Links Inc; Outstanding Service Award, Delta Sigma Theta Sorority. **Special Achievements:** Featured in national media including The Today Show, New Yorker magazine, Black Enterprises, National Geographic, Redbook, The Washington Post & New York Times.

### SAUNDERS-HENDERSON, MARTHA M.
Educator, school administrator, museum director. **Personal:** Born Dec 18, 1924, Spartanburg, SC; daughter of Milderd Ruth Clemons and Alix Pinky; married Mark Jr; children: Sondra Jo Ann Jones, Woodrene Ruth, Markette Harris, Mark III & Alexis Lillian Marion. **Educ:** Burlington City Col, AA, 1978, AS, 1979; Southern Ill Univ, BS, 1982; Cent Mich Univ, MBA, 1983; Rutgers Univ, doctoral. **Career:** Gov Island Nursery Sch, dir, 1963; Girls Scouts Far E Okinowa, coordr, 1965; NJ, Pa Dept Ed, consult, 1970; Merabash Mus, vp & mus exec, 1970-, dir prog teaching spec sch, 1987, pres, 1989; Spec Serv Sch, NJ, instr, 1983-84; Merabash Mus, pres, 1983; Beverly City Sch, instr, NJ, 1984; Spec Sch, Mt Holly, teacher, 1986-87; Burlington County Col, Pemberton, NJ, instr, 1989; African Am Preserv, Hist Sites & Hist African Am, consult, 1989; Markette & Yaneek Creative Inc, 1989. **Orgs:** Bd trustee, Merabash Mus, 1969-85; Burlington Co Cult & Heritage, NJ, 1975; consult, Nj Art Asn, 1977-78; Burlington City Col, NJ, 1980-84; hon mem, Sigma Gamma Rho Sorority, 1986; consult, Burlington Co Cult & Heritage Ft Dix Black Hist Prog; Burlington Col Alumni Hall Fame; Union Co Col Fund Raising; Community Alert, WNET/Thirteen Comt Affairs Dept; African Am Mus Asn, Contemp Educ Arts & Cult Res Black C; Nat Asn Female Execs, Nat Fedn Presswomen, Nat Comt Artist Mem. **Home Addr:** 59 Emerald Lane, Willingboro, NJ 08046-2256. **Business Addr:** President, Merabash Museum, PO Box 752, Willingboro, NJ 08046-0752, **Business Phone:** (609)877-3177.

### SAVAGE, DENNIS JAMES
State government official. **Personal:** Born Jun 28, 1944; children: Dennis Jr. **Educ:** Cheney Univ, BA, sec educ, 1966; Temple Univ, post grad. **Career:** Chester, PA, teacher; Wilmington Sch Dist, teacher; Proj 70001, DE, teacher & coordr; 70001 Ltd, vpres; St bd educ, 2003; Del Off Community Serv, Dept Health & Social Serv, Div State Serv Centers, dir, currently. **Orgs:** Del Adv Coun Career Voc Educ; Christina Sch Dist Bd Educ; Adv Coun Fund Improv Post Sec Educ; Govs Adv Coun Future Educ. **Business Addr:** Director, Delaware Office of Community Services, Carvel State Office Bldg 820 N French St 4th Fl, Wilmington, DE 19801-3509.

### SAVAGE, DR. EDWARD W., JR.
Obstetrician, physician, educator. **Personal:** Born Jul 7, 1933, Macon, GA; son of Edward Warren and Mildred Eleanor; married Carole Avonne Porter; children: Cheryl, Racheal & Edward III. **Educ:** Talladega Col, AB, 1955; Meharry Med Col, MD, 1960; St Louis Univ, postgrad, 1955; State Univ NY, USPHS; cert, Am Bd Obstet & Gynecol, 1969; Spec Competence Gynecol Oncol, cert, 1974. **Career:** St Josephs Hosp Health Ctr, internship, 1960-61; State Univ NY Health Sci Ctr Brooklyn, resident, 1963-68; State Univ NY Downstate Med Ctr, from asst instr to instr, 1964-69; Univ IL Med Ctr, asst prof, 1969-73; Charles R Drew Post grad Med Sch, assoc prof, 1973-80, chief, Div Gyncol, 1983; King/Drew Med Ctr, med dir; Univ Calif, adj assoc prof, 1977, prof, 1986; Charles R Drew Post grad Med Sch, adj prof, currently; pvt pract physician. **Orgs:** Fel Downstate Med Ctr, 1967-69; Task Force Assessment Qual Health Care Am Col Obstet/Gynaecol, 1977-80; consult, Obstet/Gynaecol Albert Einstein Eval Unit Dept Health Educ & Welfare, 1973-76; consult, Obstet/Gynaecol Drew Ambulatory Care Rev Team Dept Health Educ & Welfare, 1973-76; consult, Obstet/Gynaecol State Calif Health Care Eval Sect Alternative Health Systs Div, 1975-77; consult, Albert F Mathieu Chrioepithelioma Registry S Calif Cancer Ctr, 1975; consult, Dept Health & Human Serv, 1980; consult, Obstet/Gynaecol Nat Inst Health, 1981; fel ACS; fel LAOG; N Med Asn; Pac Coast Obstet & Gynec Soc; ed bd, J Nat Med Asn, 1981; SGO; spec reviewer Obstet/J Am Med Asn, CHEST; fel Am Cong Obstetricians & Gynecologists; fel Am Col Surgeons. **Honors/Awds:** Dean's list Meharry Med Col, 1960; USPHS Postdoctoral Fel Gynecologic Cancer, 1967-69; Best Doctors in Am 1st Ed. **Special Achievements:** Numerous publs abstracts & presentations incl Savage EW Matlock DLSalem FA & Charles EH "The Effect of Endocervical Gland Involvement On the Cure Rates of Patients with CIN Undergoing Cryosurgery" Gynecol Oncol 14, 194-198 1982; Savage E W "Cesarean Hysterectomy Abstracts of Semelweiss Waters" OB Conf Dec 30 1981; "Treat of Cervical Intraepithelial Carcinoma" Meharry Med Coll Ob/Gyn Grand Rounds Nashville TN, 1983. **Home Addr:** 3660 E Imperial Hwy, Lynwood, CA 90262, **Home Phone:** (310)631-9988. **Business Addr:** Adjunct Professor of Obstetrics and Gynecology, Charles R Drew University of Medicine and Science, 1731 E 120th St, Los Angeles, CA 90059, **Business Phone:** (323)563-4800.

### SAVAGE, FRANK
Writer, chairperson, chief executive officer. **Personal:** Born Jul 10, 1938, Rocky Mount, NC; son of Frank and Grace Vivian Pitt; married Lolita Valderrama; children: Eric, Brett, Mark, Antoine, Grace & Frank. **Educ:** Howard Univ, BA, 1962; Johns Hopkins Sch Advan Int Studies, MA, 1968. **Career:** Citi bank, Int Div, staff, 1964-70; Equico Capital Corp, pres, 1970-73; TAW Int Leasing, exec vpres, 1973-75; Alliance Capital Mgt Int, exec vpres, 1985-86, vice chmn, 1986-92, chmn, 1994-2001; Equitable Life Assurance, vpres, 1976-85, sr vpres, 1987-96; Lockheed Martin Corp, dir, 1990-95; Equitable Capital Mgt Corp, bd chmn, 1992-93, vice chmn & head, int opers, 1986-92; Alliance Capital Mgt Corp, dir, 1993; ARCO Chem Co, dir, 1993; Enron Corp, dir, 1999-2002; Qualcomm Inc, dir, 1996-2004; Arab Bankers Asn N Am, dir; QUALCOMM Spinco Inc, dir, 2000; Savage Holdings LLC, chmn & chief exec officer, 2001-; Bloomberg L.P, dir; Alliance Corp Finance Group Inc, bd chmn; US Synthetic Fuels Corp, US presidential appointee to bd dir. **Orgs:** Trustee, Johns Hopkins Univ, 1977-; Coun Foreign Rels, 1982-; dir, Boys Choir Harlem, 1985-; dir, Essence Commun, 1988-; dir, Lock heed Corp, 1990-; bd trustee, Inst Int Educ, 2001; dir, NY Philharmonic; bd trustee, Howard Univ; bd dir, Southern Africa Fund. **Special Achievements:** Book: The Savage Way: Successfully Navigating the Waves of Business and Life. **Business Addr:** Chairman, Chief Executive Officer, Savage Holdings LLC, 1414 Avenue of the Americas, New York, NY 10019, **Business Phone:** (212)750-7400.

### SAVAGE, HORACE CHRISTOPHER
Executive, clergy. **Personal:** Born Jul 30, 1941; married Carolyn Anne; children: Christopher, Nicholas & Carter. **Educ:** VA State Col, BA, 1968; Northwestern Univ, Evanston, IL, MA & PhD, 1977. **Career:** USN Naval Shipyard, personnel mgt spec, 1968-70; Northwestern Univ, res asst, 1968-69, teaching asst, 1969-70, teaching intern, 1970-71, vis lectr ed, 1971-72; Sesame St Eval Proj Ed Testing Serv, 1969; summer res Fel Princeton, 1970; Martin Luther King Jr Woodrow Wilson Fel, 1970; EMarie Johnson & Assoc, Chicago, staff, 1970-72; Chicago read Ment Health Ctr, Chicago, 1971-72; Lake Forest Col, Ill, lectr psychol, 1971-72; Howard Univ, Wash DC, lectr asst vpres & dir res & eval, 1972; George Mason Univ, assoc prof clin psychol; pvt pract, 1973. **Orgs:** Eastern region chmn, Nat Asn Black Psychol; Am Psychol Asn; Am Asn Univ Profs; Int Transactional Anal Asn; Am Correctional Asn; Am Ed Res Asn; Nat & Coun Black Child Develop; Phi Delta Kappa Prof Ed Frat; Am Asn Advan Sci; MD Pry Asn; DC Asn Black Psychol; DC Psychol Asn; Am Mgt Asn; bd psychol Examiner, Wash, DC. **Honors/Awds:** WEB Dubois Award, 1968; Univ Scholarship, Northwestern Univ, 1970; Alpha Mu Gamma National Foreign Language Honor Soc; Beta Kappa Chi Nat Sci Honor Soc. **Special Achievements:** Has written many papers and publications in his field and conducted many workshops. **Home Addr:** 1027 Langston St, Memphis, TN 38122-3358.

### SAVAGE, DR. JAMES EDWARD, JR.
Executive director, consultant, educator. **Personal:** Born Jul 30, 1941, Norfolk, VA; son of James and Thelma; children: Jeffrey, Itayo & James. **Educ:** Norfolk State Univ, BA, 1968; Northwestern Univ Evanston, MA, 1970, PhD, 1971. **Career:** Inst Life Enrichment, dir, 1979-; James E Savage, Jr & Assoc Ltd, pres, owner, 1978-; Howard Univ, asst prof, assoc prof; George Mason Univ, asst prof, assoc prof; Naval Supply Command, training consult; DC Govt, training consult. **Orgs:** Martin Luther King Jr Woodrow Wilson Fel Woodrow Wilson Fel Found, 1968-70; Educ Testing Serv Summer Res Fel Princeton, NJ, 1970; Eastern reg chmn, Nat Asn Black Psychologists, 1971; Int Transactional Anal Asn, 1972-; Am Psychol Asn, 1972-; pres, Asn Black Psychologists, 2004-05; vpres, dir res & eval, E. Marie Johnson & Assocs; chmn, Nat Asn Black Psychologists; Dc Psychol Asn; Dc Asn Black Psychologists. **Home Addr:** 1600 Myrtle St NW, Washington, DC 20012-1130. **Business Addr:** President, Owner, James E Savage Jr & Associates Ltd, 7852 16th St NW, Washington, DC 20012-1200, **Business Phone:** (202)291-5008.

### SAVAGE, JANET MARIE
Executive. **Personal:** Born Nov 12, 1960, Chicago, IL; daughter of Howard T and Ruth F; married John Fellows; children: Jared & Rachel. **Educ:** Stanford Univ, BA, eng lang & lit lett, 1982; Harvard Law Sch, JD, 1985. **Career:** Wilson, Sonsini, Goodrich & Rosati, assoc, 1985-89; Walt Disney Co, coun, 1989-91, sr coun, 1991-92; KCAL TV, gen coun, vpres & bus affairs, 1992-95; Fox Broadcasting Co, sr coun, 1996-99, vpres, legal affairs, 1999-2001, vpres, bus affairs, 2001-02; Twentieth Century FOX TV, vpres & bus affairs, 2002-04; Fox Entertainment Group Co, DirecTV, FBC, AMW.com, Flashlight 21 Prods, consult, 2004-07; Twentieth Tv Inc, vpres, bus & legal affairs, 2007-. **Orgs:** Co-founder & pres, Comt Sports & Entertainment Law, Harvard Law Sch. **Home Addr:** 2346 Veteran Ave, Los Angeles, CA 90064, **Home Phone:** (310)478-8689. **Business Addr:** Vice President, Business & Legal Affairs, Twentieth Television Inc, 2121 Avenue of the Stars Suite 21, Los Angeles, CA 90067, **Business Phone:** (310)369-1000.

### SAVAGE, DR. VERNON THOMAS
Psychologist. **Personal:** Born Sep 13, 1945, Baltimore, MD; son of Theodore and Mary Williams; married Frances Sommerville; children: Tonya, Nakia, Bariki & Jabari. **Educ:** Hagerstown Community Col, Hagerstown, Md, AA & MD, 1973; Syracuse Univ, Syracuse, NY, AB, 1974; Univ Ill, Urbana, IL, MA, 1976, PhD, clin psychol, 1981. **Career:** Marine Corps Res, 1964-70; C Psychiatrist Ctr, Eatontown, NJ, clin intern, 1978-79; Oberlin Col, Oberlin, Ohio, clin psychologist, 1979-83; Swarthmore Col, Swarthmore, Pa, assoc dean students, 1983-87; Towson State Univ, Towson, Md, psychologist & sr counr, 1987; John Hopkins Univ, Coun Ctr, assoc dir & dir outreach, 1993-. **Orgs:** Black Fac Adminr & Staff Asn, 1987-; Am Psychol Asn, 1989-; dir, Outreach Coun Ctr; founding mem, pres, Black Fac & Staff Asn, 1998-99, 2007-09. **Honors/Awds:** National Honor Fraternity for American Junior Colleges, Phi Theta Kappa, 1972; Upper Div Scholar, Ford Found, 1973; Traineeship, United State Pub Health Admin, 1974. **Home Addr:** 9605 Mendoza Rd, Randallstown, MD 21133-2502, **Home Phone:** (410)655-1819. **Business Addr:** Associate Director, Director of Outreach, Johns Hopkins University Counseling Center, 358 Garland Hall 3400 N Charles St, Baltimore, MD 21218-3225, **Business Phone:** (410)516-8278.

## SAVAGE, WILLIAM ARTHUR
College administrator. **Personal:** Born Chicago, IL; son of John and Marie; children: William Jr & Michelle. **Educ:** Univ Ill, Urbana-Champaign, BS, 1969; Ill State Univ, Norm, MS, educ, 1973, ABD. **Career:** Edu Asst Prog, Chicago, Ill, instr & counr, 1969-70; Ill State Univ, Norm, asst dir & coordr acad support servs, High Potential Stud Prog, 1970-75, lectr hist, 1971-73, advisor & coordr, Acad Advisement Ctr, 1975-77, affirmative action, 1977-80; Univ Ill, Urbana-Champaign, asst chancellor, dir, 1980-91; Univ Pittsburgh, asst chancellor, off affirmative action, dir affirmative action, currently; Savage Fine Art Asthete, art consultant. **Orgs:** Am Asn Affirmative Action; Col & Univ Personnel Asn; Nat Asn Advan Colored People; Pa Black Coun Higher Edu; Three Rivers Youth; Phi Delta Kappa; Black Art Am. **Home Addr:** 1403 N Negley Ave, Pittsburgh, PA 15206-1117, **Home Phone:** (412)661-0556. **Business Addr:** Assistant to the Chancellor, Director of Affirmative Action, University of Pittsburgh, 901 William Pitt Union, Pittsburgh, PA 15260, **Business Phone:** (412)648-7860.

## SAWYER, DEBORAH M.
Consultant. **Personal:** Born May 11, 1956, Columbus, OH; daughter of Betty P. **Educ:** Emory Univ, BA, polit sci & biol, 1978; Eastern NMex Univ, MS, petrol microbiol, 1982. **Career:** URS Consults, asst & midwest opers mgr, 1986-88; Ohio Environ Protect Agency, environ scientist II, 1986-89; URS Corporation, oparation mgr; Beling Consults Inc, Solid, Toxic and Hazardous Waste Management Division, sr vpres, bd mem, opers mgr, 1988-90; Environ S/E Inc, opers mgr, toxic & hazardous waste mgt div, 1990-91; Environ Design Int Inc, founder, pres & chief exec officer, 1991-. **Orgs:** Chicago Region Cert Hazardous Mat Mgrs, 1988-; bd mem, Joseph Corp, 1992-; Womens Bus Develop Ctr, 1992-; bd mem, Suburban Black Contractors Asn, 1993-; Evanston Bus Adv Comn, 1993-; Chem Indust Coun Ill, 1994-; pres, Nat Asn Women Bus Owners, Chicago Chap, 1996-97; Consult Engrs Coun Ill, 1996-; Rice Campus Adv Bd; Chicago land Chamber Com; Bradley Univ Col Eng; Ill Inst Technol; Lake Mich comn; bd pres, Young Women's Leadership Charter Sch, 2007-11, teacher. **Honors/Awds:** Small Minority Business of the Year Region 5, Small Bus Asn, 1994; Small Business Award, Bank Am, 1995; Woman of Achievement, Bank Am, 1996; Entrepreneur of the Yr, Nat Asn Women Bus Owners, 1996; Chicago Magazine's Green Award, 2012. **Business Addr:** President & Chief Executive Officer, Founder, Environmental Design International Inc, 33 W Monroe St Suite 1825, Chicago, IL 60603, **Business Phone:** (312)345-1400.

## SAWYER, RODERICK TERRENCE
Lawyer. **Personal:** Born Apr 12, 1963, Chicago, IL; son of Celeste C Taylor and Eugene (deceased); married Cheryll; children: Sydni Celeste & Roderick T Jr. **Educ:** DePaul Univ, BS, finance, 1985; Ill Inst Technol Chicago, Kent Col Law, JD, 1990. **Career:** SNN Inc, dba S's Lounge, pres, 1986-; Ill Com Comn, ade law judge, 1991-; Law Off Steven G Watkins Assoc, partner, 1992-; Ill Com Comn, Admin Law Judge; Ill Dept Transp & Prosecutor, spec asst atty gen; Odelson & Sterk Ltd, coun; Law Off Roderick T Sawyer, founder & managing atty, 1993-2011; City Chicago, 6th Ward, alderman, 2011-. **Orgs:** Pk Manor Neighbors Asn, 1985-; Phi Alpha Delta Law Fraternity, 1990-; Sixth Ward Dem Orgn, pres, 1990-92; Chicago Bar Asn, 1990-; CCBA-ARDC Liaison Comt, 1992-; Ill State Bar Asn; bd dir, S Shore Drill Team, eta Creative Arts Found; bd trustee, St. Mark A.M.E. Zion Church; McDade Class Sch; pres, Chatham Avalon Pk Community Coun. **Home Addr:** 7229 S Prairie Ave, Chicago, IL 60619, **Home Phone:** (773)488-0228. **Business Addr:** Alderman, Chicago City Council, 8001 S Dr Martin Luther King Jr Dr, Chicago, IL 60619, **Business Phone:** (773)635-0006.

## SAWYER, TALANCE MARCHE
Football player. **Personal:** Born Jun 14, 1976, Bastrop, LA. **Educ:** Univ Nev, Las Vegas. **Career:** Football player (retired); Minnesota Vikings, 1999, 2002-03, defensive end, 2000-01. **Home Addr:** , Cedar Hill, TX.

## SAWYER, DR. WILLIAM GREGORY
School administrator, dean (education). **Personal:** Born Nov 6, 1954, Columbus, OH; son of William Wesley and Betty Pride S. **Educ:** Mt Union Col, Alliance, OH, BA, commun & eng, 1976; Eastern NMex Univ, Portales, NM, MA, orgn commun behav, 1978; Univ N Tex, Denton, TX, PhD, higher educ admin, 1986; Harvard Univ Grad Sch Educ, MDP Prog, higher educ/higher educ admin, 1993. **Career:** Eastern New Mex Univ, teaching asst, 1977-78; Amarillo Col, Amarillo, Tex, prof commun, comun instr, 1978-80; Univ N Tex, Denton, Tex, asst dir basic commun, 1980-82, asst dir conf & facil serv, 1983, hall dir, 1983-85, coordr inter cult serv, 1985-86, from asst dean stud to dean stud, 1986-95; Sawyer Commun Consult, consult, 1982-; Fla Gulf Coast Univ, founding dean stud serv, 1995-2001; Calif Univ Channel Islands, founding vpres stud affairs, dean, 2002-. **Orgs:** Minority Caucus Advisor Unit, 1985-; adv, Progressive Black Stud Org Univ N Tex, 1985-; chmn, alumni comt, Blue Key, 1986-; advisor, Golden Key, 1987-; Gamma Beta Phi; Kappa Delta Pi; Commun chair Multicultural Issues Higher Educ, 1987-89; Alpha Lambda Delta; Tex Asn Black Prof, 1988-92; bd mem, Tex State Sickle Cell Found; vpres, 1989-90, pres, 1990-92, pres, 1992-93, Tex Asn Col & Univ Personnel Adminr; comnr, Calif Stud Aid Comn, 2013. **Special Achievements:** Author, Communication Practices and Principles: A Participants Manual, 1981. **Home Addr:** 1201 SW 44th St, Cape Coral, FL 33914-6389. **Business Addr:** Founding Vice President for Student Affairs, California State University Channel Islands, 1 University Dr, Camarillo, CA 93012, **Business Phone:** (805)437-8400.

## SAWYERS, DORRET E.
Educator. **Personal:** Born Jul 27, 1957, Clarendon; daughter of W McTaggart; children: Brian, Kareem & Akilah. **Educ:** Col Arts, Sci & Technol, dipl, 1979; Tuskegee Univ, BS, 1984; Univ Mo-Columbia, MPA, 1987; Fla Int Univ. **Career:** Knox Col, lectr, 1979-81; Tuskegee Univ, stud asst, 1982-84; Univ Mo, fiscal analyst, 1985-91; Fla Int Univ, Stud Support Serv, dir multicultural progs & serv, 1992-; Multicultural Progs MMC, dir prog admin, 20014-11. **Orgs:** Fla Asn Women Educ; Nat Alliance State Pharm Asn; comt mem, Higher Educ Adminr; co-chair, Univ wide Scholar Comt; co-chair, Div Staff Devel Comt; Diversity Day Comt, BBC; chair, SAGE Fundraising Prog Comt; Miami Found; FIU Opa-Locka Scholar Comt; Black Stud Union; Stud Orgn Coun; assoc dir, Minority Stud Serv, 1992-97. **Home Addr:** 2813 Acapulco Dr, Miramar, FL 33023-4707, **Home Phone:** (954)443-3554. **Business Addr:** Director of Multicultural Programs & Services, Florida International University, 11200 SW 8th St GC 216, Miami, FL 33199, **Business Phone:** (305)348-2436.

## SAXTON, PAUL CHRISTOPHER
Government official. **Personal:** Born Dec 14, 1970, Cleveland, OH; son of Cay and Madison. **Educ:** Ky State Univ, BA, criminal justice, 1998, MPA, pub admin, human resource mgt, 1999. **Career:** Commonwealth KY, policy analyst, 1995-99; Cabinet Families & C, policy analyst, 1999-; Ky State Univ, coordr, serv learning & community develop, 2000-01; Commonwealth KY, policy analyst; Tex Southern Univ, dir, 2002-05; Univ Ky, res adminr, 2005-06; Lone Star Col, dir grants develop, 2006-09; Tomball Col, dir res develop & grant admin, currently. **Home Addr:** Gla Reilly Rd, Frankfort, KY 40601. **Business Addr:** Director, Tomball College, 30555 Tomball Pkwy, Tomball, TX 77375, **Business Phone:** (281)351-3300.

## SAYERS, GALE EUGENE
Football player, entrepreneur. **Personal:** Born May 30, 1943, Wichita, KS; married Linda McNeil; children: Gale Lynne, Scott Aaron, Timothy Gale, Gaylon, Guy & Gary; married Ardythe Elaine Bullard. **Educ:** Kans Univ; NY Inst Finance. **Career:** Football player (retired), entrepreneur; Chicago Bears, 1970-71, running back, Halfback, Kick returner, Punt returner, 1965, Halfback, Kick returner, 1966-67, 1969, Halfback, 1968; Kansas Univ, asst to athletic dir; Southern Ill Univ, athletic dir, 1984; Chicago Daily News, columnist; Comput Supplies by Sayers, vpres, mkt; Sayers Comput Source, chmn & chief exec officer, 1982-; Sayers 40 Inc, founder, pres & chief exec officer, chmn, currently; Univ Kans Athletic Dept staff, dir, 2009. **Orgs:** Co-chmn, Legal Defense Fund, Sports Comt, Nat Asn Advan Colored People; coordr, Reach Out Prog, Chicago; hon chmn, Am Cancer Soc; comnr, Chicago Pk Dist; Kappa Alpha Psi; Triad Hosp; Am Century Funds; Marklund; Cradle Soc. **Honors/Awds:** Most Courageous Player Award, Pro Football Writers Am, 1970; Kansas Sports Hall of Fame, 1976; Pro Football Hall of Fame, 1977; Chicago's Entrepeneurship Hall of Fame, Univ Ill, 1999; Technical & Communications Entrepeneurs of the Year, Ernst & Young, 1999; Ranked number 21 on The Sporting News' list of the "100 Greatest Football Players". **Special Achievements:** Company is ranked No 26 on Black Enterprise mag's 1997 list of Top 100 Black businesses; Author, autobiography, I Am Third. **Home Addr:** 1313 N Ritchie Ct Apt 407, Chicago, IL 60610-2153, **Home Phone:** (312)624-8802. **Business Addr:** President, Chief Executive Officer, Sayers 40 Inc, 1150 Feehanville Dr, Mount Prospect, IL 60056, **Business Phone:** (847)391-4040.

## SCAFE, JUDITH ARLENE
Executive. **Personal:** Born May 14, 1961, Detroit, MI; daughter of Julious O and Mary A. **Educ:** Mich State Univ, telecommun, 1984; Wayne State Univ, comput sci, 1986, small bus mgt coursework, 1991; Cent Mich Univ, MPA, 1991-. **Career:** WDTB News Radio, reporter, 1983-84; MCI Commun, corp acct exec, 1985-86; Detroit Pub Schs, substitute teacher, 1987-88; Polimage Group Inc, proj coordr, 1988-90; Wayne County HTH Community Serv, prog coordr, 1988-92; Detroit City coul, spec proj asst, 1989-; WTVS Channel 56, City Youth, proj mgr, 1992. **Orgs:** Planning comn, United Commun Serv, 1988-92; bus united, Officers Youth, 1988-; comnr, Detroit City Coun Youth Comn, 1989-; New Detroit Inc, 1990-92; adv, Mumford Area Youth Assistance, 1990-; Detroit Urban league, 1991-92; Nat Asn Black Journalists, 1992-; Am Red Cross, 1992-.

## SCAGGS, DR. EDWARD W.
Management consultant. **Personal:** Born Mar 4, 1932, East St. Louis, IL; children: Jonathan, Gregory, Helen, Keith, Edward Jr & Patricia Jean. **Educ:** Ill State Norm Univ, BS, 1956; Univ Ill, MS, 1958; Kans State Univ, PhD, 1975. **Career:** Self employed, consult; PATCO, spec exec dir; Ten Cities DOL-HEW, exec dir; Univ Kans, asst prof; Training Corp Am, exec dir; Social Dynamics Inc; Poland Springs Eco Sys Corp, lang dir; St Paul Sch Midwest Theol Sem; Western Auto Co; Milgrams Food Chains; Builder's Assoc; Impact Studies Inc; Tex Govt Wichita Falls, currently. **Orgs:** Kans City C C, KS City Human Rel Menorah Med Ctr, Skill Upgrading Inc, Al Nellum Asn, Al Andrews & Co; dir, KC Sch Dist Bd; exec bd, Mo Sch Bds Asn; adv bd, Mo Voc Educ Bd; adv bd, Urban League; adv bd, YMCA Careers; adv bd, Niles Home C. **Honors/Awds:** Published numerous articles and manuals. **Home Addr:** 5720 Agnes Ave, Kansas City, MO 64117-7803, **Home Phone:** (816)926-9434.

## SCALES, ALICE MARIE
Educator, teacher. **Personal:** Born Nov 3, 1941, Darling, MS. **Educ:** Rust Col, BS, elem educ, 1963; Univ Mass, EdD, reading & lang arts educ, 1971; Southern Univ, MEd, elem educ, 1966. **Career:** John Hyson Elem Sch, teacher, 1963-65; Brook field Elem Sch, remedial reading teacher, 1966-67; Ware Sch Syst, reading specialist, 1966-69; Hadley Sch Syst, reading specialist, 1969-70; Univ Mass, instr & dir; Westfield State Col, instr, 1970-71; Ind Univ, asst prof educ, 1971-72; Int Col Cayman Islands, adj prof educ; Univ Pittsburgh, asst prof educ, 1972-97, prof, instr & learning, 1997-, Dept Instr & Learning, assoc chair, prof emer, currently; Reading Issue Rev, ed-in-chief & co-managing ed, currently. **Orgs:** Consult, Carnegie-Mellon Action Proj, Carnegie Mellon Univ; ESAA Sch; Banneker Contracted Curric Ctr; Int Reading Asn; Am Personnel & Guid Asn; Nat AsnAdvan Colored People; Nat Asn Black Psychologists; Alpha Kappa Alpha; Nat Alliance Black Sch Educr; Am Educ Res Asn; Nat Coun Teachers Eng; Black Women's Asn Inc; Aging & Inter generational Reading; Am Asn Adult & Continuing Educ; Phi Delta Kappa; Am Asn Univ Prof; Am Educ Res Asn. **Honors/Awds:** USA Presidential Citation, 1980; Cert Appreciation, PA Asn Adult & Continuing Educ, 1985; City of Pittsburgh Award, 1987; Distinguished Service Award, Negro Educ Rev, 1997; Henry Highland Garnet Society Award, 2007. **Special Achievements:** Publications: "Efficient Reading for Minorities Implications for Counselors", "Strategies for Humanizing the Testing of Minorities", "College Reading & Study Skills An Asses-Perscriptive Model", "A Comm Operated After Sch Rdg Prgm", "Preparing to Assist Black Children in the Rdg Act". **Business Addr:** Emeritus Professor, University of Pittsburgh, 5602 Wesley W Posvar Hall 230 S Bouquet St, Pittsburgh, PA 15260, **Business Phone:** (412)648-2115.

## SCALES, DR. JEROME C., JR.
Dentist. **Personal:** Born Nov 21, 1942, Birmingham, AL; son of J C and Annie Fancher Mason; married Sandra Wills; children: Lia, Jerome III & Marc. **Educ:** Tenn State Univ, BS, 1969; Meharry Med Col, DDS, 1973; Univ Ala Sch Dent, cert pediat dent, 1975. **Career:** US Postal Serv, lett carrier, 1965-66; Veterans Admin Hosp, dent intern, 1972; Meharry Med Col, stud res asst, 1970-73; Univ Ala Sch Dent, clin assoc prog, 1975-; pediat dent pvt pract, 1975-; C's Hosp Ala, staff. **Orgs:** Phi Beta Sigma Fraternity, 1976-; vpres, 1977, treas, 1978-90, Ala Dent Soc, Zone I, Birmingham; pres, vpres, Birmingham Pediat Dent Asn, 1981-82; bd deacons, Tabernacle Baptist Church, 1982; adv bd, Am Straight Wire Orthod Asn, 1983-84; vpres, 1988-89, pres, 1989-90, Ala Soc Pediat Dent, 1991; pres, Ala Soc Pediat Dent, 1989-90; bd dir, Dent Examiners Ala, 1997-2002; Nat Dent Asn; Am Dent Asn; Am Acad Pediat Dent; Am Orthod Soc; Ala Dent Asn; Southeastern Soc Pediat Dent; Birmingham Dist Dent Asn; Meharry Med Col Alumni Asn; Tenn State Univ Alumni Asn. **Honors/Awds:** Nominated for Martin L King Jr Award, Meharry Medical Col, 1973; best graduate student, Univ Ala Sch Dent, 1975; Certificate in Straight Wire Orthodontics, Straight Wire Technique Found, 1978, 1980; Plaque services as pres, Ala Soc Pediatric Dentistry, 1990. **Special Achievements:** First Black President of Alabama Society of Pediatric Dentistry. **Home Addr:** 3621 Chippenham Dr, Birmingham, AL 35242, **Home Phone:** (205)980-1057. **Business Addr:** Pediatric Dentist, 623 8th Ave W, Birmingham, AL 35204, **Business Phone:** (205)781-9399.

## SCALES, DR. MANDERLINE ELIZABETH WILLIS
Educator, administrator, association executive. **Personal:** Born Mar 14, 1927, Winston-Salem, NC; daughter of Shakepeare Pitts and Roxanne Pitts; married Robert Albert; children: Albert Marvin. **Educ:** Spelman Col, AB, 1949; Univ Pittsburgh, MEd; Univ Valencia, Spain; Univ NC, Greensboro, PhD, bus & mgt, 1982. **Career:** Winston-Salem State Univ, prof soc sci span; Winston-Salem Forsyth Co, Schs Forsyth Tech Inst, teacher; Asn Classroom Teachers, pres; Dist & State Levels Foreign Lang Teachers NCTA, chmn; Forsyth PTA Enrich Proj, chmn; Forsyth Co YWCA, dir bd; Winston-Salem Nat Coun Negro Women. **Orgs:** Past Loyal Lady Ruler Golden Circ; OES; Delta Sigma Theta Sor; bd dirs, Delta Fine Arts Proj; trustee, Shiloh Baptist Church; pres, Union RJ Reynolds Fel study Spain; dir, Shilohian St Peter's Corp Family Ctr, 1984-02; pres, Top Ladies Distinction Inc, 1986-89; nat pres, Nation Women Achievement Inc; Chamber Com; Allocations Community & Proj Blueprint, United Way; Chair Community Develop, Legacy 2000 Forsyth County; YWCA; pres & convener, Nat Coun Negro Women Inc; pres, Spelman Col Alumni Chap. **Honors/Awds:** Outstanding Woman in Civic & Comm Winston-Salem, 1974; Commandress of the Year, Nat Organ Daughters Isis; Hall of Justice, Community Forsyth County; Leadership Award, United Negro Col Fund; COT Leader Award, Winston-Salem Chronicle. **Special Achievements:** Past Nat Adv COM for NASA classroom of the Future; Honored by 1981 class of Winston-Salem Univ; organizer of the col Group WSSU & the Regional and Nat Levels. **Home Addr:** 4000 Whitfield Rd NE, Winston-Salem, NC 27105-3933, **Home Phone:** (336)767-4003. **Business Addr:** Convener, National Council of Negro Women Inc, 633 Pennsylvania Ave NW, Washington, DC 20004, **Business Phone:** (202)737-0120.

## SCALES, ROBERT L.
Politician. **Personal:** Born Sep 14, 1931, Wedowee, AL; married Marcia. **Educ:** Allied Inst Tech, master machinist; Univ Ill. **Career:** Maywood, village trust fourth dist; Tool & Die Maker Am Can Co; Am Fed Labor & Cong Indust Orgn, work men's compen rep; United Steel Workers Am, grieve com, 1972. **Orgs:** Bd dir, Proviso Day Care Ctr; bd mem, Proviso-Leyden Coun Comn Action; Asn Dean Polit Educ Oper PUSH; Oper PUSH; Nat Black Caucas Loc Elected Off; Polit orgn voter regist & Voter Educ; First Baptist Church Melrose Pk; bd mem, Maywood Village; Maywood Comn, 1972 pres elec; Maywood Traffic & Safety Comn; demon vote splitting; initiated comn wide newsletter Black Men Pushing, oper PUSH. **Home Addr:** 2020 Wash Blvd, Maywood, IL 60153-1479, **Home Phone:** (708)344-2816.

## SCALES-TRENT, PROF. JUDY
Lawyer, educator, college teacher. **Personal:** Born Oct 1, 1940, Winston-Salem, NC; daughter of William J Jr and Viola; children: Jason B Ellis. **Educ:** Oberlin Col, BA, fr, 1962; Middlebury Col, MA, fr, 1967; Northwestern Univ Sch Law, JD, 1973. **Career:** New Trier Twp High Sch, teacher; Ridgewood High Sch, teacher; Oberlin Col Peace Corps Training Prog, teacher, 1962-68; Off Decisions & Interpretations; legal res & writing Comn decisions novel policy issues, supvr atty; Equal Employ Opportunity Comn, supvr atty, spec asst vice chmn, 1973-79, spec asst gen coun, 1979-80, appellate atty, 1980-84; State Univ New York Buffalo Law Sch, assoc prof law, 1984-90, prof law, 1990-, St Mary's Univ Sch Law, San Antonio, TX, vis prof, 1994; Floyd H & Hilda L Hurst Fac Scholar, currently; Fac des Sci Juridiques et Politiques, vis prof; senegal grant, 2000-01; Univ Cheikh Anta Diop de Dakar, vis prof, 2001; State Univ NY, Buffalo Law Sch, prof emer, 2009-. **Orgs:** DC Bar; NY Bar; US Ct Appeals Fourth, Fifth, Sixth, Seventh, Nineth & Eleventh Circuits; Am Bar Asn; bd dir, Pk Sch Buffalo, 1985-88 Employ Mgt Working Group; co-chair, Womens Rights Sect, Nat Conf Black Lawyers, 1985-86; bd dir, Nat Women & Law Asn, 1987-91 Adv Coun Educ Opportunities Prog, 1987-92; bd trustee, Ujima Theatre Co, 1989-92; secy & mem, bd dir, Exec Comt, 1990-91; bd visitor, Roswell Pk Mem Cancer Inst, 1991-96; bd gov, Soc Am Law Teachers, 1992-95 Sect Africa Am Asn Law Schs, 2007-08; Asn Study African Am Life & Hist. **Honors/Awds:** Haywood Burns Award, 2004; Trailblazer Award, 2000, 2007; Northeast People Color Legal Scholar Conf. **Special Achievements:** Articles published: "A Judge Shapes and Manages Institutional Reform: School Desegration in Buffalo," 12 NYU Review of Law and Social Change, 1989; "Black Women and the constitution: Finding our Place, Asserting our Rights", 24 Harvard Civil Rights-Civil Liberties Law Review 9, 1989; "Women of Color and Health: Issues of Gender, Power and Community", 43Stanford Law Review 1357, 1991; "The Law as an Instrument of Oppression and the Culture of Resistance", in Black Women in America: An Historical Encyclopedia 701, 1993; "On Turning Fifty", in Patricia Bell-Scott, ed

Life Notes 336, 1994; "Equal Rights Advocates: Addressing Legal Issues of Women of Color", Berkeley Women's Law Jnl, 1998; "African Women in France: Immigration, Family, and Work", Brooklyn Jnl of Internal Law, 1999; Book published: Notes of a White Black Woman: Race, Color, Community, 1995. **Home Addr:** 352 Old Meadow Rd, East Amherst, NY 14051. **Business Addr:** Professor Emeritus, State University of New York Buffalo Law School, 317 O'Brian Hall, Buffalo, NY 14260-1100, **Business Phone:** (716)645-2093.

### SCANLAN, AGNES BUNDY

Executive, association executive. **Educ:** Smith Col, BA, 1979; Georgetown Univ Law Ctr, JD, 1989. **Career:** Fairchild Republic Co, Lobbyist, 1984-87; US Sen Budget Comt, legal coun, 1989-93; Bank Am/FleetBoston Financial, sr vpres & dir, 1994-99, chief privacy officer, 1999, managing dir, chief compliance officer, 2002-04; Bank Am, regulatory rels exec, 2004; Goodwin Procter LLP, Bus Law Dept, coun, 2005-09; TD Bank NA, 2009-11; Treliant Risk Advisor, sr advisor, 2012-15; Consumer Financial Protection Bur, regional dir, 2015-. **Orgs:** Chairwoman, Fed Res Bd Gov Consumer Adv Coun; founding chmn, pres & bd dir, Int Asn Privacy Prof, 2000-12; chair, Compliance Mgt Subcomt, Am Bar Asn; bd trustee & chair, Smith Col, 2005-14; vice chair & trustee, Bd Bryant Univ; chair, Risk Mgt Comt, Bridge Over Troubled Waters; Boston C Mus; Bars Supreme Ct Pa; Super Ct Dist Columbia; Financial Serv Prac; bd trustee, Buckingham, Browne & Nichols, 2013-. **Honors/Awds:** Bostons Power Women, CBS Boston affiliate WBZ, 2004; IAPP Synomos Vanguard Award, 2004. **Special Achievements:** Frequent speaker on government & regulatory relations, ethics, privacy & risk management matters at industry seminars, professional conferences & academic institutions. **Business Addr:** Regional Director, Consumer Financial Protection Bureau, 1700 G St, Washington, DC 20552, **Business Phone:** (855)411-2372.

### SCANTLEBURY-WHITE, DR. VELMA PATRICIA

Surgeon. **Personal:** Born Oct 6, 1955; daughter of Delacey and Kathleen; married Harvey; children: Akela & Aisha. **Educ:** Long Island Univ, Brooklyn Campus, BS, biol, 1977; Columbia Univ, Col Physicians & Surgeons, MD, 1981. **Career:** Harlem Hosp, intern & resident gen surg, 1981-86; Univ Pittsburgh Sch Med, asst prof, surg, 1988-94, fel transplantation surg, 1988-2002, assoc prof, 1989-2002; Univ S Ala, prof & asst dean community educ, 2002-08; Christiana Care Health Systs, assoc chief transplant surg, 2008-. **Orgs:** Dipl, Am Col Surgeons, 1982-90; Am Med Asn, 1987, 1991-; Nat Med Asn, 1989-; P & S Minority Alumni Asn, 1981-; Gateway Med Soc, 1991-; Am Col Surgeons, 1994; Am Soc Transplant Surgeons, 1994; med adv bd, vice-chairperson, African Am Outreach Comt; med adv bd, vice-chairperson, Nat Kidney Found Western Pa; fel Am Col Surgeons, 1994; Donate Life Am; Nat Minority Organ & Tissue Transplant Educ Prog. **Honors/Awds:** Annual Award, Outstanding Young Women Am, 1988; Outstanding Service Award, Harlem Hosp Ctr, 1988; Celebration Excellence Award, Triangle Corner Ltd, 1992; WPTT & Duquesne Light, Outstanding African Am Contribution, 1992; Distinguished Daughter of PA, 1996; Carlow Col Women of Spirit Award, 1997; Gift of Life Award, Nat Kidney Found, 1998; YWCA of Greater Pittsburgh Leadership Award in Healthcare, 2002; National Kidney Foundation Gift of Life award, 2003; UNCF Achievers Hall of Fame Award, 2003; Best Doctors in America, 2004; ASMHTP Lifetime Achievement Award, 2004; America's Top Doctors, 2004, 2007, 2008; Honorary Member of Delta Sigma Theta, 2006; YWCA WOA Lifetime Achievement Award, 2007. **Special Achievements:** First African-American female transplant surgeon in 1989. **Home Addr:** 5833 Northumberland St, Pittsburgh, PA 15217, **Home Phone:** (412)521-7318. **Business Addr:** Associate Chief of Transplant Surgery, Christiana Care Health Systems, 4735 Ogletown-Stanton Rd Suite 2224, Newark, DE 19713, **Business Phone:** (302)623-3866.

### SCANTLING, WAYNE LAMAR

Engineer. **Personal:** Born Mar 21, 1954, Greensboro, NC; son of Johnny and Ann; married Wendi; children: Whitney. **Educ:** NC Agr & Tech State Univ, BSME, 1977; Univ Cent Fla, MSME, 1999. **Career:** NASA Langely Res Ctr, 1972-77; Raytheon Electronics, corp engr, 1977-80; Lockheed Martin, sr engr, 1980-93; Walt Disney Co, mgr, principle engr, 2003-08, staff systs engr, 2008-; Ride & Show Engineering Dept, sr mech engr. **Orgs:** Vpres, SECME, NSBE-Orlando Chap, 1994-96; pres, NC A&T CEN Fla Alumni, 1992-94; Fla Engineering Soc; Am Soc Mech Engrs; Nat Soc Prof Engrs; Campus Crusade Christ; United Way Am. **Honors/Awds:** NASA Advanced Academic Awards Scholar, Nat Aeronaut & Space Admin, 1972; Amoco Production Foundation Honors Scholar, Amoco Oil Co, 1972; North Carolina Agricultural and Technical State University Presidenetial Scholar, NC A&T State Univ, 1972; Martin Marietta, Spot Award, 1985. **Special Achievements:** Publications: "Effect of Spanwise Blowing on Leading Edge Vortex Bursting of a Highly Swept, Aspect Ratio 1.18 Delta Wing", NASA Hi-Number TMX-71987, 1974; Nasa High Number TM-X; published various articles in: NSBE Bridge Mag, Black Enterprise, ASEE Prism Mag, ASME Mech Engr Mag. **Home Addr:** 7273 Branchtree Dr, Orlando, FL 32835, **Home Phone:** (407)291-9482. **Business Addr:** Staff Systems Engineer, The Walt Disney Co, 500 S Buena Vista St, Burbank, CA 91521, **Business Phone:** (818)560-1000.

### SCARBOROUGH, CHARLES S.

Educator, executive director. **Personal:** Born May 20, 1933, Goodman, MS; married Merion Anderson; children: Charles II & James II. **Educ:** Rust Col, AB, 1955; Northwestern Univ, MS, 1958; Mich State Univ, PhD, 1969. **Career:** Alcorn A&M Col, instr, 1957-59; Mich State Univ, grad teacher asst, 1959-63, instr, 1963-69, asst prof, 1969-72, asst dir, 1971-73, assoc prof, 1972, dir, 1973. **Orgs:** Am Men & Women Sci; Acad Affairs Admin; Sigma Xi; Am Asn Advan Sci; Asn Gen & Lib Studies; consumer info comm, Mich State Univ Employee Credit Union; chmn elect, Mich State Univ Black Fac & Admin Group. **Honors/Awds:** Dr. Charles S. Scarborough Endowed Scholarship, named in honor, Mich State Univ. **Home Addr:** 1903 Holly Way, PO Box 17151, Lansing, MI 48910-2542, **Home Phone:** (517)393-3708.

### SCHENCK, FREDERICK A.

Executive. **Personal:** Born May 12, 1928, Trenton, NJ; son of Frederick A Sr and Alwilda McLain; married H Quinta Chapman. **Educ:** Howard Univ, attended 1950; Rider Col, BS, com, 1958, MA, 1976. **Career:** NJ Dept Labor & Indust, personnel officer, 1960-64; NJ Off Econ Opportunities, chief admin serv, 1966-68; NJ Dept Community Affairs, chief pub employ career develop prog, 1966-68, dir admin, 1967-72; NJ Dept Inst & Agy, dir div youth & family serv, 1972-74; NJ Dept Treas, dep dir admin Div purchase & property, 1974-77; US Dept Com, reg rep sec com, 1977-78, dep under secy, 1978-79; Resorts Int Casino Hotel, Atlantic City NJ, sr vpres admin, 1979-88; Cunard Line Ltd, New York, NY, vpres, 1988-93; Bur Nat Affairs Inc, dir, currently; self employed mgt consult, Secaucus, NJ, 1995-. **Orgs:** Bd dir, Bur Nat Affairs Inc, 1946-48; Govs Task Force Serv Disabled, 1986-87; bd trustee, Sammy Davis Jr Nat Liver Inst, 1990-; adv bd, Rider Col; Am Soc Pub Admin; Nj Chamber Com Clubs. **Home Addr:** 569 Sanderling Ct, Secaucus, NJ 07094-2220, **Home Phone:** (201)330-8605. **Business Addr:** Director, The Bureau of National Affairs Inc, 1231 25th St Nw, Washington, DC 20037, **Business Phone:** (202)452-4200.

### SCHEXNIDER, DR. ALVIN J.

School administrator. **Personal:** Born May 26, 1945, Lake Charles, LA; son of Alfred and Ruth Mayfield; married Virginia Y Reeves. **Educ:** Grambling State Univ, BA, polit sci, 1968; Northwestern Univ, MA, 1971, PhD, polit sci, 1973. **Career:** Executive vice president (retired), board trustee; Owens-IL Inc, asst dir personnel, 1968; Northwestern Univ, Norman Wait Harris fel, 1971-72; Ford Found, fel, 1972; Woodrow Wilson Found, fel, 1973; Southern Univ, asst prof, 1973-74; Syracuse Univ, asst prof, 1974-77; Fed Exec Inst, sr prof, 1977-79; Va Commonwealth Univ, assoc dean, 1979-84, vice provost undergrad studies, 1987-95; Univ NC Greensboro, asst vice chancellor, 1984-87; Winston-Salem State Univ, chancellor, 1996-2000; Norfolk State Univ, interim exec vpres, 2002, exec vpres, 2003, interim pres, 2005-08; Thomas Nelson Community Col, interim pres, pres, 2008-11; Va Wesleyan Col, bd trustee; Wake Forest Univ Sch Med, Off Health Policy Develop, dir; Schexnider & Assocs LLC, pres, currently. **Orgs:** Alpha Phi Alpha, 1965-; fel Inter-Univ Sem Armed Forces & Soc, 1975-; consult, Va Munic League, 1980; pres, Va Chap, Am Soc Pub Admin, 1983-84; gov commiss Va Future, 1982-84; adv bd, Greensboro Nat Bank, 1986-87; bd visitors, Va State Univ, 1986-87; Sigma Pi Phi, 1989-; State Bd Educ, 1990-94; vice chair, Gov Adv Comn Revitalization Va's Cities; fel Nat Acad Pub Admin; Am Pol Sci Asn; Am Soc Pub Admin; Nat Conf Black Polit Sci. **Honors/Awds:** Outstanding Young Men Am US Jaycees, 1978; J Sargent Reynolds Award, Am Soc Pub Admin, 1980; Distinguished Educator of the Year Award, Alpha Phi Alpha; Distinguished Alumni Award, Grambling State Univ; Hall of Fame, Grambling State Univ. **Special Achievements:** Books: "Saving Black Colleges: Leading Change in a Complex Organization", New York: Palgrave Macmillan, 2013; Blacks and the Military, Brookings Inst. **Business Addr:** President, Schexnider & Associates LLC, 1208 Masters Row, Chesapeake, VA 23320, **Business Phone:** (757)547-4596.

### SCHMIEGELOW, TONI D.

Government official. **Personal:** married Jerome Gaskins. **Educ:** Univ Pa, BA, sociol, 1970; Columbia Univ, MA, educ coun. **Career:** US Dept Housing & Urban Develop, dir cong rels, Wash, DC, Off Multifamily Housing Develop, sr proj mgr, Richmond, VA, field off dir, Detroit, MI, sr mgt analyst, opers specialist, Richmond, VA, currently. **Business Addr:** Senior Management Analyst, US Department of Housing & Urban Development, 600 E Broad St 3rd Fl, Richmond, VA 23219, **Business Phone:** (800)842-2610.

### SCHMOKE, KURT LIDELL

President (organization), business owner. **Personal:** Born Dec 1, 1949, Baltimore, MD; son of Murray and Irene B Reid; married Patricia Locks; children: Gregory & Katherine. **Educ:** Yale Univ, BA, hist, 1971; Oxford Univ, MA, 1973; Harvard Univ Law Sch, JD, 1976. **Career:** Piper & Marbury Baltimore, atty, 1976-77, assoc, 1978-79; 1981-82; White House Domestic Policy Staff, asst dir, 1977-78; US Dept Justice, City Baltimore, asst US atty, 1978-, state's atty, 1982-87, mayor, 1988-99; US Transp Dept, 1979-81; Wilmer Cutler & Pickering LLP, partner, 1999-2002; Howard Univ Sch Law, Wash, DC, dean, 2003-12, sr vpres, 2012-13; Interim Provost, 2013-14; Univ Baltimore, pres, 2014-; Actor: Avalon, 1990; Am's War Drugs: Searching Solutions, 1995; Homicide: Movie, 2000; Wire: Its All Connected, 2006. **Orgs:** Admitted Md Bar, 1976; Govs Comn Prison Overcrowding, MD Criminal Justice Coord Coun, Task Force to Reform Insanity Defense; Alpha Phi Alpha Fraternity Hon; Am Bar Asn; trustee, Carnegie Corp; Coun Foreign Rels; Dean Am; Hillary Rodham Clinton US Senate Comt; fel, Balliol Col, 2004; trustee, Howard Hughes Med Inst, 2005-; bd dir, Nat Campaign Prevent Teen Pregnancy; Obama Am; Obama Ill; Trilateral Comn; Rhodes Scholar; mem bd, Legg Mason, 2002-; mem bd, McGraw Hill, 2003-; Greater Baltimore Comt, 2014-; Hippodrome Found, 2014-; Baltimore Community Found, 2014-; Lyric Found, 2014-. **Home Addr:** 3320 Sequoia Ave, Baltimore, MD 21215. **Business Addr:** President, University of Baltimore, 1420 N Charles St, Baltimore, MD 21201 - 5779, **Business Phone:** (410)837-4866.

### SCHOOLER, DR. JAMES MORSE, JR.

Educator. **Personal:** Born Mar 22, 1936, Durham, NC; son of James Morse Sr and Frances W Williams; married Mignon I Miller; children: Wesley G & Vincent C. **Educ:** Wittenberg Col, BA, chem, 1957; Univ Wis, MS, chem, 1959, PhD, chem, 1964. **Career:** Harvard Med Sch, res fel, Dept Physiol, 1964-66; Tuskegee Inst, asst prof, 1966-70; Duke Univ, asst prof physiol, 1970-75; NC Cent Univ, prof, chmn, chem; Duke Univ, adj assoc prof, 1975-, chair, 1976-91. **Orgs:** Am Chem Soc; Am Asn Advan Sci; Am Physiol Soc; BSA; Durham Com Black Affairs Educ Subcom; Trust White Rock Baptist Church; Sigma Xi; Beta Kappa Chi; Phi Lambda Upsilon; Phi Alpha Theta; Alpha Phi Alpha; Boys Scouts Am; asst treas, Durham Community Martin Luther King, Jr. Steering Comt Inc. **Honors/Awds:** Hillside HS Alumni Award, 1970. **Home Addr:** 4001 Colorado Ave, Durham, NC 27707-5380, **Home Phone:** (919)493-3885. **Business Addr:** Adjunct Associate Professor, Duke University, 2138 Campus Dr, Durham, NC 27708, **Business Phone:** (919)684-8111.

### SCHOONOVER, BRENDA BROWN

Ambassador. **Personal:** Born Baltimore, MD; married Richard C. **Educ:** Morgan State Univ, BA; Howard Univ, grad studies. **Career:** Ambassador (retired); Peace Corps, Philippines, vol & assoc dir, 1961; Arlington County Va, affirmative action officer, 1970; Bur Europ & Can Affairs, chief personnel, 1988-91; Off Joint Admin Serv, US Embassy, Brussels, Belg, admin Officer & dep dir, 1992-96, dep chief, 2001-04; US Ambassador Togo, 1998-2000; pres, bd dir on-line publ: Am Diplomacy, currently. **Orgs:** Alpha Kappa Alpha Sorority; Peace Corps Alumni Asn; Peace Corps All-Vol Conf, Pagala, Togo; Int Affairs Coun; chair, IntraHealth Adv Coun, Global Health Adv Coun. **Honors/Awds:** Superior Honor, State Dept; U.S. Presidential Meritorious Service Award, 2003.

### SCHULTERS, LANCE A.

Football player, football coach. **Personal:** Born May 27, 1975; married Sherrice; children: Kshawn, Kayanna & Unique. **Educ:** Nassau Comm Col; Hofstra Univ, sociol, 1998. **Career:** Football player (retired), coach; San Francisco 49ers, defensive back & free safety & safety & strong safety, 1998-2001; Tenn Titans, free safety, 2002-04; Miami Dolphins, safety & free safety, 2005 & 2007; Atlanta Falcons, defensive back & right corner back, 2006; New Orleans Saints, 2008; Bryant Univ, defensive backs coach, 2011. **Orgs:** Founder, Lance Schulters Found, 2001. **Honors/Awds:** Iron Mike Award & Hofstras Most Valuable Player, 1997; Defensive Player of the Year, WGBB Radio, 1997; Defensive Player of the Week; Pro Bowl, 1999; Ed Block Courage Award, 2001; Matt Hazeltine (Ironman) Award, 2001; All-Pro, 2002; Hofstra Athletics Hall of Fame, 2013. **Business Addr:** Defensive Backs Coach, Bryant University, 1150 Douglas Turnpike, Smithfield, RI 02917, **Business Phone:** (401)232-6000.

### SCHULTZ, MICHAEL A.

Movie director, movie producer. **Personal:** Born Nov 10, 1938, Milwaukee, WI; son of Leo and Katherine Frances Leslie; married Lauren Jones; children: 2. **Educ:** Univ Wis-Madison; Marquette Univ, BFA; Princeton Univ. **Career:** Dir & producer; Theater direction incl: Waiting Godot, 1966; Song Lusitanian Bogey, 1968; Kongi's Harvest; God a (Guess What?); Does a Tiger Wear a Necktie?; Reckoning, 1969; Every Night When Sun Goes Down, 1969; Eugene O'Neill Memorial Theatre, directed plays by new playwrights, 1969; Oper Sidewinder; Dream Monkey Mountain, 1970, 1971; Woyzeck, 1970; Three Sisters, 1973; Thoughts, 1973; Poison Tree, 1973; What Winesellers Buy, 1974; New Theater Now, dir, 1974. Films: Together Days, 1972; Honeybaby, Honeybaby, 1974; Cooley High, 1974; Billie Holliday, 1974; Honeybaby, 1974; Car Wash, 1976; Greased Lightning, 1977; Which Way Up?, 1977; Sgt Pepper's Lonely Hearts Club Band, 1978; Scavenger Hunt, 1979; Carbon Copy, 1981; Bustin' Loose, 1983; Last Dragon, 1985; Krush Groove, producer & dir, 1985; Disorderlies, dir & co-producer, 1987; Livin' Large, 1991; Phat Beach, exec producer, 1996; Adventures Young Ind Jones: Tales Innocence, 1999; Woman Thou Art Loosed 2004; Blokhedz Mission G Animated Web Ser, exec producer, 2009; Pool Boy, 2010; Adventures Young Ind Jones: My First Adventure, 2007; TV ser: To Be Young, Gifted & Black, 1972; Roll Out, 1973; Chg at 125th St, 1974; Toma, 1974; Rockford Files, 1974; Ceremonies Dark Old Men, 1975; "Starsky & Hutch", 1975; What's Happeining!!, 1976; Benny's Pl, 1982; Us Living: Medgar Evers Story, 1983; Earth, Wind & Fire Concert, 1984; Jerk, Too, 1984; Spirit, 1987; Timestalkers, 1987; Rock 'n' Roll Mom, 1988; Tarzan Manhattan, 1989; Hammer, Slammer & Slade, 1990; Jury Duty: Comedy, 1990; "Picket Fences", 1992-95; Day-O, 1992; "L.A. Law", 1993; "Adventures Brisco County Jr.", 1993; Young Ind Jones & Hollywood Follies, 1994; "Diag Murder", 1995; Shock Treat, 1995; "Sisters", 1995-96; "Chicago Hope", 1996-98; "Promised Land", 1996; Young Ind Jones: Travels with Father, 1996; Pract, 1997-2001; "Ally McBeal", 1997-2001; "JAG", 1997-2002; Killers House, 1998; "Family Law", 1999; "Felicity", 1999; "Wasteland", 1999; "Ally", 1999; My Last Love, 1999; "That's Life", 2000; "City Angels", 2000; "City Angels", 2000; Charmed, 2000-01; "Boston Pub", 2000-03; "Philly", 2001; "L.A. Law: Movie", 2002; "Everwood", dir & producer, 2002-05; "Jack & Bobby", 2004-05; "Cold Case", 2005; "Pepper Dennis", 2006; "Gilmore Girls", 2006; "October Rd", 2007; "Lincoln Heights", 2007; O.C., 2007; "Dirty Sexy Money", 2007-08; "Bros & Sisters", 2007-10; "Women's Murder Club", 2008; "Eli Stone", 2008-09; "Drop Dead Diva", 2009; "Privileged", 2009; "Chuck", 2010. **Home Addr:** PO Box 1940, Santa Monica, CA 90406. **Business Addr:** Director, William Morris Agency, 1 William Morris Pl, Beverly Hills, NY 90212, **Business Phone:** (310)859-4000.

### SCHUTZ, ANDREA LOUISE

Executive. **Personal:** Born Feb 15, 1948, Natchez, MS; married Simuel; children: Kobie & Kareem. **Educ:** Tougaloo Col, BA; Tuskegee Inst, attended 1966; Yale Univ, attended 1967; Princeton Univ, MA, 1971. **Career:** Adams-Jefferson Improve Corp, tutorial dir, 1969; Educ Found, consult, 1970; DC Redevel Land Agy, urban renewal asst, 1970; Urban Opinion Surveys Mathematica Inc, res assoc, 1971; NJ Munic & Co Govt Study Com, researcher interviewer, 1971; Princeton Univ, asst to dean grad sch, 1972-75; Mathematica Inc, personnel dir, 1975-77, vpres, 1978-84; Lenox Inc, dir hr, 1984-88; Educ Testing Ser, Hr, vpres, 1988-97; Mgt Due Diligence Inc, pres & chief exec officer, founding prin, 1997-; Mackenzie & Co, Lawrence, Kans, prin consult; Surv Admin & Surv Opers, Mathematica Policy Res, oper, surv assoc; Adams County Redevelop Asn, assoc; Southern Educ Found, consult; Dist Columbia Redevelop Land, consult. **Orgs:** Pres, Alpha Kappa Alpha Sorority Tougaloo Col, 1966-67; Asn Black Princeton Alumni, 1979; Tougaloo Col Alumni Asn, 1979-; bd mem, Princeton NJ YMCA; Nat Asn Advan Colored People Legal Defense & Educ Fund; bd trustee, Hun Sch Princeton; bd trustee, Granville Acad; Am Compensation Asn; Soc Human Resource Mgt. **Home Addr:** 28 Morgan Pl, Princeton, NJ 08540-2610, **Home Phone:** (609)921-6373. **Business Addr:** President, Chief Executive Officer, Management Due Diligence Inc, 301 N Harrison St Suite 250, Princeton, NJ 08540-3512, **Business Phone:** (609)683-4980.

### SCIPIO, DR. LAURENCE HAROLD
Physician, executive. **Personal:** Born Aug 15, 1942; married JoAnn Wilson; children: Kia Nicole & Courtney Lauren. **Educ:** Howard Univ, Col Lib Arts, BS, 1970; Howard Univ Col Med, MD, 1974. **Career:** Voc Rehab, physician, 1979-82; Birt & Howard PA, physician & urologist, 1979-80; Pvt Pract, urologist, 1980-; Northwest Community Health Care, urol consult, 1983-; Constant Care Community Health Ctr, urol consult, 1984-; Liberty Med Ctr Inc, staff; Md Gen Hosp, staff; Bon Secours Hosp, staff; Mercy Hosp, staff; N Charles Gen Hosp, staff; St Mary's Parish, pastoral Coun pres, currently. **Orgs:** Md Urol Asn; Med & Chirurgical Fac State Md, Baltimore City Med Soc; Monumental City Med Soc, 1980-; W Baltimore Community Health Ctr; Care First; Knights Columbus. **Home Addr:** 1649 Westchester Ct, Annapolis, MD 21409, **Home Phone:** (410)974-1581. **Business Addr:** Pastoral Council President, St Mary's Parish, 111 Duke Gloucester St, Annapolis, MD 21401, **Business Phone:** (410)263-2869.

### SCONIERS, HON. ROSE H.
Judge. **Personal:** Born Sep 23, 1945, Waverly, VA; daughter of Elma R Hamlin (deceased) and Arish L Hamlin (deceased); married Lester G; children: Lisa Rose & Lester Jr. **Educ:** Long Island Univ, BA, polit sci, 1969; State Univ NY, Sch Law, Buffalo, NY, JD, 1973. **Career:** New York Urban Develop Corp; City Buffalo corp coun, asst, 1975, Legal Aid Bur, exec atty, 1980-87; Buffalo City Ct, judge, 1993; NY Supreme Ct, 8th Judicial Dist, 1993, 2007, Appellate Div, Fourth Dept, assoc justice, 2010-. **Orgs:** NY Bar Found; pres, New York State Asn; chair, Franklin H Williams Judicial Comn Minorities, 2009-; emer mem, Buffalo Coun, State Univ New York; adv comt, Unified Ct Syst; pres, Univ Buffalo Law Alumni Asn; bd dir, Ny state Defenders Asn; bd dir, Erie County Bar Found; Erie County Bar Asn Grievance Comt; chmn, Lawyer Referral Serv Comt & Law Day Comt; pres, Supreme Ct Justice Asn; bd trustee, St. Mary Sch Deaf; bd dir, Buffalo Chap; Dean's Adv Coun; New York State Bar Found, fel. **Home Addr:** 46 Chatham Ave, Buffalo, NY 14216, **Home Phone:** (716)876-2019. **Business Addr:** Associate Justice, New York State Supreme Court, M Dolores Denman Courthouse, Rochester, NY 14604, **Business Phone:** (585)530-3100.

### SCOTT, ALBERT J. (AL SCOTT)
State government official, association executive, chairperson. **Personal:** married Diann B. **Educ:** Armstrong State Col. **Career:** Ga House Reps, Dist 2, rep, 1976-82; Ga State Senate, Dist 2, sen, 1982-90, comnr labor, 1990-92, Ga Legis Black Caucus, chmn; State Bd Educ; Ga Ports Authority, bd dir, secy, vice chair & chmn; Chatham County Comn, chmn, 2012-; Union Camp Corp, staff; International Paper, staff. **Orgs:** Bd mem, Goodwill Indust; bd mem, Boy Scouts Coastal Empire; bd mem, Boy Scouts Am; Hospice Operating Bd; founding bd mem, King Tisdale Museum; Beach Inst; chmn, Pub Utilities Comt; Consumer Affairs Comt; Appropriations Comt; Union Camp Corp; bd mem, Hodge Mem Day Care Bd; bd mem, Hospice Savannah Found Inc; BB & T Community Bank Bd; First Liberty Bank Bd; Southern State Energy Bd; Grad Leadership Ga; chair, Chatham County Dem Comt; pres, Savannah Br, Nat Asn Advan Colored People, currently. **Honors/Awds:** Twice voted one of the Ten Most Influential Legislators in Georgia; Recipient of numerous civic and leadership awards. **Business Addr:** Chairman, Chatham County Commission, PO Box 8161, Savannah, GA 31402, **Business Phone:** (912)652-7878.

### SCOTT, ALBERT NELSON
Government official. **Personal:** Born Nov 27, 1916, Richmond, VA; married Annie Mae Smith; children: Maxine Gill, Albert N Jr, Luana Webster, Duane, Leona, Barbara, CharleneJones, Eugene & Cynthia Henry. **Educ:** Fayette Co Schs WVa. **Career:** Local Union 2325 Coal Mine, vpres, 1971; Mine Comm, chmn, 1971-79; Beckley City Coun, city councilman, 1979-. **Orgs:** Head, deacon Holiness Church Jesus, 1965-; Raleigh Co Commitment Comm Dem Party, 1970; Recreation Bd, 1971; Citizens Adv Comt, 1972; WVa Planning Asn, 1979-84; Am Legion Post 70, 1982; St Comn, 1982-84; Nat Asn Advan Colored People, 1985; appt mem, Beckley Urban Renewal Auth, 1985. **Honors/Awds:** Working With Youths Beckley City Youth, 1981-82; Cert of Appreciation Quad Counties OIC Inc, 1982; ground breaking Water Pollution Control Proj, 1984. **Home Addr:** 212 Antonio Ave, Beckley, WV 25801. **Business Addr:** City Councilman, Beckley City Council, 820 S Fayette St, Beckley, WV 25801.

### SCOTT, ALEXIS (M ALEXIS SCOTT)
Publisher, chief executive officer, vice president (organization). **Personal:** Born Atlanta, GA; children: 2. **Career:** Atlanta Jour-Const, vpres & community affairs; Cox Enterprises Inc, reporter to vpres & dir diversity; Atlanta Daily World, publ & chief exec officer, currently. **Orgs:** St Jude's Recovery Ctr; Kenny Leon's True Colors Theater Co; Atlanta Hist Ctr; bd, High Mus Art; Atlanta Conv & Visitors Bur & Cent Atlanta Progress; Atlanta Workforce Develop Agency; presiding officer, First Congregational Church, 1982-92; Nat Asn Advan Colored People; bd dir, Atlanta Life Financial Group; bd, Hist S View Cemetery Preserv Found; Rotary Club Atlanta; global adv bd, Ctr for Civil & Human Rights & Pres's Coun Atlanta Hist Ctr. **Home Addr:** 2128 Jones Rd, Atlanta, GA 30318-5912, **Home Phone:** (404)505-1328. **Business Addr:** Publisher, Chief Executive Officer, Atlanta Daily World, 3485 N Desert Dr Suite 2109, Atlanta, GA 30344, **Business Phone:** (404)761-1114.

### SCOTT, ANTHONY R.
Consultant, police chief, executive. **Educ:** Loyola Univ, BA, bus admin, BA, criminal justice; FBI Nat Acad. **Career:** Police chief (retired), consultant; Holyoke Police Dept, chief police, 2001-11; Quad Cities Metrop Enforcement Group; Quad Cities Gang Task Force; Ill Quad Cities Law Enforcement Group; ASLEC LLC, founder & consult, currently. **Orgs:** Quad Cities Coun Police Chief's; Ill Asn Chief's Police; Agenda Black Quad Citizens; Land Lincoln Chap, Nat Org Black Law Enforcement Execs, pres; FBI Nat Acad Assocs; Int Asn Chief's Police; & FBI Law Enforcement Exec Develop Sem Assocs; Paul Harris fel Rotary Found; Retirement Roast Planning Comt. **Honors/Awds:** Outstanding Law Enforcement Professional of America, 1990; Who's Who in Law Enforcement, 1990; Charles E Dunbar Jr Career Civil Service Award; Martin Luther King Jr Community Relations Award; City Employee of the Year, Rock Island, 1996; Law Enforcement Professional for the State of Illinois, Ill Bar Asn, 2001. **Special Achievements:** First African-American appointed Chief of Police in Holyoke, MA. **Business Addr:** Chief of Police, Holyoke Police Department, 138 Appleton St, Holyoke, MA 01040, **Business Phone:** (413)536-6431.

### SCOTT, ARTIE A.
Insurance executive, association executive, executive. **Personal:** Born Mar 23, 1946, Americus, GA; daughter of Lee Decie Anthony and Cicero Anthony; children: Shujwana Smith & Gabriel Omari. **Educ:** Albany State Col, attended 1968; Fla Int Univ, BA, 1974; Ins Inst Am, HIAA, attended 1980; Life Off Mgt Inst, attended 1993; Corp Mgt Sch, attended 1991. **Career:** IllA Welfare & Pension Fund, admin clerk & examr, 1970-76; Equitable Life Assurance Soc, examr, supvr, 1976-86; Alexander & Alexander, Turner & Shepard, supvr, asst mgr, 1986-88; Nationwide Life Ins Co, benefits & claims mgr, 1988-2000; Jebel Ali Int Hotels, exec benefits mgr, 2000-04; John Perry & Assocs, sales assoc, 2004-06; The McCart Group, sr claims analyst, 2006-. **Orgs:** Am Bus Women's Asn, 1984-90; vpres, secy, Action Alliance Black Prof, 1987-; Nationwide's Civic Activities Rep, 1990; United Negro Col Fund Ann Walk-A-Thon, 1991-. **Honors/Awds:** Chmn, United Way Employee Campaign Dr, 1988; Ohio House Reps, Community Clothes Dr, 1992; Action Alliance Black Prof, Homeless Shelter Dr, 1991, 1992. **Special Achievements:** Song Dedication Ceremony for educ wing of Tabernacle Baptist Church, 1987; Contributing writer, "How to File a Claim", The Total Manager Mag, 1992; Soar Award recipient, Excellence Customer Serv, 1993-94. **Home Addr:** 1472 Fahlander Dr N, Columbus, OH 43229, **Home Phone:** (614)847-4282. **Business Addr:** Senior Claims Analyst, The McCart Group, 2405 Satellite Blvd Suite 200, Duluth, GA 30096, **Business Phone:** (770)232-0202.

### SCOTT, DR. BASIL Y.
Administrator. **Personal:** Born Jan 18, 1925; son of James and Iris; married Luna Lucille Edwards; children: Karen & Brian Y. **Educ:** City Col New York, BA, 1948; Columbia Univ, MA, 1949; Siena Col, MBA, 1952; Syracuse Univ, PhD, 1962. **Career:** Administrator (retired); State Univ New York, adj prof, 1959-68; NY Dept Motor Vehicles, staff, 1960-70, admin dir, 1970-77, dep comnr, 1977-78, Dept Educ, dep comnr, 1978-83; Kutztown, admin & finance, vpres; Kutztown Univ, adj prof, 1984-86, vpres admin & finance, 1995. **Orgs:** Phi Beta Kappa, 1948; pres, Nat Hwy Safety Adv Comn, 1969-72 & 1977-80; Bd dir, Blue Shield Northeastern New York, 1971-81; chmn bd dir, Blue Shield Northeastern New York, 1978-81; secy, Nat Motor Vehicle Safety Adv Coun, 1975-77; bd gov, Albany Med Ctr, 1975-81; bd dir, Kutztown Univ Found, 1983-89; bd dir, Concern Prof Serv C, Youth & Families, 1995-; bd pres, Concern Prof Serv C, Youth & Families, 1997-99; bd trustee, Alvernia Col, 1999-; bd trustee, Reading Berks County YMCA, 2001-; Facil & Technol Comn, 2003-. **Home Addr:** 1927 Meadow Lane, Wyomissing, PA 19610, **Home Phone:** (215)842-0428.

### SCOTT, BENJAMIN
Executive, consulting engineer. **Personal:** Born Nov 30, 1929, Maringouin, LA; son of Harry and Sarah; married Doretha; children: Benjamin E Jr & Daryl D. **Educ:** Pasadena City Col, AA, 1954; Pac State Univ, BS, 1959; Univ Calif, Los Angeles, MS, 1969. **Career:** Executive (retired); US Dept Defense, Res & Develop Lab, elec engr, 1952-69, dir sylmar, 1964-67, proj engr, 1969-74; Benjamin Scott Assocs & Co Inc, chief exec officer & consult engr, 1977-2001. **Orgs:** Chmn, Pasadena Nat Asn Advan Colored People, 1952; chmn, Pasadena Urban Coalition, 1966-1974; chmn, Watts Comm Action Comn, 1970. **Home Addr:** 1004 E Woodbury Rd, Pasadena, CA 91104, **Home Phone:** (626)398-5782. **Business Addr:** Consulting Engineer, Benjamin Scott Associates & Co Inc, 1004 E Woodbury Rd, Pasadena, CA 91104-1315, **Business Phone:** (626)798-0486.

### SCOTT, DR. BEVERLY ANGELA
Government official. **Personal:** Born Aug 20, 1951, Cleveland, OH; daughter of Winifred M Jones Smith and Nathaniel H Smith; married Arthur F; children: Lewis K Grisby III. **Educ:** Fisk Univ, BA, polit sci, 1972; Howard Univ, PhD, pub admin, 1977. **Career:** Tenn State Univ, asst prof, 1976; Metrop Transit Authority, Harris County, Tex, asst gen mgr, 1978-83; Minority Contractors Asn, exec dir, 1983-84; AO Phillips & Assocs, consult, 1984-85; New York Metrop Transit Authority, asst vpres, 1985-89, vpres, admin & personnel, 1989; RI PubTransit Authority, gen mgr; Sacramento Regional Transit Dist, gen mgr & chief exec officer, 2002-07; Metrop Atlanta Rapid Transit Authority, gen mgr & chief exec officer, 2007-; Ri Pub Transit Authority, gen mgr; Nj Transit Corp; Wash Metrop Transp Authority; Mass Bay Transp Authority, chief exec officer. **Orgs:** Am Pub Transit Asn; US Dept Transp; Nat Bus League; Women Transp Sem; RI Prof Engrs Soc; Sierra Club; Conf Minority Transp Officials; Nat Forum Black Pub Admin; Urban League; fel Ford Found 1972-76; fel Carnegie Found, 1977-78; Am Socs Pub Adminr; chairperson, Am Pub Transp Asn, 2009; vice chair, Reconnecting Am, Rail-Volution; Transp Learning Ctr; Americans Transit; exec comt, Transp Res Bd; exec comt, Nat Academies Sci. **Special Achievements:** First female Chief Executive Officer & General Manager of Metropolitan Atlanta Rapid Transit Authority. **Business Addr:** General Manager, Chief Executive Officer, Metropolitan Atlanta Rapid Transit Authority, 2424 Piedmont Rd NE, Atlanta, GA 30324-3311.

### SCOTT, BRENT
Basketball player, basketball coach. **Personal:** Born Jun 15, 1971, Jackson, MI; married Brooke; children: Brekayla & Berklee. **Educ:** Rice Univ, BA, kinesiology, 1993. **Career:** Basketball player (retired), basketball coach; AEL Larissa, Greece, 1993-95; Miami Tropics, 1995; Olitalia Forli, Italy, 1995-96; Portland Mountain Cats, Us Basketball League, 1996; Ind Pacers, Nat Basketball Asn, power forward, 1996-97; Atlantic City Seagulls, Us Basketball League, 1997; Tau Ceramica, Spain, 1997-98; Viola Reggio Calabria, Italy, 1998-99, 2000-01; Snaidero Udine, Italy, 2001-02; PAOK, Greece, 2002-03; Polaris World Murcia, 2003-04; Joventut Badalona, Spain, 2004-05; Anwil Wloclawek, 2006; AEK Athens, 2006-07; Rice Univ, asst basketball coach, 2007-08; La State Univ, asst basketball coach, 2008-12; Tex Christian Univ, asst basketball coach, 2012-. **Business Addr:** Assistant Coach, Texas Christian University, 2800 S University Dr, Fort Worth, TX 76129, **Business Phone:** (817)257-7000.

### SCOTT, BYRON ANTOM
Basketball player, basketball coach, television news anchorperson. **Personal:** Born Mar 28, 1961, Ogden, UT; married Anita; children: Thomas, LonDen & DeRon. **Educ:** Ariz State Univ, attended 1983. **Career:** Basketball player (retired), basketball coach; Los Angeles Lakers, prof basketball player, 1983-93, 1996-97; Ind Pacers, 1993-95; Vancouver Grizzlies, 1995-96; Pananthinaikos, Greece, 1997-98; Sacramento Kings, asst coach, 1998-2000; NJ Nets, head coach, 2000-03; New Orleans Hornets, head coach, 2004-09; ABC NBA telecasts, studio analyst; Am Nat Basketball Asn; Cleveland Cavaliers, head coach, 2010-2013; Los Angeles Lakers, head coach, 2014-. **Orgs:** Byron Scott Childrens Fund. **Home Addr:** 7505 Hannum Ave, Culver City, CA 90230-6162, **Home Phone:** (310)745-2801. **Business Addr:** Head Coach, Los Angeles Lakers, 555 N Nash St, El Segundo, CA 90245, **Business Phone:** (310)426-6000.

### SCOTT, CANDACE YVETTE WILLRICH
Executive, president (organization), chief executive officer. **Personal:** Born Mar 26, 1965, Dallas, TX; daughter of Theodis and Margie; married Eugene. **Educ:** Univ Tex, Austin, TX, BS, math, 1988, MBA, finance & info systs, 1990. **Career:** Comshare Inc, consult, 1991-95; Willrich Scott Consult Group, founder, chief exec officer & pres, 1995-; Willrich Innovations Inc, exec, 1995-. **Orgs:** Tex Ex Alumni Asn, 1998-; Nat Asn Female Execs, 1998-; Nat Asn Advan Colored People, 1998-; Nat Black MBA, 1990-; Women Technol, 1999-; Data Mgt Asn, 1999-. **Home Addr:** 1743 Creekbend Dr, Lewisville, TX 75067, **Home Phone:** (972)434-1732. **Business Addr:** President, Chief Executive Officer, Willrich Scott Consulting Group Inc, 3700 Forums Dr Suite 106, Flower Mound, TX 75028-1849, **Business Phone:** (972)724-1725.

### SCOTT, CARSTELLA H.
Government official. **Personal:** Born Apr 6, 1928, Thomasville, AL; married Percy Sr; children: Rosia B Grafton, Percy Jr, Maxine , Veronia, Geraldine, Katherine YParham, Christine & Roderick. **Educ:** Ruth's Poro Beauty Col, BS; Southern Beauty Cong, MA, PhD, 1984. **Career:** Englewood Elem Fairfield, pres, 1957-67; Law Comn Ala, mem, 1980; Ala Gov Comn, mem, 1983; Fairfield Dem Women, vpres; Ala Voter Educ, mem, 1985; Fairfield City Coun, coun woman; Fairfield Ala PTA, pres. **Orgs:** Pres, Missionary Cir Shady Grove, CME Church, 1973; Nat Asn Advan Colored People, Zeta Phi Lambda Sorority, Christian Women Am, 1980; execbd mem, Ala Mod Beauticans, Chamber Com, Fairfield, 1982. **Honors/Awds:** Nine Year Serv Award, CME Church, Birmingham Conf, 1984; Nominating Comn, Women's Missionary Coun; Mother of the Yr, Fairfield Sch Syst. **Home Addr:** 537 Valley Rd Wd 4, PO Box 2, Fairfield, AL 35064, **Home Phone:** (205)781-0261.

### SCOTT, CHAD OLIVER
Football player, air force officer. **Personal:** Born Sep 6, 1974, Capitol Heights, MD. **Educ:** Community Col Air Force, AA, commun applications, 2001; Univ Md, human resources mgt, 2012. **Career:** Football player (retired), executive, free agent; Pittsburgh Steelers, right corner back & left corner back & center & corner back, 1997-2004; New Eng Patriots, corner back, 2005-07; New Eng Patriots, free agt, 2005; Joint Forces Component Command-ISR/Defense Intelligence Opers Coord Ctr, opers supt, 2008-09; Usaf, air force specialty mgr, 2009-10, chief, force develop & advan training, 2010-12, 497 ISR Group, supt, 2011-12, HQ Air Combat Command, chief enlisted mgr, 2012-. **Honors/Awds:** Joe Greene Award, 1997; All-Rookie team, Assoc Press, 1997.

### SCOTT, CHARLES E.
Real estate agent. **Personal:** Born Dec 4, 1940, Macon, GA; children: Erica & Derek; married Francenia D Hall. **Educ:** Morris Brown Col, BS, music educ, 1963. **Career:** Atlanta Bd Educ, music teacher, 1963-65; IBM Corp, sales rep, 1968-71; Charles E Scott & Assoc, realtor, internet marketer, appraiser & owner, 1971-. **Orgs:** Appraisal Inst Cand, 1977-; pres, Nat Soc Real Estate Appraisers Inc, Local Satellite Chap, 1980; secy, C's Psychiat Ctr, 1979-. **Home Addr:** 931 NE 79th St, Miami, FL 33138-4727. **Business Addr:** Owner, Charles E Scott & Associates, 931 NE 79th St, Miami, FL 33138, **Business Phone:** (305)757-7111.

### SCOTT, CHARLES E.
Photojournalist. **Personal:** Born Jul 23, 1949, Houston, TX; son of Garret and Marie Johnson; married Consulla Gipson; children: Tracy, Tamara & Christopher. **Educ:** Univ Houston, Houston, TX, 1971. **Career:** KUHT, Houston, Tex, 1971-72; Independent Filmmaker, Houston, Tex, 1971-73; KPRC-TV, Houston, Tex, news camera mgr, 1972-; Video Seminars Inc, Houston, Tex, pres, 1990-. **Orgs:** NABJ, 1987-; founding mem, HABS, 1987-; NPPA, 1972-85. **Honors/Awds:** Spec Recognition, HABS, 1988; Unity Awards in Media, Lincoln Univ, 1984; UPI Tex, Texas UPI Broadcaster, 1983; PAT Weavor, MDA, Muscular Dystrophy Asn, 1980; Film Grant, ACT/Pub Television, 1973; Insite photographer of the week. **Home Addr:** 619 Kenwood St, Houston, TX 77074, **Home Phone:** (713)453-0847. **Business Addr:** Photojournalist, KPRC-TV, 8181 Southwest Fwy, Houston, TX 77074, **Business Phone:** (713)222-6397.

### SCOTT, DARNAY
Football player, football coach. **Personal:** Born Jul 7, 1972, St. Louis, MO; children: 2. **Educ:** San Diego State Univ. **Career:** Football player (retired); Cincinnati Bengals, wide receiver, 1994-2001; Jacksonville Jaguars, 2001; Dallas Cowboys, wide receiver, 2002; Mesa Col & Lincoln High Sch, community & coaching, currently. **Home Addr:** , San Diego, CA. **Business Addr:** Football Coach, 4777 Imperial Ave, San Diego, CA 92113, **Business Phone:** (619)266-6500.

**SCOTT, DAVID A.**
Government official, founder (originator), chief executive officer. **Personal:** Born Jun 27, 1946, Aynor, SC; married Alfredia Aaron; children: Dayna & Marcye. **Educ:** Fla A&M Univ, BA, finance, 1967; Univ Pa, Wharton Sch Bus, MBA, 1969. **Career:** GA House Representatives, rep, 1974-82; Dayn-Mark Advert, founder & chief exec officer, 1979-2002; GA State Sen, sen, 1982-2002; US House Representatives, US rep, comt on agr, comt on financial serv, nato parliamentary assembly, 2003-; Online gambling, staunch advocate. **Orgs:** Fin Servs Comt; co-chmn, Democratic Study Group on Nat Security; Alpha Phi Alpha; Blue Dog Coalition; New Dem Coalition. **Business Addr:** US Representative, US House of Representatives, 173 N Main St, Jonesboro, GA 30236, **Business Phone:** (770)210-5073.

**SCOTT, DR. DEBORAH ANN**
Physician. **Personal:** Born Oct 2, 1953, New York, NY; married Ralph C Martin II. **Educ:** Princeton Univ, BA, 1975; Howard Univ, Col Med, MD, 1979. **Career:** US Pub Health Serv, internal med, 1980; Carney Hosp, internal med, 1982; Howard Univ Hosp, dermat fel, 1982-83; Roger Williams Gen Hosp, dermat fel, 1984, dermat cheif resident, 1985, dermat teaching fel, 1986; Mass Inst Technol, staff physician, 1986-96; Harvard Community Healthplan, 1993-; Beth Israel Deaconess Med Ctr, 1996-; Ctr Laser Dermat & Skin Health, dir; Hair Loss Clin, co-dir; Harvard Med Sch, asst prof; Brigham & Women's Hosp, assoc physician & instr, currently; Laser & Skin Healthcare Syst, dir, currently. **Orgs:** NE Med Soc, 1983-87, Am Acad Dermat, 1986-, New England Med Soc, 1986, New England Dermatological Soc, 1987. **Honors/Awds:** Alpha Omega Alpha Hon Soc, 1979. **Home Addr:** 154 Moss Hill Rd, Jamaica Plain, MA 02130. **Business Addr:** Associate Physician, Instructor, Brigham & Women's Hospital, 850 Boylston St Suite 402, Chestnut Hill, MA 02467, **Business Phone:** (617)732-9300.

**SCOTT, DENNIS EUGENE**
Basketball player, radio host. **Personal:** Born Sep 5, 1968, Hagerstown, MD; married Rachael; children: Ryan, Dennis III & Crystal. **Educ:** Ga Inst Technol, Atlanta, GA, attended 1990. **Career:** Basketball player (retired), basketball exec, host; Orlando Magic, forward, 1990-97; Dallas Mavericks, 1997-98; Phoenix Suns, 1998; New York Knicks, 1999; Minn Timberwolves, 1999; Vancouver Grizzlies, 1999-2000; 3-D Entertainment Inc, pres; 790 Zone, host; 3-D's After Dark, host, 2005-; Am Basketball Asn, Atlanta Vision, gen mgr, 2005-; FSN, studio analyst; Atlanta Hawks, radio analyst, currently; NBA TV, studio host & commentator, currently. **Home Addr:** , Sandy Springs, GA 30328. **Business Addr:** Radio Analyst, Atlanta Hawks, Centennial Tower, Atlanta, GA 30303, **Business Phone:** (404)878-3800.

**SCOTT, DR. DONALD LAVERN**
Government official, military leader. **Personal:** Born Feb 8, 1938, Hunnewell, MO; son of William E and Beatrice Dant; married Betty Jean; children: Lloyd (deceased), Jeffrey & Mel. **Educ:** Lincoln Univ, BA, graphic arts, 1960, PhD; Troy State Univ, MA, 1982. **Career:** Military leader & government officer (retired); AUS, brig gen, 1960-91; Res & Natl Guard units s eastern US & Vi, 1988-91; City Atlanta, chief operating officer, chief staff, 1991-93, mayor; Ameri Corps Nat NCCC, Corp Nat Serv, founder & dir, 1993-96; Dep Librn Cong, 1996-2006. **Orgs:** Kappa Alpha Psi Fraternity, 1960-; Nat Asn Advan Colored People, 1991-; 100 Black Men, Atlanta Chap, 1991-94; Am Libr Asn, 1993-; Black Caucus Am Libr Asn, 1997-. **Special Achievements:** Speak Vietnamese, 1965; Air Force War Col, Leadership Thesis, 1981. **Home Addr:** 2118 Tysons Exec Ct, Dunn Loring, VA 22027, **Home Phone:** (703)698-9799.

**SCOTT, DONNELL**
Executive, interior designer, chief executive officer. **Personal:** Born Oct 25, 1947, Orange, NJ; son of Walter and Katherine Robinson; married Bessie Beckwith; children: Darrin B. **Educ:** NC Cent Univ, BA, polit sci, 1970; Seton Hall Univ, S Orange, NJ, MA, Am studies, 1973; Nova Southeastern Univ, EdD, orgn leadership. **Career:** Int Bus Mach Corp, 1976-80; NC Cent Univ, Durham, NC, dir exec MPA (EMPA), 2006-; NC Cent Univ, Dept Pub Admin, adj prof, 2006-; At Window, Sea Bright, NJ, pres, 1980-; WS Exterminating Inc, chief exec officer, currently; Duke Univ Sch Continuing Educ, teacher; K.S. Serv Consult Group Inc, Managing Partner, 1995-98; Episcopal Dist Econ Abbr Group Inc, chief admin officer, 1998-2001; Pt Consult Group, pres, 2009-; Fac Adv, Ghana Institue Mgt & Pub Admin, 2010; Am Soc Pub Admin, int dir, 2011-; J William Fulbright Foreign Scholar Bd, Fulbright Int Specialist, 2011-. **Orgs:** United Black Families Freehold Twp, 1976-; 100 Black Men Am, 1989-; int dir, ASPAs nat coun. **Home Addr:** PO Box 228, Tennent, NJ 07763-0228, **Home Phone:** (908)780-1045. **Business Addr:** Director, North Carolina Central University, 1801 Fayetteville St, Durham, NC 27707, **Business Phone:** (919)530-5192.

**SCOTT, DR. ELSIE L.**
Manager, police officer. **Personal:** Born Lake Providence, LA; daughter of John H and Alease Truly; married Irving Joyner. **Educ:** Southern Univ, BA, 1968; Univ Iowa, MA, 1970; Atlanta Univ, PhD, polit sci, 1980. **Career:** St Augustines Col, dir Criminal Justice Prog, 1977-79; NC Cent Univ, asst prof, 1979-80; Howard Univ, asst prof & res assoc, 1981-83; Nat Org Black Law Enforcement Exec, prog mgr, 1983-85, exec dir, 1985-91; NY Police Dept, dep scomnr training, 1991, asst exec dir corp support, currently; Detroit Police Dept, sr & supvry staff; Howard Univ, fac; Rutgers Univ, fac; Cent Fla Univ, fac; NC Cent Univ, fac; US Dept Homeland Security, staff; Howard Univ, Ronald W. Walters Leadership, founding dir; Howard Univ, Pub Policy Ctr, founding dir; Cong Black Caucus Found, vpres, res & progs, 2005, interim pres & chief exec officer, 2006-12. **Orgs:** Pres, Nat Conf Black Polit Scientists, 1980-81; secy, Rev John H Scott Memorial Fund, 1980; panelist, Comn Status Black Am Nat Res Coun, 1986-88; adv bd, Nat Inst Against Prejudice & Violence, 1987-93; exec bd, Nat Org Black Law Enforcement Execs, 1991-93; Am Soc Criminol; Criminal Justice Brain Trust; exec dir, Nat Orgn Black Law Enforcement Execs. **Honors/Awds:** Achievement Award, 100 Black Women, 1988; African American Women Distinction, Guardian Assoc, 1991; Black Comn Crusade C, Working Comt, 1992; Louisiana Black History Hall of Fame, 1993. **Special Achievements:** Violence Against Blacks US, 1979-81, Howard Univ, 1983; Co-author, Racial & Rel Violence, Noble, 1986. **Home Addr:** 225 Rector Pl Suite 7R, New York, NY 10280. **Business Addr:** President, Chief Executive Officer, Congressional Black Caucus Foundation, 1720 Mass Ave NW, Washington, DC 20036, **Business Phone:** (202)263-2800.

**SCOTT, COL. EUGENE FREDERICK**
Publisher, management consultant. **Personal:** Born Oct 14, 1939, Miami, FL; son of Eugene Sr and Bertha; married Patricia; children: Eugene Jr, Jacqueline, Gregory, Michael & Leta. **Educ:** Univ Okla; Fla A&M Univ, BA, polit sci, 1961. **Career:** Prin staff officer, Training & Opers, 8th Inf Div Combat Ready Forces; Chicago Defender, gen mgr, 1990, publ, 2000-01; Chicago Defender Charities, pres, gen mgr & publ; Sengstacke Enterprises, exec asst. **Orgs:** Omega Psi Phi; chmn & chair, Nat African Am Mil Mus; Armed Forces Comt; Nat Newspaper Publs Asn; Bronzeville Mil Acad; Ill Mil Flags Comn; Govs Comn Discrimination & Hate Crime; Atty Gens African Am Adv Comt; Nat Adv Comt Inst Govt & Pub Affairs, Univ Ill; Chicago Area Boy Scouts. **Honors/Awds:** Boy Scouts, Silver Beaver, 1987; Veteran of the Month, Illinois Department of Veterans Affairs, 2010. **Home Addr:** 20724 Corinth Rd, Olympia Fields, IL 60461-1835, **Home Phone:** (708)606-0599. **Business Addr:** President, Chicago Defender Charities, 700 E Oakwood Blvd 5th Fl, Chicago, IL 60653, **Business Phone:** (773)536-3710.

**SCOTT, GILBERT H., SR.**
Chief executive officer, executive, consultant. **Personal:** Born Sep 7, 1946, Richmond, VA; son of Charles and Vernell Green Dickerson; married Brenda Patterson; children: Gilbert H Jr & Cecily R. **Educ:** Hampton Univ, BS, econ, 1968; Stanford Univ, exec mkt mgr prog, 1989; Wharton Sch Bus, int forum, 1995. **Career:** Va Elec & Power Co, sales rep, 1970-71; Xerox Corp, Va, 1971, sales rep, gen mgr & vpres, 1990-96; Hurshell Assoc, founder, pres & chief exec officer, 1998-; Cyveillance, vpres sales, 1999-; Bartech Group, pres & chief operating officer; Mass Inst Technol, guest lectr; Sloan Grad Sch, guest lectr; Silanis Technol Inc. **Orgs:** Vice chmn & exec mem, Pres Cabinet, Univ Calif; corp adv bd, George Wash Univ, Va Campus; San Luis Obispo. **Honors/Awds:** Community Involvement, Asn Black Military Officers, 1987. **Business Addr:** President, Chief Executive Officer, Hurshell Associates, 10731 Hunters Pl Dr, Vienna, VA 22181-2843, **Business Phone:** (703)716-7501.

**SCOTT, DR. GLORIA DEAN RANDLE**
Educator, college president, association executive. **Personal:** Born Apr 14, 1938, Houston, TX; daughter of Freeman Randle and Juanita; married Will Braxton. **Educ:** Ind Univ, BA, zool, 1959, MA, zool, 1960, PhD, higher educ, 1965, LLD, 1977. **Career:** School administrator (retired); Inst Psych Res, res assoc genetics, 1961-63; Marian Col, col prof, 1961-65, instr biol; Knoxville Col, prof, 1965-67, dean students; NCA Tex Southern Univ, prof, 1967-76, asst to pres, 1967-68, prof, 1976-78; Nat Inst Educ, head post sec res, 1973-75; NCA Tex Southern Univ, Planning & Inst Res, dir, 1973-76; Clark Col, prof, 1978-86, vpres, 1978-86; Grambling State Univ, prof, 1987; Bennett Col, pres, 1987-2001; Scotts Bay Enterprises, owner, currently; G Randle Serv, pres, owner, currently. **Orgs:** Bd dirs, Southern Educ Found, 1971-76; pres, G Randle Serv, 1975-; owner, Scotts Bay Courts, 1972-; consult, Ford Found, Southern Educ Found, 1967-72, 76; sec, Corp PREP, 1966-82; vpres, Girl Scouts USA, 1972-75, pres, 1975-78; bd dir, Nat Urban League, 1976-82; mem & chw, Defense Community Women Servs, 1979-81; chair bd dirs, Nat Scholar Fund Negro Studs, 1984-85; contrib ed, Good Housekeeping, 1985; adv bd, Historically Black Cols, 1988-92; vchair, PRSs Adv HBCU Bd, 1976-83; vpres, United Meth Ch Black Col Fund, 1995-97, pres, 1997-99; nat bd dir, UNCF, 1990-97; bd mem, Loews, 1990-; head deleg, Women INT Forum, Beijing, China, 1995; Delta Sigma Theta Sorority; co-founder, ex-officio, Nat African Am Women's Leadership Inst. **Honors/Awds:** Woman of the Year, YMCA, 1977; Kizzie Image Award, 1979; Honarary Degrees, Ind Univ, 1977; NCA Governor's Award-Women, 1990; Drum Major for Justice Award, SCLC, 1994; Texas Woman of Achievement, Girl Scouts San JacintoCoun, 1997; numerous honarary degrees. **Special Achievements:** First African-American to get a degree in zoology from Indiana Univ; First African-American president of the Girl Scouts of the USA. Author, "A Historically Black College Perspective"; First African American instructor at Marion College. **Home Addr:** PO Box 900, Riviera, TX 78379, **Home Phone:** (361)297-5307. **Business Addr:** President, Owner, G Randle Serv, 539 S County Rd Suite 1142 Rt 1, Riviera, TX 78379.

**SCOTT, HATTIE BELL (HATTIE SCOTT)**
Real estate executive, manager. **Personal:** Born May 28, 1945, Ft. Motte, SC; daughter of Cassie Keith Weeks and Jesse Weeks; married Leonard Henry; children: Allen Leonard & Gregory Walter. **Educ:** Allen Univ, attended 1965. **Career:** Long & Foster, Camp Springs, Md, realtor assoc, 1977-81, sls mgr, 1981-88, Waldorf, Md, sr vpres & Southern Md reg mgr, 1988-. **Orgs:** Prince Georges' County Bd, Realtors Distinguished Sls Club, 1978; Prince Georges' County Fair Housing Comt, 1980-; Women's Coun, Prince Georges' County Bd Realtors, 1982-; Prince Georges' County Bd Realtors Polit Action Comt, 1987-, chmn, 1989; Prince Georges' County Arts Coun, 1990-. **Honors/Awds:** Manager of the Year, 1984; Rookie of the Year, 1978. **Home Addr:** 5221 Cottonwood Dr, Lothian, MD 20711, **Home Phone:** (301)627-1953. **Business Addr:** Senior Vice President, Regional Manager, Long & Foster Realtors, 3165 Crain Hwy Suite 200, Waldorf, MD 20603-4847, **Business Phone:** (301)932-4700.

**SCOTT, DR. HELEN MADISON MARIE PAWNE KINNARD**
Executive. **Personal:** Born Washington, DC; daughter of David and Helen T; married Victor F; children: Lenise Sharon & Monique Sherine. **Educ:** Wash Univ, BMT, 1963; Howard Univ, BA, 1971, MA, 1973; Grant Col, PA, pub admin. **Career:** Univ West I, distinguished vis prof, 1971-72; Howard Univ, liaison pres, 1971; Dr Joyce Ladner, res asst, 1972-74; Dept Comm Plan, asst prof, 1973-74; Howard Univ, Sch Social Work, adj prof, 1973-74, Sch Commun, asst admin, prof, from adj asst to mgr Cramton Aud; TV, writer, co-star, 1973; Travel Way Found, prof soc plan & policy; RLA Inc, vpres, dir Zambia (HIRD) Proj Lusaka, Zambia; Licensure Real Estate, Wash DC; LICSW Social Work, Wash DC; Am Psychol Asn, prog adminr, currently. **Orgs:** Int Manpower Dev Sem, 1972, 1974; consult, Soc Planning Cong Black Caucus, 1973; Nat Inst Ment Health Maint & Tuition, 1973; Chi Lambda Phi; State Calif Child Care Conf, 1973; state organizer, Nat Coun Negro Women, 1973; Phi Beta Kappa, 1973; coord, 7th World Law Conf, 1975; Com Human Settlements, 1976; Am Ded Radio & TV Artists; Am Planning Asn; Am Soc Plan Off, Delta Sigma Theta Sorority; Nat Acad Sci; Nat Asn Soc Workers; Nat Asn Col & Univ Concern Mgt; Nat Asn Advan Colored People; Southern Christian Leadership Conf; Nat Asn Black Educrs; Nat Asn Educ Young C; Coun Except C, Int City Mgt Asn; Howard Univ Alumni Asn; bd dirs, Freedom Bowl Alumni Comn, Asn Black Psychologists; Caribbean Am Intercult Org Inc; Caribbean Festivals Inc; Phi Delta Kappa. **Honors/Awds:** National Endowment for Arts Scholarship, 1971; Outstanding Human Service, Howard Univ MS Proj, 1971; Southern California Film Institute Award, 1973; Emmy Award, TV Show, 1973; Rockefeller Foundation Award, 1973; Bureau of Standard Award for Outstanding HS Student in Mathmatics & Science. **Home Addr:** 10 Travilah Terr, Potomac, MD 20854-1042, **Home Phone:** (301)519-2255. **Business Addr:** Program Administrator, American Psychological Association, 750 1st St NE, Washington, DC 20002-4242, **Business Phone:** (202)336-5500.

**SCOTT, HOSIE L.**
Clergy, college administrator. **Personal:** Born May 31, 1943, Clopton, AL; married Ruth. **Educ:** Kean Col, BA, MA; Brookdale Community Col. **Career:** Jersey Cent Power Co, Sayreville, NJ, technician, 1967-68; NC Mutual Life Ins Co, Newark, NJ, life underwriter counr & debit mgr, 1968-70; Red Bank YMCA, exec youth prog dir, 1970-72; Brookdale Community Col, Lincroft, NJ, coordr affirm action & personnel admin, 1972-; chaplain minister, currently. **Orgs:** NJ Col & Univ Personnel Asn; Monmouth Ocean Co Prof Personnel Dir Asn; dir affirm action, NJ Prof; Nat Coun Black Am Affairs; Am Asn Community Jr Col; Life Underwriters Asn, 1968-70; Asn Prof Dir YMCA, 1970-72; BAN-WY'S YMCA, 1970-74; Am Soc Notaries; Greater Red Bank Nat Asn Advan Colored People; bd dir, Union Co Urban League, NJ; chmn, Affirm Action Adv Comt Brookdale Col, NJ; chmn, Matawan Twp Drug Coun, NJ; adv bd, EOF Brookdale Col; Dept Higher Educ Affirm & Action Comn; adv com mem, Inst Appl Humanities Brookdale Community Col; Dr M Luther King Observance Com; exec com mem, Monmouth Co NJ Bicentennial; pres, Tri-Community Club Matawan NJ; exec comt, African Am Arts & Heritage Festival. **Honors/Awds:** Outstanding Certificate of Leadership & Achievement Award, Dept Army, 1967; Fitness Finders Award, Nat YMCA, 1972; Outstanding Leadership Award, New Shrewbury, NJ Kiwanis, 1972; Distinguished Service Award, Matawan Twp Tri-Community Club, 1973; Service Award, Greater Red Bank Nat Asn Advan Colored People, 1973. **Home Addr:** 12 Westbrook Dr, Morganville, NJ 07751, **Home Phone:** (732)536-8174. **Business Addr:** Coordinator Affirm Action, Personnel Administration, Brookdale Community College, 765 Newman Springs Rd, Lincroft, NJ 07738-1543, **Business Phone:** (732)224-2345.

**SCOTT, HUGH B.**
Judge. **Personal:** Born Apr 29, 1949, Buffalo, NY; son of Edward Nelson and Anne Braithwaite (deceased); married Trudy Carlson; children: Hugh B Jr & Everett N. **Educ:** Niagara Univ, Lewiston, NY, BA, 1971; State Univ NY, Buffalo Law Sch, JD, 1974. **Career:** Co Erie Dept Law, asst co atty, 1974-75; City Buffalo Dept Law, asst corp coun, 1975-77; Dept Justice, Buffalo, NY, asst US atty, 1977-79; NY State Dept Law, Buffalo, NY, asst atty gen, 1979-83; Univ Buffalo Law Sch, Amherst Campus, lectr, 1980-; NY State Off Ct, Buffalo City Ct, judge, 1983-; US Magistrate Judge, 1995-. **Orgs:** Vice chmn, Urban League Buffalo, 1980; Alpha Kappa Boule, 1983-; bd dir, Univ Buffalo Law Alumni Asn, 1988-; bd mgrs, Buffalo Mus Sci, 1989-; adv coun, TransAfrica Buffalo, 1990-; bd trustee, Canisius Col, chair adv bd, Off Multicultural Prog; bd trustee, Catholic Health Syst; bd mem, Nat Fedn Just Communities; bd dir, Erie Co Bar Asn Aid Indigent Prisoners Soc; dean's adv bd, Buffalo Law Sch; bd mem, Community Found Greater Buffalo; Second Circuit Judicial Conf Planning & Prog Comt. **Honors/Awds:** Lifetime Achievement Award, Rochester Black Bar Asn; Citation Award, Nat Conf Community & Justice; One Hundred Black Men of Buffalo Community Service Award; YMCA of Buffalo Toast of Buffalo Community Service Award; Law Review Distinguished Service Award, Buffalo Law Sch; Distinguished Alumnus Award, UB Law Alumni Asn; William Wells Brown Award, Afro-American Hist Asn; Judges & Police Executives Community Service Award; Man of the Year Award, Nat Asn Negro Bus & Prof Women's Clubs; Greater Buffalo Council on Alcoholism & Substance Abuse Service Award; Attorney General Robert Abrams Alumnus Award; Caritas Metal, Niagara Univ. **Special Achievements:** First African-American Assistant United States Attorney for the Western District of New York; First African American to become assistant United States Attorney, assistant corporation counsel and assistant county attorney; First African-American federal judge in Western New York History. **Home Addr:** 6242 Bridlewood Dr S, East Amherst, NY 14051-2023, **Home Phone:** (716)833-5923. **Business Addr:** Magistrate Judge, United States District Court, 2 Niagara Sq, Buffalo, NY 14202, **Business Phone:** (716)551-1860.

**SCOTT, DR. HUGH J.** **See Obituaries Section.**

**SCOTT, JACOB REGINALD**
Executive. **Personal:** Born Jun 2, 1938, New York, NY; married Merri Hinkis; children: Elaine Beatrice & Lisa Anne White. **Educ:** Lincoln Univ, BS, psychol, 1960; Inst African De Geneve, Geneva Switz, dipl African studies, 1971. **Career:** US State Dept Foreign Serv, Ethiopia, econ & comn officer, 1966-68; Seagram Africa, sales mkt dir, 1971-80; Seagram Overseas Sales NY, mkt dir Africa, 1982-83, vpres Africa, 1984-91; Seagram Europe & Africa, vpres Africa, 1992-94, vpres external affairs, 1995-. **Orgs:** Montclair Alumni Chap, Kappa Alpha Psi, 1981-83; founding mem & dir, Seagram Safrica Pty Ltd, 1994-. **Home Addr:** 3650 Environ Blvd, Lauderhill, FL 33319. **Business Addr:** Vice President External Affairs, Seagram Europe & Africa, 57 Mandeville Pl, LondonW1M 5LB.

### SCOTT, JAMES HENRY
Association executive, executive. **Personal:** Born Dec 22, 1942, St. Louis, MO; married Cora Sabeta Dillon; children: 4. **Educ:** Villanova Univ, BS, electrical engineering, 1965, MA; Wash Univ, MBA, 1970. **Career:** Guyana, S Am, Peace Corps vol, 1966-68; Citibank, acct officer, 1970-72; Gulf & Western Ind Inc, asst vpres fin, 1972-73; White House, 1978-79; TXU Corp, vpres, asst treas, sr corp planner, corp secy, exec asst to chief exec officer, interim chief operating officer; JP Morgan & Co, head banking, vpres/sr banker. **Orgs:** Ed chief, Circuit, 1964-65; co-found & sec, AFRAM Enterprises Inc, 1968-73; asst treas, Greater NY Coun Boy Scouts Am; NY Urban League; Acad Polit Sci; bd, Aid Asn Lutherans, 1998-2001; dir, Intersections Inst; exec dir, Morgan Stanley Investment Mgt, 2007-; treas, Amherst Col, 1986-90; CFA Soc Philadelphia; Am Soc Engineering Educ; Edison Elec Inst; Strategic Planning Exec Adv Comt; Nuclear Energy Inst, Commun Adv Comt; Am Soc Corp Secretaries; treas, chief financial officer, Lutheran Theol Sem; chair, Univ Tex; trustee, Gettysburg Col; United Way Metrop Dallas; Dallas Zool Soc; Augsburg Fortress Publishers; vpres, Morgan Guaranty Trust Co; vpres, Bank Morgan Labouchere NY; treas, Lutheran Theol Sem, Philadelphia; bd dir, Thrivent Financial Lutherans, 2006-; Calvary Lutheran Church. **Home Addr:** Haringvlietstraat 21, Amsterdam1078 J7. **Business Addr:** Director, Thrivent Financial for Lutherans, 4321 N Ballard Rd, Appleton, WI 54919-0001, **Business Phone:** (612)340-7000.

### SCOTT, JILL
Singer, songwriter, actor. **Personal:** Born Apr 4, 1972, Philadelphia, PA; daughter of Joyce; married Lyzel Williams. **Career:** Singer-songwriter, poet, 2000-; Vocalist, song writer. albums: In Too Deep, 1999; Who Is Jill Scott?: Words & Sounds Vol 1, 2000; Save the Last Dance, 2001; Down to Earth, 2001; Experience: Jill Scott 826, 2001; Brown Sugar, 2002; Love Don't Cost a Thing, 2003; Beautifully Human: Words & Sounds Vol2, 2004; Beauty Shop, 2005; Block Party, 2005; Something New, 2006; Hounddog, 2007; The Real Thing: Words & Sounds Vol.3, 2007; Welcome Home, Roscoe Jenkins, 2008; Obsessed, 2009; The Light of the Sun, 2011. stage appearance: Rent, Canadian touring cast; songs: "Gettining In the Way", 2000; "A Long Walk", 2001; "He Loves Me (Lyzel In E Flat)", 2002; "Golden", 2004; "Whatever", 2005; "Cross My Mind", 2005; "Day dreamin", 2006. films: Hounddog, 2007; Why Did I Get Married, 2007; Why Did I Get Married Too?, 2010; Sins of the Mother, 2010; Steel Magnolias, 2012; Second Sight, 2013; With This Ring, 2015; Snowfall, forthcoming, 2015; Coco, forthcoming, 2016. TV: "Broadway's Best", 2002; "Prophet & Loss", 2004; "A Comedy of Eros", 2004; "On the Couch", 2004; "He Loves Her, He Loves Her Not", 2004; "The Boy with an African Heart", 2009; "Problems in Moral Philosophy", 2009; "Beauty & Integrity", 2009; "A Real Botswana Diamond", 2009. **Orgs:** Founder, Blues Babe Found. **Business Addr:** Singer, Songwriter, clo Hidden Beach Recording LLC, 1802 Berkeley St, Santa Monica, CA 90404, **Business Phone:** (310)453-1400.

### SCOTT, DR. JOHN SHERMAN
Writer, educator. **Personal:** Born Jul 20, 1937, Bellaire, OH; son of Beauta and George; married Sharon A Riley; children: Jon-Jama & Jasmin Evangelene. **Educ:** SC State Univ, BA, 1961; Bowling Green Univ, MA, 1966, PhD, 1972. **Career:** Bowling Green State Univ, OH, prof ethnic studies & resident-writer, 1970, Ethnic Cult Arts, dir, prof emer, currently; Nathan Hale Auditorium, dir, 1987; Scottvisions Productions & Publ, playwright, dir & chief exec officer, 2003-; Jackson State Univ, Dept Speech Commun & Theatre, prof & chair, 2007; Ethnic Cult Arts Prog, dir; Kaleidoscope; Shorty; Lizard Ther; Tex A&M Univ, dir; HBCU Benedict Col, Dept Fine Arts, prof & chair; Fla Memorial Col, Humanities Div, prof & chair, Performing Arts, dir; Dillard Univ, Consult Artistic, dir & lectr. **Orgs:** Speech Comm Asn, 1966-73; consult, Toledo Model Cities Prog, 1969-72; Eugene O'Neill Memorial Theatre Ctr, 1970-; consult, Toledo Bd Educ; New York Dramatists League, 1971-; Frank Silvera Writer's Workshop, 1973-. **Honors/Awds:** Karma & The Goodship Credit, Richard Allen Ctr, 1978-79; Governor's Award for the Arts, State of Ohio, 1990; produced play (TV), CURRENTS, 1991, produced docu-drama (TV), Hats & Fans, 1991, PBS; Govenor's Award for The Arts. **Special Achievements:** Ride A Black Horse, Negro Ensemble Co, 1972; Pub articles Players Black Lines; plays performed, Off-Broadway, NYC; Karma's Kall, Vinette Carroll's Urban Arts Theatre; Karma, Afro-Am Total Theatre; The Good Ship Credit, Richard Allen Ctr; From The Rivers Of Our Fathers. Books: Kaleidoscope: Black Theatre Visions; Shorty: Six One-act Plays; Lizard Therapy: Poems, Songs, Monologues & Short-Stories. Author of Numerous Books. **Home Addr:** 5962 Forest Hills Ct, Maumee, OH 43537, **Home Phone:** (419)215-9348. **Business Addr:** Playwriter, Director, Scottvisions Publications & Productions, 1687 Wyandotte Blvd, Maumee, OH 43537, **Business Phone:** (567)742-7581.

### SCOTT, JOSEPH M.
Banker, president (organization). **Personal:** Born Apr 2, 1945, Vicksburg, MS; son of Pierre A Sr and Carrie Albert; children: Bettina Harding & Patrick. **Educ:** Grambling State Univ, BS, 1967; Eastern Mich Univ, MA, 1974. **Career:** Government official (retired); Nat Bank Detroit, asst br mgr, 1967-68; First Am Bank, 1971-98; First Independence Nat Bank, pres, 2004. **Orgs:** Adv bd, Detroit Med Ctr NW; United Way Community Servs; Leadership Detroit Alumni Asn; Urban Bankers Forum; Detroit Urban League; Detroit Econ Growth Corp; Sothfield Econ Develop Corp. **Honors/Awds:** Spirit of Detroit Award, 1995. **Home Addr:** 28051 Golf Pointe Blvd, PO Box 2571, Farmington Hills, MI 48331, **Home Phone:** (248)489-9089.

### SCOTT, JOSEPH WALTER
Writer, educator, association executive. **Personal:** Born May 7, 1935, Detroit, MI; son of William Felton and Bertha Colbert; children: Victor, Valli & Velissa. **Educ:** Cent Mich Univ, BS, 1957; Ind Univ, MA, sociol, 1959, PhD, sociol & anthrop, 1963. **Career:** John Hay Whitney, fel, 1960-61; Nat Insts Health, fel, 1962-63; Am Univ, lectr, 1964-65; Univ KY, asst prof sociol, 1965-67; Univ Toledo, prof sociol, 1967-70; Univ Notre Dame, Black Studies Prog, dir, 1970-72, assoc prof sociol, 1970-75, prof sociol & anthrop, 1978-85; Univ Ibadan, vis prof sociol, 1972-73; Univ Wash, prof Am ethnic studies, 1985-97, 1990-98, African Ethnic Studies, chair, 1985-90, prof sociol, prof emer sociol, currently. **Orgs:** Am Sociol Asn, 1958-; fel Inst Health, 1962-63; N Cent Sociol Asn, 1963-; State Dem Conv, 1970-; Rockefeller fel 1972-73; fel Am Coun Educ, NW Univ, 1975-76; pres, N Cent Sociol Asn, 1983-84; pres, Asn Black Sociologists, 1996-97; consult, War Poverty Prog Ind; Sunday Sch teacher Braden Meth Church Toledo; bd mem, Mt Zion Baptist Church Ethnic Sch; bd mem, Inner-City Devel Educ Action; Rainbow Coalition Organizer SB Ind; Nat Asn Advan Colored People; Pi Kappa Delta; Kappa Delta Pi. **Honors/Awds:** Scholastic Scholar, Cent Mich Univ, 1953-57; Who's Who Among Students Am Univs & Cols, 1956-57; Leadership Award, Mil Police Officers Basic Sch, 1963; Fulbright Scholar Argentina, 1967, 1969; Outstanding Grad Award, Cent Mich Univ; Outstanding Graduate Award, Carnegie Mellon Univ; Outstanding Student Senator Award; Athletic Scholar Award, Cent Mich Univ; Athletic Scholarship Award, Carnegie Mellon Univ; Centennial Award, Cent Mich Univ, 1992-93; G Pritchy Smith Multicultural Educator Award, Nat Asn Multicultural Educ; Ford Foundation Lecturer Award; Distinguished Alumni Award, Mich Univ. **Special Achievements:** Publication: The Black Revolts: The Politics of Racial Stratification. **Home Addr:** 4814 49th Ave S, Seattle, WA 98118, **Home Phone:** (206)722-2376. **Business Addr:** Emeritus Professor of Sociology, University of Washington, 211 Savery Hall, WA 98195-4380, **Business Phone:** (206)543-2051.

### SCOTT, JUDITH SUGG
Executive, lawyer. **Personal:** Born Aug 30, 1945, Washington, DC; daughter of Irvin D Sugg and Bernice Humphrey; married Robert C; children: Carmen & Nichole. **Educ:** Va State Univ, Petersburg, VA, BS, bus admin; Swarthmore Col, Swarthmore, post-bachelor degree, econs; Cath Univ Sch Law, Wash DC, JD. **Career:** Commonwealth, Va, asst atty gen, 1975-76; Va Housing Develop Authority, sr coun, 1976-82; Gov Va, sr coun, 1982-85, gen coun, 1985-91; Old Dom Univ, dir, 1991-98; Portfolio Recovery Assoc, exec vpres, secy & gen coun, 1998-. **Orgs:** Am Bar Asn; Va State Bar; Norfolk & Portsmouth Bar Asn; chmn, Govs War Drugs Task Force; fel, Rockefeller Found; bd dir, Girl Scouts Colonial Coast Coun; bd dir, United Way S Hampton Roads; bd dir, Women's Leadership Coun. **Home Addr:** 405 Pin Oak Rd, Newport News, VA 23601. **Business Addr:** Executive Vice President, General Counsel, Secretary, Portfolio Recovery Associates, 120 Corp Blvd, Norfolk, VA 23502, **Business Phone:** (757)519-9300.

### SCOTT, JULIE (JULIE ANGELYN NEWELL)
Planner. **Career:** Eli Lilly & Co, planner/architect, currently. **Home Addr:** 11325 Bear Hollow Ct, Indianapolis, IN 46229, **Home Phone:** (317)891-7567. **Business Addr:** Planner, Eli Lilly & Co, Lilly Corp Ctr, Indianapolis, IN 46285, **Business Phone:** (317)276-2000.

### SCOTT, DR. JULIUS S., JR.
President (organization), school administrator. **Personal:** Born Feb 26, 1925, Houston, TX; son of Julius Sebastian and Bertha Bell; married Ianthia Ann; children: Julius III, David K & Lamar K. **Educ:** Wiley Col, Marshall, TX, BA, 1945; Garrett Theol Seminary, Evanston Ill, BD, 1949; Brown Univ, Providence, RI, MA, 1964; Boston Univ, Boston, MA, PhD, 1968. **Career:** Mass Inst Technol, Cambridge Mass, Meth campus minister, 1960-61; Wesleyan Found, Houston Tex, chair united ministries, 1961-63; Southern Fellowships Fund, Atlanta Ga, asst dir, 1967-69; Spelman Col, Atlanta Ga, spec asst pres, 1972-74; Division of Higher Educ, Bd Higher Educ, Nashville Tenn, assoc gen secy, 1982-88; Paine Col, Augusta Ga, pres, 1975-82 & 1988-94; Albany St Col, interim pres; Wiley Col, Marshall Tex, pres, 1996-2002; Med Col Ga, interim pres, spec asst to pres diversity initiatives, currently; Albany State Univ, pres; Philander Smith Col, Little Rock, Ark, interim pres, currently. **Orgs:** Am Sociol Asn; Am Asn Univ Profs; Black Methodists Church Renewal; Soc Educ Reconstruction; United Methodists Church; exec dir, Martin Luther King Jr Ctr Nonviolent Social Chg. **Home Addr:** 1238 Beman St, Augusta, GA 30904, **Home Phone:** (404)737-6063. **Business Addr:** Interim President, Philander Smith College, 900 W Daisy Bates Dr, Little Rock, AR 72202, **Business Phone:** (501)375-9845.

### SCOTT, DR. KENNETH RICHARD
Educator. **Personal:** Born Apr 17, 1934, New York, NY; son of Howard Russell and Emma Eugenia Doby; married Elizabeth Willette Miller; children: Russell William & Preston Richard. **Educ:** Howard Univ, WA, BS, pharm, 1956; State Univ NY, Buffalo, NY, MS, pharmaceut chem, 1960; Univ Md, Baltimore, MD, PhD, org chem, 1969. **Career:** State Univ NY, Buffalo, fel grad asst, 1956-60; Howard Univ, Wash, instr, 1960-66, from asst prof to assoc prof, 1966-76, prof & interim chmn, 1976-, dir grad studies, currently; Univ Md, Baltimore, terminal pre-doctoral, 1965-66; Fulbright fel, 1989-90. **Orgs:** Pres, Howard Univ Chap, Rho Chi Pharm Hon Soc, 1963-64; pres, Howard Univ Pharm Alumni Asn, 1972-74; pres, Howard Univ Chap, Sigma Xi Sci Soc, 1975-77; Epilepsy Found Am, 1982-83; bd dir, Epilespy Found Am, 1983-89; ed adv bd, Trans Pharmaceut Scis, 1987-; Rho Chi; Am Chem Soc; Soc Neuroscience; Am Epilepsy Soc. **Home Addr:** 9816 Cottrell Ter, Silver Spring, MD 20903-1917, **Home Phone:** (301)434-7803. **Business Addr:** Professor & Interim Chairman, Director of Graduate Studies, Howard University, Dept Pharmaceut Sci Rm 309A Cooper Hall 2300 4th St NW, Washington, DC 20059, **Business Phone:** (202)806-7288.

### SCOTT, LARRY B.
Writer, actor, executive. **Personal:** Born Aug 17, 1961, Harlem, NY; son of Valerie. **Educ:** John Bowne, dipl, 1978. **Career:** Films: A Hero Ain't Nothing But a Sandwich, 1978; Karate Kid, 1984; Revenge of the Nerds, 1984; That Was Then This Is Now, 1985; Space camp, 1986; Iron Eagle, 1986; Inside Adam Swit; Extreme Prejudice, 1987; Revenge of the Nerds Part II, 1994; Thieves; Diablo II, 2000; The Cheapest Movie Ever Made, 2000; Diablo II: Lord of Destruction, 2001; 100 Kilos, 2001; Judge Koan, 2003; Business Johnson, 2007; Nobody Smiling, 2010; Spring Break '83. TV series: "Onein a Million", 1978; "Barney Miller", 1978; "Rag Tag Champs", 1978; "Roll of Thunder Hear My Cry", 1978; "The Jerk Too", 1984; "St Elsewhere", 1984-85; "Magnum PI", 1985; "The Jeffersons", 1985; "Grand Babies", 1985; "C of Times Sq", 1986; "Martin", 1996; "The Liberators", 1987; "All for One"; "The Trial of Bernard Goetz"; "Super Force", 1990; "Seinfeld", 1997; "A Mother's Testimony", 2001; "Meter Maids Need Love, Too", 2002; "The Parkers", 2002; "Getting Played", 2006. Theater: Back to Back; Eden; The Wizard of Oz; The Tempest; Stainless Steele; radio ser & writer; dir: Funny Futher muckers in Concert, Vol 1, 2001; Funny Futher muckers in Concert, Vol 2, 2001; They Are Coming: Prologue, 2010; Major Player, 2010; Grind, 2014; Producer: Cheapest Movie Ever Made, 2000; Funny Futhermuckers in Concert, Vol 1, 2001; Funny Futhermuckers in Concert, Vol 2, 2001; They Are Coming: Prologue, 2010; Grind, 2014; Larry B scott's companies, pres & chief exec officer, 1997-; LBS Productions, owner. **Honors/Awds:** Best Supporting Actor, Virgin Islands Film Festival; Outstanding Achievement in Theatre, Ensemble Perf, 1980; LA Drama Critics Award. **Home Addr:** 5200 Lankershim Blvd Suite 260, North Hollywood, CA 91601-3109. **Business Addr:** President, Chief Executive Officer, Larry B Scott's Co, North Hollywood, CA 90067.

### SCOTT, DR. LEONARD STEPHEN
Dentist, clergy. **Personal:** Born Feb 28, 1949, Indianapolis, IN; son of Nathaniel and Bernice Katherine Covington; married Christine Tyson; children: John, Bryant, Nathan, Leonard, Lynna, Melanie & Katherine. **Educ:** Ind State Univ, BS; Ind Univ Med Ctr, attended 1976; Ind Univ Sch Dent, DDS, 1973. **Career:** Leonbea Inc, pres; Tyscot Inc Rec Co, pres; pvt dent pract; Rock Community Church, pastor; Scott Dent, founder, 1973-, sr dentist, currently. **Orgs:** Amer Dent Asn; Indianapolis Dist Dent Soc; Ind State Health Facil Admin; Ind Dent Asn; Omega Psi Phi Frat; Nat Asn Advan Colored People; tst, Christ Apostolic Church; bd dir, sec Christ Ch Apostolic; AO Dent Frat; Nat Acad Rec Arts & Scis; pres, Gospel Excellence Ministries Inc; fac mem, Aenon Bible Col; founder, Scott Dent, 1973. **Honors/Awds:** Fel, Acad Gen Dent. **Home Addr:** 3402 Schofield Ave, Indianapolis, IN 46218-1136. **Business Addr:** Dentist, Scott Dentistry, 5501 E 71st St Track Suite 3, Indianapolis, IN 46220, **Business Phone:** (317)479-2340.

### SCOTT, M ALEXIS. See SCOTT, ALEXIS.

### SCOTT, MARIAN ALEXIS
Newspaper publisher, journalist. **Personal:** Born Feb 4, 1949, Atlanta, GA; daughter of William Alexander III and Marian Willis; married Marc Anthony Lewis; married David L Reeves; children: Cinque Reeves & David L Reeves Jr. **Educ:** Barnard Col, attended 1968; Spelman Col, attended 1990; Columbia Univ, Sch Journalism, attended 1974; Leadership Atlanta, 1991; Regional Leadership Inst, 1992. **Career:** Atlanta Const, Atlanta, Ga, reporter, 1974-78, copy ed, 1978; Columbia Univ Sch Journ, Michelle Clark fel, 1974; Atlanta Jour-Const, Atlanta, Ga, ed, Intown Extra, 1979-81, asst city ed, 1982-84, ed dir & video ed, 1984-86, vpres community affairs, 1986-93; Cox Enterprises, dir diversity, 1993-97; Atlanta Daily World Inc, chmn, pres, 1997-; Atlanta Daily World Newspaper, founder, publ, 1997-. **Orgs:** Atlanta Chap, Nat Asn Media Women, 1985-87; chair, Nat Asn Advan Colored People Youth Achievement Acad, 1987-90; chair, Exodus/Cities Schs, 1990-91; steering comt mem, Ga Partnership Excellence Educ, 1990-91; ad-hoc comt chair, Multi-Cult Audience Develop, High Mus Art, 1990-91; vice chair, Friends Spelman, 1990, 1991; vice chair, High Mus Art, bd dir, 1991-93; chair, Friends Spelman, 1992-94; chair, Atlanta C's Shelter, 1995-96; pres, Atlanta Press Club, 2000-01; St Judes Recovery Ctr, bd mem, Atlanta Hist Ctr; High Mus Art; Atlanta Conv; Cent Atlanta Progress; True Colors Theatre Co. **Honors/Awds:** Sch Bell Excellence Educ Reporting, Ga Asn Educr, 1977; Distinguished Urban Journ Award, Nat Urban Coalition, 1980; Nat Media Woman of the Year, Nat Asn Media Women, 1983; Top 100 Bus & Prof Women, Dollars & Sense Mag, 1986; Acad of Women Achievers, YWCA, 1989; Pioneer Black Journalist Award, Atlanta Asn Black Journalists, 1998; Citizen of the Year Award, SW Hosp, 2001; Media of the Year Award, Ga Legis Black Caucus, 2001; Grimes Fel, Cox Family Enterprise Ctr, Kennesaw Univ, 2001; Imperial Court Daughters of Isis Hall of Fame Award, 2004; TD Jake's Megafest Phenomenal Woman Award, 2004. **Special Achievements:** Appointed by Mayor Shirley Franklin to the bd Atlanta Workforce Development Agency, 2003; Named Among 20 Women Making A Mark on Atlanta, Atlanta Mag, 1998. **Business Addr:** Publisher, Journalist, Atlanta Daily World, 3485 N Desert Dr Suite 2109, Atlanta, GA 30344, **Business Phone:** (404)761-1114.

### SCOTT, DR. MARVIN BAILEY
Educator, administrator, politician. **Personal:** Born Mar 10, 1944, Henderson, NC; son of Robert B and Gertrude Bailey; married Carol A Johnson; children: Robert B & Cindy P; married Dulce M; children: Alex Costa & Marvin B Jr. **Educ:** Univ Allahabad, 1966; Johnson C Smith Univ, BA, psychol, 1966; Univ Pittsburgh, MEd, 1968, PhD, 1970. **Career:** Boston Univ Sch Educ, assoc prof, 1970-81, asst provost, 1979-80; Univ Mass, Off Pres, ACE fel, 1979-80; ATEX Comput, dir hum RRO, 1980-82; WRKO, radio talk show, Boston, host, 1982-86; Mass Bd Regents, asst chancellor prof, 1983-86; Pres St. Paul's Col, Lawrenceville, Va, 1986-88; "Cent VA Focus", TV prog, WPLZ, host, 1987-88; Marvin B Scott Assocs, pres, 1988-89; Lilly Endowment, educ prog dir, 1990; Butler Univ, spec asst pres, assoc dean educ, chair sociol & criminol dept, prof sociol, 1991-2015; U S House, 1996; cand, US Senate, 2004; Indianapolis Water Works, pres, 2011-14; Nat Coun Humanities, 2013-14. **Orgs:** Numerous mem incl vpres, Bd Int Visitors; bd dir, Black Media Coalition, Wash, DC; secy & exec bd mem, Cent Intercoll Athletic Asn; Community Adv Bd, Brunswick Correctional Ctr, Lawrence ville; 100 Black Men Indianapolis; bd dir, Indianapolis Civic Theater; bd dir, Crossroad Coun, Boy Scouts Am; bd dir, Martin Luther King Mult-Serv Ctr; ct expert, Boston Desegregation Case, 1975-82; Nat Asn Advan Colored People Sch Desegration Cases, 1981-84; Kappa Alpha Psi; Phi Delta Kappa; Alpha Kappa Mu; Alpha Kappa Delta; Phi Kappa Phi; Nat Coun Humanities Deacon, Second Presby Church, IN; sr dir, Ind Acad Soc Sci Ex Crossroads Coun; Boy Scouts Am. **Home Addr:** 11621 Cakmanor Way, Indianapolis, IN 46037, **Home Phone:** (317)288-9771. **Business Addr:** Professor, Butler University, Jordan Hall 371 4600 Sunset Ave, Indianapolis, IN 46208, **Business Phone:** (317)940-9464.

### SCOTT, MARVIN WAYNE
Educator. **Personal:** Born Jan 21, 1952, Philadelphia, PA; son of Albert and Maloy; married Marcia Annette Simons; children: Thembi L & Kori A. **Educ:** E Stroudsburg Univ, BA, phys educ, 1973; Ohio State Univ, MA, phys educ, 1974; Univ NC, Greensboro, EdD, curric theory & prog eval phys educ, 1986. **Career:** Miami Dade Community

Col, asst prof, 1974-78; Howard Community Col, assoc prof, 1979-87; Univ Md, asst prof, 1987, adj mem, currently, sr lectr, instr & coordr, currently. **Orgs:** Scholar comt, Md Asn Health, Phys Educ, Recreation & Dance, 1980, 1984; Comt investigate greater involvement, EDA Am Alliance Health, Phys Educ, Recreation & Dance, 1981; Nom Comt, Nat Asn Sport & Phys Educ, 1982; curric consult, Hampton Inst, 1982, Md State Dept Educ, 1982; progeval, Univ Md, Batlimore, 1984; Am Asn Univ Women ann conf. **Home Addr:** 7366 Broken Staff, Columbia, MD 21045, **Home Phone:** (301)381-9360. **Business Addr:** Instructor, Coordinator, University of Maryland, Rm 2347 HHP Bldg, College Park, MD 20742-2611, **Business Phone:** (301)405-2480.

### SCOTT, MELVINA BROOKS
Insurance agent, government official, executive director. **Personal:** Born Mar 19, 1948, Goodman, MS; daughter of Sabina Walker and Shed; children: Johnny F Jr, James T & Kateea P. **Educ:** Hawkeye Inst Tech, grad life underwriting assting; Univ Northern Iowa, BA, social work, 1976, masters prog; Wartsburg Col, cert, mgt objective, community law, affirmative action & substance abuse, 1985. **Career:** Area Educ Agency VII, media clerk, 1968-75; Minority Alcoholism Coun, 1975-76; Black Hawk Co, Dept Corresp Serv, probation officer, 1976-77; Royal Neighbors of America, insurance agen, 1977t; Prudential Ins Co, dist agt, 1977-81; polit consult, 1978-86; Cutler Cong, polit counr; All State Ins, 1981-85; Waterloo Comm Schs, 7th grade basketball coach, 1985-93; Nagle Cong, polit counr, 1986; Congressman David Nagle, caseworker & staff asst, 1987-93; Mel Scott Agency, Owner, currently. **Orgs:** Chairperson, dem party Black Hawk Co, 1974-78; youth adv & vpres, Black Hawk Co Nat Asn Advan Colored People, 1976-80; vpres bd, Logandate Coop Daycare, 1977-78; civic comm, mem C of C Com Delta Sigma Theta, 1977-79; pres, United Sister Black Hawk Co; polit action coun mem, Life Underwriters Asn, 1978-; comm develop, Comm Funding CMS, 1980-86; Layman Orgn Payne AME Ch; Payne AME; comm mem, Minority Drug Coun Int Women's Yr Comm Del to Houston; co mem, Third Dist Affirmative Action Comm; ward leader, Dem Party Cent Comm, 1980-86; vice chairperson, Iowa Black Caucus; bd treas, NHS, 1983-86; Mayor Rev Comm St, 1988-89; Mayor Rev Comm Area Econ Develop, 1989; exec bd mem, YWCA, 1990-96; affirmative action chairperson, Iowa Dem Party; founding mem & exec dir, African Am Hist & Cult Mus, 2004; pres, United Sisters & Reg Networkers Together Inc; Nat Women's Conf; bd dir, Waterloo Neighbour Econ Develop Corp. **Honors/Awds:** Service Award, Boys Club Waterloo, 1977; National Sale Achievement Award, 1978, 1980. **Home Addr:** 413 Oneida St, Waterloo, IA 50703, **Home Phone:** (319)234-8404. **Business Addr:** Owner, Business Developer, Mel Scott Agency, 413 Oneida St, Waterloo, IA 50703, **Business Phone:** (319)504-1204.

### SCOTT, MICHAEL W., SR.
Association executive, president (organization). **Personal:** Born Sep 4, 1949, Chicago, IL; married Diana. **Educ:** Fordham Univ, BA, urban planning. **Career:** Pyramid W Develop Corp, vpres; Lawndale People's Planning & Action Coun, dir community develop, 1978-82; Chicago Bd Edu, bd mem, 1980-81, pres, 2001-; Dept Spec Events, dep dir; spec asst mayor, dir; City Chicago's Off Cable Commun, chief cable admin; Prime Cable, gen mgr; AT&T Broadband, vpres local govt affairs; Comcast Corp, vpres regulatory affairs; Pyramidwest Develop Corp, vpres; Chicago Pk Dist Bd, pres; Michael Scott & Assocs LLC, pres, currently; Chicago Pub Schs, bd edu, bd pres; Pub Bldg Comn Chicago, Comnr, 2002-. **Orgs:** Coun Great City Sch; Chicago Olympic Comt; Mt Sinai Hosp; Better Boys Found; Chicago Hist Soc; Chicago Urban League; Build On; bd mem, YMCA USA. **Home Addr:** , IL. **Business Addr:** Board President, Chicago Board of Education, 125 S Clark St 6th Fl, Chicago, IL 60603, **Business Phone:** (773)553-1600.

### SCOTT, DR. MONA VAUGHN
Executive, educator. **Personal:** Born Jackson, MS; daughter of Birel and Nora (deceased); married Richard; children: Monika, Sean & Malaika. **Educ:** Col Pac, BA; Univ Pac, MA; Stanford Univ, PhD, 1977. **Career:** George Washington Univ, dir res soc servs, 1966; Univ Calif Dent Sch, teacher, minority admis comn, consult, 1969; Dent Sch Univ San Francisco, Gen Admis Comt, consult, 1969; Minortiy Allied Health League Concentration Motivation, founder, dir consult, 1970-75; Family Background & Family Lifestyles Minorities San Francisco, dir res, 1971-73; Inner-City Youth Orchestra, founder; Nat Med Asn, res cons; Golden State Med Asn, res cons; Black Repertory Group, Berkeley, Calif, exec dir; Wash Sch Psychiat, dir res soc servs; Scotts Int Res & Educ Consult Orgn, exec dir researcher. **Orgs:** Calif Teachers Eng Speakers Other Lang; dir, SIRECO; Bay Area Asn Black Psychologists; Nat Asn Advan Colored People; lifetime mem, ORCHESIS; bd mem, Black Repertory Group; Hon Soc Nat Mod Dance. **Honors/Awds:** Women of the Year Award, Delta Theta Nu, 1964; Tulley Knowles Scholarship Philosophy Inst; Mary R Smith Scholarship; Outstanding National Meth Student Scholarship; National Meth Scholarship; Ambassadors Award, Comm Serv Wash, DC; Dept Behavioral Technical Award, Westinghouse; Ambassadors Youth Award, Alameda County Women Hall Fame; Mayor Berkeley, Calif's Commendation. **Special Achievements:** Author: "The Efficacy of Tuition-Retention Programs for Minorities", 1968; "White Racism & Black Power", 1969; co-author: "Algerian Interview with Kathleen Cleaver", 1972; "Institutional Racism in Urban Schools", 1975. **Home Addr:** 309 Coral Ridge Dr, Pacifica, CA 94044-1432. **Business Addr:** Director, Black Repertory Group Theater, 3201 Adeline St, Berkeley, CA 94703, **Business Phone:** (510)652-2120.

### SCOTT, NELSON
Fashion model. **Personal:** Born Bronx, NY. **Career:** Ads: Guess, Banana Repub, Benetton; Ralph Lauren, runway show. **Business Addr:** Model, c/o Zoli Management, 3 W 18th St, New York, NY 10011-4610, **Business Phone:** (212)242-1500.

### SCOTT, NIGEL L.
Lawyer. **Personal:** Born Aug 23, 1940; married Monica Chasteau; children: Duane, Omar J & Rion. **Educ:** Howard Univ, BS, 1970; Howard Univ Sch Law, JD, 1973. **Career:** Eastman Kodak, patent atty, 1973-75; atty, pvt pract, 1975-79; Scott & Yallery-Arthur, law pract, atty, 1980-; Fed Courts & Local Courts. **Orgs:** DC Pa & US Patent Bars, 1975-; exec dir, Nat Patent Law Asn, 1979-; pres, Trinidad & Tobago Asn, 1977-79; adv, Human Rights Comn, Montgomery County, 1980. **Home Addr:** 8813 Leonard Dr, Silver Spring, MD 20901, **Home Phone:** (301)588-5783. **Business Addr:** Attorney, Scott & Yallery-Arthur Law Office, 7306 Ga Ave NW, Washington, DC 20012, **Business Phone:** (202)882-5770.

### SCOTT, OLYMPIA RANEE (OLYMPIA SCOTT-RICHARDSON)
Basketball player, basketball coach. **Personal:** Born Aug 5, 1976, Los Angeles, CA; daughter of Jacqueline Parker; married Al Richardson; children: BreAzia. **Educ:** Stanford Univ, BA, sociol, 1998. **Career:** Basketball player, basketball coach (retired), executive; Utah Starzz, 1998-99; Detroit Shock, ctr-forward, 2000-01; Ind Fever, ctr-forward, 2001-02, 2006-07; Super Parenting LLC, co-founder, pres & chief exec officer, 2003-; Charlotte Sting, ctr-forward, 2004; William Smith Col, head coach, 2004; Ceyhan, 2005-06; Sacramento Monarchs, ctr, 2005-06; Dynamo Moscow, 2006-07; Col Sequoias, asst coach; Phoenix Mercury, ctr, 2007; Iraklis Thessaloniki, 2007-08; Phoenix Suns, mercury player, 2007-08; A Wonderful Life! Coaching, founder, 2007-11; Mersin, 2008-10; Hatis Yerevan, 2010-11. **Orgs:** Delta Sigma Theta Sorority Inc; secy/treas, Women's Nat Basketball Players' Asn. **Business Addr:** President, Chief Executive Officer, Super Parenting LLC, PO Box 83632, Los Angeles, CA 90083.

### SCOTT, DR. OTIS L.
Dean (education), educator, administrator. **Personal:** Born Dec 27, 1941, Marion, OH; son of William and Harriett Booker; married Willie Vern Hawkins; children: William F, Byron O & David A. **Educ:** Univ Md; Eastern Wash State Col, Cheney, WA; Cent State Col, Wilberforce, OH; Calif State Univ, Sacramento, BA, 1971, MA, 1973; Union Grad Sch, Cincinnati, OH, PhD, 1982. **Career:** Calif State Univ, Sacramento, Calif, prof, 1974-, legacy, Col Soc Sci & Interdisciplinary Studies, actg dean, assoc dean, dean emer, currently; Calif State Univ Resistance, Sacramento, assoc dean social sci. Books: Veil Perspectives on Race and Ethnicity in the United States, 1994; Teaching from a Multicultural Perspective, 1994; Lines, Borders and Connections, 1997. **Orgs:** Sacramento Area Black Caucus, 1974-; Nat Coun Black Studies, 1979-; Nat Asn Ethnic Studies, 1985-; Nat Conf Black Polit Scientists, 1989-; pres, Nat Asn Ethnic Studies, 1996-98; bd mem, Smokey Robinson Found; chair, Sacramento State Ethnic Studies Dept. **Home Addr:** 10139 Malaga Way, Rancho Cordova, CA 95670, **Home Phone:** (916)363-3013. **Business Addr:** Dean Emeritus, Professor of Ethnic Studies & Government, California State University Sacramento, 6000 J St, Sacramento, CA 95819-6013, **Business Phone:** (916)278-6011.

### SCOTT, QUINCY, JR.
Clergy. **Personal:** Born Jan 11, 1944, Norfolk, VA; son of Josephine D; married Col Constance L; children: Toya Williams & Quincy III & Derek. **Educ:** Shaw Univ, BA, 1965; Vanderbilt Univ, MDiv, 1973; Boston Univ, MEd, 1976; Howard Univ, DMin, 1979; Mil Command Gen Staff Col. **Career:** Shaw Univ, chaplain dean the Thomas J Boyd Chapel, 1995-; Army Chaplain Sch, assoc prof; Pentagon, Wash, chaplain; Second Inf Div, S Korea, div chaplain; Walter Reed Army Med Ctr, staff chaplain; Edgehill United Methodist Church; Norfolk Pub Recreation. **Orgs:** Alpha Kappa Mu Hon Soc; Kappa Alpha Psi Fraternity; Nat Asn Advan Colored People; Retired Officers Asn; Nat Theol Fraternity; Mil Chaplains Asn; life mem, Shaw Alumni Asn. **Honors/Awds:** Man of the Year, Norfolk Women Dnl, 1996; The Legion of Merit, US Government. **Home Addr:** 5464 Brushy Meadows Dr, Fuquay Varina, NC 27526, **Home Phone:** (919)557-2141. **Business Addr:** Dean of the Chapel, Shaw University, 118 E S St, Raleigh, NC 27601-2399, **Business Phone:** (919)546-8454.

### SCOTT, R. LEE
Executive. **Personal:** Born Oct 8, 1943, Hollywood, AL; son of Lee J (deceased) and Jannie; married Mae Frances Kline; children: Ronald & Lynne. **Educ:** Univ Conn, BA, 1966; Univ Hartford, MBA, 1977; Cornell Univ, exec dev prog, 1984; Northwestern Univ, consumer strategy, 1989. **Career:** Aetna Life & Casualty Ins, sr underwriter, 1966-70; Southern New Eng Telecom, dist staff mgr int auditing, 1970-87, dist mkt mgr, consumer prod, 1987-, dir legis affairs, currently; Univ Hartford, adj prof, 1978-; Univ New Haven, adj prof. **Orgs:** Alpha Phi Alpha Frat, 1968; Sigma Pi Phi Frat; New Brit Nat Asn Advan Colored People; bd dir, Indian Hills Country Club Newington, Conn. **Home Addr:** 27 Hillside Pl Apt 25, New Britain, CT 06051-2571. **Business Addr:** Director Legislative Affairs, Southern New England Telecommunications, 55 Trumbull St, Hartford, CT 06111, **Business Phone:** (203)947-7034.

### SCOTT, RICHARD ELEY
Judge. **Personal:** Born Dec 25, 1945, Kilgore, TX. **Educ:** Prairie View A&M Univ, BA, 1968; Univ Tex, JD, 1972. **Career:** Pvt pract atty, 1972-; Tex Stand Rep Eddie B Johnson, legal asst, 1973; Austin Community Col, part-time instr, 1973; Travis Co Tex, Precinct One, justice peace, 1975-. **Orgs:** Nat Asn Advan Colored People; State Bar Tex, 1972; Del Dem Nat Conv, 1972; Travis County Jr Bar Asn, 1973; Nat Bar Asn, 1975; comt chmn adm State Bar Tex, 1976; E Austin Youth Found Coach, 1976; sponsoring comt, Austin Urban League, 1977; Rishon Lodge Suite 1, 1977. **Home Addr:** 6101 Easy Meadow Cove, Manor, TX 78653, **Home Phone:** (512)276-7115. **Business Addr:** Judge, Precinct One, Travis County, 4717 Heflin Lane Suite 107, Austin, TX 78721, **Business Phone:** (512)854-7700.

### SCOTT, ROBERT CORTEZ (BOBBY SCOTT)
Congressperson (U.S. federal government). **Personal:** Born Apr 30, 1947, Washington, DC; son of C Waldo and Mae Hamlin. **Educ:** Harvard Col, BA, 1969; Boston Col Law Sch, JD, 1973. **Career:** Atty at law, 1973-91; Va Gen Assembly, del, 1978-83; Va House Representatives, state rep, 1982-93; US House Rep, congressman, 1993-. **Orgs:** Newport News Old Dom Bar Asn, 1973-91; pres, Peninsula Bar Asn, 1974-78; pres, Newport News br, 1974-80, golden heritage life mem, Nat Asn Advan Colored People, 1976-; pres, Peninsula Legal Aid Ctr Inc, 1976-81; chmn, 1st Congional Dist Dem Com, 1980-85; vchmn, Va Dem Black Caucus, 1980; del, Nat Dem Conv, l980; Hampton Inst Ann Fund Com; bd mem, Peninsula Asn Sickle Cell Anemia; Peninsula Coun Boy Scouts Am; March Dimes; Alpha Phi Alpha, Sigma Pi Phi. **Honors/Awds:** Outstanding Leader Hampton Roads Jaycees, 1976; Man of the Year, Zeta Lambda Chap Alpha Phi Alpha Frat, 1977; Distinguished Community Service, Kennedy-Evers-King Memorial Found, 1977; Outstanding Achievement, Peninsula Nat Asn Negro Bus & Prof Women, 1978; Virginian of the Year award, Virginia Young Democrats, 1983; Brotherhood Citation Nat Conf Christians & Jews, 1985; Public Health Recognition Award, Va Pub Health Asn, 1986; Outstanding Legislator Award, Va Chapt & Amer Pediat Soc, 1986; Police Service Award, Virginia Fraternal Order, 1987; hon doctorate govt sci degree, Commonwealth Col, 1987; Outstanding Legislator Award, Southern Health Asn, 1989; Nat Humanitarian Hero Award, 2004; Virginia Fire & Emergency Services Award, 2005; NAMI Exemplary Legislator Award, 2006; Honorary Degree, Norfolk St Univ, 2007; Good Scouter Award, 2007; Distinguished Lifetime Award, 2007; Norvleate Downing-Gross Achievement Award, 2007; Distinguished Citizen of the Year Award, Va Peninsula Chamber Commerce, 2008. **Special Achievements:** First black member of Congress from Virginia since Reconstruction. **Home Addr:** 405 Pin Oak Rd, Newport News, VA 23601. **Business Addr:** Congressman, Member, US House of Representatives, 1201 Longworth HOB, Washington, DC 20515, **Business Phone:** (202)225-8351.

### SCOTT, ROBERT JEROME
Television actor, executive, media executive. **Personal:** Born Feb 2, 1946, San Francisco, CA; son of Robert and Mary Helen Harris Weeks; children: Siiri Sativa & Jeremy Harrington. **Educ:** Wayne State Univ, attended 1972. **Career:** Studio Theatres Detroit, supvr, 1968-69; Detroit News, staff photogr, 1969-71; Optek Photog, owner & photogr, 1971; Detroit Free Press, staff photogr & jazz critic, 1971-79; Mich Dept Com, dir mich film off, 1979-85; WTVS Channel 56, dir proj mkt, 1985-87, vpres community develop, 1987-91, vpres govt rels & support; WRCJ, sta mgr, 2005-08; Detroit Pub Tv, vpres, Foundations & Govt Rels, 2008-10; TV Ser: "Senzinina: What Have We Done to Deserve This", 1987; "Back to Detroit: Future", 1987; "Spectrum, Ser Arts Mich", 1987-90; "Gov Arts Awards Prog", 1989-92; "1991 Montreux Jazz Festival", 1991-92. **Orgs:** New Detroit Inc, comt racial & econ justice, 1986-88; bd dir, Theatre Grottesco, 1987-90; Gov Arts Awards Comt, 1989-92; bd dir, Concerned Citizens Arts Mich, 1991-92. **Honors/Awds:** Michigan Emmy Award, Nat Acad TV Arts & Sci, 1987. **Home Addr:** 14518 Abington Ave, Detroit, MI 48227-1408, **Home Phone:** (313)838-4505. **Business Addr:** Station Manager, WRCJ, 123 Selden St, Detroit, MI 48201, **Business Phone:** (313)494-6400.

### SCOTT, RUBY DIANNE
Media executive, consultant, association executive. **Personal:** Born Sep 19, 1951, New Rochelle, NY; daughter of Carmen Saunders and Clemmie; married Raymond Williams. **Educ:** Boston Univ, BS, jour, 1973; Northwestern Univ Mgt Training Ctr, 1985; Northwestern Univ, Advan Exec Prog, 1998; Kellogg Grad Sch Mgt Evanston, IL, advan exec prog. **Career:** Boston Globe, intern asst news ed, 1972-77; Chicago Tribune, copy ed, 1977-87, managing ed, 1987-90, opinion page ed, 1990-93; Tomorrow, ed, 1983-85; Sunday Mag, assoc ed, 1985-87, managing ed, 1987-90; Tribune Publ, ed resources diversity designed, 1993-99; Tribune Co, dir, diversity recruiting, 1999-2001; Nomadic Consult, sr consult, 2001-; Hewitt Assocs, sr opers mgr, 2003-04; Wallis Consult Group, sr commun consult, 2004-. **Orgs:** Nat Asn Black Journalists, 1984-; Nat Asn Minority Media Exec, 1993-; mentor, Sisters Struggle, 1993-; Am Soc Newspaper Ed Diversity Comn, 1994-; co-chair, Tribune Diversity Steering Comm, 1995-; Media Diversity Managers, 1995-; Newspaper Asn Am, recruitment & youth develop comn, 1997-; Int Asn Bus Communicators. **Honors/Awds:** Outstanding Professional Performance, Chicago Tribune, 1983; YMCA Black & Hispanic Achievers Bus & Indust, 1993. **Home Addr:** 5917 Pink Chaff St, North Las Vegas, NV 89031, **Home Phone:** (312)259-0185. **Business Addr:** Senior Consultant, Nomadic Consulting Inc, 200 E Ohio St Suite 300, Chicago, IL 60611, **Business Phone:** (312)664-1732.

### SCOTT, RUTH ELAINE HOLLAND
Management consultant, executive, government official. **Personal:** Born Aug 13, 1934, Albion, MI; daughter of Robert and Edna; married William G; children: Greg, June & Chrystal. **Educ:** Albion Col, BA, social work, 1956; Kent State Univ, ME, couns, 1961; Buffalo State, EdD, 1968; State Univ NY, cert, educ admin, 1981; Alfred Univ Hons Causa, DHL, 1997. **Career:** Cleveland Pub Schs, teacher, 1956-61; W Valley Cent Sch, NY, teacher, 1961-62; Arcade Cent Sch, NY, teacher, 1964-66; Educ Serv BOCES Cattaraugus Co, consult, 1966-70; City Sch Dist Rochester, consult nursing prog, 1971; Wilson Jr High Sch, reading lab coordr, 1974; City Sch Dist Rochester, adv specialist & human rels, 1975-77; Ford Found, consult, 1976-78; Community Savings Bank Rochester, personnel compliance coordr, 1977-, regional mgr; City Rochester, city councilwoman-at-large, coun pres, 1986-; Scott Assoc Inc, pres, chief exec officer, 1989-; Multicultural Inst, Portland, develop multi-cult workshops, 1993-. **Orgs:** Bd dir, WXXI, 1976-87; Friends Rochester Pub Libr, 1976-87; adv coun, Women's Career Ctr, 1977-; adv bd, WHEC TV-10; chairperson, Nat League Cities Community & Econ Develop, 1987; bd, Monroe County Water Authority; treas, Leadership Am Alumni Bd, 1990; bd mem, New Futures Initiative, NLC's Women Munic Govt bd pres, Rochester Community Found, 1991-96; exec secy, Rochester Area Found, pres, 1992; Phi Delta Kappa. **Honors/Awds:** Championship Debater Albion Col, 1952; Outstanding Alumni Award, Albion Col, 1975; Chamber Civic Award, Leadership Am Class, 1989; Exemplar Award, 1997; Senate Woman of Distinction Award, 2005; Outstanding Citizen-Politician-Christian Worker, Black Student Caucus local Col Divinity; Volunteer Service Award, Cert Martin Luther King Jr Greater Rochester Festival CMS. **Special Achievements:** Served as Rochester Community Savings Bank's first Community Reinvestment officer; One of the Women Builders of Communities and Dreams, honored by YWCA; One of five businesswomen, honored by prestigious Athena Award comm significant contrib bus & community; first black woman to serve on Rochester City Council. **Home Addr:** 30 Arvine Heights, Rochester, NY 14611, **Home Phone:** (716)328-3516. **Business Addr:** President, Chief Executive Officer, Scott Associates

Consulting Inc, 30 Arvine Heights, Rochester, NY 14611, **Business Phone:** (716)328-4770.

## SCOTT, SAMUEL N.

Engineer, government official. **Personal:** Born Feb 2, 1946, San Francisco, CA; married Christine Mary Harrington; children: Stephany & Sybil. **Educ:** Wayne State Univ, attended 1968. **Career:** Univ Mich Soc Res Study, coord personal, 1967-68; Studio Theaters Detroit, supvr, 1968-69; Detroit News, photo, 1969-71; Optek Photographics, dir & photo, 1971-72; Detroit Free Press, photo & jazz critic, 1972-79; Mich Film & TV Serv Mich Dept Com, exec officer, dir. **Orgs:** Mich Press Photo Asn, 1972-80; Nat Asn Film Comn, 1980. **Honors/Awds:** Honorable mental Michigan Press Photo, 1976-79; Public Service Award, Wayne Co Bd Comnrs, 1979. **Home Addr:** 5500 Eads St NE, Washington, DC 20020, **Home Phone:** (202)583-3923. **Business Addr:** 2021 Jefferson Davis Hwy Crystal City, Arlington, VA 22202.

## SCOTT, SERET

Theatrical director. **Personal:** Born Sep 1, 1947, Washington, DC; daughter of John William and Della; married Amos Augustus; children: Scott. **Educ:** NY Univ Sch Arts, attended 1969; Rutgers Univ, attended 1989. **Career:** New Haven's Long Wharf Theatre, dir, 1994-97; San Diego's Old Globe Theatre, assoc artist, dir, 1996-; Costa Mesa's S Coast Repertory, dir, 1996, 1999; NYC's Vivo Flamenco, dir, 1999; Second Line, auth. **Orgs:** Stage dir & Choreographers Union, 1990-. **Home Addr:** , Teaneck, NJ 07666. **Business Addr:** Theatre Director, Old Globe Theatre, 1363 Old Globe Way, San Diego, CA 92101.

## SCOTT, SHAWNELLE

Basketball player. **Personal:** Born Jun 16, 1972, New York, NY. **Educ:** St John's Univ, attended 1994. **Career:** Basketball player (retired), coach; Okla City Cavalry, 1994-95; Conn Pride, 1995-96, 1998-2000; Long Island Surf, 1996; Cleveland Cavaliers, ctr, 1996-98; Titanes De Morovis, Pr, 1999; Gigantes De Carolina, Pr, 2000; San Antonio Spurs, ctr, 2000-01; Denver Nuggets, ctr, 2001-02; Metis Varese, Italy, ctr, 2002-03; Teramo Basket, Italy, ctr, 2003-04; Indios De Mayaguez, Pr, 2004; Jilin Northeast Tigers, China, 2004-05; Olympia Larissa, Greece, 2004-05; Strong Island Sound, 2005-06; Millennium Brooklyn High Sch, coach, currently. **Business Addr:** Coach, Millennium Brooklyn High Sch, 237 7th Ave, Brooklyn, NY 11215, **Business Phone:** (718)832-4333.

## SCOTT, STEPHEN L.

President (organization), businessperson. **Career:** Scott-Hilliard-Kosene Inc, pres & partner, currently. **Orgs:** Indianapolis Adv Comn Indust Develop; bd dir, Greater Indianapolis Chamber Com; bd mem, Indianapolis Neighborhood Housing Partnership Inc; bd mem, Greater Ft Lauderdale Alliance; bd mem, Coalition Homelessness Intervention & Prev. **Business Addr:** President, Partner, Scott-Hilliard-Kosene Inc, 4495 Saguaro Trl, Indianapolis, IN 46268-2555, **Business Phone:** (317)290-4967.

## SCOTT, SYREETA

Founder (originator), beautician, harmonica player. **Educ:** Hampton Univ, 2000. **Career:** Duafe Holistic Hair Care Inc, founder, owner, chief exec officer & stylist, 2000-. **Orgs:** Treas, bd mem, Blues Babe Found; vol, Temple Univ, Pan Africa Studies Community Educ Prog; bd mem, Art Santuary. **Honors/Awds:** Winner of the Coalition, 100 Black Women. **Special Achievements:** Ten People Under 40 To Watch, Philadelphia Tribunes; Best of Philly Black Hair Salons 08, Philadelphia Magazines. **Business Addr:** Stylist, Owner, Duafe Holistic Hair Care, 3502 Scotts Lane, Philadelphia, PA 19130-1119, **Business Phone:** (267)297-7636.

## SCOTT, DR. TIMOTHY VAN

Ophthalmologist. **Personal:** Born Jul 12, 1942, Newport News, VA; son of William H and Janet H; married Karen Hill; children: Van, Lanita, Kevin & Amara. **Educ:** Fisk Univ, BA, 1964; Meharry Med Col, MD, 1968; Am Bd Ophthal, dipl, 1973. **Career:** Hubbard Hosp, Nashville, Ophthal Res, rotating internship, 1969; pvt pract, ophthalmologist, currently; Ophthalmologist Kaiser Hosp, staff, 1972-73; Univ Calif Glaucoma Jules Stein Eye Inst, HEED Ophthalmic Found fel, 1973, assoc prof, consult, 1973-; Ophthal Martin Luther King Jr Gen Hosp, chief div, 1973-82; Glaucoma Serv Harbor Hosp, 1973-79; Charles R Drew Post grad Med Sch, asst prof surg. **Orgs:** Am Asn Ophthal; Nat Asn Res & Interns; Omega Psi Phi Frat; Am Acad Ophthal. **Honors/Awds:** Outstanding Young Men of America, 1974. **Special Achievements:** First African American to undertake a glaucoma fellowship at the Jules Stein Eye Institute. **Home Addr:** 6175 Wooster Ave, Los Angeles, CA 90056, **Home Phone:** (310)215-3723. **Business Addr:** Ophthalmologist, Private Practice, 323 N Prairie Ave Suite 201, Inglewood, CA 90301, **Business Phone:** (310)673-5774.

## SCOTT, TODD CARLTON

Football player. **Personal:** Born Jan 23, 1968, Galveston, TX. **Educ:** Southwestern La Univ, grad. **Career:** Football player (retired); Minn Vikings, defensive back, 1991, strong safety, 1992-94; New York Jets, free safety, 1995; Tampa Bay Buccaneers, defensive back, 1995-96; Kans City Chiefs, 1997. **Honors/Awds:** Pro Bowl, 1992.

## SCOTT, VERONICA J.

Educator, physician. **Personal:** Born Feb 8, 1946, Greenville, AL; daughter of C B Jr and Mary Loys Greene (deceased). **Educ:** Howard Univ, BS, 1968; Albert Einstein Col Med, MD, 1973; UCLA Sch Pub Health, MPH, 1978. **Career:** Beth Israel Hosp, intern res med, 1973-75; UCLA prev med resident, 1976-78, W Los Angeles VAMC, geriat med fel, 1978-80; Birmingham VAMC, chief geriatrics sect, 1980-88; UAB/Med Ctr Aging, asst dir, 1980-; Meharry Consortium Geriat Educ Ctr, dir, 1990-; VA Tenn Valley Healthcare Syst GRECC, Assoc Dir, 2000; TVHS, Ethics Coordr, 2008; Meharry Med Col, ctraging, dir ctr aging, assoc prof med, currently; Geriat Res Educ & Clin Ctr, assoc dire duc & prog eval, currently. **Orgs:** Am Geriat Soc, 1978-; Geriat Soc Am, 1978-; AMR Soc Aging, 1978-; Am Pub Health Asn, 1978-; comt mem, Jeff Co Long Term Care Ombudsman Comt, 1982-84; chmn, Vis Nurses Asn, 1983; VNA Med Adv Comt, co-chairperson, 1983-; Mayors CMS Status Women, 1984-87; charter mem, Asn Heads Acad Progs Geriatrics, 1991-; NA Res Task Force Aging, 1992-; module comt chair, Dept Veteran Affairs, VA Tenn Valley GRECC. **Honors/Awds:** National Science Foundation Research Award, 1965-68; Associate Inv Award, W Los Angeles VAMC, 1980; Geriatric Medicine Academic Award, Nat Inst Aging, 1982-87; Govenor's Award, ITTG, Govenor G C Wallace, 1984. **Home Addr:** 1701 Old Hickory Blvd, Brentwood, TN 37027, **Home Phone:** (615)373-3688. **Business Addr:** Director, Meharry Medical College, 1005 D B Todd Jr Blvd, Nashville, TN 37208, **Business Phone:** (615)327-6862.

## SCOTT, WERNER FERDINAND

Marketing executive. **Personal:** Born Feb 27, 1957, Pfungstadt; son of Arthur Jr and Irene Schaffer. **Educ:** NMex State Univ, Las Cruces, BBA, human resources mgt, 1979. **Career:** Xerox Corp, Albuquerque, sales rep mgr, 1979-85, dist reg mgr, 1982-85; Advantage Mkt Group Inc, founder, pres & chief exec officer, 1985-; Advantage Lifestyle LLC, property owner, currently. **Orgs:** pres & chief executive officer, AMG Sports, 1985-; Supporter, United Negro Col Fund, 1988-91; chmn, Dallas Int Sports Comn, 1989-90, bd mem, 1990-91; Nat Asn Advan Colored People, 1990-91; founding mem, Open Doors Found; Academies Excellence; Ctr Study Sports Soc. **Honors/Awds:** Presidents Club Winner, Xerox Corp, 1980-85; Quest for Success Award, Dallas Black Chamber, Morning News, 1991. **Business Addr:** President, Chief Executive Officer, Advantage Marketing Group Inc, 10030 N MacArthur Blvd Suite 195, Irving, TX 75063, **Business Phone:** (972)869-2244.

## SCOTT, WESLEY ELLINGTON

Physician. **Personal:** Born Mar 23, 1925, Memphis, TN; married Virginia Smith; children: Stephany Scott Boyette. **Educ:** Meharry Med Col, MD, 1950; Brooklyn Hosp Ctr, internship, 1950-51; NY Univ Sch Med, Orthop Surg, resident, 1953, 1955. **Career:** Orthop surgeon, 1954-84; pvt pract, currently. **Orgs:** Omega Psi Phi Fraternity, 1950-; Am Acad Orthop Surgeons, 1960-; fel Am Col Surgeons, 1961-; Nat Asn Advan Colored People, 1969-; fel Am Col Surgeons. **Honors/Awds:** Man of the Year, Nat Asn Advan Colored People, Freeport, NY, 1959. **Special Achievements:** Certified private pilot: single engine-land, single engine-sea, multi-engine-land, helicopter, instrument rating. **Home Addr:** 2614 Princess Lane, Missouri City, TX 77459, **Home Phone:** (281)261-0262. **Business Addr:** Physician, 2614 Princess Lane, Missouri City, TX 77459, **Business Phone:** (281)261-0262.

## SCOTT, DR. WILL

Social worker, college teacher. **Career:** Stephen F Austin State Univ, Sch Social Work, prof & social worker. **Business Addr:** Professor, Social Worker, Stephen F Austin State University, 420 E Starr Ave, Nacogdoches, TX 75962-6104, **Business Phone:** (936)468-5105.

## SCOTT, DR. WINDIE OLIVIA

Lawyer. **Personal:** Born Mobile, AL; daughter of Clifford A and Vivian Pugh. **Educ:** Calif State Polytech Univ, BA, polit sci, 1974; Univ Calif, Sch Law, Davis, JD, 1977. **Career:** State Calif, Off State Controller, legal coun, 1979, staff coun, 1981-87, sr staff coun, 1987-96, tax coun III, 1996-97, chief dep to bd mem john chiang, 1997-2000, chief coun, 2000-03, dep controller, 2003-07, tax coun iii specialist, 2007-08, 2011-14, chief dep dir, 2008-11; Calif Workforce Investment Bd, chief coun, currently. **Orgs:** State Bar Calif, 1979-; Nat Bar Asn, 1980-; treas, Pan Hellenic Coun, 1982-84; pres, Wiley Manuel Bar Asn, 1984; bd mem, Calif Asn Black Lawyers, 1984-85; bd mem, Centro de Legal-Sacramento, 1984-85; City Bar Sacramento, 1984-85; County Bar Coun, 1989-92; vpres, Calif Asn Black Lawyers, 1989; pres, Women Lawyers Sacramento, 1989; exec comt, State Bar Conf Dels, 1990-93; chair, Mayor's City Affirmative Action Adv Coun, 1991-94; pres, Alpha Kappa Alpha Sorority, 1992; pres, Sacramento County Bar Asn, 1997; Black Women's Network. **Honors/Awds:** Sacramento 100 Most Influential Blacks, 1984; President Award, Wiley Manuel Bar Asn, 1985; Ernest L Robinson Jr Award, McGeorge Black Law Studs Asn, 1985; Outstanding Women Award, Nat Coun Negro Women, 1988; 25 Blacks to Watch in 1989, Observer Newspapers; Outstanding Woman of the Year, Gov/Law Sacramento, YWCA, 1990; Unit Award, Wiley Manuel Bar Asn, 1990; Mayor's Community Serv Award, 1995; Lawyer of the Year, Sacramento County Bar Asn, 2000; Bench & Bar Coalition Leadership Award; African American Community Medallion of Honor; Woman of Inspiration Award, Sacramento Observer Newspaper; Ida L. Jackson Graduate Achievement Award, Alpha Kappa Alpha Sorority Inc. **Home Addr:** 784 Clipper Way, Sacramento, CA 95831, **Home Phone:** (916)393-1497. **Business Addr:** Chief Counsel, California Workforce Investment Board, 7567 Sailfish Way, Sacramento, CA 95831, **Business Phone:** (916)324-3425.

## SCOTT-CLAYTON, DR. PATRICIA ANN

Lawyer. **Personal:** Born Oct 6, 1953, Chicago, IL; daughter of Verna and Merle; children: Robynn. **Educ:** Northwestern Univ, BA, 1975; Georgetown Univ Law Ctr, JD, 1978, ML Tax, 1986. **Career:** Dept Justice, Tax Div, trial atty, 1978-85; IRS, sr atty, 1985-89, employee plans litigation coun, 1989-93, respondent appellant, sect chief, employee benefits & exempt orgns, 1991-93; Pension Benefit Guaranty Corp, assoc gen coun, 1993-97, dep gen coun, 1997-. **Orgs:** Secy, Parents Asn, 1993-94; bd dir, Essential Theatre, 1993-96; bd trustee, Sheridan Sch, 1994-97, chmn, 1996-97; chmn, Pension Benefit Guaranty Corp, 1995; travel coord, Fund raising Comn, 1996-98; chmn, DC Jrs Volleyball Club, 1997-98; parents rep, Sidwell Friends Sch, 1997-99; bd dir, Peak Performance Volleyball Club & Peak Performance Sports Acad, 1998-99; Wash Univ Parents Coun, 2000-. **Honors/Awds:** Attorneys General's Award, Dept Justice, 1979; Special Achievement Awards, IRS, 1990, 1992, 1993. **Special Achievements:** Author: Tax Qualification of Tax Sheltered Annuities, The Tax Lawyer, Fall, 1995. **Home Addr:** 9075 Pickwick Village Terr, Silver Spring, MD 20901, **Home Phone:** (301)434-1825. **Business Addr:** Deputy General Counsel, Pension Benefit Guaranty Corp, Off Gen Coun 1200 K St NW Suite 340, Washington, DC 20005, **Business Phone:** (202)326-4020.

## SCOTT-COLEMAN, MELISSA

Executive director, manager. **Career:** Detroit Advantage Acad, prin, exec dir; A new Day Detroit, campaign mgr. **Business Addr:** Campaign Manager, A New Day in Detroit, Detroit, MI 48204, **Business Phone:** (313)850-8893.

## SCOTT-JOHNSON, ROBERTA VIRGINIA

Government official, educator. **Personal:** Born WV; married Jesse; children: Robert Jerome Patterson, Rex Lenear Patterson, Carolyn Marie Patterson & Terrence Jerome. **Educ:** Bluefield Col, BS, bus admin; Univ Mich, MA, guid & couns, 1966; Univ Edinborough, 1979. **Career:** Elkhorn High Sch, WVa, dir com ed; Saginaw City Sch Dist, teacher, counr; Econ Develop Corp, Buena Vista Township, dirship, township trustee, 1978-84, township treasurer. **Honors/Awds:** Outstanding Service Award, Jessie Rouse Sch, 1970-80; Honorary Award, Buena Vista Township, 1980. **Home Addr:** 4636 S Gregory St, Saginaw, MI 48601, **Home Phone:** (989)752-3424. **Business Addr:** Township Treasurer, Teacher, Buena Vista Char Township, 1160 S Outer Dr, Saginaw, MI 48601.

## SCOTT-RICHARDSON, OLYMPIA. See SCOTT, OLYMPIA RANEE.

## SCRANTON, BRENDA A.

Vice president (organization). **Personal:** daughter of Evelyn Arnold; married Paul; children: Shaun. **Educ:** Loyola Marymount Univ, BA; Calif State Univ, MA. **Career:** Bronx Community Col, vpres stud develop, 2002. **Business Addr:** NY.

## SCRIBNER, ARTHUR GERALD, JR.

Manager, engineer, chief executive officer. **Personal:** Born Nov 19, 1955, Baltimore, MD; son of Arthur Gerald Sr and Elizabeth Worrell; children: Lamara Chanelle, Arthur Gerald III & Milton Thomas. **Educ:** Univ Md Baltimore, BA, 1981, BS, 1981; Johns Hopkins Univ Sch Eng, MS, 1987. **Career:** Scribner Consult Inc, pres, 1985; Md Med Labs, pathol asst, 1986; Inner Harbor Sounds Inc, producer, 1986; US Dept Defense, sr syst anal & engr, 1982; A G Scribner & Assocs, pres, 1988; Consortium Inc, pres & chief exec officer, 1988. **Orgs:** Tenor & soloist Univ MD Chamber, 1978-81; pub rel consult Vivians Fashions NY, 1980-; asst instr, Univ MD, 1980-81; talent coordr, Baltimore Citywide Star Search, 1985-86; vpres, Metropolitan Entertainment Consortium Inc, 1985. **Honors/Awds:** Superior Achievement Award, Inter prof Studies Inst, Univ Md, 1982; Black Engineer of the Year, Nat Security Agency, 1993. **Home Addr:** 6820 Parsons Ave, Gwynn Oak, MD 21207-6422, **Home Phone:** (410)653-1886. **Business Addr:** Owner, Scribner & Associates, 5322 Wesley Ave, Gwynn Oak, MD 21207, **Business Phone:** (410)448-6101.

## SCRIVENS, DR. JOHN J.

Administrator, educator. **Personal:** Born Tampa, FL; married Molbert Robinson; children: J J Scrivens III, Jevin E & Janelle L. **Educ:** Fla A & M Univ, Sch Pharm, Tallahassee, FL, BS, pharm, 1972; Univ Fla, Gainesville, FL, MS, pharm, 1976; Univ S Fla, Tampa, FL, PhD, pub health, 1994. **Career:** VA Hosp, Miami, clin pharmacist; Tampa Gen Hosp, clin coordr, clin pharmacist, 1982-85; Centro Espanol Hosp, dir pharm; Univ S Fla Psychiat Ctr, dir pharm, 1987-93; Nat Prescription Serv Merck/Medco Inc, Pharmacist, 1993-95; Fla A&M Univ, Col Pharm & Pharmaceut Sci, assoc prof & dir, Tampa Pharm Pract div, 1995-; USF Psychiat Ctr Tampa, dir; Veterans Admin Hosp, resident, 1997; Hillsborough Community Col, Pharmaceut Sci Prog, proj dir, 2002-; Johnnie Ruth Clarke Community Health Ctr, Community Health Centers Pinellas Pharm Serv prog, proj dir, contract mgr, 2004-. **Orgs:** Am Pharmaceut Asn; Am Soc Health-Systs Pharmacists; treasuree, Nat FAMU Pharm Alumni Coun; Fel Am Soc Health-Systs Pharmacists, 2007; founding pres & exe dir, Asn Black Health-systs Pharmacist; Rho Chi Nat Hon Soc Pharm; Fla Soc Health-systs Pharmacists; Fla Med Dent & Pharmaceut Asn; Nat Pharmaceut Asn; Fla Pharmaceut Asn; co founder, Stud Nat Pharmaceut Asn; prolific contribr, Nat Diamondback Pharm Alumni Coun; prolific contribr, Platinum level donor. **Home Addr:** 4602 N 39th St, Tampa, FL 33610, **Home Phone:** (813)238-2628. **Business Addr:** Associate Professor, Director, Florida A & M University, 3500 E Fletcher Ave Suite 133, Tampa, FL 33613, **Business Phone:** (813)975-6500.

## SCROGGINS, BOBBY

Artist, college teacher, educator. **Personal:** Born Kansas City, MO. **Educ:** Kans City Art Inst, BFA, 1976; Southern Ill Univ, Edwardsville, MFA, sculpture, 1980. **Career:** Univ Ky, head ceramics dept, 1990-96, assoc prof & head ceramics, 1996-; Ky Gov Sch Arts, visual art fac. **Orgs:** Fel, Univ & Ford Found 1980; dir-at-large, Nat Coun Educ Ceramic Arts, 1993-95; chmn, visual art div; chmn, ceramics & sculpture pilot progs, Northwest Acad Arts, 2003-04. **Home Addr:** 3353 Otter Creek Dr, Lexington, KY 40515-5933, **Home Phone:** (859)263-5237. **Business Addr:** Associate Professor, University of Kentucky, Rm 231 Reynolds Bldg Suite 1, Lexington, KY 40506-0022, **Business Phone:** (859)257-5371.

## SCROGGINS, TRACY L.

Football player. **Personal:** Born Sep 11, 1969, Checotah, OK. **Educ:** Univ Tulsa, grad. **Career:** Football player (retired); Detroit Lions, defensive end, 1992-2001. **Honors/Awds:** Lettermen's Hall of Fame, Coffeyville Community Col, 2002.

## SCRUGGS, BOOKER T., II

Educator, college administrator. **Personal:** Born Oct 2, 1942, Chattanooga, TN; son of Mabel Humphrey and Booker T; married Johnnie Lynn Haslerig; children: Cameroun. **Educ:** Clark Col, BA, 1964; Atlanta Univ, MA, 1966. **Career:** Col adminr (retired), educr; Howard High Sch, social sci teacher, 1966; Community Action Agency, coordr res & reporting, 1966-70; WNOO Radio, prog moderator, 1973-82; Univ Tenn Chattanooga, prof sociol, asst dir Upward Bound, 1970-91, instr sociol, prog dir, currently, adj fac mem, currently. **Orgs:** Alpha Phi Alpha, Adult Educ Coun; mem bd, Chattanooga Elec Power Bd, 1975-85; vpres, Brainerd High Sch PTA, 1989-90; life mem, Nat Asn

Advan Colored People; Chattanooga Gospel Orchestra; bd mem, Methodist Stud Ctr, Univ Tenn, Chattanooga; chair mem, Wiley Methodist Church; pres, Tenn Asn Spec Prog, 1991-93; Chattanooga Clarinet Soc; Maxtiam Trio; Spectrum Jazz Ban; Bethlehem-Wiley United Methodist Church. **Special Achievements:** Released Three Gospel CDs: My Tribute; Let Not Your Heart Be Troubled; In The Spirit; Three Jazz CDs with The Maxtium Trio and the Booker T. Scruggs Ensemble: A Salute To The Duke; Live From Blue Orleans; Booker T. Scruggs Ensemble Live At 4 Bridges. **Home Addr:** 1103 Queens Dr, Chattanooga, TN 37406, **Home Phone:** (423)266-3623. **Business Addr:** Sociology Instructor, University of Tennessee, 206 Race Hall 615 McCallie Ave, Chattanooga, TN 37403, **Business Phone:** (423)425-2110.

## SCRUGGS, CLEORAH J.

Educator, founder (originator). **Personal:** Born Aug 20, 1948, Akron, OH; daughter of Cleophus and Deborah; married Paul Lawrence DeBose. **Educ:** Univ Akron, Ohio, BA, elem educ, 1970, MA, elem educ, 1977, admin cert, 1984. **Career:** Educator (retired); Flint Bd Educ, instr, 1970-2000; GED instr, 1974; Charles Harrison Mason Bible Col, instr, 1975-76; Mott Adult High Sch, Flint, Mich, workshop presenter; Scruggs & Assoc Educ Consult Serv, founder, pres. Book: Boaz Found Me, A Love Story & Companion Guide. **Orgs:** United Teachers Flint, 1987-, precinct deleg, 1990, 1994; Mich Educ Asn; Nat Educ Assoc; Nat Alliance Black Sch Educ; Silver Soror, Sorority Inc; Flint Community Schs, Supt's Adv Coun Way; United Negro Col Fund; Univ Akron, Alumni Asn; Nat Asn Advan Colored People. **Honors/Awds:** Community Service Award, Humane Soc, McCree Theater, Religious & Comm Orgn, 1975, 1988, 1990; Identification of Beginning Teachers Problems, Univ Akron, 1977; Nominee Teacher of the Year, 1987; Excellence Award, MEA IPD, Commitment Educ & Diversity, 1993; Multicultural Diversity Award, MEA Concerns Comm, 1994; Social Studies Educator of the Year, Mich Coun Social Studies, 1995; Dr Martin Luther King Jr Award, NEA, 2000; Childrens Champion Award, Priority C, 2001; Alumni Award, Univ Akron, 2002; Int Understanding Award, MEA, 2002; C.O.G.I.C. National Fine Arts Scholarship Department Award. **Home Addr:** 1963 Laurel Oak Dr, Flint, MI 48507-6038, **Home Phone:** (810)235-9393.

**SCRUGGS, FREDRO, JR.** See STARR, FREDRO.

## SCRUGGS, SYLVIA ANN

Educator, social worker. **Personal:** Born Jun 18, 1951, Akron, OH; daughter of Cleophus and Deborah. **Educ:** Univ Akron, BS, 1976; Case Western Res Univ, MS, 1990. **Career:** Univ Akron, clerk typist, 1974-77; Akron C's Med Ctr, ward secy, 1977-78; Akron Urban League, edur, 1978-82; Hawkins Skill Ctr, edur, 1983; Depart Human Serv, income maint III, 1984-. **Orgs:** Counrs asst S High Sch, 1969; Big Sister & Tutor Univ Akron, 1970; Nat Asn Advan Colored People, 1981-82; precinct comt, Community Third Ward, 1981; youth leader, Youth Motivation Task Force, 1982; vol, 1990, proj Learn, Nat Asn Social Workers, 1990; vol, Battered Women's Shelter, 1991. **Home Addr:** 1066 Orlando Ave, Akron, OH 44320, **Home Phone:** (330)836-6400. **Business Addr:** Income Maintenance III, Department of Human Services, 47 N Main St, Akron, OH 44308-1991, **Business Phone:** (330)643-8200.

## SCRUGGS-LEFTWICH, YVONNE (YVONNE SCRUGGS-PERRY)

Executive, educator, advocate. **Personal:** Born Jun 24, 1933, Niagara Falls, NY; married Edward V Jr; children: Cathryn D Perry, Rebecca S Perry-Glickstein, Tienne Davis & Edward III. **Educ:** NC Cent Univ, BA, polit sci, 1955; Free Univ Berlin, Ger Hochsch fur Politik, cert, 1956; Univ Minn, pub admin, MAPA, 1958; Univ Pa, PhD. **Career:** Fullbright fel, Ger, 1952-53; Univ Penn, Wharton Schs HRC, fac, 1970-74; Howard Univ, Dept City & Regional Planning, prof, 1974-77, Presidents Urban & Regional Policy Group, exec, 1977-78, Dept Housing & Urban Develop, Community Planning & Develop, dep asst secy, 1977-79, prof, 1979-81; NY State Div Housing & Community Renewal, regional dir, 1981-82, staff, 1982-85; YEL Corp, CSC Inc & Harlem USA Inc, chief operating officer & bd chair, 1984-90; City Philadelphia, dep mayor, 1985-87; Pryor, Govan, Counts & Co Inc, sr consult vpres, 1987-88; George Wash Univ, prof, 1987-99; Urban Policy Inst & Nat Policy Inst, Joint Ctr Polit & Econ Studies, dir, 1991-96; Black Leadership Forum Inc, exec dir & chief operating officer, 1996-2005; SUNY Col, prof; Nat Labor Col, prof, 2005-; State Univ of New York, prof, comnr; Univ of Pa, prof; News Hour, commentator. Books: Consensus and Compromise: The Making of National Urban Policy; Sound Bites of Protest and Standing with My Fist. **Orgs:** Bd mem, World Affairs Coun, 1970-73; Philadelphia Coun Community Advan, 1970-74; vpres, Penn Housing Fin Corp, 1974; trustee, Cornerstone Equity Adv; Nat Coun Negro Women; Nat Asn Advan Colored People; Greater Wash Urban League; vpres & trustee, Milton S Eisenhower Found; pres, Women Distinction; Nat Polit Cong Black Women; founding pres, Geneva B Scruggs Community Health Ctr; Am Inst Planners; comnr, Mobile Homes Community; vpres, Asn Col Schs Planning; Nat Newspaper Asn; trustee, nat Fulbright Asn; trustee, Verizon's Nat Consumer; Nat Coalition for Black Civic Participation; adv bd chair, Ctr Community & Econ Justice Inc, 2001-. **Business Addr:** Professor, National Labor College, 10000 NH Ave, Silver Spring, MD 20902, **Business Phone:** (301)431-5452.

**SCRUGGS-PERRY, YVONNE.** See SCRUGGS-LEFTWICH, YVONNE.

## SCURLOCK, MICHAEL LEE, JR.

Executive, executioner, football coach, football player. **Personal:** Born Feb 26, 1972, Tucson, AZ; married Michaela; children: 3. **Educ:** Univ Ariz, BA, media arts. **Career:** Football player (retired), football coach, exec; St Louis Rams, defensive back & corner back & safety, 1995-99; Carolina Panthers, 1999-2000; Westminster Catawba Christian Sch, athletic dir; Varsity Football, head coach; Carolina Panthers Pop Warner, tv color analyst; Architech Sports & Phys Ther, co-founder, currently; York County Sheriffs Dept, Sheriff Dep, currently. **Honors/Awds:** Ram Attitude Award, 1998. **Home Addr:** 6053 Daphne Cir, Fort Mill, SC 29708-6577. **Business Addr:** Co-Founder, Architech Sports and Physical Therapy, 8918 Blakeney Prof Dr Suite 120, Charlotte, NC 28277, **Business Phone:** (704)900-8960.

**SEA, HOUSTON.** See HOUSTON, SEAWADON L.

## SEABROOK, REV. BRADLEY MAURICE

Clergy. **Personal:** Born Mar 12, 1928, Savannah, GA; son of Bradley and Katie Lue Carpenter; married Minnie Lucile Long; children: Criss, Lilla, Tina & Lisa. **Educ:** Fla Int Univ, Miami, Fla, BT, indust technol, 1979. **Career:** Clergy (retired); Aircraft Engine Mech, USAF, Eglin AFB, Fla, 1955-58, 1961-68; Naval Aviation Engineering Serv Unit, Philadelphia, PA, 1968-83. **Orgs:** Past comdr, Am Post 193 Pensacola, Fla, 1956-58; sir knight, 4th Degree, Deluwa Assembly, 1971; life mem, Nat Asn Advan Colored People, 1975; Knights Columbus-5658, Past Grand Knight, 1975-76; dir, Off Black Cath Ministry, 1986-2003. **Honors/Awds:** Knight of the Year, Knights of Columbus Coun-5658, 1974-75; Sustained Superior Performance Award, Dept Navy, NAESU, 1983; Ordination to the Diaconate, Diocese Pensacola-Tallahassee, 1980; George Wash Honor Medal, 1995; Community Volunteer Award, Nat Asn Advan Colored People Pensacola Branch, 1995. **Home Addr:** 505 W Quintette Rd, PO Box 702, Cantonment, FL 32533-8095, **Home Phone:** (850)968-6425.

## SEABROOK, JULIETTE THERESA (TERRY SEABROOK)

Real estate agent, business owner. **Personal:** Born Jan 27, 1954, Charleston, SC; daughter of Luther and Eva Wilson; children: Gerren. **Educ:** Howard Univ, BA, 1975; Univ Md Law Sch, JD, 1978. **Career:** US Dept Health & Human Servs, staff atty, 1979-85; Space Co, preS, owner & broker-in-charge, 1986-. **Orgs:** Charleston County Planning Bd, 1993-96; adv bd, First Union Nat Bank, 1994-; adv bd, Charleston County Human Servs Comn, 1994-; adv bd, Charleston Local Citywide Develop Corp, 1994-95; adv bd, Community Found, 1995. **Honors/Awds:** The Space Co, Black Enterprise Mag, Nov, 2006. **Special Achievements:** The Space Company featured in Black Enterprise Magazine November, 2006. **Home Addr:** 220 3rd Ave, Charleston, SC 29403, **Home Phone:** (843)577-6428. **Business Addr:** President, Real Estate Broker, The Space Co, 82 1/2 Spring St Suite A, Charleston, SC 29403, **Business Phone:** (843)577-2676.

## SEABROOKS, NETTIE HARRIS

Government official, executive. **Personal:** Born Feb 22, 1934, Mt. Clemens, MI; daughter of Ivan Joseph Harris and Katherine Marshall Davis Harris; children: Victoria D & Franklyn E. **Educ:** Marygrove Col, BS, chem; Univ Mich, MLS. **Career:** Detroit Pub Libr, Technol Dept, chem librn; Tenn State Univ, instr; Gen Motors, Pub Rels Staff Libr, librn, Corp Res Opers, mgr, Pub Affairs Info Servs, dir, GM Chev-Pont, Can Group, dir govt & civic affairs, GM N Am Passenger Car Platforms, dir govt rels; City Detroit, dep mayor, chief admin officer, 1994-97, chief operating officer & chief staff, 1998; Detroit Inst Arts, sr assoc officer to dir, 2002, chief operating officer, 2002, exec advisor dir, 2008. **Orgs:** Bd mem, Mus African-Am Hist; bd trustee, Detroit Inst Arts Friends African & African-Am Art; Detroit Med Ctr; bd dir, exec comt, Karmanos Cancer Inst; bd dir, exec comt, Detroit Med Ctr; Am Asn Univ Women; hon dir, Detroit Inst Arts, 2008-; bd mem, Detroit RiverFront Conservancy. **Home Addr:** 8200 E Jefferson Ave, Detroit, MI 48214, **Home Phone:** (313)331-4296. **Business Addr:** Honorary Director, Detroit Institute of Arts, 5200 Woodward Ave, Detroit, MI 48202, **Business Phone:** (313)833-7900.

## SEABROOKS-EDWARDS, MARILYN S.

Government official. **Personal:** Born Mar 3, 1955, Allendale, SC; married Ronald Burke. **Educ:** Univ SC Saik Regional Campus, attended 1975; Ga Southern Col, AB, 1977; US Dept Agr, attended 1984; Baruch Col/City Univ NY, MPA, 1984. **Career:** City Savannah Housing Dept, spec proj coordr, 1981-83, prog coordr, 1984-85; Dept Human Serv, spec asst to dir, 1983-84, prog analyst, 1985-; Exec Off Mayor Off Secy DC, chief admin officer, 1987, chief technol officer, currently. **Orgs:** Secy WVGS Radio Bd Ga So Col, 1976 & 1977; social studies teacher Jenkins County Sch Syst, 1977-78; financial counr City Savannah Housing Dept, 1978-81; YMCA, 1983; memship Washing Urban League, 1984-85; memship Natl Forum Black Pub Admin, 1984-85; memship Intl City Mgt Asn, 1984-85; sec Wash, DC Chap natl Forum Black Pub Admin; bd mem, Notary Pub Bd, DC; hearings compliance officer Exec Off Mayor. **Honors/Awds:** John Phillip Sousa Award, 1973; Psi Alpha Theta, Ga Southern Col, 1975-77; Outstanding Young Women of Am, 1982-83; Nat Urban Fel, 1983-84. **Home Addr:** 2352 Glenmont Cir Suite 201, Silver Spring, MD 20902. **Business Addr:** Chief Technology Officer, Office of the Chief Technology Officer, 441 4th St NW Suite 930 S, Washington, DC 20001, **Business Phone:** (202)727-2277.

## SEALE, BOBBY (ROBERT GEORGE SEALE)

Educator, activist, writer. **Personal:** Born Oct 22, 1936, Dallas, TX; son of George and Thelma; married Artie; children: Malik Kkrumah Stagolee. **Educ:** Merritt Col, attended 1962. **Career:** Black Panther Party for Self-Defense, chmn, minister info & co-founder, 1966-74; Temple Univ, teacher; Advocates Scene, founder, 1974-; Films: Rude Awakening, actor, 1989; Malcolm X, actor, 1992; A Lonely Rage, actor, 2006; Reach Cinema Prod, creator & dir, currently. **Orgs:** Afro-Am Asn. **Special Achievements:** Author: Seize the Time: The Story of the Black Panther Party and Huey PNewton, Random House, 1970; A Lonely Rage: The Autobiography of Bobby Seale, 1978; Barbeque with Bobby, 1987; first member of the Black Panther Party. **Home Addr:** PO Box 26785, Elkins Park, PA 19027. **Business Addr:** Creator, Director, Reach Cinema Productions Inc, PO Box 26712, Elkins Park, PA 19027, **Business Phone:** (215)848-3554.

**SEALE, ROBERT GEORGE.** See SEALE, BOBBY.

## SEALE, SAMUEL RICARDO

Football player, scout. **Personal:** Born Oct 6, 1962; married Elizabeth D; children: Sam Jr, Samir & Shi-Ann. **Educ:** Western State Col. **Career:** Football player (retired), scout; Western Football, wide receiver, 1980-83; Los Angeles Raiders, wide receiver, 1984, kick returner, 1985, right cirnerback, 1986-87, 1992; San Diego Chargers, left cornerback, 1988, right cornerback, 1989-91; Los Angeles Rams, cornerback, 1993; Green Bay Packers, recruiting coordr, 1995-2008, col scout, 2012-. **Honors/Awds:** Hall of Fame, Western State Col, 2002; All-America honor, NAIA. **Home Addr:** 1818 Da Gama Ct, Escondido, CA 92026-1729. **Business Addr:** College Scout, Green Bay Packers, Lambeau Field Atrium 1265 Lombardi Ave, Green Bay, WI 54304, **Business Phone:** (920)569-7500.

## SEALLS, ALAN RAY

Meteorologist, educator. **Personal:** Born Mt. Vernon, NY; son of Albert and Josephine Reese. **Educ:** Cornell Univ, BS, 1985; Fla State Univ, MS, broadcast meteorol, 1987; Am Meteorol Soc, cert; Nat Weather Asn, cert; Cert Broadcast Meteorologist, cert. **Career:** Fla State Univ, Tallahassee, Fla, grad asst, 1985-87; WALB-TV, meteorologist, 1987-88; WTMJ Inc, meteorologist, 1988-92; Columbia Col, prof meteorol; WGN-TV, meteorologist; WMAQ-TV, meteorologist; Univ S Ala, instr meteorol, currently; WKRG-TV, chief meteorologist, currently. **Orgs:** Pres, Chicago Chap, Am Meteorol Soc, 1984-, counr, currently; seal chmn, counr, Nat Weather Asn, 1987-; Nat Asn Black Journalists, 1989-; Nat Asn Advan Colored People, 1989-; fel Am Meteorol Soc. **Home Addr:** , Mobile, AL 36609. **Business Addr:** Chief Meteorologist, WKRG-TV, 555 Broadcast Dr, Mobile, AL 36606, **Business Phone:** (414)332-9611.

## SEALS, GEORGE EDWARD

Executive, football player. **Personal:** Born Oct 2, 1942, Higginsville, MO; married Cecelia McClellean; children: Dan Seals. **Educ:** Univ Mo. **Career:** Football player (retired); Chicago, Bd Trade, trader; Wash Redskins, defensive tackle, 1964; San Diego Chargers, 1964; New York Giants, 1964; Chicago Bears, offensive guard, 1965-71; Kans City Chiefs, offensive tackle, 1972-73; Chicago Bd Options Exchange Bd. **Orgs:** Better Boys Found; Chicago PUSH; Bd Regents, Daniel Hale Williams Univ, 1967. **Business Addr:** Trader, Chicago Board of Trade, 141 W Jackson, Chicago, IL 60604, **Business Phone:** (312)435-3500.

## SEALS, GERALD

Educator, government official, administrator. **Personal:** Born Sep 22, 1953, Columbia, SC; son of Janet Kennerly; married Carolyn; children: Gerald II & Jelani-Akil; married Kanet. **Educ:** Univ SC, BA, govt & pub admin, 1975; Univ Denver, MA, philos, 1976; Southern Ill Univ, Carbondale, MS, ABT, 1978; Capella Univ, PhD. **Career:** Carbon dale City, Ill, admin intern, 1977-78; Village Glen Ellyn IL, asst to village admin, 1978-81; Village Glendale Heights, from asst village mgr to village mgr, 1981-84; Springfield City, from asst city mgr to city mgr, 1984-88; Corvallis City, city mgr, 1988; Living Word Church & Fel, pastor; Intergovernmental Risk Mgt Agency, chmn; Greenville County, SC, county adminr; Greenville County Econ Develop Corp, pres, currently; Newberry Col, asst prof, 2005-. **Orgs:** Vice chmn bd, Inter govt Risk Mgt, 1982-83; chmn DuPage, Reg IV Sub-Region Regionalization Comn, 1982-84; chmn bd, Inter govt Risk Mgt Agency, 1983-84; bd mem, Springfield Civic Theatre, 1985-88; bd mem, Springfield OIC 1985-; bd dir, Clark County Transp Coordinating Comn, 1985-88; State Ore Structural Code Adv Bd, 1988-; Corvallis/Benton County United Way, 1989-; bd mem, Nat Forum for Black Pub Adminr, 1989-. **Home Addr:** 230 NE Powderhorn Dr, Corvallis, OR 97330, **Home Phone:** (503)758-9123. **Business Addr:** Associate Professor, Newberry College, 2100 College St, Newberry, SC 29108, **Business Phone:** (803)947-2069.

## SEALS, MAXINE LANE

School administrator, executive, salesperson. **Personal:** Born Trinity, TX; married Frank; children: Thaddeus & Cedric. **Educ:** Houston Community Col; Tex Southern Univ. **Career:** Southwestern Bell Tel Co, mgr; Continental Airlines, reservation group sales, currently; N Forest Independent Sch Dist, 1980-86, 1994-2007; Continental Airlines Inc, part-time sales agt, part-time team leader; Bell Tel, supvr; Lane Security Co, sales agt. **Orgs:** Fontaine Scenic Woods Civic Club; pres, Tex Caucus Black Sch Bd Mems, 1984-85; dir, Gulf Coast Sch Bd Asn, currently; N Forest Bd; life mem, Nat Asn Advan Colored People; bd dir, Northeast Young Men Christian Asn; bd officer, Settegast Health Clin Coun; Fontaine Scenic Woods Civic Club; life mem, PTA; master trustee, Tex Asn Sch Boards Inc; bd trustee mem, M B Smiley high Sch; bd dir, Northeast YMCA; bd dir, LBJ Hosp Coun; bd officer, Settegast Health Clin Coun; Fifth Ward Church Christ; Nat Asn Sch Boards; bd trustee, bd pres, master trustee, N Forest Independent Sch Dist Sch Bd, currently. **Home Addr:** 5106 Nolridge Dr, Houston, TX 77016-2929, **Home Phone:** (713)631-3901. **Business Addr:** Sales Agent, Lane Security Co, 5106 Nolridge Dr, Houston, TX 77016-2929, **Business Phone:** (713)443-6767.

## SEALS, RAYMOND BERNARD

Football player, football coach. **Personal:** Born Jun 17, 1965, Syracuse, NY; married Jamesetta. **Career:** Football player (retired), coach; Tampa Bay Buccaneers, left defensive end, 1989-93; Pittsburgh Steelers, right defensive end, 1994-96; Carolina Panthers, right defensive end, 1997; Madison High Sch, coach, currently. **Honors/Awds:** Semi Pro Football Hall of Fame, Am Football Asn's, 1992; High School Football Coach of the Year, National Football League, 2009.

## SEALS, RUPERT GRANT

School administrator, educator. **Personal:** Born Aug 6, 1932, Shelbyville, KY; married Georgetta Angela Lynem; children: Rupert La Wendell, Rori LaRele, Regan Wayne & LaRita Angela. **Educ:** Fla Agr & Tech Univ, BS, hon, 1953; Univ Kent, MS, 1956; Wash State Univ, PhD, 1960. **Career:** Fla Agr & Tech Univ, instr dairy, 1954-55, dean prof sch agr & home econ, 1969-74, int prog, 1989-94; Wash State Univ, res asst dairy mfg, 1955-59; Tenn State Univ, asso prof dairy chem biochem, 1959-64; Iowa State Univ, res assoc food tech, 1964-66, asst prof food tech, 1966-69; USDA, coordrspec prog SEA/CR, 1974-76; Col Agr Univ Nev, Reno, assoc dean, 1976; Univ Nev, Reno, prof, biochem, 1982-87, prof emer, 1987-; Univ Ariz, Pine Bluff, interim dir develop, 1988-89. **Orgs:** Alpha Kappa Mu Hon Soc Fla Agr & Mech Univ, 1951; Sigma Xi Wash State Univ, 1958; chmn, Am

Fair Housing Bd Am, IA, 1967-69; pres, Men First Methodological Church, IA, 1967-68; Expert state comt policy, NASULGC, 1971-73; Overseas liaison com Am Counc Educ, Washington, DC, 1971-77; dir, FAMU Agr Res & Educ Ctr, Inst Food & Agr Sci Univ Fla, 1972-74; Alpha Phi Alpha; Gamma Sigma Delta Hon Soc, 1979; Alpha Zeta Hon Soc, 1979. **Honors/Awds:** Named Distinguished Alumnus, Fla Agr & Mech Univ, 2000; Named "Distinguished Graduate: Science, Education and Technology", Alumni Achievement Award, exemplary acad leadership, agr educ, advocacy & action creating a nat awareness vital need increased econ support & opportunities African Americans, Wash State Univ, 2003; Lifetime Achievement Award, Nat Asn Advan Colored People, 2008. **Special Achievements:** Published numerous articles. Books: Disparity: An Analysis of the Historical, Political, and Funding Factors at the State Level Affecting Black Academic Agriculture, 1998; Fifth African American to earn a doctorate from Washington State University, animal science, 1960. **Home Addr:** 1429 Foster Dr, Reno, NV 89509-1209, **Home Phone:** (303)588-6185. **Business Addr:** Professor Emeritus, University of Nevada, 1664 N Va St, Reno, NV 89557-0208, **Business Phone:** (775)784-1110.

## SEALS, THEODORE HOLLIS
Journalist. **Personal:** Born Oct 26, 1950, Chicago, IL; son of Jack H and Costello C. **Educ:** Yale Univ, BA, 1973. **Career:** Chicago Courier, ed writer, 1969-73, assoc ed, 1973-74; Chicago Sun-Times, reporter, rewriteman, 1974-78; C-BREM Commun Corp, corp secy, gen secy, 1983-2010, sr ed; Pub Rels & Commun Prof, currently. **Orgs:** Monitor, Comt Decent Unbiased Campaign Tactics, 1987; 6th Ward Econ Develop Comt; Block Club, pres, 1994-98; Community Policing Strategy Movement. **Special Achievements:** Editor, Evelyn, Vantage Press, 1995; author, The Discovery, Godfrey, The Demon Killer; freelance writer, work has appeared in Chicago Crusader, Chicago Defender, Chicago Tribune, Heritage, newsletter of American Jewish Committee. **Home Addr:** 7228 S Rhodes Ave, Chicago, IL 60619, **Home Phone:** (773)846-6882.

## SEALY, DR. JOAN RICE
Physician, surgeon. **Personal:** Born Apr 23, 1942, Philadelphia, PA; daughter of John K Rice Jr and L Beverly Daniels; children: Desa & Denice. **Educ:** Univ Chicago, BA, 1964; George Washington Univ, Sch Med & Health Sci, Wash, DC, Md, 1968; Yale Univ Sch Med, residency training psychiat; Wash Hosp Ctr, internal med. **Career:** Wash Hosp Ctr, internship, 1968-69; Yale Univ Med Ctr, resident psychiat, 1969-72; pvt pract psychiatrist; George Wash Univ Med Ctr, Dept Psychiat & Behav Scis, assoc clin prof Psychiat & Behav Scis, currently; Providence Hosp, psychiatrist. **Orgs:** Am Psychiat Asn; Wash Psychiat Soc; DC Med Soc. **Home Addr:** 6941 32nd St NW, Washington, DC 20015, **Home Phone:** (202)244-6946. **Business Addr:** Associate Clinical Professor, George Washington University Medical Center, 2300 Eye St NW Suite 713W, Washington, DC 20037, **Business Phone:** (202)994-2987.

## SEAMS, FRANCINE SWANN
Entertainer, business owner. **Personal:** Born Sep 15, 1947, Ronceverte, WV; daughter of John Calvin Sr and Virginia Caroline; married Michael Hugh; children: Scott Calvin & Coy Jvon. **Educ:** WVa State Col, attended 1967; Marshall Univ, attended 1976. **Career:** C&P Tel Co, serv supvr, 1970-77; Diamond State Tel, mkt advr, 1977-83; AT&T Info Systs, supvr, 1983-85; Aerobicize, co-owner, educ dir, 1983-87; Fitness Specialists, dir educ, 1988-92; State Delaware, telecommunications consult, 1986-; Christina Sch Dist, adult continuing educ, fitness, 1987-; Body Seams, Fitness Specialists, owner, dir, 1987-. **Orgs:** Gold certified mem, Am Coun Exercise, 1986-; educ comt, Gov's Coun Lifestyles & Fitness, appointee, 1989-; educ comt, Gov's Coun Drug Abuse, appointee, 1989-; solicitor & presenter, Am Heart Asn DanceHeart, 1989-; chair, IDEA, Asn Fitness Prof, Task Force AFA Fitness Participation, 1990-; chair, City Hope Nat Workouts, Delaware Workouts, 1992-; planner & presenter; United Cerebral Palsy Workouts, 1992-. **Honors/Awds:** Gold Certification, Am Coun Exercise, 1986; Avia Outstanding Achievers, Avia Outstanding Professional Achievement Award, 1987; Randal, winner's cup, over 40 cycle racers, 1990; Educator Honor Roll, Christina Sch Dist, Bd Educ, 1992. **Special Achievements:** Developed new exercise technique: board bounding, 1990; wrote, 40-hour Fitness Instructor Course, 1990; founded IDEA Task Force on AFA Fitness Participation, 1990; wrote ", An Instructor's Guide to Board Bounding", 1991; developed data and delivered, "Black, Bold, Beautiful-Make it Fit" series, 1992. **Home Addr:** 2416 Beaucatcher Lane, Charlotte, NC 28270-0487, **Home Phone:** (803)324-2149. **Business Addr:** Owner, Body Seams The Fitness Specialists, 237 Crystal Ct, Newark, DE 19713, **Business Phone:** (302)368-7721.

## SEARCY, LEON, JR.
Football player, football coach. **Personal:** Born Dec 21, 1969, Washington, DC; married Sonya; children: Malika-Maya & Kenya Imani. **Educ:** Univ Miami, BA, sociol, 1992. **Career:** Football player (retired), coach; Pittsburgh Steelers, offensive tackle, right tackle, 1992-95; Jacksonville Jaguars, offensive tackle, 1996-2000; Baltimore Ravens, 2001; Miami Dolphins, guard, 2002; Fla Int Univ, Miami, offensive line coach, 2004-06. **Orgs:** Founder, Leon Searcy Jr Found; spokesman, Kidney Found; Jacksonville Bone Marrow Donor Registry. **Honors/Awds:** National Champion, 1987, 1989, 1991; Best Right Tackle in Nat Football League, The Sporting News, 1999; Pro Bowl, 1999; Sports Hall of Fame, Univ Miami, 2003.

## SEARCY, LILLIE
Executive director. **Educ:** Lesley Col, BS, early childhood educ & teaching; Tufts Univ-Medford, MA, MS, pub policy; Harvard Univ Sch Bus/Hauser Ctr, cert, strategic planning, 2003; Harvard Univ Kennedy Sch Govt, cert, community develop, 2012. **Career:** Mattopan Family Serv Ctr, exec dir, 1993-2011; Neighborhood Leadership Initiative Inc, managing consult, 2011-12. **Orgs:** Mattapan Community Develop Corp; bd mem, Blue Hill Ave Coalition; Mattapan Bd Trade; Mattapan Re-Zoning Adv Comm; Action Boston Community Develop Inc; vols, Massachusetts Tax & Asset Bldg Consortium; fel Johnson & Johnson Head Start Mgt Inst Univ Calif, 1996; fel Eureka Found-Boston, Massachusetts, 2001; fel Harvard Univ Sch Bus / Hauser Ctr Nonprofit Orgn, 2003; bd dir, Mattapan Sq Main St, 2011-; Hattie B cooper Community Ctr, chief exec officer, 2012-, exec dir, currently. **Business Addr:** Chief Executive Officer, Executive Director, Hattie B Cooper Community Center, 1891 Wash St, Roxbury, MA 02118, **Business Phone:** (617)445-1813.

## SEARS, COREY ALEXANDER
Football player. **Personal:** Born Apr 15, 1973, San Antonio, TX. **Educ:** Miss State Univ. **Career:** Football player (retired); St Louis Rams, defensive tackle, 1998; Ariz Cardinals, left defensive tackle, 1999, defensive tackle, 2000; Houston Texans, 2002, defensive tackle, 2004.

## SEATON, SANDRA CECELIA
Educator, playwright. **Personal:** Born Sep 10, 1944, Columbia, TN; daughter of Albert S Browne and Hattye Evans Harris; married James E; children: Ann, James Jr, Amanda & Jeremy E. **Educ:** Univ Ill, BA, 1971; Mich State Univ, MS, creative writing, 1989. **Career:** Author, plays: The Bridge Party, 1998; The Will, 1999; Do You Like Philip Roth?, 2001; Room & Board, 2002; Sally, 2003; A Bed Made In Heaven, 2005; Martha Stewart Slept Here, 2008; A Chance Meeting, 2009; Music History, 2010; Estate Sale, 2011; The Lookout, 2013; Black for Dinner, 2014; Chicago Trilogy, 2015; Libretto for Song Cycle by Composer William Bolcom: From the Diary of Sally Hemings, 2001; Dorset Writers Colony, Hedgebrook, Writer in Resident, 1997; Cent Mich Univ, prof english, 1990-2004. **Orgs:** Dramatist's Guild; BMI; Socs Study Midwestern Lit; Theater Commun Group; Asn Fac & Staff Color; MI Educ Asn; Nat Educ Asn; African Am Bridge Club; Alpha Kappa Alpha sorority. **Home Addr:** 322 Kedzie St, East Lansing, MI 48823-3530, **Home Phone:** (517)332-6446.

## SEATON, DR. SHIRLEY SMITH
School administrator, educator. **Personal:** Born Cleveland, OH; daughter of Kibble Clarence and Cecil Stone Wright; married Lawrence; children: Eric Dean. **Educ:** Howard Univ, Wash, DC, BA, 1947 & MA, 1948; Case Western Res Univ, Cleveland, OH, MA, 1956; Univ Akron, Akron, OH, PhD, 1981; Beijing Norm Univ, Beijing, China, post doctorate, 1982. **Career:** Cleveland Bd Educ, teacher, 1950-58, asst prin, 1959-65, prin, 1966-76; WEWS-TV, Cleveland, Ohio, teacher, 1963-67; US Govt, Dept Educ, educ specialist, 1965; Cleveland State Univ, adj prof, 1977-85; Basics & Beyond Educ Consults, dir; John Carroll Univ, liaison, community affairs, 2004-06, interim assoc dir, Multicultural Affairs, 2005-07. **Orgs:** Nat Alliance Black Sch Edur; Nat Coun Social Studies; Nat Asn Sec Sch Principals; Asn Supv & Curric Develop; pres, Metrop Cleveland Alliance Black Sch Educr, 1981-; Coalition 100 Black Women, 1991-; Phi Delta Kappa 1979-; Fulbright Asn; bd mem, Western Res Hist Soc; bd mem, Retired & Sr Vol Prog; Am Asn Univ Women. **Home Addr:** 13825 Cedar Rd Apt 102, Cleveland Heights, OH 44118-2356, **Home Phone:** (216)932-1574. **Business Addr:** Liason Community Affairs, John Carroll University, Admin Bldg 20700 N Pk Blvd Suite 126, University Heights, OH 44118-4581, **Business Phone:** (216)397-4185.

## SEAVERS, DEAN
President (organization), chief executive officer. **Educ:** Kent State Univ, BBA, 1984; Stanford Univ, Grad Sch Bus, MBA, 1987. **Career:** Ford Motor Co, Advert & Prod Planning; KFC Nat Mgt Co, opers mgr, 1990-92; Flex-Tech Commun, co-owner & managing dir, 1992-96; Allied Domecq Retailing, mgr brand transformation, 1996-99; Burger King Corp, opers dir, 1999-2000; ADT Security Serv, sr vpres oper, 2000-03; SimplexGrinnell Tyco Fire & Security LLC, 2003-07, head, 2004-; GE Security, pres & chief exec officer, 2007-10; United Technologies, Fire & Security, pres global serv, 2010-11; Red Hawk Fire & Security, pres, chief exec officer, 2012-14; Nat Grid Plc, pres & exec dir, 2014-. **Orgs:** Bd dir, Nat Fire Protection Asn; lead network mem, City Light Capital, 2011-. **Honors/Awds:** National Eagle Leadership Institute, CareerFocus Eagle Award; "Black Enterprise," The 100 Most Powerful Executives in Corporate America, 2010. **Business Addr:** President US, Executive Director, National Grid PLC, 1-3 Strand, London, GL WC2N 5EH.

## SEAY, DAWN CHRISTINE
Sales manager, executive director. **Personal:** Born Jan 23, 1964, Washington, DC; daughter of Ewart and Marjorie Russell; married Geoffrey V; children: Alexandra & Ashton. **Educ:** Univ Cent Fla, BA, jour, 1986. **Career:** Wash Hilton & Towers, guest serv, 1986-87; hospity Parteners, sales mgr, 1987-89; Philadelphia Hilton & Towers, nat sales mgr, 1989-93; Philadelphia Conven Visitors Bur, conven sales mgr, dir, 1993-98; Wash Conv Ctr, dir sales. **Orgs:** Assoc mem, Nat Coalition Black Meetings Planners, 1989-; bd mem, Hospitality Sales & Mkt Asn, chap, 1990-93; chair educ comm, Multicult Affairs Cong, 1994-; dir, Am Heart asn, 2004-06; dir, Am Diabetes asn, 2006-. **Home Addr:** 2928 Ogden St, Philadelphia, PA 19130, **Home Phone:** (215)763-0439. **Business Addr:** Director, Philadelphia Convention & Visitors Bureau, 1515 Mkt St Suite 2020, Philadelphia, PA 19102, **Business Phone:** (215)636-4401.

## SEAY, NORMAN R.
School administrator. **Personal:** Born Feb 18, 1932, St. Louis, MO. **Educ:** Stowe Teachers Col, BA, 1954; Lincoln Univ, MEd, 1966. **Career:** Work-Study Coord St Louis Bd Educ, teacher, 1954-65; Jefferson Bank & Trust Co, staff, 1963; Dist OEO Officers, dir, 1965-67; Concentrated Employ Prog, dir, 1967-70; Dept Health, Educ & Welfare, equal employ opportunity specialist; Social Serv, dep gen mgr, 1970-71, proj dir, 1971-73; UMSL Off Equal Opportunity, EEO progs, 1987-2000; Univ Mo, adminr, Retirees Asn, Off Equal Opportunity, bd dir, 2006-. **Orgs:** Co-chair, Racial Polarization Task Force, 1988-; co-chair & vpres, Educ Adv Comt, 1989-; Bd Adult Welfare Serv; exec bd, MO Asn Soc Welfare; Pub Improv Bond Issue Screening Comt; chmn bd dir, Yeatman-Cent City Foods Inc; Patrolman CC Smith's C Educ Trust Fund Comt; founding mem, Cong Racial Equality; pres, Nat Asn Advan Colored People; pres, Urban League Metrop St. Louis Inc. **Honors/Awds:** Distinguished Citizen Award, St Louis Argus Newspaper, 1974; Most Distinguished Alumni Award, Harris-Stowe State Col, 1989; Outstanding Community Service, Gamma Omega Chap, Alpha Kappa Alpha; Outstanding Service, Dist St Louis Black Police Asn; Valiant Leadership, Alpha Zeta Chap Iota Phi Lambda Sor Inc; Cert Achievement United Front Cairo, IL; Outstanding Aid Law Enforcement, St Louis Police Dept; Community Service Award, St Louis CORE; Outstanding Community Service, Northside Church Seventh-Day Adventists; Outstanding Civic Work, True Light Baptist Church; Merit Service Award, HDC Credit Union. **Home Addr:** 3032 James Cool Papa Bell Ave, St Louis, MO 63106-1518, **Home Phone:** (314)533-2635. **Business Addr:** Director Emeritus, University of Missouri, 1 Univ Blvd, St Louis, MO 63121-4400, **Business Phone:** (314)516-5000.

## SEBHATU, DR. MESGUN U.
Educator. **Personal:** Born Jan 6, 1946, Monoxeito; married Almaz Yilma; children: Emnet M & Temnete M. **Educ:** Haile Selassie I Univ, BSc, physics, 1969; Clemson Univ, PhD, theoret & math physics, 1975. **Career:** NC State Univ, vis asst prof physics, 1975-76; Pensacola Jr Col, asst prof physics, 1976-78; Winthrop Col, from asst prof physics to assoc prof physics, 1978-91, Dept Chem, Physics & Geol, prof physics, 1991-2014, emer prof physics, 2014-, pre-engineering advisor, currently; NSF res grant, 1990-91; Mich State Univ, King-Chavez-Parks, vis prof physics, 1991-92. **Orgs:** Cath Church, 1946-; Nat Soc Black Physicists Am Phys Soc; Am Asn Physics Teachers; African Sci Inst fel. **Honors/Awds:** Kavli Institute Theoretical of Physics scholar, University Calif, Santa Barbara, 2002-04; Inducted, Howard Univ, 2006; Listed in Men of Achievement by the International Biography Centre, Who's Who Among African Americans. Who's Who in Science and Engineering, Who's Who in Frontiers of Science and Technology, Who's Who in American Education, Who's Who in the South and South West. **Special Achievements:** One of seven theoretical physicists selected to participate in the program of "Two Nucleon Solitary Wave Exchange Potentials"; Published articles Ill Nuovo Cimento, Acta Physica Polonica, Physics Teacher Etc; reviews physical science and physics books for major publishers. **Home Addr:** 750 Norwood Ave, Rock Hill, SC 29730-3255, **Home Phone:** (803)324-1254. **Business Addr:** Emeritus Professor, Pre-Engineering Advisor, Winthrop University, 101 Sims Bldg, Rock Hill, SC 29733, **Business Phone:** (803)323-2113.

## SEBREE-BROWN, CLAUDIA
Chief executive officer, executive. **Personal:** daughter of Aunt Minnie. **Career:** Aunt Minnies Food Serv Inc, vpres, chief exec officer & Prin, currently. **Business Addr:** Vice President, Chief Executive Officer, Aunt Minnie's Food Service Inc, 12265 Williams Rd Suite B, Perrysburg, OH 43551-6807, **Business Phone:** (419)872-4396.

## SEE, DR. LETHA A. (LEE SEE)
Educator, social worker, psychotherapist. **Personal:** Born Jan 23, 1930, Poteau, OK; daughter of Truppy Sanders and Edward Sanders; married Colonel Wilburn R; children: Terry L. **Educ:** Langston Univ, BS; Univ Okla, EdM; Univ Wis, MSW; Bryn Mawr Col, PhD, 1982. **Career:** Professor (retired), professor emeritus; US Dept Educ & labor unions, consult; Univ Ark, asst prof, 1972-77; Child Welfare Serv, agency head, 1977-80; Atlanta Univ, adj prof, 1982-83; Univ Ga, assoc prof, 1983-98, prof emer, currently; Univ WI-Madison, Title III fel, 1987. Author: Tensions and Tangles Between Afro Americans and Southeast Asian Refugees; Human Behavior in the Social Environment from an African-American Perspective; Violence as Seen Through a Prism of Color; My Mama; A Black Women of Honor. **Orgs:** US deleg Soviet Union World Cong Women, 1987; Peoples Repub China; Australia Social Welfare; Acad Social Workers; comn mem, Coun on Social Work Educ; Phi Delta Kappa prof fraternity; Delta Sigma Theta Sorority. **Home Addr:** 909 Otter Way, Marietta, GA 30068-4244, **Home Phone:** (770)971-1051. **Business Addr:** Professor Emeritus, University of Georgia, 240A Riverbend Rd, Athens, GA 30602-1511, **Business Phone:** (706)542-5286.

## SEELE, PERNESSA C.
Educator, chief executive officer, founder (originator). **Personal:** Born Oct 15, 1954, Lincolnville, SC; daughter of Charles and Luella. **Educ:** Clark Univ, BS, 1976; Atlanta Univ, MS, 1979; Col New Rochelle, NY, DHL, 2007. **Career:** Harlem Hosp, AIDS Initiative Prog, adminr; Res NY Univ, res asst, 1981-84; Drake Univ Bus Sch, instr, 1987; Interfaith Hosp, AIDS coordr, 1987-89; Narcotics & Drug Res, assoc AIDS trainer, 1988-89; NY City Health & Hosps, Drug Addiction Prog, admin, 1989-92; HCCI, vpres, 1992-94; lic minister. **Orgs:** Balm In Gilead, founder & chief exec officer, 1989-; bd mem, Harlem United, 1993-95; bd mem, AIDS Action Coun, 1996; AIDS Action Comt, 1998; hon mem, Alpha Kappa Alpha Sorority Inc; lifetime mem, Nat Coun Negro Women; founder, EveryChild USA, 2010-. **Business Addr:** Founder, Chief Executive Officer, The Balm In Gilead Inc, 130 W 42nd St Suite 450, New York, NY 10036-7802, **Business Phone:** (212)730-7381.

## SEGAR, LESLIE
Radio host, actor, dancer. **Personal:** Born Queens, NY; daughter of Leo and Ella. **Educ:** Springfield Col, BS, exercise physiol & sports med, MA; Howard Fine Actg Sch, Los Angeles, Calif, scene study; Herbert Bergdoff Actg Acad, New York, NY, tech & scene study i provisational & scene; Flushing YMCA, Flushing, NY, gymnastics & rhythmic gymnastics. **Career:** Actress, dancer, choreographer, radio personality, producer, fitness specialist & entertainer; Emmis Broadcasting, Hot 97 Radio, New York, dj; CBS Radio, V103, Atlanta, dj; Sirius Satellite Radio, Hot Jamz-Nat, Afternoon Dr, dj; Emmis Broadcasting, Power 106, Big Boy Morning Show, dj; Chancellor Media, 1000.3 The Beat-Los Angeles, dj; Radio One, Steve Harvey Morning Show, Los Angeles, dj; Premiere radio Networks, Hollywood 360, entertainment reporter clear channel affil; Big Lez Enterprises Inc, owner; Films: House Party 2, 1991; Malcolm X, 1992; Who's the Man, 1993; Black Entertainment Televisions, co-host Nj Dr, 1995; Hav Plenty, 1997; An Alan Smithee Film: Burn Hollywood Burn, 1998; 3 A.M., 2001; 142 John St, 2008. TV series: "Rap City", 1993-2000; "My Coolest Yrs", 2004; "Made You Look: Top 25 Moments of BET Hist", 2005; The Fabric of a Man, 2005; Grand Theft Auto: Vice City Stories, 2006; 142 John Street, 2008. **Orgs:** Screen Actors Guild; Am Fedn TV & Radio Asn. **Special Achievements:** Set up fitness training program for SWV, Heavy D, Andre Harrell, Puff Daddy; Choreographed & danced in videos by Whitney Houston, Michael Jackson, Bobby Brown, Salt-n-Pepa, Mary J Blige. **Home Addr:** 8306 Wilshire Blvd

Suite 293, Beverly Hills, CA 90211, **Home Phone:** (818)988-2702. **Business Addr:** Actress, c/o Talent Agency, Los Angeles, CA 90048, **Business Phone:** (323)965-5600.

## SEGREE, E. RAMONE

Fund raising consultant. **Personal:** Born Aug 23, 1949, Chicago, IL; son of Eustas Matthew and Blanche Hill; married Carmen Montague; children: Ashton Montague & Tara Montague. **Educ:** Calif State Col, BA, polit sci & educ, 1972; Pa State Univ, Middletown, MPSSC, community psychol & orgn develop, 1979; Columbia Univ, Teachers Col, EdD, adult learning & orgn leadership, 2014. **Career:** PEN NCP, Harrisburg, Pa, exec dir, 1980-82; USX CRP, Pittsburgh, pub & goval affairs rep, 1982-83; Ketchum Inc, Pittsburgh, campaign dir & Study Coun, 1983-85; United Way SW PEN, Pittsburgh, Pa, div & proj dir, 1984-86; Univ Pittsburgh, Pa, sr dir develop, 1987-89; Pittsburgh Pub Theater, Pittsburgh, vpres develop, 1989-95; Salem State Col, vpres inst advan & found exec dir, 1995-2000; Meharry Med Col, sr vpres inst advan, 2000-02; Segree Assoc, pres, 2002-09; Columbia Univ Sch Continuing Educ, fac, 2008-; LaGuardia Community Col, vpres instnl advan & found exec dir, 2009-13; Winthrop-Univ Hosp, vpres develop, 2013-; Roger Williams Univ, Univ Advan, vpres, currently. **Orgs:** Founder & co-chr, Pittsburgh Black & Jewish Dialogue, 1984-; bd mem, Pittsburgh Community TV Programming Trust, 1987; bd mem, Pittsburgh Youth Symphony Orchestra, 1991; pres bd, Hill House Asn, 1991-; chair, performing arts cmsing, Three Rivers Arts Festival, 1992; Minority Theater Panel, Penn Coun Arts, 1993; secy, Nat Found Bd, Nat Soc Fundraising Execs, 1994-; chmn, Corps & Founds Comt, St Edmunds Acad, 50th Anniversary Capital Campaign; fac mem, fundraising mgt prog, Columbia Univ; exec dir, Pa Nat Asn Adv Coloured People; chair, Int Asn Fund Raising Professionals Found Philanthrop; Int AFP's Leadership Socs AFP's Greater New York & RI Chapters; vpres & chief develop officer, Jackie Robinson Found. **Honors/Awds:** Service Award, Kappa Alpha Psi Fraternity, Harrisburg Alumni Chapter, 1980; Community Leadership Award, 100 Black Men of Pittsburgh, 1988; Service & Achievement Award, Univ Pittsburgh African Heritage Classroom Comt, 1988; Coun Fund-Raisers Citation, 1989; Certified Fund Raising Exec, Nat Soc Fund-Raising Exec, 1990; Pittsburgh Continuing Our Traditions Award, 1992; Hono AS Deg, Community Col Allegheny County, 1992; Distinguished Alumni Award, Community Col Allegheny County, 1992. **Special Achievements:** Published "Strategic Management: Leadership in Changing Times". **Home Addr:** 1067 Blackridge Rd, Pittsburgh, PA 15235, **Home Phone:** (412)243-3133. **Business Addr:** Vice President Development, Winthrop-University Hospital, 259 1st St, Mineola, NY 11501, **Business Phone:** (516)663-0333.

## SEIDENBERG, MARK

Banker. **Career:** Time Savings & Loan Asn, San Francisco, Calif, chief exec officer. **Business Addr:** Chief Executive Officer, Time Savings and Loan Association, 100 Hegenberger Rd Suite 110, Oakland, CA 94621-1447.

## SEIGLER, DEXTER E.

Football player. **Personal:** Born Jan 11, 1972, Avon Park, FL. **Educ:** Univ Miami. **Career:** Miami Dolphins, 1994-95, free agt; Seattle Seahawks, defensive back, 1996-98; Ariz Cardinals, 1998; Amsterdam Admirals, corner back, 1998-99. **Honors/Awds:** All-Star CB, 1998. **Special Achievements:** All-Star NFL Europe. 1993, 1998. **Home Addr:** 17 W 5th St, Jacksonville, FL 32206, **Home Phone:** (904)821-4809.

## SELBY, DR. CORA NORWOOD

Educator, secretary (government). **Personal:** Born Jul 15, 1920, Nassau, DE; daughter of Martha L Maull and Clarence Page; married Paul M; children: Paul MN, Clarence PN, Clyde LN, Adrian LeBlanc & Terence RN. **Educ:** Del State Col, BS, 1940; Univ Del, MEd, 1959. **Career:** Educator (retired), secretary (Government); State Bd Educ, Dover, Laurel teacher specialist, 1941-87; Ross Point Sch Dist, teacher, 1941-64, reading teacher, 1964-65, spl educ teacher, 1965-66, 2nd grade teacher, 1966-69; Indian River Sch Dist, Millsboro, ABE Inst; Headstart Follow-through Prog, fac adv, 1969-80; Migrant Educ Prog, teacher, 1981-87; Sussex Technol, ABE-GED teacher, 1991-95; Sussex County, secy. **Orgs:** LEA, DSEA, NEA Teacher Educ Org, 1941-; cert layspeaker, United Methodist Church, 1980-; secy, DE State Col, 1980-, vpres, Peninsula Delaware Conf Coun on Ministries, UM Church, 1985-; life mem, Nat PTA, 1986-; chaplain, Alpha Delta Kappa State Chap, 1986; bd trustee; pres, Laurel Sr Ctr, 1987-; Gov's Comn Post-Sec Educ; AARP-DRSPA, SCRSPA, 1987; Phi Delta Kappa; secy, bd dir, Carvel Garden Housing; Laurel Hist Soc; lay leader, Peninsula Delaware Conf, UM Church; state & nat PTA youth coun; Comn Archives & Hist, Peninsula Del Conf; Comn Area Episcopacy Peninsula Del Conf; Del Div Literacy, 1988-; Child Placement Review Bd, 1992-; First State Community Action policy coun, 2000-; pres, Carvel Gardens Housing bd, 2000-; Laurel Exchange Club, 2000; Laurel Chamber Com, 2000; vol, Read Aloud; Math Magic; pres, Sussex County Sch Personnel Asn, 2001; pres, Laurel Sr Ctr, 2001; trustee emeritus, Del State Univ. **Home Addr:** Rd 62, Laurel, DE 19956, **Home Phone:** (302)875-3790. **Business Addr:** Trustee Emeritus, Delaware State University, 1200 N DuPont Hwy, Dover, DE 19901, **Business Phone:** (302)857-6060.

## SELBY, MYRA C.

Lawyer, judge. **Personal:** Born Jul 1, 1955, Saginaw, MI; daughter of Ralph and Archie; married Bruce Curry; children: Lauren & Jason. **Educ:** Kalamazoo Col, BA, 1977; Univ Mich Law Sch, JD, 1980. **Career:** Seyfarth, Shaw, Fairweather & Geraldson, assoc, 1980-83; Ice, Miller, Donadio & Ryan, partner, 1983-93; State Ind, dir health care policy, 1993-94; Ind Supreme Ct, assoc justice, 1995-99; columnist, Indianapolis Bus J; Ice Miller LLP, atty & partner, currently; judge, US Ct, 2016-. **Orgs:** Bd dir, Nat Health Lawyers Asn; Am Inn Cts; Am Law Inst; Am Bar Asn; Chicago Med Sch, Finch Univ Health Sci, 1993-94; pres & bd dir, Alpha Nursing Home; Am Hosp Asn; bd dir, Flanner House; bd dir, Indianapolis Ballet Theatre; bd trustee, Indianapolis Mus Art; bd adv, Ind Univ, Indianapolis; bd adv, Purdue Univ, Indianapolis; chmn, Ind Supreme Ct Comn Race & Gender Fairness; Stanley K Lacy Leadership Selection Comt; bd develop comt, Big Sisters Cent Ind, 1995; Ind State Bar Asn; Nat Bar Asn; Nat Arbit Forum; fel Am Bar Found; Am Law Inst. **Honors/Awds:** Stanley K Lacy Leadership Ser Class XIII, 1989; A Breakthrough Woman Award, Coalition of 100 Black Women, 1990; Leadership Initiative, Indianapolis Chamber Com, 1992-94; Antoinette Dakin Leach Award, Indianapolis Bar Asn, 1997; listed in The Best Lawyers in America; Featured in Indiana Trailblazing Women, 2000; Touchstone Awards, Girls Inc, 2001; Distinguished Barrister, Indiana Lawyer, 2008; Indiana Super Lawyer, Health Care, 2010. **Special Achievements:** First woman and the First African American to sit on the bench of the state's highest court. **Business Addr:** Partner, Attorney, Ice Miller, 1 Am Sq, Indianapolis, IN 46282-0200, **Business Phone:** (317)236-5903.

## SELF, FRANK WESLEY

Executive, accountant, manager. **Personal:** Born Nov 2, 1949, Junction City, KS; son of Nolan and Wilma Pollet; married Shirley M Brown; children: Frank E & Shelley M. **Educ:** Univ Colo, Denver, CO, BS, acct, 1976; State Colo, Denver, CO, CPA, cert, 1979. **Career:** Ashby, Armstrong & Johnson, Denver, Colo, mgr, 1977-82; Am TV & Commun Corp, Englewood, Colo, dir, 1982; Time Warner Cable, dir invest acct, sr dir opers acct. **Orgs:** Nat Asn Black Accts, 1978; Am Inst CPAs, 1981; Colo Soc CPAs, 1981; Nat Asn Minorities Cable, 1985; Korean Tong Soo Do Karate Asn, 1989. **Honors/Awds:** Am Best & Brightest, Dollars & Sense, 1989; Young Bus & Prof Men. **Home Addr:** 17 Heritage Hill Rd, Norwalk, CT 06851, **Home Phone:** (203)846-4517.

## SELLARS, HAROLD GERARD

Banker, administrator, vice president (organization). **Personal:** Born May 27, 1953, Vass, NC; son of Frank Alfred and Bessie Mae Johnson; married Clara Scott; children: Dwight & Dwayne. **Educ:** Sandhills Community Col, 1972; NC Cent Univ, Durham, NC, BA (cum laude), bus admin, 1978. **Career:** United Carolina Bank, Whiteville, NC, sr vpres, 1977-98; Br Banking & Trust Co, vpres; Mech & Farmers Bank, Durham, NC, sr vpres lending adminr, qual assurance & security officer, 1998-2012. **Orgs:** Bd mem, Bankers Educ Soc Inc, 1985-95; adv bd, NC Small Bus Admin Adv Coun, 1990-95; bd mem, NC Rural Econ Develop Ctr, 1990-97; bd mem, NC Small Bus Tech & Develop Centers, 1989-97; bd edu, Whiteville City Schs, 1996-98; bd mem, Self Help Ventures Fund; bd mem, Durham's Partnership C, 1999-2007, bd chair, 2005-07; vice chmn, Mech & Farmers Bank. **Home Addr:** 4 Wateroaks Ct, Durham, NC 27703. **Business Addr:** Senior Vice President, Mechanics & Farmers Bank, PO Box 1932, Durham, NC 27702, **Business Phone:** (919)683-1521.

## SELLERS, JACQUELINE H.

Lawyer. **Educ:** Howard Univ, BA, Eng, sociol, 1978; Mich State Univ, Detroit Col Law, JD, 1985. **Career:** Mich Supreme Ct, law clerk, 1986-87; Lewis & Munday, pres & chief exec officer, 1987-2004; Blackwell Igbanugo, managing partner, 2004-06; Wayne County Circuit Court, mediator; Mich Atty Discipline Bd, panelist; Clark Hill PLC, mem, 2006-08, pract group leader, Litigation Mgt group & mem, Detroit off, Coun, 2008-; Col Southern Md, adj prof-legal studies, 2012-. **Orgs:** Am Bar Asn; Defense Res Inst; Nat Bar Asn, panelist; Straker Bar Asn; Wolverine Bar Asn; exec dir, bd dir & exec secy, Forgotten Harvest bd; Augustus Straker Bar; fel State Bar Mich; Renaissance Chap Links Inc, 1996-; CYOC Found, 1998-2009; Nations Third Largest Food Rescue Orgn; Michs Atty Discipline Bd; Women Lawyers Asn Mich; exec dir & secy, Forgotten Harvest, 2005-11. **Business Addr:** Of Counsel, Clark Hill PLC, 500 Woodward Ave Suite 3500, Detroit, MI 48226, **Business Phone:** (313)965-8377.

## SENBET, PROF. LEMMA W.

Executive director, research scientist, educator. **Personal:** son of Wolde. **Educ:** Haile Sellassie I Univ, Addis Ababa, BBA, 1970; Univ Calif, Los Angeles, CA, MBA, 1972; State Univ NY, Buffalo, NY, PhD, 1975. **Career:** Northwestern Univ, vis assoc prof, 1980-81; Univ Wis-Madison, assoc prof, 1980-83, prof & Dickson Bascom prof, finance, 1983-87, Charles Albright chair & prof, finance, 1987-90; J Finance, assoc ed, 1983-84; UC Berkeley, vis prof finance, 1984-85; Distinguished Res Visitor, London Sch Econ; World Bank, consult, 1989-; Univ Md, Robert H Smith Sch Bus, William E Mayer chair prof, finance & dir, ctr financial policy, 1990-, Dept Finance, chair, 1998-2006; African Econ Res Consortium, consult, 1994-, exec dir, 2013-; Int Monetary Fund, consult, 1996-; UN, consult, 1996-97 & 2002-03; Financial Mgt, exec ed, 1999-2005; Hartford Funds, dir, 2005-; J Int Bus Studies, ed, 2005-11. **Orgs:** Pres, Western Fin Asn, 1989-90; bd dir, Am Fin Asn, 1991-94, 1997-99; ed bd, Jour Finance; ed bd, Jour Financial & Quant Anal; ed bd, Financial Mgt, exec ed; ed bd, Jour Banking & Finance, 1995-99; chair, FMA Doctoral Panel; bd dir, Fortis Mutual Funds, 2000-02; fel Financial Mgt Asn Int, 2006. **Home Addr:** 3210 Rittenhouse St NW, Washington, DC 20015. **Business Addr:** William E Mayer Chair Professor of Finance, Director of Center for Financial Policy, University of Maryland, 4437 Van Munching Hall, College Park, MD 20742, **Business Phone:** (301)405-2242.

## SENEGAL, REV. NOLTON JOSEPH, SR.

Lawyer, religious leader. **Personal:** Born Mar 15, 1952, Lafayette, LA; son of Willie Floyd; married Patricia Dianne Frank; children: Nolton Joseph Jr, Anysia Nicole & Terrence Jamal. **Educ:** Southern Univ, BS, bus educ & social studies, 1973, MS, admin & supv, 1975; Southern Univ Law Sch, JD, 1984. **Career:** St Landry Parish Police Jury, 1975-77; Diocese Lafayette, 1975-77; Lafayette Regional Voc Tech Sch, 1977-81; Lafayette Parish Sch Bd, 1977-81; Acadiana Legal Serv Corp, dir, 1985-97, sr atty; Our Mother Mercy Church, deacon, 2000-; Farm workers Legal Assistance Proj, dir, currently; Roman Cath Church, deacon. **Orgs:** Alpha Phi Alpha Frat, 1977-; Phi Delta Kappa Law Frat, 1982-; pres, Stud Bar Asn Law Ctr, 1983-84; chair, Minority Involvement Sect LSBA, 1993-95; Fed Rel Network, Nat Sch Bds Asn, 1996-2007; exe dir, La Sch Bd Assoc, 2007-; pres, Acadia Parish Sch Bd; past chmn, La State Bar Asn Minority Involvement Comt; chmn & probation monitor, La State Bar Asn-Disciplinary Comts. **Special Achievements:** First African American to serve as president of the Acadia Parish School Board; first vice president of LA School Bds Assn, 1997-99. **Home Addr:** 413 Sect Ave, PO Box 564, Rayne, LA 70578-5949, **Home Phone:** (318)334-5759. **Business Addr:** Deacon, Our Mother of Mercy Church, 707 Lyman Ave, Rayne, LA 70578-0468, **Business Phone:** (337)334-3516.

## SENGSTACKE, BOBBY (ROBERT ABBOTT SENGSTACKE)

Photojournalist, photographer. **Personal:** Born May 29, 1943, Chicago, IL. **Educ:** Bethune Cookman Col. **Career:** Chicago Defender, photojournalist youth sect; Los Angeles Centennial, photojournalist; Lemont McLemore, understudy; Muhammad Speaks, staff photogr; Chicago Defender, head photogr & ed; Fisk Univ, artist resident; Memphis Tri-State Defender, gen mgr & publ; Sengstacke Stock Images & Arch, founder; Sengstacke Studio, founder. **Business Addr:** 350 N Odgen Ave Suite 450, Chicago, IL 60607, **Business Phone:** (773)744-7487.

**SENGSTACKE, ROBERT ABBOTT. See SENGSTACKE, BOBBY.**

**SENSE, COMMON. See LYNN, LONNIE RASHID, JR.**

## SERGEANT, CARRA SUSAN

Association executive, educator. **Personal:** Born Jul 16, 1953, New Orleans, LA; daughter of James Bernard and Susan Caralita Craven. **Educ:** Dillard Univ, New Orleans, LA, BA, 1976; Univ Cent Ark, Conway, AR, MS, 1978. **Career:** Ind Univ Pa, Ind, Pa, residence dir, 1978-80; Ind Coun Against Rape, Ind, Pa, dir, 1979-80; Ga Inst Technol, Atlanta, Ga, area coord, 1980-85; Metrop Develop Ctr, New Orleans, LA, active treat mgr, 1985-89; Los Angeles State Univ, Eunice, LA, coord support serv, 1989-90, coord Upward Bound, 1990-, asst dir acad assistance prog & counr, regist chair, currently. **Orgs:** Vpres, New Orleans Chap, Nat Orgn Women, 1987-89, pres, 1988-89; regional newsletter ed, Southwest Asn Stud Assistance Prog, 1989-91; comt chair, La Asn Stud Assistance Prog, 1990-, secy, 1991-, pres, 1995; Nat Asn Women Educ; regist chair, Womens Comn Southwest Las Fall Conf. **Home Addr:** PO Box 251, Eunice, LA 70535, **Home Phone:** (318)546-6830. **Business Addr:** Registration Chair, Louisiana State University Eunice, 2048 Johnson Hwy, Eunice, LA 70535, **Business Phone:** (318)457-7311.

## SERGENT, ERNEST E., JR.

Physicist, business owner. **Personal:** Born Feb 9, 1943, New Orleans, LA; married Claudette Ruth Brown; children: Sandra Michelle, Ernest III & James Richard. **Educ:** Southern Univ New Orleans, BS, math & physics, 1970; Univ MI Ann Arbor, MS ,ohysics, 1974. **Career:** Dowell Labs, 1966-70; Univ Mich Geol Dept, res assoc, 1972-74; Gen Motors Res Ctr, jr physicist, 1973; 3M Co, prod engineering specialist, 1974-2006, advan physicist, 1974-75, adv prod control engr, 1975-79, sr physicist, 1979; Sergent Enterprises, owner, 1999-. **Orgs:** Fel Univ Mich, fel, 1970-72; Afro-Am Art Soc 3M Co; bd dir, Cottage Grove Jaycees, 1978-79; Cottage Grove Human Serv Community; Cottage Grove Baseball/Softball Div; Soc Automotive Engrs; Community Vol Serv; Am Qual Asn; Proj Planning Asn; Am Phys Soc; Am Chem Soc. **Honors/Awds:** Who's Who in Black America, 1979-80; Outstanding young Minnesotan, 1979; Golden Step Award, 3M, 2001; 3M Volunteer of the Year 2003. **Home Addr:** 9119 79th St S, Cottage Grove, MN 55016-2214, **Home Phone:** (651)459-8052. **Business Addr:** Owner, Sergent Enterprises, 9119 79th St S, Cottage Grove, MN 55016-2214, **Business Phone:** (651)459-8052.

## SERMON, ERICK (ERICK ONASSIS)

Rap musician. **Personal:** Born Nov 25, 1968, Bay Shore, NY. **Career:** Singer, producer & writer; Albums: Strictly Business, 1988; Unfinished Business, 1989; Business Never Personal, 1992; No Pressure, 1993; Business as Usual, 1994; Double or Nothing, 1995; Back in Business, 1997; El Nino, 1998; Out of Business, 1999; Erick Onasis, 2000; Music, 2001; React, 2002; Chilltown, New York, 2004; Singles: Hittin' Switches, 1993; Stay Real, 1993; Bomdigi, 1995; Welcome, 1996; Why Not, 2000; I'm Hot, 2001; Love Iz, 2002; Feel It, 2004; Street Hop, 2004; Producer: Reservoir Dogs, 1999; Da Heat wave, 2000; So Fly, 2005; Goldmine, 2006; We Mean Business, 2008. Films: Juice, 1992; Who's the Man?, 1993; A Low Down Dirty Shame, 1994; Die Hard: With a Vengeance, 1995; The Show, 1995; Don't Be a Menace, 1996; Rhyme & Reason, 1997; Side, actor, 1998; Blade, 1998; Black & White, 1999; The Corruptor, 1999; In Too Deep, 1999; Nutty Professor II The Klumps, 2000; Rush Hour 2, 2001; Barber Shop, 2002; Honey, 2003; Beef II (doc), 2004; Syriana, 2005; Rock The Bells, 2006, 2008; What Happens in Vegas, 2008; Whip It, 2009; The Lincoln Lawyer, 2011. **Business Addr:** Recording Artist, Universal Motown Records, 1755 Broadway 6th Fl, New York, NY 10019, **Business Phone:** (212)373-0750.

## SERWANGA, WASSWA KENNETH

Football player. **Personal:** Born Jul 23, 1976, Kampala. **Educ:** Univ Calif, Los Angeles, BA, 2003; St Mary's Col Calif, MBA, bus admin, 2011. **Career:** Football player (retired), executive; San Francisco 49ers, defensive back, 1999; Minn Vikings, 2001, cornerback, left cornerback, 2000; Los Angeles Avengers, defensive back, 2003; Wells Fargo, Bus Banker, 2003-06, bus relationship mgr, 2006-07; Wash Mutual, vpres bus relationship mgr, 2007-08; JPMorgan Chase, vpres bus banker, 2008-10. **Honors/Awds:** Rookie of the Year, 1999. **Business Addr:** Vice President, Washington Mutual Business Banking, Washington Mutual, Seattle, WA 98101, **Business Phone:** (800)788-7000.

## SESSION, JOHNNY FRANK, JR.

Government official. **Personal:** Born Mar 2, 1949, Panama City, FL; son of Karetta Baker Alexander and Jake; married Linda Tibbs; children: Tomeka, Johnny Frank Jr & Marcus. **Educ:** Gulf Coast Jr Col, Panama City, FL, AA, 1970; Fla A&M Univ, Tallahassee, FL, BS, 1973. **Career:** Deloit, Haskins & Sells, Ft Lauderdale, Fla, staff acct, 1973-75; City Hollywood, Hollywood, Fla, staff acct, 1975-77, sr acct, 1977-81, controller, 1981-84; City Tallahassee, Tallahassee, Fla, controller, 1984-, sr financial mgr. **Orgs:** Govt Fin Officers Asn; chap pres, Nat Asn Black Accountants; Fla Inst Cert Pub Acct; Am Inst Cert Pub Acct; dir, Community Neighborhood Renaissance Partnership Inc. **Home Addr:** 2806 Sweetbriar Dr, Tallahassee, FL 32312, **Home Phone:** (904)386-8349. **Business Addr:** Senior Financial Manager, Controller, City of Tallahassee, 300 S Adams St, Tallahassee, FL 32301, **Business Phone:** (850)891-8867.

**SESSOMS, ALLEN LEE**
School administrator, physicist, association executive. **Personal:** Born Nov 17, 1946, New York, NY; son of Albert Earl and Lottie Beatrice Leff; married Csilla Manette von Csiky; children: Manon Elizabeth & Stephanie Csilla. **Educ:** Union Col, BS, math, 1968; Univ Wash, MS, physics, 1969; Yale Univ, MPhil, 1971, physics, PhD, physics, 1972. **Career:** Brookhaven Nat Lab, res assoc, 1972-73; Europ Org Nuclear Res, sci assoc, 1973-75; Ford Found Travel & Study Grant, 1973-74; Harvard Univ, assoc prof physics, 1974-81; Alfred P Sloan Found, fel, 1977-81; US Dept State, Bur Oceans & Int Environ & Sci Affairs, sr tech adv, 1980-82, Bur's Off Technol & Safeguards, dir, 1982-87, Sci & Technol Affairs, counr, 1987-89, US Embassy Mex, minister counsr polit affairs, 1989-91, dep chief mission, 1991-93; Univ Mass, exec vpres, 1993-95, vpres acad affairs, 1994-95; City Univ NY, Queens Col, pres, 1995-2000; US Secy Energy Adv Bd, 1997-2001; Bd Overseers Fermi Nat Accelerator Lab, 1998-2006; Harvard Univ, JFK Sch Gov, vis prof, 2001-03, vis scholar, 2000-01; Del State Univ, pres, 2003-; US intelligence community, consult. **Orgs:** Chair, US Dept Energy, 1996-, sec energy adv bd, 1996-; Am Phys Soc; Socs Sigma Xi; Del Coun Arts; MR Asn Advan Sci, 1973-; NY Acad Sci; 100 Black Men, 1995-; Cosmos Club. **Honors/Awds:** Tree of Life Award, Jewish Nat Fund, 1996; Meritorious & Superior Honor Awards, State DPT; Medal of Highest Honor, Soka Univ, Japan, 1999; Wilbur Lucius Cross Medal, Yale Grad Sch Asn, 1999; Officier dans l'Ordre des Palmes Academiques, 1999; Seikyo Culture Award, Japan, 1999. **Special Achievements:** Author of over 30 scientific publications in professional journals and US government policy papers. **Home Addr:** 130 Beacon St, Chestnut Hill, MA 02467, **Home Phone:** (302)264-1549. **Business Addr:** President, Delaware State University, 1200 N Dupont Hwy Suite 400, Dover, DE 19901, **Business Phone:** (302)857-6001.

**SESSOMS, DR. FRANK EUGENE**
Executive, physician, association executive. **Personal:** Born Oct 24, 1947, Rochester, PA; son of Frank L and Catherine; married Sandra Scalise. **Educ:** Bradley Univ, attended 1966; Harvard Univ, Intensive Summer Studies prog, 1968; TN State Univ, BS, 1970; Meharry Med Col, MD, 1974. **Career:** Procter & Gamble, food prods tech brand specialist, 1969; US Dept Agr, summer researcher animal health div, 1970; Procter & Gamble Miami Valley Labs, summer researcher, 1971; stud researcher, Meharry Med Col, 1971-74; St Margaret's Memorial Hosp, internship & residency family pract, 1974-77; fel Samuel Goldwyn Found, 1971-74; St John's Gen Hosp, dir emergency serv, 1977; Diplo Am Bd Family Pract, 1977; med consult psychiat dept, 1983; pvt pract physician, 1979-; Univ Pittsburgh Family Med & Proc, prof; W Penn Allegheny Health Syst, physician, 1998-; Frank E Sessoms Inc, pvt pract, currently. **Orgs:** Vpres, stud coun, Tenn State Univ, 1969-70; class pres, Meharry Med Col, 1970-71; vpres, Pre-Alumni Coun, Meharry Med Col, 1973-74; Cong Black Caucus Health Brain Trust, 1974-; mem bd, Homewood Brushton YMCA, 1979-83; chmn bd, Pittsburgh Black Action Methadone Maint Ctr, 1985-86; Nat Med Asn; med dir, Bidwell Drug & Alcohol Prog; pres, Alpha Phi Alpha, 1998-; Nat Asn Advan Colored People; Urban League, AMA; Penn Med Soc; Undersea Med Soc; Nat Asn Health Serv Execs; Pittsburgh Chap 100 Black Men; Frontiers Int; bd govs, Tenn State Univ Stud Union; Univ Counselors Tenn State Univ; Alumni Bd Mgt, Meharry Med Col; Chi Delta Mu Fraternity; Am Corner, 1987-; Gateway Med Soc; Allegheny County Med S; pres, Meharry Nat Alumni Asn, 1993-95; comnr PA, Gov Com African Am Affairs, 1992-; partic, Pres Intercultural Task Force Healthcare Reform, 1994; Guest Lectr, CCAC, 1994; Pittsburgh Pub Sch's Restructing Task Force, 1992-93; Comt African Am Stud's; Bd Mgt, Meharry Med Col, 1995-. **Honors/Awds:** Fel NY Acad Sci; patent holder High-Protein Fruit-Flavored Fat Stablized Spread, 1969; Pre-Alumni Coun Award, 1974; Hon Sgt-at-Arms, Tenn House Representatives, 1974; Presidential Citation Nat Asn Equal Opportunities Higher Educ, 1984; fel Am Acad Family Pract. **Special Achievements:** Publisher: "Effects of Ethane 1, 1 Dihydorxy Diphospanate "EHDP" on the Collagen Metabolism in the Rat" 1971 (Procter & Gamble Res Lab); scientific articles "Uses of the Soybean & Their Prospects for the Future", TN State Univ Dept of Bio-Chemistry, 1970. **Home Addr:** 2777 Shamrock Dr, Allison Park, PA 15101-3146. **Business Addr:** Physician, Medical Director, Frank E Sessoms Inc, 211 N Whitfield St Suite 610, Pittsburgh, PA 15206, **Business Phone:** (412)363-6560.

**SESSOMS, GLENN D.**
Executive, vice president (organization). **Personal:** Born Oct 20, 1953, Norfolk, VA; son of Clarence and Geraldine; married Linda D; children: Daryn L, Justin R & Adea M. **Educ:** Va State Univ, BS, 1976. **Career:** Exec (retired); Johnson & Johnson, 1976-82; Fed Express Corp, 1983-88, Supvr, Sr Mgr, managing dir, 1988-94, Southern Region AGFS, gen mgr, vpres, human resources serv, 1994-2009, chief diversity officer; GDS Inc, motivational speaker, 2009-. **Orgs:** Omega Psi Phi Fraternity, 1975; chmn, bd dir, Leadrship Memphis. **Home Addr:** 341 Riveredge Dr W, Cordova, TN 38018-7610, **Home Phone:** (901)754-4144. **Business Addr:** Board of Directors, Leadership Memphis, 119 S Main St Suite 425, Memphis, TN 38103, **Business Phone:** (901)278-0016.

**SETTLES, DARRYL STEPHEN**
Restaurateur, executive, entrepreneur. **Personal:** Born Mar 30, 1961, Augusta, GA; son of David Jr and Rebecca. **Educ:** Carnegie Mellon Univ, attended 1978; Univ Tenn, Knoxville, attended 1981; Digital Equip Corp, sales develop prog; Carnegie-Mellon Univ, summer engineering prog; Va Polytech Inst & State Univ, BS, indust engineering & opers res, 1984. **Career:** Gen Elec Co, 1979-81; Digital Equip Corp, engr, 1984-85, sls acct mgr, 1985-90, mkt exec; D'Ventures Unlimited Inc, pres, 1990-2014; Bob's Southern Bistro, owner & pres, 1990-; Darryl's Corner Bar & Kitchen (DCBK), proprietor, 1990-; Wise Urban Develop, pres, 2010-; Cataylst Ventures Develop, pres & managing partner, 2014-. **Orgs:** Boston Fel, 1991-; lead Boston, Nat Conf Community & Justice, 1991-; Greater Boston Conv & Tourism Bur, 1991-; bd mem, Mass Restaurant Asn Bd, 1992-; bd mem, Kids Fund, Boston Med Ctr; organizer, BeanTown Jazz Festival; Coun Overseers; Mass Conv Ctr Authority; assoc Comnr, Metrop Dist Comn; Berklee Col Music Adv Bd; Huntington Theater Bd; Mus Fine Arts Bd; Berklee Col Music (2008); Mass Conv Ctr Authority; Newton Econ Develop Comn; Berklee Col Music Adv Bd; Huntington Theater Bd; Mus Fine Arts Bd; Wang Ctr (currently Citi Performing Arts Ctr); Mass Restaurant Asn Bd; & Metrop Dist Comn, Assoc Comnr; Mass Black Bus Asn; Boston Black Bus Leaders; Nat Soc Black Engrs; Conv Partnership Comt; bd mem, Inclusive Econ Polit Action Comt; Black Econ Coun Mass, 2015-. **Honors/Awds:** Change Agent, Color Magazine; Legacy Award, Museum of African American History; Minority Business of the Year, City of Boston ; Business Profile Award, Black & White Boston; We Are Boston Community Leadership Award; 100 Players of Boston Nightlife (3 years); Forty Bostonians We Love, Boston Magazine; Omega Man of the Year, Omega Psi Phi Fraternity; DEC100 (Digital Sales Award; 4 years), Digital Equipment Corporation; Tiffany 10 Community Award; All-Inclusive Awards: Chg Agt, Color Mag, 2012; Leaders Diversity Award, Boston Bus J, 2014; Community Leadership Award, Jewish Alliance Law & Social Action, 2014; Harriet Tubman Community Achievement Award, United S End Settlements, 2014. **Special Achievements:** America's Best & Brightest Young Business & Professional Men, Dollars & Sense Magazine, 1992; Darryl has been named one of Boston Magazine's, Forty Bostonians We Love. **Home Addr:** 41 Ft Ave, Boston, MA 02119. **Business Addr:** Managing Partner, President, Catalyst Ventures Development, 16 John Eliot Sq, Boston, MA 02119, **Business Phone:** (617)512-9275.

**SETTLES, TRUDY Y.**
Government official. **Personal:** Born Jun 3, 1946, Springfield, OH; daughter of Nathaniel and Ruth Dennis. **Educ:** Cent State Univ, Wilberforce, OH, BS, 1968. **Career:** City Dayton, Dayton, Ohio, 1971-75; RL Polk & Co, Wash, DC, off assoc, 1975-76; Southern Calif Gas Co, Wash, DC, secy, 1976-82, govt affairs asst, 1982-94; Senate Judiciary Sub comt Immigration, staff asst, 1995-97; Columbia Gas Transmission, adv asst chief exec officer, 1997-; Wilberforce Univ, Wilberforce, Ohio, secy pres. **Orgs:** Rules comt, Wash Energy Affil, Desk Derrick Clubs, 1983-86, corresp secy, 1986, bd dir, 1986-88, chmn, prog comt, finance comt, pres, 1992-93; secy, DC Metrop Chap Am Asn Blacks Energy, Wash, 1990-92; Cancer Sociaty. **Home Addr:** 1150 Conn Ave NW Suite 717, Washington, DC 20036. **Business Addr:** Assistant to the Chief Executive Officer, Columbia Gas Transmission Corp, 12801 Fair Lakes Pkwy, Fairfax, VA 22033, **Business Phone:** (703)227-3200.

**SEUNAGAL, DEBORAH EVANS**
Librarian. **Personal:** Born Sep 30, 1959, Detroit, MI; daughter of Thomas and Irene Parks; children: 1. **Educ:** Univ Mich, AB, 1981, AMLS, 1983; Wayne State Univ, cert archival admin, 1992; Preserv Intensive Inst, Univ Calif, Los Angeles, 1994. **Career:** Dickinson, Wright, et al, law librn, 1983-84; Wayne Co Libr, librn, 1985-88; Detroit Pub Libr, field archivist, 1988-95, librn III, specialist, 1995-99; Detroit Radio Info Serv, Prog Co-Host, Co-Producer, 2000-01; Southfield Pub Libr, adult serv librn, 2001, Pres, bd trustee, 2009-; info search coach, currently; Greenfield Village, Henry Ford, Hist Presenter, 2007-; Master Presenter, 2013-, Oakland County Cs Village Sch, 2008-. **Orgs:** Am Asn Law Libr, 1983-84; Spec Libr Asn, 1983-84; Fred Hart Williams Geneal Soc, 1989-97; Mich Libr Asn, 1987-88; Oral Hist Asn, 1988-89; pres, Deborah Evans Asn, 1990-94; Am Libr Asn, 1992-94; Detroit Asn Black Storytellers, 1994-97; bd large, Fred Hart Williams Geneal Soc, 1995-96, vpres, 1996-97; Int Platform Asn, 1995-97. **Honors/Awds:** Margaret Mann Award, Univ Mich, Sch Infor & Libr Studies, 1983, Edmon Low Award, 1983; Cert Appreciation, Mich Geneal Coun, 1991; Libr Mich, Librn's Prof Cert, 1991; Scholar form Calif State Libr to attend Preserv Intensive Inst, 1994. **Special Achievements:** Presented paper: "MIC in Perspective," Local Hist Conf, 1991; MIC Archival ASN Spring Conf, panelist, 1992; published video reviews, Libr Journal, 1992; MIC AFA Symposium, Detroit MIC, conf co-chair, 1995; Developer & presenter: AFA Internet Resources Workshops, Detroit Pub Libr, 1996-97. **Home Addr:** 16028 W Eleven Mile Rd, Southfield, MI 48076, **Home Phone:** (248)569-0441.

**SEVILLIAN, CLARENCE MARVIN, SR.**
Educator, musician. **Personal:** Born Apr 23, 1945, Buffalo, NY; married Madeline Carol Cochran; children: Clarence II & Nicole Ren. **Educ:** Fla Agr & Mech Univ, BS, 1966; Eastern Mich Univ, MEd, admin, 1974. **Career:** Hoxey Job Corp Ctr, Cadillac, resident, counr, 1966-68; Saginaw Foundries, purchase agt, 1968-70; N western High Sch, Flint, staff spec; Bryant Jr High Sch, Flint, instrumental music teacher, 1970-74; Beecher Community Sch, dep prin. **Orgs:** Rec keeper Saginaw Alumni, Kappa Alpha Psi; Mich Educ Asn; NEA; United Teacher Flint; Mich Sch Band & Orchestra Asn; Music Edur Nat Conf; Adv Bryant Band & Orchestra Parents Asn. **Honors/Awds:** Outstanding Secondary Educator of America, 1974; Outstanding Young Man of America, 1974. **Special Achievements:** First vpres of Unity Urban Community Develop & Rehab Corp. **Home Addr:** 2161 Heather Way, Gladwin, MI 48624-8606, **Home Phone:** (989)426-8423.

**SEWELL, EDWARD C.**
Executive, real estate developer. **Personal:** Born Aug 18, 1946, Hanover, MD. **Educ:** Bowling Green Univ, BA; Ind Univ, MBA. **Career:** Xerox Corp, financial analyst, 1970-72; Irwin Mgt Co, asst pres, real estate developer, 1972-75; Crocker Nat Bank, vpres real estate planning, 1975-78; J P Mahoney & Co, real estate developer, 1978-; Prof Sports Ctr, pres sports agt, 1983-2001; Edward Sewell & Assocs, prin, 1990-. **Orgs:** Vice chmn & founder, Judge Joseph Kennedy Scholar Found Bay Area Minorties; fel, Consortium Grad Study Mgt, 1968-70. **Home Addr:** 1238 Cole St, San Francisco, CA 94117-4322, **Home Phone:** (415)681-0819. **Business Addr:** President, Professional Sports Center, 1238 Cole St, San Francisco, CA 94117-4322, **Business Phone:** (415)681-1335.

**SEWELL, EUGENE P.**
Executive director, business owner, association executive. **Personal:** Born Jun 20, 1962, Detroit, MI; son of Solomon and Carrie; married Adrienne; children: Christopher, Alexandria & Maya. **Educ:** Wayne State Univ, BA, commun, jour, & related progs, 1984; Univ Detroit Mercy, MA, pub rels, advert, & appl commun, 1996. **Career:** City Detroit, asst dir, 1988-94; Univ Detroit Mercy, mgr, community rel, 1994-2000; 100 Black Men Greater Detroit Inc, exec dir, 2000; St.Peters Home Boys, pres, currently; Mkt Plus Co, owner, pres & chief exec officer, 2000-. **Orgs:** Bd mem, Detroit Neighborhood Housing Serv, 1994-; adv bd, Detroit Compact, 1995; exec comt, Nat Kidney Found, 2000; NW Neighborhood Health Empowerment Ctr, 2001-; bd dir, Vpres, Franklin Wright Settlement, 2001-. **Honors/Awds:** Key to the City, City of Detroit Mayor's Office, 1989. **Home Addr:** 6129 Yorkshire Rd, Detroit, MI 48224, **Home Phone:** (313)885-7595. **Business Addr:** Board Director, Vice President, Franklin-Wright Settlements Inc, 3360 Charlevoix, Detroit, MI 48207, **Business Phone:** (313)579-1000.

**SEWELL, ISIAH OBEDIAH**
Government official, engineer. **Personal:** Born Nov 20, 1938, Lexington, SC; son of Joseph Preston and Annie Bell Sligh; married Julia Smith; children: Kevin, Kendra & Keith. **Educ:** SC State Col, BSEE, 1961; George Washington Univ, attended 1972. **Career:** US Dept Navy, elec engr, 1964-71, head utilities, 1971-75; US Dept Energy, Washington, DC, gen engr, 1975-84, hbcu liason, 1984-92, coordr minority educ progs, 1986-92; Innovative & Univ Progs, staff dir, 1992-95. **Orgs:** Past secy, trustee bd, Ward Memorial AME, 1975-; Fed Task Force Nat Power Grid Study, 1979; Lawrence Berkeley Nat Lab/Mendez Educ Found Sci Consortium, 1986-92; chmn, Fed Agency Sci & Tech Bd, 1986-92; pres, Athenians Inc Wash DC; pres, Wash Chap SC State Col Nat Alumni; Alpha Phi Alpha, Alpha Kappa Mu. **Home Addr:** 7000 97th Ave, Seabrook, MD 20706, **Home Phone:** (301)794-8940.

**SEWELL, LUTHER JOSEPH, JR.**
Executive, consultant, founder (originator). **Personal:** Born Aug 9, 1936, Chattanooga, TN; son of Luther and Minnie P Sloan; married Wilma Johnson; children: Luther J III & Lela J. **Educ:** Tenn A&I Univ, attended 1956; Duquesne Univ, attended 1958; Monterey Peninsula Col, attended 1960; Allegheny Community Col; Univ Ariz, attended 1969; Trinity Hall Col & Sem, grad, 1971. **Career:** Talk Mag, publ, 1962-; LJS Group, founder & publ, 1962-; Bus & Job Develop Corp, consult, mkt analyst, community develop coord, 1964-70; Mellon Nat Bank, consult, 1965-71; Allegheny County Civil Serv Comn, secy, 1973-; Trans World Airlines, Pa Lottery, consult, currently; LJS Publ Inc, pres & chief exec officer. **Orgs:** Bus & Job Develop Corp, 1963; Am Mkt Asn, 1968-72; vpres, LoendiLit & Social Club, 1969; rev comt, Community Chest Allegheny County, 1971-73; bd dir, Pittsburgh Goodwill Indust, 1972-; Mendelssohn Choir, 1972-; partner, vpres, A & S Securities Syst Inc, 1973-74; bd dir, Pittsburgh Chap Nat Asn Advan Colored People, 1973-; Pittsburgh Press Club; Gateway Ctr Club. **Honors/Awds:** Young Businessman of the Year, AME Gen Conf, 1965; Economic Development Award, Urban Youth Action Inc, 1972; Communications Award, Pittsburgh Club United, 1972; Martin Luther King Award, Music & Arts Club Pittsburgh, 1972; Red Cross Volunteer Award, 1973; Black Achievers Award, Ctr Ave Youth Men's Christian Asn, 1973; Publishers Award, Black Polit Action Asn, 1988; Business Award, Federal Exec Bd, 1989. **Special Achievements:** First African-American civil service commissioner in Allegheny County. **Home Addr:** 3432 Webster Ave, Pittsburgh, PA 15219, **Home Phone:** (412)683-5920. **Business Addr:** President, Chief Executive Officer, LJS Publishing Inc, 3423 Webster Ave, Pittsburgh, PA 15219-3917, **Business Phone:** (412)823-4007.

**SEWELL, STEVEN EDWARD (STEVE SEWELL)**
Football player, football coach. **Personal:** Born Apr 2, 1963, San Francisco, CA; children: Samuel, Caleb & Calah. **Educ:** Univ Okla, BA, orgn commun, 1986. **Career:** Football player (retired), football coach; Denver Broncos, running back, wide receiver, 1985-91; Grandview High Sch, asst football coach, offensive coordr; Colo State Univ, Pueblo Football Prog, asst running backs coach, 2008-15. **Orgs:** Youth Found. **Honors/Awds:** Super Bowl, 1986, 1987, 1988 & 1990; RMAC Offensive Freshman of the Year. **Business Addr:** Running Backs Coach, Colorado State University, 2200 Bonforte Blvd, Pueblo, CO 81001, **Business Phone:** (719)549-2059.

**SEYMORE, STANLEY**
Executive. **Personal:** Born Jul 2, 1951, Bronx, NY; son of Charles Bernard Clark and Ertha Mae Reese; married Julia A Williams; children: Kadeem Toure. **Educ:** Brooklyn Col, Brooklyn, NY, BA, econs, 1980. **Career:** Blue Cross Blue Shield, New York, oper auditor, 1974-79, syst coord, 1979-81, programmer, 1981-84; Morgan Guaranty Trust, New York, prog analyst, 1984-86; New York Times, New York, syst mgr, 1986-. **Orgs:** Black Data Processing Asn; Am Payroll Asn. **Home Addr:** 60 E 17th St Suite 2G, Brooklyn, NY 11226, **Home Phone:** (212)282-9025. **Business Addr:** Systems Manager, New York Times, 229 W 43rd St 7th Fl, New York, NY 10036, **Business Phone:** (212)556-1577.

**SEYMOUR, DR. BARBARA L.**
Lawyer. **Personal:** Born Columbia, SC; daughter of Leroy Semon and Barbara Youngblood. **Educ:** SC State Univ, BS, acct & econs, 1975; Georgetown Univ Law Ctr, JD, tax & corp, 1979; Harvard Bus Sch, MBA, gen bus, 1985. **Career:** Texaco Inc, White Plains, NY, tax atty, 1979-98; Equilon Enterprises LCC, asst to chief financial officer & gen coun, 1998-99, asst corp secy & counr, 1999; Shell Oil Prod US, asst secy & coun, 1999-2003; Barbara L Seymour, Atty & Counr at Law, atty, 2005-; Warner & Assocs PLLC, partner, currently. **Orgs:** Tax Sect, Am Bar Asn, 1979-; treas, Sickle Cell Asn Tex Gulf Coast, 1986-88, pres, 1988-90; Leadership Houston, 1989; Leadership Am, 1990-; Internal Revenue Serv Comnr's Adv Group, 1995-97; dir, Houston Area Urban League, 1995-, vpres, 1998-; vpres, Houston Chap Links, 1996-; Alpha Kappa Omega Chap, Alpha Kappa Alpha, 1996-; dir, Sandra Orgn Dance Co, 1999-; dir, Found Main St, 1999-; Nat Bar Asn; Houston Bar Asn; Houston Lawyers Asn; bd mem, Making Main St Happen; bd mem, Houston Grand Opera. **Honors/Awds:** Distinguished Business Alumnus, SC State Univ Sch Bus, 1991; Foremost Fashionable, Alpha Kappa Alpha, 1994; Eagle Award, Nat Eagle Leadership Inst, 1995. **Special Achievements:** One of 50 Outstanding Young Leaders, Ebony Magazine, 1983; Author: The1980 Crude Oil Windfall Profit Tax, Howard Law Journal, 1980. **Home Addr:** 5410 Del Monte Dr, Houston, TX 77056-4212, **Home Phone:** (713)626-7938. **Business Addr:** Partner, Warner & Associates PLLC, 550 Westcott Suite 415, Houston, TX 77007, **Business Phone:** (713)807-1007.

**SEYMOUR, CYNTHIA MARIA**
Clergy. **Personal:** Born Sep 1, 1933, Houston, TX; married Oliver W; children: Michael Dwight Sweet, Wendell Raynard Sweet & Eugene LaValle Sweet Jr. **Educ:** John Adams Sch Bus, bus cert, 1965. **Career:** Jones Memorial United Methodist Church, secy finance comt, 1986- . **Orgs:** Vpres, San Francisco 49ers Toastmistress, 1981-83; Nat Asn Advan Colored People; Nat Coun Negro Women; adv, Young Adult Fel; secy, Joseph P Kennedy Found; bd dir, Eleanor R Spikes Memorial; far western regional dir soror, Gamma Phi Delta Sor Inccurrently. **Home Addr:** 2535 Ardee Lane, South San Francisco, CA 94080, **Home Phone:** (650)588-7169. **Business Addr:** Director, Gamma Phi Delta Sorority, 2657 W Grand Blvd, Detroit, MI 48202-1203, **Business Phone:** (313)873-2691.

**SEYMOUR, DR. LAURENCE DARRYL**
Surgeon. **Personal:** Born Feb 1, 1935, Memphis, TN; children: Lauren Juanita & Eric Lawrence. **Educ:** Tenn State Univ, BS, 1957; Howard Univ, Md, 1961. **Career:** City St Louis Hosp, intern, 1961-62; resident, 1962-66; Boston Univ, instrurol, 1966-68; Univ Tenn, Memphis, clin assoc urol, 1969-; Med Clin Inc, vpres, 1971-. **Orgs:** Bd dir, Boys Club Memphis, 1969-; trustee Collins Chapel Hosp Memphis, 1972; Am Bluff City Med Asns; Alpha Kappa Mu; Beta Kappa Chi; Omega Psi Phi; Mason; Sigma Pi Phi Fraterniry; Memphis Unologic Soc; fel Int Col Surgeons; fel Am Asn Clin Urologists. **Home Addr:** 1662 Joanne St, Memphis, TN 38111-3718, **Home Phone:** (901)743-9382. **Business Addr:** Vice President, Medical Clinic Inc, 1325 Eastmoreland Suite 435, Memphis, TN 38104, **Business Phone:** (901)726-5073.

**SHABAZZ, KALEEM**
Association executive, government official. **Personal:** Born Jul 17, 1947, Atlantic City, NJ; son of Theodus Jowers Sr and Edna Evans Jowers; married Yolanda Dixon; children: Anjail. **Educ:** Rutgers Univ, NJ, BA, urban studies, 1971; Rutgers Univ, Camden, NJ, MPA, 1988. **Career:** Co Atlantic City, NJ, welfare care worker, 1979-81, info Atlantic, 1981-83, bus coordr, 1983-85, dir community develop, 1985-87; City Atlantic City, Atlantic City, NJ, aide city coun pres, 1987-89; Atlantic City Art Ctr, secy, actg exec dir, exec dir, 2007-; Nat Conf Christians & Jews, dir; Atlantic City, dep mayor, currently; Shabazz Assocs, 1996-. **Orgs:** Chmn, Minority Community Leaders Adv Bd, Rutgers Univ, 1987-; chmn, Inst Rev Bd Inst Human Develop, 1989-; United Negro Col Fund, 1989-; Atlantic City Chamber Com; Atlantic City Hotel & Lodging Asn; pres, Masjid Muhammad Atlantic City, 2009-; exec bd mem, Am Conf Diversity, 2010-15; pres, Bridge Faith, 2014-. **Home Addr:** 1258 Monroe Ave, Atlantic City, NJ 08401, **Home Phone:** (609)344-2590. **Business Addr:** Executive Director, Atlantic City Art Center, NJ Ave & Boardwalk, Atlantic City, NJ 08401, **Business Phone:** (609)347-5837.

**SHACK, WILLIAM EDWARD, JR.**
Automotive executive, business owner, consultant. **Personal:** Born Feb 4, 1943, Woodward, AL; married Lois D Webster; children: William Edward III, Nicole, Vincent W & Christina. **Educ:** Clark Col, attended 1962. **Career:** Thrifty Drug & Discount, mgr, 1966-72; Ford Motor Co, mgr, 1972-75; B & W Rent A Car, owner, 1974-75; BFLMDA, pres, 1980; Miramar Lincoln-Mercury, San Diego, Future Ford Banning, pres, owner 1983-; Cooper Hill Homes, Yucca Valley, Calif, pres, 2002; Queen City Ford; Manhattan Beach Ford; Miramar Lincoln Mercury Yucca Valley Ford Future Ford, pres & owner; Rainbow-PUSH; Int Trade Bur; Shack-Woods & Assocs, Long Beach, Calif, chief exec officer, currently; Shack-Findlay Honda, co-owner, 1998-. **Orgs:** Dir, United Way, 1977-83; Yucca Valley Lions, 1977-84; dir, Inland Area Urban League, 1977-83; pres, Black Ford Lincoln Mercury Dealer Coun, 1979-85; pres, PUSH Int Trade Bur, 1985; dir, Jackie Robinson YMCA, San Diego; comnr, San Diego City & County Int World Trade Comn; bd trustee, Clark Atlanta Univ; founding pres, Nat Asn Minority Auto Dealers; Sr Adv Bd, Nat Urban League; polit action comt. **Home Addr:** 7842 Balsa Ave, Yucca Valley, CA 92284-2334, **Home Phone:** (760)365-2994. **Business Addr:** Co-Owner, Shack Findlay Honda, 933 Auto Show Dr, Henderson, NV 89014, **Business Phone:** (702)568-3500.

**SHACKELFORD, BILL.** **See SHACKELFORD, WILLIAM G, JR.**

**SHACKELFORD, GEORGE FRANKLIN**
Sales manager, executive, manager. **Personal:** Born Jun 3, 1939, Baltimore, MD; son of George and Doris; married Barbara Janice; children: Shawn, Terrence, Kymberly, Tanya & George. **Educ:** Univ Md, prog mgt develop; Harvard Univ. **Career:** Amoco Oil Co, dir acquistions, gen mgr, lubricants, bus mgr light oils, capital investment mgr, mgr advert & consumer affairs, dir mktg res, dirmkt strategies, mgr spec acct, dist mgr, mgr mdsg, spec proj develop, pricing spec, fld sales mgr, term mgr, territory mgr, equip clerk, mail boy, 1965. **Home Addr:** 55 Stratham Cir, North Barrington, IL 60010, **Home Phone:** (847)382-3885.

**SHACKELFORD, LOTTIE HOLT**
Executive. **Personal:** Born Apr 30, 1941, Little Rock, AR; daughter of Curtis (deceased) and Bernice Linzy; married Calvin; children: Russell, Karen & Karla. **Educ:** Broadway Sch Real Est, dipl, 1973; Philander Smith Col, BS, 1979, DHL, 1988; Shorter Col, DHL, 1987. **Career:** Urban League Greater Little Rock, educ dir, 1973-78; City Little Rock, city dir, 1978-87; Ark Regional Minority Purchasing Coun, exec dir, 1982-92; Little Rock City, mayor, 1987-91; Dem Nat Comt, vchmn, 1989-2009; Overseas Pvt Investment Corp, dir, 1993-2002; Global Us Am Inc, sr exec vpres, currently; Del Ital Econ Trade Mission, 1987; Us-Soviet Women's Wilderness Dialogue, Union Soviet Socialist Republics, 1987; Harvard Univ Inst Polits, panelist. **Orgs:** Youth dir, St. Peter's Baptist Church, 1969-73; pres, Little Rock Parent-Teachers Asn Coun, 1973; fel Ark Inst Polit, 1975; coordr, human & civil rights workshops, 1975-77; regional bd dir, Nat Black Caucus Local Elected Officials, 1979-92; co-chair, Del Dem Nat Conv, 1980, 1984, 1988, 1992, 2000, 2004 & 2008; pres, S Reg Coun, 1980-; from sec to chair, Ark Dem St Comm, 1982-90; co-chair platform comt, Dem Nat Comt, 1984; bd mem, Nat League Cities, 1984-86; bd dir, pres, 1988-90; Southern Regional Coun, vice chmn, Dem Nat Comn, 1989-92; bd dir, Medicis Pharmaceut Corp, 1993-; Southern Youth Leadership Inst, 2008-; bd dir, Overseas Pvt Investment Corp; reg dir, Nat Black Caucus Locally Elected Off; bd dir, Nat Urban League; bd mem, Womens Pol Caucus; Delta Sigma Theta Sorority; bd dir, Links Inc; First Baptist Church, Little Rock; Nat Asn Advan Colored People; bd dir, Little Rock Advert & Prom; bd dir, Econ Opportunity Agency; bd dir, Little Rock Job Corps; bd dir, Elizabeth Mitchell's C Ctr; bd dir, Phoenix. adv comt, Ark Voc & Technol Educ; adv comt, Sta KARK-tv; Dem Policy Comn; bd dir, Ark Munic League; bd dir, Ark Women's Polit Coun; bd dir, Am Red Cross; bd dir, Ark Parent-Teachers Asn; bd dir, Young Women's Christian Asn; Gamma Phi Delta; Alpha Kappa Mus. **Home Addr:** 1720 Abigail, Little Rock, AR 72204. **Business Addr:** Executive Vice President, Global USA Inc, 1990 M St NW Suite 200, Washington, DC 20036, **Business Phone:** (202)296-2400.

**SHACKELFORD, WILLIAM G., JR. (BILL SHACKELFORD)**
President (organization), consultant, founder (originator). **Personal:** Born Mar 30, 1950, Chicago, IL; married Renee Nuckols; children: Dionne Deneen, Lenise Yvonne & Andre' Tarik. **Educ:** Clark Atlanta Univ, BS, physics, 1971; Ga Inst Tech, MS, appl nuclear sci, 1974; Wake Forest Univ Babcock Ctr Mgt Develop, mgt training. **Career:** Babcock & Wilcox Navl Nuclear Fuel Div, Va, qual control engr, 1972-73; Clark Col, assoc res phys dept, 1973-74, coop gen sci prog phys dept; Nat Ctr Atmospheric Res Co, vis res, 1975; Cent Intel Agency, analyst, 1975-77; Nuclear Assurance Corp, proj mgr, 1977-79; Atlanta Univ Ctr, dir dual degree engineering prog, 1980-86; Knox Consults, mkt mgr, 1986-87; IEC Enterprises Inc, pres & founder, 1988; ACTA, managing partner, 2000-; GlobalOrg Solutions LLC, pres, 2010-; Cultivate A Bus Legacy, pres, 2014-. **Orgs:** Beta Kappa Chi Nat Hon Soc Joint Mtng, 1971; chmn, Spectrum Club Comn, 1974; Leadership Ga Partic, 1982; bd dir, Atlanta Camp Fire; regional pres & nat mem chmn, Nat Asn MNY Engineering Prog ADRs; Soc Human Resource Mgt; pres, Greater Atlanta Chap Am Soc Training & Develop, 1997-. **Honors/Awds:** Roster Listee, Blacks Physics Second Awards Ceremony; Outstanding Black Physics, 1975; First Prize for Paper Presented, Nat Sci Found. **Special Achievements:** Author of the book "Minority Recruiting, Building the Strategies & Relationships for Effective Diversity Recruiting," published in the Society of Human Resources Management (SHRM) Journal, the Journal of Staffing & Recruiting, Bureau of National Affairs, Resources Management, Recruiting Trends and he Black Collegian; Judge DeKalb Co Dist Sci Fair, 1974-75, 1978-84. **Business Addr:** President, Founder, IEC Enterprises Inc, 5439 Golforest Circle, Stone Mountain, GA 30088, **Business Phone:** (678)995-8677.

**SHACKLEFORD, CHARLES EDWARD**
Basketball player. **Personal:** Born Apr 22, 1966, Kinston, NC. **Educ:** NC State Univ, attended 1988. **Career:** Basketball player (retired); NJ Nets, forward-ctr, 1988-90; Phonola Caserta, Italy, 1990-91; Philadelphia 76ers, forward-ctr, 1991-93; Onyx Caserta, Italy, 1993-94; Minn Timberwolves, forward-ctr, 1994-95; Ulkerspor, Turkey, 1995-96; Aris, Greece, 1996-97; PAOK, Greece, 1997-98; Idaho Stampede, 1998-99; Charlotte Hornets, 1998.

**SHADE, DR. BARBARA J.**
Consultant, educator, executive. **Personal:** Born Oct 30, 1933, Armstrong, MO; daughter of Murray K Robinson and Edna Bowman; married Oscar DePreist; children: Christina Marie, Kenneth E & Patricia Louise. **Educ:** Pittsburg State Univ, BS, 1955; Univ Wis Milwaukee, MS, 1967; Univ Wis Madison, PhD, 1973. **Career:** Univ Wis, Dept Afro-Am Studies, asst prof, 1975; Dane Co Head Start, exec dir, 1969-71; Milwaukee Wis Pub Schs, teacher, 1960-68; Consult, parent Develop Regn, V, 1973-75; Dept Pub Instr Wis, urban educ consult, 1974-75; Univ Wis Parkside, assoc prof & chmn div educ, prof & dean emer, currently. **Orgs:** Delta Sigma Theta Sor, 1952-; Am Psychol Asn; bd pres, St Mary's Hosp Med Ctr, 1978; vpres, Priorities Dane Co United Way, 1979; Asn Black Psychologists, Am Educ Res Asn. **Honors/Awds:** Postdoctoral Fel, Nat Endowment Humanities, 1973-74. **Home Addr:** 530 Mulberry Lane, Racine, WI 53402. **Business Addr:** Dean Emeritus, University of Wisconsin Parkside, 900 Wood Rd, Kenosha, WI 53141-2000, **Business Phone:** (262)595-2345.

**SHADE, DR. GEORGE H., JR.**
Physician. **Personal:** Born Jan 4, 1949, Detroit, MI; son of George H Sr and Julia M Bullard; married Carlotta A; children: Carla N & Ryan M. **Educ:** Wayne State Univ, BS, 1971, MD, 1974. **Career:** Detroit Med Ctr, specialist cheif; Wayne State Univ Affiliated Hosps, Obstet & Gynec residency, 1974-78, chief resident gynec, 1977-78; Southwest Detroit Hosp, chief gynec, 1981-84; Detroit Receiving Hosp, vice chief gynec, 1982-87; Wayne State Univ Sch Med, clin instr gynec, 1983-87, clin asst prof, 1987-; St John Detroit Riverview Hosp, dir resident educ gynec, 1991-, chief obstet & gynec dept, 1995-, Interim Sr Vpres Med Affairs, Chief Med Officer; OHEP, course instr, 1996-98; Mich State Univ, asst clin prof, 2000; Phy Leadership Coun St John Health Sys, chmn, 2001-; Sinai-Grace Hosp, vpres med affairs, 2005-, chief obstet & gynec; Wayne County Med Soc, pres; Detroit Med Ctr, sr vpres & chief qual officer; St. Vincent Indianapolis Hosp, Chief Med Officer; Wayne State Univ, Chmn Obstet & Gynec, dept Chmn Obstet & Gynec, Dept Obstet & Gynec, assoc prof; pvt pract, currently. **Orgs:** Am Med Asn; Nat Med Asn; Mich State Med Soc; Wayne County Med Soc; Detroit Med Soc; bd dirs, Detroit-Macomb Hosp Corp, 1996-; bd dirs, Wayne State Univ Alumni Asn, 1983-87; bd, Omnicare Health Plans; pres, Wayne County Med Soc Southeast Mich, currently; chmn, vchmn, Mich State Bd Med, 2009-. **Honors/Awds:** Am Legion Scholar Award; 'David S Diamond Award Obstet & Gynec'; Chrysler Youth Award; Outstanding Sr Residence Award, Obstets & Gynec; Boy Scouts Am, Eagle Scout Award; Serv Award, Detroit Med Soc; fel, Am Soc Laser Med & Surg; fel, Am Col Physician Execs; fel, Am Col Obstet & Gynecs. **Special Achievements:** Presentations: "Paradoxical Pelvic Masses", Hutzel Hospital, 1986; "Viral Infections in Obstet & Gynec",Detroit Riverview Hospital, 1992; "Urinary Stress Incontinence",Detroit Riverview Hospital, 1992; "Pelvic Endometriosis: Diagnostic Challenges",Henry Ford Hospital, 1993; "Endoscopy in Modern Gynecology",The Detroit Medical Society, 1995. **Home Addr:** 31555 Franklin Fairway, Farmington Hills, MI 48334, **Home Phone:** (734)626-8493. **Business Addr:** Physician, 26400 W 12 Mile Rd Suite 140, Southfield, MI 48034, **Business Phone:** (248)352-8200.

**SHADE, SAMUEL RICHARD**
Football player, football coach. **Personal:** Born Jun 14, 1973, Birmingham, AL; married Jacquetta; children: Justin, Jacoby, Jaila & Jamyia. **Educ:** Univ Ala, BA, finance gen. **Career:** Football player (retired), commentator, football coach; Cincinnati Bengals, defensive back, 1995-96, strong safety, 1997-98; Wash Redskins, strong safety & safety, 1999-2001, defensive back, 2002; MBC Network, color commentator, 2003-04; Shade Holdings LLC, pres & chief exec officer, 2004-; Wealth Mgt Partners LLC, corner backs coach, financial consult, 2006-; Briarwood Christian Sch, vol coach; Samford Univ, asst football coach, 2009-. **Honors/Awds:** Redskins' Unsung Hero Award, 2000; Named Bryant-Jordan Scholar Athlete. **Business Addr:** Financial Consultant, Wealth Management Partners LLC, 600 S Ct St, Montgomery, AL 36104-4106, **Business Phone:** (334)230-9677.

**SHAFT, JOHN.** **See CAGE, MICHAEL JEROME, SR.**

**SHAKESPEARE, EASTON GEOFFREY**
Consultant, president (organization). **Personal:** Born Mar 20, 1946, Kingston; son of Easton G and Leone Williams-Phillips; married Maria A; children: Christopher G & Collin M. **Educ:** Col Arts, Sci & Technol, attended 1960; Senera Col, attended 1969; Col Ins, attended 1992; Am Co, Calif Lutheran Univ, CHFC, 1993. **Career:** Island Life Ins Co-Kingston Jamaica, rep, 1974-77; Guardian Life Ins Co, group rep, 1978-87; Easton Shakespeare & Asn, ins broker, 1987-; ERA Realtors, real estate Asn, 1990-91; FF&G Inc, Newark, NJ, vpres & treas, 1991-93; Fin Supermarket Ins Sch, partner & instr, 1992-; Capital Employee Benefit Servs Inc, pres, 1993-97; EMCC Mkt Corp, pres, 1997; Blue Cross & Blue Shield Asn, currently; EMCC Benefits LLC, owner, pres & instr, 2005-; EMCC Ins Training, instr, 2005-. **Orgs:** Am Soc Chartered Life Underwriters & Chartered Fin Consult, 1983-; NJ Soc Calif Lutheran Univ & ChFC, 1985-; NY Soc CLU & CHFC, 1983-85; Monmouth County, NJ Bd Realtors, 1990-; Nat Asn Life Underwriters, 1988; Nat Asn Health Underwriters; Soc Fin Servs Prof. **Business Addr:** Manager, Blue Cross & Blue Shield Association, PO Box 55, Lithonia, GA 30058, **Business Phone:** (404)312-4141.

**SHAKIR, DR. ADIB AKMAL**
School administrator. **Personal:** Born Jun 15, 1953, Richmond, VA; married Annette Goins; children: Ameenah N & Yusuf S. **Educ:** Morehouse Col, BA (cum laude), 1976; Norfolk State Univ, MA, community & clin psychol, 1980; Fla State Univ, PhD, coun & human systs, 1985. **Career:** Fla A&M Univ, instr psychol, 1981-83; Bethune-Cookman Col, sr adminr, dir coun ctr, 1983-85, asst to pres govt affairs, 1985-86, interim vpres acad affairs & dean fac, 1986-88; Tougaloo Col, Jackson, Miss, lectr & pres, 1988-94; Norfolk State Univ, exec asst to pres, 2007-, asst prof psychol; Cassidy & Assocs Inc, sr vpres mgt consult; Educ Consults LLC, owner & pres; Mattox Woolfolk LLC, sr consult & sr adminr. **Orgs:** E Cent FL Consortium Higher Educ Indust; Nat Coun Black Studies; Nat Asn Black Psychologists; N FL Chap Asn Black Psychologists; bd dir, Miss Mus Art; bd dir, United Negro Coll Fund; bd dir, Amistad Res Ctr; Asn Black Psychologists; 100 Black Men; Sigma Pi Phi Fraternity; US Pres's Bd Advisors, Historically Black Cols & Univs, 1992-2000; bd mem, Am Coun Educ; bd mem, Nat Asn Independent Cols & Univs; bd mem, Col Fund & UNCF; co-chair, Consortium Practicum & Res Minority Males & Minority Males Consortium. **Home Addr:** PO Box 1504, Daytona Beach, FL 32115. **Business Addr:** Executive Assistant, Assistant Professor Psychology, Norfolk State University, 700 Pk Ave, Norfolk, VA 23504, **Business Phone:** (757)823-8600.

**SHAKOOR, HON. ADAM ADIB**
Lawyer. **Personal:** Born Aug 6, 1947, Detroit, MI; son of Harvey Caddell and Esther (Hart); married Gayle Lawrence; children: Sahir, Lateef (deceased), Keisha, Malik, Khalidah, Koya, Kareena & Jelani. **Educ:** Wayne State Univ, cert, local union admin, 1969, BS, 1971, MEd, 1974, JD, educ sociol, 1976; King Abdul Aziz Univ Saudi Arabia, cert, 1977. **Career:** Wayne Co Community Col, Detroit, Mich, prof bus law & black studies, 1971-93; US Dept Housing & Urban Develop, Grand fel, 1971-73; SE Mich Coun Govt, fel, 1971-73; Pitts, Mann & Patrick PC, assoc atty, 1977-79; Common Pleas Ct Judge, Wayne Co, judge & pub adminr, 1981-89; 36th Dist Ct, Detroit, Mich, judge, 1982-85, chief judge, 1985-89; Marygrove Col, Detroit, Mich, prof real estate law, 1984; City Detroit, dep mayor & chief admin officer, 1989-93; Reynolds, Beeby & Magnuson, PC, managing partner, 1994-97; Shakoor, Grubba & Miller PC, managing shareholder, partner & founder, 1997-2004; Cluster Leaders Mgt Group, chmn; Wayne County Community Col, prof bus law, 1971-; Adam Shakoor & Assocs PC, 2004-. **Orgs:** Consult community affairs, New Detroit Inc, 1973-74; pres, Black Legal Alliance, 1975-76; founding mem, Nat Conf Black Lawyers Detroit Chap, 1975; Shakoor & Assocs, 1977-78; Ashford, Cannon, Lumumba, Edison & Shakoor, 1978-81; club pres, Optimist Club Renaissance Detroit, 1982-83; pres, Asn Black Judges Mich, 1985-86; Detroit Alumni Chap, Kappa Alpha Phi; pres bd, Boysville Inc, 1994; founder, Nat Day Freedom Inc, 1996; Wills & Probate Law, Carolyn Kilpatrick Supporter; Mich Dist Judges Asn; State Bar Mich; Wolverine Bar Asn; pres, Wayne County Probate Bar Asn. **Honors/Awds:** Scholar, Nat Bar Asn, 1975; Certificate of Distinction, Comt Stud Rights, 1979; Certificate of Merit Exceptional Achievement, Govt Affairs MI State Legis, 1980. **Home Addr:** 500 Rosewood Trl, Grayson, GA 30017, **Home Phone:** (313)865-7027. **Business Addr:** Attorney at Law, Adam Shakoor & Associates PC, 615 Griswold St Suite 1402, Detroit, MI 48226-3989, **Business Phone:** (313)961-2720.

**SHAKOOR, DR. WAHEEDAH AQUEELAH (SANDRA SHORT ROBERSON)**
School administrator, government official. **Personal:** Born Feb 11, 1950, Washington, DC; children: Barella Nazirah. **Educ:** Wilberforce Univ, attended 1971; Univ Cincinnati, BS, spec educ & teaching, 1973; Univ DC, BS, reading teacher educ & MEd, 1980; Trinity Col, attended 1984; Wash Univ, EdD, curric & instr eng second lang, 2006. **Career:** Cin Recreation Comn, prog dir, ment retarded, 1973;

Cin Pub Sch, teacher spec educ, 1973-74; Univ Islam, teacher, elem educ, 1974-75; Charles County Schs, teacher spec educ, 1976-79; Dist Columbia Pub Schs, teacher, dept chairperson spec educ, 1979-85 & 2014-; Francis L Cardozo Sr High Sch, teacher, chairperson & dir Eng Lang dept, currently. **Orgs:** Counc Except C, 1971-84; coach spec, Olympics, 1974-77; Marshall Hts Civic Asn, 1981-84; adv neighborhood & comn, DC Govt, 1981-83; Capitol View Civic Asn, 1981-85; consult brd educ, Sis Clara Muhammad Sch, 1981-85; exec bd mem, Marshall Hts Community Devel Org, 1981-84; educ pres, Wash Saturday Col, 1982-85; pres, Bilal Entr Inc, 1983-85; Friends DC Youth Orchestra, 1985-; pres bd dir, African Immigrant & Refugee Found, 2010-. **Home Addr:** 3510 Sunflower Pl, Bowie, MD 20721-2462, **Home Phone:** (301)860-0316. **Business Addr:** Chairperson, ESOL Director, Francis L Cardozo Senior High School, 1200 Clifton St NW, Washington, DC 20009, **Business Phone:** (202)673-7385.

**SHAMBERGER, JEFFERY L.**
Automotive executive, business owner, consultant. **Personal:** Born Jan 1, 1949; married Regina; children: Jason & Jessica. **Educ:** Wilberforce Univ, BS, 1971. **Career:** Ford Motor Co, sr mgr, 1971-88; Shamrock Ford-Lincoln-Mercury, owner, pres, 1988-2005; Champion Ford Inc, pres, 2006-07; Automotive Consult/Finance Officer, owner & pres, 2007-. **Business Addr:** Owner, President, Shamrock Ford-Lincoln-Mercury, 829 Tecumseh Rd, Clinton, MI 49236, **Business Phone:** (517)456-7414.

**SHAMBORGUER, NAIMA**
Singer. **Personal:** Born Detroit, MI; daughter of Julian Thomas and Cleopatra Davis Jones; married George L G; children: Michael Julian Griffin, David William Griffin & James Keith Griffin. **Educ:** Peralta Jr Col, attended 1966; Highland Pk Community Col, attended 1970; Wayne State Univ, attended 1976, attended 1985. **Career:** Jazz vocalist; Vernor Pre-Sch, head teacher, 1968-72, 1977-79; Story Bk Nursery, head teacher & dir, 1972-73; Grand Circus Nursery, head teacher supvr summer, 1974; Greenfield Peace Lutheran Sch, prog dir, 1979-80; Action Head Start, parent involvement coordr, 1980-85; Detroit, Montreux Jazz Festival, performer, 1980-96; Clark & ASC, psychologist asst, 1986-93; Art serve, MI, creative artist grant; Skyline Club, performer, 1988-89; Renaissance Club, house performer, 1989-; Montreux Jazz Festival, performer, 1980-2000; Shambones Music, owner, currently; Recordings: Naima's Moods; A Blossom Sings; Negre Con Leche; Tirbute to Louis Armstrong; Hope for Christmas; Songs: "A Blossom Sings"; "Land of Illusion"; "Puerto Vallarta"; "Music In The Air"; "Willy Nilly"; "Yesterday's Everyday"; "I Will Never Walk Away". **Orgs:** Bd mem, Jazz Alliances MIC; bd mem, Ctr Musical Intelligence; Int Asn Jazz Educrs; Jazz Vocal Coalition. **Honors/Awds:** Spirit of Detroit Award, City Detroit, 1984; Outstanding Service Award, Societies Culturally Concerned, 1992; Best Jazz Video, BET Jazz Discovery, 1994; Artisans Award, Friends Sch C's Festival, 1995; Special Volunteer, Nat Soc Fund Raising Exec, 1997. **Special Achievements:** Michigan Heart Assn Fund raiser, Opening act for Phyllis Diller/Ruda Lee, 1988, Michigan Cancer Foundation Fund raiser, Opening act for Lainie Kazan, 1988, Vocal Workshop, Technique and Song, 1989-, voted number 1 female vocalist by the Southeastern Jazz Assn Musicians Poll, 1989, Featured Black History Month WEMU, Eastern Michigan University Radio, co-wrote" Sands of Love", "The Only Blessing That I Have Is You", "It's Good to be home Again", performances with: Steve Turre, Geri Allen, Michigan Jaxx Masters Marcus Blegrave, Donald Walden, Harold Mckinney, Wendell Harrisoin, Teddy Harris, Jr, Marion Hayden, James Carter, Rayse Biggs, George (Sax Man) Benson Donald Byrd, Kenny Burrell, Berry Harris, Rodney Whittaker, Ken Cox, Charlie Gabriel and Lewis Smith, Jonny Turdell, Jimmy Wilkins, Erine Rodgers and the African American Black Caucus Band. **Home Addr:** 19760 Hartwell Ave, Detroit, MI 48235-1172, **Home Phone:** (313)863-7168. **Business Addr:** Owner, Shambones Music, 19760 Hartwell Ave, Detroit, MI 48235-1172, **Business Phone:** (313)863-7168.

**SHAMMGOD, GOD**
Basketball player. **Personal:** Born Apr 29, 1976, New York, NY. **Educ:** Providence Col, attended 1997. **Career:** Basketball player (retired); Wash Wizards, guard, 1997-99; La Crosse Bobcats, guard, 1999-2000; Brok Czarni Slupsk, 2000-01; Fla Sea Dragons, 2001-02; Zhejiang Horses, 2001-02; Al Ittihad (KSA-D1), guard, 2001-02; Zhejiang Horses, 2002-03; Zhejiang Wanma Cyclones, 2003-04, 2007-08; Al-Ittihad Jeddah, Saudi Arabia, 2003-05; Al Ittihad, guard, 2004; Shanxi Yujun, China, 2006-07; Portland Chinooks, 2007, 2009; Al Kuwait, 2007; Cedevita Zagreb, 2008; Ore Waves, 2009.

**SHAMSID-DEEN, WALEED**
Executive. **Personal:** Born Jul 31, 1972, Brooklyn, NY; son of Edith and Lawrence; children: Naim, Layla & Siraj. **Educ:** Fla Agr & Mech Univ, BS, bus econs, 1994; Walden Univ, MBA, finance, 2010. **Career:** Supreme Fish Delight, vpres, 1994-2001; Shamsid-Deen & Assocs, pres & chief exec officer, 2000-; AVF Inc, managing partner, 2001-; Drumline Live, producer, 2005-13; Allen Entrepreneurial Inst, dir opers, 2012-14; Supreme Foods Worldwide, pres & chief exec officer, 2015-; Shamsid-Deen & Assocs, pres & chief exec officer, currently; Jackie Alexander Productions, producer, currently; Abdur-Rahim Enterprises Inc, managing partner, currently. **Orgs:** Chmn, Youth VIBE Inc, exec dir, founder, 1996-; Rotary Int; S Dekalb Bus Asn; Leadership Dekalb; adv bd, DeKalb Co Develop; S DeKalb Bus Asn. **Honors/Awds:** Rotary Serv Above Self, 1998; Business Man of the Year, S Decatur Bus Asn, 1998; People to Watch Award, SDBA, 1999; Community Service Award, The Winning Circle, 1999; Youth Vibe Award, SDBA, 2000; Young Adult of the Year Award, Muslim Soc, 2001; Youth Summit Award, Islamic, 2001; Economics Award, UJAAMA Collective, 2002; Amercian Leader Under 30, Ebony Mag, 2003; Outstanding Citizen, GA Secy State, 2003; Rising Star Award; Champion Award. **Special Achievements:** Author: Excellence at a Minimum: The Plight of an Entrepreneur, 2014-. **Home Addr:** 2941 Crabapple Cir, Decatur, GA 30034-4514, **Home Phone:** (678)414-2174. **Business Addr:** Executive Director, Founder, Youth VIBE Inc, 1827 Columbia Dr, Decatur, GA 30032, **Business Phone:** (404)254-4374.

**SHAMWELL, PROF. RONALD L.**
Educator, executive director, chairperson. **Personal:** Born Nov 8, 1942, Philadelphia, PA; married Jean; children: Nathan & Monique. **Educ:** Winston-Salem St Univ, BS, phys educ & hist, 1969; Temple Univ, MSW, social work admin, 1973; Capella Univ, MEd, educ, 2011; cer, BCIA, distance educ, webmaster, & e-com. **Career:** Philadelphia Sch, teacher, 1970-71; asst exec dir, 1973; Antioch Col, instr, 1974; Wharton Ctr, exec dir, 1974; Educ Opportunity Ctr, exec dir; NJ State Dept Higher Educ, prog officer; Community Col Philadelphia, facilitator & instrnl designer, 2001-12, adj prof, currently. **Orgs:** Asn Black Social Workers; Nat Fed Settlements; bd mem, Urban Priorities; chmn bd, N Cent Dist Youth & Welfare Coun; Del Valley Asn Dirs Vol Prog; bd mem, Community Concern; Rotary Club; consult, Temple Univ Massiah Col; consult, Antioch Col; chmn, Youth Task Force N Cent Philadelphia; Philadelphia Chap Oper Bread basket; Am Social Asn; Asn Training & Develop; Eastern Asn Training & Develop; exec dir, United Way affiliated agency. **Honors/Awds:** Honor Award, Temple Univ; Merit Award, Antioch Col. **Home Addr:** 7946 Forrest Ave, Philadelphia, PA 19150-2107, **Home Phone:** (215)224-8028. **Business Addr:** Adjunct Professor, Community College of Philadelphia, 1700 Spring Garden St, Philadelphia, PA 19130-3936, **Business Phone:** (215)751-8000.

**SHANGE, NTOZAKE (PAULETTE WILLIAMS)**
Poet, playwright, writer. **Personal:** Born Oct 18, 1948, Trenton, NJ; daughter of Paul T and Eloise. **Educ:** Barnard Col, BA, 1970; Univ Southern Calif, MA, 1973. **Career:** Mills Col, teacher; Sonoma St Univ, teacher; Medgar Evers Col, teacher; Univ Calif, Berkeley, teacher, 1972-75; Univ Houston, drama instructor, 1983-; Plays: For Colored Girls Who Have Considered Suicide When the Rainbow Is Enuf, 1976; Sassafrass: A Novella, 1976; A Photograph: Lovers-in-Motion, 1977; Nappy Edges, 1978; Boogie Woogie Landscapes, 1979; Spell #7, 1979; Three Pieces, 1981; Cypress & Indigo, 1983; A Daughter's Geography, 1983; From Okra to Greens, 1984; Betsey Brown, 1985; Ridin' the Moon in Texas, 1988; Daddy Says, 1989; If I Can Cook, You Know God Can, 1998; Float Like a Butterfly: Muhammad Ali, 2002; Ellington Was Not a Street, 2003; Poems: "I Live inMusic", 1994; "Whitewash", 1997; "How I Come By This Cryin' Song", 2006; "Blood Rhyhms"; "Poet Hero". Novels: For Colored Girls Who Have Considered Suicide/When the Rainbow is Enuf, 1976; Sassafrass, Cypress & Indigo, 1982; Betsey Brown, 1985; The Black Book, 1986; Liliane, 1994; Some Sing, Some Cry, 2010. Children's Books: Float Like a Butterfly, 2002; Daddy Says, 2003; Ellington Was Not a Street, 2003; Coretta Scott, 2009. **Orgs:** Poets & Writers Inc; New York Feminist Art Guild; Inst Freedom Press; fel Guggenheim Found; fel Lila Wallace-Reader's Dig Fund. **Honors/Awds:** Outer Critics Circle Award, 1977; Obie Award, 1977, 1981; Audelco Award, 1977; Frank Silvera Writers Workshop Award, 1978; Pushcart Prize; Mademoiselle Award; Los Angeles Times Book Prize for Poetry, 1981; Medal of Excellence, 1981; Nori Eboraci Award; Lila Wallace-Reader's Digest Fund Annual Writer's Award, 1992; Paul Robeson Achievement Award, 1992; Arts and Cultural Achievement Award; Living Legend Award, 1993; Claim Your Life Award; Monarch Merit Award; St. Louis Walk of Fame. **Business Addr:** Instructor, University of Houston, 4800 Calhoun Rd, Houston, TX 77004, **Business Phone:** (713)743-2611.

**SHANK, SUZANNE F.**
Founder (originator), president (organization), chief executive officer. **Personal:** Born Jan 1, 1962; children: Devin & Camryn. **Educ:** Univ Pa, Wharton Sch, MBA, finance, 1987; Ga Inst Technol, BS, civil engineering. **Career:** Siebert Brandford Shank & Co LLC, founder, pres, chairwoman, chief exec officer, partner & co-owner, 1996-; Gen Dynamic, Elec Boat Div, design engr; WAVE, vpres. **Orgs:** Bd mem, Munic Securities Rulemaking Bd; bd mem, Nat Asn Securities Professionals; founder, Detroit Summer Finance Inst; bd dir, Detroit Inst Arts; bd dir, Detroit Regional Chamber; bd dir, Citizens Budget Comn; bd dir, New Econs Initiative; bd dir, Women Pub Finance; SIFMA; bd dir, Bond Mkt; dir, Securities Indust & Financial Markets Asn; bd mem, Caribbean Am Mission Educ Res Action; mem bd dir, Invest Detroit. **Honors/Awds:** Most 75 Powerful Blacks on Wall Street, 2005-06; 50 Most Influential Black Women in Business, Black Enterprise Mag, 2006; Top 25 Nonbank Women in Finance, US Banker Magazine, American Banker Magazine, 2009-10; Top 50 Women in Wealth Management for 2010, WealthManagerWeb.com; Maynard H Jackson Award, Nat Asn Securities Professionals, 2013; National Entrepreneur of the Year, Madame CJ Walker Ctr; Metropolitan Detroit's Most Influential Black Women, Women's Informal Network; Academy of Engineering Alumni, Ga Tech; Entrepreneur of the Year, Nat Asn Securities Professionals, She's Our Hero Award, Women Pub Finance. **Special Achievements:** Recognized by Crain's Detroit Business as one of the 40 outstanding leaders under 40, as the National Entrepreneur of the year by Madame CJ Walker Center and by the Women's informal Network of Detroit and Wayne County. **Business Addr:** Chief Executive Officer, President, Siebert Brandford Shank & Co LLC, 100 Wall St 18th Fl, New York, NY 10005, **Business Phone:** (646)775-4850.

**SHANKS, JAMES A.**
Mayor, educator, secretary general. **Personal:** Born Feb 7, 1912, Tutwiler, MS; son of T A and Dora; married Willye B Harper. **Educ:** Miss Valley State Col, BS, Ed, 1958; Univ St Louis, attended 1961; Miss State Univ, attended 1965. **Career:** Coahoma County Sch Syst, teacher, 1938-77; Town Jonestown, mayor, 1973, alderman, 1973. **Orgs:** Deacon/supt & teacher, Met Baptist Church, 1942; secy & treas, Nat Asn Advan Colored People, 1944; MACE, 1944; Elks Club, 1946; exec comt, Dem Party County & Dist, 1974; asst prog, Elderly Housing Inc/Manpower Proj, Clarksdale, 1978; Nat Conf Black Mayors; Miss Conf Black Mayors. **Honors/Awds:** Outstanding Achievement Pub Service Award, Miss Valley State Col, Itta Bena, 1977; Miss Internal Develop System, Govt Miss, 1978. **Special Achievements:** Town of Jonestown, Mississippi elected its first black Mayor, 1973. **Home Addr:** 616 Main St, Jonestown, MS 38639, **Home Phone:** (662)358-4429.

**SHANKS, TRINA R.** See WILLIAMS, DR. TRINA RACHAEL.

**SHANKS, WILHELMINA BYRD**
Executive. **Personal:** Born Jul 19, 1951, Atlanta, GA; daughter of T J Watkins Sr and Annie Byrd Watkins; children: Harold Jerome Jr. **Educ:** Morris Brown Col, Atlanta, GA, BA, eng & jour, 1973; Ga State Univ, Atlanta, GA, 1974. **Career:** Rich's, Atlanta, Ga, sales mgr, 1973-75, buyer, 1975-78; Jordan Marsh, Ft Lauderdale, Fla, div mgr, 1978-80; Macy's S, Atlanta, Ga, merchandise mgr, 1980-84, store mgr, 1984-, vpres, 1986-, vpres & admin, 1986-90; Foley's, Dallas, Tex, vpres & gen mgr, 1990-92; Ashford Mgt Group, Atlanta, geo, retail acct exec, 1992-94; Shanks & Assoc Exec & Temp Placement Servs, pres, 1994-; Atlanta Com Olympic Games, dir merchandising, 1996; Reebok Int, vpres apparel forecasting & inventory mgt, 1996-98; Class A Consults, exec consult, 1998-2000; Atlanta Pub Schs, Eng teacher, 2009-; St Stephen Christian Acad, prin. **Orgs:** Bd dir, Family Life Serv, 1986; Am Bus Women's Asn; ex bd, Romar Acad; AKA; Hundred Black Women, Atlanta Chap; bd dir, Bethel Acad Advan Career Training; Nat Coalition Black Women; bd dir, JSCF Inc. **Home Addr:** 2750 Veltre Terr, SE Atlanta, GA 30311. **Business Addr:** Principal, St. Stephen Christian Academy, 2670 Hogan Rd, New York, NY 30344, **Business Phone:** (404)305-8200.

**SHANNON, JOHN WILLIAM**
Army officer, business owner, government official. **Personal:** Born Sep 13, 1933, Louisville, KY; son of John Henry and Alfreda Williams; married Jean Rheta Miller; children: John W Jr. **Educ:** Cent State Univ, BS, 1955; Shippenburg Col, MS, 1975, AUS War Col, Carlisle, PA, 1975. **Career:** AUS, second lt, comdr, staff officer, col, 1955-78, Off Sec, Army, Wash, cong liaison officer, 1972-74, Dept Dir Manpower & Res Affairs Off, asst secy defense LA, 1975-78, Dept Army Wash, dep dir manpower & res affairs, 1978-81, Off Asst Secy Defense Legis Affairs, spec asst manpower res affairs & logistics, 1978-81, dep under secy, 1981-84, asst secy installations & logistics, 1984-89, under secy army, 1989-93; actg secy army, 1993; Shannon Consult Serv, owner, operator. **Orgs:** Kappa Alpha Psi Fraternity. **Honors/Awds:** Legion of Merit; Bronze Star; Combat Infantry Badge; Distinguished Civilian Service Award, Dept Army; Secretary of Defense Award for Outstanding Public Service; Defense Superior Service Award; Roy Wilkins Meritorious Service Award.

**SHANNON, MARIAN L. H.**
Counselor. **Personal:** Born Oct 12, 1919, Escambia County, FL; daughter of James Henry Harris and Lacey Sinkfield Harris; married T J. **Educ:** Hampton Inst, BS, 1944; Univ Miami, MEd, 1964. **Career:** Counselor (retired); Dade Co Pub Sch, sch counr; Dade County Pub Sch, Stud Serv Guid & Testing, chairperson; Booker T Wash Jr High Sch; Curr Writer Fed Proj, "Self Concept", "Images in Black" & "Coun the Minority Stud"; Bus Educ Courses Social Studies Courses, teacher & test chmn. **Orgs:** Miami Chap March Dimes Found; vpres, Black Arch Hist & Res Found, S Fla; 1987-91; proj coordr, Thedore R Gibson Oratorical & Declamation Contest, 1989-; partic, Intergenerational Proj Dade Pub Schs, 1993-97; Zeta Phi Beta Sorority, 1995-2003; historian emer, Southeastern Region, Zeta Phi Beta Sorority; sr adult ministry, Greater Bethel Am, 1996; Hist Beta Tau Zeta Chap, 1999-2003; couns & res consult, Sr Citizens & Youth. **Honors/Awds:** Hon doctorate, EWD Waters Col, 1954; Outstanding Citizen, Omega Psi Phi Frat, 1967; Meritorious Service Award, Zeta Phi Beta Sorority, 1965 & 1970; Outstanding Service Award, Prof Orgns, 1971-73; Shannon Day, Miami City & Dade Co, 1984; Zeta Hall of Fame, Fla, 1986; Educator Trail Blazer Award, Delta Sigma Theta Sorority, 1990; Dade County Woman of Impact Honoree; Dade County Co Women Award, 1995. **Home Addr:** 2191 NW 58 St, Miami, FL 33142-7816.

**SHANNON, ODESSA M.**
County government official, executive director. **Personal:** Born Jul 4, 1928, Washington, DC; daughter of Gladys McKenzie and Raymond McKenzie; children: Mark V & Lisa S. **Educ:** Smith Col, BA, 1950. **Career:** EEOC, dep dir field serv, 1979-81; prog planning & eval, dir, 1981-82; nat prog dir, 1982-84; Off Res, exec asst; Bur Census, comp syst analyst; Baltimore Pub Sch, teacher; spec asst to county exec, 1984-86; Montgomery County, MD, spec asst to county exec, human serv coord & planning, dir, 1986-89, dep dir family resources, 1990-94, Off Human Rights, exec dir human rights comn, 1995-2008. **Orgs:** Regional bd dir, Nat Conf Christians & Jews, 1980-89; elected mem bd ed, Montgomery County, MD, 1982-84; Local Coun; United Way; Alpha Kappa Alpha Sor; Nat Asn Advan Colored People; bd dir, Nat Polit Cong Black Women, 1985-86; chmn bd dir, Regional Inst C & Adolescents; bd dir, Montgomery County Arts Coun; chmn bd, Coalition Equitable Representation Govt, 1986-; bd dir, Montgomery Housing Partnership; bd dir, Nat Coalition 100 Black Women, Montgomery County, 1989-; bd dir, Christmas April, 1989-; bd dir, Round House Theatre, 1990-92; bd dir, Metrop Boys & Girls Clubs, 1990-92; bd dir, Positive Shades Black; founder, Montgomery County Human Rights Hall Fame, 2001; Coalition Opposed to Violence & Extremism; sr exec serv, nat prog dir, Equal Employ Opportunity Comn. **Honors/Awds:** Omega Psi Phi, 1977; Alpha Phi Alpha, 1978; Kappa Alpha Psi, 1982; Outstanding Achievements in Human Rights, Tex State, NAACP, 1983; Outstanding Public Service, Am Asn Pub Admin, 1984; Exceptional Achievements, Nat Asn Advan Colored People Legal Def & Ed Fund, 1984; Outstanding Public Service, AKA, 1984; International Book of Honor, 1986; Hall of Fame, Int Prof & Bus Women, 1994; Woman of Distinction, Comn Women, 1997; Leadership Montgomery, 1997; Archives of Women of historical importance, Montgomery County, comm Women, 2002; Hornbook Award; Women of Vision Award, Montgomery County Commission for Women. **Special Achievements:** First African American woman to have been elected to a policy-making political position in Montgomery County; First woman to hold the post of Special Assistant to the Montgomery County Executive, is honored as One of Nine Montgomery County Women at Women of Achievement Gala, 2006. **Home Addr:** 13320 Bea Kay Dr, Silver Spring, MD 20904. **Business Addr:** Executive Director, Montgomery County Human Rights Commission, 21 Maryland Ave Suite 330, Rockville, MD 20850, **Business Phone:** (240)777-8450.

**SHARP, CHARLES LOUIS**
Executive, educator. **Personal:** Born May 19, 1951, Madisonville, KY; son of Macindy and Charlie. **Educ:** Millikin Univ, BS, mkt mgt,

1973; Wash Univ, MBA, mkt mgt, 1975; Univ Wis-Madison, Madison, WI, PhD, mkt, 1996. **Career:** RJ Reynolds Tobacco Co, Winston-Salem, NC, asst brand mgr & mkt asst, 1975-77, Camel Flavor Brands, Salem Lights, brand mgr, 1977-80, brand mgr spec mkts, 1980-83, prom mgr, 1984-89, group mgr financial control & admin, 1986-89; Southern Ill Univ, Edwardsville, Ill, part-time instr, 1974-75; Winston-Salem State Univ, Div Bus & Econs, from part-time instr to instr, 1982-90; Univ Louisville, Sch Bus, instr, 1990; Upper Iowa Univ, adj prof, 1992; Univ Wis-Madison, Wis, Sch Bus, teaching asst & lectr, 1991-96; Univ Louisville, Col Bus & Pub Admin, asst prof, 1997-. **Orgs:** Big Bro & Big Sister, 1983-87; Young Men Christian Asn, 1984-; treas, Civic Develop Coun, 1987; Entrepreneurship Fac Res Team, 1996-99; fel Decanal Rev Comt, 1998; bd dir, Tidy Maid Cleaning & Janitorial Serv Inc, 1998-2001; Int MBA Team, 1999-2002; MBA Prog Comt, 1999-2003; Hon & Awards Comt, currently; fac adv, Alpha Kappa Psi Prof Bus Frat, Omicron Phi Chap; fac adv, Stud Mkt Asn; Fac Grievance Rev Comt; fac lectr, Proj BUILD; Integrated MBA Comt, currently; Stud Recruitment & Retention Comt, currently; Am Mkt Asn; Asn Consumer Res; Acad Mkt Sci; ed rev bd, Mkt Educ Rev; adv bd, Portland Child Develop Ctr, 2000-03; fel Univ Diversity Comt, 2001-02; fel Col Bus & Pub Admin Dean Search Comt, 2002-03; fel Presidential Search Fac Adv Comt, 2002; fel Pres Planning & Budget Adv Comt, 2003-; sub comt mem, Press Comn Diversity & Racial Equality, 2003-; adv, Coun Diversity & Racial Equality; bd dir, Nat Mult Sclerosis Soc; Metro United Way, currently; fel Louisville Urban League; fel Gen Motors; fel Nat Consortium Educ Access; fel Advan Opportunity; Broadway Temple Church & African Methodist Episcopal Church; bd trustee & chmn, Hickory Grove African Methodist Episcopal Church. **Home Addr:** 129 Gardiner Lake Rd, Louisville, KY 40205-2791, **Home Phone:** (502)458-1299. **Business Addr:** Assistant Professor of Marketing, University of Louisville, Rm 153, Louisville, KY 40292, **Business Phone:** (502)852-7565.

### SHARP, DR. J. ANTHONY

Consultant, school administrator. **Personal:** Born Dec 27, 1946, Norfolk, VA; son of James A and Viola Brown; married Khalilah Z; children: Tahmir T & Aleem S. **Educ:** Yavapai Col, Prescott, AA; Long Island Univ, NY, BA, polit sci, 1971; NY Univ, MA, polit sci, 1972; Univ Miami, Coral Gables, PhD, higher educ leadership. **Career:** United states Air Force, aircraft mech & flight crewmember, 1964-68; Embry-Riddle Aero Univ, flight instr & flightsupvr, 1978-81; Hawthorne Aviation, contract & charter pilot, 1982-83; Jersey City State University, New Jersey; Union College in Schenectady, New york; Pima Community College, Tucson; Ohio University, Athens; Elizabeth City State Univ, adj instr airway sci, 1986; Hampton Univ, asst prof airway sci, 1986-89; Fla Memorial Col, Div Airway & Comput Scis, chp, 1989-94; Nova Southeastern Univ, prof technol, 1994-96; FlightSafety Int, Wichita, KS, prog mgr, 1999-2005; Ohio State Univ, Dept Aviation, chmn, 2005-07; consult currently; Elizabeth City State Univ, Dept Aviation Sci, dir, 2007-14; Prof Minority Aviation Consults, chief exec officer & pres, 2014-. **Orgs:** Aircraft Owners & Pilot Asn, 1976-; pres, Nat Asn Minorities Aviation, 1976-; Tuskegee Airmen Inc, 1987-90; secy, Univ Aviation Asn, 1989; Negro Airmen Int, 1990-; 100 Black Men S Fla, 1991-; Am Inst Aeronaut & Astronaut, 1989-; bd mem, Magnet Educa Choice Asn Inc, Dade County, 1992; Nat Asn Advan Colored People; Northeast Acad Aerospace & Advan Technol. **Home Addr:** 1845 Chateau St, Wichita, KS 67207, **Home Phone:** (316)618-6643.

### SHARP, JAMES ALFRED, JR.

Executive. **Personal:** Born May 28, 1933, New York, NY; married Tessie Marie Baltrip; children: Owen, Jacqueline H, James A III & LaTanya M. **Educ:** Univ Calif, San Diego; John F Kennedy Sch. **Career:** US Senate, Senator Donald Riegle Jr, mgr state serv; City Flint Mich, mayor, 1983-87; Dem Nat Conv, alt deleg; City Mgt Corp, vpres community & govt affairs, 1988-98. **Orgs:** Bd trustee, Oakland Univ Found; chmn, Detroit Inst Art, 1998-2000, bd dir, currently. **Business Addr:** Vice President Community and Government Affairs, City Management Corp, 19200 W 8 Mile Rd, Southfield, MI 48075, **Business Phone:** (248)386-4242.

### SHARP, JEAN MARIE

School administrator. **Personal:** Born Dec 31, 1945, Gary, IN. **Educ:** Ball State Univ, BA, 1967; Ind Univ, MA, teaching, 1969; Columbia Univ, Teachers Col, EdM, 1975, EdD, 1976. **Career:** Froebel HS Gary, Ind, teacher, 1966-68; W Side HS Gary, Ind, dept chmn & teacher, 1969-72; Doctoral Prog Educ Leadership, Ford Found fel, 1973-76; Gen Asst Ctr, Columbia Univ, field specialist, 1976; Off Human & Develop Serv, spec asst to asst secy, 1977; Rockefeller Found fel, 1977; Montclair Bd Educ, dir pupil, 1978-, asst supt admin serv, 1978. **Orgs:** Am Asn Sch Admin, 1980; Black Child Develop Inst, 1980; Kappa Delta Pi, 1980; coord, 1st & 2nd Ann Black Representation Orgn Symp, 1973-74; UhuruSasa Sch Brooklyn, 1975; vpres, Nu Age Ctr Harlem, 1979-. **Honors/Awds:** Outstanding Young Women of the Year, United Fedn Women, 1971; Stud Senate Award, Columbia Univ, NY, 1974. **Home Addr:** 106 Morningside Dr Suite 34, New York, NY 10027-6027, **Home Phone:** (212)663-2859. **Business Addr:** Director, Montclair Board of Education, 22 Valley Rd, Montclair, NJ 07042, **Business Phone:** (973)509-4000.

### SHARP, SAUNDRA PEARL

Writer, movie director, actor. **Personal:** Born Dec 21, 1942, Cleveland, OH; daughter of Faythe McIntyre and Garland Clarence. **Educ:** Bowling Green State Univ, Bowling Green, Ohio, BS, 1964; Los Angeles City Col, Los Angeles, Calif, attended 1989. **Career:** Black Persuasion; "Sharp writes"; "Put that white girl back where you got her"; 'Cause Iiii got the power to make you the 8th wonder'; Come get some of the magic B. P. / Positive B.P. / Strong B.P. / womanly, / Powerful, / soft, soft Black Persuasion"; Plays: "Black Girl", "To Be Young, Gifted & Black, " "Hello, Dolly!"; Playwright: "The Sistuhs"; Voices Inc, Los Angeles, CA, head writer, 1988; Black Film Rev, former asn ed; Black Anti-Defamation Coalition, newsletter, ed; publ & ed: The Black Hist Film List; Poets Pay Re Too, 1989. Books: Typing in the Dark, 1991; From The Windows of My Mind, 1970; In the Midst of Chg, 1972; Soft Song, 1978; Black Women For Beginners, 1993. TV series: "The Jeffersons", 1977; The Greatest Thing That Almost Happened, 1977; "Wonder Woman", 1977-79; Minstrel Man, 1977; "Good Times", 1978; "Charlie's Angels", 1978-80; "Barnaby Jones", 1978-79; Night Cries, 1978; Lou Grant, 1978; "The White Shadow", 1979-81; Hollow Image, 1979; "The Incredible Hulk", 1980; "Different Strokes", 1981; "Benson", 1981; "NBC Spec Treat", 1984; "St. Elsewhere", 1984-87; "Knots Landing", 1985; "T.J. Hooker", 1985. Films: The Learning Tree, 1969; Back Inside Herself, producer, writer & dir, 1984; Picking Tribes, dir, ed, writer & producer, 1989; The Healing Passage: Voices from the Water, exec producer, writer & dir, 2004; Dilemma, producer, 2006; Redeemer, 2011. **Orgs:** Black Am Cinema Soc; Reel Black Women; Atlanta African Film Soc; co-founder, Black Anti-Defamation Coalition. **Honors/Awds:** First place film production, Black American Film Soc, 1984 & 1989; First Place, San Francisco Poetry Film Festival, 1985; Heritage Magazine Award for outstanding journalism, 1988; Paul Robeson Award, Newark Black Film Festival, 1989; Artist Grant, Calif Arts Coun, 1992; Best Script Award, Black Filmmakers Hall of Fame, 1992; Poet of Los Angeles' Watts Towers Arts Center, 2006-07. **Business Addr:** Actress, c/o Allen & Associates, 5417 Whitesept Ave, North Hollywood, CA 91607, **Business Phone:** (213)462-6565.

### SHARPE, DR. AUDREY HOWELL

Educator, school principal, physician. **Personal:** Born Dec 14, 1938, Elizabeth City, NC; daughter of Simon and Essie Griffin; married Willie M; children: Kimberly Y. **Educ:** Hampton Inst, BS, 1960; Northwestern Univ, MA, 1966; Ball State Univ, EdD, psychol, 1980. **Career:** Educator (retired); State Ind Ft Wayne, speech & hearing therapist, 1960-62; State Ill Dixon, hearing & speech specialist, 1962-64; Ft Wayne, speech & hearing therapist, 1964-65; Univ Mich C Psychiat Hosp Ann Arbor, educ diagnostician lang pathologist, asst prin, 1965-68; E Wayne St Ctr Ft Wayne, head start dir, 1968-69; Purdue Univ, lectr educ, 1968-69; E Allen Co Sch, title I teacher, 1973-74, title I coordr, 1974, prin; Village Woods Jr High, asst prin, 1980-81; Village Elem Sch, prin, 1981-84; Sch & Community Rels, dir, 1994-96; Hoagland Sch, prin, 1996-98. **Orgs:** Am Speech & Hearing Asn, 1961-74; Asn C with Learning Disabilities, 1968; bd dir, Three Rivers Asn C with Learning Disabilities, 1969-72; DST; Alpha Kappa Mu; Kappa Delta Pi; Morrow Presby Ch Morrow, Ga; Delta Sigma Theta Sorority; Leadership, Ft Wayne; bd dir, YWCA, 1984-87; Jr League. **Honors/Awds:** Woman of the Year, DST, 1973; Florene Williams Service Award, 1986; EDR of the Year, Phi Beta Sigma, 1987; Dual Service Award, 1988; Service Award, KAP Fraternity, 1984-85. **Special Achievements:** ISHA, Spring 1969; Author: "Effects of assertive discipline on Title I students in the areas of reading and mathematics achievement ", 1980. "Another View of Affective Education: The Four H's-Honesty,Humaneness, Humility, and Hope", Principal, Fall 1984; Principal, Fall 1985; "Language Training in Headstart Programs", "Pass Me That Language Ticket", Principal, Spring 1986; "Physical Education, A No Frills Component to the Elementary Curriculum", guest columnist: Fort Wayne News-Sentinel; Frost Illustrated. **Home Addr:** 5415 Emily Cir, Ellenwood, GA 30294-4327, **Home Phone:** (678)422-5741.

### SHARPE, PROF. CALVIN WILLIAM

Lawyer, educator. **Personal:** Born Feb 22, 1945, Greensboro, NC; son of Mildred Johnson and Ralph David; married Janice McCoy Jones; children: Kabral, Melanie & Stephanie. **Educ:** Clark Col, BA, philos & relig, 1967; Northwestern Univ, Law Sch, JD, 1974; Chicago Theol Sem, MA, philos, relig & polit sci, 1996. **Career:** Intermediate Sch 55, Brooklyn, New York, hist teacher, 1968-69; Univ Chicago, Ford Training & Placement Prog, researcher & evaluator, 1970-72; Hon Hubert L Will US Dist Ct, law clerk, 1974-76; Cotton Watt Jones King & Bowlus Law Firm, assoc, 1976-77; Nat Labor Rels Bd, trial atty, 1977-81; Univ Va, Law Sch, asst prof, 1981-84; Clark Col, Hon Woodrow Wilson fel; Wake Forest Univ, vis assoc prof law, 1982-83; Case Western Res Univ, vis assoc prof law, 1983-84, assoc prof law, 1984-88, prof law, 1988-, John Deaver Drinko-Baker & Hostetler, chmn, 1990-, assoc dean acad affairs, 1991-92, John Deaver Drinko-Baker & Hostetler prof law, 1999-, Ctr Interdisciplinary Study Conflict & Dispute Resolution, dir, 2013; Ariz State Univ Col Law, scholar residence, 1990; George Wash Univ, Nat Law Ctr, DC, vis prof, 1991; DePaul Univ Col Law, distinguished vis prof, 1995-96; Chicago-Kent Col Law, vis scholar; Cleveland State Univ Marshall Sch Law, assoc prof. **Orgs:** Labor, Am Arbit Asn, 1984-; bd trustee, Cleveland Hearing & Speech Ctr, 1985-89; OH State Employ Rels Bd Panel Neutrals, 1985-; chmn-evidence sect, Asn Am Law Schs, 1987; exec bd, Pub Sector Labor Rels Asn, 1987-89; Fed Mediation & Conciliation Serv Roster Arbitrators, 1987-; OH Health Care Employees Asn Dist, 1199, 1987-92; AFSCME & OCSEA, 1987-92; Fedn Police, 1988-92; State Coun Prof Educr OEA & NEA, 1989-; Youth Serv Subsid Adv Bd Comnr, Cuyahoga Co, Ohio, 1989; Nat Acad Arbitrators, 1991-; Asn Am Law Schs Comn Sect & Ann Meeting, 1991-94; convener & first chair, Labor & Employ Law Sect IRRA, 1994-96; Univ Minn Panel Arbitrators, 2000-; Phoenix Employ Rels Bd Panel Neutrals; Los Angeles City Employee Rels Bd Panel Neutrals; Permanent Arbitrator State Ohio; Am Bar Asn; Indust Rels Res Asn; Int Socs Labor Law & Social Security; bd dir, JustPeace ctr. **Business Addr:** John Deaver Drinko-Baker & Hostetler Professor, Director, Case Western Reserve University, 11075 E Blvd, Cleveland, OH 44106, **Business Phone:** (216)368-5069.

### SHARPE, FELIX

Government official. **Personal:** married Lisa Webb; children: Felix II, Justen & Alexandra. **Career:** Detroit City, from legis asst to Detroit Mayor Dennis Archer; archiveher's staff, ending, 1999; DeMaria Bldg Co, dir bus develop & govn rels; Strategic Staffing Solutions, vpres corp mkt, currently. **Orgs:** Detroit Regional Chamber of Com. **Business Addr:** Vice President of Corporate Marketing, Strategic Staffing Solutions, 645 Griswold St Suite 3446, Detroit, MI 48226, **Business Phone:** (313)965-1110.

### SHARPE, SHANNON

Television show host, football player. **Personal:** Born Jun 26, 1968, Chicago, IL. **Educ:** Savannah State Univ, criminal justice. **Career:** Football player (retired), television show host; Denver Broncos, tightend, 1990-99 & 2002-03; Baltimore Ravens, tightend, 2000-01; CBS Sports, commentator, 2014; CBS TV Network, studio analyst, 2004-. Sirius NFL Radio'sOpening, hosts, currently; FitnessRX Men Magazine, columnist & spokesperson, 2013. **Honors/Awds:** Super Bowl Champion; SIAC Player, 1987; Division II, Football Hall of Fame, 2009; Pro Bowl, 1992; Pro Bowl, 1992; Pro Bowl, 1993; Pro Bowl, 1994; Pro Bowl, 1995; Pro Bowl, 1996; Pro Bowl, 1997; Pro Bowl, 1998; Pro Bowl, 2001; Pro Football Hall of Fame, 2011. **Special Achievements:** Played in World Series of Poker, 2005; appeared in SIRIUS NFL Radio's Movin' The Chains & writes a column on NFL. com. finalists, Pro Football Hall of Fame, 2009. **Home Addr:** Atlanta, GA. **Business Addr:** Studio Analyst, CBS Sports, 2200 W Cypress Creek Rd, Ft. Lauderdale, FL 33309, **Business Phone:** (954)351-2120.

### SHARPE, V. RENEE

Consultant. **Personal:** Born Oct 24, 1953, Jackson, TN; daughter of Vermon Huddleston Cathey and Marvin Cathey. **Educ:** Memphis State Univ, Memphis, TN, BBA, 1974, MBA, 1979; St tech inst, Memphis, TN, AAS, 1976. **Career:** Transamerica Ins, Los Angeles, Calif, proj leader, 1979-81; FedEx, tech consult, 1981-2001. **Orgs:** Stud tutor, Neighborhood Christian Ctr, 1982-95; Asn Female execs, 1986-95; pres, Memphis chap, Black Dp asn, 1989-90; Nat Asn Advan Colored People, 1989-90; nat corrections secy, Black Dp Asn, 1991-92; allocations comt, United Way Greater Memphis. **Home Addr:** 3144 Mackham Ave, Memphis, TN 38118-6747, **Home Phone:** (901)366-4392.

### SHARPLESS, HON. MATTIE R.

Federal government official. **Personal:** Born Jul 1, 1943, Hampstead, NC; daughter of James and Lecola. **Educ:** NC Cent Univ, Durham, NC, BS, bus educ, 1965, MBA, bus admin & econs, 1972. **Career:** USDA Foreign Serv, Off Agr Affairs, Geneva & Bern, Switz, US Mission Europe Union, Brussels, Belg, Rome, Italy, Paris & France, Foreign Agr Serv, agr minister counr, 1995-99, actg adminr, spec asst dep under secy, 2003-06, USDA, ambassador, 2001-03. **Orgs:** Chair, N Carolina Cent Univ External Adv Bd; Trade Adv Comt Africa; Alpha Kappa Alpha Kappa Sorority. **Home Addr:** 700 7th St SW Suite 614, Washington, DC 20024-2452, **Home Phone:** (202)554-5112. **Business Addr:** Ambassador, USDA, 1400 Independence Ave SW, Washington, DC 20250-0237, **Business Phone:** (202)690-1177.

### SHARPP, NANCY CHARLENE

Social worker. **Personal:** Born Pine Bluff, AR; married Tilmon Lee; children: Tilmon Monroe. **Educ:** Wayne State Univ, BA, 1961; Govs State Univ, MA, 1976. **Career:** Ill Dept Corrections Juv Div, supvr, admin, 1966-79; Ill Dept C & Family Servs, mgr support servs, 1979-81, case rev admin, 1981-; W Maywood Pk Dist, pres bd commrs. **Orgs:** Panelist Panel Am Women, 1968-72; founder & pres, Chicago Area Club-Nat Asn Negro Bus & Prof Womens Clubs, 1977-82; founder, Ascension Manhood, 1982; life mem, Nat Asn Negro Bus Prof Womens Clubs; comdr, W May wood Pk Dist, 1981. **Honors/Awds:** Nat Presidents Award, Nat Asn Negro Bus & Prof Womens Clubs, 1977; Sperry-Hutchins Community Serv Award, Sperry-Hutchins Corp & NANBPW, 1981; Community Image Award, Fred Hampton Mem Scholarship Fund Inc, 1983. **Home Addr:** 35 S 20th Ave, Maywood, IL 60153-1232. **Business Addr:** President, West Maywood Park District, 16th & Wash, Maywood, IL 60153.

### SHARPTON, REV. ALFRED CHARLES, JR. (AL SHARPTON)

Activist, politician, clergy. **Personal:** Born Oct 3, 1954, Brooklyn, NY; son of Alfred C Sr and Ada Richards; married Kathy Jordan; children: Dominique & Ashley. **Educ:** Brooklyn Col, attended 1975. **Career:** SCLC Oper Breadbasket, NY, youth dir, 1969-71; Nat Youth Movement Inc, founder, pres, 1971-86; singer James Brown, rd mgr, 1973-80; State Senate cand, 1978; Wash Temple Church God Christ, jr pastor; Nat Action Network Inc, founder, pres, 1991-; NYC Mayoral cand, 1997; presidential cand, 2004; Part activist & part entertainer; Nat Youth Movement, founder; U.S, pres, 2004. **Orgs:** Founder & dir, Nat Youth Movement, 1971-88; founder, Nat Action Network, 1991; nat coordr, Nat Rainbow Coalition's Minister Div, 1993-; assoc minister, Bethany Baptist Church, Brooklyn, 1994-; co-founder, Second Chance, 1999; Phi Beta Sigma; preacher, Wash Temple Church God. **Home Addr:** 1902 Ditmas Ave, Brooklyn, NY 11226. **Business Addr:** President, National Action Network Inc, 106 W 145th St, New York, NY 10039, **Business Phone:** (212)690-3070.

### SHARPTON, DENISE

Public relations executive. **Personal:** Born Jul 18, 1958, Vero Beach, FL; daughter of Raymond. **Educ:** Fla A&M Univ, attended 1978; Fla State Univ, BS, 1979. **Career:** KKDA Radio, news anchor, pub affairs host; Ed, Mind Health blog.com; SHARP/PR, pres, currently. **Orgs:** Chmn & founder, Multi-Ethnic Heritage Found, 1990; Delta Sigma Theta Sorority. **Honors/Awds:** Businesswoman of the Year, Iota Phi Lambda, 1993. **Home Addr:** 1500 Venera Ave Suite U2, Coral Gables, FL 33146. **Business Addr:** Founder, Multi-Ethnic Heritage Foundation, PO Box 710452, Dallas, TX 75371-0452.

### SHATTEEN, WESTINA MATTHEWS

Executive. **Personal:** Born Nov 8, 1948, Chillicothe, OH; daughter of Wesley Smith Matthews; married Alan. **Educ:** Univ Dayton, BS, 1970, MS, 1974; Univ Chicago, PhD, philos educ, 1980. **Career:** Mills Lawn Elem Sch, Yellow Springs, OH, teacher, 1970-76; Stanford Res Inst, Menlo Pk, Calif, admin asst, 1976-77; Northwestern Univ, postdoctoral fel, 1981; Univ Wis, Madison, postdoctoral fel, 1982; Chicago Community Trust, Chicago, Ill, sr prog officer, 1982-85; Merrill Lynch, managing dir, 1985-2009; philanthropic progs, dir, 1985-97, first vpres, global diversity, 1997-2000, sr vpres, community develop serv, 2000-01, first vpres, community leadership, global pvt client group, 2001-03, first vpres, community leadership, chief financial officer, 2003-; Harvard Univ, fel, weatherhead ctr int affairs, 2011; Jackie Robinson Found, vpres & chief prog officer, 2012-15, vpres New Progs, 2015-. **Orgs:** New York Bd Educ, 1990-93; chair, outstanding trustee comt, Asn Gov Boards Univs & Cols, 1995-2000; Bd mem, Exec Leadership Coun, 1997-; New York Women's Forum, 1997-; trustee, Bank St Col Educ, 1999-2006; trustee, Merrill Lynch Found; trustee, Univ Dayton, 2002-11; pres, New York Women's Forum, 2006-08; dir, Int Women's Forum, 2006-12; adj prof, Gen Theol Sem, 2009-; dir, Berkeley Divinity Sch, Yale, 2010-12; Trinity Wall St, 2011; vpres & chief prog officer, Jackie Robinson Found, 2012-. **Business Addr:** Chief Program Officer, Vice President, Jackie Robinson Foundation, 1 Hudson Sq, New York, NY 10013-1917, **Business Phone:** (212)290-8600.

## SHAVERS, DR. CHERYL L.

Chairperson, scientist, chief executive officer. **Personal:** Born Jan 1, 1953, Phoenix, AZ; married Joe Agu; children: Cecily. **Educ:** Ariz State Univ, BS, chem, 1976, PhD, solid state chem, 1981. **Career:** Motorola, prod engr, 1976; Libr Cong, US Patent & Trademark Off Dept Comn, regist patent agt, 1984-; Aspen Inst, Henry Crown fel, 1998; Under Secy Comn Technol, US Dept Comn, staff, 1999-2001, sr advisor; Bit Arts, chair, 2001-; Global Smarts Inc, chmn, chairwoman & chief exec officer, 2001-; Hewlett-Packard, process engr; Wiltron Co, microelectronics sec mgr; Varian Assocs, thing films appln mgr; Intel Corp, Technol & Mfg Grp, gen mgr advan technol oper, Microprocessor Prod Grp, Dir Emerging Technol, patent agt; ATMI Inc, dir, 2006-; Santa Clara Univ, prof. **Orgs:** Fel US-Israel Sci & Technol Comn; fel USISRC; bd dir, US-Israel Sci & Technol Found; co-chair, Technol Subcomt, US-Egypt Partnership Econ Growth; Technol Comt, US-China Joint Mgt Comt; US-Japan Joint High Level Comn; Media Tech Capital Partners; bd dir, Am Red Cross; Am Vacuum Soc; rep, Nat Sci & Technol Coun's Comt; trustee, San Jose Tech Mus Innovation; adv bd, EW Scripps; chmn bd, BitArts, 2001-03; bd mem, Rockwell Collins, 2002-; bd mem, ATMI Inc, 2006-; assoc mem, Libr Cong; bd mem, Anita Borg Inst; Dept Coms rep Nat Sci & Technol Coun Comt Nat Security; Comt Int Sci, Engrg & Technol; Comt Technol; mem, bd dir, San Jose Tech Mus Innovation; Aspen Inst Henry Crown Fel. **Business Addr:** Chairman, Chief Executive Officer, Global Smarts Inc, 3333 Bowers Ave Suite 130, Santa Clara, CA 95051, **Business Phone:** (408)844-9099.

**SHAW, DR. ANN.** **See Obituaries Section.**

## SHAW, BERNARD

Television news anchorperson, journalist. **Personal:** Born May 22, 1940, Chicago, IL; son of Edgar and Camilla Murphy; married Linda Allston; children: Amar Edgar & Anil Louise. **Educ:** Univ Ill, Chicago Circle, hist, 1968; Ind Univ. **Career:** Television news anchorperson (retired), journalist; WYNR/WNUS-Radio, Chicago IL, reporter, 1964-66; Westinghouse Broadcasting Co, Chicago IL, reporter, 1966-68; corresp, WA, DC, 1968-71; Columbia Broadcasting Syst, WA, DC, tv reporter, 1971-74, corresp, 1974-77; Am Broadcasting Co, Miami, FL, corresp & chief Latin Am bur, 1977-79; Cable News Network, WA, DC, tv news anchor, 1980-2001, co-anchored, 2005, chief anchor. **Orgs:** Nat Press Club; Sigma Delta Chi; fel Soc Prof Journalists. **Honors/Awds:** Hon Doctorate, Marion Col, 1985; Distinguished Service Award, Cong Black Caucus, 1985; Lowell Thomas Electronic Journalism Award, 1988; Golden Award for Cable Excellence, Nat Acad Cable Programming; Best New Anchor, 1988; Journalist of the Year, Nat Asn Black Journalists, 1989; George Foster Peabody Broadcasting Award, 1990; Golden Award for Cable Excellence, Nat Acad Cable Programming, ACE, 1991; Gold Medal, Int Film & TV Festival; Nat Headliner Award; Overseas Press Club Award; Best Newscaster, 1991; Cultural Journalistic Award, Eduard Rhein Found, 1991; President's Award, Italian Government, 1991; David Brinkley Award for Excellence in Communications, Barry Univ, 1991; Chairman's Award for Outstanding Journalistic Excellence, NAACP, 1992; Best Newscaster of the Year, Award for Cable Excellence, 1992 & 1993; Honor Medal for Distinguished Service in Journalism, Univ Mo, 1992; Emmy Award, Nat News & Documentary Competition, 1992; Best Newscaster, 1993; Dr Martin Luther King Jr Award for Outstanding Achievement, Cong Racial Equality, 1993; Dr Martin Luther King Jr Award for Outstanding Achievement, Cong Racial Equality, 1993; Hon Doctor of Humane Letters Degree, Univ Ill, 1993; William Allen White Medallion for Distinguished Service, Univ Kans, 1994; Nat Headliner Award, Nat Conf Christians & Jews-Miami Region, 1994; Hon Doctorate, Northeastern Univ, 1994; Emmy Award, Instant Coverage of a Single Breaking News Story, 1996; Edward R Murrow Award, Best TV Interp or Documentary on Foreign Affairs, 1996; Paul White Life Achievement Award, 1996; Best Newscaster of the Year, Award for Cable Excellence, 1996; Trumpet Award, 1997; Chicago Journalists Hall of Fame, 1997; Tex McCrary Award for Journalism; Congressional Medal of Honor Society; Broadcasting & Cable Hall of Fame, 1999; Hubert M Humphrey 1st Amendment Freedom Prize, Anti-Defamation League, 2001; Pioneer in Broadcasting Award, Nat Asn Black Owned Broadcasters, 2001; Edward R Murrow Lifetime Achievement Award, Washington State Univ, 2001. **Special Achievements:** Presidential debate moderator, second debate in Los Angeles, 1988; Named to top ten outstanding business and professional honorees list, 1988; Held exclusive interview with Saddam Hussein, Operation Desert Storm, October 1990; Bernard Shaw Endowment Fund established, Univ of IL Foundation, 1991; Democratic presidential candidates' debate moderator, third debate, 1992; first correspondent/anchor to break the news of Jan17, 1994, Los Angeles earthquake; anchored CNN's live coverage of President Bill Clinton's first Economic Summit from Tokyo, 1993; Moderated vice presidential debate, 2000.

## SHAW, BOOKER THOMAS

Judge, educator, association executive. **Personal:** Born Sep 14, 1951, St. Louis, MO; married Jane; children: 3. **Educ:** Southern Ill Univ, Carbondale, BA, govt, 1973; Cath Univ Am, DC, JD, 1976; MO Bar, 1976; Nat Judicial Col, attended 1983; Am Acad Judicature, attended 1989. **Career:** US dept justice, 1974; Fed Trade Comn, law clerk, 1975; Columbus Comm Legal Servs, Wash, DC, law clerk, 1975-76; Circuit Atty Off, asst circuit atty, 1976-83; Twenty-Second Circuit Ct Mo, assoc judge, circuit judge, 1983-2002; Wash Univ Sch Law, adj prof trial advocacy, 1995-; Nat Inst Trial Advocacy, instr, 1999-; Eastern Dist Ct Appeals, MO, judge, 2002-09; Eastern Dist Ct Appeals, MO, judge, 2006-; Emory Trial Tech Prog; Miss Bar CLE prog; Thompson Coburn LLP, partner, 2009-. **Orgs:** Mound City Bar Asn; Metro Bar Asn; St John AME Church; trustee; Nat Bar Asn; Second Presbyterian Church; Nat Asn Advan Colored People; Am Bar Asn; Lawyer's Asn St. Louis; Mo Bar Asn. **Honors/Awds:** Scholar Award in Music, Southern Ill Univ, 1970-72; Spirit of St Louis Scholar Award, 1975; Am-Jur Bk Award, 1976; Distinguished Service, Mound City Bar, 1983; Distinguished Service, Circuit Atty, St Louis, 1983; Outstanding Service, Black Law Studs, Wash Univ, 1989; Outstanding Service, Judicial Coun, Nat Bar Asn, 1992; Legal Legend Award, Mound City Bar Association; Judicial Conference Award, National Bar Association; Award of Excellence, Mound City Bar Association; Career Achievement Award, Circuit Attorneys Office; Black Law Students Association Award, Washington University; Sentinel Newspapers Editorial Honoree. **Business Addr:** Adjunct Professor, Washington University School of Law, 1 Brookings Dr, St. Louis, MO 63130-4899, **Business Phone:** (314)935-6400.

## SHAW, BRIAN K.

Basketball coach, basketball player. **Personal:** Born Mar 22, 1966, Oakland, CA; married Nikki; children: 2. **Educ:** St Marys Col, attended 1985; Univ Calif, Santa Barbara, CA, attended 1988. **Career:** Basketball player (retired), basketball coach; Boston Celtics, guard, 1988-89, 1990-92; Il-Messaggero, Italy, 1989-90; Virtus Roma, 1989; Miami Heat, 1992-94; Orlando Magic, 1994-97; Golden State Warriors, 1997-98; Philadelphia 76ers, 1998; Portland Trail Blazers, 1999; Los Angeles Lakers, guard, 1999-2003, asst coach, 2005-11; Ind Pacers, asst coach, 2011-13; Denver Nuggets, head coach, 2013-15. **Business Addr:** Head Coach, Denver Nuggets, 1000 Chopper Cir, Denver, CO 80204, **Business Phone:** (303)405-1100.

## SHAW, CARL BERNARD

Restaurateur, entrepreneur, teacher. **Personal:** Born Jan 4, 1964, Detroit, MI; son of Cyrus and Louise. **Educ:** Eastern Mich Univ, BA, bus & info syst, 1990; Lawrence Technol Univ, cert, lean health care systs, 2009. **Career:** Detroit Pub Schs, adult educ teacher, 1985-87; Automatic Data Processing, sr comput operator; Stroh Brewey Co, bus analyst, 1987; Cafe Mahogany Inc, pres; Black & Veatch Solution Group, proj mgr, 1999-2001; Gen Motors, proj mgr, 2002-05, sr consult, 2005-07; Comput Consults Am, proj mgr, scrum master, 2007-12; IBM, iteration mgr, 2009; Jawood, iteration mgr, 2009; Sogeti, iteration transformation mgr, 2009-10; GE Healthcare, prog mgr, 2010-14; API Healthcare, prog mgr/fastworks coach, 2014-. **Orgs:** Alpha Phi Alpha Fraternity Inc, 1984; Agile Proj Mgt Group; GE Healthcare Unofficial Forum; Eastern Mich Univ Alumni Asn; Global Prog & Proj Networking Group; Big Bros Big Sisters, 2014; GE Speaks Toastmasters, 2014. **Home Addr:** 18960 Woodingham Dr, Detroit, MI 48221-2160, **Home Phone:** (313)863-9345.

## SHAW, CHARLES ALEXANDER

Judge. **Personal:** Born Dec 31, 1944, Jackson, TN; son of Alvis and Sarah; married Kathleen Marie Ingram; children: Bryan. **Educ:** Harris Stowe State Col, BA, 1966; Univ Mo, MBA, 1971; Cath Univ Am, Columbus Sch Law, JD, 1974. **Career:** Berlin Roisman & Kessler, law clerk, 1972; Dept Justice, Law Enforcement Asst Admin, law clerk, 1972-73; Off Mayor, DC, assigned DC pub sch, hearing officer, 1973-74; Nat Labor Rels Bd, Enforcement Litigation Div, DC, atty, 1974-76; Lashly-Caruthers-Thies-Rava & Hamel, atty, 1976-80; Danforth Found, St Louis Leadership fel, 1978-79; Dept Justice, E Dist Mo, asst US atty, 1980-87; State Mo, circuit judge, 1987-93; US Dist Ct, Eastern Dist Mo, judge, 1993-2009, sr judge, 2009-. **Orgs:** Chairperson, Labor Mgt Rels Comn, Am Bar Asn Young Lawyers Div, 1976-77; Mound City Bar Asn, 1976-; Mo state vice chairperson, Econ Law Sect, Am Bar Asn, 1976-77; United Negro Col Fund, 1978-80; commr, Lawyers Fee Dispute Comn, St Louis Met Bar Asn, 1979-80; Am Bar Asn; MO Bar Asn; DC Bar Asn; MO State & Corp Comn; Nat Asn Advan Colored People; Cath Univ Law Sch Alumni Asn; Harris-Stowe Col Alumni Asn; bd mem, St Louis Black Forum, 1979-80; bd trustee, St Louis Art Mus, 1979-80, 1992-96; Sigma Pi Phi Fraternity, 1988-; St Louis Metro Amateur Golf Asn, 1993-; Asn Guardsmen, 1994-. **Honors/Awds:** Distinguished Service Citation, United Negro Col Fund, 1979; St Louis Public Schools Law & Education Service Award, 1984; Wellston School District Service Award, 1987-; Distinguished Alumni Award, Harris Stowe State Col, 1988; BLSA Distinguished Alumni Award, Catholic Univ, 1994; Catholic Univ Alumni Achievement Award, 2001. **Home Addr:** 4426 Westminster Pl, Saint Louis, MO 63108-1813, **Home Phone:** (314)652-2901. **Business Addr:** Senior Judge, US District Court, 111 S 10th S Suite 12-148, Saint Louis, MO 63102, **Business Phone:** (314)244-7480.

## SHAW, CURTIS MITCHELL

Lawyer. **Personal:** Born Apr 13, 1944, Jacksonville, FL; married Ann; children: Caja, Curtis Jr & Alexis. **Educ:** Univ NMex, BS, 1967; Loyola Univ, La, JD, 1975. **Career:** Pvt pract atty; Musical Entertainers & Motion Picture Personalities, rep; Denver Pub Schs, educr. **Orgs:** Dir, Num Motion Picture & Prod Co; Los Angeles Unified Sch Dist Bd; Hollywood Chamber Com; Los Angeles Co Bar Asn; Langston Law Club; Am Bar Asn; Beverly Hills Bar Asn; State Bar Calif, 1975. **Home Addr:** 433 N Camden Dr Suite 600, Beverly Hills, CA 90210, **Home Phone:** (310)288-1826.

## SHAW, FERDINAND

Educator. **Personal:** Born May 30, 1933, McDonough, GA; children: Mark & Gail. **Educ:** Ohio State Univ, BS, nursing, 1955; Boston Univ, MS, 1957; Union Grad Sch, PhD, 1980. **Career:** Cincinnati Gen Hosp, staff nurse, asst head nurse, 1955-56; Ohio State Univ, instr, asst prof, 1957-73; Ohio State Univ Sch Nursing, assoc prof, 1973. **Orgs:** Consult & rev panel mem, Div Nursing Dept HEW, 1965-74; bd mem, Sex Info & Educ Coun US, 1971-74; adv comt, Am Nurses Asn RN Maternity Fel Prog, 1973-; vpres, Am Nurses Asn, 1974-76; chair, Am Nurses Asn Comn Human Rights, 1976-; consult, Womens Res Staff Nat Inst Educ Dept HEW, 1975. **Home Addr:** 1327 York Ave, Glendora, CA 91740. **Business Addr:** 830 K St Mall, Sacramento, CA 95814.

## SHAW, HAROLD LAMAR

Football player. **Personal:** Born Sep 3, 1974, Magee, MS; son of Josephine. **Educ:** Southern Miss Univ. **Career:** New Eng Patriots, 1998-2000; Grand Rapids Rampage, 2001-02; New Eng Surge, running back, 2007-08.

**SHAW, LEANDER JERRY, JR.** **See Obituaries Section.**

## SHAW, REV. MARTINI

Tutor, clergy. **Personal:** Born Nov 6, 1959, Detroit, MI; son of Melton and Joyce. **Educ:** Wayne State Univ, BS, psychol, 1983, BA, biol, 1983; McCormick Theol Sem, MDiv, 1988; Seabury-Western Theol Sem, cert, Anglican Studies, 1988; Oxford Univ, Eng, Grad Theol Found, Doctor Ministry , 2008. **Career:** Detroit Pub Schs, teacher, 1983-85; St. John Evangelist Episcopal Church, Episcopal Priest, 1988; St Johns Church, asst to rector, 1988-90; St Thomas Church, rector, 1990; S Diocesan Deanery, dean, 1999; The African Episcopal Church, St. Thomas, rector, currently; Ill 3rd Legis Senate Dist, dem cand. **Orgs:** Alpha Phi Alpha Fraternity Inc, 1985-; Chicago Urban League, 1986-; bd dir, vpres, Chase House Child Care, 1988-; Community Develop Adv Comn; exec bd, Nat Asn Advan Colored People, 1988-; chair, Church Fedn Chicago, Ecumenical Affairs, 1988-90; Cook County Dem, 1990-; Ill Comn Afr Am Males, 1992-; diocesan secy, Union Black Episcopalians, 1993; chair, Desegregation Monitoring, Chicago educ bd; Community Develop Adv Comn; Chicago Anti-Hunger Fedn; Chicago Human Rels Comn; Episcopal Diocese's Comn; Episcopal Church Bldg Fund; Adv Bd Black Ministries Episcopal Church; Ill Coun Against Handgun Violence; Alpha Phi Alpha Fraternity Inc, N.A.A.C.P & Union League Club Philadelphia. **Home Addr:** 3312 S Ind Ave, Chicago, IL 60653, **Home Phone:** (312)791-1289. **Business Addr:** Rector, The African Episcopal Church Saint Thomas, 6361 Lancaster Ave, Philadelphia, PA 19151, **Business Phone:** (215)473-3065.

## SHAW, MELVIN B.

Fund raising consultant, executive. **Personal:** Born Dec 23, 1940, Memphis, TN; married Pearl; married Gwendolyn; children: Remel, Dana, Randall & Renee. **Educ:** Lane Col, BS, bus educ, 1962; Univ Memphis, MBEd, 1968; Harvard Bus Sch, cert, educ mgt & bus admin, 1971. **Career:** Shelby City Bd Ed, teacher, 1962-68; Lane Col, dir develop, 1968; Tex Asn Develop Cols, exec dir, 1968-79; United Negro Col Fund, vpres mkt, 1979-93; Shaw & Co, founder & chief exec officer, 1995-2002; Great Urban Escape, co-founder; Saad & Shaw, founder & prin, 2002-. **Orgs:** Omega Psi Phi, 1959; bd mem, Asn Fundraising Prof Golden Gate Chap; adv coun, MultiCultural Alliance; Develop Exec Roundtable; First AME Church; bd mem, Lincoln Child Ctr, 2000-09; campaign coun, Destiny Arts Ctr, 2008-2009. **Home Addr:** 40 Sutton Pl Suite 8G, New York, NY 10022. **Business Addr:** Founder, Principal, Saad & Shaw, 715 Harbor Edge Cir Suite 102, Memphis, TN 38103, **Business Phone:** (901)522-8727.

## SHAW, NANCY H.

Executive director. **Personal:** Born Sep 24, 1942. **Educ:** Jarvis Christian Col, BA, 1965. **Career:** Flanner House, res asst, 1965-66; VISTA Training Prog, counr, 1966; Manpower Training Prog, employ counr, 1966-67; Bd Fundamental Educ, adminr asst dir & educ, 1967-68, mgr adminr servs, 1968-69, spec asst pres, 1969-70; Indianapolis Bus Dev Fed, vpres; Comn Action Against Poverty, vpres; Ind Civil Rights Comn, dep dir, 1970-71; Human Rights Comn Indianapolis & Marion Co, exec dir, 1971-. **Orgs:** Comp Health Planning Coun; Citizens Comn Full Employ; bd dir, Comn Serv Coun Gr Indianapolis; racism com Episcopal Diocese So Ind; All Saints Epi Sch; bd mem, YMCA Greater Indianapolis. **Home Addr:** 1064 W 37 St, Indianapolis, IN 46208. **Business Addr:** Associate, Lilly Eli & Co, Lilly Corporate Center Drop 1017, Indianapolis, IN 46285.

## SHAW, NINA L.

Lawyer. **Personal:** Born Jan 1, 1956?, Harlem, NY; children: 2. **Educ:** Barnard Col, BA; Columbia Law Sch, JD, 1979. **Career:** O'Melveny & Meyers, Entertainment Dept, atty, 1979-81; Dern, Mason, Swerdlow & Floum, atty, 1981-89; Del, Shaw, Moonves, Tanaka, Lezcano & Finkelstein Law, founding partner, 1989-. **Orgs:** Beverly Hills Bar Asn; bd mem, Independent Sch Alliance Minority Affairs; Columbia Law Sch W Coast Adv Bd. **Honors/Awds:** Women in Film, Crystal Award, 2005; "Hollywood Reporter," Women in Entertainment Power 100, 2011-13; Entertainment Lawyer of the Year, Beverly Hill's Bar Asn, 2013; "Black Enterprise", America's Top Black Lawyers; "Savoy", The 100 Most Influential Blacks in America; . **Business Addr:** Partner, Del, Shaw, Moonves, Tanaka, Lezcano & Finkelstein Law, 2120 Colorado Ave Suite 200, Santa Monica, CA 90404, **Business Phone:** (310)979-7920.

## SHAW, SEDRICK ANTON

Football player. **Personal:** Born Nov 16, 1973, Austin, TX; son of Charles and Sandrea; married Felicia Peoples. **Educ:** Univ Iowa, grad. **Career:** Football player (retired); New England Patriots, running back, 1997-98; Cincinnati Bengals, running back, 1999; Cleveland Browns, running back, 1999; Sask Roughriders, running back, 2002-03.

## SHAW, TALBERT OSCALL

Educator. **Personal:** Born Feb 28, 1928; married Lillieth H Brown; children: Patrick Talbert & Talieth Andrea. **Educ:** Andrews Univ, BA, 1963, MA, 1961, BD, 1963; Univ Chicago, MA, 1968, PhD, 1973. **Career:** Educator (retired), president emeritus; Oakwood Col, Huntsville, Ala, prof chris ethics, 1965-72, dean stud; Howard Univ, dean, 1971-76; Sch Relig Howard Univ, actg dean & assoc prof ethics, 1972-81, prof, adminr; Cath Univ Am, vis prof, 1973-74; Bowie State Col, vis prof, 1974; Princeton Theo Sem, vis prof, 1975; Col Lib Arts Morgan State Univ Baltimore, dean, 1976-87; Shaw Univ, pres, 1987-2003, pres emer, 2003-. **Orgs:** Exec bd, Nat Com Prev Alcoholism; exec com, Wash Theo Consortium; exec com, Howard Univ; fac mem, Soc Study Black Religions; Am Acad Relig; Am Soc Chris Ethics, 1972. **Honors/Awds:** Voted Distinguished Teacher of the Year, Howard Univ Sch of Religion, 1974; Talbert O Shaw endowment Fund, NC Community Found, named in honor. **Home Addr:** 6711 Newport Lake Cir, Boca Raton, FL 33496-3004, **Home Phone:** (561)241-2809. **Business Addr:** President Emeritus, Shaw University, 118 East South St, Raleigh, NC 27601, **Business Phone:** (919)546-8200.

## SHAW, TERRANCE BERNARD

Association executive, football player, football coach. **Personal:** Born Jan 11, 1973, Marshall, TX; married Shawneeque Bowers; children: Ashley, Terrance Jr, Teris, Thomas, Trysten, Tierney & Trinity. **Educ:** Stephen F Austin State Univ. **Career:** Football player (retired), coach; San Diego Chargers, right corner back, 1995-99; Miami Dolphins, corner back & middle line backer, 2000; New Eng Patriots, defensive back & free safety & corner back, 2001; Oakland Raiders, corner back & free safety & strong safety, 2002-03; Minn Vikings, left corner back & right corner back, 2004; Titans, youth league coach, currently. **Orgs:** Phi Beta Sigma Fraternity; Stephen F Austin State

Univ. **Special Achievements:** Second round/34th overall NFL draft pick, 1995.

**SHAW, THEODORE MICHAEL**
College teacher, lawyer. **Personal:** Born Nov 24, 1954, New York, NY; son of Theodore (deceased) and Jean Audrey Churchill (deceased); married Cynthia E Muldrow; children: T Winston & Zora Jean. **Educ:** Wesleyan Univ, BA, social studies, 1976; Columbia Univ Sch Law, JD, 1979. **Career:** US Dept Justice, Civil Rights Div, trial atty, 1979-82; Nat Asn Advan Colored People Legal Defense & Educ Fund Inc, asst coun, 1982-87, western regional coun, 1987-90, assoc dir-coun, 1993, dir coun & pres, 2004-; Columbia Univ Sch Law, adj prof, 1993-, prof, 2008-14; Univ Mich Sch Law, asst prof law, fac, 1990-93; Prof Pract, prof; Fulbright & Jaworski LLP, coun; Obama Transition Team, team leader; Temple Law Sch; CUNY Sch Law. **Orgs:** Bd mem, Greater Brownsville Youth Coun, 1982-; bd trustee, alumni elected trustee, 1986-89, charter mem, 1992-2003, vice chmn bd, trustee, Wesleyan Univ, 1999-2003; bd visitor, Columbia Law; bd mem, Poverty & Race Res Action Coun, 1990-; bd mem, Archbishop's Leadership Proj, 1994-; Haywood Burns Chair Civil Rights, CUNY Law Sch, 1997-98; adv bd mem, Europ Roma Rights Ctr, Budapest, Hungary, 1998-; bd mem, Nat Res coun Bd Testing & Assessment Farrlest, 1999-; Nat Bar Asn; Am Bar Asn; Am Const Soc; bd mem, Deacons Abyssinian Baptist Church City; legal adv, Europ Roma Rights Coun. **Home Addr:** 63 Lefferts Pl, Brooklyn, NY 11238, **Home Phone:** (718)783-6937. **Business Addr:** Professor, Columbia Law School, 435 W 116th St Mail Code 4004, New York, NY 10027, **Business Phone:** (212)854-2640.

**SHAW, TODD ANTHONY. See TOO SHORT.**

**SHAW, REV. DR. WILLIAM J.**
Clergy. **Personal:** Born Jan 1, 1934, Marshall, TX; married Camellia Lottie; children: Tim. **Educ:** Bishop Col, BA; Union Theol Sem, MA; Colgate Rochester Divinity Sch, DMin. **Career:** White Rock Baptist Church, Philadelphia, actg pastor, pastor, 1956-, sr pastor; Pa Baptist St Conv, pres, 1978-82; Opportunities Industrialization Centers, exec dir; Nat Cong Christian Educ, dir ministers div, 1981-94; Nat Baptist Conv, USA Inc, past pres, 1999-; US Comn Int Relig Freedom, comnr, 2010-. **Orgs:** Bd mem, Community Legal Serv Philadelphia; Med Ctr Univ Penn; Presby Hosp Med Ctr; Philadelphia Airport Adv Bd Greater Philadelphia Urban Affairs Coalition & Martin Luther King FelsBlack Studies; pres, Baptist Ministers Conf Philadelphia & Vicinity; pres, Metrop Christian Coun Philadelphia; Union Theol Sem Nat Alumni Asn; pres, Pa State Baptist Conv. **Honors/Awds:** Unitas Award, Alumni Asn Union Theol Sem; T. B. Maston Foundation Christian Ethics Award, Southwestern Baptist Theol Sem. **Business Addr:** Pastor, White Rock Baptist Church, 5240 Chestnut St, Philadelphia, PA 19139, **Business Phone:** (215)474-1738.

**SHAW, DR. WILLIE G.**
Athletic director. **Personal:** Born Mar 29, 1942, Jackson, TN; son of Verneil S and Morgan Curtis; married Brenda Joyce Robinson; children: Stacey Alexis & Daricus; married Linda M Johnson. **Educ:** Lane Col, BS, 1964; Univ Tenn, Knoxville, MS, 1968; Mid Tenn State Univ, DA, 1975; Memphis State Univ, attended 1984. **Career:** New York Astronauts, 1964-65; Lane Col, asst football coach, 1965-71, basketball coach, 1976-79; City Jackson TN, gymnastics instr, 1976-79; Lane Col Nat Youth Sports Prog, proj activ dir, 1976-80; Lane Col, dir athletics; Nc Cent Univ, adminr, 1987-91; Elizabeth City State Univ, athletic dir & dept chmn, 1991-93; Shaw Cons, pres, 1993. **Orgs:** Chmn, s reg Nat Col Athletic Assoc Div III Basketball Comm, 1977-; Nat Coll Athletic Assoc Comm on Comts, 1979-81; proj admin, Lane Coll Nat Youth Sports Prog, 1980-; bd mem, Jackson-Madison Cty Airport Auth Bd Dir, 1980-; Nat chmn, Nat Coll Athletic Assoc Div III Basketball comm, 1981-; bd chmn, Jackson Housing Auth Anti-Crime Comm, 1982; NABC, NIRSA, NAHPERD. **Honors/Awds:** Basketball Coach of the Year, 1969, 1978, 1982, 1994-2001; State Fellow, Middle Tenn State Univ, 1972, 73. **Special Achievements:** Col div Basketball Scoring Leading Natl Assn of Inter col Athletic Natl Col Athletic Assn, 1962, 64; Basketball All Amer Natl Asn of Inter col Athletics Asn Press United Press Intl, 1963-64. **Home Addr:** 149 Commanche Trail, Jackson, TN 38305.

**SHAWNEE, LAURA ANN**
Executive, manager. **Personal:** Born Sep 18, 1953, Merced, CA. **Educ:** Univ Santa Clara, BA, hist, 1975, MA, educ admin; Stanford Univ, cert managing innovation. **Career:** NASA Ames Res Ctr, Col recruitment coordr, 1975-83, personnel mgr, 1975-84, handicapped prog mgr, 1982-84, dep chief off equal opportunity prog, mgr informal educ prog, educ div, strategic commun & develop, educ specialist, currently. **Orgs:** Admin asst, 1975-, church treas, 1975-, Cumming Temple Christian Methodist Episcopal Church; pres, Missionary Soc, 1985; Nat Asn Minority Engineering Prog Adminr, 1985-; Community Life & Witness, 1986; Christian Methodist Episcopal Church; bd dir, Imperative Comt Eliminate Racism, 1987; Mid Peninsula Leadership Coun YWCA; Nat Asn Female Exec. **Honors/Awds:** Achievement Award, Bank Am, 1971; Agency Group Achievement Award, Summer Med Stud Intern Prog NASA, 1976; Special Achievement Award, NASA, 1980. **Home Addr:** 365 Wilton Ave, Palo Alto, CA 94306-2857, **Home Phone:** (650)799-1756. **Business Addr:** Education Specialist, NASA Ames Research Center, EN 226 8, Moffett Field, CA 94035-1000, **Business Phone:** (650)604-5000.

**SHEAD, KEN (KENNETH W SHEAD)**
Executive. **Personal:** Born St. Louis, MO; married Cassandra. **Educ:** St Benedicts Col, bus admin. **Career:** Xerox; Exxon; Sperry/Unisys; IQ Media Inc, chief exec officer; Drew Pearson Co, bd mem, founder, pres, 1985-; Nat Black Col Licensing Co; Cassandra Shead & Assocs, partner. **Orgs:** Nat Minority Develop Coun. **Home Addr:** PO Box 1553, Addison, TX 75001.

**SHEALEY, RICHARD W.**
Banker, president (organization), chief executive officer. **Educ:** DePaul Univ, Charles H. Kellstadt Grad Sch Bus, BSc, finance & financial mgt services, MBA, finance & financial mgt services, 1971. **Career:** Continental Ill Nation Bank, vpres & asst gen mgr, 1971-83; Independence Bank Chicago, pres, 1983-88; Infinite Grace Ministries, pastor rich, 1987-; Sylvanus Corp, pres, 1988-91; First Independence Nat Bank, pres & chief exec officer, 1991-96; Daniele Co LLC, exec vpres, chief financial officer, 1996-; Ctr Exec Coaching, cert exec & small bus coach, 2009-13; Optimal Human, auth, 2011-; Faulkner/Haynes & Assocs Inc, gen mgr, financial dir, 2013-. **Orgs:** Ctr Exec Coaching. **Special Achievements:** Author: "Transformational Change Agent"; "Visionary Independent Thinker"; "Creative Synergistic Coach". Publication: The End of Race and Racism, 2016. **Business Addr:** Financial Director, Faulkner/Haynes & Associates Inc, 4365 Dorchester Rd Bldg 100 Suite 107, Charleston, SC 29405, **Business Phone:** (843)884-3554.

**SHEARD, REV. JOHN DREW**
Clergy. **Personal:** Born Jan 1, 1959, Detroit, MI; son of John H and Willie Mae; married Karen Clark; children: Kierra Valencia & John Drew II. **Educ:** Wayne State Univ, BS, educ, 1982, MEd, maths, 1988; St Thomas Christian Col, DDiv. **Career:** Detroit Pub Sch, teacher, 1982-93; Mich Dept Health, supvr, 1985-86; COGIC, Greater Emmanuel Inst, sr pastor, 1988-, dist supt, 1994-, spec asst to Bishop, 1996-2005, AIM Conv exec sec, 1995-2005, youth dept int pres, 1997-2000; Church Of God In Christ Inc, pastor, 2002; AIM Conv, chmn, 2005-, first admin asst to Bishop, 2005-. **Orgs:** Exec dir, Southern Christian Leadership Conf, 1985-87; supvr, Mich Youth Employ, 1985-86; founder, C D Owens Scholar; bd Preachers, prestigious Morehouse Col Martin Luther King Jr; Greater Emmanuel Men's Socs. **Honors/Awds:** Mich Chptr Pastor of the Year, SCLC, 2006; J Barett Lee Award, Martin Luther King Jr, Board of Preachers, 2008. **Home Addr:** 6286 Branford Dr, West Bloomfield, MI 48322-1088, **Home Phone:** (248)668-1301. **Business Addr:** Senior Pastor, Greater Emmanuel Institutional COGIC, 19190 Schaefer Hwy, Detroit, MI 48235, **Business Phone:** (313)864-7170.

**SHEARIN, KIMBERLY MARIA**
Journalist. **Personal:** Born Apr 1, 1964, Baltimore, MD; daughter of Matthew and Mary James Withers. **Educ:** St Mary's Col, St Mary's City, MD, BA, eng, 1986; Boston Univ, Boston, MA, MS, jour, 1987. **Career:** The Associated Press, Providence, RI, staff reporter, 1985, 1987-89; New Haven Regist, New Haven, Conn, staff reporter, 1989-; Atty, currently. **Orgs:** Nat Asn of Black Journalists, 1987-. **Honors/Awds:** National Dean's List, 1983, 1985; Helped launch St Louis Sun newspaper, 1989. **Home Addr:** 7918 Dunhill Village Ctr Suite 201, Baltimore, MD 21207-3629, **Home Phone:** (410)931-9544. **Business Addr:** Reporter, New Haven Register, 40 Sargent Dr, New Haven, CT 06511, **Business Phone:** (203)789-5714.

**SHEATS, JAMAAL B.**
Artist, college teacher. **Personal:** married Marcya Carter. **Educ:** Fisk Univ, BA, fine art; Tufts Univ, MFA, studio art, 2011. **Career:** Sheats Repousse, founder; Charlotte Art Proj, founder, 2015-; Fisk Univ, Art Dept, adj prof. **Honors/Awds:** Boston Globe, Artists to Watch. **Special Achievements:** Specializes in metal relief sculpture, painting, and mixed media; named SMFA Teaching Fellow; Tennessee Art Commission, Commissioned to produce works for Nashville's historic "Music City Center"; guest lecturer at Tugaloo University Art Colony and Alabama A&M University. **Business Addr:** Adjunct Professor, Fisk University, Basic College Bldg, Nashville, TN 37208.

**SHEATS, MARVIN ANTHONY**
Association executive, consultant. **Personal:** Born Nov 22, 1958, Detroit, MI; son of Marvin and Evelyn Flacks. **Educ:** Wayne County Community Col, lib arts, 1981; Comput Skills Training Ctr, cert, comput oper, 1985; EDS, cert, comput oper, 1986. **Career:** Electronic Data Syst, comput operator, 1985-88; Wayne County Pub Serv, comput operator II, 1988-99; Mac Training & Design Inc, vpres, owner, consult, 1990-95; Campbell-ewald Advert, user support analyst, 1999-2000; J. Walter Thompson, sr helpdesk technician, 2000-03; Global Hue Advert, info technol mgr, 2003-04; H&R Block, seasonal tech support specialist, 2010-11. **Orgs:** MacGroup Detroit, vpres, 1990-. **Honors/Awds:** Achievement Award, Comput Skills Training Ctr, 1992. **Home Addr:** 12008 Rossiter St, Detroit, MI 48224-1185, **Home Phone:** (313)527-4881. **Business Addr:** Vice President, Mac Training & Design Inc, 15900 W 10 Mile Rd Suite 106, Southfield, MI 48075, **Business Phone:** (313)557-0750.

**SHEDD, KENNY (KENDRICK DWAYNE SHEDD)**
Football player, police officer. **Personal:** Born Feb 14, 1971, Davenport, IA. **Educ:** Northern Iowa Univ, grad. **Career:** Football player (retired), police officer; New York Jets, wide receiver, 1993-96; Chicago Bears, 1994; Oakland Raiders, wide receiver, 1996-99; Wash Redskins, 2000; San Leandro Police Dept, law enforcement officer, currently. **Business Addr:** Law Enforcement Officer, San Leandro Police Department, 835 E 14th St, San Leandro, CA 94577-3767, **Business Phone:** (510)577-0663.

**SHEDROFF, JOSHUA. See REDMAN, JOSHUA.**

**SHEFFEY, DR. RUTHE T.**
Educator, association executive, administrator. **Personal:** Born Essex County, VA; married Vernon R; children: Illona Cecile Sheffey Rawlings & Renata Gabrielle Sheffey Strong. **Educ:** Morgan State Univ, BA, 1947; Howard Univ, MA, 1949; Univ Pa, PhD, 1959. **Career:** Howard Univ, grad asst eng, 1947-48; Claflin Col, instr eng & fr, 1948-49; Morgan State Col, asst prof to assoc prof, 1959-70; Morgan State Col, Eng Dept, chairperson, 1970-74; Morgan State Univ, Dept Eng, prof, 1975, chair eng lit, emer. **Orgs:** Commun Comt, United Fund Md, 1972-74; Md Coun Humanities, 1990-96; Col Eng Asn; Col Lang Asn; Mod Lang Asn; Nat Coun Teachers Eng; Eighteenth Century Studies Asn; Mid Atlantic Writers Asn; vpres, pres, Langston Hughes Soc; founder & pres, Zora Neale Hurston Soc, 1984; ed, Zora Neale Hurston Forum; Asn Study Aro Life & Cult; Kings Kids Mentor, Heritage United Church Christ; Mayor's Coun Women's Rights; deleg, White House Conf Women Econ Equals; Morgan State Univ Alumni Asn, Howard Univ Alumni Asn, Univ Pa Alumni Asn; comnr & vice chair, Baltimore Co Human Rels Comn; Md state deleg, Paula Hollinger's Scholar Award Panel. **Honors/Awds:** Creative Achievement Award, Col Lang Asn, 1974; Award Community Serv, United Fund, 1975; Community Service Award, Jack & Jill Am, 1979; Distinguished Alumni Citation, Nat Asn Equal Opportunity, 1980; Achievement Award, African Am History Culture, 1984; Distinguished BlackWoman Am, Towson State Univ, 1984; Morgan State University Women Award, 1985; Alumna of the Year, Howard Univ, Baltimore Chapter, 1987; Faculty Member of the Year Award, Md Asn Higher Educ, 1994; Hall of Fame, Morgan State Univ, 1998. Named honor: "The Ruthe T. Sheffey Award", Morgan State Univs Dept Eng Lang, 1998. **Special Achievements:** Author of numerous books, articles, and reviews. Books: Impressions in Asphalt, Charles Scribner s Sons, 1969; Rainbow Round My Shoulder: The Zora Neale Hurston Symposium Papers, 1982; Trajectory: Fueling the Future and Preserving the African-American Literary Past Essays in Criticism (1962-1986), 1989; First on the campus of any American college or university. **Home Addr:** 7126 Minna Rd, Baltimore, MD 21207-4457, **Home Phone:** (410)944-6395. **Business Addr:** Professor of English, Morgan State University, 1700 E Cold Spring Lane 202 Holmes Hall, Baltimore, MD 21251, **Business Phone:** (443)885-3165.

**SHEFFIELD, GARY ANTONIAN**
Baseball player, baseball manager. **Personal:** Born Nov 18, 1968, Tampa, FL; son of Betty Jones; married Deleon Richards; children: Ebony, Carissa & Jaden Amir. **Career:** Baseball player (retired), baseball coach; Milwaukee Brewers, infielder, 1988-91; San Diego Padres, third baseman, 1992-93; Fla Marlins, 1993-98; Los Angeles Dodgers, 1998-2001; Atlanta Braves, 2002-03; New York Yankees, right fielder, 2004-06; Detroit Tigers, 2007-08; New York Mets, 2009; sports agt, currently. **Orgs:** Gary Sheffield Found, 1995-; Sheff's Kitchen. **Special Achievements:** Film: Knuckleball, 2012. **Home Addr:** 6731 30th St S, St Petersburg, FL 33712. **Business Addr:** Professional Baseball Player, Detroit Tigers, 2100 Woodward Ave, Detroit, MI 48201, **Business Phone:** (313)962-4000.

**SHEFFIELD, REV. HORACE L., III**
Baptist clergy, association executive. **Personal:** son of Horace Jr. **Career:** Nat Action Network, Mich Chap, pres; Nat Asn Black Orgn, chief exec officer; New Galilee Missionary Baptist Church, pastor, currently; Detroit Cares Alternative Acad, pastor & founder; New Destiny Baptist Church, minister. **Orgs:** Del, Dem Nat Conv, 2004; exec dir, Detroit Asn Black Orgn; chair & bd dir, Nat Black Leadership Comn AIDS. **Home Addr:** 12048 Grand River Ave, Detroit, MI 48204, **Home Phone:** (313)491-0003. **Business Addr:** Chairperson, Board of Director, National Black Leadership Commission on AIDS Inc, 120 Wall St Suite 2303, New York, NY 10005-3904, **Business Phone:** (212)614-0023.

**SHEFTALL, DR. WILLIS B., JR.**
School administrator, lecturer, association executive. **Personal:** Born Dec 12, 1943, Macon, GA. **Educ:** Morehouse Col, BA, 1964; Atlanta Univ, MA, 1969; Ga State Univ, PhD, 1981. **Career:** Ala State Univ, instr econ, 1969-71; Atlanta Univ, res assoc, 1978-80; Ga State Univ; Morehouse Col, asst prof econ, 1976-81, prof, 2002-07, sr vpres acad affairs, pres, 1998; Hampton Univ, chmn econ dept, 1981-82, dean Sch bus; Piedmont Med Ctr, bd dir, 2001; Morehouse Col, prof econs, currently. **Orgs:** Consult, City Atlanta, State Ga; Commonwealth Va; Gen Serv Admin; Am Econ Assoc; Nat Econ Assoc; Int Assoc Black Bus Ed; Assoc Social & Behav Sci; past pres, Nat Urban League; Nat Advan Asn Colored People. **Special Achievements:** Published articles in the areas of local public finance & urban economics; Merrill Foreign Study Travel Scholar 1968-69. **Home Addr:** 53 Bainbridge Ave, Hampton, VA 23663. **Business Addr:** Professor of Economics, Morehouse College, 830 Westview Dr SW, Atlanta, GA 30314, **Business Phone:** (404)681-2800.

**SHEHEE, RASHAAN A.**
Executive, football player. **Personal:** Born Jun 20, 1975, Los Angeles, CA; married Rukiya; children: Kailynn & RJ. **Educ:** Univ Wash. **Career:** Football player (retired), executive; Kans City Chiefs, 1998, running back, 1999; Xtreme Football League, Los Angeles Xtreme, running back, 2001; Bakersfield High Sch, teaching health, currently; Catch 22 Xtreme Fitness, founder, currently. **Orgs:** Youth Friends Prog. **Honors/Awds:** Big-Game Playmaker, Jacque Robinson, 1980; Doak Walker Award winner, Greg Lewis, 1990; Rookie of the Year, 1998. **Home Addr:** 6120 Bay Club Ct, Bakersfield, CA 93312-6212, **Home Phone:** (661)589-2879. **Business Addr:** Founder, Catch 22 Xtreme Fitness, Bakersfield, CA.

**SHELBY, KHADEJAH E.**
Government official. **Personal:** Born Feb 15, 1929, Dayton, OH; daughter of Eloise Evans and Artman; children: Elizabeth Diane Lugo. **Educ:** Baldwin-Wallace Col, Berea, OH, 1949; NCA Univ, grad, 1986; Wayne State Univ Prof Mgt & Develop Sch, Am Asn Zool Parks & Aquariums, 1989. **Career:** NY Univ Med Ctr, exec asst, 1958-69; City Detroit, adr, 1975-82, Zool Parks Dept, admin, dep dir, actg dir, 1982-. **Orgs:** Fel Am Asn Zool Parks & Aquariums, 1982-; Friends African Art, 1972-; Detroit Inst Arts, Founders Soc, 1972-; Nat Asn Advan Colored People. **Home Addr:** 16835 Sorrento, Detroit, MI 48235-4209, **Home Phone:** (313)863-9575. **Business Addr:** Deputy Director, Detroit Zoological Parks Department, 8450 W Ten Mile Rd, Royal Oak, MI 48068-0039, **Business Phone:** (313)398-0903.

**SHELL, ARTHUR, JR. (ARTHUR LEE SHELL)**
Football coach, football player. **Personal:** Born Nov 26, 1946, Charleston, SC; son of Arthur Sr and Gertrude; married Janice; children: Arthur II & Christopher. **Educ:** Md State-Eastern Shore Col, BS, indust arts educ, 1968. **Career:** Football player (retired), football coach; Oakland Raiders, player, 1968, tackle, 1969, left tackle, 1970-80, coach, 2006-07; Los Angeles Raiders, tackle, 1982, coach, 1983-94; Kans City Chiefs, offensive line coach, 1995-96; Atlanta Falcons, 1997-2000; NFL, sr vpres football opers & develop, 2001-05. **Orgs:** Alpha Phi Alpha. **Honors/Awds:** Played in Pro Bowl, 1972-78, 1980; Football Hall of Fame, 1989; Pro Football Weekly Coach of the Year,

1990; Coach of the Year, Maxwell Football Nat Football League, 1990; UPI Coach of the Year, 1990; Coach of the Year, Asniated Press, 1991; South Carolina Sports Hall of Fame; College Football Hall of Fame, 2013. **Special Achievements:** First black head football coach in National Football League.

### SHELL, DR. JUANITA (JUANITA SHELL PETERSON)

Educator, psychologist. **Personal:** Born Apr 21, 1939, Winston-Salem, NC; daughter of Douglas and Sallie Sanders; married Alonza Peterson; children: Lisa S & Jason. **Educ:** City Col NY, BA, 1971; City Univ NY, Clin Psychol Prog, PhD, 1978, postdoc, 1991. **Career:** Fel, Black Analyst Inc, 1975-76; Brooklyn Com Counl Ctr, staff psychol, 1976-84; Brooklyn Col, adj prof 1976-78; New York Univ, Bellevue Med Ctr, staff psychol, 1978-2011, clin asst prof, currently; pvt pract psychoanalyst, currently. **Orgs:** Am Psychol Asn, 1975-; Mayors Adv Sub-comt Ment Retard & Dev Disabilities, 1978-; chairperson, Health Comn Community Bd dist 4, 1979-81; NY Acad Sci, 1981-; vpres, Metrop Chap Jack & Jill Am, 1984-86, pres, 1987-89, 1990-; cofounder, Metrop Jack & Jill Alumnae Inc, 1990-; consult, Shelter & Arms Child Serv, 1984; New York Univ, Bellevue Psychiat Soc; Ny Div Women Comt; trustee, Schomburg Corp; secy, bd dir, Coun Greater Harlem Inc, 1994-99. **Home Addr:** 906 Gerard Ave, Bronx, NY 10452-9404, **Home Phone:** (718)681-7562. **Business Addr:** Clinical Assistant Professor, New York University Medical Center, New Bellevue 22 20W40 462 1st Ave, New York, NY 10016, **Business Phone:** (212)562-4509.

### SHELL, THEODORE A., SR.

Dentist. **Personal:** married Juanita Hamlin; children: Gail & Theodore Jr. **Educ:** Miles Mem Col, AB; Wayne State Univ, MBA; Calif Lutheran Univ, Am Col Life Underwriters. **Career:** Great Lakes Mutual Ins Co, debit mgr, asst mgr & mgr, 1934-44; Great Lakes Mutual Life Ins Co, exec vpres, 1944-59; Golden State Minority Found, pres; pvt pract, dentist, 2007-. **Orgs:** Vice chmn bd, Golden State Mutual Life Ins Co, 1960-. **Honors/Awds:** Olive Crosthwait Award, Chicago Ins Asn; Special Service Award, Nat Ins Asn, 1973. **Business Addr:** Dentist, Private Practice, 4326 Westover Pl NW, Washington, DC 20016-5551, **Business Phone:** (202)363-2446.

### SHELTON, BRYAN

Tennis player, athletic coach. **Personal:** Born Dec 22, 1965, Huntsville, AL; married Lisa; children: Emma & Benjamin. **Educ:** Ga Inst Technol, BA, indust engineering, 1989. **Career:** Tennis player (retired), athletic coach; Yellow Jackets, Georgia Tech, 1985-88; Prof tennis player, Georgia Tech, 1989-97; two singles titles, ATP Tour, Newport, 1991, 1992; MaliVai Wash, coach; US Tennis Asn, nat coach, 1998-99; Ga Tech Athletic Asn, womens tennis team, head coach, 1999-; head coach, Fla Gators, currently. **Honors/Awds:** Athletic Hall of Fame, Ga Tech, 1993; Hall of Fame, Ga Tennis, 2002; ACC Coach of the Year, 2002, 2005 & 2007; Huntsville-Madison County Hall of Fame Inductee, 2006; USTA/ITA National Coach of the Year, 2007. **Special Achievements:** First African American to win an ATP event. **Home Addr:** , Smyrna, GU. **Business Addr:** Head Coach, Georgia Tech Athletic Association, 150 Bobby Dodd Way NW, Atlanta, GA 30332-0455, **Business Phone:** (404)894-0458.

### SHELTON, CHARLES E.

Newspaper executive, vice president (organization), manager. **Personal:** Born Oct 5, 1945, New York, NY; son of Edward and Fredrine Bolden; married Sylvina Robinson; children: Helen, Charmaine & Mia. **Educ:** Northeastern Univ, Boston, MA, 1965; Pace Univ, attended 1984; Stanford Univ, grad sch, attended 1991; Dartmouth, tuck exec prog, 1994. **Career:** New York Times, New York, NY, budget analyst, 1967-79, consumer mkt rep, 1979-81, city circulation mgr, 1981-83, metro circulation mgr, 1983-87, metrop home delivery dir, 1987-88, single copy sales dir, 1988-89, dir, 1989, group dir, sales & opers, 1992, vpres circulation sales, vpres distrib, 1995-98, vpres human resources workforce develop, 1998-. **Orgs:** Soc Human Resources Mgt. **Honors/Awds:** Black Achiever Award, Harlem YMCA br, 1982. **Business Addr:** Vice President for Human Resources, Workforce Development, The New York Times Co, 229 W 43rd St, New York, NY 10036, **Business Phone:** (212)556-1234.

### SHELTON, CORA R.

Counselor, social worker. **Personal:** Born Mar 5, 1925, Monroe, MI; married Jean C Mitchell; children: Deborah, Mark & Janice. **Educ:** Wayne State Univ, Detroit, attended 1960; Wayne County Community Col, attended 1969; Univ Mich, Detroit, attended 1972. **Career:** Detroit State & Rys, transp equip operator, 1946-73; Met Life Ins Co, sales rep, 1973-79; Kent Barry Eaton Connecting Ry Inc, corp dir, pres gen mgr, 1979. **Orgs:** Dist rep, Div 26 Street car & Bus Oper, 1960-62; vice chmn, City-Wide Polit Action Group, 1961-63; pres, St Cecelia Church Dad's Club, 1968-70; Nat Fedn Independent Bus, 1979; South-central Mich Transp Planning Comn, 1980. **Honors/Awds:** Man of the year award, Nat Life Underwriters, 1974. **Home Addr:** 183 E 98 St Apt 7g, New York, NY 10029, **Home Phone:** (212)722-3418.

### SHELTON, DAIMON

Football player. **Personal:** Born Sep 15, 1972, Duarte, CA; married Stephanie; children: Aliya. **Educ:** Sacramento State Univ; Fresno City Col, rctrn admin, 1994. **Career:** Football player (retired); Jacksonville Jaguars, 1997, fullback, 1998-2000; Chicago Bears, fullback, 2001-02; Buffalo Bills, fullback, 2004-07; San Jose SaberCats, 2008. **Honors/Awds:** Co-Most Valuable Player, Cent Valley Conf, 1994; Rookie of the Year, 1997. **Home Addr:** 9069 Quail Feather Way, Elk Grove, CA 95624-4037. **Business Addr:** Football Player, San Jose SaberCats, 525 W Santa Clara St, San Jose, CA 95113, **Business Phone:** (408)573-5577.

### SHELTON, HAROLD TILLMAN

Physician, surgeon general. **Personal:** Born May 4, 1941, Lake Charles, LA; married Dolores Hayes; children: Keith, Sherry & Stephanie. **Educ:** McNeese St Univ, BS, 1970; La St Univ Med Sch, Md, 1974. **Career:** La State Univ Med Ctr, Charity Hosp, intership, 1975, residency gen surg, 1975-79, clin instr, 1980; Lake Charles Mem Hosp, staff mem, 1979; St Patrick Hosp, staff mem, 1979; pvt pract gen surg, 1979-; emergency physician, currently. **Orgs:** Regional dir, Region III Ctr Nat Med Asn, 1973; cand group Am Col Surgeons, 1979; AMA; La State Med Soc; Calcasieu Parish Med Soc, 1979; ACS; CPMS; Latin Am Sch Med Sci; diplo, Am Bd Surg, 1980. **Special Achievements:** Publisher: "Evaluation of Wound Irrigation by Pulsatile Jet & Conventional Methods" Annals of Surgeons, Feb, 1978. **Business Addr:** General Surgeon, 511 Hodges St, Lake Charles, LA 70601, **Business Phone:** (337)309-1428.

### SHELTON, DR. HARVEY WILLIAM

Administrator, executive director. **Personal:** Born Jan 18, 1936, Charlottesville, VA; married Mary Etta; children: Renee & Harvey Jr. **Educ:** Va State Univ, BS, 1960; NC State Univ, cert pub policy, 1967; NC State Univ, Adult Educ 1969; VPI & SU, EdD adult & continuing educ, 1976. **Career:** Administrator (retired); Pittsylvania Co Va, exten agt, 1963-69; VPI & SU, area resource develop agt, 1969-70; Comn Resource Develop VPI & SU, prog leader, 1970-78; Comn Resource Devel & Energy MD Coop Ext Serv, asst dir, 1978-86; MD Coop Exten Serv, asst dir, 1986-93. **Orgs:** Fel Kellogg Found, 1966-67; Big Bros Asn, 1971-73; Adult Educ Asn USA, 1972-80; fel Ford Found, 1974-75; Phi Kappa Phi Hon Soc, 1975-80; Boy Scout Coun, 1976-78; treas, Roanake Nat Asn Advan Colored People, 1976-78; chmn, prof improv comt, Comn Develop Soc Am, 1979-83; MD Asn Adult Educ, 1980. **Honors/Awds:** Epsilon Sigma Phi Outstanding Achievement Award, Va Pol Inst & State Univ, 1978; US Senator Mac Mathis Award, 1983; Community Develop Soc Service Award, 1985. **Home Addr:** Rte 1, PO Box 2236, Buckingham, VA 23921.

### SHELTON, HELEN C.

Executive, association executive. **Educ:** Dartmouth Col, BA, hist & govt; Boston Univ, MS, jour & commun. **Career:** City Chicago, asst, 1991-92; Human Resources Develop Inst Inc, dir commun & pub affairs, 1992; Resnicow Schroeder Assocs Inc, acct supvr, 1992-93; Mingo Group/plus Inc, dir pub rels, 1993-96; Ruder Finn, exec vpres arts & commun counselors, 1996-2007, Multicultural & Image Mkt Group, exec vpres, 2006-11; Judith Leiber, mkt commun consult, 2003-05; Remy Cointreau USA, corp & entertainment commun consult, 2004-06; Finn Partners, sr partner, 2011-; WRKS-FM Radio, NY, promotions & pub rels; Seventeen Mag, promotions & pub rels. **Orgs:** Bd mem, Support Network Inc; founding mem, Pi Theta Chap, Delta Sigma Theta Sorority Inc; bd mem, ReadNet Inc; bd dir, ColorComm, 2013-; Greater New York Chap Links Inc, 2013-. **Honors/Awds:** Under 40 Award, The Network Jour, 2004; Outstanding Woman in Communications Award in Public Relations, Ebony Mag, 2006; Support Network's Woman of the Year; ColorComm Circle Award, 2016. **Business Addr:** Senior Partner, Finn Partners, 301 E 57th St, New York, NY 10022, **Business Phone:** (212)715-1600.

### SHELTON, HILARY O.

Executive, politician. **Personal:** Born Aug 12, 1958, St. Louis, MO; married Paula Young; children: Caleb Wesley, Aaron Joshua & Noah Ottis. **Educ:** Howard Univ, Wash, DC, BA, polit sci; Univ Mo, St Louis, MO, MA, commun; Northeastern Univ, Boston, MA, legal studies. **Career:** United Negro Col Fund, fed liaison & asst dir, govt affairs dept; US Congress. **Orgs:** Fed Policy Prog dir, United Methodist Church's Gen bd Church & Socs; Fed Liaison/asst. dir Govt Affairs dept United Negro Col Fund; dir, Nat Asn Advan Colored People Wash Bur; bd dir, Leadership Conf Civil Rights; Ctr Dem Renewal; Coalition to Stop Gun Violence; Cong Black Caucus Inst; wash bur dir & sr vpres advocacy, Nat Asn Advan Colored People. **Business Addr:** Director to the NAACP Washington Bureau, Senior Vice President for Advocacy & Policy, National Association for the Advancement of colored People, 1156 15th St NW Suite 915, Washington, DC 20005, **Business Phone:** (202)463-2940.

### SHELTON, JOHN W.

Vice president (organization), executive. **Personal:** Born Dec 16, 1958, Buffalo, NY; son of John and Joyce Hargrave; married Martha Zehnder; children: John Bradford & Nicholaus Edwin. **Educ:** Valparaiso Univ, Valparaiso, IN, BS, bus admin, mgt & mkt, 1980. **Career:** MGM Grand Hotel, Las Vegas, Nebr, reservations, 1981-82; Flamingo Hilton Hotel, Las Vegas, Nebr, front off, 1982-83; Hyatt Regency Oakland, Oakland, Calif, sls mgr, 1984-87; Hyatt Regency Atlanta, Atlanta, Ga, sls mgr, 1987-88; Hyatt Regency Flint, Flint, Mich, dir sls, 1988-90; Zehnder's Frankenmuth, Frankenmuth, Mich, dir sls, vpres sls & mkt, currently; Zehnder's Snowfest, 2010, chmn, currently. **Orgs:** Chmn, Soc Govt Meeting Planners, 1987; Big Bros/Big Sisters E Bay, 1987; Rotary Int, 1989; Nat Coalition Black Meeting Planners; Mich Soc Asn Execs; Ment Illness Res Asn. **Home Addr:** 7320 W Ronrick Pl, Frankenmuth, MI 48734, **Home Phone:** (989)652-3478. **Business Addr:** Vice President of Sales & Marketing, Zehnder's of Frankenmuth, 730 S Main St, Frankenmuth, MI 48734, **Business Phone:** (989)652-0400.

### SHELTON, JOSEPH B., JR.

Executive, construction manager. **Personal:** Born Oct 12, 1946, Vicksburg, MS; son of Charlene (deceased) and Joseph B (deceased); married Valeria D Bledsoe; children: Robert Waites Jr, Tamara, Joseph III & Jonathan B. **Educ:** Hampton Inst, BS, bldg construct engineering, 1969. **Career:** Darin & Armstrong, field engr, 1969-70, coordr, 1970-75, proj engr, 1975-78, proj mgr, 1978-84; Walbridge Aldinger Co, proj mgr, 1984-91, proj dir, 1991, vpres, 2007. **Orgs:** Eng Soc Detroit, 1976-; admis comn, St Gerard's Church, vpres, 1989-92; vpres, St Gerard's Sch, sch bd, 1987-90; pres, N Huntington Block Club, 1982-88. **Honors/Awds:** Minority Achiever in Industry, Young Men's Christian Asn, 1980. **Home Addr:** 24351 Morton St, Oak Park, MI 48237-1676. **Business Addr:** Vice President, Walbridge Aldinger Co, 777 Woodward Ave Suite 300, Detroit, MI 48226-2521, **Business Phone:** (313)963-8000.

### SHELTON, MILLICENT BETH

Administrator, executive, screenwriter. **Personal:** Born Jan 29, 1966, St. Louis, MO; daughter of Earl W and Mildred E; married Donald Samuel; children: 2. **Educ:** Princeton Univ, BA, eng, 1988; NY Univ, MFA, 1993. **Career:** Forty Acres & a Mule Film works, wardrobe asst, 1988; Cosby Show, wardro beasst, 1988-89; Idol makers Films & Fat Productions, dir, 1989-92; Fat Film Productions, pres & dir, 1992. dir: "The Bernie Mac Show", 2005; "Barbershop", 2005; "Dance Like We Do", 2005; "Big Day", 2006; My Name Is Earl, 2006; "Everybody Hates Chris", 2006-09; "Cavemen", 2007; "Girlfriends", 2007; "Lincoln Heights", 2007; "The Loop", 2007; "Apollo, Apollo", 2009; "30 Rock", 2009-10; "Ruby & the Rockits", 2009; "Parks and Recreation", 2009; "Men of a Certain Age", 2009-11; "Saving Grace", 2009; "Cougar Town", 2010; "My Boys", 2010; "90210", 2010-11; "Zeke and Luther", 2010; "Leverage", 2010; "Castle", 2011; "Awkward", 2011; "Single Ladies", 2011; "Free Agents", 2011; "Warehouse 13", 2011-13; "Pan Am", 2011; "Californication", 2012; "Harry's Law", 2012; "Jane by Design", 2012; "Go On", 2012; "Parenthood", 2012-13; "The Hustle", 2013; "Dallas", 2013-14; "The Fosters", 2013-14; "Hit the Floor", 2013-14; "Things You Shouldn't Say Midnight", 2014; "The Mysteries of Laura", 2014; "The Flash", 2014; "Switched at Birth", 2014-15; "The Divide", 2014; "Girlfriends' Guide to Divorce, 2015; "Dig", 2015; "American Crime", 2015; "Proof", 2015; "Dominion", 2015; "Rosewood", 2015; "Black-ish", 2015; Production Assistant:Spike Lees, "Do The Right Thing", The Cosby Show. **Special Achievements:** First African-American woman to earn a Primetime Emmy Award nomination for Outstanding Directing for a Comedy Series for the episode "Apollo, Apollo".

### SHELTON, REP. O. L.

State government official. **Personal:** Born Feb 6, 1946, Greenwood, MS; son of Idell McClung and Obie; married Linda Kay; children: Eric, Shron, Jaimal & Kiana M. **Educ:** Lincoln Univ, AB, 1970. **Career:** Mo Exten Serv, St Louis, youth specialist, 1972-82; Mo State Legis, state rep, 1982-2000. **Orgs:** William Community Sch Bd; chmn, Ville Area Neighborhood Housing Asn Inc; chmn, St Louis Dem Cent Comn; Early Childcare Develop Corp. **Home Addr:** 1803 Cora Ave, St Louis, MO 63113-2221, **Home Phone:** (314)533-0823. **Business Addr:** Representative, MO House of Representatives, Rm 407B 201 West Capitol Ave, Jefferson City, MO 65101, **Business Phone:** (573)751-2198.

### SHELTON, ESQ. REUBEN ANDERSON, III

Lawyer. **Personal:** Born Dec 6, 1954, St. Louis, MO; son of Sedathon and Elizabeth; married D; children: Christian & Heather. **Educ:** Univ Kans, BS, jour, 1977; St Louis Univ Sch Law, JD, 1981; Wash Univ, MBA, 1991. **Career:** US Dist Ct, law clerk, 1978-83; Legal Serv Eastern Mo, atty, 1980-81; Husch, Eppenberger, Donohue et al, litigation atty, 1983-84; Union Elec Co, house atty, 1984-; Kappa Alpha Psi Fraternity Inc, Past Prov Polemarch, gen coun, currently. **Orgs:** Bd dir, Kappa Alpha Psi Fraternity Inc, 1974-; chair atty comn, United Negro Col Fund, 1983-; task force dir, Bar Asn Metro St Louis, 1984; pres, Mound City Bar Asn, 1985-86; dir, Child haven Autistic Childcare, 1986-; YMCA, 1986-; CRWLC Comn, Mem Intake Comt; Nat Asn Advan Colored People; Mo Lottery Comn; trustee, Antioch Baptist Church; Pres, Mo Bar Asn, currently; Vice Chmn, Mo Develop Finance Bd, currently. **Honors/Awds:** Law Student of the Year, St Louis Chap, Black Am Law, 1981; Lifetime Achievement Award; Legal Services Equal Access to Justice Award; Professional Award, Dollars and Sense Mag. **Special Achievements:** Named one of Ten Outstanding St. Louisans by the Junior Chamber of Commerce; the first African American ever elected as president of the Bar Association of Metropolitan St. Louis, and the St. Louis Bar Foundation. **Home Addr:** 5155 Westminster Pl, Saint Louis, MO 63108-1120, **Home Phone:** (314)367-2077. **Business Addr:** General Counsel, St Louis Alumni Chapter, Board of Director, Kappa Alpha Psi Fraternity Inc, 800 N Lindbergh Blvd Suite E2NE, St. Louis, MO 63141-7843, **Business Phone:** (314)694-8998.

### SHELTON, ROY CRESSWELL, JR.

School administrator, electrical engineer, manager. **Personal:** Born Jun 30, 1941, Toledo, OH; son of Celestine B Campbell and Roy C; married Patricia Lee Little; children: Kevin Lamont, Kelly Marie, Roy C III, James Phillip & Katherine Celestine. **Educ:** Cent State Univ, pre-eng, 1961; Univ Toledo, BSEE, 1964, MSEE, 1967; Univ Detroit, doctorate eng, 1972, 1991. **Career:** Lawrence Technol Univ, assoc prof, elec eng, chmn, Dept Eng; Badgett Indust Inc, proj mgr, currently. **Orgs:** Tau Beta Pi, 1963-; Eta Kappa Nu, 1964-; Fac adv, Nat Soc Black Engrs, 1983-. **Honors/Awds:** Black Educator of the Year, Peace Corps, 1990. **Home Addr:** 15748 St Marys, Detroit, MI 48227, **Home Phone:** (313)838-9143.

### SHELTON, SILHOUETTE ANITA LAVERNE MCCOLLUM. See MCCOLLUM, ANITA LAVERNE.

### SHELTON, ULYSSES

State government official. **Personal:** Born Jul 1, 1917, St. Petersburg, FL; son of Wright and Leila Arline; married Pearl A Daniels; children: Charles & Frederick. **Educ:** Mastbaum Voc Sch. **Career:** Pa, mem, 1961-68, House Rep 181 Dist, dem mem, 1969-78; US Congressman Bradley, magistgrate's clerk, dept rec, clerk, aide; beer distribr; Yorktown Civic Asn, club owner. **Orgs:** N Philadelphia Model City Prog. **Business Addr:** Owner, Yorktown Civic Association, 1132 W Jefferson St, Philadelphia, PA 19122.

### SHEPARD, BEVERLY RENEE

Journalist, lawyer. **Personal:** Born Nov 30, 1959, Jacksonville, NC; daughter of Odis and Ruth Pearson. **Educ:** Univ NC, BA, journ, 1982, JD, 1985. **Career:** Atlanta J-Const, reporter legal affairs, 1991-93, news res mgr, 1993-95, advert mkt mgr, 1995-99; Manheim Interactive, mkt dir, 1999-2001; Cox Newspaper Div, spec proj, 2001-02; Virginian-Pilot, Mkt & Brand Mgt, mgr, 2003-09; Community Personal Care Inc, dir mkt, 2009; ValueOptions, dir mkt, 2009-12; Capital One, sr commun specialist, 2012; Coca-Cola Enterprises, proj mgr, it portfolio mgt & commun, 2012; Contracted Prof, commun & mkt, 2013; ICF Int, sr health ed, 2014; Centers DisControl & Prev, health commun specialist, 2015-. **Orgs:** Atlanta Chap, Nat Coalition 100 Black Women, 2001-03; bd Mem, Va Social Ventures, 2005-07; Nat Asn Black Journalists; Hampton Roads Black Media Profs; bd mem, vpres mkt, Hampton Roads Chap, Am Mkt Asn, 2008-11; Pub Rels Soc Am; Am Mkt Asn; Am Mkt Asn; Atlanta Asn Black Journalists;

Nat Asn Prof Women; United Way; Gwinnett County Bd Elections Poll Worker. **Honors/Awds:** Team winning First Place In A Series for project concerning the Year of the Child, Va Press Asn, 1990; First Place, news writing, Va Press Women's Asn, 1990; Second Place, overall news coverage among staff, The Virginian-Pilot & Ledger-Star, 1990; Hon Mention, News Writing, Nat Fed Press Women, 1990; Algernon Sydney Sullivan Award; Soc Hellenas for contributions to sorority life; Holderness Moor Court, Univ NC Law Sch; Winner, Regional Team Competition, Black Law Studs Asn; Certification, cpr, American Red Cross, 2012; Certification, mediation, Supreme Court of Georgia's Commission on Dispute Resolution, 2013; Glory Foods Women of Distinction; Marketing Campaign Awards, Newspaper Asn Am; Certification, CPR, Am Red Cross, 2012; Certification Mediation, Supreme Ct Ga's Comn Dispute Resolution, 2013. **Home Addr:** 4711 Goldeneye Ct, Virginia Beach, VA 23462, **Home Phone:** (804)490-4572.

**SHEPARD, GREGORY**
Executive, association executive. **Personal:** Born Mar 7, 1961, Trenton, NJ; son of George Jr and Evelyn M. **Educ:** Rensselaer Polytech Inst, BS, elec engineering, 1983; Wharton Sch, Univ Pa, MBA, 1985. **Career:** Shepard-Patterson & Assocs, chief exec officer, 1986-95; Britton Financial Group, Investment Banking, prin, 1995-97; US Web Page Co, chief exec officer, 1997-. **Orgs:** Alpha Phi Alpha, 1982-; chmn, Osayande Partners, 1991-; pres, Rensselaer Alumni Club Wash, DC, 1992-; chmn, Leadership Cong 21st Century, 1994-. **Honors/Awds:** Leadership fel, Johnson & Johnson, 1983; Director Award, Rensselaer Polytech Inst, 1994. **Special Achievements:** Pvt Pilot Cert, 1993. **Home Addr:** 5709 16th St NW, Washington, DC 20011, **Home Phone:** (301)495-9653.

**SHEPARD, LINDA IRENE.** **See Obituaries Section.**

**SHEPHERD, BENJAMIN ARTHUR**
Educator. **Personal:** Born Jan 28, 1941, Woodville, MS; married Ann Marie Turner; children: Benjamin III & Amy Michelle. **Educ:** Tougaloo Col, BS, biol, 1961; Atlanta Univ, MS, biol, 1963; Kans State Univ, PhD, zool, 1970. **Career:** Professor (retired); Atlanta Univ, teacher, 1962-63; Tougaloo Col, instr, 1963-65; Kans State Univ, teacher asst, 1966-69; Southern Ill Univ, asst prof, 1970-73, assoc prof, 1973-75, asst dean grad sch, 1973-74, asst chmn, zoo, 1976-79, prof zoo, assoc vpres, acad affairs & res, 1979, vpres, acad affairs & res, 1988, vice-chancellor, acad affairs & provost, 1992-96, prof emer, currently. **Orgs:** Omega Psi Phi Fraternity; Am Soc Zoologists; Am Asn Anatomists; Ill Acad Sci; Ny Acad Sci; AAAS; Sigma Xi; Soc Study Reproduction; Nat Asn Advan Colored People; life mem, Tougaloo Col Nat Alumni Asn. **Special Achievements:** First person to be named provost at SIUC. **Home Addr:** 4009 Old US Hwy 51 S, Makanda, IL 62958-2201. **Business Addr:** Professor Emeritus, Southern Illinois University, Life Sci Bldg II 354C Rm 351, Carbondale, IL 62901-6501, **Business Phone:** (618)536-2314.

**SHEPHERD, BERISFORD (SHEP SHEPHERD)**
Drummer, musician. **Personal:** Born Jan 19, 1917; married Pearl E Timberlake; children: Roscoe, Synthia & Keith. **Career:** Jimmy Gorham's Orchestra Philadephia, drummer, 1932-41; Benny Carter & Artie Shaw, 1941-42; AUS Bands, 1943-46; Cab Calloway, 1946; Buck Clayton Sextet, 1947; Earl Bostic Philadelphia, 1950-52; Bill Doggett Combo, freelancer, 1952-59; Mr Kicks & Co, Am Be Seated, Jerico Mim Crow, Here's Love; Sy Oliver Orchestra, 1964; Erskine Hawkins Orchestra; Honky-Tonk, co-writer; Berisford San Francisco, owner, designer & builder fine furniture; N Peninsula Wind & Percussion Ensemble, Second Trombone; John Cordoni, Big Band, drummer; Charles Brown Combo, W Coast Only, sub drummer. **Orgs:** Pres, Friendly World Sound Swoppers; hon mem, Friendly Fifty. **Honors/Awds:** Men of Distinction, British Publ; Listed in the Biographical Encyclopedia of Jazz; Who's Who Among Black Americans. **Home Addr:** Casa Del Sol 27892 Via Granados, Mission Viejo, CA 92692. **Business Addr:** Owner, Fine Furniture by Berisford of San Francisco, 195 Elmira St, San Francisco, CA 94124, **Business Phone:** (415)468-4426.

**SHEPHERD, ELMIRA**
Accountant. **Personal:** Born Sep 9, 1959, Birmingham, AL; daughter of Fred and Cordell Johnson. **Educ:** Clerical cert, 1980; Booker T Wash Jr Col, Birmingham, Ala, attended 1987; Southern Jr Col, Birmingham, Ala, BBA, 1989. **Career:** Lakeshore Clerical Training, Birmingham, Ala; Church sch teacher, Bethel African Methodist Episcopal Church, 1983-91; YMCA, Birmingham, Ala, tutor, 1984-85; Lakeshore Hosp Work Lab, Birmingham, Ala, microfilm aide, 1984-85; Goodwill Industs, Birmingham, Ala, bk sorter, 1986-88; Div Four Inc, Birmingham, Ala, bookkeeper, 1991; S Birmingham Huntsville Bessemer Dist, supt, currently. **Honors/Awds:** Valadictorian, Southern Jr Col, 1990. **Home Addr:** 13-14th Ave SW, Birmingham, AL 35203, **Home Phone:** (205)324-9671. **Business Addr:** Superintendent, South Birmingham Huntsville Bessemer District, PO Box 22346, Huntsville, AL 35814, **Business Phone:** (256)585-1521.

**SHEPHERD, GRETA DANDRIDGE.** **See Obituaries Section.**

**SHEPHERD, LESLIE GLENARD**
Football coach, football player. **Personal:** Born Nov 3, 1969, Washington, DC; married Monica; children: Khalek. **Educ:** Temple Univ, grad. **Career:** Football player (retired), football coach; Wash Redskins, 1994, 1999, wide receiver, 1995-98; Cleveland Browns, wide receiver, 1999; Miami Dolphins, wide receiver, 2000; Gwynn Pk High Sch, coach, currently. **Business Addr:** Coach, Gwynn Park High School, 13800 Brandywine Rd, Brandywine, MD 20613, **Business Phone:** (301)372-0140.

**SHEPHERD, DR. LEWIS A., JR.**
President (organization), clergy, dean (education). **Personal:** married Joycemarried Colson. **Educ:** Ouachita, BA, relig, 1980; Okla Baptist Univ, MS, educ, 1982; Univ Ark, EdD, 1997. **Career:** Ark State, police comnr; Greater Pleasant Hill Baptist Church, pastor; Ouachita Baptist Univ, asst dean, 1980, dir, 1987-98, asst to pres spec prog & univ compliance officer; Henderson State Univ's Southwest Ark Technol Learning Ctr & Extern Progs, vpres, 2009-. **Orgs:** Bd dir, S Ark Develop Corp bd; bd dir, Economic Develop Corp Clark County; bd dir, Summit Bank. **Business Addr:** Vice President, Henderson State University, 1100 Henderson St, Arkadelphia, AR 71999-0001, **Business Phone:** (870)230-5081.

**SHEPHERD, MALCOLM THOMAS**
Executive, consultant, president (organization). **Personal:** Born Sep 27, 1952, Chicago, IL; son of Chester and Christine; married Thelma Jones; children: Monica, Malcolm Jr, Marlon, Maxwell & Makalen. **Educ:** Jackson State Univ, BA, 1976, MPA, 1981; Bernard M Baruch Col, New York, NY, MPA, 1985. **Career:** St New York Mortgage Agency, New York, NY, spec asst pres, 1984-85; Dept Econ Develop, Jackson, Miss, financial consult, 1985-88; Governor's Off, St Miss, Jackson, Miss, econ develop policy analyst, 1988-89; Madison Madison Int, Jackson, Miss, mgr, 1989-93; MTS Ltd Inc, pres & dir, 1993-. **Orgs:** Nat Asn Advan Colored People, 1977; Nation Urban Fel, 1985-; pres, Miss Chap-Nat Bus League, 1990-91; chmn, Jackson State Univ Small Bus Develop Ctr, 1990-91; Nat housing & urban develop Fel. **Home Addr:** 773 Woodlake Dr, Jackson, MS 39206, **Home Phone:** (601)362-8278. **Business Addr:** President, Director, MTS Ltd Inc, 430 Bounds St, Jackson, MS 39207-2542, **Business Phone:** (601)366-0290.

**SHEPHERD, SHEP.** **See SHEPHERD, BERISFORD.**

**SHEPHERD, SHERRI EVONNE.** **See SHEPHERD-TARPLEY, SHERRI.**

**SHEPHERD, VERONIKA E.**
Government official. **Personal:** Born Apr 9, 1947, Cincinnati, OH; daughter of Carl Nathenial Oliver and Leola Oliver Gibson (deceased); married David Louis; children: Kevin, Willie, Bryan, Athena & Deja Dewberry. **Educ:** Ohio State Univ, Columbus, OH, AA, social work, 1975. **Career:** Government official (retired); State Ohio, Columbus, training coordr, 1974-75, head start admin coordr, 1975-79, grants adminr, 1979-82, CCA/CSA/state adminr, 1982-84, geriat admin specialist, 1985, personnel adminr, 1985-86; Village Urban crest, mayor, 1987-91, mem coun. **Orgs:** First vice chair, Nat Chap Black Mayors Inc, Black Women Caucus, 1990-91; Unicare Develop Bd, Village Urban crest, 1990-94; Southwestern City Sch Dist Bus Comput Prog Adv Comt, Hayes Tech High Sch, 1990-91; Franklin County Headstart Policy Comt, 1991-93; Franklin County Right From Start Community Forum Bd, 1991-93; comnr, State Ohio Women Res Policy Comn, 1991-93; Mid-Ohio Regional Planning Bd, 1991-94; pres, Ohio Chap Black Mayors Inc; first vpres, Columbus Metrop Area Community Action Orgn. **Home Addr:** 2876 Vine St, Grove City, OH 43123-1915, **Home Phone:** (614)875-2548.

**SHEPHERD-TARPLEY, SHERRI (SHERRI EVONNE SHEPHERD)**
Actor, television actor. **Personal:** Born Apr 22, 1970, Chicago, IL; married Jeff Tarpley; children: Jeffrey Charles Tarpley; married Lamar Sally; children: 1. **Educ:** Trade col. **Career:** Films: King of the Open Mic's, 2000; Pauly Shore Is Dead, 2003; Cellular, 2004; Guess Who, 2005; Beauty Shop, 2005; Who's Your Caddy, 2007; Push, 2008; Madagascar: Escape 2 Africa, 2008; Precious: Based on the Novel Push by Sapphire, 2009; Madea Goes to Jail, 2009; Big Mommas: Like Father, Like Son, 2011; One for the Money, 2012; Think Like a Man, 2012; Top Five, 2014. TV series: "Cleghorne!", 1995; "Claude's Crib", 1997; "Holding the Baby", 1998; Rewind, 1997; "The Jamie Foxx Show", 1998-2000; "Everybody Loves Raymond", 1998-2001; "Suddenly Susan", 1996; "Emeril", 2001; "Wednesday 9:30 (8:30 Central)", 2002; "Less Than Perfect", 2002-06; "Holla", 2002; "Joan of Arcadia", 2003; "Kim Possible", 2004-07; "Brandy & Mr.Whiskers", 2005-06; "Capitol Law", 2006; "The View", 2008; "The Wedding Bells", 2007; "30 Rock", 2007-12; "Entourage", 2008; "Sherri", 2009; "Hot in Cleveland", 2011; "Rip City", 2011; "The Soul Man", 2012; "Abducted: The Carlina White Story", 2012; "How I Met Your Mother", 2013; "It's My Time to Talk", exec producer, 2013. **Honors/Awds:** BET Comedy Award Nominee for Outstanding Supporting Actress in a Comedy Series for: "Less Than Perfect" (2002), 2005; Daytime Emmy Award, 2009; BSFC Award, Boston Soc Film Critics, 2009; Gracie Allen Award, 2010, 2013. **Business Addr:** Actress, c/o AKA Talent, 6310 San Vicente Blvd Suite 200, Los Angeles, CA 90048, **Business Phone:** (323)965-5600.

**SHEPPARD, DONALD**
Educator, association executive, social worker. **Personal:** Born Nov 26, 1950, Houston, TX; son of L K and Blanche; married Donna Marie; children: Ahmad, Wali, Aisha, Jamilah, LaChande & LaLyssa. **Educ:** Houston Community Col, AA, 1976; Tex Southern Univ, BA, social work, 1979; Univ Chicago, Sch Social Serv Adm, AM, 1988; Tex A&I Univ. **Career:** Pub Welfare Coalition, prog coord, 1987-88; Tex Southern Univ, asst prof, social work, 1988-91, prof, 2009-11; Houston Endowment Inc, grant officer, currently. **Orgs:** Coun Founds, 1993-; Conf Southwest Founds, 1993-; Asn Black Found Exec, 1995-; Nat Asn Social Workers; Nat Asn Black Social Workers; Phi Beta Sigma Fraternity Inc; Coun Advan & Support Educ. **Honors/Awds:** Presidents Award, Nat Asn Advan Colored People, Houston Br, 1998. **Business Addr:** Grant Officer, Houston Endowment Inc, 600 Travis Suite 6400, Houston, TX 77078, **Business Phone:** (713)238-8100.

**SHEPPARD, STEVENSON ROYRAYSON**
Government official, school administrator. **Personal:** Born Jan 10, 1945, Bunkie, LA; married Diana Lewis; children: Stephen & Steven. **Educ:** Grambling State Univ, BS, 1967; Southern Univ, MEd, 1974; Northwestern State Univ, MA, 1976. **Career:** Rapides Parish Sch Syst, teacher, 1967; Aroyelles Parish Sch Syst, teacher& coach, 1968; Aroyelles Progress Action Comt, athletics dir, 1968; Sheppard & Jones Reading Clin, dir; Town Bunkie, alderman-at-large. **Orgs:** Wm Progressive Lodge No 217, 1975; chmn bd, Amazon Baptist Church, 1982; dir & vpres, Zach & Shep's Skate-Arama Inc, 1983. **Home Addr:** 312 Hickory St, Bunkie, LA 71322, **Home Phone:** (318)346-6436.

**SHEPPHARD, DR. CHARLES BERNARD**
Civil rights activist, business owner, educator. **Personal:** Born Sep 26, 1949, Port Gibson, MS; married Brenda Joyce Stone; children: Charles Kwame & Tenopra Me. **Educ:** Alcorn State Univ, BS, 1970; Southern Univ, JD, 1973; MS Col, JD, 1977. **Career:** Shepphard & Assoc, consult; Alcorn State Univ, prof hist & polit sci, 1977; MS House Rep, 1980-96; Fayette Chronicle Newspaper, owner, publ; Alcorn State Univ(retired), exten specialist, community resource develop specialist. **Orgs:** Am Hist Asn; Southern Growth Policy Bd; Am Mgt Asn; Int Affairs Asn; chmn, Nat Asn Advan Colored People-Fair Share Comt; chmn, Local Polit Party Activ; coordr, Polit Sci Internship Prog, Black Polit Sci Soc. **Honors/Awds:** Outstanding Young Men Award; Progressive Young Legislator of Miss. **Home Addr:** 158 McDonald Rd, Lorman, MS 39096-5502, **Home Phone:** (601)437-3722. **Business Addr:** CRD Specialist, Program Leader, Alcorn State University, 1000 ASU Dr Suite 479, Alcorn State, MS 39096-7500, **Business Phone:** (601)877-6100.

**SHERIDAN, EDNA K.**
Contractor, lawyer, army officer. **Personal:** Born Feb 20, 1951, Huntsville, AL; daughter of Willie Ed Fletcher and Beulah Ford; children: Daryl Andrae & Renita LaKaye Kimbrough. **Educ:** Ala A&M Univ, BS, 1980, MBA, 1982; Fla Inst Technol, MS, 1993. **Career:** USAR, sr instr, 1976-; AUS Corps Engrs, chief contracting div, currently, contracting officer; Saudi Arabian Nat Guard PARC Off, contracting officer, currently; Contract specialist over 20 yrs. **Orgs:** Pres, Alpha Kappa Alpha Sorority Inc, Rho Chi Omega Chap, 1994-97, S Eastern Region, cluster coordr, 1999-2002; bd mem, Am Red Cross, Madison & Marshall Co Chap, 1996-; Nat Contract Managers Asn, 1999-; pres, Fun-Set Social & Charity Club, 1999-2002; life mem, Nat Asn Advan Colored People; bd mem, Calhoun Community Col Ctr Polit Cult. **Honors/Awds:** South Eastern Region President of the Year, Alpha Kappa Alpha, 1995; 20 Distinguished Men, Community Serv/Leadership, 1996; Resolution, Leadership, City Huntsville, 1997; Resolution, Community Leadership, City Madison, 1997; Leadership Award, Women Studies Group, 1997; Presidential Excellence Award, Nat Asn Advan Colored People, Madison County Br, 1998; Resolution, Community Leadership Award, State Ala; South Eastern Region Member of the Year, 1998; Woman of the Year, AUS Corp Engrs, Huntsville Ctr, 2000; Army Acquisition Excellence Award, U.S. Army Acquisition Corps Ann Awards Ceremony, 2009. **Home Addr:** 3238 Delicado Dr NW, Huntsville, AL 35810-2963, **Home Phone:** (256)859-3023. **Business Addr:** Contracting Officer, Saudi Arabian National Guard PARC Office.

**SHERMAN, BARBARA J. (BARBARA JEAN SHERMAN-SIMPSON)**
Financial manager, vice president (organization), stockbroker. **Personal:** Born Jul 20, 1944, Los Angeles, CA; daughter of Ernest and Estelle; married Mike O Simpson. **Educ:** Calif State Univ, attended 1961; Mesa Community Col, attended 1971; Ariz State Univ, MBA, gen, 1974; Calif State Univ Northridge, MBA, gen. **Career:** Merrill Lynch, Phoenix, acct exec, 1975-77; Dean Witter, acct exec, 1977-80; Merrill Lynch, acct exec, 1980-84; Prudential Securities, vpres, investments, 1984-; Piper Jaffray; Morgan Stanley Smith Barney LLC, sr vpres, financial advisor, 2007-. **Orgs:** Ariz Bd Realtors, 1972-; Stockbroker's Soc, 1975-; City PhoenixMayor's Comn Status Women, 1979-82; Valley Big Sisters, 1983-86; chairperson, Black Republican Coun-Phoenix, 1985; Black Jewish Coalition, 1986-; Ariz state chairperson, United Negro Col Fund, 1987-88; bd mem, Am Red Cross Cent Ariz Chap, 1988-; Mayor's Comn Status Women-City Phoenix; Nat Asn Advan Colored People; Phoenix Urban League. **Honors/Awds:** Woman of the Year in a Non-traditional role, Delta Sigma Theta Inc, Phoenix, AZ Chapter, 1983; numerous performance awards, Merrill Lynch and Prudential-Securities; 100 of the most promising Black women in corporate America, Ebony Mag. **Home Addr:** 1010 W Claremont St, Phoenix, AZ 85013. **Business Addr:** Vice President Investments, Prudential Securities Inc, 17220 N Boswell Blvd, Sun City, AZ 85373-2000, **Business Phone:** (623)876-4800.

**SHERMAN, C. A. (TONY SHERMAN)**
Writer, lecturer, sculptor. **Personal:** Born Crockett, TX; married Teri; children: 3. **Career:** The American Black Cowboy: & Present, auth, 1988; Tex Comn Arts, comnr, 1997-2003; Black Cowboys of Texas, contrib auth, 2000; Coun Elders, founder, 2000-; Tony Sherman's Sch Art & Gallery, owner, artist & sculptor, currently. **Orgs:** Tex Arts Comn. **Business Addr:** Owner, Artist, Tony Sherman's Sch Art & Gallery, 2420 Cartwright Rd Suite C, Missouri City, TX 77489-6000, **Business Phone:** (281)499-9958.

**SHERMAN, EDWARD FORRESTER (ED SHERMAN)**
Photographer. **Personal:** Born Jan 17, 1945, New York, NY; married Audrey Johnson; children: Edward F. **Educ:** Amsterdam Photog Workship, attended 1960; Bronx Community Col, attended 1964; Univ S Marine Corps, attended 1966; New Sch Soc Res Spring, attended 1969; Brooklyn Col, attended 1973. **Career:** Freelance photogr, 1962-65; still photogr, USMC, 1965-67; Photo-Lab Tech, 1968-69; New Dimensions Assocs, dir, 1968; Freelance Photogr, 1969; Photog Prog, dir, 1970; Comm Corp Lower W Side, art instr, 1972; NCA New Jour, assoc ed, 1973. **Orgs:** Co-chmn, Collective Black Photogrs, 1971; chmn, Benin Enterprises Inc, 1975.

**SHERMAN, RAY**
Football coach. **Personal:** Born Nov 27, 1951, Berkeley, CA; married Yvette; children: 3. **Educ:** Laney Jr Col; Fresno State Univ; San Jose State, educ, 1975. **Career:** Football player (retired), coach; San Jose State Univ, grad asst, 1974; Univ Calif, defensive backs, 1975, 1981; Mich State Univ, tight ends, 1976-77; Wake Forest Univ, coaching staff, 1978-80; Purdue Univ, running backs, 1982-85; Ga Univ, wide receivers, 1986-87; Houston Oilers, running backs coach, wide receiv-

ers, 1988-89; Atlanta Falcons, asst head coach, 1990; San Francisco 49ers, running backs, 1991, wide receivers, 1992-93; New York Jets, offensive coordr, 1994; Minn Vikings, quarterbacks, 1995-97, offensive coordr, 1999; Pittsburgh Steelers, offensive coordr, 1998; Green Bay Packers, wide receivers coach, 2000-04; Titans Radio, wide receivers coach, 2004-07; Tenn Titans, wide receiver, 2005-06; Dallas Cowboys, wide receivers coach, 2007-10; St Louis Rams, wide receivers coach, 2012-15. **Orgs:** Am Football Asn. **Business Addr:** Coach, St Louis Rams, 1 Rams Way, Earth City, MO 63045, **Business Phone:** (314)982-7267.

### SHERMAN, THOMAS OSCAR, JR.

Administrator, engineer. **Personal:** Born May 29, 1948, Elberton, GA; son of Thomas Sr and Edna Murray; married Joyce Chestang; children: Alfred, Morris & Katherine. **Educ:** NC A&T State Univ, BSEE, 1971; Golden Gate Univ, MBA, 1979. **Career:** USAF Strategic Air Command, ATC, capt ewo instr, 1971-80; 129th Commun Flight Calif Air Nat Guard, oper officer, capt, 1980-83; Ford Aerospace, sr syst engr, 1980-83, mgr comput syst, 1983-84, mgr TREWS engrg, 1984-88, SDDS/TREWS Prog Mgr, 1988-90; 129th Info Syst Flight Calif Air Nat Guard, comdr, major, 1983-87; 129 Mission Support Squadron Calif Air Nat Guard, comdr, lt col, 1987-94; Loral SRS, Ridgecrest, Calif, dir E W prog, 1990-91, dep engineering dir, 1991-95; 129th Support Group, col, comdr, 1994-98; Lockheed Martin SRS, chief engr, dir, 1996-. **Orgs:** Asn Old Crows, 1976-; Nat Guard Air Force Asn, 1980-; Union Baptist Church Ridgecrest Calif; adult bible teacher, Union Baptist Church, 1987, choirmem, Union Baptist Church, 1986-94; chmn, Kiwanis Club Ridgecrest, Calif, 1990-91; adult bible teacher, Emanual Baptist Church, 1994-. **Home Addr:** 1100 Creek Ridge Ct, Roseville, CA 95747-7912, **Home Phone:** (916)782-7158. **Business Addr:** Chief Engineer, Director, Lockheed Martin Western Development Labs, 1260 Crossman Ave, Sunnyvale, CA 94089, **Business Phone:** (408)734-6500.

### SHERMAN, TONY. See SHERMAN, C. A.

### SHERMAN-SIMPSON, BARBARA JEAN. See SHERMAN, BARBARA J.

### SHERRELL, REV. CALVIN L.

Executive. **Career:** Rural Christian Mission, pres. **Orgs:** St Lukes Evangel Lutheran Church. **Business Addr:** Member, St Lukes Evangelical Lutheran Church, 4051 King Wilkinson Rd, Lincolnton, NC 28092, **Business Phone:** (704)735-2968.

### SHERRELL, CHARLES RONALD, II

Executive, broadcaster, president (organization). **Personal:** Born May 10, 1936, Gary, IN; son of George Wesley Jr and Beatrice Mariner; married Trutie Thigpen. **Educ:** Mex City Col, BA, 1958; Roosevelt Univ, Chicago, IL, MA, 1963; Univ Chicago, PhD, 1975. **Career:** Gary Pub Schs, Gary, Ind, foreign lang teacher, 1961-65; US Steel, Gary, Ind, foreman, 1965-67; Globe Trotter Commun, Chicago, Ill, sales mgr, 1967-71; Bell & Howell Schs, Chicago, Ill, vpres, 1971-74; Mariner Broadcasters Inc, Chicago, Ill, chief exec officer, 1974-; CD 1570-AM Radio Sta, pres. **Orgs:** Radio Advert Bur, 1974-; pres, Am Soc Linguists, 1978-80; chmn mem comt, Black Hisp Asn, 1979-84; reading educ comn, New Fronteirs Inc, 1981-82; chmn, Nat Asn African-Am Anthropologists, 1983-85; chmn, Cable TV Comn, 901 Condo Bd Asn, 1987-89; pres, 1988-90; chmn, Nat Asn Black-Owned Broadcasters Inc, 1990-; pres, Chatham Bus Asn Chicago; pres & chmn, Nat Inst Corp Responsibility. **Home Addr:** 1098 N Ave, Highland Park, IL 60035-1132, **Home Phone:** (312)461-9247. **Business Addr:** President, Chief Executive Officer, Mariner Broadcasters Inc, 15700 Campbell Ave, Harvey, IL 60426, **Business Phone:** (708)331-7840.

### SHERROD, REV. CHARLES M.

Chaplain, clergy. **Personal:** Born Jan 2, 1937, Petersburg, VA; son of Raymond and Martha Walker; married Shirley M; children: Russia & Kenyatta. **Educ:** Va Union Univ, AB, 1958, Sch Rel, BD 1961; Union Theol Sem, sacred theol, 1967; Univ Ga, cert community develop. **Career:** Interdenominational, minister, 1956-; SNCC, Field Secy, 1961-67; SW Ga Proj Community Educ, dir, 1961-87; New Community Inc, dir, 1969-85; City Albany, city comnr, 1976-90; Ga State Senate, 1996; Ga State Prison, Homerville, Ga, chaplain, currently. **Orgs:** First SNCC Field Organizer, 1961; Freedom Ride Coord Comn, 1963; pres, SW Ga Proj, 1967-85; bd, National Association for the Advancement of Colored People, 1970-85; US Govt OEO, 1974; Fel Inst Policy Studies, 1974; consult, Nat Coun Churches, 1978; bd, Slater King Ctr, 1975-85; bd, SW Ga Planning Comn, 1978-85; bd mem, Fed Southern Coop, 1979-87; Ga Coalition Housing, 1983-85. **Honors/Awds:** Omega Man of the Year, Lambda Chap, Richmond, 1958; Hons Civil Rights, Nat Lawyers Guild, 1985; Delegate, Nat Dem Party Conv, 1984. **Home Addr:** 201 Garden Hill Dr, Albany, GA 31705, **Home Phone:** (912)432-1338. **Business Addr:** Chaplain, Homerville State Prison, 700 Reddick St, Homerville, GA 31634, **Business Phone:** (912)487-3052.

### SHERROD, EZRA CORNELL

Executive. **Personal:** Born Jul 25, 1950, Wilson, NC; son of John and Mary Hester Worsely; married Charlotte Pye; children: Derrick Cornell. **Educ:** Lear Siegler Inst, AA, 1971; Univ DC, BA, 1977; proj mgt seminars, 1980; People & Resources Mgt Seminars, 1986. **Career:** Woodard & Lothrop, comput specialist, 1970-72; Int Bus Serv Inc, proj mgr, 1972-80; Automated Datatron Inc, proj mgr, 1980-86; Sherrod Security Co, pres, owner, 1986; Wilkins Systs Inc, facil mgr, 1986-; Hecht's, comm sales, prof sales exec, 1990-91; Advantage Mortgage Serv, vpres, 1993-. **Orgs:** Pres, Hist Club Univ DC, 1974-76; Univ DC Alumni, 1984; Minority Bus Comn, 1986; Evangel Assembly Church Camp Springs MD; Bus Network Wash DC; Phys & Ment Self-Improv Prog. **Honors/Awds:** Diamond Club Mem, Top Sales Level Hecht's, 1991. **Special Achievements:** Top Five Managers of Year Automated Datatron Inc, 1985; Author letter of intro "Saga of Sidney Moore, " 1985; Top candidate for major exec position involving a major computer network w/Wilkins Systems Inc, 1987. **Home Addr:** 6064 Thoroughbred Ct Unit D, Waldorf, MD 20603-3328, **Home Phone:** (301)418-0626.

### SHERWOOD, HON. O. PETER

Lawyer, judge, executive. **Personal:** Born Feb 9, 1945, Kingston; son of Leopold and Gloria Howell; married Ruby Birt; children: 1. **Educ:** Brooklyn Col, BA, 1968; NY Univ Sch Law, JD, 1971. **Career:** NY Civil Ct, law secy to Hon Fritz W Alexander II, 1971-74; Nat Asn Advan Colored People, Legal Def & Educ Fund Inc, asst coun, 1974-84; NY Univ Sch Law, adj asst prof law, 1980-87; State NY Ethics Comn, solicitor gen, 1986-91; City New York, corp coun, 1991-93; Kalkines, Ark, Zall & Bernstein, partner, 1994-2002; City Univ NY Law Sch, vis prof, 1994; Manatt, Phelps & Phillips, litigation partner, 1994-2008; Appellate Pract II Circuit, NY State Bar Asn, lectr, 1996; NYS Ethics Comn, comnr, 1998-2003; NY State Judicial Inst Professionalism Law, 1999-; Supreme Ct, Civil Br, New York County, judge, 2008-. **Orgs:** Comt Gen Aptitude Test Battery, Nat Res Coun, 1987-90; Trustee, NY Univ Law Ctr Found; 100 Black Men; Metro Black Bar Asn; Nat Bar Asn; New York Procurement Policy Bd, 1991-94; secy, Asn Bar City New York, 1992-97; NY State Bar, 1972; arbitrator, Am Arbit Asn; Bd Deleg, NY State Bar Asn; Fed Bar Asn; Inns Ct; Am Acad Appellate Lawyers; panelist, Ctr Policy Rev, Panel Distinguished Neutrals; Law Ctr Found, NY Univ Sch Law. **Home Addr:** 255 Lyncroft Rd, New Rochelle, NY 10804. **Business Addr:** Litigation Partner, Supreme Court Civil Branch New York County, Rm 615 60 Ctr St, New York, NY 10007, **Business Phone:** (646)386-3807.

### SHERWOOD, WALLACE WALTER. See Obituaries Section.

### SHIELDS, DR. CLARENCE L., JR.

Physician. **Personal:** Born Jul 19, 1940, Helena, AR; married Barbara Wilson; children: Brian, Christopher & Angela. **Educ:** Loyola Univ, Los Angeles, 1962; Creighton Univ Sch Med, Omaha, Nebr, MD. **Career:** Univ Calif, Los Angeles Med Ctr, surg intern, 1966-67; Univ Southern Calif Med Ctr, orthop surg residency; Southwestern OrthopMed Group, orthop surg, 1973; Daniel Freeman Hosp, staff, 1973; LosAngeles Rams, team physician, 1973-95; Viewpark Community Hosp, staff, 1973; Martin Luther King Hosp, staff, 1973; Charles Drew Sch Med, asst clin prof, 1973-; Rancho Los Amigos Hosp, staff, 1976; Los Angeles Dodgers, LosAngeles Lakers, Los Angeles Kings, Calif Angels, orthop consult, currently; Univ Southern Calif Sch Med, asssoc clin prof, 1976-; Nat Football League, neutral physician; Univ Calif Irvine Med Ctr, consult; Kerlan-Jobe Orthopaedic Clin, sports med fel, orthopaedic Surgeon, assoc, vpres; pvt pract, currently. **Orgs:** AMA; Am Orthop Soc Sports Med; Am Bd Orthop Surg; Am Acad Orthop Surgeons; dipl, Nat Bd Med Examrs; bd dirs, Western Orthop Asn, 1979; Los Angeles County Med Asn; Charles Drew Med Soc; Calif Med Asn; Western Orthop Asn; chmn, Orthop Rev Comm, 1978-, orthop Comm & Credential Comn, Centinela Hosp; adv bd, 1973-, chmn, Fel Comm, 1973-; Nat Athletic Health Inst; Alpha Omega Alpha; Herodicus Soc; Calif Orthop Asn; Pan Pac Surg Asn; Am Col Sports Med; Int Soc Knee; Int Arthroscopy Asn; Arthroscopy Asn N Am; Founder & med dir, Team HEAL Found, 1994-; bd trustee, Loyola Marymount Univ, 1995-05, Chair, Stud Life Comt, 2000-05; Pres, secy & Bd Dir, Am Orthopaedic Socs Sports Med, 2001-02. **Honors/Awds:** Presidential Medallion, Am Orthopaedic Socs Sports Med, 2001; Godfather, Am Orthopaedic Socs Sports Med, 2004; Mr. Sports Medicine, Am Orthopaedic Socs Sports Med, 2006. **Special Achievements:** Authored more than 40 publications, 5 book chapters, 1 book, and 3editorials and has been a facilitator for over 200 lectures. **Business Addr:** Physician, Kerlan-Jobe Orthop Clinic, 6801 Pk Ter Dr Suite 400, Los Angeles, CA 90045, **Business Phone:** (310)665-7200.

### SHIELDS, CLARESSA

Boxer. **Personal:** Born Mar 17, 1995, Flint, MI; daughter of Bo Shields. **Educ:** Olivet College, Attending. **Career:** Boxer, Middleweight Division. **Honors/Awds:** Junior Olympic National Champion, 2011; National Police Athletic League Championships, Middleweight Title and named Top Overall Fighter, 2011; U.S. Olympics Team Trials Champion and Outstanding Boxer, 2012; Women's Continental Champion, 2012; Olympics, Gold medal, 2012; TheGrio.com, 100 Making History Today, 2012; USA Boxing Youth National Champion, 2013. **Special Achievements:** First American woman to win a gold medal in Olympic boxing, 2012.

### SHIELDS, CYDNEY ROBIN

Manager, auditor. **Personal:** Born Feb 24, 1957, Jamaica, NY; daughter of Waddel and Sylvia. **Educ:** Ind Univ Pa, BA, Eng, 1980; Univ Md, MA, technol mgt & MBA. **Career:** Lockheed Mgt Info Systs, internal auditor, analyst, 1982-84, control mgr, 1984-87, regional off mgr, 1987-; Claims Admin Corp, div mgr audit serv, 1989; Coventry Health Care, dir; Prin Health Care, dir & proj support, 1993-98; Prin Financial Group, dir, bus support, 1994-98; UUNET, mgr, billing integration proj, 1999-2004; Verizon Bus, IT Sox Compliance mgr, prog proj mgt, 1999-; MCI, proj mgr, 2000-04. **Orgs:** Delta Sigma Theta, 1977; founder, Black Women Who Win, 1986-; vpres, Am Bus Women's Asn, 1988; Black Women's Adv Bd, 1989; Nat Comn Working Women Wider Opportunities Women, 1992-; Nat Asn Female Execs; Project Mgt Inst; ISACA; Women Technol. **Honors/Awds:** Hundred Heroes Award; IT Strategic Pillar Award; Woman of the Year Award, Am Bus Women's Asn, Wash, DC chap. **Special Achievements:** Co-author, Work, Sister, Work: The Right Moves on Your New Job, Women in Business, 1991; Why Black Women Can't Get Ahead, 1992; Managing Your Writing, Mgt World, 1992; Mounting a Career Climb, Career Focus Magazine, 1992; Author: Career Decisions: the Art of Soaring to the Top. **Home Addr:** 604 Sunnybrook Terr Suite 1012, Gaithersburg, MD 20877, **Home Phone:** (301)590-0119. **Business Addr:** IT Manager, Verizon Business, 140 W St, New York, NY 10007, **Business Phone:** (301)517-2165.

### SHIELDS, REV. DEL PIERCE

Radio host, clergy. **Personal:** Born Apr 29, 1933, New York, NY; son of Judge and Daisy Hite; children: Leslie, Allyson, Cydney, Cynthia & Stacy. **Educ:** Nat Theol Sem, BS, 1978, MA, 1982, MDiv, 1984; Univ Santa Barbara, PhD, 1989. **Career:** WLIB, radio host, 1965-68; Independent Network-WLIB, WRVR, WWRL, radio host, 1968-70; Jemmin Inc, asst vpres, 1970-77; Avant-Garde Broadcasting Inc, vpres & gen mgr, 1975-77; Zion Gospel Church, pastor, sr pastor, 1980-; Unity Broadcasting WWRL, Morning Fel host, 1986-91, Drivetime Dialogue commentator. **Orgs:** Exec vpres, 1971-73, exec dir, 1974-78, Nat Asn TV & Radio; Church God Christ, Inc, 1999. **Honors/Awds:** Blanton Peale, Grad Inst, 1981. **Special Achievements:** Moments in Meditation, 1991-92. **Home Addr:** 112-11 Dillon St, Jamaica, NY 11433, **Home Phone:** (718)658-2420.

### SHIELDS, KAREN BETHEA (KAREN LOUISE BETHEA-SHIELDS)

Lawyer. **Personal:** Born Apr 29, 1949, Raleigh, NC; daughter of Bryant W and Grace Louise; married Kenneth R Galloway; married Linwood B. **Educ:** E Carolina Univ, AB, psychol, 1971; Duke Univ, Sch Law, JD, 1974. **Career:** Paul Keenan Rowan & Galloway, partner, 1974-77; Loflin Loflin Galloway & Acker, partner, 1977-80; 14th Judicial Dist Durham Co, judge, 1980-85; Karen Bethea-Shields law firm, sole practr, 1986-; atty & counr-at-law, currently; Juv Crime Prev Coun, atty. **Orgs:** Am Bar Asn; Nat Conf Black Lawyers; judiciary coun, NBA, Nat Judicial Col; ACL; fac mem, Nat Inst Trial Advocacy; trial pract instr, training lawyers; Nat Col Criminal Defense Lawyers NACDA; Nat Asn Women Judges; Am Judicature Soc; guest lectr & workshop panel mem, Nat Acad Trial Lawyers, Toronto, Can, 1982; Nat Judicial Col Search & Seizure & Grad Evidence Spec Sessions, 1983; fac mem, Women Trial Lawyers Advocacy Clin, San Francisco, Calif, 1984; Int Platform Asn, 1988-89; NCW, 1989; vice chairperson, Educ Comn, Durham Comn Affairs Black People, 1989-; bd mem, Edgemont Community Ctr, 1990-; bd mem, Hayti Develop Corp; bd mem, Durham Community Shelter HOPE; NC State Bar. **Honors/Awds:** Joann Little Defense Team, 1974-75; Lawyer of the Year, Nat Conf Black Lawyers, 1976; Outstanding Service Award, Raleigh Chap, Delta Sigma Theta, 1977; Certificate of Appreciation, NC State Asn Black Social Workers, 1979; Outstanding Young Woman of the Year, 1983; Distinguished Achievement Award, Nat Asn Advan Colored People, 1981; Runner-up, NEXT Mag, 100 Most Powerful People for the 80's; Certificate for 1982, NC Juvenile Ct Judges, 1984; Outstanding Service, Community Service, Excellence in Education, Sister Clara Muhammad Schs Educ Fund NC, 1989. **Special Achievements:** First African American female and first female Dist Court Judge in Durham County; Second African American female judge in North Carolina; First African American Woman Graduate From Duke Law School. **Home Addr:** 3221 Apex Hwy 55, Durham, NC 27713-1598, **Home Phone:** (919)361-0228. **Business Addr:** Attorney, 123 Orange St, Durham, NC 27702, **Business Phone:** (919)682-0383.

### SHIELDS, WILL HERTHIE

Football player. **Personal:** Born Sep 15, 1971, Ft. Riley, KS; married Senia; children: Soloman, Sanayika & Shavon. **Educ:** Univ Nebr, BA, commun. **Career:** Football player (retired); Nebr Cornhuskers football, 1989-92; Kans City Chiefs, guard, 1993-2006; Pro Bowl, 1995-2006; Walter Camp Football Found, offensive guard, 1999. **Orgs:** Bd mem, Marillac Ctr C; founder, Will to Succeed Found, 1993; spokesperson, United Way, 2003-06; fel track squad. **Home Addr:** , Overland Park, KS 66204. **Business Addr:** Founder, Will to Succeed Foundation, PO Box 26104, Overland Park, KS 66225-6104.

### SHIELDS-JONES, ESTHER L. M.

Nutritionist, consultant, executive. **Personal:** Born Beatrice, AL; daughter of Marshall A Montgomery Sr (deceased) and Annie Gertrude Ishman Montgomery; children: Reginald A & Darryl K. **Educ:** Tuskegee Univ, Tuskegee Inst, Ala, BS, 1963; Tex Southern Univ, Houston, Tex, MS, 1976; Univ Minn, Minneapolis, Minn, nutrit admin, 1989. **Career:** Tuskgee Univ, dietetic intern, 1966-67; Veterans Admin Hosp, Tuscaloosa, Ala, clin dietician, 1976-78; Jefferson County Health Dept, Birmingham, Ala, nutrit consult, 1978-84; Elba Gen Hosp, Elba, Ala, dir dietary serv, 1984-85; Univ Ala, Birmingham, Ala, clin instr, 1985-86; Hillhaven Corp, Nashville, Tenn, staff dietician, 1985-87; Beverly Enterprises Inc, Atlanta, Ga, dietary consult, 1987-91; Consult Dietician Community Dialysis Ctrs, Salem Nursing Home & Rehab Ctr, Ala Dialysis Inc, 1993-96; Prof Directions, Consult Dietician Group, 1996-; Healthcare Partners, Med Group, nutrit educr, 1996; Inglewood Unified Sch Dist, Food Serv Dept, dir food serv; pvt pract dietician, currently. **Orgs:** Am Dietetic Asn, 1968-; Ala Dietetic Asn, 1967-; Birmingham Alumnae Chap, Delta Sigma Theta Sorority, 1984-; Consult Dietitians Health Care Facil, 1988-; Birmingham Metrop Chap, Top Ladies Distinction, 1989-. **Honors/Awds:** Outstanding Dietitian Nominee, Birmingham Dietetic Asn, 1982. **Business Addr:** Dietician, 4581 Don Felipe Dr, Los Angeles, CA 90008-2853, **Business Phone:** (323)299-9026.

### SHIFFLETT, LYNNE CAROL

Administrator, association executive, journalist. **Personal:** Born Jan 1, 1940?, Los Angeles, CA; daughter of James Hubbard and Carolyn Ellen Larkin. **Educ:** Govt, Polit Sci, La State Col, BA; Univ Wis, MA. **Career:** NBC, admin; Neighborhood Adult Participation Proj, watts ctr dir; Sch Workers, Univ WI, instr; Commun Rel Social Develop Comn, Milwaukee Co, urban planner, 1969-71; KMOX-TV, cbs, news writer, 1971-72, news producer, 1972-73; Columbia Univ Summer Prog Broadcast Jour Minority Groups, consult & tchr, 1973; WNBC-TV News Ctr 4, weekend news producer, 1973-75, NBC Loan Community Film Workshop, trng dir & tchr, 1975, WNBC-TV news field, producer & writer, 1975-85; Shifflett Gallery, art dir, 1985-; Sr newswriter, KCOP Tv News, 1989-91; Eng & Soc Studies, Horace Hann Mid Sch, La, tchr, 2000, Chess Club, fac adv; Fel Opers Crossroads Africa; House representatives, congressman, 2002. **Orgs:** Delegate 8th Nat Conf US Nat Com UNESCO, 1961; Cert Comn Leadership Sch Pub Admin USC, 1966; bd dir, Triad Inc, 1977; bd dir, Henry St Settlement, 1978; adv comn Edwin Grould Serv Children, 1985; Golden Life Mem, Delta Sigma Theta Sorority; Am WomenRadio & TV; Nat Acad Television Arts & Sci; Nat Asn Black Journalists. **Home Addr:** 2214 W 20th St, Los Angeles, CA 90018, **Home Phone:** (323)732-2355. **Business Addr:** Art-Director, Shifflett Gallery, 8033 Sunset Blvd Suite 877, Los Angeles, CA 90028, **Business Phone:** (323)737-6900.

**SHINE, THEODIS (TED SHINE)**
Educator. **Personal:** Born Apr 26, 1931, Baton Rouge, LA; son of Theodis Wesley and Bessie Herson. **Educ:** Howard Univ, Wash, DC, BA, 1953; Univ Iowa, 1958; Univ Calif, Santa Barbara, CA, PhD, 1973. **Career:** Dillard Univ, New Orleans, LA, instr drama & eng, 1960-61; Howard Univ, Wash, DC, asst prof drama, 1961-67; Prairie View A&M Univ, Prairie View, Tex, prof & head dept drama, 1967, Dept Musin & Drama, adj Prof; prof emer, currently. **Orgs:** Omega Psi Phi; Nat Theatre Conf, Nat Conf African Am Theatres; South west Theatre Asn; Tex Educ Theatre Asn; bd mem, Tex Non-Profit Theatres; AmTheatre Asn. **Home Addr:** 10717 Cox Lane, PO Box 2082, Dallas, TX 75229, **Home Phone:** (214)357-6780. **Business Addr:** Professor Emeritus, Prairie View A & M University, PO Box 2779, Prairie View, TX 77446-0519, **Business Phone:** (936)857-2817.

**SHIPE, JAMESETTA DENISE HOLMES**
Journalist. **Personal:** Born May 30, 1956, Knoxville, TN; daughter of James Edward and Lavonia Thompson; married Abie; children: Kristen Janan. **Educ:** Univ Tenn, BS, commun & jour, 1980; Cooper Bus Sch, AS, bus, 1982; Tenn Inst, Electronics, attended 1990; Nat Col Bus & Technol, assoc, pharm, 2010. **Career:** FBI Off Cong & Pub Affairs, writer, pub release rep, 1982-83; BWXT Y-12 Nat Security Complex, comput maintenance customer serv, 1983-2005; Martin-Marietta Energy Systs Inc, Comp Electronics Serv, customer rels rep, 1983-; Jewelry Tv, customer serv agt, 2006-09. **Orgs:** Sigma Delta Chi Soc Prof Journalists, 1975-; Pub Rels Soc Am, 1977; pub affairs, press consult, Knoxville Women's Ctr, 1979-80; Phi Beta Lambda Soc Bus, 1982; Smithsonian Inst, 1987-; Nat Asn Advan Colored People, 1988-; Soc Pub Rels Professionals. **Home Addr:** 206 Northwestern Ave, Oak Ridge, TN 37830, **Home Phone:** (615)481-3244. **Business Addr:** Public Relations Assistant, Martin-Marietta Energy Systems Inc, Y-12 Plant, Oak Ridge, TN 37831-8103, **Business Phone:** (615)574-6528.

**SHIPLEY, REV. ANTHONY J.**
Clergy, educator, association executive. **Personal:** Born May 19, 1939, New York, NY; son of Oscar and Lillian Hawkins; married Barbara McCullough; children: Cornelia Jean. **Educ:** Drew Univ, BA, 1961; Garrett Sem, DMin, 1964; Adrian Col, DD, 1974; Am Mgt Asn, pres course, 1975. **Career:** Christ United Methodist Church, coun dir, 1971-82, Detroit W Dist, supt, 1982-87; Gen Bd Global Ministries, dep gen secy, 1991-93, sr pastor, 1994-; Scott Church, pastor, 1987-; Garrett Evangel Theol Sem, adj prof; Church Admin N MS Pastors Sch, lectr; Harvard Univ, fel, 1999. **Orgs:** Vpres & founder, Chandler Pk Acad, 1997-; Deleg, Gen Conf United Methodist, 1980; consult, NCJ Urban Network; bd dir, Adrian Col; chmn, Develop Comn Nat Black United Fund; pres, Asn Am Mgt Asn; Inst Adv Pastoral Studies; pres, Nat Fel Conf Coun; dir, Detroit Coun Churches; Mich State United Ministries Higher Educ; Nat Bd Higher Educ & Min; mgt consult, Charfoos Christenson Law Firm; bd dir, Methodist Theol Sch, OH; founder, McKenzie High Sch & Adrian Col Bound Prog; bd dir, Barton McFarland Neighborhood Asn; cert trainer, Cuvy Leadership Ctr, 7 Habits Highly Effective People; chair bd, U-Snap-Back Community Develop Corp; chair, Phoenix Dist Boy Scouts Am; founder, Black MethodistsChurch Renewal; bd dir, Detroit Urban League. **Honors/Awds:** Distinguished Alumnus, Garrett-Evangel Theol Sem, 1993. **Special Achievements:** Author: The Care & Feeding of Cliques in the Church, Interpreter Mag 1975, The Self Winding Congregation, Interpreter Mag 1975, Everybody Wants to Goto Heaven But Nobody Wants to Die, Christian Century 1976, The Council on Ministries as a Support System, Letter Ctr for Parish Developmet, LongRange Planning in the Local Church, MI Christian Advocate, Something forNothing, MI Christian Advocate, Fable of Disconnection, MI Christian Advocate. **Home Addr:** 19505 Canterbury Rd, Detroit, MI 48221-1876. **Business Addr:** Senior Pastor, Christ United Methodist Church, 15932 E Warren Ave, Detroit, MI 48224-3222, **Business Phone:** (313)882-8547.

**SHIPMAN, REV. DR. SHELDON R.**
Clergy, executive. **Personal:** Born Durham, NC; son of F George; married Teresa L McNair; children: Joshua McKoy & Jamiel Baker. **Educ:** Univ NC-Charlotte, BS, relig studies & polit sci; Livingstone Col, Hood Theol Sem, Mdiv; Va Union Univ, Samuel DeWitt Proctor Sch Theol, PhD. **Career:** IBM Corp, news reporter & sales acct mgr; Greenville Mem African Methodist Episcopal Zion Church, sr pastor, currently; Walls Memorial African Methodist Episcopal Zion Church, pastor, currently; Church Frederick Douglass, pastor, currently; Silvanus Enterprises Inc, vpres, sec & dir, 2005-. **Orgs:** United Way; Urban League; Nat Asn Advan Colored People; Kappa Alpha Pai Fraternity Inc; UNCC Alumni Asn; bd trustee, Hood Theol Sem. **Home Addr:** 8804 Walden Ridge Dr, Charlotte, NC 28216-2165, **Home Phone:** (704)697-0885. **Business Addr:** Senior Pastor, Greenville Memorial African Methodist Episcopal Zion Church, 6116 Montieth Dr, Charlotte, NC 28213, **Business Phone:** (704)596-4742.

**SHIPP, ETHELEEN RENEE**
Columnist, educator. **Personal:** Born Jun 6, 1955, Conyers, GA; daughter of Johnny Will Sr and Minnie Ola Moore. **Educ:** Ga State Univ, BA, jour, 1976; Columbia Univ, MS, jour, 1980, JD, 1980, MA, hist, 1994. **Career:** NY Times, nat corresp, legal corresp, asst metrop ed, 1980-92; NY Daily News, columnist, 1994-2006; Columbia Univ Grad Sch Jour, asst prof, 1994-2005; Wash Post, ombudsmen, 1998-2000; Hofstra Univ, Dept Jour Media Studies & Pub Rels, distinguished prof, spec assoc prof, 2005-. **Orgs:** Nat Asn Black Journalists, 1983-, 1986-. **Business Addr:** Distinguished Professor, Special Associate Professor, Hofstra University, 405 NAB, Hempstead, NY 11549-1000, **Business Phone:** (516)463-6600.

**SHIPP, HOWARD J., JR.**
Educator, athletic coach. **Personal:** Born Oct 2, 1938, Muskogee, OK; married Jeanetta Combs; children: Jackie. **Educ:** Langston Univ, BS, 1962; Northeastern State Col, MS, 1966; Okla State Univ, post grad. **Career:** Muskogee Pub Schs, teacher, football coach; Douglas HS Okla City, teacher football coach; Northeast HS Okla City, asst prin; Prof Baseball Player, 1958-59; Prof Barber, 1966-71; Univ Coun Ctr, counr, 1971; Okla State Univ, dir the Multicultural Develop & Assessment Ctr, 2005. **Orgs:** Okla City Classroom Teacher Asn; Okla City C C; Okla Educ Asn; Nat Asn Educ; Am Pub Gardens Asn; Nat Asn Advan Colored People; Okla Coun Pub Affairs, Bd Community Action Prog Still water, Okla; treas, Mid Scope; chmn, Minority Scholar Comt; Inst Scholar Comt; fac advr, Okla State Univ, Afro-Am Soc; sponsor, Kappa Alpha Phi. **Special Achievements:** First African American counselor at Oklahoma State University in 1971. **Home Addr:** 2005 N Glenwood Dr, Stillwater, OK 74075-2808, **Home Phone:** (405)372-6746.

**SHIPP, DR. MELVIN DOUGLAS**
Educator. **Personal:** Born Aug 10, 1948, Columbus, GA; son of Gene T and Doris O; married Michele Pierre Louis; children: Gael & Elizabeth. **Educ:** Ind Univ Sch Arts & Sci, BS, 1970; Ind Univ Sch Optom, OD, 1972; Harvard Univ Sch Pub Health, MPH, 1980; Univ Mich, Sch Pub Health, DrPH, 1996. **Career:** Naval Hosp Port Hueneme, Calif, chief optom serv, 1972-76; Univ Ala, Birmingham, asst prof, 1976-83, dir optom technician prog, 1976-79, asst dean clin serv & dir clin, 1980-86, Univ Ala, from assoc prof to prof, 1983-04; Sen Donald W Reigle Jr, health legis asst, 1989-90; Robert Wood Johnson Health Policy, Fel, 1989-90; Univ Ala, assoc prof to prof, 1983-04; OH State Univ, prof & dean, 2004-14. **Orgs:** Panelist, Nat Asn Minority Med Educr, 1994; Fel Am Acad Optom; Am Optom Asn; bd mem, pres, Asn Sch & Col Optom; Bur Health Professions; Food & Drug Admin; Nat Bd Examiners Optom; Nat Eye Inst; Nat Optom Asn; Prevent Blindness Am; Transp Res Bd; exec Bd mem, Am Pub Health Asn, 1999-2007, treas, 2000-07, pres, 2010-; chair, Am Acad Optom, 1999-2001; Nation's Health Adv Comt; chair, Ad-Hoc Nomination & Campaign Rev Comt. **Home Addr:** 5481 Heathrow Dr, Powell, OH 43065.

**SHIPP, DR. PAMELA LOUISE (PAM SHIPP)**
Psychologist. **Personal:** Born Feb 18, 1947, St. Louis, MO; daughter of Mall B and Lovia L Falconer. **Educ:** Colo Col, BA, 1969; George Wash Univ, MA, 1973; Denver Univ, PhD, coun psychol, 1985. **Career:** Irving Jr HS, dean studs, 1975-77, counr, 1977-83; Southern Ill Univ, Coun Ctr, therapist, 1983-84; Palmer HS, counr, 1984-85; Colo Col, therapist, 1985-, Lic Clin Psychologist, counr, currently; Pikes Peak Psychol Ctr, therapist, 1985-; Leadership Peak, fac; Founds Coaching, fac; pub Sch Adminr; bus mgt consult; exec coach; Denver Univ, Grad Prog Couns Psychol, adj prof, currently; Ctr Creative Leadership, adj fac, currently. **Orgs:** Alumni, Kappa Kappa Gamma Sorority, 1966-87; Am Psychol Asn, Div 16, 1985-87; consult, Ctr Creative Leadership, 1986-; pres, vice chair, Asn Black Psychol; pres, Denver/Rocky Mountain Chap, 1986-87; bd dir, Boys & Girls Club Pike Peaks Region, 1988-91; bd dir, World Affairs Coun, Colo Springs, 1988-91; mem adv bd, El Pomar Found, bd dir, Colo Springs C's Mus; Colo Springs Human Rels Bd; Assoc Black Psychol; bd dir, Penrose St. Francis Hosp; co-founder & pres, Colo Springs Black Leadership Forum; bd dir, Pikes Peak Community Found. **Honors/Awds:** Community Service Award, Nat Asn Advan Colored People. **Special Achievements:** Author: Counseling Blacks: A Group Approach; The Personnel and Guidance Journal, Oct. 83; Managing Diverse Work Teams: Leaders in Action, Jan/Feb01, Vol. 20; Building Communities For Tomorrow, One Person At A Time, 2002; recognized in Who's Who in Black Colorado Springs; featured in the Gazette Telegraph's Women at the Top. **Home Addr:** 1510 Witches Willow Lane, Colorado Springs, CO 80906-6207, **Home Phone:** (303)579-6878. **Business Addr:** Adjunct Faculty, Consultant, Center for Creative Leadership, 850 Leader Way, Colorado Springs, CO 80906-1353, **Business Phone:** (719)633-3891.

**SHIPPY, JOHN D.**
Government official. **Personal:** Born Gaffney, SC; son of John H and Hattie M Gibbs; married Carmen L Richardson; children: Angela A, Tamar S & Stearmen R. **Educ:** USAF, cert master instr, 1975; Culver-Stockton Col, Canton, MO, BA, polit sci, 1978; Webster Univ, St Louis, MO, MA, personnel mgt, 1986; St Mary's Univ; Our Lady Lake Univ; AHMA, cert conv serv mgr, 1988; Dept State Admin Officer Course. **Career:** USAF officer (retired); USF, MacDill AFB, cook, 1964-65; MACV, Compound, Pleiku AB, Vietnam, cook, 1965-66; High Wycombe Air Sta, Eng, storeroom supvr, 1967-69; 12th TFW Alert Facil, Cam Ranh Bay AB, Vietnam, supvr, 1969-70, Offr's op en mess, suv, 1970-71; 4th TFW Hosp, Seymour Johnson AFB, shift supvr, 1970; Bien Hoa AB, Vietnam, shift suv, 1970; Lackland AFB, mil training inr, 1971-76; Royal Saudi Air Force, info progr, 1976-77, ATC Master Instr, 1971-78; mil training instr, 1977-79; Offutt AFB, serv opers off, 1979-81; Air Force recruitment off, 1981-83; Off Recruitment Br, chief, 1983-85; Kunsan AB, Korea, serv opers officer, 1985-86; Cent Tex Col, Pac Div, human Rels mgt instr, 1985-86; Kelly AFB, Base Servs Div, chief, 1986-88; Raf, 20th Serv Squadron, Upper Hayford, Eng, comdr, 1988-91, spec asst, 1991-93; Army Air Force Exchange Serv Hq, planning officer, USAF off, Dept State, Foreign Serv Off, 1994; US Am Embassy, Lima Peru; Dept State, recruiter, currently. **Orgs:** Mil Training Instr Asn, 1971-; Veterans Foreign Wars, 1972-; Air Force Asn, 1978-; Vietnam Veterans Am; Am Legion Servs Soc; Hq AAFES Food Inspection & Eval Prog; Servs Soc, 1985-; Retired Off Asn, 1985-; vpres, Black Awareness Comt, 1990-91; bd Govs, Hq AAFES Officers' Club, 1991-92. **Home Addr:** , DC. **Business Addr:** DC.

**SHIRLEY, DR. GEORGE IRVING**
Opera singer, educator. **Personal:** Born Apr 18, 1934, Indianapolis, IN; son of Irving Ewing and Daisy; married Gladys Lee Ishop; children: Olwyn & Lyle. **Educ:** Wayne State Univ, BS, music educ, 1955, grad study, 1956. **Career:** Detroit Bd Edu, music teacher, 1955-56; Univ Md, voice prof, 1981-87; Univ Mich, prof voice, 1987-92; Joseph Edgar Maddy Distinguished Univ prof voice, 1992-2007; dir Vocal Arts Div, 1999-2007; Joseph Edgar Maddy Distinguished Univ emer prof voice, currently. **Orgs:** Nat Asn Teachers Singing; Am Guild Musical Artists; AFTRA; Nat Asn Negro Musicians; Wayne State Univ Alumni Asn; Univ Mich Musical Soc, adv bd; Alpha Phi Alpha; Phi Mu Alpha; Phi Kappa Phi; Omicron Delta Kappa; Pi Kappa Lambda, Nat Opera Asn; Santa Fe Opera; Voice Found; Sullivan Found. **Honors/Awds:** Nat Arts Club Award, 1960; Grammy Award, for performance in recording Mozart's Cosi Fan Tutte, 1968; Named one Distinguished Teachers, Univ Md, 1985-86; Multiple Alumni Achievement Awards, Wayne State Univ; Black Alumni Achievement Award, Wayne State Univ; Honorary doctorates: Montclair Col, 1984; Wilberforce Univ, 1987; Lake Forest Col, 1988; Univ Northern Iowa, 1997; Lift Every Voice Legacy Award, Nat Opera Asn, 2003; Honorary degrees from New Eng Conserv Music, Lake Forest Col, Univ Northern Iowa, Montclair State Col, Wilberforce Univ; DHL, Wayne State Univ, 2013; National Medal of Arts Award, 2015. **Special Achievements:** First African-American high school music teacher in Detroit; Appeared in over 80 opera productions world wide; First African-American tenor and second African-American male to sing leading roles with the Metropolitan Opera; First African-American member of the United States Army Chorus in Washington, DC. **Home Addr:** 2723 Provincetown Ct, PO Box 1916, Ann Arbor, MI 48103-2355, **Home Phone:** (734)665-0312. **Business Addr:** Joseph Edgar Maddy Distinguished University Emeritus Professor of Voice, University of Michigan, 1100 Baits Dr 3027 Moore, Ann Arbor, MI 48109-2085, **Business Phone:** (734)417-3079.

**SHIRLEY, DR. OLLYE L. BROWN. See Obituaries Section.**

**SHIVER, JUBE**
Journalist. **Personal:** Born May 30, 1953, South Boston, VA; son of Jube Sr and Mildred Leigh; married Tadasha Culbreath. **Educ:** Syracuse Univ, Syracuse, NY, BS, 1975; Antioch Sch Law, Wash, DC, JD, 1978; Univ Southern Calif, Los Angeles, CA, MA, int jour 1988. **Career:** Wilmington News-J, Wilmington, Del, staff writer, 1977-79; Wash Star, Wash, DC, staff writer, 1979-81; Wash Post, Wash, DC, staff writer, 1981-82; USA Today, Arlington, Va, staff writer, 1982-83; Sch Commun, adj instr; Shiver Mgt Group, property mgt firm, pres; Los Angeles Times, Los Angeles, Calif, staff writer, 1983-, Wash, DC, nat corresp, jornalists, currently. **Orgs:** Wash Asn Black Journalists; Nat Asn Black Journalist. **Honors/Awds:** Wash/Baltimore Newspaper Guild Award, 1981; Int Journ, fel Univ SC, 1987; Los Angeles Press Club Award, 1992. **Special Achievements:** Author, Horizons East, 1974. **Business Addr:** Journalists, Los Angeles Times, 1875 I St NW Suite 1100, Washington, DC 20006, **Business Phone:** (202)293-4651.

**SHIVERS, AUDRA BARRETT. See BARRETT, AUDRA.**

**SHIVERS, P. DERRICK (PETER DERRICK SHIVERS)**
Media executive. **Personal:** Born Oct 30, 1964, Kansas City, MO; son of Isiah and Alice L Perry. **Educ:** Maplewoods Community Col, attended 1984; Pa Valley Community Col, AS, 1986; Univ MSR, Kansas City, attended 1988. **Career:** PDS Universal Entertainment Group Inc, pres, 1989-92; Paradigm Entertainment, consult, 1990-; PDS Communs Inc, chmn, chief exec officer, 1992-; SS Gear Int Ltd, vpres & gen mgr, 1994. **Orgs:** BMI, 1989; Am Soc Composers, Authors & Publ, 1989; consult, Truth Orgn, 1990; Nat Asn Rec Merchants, 1990; Nat Asn Ind Rec Distribr, 1990; RIAA, 1991; UCC, 1991. **Honors/Awds:** Outstanding Achievement, Black Bus Asn, 1990-91. **Special Achievements:** Image Magazine, Kans City, Entertainment Indust Top Ten, 1990. **Business Addr:** Chairman, Chief Executive Officer, PDS Communications Inc, Dept A1, Kansas City, MO 64141-2477, **Business Phone:** (800)473-7550.

**SHIVERS, S. MICHAEL**
Government official, business owner, scientist. **Personal:** Born Mar 20, 1935, Madison, WI; son of Dimetra C Taliaferro and Stanley M; married Jacklyn Lee Gerth; children: Steven Michael, David Wallace & Julie Ann. **Educ:** Univ Wis, BS, 1958. **Career:** Government, business owner, scientist (retired); City Madison, alderman17th dist, 1971-73, 1975; soil scientist, entrepreneur & politician. **Orgs:** Wis Soc Prof Soil Scientists, 1958-78; Equal Opportunities Comn; Bd Pub Works; City Parks Comn; Transp Comn; Legis Comn; Madison Water Utility, Health Comn; Dane County Parks Comn; Common Coun Orgn Comn; City-County Bldg Comn; Nat Asn Advan Colored People; Urban League; City County Liaison Comn; City MATC Liaison Comn; sr mem, Madison Common Coun; bd dir, WIBA. **Honors/Awds:** Distinguished Service Award, N Madison Jaycees, 1977-78. **Home Addr:** 3554 Ridgeway Ave, Madison, WI 53704, **Home Phone:** (608)249-8091.

**SHOCKLEY, ANN ALLEN**
Librarian, educator, writer. **Personal:** Born Jun 21, 1927, Louisville, KY; daughter of Bessie Lucas and Henry Allen; married William; children: William Leslie Jr & Tamara Ann. **Educ:** Fisk Univ, BA, 1948; Case Western Res Univ, MSLS, 1959. **Career:** Del State Col, freelance writer, 1959-60, asst lib, 1959-66, assoc lib, 1966-69, African Am Collections, cur, currently; Univ Md, Eastern Shore, lib, 1969, assoc lib pub serv & dir oral hist, Libr Admin Devel Inst fel, 1974, cur, currently; Fisk Univ, assoc lib spec collections & univ archivist, assoc prof lib sci, 1970-98, cur, 1999-; Books: Living Black Am Authors: A Biog Dir, 1973; Handbook of Black Librarianship, 1977; History of Public Library Service to Negroes in the South; An Anthology and Critical Guide, 1988. **Orgs:** Authors Guild; Am Lib Asn Black Caucus; Tenn Archivists; founder, Black Oral Hist Prog. **Honors/Awds:** Additional Awards, Cent High Sch, Louisville, KY, 1944; Short Story Award, Asian Am Writers Workshop, 1962; Faculty Research Grant, Fisk Univ, 1970; ALA Black Caucus Award, 1975; First Annual Hatshepsut Award for Literature, CVOBW, 1981; Martin Luther King Black Author's Award, 1982; Susan Koppelman Award for Best Anthology, Popular & Am Cult Asn, 1989; Outlook Award, 1990; Achievement Award for Extraordinary Achievement in Professional Activites, Black Caucus Am Libr Asn, 1992; 1/2 Success Recognition Award Librarian/Author, 1997; Crossroad to Freedom Award, 2005. **Special Achievements:** Loving Her, Bobbs-Merrill Inc, 1974; Living Black Am Authors, 1973; A Handbk for Black Librarianship, 1977; The Black and White of It, Naiad Press, 1980; Say Jesus and Come to Me, Avon Bks, 1982; An Anthology and Critical Guide, G K Hall, 1988; written several reference books for the library; author of numerous articles. **Home Addr:** 5975 Post Rd, Nashville, TN 37205-3232, **Home Phone:** (615)353-0771. **Business Addr:** Curator, Fisk University, 1000 17th Ave N, Nashville, TN 37208-3051, **Business Phone:** (615)329-8500.

**SHOCKLEY, LINDA WALLER**
Administrator, president (organization). **Personal:** Born NJ. **Educ:** Univ Bridgeport, BA, jour, 1976. **Career:** Gannett Co, reporter, news ed, bur chief & city ed; Lawnside Hist Soc Inc, pres, currently; Dow Jones Newspaper Fund, asst to dir, 1988-92, dep dir, 1992-2014; Lawnside Hist Soc Inc, pres, 1994-; Preserv Nj, secy, 1995-98; Dow Jones News Fund, managing dir, 2014-. **Orgs:** Trustee, Lawnside Hist Soc Inc; chair, Minority Affairs Comt, Gannett Co; NABJ, 1984-; Nat Asn Black Journalists, conv co-chair, 1987-89; Journalism Educ Asn, 1988-2010. **Home Addr:** , NJ. **Business Addr:** President, Lawnside Historical Society Inc, PO Box 608, Lawnside, NJ 08045-0608, **Business Phone:** (856)546-8850.

**SHOEMAKER, VERONICA SAPP (SAPP V SHOEMAKER)**
Clergy, government official, gardener. **Personal:** Born Jun 23, 1929, Ft. Myers, FL; daughter of Henry L Sapp and Lillian Sapp; married Bennie; children: Mattie, Bennie & Duane E (deceased). **Educ:** Edward Waters Col, Jacksonville, FL, attneded 1951; Edison Comm Col, Ft Myers, FL, attended 1972. **Career:** Fla Health & Rehab Servs, foster care home, 1974-83; Sunland Develop Ctr, resident training instr; City E Ft Meyers, city coun woman, 1982-2002; Veronica Shoemaker Florist, owner & designer, 1974-. **Orgs:** Area dir, Southwest Fla State Conf, Nat Asn Advan Colored People; vol prog, Lee County RSVP Comn; Hisp Am Soc; mem bd, Lee County Cemetary; sch bd mem, Lee County Sch Bd ESAA Comn; bd mem, charter mem Dunbar Merchants Asn Inc; Greater Ft Myers Chamber Com; Fla Conf C & Youth; Lee County Charter Comn; Lee County Hosp Study Comn; Lee County Human Rels Comn; chmn, Lee County Bi-Racial Comn; Lee County Ment Health Asn; pres, Dunbar HS & Elem PTA; Lee County Coun PTA; pres & charter mem, Dunbar Little League; past charter Ebony Parent Club; past mem, Dunbar Easter Club; past charter mem, vpres, Fla Women's Polit Caucus; past charter mem, Southwest Fla Women's Polit Caucus; past mem Lee County League Women Voters, Overall Econ Devel Comm; pres & charter mem, Dar Improv Asn, 1979-; bd dir, Nat League Cities, Goodwill Indust, Metro Org, SW Fl League Cities, Women in Munic Govt; founder & dir, Source Light & Hope Develop Ctr Inc, 1988; pres, Veronica S Shoemaker Charity Serv Inc; pres, Nat Asn Advan Colored People. **Honors/Awds:** Woman of the Year, Zeta Phi Beta; SROP for Comm Serv Plaque; Nat Asn for the Advancement of Colored People Award FL; Presidential Award, Dunbar Little League; Honor & Award, Edison Comm Col Black Student Union; High Honor Heart of Gold Gannett Found; Martin Luther King Jr Human & Civil Rights Award, FTP & Nat Educ Asn, 1992; Luminary Award, Hodges University. **Special Achievements:** Honored 3 Mile Street Named "Veronica S Shoemaker" Blvd, 2002; Shoemaker Lane, 1998; first black council member; First African American elected official in Fort Myers. **Home Addr:** 3054 Mango St, Fort Myers, FL 33916-1920, **Home Phone:** (239)332-7206. **Business Addr:** Owner, Veronica Shoemaker Florist, 3510 Martin Luther King Blvd, Fort Myers, FL 33916, **Business Phone:** (239)332-1802.

**SHOFFNER, GARNETT WALTER (GUS SHOFFNER)**
Counselor. **Personal:** Born Jul 12, 1934, Greensboro, NC; son of Robert and Hortense; married Doris Cole; children: Joseph, Robin & Debra. **Educ:** Bellevue Col, BS, 1972; Univ Nebr, MPA, 1975; Creighton Univ, MS, 1988. **Career:** Employee Develop Ctr, Enron Corp, dir, 1979-87; Great Plains Coun Ctr, counr, 1988-90, dir, 1990-; prof counr, 1991-2004; ment health practr, 1994-2004. **Orgs:** Bd vpres, Nova Therapeut Community; bd mem, Sarpy County Ment Health; bd mem, Bryant Res Community Ctr; steering comt, Omaha Temp Organizing; Rotary Int; Nat Asn Advan Colored People; Urban League; Family Life Ministry, Creighton Univ, 1990-. **Honors/Awds:** Great American Family Midlands, State Nebr, 1990. **Home Addr:** 606 Laurel Dr, Bellevue, NE 68005, **Home Phone:** (402)291-5289. **Business Addr:** Counselor, Co-owner, Great Plains Counsel Center, 205 N Galvin Rd Suite B, Bellevue, NE 68005-4852, **Business Phone:** (402)292-7712.

**SHOFFNER, JAMES PRIEST**
Chemist, counselor. **Personal:** Born Jan 14, 1928, New Madrid, MO; married Cornelia Dow; children: Stuart, Karen & Andrew. **Educ:** Lincoln Univ, BS, 1951; DePaul Univ, MS, org chem, 1956; Univ Ill Med Ctr, PhD, org chem, 1965. **Career:** Chemist (retired), counselor; Post Off, Chicago; CPC Internat, res chmn, 1956-61; UOP Inc, res chemist, 1993; ACS, counr, 1974; Inst Sci Educ & Sci Commun Columbia Col, sci prof & educ consult, 2004; Am Chem Soc Depart Diversity Prog, consult, currently; PBS NOVA prog, consult, 2007-. **Orgs:** Am Chem Soc; Catalysis Soc; Chicago Chem Club; Ill Acad Sci; Nat Counr Am Chem Soc; chmn, Chicago Am Chem Soc, 1976-77; bd mem, NW Suburban SCLC; Dist 59 Sch Community Coun; Omega Psi Phi. **Honors/Awds:** Black Achievers Award, YMCA, 1975; Encouraging Disadvantaged Students into Careers in the Chemical Sciences Award, Henry Hill Award, Am Chem Soc, 2002; 30 year councilor plaque, Am Chem Soc, 2004; ACS Award. **Special Achievements:** Pub Papers in Num Sci Jours Patents; first in 1968 to chair (with Dr Joe Arrigo) the pilot of Project SEED. **Home Addr:** 296 Parkchester, Elk Grove Village, IL 60007. **Business Addr:** Counselor, American Chemical Society, 1155 16th St NW, Washington, DC 20036, **Business Phone:** (202)872-6243.

**SHOPSHIRE, DR. JAMES MAYNARD, SR.**
Educator, clergy. **Personal:** Born Oct 7, 1942, Atlanta, GA; son of James Nathaniel and Esther Pickett; married Berlinda Kay Brown; children: James Jr, Anika Diarra & Ekerin Ayobami. **Educ:** Clark Col, BA, 1963; Gammon Theol Sem Interdenominational Theol Ctr, BD, 1966; Northwestern Univ, PhD, 1975. **Career:** Interdenominational Theol Ctr, asst prof, 1975-80, chair church & soc dept, 1978-80; Wesley Theol Sem, Wash, DC, assoc prof, 1980-83, assoc dean, 1980-85, prof, sociol relig, 1983-. **Orgs:** Minister Bethlehem United Methodist Church, 1964-66, Burns United methodist Church, 1966-71, Ingleside-Whitfield United Meth Church, 1974-75. **Home Addr:** 6215 Sligo Mill Rd NE, Washington, DC 20011, **Home Phone:** (301)899-6417. **Business Addr:** Professor, Wesley Theological Seminary, 4500 Massachusetts Ave NW, Washington, DC 20016, **Business Phone:** (202)885-8600.

**SHORT, PROF. KENNETH L.**
Educator. **Personal:** Born Aug 21, 1943, Chicago, IL. **Educ:** Howard Univ, BSEE, 1966; State Univ NY, Stony Brook, MS, 1969, PhD, 1972. **Career:** State Univ New York, Stony Brook, Dept Elec Sci, 1968, asst prof, 1985, Dept Elec & Comput Engineering, dir, prof, currently; Nat Eng Consortium Inc, Schmitt Scholar fel, 1974. **Orgs:** Inst Elec & Electronic Engrs, 1964-; NY State Soc Prof Engrs, 1970-; NY Karate Asn, 1970-. **Honors/Awds:** Chancellor' Award for Excellence in Teaching, State Univ New York, Stony Brook, 1985; President's Award for Excellence in Teaching, State Univ New York, Stony Brook, 1985; Frederick Emmons Terman Award, 1987; Deans Award for Extraordinary Service, Col Engineering, State Univ New York, 1994; Excellence in Teaching Award, Col Engineering, 1994; Award of Honor for Excellence in Teaching, Elec Engineering Dept, State Univ New York, 1997. **Special Achievements:** Published 14 articles Author: Embedded Microprocessor Systems Design: Microprocessors and Programmed Logic, 1980, An Introduction Using the Intel 80C188EB, Prentice Hall, 1998, VHDL for Engineers, 2008. **Home Addr:** 5 Dale Rd, Stony Brook, NY 11790-1617. **Business Addr:** Professor, Stony Brook University, Light Engineering Bldg 229, Stony Brook, NY 11794-2350, **Business Phone:** (631)632-8403.

**SHORT, LESLIE**
Businessperson, chief executive officer. **Educ:** IMCR Dispute Resolution Ctr, mediation. **Career:** J. Men's Tokyo, owner; Montel Williams Show, assoc producer, 1994-96; Thirteen/WNET, music coordr; Macy's Dept Store, spec events mgr, 1996-97; KIM Media, pres & ceo, 2000-; FUBU, pres mkt, advert & pub rels, 1997-2007; Event Mgt USA, head trainer; K.I.M. Media LLC, owner, 2000-; Shark Branding, head, global initiatives & spec proj, 2012-15; Ascend Bereavement Mgt, owner, 2012-. **Orgs:** Adv bd mem, Chief Mkt Officers Coun; ISES-Int Spec Events Soc; Int Wedding Alliance Hong Kong; IMCR Mediation Ctr Bronx NY; chaplain, Ny Chaplain Task Force; global corresp, I-Meets; N Am Adv bd; adv bd pastoral care, Hofstra Univ; pastoral care vol, pastoral adv bd, Brooklyn Hosp Ctr. **Business Addr:** President, Chief Executive Officer, K I M Media LLC, 139 Cambridge Pl 2nd Fl, Brooklyn, NY 11238, **Business Phone:** (917)627-6974.

**SHOTWELL, ADA CHRISTENA**
Educator. **Personal:** Born Sep 5, 1940, Helena, AR; married Roy Edward. **Educ:** Southern Univ, Baton Rouge, BA, 1961; Univ Calif, Berkeley, teaching cert, 1962; Memphis State Univ, MEd, 1974; Univ Miss, PhD, 1986. **Career:** Clover Park Sch Dist, teacher, 1964-67; Memphis City Sch, teacher, 1968-75; State Tech Inst, teacher, 1975; State Tech Inst, dept head, develop studies, 1976-78; State Tech Inst Memphis Correctional Ctr, div head, correctional educ, 1978-; SW Tenn Comm Col, Lib studies & educ, prof, dean & prof emer, currently. **Orgs:** AVA, 1976-; TVA, 1976-; ATEA, 1976-; TTEC, 1976-; WTEA, 1976-; MACBE, 1976-; Nat Asn Black Amns Voc Educ, 1979-80; chap, bd dir, Black Black Crime Task Force, 1985;Nat Asn Advan Colored People, 1985; PUSH, 1985; Pierian Soc. **Home Addr:** 4506 Paula Dr, Memphis, TN 38116-7254, **Home Phone:** (901)398-1263. **Business Addr:** Dean, Liberal studies and education, 5983 Macon Cove Sulcer 220, Memphis, TN 38134, **Business Phone:** (901)333-4612.

**SHOWELL, HAZEL JARMON**
Educator. **Personal:** Born Apr 5, 1945, Macon, GA; children: Angela & Patrick. **Educ:** Del State Col, BA, eng, 1968; Univ Bridgeport, MA, guid, 1973. **Career:** Wm Henry Mid Sch, Dover, Del, teacher humanities, 1968-73, assoc prin, 1973-76; Univ Del, consult staff leadership, 1975; Dept Pub Instr, state supt, adult educ, 1976-; State Va, consr & evaluator, 1978; State Del, cons & police training, 1979; Groves Adult High Sch, Middletown, Del, prin, currently; Del Coalition Literacy Inc, dir, prin, currently; Appoquinimink Sch Dist, Appoquinimink Adult Continuing Educ Progs Sch, prin, 2004-. **Orgs:** Delta Sigma Theta, 1968; Women Vision Daring to Venture, Delta Sigma Theta Sor, Dover, DE, 1974; pres, Peninsula Sect Nat Coun Negro Women, 1976-79; chairperson, Social Justice Comn, NAPCAE, 1978; Dir, Comnof Affil Orgn (CAO), AAACE Leadership; bd mem, Am Asn Adult & Continuing Educ. **Business Addr:** Principal, James H Groves Adult High School, 504 S Broad St, Middletown, DE 19709, **Business Phone:** (302)378-5037.

**SHOWELL, MILTON W.**
Army officer, military leader. **Personal:** Born Apr 19, 1936, Baltimore, MD; married Alberta Graves; children: Keith & Kimberly. **Educ:** Morgan St Col, BS, 1958. **Career:** Logistic Vietnam, mgr med serv, 1966-67; Korea, 1971-72; AUS Europe, implemented race rels prog; Seminars Drug Abuse; Auth Bk; Dept Def Race Rels Inst, grad; Patrick AFB, FL, 1974. **Special Achievements:** First African American to win All Europe Winner Toastmaster's Dist Speech Contest, 1975. **Home Addr:** 7224 Easy St, Temple Hills, MD 20748-4117, **Home Phone:** (301)449-5735.

**SHOWS, MARK D.**
Meeting planner, chief executive officer. **Educ:** Wayne State Univ, BASc, acct, 1990; Univ Mich, Stephen M Ross Sch Bus, MBA, finance & gen, 1994. **Career:** Gen Motors, finance, 1994-99; Ford Motor Co, Purchasing, prog mgr, 2000-06; Selective Serv Syst, area coordr, 2002-06; New Detroit Real Estate Mgt, managing partner, 2002-07; ThyssenKrupp Mat NA, vpres, cent region, 2006-08; L&H Diversified Mfg, vpres sales & mkt, 2008; Link Resource Partners, partner, 2009-13; GIB Americas MI LLC, managing parter, 2013-. **Business Addr:** ManagingPartner, GIB Americas MI LLC, 1180 Franklin Rd SE, Marietta, GA 30067-8900.

**SHROPSHIRE, HARRY W.**
Financial manager, consultant. **Personal:** Born Apr 13, 1934, Asbury Park, NJ; married Kathleen Rae Nelson. **Educ:** Moravian Col, BS, econs & bus admin, 1957; Advan Training Mgt Prog, cert, 1972; Foreign Affairs Exec Studies Prog, cert, 1974; Financial & Econ Anal, 1976. **Career:** Emerson Radio & Phonograph Corp, NJ, acct, 1957-62; Hess Oil & Chem Corp, NJ, acct, 1962-65; US Dept State AID, auditor, 1965-70, acct mgr, 1970-75; foreign serv controller, 1975-86; Self-employed, financial mgt consult, 1986-. **Orgs:** Asn Govt Accountants, 1966-; Am Mgt Asn, 1976-; BYC Lounge. **Honors/Awds:** Certificate of Appreciation, US Dept State AID, 1974. **Home Addr:** 592 Trout Lake Dr, Bellingham, WA 98226-9032, **Home Phone:** (360)676-4683.

**SHUFORD, HUMPHREY LEWIS**
School administrator, dean (education), association executive. **Personal:** Born Nov 18, 1945, Wetumpka, AL; son of Robert and Cora; children: M Shondia & Monique. **Educ:** Ala A&M Univ, BS, 1969; Troy State Univ, advan studies, attended 1973; Univ Southern Ala, advan studies, attended 1974; Auburn Univ, advan studies, attended 1976; Ala State Univ, MS, 1978. **Career:** Atmore State Tech Col, coordr stud personnel; State Ala postsecondary educ syst, employee; Jefferson Davis St Jr Col; part time Sociol Inst; Jefferson Davis Community Col, dean extended servs. **Orgs:** Ala Col Personnel Asn, 1980-86; Ala Counsr Asn, 1980-86; Atmore State Tech Col Educ Asn, vpres, 1982-84, pres, 1984-86; vpres, pres, Progressive Civic Club, 1982-83; vpres, 1983, pres, 1985, Atmore Alumni Chap, Kappa Alpha Psi; bd mem, Atmore Chamber Com; Ala Educ Asn, 1986; Nat Educ Asn, 1986; Am Asn Coun, 1986, Ala Dem Conf, Hermon Lodge No 260; vice chmn bd, Escambia County Sch Bd, Atmore, Ala. **Honors/Awds:** Achievement Award, Progressive Club, 1979; Polemarch Award, 1981, Achievement Award, Atmore Alumni Chap Kappa Alpha Psi, 1981; Achievement Award, State Testing Prog, 1982; Special Service Award, Atmore Alumni Chap Kappa Alpha Psi, 1982; Southern Province Achievement Award, Kappa Alpha Psi, 1986; Chapter of the Year Award, Kappa Alpha Psi Frat, 1986. **Home Addr:** PO Box 902, Atmore, AL 36504, **Home Phone:** (251)368-2985. **Business Addr:** Dean, Jefferson Davis Community College, 220 Alco Dr, Brewton, AL 36426, **Business Phone:** (251)867-4832.

**SHULER, ADRIENNE**
Basketball player, basketball coach. **Personal:** Born Apr 24, 1969, Bowman, SC. **Educ:** Univ Ga, social work; Bellevue Univ, leadership. **Career:** Basketball player (retired), basketball coach; Univ Ga, pt guard, 1987-91; Lady Bulldogs, capt, 1990, 1991; Ind Fever; Marshall Univ, grad asst coach; Okaloosa-Walton Comm Col, asst coach, 1993-94; Ga Col & State Univ, 1994-95; Wash Mystics, guard, 1998; CSTV Networks Inc, women's basketball coach; Furman Col, asst coach, assoc head coach; Appalachian State Univ, Appalachian Mountaineers, head coach, 2002; Lady Pirates, asst coach, currently. **Business Addr:** Assistant Coach, Lady Pirates, Reedley High Sch, Reedley, CA 93654, **Business Phone:** (559)305-7100.

**SHUMATE, GLEN**
Executive. **Personal:** Born Sep 9, 1958, Sandusky, OH; son of John Wesley and Annie Ruth Henson; children: Darrin Wesley. **Educ:** Univ Toledo, Toledo, OH, BS, stud serv, 1982; Cleveland State Univ, urban affairs, 1989; Case Western Res Univ, Weatherhead Sch Mgt, attended 2007. **Career:** Cleveland State Univ & Case Western Res Univ, bus training; Univ Toledo, Toledo, Ohio, activ coordr, 1980-82, counr asst, 1982-83; Burlington Northern, Holland, Ohio, opers agt, 1983-84; Cimmaron Express, Genoa, Ohio, opers mgr, 1984-86; Hillcrest Hosp, Mayfield, Ohio, mgr patient support serv, 1986-88; Cleveland Indians, dir community rels, 1987-95; Cleveland Conv & visitors Bur, vpres tourism Sales & Mkt, 1995-2004; World Travel Mkt, pres, 2005-06; Call & Post, pres, 2006-08; COMMASA, commun, mkt & training consult, 2008-; Construct Employers Asn, vpres, pub affairs & educ, 2008-; Contractor Assistance Asn, exec dir. **Orgs:** Rainbow Hosp; Sickle Cell Anemia Advi Bd, 1989-95; coordr, United Way Campaign, 1990-93; bd mem, Esperanza Inc, 1991-95; C's Mus Cleveland, 1997-2002; bd dir, Leadership Cleveland, 1999; Am Bus Asn, 2001-05; bd dir, Tri C Jazzfest Cleveland; Cleveland Advert Asn; Stud Youth Travel Asn, 2001-05; bd dir, treas, Travel Professionals Color, 2006; Urban Scholastic Media Initiative, 2012; chmn, Diversity Comt; Nat Asn Mkt Developers; Ohio Travel Asn. **Business Addr:** Vice President, Construction Employers Association, 950 Keynote Cir Suite 10, Cleveland, OH 44131-1802, **Business Phone:** (216)398-9860.

**SHUMPERT, TERRANCE DARNELL (TERRY SHUMPERT)**
Baseball player. **Personal:** Born Aug 16, 1966, Paducah, KY; married DeQuita; children: 5. **Educ:** Univ Ky. **Career:** Baseball player (retired); Kans City Royals, infielder, 1990-94; Boston Red Sox, 1995; Chicago Cubs, 1996; San Diego Padres, 1997; Colo Rockies, 1998-2002; Omaha Royals, 2001; Los Angeles Dodgers, 2003; Tampa Bay Devil Rays, 2003.

**SHURNEY, DR. DEXTER WAYNE**
Executive, physician, association executive. **Personal:** Born Jul 15, 1958, Loma Linda, CA; son of Dr Green and Juanita; married Wanda Whitten; children: Simone J & Cameron. **Educ:** Loma Linda Univ, BS, biol, 1979; Howard Univ Col Med, MD, med, 1983; Univ Detroit Mercy, MBA, int finance, 1990; Med Col Wis, MPH, prev med & pub health, 1999. **Career:** Westland Med Ctr, surg staff physician, 1986-90; Blue Cross Blue Shield Mich, case mgmt dir, 1987-90, Network, HMO, med dir, 1990-92, planning sr assoc med dir, 1992-95, vp corp med dir, 1996, chief med officer, 1996-99; BCN, med dir, 1990-92; AMA, ACMQ deleg, 1999-; Am Health ways Inc, vpres & nat bus med dir, currently; Amgen, Chief Managed Care Govt Affairs Strategist, 2003-05; Healthways, sr vpres & chief med officer, 2005-08; Vanderbilt Univ, Grad Sch Bus, chief med dir-hr benefits, asst prof health policy, adj prof owen, 2009-13; Onlife Health, sci advisor, 2010-11; Cummins Inc, chief med dir & exec dir global health/wellness, 2013-. **Orgs:** Am Med Asn, 1988-; Hospice Southeast Mich, 1995-; Mich AIDS Fund, 1995-; Mich Environ Coun, 1997-; ed bd, JMgr Care, 1997-; steering comt, Drug-Free Mich Comn, 1997-; adv panel, Fed Int Health Funds, 1998-; co chair, Kids Immunization Initiative Detroit/Southeast Mich, 1998-; bd dir, Care Continuum Alliance, 2009-13; bd mem, Am Col Lifestyle Med, 2009-; bd mem, Integrated Benefits Inst, 2011-. **Honors/Awds:** Detroit Med Soc, Community Service Award, 1998. **Home Addr:** 2525 W End Ave Suite 500, Nashville, TN 37203, **Home Phone:** (615)343-3825. **Business Addr:** Chief Medical Director, Executive Director, Cummins Inc, 500 Jackson St, Columbus, IN 47201, **Business Phone:** (812)377-5000.

**SIDBURY, HAROLD DAVID**
Business owner, executive. **Personal:** Born Sep 15, 1940, Hampstead, NC; married Vivian Ann Radd; children: Timothy, Channeta, Felicia, Colette, Harold Jr, Jarvis & Ingar. **Educ:** Cape Fear Tech, attended 1960, Kittrell Col, attended 1966. **Career:** African Methodist Episcopal Church, pastor, 1966-87; Gen Contractor, 1974-87; SCC Construct Co, owner, 1974-2013, pres. **Orgs:** Chmn, Coun Bd Educ Pender co, 1960-85; E Gate Masonic Lodge No 143, 1965-; chmn bd trustee, Grand United Order Salem, 1978-85, chmn bd dir, 1985-87. **Honors/Awds:** Appreciation Award, Neighborhood Housing Develop Wilmington Chap, 1979; Designing & Building Award, Grand United Order Salem Bldg, 1982; Most Outstanding Minister of Year, Black Caucus Robeson Co, 1984. **Home Addr:** 367 Union Bethel, Hampstead, NC 28443, **Home Phone:** (910)324-5670. **Business Addr:** President, SCC Construction Co, 1301 Castle St, Wilmington, NC 28401-5422, **Business Phone:** (919)762-5353.

**SIEVERS, ERIC SCOTT**
Football coach, executive, football player. **Personal:** Born Nov 9, 1957, Urbana, IL. **Educ:** Univ Md, attended 1980. **Career:** Football player (retired), football coach, executive; San Diego Chargers, tight end, 1981-88; Los Angeles Rams, 1988; New Eng Patriots, tight end, 1989-90; Langley High freshmen team, asst football coach; Gen Motors Corp, mgr, 2008; Lindsay Cadillac, sales mgr, currently. **Orgs:** Numerous memships including, Arlington Better Sports Club, 1991; Wash-Lee High, 2002. **Honors/Awds:** Numerous awards including Maryland's Offensive Lineman of the Year; Outstanding Senior Award; AV Williams Award, 1980; played in AFC Championship Game, post-1981 season; Virginia High School Hall of Fame, 1997. **Business Addr:** Sales Manager, Lindsay Cadillac of Alexandria, 1525 Kenwood Ave, Alexandria, VA 22302, **Business Phone:** (703)998-6600.

**SIFFORD, DR. CHARLES L. See Obituaries Section.**

**SIGLAR, RICKY ALLAN**
Executive, football player. **Personal:** Born Jun 14, 1966, Albuquerque, NM; married Janice; children: Jovante O'Neill. **Educ:** San Jose State Univ, attended 1988. **Career:** Football player (retired), business owner; San Francisco 49ers, tackle, 1990; Kans City Chiefs, right tackle, 1993-96, 1998; New Orleans Saints, tackle, 1997-98; Carolina Panthers, 1998; Tri-Union & Assocs, owner; Myotraining, trainer, co-owner, currently. **Orgs:** Chmn, Kans City Ambassadors, 2006-; Caring Athletes Touching Children's Hearts; Urban Youth Develop; youth care &counr, Gillis Ctr. **Home Addr:** 10408 Eden Dr NE, Albuquerque, NM 87112, **Home Phone:** (505)296-5110. **Business Addr:** Owner, Tri-Union & Associates, 12721 Outlook, Shawnee Mission, KS 66209-3667, **Business Phone:** (913)915-8659.

**SIGLER, I. GARLAND**
Executive. **Personal:** Born Dec 7, 1932, Bessemer, AL; married Bertha; children: Glenn Garland & Ennis Stevenson. **Educ:** Pa State Univ; Temple Univ. **Career:** SE PA Transp Authority, ino agt, 1960-; Philadelphia HS Girls, instr, 1967-; Sigler Travel Serv & Ticket Agency, pres, owner; Comn Serv Ctr, exec dir, 1970-; Teamster Local 161 Intl Brotherhood Teamster, vpres, 1972-. **Orgs:** C's pgm dir, Nat Med Assoc, 1971; pres, Transit Roundtable Philadelphia; pres, York 15 Home Assoc; life mem, Nat Asn Advan Colored People; dir, N Philadelphia Br, 1972-73. **Home Addr:** 6240 N 15 St, Philadelphia, PA 19141. **Business Addr:** President, Owner, Sigler's Travel Svc, 1318 W Olney Ave, Philadelphia, PA 19141-3107, **Business Phone:** (215)924-1330.

**SIGUR, WANDA ANNE ALEXANDER**
Engineer. **Personal:** Born May 26, 1958, New Orleans, LA; daughter of Alvin Maurice and Louella Clara Boyd; married Michael Gerard; children: Michael Jr & Gregory. **Educ:** Rice Univ, Houston, Tex, BS, mech & mat sci engineering, 1979; Tulane Univ, MBA. **Career:** Gen Elec, Houston, Tex, lab technician, 1977-79; Martin Marietta Manned Space Systs, New Orleans, La, sect chief & mat engr, 1979-; Gen Elec, lab technician; Lockheed Martin Corp, mgr, Design & Anal, 1996, dir, Engrg & Technol Labs, 2000, vpres, External Tank Proj, currently. **Orgs:** Soc Advan Mat & Process Engrg, 1983-90; Treas, Am Inst Aerospace & Astronaut, 1988-90. **Honors/Awds:** R&D Investigator Award, Martin Marietta Corp, 1986; Author Award, Martin Marietta Corp, 1987; Author Award, AIAA, 1988; Technology Disclosure Award, US Patent & Technology Disclosure Office, 1989; Principal Investigator of the Year, Martin Marietta Corp, 1989. **Home Addr:** 6828 Glengary Rd, New Orleans, LA 70126, **Home Phone:** (504)246-4825. **Business Addr:** Vice President, External Tank Project, Lockheed Martin Corp, 1401 Del Norte St, Denver, CO 80221-6910, **Business Phone:** (303)430-2004.

**SILAS, DENNIS DEAN**
President (organization). **Personal:** Born Jul 4, 1954, Beulah, MS; son of Flossie Bowie; married Brenda; children: Angela Denise. **Educ:** Delta State Univ, BS, 1976, MS, 1981. **Career:** Drew High Sch, sci teacher, 1976-92; Hunter Mid Sch, prin, 1992-94; Drew Sch Dist, technol coordr, asst supt, 1994, supt. **Orgs:** Friends Libr, 1988-2000; MAE, 1992-94; MECA, 1993-2000; chap pres, Phi Delta Kappa, 1994-2000; Miss Prof Educr, 1997-2000; area dir, bd dir & pres, Miss Prof Educr. **Honors/Awds:** Star Teacher, Miss Econ Coun, 1981, 1982, 1988 & 1992; SERVE, Prog Excellence, 1990; Administrator of the Year, Drew Sch Dist, 1995; Spotlight School, Miss Dept Educ, 1999; Exemplery Program Award, Nat Rural Educ Asn, 2000. **Home Addr:** 1117 Morgan St, Cleveland, MS 38732, **Home Phone:** (662)608-6677. **Business Addr:** Board of Director, Mississippi Professional Educators, 1117 Morgan St, Cleveland, MS 38732-3513, **Business Phone:** (662)745-6657.

**SILAS, PAUL THERON, SR.**
Basketball coach, basketball player. **Personal:** Born Jul 12, 1943, Prescott, AR; married Carolyn E; children: Paula & Stephen. **Educ:** Creighton Univ, Omaha, NE, 1964. **Career:** Basketball player, basketball coach (retired); St Louis Hawks, forward, 1964-68; Atlanta Hawks, 1964-69; Phoenix Suns, 1969-72; Boston Celtics, 1972-76; Denver Nuggets, 1976-77; Seattle Supersonics, forward, 1977-80; San Diego Clippers, head coach, 1980-83; NJ Nets, asst coach, 1988-89, 1992-95; New York Knicks, asst coach, 1989-92; Phoenix Suns, asst coach, 1995-97; Charlotte Hornets, asst coach, 1997-99, head coach, 1999-2002; New Orleans Hornets, head coach, 2002-03; Cleveland Cavaliers, head coach, 2003-05; Charlotte Bobcats, head coach, 2010-12; Entertainment & Sports Programming Network, analyst. **Orgs:** Pres, NBA Players Asn, 1974-80. **Honors/Awds:** NBA Draft, 1964; NBA All-Star Team, 1972 & 1975; NBA All-Defensive Team. **Home Addr:** 2463 Peninsula Shores Ct, Denver, NC 28037-7655.

**SILAS-BUTLER, ESQ. JACQUELINE ANN**
Lawyer. **Personal:** Born Aug 20, 1959, Middletown, OH; daughter of Frank and Elizabeth Peterson; married Lawrence Berry Jr. **Educ:** Ohio State Univ, BA, hist & polit sci, 1981; Univ Akron Sch Law, JD, 1984. **Career:** Parms, Purnell, Stubbs & Gilbert, law clerk, 1982-83; Jones Day Reavis & Poque, law clerk, 1983-84; Akron Metro Housing Auth, legal intern & Hearing officer, 1983-84; Summit Co Prosecutor's Off, asst prosecuting atty, 1984-87; Parms Purnell Gilbert & Stidham, assoc, 1985-86; Robinson Smith & Silas Law Firm, atty & partner, 1986-87; Akron Metrop Housing Authority, Akron, Ohio, chief legal coun, 1987-89; pvt pract atty, 1989-91; Univ Akron Sch Law, assist admis dir, 1990, adj prof; Summit Co Juv Ct, ct referee, 1991-; Proj GRAD Akron, exec dir, 2006-; Summit Co Domestic Rels Ct, magistrate. **Orgs:** Vip, Black Law Students Asn, 1981-84; Akron Alumnae Chap, Dist Sorority, 1984-, pres, 1990-; Akron Barristers Club, 1984-; vip, 1985-87, pres, 1987-90; bd mem, Akron Area YWC, 1987-90; Young Lawyers Comn, 1986-87; Akron Bar Asn, 1986-91, Judicial Eval Comn, 2014-, Strategic Planning Comn, 2015-; Nat Bar Asn, 1986-91; Nat Asn Black Women Atty, 1986-90; OH State Bar Asn, 1986-90; Bus Network Connection, 1986-88; bd mem, secy, E Akron Ct House, 1986-88; bd mem, Western Res Girl Scout Coun, 1989-; Jr League Akron, 1989-; bd mem, Akron Summit Community Action Agency, 1991-; Wesley Temple AME Zion Church; bd mem, Summit Co Am Red Cross, 1992-; NCW, 1992-; bd dir, Akron Roundtable, 2009, pres, 2014-15, vpres, 2013-14, chair, fund develop comt, 2013-14, chair, governance comt, 2015-; Akron Br, Nat Asn Advan Colored People; pres, Univ Akron Law Alumni Asn; pres, Akron Barristers Asn; Leadership Akron Alumni Asn; bd dir, United Way Summit Co; chap pres, Delta Sigma Theta Sorority Inc. **Honors/Awds:** Member of the Year, Black Law Students Asn, 1984; Senior Award, Black Law Students Asn, 1984; Delta Service Award, DST Inc, Akron Alumnae Chap, 1989; Community Service Award, DST Inc, 1988. **Home Addr:** 2081 Larchmont Rd, Akron, OH 44313, **Home Phone:** (330)867-4889. **Business Addr:** Executive Director, Project GRAD Akron, 400 W Market St Suite 1, Akron, OH 44303-2060, **Business Phone:** (330)761-3113.

**SILBERSTEIN, TRACEE JOY. See ROSS, TRACEE ELLIS.**

**SILER, BRENDA CLAIRE**
Public relations executive, association executive, executive. **Personal:** Born Oct 3, 1953, Washington, DC; daughter of Helen G and Floyd Howard. **Educ:** Spelman Col, BA, Eng, 1975. **Career:** Natl Ctr Vol Action, resource specialist, 1978-79; United Way Metro Atlanta, comm assoc, 1979-82; Rafshoon Shivers Vargas & Tolpin, acct exec, 1982; Siler & Assocs, owner pres, 1982-83; Am Red Cross Metro Atlanta Chap, asst dir pub rel, dir chap commun & dir external communs, 1983-89; AARP, communs rep, 1989-94, assoc state dir-commun, 2013-; Coun Competitiveness, dir communs, 1994-99; Am Speech-Lang-Hearing Assn, dir Pub Rels, 1999-2005; Independent Sector, dir Commun & Mkt, 2008-09; Best Commun Strategies, pres, owner & proj dir, 2005-; Prof Outplacement Assistance Ctr, Beltway Regional Affinity Group, facilitator, 2012-. **Orgs:** Chairperson, 1980, publicity chair, 1983, prof stand chair, 1984, Atlanta Asn Black Journalists; pub comn, Minority Bus Awareness Week, 1982; Bronze Jubilee Task Force, WETV, 1982-83; chaplain, Nat Asn Media Women, Atlanta, 1983; adv coun, United Ways Vol Atlanta, 1983-; second vpres, Nat Asn Media Woman, 1984-85; team capt, High Mus Mem Comt, 1985; bd mem, 1985-86, vpres, 1987, Atlanta Womens Network; Nat Asn Mkt Developers; vpres, int bd dir-at-large & int chairwoman, Int Asn Bus Communicators, 1990-99; Capital Press Club, 1995-; bd advisor, judge, PR News, 2003-; pub rels dir, Speech-Lang-Hearing Asn, 1999-2005; nat dir commun & mkt, United Negro Col Fund, 2005-08; co-chair commitee, Nat Alumnae Asn Spelman Col, 2007-; vpres-commun & mkt, Independent Sector, 2008-09; vol advisor, Ctr Stud Opportunity, 2011-12; POAC-Beltway Reginal Affinity Group, co-facilitator, 2011-; elections judge, Bd Elections Montgomery County, 2012; corresp secy & chairperson-commun Chmn, Andrew Rankin Chapel, 2013-. **Honors/Awds:** Gold Award for Annual Report Writing, United Way, 1980; Outstanding Achievement in Public Relations, Nat Asn Media Women, 1980; Outstanding Young Women in America, 1981; President's Award, Nat Asn Media Woman, 1983-85; Chairman's Award, Atlanta Asn Black Journalists, 1984; hon mention for Annual Report Writing, Am Red Cross Commun Excellence, 1987; hon mention for Exhibits, Am Red Cross Commun Excellence, 1989; Outstanding Atlanta Hon, 1989; President's Award, Int Asn Bus Communicators, 1990; Award of Merit for Press Kits, Pub Rels Soc Am, Georgia Chap; Communicator of the Year Award, IABC. **Special Achievements:** First African American woman to be named chairwoman of the International Association of Business Communicators; contributed a chapter titled, "Research and Evaluation on a Shoestring" for the PR News guidebook titled, "Lessons Learned in the PR Trenches, " 2004. **Home Addr:** 1400 E W Hwy Suite 1020, Silver Spring, MD 20910-3260, **Home Phone:** (301)587-0027. **Business Addr:** Board Advisor, 9211 Corporate Blvd, Rockville, MD 20850, **Business Phone:** (800)777-5006.

**SILER, DR. JOYCE B.**
Educator, vice president (organization), president (organization). **Personal:** Born Jun 1, 1947, Siler City, NC; daughter of Ross and Juanita Womble; married Lloyd G Flowers; children: Rashad Flowers. **Educ:** NC Cent Univ, BS, 1967; Hunter Col, MS, 1976; Manhattan Col, MBA, 1983; Columbia Univ, Teachers Col, EdD, 1991. **Career:** Educator (retired); Nc Cent Univ. **Orgs:** Pres & vpres, New York Metrop Chap Nc Cent Univ Alumni Asn. **Home Addr:** 700 Columbus Ave Apt 11G, New York, NY 10025-6678, **Home Phone:** (212)866-7635. **Business Addr:** NY.

**SILVA, DR. OMEGA C. LOGAN**
Endocrinologist, president (organization). **Personal:** Born Dec 14, 1936, Washington, DC; daughter of Louis Jasper and Mary Ruth Dickerson; married Harold Bryant Webb; children: Frances Cecile. **Educ:** Howard Univ, BS (cum laude), 1958, chem, MD, 1967. **Career:** Physician, president (retired); NIH, chemist, 1963; Veterans Admin Med Ctr, intern med, 1967-68, resident 1968-70, res assoc, 1971-74, clin investr, 1974-77, asst chief endocrinol, Diabetic Clin, chief, 1977-96; Howard Univ, assoc prof to prof oncology, 1977-97; George Washington Univ, from asst prof to prof med, 1975-97, prof emer med, 1999. **Orgs:** Fel endocrinol, George Washington Univ, 1970-47; consult, FDA Immunol Panel, 1981-89; pres, Howard Univ Med Alumni, 1983-88; VA Adv Comn Women Veterans, 1983-88; gen res support review comt, NIH, 1984-89; pres, Am Med Womens Asn Br I, 1987-88; Am Med Women's Asn, vpres progs, 1997-99, pres, 2000-02; bd trustee, Howard Univ, 1991-97; bd dir, Health Care Coun; Nat Capital Area, 1995-. **Special Achievements:** First African American to awarded a Clinical Investigatorship in the Department of Veterans Affairs, 1974; First woman to be appointed president of the Howard University Medical Alumni; 1983. **Home Addr:** 354 N St SW, Washington, DC 20024, **Home Phone:** (202)554-9428.

**SILVER, DR. JOSEPH HOWARD, SR.**
Educator, administrator. **Personal:** Born Oct 19, 1953, Goldsboro, NC; son of Joel Sr and Augusta King; married Rosalyn Smalls; children: Crystal & Joseph H Jr. **Educ:** St Augustine's Col, BA, 1975; Atlanta Univ, MA, 1977, PhD, 1980. **Career:** Kennesaw State Col, Marietta, Ga, prof polit sci, 1977-83, dir minority affairs & prof, polit sci, 1983-85; Ga bd regents, Atlanta, Ga, asst vice chancellor acad affairs, 1985-97; Savannah State Univ, vpres acad affairs, 1997-2007, prin investr, 2003-; Clark Atlanta Univ, provost & vpres acad affairs, currently; Ala State Univ, pres, 2012-. **Orgs:** Pres, Kathryn R Woods Scholar Fund, 1987-; pres, St Augustine's Col Alumni Asn, 1988-; pres & bd dir, Girls Inc Cobb County, 1990-92; pres, Nat Conf Black Polit Scientists, 1990-92; nat bd dir, Girls Inc; Am Red Cross Metro Chap, 1991-; vpres comn cols, Southern Asn Cols & Schs, 2006. **Home Addr:** PO Box 14592, Savannah, GA 31416, **Home Phone:** (912)898-1308. **Business Addr:** Provost, Vice President for Academic Affairs, Clark Atlanta University, 223 James P Brawley Dr SW, Atlanta, GA 30314, **Business Phone:** (404)880-8000.

**SILVER-PARKER, ESTHER**
Executive, president (organization), chief executive officer. **Educ:** NC Cent Univ, BA, polit sci; Columbia Univ, MA, jour; Pa State Univ, exec mgt prog. **Career:** Essence Mag, journalist; Rev Polit Econ, journalist; New World Outlook, journalist; NY telephones, pub rels officer; AT&T, entry level pub rels position, vpres corp affairs, found pres; Wal-Mart Stores Inc, vpres external diversity & vpres diversity rels, sr vpres corp affairs, 2003-10; SilverParker Group, founder, pres & chief exec officer, 2010-. **Orgs:** Pres, Int Womens Forum; bd, Nat Asn Advan Colored People Spec Contrib Fund; Atlanta Diversity Roundtable; Northwest Ark Diversity Coun; fel Dwelling Pl Church; pres, AT&T Found; bd mem, Global Food Banking Network, currently; bd mem, Spelman Col, currently; bd mem, Ark Women's Found, currently. **Honors/Awds:** Black Achiever in Industry Award, Harlem YMCA, 1998; Hon DHL, Benedict Col; 2007 Humanitarian Award, Just Communities; Catherine Cleary Award; Outstanding Women in Corporate Marketing, Ebony Magazine; Congressional Black Caucus Unsung Hero Award; DECA Award; Community Service Award; Atlanta Business League's Outstanding Corporate Person Award; 100 Black Men of America's Corporate Excellence Award; National AIDS Fund's Leadership Award; Asian Pacific Islanders Women's Leadership Starfish Award; Alpha Kappa Alpha President's Award; Northwest Arkansas' Just Communities Humanitarian of the Year Award; The New York Links Spirit Award; Alpha Kappa Alpha Corporate Citizen Award; Wal-Mart Unity Trailblazer Award; The National Coalition of 100 black Women Torchbearer Award; Links Spirit Award; Received more than 70 awards from national civic and leadership organizations. **Special Achievements:** Books: "Yes I Can Do That"; "Do You Giving While Living & Organizational Champions". **Home Addr:** , AR. **Business Addr:** Chief Executive Officer & Founder, President, The SilverParker Group, 105 NW 2nd St, Bentonville, AR 72712, **Business Phone:** (479)366-7205.

**SIMEUS, DUMAS M.**
Chief executive officer, executive. **Personal:** Born Jan 1, 1939, Pont Sonde; son of Mecene and Bonne; children: 3. **Educ:** Fla Agr & Mech Univ; Howard Univ, Wash DC, BS, 1966; Univ Chicago, MBA, 1972. **Career:** Stand Oil Corp, elec design engr; TLC Beatrice Int Holdings Inc, pres & chief exec officer, 1982-94; Simeus Foods Int, chief exec officer, chmn & founder, 1996-2004, bd dirs, 2008, investor; DMS Food Group, founder; Pacesetter Capital Group, operating partner; TLC Beatrice Foods, pres, chief operating officer, bd mem; Rockwell Int, financial analyst; KB Home, financial analyst; Bendix Latin Am Oper, dir; Hartz Pet Food, gen mgr; Atari Inc, exec staff; New Century Packaging, owner, chmn & chief exec officer, 2006-; Frontier Oilfield Serv, dir, 2013-14. **Orgs:** Bd mem, Greater Dallas Chamber Com; TGI Friday's; bd mem; Nat Org Advan Haitians; Dallas Forth Worth Minority Bus Develop Coun; pres, Simeus Found; bd Int Foodservice Manufacturers Asn; chmn, Caribbean Am Leadership Coun; fel Haitian Am Bus Develop Coun; Nat Orgn Advan Haitians; Dallas Urban League Inc; DF W Minority Bus Develop Coun; bd mem, BiGAustin; founder, Saving Lives, 2000; adv bd mem, Inter-Am Found, 2005-12; adv bd mem, UNT-Dallas, 2011-12. **Business Addr:** Chairman, Owner, New Century Packaging Systems, 9900 Pflumm Rd Suite 38, Lenexa, KS 66215, **Business Phone:** (913)227-0866.

**SIMIEN, TRACY ANTHONY**
Football player, football coach. **Personal:** Born May 21, 1967, Bay City, TX. **Educ:** Tex Christian Univ. **Career:** Football player (retired), coach; Pittsburgh Steelers, 1989; New Orleans Saints, 1990; Montreal Mach, 1991; Kans City Chiefs, left inner linebacker & mid linebacker, right inner linebacker, 1991-97; San Diego Chargers, linebacker, 1999; Cologne Centurions, defensive line coach, 2005-06, 2007; Houston

Texans, asst defensive line coach, 2006; Cologne Centurions, defensive line coach, 2007. **Orgs:** Simien Seniors Found.

### SIMMELKJAER, ESQ. ROBERT T.
Lecturer, lawyer, educator. **Personal:** Born New York, NY; son of Lenora and Carl; married Gloria J Foster; children: Robert Jr & Mark Allen. **Educ:** City Col NY, BS, polit sci, 1962, MA, polit sci, 1964; Columbia Univ, Teachers Col, EdD, admin sci, 1972, Bus Sch, MBA, indust rels/labor econs, 1977, PhD, pub admin; Fordham Univ Sch Law, JD, labor & employ, 1978. **Career:** Inst Educ Develop, exec asst to pres, 1969-71; New York Bd Educ, prin, 1971-74; City Col NY, prof ed admin, 1974-79, dean gen studies & vice provost acad admin, 1979-86; atty & arbitrator; Gov Adv Cms Black Affairs, exec dir, 1986-88; New York Transit Authority, admin law judge, 1988-90; Joint Comn Integrity Pub Schs, dep chief coun, 1989-90; Inst Mediation & Conflict Resolution, pres, chief exec officer, 1991-; Cornell Univ, adj fac; NJSBA, coordr; Sidney Reitman Employ Law Inn Ct, bencher; Labor Arbit Inst, Off-Duty Misconduct & Absenteeism Cases, lectr; George Meany Ctr Labor Studies, adj fac; NYSBA, secy, chair; Metrop Transit Authority, trial bd hearing officer; Govt Accountability Off, vice chair, personnel appeals bd; NYC Intermediate Sch, prin; Lincoln Tool Parts, machinist. **Orgs:** PERC, OCB, 1977-; minority sch fin network, Urban League & Nat Asn Advan Colored People, 1980-83; bd dir, Inst Mediation & Conflict Resolution, 1980-84; New York Task Force Equity & Excellence; Urban Coalition Local Sch Develop, 1980-83; bd dir, Inst Mediation & Conflict Resolution, 1980-92; vice chmn, Personnel Appeals Bd, US Acct Off, 1981-84; speaker, consult US Info Agency, 1981-84; consult, New York Univ Sch Bus, 1982-83; chmn, bd dir, Nat Acad Arbitrators, 1988-; consult, Ford Found, Nat Sch Fin Proj; Bar Asn City New York; DC Bar Asn; fel Col Labor & Employ Lawyers; pres, LERA, NJ Chap. **Honors/Awds:** New York State Regents Scholarship, 1957; US OE Ed fellowship, 1969-70; Great Cities res fel, 1971. **Special Achievements:** Chapter in a Quest for Ed Opportunity in a Major Urban School District, The Case of Washington DC, 1975; Finality of Arbitration Award, The Arbitration Forum, Fall, 1989; State Aid to Substantially Black School Districts, in Crisis and Opportunity Report New York; Federal Civil Service Lawand Procedure, Wash, DC, 1990: two chapters on collective bargaining and arbitration; author: From Partnership to Renewal, Evolution of an Urban Ed Reform, The Ed Forum, 1979; State Aid to Substantially Black School Districts, Crisis and Opportunity; Collective Bargaining Impasses in Federal Civil Service Law and Procedures, BNA, 1990. **Home Addr:** 29 Chestnut St, Haworth, NJ 07641-1905, **Home Phone:** (201)387-6397. **Business Addr:** President, Chief Executive Officer, Institute for Mediation & Conflict Resolution, 384 E 149th St Suite 330, Bronx, NY 10455, **Business Phone:** (718)585-1190.

### SIMMONS, ANTHONY LAMONT
Football player. **Personal:** Born Jun 20, 1976, Spartanburg, SC. **Educ:** Clemson Univ, mkt, 1998. **Career:** Football player (retired); Seattle Seahawks, linebacker & mid linebacker & left outside linebacker, 1998-2004; New Orleans Saints, 2006. **Honors/Awds:** Rookie of the Year; National Freshman of the Year, United Press Int; Consensus All-American, 1997.

### SIMMONS, BRIAN EUGENE
Football player. **Personal:** Born Jun 21, 1975, New Bern, NC. **Educ:** Univ NC, BS, sociol. **Career:** Football player (retired); Cincinnati Bengals, linebacker & left inside linebacker & mid linebacker, 1998-2000-02 & 2006, weak side linebacker, 2003, right line backer, 2004-05; New Orleans Saints, linebacker, 2007. **Orgs:** Univ NC 15 player Leadership Comm; hon chmn, Greater Cincinnati Northern Ky Walk Am, 2002. **Honors/Awds:** Consensus All-American, 1997; Defensive Player of the Week, Am Football conf, 2005; First All American Honors, Walter Camp Found.

### SIMMONS, DR. CHARLES WILLIAM
School administrator, founder (originator), president (organization). **Personal:** Born Jun 17, 1938, Baltimore, MD; son of Floyd Mays and Vivian Jordan; married Brenda Leola Hughes; children: Dominic, Natalie Bohannan, Wanda Williams, Anthony, Kojo, Rashida & Tacuma. **Educ:** Antioch Univ, AB, 1972; Union Grad Sch, PhD, admin higher educ, 1978; Harvard Univ, MA, 1984; Morgan State Col; Antioch Col, MA, hist & polit sci, urban develop & sociol. **Career:** Int Brotherhood Teamsters, field rep, 1964-67; Baltimore City Health Dept, dir health, educ & community orgn, 1967-74; Antioch Univ, Homestead Montebello Ctr, co-dir, 1972-80; Sojourner-Douglass Col, pres & founder, 1980-. **Orgs:** Nat Asn Advan Colored People, African-Am Empowerment Proj; Marine Corps AEC; bd dir, secy & bd mem, Nat Asn Equal Opportunity Higher Educ; co-founder & bd mem, Left Bank Jazz Soc, 1964-87; secy & bd dir, Nat Asn Equal Opportunity Higher Educ; Greater Baltimore Comt, 2000; Md Leadership, 2001; Coun Advan Experiential Learning; Cong Black Caucus Educ & Bus Brain Trusts; Asn Community Based Educ; Greater Baltimore Comt. **Special Achievements:** Sojourner-Douglass College first and only president. **Home Addr:** 100 Harbor View Dr, Baltimore, MD 21230, **Home Phone:** (410)347-3347. **Business Addr:** President, Founder, Sojourner-Douglass College, 200 N Cent St Suite 103, Baltimore, MD 21202, **Business Phone:** (410)276-4101.

### SIMMONS, CLAYTON LLOYD
Law enforcement officer, social worker. **Personal:** Born Sep 11, 1918, New York, NY; son of William Arthur (deceased) and Florence Albertha Forde (deceased); married Angela L Petioni; children: Janet, Sandra, Angela & Rene. **Educ:** Columbia Univ, BS, 1954, MS, 1969. **Career:** New York Dept Probation, probation officer, supv probation officer, proj coordr, equal employ opportunity officer, 1960-82; freelance pianist & keyboardist, 1983-; Upjohn Health Care Serv, contract social worker, 1984-85; ABC Home Health Fla Inc, social work consult, 1987-89; Best Western Hotel, pianist, 1988-92. **Orgs:** Nat Coun Crime & Delinq, 1962-83; chmn, bd dir, Youth Activ Community Inc, 1972-82; Rockland County, NY, Bd Commissioners Sewer DistNo 1, 1974-78; bd dir, Columbia Univ Sch Social Work, 1977-80; Rockland County, NY, Bd Gov Health Facil, 1977-79; jr warden, St Paul's Episcopal Church, 1977-82; vice chmn, Spring Valley, New York Dem Community, 1978-80; bd trustee, Village Spring Valley, NY, 1979-82; pres, Martin Luther King Jr Multi-Purpose Ctr, 1980-82; Vestry St Stephen's Episcopal Church, Silver Spring Shores Fla, 1984-88, 1995-; Comn Church Soc Cent Fla Episcopal Diocese, 1984-88; pres, St Stephen's Episcopal Church Men's Club, Ocala, Fla, 1987, 1988 & 1991; second vice comdr, Post 284 Am Legion, Belleview, Fla, 1988. **Honors/Awds:** Plaque, Club Personality Magnificent Job, Pres Spring Valley Nat Asn Advan Colored People, 1973-79; Cert Merit, Roberto Clemente Social & Cult Club Inc, 1974; Plaque, Carlton & Surrey Apts serv tenants, 1977; Guardsman Award, Nat Guard Bur, 1977; Distinguished Service Award, Rockland County, 1977, 1979 & 1982; Plaque for Outstanding Leadership & Intensified Struggle Minorities, First Baptist Church, 1978; Certificate of Apppreciation, Off Dist Atty Rockland County, 1980; New York State Senate Achievement Award, 1981; Cert Merit, New York State Assembly, 1981; Plaques, Outstanding Serv Village Spring Valley, NY, 1982; Plaque, Outstanding & Dedicated Serv Nat Asn Advan Colored People & Community, Nat Asn Advan Colored People, 1982; Plaque, Haitian-Am Cult & Social Orgn Serv Community, 1982; Certificate of Apppreciation, 26th Cong Dist, 1982; CertMerit, Spring Valley, NY, Youth Coun Nat Asn Advan Colored People, 1982; Martin Luther King Jr, Multi-Purpose Ctr Inc, 1982; Award Clock, Black Dem Comt Men, 1982; Plaque, Black Polit Caucus Rockland County, NY, 1984; Cert Participation, Am Legion Post 284 Bellview, Fla, 1986; Cert Appreciaton, Off Gov State Fla, 1986. **Home Addr:** PO Box 7487, Ocala, FL 34472-7487.

### SIMMONS, CLYDE, JR.
Football player, football coach. **Personal:** Born Aug 4, 1964, Lane, SC; married Sandra; children: Jaison, Corey & Janaya. **Educ:** Western Carolina Univ, BA, indust distrib, 1996. **Career:** Football player (retired), football coach; Philadelphia Eagles, 1986, right defensive end, 1987-93; Ariz Cardinals, right defensive end, 1994-95; Jacksonville Jaguars, right defensive end, 1996-97; Cincinnati Bengals, right defensive end, 1998; Chicago Bears, 1999, defensive end, 2000; New York Jets, coach, 2010; Los Angeles Rams, asst defensive line coach, 2012-. **Orgs:** Omega Psi Phi Fraternity Inc. **Honors/Awds:** Pro Bowl selection, 1991, 1992; First-Team All-Pro selection, 1991, 1992, National Football League Sacks Leader, 1992. **Business Addr:** Assistant Defensive Line Coach, Los Angeles Rams, 29899 Agoura Rd, Agoura Hills, CA 91301, **Business Phone:** (314)982-7267.

### SIMMONS, CRAIG, SR.
Executive, vice president (organization). **Personal:** Born Sep 2, 1962, Riverside, NJ; son of William and Joan; married Dail St Claire; children: Rachel & Craig. **Educ:** Amherst Col, BA, 1984; Doshisha Univ, exchange stud. **Career:** Credit Suisse First Boston Corp, analyst, corp finance, 1984-85; Sumitomo Bank NY, asst treas, pub finance, 1985-87; asst vpres, int sales, 1987-90; Kankaku Securities Am Inc, vpres, fixed income, 1990-96; Cantor FitzgeraldCo, vpres; Ashland Capital Holdings, vice chmn, currently; Drexel Hamilton LLC, managing dir, capital markets, currently. **Orgs:** Campership steering comt, Boy Scouts Am, 1987-; vpres bd dir, One Hundred Black Men Inc, 1989-; bd vestry, St Bartholomew's Church, 1994-; adv bd, St Bartholomew's Community Preschool, 1994-; adv bd, Nat Asn Advan Colored People, 1994-95; vpres bd dir, Fifth Ave Tower Condominium, 1994-97. **Home Addr:** 445 5th Ave, New York, NY 10016. **Business Addr:** Vice Chairman, Ashland Capital Holdings LLC, 380 Lexington Ave 11th Fl, New York, NY 10168, **Business Phone:** (212)587-7666.

### SIMMONS, EARL
Rap musician, actor. **Personal:** Born Dec 18, 1970, Baltimore, MD; married Tashera; children: Tacoma, Xavier, Praise Mary Ella & Shawn. **Career:** Columbia Rec, rapper; Sony BMG, currently; Bloodline Rec, founder; Def Jam Rec; Albums: It's Dark and Hell is Hot, 1998; Flesh of My Flesh, Blood of my Blood, 1998; .. And Then There Was X, 1999; The Great Depression, 2001; Grand Champ, 2003; Year of the Dog.. Again, 2006; Walk With Me Now, You 'll Fly with Me Later, 2009; Redemption of the Beast, 2011; Undisputed, 2012. Films: Belly, 1998; Romeo Must Die, 2000; Exit Wounds, 2001; Cradle 2 The Grave, 2003; Never Die Alone, actor & producer, 2004; Lords of the Street, 2008; Last Hour, actor & assoc producer, 2008; Death Toll, actor & exec producer, 2008; Jump Out Boys, exec producer, 2008; The Bleeding, 2009; King Dog, 2013; Blame It On The Hustle, 2013. TV series: "Eve", 2003; "Third Watch", 2003; "Chappelle's Show", 2004; "DMX: Soul of a Man", actor & producer, 2006; "Couples Therapy", 2012; "Iyanla, Fix My Life", 2013. Songs: "Born Loser", 1993; " Time To Build", 1995; "Usual suspects", 1997; "Money, Power & Respect", 1998; "We Got This", 1998; "Dog & A Fox", 1999; "Scenario 2000", 1999; "Tales from the Darkside", "Get it Right", 2000; "Scream Double R", 2001; "Walk with Me", 2001; "Most High", 2002; "Deeper", "What's Really Good?", 2003; "Lets Get Crazy", "Put Your Money", 2004; "Get Wild", 2005; "Innocent Man", 2006; "Gonna Get Mine", 2007; "Bad Boys", 2008; "Intro", 2008; "Who's Real", 2009. **Honors/Awds:** American Music Award, Favorite Rap/Hip-Hop Artist, 2000. **Business Addr:** Musician, Def Jam Recordings, 160 Varick St 12th Fl, New York, NY 10013, **Business Phone:** (212)229-5200.

### SIMMONS, DR. ELLAMAE
Physician. **Personal:** Born Mar 26, 1919, Mt. Vernon, OH; daughter of G L and Ella Cooper; children: Delabian, Diana, Daphne & Debra. **Educ:** Hampton Inst, RN, 1940, MA, 1950; Meharry Med Col, grad stud, 1955; Howard Univ, MD, 1959; Ohio State Univ, BS, 1948; Ohio State Univ, MA, 1958. **Career:** Physician (retired); Practiced nursing at var hosps, 1940-42, 1950-51; Bellevue Hosp, med social worker, 1951-53; Wayne Co Hosp, intern; Univ Co Med Ctr, resident, 1962-63; Nat Jewish Hosp, resident chest med & allergy, 1963-65; Kaiser Found Hosp, allergist. **Orgs:** AMA; Admis Com Univ Calif Sch Med, 1974-79; Calif & San Francisco Med Soc; John Hale Med Soc; Am Acad Allergy; Am Med Womens Asn, CA; Mutual Real Estate Investment Trust; No Calif Med Dent Pharmaceut Asn; Univ CA, San Francisco Sch Med Admis Com, 1974-79; Nat Asn Advan Colored People, Urban League. **Honors/Awds:** Certifcate of Recognition, CA State Senate & CA Legislature Assembly, 1990; Women of Distinction, Soroptomist Int, 1995; Award for Dedication & Commitment to Service, Martin Luther King Family Health Ctr, 1994; Presidential Citizenship Award, Hampton University, 2007. **Special Achievements:** First African American woman physician hired at Kaiser Permanente. **Home Addr:** 3711 Clay St, San Francisco, CA 94118, **Home Phone:** (415)386-5257.

### SIMMONS, ESMERALDA
Lawyer, school administrator, executive. **Personal:** Born Dec 16, 1950, Brooklyn, NY; daughter of Frank V and Esmeralda Benjamin; married Lesly Jean Jacques; children: 3. **Educ:** Hunter Col, City Univ NY, BA, 1974; Brooklyn Law Sch, JD, 1978. **Career:** NY Col Law Dept, hons atty, civil rights employ unit, 1978-79; US Dist Ct US Dist Judge Henry Bramwell, law clerk, 1979-80; US Dept Educ Off Civil Rights, reg civil rights atty, 1980-82; NY Dept Law Atty Gen's Off, asst atty gen, 1982-83; NY State Div Human Rights, first dep comnr, 1983-85; Medgar Evers Col, Ctr Law & Social Justice, exec dir, currently. **Orgs:** Nat Conf Black Lawyers, 1975-; Nat Bar Asn, 1979-; pres, Bedford Stuyvesant Lawyers Asn, 1981-84; legal comt chair, Coalition Community Empowerment, 1983-91; bd dir, Metro Black Bar Asn, 1984-91; vice chair, NY City Districting Comn, 1990-92; bd mem, Fund City NY, 1990-00; NYC Bd Ed, 1993-94; Appl Res Ctr, 1997; bd dir, Vallecitos Mountain Refuge; Poverty & Race Res Action Coun. **Home Addr:** 272 Hancock St, Brooklyn, NY 11216, **Home Phone:** (718)789-9609. **Business Addr:** Executive Director, Founder, Medgar Evers College, 1150 Carroll St, Brooklyn, NY 11225, **Business Phone:** (718)804-8893.

### SIMMONS, FRANK
Automotive executive. **Career:** Hill Top Chrysler Plymouth, pres, currently. **Orgs:** Bd mem, Chrysler Minority Dealer Asn; vice chmn, bd Vols Am; Coun Better La. **Business Addr:** President, Hilltop Chrysler & Plymouth Inc, 940 N Beckley St, Lancaster, TX 75146, **Business Phone:** (972)230-2300.

### SIMMONS, FREDDIE SHELTON WAYNE
Social worker. **Personal:** Born Jun 14, 1966, Allendale, SC; son of Ella Mae. **Educ:** Univ SC, Columbia, SC, BS, psychol, 1988; Grad Sch Columbia, SC, attended 1997. **Career:** Univ SC, Col Pharm, res asst, 1986-87; SCA Prog, asst line, Off Lt Gov Nick Theodore, data entry specialist, 1987-88; SCA Dept Social Serv, social servs specialist II, 1988-93, self sufficiency case mgr, 1996-; Carolina Boys Home, prog dir, 1999-2000; Verizon Wireless Corp, corp employee trainer, 2001-. **Orgs:** Bd Social Work, licensed bac caulaureate, social work, 1989; bd mem, SCA State Employees Asn, Allendale Chap, 1989-93; adult choir, pres, Macedonia Christian Methodist Episcopal Church, Sunday Sch, 1996-, supt, 1998-, trustee, 1998-. **Honors/Awds:** Meritorious Biology Society, Omni Biol Soc, 1982; Honor Student, Psi Chi Honor Society, Univ SC, Columbia, 1986; Outstanding College Students of America, Outstanding College Student Award, 1987; Outstanding Young Americans, Outstanding Young American Award, 1998. **Home Addr:** 2020 Memorial Dr, Cayce, SC 29033, **Home Phone:** (803)796-8347. **Business Addr:** Corporate Employee Trainer, Verizon Wireless Corp, 398 Barnvell, Columbia, SC 29204, **Business Phone:** (803)400-4000.

### SIMMONS, GERALDINE CROSSLEY
Lawyer. **Personal:** Born Feb 17, 1939, Chicago, IL; daughter of Ivey Moore and Hosea H Crossley Sr; children: Stacey Elizabeth. **Educ:** Roosevelt Univ, BA; John Marshall Law Sch, JD, 1981. **Career:** Scott Foresman & Co, dir copyrights & permission contracts, 1965-80; Ill Appellate Ct, judicial law clerk, 1981; US Ct Appeals 7th Circuit, staff atty, 1981-83; Wash, Kennon, assoc, 1983-84; Law Off Geraldine C Simmons, atty, 1984-; Roosevelt Univ Paralegal Prog, instr, 1985-86. **Orgs:** Bd mem, Cook County Bar Asn, 1985-2009, pres, 1989-90; Nat Bar Asn, 1985-2010; pres, bd mem, bd mem emer, John Marshall Law Sch Alumni Asn, 1990-2011; Alpha Gamma Phi, 1992-2010; Am Bar Asn; Women's Bar asn; Black Women Lawyers Asn, 1994-2009; Ill State Bar Asn; Chicago Bar Asn; Sojourner's Polit Action Comt; adv bd, State Literacy; Pkwy Community House. **Honors/Awds:** Nathan Burkan Copyright Competition, John Marshall Law Sch, 1979; Law Review, John Marshall Law Sch, 1981; Distinguished Serv Award, Cook County Bar Asn, 1985, 1995, 1996, 1997; Businesswoman of the Year, Pkwy Community Ctr, 1986; Distinguished Service Award, John Marshall Law Sch, 1990; Nat Bar Asn Award, 1996; Presidential Award; Numerous awards, CCBA. **Business Addr:** Attorney, Law Office of Geraldine C Simmons, 7316 S Cottage Grove Ave, Chicago, IL 60619-1910, **Business Phone:** (773)994-2600.

### SIMMONS, HENRY OSWALD, JR.
Actor. **Personal:** Born Jul 1, 1970, Stamford, CT; son of Henry and Aurelia; married Lauren Sanchez; married Sophina Brown. **Educ:** Franklin Pierce Col, BA, bus, 1992. **Career:** Fortune 500; Films: Above the Rim, 1994; On the Q.T., 1999; Let It Snow, 1999; Snow Days, 1999; A Gentlemen's Game, 2002; Taxi, 2004; Are We There Yet, 2005; Something New, 2006; Madea's Family Reunion, 2006; The Insurgents, 2006; South of Pico, 2007; World's Greatest Dad, 2009; From the Rough, 2013; No Good Deed, 2014; TV series: "Saturday Night Live", 1994; "The Cosby Mysteries", 1994; "New York Undercover", 1994-95; "One Life to Live", 1997; "Another World", 1997-99; "NYPD Blue", 2000-05; Spartacus, 2004; Lackawanna Blues, 2005; "Pepper Dennis", 2006; "Shark", 2006-08; "The Cleaner", 2009; Georgia O Keeffe, 2009; "CSI: Miami", 2009; "Raising the Bar", 2009; "Man Up", 2011; "Let's Stay Together", 2011; "Common Law", 2012; "Coogan Auto", 2013; "Bones", 2013; "Second Generation Wayans", 2013; "Stalkers", 2013; "Ravenswood", 2014; "Agents of S.H.I.E.L.D., 2014"; "Law & Order: Special Victims Unit", 2014; "Reckless", 2014; "Transparent ", 2014; "Saint Francis", 2014. **Honors/Awds:** The 16th Annual Soap Opera Awards, 2000; Grand Jury Prize, Am Black Film Festival, 2007. **Business Addr:** Actor, c/o Gersh Agency Incorporation, 232 N Canon Dr, Beverly Hills, CA 90210, **Business Phone:** (310)274-6611.

### SIMMONS, DR. HOWARD L.
School administrator, educator. **Personal:** Born Apr 21, 1938, Mobile, AL; son of Eugene and Daisy. **Educ:** Spring Hill Col, BS, sec educ & span, 1960; Ind Univ, MAT, slavic lang & lit, 1965; Fla State Univ, PhD, design & mgt post sec educ, 1975. **Career:** Educator (retired); Lake Shore High Sch, Fla, span & eng instr, 1960-61; Cent High Sch, Ala, russ & span instr, 1961-63; Ind Univ, NDEA fel, 1963-64; Forest Pk Community Col, Mo, chmn foreign lang dept, 1964-69; Northampton County Area Community Col, Pa, dean instrnl serv, 1969-74; Fla State Univ, EPDA fel, 1973-75; Comm Higher Educ, Mid States Asn, assoc dir, 1974-88, exec dir, 1988-95; Ariz State Univ, Div Educ Leadership & Policy Studies, prof & assoc dean, 1995-99, prof emer, 2000; Mor-

gan State Univ, Dept Advan Studies, advan studies, leadership, policy, chmn & prof, 2000-08; Sojourner Douglass Col, exec vpres, 2008-12; St Louis Community Col, fac; Northampton Community Col, fac; Lafayette Col, fac. **Orgs:** Bd mem, St Louis Teachers Credit Union, 1965-69; consult, 1969-; staff assoc, Am Asn Community & Jr Col, 1972-73; Phi Delta Kappa, 1972-; fel Am Coun Educ, 1972-73; exec dir & assoc dir, Mid States Comn Higher Educ, 1974-95; bd dir, Am Asn Higher Educ, 1974-75; Kappa Delta Phi, 1974-; sr researcher & vis scholar, Nat Ctr Postsecondary Governance & Fin Res Ctr Ariz State Univ, 1986-87; consult, Asn Dominican Univ Chancellors, Santo Domingo, 1987-; exec bd, Am Asn Higher Educ Black Caucus, 1989-92; Ariz State Bd Behavl Health Examiners, 1996-99; Coun Chiropractic Educ Comm Accreditation, 1999-; Accreditation Comm Acupuncture & Orient Med, 2002-; Nat Forum Info Literacy, 2003; adv coun, Am Psychol Asn, BEA, 2003-; Asn Study Higher Educ, 2000-; pub mem & chairperson, Accreditation Comn Acupuncture & Orient Med, 2003-; secy, Nat League Nursing Accreditation Comn, 2005-, policy bd, Nat Info Literacy Res Comt, 2006; fel Am Coun Exercise; fel Asn Am Indian Physicians. **Honors/Awds:** Grad Made Good Distinguished Alumnus, Fla State Univ, 1988; First Annual Diversity Award, Am Asn Higher Educ Caucuses, 1992; LHD, Sogourner-Douglas Col, MD, 1995; HHD, King's Col, PA, 1998; ETS-HBCU Research Scholar, 2003-; hon deg, Kings Col. **Special Achievements:** Published study "Involvement & Empowerment of Minorities and Women in the Accreditation Process," 1986, various articles in professional journals. **Home Addr:** 218 N Charles St Suite 604, Baltimore, MD 21201, **Home Phone:** (410)659-4197. **Business Addr:** Professor, Chairman, Morgan State University, 1700 E Cold Spring Lane, Baltimore, MD 21251, **Business Phone:** (443)885-1969.

### SIMMONS, JAMES, JR.
Chief executive officer, president (organization). **Personal:** Born Houston, TX. **Educ:** Kellogg Grad Sch Mgt; Tuck Sch Bus, Dartmouth, minority bus exec prog; Univ Houston, BBA, 1975. **Career:** Allied Bank Tex, vpres, 1971-82; Threading Serv, pres, 1982-90; Total Premier Serv Inc, chmn & chief exec officer, 2004-. **Orgs:** Prairie View A & M Univ; Tex Southern Univ; bd mem, Am Petrol Inst. **Business Addr:** Chairman, Chief Executive Officer, Total Premier Services Inc, 2211 Norfolk Suite 1100, Houston, TX 77028, **Business Phone:** (713)610-1100.

### SIMMONS, JAMES RICHARD
Administrator. **Personal:** Born Mar 1, 1939, Chicago, IL; son of Phyllis Isbell Jones and Oscar Lee; married Judith Marion Albritton; children: James Jr & David. **Educ:** Grinnell Col, BA, 1961; Univ Chicago, Sch Social Serv Admin, MA, 1964; Brandeis Univ, Heller Sch Advan Soc Policy, MM, 1984. **Career:** Ill Youth Comn, caseworker & team moderator, 1964-66; Ill C's Home & Aid Soc, caseworker & psychotherapist, 1966-69; Vols Am, state & exec dir & dir c's serv, 1969-71; Dept Polit Sci at Univ Wis Oshkosh, prof, chair; Chicago United Inc, dep dir, vpres & admin, 1984-. **Orgs:** Nat Asn Social Workers, 1964-72; Acad Cert Social Workers, 1966-72; deleg ill, White House Conf C, 1970; Nat Asn Black Social Workers, 1973-75; vpres, Grinnell Col Alumni Bd, 1973; bd mem, Planning Consortium C, 1973-75; bd mem, Ill Child Care Asn, Ill, 1975-76; Nat Social Welfare Sec Vol Am, 1980; dir, Pub Admin Prog; Nat Asn Blh Alumnack MBA's, 1986; pres, Hellen Sci, Brandeis Univ, 1986-. **Honors/Awds:** Minority Advocate-IL, US Small Bus Admin, 1989. **Home Addr:** 1218 W Albion Ave, Chicago, IL 60626, **Home Phone:** (773)262-5984. **Business Addr:** Vice President, Chicago United Inc, 300 E Randolph St E Pedway Dr, Chicago, IL 60601-5083, **Business Phone:** (312)977-3068.

### SIMMONS, PROF. JOHN EMMETT, III
Educator. **Personal:** Born Feb 6, 1936, St. Petersburg, FL. **Educ:** Morehouse Col, BS, 1957; Syracuse Univ, MS, 1961; Colo State Univ, PhD, 1971. **Career:** Educator (retired), professor emeritus; Univ Iowa; Albany State Col, Albany, Ga; Syracuse Univ; Rutgers Univ; Univ Cincinnati; Western Col Women, asst prof biol, 1965-68; George Wash Univ, Wash Hosp Ctr, res assoc, 1968-70; CO State Univ, asst prof physiol, 1971-72; Trinity Col, assoc prof biol, 1972-82, prof biol, 1982-97, prof emer biol, 1997-; Kuwait Univ, vis prof dept biol, 1974-75. **Orgs:** Soc Neuroscience; Endocrine Soc. **Home Addr:** 31 Woodland St Apt 5-P, Hartford, CT 06105, **Home Phone:** (860)522-6810. **Business Addr:** Professor Emeritus of Biology, Trinity College, 300 Summit St, Hartford, CT 06106, **Business Phone:** (860)297-2000.

### SIMMONS, JOYCE HOBSON (JOYCE ANN HOBSON-SIMMONS)
Accountant. **Personal:** Born Aug 1, 1947, Port Jefferson, NY; daughter of Nathan Edward Sr and Ada Rebecca Townes; married Leroy Jr; children: Leroy III & Victor. **Educ:** Essex City Community Col, attended 1971; Indian River State Col, AA, 1973; Am Inst Banking, basic cert, 1973; Fla Atlantic Univ, BBA, 1975. **Career:** Port NY Authority, personnel dept, police recruitment, world trade ctr, bldg construct dept, toll collector, 1969-71; First Nat Bank & Trust Co, auditor com loan dept, supv proof dept, 1971-75; Homrich Miel & Mehlich, staff acct, 1976-77; Westinghouse Comn Develop Group, staff supvr, 1977; JA Hobson Acct & Tax Serv, sole proprietor, 1978-95; Fla Dept Educ, dirbus & citizens partnerships, dir, 1995-97, Div Admin, dir, 1997. **Orgs:** Stuart/Martin City Chamber Com, 1980-82, 1992-95; pres, Am Bus Women's Asn, 1981-82; Martin Co Sch Bd, 1982-86, 1990-95; chmn, Martin City Sch Bd, 1982-86, 1993-94; dir, Girl Scouts Am Palm Glade Coun, 1982-86; FAU Alumni Asn, 1982-88; IRCC Adv Coun Acct & Fin, 1984-86; Martin Cty 4-HFound, 1984-86; bd trustee, IRCC, 1987; dir, C Serv Coun, 1988; dir, United Way Martin Co, 1990-95; Grad Leadership Martin Co, 1991-92; treas, Fla Sch Bd Asn, 1992-93, pres-elect, 1993-94, pres, 1994-95; Martin Mem Found Hosp Comm Coun, Am Acct Asn; pres, 1993-94, S Fla Consortium Sch Bd; Martin County Econ Coun; Republican Club; Exec Comt Coun 100; Fla Comn Community Serv Found; Fla Educ Found, 1997. **Home Addr:** 2322 Tina Dr, Tallahassee, FL 32301, **Home Phone:** (904)216-1702. **Business Addr:** Director, Florida Department of Education, 325 W Gaines St Suite 1532, Tallahassee, FL 32399, **Business Phone:** (850)245-0445.

### SIMMONS, JUANITA
Business owner, association executive, president (organization). **Personal:** Born Oct 4, 1950, Columbus County, NC; daughter of Raymond and Ethel; children: Karen Y. **Educ:** York Col, BA, speech, 1993; Toastmasters, pub speaking, 2012. **Career:** Salomon Bros, commun specialist, 1980-97; Goldman Sachs, commun specialist, 1980-2000; Mind Body Soul Connection, pub tv producer, 1995; Goldman Sachs, clientrep, 2000; Body Connections Health Club, personal trainer, aerobics instr, chief exec officer, owner, pres, 2000-; Salmon Smith Barney, staff. **Orgs:** Founder & vpres, Women Maintenance Orgn, pres, 1999-; dir, Neighborhood Housing Serv New York. **Home Addr:** 11311 209th St, Queens Village, NY 11429-2211, **Home Phone:** (718)479-0373. **Business Addr:** Chief Executive Officer, President, Body Connections Health Club, 18820 Linden Blvd, St. Albans, NY 11412-4028, **Business Phone:** (718)723-4060.

### SIMMONS, KELVIN
Executive, government official. **Personal:** Born Oct 4, 1963, Kansas, MO; son of Thurman (deceased) and Inez; married Lisa; children: Avery, Stepson & Bradley. **Educ:** Univ Mo, Columbia, BA, commun, BA, interdisciplinary studies, 1986; Univ Mo, Kans City, EMBA, 1999. **Career:** Kans City Coun, coun mem, 1997-2000; Mo Pub Serv Comn, comnr & chmn, 2001; Mo Dept Econ Develop, dir econ develop, 2003-; Swope Community Builders, pres & chief exec officer, 2006-; AM Develop LLC, founder, owner & chief exec officer, 2006-; State Mo Govt, chief admin oper officer, Comnr, 2009-; Gov Mel Carnahan, sr staff mem. **Orgs:** Vpres govt affairs, Swope Health Serv, 2005; Univ Mo-Columbia Alumni Asn; bd mem, Nat Asn Chief State Admin Officers; bd trustee mem, Mo State Employee Retirement Syst; bd mem, Mo Consol Health Care Plan; bd mem, Minority Bus Advocacy Develop Comn; Nat Asn Regulatory Utility Commissioners; Nat League Cities; Mo Munic League. **Home Addr:** . **Business Addr:** Chief Executive Officer, A M Development LLC, 2928 S Brentwood Blvd, St Louis, MO 63119, **Business Phone:** (314)963-1212.

### SIMMONS, KIMORA LEE
Fashion designer. **Personal:** Born May 4, 1975, St. Louis, MO; daughter of Vernon Whitlock Jr and Joanne (Perkins) Kyoko Syng; married Russell Simmons; children: Ming Lee & Aoki Lee; married Djimon Hounsou; children: Kenzo Lee Hounsou. **Educ:** Univ Calif, Los Angeles. **Career:** Model, 1989-; Baby Phat, chief exec officer & head design, 1999-2010; Feb 2007 launched Simmons Barbie doll; launched couture line, KLS, Fall, 2007-; launched four perfumes, Goddess, Golden Goddess, Seductive Goddess & Baby Phat Fabulosity; Diamond Diva jewelry line, 2004-; Phat Fashions. Pres & creative dir, 2007; JustFab, pres/creative dir, 2011. **Orgs:** EstabKimora Lee Simmons Scholar Fund at Lutheran High Sch N; active mem youth advocacy orgn Amfar, G&P Found, Keep a Child Alive, & Hetrick-Martin Inst; onBd Dirs at Rush Philanthropic. **Honors/Awds:** Tony Award, for Russell Simmons Def Poetry Jam (executive producer), 2003. **Special Achievements:** Book, Fabulosity: What It Is and How To Get It; presented by the mayor with the key to the city and March 18 2008 was named "Kimora Day" in St. Louis. **Business Addr:** President, Phat Fashions LLC, 512 7th Ave, New York, NY 10018, **Business Phone:** (212)391-3100.

### SIMMONS, MAURICE CLYDE
Marketing executive, executive director. **Personal:** Born Feb 15, 1957, Washington, DC; son of Clyde T (deceased) and Ada Blaylock (deceased); married Vicki Baker; children: Marcus & Shaun. **Educ:** Dartmouth Col, AB, 1979; Univ Pa Wharton Sch, MBA, 1986. **Career:** Procter & Gamble, sls rep, 1979-81, dist field rep, 1981-82, unit mgr, 1982-84; McNeil Consumer Prod Co, from asst prod dir to prod dir, mgr, customer support; Johnson & Johnson CFT, mkt mgr; Methodist Action Prog, exec dir, currently. **Orgs:** Nat Black MBA Asn, Philadelphia Chap, 1984-; reg coordr, Black Alumni Dartmouth, 1984, 1987; pres, Wharton Black MBA Asn, 1985; co-chmn prog develop, Nat Black MBA, 1987 Conf Comn. **Home Addr:** 5963 Woodbine Ave, Philadelphia, PA 19131-1206, **Home Phone:** (215)477-9683. **Business Addr:** Executive Director, Methodist Action Program, 100 W 10th St Suite 701, Wilmington, DE 19801, **Business Phone:** (302)225-5627.

### SIMMONS, NORBERT
Executive. **Career:** Atty & real estate developer; First Commonwealth Securities Corp, pres & chief exec officer, 1987-; Ballys Casino Lakeshore Resort, owner, 1991-. **Business Addr:** Owner, Bally Casino Lakeshore Resort, 1 Stars & Strips Blvd, New Orleans, LA 70126, **Business Phone:** (504)248-3200.

### SIMMONS, PAUL A.
Judge. **Personal:** Born Aug 31, 1921, Monongahela, PA; son of Perry C and Lilly P; married Gwendolyn; children: Paul Jr, Gwendolyn & Anne. **Educ:** Univ Pittsburgh, BA, 1946; Harvard Law Sch, JD, 1949. **Career:** Judge (retired); Pa RR, employee, 1941-46; SC Col Law, prof law, 1949-52; NC Col Law, prof law, 1952-56; gen pract, 1956-58; Monongahela, Pa, pvt pract, 1956-73; Clyde G Tempest, 1958-70; Hormell Tempest Simmons Bigi & Melenyzer, law partner, 1970-73; Common Pleas, Wash County, PA, judge, 1973-78; US Dist Ct, W Dist Pa, judge, 1978-90. **Orgs:** Am Bar Asn; Am Trial Lawyers Asn; Am Judicature Soc; Pa Bar Asn; Wash County Bar Asn; NC State Bar; Nat Asn Advan Colored People; Ind Benevolent Protective Order Elks World; Pa Human Rel Comn; Commonwealth Pa Minor Judiciary Educ Bd; Bethel AME Church; Alpha Phi Alpha; bd dir, Mon Valley United Health Serv; past grand atty, State Pa Most Worshipful Prince Hall Grand Lodge F&AM, PA. **Honors/Awds:** Two Human Rights Awards, Nat Asn Advan Colored People; Meritorious Community Service Award, Most Worshipful Prince Hall Grand Lodge; Lifetime Achievement Award, Pa Bar Asn, Minority Bar Comt, 1992; Hall of Fame, Nat Bar Asn, 1994. **Special Achievements:** First African-American in Pennsylvania to sit regularly as a Common Pleas Orphans Court judge; First African-American to become a U.S. District Judge for the Western District of Pennsylvania (1978; He was President Carter's First African-American judicial nominee). In 1965, was the First African-American to run statewide for a judicial office in Pennsylvania, and in 1975 was appointed judge of the Court of Common Pleas of Washington County (nominated by both parties in 1975 and elected to a full term). **Home Addr:** 700 Meade St, Monongahela, PA 15063-2200, **Home Phone:** (724)258-5079.

### SIMMONS, ROBERT L.
Football coach. **Personal:** Born Jun 13, 1948, Livingston, AL; son of Fred and Annabelle; married Linda Davidson; children: Brandon, Nathan & Lelanna. **Educ:** Bowling Green Univ, BS, phys educ, 1971, MS, stud personnel, 1972. **Career:** Football player (retired), coach; Bowling Green Univ, receivers coach, 1972-76; Univ Toledo, outside linebackers coach, 1977-79; WVa Univ, linebackers coach, asst coach, 1983-87; Colo Univ, outside linebackers coach, 1988-91, D-line coach, 1992-93, asst coach, 1993-94; Okla State Univ, head football coach, 1995-2000; Big XII Conf, vol consult, 2001; Notre Dame, 2002-04; Univ Wash, 2005-07; Boulder High Sch, head coach, 2013-. **Honors/Awds:** Big XII Conference Coach of the Year, 1997; Salt & Light Award, 1998; Distinguished Citizen Award, Boy Scouts Am, 1998. **Home Addr:** 4169 E 139th Pl, Thornton, CO 80602-8816, **Home Phone:** (574)243-6010. **Business Addr:** Head Coach, Boulder High School, 1604 Arapahoe Ave, Boulder, CO 80302, **Business Phone:** (720)561-2200.

### SIMMONS, RON
Wrestler, football player. **Personal:** Born May 15, 1958, Perry, GA; married Michelle Golden; children: 4. **Educ:** Fla State Univ. **Career:** Football player, wrestler, (retired); Cleveland Browns, Nat Football League, 1981-82; Tampa Bay Bandits, US Football League, 1984-85; Memphis Showboats, 1985; Prof wrestler: Extreme Championship Wrestling, 1994-95; World Wrestling Entertainment, 1996-2009. **Honors/Awds:** College Football Hall of Fame, 2008, Consensus All-American, 1979 & 1980. **Special Achievements:** First African American to win the WCW World Heavy weight Championship, & was thus the first officially recognized African American world heavy weight champion; TV Movie: Fully Loaded, 1998, 2000; No Way Out, 1998, 2000. **Business Addr:** Professional Wrestler, World Wrestling Entertainment, 1241 E Main St, Stamford, CT 06902, **Business Phone:** (203)352-8600.

### SIMMONS, RUSSELL WENDELL
Executive, music producer. **Personal:** Born Oct 4, 1957, Queens, NY; son of Daniel and Evelyn; married Kimora Lee; children: Ming & Aoki. **Educ:** City Col NY, Harlem Br, sociol, 1979. **Career:** Rush Producers Mgt, owner; Rush Model Mgt, partner; Krush Groove, film co-producer; Tougher Than Leather, film co-producer; Rush Artist Mgt, owner, Phat Fashion, developer, Russell Simmons' Def; Def Jam Rec, co-founder, owner, 1983-; Comedy Jam, producer HBO, 1992-; Nutty Prof, coproducer, 1996; Waist Deep, 2006, exec producer; Hip-Hop Summit Action Network, founder; Russell Simmons Music Group, owner, 2005-; Rush Commun, chmn & chief exec officer, 1991-; Global Grind.com, ed chief, 2009-; UN Slavery Memorial, Goodwill Ambassadors, 2009. **Orgs:** Chmn bd, Found Ethnic Understanding, 2001; Somaly Mam Found. **Business Addr:** Founder, Chief Executive ofìcer, Rush Communications Inc, 512 7th Ave Suite 43-45, New York, NY 10018-4603, **Business Phone:** (212)840-9399.

**SIMMONS, DR. S. DALLAS. See Obituaries Section.**

### SIMMONS, SHIRLEY DAVIS
Government official. **Personal:** Born Sep 3, 1941, Vaughn, MS; married Princeton G; children: Brenda S Gooden, Vernadette S Gipson, Princeton Jr, Katrina & Makeba. **Educ:** Tougaloo Col, cert AA; Jackson State Univ, cert; Mary Holmes Col, cert. **Career:** Madison County Sch, secy, currently. **Orgs:** First vpres, Nat Coun Negro Women, 1978; Summer Feeding Prog, coordr, 1979; chmn redress, Nat Asn Advan Colored People, 1980-82; publicity chmn, Women Progress, 1982; chmn personnel, Madison-Yazoo-Leake Health Clin, 1984; Energy Assistance, coordr, 1984; Madison County Sch Bd, 1984-; Proj Unity, 1985. **Honors/Awds:** Outstanding Contribution to Youth Award, Project Unity, 1983. **Home Addr:** Rte 3, PO Box 327, Canton, MS 39046. **Business Addr:** School Board Member, Madison County School, 1435 Way Rd, Canton, MS 39046, **Business Phone:** (601)859-5669.

### SIMMONS, STEPHEN LLOYD
Restaurateur. **Personal:** Born Aug 4, 1958, Boston, MA; son of Herbert and Sylvia; married Elizabeth; children: Alexander Charles. **Educ:** City Col San Francisco, hotel restaurant mgt, 1984. **Career:** Stanford Ct Hotel, roundsman, 1980-83; Campton Pl Hotel, chef de cuisine, 1983-86; Casa Madrona Hotel, exec chef, 1986-88; SS Monterey Cruise Ship, exec chef, 1988-89; One Mkt Restaurant & Lark Creck Inn, chef & partner, 1989-94; San Franciscos Stanford Ct hotel; Bubba's Diner, owner & chef, currently. **Orgs:** Bd mem, City Col Adv Bd, 1992-; bd mem, Full Circle Progs, 1993-96. **Honors/Awds:** James Beard House, Rising Star Chef, Am Cuisine, 1989; Cornell Univ, Cross Country Dining Prog, 1989; 100 Black Men, Top Black Chefs, 1993; Celebrated Chef World Pork Expo, Nat Pork Producers Coun, 1999. **Special Achievements:** Published Recipes include : Detroit Free Press, 1984-95, San Jose Mercury News, San Francisco Chronicle, Marin Independent Jour; presently working on cookbook; Nat Pork Producers Coun announced Stephen Simmons, chef & owner as a Celebrated Chef at the 1999 World Pork Expo in June. **Home Addr:** 182 Floribel Ave, San Anselmo, CA 94960, **Home Phone:** (415)459-7163. **Business Addr:** Owner, Bubba's Diner, 566 San Anselmo Ave, San Anselmo, CA 94960, **Business Phone:** (415)459-6862.

### SIMMONS, DR. SYLVIA Q. (SYLVIA JEANNE QUARLES SIMMONS)
Educator, administrator, association executive. **Personal:** Born May 8, 1935, Boston, MA; daughter of Lorenzo C Quarles and Margaret M Thomas Quarles; married Herbert G Simmons Jr; children: Stephen, Lisa & Alison. **Educ:** Manhattanville Col, BA, 1957; Boston Col, MED, 1962, Lynch Sch Educ, PhD, 1990. **Career:** ABCD Headstart Prog, soc serv suprv, 1965; Charles River Pk Nursery Sch, Montessori, teacher, 1965-66; Boston Col, reg sch mgt, 1966-70; Harvard Univ, assoc dean admis & financial aid, fac arts & sci, 1974-76; Radcliffe Col, assoc dean admis, financial aid & womens educ, dir financial

aid, 1972-76; Univ Mass Cent Off, assoc vpres acad affairs, 1976-81; Mass Higher Educ Asst Corp, sr vpres, 1982-; Am Stud Assistance Corp, exec vpres, 1992-95, pres, 1995-96, chief exec officer; Boston Univ, lectr educ, assoc trustee; Am Stud Assistance Serv Corp, pres; Boston Univ, lectr educ, currently; Exec Serv Corps New Eng, consult, currently, Educ Resources Inst Inc, vice chair, currently. **Orgs:** Exec Coun Nat Assoc Stud Fin Aid Admin; vpres, Eastern Assoc Fin Aid Admin; Mass Asn Col Minority Admin; consult, Dept Hew Off Educ Reg I; consult, Col Scholar Serv, Mass Bd Higher Educ; Rockefeller Selection Comn Harvard Univ; Delta Sigma Theta Nat; bd mem, Family Serv Assoc Boston, Wayland Fair Housing, Concerts Black & White, pres, Newton Chap Jack & Jill Inc, Boston Chap Links Inc, Boston Manhattanville Club; bd trustee, Manhattanville Col; bd trustee, Rivers Co Day Sch; bd mem, Cambridge Ment Health Asn; bd trustee, Simons Rock Col; chmn bd trustee, N Shore CC; pres, William Price Unit Am Cancer Soc; bd dir, MA Div1-90, Am Cancer Soc; bd trustee, Boston Col; mem bd, Mass Found Humanities, 1990-91; bd trustee, Merrimack Col; bd overseers, Mt Ida Col; bd dir, Grimes-King Found; bd trustee, Regis Col; bd mem, Anna Stearns Found; bd dir, Exec Serv Corps; bd trustee, Mt Ida Col, currently. **Honors/Awds:** Women Politics; Outstanding Young Leader Boston Jr Chamber Commerce, 1971; Boston College Bicentennial Award, 1976; Black Achiever Award, 1976; President's Award, Mass Educ Opportunity Prog, 1988; Human Rights Award, Mass Teachers Asn, 1988; Recognition of Contributions to Higher Education, Col Club, 1988; Educator of the Year, Boston Chap Asn Negro Bus & Prof Women's Club, 1989; Sojournore Daughters, 25 AFA Women Who Have Made A Difference, 1990; Honorary Degree, St Joseph's Col, 1994; Bishop James Healey Award, 1997; Honorary Degree, Merrimack Col; DHL, Boston Col. **Special Achievements:** First African-American female administrator at Boston College. **Home Addr:** 19 Clifford St, Roxbury, MA 02119-2120, **Home Phone:** (617)445-5014. **Business Addr:** Trustee Associate, Boston College, 140 Commonwealth Ave, Chestnut Hill, MA 02467, **Business Phone:** (617)552-8000.

### SIMMONS, THELMA M.
Executive, manager. **Personal:** Born Aug 10, 1942, Bastrop, LA; daughter of Charlie Cross and Leona Averitt Cross; married Arthur; children: R Stevonne, Eric & Brenda. **Educ:** Western Wash State Col, human resources, 1979. **Career:** Pac Nw Bell, Seattle, supvr, mgr, 1965-76, staff mgr, 1976-79, mgr, operator serv, 1979-82, exec asst, 1982-84; AT&T, Seattle, carrier selection mgr, 1984-85, Oakland, Calif, reg diversity mgr, 1985-88, San Francisco, Calif, reg compensation mgr, 1988-. **Orgs:** Lifetime mem, Nat Asn Advan Colored People, 1965-; Delta Sigma Theta, 1979-; Seattle Women's Comm, 1981-83; chairperson, human resource comm, Oakland Pvt Indust Coun, 1987-. **Honors/Awds:** Future Black Leaders of the 80's, Black Elected Officials, Wash State, 1980; Certificate of Appreciation, Mayor of Oakland, 1990. **Home Addr:** 153 Mountain Valley, Oakland, CA 94605, **Home Phone:** (510)430-8884. **Business Addr:** Regional Compensation Manager, Human Resources, AT&T Western Region, Rm 2147 795 Folsom St, San Francisco, CA 94107, **Business Phone:** (415)442-2902.

### SIMMONS, TONY DEANGELO
Football coach, football player. **Personal:** Born Dec 8, 1974, Chicago, IL. **Educ:** Univ Wis-Madison, BS, construct admin. **Career:** Football player (retired), coach; New Eng Patriots, wide receiver, 1998-2000; Barcelona Dragons, 2001; Indianapolis Colts, 2001; Cleveland Browns, 2001; Houston Texans, 2002; New York Giants, 2002; Edmonton Eskimos, 2004; BC Lions, wide receiver, 2005-07; Triangle Razorback, Vejle, Denmark, wide receiver, offensive coordr & spec-teams coach, 2010; Bekescsaba Raptors, Hungary, head coach, offensive coordr, defensive coordr, spec-teams coordr, strength/speed coach & wide receiver, 2011; Elite Football League India, coach, offensive coordr, defensive coordr, spec-teams coordr & strength/speed coach, 2012; Amstetten Thunder, Austria, head coach, offensive coordr, defensive coordr, spec-teams coordr & strength/speed coach, 2012; Cagliari Crusaders, Italy, head coach, offensive coordr, defensive coordr, spec-teams coordr & strength/speed coach, 2013; E Sao Paulo, Brazil, head coach, offensive coordr, defensive coordr, spec-teams coordr & strength/speed coach, 2013; Kouvola Indians, Finland, head coach, offensive coordr, defensive coordr, spec-teams coordr, strength/speed coach & coaching consult, 2014. **Honors/ Awds:** Rookie of the Year, 1998; Direct TV NFL Play of the Week Award, 2000; St Rita High Sch Hall of Fame, 2011. **Home Addr:** 8844 S Winchester Ave, Chicago, IL 60620.

### SIMMONS, WILLIE, JR.
Banker, chief executive officer, manager. **Personal:** Born May 23, 1939, Meridian, MS; son of Gussie (deceased) and Willie (deceased); married Vernocia Neblett; children: Michael Anthony & Kevin Lawrence. **Educ:** Mil Police Officer, advan course, 1970; Univ Tampa, BS, criminol, 1975. **Career:** AUS, police officer, 1958-78; Ingalls Memorial Hosp, Harvey, dir security, 1978-80; First Chicago Security Serv Inc, chmn & chief exec officer, 1985-; First Nat Bank Chicago, security chief, mgr protection & security, 1980-85, dir corp security, 1985-. **Orgs:** Pres, IL Security Chiefs Asn, 1982; speaker Proj We Care, 1982-; chmn, Deacon Bd Truevine MB Church, 1982-; Am Soc Industl Security, 1984-; chmn, Bd Christian Educ Truevine MB Church, 1985-; vice chmn, Crime Stoppers Plus, 1986-; Int Org Black Security Execs; chair, BAI Security Comm, 1992. **Home Addr:** 10019 S Beverly Ave, Chicago, IL 60643-1346. **Business Addr:** Director/First Vice President, Chicago NBD Corp, 1 First Natl Plz, Chicago, IL 60670, **Business Phone:** (312)732-3343.

### SIMMONS-EDELSTEIN, DEE
Executive. **Personal:** Born Jul 1, 1937, New York, NY; daughter of Gertrude and Tonsley. **Educ:** City Col NY, BA, psychol & bus admin; Manhattan Community Col, entrepreneurship. **Career:** Fashion commentator; Grace Del Marco, prof com model, vpres & exec dir; WNJR-AM, NJ, Dee Simmons Radio Show, host; Nat Shoes, New York, statist bookkeeper; mag cover girl; New York Images & Voices, host, currently; Dee Luxe Talent Productions, owner; ESB Productions Inc, Artra Cosmetics, Prin; Dee Simmons TV Show, producer & host, currently; talent agt, 2001-; Ophelia DeVore Assocs Inc, exec dir & vpres, currently. **Orgs:** Am Fedn TV & Radio Asn; Nat Asn Women Media; 100 Coalition Black Women; Affairs Comt Freedom Fund Dr;Nat Asn Advan Colored People; Nat Dr Cerebral Palsy Telethon. **Special Achievements:** First model of color to be a principal in a TV commercial in the United States for Artra Cosmetics. **Home Addr:** 345 E 93rd St Suite 28H, New York, NY 10128. **Business Addr:** Vice President, Executive Director, Ophelia DeVore Associates Inc, Empire State Bldg, New York, NY 10118, **Business Phone:** (212)629-6400.

### SIMMS, PASTOR ALBERT L.
Clergy. **Personal:** Born Jan 21, 1931, Claremont, WV; son of Robert T; children: Div. **Educ:** N Gate Bible Col, BA. **Career:** First Baptist Church, Harlem Heights, pastor; Newcastle Southern Baptist Church, pastor, currently. **Orgs:** Int Gov Club, 2000-; past treas, New River Valley Missionary Baptist Asn; asst dir, Hill Baptist Ext Sem; historian, New River Valley Baptist Asn; Hist Comn WV Baptist State Conv; chair, Dist Asn New River Educ Com; adv bd, Hill Top Baptist Ext Sem; WV Baptist Minister Conf; past vpres, Fayette County Community Action; Crippled C Div Asn; youth counr, Active Bible Integrated Camps & 4H Camps. **Honors/Awds:** Award of Merit, Profiles Christian, 1972; Selected one of Outstanding People of 20th Century, Int Biog, 1999; Distinguished Leadership Hall of Fame, 2000; International Man of the Year, Intl Biog, 2000, 2001; Int Dipl of Hon. **Home Addr:** 216 Broadway Ave, Oak Hill, WV 25901. **Business Addr:** Pastor, Newcastle Southern Baptist Church, 110 Stampede St, Newcastle, WY 82701, **Business Phone:** (307)746-4231.

### SIMMS, BILL. See SIMMS, WILLIAM E.

### SIMMS, BOB. See SIMMS, ROBERT H.

### SIMMS, REV. JAMES EDWARD
Executive director, secretary (government), clergy. **Personal:** Born Dec 14, 1943, Richmond, VA; married Emma jane Miller; children: Rachael Couch, Eboni Talley & James C (deceased). **Educ:** Va Union Univ, BA, 1967; Pittsburgh Theol Sem, Mdiv, 1972, Dr ministry, 1974. **Career:** Pittsburgh Human Rels Comn, exec dir, 1972; Allegheny County Comn Col, stud serv coord, 1973; Chatham Col, instr, 1974; Comn Release Agency, exec dir, 1974; Comn Action Pittsburgh Inc, neighborhood admin, 1977; City Pittsburgh, Off Mayor, asst exec secy. **Orgs:** Chmn, United Negro Col Fund Telethon, 1983; pastor, St Paul Baptist Church; pres, Am Baptist Theol Sem; chmn, Munic Campaign United Way; Nat Forum Black Pub Admin; pres, Homer S Brown Alumni Asn Va Union Univ; pres, bd dir, Hill House Community Serv Inc; bd dir, Hill House Asn; bd dir, Vol Action Ctr; bd dir, Action Housing; Bd Garfield Jubilee Housing Inc; chairperson, Budget & Finance Comt, County Council; pres, Allegheny County Coun. **Home Addr:** 4337 Andover Terr, Pittsburgh, PA 15213, **Home Phone:** (412)621-7955. **Business Addr:** President, Allegheny County Courthouse, 436 Grant St Rm 119, Pittsburgh, PA 15219, **Business Phone:** (412)350-6490.

### SIMMS, DR. MARGARET CONSTANCE
Economist. **Personal:** Born Jul 30, 1946, St. Louis, MO; daughter of Frederick T and Margaret E. **Educ:** Carleton Col, Northfield, MN, BA, 1967; Stanford Univ, MA, econs, 1969, PhD, econs, 1974. **Career:** Univ Calif, Santa Cruz, actg asst prof, 1977-78; Atlanta Univ, asst prof Sch Bus, 1972-81, Econ Dept, assoc prof & dept chair, 1976-81; Urban Inst, sr rsch assoc, 1979-81, dir minorities & social policy prog, 1981-86; Joint Ctr Polit Studies, dep dir res, 1986, dir res progs, 1991-97, vpres res, 1997, sr vpres res, 2003-, interim pres & chief exec officer, 2006-. **Orgs:** Ed, Rev Black Polit Econ, 1983-88; Nat Econ Asn, 1971-, pres, 1978-79; bd mem, Coun Econ Priorities, 1979-85; Black Enterprise Bd Economists, 1987-; Inst Women's Policy Res, bd mem, 1991-99, bd chair, 1993-98; bd, Partners Dem changes, 1999-; Fed Adv Panel Fin Elem & Sec Educ, 1979-82; brooking econ policy fel, US Dept Housing & Urban Develop; Nat Urban League; Nat Inst Educ; Nat Urban Coalition; consult, US Dept State & Rockefeller Found; sr res assoc, Urban Inst Prog Res Women & Family Policy; adv, Cong Adv Panel; vpres bd dir, Nat Acad Social Ins, 1994-; consult, Annie E Casey Found; pres, Nat Acad Social Ins, 2007-09; Am Acad Arts & Sci; mem bd dir, Partners Dem Chg, currently. **Honors/Awds:** Samuel Z. Westerfield Award, Nat Econ Asn, 2008; hon doctor of laws degree, Carleton Col, 2010. **Special Achievements:** Selected Publications editor: Black Economic Progress: An Agenda for 1990s, Julianne M Malveaux, Slipping Through the Cracks; The Status of Black Women, 1986, Kristin A Moore & Charles L Betsey, Choice & Circumstance, Racial Differences in Adolescent Sexuality & Fertility (New Brunswick, NJ, Transaction Books, 1985); Economic Perspechives on Affirmative Action, 1995; Young Black Men in Jeopardy, 1994; One of four African-American during her freshman year in Carleton College. **Home Addr:** 212 G St NE, Washington, DC 20002. **Business Addr:** Interim President, Chief Executive Officer & Senior Vice President, Joint Center for Political and Economic Studies, 1090 Vt Ave NW Suite 1100, Washington, DC 20005, **Business Phone:** (202)789-3522.

### SIMMS, ROBERT H. (BOB SIMMS)
Consultant, executive. **Personal:** Born Oct 2, 1927, Snow Hill, AL; son of Harry and Alberta; married Aubrey Watkins; children: Leah Aliece Graham & David Michael. **Educ:** Xavier Univ, BS, 1949; Tuskegee Inst; NY Univ, Advan Study; Univ Miami; Univ Mass. **Career:** Macon Co Bd Educ, teacher, 1949-50, 1952-53; Dade Co Bd Educ, teacher, 1953-65; Small Bus & Develop Ctr, exec dir, 1965-66; US Dept Defense Race Rels Inst, Patrick Afb, contractor; Metro Dade Community Rels Bd, dep dir, 1967-68; exec dir, 1968-83; Bob Simms Assoc Inc, pres & chief exec officer. **Orgs:** Creator Inner City & Minority Experience Defense Depts Race Rels Inst, 1972; founder, Miami Varsity Club; Orange Bowl Com; Kappa Alpha Psi; Sigma Pi Phi; trustee emer, Univ Miami; founding mem, Church Open Door. **Special Achievements:** He was featured in the April 1988 Conference of the American Society of Newspaper Editors and "Presstime, " the journal of the American Newspaper Publisher's Association. **Home Addr:** 39 Storm Cove Lane, Miami Poland, ME 04274, **Home Phone:** (207)786-3922.

### SIMMS, STUART OSWALD
Government official, lawyer, politician. **Personal:** Born Jul 17, 1950, Baltimore, MD; married Candace Otterbein; children: Marcus & Paul. **Educ:** Dartmouth Col, BA, 1972; Harvard Law Sch, JD, 1975. **Career:** Semmes, Bowen & Semmes, assoc atty, 1975-77; Baltimore City, dep's state atty, 1983, state's atty; Baltimore state's atty, 1987-95; US Attny's Off US Courthouse, atty; Md Dept Juv Servs, secy, 1995-97; Md Dept Pub Safety & Correctional Servs, secy, 1997-2003; Brown, Goldstein, Levy LLP, partner & atty, currently; Dem Party, mem, currently. **Orgs:** Citizens Planning & Housing Asn, 1975-77; Pres, Black Alumni Asn, 1979-81; co-chair, Md Mentoring Partnership, 1996-2010; Nat Asn Advan Colored People, 1990-92; Baltimore Educ Scholar Trust, 1990-; Baltimore Mus Art, 1988-; Sinai Hosp, 1987-; Baltimore Zool Soc, 1984-85; Am Bar Asn, 1990; Md State Bar Asn; Monumental City Bar Asn; bd mem, Gilman Sch; bd mem, Baltimore Symphony Orchestra, 1988-; Baltimore City Bar Asn; Urban League; Md Judicial Campaign Conduct Comt, 2005-09; Greater Baltimore Med Ctr, 2005; adv bd, Univ Baltimore Sch Law; bd trustees, Baltimore Community Found, 2007. **Honors/Awds:** Nelson A Rockefeller Distinguished Service Award, Rockefeller Ctr, Dartmouth, 1998; Daniel Webster Distinguished Service Award, Dartmouth Club Washington, DC, 2003; Founder Award, Baltimore Child Abuse Ctr, 2012; Maryland Leadership in Law Award, 2013; Child Abuse Center's first Founder's Award; Leadership in Law Award, The Daily Rec, 2013; Whitney M. Young, Jr. Service Award, Boy Scouts Am, 2014. **Home Addr:** 3511 Cedardale Rd, Baltimore, MD 21202. **Business Addr:** Partner, Attorney, Brown, Goldstein & Levy LLP, 120 E Baltimore St Suite 1700, Baltimore, MD 21202, **Business Phone:** (410)962-1030.

### SIMMS, WILLIAM E. (BILL SIMMS)
Insurance executive, business owner, association executive. **Personal:** Born Aug 23, 1944, Indianapolis, IN; son of Frank T Sr (deceased) and Rosa Lee Smith (deceased); married Maxine A Newman; children: Terry Denise Reddix & Randall L; married Johanna Marie Gaines. **Educ:** Univ Southern Calif, Los Angeles, Calif, BS, bus admin, 1971, MBA, mkt, 1976. **Career:** Transamerica Occidental Life, Los Angeles, Calif, mgr, 1969-77, vpres reinsurance mkt, 1980-84, vpres sales & admin, 1984-86, vpres reinsurance, 1987, sr vpres reinsurance, 1988; Lincoln Nat Reinsurance Co, Ft Wayne, Ind, second vpres, 1977-80; Transamerica Life Co, reinsurance div, pres, 1997-; Carolina Panthers, owner, currently. **Orgs:** Pres & chief exec officer, 100 Black Men Am, 2001-; Calif Life Ins Co Asn; Los Angeles Jr Chamber Com; Nat Urban Leauge; bd trustee, Los Angeles Summer Games Found; Los Angeles Open Gulf Found; adv bd, United Negro Col Fund. **Special Achievements:** Second African American member of the exclusive Augusta National Golf Club, 1995; Won an Olympic Gold medal in the 1968 Olympics. **Home Addr:** 212 Perrin Pl, Charlotte, NC 28207. **Business Addr:** Owner, Carolina Panthers, 800 S Mint St, Charlotte, NC 28202, **Business Phone:** (704)358-7000.

### SIMON, COREY JERMAINE
**Personal:** Born Mar 2, 1977, Boynton Beach, FL; married Natasha; children: Corey Jr. **Educ:** Fla State Univ, BA, info studies. **Career:** Football player (retired); Philadelphia Eagles, defensive tackle, 2000-04; Indianapolis Colts, defensive tackle, 2005-06; Tenn Titans, 2007. **Orgs:** Founder, Corey Simon Success Ctr. **Honors/Awds:** BCS National Championship, 1999; Howie Long Tough Guy Team, 2000; Football Digest Top 16Rookies, 2000; Defensive Rookie of the Month, National Football League, 2000; Football Digest All NFL, 2001; Pro Bowl, 2003. **Special Achievements:** Finalist, Lombardi Award and Outland Trophy. **Home Addr:** 6089 Leigh Read Rd, Tallahassee, FL 32309-8929.

### SIMON, DR. ELAINE (ELAINE C SIMON)
Beautician. **Personal:** Born Nov 30, 1944, St. Johns; daughter of Rosalyn Richards Jarvis and Hubert Phillips; children: Denise, Francine & Sheldean. **Educ:** Bay Col, Baltimore, Md, AA, 1976; Univ Baltimore, attended 1978; Catinsville Community Col, cert, 1982; Cent State Univ, Columbus, OH, cert, 1985; Coppin State Col, cert, 1985; Nat Beauty Culturist League, Wash, DC, PhD, 1987. **Career:** Bay Col Md, lounge mgr, 1975-76; Touch Paris Coiffure, owner, mgr, 1978-; Johnsons Prod Co, lectr, technician, 1979-85. **Orgs:** Pub rels dir, Nat Beauticulturist League, Baltimore, Md, 1978-89; exec dir, Nat Black Women Consciousness Raising Asn, 1980-89; pub rels dir, Master Beautician Asn, 1982-89; educ dir, Md State Beauty-Cult Asn, 1982-89; pub rels dir, Theta Mu Sigma Nat Sorority, Zeta Chap, 1985; exec, pres, Caribbean Am Carnival Asn Baltimore, chief exec officer, currently. **Honors/Awds:** Civil Rights Humanitarian Award, Md Spec Inaugural Comn, 1981; Governor's Citation, Gov Md, 1983; Econ Stress Threaten Black Salon, shop talk mag, 1983; "Pocket News Paper", 1983; Resolution, City Coun Baltimore, 1989; Booker T Washington Citation Honor, Bus League Baltimore, 1989; Business Award, Mayor Baltimore City, 1994; Nat Black Women Consciousness Raising Asn Inc; nat exec dir, Baltimore Response Asn; admin adv, Rosa Pryor Music Scholarship Fund. **Home Addr:** 20 N Kossuth St, Baltimore, MD 21229-3751. **Business Addr:** President, Chief Executive Officer, Caribbean American Carnival Association of Baltimore, PO Box 31424, Baltimore, MD 21216, **Business Phone:** (443)869-1853.

### SIMON, DR. KENNETH BERNARD
Surgeon. **Personal:** Born Sep 29, 1953, San Francisco, CA. **Educ:** Univ Ariz, Tucson, BS, 1976; Meharry Medical Col, MD, 1980; Kennesaw State Univ, MBA, 1999. **Career:** Howard Univ, internship, 1980-81, resident, 1981-85; DC Gen Hosp, staff surgeon & instr surg, 1985-86; Univ Alta Hosps, resident cardiac surg, 1986-87; Univ Miss, Jackson, Miss, asst prof surg, 1987-90; Va Hosp, Jackson, Miss, staff surgeon, 1987-90; Cleveland Clin, Cleveland, Ohio, fel vascular surg, 1990-91; Va Hosp, chief surg serv; Univ Miss Med Ctr, asst prof surg, 1992-; US Dept Health & Human Serv, Medicare & Medicaid Ctr, med officer & exec dir, currently; Gulf Coast Med Ctr. **Orgs:** Am Col Surgeons; Asn Acad Surgeons; Nat Med Asn; Asn Va Surgeons. **Honors/ Awds:** Kim Meche Scholar, Univ Ariz, 1974-75. **Home Addr:** 1500 E Woodrow Wilson Dr, Jackson, MS 39206, **Home Phone:** (601)982-0128. **Business Addr:** General Surgeon, 400 Veterans Ave, Biloxi, MS 39531, **Business Phone:** (228)523-5000.

**SIMON, MATT**
Athletic coach, football player, football coach. **Personal:** Born Dec 6, 1953, Akron, OH. **Career:** Eastern NMex Univ, Grad Asst, 1972-75, 1977; Borger High Sch, Borger, Tex, asst coach, 1978; Univ Tex-El Paso, Tight Ends, Linebackers, 1979-81; Univ WA, Running Backs, Kicking, 1982-91; Univ NMex, Offensive Coordr, 1992-93; Univ N Tex, head football coach, 1994-97; Baltimore Ravens, running back coach, 1999-2005; San diego chargers, running back coach, 2007; Gilmour Acad, consult, head coach, 2009-10; Univ at Buffalo, running backs coach, 2011-. **Honors/Awds:** Hall of Fame, Univ Wash; Coach of the Year, Southland Conf; Coach of the Year, Black Coaches Asn Nat Football; Coach of the Year, AFCA Region 4. **Business Addr:** Running Backs Coach, University at Buffalo, 12 Capen Hall, Buffalo, NY 14260-1660.

**SIMON, MILES JULIAN**
Basketball player, basketball coach. **Personal:** Born Nov 21, 1975, Stockholm; son of Walter. **Educ:** Univ Ariz, BS, 1998. **Career:** Basketball player (retired), basketball coach; Ariz Wildcats, 1994-98, guard, asst coach, 2005-08; Orlando Magic, guard, 1998-99; Maccabi Raanana, 2000-01; Mabo Livorno, 2001; Dakota Wizards, 2001-03; Metis Varese, 2002; Seattle SuperSonics, 2002-03; Tuborg Pilsener, 2004; ESPN, analyst, 2010-11.

**SIMONS, EGLON E.**
Advertising executive. **Personal:** Born Mar 7, 1946, Bermuda; son of Edward H and Ivy S; married Renee V H; children: Kimberly, Cameron & Kourtney. **Educ:** City Col New York, BA, art design, 1968; Harvard Bus Sch, MBA, gen mgt & mkt, 1976. **Career:** CBS Inc, financial analyst & corp control anal, 1976-77, acct exec & nat sales serv mgr, 1977-81, acct exec/nat sales, 1980-81, WCBS-TV, nat sales mgr/sports sales mgr, 1981-82, KMOX-TV, dir sales, 1982-84, CBS Tv Stas, vpres sales & mkt, 1984-89; Cablevision Systs Corp & Rainbow Advert Sales, NY Interconnect, dir sales, 1990-91, vpres & gen mgr, 1992-95, sr vpres & gen mgr, 1995-2002, exec vpres, 2002-11; Exec Sales Mgt, currently. **Orgs:** Omega Psi Phi Fraternity; bd dir, Westchester ARC, 1994-2002; bd dir, Nat Down Syndrome Soc, 1998-2003; pres & chief exec officer, Nat Asn Multi-ethnicity Commun, 2014-. **Honors/Awds:** President's Award, Cable Advert Bur, 2003. **Home Addr:** 25 Hemlock Hills, Chappaqua, NY 10514, **Home Phone:** (914)238-9645. **Business Addr:** President, Chief Executive Officer, National Association for Multi-ethnicity in Communications, 50 Broad St Suite 1801, New York, NY 10004, **Business Phone:** (646)545-2503.

**SIMONS, RENEE V. H.**
Executive, consultant. **Personal:** Born May 27, 1949, New York, NY; daughter of Charles Leroy Moore and Phyllis Harley Phipps; married Eglon E; children: Kimberly, Cameron H & Kourtney. **Educ:** Hunter Col, New York, NY, BA, urban affairs, 1971; Fordham Grad Sch Educ, New York, NY, MS, educ planning, 1974; Columbia Grad Sch Bus, New York, NY, MBA, mkt gen mgt, 1978. **Career:** Gen Foods Corp, White Plains, NY, asst brand mgr, Kool-Aid, 1978-80; Am Can James River, Greenwich, Conn, brand mgr, Dixie Northern, 1980-83; Seven-Up Co, St Louis, Mo, brand mgr, 1983-85; Philip Morris USA, NY, exec asst exec vpres, 1985-86, brand mgr, mkt & sales mgt, 1986-89; Philip Morris Mgt Corp, NY, dir, spec proj, 1989-91, group dir mkt, 1991, Trade Mkt, Sales Promotions & Info, dir, 1991-93, mkt, dir consumer mkt serv, 1993-94, mkt, dir media, 1994-98; JP Morgan Chase, vpres, corp mkt & commun, 1998-2000, sr vpres, ETECH Mkt & Commun, 2000-01; Global Investment Banking bus; JP Morgan Chase, managing dir mkt & commun; Harley Simons Group, founder; Clear Peak Commun, chair, 2008, consult, currently. **Orgs:** Delta Sigma Theta Sorority, 1968-; Links Inc, 1990-; pres, bd dir & vpres bd trustee, Ad Club NY; chair & past pres bd dir, ADVERT CLUB; vice chair bd dir, Covenant House New York; pres, Greater Hudson Valley Chap Links Inc. **Honors/Awds:** Fel, COGME, 1976-78; Black Achievers Award, YMCA, 1981-82; Outstanding Professional Women in Advertising Award, Dollars & Sense, 1989; 21 Women of Power & Influence, Black Enterprise mag, 1991. **Home Addr:** 80 Riverside Blvd Apt 14e, New York, NY 10069-0314, **Home Phone:** (631)725-2674. **Business Addr:** Consultant, Clear Peak Communications, 167 W 21st 3rd Fl, New York, NY 10011-3201, **Business Phone:** (646)336-7566.

**SIMPKINS, DR. CUTHBERT ORMOND, SR.**
Dentist, state government official. **Personal:** Born Jan 13, 1925, Mansfield, LA; son of Oscar and Olivia Gardner; married Elaine Joyce Shoemaker; children: Cuthbert Ormond Jr, Deborah, Eric, Cheri Gardner & Alicia Ritchens; married Dorothy Herndon. **Educ:** Wiley Col; Tenn State Univ; Meharry Med Col, DDS, 1948. **Career:** Dentist pvt pract. **Orgs:** Nat Soc Dent Practitioners; Nat Dent Asn; Acad Gen Dent; Am Analgesic Soc; Am Dent Asn; NY State Dent Soc; Queens County Dent Soc; Queens Clin Soc; Alpha Phi Alpha Fraternity; charter mem, Inst Continuing Dent Educ Eleventh Dist; Biracial Comn; fourth vpres, Southern Christian Leadership Conf; Sigma Pi Phi Fraternity; bd dir, Grambling Black & Gold Found. **Home Addr:** 1819 Willow Point Dr, Shreveport, LA 71119, **Home Phone:** (318)631-5243. **Business Addr:** Dentist, Private Practitioner, 4001 Lakeshore Dr, Shreveport, LA 71109-1927, **Business Phone:** (318)635-2382.

**SIMPKINS, DICKEY. See SIMPKINS, LUBARA DIXON.**

**SIMPKINS, J. EDWARD**
Educator. **Personal:** Born Oct 18, 1932, Detroit, MI; married Alice Marie Mann; children: Edward, Evelyn & Ann Marie. **Educ:** Wayne State Univ, BA, 1955, EdM, 1961; Harvard Univ, CAS, 1969, EdD, 1971. **Career:** High Sch Eng J Hist, teacher, 1956-65; Detroit Fedn Teachers, exec vpres, 1966-68; Harvard Univ fel; Hist Dept, Tufts Univ, lectr, 1969-71; fac & exec dir, Ctr Urban Studies, Harvard Grad Sch Educ, asst & dean, 1970-71; Penn Pub Schs, chief negotiator & dir labor rel, 1971-72; Wayne State Univ, Ctr Black Studs, 1972-74, Col Educ, dean, 1974-86, Div admin & Orgn Studies Col Educ, adminr & arbitrator prof; Baltimore Pub Schs, chief negotiator & dir labor rel, 1973-74. **Orgs:** Am Arb Asn; Ind Rel Res Asn; Woodrow Wilson Found; Phi Delta Kappa; pres, Asn Study Afro Am Life & Hist State Mich; Fed Mediation & Conciliation Serv. **Honors/Awds:** Human Rights Award, 1968; Spirit of Detroit Award, 1974; Martin Luther King Award. **Home Addr:** 4255 W Outer Dr, Detroit, MI 48221-1459, **Home Phone:** (313)805-5764. **Business Addr:** Arbitrator, PO Box 21609, Detroit, MI 48221, **Business Phone:** (313)864-6243.

**SIMPKINS, LUBARA DIXON (DICKEY SIMPKINS)**
Basketball player, basketball coach, executive. **Personal:** Born Apr 6, 1972, Washington, DC. **Educ:** Providence Col, BA, mkt & art, 1994. **Career:** Basketball player, (retired), basketball coach, executive; Chicago Bulls, point forward, 1994-97, 1998-2000; Golden State Warriors, point forward, 1997-98; Makedonikos, Greece, 2000-01; Atlanta Hawks, 2001-02; Maroussi, Greece, 2001-02; Continental Basketball Asn, Rockford Lightning, 2001-02; Criollos de Caguas, Pr, 2001-02; Unics Kazan, Russia, 2002-03; Lietuvos Rytas, Lithuania, 2003-04; Leones de Ponce, Pr, 2003-04; Continental Basketball Asn, Dakota Wizards, 2004-05; Plus Pujol Lleida, Spain, 2004-05; Alaska Aces, Philippines, 2004-05; Blue Stars, Lebanon, 2005-06; Blose Bamberg, Ger, 2005-06; Lake Forest Acad Prep Sch, basketball skill develop consult, 2006-11; Entertainment & Sports Programming Network, col basketball analyst, 2007-12; Next Level Performance Inc, founder, pres & head trainer, 2006-12; Charlotte Bobcats, scout, 2010-; FOX Sports, analyst, 2013-; nat motivational speaker. **Honors/Awds:** Washington, DC Area Championship, 1987, 1989 & 1990; McDonalds Capitol Classic Team, 1990; Gold Medal, Olympic Festival, 1991; Champion, Nat Basketball Asn, 1996, 1997, 1998. **Business Addr:** Scout, Charlotte Bobcats, 333 E Trade St, Charlotte, NC 28202, **Business Phone:** (704)688-8600.

**SIMPSON, CARL WILHELM**
Football player. **Personal:** Born Apr 18, 1970, Vidalia, GA. **Educ:** Fla State Univ, BS. **Career:** Football player (retired); Chicago Bears, defensive tackle & left defensive tackle & right defensive tackle, 1993-97; Ariz Cardinals, defensive tackle, 1998-99; Las Vegas Outlaws XFL, 2001.

**SIMPSON, CAROLE**
Radio host, journalist, educator. **Personal:** Born Dec 7, 1940, Chicago, IL; daughter of Lytle Ray and Doretha Viola Wilbon; married James Edward Marshall; children: Malika Hurd & Adam. **Educ:** Univ Ill, attended 1960; Univ Mich, BA, 1962; Univ Iowa, attended 1965. **Career:** Northwestern Univ's Medill Sch, instr journalism; Tuskegee Inst, instr journalism; WTTW, commentator; WCFL Radio, news reporter, 1965-68; WBBM Radio, news reporter & anchor, 1968-70; WMAQ-TV, news reporter, 1970-74; NBC Nighty News, news corresp, 1974; ABC News, news corresp, 1982, sr corresp, 1982-, weekend anchor, 1988-2003; ABC News Women's Adv Bd, chair; Carole Simpson Leadership Inst African Women's Ctr Dakar, senegal, 1998; Emerson Col, leader-in-residence, 2007; World News Tonight Sunday, anchor, currently. **Orgs:** Radio-TV Corresps Asn; Theta Sigma Phi; Nightline, S Africa; chair, ABC News Women's Adv Bd; vice chair, Int Women's Media Found; bd dir, Nat Comn Working Women; bd trustees, Radio & TV News Dirs Found; Nat Acad Scis' forum Future C & Families; Nat Press Found. **Honors/Awds:** Media Journalism Award, AMA; Outstanding Woman in Communications, YWCA Metro Chicago, 1974; Journalist of the Year, Nat Asn Black Journalist, 1992; Star Award, Am Women Radio & TV; Carole Simpson scholar, Radio-TV News Dirs Found; Trumpet Award, Turner Broadcasting; Emmy Award, ABC News; Milestone in Broadcasting Award, Nat Comn Working Women; Leonard Zeiden berg First Amendment Award, Radio-TV News Dirs Found; Nat Organization of Women Legislators Nat Media Award; Joseph Medill Distinguished Journalism Award, Chicago Hist Soc;University of Iowa Communications Hall of Fame. **Special Achievements:** First African-American female to broadcast news; First African-American female television reporter. **Business Addr:** Senior Correspondent, ABC News, 1717 DeSales St NW, Washington, DC 20036, **Business Phone:** (617)824-8500.

**SIMPSON, DARLA**
Basketball player. **Personal:** Born Apr 11, 1969. **Educ:** Univ Houston. **Career:** Atlanta Glory, forward, 1997-98; Colo Xplosion, forward, 1998; Women's Nat Basketball Asn, Shock, free agt, 2000-10; Sacramento Monarchs, 2002; Houston Jaguars, ctr, 2003-04.

**SIMPSON, DR. DAZELLE DEAN**
Physician. **Personal:** Born Aug 28, 1924, Miami, FL; married George Augustus Simpson Sr; children: George Jr, Gregory & Gary. **Educ:** Fisk Univ, BA, 1945; Meharry Med Col, MD, 1950. **Career:** Physician (retired); Pvt pract. **Orgs:** Dipl Am bd Pediat, 1957; Delta Sigma Theta Sor Head Start Consult Force Pediat Educ, 1974-78; fel Am Acad Pediat; chmn pediat sec, Nat Med Asn, 1975-77; nat pres, Meharry Alumni Asn, 1976-77; bd trustee, Meharry Med Col, 1977-; life mem, Nat Asn Advan Colored People; task mem, Am Acad Ped Miami Childrens Hosp, bd dir, 1988; pres, James Wilson Bridges MD Med Soc; treas, James Wilson Bridges, MD Med Soc. **Honors/Awds:** Alumnus of the Year, Meharry Col, 1974; Contributing editor, Current Therapy, 1980. **Special Achievements:** First African American pediatrician in Florida; Inducted in to GW Carver High School in Coral Gables Hall of Fame, 2010. **Home Addr:** 3619 Percival Ave, Miami, FL 33133-4909, **Home Phone:** (305)461-5371. **Business Addr:** FL.

**SIMPSON, DIANE JEANNETTE**
Counselor, social worker. **Personal:** Born Sep 20, 1952, Denver, CO; daughter of Arthur H and Irma Virginia Jordan; children: Shante Nicole. **Educ:** NE Wesleyan Univ, BS, 1974; Univ Denver Grad Sch Social Work, MSW, 1977. **Career:** Girl Scouts Mile Hi Coun, summer asst, 1971-77; Denver Pub Sch, social worker asst, 1974-75, social worker, 1977-; Univ Denver Grad Sch Soc Work, field instr, 1984; Adoption Home, study work Denver, Dept Human Serv. **Orgs:** Nat Assoc Black Soc Workers, 1980-86, Nat Asn Social Workers; sec bd trustee, Warren Village Inc, 1982-83; nominations & personnel comm, Christ United Methodist Ch, 1981-84; Denver Chap Black Geneal Org, 1981-87; chairperson minority adult recruitment team Girl Scouts Mile Hi Coun, 1982-84; Black Women's Network, 1983-86; nat coun deleg Girl Scouts, 1984-87; chairperson plng comm, Creative Ctr C, 1984, adv bd, 1984-86, Christ United Meth Ch; Denver Sister Cities Inc, 1984; admin bd, staff, parish rels, Coun Ministries Christ United Methodist Church, 1984-87; vpres, United Methodist Women, Christ United Methodist Ch, 1989-91; Educ Scholar Comm Shorter African Methodist Episcopal Ch; Shorter AME Ch, Breast Cancer Support Ministry, 2001-; Denver Child Fatality Rev Bd, 1998-. **Honors/Awds:** Selectee to Ghana West Africa Girl Scouts of the USA/ Oper Crossroads Africa, 1974; Crusade Scholar Bd of Global Ministries, United Methodist Church, 1976-77; Spec Mission Recognition United Methodist Women, United Methodist Church, 1982; Elizabeth Hayden Award for Outstanding Serv Girl Scouts Mile Hi Council, 1983; Young Alumni Loyalty Award, NE Wesleyan Univ, 1985; Woman of the Year Award Aurora Area Business & Professional Women's Org, 1986; Excellence in Education Award, Black Educators United, Denver Public Schools, 1990. **Home Addr:** 1824 S Pontiac Way, Denver, CO 80224-2269, **Home Phone:** (303)758-4609. **Business Addr:** Social Worker, Denver Public Schools, 900 Grant St, Denver, CO 80204, **Business Phone:** (303)322-5080.

**SIMPSON, DONNIE (DR. GREEN EYES)**
Radio host. **Personal:** Born Jan 30, 1954, Detroit, MI; son of Calvin and Dorothy; married Pamela Gibson; children: Donnie Jr & Dawn. **Educ:** Univ Detroit, BA, communs. **Career:** WJLB Detroit, air personality, 1969-77; WKYS Wash, radio host & prog dir, 1977-93; Black Entertainment TV, host, "Video Soul"; WRC-TV, sports anchor, 1981; George Michael Sports Mach, host, 1981; BET, host Video Soul, 1983; WPGC Radio, on-air personality, 1993-2010; WMMJ-FM, host, 2015-. **Orgs:** Supporter, United Negro Col Fund, Donnin Pam Simpson Scholar Fund; Hon Chmn; NatBlack Family Reunion. **Honors/Awds:** Program Dir of the Year, Billboard Mag, 1982; Superstar of the Year, The Nat Urban Coalition, 1989; Personality of the Year, Billboard Mag, 1999; BET Walk of Fame, 2004. **Special Achievements:** Films: Krush Groove, 1985; Disorderlies, 1987. TV series: "Video Soul", 1981; "Martin", 1996; "The Jamie Foxx Show", 1997; "The 10th Annual Walk of Fame Honoring Smokey Robinson", 2004; "Mayor for Life", 2011. **Business Addr:** Radio Host, WMMJ-FM 102.3, 8515 Ga Ave 9th Fl, Silver Spring, MD 20910, **Business Phone:** (301)306-1111.

**SIMPSON, INDIA ARIE**
Songwriter, singer. **Personal:** Born Oct 3, 1975, Denver, CO; daughter of Ralph and Joyce. **Educ:** Savannah Col Arts & Design, jewelry making. **Career:** Singer & songwriter, currently; Albums: Acoustic Soul, 2001; Voyage to India, 2002; Brown Sugar, 2002; I Am Not My Hair, 2005; Testimony Vol 1, Life & Relationship, 2006; Testimony Vol 2, Love & Politics, 2009; Films: Radio, 2003; SharkTale, 2004; "The Tyra Banks Show", 2005; Singles: "Ready For Love", 2001; "Little Things", 2002; Beautiful Flower, 2007; Words, 2008; Chocolate High, 2008; Pearls, 2010; Imagine, 2011. TV Series: "Motown Christmas", 2002; "Act of contrition", 2003; "American Dreams", 2003. Films: American Dreams, 2003; The Bernie Mac Show, 2003; One on One, 2006; Pastor Brown, 2009; Being Mary Jane, 2015. **Home Addr:** , NY. **Business Addr:** Recording Artist, Universal Motown Records, 1755 Broadway Fl 6, New York, NY 10019-3743, **Business Phone:** (212)841-8000.

**SIMPSON, JAMES ARLINGTON. See SIMPSON, NORVELL J.**

**SIMPSON, DR. JOHN O.**
School administrator, school superintendent, educational consultant. **Personal:** married Rita; children: John. **Educ:** W Chester Univ, BS, music educ, 1970, MM, vocal pedag, MEd, 1975; Univ Del, educ leadership, 1981; Univ Mich, PhD, educ policy, planning & admin, 1983. **Career:** Philadelphia pub sch, teacher, 1970-72; New Castle County Schs, teacher, 1972-81, teacher & dept chair, 1983-84; Newark, DE, Philadelphia, music teacher; Wash, asst jr high prin, 1984-86, elem prin, 1986-88; Okla City, 29 pub elem sch, dir, 1988-91; N Chicago Pub Schs, supt, 1993; Ann Arbor Bd Educ, supt, 1993-98; Norfolk pub schs, supt, 1998-2004; Broad Superintendents Acad, supt in residence, currently; Large City Sch Superintendents, pres; Horace Mann League, pres; Hazard, Young & Attea LLC, assoc. **Orgs:** Rotary Club; bd dir, Hands-Mus, Washtenaw Co Red Cross, Univ Musical Soc; Am Asn Sch Adminr; bd mem, Broad Prize Rev; Nat Asn Black Sch Educrs; Mich Asn Sch Adminrs; adv, sr exec & dir, Stupski Found, 2007; bd visitors, Eastern Va Med Col; advisor, Broad Superintendents Acad. **Home Addr:** 3248 Bellflower Ct, Ann Arbor, MI 48103. **Business Addr:** Superintendent in Residence, Broad Superintendents Academy, 10900 Wilshire Blvd 12th Fl, Los Angeles, CA 90024, **Business Phone:** (310)954-5000.

**SIMPSON, DR. JOHN RANDOLPH**
Educator, college administrator. **Personal:** Born Jun 27, 1946, Elloree, SC; son of Arthur H and Geneva; children: Stephanie C. **Educ:** Tuskegee Univ, BS, 1972; Atlanta Univ, MA, 1973; Ohio State Univ, PhD, 1981. **Career:** Social Security Admin, claims rep, 1974-77; Ky State Univ, dir govt rels, 1977-78; Univ SC, Beaufort, assoc prof, 1978-86; SC State Univ, dean & sociol prof, 1986; Philander Smith Col, dean acad affairs, 2005-06. **Orgs:** Kappa Delta Pi, 1977; Phi Kappa Phi, 1980; Gamma Sigma Delta, 1981; Southern Sociol Soc, 1982-; Asn Behav & Social Scientists, 1986-; Rural Sociol Soc, 1988-. **Home Addr:** 420 Hodges Dr NW, Orangeburg, SC 29118, **Home Phone:** (803)531-2176.

**SIMPSON, LORNA**
Artist. **Personal:** Born Aug 13, 1960, Brooklyn, NY; daughter of Elian and Eleanor; married James Casebere; children: Zora. **Educ:** NY Sch Visual Arts, BFA, photog, 1982; Univ Calif, San Diego, Calif, MFA, 1985. **Career:** Group exhibits: Whitney Mus Am Art; Studio Mus, Harlem, 1989; solo exhibits: Mus Modern Art, NY, 1990; Cameos & Appearances, Whitney Mus Am Art, 2002; Am Fedn Arts traveling show, Mus Contemp Art, 2006; Miami Art Mus, artist. **Orgs:** Fel Nat Endowment Arts, 1985. **Honors/Awds:** Louis Comfort Tiffany Award, 1990; Col Art Asn grant, 1994; Am Art Award, Whitney Mus, 2001; ICP Infinity Award, International Center of Photography, 2010. **Special Achievements:** First African American woman to have works exhibited at the Venice Biennale, Venice, Italy, 1990. **Business Addr:** Artist, c/o The Miami Art Museum, 101 W Flagler St, Miami, FL 33130, **Business Phone:** (305)375-3000.

**SIMPSON, NORVELL J. (JAMES ARLINGTON SIMPSON)**
Administrator. **Personal:** Born Mar 25, 1931, Rochester, NY; son of Frank Douglas and Martha Perlina Jentons; married Alice Elizabeth Saxton; children: Gary A, Sharon R & Leslie A. **Educ:** Pk Col, BA, econ & bus admin, 1970; Univ Colo, MA, cand guid & couns, 1981. **Career:** Administrator (retired); USAF, sr mstr sgt, 1949-71; Pikes Peak Comm Action Prog, exec dir, 1972-79; El Paso City co, dir comm serv dept, 1974-79, dept head; TRW/EPI, prop control & serv mgr, bus adminr, 1979-86; Colo Springs Pub Schs Dist 11, human rels adminr, external affairs & affirmative action coordr, 1986-94; vpres, Lota Omicron Lambda Chapter. **Orgs:** Exec bd, United Way Pikes Peak Reg, 1978-93; Sch Dist 11, 1975-85; CO Asn Sch Bd, 1983-84; comm Colo Sprngs Human Rel, 1973-79; Alpha Phi Alpha; Kadesia Shrine Temple; jr achievement bd dir, Citizen's Goals Colo Springs comt; youth employ adv comt; Pikes Peak Ment Health Adv comt; Clean Air Task Force; Colo Martin Luther King Jr State Holiday Comn; Colo State educ Accountability comt; dir, Pikes Peak Community Action Agency; chmn, Colo Springs Pub Schs Dist 11; Non Comn Officiers Asn; Community Sch Adv Coun. **Honors/Awds:** Citizen of the Year, Alpha Phi Alpha, 1979, 1981, 1982; Omega Psi Phi, 1978; TRW Leadership Award, TRW, 1979; The Colorado Education Association Lion II Award, The Norvell Simpson Community ctr. **Special Achievements:** First African American elected to the Colorado Springs School District 11 Board of Education; First African American director of the Pikes Peak Community Action Agency; named "The Norvell Simpson Community Center" at Hillside Community Center. **Home Addr:** 13518 E 53rd Lane, Yuma, AZ 85367, **Home Phone:** (928)342-6588.

**SIMPSON, RALPH DEREK (RALPH SIMPSON)**
Basketball player. **Personal:** Born Aug 10, 1949, Detroit, MI; married Joyce McMullen; children: India Arie & J'On. **Educ:** Mich State Univ, attended 1973. **Career:** Basketball player (retired); Denver Rockets, 1970-74; Denver Nuggets, 1974-76, 1977-78; Detroit Pistons, 1976-77; Philadelphia 76ers, 1978-79; Nj Nets, 1978-80. **Home Addr:** , Denver, CO.

**SIMPSON, REV. DR. SAMUEL G.**
Clergy, writer. **Personal:** Born Dec 6, 1931, Jamaica; married Lola Campbell; children: Erica, Stephen & Kim. **Educ:** BRE, 1967; MDiv, NY Theol Sem, MPS. **Career:** Pastor (retired); Jamaica, civil servant treas, 1955-59; Bronx Baptist Church, founding pastor, 1964-; Southern Baptist Churches, pastor dir; Carib News, weekly column writer; Wake-Eden Community Baptist Churches, pastor, 1972. **Orgs:** Exec bd mem, Northeastern Bible Col, 1974; pres, E Tremont Church Coun; vpres, Coun Church Bronx Div; vpres, Meterop NY Baptist Asn; vpres, Baptist Conv NY, pres; chmn, Nominating Comt, Coun Chairs, NY City Sec Comt Planning Bd No 6 Bronx; treas, Twin Parks Urban Renewal Bronx; Honeywell Baptist Chapel; Grace Baptist Chapel; founding mem, Shepherds Restoration Corp; moderator, Metrop New York Baptist Asn; pres, bd chmn, Coun Churches; founding mem, Clergy Coalition 47th Precinct, pres; fel Harvard Divinity Sch; sr common fel Regents Pk Col; pres, Baptist Conv New York; merrill fel Harvard Divinity Sch. **Honors/Awds:** Award for Baptist Convention, MD; Air Jamaica National Airlines Award of Excellence; Alumni of the Year, Northeastern Bible Col; Bishop of the Bronx; Man of the Year, Bronx Coun Churches; Hon, Asia Bible Col; Hon, Marthas Vineyard Theol Sem. **Special Achievements:** Books: "What God did for Me"; "Architect of Hope"; "To Dream the Impossible Dream"; "Wake Eden Community Baptist Churches"; Proclamation from Congressman Elliot Engle. **Home Addr:** 4065 Hill Ave, Bronx, NY 10466-2301, **Home Phone:** (718)231-3436. **Business Addr:** Founding Pastor, Bronx Baptist Church, 331 E 187th St, Bronx, NY 10458, **Business Phone:** (718)933-4095.

**SIMPSON, STEPHEN WHITTINGTON**
Executive, lawyer. **Personal:** Born Mar 14, 1945, Philadelphia, PA; married Audrey C Murdah; children: Stephen Jr & Christopher Lindsey. **Educ:** Harvard Univ, AB, 1966; Univ Pa, JD, 1969. **Career:** Pa Super Ct, law clerk, 1969-70; Dechert, Price & Rhoades, atty, 1970-73; Goodrs Greenfield, atty, 1973-77; Suns Co Inc, chief coun, 1978-87; Vance, Jackson, Simpson & Overton, atty, currently; Arnelle & Hastie, partner. **Orgs:** Am Bar Asn; Philadelphia Bar Asn; Barristers Club. **Home Addr:** 239 W Allens Lane, Philadelphia, PA 19119-4103. **Business Addr:** Attorney, Vance Jackson Simpson & Overton, 1429 Walnut St Fl 8, Philadelphia, PA 19102-3218, **Business Phone:** (215)665-8082.

**SIMPSON, VALERIE**
Singer, songwriter, restaurateur. **Personal:** Born Aug 26, 1946, Bronx, NY; married Nicholas; children: Nicole & Asia. **Career:** Motown Records, Songwriter & singer; Albums: Ain't No Mountain High Enough; Let's Go Get Stoned, 1964; Tamla; Can't It Wait Until Tomorrow, 1971; Silly Wasn't I, 1972; (I'd Know You) Anywhere, 1974; It'll Come, It'll Come, 1976; Somebody Told a Lie, 1976; Over & Over, 1977; Send It, 1977; So So Satisfied, 1977; Tried, Tested & Found True, 1977; By Way Of Love's Express, 1978; Don't Cost You Nothing, 1978; It Seems to Hang On, 1978; Flashback, 1979; Found a Cure, 1979; Is It Still Good to Ya, 1979; Nobody Knows, 1979; Happy Endings, 1980; Love Don't Make It Right, 1980; Get Out Your Handkerchief, 1981; It Shows in Your Eyes, 1981; Love It Away, 1982; Street Corner, 1982; High-Rise, 1983; It's Much Deeper, 1983; I'm Not That Tough, 1984; Solid, 1984; Babies, 1985; Outta the World, 1985; Count Your Blessings, 1986; I'll Be There for You, 1989; Hungry for Me Again, 1990; Been Found, 1996; What If, 1997; We Are Family, 2001; Dinosaurs Are Coming Back Again, 2012; Ashford & Simpson's Sugar Bar, co-owner, 1996-. **Business Addr:** Co Owner, Ashford & Simpson's Sugar Bar, 254 W 72 St Suite 1A, New York, NY 10023, **Business Phone:** (212)579-0222.

**SIMPSON, DR. WILLA JEAN**
Manager. **Personal:** Born May 15, 1943, Little Rock, AR; married Earl Henry; children: Desiree, Jill & Earla. **Educ:** Kennedy King Col, AA, 1969; Chicago State Univ, BS, 1974; Gov State Univ, MA, 1975; Fielding Inst, PhD, 1981. **Career:** Golden Gate Consult, child family therapist, 1981-; Malcolm X Col, Chicago, Ill, instr, 1981-84; BCDI Chicago affil, rec secy, 1982-85; Dept Army Savanna Ill, educ spec, 1984; AUS Dept Defense Rock Island Arsenal, child develop serv coordr; Ft Hood Army Base, child develop serv coordr, 1987-; AUS Materiel Command, Youth Serv div, 1991-93; US Dept HTH & Human Serv, Ed Prog Specialist, 1993-2003; Trinity Col, adj prof, 1995-2003. **Orgs:** Pres, bd bir, Golden Gate, 1971-81; dep dir, CEDA Chicago, 1976-78; spec needs mgr, Ebony Mgt Asn Chic, 1980-82; Handicap coordr, Dept Human Srv Chicago Ill, 1982-83; Nat Black Child Develop Inst, 1982-2000; Nat Phi Delta Kappa Inc, 1983; Pi Lam Theda, 1985-; Nat Asn Ed Young C; chmn, Dale City Christian Support Group, 1993-2000; Nat Polit Cong Black Women, Prince William Chap, 1995; Potomac Hosp Cancer Support Group, 1995-2000. **Honors/Awds:** Biog study Black Educ PhD Dissertation GGDCC Pub, 1981; Service Award, Harris YWCA Chic, 1974; Holy Cross Child Care Ctr, 1984; Gldn Gate Day Care Ctr Chic, 1984; Special Act Award, Rock Island Arsenal, 1985; Exceptional Performance Award, Rock Island Arsenal, 1986; ACYF Service Award, Early Head Start Team, 1997; Holy Family Cath Church Outreach Award, 2000; presenter, Nat Asn Ed Young Conf, 2000, 2001, 2003; Nat Black Child Develop Inst, 2000, 2001, 2002. **Home Addr:** 10726 S King Dr, Chicago, IL 60628. **Business Addr:** Children Development Service Coordinator, Fort Hood Army Base, PO Box 2272, Woodbridge, VA 22193.

**SIMPSON-CHILES, SANDRA.** **See SIMPSON-MITCHELL, SANDRA.**

**SIMPSON-MITCHELL, SANDRA (SANDRA SIMPSON-CHILES)**
Executive. **Personal:** Born Oct 4, 1955, Laurel, MS; daughter of Charles and Annie; children: Charles & Justin. **Educ:** Southern Univ, BS, acct, 1977; Univ Wis, MBA, mkt, 1980; Col Bus. **Career:** Peak, Marwick & Mitchell asst acct, 1977-79; Gen Mills, asst brand mgr, 1980-82; HBO, acct exec & vpres, 1982-98, reg mgr, reg dir, sr vpres, 1999-, gen mgr, affil sls, currently. **Orgs:** Delta Sigma Theta, 1974-; Nat Asn Minorities Cable, 1980-; TV bd mem, Mkt Soc Cable TV & Telecom Indust, 1987-, Women Cable & Tv; Jack & Jill Am Inc; Asn Mkt & Advert Professionals. **Home Addr:** 18012 Benchmark Dr, Dallas, TX 75252, **Home Phone:** (972)250-3836. **Business Addr:** Senior Vice President, General Manager, HBO, 1100 Avenue of the Americas, New York, NY 10036, **Business Phone:** (212)512-1000.

**SIMPSON-TAYLOR, DR. DOROTHY MARIE**
Educator. **Personal:** Born Jun 25, 1944, Pickens, MS; daughter of Willie Andrew and Mary Jane Young; married Harold J; children: Harold Duane & Robert Lance. **Educ:** Univ Nebr, Omaha, BGS, urban studies, 1972, MS, guid & coun, 1974; Univ Denver, PhD, coun psychol, 1988. **Career:** Pikes Peak Coun Ctr, ment health therapist, 1978-83; Iowa State Univ, psychol intern, 1984-85; Va Veterans Readjustment Ctrs, team leader & coun, 1985-88; Univ Northern Colo, asst prof, coun psychol, 1988-90; Ind State Univ, asst prof, africana studies, 1990; Ethnic Diversity, spec asst pres, 1995. **Orgs:** Gov affairs, Ind Asn Blacks Higher Edu, 1991-93; prog rev bd, Ind State Bd Health, 1991-93; Vigo County AIDS Task Force, 1991-93; steering com, Wabash Valley Critical Incident Stress Debriefing Team, 1992-93; Nat Asn Black Psychologists; Nat Black Storytellers Asn. **Home Addr:** 3700 N Capitol St, Washington, DC 20011, **Home Phone:** (812)237-3609.

**SIMPSON-WATSON, DR. ORA LEE**
Educator. **Personal:** Born Jul 7, 1943, East Chicago, IN; children: Ronald Damon & Kendyl Joi. **Educ:** Ball State Univ, Muncie, IN, BA, 1965; Purdue Univ, MA, 1969, PhD, 1977. **Career:** Dallas Independent Sch Dist, dir learning, 1977-80, dean instr, 1981-83; Dallas County Community Col, N Lake Col, div chair 1983-; Keep's Sake Inc, chmn & dir; Lake Forest Estate, secy. **Orgs:** Sch bd trustee, Dallas Independent Sch Dist; Nat Asn Black Sch Educs; Alpha Kappa Alpha; Links Tex Asn Sch Bd; consult Rep Suri Name, 1986; Child Care, Dallas, 1986. **Home Addr:** 6840 Talbot Pkwy, Dallas, TX 75232. **Business Addr:** Chairman, Director, For Keep's Sake Inc, 909 Liberty St, Dallas, TX 75204.

**SIMS, BARBARA MERRIWEATHER**
Judge. **Personal:** Born Buffalo, NY; daughter of Frank and Carmelita; married William; children: Frank William & Sue Cynthia. **Educ:** State Univ Col Buffalo, BS; State Univ NY, Buffalo Law Sch, JD. **Career:** Erie Co Off, asst dist atty, 1964-68; State Univ NY, Buffalo, asst to pres, 1969-74, Law Sch, lectr; City Buffalo Parking Violations Bur, hearing officer, 1975-77; City Ct Buffalo, city ct judge, 1977-; Univ at Buffalo Law Sch; Minority & Women's Affairs, Asst to Pres; dir, Equal Opportunity; coun, Buffalo Criterion weekly newspaper, currently. **Orgs:** Nat Bar Asn; Women's Polit Caucus; nat vpres, Nat Asn Black Women Attys, 1975-80; Erie Co Bar Asn; pres, vpres, secy & treas, Women Lawyers W NY; bd dir, Nat Asn Advan Colored People; bd dir, BC/BS W NY; United Fund Nat Fund Birth Defects; Nat Asn Negro Bus-Prof Women Buffalo Chap; deleg, Nat Women's Yr Conf Houston, 1977; African Am Community Builders. **Honors/Awds:** Recipient Community Service Award, 1968; Fight for Freedom Award, 1968; Distinguished Achievement Award, 1968; Distinguished Service Award, Grand United Order Odd fellows, 1978. **Special Achievements:** Chosen as one of 100 Black Women in Chicago Convention, 1972; First African American women to receive a law degree at UB; First African American women Assistant District Attorney in Erie County; Recipient of more than fifty awards. **Home Addr:** 280 Humboldt Pkwy, Buffalo, NY 14214, **Home Phone:** (716)881-1322. **Business Addr:** Counsel, Buffalo Criterion Weekly Newspaper, 623-625 William St, Buffalo, NY 14206, **Business Phone:** (716)882-9570.

**SIMS, CALVIN GENE**
Journalist. **Personal:** Born Dec 17, 1963, Compton, CA; son of Calvina Odessa Borders and Lonnie Gene. **Educ:** Yale Univ, New Haven, CT, BA, 1985; Univ Calif, attended 2005. **Career:** New York Times, New York, NY, reporter, 1985, ed producer, 2003, dir tv develop & foreign corresp, 2005-07; Poynter Fel, jour, 1985; Am Univ, consult, 2002-04; Princeton Univ, ferris prof journalism, 2002-03; Ford Found, vice chair, prog officer, 2007-2013. Edward R Murrow Press Coun Foreign Rels, fel; Int House, pres, chief exec officer, 2013-. **Orgs:** Fel Am Asn Advan Sci, Mass Media, 1984; Scroll & Key, 1985-; staff worker, Coalition Homeless, 1985-87; trustee, Overseas Press Club; trustee, Nat Bk Found; trustee, Harlem Educ Activ Fund. **Honors/Awds:** New York Times Publisher's Award, 1990. **Business Addr:** Director, The New York Times, 620 8th Ave, New York, NY 10018, **Business Phone:** (212)556-1234.

**SIMS, CARL W.**
Newspaper editor. **Personal:** Born Apr 29, 1941, Washington, DC; married Barbara Lindsey; children: 1. **Educ:** Howard Univ, attended 1962; Univ Minn, attended 1987. **Career:** Peace Corps Sierra Leone, vol, 1962-63; Wa Post, reporter, 1965-70; Boston Globe, copy ed, 1970; Bay State Banner Boston, ed, 1970-72; Newsweek, assoc ed, 1973-74; Minneapolis Star Tribune, nat ed, asst news ed, 1992. **Orgs:** Capital Press Club, 1966-69, Harvard Club Minn; Nat Asn Black Journalists, 1990-. **Honors/Awds:** Nieman Fel, Harvard Univ, 1972-73. **Home Addr:** 2770 Thomas Ave S, Minneapolis, MN 55416. **Business Addr:** National Editor, Assistant News Editor, Minneapolis Star Tribune, 425 Portland Ave, Minneapolis, MN 55488, **Business Phone:** (612)673-7276.

**SIMS, DELORIS**
Entrepreneur. **Personal:** married Isaiah; children: Elise & Annette. **Educ:** Univ SC, Moore Sch Bus; Marquette Univ Bus Admin, Kohler Ctr Entrepreneurship Owner-Mgr Prog, cert achievement; MATC, bus admin. **Career:** US Small Bus, vice chair; Firstar Bank, part-time teller br, part-time teller, vpres; Legacy Bancorp Inc, pres & treas; Legacy Banks Bd Dirs, chair, vice chair; Legacy Bank inc, pres & chief exec officer, currently; Legacy Bancorp Inc, pres & chief exec officer, currently. **Orgs:** Mem bd dir, Legacy Found; bd dir, Nat Bankers Asn; bd dir, Milwaukee Art Mus; bd dir, State Wis Investment Bd; bd dir, Wis African-Am Women LTD, 1997; bd dir, 1290 Scholar Fund; bd dir, Bus Coun-MMAC; bd dir, Milwaukee Boarding Sch Partnership with SEED Found; bd dir, Generation Growth Capital Inc; bd dir, Great Lakes Scholar Fund; bd dir, adv bd mem, Joe Zilber, Zilber Found; founder, Wis Urban Bankers Asn; founder, Wis African-Am Womens Ctr; bd dir, Legacy Redevelop Corp, bd mem; Metrop Milwaukee Asn Com, bd mem; Next Door Found, bd mem. **Honors/Awds:** Ernst & Young Entrepreneur of the Year in Financial Services, 2003. **Business Addr:** Chief Executive Officer, President, Legacy Bank Inc, 2102 W Fond du Lac Ave, Milwaukee, WI 53206, **Business Phone:** (414)343-6900.

**SIMS, DR. EDWARD HACKNEY**
Surgeon, physician. **Personal:** Born Sep 5, 1944, Atlanta, GA; children: Jessica Carolyn. **Educ:** Morris Brown Col, Atlanta, BS, 1965; Meharry Med Col, Sch Med, MD, 1972. **Career:** United Hosps Inc, internship, 1972-73; Los Angeles County King-Drew Med Ctr, resident, 1973-78; King/Drew Med Ctr, chief gen surg, 1983-87; St. Francis Med Ctr; Lakewood Regional Med Ctr; pvt pract, currently. **Orgs:** Fel Am Col Surgeon. **Home Addr:** 2624 N Commonwealth Ave, Los Angeles, CA 90027-1210, **Home Phone:** (323)522-6274. **Business Addr:** General Surgeon, 3625 E Martin Luther King Jr Blvd Suite 9, Lynwood, CA 90262, **Business Phone:** (310)631-9073.

**SIMS, ESAU, JR.**
Executive, association executive. **Personal:** Born Apr 14, 1953, Barberton, OH; son of Esau Sr and Eleanor; married Sarah Harris; children: Esau Jaques, Rashawn & Jeffrey. **Educ:** Nat Col Educ, BS, 1972. **Career:** Arthur Treacher's Fish 'n Chips, dist mgr, 1973-75, area mgr, 1975-78, asst dir franchise opers, 1978-79; Burger King, dist mgr, 1979-83, area mgr, 1985, vpres opers, 1989, vpres franchise sales & serv div, pres; Pro Mgt Group LLC, staff, currently. **Orgs:** Vpres, Swift Creek Athletic Asn, 1986-92; vpres, Chesterfield County Athletic Asn, 1991; chair, trustee, Spring Creek Baptist Church, 1992-93. **Home Addr:** 16008 Langhorne Ct, Tampa, FL 33647, **Home Phone:** (813)744-9342. **Business Addr:** Staff, Pro Management Group LLC, 44 Broad St NW Suite 510, Atlanta, GA 30303, **Business Phone:** (678)705-7217.

**SIMS, GENEVIEVE CONSTANCE**
Lawyer, founder (originator). **Personal:** Born Nov 4, 1947, Baltimore, MD; daughter of Joe and Fannie. **Educ:** NC State Univ, BA, econs, 1969; Univ Southern Calif, MPA, 1976; NC Cent Univ, JD, 1986. **Career:** Off State Personnel, NC State Govt, econ analyst, 1969-72; US Civil Serv Comn, personnel mgt specialist, 1972-76; Off Mgt & Budget Exec Off Pres, mgt analyst, 1976-77; US Civil Serv Comn, spec asst comnr, 1977-78; Merit Sys Protection Bd, spec asst, 1979-81; NC State Univ, Raleigh, NC, asst prof, 1982-93; NC Cent Univ, Durham, NC, vis instr, 1982-92; Genevieve C Sims Law Off, owner, lawyer, 1987-. **Orgs:** Bd dir, YWCA Wake County; bd adjustments, Wake County; NC Bar Asn; bd, United Black Fund Wash, 1976-81; chmn, bd dir, Shelley Sch; bd dir, NC Asn Black Lawyers, 1989-92; bd, NC Acad Trial Lawyers, 1995-2000; NC State Bd Elections; bd dir, Summit House Raleigh, 1996-2001, bd mem, 2001-09; NC State Bar; SC Bar; Wake County Bar Asn. **Honors/Awds:** Award, NC Special Olympics, 1982. **Home Addr:** 3923 Napa Valley Dr, Raleigh, NC 27612-7391, **Home Phone:** (919)785-3238. **Business Addr:** Attorney, Owner, Offices of Genevieve C Sims PC, 4024 Barrett Dr Suite 204, Raleigh, NC 27609, **Business Phone:** (919)834-7775.

**SIMS, GRANT**
Administrator, president (organization). **Career:** AAA Michigan, asst vpres, pres. **Business Addr:** Assistant Vice President, President, AAA Michigan, 1 Auto Club Dr, Dearborn, MI 48126, **Business Phone:** (313)336-1920.

**SIMS, HAROLD RUDOLPH**
Executive, writer. **Personal:** Born Jul 25, 1935, Memphis, TN; son of Benjamin Webster and Geraldine Rayford; married Lana Joyce Taylor; children: Douglass D & Kimberly J. **Educ:** Univ Poona, Poona, India, cert, int rels, 1956; Southern Univ, BR, LA, BA, 1957; Johns Hopkins Univ, Baltimore, grad study, 1962; Yale Univ, cert; George

Washington Univ, MS, 1967; King Memorial Col, DHL, 1977. **Career:** Owner (retired); Off Econ Opportunity Exec Off Pres White House, exec sec, 1968-69; Nat Urban League, dep exec dir, 1969-71, exec dir, pres, 1971-72, actg dir; Johnson & Johnson, vice pres corp affairs, 1972-79; Sims & Assoc/Sims Int, pres, 1979; Sound Radio WNJR, chief exec officer, gen mgr, pres, 1984-92; MLK Jr NJ Comn, Off Gov, exec dir, 1985-86; Ebony Mag, sr acct exec, 1986-87; Uni-Med Consult, chmn, exec comt, beginning 1992; Centennial Concepts. **Orgs:** Adv bd, Princeton Univ, 1971-82; vpres, Oper PUSH, Eastern Region, 1972-74; bd dir, Martin Luther King Jr Ctr, 1972-; sr int adv & UN rep, 1972-96; chair, Friends Cong Black Caucus, 1973-78; asst vpres, St Louis Univ, 1974-84; pres, Nat Asn Mkt Develop, NY Chap, 1974-76; bd dir, Near E Found, 1976-; int bd adv, African-Am Inst, 1976-; nat adv bd, Nat Sci Found, 1977-82; pres, Sims-Sutton Indust Develop Group, 1982-; exec vpres, Gibson-Wonder Film Co/Jos P Gibson Found, 1983-; comnr, NJ MLK Jr Comn, 1984-86; co-founder, King-Luthuli S African Transformation Ctr, 1989-; Sharon Baptist Church, deacon, 1989-; AUS Spec Forces Asn, 1996-; life mem, Alpha Phi Alpha Fraternity; Nat Asn Advan Colored People. **Home Addr:** 1 Lincoln Pl Suite 27K, North Brunswick, NJ 08902, **Home Phone:** (732)940-9917.

## SIMS, JOHN LEONARD

Computer executive, president (organization), chemist. **Personal:** Born Jul 1, 1934, Wilmington, DE; son of Thomas A and Ella Gibbs; married Shirley; children: John Jr, Kevin & Joe. **Educ:** Del State Col, Dover, Del, BS, 1962; Ohio State Univ, Columbus, OH, Grad Work; Columbia Univ, New York, NY, Mgt Training Courses. **Career:** E I Du Pont de Nemours Co Inc, mgt positions, chemist; WFD SafricA Free Elections Fund & Digital Equip Corp, sr exec; Champion Int Corp, mgt positions, govt rels; Digital Equip Corp, Maynard, MA, corp mgr EEO/AA, 1974-75, dir manf personnel, 1975-81, corp staff mgr, 1981-84, vpres personnel, 1984-87, vpres strategic resources, 1987-93; John L Sims Consul, pres, currently. **Orgs:** Bd dir, Boston Bank Com, 1983-; bd govs, ASTD, 1987-; chmn, Freedom House, 1987-; bd govs, Boston Chamber Com, 1992-; Nat Nat Asn Advan Colored People; Boston Pvt Indust Coun; exec leadership coun, Northeast Human Resources Asn; bd trustee, Nat Urban League; SBI Roundtable Fla A&M; chair bd, Cambridge Col; bd dir, ABW Mfg Co; bd dir, Am Socs Training & Develop; bd dir, Roxbury Community Col found; bd dir, Bay State Skills Corp; vice chmn, OneUnited Bank. **Honors/Awds:** Award for Contributing, Nat Urban League, 1988; Award for Service, Freedom House; Award for Service, Alpha; Award for Achievements, Several Colleges & Minority Organizations; Image Award, Nat Asn Advan Colored People; National Urban League Achievement Award. **Special Achievements:** Top 25 Most Powerful Black Managers, Black Enterprise Magazine, 1988. **Home Addr:** 356 N Spaulding Cv, Lake Mary, FL 32746-4323, **Home Phone:** (407)833-8506. **Business Addr:** President, John L Sims Consulting, 100 Frankflin St, Boston, MA 02110, **Business Phone:** (617)457-4400.

## SIMS, KEITH ALEXANDER

Football player, entertainer. **Personal:** Born Jun 17, 1967, Baltimore, MD; married Tia; children: Cairo, Storm, Keith Jr, Jayson & Jayson. **Educ:** Iowa State Univ, BS, indust technol, 1993. **Career:** Football player (retired), radio sideline reporting; Miami Dolphins, guard & left guard, 1990-97; Wash Redskins, guard & left guard & right guard, 1998-2000; Miami Dolphins Radio Network, sideline reporting, currently; Dunkin Donuts, Franchise owner. **Honors/Awds:** Pro Bowls, 1993-95; Hall of Fame, Iowa State, 2006. **Special Achievements:** Films: 1990 NFL Draft, 1990; 1992 AFC Championship Game, 1993. TV Series: "NFL Monday Night Football", 1992-95; "ESPN's Sunday Night Football ", 1992-95; "The NFL on NBC". 1995. **Business Addr:** Franchise Owner, Dunkin Donuts, 5701 N Pine Island Rd 300, Tamarac, FL 33321, **Business Phone:** (954)721-4332.

## SIMS, LOWERY STOKES

Museum director. **Personal:** Born Feb 13, 1949, Washington, DC; daughter of John Jacob Sr and Bernice Banks. **Educ:** City Univ NY, Queens Col, BA, art hist, 1970; Johns Hopkins Univ, MA, art hist, 1972; City Univ NY, MA, philosphy, 1990, Grad Sch, PhD, art hist, 1995. **Career:** Metro Mus Art, asst mus educr, staff, 1972-75; Queens Col Dept Art, adj instr, 1973-76; Sch Visual Arts, instr, 1975-76, 1981-86; Metro Mus Art, assoc cur, 1979-95, cur, 1995-99; Studio Mus Harlem, pres, exec dir, Permanent Collection, adj cur, 2000-07; Queens Col, vis prof, 2005; Hunter Col, New York, vis prof, 2006; Nat Mus Am Indian, gen ed & essayist, 2008; Univ Minn, Dept Art, vis scholar, 2007; Clark Art Inst, fel, 2007; Mus Arts & Design, cur, 2007-; MAD, co-curated, "Remixing the Ordinary", 2008, "Dead or Alive", 2010. **Orgs:** Fel Black Doctorate Students, Ford Found, 1970-72; Am Sect Int Art Critics Asn, 1980-; Col Art Asn, 1983-; coun mem, NY State Coun Arts, 1987-92; bd, Col Art Asn, 1994-97; bd, Tiffany Found, 1995-97; adv bd, Ctr Curational Studies, 1995-; selection jury, World Trade Ctr memorial, 2003-04; ArtTable Inc; Tiffany Found & Art Matters Inc; Asn Art Critics; lectured, Nat Gallery Kingston, Jamaica, 2004; lectured, Cleveland Mus Art, 2006; lectured, New York Hist Soc, 2006; lectured, Driskell Ctr at Univ Md, Col Pk, 2009. **Honors/Awds:** Employee Travel Grant, Metrop Mus Art, 1973; DHL, Md Inst Col Art, 1988; Frank Jewett Mather Award, Col Art Asn, 1991; hon degrees, Moore Col Art & Design, 1991; Lifetime Achievement Award in the Arts, Queens Mus Art, 1998; Hon Doctorate, Parsons Sch Design, New Sch Univ, 2000; Hon Doctorate, Arts, Atlanta Col Art, 2002; Hon Doctorate, Col New Rochelle, 2003; Hon Doctorate, Brown Univ, 2003. **Special Achievements:** One of Crain's Mag Top 100 Minority Executives, 1998, 2003; One of 50 Women Who Have Changed the World, Essence Magazine, 2003; Numerous publications; American Artists and Exhibition catalogs. **Home Addr:** 1125 Lexington Ave, New York, NY 10075, **Home Phone:** (212)734-8385. **Business Addr:** Curator, Museum of Arts And Design, 2 Columbus Circle, New York, NY 10019, **Business Phone:** (212)299-7777.

## SIMS, PETE, JR.

Executive. **Personal:** Born May 11, 1924, El Dorado, AR. **Educ:** Atlanta Col Mil Sci, 1950. **Career:** El Dorado Housing Authority, pres, 1970-; Sims Enterprises, pres, 1973-; Ark Fun dir & Mrtcns Asn, pres, 1974; NFDMA Ark St Funeral dir, pres dist gov; C E U Instr, Funeral Serv State Ark; Sims Mortuary Inc, chief exec officer, pres, funeral dir & mortician, currently. **Orgs:** Bd mem, Nat Funeral dir & Morticians Inc; Nat & State Funeral dir Asn; Ark Off Asn; Nat Asn Advan Colored People; Oper PUSH; DeSota Area Coun Boys Scouts; Ex-Ruler, IBPOE W; Chamber Com, El Dorado, Ark; chmn, First Baptist Church; Nat Ex-Ruler Coun Elks; state pres, Ark State Elk Asn; Dist, Gov, Dist VI; Exchange Club; bd mem, State Bd Burial Asn; Ark Funeral dir Asn; N E La Funeral dir Asn; pres, Booker T Wash Alumni Asn; Union County Community Found Bd; Barton Libr Bd; Ark Funeral Serv Educ Bd; Trustee Bd First Baptist Church; Lion Oil Community Adv Panel; Nation Funeral Ethic Asn. **Business Addr:** Chief Executive officer, President, Sims Mortuary Inc, 432 Liberty St, El Dorado, AR 71730-4531, **Business Phone:** (870)862-4266.

## SIMS, ROBERT

Musician, college teacher. **Personal:** Born Oct 10, 1965, Chicago, IL. **Educ:** Oberlin Conserv, cert; State Univ NY, Binghamton, cert; Northwestern Univ, artistic dipl; Music Acad W, cert. **Career:** Baritone focusing in African American folk songs and spirituals: Community Concerts and Live On Stage Series, more than 150 recitals across the United States; Pacific Music Festival, toured Japan including a nationally televised performance of Bernstein's "Opening Prayer"; Appeared with Mercedes Ellington and David Baker in Duke Ellington's "My People"; National tours with the Three Generations trio; Northern Ill Univ, Sch Music, fac. **Honors/Awds:** American Traditions Competition, Gold Medal Winner; Friedrich Schorr Opera Award, Winner. **Special Achievements:** Made recital debut at Carnegie Hall in 2005; Participated in Jessye Norman's "Honor! A Celebration of the African American Cultural Legacy at Carnegie Hall" in March 2009; Four CDs by producer Canti Classics: "Soul of a Singer," "Sims Sings Copland," "Spirituals, In The Spirit," and "Three Generations"; guest on recordings with Moses Hogan Chorale: "Deep River" and "Gotta Home in Dat Rock". **Business Addr:** Professor, Northern Illinois University, College of Visual and Performing Arts, DeKalb, IL 60115, **Business Phone:** (815)753-0537.

## SIMS, RONALD CORDELL (RON SIMS)

Government official. **Personal:** Born Jul 5, 1948, Spokane, WA; son of James C Sr and Lydia T Ramsey; married Cayan Topacio; children: Douglas, Daniel & Aaron; married Topacio. **Educ:** Cent Wash State Univ, Ellensburg, Wash, BA, psychol, 1971. **Career:** Wash State Atty Gen, Seattle, Wash, investr, 1971-72; Fed Trade Comn, Seattle, Wash, sr investr, 1972-78; City Seattle Dept Human Resources, mgr youth serv, 1979-81; Wash State Senate, Olympia, Wash, leadership coordr, 1981-86; King County Coun, Seattle, Wash, counman, 1986, exec, 1996-09, 2001, 2005; US Dep Housing & Urban Devp, dep secy, 2009-. **Orgs:** Pres, Comn trade & investment policy Asia; Seattle Human Rights Comn, 1984-86; vol, Meany Mid Sch; lay minister, Oper Night watch; pres, Rainier Dist Youth Athletic Asn; bd dir, Planned Parenthood; bd mem, Families First C's Home Soc; dir, S E Effective Develop. **Honors/Awds:** World Affairs Fel, James Madison Found, 1986-87; Humanitarian of the Year Award, Progressive Animal Welfare Soc, 1993; Robert L Woodson Jr Affordable Communities Award, Housing & Urban Develop, 2005; One of Gov Mag's Govt Officials of the Year, 2007; Leader of the Year, Am City Mag, 2008; Leader of the Year, County Mag, 2008; Health Quality Award, Nat Comt Qual Assurance, 2008; Honored with national awards from the Sierra Club, the Environmental Protection Agency. **Special Achievements:** Most powerful post yet attained by an African American in Washington; First African American elected to the King County Council. **Home Addr:** 3227 Hunter Blvd S, Seattle, WA 98144-7029, **Home Phone:** (206)722-7467. **Business Addr:** Deputy Secretary, US Department of Housing and Urban Development, 451 7th St S W, Washington, DC 20410, **Business Phone:** (202)708-1112.

## SIMS, PROF. RONALD R. (RON SIMS)

Educator, consultant. **Personal:** Born Apr 27, 1949, Steubenville, OH; married Serbrenia J; children: Nandi, Dangaia & Sieya. **Educ:** Univ Steubenville, BA, sociol, 1971; Univ Md, Baltimore, MSW, sch social work & community planning, 1972; Case Western Reserve Univ, PhD, orgn behav, 1981. **Career:** Ohio Dept Ment Retardation, dir social work serv, 1975-77; Crisis Intervention Ctr, social worker, 1977-80; Cent Nat Bank, internal orgn develop consult, 1978-80; Ronald R Sims & Assocs, orgn & mgt consult, 1981-; Auburn Univ, Montgomery, asst prof, 1981-86, consult, currently; Ala State Univ, Col Bus Admin, adj prof; Col William & Mary, Mason Sch Bus, prof, Sch Bus Admin, assoc prof, 1986-92, Floyd Dewey Gottwald, sr prof bus admin & orgn behav, co-chair, 1992-, dir, Masters Bus Admin, 1994-95; TRI Corp, associate, 1995-2000. **Orgs:** Acad Mgt, 1981-; Asn Bus Simulation & Experiential Learning, 1983-97; comt mem, Col William & Mary; bd dir, BoundlessNetworks & 3Tango, 1988-2001; chair, Oversight Committee; 1992-94. **Business Addr:** Floyd Dewey Gottwald Sr Professor of Business Administration, College of William & Mary, Rm Tyler 318A 102 Richmond Rd, Williamsburg, VA 23187-8795, **Business Phone:** (757)221-2855.

## SIMS, THEOPHLOUS ARON, SR.

Pharmacist, school administrator, president (organization). **Personal:** Born Mar 17, 1939, Jefferson, TX; married Nancy Jayne Wattley; children: 3. **Educ:** Tex Southern Univ Sch Pharm, BS, pharmy & health sci, 1961, MS; Nat Asn Retail Druggists, doctor pharm cert, 1984. **Career:** Sims Enterprises Inc, pres, currently; Forth Worth Independent Sch Dist 4, bd mem, 1983-, bd vpres & secy, currently; pharmacist, currently; Sims Prof Pharm; second vpres, Dist 4. **Orgs:** Nat Asn Retail Druggist; life mem, Kappa Alpha Psi; Alpha Phi Alpha, 1983; bd mem, Tex Enterprise Found, 1984; adv comt, Tex Girls Choir, 1984; NIH, 1984-; Ft Worth Metrop Black Chamber Com; Nat Asn Sch Bd; Rolling Hills Civic League Club; Tarrant County Health Planning Coun; Campus Dr United Methodist Church; Kappa Alpha Fraternity; Chi Delta Mu Med Fraternity; Tex Pharmaceutl Asn; Am Pharmaceutl Asn; Tarrant County Pharmaceut Asn; vpres, Nat Alumni, Tex Southern Univ; life mem, Nat Asn Advan Colored People; life mem, Prairie View Interscholastic League Coaches Asn; Ft Worth Metrop Black Chamber Com; Glencrest Civic League Club. **Honors/Awds:** Personalities of the South Award; Maroon & Grey Club Service Award; Eminent Man Outstanding Leadership Award; Street named for Dr Sims in New Rollings Addition. **Special Achievements:** Honored with naming of T. A. Sims Elementary School, 1989; Originator of FWISD Scholar Athlete Award Program; FW Black Achievers; First African-American School Board President. **Home Addr:** 4421 Kingsdale Dr, Ft Worth, TX 76119-4529, **Home Phone:** (817)534-7467. **Business Addr:** Vice President, Board Secretary, Fort Worth Independent School District 4, 100 N Univ Dr, Ft. Worth, TX 76107-1360, **Business Phone:** (817)871-2000.

## SIMS-DAVIS, EDITH R.

School administrator. **Personal:** Born Dec 24, 1932, Marion, LA; daughter of Rich Louis Robinson and LuEllen Nelson; married Samuel C; children: Cynthia Laverne Sims & William Sims Jr. **Educ:** AM&N Col, BS, 1955; Tuskegee Inst, MS, 1960; Univ Buffalo, PhD, 1962; Chicago State Univ, Chicago, Ill, attended 1966. **Career:** Principal (retired), consultant; Merrill High Sch, teacher, 1955-59; Englewood High Sch, 1961-66; counr, 1966-68; Fenger High Sch, fac, 1968-69; Calumet High Sch, asst prin, actg prin, 1969-71; Caldwell & McDowell Sch, prin, 1971-82; Corliss High Sch, prin, 1982-96; Bryn Mawr Col, interim prin; Sch Bd, consult, currently. **Orgs:** Delta Sigma Theta Sorority, 1953-; Univ Ark Alumni Asn, 1969-; Samuel B Stratton Asn, 1980-; Chicago Bd Educ; Ill Prin Asn; Chicago Prin Asn; Ella Flagg Young Chap Nat Alliance Black Sch Educations; Nat Coun Admin Women Educ; Chicago Urban League; Beta Kappa Chi Sci Frat; Nat Coun Negro Women; Metrop Cluster. **Honors/Awds:** Univ Ark Alumni Asn, Pine Bluff "Miss Alumni", 1955; Alpha Kappa Mu Nat Honor Soc; Roseland Comt Grit Award, 1986; Outstanding Chicago Prin Award Dist 33, 1986; Outstanding Principal Award, Supt Sch Chicago Bd Educ, 1986; Distinguished Alumni Award, Univ Ark, Pine Bluff, 1987; Whitman Award, Excellence Educ Mgt, Whitman Corp, 1990; Phi Delta Kappa Award, 1992. **Home Addr:** 21 E Huron St, Chicago, IL 60611, **Home Phone:** (312)649-1425.

## SIMS-PERSON, LEANN MICHELLE

Banker. **Personal:** Born Aug 14, 1972, Ft. Worth, TX; daughter of William and Mildred (deceased); married Marc A; children: Austin Person. **Educ:** Tex Christian Univ, BBA, 1994; Tex Wesleyan Univ, MBA, 2000. **Career:** Chase Bank Tex, human resources recruiter, 1994-, asst vpres, currently; songwriter. **Orgs:** Financial asst, Delta Sigma Theta Sorority, 1992; youth teacher & choir mem, Campus Dr United Methodist Church; bd mem, Minority Leaders & Citizens Coun, 1996-99; Young Bankers Asn, 1996-2000; Consumer Skills Comm, Tex Agr Exten Serv, 1996-2000; Finance Comm, Neighborhood Housing Serv, 1997-99; United Way, Increasing Self-Sufficiency Community, 1998-2000; Heritage Coun, FW Conv & Visitors Bur, 1998. **Honors/Awds:** The 50 Future Leaders, Ebony Mag, 1994; Doer's Award, City Ft Worth, 1997. **Home Addr:** 2916 Patino Rd, Fort Worth, TX 76112, **Home Phone:** (817)496-0670.

## SIMTON, CHESTER

Librarian. **Personal:** Born Jan 28, 1937, Longstreet, LA; son of Jim and Umie Lee; married Peggy I Nabors; children: Annelle M & Mary Lee; married Dorothy M Powell; children: Jessica & Jennifer. **Educ:** Univ Calif, Berkeley, BS, 1976, MLS, 1977; Matanuska Susitna Community Col, Palmer, AK; Norton Sound Col, Nome, AK; Univ Anchorage, Anchorage, AK. **Career:** Matanuska Susitna Bor Sch Dist, Palmer, AK, librn media, 1973-; Nome Pub Sch Dist, Nome, AK, libr & media specialist, 1980-83; King Cove City Sch Dist, King Cove, AK, libr & media specialist; Wasilla Pub Libr, dir, currently. **Orgs:** Media Round Table, Alaska Libr Asn, 1987-88; Diversified Occup Palmer High Sch, 1987-90; Teachers Right Comt, Exec Bd, NEA Alaska, 1989-; multicultural chair, State of Alaaska, 1992-93. **Home Addr:** 4144 E Country Fld Cir, Wasilla, AK 99654, **Home Phone:** (907)373-6557. **Business Addr:** Director, Wasilla Public Library, 391 N Main St, Wasilla, AK 99654, **Business Phone:** (907)376-5913.

## SINCLAIR, BENITO A.

Engineer. **Personal:** Born Aug 18, 1931, Colon; son of Arthur Donovan and Isabel Darshville; married Helen Rahn; children: Marcia Yvette & Shana Elida. **Educ:** Calif Polytech State Univ, San Luis Obispo, CA, BS, archit engineering, 1957. **Career:** Benito A. Sinclair Assocs, owner; consult engr & construct mgr. **Orgs:** Dir, Struct Engrs Asn Calif, 1982-84; Los Angeles city comnr, Bldg & Safety, 1984-94; founding mem, pres, Los Angeles Coun Black Prof Engrs; founding mem, pres, Calif Asn Minority Consult Engrs; Nat Asn Black Consult Engrs; Am Soc Civil Engrs; Am Coun Eng Co; Earthquake Eng Res Inst. **Honors/Awds:** Distinguished Alumnus, Calif Polytech Univ Arch Engr, 1969; Outstanding Contributions to Community, Am Soc Civil Engrs, 1976; Excellence in Design, AM Inst Architects, 1984; Tom Bradley Terminal, LAX, Prestressed Conc Inst, 1987; Special Honoree, Los Angeles Coun Black Prof Engrs, 1987. **Special Achievements:** First Black Graduate from School of Architecture and Environmental Design, Calif Polytechnic State Univ, 1957; First Black Registered Structural Engineer in California. **Home Addr:** 5636 Tuxedo Terr, Hollywood, CA 90068, **Home Phone:** (323)219-9390. **Business Addr:** President, Chief Executive Officer, B A Sinclair & Assoc Inc, 5601 W Wash Blvd, Los Angeles, CA 90016, **Business Phone:** (213)933-5581.

**SINCLAIR, CLAYTON, JR.** **See Obituaries Section.**

**SINCLAIR, FLOYD JOY.** **See MAYWEATHER, FLOYD, JR.**

## SINCLAIR, MICHAEL GLENN

Football player, football coach. **Personal:** Born Jan 31, 1968, Galveston, TX; married Betty; children: Michael, Michaela & Johnnie Glenn. **Educ:** Eastern NMex Univ, BS, phys educ. **Career:** Football player (retired), football coach; Seattle Seahawks, defensive end, 1991-94, left defensive end, 1995-2001; Sacramento Surge, 1992; Philadelphia Eagles, defensive end, 2002; W Tex A&M Univ, asst coach defensive line, 2005-06; Hamburg Sea Devils, defensive line coach, 2007; Montreal Alouettes, defensive line coach, 2008-12; Sask Roughriders, asst head coach, defensive line coach, 2013; Chicago Bears, defensive line coach, 2013-14. **Honors/Awds:** Pro Bowl, 1996, 1997, 1998; Steve Largent Award, 1998; Sack Leader, Nat Football League, 1998; Second-team All Pro, 1998; World Bowl, Hamburg Sea Devils, 2007.

### SINDLER, MICHAEL H.
Executive director. **Personal:** Born May 15, 1943, DC; married Louise Bates. **Educ:** Georgetown Sch Foreign Serv, BS, 1965; Georgetown Law Sch, JD, 1968. **Career:** DC Legis & Opinions Div, asst corp coun, 1969-73; Motor Vehicles DC, asst dir, 1973-74, spl asst dir, 1974-. **Orgs:** Wash Bar Asn; DC Bar Asn; Fed Bar Asn; DC Munic Officers Club, 1973-. **Honors/Awds:** American Jurisprudence Award. **Home Addr:** 4548 Linnean Ave NW, Washington, DC 20008. **Business Addr:** 301 C St NW, Washington, DC 20001.

### SINGLETARY, DEBORAH DENISE
Artist, consultant, educator. **Personal:** Born Apr 27, 1952, Brooklyn, NY; daughter of Peter and Doris. **Educ:** City Univ NY, Hunter Col, attended 1973. **Career:** Elva McZeal Comput Learning Ctr, instr, 1996-; Vision Carriers, painter & multi-media artist, pres, publ, 2004-; Mama Found Arts, prog coordr, 2001-, dep exec dir, 2012-. **Orgs:** Coord coun, Entitled Black Women Artists, 1999-; Nat Coun Artists, 2000-. **Honors/Awds:** Exemplary Serv Award, US Dept Justice Off USA, 2001; Award, Art Matters Inc. **Business Addr:** Publisher, Painter & Multi-Media Artist, Vision Carriers, 360 Clinton Ave Suite 1R, Brooklyn, NY 11238, **Business Phone:** (718)398-4616.

### SINGLETARY, REGGIE LESLIE
Executive, football player. **Personal:** Born Jan 17, 1964, Whiteville, NC; son of Dan Arron and Notredane Pridgen; married Janice Jeffires; children: 2. **Educ:** NC State Univ. **Career:** Football player (retired), employee; Philadelphia Eagles, 1987-89, guard & offensive tackle, Right defensive tackle, 1986, Right Guard, 1988, Right tackle, 1990; Green Bay Packers, 1991; Gen Elec, Burlington, staff, currently. **Honors/Awds:** Dick Christy Award, NC State Univ, 1985; All Rookie Team Defense, NFL, 1986. **Home Addr:** 3434 N NC 49, Burlington, NC 27217, **Home Phone:** (336)578-3614. **Business Addr:** Staff, General Electric Co, 510 E Agency Rd, West Burlington, IA 52655-1649, **Business Phone:** (319)753-8400.

### SINGLETON, ALSHERMOND GLENDALE (AL SINGLETON)
Football coach, executive, football player. **Personal:** Born Aug 7, 1975, Newark, NJ. **Educ:** Temple Univ, BS, sport recreation mgt. **Career:** Football player (retired), coach, owner; Tampa Bay Buccaneers, 1997-99, 2001, linebacker, 2000, 2002; Dallas Cowboys, linebacker, 2003-06; free agent; dry cleaners store owner; Tampa Bay Buccaneers, coaching intern, 2015-. **Business Addr:** Intern Coach, Tampa Bay Buccaneers, 1 Buccaneer Pl, Tampa, FL 33607.

### SINGLETON, BENJAMIN, SR.
Police officer, business owner. **Personal:** Born Dec 17, 1943, Summerville, SC; son of Clement Addison Sr and Catherine Fludd; married Dorothy Abraham; children: Benjamin Jr. **Educ:** Voc Training, Columbia SC, cert, 1981; Atlanta Univ, Criminal Justice Inst, Miami, FL, cert, 1985. **Career:** Dorchester County Sheriffs Dept, St George SC, lt, deputy sheriff, 1971-95; County Public Defenders Office, deputy coroner, coordinator; Ga Police Dept, unpaid reserve officer; Knights ville Dry Cleaners, Summer ville SC, owner, 1986. **Orgs:** Life mem, Cannan United Methodist Church, United Methodist Mens Club; New Eden Lodge 32, 1984; Nat Asn Advan Colored People, 1985; Upper Dorchester Civic Club, 1985; vpres, Palmetto State Law Enforcement Off Asn, 1985-87, pres, 1987-89; First Cong Dist Black Caucus, 1986-90; SC Atty Gen Adv Bd State Grand Jury, 1988-92, Univ SC Police Census, 1988-92. **Honors/Awds:** Sponsor, Ann sr Citizens Dinner Tri-County; Co-Sponsor, Dixie League Baseball Team Community, 1967-; Co-Founder, The Berkeley-Dorchester Chap PSLEOA, 1977; Outstanding Servs, Palmetto State Law Enforcement, 1982; Sponsor, Dixie League Baseball Team, 1984; Speaker varied church youth groups on law enforcement, 1985-90; Community Serv, Berkeley-Dorchester Chap, 1989. **Home Addr:** 406 E Old Orangeburg Rd, Summerville, SC 29483, **Home Phone:** (803)873-9638. **Business Addr:** Owner, Knightsville Dry Cleaners, 1580 Cent Ave, Summerville, CA 29483, **Business Phone:** (843)875-5132.

### SINGLETON, CHRIS
Football player, sports manager. **Personal:** Born Feb 20, 1967, Parsippany, NJ. **Educ:** Univ Ariz, sociol maj, 1989. **Career:** Football player (retired), manager; New Eng Patriots, outside linebacker, right outside linebacker, 1990-93; Miami Dolphins, left linebacker, right linebacker, 1993-96; Merck, pharmaceut sales rep, 2001-03; Bristol-Myers Squibb, territory bus mgr, 2003-05; Novartis, sales consult, 2005-06; Isotis Orthobiologics, orthobiologic specialist, 2006-08; OptumRx, diabetes acct mgr, 2008-13; Vanderbilt Univ, asst equip mgr football, 2013-; Credit Relief USA, sr acct mgr, 2014-15; Purdue Pharma L.P, territory bus mgr, 2015-. **Honors/Awds:** Two time All Pac 10 selection; Second team All Am, Sporting News, 1989. **Business Addr:** Assistant Equipment Manager Football, Vanderbilt University, 2601 Jess Neely Dr, Nashville, TN 37212, **Business Phone:** (615)322-4653.

### SINGLETON, CHRISTOPHER VERDELL
Baseball player, media executive. **Personal:** Born Aug 15, 1972, Martinez, CA; married LaShunda Gray. **Educ:** Univ Nev. **Career:** Baseball player (retired), media executive; San Francisco Giants, 1993; Chicago White Sox, outfielder, 1998-2001; Baltimore Orioles, ctr fielder, 2002; Oakland Athletics, ctr fielder, 2003; Pittsburgh Pirates, 2004; Tampa Bay Devil Rays, ctrfielder, 2005; Chicago White Sox, commentator, 2006-07, color analyst, 2006-08; ESPN, baseball tonight, currently. **Orgs:** Chris Singleton Fund, founder, currently. **Business Addr:** Baseball Tonight, ESPN, ESPN Plz, Bristol, CT 06010.

### SINGLETON, ERNIE
Consultant, executive, president (organization). **Personal:** Born New Orleans, LA. **Educ:** Southern Univ New Orleans. **Career:** Radio Sta, New Orleans, host; Radio Sta, Jackson ville, host, music dir, prog dir, morning newsman; Fantasy, Mercury Recs, regional prom mgr; Casablanca Recs, regional prom mgr, nat prom dir; Poly Gram Recs, nat prom dir, 1978-83; Warner Bros Recs, sr vpres, Reprise Recs Prom, staff head, 1987; Urban & Jazz Music Prom, v pres, Black Music Div, pres, 1990-; MCA Recs, Black Music Div, black music prom nat dir, pres urban music, 1990-97; Singleton Entertainment Corp, chief exec officer, 2008-. **Orgs:** Young Black Prgm Coalition, 1989, founding mem, 1990. **Honors/Awds:** Bobby Poe Executive of the Year Award, 1985; Award of Excellence, Young Black Programmers Coalition, 1987; Executive of the Year, Urban Network, Impact, Black Radio Exclusive, 1990. **Business Addr:** Chief Executive Officer, Singleton Entertainment Corp, 18341 Sherman Way Suite 206, Reseda, CA 91335, **Business Phone:** (818)774-0818.

### SINGLETON, HAROLD, III
Executive, financial manager. **Personal:** Born Apr 11, 1962, Chicago, IL; son of Harold Jr and Ruth Ann; married Saundra R; children: James D Butler, Juliana L & Deana J. **Educ:** Ill Inst Technol, BS, chem engineering, 1983; Univ Chicago, Booth Sch Bus, MBA, finance, 1989. **Career:** Atlantic Richfield Co, assoc chem engr hydroprocessing & coking res & develop, 1980-83; RR Donnelley & Sons, mfg supvr, 1984-90; First Chicago Corp, Transp Div, corp banking officer, 1990-93; Zaske Sarafa & Assoc, managing analyst, portfolio mgr, equity analyst, 1993-95; Fifth Third Bank NW Ohio, sr portfolio mgr, 1995-96; Brinson Partners Inc, partner, 1996-2000; Metrop W Capital Mgt LLC, sr vpres, small cap value portfolio mgr & investment analyst, 2000-03; UBS Global Asset Mgt, exec dir, co-mgr small cap value equity & sr investment analyst, 2003-06; Perspectives Charter Sch, Oper & Finance Comt, bd dir; PineBridge Investments, managing dir, equity prod specialist & client portfolio mgr, 2007-10, global head equity & fixed income prod specialists, 2009-10, head asset mgt co & global head retail & intermediary sales, 2010-12; NexTier Capital Solutions LLC, sr consult prin, 2013; Lincoln Financial Group, vpres, head client portfolio mgt, 2014-16, head mgr selection & portfolio construct, 2016-. **Orgs:** Nat Black MBA Asn, 1990-; Nat Asn Securities Prof, 1992-; Asn Investment Mgt & Res, 1993-; Orange Co Soc Investment Mgr, 2000-; bd dir, Loretto Hosp Found; Investment Analyst Soc Chicago; Global Equity Team; Metrop W Capital Mgt LLC; Am Bridge Asn Educ & Charitable Found; New York Soc Security Analys; Ill Inst Technol; present chmn, PineBridge Investments Mgt Taiwan Ltd; Perspectives Charter Sch; bd dirs, Vantagepoint Funds, 2013-14. **Honors/Awds:** Chartered Financial Analyst, Asn Investment Mgt & Res, 1995. **Special Achievements:** Savoy Mag's 2012 Top 100 Most Influential Blacks Corp Am. **Home Addr:** 5320 Chariton Ave, Los Angeles, CA 90056, **Home Phone:** (323)291-9410. **Business Addr:** Head Manager, Portfolio Construction, Lincoln Financial Group, 1300 S Clinton St, Fort Wayne, IN 46802, **Business Phone:** (781)395-1219.

### SINGLETON, ESQ. HARRY M.
Lawyer, real estate agent, association executive. **Personal:** Born Apr 10, 1949, Meadville, PA; son of GT and Rose A Fucci; children: Harry Jr & Leah. **Educ:** Johns Hopkins Univ, BA, 1971; Yale Law Sch, JD, 1974. **Career:** Houston & Gardner Law Firm, assoc, 1974-75; Consult, Am Enterprise Inst, 1975; Off Gen Coun & Fed Trade Comn, atty, 1975-76; Covington & Burling Law Firm, assoc, 1976-77; Com Dist Columbia, US House Reps, dep minority coun, 1977-79, minority chief coun & staff dir, 1979-81; Off Congional Affairs, US Dept Com, dep asst secy, 1981-82; US Dept Ed, asst secy, 1982-86; Harry M Singleton & Assocs Inc, pres, 1986-91; pvt pract atty, 1991-; Remax Allegiance, chief exec officer. **Orgs:** Pres & bd trustee, Barney Neighborhood House, 1978-80; corp bd dir, C's Hosp Nat Med Ctr, 1984-88; bd dir, DC Chap, Republican Nat Lawyers Asn, 1990-91; bd dir, Coun 100 Black Republicans, 1991-92; DC Black Republican Coun, 1991-93; chmn, DC Black Republican Coun, 1992-93; Republican Nat Hisp Assembly DC, 1991-93; DC Republican Comt, 1991-; Republican Nat Comt man, DC, 1992-2000; Republican Nat Comt Exec Coun, 1993-95; Republican Nat Comt, Resolutions Community, 1997-2000; Lions Club, Dist 22-C, 1991-97; Nat chmn, Republican Nat African-Am Coun, 1993-2000; chmn, DC Chap Republican Nat African-Am Coun, 1993-2000; Boys & Girls Clubs Greater Wash, 1994-97. **Honors/Awds:** Distinguished Honorary Alumnus Award, Langston Univ, 1984; Montgomery College Faculty Excellence Award, 2010-13. **Home Addr:** 604 Butternut St NW, Washington, DC 20012, **Home Phone:** (202)841-3490. **Business Addr:** Owner, Attorney, Harry M Singleton & Associates, 1250 Conn Ave Nw, Washington, DC 20036, **Business Phone:** (202)291-1781.

### SINGLETON, JAMES MILTON (JIM SINGLETON)
Consultant, government official, teacher. **Personal:** Born Jan 1, 1931, Hazlehurst, MS; married Allie Mae Young; children: James Jr & Allie. **Educ:** Southern Univ Baton Rouge LA, BS; Xavier Univ, New Orleans, health planning; Loyola Univ; Univ Okla. **Career:** Government official (retired); Orleans Parish Sch Bd, teacher, 1956-70; Nat Urban Health, New Orleans, consult, 1970-71; City New Orleans Mayors Off, spec consult health, 1971-78; City New Orleans, city councilman, 1977, councilmember Dist B, 1994-2002, coun pres, mayors designated rep. **Orgs:** Pres, Cent City Econ Corp, 1965-78; Total Comm Action Inc, 1975; founder, Dryades YMCA; chmn, Heritage Aq Adv Comm, Bd; LA Health Plan; chmn bd, Total Comm Action Inc; prime mover BOLD; New Orleans City Coun; La Gaming Comn; Nat Urban League; Nat Asn Advan Colored People; Black Orgn Leadership Develop; chmn, Master Plan Adv Comt; Cent City Econ Opportunity; Broadmoor Improv Asn. **Honors/Awds:** President Award, Total Comm Action Inc, 1976; President Award, Dryades St, YMCA, 1977. **Home Addr:** 3816 General Taylor St, New Orleans, LA 70125-3733, **Home Phone:** (504)821-3429. **Business Addr:** Founder, Dryades YMCA, 2220 OC Haley Blvd, New Orleans, LA 70112, **Business Phone:** (504)299-4310.

### SINGLETON, JOHN DANIEL
Screenwriter, movie director. **Personal:** Born Jan 6, 1968, Los Angeles, CA; son of Danny and Sheila Ward Johnson; married Vestria Barlow; children: Maasai Mohandas & Cleopatra; married Akosua Busia; children: Hadar. **Educ:** Univ Southern Calif, Sch Cinema-TV, BA, 1990. **Career:** Director; film producer; actor; Films: Boyz n the Hood, writer & dir, 1991; Poetic Justice, producer, 1993; Beverly Hills Cop III, 1994; Higher Learning, producer, 1995; Rosewood, 1997; Woo, exec producer, 1998; Shaft, producer, 2000; Baby Boy, producer & music supvr, 2001; 8 Mile, actor, 2002; 2 Fast 2 Furious, dir, 2003; How to Get the Man's Foot Outta Your Ass, 2003; Four Brothers, dir, 2005; Hustle & Flow, producer, 2005; Black Snake Moan, producer, 2007; Illegal Tender, producer, 2007; Abduction, dir, 2011; Videos: "Remember the Time", 1995; Columbia Studios, internship. **Special Achievements:** Oscar nominee, Best Original Screenplay, Best Dir, Boyz N the Hood, 1992. **Business Addr:** Filmmaker, Creative Artists Agency, 2000 Ave of the Stars Suite 100, Los Angeles, CA 90067, **Business Phone:** (424)288-2000.

### SINGLETON, KENNETH WAYNE (KEN SINGLETON)
Baseball player, television broadcaster. **Personal:** Born Jun 10, 1947, New York, NY; married Susan McCarthy; children: 4. **Educ:** Hofstra Univ, Hempstead, NY. **Career:** Baseball player (retired), commentator; New York Mets, outfielder, 1970-71; Montreal Expos, outfielder, 1972-74; Baltimore Orioles, outfielder, 1975-84; WJZ-TV, sportscaster, 1980; Sports Network, tv color commentator; Montreal Expos broadcasts, radio color commentator; Fox Sports, color commentator; Sports Network Can, analyst; New York Yankees, YES Network, commentator, currently. **Orgs:** Bd dir, Cool Kids Campaign, Currently. **Home Addr:** 10 Sparks Farm Rd, Sparks, MD 21152-9300. **Business Addr:** Commentator, YES Network, Chrysler Bldg 405 Lexington Ave 36th Fl, New York, NY 10174-3699, **Business Phone:** (646)487-3600.

### SINGLETON, LEROY, SR.
Funeral director. **Personal:** Born Oct 8, 1941, Hempstead, TX; son of Oscar (deceased) and Rosie Lee; married Willie E Franklin; children: LaRonda K, Leroy Jr, Kaye, Erica, Kareen & Garard W. **Educ:** Prairie View A&M Univ, Prairie View, Tex, BS, indust art educ, 1968, MEd, coun & guid, 1971; Commonwealth Sch Mortician, Houston, Tex, dipl, mortuary sci, 1984. **Career:** Dallas ISD, Dallas, Tex, teacher, 1968-69; Prairie View A&M Univ, Prairie View, Tex, assoc teacher, 1971-75; Singleton Trucking, owner & mgr, 1975-82; Singleton Funeral Home, Hempstead, Tex, dir, co-owner & lic ins agt, 1982-; Hempstead, Tex, mayor, 1984-90; county comnr, 1997-2005. **Orgs:** Am Legion Post 929, 1966-; charter mem, Lion Tamer, Lion's Club, 1972-; Lone Star Masonic Lodge No 85, 1980-; Tex State Rev Bd, 1986-89; Appraisal Licensing & Cert Bd, 1991-94; Independent Funeral dir Asn, Tex Independent Funeral dir Asn; Kiwanis Int; Nat Conf Black Mayors, World Conf Mayors; Am Personnel & Guid Asn; Am Col Personnel Asn; Admin Stud Personnel; Piarie View Alumni Asn; Asn Counr Educ & Supv; Am Sch Counr Asn; Tex Admin Stud Personnel; Phi Delta Kappan; Omega Psi Phi Fraternity Inc; Tex Coalition Black Dem; Nat Asn Advan Colored People. **Honors/Awds:** Plaque, Boy Scouts Am, 1985; Plaque, Vocational Guidance Serv, 1986; Houston Chap Community Serv Award, Nat Tech Asn; Outstanding Serv Award, First Black Mayor Hempstead, Tex. **Special Achievements:** First Black Mayor, Lone Star Lodge No 85, 1985. **Home Addr:** PO Box 344, Hempstead, TX 77445. **Business Addr:** Director, Co-Owner, Singleton Funeral Home, 616 7th St, Hempstead, TX 77445, **Business Phone:** (979)826-2425.

### SINGLETON, NATE, III (NATHANIEL SINGLETON, III)
Football player, athletic trainer. **Personal:** Born Jul 5, 1968, New Orleans, LA. **Educ:** Grambling State Univ. **Career:** Football player (retired), trainer; San Francisco 49ers, wide receiver, 1993-96; Baltimore Ravens, 1997; Tenn Oilers, 1997; Mackie Shilstone's PEP Prog, athletic trainer; E Jefferson Gen Hosp Fitness Ctr, staff; Nat Football League, wide receiver, currently. **Business Addr:** Wide Receiver, National Football League, 345 Pk Ave, New York, NY 10016, **Business Phone:** (212)450-2000.

### SINGLETON, RICKEY
Executive, teacher, president (organization). **Personal:** Born Nov 13, 1959, Chicago, IL; son of Isaac and Juanita; married Diane; children: Sean Marcus, Corey & Taranikqa. **Educ:** Friends Int Christian Univ, DDiv, 1996. **Career:** Entrepreneur; Whole Truth Pentecostal Church God Harvey, Ill, founder; S End Conserv Music, owner & teacher, 1979-84; Word Faith Fel, sr pastor, 1984-96; WEMG-FM Radio, owner & gen mgr, 1993-96; Grace Church Int, sr pastor, 1996-; Ditacore Nutrit Foods Distrib Co, owner, 1998-, Richards Super Premium Ice Cream, chief exec officer, 1999-; King Richard's Deli, chief exec officer, 2002-; Golden Kernel Popcorn Co, founder & owner, 2002-; Richard's Rolling Stores, owner, 2004-; Supernatural Empowerment Radio, pres & owner, 2010-; Spirit Grace Church, pastor & teacher, currently. **Orgs:** Word Faith Fel; Pres & ceo, Covenant Entrepreneur's Network, 1997-; Grace Message & manifestations personal empowerment; Pres & ceo, Covenant Entrepreneur's Network, 1997-. **Home Addr:** 1720 Richards Ct, Flossmoor, IL 60422, **Home Phone:** (708)799-8238. **Business Addr:** Pastor, Grace Church International, 13957 S Marquette, Burnham, IL 60633-1914, **Business Phone:** (708)891-4800.

### SINGLETON, DR. ROBERT
Association executive, educator. **Personal:** Born Jan 8, 1936, Philadelphia, PA; son of Walter and Julia Margaret Cloud; married Helen; children: Robby, Damani & Malik. **Educ:** Univ Calif, BA, polit sci, 1960, MA, int econs, 1962, PhD, urban econs & labor econs, 1983. **Career:** Pac Hist Rev Univ Calif, asst ed, 1958-60; Univ Calif, res asst, 1961-63; Univ Calif Inst Indus Rels, chief res economist, 1963-64, res economist, 1967-69; Afro-Am Studies Ctr, founding dir, prof, 1969-70, economist, 1969-71; John Hay Whitney fel, 1963; US Labor Dept, res economist, 1964-66; US Dept Labor Grant support dissertation, 1966; Educ Asn Inc, Wash, consult; Robert Singleton & Assocs, partner, 1976-, pres, 1979-; Loyola Marymount Univ, Dept Econ, assoc prof, 1980, chmn, prof, 1982-. **Orgs:** Founding dir, Univ Calif Los Angeles, Ctr Afro-Am Studies, 1969-71; Social Sci Res Coun, Comt Afro-Am Studies, 1969-75; mem bd dir, Am Educ Fin Asn, 1969-78; founder, chmn J Black Studies mem, bd dir, Am Civil Liberties Union, Southern Calif Chap, 1970-72; Am Econ Asn, 1979-; Western Econ Asn, 1980-; Int Atlantic Econ Soc, 1985-; Western Regional Sci Asn, 1986-; Econ Asn, 1988-; pres, Univ Calif Los Angeles, Nat Asn Advan Colored People; chmn, Santa Monica Venice Cong Racial Equality; Chancellors Adv Com Discrimination, Am Civil Liberties Union, Soc Sci Res Coun Com Afro-Am Studies; consult staff Senate Select Subcom, OP-EN; HEW; Urban Educ Task Force; Nat Urban League Educ Task Force; Nat Asn Planners. **Home Addr:** 9208 S Vail Way, Inglewood, CA 90305-1894, **Home Phone:** (918)599-0123. **Business**

**Addr:** Professor, Loyola Marymount University, University Hall, Los Angeles, CA 90045-2659, **Business Phone:** (310)338-7373.

### SINGLEY, ELIJAH
Librarian. **Personal:** Born Jan 29, 1935, Bessemer, AL; son of Daniel; married Yvonne Jean; children: Jennifer M. **Educ:** Miles Col, BA, social sci, 1958; Atlanta Univ, MS, libr sci, 1959; Sangamon State Univ, MA, sociol & anthrop, 1980; Ill State Univ, ABD, Am hist, 1998. **Career:** Librarian (retired); Va State Col, asst ref librn, 1960; Ala State Univ, dir, libr serv, 1963-71; Lincoln Land Community Col, asst librn, 1971-2000. **Orgs:** Fel Vinegar Hill Neighborhood Asn; Alpha Phi Alpha Frat; Am Numis Asn; Nat Urban League; Ill Sociolog Asn; Ill Libr Asn; White House Conf Libr & Info Serv, 1978-79; Nat Asn Advan Colored People; Antique Advert Asn Am; Orgn Am Historians; Am Libr Asn; Am Legion. **Home Addr:** 2301 S Noble Ave, Springfield, IL 62704-4343, **Home Phone:** (217)546-5143.

### SINGLEY, YVONNE JEAN
School administrator, vice president (organization). **Personal:** Born Jun 18, 1947, Gary, IN; daughter of William Webb and Mary Williams; married Elijah; children: Jennifer. **Educ:** Univ Memphis, BA, latin, 1969; Univ Ill, Urbana, MUP, 1974, doctoral studies, higher educ leadership; Capella Univ, PhD, educ leadership, 2011. **Career:** Ind Univ-Northwest, social researcher, 1969-72; Opportunities Indust Ctr, Manpower Training, CETA, educ coordr, 1974-75; Div Voc Rehab, Prog Eval Unit, methods & procedures adv, 1975-78; Ill Dept Pub Aid, Title XX Prog, social serv planner, 1978-79; Ill Bd Educ, Acad & Health Affairs, asst dir, 1979-87; Ill Co Col Bd, asst dir, 1983-91, sr dir stud & inst develop, sr dir, 1991-2004; Diversity Works Inc, vpres, owner, 2004-; Univ Ill, Grad Col, grad fel; Univ Ill Champaign. **Orgs:** Bd mem, Springfield Urban League, 1977-80; bd mem, Springfield League Women Voters, 1979-84; pres, Access Housing, 1981-86; YMCA, 1985-91; bd mem, Springfield Jr League, 1987-88; vol, Springfield Magical Event, 1991; Kappa Delta Pi, Int Hon Soc, 1995; co-founder, Ill Comt Black Concerns Higher Educ; Am Asn Women Community Cols, State Exec Comt; Phi Theta Kappa Hon Soc; regional dir nat bd, Am Asn Women Community Cols; Am Asn Women Community Cols; Opportunities Industrialization Ctr; Ilinois Community Col Bd; Higher Learning Comn-N Cent Accreditation; Am Health Info Asn; Ill State Bd Educ. **Home Addr:** 2301 S Noble Ave, Springfield, IL 62704-4343, **Home Phone:** (217)546-5143. **Business Addr:** Vice President, Owner, Diversity Works Inc, 44 E Main St Suite 508, Champaign, IL 61820-3649, **Business Phone:** (217)378-5135.

### SINKFORD, REV. WILLIAM GEORGE
Clergy, minister (clergy). **Personal:** Born Jun 15, 1946, San Francisco, CA; son of William Johnson and Kathryn Love; married Maria; children: William James & Danielle Shay. **Educ:** Harvard Col, BA, 1968; Starr King Sch Ministry, Mdiv, 1995. **Career:** Sink ford Restorations Inc, 1981-92; Creating Safe Congregations: Toward Ethnic Right Rels, co-ed; First Unitarian Church, sr minister. **Orgs:** Dir, Unitarian Universalist Asn; pres, Congregational Dist Exten Serv, 2001-09. **Home Addr:** 3435 NW Luray Terr, Portland, OR 97210. **Business Addr:** Senior Minister, First Unitarian Church, 1034 SW 13th Ave, Portland, OR 97205, **Business Phone:** (617)318-6010.

### SINNETTE, DR. CALVIN HERMAN
Physician. **Personal:** Born Aug 30, 1924, New York, NY; son of Norman J and Frances; married Elinor Kathleen DesVerney; children: Caleen S Jennings & Darryle S Craig. **Educ:** City Col NY, BS, 1945; Howard Univ Col Mede, MD, 1949. **Career:** Physician (retired), educator; Univ Ibadan & Zaria Univ, prof pediat, 1964-70; Columbia Univ, prof pediat, 1970-75; Univ Nairobi Kenya, prof pediat, 1975-77; Sch Med Morehouse Assoc, dean clin affairs, 1977-79; Howard Univ, asst to vpres health affairs, 1979-88, asst vpres health affairs, 1988-91, prof, emer prof pediat. **Orgs:** Nat Med Asn, 1977; Alpha Omega Alpha, 1978; bd dir, Trans Africa, 1981-89; assoc mem, Nat Minority Golf Scholar Asn. **Honors/Awds:** Magnificent Prof Award, Howard Univ Col Med, 1996; Leadership Award, Arthur Ashe Athletic Asn, 1998. **Home Addr:** 1016 S Wayne St Apt 409, Arlington, VA 22204-4435, **Home Phone:** (703)521-2515. **Business Addr:** Professor Emeritus, Howard University College of Medicine, 2400 Sixth St, Washington, DC 20059, **Business Phone:** (202)806-6100.

### SINNETTE, DR. ELINOR DESVERNEY
Librarian, college teacher. **Personal:** Born Oct 8, 1925, New York, NY; daughter of James C DesVerney (Deceased) and Elinor Adams Calloway (Deceased); married Calvin H; children: Caleen Jennings & Darryle Craig. **Educ:** Hunter Col City Univ NY, AB, 1947; Pratt Inst Sch Libr Serv, MLS, 1959; Columbia Univ Sch Libr Serv, DLS, 1977. **Career:** Librn (retired); NY City Pub Libr, librn, 1947-54; NY City Bd Educ, sch librn, 1960-65; Inst African Studies, Univ Ibadan, Nigeria, lectr, Ist Librn ship, 1965-69; Ahmadu Bello Univ, Zaria, Nigeria, lectr, 1969-70; Howard Univ, Moorland-Spingarn Res Ctr, dir, 1980; Black Bibliophiles & Collectors, ed. **Orgs:** Oral Hist Asn, Oral Hist Mid Atlantic Region; Black Caucus Am Libr Asn. **Home Addr:** 1016 S Wayne St Apt 409, Arlington, VA 22204-4435, **Home Phone:** (703)521-2515.

### SKEENE, LINELL DE-SILVA
Physician, pediatrician. **Personal:** Born Nov 6, 1938, Brooklyn, NY; daughter of Gilbert M (deceased) and Odessa; married Henry Mark Hunter. **Educ:** Temple Univ, BA, 1959; Meharry Med Col, MD, 1966. **Career:** Maimonides Med Ctr, resident gen surg, 1969-71, attend surgeon; Metro Hosp, 1971-72; NY Med Col, instr surgeon, 1971-72; Brookdale Med Ctr Hosp, attend surgeon, emergency med, currently. **Orgs:** AMA; Am Med Women's Asn; NY St Med Soc; Nat Coun Negro Women; Nat Advan Asn Colored People; Nat Med Asn. **Honors/Awds:** Outstanding Young Women of America, 1974. **Business Addr:** Physician, Brookdale Med Center Hospital, 1 Brookdale Plz Suite 300chc, New Hyde Park, NY 11040, **Business Phone:** (718)240-6504.

**SKELETON, DEBRA RENEE WILSON. See WILSON, DEBRA.**

### SKILLERN, GWENDOLYN D.
Vice president (organization), auditor. **Personal:** Born Nacogdoches, TX. **Educ:** Univ Calif, Berkley, CA, BA, acct, 1976; Stanford Univ, MBA, 1976. **Career:** Deloitte & Touche LLP, audit mgr, sr auditor & staff auditor, 1976-83; Crown Zellerbach, group financial mgr, 1983-86; GWENDOLYN D. SKILLERN, CPA, chief exec officer, 1986-92; Williams, Adley & Co-DC LLP, partner, 1992-93; Kaiser Found Health Plan, dir internal audit, Northern Calif region, 1993-95, dir internal audit, Northwestern hub, 1995-98; Bass Hotels & Resorts, vice pres internal audit, 1998-99, vice pres & controller, 1999-2000; CareFirst BlueCross BlueShield, sr vpres, gen auditor, 2000-. **Orgs:** Past nat pres & chief exec officer, Nat Asn Black Accountants, 2006-08. **Business Addr:** Senior Vice President, General Auditor, CareFirst BlueCross BlueShield, 10455 & 10453 Mill Run Cir, Owings Mills, MD 21117.

### SKINNER, BRIAN
Basketball player. **Personal:** Born May 19, 1976, Temple, TX; son of James and Gladys; married Rebecca; children: Madisen & Avery. **Educ:** Baylor Univ, environ studies, 1998. **Career:** Los Angeles Clippers, forward, 1998-2001, 2008-10, free agt, currently; Cleveland Cavaliers, forward-ctr, 2001-02; Philadelphia 76ers, forward-ctr, 2002-03; Milwaukee Bucks, 2003-04, 2006-07, 2010-11; Sacramento Kings, 2005-06; Portland Trail Blazers, 2006; Phoenix Suns, 2007-08; Benetton Treviso, 2010-11; Memphis Grizzlies, 2011-12. **Business Addr:** Free Agent, Los Angeles Clippers, 1111 S Figueroa St Suite 1100, Los Angeles, CA 90015, **Business Phone:** (888)895-8662.

### SKINNER, DR. EWART C.
Educator. **Personal:** Born Jan 2, 1949. **Educ:** Univ Hartford, Hartford, CT, 1969; Tarkio Col, Tarkio, MO, BA, 1971; Am Univ Cairo, Cairo, Egypt, MA, 1974; Mich State Univ, E Lansing, MI, PhD, 1984. **Career:** Self-employed media consult, Trinidad & Tobago, 1975-79; MI State Univ, E Lansing, MI, instr, 1983-84; Purdue Univ, W Lafayette, IN, asst prof, 1984-; Caribbean Mass Media Systs & Int Media, specialist; UNESCO, Trinidad& Tobago, Wi, 1987; Bowling Green State Univ, assoc prof telecom & chair, currently. **Orgs:** Int Asn Mass Communs Res; Int Commun Asn; Int Peace Res Asn; Semiotics Soc Am; Asn Educ Jour & Mass Commun; Caribbean Studies Asn. **Home Addr:** PO Box 2497, Evansville, IN 47728-0497, **Home Phone:** (317)497-1278. **Business Addr:** Associate Professor, Chair, Bowling Green State University, 323 W Hall, Bowling Green, OH 43403-0001, **Business Phone:** (419)372-8646.

**SKINNER, ROBERT L, JR. See Obituaries Section.**

### SKIPPER, CLARENCE, III
Restaurateur. **Personal:** Born Jul 5, 1971, Lafayette, LA; son of Philomena and Clarence; children: Travion. **Educ:** Southern Univ, A&M Col, BS, comput sci. **Career:** JC Penney Life, systs analyst, 1994-96; Neiman Marcus, programmer analyst, 1996; Midwest Consult, contract programmer, 1996-97; Systware, contract programmer, 1997-98; Creole Cafe, owner, currently. **Home Addr:** 18702 Platte River Way, Dallas, TX 75287-2013, **Home Phone:** (972)307-5218. **Business Addr:** Owner, Creole Cafe, 2717 E Belt Line Rd Suite 111, Carrollton, TX 75006, **Business Phone:** (972)478-7176.

### SLADE, CHRISTOPHER CARROLL (CHRIS SLADE)
Football player, broadcaster, football coach. **Personal:** Born Jan 30, 1971, Newport News, VA; married Talisa Marie; children: 2. **Educ:** Univ Va, grad. **Career:** Football player (retired), coach; New Eng Patriots, right outside linebacker, 1993-95, left linebacker, 1996-98, line backer, 1999, linebacker, right outside linebacker & left outside linebacker, 2000; Carolina Panthers, linebacker, 2001; Univ Va, sports broadcaster & sideline reporter; Pace Acad, head football coach, 2013-; high school coach. **Honors/Awds:** Defensive Player of the Year, 1992; Defensive Most Valuable Player, 1990, 1776 Quarterback Club, 1994; Pro Bowl Alternate, 1995; Pro Bowl Selection, 1997; All-Pro, 1997; 1 Time AA Georgia High School Football Champion, 2015. **Special Achievements:** Films: 1996 AFC Championship Game, 1997; Super Bowl XXXI, 1997. **Business Addr:** Head Football Coach, Pace Academy, 966 W Paces Ferry Rd NW, Atlanta, GA 30327, **Business Phone:** (404)262-1345.

### SLADE, DR. JOHN BENJAMIN, JR.
Physician. **Personal:** Born Dec 20, 1950, Columbus, OH; son of John Benjamin Sr and Betty Buckner; married Rischa Ann Williams; children: Danielle & Alana. **Educ:** USaF Acad, BS, 1972; Case Western Res Univ, MD, 1978; David Grant USAF Med Ctr. **Career:** David Grant Med Ctr, internship, 1978-79, resident family pract, 1979-81; USAF, Beale AFB, Family Pract Clin, chief, 1981-84, Sch Aerospace Med, fel, hyperbaricmed, 1988-89; David Grant Med Ctr, Travis AFB, resident; family pract staff, 1984-86, chair, Dept Hyperbaric Med, 1989-96, chief med staff, 1996-97; Iraklion Air Sta, Crete, Greece, chief, hosp servs, 1986-88; Doctors Med Ctr, San Pablo, Calif, assoc med dir, med dir, currently; NorthBay Healthcare, Northbay Ctr Wound Care, hyperbaric physician, currently; Sutter Med Group, Sutter Solano Med Ctr, physician, currently. **Orgs:** Am Acad Family Pract, 1981-; Aerospace Med Asn, 1989-; Wound Healing Soc, 1990-; treas, Undersea & Hyperbaric Med Soc, pres, 1999-2000; Hyperbaric Oxygen Ther & Educ Comt. **Home Addr:** 131 Blackwood Ct, Vacaville, CA 95688-1058, **Home Phone:** (510)970-5343. **Business Addr:** Medical Director, Hyperbaric Medicine, Doctors Medical Center, 2000 Vale Rd, San Pablo, CA 94806, **Business Phone:** (510)235-3483.

### SLADE, KAREN E.
Executive. **Personal:** Born Oct 18, 1955, Cleveland, OH; daughter of Charles and Violette Crawford. **Educ:** Ky State Univ, BS, telecommunications, 1977; Pepperdine Univ, MBA, 1991. **Career:** Xerox Corp, acct exec, 1978, mkt consult, proj mgr, dealer sales mgr, regional sales mgr, 1988-89; Taxi Productions Inc, vpres & gen mgr, 1989; KJLH-FM, Radio, sr vpres & gen mgr, currently. **Orgs:** Alpha Kappa Alpha Sorority; bd mem, Los Angeles Urban League, 1989-95; MOSTE, mentoring prog w/jr high sch students, 1989-; Black Media Network, 1989-; Nat Asn Black Owned Broadcasters, 1989-; Stephanie Starks HOPE Found. **Home Addr:** 1148 S Citrus Ave, Los Angeles, CA 90019, **Home Phone:** (213)934-8371. **Business Addr:** Senior Vice President, General Manager, Taxi Productions Inc, 161 N La Brea Ave, Inglewood, CA 90301-1707, **Business Phone:** (310)330-2200.

### SLADE, PHOEBE J.
Sociologist, educator. **Personal:** Born Oct 17, 1935, NY; married Robert H; children: Robert & Paula. **Educ:** Hunter Col, attended 1954; Bellevue Nursing Sch, RN, 1957; Jersey City State Col, BS, 1958; Columbia Univ, Teachers Col, MA, 1960, EdD, 1976. **Career:** New York Dept Health, pub health nurse, 1959-61; NJ State Dept Health, consult, 1961-63; Hunter Col, lectr, 1965-71, asst dir, dorm, 1966-67, chmn, health scis dept, 1968-69; Jersey City State Col, asst prof, 1963-74, assoc prof, 1975-77, prof, 1977, chair, sociol & anthrop dept, 1985, prof emer, currently. **Orgs:** Delta Sigma Theta, 1954-; Nat Asn Advan Colored People, 1960-; Am Pub Health Asn, 1962-; Jersey City State Col Fac Asn, 1963-; Asn NJ Col Fac, 1963-; Nat Coun Family Rels, 1966-; Tri-State Coun Family Rels, 1968-; Royal Soc Health, London, Eng, 1969-; Jersey City Pub Lib, 1970-74; Jersey City Com Criminal Justice, 1970-75; Jersey City Bd Ed, 1971-74; Mayors Task Force Ed, Jersey City, 1972-; Nat Educ Asn, 1972-; Teaneck & Together, 1973-; Jersey State Col, 1975-; Bd Ethics, Teaneck, 1976-; Archdiocean Bd Educ, 1976-; vpres, Hawthorne's PTA, 1977; Afro-Amer Comm Polit Act, 1985; Mayors Spl Task Force Res, Teaneck, 1985; ANSS-CF; HCEA; Nat Geog Soc; Mus Nat Hist; Nj State Bd Human Servs, 1991-; Zonta Int, 1994-; State Bd Human Serv; Archdiocese Newark; Jersey City Bd Educ; NJ State Dept Health-Cardiovasc Health Adv Panel; NJ State Bd Human Serv; Hudson County Task Force Foster Care &Hudson County Serv Comn. **Honors/Awds:** Pi Lamda Theta, National Scholastic Organization for Women in Education, 1967; Citation Award, Comm Civil Rights Met, New York, 1963; Jersey City Public Library, Board of Trustee's Service Award, 1975; Tribute to Mother's Award, Hudson County Sickle Cell Anemia Asn, 1989; Teaneck Pioneer Recognition Award, Teaneck Centennial Comt 100+, 1995; Dr. Slade received Merit, Research, and Civil Rights Awards. **Special Achievements:** Author: "Evaluating Today's Schools: Relevancy of the Open Classroom, " NJE Pac, May 1978; co-author: The Complete Guide to Selected Health and Health Related Careers, 1980. **Home Addr:** 765 Salem St, Teaneck, NJ 07666-5320, **Home Phone:** (201)833-2581. **Business Addr:** Professor Emeritus, Jersey City State College, 2039 Kennedy Blvd, Jersey City, NJ 07305-1527, **Business Phone:** (201)200-2000.

### SLADE, DR. PRISCILLA DEAN
School administrator. **Personal:** children: Al & Maurice. **Educ:** Miss State Univ, BS, bus admin; Jackson State Univ, MS, prof acct; Univ Tex, Austin, PhD, acct, 1985. **Career:** Tougaloo Col, asst prof acct, 1979-80; Jackson State Univ, MPA coordr, 1980-81, adminr & part fac mem, 2009-; Univ Tex, asst acct instr, 1981-85; FL A&M Univ, asst prof acct, 1985-91; Tex Southern Univ, assoc prof acct, 1991, chair Acct Dept, 1991-93, Jesse H Jones Sch Bus, dean, 1992-99, actg pres, 1999, pres, 1999-2006. **Orgs:** Bd mem, Qual Rev Oversight Bd State TX; bd mem, Fin Comn, Houston Area Urban League; bd mem, Am Asn Col Sch Bus; Am Acct Asn; Am Asn Univ Women; Am Coun Educ; Am Soc Women Acct; Beta Alpha Psi; Coun Pub Univ Pres & Chancellors; Nat Asn Equal Opportunity Higher Educ; Prof Black Women's Enterprise; bd dir, Fed Res Bank-Houston Br; Greater Houston Partnership; bd dir, Houston Super Bowl, 2004; Houston 2012 Found; Houston Technol Ctr; INROADS Houston Inc; Jr Achievement; Houston Forum; YMCA Greater Houston Area; HISD HU-LINC Gov Bd; Telecom Opportunity Inst, Jackson State Univ.

### SLASH, JOSEPH A. (JOE SLASH)
President (organization), executive, accountant. **Personal:** Born Aug 25, 1943, Huntington, WV; son of Joseph Autumn and Clara Rose; married Meredith; children: Alexandria Dawson & Adrianne Letetia. **Educ:** Marshall Univ, BBA, acct, 1966. **Career:** Sears Roebuck & Co, comptroller asst, 1966; Arthur Young & Co, Staff Acct, audit mgr, 1968-78; City Indianapolis, Ind, dep mayor, 1978-89; Indianapolis Power & Light Co, Indianapolis, Ind, vpres, 1989-2001; Indianapolis Urban League, pres & chief exec officer, 2002-14. **Orgs:** United Way Greater Indianapolis; Ind Asn CPA's Adv Forum, 1976-78; Am Inst CPA; Ind Asn CPA; bd dir, Indianapolis Chap Ind Asn CPA; Kappa Alpha Psi; Alpha Eta Boule; Sigma Pi Phi; bd dir, United Way Cent Ind, 1985-; exec comt, Comn Downtown, 1991-; exec comt, Ind Sports Corp, 1991-; co-chair, Indy Counts community; Ind Humanities Coun; bd dir, Greater Indianapolis Progress Comn; adv bd, Marshall Univ Lewis Sch Bus; bd dir, CtrLeadership Develop Columbia Club, Downtown Kiwanis Club; mem bd dir, Fifth Third Bank Cent Ind & Nat Govt Serv; Indianapolis Metrop Police Dept Merit Bd; bd dir, Greater Indianapolis Progress Comt (GIPC); bd dir, & Secy Ctr Leadership Develop; Columbia Club; Indianapolis SuperBowl Host Comt, 2012; former Dir & mem Exec Comt Ind Sports Corp; exec coordr, Circle City Classic; Ind Sports Corp; exec comt, NCAA Proj, 2000, Nat Col Athletic Asn; Men's Basketball Final Four Organizing Comt; Exec Comt 2001 World Police & Fire Games; past chmn Indianapolis Pvt Indust Coun; Bd Dirs & Adv Bd Indianapolis Urban League; co-chmn, Race Rels Leadership Network; chmn, adv bd, Ind Univ-Purdue Univ Indianapolis, 2005-08; trustee, treas, N Indianapolis First Baptist Church; Treas, Indy Partnership Inc; adv council, IndyHub Inc. **Honors/Awds:** Kappa of the Month, Kappa Alpha Psi, 1978; Outstanding Black Alumni, Marshall Univ, 1986; Professional Achievement Award, Ctr Leadership Develop, 1987; Outstanding Young Man of the Year, Jaycee; Sagamore of The Wabash; Who's Who in Black America; United Way of Central Indiana's Outstanding Service Award; Marshall University Outstanding Alumni Award. **Special Achievements:** First African American Deputy Mayor of the City of Indianapolis in the Hudnut administration. **Home Addr:** 1140 Fox Hill Dr, Indianapolis, IN 46228-1367, **Home Phone:** (317)257-2780. **Business Addr:** Treasurer, Indy Partnership Inc, 111 Monument Circle, Indianapolis, IN 46204, **Business Phone:** (317)236-6262.

### SLATER, JACKIE RAY
Football player, executive. **Personal:** Born May 27, 1954, Jackson, MS; married Annie; children: Matthew & David. **Educ:** Jackson State

Univ, BA; Livingston Univ, MS. **Career:** Football player (retired), coach, exec; Los Angeles Rams, offensive tackle, right tackle, 1976-94; St Louis Rams, offensive line, tackle, 1995; Oakland Raiders, co-offensive lineman coach, 2006; Saddleback Community Col, asst offensive line coach, 2007-09; Slater Enterprises LLC, owner, currently; El Modena High Sch Varsity team, head offensive lineman coach, currently; Azusa Pac Univ, offensive line coach, currently. **Orgs:** Rams Speakers Bur; Pro Football Hall Fame, 2001. **Honors/Awds:** Walter Payton Phys Educ Award, Jackson State Univ; All-NFC, First Team, 1983, 1986-87, 1989, Second Team, UPI, 1985, 1988, 1990, Football News, 1985; Pro Bowl, 1983, 1985-90; First Team All Pro, 1987-89; Second team All Pro, 1983, 1985; Bart Starr Man of the Year Award, 1995; Inducted into the Pro Football Hall of Fame, 2001. **Special Achievements:** First recipient of Walter Payton Physical Education Award, Jackson State University. **Home Addr:** PO Box 6411, Orange, CA 92863-6411. **Business Addr:** Owner, Slater Enterprises LLC, 9203 Bent Spur Lane, Houston, TX 77064, **Business Phone:** (281)469-0818.

## SLATER, REGGIE DWAYNE

Basketball player, executive. **Personal:** Born Aug 27, 1970, Houston, TX; married Katie; children: 3. **Educ:** Univ Wyo, BA, lib arts, 1992. **Career:** Basketball player (retired), executive; Argal Huesca, Spain, forward, 1992-93; Girona, 1993-94; Denver Nuggets, power forward, 1994-95, 1996; Portland Trail Blazers, power forward, 1995-96; Dallas Mavericks, power forward, 1995-96; Chicago Rockers, Continental Basketball Asn, 1995-96, 1996-97; Ulkerspor, Turkey, 1996; Toronto Raptors, power forward, 1996-99, 2001-02; Minn Timberwolves, power forward, 2000-01, 2002-03; NJ Nets, 2001; Atlanta Hawks, 2001-02; Kans City Knights, Am Basketball Asn, 2002; Basket Livorno, Italy, 2002; Caja San Fernando, Spain, 2003; Unicaja Malaga, Spain, 2003; Slater's Sports Zone, founder, currently. **Home Addr:** , south Houston, TX. **Business Addr:** Founder, Slater Sports Zone, 727 Plantation Dr, Richmond, TX 77406, **Business Phone:** (281)341-0200.

## SLATER, RODNEY E.

Government official. **Personal:** Born Feb 23, 1955, Marianna, MS; son of Earl Brewer and Velma Brewer; married Cassandra Wilkins; children: Bridgette & Josette. **Educ:** Eastern Mich Univ, BS, 1977; Univ Ark, LLB; Univ Ark, JD, 1980. **Career:** State Atty Gen Off, asst atty, 1980-82; Ark Gov Bill Clinton, staff spec asst, 1983-85, exec asst, 1985-87; Ark State Univ, dir govt rels, 1987; US Fed Hwy Admin, fed hwy adminr, 1993-96; Secy Transp, 1997; Kans City Southern Inc, dir, 2001; Ark Hwy & Transp, comnr; Global Options Group Inc, sr vpres, 2006-; Patton Boggs LLC, partner & atty, currently; Transurban Group, 2009; Verizon, dir, 2010-; Delta Air Lines inc, dir; ICx Technologies Inc, dir; Atkins plc, dir. **Orgs:** Campaign mgr, Gov Bill Clinton's Staff, 1982-86; Ark State Hwy Comn, 1987-92; pres, W Harold Flowers Law Soc; founding mem, Ark C's Hosp Community Future; bd mem, GW Carver YMCA Little Rock; John Gammon Scholar Found Ark; bd mem, United Cerebral Palsy Cent Ark; vol &supporter, Boy Scouts Am; Gyst House; March Dimes; Sickle Cell Anemia Found; Thurgood Marshall Scholar Fund; United Negro Col Fund; Eastern Ark Area Coun; bd dir, Ark Advocates C & Families; secy-treas, Ark Bar Asn; Comn Ark Future; bd mem, John Gammon Scholar Found Ark; Fed Judge Henry Woods, mem Eastern Dist Ark Comn Bicentennial US Const; Dir, Parsons Brinckerh off Inc., 2008-; Martin Luther King, Jr. Fed Holiday Comn; Corp Governance & Policy Comt; Human Resources Comt. **Home Addr:** 2117 Brown, Jonesboro, AR 72401, **Home Phone:** (501)932-9221. **Business Addr:** Partner, Attorney, Patton Boggs LLC, 2550 M St NW, Washington, DC 20037, **Business Phone:** (202)457-5265.

## SLATON, GWENDOLYN C.

Librarian. **Personal:** Born Jun 19, 1945, Philadelphia, PA; daughter of George Alexander Childs and LaFronia Delorial Dunbar Childs; married Harrison Allen; children: Kimberly Dawn & Leigh Alison. **Educ:** Pa State Univ, PA, BA, hist, 1970; Seton Hall Univ, NJ, MA, educ, 1975; Rutgers Univ, NJ, MLS, 1982. **Career:** Essex County Col, Newark, NJ, staff, 1970-, librn, 1976-81, libr admin, 1981-97, exec dir & assoc dean, learning resources, 1997-. **Orgs:** Bd dirs, Family Serv Child Guid Ctr, 1977-83; adv bd, Youth Ctr, S Orange-Maplewood, 1983-89; exec bd, Essex-Hudson Reg Libr Coop, 1986-91; sec, Maplewood Cult Comn, 1986-91; Delta Sigma Theta Sorority, 1966-; pres, Delta Sigma Theta Sorority, N Jersey Alumnae Chap, 1993-95; Mid-Atlantic Innovative Users Grp. **Home Addr:** 620 Prospect St, Maplewood, NJ 07040, **Home Phone:** (973)763-3668. **Business Addr:** Associate Dean, Executive Director, Essex County College, 303 Univ Ave, Newark, NJ 07102-1798, **Business Phone:** (973)877-3233.

## SLAUGHTER, CAROLE D.

School administrator, association executive. **Personal:** Born Jul 27, 1945, Chattanooga, TN; daughter of Preston Jones and Rebecca Jones; married Thomas F Jr; children: Kelli & Eric. **Educ:** Douglass Col, Rutgers Univ, BA, 1972; Princeton Univ, MA, 1975. **Career:** Educ Testing Services, assoc examr, 1974-79, grad record exams assoc prog dir & dir develop, 1979-86, coll & univ prog, prog dir, 1986-87, off corp Secy, dir, 1987. **Orgs:** Chairperson ETS Comt Personnel Equity, 1983-85; chair person, League Women Voters Women's Rights Study Group; Highland Park NJ Sch Bd. **Honors/Awds:** Ford Foundation Fel, 1972-76; Test Preparation Specialist. **Home Addr:** 254 Lawrence Ave, Highland Park, NJ 08904, **Home Phone:** (732)249-5363. **Business Addr:** Director, Educational Testing Service, 1425 Lower Ferry Rd, Ewing, NJ 08618-1414, **Business Phone:** (609)895-0536.

## SLAUGHTER, ATTY. FRED L.

Educator, lawyer. **Personal:** Born Mar 13, 1942, Santa Cruz, CA; married Kay Valerie Johnson; children: Hilary Spring & Fred Wallace. **Educ:** Univ Calif, Los Angeles, BS, 1964, MBA, 1966; Columbia Univ, JD, 1969. **Career:** Spec asst chancellor, 1969-71; Practicing atty, 1970-; Sch Law, Univ Calif, Los Angeles, asst dean, lectr, 1971-80, assoc campus advocate, 1971-72, real estate broker, 1974-. **Orgs:** La Co, Calif St Am Bar Asn; US Fed Cts, Calif St Cts; life mem, UCLA Alumni Asn. **Home Addr:** 464 19th St, Santa Monica, CA 90402-2432. **Business Addr:** Attorney Law, PO Box 3522, Santa Monica, CA 90408-3522, **Business Phone:** (310)393-3522.

## SLAUGHTER, DR. JOHN BROOKS

President (organization), executive, school administrator. **Personal:** Born Mar 16, 1934, Topeka, KS; son of Reuben Brooks and Dora; married Ida Bernice Johnson; children: John II & Jacqueline Michelle. **Educ:** Kans State Univ, BS, elec engineering, 1956; Univ Calif Los Angeles, MS, engineering, 1961; Univ Calif, San Diego, PhD, engineering sci, 1971. **Career:** President (retired), president emeritus; Gen Dynamics Corp, electronics eng, 1956-60; Naval Elec Lab Ctr, engr & dept head, 1960-75, div head, 1965-71, dept head, 1971-75; Wash Univ, Appl Physics Lab, dir, prof elec engineering dept, 1975-77, acad vpres & provost, 1979-80; Nat Sci Found, Astron, Atmospheric, Earth & Ocean Sci, asst dir, 1977-79, dir, 1980-82; Univ Md Col Pk, chancellor, 1982-88; Occidental Col, pres, 1988-89, pres emer; Univ Southern Calif, prof; Irving R. Melbo Prof Leadership Educ, 1999-2000. **Orgs:** Pres, Zeta Sigma Lambda Chap Alpha Phi Alpha, 1956-60; bd mem, San Diego Urban League, 1962-66; San Diego Transit Corp, 1968-75; bd dir, Comm Credit Co, 1983-88; bd mem, Monsanto CPN, 1983-; AAAS, 1984-; bd mem, Baltimore Gas Elec Co, 1984-88; bd dir, Sovran Bank, 1985-88; Med Mutual Liability Ins Soc, 1986-88; chmn pres comn, Nat Col Athletic Asn, 1986-88; bd mem, Martin Marietta Corp, 1987; bd dir, Int Bus Mach, 1988-; bd mem, Avery Dennison, 1989-; bd mem, Atlantic Richfield, 1989-; bd dir, Los Angeles World Affairs Coun, 1990-96; Town Hall Calif, 1990-94; bd dir, Northrop Grumman & Solutia Inc, 1993-; pres & chief exec officer, Nat Action Coun Minorities Eng, 2000; Inst Elec & Electronic Engrs; Am Acad Arts & Scis; Tau Beta Pi Hon Eng Soc; Eta Kappa Nu Soc; Nat Acad Engineering. **Home Addr:** 700 S Orange Grove Blvd, Pasadena, CA 91105-1713. **Business Addr:** President Emeritus, Occidental College, 1600 Campus Rd, Los Angeles, CA 90041, **Business Phone:** (323)259-2500.

## SLAUGHTER, DR. PETER

Physician, pediatrician. **Personal:** Born May 15, 1928, Detroit, MI; married Geraldine; children: Chevon, Karen & Tracy. **Educ:** Wayne Univ, BS, 1955; Univ MI Med Sch, MD, 1963. **Career:** Samaritan, med dir; Clin Opers, Dmic-Prescad, dir; Henry Ford Hosp; pvt pract pediat, currently. **Orgs:** Fel Am Acad Ped; Detroit Ped Soc; Am Acad Pediat, 1973. **Honors/Awds:** Special Achievement Award, Galen's Honorable Society, 1961. **Home Addr:** 18254 Pennington Dr, Detroit, MI 48221-2142, **Home Phone:** (313)862-7480. **Business Addr:** Medical Director, Samaritan, 10201 E Jefferson, Detroit, MI 48221, **Business Phone:** (313)824-7866.

## SLAUGHTER, WEBSTER MELVIN

Football player. **Personal:** Born Oct 19, 1964, Stockton, CA. **Educ:** San Joaquin Delta Col, attended; San Diego State Univ. **Career:** Football player (retired); Cleveland Browns, wide receiver, 1986-91, punt returner, 1991; Houston Oilers, wide receiver, 1992-94, punt returner, 2002; Kans City Chiefs, wide receiver, 1995; New York Jets, wide receiver, 1996; San Diego Chargers, wide receiver, 1998. **Honors/Awds:** Pro Bowl, 1989, 1993; All Pro, 1989.

## SLAUGHTER-TITUS, REV. LINDA JEAN

Clergy. **Personal:** Born Aug 5, 1948, Albany, GA; daughter of Howard Mitchell and Burniece Jackson-Thomas (deceased); married Phylemon Depriest; children: Henry Lee Jr, Duane Dushaun & Faouly-Sekou. **Educ:** Highland Pk Community Col, AA, 1979; Wayne State Univ, BA, 1989; United Theol Sem, MDiv, 1997. **Career:** Golden State Ins, agt, 1973-82; Merrill Lynch Brokers, acct asst, 1982-85; Thoburn United Methodist Church, pastor, 1985-90; Jefferson Ave United Methodist Church, pastor, 1990-91; Oak Park Faith United Methodist Church, pastor, 1991-97; Cass Cot United Methodist Church, assoc pastor, 1995-97; Henderson Mem United Methodist Church, pastor, 1997; Berkley First United Methodist Church, pastor, currently. **Orgs:** Black Psychol Alumni, Wayne State Univ, 1985-; bd dir, Oakland Co Nat Asn Advan Colored People, 1992-97; ABATE-JWA, Nat Asn, 1995-; Black United Fund Mich, CTOB 100, 1997-; Mich Emmaus; bd dir, Nat Black Methodist Church Renewal; chair, Women's Concern, Pastor's Inst. **Special Achievements:** First Black Chair Annual Conf on Religion/Race, Detroit, 1980-84; First Black Female licensed in Health/Life/Property/Casualty in Michigan, 1983; New Church Developers, 1989; Mediation Certification, 1996. **Home Addr:** PO Box 47627, Oak Park, MI 48237. **Business Addr:** Pastor, Berkley First United Methodist Church, 2820 W 12 Mile Rd, Berkley, MI 48072, **Business Phone:** (248)399-3698.

## SLEDGE, CARLA

Government official. **Personal:** Born Jul 20, 1952, Detroit, MI; daughter of Thomas Griffin Sr and Zephrie; married Willie F; children: Arian Darkell & Ryan Marcel. **Educ:** Eastern Mich Univ, BA, 1978, MA, 1981; Wayne State Univ, BS, acct, 1989. **Career:** Taylor Bd Educ, teacher, 1974; Deloitte & Touche LLP, audit mgr, 1986-95; Metrop Youth Found, instr, 1986; Charter County of, Mich, chief dept financial officer, 1995-02, chief financial officer, 2002, 2005-13, key advisor to chief exec officer & mem sr exec team, 2003-05, Dept Mgt & Budget, dir mgt & budget, currently; Charter County Wayne, chief financial officer, 1995-; Robert A Ficano Admin, chief dep financial officer, 2003-. **Orgs:** Treas, Mich Munic Finance Officers Asn, 1995-; Black Caucus, 1995-; Women's Network, 1995-; Spec Rev Comt, 1996-; Am Inst Cert Pub Accountants, 1996-; Asn Govt Accountants, 1996-; Mich Inst Cert Pub Accountants, Mem Standing Comt, 1996-; bd dir, COBRA Comt, 1997-; co-chmn, 1998-, Nat Asn Black Accountants Inc; pres, Govt Finance Offices Asn; Mem Comt, Women's Econ Club, 1999-; treas, C's Outreach, 1999-; trustee, Rochester Col, 2000-; GFOA, pres, 2005-06. **Honors/Awds:** Outstanding Professional Achievement in Govt, Nat Asn Advan Colored People, 1996-97; Nat Achievement in Govt, 1999; Outstanding Cert Pub Acctin Government Award, AICPA, 2006; National Association of Black Accountants Award, 1999; CFO Award, Crain's Detroit Bus, 2011. **Special Achievements:** The 30 Most Influential Black Women in Metro Detroit, Women's Informal Network, 1999. **Home Addr:** 18653 Tracey St, Detroit, MI 48235-1760, **Home Phone:** (248)737-6929. **Business Addr:** Director, Wayne County, 600 Randolph St 3rd Fl, Detroit, MI 48226, **Business Phone:** (313)224-0420.

## SLEET, GREGORY MONETA

Judge. **Personal:** Born Mar 8, 1951, New York, NY; son of Moneta Jr; married Mary G; children: Moneta & Kelsi. **Educ:** Hampton Univ, BA, 1973; Rutgers Univ Sch Law, JD, 1976. **Career:** Defender Asn Philadelphia, asst pub defender, 1976-83; Pvt prac lawyer, Philadelphia, Pa, 1983-90; Dept Justice, Del state, dep atty gen, 1990-92; Hercules Inc, coun, 1992-94; US Dist Ct Del, dist atty, Judge, 1994-98. **Orgs:** Del Bar Asn; Penn Bar Asn; Ny Bar Asn; Am Bar Asn; Nat Bar Asn; bd dir, St Michael's Day Sch & Nursery; Dist Ct Adv Comt; bd mem, Widener Univ Sch Law, currently; bd mem, Criminal Justice Coun State Del. **Business Addr:** Judge, US District Court, 844 N King St, Wilmington, DE 19801-3570, **Business Phone:** (302)573-6470.

## SLIE, PASTOR SAMUEL N.

Educator, clergy. **Personal:** Born Jun 8, 1925, Branford, CT; son of Robert and Hannah Brown. **Educ:** Springfield Col, Mass, BS, group work & community orgn, 1949; Wilberforce Univ, Ohio; Yale Divinity Sch, BD, relig & higher educ, 1952, STM, roman cath ecumenical thought, 1963; NY Sem, DMin, 1985; Yale Divinity Sch, lectr. **Career:** YMCA, southern area staff, 1952-55; New Eng Stud Christian Movement, United Church Christ, regional dir, 1955-65; Southern Conn State Univ, dir united ministry higher educ, 1976-86; Downtown Coop Ministry, New Haven, coordr, 1986-94; Church Christ Yale Univ, assoc pastor & lectr higher educ, emer, 2004-. **Orgs:** United Church Christ Task Force World Hunger, 1972-73; corp mem, United Church Bd World Ministries, 1973-81; past pres, Nat Campus Ministers Asn, 1973-74; Theol Community Worlds Alliance YMCA's, 1981-86; treas, Conn Un Asn USA, 1984-92; Adv coun Nat Ecumenical Stud Christian Coun, 1984-86. **Honors/Awds:** Distinguished Service Award, Alpha Phi Omega, Gamma Eta Chap, Springfield Col, 1949; International Distinguished Service Award, Nat YMCA, Boston, 1981; Elm-Ivy Award Contribution Town-Govt Rels, Mayor New Haven & Pres of Yale Univ, 1985; Distinguished Educational Service Award, Dixwell Community House, 1989; Man of the Year, Nat Negro Prof & Bus Women, New Haven Chapter, 1991; Distinguished Alumnus Award, Yale Divinity Sch, 1993; Gandhi, King, and Ikeda, 2005. **Special Achievements:** Articles: "The New Naionall Ecumenical Journal", 1981; "The Black Church", "Identity in the United Church of Christ," Theol, 1990. **Home Addr:** 188 W Walk, West Haven, CT 06516-5961, **Home Phone:** (203)933-8238. **Business Addr:** Associate Pastor, Emeritus, The Church of Christ in Yale University, 300 College St, New Haven, CT 06511-8960, **Business Phone:** (203)432-1130.

## SLOAN, MACEO KENNEDY

Financial manager. **Personal:** Born Oct 18, 1949, Philadelphia, PA; son of Maceo Archibald and Charlotte; married Melva Iona Wilder; children: Maceo S & Malia K. **Educ:** Morehouse Col, BA, 1971; Ga State Univ, MBA, 1973; NC Central Univ Law Sch, JD, 1979. **Career:** NC Mutual Life Ins Co, investment analyst trainee, 1973-75, chief investment officer, 1973-86, investment analyst, 1975-77, asst treas, 1977-78, asst vpres, 1978-83, treas, 1983-85, vpres, pres, 1985-86; NC Cent Univ, adj vis prof, 1978-86; Sloan & Assocs, atty, 1979-2016; NCCU Sch Law, adj vis prof, 1979-86; Study Sem Financial Analysts, workshop rev leader, 1980-; Moore & Van Allen Attorneys Law, couns, 1985-86; NCM Capital Mgt Group Inc, pres & chief exec officer, 1986-91; Sloan Financial Group Inc, chair, pres & chief exec officer, 1991-; NCM Capital, chmn, chief exec officer & chief investment officer, 1991-; SCANA Corp, bd dir, 1997-; Sc Elec & Gas Co, dir, 1997; Pub Serv Co NC, dir; Graphics Technologies Inc, dir, 1999-; NCM Capital Adv Inc, chmn, chief exec officer & co-chief investment officer; NCM Capital Investment Trust, chmn & chief exec officer; NCM Capital Mid-Cap Growth Fund, chmn & chief exec officer; Wilshire Mutual Funds Inc, chmn & chief exec officer; Wilshire/MAXAM Diversity Fund, chmn & chief exec officer. **Orgs:** Fin Analysts Fedn, 1974-; Durham Chamber Com, 1974-; vpres NC Soc Fin Analysts, 1977-78; bd visitors NCCU Sch Law, 1979-86; NC State Bar, 1979-; bd dirs Mech & Farmers Bank, 1979-, chmn trust comt, 1979-93, chmn, 2005-08; bd dirs, Nat Ins Asn, 1980-; bd dirs, United Way Durham, 1980-89; vice chmn, treas, Urban Ministries Durham, 1983-88; Univ Club, 1986-; Georgetown Club, 1988-; founder & chair, Nat Investment Managers Asn; bd trustee & chmn, Col Retirement Equities Fund, 1991-; bd trustee, Employee Retirement Income Security Act Adv Coun US Dept Labor, 1991-93; bd mem, Teachers Ins & Annuity Asn, 1991-; bd dir, Observer Pub Co. **Honors/Awds:** Outstanding Service as Pres Better Business Bureau, 1980; Freedmon Guard Award, Durham Jaycees, 1981; Outstanding Leadership Award, United Way Durham, 1984; Resolution in Appreciation, The Durham City Coun; Cert Serv. **Special Achievements:** Featured on "Bridge builders, " 1998. **Home Addr:** 24000 S Lowell Rd, Bahama, NC 27503, **Home Phone:** (919)471-3068. **Business Addr:** Chairman, Chief Executive Officer & Chief Investment Officer, NCM Capital, 2634 Durham-Chapel Hill Blvd, Durham, NC 27707-2875, **Business Phone:** (919)688-0620.

## SLOCUMB, HEATHCLIFF (HEATH SLOCUMB)

Baseball player. **Personal:** Born Jun 7, 1966, Jamaica, NY; son of Karl Paul and Mattie Louise; married Deborah; children: Jessica & Heather. **Career:** Baseball player (retired); Chicago Cubs, pitcher, 1991-93; Cleveland Indians, pitcher, 1993; Philadelphia Phillies, pitcher, 1994-95; Boston Red Sox, pitcher, 1996-97; Seattle Mariners, pitcher, 1997-98; Baltimore Orioles, pitcher, 1999; St Louis Cardinals, pitcher, 1999-2000; San Diego Padres, pitcher, 2000. **Home Addr:** 130-14 97th Ave, Jamaica, NY 11419.

## SLOCUMB, JONATHAN

Comedian. **Personal:** Born Atlanta, GA. **Educ:** Oakwood Col, Huntsville, AL, BS, broadcast jour. **Career:** TV series: "Def Comedy Jam"; "The Big One's Back: The Sanford & Son Reunion"; "The Steve Harvey Show", 1996-2001; "When the Funk Bites the Dust", 1997; "When the Funk Hits the Rib Tips", 1997; "White Men Can Funk", 1998; "Meet the Browns", 2008; "Addicted to Love and Whatnot", 2001; "No Free Samples", 2001; "BET's Comicview", 2004; "Jamie Foxx Presents Laffapalooza", 2006; "Baisden After Dark", 2008; "The Mo'Nique Show", 2010; "Comedy.TV", 2012; Writer:"Jamie Foxx Presents Laffapalooza", 2003; Album: Laugh Yo Self 2 Life, 1997. **Special**

**Achievements:** Co-hosted the Annual Stellar Awards for two consecutive years and 28th Annual NAACP Image Awards. **Business Addr:** Comedian, Warner Alliance Music Group, 20 Music Sq E, Nashville, TN 37203, **Business Phone:** (615)748-8000.

## SMALL, DR. CLARA LOUISE

Educator. **Personal:** Born May 17, 1946, Plymouth, NC; daughter of Tarlton (deceased) and Doris Skinner (deceased). **Educ:** NC Cent Univ, Durham, NC, BA, 1969, MA, 1971; St John's Col, Sante Fe, NM, MA, 1974; Univ Mo, Columbia, MO, doc hist; Univ Del, PhD, 1990. **Career:** Professor (retired); St Paul's Col, hist instr, 1970-72; Chambers Child Develop Ctr, headstart teacher, 1972-73; Lincoln Univ, instr hist, 1973-77; Salisbury Univ, prof hist, 1977-2013; Shore-Up Inc, counr, 1980. **Orgs:** Adv, Phi Alpha Theta, 1977-2003; chancellor, N Eastern Region, bd trustee, 1991-, vpres, Pi Gamma Mu; historian, Buffalo Soldiers, Thomas E Polk Sr Chapt, 1999-; Princess Anne Chap Links Inc, 2002-; bd mem, Lower Eastern Shore Heritage Comt; bd mem, Pemberton Manor; chair, Commemoration Comt; By-Laws Comt; Hist Sites Comt; Outreach & Initiative Comt; Resources Preserv Comt; Tourism & Equity Oversight Comt.

## SMALL, ERIC

President (government), chief executive officer, executive. **Educ:** Georgetown Univ McDonough Sch Bus, BS, finance, 1976; Hult Int Bus Sch Arthur D Little Sch Mgt, MSM, int mgt, 1980. **Career:** Harris Bank, com lending officer, 1976-79; Arthur D Little, mgt consult, 1979-84; Aetna Life & Casualty, sr investment dir, 1984-92; SBK-Brooks Investment Corp, pres & chief exec officer, 1994-2009; Maxine Goodman Levin Col Urban Affairs, Cleveland State Univ, adj Prof, finace & econs, 1996-2001; Rapid Charge Technologies, LLC, dir, 2010-12; CastleOak Securities LP, sr managing dir, 2011-12; Wellness Integrated Network LLC, interim chief financial officer, 2012-13; Pub Finance & Energy Advisors, sr managing dir, 2012-; IFS Securities Inc, sr vpres, 2014-. **Orgs:** Mem bd trustee, treas & mem exec comt, Northeast Coun Higher Educ, 2001; mem bd dir, Cleveland 2030 Dist, 2013; life mem, Alpha Phi Alpha Fraternity Inc; life mem, NAACP Cleveland Chap; partic, Leadership Cleveland; mem bd trustee, Black Men; Blaylock & Partners LP, managing dir. **Honors/Awds:** Weatherhead 100 Award, 1999. **Special Achievements:** Bank listed No 9 on Black Enterprise's list of top investment banks, 1998, No 5, 1999, No 8, 2000, ranked as the top co-underwriter of municipal bonds in Ohio & among the top 50 in the US. **Business Addr:** Senior Vice President, IFS Securities Inc, 3414 Peachtree Rd NE Suite 1020, Atlanta, GA 30326, **Business Phone:** (404)382-5223.

## SMALL, ISADORE, III

Salesperson. **Personal:** Born Apr 27, 1944, Pontiac, MI; married Earline Olivia Washington; children: Michael, Brian & Vanessa. **Educ:** Univ Mich, BS, elec Engr, 1967; Wayne State Univ, MBA, 1981. **Career:** Cutler-hammer Inc, Milwaukee Wis, design engr, 1967-74; Detroit Mich, sales engr, 1974-82; Eaton Corp Southfield Mich, sales mgr, 1982-83; Eaton Corp Grand Rapids Mich, sales engr, 1984. **Orgs:** Soc Automotive Engrs, 1966-67; Asn Iron & Steel Engrs, 1974-84; Elect Mfg Rep Asn, 1979-; state youth dir, Church God Wis, 1969-74; Alpha Pi Omega Fraternity, 1966-67; chmn, bd trustee, Metrop Church God, 1974-84; chmn, Bus Assembly; Men Church God, 1983-90; parent adv, Kentwood Sch Legis Comt, 1986-91; church coun chmn, Orchard View Church God, 1987-93; chmn, Div Church Exten, 1988-94; Nat Div Church Exten, Church God, 1994-. **Honors/Awds:** Electronic Patent US Patent Off, 1972, 1974; Eaton Soc Inventors, 1980; Man of the Year, 1984. **Home Addr:** 8754 Grainery Ct SE, Caledonia, MI 49316-8142, **Home Phone:** (616)891-8960.

## SMALL, ISRAEL G.

Manager. **Personal:** Born Feb 26, 1941, Rincon, GA; married Jenetha Jenkins; married Wanda; children: 4. **Educ:** Savannah State Univ, BA, health & phys educ, 1963; Ft Valley St Col; Ga Col & State Univ, MPA, 1984; Comm Planning & Eval Inst, Wash DC. **Career:** City Savannah, model cities admin, model cities prog, 1970, asst city mgr, 1998-2007; City Macon, city mgr, 1983-98; Bur Pub Dev, Savannah, dir, hum serv, 1985; Small Group LLC, pres & chief exec officer, 2007-. **Orgs:** Kappa Alpha Psi; Ga Tchrs Ed Asn; Nat Ed Asn; Am Tchrs Asn; YMCA; Savannah Drug Abuse Adv Cncl; Nat Asn Advan Colored People; People United to Save Humanity; completed training Munic & Comm Planning; vpres, Black Pub Adminr Savannah Metrop Ctr; bd mem, Memorial Health Univ Med Ctr; bd mem, United Way; bd mem, Hist Savannah Found Inc; mem bd trustee, Hist Savannah Found Inc; bd mem, Savannah Develop Renewal Authority; Community Housing Serv Agency; chief exec officer, Savannah State Col Community Booster Club, currently; dd mem, Chatham County Hosp Authority, currently. **Home Addr:** 146 Steeplechase Rd, Savannah, GA 31405-1049, **Home Phone:** (912)232-2479. **Business Addr:** Chief Executive Officer, Savannah State Col Community Booster Club, 3206 Col St, Thunderbolt, GA 31404.

## SMALL, KENNETH LESTER

Association executive, lobbyist. **Personal:** Born Oct 1, 1957, New York, NY; son of Julius and Catherine Johnson; children: Catherine Louise. **Educ:** Fordham Univ, BA, econs, 1979; Long Island Univ, MA, econs, 1981. **Career:** Long Island Univ, res asst, 1979-80, adj prof, 1995; Bur Labor Statist, US Dept Labor, economist, 1980-81; NY Pub Libr, info asst, 1981-84; Nat Urban League Inc, New York, NY, prog evaluator, 1984-86, asst dir, 1985-86, exec asst, 1986-89, strategic planner, 1986-95, assoc dir, res & eval, 1994-95, dir planning & eval; Sphinx Communs Grp, assoc consult, 1989-95; KTL Asn, prin consult, 1990-; Citizen Advice Bur, dev dir; BronxWorks Inc, lobbyists, 2012, dev dir, currently; US Dept Labor's Bur Labor Statist, res asst & economist; Citizens Advice Bur, develop dir. **Orgs:** NY Urban League; Nat Econ Asn, 1990-; Co-op Am; Friends Black Scholar; Hunger Action Network Ny, bd mem, 1993-99, 2001-02; Nat Coalition Blacks Reparations Am, 1993-99; Nat Urban League Guild, 1999-; Imani House Int, 1998; Urban League Essex County; bd mem, Bethex Fed Credit Union, 1999-2003; Nat Electronic Communs Network, bd mem, 2001-02; bd mem, Maa Sa-Akhi Performing Arts Acad, currently. **Honors/Awds:** Connolly Sch Grad Asst, Long Island Univ, 1979-80; HW Wilson Scholar, Pratt Inst, 1990. **Home Addr:** 3520 Tryon Ave Suite 704, Bronx, NY 10467-1592, **Home Phone:** (718)881-5265. **Business Addr:** Development Director, BronxWorks Inc, 60 E Tremont Ave, Bronx, NY 10453, **Business Phone:** (646)393-4000.

## SMALL, LILY B.

Executive, educator. **Personal:** Born Sep 1, 1934, Trelawny; married Sylvester; children: Dale Andrew & Donna Marie. **Educ:** Calif State Univ, Fresno, BA, Eng, 1970, MA, eng, 1971; Univ Pac, Stockton, EdD, curric & instr, 1976. **Career:** Calif State Univ, Fresno, assoc prof & affirmative action coordr, 1972, Univ Affirmative Action, dir, 1977-82, acad specialist, 1977-82, from assoc prof ethnic studies prog to prof ethnic studies prog, 1978-2003, dir proj enhancement, 1989-90 & 1992-93, Ethnic Studies Prog, chair, 1990-98, prof emer ethnic studies prog, 2003-; Stockton Univ Sch Dist, Stockton, reading specialist, 1973-74; Ministry Educ, Kingston, Jamaica, teacher. **Orgs:** Am Asn Affirmative Action; Am Asn Univ Women; San Joaquin Reading Asn; chap secy, Phi Kappa Phi, 1978-80; Pres, Phi Kappa Phi Nat Acad Hon Socs, 1980-81; teacher, supvr, Sun Sch Church God; Black Fac & Staff Asn; Nat Acad Hon Soc; Human Rels Comn, Calif State Univ, Fresno, 1995-96; Athletic Behav Rev Comt, 1995-96; founder & pres, FCPW Investment Club. **Honors/Awds:** Cited in Whos Who in the West and Mid-West, 1973; Community Service Award, Church Living God & Living Heritage Drama Group, 1999; Rosa Parks Award for Service and Dedication to the African American Community, 1999; Human Relations Commission Community Recognition Award, City of Fresno, 1999; Honorary Member Award, Africana Students United, 2003. **Special Achievements:** Nominated for the Fresno Bee/Channel 30/YWCA Top Ten Business/Professional Women of the Year, 1994. **Home Addr:** 7216 N Belvedere Ave, Fresno, CA 93722-3407, **Home Phone:** (559)277-9389. **Business Addr:** Professor Emeritus, California State University, Fresno, 5241 N Maple Ave, Fresno, CA 93740, **Business Phone:** (559)278-4240.

## SMALL, STANLEY JOSEPH

School administrator. **Personal:** Born Jun 1, 1946, Weeks Island, LA; married Dorothy Collins; children: Keith V, Keisha L & Kory K. **Educ:** Southern Univ Baton Rouge, BS, math & sci, 1968, MS, admin & supv, 1973. **Career:** New Iberia Middle Sch, teacher, 1968-70, asst prin; Anderson Middle Sch, teacher, 1970-81, prin, 1992; Iberia Parish Coun, elected parish off, 1984; Lee Street Elem Sch, prin, 1989-92; Iberia Parish govt, dir housing. **Orgs:** Nat Educ Asn, 1969-85; pres, Neighborhood Community Serv Coalition, 1978-85; Los Angeles Asn Educ/Polit Action Comt, 1979-85; chmn, Human Serv Comt Iberia Parish Coun, 1984; NACO Human Serv Steering Comt, 1984; Parish Bd Comt Action Agency, 1984. **Honors/Awds:** Outstanding Teacher of the Year, Asn Classroom Teachers, 1978; Principal of the Year. **Special Achievements:** Developed and implemented motivation program for students New Iberia Middle School in 1981. **Home Addr:** 514 Astor Pl Dr, New Iberia, LA 70563-2232, **Home Phone:** (337)380-3354.

## SMALL, TORRANCE RAMON

Football player. **Personal:** Born Sep 4, 1970, Tampa, FL; married Denise; children: Devante & Kayla. **Educ:** Alcorn State Univ, gen studies, 2000. **Career:** Football player (retired); New Orleans Saints, wide receiver, 1992-96; St.Louis Rams, 1997; Indianapolis Colts, 1998-99; Philadelphia Eagles, 1999-2000; New Eng Patriots, wide receiver, 2001. **Home Addr:** , Kenner, LA.

## SMALL, WILLIAM

Administrator. **Personal:** Born Dec 5, 1940, Elizabeth, NJ; married Carolyn; children: William & Michael. **Educ:** Howard Univ, AB, 1962, JD, 1965. **Career:** Domar Buckle Mfg Corp, laborer, 1959; Astro Air Prod Corp, laborer, 1960-61; Western Elec Corp, laborer, 1962; Union Co Legal Serv Corp, chief investr, 1968-69; Promethean vpres Summer Serv Corp, pub & circulation mgr, 1969; CAFEO, dep dir, actg exec dir, 1969; William Patterson Col, asso prof, 1970, dir acad serv, 1971; Newark St Col, instr, 1970; Contract Admin, dir, 1975-; Title 1, asv com; Plans Progress Task Force Youth Motivation, part; Mayors Task Force; Polit Sci Soc. **Orgs:** Bd trustee, Urban League Eastern Union Co; Concern Inc; adv, var comn based youth groups; SPS conflict mgt educ consult firm. **Honors/Awds:** Outstanding Achievement Award, Fed Jurisdiction; Outstanding Service Award, William & Paterson Col Student Govt Asn; Service Award, Nat Headquarters Boy Scouts Am, 1974-75; Outstanding Trainee, Univ Co 3re BCTBde; Outstanding Trainee, postwide competition; National Defence Service Medal; Vietnamese Service Medal; Vietnamese Campaign Medal; Good Conduct Medal; Army Commedation Medal. **Business Addr:** Dean of Social Sciences, William Patterson College, 300 Pompton Rd, Wayne, NJ 07470, **Business Phone:** (877)978-3223.

## SMALLEY, PAUL

Manager. **Personal:** Born Dec 8, 1935, Gay Head, MA; children: Polly & Patrick. **Career:** Comn Rel NE; Gen Dynamics, 1958-69; Adv Com OIC Nat Tech V. **Orgs:** Vice chmn, Reg Bd Ed, 1973-79; chmn, OIC Reg I; chmn, Deep River Dem Town, 1980-82; Conn Nat Asn Advan Colored People St Bd Fin; mem bd dir, Urban League Gr Hartford; min adv bd chmn, WFSB-TV-3. **Home Addr:** 24 Hemlock Dr, Deep River, CT 06417.

## SMALLS, CHARLEY MAE

Scientist. **Personal:** Born Oct 22, 1943, Charleston, SC; daughter of Charles A Sr and Ida Mae White (deceased). **Educ:** Knoxville Col, BS, 1965; Univ Md, MS, zool, 1972. **Career:** Med Univ SC, Dept Anat, lab technician, 1965-68; Johns Hopkins Univ, Dept Path, res technician, 1968-70; Dept Zool, Univ Md, grad asst, 1970-72; Dept Anat Milton S Hershey Med Ctr, res asst, 1973-79; US EPA, EPA asst, 1980-81, environ scientist, 1981-88, HMC/EPA Environ Monitoring Lab, environ radiation specialist, 1988-90, environ radiation specialist, 1990-94, div health physics. **Orgs:** Deacon, 1986-90, elder, 1992, Capital Presb Church-; Micros Soc Am; Pa Alliance Environ Educ; Susquehanna Valley Health Physics Soc; Alpha Kappa Alpha Sorority. **Honors/Awds:** CM Smalls & MD Goode, 1977; "Ca2 Accumulating Components in Dev Skeletal Muscle" J Morph, 1977; Bronze Medal, US Environ Protection Agency, 1980, 1988; 'Award for Excellence', Commonwealth Pa, Dept Environ Protection, 2001. **Home Addr:** 1901 Herr St, Harrisburg, PA 17103-1622, **Home Phone:** (717)232-3141.

## SMALLS, DIEDRE A.

Executive, executive director. **Educ:** Syracuse Univ, Utica Col, BS, bus admin & mkt, 1989; Columbia Univ City New York, cert wellness-holistic health coun, 2008. **Career:** Draftfcb, acct exec, 1991-96; UniWorld Group Inc, sr acct exec, 1996-98; Grey Global Group, vpres & group mgt supvr, 1997-2005; Publicis, vpres group mgt supvr, 2006; Footsteps, group acct dir, 2006-10; mkt commun consult, 2010-11; Multicultural Mkt Resources, IPG Mediabrands, exec vpres, managing dir, 2011-. **Orgs:** New Prof Theatre; bd mem, YMCA, 2006-08. **Honors/Awds:** Outstanding Women in Marketing & Communication, Ebony Mag, 2003. **Special Achievements:** Featured in various magazines including EBONY, ESSENCE. **Business Addr:** Managing Director, Executive Vice President, Multicultural Mkt Resources, 100 W 33 St, New York, NY 10010, **Business Phone:** (917)576-4322.

## SMALLS, DOROTHY M. (DOROTHY SMALLS TAYLOR)

Educator. **Personal:** Born Jan 2, 1920, Georgetown, SC; children: Eleanor J, Carla S & Lois D. **Educ:** SC State Col, BS, 1940, MS, 1960; Univ SC; Univ Chicago. **Career:** Bd End Georgetown, eng teacher; JB Beck Elem Georgetown, elem sch teacher; Kensington Sch Georgetown, reading consultant; Wm C Reavis Sch Chicago, teacher; Beck Jr High Sch Georgetown, teacher engl reading. **Orgs:** United Teaching Prof; Pee Dee Reading Coun; Nat Coun Reading; pres, SC State Alumni; secy, GC Educ Asn; pres, Dis Missions; Nat Asn Advan Colored People; Voter Regist; Home Missions. **Home Addr:** 409 Orange St, Georgetown, SC 29440, **Home Phone:** (843)546-4278.

## SMALLS, EVELYN F.

President (organization), chief executive officer. **Educ:** NC Univ, BA, bus admin. **Career:** Human Resources & Compliance, sr vpres; United Bank Philadelphia, sr vpres, 1993-2000, pres, chief exec officer & dir, 2000-. **Orgs:** Bd mem, Trustee Certain Voting Trust Agreements, United Bancshares Inc, Ohio; bd mem, Communities; bd mem, Forum Exec Women. **Business Addr:** President, Chief Executive Officer, United Bank of Philadelphia, 30 S 15th St, Philadelphia, PA 19102, **Business Phone:** (215)351-4600.

## SMALLS, DR. JACQUELYN ELAINE (JACQUELINE E SMALLS-GOODNIGHT)

Consultant, pathologist. **Personal:** Born Nov 16, 1946, Charleston, SC; daughter of Charles Augustus Sr and Ida Mae White (deceased); married Willard Goodnight Jr. **Educ:** Hampton Inst, BA, 1968; Pa State Univ, MA, 1976; Howard Univ, MS, 1980, PhD, 1984. **Career:** Grad fel, Pa St Univ, 1970, 1971 & 1973; fel, Howard Univ, 1978-83; York City Pub Sch, speech pathologist, 1968-78; Blast IU 14, coordr, 1975-76; Pub Sch Prog, consult, prog evaluator, 1982; DC Pub Schs, speech pathologist, 1982; Ment Retarded C & Adults, consult, 1987; Functional Commun Assocs Inc, partner. **Orgs:** Consult, Nat Educ Asn, 1975; Philadelphia Pub Sch, 1982; Am Speech Lang & Hearing, 1982; Sgt Memorial Presby Church, 1983. **Honors/Awds:** Distinguished Am. **Special Achievements:** MD Licensure, 1995. **Home Addr:** 2803 Henderson Ave, Silver Spring, MD 20902-2113, **Home Phone:** (301)933-3369.

## SMALLS, MARCELLA E.

Administrator, executive. **Personal:** Born Sep 30, 1946, McClellanville, SC; children: Marcus. **Educ:** Durham Col, BA, 1968. **Career:** South Santee Germantown Action Group, fin secy, 1980-83; SC Charleston Chap Nat Sec Asn, name tag comnr, 1982; South-Santee Comm Ctr, bd dir, 1983; Howard AME Church, asst secy, 1982-; Amoco Chem Co, acct; Sewee Santee CDC, adminr, currently. **Orgs:** Treas, Amoco Chem Recreation Club, 1983; secy, trustee Bldg Fund Howard AME Church; fin adv, Jr Achievement Cainhoy HS, 1986-87; chmn, March Dimes, Amoco Chem Co, 1989-91; March Dimes Ad Bd, Charleston Chap; treas, PTA, St James Santee Elem Sch, McClellanville, SC; past chmn, Qual Awareness Recognition Sub comt; Amoco Cooper River Wellness Focus Comn, Amoco Bonner & Moore; COMPASS implementation team mem. **Honors/Awds:** Employee of the Month, 1989; Opportunity for Improvement Winner, 1991. **Home Addr:** 1940 Hill Rd, McClellanville, SC 29458, **Home Phone:** (843)546-3209. **Business Addr:** Administrator, Sewee to Santee CDC, 405 Pinckney St, McClellanville, SC 29458, **Business Phone:** (843)887-4453.

## SMALLS, MARVA A.

Executive. **Educ:** Univ SC, BA, polit sci, MA, pub admin; Francis Marion Univ, hon doctorate humanities; Coker Col SC, hon doctorate humanities. **Career:** MTV Networks Co, exec vpres global inclusion strategy, 2006-; Nickelodeon/MTVN Kids & Family Group, exec vpres, pub affairs & chief staff, currently; Nat Bank SC, dir; Gov Richard Riley, SC Pvt Indust Coun, staff dir; Congressman Robin Tallon, chief staff. **Orgs:** Nat Asn Advan Colored People; Nat Dem Inst; Northside Ctr Child Develop; Big Bros Big Sisters Am; Nat Bank SC; SC Educ TV Endowment Comn; Univ SC Educ Found; Nat Alumni Coun; Bd Noggin; Exec Leadership Coun; Alpha Kappa Alpha Sorority; Trinity Baptist Church; bd mem, Brookgreen Gardens Sc; bd mem, Nat Coun Families & Tv; bd mem, C Affected by AIDS Found. **Honors/Awds:** George C Peabody Award; Golden CableAce Award; NAMIC prestigious L Patrick Mellon Mentorship Award; Nat Action Network Triumph Award; T Howard Found Champion Diversity Award. **Business Addr:** Executive Vice President, Chief Staff, Nickelodeon/MTVN Kids & Family Group, 1515 Broadway 38th Fl, New York, NY 10036, **Business Phone:** (212)258-8000.

## SMALLS, O'NEAL

Educator. **Personal:** Born Sep 7, 1941, Myrtle Beach, SC. **Fduc:** Tuskegee Inst, BS, 1964; Harvard Law Sch, JD, 1967; Georgetown Univ, LLM, 1975. **Career:** Am Univ, assoc prof, 1969-76; Syst & Appl Sci Corp, bd dir, 1974-85; George Washington Univ Sch Law, prof law, 1976-79; Am Univ, prof law, 1979-88; Univ SC Sch Law, fac, 1989-2006, distinguished prof emer law, currently. **Orgs:** Asst dir, Harvard

Law Sch Summer Prog Minority Stud, 1966; Harvard Law Sch Res Comn, 1966-67; dir admis & chmn Comt Admis & Scholars, Am Univ, 1970-74; DC, Nat Am Bar Asns; serv comn & bd trustees, Law Sch Admis Coun Princeton, 1972-76; adv comn, Legis Serv Plan Laborers Dist coun Wash DC, 1973-75; bd dir, Syst & Appl Sci Corp, 1974-85; chmn bd dir, Skyanchor Corp; exec bd, DC Bapt Conv; pres & chmn bd, Freedoms Found, Myrtle Beach, SC, 1987-. **Special Achievements:** Articles "Class Actions Under Title VII", Am Univ Law Rev, 1976; "The Path & The Promised Land", Am Univ Law Rev, 1972; booklets "New Directions, An Urban Reclamation Program for the Dist of Columbia", 1982; "Manhood Training An Introduction to Adulthood for Inner City Boys Ages 11-13", 1985. **Home Addr:** 900 Veterans Rd, Columbia, SC 29209-2332, **Home Phone:** (803)776-8072. **Business Addr:** Distinguished Professor Emeritus of Law, University of South Carolina, 701 Main St, Columbia, SC 29208, **Business Phone:** (803)777-4155.

### SMALLS-GOODNIGHT, JACQUELINE E. See SMALLS, DR. JACQUELYN ELAINE.

### SMALLWOOD, RICHARD
Gospel singer, musician. **Personal:** Born Nov 30, 1948, Atlanta, GA. **Educ:** Howard Univ, grad, ethnomusicology; Howard Univ Divinity Sch. **Career:** Gospel vocalist, pianist, composer: Richard Smallwood Singers, founder, 1977; Vision, mem; Albums with Richard Smallwood Singers: Richard Smallwood Singers, 1982; Psalms, 1984; Textures, 1986; Vision, 1988; ortrait, 1990; Testimony, 1992; Live at Howard Univ, 1993; Albums with Vision: Adoration: Live in Atlanta, 1996; Rejoice, 1997; Healing: Live in Detroit, 1999; Persuaded: Live in D.C., 2001; The Walter Hawkins Tribute Concert, 2011; Journey: Live in New York, 2007; Promises, 2011; Compilations: Gospel Greats, 1994; Memorable Moments, 1999; Praise & Worship Songs of Richard Smallwood With Vision, 2003; Quintessential Collection, 2007; "Center of My Joy", 2007; Run To Him, 2008; Metrop Baptist Church, assoc minister, currently; Metrop Music Ministry Metrop Baptist Church, artist-in-residence, currently. **Honors/Awds:** Numerous honors & awards including Distinguished Achievement Award, Howard Univ; Stellar Award, 1992, 2000 & 2002; Gospel Music Hall of Fame, 2006. **Business Addr:** Gospel Vocalist, c/o The Alliance Agency, 1035 Bates Ct, Hendersonville, TN 37075, **Business Phone:** (615)822-5308.

### SMALLWOOD, WILLIAM LEE
School administrator, city council member. **Personal:** Born Sep 2, 1945, York, PA; son of Herman L (deceased) and Vera Horton; married Janis M Rozelle; children: Yolanda M Sherrer, Aundrea L & Liza D. **Educ:** USAF Personnel Tech Sch, personnel cert, 1963; LaSalle Exten Univ, cert, acct, 1968; Pa State Univ, attended 1971; Empire State Col-State Univ NY, attended 1983. **Career:** US Civil Serv, acct clerk, 1967-68; LIAB Aircraft Corp, admin, 1968-69; WJ Grant Co, credit mgr, 1969-70; Caterpillar Inc, track press operator & mat handler, 1970-71; Community Progress Coun Inc, bus mgr, 1971-74; Pa Dept Community Affairs, admin officer, 1974-79; York City Coun, 1977-80, pres, 1984-2007, councilman, 2007-08, Bus Admin Comt Coun, chair, 2008; York Co Off Employ & Training, exec dir, 1979-80; Crispus Attucks Asn Inc, housing financial coordr, 1980-88. **Orgs:** Founder & pres, Minority Bus Asn Inc, 1983-; bd dir, Leadership York, 1983-87; co-chair, Off Minority Bus Develop, 1990-; pres & bd dir, William C Goodridge Bus Resource Ctr, 1993; York Co Indust Dev Corp, 1994-; S Pershing Community Develop Corp, 1994-; bd mem, York Area Develop Corp; bd mem, Crispus Attucks Asn Inc; bd mem, York City Citizens Adv Comt; bd mem, Minority Police Recruitment Steering Comt; bd mem, Community Caucus York; bd mem, York Area Chamber Coms; bd mem, Strand-Capitol Performing Arts Ctr Inc; charter mem, S York Lions Club; Prof Develop Comt; Pa Asn Continuing Educ; Educ Comt York 2000. **Home Addr:** 53-51 S Newberry St, York, PA 17404-3851, **Home Phone:** (717)845-1901. **Business Addr:** Councilman, Office of York City Council, 1 Marketway W 3rd Fl, York, PA 17401-1231, **Business Phone:** (717)849-2246.

### SMASHUM, OLIVIA
Vice president (organization). **Educ:** Hampton Univ, BA; Columbia Univs Sch Bus, MA, mkt & finance. **Career:** Home Box Off Inc, exec vpres, affil mkt, assoc mkt mgr, 1980-. **Business Addr:** Executive Vice President, Home Box Office Inc, 1100 6th Ave, New York, NY 10036, **Business Phone:** (212)512-1000.

### SMEDLEY, ERIC ALAN
Football player. **Personal:** Born Jul 23, 1973, Charleston, WV. **Educ:** Ind Univ. **Career:** Football player (retired); Buffalo Bills, 1996, 1998, defensive back, 1997; Indianapolis Colts, 1999. **Honors/Awds:** Rookie of the Year, 1996.

### SMILEY, DR. EMMETT L.
Dentist. **Personal:** Born Jun 14, 1922, Montgomery, AL; son of George Washington (deceased) and Hattie Dabney (deceased); married Mary Jo Carter; children: Lynn S Hampton, Karen J, Kim A & George Wesley. **Educ:** AL State Univ, BS, 1945; Prairie View Univ, Hempstead, Tex; Univ Florence, Florence Italy; Meharry Med Col, DDS, 1950. **Career:** Pvt pract dentist, 1950-; Columbia Univ, Col Physicians & Surgeons, chief resident; Smiley Dent Assocs Inc, owner, currently. **Orgs:** Pres, Ala Dent Soc, 1964-66; exec bd, Ala Dent Soc, 1966-; pres, Capitol City Med Soc, 1968-70; Nat Dent Asn; Mid-century Dent Asn; Ewell Neil Dent Soc; Delta Dent Care Inc; adv bd, Urban League Montgomery Area C C; Mayors Com Comm Affairs, 1964-70; Montgomery Improv Asn; pres, Alpha Phi Alpha Frat; pres, Cligue Social Club; Cleveland Ave Br YMCA; Century Club; Phi Boule. **Honors/Awds:** Listed in AL Dept of Archives History under "Men of Prominence"; Service Award, Alabama Dental Soc, 1990. **Home Addr:** 4601 Lawnwood Dr, Montgomery, AL 36108, **Home Phone:** (205)263-7418. **Business Addr:** Owner, Smiley Dental Associates Inc, 2026 Clifton Ave, Nashville, TN 37203-1910, **Business Phone:** (615)321-5600.

### SMILEY, TAVIS
Television journalist. **Personal:** Born Sep 13, 1964, Gulfport, MS; son of Joyce M and Emory G. **Educ:** Ind Univ, attended 1986. **Career:** Mayor Tomilea Allison, asst mayor, 1984-85; Pat Russell, coun pres & coun aide, 1987; Southern Christian Leadership Conf, La, spec asst exd, 1978-88; Mayor Tom Bradley, ade aide, 1988-90; self-employed; Smiley Report, radio & tv commentator, 1990-2001; BET Tonight, host, 1996-2001; ABC TV, spec corresp, 2001-; Tavis Smiley (talk show), chief exec officer, 2004-; Books: Black America Better; Leading African Americans Speak Out, 2001; What I Know for Sure, 2006. **Orgs:** Chmn, Opers Comt, LA's Young Black Profs, 1988-90; steering comt, United Way Greater Los Angeles, 1989-90; adv bd, Inner City FND Excellence Edu, 1989-91; bd dir, Challengers Boys & Girls Club, 1989-; adv bd, After Class Scouting, Scouting USA, 1991; bd dir, Los Angeles Black CLG Tour, 1991-; KAP; adv bd, Martin Luther King Jr Ctr Non-violent Soc Chg, 1992-93; founder, Tavis Smiley Found, 1999. **Honors/Awds:** Outstanding Business & Professional Award, Dollars & Sense Mag, 1992; Hall of Fame, Vanity Fair, 1996; PRS Image Award, NCP, 2000; Image Award, Best News Talk or Info Series, 1999; Mickey Leland Humanitarian Award, Nat Asn Minorities Commun, 1998; NAACP Image Award. **Special Achievements:** US Debate Team, "International Dialogue", 1986; Author: Straight Talk About the Wrongs of The Right, Anchor & Doubleday. **Home Addr:** 4150 6th Ave, Los Angeles, CA 90008, **Home Phone:** (323)295-3543. **Business Addr:** Organiser, The Smiley Group Inc, 3870 Crenshaw Blvd Suite 391, Los Angeles, CA 90043-1208, **Business Phone:** (323)290-4690.

### SMILEY-ROBERTSON, CAROLYN
Systems analyst, counselor, consultant. **Personal:** Born Aug 26, 1954, Cincinnati, OH; daughter of James W and Lillian Anderson; married Tommie L; children: Kevin James & Michael John. **Educ:** Wellesley Col, BA, econs, 1976; Xavier Univ, MBA. **Career:** Western Southern Life Ins, programmer, 1976-78; AT&T, systs develop specialist, 1978-83, dist mgr, systs analyst, 1984-85, mgr, info mgmt, 1985-96, dist mgr, 1996-2002; Village Woodlawn, ambassador, 1980; Village Woodlawn, vice mayor, 1982; Village Woodlawn, econ consult, 1984-; Village Woodlawn, coun mem, 1978-84; Village Evendale, pres coun, 2003-; consult, currently. **Orgs:** Woodlawn Bd Zoning Appeals, 1978-82; Woodlawn Planning Comn, 1978-84; trustee, Woodlawn Community Improv Corp, 1981-; vice chair, Recreation Comn, 1998-2001; Charter Rev Comt, 2002. **Honors/Awds:** YMCA Black Achiever, Cincinnati, OH, 1983. **Home Addr:** 9620 Otterbein Rd, Cincinnati, OH 45241, **Home Phone:** (513)733-1050. **Business Addr:** President of Council, Village of Evendale, 10141 Woodlawn Blvd, Woodlawn, OH 45215, **Business Phone:** (513)771-6130.

### SMIRNI, ALLAN DESMOND
Lawyer, executive. **Personal:** Born Aug 27, 1939, New York, NY; son of Donald W and Ruby M (King) S; married Barbara; children: Amie Joy. **Educ:** City Univ NY, Brooklyn Col, BA, 1960; Univ Calif, Sch Law, Berkeley, JD, 1971. **Career:** Brobeck, Phleger & Harrison, assoc atty, 1971-74; Envirotech Corp, asst gen couns, asst secy, 1974-81; Televideo Systs Inc, chief coun & secy, 1982-86; Memorex Corp, vpres, gen coun & secy, 1987-89; Pyramid Technol Corp, Siemens Pyramid Info Systs Inc, vpres, gen coun, 1989-, secy, 1992-93. **Orgs:** State Calif Job Training & Develop, 1970-72; State Bar Calif, 1972-; Charles Houston Bar Asn, 1972-; Am Soc Corp Secy, 1976-; trustee, Envirotech Found, 1978-81; Am Corp Coun Asn, 1982-; trustee, Tele Video Found, 1983-; adv bd dir, Social Advocates Youth, 1985; Soc Corp Secretaries & Governance Prof. **Home Addr:** 1363 Lennox Way, Sunnyvale, CA 94087. **Business Addr:** Vice President, General Counsel, Siemens Pyramid Info Systems Inc, 3860 N 1st St, San Jose, CA 95134-1702, **Business Phone:** (408)428-9000.

### SMITH, AL FREDRICK
Football player, president (organization). **Personal:** Born Nov 26, 1964, Los Angeles, CA; children: 3. **Educ:** Utah State Univ, BS, sociol, 1987; Tenn State Univ, MS, sports admin. **Career:** Football player (retired), director; Houston Oilers, linebacker, 1987-96; Tenn Titans, dir player develop & pro personnel, 1998-2002; Masterplan Group, Player Personnel & Partner Football Opers, dir, currently. **Business Addr:** Director of Player Personnel, Partner Football Operations, Masterplan Group International LLC, 122 S Michigan Ave Suite 1220, Chicago, IL 60603, **Business Phone:** (312)880-0340.

### SMITH, ALFRED J., JR.
Educator. **Personal:** Born Jul 9, 1948, Montclair, NJ; married Judith Moore. **Educ:** Boston Univ, BFA, 1970, MFA, 1972. **Career:** Natl Ctr Afro-Amer Art, instr art, 1969-72; Boston Univ Afro-Amer Ctr, dir cult affrs, 1970-71; Boston Univ, asst instr, 1970-72; Norfolk Correct Inst, instr art, 1970-72; Howard Univ, assoc art, 1972, chair, 2001-07, prof & coordr, currently. **Orgs:** Nat Conf Art. **Home Addr:** 10901 Little Patuxent Pkwy, Columbia, MD 21044, **Home Phone:** (410)772-4800. **Business Addr:** Professor, Howard University, 2455 6th St NW, Washington, DC 20059, **Business Phone:** (202)806-7047.

### SMITH, BISHOP ALFRED M.
Clergy. **Personal:** Born Sep 7, 1930, Detroit, MI; son of Bishop Alfred (deceased) and Minnie J; married Roberta Williams; children: Daryl Michael, Beverly Gail Otis & Marsha Renee Brown. **Educ:** Detroit Bible Col, attended 1956; Univ Mich; Wayne State Univ. **Career:** Indiane Ave COGIC, asst pastor, 1957; Shiloh Chapel COGIC, founder & pastor, 1962-; Sunday Sch, supt, 1970, bd elders, chair, 1971, admin asst, 1975, sr admin asst, 1995; Penecostal Tabernacle COGIC, 1972; Gen Motors Corp, 1988. **Orgs:** Exec secy, Great Lakes Jurisdiction COGIC, 1966-93; Church God Christ, Nat Regist Dept; Nat Ways & Means Comn; Nat Stand & Jurisdiction Exten Comn; Gen Assembly Exec Comn; Nat Const Comn; Am Mgt Asn; coordr, United Found Gen Motors Corp, 1972-83; United Way Mich, Finance Allocation Comn, 1978-80. **Business Addr:** Pastor, Shiloh Chapel Church of God in Christ, 14841 Eastburn Ave, Detroit, MI 48205, **Business Phone:** (313)527-5400.

### SMITH, ALICE B
School administrator, association executive. **Educ:** Ft Valley State Col, BA, fr lit, 1968; Atlanta Univ, MA, fr lit, 1969; Yale Univ, New Haven, Conn, cert, Intensive Lang & Lit, 1970; Mich State Univ, fr lit, 1972; Sorbonne, Paris, France, cert, mod fr lit, 1973; Columbia Univ, New York, cert, Ger Lang, 1973; Univ Mass, PhD, fr lit, 1978. **Career:** Hawkinsville HS, instr, 1967; Fort Valley State Col, instr, 1969-71; Univ Mass, teaching asst, 1973-77, placement counr, 1979-80, dir resource ctr, 1979-81, asst dir, placement servs, 1979. **Orgs:** Mem Alpha Kappa Mu Nat Hon soc, Alpha Kappa Alpha, 1969-72; Phi Delta Kappa, 1980. **Honors/Awds:** Academic Scholarship, Paris France, 1966; Nat Defense Scholarship, Fort Valley State Col, 1964-68; The Atlanta Univ Fellowship, 1968-69; Nat Fellowships Fund, 1976-78. **Home Addr:** PO Box 1934, Moultrie, GA 31776-1934.

### SMITH, DR. ALLEN JOSEPH, SR.
School administrator. **Personal:** Born Mar 10, 1936, Chicago, IL; children: Allen J Jr, Wendy M & Anthony R. **Educ:** Roosevelt Univ, BA, 1960, MA, 1966; Nova Univ, EdD, 1981. **Career:** Chicago Bd Educ, teacher, 1960-67, adult educ teacher, 1964-67, counr, 1967-69, guid coordr, 1969-82, dir bur guid, 1982; Kappa Leadership Inst, dean. **Orgs:** Bd dir, Parliamentarian Asn Multicultural Couns & Develop, 1978-82 &1985-86; bd dir, Human Resource Develop Inst, 1984-; supt schs, Bellwood Sch Dist. **Home Addr:** 6832 S Paxton Apt 1B, Chicago, IL 60649. **Business Addr:** Director Bureau of Guidance, Kappa Leadership Institute, 1507 E 53rd St 450, Chicago, IL 60615, **Business Phone:** (312)275-5722.

### SMITH, DR. ALONZO NELSON
College teacher. **Personal:** Born Oct 11, 1940, Washington, DC; son of Alonzo de Grate and Marie Wright; married Susan T Cramer; children: Anne Marie & Alexander. **Educ:** Georgetown Univ, BS, foreign serv, 1962; Howard Univ, MA, African hist, 1967; Univ Calif, Los Angeles, CA, PhD, Afro Am hist, 1978. **Career:** Peace Corps, vol; Ivory Coast Ministry Nat Educ; Ivory Coast Repub, sch teacher; Los Angeles City Col; Black Studies Ctr Claremont Col, lectr, 1970-75; Cal Poly State Univ, inst hist, 1976-77; Univ Nebr, asst prof, 1978-86; Urban League Nebr, social worker, 1986-91; Africare, Sierra Leone, prog dir & country mgr, 1991-92; Hampton Univ, Hampton, Va, prof, 1992-93; Smithsonian Inst, res historian & assoc cur, 1994-2005; Montgomery Col, Rockville, Md, adj prof, 1998-2005; Montgomery Col, Rockville, Md, prof, 2005-. **Orgs:** Omaha Nat Asn Advan Colored People, 1985; Cent Comm Nebr State Dem Party, 1985; Urban League, Nebr, 1989. **Business Addr:** Professor, Montgomery College, 51 Mannakee St, Rockville, MD 20850, **Business Phone:** (240)567-7283.

### SMITH, ALPHONSO LEHMAN
School administrator, dean (education), college teacher. **Personal:** Born Feb 27, 1937, Memphis, TN; children: Angela, Anthony & Audrey. **Educ:** Fisk Univ, attended 1957; Ohio State Univ, BS, 1959, MS, 1964. **Career:** Wright State Univ, math instr, 1964-68, asst prof math, 1970-93, asst dir affirmative action fac, 1972-73, dir affirmative action progs, 1973, pres fac, 1987-91, asst dean, Col Sci & Math, 1991-93, Dept Math & Statist, asst prof prof emer, 1993-. **Orgs:** Fel NSF, 1956-72; Pi Mu Epsilon, 1958-; Phi Beta Kappa, 1960-; Am Math Soc, 1961-; chmn, Ohio Affirmative Action Officers Asn, 1973-; Yellow Springs Title, IX Adv Comt, 1976-77; United Way, 1982-87; Phi Kappa Phi, 1992-. **Home Addr:** 1750 Randall Rd, Yellow Springs, OH 45387-1226, **Home Phone:** (937)767-7446. **Business Addr:** Assistant Professor Emeritus, Wright State University, 120 Math & Microbiol Sci, Dayton, OH 45435, **Business Phone:** (937)775-3927.

### SMITH, ANDRE RAPHEL
Conductor (music). **Personal:** Born Durham, NC. **Educ:** Univ Miami, BMus, trombone; Yale Univ, MMus; Curtis Inst Music, dipl, conducting; Julliard Sch Music, Advan Cert, orchestral conducting. **Career:** Bruno Walter Memorial Scholar, Juilliard Sch; Norwalk Youth Symphony, music dir, 1990; St Louis Symphony Orchestra, asst conductor, In Unison Program, 1991-94; Philadelphia Orchestra, asst conductor, 1994-2000; Kurt Masur, New York Philharmonic, asst conductor, 2000-02; Wheeling Symphony Orchestra, music dir, 2003-; Neubrandenburger Philharmonie, guest conductor, 2005. **Orgs:** In Unison. **Home Addr:** PO Box 41091, Philadelphia, PA 19127. **Business Addr:** Music Director, Wheeling Symphony Orchestra, 1025 Main St Suite 811, Wheeling, WV 26003, **Business Phone:** (304)232-6191.

### SMITH, PROF. ANDREW W.
School administrator, singer. **Personal:** Born Aug 24, 1941, Lexington, KY; married Yvonne Bransford; children: Antron William, Avrom Willon & Ahira Yvonne. **Educ:** Ky State Univ, Frankfort, Ky, BS, 1964; Roosevelt Univ, Chicago, M Mus, 1970. **Career:** Chicago Brd Educ, teacher, 1964-70; City Markham, dir urban develop, 1971, actg city mgr, 1972-74; Markham Roller Rink Markham, Ill, asst mgr & co-owner, 1972-79; Met Opera, opera singer, 1976-; Opera Orchestra New York, 1979-; Ky State Univ, Dept Music, asst prof, prof & dir, 1996-. **Orgs:** Opera singer New York Opera, 1977-79; Houston Grand Opera; Mich Opera; Boston Opera; Atlanta Symphony; Grand Pk Summer Festival; Art Pk Music Festival; Chicago Sinai Congregation Cantorial Soloist 7 Yrs; Kappa Alpha Phi; Concert Choir; Conn Opera; Mich Opera Theatre; Oakland Opera; Palm SpringsConcert Choir; Pittsburg Opera; Nj State Opera. **Honors/Awds:** Winner Of Chicago land Music Festival, 1965; WGN Audition Air Met Audition; Emmy Award, 1977; Tony Award. **Home Addr:** 3280 Brighton Pl Dr, Lexington, KY 40509, **Home Phone:** (859)225-0374. **Business Addr:** Professor, Director, Kentucky State University, 400 E Main St, Frankfort, KY 40601, **Business Phone:** (502)597-6000.

### SMITH, ANGELA L. D.
Accountant. **Home Addr:** 530 Birchberry Ter, Atlanta, GA 30331-8495.

### SMITH, DR. ANN ELIZABETH
School administrator. **Personal:** Born Aug 17, 1939, Poplar Bluff, MO; daughter of Leland G (deceased) and Hallie W (deceased).

**Educ:** Lincoln Univ, BA, 1960; Univ Iowa, MA, 1962; Union Inst, PhD, 1974. **Career:** Eng Cent High Sch, instr, 1960; E Ill Univ, instr, 1962-66; Univ Ind Black Theatre, lectr, 1971; Northeastern Ill Univ, vpres acad affairs, actg vpres, Speech & Performing Arts, assoc prof, 1975-77, asst to pres, 1969-75, instr, 1966-69; Prudential Ins Co, sales mgr, 1978; Endow Inc, Chicago, Ill, vpres, 1978-88; Stratton & Co, dir mkt cook, 1981; Univ Ill, Chicago, assoc chancellor community affairs, 1988, asst chancellor, dir community rels; Gamaliel Found, pres, 2011, retired. **Orgs:** Delta Sigma Theta Sorority, 1957; prod coordr, Orgn Black Am Cult, 1967-; consult, Women's Prog Reg Off HEW & HUD, 1972-73; nat policy bd mem, Union Grad Sch, 1972-75, chairperson, 1974-75; Improving Col & Univ Teaching, 1974; bd mem, League Black Women, 1976-80; bd mem, PUSH Womens Benefit Bd, 1979-90; bd trustee, Univ Ill, 1985-88; bd mem, Chicago Access Corp, 1989-; bd mem, Gamaliel Found, 1990; consult, Dramatic Art; City Col, Commuters & Community Houses; vpres bus & prof people pub interest, W Cent Asn; Ill Arts Alliance & Found; Nat Adv Coun; nat adv coun, Nat Asn Advan Colored People; Duncan YMCA; Marcy Newberry Asn; Southside Community Arts Ctr; Boards Joel Hall Dancers; Ill Comt Black Concerns Higher Educ; Am Col. **Honors/Awds:** International Women's Year Award, Nebr Ill Univ, 1975; PUSH Excellence Award, 1977; Legionaire Award, Prudential Ins Co, 1978-79; Presidential Citation, Prudential Ins Co, 1979; Million Dollar Roundtable Prudential Ins Co, 1980; HDL, Lincoln Univ, 1987; Top 100 Black Business & Professional Women, Dollars & Sense Mag, 1988; Honorary Doctorate, Lincoln Univ. **Special Achievements:** First African American women to be elected to the board of trustees; First African American appointed as a full-time professor at Eastern Illinois University. **Home Addr:** 505 N Lake Shore Dr, Chicago, IL 60611, **Home Phone:** (312)828-0507.

### SMITH, ANNA DEAVERE

Playwright, actor, educator. **Personal:** Born Sep 18, 1950, Baltimore, MD; daughter of Deavere Young Jr and Anna Rosalind Young. **Educ:** Beaver Col, BA, 1971; Am Conserv Theatre, MFA, 1976. **Career:** Carnegie-Mellon Univ, asst prof theater, 1978-79; Yale Univ, vis artist, 1982; New York Univ, teacher actg, 1983-84, univ prof; Performance Studies Tisch Sch Arts, art & pub policy affil; Nat Theatre Inst, vis teacher, 1984-85; Am Conserv Theatre, master teacher actg, 1986; Stanford Univ, Drama Dept, prof, 1990-2000; Harvard Univ, Inst Arts & Civic Dialogue, founder & founding dir, 1997-; Twilight: Los Angeles, writer & producer, 2000; Univ Southern Calif, Los Angeles, asst prof actg; Lincoln Ctr Inst, teaching artist, New York Univ, Tisch Sch Arts, Dept Performance Studies, univ prof, prof, New York Univ Sch Law, affil; Anna Deavere Smith Works Inc, founder & founding dir; Writings: On the Road (play), 1983; Aye, Aye, Aye, I'm Integrated (play), 1984; Piano (play), 1989; Fires in the Mirror: Crown Heights, Brooklyn & Other Identities (play), 1993; Twilight: Los Angeles, 1994; Talk to Me: Listening between the Lines, 2000; House Arrest: A Search for American Character in & around the White House, Past & Present (play), 2003; Letters to a Young Artist: Straight-up Advice on Making a Life in the Arts, 2006; Films: Soup for One, 1982; Unfinished Business, 1987; Dave, 1993; Philadelphia, 1993; The American President, 1995; The Human Stain, 2003; The Manchurian Candidate, 2004; Cry_Wolf, 2005; Rent, 2005; The Kingdom, 2007; Rachel Getting Married, 2008; TV Series: "All My Children", 1970; Fires in the Mirror, writer, 1993; "The West Wing", 2000-06; "The Practice", 2000; "100 Centre Street", 2001; "Presidio Med", 2002; Expert Witness, 2003; Numb3rs, 2005; Life Support, 2007; "Nurse Jackie", 2009-15; "The Surgeon General", 2013; "Anna Deavere Smith: A YoungArts Masterclass", 2014; "Black-ish", 2015-16; "Law & Order: Special Victims Unit", 2016; "Legends of Tomorrow", 2016. **Orgs:** MacArthur Fel, 1994; Fletcher Found Fel, 2006; Dramatists Guild; Am Fedn TV & Radio Artists; Screen Actors Guild; Actors Equity Asn. **Honors/Awds:** Obie Award Special Citation, 1991-92; Drama Desk Award, Solo Performance, 1992, 1993; Los Angeles Drama Critics Award for Distinguished Achievement, 1993; Obie Award for Best Play, 1993-94; Drama Desk Award, Outstanding Solo Performance, 1993-94; Los Angeles Drama Critics Circle Award, 1993; NAACP Image Award, 1994; Lucille Lortel Award, 1994; New York Drama Critics Circle Special Citation, 1994; The MacArthur Award, 1994; Genius Award for Theater Work, John D & Catherine T Mac Arthur Found, 1996; Radcliffe Medal of Honor, 1997; Wisconsin Association of Family & Children's Agencies Award, 2003; Black Reel Award, 2004; Helen Hayes Award; National Association for the Advancement of Colored People Award. Honorary Doctorates: Univ Nc, Chapel Hill, 1995; Wheelock Col, 1995; Beaver Col, 1995; Calif State Univ, Sacramento, 1996; Colgate Univ, 1997; Wesleyan Univ, 1997; Sch Visual Arts, 1997; Holy Cross Col, 1997; Pratt Inst, 1998; Occidental Col, 1999; Matrix Award, New York Women CommunInc, 2008; Fellow Award, Theater Arts from Us Artists, 2009; Outstanding Solo Performer Award, United Solo Theatre Festival Bd Awards, 2010; Theatre World Award. **Business Addr:** University Professor, Professor, New York University, Rm 519 721 Broadway Sixth Fl, New York, NY 10003, **Business Phone:** (212)998-1812.

### SMITH, ANNE STREET

Social worker. **Personal:** Born Mar 19, 1942, Spartanburg, SC; daughter of Willie L Amos and Sallie McCracken Amos; married Douglas M; children: Michael D Street, Jerome & Jared. **Educ:** Howard Univ, BA, 1964, MSW, 1969; Ctr Grp Studies, 1974. **Career:** Dept Hr, social worker, 1969-72; Howard Univ Hosp, Psychol & Social Serv Dept, social worker/instr, 1972-80, Social Work Serv Dept, assoc dir, 1980-86, dir social servs, 1986-93, social worker, 1994-; Sabbatical Leave, 1993-94. **Orgs:** Gamma Sigma Sigma Nat Serv Sorority, 1963-; Nat Asn Social Workers, 1969-; rec secy, historian, DC Hook-Up Black Women, 1980-84; corresp secy bd dir, Ionia R Whipper Home Inc, 1984-85; Soc Hosp Social Work Dirs Am Hosp Asn, 1986-93; Am Pub Health Asn, 1986-; realtor assoc, Jackson Realty, 1989-91; Nat Inst Ment Health. **Honors/Awds:** Training Student, Nat Inst Mental Health, 1967-69; Fellowship Grant, Nat Endowment for Humanities, 1980; Prestigious Meritorious Award, DC Hook-Up Black Women, 1983. **Home Addr:** 601 G St, Washington, DC 20024, **Home Phone:** (202)865-6731. **Business Addr:** Social Worker, Howard University Hospital, 2041 Ga Ave NW Rm 2023, Washington, DC 20060, **Business Phone:** (202)865-6731.

### SMITH, ANTHONY EDWARD

Manager, engineer. **Personal:** Born Nov 14, 1961, Harvey, IL. **Educ:** Univ Ill, Urbana-Champaign, BS, Eng, gen, 1983. **Career:** Owens-Corning Fiberglas, coop, eng intern, 1981-82; Ill Bell Tel Co, asst mgr, 1983-86, area mgr, 1986-. **Orgs:** Am Youth Found; pres, Black Stud Union Univ Ill, 1980-81; Ill Soc Gen Engrs, 1982-83; Rotary Int Harvey Club, 1986-; Nat Black MBA Assoc. **Honors/Awds:** Larson Award, Univ Ill, 1983.

### SMITH, ANTHONY TERRELL. See LOC, TONE.

### SMITH, ANTOWAIN DRURELL

Football player. **Personal:** Born Mar 14, 1972, Millbrook, AL. **Educ:** E Miss Community Col; Univ Houston, kinesiol. **Career:** Football player (retired); Buffalo Bills, running back, 1997-2000; New Eng Patriots, running back, 2001, tight end, 2002, punter, 2003; Tenn Titans, running back, 2004; New Orleans Saints, running back, 2005; Houston Texans, 2006. **Honors/Awds:** Super Bowl champion, XXXVI, XXXVIII.

### SMITH, ARTHUR D.

School administrator. **Personal:** son of Augusta Banks and Adolphus. **Educ:** Kent State Univ, BS, 1957, MA, 1962; Yale Univ, PhD, 1973. **Career:** Yale Univ, Transitional Prog, dir, 1968-70, Yale Child Study Ctr, Baldwin-King Prog, dir, 1970-73, asst dean, 1973-74; Northwestern Univ, assoc prof, 1974-78, interim dean, 1979-80, assoc provost, 1981-86, dir planning, 1986, dir opers, 1992. **Orgs:** Educ consult, Am Friends, 1974-; chmn bd, Northcare, 1976; assoc provost, Northeastern Univ, 1980-; prog vol evaluator, United Way Boston, 1979-80. **Honors/Awds:** John Hay Fellow, John Hay Whitney Found, 1964; Branford College Fellow, Yale Univ, 1972. **Home Addr:** 10901 Johnson Blvd Suite 306, Seminole, FL 33772, **Home Phone:** (727)546-5065.

### SMITH, AUBREY CARL

Manager, chemist. **Personal:** Born Mar 12, 1942, Clarksdale, MS; son of Aubrey Carl Sr and Mattye Alice Johnson; married Marie Joyce; children: Nicole Denise & Aubrey Brian. **Educ:** Univ Ill, BS, chem, 1963; Thornton Community Col, Harvey, AA, sci, 1968; Ill Inst Technol, Chicago, BA, chem, 1972. **Career:** Manager (retired); A B Dick Co, Niles, toner chemist, 1972; Arco Petrol Prod Co, Harvey, anal chemist, 1974, lubricants chemist, 1983, supvr, health, safety & environ protection, 1985; Argonne Nat Lab, Argonne, supvr, waste mgt opers, 1986, lab environ compliance officer, 1988, mgr, waste mgt opers, 1988, Mat & Components Technol & Mat Sci Div, dep bldg mgr, environ compliance rep, 1990-92, bldg mgr, environ compliance off, 1992-. **Orgs:** Am Chem Soc, 1983-; Am Soc Lubrication Engs, 1983-85; Soc Automotive Eng, 1983-85; Chicago Nat Safety Coun, 1983-85; Am Soc Testing Mat, 1983-85. **Honors/Awds:** Elected to Dwight D Eisenhower High School Hall of Fame, Blue Island, Ill; Selected by Ebony & Jet Magazines "Speaking of People" Sections, 1989; First black person to hold the following positions at Argonne Nat Laboratory: Laboratory Environmental Compliance Officer. **Home Addr:** 880 Honey Lane, Crete, IL 60417, **Home Phone:** (708)672-9231.

### SMITH, AUDREY S.

Executive, educator. **Personal:** Born Feb 24, 1940, Upper Marlboro, MD; daughter of Frank Spriggs and Mary Henry Spriggs; married Lynn H; children: Michael & Lisa Miller. **Educ:** Roger Williams Col, Bristol, RI, BS, 1976; Univ Md, MS, gen admin. **Career:** Educator, Executive (retired); Brown Univ, Providence, RI, training asst, 1971-73, dir employ & employee rels, 1973-75, from assoc dir personnel to dir personnal, 1975-81; Montgomery Col, Rockville, Md, dir personnel, 1981-89; Princeton Univ, Princeton, NJ, vpres human resources, 1989-96. **Orgs:** Urban League, 1963-; Col & Univ Personnel Asn, 1975-; ACE, 1975-; NIP, 1975-; comt status women, Princeton Univ, 1989-; Multicultural Studies Proj, 1990-; Am Coun Educ; Nat Identification Prog; Diversity Leadership Coun. **Home Addr:** 18 Lake Lane, Princeton, NJ 08540.

### SMITH, BARBARA

Writer. **Personal:** Born Nov 16, 1946, Cleveland, OH; daughter of Hilda. **Educ:** Mt Holyoke Col, BA, 1969; Univ Pittsburgh, MA, 1971; Univ Conn, ABD, 1981. **Career:** Univ Mass, instr, 1976-81; Barnard Col, instr, 1983; NY Univ, instr, 1985; Univ Minn, vis prof, 1986; Hobart William Smith Col, vis prof, 1987; Mt Holyoke Col, vis prof, 1988; Kitchen Table Women Color Press, dir, 1981-95; Bks: This Bridge Called My Black: Writings by Radical Women Color, 1981; All Blacks Are Men, But Some Us Are Brave: Black Women's Studies, 1982; Home Girls: A Black Feminist Anthology, 1983; Yours Struggle: Three Feminist Perspectives Anti-Semitism & Racism, 1984; Truth That Never Hurts: Writings Race, Gender & Freedom, 1998. **Orgs:** Founder, Combahee River Collective, 1974-80; artist-in-residence Hambidge Ctr Arts & Sci, 1983, Millay Colony Arts, 1983, Yaddo, 1984, Blue Mountain Ctr, 1985; bd dir, NCBLG, 1985-88; Nat Asn Advan Colored People, Black Radical Cong, Feminist Action Network, Nat Writers Union; Bunting fel, 1996-97. **Home Addr:** 15953 Whitcomb Rd, Cleveland, OH 44110, **Home Phone:** (216)541-6262.

### SMITH, BARBARA

Restaurateur. **Personal:** Born Aug 24, 1949; daughter of William H and Florence; married Donald Anderson; children: Dana; married Dan Gasby. **Educ:** John Robert Powers Modeling Sch, attended 1967. **Career:** Former model & actress: Wilhelmina Modeling Agency, model, 1967; Ebony Fashion Fair, 1969; Ark's Am, hostess & floor mgr; TV host; B Smith's restaurant, owner, 1986-; TV culinary hostess, 1997; B Smith Restaurant Group, owner, 1998-; B Smith Style Home Collection, 2001-; B Smith Jewelry Collection, currently; Oil of Olay & Colgate Palmolive Oxy prod, spokesperson; TV shows: "The Oprah Winfrey Show", ABC's "Good Morning Am", "The Cosby Show", "The Cosby Mysteries", "The View" & NBC's "The Today Show". **Orgs:** Trustee, Culinary Inst Am; Feminist Press; founding mem, Times Sq Bus Improv Dist; New York Women's found. **Honors/Awds:** First Black Woman on Cover, Mademoiselle, 1976; Harvard Business School's Dynamic Women in Business Conference; Earl Graves Entrepreneurial Award, 2008; BET Honors Award for Entrepreneurship, 2009; Black Enterprise Legacy Award, 2010; Visionary Leader Award, National Kidney Foundation, Chamber of Commerce, 2011. **Special Achievements:** B Smith's Entertaining and Cooking for Friends, Artisan, 1995; B. Smith: Rituals and Celebration; B. Smith Cooks Southern-Style; hosted the lifestyle television show B Smith with Style; graced the covers of 15 magazines including Mademoiselle 's first ever featuring an African-American woman, 1976; author of two tabletop books on entertaining the host of B. Smart Tips for a Better Life heard on New York 's WBLS-FM, and a columnist for Soap Opera Digest; first black Miss Triad, Queen of the Three Rivers. **Business Addr:** Founder, Chief Executive Officer, B Smiths Restaurant, 320 W 46th St, New York, NY 10036, **Business Phone:** (212)315-1100.

### SMITH, DR. BARBARA WHEAT

School administrator, educator. **Personal:** Born May 28, 1948, Mobile, AL; daughter of Sidney W Wheat and Rosetta W Wheat; children: Daryl E, Yuri J, Afra S & Mastaki A. **Educ:** Tuskegee Univ, BA, 1969; Univ Wis, MA, 1972, PhD, 1982. **Career:** Univ Wis, Sch Nursing, Equal Opportunities Prog, dir, 1973-75, acad adv, 1976, col Agr & Life Sci, 1978-80, asst dean, 1991-; dir edu diversity prog, currently; BJ Smith Co Inc, Mobile, Ala, pres, 1982-88; Us Census Bur, Mobile, Ala, recruiting opers mgr, 1990; Searcy Hosp, psychiat rehab counr, 1990-91. **Orgs:** Nat Asn Minorities Agr; Nat Resources & Related Sci; historian, Madison Metrop Links Inc; bd dir, State Ala Ment Health Technicians; bd dir, Progressive League Inc; bd dir, Nat Assault Illiteracy; coop bd adv, Asn Women Agr; Nat Conf Black Mayors, Guyana, S Am; Am Ethnic Sci Soc; Nat Coun Negro Women; Ala state prs; Delta Sigma Theta Sorority; Pi Lamba Theta, 1976. **Home Addr:** 801 Wellington St, Mobile, AL 36617-2740. **Business Addr:** Assistant Dean Academic Student Affairs, Director of Educational Diversity Programs, University of Wisconsin, 116 Agriculture Hall 1450 Linden Dr, Madison, WI 53706, **Business Phone:** (608)262-3003.

### SMITH, BENJAMIN JOSEPH

Football player. **Personal:** Born May 14, 1967, Warner Robins, GA; son of Bennie Joe. **Educ:** Univ Ga, social work; Northeastern Okla A&M Univ. **Career:** Football player (retired); Philadelphia Eagles, free safety & left corner back, 1990-93; Denver Broncos, left corner back, 1994; Ariz Cardinals, defensive back, 1995-96. **Honors/Awds:** Defensive Most Valuable Player, 1989.

### SMITH, BEVERLY EVANS

Business owner. **Personal:** Born Apr 12, 1948, Massillon, OH; daughter of Louie Edward and Willa Dumas; married Stephen J; children: Brian S & Stacy N. **Educ:** Bowling Green State Univ, OH, BS, 1970; Kent State Univ, OH, MEd, 1973; Babson Col, Wellesley, MA, Exec Develop Consortium, 1987; St Catherine's Episcopal Church, cert Stephen Minister, 1991. **Career:** Garfield High Sch, teacher, speech, 1971-72; Kent State Univ, Kent, OH, asst dir, Financial Aids, 1972-74, dir, Upward Bound, 1974-76; GA State Univ, Atlanta, GA, asst dean, stud life, 1976-78; Southern Bell, Atlanta, GA, staff mgr, 1978-83; AT&T, Atlanta GA, dist mgr, 1984-96; Delta Sigma Theta, Wash, DC, exec dir, 1988-90; Riverside Bank, adv bd; Chattahoochee Tech Col, bd dir; HR Group Inc, vpres, exec dir tech col syst & sr partner, currently. **Orgs:** Nat secy, Delta Sigma Thetha Sorority; chair, Cobb County Ga Bd Elections; past exec dir, Delta Sigma Theta Sorority; 1967; past pres, Jack & Jill, N Suburban Atlanta Chap, 1981-84; state commr, Ga Clean & Beautiful Comn, 1984-88; chair, Adult Educ, St Catherine's Episcopal Church, 1986-88; Cobb County Ga gov bd, Leadership Cobb, 1987-91; Proj Mgt Inst, 1987-89; Asn Chief Exec Coun, 1988-89; bd mem, Women Meaningful Summit, 1989; adv bd, United Way, Cobb County, 1991-95; bd dir, Girls Inc, 1992-94; chairperson, Leadership Cobb, 1997-98; Cobb Exec Women, 1998-; adv bd, Riverside Bank; bd trustees, chair, Strategic Planning Comn, Bowling Green State Univ; Soc Human Resource Professionals; exec bd, Atlanta Human Resources Asn; Nat Asn African Americans Human Resources. **Honors/Awds:** Named AA History-Makers; Outstanding Freshman & Senior Woman, Bowling Green State Univ, 1967, 1970; Mortar Bd Honor Soc, 1969; Omicrom Delta Kappa Honor Soc, 1977; Georgia Woman of the Year in Business, Cobb County Georgia, 1984; Outstanding Business Professional, Washington DC Business Professional Asn, 1988; Salute to Women Achievement Award, YWCA, 1995. **Home Addr:** 1152 Clarendon Dr, Marietta, GA 30068, **Home Phone:** (404)998-7369. **Business Addr:** Executive Director, Stewardship & Development, The Technical College System of Georgia, 1800 Century Pl NE, Atlanta, GA 30345, **Business Phone:** (404)679-1704.

### SMITH, BOBBY (ROBERT EUGENE SMITH)

Baseball player. **Personal:** Born May 10, 1974, Oakland, CA. **Career:** Baseball player(retired); Tampa Bay Devil Rays, infielder, 1998-2002; Milwaukee Brewers, 2003; New York Yankees, 2003; Chicago White Sox, 2003-04, 2006; Oakland Athletics, 2005.

### SMITH, BOBBY ANTONIA

Government official. **Personal:** Born Feb 12, 1949, West Palm Beach, FL; daughter of Will and Ida Mae; children: Antonia & Erika. **Educ:** Fla A&M Univ, BS, 1970; Fla State Univ, MPA, 1972; Nova Univ, attended 1983. **Career:** Broward County Sch Dist, Pompano Beach, Fla, instr, 1970-73; Fla Dept Community Affairs, Tallahassee, Fla, local govt spec II, 1973-75; Fla W Palm Beach, asst county adminr, 1975; Fla Wildlife Unlimited Inc, pres, currently. **Orgs:** Nat Asn Advan Colored People; Urban League Palm Beach County. **Home Addr:** 901 NW 2nd St, Delray Beach, FL 33444, **Home Phone:** (561)278-3522. **Business Addr:** President, Florida Wildlife Unlimited Inc, PO Box 2523, Wauchula, FL 33873, **Business Phone:** (863)767-0930.

### SMITH, BRUCE BERNARD

Football player, businessperson. **Personal:** Born Jun 18, 1963, Norfolk, VA; married Carmen; children: Alston. **Educ:** Va Polytech Inst & State Univ, sociol. **Career:** Football player (retired), businessperson; Buffalo Bills, defensive end & right defensive end, 1985-99; Wash Redskins, defensive end, 2000-03; Bruce Smith Enterprise LLC, founder, 2004-; Legends Energy Group, co-owner, currently. **Orgs:** Queen St Baptist Church; St Jude's C's Hosp; Oper Smile; bd vis, Va Tech. **Honors/Awds:** Outland Trophy, 1984; Pro Bowl, 1987-90 &

1992-98; AFC Defensive Player of the Year, Nat Football League Players Asn, 1985; Pro Bowl MVP, 1987; UPI AFL-AFC Player of the Year, 1987, 1988, 1990, 1996; Defensive Lineman of the Year, Nat Football League, 1987; George Halas Trophy, Newspaper Enterprise Asn, 1990, 1993; Defensive Player of the Year, Nat Football League, 1990, 1993, 1996; Ed Block Courage Award, 1992; Independence Bowl Hall of Fame, 1996; Mackay Award, 1996; Record for NFL Sacks in a Career, 2000, 2003-; Virginia Tech Hall of Fame, 2005; Col Football Hall of Fame, 2006; Hampton Roads Sports Hall of Fame, 2008; Buffalo Bills Wall of Fame, 2008; Pro Football Hall of Fame, 2009. **Business Addr:** Founder, Bruce Smith Enterprise LLC, Virginia Beach, VA.

### SMITH, BRUCE L.
Automotive executive, president (organization). **Personal:** Born Oct 15, 1962, McKeesport, PA. **Educ:** Carnegie-Mellon Univ, BS, mech engineering, 1985; Harvard Univ, MBA, 1989; USAF Acad, engineering, 1980. **Career:** Delphi, Gen Motors maintenance supvr, 1985-86, mfg eng, 1989, mfg gen supvr, 1989-90; ITT, mgr mfg syst, 1993-94, exec asst ceo, 1994-95, plant mgr, 1995-96; Diesel Technol Co, pres & chief exec officer, 1996-98; Am Nat Can, dir mfg, 1998-2001; United Plastics Group Inc, pres & chief operating officer, 2001-03; Piston Automotive LLC, vpres, chief exec officer, 2003-05; guilford, chief operating officer, 2005-09; Elyria & Hodge Foundries, pres & chief exec officer, 2009-. **Home Addr:** 4400 N Scottsdale Rd Suite 258, Scottsdale, AZ 85251-3331. **Business Addr:** President, Chief Operating Officer, United Plastics Group Inc, 900 Oakmont Lane Suite 100, Westmont, IL 60559, **Business Phone:** (630)321-5500.

### SMITH, C. MILES
Television journalist. **Personal:** Born Apr 2, 1950, Atlanta, GA; son of Margaret N and C Miles; children: Calvin Miles III, Nina Patrice & Che Lena. **Educ:** Morehouse Col, BS, 1979. **Career:** WGST-AM, News Radio 640, talk show host; Radio One Corp magnate Cathy Hughes, Radio One 1450 am, talk show host, 1998; Talk How You Like Underground Posse Line Show, host, currently; Radio Diary, host, currently. **Orgs:** Omega Psi Phi, Psi Chapt, Morehouse, 1969. **Home Addr:** 1216 New Hope Rd, Atlanta, GA 30331, **Home Phone:** (404)703-1089. **Business Addr:** Host, Radio Diary, PO Box 71061, Washington, DC 20024, **Business Phone:** (301)808-0833.

### SMITH, DR. CALVERT H.
College president, educator. **Educ:** Winston-Salem State Col, BA, 1959; DePaul Univ, MA; Northwestern Univ, PhD, 1964. **Career:** Morris Brown Col, pres; Cincinnati Pub Schs, dep supt, 1992; Univ Cincinnati, Col Educ, Criminal Justice & Human Serv, adj prof, prof emer, currently; Winston-Salem State Univ, bd visitors, currently. **Orgs:** Pres, Cincinnati Br Nat Asn Advan Colored People, 2002. **Home Addr:** 930 Goss Rd, Cincinnati, OH 45229, **Home Phone:** (513)470-8104. **Business Addr:** Professor Emeritus, University of Cincinnati, PO Box 210002 Teachers/Dyer Hall, Cincinnati, OH 45221, **Business Phone:** (513)556-3646.

### SMITH, CARL WILLIAM
Administrator. **Personal:** Born Jun 8, 1931, Raleigh, NC; married Pearl Mitchell Wilson; children: Wanda & Wendi. **Educ:** St Augustine Col, BA, 1954; NC Cent Univ, MSC, 1962; Univ Wis-Madison, attended 1965; Exec Prog Univ NC-Chapel Hill, cert, 1981. **Career:** Administrator (retired); CE Perry HS, asst prin & teacher, 1954-55; St Augustine's Col, adminr & instr, 1955-60; PPG Indust, consult, 1969-71; NC Cent Univ, asst chmn & fac, 1961-72; Univ NC-Chapel Hill, asst to the provost, 1972-95. **Orgs:** Am Mgmt Asn; Am Mktg Asn; Am Asn Higher Educ. **Home Addr:** 5825 N Beaver Lane, Raleigh, NC 27604, **Home Phone:** (919)850-9912.

### SMITH, DR. CARLOS F.
Physician. **Educ:** Monmouth Col, Monmouth, IL, BA, 1990; Dr William M Scholl Col Podiatric Med, Chicago, IL, BS, 1994, DPM, 1994; Am Bd Podiatric Orthop & Primary Podiatric Med, dipl; Am Bd Podiatric Surg, dipl. **Career:** Univ Tex Health Sci Ctr, San Antonio, Tx, intern, 1995; Bellaire Med Ctr, Harris Co Podiatric Surg Prog, Houston, Tx, resident PSR-1924, 1997; Dr William M Scholl Col Podiatric Med, Dept Med & Surg, clin fac, asst prof, 1997-; Ill Masonic Med Ctr, Dept Surg, clin fac, 1997-; pvt pract, 1997-; Dr. William M Scholl Coll Podiatric Med, Off Minority Stud Affairs, actg dir, 1997-2001; Mary Hosp & Med Ctr, physician; Mercy Hosp & Med Ctr, physician; Advocate Trinity Hosp, physician; Advocate Christ Med Ctr, physician; St. Joseph Hosp, physician; Mt Sinai Hosp Med Ctr, Dept Surg, clin fac, 1998-; Loyola Univ Med Ctr, Dept Orthop Surg & Rehab, lectr, 1999-; Ctrs Foot & Ankle Care, chief exec officer & med dir, currently. **Orgs:** Am Diabetes Asn; Am Podiatric Med Asn; Ill Podiatric Med Asn; Durlacher Podiatric Hon Soc, 1991; pres, Cook Co Podiatric Med Asn, 1998-; alumni bd, Monmouth Col, 1998-; bd dir, Nat Podiatric Med Asn, 1999-; bd trustees, Monmouth Col, 2001-; fel Am Col Foot & Ankle Surgeons; fel Am Col Foot & Ankle Orthop & Med; Am Bd Podiatric Med; Am Bd Foot & Ankle Surg. **Honors/Awds:** Scholl Col Half-Tuition Scholar, 1991, 1992; Durlacher Podiatric Hon Soc, 1991; Philip R Brachman & Alumni Scholar, 1992, 1993; listed, Who's Who Among Students, Am Univs & Cols, 1992, 1993, 1994; Ill State Podiatric Med Full-Tuition Scholar, 1993, 1994. **Special Achievements:** Publications: Ingrown Toenails and Other Selected Nail Diseases, 1994; Pes Planus Deformity: Etiology, Evaluation, and Non-Operative Treatment, 1995; Clinical Evaluation of the Diabetic Foot, 1996; Computed Tomography of the Lower Extremity, 1997; Charcot Arthropathy, 1997; Diabetic Foot Care, 1998; Current Trends in Onychomycosis, 1999; Current Trends in Onychomycosis, 1999; Posterior Tibial Tendon Dysfunction, 1999; Achilles Tendon Ruptures, 2001. **Business Addr:** Chief Executive Officer, Medical Director, Centers for Foot & Ankle Care, 711 W N Ave Suite 210, Chicago, IL 60610, **Business Phone:** (312)642-3440.

### SMITH, CAROL BARLOW
Government official, chairperson. **Personal:** Born Mar 9, 1945, Atlanta, GA; married Douglas; children: Eric Douglas. **Educ:** Ark Bus Col; Wayland Baptist Univ, BA, 1996. **Career:** Gr Anchorage Area Comm Action Agency Northwest Rep Women's Caucus, pub info specialist; BLM Anchorage, asst to chief br field surveys; City Anchorage, eeo officer; Municipality Anchorage, Dept Employee Rels, affirmative action compliance officer & personnel specialist, compliance mgr, currently. **Orgs:** Int Asn Off Human Rights Agencies; bd dir, Ark Presswomen; Coun Drug Abuse; Coun Planned Parenthood; bd dir, Citizens Consumer Protection; YWMU; pres, New Hope Baptist Ch; mem bd comnrs, Ark State Human Rights Comn; 2nd vpres, Nat Asn Advan Colored People; Ark Presswomen; Anchorage Bicentennial Comn; chmn, Ark State Human Rights Comm, 1976; Anchorage Equal Rights Asn; chmn, Nat Asn Advan Colored People, Freedom Fund Banquet, 1972; vice chmn, Ark State Human Rights Comn; trustee, bt trustee, Southern Baptist Conv. **Honors/Awds:** Bus Leader of the Day, 1974; Outstanding Stud Award, Wayland Baptist Univ. **Home Addr:** 3641 Amber Bay Loop, Anchorage, AK 99517. **Business Addr:** Personnel Specialist, Affirmative Action Compliance Officer, Municipality of Anchorage, 632 W 6th Ave Suite 620, Anchorage, AK 99501, **Business Phone:** (907)343-4896.

### SMITH, CAROL J. See Obituaries Section.

### SMITH, CAROLYN LEE
Executive. **Personal:** Born Nov 14, 1942, Lakewood, NJ; daughter of Davis Lee and Arline Erwin Knight; married Vernon; children: Soniab & Angela. **Educ:** Howard Univ, BA, 1965; Univ Md, MBA, 1994. **Career:** United Planning Orgn, specialist, 1965-66; Cooper & Lybrand, audit mgr, 1971-77, 1982-85, nat inst comm dev, vpres financial mgt, 1972-73, dir, mgmt consult 1985-86; DC Dept Fin & Revenue, dir govt dc, tres, 1977-79, 1979-82; Pricewaterhouse Coopers, partner 1986-. **Orgs:** Pres, Met Wash DC Chapt, 1977-79; Greater Wash Bd Trade, 1983-; treas, Pub Access Bd, 1985-87; chmn, DC Bd Accountancy, 1985-88; bd gov DC Inst CPAs, 1985-87; DC Retirement Bd, 1988-92; chmn, DC Retirement Bd, 1990-92; Nat Asn Black Accts. **Home Addr:** 2600 Keating St Apt 418, Temple Hills, MD 20748-1520, **Home Phone:** (301)430-0236. **Business Addr:** Partner, Pricewaterhouse Coopers, 1616 N Ft Myer Dr, Arlington, VA 22209, **Business Phone:** (703)741-1077.

### SMITH, CARSON EUGENE
School administrator. **Personal:** Born Dec 23, 1943, Louisville, KY; son of Fred Eugene and Louise Bernadine Carson; married Gleneva McCowan; children: Mark, Shanna, Angela & Andrew. **Educ:** Ky State Univ, BA, hist & polit sci, 1965; Univ Ky, MA, polit sci, 1972, Dissertation Stage, 1973. **Career:** Office for Policy & Mgmt State Govt, policy adv for higher educ, 1973-74; Coun on Higher Educ, coordr for fin planning, 1974-77; Univ Ky, asst budget dir, 1977-80; Univ Mo, asst dir budget, 1980-83; Ky State Univ, Frankfort, Ky, vpres, admin servs, fin & admin; Univ Ky, Col Medicine, Lexington, Ky, bus mgr; State Univ New York, Canton, vpres, Admin Servs, 2001-. **Orgs:** Central Assoc Col & Univ Bus Officers, Southern Assoc Col & Univ Bus Officers, Nat Assoc Col & Univ Bus Officers, 1999-2000, EDUCAUSE, Alpha Phi Alpha, 1962-; State Univ New York Bus Officers Asn, 2003; Nat Asn Col & Univ Bus Officers. **Home Addr:** 34 State St, Canton, NY 13617-1014, **Home Phone:** (315)379-0772. **Business Addr:** Vice President for Administrative Services, State University of New York, 34 Cornell Dr, Canton, NY 13617, **Business Phone:** (315)386-7103.

### SMITH, CEDRIC DELON
Football player, football coach. **Personal:** Born May 27, 1968, Enterprise, AL; married Nicole; children: Cole, Chandler & Canyon. **Educ:** Univ Fla, BS, pub health, 1990, rehabilitative coun, 1993. **Career:** Football player (retired), football coach; Fla Minn Vikings, fullback, 1990; New Orleans Saints, 1991; Wash Redskins, fullback, 1994, 1995; Ariz Cardinals, fullback, 1996-97; Ment Hosp, Gainesville; Denver Broncos, asst strength & conditioning coach, 2001-06; Kans City Chief, strength & conditioning coach, 2007; Houston Texans, strength & conditioning coach, currently. **Honors/Awds:** Southeastern Conference (SEC) Academic Honor, 1987, 1988, 1989. **Home Addr:** , Parker, CO. **Business Addr:** Strength & Conditioning Coach, Kansas City Chief, 1 Arrowhead Dr, Kansas City, MO 64129, **Business Phone:** (816)920-9300.

### SMITH, CHARLES ANTON. See SMITH, TONY.

### SMITH, CHARLES CORNELIUS
Basketball player. **Personal:** Born Aug 22, 1975, Ft. Worth, TX. **Educ:** NMex State Univ, attended 1997. **Career:** Basketball player (retired); Miami Heat, guard, 1997-98; Los Angeles Clippers, 1998-99; Rockford Lightning, 1999-2000; Amatori Basket Udine, 2000-01; Snaidero Udine, 2000-01; San Antonio Spurs, 2001-02; Portland Trail Blazers, 2002-03, 2005-06; Makedonikos Kozani, 2003; Carisbo Castelmaggiore, 2003-04; Virtus Bologna, 2003-04; Scavolini Pesaro, 2004-05; Denver Nuggets, 2006; Efes Pilsen Istanbul, 2006, 2008-10; Real Madrid, 2006-08; Turkish Basketball League, 2008-09; Efes Pilsen, 2008-10; Lottomatica Roma, 2010-11.

### SMITH, CHARLES DANIEL
Association executive, chief executive officer, basketball player. **Personal:** Born Jul 16, 1965, Bridgeport, CT; son of Charles D and Dorthy J Childs Lee; married Lisa Johnson; children: 1. **Educ:** Univ Pittsburgh, BA, commun & lib studies, 1988; Stanford Univ Grad Sch Bus, exec prog, entrepreneurship, 2006; Seton Hall Univ, MBA, mgt, 2011. **Career:** Basketball player (retired), association executive, chief executive officer; US nat team, 1986; Los Angeles Clippers, ctr-forward, 1988-92; Fluid Sports & Entertainment, founder/pres, 1989-94; New York Knicks, ctr-forward, 1992-96; Fla Beachdogs, 1996; San Antonio Spurs, ctr-forward, 1996-97; Simply TV, pres, 1996-98; New Media Technol, founder, chief exec officer, prin, 1997-; Charles Smith Educ Ctr, Bridgeport, Conn, owner, founder; Players Capital Mgt, co-founder; Nat Basketball Players Asn, regional mgr, 2006-08; Prof Basketball Alumni Asn, chief exec officer, 2011-. **Orgs:** Founder, chmn, Charles D Smith Jr Found, 1989-2007; vpres, NBA Players Asn; regional rep, Nat Basketball Players Asn, 2006-08; exec dir, Nat Basketball Retired Players Asn, 2008-10. **Home Addr:** 6 Colonial Dr, Trumbull, CT 06611, **Home Phone:** (203)335-5751. **Business Addr:** Chief Executive Officer, Professional Basketball Alumni Association, 5 Penn Plz 23rd Fl, New York, NY 10001, **Business Phone:** (212)896-3984.

### SMITH, CHARLES EDISON
Lawyer, consultant, educator. **Educ:** Calif Polytech Univ, BS, 1965; Georgetown Univ, Wash, DC, JD, 1972; Duke Univ, LLM, 1983. **Career:** US Patent & Trademark Off, Wash, DC, patent examr, 1967-69; Xerox Corp, Patent Atty, 1972-75; Bechtel Corp, Patent Atty, 1975-78; Golden Gate Univ, asst prof law, 1977-79; Con Edison, consult, 1987-; NC Cent Univ Sch Law, Durham, NC, prof law, biotechnology & Pharmaceut Law Inst, founding dir, 2006, currently. **Orgs:** Arbitrator, Am Bar Asn, 1979-, St reporter, ABA LP Laws, 1986-; Delta Theta Phi Law Frat, 1970-; comnr, NC Statutes Comn, 1987-; atty vol, AIPLA Inventor Consult Serv, 1985-; St reporter, ABA LLC Act, 1993-; Am Arbit Asn; Am Intellectual Property Law Asn; Panel Com Arbitrators; New York Acad Sci; Nat Bar Asn. **Home Addr:** 105 Get-a-Way Lane, Bahama, NC 27503, **Home Phone:** (919)477-4213. **Business Addr:** Professor, North Carolina Central University School of Law, 640 Nelson St, Durham, NC 27707, **Business Phone:** (919)641-0086.

### SMITH, DR. CHARLES FRANK, JR.
Educator. **Personal:** Born Jan 5, 1933, Cleveland, OH; son of Charles Frank Sr and Julia Anna W; married Lois Thompson; children: Carolyn Adelle & Charles Frank III. **Educ:** Bowling Green State Univ, BS, 1960; Kent State Univ, EdM, 1963; Harvard Univ, Grad Sch Ed, CAS, 1965; Mich State Univ, EdD, 1969. **Career:** Professor (retired): Elem Sch Teacher Lorain, OH, 1960-62; Peace Corps Field Training Ctr, Pr, acad dir, 1962-63; Peace Corps, Wash, DC, spec asst, 1963; Flint Pub Schs, asst dir elem educ, 1965-66; Mich State Univ, instr educ, 1966-68; Boston Col, Teacher Corps Prog, dir, 1968, instr, 1968, Lynch Sch Educ, assoc prof educ, assoc prof emer, 1996-. **Orgs:** Danforth Asn, 1974; bd dir, Nat Coun Social Studies Supvrs Asn; bd dir, Mass Coun Social Studies; Am Asn Univ Prof; Am Asn Col Teachers; Am Asn Sch Adminrs; Asn Supv & Curric Develop; Dept Elem Sch Prins; Nat Coun Social Studies; Phi Delta Kappa emer, 1998; chmn, Newton, Mass Area Welfare Bd; vice chmn, Black Citizens Newton, Mass; founder & chmn, Coun Black Fac, Staff & Adminrs Boston Col; Numerous fels representing US humanitarian goodwill missions Incl Jamaica, BWI, 1953; W Ger, 1954; Can, 1957; Fr Cameroon, 1958; Nigeria, 1960; ed goodwill tours Incl Egypt, 1990; Russia, 1995; China, 1996; Australia, 1997; Nz, 1997. **Home Addr:** 194 Parker St, Newton Centre, MA 02459, **Home Phone:** (617)552-6295. **Business Addr:** Professor Emeritus, Boston College, Campion Hall 140 Commonwealth Ave, Chestnut Hill, MA 02467, **Business Phone:** (617)552-4246.

### SMITH, CHARLES HENRY, III (CHUCK SMITH)
Football coach, football player, radio host. **Personal:** Born Dec 21, 1969, Athens, GA; married Mynique; children: Giavani, Chuckie & Maddox. **Educ:** Univ Tenn, attended 1991. **Career:** Football player (retired), radio host, coach; Atlanta Falcons, defensive end & right defensive end & left defensive end & linebacker, 1992-99; Carolina Panthers, defensive end, 2000; Ryan Cameron Morning Show, co-host; Fox Sports Net, host; Media One Cable Network, host; Frank & Wanda Morning Show, co-host & sports dir; WQXI AM, Sports Radio 790 Zone, radio co-host; Univ Tenn, defensive line coach, 2010-11; Defensive Line Inc, fitness trainer, currently. **Honors/Awds:** Most Valuable Player, Senior Bowl; Best Defensive Lineman, Atlanta Falcon Fans; NFL Quarter back Award; All-Pro Selection, 1997; NFL Unsung Hero Award, 1998; Howie Long Tough Guy Award. **Business Addr:** Radio Co-Host, WQXI AM, 3350 Peachtree Rd Suite 1610, Atlanta, GA 30326, **Business Phone:** (404)237-0079.

### SMITH, CHARLES LEON
Automotive executive. **Personal:** Born Feb 7, 1953, Charleston, WV; son of James and Frances Elizabeth Brown; married Emma Ruth Witten; children: Charles & Andrew. **Educ:** WVa Wesleyan Col, Buckhannon, WVa, BS, bus adminr, 1976; WVa Sch Banking, Charleston, WVa, banking degree, 1983; Nat Automobile Dealers Asn Dealer Acad, 1986; Ford Motor Co Dealer Acad Prog, Detroit, MI, 1988. **Career:** CL Smith Enterprises, Clarks Summit, PA, pres & owner, 1977-; Kanawha Banking & Trust, Charleston, WVa, vpres loans, 1978-85; Ford Motor Co., Detroit, Mich, dealer cand, 1985-88. **Orgs:** Treas, Charleston Prof & Bus Club, 1978-85; bd mem & treas, Charleston Housing Bd, 1979-83; bd dir, Optimist Club, 1980-85; W Va State Senate Small Bus Adv Bd, 1982-85; selective serv bd mem, Charleston, WV, 1982-85; adv bd mem, W Va State Community Col, 1982-85; vpres, Lackawanna Valley Auto Dealers Asn, 1988-; Black Ford Lincoln Mercury Dealers Asn, 1988-; Kiwanis Club, 1990; Scranton Chamber Com. **Home Addr:** 4420 Greenwar Dr N, Little Rock, AR 72116, **Home Phone:** (717)586-5104.

### SMITH, DR. CHARLES U. See Obituaries Section.

### SMITH, CHARLOTTE
Basketball player. **Personal:** Born Aug 23, 1973, Shelby, NC; daughter of Ulysses and Falonda; married Johnny Taylor. **Educ:** Univ NC, BA, sociol, 1999. **Career:** Basketball player (retired), basketball coach; Shelby High Sch, basketball player; Colo Xplosion, 1996-97; San Jose Lasers, forward, 1997-98; Charlotte Sting, 1999-2004; US Sports Mgt, 2001-02; Univ NC, asst coach, 2002-03; Univ Nc, assitant coach, 2002-11; Wash Mystics, 2005; Ind Fever, 2006; Elon Univ, head women's basketball coach, 2011-. **Home Addr:** 6917 Rodling Dr Suite C, San Jose, CA 95138. **Business Addr:** Head Women Basketball Coach, Elon University, 100 Campus Dr, Elon, NC 27244, **Business Phone:** (336)278-6800.

### SMITH, CHELSI MARIAM PEARL. See CHELSI, CHELSI.

### SMITH, CHESTER B.
Government official. **Personal:** Born Jul 1, 1954, Mound Bayou, MS. **Educ:** Tufts Univ, BA, 1975; Northwestern Univ, MBA, 1977, JD, 1980. **Career:** Delta Capital Corp, vpres, 1980-84; vis prof, Black Exec

Exchange Prog, 1981-83; New Memphis Dev Corp, dir, 1981-84; Ctr Econ Growth, founder, 1982; pvt pract atty, 1983-86; Pro-Mark Inc, financial consult, 1984-85, vpres; US Dept Com, Minority Bus Develop Agency, Wash, DC, asst dir prog develop, 1986. **Orgs:** Consult, Proj Bus, 1982-85; Miss State Bar Asn, 1982-87; consult, Tenn Valley Authority, 1985-86. **Home Addr:** PO Box 2746, Arlington, VA 22202, **Home Phone:** (703)751-4078.

## SMITH, CHRISTOPHER GERARD (CHRIS SMITH)

Executive, basketball player. **Personal:** Born May 17, 1970, Bridgeport, CT; children: Christopher G II & China Elizabeth. **Educ:** Univ Conn, BA, bus admin, 1992. **Career:** Basketball player (retired), exec; Minn Timber wolves, guard, 1992-95; Caceres, Spain, 1995-96; Capitalinos de San Juan, 1996; Echo Houthalen, 1996-97; Grand Rapids Hoops, 1997-98; CSP Limoges, 1997; Bnei Herzliya; La Crosse Bobcats, 1998; Maccabi Ra'anana, 1998; Ft Wayne Fury, 1999; Rockford Lightning, 1999; Sioux Falls Skyforce, 1999-2000; Mortgage Co, loan officer; Beardsley, Brown & Basset, bus develop officer, 2003-. **Honors/Awds:** Bronze Medal, FIBA World Championship, 1990; Silver Medal, Goodwill Games, 1990. **Business Addr:** Business Development Officer, Beardsley Brown & Bassett, 850 Main St Suite 2, Bridgeport, CT 06604, **Business Phone:** (203)338-7900.

## SMITH, CLARENCE O.

Music publisher, publishing executive. **Personal:** Born Mar 31, 1933, Bronx, NY; son of Clarence (deceased) and Millicent Fry (deceased); married Elaine Goss; children: Clarence & Craig. **Educ:** Baruch Sch Bus, attended 1961. **Career:** Prudential Ins Co Am, NY, spec rep, 1963-69; Investors Planning Corp, NY, regist rep, 1966-69; Essence Commun Inc, NY, co-founder, chief exec officer & pres, 1969-2002, pres emer, 2003-; Avocet Travel LLC, founder, chmn & chief exec officer; You Entertainment LLC, founder & chmn, chief exec officer, currently; Rec: CD Love Pages, 2005. **Orgs:** Asst treas, Am Advert Found; Chmn, African Am Mkt & Media Asn, 1991; dir-at-large, Advert Coun; Am Mgt Asn; bd dirs, Cosmetic, Toiletry & Fragrance Asn; African Am Task Force Media-Advert Partnership Drug-Free Am; bd dirs, Teach Am; trustee, TransAfrican Forum; Nat Asn Mkt Developers. **Honors/Awds:** Annual Achievement Award, Black Enterprise Mag, 1980; Black Achievement Award, The Equitable Assurance Soc US, 1985; Prin's Award, Henry Highland Garnet Sch Success, 1988-89; Communicator of the Year, Nat Asn Mkt Developers, 1990; Meritorious Service Award, UNCF, 1990; President's Award, One Hundred Black Men Am, 1995; A G Gaston Lifetime Achievement Award, Black Enterprise & Nations bank Entrepreneurs Conf, 1997; Fred Luster Sr Image Award, Luster Prod Black Heritage Found, 1997. **Special Achievements:** Annual Achievement Award, Black Enterprise Mag, 1980; Black Achievement Award, The Equitable Assurance Soc US, 1985; Prin's Award, Henry Highland Garnet Sch Success, 1988-89; Communicator of the Year, Nat Asn Mkt Developers, 1990; Meritorious Service Award, UNCF, 1990; Entrepreneur of Year Award, Ernst and Young, 1994; President's Award, One Hundred Black Men Am, 1995; A G Gaston Lifetime Achievement Award, Black Enterprise & Nations bank Entrepreneurs Conf, 1997; Fred Luster Sr Image Award, Luster Prod Black Heritage Found, 1997. **Business Addr:** Chief Executive Officer, Chairman, YOU Entertainment LLC, 304 Park Ave S Fl 10, New York, NY 10010, **Business Phone:** (310)828-0116.

## SMITH, CLIFFORD

Rap musician, actor, music director. **Personal:** Born Apr 1, 1971, Hempstead, NY; children: 3. **Career:** Wu-Tang Clan, rapper; Group albums: Enter the Wu; Wu-Tang Forever, 1997; Solo Albums: Tical, 1995; Blackout, 1999; Blackout (Bonus Track), 2003; Tical 0: The Prequel, 2004; 4:21... The Day After, 2006; Blackout! 2, 2009; Wu-Massacre, 2010; Films: Batman Forever, 1995; High School High, 1996; Space Jam, 1996; Hav Plenty, 1997; Soul in the Hole, 1997; Copland, 1997; Belly, 1998; Bulworth, 1998; In Too Deep, 1999; Shaft, 2000; Boricula's Bond, 2000; How High, 2001; Save the Last Dance, 2001; The Fast and the Furious, 2001; Pootie Tang, 2001; How High, 2001; Paid in Full, 2002; All About the Benjamins, 2002; My Baby's Daddy, 2004; Soul Plane, 2004; Venom, 2005; The Wackness, 2008; Meet the Spartans, 2008; Sinners & Saints, 2010; The Sitter, 2011; The Mortician, 2011; Red Tails, 2012; Chozen, 2014; Mob Wives, 2014; The Cobbler, 2014; Staten Island Summer, 2014; Lucky N#mbr, 2014. TV series: "Wonderland", 2000; "Oz", 2001; "Boston Public", 2003; "The Wire", 2003-09; "Method & Red", exec producer, 2004; "The Fairly OddParents", 2004; "CSI: Crime Scene Investigation", 2006-08; "Burn Notice", 2008; "The Good Guys", 2010; "The Good Wife", 2011; "Scorpion", 2014. **Honors/Awds:** Grammy Award, 1996.

## SMITH, DR. CLIFFORD V., JR.

School administrator. **Personal:** Born Nov 29, 1931, Washington, DC; son of Clifford V Sr; married Nina Marie Singleton; children: Sharon Jones, Debra McKee & Tricia Pausz. **Educ:** State Univ Iowa, BS, civil & sant engineering, 1954; John Hopkins Univ, MS, environ, sant engineering & water res, 1960, PhD, radiol sci & sant engineering, 1966. **Career:** Pa Dept Health, chief engr water supply sect, 1959-61; Univ Conn, asst prof, 1961-63; Johns Hopkins Univ, res & teaching asst, 1963-65; Univ Mass, asst prof, 1965-66; Tufts Univ, asst prof, 1966-68; Dorr-Oliver Inc, Stamford, Conn, sanit technol mgr, 1968-70; City Col NY, asst prof, 1970-72; US Environ Protection Agency, Seattle, regional adminr, Boston, dep regional adminr, 1972-74; Bechtel Corp, San Francisco, Advan Technol Div, exec engr, prog mgr & bus develop mgr; Ore State Syst Higher Educ, State Syst Sci Technol & Econ Develop, spec asst to chancellor, Coun Advan Sci, Engineering Educ & Res Indust, dir; Univ Wis-Milwaukee, chancellor & pres, 1986-90; US Nuclear Regulatory Comn, asst secy level; Ore State Univ, vpres, admin, dir, Radiation Ctr & Inst Nuclear Sci & Engineering, head, dept nuclear engineering; Gen Elect Found, Fairfield, pres, 1997; Inst Int Educ Inc, trustee, currently. **Orgs:** New Eng Health Physics Soc; Am Water Works Asn; Water Pollution Control Fed; Int Asn Water Pollution Res; treas, Kappa Alpha Psi; treas, stud br, Am Soc Civil Engrs; Radiation Adv Comt, US EPA Sci Adv Bd; US NASA Adv Coun; consult, Energy Res Adv Bd, US Dept Energy; consult, US Nuclear Regulatory Comn; consult, Bechtel Corp; consult, Rockwell Int; Engineering Builiding Campaign Steering Commitee; Alumni Asn; Col Eng Develop Coun; pres, G E Found; consult, Nsf; bd dir, UI Found Bd; Pres's Club. **Special Achievements:** First African American four-year college chancellor in the University of Wisconsin System. **Business Addr:** Trustee, The Institute of International Education Inc, 809 UN Plz Fl 7, New York, NY 10017, **Business Phone:** (212)984-5367.

## SMITH, DANTE TERRELL. See MOS DEF.

## SMITH, DANYEL

Writer, journalist. **Personal:** Born Jan 1, 1966, Oakland, CA. **Educ:** Univ Calif, Berkeley, 1986; New Sch Univ, MFA, creative writing & fiction, 2006. **Career:** Freelance music writer, 1989-91; SF Weekly, music ed, 1990-91; San Francisco Bay Guardian, columnist & critic, 1991-93; Billboard mag, R&B ed, 1993, ed, 2011-12; Spin Mag, columnist & critic, 1992-94; NY Times, pop music critic, 1992-94; Vibe Mag, music ed, 1994-96, ed chief, 1997-99; Time Inc, ed at large, 1999-2001; New Sch, Adj Fac, 1999-2006; St Mary's Col Calif, guest fac, 2004; Skidmore Col, writer, 2005; novelist, 2003-; VIBE Media Group, chief content officer, 2006-09; Journalism fel, Stanford Univ, 2013-14; HRDCVR, co-founder, 2014-; Bks: More Like Wrestling, 2003; Bliss, 2006; Articles: "Vibe"; "San Francisco Bay Guardian"; "New York Times"; "Rolling Stone"; "Village Voice"; "Spin & New Yorker".

## SMITH, DARRIN ANDREW

Football player, executive. **Personal:** Born Apr 15, 1970, Miami, FL; children: 2. **Educ:** Univ Miami, BS, bus mgt, 1991, MS, mkt, 1993. **Career:** Football player (retired), exec; Dallas Cowboys, linebacker, 1993-96; Philadelphia Eagles, left linebacker, 1997; Seattle Seahawks, left linerbacker, 1998, linebacker & left outside linebacker, 1999; New Orleans Saints, mid linebacker, 2000, 2003, linebacker, 2001-03, right outside linebacker, 2001, defensive end, 2003, 2004; bondsman, currently; Real Estate Investment/Develop Co, owner, currently. **Orgs:** Founder & pres, Int Asn Black Millionaires; head, Athletes Christ Bible Study Ministry, Fountain Pembroke Pines, currently. **Honors/Awds:** Col Football Nat Championship, 1989, 1999; Super Bowl, XXVIII & XXX, 1993, 1995; Miami Sports Hall of Fame, 2006. **Business Addr:** Member, Head, The Fountain of Pembroke Pines, 4601 NW 167th St, Miami Gardens, FL 33055, **Business Phone:** (305)622-3123.

## SMITH, DARRYL C.

Manager, lecturer, executive director. **Personal:** Born Aug 1, 1966, MD; married Pheorma N Davis. **Educ:** Towson Univ, BA, 1989; Univ Mo, Sch Jour, MA, journ & media mgt; Univ Mo, Sch Law, JD. **Career:** Mo Supreme Ct Off State Cts admin, mgr; WJHU FM, opers mgr, 1988-90; WETA FM, ops mgr, 1990-91; KL UM-FM/KJLU FM, gen mgr, 1991-; Univ W Fla, Dept Commun Arts, lectr & dir grad studies, 2000-. **Orgs:** Am Mensa; Commn Arts Graduate Prog. **Honors/Awds:** President's Award, 2009-10. **Business Addr:** Lecturer of Communication & Arts, Director, University of West Florida, Rm 183 Bldg 36 11000 Univ Pkwy, Pensacola, FL 32514, **Business Phone:** (850)474-2064.

## SMITH, DAWN C. F. (DAWN CAROL FABIOLA SMITH)

Marketing executive. **Personal:** Born Dec 23, 1960, London; daughter of George and Mavis Collier; married Elbert L Robertson; children: Erica Saran. **Educ:** Brown Univ, BA, Econs, 1982; Univ Mich, MBA, 1985. **Career:** Black Stud's Guide Col, co-mng ed, 1982; MBA Consortium fel, 1983-85; Gen Mills, mkt res internal, 1984; Colgate Palmolive, asst brand mgr, 1985-87; Kraft Inc, assoc brand mgr, 1987-88; Jacobs Suchard, brand mgr, 1988-90; Citicorp's Diners Club, Corp Travel Div, dir mktg, 1990-. **Orgs:** Nat Black MBA Asn, 1983-; Nat Alumni Schs Prog, Brown Univ, 1984-. **Honors/Awds:** National Black MBA Scholar, 1984. **Home Addr:** 4800 S Lake Shore Dr, Chicago, IL 60615, **Home Phone:** (312)373-7850. **Business Addr:** Director, Citicorp Diners Club, 8430 W Bryn Mawr Suite 700, Chicago, IL 60607, **Business Phone:** (773)380-5160.

## SMITH, DEBBIE A.

Association executive. **Personal:** Born Apr 12, 1959, Washington, DC. **Educ:** Cath Univ Am, BA, elem & spec educ, 1981; Howard Univ, MBA, 1985. **Career:** Xerox, mktg rep, 1985-87; Riggs Nat Bank, credit lending officer, 1987-90; Signet Bank, credit lending officer, 1990-93; US House Reps, staff dirs mall bus, sub comt, 1993-95; Nat Asn Invest Co, vpres, 1994-95; Nat Asn Urban Bankers, exec dir, 1995-98; Int Franchise Asn, Pub Affairs & Emerging Markets, vpres, 1998-2001; Allfirst, sr vpres diversity, 2001-04; Walter Kaitz Found, exec dir, 2004-06; Discovery Commun, named vpres diversity & human resources serv, vpres global diversity & inclusion, 2006-11; Discovery Commun, Human Resource Dept; Smith Rayford Consult, prin, 2012-; Wellness Corp Solutions LLC, chief mkt & diversity officer, 2012-15; Internal Revenue Serv, off equity, dir diversity & inclusion, 2015-. **Orgs:** Mayor's Cong Affairs Adv, Wash, DC, 1991-; adv bd, Orgn New Equality, 1996. **Honors/Awds:** Pioneer Award, Orgn New Equality, 1997; Top Executive in Diversity, Black Enterprise; Inspiration Touchstones Award, Women Cable Telecommunications. **Business Addr:** Director, Internal Revenue Service, 1111 Constitution Ave NW, Washington, DC 20224, **Business Phone:** (202)622-8229.

## SMITH, DEHAVEN L.

Lawyer. **Personal:** Born Aug 10, 1928, Baltimore, MD; married Gertrude Jackson; children: Rubye. **Educ:** Va Union Univ, BA, 1949; Univ Md, Sch Law, JD, 1958. **Career:** Williams, Smith & Murphy, atty; pvt pract atty, currently. **Orgs:** Am Bar Asn; Nat Bar Asn; Monumental City Bar Asn; Baltimore City Bar Asn Judicature Soc; World Peace Law Comn; Nat Asn Advan Colored People. **Business Addr:** Attorney, 1212 Winston Ave, Baltimore, MD 21239-3411, **Business Phone:** (410)433-8783.

## SMITH, DENNIS

Football player. **Personal:** Born Feb 3, 1959, Santa Monica, CA; married Andree; children: Tiffany Diamond & Armani Joseph. **Educ:** Univ Southern Calif, attended 1980. **Career:** Football player (retired); Denver Broncos, safety & free safety & defensive back, 1981-94. **Orgs:** Make-A-Wish Found; Covenant House. **Honors/Awds:** Most Inspirational Player, 1992; Ring of Fame, 2001; Colorado Hall of Fame, 2006; Santa Monica High School Hall of Fame. **Special Achievements:** Films: Super Bowl XXII, 1988; Super Bowl XXI, 1987; Super Bowl XXIV, 1990; Acted in video Hopelessly Awkward, 2009. **Business Addr:** 2450 Achilles Dr, Los Angeles, CA 90046-1626.

## SMITH, DENVER LESTER

Insurance agent. **Personal:** Born Sep 21, 1946, Detroit, MI; son of Henry L and Hattie M. **Career:** Denver L Smith Ins Agency Inc, pres, currently. **Home Addr:** 19967 Birwood St, Detroit, MI 48221-1035, **Home Phone:** (313)341-2096. **Business Addr:** President, Denver L Smith Insurance Agency Inc, 28475 Greenfield Rd, Southfield, MI 48076, **Business Phone:** (248)559-9834.

## SMITH, DETRON NEGIL

Football player. **Personal:** Born Feb 25, 1974, Dallas, TX. **Educ:** Tex A&M Univ, attended 1995. **Career:** Football player (retired); Denver Broncos, running back, 1996-2001; Indianapolis Colts, fullback, 2002-03. **Honors/Awds:** Pro Bowl, 1999; Champion, Super Bowl, XXXII, 1997, XXXIII, 1998. **Home Addr:** 9601 Mdl Fiskville R, Austin, TX 78753, **Home Phone:** (512)836-9449.

## SMITH, DIANE L.

Government official. **Personal:** Born Nov 2, 1962, Hartford, CT; married LaMont Andrews; children: Derek L. **Educ:** Univ Conn, BA, 1986; Trinity Col. **Career:** State Conn, Off Policy & Mgt, policy & prog analyst, 1988-92, mgr bus devel, 1992-93; Dept Econ Devel, spec proj mgr, 1993-96; Dept Econ & Community Develop, bus develop mgr, devel specialist, 1996-98, exec dir, 1998-; Conn Housing Finance Authority, community & prog develop officer. **Orgs:** Steering comt, Hartford Neighborhood Support Collab, 1996-; bd mem, Greater Hartford Bus Devel Ctr, 1997-99; bd mem, Waterbury Partnership, 2000, 1998-2000; bd mem, Literacy Vols Greater Hartford, 1999-; col steering comt, Hartford Studies Proj Trinity. **Home Addr:** 226 Deerfield Rd, Windsor, CT 06095, **Home Phone:** (860)687-1903. **Business Addr:** Director Community, Housing Development, Department of Economic & Community Development, 505 Hudson St 4th Fl, Hartford, CT 06106, **Business Phone:** (860)270-8223.

## SMITH, DOLORES J.

Executive, radio producer. **Personal:** Born Feb 10, 1936, Lockport, IL; daughter of Ernest Gill Jones and Mira Ellen Bills Jones-Spinks; married Paul R; children: Kathleen, Robert, Debra, Alan, Paul II & Dolores II. **Educ:** Princeton Univ, cert, orgn develop, 1970; Univ Mich, cert, mgt by objectives, 1971; Nat Training Lab, cert, sensitivity training interpersonal rels, 1972; Roosevelt Univ, Chicago, Ill, BS, bus admin, 1979; Ohio Univ, Athens OH, MA, commun, 1983; Gestalt Inst, Cleveland, OH, cert, orgn & systs, 2000; DePaul Univ Col Law, cert, mediation, 2007. **Career:** Smiths Off Serv, owner/mgr, 1959-65; Suburban Echo Reporter, advert mgr, 1965-67; Jewel Food Stores, area personnel mgr, human resources generalist, 1967-79; Bausman Assocs, mgt consult, 1979-80; WTTW Chicago, dir admin serv, 1980-82; Ohio Univ, instr/grad asst, 1982-83; Columbia Col, Chicago, Ill, adjunt fac, 1983-; D J Smith Enterprises, consult, owner & pres, 1983-; NBC WKQX Radio, producer/host, 1983-86; Lewis Univ, Romeoville, Ill adjunt fac, 2004-. **Orgs:** Exec comm bd dir, Midwest Women's Ctr, 1977-87; Gov Adv Coun Employ & Training, 1977-82; Nat Asn Advan Colored People, Soc Human Resources Mgt; Soc Training & Develop; trustee, Wieboldt Found, 1982-92; bd dir, Exec comm bd dir, Midwest Women's Ctr, 1977-87; Gov Adv Coun Employ & Training, 1977-82; Nat Asn Advan Colored People, Soc Human Resources Mgt; Soc Training & Develop; trustee, Wieboldt Found, 1982-92; bd dir, Women & Founds Corp Philanthropy, 1984-88; exec comm bd dir, Lambda Alpha Omega Chap; Alpha Kappa Alpha Sorority, 1986-87; Soc Intelletual Educ, Training & Res. **Honors/Awds:** Corp Public Broadcasting Scholar, Ohio Univ, 1982-83. **Business Addr:** President, Owner, DJ Smith Enterprises, 1150 N Lake Shore Dr Suite 7F, Chicago, IL 60611, **Business Phone:** (312)335-8268.

## SMITH, DR. DONALD HUGH

Teacher, executive director, educator. **Personal:** Born Mar 20, 1932, Chicago, IL; son of William H and Madolene. **Educ:** Univ Ill, AB, 1953; DePaul, MA, 1959; Univ Wis, PhD, 1964. **Career:** Chicago Pub Sch, teacher, 1956-63; Ctr Inner City Studies Northeastern Ill Univ, asst prof, asso prof, dir, 1964-68; Univ Comm Educ Prog Univ Pitts, prof, dir, 1968-69; Nat Urban Coalition Wash DC, exec assoc, 1969-70; Baruch Col, prof, chmn, dept educ, prof dir, 1970-97, assoc provost, sr vpres academic affairs, prof emer. **Orgs:** Fel Chicago Bd Educ, 1962; fel Univ Wis, 1963; Nat Adv Counc Voc Educ, 1968-70; Inter Am Cong Psychol, 1972-; Nat Study Comn Teacher Educ, 1972-75; exec dir, Chancellor's Task Force SEEK City Univ NY, 1974-; adv Doctoral Prog Educ Admin Atlanta Univ, 1975; founder, NY Alliance Black Sch Educ, 1981; pres, Nat Alliance Black Sch Educr, 1983-85; chmn, Black Fac City Univ NY, 1989-92; adv Martin Luther King JrCtr Social Chg; chmn, task force NY State Dropout Prob; bd dir, NY Serv Older People; adv bd, African Heritage Studies Asn; founding mem, Bd Educ People African Ancestry; chmn, New York Bd Educ Comn Stud African Descent; pres, Nat Alliance Black Sch Educr; bd mem, BEPAA; chmn, col's educ dept & chmn, col's Black & Latino Fac Asn. **Special Achievements:** Baruch College first black administrator. **Home Addr:** 250 W 103rd St Apt 4A, New York, NY 10025.

## SMITH, DONALD M.

Manager, executive. **Personal:** Born Jul 12, 1931, Elgin, IL; married Jeanette M; children: Tracy & Tiffany. **Educ:** Purdue Univ, BA, 1956, MA, 1961. **Career:** Hills McCanna, shop supt, 1960-69; Hemmenns Auditorium, gen mgr, 1969-80; Rockford Metro Ct, oper mgr, 1980-. **Orgs:** Int Asn Aud Mgr, 1964; Am Legion, 1969-; founder, Performing Arts Young People, 1969-80; founder, Elgin Area Arts Coun, 1969-80; Prince Hall Masons, 1980-. **Home Addr:** 3202 Prairie Rd, Rockford, IL 61102.

## SMITH, DR. DOROTHY LOUISE WHITE

Educator. **Personal:** Born Sep 28, 1939, Memphis, TN; daughter of Theodore and Classy; married Carl; children: Carlton Edward & Sharian Lott. **Educ:** Cuyahoga Community Col, attended 1964; Case Western Res Univ, BA, eng, 1966; Calif State Univ, MA, eng, 1969;

Univ Southern Calif, EdD, educ leadership & intercult educ, 1992. **Career:** Glenville High Sch, instr eng, 1966-67; Millikan High Sch, instr eng, 1969-70; Long Beach City Col, prof eng, 1970-73; Grossmont Col, prof; San Diego City Col, Prof, Eng & African Am lit, 1973-97; Women Inc; San Diego Unified Sch Dist, bd educ, 1981-88; San Diego St Univ Sch Teacher Educ, 1989-91; San Diego Pub Sch Bldg Corp; educ consult; Grio Press, writer & pres; Bks: My face to rising Sun, 1999. **Orgs:** Alpha Kappa Alpha Sorority, 1958-; adv comt mem, Allensworth St Hist Pk, 1977-86; pres, vpres, Bd Educ San Diego City Schs, 1981; del assembly, Nat Sch Bds Asn, 1983-85; pres, San Diego Bd Educ, 1984, 1988; steering comt, Coun Urban Bds Educ, 1985-88; Calif Mid Grades Task Force, 1986-87; pres, bd dir, San Diego Sch Success, 1989-98; Ctr City Develop Comt, Martin Luther King Promenade, 1991-; Ctr City Develop Corp Black Hist Dist Adv Comt; City San Diego Ethics Comt, 2001-; pres, City San Diego Ethics Comn, 2003-05; adv comt, adv bd, Univ San Diego Sch Leadership & Educ Sci, 2004-; Common Ground Theatre, 2004-; Golden Soror, 2008. **Home Addr:** PO Box 152443, San Diego, CA 92195, **Home Phone:** (619)263-3651.

### SMITH, DOROTHY O.

Mayor, government official. **Personal:** Born May 28, 1943, Lawrence County, AL; daughter of James Samuel Owens Sr (deceased) and Cornelia Swoope Owens (deceased); children: Derra S Jackson, Leo D Jr & Kathleen S Goodlaw. **Educ:** John C Calhoun, Decatur, bus, 1969. **Career:** S Cent Bell, Decatur, network, 1971; City Hillsboro, Hillsboro, mayor, 1986-2000. **Orgs:** Secy, Black Mayors Conf, 1988; Nat Black Women Mayors Caucus, 1988; Martin Luther King Jr Profiles Courage, ADC, Lawrence County Chap, 1988. **Home Addr:** 200 Oakdale Ave, Hillsboro, AL 35643-3963, **Home Phone:** (256)637-8111.

### SMITH, DOUG (DOUGLAS SMITH)

Basketball player. **Personal:** Born Sep 17, 1969, Detroit, MI. **Educ:** Univ Mo, attended 1991. **Career:** Basketball player (retired); Dallas Mavericks, forward, 1991-95; Boston Celtics, forward, 1995-96; Okla City Cavalry, 1996-97; Quad City Thunder, 1997-99; St Louis Swarm, 1999-2001; Kans City Knights, 2001-02; Great Lakes Storm, Continental Basketball Asn, 2004-05. **Honors/Awds:** Silver Medal, FIBA Americas Championship, 1989; Bronze Medal, World Championship, 1990; Silver Medal, Goodwill Games, 1990; Big Eight Player of the Year, 1991; Univ MO Hall of Fame, 1996; CBA Champion, 1997, 1998, 1999; Silver Medal, Pan American Games, 1999; IBL Most Valuable Player, 2000; IBL Champion, 2000, 2001. **Home Addr:** 21930 Windchester, Southfield, MI 48076.

### SMITH, DOUGLAS M.

Journalist. **Personal:** Born Apr 18, 1942, Hampton, VA; son of Samuel R and Virginia Jones; married Shirley Thomas; children: Jerome & Jared; married Anne Street. **Educ:** Hampton Univ, Hampton, VA, BA, math, 1964. **Career:** Journalist (retired); Newsday, Garden City, NY, reporter & ed, journalist, 1970-77; New York Post, New York, NY, reporter & ed, 1977-78; Newark Bd Educ, Newark, NJ, pub rels specialist, 1978-79; Howard Univ Hosp, Wash, DC, ed & writer, 1980-85; USA Today, Arlington, Va, reporter & tennis writer, 1986-2001; Hampton Univ, Dept Mass Media Arts, journalist-in-residence, 1993-94. **Orgs:** Am Tennis Asn, 1979-86; US Tennis Asn, 1979-88; US Tennis Writers Asn, 1990-; Nat Asn Black Journalists, 1990-; pres, USTWA, 1990-92, vpres, 1994-95; Black Col Commun Asn, 1993. **Honors/Awds:** Appreciation Award, Am Tennis Asn, 1985; Lifetime Achievement Award, US Tennis Asn, 1988; Media Person of the Year, Women's Int Tennis Asn, 1989; Great Am Tennis Writing Award, Tennis Week, 1990; Deadline Writer of the Year, Tennis Week, 2000. **Special Achievements:** Co-author with Zina Garrison of My Life as a Tennis Pro, 2001. **Home Addr:** 601 G St SW, Washington, DC 20024, **Home Phone:** (202)554-9322.

### SMITH, DR. EARL BRADFORD

Social worker, teacher. **Personal:** Born Sep 28, 1953, St. Louis, MO; married Treva Talon. **Educ:** Thiel Col, BA, ssych & sociol, 1977; Marywood Col, MSW, 1979; Univ Pittsburgh, PhD, cand educ. **Career:** Vet Admin Hosp, social work assoc, 1976-78; Lackawanna Cty Child & Youth Serv, social worker II, 1979-82; Susquehanna Human Serv, human resources spec; Pittsburgh Bd Educ, sch social worker; Pt Pk Univ, adj fac; Univ Phoenix, adj prof; Robert Morris Univ, W Allegheny Sch Dist, asst prin, adj fac & adminr, 2009. **Orgs:** Nat Asn Social Workers; lector, St Peters Cathedral Soc, 1977-82; lector, St Benedicts & St Marys Lectureship Soc. **Honors/Awds:** Dance Awards, Modern Dance-Jazz Performances. **Home Addr:** 104 Jessica Dr Suite 5648, Pittsburgh, PA 15237, **Home Phone:** (412)795-2228.

### SMITH, EDDIE D., SR.

Clergy. **Personal:** Born Jun 8, 1946, Macon, GA; son of Rev Jack Jr (deceased) and Mattie Mae; married Verlene Fields; children: Charlitha S Austin, Edwanna L, Eddie Jr, Corey & Alvy (deceased); married Martha Kate. **Educ:** Ft Valley State Col, BS, 1968, MS, 1971; Universal Bible Col, Alamo, TN, Ddiv. **Career:** Bibb Co Sch, teacher, 1968-82, media specialist; Macedonia Missionary Baptist Church, pastor, 1972-; City Macon, coun man, 1975-78; Bibb Co, bd educ, 1985-. **Orgs:** Bd dir, United Way; Am Cancer Soc; Macon Ministerial Asn; dir, Disting Am, 1981. **Honors/Awds:** Cert of Appreciation, Bibb Co Voter's League, 1977; Dr E D Smith Day Proclamation, City Macon, 1977; Citizens Award, Macon Courier, 1977; Nat Alumni Cert of Achievement, Ft Valley State Col, 1978; 3 Year Service Award for City Coun, City Macon, 1979; Medgar Malcolm Martin's Award, SCLC, 1979; Minister of the Day GA State Legis, 1981. **Home Addr:** 5798 Kentucky Downs Dr, Macon, GA 31210, **Home Phone:** (912)742-4953. **Business Addr:** Pastor, Macedonia Missionary Baptist Church, 928 Anthony Rd, Macon, GA 31204, **Business Phone:** (912)746-2151.

### SMITH, DR. EDGAR EUGENE

Educator. **Personal:** Born Aug 6, 1934, Hollandale, MS; son of Augusta McCoy and Sam; married Inez Wiley; children: Edwin D, Anthony R, Stephen S & Gregory S. **Educ:** Tougaloo Col, Tougaloo, BS, 1955; Purdue Univ, Lafayette, IN, MS, 1957, PhD, biochem, 1960. **Career:** Educator (retired): Purdue Univ, Dept Biochem, Lafayette, Ind, res asst, 1955-58, teaching asst, 1958-59; Harvard Med Sch, Boston, MA, res fel surg biochem, 1959-61, res assoc surg biochem, 1961-68; Beth Israel Hosp, Boston, MA, assoc surg res, 1959-68; Boston Univ Sch Med, Boston, MA, from asst prof surg chem to assoc prof surg chem, 1968-73, assoc dean; Univ Mass Med Ctr, provost & assoc prof, 1974-83, fel, 1977-78; Univ Mass syst, vpres, 1983-91, prof emer, biochem & molecular biol, 1991, assoc dean; Nellie Mae, vpres, 1991-93; Tougaloo Col, interim pres, consult, 1993-97, actg pres, 1994-95, sr adv pres, 2002, Search Comn, chair, emer, currently; MS AHEC, founding dir, 1998-2000; Univ Miss Med Ctr, Statewide Area Health Educ Centers, founding prog dir & prof, Family Med. **Orgs:** Fel Nat Found, Purdue Univ, Lafayette, Ind, 1958; trustee, Tougaloo Col, 1968-90; trustee, Metco Scholar Fund, 1969-86; trustee, Morehouse Sch Med, 1976-89; fel Robert Wood Johnson Health Policy, Inst Med, 1977-78; gov bd, Rob Wood Johnson Health Policy Fel Prog, 1978-85; Am Soc Biol Chemists; consult, NIH; trustee, Alcohol Bev Med Res Found, 1982-94; bd dir, Planned Parenthood, Mass, 1984-90; Am Asn Higher Educ; chief acad officer, Nat Forum Syst; Nat Asn State Univ & Land-Grant Col Coun Acad Affairs; Am Soc Biol Chemist; Am Chem Soc; Aaas; NY Acad Sci; Am Asn Cancer Res; fel Am Inst Chem; Boston Cancer Res Asn; Sigma Xi; Phi Lambda Upsilon; Nat Chem Hon Soc; Am Pol Sci Asn; Nat Asn Minority Media Exec; chmn, Deans Adv Hoc Com Black Grad Students; admin comt, Sch Med; chmn, Black Fac Caucus; ed bd, Centerscope; comnr, Am Cancer Ins Grant; liaison, Div Med Sci Biochem; consult, NSF; consult, Asn Am Med Cols; consult, Pew Found; consult, Macy Found; consult, Am Asn Cols. **Home Addr:** 5934 Paddock Pl, Jackson, MS 39206-2135, **Home Phone:** (601)713-2756. **Business Addr:** Trustee Emeritus, Tougaloo College, Edward Blackmon Admin Bldg 500 W Co Line Rd, Tougaloo, MS 39174, **Business Phone:** (601)977-7730.

### SMITH, EDITH B.

Broadcaster, manager. **Personal:** Born Jan 18, 1952, Norfolk, VA; daughter of Elijah J Billups and Nannie Ruth Winstead Codrington; married Joseph; children: Kelley N. **Educ:** Norfolk State Univ, BA, 1974. **Career:** The Virginian-Pilot, reporter, 1972-80; WHUR Radio, promotions dir, 1981-84; Mondale-Ferraro Campaign, advan press person, 1984; WDCU-FM Radio, Wash, gen mgr, 1985; WPFW-FM 89.9, sta gen mgr. **Orgs:** Capitol Press Club, 1994-95. **Honors/Awds:** Nat Black Media Coalition, for achievements in broadcasting, 1994. **Business Addr:** General Manager, WDCU-FM Radio, Rm A-03 Bldg 38 4200 Conn Ave NW, Washington, DC 20008, **Business Phone:** (202)274-5090.

### SMITH, DR. EDWARD NATHANIEL, JR.

Physician, educator. **Personal:** Born Jul 28, 1955, Elizabeth City, NC; son of Edward Nathaniel Sr and Georgia Long; married Mona LaMothe; children: Edward N III & Arianne LaMothe. **Educ:** Morehouse Col, BS, 1976; Howard Univ Col Med, MD, 1980; Am Bd Radiol, cert. **Career:** US Pub Health Serv, med officer, 1980-82; Emory Univ Sch Med, clin assoc, 1982-84; Howard Univ Hosp, fel, radiol resident, 1984-87, asst prof radiol, 1988-, fel interventional/cross sectional imaging; Progressive Radiol, radiologists, currently. **Orgs:** Omega Psi Phi Frat, 1974-; Am Cancer Soc, 1980-; bd dir, Omega Diversified Investment Corp, 1982-; Piney Br Sligo Civic Orgn, 1984-; vice chmn, Nat Med Assoc Radiol Sect, 1985-; Radiol Soc N Am, 1985-; Am Roentgen Ray Soc, 1988-; Am Col Radiol, 1989-; Am Heart Asn, 1990-; Soc Cardiovasc & Inerventional Radiol, 1991-, adv comt mem, Nat Med Asn, vice chmn; bd dir, Homemaker Health Aide Serv, Wash, DC, 1992-. **Home Addr:** 9119 Sudbury Rd, Silver Spring, MD 20901, **Home Phone:** (301)585-5723. **Business Addr:** Radiologists, Progressive Radiology, 7799 Leesburg Pke Suite 1000 N, Falls Church, VA 22043, **Business Phone:** (703)667-8600.

### SMITH, ELAINE MARIE

Government official. **Personal:** Born Nov 30, 1947, Mobile, AL; married Vernon Leon York; children: Vernon Leon York Jr. **Educ:** Ala A&M Univ, BS; Merced Col, AA, 1972. **Career:** USAF, staffing asst, 1976-77, personnel staffing spl, 1977-78; AUS Corps Engrs, staffing asst, 1978, affirmative action recruiter, 1978-. **Orgs:** Youth Motivation Task Force, 1980-86; vpres, secy Blacks Govt, 1980-86; secy, Carver State Tech Col Adv Bd, 1982-86; Southern Col Placement Asn, 1982-86; Southeastern Fed Recruiting Coun, 1982-86; Black Execs Exchange Prog, 1986. **Home Addr:** 5821 Wood Gate Rd, Mobile, AL 36609. **Business Addr:** Affirmative Action Recruiter, US Army Corps of Engineers, PO Box 2288, Mobile, AL 36628.

### SMITH, DR. ELEANOR JANE

School administrator. **Personal:** Born Jan 10, 1933, Circleville, OH; daughter of John A Lewis (deceased) and Eleanor J Dade Lewis (deceased); married Paul M Jr; children: Teresa Marie Banner. **Educ:** Capital Univ, BSM, 1955; Ohio State Univ, MEd 1966; Union Grad Sch/UECU, PhD, 1972. **Career:** School administrator (retired); Bd Educ, Columbus, Ohio, 2nd-6th grad teacher, 1956-64; Bd Educ, Worthington, Ohio 6 & 7th grad teacher, 1964-69; Univ Cinn, prof, Afro-Am Studies, 1972-88; vice provost Fac & Acad Affairs; Smith Col, dean instnl affairs & prof, Afro-Am hist, 1988-90; William Paterson Col, vpres acad affairs & provost, 1990-94; Univ Wis-parkside, chancellor, 1994-97. **Orgs:** Asn Black Women Historians, Nat co-founder & co-director, 1978-80; Nat Coun Black Studies, 1982-88; Nat Asn Women Educ, 1986-; Am Asn Higher Educ; Am Coun Educ; Am Asn State Cols & Univs. **Special Achievements:** First African American chancellor to lead UW-Parkside. **Home Addr:** 40 Harborview Dr, Racine, WI 53403.

### SMITH, REV. ELIJAH, SR. (WYRE SMITH)

Business owner, clergy. **Personal:** Born Dec 28, 1939, Peach County, GA; son of Samuel Lee and Ola Mae John; married Janet Broner; children: Audrey Maria Diamond, Elijah Jr, Sonja A, Avice D, Richard A, Mark A, D'ete, LaShaunda R Thomas & Velecia Thomas. **Educ:** Turner Theol Sem, dipl theol, 1975. **Career:** Blue Bird Body Co, utility man, 1964-66; Robins Afb Ga, electronic repairman, 1966-75; Eastman Circuit Eastman Ga, pastor, 1967-71; Allen Chapel & Mountain Creek AME Churches, pastor, 1971-84; D&S Florist, owner, 1974-76; St John AME Church, pastor; Eastern Dist Southwest Ga, Sixth Episcopal Dist African Methodist Episcopal Church, host presiding elder to sr presiding elder, currently. **Orgs:** Columbus & Phoenix City Ministerial Alliance, 1984-; Masonic Lodge 134 Powersville Ga, 1965-; Columbus Br Nat Asn Advan Colored People, 1984-; Pub Affairs Coun, Columbus, 1984-; AME Church Ministers Alliance Columbus; S Columbus Exchange Club, 1989; A J McClung YMCA; Columbus Urban League. **Honors/Awds:** Oscar Maxwell Award, Man of the Year, Americus Boy Scouts, 1978; Minister of the Year, Black Youth Action, 1979; Tomorrow's Leaders Award, Ga Power, 1979; Outstanding Public Service Award, Sumter Co Bd Gov of C, 1980; Outstanding Service & Dedication Award, Kent Hill Youth Devel Prog, 1984; Distinguished & Devoted Service Award, Americus-Sumter Co Nat Asn Advan Colored People, 1984; Community Service Award, Mayor City Americus, 1984; Service Award, Chief Police Americus, Ga, 1984; Outstanding & Dedicated Service Award, Americus Police Dept & Comm Americus & Sumter Co, 1984; Devoted Leadership Service to St John & Community, St John AME Church, 1989; The Martin Luther King Sr, Minister's Community Service Award, PUSH, 1991; Pastor of the Year, The Sons of Allen of the Southwest Ga Ann Conf AME Church, 1992; Pastor of the Year, Lay Orgn Southwest Ga, Ann Conf AME Church, 1992. **Home Addr:** 1938 Armory Dr, Americus, GA 31709-2110, **Home Phone:** (912)928-9727. **Business Addr:** Senior Presiding Elder, Eastern District African Methodist Episcopal Church, 2008 Armory Dr, Americus, GA 31719, **Business Phone:** (229)928-9727.

### SMITH, ELISA C. NEWSOME

Journalist. **Personal:** Born Jul 6, 1964, Detroit, MI; daughter of William York and Gwendolyn; children: Andrew I Lee. **Educ:** Miami Dade Community Col, Miami, FL, AA & AS, 1986; Univ Miami, Coral Glades, FL, BS, commun, 1988; Acupuncture & Massage Col, cert, massage ther & therapeut massage, 2010. **Career:** Palm Beach Post, W Palm Beach, Fla, reporter, journalist, 1989-92; Miami-Dade County, commun admin, 1994-2007; Abide Chi, massage therapist & tai chi & qigong instr, 1995-. **Orgs:** Nat Asn Black Journalists, 1987-; Am Tai Chi Asn; Tai Chi Health Community Health Preserv Asn. **Home Addr:** 20101 NW 28 Ct, Carol City, FL 33055, **Home Phone:** (305)628-1402. **Business Addr:** Massage Therapist, Tai Chi & Qigong Instructor, Abide in Chi, 6600 SW 62 Ave, South MIami, FL 33143, **Business Phone:** (305)343-6365.

### SMITH, DR. ELMER G., JR.

Physician. **Personal:** Born May 22, 1957, Chicago, IL; son of Elmer and Joyce; married Ingrid S P; children: Brittany Francoise, Harrison Monfort, Samantha Dominique & AlexanderJean-Marc. **Educ:** Univ Ill-Chicago, BS, 1980; Howard Univ Col Med, MD, 1983. **Career:** Norwalk/Yale Hosp, resident physician, 1983-86; Northwestern Med Sch, clin med instr, 1989; Northwestern Memorial Hosp, active attend, 1990; Cook County Hosp, med consult, 1988-93, dir ambulatory screening, 1993-; pvt pract, currently; N Hills Internal Med. **Orgs:** Alpha Phi Alpha Frat Inc, 1980-; Am Med Asn, 1980-; Am Col Physicians, 1985-; Ill State Med Soc, 1986-; Chicago Med Soc, 1986-; pres, Am Cancer Soc, Ill Div, Austin Unit, 1987-89; Soc Gen Internal Med, 1991; ASIM. **Honors/Awds:** VPres, Pub Relations, Sr Class, Howard Univ, 1982-83; Psychiatry Res Award, Howard Univ Col Med, 1983; Dipl Am Bd Internal Med, 1986; Chicago's Caring Physicians Award, Metropolitan Chicago Health Care Council, 1987; Cook County Hosp, Acute Pharyngitis, 1989, syphilis, 1990; WVAZ, Heat Syndromes, 1991. **Home Addr:** 4351 Booth Calloway Rd Suite 311, North Richland Hills, TX 76180, **Home Phone:** (817)595-4949. **Business Addr:** Physician, North Hills Internal Medical, 4351 Booth Calloway Rd Suite 311, North Richland Hills, TX 76180, **Business Phone:** (817)595-4949.

### SMITH, ELSIE MAE

Nurse. **Personal:** Born Feb 27, 1927, Erin, OK; daughter of Isadore Brooks and Laura Latour; married James Almer Jr; children: James, Roger, Margo & Melanie. **Educ:** St Marys Sch Nursing, St Louis, Mo; Am Int Col. **Career:** Nurse (retired); Bay State Med Ctr, gastroenterol, staff RN, 1973-90. **Orgs:** Links, Greater Springfield Chap Inc; docent, Mus Fine Arts, Springfield, MA; cooperator, Springfield Mus & Libr Asn; pres, 1980-82, Springfield Chap Girl Friends; bd dir, secy, Springfield Girls Club Family Ctr; bd dir, Conn Valley Girl Scouts; pres, Springfield Alpha Wives, 1961-63; world traveler; vol, Housing Habitant; vol, Springfield Tech Community Col, Tutor students foreign taking Eng; African Hall Steering Comt, Sci Mus, Springfield, MA; Cooperator Bay State Med Ctr; Comt St Michaels Cathedral. **Honors/Awds:** Achievement Award, McKnight Neighborhood; Certificate of Training, Springfield Libr & Museum Asn, 1989. **Home Addr:** 936 Grayson Dr Apt 325, Springfield, MA 01119-1546, **Home Phone:** (413)737-7161.

### SMITH, EMMITT J., III

Executive, football player. **Personal:** Born May 15, 1969, Pensacola, FL; son of Emmitt Jr and Mary Clements; married Patricia Southall; children: Emmitt IV, Rheagen, Jasmin & Skylar. **Educ:** Univ Fla, BA, pub recreation, 1989. **Career:** Football player (retired), analyst, executive; Dallas Cowboys, running back, 1990-2002; Ariz Cardinals, running back, 2003-04; Nat Football League Network, Nat Football League Total Access, studio analyst, 2005-07; Entertainment & Sports Programming Network, Nat Football League studio analyst, 2007-; ESmith Legacy, partner, co-founder, co-chair, chief exec officer, 2000-; EJSmith Construct, owner & chmn, 2010-; E Smith Realty Partners, chmn, 2013-; Smith/Cypress Partners LP, co-founder; EJ Smirth Enterprises LLC, owner, currently; Gents Pl, co-owner, 2016-. **Orgs:** Make a Wish Found; founder, Emmitt Smith Scholar Prog; spokesperson, Just Say No Anti-Drug Campaign, 1986; Phi Beta Sigma; Col Football Hall Fame; Tex Sports Hall Fame; Fla Sports Hall Fame; founder, Emmitt Smith Charities Inc, 2006-. **Honors/Awds:** High School Player of the Year, USA Today, Parade Mag, 1986; National Freshman of the Year, UPI, Sporting News, 1987; SEC Most Valuable Player, 1989; AP NFL Offensive Rookie of the Year, 1990; Pro Bowl, 1991, 1992-98; Miller Lite NFL Player of the Year, 1993; Most Valuable Player Award, Nat Football League, 1993; Super Bowl XXVIII Most Valuable Player, 1993, 1994, 1996; Super Bowl, 1993; Super Bowl Most Valuable Player Award, 1993; NFL MVP Award, 1993; AP NFL Most Valuable Player, 1993; Four Nat Football League, Rushing Titles; holder of numerous Cowboys & NFL records; all-time NFL leading rusher; Two consecutive Jim Thorpe Football Awards; Bert Bell Award, 1993; inducted, Dallas Cowboys Ring of Honor, 2005; inducted, College Football Hall of Fame; inducted, Gator Football Ring of Honor; mem, Florida High School All-Century Team; Florida High School Athletic Association Player of the Century; Pro Football Hall of Fame, 2010. **Special Achievements:** Surpassed the 1, 000-yard rushing mark earlier than any other player in Col football hist; He is the only running back to ever win a Super Bowl championship; Co-author: Autobiography, The Emmitt Zone, Crown Pub, 1994; Univ Florida Athletic Hall of Fame, Gator Great, 1999; first Dallas Cowboy Player to lead the league in rushing; football field named and holiday created in his hon, Escambia HS, Pensacola, FL, 2003; Gator Football Ring of Honor, 2006; College Football Hall of Fame, 2006; Escambia High Sch Sports Hall of Fame, 2010. **Home Addr:** , Dallas, TX. **Business Addr:** Owner, EJSmith Enterprises LLC, 5495 Belt Line Rd Suite 110S, Dallas, TX 75254, **Business Phone:** (972)701-8222.

### SMITH, DR. ERNEST HOWARD

Physician, cardiologist, pediatrician. **Personal:** Born Nov 9, 1931, Bethlehem, PA. **Educ:** Lincoln Univ, BA, biol, 1953; Howard Univ, MD, 1957. **Career:** C Hosp Philadelphia, DC Gen Hosp, resident pediatrist; C Hosp Philadelphia, Henry Ford Hosp Detroit, fel pediat cardiol USPHS CheyenneSioux Reservation Eagle Butte SD, med officer incharge, 1958-61; Detroit, priv prac pediat cardiol, 1964-68; Henry Ford Hosp, staff pediat cardiologist, 1965-71; Univ Calif, Los Angeles, assoc prof pediat King Charles RDrew Med Sch, Los Angeles, Calif, asst prof pediat, dir pediat cardiologist & head community pediat, 1972-2004; WGPA radio, piano broadcast; Compton Sickle Cell Ctr, co-dir; Martin Luther King Gen Hosp, assoc prof pediat cardio, currently; King/Drew Med Univ, assoc prof pediat, currently. **Orgs:** Catalytic Community Asn, Detroit, 1968-70; S Cent Planning Coun, Los Angeles, 1973-; SE Ment Health Liason Coun, 1973-; Cit Youth Employ, 1973-; organist, Pilgrim Congregational Ch Eagle Butte, SD; Christ United Church Christ, Detroit; Hartford Ave Baptist Church Detroit; First Baptist Church Warrenton, VA; St Pauls Baptist Church, Bethlehem, PA; accompanist, Lincoln Univ Glee Club, PA; select comt, World C; fel pediat cardiol, C's Hosp Philadelphia; Bethlehem Conserv Music; minister, Baptist Church; minister, United Church Christ. **Honors/Awds:** Quinland Prize For Biology, Lincoln Univ, 1953; Award, Kappa Alpha Psi Mu Chap, 1953; Cheyenne Sioux Tribal Citation, 1961; President's Award, S Cent Planning Coun, 1974; Education Fraternity Award, Phi Delta Kappa, 1975. **Home Addr:** 1201 S Gramercy Pl, Los Angeles, CA 90019. **Business Addr:** Associate Professor, Martin Luther King General Hospital, 12021 S Wilmington Ave, Los Angeles, CA 90059.

### SMITH, DR. ESTELLA W.

Executive. **Educ:** Ind Univ, Bloomington, BS, educ; Memphis State Univ, MS, PhD, educ. **Career:** Duquesne Light Co, dir invest & bank rels, community rels mgr, 1991, pub affairs, gen mgr(retired); Univ Pittsburgh, asst prof educ; Memphis State Univ, instr; Heritage Nat Bank, pres & chief exec officer; sch systs Ind & Tenn, educr; Port Authority Allegheny County, dir, 2001-06, Finance & Admin Comt, chmn; Hill Community Develop Corp, chairperson. **Orgs:** Adv bd, Urban League; mem develop adv & african-am develop comt, Extra Mile Educ Found; bd mem, UPMC Health Syst & Magee Womens Hosp; adv bd & bd trustee, Community Col Allegheny County Educ Found. **Home Addr:** 6393 Penn Ave, Pittsburgh, PA 15206.

### SMITH, DR. ESTUS

Foundation executive. **Personal:** Born Oct 13, 1930, Crystal Springs, MS; son of David and Margaret; married Dorothy Triplett; children: Donald Gregory. **Educ:** Jackson State Univ, BS, 1953; Ind Univ, MM, 1961; Univ Iowa, PhD, 1970; Eastman Sch Music, addn studies. **Career:** Foundation executive (retired); Sch Lib Studies, dean, 1968-73; Jackson State Univ, dean, vpres acad affairs, prof music, 1973-84; Charles F Kettering Found, prog officer, dir opers, vpres & chief operating officer emer. **Orgs:** Univ Iowa Alumni Asn; fel Am Coun Higher Educ, 1969; gov bd, trustee, Dayton Found, 1990-; bd trustee, Centerville/Wash Twp Educ Found, 1990-; Nat Conf Community, 1995; bd trustee, bd dir, Knowledge Works Found, 1999-; bd trustee, Cent State Univ, 2001-06, chmn bd, 2002; former chmn Comn, Miss Humanities; former bd trustee, Dept Arch & Hist State Miss; pres, vpres, Southern Conf Deans Fac & Acad; chmn bd dir, State Mutual Fed Savings & Loan Asn; pres, Opera/S Co; Nat Asn Advan Colored People; Omega Psi Phi; Phi Delta Kappa; Phi Kappa Phi; Beta Beta Beta; bd dir, Dayton Coun World Affairs; exec bd, Miami Valley Leadership Acad; Sigma Pi Phi Frat; Alpha Lamba Delta; Phi Kappa Phi Frat; Kappa Psi Frat; trustee, St George's Episcopal Church; emer mem, bd dir, African Am Community Fund; bd dir, Dayton Area Chap Am Red Cross; treas, Episcopal Diocese Southern Ohio; bd trustee, Alliance Community Schs Inc. **Honors/Awds:** Numerous awards including Episcopalian Outstanding American, 1970; Outstanding Alumni & Scholar, 1970; Outstanding Educator of America; Jackson State University Sports Hall of Fame, 1980; Distinguished Service Award, Nat Gov Asn, 1981; Archon of the Year, Sigma Pi Phi Frat, 1988; ten top African American Males Award, Parity 2000, Dayton. **Home Addr:** 398 Grassy Creek Way, Centerville, OH 45458-9249.

### SMITH, EUGENE, JR.

Executive, manager. **Personal:** Born Aug 13, 1938, Alquippa, MT; married Jacquelyn L; children: Charmaine, Deborah & Carlton. **Educ:** Geneva Col; Univ Duquesne. **Career:** Munic Water Authority Aliquippa, asst mgr, gen mgr, currently. **Orgs:** Bd mem, vpres, Alquippa Pub Sch Dist; bd mem, Beaver Co Hosp Authority; mem bd dir, PA Minority Bus develop Comn; US Mil Selection Com; Zion Hope Lodge; St Cyprian Consistory; Sahara Temple. **Home Addr:** 124 Wilker Ave, Aliquippa, PA 15001-3451, **Home Phone:** (724)203-2620. **Business Addr:** General Manager, Municipal Water Authority of Aliquippa, 160 Hopewell Ave, Aliquippa, PA 15001, **Business Phone:** (724)375-5525.

### SMITH, EUGENE DUBOIS (GENE SMITH)

Athletic director, executive, association executive. **Personal:** Born Dec 18, 1955, Cleveland, OH; son of Theodore and Elizabeth DuBois; married Sheila; children: Matt, Nicole Dawn, Lindsey Rose & Summer Denise. **Educ:** Univ Notre Dame, Ind, BBA, 1977. **Career:** Irish, defensive end; Assoc Press nat championship team, 1973; Univ Notre Dame, Ind, asst football coach, 1977-81; IBM, S Bend, Ind, mkt rep, 1981-83; Eastern Mich Univ, Ypsilanti, Mich, from asst athletic dir to athletic dir, 1983-93; Iowa State Univ, athletic dir, 1993-2000; Ariz State Univ, athletic dir, 2000-05; Ohio State Univ, athletic dir, vpres, 2005-; Div 1-A Athletic Dirs Asn, pres, 2007. **Orgs:** Bd mem, Nat Col Athletic Asn Track & Field Rules Comt, 1987-89; Nat Asn Advan Colored People; Ypsilanti Chap, 1988-; bd mem, Chamber Com, Ypsilanti, Mich, 1989-; exec bd, Nat Assoc Col Dirs Athletics, 1990-; Kids Unlimited Nat Adv Bd; NCAA Mgt Coun; NCAA Comt Infractions; NCAA Exec Comt; NCAA Football Rules Comt; Pres's Comn Liaison Comt; NCAA Baseball Acad Enhancement Task Force; Nat Football Found Hons Ct; chair, NCAA Men's Basketball Comt, 2010-11; NCAA Div I Admin Cabinet, 2011-. **Honors/Awds:** Athletic Administrator of the Year, Black Coaches Association, 2007; John L. Toner Award, 2008; Carl Maddox Sports Management Award, 2010; Sport Business Journal Athletic Director of the Year, 2010; National Association for Athletics Compliance Award, 2013. **Special Achievements:** Identified in the March 2005 issue of Black Enterprise magazine as one of the 50 Most Powerful African Americans in Sports; First African American to hold the athletics director position at Ohio State University; First African American president of the National Association of Collegiate Directors of Athletics. **Home Addr:** 44155 Applewood, Canton, MI 48188, **Home Phone:** (313)397-3474. **Business Addr:** Director of Athletics, Associate Vice President, Ohio State University, 281 W Lane Ave, Columbus, OH 43210, **Business Phone:** (614)292-2477.

### SMITH, FERNANDO DEWITT

Football player. **Personal:** Born Aug 2, 1971, Flint, MI; children: Quantiash & Tyna. **Educ:** Jackson State Univ, attended 1994. **Career:** Football player (retired); Minn Vikings, defensive end & left defensive end, 1994-97, 2000; Jacksonville Jaguars, defensive end, 1998; Baltimore Ravens, defensive end, 1999; St Louis Rams, defensive end, 2000; Carolina Panthers, defensive end, 2002.

### SMITH, FRANCES C.

Funeral director. **Personal:** Born Williamston, NC; daughter of Leo Cherry (deceased) and Omenella Riddick Cherry; married Alfred J Jr; children: Randy & Trent. **Educ:** McAllister Sch Embalming; Am Acad Sch Embalming, grad studies. **Career:** Garden State Funeral dir Asn, secy; Smith Funeral Home, owner & funeral dir, currently. **Orgs:** Gov Comn Qual Educ State NJ, 1991-; NJ State Bd Mortuary Sci; Elizabeth Develop Co; Garden State Funeral dir; past pres, Urban League Guild; past matron, Lincoln Chap OES; pres, Union Co Unit Nat Asn Negro Bus & Prof Women's Clubs; past pres, Women's Scholar Club Elizabeth; Elizabeth Bd Educ; Soroptimist Int Eliz; Union Co Asn Women Bus Owners; New Zion Baptist Church; Sr Choice & Missionaries; Nat Asn Advan Colored People; Womens Scholar Club; Girl Scouts; Gay Parisiennes Social Club; bd mem, Vis Nurses Asn; bd mem, Summit Trust Co & Elizabeth Develop Asn. **Honors/Awds:** Achievement Award, Urban League Eastern Union Co; Professional Woman of the Year Award, NJ Unit Nat Asn Negro Bus & Prof Women's Clubs; Appreciation Award, Elizabeth Br Nat Asn Adv Colored People, 1980; Business Woman of Year Award, Union Co Nat Asn Negro Bus Women & Prof Women's Clubs. **Special Achievements:** First Black Board Member in Egenolf Day Nursery in Elizabeth & Presently on advisory board of nursery; Honored by receiving 'Key to City' by Mayor and the First Black woman to receive such an honor; First African-American to serve on the New Jersey State Board of Mortuary Science. **Home Addr:** 45 Cherry St, Elizabeth, NJ 07202, **Home Phone:** (908)352-9114. **Business Addr:** Owner, Director, Smith Funeral Home, 45 Cherry St, Elizabeth, NJ 07202, **Business Phone:** (908)352-1855.

### SMITH, DR. FRANK, JR.

Executive director, government official, chief executive officer. **Personal:** Born Sep 17, 1942, Newnan, GA; married Jean. **Educ:** Morehouse Col, attended 1959; Union Inst, OH, PhD, 1980. **Career:** Commentator, civil rights activist, politician, speaker; Morehouse Col, SNCC, founding mem, 1959-62, Miss, AL organizing & registering African Am voters, 1962-68; Inst Policy Studies, researcher, adv neighborhood comnr, 1968; City Washington, DC, city councilman; Dist Columbia City, coun, 1983-99; African Am Civil War Memorial Freedom Found & Mus, founding exec dir & chief exec officer, 1998-. **Orgs:** Chair, Civil War Found; New Farmers Am; chmn bd, African Am Civil War Memorial Found & Mus, 1998-. **Home Addr:** 330 T St NW, Washington, DC 20001-1843, **Home Phone:** (202)232-8379. **Business Addr:** Chief Executive Officer, Executive Director, African American Civil War Memorial Museum, 1925 Vermont Ave NW, Washington, DC 20001, **Business Phone:** (202)667-2667.

### SMITH, FRANKIE LEE

Football player, football coach, teacher. **Personal:** Born Oct 8, 1968, Ft. Worth, TX. **Educ:** Baylor Univ, grad. **Career:** Football player (retired), coach, teacher; Miami Dolphins, defensive back, 1993-95; San Francisco 49ers, 1996-97; Chicago Bears, safety, 1998-2001; Groesbeck (Tex) High Sch, asst football coach; Mexia Independent Sch Dist, coach & health teacher, currently. **Special Achievements:** Film: 1992 NFL Draft, 1992. **Business Addr:** Coach, Health Teacher, Mexia Independent School District., 616 N Red River, Mexia, TX 76667, **Business Phone:** (254)562-4000.

### SMITH, FRONSE WAYNE, SR.

Association executive, executive, painter (artist). **Personal:** Born Aug 11, 1946, Chicago, IL; son of Elmer and Floy; married Germaine; children: Alonda Fleming, Lehia Franklin, Fronse Jr, Gamal-Azmi & Julius. **Educ:** Univ Ill, Chicago, BS, org chem, 1970; Grand Valley State Univ, MBA, int new ventures, 1980. **Career:** Glidden Co, qual control technician, 1965-67; DeSoto Inc, res chemist, 1968-75; W-L Co, Parke Davis Div, Paints, anal chemist, 1977-81; Warner Lambert Co, Pharmaceut, sr buyer, 1981-83, purchasing mgr, 1983-2002; Sterile Prod, purchasing agt, 1988-92; May Day Chem Co Inc, gen mgr, chem distrib, 1992-96; BPS Int Ltd, Consults Africa Chem Procurement & Bus Match-making, pres, educ advocate, 1970-2008, facilitator, 1980-2012; Christian Reformed Church N Am, 2nd elder deleg, holland classis, 2011. **Orgs:** Deacon & elder, Hope Reformed Church, 1977-96; Steward, Bethel AME Church, 1982-83; master mason, Prince Hall, FAM, Tyrian Widows & Sons Lodge 34, 1987; co-founder, Holland Coalition, People Color, 1989; nat assoc mem, Nat Asn Purchasing Mgr; Univ Ill, Chicago, Black Alumni Asn; life mem, Univ Ill Alumni Asn; fel African Sci Inst, 2013-. **Honors/Awds:** Eagle Scout with Bronze Palm, Boy Scouts Am, 1962; Certified Volunteer, State Mich, Dept Corrections, 1979-82. **Special Achievements:** Contributor, "Dew Freeze Vacuum, Wet Adhesion Test", Journal of Coatings Technology, 1973; amateur painter & exhibitor in Holland, MI, 1981. **Business Addr:** Officer, Bps International Ltd, 601 Douglas Ave, Holland, MI 49424-2783, **Business Phone:** (616)396-1082.

### SMITH, ESQ. G. ELAINE

Executive, association executive. **Career:** Am Baptist Churches Us Am, pres, 1996-97, vice chair. **Orgs:** Tenn Bar Asn; PA Bar Asn; NJ Bar Asn; Alpha Kappa Alpha Sorority; Death Penalty Initiative; Const Proj. **Honors/Awds:** Hon Doctorate, Ottawa Univ. **Special Achievements:** First African American female president of the American Baptist Churches USA. **Business Addr:** Member, Constitution Project, 1025 Vermont Ave NW Suite 1000, Washington, DC 20036, **Business Phone:** (202)580-6920.

### SMITH, GENE. See SMITH, EUGENE DUBOIS.

### SMITH, GEORGE BUNDY

Judge. **Personal:** Born Apr 7, 1937, New Orleans, LA; married Alene Jackson; children: George Jr & Beth. **Educ:** Inst d'Etudes Politiques Paris, CEP Inst, 1958; Yale Univ, BA, 1959; Yale Law Sch, LLB, 1962; NYU, MA, polit sci, 1967, PhD, 1974; Univ Va Sch Law, LLM, 2001. **Career:** Civil Ct Judge Jawn Sandifer, law secy, 1964-67; New York Civil Ct, judge, 1975-79; Horace Mann-Barnard Sch, trustee, 1977-99; Supreme Ct State NY, justice, 1980-86; Supreme Ct, Appellate Div State NY, first dept assoc justice, 1987-92; NY State Ct Appeals, assoc judge, 1992-2006; Fordham Univ Law Sch, adj prof law, 1981-; NY Law Sch, adj prof law, 2001-; Chadbourne & Parke LLP, partner, 2006-11. **Orgs:** Chartered Inst Arbitrators; Am Arbit Asn; mem bd dir, founding mem, Metrop Black Bar Asn, chmn bd, 1984-88; Phillips Acad, trustee, 1986-90; vpres, Asn Bar City New York, 1988-89; pres, Harlem Lawyers Asn; commr, NY State Ethics Comn Unified Ct Syst, 1989-2001; Judicial Friends; Nat Bar Asn Judicial Coun; dir, Harlem-Dowling Westside Ctr C & Family Serv; chair, bd trustee, Grace Congregational Church. **Honors/Awds:** Honorary Doctor of Laws, Fordham Univ Sch Law, 2004; hon PhD, Albany Law Sch Union Univ, 2006; Lifetime Public Service Award, The Fund for Modern Courts, a private, nonprofit, nonpartisan organization dedicated to improving the administration of justice in New York, 2007; William Brennan Award for Outstanding Jurist, NY State Asn Criminal Defense Lawyers, 2007; Honorary Doctor of Laws, Brooklyn Law Sch, 2008; Spirit of Excellence Award, American Bar Association Commission on Racial and Ethnic Diversity, 2008. **Home Addr:** 549 W 123 St Apt 13 F, New York, NY 10027. **Business Addr:** Partner, Chadbourne & Parke LLP, 30 Rockefeller Plz, New York, NY 10112, **Business Phone:** (212)292-0195.

### SMITH, DR. GEORGE EDMOND

Writer, educator. **Career:** Family Pract Physician; Hahnemann Sch Med, Philadelphia, PA, asst clin prof family med, currently. Author: More Than Sex: Reinventing The Black Male Image, 2000; Weight Loss for African American Women, 2001; Walking Proud: Black Men Living Beyond the Stereotypes, 2001; Weight Loss for African-American Women: An Eight-Week Guide to Better Health, 2001; Taking Care of Our Own: A Family Medical Guide for African Americans, 2004. **Orgs:** Am Cancer Soc Inc; Am Diabetes Asn; Am Heart Asn. **Business Addr:** Assistant Clinical Professor, Hahnenmann School of Medicine, Broad & Vine, Philadelphia, PA 19102, **Business Phone:** (215)762-7000.

### SMITH, HON. GEORGE S.

Government official. **Personal:** Born Jan 6, 1940, Terry, MS; children: George Jr, Tosha, Eric & Carol. **Educ:** Utica Jr Col, AA; Jackson State Univ. **Career:** Smith Enterprises, owner & operator, 1965-; Gov Miss, sr staff, 1966; State Miss, sr staff mem & advisor econ develop, 1975-80; State Medicaid Comt, comt mem, 1966; State Bldg Comn, supvr, 1979; Hinds Cty Dist Five, supvr, 1980-, pres 1984-; Ins agt, 1988-. **Orgs:** TC Almore Lodge 242; Jackson Chap Nat Bus League; Jackson Urban League; Nat Asn Advan Colored People; bd dir, Smith-Robertson Comn; Metrop Young Men Christian Asn; Goodwill Indust; Cent MS Planning & Develop Dist Adv Coun Aging; Ctr S Indust Develop Group; Jackson Chamber Com; 100 Black Men Jackson; Hinds County Pvt Indust Coun; vice chmn, Nat Asn Counties; vice chmn, Agr & Rural Affairs Steering Comt, Nat Asn Black County Officials; Nat Urban Leag; Miss Consortium for Int Dev; Hinds County Pvt Ind Coun; Americ Red Cross; Collis Hill Church Christ Holiness; Oper Heartbeat Am Heart Asn; Miss Rural Develop Coun; Miss Hall Fame Sports Found; Miss Consortium Int Develop; Miss Ballet Int USA Inc; John Bell Williams Airport Authority; Hinds Community Col Develop Found; Gov's Comn Electronic Govt; Downtown Conv Adv Comt; Jackson State Univ Nat Youth Sport Prog; Hinds County Health Alliance; Jackson State Univ Pkwy Comn; Jackson State Univ E-City Comt; Miss State Comt Taxation; Delta Regional Authority; Jackson Metro Housing Partnership; Nat Asn Advan Colored People; W Jackson Community Develop Corp; Metro YMCA; Goodwill Industs; Oper Heartbeat Am Heart Asn; Nat Bus League. **Honors/Awds:** Spec Recog Award, Jackson St Univ/Outstanding Alumni, 1985; Spec Recog Award for Outstanding Achiev in Govt, Jackson St Univ/Nat Alumni, 1986; Trailblazer Award; Proven Leader through the New Millennium, MAS Mag, 2000; Elliott Fel- Governing in the Global Age, George Wash Univ, 2002; Hinds Community College, Utica Campus, Distinguished Alumnus Award, 2003. **Special Achievements:** First black appointed to the State Building Commission; First black to be senior staff member to Governor of Mississippi; First black to be appointed as commn of State Med Commn; One of two blacks to be elected as supervisor of Hinds County Dist Five 1979, re-elected supvr, 1983; First black to serve as president of Hinds County Board of Supervisors, 1984; First black President of the Mississippi Association of Supervisors in 1999. **Home Addr:** 1519 Jones Ave, Jackson, MS 39204, **Home Phone:** (601)354-2665. **Business Addr:** President, Supervisor, Hinds County Board of Supervisors, PO Box 686, Jackson, MS 39205-0686, **Business Phone:** (601)968-6795.

**SMITH, REV. GEORGE WALKER**
Executive, clergy. **Personal:** Born Apr 28, 1929, Hayneville, AL; married Elizabeth; children: Anthony, Carolyn & Joyce. **Educ:** Knoxville Col, BS, 1951; Pittsburgh Theol Sem, MDiv; Ala State Univ, MA. **Career:** Pastor (retired), executive; Ala State Univ; Christ United Presby Church San Diego, pastor, minister & founder, 1956-2000; Wayman Chapel, pastor; Catfish Club, founder & bd dir, 1970-. **Orgs:** Pres, Coun Great City Schs; pres, Nat Sch Bd Asn, 1976, secy, treas & vpres; App, Calif Ad Hoc Comn; app, Calif Savs & Loan Leag; San Diego Bd Educ; dir & vpres, Pac Coast Bank; Kappa Alpha Psi; Social Club; charter mem, San Diego Chap Alpha Pi Boule; Sigma Pi Phi Nat Adv Comn Juv Justice & Delinq Prev White House Conf C & Youth; Calif Sch Bd Asn; bd trustee, San Diego Community Col Dist; Calif Jr Col Asn; Kiwanis Club; bd mem, Calif Legis Black Caucus Found Inc. **Honors/Awds:** San Diego's Outstanding Young Clergyman; Phi Delta Kappa Lay Citizen Award; Gentleman of Distinction of the Women's Guild of Temple Emanuel; Distinguished Alumni of Pittsburgh Theological Seminary, 1985; Allen Temple Leadership Institute Award, 2000; Doctor of Humane Letters, San Diego State Univ; Annual Civic Service Award, 2004; Distinguished Alumni of Knoxville College, 2004. **Special Achievements:** First Presbytery of San Diego so honored moderator of the General Assembly; He became the first member of the local Kiwanis Club; The first African American to join the National School Board. **Home Addr:** 610 Gateway Ctr Way, San Diego, CA 92102, **Home Phone:** (619)266-7278. **Business Addr:** Founder, Board of Director, The Catfish Club, 2131 Pan America Pl, San Diego, CA 92101, **Business Phone:** (619)266-7278.

**SMITH, GERALD B. (GERALD BERNARD SMITH)**
Founder (originator), chairperson, chief executive officer. **Personal:** married Anita; children: Marcus, Jackson, Jordan & Joy. **Educ:** Tex Southern Univ, BBA, finance. **Career:** Dillon Read & Co, vpres; Underwood Neuhaus & Co, sr vpres & dir fixed income; Westcap Corp, first sr vpres & dir mkt & sales; Cooper Industs, dir; Robeco Group, dir; Smith, Graham & Co Investment Advisors LP, co-founder, chmn & chief exec officer, 1990-; Viking Gas Transmission Co, dir; Pennzoil-Quaker State Co, dir; New York Life Ins Co, dir, 2012-; New York Life Ins Co, dir, 2012-; Eaton Corp, dir, 2012-. **Orgs:** Trustee, Schwab Capital Trust, 2000-; dir, ONEOK Partners LP, 2006-; dir & bd trustee, Charles Schwab Family Funds; dir, ONEOK Partners GP LLC, 2009-13; bd dir & trustee, Mus Fine Arts-Houston; bd dir, Greater Houston Partnership; vice chmn bd dir, Houston Metrop Transit Authority (METRO); bd visitor, Md Anderson Cancer Ctr; chmn, Tex Southern Univ Found; audit comt chmn, Northern Border Partners LP; bd dir, Cooper Industs; founding chmn, Houston Mus African-Am Cult; founding mem, New York Futures Exchange; Fed Res Bank; treasure, Nat Asn Securities Professionals. **Honors/Awds:** National Black College Alumni Hall of Fame, Inductee; Maynard Holbrook Jackson Jr Award, Nat Asn Securities Professionals (NASP); United Way Volunteer of the Year; National Black MBAs Leadership Empowerment Award; YMCA Annual Tribute to Leadership Award; Father of the Year Award, Community Partners; 75 Most Powerful Blacks on Wall Street, "Black Enterprise", 2011. **Special Achievements:** One of the Most Influential Blacks on Wall Street, Black Enterprise; National Black College Alumni Hall of Fame for achievements in the field of Business. **Business Addr:** Chairman, Chief Executive Officer, Smith, Graham & Company Investment Advisors LP, 6900 JPMorgan Chase Tower, Houston, TX 77002, **Business Phone:** (713)227-1100.

**SMITH, DR. GERALD LAMONT**
Clergy, educator, college administrator. **Personal:** Born Apr 8, 1959, Lexington, KY; married Teresa Turner; children: Elizabeth & Sarah. **Educ:** Univ Ky, BA, 1981, MA, 1983, PhD, urban & African Am hist, 1988. **Career:** Author, editor; Univ Ky, teaching asst, 1985-86, instr, 1986-88, asst prof hist, 1993-, African American Studies & Res Prog, dir, 1997-; Univ Memphis, asst prof, 1988-93; Farristown Baptist Church Berea, Kentucky, pastor; Pilgrim Baptist Church, pastor; dir, African Am Studies & Res Prog, 1997-2005; General hist African Am, writer, currently; Theodore A Hallam Professorship, 2015-17; Martin Luther King Ctr Scholar-Residence, 2015-17; Editor: The Papers of Martin Luther King, Jr: Advocatge of the Social Gospel; Black America Series: Lexington, Kentucky, 2001; Kentucky African American Encyclopedia, 2015; Author: A Black Educator in the Segregated South: The Life and Times of Rufus B Atwood, 1987-1983, 1994. **Orgs:** Greater Lexington Chamber Com, Minority Bus Develop Adv Bd, 1999; Univ Ky Libr Assocs, Exec Comt, 1999; Univ Press KY Comt; assoc minister, Consol Baptist Church; bd trustee, Lexington Hist Mus; Ky Hist Mus; bd dir, Univ Ky Athletic Asn; chair, Ky African Am Heritage Comn. **Home Addr:** 2416 Pierson Dr, Lexington, KY 40505-1815, **Home Phone:** (859)523-2196. **Business Addr:** Associate Professor of History, University of Kentucky, 1773 Patterson Off Tower, Lexington, KY 40506-0027, **Business Phone:** (859)257-1357.

**SMITH, GERALD WAYNE**
Television director, television show host. **Personal:** Born Jul 26, 1950, Detroit, MI; son of Jacob M and Antoinette T Howard; children: Adanna Nekesa. **Educ:** Highland Pk Community Col, Highland Pk, Mich, attended 1969; Univ Detroit, Detroit, Mich, BA, 1974, grad studies, 1975; Am Soc Indust Security, Detroit Chap, cert, 1983; Real Estate Inst, Sch Continuing Educ, NY Univ, New York, NY, Cert, 1984. **Career:** New Detroit Inc, Detroit, Mich, admin serv asst, 1968-69; City Detroit Model Neighborhood Agency, Detroit, Mich, community organizer, 1969-71; Wayne Co Community Col, Detroit, Mich, instr, 1972-80; Wayne Co Circuit Ct, Probation Dept, Detroit, Mich, social serv worker, 1974-75; Wholesale Distrib Ctr, Citizens Dist Coun, Detroit, Mich, adminr, 1976-80; Eastern Mkt, proj dir; Seven Mile-Livernois, proj dir; Millender Ctr proj, proj dir; Detroit Econ Growth Corp, develop assoc & proj dir, 1980-85; Wayne State Univ, Dept Africana Studies, asst prof, 1980; TV/Radio Host, "Back to Back", Detroit Pub TV/WQBH AM 1400, dir, community & proj develop, 1992; Comcast Cable Commun Inc, area dir, corp affairs, currently. **Orgs:** Bd mem, Big Bros/Big Sisters, 1997; secy, bd dir, Cent Educ Network, Chicago, Ill, 1996-97; chmn, Detroit Cable Commun Comt, 1994-; chmn, Friends African Art, 1988-90; trustee, Detroit Inst Arts, 1988-90; Move Detroit Forward, 1980-; Arab-Am Community Ctr; bd govs, Nat Acad TV Arts & Scis, 2001-; bd mem, Access; Pres's Regional Adv Bds; bd trustee, Madonna univ; bd trustee mem, Detroit Jazz Festival. **Honors/Awds:** Numerous honors & awards including Spirit of Detroit Award, 1978; Afro-American Benefactor's Award, 1980; Crime Prevention Citation, 1982; Mayor's Award of Merit, 1982; Wayne County School District Merit Awards, 1984, 1985; Michigan Legislative Resolution, 1986; Michigan Senate Tribute, 1986; Certificate of Appreciation, Literacy Vols Am, 1986; Certificate of Appreciation, Greater Detroit Community Outreach Ctr, 1986; Carter G Woodson Award, Educator of the Year, Creative Educ Concepts, 1987; Certificate of National Recognition, 7 Mile-Livernois Project, US Dept Housing & Urban Develop, 1986; Arab Community Center for Economic & Social Services Award, 1990; Haitian American Award, 1990; Black Educator of the Year, US Peace Corps, 1990; author, Arab-American Directory, 1990; Spirit of Detroit Award, 1991; Mich Minority Women's Network, Man of the Year, 1993; Public Television's Gold Award, 1993; Commitment of Youth Award, W K Kellogg Found, 1994; Emmy nominations, 1995, 1996 & 1997; Testimonial Resolution, City of Detroit, 1999; Spirit of Detroit Award, 1999. **Home Addr:** 1300 E Lafayette Blvd Suite 109-110, Detroit, MI 48207-2918, **Home Phone:** (313)259-4546. **Business Addr:** Area Director of Corporate Affairs, Comcast Cable Communications Inc, 12775 Lyndon St, Detroit, MI 48227, **Business Phone:** (313)646-4202.

**SMITH, GERALDINE T.**
Social worker. **Personal:** Born Sep 14, 1918, Cave Spring, GA; daughter of Dallas C and Cora L Johnson Turner; children: Karen T Watts (deceased). **Educ:** Hunter Col, BA, 1943; Columbia Univ, MA, 1947; Smith Col, Sch Social Work, MSS, 1952. **Career:** Social worker (retired); Bur Child Welfare, social worker, 1952-57; Pittsburgh Pub Schs, social worker, 1957-58; Western Psychiat Inst, sr psychiat social worker, 1958-68; Univ Pittsburgh, asst prof, 1965-87; Neighborhood Psychiat Unit & Coun Serv, 1966-68; Pittsburgh Model Cities Agency, consult, 1968-69; Western Psychiat Inst, Univ Pittsburgh, dir social work, 1968-75; Pittsburgh Model City Agency, consult, 1968-69; Dixmont State Hosp Social Serv, consult, 1973-74; CMH/MRC, asst dir educ, 1975-78; Western Psychiat Inst & Clin Hill Satellite Ctr, Western Psych Inst, Univ Pittsburgh, dir, 1979-87. **Orgs:** Secy adv bd, New OpportunitiesAging, 1984; Nat Asn Social Workers; Acad Cert Social Workers; Coun Social Work Educ; Nat Conf Social Welfare; dir, Soc Hosp Social Work; United Ment Health Allegheny County; bd mem, Bethesda Ctr, 1988-94. **Home Addr:** 1710 Swissvale Ave, Pittsburgh, PA 15221, **Home Phone:** (412)371-9398.

**SMITH, GLORIA DAWN**
Hospital administrator, vice president (organization). **Personal:** Born Oct 2, 1947, Jones, LA; daughter of Alvin and Hazel; children: Lawonda & Orlando. **Educ:** Univ San Francisco, BS, orgn leadership, 1982; Golden Gate Univ, MBA, 1985. **Career:** Real Estate Consult, 1984-87; Stanford Univ, human resources mgr, 1968-85; C's Hosp Stanford, dir personnel, 1985-88; Woodland Mem Hosp, vpres human resources, 1988-91; C's Hosp, Oakland Calif, dir personnel, 1991-93; Univ Health Ctr Tyler, vpres human resources, 1993-; Ins & Human Resources Consult Serv, owner, agt, 2004. **Orgs:** Bur Nat Affirs Forum, 1995-97; Parkinsonian, Tyler, TX, 1994-; Child Care Comn City Woodland, Ca, 1990-91; bd dir, YMCA, Woodland, Calif, 1989-91; Neighborhood Housing, Menlo Pk, Calif, pres, 1980-82; Nat Asn Advan Colored People, 1995; Dem Cent Comt, 1990-91; Prof Woman Asn, 1995. **Home Addr:** 516 Denise St, Saginaw, TX 76179, **Home Phone:** (817)306-0131. **Business Addr:** Assistant Director, University of Texas, Health Center, PO Box 2003, Houston, TX 75710, **Business Phone:** (903)877-7748.

**SMITH, GREG**
Radio host. **Personal:** Born Mar 25, 1964, Bay Springs, MS; son of Jim and Adelia Barnes; married Terri Nealy; children: Greg Jr, Donovan & Berkeley. **Educ:** Ariz State Univ, BA, broadcasting, 1986. **Career:** Wall St J; New York Times; New York Times Mag; CBS News; Nat Pub Radio; KTAR/K-Lite Radio, dir res & sales prom, 1987-92; AccessLife.com, consult, 2000-01; On a Rol Commun, radio prog, founder & host, 1992-2006, A Roll Commun, host, founder, 2003-; Talk Radio Life & Disability, prof speaker, host & founder, 2003-; Ariz State Univ, Strength Coach, host, 2013; Coun Except C, 2013; Phoenix Union High Sch Dist, 2014; Am Asn State Hwy & Transp Officials, 2014; Kennesaw State Univ, 2014; WebTalkRadio.net, host, 2014-. **Orgs:** Nat Asn Black Journalists; Pres's Comm Employ People with Disabilities, Communs Subcomt; Media Adv Bd, Am Asn People Disabilities; bd dir, Nat Asn Alcohol, Drugs & Disabilities Inc; Nat Speakers Asn, 2002; Omega Psi Phi Fraternity Inc. **Honors/Awds:** Exceptional American, Nat Liberty Mus; Twenty Leaders Award in the Disability Community, Access Ctr for Independent Living, 20 Yrs, 2000; Second Place Award for Commentary about the movie Toy Story 2, Pub Radio News Dirs Inc, 2000. **Business Addr:** Founder, Host, On A Roll Communications, 3625 Perryman Rd, Ocean Springs, MS 39566, **Business Phone:** (877)331-7563.

**SMITH, DR. GREGORY ALLEN**
Gynecologist, obstetrician. **Personal:** Born Sep 12, 1952, Detroit, MI; married Jennifer; children: Amber & Camille. **Educ:** Mich State Univ, BS, 1974; Howard Univ, MD, 1978. **Career:** Wayne State Univ, resident, 1978-82; AMI Doctors Med Ctr, chief, 1987-88; Assoc Women's Care Tulsa, pres; Atlanta Med Ctr, physician; pvt pract, currently. **Orgs:** Nat & Am Med Assoc, Okla State Med Soc, Tulsa Co Med Soc; adv bd, Sickle Cell Anemia Res Found, Okla. **Honors/Awds:** Diplomate, Am Bd of Obstetrics-Gynecology. **Business Addr:** Physician, Private Practitioner, 315 Blvd NE Suite 336, Atlanta, GA 30312, **Business Phone:** (404)522-4888.

**SMITH, DR. REV. GREGORY ROBESON, SR.**
Clergy, executive, association executive. **Personal:** Born Sep 22, 1947, Philadelphia, PA; son of William Drew Robeson and Maria Louisa Bustill; married Brenda Lee Galloway; children: Gregory Robeson Jr, Avery Vaughn & Whitney DeAnna. **Educ:** Dewitt Clinton High Sch, Bronx, NY, dipl, 1954; Livingstone Col, BA, 1969; Univ Wis, MBA, mkt & finance, 1972; Union Theol Sem, MA, divinity, 1985; Columbia Univ; PhD higher educ admin & finance; PhD ministries. **Career:** Lever Bros, prod mgr, 1975-77; Revlon Inc, mkt mgr, Group I Classic Revlon, mkt mgr, 1977-80; Polished Ambers, 1977-79; Classic Revlon, 1979-80; Joseph E Seagram & Sons Inc, nat prod mgr, 1980-82; Nat Coun Churches, Church World Serv, dir disaster relief, 1983-88; Mt Hope AME Zion Church, pastor, 1986-; Antonovich Inc, dir mkt, 1988-91; African Develop Found, pres & chief exec officer, 1991-95; Mother AME Zion Church, sr pastor, currently. **Orgs:** Omega Phi Psi Fraternity Inc; Beta Alpha Alpha Chap; dep grand master, Prince Hall Masons; presiding pres, Elder's Coun; pres, Prince Hall Temple Assocs Inc; exec comt, Connectional Budget Bd; exec secy, AME Zion Church Ministers & Lay Asn; grand master, Most Worshipful Prince Hall Grand Lodge, 2009-. **Honors/Awds:** No 17, Holy Royal Arch Masons, King David Consistory; No 3, ASSR 33 Degree Mason; Delegate, 14th Session of the World Methodist; White House Fellow, Nat Finalist, 1976. **Special Achievements:** First African American in New York State to be selected by a major political party as their mayoral candidate. Author, thesis: "Ghetto as a Marketing Segment, "; "Towards a more Perfect Union between the AME, AME Zion, and CME Denominations, "; AME Zion Church, youngest person in history, elected in 1976; One of the Outstanding Men of America, The History Makers, 2007. **Home Addr:** 5 Stanley Rd, White Plains, NY 10605-2909, **Home Phone:** (914)428-9400. **Business Addr:** Senior Pastor, The Mother AME Zion Church, 140 6 W 137th St, Harlem, NY 10030, **Business Phone:** (212)234-1545.

**SMITH, GUY LINCOLN**
Executive. **Personal:** Born Mar 16, 1949, New Orleans, LA; son of Guy Lincoln III and Laura Louise Orr; married Marjorie Whaley Russell; children: Abigail, Guy & Laura. **Educ:** Bowling Green State Univ, attended 1968; Univ Tenn, attended 1970; Am Univ, attended 1971; US Dept Agr Grad Sch, attended 1971. **Career:** Knoxville Jour, reporter, 1967-68, asst city ed, 1968-70; Appalachian Regional Comn, Wash, DC, asst dir info, 1970, dir info, 1970-72; City Knoxville, press secy, 1972-76; Miller Brewing Co, Milwaukee, WI, mgr corp affairs, 1976-79; Philip Morris Co Inc, vpres corp affairs, 1975-92, sr pub rels, pub rels officer, 1992; Hill & Knowlton Int Pub Rels, chief operating officer, 1992-93; Smith Worldwide Inc, 1994-96; Pres Clinton, spec adv, 1998-99; Hawthorn Group, 1999-2000; Diageo, exec vpres, 2000-05; Intellicheck Mobilisa Inc, independent dir, chmn compensation comt & mem audit comt, 2005-; Fire Dept New York, hon battalion chief; Tobacco Itute, Commun Comt, chair; Seven-Up Co, St Louis, Mo, vpres corp affair. **Orgs:** Bd dir, Laumeir Int; bd dir, Jackie Robinson Found; bd dir, Opera Theatre St Louis; chmn, Barrier Island Trust; bd advisor, Mt Vernon, George Wash's home outside Wash; chmn, Compensation Comt, Intelli-Check Inc; Corp Governance & Nominating Comt, Intelli-Check Inc. **Honors/Awds:** Excellence in News Writing Award, William Randolph Hearst Found, 1970; Award for Communication Excellence to Black Audiences, Black Commun Inst, 1982. **Business Addr:** Independent Director, Chairman, Intellicheck Mobilisa Inc, 100 Jericho Quadrangle Suite 202, Jericho, NY 11753, **Business Phone:** (516)992-1900.

**SMITH, GWENDOLYN ILOANI**
Association executive, president (organization), chief executive officer. **Educ:** Colgate Univ, BA; Univ Hartford, MBA. **Career:** Aetna Inc Investment Dept, managing dir; Conn Mutual, mgt trainee; investment dept, investment analyst; Smith Whiley & Co, chief investment officer, pres & chief exec officer, currently. **Orgs:** Life mem, Nat Asn Advan Colored People; Chairperson, Audit Comt; bd mem, Nat Asn Investment Com; bd mem, Conn; bd mem, Country Roads Bd Car Club Inc; Smith Whileys Exec Comt; chmn, Firms Investment Comt; Aetnas Investment Comt; founding mem, Smith Whiley; Aetna's Investment Comt; bd mem, Nat Asn Advan Colored People Spec Contrib Fund & Crisis mag; Fed Res Bd; trustee, Univ Conn Found; bd trustee, Colgate Univ; emer trustee, currently. **Business Addr:** President, Chief Executive officer, Smith Whiley & Co, 242 Trumbull St 8th Fl, Hartford, CT 06103, **Business Phone:** (860)548-2513.

**SMITH, H. RUSSELL**
Entrepreneur, lawyer, founder (originator). **Personal:** Born Oct 8, 1957, Detroit, MI; son of Oliver H and Mildred A. **Educ:** Univ Mich, BBA, 1979; Northwestern Univ, MBA, MM, 1983, JD, 1983. **Career:** Dykema, Gossett, atty, 1983-85; Burroughs crp & Unisys, atty, 1985-87; Growth Funding Ltd, atty, consult, 1987-88; H Russell Smith Esq, atty, 1988-89; Lewis, White & Clay PC, sr atty, 1989-92; Blacks Factor Inc, pres & founder, 1992-; Venture Law PLLC, atty. **Orgs:** Wolverine Bar Asn; Detroit Bar Asn; Mich Bar Asn. **Business Addr:** Attorney, Venture Law PLLC, 18660 Mendota St, Detroit, MI 48221-1912, **Business Phone:** (313)862-7287.

**SMITH, REV. HAROLD GREGORY**
Clergy. **Personal:** Born Chicago, IL; son of Harold and Mable Lee Cline Jenkins. **Educ:** Bradley Univ, BS, music & elem educ, 1974; Nashotah House Theol Sem, MDiv, 1980. **Career:** Am Nat Red Cross, Wash, DC, spec asst to nat dir youth serv progs, 1974-76; US Pres Exec Off, staff writer, 1976-77; Church Holy Cross, rector, 1980-85; St Simon Episcopal Church, rector, 1985-88; St Simon Cyrene, rector, 1988-90; St Timothy Episcopal Church, rector, 1990-93; Church Holy Redeemer, rector, 1993-; Church St Luke, rector, currently. **Orgs:** Bd mem, Rochester Soc Prev Cruelty C, 1985-88; bd mem, Ore-Leopold Day Care ctr, 1988-90; Judicial Process Comn; bd mem, Bishop Sheen Ecumenical Housing Found; bd mem, Episcopal Church Home; bd mem, Am Cancer Soc, Rochester Chap; bd mem, Am Heart Asn, Rochester Chap; vol, Proj Open Hand; chair, Pl Ministry; Chaplain, Col State House Representatives; econ adv bd, comnr, Denver City. **Honors/Awds:** Honorary canon of the Anglican cathedral, Accra, Ghana. **Home Addr:** , Philadelphia, PA 19019. **Business Addr:** Rector, St Luke's Episcopal Church, 5421 Germantown Ave, Philadelphia, PA 19144, **Business Phone:** (215)844-8544.

**SMITH, HAROLD TELIAFERRO, JR.**
Lawyer. **Personal:** Born Apr 10, 1947, Miami, FL; son of Harold and Mary; children: Katrell & Talia. **Educ:** Fla A&M Univ, BS, math, 1968; Univ Miami Law Sch, JD, law, 1973. **Career:** Dade County Pub Defenders, asst pub defender, 1973-76, atty, 1976-77; Dade County Attys Off; Long & Smith PA, pract atty, 1977-81; HT Smith PA, founder, 1981-, atty, 2001, pres, currently. **Orgs:** Kappa Alpha Psi Fraternity, 1983-; chair, Coalition Free S Africa, 1985-90; exec comt, Miami Dade Br, Nat Asn Advan Colored People, 1990-; co-spokesperson, Boyscott Miami Campaign, 1990-93; co-chair, MiamiPartners Progress, 1993-; secy, Inroads/Miami, 1993-; Community Partnership Homeless,

1993-94; pres, Nat Bar Asn, 1994-; founding pres, Black Lawyers Asn Dade County; Virgil Hawkins Fla Chap Nat Bar Asn. **Honors/Awds:** Service Award, Nat Conf Black Lawyers, 1991; Charles Whited Spirit of Excellence Award, Miami Herald, 1993; Best Lawyers in America, 1995-96; Bronze Star (valor), AUS; Vietnam Service, AUS; Honorable Discharge, AUS, 1970; Pioneer Award; Top Scholars Award. **Special Achievements:** Wrote numerous articles for publication & gave hundreds of speeches & seminars. He is listed in The Best Lawyers in America, Florida Superlawyers & Law & Leading American Attorneys. Also, the National Law Journal has recognized H. T. as one of the top trial lawyers in America; First African-american Assistant Public Defender &Then As The County's First African-american Assistant County Attorney. **Business Addr:** Professor, Director of the Trial Advocacy Program, Florida International University, 11200 SW 8th St Rafael Diaz Balart Hall, Miami, FL 33199, **Business Phone:** (305)348-7189.

**SMITH, HEMAN BERNARD, JR.**
Lawyer, educator. **Personal:** Born Aug 20, 1929, Alexandria, LA; son of Heyman and Rosa; married Ina Jean Washington; children: Heman III, Lanie C & Paula Barnes. **Educ:** Univ Md, attended 1960; Univ Pac, McGeorge Sch Law, JD, 1971. **Career:** Smith, Hanna, de Bruin & Yee, Sacto, partner & sr atty, 1971-78; Smith & Yee, Sacto, partner, 1978-84; Smith & Assoc, Sacto CA, sr atty, 1984; Univ Northern Calif, L P Sch Law, Sacto, exec dean & founder, 1988; Univ Northern Calif, L P Sch Law, dean studs; Univ Northern Calif, Lorenzo Patino Law Sch, founder, emer fac, currently. **Orgs:** Bd mem, Am Red Cross, Sacto, 1980-87; Minority Steering Comt Calif Youth Authority, 1985-87; Wiley Man Bar Asn, 1988-; Calif State Bar Asn, 1971-; bd trustee, Sacramento Urban League; Nat Asn Advan Colored People; arbitrator, Sacramento Co Bar Asn Atty Client Dispute. **Home Addr:** 6370 Havenside Dr, Sacramento, CA 95831-1502, **Home Phone:** (916)422-6296. **Business Addr:** Emeritus Faculty, University of Northern California, 1012 J St, Sacramento, CA 95814, **Business Phone:** (916)441-4485.

**SMITH, DR. HENRY THOMAS**
Consultant, physician. **Personal:** Born Mar 31, 1937, Portsmouth, VA; son of Julius; married Diane; children: Robert & Alicia. **Educ:** Howard Univ, BS, 1957; Univ Rochester, Sch med & dent, MD, 1961. **Career:** Minn Gen Hosp, internship, 1961-62; Hennepin County Gen Hosp, med resident, 1964-67, fel, 1967-69; Hennepin Co Med Ctr, asst dir, chronic dialysis unit, 1967-69; Pilot City Med Ctr, physician, 1969-71; Mod Med Jour, assoc ed, 1970-72; Geriatrics Jour, abstr ed, 1970-72; Pk Nicollet Med Ctr, physician, 1971-94, med dir hypertension mgt prog, chief nephrology; Nephrology Mod Med Jour, consult, 1975-77; Univ Minn, Sch Med, from assoc clin prof to clin prof, 1975-95; Hennepin Fac Assocs, HFA Div Internal Med, dir, 1994-, clin med dir, 1996-, chief, currently. **Orgs:** Sister Kenny Inst, 1972-75; Minn Heart Asn, 1974-76; pres, Nat Kidney Found Upper Midwest, 1982-84; Minneapolis Soc Internal Med; Nat Med Asn; charter mem, Am Soc Hypertension; fel Am Col Physicians; bd dir, Am Heart Asn, Minn Affil; Hennepin County Med Soc; adv bd, Nat Kidney Found Upper Midwest; chief, HFA Div internal med, Hennepin Fac Assocs; exec comt, Hennepin County Med Ctr, 1994-97; bd gov, Univ Minn Health Syst, 1994-96; bd trustee, Minn Med Asn; bd dir, Turning Pt Community Health Care Ctr, 1997-99; AMA; Am Soc Internal Med; Minn Asn Black Physicians; Minn State Med Asn. **Honors/Awds:** Commanding General Award for Medical Service, 1964; Cert Internal Med, 1969, Nephrol, 1974; Phi Beta Kappa; Best Doctors in America: Central Region, 1996-97; Award of Excellence, Communities Color, 1997; President's Award, Minn Med Asn, 1999; Best Doctors in America, 2000; Laureate Award, ACP-ASIM, Minn chap, 2001; designated specialist in hypertension, ASH, 2001; Minority Service Award, Minn Asn, 2002; Top Doctors list: Minneapolis, St. Paul Mag annual survey, 2003. **Special Achievements:** Author, Modern Medicine Practice Guide, VIAGRA: Study to Assess the Effectiveness and Safety of Viagra in Men with Erectile Dysfunction Who Are Taking 2 or More Blood Pressure Medications. **Home Addr:** 6717 Cahill Rd, Edina, MN 55439. **Business Addr:** Medical Director, Chief, Hennepin Faculty Associates, 825 S 8th St Suite 206, Minneapolis, MN 55404, **Business Phone:** (612)347-7534.

**SMITH, DR. HERMAN BRUNELL, JR.**
Executive, consultant, association executive. **Personal:** Born Feb 12, 1927, Mansfield, OH; married Annie Mae Lavender; children: Gregory B & Terri Lynne. **Educ:** Knoxville Col, Knoxville, TN, BA, 1948; Univ Wis, Madison, WI, MS, 1955, PhD, 1960. **Career:** Consultant (retired); Southern Educ Found, Atlanta, Ga, consult, 1966-68; Nat Asn Land Grant Cols, Wash, DC, dir, 1968-74; Univ Ark, Pine Bluff, Ark, pres, 1974-81; Atlanta Univ, Atlanta, Ga, vpres, 1981-82; Kettering Found, Dayton, Ohio, consult, 1982-89; Univ Ga, Athens, Ga, consult to pres, 1985-88; Jackson State Univ, Jackson, Miss, interim pres, 1991-92; Cent State Univ, interim pres, 1995-96. **Orgs:** Vpres, W End Rotary Club; pres, Knoxville Col Nat Alumni Asn, 1988-91. **Honors/Awds:** Distinguished Alumnus, Univ Wisconsin Alumni Asn, 1988; Outstanding Service Award, City Knoxville, TN, 1986; Outstanding Service Award, Sigma Pi Phi, 1986; Outstanding Service Award, Phi Delta Kappa, Atlanta Univ, 1989; Doctor of Laws Degree, Stillman Col, Tuscaloosa, Alabama, 1991; School Education Alumni Achievement Award, Univ Wisconsin, Madison, 1992; Distinguished Graduate Award, Univ Wisconsin Sch Educ, 1992. **Home Addr:** 3380 Benjamin E Mays Dr SW, Atlanta, GA 30311-2238, **Home Phone:** (404)696-6240.

**SMITH, HOWLETT P.**
Musician. **Personal:** Born Feb 28, 1933, Phoenix, AZ; son of Howard Lowell and Josephine Cox; married Judith Celestin; children: Juliette, Rachel, Mark, April, Sandra & Peter. **Educ:** Univ Ariz, BM, 1955. **Career:** Composer, pianist, singer, arranger, vocal coach, music teacher, whistler, performer & instr; Inter-Cult Awarness Prog, LA Unifiead Sch dist, church pianist, organist & numerous pub appearances; lectr & demonstrations concerning use jazz in church; Songs: Me & Bessie, dir; A Candle in the Dark, composer; Raven Rec, pianist, currently; Piano & Vocals: "Funny Side Up"; "Ugly Woman"; "Sin Around Here"; "Pennies From Heaven"; "Gail, All About Love"; "Equal Opportunity Lover"; "Chitlins in the Whitehouse"; "Ebonically"; "He Sho' Did Preach"; "Are We Havin' Fun Yet?"; "Truth; Gender Bender Blues"; "Let's Go Where The Grass Is Greener"; "It's The Last Day of Summer"; "Little Alter Boy"; "Shoes"; "Would Anybody Care?"; "Almost Human"; "Tired of Bein' White"; "You Punched A Hole In My Dreams"; "I Used To Be Colored"; "Shoes & Laughin' To Keep From Cryin". **Orgs:** Life mem, Psi Mu Alpha; Univ Ariz Alumni Asn; Kappa Psi; Newman Club; Camino Col Fac. **Honors/Awds:** Named Mr Newmanite, Univ Ariz, 1955; Hall of Fame. **Special Achievements:** Composer of popular & religious works, numerous recording tapes/CDs, featured performer at Bob Burns Restaurant, Santa Monica, CA, for 20years, listed in April 1994 issue of LA Mag as "One of the reasons toremain in LA", composer of special masses, musicals, and cantatas; Appearances in TV and movies, The Sch for the Deaf & Blind, Tueson, AZ, 2002, awarded a Scroll of Recognition from the Los Angeles County Bd of Supvrs for cultural & humanitarian contributions to the greater Los Angeles area community, 2002. **Home Addr:** 3525 Jasmine Ave Apt, Los Angeles, CA 90034-4933. **Business Addr:** Pianist, Raven Records, 1821 Wilshire Blvd, Santa Monica, CA 90403.

**SMITH, DR. IAN K.**
Physician, journalist, writer. **Personal:** Born Jul 15, 1969, Danbury, CT; married Shelby. **Educ:** Harvard Col, BA, 1992; Columbia Univ, MS, 1993; Dartmouth Med Sch, MD; Chicago Univ, Pritzker Sch Med. **Career:** Albert Einstein Col, Med Hosp, surg intern, orthop; NBC News Network News Channel 4, NY, med corresp; New York Daily Men's Health Mag, med columnist; WNBC's Today, NY, reporter; News week Mag, med columnist; VH1's Celebrity Fit Club, med/diet expert, currently; NPR's Tavis Smiley Show & nationally Syndicated View, commentator, currently; Celebrity Fit Club, med diet expert, currently; 50 Million Pound Challenge, founder, 2010-; Author: Extreme Fat Smash Diet; The 4 Day Diet; The Fat Smash Diet; The Blackbird Papers, 2005; Dr Ian Smith's Guide to Med Websites; The Take-Control Diet; Happy, 2010; Broadcasting: The View; The Tyra Banks Show; Larry King Live; Anderson Cooper 3600; Showbiz Tonight; The Verdict with Dan Abrams. **Orgs:** Bd mem, New York Mission Soc; bd mem, Cancer Res Found Am; bd mem, Am Coun Exercise; bd mem, N Shore-Long Island Jewish Res Inst; bd mem, Henry H Kessler Found, Bldg with Bks; Nat Acad Tv Arts & Sci; New York Coun Humanities. **Honors/Awds:** Nat Acad TV Arts & Sci, 2001; The Blackbird Papers BCALA fiction Honor Book Award winner, 2005; Trauma: Life in the ER, NY Asn Black Journalists; BCALA Fiction Honor Book Award Winner, 2005. **Special Achievements:** Featured in several publications including: People, Ebony, Cosmopolitan, JET, Univ Chicago Med on the Midway. **Home Addr:** 235 E 40th St, New York, NY 10112. **Business Addr:** Medical Contributor, The View, PO Box 765, New York, NY 10150.

**SMITH, IRVIN MARTIN**
Radio host, football player. **Personal:** Born Oct 13, 1971, Trenton, NJ. **Educ:** Univ Notre Dame, mkt. **Career:** Football player (retired), radio host; New Orleans Saints, tight end, 1993-97; San Francisco 49ers, tight end, 1998; Cleveland Browns, tight end, 1999; EZ Sports Talk, co-host, currently. **Honors/Awds:** Rookie of the Year, 1993. **Business Addr:** Co-Host, EZ Sports Talk, 18402 N 19th Ave Suite 236, Phoenix, AZ 85023, **Business Phone:** (623)329-1911.

**SMITH, REV. DR. J. ALFRED, SR.**
Clergy, college teacher. **Personal:** Born May 19, 1931, Kansas City, MO; son of Amy; married Joanna Goodwin; children: J Alfred Jr, Craig, Anthony, Amy Jones, Shari Rigmaiden & Ronald Craig. **Educ:** Western Baptist Col, BS, elem educ, 1952; Mo Sch Relig, Univ Mo, 1959; Pac Sch Relig, attended 1962; Inter-Baptist Theol Ctr, Church & Community, MTh, 1966; Am Baptist Sem W, MTh, 1972; Golden Gate Baptist Theol Sem, DMin, 1975; ABSW, DHL, 1990. **Career:** Lic minister, 1948-; ordained minister, 1951-; Allen Temple Baptist Church, sr pastor, 1970-2006, pastor emer, 2006-; Am Baptist Sem W, actg dean, 1975-87, prof, 1975-; Grad Theol Sem, prof; Fuller Theol Sem, vis prof, currently; Hampton Univ, lectr, 1979; Fuller Sem, instr, 2009; Gardner-Webb Univ, scholar residence. **Orgs:** Pes, Baptist Pastors & Ministers Conf, Oakland & Easy Bay, 1986-; pres, Progressive Nat Baptist Conv, 1986-88; bd dir, Metrop YMCA; bd bir, Nat Coun Churches; bd dir, Cong Nat Black Churches; Bread World; Nat Conf Black Seminarians; Howard Thurman Educ Trust; Bishop Col Renaissance Campaign; adv bd, Howard Univ Sch Divinity; adv bd, United Theol Sem; adv bd, Univ Calif, Berkeley, county; rep, Am Baptist Churches USA; founding chairperson, Bay Area Black United Fund; AFRICARE; APA; pres & actg dean, Am Baptist Sem W.f; Ministers & Missionaries Benefit Bd; pres, Am Baptist Churches W. **Honors/Awds:** Outstanding Citizen of the Year, Oakland Tribune; Martin Luther King International Chapel, Morehouse Col; Prince of Hall, Free & Accepted Masons; Man of the Year Award, Golden West Mag, LA, 1976; Award for Outstanding Accomplishments, Grass Roots Level New Oakland Community, 1976; Man of the Year Award, Sun-Reporter & Metro Reporter, 1976; Recognition Distinguished Service, Boy Scouts Am, 1986; Bishop Col Renaissance Campaign; Earl Lect, Pac Sch Relig, 1989; Hay Lect, Drake Univ, 1989; Addressed United Nations S African Apartheid, 1989; bd mem, CA Bd of Gov meeting, 2009; Most Influential Black Americans, Ebony Mag; Lifetime Achievement Award, Greenlining Inst; Humanitarian of the Year Award, E Bay Area Agency C; Agape Award, Women's Ministry Shiloh Baptist Church; Gandhi Ikeda Award, Morehouse Col. **Special Achievements:** Co-author, works include: Giving to a Giving God: Basic Bible Sermons; The Study Bible, Holman Bible Publishing; Preaching As a Social Act; Guidelines for Effective Urban Ministry; listed in Ebony Magazine as one of the fifteen greatest African American preachers in America; He is the author of over fifteen books including "On the Jericho Road" & served as editor of "No Other Help I Know: Sermons on Prayer & Spirituality", & "Outstanding Black Sermons", both from Judson Press; Elevated 33rd Degree; Three awards named in honor. **Home Addr:** 8453 Aster Ave, Oakland, CA 94605, **Home Phone:** (510)569-0262. **Business Addr:** Emeritus Pastor, Allen Temple Baptist Church, 8501 International Blvd, Oakland, CA 94621, **Business Phone:** (510)544-8910.

**SMITH, DR. J. CLAY, JR.**
Lawyer, government official, educator. **Personal:** Born Apr 15, 1942, Omaha, NE; son of John Clay Sr and Emily V Williams; married Patti Jones; children: Stager, Michael Laurel, Michelle Lori & Eugene Douglas. **Educ:** Creighton Univ Omaha, Nebr, AB, 1964; Howard Law Sch, Wash, DC, JD, 1967; George Washington Univ Law Sch, Wash, DC, LLM, 1970, SJD, 1977. **Career:** Educator, lawyer, government offical (retired); AUS Judge Advocates Gen Corp, capt lawyer, 1967-71; Arent Fox Kintner Plotkin & Kahn Wash, DC, assoc, 1971-74; Fed Commun Comn, Cable TV Bur, dep chief, 1974-76, assoc gen coun; Fed Communs Comn, assoc gen counr, 1976-77; Equal Employ Opportunity Comn, us comnr, 1977-82, actg chmn, 1981-82; Howard Univ Sch Law, prof law, 1982-86, dean & prof law, 1986-88, prof, 1988-2004. **Orgs:** NE Bar Assoc, 1967; Howard Law Sch Alumni Asn, 1967-; Dist Columbia Bar, 1968; pres bd dir, Wash Bar Asn, 1970; US Supreme Ct, 1973; adv pres, Nat Bar Asn, 1973-; Nat Asn Advan Colored People, 1975-; Urban League, 1975-; pres, founder, Wash Bar Asn, 1978; nat pres mem, Fed Bar Asn, 1979; Utility Spec Pub Serv Comm, 1982-84; Am Bar Asn, 1982-; mem ed bd, ABA Compleat Lawyer, 1984-87; Adv Comm, DC Bar Exam; bd mem, Nat Lawyers Club; planning comm Task Force Black Males, Am Psyh Asn, 1986-90; Am Law Inst, 1986-88; chairperson, Nat Bar Asn Comm Hist Black Lawyers; legal coun Elderly Policy Bd, 1986-88; Verizon Consumer Adv Bd, 2000-; dir, Nat Lawyers Comt Civil Rights Under Law; Clinton-Gore Presidential Transition Team. **Honors/Awds:** Ollie May Cooper Award, 1986; C Francis Strad ford Award, 1986; Outstanding Alumni Achievement Award, Howard Univ, 1981; Outstanding Alumni Achievement Awards, Creighton Univ, 1989; Outstanding Alumni Achievement Awards, George Wash Univ, 1990; National Book Award, Nat Conf Black Political Scientist, 1995; Distinguished Faculty Author Award, Pres the Univ, 2001 & 2002; Political Science Book Award. **Special Achievements:** First African American Governor of Boys State NE and nation in 1959, has published Fed Bar Assn Natl Pres Messages, Fed Bar News, CIVICS LEAP, Law Reason & Creativity, Mgng Multi ethnic Multi racial Workforce Criminal, Chronic Alcoholism Lack of Mens Rea A Dfns Pblc Intoxication 13 Howard Law Journal, An Investment in a New Century, Wash Afro Am; The Black Bar Assn & Civil Rights, A Black Lawyers Response to the Fairmont Papers, Memoriam: Clarence Clyde Ferguson, Jr, Harvard Law Rev, Forgotten Hero:Charles H Houston, Harvard Law Rev, Justice & Juris prudence & The Black Lawyer, Notre Dame Law Rev, Emancipation: The Making of The Black Lawyer, 1844-1944, 1993; Rebels in Law: Voices in History of Black Women Lawyers, 1998, Served on the transition team of president Clinton and Vice president Pgore, 1992; first African American elected as national president, Fed Bar Asn in 1980-81; Supreme Justice: The Writings and Speeches of Thurgood Marshall, 2003, editor; First black lawyer to lead a national white bar association in the nations history; He was the first black appointed to a staff policy position in the history of the Federal Communications Commission. He is the author of "one hundred year study of black lawyers : Emancipation: The Making Of The Black Lawyer". **Business Addr:** Director, National Lawyers Committee for Civil Rights Under Law, 1401 New York Ave NW Suite 400, Washington, DC 20005, **Business Phone:** (202)662-8600.

**SMITH, J. THOMAS**
Lawyer, broadcaster, consultant. **Personal:** Born Wayne, MI; son of Marjorie and Louis. **Educ:** Univ State New York, BS, lib studies, commun, 1988; Vt Col, Norwich Univ, MA, coun psychol, 1988; Univ San Jose, Costa Rica, PhD, behav sci, 1995; Tex Southern Univ, Thurgood Marshall Sch Law, JD, 1999; Calif Coast Univ, PsyD, 2005. **Career:** Houston Community Col Syst, assoc campus dir, instr, 1982-87; Mind Sci Primer, auth, 1986; City Univ Los Angeles Sch Law, interim dean, 1989-90; Atlanta Metrop Col, 1990-91; Columbia & HCA Spring Br Med Ctr, dir John Lucas Treat & Rec Ctr, 1991-93; Tex Southern Univ, Sch Cont Ed, adj prof, 1993-97; Prairie View A & M Univ, dir coun & multicultural servs, 1993-97; "Ask Doctor", NPR Syndicated, "Sisters & Friends", radio prog, 1997-2001; Anderson & Smith, PC, law clerk, 1998-2000; Columist, "Ask Doctor", Majic Mag, KMJQ Com, 1999-2002; gen fed law pract, atty law; Dr. J Thomas Smith & Assoc, ment health consult, 1991-, pres & chief exec officer, 2005-; KMJQ-FM, air talent, 1994-; Tax Defense USA, chief exec officer, 2013-; J Thomas Smith Motivational Speaker, chief motivator, 2015-. **Orgs:** Am Fed TV & Radio Artists, Ethnic Minority Comm, chair, 1983-87; Am Ment Health Counr asn, bd dir, CCMH, liaison, 1993-96; Nat Bd Cert Counors, Exam Comm, 1994-99; Nat Comm Ment Health, bd dir, 1995-96; Phi Alpha Delta Legal Fraternity, 1997-; Nat Asn Alcoholism & Drug Abuse Counors; Screen Actors Guild; State Bar Tex, Law Stud Div, campus dir, 1999-2000; United Clergy Relig Sci; Am Bar asn; Fed Bar asn; Houston Bar asn; Am Immigration Lawyers asn; Fed Commun Bar Asn, 2013-; Am Bar Asn, 2013-. **Honors/Awds:** Black Radio Exclusive, Air Personality of the Year on Pop Radio, 1983; Top 50 Black Attorney, D-Mars.Com Bus J, 2013; Houston Sun Beacons of Light: Men of Valor and Purpose, Houston Sun Newspaper, 2013. **Home Addr:** PO Box 68113, Houston, TX 77268-1113, **Home Phone:** (713)529-9800. **Business Addr:** Attorney, Counselor at Law, Law Offices of J Thomas Smith JD PhD, 11500 Northwest Fwy Suite 280, Houston, TX 77092, **Business Phone:** (877)978-3687.

**SMITH, JADA PINKETT (JADA KOREN PINKETT)**
Songwriter, actor, singer. **Personal:** Born Sep 18, 1971, Baltimore, MD; daughter of Robsol Jr and Adrienne Banfiled; married Will; children: Jaden, Willow & Trey. **Educ:** Baltimore Sch Arts, dance & theatre, 1989; NC Sch Arts. **Career:** TV series: "Moe's World", 1990; "A Different World", 1991-93; "If These Walls Could Talk", 1996; "Maniac Magee", 2003; "Hawthorne", 2009-11; "Gotham", 2014-15; Films: Menace II Society, actress, 1993; The Inkwell, actress, 1994; A Low Down Dirty Shame, actress, 1994; Jason's Lyric, actress, 1994; Demon Knight, actress, 1995; The Nutty Professor, actress, 1996; Set It Off, actress, 1996; Scream 2, actress, 1997; Woo, actress, 1998; Return to Paradise, actress, 1998; Bamboozled, actress, 2000; Kingdom Come, actress, 2001; Ali, actress, 2001; The Matrix Reloaded, actress, 2003; The Matrix Revolutions, actress, 2003; Collateral, actress, 2004; Madagascar, actress, 2005; Reign Over Me, actress, 2007; The Women, 2008; The Human Contract, actress, 2008; Merry Madagascar, 2009; Madagascar 3: Europe's Most Wanted; 2012; Madly Madagascar, 2013; Magic Mike XXL; 2015; Theater roles: August's Wilson's Joe Turner's Come & Gone; The Nutcracker; Carol's Daughter, co-owner; Planet Hollywood, owner, 1998-. **Orgs:** Alpha Kappa Alpha Sorority Inc; co-founder, Will & Jada Smith Family Found. **Business Addr:** Actress, United Talent Agency, 9560 Wilshire Blvd Fl 5, Beverly Hills, CA 90212, **Business Phone:** (310)273-6700.

## SMITH, DR. JAMES ALMER, JR.

Physician, educator. **Personal:** Born May 30, 1923, Montclair, NJ; son of James A and Carrie Elizabeth Moten; married Elsie Brooks; children: James A III, Roger M, Margo A & Melanie K. **Educ:** Howard Univ, BS, 1947, MD, 1948. **Career:** Homer G Phillips Hosp, intern, 1948-49, res psychiat, 1949-51; Wash Univ, child psychiat, 1952-53; Ment Hygiene Clin Group Co, 1953-55; Hartley Salmon Child Guidance Clin, staff psychiat, 1955-60; Children's Serv Conn, 1956-60; Juv Ct, Hartford, consult, 1956-61; Bay State Med Ctr, asst vis psychiat, 1960; Childrens Study Home, consult, 1960; Springfield Child Guidance Clin, assoc psychiatrist, 1960-83; Tufts Sch Med, asst clin prof, 1977; Kolburne Sch New Marlborough, med dir. **Orgs:** Human Rel Comn Springfield, 1961-62; Am Psychiat Asn; fel Am Ortho Psychiat Asn; Bd Negro Cath Scholar Fund, 1980-; Am Asn Psychoanal Physicians Inc; fel Am Soc Psychoanal Physicians, 1987-; Sigma Pi Phi. **Honors/Awds:** American Academic Human Service Award, 1974-75; Community Leaders & Noteworthy Americans Award, 1978; Int Directory Distinguished Psychotherapists, 1981, 1982; Dr Anthony L Brown Award, WW Johnson Ctr, 1987. **Home Addr:** 3000 Falstaff Rd, Springfield, NC 01109, **Home Phone:** (919)250-1500.

## SMITH, DR. JAMES ALMER, III

Psychiatrist. **Personal:** Born May 24, 1950, St. Louis, MO; married Sandra Wright; children: Anthony, Jason & Brian. **Educ:** Howard Univ, BS, 1972, MD, 1976. **Career:** Harlem Hosp Ctr, intern, 1976-77; Walter Reed Army Med Ctr, resident, 1977-80; AUS Ft Bragg, in-patient chief psychologist, 1980-81, out-patient chief psychologist, 1981-82; Cent Prison Hosp, chief psychiatrist; Cent Prison Dept Corrections, staff psychologist, 1982-85, clin dir, 1985-87; Wake Co Alcoholism Treat Ctr, out-patient psychologist, 1983-87; Duke Univ Med Ctr, clin instr psychiat, criminal adj prof, 1989-91; NC Dept Corrections, clin dir ment health; Duke Med Ctr, Dept Psychiat, consult assoc; Univ Nc Chapel Hill, clin adj prof psychiat; pvt pract, currently; Carolina Partners Ment HealthCare PLLC, managing partner, 2005-. **Orgs:** Bd dir, Drug Action Wake Co, 1986-87; pres, La Scruggs Med Soc, 1989-91, 1993-; chair, Healthy Wake Co, 2000; bd dir, Usher bd; bd dir, Cath Social Ministries & Usher Bd; speaker, NC Minority Bus Leader Conf; NC Psychiat Asn; distinguished fel Am Psychol Asn; NC Psychiat Asn. **Home Addr:** 209 Worham Dr, Raleigh, NC 27614. **Business Addr:** Managing Partner, Carolina Partners in Mental HealthCare PLLC, 1055 Dresser Ct, Raleigh, NC 27609, **Business Phone:** (919)876-3130.

## SMITH, JAMES CHARLES

Engineer, computer executive. **Personal:** Born Jul 27, 1936, Winnfield, LA; son of Annie Lee Rush; children: Rodney D, Michael D, Wanda T & Donna M Murphy. **Educ:** Southern Univ A & M Col, BA, 1960; St Mary's Univ, MBA, 1971; GE Mgt Develop Inst, attended 1985. **Career:** AUS, Mil Award Br, chief, 1977-79, Comput Syst Cmd, dir personnel & admin, 1979-81; Gen Elec Co, sr syst engr, 1981-83, mgr, 1983-86; Syst Eng & Mgt Assocs Inc, founder, pres, chief exec officer, 1986-. **Orgs:** Omega Psi Phi Fraternity, KRS, Basielus, 1985-87; INROADS-Greater WashInc, 1991-92; Adv Bd, George Wash Univ, 1992-93; comnr, Va Govs Comt Defense Conversion, 1992; Va Gov's Task Force Workforce, 2000, 1992-93; NASA Minority Bus Resource Adv Coun, 1993-94; bd dir, Va Venture Fund Found, 1993-94; bd dir, DC Math Sci Tech Inst, 1993; Kauffman Found. **Honors/Awds:** Chapter Man of the Year, Omega Psi Phi Fraternity, 1984; Chapter & District Citizen of the Year, Omega Psi Phi Fraternity, 1988, 1990; Mentor of the Year, N Va Minority Bus Asn, 1989; Small Bus of the Year, Defense Comt Agency, 1989; Outstanding Vendor Award, Teledyne Brown Engr, 1989; New Bus of the Year, Fairfax Co Chamber Com, 1990; Jump Start Recognition, Wash Tech Mag, 1990, 1991; Entrepreneur of the Year, Merrill Lynch Inc, Ernst & Young & Wash Bus Jour, 1991; 50 most important African American technologists, Templeton, 2009. **Special Achievements:** Top 10 Fastest Growing Govt Contractors, Govt Comput News, 1989, 1992; First African American to be appointed by Gov L Douglas Wilder to the three member Bd of Vistors, Gunston Hall, home of Geoorge Mason, author of the US Constitution, 1990; Profiled on the CBS local affiliate's TV show "Success Stories", 1991, 1992; Fast 50 Fastest Growing Companies, Wash Tech Mag, 1992-93; Inc 500 Fastest Growing Co, Inc Mag, 1993; Top 100Black Owned Cos in US, Black Enterprise Mag, 1994. **Home Addr:** 5145 Heritage Lane, Alexandria, VA 22311-1327, **Home Phone:** (703)821-5380. **Business Addr:** President, Chief Executive Officer, Systems Engineering Management Associates Inc, 1515 Poydras St Suite 2200, New Orleans, LA 70112-3752, **Business Phone:** (504)299-8288.

## SMITH, JAMES RUSSELL

Government official, air force officer, insurance executive. **Personal:** Born May 2, 1931, Tupelo, MS; married Madie Ola; children: Rickey Young, Robert Young, Anita Young, Bonita Tate, Valeria Wedley & Richard. **Educ:** Jackson State Jr Col, BA, 1979. **Career:** Airforce officer, government official insurance executive (retired); Golden Circle Life Ins Co, salesman, 1972-85. **Orgs:** Pres, Humboldt Chap Nat Asn Advan Colored People, 1975-80; bd mem, Humboldt City Schs, 1982-85. **Home Addr:** 301 S 3rd Ave, Humboldt, TN 38343-3111, **Home Phone:** (731)784-7189.

## SMITH, JAMES TODD. See LL COOL J.

## SMITH, JAMIL

Writer, television producer. **Educ:** University of Pennsylvania, B.A. in English, 1997. **Career:** William Morris Agency, Agent Asst., 1997-02; CNN, Production Asst., 2002-03; HBO Sports, Asst. to the Producer, 2003-04; National Football League, NFL Films Associate Producer, 2004-10; MSNBC's "The Rachel Maddow Show," Segment Producer and Blogger, 2010-12; MSNBC's "Melissa Harris-Perry Show," Segment and Digital Producer, 2012-. **Honors/Awds:** Sports Emmy Award (segment producer), Outstanding Studio Show, Weekly for "Inside the NFL" (HBO), 2005 and (Showtime) 2008; Sports Emmy Award (segment producer), Outstanding Edited Sports Series or Anthology for "Hard Knocks: Training Camp with the Cincinnati Bengals" (HBO), 2009; "The Root" Magazine, The Root 100 Honorees, 2013.

## SMITH, DR. JANE E.

Educational consultant, executive director. **Personal:** Born Jul 27, 1946, Atlanta, GA; children: 2. **Educ:** Spelman Col, BA, sociol; Emory Univ, MA, sociol; Harvard Univ, PhD, social policy anal. **Career:** Spelman Col, asst prof sociol & dir freshman studies, 1975, Ctr Leadership & Civic Engagement, exec dir, 2004-; Atlanta Univ, asst vpres develop; INROADS, Atlanta & Detroit, managing dir, 1981-94; Martin Luther King Ctr Noviolent Social Chg, dir develop, 1991-94; Carter Ctrs Atlanta Proj, dir, 1994-98; Nat Coun Negro Women Inc, pres & chief exe cofficer, 1998-2002; Bus & Prof Women & USA, chief exec officer, 2002. **Orgs:** Delta Air Lines Bd Curators; Am Inst Pub Serv; Us Women's Chamber Com; Nat Judging Panel Nat Women's Hall Fame Inductees; Us Women's Chamber Com; US Chamber Com Comt 100; judge, Lifetime Tv's Lifetime Achievement Awards; bd mem, Alliance Digital Equality & Ga Ctr Child Advocacy; Delta Sigma Theta Sorority Inc; fel Am Coun Educ; baby boomer; Higher Educ Resource Serv; Univ Dc; Un Beijing Plus Five Conf deleg; bd mem, Pub Leadership Educ Network; bd mem, Maynard Jackson Youth Found; Int & Ga Women's Forums; Nat Pk Serv's hon comt. **Business Addr:** Executive Director, Spelman College, 350 Spelman Lane, Atlanta, GA 30314, **Business Phone:** (404)681-3643.

## SMITH, CAPT. JANET K.

Government official, police officer. **Career:** New Castle County Police Dept, police officer, lt, capt, 1973, maj, 1997. **Special Achievements:** First minority to be elevated to the rank of Major, 1996.

## SMITH, JANET MARIA

Publisher. **Personal:** Born Bluefield, WV; daughter of John H and Edith P; children: Tiffany A & Taashan A. **Educ:** Franklin Univ, attended 1987. **Career:** J M Smith Commuss, pres; The Blue Chip Profile Inc, publ & chief exec officer. **Orgs:** Co-chair, regional conf, Columbus Asn Black Journalists, 1992; Nat Asn Mkt Developers; Columbus Urban League; NCP, Columbus. **Special Achievements:** Publisher, Blue Chip Profile, Resource guide for African American, annual, 1991; Founder, Blue Chip Awards, honoring African Americans, 1992. **Home Addr:** 122 Wagnalls Ct, Pickerington, OH 43147, **Home Phone:** (614)834-8771. **Business Addr:** Chief Executive Officer, The Blue Chip Profile Inc, 4315 Donlyn Ct, Columbus, OH 43232, **Business Phone:** (614)861-0772.

## SMITH, JANICE EVON

Association executive, public relations executive, president (organization). **Personal:** Born Feb 21, 1952, Warsaw, NC. **Educ:** NC A&T State Univ, BS, 1974; Ohio State Univ, MA, 1975; Howard Univ, PhD, mass commun/media studies, 2013. **Career:** Greensboro Daily News-Rec, reporting intern, 1974; Charlotte News, daily newspaper reporter, 1975-79, reporter & ed, 1980; Nat Urban League Wash Opers, comn assoc, 1981-83; DC Off Human Rights, spec asst dir, 1987-91; JES Commun, pres, 1991-96; Montgomery Col, adj prof, 1992-93; Prince George's Community Col, adj prof, 1993-95; Greater Wash Urban League Inc, chief staff & commun dir, 1996-2010, gala coordr & chief operating officer, 2010-; Morgan State Univ, adj prof commun, 2014-. **Orgs:** Chmn, Dist III NC Press Womens Assoc, 1977; publicity chmn & bd dir, Charlotte Mecklenburg Afro-Am Cult Ctr, 1978-80; forum coord, Wash Assoc Black Journalists, 1982; Capital Press Club, 1982-85; Nat Asn Advan Colored People, 1983-84; comn chmn, Nat Capital Chap Pub Rels Soc Am, 1986-87. **Home Addr:** 3104 Banneker Dr NE, Washington, DC 20018, **Home Phone:** (202)529-0352. **Business Addr:** Chief Operating Officer, Greater Washington Urban League Inc, 2901 14th St NW, Washington, DC 20009, **Business Phone:** (202)265-8200.

## SMITH, ESQ. JERALDINE WILLIAMS

President (organization), executive, lawyer. **Personal:** Born Jan 14, 1946, Tampa, FL; married Walter L; children: Salesia Vanette & Walter Lee II. **Educ:** Univ Fla, BS, jour, 1967; Atlanta Univ, MBA, 1970; Fla State Law Sch, JD, 1981. **Career:** Bus consult, journalist, exec & lawyer; Freedom Savings, bank mgr, 1973-75; Digital Equip Corp, admin mgr, 1975-77; Fla Dept Ins, lawyer 1983-; Capital Outlook Weekly Newspaper, pub, 1983-91; George E. Shaw Bail Bonds Inc, Smith-Phoenix Global Enterprises Inc, dir; The Middleton Sr High Sch Alumni Asn Inc, Law Off Jeraldine Williams-Shaw, P.A, Smith & Smith of Tallahassee Inc, Pres. **Orgs:** Am Bar Asn; Fla Bar Asn, 1982-; Nat Newspaper Pub Asn; Fla Press Asn. **Home Addr:** 2504 E 12th Ave, Tampa, FL 33605, **Home Phone:** (813)248-8060.

## SMITH, DR. JESSE OWENS

Educator. **Personal:** Born Dec 5, 1942, Comer, GA; son of Victor C and Lena Mae Corbitt; married Rhoda Lee Crowe; children: Rhonda, Karla & Seaton. **Educ:** Calif State Univ, Los Angeles, BA, jour, 1971; Univ Chicago, IL, MA, polit sci, 1973, PhD, polit sci, 1976. **Career:** Univ Wis, Oshkosh, Wis, prof, 1974-76; San Diego State Univ, San Diego, prof, 1977-84; Calif State Univ, Fullerton, Dept African Am Studies, Afro-Ethnic Studies, prof emer, 1984-. **Orgs:** Nat Conf Black Polit Scientists, 1972-; Nat Coun Black Studies, 1976-; Am Polit Sci Asn, 1976-; Calif Black Fac & Staff Asn, 1978-; Nat Asn Advan Black Studies. **Home Addr:** 11347 La Verne Dr, Riverside, CA 92505, **Home Phone:** (714)785-4037. **Business Addr:** Professor Emeritus, California State University, H-332 800 State Col Dr, Fullerton, CA 92831, **Business Phone:** (657)278-3677.

## SMITH, DR. JESSIE CARNEY

Educator, librarian. **Personal:** Born Sep 24, 1930, Greensboro, NC; daughter of James Ampler Carney and Vesona Bigelow Graves; children: Frederick Douglas Jr. **Educ:** NC Agr & Tech State Univ, BS, home econ, 1950; Cornell Univ, attended 1950; Mich State Univ, MA, child develop, 1956; George Peabody Col Teachers, MA, libr sci, 1957; Univ Ill, PhD, libr sci, 1964. **Career:** Nashville City Schs, teacher, 1957; Tenn State Univ, head cataloger & instr, 1957-60, coordr libr serv, asst prof, 1963-65; Univ Ill, teaching asst, 1961-63; Fisk Univ, univ librn & prof, 1965-, dean libr, 2010, fedrel officer, dir, fed progs, 1975-77, William & Camille Cosby prof humanites & librn, currently; Vanderbilt Univ, Dept Libr Sci, lectr, 1969-, vis prof, 1980-84; Atlanta Univ, Workshop Intern Prog Librns Predominately Negro Col, assoc dir, 1969, 1970; Fisk Univ, Inst Selection Orgn & Use Mat & About Negro, dir, 1970; Ala A & M Univ, assoc prof, consult, 1971-73; Develop Collections Black Lit, dir, 1971; African-Am Mat Proj, coordr, 1971-74; Internship Black studies Librarianship, dir, 1972-73; Univ TN Sch Libr Sci, vis lectr, 1973-74; Mini-Inst Ethnic Studies Librarianship, dir, 1974; Internship Ethnic Studies Librarianship, dir, 1974-75; Res Prog Ethnic Studies Librarianship, dir, 1975; Libr Study, Tenn Higher Educ Comn, dir, 1975-76; Inst Ethnic Geneal Librns, dir, 1979; Race Rels Collection Proj, dir, 1980-81; Images Black Artifacts, dir, 1980-81; Learning Libr Prog, dir, 1980-84; I've Been Mountain Top: A Civil Rights Legacy, dir, 1984-86; Metrop Nashville Schs, teacher, 1987; Chicago Renaissance Proj, dir, 1988-89. **Orgs:** Episcopacy Comt, United Methodist Church, 1984-88; Metro Hist Comn, Nashville, 1984-88; Nat Comt Bicentennial Scholars Prog, United Methodist Church, 1985-87; adv coun, Black Col Libr Improv Proj, Southern Educ Found, 1985-; bd dir, C Int Educ Ctr, 1986-; bd dir, Hist Nashville, 1986-89; Tenn Adv Coun Libr, 1990-; chair, bd dir, Coop Col Libr Ctr, 1990-99; bd trustee, Gammon Theol Sem, 1998-; bd trustee, Fisk Univ, 2000-; Am Libr Asn; Tenn Libr Asn; SE Libr Asn; Asn Col & Res Lib ALA; Lib Admin Div ALA; Lib Educ Div ALA; Am Asn Univ Profs. **Honors/Awds:** Martin Luther King Jr Black Authors Award, 1982; Academic or Research Librarian of the Year Award, Asn Col & Res Libr, Am Libr Asn, 1985; Certificate of Commendation, State Tenn, 94th Gen Assembly, House & Senate Concurring, 1985; Distinguished Scholars Award, United Negro Col Fund, 1986; Distinguished Alumni Award, Dept Libr Sci, Peabody Col Vanderbilt Univ, 1987; Distinguished Alumni Award, Grad Sch Libr & Info Sci, Univ Ill, 1990; National Womens Book Association Award, 1992; Candace Award, Nat Coalition 100 Black Women; Anna J. Cooper Award, Sage Mag; Black Caucus of the American Library Association Achievement Award. **Special Achievements:** First African American to earn a Ph.D. in library science from the University of Illinois.Writings includes: A Handbook for the Study of Black Bibliography, 1971, Ethnic Genealogy: A Research Guide, 1983, Images of Blacks in Amer Culture: A Reference Guide to Info Sources, 1988, Black Heroes, ed, 2001; Black Firsts: 4,000 Ground-Breaking & Historical Events, 2003; Notable Black American Women: Book III, 2003; Book: Epic Lives: One Hundred Black Women Who Made A Difference; Powerful Black Women. **Home Addr:** 146 Jefferson Sq, Nashville, TN 37215. **Business Addr:** Dean of the Library, William and Camille Cosby Professor in the Humanities, Fisk University, 1000 17th Ave N, Nashville, TN 37208-3051, **Business Phone:** (615)329-8730.

## SMITH, DR. JOANNE HAMLIN

School administrator, association executive. **Personal:** Born Oct 19, 1954, Pittsburgh, PA; daughter of Robert E and Helen Rogers; married James E Jr. **Educ:** Edinboro Univ Pa, BS, elem educn, 1976; Wichita State Univ, MEd, coun & stud Personnel, 1979; Kans State Univ, PhD, stud personnel admin, 1986. **Career:** McPherson Col, dir residence life, judicial affairs & orientation, 1976-86; Ariz State Univ, asst dir residence life, 1986-91; Southwest Tex State Univ, dir residence life, 1992-2000, assoc vpres stud affairs & dir enrollment mgt, 2000-04, dir residence life, interim vpres stud affairs, asst prof coun & guid, vpres stud affairs, 2004-. **Orgs:** Accompanist First United Methodist Church, 1987; Am Acad Cosmetic Dent; Phi Delta Kappa, 1976-; cert counr, Nat Brd Cert Counrs, 1980-; treas, pres elect & pres, Ariz Col Personnel Assn, 1986-91; Am Col Personnel Assn, 1986-; Southwest Assn Col & Univ Housing Officers, 1986-, pres, 1999-2001. **Honors/Awds:** Award for Outstanding Contributions, NASPA Region IV W, 1978; Women Helping Women Honoree, Soroptomist Int, 1979. **Home Addr:** 13438 Forum Rd, Universal City, TX 78148-2801, **Home Phone:** (210)945-9089. **Business Addr:** Vice President for Student Affairs, Southwest Texas State University, 601 Univ Dr, San Marcos, TX 78666, **Business Phone:** (512)245-2152.

## SMITH, JOE (JOSEPH LEYNARD SMITH)

Basketball player. **Personal:** Born Jul 26, 1975, Norfolk, VA; married Yolanda; children: Alanna, Jamie & Cameron. **Educ:** Univ Md, attended 1995. **Career:** Basketball player (retired); Golden State Warriors, forward, 1995-98; Philadelphia 76ers, 1998, forward, 2006-07; Minn Timberwolves, 1999-2000, 2001-03; Detroit Pistons, 2000-01; Milwaukee Bucks, forward, 2003-06; Denver Nuggets, 2006; Chicago Bulls, 2007-08; Cleveland Cavaliers, 2008-09; Okla City Thunder, 2008-09; Atlanta Hawks, 2009-10; Nj Nets, 2010; Los Angeles Lakers, power forward, 2010-11, forward-ctr, 2011; Albums: "Joe Beast"; "Murda Kapital"; "I Does This". **Orgs:** Joe Smith Found. **Business Addr:** Professional Basketball Player, Los Angeles Lakers, 555 N Nash St, El Segundo, CA 90245, **Business Phone:** (310)426-6000.

## SMITH, DR. JOE LEE

School administrator. **Personal:** Born May 29, 1936, Cocoa, FL; married Altamese Edmonson; children: Chyrell, Trina, Sharon & Twila. **Educ:** Fla A&M Univ, BS, 1959, MEd, 1963; Univ Fla, EdS, 1973, EdD, admin & supv higher educ, 1974. **Career:** President (retired); Brevard City Pub Sch, instr, 1959-63; Ft Lauderdale Broward City Pub Sch, instr, 1963-67; Miami Dade Community Col, instr, 1967-69; Cocoa High Sch, asst prin, 1969-70; Brevard Community Col, dir stud activ, 1970-72, dir placement, 1974-75, dir coop educ placement & follow-up, 1975-77, dean stud serv, provost, Ambassador, currently; Univ Fla, res asst assoc dir inst res coun, 1972-73; Brevard Community Col, Cocoa Campus, pres, campus pres emer, currently; City Coun, chmn. **Orgs:** Bd dir, United Way of Brevard Co; bd dir, Deveraux Fla; bd dir, Wachovia Bank; bd dir, Salvation Army; bd dir, Brevard Literacy Coun; bd dir, Circles Care; Space Coast Civilian Mil Coun; Cocoa Rockledge Civic League; Rockledge High Sch Raiders Quarterback Club; Child Care Asn Policy Coun; Alco Rest Treat Shelter Ctr; Leadership Brevard Educ Comt; Friends Taylor Park Rockledge; Rockledge Heritage Found; Phi Delta Kappa, 1963; Omega Psi Phi Frat, 1969; vchmn, Rockledge City Coun; life mem, Fla Assoc Community Col, 1974; sunday sch teacher, Zion Orthodox Primitive Baptist Chruch; Life Mem, Fla A & M Univ Nat Alumni Asn. **Honors/Awds:** Citizen of the Year, Alpha Phi Alpha Frat, 1972; Outstanding Educator of American, 1975; Sports Hall of Fame, Fla A & M Univ, 1986; BCC Melbourne Campus has a newly-named building: The Dr. Joe Lee Smith Teaching Center. **Special Achievements:** Recreation ctr named Joe Lee Smith Recreation Ctr 1973; Article "27 Stepsto Better Discipline", 1974. **Home Addr:** 918 Levitt Pkwy, Rockledge, FL 32955-4032, **Home Phone:** (321)636-2166. **Business Addr:** Ambassador, Brevard Community College, 1519 Clearlake Rd, Cocoa, FL 32922, **Business Phone:** (321)433-7306.

### SMITH, JOHN B., SR.

Publisher, chief executive officer, teacher. **Personal:** Born LaGrange, GA; son of John Watson and Pressarene Whitfield; married Frances M Evans; children: Pamela D, Lori A & John Jr. **Educ:** Morehouse Col, BS, math, 1958; Atlanta Univ, MA, admin, MA, math. **Career:** Educator, ed, publ; Black Press Arch, chmn; Atlanta Pub Schs, math teacher, chmn mathmatics dept, actg prin, 1960-91; The Atlanta Inquirer, advert salesman, 1961, publ & chief exec officer, currently. **Orgs:** Past chmn, Nat Newspapers Publ Asn, 2005-09; Omega Psi Phi; bd dir, Atlanta Fair & Expos; bd dir, Grade Homes Boys Club; bd dir, Boy Scouts Am; Atlanta Chamber Com; vpres, Nat Newspapers Publ Asn; Bus Group Community Rels Comn; first vice chmn, Nat Newspapers Publ Asn, 2009-. **Home Addr:** 3153 Mangum Lane SW, Atlanta, GA 30311-3045, **Home Phone:** (404)794-4747. **Business Addr:** Publisher, Chief Executive Officer, The Atlanta Inquirer, 947 Martin Luther King Jr Dr NW, Atlanta, GA 30314-2367, **Business Phone:** (404)523-6086.

### SMITH, JOHN B., JR.

Accountant. **Home Addr:** 530 Birchberry Ter, Atlanta, GA 30331-8495.

### SMITH, JOHN L., JR. (JACK SMITH)

School administrator, educator. **Personal:** Born Sep 14, 1938, Bastrop, LA; son of John L Sr and Julia S; married Juel Shannon; children: Kenneth, Babette, Angela, Gina, Lisa, Michael & Eva. **Educ:** Lincoln Univ, BME, 1959; Univ Ind, MME, 1961, performance cert, 1961; Univ Mo, Kans City, DMA; Harvard Univ, post-doctoral study, 1992. **Career:** Firman Settlement House, dir, 1964-66; Black Liberated Arts Ctr Inc, founder, pres, 1969-72; Langston Univ, Fine Arts Ser, dean, 1969-72, Music dept, chair, 1969-72; Univ S Fla, Music dept, actg asst chair, 1973-74, asst dean, coordr adv, 1977-86, actg dean, 1986-88, Fine Arts Col, dean, 1988-98; FLA Orchestra Brass Quintet, 1978-; Fisk Univ, pres, 1999-2001. **Orgs:** Bd dir, Hillsborough County Arts Coun, 1986-; bd dir, African Arts Coun, 1988-90; bd dir, Fla Orchestra, 1989-; comn arts, Nat Asn State Univs & Land Grant Cols, 1989-92; chair, Community Cult Diversity & Inclusion Arts, 1989-92; bd trustee, Fla Cult Action & Educ Alliances, 1990-; Mayor's Task Force Arts, 1991-92; chair, Fla Higher Educ Arts Network, 1992-94; pres, Int Coun Fine Arts Deans, 1997-98; Pi Kappa Lambda. **Home Addr:** 13820 Cherry Brook Lane, Tampa, FL 33618, **Home Phone:** (813)961-8068.

### SMITH, DR. JOHN RAYE (JOHN RAYE)

Journalist, chief executive officer, president (organization). **Personal:** Born Jan 30, 1941, Gibson, LA; son of Paul and Vera Phillips; married Rosie King; children: Michelle & Dexter Renaud. **Educ:** Southern Univ, BS, 1964; Columbia Univ, jour, 1967; Wash Jour Ctr, attended 1968. **Career:** Albany Springfield High Sch, instr, gen scis, chem, biol, 1963-64; US Dept Agri, McMinniville, soil conversationist, 1964-66; Valley Migrant League, voc counr, 1966-67; Moses Lakes Job Corps Ctr, 1967-68; KREM-TV; King TV-Seattle; WNBC-TV; WTTG-TV; TV reporter/anchor-producer, 1968-79; US Census Bur, 1979-83; Majestic Eagles Inc, pres, chief exec officer, founder, 1983-; John Raye & Assocs, pres, chief exec officer, founder, 1983-; Compro Tax, regional dir; MATAH Network Inc, regional dir; Forever Living Prod, sr mgr, currently. Author:; Starting Your Own Business; Producer: Dreamtime; Finding Success In America; Host: 21st Century Underground Railroad: A Video Magazine. **Orgs:** Dir, Funds Secure Majestic Eagles headquartes bldg.; Ubiquitous Comput & Monitoring Syst; co-founder, Nat Black Alliance Network. **Special Achievements:** First black television anchormen at prominent broadcast stations in Seattle, New York and Washington, DC. **Home Addr:** 9805 Betteker Lane, Potomac, MD 20854, **Home Phone:** (301)340-9144. **Business Addr:** President, Chief Executive Officer, Majestic Eagles Inc, 2029 Rhode Island Ave NE, Washington, DC 20018, **Business Phone:** (202)635-0154.

### SMITH, DR. JOSEPH EDWARD

Chemist, dentist. **Personal:** Born Sep 13, 1938, Jacksonville, FL; married Mildred; children: Daryl, Ivan & Jomila. **Educ:** Allen Univ, BS, 1960; Howard Univ, Col Dent, DDS, 1970. **Career:** Dentist self; Roxbury Health Ctr, chemist, 1966-67; Boston Univ, Grad Sch Dent, asst prof, 1970-74; Jacksonville Health Ctr, 1974-76; Smith & Smith Dent Assocs, Fla, chief dent, currently. **Orgs:** US Bur Mines, 1964-66; Ribault Jr HS, 1975; secy, treas, Denticare Prepaid Dent Plan Fla, 1976-77; Jacksonville Opt Ind Ctr, 1976-77; dir, Denticare Prepaid Dent Plan, 1976-77; Small Bus men's Serv Asn, 1976-77; Nat Dent Asn; Am Dent Asn; Fla Dent Asn; VI Dent Asn; New Bethel AME Ch; stewart, pres Kenneth White Gospel Chorus; 3rd Sunday supt Sunday Sch; dir, Northside Boys Club; bd mem, Youth Cong Sickle Cell Anemia Prog; life mem, Nat Asn Adv Coloured People; Sunshine State Dent Asn. **Home Addr:** 3905 Ernjo Rd, Jacksonville, FL 32209. **Business Addr:** Chief Dentist, Smith & Smith Dental Associates, 1190 W Edgewood Ave Suite B, Jacksonville, FL 32208, **Business Phone:** (904)764-4549.

### SMITH, JOSEPH F.

Educator, government official. **Personal:** Born Aug 22, 1945, Jacksonville, FL; son of Hazel Hall and Joe; married Mary Townsend; children: Joseph Cordell & Karina Sharon. **Educ:** T Valley State Col, BA, 1967; Ft Valley State Col, Ft Valley, GA, BA, 1967; Howard Univ, Sch Law, Wash, DC, JD, 1970. **Career:** WRC/NBC, Consumer Guidelines, moderator, 1971-74; Dept Housing & Urban Develop, Wash, DC, actg asst secy admin, dir inter govt affairs, 1980-85, dir econ anal & eval, 1985-89, dep dir, off policy, 1989, dep off healthy homes & lead hazard control; Off Chief Human Capital Off, miscellaneous admin & prog, 2015; Consumer Liaison Div Consumer Affairs Dept HUD, dir; Nat Consumer Info Ctr, producer & exec dir; WRC/NBC, It's Your World, exec producer & moderator; Am Univ, prof; Howard Univ, prof; numerous consumer manuals, econ & polit articles, ed & lct pub. **Orgs:** Fed Trade Comn, 1968-; mem & consult, Off Consumer Affairs, 1969-; OEO, 1970-; Atty Gen Off MA, DC & WI, 1970-74; Nat Inst Educ Law & Poverty, 1970; Am Bar Asn, 1971; Nat Legal Aid & Defender's Asn, 1972; Consumer Adv Comm Fed Enery Off, 1972-74; NY NV Consumer Off, 1973-74; Ohio C C, 1973; Off Gov, 1973-; Cost Living Coun Asn, 1974; Asn Home Appliances Mfg, 1974; secy, Class 23 Fed Exec Inst, 1984-86; treas, Reid Temple AME, 1987-; Nat Asn Atty Gen; Alpha Phi Alpha; Nat Asn Advan Colored People; Consumer Fedn Am; Nat Conf Black Lawyers; Cong Staff; Black Caucus; Housing & Urban Dev; Social Rehab Serv; Howard Univ Law Sch Alumni Asn. **Honors/Awds:** Outstanding Executive, 1988, Certificate of Merit, 1989, Federal Executive Institute Award, 1995, Dept Housing & Urban Develop. **Home Addr:** 5600 Signet Lane, Riverdale, MD 20737-3514, **Home Phone:** (301)345-0529. **Business Addr:** Director, Office of Executive Services, 451 7th St SW, Washington, DC 20410-4500.

### SMITH, JOSHUA ISAAC

Executive. **Personal:** Born Apr 8, 1941, Garrard County, KY; married Jacqueline Jones; children: Joshua I II. **Educ:** Cent State Univ, BS, biol & chem, 1963; Univ Akron Sch Law, grad studies, 1968; Univ Del, asn mgt, 1975; Cent Mich Univ, grad studies, bus mgt, 1977. **Career:** Plenum Publ Corp, mgr databook div, 1969-70; Am Soc Info Sci, exec dir, 1970-76; Herner & Co, vpres, 1976-78; MAXIMA Corp, pres & chief exec officer, 1978-98; FedEx Corp, dir, 1989-2013; Allstate Ins Corp, dir, 1997-2013; Coaching Group, chmn & managing partner, 1998-; iGate Inc, vice chmn, pres, chief develop officer, 2000-01; Caterpillar inc, dir, 1993-2013; Datawind Ltd, advisor; Biz Talk With Josh, host; Fed Express Corp, dir; Sting Free Co, dir; Sting Free Technologies Co, dir; Cardio Comm Solutions Inc, dir; Cardiocomm Solutions Inc, dir, 2000-. **Orgs:** Chmn, United Way Fundraising Campaign, 1984; chmn, US Comn Minority Bus Develop, 1989-92; chmn bd, Nat Bus League Montgomery Co; mem bd dir, Int Asn Studs Bus Mgt & Econs; Minority Bus Enterprise Legal Defense & Educ Fund; chmn, Nat Urban Coalition; dir, TN Tech Found; Citizens Adv Comt Career & Voc Educ; Corp Round Table; mem adv bd, Grad Sch Libr & Info Sci Univ TN; mem adv bd, NC Cent Univ Sch Libr Sci; Am Asn Advan Sci; Am Libr Asn; exec dir, Am Soc Info Sci; Black Presidents Roundtable Wash; Engineering Index Inc; Info Indust Asn Long Range Planning Comn; Nat Bus League Montgomery Co; mem adv bd, Sodexo Inc, 2004-; vice chmn, Advanzeon Solutions Inc, 2009-; vice chmn, Comprehensive Behav Care Inc, 2009-; mem adv bd, Essential Reality Inc, 2001-; bd trustee, John F. Kennedy Ctr Performing Arts; bd trustee, George H.W. Bush Memorial Libr; Md Stadium Authority; bd dir, Nat Black Chamber Com; bd dir, Village Found. **Honors/Awds:** Minority Businessperson of the Year, Small Bus Admin; Distinguished Corporate Award, US Dept Com Minority Bus Develop Agency; Special Recognition Award for Valuable Commitment, US Dept Com Minority Bus Develop Agency; Man of Achievement Award, Anti-Defamation League. **Special Achievements:** Numerous publications. **Home Addr:** , Washington, DC. **Business Addr:** Managing Partner, The Coaching Group LLC, 8401 Colesville Rd Suite 640, Silver Spring, MD 20910-3349, **Business Phone:** (301)589-9800.

### SMITH, DR. JOSHUA L.

Educator. **Personal:** Born Dec 11, 1934, Boston, MA; son of Joshua and Lorina A Henry. **Educ:** Boston Univ, BA, 1955; Harvard Univ, MA, 1959, EdD, 1967. **Career:** Educator (retired); Pittsburgh Pa, admin asst supt sch, actg vice prin, 1966-68; Ford FND, prog officer, asst prog off, proj specialist, 1968-74; City Col, City Univ, New York, prof educ, 1974-76, dean, sch educ, 1976-77; Boro Manhattan Community Col, actg pres, 1977-78, pres, 1978-85; St Calif Community Cols, chancellor, 1985-87; Brookdale Community Col, pres, 1987-90; Baruch Col, City Univ NY, Dpt Educ, prof, 1990, interim chmn, 1992; New York Univ, chmn, dir, Prog Higher Educ & Ctr Urban Community Col Leadership, 2000, prof emer. **Orgs:** Bd trustee, Pub Educ Asn, 1974-; bd trustee, Mus Collab Inc, 1974-; bd trustee, Nat Humanities Fac, 1974-; chmn, Nat Asn Advan Colored People Task Force Qual Educ, 1977-; bd deacon, Riverside Church, NY, 1977-82, bd trustee, 1988-; AACJC Comn Govt Affairs, 1978-; rep, CUNY Big City Community Col Pres & Chancellors, AACJC, 1978-; New York Co Local Develop Corp Inc, 1980; bd dir, AACJC, 1980; vice chmn, Joint Comn Fed Rel AACJC ACCT, 1982, chmn, 1983; bd dir vice chmn, 1983-84, bd dir chmn, AACJC, 1984-85; bd overseer, Univ St New York Regents Col Degrees & Exam, 1985-; golden heritage mem, Nat Asn Advan Colored People; bd trustee, Excelsior col. **Honors/Awds:** Phi Delta Kappa Award of Achievement for Outstanding Service to the Field of Educ, AL A&M Univ, 1972; Distinguished Service Award, Bilingual Vol Am, 1973; Distinguished Service Award, Harlem Prep Sch, 1973-75; Award of Appreciation, Support Develop S Leadership Develop Prog, So Region Coun, 1974. **Home Addr:** 315 W 70th St Apt 12k, New York, NY 10023-3516, **Home Phone:** (212)721-4063. **Business Addr:** Professor Emeritus, New York University, 100 Wash Sq E, New York, NY 10003.

### SMITH, JUANITA

Government official. **Personal:** Born Jun 28, 1927, St. Petersburg, FL; daughter of Ruffin Sr and Annabelle Momoan; married Thomas H; children: Carol Tracey. **Educ:** Gibbs Jr Col, elem educ; Tuskegee Inst, indust arts, 1947; Fla Int Univ, BS, polit sci, 1974. **Career:** AL Lewis Elem Sch, teacher; Homestead Jr HS, teacher; Dade County Bd Pub Instr, teacher, 1967-; Fla City, comnr, vice mayor. **Orgs:** Dade County Crime Comm Ct Aide; Am Red Cross; United Heart Fund; Dade County Cancer Soc; March Dimes; Dade County Comn Action Ctr; Dade County Dept Pub Health; Hills bor Co Juv Home; vpres, Dade County Voters League; vpres, A L Lewis PTA; adv bd, Protestant Christian Comm Serv Agency; adv bd, Fla City Parks & Rec; chair person Pub Rel Bd A L Lewis Elem Sch; Comm Block Club; Nat Coun Negro Women; Crime Stoppers; C's Libr Club; youth leader, welfare worker Seventh Day Adventist Church; bd mem, Greater Miami Urban League, 1984-; bd mem, Community Health S Dade County, 1985-; Nat Asn Advan Colored People, 1986-; bd mem, Dade County League Cities, 1987- treas, 1992; Am Civil Liberties Union Fla; vol, Homestead Soup Kitchen. **Honors/Awds:** Woman of the Year, Links Inc, 1985; Award of Appreciation, Naval Security Group Activity, 1985; Certificate & Award of Service, Dade County Community Action Ser, 1985; Woman of the Year, Zeta Phi Beta, 1985; Woman of the Year, Bethel Seventh Day Adventist Church. **Home Addr:** 706 NW 3rd St, Florida City, FL 33034, **Home Phone:** (305)246-1579. **Business Addr:** Commissioner, City Hall, 404 W Palm Dr, Florida City, FL 33034-3346, **Business Phone:** (305)247-8221.

### SMITH, DR. JUDITH MOORE (JUDI MOORE LATTA)

Executive director, educator. **Personal:** Born Aug 3, 1948, Tallahassee, FL; daughter of Oscar and LaVerne; married Joseph; children: 2. **Educ:** Hampton Inst, BS, eng educ, 1970; Boston Univ, MA, eng lit, 1971; Univ Md, PhD, 1999. **Career:** Cambridge High & Latin Sch, instr eng, comt, 1971-72; Univ DC, Dept Commun, asst prof, 1972-80, Van Ness Campus Fac Senate, chairperson, 1977-78, asst prof communicative & performing arts, FM Radio Proj, communs cons, bd mem's newsletter, 1978-80; African Heritage Dancers & Drummers, lead dancer, 1973-; WAMU-FM Radio, prod, writer, series host, 1977-78; WETA-TV/FM, producer, 1978-79; Pub Radio Syst, producer, 1980-88, reporter, 1988, exec producer, sr producer, 1992; Howard Univ, Dept Radio, Tv & Film, from asst prof to assoc prof, 1984-2000, prof, 2000-, dept chair, 2000-02, dep gen mgr, 2002-03, WHUT-TV, interim gen mgr, 2003-, exec dir, 2009-, pres exec leadership cabinet, 2012; WUSA-TV, reporter, producer, 1990-92; WRC-TV, producer, 1992; Womens Studies, co-chair, 2005-11; WHUR-WORLD, dir, 2006-09; Grad Cert Women Studies, co-dir, currently. **Orgs:** Bd dir Friendship House, 1975-; Nat Coun Negro Women, 1977; Nat Commun Asn; Am Fed Television & Radio Artists; People's Community Baptist Church; Am Studies Asn; Links Inc; Olive Br Community Church. **Special Achievements:** First woman to serve in the role of interim general manager of Howard University's WHUT-TV, 2002. **Home Addr:** 14744 Silverstone Dr, Silver Spring, MD 20905, **Home Phone:** (301)384-2859. **Business Addr:** Executive Director, Howard University, 2225 Ga Ave NW Suite 603, Washington, DC 20059, **Business Phone:** (202)238-2338.

### SMITH, JUDY SERIALE

Government official, social worker. **Personal:** Born Mar 10, 1953, Lafayette, LA; daughter of Joseph Seriale and Vernice Bellard; married Sylvester Lee Smith Jr; children: Sylvester Lee III & Joseph Seriale. **Educ:** Grambling State Univ, BA, social work, 1974. **Career:** S Cent Ark Community Action, Camden, Ark, community serv coordr, 1980-84; PAC Inc, exec dir, 1984-2002; Ark House Representatives, dep majority leader, House Pub Health, Welfare & Labor Comt, vice-chair, Human Serv sub-comt, chair, 1990-97; Ark Minority Health Comn, exec dir, 2002-07; Dept Workforce Educ & Ark Re-habilitation Serv, transition serv dir, 2007-; Ark, state legislator; Ark Career Training Inst, interim adminr. **Orgs:** Bd mem, Ouachita County Emergency Food & Shelter Bd, 1986-; bd mem, Women's Crisis Ctr Camden, 1988-; SAU Tech Br Adv Bd, 1988-; exec dir, Ark Drug Free YouthCamden, 1984-2002; bd mem, Ark Child Abuse Prev, 1989-; regional coordr, Ark Drug Free Youth, 1990-; Ark Rehab Serv; Sigma Beta Omega Chap Alpha Kappa Alpha Sorority Inc. **Honors/Awds:** Delegate to Japan, ACYPL, 1992; Top Ten Legislative Hall of Fame, 1993; Arkansas Democrat Gazette; Woman of Distinction, Ark Bus Weekly; Top 100 Women in Arkansas; Flemming Fellow, Leadership Inst, 1995. **Home Addr:** PO Box 1011, Camden, AR 71711, **Home Phone:** (501)836-3945. **Business Addr:** Transition Service Director, Arkansas Department of Workforce Education, 525 W Capitol Ave, Little Rock, AR 72201, **Business Phone:** (870)862-5451.

### SMITH, KATRINA MARITA

Chiropractor. **Personal:** Born Oct 1, 1958, Kosciusko, MS. **Educ:** Palmer Jr Col; E Carolina Univ; Univ Northern Iowa; Palmer Col Chiropractic, DC, 1984; W Coast Col Massage Ther, Vancouver, grad. **Career:** Pvt pract, chiropractor, currently; Thrive Chiropractic Wellness Ctr, chiropractic physician, currently; Diamond Hill Jarvis High Sch, asst prin, currently. **Orgs:** Bd mem & secy, Independent Sch Dist Sch; Sigma Phi Chi, 1984; Int Chiropractic Asn, 1984; Am Chiropractic Asn, 1984; secy, Black Chiropractic Asn, 1984. **Home Addr:** 30 N Hill Pkwy Apt A 8, Jackson, MS 39206. **Business Addr:** Chiropractic Physician, Thrive Chiropractic Wellness Center, 1546 W Second Ave, Vancouver, BC V6J 1H2, **Business Phone:** (604)730-0111.

### SMITH, KEITH DRYDEN, JR.

School administrator. **Personal:** Born Jun 8, 1951, New York, NY; son of Keith Dryden Sr and Marion B Sutherland; married Heather Y Duke; children: Mitchell Duke & Ally Megan Lusk. **Educ:** State Univ NY, BA, MA, 1973; Syracuse Univ, MS, 1978. **Career:** Red Creek Cent Sch, sci teacher, 1974-75; Syracuse Univ, Utica Col, counr, 1975-77, coordr acad & supportive serv, 1977-79, Educ Opportunity Prog dir, 1979-81; Am Asn Univ, prof, 1975-81; State Univ NY, Plattsburgh, Educ Opportunity Prog dir, 1981-92, lectr Afro-Am studies, 1984-86, Cortland, sr prog counr, adj instr, 1993, lectr African-Am studies, Educ Opportunity Prog, dir, 1992-10, dir emer, currently. **Orgs:** United Univ Profs, 1981-; secy, affirmative action comt, State Univ NY, Plattsburgh, 1983-85, chair, Cortland, 1992-98; inst planning comt, State Univ NY Off Spec Prog, 1985-87; human rights chair, Col Stud Personnel Asn NY Inc, 1986-87; cert mediator, Unified Ct Syst NY, Community Dispute Resolution Prog, 1987-; secy & dir, State Univ NY, 1988-90, treas, 1994-95, Coun Educ Opportunity Prog; sen, State Univ NY, Plattsburgh, 1990-92; chmn, State Unvi NY, Plattsburgh Pres Adv Comt Affirmative Action, 1990-92; curric rev comt, State Univ NY, 1992-95; State Univ NY, Cortland, Stud Support Comt, 1992-93, 1994-95; secy & bd dir, 1997-99, treas, bd dir, 1999-2004, State Univ NY, Cortland C's Ctr. **Home Addr:** 100 Halseyville Rd, Ithaca, NY 14850, **Home Phone:** (607)272-5304. **Business Addr:** Director Emeritus Educational Opportunity Program, State University of New York College at Cortland, 3745 Stratton Dr, Cortland, NY 13045-0900, **Business Phone:** (607)753-2011.

### SMITH, KELLITA

Actor. **Personal:** Born Jul 11, 1929, Chicago, IL; daughter of Honey. **Educ:** Santa Rosa Jr Col, AA, polit sci, 1989. **Career:** Films: House Party 3, 1994; The Crossing Guard, 1995; Q: The Movie, 1999; Retiring Tatiana, 2000; Kingdom Come, 2001; Hair Show, 2004; Fair Game, 2005; King's Ransom, 2005; Roll Bounce, 2005; Three Can Play That Game, 2007; Feel the Noise, 2007; Three Can Play That Game, 2007; Conspiracy X, 2009; From Cape Town with Love, 2010; Conspiracy X, 2010; She's Not Our Sister, 2011; Gang of Roses 2, 2012; The Love Section, 2013; TV series: In Living Color", 1993; "Living Single", 1993; "Hangin' with Mr. Cooper", 1994; Martin, 1994-95; "Sister, Sister", 1995; "The Wayans Bros", 1996; "Moesha", 1996; "Dangerous Minds", 1996; "The Parent 'Hood", 1997; "High Incident", 1997; "Malcolm &

Eddie", 1997; "The Jamie Foxx Show", 1997-99; "The Parkers", 1999; "The Steve Harvey Show", 1999; "For Your Love", 2000; "Masquerade", 2000; "The Bernie Mac Show", 2001-06; "Nash Bridges", 2001; "NYPD Blue", 2001; "The Bernie Mac Show", 2001-06; "She's Still Not Our Sister", 2011; "The First Family", 2012-13; "Kimmie's Kitchen", 2013; " Z Nation", 2014; Theatre performance: Tell It Like It Tiz; No Place To Be Somebody; Feelings; Strange Fruit, owner, 2001-. **Business Addr:** Actress, c/o Fox Broadcasting Co, 10201 W Pico Blvd, Los Angeles, CA 90035, **Business Phone:** (310)369-1000.

### SMITH, KELLY MILLER, JR.

Minister (clergy). **Personal:** son of Kelly Miller Sr and Alice C; married Sue Hall Smith; children: Sharanda, Valerie & Kelly Miller III. **Educ:** Morehouse Col, BA, 1976; Morehouse Sch Relig Interdenominational Theol Ctr, Mdiv, 1983; United Theol Sem, DMin, 1993. **Career:** Berean Baptist Church, Nashville, TN, pastor, 1985-91; Mt Olive Baptist Church, Knoxville, TN, pastor, 1991-2010; Am Baptist Col, Nashville, dir continuing educ; Nat Baptist Conv, USA Inc, exec eirector Sunday sch publ bd, 1997-2013; First Baptist Church, Capitol Hill, pastor, 2010-. **Orgs:** Tenn Baptist Missionary & Educ Conv, vpresident at large; Sigma Pi Phi. **Special Achievements:** Licensed to preach, 1974; ordained at First Baptist Church, Capitol Hill, Nashville, TN, 1979. **Business Addr:** First Baptist Church, Capitol Hill, 625 Rosa Parks Blvd, Nashville, TN 37203.

### SMITH, KEVIN L.

Executive. **Career:** SC Security Inc, Charlottesville, pres, owner, currently. **Business Addr:** President, Owner, SC Security Inc, 125 Riverbend Dr Suite 6, Charlottesville, VA 22911, **Business Phone:** (434)293-8164.

### SMITH, KEVIN REY

Football player, executive. **Personal:** Born Apr 7, 1970, Orange, TX. **Educ:** Tex A&M Univ. **Career:** Football player (retired), executive; Dallas Cowboys, defensive back, left defensive back, 1992-2000, defensive back, 1995; Tex A&M Football Games, color commentator; First Plus Financial Group, vpres bus develop, currently. **Honors/Awds:** Champion, Super Bowl, XXVII, XXVIII, XXX; All-Pro, 1996; Athletic Hall of Fame, Tex A&M Univ, 1997. **Business Addr:** Vice President of Business Development, First Plus Financial Group, 3965 Phelan Blvd Suite 209, Beaumont, TX 77707, **Business Phone:** (409)363-0695.

### SMITH, LAFAYETTE KENNETH

Executive, administrator. **Personal:** Born Dec 17, 1947, Memphis, TN; son of Joseph and Elizabeth Berniece Hodge. **Educ:** Howard Univ, Wash, DC, BS, 1971; Bernard M Baruch Col, New York, NY, MPA, 1984. **Career:** Opportunities Industrialization Ctr, Wash, DC, job placement specialist, 1972-75, job placement supvr, 1975-76, prog supvr, 1976-78, br mgr, 1978-81, prog coordr, 1981-82; Chicago Pub Schs, Chicago, Ill, spec asst gen supt, 1982-83; Wash, DC Govt, Dept Human Serv, Contracts Div, asst chief, 1984-87; Youth Serv Admin, contract adminr, 1987-91; DC Dept Human Servs, Wash, DC, sr contract specialist, 1993-98; DC Off Contracting & Procurement, supv contract specialist, 1999, contracting officer, currently. **Orgs:** Nat Asn Advan Colored People, 1970-; Howard Univ Alumni Asn, 1971-; Big Bros, Wash, DC, 1975-82; Prince Georges County, Pvt Indust Coun, 1979-81; State Md Occup Info, 1980-81; bd mem, Wash DC Pub Schs, 1980-82; scout master, Boy Scouts Am, 1981-81; Am Soc Pub Admin, 1982-; Chicago Urban League, 1982-83; Baruch Col Alumni Asn, 1984-; Nat Forum Black Pub Admin, 1985-; bd mem, Nat Urban Fels Alumni Asn, 1986-; Concerned Black Men Inc, 1986-95. **Home Addr:** 2400 16th St NW Suite 423, Washington, DC 20009-6627, **Home Phone:** (202)232-4464. **Business Addr:** Contracting Officer, District of Columbia, 1 Judiciary Sq 441 4th St NW Suite 700 S, Washington, DC 20001, **Business Phone:** (202)724-4014.

### SMITH, LAMAR HUNTER

Football player. **Personal:** Born Nov 29, 1970, Ft. Wayne, IN. **Educ:** Northeastern Okla A&M Col; Univ Houston. **Career:** Football player (retired); Seattle Sea hawks, running back, 1994-97; New Orleans Saints, half back & running back, 1998-99, 2003; Miami Dolphins, half back, 2000-01; Carolina Panthers, half back, 2002; Nat Football League Europe, coaching internship prog, 2007.

### SMITH, LARRY

Basketball coach, basketball player. **Personal:** Born Jan 18, 1958, Rolling Fork, MS; married Belinda; children: Larry Jr, Tiffany & Torri. **Educ:** Alcorn State, BS, recreation admin & MS, athletic admin, 1980. **Career:** Basketball player (retired), basketball coach; Golden State Warriors, 1980-89; Houston Rockets, 1989-92; San Antonio Spurs, 1992-93; Houston rockets, asst coach, 1993-2003; Atlanta Hawks, asst coach, 2003-04; Los Angeles Lakers, asst coach, 2004-05; Albuquerque Thunderbirds, asst coach, 2005-06; Anaheim Arsenal, head coach, 2006-07; Austin Toros, asst coach, 2006-07; Los Angeles Sparks, asst coach, 2008; Alcorn State Univ, head coach, 2008-11; Alcorn State Univ, dir athletic develop, 2011-. **Business Addr:** Director of Athletic development, Alcorn State University, 1000 Asu Dr Suite 359, Lorman, MS 39096, **Business Phone:** (601)877-6100.

### SMITH, LASALLE S., SR.

Law enforcement officer. **Personal:** Born Oct 13, 1947, Lithonia, GA; son of Ollie Tuggle and Link; married Evelyn Peek; children: LaSalle Jr, Evita L & Erika. **Educ:** Md Sch Music, Wash, DC, 1966; Police Lt, 1998; LaSalle Exten Univ, Chicago, acct, 1968; Dekalb Community, Clarkston, GA, 1977; Brenau Col, Gainesville, GA, 1985; Ga Bur Invest, trainer, analyst, 2000; United Christian Ministries, IN, BA, bibl educ; Columbus State Univ, Ga Law Enforcement Command Col, MA, pub admin. **Career:** Fed Bur Invest, Wash, DC, finger print sect, 1965-66; Atlanta Police Dept, patrol squad, 1968, detective, 1971, police sgt, 1973-74, police lt, 1974-80, Off Mayor, Atlanta, exec protection comdr, 1980-84, Off Comnr Pub Safety, Internal Affairs Unit, comdr, 1984-86, Off Chief Police, comdr numerous task forces, 1986-90, Chaplaincy Corp, dir, 1991-98; Ga Bur of Invest, trainer, analyst, 1998-2000; Ga Security Prof LLC, owner, pres & chief exec officer, 2005-. **Orgs:** Nat Orgn Black Law Enforcement Exec, 1984-; Nat Forum Black Pub Adminr; Nat Black Police Asn; Fulton County Task Force Drugs & Crime; Wings Hope Anti-Drug & Anti-Gang Task Force; Ga Asn Chiefs Police; Beautiful Blessings Christian Ministries. **Home Addr:** 4553 Lionshead Cir, Lithonia, GA 30038-2288, **Home Phone:** (770)987-7586. **Business Addr:** President, Chief Executive Officer, Georgia Security Professionals LLC, 8075 Mall Pkwy Suite 101-354, Lithonia, GA 30038, **Business Phone:** (770)605-9937.

### SMITH, LAWRENCE JOHN, JR.

Executive. **Personal:** Born Dec 20, 1947, New York, NY; son of Jeanne Henderson and Lawrence John; married Ernestine Randall; children: Karyn Jennifer & Lawrence John III. **Educ:** Univ Notre Dame, Notre Dame, BBA, mkt & psychol, 1969; Harvard Univ, Grad Sch Bus Admin, Boston, MBA, finance & gen mgt, 1971; Columbia Univ, Columbia Bus Sch, exec prog bus, 1988; Venture Capital Inst, attended 1993. **Career:** Honeywell Info Syst, Waltham, Mass, sr financial analyst, 1972-74; Digital Equip Corp, Maynard, Mass, prod line controller, 1974-79; Pizza Hut Inc, Wichita, Kans, US Controller, 1979-81; Wang Lab Inc, Lowell, Mass, chief exec officer software subs, 1982-89; TM Group, founder & ceo, pres, 1988-07, pres, 1994-; Philip Morris Inc, corp planning analyst; TM Group, founder & chief exec officer, 1988-2007; Transnational Mgt Asn, Grafton, Mass, pres & managing dir, 1989-90; Venture Capital Inst, trainer; Mass Ind Fin Agency, Boston, Mass, chief financial officer, 1990-95; Mass Growth Ventures LP, pres, 1993-94; Babson Col, Lectr Mgt, 1997-2012; Inner Circle Logistics Inc, Net-Centric Supply Chain Software & Serv, chief financial officer, currently; Masonic Educ & Charity Trust, Grand Lodge Mass, treas & chief financial officer, 2007-12; Wisdom4Hire, ceo & founder, 2012-; Middlesex Bank Incorporator & dir. **Orgs:** MENSA, 1982-; Harvard Bus Sch Asn Boston, 1988-; trustee, Dimock Community Health Ctr, 1990, bd vice chmn & finance comt chmn, 1997-2009; Harvard Club Boston, 1990-; trustee, Boston Opera Theatre, 1990-; dir, N Am Consult Inc, 1994-; dir, Metro W Med Ctr, 1994-; bd mem, Inner Circle Logistics Inc; Nat Asn Corp dir; bd gov, Cs Dyslexia Ctr Boston; bd mem, Boston Lyric Opera Forum; Beta Beta Boule Sigma Pi Phi; Masonic Health Systs Inc, C's Dyslexia Ctr Greater Boston. **Home Addr:** 46 Hinckley Rd, Milton, MA 02186-1634, **Home Phone:** (617)696-2261. **Business Addr:** Chief Executive Officer, Founder, Wisdom4Hire, 46 Hinckley Rd, Milton, MA 02186-1634, **Business Phone:** (617)696-7792.

### SMITH, LEE ARTHUR

Baseball player. **Personal:** Born Dec 4, 1957, Shreveport, LA; married Diane; children: Nikita, Lee Jr & Dimitri; married Cheryl; children: Nicholas & Alana. **Educ:** Northwestern State Univ, Natchitoches, La. **Career:** Baseball player (retired), baseball coach; Chicago Cubs, pitcher, 1980-87; Boston Red Sox, pitcher, 1988-90; St Louis Cardinals, pitcher, 1990-93; New York Yankees, pitcher, 1993; Baltimore Orioles, pitcher, 1994; Calif Angels, pitcher, 1995-96; Cincinnati Reds, pitcher, 1995-96; Cincinnati Reds, pitcher, 1996; Montreal Expos, pitcher, 1997; San Francisco Giants, pitching instr, 2000; SafricA Nat Baseball Team, pitching coach, 2006; Maj League Baseball Int, coach, 2007. **Orgs:** Baseball Writers Asn Am. **Home Addr:** 2124 Hwy 507, Castor, LA 71016-4069.

### SMITH, LEONARD PHILLIP

Football player. **Personal:** Born Sep 2, 1960, New Orleans, LA. **Educ:** Mc Neese State Univ; Fla State Univ. **Career:** Football player (retired); Am football, defensive back; St Louis Cardinals, strong safety, 1983-88; Phoenix Cardinals, defensive back, 1988; Buffalo Bills, strong safety, 1988-91. **Honors/Awds:** All-Pro, 1986; Super Bowl, 199; College Football Hall of Fame, 2014; Louisiana Sports Hall of Fame, 2015.

### SMITH, LEROI MATTHEW-PIERRE, III

Social worker. **Personal:** Born Jan 11, 1946, Chicago, IL; son of Norma and LeRoi Jr; children: Le Roi IV. **Educ:** Idaho State Univ, BA, psychol, 1969, MEd; WA State Univ, PhD, psychol, 1977. **Career:** Idaho State Univ, lectr, 1969-70; Wash State Univ, lectr, 1970-71; Evergreen State Col, prof, 1971-81; Port Seattle, dir, Diversity Progs; Thomas Edison State Col, mem fac, 1968-95. **Orgs:** Bd dir, Thurston Mason Co Ment Health, 1974-81; Nat Asn Black Psychologists, 1974-80; Tacoma-Pierce Co OIC, 1979-81; consult, Seattle Pub Schls, 1976-85; Am Soc Personnel Admin, 1981-; Am Psychol Asn. **Honors/Awds:** US Dept Educ, 1969; Nat Sci Found, 1976; Danforth Found, 1978; Fellowship, Lilly Found, 1981. **Home Addr:** PO Box 2903, Blaine, WA 98231-2903. **Business Addr:** Faculty Member, Thomas Edison State College, 101 W State S, Trenton, NJ 08608-1176, **Business Phone:** (609)984-1181.

### SMITH, LILA B.

Scientist. **Personal:** Born Memphis, TN. **Educ:** Lemoyne Col, BS, math, 1957; Howard Univ, MS, physics, 1959. **Career:** American scientist; Fla A&M Univ, asst prof physics, 1959-62; LeMoyne Col, asst prof math, 1962-63; US Atomic Energy Comn, sci analyst, 1963-76; Tech Info Ctr US Dept Energy, chief conserv & solar br, 1976-83, chief nuclear eng & physics br, OSTI & USDOE. **Orgs:** Pres & charter mem, Blacks Govt Oak Ridge Chap, 1984; vpres, Region IV Blacks Govt Inc, 1984-; vpres, Xi Iota Omega Chap Alpha Kappa Alpha Sor, 1985; Am Solar Energy Soc Inc; Nat Forum Black Pub Admis; Altrusa Inc, Oak Ridge Chap; Nat Asn Advan Colored People; Fed Employed Women Inc; Negro Bus & Prof Women's Clubs; TN Coun Human Rels; Oak Valley Baptist Church; Toastmasters Int. **Home Addr:** 4256 Woodcrest Dr, Memphis, TN 38111-8140, **Home Phone:** (901)745-4694.

### SMITH, LONNIE

Baseball player. **Personal:** Born Dec 22, 1955, Chicago, IL; married Pearl; children: Yaritza LaVonne & Eric Tramaine. **Career:** Baseball player (retired); Philadelphia Phillies, 1978-81; St Louis Cardinals, 1982-85; Kans City Royals, 1985-87; Atlanta Braves, 1988-92; Pittsburgh Pirates, 1993; Baltimore Orioles, 1993-94. **Home Addr:** 145 Baybeery Run, Fairburn, GA 30213.

### SMITH, LORETTA GARY

Banker, vice president (organization). **Personal:** Born Mar 27, 1949, Detroit, MI; daughter of Luther (deceased) and Doris Gary; married William J; children: Stacey Espie, Stephanie & Ashley. **Educ:** Univ Detroit-Mercy, bus admin. **Career:** JL Hudson, clerk, 1966-67; Comerica Inc, vpres, pub affairs, 1968-, community reinvestment mkt mgr mich. **Orgs:** Bd dir, Detroit & Pontiac Neighborhood Housing Serv Inc; Habitat Humanity, Metro-Detroit, bd dir; Univ Detroit Mercy, Leadership dev inst, adv bd mem; Cornerstone Schs, partner, tutor; Tri City Dev Corp; New Mt Hermon Baptist Church; adv bd mem, United Negro Col Fund; treas & bd dir, Plymouth Educ Ctr; Community Reinvestment Act Asn Mich; ProLiteracy Detroit & Detroit Neighborhood Housing Serv Inc; adv bd, James Tatum Found Arts; lifetime mem, Nat Asn Advan Colored People; City Planning Comn DOCTOR Prog; bd dir, Lighthouse Oakland County Develop Corp; bd dir, H. P. Devco & Reading Works; chair & adv bd, UNCF Bk Smart 2001 Scholar. **Home Addr:** 19345 Santa Rosa, Detroit, MI 48221, **Home Phone:** (313)345-2152. **Business Addr:** Vice President Public Affairs, Comerica Inc, 500 Woodward Ave, Detroit, MI 48275-3352, **Business Phone:** (313)222-6987.

### SMITH, LOVIE LEE

Football coach. **Personal:** Born May 8, 1958, Gladewater, TX; married MaryAnne; children: Mikal, Matthew & Miles. **Educ:** Univ Tulsa. **Career:** Big Sandy High Sch, defensive coordr, 1980; Cascia Hall Prep, asst coach, 1981-82; Tulsa, linebackers coach, 1983-86; Univ Wis, 1987; Ariz State Univ, linebackers coach, 1988-91; Univ Ky, linebackers coach, 1992; Univ Tenn, defensive backs coach, 1993-94; Ohio State Univ, defensive backs coach, 1995; Tampa Bay Buccaneers, linebackers coach, 1996-2000, head coach, 2014-; St. Louis Rams, defensive coordr, 2001-03; Chicago Bears, head coach, 2004-12. **Orgs:** Founder, Lovie Smith MaryAnne Smith Found; Am Diabetes Asn. **Home Addr:** 601 Carlson Pkwy Suite 610, Minnetonka, MN 55305. **Business Addr:** Founder, Lovie & Mary Anne Smith Foundation, 736 NW Ave Suite 209, Lake Forest, IL 60045, **Business Phone:** (847)563-8431.

### SMITH, DR. LUTHER EDWARD, JR.

Educator, clergy, association executive. **Personal:** Born May 29, 1947, St. Louis, MO; son of Luther and Clementine; married Helen Pearson; children: Luther Aaron & Nathan. **Educ:** Wash Univ, BA, 1969; Eden Theol Sem, MDiv, 1972; St Louis Univ, PhD, 1979. **Career:** E St Louis Welfare Rights Org, coordr, 1970-72; Educ Black Urban Ministers, exec coordr, 1972-79; Lane Tabernacle CME Church, asst pastor, 1972-79; St Louis Univ, Black Church Leaders Prog, coordr, 1975-79; Emory Univ, Candler Sch Theol, fac, 1979-, Univ Senate, pres, Fac Coun, pres, candlers assoc dean, prof church & community, prof emer church & community, currently; Christian Methodist Episcopal Church, elder, currently. **Orgs:** Northside Team Ministries, 1973-79; vpres, Mo Asn Soc Welfare St Louis Div, 1973-79; Metrop Ministerial Alliance, St Louis, 1975-79; Urban Churches Community Develop Prog, 1978-79; Urban Training Org, Atlanta, 1980-; Inst World Evangelism, 1982-; Int Soc Theta Phi, 1987; Omicron Delta Kappa, 1991; Families First, 1992; Eden Theol Sem; founder, Interfaith Childrens Movement. **Honors/Awds:** Service Award, St Louis & Mid St Louis City Jaycees, 1975; Inducted, Martin Luther King Jr Collegium Scholar, Morehouse Col; Distinguished Volunteer Award, Prevent Child Abuse Ga, 2007; Bishops Thomas Hoyt and Paul Stewart Institutional Ministry Award, Phillips Sch Theol, 2009; Big Voice for Georgias Children Award, Voices Georgias C Inc, 2009; Emory Williams Distinguished Teaching Award, Emory Univ, 2010. **Special Achievements:** Co-author, actor: "What's Black," televised KFTC, 1970, "Earth Day, "televised PBS, 1970; "Howard Thurman, the Mystic as Prophet," 1981; "Intimacy & Mission: Intentional Community as Crucible for Radical Discipleship", 1994; Howard Thurman: Essential Writings, 2006. **Home Addr:** 1956 Mountain Creek Dr, Stone Mountain, GA 30087-1018. **Business Addr:** Professor Emeritus of Church & Community, Emory University, 1531 Dickey Dr, Atlanta, GA 30322, **Business Phone:** (404)727-6326.

### SMITH, DR. MARIE EVANS

Child psychologist. **Personal:** Born Oct 21, 1928, Philadelphia, PA; daughter of Frederick and Mamie Pace; married Charles N; children: Dianne S Partee, Dionne S Jones & Deborah S. **Educ:** Temple Univ, BS, 1972; Antioch Univ, MEd, 1974; Kensington Univ, PhD, 1985. **Career:** Greentree Sch, teacher, 1960-65; Inst Human Potential, asst dir, 1965-70; Pkwy Day Sch, perceptual motor spec, 1970-74; Hahnemann Med Col & John F Kennedy Ment Health Ctr, instr & supvr, 1974-; John F Kennedy Ment Health/Ment Retardation Ctr, pa clin psychologist, 1974-, site dir, 1988-; Int Biog Asn, fel, 1989. **Orgs:** Pres, Wellesley Civic Asn, 1965-; Temple Univ Alumni Asn, 1973-87, Antioch Univ Alumni Asn, 1974-87; ment health consult, Sch Dist Philadelphia, 1974-; Coun Int Visitors Mus Civic Ctr, 1983-87; Coun Asn Greater Philadelphia, 1985-, Nat Geog Soc, 1985-; mem at large, Nat Asn Advan Colored People, 1985-; Afro-Am Hist Cult Mus, 1985-87; bd mem, Am Black Women's Heritage Soc, 1986-87; Zeta Phi Beta, 1986-; consult & child psychologist, Minority Ment Health Advocacy Task Force; founding mem, Am Legion Aux Henry Hopkins Post 881; Urban League Philadelphia, 1990-; Nat Polit Cong Black Women, 1989-; Philadelphia Mus Art, 1990; fel & dipl, Am Bd Med Psychotherapist, 1990; golden life mem, Zeta Phi Beta Sorority, 1990. **Honors/Awds:** Legions of Honor Membership Chapel of Four Chaplains Award, 1965; Service to Children Award, parkway Day Sch, 1974; Certificate of Service Award, Hahnemann Med Col, 1980; Certification of African Cultures, Am Forum Int Study, 1981; Certificate of Merit, Sch Dist Philadelphia, 1983; Recognition of Achievement, Providence Baptist Church, 1985; John F Kennedy Community Service Award, Philadelphia PA, 1985, 1986; Certificate of Achievement, Behavioral Ther Temple Univ; Womens Hist Month NJ Black Women's Educ Alliance, 1989; Recognition of Service, John F Kennedy Ment Health/Ment Retardation Ctr, 1988; Top Ladies of Distinction, 1995. **Home Addr:** 518 Wellesley Rd, Philadelphia, PA 19119, **Home Phone:** (215)247-7123. **Business Addr:** Site Director, John F Kennedy Mental Health-Poplar Guidance Clinic, 321 W Girard Ave, Philadelphia, PA 19123, **Business Phone:** (215)235-6250.

### SMITH, MARIE F.
Association executive. **Personal:** Born Mar 12, 1939, East St. Louis, IL; daughter of David and Christina Ford; married Richard Stanley. **Educ:** Fisk Univ, BS, biol & premed studies, attended 1961; Stanford Univ, pub affairs. **Career:** Women's Initiative Prog, spokesperson, nat pres, 2004-06; freelance writer; Social Security Adv Bd, 2011-; real estate consult; US Social Security Admin, claims rep, dir manpower mgt & orgn planning, off mgr & mgt analyst. **Orgs:** Treas, nat pres & spokesperson, 2002-04, Bd dir, AARP, Nat Legis Coun, chair; Maui Vol Ctr; Maui Adult Day Care Ctr; Interfaith Vol Caregivers; pres, African Am Heritage Found Maui; local chap, Nat Asn Retired Fed Employees; Zonta Int, Wash, DC; adv bd, County Off Aging; comnr, Status Women, Gov Hawaii. **Honors/Awds:** Listed in Who's Who in American Women, 2004; Cited as one of America's 100 most influential African American leaders, Ebony magazine, 2004; Woman of Excellence Award, Comn Status Women; Circle of Women Award, County Comt Status Women; Commissioner's Citation, Social Security Admin.. **Business Addr:** Advisory Board Member, Social Security Advisory Board, 400 Va Ave SW Suite 625, Washington, DC 20024, **Business Phone:** (202)475-7700.

### SMITH, MARK ANTHONY
Football player. **Personal:** Born Aug 28, 1974, Vicksburg, MS. **Educ:** Auburn Univ, grad. **Career:** Football player (retired); Ariz Cardinals, 1999, defensive end, defensive tackle, 1997, right defensive tackle, 1998, right defensive tackle, left defensive tackle, 2000; Cleveland Browns, 2002, right defensive tackle, 2001.

### SMITH, MARQUETTE
Football player, football coach, executive. **Personal:** Born Jul 14, 1972, Casselberry, FL; married Dontonya; children: Whitney. **Educ:** Fla State Univ, AA, bus, 1993; Univ Cent Fla, BA, orgn commun, 1995; Madison Univ, MBA, bus admin, 2005. **Career:** Football player (retired), football coach, executive; Carolina Panthers, running back, 1996-97; Rhein Fire, NFL Europe; Winnipeg Blue Bombers, CFL; Shreveport Knights, RFL; Green Bay Bombers, IFL; Iowa Barnstormers, AFL; Lacrosse Knight Train, NIFL; Carolina Stingrays, NIFL; alma mater, running back coach, 2000; Winter Springs High Sch, offensive coordr, 2001; ghostriders, head coach & dir football opers, currently; First Step Adolescent Serv Inc, prog mgr, 1999-2001, dir staff develop & internal invests, 2001-08; Rsight Invests, surveillance & siu field investr, 2008-09; SmithGroup Invests Inc, chief exec officer, 2009-; Global Options, opers mgr, 2011-13. **Honors/Awds:** Second team All-Am honors, 1995; honorable mention selection, Orlando Sentinel's 25th Anniversary Football Team. **Business Addr:** Chief Executive Officer, Smithgroup Investigations Inc, 37 N Orange Ave Suite 500, Orlando, FL 32801, **Business Phone:** (407)568-0057.

### SMITH, MARVIN PRESTON
Police officer, vice president (organization). **Personal:** Born May 5, 1944, Grand Rapids, MI; son of Maxine and Isaiah; children: Micheal, Debbie, Tracey, Preston & Marika D. **Educ:** Jackson Ct Col, cert, Mich law enforcement, 1975. **Career:** Police officer (retired), vice president; Grand Rapids Police Dept, police officer, 1975-92; Grand Rapids Bd Educ, bldg safety rep; Proj ReHab Com Alternative Prog, resident counr, 1992, residential supv; Recovery Rd LLC, vpres, currently. **Orgs:** Pres, Officers Shield, 1988-; deleg, Nat Black Police Officer Asn, 1989-; Wealthy St Ctr, 1990-. **Home Addr:** 142 Alger St SE, Grand Rapids, MI 49507, **Home Phone:** (616)452-2039. **Business Addr:** Vice President, Recovery Road LLC, 4362 Northlake Blvd Suite 109, Palm Beach Gardens, FL 33410, **Business Phone:** (561)899-4388.

### SMITH, MARY ALICE. See ALICE, MARY.

### SMITH, MARY LEVI
College president. **Personal:** Born Jan 30, 1936, Hazlehurst, MS; daughter of William Levi and Byneter Markham; married LeRoy; children: Darryl, Angela Williams & Danee. **Educ:** Jackson State Univ, BS, 1957; Univ Ky, MA, 1964, EdD, 1980. **Career:** Tenn Elem Grade Schs, teacher, 1957-64; Tuskegee Inst, asst dir reading clin, 1964-70; Ky State Univ, asst coordr, assoc prof educ, 1970, chair, dept educ, 1981-83, Col Appl Sci, dean, 1983-88, vpres acad affairs, 1988-89, interim pres, 1989-90, spec asst to pres, prof educ, 1990-91, pres, 1991-98, pres emer & fac emer, currently. **Orgs:** Comnr, Comn Cols Southern Asn Cols & Schs, 1992-97; bd dir, Nat Asn State Univs & Land Grant Col; Nat Asn Equal Opportunity Higher Ed; Am Asn Cols Teacher Educ; United Way Frankfort; Frankfort & Franklin Co Comt Educ, Govt Servs Ctr Common wealth Ky; Am Coun Educ Comt Women Higher Educ; Nat Bd Examrs, Nat Coun Accreditation Teacher Educ; Delta Sigma Theta Sorority; bd mem, Capital City Mus; St John AME Church; Ky Hist Soc; Nat Asn Advan Colored People. **Honors/Awds:** Outstanding Faculty of the Year, Ky State Univ, 1986; Outstanding Alumnus Award, Jackson State Univ, 1988; Torchbearers & Trail bearers Award, Pi Lambda Omega Chapter of Alpha Kappa Alpha Sorority, 1989; Women of Achievement Award, Young Women's Christian Asn Lexington, 1990; Woman of the Year Award, Nat Asn Advan Colored People, Frankfort Chap, 1990; Citizens Award, Delta Sigma Theta, Frankfort Alumnae Chap, 1990; Alumni Hall of Fame, Univ Ky, 1992; Professional Achievement Award, Louisville Defender; Woman of Achievement Award, Frankfort Bus & Prof Women, 1994; Inducted to Hall of Distinguished Alumni by Ky State Univ, 1995. **Special Achievements:** First Female President of Kentucky State University; author, In Spite of the Odds: Using Roadblocks, Potholes, & Hurdles as Stepping Stone to Success. **Home Addr:** 410 Col Pk Dr, Frankfort, KY 40601. **Business Addr:** President Emeritus, Kentucky State University, 400 E Main St, Frankfort, KY 40601, **Business Phone:** (502)597-6000.

### SMITH, MARZELL L.
Educator, consultant. **Personal:** Born Aug 14, 1936, Conehatta, MS; married Albertine B. **Educ:** Jackson State Col, BS, 1958; TN A&I State Univ, MEd, 1964; Univ Miami, 1969; Univ Miami, Ed.D, 1973. **Career:** Allen Carver Jr Sr HS, 1958-64; Jim Hill Jr Sr HS, teacher, 1964-66; GN Smith Elem Sch, asst prin, 1966-69; Univ Miami, fel, 1969-70; FL Sch Desegregation Univ Miami, staff consult, 1970-; Douglas Elem, coordr, 1971-72; Alachua Co, 1972; Dept Found FL Atlantic Univ, 1975; Monreo Co Sch Syst; Collier Co. **Orgs:** Am Educ Res Asn; Nat Asn Sch Adminr; BSA; Nat Asn Sec Sch Prin; Col Hill Bapt Ch; Jackson Bd Cert Officials; Phi Delta Kappa; SW Officials Asn; Kappa Alpha Psi Frat; Urban League; MTA-JTA-CTA; Miami Chap Nat Alliance Black Sch Edr; Fla Asn Dist Sch Supt; So Asn Black Adminstrv Personnel; Univ Miami Black Fac Adminr; bd dir, Miami Black Arts Gallery &Workshop; Dept Adminr Curric & Instr; NEA; Nat Alliance Black Sch Educ; Poverty Law Ctr; Nat Asn Advan Colored People. **Home Addr:** 6355 NW 200 St, Miami, FL 33015-2185, **Home Phone:** (305)625-9757.

### SMITH, MATT JERMAINE
Football player. **Personal:** Born Feb 3, 1972, Augusta, GA. **Educ:** Univ Ga. **Career:** Football player (retired); Green Bay Packers, defensive tackle, 1997-2000; NJ Hitmen, 2001; Las Vegas Outlaws, 2001; Ga Force, 2002-03, defensive lineman, 2005-08; Orlando Predators, 2004, 2013; Tampa Bay Storm, 2010-11; San Jose SaberCats, 2012; free agt, currently. **Special Achievements:** Ranked first in club history in career sacks with 26.0 and ranks second for sacks in a single-season with 7.5, 2007. **Business Addr:** Defensive Tackle, Tampa Bay Storm, 401 Channelside Dr, Tampa, FL 33602, **Business Phone:** (813)276-7300.

### SMITH, MICHAEL
Basketball executive, basketball coach. **Personal:** Born Feb 5, 1955, Memphis, TN. **Career:** Basketball coach (retired), basketball referee; MBCC Church League, coach; Nat Basketball Asn, referee, currently. **Orgs:** Nat Basketball Referees Asn. **Honors/Awds:** Schick Rookie Game, 1997; McDonalds High School All-American Game, 1999; Mexico Challenge, 2000; NBA Europe Games, 2003; Vanguard Club Achievement Award. **Special Achievements:** Volunteered to work with Mid-South Junior Golf Association, 1996-99. **Business Addr:** NBA Official, National Basketball Referees Association, The Willard Offices 1455 Pa Ave NW Suite 225, Washington, DC 20004, **Business Phone:** (202)638-5090.

### SMITH, MICHAEL JOHN
Basketball player. **Personal:** Born Mar 28, 1972, Washington, DC. **Educ:** Providence Col, attended 1994. **Career:** Basketball player (retired); Sacramento Kings, power forward, 1994-98; Vancouver Grizzlies, power forward, 1998-99; Wash Wizards, power forward, 1999-2001; Snaidero Udine, 2001-02; Idaho Stampede, Continental Basketball Asn, 2002-03; Dakota Wizards, Continental Basketball Asn, 2003-04.

### SMITH, DR. MILDRED BEATTY
Educator, elementary school teacher. **Personal:** Born Feb 3, 1935, SC. **Educ:** SC State Col, BS; Mich State Univ, MA, PhD. **Career:** Curric coordr; elem teacher; elem dir; vis lectr; consr; Flint Bd Educ, elem dir. **Orgs:** Bd dir, First Independence Nat Bank Detroit; bd regent, Eastern Mich Univ, 1964-77. **Special Achievements:** Author: "Home & Sch Focus on Reading", 1971; co-author: "Reading Systems & Open Highways", 1971-74. **Home Addr:** 922 Maxine St, Flint, MI 48503-5319, **Home Phone:** (810)233-6252.

### SMITH, MONICA LAVONNE
Editor, journalist. **Personal:** Born Jan 26, 1966, New Haven, CT; daughter of Hulee Evans and Erma J. **Educ:** Va State Univ, BA, 1988. **Career:** Comtex Scientific Corp, copy ed, 1989-90, sr ed, 1990-. **Orgs:** NAB, 1990-; Nat Asn Negro Bus & Prof Womens Clubs Inc, 1990-; NCP, Greater New Haven Br, election supvr comn; Hill Neighborhood Tutoring Prog, 1991-. **Business Addr:** Senior Editor, Comtex Scientific Corp, 911 Hope St, Stamford, CT 06907, **Business Phone:** (203)358-0007.

### SMITH, MORRIS LESLIE
Research scientist. **Personal:** Born May 29, 1933, Camden, NJ; son of William E and Tamar H; married Alice Marie Gray; children: Morris G, Wesley E & Stephen J. **Educ:** Mich State Univ, BS, 1959; Temple Univ, MBA, 1978. **Career:** Magna Bond Inc, res chemist, 1959-61; EL Conwell Inc, anal chemist, 1961; Scott Paper Co, Philadelphia, res chemist, 1961-65, sr res proj chemist, 1965-74, sect leader, 1974-78, sr res leader, 1978, technol mgr; The ML Smith Group Inc, pres, currently. **Orgs:** Pres, Echelon Br Camden Co, YMCA, 1983-86; exec large Int Soc African Scientists, 1984-; chmn, bd dir, Camden Co, YMCA, 1990-; chmn, vice chr, bd pensions, TV Mins Comm, Southern NJ Ann Conf United Methodist Church; treas parade marshal Lawnside 4th of July Comm Inc; pres, United Methodist Homes NJ Found; NJ Supreme Ct Commt Minority Concerns, 1996; vice chmn, Southern NJ Ann Conf United Methodist Church, Bd Pensions. **Home Addr:** 307 Tillman Ave, Lawnside, NJ 08045-1019, **Home Phone:** (856)546-8733. **Business Addr:** President, ML Smith Group Inc, 307 Tillman St, Lawnside, NJ 08045, **Business Phone:** (856)546-8733.

### SMITH, NATHANIEL, JR.
Executive. **Personal:** son of Nathaniel and Lena; married Jannie. **Career:** Ver-Val Enterprises, Ft Walton Beach, Fla, owner, secy, pres, chief exec officer, 1979-. **Business Addr:** Owner, President, Ver-Val Enterprises, 646 Anchors St Suite 8, Fort Walton Beach, FL 32549, **Business Phone:** (904)244-7931.

### SMITH, NEIL
Football player, sports team owner. **Personal:** Born Apr 10, 1966, New Orleans, LA; married Sheri; children: Joshua, Nesha & Ne. **Educ:** Univ Nebr. **Career:** Football player (retired), owner; Sporting News Coll All-Am Team, defensive lineman, 1987; Kans City Chiefs, defensive end & left defensive end, 1988-94, 1996, right defensive end, 1995; Denver Broncos, left defensive end, 1997-98, defensive end, 1999; San Diego Chargers, 2000; Kans City Brigade Arena Football League, vpres abbr, co-owner, 2006-08. **Orgs:** Nat spokesman, Yes I Can Found. **Honors/Awds:** Pro Bowl, 1991-97; Super Kans Citian Award, S KC Chamber Com; Outstanding Learning Disabled Achievers Award, Lab Sch Wash; Ed Block Courage Award, 1994; 10 Outstanding Ams Award, US Jr Chamber Com, 1996; Super Bowl, Denver Broncos, 1998; Chiefs' Hall of Fame, 2006; Missouri Sports Hall of Fame, 2008. **Business Addr:** KS.

### SMITH, DR. NELLIE J.
Educator. **Personal:** Born May 15, 1932, Meridian, MS; daughter of Booker T Johnson and Nettie B Johnson; married Elder Levi; children: Bobby, Paula, Perry & Joseph. **Educ:** Rust Col Holly Spring, BS, bus, 1954; Kans State Teachers Col, Emporia, MS, grad prog bus, 1956; Univ NDak, PhD, bus educ, 1973. **Career:** Rust Col, secy pres, 1954-55, chair person div bus, bus instr, 1962-63, assoc prof bus educ, 1970-2002, prof bus educ, 1970-; Int Bros Teamsters, stenographer/bookkeeper, 1960-62; Wilberforce Univ, Xenia, OH, secy; Harris High Sch, bus instr, 1963-64; Miss Valley State Col, asst prof, bus teacher, 1964-70; Star Inc, Bus Teacher & Co-Dir Bus Prog, 1966-67; Memphis State Univ, Off Admin Dept, 1984. **Orgs:** Nat Coun Negro Women; Social Bus Educ Asn, UMC, 1942-, Cappella Choir Rust Col, 1950-55; voice recital MS Valley State Col, 1969; Asbury United Methodist Church, 1970-; choral union, Univ Ndak, 1971-73, Nat Bus Educ Asn, Delta Pi Epsilon, Pi Omega Pi, PhiBeta Lambda; Marshall Co Republican Women's Group, 1982; Marshall Co Election Comn, 1993-97; Miss Arts Comn, 1994-98; app gov, Pvt Indust Cou, & Comn Temp Assistance Needy Families, 1997-2001; adv, Adult Pathway Prog. **Special Achievements:** Book: A Comparative Analysis of National Employment Patterns as Perceived by Minority and Non-Minority Bachelor-degree Business Education Graduates of 1972, 1973. **Home Addr:** 30 McMillan Dr, Holly Springs, MS 38635-1124, **Home Phone:** (662)252-1968. **Business Addr:** Professor of Business & Secondary Education, Rust College, 150 Rust Ave, Holly Springs, MS 38635, **Business Phone:** (601)252-8000.

### SMITH, NICK
Actor. **Educ:** Santa Rosa Jr Col, AA, commun, 1996; Univ Calif, Berkeley, CA, BA, polit sci, 1999; Emerson Col, Boston, MA, commun mgt, 2002. **Career:** WPRI, photogr & truck operator; E! Entertainment TV, entertainment reporter & host; Weather Channel; World News Now, "Live! With Regis & Kelly", host; ABC, host; Fox News Channel, field producer, 2000-02, Fox Networks Group, news anchor, 2004-06, FOX 29, "Good Day Philadelphia", co-anchor, 2005-06, actor, 2010; WLFL-TV, photogr, 2002-03; WTVD-TV, reporter, 2002-04; KGO-TV, coresp, 2006-11; ABC7 News, corresp, 2004, 2006-11, host & reporter, 2006-07, ABC TV, corresp & substitute anchor, 2006-, ABC Network, "Am Inventor", reporter & host, 2007; FremantleMedia, host, 2007; Imagine Tv, actor, 2009; Tremendous Entertainment, host, 2010-13. **Business Addr:** Correspondent, ABC TV, 7 Lincoln Sq, New York, NY 10023, **Business Phone:** (212)877-0588.

### SMITH, NORMAN RAYMOND
Publisher. **Personal:** Born Nov 17, 1944, New Orleans, LA; married Patricia A; children: Corey Norman & Christopher Jude. **Educ:** Southern Univ, New Orleans, BA, hist, 1964; Commonwealth Col Sci, mortuary sci, 1966. **Career:** Treme Improv Polit Soc, pres & chmn bd, 1970-; Forget-Me-Knots Inc, pres & chmn bd, currently; Treme Cult Enrichment Progs, secy. **Orgs:** New Orleans Embalmers Asn, 1966-; fel, Loyola Univ Inst Polit, 1979; Upper Pontalba Bldg Comn, 1980-88; Armstrong Pk Adv Comn, 1983-88; grand knight, Knights Peter Claver-Thomy Lafon Coun 240, 1986-89; treas, Greater New Orleans Black Tourism Ctr, 1986; exec bd mem, LA Black Cult Commn, 1984-88; exec dir, Treme Community Educ Prog, 1996-. **Home Addr:** 1615 St Philip St, New Orleans, LA 70116-2936, **Home Phone:** (504)581-4411. **Business Addr:** President, Forget-Me-Knots Inc., LLC, PO Box 7332, New Orleans, LA 70186, **Business Phone:** (504)304-0127.

### SMITH, OBRIE, SR.
Association executive, president (organization). **Personal:** married Cora; children: Kyle & Obrie Jr. **Educ:** Lincoln Univ, BS, MA. **Career:** NC A&T Found Inc, chmn, bd dir & pres, currently; Greensboro Int Civil Rights Ctr & Mus, bd treas, currently. **Orgs:** Vpres & bd mem, Waukesha County; Nat Asn Advan Colored People; bd mem, United Way; Nat Hisp Univ; Milwaukee Enterprise Ctr; Charlotte Meckleburg Ministries; Friendship Baptist Church, NC. **Home Addr:** 1338 Manicott Dr, Matthews, NC 28105. **Business Addr:** President, Board Director, North Carolina A&T Foundation Inc, Alumni Found-Event Ctr 200 N Benbow Rd, Greensboro, NC 27411, **Business Phone:** (336)433-5576.

### SMITH, ORLANDO. See SMITH, TUBBY.

### SMITH, OSCAR A., JR.
Business owner, chief executive officer, executive. **Educ:** Morgan State Univ, BS, bus admin & mgt, 1973. **Career:** Community Foods Inc, chief exec officer, owner & pres, 1992-2000. **Orgs:** mem, Omega Psi Phi Fraternity. **Honors/Awds:** CPN, ranked 18, BLK Enterprise mag list of top 100 indust & serv companies, 1992. **Business Addr:** Chief Executive Officer, Owner, Community Foods Inc, 2936 Remington Ave, Baltimore, MD 21211, **Business Phone:** (410)235-9800.

### SMITH, OTIS, III
Football player, football coach. **Personal:** Born Oct 22, 1965, New Orleans, LA; married Sandy; children: LaKeitha, Chanel, Ciara & Chloe. **Educ:** Univ Mo. **Career:** Football player (retired), football coach; Philadelphia Eagles, defensive back, 1991-94, asst sec coach, 2008-09; New York Jets, right cornerback, 1995, 1997-99; New Eng Patriots, right cornerback, 1996, 2000-02, free safety, asst coach, 2006-07; Detroit Lions, left cornerback, 2003; Kans City Chiefs, defensive qual control coach, currently. **Orgs:** Mem, Patriots orgn. **Honors/Awds:** Defensive Player of the Week; Kyle Clifton Good Guy Award, 1998; Super Bowl champion (XXXVI). **Business Addr:** Assistant Coach, Kansas City Chiefs, 1 Arrowhead Dr, Kansas City, MO 64129, **Business Phone:** (816)920-9300.

### SMITH, REV. OTIS BENTON, JR.
Clergy. **Personal:** Born Nov 5, 1939, Lexington, KY; son of Otis B Sr (deceased) and Hattie Bibbs (deceased); married Bertha Odessa Stevenson; children: Otis III, Patrick Tyrone & Kenise Lynette. **Educ:** Cent State Univ, BS, 1960; Southern Baptist Theol Sem, MDiv, 1969;

Univ N Ala; Certi Continuing Educ, 1985; Selma Univ, DDiv, 1991. **Career:** Nat Jewish Hosp, Pediat Sect, recreation supvr & counr, 1964-65; E Moline State Hosp, recreation supvr, 1965-66; WVa Hosp Dayton, recreation spec, 1966; Fifth St Baptist Church, Louisville, asst pastor, 1966-69; First Baptist Church, pastor & secy 1969-; Sch Relig N Ala Baptist Acad-Courtland Ala, instr, 1970-73; N Ala Bapt Ministers Conf, lectr & Secy, 1976-79; Ala Bapt State Conv Ministers Sem, lectr, 1980-. **Orgs:** Exec mem & bd dir, Muscle Shoals Area Ment Health, 1971-2001; conv mem & bd trustee, Selma Univ, 1973-86; exec mem, bd dir, Colbert Lauderdale Comn Action Agency, 1973-79; pres, Muscle Shoals Baptist SS & BTU Cong, 1981-90; vice moderator, Muscle Shoals Baptist Dist Asn Ala, 1983-85; vice chmn & bd dir, Muscle Shoals Area Ment Health Ctr, 1983-85; chmn, bd dir, Riverbend Ment Health Ctr, 1985-87; adv coun, Shoals Community Col, 1987-; asst sec, Nat Baptist Conv, USA INC, 1988-94, 2001-; gen secy, Ala State Missionary Baptist Conv, 1995-; Nat Asn Advan Colored People; Kappa Alpha Psi; Ala Baptist State Conv; NBC Inc; bd dir, Roster, currently. **Honors/Awds:** Minister of the Year, Nat Asn Advan Colored People, Muscle Shoals, Ala, 1976; Minister of the Year, Alpha Pi Chap Omega Psi Phi, 1979; Special Cert Recognition, Tri County Branch, Nat Asn Advan Colored People, 1979; Citizen of the Year, Alpha Pi Chap Omega Psi Phi, 1983; Cert Merit, 1984; Minister of the Year, Top Hatters Club Inc, 1987. **Special Achievements:** First Black member & board directors in Shoals Hospital from 1980-82. **Home Addr:** 1022 Hemlock St, PO Box 544, Tuscumbia, AL 35674, **Home Phone:** (256)381-3459. **Business Addr:** Pastor, Secretary, First Baptist Church, 611 S High St, Tuscumbia, AL 35674, **Business Phone:** (205)383-8818.

### SMITH, OTIS FITZGERALD

Founder (originator), basketball player, basketball executive. **Personal:** Born Jan 30, 1964, Jacksonville, FL. **Educ:** Jacksonville Univ, BA, mkt & mgt, 1986. **Career:** Basketball player (retired), basketball executive, founder; Denver Nuggets, 1986-87; Golden State Warriors, 1987-89; Orlando Magic, 1989-92; Solna Vikings, Sweden Prof League, 1996-97; Orlando Magic, dir community rels, 1997-99, asst gen mgr to gen mgr, 2005-12; Boys & Girls Club, vpres mkt & community rels, 1998-99; Golden State Warriors, dir community rels, 1999-2002, exec dir basketball opers, 2002-03; Otis Smith Kids Found, founder, currently. **Orgs:** Founder & pres, Otis Smith Kids Found, 1989-; Orlando Magic, 1989. **Special Achievements:** Official Torch Bearer of the Olympic Flame for the Summer Olympics in Atlanta, 1996. **Home Addr:** 112 W Adams, Jacksonville, FL 32209. **Business Addr:** Founder, Otis Smith Kids Foundation, 9526 Argyle Forest Blvd Suite 2, Jacksonville, FL 32222, **Business Phone:** (904)880-6847.

### SMITH, DR. OTRIE B. HICKERSON

Psychiatrist. **Personal:** Born Mar 17, 1936, Coffeyville, KS; married Robert A Sr; children: Claude, Donna & Robert Jr. **Educ:** Howard Univ, BS, 1958; Howard Univ Col Med, MD, 1962. **Career:** Kings Co Hosp, internship, 1963; Menatl Health Inst, resident, 1966; Menninger Found, staff mem, 1966-67; Area B Comm Health Ctr, chf, 1967-69; Univ Med Ctr, instr, 1969-; Tougaloo Col, 1969-72; VA Ctr, staff mem, 1969-70; Jackson-hinds Comprehensive Health Ctr, dir ment, 1970-; Tougaloo Col, consult; Jackson State Univ, instr; Am & Psychiat Asn, obsvr consult, 1974-75; pvt pract, currently. **Orgs:** Minority Ment Health Ctr; Nat Inst Ment Health; Nat Med Asn; AMA; Am Psychiat Asn; Community Black Psychiat; MS Med Asn; MS State Dept Ment Health; Delta Sigma Theta Sorority; Friends C MS Head Start Proj; bd mem, Hinds Co Proj Head Start. **Business Addr:** Psychiatrist, 1134 Winter St, Jackson, MS 39204-2841, **Business Phone:** (601)948-5572.

### SMITH, OZZIE (OSBORNE EARL SMITH)

Baseball player, business owner, broadcaster. **Personal:** Born Dec 26, 1954, Mobile, AL; son of Clovi and Marvella; married Ethel Denise Jackson; children: Osborne Earl Jr, Dustin & Taryn. **Educ:** Calif Poly Tech State Univ, attended 1977. **Career:** Baseball player (retired), broadcaster, business owner; San Diego Padres, shortstop, 1978-81; St Louis Cardinals, shortstop, 1982-96; TV Show, host; "This Week in Baseball", 1997-98; CNN News Group, baseball analyst, 1999-2002; Nat Baseball Hall Fame, educ ambassador, currently; Ozzie's Restaurant & Sports Bar, owner, currently. **Orgs:** Red Cross, Mult Sclerosis, March Dimes & Annie Malone C Home; pres, Coun Drug Abuse; nat spokesman, CPR; pres, Gateway PGA Found. **Home Addr:** PO Box 8787, St. Louis, MO 63102. **Business Addr:** Owner, Ozzie's Restaurant & Sports Bar, 645 Westport Plz, St. Louis, MO 63146, **Business Phone:** (314)434-1000.

### SMITH, PATRICIA GRACE

Executive. **Personal:** Born Nov 10, 1947, Tuskegee, AL; daughter of Douglas Jones Sr and Wilhelmina R Griffin Jones; married J Clay Jr; children: Stager C, Michelle L, Michael L & Eugene Grace. **Educ:** Wesleyan Col, acad exchange prog, 1964; Univ Mich, acad exchange prog, 1965; Tuskegee Inst, BA, eng, 1968; Auburn Univ, grad courses masters prog eng, 1971; Harvard Univ, Grad Sch Bus Admin, broadcast mgt dev course, 1976; George Washington Univ, telecommunication policy course, 1984; Fed Exec Inst, attended 1997. **Career:** Tuskegee Inst, instr dept eng, 1969-71; Curber Assoc, mgr prog, 1971-73; Nat Asn Broadcasters, dir placement, 1973-74, dir comm affairs, 1974-77; Group W Westinghouse Broadcasting Co WJZ TV, from assoc producer to producer, 1977-78; Sheridan Broadcasting Network, dir affil rels programming, 1978-80; FCC, Off Pub Affairs, chief consumer assist & small bus div, 1980-92, assoc managing dir pub info, ref serv & dep dir policy, 1992-94; US Dept Transp, Off Com Space Transp, assoc managing dir, 1994-95; Fed Aviation Admin Off, assoc admin com space transp, actg assoc adminr, 1995-98; SpaceDev, bd dir, 2008-. Patti Grace Smith Consult, aerospace consult. **Orgs:** Am Women Radio TV, 1973-77; interim chairperson, Int Broadcasting Comm Nat Asn TV Radio Artists, 1974; Cert Prog Commun Mgt Tech, 1974-76; vice chairperson, Nat Conf Black Lawyers Task Force Commun, 1975-81; trustee, Nat Urban League, 1976-81; Jour Commun Adv Coun Auburn Univ, 1976-78; comm, Comm Cancer Coord Coun, 1977-84; adv bBd, Black Arts Celebration, 1978-83; Ala State Soc, 1984-92; Wash Urban League, 1983-87; Nat Asn Advan Colored People, 1983-; comnr, Dist Columbia Comn Human Rights, 1986-87, chairperson, 1987-91; bd adv, Salvation Army, 1992-2001; bd dir, Broadcasters Club; Nat Adv Comm Women Commun Inc; Lambda Iota Tau Int Hon Soc. **Home Addr:** 4010 16th St NW, Washington, DC 20011, **Home Phone:** (202)267-7793. **Business Addr:** Board of Directors, SpaceDev Inc, 13855 Stowe Dr, Poway, CA 92064, **Business Phone:** (858)375-2000.

### SMITH, REV. DR. PAUL

Executive, clergy, administrator. **Personal:** Born Sep 20, 1935, South Bend, IN; married Frances Irene Pitts; children: Kathleen, Heather & Krista. **Educ:** Talladega Col, AB, 1957; Hartford Sem, MDiv, 1960; Eden Theol Sem, DMin, 1977. **Career:** Clergy (retired), executive; Wash Univ, administrator, 1970-78, assoc vice chancellor, 1974-78; Morehouse Col, vpres, 1978-79; Columbia Theol Sem, adj prof, 1979-; Candler Sch Theol, adj prof, 1979-; Hillside Presby Church, pastor; Henry St's First Presby Church, sr minister; Macy's Federated Stores, minority & diversity consult; Am Honda Motors, minority & diversity consult; Second Presby Church, assoc pastor; Berea Presby Church, co-pastor; Morehouse Med Sch, fac; Healthy Families, Brooklyn, exec dir, currently. **Orgs:** State Adv Comt US Civil Rights Comn, 1977-83; trustee, Presby Sch Christian Educ, 1981-; Metro Fair Housing Serv Inc, 1981-; Leadership Atlanta, 1981; consult, Howard Thurman Educ Trust, 1982; bd mem, Child Serv Family Coun, 1983-; Coun Atlanta Pres; Union Sem; Compassion & Choices; Brooklyn Acad Music; Long Island Univ; trustee, bd dir, Continuum Health Partners Inc; longtime mem & chairperson, pastor emer, First Presby Church; bd dir, State Univ New York Downtown Med Ctr, Arthur Ashe Inst Urban Health; trustee, Long Island Col Hosp. **Honors/Awds:** National Endowment for the Humanities, 1982; Women United in Philanthropy. **Special Achievements:** Book: "Theology Computerized World", 1985-86; Public Unity in Diversity, Inclusiveness, 1985; Facing Death: The Deep Calling to the Deep, 1999. First black minister of all-white Hillside Presbyterian Church in Decatur, Georgia, outside Atlanta; First black pastor of a predominantly white church in existence since 1823. **Home Addr:** 300 Missionary Dr, Decatur, GA 30030.

### SMITH, REV. PERRY ANDERSON, III

Clergy. **Personal:** Born May 16, 1934, Mound Bayou, MS; son of Perry and Elease Wilson; married Constance. **Educ:** Howard Univ, BA, 1955, Divinity Sch, MDiv, 1958. **Career:** Pastor (retired); 19th St Baptist Church, stud asst; First Baptist Church Inc, pastor, 1958-2010, sr pastor; Comt Action PG County, Md, exec dir, 1965-69; Nat Civil Serv League, assoc dir, 1969-72; Univ Md, chaplain, 1975-82. **Orgs:** Treas, Prog Nat Baptist Conv, 1974-76, auditor, 1978-80; bd dir, Nat Asn Advan Colored People, Prince George's County, MD; bd dir, Minster Blacks Higher Educ; vpres, Nat Conf Black Churchmen; adv bd mem, Family Serv Prince George's County; Ministries to BlacksHigher Educ; Concerned Clergy Prince George's County. **Honors/Awds:** Martin Luther King Jr Award, Black Student Union, Univ Md Col Park, 1976; Hester V King Humanitarian Award, 1985; Brotherhood/Sisterhood Award, NCCJ, 1998; The Benjamin E Mays Award, Howard Univ Div Sch; Outstanding Community Serv, Prince George's County, Maryland Nat Asn Advan Colored People; Outstanding Community Serv, Progressive Baptist Laymen of Washington DC; Outstanding Community Serv, Frontiers Int; Outstanding Community Serv, Metropolitan Washington Health & Welfare Coun; Outstanding Serv, Univ Md, Nat Asn Advan Colored People; Outstanding Serv, DC Women Ministers Asn; Outstanding Serv, Community Action Prince George's County Md; Achievement Award, Combined Communities Action, Prince George's County, Maryland; Metropolitan Service Award, Iota Upsilon Lambda Chap, Alpha Phi Alpha Fraternity Inc. **Home Addr:** 2908 Native Dancer Ct, Bowie, MD 20721, **Home Phone:** (301)277-4742.

### SMITH, DR. PHILLIP M.

Educator, writer. **Personal:** Born Jan 24, 1937, Ann Arbor, MI; son of Robert and Bernice Whaley; married Gloria J; children: Phillip Jr & Jeffrey M. **Educ:** WVa State Col, BS, zool & math & chem, 1958; City Univ NY, MA, 1969; Educ Admin, dipl; Hofstra Univ, attended 1970; Univ MA, EdD, 1987. **Career:** New York Dept Welfare, Childrens counr, 1958-59; New York Dept Parks, recreation leader, 1959-60; New York Dept Hosp, recreation & dir, 1960-82; Wilkyck Sch Boys, child care specialist, supvr, 1962-66; Neighborhood Youth Corps, curric specialist, 1965-66; Roosevelt Jr & Sr High Sch, sci teacher, 1966-69, dir adult educ, 1969-70, dir reading prog, 1969-70, asst prin, 1969-79, Multi-level Alternative Prog, dir, 1973-74, prin, 1979-88; Roosevelt Sch Dist, dist dir supporting servs, 1988-92; St John's Univ, Queens, adj prof, 1993; Five Towns Col, currently. **Orgs:** Life mem, Nat Asn Advan Colored People; life mem, Kappa Alpha Psi; Nat Asn Black Sch Educrs; Nat Asn Sec Sch Prin; Sch Adminr Asn NY State; Roosevelt Adminrs Asn; vpres, pres, exec bd, PLUS Group Homes Inc, 1980; adv bd, House Good Coun, 1987-; vpres, exec bd, Long Island Asn Supv & Curric Develop, 1988-; trustee, Uniondale Sch Bd, 1991-; bd trustee, Five Towns Col; exec comt, Nassau Suffolk Sch Bd Asn, 1995-. **Honors/Awds:** Fifteen Years Service Award, Health & Hosp Corp; listed in Whos who among students in American Colleges and Universities; listed in Whos who in American Education; listed in Whos who among Black Americans. **Special Achievements:** Cover photo for feature article "Black tennis" Tennis Mag, 1974. **Home Addr:** 857 Northgate Dr, Uniondale, NY 11553-3047, **Home Phone:** (516)483-0799. **Business Addr:** Trustee, Five Towns College, 305 N Service Rd, Dix Hills, NY 11746-6055, **Business Phone:** (631)424-7000.

### SMITH, DR. QUENTIN TED

Educator, health services administrator. **Personal:** Born May 1, 1937, Seaford, DE; son of Carlton and Elizabeth Holland; married Marjorie McCoy; children: Candace, Jason & Michael. **Educ:** Fisk Univ, BA, psychol, 1961; Howard Univ, MD, 1967. **Career:** Univ Chicago, Woodrow Wilson fel, 1961-62; Howard Univ, Nat Med fel, 1963-67; WMHC Fulton City, dir, 1974-75; Ment Health Grady Hosp, dir outpatient child & adolescent, 1977-82; Morehouse Sch Med, prof clin psychiat, course dir, Psychiat & Behav Sci, vice chair & prof, currently, dir third psychiat clerkship & fourth yr child & adolescent psychiat elective; Ridgeview Inst, pvt pract & dir child & adolescent serv & supr psychiat residents & child fel; Emory Univ, assoc prof; Cork Inst, Black Alcohol Studies, vice chair psychiat educ & med dir; Univ Hosps Cleveland Ohio, Child & Adolescent Psychiat fel. **Orgs:** Fel Am Psychiat Asn, 1971-; Am Acad Child Psychiat, 1974-; Pub Affairs Comt, Ga Psychiat Asn, 1986-95; Ridgeview Inst, Peer Rev Subcomt, Nominating Comt; Morehouse Sch Med, Stud Acad Affairs & Prom Comt, Residency Training Comt, Stud Appeals Comt; C's Trust Fund Comt State Ga; Clin Adv Comt, Ridgeview Inst; 100 Black Men Atlanta Inc, Community Involvement Comt; Am Ortho psychiat Asn; Doctors Med Stud Educ Psychiat; Am Coun Alcoholism Psychiatrists Alcohol & Addictions; Nat Med Asn; Ga Psychiat Physicians Asn; Ga Coun Child & Adolescent Psychiat; Black Psychiatrists Am; Guate Educ Biomed Sci Coun; pres, Atlanta Chap Black Psychiatrists Am; Am Acad Addiction Psychiatrists; Am Asn Adolescent Psychiat; Am Acad Addiction Psychiatrists; Am Bd Psychiat & Neurol; Alpha Omega Alpha Med Hon Soc. **Honors/Awds:** Phi Beta Kappa, Fisk Univ, Nashville, TN, 1961; Beta Kappa Chi, 1961; Man of the Year Award, Fisk Univ, 1961, Community Service Award, 2000; Outstanding Teaching Award; Master Teacher Award; Outstanding Service Award, Fisk Univ; Outstanding Service Award, Howard Univ Col Med Dean's; Outstanding Alumnus Award, United Negro Col Fund. **Special Achievements:** Authored Numerous Publication. **Home Addr:** 2750 Ridge Valley Rd NW, Atlanta, GA 30327-1826. **Business Addr:** Professor of Clinical Psychiatry, Course Director & Vice Chairperson, Morehouse School of Medicine, 720 Westview Dr SW Suite 212, Atlanta, GA 30310, **Business Phone:** (404)756-1440.

### SMITH, REGINALD D, SR. See Obituaries Section.

### SMITH, REV. REGINALD EDWARD

Clergy. **Personal:** Born Jan 10, 1967, Detroit, MI; son of Major E and Edith; married Tracy Geneen; children: Tkhari Gamal, Tyre Gavon-Major & Tavis Geremiah. **Educ:** Ala State Univ, BS, 1991; Samuel Dewitt Proctor Sch Theol, Va Union, MDiv, 1997; Univ Mich, Dearborn, continuing educ studies. **Career:** Union Grace Missionary Baptist Church, pastor, sr pastor, currently. **Orgs:** Alpha Phi Alpha Fraternity Inc, 1989; mem comt, Coun Baptist Pastors Detroit & Vicinity; exec dir, Union Grace Community Develop Corp; exec mem, Kingdom Builders Pastor & People Int Conf; exec mem, Drum Majors; Merrill Lynch Exten Bd. **Home Addr:** 1823 Fleetwood, Troy, MI 48098, **Home Phone:** (313)894-2501. **Business Addr:** Senior Pastor, Union Grace Missionary Baptist Church, 2550 W Grand Blvd, Detroit, MI 48208, **Business Phone:** (313)894-2500.

### SMITH, REGINALD KEITH

School administrator. **Personal:** Born Mar 3, 1960, Kenansville, NC; son of Rayford and Willie Lucille Miller; married Lisa L Nelson. **Educ:** NC Cent Univ, Durham, NC, BA, pub admin & polit sci, 1982; Univ Del, Newark, DE, MPA, 1984. **Career:** Dept Health & Human Serv, Rockville, Md, pub health analyst, 1981; State NC Gov's Off, Durham, minority affairs asst, 1982; Univ Del, Newark, dorm residence dir & nutrit monitor, 1982; NC Cent Univ, Durham, adj asst prof, spec asst & internship coordr, 1984-87, assoc dean, 1998-2003, higher educ adminr & outreach dir, currently, SUSI prog, managing dir, currently; Durham County Govt, NC, asst county mgr, 1987-88; NC Univ, Durham, bus opers mgr; Pub Educ Network, Durham Pub Schs, Durham, NC, interim exec dir, 2005-07. **Orgs:** Parliamentarian & pub rels chairperson, NCCU Alumni Asn, 1984-88; zone chmm, Durham Scouting Roundup, 1984, 1986; bd dir, Salvation Army Boys Club; Youth Serv Adv Comm, 1985-; Rockefeller Fel Duke UNC Women Studies, 1985-86; contrib founder, Acad Help Ctr, 1986-89; Durham Pub Schs Budget Adv Comt, 2006-07; advisor, Alpha Phi Alpha Fraternity Inc, currently. **Home Addr:** 3200 Victor Ave, Durham, NC 27707, **Home Phone:** (919)490-1701. **Business Addr:** Higher Education Administrator, Outreach Director, North Carolina Central University, 1801 Fayetteville St, Durham, NC 27707, **Business Phone:** (919)530-6445.

### SMITH, DR. RICHARD ALFRED

Physician. **Personal:** Born Oct 13, 1932, Norwalk, CT; son of Julius and Mabel; married Lorna Carrier; children: Dirk Devi, Rik Balakrishna, Erik Dibnarine, Blake Andrew & Quintin Everett. **Educ:** Howard Univ, BSc, 1953, MD, 1957; Columbia Univ, Sch pub health, MPH, 1960. **Career:** Columbia Univ's Sch Pub Health, resident; US Pub Health Serv, med dir, 24 yrs; Peace Corps Nigeria, 1961-63; Wash, DC, dep med dir, 1963-65; Indian Health Serv Ariz; Am Health Care Syst, physician asst; Peace Corps physician Nigeria; Dept Health & Human Serv, Off Int Health, chief off planning, 1965-68, dep dir; Univ Wash, MEDEX Prog, prof & dir, 1968-72; Univ Hawaii, Sch Med, MEDEX Group, clin prof & dir, 1972-, primary care & health specialist, currently. **Orgs:** Fel Am Col Preventive Med, 1961-; Am Pub Health Asn, 1963-; Inst Med Nat Acad Sci, 1972-; consult World Health Org, 1972-; dir, Peace Corp; dir staff, Health & Human Serv; Inst Med Nat Acad Sci; Who expert comts; Physician Asst Hist Soc. **Honors/Awds:** William A Jump Award, Dept Health, Educ & Welfare; Gerard B Lambert Award, Lambert Found, 1971; Rockefeller Public Service Award, Princeton Univ, 1981; Outstanding Service Award, Region IX, Dept Health & Human Servs for Leadership in Developing the Physician Asst & Nurse Practitioners Movement USA, 1992. **Business Addr:** Clinical Professor, Director, University of Hawaii, 95-390 Kuahelani Ave, Mililani, HI 96789, **Business Phone:** (808)533-6492.

### SMITH, REV. ROBERT, JR.

Clergy. **Personal:** Born Oct 5, 1951, Pensacola, FL; son of Robert Sr (deceased) and Ollie Mae Hale; married Cynthia Perkins; children: Sherique Moshelle Ransby (Olander), Conderidge & Terique Moshelle Parker (Gary). **Educ:** Lawson St Jr Col, Birmingham, Ala; Jefferson St Jr Col, Birmingham, Ala; Miles Col, Birmingham, Ala, BA, 1974; New Orleans Baptist Theol Sem, New Orleans, LA, Mdiv, 1976; Drew Univ, DMin. **Career:** New Bethel Baptist Church, Detroit, MI, co-pastor, 1982-84, pastor, 1984, sr pastor & chief exec officer, currently; Eastern Star Baptist Church, Birmingham, AL, pastor; Mt Tabor Baptist Church, Brent, AL, pastor; First Baptist Church, Mason City, Birmingham, AL, pastor; Bethel Baptist Church, Pratt City, Birmingham, AL, pastor; rec artist; Mich Dist Baptist Asn, moderator at large; Haiti Mission Alliance, founder & chair. **Orgs:** Chmn, Mayor Young's, 1989; Re-election Comm; bd mem, Greater Opportunities Industrialization Ctr; Continuing steering comt, Nat Bank Detroit; Detroit Econ Club; prog coordr, SCLC, Detroit Chap; vpres, Detroit Chap Nat Asn Advan Colored People; exec bd mem, Mich Chap, Southern Christian Leadership Conf. **Honors/Awds:** Councilman David Eberhard Outstanding Community Award, 1989; Outstanding Achievement Award, 1982; Sermon Album of the Year,

Singing Preacher of the Year, WENN Radio & Clergy That Care, 1982; SCLC Minister of the Year Award, 1992. **Home Addr:** 19301 Warrington, Detroit, MI 48221, **Home Phone:** (313)864-8577. **Business Addr:** Senior Pastor, Chief Executive Officer, New Bethel Baptist Church, 8430 C L Franklin Blvd, Detroit, MI 48206, **Business Phone:** (313)894-5788.

**SMITH, PROF. ROBERT CHARLES**
Educator. **Personal:** Born Feb 12, 1947, Benton, LA; son of Martin and Blanch Tharpe; married Scottie Gibson; children: Blanch & Jessica Scottus-Charles. **Educ:** Los Angeles City Col, CA, AA, 1967; Univ Calif, Berkeley, CA, BA, 1970; Univ Calif, Los Angeles, CA, MA, 1972; Howard Univ, Wash, DC, PhD, 1976. **Career:** State Univ New York Col, Purchase, NY, asst prof, 1975-80; Columbia Univ, New York, NY, res assoc, 1976-80; Howard Univ, Wash, DC, assoc prof, 1980-89; Prairie View A&M Univ, Prairie View, Tex, prof, 1989-90; San Francisco State Univ, San Francisco, Calif, prof, 1990-. **Orgs:** Fel Ford Found, 1973-76; Am Polit Sci Asn, 1976-; Acad Polit Sci, 1976-; Nat Conf Black Polit Sci; Nat Cong Black Fac, 1988-; CA Black Fac, 1990-; Western Polit Sci Asn; Nat Asn Advan Colored People; San Francisco County Slavery Disclosure Ordinance, 2006. **Special Achievements:** Author of twelve books on race and African American politics and the Encyclopedia of African American Politics; Editor of the State University of New York Press series in African American Studies. **Home Addr:** 5044 Santa Rita Rd, Richmond, CA 94803-3236, **Home Phone:** (510)222-7273. **Business Addr:** Professor, San Francisco State University, 1600 Holloway Ave, San Francisco, CA 94132, **Business Phone:** (415)338-7524.

**SMITH, ROBERT D.**
Businessperson, artist. **Personal:** Born Apr 3, 1932, Chicago, IL; son of Henry D and Lois Etta Bullock; married Rosemary Booker; children: Laura Susan, David Bernard & Stacy Donnell. **Educ:** E Los Angeles Col, LA, Calif, AA, 1952; Calif Sch Art, Los Angeles, Calif, 1948; Art Ctr Sch Design, Los Angeles, Calif, BPA, 1958. **Career:** Merville Studios, illusr, 1959-60; ACP Graphic Art Studio, illusr, 1960-62; freelance illusr, 1962-67; Tri-Arts Studio, illusr, 1967-75; freelance Illusr, 1975-; Blacksmiths Cards & Prints, owner, pres, 1980-. **Orgs:** Los Angeles Soc Illusr, 1958-; Graphic Arts Guild; adv comn, Los Angeles Trade Tech Col. **Honors/Awds:** CEBA Award of Distinction, World Inst Black Commun, Graphics Annual Int Annual Advert & Ed Art, 1979-80; Best Black & White Illustration, Soc Illusr, 1960; Exhibitor, Int Exhib Media Arts Commun Arts Mag, 1976, 1978, 1979. **Home Addr:** 1024 Royal Oaks DR Apt 908, Monrovia, CA 91016-5405, **Home Phone:** (213)681-1446. **Business Addr:** Owner, Blacksmiths Cards & Prints, PO Box 623, Altadena, CA 91003, **Business Phone:** (818)794-1167.

**SMITH, ROBERT EUGENE.** **See SMITH, BOBBY.**

**SMITH, ROBERT F.**
Founder (originator), chairperson, chief executive officer. **Educ:** Cornell Univ, BS, chem engineering; Columbia Bus Sch, MBA, finance & mkt. **Career:** Kraft Gen Foods, strategic planning & develop; Goldman, Sachs & Co, vpres & co-head of Investment Banking Div, 1994-2000; Vista Equity Partners LLC, founder, chmn & chief exec officer, 2000-; Enterprise Systs & Storage, co-head. **Orgs:** Young Pres's Orgn, chmn, Robert F Kennedy Ctr Justice & Human Rights. **Honors/Awds:** Beta Gamma Sigma honors, Columbia University; Robert F Kennedy Center for Justice & Human Rights, Ripple of Hope Award, Recipient, 2010; "Black Enterprise", 75 Most Powerful Blacks on Wall Street, 2011; Reginald F. Lewis Achievement Award; Humanitarian of the Year Award, Robert Toigo Found; Ripple of Hope Award, Robert F. Kennedy Ctr Justice & Human Rights; Award of Excellence, Nat Asn Investment Co; Columbia University BBSA Distinguished Alumni Award. **Special Achievements:** Principal inventor on two US and two European patents. **Business Addr:** Founder, Chairman, Vista Equity Partners LLC, 401 Congress Ave Suite 3100, Austin, TX 78701, **Business Phone:** (512)730-2400.

**SMITH, DR. ROBERT H.**
College administrator, chancellor (education). **Career:** Southern Univ, Shreveport, La, exec, chancellor, 1987-92.

**SMITH, DR. ROBERT P., JR.**
Educator, college teacher. **Personal:** Born Oct 12, 1923, New Orleans, LA; son of Robert Sr (deceased) and Leola Mitchell (deceased); married Arlette Marie Carlton; children: Arlette Therese. **Educ:** Howard Univ, BA, 1948; Univ Chicago, MA, 1950; Univ Bordeaux, France, attended 1953; Univ PA, PhD, 1969. **Career:** DEU CEF Univ de Bordeaux, France, fulbright fel, 1952-53; Talladega Col, instr fr span & ger, 1953-54; Fisk Univ, asst prof fr & span, 1954-58; John Hay Whitney Found, fel, 1958-59; Rutgers Univ, instr, asst prof, assoc prof, Fr Dept, chmn, 1965-73, assoc dean acad affairs, 1973-79, prof, 1984-89, prof emer, 1987-; NEH Summer grant, 1981. Books: The Case of the Socialist Witchdoctor and Other Stories. **Orgs:** Treas, Col Lang Asn, 1986-98; Alpha Phi Alpha; Am Asn Univ Prof; Am Asn Teachers Fr; Mod Lang Asn; African Lit Asn; Col Lang Asn. **Special Achievements:** Published articles Fr Rev, Col Lang Assn J, Langston Hughes Rev, Le Petit Courier, Celacef Bull, World Lit Today, Celfan Rev. **Home Addr:** 1189 Elberta, Bensalem, PA 19020, **Home Phone:** (215)632-0478.

**SMITH, ROBERT SCOTT**
Football player, executive. **Personal:** Born Mar 4, 1972, Euclid, OH. **Educ:** Ohio State Univ. **Career:** Football player (retired), executive; Minn Vikings, running back, 1993-2000; Nat Football League Network, analyst, currently. **Orgs:** Founder, Robert Smith Found. **Honors/Awds:** Ohio's Mr. Football Award, 1988, 1989; Pro Bowl, 1998, 2000; Alumni Running Back of the Year, Nat Football League, 2000. **Special Achievements:** Films: 1998 NFC Championship Game, 1999; 2010 R+L Carriers New Orleans Bowl, 2010. TV Series: "Mystery Science Theater 3000", 1997. Book: "The Rest of the Iceberg: An Insider's View on the World of Sport & Celebrity", 2004; Appearing as a guest on the ESPN news program Outside the Lines; Amateur astronomer featured in science writer Timothy Ferris's PBS program, 2007. Ohio State buckeyes starting tailbacks, 1990; The Mole People. **Business Addr:** Analyst, NFL Network, 10950 Wash Blvd, Culver City, NY 90232, **Business Phone:** (310)280-1132.

**SMITH, ROBIN**
Executive director, association executive. **Educ:** Harvard Bus Sch, 1988. **Career:** Goldman, Sachs & Co, corp financial assoc, 1988; One to One Partnership, exec dir, co-founder, 1992-93, vpres local mobilization, currently; Beacon Group LLC, admin dir, 1997-. **Orgs:** Bd dir, Dreyfus Corp. **Special Achievements:** First African American female & youngest member to serve on the Dreyfus Corp board of directors. **Business Addr:** Co-Founder, One to One Partnership, 399 Pk Ave 17th Fl, New York, NY 10022, **Business Phone:** (212)339-9112.

**SMITH, ROD**
Entrepreneur, football player. **Personal:** Born May 15, 1970, Texarkana, AR; children: Devin, Roderick Jr & Vanessa. **Educ:** Mo Southern State Univ, bus, econs, bus admin, econ, 1994. **Career:** Football player (retired); Denver Broncos, wide receiver, 1994-2006; Rod Smith Develop, owner, currently. **Orgs:** Spokesman, Ann Denver Broncos Community Blood Dr.

**SMITH, RODNEY MARC (ROD SMITH)**
Football player, broadcaster. **Personal:** Born Mar 12, 1970, St. Paul, MN. **Educ:** Univ Notre Dame, BA, econs, 1992; Pfeiffer Univ, MBA, orgn managment, 2003. **Career:** Football player (retired), manager, broadcaster; New Eng Patriots, defensive back & left corner back, 1992-94; Carolina Panthers, right corner back, 1995-98; Minn Vikings, 1996; Green Bay Packers, 1998; ESPN Regional, studio analyst, currently; NFL Alumni, Carolinas Chap, pres, 2004-; Fox Sports, broadcaster, 2007-; Bldg Ctr Inc, OSR, 2011-. **Orgs:** Adv bd mem, Pt Lake & Golf Club. **Honors/Awds:** New England Rookie of the Year, 1992. **Home Addr:** 821 W 4th St, Charlotte, NC 28202. **Business Addr:** OSR, The Building Center Inc, 10201 Industrial Dr, Pineville, NC 28134, **Business Phone:** (704)889-8182.

**SMITH, RODNEY STACEY**
Wrestler, athlete. **Personal:** Born Apr 13, 1966, Washington, DC. **Educ:** BS, criminal justice, 1988; Western New Eng Col, attended 1989. **Career:** US Olympic Team, Wrestling Team, athlete, 1992, 1996; Olympics, Sydney, Australia, asst coach, 2000; Western New England Col, asst coach, currently, Hampden Charter School of Science, coach, currently. **Honors/Awds:** Greco-Roman wrestling, Bronze, 1992. **Business Addr:** Assistant Coach, Hampden Charter School of Science, 20 Johnson Rd, Chicopee, MA 01022, **Business Phone:** (413)593-9090.

**SMITH, ROGER LEROY**
Electrical engineer. **Personal:** Born May 15, 1946, New York, NY; children: Kim M, Lisa R & Shawnee L. **Educ:** Criminal Justice Nassau Community Col, AA, 1975. **Career:** US Customs Bur, 1971-74; Fed Aviation Admin, air traffic controller, 1974-76; Fed Aviation Admin & Flight Inspec, electronic technician, 1976-; US customs, sec & patrol off skymarshal. **Honors/Awds:** Comm pilot only black airborne technician FAA Flight Inspec Div; First All Black Flight Insp Crew. **Home Addr:** 621 Winthrop Dr, Uniondale, CA 11553.

**SMITH, DR. ROLAND BLAIR, JR.**
School administrator. **Personal:** Born Mar 21, 1946, Washington, DC; son of Roland B Sr and Annie Louise; married Valerie V Peyton; children: Rovelle Louise & Roland Blair III. **Educ:** Bowie State Col, BA, anthrop & sociol, 1969; Univ Notre Dame, attended 1970; Ind Univ Sch, MPA, pub & environ affairs, 1976; Univ Notre Dame, attended 1980; Harvard Univ, EdD, teaching, curric & learning environ/qual res methods, 1988. **Career:** Bowie St Col, Sociol-Anthrop Dept, fac asst, 1968-69; US Senate, internres asst, 1970; PSC S Bend Ind, dir youth employ, 1970-71; City SBend, Ind, Pub Serv Careers Off, job coach, 1970-71, Summer Youth Employ Prog, dir, 1971, Mayor's Manpower Planning Coun, Systs Coordr, 1971-73; MAPC S Bend Ind, manpower systs coord, 1971-73; Univ Notre Dame Proj Upward Bound, asst dir, 1973-76, dir, 1976-80, exec asst to pres, concurrent assoc prof sociol; Univ Norte Dame, S Bend, Ind, from asst dir to dir, Upward Bound, 1973-83, 1986-88, from asst prof to assoc prof specialist fac urban studies, 1976-96, Inst Urban Studies, Ctr Educ Opportunity, founding dir, 1980-83, 1986-96, exec asst to pres, freshman writing instr, 1989-92, concurrent assoc prof sociol, 1991-96, Urban Inst Community & Educ Initiatives, dir, 1992-95; Ctr Educ Opportunity Inst Urban Studies, founding dir; Ctr Educ Opportunity, dir, 1980-83, 1986-92; Harvard Grad Sch Educ, admin intern & researcher, 1983-84, acad counsr, 1984-86, Off Asst Dean, grad asst, 1984-86, teaching, 1985; Rice Univ, Houston, assoc provost, 1996-, lectr educ, 1996-2000, Mellon Mays Undergrad Fel Prog, prin investr & coordr, 1998-, adj prof educ, 2000-; consult; Univ's Educ Outreach Coun, chair. **Orgs:** Lambda Alpha Nat Anthrop Hon Soc, 1969; Field reader DHEW US Off Educ, 1977; bd dir, Mid-Am Asn Educ Opportunity Prog Personnel, 1979-81; pres, Ind Asn Educ Opportunity Prog Personnel, 1979-80; ed bd, Harvard Educ Rev, 1984-; exec bd, Youth Serv Bur St Joseph County, 1972-77; pres, S Bend Br, Nat Asn Advan Colored People, 1975-76; Ind Adv Com US Civil Rights Comn, 1979-83; Ed bdHarvard Educ Rev, 1984-86; bd mem, pres, Am Asn Blacks Higher Educ, 1986; Phi Delta Kappa Harvard Chap, 1986; vpres, Pvt Indust Coun St Joseph County, 1990-92; exec comt Community Educ Round Table, 1988-91; chair, prog comt, Minority Bus Develop Coun, 1990-92; MLK Fed Holiday Comm, 1993-94; chair, Univ Comt Cult Diversity, 1993-96; chair, Nat Asn Presidential Assist Higher Educ, 1994-95; bd dir, Harvard Alumni Asn, 1995-; vice chair, Black Caucus, Am Asn Higher Educ, 1995-97, chair, 1997-99; bd visitors, Bowie State Univ, 1998-; bd dir, Houston INROADS, 1997-; bd dir, Houston Nat Black MBA Asn, 1999-; bd dir, Life Gift Organ Donation Ctr, 2000-; bd dir, lifegift organ donation ctr, 2000-; past chair, bd dir, Life Gift Organ Donation Ctr, 2010-12; life mem, Tex Asn Black Personnel Higher Educ, 2003-; bd dir, Am Conf Acad Deans; Martin Luther King, Jr Fed Holiday Comn Press Coun Minority Affairs; pres, Col Chap Nat Asn Advan Colored People; chmn, Nat Asn Presidential Assts Higher Educ; Ind Adv Bd to US Civil Rights Comn; chmn, Black Caucus Am Asn Higher Educ; Bowie State Univ Bd Visitors; Ind Univ Sch Pub & Environ Affairs Alumni Adv Bd; Martin Luther King Jr Fed Holiday Cong Comn. **Honors/Awds:** MD State Senatorial School Award, 1968; Distinguished Service Award, United Negro Fund, 1974; Outstanding Achievement Award, Kappa Alpha Psi South Bend Alumni Chap, 1976; President Citation, Bowie State Col, 1977; Distinguished Alumni Award, Ind Univ South Bend Sch Pub & Env Aff, 1983. **Home Addr:** 3356 Lakeway Lane, Pearland, TX 77584. **Business Addr:** Adjunct Professor, Associate Provost, Rice University, Rm 313A Lovett Hall 6100 S Main St, Houston, TX 77005-1892, **Business Phone:** (713)348-5688.

**SMITH, DR. ROULETTE WILLIAM**
Educator, association executive. **Personal:** Born Jan 19, 1942, New York, NY; married Norma Abe; children: Nicole Michelle & Todd Roulette. **Educ:** Morehouse Col, BS, mathematics, 1961; Stanford Univ, MS, mathematics, 1964, MS, comput sci, 1965, PhD, math models educ processes, 1973; Univ Calif, Sch Med, San Francisco, MEd, 1980. **Career:** NMex Highlands Univ, res asst, 1961; IBM, assoc programmer, 1965-66; Stanford Univ, res asst, 1966-70, vis scholar, Inst Math Studies Social Sci, 1981-82, sch med, miscellaneous prof, 1982-83; Univ Calif Santa Barbara, asst prof psychol & educ, 1970-75; Elsevier Publ Co, Exec Ed, 1970-83; Inst Human Potential Psychol, co-founder, 1970-; Carnegie-Mellon Univ, Pittsburgh, vis asst prof, 1974-75; Math Lab Cherry Chase Sch, Sunnyvale, mgr, 1985-87; Inst Postgrad Interdisciplinary Studies, Palo Alto, CA, dir, 1985-; Humanized Technologies, dir, 1985-; Rosebridge Grad Sch Integrative Psychol, Concord, adj fac, 1993-98; San Jose State Univ, assoc dir testing & eval, 1995-99; Inst Transpersonal Psychol, Palo Alto, adj res fac mem, 1996-2001, assoc prof, 2001-05; San Jose State Univ, prof, 1998-99; Calif State Univ, Dominguez Hills, testing off, head, 1999-2003, assoc prof Psychol, 2002-05. **Orgs:** Consult Rand Corp, 1970-74; sales mgr, Stanford Europ Auto, 1970-74; ed Instrnl Sci, 1971-83; Value Engineering Co, 1973; assoc ed, Health Policy & Educ, 1979-83; mem bd dir, Inst Human Potential Psychol; statist consult, Asn Support Grad Students, 1990-2011. **Home Addr:** PO Box 19061, Stanford, CA 94309-9061, **Home Phone:** (650)493-0200. **Business Addr:** Director, Humanized Technologies, PO Box 60846, Palo Alto, CA 94306-0846.

**SMITH, RUFUS HERMAN**
Government official. **Personal:** Born Jun 23, 1950, Loudon, TN; married Patricia Ann Howse; children: Rufus H Jr & Courtney Danielle. **Educ:** Tenn State Univ, BS, 1972; Univ Tenn, Knoxville, MS, 1978. **Career:** TN Valley Authority, equal opportunity staff, 1978-83; US Dept Energy, equal opportunity mgr, 1983, diversity progs mgr & Employee Concerns Mgr, currently. **Orgs:** Mgr, affirmative action prog Fed employees & direct minority educ assistance progs Including specifically related historically black cols & univs. **Home Addr:** 304 Long Bow Rd, Knoxville, TN 37934-1300, **Home Phone:** (865)675-2452. **Business Addr:** Diversity Programs Manager & Employee Concerns Manager, United States Department of Energy, 200 Admin Rd, Oak Ridge, TN 37831, **Business Phone:** (865)576-4988.

**SMITH, SALAAM COLEMAN**
President (organization), media executive. **Personal:** married Christopher; children: 2. **Educ:** Stanford Univ, BS, indust engineering. **Career:** Andersen Consult (now Accenture), mgt consult; MTV Networks, Nickelodeon/Nick, vpres programming, 1993-2003; Comcast Entertainment Group, E!Networks, sr vpres programming, 2003-08, Style Media, exec vpres, 2006-08, pres, 2008-13, NBCUniversal, Strategic Initiatives, pres, 2013-14; Disney ABC Tv Group, ABC Family & Freeform, exec vpres, 2014-. **Orgs:** Dress Success, 2009-14; Women Cable Telecommunications, 2010-12; co-chair, exec leadership coun, Women's Leadership Forum, 2010-; Nat Bd Mem; Worldwide Bd Mem. **Honors/Awds:** Walter Kaitz Foundation Fellow; Betsy Magness Leadership Institute Class XV Fellow; Lifetime Achievement Award, Women Cable Telecommunications, 2009; "Fortune" Magazine, 40 Under 40--8 to Watch; "Black Enterprise" Magazine, Top 50 Black Hollywood Powerbrokers; CNN Money, Fast Risers Under 40--8 to Watch, 2009; TheGrio.com, 100 Making History Today, 2012. **Business Addr:** Executive Vice President, Disney ABC TV Group, Burbank, CA 91501.

**SMITH, SHERMAN, SR.**
Manager, mayor, teacher. **Personal:** Born Apr 26, 1957, Earle, AR; married Odessa Pitchford; children: Margual & Sherman Jr. **Educ:** Draughon Bus Col, assoc bus mgt, 1977. **Career:** Earle Jr High Sch, sub-teacher, 1977-78; Halstead Indus Prod, store room supvr, 1981; Arkan Munic League, mayor. **Orgs:** Youth dept pres Earle Church God Christ; pres, Student Govt, 1976-77; Alderman City Earle, 1983; Minister Gospel Earle Church God Christ, 1983. **Honors/Awds:** Cert income tax preparer cert HR Block, 1978. **Home Addr:** 215 Ala St, Earle, AR 72331-1805, **Home Phone:** (870)792-8454.

**SMITH, SHEVIN JAMAR**
Football player. **Personal:** Born Jun 17, 1975, Miami, FL; children: 3. **Educ:** Fla State, BA, finance. **Career:** Football player (retired), educator; Tampa Bay Buccaneers, defensive back, 1998-99; St Louis Rams, safety; Tampa Bay Storm, wide receiver & defensive back, 2004; high sch teacher, currently.

**SMITH, SHIRLEY HUNTER**
Entrepreneur, consultant, educator. **Personal:** Born Sep 22, 1940, Macon, GA; daughter of E Willie Hunter Sr; married Charlie Haskins; children: David Asher. **Educ:** Morris Brown Col, BS, 1962; Fisk Univ, NSF, MS, 1967; City Col NY, prof dipl, 1972; NY Univ, PhD, 1983; Hunter Col & City Univ NY, MS, 2001; Columbia Univ Bus Sch, exec mgt not-for-profit cert prog, 2002; Harvard Univ, Col Admissions Inst, 2003. **Career:** Carver High Sch, Columbus, Ga, physics & gen sci teacher, 1962-66; Morris Brown Col, Atlanta, Ga, asst prof, sci ed, asst dir teacher training, 1967-68; IS 201, NY, gen sci teacher, 1969-74; NY Pub Schs, asst prin & teacher, 1974-88; NYC Bd Educ, Cent Bd, Off Appeals & Reviews, hearing officer, 1988-92; Medgar Evers Col & CUNY, dir SEEK, 1993-95; Hostos Community Col & CUNY, asst dir coun, 1995-97; Bronx Community Col & CUNY, dir coun & col

discovery, 1997-99; NJ Pub Schs, asst supdt & dir sci, 1999-2000; US Dept Educ, Settlement Col Readiness Trio, dir & consult, currently; Sch Admin & Supv & Training Prins, assoc adj; UFT Teacher's Ctr; SUNY & Stony Brook; Col New Rochelle. **Orgs:** Delta Sigma Theta Sorority Inc; Am Coun Asn; Kappa Delta Pi; Nat Sci Teachers Asn; AAAS; NY Acad Scis; Black Psychologist Inst; dir, NYC, Clin Educ; Jack & Jill Am Inc; Asn Supv & Curric Develop; Am Asn Univ Women; Phi Delta Kappa; NACAC; NASACAC; bd trustee, UMEZ; Manhattan & BronxMental Health Coun; co-chair, Youth Comn, Community Bd #2 Manhattan; mentor, Int House Women in Leadership; United Univ Profs; comnr, NYS, Educ Parent Adv; bd mem, Lewis H Latimer Fund; Manhattan Bor Pres's Educ Adv Panel. **Home Addr:** 3 Wash Sq Village Apt Suite 3J, New York, NY 10012, **Home Phone:** (212)228-9719. **Business Addr:** Director, Consultant, Settlement College Readiness, 1775-1777 Third Ave Flr 1, New York, NY 10029, **Business Phone:** (212)828-6138.

### SMITH, SHIRLEY LAVERNE
Government official, manager. **Personal:** Born Apr 2, 1951, Midlothian, VA; daughter of Walter and Thelma Draper. **Educ:** Va Commonwealth Univ, BS, 1973. **Career:** Internal Revenue Serv, clerk/tax examr, 1974-79, tax rep/tax specialist, 1979-81, EEO specialist, 1981-84, EEO officer, 1984-88, recruitment coordr, 1988-92, personnel mgt specialist, 1992-94, IRS Workers Compensation Ctr, mgr, 1994, chief, currently. **Orgs:** NE Region Undergrad Chap Coor Sigma Gamma Rho, 1986-88; Nat Coun Negro Women; NE regional dir, 1988-92, int secy, 1992-94, grand anti-grammateus, Sigma Gamma Rho Sorority, 1992-; int bd dir, Sigma Gamma Rho Sorority, 1986-92; Federally Employed Women; Int Training Commun Clubs; Urban League Guild; YWCA; Nat Asn Advan Colored People; Richmond Jazz Soc; Asn Improv Minorities-IRS. **Home Addr:** 14421 Tanager Wood Trl, Midlothian, VA 23114, **Home Phone:** (804)794-8703. **Business Addr:** Chief, Internal Revenue Service, 1111 Constitution Ave Nw Rm 5408, Washington, DC 20224, **Business Phone:** (202)622-5000.

### SMITH, ESQ. STANLEY G.
Lawyer, manager, executive. **Personal:** Born Jul 21, 1940, Brooklyn, NY; married Ruth Grey; children: Craig & Carl. **Educ:** Rutgers Univ, BS, acct, 1964; Seton Hall Univ, JD, 1970. **Career:** Housing Develop City Newark, dir; RCA, 1964-68; Fidelity Union & Trust Co, fed asst, code enforcer, financial analyst, 1968-70; Voice Newspaper, bd dir, 1971-72; City Newark, NJ, asst corp coun, 1972; Lofton Lester & Smith, atty law partner, 1985; Seton Hall Univ Sch Law, assoc, prof; Newark Housing Develop & Rehab Corp, pres, chief exec officer; Urban Develop Res Inc, pres; Asbury Pk Housing Authority, exec dir; City Nat Bank, vp; Atty, gen pract, currently; Smith Lawson Inc, pres, currently; Smith & Forbes, atty, currently. **Orgs:** Nat Bar Asn; concerned legal asn mem, bd dir, Neighbourhood Health ServCorp, 1972; vpres, Phi Sigma Delta, 1960; Nj State Bar Asn, 1990-91; trustee, Shiloh Baptist Church. **Honors/Awds:** State Scholarship, Rutgers Univ, 1957; Hall of Fame, Asbury Pk High Sch, 2003; Honarary Scholarship, NJ Bell Elks Club; Who's Who in Black America. **Home Addr:** 1650 Forest Hill, Plainfield, NJ 07060. **Business Addr:** Attorney, Smith & Forbes, 1032 S Ave Suite 242, Plainfield, NJ 07062, **Business Phone:** (908)755-0001.

### SMITH, STEVEN DELANO (STEVE SMITH)
Basketball player, broadcaster, executive. **Personal:** Born Mar 31, 1969, Highland Park, MI; son of Donald and Clara Bell (deceased); married Millie; children: Brayden & Davis. **Educ:** Mich State Univ, attended 1991. **Career:** Basketball player (retired), business owner, color analyst; Miami Heat, shooting guard, 1991-94, 2004-05; Atlanta Hawks, shooting guard, 1994-99, announcer, 2008; Portland Trail Blazers, shooting guard, 1999-2001; San Antonio Spurs, shooting guard, 2001-03; New Orleans Hornets, shooting guard, 2003-04; Charlotte Bobcats, shooting guard, 2004-05; Fox Sports, color analyst, currently; Steve Smith Charitable Fund, owner, currently; Big Ten Network, col basketball analyst. **Orgs:** Bd Dir, Nat Bd Reading Fundamental; Boys & Girls Club; Nat Alumni Bd Mich State Univ; Nat Develop Bd Mich State Univ. **Honors/Awds:** Gold Medal, Summer Universiade, 1989; NCAA All-American Second Team, 1991; NBA All-Star, 1998; Miami Heat, Most Valuable Player, 1993; Gold Medal, FIBA Americas Championship, Canada, 1994; J Walter Kennedy Citizenship Award, 1998; Gold Medal, FIBA Americas Championship, 1999; Gold Medal, Summer Olympics, 2000; Michigan State University Athletic Hall of Fame, 2001; NBA Sportsmanship Award, 2002; Joe Dumars Sportsmanship Award, 2001-02; NBA champion, 2003; World Sports Humanitarian Hall of Fame, 2006; Dick Enberg Award, 2009; Michigan Sports Hall of Fame, 2013. **Special Achievements:** Clara Bell Smith Student-Athlete Academic Center, 1998; Tribute by holding "Steve Smith Day" in September 2001. **Business Addr:** Owner, Steve Smith Charitable Fund, PO Box 16248, Lansing, MI 48901, **Business Phone:** (313)866-7700.

### SMITH, STEVIN L.
Basketball player, baseball executive. **Personal:** Born Jan 24, 1972, Dallas, TX. **Educ:** Ariz State Univ, attended 1994. **Career:** Basketball player (retired); Somontano Huesca, 1994; Grand Rapids Hoops, Continental Basketball Asn, 1994-95, 1995-96; Sunkist Orange Juicers, 1995; Sioux Falls Skyforce, D-League, 1996-97; Dallas Mavericks, shooting guard, 1997; Olympique Antibes, 1997-98; Kusadasi, 1998-99; Olympique Antibes, 2000-01; SLUC Nancy, 2001-02; ASVEL Villeurbanne, 2002-03; Ironi Nahariya, 2003-04; Dynamo Moscow Region, 2004-06; Scafati Basket, 2006-07; Lukoil Acad, 2007-08; NOW Prog, vpres. **Orgs:** Vpres, Nat Orgn Women. **Business Addr:** Professional Basketball Player, PBC Lukoil Akademik Sophia, Postoyanstvo 67A, Scafati84018, **Business Phone:** (359)2917-423.

### SMITH, SUNDRA SHEALEY
Health services administrator. **Personal:** Born Feb 9, 1948, Birmingham, AL; daughter of John Shealey (deceased) and Eddie Griggs Harrell; married Marcellus L Jr; children: Sonja Q & Stephanie M. **Educ:** Tuskegee Inst, Tuskegee, AL, BS, 1970; Southern Ill Univ, Carbondale, IL, MS, 1973; Univ Ala, Birmingham AL, MPH, 1984. **Career:** Progressive Enterprises, Birmingham, AL, owner, 1976-80; Ala Christian Col, Birmingham, AL, instr, 1981-83; Univ Ala, Sch Pub Health, Birmingham, AL, med researcher, 1982-84; Lawson State Jr Col, Birmingham, AL, instr, 1983-86; Geriat Med, coordr, 1984-86; Birmingham Reg Plan Comn, Birmingham, AL, mgr, Medicaid Waivers, 1987-90; AIDS Task Force Ala Inc, exec dir; A Plus Sem & Coun, coun, currently. **Orgs:** Nat Asn Negro Bus & Prof Womens Clubs Inc, 1974-; gov, SE Dist; Omicron Omega Chap, Alpha Kappa Alpha Sorority; secy, Birmingham Rose Soc; arbitrator, Birmingham Better Bus Bur, 1981-; Am Pub Health Asn, 1982-; Ala Pub Health Asn, 1986-; Ala Geront Soc, 1986-; Brown & Williamson, Kool Achiever Awards Screening Comt, 1986-89; Birmingham News Adv Bd, 1986-88; Birmingham League Women Voters, 1988. **Home Addr:** 1569 Fairway View Dr, Birmingham, AL 35244-1316, **Home Phone:** (205)985-7360. **Business Addr:** Consultant, A Plus Seminar & Counseling, 1100 E Pk Dr 200, Birmingham, AL 35235, **Business Phone:** (205)838-7031.

### SMITH, SYMUEL HAROLD
Executive. **Personal:** Born Jun 1, 1922, Port Tampa City, FL; children: Cynthia D, Celeste D & Carmen D. **Educ:** St Louis Univ, St Louis, AA, pub admin, 1943; Wash Univ St Louis, BS, bus finance, 1961, MS, hosp admin, 1965. **Career:** City St Louis Dept Health, 1950-52; Homer G Phillips Hosp, St Louis, asst adminis, 1952-63; Flint-goodridge Hosp New Orleans, adminis resi & adminis asst, 1964-65; Bronx Muni Hosp Ctr Bronx, asst admin, 1965-66; NY State Dept Health NY, hosp admin consult, 1966-67; Edgecombe Rehab Ctr NY State Narcotic Addiction Control Community NYC, dir, 1967-68; Morisania City Hosp Bronx, exec dir, 1968-74; Wayne Co Gen Hosp Mich, exec dir, 1974-78; Detroit Gen Hosp, dir hosps & chief exec officer, 1978; Milwaukee Co Inst & Dept Wis, dir beginning 1978; ARSMARK Group Ltd, chief exec officer & founder, 1986-; Group Limited, Sales & Consult, pres, currently. **Orgs:** Omicron Chap, 1970; Am Hosp Asn; fel, Am Pub Health Asn; Am Col Hosp Admin; Nat Asn Health Serv Execs; vpres, Hosp Exec Club NY; exec comt, Greater Detroit Area Hosp Coun; Mich State Arbit Comt; Hosp admin consult, City St Louis MO;Nat Asn Advan Colored People; Gov Coun Pub Gen Hosp; secy, AHA; Cita Chi Eta Phi Sorority Inc. **Home Addr:** 3460 N Dousman St, Milwaukee, WI 53212, **Home Phone:** (414)962-1381.

### SMITH, TANGELA NICOLE
Basketball player. **Personal:** Born Apr 1, 1977, Chicago, IL. **Educ:** Univ Iowa, cult studies & sports, 1998. **Career:** Basketball player; Sacramento Monarchs, forward, 1998-2004; Italy, Israel, S Korea & Turkey, prof basketball player; Turkish league crown, Botasspor squad, 2001; Korean league, Shinsegae Coolcats, 2002; Charlotte Sting, forward & ctr, 2005-06; Phoenix Mercury, forward, 2007-10; Ind Fever, 2011; San Antonio Silver Stars, 2012-; Hat-agro Uni Gyor, 2013-; Studio 5027, co-owner, currently. **Business Addr:** Co owner, 5027 Studio, 579 Main St, Palmetto, GA 30268, **Business Phone:** (770)463-4129.

### SMITH, TARIK
Football player, football coach. **Personal:** Born Apr 16, 1975, Agoura, CA. **Educ:** Univ Calif, Los Angeles, grad. **Career:** Football player (retired); Dallas Cowboys, running back, 1998-99; Concord High Sch, coach. **Home Addr:** 8825 Rodeo Dr Suite 348, Irving, TX 75063. **Business Addr:** Coach, Concord High Sch, 4200 Concord Blvd, Concord, CA 94521, **Business Phone:** (925)687-2030.

### SMITH, THELMA J.
Executive. **Career:** Ill Serv Fed Savings & Loan Asn Chicago, Chicago, Ill, vpres, secy, exec vpres, pres, chief exec officer & asst secy, currently; Nc Mutual Life Ins Co, dir, 1990-. **Orgs:** Chicago Theol Sem; Community Renewal Soc; bd mem, chair, audit comt, NC Mutual Comt; bus adv coun, NC Mutual Univ Ill; Chicago Network; Links Inc, Chicago Chap; bd dir, Ill Serv Fed Savings & Loan Asn; bd trustee, Chicago Sunday Eve Club; equal opportunity adv coun, Chicago Area Ill Nat Guard & Comm Ctr Influence; bd trustee, Chicago Acad Sci; prin, Chicago United; Union League Club; Congregational Church Pk Manor. **Business Addr:** President, Chief Executive Officer, Illinois Service Federal Savings & Loan Association, 4619 S King Dr, Chicago, IL 60653, **Business Phone:** (773)624-2000.

### SMITH, THOMAS LEE, JR.
Football player. **Personal:** Born Dec 5, 1970, Gates County, NC. **Educ:** Univ Nc, BS, bus admin & mgt gen, 1993; Ind Univ Bloomington, MBA, bus admin, mgt & opers, 2015-. **Career:** Football player (retired); Buffalo Bills, defensive back, 1993, right cornerback, 1994-99, cornerback, 1999, defensive back, 2000; Chicago Bears, right cornerback & cornerback, 2000, defensive back, 2001; Indianapolis Colts, defensive back, 2001; Tytcover Inc, pres & chief investment officer, 2002-08; J.B. Hunt Transp Inc, acct mgr, 2008-10; Tr Transp Network, owner, 2010-14; Bel Air Honda, sales & leasing consult, 2014-15; Athletic Scholar Corp, scouting dir, 2015-; Property Mgt Inc, chief exec officer & owner, 2015-. **Orgs:** Mountain Christian Church. **Special Achievements:** Film: Super Bowl XXVIII, 1994; E-Book: "The Power of Mentorship - Back in the Game", 2014. **Business Addr:** Owner, Chief Executive Officer, Property Management Inc, 2940 Maple Loop Dr Suite 104, Lehi, UT 84043, **Business Phone:** (801)407-1301.

### SMITH, DR. TOMMIE
Athlete, lecturer, activist. **Personal:** Born Jun 6, 1944, Clarksville, TX; son of Richard and Dora; married Delois Jordan. **Educ:** San Jose State Univ, BA, soc sci; Goddard-Cambridge, Boston, MA, sociol; MS, phys educ & soc. **Career:** Athlete (retired), football player, lecturer; Cincinnati Bengals, wide receiver; Prof Athlete, sprinter; Oberlin Col, Ohio, track coach, sociol fac; Santa Monica Col, Santa Monica, CA, fac mem, 1978-2005; Delo 2K Enterprise, educr & lectr, currently. **Orgs:** Nat Track & Field Hall Fame, 1978. **Special Achievements:** Released his autobiography Silent Gesture, 2007. **Home Addr:** 1800 Lilburn Stone Mountain Rd, Stone Mountain, GA 30087-1720, **Home Phone:** (770)564-3658. **Business Addr:** Educator, Lecturer, DELO2K Enterprises, PO Box 870010, Stone Mountain, GA 30087, **Business Phone:** (818)618-0553.

### SMITH, TONI COLETTE (TONI COLETTE SMITH-ALSTON)
Government official. **Personal:** Born Oct 31, 1952, Columbus, OH. **Educ:** Ohio State Univ, BA, 1974, mgt courses; Ohio State Univ, Columbus, attended 1976; Univ Dayton, MS, 1993. **Career:** Ohio State Human Servs, consult, 1974-75; Franklin County Human Servs, caseworker, 1976-79, supvr, 1979-86, adminr, 1986-91, asst dep dir, depdir, 1996-98; Columbus State Community Col, instr, 1990-91; Human Servs, dep dir, 1996-; Best Inc, bus consult & vpres, 1998-; Tex Lottery Comn, chief exec officer, 1998-, mkt dir, 2000-03. **Orgs:** Corresponding secy, Am Asn Univ Women, 1988-; vpres, Berwick Civic Asn, 1989-91, pres, 1991-; pres, exec bd, Syntaxis Residental Care for Youth, 1990-92, 1996-98; admis exec bd, United Way, 1990-; Franklin County Ment Health Asn. **Home Addr:** 6740 Temperance Point St, Westerville, OH 43082-8747, **Home Phone:** (614)891-6645. **Business Addr:** Market Director, Texas Lottery Commission, 6740 Temperance Pt St, Westerville, OH 43082, **Business Phone:** (614)891-6645.

### SMITH, TONY (CHARLES ANTON SMITH)
Basketball player. **Personal:** Born Jun 14, 1968, Wauwatosa, WI. **Educ:** Marquette Univ, Milwaukee, WI, BS, mech engineering & orgn leadership, 1990. **Career:** Basketball player (retired), executive; Los Angeles Lakers, 1990-95; Miami Heat, 1995-96; Phoenix Suns, 1995-96; Charlotte Hornets, 1996-97; Milwaukee Bucks, 1997-98; Tau Ceramica, 1997; Atlanta Hawks, guard, 2000-01; Rockford Lightning, 2000-01; San Lazaro, 2001; Am Basketball Asn, Phoenix Eclipse, 2002; Marquette Univ, player; Time Warner Cable, guest roundtable sports 32, 2007-; RAS Milwaukee, founder & prog dir, 2007-; Fox Sports Wis, pre & post analyst milwaukee bucks, 2008-; Platypus Advert + Design, dir scouting & recruitment, 2009-; seacret agt, 2012-. **Business Addr:** Director of Scouting and Recruitment, Platypus Advertising and Design, N29 W23810 Woodgate Ct W Suite 100, Pewaukee, WI 53072, **Business Phone:** (262)522-8181.

### SMITH, TORRANCE
Football player. **Personal:** Born Sep 4, 1970, Tampa, FL; married Denise; children: Kayla. **Educ:** Alcorn State Univ. **Career:** New Orleans Saints, wide receiver, 1992-96; St Louis Rams, wide receiver, 1997; Indianapolis Colts, wide receiver, 1998; Philadelphia Eagles, wide receiver, 1999-2000; New Eng Patriots, wide receiver, 2001.

### SMITH, TRACY K.
College teacher, poet. **Personal:** Born Apr 16, 1972, Falmouth, MA; children: 1. **Educ:** Harvard Univ, BA, eng, Am lit & Afro-Am studies, 1994; Columbia Univ, MFA, creative writing, 1997. **Career:** Poet; City University of New York, the University of Pittsburgh and Columbia University, instr; Princeton University, creative writing teacher, 2006-. **Special Achievements:** Author, "The Body's Question (2002), "Duende" (2007), "Life on Mars" (2011), "Ordinary Light" (2015); literature protege of the Rolex Mentor and Protege Arts Initiative, 2009-11 cycle. **Business Addr:** Princeton University, New South Bulding 6th Fl, Princeton, NJ 08544, **Business Phone:** (609)258-8561.

### SMITH, TREVOR TAHIEM, JR. See RHYMES, BUSTA.

### SMITH, TUBBY (ORLANDO SMITH)
Basketball coach, founder (originator). **Personal:** Born Jun 30, 1951, Scotland, MD; married Donna; children: GG, Saul & Brian. **Educ:** High Pt Col, BS, health & phys educ, 1973. **Career:** Great Mills High Sch, phys educ teacher, coach; Hoke County High Sch, phys educ teacher, coach; Va Commonwealth Univ, asst coach, 1979-86; Univ SC, asst coach, 1986-89; Univ KY, 1989-91; Univ Tulsa, Tulsa Golden Hurricane, men's basketball coach, 1991-95; Univ Ga, Ga Bulldogs, men's basketball coach, 1995-97; Univ Ky, Ky Wildcats, head basketball coach, 1997-2007; Univ Minn, Golden Gophers, head coach, 2007; Tex Tech Univ, head coach, 2013; Univ Memphis, head coach, 2016-. **Orgs:** Founder, Tubby Smith Found; bd dir, Nat Asn Basketball Coaches, 2000. **Honors/Awds:** MVC Coach of the Year, 1994, 1994; SEC Coach of the Year, 1998, 2003, 2005; AP College Coach of the Year, 2003; Henry IBA Award, 2003; Naismith College Coach of the Year, 2003; NABC Coach of the Year, 2003; Jim Phelan Coach of the Year, 2005; Big 12 Coach of the Year, 2016; John R Wooden Legends of Coaching Award, 2016; National Coach of the Year, Sporting News, 2016; District 8 Coach of the Year, NABC, 2016. **Special Achievements:** First African American head coach at the Univ GA-Athens; guided the Univ Tulsa's Golden Hurricane to the Sweet 16 in the NCAA men's basketball Tournament; First African American Coach at the Univ KY; First African American & First Rookie Coach to win a championship at KY; Second Coach in History to Lead Five Different Teams to the NCAA Tournament. **Business Addr:** Head Coach Men, Golden Gophers, University of Minnesota, 267 19th Ave S, Minneapolis, MN 55414, **Business Phone:** (612)624-4300.

### SMITH, VALERIE
College president, college teacher. **Personal:** daughter of W Reeves and Josephine. **Educ:** Bates Col, BA, eng; Univ Va, MA, PhD. **Career:** Princeton Univ, asst prof, 1982-86, assoc prof, 1986-89, vis prof, 2000-01, Woodrow Wilson Prof Lit, prof, 2001-15, dir Prog African Am Studies, 2002-06, dir Ctr African Am Studies, 2006-09, dean, 2011-15; Univ Calif Los Angeles, vis res assoc Ctr African-Am Studies, 1986-87, assoc prof, 1989-94, prof, 1994-2001, vice chair grad studies, 1994-97, co-dir Cult Studies African Diaspora Proj, 1996-2000, chair Interdepartmental Prog African-Am Studies, 1997-2000; Columbia Univ, vis fac mem, 1989; Univ Calif, Berkeley, Beckman vis prof, 1997; Swarthmore Col, pres & prof, 2015-. **Orgs:** Phi Beta Kappa, mem, 1975; Eng Inst, mem supv comt, 1991-94; Univ Calif Humanities Res Inst, convenor, 1992-93. **Special Achievements:** First African American president of Swarthmore, 2015-; author, "Self-Discovery and Authority in Afro-American Narrative" (1987), "Not Just Race, Not Just Gender: Black Feminist Readings" (1998), "Toni Morrison: Writing The Moral Imagination" (2012); contributor to books, "Cambridge Companion to Frederick Douglass" (2009), "The Cambridge Companion to American Novelists" (2012); contributor to periodicals including American Literary History, PMLA, Journal of Presbyterian History, and Women's Studies Quarterly. **Business Addr:** Swarthmore College, 500 College Ave, Swarthmore, PA 19081.

### SMITH, VERNEL HAP
Manager, teacher, government official. **Personal:** Born Nov 12, 1924, Waycross, GA; children: Randy & Kevin. **Educ:** Ohio State Univ, BS, social admin, MA, social admin. **Career:** US & Overseas Social Welfare, admin, lectr, teacher, trainer; City Oakland, mgr recreation serv, 1966-74, supvr recreation, dir off pk & recreation, 1974-; Canton Urban League, leader. **Orgs:** Slitant bovs work secy, associate phys dir & swim Instr & examr, Young Mens Christian Asn. **Honors/Awds:** Outstanding & Dedicated Service Award, Nat Recreation & Pk Asn Ethnic Minority Soc, 1984. **Business Addr:** Director, City of Oakland, 1520 Lakeside Dr, Oakland, CA 94612.

### SMITH, VERNICE CARLTON
Football player. **Personal:** Born Oct 24, 1965, Orlando, FL; married Era; children: Alexandria, Vernice Jr & Mitchell. **Educ:** Fla Agr & Mech Univ, BS. **Career:** Football player (retired); Phoenix Cardinals, guard, 1990-92; Chicago Bears, guard, 1993; Wash Redskins, guard, 1993-95; St Louis Rams, guard, 1997.

### SMITH, VERNON G.
Educator, state government official. **Personal:** Born Apr 11, 1944, Gary, IN; son of Albert J and Julia E. **Educ:** Ind Univ, BS, 1966, MS, 1969, EdD, elem educ & elem admin, 1978, post-doctoral work, 1990; Purdue Univ, post-doctoral work. **Career:** Ind Pub Sch Systs, teacher, 1966-71, resource teacher, 1971-72; Ind Univ Northwest, part-time counr, 1967-69, adj lectr, 1987-92, asst prof, 1992-, assoc prof educ, currently; Gary Urban League's Oper Jobs, asst dir, 1966; Gary, Pub Sch Syst, teacher, 1966-71, resource teacher, 1971-72; OEO's Oper Sparkle, asst dir, 1967; John Will Anderson Boys Clb, staff asst, 1967-68; Gary Crusader Newspaper, columnist, 1969-71; Ivanhoe Sch Gary, Ind, asst prin, 1972-78; City Gary, Ind, 4th dist councilman, 1972-90; Nobel Sch Gary, Ind, prin, 1978-85; Williams Sch Gary IN, prin, 1985-92; Develop Training Inst, speaker, 1986-; Ind House Rep, rep, 1990-; New Hope Missionary Baptist Church, deacon. **Orgs:** Pres & tres, Gary Downtown Merchants Asn; Gary Brnch Nat Asn Advan Colored People; Univ Alumni Asn; mega Psi Phi Frat; founder & pres, IU Gents Inc; founder & pres, IU Dons Inc; founder & sponsor, Focus Hope; founder & sponsor, Young Citizens League; founder sponsor, Youth Ensuring Solidarity; Phi Delta Kappa Frat; pres, Gary Comt Ment Health Bd; deacon, trustee, & teacher, Pilgrim Baptist Church; pres, Gary Common Coun, 1976, 1983-84, 1988, vpres, 1982, 1985-87; founder & chmn, City-wide Festivals Comt Inc; Handgun Control Inc; Gary Reading Coun-State Reading Asn; Asn Sch Principals; founder, NorthernAsn Black Sch Educrs; founder & bd pres, African-Am Achievers Youth Corps Inc; bd trustee, Criminal Justice Inst; Gov's Comn Drug Free IN; chmn, Comn Social Status Black Males; founder & sponsor, Vernon Stars; bd dir, Northwest Ind Urban League; Omega Psi Phi Fraternity; Ind Univ Northwest Chap, Am Asn Univ Professors; Bros Keepers Shelter Homeless Men; chair, Ind Black Legis Caucus, 2006-08; treas, Ind Asn Elem & Mid Sch Principals; pres, Gary Elem Principals Asn; Gary Young Dem; Little League World Ser Bd; Gary's Educ Talent Search Bd; Northwest Ind Urban League Adv Bd; Med Ctr Gary; founder, sponsor, Youth Ensuring Solidarity. **Honors/Awds:** Omega Psi Phi 10th District Citizen of the Year, 1972, 1989; Omega Man Year, 1974; Gary Jaycees, Good Govt Award, 1977; Club FAB Outstndg Achvmnt citation Ebony mag most eligible bachelor, 1977; Club FAB Outstanding Achievement Citation, 1978; Gary Downtown Merchants Businessman of the Year Award, 1979; Young Democrat's outstanding Service Award, 1979; Mahalia Jackson Special Achievement award, 1980; Alpha Chi Chap Citizen of the Year Award, Omega Psi Phi, 1980; Appreciation Award, Gary Community Mental Health Ctr, 1981; GOIC Dr Leon H Sullivan Award, 1982; Youth Award, 1983; Outstanding Citizen of NW IN & Outstanding Education Award, Info Newspaper, 1984; Blaine Marz Tap Award, Post Tribune, 1984; 10th Year Service Award, 1985; Focus Hope Dedication in Action Award, 1987; Gary Educator for Christ Administrator Leadership Award, 1988; Omega Psi Phi Citizen of the Year, 10th District, 1989; Froebel High Scl Alumni Appreciation Award; Phi Delta Kappa Northwest IN Chapter 25 Year Award; IU Northwest Alumni Asn Chiefs Police Appreciation Award; Methodist Hosp Child & Adolescent Prog Mr G's Service Award; IUSAA Founding Member Award; Gary Community Schs Presenter's Award; Omega Psi Phi's Omicron Rho Appreciation Award, 1991; IU Northwest Alumni Asn Chiefs Police Appreciation Award; Methodist HospChild & Adolescent Prog Appreciation Award; Brothers Keeper AppreciationAward; IN Asn Elem & Middle Schl Principals Service Award, 1992; Northwest IN Black Expo's Senator Carolyn Mosby Above & Beyond Award, 1995; Gary Community Sch Corp, Parent Involvement Program Presenters Award; Nat Coun Negro Women In The Bethune Tradition Award, 1996; Froebel High Scl Alumni Appreciation Award; IN Chapt Nat Asn Social Workers, Citizen of the Year; Pittman Square Sch Appreciation Award, 1997; recipient of over 125 awards & citations. **Home Addr:** PO Box 64622, Gary, IN 46401, **Home Phone:** (219)887-2046. **Business Addr:** State Representative, Indiana House of Representatives, 200 W Washington St, Indianapolis, IN 46204-2786, **Business Phone:** (800)382-9842.

### SMITH, VIDA J.
Meeting planner. **Personal:** Born Lynchburg, VA; daughter of Leo Jones and Mary. **Educ:** Cent State Univ, elem educ, 1972; Univ DC, attended 1992. **Career:** Nat Black Media Coalition, dir, black radio proj, 1985-88; Delta Sigma Theta Sorority, Inc, meeting planner, 1989-; Traci Lynn, consult, partner, 2012-. **Orgs:** NCBMP; GWSAE; bd mem, Nat Coalition Black Meeting Planners; ASAE. **Honors/Awds:** Meeting Planner of the Year, Coalition of Black Meeting Planners, 1996; Meeting Prof To Watch, Convention South mag, 2001, 2003. **Home Addr:** 1536 E Warner Ave Suite E, Santa Ana, CA 92705-5474. **Business Addr:** Meeting Planner, Delta Sigma Theta Sorority Inc, 1707 NH Ave NW, Washington, DC 20009-2501, **Business Phone:** (202)986-2400.

### SMITH, VINSON ROBERT
Football player, broadcaster, business owner. **Personal:** Born Jul 3, 1965, Statesville, NC; married Anne Oliver; children: Jayme, Payton & Christian; married Maria Robinson; children: 5. **Educ:** E Carolina Univ, BS, commun, 1989. **Career:** Football player (retired), football coach, owner; Atlanta Falcons, linebacker, 1988; Dallas Cowboys, linebacker, 1990-92, 1997; Chicago Bears, linebacker, 1993-96; New Orleans Saints, linebacker, 1998-2000; JPC LOC, owner, currently; Game Day broadcaster, owner, currently; Piedmont Christian Paladins, Statesville, head coach, currently. **Orgs:** Big Brothers & Big Sisters; United Way.

### SMITH, HON. VIRGIL CLARK, JR.
Judge, lawyer. **Personal:** Born Jul 4, 1947, Detroit, MI; son of Virgil Columbus and Eliza (Boyer) S; married Evelyn Owens; married Elizabeth Ann Little; children: Adam, Virgil Jr, Anthony L & Jordan P. **Educ:** Mich State Univ, BA, polit sci, 1969; Wayne State Law, JD, 1972. **Career:** Justice Wade McCree US Appeals Ct, stud clerk; Wayne Co Legal Servs, legal adv, 1972-73; Wayne County Legal Serv, supv atty, 1973-74; City Detroit, sr asst corp coun, 1974-75; Model Cities Drug Clin; Corp Coun City Detroit; Mich House Representatives, state rep, 1977-88, mem; Mich State Senate, sen, dem floor leader, 1988-2001, mem; Third Judicial Circuit Mich, Family Div Juv Sect, presiding judge, chief judge, 2009-. **Orgs:** Former finance, Family Law, Criminal Law & Corrections, & Reapportionment Cmtes; Law Rev Cmsn; Legis Black Caucus; appropriations, sub committes Capital Outlay, Regulatory &Transp; Families Ment Health & Human Svcs, judiciary, legis Coun. **Honors/Awds:** Legislator of the Year, Police Officers Asn Mich & Mich Judges Asn, 1996. **Home Addr:** 19316 Norwood, Detroit, MI 48234, **Home Phone:** (313)366-2260. **Business Addr:** Chief Judge, The Third Judicial Circuit Michigan, Lincoln Hall of Justice 1025 E Forest Ave, Detroit, MI 48207, **Business Phone:** (313)224-5261.

### SMITH, VIRGINIA M.
Educator. **Personal:** Born May 9, 1929, El Dorado, AR; daughter of Henry Burks and Annie Burks; children: Marcia Green Hamilton, Gregory Green & Dana Paul Green. **Educ:** Am&N Col, BA, 1950; Univ Ill, MEd, 1955; Univ Ark, attended 1963. **Career:** Educator (retired); Ark Pub Sch, teacher, 1950-60; Southern Univ, asstprof, 1963-65; El Dorado, counr, 1965-70; Henderson State Univ, personnel dean, 1971-81, dir spec serv disadvantaged stud, 1982-86; Ark Baptist Col, teacher, admin asst pres, 1986-95. **Orgs:** Local Bd Church Women United, 1998 bd dir, Clark Co Community Found, 2002; mem chmn, Clark Co Retired Teachers Asn, 2002; Delta Sigma Theta Sorority Inc; Nat Asn Advan Colored People; Arka delphia Women's Develop Coun; life mem, UAPB Alumni Asn. **Honors/Awds:** Teacher of the Year, Ark Baptist Col, 1989-90. **Special Achievements:** First African American staff member in Henderson St University, 1971. **Home Addr:** 110 S Austin St, PO Box 274, Arkadelphia, AR 71923-5717, **Home Phone:** (870)246-3240.

### SMITH, VOYDEE
Banker. **Personal:** Born Feb 14, 1949, Barton, FL; son of Voydee and Fannie Colson; married Saundra Johnson; children: Daryl, Allen, Eric, Jason & Steven. **Educ:** NC AT&T State Univ, BS, 1973. **Career:** US Dept Treas, asst bank examr, Off Controller Currency, nat bank examr, 1973-85; IDL Bank Wash, sr vpres, loan admin, 1985-95; Consol Bank & Trust Co, sr vpres, chief credit officer, & loan adminr, 1995-. **Orgs:** IDL Bank, Loan Officers Comn, chmn, 1985, loan & discount comt, 1985, mgt comt, 1986; Wash Area Bankers Asn, 1987; Nat Bankers Asn, 1989; bd mem, Richmond Metrop Bus League. **Home Addr:** 5356 Lake Normandy Dr, Fairfax, VA 22030. **Business Addr:** Senior Vice President, Chief Credit Officer, Consolidated Bank & Trust Co, 320 N 1st St, Richmond, VA 23240, **Business Phone:** (804)771-5200.

### SMITH, REV. DR. WALLACE CHARLES
Educator, clergy. **Personal:** Born Nov 6, 1948, Philadelphia, PA; married G Elaine Williams; children: Christen Ann. **Educ:** Villanova Univ, BA, 1970; Eastern Bapt Sem, MDiv, 1974; Eastern Bapt Sem, DMin, 1979. **Career:** Calvary Baptist Church, Chester, PN, minister, 1974-85; Eastern Baptist Sem, dir alumni affairs & asst dir field educ, 1979-85; Prog Nat Baptism, home mission bd, 1979; Eastern Baptist Theol Sem, asst prof practical theol, 1979-85; First Baptist Church-Capitol Hill, Nashville, TN, minister, pastor, 1985-91; Vanderbilt Divinity Sch Pract Ministry, prof, 1988-91; Shiloh Baptist Church, Wash, DC, pastor, 1991-, sr minister, currently; Palmer Theol Sem Eastern Univ, pres, 2006-06; MMBB, bd mgr, 2007-; Howard Divinity Sch, adj fac mem; Wesley Theol Sem, adj fac mem; ABCUSA, ordained minister; Progressive Nat Baptist Conv, ordained minister; Baptist World Alliance, vpres; Palmer Theol Sem, Wallace Charles Smith Sch Christian Ministries, dean, currently. **Orgs:** Exec bd, Chester Br Nat Asn Advan Colored People, 1974-; pres, Chester Clergy Asn, 1977-79; pres, Chester Comm Improv Proj, 1979-; mem bd, Eastern Baptist Sem; Gen Coun Baptist World Alliance; chmn, Spl Comn Baptists Against Racism; 1994 Class Leadership Wash; bd mem, Interfaith Coun Wash Vicinity; United Black Fund Nat Capitol Area United Way; Adv Bd Riggs Nat Bank; chmn, Proj Koinonia DC Baptist Conv; Progressive Nat Baptist Conv, USA Inc; trustee, Bd Home Missions; Ministers & Missionaries Benefit Bd. **Honors/Awds:** Distinguished Service Award, Anti-Defamation League B'nai Brith, 1994; Honorary doctorate, Alderson-Broaddus Univ W Va, 1997. **Special Achievements:** First African American to be appointed to full time Faculty status in Eastern Baptist Theological Seminary. Contributing editor of The Pulpit Digest, he has written numerous articles, including guest editorials for the Washington Post, is the author of a book, The Church in the Life of the Black Family. **Home Addr:** 2428 Edgmont Ave, Chester, PA 19013. **Business Addr:** Pastor, Senior Minister, Shiloh Baptist Church, 1500 9th St NW, Washington, DC 20001-3318, **Business Phone:** (202)232-4288.

### SMITH, DR. WALTER L.
Educator. **Personal:** Born May 13, 1935, Tampa, FL; married Barbara; children: John, Andre V Gordon, Salesia & Walter II. **Educ:** Gibbs Jr Col, St Petersburg, FL, AA; Fla A&M Univ, BA, biol & chem, 1963, MEd, admin & supv, 1966; Fla State Univ, PhD, higher educ admin, 1972. **Career:** Educator (retired); Nat Educ Asn, assoc regional dir, 1969-70; Fla Educ Asn, admin asst, 1970, asst exec secy, 1970-73; Hillsborough Community Col, colegium dir, 1973, dean employee rels, 1973-74, provost, 1974; Roxbury Community Col, pres, 1974-77; Fla A&M Univ, pres, 1977-85, pres emer, currently; Univ Malawi, Chancellor Col, Nat Championship Team, head baseball coach, 1985-86; Univ Fla, vis prof, 1995-2002; Educ Develop S Africa, int team leader; Funda Community Col, S Africa, founding dir. **Orgs:** Chairperson, Fla Supreme Ct Judicial Nominating Comt, 1980-83; bd dir, Am Asn State Col & Univs, 1980-83; chmn, State Bd Educ Adv Comn, 1982-85; bd dir, Nat Asn Equal Opportunity HE, 1982-84; Fla Supreme Ct Article Vice Comn, 1983; US Dept Interior, 1984; Urban League, 1992-95; counr, Sons Allen men's ministry, AME church; Dr. Walter L. Smith Libr, 2002. **Special Achievements:** Book: The Magnificent Twelve: Florida's Black Junior Colleges. **Home Addr:** 1940 Cypress St, Tampa, FL 33606. **Business Addr:** President Emeritus, Florida A&M University, 1700 Lee Hall Dr, Tallahassee, FL 32307, **Business Phone:** (850)599-3183.

### SMITH, ESQ. WAYMAN F., III
Executive, vice president (organization), judge. **Personal:** Born Jun 18, 1940, St. Louis, MO; son of Wayman Flynn and Edythe; children: Kymberly Ann. **Educ:** Wash Univ, attended 1959; Monmouth Col, BA, 1962; Howard Univ Sch Law, JD, 1965. **Career:** Executive, vice president (retired); Mo Comn Human Rights, dir concilliation, 1966-68; Law Firm Wilson Smith Smith & McCullin, partner, 1969; St Louis City Coun, three-term alderman; City St Louis munic ct, judge, 1973-75; Anheuser-Busch Co Inc, vpres corp affairs, 1980-2000; Smith Partnership PC, sr partner; Howard Univ, chmn emer, currently. **Orgs:** Bd alderman, City St Louis, 1975-; bd dir, Anheuser-Busch Co Inc, 1981-2000; coordr, Lou Rawls Parade Stars fund-raising telethon which benefits United Negro Col Fund; bd admis, US Dist Ct Eastern Dist Mo; ABA; Nat Bar Assoc; Mound City Bar Assoc; Bar Asn Metro St Louis; bd trustee, Howard Univ Hosp, 1989-, chmn, 1991-95; Howard Univ, trustee; chmn bd regents, Harris Stowe State Col; Cong Black Caucus Found; Nat Urban League; Nat Asn Sickle Cell DisInc; St Louis Symphony; St Louis Metrop YMCA; Am Bar Asn; Nat Bar Asn. **Home Addr:** 3910 Lindell Blvd, St. Louis, MO 63108, **Home Phone:** (314)371-2600. **Business Addr:** Chairman Emeritus, Howard University, 2400 6th St NW Suite 440, Washington, DC 20059, **Business Phone:** (202)806-2250.

### SMITH, WAYNE FRANKLIN
Association executive, executive director. **Personal:** Born Feb 17, 1951, Providence, RI; married Debra Petrarca; children: Marah Elizabeth Ann. **Educ:** Union Experimenting Cols & Univs, BA, psychol, 1977. **Career:** Vietnam Veteran Readjustment Coun Ctr, counr, 1979-86; Vietnam Veterans Am, dir mem, 1987-91; Vietnam Veterans Memorial Fund, dir develop, 1991-94; Black Revolutionary War Patriots Found, pres & exec dir, 1994-99; Justice Proj, exec dir & pres, 2000-04; Kerry-Edwards 2004 Presidential Campaign, dir, 2004; Black Patriots Found Inc, exec dir, pres; human rights advocate, currently. **Orgs:** Bd dir, Vietnam Veterans Am Found, spec asst pres, 2004; civil liberties prog dir, Unitarian Universalist Serv Comt, 2005-11; bd dir, Nat Veterans Legal Serv Proj; bd dir, Friends Vietnam Veterans Mem; Nat Asn Advan Colored People. **Special Achievements:** Vietnam Veterans of America Foundation, co-recipient of Nobel Peace Prize, 1997; guest appearances on numerous television news & radio programs, including CBS News, ABC News, NBC Nightly News, C-SPAN, CNN, BBC, & National Public Radio; subject in documentaries "Black American Participation in the US Military"; "Fields of Armor & Race Relations during the Vietnam War". **Business Addr:** Director, Vietnam Veterans Memorial Fund, 2600 Virginia Ave NW Suite 104, Washington, DC 20037, **Business Phone:** (202)393-0090.

### SMITH, WILL (WILLARD CHRISTOPHER SMITH, JR.)
Actor, singer, movie producer. **Personal:** Born Sep 25, 1968, Philadelphia, PA; son of Willard Sr and Caroline; married Sheree Zampino; children: Willard III; married Jada Pinkett; children: Jaden & Willow Camille Reign. **Career:** Actor, producer, writer, dir & singer; Member duo DJ Jazzy Jeff & the Fresh Prince, 1986; Albums: Rock the House, 1987, 1989; He's the DJ, I'm the Rapper, 1988; Andin This Corner, 1989; Homebase, 1991; Solorapper: Big Willie Style, 1997; Willennium, 2000; Lost & Found, 2005; Actor, Seven Pounds, 2008; Hancock, 2008; Men in Black III, 2012; After Earth, 2013; Producer: Show Time, exec producer, 2002; Ride or Die, exec producer, 2003; "All of Us", exec producer, 2003-07; Saving Face, 2004; The Seat Filler, exec producer, 2004; ATL, 2006; Lakeview Terrace, producer, 2008; The Human Contract, exec producer, 2008; The Secret Life of Bees producer, 2008; Hancock, producer, 2008; Seven Pounds, producer, 2008; The Karate Kid, producer, 2010; This Means War, producer, 2010; Free Angela and All Political Prisoners, exec producer, 2010; After Earth, producer, 2013; "The Queen Latifah Show", producer, 2013; Annie, 2014. Films: Where the Day Takes You, 1992; Made in America, 1993; Six Degrees of Separation, 1993; Bad Boys, 1995; Independence Day, 1996, Men in Black, 1997; Enemy of the State, 1998; Wild Wild West, 1999; Welcome to Hollywood, 2000; The Legend of Bagger Vance, 2000; America: A Tribute to Heroes, 2001; Ali, 2001; Men in Black 2, 2002; Bad Boys II, 2003; I, Robot, exec producer, 2004; Hitch, 2005; The Pursuit of Happyness, 2006; I Am Legend, 2007; Hancock, 2008; The Secret Life of Bees, 2008; Lakeview Terrace, 2008; Seven Pounds, 2008; The Karate Kid, 2010; This Means War, 2012; After Earth, 2013; Anchorman 2: The Legend Continues, 2013; Winter's Tale, 2014. **Honors/Awds:** Grammy Award; Numerous honors and awards including 2 Oscar nominations; Blimp Award, 1991, 1998, 2000, 2005-06 & 2009; ASCAP Awards, 1994, 1998 & 2000; ShoWest Award, 1995, 1997, 1999 & 2002; Universe Reader's Choice Award, 1996; Blockbuster Entertainment Award, 1997-99; Hall of Fame, Kids' Choice Awards, 1997; MTV Movie Award, 1997, 1999, 2002 &2008; Special Award, Nat Asn Advan Colored People, 1999; Razzie Award, 2000 & 2014; BET Award, 2002 & 2009; Jupiter Award, 2002 & 2005; Wannabe Award, 2003; NRJ Cine Award, 2004-05 & 2007; Honorary Cesar Award, 2005; Teen Choice Award, 2005, 2007 & 2008; People's Choice Award, 2005 & 2009; Modern Master Award, 2007; Saturn Award, 2008; Image Award, Nat Asn Advan Colored People, 2009. **Special Achievements:** First hip-hop artist to be nominated for an Academy Award. **Business Addr:** Actor, c/o Creative Artists Agency, 2000 Ave of the Stars, Los Angeles, CA 90067, **Business Phone:** (310)288-4545.

### SMITH, WILLIAM FRED
Executive, manager. **Personal:** Born Mar 22, 1938, Savannah, GA. **Educ:** Savannah State Col; Calif State Univ. **Career:** Litton Guid & Control Sys, mgr, affirmative action, 1972-76; EEO Comput Sci Corp, corp mgr, 1976-78; Litton Date Syst, mgr affirmative, 1978-80; Bunker Ramo Corp, mgr personnel, 1980; Contel Fed Syts, dir, human resources, 1986-91; Gen Tel & Electronics Corp, dir, human resources, 1991-94. **Orgs:** Valley Pref Employee Comm; Kappa Alpha Psi Frat; PMAA; LA Basin EEO; Nat Asn Advan Colored People; Employ Mgt Asn; Soc Human Resources Mgt; bd dir, Westlake Village Chamber Com; Nat Employee Serv & Recreation Asn; Human Rel Comn; W Covina City, 1970-74; Aerospace indust, EEO Comn, 1970-93; personnel mgt asn, Aztian, 1974-93; Soc Human Resources Mgt, 1980-94; Calif Chap Family Motor Coach Asn, 1980-; Employ Mgt Asn, 1984-; JTPC/Pvt Indust Coun, Ventura Co, CA, 1987-94; community police adv bd, Los Angeles Police Depart, 1994-; adv bd, Thousand Trails NACO/Leisure Time, 2001-. **Honors/Awds:** Selective syst bd mem adv appointed by Pres, 1971; Community Service Award, 1971; Community Service Award, Los Angeles Co Human Relations Comn, 1972; National Media Women Communication Award, 1973; appointed to Calif Gov Comm Employ Handicapped, 1978; San Fernando Concerned Black Womens Award, 1979; invited to White House by Pres Carter, 1980; Society of Black Engineers, Calif State Univ Northridge, 1980. **Home Addr:** 10611 Ledeen Dr, Lake View Terrace, CA 91342.

### SMITH, WILLIAM FRENCH
Engineer, consultant. **Personal:** Born Nov 30, 1941, Bay City, TX; son of William III Sr and Willie Mae Perry; married Sylvia Knight; children: William III & Maurice. **Educ:** Tuskegee Univ, BS, 1964; Wash Univ, St Louis, MO, Grad Study, 1970. **Career:** Boeing Co, Huntsville, AL, equip engr, 1964-67; McDonnell Douglas Corp, St Louis, MO, plant design engr, 1967-69; St Louis County Govt, proj engr, 1969-72; E I DuPont de Nemours & Co Inc, div engr, Wilmington, DE & Victoria, TX, 1972-74; Westinghouse Corp, Millburn, NJ, engineering mgr, 1974-76; Denver Pub Schs, bldg safety engr, 1976-, proj adminr, 1977-, energy conservationist, 1978-; Tuskegee Univ, Denver, CO, mgr hazardous mat, 1985-88, environ safety engr, 1988-, safety engr, mgr environ safety, 1992-; Wm Fr Smith Consult, chief exec officer, currently. **Orgs:** Bd dir, Denver Opportunity Ind Ctr, 1979-80, Nat Comn Future Regis Col; Mayor's Citizens Adv Comn Energy, 1980-; Am Soc Safety Engrs, Colo Asn Sch Energy Coordrs, Am Asn Blacks Energy, treas, Denver Pub Schs Black Admin & Supvs Asn; Colo Environ Health Asn, Nat Asbestos Coun, Colo Hazardous Waste Mgmt Soc, Colo Hazardous Mat Asn, Nat Asn Minority Contractors, Rocky Mountain Hazardous Mat Asn, Tuskegee Univ Alumni Asn; vpres, Rocky Mountain Poison & Drug Ctr, 1990-; vpres, Hazardous Mat Asn; Colo Emergency Planning Comn; Colo Alliance Environ Educ; Nat Black Environ Asn; Denver Emergency Planning Comn; Sr Citizens Adv Bd; City Lakewood, CO, bd Appeals; Community Rels Rep Fed Emergency Mgmt Agency; bd mem, Colo Alliance Environ Educ. **Honors/Awds:** Black Engineer of the Year, Career Community Group Inc, 1990, 1991, 1992; Registered Environ Assessor; Certified Environmental Inspector; Juanita Gray Community Service Award; President's Award on Energy Conservation. **Home Addr:** 102 S Balsam St, Lakewood, CO 80226-1334, **Home Phone:** (303)233-3335. **Business Addr:** Safety Engineer & Energy Czar, Special Project Manager, Denver Public Schools, 102 S Balsam St, Denver, CO 80226-1344, **Business Phone:** (303)575-4126.

### SMITH, WILLIAM GENE
Banker. **Personal:** Born Jan 23, 1955, Windsor, NC; son of James L (deceased) and Mattie S; children: Byron Eugene & Antoine A. **Educ:** NCA Cent Univ, BA, 1977; Univ NC, Sch Banking, mid mgt, 1985. **Career:** First Union, br mgr, 1977-81, asst consumer bank mgr, 1984-85, durham, consumer bank mgr, 1985-88, raleigh, consumer bank mgr, 1988-90, regional consumer bank exec, 1990-92, durham, city area exec, 1992-2001; Mutual Community Savings Bank, pres & chief exec officer, 2001-. **Orgs:** InRoads, 1986-92; bd mem & treas, NCCU Found, 1990-; treas & bd mem, Wake Opportunities; chmn, NC Cent Univ Bd Trustees; adv bd chair, Nat Asn Urban Bankers; bd mem, Greater Durham Chamber Com; bd mem, Durham Black Achievers Prog; bd mem, United Way; Phi Beta Sigma; Alpha Tan Blvd; 100 Black Men Am; Oakland African Am Chamber Com. **Honors/Awds:** Consumer Banking Manager of the Year, 1986; Consumer Credit Sales Manager of the Year, First Union Nat Bank, 1993; Outstanding Chapter Member, NC Asn Urban Bankers, 1994; Positive Image Award, Pee Dee Newspaper Group, 1996. **Special Achievements:** Dollars & Sense Magazine, honored as one of Americas Best and Brightest Executive, 1992. **Home Addr:** 2021 Matilene Ave, Durham, NC 27707, **Home Phone:** (919)596-8858. **Business Addr:** President, Chief Executive Officer, Mutual Community Savings Bank, 315 E Chapel Hill St, Durham, NC 27701-3317, **Business Phone:** (919)688-1308.

### SMITH, WILLIAM JAMES
Lawyer. **Personal:** Born Mar 5, 1946, Fresno, CA; married Joy E Johnson; children: Danielle, Nicole, Seth & Kira. **Educ:** Univ Calif, Los Angeles, BA, polit sci, 1968; Univ Calif, Sch Law, Los Angeles, JD, law, 1972. **Career:** County San Diego, Chief Dep County Coun, 1974-2010, Mem, Assessment Appeals Bd, 2010-; Trust Admin Union Bank, Univ Calif Los Angeles football; Nat Labor Rels Bd, atty; Brundage Reich & Pappy Labor Spec, atty; W J Smith & Assoc, partner, currently; State Ctr Community Col, pres, 1990-, Bd Trustees, bd dir; William D. Smith, Consult Drafting Legis, Pub Retirement Law, Local Govt Law, 2010-. **Orgs:** Nat Conf Black Lawyers; bd dir, Black Law Journ; Los Angeles County Bar Asn; Beverly Hills Bar Asn; Asn Trial Lawyers Am; Calif Bar Asn; Langston Law Club; Pro Bono Cases Labor Law; Col Labor & Employ Lawyers; active mem, Am Bar Asn; exec bd mem, Nat Employ Lawyers Asn; co-chair, Sexual Harassment Comt; exec & bd mem, Calif Employ Lawyers Asn; Fed Bar Asn; chair, Civil Rights Comt; Inns Ct; pres, Fresno County Bar Asn; pres, 1980; pres, bd dir, Cent Calif Legal Serv; bd trustee, State Ctr Community Col Dist; Mediator & arbitrator, Calif State Mediation & Conciliation Serv. **Honors/Awds:** Outstanding employ lawyers in Calif, Calif Law Bus. **Home Addr:** 3189 W La Costa Ave, Fresno, CA 93711-0225. **Business Addr:** Attorney, W J Smith & Associates, 2350 W Shaw Ave Suite 132, Fresno, CA 93711, **Business Phone:** (559)432-0986.

### SMITH, WILLIAM XAVIER
Banker. **Personal:** Born Dec 9, 1934, Livingston, AL; son of Elijah and Daisy Jones; married Cynthia Wright; children: Molina, Xavier Gerard, Dianna & April. **Educ:** Bryant Col, BS, acct & finance, 1960; AIB basic & stand cert, cert, 1974; Univ Wis, Sch Bank Admin, dipl, 1975. **Career:** Liggett Drug Co, jr acct, 1960-62; Wonstop Auto Serv, acct, 1962-63; US Treas Dept, intl revenue agt, 1963-67; GAC Corp, tax res supvr, 1967-70; Unity Bank & Trust, asst treas, 1970-72; Peoples Bank Vi, vpres cashier, 1972-77; Am State Bank, vpres oper, 1977-82, pres & dir, 1982-; Gateway Nat Bank, St Louis, Mo, pres, dir 1990-95; United Bank Philadelphia, exec vpres, chief operating officer, 1995-98; Community Bank Bay, vpres, compliance officer, 1998-, sr vpres & chief risk officer, 2008-. **Orgs:** Dir & treas, Boy Scouts Am, Vi, 1974-77; pres, Greenwood Chamber Comn, 1984-; dir, Tulsa Comn Action Agency, 1985-; dir, Monsanto, YMCA, St Louis, Mo, 1991-. **Home Addr:** 5563 Pershing Ave Suite 2 W, Saint Louis, MO 63112-1773, **Home Phone:** (314)367-6916. **Business Addr:** Senior Vice President, Chief Risk Officer, Community Bank of the Bay, 1750 Broadway, Oakland, CA 94612, **Business Phone:** (510)433-5403.

### SMITH, WILLIE A. See WILSON-SMITH, WILLIE ARRIE.

### SMITH, WILLIE B.
Educator. **Personal:** Born Mar 30, 1941, Doddsville, MS; daughter of Cato Willis and Flora; married Reubin K; children: Wilton Reubin. **Educ:** Miss Valley State Univ, BS, elem educ, 1961; Delta State Univ, MEd, elem educ, elem supv, 1969; Ala A&M Univ, adult educ cert, 1976. **Career:** Caohoma Community Col, basic adult teacher; Ruleville Cent High Sch, teacher, 1961-67; Friars Pt Elem Sch, teacher, 1967-91; New Bethel HOP, teacher, 1998-. **Orgs:** Nat Asn Advan Colored People, 1972-91; sunday sch teacher, New Bethel Baptist Church, 1976-2000; prog comt, chmn, Delta Sigma Theta Sorority, 1996-; jr matron, Heroines Jericho, 1986-2000; vpres, Women Missionary Soc, 1998-2000. **Home Addr:** PO Box 434, Clarksdale, MS 38614-0434, **Home Phone:** (662)627-5333. **Business Addr:** Teacher, Librarian, New Bethel H O P (Helping Other People), 101 18th St, Clarksdale, MS 38614, **Business Phone:** (662)624-5373.

### SMITH, WILSON WASHINGTON, III
Association executive, fashion designer, executive. **Personal:** Born Oct 2, 1957, Portland, OR; son of Wilson Jr. **Educ:** Univ Ore, Sch Architect, BArch, 1980. **Career:** Skidmore, Owings & Merrill, architect, 1981-82; self-employed, map designer & freelance architect, 1982; Portland Gen Elec, CAD, 1982-83; Planning Bur, urban planner, 1983; SouthLake Foursquare Church, worship leader, 2001-11; NIKE Inc, interior designer, 1983-86, prod designer footwear, 1986-90, sr prod designer & creative dir, 2003-. **Orgs:** Music minister & worship coordr, Portland Foursquare Church, 1987-; coordr, Worship Servants, Portland, 1989-; music minister, S Lake Foursquare Church, Lake Oswego, Ore, currently. **Honors/Awds:** Outstanding Business & Professional Award, Dollars & Sense Mag, 1993; One of America's Top Black Designers, Black Enterprise Mag. **Special Achievements:** Appeared in numerous television series including 20/20, Presentation on NIKE Design, 1988; Breakfast Club, FX Network, "NIKE Design", 1994; "How'd They Do That", Presentation on NIKE Design, 1994; Music Director Summit, 1991, (6000 Youth, 3 day, 1988), National Four Square Youth Convention, 1988; Creator of many athlete-endorsed products including Andre Agassi's signature line, 1997; First dedicated Senior Footwear Designer for Brand Jordan; Collaborating with Michael Jordan created the industry leading Air Jordan 16 & 17, 2003. **Home Addr:** 6055 SW Sequoia Dr, Tualatin, OR 97062-6836. **Business Addr:** Senior Product Designer, Creative Director, NIKE Inc, 1 Bowerman Dr MJ4, Beaverton, OR 97005, **Business Phone:** (503)671-6453.

### SMITH, ZACHARY
Chef. **Personal:** Born Jul 1, 1951, Detroit, MI; son of Jame Z and Leola; married Donna J Alex; children: Chelsea & Christina. **Career:** Battery Pt, chef; Hyatt Regency, San Francisco, sous chef; Benbow Inn, exec chef; Lansdowne, exec chef; Restaurant OneTwentyThree, exec chef; five star hotels & restaurants, exec chef; Zachary Cafe, owner, currently. **Orgs:** Chef Asn. **Honors/Awds:** One of best the chefs in Michigan. **Special Achievements:** Cooking demonstration Baccat Sch; 4-star rating, Restaurant One Twenty Three, in Restaurants Detroit, 6th edition, by Molly Abraham. **Home Addr:** 908 Neff, PO Box 231155, Grosse Pointe, MI 48230. **Business Addr:** Owner, Zachary Cafe, 9415 Hwy 64, Zachary, LA 70791, **Business Phone:** (225)654-3354.

### SMITH-ALSTON, TONI COLETTE. See SMITH, TONI COLETTE.

### SMITH-CROXTON, TERRI (TEARETHA SMITH-CROXTON)
Executive. **Educ:** BA, 1979. **Career:** Ralston Purina, Monsanto & Pyramid Inc, human resource; JD & Assoc Inc, Arlington, Tex, pres & chief exec officer, 1980-. **Orgs:** Vpres, Links Inc, chaplain; League Women Voters; WIB; Boys & girls Club; Chamber com; chair bd, Ft Worth Econ Develop Inc; Arlington African Am Chamber Com; Arlington Philharmonic; YWCA. **Home Addr:** 2315 Table Rock Ct, Arlington, TX 76006. **Business Addr:** President, Chief Executive Officer, JD & Associates Inc, 609 E Main St, Arlington, TX 76006-8391, **Business Phone:** (817)265-4721.

### SMITH-EPPS, E. PAULETTE
Librarian. **Personal:** Born Mar 6, 1947, Atlanta, GA; daughter of William Chauncey Sr and Viola Williams (deceased); married William Given Sr. **Educ:** Spelman Col, Atlanta, Ga, BA, 1968; Atlanta Univ, Atlanta, Ga, MSLS, 1971. **Career:** Librarian (retired); Atlanta Univ, Atlanta, Ga, circulation librn, 1972-73; Atlanta-Fulton Pub Libr, Atlanta, Ga, ref librn, 1973-76, br mgr, 1976-82, asst br servs admin, 1982-86, br servs admin, 1986-91, cent libr admin, 1991-92, proj mgr, 1992, outreach servs advr, 1992-95, learning assistance bus officer, 1995-96, pub servs adminr, 1996-97, asst dir pub servs, 1997-2000; Heards Ferry Elem Sch, asst teacher Pre-K, currently. **Orgs:** Spelman Col Alumnae Asn, 1968-; Clark Atlanta Univ Alumni Asn, 1971-; Metro-Atlanta Libr Asn, 1971; Am Libr Asn, 1974-; Black Caucus Am Libr Asn, 1976-; Episcopal Diocese Atlanta. **Home Addr:** 5160 Bruce Pl SW, Atlanta, GA 30331, **Home Phone:** (404)349-0607. **Business Addr:** Assistant Teacher, Heards Ferry Elementary School, 1050 Heards Ferry Rd NW, Sandy Springs, GA 30328-4730, **Business Phone:** (770)933-6190.

### SMITH-GASTON, LINDA ANN
Executive, administrator. **Personal:** Born Jan 17, 1949, Kingstree, SC; daughter of George and Frances Latimer Montgomery; married Anthony R; children: Taylor Aderemi Humphries & Leigh Jamila. **Educ:** Univ Calif Los Angeles, BA, 1970; Calif State Univ, MA, 1984. **Career:** KTTV-TV, Los Angeles, Calif, host, 1978-80; Drew Post Grad Med Sch, Los Angeles, Calif, prog specialist, 1979-80; Consumer Credit Counrs, Los Angeles, Calif, counr, 1981-82; ARCO, Los Angeles, Calif, consumer affairs specialist, 1982-84; Southern Calif Gas Co, Los Angeles, Calif, sr consumer affairs specialist, 1984-. **Orgs:** Chairperson, KCET Community Adv Bd, 1987-88; pres, Soc Consumer Affairs Profs Bus, 1989; bd mem, Los Angeles County Comn Local Govt Serv, 1990-; state coordr, Calif Agenda Consumer Educ, 1990-; bd mem, Nat Coalition Consumer Educ, 1991-. **Home Addr:** 1620 Corning St, Los Angeles, CA 90035. **Business Addr:** Senior Consumer Affairs Administrator, Southern California Gas Co, 810 S Flower St ML 301V, Los Angeles, CA 90017, **Business Phone:** (213)689-3176.

### SMITH-GRAY, CASSANDRA ELAINE
Government official, manager, executive director. **Personal:** Born Mar 7, 1947, Detroit, MI; married Charles A; children: David Charles. **Educ:** Wayne State Univ, BS, 1971. **Career:** Detroit Pub Sch, ed, 1970-74; City Detroit Youth Dept, dir, 1974-76; City Detroit Bd Assessors, assessor, 1976-82; City Detroit Neighborhood Serv, exec dir; Detroit Housing Comn, exec dir, currently. **Orgs:** Nat Asn Negro Bus & Prof Women; campaign mgr, Mayor Young's Re-election, 1981; state cent mem alt, Mich Dem Party, 1982-; bd mem, Mayor's Anti-Crime Proj, 1982; trustee, Ctr Humanist Studies, 1983-; bd mem, Wayne City Child Care Coun, 1983-; life mem, Nat Adavn Asn Colored People; det campaign mgr, Mondale-Ferrarro Campaign, 1984; deleg, Dem Nat Conv, 2004-. **Honors/Awds:** First Black Woman Assessor Cert, MI, 1979. **Home Addr:** 2112 Hyde Park Dr, Detroit, MI 48207. **Business Addr:** Director, Detroit Housing Commission, 1301 E Jefferson Ave, Detroit, MI 48207, **Business Phone:** (313)877-8639.

### SMITH-GREGORY, DEBORAH P.
Educator, journalist. **Personal:** Born May 6, 1951, Dayton, OH; daughter of John Pridgen and Mae Mack Pridgen; married Carl; children: Rahsaan & Hakim. **Educ:** Univ Calif, Berkeley, CA, cert jour; Seton Hall Univ, S Orange, NJ, BS, eng, hist, sec educ; Montclair State Col, Montclair, NJ, post grad studies. **Career:** Newark Bd Educ, Newark, NJ, educr & advisor, 1974-; NJ Afro-Am newspaper, Newark, NJ, journalist, 1984-89, reporter, 1985-88, resident ed, 1988-89; NJ Perspectus News Mag, founding ed, 1989-94; DP Smith Assoc, Pub Rels, Publ Co, pres, 1994-. **Orgs:** Life mem, 1989-, pres, chair, Nat Asn Advan Colored People; Nat Asn Black Journalists, 1989-; Garden State Asn Black Journalists, 1990-; pres & bd dir, United Acad, 1990-; chair person, Newark Afro Acad, Cult, Technol prog; fel Metrop Baptist Church; chairperson, Nj State ACT-SO Prog. **Home Addr:** 800 S 11th St, Newark, NJ 07108, **Home Phone:** (201)563-0868. **Business Addr:** President, Chair, NAACP New Jersey State Conference, PO Box 1262, Newark, NJ 07101-1262, **Business Phone:** (973)624-6400.

### SMITH-HENDRICKS, CONSTANCE KASANDRA. See HENDRICKS, DR. CONSTANCE SMITH.

### SMITH-SMITH, PEOLA
School principal, president (organization). **Personal:** Born New Orleans, LA; married Vernell; children: Vania & Vallyn. **Educ:** MSED; BA, health & phys educ, 1971; Monmouth Col, MA, coun & guid, 1979. **Career:** School principal (retired), president; Neptune Mid Sch, prin, chairperson, coun/guid dept. **Orgs:** Nat pres, Nat Asn Negro Bus & Prof Women's Clubs Inc, 2003-07; Delta Sigma Theta Sorority; Nat Coun Negro Women. **Home Addr:** 1101 Fordham Rd, Neptune, NJ 07753-4321, **Home Phone:** (732)774-1287. **Business Addr:** Chair-Person, Counseling/Guidance, Neptune High School, 55 Neptune Blvd, Neptune City, NJ 07753, **Business Phone:** (732)776-2200.

### SMITH-SURLES, DR. CAROL DIANN
School administrator, president (organization). **Personal:** Born Oct 7, 1946, Pensacola, FL; children: Lisa Ronique & Philip. **Educ:** Fisk Univ, BA, 1968; Chapman Col, MA, 1971; Univ Mich, PhD, 1978. **Career:** Counr; Santa Barbara County, social worker, 1968-69; Allan Hancock Col, instr, 1971-72; Univ Mich, personnel rep, 1971-77; Univ Cent Fla, dir eeo, 1978-84, exec asst to pres, 1982-84, assoc vpres, 1984; Jackson State Univ; Calif St Univ, vpres admin & Bus affairs, 1992-94; Tex Woman's Univ, pres, 1994-99; Tex-NMex Power Co, dir, 1995; TNP Enterprises Inc, dir, 1995-; Eastern Ill Univ, pres, 1999-2001. **Orgs:** Pi Lambda Theta Hon Soc, 1977; Nat Asn Advan Colored People; mem bd trustee, WMFETV & FM radio, 1984-; bd mem, Orlando Human Rels Bd, 1984-; pres, Orlando Leadership Coun Orlando Chamber Com, 1985; bd dir, First St Bank, 1995-; Am Asn Univ Professors; Am Asn Univ Women; Golden Key Hon Soc; League Women Voters; Nat Urban League. **Honors/Awds:** Outstanding Scholars Award Delta Tau Kappa Int Social Sci Hon Soc, 1983; United Auto Workers Award; Leadership Orlando Presidential Award. **Special Achievements:** First African American to hold the position as president in Eastern Illinois University. **Home Addr:** 3115 Loren Lane, Charleston, IL 61920, **Home Phone:** (217)345-2605. **Business Addr:** Director, TNP Enterprises Inc, 4100 Int Plz, Ft Worth, TX 76113, **Business Phone:** (817)731-0099.

### SMITH-TAYLOR, REV. DONNA LYN
Clergy. **Personal:** Born Jan 1, 1949, Detroit, MI; daughter of Roger Brook Smith and Georgia O. **Career:** Carl Byoir & Assocs Inc, supvr,

acct payable, acct adminr, 1978-85; Memorial Baptist Church, asst pastor, admin asst, 1985-88; Kenilworth Baptist Church, pastor, 1988-90; Empire Baptist State Conv, Empire Chronicle Newspaper, asst ed, currently; New Progressive Missionary Baptist Church, pastor; Shiloh Baptist Church, pastor, currently. **Orgs:** Recording secy, Central Hudson Baptist Asn, 1989-; asst fin secy, Empire Baptist State Conv, 1989-; Black Ministerial Alliance, 1991-. **Home Addr:** 51 E Strand St Suite 33A, Kingston, NY 12401-6067, **Home Phone:** (914)339-8271. **Business Addr:** Pastor, Shiloh Baptist Church, 90 N Wash St, Tarrytown, NY 10591, **Business Phone:** (914)631-4197.

## SMITHERMAN, ESQ. CAROLE CATLIN

Judge, educator, lawyer. **Personal:** Born Sep 25, 1952, Birmingham, AL; daughter of Jerry and Thelma; married Rodger; children: Rodger, Tonya, Mary & Crystal. **Educ:** Spelman Col, BBA, polit sci, 1973; Miles Law Sch, JD, 1979. **Career:** Miles Law Sch, prof, 1982-; pvt pract atty; State Ala, Jefferson County, circuit ct judge, 1991-93; Birmingham City Coun, dist 6 rep, 2001-13, coun pres, 2005-09. **Orgs:** Founder, C Village; Econ Develop & Educ Comt; Birmingham Bar Asn; Nat Asn Advan Colored People; bd dir, Police Athletic Teams, 1989; chairperson, Admin/Budget & Fin Comt, currently. **Home Addr:** 928 Ctr Way SW, Birmingham, AL 35211. **Business Addr:** Council President, Birmingham City Council, 710 20th St N, Birmingham, AL 35203-2216, **Business Phone:** (205)254-2359.

## SMITHERMAN, DR. GENEVA

Educator. **Personal:** Born Dec 10, 1940, Brownsville, TN; daughter of Harry Napoleon; married Jeff R Donaldson; children: Robert Anthony. **Educ:** Wayne State Univ, BA, 1960, MA, 1962; Univ Mich, PhD, sociolinguistics & educ, 1969. **Career:** Detroit Pub Schs, teacher, 1960-65; Eastern Mich Univ, instr, 1965-71; Wayne St Univ, instr, 1965-71, asst prof, prof, 1973-; Harvard Univ, Afro-Am studies lectr, 1971-73; Univ Mich, adj prof, 1971; Mich St Univ, actg dir, African Am & African Studies, 2009-10, univ distinguished prof Emerita eng, currently. **Orgs:** Oral Hist Comt, Afro Mus, 1967-68; Wayne County Community Col, curric consult & instr, 1969-71; Exefc Comt Conf Col Compos Commun, 1971-73; chmn, Black Lit Sec, Midwest Lang Asn, 1972; judge, Scholastic Writing Awards Contest, 1975; Mod Lang Asn Comt, Minorities, 1976-77; founding mem, African-Am Heritage Asn, 1976; adv bd, Ethnic Awareness Proj, 1977-78; Nat Coun Teachers Eng, lang comn, 1979-82; chair, Lang Policy Comt, 1987-2010; chair, Tenure Comt, 1997-98; Standing Comt Res, Nat Coun Teachers Eng, 2000-03; co chair, African Am Lit & Cult Search Comt, 2001-06; chair & organizer, Panel African Am Eng, Am Dialect Soc, 2001; chair, Lang & Ling Sect, African Studies Asn, 2001; co-founder & mem, African Am Lit & Cult Comt, 2007; Mod Lang Asn Teagle Found Task Force, 2007-08; adv bd mem, ABC Connects, 2007-11; dir, African Am Lang & Literacy Prog, Mich St Univ, 1989-2011; grant proposal reviewer, Nat Res Found, SafricA, 2013. **Honors/Awds:** Richard Wright-Woodie King Award; Honored Woman of Wayne, Wayne State Univ; Outstanding Woman of the Year, Nat Asn Negro Bus & Prof Womens Young Adult Club; Dean List of Hon Students, Wayne St Univ; Award for Scholarly Leadership in Lang Arts Instr, 1980; W E B DuBois Scholar Award, Phylon Soc, Wayne St Univ; Zora Neale Hurston Anthrop Award, Ctr Black Studies, Wayne St Univ; James B Hamilton Award, Mid-Am Asn Educ Opportunity Prog Personnel, 1994; Ernest A Lynton Award, 1997; Educational Press Association Award; Exemplar Award, Conf Col Compos & Commun, 1999; Distinguished Fac Award, Mich St Univ, 2000; David H Russell Res Award, Nat Coun Teachers Eng, 2001; James R. Squire Award, Nat Coun Teachers Eng, 2005; MSU Lifetime Diversity Award, 2009; 50th Anniversary Award, Marcus Garvey Found, 2011; Distinguished Researcher Award, Nat Conf Res Lang & Literacies, 2012; Advancement of People of Color Leadership Award, Nat Coun Teachers of Eng, 2012. **Special Achievements:** Published many books, authored more than 100 articles and essays about Black speech, rhet & wrote the award winning article; Article: Soul n Style, The Eng J column; "My Bros Keeper", co-founder, dir, Mich State Univ; Publ: Talkin and Testifyin, 1977, 1986; Black Talk, 1994, 2000; CCCC Exemplar Award, 1999; Talkin That Talk, 2000; Lang and Democracy in the Us of Am and S africa, 2001; NCTE James R. Squire Award, 2005. **Home Addr:** 6634 Oakman Blvd, Detroit, MI 48228. **Business Addr:** University Distinguished Professor of English, Michigan State University, 221 Morrill Hall, East Lansing, MI 48824, **Business Phone:** (517)353-9252.

## SMITHERMAN, RODGER M.

Lawyer, government official. **Personal:** Born Mar 2, 1953, Montgomery, AL; son of Ralph and Mary; married Carole Catlin; children: Rodger II, Tonya Renee, Mary Elaine & Crystal Nicole. **Educ:** Univ Montevallo, BBA, 1976; Miles Law Sch, JD, 1986. **Career:** Southern Jr Col, dean Students; State Ala, 18th Dist, state sen, 1994, 2009-; Miles Law Sch, prof law, currently. **Orgs:** Dem & elder, Westimister Presby Church; bd dir, Western Area YMCA; youth & govt coach, W End High Sch; adv bd, Camp Birmingham; Vulcan Kiwanis; Birmingham Tip Off Club; vol basketball coach, Amateaur Athletic Union; Police Athletic Team; Ala State Bar Asn; Birmingham Bar Asn; Birmingham Chamber Com; Ala Trial Lawyers Asn; bd dir, Metro YMCA; Exec Comt Southern Legis Conf; Nat Energy Coun; chmn, Jefferson County Senate Deleg; pres, Ala Legis Black Caucus; pres, Pro Tempore Ala Senate, 2009-10. **Home Addr:** 224 16 Ave SW, Birmingham, AL 35211, **Home Phone:** (205)322-3768. **Business Addr:** Senator, Alabama State Senate, 2029 2nd Ave N, Birmingham, AL 35203, **Business Phone:** (205)322-0012.

## SMITHERS, ORAL LESTER, JR.

Engineer. **Personal:** Born Jul 12, 1940, Columbus, OH; son of O Lester Sr and Mildred H; married Priscilla; children: Sheila & Lisa. **Educ:** Ohio State Univ, BCE, 1963; Sacramento State Col, MEngr, Mech; Cent Mich Univ, MA, 1982; Mass Inst Technol, Cambridge, MA, MS, 1985. **Career:** Aerojet Gen Corp, design engr, 1963-68; USF, aerospace engr, 1968-85; Dept Air Force, Wright Patterson Afb, F-16 dir eng, 1985-89, dir flight syst eng, 1989-92; Wright Lab, dep dir, 1992-97, dir eng, 1997-. **Orgs:** Ohio Soc Prof Engrs, Am Asn Aeronaut & Astronaut; Clark & Champaign County Soc Prof Engrs; bd dir, Armed Forces Communs & Electronics Asn; Clark State Col Bd trustees; Clark County, Springfield Plng Comn; past mem, steward bd, St Andrews AME Church; New N St AME Church; Omega Psi Phi Fraternity. **Honors/Awds:** Meritorious Civil Service Award, Air Force Sys Command; Civil Engineering Hon, Chi Epsilon; Sloan Fel, MIT, 1984-85; 4th District Man of the Year, Omega Psi Phi Fraternity, 1984; Senior Engineer of the Year, USAF Aeronaut Systems, 1989; Senior Exec Service Asn; Exceptional Civilian Service Award, 1993; Air Force EEO Management Award, 1995; Distinguished Alumni Award, Ohio State Univ, 1998; Prof Distinguished Exe Award, 2000. **Home Addr:** 1933 Sagamore St, The Villages, FL 32162, **Home Phone:** (937)864-2754. **Business Addr:** Director of Engineering, Wright Patterson AFB, Dayton, OH 45433, **Business Phone:** (937)255-3208.

## SMITHERS, PRISCILLA JANE

Association executive. **Personal:** Born Jan 2, 1942, Parkersburg, WV; daughter of Robert D and Mildred Burke; married O Lester Jr; children: Sheila & Lisa. **Career:** Mountain State Col, exec secy, 1960; Cont Cable Springfield, comn serv dir, prod, hostess weekly TV show, 1973-78; City Springfield, city clerk, 1978-87; United Way, Springfield, campaign assoc, 1987-91, Alcohol, Drug & Ment Health Bd, exec dir, 1991-96, dir resource develop; Clark Co Family Coun, exec dir, 1995-96. **Orgs:** Chmn, Civil Serv Comn, City Springfield, 1973-78; bd dir, United Way, 1976-87; Ohio Munic Clerks Asn, 1978-87; bd dirs, Alcohol Drug Ment Health Bd, 1986-91; vpres, Wittenberg Univ & Col Leadership Acad Alumni, 1988-90; Springfield Rotary Club, 1993-; cent comt, Clark Co Republican Party, 1994-; mediation bd, City Springfield, 1994-; Key Corp, Bank Comn Adv Comt, 1995-; Enon Hist Soc, 1995-; Ohio Dept Educ; LINCCS Data Mgt Coun. **Honors/Awds:** Citizen of the Year, Fraternity Int, 1978; Citizen of the Year, Black Women Leadership Caucus, 1979; Black History Award, St John Miss Church, 1990; Community Leadership Award, Springfield Comn Leadership Alumni Asn, 1990; Nat Citizen of the Year, Omega Phi Psi, 1994; Employee of the Year, ADMH, 1994. **Home Addr:** 15 Bobwhite Dr, Enon, OH 45323, **Home Phone:** (937)864-2754. **Business Addr:** Director of Development, United Way of Clark & Champaign Counties, 616 N Limestone St, Springfield, OH 45503, **Business Phone:** (513)324-5551.

## SMOTHERS, RONALD

Executive. **Educ:** Univ Calif, Los Angeles. **Career:** Burger King, Los Angeles, owner; Dennys, Crenshaw, owner, 2006; Fastaurants Inc, Los Angeles, Calif, pres & chief exec officer. **Business Addr:** President, Chief Executive Officer, Fastaurants Inc, 3700 Coliseum St, Los Angeles, CA 90016-5802, **Business Phone:** (323)298-1628.

## SMOTHERS, RONALD ERIC

Journalist. **Personal:** Born Sep 3, 1946, Washington, DC; son of Emily M and Warren (deceased); married Brenda; married Diane Marie Weathers. **Educ:** Hobart Col, BA, 1967. **Career:** Comm News Serv, ed, 1969-72; Newsday, 1968-69; Wash Post, 1967-68; New York Times, reporter, currently. **Business Addr:** Reporter, The New York Times, 111 Mulberry St, Newark, NJ 07102, **Business Phone:** (973)623-3904.

## SMOTHERSON, REV. DR. MELVIN

Clergy. **Personal:** Born Nov 6, 1936, Hattiesburg, MS; son of Melvin and Estella S Rogers; married Geraldine Jackson; children: Charles, Bwayne, Pamela & Darren. **Educ:** Mont Baptist Col, BA, 1974; Cent Baptist Theol Sem, DD, 1975; Webster Col, MA, 1980. **Career:** First Baptist Church, Creve Coeur, pastor, 1962-71; Baptist State Sunday Sch & BTU Cong, historian, 1974-75; Ministers Union Greater, St Louis, vpres, 1977-79; Wash Tabernacle Baptist Church, pastor, 1971-80; Cornerstone Inst Baptist Church, founder, pastor, 1980. **Orgs:** Grand jrwarden & grand chaplain, dep grand master, Most Worshipful Prince Hall Grand Lodge; hon mem, Mich Grand Lodge F&AM; exec comt, Nat Asn Advan Colored People; Most Worshipful Grand Master- MWPHGL Mont, 1988-90; dep imp chaplain, Ancient Egyptian Arabic Order, Nobles Mystic Shrine N & S Am & Jurisdiction, 1985-. **Honors/Awds:** Minister of the Year Award, Baptist Church, 1973; Cert of Merit, Nat Asn Advan Colored People, 1974; Doctor of Divinity, Cent Baptist Theol Sem, 1975; Citizen of the Year Award, George Wash Carver Assoc, 1979; Citizen of the Year Award, Grand Chap OES; speaker in Trinidad WI, Seoul Korea, Rome, Italy, 1987-88; Knight Grand Comdr of Humanity Re pub of Liberia, 1989; Chief of B bandi Tribe Lofa Dist, Monrovia, Liberia. **Home Addr:** 1247 Purdue Ave, St Louis, MO 63130-1843, **Home Phone:** (314)721-0936. **Business Addr:** Pastor, Cornerstone Institutional Baptist Church, 4700 Wash Blvd, St Louis, MO 63108, **Business Phone:** (314)367-8000.

## SMYRE, CALVIN

State government official, executive. **Personal:** Born May 17, 1947, Chattahoochee County, GA. **Educ:** Ft Valley State Univ, BS, bus admin, mgt & opers, 1970. **Career:** Exec & state rep; Synovus Financial Corp, Columbus Bank & Trust Co, asst vpres & mkt officer, 1976-84, asst vpres, vpres corp admin, 1984-90, sr vpres & asst to chmn community affairs, 1990-99, exec vpres corp affairs, 1999-2014; Ga Gen Assembly, state rep, dean house, 1974-2015; Synovus Found Inc, chmn & chief exec officer, currently; Dem Party, chmn, 2006. **Orgs:** Deleg, Dem Nat Party Conf, 1978; chmn, Ga Legis Black Caucus, 1979-80; deleg, Dem Nat Conv, 1980-; pres, Ga Asn Black Elected Officials, 1982-88; secy, pres, Nat Black Caucus State Legisrs; bd trustee, Morehouse Sch Med, Med Col Ga Found; Jack D Hughston Sports Med Hosp Found; chair, Ft Valley State Col Found; adv, vpres Al Gore, Gore's run pres, 2000; bd chair, River Ctr Bd, 2002-04; life-long mem, Ward Chapel AME Church; State house comts; Chmn, House Rules Comt; Liberty Theater Cult Ctr Inc. **Business Addr:** Executive Vice President, Synovus Financial Corp, PO Box 120, Columbus, GA 31902, **Business Phone:** (706)649-2311.

## SMYTHE, VICTOR N.

Librarian. **Personal:** son of Constantine (deceased) and Agnes L Scott (deceased). **Educ:** NY Univ, BA, psychol, 1964; Columbia Univ Sch Jour, 1964, Sch Libr Serv, MS, 1984; Modern Archives Inst, Nat Arch, Wash, DC, cert, 1989. **Career:** Librarian (retired); Int Circulating Exhibitions, Mus Mod Art, New York, NY, spec asst; Daniel Yankelovich Inc, field supvr; Post Exchange Servs, US Fort Clayton, internal auditor; S Bronx Proj, community liaison; Brooklyn Col, Dept Educ Serv, chief admin officer; NY Pub Libr, librn; Schomburg Cr Res Black Culture, heritage proj, archivist, librn, 1989; Art & Artifacts Div, Schomburg City, curator. **Orgs:** Am Libr Asn; Arch Roundtable Metrop NY; Mid-Atlantic Regional Arch Conf; dir, Caribbean/Am Media Studies Inc; dir, Coalition Caribbean Interests; bd mem, exec dir, 1990-97, chmn exec comt, 1982-97, Ethiopian Orthodox Church; dir, Western Hemisphere Abyssinian Cultural Ctr, 1993-97. **Special Achievements:** Editor, Black New York Artists of the 20th Century. **Home Addr:** 327 St Nicholas Ave, New York, NY 10027, **Home Phone:** (212)316-1734.

## SNEAD, CHERYL WATKINS

President (organization), administrator. **Educ:** Univ Mass, BSME, mech engineering, 1981; Purdue Univ, Krannert Sch Mgt, MBA/MSIA, bus admin & mgt, gen, 1987; Bryant Univ Grad Sch Bus, Hon Doctorate, bus admin & mgt, gen, 2006. **Career:** Gen Elec, mgt; Peerless Precision, Lincoln, owner; Banneker Indust Inc, pres, chief exec officer & owner, 1991-. **Orgs:** State deleg, US Small Bus Admin Nat Adv Coun; Textron Chamber Sch; bd dir, Bank Ri, 1995-2012; bd dir, Amica Mutual Ins Co, 2000-; bd trustee, Bryant Univ, 2007-; bd dir, Waterfire Providence, 2008-12; bd dir & forum vice chair, Women's Bus Enterprise Nat Coun, 2012-. **Business Addr:** President, Chief Executive Officer, Banneker Industries Inc, 582 Great Rd Suite 101, North Smithfield, RI 02896, **Business Phone:** (401)534-0027.

## SNEAD, DR. DAVID LOWELL

School superintendent. **Personal:** Born Oct 15, 1943, Detroit, MI; son of Herman and Edith; married Sharon McPhail; children: Deborah, David II, Brandon L, Erika & Angela. **Educ:** Tuskegee Univ, BS, 1968; Univ Mich, MA, urban educ, 1970, PhD, educ admin, 1984. **Career:** Detroit Pub Sch, sec sch educ cent off supvr, 1985, from asst prin to prin, 1985-93, interim asst supt, 1993, exec dep interim gen supt, 1993, gen supt, 1993-97; Madison Tech High Sch, headmaster; Waterbury Pub Schs, CT, supt, 2000-11. **Orgs:** Am Asn Sch Admin; Detroit Police Athletic League; bd mem, Health Alliance Plan, 1990-92; brd trustees, New Detroit Inc, 1994; Metro Detroit Alliance Black Sch Educr, 1994; brd trustees, exec comt, Coun Great City Sch, 1994; commun adv brd, Jr League Detroit, 1994; Nat Asn Advan Colored People; adv bd, WTNH Channel 8 New Haven. **Honors/Awds:** Man of the Year & Award of Merit, Alpha Phi Alpha, 1994; Michigan Superintendent of the Year, Mich Asn Sch Admin, 1994; Outstanding Leadership & Service Award, Mich Coun Deliberation Scholar Found, 1994; Editorial Award, Bus United With Officers Youth, 1994; Septima Clark Natl Editorial Award, Southern Christian Leadership Conf, 1995; Outstanding Academic Leadership Award, Conn Asn Urban Superintendents, 2002-03; Whitney M Young Jr Service Award, Boy Scouts Am, 2006. **Special Achievements:** Author: Dissertation, The Effects of Increased Grade Point Standards for Student Athletes, Univ of Mich Press, December 1984; Recommended Public School Finance Reforms, Detroit Free Press, March 1988; From Coach to Admin, It's All The Same, Secondary Education Today, Vol 29, No 3, Spring 1988; Educ Career Directory, Teaching in Urban Sch, Gale Research Copyright Inc, 1994; One of the top ten Administrators in the United States. **Home Addr:** 20071 Cherokee St, Detroit, MI 48219-1108, **Home Phone:** (313)255-3289.

## SNEAD, DR. WILLIE T., SR.

Clergy. **Personal:** children: Willie Terrell II. **Educ:** Calif Baptist Univ, Riverside, Calif, BS, bus admin; Golden Gate Theol Sem, Mill Valley, Calif, MS, christian educ; Reed Christian Col-Western Theol Sem, Los Angeles, Calif, PhD. **Career:** Greater Temple God Missionary Baptist Church, pastor & teacher, 1967-. **Orgs:** Pres, Nat Missionary Baptist Conv Am; lifetime mem, Nat Asn Advan Colored People, Los Angeles Chap; vice chmn, bd dir, Cong Nat Black Churches; former vice chmn & bd dir, Southern Calif Affil CNBC; Police Booster Club; former co chmn, Calif Comt Environ Justice; moderator emer, Pac Dist Missionary Baptist Asn; COPS - Los Angeles Sheriff's Dept; former ambassador, Union Rescue Mission; pres, Calif Missionary Baptist State Conv NAACP Los Angeles (Watts) Chap. **Honors/Awds:** Mdiv, christian educ, Golden Gate Theol Sem, Mill Valley, CA; Doctor Lett relig, St Stephens Educ Bible Col, Los Angeles, CA; DHL, Liberty Baptist Col, Muskogee, Okla; Pastor Yr; Moderator Yr; Relig Broadcast Yr, ACC News Pauline Awards. **Business Addr:** Pastor, Teacher, Greater Temple of God Missionary Baptist Church, 1404 Firestone Blvd, Los Angeles, CA 90051-0096, **Business Phone:** (323)582-7344.

## SNEED, GREGORY J.

Executive. **Educ:** Adelphi Univ, BBA, acct, 1979. **Career:** Coopers & Lybrand aka Price water house Coopers, supvr, auditing, 1979-83; Columbia Pictures & Coca Cola Co, mgr, corp audit, 1983-87; Twentieth Century Fox Film Corp, vpres finance & admin, 1987-95; Forty Acres & Mule Filmworks Inc, pres & chief operating officer, 1995-96; Home Box Off, vpres, asst controller, 1997-2000; Rainbow Media Holdings, vpres financial planning, 2000-02; Nautical Network, owner, consult, instr, 2002-09; FFSI Ins Serv Inc, regional mkt dir, 2010-13; GJS Financial & Ins Serv, financial advisor & independent life ins agt, 2010-; Retirement Choices Calif, sr financial consult, 2012-; Pac Advisors, financial agt, 2014-. **Orgs:** Am Inst Cert Pub Accountants; life mem, Alpha Phi Alpha Fraternit; Deanss List & Acct Hon Soc; Million Dollar Roundtable; First AME Church Los Angeles. **Business Addr:** Senior Financial Consultant, Retirement Choices of California, 155 W Wash Blvd Suite 1114, Los Angeles, CA 90015, **Business Phone:** (213)765-0089.

## SNEED, MICHAEL E.

Association executive, manager, vice president (organization). **Personal:** children: 3. **Educ:** Macalester Col, MN, BA, 1981; Dartmouth Col, Tuck Sch, MBA, 1983. **Career:** Johnson & Johnson Consumer Co, mkt asst, 1983, mkt mgr, 1990, Vision Care, group chmn, 2007-, vpres global corp affairs, 2012-; McNeil Consumer Prod, group prod dir, 1991-95, vpres, 1995, Nutrit Europe, managing dir, 1998-2000, Nutrit Worldwide, pres, 2000-02; Personal Prod Co, global pres, 2002, chmn, 2004. **Orgs:** Med Devices & Diag Group Operating Comt; bd mem, Family Serv Asn Bucks Co, Pa; bd trustee, Macalester Col, St Paul, Minn; mem adv bd, La Salle Univ; dir, Advert Coun Inc, 2012-; bd advisors, Nat Coun La Raza Inc; Exec Comt Ad Coun; Corps Mgt Comt. **Business Addr:** Vice President of Global Corporate Affairs, Johnson & Johnson Services Inc, 1 Johnson & Johnson Plz, New Brunswick, NJ 08933, **Business Phone:** (732)524-0400.

### SNEED, PAULA ANN

Executive. **Personal:** Born Nov 10, 1947, Everett, MA; daughter of Thomas E and Furman Mary Turner; married Lawrence P Bass; children: Courtney J Bass. **Educ:** Simmons Col, BA, lib arts, 1969; Harvard Univ, MBA, 1977; Johnson & Wales Univ, DBA, 1991. **Career:** Outreach Prog Prob Drinkers, educ supvr, female coordr, 1969-71; Ecumenical Ctr, dir plans, prog develop & eval, 1971-72; Boston SickleCell Ctr, prog coordr, 1972-75; Gen Foods Corp, asst prod mgr, assoc prod mgr, 1977-80, prod mgr, 1980-83, prod group mgr, 1983-85, category dir, 1985-86, vpres consumer affairs, 1986-90, sr vpres, Food serv Div, pres, 1990-91, Desserts Div, exec vpres & gen mgr, 1991-94; Kraft Foods Inc, sr vpres mkt servs, 1995-99, exec vpres, 1997-2007; chief mkt officer, 1999, E Com Div, pres, 1999-2000, group vpres, E-com & Mkt Servs, pres, 2000-04, Global Mkt Resources & Initiatives, exec vpres, 2005-06; Tyco Electronics Group, dir, 2007-; Phelps Prescott Group LLC, chmn & chief exec officer, 2008-; Communispace Corp, dir, 2009-. **Orgs:** Am Asn Univ Women, 1980-96; Coalition 100 Black Women, 1982-92; Nat Asn Negro Bus & Prof Women, 1983-95; adv coun to dean, Howard Univ Bus Sch, 1991-96; bd dir, Westchester & Fairfield Inroads, 1993-; bd dir, Hercules Inc, 1994-2002; Exec Leadership Coun, 1994-; bd dir, Airgas, 1999-2016; bd trustee, Chicago C's Mus, 2000-; bd trustee, Ill Inst Tech, 2000-; bd trustee, Simmons Col, 2001-; bd dir, Charles Schwab Corp, 2002-; bd dir, trustee, vice chmn, Teach Am Inc, 2003-; dir, Am Mkt Asn, 2010; partner & mem bd, Social Venture Partners Chicago, 2012-; bd dir, Family Independence Initiative, 2013-; int bd dir, Right To Play, 2015-; bd dir, Turnaround C, 2015-; dir, NewSchools Venture Fund, Investment Arm. **Honors/Awds:** Black Achiever, Harlem YMCA, 1982; MBA of the Year Award, Harvard Bus Sch Black Alumni Orgn, 1987; Benevolent Heart Award, Graham-Windham, 1987; Academy of Women Achievers, NY YWCA, 1990; listed in "Top 100 Black Women in Corp America, " Ebony Mag, 1990, 1991; "Very Important Prestigious Woman, " Corp Achievers, Dollars & Sense Mag, 1990, 1993; listed in "21 Most Influential African American Women in CorpAmerica", Black Enterprise Mag, 1991, 1997; listed in "40 most influential African American in Corp America", 1993; listed in "Breakthrough 50" Exec Female Mag; 1992 America's 50 Most Powerful Woman Managers, 1994; "25 Most Influential Mothers Working, " Mother's Mag, 1998; Most Influential African American in Corp America, Fortune Mag, 2002. **Home Addr:** 1755 Paddock Lane, Lake Forest, IL 60045, **Home Phone:** (847)735-8522. **Business Addr:** Director, Charles Schwab & Co Inc, 5190 Neil Rd Suite 100, Reno, NV 89502-8532.

### SNELL, JOHNNA M.

Executive, business owner, designer. **Educ:** New River Community Col, gen studies, 1987; Va Polytech Inst & State Univ, commun, 1993. **Career:** Coca-Cola Bottling Co Consol, vending acct mgr & proj mgr, 1995-2000; Aramark Refreshment Serv, vending sales dir, 2000-01; Abarta Media Group, sr acct exec, 2001-02; Am Heart Asn-Mid Atlantic Affil, youth mkt dir, 2002-08, Originalz creative custom jewelry, jewelry designer & owner, 2003-; Am Heart Asn, Corp Rels/ Workplace Giving-Atlanta Metro, sr dir, 2008-12; Sodexo, vpres nat health systs, 2012-. **Orgs:** Dir, Am Heart Asn. **Honors/Awds:** Outstanding Achievement Award, Am Heart Asn, 2008; National Top Youth Market Director, Am Heart Asn, 2008; National Staff (Affiliate) of the Year, Am Heart Asn, 2011. **Business Addr:** Vice President National Health Systems, Sodexo, 9801 Washingtonian Blvd, Gaithersburg, MD 20878, **Business Phone:** (301)987-4000.

### SNIPES, LOLITA WALKER

Writer, opera producer, playwright. **Personal:** Born Atlanta, GA. **Educ:** Ga State Univ, Atlanta, BA, bus mkt; Valencia Col, Film & Theater Prod Technol Prog, Orlando, Fla. **Career:** Hollywood Pictures; Epic Rec; Atlantic Rec; Good God AlMighty, writer, producer, dir; Universal Funny-Bone, writer, producer, dir; Yes-Amen, writer, producer, dir; Up With the JonZes, producer, dir; God Don't Like Ugly, writer, producer, dir; Xenon Pictures & Universal Studios, Fla, mag ed, producer; book: Peace in passing: how to find peace in the passing of someone you love, Roman Publ Inc, pres, auth, 2000; Upscale Mag, ed. **Honors/Awds:** National Association Advanced Colored People IMAGE Awards. **Special Achievements:** First comedy show with a successful line up of new-to-scene comedians, The Comedy House Jamms. **Business Addr:** Author, Roman Publishing Inc, PO Box 691657, Orlando, FL 32869.

### SNIPES, WESLEY TRENT

Actor. **Personal:** Born Jul 31, 1962, Orlando, FL; son of Wesley Rudolph and Maryann (nee Long); married April Dubois; children: Jelani Asar; married Nakyung Park; children: 4. **Educ:** State Univ NY, Purchase, theatre & dramatic art, 1985. **Career:** Actor, theatre appearances: Execution of Justice; The Boys of Winter; Death & the King's Horseman; TV: "Wild Cats", 1985; "Sts of Gold"; Michael Jackson's "Bad", video; Major League; HBO's "Vietnam War Story"; Mo "Better Blues"; King of New York; New Jack City, 1990; Jungle Fever, 1991; White Men Can't Jump, 1992; Water dance, 1992; Passenger 57, 1992; The Rising Sun, 1993; Demolition Man, 1993; Drop Zone, 1994; To Wong Foo; Thanks for Everything; Julia Newmar; Waiting To Exhale; Murder At 1600, 1997; One Night Stand, 1997; US Marshals, 1998; Down In The Delta, 1998; Blade, 1998; Liberty Stands Still, 2002; Zigzag, 2002; Blade II, 2002; Undisputed, 2002; Godforsaken, 2003; John Doe, 2004; prod, actor: The Big Hit; co-prod: Art of War, 2000; Disappearing Acts, HBO, 2000; Amen Ra Films, founder: The Marksman, 2005; The Detonator, 2006; Chaos, 2006; Hard Luck, 2006; The Contractor, 2007; The Art of War II: Betrayal, 2008; Brooklyn's Finest, 2009; Game of Death, 2010; Gallowwalkers, 2012; The Expendables 3, 2014, Chi-Raq, 2015, Temple, 2016; The Recall, 2017. **Honors/Awds:** WorldFest Houston, 1992; Image Award, 1993 & 1997; Volpi Cup, 1997; Hollywood Walk of Fame, 1998; Blockbuster Entertainment Award, 1999; CableACE, 1989; Won Victor Borge Schola; Best Actor, Venice Film Fes, 1997; Cable ACE Awards; Blockbuster Entertainment Award, 1998; Black Reel Award, 2011. **Business Addr:** Actor, William Morris Agency, 9601 Wilshire Blvd, Beverly Hills, CA 90210, **Business Phone:** (310)285-9000.

### SNODDY, ANTHONY L.

Executive. **Personal:** Born Longview, TX; children: 3. **Educ:** Eastern Mich Univ, BS, indust technol grad, 1973; Cent Mich Univ, bus; Harvard Bus Sch & Northwestern Univ, exec mgt training. **Career:** Gen Motors Corp, mats & purchasing mgt, 1991; Exemplar Mfg Co, pres, chmn, chief exec officer, 1991-; MAThread Inc, owner; Green Moxie LLC, owner, currently; Get Etched LLC, chmn, dirs & owners, currently. **Orgs:** Bd dir, chmn MIC mfg sector, Mich Minority Bus Develop Coun; Nat Asn Indust Technol; Daimler Chrysler Diversity Coun; Gen Motors Diversity Coun; bd trustee, Eastern Mich Univ; bd mem, Best Batch Found; bd mem, Focus Hope; bd mem, St. Mary's Prep Orchard Lake; bd mem, Mich Minority Bus Develop Coun; bd mem, Daimler Chrysler Diversity Coun; bd mem, Citizen Bank; bd mem, Washtenaw United Way; bd mem, Real Life 101 Scholar Fund; bd mem, Eastern Mich Univ Found Bd; UNCF; NAACP; St. Joseph Mercy Hosp. **Honors/Awds:** Outstanding Industrial Technologist, Nat Asn Indust Technol, 1998; Diamond Award, Mich Minority Bus Develop Coun; Inducted Entrepreneur Hall of Fame, EMU Bus Sch. **Special Achievements:** Black Enterprise's Top 100 Industrial/Service Companies, company ranked 38, 1998; company ranked 6, 1999. **Home Addr:** , Ann Arbor, MI. **Business Addr:** President, Chief Executive Officer, Exemplar Manufacturing Co, 506 S Huron St, Ypsilanti, MI 48197-5455, **Business Phone:** (734)483-5070.

### SNORTON, TERESA E.

Executive director, bishop. **Personal:** children: 2. **Educ:** Vanderbilt Univ, BA; Louisville Presby Theol Sem, Mdiv; Southern Baptist Theol Sem, MA, theol pastoral care; Va Commonwealth Univ, post-grad cert, patient coun; United Theol Sem, DMin. **Career:** Va Union Univ, Sch Theol; Louisville Presbyterian Theological Seminary, adj fac; Psychiatric Staff Chaplain Louisville; Emory Univ, Candler Sch, Pastoral Care, adj instr; Crawford Long Hospital, Pastoral Services, dir; Emory Ctr Pastoral Serv, exec dir; Nat Asn Clin Pastoral Educ Inc, exec dir; Fifth Episcopal District of the Christian Methodist Episcopal (CME) Church, assoc minister & bishop, 2010; Nat Asn Clin Pastoral Educ Inc, exec dir; Ky, pastor; Women Out of Order: Risking Change and Creating Care in a Multi-Cultural World, co-ed, 2009; Courageous Conversations: The Teaching and Learning of Pastoral Supervision, co-ed, 2010. **Orgs:** Miles College, chair bd trustee; chair, Christian Methodist Episcopal Church, Lay Ministries; Pan-Methodist Comn, chair, Family Life Comt World Methodist Coun; fac mem, Va Union Univ, Sch Theol; fac mem, Med Col Va, Patient Coun Prog; Pastoral Theol; Alpha Kappa Alpha Sorority; Christian Methodist Episcopal Comn, Women Ministry.

### SNOW, ERIC

Executive, basketball player. **Personal:** Born Apr 24, 1973, Canton, OH; married DeShawn; children: EJ, Darius & Jarren. **Educ:** Mich State Univ, attended 1995. **Career:** Basketball player (retired), executive; Seattle Supersonics, pt guard, 1995-98; Philadelphia 76ers, pt guard, 1998-2004; Cleveland Cavaliers, pt guard, 2004-08, shooting guard, 2004-05, captian, 2007-08; Southern Methodist Univ, dir player develop, 2012-14; Nat Basketball Asn TV, studio analyst, currently; Fla Atlantic Owls men's basketball, asst coach, 2014-. **Honors/Awds:** Big Ten Defensive Player of Year; Atlantic Division winner, Sportsmanship Award, Nat Basketball Players Asn, 1998, 1999; Sportsmanship Award, Nat Basketball Asn, 1999, 2000; Good Guys, Sporting News, 2002-04; J Walter Kennedy Citizenship Award, Prof Basketball Writers Asn, 2005; Community Contrib Award, Nat Basketball Players Asn, 2005. **Business Addr:** Assistant Coach, Florida Atlantic University, 777 Glades Rd, Boca Raton, TX 33431, **Business Phone:** (561)297-3000.

### SNOW, KIMBERLY

Marketing executive, manager. **Educ:** Adelphi Univ, BA, commun, 1998. **Career:** Mecca USA, prod mgr, dir mkt, 1998-2004; Snowstorm Inc, founder, consult, 2003-; Marc Ecko Enterprises, sr dir, mgr mkt & pub rels, 2004-08; PASTRY, dir mkt & pub rels, 2008-10; 3PM, mkt assoc, 2010-. **Business Addr:** Director of Marketing, Mecca USA, 31 W 34th St, New York, NY 10001-3009, **Business Phone:** (212)563-1233.

### SNOW, PERCY LEE

Football player. **Personal:** Born Nov 5, 1967, Canton, OH. **Educ:** Mich State Univ, BA, criminal justice, 1989. **Career:** Football player (retired); Kans City Chiefs, linebacker & left inside linebacker, 1990-92; Chicago Bears, linebacker, 1993; Rhein Fire, linebacker, 1996. **Honors/Awds:** First team All-Big Ten, 1987; Sporting News first team All-Am, first team All-Big Ten, 1988; first team All-Am & All-Big Ten, Lombardi Award, 1989; Dick Butkus Award, 1989; Big Ten Defensive Player of the Year, 1989; College Football Hall of Fame, 2013. **Special Achievements:** One of only two players in college football history to win both the Butkus Award and Lombardi Award.

### SNOWDEN, FRANK WALTER

Scientist. **Personal:** Born Nov 5, 1939, New Orleans, LA. **Educ:** Xavier Univ, New Orleans, BS, 1960; Howard Univ, Wash, DC, 1963; Univ New Orleans, PhD, chem, 1975. **Career:** US Dept Agri, Southern Regional Res Lab, stud trainee, 1957-60, chemist, 1960-73, res chemist, 1963-73; Howard Univ, teaching fel, 1960-63; Univ New Orleans, res & teaching, 1970-73; 3M Cent Res Lab, sr res chemist, 1973-78, sr tech serv engr, 1973-83, global prof serv specialist, 1983-90; Med Video Prod, Video J Ophthamol, med ed, 1990-93; Univ Minn, Inst Technol, Chem Engineering & Mat Sci Dept, asst prof, 1991-93, Gen Col, fel, 1993-97, Chem Engineering & Mat Sci Dept, prof, 1997-, Multicultural Undergrad Res Prog, dir, 1997-01, Pres Distinguished Fac Mentor Prog, dir & chmn, 1997-01, Educ & Human Resources, assoc dir, 1998-, sr tech serv engr, assoc dir, Educ & Human Resources, currently; Kirby Puckett & Jackie Robinson Found Scholar Comt, chmn; Community Scholars Prog, dir, 1998, 2000-; Acad Prog Excellence Engineering & Sci, Dir, 2000-. **Orgs:** Am Chem Soc, 1960-; Am Pub Transit Asn, 1977-93; Comnr Mr Met Transit Comn Twin Cities, 1977-93; Alpha Phi Alpha Frat; Partnerships Res & Educ Mat. **Honors/Awds:** Volunteer of the Year, Sci Mus Minn, 1998; Award of Excellence, 3M/Vision Care Lab. **Special Achievements:** Several Patents, Research Publications & Presentations. **Home Addr:** 9812 Cove Dr, Minnetonka, MN 55305-5800. **Business Addr:** Professor, Director of Education & Human Resources, University of Minnesota, 401 Amundson Hall 421 Wash Ave SE, Minneapolis, MN 55455, **Business Phone:** (612)626-2207.

### SNOWDEN, GAIL

Banker, vice president (organization). **Personal:** Born Jul 5, 1945, New York, NY; daughter of Muriel Sutherland and Otto; children: Leigh Trimmier. **Educ:** Radcliffe Col, BA, sociol, 1967; Harvard Col; Simmons Col, Grad Sch Mgt, MBA, 1978. **Career:** First Nat Bank Boston, br officer, 1971-76, br credit officer, 1977-79, loan officer, 1980, asst vpres, 1981-83, vpres, 1984-86, div exec, 1986-88, sr credit officer, 1989-90; dir, Boston First Banking/Bank Boston, 1990-92, managing dir, 2000-04; Fleet Boston Financial Corp, pres, 1992-, exec vpres & managing dir, currently; Bank Am, exec vpres; FleetBoston Financial Community Investment Group, exec vpres & managing dir. **Orgs:** Nat Asn Bank Women, 1971-; treas, Radcliffe Club Boston, 1976; asst dir, Boston Urban Bankers Forum, 1979-80; conf steering comm, Simmons Grad Prog Man Alumnae Asn, 1979-80; steering comm family Govt Comm C & Family, 1980; vpres, Nat Asn Urban Bankers, 1984-85; vpres, chief financial officer, Boston Found; bd chair, Freedom House, 1996-2001, chair emer, 2001-08, chief exec officer, 2008-13; pres, Fleet Found; bd mem, Boston Found, chief financial officer & vpres finance & opers, 2004-07; Northeastern Univ, Corp Bd; Simmons Col; Efficacy Inst. **Honors/Awds:** Banker of the Year, Nat Asn Urban Bankers, 1989; Outstanding Alumna, Simmons Grad Sch Mgt, 1989; Big Sister, Women of Achievement, 1992; Bus Advocate of the Year, Small Bus Admin, Minority, 1992; Prof Women's Award, Dollars & Sense Mag, 1992. **Home Addr:** 241 Perkins St Suite J302, Jamaica Plain, MA 02130. **Business Addr:** Executive Vice President, Managing Director, Fleet Boston Financial Corp, 100 Fed St, Boston, MA 02110, **Business Phone:** (617)434-5105.

### SNOWDEN, PHILLIP RAY

Engineer. **Personal:** Born Dec 9, 1951, Shreveport, LA; son of Harold Phillip and Nevada Swift; married Mary Ann Robinson; children: Tamara Sheniki & Tariot-Phillip Ramona. **Educ:** La Tech Univ, Ruston, BSEE, 1974; Xavier Univ, Cin, MBA, 1976. **Career:** Gen Elec Co, Stamford, corp mgt trainee-Engr, 1974-78; Gen Motors Corp, Detroit, engr, 1978-83; Kent State Univ, Warren, technol, energy instr, 1981-82; Entergy Corp, New Orleans, engr-nuclear safety. **Orgs:** Chmn, Comput Soc Inst Electronic Engrs, New Orleans Sect, 1990-; pres, LaChap Am Asn Blacks Energy, 1991-; pres, Nat Asn Acct, New Orleans Chap, 1991; pres, Your Metrop Bus & Civic Club, 1991. **Honors/Awds:** Salutatorian, Hopewell High Sch, 1969; Peak Performer Award, La Power & Light, Waterford 3, 1989; Black Achievers Award, Dryades YMCA, 1989. **Home Addr:** PO Box 1559, Gretna, LA 70053, **Home Phone:** (504)341-7460.

### SNOWDEN, RAYMOND C.

Insurance executive, business owner, manager. **Personal:** Born Aug 5, 1937, McNary, AZ; son of Loretta Hockett Banks and Clarence; married Bettye; children: Joni, Brian & Eric. **Educ:** Los Angeles City Col, AA, psychol, 1962. **Career:** Safe Way Stores Inc, store mgr, 1965-67; Continental Assurance Co, assoc mgr, 1969; Trans Am Occidental Life, 1971; Ray Snowden Ins, owner, currently. **Orgs:** Pres, Kiwanis Club SW La, 1976-77; Inglewood Calif C C; Salvation Army Youth Adv Coun, 1978; bd chmn, New Testament Church Trustee, 1978-2000; Life Underwriters Asn; dir, Inglewood C C, 1978-80, pres, 1982-84; pres, Crenshaw-Imp Sect Inglewood C C, 1978-80; citizen adv com, Centenila Hosp, 1980-86; pres, Imp-Crenshaw Kiwanis Club, 1982-83; lt gov, Kiwanis Int, 1991-92. **Honors/Awds:** First black gen agent, Trans Am Occidental Life Calif, 1971, New Agency of the Year Award, 1972; Featured in issue Sports Illus in Occidental Life's adver June 11, 1974; Kiwanis Int Award Community Serv, 1974; Commendation Inglewood City Coun Community Serv, 1984. **Home Addr:** 308 Queen St Suite 16, Inglewood, CA 90301, **Home Phone:** (310)419-5988. **Business Addr:** Owner, Ray Snowden Insurance, 6245 Bristol Pkwy Suite 161, Culver City, CA 90230, **Business Phone:** (310)365-6642.

### SNOWDEN, SYLVIA FRANCES

Artist, educator. **Personal:** Born Apr 21, 1944, Raleigh, NC; daughter of George; children: Shell Butler & John Malik Butler. **Educ:** Howard Univ, Wash, DC, BA, MFA; Grants People Inc, Cult Alliance, Wash, DC, Mkt Arts & People, cert; Skowhegan Sch Painting & Sculpture, Skowhegan, Maine, cert; Le Grande Chaumier, Paris, cert. **Career:** Yale Univ, Norfolk, Conn, lectr & instr, 1991-92; Brandywine Workshop, Philadelphia, vis artist, 1994; Corcoran Gallery art, vis artist, Washington, DC, 1995; Howard Univ, vis artist, 1995; Hirshhorn Mus & Sculpture Garden Figurative Painting, Teresia Bush, Washington, DC, panelist, 1997; Cornell Univ, artist-in-residence. **Home Addr:** 465 M St NW, Washington, DC 20001, **Home Phone:** (202)347-5576.

### SNYDER, VANESSA W.

Editor, writer. **Personal:** Born Oct 19, 1964, Washington, DC; daughter of Alvin and Dorothy Williams; married Deron K; children: Sierra Ngozi & Sequoia Elon. **Educ:** Univ Md, BS, jour, 1986; Walden Univ, MS, educ, 2008. **Career:** Gannett News Serv, ed/writer, copy ed, 1986-99; Urban Ministries, freelance writer & columnist, 1995-2005; Gospel Today Mag, contrib ed, freelance writer, columnist, 1995-99; Excellence Mag, writer, ed, teacher, 1999-; Faith Hope Christian Acad, teacher, 1999-2000; Mt Hermon Christian Sch, teacher, 2000-02; Mariner High Sch, instr, 2002-05; Lee County Govt, teacher, 2005; S Ft Myers High Sch, reading dept chair & instr, 2005-09; Moody Publishers, writer, 2008-09; BlackDoor Ventures Inc, pres, 2009-; Duke Ellington Sch Arts, teacher, 2009-; First Baptist Church Glenarden, sr commun specialist. Author: 50 Ways To Put Christ Back Christmas; The Second First Lady, 2010. **Orgs:** Nat Asn Black Journalists; prog mem, Emerge Md, 2013-. **Home Addr:** 3716 Agualinda Blvd, Cape Coral, FL 33914-5580. **Business Addr:** Teacher, Duke Ellington School of the Arts, 2001 10th St NW, Washington, DC 20001-4007, **Business Phone:** (202)282-0123.

### SOARES, BEA T.

High school principal. **Career:** Guild, prin; Gray Elem Sch, prin, 1999; William K Moore Elem Sch, prin, 2000-07. **Home Addr:** 133 Carriage Way W, Henderson, NV 89014-2721. **Business Addr:** Principal, William K Moore Elementary School, 491 N Lamb Blvd, Las Vegas, NV 89110, **Business Phone:** (702)799-3270.

### SOARIES, BUSTER. See SOARIES, REV. DR. DEFOREST BLAKE, JR.

### SOARIES, REV. DR. DEFOREST BLAKE, JR. (BUSTER SOARIES)

Clergy, public speaker, state government official. **Personal:** Born Aug 20, 1951, Brooklyn, NY; son of DeForest B Sr and Mary M; married Margaret Donna Pleasant; children: Malcolm & Martin. **Educ:** Fordham Univ, BA; Princeton Theol Sem, MA, divinity; United Theol Sem, PhD, divinity. **Career:** Kean Col, Union, NJ, vis prof; Shiloh Baptist Church, assoc pastor, 1987-90; Mercer County Community Col, asst prof, 1989-91; First Baptist Church-Lincoln Gardens, sr pastor, 1991-; Drew Univ Theol Sch, vis prof, 1997-99; NJ Secy State, 1999-2002; US Election Assistance Comn, chmn, comnr, 2003-05; Fed Home Loan Bank NY. dir, currently; Corp Community Connections, chief exec officer, currently. **Orgs:** Chmn bd, First Baptist Community Develop Corp; chair, Community Reinvestment Comt; dir, New Era Bank, 1986-98; judicial Vols Prog, NJ Super Ct, 1993; independent dir, Independence Realty Trust. **Business Addr:** Director, Federal Home Loan Bank of New York, 101 Pk Ave Suite 5, New York, NY 10178, **Business Phone:** (212)949-0220.

### SOBERS, WAYNETT A., JR.

Association executive, executive, consultant. **Personal:** Born Feb 15, 1937, Bronx, NY; son of Athlene Ghyll and Waynett; married Yvonne C Barrett; children: Loren, Julian & Stephanie. **Educ:** City Col NY, BS, 1959; Sobelsohn Sch Ins, 1965; Baruch Col, MBA, 1972; Gen Motors Dealer Develop Acad, attended 1988. **Career:** Meteorologist, 1959-69; US Weather Bur, meteorologist & tech specialist; WA Sobers Assoc Inc, pres, 1965-69; Johnson Publ Co, advert rep, 1969-71; Black Enterprise Mag, Mkt Serv, mgr, 1971-73, Advert & Mkt, vpres, 1973; EGG Dallas Broadcasting Inc, vpres, 1977; BCI Mkt Inc, pres; Earl G Graves Ltd, exec vpres, 1980-87, vpres corp commun, 1998; Sobers Chevrolet Inc, owner, pres, gen mgr, 1988-90; Wayvon Consult, sr consult & owner, 1990-; Bedford Stuyvesant Restoration Corp, exec vpres, 1995-97; Wachovia Bank, customer relationship mgr & financial ctr mgr; Energy Leadership Index, master practr & cert prof coach, currently. **Orgs:** Pres, Chappaqua Ridge Asn, 1977; secy, Chappaqua Rotary Club, 1992-95, vpres, 1995-96; bd dir, Equitable Variable Life Ins Co; Am Mgt Asn; Am Mkt Asn; City Col New York Alumni Asn; City Col New York Black Alumni Asn; Bernard M Baruch Col Alumni Asn; bd mem & treas, Nat Asn Black Owned Broadcasters NABOB; bd mem, St Peters Union Free Sch Dist; bd mem, St Peters Sch Bd Educ. **Honors/Awds:** Salesman of the Year, Ebony, 1971; Exemplary Service Award, St Luke's Epis Church, 1976; Broadcaster of the Year, Nat Asn Black-Owned Broadcasters, 1984. **Home Addr:** 55 N Broadway Apt 3-20, White Plains, NY 10601-1646. **Business Addr:** Master Practitioner, Coach, Energy Leadership Index, 149 Ave Common Suite 202, Shrewsbury, NJ 07702, **Business Phone:** (914)946-3819.

### SOCKWELL, OLIVER R., JR.

Executive director. **Personal:** Born Jul 27, 1943, Washington, DC; son of Janet and Oliver; married Harriet E; children: Kristine, Brian & Jason. **Educ:** Howard Univ, BS, physics, 1965; Columbia Univ, Grad Sch Bus, MBA, finance, 1972. **Career:** Bell Syst, commun engr, 1965-67; IBM, mkt rep, 1967-70; Smith Barney & Co, investment banker, 1972-74; Sallie Mae, Stud Loan Mkt Asn, vpres mkt, 1974-83, sr vpres oper, 1983-84, exec vpres finance, 1984-87; Connie Lee Ins Co, pres & chief exec officer; Construct Loan Ins Corp, pres & chief exec officer, 1987-97; SLM Corp, exec vpres finance; Columbia Univ, Grad Sch Bus, exec residence, 1997-; RR Donnelley & Sons Co, dir, 1997-; Liz Claiborne Inc, dir, 2002-. **Orgs:** Bd mem, Lizz Claiborne Inc; bd mem, Columbia Univ Grad Sch Bus; bd dir, RR Donnelley & Sons, 1997-; bd mem, Eugene Lang Entrepreneurial Initiative Fund; bd mem, Atlas Performing Arts Ctr; bd mem, Gail Spot; Mgt Leadership Tomorrow; dir, Fifth & Pac Co Inc, 2002-09; dir, Wilmington Trust Corp, 2007-10. **Home Addr:** 1685 Myrtle St NW, Washington, DC 20012-1129, **Home Phone:** (202)829-0837. **Business Addr:** Director, Liz Claiborne Inc, 1441 Broadway Fl 22, New York, NY 10018, **Business Phone:** (212)354-4900.

### SODEN, RICHARD ALLAN

Lawyer. **Personal:** Born Feb 16, 1945, Brooklyn, NY; son of Hamilton David and Clara Elaine Seal; married Marcia LaMonte Mitchell; children: Matthew Hamilton & Mark Mitchell. **Educ:** Hamilton Col, BA, 1967; Boston Univ Sch Law, JD, 1970. **Career:** US Dist Ct Dist Mass, pract atty; US Courts Appeals First & Sixth Circuits, pract atty; Hon Geo Clifton Edwards Jr US Ct Appeals 6th Circuit, law clerk, 1970-71; Boston Col Sch Law, fac, 1973-74; MIT Sloan Sch Mgt, lect; Goodwin Procter LLP, assoc, 1971-79, partner, 1979-2006; Goodwin Procter LLP, partner, Bus Law Dept, coun, 2006-. **Orgs:** Overseers Adv Bd WGBH; overseer, New Eng Aquarium; pres, Boston Minuteman Coun BSA; chmn, Steering Comt Boston Lawyers Comt Civil Rights Under Law; pres, Boston Bar Found; Mass IOLTA Comt; Mass Access Justice Comn; trustee, Social Law Libr; chmn, Supreme Judicial Ct Mass Lawyers Concerned Lawyers Oversight Comt; chmn, emer, trustee, Judge Baker Guid Ctr, 1974-; pres, United S End Settlements, 1977-79; adv coun, Suffolk Univ Sch Mgt, 1980-; fac, Mass Continuing Legal Educ, 1980-; pres, Mass Black Lawyers Asn, 1980-81; Nat Bar Asn; Adv Task Force Securities Regulation; secy, State Commonwealth Mass, 1982-; adv comn, Legal Educ Supreme Judicial Co Mass, 1984-; co-chmn, Lawyers Comt Civil Rights Under Law, 1991-93; Mass Minority Bus Develop Comn; pres, Boston Bar Asn, 1994-95; bd visitors, Boston Univ Goldman Sch Grad Dent; trustee, Boston Univ, 1995-; mem-at-large, Am Bar Asn; house deleg, Am Bar Asn, 1995-97, chair, Standing Comn Bar Activ & Servs, 1998-; chmn, Boston Munic Res Bur, 1996-98; pres, Greater Boston Coun, Boy Scouts Am, 1997-99; Am Bar Found; pres, United S End Settlements; pres, Am Bar Asn, 2008. **Honors/Awds:** Silver Beaver Award, Boy Scouts Am; Community Youth Service Award, Heritage Dist, Boy Scouts Am; Theodore L Storer Award, Boy Scouts Am; Silver Shingle Award, Boston Univ, Sch Law; Community Service Award, Mass Bar Asn; UNICEF-Boston Local Hero Award; Camille Cosby World Children Medallion; Spirit of Excellence Award, Am Bar Asn, 2009. **Special Achievements:** Author of the Chapter on Acquisitions in Massachusetts Business Lawyering. **Home Addr:** 42 Gray St, Boston, MA 02116-6210, **Home Phone:** (617)423-4546. **Business Addr:** Partner, Counsel, Goodwin Procter LLP, Exchange Pl 53 State St, Boston, MA 02109-2881, **Business Phone:** (617)570-1533.

### SOGAH, DR. DOTSEVI YAO

Educator. **Personal:** Born Apr 19, 1945, Tegbi; son of Fiawosinu Kwawudzo and Ahiati K; married Monica Adzo Selormey; children: Senanu, Dodzie K & Esinam. **Educ:** Univ Ghana, Legon Accra, Ghana, BSc, chem, 1971; Univ Calif, Los Angeles, MS, org chem, 1974, PhD, org chem, 1975, Santa Barbara, postdoctoral assoc, bioorganic chem, 1977. **Career:** Univ Calif, Santa Barbara, postdoctoral fel, 1975-77; Univ Calif, res assoc, 1977-80, adj prof, 1978-81; Du Pont Co, res chemist, 1981-83, group leader, 1983-84, res supvr, 1984-90, res mgr, 1990-91, consult; Columbia Univ Spring, vis prof, 1984; Cornell Univ, Ithaca, NY, prof chem, 1991-; Revlon, consult; Toxgon, consult; Vistacon J & J, consult. **Orgs:** Bd dir, 1982-84, chmn comt, 1984-85, exec Comm mem, 1994-97, Am Chem Soc Del, Wilmington; chmn proj comt, Inst S Asian Studies, 1985-; pres, Int Soc African Sci, 1987-90; vis comt mem, Lehigh Univ Chem Dept, 1989-; ed bd, Sci & Eng Composite Mat, 1989-; Ny Acad Sci; Sigma Xi Res Soc; AAAS; exec comt, Cornell Ctr Mat Res, 1999-; Inst African Develop; Polymer Outreach Prog; Cornell Ctr Mat Res; Nanobiotechnology Ctr. **Home Addr:** 39 Rosina Dr, Ithaca, NY 14850-9765, **Home Phone:** (607)257-5672. **Business Addr:** Professor of Chemistry, Cornell University, 760A Spencer T Olin Lab, Ithaca, NY 14853-1301, **Business Phone:** (607)255-4205.

### SOLIUNAS, FRANCINE STEWART

Lawyer, educator. **Personal:** Born Feb 14, 1948, Chicago, IL; daughter of Wilborn Stewart and Juanita Jeanette Harris; married Jonas; children: Lukas (deceased) & Mikah. **Educ:** DePaul Univ, Chicago, Ill, BS, math, 1970; DePaul Univ Col Law, Chicago, Ill, JD, 1973. **Career:** Lawyer (retired), educator; State Appellate Defender, Chicago, Ill, staff atty, 1974-76; Equal Employ Opportunity Comn, Chicago, Ill, supv atty, 1976-80; Ill Bell Tel Co, Chicago, Ill, sr atty, 1980-88, sr dir labor rels, 1988-90, sr atty labor, 1990-92; Ameritech, coun employ, 1980-2000, sr dir labor rels, labor-related litigation & arbit, 1992-2000; Ill Inst Technol, Chicago Kent Col Law, prof law, asst dean strat, 2003-12, prof develop & Inst law & Workplace, exec dir, currently; DePaul Univ Col Law, dean strategic & community alliances, 2012-; DePaul Univ, chief staff, 2013-, Diversity Advocate Col Law, 2013-, Diversity & Inclusion, dir alumni engagement, currently; Cook County, asst state atty. **Orgs:** Cook Co Bar Asn, 1972-; Iowa State Bar Asn, 1974-86; Sickle Cell Anemia Vol Enterprise, 1980-; Nat Bar Asn, 1982-; trustee, St Thomas Theol Sem, 1985-88; vpres, Sickle Cell Anemia Vol Enterprise, 1985-87; dir, DePaul Univ Press's Club, 1986-; Chicago Bar Asn Judicial Eval Comn, 1987-; bd dir, DePaul Univ Col Arts & Scis Adv Coun, 1987-; dir, S Cent Community Serv, 1988-2000. **Honors/Awds:** Outstanding Corporate Achiever, YMCA-Chicago Tribune, 1987; Distinguished Alumni, DePaul Univ, 1988; Black Rose Award, League Black Women, 1988; Leadership Greater Chicago, 1994; Leadership America, 1995; DePaul Alumni Award, 1999. **Special Achievements:** Hundred Most Influential Black Women in Corporate America, Ebony Magazine, 1990. **Home Addr:** 2666 N Orchard St, Chicago, IL 60614, **Home Phone:** (773)549-3634. **Business Addr:** Chief of Staff, Director of Alumni Engagement, DePaul University, 1 E Jackson Blvd, Chicago, IL 60604, **Business Phone:** (312)362-7402.

### SOLOMON, BARBARA J.

Educator. **Personal:** Born Sep 10, 1934, Houston, TX; daughter of Willie Bryant and Malinda Edmond Bryant Stinson; married Donald; children: Hugo, Edmund, Jeffrey & Marcia. **Educ:** Howard Univ, BS, psychol, 1954; Univ Calif, Berkeley, MSW, social welfare, 1956; Univ Southern Calif, PhD, social work, 1966. **Career:** Alameda Co Med Inst, clin social worker, 1956-57; Va Hosps, Houston & Los Angeles, clin social worker, 1957-63; Univ Tex, Sch Social Work, field instr, 1958-60; Univ Calif, Los Angeles, Sch Social Welfare, field instr, 1962-63; Univ Southern Calif, Sch Social Work, from asst prof to prof, 1966-77, vice provost grad studies & dean grad sch, 1988-93, vice provost fac affairs & minority affairs, 1994-98, vice provost fac diversity, Stein/Sachs prof ment health, 2004, prof emer, currently; Univs Us, guest lectr & vis scholar; Chinese Univ, vis examr, Dept Social Work. **Orgs:** Nat Asn Social Workers, 1977; Coun Social Work Educ; Coun Grad Schs; Am Asn Higher Educ; bd dir, Greater LA Partnership Homeless; Sickle Cell Found; Calif Pediat Ctr; United Way LA; Alpha Kappa Alpha; bd mem, Links Inc; chair, acad affairs comt & bd dir, Walden Univ, 1990-; bd dir, Drew Child Develop Corp; bd dir, Care Found. **Special Achievements:** First African-American dean at the University of Southern California. **Home Addr:** 5987 Wrightcrest Dr, Culver City, CA 90232, **Home Phone:** (213)559-3581. **Business Addr:** Professor Emeritus, University of Southern California, Rm 202 Admin Bldg, Los Angeles, CA 90089-4015, **Business Phone:** (213)740-5883.

### SOLOMON, DAVID

Government official. **Personal:** Born May 19, 1944, Wilmington, NC; son of Vester and Helen Spaulding. **Educ:** NC A&T State Univ, Greensboro, NC, BS, 1966; St Louis Univ, St Louis, MO, MBA, 1976. **Career:** McDonnell Douglas, St Louis, Mo, supvr, 1970-72; Monsanto, St Louis, Mo, supvr, 1972-85; self-employed, Mt Laurel, NJ, pres, 1985-88; NC Dept Econ& Community Develop, Raleigh, NC, dir, MBDA, 1988-91; NC DPT Transp, drr civil rights, 1991-93; US Dept Housing & Urban Dev, Wash, DC, EO specialist, 1994-96; US Dept Transp, Fed Transit Admin, regional civil rights Officer, fed hwy admin, proj mgr, currently; Ore Dept Transp, employee safety & risk mgr. **Home Addr:** 1027 Southern Artery Apt 407, Quincy, MA 02169, **Home Phone:** (617)472-3343. **Business Addr:** Regional Civil Rights Officer, US Department of Transportation, 55 Broadway Suite 920, Cambridge, MA 02142, **Business Phone:** (202)366-6718.

### SOLOMON, DONALD L., SR.

Executive. **Personal:** Born Feb 13, 1932, Birmingham, AL; married Clarice (deceased); children: Donald Jr, Walter Lynn & Gerald. **Educ:** Miles Col, BA; Life Ins Mgt Course; LUTC; Ohio State Univ; Savannah State Col, US Armed Forces Inst; Univ Calif. **Career:** Booker T Wash Ins Co, sr vpres mkt, currently; Lily Grove Baptist Church, pastor; Sisters Serenity Ministry Inc, exec dir & founder; These Are They Ministies, pastor; AG Gaston Interests, dir pub rels. **Orgs:** Indus develop bd dir Birmingham; Omega Psi Phi Frat; Triune Lodge 430 FAM; bd mem, African-Am Emergency Task Force, City Houston. **Home Addr:** 816 Brandy Lane, Birmingham, AL 35214-3933, **Home Phone:** (205)798-9388. **Business Addr:** Senior Vice President, Booker T Washington Insurance Co, 2724 35th Ave N, Birmingham, AL 35207, **Business Phone:** (205)458-3767.

### SOLOMON, FREDDIE LEE, JR.

Football player. **Personal:** Born Aug 15, 1972, Gainesville, FL. **Educ:** SC State Univ, grad. **Career:** Football player (retired); Philadelphia Eagles, free agent, 1995, wide receiver, 1996-98; Cleveland Browns, wide receiver, 1999; Tampa Bay Storm, wide receiver, 2003-06; Columbus Destroyers, wide receiver, 2007.

### SOLOMON, JIMMIE LEE

Baseball executive. **Personal:** Born Jan 1, 1947, Thompsons, TX; son of Jimmie and Josephine; children: Tricia. **Educ:** Dartmouth Col, BA, hist, 1978; Harvard Law Sch, JD, 1981. **Career:** Onyx Travel Serv Inc, pres & co-owner, 1987-95; Baker & Hostetler, atty, 1981-90, partner, 1990-91; Maj League Baseball, Minor League Opers, dir, 1991-94, exec dir, 1995-2000, sr vpres baseball opers, 2000-05, exec vpres, 2005-10, Baseball Develop, exec vpres, 2010-12; Sign Whale, co-owner, 1991-97; Dartvard LLC Sports Consult Agency, chief exec officer & pres, 2012-; Johnson Petrov LLP, coun, 2016-. **Orgs:** Nat Cong Award Found; Alpha Phi Alpha Fraternity Inc; vice chmn, Citizenship Through Sports Alliance; bd dir, Triplecrown Acquisition Corp; bd dir, Minor League Players Ins Trust; bd dir, Baseball Tomorrow Fund; bd dir, Nat Asn Advan Colored People Legal Defense Fund; founder, Jimmie Lee Solomon. **Honors/Awds:** Alumni Award, 1980; Sports Illustrated 101 Most Influential Minorities in Sports, 2003; Black Enterprise 50 Most Powerful African Americans in Sports, 2005; Career Gear Sportsman of the Year, 2008; Negro Leagues Baseball Museum John Henry "Pop" Lloyd Legacy Award, 2008; Rainbow PUSH Coalition Jesse Jackson Sports Person of the Year, 2008; Overall Sports Business Entrepreneur & Community Service Award, June Family Found, 2009; Ebony Sports Power 150, 2009; Congressional Horizon Award, 2009; Ebony Power 100, 2010; Triumph Award, Nat Action Network, 2011. **Special Achievements:** Included in Sports Illustrated's list of the 101 Most Influential Minorities in Sports, 2003. **Business Addr:** Executive Vice President, Jimmie Lee Solomon, America Tr 2929 Allen Pkwy Suite 3150, Houston, TX 77019, **Business Phone:** (713)489-8977.

### SOMERSET, LEO L., JR.

Executive. **Personal:** Born Aug 27, 1945, Memphis, TN. **Educ:** Memphis State Univ, BBA, 1968; Ind Univ, MBA, 1973. **Career:** Citicorp Real Estate Inc & Citibank NA, vpres, 1973-83; Colwell Financial Corp, vpres & mgr, 1983-; Intersolidated Commun Inc, pres. **Honors/Awds:** Noyes Fel Consortium Grad Study, Mgt Ind Univ, 1971. **Home Addr:** 908 S Ridgeley Dr, Los Angeles, CA 90036-4706, **Home Phone:** (323)931-0421. **Business Addr:** Vice President, Colwell Financial Corp, 3223 W 6th St, Los Angeles, CA 90020, **Business Phone:** (213)380-3170.

### SOMERVILLE, PATRICIA DAWN

Manager. **Personal:** Born Nov 24, 1956, Leonardtown, MD; daughter of James Mitchell Norris and Agnes Elizabeth Stevens. **Educ:** Univ Md, Princess Anne, MD, 1978; Howard Univ, Wash, DC, BS, phys ther, 1980; Troy State Univ, Troy, Ala, MS, mgt, 1983. **Career:** St Francis Hosp, Columbus, Ga, cardiac phys therapist, 1980-81; AUS Inf Ctr, Ft Benning, Ga, admin, 1981-84; Hq Commun-Electronics Command, Ft Monmouth, NJ, personnel mgr, 1994-. **Orgs:** Alpha Kappa Alpha Sorority. **Honors/Awds:** Most Studious Student, University of Maryland, 1976. **Home Addr:** 5 Charles Dr, Tinton Falls, NJ 07753-7902, **Home Phone:** (732)996-8465. **Business Addr:** Personnel Management Specialist, Communications-Electronics Command (AMSEL-PT-PL-3), Ft. Monmouth, NJ 07703, **Business Phone:** (732)532-8700.

### SOMMERVILLE, JOSEPH C.

Educator, college teacher. **Personal:** Born Dec 28, 1926, Birmingham, AL; married Mattie Cunningham; children: Joseph Jr & Barry C. **Educ:** Morehouse Col, BS, 1949; Univ Mich, MS, 1956, MA, EdS, 1966, PhD, 1970. **Career:** Douglass & Woodson Sch, Inkster, MI, teacher, 1949-61, prin, 1961-68; Wayne Co Intermediate Sch Dist, Asst Ctr, staff develop specialist, 1968-70; Univ Toledo, prof educ, dir admin internships, 1970-75; Univ Toledo, Col Educ, prof, 1970-92, prof emer, 1992-; Ohio AARP, pres, 1996; Dept Educ Leadership, dept chair, prof admin & supv. **Orgs:** State pres, Ohio AARP; Asn Sch Curric Develop; Phi Kappa Phi; pres, bd trustee, Toledo-Lucas Co Libr; W moreland Asn; Phi Delta Kappa; Sigma Pi Phi Fraternity; scholar comt chmn, Omega Psi Phi. **Honors/Awds:** Citation Outstanding Serv, Wayne Co; Speaker many National & local Professional Conferences. **Special Achievements:** Author numerous articles in natl & state journals & books. **Home Addr:** 7300 Clipper Ct, Maumee, OH 43537-8680, **Home Phone:** (419)441-2204. **Business Addr:** Professor Emeritus, University of Toledo, 2801 W Bancroft St, Toledo, OH 43606-3390, **Business Phone:** (800)586-5336.

### SOREY, HILMON S., JR.

Banker, executive, association executive. **Personal:** Born Jan 14, 1935, Bascom, FL; son of Hilmon S Sr and Bricy Wilson; married Martha; children: Carla-Maria & Hilmon III; married Martha Braden; children: Megan & Mollie. **Educ:** Fla A&M Univ, BS, bus admin, 1957; Univ Chicago, MBA, health serv mgt, 1969. **Career:** Executive, association executive (retired), banker; Fla A&M Univ Hosp, adminr, 1965-67; Cleveland Metro Gen Hosp, assoc dir, 1969-71; Michael Reese Health Plan, exec dir provident med ctr & founding exec, fed exec, 1971-75; Kellogg Sch, HHSM Prog, Northwestern Univ, prof, grad prog dir, 1976-87; Hilmon S Sorey Assoc, pres, 1987-90; Hawthorn Mellody Inc, pres & chief exec officer, 1990-93; Northwestern Memorial Hosp, vpres community rels & vpres support servs, 1993-97; Fla Black Bus Bd, 2000-06; ShoreBank, vpres & mgr, 2008-10; Urban

Partnership Bank, relationship banker, 2010-; Fla Black Bus Investment Bd, pres; Newman Club, founder & pres; Cleveland Metrop Gen Hosp; Evanston Technol Partners Inc, advisor, consult & dir, currently. **Orgs:** Mem bd dir, Christian Community Health Ctr, 2016; Traffic Club Chicago; Coun Logistics Mgt; Am Col Health care Execs; Nat Asn Health Serv Execs; consult, Robert Wood Johnson Found; consult, Amoco Found; consult, Sears Found; consult, Ill Dept Pub Health; consult, US Dept Health & Human Serv; consult, Ill State Med Soc; consult, Am Cancer Soc; St Eugenia Cath Church Mem; FAMU Serv Fraternity; Black MBA Asn. **Home Addr:** 1425 Oldfield Dr, Tallahassee, FL 32312. **Business Addr:** Advisor, Consultant & Director, Evanston Technology Partners Inc, 3619 S State St Suite 300, Chicago, IL 60609, **Business Phone:** (847)440-3230.

### SOSA, SAMUEL PERALTA (SAMMY SOSA)

Baseball player, executive. **Personal:** Born Nov 12, 1968, San Pedro de Macoris; son of Juan Bautista Montero and Lucrecia; married Sonia Rodriguez; children: Keysha, Kenia, Sammy Jr & Michael. **Career:** Baseball player (retired), executive, owner; Tex Rangers, right fielder, 1989, 2007; Chicago White Sox, outfielder, 1989-91; Chicago Cubs, 1992-2004; Baltimore Orioles, right fielder, 2005; Sammy Sosa Restaurant, owner, currently; free agt, currently. **Orgs:** Founder, Sammy Sosa Charitable Found. **Home Addr:** Mello Centro, San Pedro de MacorisZ-77. **Business Addr:** Free Agent, 1060 W Addison St, Chicago, IL 60613-4397.

### SOULCHILD, MUSIQ (TALIB JOHNSON)

Singer, songwriter. **Personal:** Born Sep 16, 1977, Philadelphia, PA. **Career:** Studio albums: Aijuswanaseing, 2000; Juslisen, 2002; Soulstar, 2003; Luvanmusiq, 2007; OnMyRadio, 2008; MusiqInTheMagiq, 2011; 9ine, 2013. Singles: "Just Friends (Sunny)", 2000; "Love", 2000; "Girl Next Door", 2001; "Halfcrazy", 2002; "Dontchange", 2002; "Forthenight", 2003; "Whoknows", 2004; "B.U.D.D.Y.", 2007; "Teachme", 2007; "Makeyouhappy", 2007; "Radio", 2008; "IfULeave", 2008; "SoBeautiful", 2009; "Silky Soul", 2010; "Anything", "Yes", 2011; "Feel the Fire", 2013. Featured singles: "Break You Off", 2002; "Why Me", "Chocolate High", 2008; "Forever", 2010; "Hope for Haiti", 2010; "Ah Yeah", 2012; "Still Believe in Love", 2013. TV series: "The Hot 10", 2010; "In the Meantime", 2013. **Honors/Awds:** Numerous honors and awards including Best Male R&B Artist, Best New Artist, BET, 2001; Source Award, R&B Artist of the Year, 2001; NAACP Image Award, Outstanding New Artist, 2001; Soul Train Award, Best R&B Single, 2002; NAACP Image Award, Best Song, 2002; Billboard R&B/Hip-Hop Awards; Top R&B/Hip-Hop Artist. **Special Achievements:** Grammy nomination, Best Male R&B Vocal Performance, 2002. **Business Addr:** Singer, Songwriter, c/o Universal Music Group, 2220 Colorado Ave, Santa Monica, CA 90404, **Business Phone:** (310)865-5000.

### SOUTH, LESLIE ELAINE (LESLIE ELAINE JACKSON)

Judge. **Personal:** Born Jan 4, 1949, Chicago, IL; daughter of Mildred Nash and Wesley; married Arthur Jackson; children: Wesley Jackson & Christopher Jackson. **Educ:** Loyola Univ Chicago, BA, 1976; Northwestern Univ Sch Law, JD, 1978. **Career:** Cook Co State atty, asst prosecutor, 1978-82; Chicago Transit Authority, 1984-88; State Ill, Circuit Ct Cook Co, assoc judge, 1988, judge 1992-; Appellate Ct, First dist, judge, 1996-. **Orgs:** Chairperson elect, currently, bd mem, Ill Judicial Coun, 1988-, chmn, AFA Hist Month Comn, 1988-; Ill Judges Asn, 1988-; S Suburban Bar Asn, 1989-; Womens Bar Asn, 1992-; Ill State Bar Asn, 1992-. **Honors/Awds:** Distinguished Sfs, Black Prosecutors Asn, 1991; Judicial Sfs, Ill Judicial Coun, 1992. **Home Addr:** 1412 Heather Hill Cresent, Flossmoor, IL 60422, **Home Phone:** (708)957-5524. **Business Addr:** Judge, State of Illinois, 160 N LaSalle St Suite N-1607, Chicago, IL 60601, **Business Phone:** (312)793-5450.

### SOUTHERLAND, ELLEASE (EBELE OSEYE)

Educator, writer, poet. **Personal:** Born Jun 18, 1943, Brooklyn, NY; daughter of Ellease Dozier and Monroe Penrose. **Educ:** Queens Col City Univ NY, BA, 1965; Columbia Univ, MFA, 1974. **Career:** New York, Dept Social Serv, caseworker, 1966-72; Columbia Univ, instr eng, 1973-76; Bor Manhattan Comm Col City Univ New York, adj asst prof black lit, 1973-; Pace Univ, adj prof, prof lit african peoples & creative writing, 1975. **Orgs:** Fel Inst African Studies Univ Nigeria, 1989; Harlem Writers Guild; Schomburg Soc; Asn Study Class African Civilizations; Nat Asn Advan Colored People; MLA; NCTE Black Caucus; Acad Am Poets; New York African Studies Asn; Inst Res African Am Studies; Asn Nigerian Auth. **Honors/Awds:** John Golden Award for Fiction, Queens Col City Univ New York, 1964; Gwendolyn Brooks Poetry Award, Black World, 1972; Woman of the Year, Delta Beta Zeta Chapter, Zeta Phi Beta Sorority, 1989; Literacy Achievement, Borough Pres Claire Schulman, 1990; Listed in Oxford Companion To Women Writing In The United States, 1992. **Special Achievements:** Author of novella White Shadows, 1964, author of poetry collection The Magic Sun Spins, Paul Breman, 1975, author of autobiographical novel Let the Lion Eat Straw, Scribner, 1979, wrote the novel "A Feast of Fools", Africana Legacy Press, 1998, Opening Line: The Creative Writer, Eneke Publications, 2000, contributor of stories, essays, and poems to anthologies and periodicals. **Home Addr:** 160-27 119th Dr, Jamaica, NY 11434. **Business Addr:** Professor, Pace University, Rm 1507 1 Pace Plz, New York, NY 10038, **Business Phone:** (212)346-1657.

### SOUTHERN, HERBERT B.

Architect. **Personal:** Born May 21, 1926, Washington, DC; son of Albert and Mildred R; married Mary Ann. **Educ:** Howard Univ, BS, 1950; Cath Univ, addn grad archit study. **Career:** Newark, NJ, draftsman, 1951-53; Pvt Practice, architect; Southern Assocs, architect, currently. **Orgs:** Am Inst Architects; NJ Soc Arch; bd dir, Harmonia Savings Bank; Nat Advan Asn Colored People; Urban League; chmn, Piscataway, NJ Planning Bd; City architect design Rahway Pub Libr, 1967. **Home Addr:** 571 E Hazelwood Ave, Rahway, NJ 07065, **Home Phone:** (732)388-5298. **Business Addr:** Architect, Southern Assocs Architects, 571 E Hazelwood Ave, Rahway, NJ 07065-5403, **Business Phone:** (908)338-5298.

### SOUTHERN, JOSEPH

Educator. **Personal:** Born Nov 21, 1919, Indianapolis, IN; son of John and Mary; married Eileen Jackson Southern (deceased); children: April Myra & Edward Joseph. **Educ:** Lincoln Univ, BS, 1941; Univ Chicago, MBA, 1945. **Career:** Educator (retired); Prairie View State Col, asst registr, 1941-42; Southern Univ, asst prof, 1944-45; Alcorn Col, bus mgr, 1945-46; Claflin Univ, bus mgr, 1946-49; KY State Col, prof, 1950-53; Community Fin Corp, NY, mgr, vpres, 1953-57; NY Pub Sch, teacher, 1957-71; La Guardia Col, City Univ NY, prof, 1971-85. **Orgs:** Pres, Fedn Res Afro-Am Creative Arts Inc, 1971-; co-founder & mgt ed, Black Perspective Music, 1973-; Asn Study Afro-Am Life & Hist; Kappa Alpha Psi; life mem, Nat Asn Advan Colored People; scout leader, Boy Scouts Am. **Honors/Awds:** Award Boy Scouts Am, 1960. **Home Addr:** 115 179th St, Jamaica, NY 11434.

### SOUTHGATE, MARTHA

Writer, educator. **Personal:** Born Dec 10, 1960, Cleveland, OH; children: 2. **Educ:** Smith Col, Northampton, BA (cum laude), anthrop, 1982; Radcliffe Col, Harvard Univ, Cambridge, MA, Radcliffe pub procedures course, 1985; Goddard Col, Plainfield, VT, MFA, creative writing, 1994. **Career:** Essence Mag, bks ed, 1989-98; Scribner, auth, 1998-2002; Goddard Cols, MFA writing prog, adj prof, 2003-04; New York Univ, sch continuing & prof studies, adj prof, 2003; New Sch Univ, Eugene Lang Col, New York, assoc chair writing dept, 2004-05; Brooklyn Col, MFA writing prog, adj assoc prof, adj prof, 2005-09; novelist, 1996-; New York Found Arts, fel, 2002; Novels: Houghton Mifflin, 2001-06, "Another Way to Dance"; "The Fall of Rome", "Third Girl From The Left", "The Taste of Salt"; Articles: "Writers Like Me". **Orgs:** Fel MacDowell Colony, 1998-, Breadloaf Writers Conf & Va Ctr Creative Arts; PEN Am, Assoc Writing Progs. **Special Achievements:** Her essay "Writers Like Me" received considerable notice and appears in the anthology Best African-American Essays 2009. **Home Addr:** , Brooklyn, NY. **Business Addr:** Fellow, MacDowell Colony, 100 High St, Peterborough, NH 03458, **Business Phone:** (603)924-3886.

### SOWELL, JERALD MONYE

Football player. **Personal:** Born Jan 21, 1974, Baton Rouge, LA; married Kimberly; children: Jillian & Jordyn. **Educ:** Tulane Univ. **Career:** Football player (retired); New York Jets, 1997, 1999-2002, running back, 2005, 2003-05; Tampa Bay Buccaneers, 2006. **Special Achievements:** Kid Reporter of the Week Program with The Star Ledger. clothing model for the JWO Fashion Show that raised more than $20, 000 for St. Marys Children and Family Services. **Home Addr:** 201 Stockton Dr, Southlake, TX 76092-2225, **Home Phone:** (682)831-1585.

### SOWELL, THOMAS

Educator. **Personal:** Born Jun 30, 1930, Gastonia, NC; married Alma Jean Parr; children: John & Lorraine. **Educ:** Harvard Univ, Cambridge, BA, AB, econ, 1958; Columbia Univ, NY, MA, econ, 1959; Univ Chicago, IL, PhD, econ, 1968. **Career:** US Dept Labor, economist, 1961-62; Rutgers Univ, instr econs, 1962-63; Howard Univ, lectr econs, 1963-64; Am Tel & Tel Co, econ analyst, 1964-65; Cornell Univ, asst prof econs, 1965-69; Brandeis Univ, assoc prof econs, 1969-70; Univ Calif Los Angeles, assoc prof econs, 1970-72, prof econs, 1974-80; Urban Inst, WA, DC, proj dir, 1972-74; Amherst Col, vis prof econs, 1977; Author: Says Law, An Hist Anal, 1972; Race and Econs, 1975; Knowledge and Decisions, 1980; Ethnic Am: A Hist, 1981; Markets and Minorities, 1981; The Econs and Polit of Race, 1983; Civil Rights: Rhet or Reality, 1984; Marxism: Philos and Econs, 1986; A Conflict of Visions: Ideological Origins of Polit Struggles, 1987; Compassion Vs Guilt and Other Essays, 1987; Inside Am Educ, 1993; Race and Cult: A World View, 1995; Migrations and Cultures: A World View, 1996; The Vision of the Anointed: Self-Congratulation As a Basis for Social Policy, 1996; Conquests and Cultures: An Int Hist, 1998; The Einstein Syndrome: Bright C Who Talk Late, 2002; Controversial Essays, 2002; A Personal Odyssey, 2002; The Quest For Cosmic Justice, 2002; Appl Econs: Thinking Beyond Stage One, 2003; Affirmative Action Around the World: An Empirical Study, 2004; Basic Econs: A Citizens Guide to the Econ, 2004; Black Rednecks and White Liberals: And Other Cult And Ethnic Issues, 2005; On Class Econs. New Haven, 2006; Ever Wonder Why And Other Controversial Essays, 2006; Econ Facts and Fallacies, 2007; Basic Econs: A Common Sense Guide to the Econ, 2007; A Man of Lett. San Francisco: Encounter Bks, 2007; Appl Econs: Thinking Beyond Stage One, 2009; The Housing Boom and Bust, 2009; Dismantling Am, 2010; Intellectuals and Socs, 2010; Basic Econs: A Common Sense Guide to the Econ, 2011; Intellectuals & Race, 2013. **Orgs:** Fel Ctr Advan Study Behav Sci, Stanford, CA, 1976-77; sr fel Rose & Milton Friedman Consult, Urban Coalition, Rockefeller Found, Urban Inst; Ctr Advan Study Behav Sci, 1976-77; Rose & Milton Friedman sr fel Hoover Inst, Stanford Univ, CA, 1977, 1980-; Pub Policy, 1980; Am Philos Soc. **Honors/Awds:** Francis Boyer Award, Am Enterprise Inst, 1990; Sydney Hook Award, Nat Asn Scholars, 1998; W Glenn Campbell Uncommon Book Award, 1998; Rita Ricardo-Campbell Award, 1998; National Humanities Medal, 2002; Bradley Prize, 2003; Lysander Spooner Award, 2004; Abstract Award, 2008. **Special Achievements:** Author of Numerous Books. **Business Addr:** Rose & Milton Friedman Senior Fellow on Public Policy, Hoover Institution, 434 Galvez Mall, Stanford, CA 94305-6003, **Business Phone:** (650)723-1754.

### SPAIN, DR. HIRAM, JR.

Lawyer, administrator. **Personal:** Born Aug 22, 1936, Conway, SC; son of Hiram and Gladys; married Doris Bush; children: Hiram & Nicole. **Educ:** SC State Col, BS, 1961; Howard Univ, JD, 1971; Columbia Inte Sem, MDiv; Lenoir-Rhyne Univ, Lutheran Theol Southern Sem, MDiv. **Career:** Teacher, 1961-68; legal intern, Greenville, 1971-72; Off Gov John C W, SC, proj dir, 1972-74; Columbia Urban League, chief exec officer, 1974-; St Mark Baptist Church, Columbia, pastor, 1999-. **Orgs:** Health Policy Coun, Gov John W, 1974; NABSW Bus Conf, 1975; Delta Psi Omega; consult, HEW, 1977; first exec secy, Baptist Educ & Missionary Conv SC, 2000; Nat Asn Advan Colored People; Kappa Alpha Psi; Masons; Columbia Black Lawyers Asn; Notary Pub, SC; Delta Psi Omega; Nat Coun Urban League; exec bd, Gethsemane Baptist Asn; Interdenominational Ministerial Alliance Greater Columbia; bd mem, I. D. Quincy Newman Inst; Minority Adv Coun U. S. Congressman; United Black Fund Midlands; Nat Asn Black Soc Workers; Delta Theta Phi Lavy Fraternity; S Carolina Christian Action Coun; bd mem, Communities Schs S Carolina; bd mem, Partnership S Carolina. **Honors/Awds:** Outstanding Soldier, Bussac, France, 1956; Outstanding Business Student Award, UBEA, 1961; Outstanding Employee Award, NCIC, 1971; recognized by Who's Who in American Colleges and Universities of the South, in the South East, in Black America. **Special Achievements:** First African American bureau chief of South Carolina Department of Social Services. **Home Addr:** 711 Delverton Rd, Columbia, SC 29203, **Home Phone:** (803)754-3459. **Business Addr:** Executive Assistant, State Department of Social Services, 3150 Harden St 202, Columbia, SC 29212, **Business Phone:** (803)737-5916.

### SPAND, REV. DR. MARGOT

Association executive. **Career:** The Women Color Found & Health Ministries Inc, mem & bd dir. **Business Addr:** Member, Board of Directors, The Women of Color Foundation & Health Ministries Inc, PO Box 3835, Southfield, MI 48037, **Business Phone:** (248)569-3532.

### SPANN, REV. PAUL RONALD

Clergy. **Personal:** Born Nov 7, 1943, Ann Arbor, MI; son of Paul Leon and Ruth Ann Green; married Jacqueline Graves; children: Shannon Lyn MacVean-Brown & Seth David. **Educ:** Kalamazoo Col, BA, 1965; Univ Rochester, 1966; Episcopal Divinity Sch, MDiv, 1970. **Career:** Director (retired); St Timothys Church, asst, 1970-71; Church Messiah, rector, 1971; St Cyprians Episcopal Church, consult & spiritual dir, 1996; Lic PRH educr, 1998; Christ Church Spirituality Ctr, dir; CREDO, spirituality fac; Ecumenical Theol Sem, Detroit, adj. **Orgs:** Union Black Episcopalians, 1976-; pres, founder, vpres, Island View Village Develop Corp, currently; standing comt, Diocese Mich, 1988-92; nat secy, Christian Community Develop Asn, 1989-93. **Honors/Awds:** Fel, Woodrow Wilson Found, 1965-66; Malcolm Dade Lectureship, St Cyprians Episcopal Church, 1989; Econ Justice Comn Award, Diocese Mich, 1993. **Special Achievements:** Sojourners Liturgy Mag, "Wholeness & Community," July 1991, "Oblivion & the Ghetto", 1987, Chapter on "Co-operative Housing" in book, Making Housing Happen, 2007, Chalice Press. **Home Addr:** 2971 Iroquois St, Detroit, MI 48214-1837, **Home Phone:** (313)571-5145.

### SPARKS, PHILLIPPI DWAINE

Football player. **Personal:** Born Apr 15, 1969, Oklahoma City, OK; married Jodi; children: Phillippi Jr & Jordin. **Educ:** Glendale Community Col; Ariz State Univ. **Career:** Football player (retired); New York Giants, defensive back, 1992-93, left cornerback, 1994-99, right cornerback & free safety, 1999; Dallas Cowboys, left cornerback & strong safety, 2000. **Orgs:** Sigma chi fraternity, Ariz State Univ.

### SPARROW, RORY DARNELL

Basketball player, baseball manager. **Personal:** Born Jun 12, 1958, Suffolk, VA. **Educ:** Villanova Univ, BS, 1980. **Career:** Basketball player (retired); NJ Nets, 1980-81; Atlanta Hawks, 1981-83; New York Knicks, 1983-87; Chicago Bulls, 1987-88, 1991; Miami Heat, 1988-90; Sacramento Kings, 1990-91; Los Angeles Lakers, 1991-92; NBA, prog mgr, 1994. **Orgs:** Founder, Rory F Sparrow Found. **Home Addr:** 111 Valley Rd, Montclair, NJ 07042-2322. **Business Addr:** Player Programs Manager, National Basketball Association.

### SPAULDING, AARON LOWERY

Investment banker. **Personal:** Born Mar 16, 1943, Durham, NC. **Educ:** NC Cent Univ, Durham, BS, 1964; Univ Pa, Wharton Grad Sch Finance & Com, Philadelphia, MBA, 1968; Dirs Col; Advan Dirs Col. **Career:** Re-Con Serv Inc, dir & co-founder, 1968; JFK Ctr Performing Arts, comptroller, 1972-74; Boyden Bd dir Servs, exec dir, 1974; B&C Assoc Wash, dir bus develop & consult, 1974; Exec Off Pres White House, assoc dir pres personnel off, 1974-77; Salomon Bros Inc, vpres, 1977; WR Lazard & Co, prin-in-charge, Investment Banking; Rev Leon H Sullivan's Progress Mgt, econ develop analyst; Econ Develop Proj Philadelphia, PA, Analyst; Galaxy Travel Group Inc, chmn, pres & chief exec off, currently; M & F Bancorp Inc, dir, currently. **Orgs:** Pres, Wharton MBA Asn; res asst, Dept of Industry & the Placement Off, Univ Pa. **Honors/Awds:** Outstanding Academic Achievement Award, NC Cent Univ, 1964. **Business Addr:** Director, M & F Bancorp Inc, 2634 Durham Chapel Hill Blvd, Durham, NC 27702-2800, **Business Phone:** (919)687-7800.

### SPAULDING, JEAN GAILLARD

School administrator. **Personal:** Born Feb 23, 1947, Birmingham, AL; children: Chandler & Courtney. **Educ:** Barnard Col, BA, biol, 1968; Duke Univ Sch Med, MD, psychiat, 1972. **Career:** Duke Univ Med Ctr, fel Dept Psychiat, adj fac, 1990-92, vice chancellor health affairs, 1998-2002, assoc consult prof, currently; pvt psychiat pract, 1977-, clin consult, 1977-90, assoc clin consult, 1998-; Lilly Res Labs, consult, 1997; WNCU Pub Radio, co-host weekly radio show, 1997-; WTVD Newschannel 11, consult, 1997-; Duke Endowment, trustee, currently; Cardinal Health Corp, dir, currently. **Orgs:** Nc Mus Hist, 1986-92; Alpha Omega Alpha Hon Soc; Am Psychiat Asn; AMA; Nat Med Asn; Am Asn Psychiat Servs C; Am Col Forensic Examrs; NC Neuro-Psychiat Asn; NC Coun Child Psychiat; Durham-Orange County Med Soc; NC Med Soc; Old N State Med Asn; bd trustee, Duke Univ, 1993-97; Res Triangle Found, bd trustee, 1993-97; bd dir, Wachovia Bank NC, 1995-; adv bd, Bright Horizons; bd dir, NC Biotechnology Ctr; Wells Fargo Bank; chair, Nc African Am Heritage Comn; bd dir, City Med Exec Comt, 1997-99; bd dir, Duke Univ Health Syst, 1998; Hon Co-Chair, 1999; bd dir, 1990, vpres, 1995, Josiah Charles Trent Memorial Found Inc; Bi-Nat Health Comn, 2001; Durham Pub Educ Network; March Dimes Walk Am. **Home Addr:** 2 Green Mill Lane, Durham, NC 27707. **Business Addr:** Trustee, The Duke Endowment, 100 N Tryon St Suite 3500, Charlotte, NC 28202-4012, **Business Phone:** (704)376-0291.

### SPAULDING, ESQ. LYNETTE VICTORIA

Lawyer. **Personal:** Born Dec 21, 1954, Bronx, NY; daughter of Aaron M and Gertie Mae. **Educ:** State Univ NY, Stony Brook, BA, 1976; Syracuse Univ Col Law, JD, 1979. **Career:** Syracuse Univ Law Sch, secy, 1976-79; Bristol Lab, law clerk, 1977-79; Reginald Heber Smith Comn, lawyer fel prog, 1979; Legal Aid Soc Westchester Co, atty, 1979-, Criminal Div, sr atty & dep bur chief, 1987-. **Orgs:** Treas, Nat Asn Advan Colored People, Stony Brook, 1975-76; comn chairperson, Black Am Law Stud Asn, 1976-79; justice, Judicial Bd, Syracuse Univ Col, 1976-79; bd dir, Nat Asn Black Women Attys, 1978-82; Moot Ct Bd, Col Law, 1979; chairperson & bd trustee, Divine Light USDA Church, 1985-; bd dir, Westchester Black Bar Asn, Inc, 1997; NY Bar; NY Defenders Asn; Black Boys Westchester Asn. **Honors/Awds:** Special Recognition, BALSA & Womens Law Caucus Law Day, 1977; Frederick Douglass Moot Court, BALSA Nat, 1979; Listed, Cambridge Who's Who. **Special Achievements:** Subject of article in Defender's Digest. **Home Addr:** 91 Boerum St Apt 10Q, Brooklyn, NY 11206-2522, **Home Phone:** (718)599-6776. **Business Addr:** Board of Director, Westchester Black Bar Association Inc, 333 Mamaroneck Ave, White Plains, NY 10605.

### SPAULDING, ROMEO ORLANDO

Firefighter, president (organization). **Personal:** Born Aug 27, 1940, Whiteville, NC; son of Ralph and Sarah George; married Annette Richardson; children: Valerie G, Bernardine E, Alva G, Karen R & Kevin R. **Educ:** Howard Univ, Wash, DC, math, 1962; Univ DC, Wash, DC, fire serv, 1970; Univ Md, College Park, MD, Nat Staff & Command Sch, attended 1981. **Career:** Kenwood Golf & Country Club, Bethesda, Md, food serv, 1958-59; Columbia Hosp Women, Wash, DC, procurement, 1959-65; DC Fire Dept, Wash, DC, dir community rels/lt, 1965-92. **Orgs:** Supt, Sunday Sch Bethel Bible Church, 1976-; treas, PG County PTA, 1976-80; pres, Progressive Fire Fighter Asn, 1981-85; exec bd mem, Nat Black Leadership Roundtable, 1981-90; pres, 1988, exec dir, Int Asn Black Prof Fire Fighters, 1996-02. **Honors/Awds:** Cong Commendation, US Cong, 1985; Community Service Award, DC Govt, 1986 & 1987; Firefighter of the Year, Firehouse Mag, 1989; National School Volunteer of the Year, 1989; Christian Man of the Year, Bethel Bible Church, 1989. **Home Addr:** 4204 Vine St, Capitol Heights, MD 20743-5620, **Home Phone:** (301)794-0790.

### SPAULDING, WILLIAM RIDLEY

Government official, educator, administrator. **Personal:** Born Clarkton, NC; married Dolores Hinton; children: Angelyn Flowers, Michelle & Deirdre. **Educ:** Howard Univ, BS, mech engineering, 1947. **Career:** DC Pub Schs, instr, 1947-52; Howard Univ, instr, 1950-60; Nat Security Agency, engr, 1952-74; Univ DC, instr, 1980; DC City Coun, legislator, coun mem; DC Ct Syst, Dept Admin Serv, dir, 2005, adminr. **Orgs:** Chair, Ft Lincoln Found; bd mem, Kidney Found; bd mem, Am Heart Asn; chair, Talent Search Inc. **Honors/Awds:** Producer, Metro Talent Search, 1978-85. **Home Addr:** 1905 Randolph St NE, Washington, DC 20018, **Home Phone:** (202)526-1973. **Business Addr:** Council Member, Legislator, City Council, 14th E Sts NW, Washington, DC 20004.

### SPEARMAN, LARNA KAYE

Engineer. **Personal:** Born May 7, 1945, Kokomo, IN; married Sarah Jewell Busch; children: Angela & Derek. **Educ:** Purdue Univ, BS, 1967; Ind Univ Law Sch, 1971. **Career:** Detroit Deisel Allison, engr, 1967-71; Eli Lilly & Co, supr, 1971-76, personnel; Mayor, coordr, 1976-77; Nat Asn Civilian Oversight Law Enforcement, secy. **Orgs:** Minority Contractors Adv Coun, 1970-71; Indianapolis Police Merit Bd, 1970-74; Guest lectr, Nat Crime Prev Inst; Sch Police Adminr, Univ Lousiville; vchmn, Human Rights Comn Indianapolis & Marion Co; secy, Indianapolis Settlements Inc; bd mem, Indianapolis Chap Nat Advan Asn Colored People; Indianapolis Black Rep Coun; Indianapolis Citizens Police Complaint Bd; Ind United Methodist C's Home Inc. **Honors/Awds:** Distinguished Service Award, Indianapolis Jaycees, 1977; Outstanding Young Hoosier Award, Ind Jaycees, 1977; Citz Award, Police League Ind, 1977. **Home Addr:** 3530 Watson Rd, Indianapolis, IN 46205-3546, **Home Phone:** (317)925-0305. **Business Addr:** Secretary, National Association for Civilian Oversight of Law Enforcement, 638 E Vt St, Indianapolis, IN 46202, **Business Phone:** (866)462-2653.

### SPEARMAN, VENITA

Accountant. **Educ:** Roosevelt Univ; DePaul Univ, Charles H Kellstadt Grad Sch Bus. **Career:** United Way Metrop Chicago, mgr, Spec Events & Recognition, community outreach coordr, 1991-99, prog mgr, 1999-2004, mgr spec events & recognition, 2004-09; Spyce Mkt, chief event strategist, 2011-12; HOPE worldwide, disaster case mgt coordr, 2012-13. **Orgs:** African Am Outreach Comt. **Business Addr:** Disaster Case Management Coordinator, HOPE worldwide, 1285 Drummers Lane Suite 105, Wayne, PA 19087, **Business Phone:** (773)298-0543.

### SPEARS, ANGELENA ELAINE

Journalist. **Personal:** Born Jun 28, 1955, Lansing, MI; daughter of George and Louise Owens; married Charles; children: Carmen, Jason, George & Lydia. **Educ:** Northwestern Univ, BS, jour & hist, 1978; George Washington Univ, MBA, healthcare, 2011. **Career:** Meridian Bank, direct mail adminr, 1994-97; Reading Eagle/Times, corresp, 1996-; PharmaForce Int, dir customer commun, 1999-2011; Spears-Harambee Co, owner, 1996-; Today's Healthcare Mkt, owner, 2011-. **Orgs:** Bd mem, Cent Pa African Am Mus, 1999-; Bethel AME Church. **Home Addr:** 420 Lincoln Dr, Wernersville, PA 19565, **Home Phone:** (610)678-0108. **Business Addr:** Owner, Spears-Harambee Co, 420 Lincoln Dr, Wernersville, PA 19565, **Business Phone:** (610)678-0108.

### SPEARS, MARCUS RAISHON

Football player. **Personal:** Born Sep 28, 1971, Baton Rouge, LA. **Educ:** Northwestern State Univ, grad. **Career:** Football player (retired); Chicago Bears, linebacker, 1994-96; Kans City Chiefs, 1997-2003; Houston Texans, 2004; Dallas Cowboys, defensive end, 2005-12; Baltimore Ravens, defensive end, 2013. **Orgs:** Omega Psi Phi Fraternity. **Special Achievements:** TV Series: "Rome Is Burning", 2009. **Home Addr:** , TX.

### SPEARS, RICHARD JAMES

Real estate agent, executive. **Personal:** Born Mar 5, 1962, Holyoke, MA; son of James and Janet; married Sheri D; children: Armand & Brandon. **Educ:** Syracuse Univ, BS, mkt/commun, 1984; NY Univ, dipl, real estate investment anal, 1991. **Career:** Gold Coast Realty, proj mgr sales, 1987-90; Powerhouse Realty, pres, owner, broker rec, 1990-; Onyx Ventures LLC, pres, owner, 2000-. **Orgs:** Alpha Phi Alpha, 1981-; pres, pres, 100 Black Men NJ, 1998-2000; NJ Asn Real Estate Brokers, 1998-2001; bd mem, Big Bros Big Sisters, Essex Co, 1999-. **Honors/Awds:** Who's Who in Real Estate, 1984; Outstanding Young Men of America, 1984; NAREB Million Dollar Sales Club, 1998. **Special Achievements:** Hundred Most Influential, City News, 1998; Top 20 African-American Business People, NJ Bus News, 1999; Contributor, NJ Star Ledger; Jersey Jour; Bergen Record; Black Collegian Mag. **Home Addr:** 310 W S Orange Ave, South Orange, NJ 07079-1441, **Home Phone:** (973)378-5789. **Business Addr:** President, Owner, Powerhouse Realty LLC, 2274 John F Kennedy Blvd Suite 1, Jersey City, NJ 07304, **Business Phone:** (973)763-5033.

### SPEARS, SANDRA CALVETTE

Marketing executive. **Personal:** Born Aug 9, 1964, Pontiac, MI; daughter of Calvin and Sandra Wilkerson Lockett. **Educ:** Eastern Mich Univ, Ypsilanti, Mich, BS, 1986. **Career:** Total Health Care Inc, Detroit, Mich, mkt rep, 1987-89, mkt develop coord, 1989, new provider & mkt develop coord, 1989-90, acct exec, 1990, asst pub mkt mgr, 1994-. **Orgs:** Nat Asn Advan Colored People, 1986; Booker T Wash Bus Asn, 1986; Eastern Mich Univ Alumni Asn, 1986; Nat Asn Health Serv Exec, 1987; Southeastern Mich Health Exec Forum, 1987. **Honors/Awds:** Top Sales Achiever, Total Health Care, 1987-90. **Home Addr:** 21050 Rampart Cir Suite 241, Southfield, MI 48033, **Home Phone:** (248)426-8983. **Business Addr:** Assistant Public Marketing Manager, Total Health Care Inc, 3011 W Grand Blvd, Detroit, MI 48202, **Business Phone:** (313)871-7805.

### SPEARS, STEPHANIE

Consultant, manager. **Personal:** Born Dec 9, 1949, San Francisco, CA; daughter of Richard McGee and Thadyne Black; married John; children: Mikele Adriana & Julian Richard. **Educ:** Univ Calif, Berkeley, BA, 1972. **Career:** Scenery United Ltd Tours, travel consult, 1968-82; Empire Tours, retail off mgr, 1982-83; Blue World Travel, travel consult, 1983-88, dir opers, treas, 1998-; Adventure Express & Rascals Paradise, opers mgr, 1988-98. **Orgs:** Pres, San Francisco Women Travel, 1995-96; travel agt adv bd, Govt Bahamas, 1996-99; pac gov, Int Fed Women's Travel Org, 1997-99; bd mem, AFA hist & cult soc, 1997-99; co-chair, Marriage Ministry; adv bd, Travel Dept Berkeley Community Col; mem exec bd, founding bd dir, San Francisco Women Travel, 2007. **Special Achievements:** First Black Women President of the 67 year-old San Francisco Women in Travel Group; Portion of essay published in Travel Guide for AFA Women, 1997. **Home Addr:** 377 Palm Ave Apt 208, Oakland, CA 94610-3318, **Home Phone:** (510)891-1515. **Business Addr:** Treasurer, Operations Manager, Blue World Travel Corp, 50 First St Suite 411, San Francisco, CA 94104, **Business Phone:** (415)882-9444.

### SPEED, JAMES H., JR.

President (organization), chief executive officer. **Personal:** Born Jun 13, 1953, Oxford, NC. **Educ:** NC Cent Univ, BS, 1975; Atlanta Univ, MBA, 1979; Deloitte & Touche, cert pub acct, 1979. **Career:** Pittsburgh Plate & Glass, staff auditor; Deloitte & Touche, staff acct, 1979-87, sr audit mgr, 1987; Hardee's Food Systs Inc, vpres, 1991-95, sr vpres, 1995-96, chief financial officer & treas, 1996-2000; Speed Financial Group, pres, 2000; NC Mutual Life Ins Co, sr vpres & chief financial officer, 2002-03, pres & chief exec officer, 2003-. **Orgs:** Am Inst Cert Pub Acct; Inst Mgt Accountants; Nat Asn Black Accountants; bd dir, RBC Centura Funds Inc; bd dir, Nottingham Investment Trust II; comn, Bus Laws & Econ; NC Pub Schs Adminr Task Force; bd dir, N Carolina State Bd Communities Schs; bd dir, Communities Schs Rocky Mt Region; bd dir, Cent C's Home N Carolina; trustee, Starboard Investment Trust; NC Chamber Com; Durham Chamber Com; NC Cent Univ Sch Bus; United Way Greater Triangle; UNC Healthcare Systs; Communities Schs NC; Cent C's Home NC Inc; Beta Gamma Sigma Hon Soc, Atlanta Univ; independent trustee, Brown Capital Mgt Mutual Funds, 2002-; dir, Mech & Farmers Bank, 2009-; independent trustee, New Providence Investment Trust, 2009-11; dir, Investors Title Co, 2010;Beta Gamma Sigma Hon Soc. **Business Addr:** President, Chief Executive Officer, North Carolina Mutual Life Insurance Co, 411 W Chapel Hill St, Durham, NC 27701, **Business Phone:** (919)682-9201.

### SPEEDE-FRANKLIN, WANDA A.

School administrator, executive director. **Personal:** Born Aug 1, 1956, Bronx, NY; married Melvin L; children: Ihsan K. **Educ:** Princeton Univ, BA, 1978, cert prof African- Am Studies, 1978; N Western Univ, MA, 1980. **Career:** Princeton Univ, res asst comput ctr, 1974-78, asst dir third world ctr, 1974-78; N western Univ, grad fel, 1978-79; Chicago Metro Hist Fair, assoc dir progs & opers, 1980-82; Nat Asn Independent Schs, dir, minority affairs & info serv, 1982-87; Mass Bay Transp Authority, asst dir admin pub affairs, 1987-88; Newton Metco Prog, dir; Needham Pub Schs, dir. **Orgs:** Trustee, Proj Match Minority Stud Talent Search Agency, 1984-; Nat AsnBlack Sch Educr; Am Asn Affirmative Action; Nat Asn Negro Women; bd mem, Metro Coun Equal Opportunity, 1985-. **Special Achievements:** Co-Author, Visible Now: Blacks in Private Schools, 1988. **Home Addr:** 31 Tonawanda St, Dorchester, MA 02124, **Home Phone:** (617)265-7227.

### SPEIGHT-BUFORD, DR. VELMA R.

School administrator. **Personal:** Born Nov 18, 1932, Snow Hill, NC; daughter of John Thomas Speight and Mable Edwards Speight; married William M; children: T Chineta Kennedy Davis. **Educ:** NC Agr & Tech State Univ, NC, BS, 1953; Univ Md, MEd, guid, 1965; PhD, coun personnel serv, 1976. **Career:** Administrator (retired), association executive; Kennard High Sch, teacher, 1954-60; Morgan State Col, NSF fel, 1956; Univ Md, NSF fel, 1957; Va State Col, NDEA fel, 1963; Kennard High Sch, Queen Anne's Co High Sch, counr, 1960-68; Queen Anne's County High Sch, co-ordr guid dept, 1966-68; Nat Defense Educ Act Inst Disadvantaged Youth; Univ Md, Eastern Shore, staff consult, 1967, Dept Couns Educ, chair, 1986-87, Dept Educ, chair, 1989-93, coord grad prog; Family Life & Sex Educ, Caroline, Kent, Queen Anne's & Talbot County, curric res specialist, 1969; Univ Md, Johns Hopkins Univ, vis prof & assoc prof; Univ Md, Equal Opportunity Recruitment Prog, dir, 1972; Md State Dept Educ, Compensatory Urban & Suppl Prog, asst supr, 1969-72, specialist guid, 1972-76, adminr, 1976, asst state supt, 1982-86; E Carolina Univ, Dept Couns & Adult Educ, chair, 1987; NC Agr & Tech State Univ, dir alumni affairs, 1993-97, bd trustees, 1998-, chmn bd trustee, 2005-. **Orgs:** Life mem, Md State Teachers Asn; Nat Educ Asn; pres, Queen Anne's County Teacher Asn & Educ Asn; Md Asn Counr Educ & Supvr; Md Sch Counr Asn; Am Personnel & Guid Asn; Md Asn Curric Develop, Am Asn Sch Bus Officials; Delmarva Alumni Asn, A&T State Univ; Study Group Mothers Prevent Dropouts; teacher, Summer Courses Black Stud; organizer & chmn, Youth Group Study Probs Integration; Queen Anne's, Kent & Talbot County Comn Action Agency Bd; Md & Nat Cong Parents & Teachers; Nat Asn Advan Colored People; organizer & chmn, Parent Educ Group Commun Rather Than Confrontation; chmn, Christian Social Rels Comt, Weslyan Serv Guild; Asn Sup & Curric Develop; Am Asn Coun & Develop; Asn Counr Educ & Sup; Nat Career Develop Asn; Sch Counr Asn; Am Rehab Coun Asn; Asn Meas & Eval Coun & Develop; Asn Multicultural Coun & Develop; Md Asn Coun & Develop; Md Career Develop Asn; Md Asn Multicultural Coun & Develop; organizer, Black Churches Educ Excellence, 1987-; bd mem, Chancellor Search Comt; Alpha Kappa Alpha Sorority. **Honors/Awds:** Woman of the Year, Negro Bus & Prof Women's Orgn; Alumni Achievement Award, A&T State Univ, 1974; Phi Delta Kappa; Alumni Excellence Award, A&T State Univ, 1982; Presidential Citation to Distinguished Alumni, Nat Asn Equal Opportunity Higher Educ, 1985; Minority Achievement Award, Md State Teachers Asn, 1988; Teacher of the Year, Univ Md Eastern Shore, 1992; Administrator of the Year, NC A&T State Univ, 1997; Hon, DHL, 2006. **Special Achievements:** Author of "Improving the Status of the Culturally Different and Disadvantaged Minority Students" in Gifted Programs, 1988-89. **Home Addr:** 11 Carissa Ct, Greensboro, NC 27407, **Home Phone:** (336)454-8125. **Business Addr:** Chairman, North Carolina Agricultural and Technical State University, 1601 E Mkt St, Greensboro, NC 27411, **Business Phone:** (336)334-7500.

### SPEIGHTS, ESQ. NATHANIEL H.

Lawyer. **Personal:** Born Nov 24, 1949, Bellaire, OH; son of Nathaniel H and Ollie; married Grace E, May 21, 1984; children: Ashley & Nathaniel IV. **Educ:** Col Wooster, Ohio, BA, 1972; Univ Miami, Fla, JD, 1976. **Career:** Speights & Mitchell, partner, atty, currently. **Orgs:** Pres, Wash Bar Asn, 1986-88. **Home Addr:** 3130 Rittenhouse St NW, Washington, DC 20015-1615, **Home Phone:** (202)362-4713. **Business Addr:** Attorney, Partner, Speights & Mitchell, 2600 Va Ave NW Suite 105, Washington, DC 20037-1905, **Business Phone:** (202)337-9800.

### SPELLER, DR. CHARLES K.

Orthopedic surgeon. **Personal:** Born Feb 25, 1933, Windsor, NC; married Virginia S. **Educ:** NC Cent Univ, attended 1954; Meharry Med Col, MD, 1966. **Career:** Monmouth Med Ctr, Long Br, resident; Ill Masonic Hosp, resident; Columbia Univ, internship; pvt pract, surgeon, orthopedician, 1971-. **Orgs:** Harris County Med Soc; Houston Med Forum; Nat Med Asn; Nat Trauma Soc; Sovereign Grand Insp Gen, 33rd & last deg Ancient & Accept Scottish Rite, Free masonry Gen Corp, 1954-56. **Home Addr:** 5035 Heatherglen Dr, Houston, TX 77096-4215, **Home Phone:** (713)721-4645. **Business Addr:** Surgeon, Orthopedician, Private Practice, 5445 Almeda Rd Suite 302, Houston, TX 77004, **Business Phone:** (713)781-7878.

### SPELLMAN, ALONZO ROBERT

Football player, boxer. **Personal:** Born Sep 27, 1971, Mt. Holly, NJ; married Lizzie; children: 3. **Educ:** Ohio State Univ. **Career:** Football player (retired), mixed martial arts fighter; Nat Football League, Chicago Bears, Defensive lineman, 1992-97; Nat Football League, Dallas Cowboys, Defensive lineman, 1999-2000; Nat Football League, Detroit Lions, Defensive lineman, 2001; Arena Football League, Las Vegas Gladiators, Defensive lineman, 2006; Mixed martial arts fighter, currently. **Business Addr:** Mixed Martial Arts Fighter, Chicago, IL 48101.

### SPENCE, DR. DONALD DALE

Dentist. **Personal:** Born Dec 6, 1926, Philadelphia, PA; married Theresa Seltzer; children: Kenneth, Donna, Rosalynn & Melanie. **Educ:** Morris Col, Atlanta, Ga, attended 1950; Howard Univ Sch Dent, DDS, 1960. **Career:** Baptist Univ, Sacred Heart Hosp, staff; pvt pract dentist, currently; First Pensacola Develop Co, vpres. **Orgs:** Bd dir, Pensacola C C. **Special Achievements:** Appointed by the Government of Reubin Asken to Escambia County School Board & is the highest ranking Black Official NW Florida in 1975. **Home Addr:** 1042 Stillbrook Rd, Pensacola, FL 32514-1628. **Business Addr:** Vice President, First Pensacola Development Co, 2280 N 9th Ave, Pensacola, FL 32593.

### SPENCE, REV. JOSEPH SAMUEL, SR.

Lawyer, educator. **Personal:** Born Dec 20, 1950; son of Olive Maud Bambridge and Kenneth John; married Attorney Sheila M; children: Joseph Jr, Joselyn Maria, Jonathan Clarence & Parrish. **Educ:** Pikes Peak Col, AA; Univ Md, BSc; Webster Univ, MA; Washburn Univ Law Sch, 1989; Topeka, KS, JD; Brunnel Univ W London, Brunnel, Eng, int comparative law. **Career:** Century 21 Real Estate, realtor assoc, 1978-80; AUS, capt, 1980-86; Riley County Dist Atty's Off, 1987; City Topeka Atty's Off, 1988-89; Kans State Senate, 1988-89; Milwaukee Area Tech Col, instr, 1991-; Spence Law Offices, Milwaukee, 1992-; Bryant & Stratton Col, instr, currently. **Orgs:** Founder & chapter pres, Lambda Alpha Epsilon Criminal Justice Frat, 1974; Alpha Phi Alpha; Rep-at-large, Frederick Douglass Ctr Manhattan KS, 1986-87, WSBA Washburn Law Sch, 1986-87; Kiwanis Int, 1986-87; marshal, Phi Alpha Delta Law Fraternity, 1986-87; founder & charter pres, Nat Asn Advan Colored People Manhattan KS, 1986; founder & legal adv, Lex Explorer, Washburn Law Sch, 1988; assoc minister, St Mark AME Church; chairperson, Legal Redress Comt Nat Asn Advan Colored People KS, 1987-89; Manhattan KS Chamber Com, 1987-89; Manhattan KS Am Red Cross, 1988-89; Comnr-at-large, Am Bar Asn, 1987-89; Christian Lawyers Asn, 1987-; Christian Legal Soc, 1987-; Ams

United Seperation Church & State, 1987-; Am Bar Asn, 1989-; Nat Bar Asn, 1992-; Am Trial Lawyer Asn, 1993-; Wis Acad Trial Lawyers; Nat Voc Tech Honor Soc, 1999; dist comnr, Boy Scouts Am, 2000; Int Soc Poets; World Haiku Asn. **Home Addr:** PO Box 26342, Milwaukee, WI 53226. **Business Addr:** Instructor, Bryant & Stratton College, 310 W Wisconsin Ave Suite 500 E, Milwaukee, WI 53203, **Business Phone:** (414)276-5200.

### SPENCER, ANTHONY LAWRENCE
Government official. **Personal:** Born Aug 10, 1946, New York, NY; son of Gladys Harrington; married Jeanette Butler; children: Anthony. **Educ:** State Univ NY, BS, polit sci, 1975; Command & Gen Staff Col, attended 1984. **Career:** Inst Mediation & Conflict Resolution, spec asst to pres, 1970-74; State Charter Rev Comm NYC, asst to dir community rels, 1973-74; J P Stevens & Co, tech sales rep, 1975-79; New York Dept State, spec asst to sec state, 1979-85, dep dir gov black affairs adv comm, 1985; State New York Banking Dept, proj dir; Black United Fund New York, vpres corp develop & govt affairs; New York Campaign Finance Bd, 7th Coun Dist, city coun, currently. **Orgs:** Pres, stud body City Col New York, 1972-73; vpres, Christmas Tree Harlem, 1981; bd mem, ML Wilson Boys Club Harlem, 1982-; vpres, Community Bd 9 New York, NY, 1983-84; Men Who Cook; bd dir, Harlem Little League; bd dir, New York Urban League; vpres community develop & eval, Nat Black Leadership Comn AIDS, dir, currently; 100 Black Men Am; 369th Veterans Asn; 555th Parachute Inf Asn Inc; vpres, dir, Hamilton Heights W Harlem Community Preserv Orgn; Dem State Comt, currently. **Honors/Awds:** Distinguished Service Citation, United Negro Col Fund, 1981. **Home Addr:** 470 Lenox Ave Suite 8E, New York, NY 10037. **Business Addr:** City Council, New York City Campaign Finance Board, 100 Church St 12th Fl, New York, NY 10007, **Business Phone:** (212)409-1800.

### SPENCER, BRENDA L.
Industrial engineer, administrator. **Personal:** Born Jul 7, 1951, Youngstown, OH; daughter of Walter and Flonerra; children: Ebony Ayana. **Educ:** Ky State, BS, indust engineering, 1978; Malone Col, BA, bus, 1986. **Career:** Gen Motors, acct, 1973-76; BL Unlimited Engineering & Consult Corp, owner; Repub Steel, indus engr; ITT Tech Inst, dir placement, 1987, dir career serv, 2003. **Orgs:** Nat youth leader, Nal Asn Negro Bus & Prof Women, 1978-80; nat dir, Youth& Young Adults, 1980-82; nat vpres, Prof Women & Young Adults, 1982-85; treas, Kappa Nu Zeta, 1983-85; treas, Zeta Phi Beta, 1983-85; mem chmn, Am Inst Engrs, 1983-84; Nat Coalition Black Meeting Planners; Relig Meeting Planners Conv; Leadership Mahoning Valley. **Home Addr:** 448 Ferndale Ave, PO Box 5814, Youngstown, OH 44511-3206. **Business Addr:** Director of Placement, ITT Technical Institute, 1030 N Meridian Rd, Youngstown, OH 44509, **Business Phone:** (330)270-8333.

### SPENCER, COLLINS ROBERT, III
Television news anchorperson. **Personal:** children: 1. **Educ:** Howard Univ, BA, commun, 1987; Kellogg Sch Mgt, exec mgt prog. **Career:** Miller Brewing Co, commun/PR specialist, 1990-92, state Llobbyist, 1992-93; Capitol Hill, lobbyist, 1993-97; WJLA-TV, ABC, freelance news reporter, 1997, 1999-2000; WTVR-TV, CBS, news anchor/ reporter, 1997-99; Fox News, news corresp, 2000-03; CNN Headline News, news anchor, 2003-05; WSB-TV, Channel 2 Action News This Morning & Channel 2 Action News at Noon, news anchor, 2005-07; Fidelity Int, sr vpres & dir; Aetna Inc, vpres Capital Mgt; Strategic Commun LLC, founder & chief exec officer, 2007-10; Spencer Tyson, Partner & chief exec officer, 2010-11; Spencer Davis LLC, founder, chief consult & chief exec officer, 2010-; Spencer Partners LLC, partner, currently. **Orgs:** Kappa Alpha Psi Fraternity fel; Pub Rels Socs Am; Nat Asn Black Journalists, fel; Big Bros; Habitat Humanity; Cancer Awareness; Mentor Young Entrepreneurs metro Atlanta; 100 Black Men Atlanta; Nat Coalition 100 Black Women/Atlanta; Hosea Feed Hungry & Homeless; St. Jude C's Res Hosp; Juma Ventures; Va Tech Intellectual Property Inc; Nat Asn Securities Professionals. **Business Addr:** Partner, Spencer Partners LLC, PO Box 7333, Bloomfield, CT 06002-7333, **Business Phone:** (888)530-5551.

### SPENCER, FELTON LAFRANCE
Basketball player. **Personal:** Born Jan 5, 1968, Louisville, KY. **Educ:** Univ Louisville, attended 1990. **Career:** Basketball player (retired); Minn Timber wolves, ctr, 1990-93, 1999; Ut Jazz, 1993-96; Orlando Magic, 1996; Golden State Warriors, 1996-99; San Antonio Spurs, 1999-2000; New York Knicks, 2000-02; Spalding Univ, asst coach, 2011; TV Series: "ESPN SportsCentury". **Home Addr:** 4102 Nicholas Roy Ct, Prospect, KY 40059-8209.

### SPENCER, GREGORY RANDALL
Executive. **Personal:** Born Dec 31, 1948, Washington, PA; son of William H and Anna Mae; married Janet O; children: Tammy Michelle & Michael. **Educ:** Univ Pittsburgh, BA, pub admin, 1980; St Francis Col, MA, indust rels, 1984. **Career:** US Steel, gen mgr human resources, 1971-93; AMSCO Int Inc, vpres human resources, 1993-94; Equitable Resources Inc, sr vpres & chief admin officer, 1994-2003; Minority Enterprise Corp, bd dirs, 1997; Eric Dickerson Assocs LLC, adv comt; Randall Enterprises LLC, pres & chief exec officer, 2004-. **Orgs:** Past chmn, African Am Chamber Com Western Pa; bd dir, Pittsburgh Found; Leadership Pittsburgh, 1997; bd dir, Inst Transfusion Med, 1998-; bd trustee, Robert Morris Univ; bd trustee, St. Paul AME Church; bd dir, Urban League Pittsburgh; chmn bd, pres, Hill House Asn; bd dir, NEED; chmn, Minority & Women Educ Labor Agency; exec dir, Manchester Youth Develop Ctr; Urban Youth Action Inc; Chester Engineers Inc; trustee, Propel Schs; chmn, Iota Phi Found Omega Psi Phi Fraternity. **Home Addr:** 1020 Devonshire Rd, Pittsburgh, PA 15217, **Home Phone:** (412)687-8061. **Business Addr:** President, Chief Executive Officer, Randall Enterprises LLC, 1401 Forbes Ave Forbes & Stevenson Suite 201, Pittsburgh, PA 15219, **Business Phone:** (412)281-6903.

### SPENCER, JAMES RANDOLPH
Judge. **Personal:** Born Mar 25, 1949, Florence, SC; married Margaret Poles; children: 3. **Educ:** Clark Col, Atlanta, GA, BA, 1971; Harvard Law Sch, JD, 1974; Howard Univ, Mdiv, 1985. **Career:** Atlanta Legal Aid Soc, staff atty, 1974-75; Dist Columbia, asst US atty, 1978-83; Eastern Dist Va, asst US dist atty, 1983-86, US Dist judge, 1986-04, chief judge, 2004-. **Orgs:** Omega Psi Phi; Sigma Pi Phi; Phi Beta Kappa; Alpha Kappa Mu. **Business Addr:** Chief Judge, United States District Court, 1000 E Main St No 307, Richmond, VA 23219-3525, **Business Phone:** (804)916-2700.

### SPENCER, JIMMY, JR. (JAMES ARTHUR SPENCER)
Football player, football coach. **Personal:** Born Mar 29, 1969, Manning, SC. **Educ:** Univ Fla. **Career:** Football player (retired), football coach; New Orleans Saints, defensive back, 1992-93, left cornerback, 1994-95; Cincinnati Bengals, right cornerback, 1996-97; San Diego Chargers, defensive back, 1998, right & left defensive back, 1999; Denver Broncos, corner back & left cornerback, 2000, right cornerback, 2001, 2002, linebacker & right cornerback, 2003, left cornerback, asst defensive backs coach, asst defensive back coach, 2005-06. **Home Addr:** , Parker, CO.

### SPENCER, LARRY LEE
Manager, administrator, executive director. **Personal:** Born Jan 1, 1948?, Columbus, OH; son of Hezekiah and Elizabeth; children: Tangelia Spencer Palmer, Mark & Sharese. **Educ:** Franklin Univ, BS, bus admin, 1983. **Career:** Franklin C Dept Human Servs, contract negotiator, 1976-88; Ohio Dept Ment Health, mgt analyst, 1988; United Way Franklin C, sr mgr, Proj Diversity, proj dir, currently. **Orgs:** Bd mem, Westside/Eastside Child Care Ctr Asn, 1988-90; bd mem, Leadership Worthington, 1991-; outreach comt mem, Nat Black Programming Consortium, 1991-; Dept Health, Minority AIDS Comt, 1992-; Ment Health State Afro Centric Conf Planning Comt; Worthington Community Multicultural Comt; Worthington Community Rels Comn, 1994-; chair, Players Theatre Adv Comt. **Home Addr:** 7341 Downey Dr, Columbus, OH 43215, **Home Phone:** (614)766-0703. **Business Addr:** Project Director, United Way of Franklin County, 360 S 3rd St, Columbus, OH 43215, **Business Phone:** (614)227-2740.

### SPENCER, LITA. See RICHARDSON, LITA RENEE.

### SPENCER, PROF. MARGARET BEALE
Educator, psychologist. **Personal:** Born Sep 5, 1944, Philadelphia, PA; daughter of Junius Alton and Elizabeth Rebecca Beale; married Charles L; children: Tirzah Renee, Natasha Ann & Charles Asramon. **Educ:** Temple Univ Col Pharm, BS, 1967; Univ Kans, MA, psychol, 1970; Univ Chicago, PhD, child & develop psychol, 1976. **Career:** Univ Kans Med Ctr, regist pharmacist, 1967-69; Univ Chicago, res proj dir, 1974-77, Dept Comparative Human Develop, Marshall Field IV prof urban educ & prof, 2009-; Morehouse Sch Med, clin assoc prof, 1982-89; Emory Univ, fac, 1977-93; Univ Pa, endowed chair, bd overseers, prof educ, 1993-; fel, 2006 Fletcher, US supreme courts brown V bd Educ. **Orgs:** Consult & comt, Found Child Develop, 1981-85, trustee, 1997-; consult, Fulton County, Ga Health Dept, 1983-89; bd exec comt, Fulton County Black Family Proj, 1983-88; bd, S DeKalb County, YMCA, 1984-86; WT Grant Found, 1986-93; Nat Black Child Develop Inst, bd mem, 1986-92; Ctr Successful Child Develop, 1986-88; comt chmn, Soc Res Child Develop, 1987-89; trustee & bd mem, White-Williams Found, 1994-; ed rev bd mem, J Appl Develop Psychol, 1992-; ed rev bd mem, Cambridge Univ Press, Develop & psychopath, 1994-; bd sci affairs, Am Psychol Asn, 1991-94; ed adv bd, C, Youth & Chg: Sociocultural Perspectives, 1994-; adv bd, Ctr Study Context, Generations, & Ment Health, 1994-; adv bd, Ctr Youth Develop & Policy Res; bd mem, Acad Educ Develop, 1993; adv bd, CRESPAR, 1997; dir, Ctr Health, Achievement, Neighborhood, Growth & Ethnic Studies (CHANGES); dir, W E B Dubois Collective Res, U Penn. **Honors/Awds:** Grant Research Support, Spencer, Ford, Commonwealth & WT Grant Found, 1984-87; Award for Service, DeKalb County, GA, YMCA, 1985; Outstanding Service Award, Delta Sigma Theta Sorority, Decatur Alumnae Chap, 1986; Fellow Status, Div 7, 15, 45, Am Psychol Asn. **Special Achievements:** Author: Beginnings: The Affective and Social Development of Black Children, LEA Publishing, 1985; Ethnicity & Diversity: Minorities No More, LEA, in press; Over 100 published approximately articles & chapters; Authored Several Books. **Home Addr:** 737 Cornelia Pl, Philadelphia, PA 19118-4108, **Home Phone:** (215)242-9507. **Business Addr:** Professor of Education and Psychology, Marshall Field IV Professor, The University of Chicago, Rm 418 Off 103 1126 E 59th St, Chicago, IL 60637, **Business Phone:** (773)702-3971.

### SPENCER, MARIAN ALEXANDER
Activist. **Personal:** Born Jun 28, 1920, Gallipolis, OH; married Donald Andrew Sr; children: Donald Jr & Edward Alexander. **Educ:** Univ Cincinnati, BA, Eng, 1942. **Career:** Cincinnati City Coun, Law Comn, City Planning Comn, vice chairperson, vice mayor, 1983; Community servant & civil rights activist, currently. **Orgs:** Life mem, Nat Asn Advan Colored People, chair; Chairperson, Human Resources Comn, Urban Develop Planning Zoning & Housing Comn, life mem, Alpha Kappa Alpha Sor; pres, Cincinnati Chap Links Inc, 1968-70; pres, Woman's City Club; trustee, Univ Cincinnati, 1975-79; Greater Cincinnati Occup Health Ctr Bd; adv bd, WGUC Radio Sta; pub rels comn & personnel comn, Planned Parenthood; Mt Zion United Methodist Church; vpres, Housing Opportunities Made Equal Bd; chairperson, sub comt, Discipline Task Force, Cincinnati Pub Schs; bd mem, Ctr Voting & Democracy; Nat Hon Soc. **Honors/Awds:** Career Woman of Achievement Award, YWCA, 1984; Community Activist Award, A Phillip Randolph Inst Greater Cincinnati, 1992; Jacob E Davis Vol Award, Greater Cincinnati Found, 1993; Glorifying the Lions Club, Urban League, 1994; Award recipient, Ctr Voting & Democracy, 1995; Brotherhood Award, Nat Conf Christians & Jews; Woman of the Year Award, Cincinnati Enquirer; Black Excellence Award, PUSH; Ethelrie Harper Award, Cincinnati Human Rels Comn; Distinguished Alumna Award, Alumna Asn Univ Cincinnati; State of Ohio Award, ACLU; Humanitarian Award, Freedom Heritage Found; Cincinnati Enquirer Woman of the Year Award; Hon Doctorate Humane, Univ Cincinnati, 2006. **Special Achievements:** Recognized by the Cincinnati Post as one of the 12 Most Influential Women in the City of Cincinnati, recently inducted into the OH Women's Hall of Fame, first African American woman elected to the Cincinnati City Council, First female president of the Cincinnati branch, NAACP, honored by Black Career Women. **Home Addr:** 940 Lexington Ave, Cincinnati, OH 45229.

### SPENCER, DR. MICHAEL GREGG
Engineer, college teacher. **Personal:** Born Mar 9, 1952, Detroit, MI; son of Thomas and Laura Lee; children: Thomas Lewis. **Educ:** Cornell Univ, Ithaca, NY, BS, elec engineering, 1974, ME, elec engineering, 1975, PhD, elec & commun engineering, 1981. **Career:** Gen Elec, Syracuse, NY, co-op engr, 1972-73; Bell Lab, Whippany, NJ, mem tech staff, 1974-77; Howard Univ, Wash, DC, asst prof, 1981-85, assoc prof, 1985, prof, currently, dept Elec Engineering, Mat Sci Res Ctr Excellence, dir, 1987-; SIMNET Lab, co-dir, 1987-; Cornell Univ, Col Eng, asst dean, prof, 2005-, Ctr Nanoscale Systs, Cornell Ctr Mat Researc, Nanobiotechnology Ctr. **Orgs:** Officer, Nat Soc Black Engrs, 1977-; Nat Sci Found proposal rev comm, 1984-, adv coun Elec Engineering & comput systs, 1988, adv comm mat res, 1989-; Am Vacuum Soc, 1985-; officer, Electron Device Soc Inst Elec & Electronics Engrs, 1987-; fac fel, David R. Atkinson Ctr for a Sustainable Future, Atkinson Ctr. **Home Addr:** 1006 Urell Pl NE, Washington, DC 20017-2139, **Home Phone:** (202)832-3557. **Business Addr:** Professor, Cornell University, 418 Phillips Hall, Ithaca, NY 14850, **Business Phone:** (607)254-636.

### SPENCER, OCTAVIA
Actor. **Personal:** Born May 25, 1972, Montgomery, AL. **Educ:** Auburn Univ, BS, lib arts, 1994. **Career:** Films: A Time to Kill, staff asst, 1996; The Sixth Man, 1997; Sparkler, 1997; Never Been Kissed, 1999; American Virgin, 1999; Being John Malkovich, 1999; Blue Streak, 1999; Everything Put Together, 2000; What Planet Are You From?, 2000; Big Momma's House, 2000; Four Dogs Playing Poker, 2000; The Journeyman, 2001; The Sky is Falling, 2001; Spider-Man, 2002; Legally Blonde 2: Red, White & Blonde, 2003; S.W.A.T., 2003; Sol Goode, 2003; Bad Santa, 2003; Win a Date with Tad Hamilton!, 2004; Breakin' All the Rules, 2004; Coach Carter, 2005; Pretty Persuasion, 2005; Marilyn Hotchkiss' Ballroom Dancing & Charm School, 2005; Miss Congeniality 2: Armed and Fabulous, 2005; Beauty Shop, 2005; Wannabe, 2005; Pulse, 2006; The Nines, 2007; Next of Kin, 2008; Pretty Ugly People, 2008; Seven Pounds, 2008; Love at First Hiccup, 2009; Drag Me to Hell, 2009; Jesus People: The Movie, 2009; The Soloist, 2009; Just Peck, 2009; Halloween II, 2009; Herpes Boy, 2009; Small Town Saturday Night, 2010; Dinner for Schmucks, 2010; Peep World, 2010; Girls! Girls! Girls!, 2011; Flypaper, 2011; The Help, 2011; Blues for Willadean, 2012; Smashed, 2012; Fruitvale Station, 2013; Lost on Purpose, 2013; Snowpiercer, 2013; Percy Jackson: Sea of Monsters, 2013; Paradise, 2013; Get on Up, 2014; Black and White, 2014. TV series: "Moesha", 1998; "To Have & to Hold", 1998; "ER", 1998; "Brimstone", 1999; "Lansky", 1999; "L.A. Doctors", 1999; "Chicago Hope", 1999; "Roswell", 1999; "The X-Files", 1999; "Chicken Soup for the Soul", 2000; "Missing Pieces", 2000; "Just Shoot Me!", 2000; "Becker", 2000; "Malcolm in the Middle", 2000; "City of Angels", 2000; "Grounded for Life", 2001; "Follow the Stars Home", 2001; "Dharma & Greg", 2001; "The Chronicle", 2001-02; "Titus", 2001-02; "Little John", 2002; "NYPD Blue", 2002-05; "LAX", 2004-05; "CSI: NY", 2005; "Medium", 2005; "Huff", 2006; "Ugly Betty", 2007; "Halfway Home", 2007; "The Minor Accomplishments of Jackie Woodman", 2006-07; "Wizards of Waverly Place", 2008; "CSI: Crime Scene Investigation", 2008; "The Big Bang Theory", 2008; "Faux Baby", 2008; "Worst Week", 2009; "Dollhouse", 2009; "Raising the Bar", 2009; "Hawthorne", 2010; "Family Practice", 2011; "The Looney Tunes Show", 2011; "30 Rock", 2013; "American Dad!", 2013; "Call Me Crazy: A Five Film", 2013; "Mom", 2013-14; "Red Band Society", 2014. **Honors/Awds:** Outstanding Performance by a Cast in a Motion Picture, Outstanding Performance by a Female Actor in a Supporting Role, Screen Actors Guild Awards, 2011; Best Performance by an Actress in a Supporting Role, Oscar, 2011; Best Supporting Actress, BAFTA Awards, 2011; Best Performance by an Actress in a Supporting Role in a Motion Picture, Golden Globe, 2012. **Special Achievements:** Co-author of children's mystery book, "The Rock Holler Gang: Junior Detectives," 2002; 25 Funniest Actresses in Hollywood, Entertainment Weekly, 2009.

### SPENCER, SHARON A.
Physician, educator. **Personal:** Born Birmingham, AL; daughter of Otis Sr and Annie M Rice. **Educ:** Birmingham Southern Col, Birmingham, AL, BS, chem, 1979; Univ Ala Sch Med, Birmingham, AL, MD, 1983. **Career:** Univ Ala, Birmingham, AL, resident, 1983-87, asst prof, 1989-; Univ Ala Hosp, Dept Radiation Oncol, clin dir, prof & Ruby Meredith Outstanding Clinician Endowed chair, currently; Am Socs for Radiation Oncol, Mgt of Post Oper Head, Neck & Reirradiation. **Orgs:** Am Bd Radiol; Phi Beta Kappa, 1979; Therapeut Radiol, 1988; fel Am Col Radiation Oncol, 2000. **Business Addr:** Professor, University of Alabama at Birmingham, Wallace Tumor Inst 114, Birmingham, AL 35233, **Business Phone:** (205)934-5670.

### SPENCER, TRACIE MONIQUE
Singer, actor. **Personal:** Born Jul 12, 1976, Waterloo, IA. **Career:** Albums: Tracie Spencer, 1988; Make the Difference, 1990; Love High, 1998; Tracie, 1999; The Longest Yard, 2005; Film; A Tale of Two Sisters, 2004; TV series: "ZDF Hit parade", 1988, "It's Show time at the Apollo", 1989; "Ebony/Jet Showcase", 1989-91; "1991 Billboard Music Awards", 1991; "NBA All-Star Stay in School Jam", 1992; "Family Matters", 1993; "VH-1 Where Are They Now?", 2002; Singles: "Symptoms of True Love", 1988; "Hide and Seek", 1988; "Imagine", 1989; "Save Your Love", 1990; "This House", 1990; "This Time Make It Funky", 1991; "Tender Kisses", 1991; "Love Me", 1992; "It's All About You (Not About Me)", 1999; "Still in My Heart", 2000. **Honors/Awds:** Martin Luther King Christian Leadership Award. **Special Achievements:** Has appeared on "The Arsenio Hall Show" & "Star Search"; toured with New Kids on the Block & Kid N' Play. **Business Addr:** Singer, c/o Capitol Records Incorporation, 1750 N Vine St, Hollywood, CA 90028, **Business Phone:** (213)462-6252.

### SPICER, KENNETH, SR.
Government official, president (organization), chief executive officer. **Personal:** Born Aug 21, 1949, Jacksonville, FL; son of Reba McKinney; married Patricia A Baker; children: Kenneth, Sherry & Michelle. **Educ:** Bethune Cookman Univ, BS, bus admin, 1971; Univ Mass, MS, pub affairs, 1992; N eastern Univ, PhD, law policy & soc, 1993; Har-

vard Univ, JFK Sch Govt, attended 1994. **Career:** S Fla Employ Training Consortium, dir pub serv employ, 1980, diropers, 1980-81; Dade County JMH Community Ment Health Ctr, dir opers & finance, 1981; Dade County Haitian Am Community Health Ctr, exec dir, 1982-85; Off city mgr, dir minority bus enterprise, 1985-86; EOCD, Off Secy, asst to cabinet secy affirmative action, 1986-91; Commonwealth Mass, Dept Housing & Community Develop, Off Affirmative Action, dir, 1986-91, Bur Neighborhoods, dir, 1991-99, Div Neighborhoods, assoc dir, 1999-2001; Ctr Health & Develop Inc, pres & chief exec officer, 2001-11; Medicaid & MassHealth, dir, 2014-. **Orgs:** Alpha Phi Alpha Fraternity, 1971-; founding mem, Boston Chap, Nat Forum Black Pub Admin Inc; Equal Opportunity, diversity consult, Oxf am Am, Boston Off. **Honors/Awds:** Appreciation Award, Boston Chap, Nat Forum Black Pub Admin, 1989; Appreciation Award, State Mass, 1989; Gov Quality Control Comt, 1993; Urban Edge Community Service Award, 1994; Self Sufficiency Award, Mass County Action Prog Exec Dir Asn, 1998; Grove HAV CDC Supporter of the Year Award, 1999; Recognition Award, Chelsea's Comn Hosp Affairs, 1999. **Home Addr:** 804 Norwest Dr, Norwood, MA 02062-1485, **Home Phone:** (781)352-0578. **Business Addr:** Director, MassHealth Customer Service, PO Box 9162, Canton, MA 02021, **Business Phone:** (800)841-2900.

### SPICER, OSKER, JR.
Journalist. **Personal:** Born Apr 12, 1949, Memphis, TN; son of Rosa Hall Sias; married Marion Wilson; children: Aki L. **Educ:** Lincoln Univ, Jefferson City, MO, jour maj, 1969; Morehouse Col, Atlanta, GA, BA, 1972; Columbia Univ, New York, NY, summer prog minority journalists, 1973; Atlanta Univ, Atlanta, GA, grad studies afro-am studies, 1984. **Career:** Atlanta Daily World, Atlanta, Ga, reporter & night city ed, 1970-72, 1976-77; Pittsburgh Courier, Pittsburgh, Pa, city ed, 1974-75; WCLK Radio, Atlanta, Ga, producer & announcer & news dir, 1976-81; Clark Col, Atlanta, Ga, jour instr, 1978-81, 1984; Charlotte News-Observer, Charlotte, NC, reporter, 1982-84; The Dem, Tallahassee, Fla, reporter & columnist, 1984-87; The Oregonian, Portland, Ore, copy ed & columnist, 1987-. **Orgs:** Morehouse Alumni Asn; Inst Jour Educ; bd mem, local chap, Soc Prof Journalists, 1980-; Asian-Am Journalists Asn; bd mem & charter mem, Portland Asn Black Journalists, 1990-; dir, Region X, Nat Asn Black Journalists; Int Fedn Journalists, 1990-; IRE; bd mem, W Coast Regional dir, Nat Asn Black Journalists, 1995-97; nat bd mem, 9th & 10th Cav Asn The Buffalo Soldiers, chap pres. **Honors/Awds:** Producer of the Year, WCLK Radio, 1979; Journalistic Excellence, Tallahassee Chamber, 1986-87. **Home Addr:** 8640 SE Causey Ave Suite N202, Portland, OR 97266, **Home Phone:** (503)654-4406. **Business Addr:** Copy Editor-Columnist, The Oregonian, 1320 SW Broadway, Portland, OR 97201, **Business Phone:** (503)221-8570.

### SPIGHT, BENITA L.
Executive. **Personal:** Born Apr 21, 1963, Detroit, MI; daughter of James Easterling Jr and Margaret Louise Lindsey McCray; married Brian Wesley; children: Richard Allen II & Brandon Noah. **Educ:** Univ Mich, psychol, 1985, Sch Bus Admin, cert, 1990; Univ Denver, Pub Inst, cert, 1991. **Career:** Consol Data Tech, Dearborn, Mich, clerical supvr, 1986-88; Thomson Gale Group Inc, Detroit, Mich, sr credit & acct serv rep, 1988-90, data entry supvr, 1990-93, mgr, 1993-95, corp team & work redesign, trainer, 1993-98 & dir, human resources, 1995-99; Int Thomson Publ, leadership trainer & facilitator, 1995, hr mgr corp redesign implementation, 1996-99, dir, ed serv, 1999-2002, vpres & ed serv; Menttium, alumni, 2000-; Thomson Learning & Reuters, vpres, ed serv, 2000-05; Cengage Learning, exec dir, global rights & permissions, 2006-09; Am Soc Picture Professionals, 2012; Houghton Mifflin Harcourt Publ, vpres, permissions licensing & image serv, 2010-13 & sr vpres, content develop shared serv, 2013-; Software & Info Indust Assoc, Copyright & Licensing Working Group, 2013; Global Intelligence, procurement leader, 2014; Int Assoc Contract Mgt, 2014-. **Orgs:** Nat Asn Advan Colored People, Univ Mich Br, 1982-83; Data Entry Mgt Asn, 1990-93; Detroit Zool Soc, 1992-; Asn Work Process Improv, 1993-95; Am Soc Training & Develop, 1998-; AIIM, 2000-; N Am Serials Interest Group, 2002-; Rights & Permissions Adv Coun, 2012; bd mem, Bookbuilders Boston, 2015-. **Business Addr:** Senior Vice President, Houghton Mifflin Harcourt, 1900 S Batavia Ave, Geneva, IL 60134-3399, **Business Phone:** (630)232-2550.

### SPIGNER, DR. CLARENCE
Research scientist, teacher. **Personal:** Born Mar 19, 1946, Orangeburg, SC; son of Willie and Carrie McDonald; married Jennifer Rosario. **Educ:** Santa Monica Col, Santa Monica, CA, AA, social studies, 1976; Univ Calif, Berkeley, CA, AB, sociol, 1979, MPH, behav sci, 1982, DrPH, behav sci, 1987. **Career:** Nat Health Serv, London, Eng, researcher, planner, 1982-83; Univ Calif, Berkeley, CA, fitness supvr, 1983-86, teaching asst, fel, lectr, 1984-88, Chancellor's fel, 1987; Univ Ore, Eugene, OR, asst prof, 1988-94; Univ Wash, Dept Health Servs, assoc prof, MIRT Prog, co-dir, currently, adj assoc prof, Am Ethnic Studies, London Study Abroad Prog, dir, adj prof am ethnic studies & global health, currently. **Orgs:** Phi Beta Kappa Hon Soc, 1979-; evaluator, Am Heart Asn, Marin, CA, 1981-82; steering comt mem, Clergy & Laity Concerned, 1990-94; Friars Sr Hon Soc, Univ Ore, 1990; Univ Ore, Substance Abuse Adv Bd, 1990-92, Affirmative Action Task Force, 1990-, chmn, Coun Minority Educ, 1990-91; chmn, Spec Comn Minority Fac, Univ Wash, 1996-99; chmn, Minority Int Res Training Prog, 2002-5, Dir Study Abroad, 2007-. **Honors/Awds:** Henrik Blum Distinguished Service Award, Univ Calif, Berkeley, 1987; Outstanding Faculty Award, Off Multicultural Affairs, Univ Ore, 1990. **Special Achievements:** More than 50 publications in peer-reviewed health journals; Professor of Public Health; Study Abroad director. **Home Addr:** 6029 38th Ave NE, Seattle, WA 98115. **Business Addr:** Professor, Adjunct Professor, University of Washington, H692 Health Sci Bldg 1959 NE Pac St, Seattle, WA 98195-7660, **Business Phone:** (206)616-2948.

### SPIGNER, DR. DONALD WAYNE
Physician. **Personal:** Born Feb 14, 1940, Tyler, TX; son of Jessie Lee McCauley and Kermit; married Carol Wilson; children: Nicole Adeyinka & Danielle Khadeja. **Educ:** Univ CA Riverside, BS, 1962; Univ CA San Francisco, MD, 1966; Acad Family Pract, bd cert. **Career:** Los Angeles City Govt Hosp, Internship, 1967; Los Angeles Co-Usc Med Ctr, resident; US Peace Corp, physician, 1967-69, med dir, Africa Div, 1969-70; Pilot City Health Ctr, proj dir, 1970-73; Univ MN Sch Med, assoc prof, 1973-75; Univ MN Sch Pub Health, lectr, 1973-75; Hamilton Health Ctr, med dir, 1975-87; Comm Med Assoc, pres; Univ PA Hershey Med Ctr, assoc prof, 1975-; City Harrisburg, city health officer, 1977-80; Keystone Peer Rev, part-time reviewer, 1986-; Blue Shield PA, med dir. **Orgs:** Bd mem, Pa Med Soc Liability Ins Co; Consult Africa Care, 1975-85; partner, 3540 N Progress Assoc, 1980-; Boys Club, 1982-; partner, Keystone Assocs, 1984-; pres, Dauphin Cty Med Soc, 1984-; Dauphin City MH 7 MR Bd, 1984-86; St Paul Baptist Church; Adv Bd Pa State Univ, Harrisburg Campus; Pa State Bd Podiatry; bd dir, founder, S Cent Pa Sickle Cell Coun. **Honors/Awds:** Selected to represent Univ of CA Riverside on Project India, 1961. **Special Achievements:** Videotape on African & Amer Folk medicine, 1977. **Home Addr:** 2406 Valley Rd, Harrisburg, PA 17104, **Home Phone:** (717)234-9425. **Business Addr:** President, Community Medical Association, 3601 N Progress Ave Suite 100, Harrisburg, PA 17110, **Business Phone:** (717)652-7266.

### SPIGNER, MARCUS E.
Government official. **Career:** US Postal Serv, postmaster, 1997-. **Orgs:** PHA-Masons; treas, Sabre League No 7. **Business Addr:** Postmaster, United States Postal Service, 141 N Palmetto Ave, Eagle, ID 83616, **Business Phone:** (208)939-7982.

### SPIKES, DR. DELORES RICHARD. See Obituaries Section.

### SPIKES, IRVING E., SR.
Football player, football coach. **Personal:** Born Dec 21, 1970, Ocean Springs, MS; married Stacey; children: Ices & Irving Jr. **Educ:** Ala Univ; Univ La Monroe. **Career:** Football player (retired), coach, teacher; Miami Dolphins, running back, 1994, 1995, kick returner, 1996-97; Resurrection Cath Sch, substitute teacher & vol asst football coach. **Business Addr:** Substitute Teacher, Volunteer Assistant Football Coach, Resurrection Catholic School, 520 Watts Ave, Pascagoula, MS 39567, **Business Phone:** (228)762-0282.

### SPIKES, TAKEO GERARD
Football player. **Personal:** Born Dec 17, 1976, Augusta, GA; son of Jimmie (deceased) and Lillie; children: Jakai. **Educ:** Auburn Univ, BA, lib arts. **Career:** Cincinnati Bengals, right inside linebacker, 1998-99, linebacker, 1999-2002; Buffalo Bills, linebacker, 2003-06; Philadelphia Eagles, linebacker, 2007-08; San Francisco 49ers, linebacker, 2008-10, left inside linebacker, 2008; San Diego Chargers, linebacker, 2011-13; NBC Sports Network, football analyst, currently, SiriusXM NFL progs, co-host, currently. **Honors/Awds:** Georgia Player of the Year, Atlanta Jour-Const; Defensive Player of the Year, Football News, 1997; All-American, Parade & US Today; Mr. Football; Pro Bowl, 2003, 2004; All-Pro, 2003, 2004; Ed Block Courage Award, 2006. **Special Achievements:** TV appearance: V.I.P., 2002; Bell Rung, 2012; Bizarre Bracket Behavior, 2013. **Business Addr:** Football Analyst, NBC Sports Network.

### SPINDERELLA, DJ. See ROPER, DEIDRE MURIEL.

### SPINKS, MICHAEL
Boxer. **Personal:** Born Jul 13, 1956, St. Louis, MO; married Sandy Massey; children: Michelle. **Career:** Boxer (retired), actor; prof boxer, 1976-88; actor. **Home Addr:** , St. Louis, MO.

### SPIRES, GREGORY TYRONE
Football player. **Personal:** Born Aug 12, 1974, Marianna, FL; married Alzadia Jordan; children: Leila. **Educ:** Fla State Univ, grad. **Career:** Football player (retired); New Eng Patriots, defensive end, 1998-2000; Cleveland Browns, defensive end, 2001; Tampa Bay Buccaneers, left defensive end, 2002-07, defensive tackle, 2004; Oakland Raiders, 2008. **Honors/Awds:** District Player of the Year; All-Region hons; Super Bowl Champion (XXXVII). **Home Addr:** , Cypress, TX.

### SPIVA, DR. ULYSSES VAN. See Obituaries Section.

### SPIVEY, DR. DONALD
Educator. **Personal:** Born Jul 18, 1948, Chicago, IL; married Diane Marie; children: 2. **Educ:** Univ Ill, BA, hist, 1971, MA, hist, 1972; Univ Calif, PhD, hist, 1976. **Career:** Univ Ill, dept elem educ, res asst, 1971-72; Univ Calif, dept hist teaching asst, 1972-74; Sacramento CA, music instr, 1972-74; Univ Calif, Davis, lectr hist, 1975-76; Wright State Univ, asst prof hist, 1976-79; Univ Mich, vis asst prof hist, 1978-79; Univ Conn, from assoc prof to prof hist, 1979-90, dir, Inst African-Am Studies, 1990-; Am Coun Learned Socs, res grant, 1980; Univ Conn, res found grant, 1983-84; Univ Miami, chmn dept, prof hist, 1993-. **Orgs:** Pres Comm Human Rels, Univ Conn, 1984-85; Asn Study Afro-Am Life & Hist; Orgn Am Historians; Am Hist Asn; Popular Cult Asn; Southwest Social Sci Asn; Nat Coun Black Studies; Southern Hist Asn; N Am Soc Hist Sport; bd trustee, Conn Hist Soc; Conn Acad Arts & Sci; Phi Beta Kappa; Phi Kappa Phi. **Home Addr:** 169 N Canaan St, Hartford, CT 06112. **Business Addr:** Director, University of Connecticut, Rm 610 Ashe, Storrs, CT 06268, **Business Phone:** (305)284-2737.

### SPOONER, ALLAN M.
President (organization). **Educ:** Dartmouth Col, AB, engineering sci, 1989; Univ Chicago, MBA, finance & policy studies, 1994. **Career:** St John Providence Health Syst, vice pres bus & corp develop, 2003-07; St John Hosp & Med Ctr, vpres bus develop, currently; Cath Healthcare W, chief strategy officer, 2007-13, vpres Strategy & Bus Develop; Dignity Health, pres & chief exec officer, 2011-12; Columbia St. Mary's, pres, Hosp Div, 2012-; St Rose Dominican Hospita, interim pres & chief exec officer, 2011-; Ascension Health, vpres; Tenet Health System, tenure; KPMG Peat Marwick, consult. **Orgs:** Bd mem, Detroit Pub Sch, 2005-. bd mem, Am Red Cross; bd mem, Family Ctr. **Business Addr:** President, Columbia St. Mary's Hospitals, 2301 N Lake Dr, Milwaukee, WI 53211, **Business Phone:** (414)291-1000.

### SPOONER, RICHARD C.
Lawyer. **Personal:** Born Jul 3, 1945, New York, NY. **Educ:** NY Univ, BA, 1970; Fordham Univ Sch Law, JD, 1975. **Career:** Community Develop Agency, dir prog plan, 1970-71; Human Resources Admin NYC, spec asst to gen coun, 1972-75; Carroll & Reid, assoc, 1975-77; Chem Bank, vpres & sr coun. **Orgs:** Am Bar Asn, 1977-; Nat Bar Asn, 1979-; bd dir, Urban Bankers Coalition, 1980-84, gen coun, 1981-85, int vpres, 1983; vpres finance, Metro Black Bar Asn, 1985. **Business Addr:** Vice President, Counsel, Chemical Bank, 380 Madison Ave, New York, NY 10016, **Business Phone:** (212)309-4138.

### SPOONER, COL. RICHARD EDWARD
Military leader. **Personal:** Born Sep 15, 1946, Dayton, OH; son of Marie and Lavoy; married Cora; children: Angela & Tracey. **Educ:** USAF Acad, Colo, BS, engineering, 1969; Univ Utah, MS, human resource mgt, 1977; Air Command & Staff Col, attended 1980; Nat Security Mgt Course, 1989; Harvard Univ, Cambridge, MA, nat & int security mgt, 1996. **Career:** Director (retired), military leader; Mather Afb, Calif, stud, navigator training, 1970-71; Castle Afb, Calif, stud, combat crew training, 1971; Barksdale Afb, La, KC-135 navigator, 1971-73; George Afb, Calif, F-4 weapons systs officer training, 1973-74; Ubon Airfield, Thailand, F-4 weapons systs officer, 435th Tactical Fighter, 1974; Udorn Royal Thai Afb, Thailand, F-4 squadron instr weapons systs officer, 13th Tactical Fighter Squadron, 1974-75; Raf Sta, Lakenheath, Eng, chief training, weapons systs officer, 1975-76; Luke Afb, Ariz, chief acad scheduling, 1976-78, squadron asst oper officer F-4, 1978-79; Andrews Afb, Md, wing electronic warfare officer, F-105, 1979-81, F-4 navigator instr, 1981-84, F-4 weapons systs officer, 1984-86, asst opers officer, 1986-88, F-4 flight comdr instr weapons systs officer, 1988-89, dep comdr support, 1989-91, dep comdr support, 113th Fighter Wing, 1991-93, dep comndg gen, 1993-2000; Lockheed Martin, dir, 1995-2003; Nat Guard Bur, Arlington, Va, dir, 2003-. **Orgs:** Tuskegee Airmen Inc; Air Force Asn; Nat Mil Intel Asn. **Honors/Awds:** Distinguished Service Medal; Legion Merit; Meritorious Service Medal with two oak leaf clusters; Air Medal; Air Force Commendation Medal with one oak leaf cluster; Combat Readiness Medal with one silver oak leaf cluster; National Defense Service Medal with one bronze star; Vietnam Service Medal; Republic Vietnam Gallantry Cross with Palm; Republic Vietnam Campaign Medal with Bronze Star; Who's Who/Black Engineers of America, Howard Univ, 1972. **Home Addr:** 15447 Silvan Glen Dr, Montclair, VA 22026, **Home Phone:** (703)670-6832. **Business Addr:** Director C4 Systems Division, National Guard, 1411 Jefferson Davis Hwy, Arlington, VA 22202-3231, **Business Phone:** (703)607-5900.

### SPRADLEY, FRANK SANFORD
Educator. **Personal:** Born Oct 7, 1946, New Rochelle, NY; son of Frank and Mary Williams Baker; married Patricia A Jones; children: Ayinde, Omolara, Ife & Naima. **Educ:** Southern Ill Univ, Carbondale, IL, BS, acct, mkt, 1970; Brooklyn Col, New York, NY, MA, educ, 1975, admin, supv advan cert, 1981; Fordham Univ, New York, NY, PhD. **Career:** Bd Educ, PS 137K, Brooklyn, NY, teacher, 1970-83, prin, 1983-2006; Shaw Univ, NC, instr curric writer, 1972; Col New Rochelle, New York, NY, adj prof, 1989-; Bd Educ, Brooklyn, NY, instr new teacher workshops, human rel courses; Community Sch Dist, dep supt. **Orgs:** Polit chmn, Nat Alliance Black Sch Educr; treas, Coalition Concerned Black Educr; Coun Supvr & Adminr; Coach & facilitator, NYC Leadership Acad, 2006-. **Home Addr:** 117 15 224th St, Jamaica, NY 11411, **Home Phone:** (718)525-3295. **Business Addr:** Coach, Facilitator, NYC Leadership Academy, 45-18 Court Sq 3rd Fl, Long Island City, NY 11101, **Business Phone:** (718)752-7365.

### SPRAGGINS, DR. STEWART
Administrator, chairperson. **Personal:** Born May 17, 1936, Pheba, MS; married Jean Caldwell; children: Renee Ericka & Stewart II. **Educ:** Mary Holmes Col, AA, 1958; Knoxville Col, BA, 1962; Fairfield Univ, MA, 1972. **Career:** YMCA Greater Bridgeport, exec mem & phys educ, 1962-70; YMCA Greater OK City, metro outreach exec, 1970-72; YMCA Oranges, exec dir, 1972-74; YMCA Greater NY, exec dir, 1974-77; JP Stevens & Co Inc, corp mgr, urban affairs, dir comn affairs, 1977-. **Orgs:** Bd mem, Mary Holmes Col, 1983; bd mem, NY March Dimes, 1983; bd mem, Accent Mag, 1984; bd mem, Inst NJ, 1984; chmn, Counc Concerned Black Exec; exec comt, Edges Group Inc; treas, Nat Urban Affairs Counc Corp Coordinators Vols Counc. **Honors/Awds:** Outstanding Black American, Nat Asn Advan Colored People & City of Bridgeport, 1968; Past State President Elks of North America & Canada, 1969; Board Member of the Year, Okla City Comt Action Prog, 1970; DHL, Miles Col, 1983. **Home Addr:** 18 Maplewood Ave, Maplewood, NJ 07040, **Home Phone:** (973)763-4126. **Business Addr:** Director Community Affairs, J P Stevens & Co Inc, 1185 6th Ave, New York, NY 10036, **Business Phone:** (212)930-2000.

### SPRATLEN, THADDEUS H.
Consultant, educator. **Personal:** Born May 28, 1930, Union City, TN; son of John B and Lela C Dobbins; married Lois Price; children: Pamela, Patricia, Paula, Thadd Price & Townsand Price. **Educ:** Ohio State Univ, BS, 1956, MA, 1957, PhD, 1962. **Career:** W WA State Col, inst, asst prof & assoc prof, 1961-69, Ethnic Studies Prog, actg dir, 1969; Univ Calif, Berkeley, lectr, 1965; Univ Calif, Los Angeles, 1969-72; Black Economists Devel Proj, dir, 1970-74; Univ Calif Los Angeles, consult, adj & assoc prof, 1972-75; Univ Wash, assoc prof, 1972-75, prof, Black Studies Prog, assoc dir, 1979-80, Afro-Amer Studies, actg dir, 1980-81, prof emer mkt, 2002-, Bus & Econ Develop Ctr, founding fac dir, 1995-; Howard Univ, Sch Bus Admin, vis res prof, 1986-87. **Orgs:** Beta Gamma Sigma, 1956; United Negro Col Fund, lectr, 1971, 1974; Wa State Adv Comm Minority Bus, 1974-76; US Census Adv Comm Am Mkt Asn, 1975-81; Nat Econ asn; Caucus Black Economists; Am Mkt Asn. **Honors/Awds:** John Hay Whitney Fellow, 1958-59; Doctoral Consortium Faculty, Am Mkt Asn, 1976; Frederick Douglass Scholar Award, Nat Council for Black Studies, Pacific Northwest Region, 1986; Andrew V Smith Faculty Development Award, 1993 & 1999; Dean's Citizenship Award, 2004; Special Distinguished Award; Thaddeus H Spratlen Endowment for the Business and Economic Development Center. **Special Achievements:** First African American professor hired at the Foster School of Business. Publications/Author of Numerous Books. **Home Addr:** 725 9th Ave, Seattle, WA 98104-2051, **Home Phone:** (206)365-0956. **Business**

**Addr:** Professor Emeritus Marketing, Faculty Director, University of Washington, 308 Mackenzie Hall, Seattle, WA 98195-3200, **Business Phone:** (206)543-4778.

## SPRAUVE, DR. GILBERT A.

Educator. **Personal:** Born Jun 9, 1937, St. Thomas; son of Eunice and Gehardt; married Alvara Eulalia Ritter; children: Masserae, Margaret, Janine & Singanu. **Educ:** Brooklyn Col, BA, 1960; Univ Pr, BA; Univ Southern Calif, MA, 1965; Princeton Univ, PhD, 1974; Univ Madrid, dipl de cult espanola. **Career:** Lyce Donka Guinea, Span, Eng teacher, 1960-61; Albert Acad Sierra Leone, Fr, Span teacher, 1961-63; La City Schs Calif, Fr, Span teacher, 1963-67; Univ VI, humanities prof, prof, linguist, assoc prof mod lang, prof mod lang, 1967-2010; Rockefeller Found grad black studies fel, 1971-74; Third Const Conv VI, del, 1977; 14th Leg VI, sen at-large, vpres, 1981-82; Smithsonian Inst, Festival Am Folklife, VI Sect, gen adv & res, 1990, Off Folklife Prog, sr vis scholar, 1990-91; Independent Writing & Editing Prof, currently. **Orgs:** VI Bd Educ, 1978-; adv bd mem, Caribbean Fishery Mgt Coun, 1979-; St Thomas Racquet Club. **Home Addr:** PO Box 913, St John00831. **Business Addr:** Faculty Member For Summer Institute, Culture and Communication, University of the Virgin Islands, 2 John Brewer's Bay, St. Thomas00802-9990, **Business Phone:** (340)776-9200.

## SPREWELL, LATRELL FONTAINE

Business owner, basketball player. **Personal:** Born Sep 8, 1970, Milwaukee, WI; son of Pamela and Latoska Field; children: Aquilla, Sher, Page, Latrell II, Ray & Billy. **Educ:** Three Rivers Community Col; Univ Ala, social work. **Career:** Basketball player (retired), business owner; Golden State Warriors, shooting guard, 1992-98; New York Knicks, small forward, 1998-2003; Minn Timberwolves, guard, 2003-05; Sprewell Racing, owner, currently. **Orgs:** Make-A-Wish Found; Starlight Found. **Honors/Awds:** Met Life Community Assist of the Month Award, 1999; NBA All-Star, 1994, 1995, 1997, 2001. **Business Addr:** Owner, Sprewell Racing, 1001 S San Gabriel Blvd, San Gabriel, CA 91776, **Business Phone:** (626)309-1771.

## SPRIGGS, EDWARD J.

Government official, administrator. **Personal:** Born May 22, 1947, Minneapolis, MN; married Leah; children: Lesley D. **Educ:** Univ Calif, San Diego, BA, econ, 1970; NY Univ Sch Law, JD, 1975. **Career:** Int Corp Law, pvt pract; US Foreign Serv, coun; US Dept Housing & Urban Develop, community develop rep, 1970-72; Arnold & Porter, assoc atty, 1975-79; US Agency Int Develop, E Africa Affairs, dir, 1982-85, regional legal adv, 1986-88, asst gen coun Africa, 1988-94, mission dir, Namibia, 1994-98, regional dir Southern Africa, Gabon, Botswana, 1998-2001; Univ Calif, San Diego, assoc vice chancellor resource admin, 2001-14, int assoc vice chancellor resource admin, 2007; City Imp Beach, coun mem, 2010-; UC San Diego Black Alumni Coun, Chairperson 2014-. **Orgs:** Nat Bar Asn, 1975-; Int Law Sect, 1975-; Am Soc Int Law, 1975-; DC Bar Asn, 1975-; bd mem, San Diego World Affairs Coun; regional legal advisor, U.S. Aid. **Home Addr:** 1442 Seacoast Dr Unit 8, Imperial Beach, CA 91932-3180, **Home Phone:** (619)429-6593. **Business Addr:** Associate Vice Chancellor, Resource Administration, University of California San Diego, 9500 Gilman Dr, La Jolla, CA 92093, **Business Phone:** (858)534-3475.

## SPRIGGS, MARCUS (THOMAS MARCUS SPRIGGS)

Football player. **Personal:** Born May 30, 1974, Hattiesburg, MS. **Educ:** Univ Houston. **Career:** Football player (retired); Buffalo Bills, 1997-98, right tackle & tackle, 1999, left tackle & right tackle, 2000; Miami Dolphins, left tackle, 2001-02; Green Bay Packers, offensive tackle, 2003.

## SPRIGGS, OTHA T. SKIP, III

Executive, vice president (organization). **Educ:** Towson State Univ, BS, bus admin. **Career:** UPS, 1982-96; Levi Strauss & Co., 1996-98; vpres, Home Depot, Mid-S Div 1999; vpres, human resources, Home Depot, EXPO Div, 2000-01; Catalent Pharma Solutions Inc; Cigna Corp, sr vpres human resources, 2001-09; Integrated People Solutions, pres, 2009-10; Boston Sci, sr vpres global human resources, exec comt mem, 2010-12; TIAA-CREF, exec vpres & chief human resources officer, 2012-. **Orgs:** Pres, Boston Sci Found; human resources adv bd mem, Univ Sc's Moore Sch Bus; chmn bd, Urban League Philadelphia, 2002-09; bd mem, Savannah State Univ, Col Bus Admin, 2008-; Univ S Carolina, bd mem, 2009; chmn bd, Exec Leadership Coun; bd mem, Inst Corp Productivity (i4cp), 2013-; bd mem, Pinnacol Assurance, 2015-; bd mem, TIAA-CREF Trust Co., FSB, 2015-.

## SPRIGGS, THOMAS MARCUS. See SPRIGGS, MARCUS.

## SPRIGGS, DR. WILLIAM

Economist, educator, association executive. **Educ:** Williams Col, BA, econs & polit sci, 1977; Univ Wis-Madison, MA, econs, 1979, PhD, econ, 1984. **Career:** UN Develop Prog, NY, Prog Policy Div, intern, 1976; US Agency Int Develop, Wash, DC, Africa Bur, intern, 1978; NC Agr & Tech State Univ, Greensboro, NC, Dept Econs, asst prof, 1984-83; Norfolk State Univ, Norfolk, VA, Dept Mgt & Dir, Hons Prog, asst prof, 1984-90; Econ Policy Inst, Wash, DC, economist, 1990-93, sr fel, 2004-05; Nat Commn Employ Policy, Wash, DC, dir, designate, 1993-94; Joint Econ Comt, US Cong, Wash, DC, sr economist, 1994-97; Econs & Statist Admin, US Dept Com, Wash, DC, sr adv & economist, 1997-98; Off Gov Contract & Minority Bus Develop, US Small Bus Admin, Wash, DC, sr adv, 1998-2004; Econ Policy Inst, sr fel, 2005-; Howard Univ, Dept Econs, prof & chair, econ dept, 2005-; Dept Labor, asst secy, 2009-; AFL-CIO, chief economist. **Orgs:** Nat Sci Found Minority grad fel, 1979-84; co-pres, Am Fed Teachers, Local 3220 AFL-CIO, Madison, WI, 1980-81; exec dir, Nat Urban League Inst Opportunity & Equality, 1988-2004; Nat Neighborhood Asn, 1999-2003; pres, Nat Econs Asn; Org Prof Black Economists; co-pres, Am Fedn Teachers; Black Enterprise mag bd Economists; Time Mag Bd Economists; Nat Acad Social Ins; Nat Acad Pub Admin; vice chmn, Cong Black Caucus Inst Leadership & Polit Educ; sr fel Econ Policy Inst; chmn, UAW, Independent Health Care Trust, 2006-; chmn, UAW Retirees Dana Corp Health & Welfare Trust, 2006-. **Honors/Awds:** Harold Graves Essay Prize, Univ Wis-Madison, Dept Econs, 1980; Dissertation Award, Nat Econs Asn, 1985; Winn Newman Award, Nat Comt Pay Equity, 2001; Chairman's Award, Cong Black Caucus, 2003. **Special Achievements:** Has numerous publications, has presented at several international conferences, and has done consulting work for various state, local, and international agencies; Frequent guest on various television and radio news programs. **Business Addr:** Professor, Chair, Howard University, 2400 6th St NW, Washington, DC 20059, **Business Phone:** (202)806-6717.

## SPRINGER, ERIC WINSTON

Lawyer, executive. **Personal:** Born May 17, 1929, New York, NY; son of Owen W and Maida S; married Cecile Marie Kennedy; children: Brian & Christina. **Educ:** Rutgers Univ, BA, 1950; NY Univ Sch Law, LLB, 1953. **Career:** Justice NY St Supreme Ct, law clerk, 1955-56; Univ Pittsburgh, res assoc, 1956-58, asst prof law, 1958-64, assoc prof law, 1965-68, dir compliance equal employ opportunity comn, 1967; Aspen Systs Corp, Pittsburgh, vpres, dir, publ, 1968-71; Horty, Springer & Mattern PC, founding partner, 1971-82, prin, 1982-, coun, currently; Estes Pk Inst, faculty. **Orgs:** Trustee emer, Presby Univ Hosp, 1967; dir, Duquesne LightCo, 1977; NY Bar; PA Bar; ABA, NBA, Allegheny City Bar Asn; Nat Asn Advan Colored People; pres, Allegheny County Bar Asn; Neurol Dis & Stroke Coun; nat adv, trustee, Montefiore Univ Hosp, Pittsburgh, Pen; trustee, Univ Pittsburgh Med Ctr; Estes Pk Inst; Am Col Hosp Exec; charter mem, Am Acad Hosp Attys; fel Am Pub Health Asn; trustee emer, Presby-Univ Hosp Pittsburgh; Audit, Corp Governance, Employ & Community Rels Comts; trustee, Maurice Falk Med Fund. **Honors/Awds:** Hon Fel, Am Col Healthcare Execs, 1978; Hall of Fame, Nat Bar Asn, 1993. **Special Achievements:** Author, "Group Practice and the Law", 1969; Ed, "Nursing and the Law", 1970; "Automated Medical Records and the Law", 1971; contributing editor of monthly newsletter "Action-Kit for Hospital Law", 1973. Editor & Author of numerous books. **Home Addr:** 5665 Bartlett St, Pittsburgh, PA 15217, **Home Phone:** (412)421-8308. **Business Addr:** Counsel, Founding Partner, Horty Springer & Mattern PC, 4614 5th Ave Suite 200, Pittsburgh, PA 15213-3663, **Business Phone:** (800)245-1205.

## SPRINGER, REV. LLOYD LIVINGSTONE

Clergy. **Personal:** Born Apr 28, 1930, Barbados; son of Oscar (deceased) and Olive; married Ottwritta L Philips; children: Addison. **Educ:** Codrington Col, GOE Dipl, 1963; New York Theol Sem, STM, 1975; New York Univ, MA, 1982; Acad Geront Educ & Develop, cert. **Career:** Clergy (retired); St Martin Episcopal Church, asst, 1971-73; St Edmund Episcopal Church, rector, 1973-2000; Episcopal Mission Soc House Holy Comforter, chaplain, 1980-86; Bronx Lebanon Hosp, part time chaplain. **Orgs:** Pres, Mt Hope Housing Corp, 1987-96; North West Bronx Clergy & Comn Orgn; pension comt, Ecumenical Comn, New York diocese; Walton Family Health Ctr. **Honors/Awds:** Bronx Borough President's Award; Vestry Appreciation Award, St Edmund Episcopal; Appreciation Award, Mt Hope Organization & Community; Bronx Community Board Award, New York; Honored Citizen New York State; Immigrant's Alien Award. **Home Addr:** 1358 N Normandy Blvd, Deltona, FL 32725-8432, **Home Phone:** (386)860-0177.

## SPRINGS, LENNY F., II

Chief executive officer, executive director, president (organization). **Personal:** Born Apr 25, 1947, Edgefield, SC. **Educ:** Voorhees Col, BA, 1968; Honoris Causa, DHL. **Career:** Director(retired), pres, chief executive officer; Greenville Urban League, proj dir, 1976-79, dep dir, 1979-82, exec dir, 1982-83; Southern Bank, comn rels officer, 1983-85; Wachovia Corp, asst vpres, corp rels div, sr vpres strategic partnership, dir supplier diversity, 1985-07; S-Group Inc, pres & chief exec officer, 2007-; Queen city ventures partners, pres, currently; Mech & Farmers Bank, dir. **Orgs:** Nat bd, Nat Asn Advan Colored People, 1976-, chair, bd trustee, Spec Contrib Fund; Bd dir, Boy Scouts Southern Region; pres admin, US Dept Treas Bank Secrecy Adv Group; vice chair, SC Human Affairs Comn; pres, founder, & bd mem, Charlotte Chap, Hundred Black Men Am; bd mem, Cent Carolina Urban League; Southeast Reg Bd Nat Alliance Bus; Bus Policy Rev Coun; bd dir, Carolinas Minority Supplier Develop Coun Inc; pres, bd trustee, Voorhees Col Nat Alumni Asn; Nat Urban Bankers Asn; bd visitors, Barber-Scotia Col; bd visitors, Johnson C Smith Univ; bd trustee, Elizabeth City State Univ; bd dir, Fla Mem Col; bd dir, SC State Univ Found; bd dir, Spirit Sq; Bd dir, Mech & Farmers Bank; Bd dir, Nat Asn Advan Colored People; Bd trustee, Nat Asn Advan Colored People Spec Contrib Fund Bd; chmn, bd dir, Veritas one consult; Nat Adv, Sen Barack Obamas Presidential campaign; bd trustee, bd dir, Historically Black Cols. **Home Addr:** 10911 Tavernay Pkwy, Charlotte, NC 28273, **Home Phone:** (704)594-9260. **Business Addr:** President, Chief Executive Officer, The S Group Inc, 308 SW 1st Ave Suite 200, Portland, OR 97204, **Business Phone:** (503)328-0160.

## SPRINGS, SHAWN

Chief executive officer, football player. **Personal:** Born Mar 11, 1975, Williamsburg, VA; son of Ron (deceased); married Lily; children: Shawn II. **Educ:** Ohio State Univ, BS, sociol, 1997. **Career:** Football player (retired), executive; Seattle Sea hawks, left corner back, 1997-98 & 2002-03, corner back & left corner back, 1999, left corner back, 2000, right corner back & left corner back, 2001; Wash Redskins, left corner back & right corner back & strong safety, 2004-08; Comcast SportsNet/NBC Sports, sports commentator, 2004-; New Eng Patriots, left corner back, 2009-10; Windpact Inc, chief exec officer, 2010-. **Honors/Awds:** Big Ten Defensive Player of the Year, 1996; Pro Bowl, 1998; Consensus All-American, 1996; All-Pro, 2004. **Special Achievements:** NFL Draft, First round pick, Rank 3, 1997; speaker, The Wash Post's ann All-Met dinner, 2004. **Home Addr:** . **Business Addr:** Chief Executive Officer, Windpact Inc, 1503 Edwards Ferry Rd NE Suite 201, Leesburg, VA 20176, **Business Phone:** (571)291-2222.

## SPRINKLE-HAMLIN, SYLVIA YVONNE

Librarian. **Personal:** Born Apr 25, 1945, Winston-Salem, NC; daughter of Arthur William Henry Sprinkle Jr and Thelma Norwood Holtzclaw; married Larry Leon. **Educ:** Winston-Salem State Univ, Winston-Salem, NC, BS, educ, 1967; Clark Univ, Atlanta, GA, MLS, libr sci, educ admin, 1968; Cheyney State Univ, Cheyney, PA, inst advan study, 1976; Univ NC, Chapel Hill, NC, cert county admin, 1987. **Career:** Free Libr Philadelphia, c's librn; Philadelphia Pub Schs, Philadelphia, PA, info specialist, 1970-73, instrnl media ctr dir, 1973-77; Fashion Two Twenty Cosmetics, Winston-Salem, NC, studio owner, 1977-81; Winston-Salem State Univ, Winston-Salem, NC, asst librn, asst dir univ libr, 1978-79; Forsyth County Pub Libr, Winston-Salem, NC, head, c's outreach, 1979-80, asst dir-exten, 1980-84, dep libr dir, 1984, dir, 2000-; W.H. Roberts & Assocs, libr consult. **Orgs:** Secy, NC Black Repertory Co, 1983-, pres, bd dir, 2010; dir large, mem comt, NC Libr Asn, 1989-91; vpres, Nat Women Achievement, 1989-91; nat plng chair, Nat Conf African Am Librarians, 1990-92; pres, Youth Opportunity Homes Inc, 1990-93; bd dir, Nat Black Theatre Festival, 1991, exec producer, 2007; pres, Black Caucus Am Libr Asn, 1996-; bd mem, Coun Status Women; bd mem, Winston-Salem State Univ Diggs Gallery; pres, BCALA, NC; bd dir, Family Serv; bd dir, Forsyth County Smart Start; bd dir, Shepherd Ctr Greater Winston-Salem; coun mem, Am Libr Asn; bd mem, Pub libr Asn; chmn, African Am Issues Roundtable Southeastern Libr Asn. **Honors/Awds:** Annette Lewis Phinazee Award, NC Cent Univ, 1986; Ethnic Minority Roadbuilder's Award; The Chronicle Women of the Year Award; DEMCO/ALA Black Caucus Award. **Home Addr:** 3430 Willow Wind Dr, Pfafftown, NC 27040-9244, **Home Phone:** (336)924-8477. **Business Addr:** Library Director, Forsyth County Public Library, 660 W 5th St, Winston-Salem, NC 27101, **Business Phone:** (336)703-2665.

## SPROUT, PROF. FRANCIS

Artist, educator. **Personal:** Born Mar 5, 1940, Tucson, AZ; son of Pearl Mae Greene; married Lucinda Gedeon. **Educ:** Univ Ariz, BFA, art educ, 1967; Univ Calif, San Diego, MFA, studio art, 1972; Univ Calif, Los Angeles, MA, African studies, 1990. **Career:** Ford Found Fel, 1971-72; Univ Denver, asst prof, painting & drawing, 1972-75; Metrop State Col, assoc prof, Painting, 1976-87; Hamline Univ, Fac Inst Africa, Fel, 1978; Unic Calif, Grad African Studies, fac, 1985, grad fel/summer lang inst, 1985; Ariz State Univ, fac assoc, 1987-90; State Univ New York, fac, 1991-95; Manhattanville Col, adj fac, 1993-2004; Pratt Inst, adj assoc prof, 1996-2004; Indian River Community Col, fac, adj instr, 2004-12; Vero Beach Mus Art, instr, 2004-. **Orgs:** Alliance Contemp Art Denver Art Mus, 1980; African Studies Asn, 1984; grant rev panel, Coun Arts & Humnts, 1984-85; Col Art Asn, 1990-; Cult Coun Indian River County, 2004-; Vero Beach Art Club, 2009-. **Home Phone:** (772)324-6041. **Business Addr:** Artist, 921 Oyster Shell Lane, Vero Beach, FL 32963, **Business Phone:** (772)360-5108.

## SPRUCE, DR. KENNETH L.

Educator. **Personal:** Born Mar 6, 1956, Toledo, OH; son of George Jr and Helen E Jordan; children: Sierra Monique. **Educ:** Univ Cincinnati, Cincinnati, OH, BA, 1980; Am Univ, Wash, DC, attended 1981; Univ Toledo, Toledo, OH, MPA, 1982; Clark Atlanta Univ, Atlanta, GA, PhD, 1991. **Career:** Univ Toledo, Toledo, Ohio, grad teaching asst, 1981-82; Toledo J Newspaper, Toledo, Ohio, columnist writer-reporter, 1982-85; State Ohio, Bur Employ Serv, Toledo, Ohio, personnel counr, 1983-91; Morris Brown Coll, Polit Sci Prog, Atlanta, Ga, adj instr, 1993; Clark Atlanta Univ, Polit Sci Dept, grad teaching asst, 1993-94; Floyd Col, Rome, Ga, asst prof polit sci, 1993-97, assoc prof, 1998-. **Orgs:** Nat Conf Black Polit Scientists, 1990-95; Am Polit Sci Asn, 1992-95; Am Asn Univ Prof, 1994-95; Ga Polit Sci Asn, 1994-95. **Home Addr:** PO Box 6416, Cincinnati, OH 45206. **Business Addr:** Associate Professor, Floyd College, 5198 Ross Rd SE, Acworth, GA 30102, **Business Phone:** (770)975-4088.

## SPRUELL, SAKINA P.

Editor. **Personal:** Born Jun 19, 1970, Jersey City, NJ; married Carroll Charles Cole; children: 2. **Educ:** Rutgers Univ, BA, commun, 1993; Columbia Grad Sch Journalism, MS. **Career:** Founder, Cole Media Inc; WBLS, res dir, 1993; WHYY Nat Pub Radio, weekend news anchor; Home News Tribune, staff writer; CNN financial network, NJ Local Ed, reporter, producer & freelance writer; Columbia Univ, New York, instr; Gannet daily newspaper, staff writer; Black Enterprise mag, personal-finance freelance contribr, 1998, bus news ed, 2000, sr ed, currently, Black Enterprise's Teenpreneur, founding ed. **Orgs:** Vpres, Rutgers African Am Alumni Alliance, 1998; bd dir, Achievement Radio Awards, 1999; co-chair, Nat Asn Black Journalists, 1999-; Soc Bus Ed & Writers, 2000-. **Honors/Awds:** Griot Award for Excellence, New York Chap NABJ, 2000. **Business Addr:** Senior Editor, Black Enterprise, 260 Madison Ave 11th Fl, New York, NY 10016, **Business Phone:** (212)242-8000.

## SPURLOCK, DOROTHY A.

Administrator. **Personal:** Born Mar 18, 1956, Kalamazoo, MI; daughter of Jimmie Sr and Della A Watson. **Educ:** Western Mich Univ, Kalamazoo, MI, BS, pub admin, 1979, MA, commun, 1983. **Career:** Western Mich Univ, Kalamazoo, Mich, mgr, employ serv, sr compensation analyst & coordr, legisl affairs, 1979-84; Popcorn Station, Kalamazoo, Mich, owner & mgr, 1984-88; Urban League Greater Muskegon, Muskegon, Mich, exec dir, 1988-91; Nu-Way Consulting Inc, Kalamazoo, Mich, vpres oper, 1989; Eastern Mich Univ, assoc dir, off res develop; Univ Toledo, dir, res & sponsored progs, 2002-. **Orgs:** Coun mem, City Kalamazoo, 1983-87; bd mem, Nat Coun Univ Res Adminr. **Home Addr:** PO Box 51314, Kalamazoo, MI 49005, **Home Phone:** (616)372-1399. **Business Addr:** Director, University of Toledo, 2801 W Bancroft St, Toledo, OH 43606-3390, **Business Phone:** (419)530-4723.

## SPURLOCK, DR. JAMES B., JR.

Public relations executive. **Personal:** Born Jan 20, 1936, Roanoke, VA; married Nancy H; children: James B III, Deborah G & Kenneth L. **Educ:** NC Agr & Tech State Univ, BS, 1959; Personnel Adm Personnel Mgt, dipl, 1960, 1962; Mgt Training Course, attended 1968; Univ Mich, BA, advan mgt prog, 1970. **Career:** Manager (retired); AT&T, public relations mgr, treas; Norfolk State Univ Found Inc, pres, currently. **Orgs:** Va State C C; bd deacons, First African Baptist Ch; Roanoke City Sch Bd; bd visitors, James Madison Univ; Richmond Metro COC; Richmond Nat Asn Advan Colored People; Richmond Urban League; RAPME; dir, C W Anderson Male Chorus; vpres, Norfolk State Univ found bd; bd visitors, Radford Univ; Outstanding Serv

Bd Dir Va Col Placement Asn; Outstanding Comn Ldr Burrell Memorial Hosp; Sigma Rho Sigma Nat Hon Soc, treas. **Honors/Awds:** Outstanding Citizen's Award; Father Year Inter-Faith Comm Choir; Cert Merit, City Council Roanoke; Cert Recog, Nat Alliance Busman Serv, Youth Motivation Task Force; Cert appreciation, State Dir Selective Serv; The Army Commendation medal; Vietnam Serv medal, Good Conduct medal. **Special Achievements:** Published articles, "Obsolescence or Change"; "Recruiting the Qualified Minority Grad", author. **Home Addr:** 7802 Antionette Dr, Richmond, VA 23227-2038, **Home Phone:** (804)264-8587. **Business Addr:** President, Norfolk State University Foundation Inc, 700 Pk Ave Suite 410, Norfolk, VA 23504-8003, **Business Phone:** (804)266-1573.

### SPURLOCK, DR. LANGLEY AUGUSTINE

Association executive, executive. **Personal:** Born Nov 9, 1939, Charleston, WV; son of Langley A and Eunice P. **Educ:** WV State Col, BS, 1959; Wayne State Univ, PhD, org chem, 1963. **Career:** Professor (retired), artist, consultant; Wayne State Univ, NIH predoctoral fel, 1961-63; Harvard Univ, NIH Postdoctoral fel, 1966; Brown Univ, assoc prof chem, 1969-73; Alfred PSloan fel, 1973-75; Am Coun Educ, asst pres, 1973-76; US Dept HEW, HEW fel, 1976-77; Nat Sci Found, sr staff assoc, 1977-82; Chemstar Div, 1982-94, vpres, 1994, Subcomt Minorities, liaison; Chem Mfg Asn, dir. **Orgs:** Am Chem Soc; Am Soc Asn Execs; Am Asn Advan Sci; Phi Lambda Upsilon Hon Chem Soc; Soc Sigma Xi; Beta Kappa Chi Hon Sci Soc; Alpha Kappa Mu Hon Sch Soc; Delta Phi Alpha Hon Ger Soc; Kappa Alpha Psi; chair, SeniorNet's Bd; bd dir & corp secy, Coun Environ Professionals; bd dir, Sr Serv Am Inc. **Honors/Awds:** Cert Asn Exec, 1989-. **Special Achievements:** Author 34 publications & 3 patents. **Business Addr:** Board Director, Senior Service America Inc, 8403 Colesville Rd Suite 1200, Silver Spring, MD 20910.

### SPURLOCK, LAVERNE BEARD

Educator. **Personal:** Born Feb 23, 1930, Richmond, VA; daughter of Joseph C and Mabel M Matney; married Charles T; children: Carla S Harrell. **Educ:** Va State Col, BS, 1950; Columbia Univ, MA, 1954; Univ Va, advan study, 1974; VPI & SU Blacksburg, VA, EdD, 1984. **Career:** Educator (retired); Maggie L Walker HS, teacher, 1951; Richmond Pub Schs, Guid Dept, co ordr, 1970-91, supvr guid, 1986-91; John Marshall HS, guid dept head, 1970-86. **Orgs:** Va Asn Non-White Concerns; pres, Va Sch Counr Asn; dir, educ & vpres educ Richmond Personnel & Guid Asn; VPGA; vol listener Youth Emergency Servs; bd mem, Richmond Area Psychiat Clin; Bd Christian Educ Ebenezer Bapt Ch; Personnel Com Ebenezer Bapt Ch; trustee, Ebenezer Bapt Ch; pres, Richmond Alumnae Chap Delta Sigma Theta; first vpres, Richmond Chap Nat Coalition 100 Black Women; secy, Henrico Area Ment Health Serv Bd, Human Rights Comn; proj dir, SECME; pres, Va Heroes Inc; Pi Lambda Theta; assoc dir, AVID; Delicadas Inc; Moles; Links Inc; bd dir, emer bd mem, Partnership Future, currently. **Home Addr:** 1611 Forest Glen Rd, Henrico, VA 23228-2305, **Home Phone:** (804)266-0201. **Business Addr:** Board of Director, Emeritus Board Member, Partnership Future, 4501 Highwoods Pkwy, Glen Allen, VA 23060, **Business Phone:** (804)967-2503.

### SPURLOCK, DR. OLIVER M.

Judge. **Personal:** Born Feb 28, 1945, Chicago, IL; son of Thomas L and Anna P; children: Stacey, Brandon & Marc. **Educ:** Univ Ill, BA, 1969; Northwestern Univ Law Sch, JD, 1972. **Career:** Cook County State's Atty, asst, 1972-75; pvt pract atty, 1975-88; Cook County Circuit Ct, assoc judge, 1988-01, Criminal Ct, judge. **Home Addr:** 1376 E Madison Pk, Chicago, IL 60615-2917, **Home Phone:** (773)538-7223.

### SPURLOCK, RACQUEL

Basketball player. **Personal:** Born May 25, 1973, Mesquite, TX. **Educ:** La Tech, attended 1996. **Career:** Basketball player (retired); Houston Comets, ctr, 1997.

### SPURLOCK-EVANS, KARLA JEANNE

College teacher, college administrator. **Personal:** Born Jun 30, 1949, Willimantic, CT; daughter of Odessa Fuller and Kelly M; married Booker; children: Mariama Ifetayo & Booker Theodore Jr. **Educ:** Barnard Col, BA, polit sci, 1971; Emory Univ, MA, 1972, PhD, African studies. **Career:** State Univ New York, Albany, asst prof, 1975-77; Haverford Col, dir minority affairs, assoc dean & affirmative action officer, 1977-80; Lake Forest Col, asst dean students 1981-85; Northwestern Univ, assoc dean students, dir Afro-Am stud affairs, 1985-99; Trinity Col, dean multicultural affairs & dir affirmative action, 1999- . **Orgs:** Bd mem, Assoc Advan Creative Musicians, 1981-83; Ill Col Personnel Asn; Ill Community Black Concerns Higher Educ; Nat Asn Women Deans Adminr & Coun; ed bd, Chicago Reporter; Nat Asn Stud Personnel Adminrs. **Home Addr:** 154 Lasalle Rd, West Hartford, CT 06107-2308, **Home Phone:** (860)236-2442. **Business Addr:** Dean of Multicultural Affairs, Director of Affirmative Action, Trinity College, 300 Summit St, Hartford, CT 06106, **Business Phone:** (860)297-2000.

### SQUIRE, CAROLE RENEE

Judge. **Personal:** Born Jul 21, 1953, Springfield, OH; daughter of Robert Hutchins and Reva; married Percy; children: Reva Marie & Deidra Renee. **Educ:** Ohio State Univ, BA, Eng, 1974; Ohio State Univ Col Law, JD, 1977. **Career:** Franklin Co Domestic Rels Ct, juv unit, asst prosecutor, juv unit magistrate, 1991-94; Off Ohio Atty Gen, asst atty gen; pvt law pract family law area; Am Univ, col instr; Off Gen Coun Navy, atty advisor, contracts; Youth Alternative Proj, asst dir; Ohio Legal Rights Serv, staff atty; Phonics READ, founder; Am Univ, Juv & Law Teacher; Nat Youth Alternatives Proj, asst proj mgr; Univ Md Overseas; Temple Univ Overseas; Franklin Co Ct, Div Domestic Rels & Juv Br, judge, currently. **Orgs:** Community Mediation Serv, 1988-92; Former Youth Advocate Serv, 1989-92; Seal Ohio Girl Scout Coun, 1991-93; Columbus Bar Found, 1992; Asn Female Exec, 1993; Art Child Safe Am, 1999-; Shiloh Baptist Church; Nat Conf Black Lawyers; Ohio State Bar Asn; Nat Asn Juv Ct Judges; Women Lawyers Franklin Co. **Home Addr:** 547 Mohawk St, Columbus, OH 43206. **Business Addr:** Judge, Franklin County Court, 373 S High St 6th Fl, Columbus, OH 43215-4598, **Business Phone:** (614)462-5223.

### SQUIRES, RENEE BUROSE. See BUROSE, RENEE.

### ST ETIENNE, GREGORY MICHAEL

Banker. **Personal:** Born Dec 24, 1957, New Orleans, LA; son of Emanuel and Geraldine; married Valencia Ann Tanner. **Educ:** Loyola Univ, BS, acct, 1980, MBA, 1981; Grad Sch Banking S, cert, 1988. **Career:** Laporte, Sehrt, Romig & Hand, CPA's, sr auditor, 1981-85; Liberty Bank & Trust Co, exec vpres, chief operating officer, 1985-2005; First Independence Bank, Detroit, vice chmn & chief exec officer, 2005-06; FFC Capital Mgt, managing dir, 2006-07; Ultimate Tech Solutions, Inc, chief operating officer, 2007-08; Citizens United Econ Equity, chief exec officer, pres, 2008-10; financial advisor, 2010-. **Orgs:** Pres, Kingsley House, 1986; St Thomas, Irish Channel Consortium, 1990-; secy, Nat Bankers Asn, 1991-; pres, New Orleans Urban Bankers Asn, 1992; 100 Black Men, New Orleans Chap, 1992; secy, pres, Inst Ment Hyg, 1994-; dir, La State Mus Ound, 1996-; pres bd, FirstLine Schs Inc; mem bd, Minbanc Found, Wash, DC; mem bd, Delgado Community Col Found; pres bd, Liberty House; mem bd, Bur Govt Res; dir, Loyola Univ Sch Bus Admin's Vis Comt; Fannie Mae Housing Impact Adv Comt; mem bd, Am Bankers Asn; dep mayor opers, City New Orleans, 2010. **Home Addr:** 7641 Crestmont Rd, New Orleans, LA 70126, **Home Phone:** (504)244-6184. **Business Addr:** President, Citizens United for Economic Equity, New Orleans, LA 70112.

### ST JULIEN, MARLON

Jockey. **Personal:** Born Feb 13, 1972, Lafayette, LA; married Denise; children: Jasmin. **Career:** Thoroughbred Horse Racing; Evangeline Downs, 1989; Delta Downs, leading rider, 1993-94; Lone Star Pk, leading rider, 1997-98; three-win day, Keeneland, leading rider, 1999; Ky Downs, leading rider, 1999-2000; Fayette Stakes, 1999-2001; Ky Derby, 2000; Selene Stakes, 2000; Arlington-Wash Lassie Stakes, 2001; Pocahontas Stakes, 2001; Arlington Sprint Handicap, 2001. **Honors/ Awds:** Numerous honors including Won his first stakes event, 1992; Won $100, 000 stakes aboard Caro's Royalty in the Grand Prairie Gold Cup, Lone Star, 1997; Won his 1000th winner, 1998; 2000 has seen him capture five stakes; The Selene Stakes (Zoftig); The Grand Prairie Turf Challenge Stakes (Four On the Floor); The Lone Star Park Turf Spring (Caro's Royalty); The Pippin Stakes (Really Polish); & the Assault Stakes (Lightening Ball); Leading rider at Delta Downs, 1993-94; Leading rider at Lone Star Park, 1998; Leading rider at Kentucky Downs, 1999. **Special Achievements:** ABC Sports celebrated Black History Month with "Raising the Roof: Seven Athletes for the 21st Century," which aired Feb 5 2000, and featured St Julien, golfer Tiger Woods, & five other athletes; First African-American jockey since 1921 to ride in the Kentucky Derby in 2000; First African-American jockey to race the Kentucky Derby since Henry King, 1921. **Business Addr:** Jockey, Kentucky Derby, 1001 S Third St, Louisville, KY 40203, **Business Phone:** (502)366-7460.

### ST-PIERRE, DR. MAURICE

Educator. **Educ:** London Univ, BS, sociol, minor concentration econs, 1964; McGill Univ, MA, sociol, 1969; Univ Wis, PhD, sociol. **Career:** Univ Guyana; Univ WI, Jamaica; Univ Md Baltimore County; Brit Guianas Civil Serv; Ministry Econ Develop, 1969-70; Morgan State Univ, Dept Sociol & Anthrop, prof & chmn, currently. **Home Addr:** 1304 Heather Hill Rd, Baltimore, MD 21239-1414, **Home Phone:** (410)321-0037. **Business Addr:** Professor, Chair, Morgan State University, Jenkins Behavioral Science Bldg Rm 439-A, Baltimore, MD 21251, **Business Phone:** (443)885-3338.

### ST. JOHN, KRISTOFF (CHRISTOFF ST JOHN)

Actor. **Personal:** Born Jul 15, 1966, New York, NY; son of Christopher and Maria; married Mia; children: Julian & Paris; married Allana Nadal; children: Lola. **Career:** Films: The Champ, 1979; Pandora's Box, 2002; Carpool Guy, 2005; Spiritual Warriors, 2007; 20 Ft Below: The Darkness Descending, 2014; TV series: "That's My Mama", 1975; "Happy Days", 1976; "Wonder Woman", 1977; "Roots: The Next Generations", 1979; "The Bad News Bears", 1979; "Beulah Land", 1980; "Foul Play", 1981; An Innocent Love, 1982; Sister, Sister, 1982; "CBS Afternoon Playhouse", 1982; "The Cosby Show", 1984; "The Atlanta Child Murders", 1985; "ABC Afterschool Specials", 1985; "Charlie & Co.", 1985; "What's Happening Now!", 1987; "A Different World", 1988; Finish Line, 1989; "Generations", 1989; "Jake & the Fat man", 1991; "The Young & the Restless", 1991-2014; "Diagnosis Murder", 1994; "Hangin' with Mr. Cooper", 1994-95; "Martin", 1996; "The Jamie Foxx Show", 1997; "Living Single", 1997; "Pensacola: Wings of Gold", 1998; "Family Matters", 1998; "Suddenly Susan", 1998; "For Your Love", 1999; "Get Real", 1999; "Arli$$", 2002; "Family Time", 2012-14; "The First Family", 2013; "General Hospital", 2013; "Love That Girl!", 2014. **Honors/Awds:** Daytime Emmy Award, 1992, 2008; Image Award, Nat Asn Advan Colored People, 1994-97, 2003-08 & 2013-14; Golden Palm Award, 2014. **Business Addr:** Actor, c/o William Morris Agency, 151 El Camino Dr, Beverly Hills, CA 90212, **Business Phone:** (310)859-4000.

### ST. JOHN, PRIMUS

Teacher, consultant, educator. **Personal:** Born Jul 21, 1939, New York, NY; son of Marcus L and Pearle E; married Barbara Jean Doty; children: Joy Pearle & May Ginger. **Educ:** Univ Md; Lewis & Clark Col. **Career:** Mary Holmes Jr Col, West Point, Miss, teacher; Univ Utah, teacher; Portland State Univ, Portland, Ore, prof Eng, 1973-; Portland Arts Comn, mem, 1979-81; Portland State Univ, Dept Eng, fac, 1973, prof Eng, currently; educ consult. Poems: Zero Makes Me Hungry, 1976; Skin on the Earth, 1976; It is a Light, 1982; Dreamer, 1990; From Here We Speak, 1993. **Orgs:** Fel Nat Endowment Arts, 1970, 1974, 1982; bd dir, Copper Canyon Press; bd dir, Fishtrap Found; adv bd, Oreg Heritage Asn. **Home Addr:** 2064 Sunray Cir, West Linn, OR 97068-4802. **Business Addr:** Professor of English, Portland State University, 485 NH, Portland, OR 97207, **Business Phone:** (503)725-3578.

### ST. OMER, DR. VINCENT V. E.

Administrator, educator, pharmacologist. **Personal:** Born Nov 18, 1934, St. Lucia; married Margaret Muir; children: Ingrid, Denise, Jeffrey & Raymond. **Educ:** Ont Vet Col, DVM, 1962, PhD, pharmacol & toxicol, 1969; Univ Man, MSc, 1965. **Career:** Veterinary pharmacologist, researcher, educator, administrator (retired); Hamilton & Dist Cattle Breeders Asn, field vet, 1962-63; Ont Vet Col, Univ Guelph, lectr, 1965-67; Univ KS, Bur Child Res, res assoc, 1968-71, adj prof, 1970-73; KS State Univ, Bur Child Res, adj res assoc, 1972-74; Univ Med, Sch Med, asst prof, 1974; Univ MSR, Col Vet Med, Depart Vet Biomed Scis, assoc prof, 1974-83, prof, dir grad studies, 1976-79, MNY High Sch Stud Res Apprentice Prog, dir, 1986-89; Univ W Indies, Sch Vet Med, spec leave Univ MSR, prof & dir, 1989-91; Univ Mo; Tuskegee Univ, Sch Vet Med, dir, prof & assoc dean acad affairs, Depart Biomed Scis, prof pharmacol, EHTRP prin investr; Univ Wi. **Orgs:** Sigma Xi; Am Soc Vet Physiologists & Pharmacologists; Soc Neuroscience; MSR Vet Med Asn; CNF Res Workers Animal Dis, NYK ACA Scis; Behav Teratology Soc; Caribbean ACA Scis; adv comt mem, Rotary Club Columbia; Knights Columbus; Minority Men's Network; First Chance C; bd mem, Ns Educ Leadership Consortium. **Honors/Awds:** Honarary Fellow, Am ACA Vet Pharmacol & Therapeutics. **Home Addr:** 1355 Commerce Dr Suite 407, Auburn, AL 36830. **Business Addr:** Principal Investigator, Professor, Tuskegee University, 1200 W Montgomery Rd, Tuskegee, AL 36088, **Business Phone:** (678)904-4217.

### ST. PATRICK, MATTHEW

Actor. **Personal:** Born Mar 17, 1968, Philadelphia, PA; children: Tommy. **Career:** Films: Steel Sharks, 1996; Surface to Air, 1997; Ruby's Tuesday, exec producer, 2005; War, 2007; Sleepwalking, 2008; Ball Don't Lie, 2008; Alien Raiders, 2008; Sleepwalking, 2008; Ball Don't Lie, 2008; Alien Raiders, 2008; Kristy, 2014. TV Series: "NYPD Blue", 1996-98; "General Hospital", 1997; "Mike Hammer, Private Eye", 1998; "All My Children", 1998-2000; "Six Feet Under", 2001-05; "Danny Phantom", 2004; "Reunion", 2005; Tides of War, 2005; Policeman Hero, 2005-06; "Higglytown Heroes", 2005-06; "Law & Order: Special Victims Unit", 2006; Backyards & Bullets, 2007; "Private Practice", 2009; "Saving Grace", 2009-10; " Emily Owens M.D.", 2013; "NCIS", 2013; "Sons of Anarchy", 2014. **Honors/Awds:** Screen Actors Guild Award, 2003, 2004. **Business Addr:** Actor, HBO Studio Productions, 120 E 23rd St Suite A, New York, NY 10010, **Business Phone:** (212)512-7800.

### STAATS, DR. FLORENCE JOAN

School administrator. **Personal:** Born Nov 18, 1940, Newark, NJ; daughter of Jay M and Florence Wheatley. **Educ:** Parsons Sch Design cert, 1961; NY Univ, BS, 1968; Pratt Inst, MFA, 1970; Columbia Univ Teachers Col, EdD, 1978. **Career:** Newark Pub Libr, exhib artst, 1965-68; Essex Co Col, fine arts instr, 1972-78, asst prof, coordr Art prog, 1978-81; Dutchess Comm Col, asst dean, 1982-84, asst pres, 1984-; Bloomfield Col, assoc dean, 1985-86; Rockland Community Col, assoc dean, 1986-88; NY African Am Inst State Univ NY, actg dir, 1988-89; State Univ NY Ulster Co Community Col, dir, COPE, proj coordr, 1989-99, Res & Proj Develop, pres, distinguised staff mem; Florence J Staats DR Mgt Consult Serv, founder, 1998; FJS Designs, creatice dir, currently. **Orgs:** Bd dir, Clearwater Inc, 1983-; rep, ACE/NIP Instnl Am Coun Educ Mid Hudson Chap, 1983-; exec bd, dir, Ulster Co Coun Arts, 1983-85; creative dir, pres, Arts Connection, 1984-; pres, Arts & Commun Network Inc, 1985-; bd dir, Creative Res African Am Life, 1986-; bd dir, Ulster Co Girl Scouts, 2000-; Ulster Co Off Agung, exec adv Comt, 2002; exec bd, chairperson, UlsterCounty Nat Asn Advan Colored People Educ Comt; Rosendale Environ Comn; bddir, vpres, Ulster Arts Alliance. **Honors/Awds:** OE Grant Fulbright G7 Community Col Sem Poland, 1974; NEH Grant Black Exprnc Am, 1977; CBS EEC Award for Market Planning, 1984; Summer Res Grant, NY African Am Inst, 1987; Grant Award, New York State Coun Arts, 1989; Martin Luther King Jr Award for Community Service, Ulster County Multi Serv, 1995; Recycled Design Award, Hudson Valley Material & Exchange, 2002. **Home Addr:** 128 Mossy Brook Rd, PO Box 254, Highfalls, NY 12440-5000, **Home Phone:** (845)687-4568. **Business Addr:** Creative Director, FJS Research & Designs, PO Box 254, High Falls, NY 12440, **Business Phone:** (914)687-0767.

### STACKHOUSE, JERRY DARNELL

Basketball player, broadcaster. **Personal:** Born Nov 5, 1974, Kinston, NC; son of George and Minnie; married Ramirra Marks; children: Jaye, Alexis & Antonio. **Educ:** NC Univ, BA, 1995. **Career:** Philadelphia 76ers, forward-guard, 1995-98; Detroit Pistons, 1998-2002; Wash Wizards, 2002-04; Rehab Inst Mich, bd trustee; Dallas Mavericks, 2004-09; Memphis Grizzlies, 2009; Milwaukee Bucks, 2010; Miami Heat, 2010; Atlanta Hawks, 2011-12; Brooklyn Nets, 2012-13; Toronto Raptors, asst, 2015-; NBA TV, analyst & free agt, currently. **Business Addr:** Analyst, Free Agent, NBA Media Ventures LLC, 645 5th Ave, New York, NY 10022, **Business Phone:** (212)407-8000.

### STAFFORD, DERRICK

Basketball executive. **Personal:** Born Nov 29, 1956, Atlanta, GA. **Educ:** Morehouse Col, attended 1979. **Career:** US Postal Serv, delivery, supv; labour rel; human resources; mkt; Nat Basketball Asn, referee, currently. **Orgs:** Exec bd mem, Nat Basketball Referees Asn; chmn, I Can Do Anything Found; founder, dir, Don't Foul Out Found Inc. **Honors/Awds:** Co-most valuable player baseball, 1976; NBA All-Star Game, 2002. **Special Achievements:** Officiated the McDonalds Championship game in Paris, France and the Legends All-Star Game in Orlando, 1997; volunteered at the Zion Hill Baptist Church. **Home Addr:** , Fayetteville, GA. **Business Addr:** Member, National Basketball Referees Association, 1455 Pennsylvania Ave NW Suite 225, Washington, DC 20004, **Business Phone:** (202)638-5090.

### STAFFORD, DON A. (DONALD STAFFORD)

Law enforcement officer. **Personal:** Born Dec 14, 1934, Rusk, TX; son of L V Mitchell and Chilton; married Geraldine Doughty. **Educ:** Butler Col, Tyler, TX, BS, 1956. **Career:** Law Enforcement officer (retired); Dallas Police Dept, Dallas, Tex, asst chief police, 1982-88, dist chief, exec asst chief, 1988-91. **Orgs:** Black Chamber Com; Urban League; Int Police Asn; Blacks Law Enforcement. **Home Addr:** 2913 S Houston Sch Rd, Lancaster, TX 75146-4527, **Home Phone:** (214)372-6457.

**STAFFORD, EARL W.**
Executive. **Personal:** Born Jan 1, 1948?, Mt. Holly, NJ. **Educ:** Univ Mass, BA, bus; Southern Ill Univ, MBA; Harvard Bus Sch, opm exec prog. **Career:** Universal Systs & Tech Inc, chief exec officer & chmn, 1988-09; Stafford Found, chmn & chief exec officer, 2010-; The Wentworth Group, ceo; entrepreneur, philanthropist; The Peoples Inaugural Project, 2009; Stafford Foundation Inc, chmn, 2010. **Orgs:** Bd, Joint Ctr Polit & Econ Studies; bd, Drexel Univ; bd, Bus Execs Nat Security; Horatio Alger Asn, Wesley Theol Sem, Venture Philanthropy Partners, Apollo Theater Found, Nat Symphony Orchestra & Morehouse Col Andrew Young Ctr Global Leadership; Bd Advisors Historically Black Cols & Univs. **Business Addr:** Chief Executive Officer, Chairman, The Stafford Foundation, PO Box 2665, Reston, VA 20195, **Business Phone:** (703)476-1000.

**STAFFORD-ODOM, TRISHA**
Basketball coach, basketball player. **Personal:** Born Nov 11, 1970, Los Angeles, CA; married DeWayne Odom; children: Amari & Trajen. **Educ:** Univ Calif, Berkeley, attended 1992. **Career:** Basketball player (retired), basketball coach; Calif Women's Basketball, 1988-92; San Jose Lasers, forward, 1997-98; Long Beach Stingrays, 1998; Houston Comets, 2001; Miami Sol, forward, 2002; Westchester High Sch, head girls' basketball coach, 2002-05; UnivCalif, Los Angeles, UCLA Bruins, asst coach, 2005-08, recruiting coord, 2007-08; Duke Univ, asst coach, 2009-11; Univ Nc, asst coach, 2011-; Concordia Univ Irvine, asst coach, 2013-. **Orgs:** Co-founder, Play Mode Found Inc. **Home Addr:** , Durham, NC. **Business Addr:** Head Coach, Concordia University Irvine, 1530 Concordia W Gym 200 E, Irvine, CA 92612-3203, **Business Phone:** (949)214-3232.

**STAGGERS, ROBIN L. (ROBIN CHANDLER-STAGGERS)**
Manager. **Personal:** Born Jan 24, 1958, Chicago, IL; daughter of Robert L Chandler and Ollie M Williams; children: Barrett Chandler & Davia Anaia. **Educ:** Ill State Univ, BS, bus admin, 1979; Roosevelt Univ, BS & BA, 1986, paralegal cert, 1992; DeVry Univ, Keller Grad Sch, Chicago, MS, human resource mgt, 2001. **Career:** Quaker Oats Co, community affairs, community rels coordr, 1981-86; Chicago Transit Authority, legal exec, asst gen coun, 1986-95, human resources analyst, 1995; Ill Dept Children & Family Serv, actg dep dir, dep dir human resources, 2003-05, chief staff, 2007-09; Designed2FitYou, dir & consult, 2009-; Cook County, analyst, 2011-13; Cook County Recorder Deeds, Govt Rels, spec exec asst to recorder, 2013-. **Orgs:** Lead coordr, Sweet Holy Spirit FGBC, Wedding Coordrs Ministry, 1993-. **Home Addr:** 7648 S St Lawrence Ave, Chicago, IL 60619-2420, **Home Phone:** (773)783-0417. **Business Addr:** Special Executive Assistant, Cook County Recorder of Deeds, 118 N Clark St, Chicago, IL 60602, **Business Phone:** (312)603-5050.

**STAHLY-BUTTS, MARBRE**
Advocate, activist. **Personal:** daughter of Burvell and Geraldine Butts-Stahly. **Educ:** Columbia Univ, BA; Oxford Univ, MA; Yale Law Sch, JD, 2013. **Career:** Community organizer Zimbabwe; teacher S Africa; Bronx Defenders, Equal Justice Initiative, 2010-13; Ctr Popular Democracy, fel & policy advocate, 2013-; Open Soc Found, prog organizer, 2013-15. **Honors/Awds:** Soros Justice Fellow, Center for Popular Democracy, 2013. **Business Addr:** Center for Popular Democracy, 449 Troutman St Suite A, Brooklyn, NY 11237, **Business Phone:** (347)985-2220.

**STAHNKE, WILLIAM E.**
Banker. **Career:** First Tex Bank, Dallas, pres & chief exec officer, 1987-97; BOK Financial; Am Bank Tex, NA, vice chmn, exec vpres; Citizens Nat Bank, Arlington, pres. **Orgs:** Pres, IBAT Leadership.

**STALEY, DAWN MICHELLE**
Basketball coach, basketball player. **Personal:** Born May 4, 1970, Philadelphia, PA; daughter of Estelle and Clarence. **Educ:** Univ Va, Charlottesville, VA, BA, rhet & commun studies, 1992. **Career:** Basketball player (retired), basketball coach, executive; Brazil, Spain, France, played prof basketball, 1992-95; Philadelphia Rage, guard, 1996-98; Charlotte Sting, guard, 1999-2005; Temple's Univ, head coach, 2000-08; Houston Comets, guard, 2005-06; USA Basketball Sr Nat Team, asst coach, 2006; Univ SC, womens head basketball coach, 2008-. **Orgs:** Founder, Dawn Staley Found, 1996-. **Special Achievements:** Elected to carry the United States flag at the opening ceremony of the Summer Olympics, 2004. **Business Addr:** Head Coach, University of South Carolina, 1714 Col St, Columbia, SC 29208.

**STALEY, DUCE**
Football coach, football player, broadcaster. **Personal:** Born Feb 27, 1975, Tampa, FL; son of Tena; children: Shakia, Damani Zihir & Kingson. **Educ:** Univ SC, sociol. **Career:** Football player (retired), coach, host; Philadelphia Eagles, kickoff returner, 1997, running back, 1998-2003, spec teams qual control coach, 2011-12, running backs coach, 2013-; Pittsburgh Steelers, 2006, running back, 2004-05; Gamecock Sports Radio Net, sideline reporter, currently; 107.5FM sports Radio, show host, currently. **Orgs:** Eagles Youth Partnership, Philadelphia; First Steps Prog; Variety Club; Direct Care Kids; founder, Catch 22 Found. **Honors/Awds:** Super Bowl champion XL; Eagles Ed Block Courage Award, 2001; ADDY Award, 2001; Neighborhood MVP Award, 2004; South Carolina's Athletic Hall of Fame, 2012. **Business Addr:** Running Backs Coach, Philadelphia Eagles, 1 Novacare Way, Philadelphia, PA 19145, **Business Phone:** (215)463-2500.

**STALEY, PASTOR KENNETH BERNARD**
President (organization), chief executive officer, businessperson. **Personal:** Born Dec 31, 1948, Philadelphia, PA; son of Kinzy and Bernice; married Shelia Keeys; children: Tabbatha, Christina & Harrison. **Educ:** Villanova Univ, BSCE, 1971; Miller Theol Sem, MDiv, 1975, DD, 1978; Am Asn Marriage & Family Therapist, clin, 1983. **Career:** Jos A McCollum Inc, engr training, 1966-69; RV Rulon Co, field engr, 1969; United Engrs & Constructors Inc, field engr, 1971-72; Kinzy Staley & Sons Inc, vpres, 1972-90, pres & chief exec officer, 1992-93; Summer Sch, prin, 2003; Christian Stronghold Baptist Church, assoc pastor; Covenant Group Inc, pres, prin, proj mgr, currently. **Orgs:** Bd mem, Kinzy Staley & Sons Inc, 1972-; bd mem, Christian Res & Develop, 1980-; bd mem, Mendenhall Ministries, 1981-; steering comn, Philadelphia Leadership Found, 1985-; bd mem, Greater Germantown Develop Corp, 1988-89; fel Christian Athletes, Pa state bd, 1992; steering comm, Billy Graham Crusade Philadelphia, 1992; Nat Soc Prof Engrs; Asn Cost Engrs; Am Arbit Asn; Am Ceramic Soc; Am Concrete Inst; Alpha Phi Alpha. **Honors/Awds:** Outstanding Young Man in America, US Jaycees, 1980-81, 1983. **Home Addr:** 1130 Lakeside Ave, Philadelphia, PA 19126-2308, **Home Phone:** (215)549-0758. **Business Addr:** Principal, Project Manager, Covenant Consulting Corp, 1130 Lakeside Ave, Philadelphia, PA 19004, **Business Phone:** (215)549-7271.

**STALKS, LARRIE W.**
Government official, secretary (office). **Personal:** Born Sep 28, 1925, Newark, NJ; married Frederick. **Educ:** Rutgers Univ; NY Univ. **Career:** Dept Health & Welfare City Newark, dir, 1966-70; Cent Planning Bd City Newark, exec secy, secy; Congressman Hugh J Addonizio, home dist secy. **Orgs:** Bd trustees, Cent Ward Girls Club; Edmund L Houston Found Rutgers Univ; Essex Co Youth House; pres, Metro Urban Social Serv; vpres, OMEGA Investment Corp; counr, Munic Career women Newark; founder, secy, Newark Comn Housing Corp; secy, Peoples Develop Corp; former pres, Esqui-Vogues Northern; vpres, Shanley Ave Civic Asn; life mem, chmn, Nat Advan Asn Colored People, Newark Br; state bd dir, Nat Advan Asn Colored People State Conf; past pub affairs chmn, Negro Bus & Prof Womens Club; past Ed, Citizenship; chmn, Newark Chap Coun Negro Women; Nat Planning Asn; Am Soc Planning Officials; vchmn, Newark Cent Ward; co-chmn, Newark Essex Co Meyner, Gov Club; Essex Co Rep Young Dem Conv; Newark Liaison All Co Campaigns; founder, onizer, adv Cent Ward Young Dem; Cong Liaison Kennedy Air-Lift; exec dir, Hugh Jaddonizio Civic Asn; chair, Essex County Dem Party; Minorities Affairs; chmn, Dem Party Co State; Essex County Regist Deeds. **Honors/Awds:** Community Service Award, Afro Am Newspaper, 1952; Achievement Award, Iota Phi Lamba, 1956; Achievement Award, Frontiers Am, 1957; Newark Br Nat Advan Asn Colored People Service Award, 1960; Associaiton Service Award, Stephen P Teamer Civic, 1962; Achievement Award, Negro Bus & Prof Women, 1963; Service Award, Metro Civic Asn, 1965; Service Award, ILA Local 1233, 1965; Ballantine Award, 1965; Laura Grant Award, 1965; Woman of the Year, Deomart Enterprises, 1965; Appreciation Award, Cent Planning Bd, 1967; Outstanding Women, Iota Phi Chap Sorority, 1968; Service Award, S Ward Little League, 1968; Achievement Award, Am Negro Assembly, 1968; Achievement Award, Municipal Career women Newark, 1968; Abraham Yecies Award, 1972; Service Award, After Hours Magazine, 1974. **Special Achievements:** First African American woman elected Essex County Register of Deeds and Mortgages. **Home Addr:** 131 Raymond Ave, South Orange, NJ 07079-2339, **Home Phone:** (973)763-4205.

**STALLING, RONALD EUGENE**
Police officer. **Personal:** Born Mar 11, 1946, Daytona Beach, FL; son of Lloyd George and Helen Katherine Bolden; married Paulette Marian Robinson; children: Kali & Dana. **Educ:** Southeastern Univ, Wa, DC, 1970; Am Univ, Wa, DC, 1974. **Career:** US Dept State, Wa, DC, admin asst, 1964-66, 1968-70; US Secret Serv, Clarksville, Md, Uniform Division, fed law enforcement officer, 1970-02. **Orgs:** Judge Advocate, Nat Black Police Asn, 1989-; secy, Alliance Black Fed Officers Inc, 1989-. **Honors/Awds:** Sustained Superior Performance Award. **Home Addr:** 13765 Triadelphia Mill Rd, Clarksville, MD 21029-1033. **Business Addr:** Judge Advocate, National Black Police Association Inc, 13765 Triadelphia Mill Rd, Clarksville, MD 21029, **Business Phone:** (301)854-1683.

**STALLINGS, REV. GEORGE AUGUSTUS, JR.**
Clergy, chief executive officer. **Personal:** Born Mar 17, 1948, New Bern, NC; son of George Sr and Dorothy Smith; married Sayomi Kamimoto; children: Shin Young III & Young Pal Marcus Mosiah. **Educ:** St Pius X Sem, BA, philos, 1970; Pontif Univ St Thomas Aquinas, STB, 1973, MA, pastoral theol, 1974, STL, 1975. **Career:** Ordained Roman Cath priest, 1974-89; Our Lady Queen Peace, Wash, DC, assoc pastor, 1974-76; St Teresa Avila, Wash, DC, pastor, 1976-88; Arch diocese Wash, DC, dir evangelism prog, 1988-89; Imani Temple African-Am Cath Congregation, founder, 1989-, pastor, 1989, bishop, 1990-91, sr pastor, archbishop, 1991-; SKS Press, pres & chief exec officer, currently. **Orgs:** Nat co-pres, Am Clergy Leadership Conf. **Honors/Awds:** Award for Meritorious Service, Mayor Wash; Outstanding Teaching Award, JL Francis Elem Sch, 1983-86; Doctor Sacred Theol, Eastern Theol Sem, Lynchburg, VA, 1993. **Special Achievements:** Featured on international television and radio programs, and in print media, since the founding of Imani Temple African-American Catholic Congregation, Stallings? appearances include the Oprah Winfrey Show, Larry King Live, 50 Minutes, the Phil Donahue Show, CNN, the British Broadcasting Network (BBC) and the Mario Costanza Show in Rome, Italy; First black "Golden Boy," Boy's Club of Richmond, 1972. **Business Addr:** Founder, Archbishop, Imani Temple African-Am Catholic Congregation, 609-611 Maryland Ave NE, Washington, DC 20002, **Business Phone:** (202)388-8155.

**STALLINGS, GREGORY RALPH**
Educator. **Personal:** Born Dec 28, 1957, Richmond, VA; son of Steward B Sr; married Mitzi Keyes; children: Brittny Jean. **Educ:** Col William & Mary, BA, geol, 1980; Univ Va, MA; Va Commonwealth Univ, MA; Va State Univ, MA. **Career:** Educator (retired); Boys Club Richmond, unit dir, 1980-81; Richmond Pub Schs, teacher, 1981-86, coordr intervention progs, 1986-88, instrnl leader, 1988-91, teacher specialist, 1991-95, J L Francis Elem Sch, teacher, 2004-; dir educ affairs, pres, Xi Delta Lambda, Alpha Phi Alpha, 1985-90; Summerbridge Richmond, acad dean, 1995-2010; Learning Bridge Prog, dean fac & students, 1998-2010. **Orgs:** Col adv, Theta Rho Chap, Alpha Phi Alpha, VA Common wealth Univ; treas, pres male usher bd & chmn trustee bd, First Union Baptist Church; basketball coach Recreation Dept; area dir, VACAPAF; instr, VA Ctr Educ Leadership. **Home Addr:** 5146 Snead Rd, Richmond, VA 23224, **Home Phone:** (804)745-3702.

**STALLINGS, JAMES RAIFORD**
Administrator, teacher. **Personal:** Born Oct 9, 1936, Augusta, GA; married Geneva Butler; children: Sylvia B (deceased) & James R. **Educ:** Allen Univ, BS, 1959; So Ill Univ, MS, 1968. **Career:** Richmond Co Bd Educ, math teacher, 1959-71; C&S Nat Bank, loan officer & asst br mgr, 1971-75; Augusta Col, dir financial aid, 1975. **Orgs:** Nat Bankers Asn, 1971-75; Bank PAC, 1973; Alpha Phi Alpha; hon mem, Ga Asn Stud Fin Aid Adminr; Nat Asn Stud Fin Aid Adminr; Southern Asn Stud Fin Aid Adminr. **Home Addr:** PO Box 14905, Augusta, GA 30919, **Home Phone:** (706)733-0939.

**STALLINGS, RAMONDO ANTONIO**
Football player, executive. **Personal:** Born Nov 21, 1971, Winston-Salem, NC. **Educ:** San Diego State Univ, 1994. **Career:** Football player (retired), owner; Cincinnati Bengals, defensive end, 1994-97; BC Lions, 2000; Edmonton Eskimos, 2000; Los Angeles Xtreme, defensive end, 2001-02; Arena Football, 2002-03; Am Mortgage Specialist, 2003-05; Nat Wholesale Mortgage, 2005-07; Your Needs 1st, owner, 2007-. **Business Addr:** Owner, Your Needs 1st LLC, 8912 E Shangri La Rd, Scottsdale, AZ 85260.

**STALLS, DR. MADLYN A.**
Educator, manager. **Personal:** Born Oct 22, 1947, Metropolis, IL; daughter of Robert A and Freda Mae Houston; children: Robert C Goodwin. **Educ:** Southern Ill Univ, BA, 1970, MS, 1976, PhD, 1991, MSW, 2002. **Career:** Ill Dept C & Family Servs, child welfare worker, 1970-75; Ill Farmers Union, manpower coordr, 1976-78; Southern Ill Univ Carbondale Sch Tech Careers, res & serv coordr, 1978-80, vpres, develop skills training specialist, currently; Ctr Basic Skills, coord supple inst, develop skills supt inr, vis asst prof, Black Am studies, develop skills training specialist, currently. **Orgs:** Founder & coordr, Black Women's Coalition, 1983; mentor, Develop Proj Magic, 1984-; consult, Jack Co Pub Housing Initiatives Training Prog, 1985; steering comt, 2002, Ill Comn Black Concerns Higher Educ, 1985-, vice chair, Southern Region, 1997-98; fel Ill Comn Black Concerns Higher Educ, 1984; consult, Southern Ill Univ Carbondale Women's Studies Film Proj, 1986-; Am Asn Couns & Devel; Nat Coun Black Studies; Kappa Delta Pi, 1987; exec dir, Star Human Serv Develop Corp Inc, 1987-; founder & convener, Assembly African Am Women, 1989; Am Asn Univ Women; Southern Ill Univ Alumni Asn. **Home Addr:** 407 N Robert A Stalls Ave, Carbondale, IL 62901-1609. **Business Addr:** Vice President, Developmental Skills Training Specialist, Southern Illinois University Carbondale, Ctr Acad Success Woody Hall Rm C7 900 S Norm Ave, Carbondale, IL 62901-4720, **Business Phone:** (618)536-6646.

**STALLWORTH, HON. ALMA G.**
Government official. **Personal:** Born Nov 15, 1932, Little Rock, AR; married Thomas F Jr; children: Thomas III & Keith. **Educ:** Highland Park Jr Col, AS, health educ & prom, 1949; Wayne State Univ, MA, health educ & prom, 1951; Chelsea Univ, attended; Merrill Palmer Inst, attended 1965. **Career:** Parent Involvement Prog Head start Archdiocesan Detroit, cord, 1964-68, dir vol serv, 1968-69; US Bur Census, community, serv specialist; Ctr Study Pub Policies Young C, policy assoc; High-Scope Educ Res; St John's Day Care Ctr, dir, 1969-70; Oak Grove Day Care Ctr; ran state Sen 7th Dist, 1974; Hist Dept City Detroit, dep dir, 1978; State Mich, Mich 8 Dist, rep, 1970-74, 1982-96, chair & rep, 1996-2005; Telecommunications, State-Fed Assembly, NCSL, vice chair, currently. **Orgs:** Oak Grove AME Ch; Demo Party; Natl Order Women Legislators; secy & chmn, Mich Legis Black Caucus, 1985-; Mayor's Citizens Task Force; Natl Orgn Women Detroit Sect; State Training Sch Adv Coun; Natl Inst Women's Wrongs; Wayne Co Juv Justice Commn; exec comm, United Negro Col Fund, Natl Conf State Legis; hon, Alpha Kappa Alpha Sorority; brd dir, Woman gov; Heat & Warmth Fund, Wayne City Task Force Infant Mortality; founder, pres emer, Black Child Develop Inst; founder & interim exec dir, Black Caucus Found, 1985; sch bd mem, Detroit, currently; chair, Mich Legis Black Caucus; exec bd mem, Lula Belle Stewart Ctr Inc. **Home Addr:** 19793 Sorrento St, Detroit, MI 48235-1149, **Home Phone:** (313)863-9895. **Business Addr:** State Representative, Michigan 8 District, Rm N 687 Cora B Anderson House Off Bldg, Lansing, MI 48909, **Business Phone:** (517)373-2276.

**STALLWORTH, ANNIE P.**
Government official, manager, chief executive officer. **Personal:** Born May 15, 1932, De Kalb, TX; children: Charles, Patricia Banks, Lilye Chaffin, Rachel Carr, Allen O Jr & Eric Darrel. **Educ:** Langston Univ, bus admin; Delta Col, unit comput sci; Stockton Jr Col, grad, 1949. **Career:** Government official (retired); Pac Tel, tel operator, supvr, asst operating mgr, 1963-68, personnel, employ, recruiting & coun, develop affirmative action plan, 1968-72, customer servs, educ & training, 1972-83, mkt adminr, sales, 1982-83; AT&T Info Systs, techn consult, mkt, 1983-85; trade SOURCES, mgr, chief exec officer, 1986-95. **Orgs:** Educ comt, Nat Asn Advan Colored People, 1970-94; credential comt, Dameron Hosp Bd Mem, 1970-; Bd Ed, Stockton Unified Sch Dist, 1973-90; Co-founder, first vpres, pres, chair bylaws, nominating comt, Calif Coalition Black Sch Bd, 1974-90; bd dir, usher bd, Christ Temple Church, 1975; treas scholar fund, 1978-86; pres, 1986-90, vpres, 1984-86; Stockton Chapt Links. **Honors/Awds:** Hon Life Mem James Monroe PTA, 1964; Commendation voc Ed Dr Wilson Riles Supt Pub Instr State CA, 1974; Black Woman Ed Stockton Comn, 1974; Nominee Soroptimist Woman of the Year Award, 1978; Women of Achievement Award, Nat Asn Advan Colored People, 1992; Girl Scout Role Model, 1994. **Home Addr:** 8250 Toulouse Way, Stockton, CA 95210.

**STALLWORTH, OSCAR B., SR.**
Executive, manager. **Personal:** Born Dec 5, 1944, Mobile, AL; married Elsie Thigpen; children: Oscar Jr & Brett. **Educ:** BS, mech, 1966. **Career:** Castings & Brake Components Motor Wheel Corp, jr proj engr motor wheel, 1967-68, prod engr passenger car brakes & wheels, motor wheel, 1968-71, mgr, 1971; Coland Inc, pres. **Orgs:** Alpha Phi Alpha Frat, 1964; Soc Automotive Engrs, 1967; Am Soc Metals, 1967; Am Foundryman's Soc, 1967; adv, solicitor Jr Achievement, 1968; Boys Club Lansing; vice chmn, Ingham Co Dem Party, 1970-72; mgr, Field Opers Polit Campaigns, 1970; chmn, Voter Regis A Phillip Randolph Inst, 1972. **Home Addr:** 451 McPherson Ave, Lan-

sing, MI 48915-1157, **Home Phone:** (517)482-4378. **Business Addr:** President, Coland Inc, 451 McPherson Ave, Lansing, MI 48915-1157, **Business Phone:** (517)482-4378.

### STALLWORTH, YOLANDA W.
Administrator. **Personal:** Born Jan 16, 1959, Mobile, AL; daughter of Henry and Mattie Webb; married Alfred L; children: Warren H & Sascha E. **Educ:** Tenn State Univ, BS, 1981; Xavier Univ, MA, 1997; Ohio Supt Leadership Develop Class, grad. **Career:** San Antonio State Sch, psych asst, 1986-90; Montgomery County Bd Ment Retardation & Develop Disabilities, asst dir, 1990-96; Hamilton County Bd Ment Retardation & Develop Disabilities, asst to supt, dir, 1996-. **Orgs:** Charter mem, Zeta Phi Beta Sorority Inc; vpres, Pi Sigma Zeta, 1992-; adv bd mem, Wright State Univ, Biomed Rehab Eng; bd mem, Norcen Behav Health Systs. **Home Addr:** 797 Cedarhill Dr, Cincinnati, OH 45240-1331, **Home Phone:** (513)825-8730. **Business Addr:** Assistant to the Superintdent, Hamilton County Board of Mental Retardation & Developmental Disabilities, 1520 Madison Rd, Cincinnati, OH 45206-1747, **Business Phone:** (513)794-3300.

### STAMPER, HENRY J.
Executive. **Career:** First Federal Savings & Loan Asn Scotlandville, Baton Rouge, La, chief exec; Henry J Stamper & Assoc, chief exec officer, currently. **Business Addr:** Chief Executive Officer, Henry J Stamper & Associates, 1287 Elysian Dr, Baton Rouge, LA 70810-2625, **Business Phone:** (225)769-0834.

### STAMPLEY, GILBERT ELVIN
Vice president (organization), lawyer. **Personal:** Born May 24, 1943, Baton Rouge, LA; married Ester J Francis. **Educ:** Grambling State Univ, BA, 1965; Tulane Univ Sch Law, JD, 1972. **Career:** Men's Affairs Jarvis Christian Col, dep dir, 1965-67; EEO Comn, case analyst, 1970-72; Smith & Stampley, atty, 1972-75; Harris Stampley Mckee Bernard & Broussard, atty; Orleans Parish Prog Voters League, vpres; Young Dem Am; Urban League; atty, currently. **Orgs:** La State Dem Cent Com Dist, 1962; Earl Warren Fel, 1971-72; City Planning Comn New Orleans, 1976-81; Am Bar Asn; Martinet Soc; La State Bar Asn; Nat Bar Asn; Nat Conf Black Lawyers Exec Comt; Nat Asn Advan Colored People; Palm-air Civil Improv Asn. **Home Addr:** 616 Baronne St, New Orleans, LA 70112-2457, **Home Phone:** (504)566-1393. **Business Addr:** Lawyer, 1100 Tulane Ave, New Orleans, LA 70112-1909.

### STAMPS, DR. DELORES BOLDEN
Chief executive officer, school administrator, consultant. **Personal:** Born Mar 16, 1947, Monticello, MS; daughter of Balene Sutton and Peter James; married Alvin; children: Tiffany & Katrina; married Alvin; children: Keceya Campbell & Jason Campbell. **Educ:** Tougaloo Col, BA, 1968; Univ Southern Miss, MS, 1972, PhD, 1985; Harvard Univ, MA, 1974. **Career:** Jackson State Univ, asst prof educ, 1985-88, acad skills ctr, dir, 1976-88; Tougaloo Col, dir instnl res, 1988-89, vpres & instnl advan; Piney Woods Sch, Off Instnl Advan, vpres; Found Educ & Econ Develop, pres; Southern Area Links Inc, coordr; DB Stamps Enerprises Inc, pres & chief exec officer, currently. **Orgs:** Unit leader, League Women Voters, 1975-; chairperson, Spec Events Comn, UNCF, 1985-; partic, Leadership Jackson, Jackson Chamber Comm, 1988; chair, Southern Area Links Inc; bd trustee, Miss Mus Art, 1989-; dir, capital campaign; Black Issues Higher Educ; Southern Initiative Algebra Proj; Mid-S Delta Consortium; Kellogg Found; founding exec dir, Medgar Evers Inst; Int vol serv orgn;Comn Childhood Obesity Prev. **Home Phone:** (601)366-8417. **Business Addr:** President, Chief Executive Officer, DB Stamps Enerprises Inc, 1210 Holbrook Cir, Jackson, MS 39206-2031, **Business Phone:** (601)362-6391.

### STAMPS, JOE, JR. See Obituaries Section.

### STAMPS, LEON PREIST
Government official, auditor. **Personal:** Born Dec 29, 1953, Bronx, NY; married Barbara Logan. **Educ:** Boston Col, BS, acct, 1975; Northeastern Univ, MBA, bus policy, 1976. **Career:** Government official, auditor (retired); Arthur Anderson & Co, acct, 1977-79; Roxbury Comm Col, acct prof, 1979; Xerox Corp, equip control mgr, 1979-81, ne reg control mgr, 1981-84; City Boston, city auditor controller, 1984. **Orgs:** Bd dir, Boston Col Alumni Asn, 1975-; Acct Internship Continental Group Inc, 1976; consult dir pub serv, Blue Cross & Blue Shield, 1976; Nat Asn Black Accountants, 1984-; Boston Black Media Coalition, 1985. **Home Addr:** 955 Ctr St, Jamaica Plain, MA 02130-3023, **Home Phone:** (704)442-0638.

### STAMPS, REV. LYNMAN A., SR.
Clergy, army officer. **Personal:** Born May 31, 1940, Utica, MS; son of Milton and Emma Ross; married Margarett C Donaldson; children: Lynman A Jr. **Educ:** Lane Col Jackson, BA, 1968; Webster Univ, MAT, 1972; US Dept Justice, cert jail opers; Nat Inst Correct Admin Studies. **Career:** Ill State Sch Boys, cottage parent, 1960-62; Chicago Parent Soc Adj Sch Boys, family instr, 1962-63; AUS, MP, 1963-65; Trinity Temple CME Church, 1964-66; Martin Tabernacle CME Church, pastor, 1966-69; Parkers Chapel CME Church, pastor, 1969-70; Clark Jr HS E St Louis, Ill, civic teacher, 1968-71; Pilgrim Temple CME Church, pastor, 1970-74; E St Louis, civil serv comnr, 1971-74; St Louis Correc Inst, supt, 1972-76; Radio Sta WESL E St Louis, mgr part owner, 1972-78; Coleman Temple CME Church, pastor, 1974-83; Normandy Jr HS Normandy, Mo, teacher, 1981-84; Parrish Temple CME Church, pastor, 1983-84; First Christian Methodist Independent Church, St Louis, pastor, founder, 1983-; Marion Comn, managing partner; St Louis Bd Educ, mil specialist, 1988-89; Pruitt Mil Acad, St Louis, mil specialist, 1988-2003; Trenton Civic League Trenton, TN, founder, pres. **Orgs:** Life mem, Nat Asn Advan Colored People; Am Correct Asn; exec bd mem, E St Louis Madison St Clair Co Urban League, 1972-73; exec bd mem, E St Louis Model City Agency, 1972-73; vpres, Downtown Merchant Columbus, MS, 1985. **Honors/Awds:** Certificate of Honor, Utica Inst Jr Col, 1956; Good Conduct Medal, AUS, 1963-65; Award Plaque, Offenders Chap AA, 1974; Man of the Year Award, Afro-Am Club Columbus, MS, 1985; Certificate Award, Outstanding Achievements Jobs Workshop Ex Offender Prog Human Dev Corp Prog Metro St Louis, 1976; Certificate of Appreciation, Gateway Jaycees & US Jaycees, 1976. **Home Addr:** 12031 Mereview Dr, St Louis, MO 63146, **Home Phone:** (314)567-3805. **Business Addr:** Pastor, Founder, First Christian Methodist Independent Church, 6765 St Charles Rock Rd, Pagedale, MO 63133-1705, **Business Phone:** (314)383-6227.

### STAMPS, SPURGEON MARTIN DAVID
Educator, school administrator. **Personal:** Born Jul 16, 1937, Nashville, TN; son of Spurgeon Martin David Sr and Nina Bessie Dobbins; married Miriam Cunningham Burney; children: Monique Yvonne & Spurgeon Martin David III. **Educ:** Tenn State Univ, BS, sociol, 1960; Wash State Univ, MA, sociol, 1965, PhD, sociol, 1967. **Career:** Dean (retired); Cameron High Sch, teacher, counr, 1960-62; Wash State Univ, teaching asst, 1962-67; Norfolk State Univ, asst prof, 1967-77; Syracuse Univ, assoc procto prof, sociol, 1977-82; Univ S Fla, assoc dean & pro sociol, 1982-95, interim dean, Col Arts & Scis, 1995-96, dean, Col Arts & Scis, prof sociol, interim provost, 2000-01, provost & vpres acad affairs, 2001-03, Prof Sociol, 2003-. **Orgs:** Kappa Delta Pi, 1957-; Alpha Kappa Delta, 1965-; Southern Socioll Asn, 1982-; Manpower Utilization Tidewater, Hampton Roads, VIR, 1969; estab & served ed, Rev ARO Issues & Cult, 1978-82; Participation High Sch Adolescents Vol Activ, 1979; Black Elderly Presbyterians, New York, 1982; Pi Gamma Mu, 1983-; Tampa-Hillsborough County Human Rights Coun, 1988-; Fla Ctr C & Youth, exec com, 1990-; Literacy Vols Am, Fla, vip, 1990-; Golden Key Hon Soc, 1990-. **Home Addr:** 6102 Soaring Ave, Temple Terrace, FL 33617-1375, **Home Phone:** (813)988-8607.

### STANCELL, DR. ARNOLD FRANCIS
Executive, educator. **Personal:** Born Nov 16, 1936, Harlem, NY; son of Francis and Maria Lucas; married Constance Newton; children: Christine. **Educ:** City Col NY, BS (magna cum laude), chemical engineering, 1958; Mass Inst Technol, DSc, chem engineering, 1962. **Career:** Educator, executive (retired); Mobil Oil Corp, Edison, NJ, scientist & res mgr, 1962-72, NY, plng mgr, 1972-76, vpres chem div, 1976-80, mgr corp plng, 1980-82, Eng, vpres, reg exe mkt & refining, 1982-84, NY, plng vpres, mkt & refining, 1985-86, vpres US oil & natural gas bus, 1987-88, vpres int area, 1993; Mass Inst Technol, fel, assoc prof chem engrg, 1970-71; VIR, vpres, Int Oil & Natural Gas Bus, 1989-93; GEO Tech, Ga Inst Technol, prof chem engr, turner prof chem & biomolecular engineering, 2001, prof emer, 2004. **Orgs:** Am Inst Chem Eng, 1962-; Sigma Xi, 1965-; adv comt, Mass Inst Technol, 1976-; vis comt, Dept Chem Engrg, Mass Inst Technol, 1985-; adv bd, Col Engrg City Col New York, 1990-; adv comt, Carnegie-Mellon, 1999; Nat Acad Engrg; co-chair, Bd Chem Sci & Technol NRC, 2003-; pres, Nat Sci Bd, 2011; gov bd, Nat Res Coun. **Special Achievements:** First African American to earn his Ph.D. degree from MIT in chemical engineering in 1962. **Home Addr:** 15 Woodside Dr, Greenwich, CT 06830, **Home Phone:** (203)622-7135. **Business Addr:** Professor Emeritus, Turner Servant Leadership Chair Emeritus, Georgia Institute of Technology, 311 Ferst Dr NW, Atlanta, GA 30332-0100, **Business Phone:** (404)894-1838.

### STANCELL, DR. DOLORES WILSON PEGRAM
Nurse, lawyer. **Personal:** Born Oct 26, 1936, New York, NY; married Vernon H; children: Timothy & Vernon. **Educ:** Rutgers Univ, BA, 1970; Rutgers Sch Law, JD, 1974; Mich State Univ, Ann Regulatory Studies Prog, 1976. **Career:** Fordham Hosp, staff nurse, 1957-58; Beth Israel Hosp, staff nurse, 1958-62; Head Start, nurse, 1966; Head Start MCEOC, nurse, 1967; Rutgers Urban Studies Ctr, rsch asst, 1968; Middlesex County Legal Serv, legal intern, 1970; Jersey Shore Med Ctr, nurse, 1972; Rutgers Univ Rutgers J Comput & Law, admin, 1973; Hon David D Furman Super Ct Chan Div NJ, law secy, 1974-75; NJ Dept Pub Adv, Div Rate Coun, asst dep pub adv; Camden Regional Legal Serv, supv atty. **Orgs:** Am Nurses Asn; NJ State Nurses Asn; vol, urban agt Rutgers Urban Studies Ctr, 1967-68; coord, Rutgers-Douglass Col Elem Sch Tutorial Prog, 1967-68; Pub Policy Forum Civil Dis & Forum Future NJ Rutgers Univ, 1968; trustee, Unitarian Soc, 1970-72; bd mem, Parents Asn Rutgers Prep Sch, 1970-71; vol, Ocean-Monmouth Legal Serv, 1972; Nb YWCA; Urban League; Nat Asn Advan Colored People; Gen Pract, 1976-77; Health League & Health Planning Serv Comt, 1976-78; Monmouth Bar Asn; Criminal Pract Comn, 1976-78; Med Costs, Breath Life, 1977; Acad Adv Comt, 1977-78; Am Bar Asn, Sect Legal Educ & Admis Bar, 1977-78; Forum Comn Health Law, 1977-78; vpres, Women's Div, Nat Bar Asn, 1977-78, chair, 1980-82, pres, 1986-87; vpres, Civil Trial Advocacy Sect, 1977-78; Legis & Uniform & State Laws Comn, 1977-78; Fed Bar Asn; Garden State Bar Asn; NJ State Bar Asn; treas, Asn Black Women Lawyers, NJ, 1981-83; pres, rec secy, Nat Conf Women's Bar Associations, currently; Rutgers Law Sch Alumni Asn; secy, Am Asn Nurse Attorneys; Rutgers Univ Alumni Asn; panelist, MRC-TV, NY Prog. **Honors/Awds:** Human Rels Award, Fordham Hosp, 1957. **Special Achievements:** First Vice-president of the Womens Division of the National Bar Association; Articles Wilson, Computerization of Welfare Recipients, Implications for the Individual & The Right to Privacy for Rutgers Journal of Computers and The Law 163 (1974); Minority Workers 1 Womens Rights Law Reporter 71, (1972-73). **Home Addr:** 52 Sabina Terr, Freehold, NJ 07728. **Business Addr:** Recording Secretary, National Conference of Women's Bar Associations, PO Box 82366, Portland, OR 97282, **Business Phone:** (503)775-4396.

### STANDIFER, BEN H.
Educator. **Personal:** Born Aug 24, 1934, Itasca, TX; son of Nathaniel C and Emma Jean; married Esther; children: Sonceria, Fawn, Ben Jr & Corey. **Educ:** Prairie View A&M Col, BS, 1959; Carleton Col, attended 1965; Univ Tex, attended 1968; Ill Inst Tech, 1969; Cornell Univ, attended 1970; Tex Christian Univ, MA, 1972, cert supv, 1973; Tex Wesleyan Col, attended 1974; Northern Tex State Univ, cert admin, 1975. **Career:** Ft Worth Pub Sch, math teacher, 1959-73, math improv specialist, 1974-; FWISD, math instrnl improv specialist, 1973-74; Dunbar Sr High Sch, Ft Worth Indep Sch Dist, prin, 1980-81; Our Lady Victory Priv Sch Bd, pres. **Orgs:** Organized Parent Stud Study Group Como High Community, 1960; pres, Home & Sch Asn; vpres, PTA, 1973; Ft Worth Classroom Teacher Asn; Tex Classroom Teacher Asn; Nat Educ Asn; Tex Indust Educ Asn; Phi Delta Kappa Frat; Ft Worth Area Coun Teacher Math; Task Force Team Lay Acad United Meth Ch; bd mem, Ft Worth-tarrant Co Community Develop Fund Inc; steering com mem, Conf Advan Math Teaching. **Honors/Awds:** Received numerous awards; Outstanding Teacher & State Teacher of the Year Award, 1972; Headliner in Education Award, Ft Worth Press Club. **Special Achievements:** Published books: "A Practical Guide to Good Study Habits", McGraw Hill Inc, 1957; created program at Western Hills HS in Audio Tutorial Instruction, 1970; organize ed tutorial program to help students in Wester Hills Eidglea Como Arlington Heights Communities, 1971; Published book of Audio Tutorial Instruction, 1972; Publication Improvement of Curricular/Instructional System, 1974. **Home Addr:** PO Box 1090, Alvarado, TX 76009, **Home Phone:** (817)366-1831. **Business Addr:** Principal, Fort Worth Independent School District Public Schools, 3210 W Lancaster, Ft. Worth, TX 76104, **Business Phone:** (817)871-3126.

### STANISLAUS, REV. GREGORY K.
Educator, clergy. **Personal:** Born Jun 9, 1957, New York, NY; son of Eula James and Gregory Talbert; married Ruth Y Dyer; children: 5. **Educ:** Univ Southern Calif, Los Angeles, CA, BS, biol, 1981; Western State Univ Sch Law, Fullerton, CA, JD, 1985; NY Theol Sem, NY, Mdiv, 1987. **Career:** McCutchen, Verleger & Shea, Los Angeles, Calif, legal researcher, 1981-86; Bd Educ, Brooklyn, New York, sci teacher, 1986-; Bethel Baptist Church, Brooklyn, New York, youth minister, 1988; St John Baptist Church, New York, pastor, sr clergy, currently. **Orgs:** Founder, Stanislaus Theatrical Group, 1985; staff, Brooklyn Ctr Urban Environ, 1987-; Nat Asn Advan Colored PeopleBrooklyn), 1989-91; Kings County Adv Bd, 1990-91; supt, Bethel Baptist Church Sunday Sch, 1990-; founder, Youth United Change World Int. **Home Addr:** 104 Clarken Dr, West Orange, NJ 07052, **Home Phone:** (973)736-9213. **Business Addr:** Pastor, Senior Clergy, St John Baptist Church, 4 Henry St, Inwood, NY 11096, **Business Phone:** (516)371-3408.

### STANLEY, CAROL JONES
Educator, secretary (office). **Personal:** Born Mar 16, 1947, Durham, NC; daughter of Doctor Young and Willie Ruth Lyons (deceased); married Donald Andrew. **Educ:** NC Cent Univ, Durham, NC, BS, 1969, Sch Law, 1974, MS, 1975; Univ NC, Greensboro, NC, attended 1990. **Career:** Educator (retired); NC Cent Univ, res asst, 1980-81, Sch Bus, Div Acad Affairs, adj instr, 1989, Sch Law, admin secy, 1991-94, asst dir recruitment, 1994, support staff fac serv; Fayetteville State Univ, adj instr, 1985-87. **Orgs:** NC Bus Ed Assoc, 1990-91; chairperson, Publicity Comt, N Cent Bus Educ Asn, 1990; tutor vietnamese, Immaculate Conception Church, 1990; regist reader, Delta Sigma Theta Sorority; Asn Supv & Curric Develop; Nat Bus Educ Asn; Carolina Stud Info Syst. **Honors/Awds:** Delta Sigma Theta Scholarship, 1988-89; Law Office Mgt; NC Cent Univ. **Home Addr:** 1611 Duke University Rd Apt 8F, Durham, NC 27701.

### STANLEY, MAJOR GEN. CLIFFORD LEE
Executive, military leader. **Personal:** Born Mar 31, 1947, Washington, DC; married Rosalyn Hill; children: Angela Yvonne. **Educ:** SC State Univ, BS, psychol, 1969; Johns Hopkins Univ, MS, coun, 1977; Amphibious Warfare Sch, 1978; Naval War Col, 1983; USMC Command Staff Col, 1984; Nat War Col, attended 1988; Univ Pa, EdD; Spalding Univ, LLD. **Career:** Major general (retired); Marine Corps Air Ground Combat Ctr, comndg gen, maj genera, 1998-2002, dep comndg gen; Univ Pa, exec vpres, chief operating off, 2002-03; Scholar Am, pres, 2004-09; US under secy Defense Personnel & Readiness, 2009-11; US Naval Acad, psychol & leadership instr; Marine Corps Inst, exec officer; Marine Barracks, parade comdr; Asst Secy Navy, spec asst & marine corps aide; Off Asst Secy State E Asian & Pac Affairs, Pentagon, desk officer; Marine Corps Recruit Depot Parris Island, depot inspector & comdr; dir Fed Bur Invest, spec asst; US Second Fleet, fleet marine officer; Marine Corps, Washington, dir pub affair. **Orgs:** Bd dir, White House Fel Asn; McCormic Educ Found; life mem, Kappa Alpha Psi Fraternity; bd trustee, Spalding Univ; bd gov, Civil War & Underground Rr Mus, Philadelphia; vice chmn, SC State Univ Found; pres, Philadelphia Alumni Chap, SC State Univ Alumni Asn; pres, Scholar Am; bd dir, McCormick Educ Found; US Naval Inst; dist chair, Northern Dist Boy Scouts Am. **Honors/Awds:** Legion of Merit; Defense Meritorious Service Medal; Meritorious Service Medal with Gold Star; Navy Commendation Medal; Navy Achievement Medal; Civilian Award, Nat Asn Advan Colored People; Meritorious Service Award, Nat Asn Advan Colored People; Roy Wilkins Award, Nat Asn Advan Colored People; American Legion Award. **Special Achievements:** First-ever African-American regimental commander. **Home Addr:** 2029 Stone Ridge Lane, Villanova, PA 19085-1735, **Home Phone:** (610)525-1968.

### STANLEY, CRAIG A.
State government official. **Personal:** Born Nov 20, 1955, Newark, NJ; married Debra; children: Camille, Christina & Cathryn. **Educ:** Univ Hartford, BA, polit sci, 1978; Baruch Col, MPA, 1999. **Career:** Essex County Col, prof; Wangtabs Inc, sales admin, regional mgr, 1980-85; Urban Data Systs, sales exec, 1985-88; Twenty Eigth Assembly Dist, assemblyman, 1996-2008. **Orgs:** Nat Asn Advan Colored People; Omega Phi Epsilon Fraternity; dir corp progs, YMWCA Newark & Vicinity. **Home Addr:** 137 Carolina Ave, Irvington, NJ 07111-2663, **Home Phone:** (973)375-8848. **Business Addr:** NJ.

### STANLEY, DONNA JONES
Executive. **Personal:** Born Nov 19, 1955, KY; daughter of Jane Dance; children: Stephanie Marie Reynolds; married Jerry; children: Stephanie. **Educ:** Murray State Univ, BS, social work, 1977; Univ Baltimore, MBA, 1986; Aspen Inst Humanistic Studies & Univ Md Nonprofit Mgt Inst, cert, 1988; Harvard Univ, cert, 1996. **Career:** Westvaco Corp, Wickliffe, Ky, asst buyer, 1977-79; The Chimes Inc, asst dir adult training serv, 1980-81; United Way Cent Md, dept dir, 1984-89. **Orgs:** DST Sorority, 1976; br dir, Vol Action Ctr, Cent Md Inc, 1981-84; chmn, Asn Baltimore Area Grantmakers; chmn, MD State Sch-Based Health Ctr Initiative; Asn Black Found Exec; Nat Asn Black Found Exec; exec dir, Assoc Black Charities, 1989-2003; pres, chief exec officer, Urban League Greater Cincinnati, 2003-; co-chair, PULSE; bd mem, Greater Cincinnati Chamber Com; bd mem, Downtown Cincinnati Inc; Delta Sigma Theta Sorority. **Business Addr:** President, Chief Executive Officer, Urban League of Greater Cincinnati, 3458 Reading Rd, Cincinnati, OH 21201-5515, **Business Phone:** (513)281-9955.

### STANLEY, ELLIS M., SR.
Government official. **Personal:** Born Jun 13, 1951, Shallotte, NC; son of Lewis A and Mae Belle Bryant; married Iris M White; children: Ellis M Jr & Christopher J. **Educ:** Univ NC, Chapel Hill, BA, polit sci, 1973. **Career:** Brunswick County Govt, Bolivia, NC, dir emergency mgt, 1975-82; Durham-Durham County Govt, Durham, NC, dir emergency mgt, 1982-87; Atlanta-Fulton County Govt, Atlanta, GA, dir emergency mgt, 1987-97; City Los Angeles, asst CAO, emergency prepardness div, 1997-2000, gen mgr, 2000-07; Western Emergency Mgtt Servs, dir, 2007; DNC Planning City & County Denver, dir, 2009-; St. Petersburg Col Terrorism Sch, adj; Multidisciplinary Ctr Earthquake Engineering Res, advisor, currently; City Los Angeles Emergency Preparedness Dept, gen mgr, currently. **Orgs:** Pres, Nat Forum Black Pub Admin, Atlanta Chap; pres, Nat Coord Coun Emergency Mgt, 1985, state rep, 1988-; Fulton Red Cross Adv Comt, 1987-; Red Cross Emergency Community Serv Comn, 1987-; Hazardous Mat Adv Coun, 1988-; Leadership Atlanta, 1990; pres, Nat Defense Transp Asn, Atlanta Chap; NCCEM Cert Counselors; bd natural disasters, Nat Weather Svc; Modernization Transition Comt; pres, Int Asn Emergency Managers; vpres, Bus & Indust Coun Emergency Planning & Preparedness; bd mem, Nat Inst Urban Search & Rescue; adj instr, Nat Terrorism Preparedness Inst; La Chap Am Red Cross, Disaster Preparedness Comn; comnr, Emergency Preparedness Comn Los Angeles; Bd Visitors Emergency Mgt Inst; Calif Forensic Sci Inst; Southern Calif Emergency Servs Asn; Los Angeles Transp Found; Nat Acad Pub Admin, 2007-; Am Soc Prof Emergency Planners; vice chair, Asn Contingency Planners; chair, Cert Emergency Managers Cert Comn; vice chmn, Am Red Cross; bd visitor, FEMA's Emergency Mgt Inst. **Honors/Awds:** Presidential Citation, US Civil Defense Asn, 1983; testified several times before the US Congress on Emergency Mgmt, 1985-86; lead Delegation to China to study Emergency Mgt, 1988; presented at 1st Security Sem, Caribbean, 1988; adj instr, Nat Emergency Training Ctr; Certified Emergency Mar; Post Naval Grad Sch, Grad Exec Leadership Prog; John F Kennedy Sch Govt Nat. **Home Addr:** 121 S Hope St Suite 305, Los Angeles, CA 90012-5005, **Home Phone:** (213)613-1060. **Business Addr:** General Manager, City of Los Angeles Emergency Preparedness Department, 200 N Main St Suite 1500, Los Angeles, CA 90012, **Business Phone:** (213)485-3469.

### STANLEY, THORNTON, SR.
Entrepreneur. **Personal:** Born Jan 1, 1937; children: 4. **Educ:** Ala A&M Univ, agr & landscape design, 1957. **Career:** Stanley Construct Co Inc, founder, 1961-; Stanley Construct Co Inc, pres, currently. **Orgs:** Bd dir, Top Ala Regional Coun Govt; pres, Top Ala Regional Coun Govt, currently. **Honors/Awds:** Small Business Person of the Year, US Small Bus Admin, 2001. **Special Achievements:** Awarded by Pres George W Bush, 2001. **Home Addr:** 1807 Lydia Dr NW, Huntsville, AL 35816, **Home Phone:** (256)518-9824. **Business Addr:** President, Senior Executive Vice President-Operations, Stanley Construction Co Inc, 4410 Evangel Circle NW A, Huntsville, AL 35816-2751, **Business Phone:** (256)837-6850.

### STANLEY, REP. WOODROW
Mayor. **Personal:** Born Jun 12, 1950, Schlater, MS; son of Sam and Bessie Mae; married Reta Venessa James; children: Heather Venessa & Jasmine Woodrina. **Educ:** Mott Community Col, attended 1971; Univ Mich, BA, polit sci, 1973, MPA. **Career:** Whitney M Young St Acad, counr, 1974-77; Greater Flint OIC, asst serv coordr, 1977-79, case mgt coordr, 1979-83, job club coordr, 1983-91; Flint City Coun, 1982, 2nd Ward Councilman, 1983-91; Mayor, Flint, MI, 1991-2002; MI St rep, 2008-; McCree Theatre, bd dir; Pub Sector Network Consult Group, consult, currently; Genesee County, bd comn, 2004-08, chair, 2008; state rep, 2008-. **Orgs:** Flint Human Rels Comt, 1973-76; bd mem, McCree Theatre & Fine Arts Centre, 1975-90; bd mem, YMCA, 1976-77; bd dir, Valley Area Agency Aging, chair, 1982-91; bd mem, Econ Develop Corp, 1983-, chair, 1991; adv bd mem, Univ Mich Flint African-Afro Am Studies Prog, 1983-; steering comt, Coalition Greater Flint African Relief Fund, 1984-85; Nat Black Caucus Local Elected Officials, 1987-; bd dir, Mich Munic League, Legisl & Urban Affairs Comn, 1988-91, pres; comt mem, Nat League Cities Human Develop Steering Comt, 1989-90, chair; pres, MML, 1990; bd dir, Nat League Cities, 1992-, adv coun, 1994-; bd dir, Mich Asn Mayors, 1992-94, pres, 1995; convener, Tri-County Coun Mayors, 1992; Nat Asn Advan Colored People; vice chair, Mich Dem Party; Genesee County Bd Commissioners, comnr; Ombudsman Adv Bd; bd mem, Foss Ave Christian Sch; alt trustee, Flint Retirement Bd; bd mem, Big Bros/Big Sisters Greater Flint; bd dir, New Paths; vchair, Mich Dem Party; Vernon Chapel African Methodist Episcopal Church. **Honors/Awds:** Cert Achievement, Leadership Flint, 1975-76; Volunteer Service Award, Urban League Flint, 1981; Award of Recognition, Mott Adult High School, 1982; Distinguished Community Service Award, Foss Ave Baptist Church, 1983; Community Service Award, Eureka Lodge F&AM, 1986; Senator Donald Riegle Community Service Award, Flint Jewish Fed, 1993; Mayor of the Year, Minority Women's Network Partners Community, 1994; Service Award, Black Caucus Found Mich, 1994; Booster of the Year, Sales & Mkt Execs Flint, 1995; African Am Man of Achievement Award, Dozier CME Church, 1996; Pioneer Award, Forum Mag, 1996; Honorary Doctorate Degree, Detroit Col Business; Good Scout Award, Tall Pine Boy Scout Coun; Community Leadership Award, Arab Am Heritage Coun; Alumni of the Year, Mich Community Col Asn; Hon Life Mem, Mich Munic League. **Special Achievements:** Host of radio show "Words with Wood" on WOWE. **Home Addr:** 2211 Brownell Blvd, Flint, MI 48504-7185, **Home Phone:** (810)239-7981. **Business Addr:** State Representative, Michigan House Democrats, PO Box 30014, Lansing, MI 48909-7514.

### STANLEY-TURNER, LANETT L.
State government official, consultant. **Personal:** married Rodney. **Educ:** Univ Tenn, Knoxville, BS, jour; Harvard Univ, John F Kennedy Sch Govt, attended; Carver Bible Col. **Career:** Commun consult, currently; Ga State, House Rep, rep, 1987-, Dist 33, rep, Cist 53, rep, currently; House Democratic Caucus, secy, currently. **Orgs:** Fulton County Youth Democrats Nat Org State Legislators; secy, Rules Comt; dir, Mt. Vernon Baptist Church Daycare Acad. **Home Addr:** 712 Gary Rd NW, Atlanta, GA 30318-6216, **Home Phone:** (404)794-4434. **Business Addr:** Representative, Georgia House of Representatives, Coverdell Rm 612 Legis Off Bldg, Atlanta, GA 30334, **Business Phone:** (404)656-0325.

### STANMORE, DR. ROGER DALE
Physician. **Personal:** Born Jan 20, 1957, Atlanta, TX. **Educ:** Southwestern Union Col, BS, 1979; Meharry Med Col, MD, 1984. **Career:** DC Gen Hosp, resident physician surg, 1984-85; Methodist Hosp, State Univ NY, resident physician, 1985-86; Dept Justice, chief med staff; Jacksonville Med Ctr, Jacksonville, AL, emergency room med dir, 1989-91; Pkwy Med Ctr, med dir, emergency servs, 1991-96; Decatur Emergency Med Servs Inc, pres & chief exec officer, 1996-; Gadsden-Etowah Emergency Med Servs, pres & chief exec officer, 1998-; Urgent Med Care, pvt pract, currently. **Orgs:** Am & Nat Med Asns, 1980-87; Technol Transfer Soc, 1982-87; N Ala Emergency Med Serv, adv bd, 1991-95; Am Asn Physician Specialists, 1997-99. **Honors/Awds:** Am Col Surgeons Scholar, 1983; rep, Joint Comn Med Educ, 1983. **Home Addr:** 46 Shields Rd, PO Box 18513, Huntsville, AL 35811-7800, **Home Phone:** (256)382-3680. **Business Addr:** Physician, Urgent Medical Care, 7583 Wall Triana Hwy Suite A, Madison, AL 35757, **Business Phone:** (256)830-5777.

### STANSBURY, DR. CLAYTON CRESVELL, JR.
Educator. **Personal:** Born Mar 20, 1932, Havre de Grace, MD; married Catherine Laverne Posey. **Educ:** Morgan State Univ, BS, 1955; Howard Univ, MS, 1962; Univ Md, PhD, 1972. **Career:** Howard Univ, instr psychol, 1962-63 & 1965-67; Univ Md, teaching asst psychol, 1963-65; Morgan State Univ, Baltimore, MD, asst dean freshman prog, 1970-73, Psychol Dept, chmn, 1973-75, actg dean stud affairs & dir, 1975-77, dir freshmen prog, 1975, prof psychol, 1975-96, vpres stud affairs, 1977-80, Stud Serv, vpres, 1978-96, dir hons prog, 1980-96, emer dir univ hons prog, prof emer, 1996-. **Orgs:** Am Psychol Asn; Md Psychol Asn; Psi Chi Nat Hon Soc; Alpha Phi Alpha Fraternity; Urban League; life mem, Nat Asn Advan Colored People; bd dir, YMCA; Little League Baseball; Boy Scouts Am; United Meth Men; Proj Upward Bound; Morgan ROTC; hon mem PKT; Epworth United Methodist Church; Howard L. Cornish MSU Alumni Chap. **Honors/Awds:** Alumnus of the Year, Morgan State Univ; Distinguished Alumni Award, Nat Asn Equal Opportunity. **Special Achievements:** Author Portrait of a Colored Man. **Home Addr:** 3215 Elba Dr, Baltimore, MD 21207-4402, **Home Phone:** (410)265-8655. **Business Addr:** Professor Emeritus, Morgan State University, 1700 E Cold Spring Lane, Baltimore, MD 21251, **Business Phone:** (443)885-3290.

### STANSBURY, KEVIN BRADLEY
Writer, educational consultant, educator. **Personal:** Born Aug 29, 1954, Morristown, NJ; son of Frederick Hartley and Muriel Hiller; married Renee Washington; children: Hartlei Imani. **Educ:** Brookdale Col, AA, 1991; Col St Elizabeth, BA, eng lit, 1994; NJ City Univ, MA. **Career:** Bell Commun Res, Admin Servs, mgr, 1982-93; Ami Corps, 1994-95; Red Bank Bd Educ, teacher, 1994-95, educ consult, 1997; Long Br Bd Educ, Eng lit teacher, 1995-; Freshman Success Acad Plainfield High Sch, vice prin, currently. **Orgs:** Sigma Tau Delta, Int Eng Hon Soc, 1994-; Kappa Gamma Pi, Nat Eng Hon Soc, 1994-; Nat Educ Asn, 1995; Nat Asn Advan Colored People; Lafayette 4-H Club, coordr, Morristown, 1997; Neptune Bd Educ, Bd dir, Nj, 1988-91. **Home Addr:** 167 Cheyene St, Tinton Falls, NJ 07701, **Home Phone:** (732)224-1398. **Business Addr:** Vice Principal, Freshman Success Academy, 950 Pk Ave, Long Branch, NJ 07060, **Business Phone:** (908)731-4390.

### STANSBURY, MARKHUM L.
Administrator. **Personal:** Born Apr 5, 1942, Memphis, TN; son of Willie (deceased) and Eliza Markhum (deceased); married Imogene Sayles; children: Markhum Jr & Marlon B. **Educ:** Lincoln Univ, Jefferson City, Mo, 1960; Lane Col, Jackson, Tenn, BA, 1966; Memphis State Univ, Memphis, Tenn, 1965. **Career:** WDIA Radio, Memphis, TN, announcer, 1958-; Lane Col, Jackson, TN, PR dir, 1966-69; Holiday Inns Inc, Memphis, TN, PR mgr, 1969-83, community rels mgr, through 1981; Union Cent Life Ins Co, agt, 1983-84; Am United Ins Co, agt, 1984-87; State TN, spec asst to gov, 1987-89; Memphis State Univ, Memphis, TN, asst to pres, 1989-2008; LeMoyne-Owen Col, vpres advan; Shelby State Community Col, interim pres; Memphis World, photogr; Tri-State Defender, photogr; Com Appeal, reporter & copy ed. **Orgs:** Vice chair, Emergency 911 Bd; vice chair, trustee, St Andrew AME Church; bd mem, YMCA; YWCA; bd mem, Goals Memphis; WDIA Goodwill Fund; Hooks Inst; Shelby Farms; Nat Asn Advan Colored People, Freedom Fund Gala, coordr; Shelby County Hist Comn; adv bd mem, S Cent Bell; Memphis Race Rels & Diversity Inst; Univ Memphis Found, pres, Soc Am-Memphis Chap; United Negro Col Fund Hall Fame. **Honors/Awds:** Special Recognition Award, Rotary Club, 1988; Delegate to General Conference, AME Church, 1988, 1992, 2000; Tenn Child Care Facilities, 1989; Outstanding Service to Youth in Schools; Award of Merit, Mayor, 1989; Campus Unity Award, Univ Memphis, 1993; Martin Luther King Jr Award; Humanitarian of the Year Award; Arthur S Holmon Lifetime Achievement Award; Lane College Alumni Recognition Award; Tri-State Defender Award of Excellence. **Special Achievements:** Honors from Congressman Harold E Ford, Jr and Congressman Steve Cohen. **Home Addr:** 8505 Turweston CV, Memphis, TN 38125, **Home Phone:** (901)755-9799. **Business Addr:** Assistant to the President, University of Memphis, Admin Bldg Suite 341, Memphis, TN 38152-3370, **Business Phone:** (901)678-5613.

### STANSBURY, VERNON CARVER, JR.
Businessperson, chief executive officer. **Personal:** Born Jul 13, 1939, Lexington, MS; children: Nicole Elaine & Vernon III. **Educ:** Roosevelt Univ, BS, 1962; Kent Col Law, attended 1964; Harvard Bus Sch, MBA, 1973. **Career:** Int Bus Mach, sr systs engr, 1962-67; Exxon Int, head fleet anal, 1967-71; Cummins Engine Co, gen mgr serv tools, 1973-78; Dept Com, dir export dept, 1978-81; Sci & Com Syst Corp, pres, 1981-, chief exec officer, currently. **Orgs:** Kappa Alpha Psi Fraternity; Chmn, AASU-Harvard Bus Sch, 1972; chmn, William R Laws Found, 1974; chmn, Columbus United Negro Col Fund, 1977; chmn, ERB-Sr Exec Serv, 1979; charter mem, Sr Exec Serv US, 1979; pres, DC Chap Harvard Black Alumni, 1980; mem bd dir, Intelligent Transp Syst Consortium; mem bd dir, Minority Bus Technol Transfer Consortium; mem bd dir, Contract Serv Asn Am; mem bd dir, Black Pres's Roundtable Asn. **Honors/Awds:** Goldman Sachs Award, Harvard Bus Sch, 1974; Awarded, Kids At Heart, 2007. **Special Achievements:** Outstanding Contributor White House Conference on Small Business, 1980. **Home Addr:** 6907 Rochambeau Pl, Springfield, VA 22153-1427, **Home Phone:** (703)644-1022. **Business Addr:** President, Chief Executive Officer, Scientific & Commercial Systems, 7600 Leesburg Pke E Bldg Suite 400, Falls Church, VA 22041, **Business Phone:** (703)917-9171.

### STANTON, JANICE D.
Counselor, executive. **Personal:** Born Jun 26, 1928, Beaumont, TX; daughter of Joseph Dewey Splane and Myrtle Trimble Splane; married Rufus H Stanton Jr; children: Rufus H III, Deborah Stanton Burke & Robert T. **Educ:** Wiley Col, attended 1944. **Career:** Counselor (retired). **Orgs:** Pres bd trustee, Gulf Coast Regional Ment Health-Ment Retardation Ctr, 1980-82; bd counr, St Mary's Hosp, 1980-86; adv bd, Galveston Historical Found, 1984; vpres, United Way Galveston, 1985-87; Grievance Comt, District 5B, State Bar Texas, 1988-90; bd dir, Lone Star Hist Drama Asn, 1989-92; pres, Texas Asn Community Col Bd Mems & Adminrs, 1990; adv bd, Children's Hosp, Univ Texas Med Br (UTMB) Galveston, 1992-; bd regents, Galveston Col, 1983-2004. **Honors/Awds:** Image Award, Galveston Branch Nat Asn Advan Colored People, 1983; Community Achievement Award, Zeta Phi Beta Sorority, 1983; Outstanding Citizen of the Year, Gamma Pi Lambda Chap, Alpha Phi Alpha, 1990; Steel Oleander Award, 1997. **Home Addr:** 3615 Ave O, Galveston, TX 77550-6738, **Home Phone:** (409)763-4454.

### STANTON, ROBERT G.
Government official, consultant, association executive. **Personal:** Born Sep 23, 1940, Ft. Worth, TX; children: 2. **Educ:** Huston-Tillotson Col, BS, hon doctorate sci, 1963; Unity Col, hon doctorate environ stewardship; Southern Univ, A&M Col, hon doctorate pub policy; George Washington Univ, attended. **Career:** Grand Teton Nat Pk, pk ranger, 1962-63; Huston-Tillotson Col, dir; Pk Serv, Atlanta, dep regional dir; Nat Pk Serv, personnel mgt & pub info specialist, 1966-69; Nat Capital Parks-Cent, mgt asst, 1969-70; Nat Parks-E, Washington, DC, supt, 1970-71; VI Nat Pk, supt, 1971-74; Southeast Region Atlanta, dep regional dir, 1974-76; Wash DC Hq, asst dir, resource mgmt, 1976; Wash DC Hq, asst dir, pk oper, 1977-78; Nat Capital Region, dep regional dir, 1979-87; Nat Capital Region, assoc dir, 1987-88, regional dir, 1988; Nat Pk Serv, dir, 1997-2001; Tex A&M Univ, exec prof, 2001-; Yale Univ, sch forestry & environ studies, McCluskey vis fel conser, res affiliate, 2002; Nat Resources Coun Am, consult; Howard Univ, Dept Hist Pub Prog, vis prof, 2005, 2007; Yale Univ, vis prof; US Dept Interior, dep asst secy policy, mgt & budget, 2009-. **Orgs:** Student Conserv Asn Inc; Nat Audubon Soc; Accokeek Found Piscataway Pk, Unity Col; Woods Hole Res Ctr; Eastern Nat &Guest Serv Inc; fel, Am Acad Pk & Recreation Admin; Stud Conserv Asn Inc; chmn trustee, Nat Pk Found; Accokeek Found at Piscataway Pk; Unity Col; Woods Hole Res Ctr; Eastern Nat & Guest Serv Inc; fel Am Acad Park & Recreation Admin; fel Assoc Roundtable Assocs Inc. **Business Addr:** Deputy Assistant Secretary, The Office of the Secretary, 1849 C St NW, Washington, DC 20240, **Business Phone:** (202)208-6416.

### STANYARD, HERMINE P.
Teacher. **Personal:** Born May 7, 1928, Charleston, SC; daughter of Samuel Payne (deceased) and Mabel Comfort Washington (deceased); married George Dewey Sr; children: Geormine Deweya & George Dewey Jr. **Educ:** SC State Col, BA, 1949; NY Univ, MA, 1952; Citadel Col, attended 1967, 1980. **Career:** Teacher (retired); Barnes Elem Sch, Georgetown, teacher, 1949-50; Wilson High Sch, eng teacher, 1952-56; Laing High Sch, eng teacher, 1956-59, guid counr, 1959-67, eng & reading teacher/reading coordr, 1967-85. **Orgs:** Campaigner, Greater Chas YWCA, 1966-86; vol, Laubach Reading Teacher; chmn, SAT prog, 1976-82; pres, Charleston County Coun Int Reading Asn, 1977-79; chmn, Nominating Comt, SC State Reading Asn, 1979-81; chmn, Distinguished Teacher Mem, 1981-85; vol teacher, Morris St Baptist Church, Tutorial Prog, 1982-83, 1986; chmn, Elem & Mid Sch Tutoring, 1986-; co-chair, Poetry & Storytelling Ser Moja Arts Festival, 1991-96; Int Soc Poets, 1994-; chair, Sundown Poetry Ser Piccolo Spoleto, 1995, 1996; Delta Sigma Theta Sorority Inc; Avery Institite. **Home Addr:** 17 Charlotte St Apt A, Charleston, SC 29403, **Home Phone:** (803)577-2792.

### STAPLES, GRACIE BONDS
Journalist. **Personal:** Born Oct 27, 1957, McComb, MS; daughter of Sula and Freddie Felder; married Jimmy; children: Jamila Felder & Asha Dianne. **Educ:** Southwest Miss Jr Col, Summit, MS, AA, 1977; Univ Southern Miss, Hattiesburg, MS, BA, jour, 1979. **Career:** Enterprise-Jour, McComb, Miss, 1979-80; Delta Dem-Times, Greenville, Miss, 1980-82; Miss dailies; Raleigh Times, Raleigh, NC, reporter, 1983-84; Sacramento Bee, Sacramento, Calif, reporter, 1984-90; Ft Worth Star-Telegram, Ft Worth, Tex, reporter, 1990; Atlanta J-Const, reporter, writer, columnist, currently. **Orgs:** Nat Asn Black Journalists, 1980-; Fel Southern Style. **Honors/Awds:** Maggie Award, Planned Parenthood Sacramento Valley, 1986; Calif Educ Writers Asn Award, 1988; Cert Merit, Am Bar Asn, 1993; Black Image Award, Kappa Alpha Psi Fraternity, 1995; YMCA Minority Achiever, 1997; Frederick Douglas Award for Jour, Nat Asn Advan Colored People, 1997; Vivian Castleberry award, 1999. **Special Achievements:** Award named in his honor: The Gracie Bonds Staples Community Organizer Award. **Home Addr:** 7705 Bellemont Ridge, Duluth, GA 30097-1960, **Home Phone:** (678)584-9714. **Business Addr:** Reporter, Journalist, Atlanta Journal-Constitution, 72 Marietta St NW, Atlanta, GA 30303, **Business Phone:** (770)263-3621.

### STAPLES, LELA ROCHON. See ROCHON, LELA.

### STAPLES, MAVIS
Singer. **Personal:** Born Jul 10, 1939, Chicago, IL; daughter of Roebuck and Oceala. **Career:** Staple Singers, R&B singer, 1951-; Albums: Mavis Staples, 1969; Only for the Lonely, 1970; A Piece of the Action, 1977; Oh What A Feeling, 1979; Mavis Staples, 1984; Time Waits for No One, 1989; Don't Change Me Now, 1990; The Voice, 1993; Mavis Staples & Lucky Peterson Spirituals & Gospel: Dedicated to Mahalia

Jackson, 1996; Have A Little Faith, 2004; We'll Never Turn Back, 2007; Live: Hope at the Hideout, 2008; You Are Not Alone, 2010; One True Vine, 2013. Singles: "Crying in the Chapel"; "I Have Learned to Do Without You"; "Endlessly"; "A House Is Not a Home"; "A Piece of the Action"; "The Weight on the The Last Waltz", 1976; "Oh What a Feeling", 1979; "Tonight I Feel Like Dancing", 1979; "Love Gone Bad", 1984; "Show Me How It Works", 1986; "20th Century Express", 1989; "Time Waits for No One", 1989; "Jaguar", 1989; "Melody Cool", 1991; "The Voice", 1993; "Blood Is Thicker Than Time", 1993. TV series: "The Cosby Show", 1990; "Graffiti Bridge", 1990; "Great Performances", 2007. **Honors/Awds:** Rock & Roll Hall of Fame, 1999; Grammy Award, 2005; AMA "Spirit of Americana" Free Speech Award, First Amendment Ctr, 2007. **Special Achievements:** Ranked No 57 on VH1's 100 Greatest Women of Rock N Roll; Films: Graffiti Bridge, 1990; The Sacrifice of Victor, 1995; TV: "The Cosby Show", 1990; Blind Boys of Alabama: Go Tell It on the Mountain, 2004. **Business Addr:** Recording Artist, The Rosebud Agency, PO Box 170429, San Francisco, CA 94117, **Business Phone:** (415)386-3456.

### STAPLES, ROBERT E.

Educator. **Personal:** Born Jun 28, 1942, Roanoke, VA; son of John Ambrose and Anna Theresa. **Educ:** La Valley Col, AA, gen educ, 1960; Calif State Univ, Northridge, AB, sociol, 1963; San Jose St Univ, MA, sociol, 1965; Univ Minn, PhD, family sociol, 1970. **Career:** St Paul Urban League, dir res, 1966-67; Bethune-Cookman Col, Daytona Beach, assoc prof sociol, 1967-68; Calif St Univ, asst prof sociol, 1968-70; Fisk Univ, vis prof, 1969-70, asst prof sociol, 1970-71; Univ Md, adj prof, 1971-73; Howard Univ, assoc prof sociol, 1971-73; Univ Calif, San Francisco, prof sociol, 1973-84, prof emer, 1984-; Tougaloo Col, Tougaloo, vis prof sociol, 1975; Fla State Univ, vis prof sociol, 1977; Univ Mich, vis prof sociol, 1979; Univ Hawaii, prof sociol, 1983; Univ Minn, vis prof african studies, 1984. **Orgs:** Nat Teaching Fel, 1967-68; Nat Coun Family Rels, 1970-72; ed & contribr, Black Family, 1971; bd dir, SERICO Res Corp, 1976-; ed, Western Jour Black Studies, 1978-; bd dir, Black World Found, 1980-; vis fel Inst Family Studies, Australia, 1982; vis res fel Centre Australia Indigenous Studies, Monash Univ, Melbourne, Australia; Am Acad Polit & Social Sci; Am Asn Univ Prof; African Heritage Studies Asn; Am Sociol Asn; Asn Social & Behav Sci; Groves Conf Marriage & Family Nat Coun Family Rels; Pac Sociol Asn; Sex Info & Educ Coun US; fel Soc Sci Study Sex; Asn Black Nursing Fac; Asn Black Sociologists. **Honors/Awds:** Distinguished Achievement, Howard Univ, 1979; Simon Bolivar Lecture, Univdel Zulia, Maracaibo, Venezeula, 1979; Distinguished Achievement, Nat Coun Family Rels, 1982; Marie Peters Award, Nat Council Family Rels, 1986; Publisher of the Year Award, Asn Black Nursing Fac, 1992. **Special Achievements:** Author: The Lower-Income Negro Family in Saint Paul, 1967; The Black Woman In America, 1973; Introduction to Black Sociology, 1976; World of Black Singles, 1981; Black Masculinity, 1982; The Urban Plantation, 1987; Black Families Essays, 1991; Black Families at the Crossroads, 1993; Authored Numerous Books, Papers & Articles. **Home Addr:** 1895 Jackson St Apt 406, San Francisco, CA 94109-2882. **Business Addr:** Professor Emeritus, University of California, Laurel Heights 455 3333 Calif St, San Francisco, CA 94143-0612, **Business Phone:** (415)476-3964.

### STAPLETON, MARYLYN A.

Government official, transportation consultant. **Personal:** Born Sep 25, 1936, St. Thomas; daughter of Aletha C Callender John and Lambert George; married Frank; children: Linda Elaine. **Educ:** Wash Bus Inst, New York, NY, AS, 1959; Hunter Col, NY. **Career:** Caribair Airline, St Thomas, VI, reservation agt, 1954-56; Macy's Dept Store, New York, NY, salesclerk, 1956-57; Gift Shop, New York, NY, salesclerk, 1957-63; Eastern Airlines Inc, NY, supvr, 1967-86; Caribbean Travel Agency, St Thomas, VI, travel agt, 1986-87; Gov VI, St Thomas, VI, dep comnr, 1987-91, asst comnr, 1991-95; Melvin Jones fel Lioness Club, 1989; Small Bus Environ Asst Prog, environ prog mgr, 1995-, assistance prog & coordr, currently; Inter nat Asn Plumbing Mech Officials, state exec dir, 1999, regional manager, currently; Dept Planning & Nat Resources & environ prog mgr, 2004-; Vi Conv Deleg, vice chair. **Orgs:** State-chair, Dem Party, 1986-99; Lioness Club, 1987-88; treas, Lioness Club, 1985-86; pub rels off, Nevis Benevolent Soc, 1966-85; mem chair, Lioness Club STT, 1988-89; pageant chair, Lioness Club STT, 1986-87. **Home Addr:** PO Box 3739, St. Thomas00803, **Home Phone:** (809)775-9443. **Business Addr:** Environmental Program Manager, Coordinator, Small Business Environmental Assistance Program, Terminal Bldg 2nd Fl Cyril E King Airport, St. Thomas00802, **Business Phone:** (340)714-9529.

**STARGELL, ANTHONY L. See STARGELL, TONY.**

### STARGELL, TONY (ANTHONY L STARGELL)

Football player. **Personal:** Born Aug 7, 1966, LaGrange, GA. **Educ:** Tenn State Univ, health & phys educ, 1986. **Career:** Football player (retired); New York Jets, left cornerback, 1990-91; Indianapolis Colts, defensive back, 1992-93; Tampa Bay Buccaneers, defensive back, 1994, cornerback, 1995; Kans City Chiefs, defensive back, 1996; Chicago Bears, 1997. **Business Addr:** Free Agent, Kans City Chief, 1 Arrowhead Dr, Kansas City, MO 64129, **Business Phone:** (816)920-9300.

### STARKEY, DR. FRANK DAVID

Labor relations manager, educator. **Personal:** Born Aug 6, 1944, Indianapolis, IN; married Gunilla Emilia Ekstedt; children: Michael & Julia. **Educ:** Wabash Col Ind, AB 1966, BA, chem; Brown Univ, PhD, chem, org chem, 1973. **Career:** Ill Wesleyan Univ, prof, 1971-80, Chem Dept, head, Res & Develop Ctr, admin, 1980; Gen Elec Co, mgr, 1980-82, adminr human resource prog, 1982. **Orgs:** Pres, Wabash Coun Racial Equality, 1965; chmn, Afro Am Soc, Brown Univ, 1967-71; mem state coun, Am Asn Univ Prof, 1972; mem grant rev panel, NSF, 1980; GE Found Minority Eng Comt, 1980; comt mem, Am Chem Soc, 1983-85; bd mem, Selection Comt, Nat Assoc Biol Teachers, 1986. **Honors/Awds:** Alfred P Sloan Scholar, Wabash Col, 1962-66; NSF Traineeship, Brown Univ, 1966-70; Kemp Foundation Award, Ill Wesleyan Univ, 1976, Teacher of the Year, Ill Wesleyan Univ, 1978; Outstanding Young Man of America, 1979; GE Honarary Black Achiever Indust Harlem, YMCA, 1986; Outstanding State Biology Teacher Award, Nat Asn Biol Teachers, 1986. **Home Addr:** 1274 Regent St, Niskayuna, NY 12309-5351, **Home Phone:** (518)393-0043.

### STARKS, DORIS NEARROR

Administrator, educator. **Personal:** Born Jul 30, 1937, Conecuh County, AL; daughter of Cleveland H Jenkins and Virgie G; married Wilbert L Sr; children: Wilbert L Jr & Garrick Edward. **Educ:** Tuskegee Univ, BSN, 1958; Cath Univ Am, MSN, 1965; Union Grad Sch, PhD, nursing, 1978. **Career:** Educator, administrator (retired); Veterans Admin Hosp Ctr, staff nurse, 1958-61, in-serv educ instr, 1965-1966; Wash Hosp Ctr, staff nurse, 1963-1965; Tuskegee Univ, asst prof nursing, 1966-68; County Col Baltimore, 1968-91; Dept Nursing, Pro Med Surg Nursing, 1968-80, asst chap, 1980-84, chap, 1984-86, Dept Nursing & Health Sci, chair, 1986-89, dir nursing & dir, prof, 1989-90; Coppin State Col, Helene Fuld Sch Nursing, asst dean, 1990-91, dean, 1991-98. **Orgs:** Chi Eta Phi, 1956-; Tuskegee Univ Nurses Alumni Asn, 1958-; chair, Baltimore City Community Col, 1968-91; Sigma Theta Tau Int Hon Soc Nurses, 1977-; Alpha Kappa Alpha, 1980-; Nat Asn Black Nursing Fac, 1990-; Nat Coalition 100 Black Women, 1991-; Epicureans, 1991-; Club Dejour, 1992-; vpres, Continental Soc Inc, Columbia, MD Chap, 1992-; fel Am Acad Nursing, 1997-; Am Nurses Asn. **Home Addr:** 9068 Bellwart Way, Columbia, MD 21045, **Home Phone:** (410)997-8036.

### STARKS, DUANE LONELL

Football player. **Personal:** Born May 23, 1974, Miami, FL. **Educ:** Univ Miami, lib arts. **Career:** Football player (retired); Baltimore Ravens, right corner back, 1998, right corner back, corner back, 1999, right corner back, left corner back, 2000, left corner back, 2001; Ariz Cardinals, left corner back, 2002-04; New Eng Patriots, corner back, right corner back, 2005; Oakland Raiders, cornerback, 2006-08. **Orgs:** Founder, Starks Charitable Found, 1998. **Honors/Awds:** Super Bowl champion (XXXV); James Browm Award, CBS Sports; Presidents Award, 2007. **Business Addr:** Founder, Starks Charitable Foundation, PO Box 170103, Hialeah, FL 33017, **Business Phone:** (305)816-5828.

### STARKS, JOHN LEVELL

Basketball coach, basketball player, founder (originator). **Personal:** Born Aug 10, 1965, Tulsa, OK; son of Irene; married Jacqueline; children: John Jr & Chelsea. **Educ:** Okla State Univ, attended 1988. **Career:** Basketball player (retired) basketball coach; Golden State Warriors, guard, shooting guard, 1988-89, 1999-2000; Cedar Rapids Silver Bullets, 1989-90; New York Knicks, shooting guard, 1990-98, advisor, 2003; Memphis Rockers, 1990; Chicago Bulls, 1999-2000; Utah Jazz, guard, shooting guard, 2000-02; Westchester Wildfire, US Basketball League, head coach, 2003-04; MSG Networks home Knicks, pre & post game analyst. **Orgs:** Boys Brotherhood Repub; founder, John Starks Found, 1994-. **Honors/Awds:** NBA All-Defensive Second Team, 1993; NBA All-Star, 1994; NBA Sixth Man Award, 1996; Hank Iba Citizen Athlete Award, 1997; Good Guy Award, NY Press Photographers Asn, 1997. **Special Achievements:** Author: John Starks: My Life; First player in NBA history to make 200 three-pointers in one season. **Business Addr:** Founder, John Starks Foundation, 1127 High Ridge Rd Suite 331, Stamford, CT 06905, **Business Phone:** (203)322-7788.

### STARKS, RICK H.

Manager, government official, vice president (organization). **Personal:** Born Apr 16, 1948, Scottsville, KY; son of Ruby and L C; married Saundra Hardin; children: Derrick D & Shannon M. **Educ:** Western Ky Univ, BS, pub serv, 1971, MPS, 1975; Univ Okla, Econ Develop Inst, attended 1988. **Career:** Bowling Green Parks & Rec Ctr, dir, 1971-72; Mammoth Cave Nat Pk, tour guide, 1971; Barren River Area Develop Dist, recreation planner & proj supt, 1972-80; Tenn Valley Authority, Bowling Green, KY, sr econ develop supvr, regional mgr, 1994-2003, sr specialist, currently. **Orgs:** Vpres, Big Bros/Big Sister, 1978-79; Bowling Green Human Rights Comn, 1978; vice polemarch, 1978-79, keeper recs, 1989-96, KAP Frat; chmn action comm, 1979-81, spec proj adv, 1988, Bowling Green Nat Asn Advan Colored People; developer, Nat Asn Advan Colored People Youth Improv Grant, 1987; chmn, BRADD Econ Develop Comm, 1988; Ky Indust Develop Coun, 1989; bd dirs, UPPRE Inc, 1989-91; Bradd Pvt Indust Coun, 1989-; trustee bd, Taylor Chapel AME Church, 1996-98; Gov's Ky Infrastructure Authority, 1996-2000; Gov's Comn Women, 1998-; vpres mem serv & econ develop, Warren Rural Elec Coop Corp, econ develop consult; bd dir, Greenview Hosp; chair, Ky Econ Develop Asn Sponsorship Comt; Ky Comn Women; Bowling Green Area Chamber Com; Hopkinsville Christian County Chamber; Scottsville-Allen County Chamber; Bd dir, Farmers Nat Bank, currently. **Honors/Awds:** Big Brother of the Year Award, Big Brothers Agency, 1979; Civitan Service Award, Bowling Green Noon Civitan, 1979; AWARE, Meritorious Service Award, 1980; Governor's Economic Development Leadership Award, 1997; James N. Gray Award, 2004. **Home Addr:** 2432 Tam-O Shanter Ct, Bowling Green, KY 42104, **Home Phone:** (502)782-3819.

### STARKS, ROBERT TERRY

Educator. **Personal:** Born Jan 24, 1944, Grenada, MS; son of Lula Ella and Vernon; married Judith Ann Minor; children: Kenya Mariama & Robert Willis. **Educ:** Loyola Univ, BS, polit sci, 1967, MA, urban studies, 1972; Univ Chicago, PhD, polit sci, 2010. **Career:** Professor (retired), Emeritus professor; Booz-Allen & Hamilton Inc, mgt & consult, 1968-69; Chicago Urban League, res specialist, 1969-70; Northern Ill Univ, dir black studies, 1970-72, assoc prof, 1972-; Horace H Rackham Sch Graduation Studies, Univ Mich, vis scholar, 1976; Kellogg Found, res fel, 1978-80; Robert T Starks & Assoc, founder & pres, 1982-; Mayor Harold Wash & City Chicago, issues consult, 1982-87; Goethe Inst, Berlin, Ger, lang fel, 1986; Diversity Insts & Corps, consult & lectr, 1987-; N'digo Newspaper, Hartman Group Publ Ltd, columnist & polit ed, 1991-; Urban Affairs Rev, ed bd, 1992-95; WRON Radio, Chicago, talk show host, 1995; Harold Wash Inst Res & Policy Studies, founder, dir, 2005-; NEIU, prof emer, 2012. **Orgs:** Coun, Nat Conf Black Polit Scientists, 1979-81; DuSable Mus Afro-Am Hist, 1980-; vpres, PUSH, Int Trade Bur, 1981-82; issues consult, Rev Jesse L Jackson Nat Rainbow Coalition & Oper, PUSH, 1981-; founder, chmn, Task Force Black Polit Empowerment, 1982-; bd dir, S Side Comt Art Ctr, Chicago, 1982-; founder, chmn, Free S Africa Movement Chicago, 1985-; fel Leadership Greater Chicago, 1986-87; bd mem, Third World Conf Found, 1986-87; bd mem, Ill Chap, Am Civil Liberties Union, 1987-88; vice chmn, Nat Black United Fund, 1987, chair, 1990-10; deutscher akademischer austausch dienst, Interdisciplinary Ger Studies, Sem, Phillips Univ, 1987; chmn bd, Ill Black United Fund, 1990-; bd dir, African Am Family Comn Ill, 1995-; bd mem, Can TV, 2008-10. **Home Addr:** 6700 S Crandon Ave Apt, Chicago, IL 60649, **Home Phone:** (773)684-1732. **Business Addr:** Professor Emeritus, Northeastern Illinois University, 700 E Oakwood Blvd, Chicago, IL 60653, **Business Phone:** (773)268-7500.

### STARR, FREDRO (FREDRO SCRUGGS, JR.)

Rap musician, actor. **Personal:** Born Apr 18, 1971, Queens, NY; married Korina Longin. **Career:** Actor & singer; Onyx, rap group mem, 1993-; Albums with ONYX: Bacdafucu, 1993; All We Got Iz Us, 1995; Shut 'Em Dow, 1998; Bacdafucup Part II, 2002; Triggernometry, 2003; Cold Case Files, 2008; Solo Albums: That B Them, 2000; Firestarr, 2001; Don't Get Mad, Get Money, 2003; Last Dayz, 2008; Made In The Streets, 2014. Films: Clockers, The Addiction, 1995; Sunset Park, 1996; Ride, 1998; Black & White, Light It Up, 1999; Save the Last Dance, Flossin, 2001; Vegas Vampires, 2003; Torque, Almost Gangsta, 2004; Forbidden Fruits, My Brother, 2006; A Day in the Life, 2007; Show Stoppers, Queen of Media, Darling Nikki: The Movie, The Next Hit, actor & producer, 2008; The Eddie Black Story, Busted, A Day in the Life, 2009; Queen of Media, 2011; Comrades, 2011; After Hours: The Movie, 2011; Duke, 2013; Deceitful, 2013. TV series: "Strapped", 1993; "Law & Order", 1994; "NewYork Undercover", 1995; "Moesha", 1996-2000; "Dangerous Minds", 1996; NYPD Blue", 1998-2002; "Promised Land", "In the House", 1998; "Commitments", 2001; "One Arrest", 2002; The Wire, 2002-03; "Justice", "Karen Sisco", 2003; "Dance 360", 2004; Title Racer, 2005; "Bloodlines", "Blade: The Series", 2006; "CSI: Miami", 2009; "CSI: NY", 2009; "Ultimate MC", 2011; "The Eric Andre Show", 2013. **Honors/Awds:** Best Supporting Actor, Cable ACE nomination. **Special Achievements:** Co-hosted Dance 360, Paramount Domestic Television's daily. **Business Addr:** Artist, c/o William Morris Agency, 151 El Camino Dr, Beverly Hills, CA 90212, **Business Phone:** (310)859-4000.

**STARR-WHITE, DEBI. See LIVINGSTON-WHITE, DR. DEBORAH J. H.**

### STATEN, EVERETT R.

Founder (originator), executive, chief executive officer. **Personal:** Born Jun 17, 1951, Philadelphia, PA; son of Harris L and Juanita A; children: Kharee Harris. **Educ:** Temple Univ, BA, 1980. **Career:** Bell Pa, sales consult, 1968-76; Metro Atlanta Black Pages, assoc pub, 1981-85; Black Enterprise Mag, sr account exec, 1986-88; Emerge Mag, co-founder & adv dir, 1988-91; Black Expo USA, vpres, managing partner, 1991-96; Inner City Events, pres, 1991; The Staten Group Inc, chief exec officer, 1991; The Mobil Nat African Am Cult Expo, Founder & ceo, currently; Everett & Assocs Inc. **Orgs:** Nat Asn Mkt Dev, 1980-; Nat Coalition Black Meeting Planners, 1994-; African-Am Chamber Cong Philadelphia, 1994-; Philadelphia Multicultural Affairs Cong, 1994-; Int Asn Expos Mgt, 1995; Nat Asn Consumer Shows, 1996; founder, Black Hist Showcase; founder, African Am Cult Expo; Proud African Am Found. **Business Addr:** Founder, Chief Executive Officer, The Mobil National African American Cultural Expo, 6228 N 8th St, Philadelphia, PA 19126, **Business Phone:** (215)549-1600.

### STATEN, MARK EUGENE

Banker. **Personal:** Born Jan 22, 1963, Stuttgart; son of Walter (deceased) and Janette; married Barbara Sandy; children: Marylynn. **Educ:** Langston Univ, attended 1986. **Career:** Am State Bank, asst vpres, 1981-. **Orgs:** Kappa Alpha Psi; worshipful master, Masonic Lodge, Pyramid Lodge No 69; Nat Asn Advan Colored People. **Home Addr:** 652 N Osage Dr, Tulsa, OK 74106-6902, **Home Phone:** (918)587-4604. **Business Addr:** Assistant Vice President, American State Bank, 3816 N Peoria Ave, Tulsa, OK 74106, **Business Phone:** (918)428-2211.

### STATES, LAUREN C.

Vice president (organization). **Personal:** married Kenneth J Creary; children: Rachel Creary. **Educ:** Univ Pa Wharton Sch, BS, econs; Columbia Univ, Bus Sch, Exec Educ Prog, cert, bus excellence. **Career:** IBM, vpres tech sales & software group enablement, systs engr, vpres cloud comput, vpres technol, strategy growth initiatives & chief technol officer cloud comput, currently; D'Amore-McKim Sch Bus Northeastern Univ, exec in residence. **Orgs:** Co-chair, IBM's Women's Coun; chair, Multicultural Women Technol; bd visitors, Northeastern Univ Col Bus; Exec Leadership Coun; Advan Leadership Harvard Fel, 2015. **Business Addr:** Vice President, IBM, 60 Hudson St, New York, NY 10013, **Business Phone:** (212)791-7952.

### STATES, ROBERT ARTHUR

Executive, president (organization). **Personal:** Born Mar 19, 1932, Boston, MA; son of Earl H and Rosita A; married Eva D Smith; children: Lauren (Kenneth Creary), Lisa (Kevin Hamel) & Robert Jr. **Educ:** Boston Univ, BS, 1953; Bentley Col, cert, 1957; Western New Eng Col, JD, 1968; NY Univ Grad Law Sch, attended 1971. **Career:** US Veterans ADM, acct, 1961-62; US Internal Revenue Serv, IRS agt, 1962-69; Aetna Life & Casualty Income taxes & tax audits, dir, 1969-91; Triple Check Financial & Bus Servs, owner, pres, currently. **Orgs:** Town E Hampton, Water & Sewer Authority, 1967-87; Econ Develop CMS, 1992-; Am Bar Asn, 1977-; Nat Soc Enrolled Agts, 1991-; Conn Soc Enrolled Agts, 1991-; Nat Asn Tax Practitioners, 1992-. **Home Addr:** 49 Wangonk Trl, PO Box 238, East Hampton, CT 06424, **Home Phone:** (203)267-9408. **Business Addr:** President, Owner, Triple Check Financial & Business Services, 11 S Main St Suite 4, Marlborough, CT 06447, **Business Phone:** (860)295-0729.

### STATHAM, CARL

Executive, executive director. **Personal:** Born Dec 9, 1950, Macon, GA; son of Carl and Marie; married Gloria Marie Long; children:

Stephanie & Christopher. **Educ:** Tuskegee Inst, BS, 1973. **Career:** Gen Motors, bus consult, 1973-77; Ford Motor Co, acct rep, 1977-80, mgr acct reps, 1980-83; Southside Ford Truck Sales, chief exec, acct gen mgr, 1983-84, pres, 1984-; Midwest Bus Serv Inc, pres. **Orgs:** Co Ford Hwy Truck Dealer Coun, 1989; Devon Homeowners Asn. **Honors/Awds:** Top 100 Black Buss, Black Enterprise, 1984-88; Top 300 Dealers Parts & Service Volume, Ford Motor Co, 1984-88; Distinguished Service Award, Ford Motor Co, 1984-87. **Home Addr:** 4 Devon Ct, Burr Ridge, IL 60521. **Business Addr:** President, Southside Ford Truck Sales Inc, 310 W Pershing Rd, Chicago, IL 60609, **Business Phone:** (773)247-8662.

## STATON, CANZETTA MARIA (CANDI STATON)

Singer. **Personal:** Born Mar 13, 1940, Hanceville, AL; daughter of Ursie and Rosa; married Clarence Carter; children: Clarence Carter Jr; married Joe Williams; children: Marcus Williams, Marcel Williams, Terry Williams & Cassandra Hightower; married John Sussewell. **Career:** Capitol Rec, rec artist, 1969-71; United Artists, rec artist, 1972-73; Wagner Bros rec, rec artist, 1974-80; La rec, rec artist, 1981; Sugar hill Rec, rec artist, 1982; Beracah Rec, rec artist, 1983; Trinity Broadcasting Network, tv host, 1986; singer, currently; Albums: I'm Just a Prisoner, 1969; Stand By Your Man, 1971; Candi Staton, 1972; Candi, 1974; Young Hearts Run Free, 1976; Music Speaks Louder Than Words, 1977; House of Love, 1978; Chance, 1979; Candi Staton, 1980; Nightlites, 1982; Suspicious Minds, 1982; Make Me An Instrument, 1983; The Anointing, 1985; Sing A Song, 1986; Love Lifted Me, 1988; Night lites, 1989; Stand Up & Be A Witness, 1990; Standing On The Promises, 1991; I Give You Praise, 1993; It's Time, 1995; Cover Me, 1997; Outside In, 1999; Here's a Blessing, 2000; Christmas In My Heart, 2000; Glorify, 2001; Proverbs 31 Woman, 2002; His Hands, 2006; The Ultimate Gospel Collection, 2006; I Will Sing My Praise To You, 2008; Who's Hurting Now?, 2009; Singles: "I'd Rather Be An Old Man's Sweetheart, 1969; "I'm Just A Prisoner", 1969; "Sweet Feeling", 1970; "Stand By Your Man", 1970; "He Called Me Baby", 1971; "Do It In The Name Of Love", 1973; "As Long as He Takes Care of Home", 1974; "Young Hearts Run Free", 1976; "Destiny", 1976; "Nights On Broadway", 1977; "Honest I Do Love You", 1978; "Victim", 1978; "When You Wake Up Tomorrow", 1979; "Suspicious Minds", 1982; "You Got The Love", 1986, 1991, 1997, 2005 & 2006; "Love On Love", 1999; "I Just Can't Get To Sleep At All", 2000; "Love Sweet Sound", 2007; "Wilder Side", 2010; "The Award Goes To: A Look Back at the Legends", 2010; "White Heat", 2012; "Accused", 2012. **Orgs:** Nat Acad Rec Arts & Sci, 1970. **Special Achievements:** Grammy nominations: 1971, 1973, 1984, 1987. **Home Addr:** 6795 Blantyre Blvd, Stone Mountain, GA 30087, **Home Phone:** (770)469-8868. **Business Addr:** Singer, Beracah Ministries, Cassandra Hightower, Stone Mountain, GA 30087, **Business Phone:** (770)266-0718.

## STATON, DONNA HILL

Lawyer. **Personal:** Born Dec 5, 1957, Chester, PA; daughter of Donald B and Ethel B Hill; married Kerry D; children: 2. **Educ:** Princeton Univ, BA, Eng, 1979; George Washington Univ, Sch Law, JD, 1982. **Career:** Judge (retired); Hon Joseph C Howard, US Dist Ct Dist Md, judicial law clerk, 1982-83; Piper & Marbury, assoc, 1983-92, litigation partner, 1993-95; Md, circuit ctjudge, 1995; Howard County Circuit Ct, Fifth Judicial Circuit, assoc judge, 1995-96; Md state, dep atty gen, 1997-2007, actg dep atty gen, currently; Univ Md, adj prof, 2008; Howard Bancorp & Howard Bank, dir, 2009-. **Orgs:** Bd dir, Howard County Sexual Assault Ctr, 1982-86; Alpha Kappa Alpha Sorority, 1983-; vpres, Alliance Black Women Attys, 1986-87, pres, 1987-88; bd gov, Md State Bar Asn, 1988-90; bd dir, Peoples Pro Bono Action Ctr, 1990-92; comnr, Atty Grievance Comt MD, 1991-95; adv comt, US Dist Ct, Dist MD, 1991-95; bus adv bd, Col Notre Dame Md, 1993; William T. Walters Asn, 1994-; Beyond Bars Community Adv Comt, Girl Scouts, 1995; bd dir, Leadership Howard County, 1997-2003; trustee, McDonogh Sch, 1999-2007; bd mem, Md State Bd Educ, 2009-15; trustee, Client Protection Fund Bar Md, 2012-; bd dir, McDonnogh Sch; fel Md Bar Found; Nat Bar Asn; Am Bar Asn; Howard County & Monumental City Bar Asn; trustee, Client Protection Fund Md; Daily Rec Ed Adv Bd. **Honors/Awds:** Honoree, AFRAM Expo Salute Black Women, 1992; Honoree, Alliance BlackWomen Atty, 1994; MD Top 100Women, 2000; Maryland Leadership in Law Award, Daily Record, 2012; Trailblazer Award, NAACP, 2010; 100 Outstanding Black Women of Baltimore, EmmanuelChristian Comm Church; Distinguished Black Marylanders Award, Towson Univ; Trailblazer Award, Alliance Black Women Attys; Community Service Award, Alpha Kappa Alpha Sorority; Distinguished Black Marylander Award, Towson Univ. **Special Achievements:** First African American circuit court judge in Howard County, MD; First African American woman deputy attorney general in MD; Marylands Top 100 Women, Daily Records. **Home Addr:** 13827 Lakeside Dr, Clarksville, MD 21029, **Home Phone:** (410)531-3914. **Business Addr:** Director, Howard Bancorp Inc, 6011 Univ Blvd, Ellicott City, MD 21043, **Business Phone:** (410)750-0020.

## STATON, KERRY D.

Businessperson, lawyer. **Personal:** Born Aug 30, 1954, New Rochelle, NY; son of James and Marie; married Donna Hill; children: Brooke Avery & Lindsey Simone. **Educ:** Oberlin Col, BA, Eng, 1976; Univ Md Sch Law, JD, 1980. **Career:** Legal Aid Bur Inc, staff atty, 1980-82; Ellin & Baker, assoc, 1982-84; Schochor, Federico & Staton, founding partner, 1984-. **Orgs:** Phi Alpha Delta, 1979-; Am Bar Asn, 1980-; Md State Bar Asn, 1980-; Monument City Bar Asn, 1982-; Bar Asn Baltimore City, 1982-; fel Reginald Heber Smith Fel, 1980-82; Asn Trial Lawyers Am, 1984-; Am Judicature Soc, 1984-; Md State, Spec Comt Audit Procedures, 1985-86, Common Minorities Legal Prof, 1988-89; inquiry panel, Atty Grievance Comn Md, 1987-92; Rev Bd, 1992-97, vchmn, 1995-96, chmn, 1996-97, peer rev panel, 2000-10, comnr, 2010-; bd govs, Md Asn Justice, 1988-95; lect, Nat Bar Asn, 1990-; Comn Civilty, 1996; Am Bd Trial Advocates, 2005-; fel Am Col Trial Lawyers, 2010-; fel Int Soc Barristers, 2014-; Nat Black Lawyers Top 100, 2014-; Fourth Circuit Judicial Conf; Trial Lawyers Pub Justice; Am Bd Trial Advocate; fel Md Bar Found; fel Howard County Bar Found; Reginald Heber Smith Law fel; Md State Deleg & Minority Caucus; Comt Civility Baltimore City Bar Asn; Monumental City Bar Asn Judicial Nominating Comt; Phi Alpha Delta Law Fraternity; Am Judicature Soc; bd gov, Md Trial Lawyers Asn; Md State Deleg & Minority Caucus Mem; fel Md Bar Found; fel Howard County Bar Found; fel Reginald Heber Smith Law Fel; vice-chmn, chmn, Rev Bd; lifetime mem, Strathmores Whos Who; Am Asn Justice. **Honors/Awds:** Super Lawyer, Schochar, Federico & Staton, 2007; Best Lawyers in America, 2008-12. **Home Addr:** 13827 Lakeside Dr, Clarksville, MD 21029, **Home Phone:** (410)531-3914. **Business Addr:** Partner, Schochar, Federico & Staton PA, 1211 St Paul St, Baltimore, MD 21202, **Business Phone:** (410)234-1000.

## STATON, RHONDA BAILEY

Manager. **Educ:** Univ Tex, Austin, BA, elem educ & teaching, 1977. **Career:** The Seattle Times Co, retail advert sales mgr, 1989-, travel advert sales mgr, 2000-03, display sales mgr, metro, currently; Atlantic St Ctr, bd dir, 2008-. **Business Addr:** Display Sales Manager, The Seattle Times Co, 1120 John St, Seattle, WA 98109, **Business Phone:** (206)223-2769.

## STEANS, EDITH ELIZABETH

Executive. **Personal:** Born Sep 4, 1929, Anderson, IN; daughter of Ernest J Downing (deceased) and Mary L Adams Downing (deceased); children: Bruce, Judith, Carol & Stacy. **Educ:** Anderson Col, BA, 1976; Ball State Univ, MAS, 1978. **Career:** Madison Co Dept Pub Welfare, caseworker, 1969-72; Madison County Super Ct II, chief juv probation officer, 1973-79; State Ind, affirmative action dir, 1979-82; City Anderson, affirmative action & human rel dir, 1982-89; Univ Nebr Med Ctr, affirmative action & equal employ opportunity dir, 1989-95. **Orgs:** Urban League, 1955-90; Nat Asn Advan Colored People, 1955-90; bd dir, Comm Justice Ctr, 1970-88; YWCA, 1973-; Alpha Kappa Alpha Sorority, 1978-; instr, Anderson Col, 1978-88; comnr, Mayor's Econ Develop, 1982-86; bd dir, St John's Hosp Chem Dependency, 1982-88; bd dir, Enterprize Zone Asn, 1984-87; St Mary's Church. **Honors/Awds:** Outstanding Citizen, Nat Asn Advan Colored People, 1983. **Home Addr:** 1619 W 15th St, Anderson, IN 46016-3205, **Home Phone:** (765)642-3744.

## STEBBINS, ESQ. DANA BREWINGTON

Government official, administrator. **Personal:** Born Nov 2, 1946, Baltimore, MD. **Educ:** Howard Univ Sch Law, BA, psychiat social work, 1967; Howard Univ, MSW, 1970; Howard Univ, JD, 1975. **Career:** Super Ct, DC, judicial clerk, 1975-77; Commodity Futures Trading Comn, atty/adv/spl asst, 1977-78; Nat Bar Asn, dir com law proj, 1978-80; Small Bus Admin, spl asst to assoc adminr minority small us, 1980-; US, Legis Coun, spec asst & white house liaison, sr coun, confidential asst, Small Bus Admin, pres; Wilkes, Artis, Hedrick & Lane, partner; Law Off Dana B. Stebbins Esq, pres; Cornelius Group, TCG, prin & chief exec officer, currently; Md, dir legis affairs. **Orgs:** Am Bar Asn; Nat Asn Black Women Attys; Nat Bar Asn; Nat Asn Black Social Workers; Delta Theta Phi Legal Fraternity; Nat Asn Social Workers; Nat Conf Black Lawyers; pres, Dist Columbia Chamber Com, bd, Metrop YMCA; bd, Lab Sch; Parren J Mitchell Found; trustee, Fed City Coun; Md Econ Develop Corp; chair, DC Chamber Com; Nat Asn Women Attorneys; J. Franklyn Bourne Bar Asn; Wash Bar Asn; gen coun, Nat Asn Women Bus Owners; gen coun, Latin Am Contractors Asn; chair, DC Agenda Support Corp Comt Econ Develop; chair, Prince George's Group. **Honors/Awds:** Hundred Most Powerful Women in Washington, Wash Mag. **Home Addr:** 11818 Bishops Content Rd, Bowie, MD 20721-2569, **Home Phone:** (301)390-7495. **Business Addr:** Chief Executive Officer, The Cornelius Group, 1350 Conn Ave NW Suite 303, Washington, DC 20036, **Business Phone:** (202)861-1971.

## STEED, JOEL EDWARD

Football player. **Personal:** Born Feb 17, 1969, Frankfurt; married DAngela; children: Traicee Eileen. **Educ:** Univ Colo, BA, 1992. **Career:** Football player (retired); Pittsburgh Steelers, nose tackle, 1992-99; Nat Football League, free agt, currently. **Honors/Awds:** Pro Bowl alternate, 1996. **Special Achievements:** Films: 1994 AFC Championship Game, 1995; 1995 AFC Championship Game, 1996; Super Bowl XXX, 1996; 1997 AFC Championship Game, 1998. **Business Addr:** Free Agent, National Football League, 345 Pk Ave, New York, NY 10154, **Business Phone:** (212)450-2000.

## STEED, TYRONE

Health services administrator, spokesperson. **Personal:** Born Aug 18, 1948, Norfolk, VA; married Irene; children: Kenyatta Uniquegu. **Educ:** Northeastern Fashion Inst Techol, AAS, interior design, 1973; Thomas Edison Col, BA, 1976; Kean Col, NJ, MA, org develop, 1981. **Career:** New Horizons Inc, dist mgr, asst vpres, 1976-77; Girl Scouts Am, counfield rep, 1977-79; St Charles Kids Sch, teacher, 1979-80; Newark Office Aging, sr commun rel spec, 1980-; VA Med Ctr, Chief Crystal Grace, dir pub rel, spokesman, Dept Veterans Affairs, vol serv asst/mgr, currently. **Orgs:** Am Hosp Asn, 1981-; NJ Hosp Asn 1981-; pub rel dir, Am Hosp Asn Soc, 1982-; Seton Hall Univ Geront Adv Comt, 1982-; dir vol serv, NJ Asn, 1983. **Home Addr:** 88 Schuyler Ave, Newark, NJ 07112. **Business Addr:** Voluntary Service Assistant, Spokesman, VA Medical Center, Tremont Ave & S Ctr St, East Orange, NJ 07019, **Business Phone:** (973)395-7258.

## STEELE, BOBBIE L.

Government official, educator. **Personal:** Born Oct 18, 1937, Cleveland, MS; daughter of Mary Rodges; married Robert P; children: 7. **Educ:** Ala AMA Col, attended 1956; Chicago's Teacher's Col, elem educ, 1966; Roosevelt Univ, MS, supv admin educ, 1982. **Career:** Educator, commissioner (retired); Chicago Bd Educ, sch teacher, 1966-86; Cook County Bd Commissioners, comnr, 1986-06, interim pres, pres, 2006; Author: Woman of Steele: A Personal & Political Journal, 2011. **Orgs:** Pres, Nat Asn Black County Officials; chairperson, Nat Asn County Officials Deferred Compensation Adv Comt; Nat Coun Negro Women; League Women Voters; Lake Shore Links Inc; United Missionary Baptist Church; Cook County Dem Women; bd mem, Oper Brotherhood; Alpha Kappa Alpha Sorority; chairperson finance comt, Forest Preserve Dist Chicago; Ill Counties Bd dir; Ill Women Leadership Bd dir; bd dir, Lawndale Christian Develop. **Home Addr:** 2116 S Springfield, Chicago, IL 60623, **Home Phone:** (312)762-2798.

## STEELE, CAROLYN ODOM

Executive, consultant. **Personal:** Born Aug 31, 1944, Augusta, GA; daughter of P C Odom and Marjorie Odom. **Educ:** Spelman Col, BA, 1966; Am Univ, MA, comm, 1970. **Career:** Col Med & Dent NJ, mat developer, 1970; Minority Econ Develop Corp, admin asst educ, 1971; New York Addiction Serv Agency, dep dir pub rels & community info, 1972-76; Nat Health Coun, asst dir, commun coordr, 1976-77; Earl G Graves Ltd, dir pub affairs, 1977-83, corp commun, vpres, sr vpres; AT&T, corp affairs dir pub rels; mkt commun consult, currently. **Orgs:** Bd dir, Nat Black Child Devel Inst; co-chair Corp Women's Roundtable, Spelman Col; EDGES Group; Women Commun; bd mem, Nat Coalition 100 Black Women. **Honors/Awds:** Nat French Hon Soc Pi Delta Phi, 1963; YWCA Acad Women Achievers, 1984; publications: "Talking with the Inner City", Public Relations Journal, 1969, "The Enigma of Drug Abuse", Journal of Practical Nursing, 1974. **Business Addr:** Consultant, 209-45 Bardwell Ave, Queens Village, NY 11429.

## STEELE, DR. CLAUDE MASON

Educator, association executive, administrator. **Personal:** Born Jan 1, 1946, Chicago, IL; married Dorothy Munson; children: Jory Claire & Benjamin. **Educ:** Hiram Col, Hiram, OH, BA, psychol, 1967; Ohio State Univ, MA, social psychol, 1969, PhD, social psychol, 1971. **Career:** Univ Utah, asst prof psychol, 1971-73; Univ Wash, asst prof psychol, 1973-77, assoc prof, 1977-85, prof psychol, 1985-87; Univ Mich, prof psychol, 1987-91, inst social res, res scientist, 1989-91; Stanford Univ, prof psychol, 1991-2009, chmn dept psychol, 1997-2000, Lucie Stern prof social sci, 1997-2009, co dir res inst comparative studies race & ethnicity, 1999-2002, dir ctr comparative studies race & ethnicity, 2002-05, fac diversity coun, 2001-02, fac senate steering comm, 2002-02, fac senate, 2000-02, emer prof, currently. **Orgs:** Bd, Black Stud Psychol Asn, 1968-71 Nat Inst Alcohol Abuse & Alcoholism, Psychosocial Res Study Sect, 1984-88; sec treas, 1987-88, Soc Exp Social Psychol, chmn, 1988-89; mem & bd dir, Am Psychol Soc, 1996-97; Am Psychol Asn Div 8 Exec Comm, 1988-91; fel Ctr Adv Study Behav Sci, 1994-95; pres, Western Psychol Asn, 1996-97; Presidential Search Comm, 1999-2000; pres, Soc Personality & Social Psychol, 2002-03; bd, Trustees Develop Comm, Stanfort Univ, 2002-; pres, Soc Personality & Social Psychol, 2002-03; trustee, John D. & Catherine MacArthur Found, 2008-; trustee, Russell Sage Found, 2010-. **Honors/Awds:** Deans Teaching Award, Stanford University, 1995; Gordon Allport Prize in Social Psychology, Soc Psychol Study Social Issues, 1997; Distinguished Scientific Contribution Award, Am Psychol Asn, 1998; Honorary Doctorate, Univ Chicago, 2000; William James Fellow Award for Distinguished Scientific Career Contribution, Am Psychol Soc, 2000; Donald Campbell Award, Soc Personality & Social Psychol, 2001; Honorary Doctorate, Yale Univ, 2002; Kurt Lewin Memorial Award, Soc Psychol Study Social Issues, 2002; Senior Award for Distinguished Contributions to Psychology in the Public Interest, Am Psychol Asn, 2002; Honorary Doctorate, Princeton Univ, 2003; Columbia Teachers College Medal, 2004; Honorary Doctorate, Univ Mich, 2006; Distinguished Scientific Impact Award, Soc Exp Social Psychol, 2007; Honorary Doctorate, Northwestern Univ, 2010; Elizabeth Hurlock Beckman Award, 2010; Honorary Doctorate, Claremont Grad Univ, 2011; Honorary Doctorate, DePaul Univ, 2011; Alexander George Book Award, Int Soc Polit Psychol, 2011; Service Award, 2012; Social Psychology Award, 2012. **Special Achievements:** Associate editor of Personality and Social Psychology Bulletin in 1984-87. **Business Addr:** Emeritus Professor, Stanford University, 485 Lasuen Mall, Stanford, CA 94305-3096, **Business Phone:** (650)723-2109.

## STEELE, JOYCE YVONNE

Beautician. **Personal:** Born Dec 8, 1930, St. Johns; daughter of William Isaac and Agatha Isaac; married Richard Biddy; children: Richard Biddy & Mark Biddy; married Edgar S. **Educ:** Hopes Beauty Sch, London, eng, dipl, 1961; Loriel Beauty Sch, Paris, France, dipl, 1968; Lee Col Sch Cosmetology, Baytown, TX, dipl, 1982. **Career:** Dame Yvonne Beauty Sch, leister, eng, owner, 1958-74; Am Caribbean Beauty Prod, Baytown, Tex, owner, 1982-; Ultra Elegance Salon, Baytown, Tex, owner, 1982-. **Home Addr:** 509 Stimpson, Baytown, TX 77520, **Home Phone:** (713)420-1822. **Business Addr:** President, Ultra Elegance Salon, 823 S Pruett, Baytown, TX 77520, **Business Phone:** (713)422-5100.

## STEELE, LAWRENCE

Fashion designer. **Personal:** Born Jul 7, 1963, Hampton, VA; son of William Anderson and Winifred Delores. **Educ:** Sch Art Inst Chicago, BA, fine art, 1985. **Career:** knitwear aficionados Jan & Carlos, Japan, 1975-80; Franco Moshino, design asst, 1985-90; Miuccia Prada, design asst, 1990-94; Lawrence Steele Design, designer, 1994-. **Special Achievements:** Participated in Florence Biennale, 1998; Designed wedding dress Jennifer Aniston, 2000; Collaborated with artist Vanessa Beecroft for her performance, VB48, Genoa, Italy, 2001. **Business Addr:** Designer, Lawrence Steele Design, Via Seprio 2, Milan20149, **Business Phone:** (390)24819-51.

## STEELE, MICHAEL STEPHEN

Government official, politician. **Personal:** Born Oct 19, 1958, Prince George's County, MD; son of William (deceased) and Maebell; married Andrea Derritt; children: Michael II & Drew. **Educ:** Johns Hopkins Univ, BA, int rels, 1981; Augustinian Friars Sem, Villanova Univ; Georgetown Univ Law Sch, JD, 1991. **Career:** Cleary, Gottlieb, Seen & Hamilton Law Offs, lawyer, 1991-97; Steele Group, founder & chief exec officer, 1998-; Md Republican Party, chair, 2000-02; Md lt gov, 2002-; Pope Benedict XVI, Vatican City, 2005-; CNN, "The Situation Room", polit pundit, currently; A 12-Step Program for Defeating the Obama Agenda, 2010; MSNBC, polit analyst, 2011-; Malvern Prep Sch, teacher. **Orgs:** Bd Trustee, Johns Hopkins Univ, 1981-85; assoc, Cleary, Gottlieb, Steen & Hamilton, 1991-97; Prince Georges County Md Black Republican Coun, 1992; chair, Prince Georges County Republican Cent Comt, 1994-2000; chair, Md State Minority Outreach Task Force, 1995-97; deleg, Republican Party Nat Conv, 2000 & 2004; chair, Republican Party State Cent Comt, 2000-02; Nat Comn Fed Election Reform, 2001; bd visitors, US Naval Acad, 2002-05; Govs Exec Coun, 2003-; chair, State House Trust, 2003-; chair, Gov's Comn Minority Bus Enterprise Reform, 2003; Lt Gov Md, 2003-07; chair, Gov's Comn Qual Educ, 2004-05; State Planning Comt Higher Educ,

2004-; Gov's Sub cabinet Int Affairs, 2005-; chmn, Republican Nat Comt, 2009-11; Nat Asn Advan Colored People; co-chair & nat bd, Republican Leadership Coun; Tau Epsilon Phi Fraternity. **Business Addr:** Political Analyst, MSNBC, 30 Rockfeller Plz, New York, MD 10112, **Business Phone:** (212)664-4444.

### STEELE, DR. RUBY L.

Consultant, nurse, educator. **Personal:** Born Marion, AL; daughter of Alexander Williams and Mamie Whitehead; married George W; children: Jocelyn, Sonya, George & Christopher. **Educ:** Am River Col, Sacramento, CA, AA, 1970; Metrop State Col, Denver, CO, BS, 1974; Southern Ill Univ, Edwardsville, IL, MS, 1979; St Louis Univ, St Louis, MO, PhD, 1988. **Career:** Belleville Memorial Hosp, Belleville, Ill, nurse, 1975-78; NIMH Traineeship Grad Study, 1977; Belleville Area Col, Belleville, Ill, instr, 1977-78; Southern Illi Univ, Edwardsville, Ill, instr, asst prof, 1979-87; Webster Univ, St Louis, Mo, asst prof, 1987-90; Southeast Mo State Univ, Cape Girardeau, Mo, assoc prof, 1990-94; Ft Valley State Col, pro & dir nursing prog, 1994; Independent consult, vol, currently. **Orgs:** House Delegates, ANA, 1971-; Steering Comt, INA, 1975-; Sigma Theta Tau, Nursing Hon Soc, 1980-; Asn Black Nursing Fac, 1987-; bd dir, St Louis Univ Alumni; YWCA; Belleville News Dem. **Home Addr:** 537 Windrift Dr, Belleville, IL 62221-5847, **Home Phone:** (618)277-5978.

### STEELE, DR. SHELBY

Educator, writer, columnist. **Personal:** Born Jan 1, 1946, Chicago, IL; son of Shelby Sr and Ruth; married Rita; children: 2. **Educ:** Coe Col, Cedar Rapids, Iowa, BA, polit sci; Southern Ill Univ, MA, sociol; Univ Utah, PhD, Eng, 1974. **Career:** San Jose State Univ, prof eng, 1974-91; Hoover Inst, sr res fel, Robert J & Marion E Oster sr fel, currently; Harper's mag, contrib ed, currently; writer; columist; Books: The Content of Our Character: A New Vision of Race in America, 1991; A Dream Deferred: The Second Betrayal of Black Freedom in America, 1999; White Guilt: How Blacks & Whites Together Destroyed the Promise of the Civil Rights Era, 2006; A Bound Man: Why We Are Excited About Obama & Why He Can't Win, 2007. **Orgs:** Nat Asn Scholars; Am Acad Lib Educ; Univ Accreditation Asn; nat bd mem, Ctr New Am Community, Manhattan Inst; sr res fel Stanford Univ. **Honors/Awds:** National Book Critics Circle Award, 1991; Emmy Award, 1990; Nat Humanities Medal, 2004; Bradley Prize, 2006; Writer's Guild Award; San Francisco Film Festival Award. **Special Achievements:** Host, PBS spec, Seven Days in Benson hurst. **Business Addr:** Senior Research Fellow, Hoover Institution, Stanford Univ 434 Galvez Mall, Stanford, CA 94305-6010, **Business Phone:** (650)723-1754.

### STEELE, TOMMY

Writer, government official, clergy. **Personal:** Born Jul 26, 1950, Portsmouth, VA; son of Dr Thomas Melvin and Elizabeth Wood; married Gail White; children: Tommy Jr & Tiffany Gail; married Tonda Bostick; children: Gary & Joshua. **Educ:** Norfolk State Univ, BA, hist, 1977; Jameson Bible Inst, MDIV, 1978; Jameson Christiam Col, PhD, 1986; E NC Theol Inst, STB, 1995. **Career:** New Ahoskie Baptist Church, 1970-78; First Baptist Church, 1978-81; First Ledge Rock Baptist Church, sr pastor, 1981-83; Hardie Grove Baptist Church, sr pastor, 1981-83; Jerusalem Baptist Church, sr pastor, 1983; New Life Baptist Church, sr pastor, currently. **Orgs:** Home mission bd, Nat Baptist Conv; adv bd, Rider Univ; past chaplain, bd dir, Kappa Alpha Psi; chaplain, Trenton Police Dept; bd trustee, E NC Theol Inst; life mem, Elizabeth City State Univ Alumni Asn; life mem, NAACP; bd trustee, Apex Sch Theol; past bd dir, Kiwanis Club; Frontier Intl; Epsilon Delta Chi. **Honors/Awds:** Hon Dr Theol; More than 200 community, civic & religious awds. **Special Achievements:** First African American Chaplain of the Trenton Police Dept. **Home Addr:** 218 Kensington Ave, Trenton, NJ 08618-3332, **Home Phone:** (609)394-1778. **Business Addr:** Sr Pastor, New Life Baptist Church, 1281 Biscayne Dr, Concord, NC 28027, **Business Phone:** (704)782-6215.

### STEELE-ROBINSON, ALICE LOUISE

Educator. **Personal:** Born Mar 27, 1943, Concord, NC; daughter of Andrew A and Neomia Pharr; married Harold O. **Educ:** Barber-Scotia Col, Concord, NC, BS, 1965; Appalachian State Univ, Boone, NC, MA, 1977; Univ NC-Charlotte, curric specialist, 1988. **Career:** Educator (retired): Moore County Schs, teacher, 1965-67; Concord City Schs, teacher, 1967-77, K-12 Reading & Lang Arts, coordr, 1977-85, Head Start, dir, 1983-85; Cabarrus County Schs, Elem Educ Chap 1, ESEA, dir, 1986-95; Acad Learning Ctr, dir, exec dir. **Orgs:** Delta Kappa Gamma Int Hon Soc Women Educ, 1979-; United Way Cabarrus County, Adv Panel, 1983-99; Rowan Community Col, Early Childhood Adv Bd, 1985-95; bd dir & chmn, Cabarrus County Red Cross, 1986-95; bd mem & chmn, Cabarrus Victim Assistance Network, 1989-2000; Prince Hall Affil Order Eastern Star, 1989-2000; bd trustee, Rock Hill AME Zion Church, Concord, NC, 1989-2000; basileus, Zeta Phi Beta Sorority, Gamma Epsilon Zeta Chap, 1991-2000; secy, ACT-SO, chmn, Cabarrus County Nat Asn Advan Colored People, 1992-98; precient chief judge, Cabarrus County Bd Elections, 1992-2000; exec secy, African Methodist Episcopal Zion Church, Woman's Home& Overseas Missionary Soc, 1995-2000; exec adminr, Woman's Home & Overseas Missionary, African Methodist Episcopal Zion Church Carol Werchan; Cabarrus County Sch Facil Blue Ribbon Comt. **Home Addr:** 3735 Rock Hill Ch Rd, Concord, NC 28027, **Home Phone:** (704)786-9550.

### STEGER, DR. C. DONALD (C DON STEGER)

Government official. **Personal:** Born Aug 27, 1936, Huntsville, AL; son of Fred and Lula Cliff; married Elizabeth Sutton; children: Lisa Monique. **Educ:** Bethune Cookman Col, BS, psychol, 1964; Gammon Theol Sem, BD, 1968, MS, psychol & theol; Univ S Fla, PhD, statist & behav res, 1972. **Career:** WOBS Radio Jacksonville, announcer, 1960-64; Tampa Inner City Progs, dir, 1968-71; McCabe Black Community Develop, dir, 1972-75; Gen Elec Co, consult, 1972-74; Pinellas Co Sch, Clearwater, dir res proj, 1973; Honeywell, consult, 1975-77; Pinellas County Fla Schs, adminr, 1975-77; City St Petersburg, Fla, dep city mgr, 1977-79; City Charlotte, asst city mgr, 1979-95; Carolina HealthCare Syst, vpres corp health serv, 1995-2000; Reeder Memorial Baptist Church, sr pastor, currently. **Orgs:** Consult, US Civil Serv Comn, 1969-78; bd dir, Rotary Club Charlotte, 1975-; pres bd, Bethlehem Ctr Charlotte, 1985-86; chmn, Campaign Charlotte Meckenburg United Way, 1986; dir, Found Carolinas, 1986; Pub Libr Charlotte & Mecklenburg County, bd chair. **Home Addr:** 6517 Hunter Pine Lane, Charlotte, NC 28270, **Home Phone:** (704)365-1129. **Business Addr:** Senior Pastor, Reeder Memoiral Baptist Church, 3725 Beatties Ford Rd, Charlotte, NC 28226, **Business Phone:** (704)398-2914.

### STEIB, REV. JAMES TERRY

Clergy, bishop, college teacher. **Personal:** Born May 17, 1940, Vacherie, LA; son of Vivian Jones and Rosemond. **Educ:** Divine Word Sem, theol deg, 1967; Xavier Univ, MA, guid & coun, 1973. **Career:** Priesthood, ordained, 1967; Divine Word Sem, asst dean stud, 1967-69, prov super, 1976-83; St Stanislaus High Sch, prof, 1967-76; Archdiocese St Louis, auxiliary bishop, 1984; Cath Diocese Memphis, bishop, 1993-; Titular Bishop Britonia. **Orgs:** Prov super, Socs Divine Words; vpres, Conf Maj Superiors Men, 1979-83; consult, African Am Cath Comt, Nat Conf Cath Bishops; bd dir, Cath Exten Soc, currently; bd dir, Cath Univ Am; bd dir, Cath Relief Serv; USCCB Comt Clergy & Consecrated Life & Vocations, currently; consult, USCCB Comt Cult Diversity, currently; Comn Relig Life & Ministry, currently; Sub Comt Cath Campaign Human Develop, currently. **Special Achievements:** Named 4th Bishop of Memphis, 1993. **Business Addr:** Bishop, The Catholic Diocese of Memphis, 5825 Shelby Oaks Dr, Memphis, TN 38134-7316, **Business Phone:** (901)373-1200.

### STEINER, K LESLIE. See DELANY, SAMUEL RAY, JR.

### STENT, MADELON DELANY

Educator. **Personal:** Born Sep 22, 1933, Washington, DC; children: Michelle, Nicole & Evan. **Educ:** Sarah Lawrence Col, BA; Wellesley Col, MA; Columbia Univ, EdD, 1965; Teachers Col, grad. **Career:** City Univ New York, City Col, prof educ, 1963-, Fordham Univ Sch Educ, vis prof, 1969-71, Div Interdepartmental Studies, dir, 1981-94, prof emer, currently; Univ Dist Columbia, actg vpres acad affairs, 1977-78; Teachers Col, fac; Columbia Univ, fac; Queens Col, fac; Mills Col, fac; Random House/Knopf Mag, journalist & auth. **Orgs:** Educ con planner Voices Inc, 1966-; Nat Asn Black Sch Educrs, 1971-; Am Educ Res Asn, 1973-; nat chairperson, Higher Ed Comm Nat Alliance Black Sch Educrs; consult; HARYOU-ACT; Kappa Delta Pi Hon Educ Soc; US Off Educ; Univ Peurto Rico; Univ Calif; bd trustee, Int Partnership Serv Learning & Leadership; trustee, Roehampton Univ. **Honors/Awds:** Student Ambassador Award, Spain, 1952; Community Service Society Award, 1964; Ford Found Research Grantee, 1973; Ford Found Grantee, 1974; Rockefeller Scholar, Re Bellagio, Italy, 1975. **Special Achievements:** Co-Edited, "Cultural Pluralism in American Higher Education", 1973; Minority Enrollment & Rep in Institute of Higher Education, Praeger Press, Special Studies International, 1974, 1976. **Home Addr:** 5700 Arlington Ave Suite 5B, Riverdale, NY 10471. **Business Addr:** Professor of Education, Professor Emeritus, City College of New York, 160 Convent Ave, New York, NY 10031, **Business Phone:** (212)650-7000.

### STENT, DR. NICOLE M.

Government official, health services administrator. **Personal:** Born Jul 22, 1960, New York, NY; daughter of Theodore R and Madelon Delany; married Mark A Graham; children: Imani Simone & Mark Anthony. **Educ:** Dartmouth Col, Hanover, NH, BA, 1982; Howard Univ Sch Law, Wash, DC, JD, 1985. **Career:** US House Rep, Cong Black Caucus, fel, 1983; Leftwich, Moore & Douglass, Washington, DC, legal intern, 1985; NYK Supreme Ct, law asst, 1986; NYC Financial Servs Corp, Sr proj mgr, 1987-88; City NYK, Mayor's Off African Am & Caribbean Affairs, dep dir, actg dir, 1988-90; NYC Offtrack Betting Corp, asst gen coun, 1991; NYC HTH & Hosps Corp, Affirmative Action & EEO, asst dir, 1992-97, exec asst, CRE Planning, Cot Health Inter Govt Rels, 1998-, dist mgr, currently; Bronx Community Bd 8, dist mgr, 2007-. **Orgs:** Dartmouth Lawyers Asn, 1985-; New York Urban League, 1990-; bd mem, Paage Et Cie Ltd. **Home Addr:** 6015 Independence Ave, Bronx, NY 10471, **Home Phone:** (718)549-2457. **Business Addr:** Board Member, Paage Et Cie Ltd, 59 Beech Hill Rd, Scarsdale, NY 10583, **Business Phone:** (914)725-0343.

### STEPHEN, JOYCE A.

Police chief. **Personal:** Born Sumter, SC; children: Bruce. **Educ:** John Jay Col Criminal Justice, BS, criminal justice, 1981. **Career:** Dep chief (retired); New York Police Dept, 46th Precinct, Bronx, 1981, capt, dep inspector, 28th Precinct, Manhattan, comndg officer, dep chief, 2005. **Orgs:** John Jay Col Alumni Asn. **Special Achievements:** First African American woman deputy chief of the New York police department; First African-American female Captain. **Business Addr:** Deputy Chief, New York Police Department, 2271-89 Frederick Douglass Blvd, New York, NY 10027, **Business Phone:** (212)678-1611.

### STEPHENS, BOOKER T.

Judge. **Personal:** Born Nov 3, 1944, Bluefield, WV; son of Robert L (deceased) and Estella (deceased); married Gloria M Davis; children: Ciara Midori & Booker Taliaferro. **Educ:** WVa State Col, BA, polit sci & span, 1966; Howard Univ, JD, 1972. **Career:** Wva Univ Col Law, adj instr; Bluefield State Col, adj instr; Nat Judicial Col, fac; Asst prosecuting atty, 1977-78; WV House Deleg, 1979-82; Circuit Ct McDowell County, 1984, chief judge, 1990-; State WV, Circuit Ct, Eighth Judicial Circuit, chief judge. **Orgs:** Life mem, Nat Asn Advan Colored People, Earl Warren fel, legal defense fund, coop atty; Alpha Phi Alpha Fraternity; chmn, Standing Comt Polit Subdivisions, 1980; WV Judicial Asn; Am Bar Asn; WV State Bar Asn. **Business Addr:** Chief Judge, Eighth Judicial Circuit, State of West Virginia Circuit Court, County Courthouse, Welch, WV 24801-0310, **Business Phone:** (304)436-8535.

### STEPHENS, BRENDA WILSON

Librarian. **Personal:** Born Oct 22, 1952, Durham, NC; daughter of Leroy Wilson and Lucy Umstead; married Gregory; children: Seth & Sara. **Educ:** Vincennes Univ, Vincennes, Ind, 1971; Winston-Salem State Univ, Winston-Salem, NC, BS, 1974; NC Cent Univ, Durham, NC, MLS, 1981. **Career:** Orange County Pub Libr, Hillsboro, NC, libr asst, 1976-81, asst county librn, 1981-90, county librn, 1990-91, regional libr dir, 1991-. **Orgs:** NC Libr Asn, Pub Libr Sect, 1983-85; chair, adult serv, NCLA, Pub Libr Sect, 1987-93; pres, PTO-Cameron Pk Sch, 1988-89; pres, Kiwanis Club, 1990-; bd mem, United Way Greater Orange County, 1991-94; pres, Al Stanback Mid Sch; bd educ, Orange County Sch, 1998-. **Honors/Awds:** Homecoming Queen, Vincennes Univ, 1970-71; Roadbuilders' Award, NC Library Asn Roundtable, 1997. **Home Addr:** 5807 Craig Rd, Durham, NC 27712-1008, **Home Phone:** (919)309-0919. **Business Addr:** Regional Library Director, Orange County Public Library, 300 W Tryon St, Hillsborough, NC 27278, **Business Phone:** (919)220-5429.

### STEPHENS, BROOKE MARILYN

Financial manager, writer. **Personal:** Born Jan 1, 1944, Atlanta, GA; daughter of Charles W Jr and Grace Anne. **Educ:** Fisk Univ, BA, 1963; Western Mich Univ, MA, libr res, 1965; Harvard Bus Sch, finance & mkt, 1973; Adelphi Univ, CFP, 1986. **Career:** Chase, W Africa, int trade officer; Sweet Lantana, freelance designer & owner; Citicorp Investment Servs, New York, sr investment consult; Financial writer & investment adv, pvt pract, currently; stockbroker & insurance agent; Author: Brooke Stephens Wealth Building Journal; Talking Dollars & Making Sense: A Wealth-Building Guide for African-Americans; It's Your Money: Everything You Need to Know to Be Your Own Financial Planner; Wealth Happens One Day At A Time 365 Days To A Brighter Financial Future; Men We Cherish: African American Women Praise The Men In Their Lives; Published works: Just Frienda; Talking Dollars and Making Sense: A Wealth-Building Guide for African-Americans. **Orgs:** Financial Women's Asn New York; adv bd, chairs, econ literacy comt, Girls Inc; NY Soc Cert Financial Planners; Am Mgt Asn; Nat Asn Black Journalists. **Home Addr:** , NY. **Business Addr:** Financial Advisor, Author, Private Practice, 314 W 231st St Suite 470, Bronx, NY 10463, **Business Phone:** (718)875-2575.

### STEPHENS, CYNTHIA DIANE

Judge. **Personal:** Born Aug 27, 1951, Detroit, MI; daughter of Nathaniel Otis and Diane Shand; married Thomas Oliver Martin; children: Imani Diane. **Educ:** Univ Mich, BA, 1971; Atlanta Univ, postgrad, 1972; Wayne State Univ Law Sch; Detroit Col Law & Univ; Emory Law Sch, JD, 1976. **Career:** Neighborhood Youth Corps Econ Opportunity, proj coordr, 1972-73; Clark Col, adj fac, 1975-77; Nat Conf Black Lawyers, southern regional dir, 1976-77; Nat League Cities, coordr, 1977-78; Pan-African Orthodox Christian Church, gen coun, 1978-82; Mich Senate, assoc gen coun, 1979-81; Wayne Co Charter Comn, vice-chmn, 1980-81; Law Off Cynthia D Stephens, atty, 1981-82; 36th Dist Ct, judge, 1982-85; Landlord Tenant Div, 1983-84; Wayne Co Community Col, instr, 1984-92; Wayne Co Circuit Ct, judge, 1985-; Univ Detroit Mercy Law Sch, adj prof, 1986; Wayne State Univ Law Sch, adj fac, 1990-91; Detroit Col Law, adj prof, 1992-95; Nat Judicial Col, fac, 1994; Third Circuit Ct, chief pro-tempore judge, currently. **Orgs:** Nat Conf Black Lawyers, 1970-; Wolverine Bar Asn, 1979; bd mem, Wayne Co Neighborhood Legal Serv, 1980; New Detroit Inc, 1981-; Adv Comt, Am Corp Coun Pro-Bono, 1982-88; bd mem, Asn Black Judges Mich, 1982-89; Mich Dist Judges Asn, 1982-85; Greater Detroit Health Care Coun, 1983-85; Univ Mich Symp Ser Ctr African & Afro-Am Studies, 1984; Adv Bd, African Diaspora Proj Delta Inst, 1984-88; mem-at-large, City Wide Sch Comm Org, 1984-86; Delta Manor LDHA, 1984-, YMCA Downtown Detroit, 1984; Am Bar Asn Comm Judicial Eval, 1984-85; Delta Sigma Theta Detroit Alumni, 1984-85; Adv Bd, Mich Bar J, 1985-; bd comnrs, State Bar Mich, 1986-; Nat Asn Women Judges; Mich Judges Asn; Nat Bar Asn; State Bar Mich; Acad Adv Comt, Mich Judicial Inst. **Honors/Awds:** Outstanding Woman Award, Woodward Ave Presbyterian Church, 1982; Distinguished Service Award, Region 5 Detroit Pub Sch, 1983; Wolverine Bar member of the Year, 1984; Golden Heritage Award for Judicial Excellence, Little Rock Baptist Church, 1984; Outstanding Woman in Law, Hartford Mem Baptist Church, 1985; Distinguished Alumni Award, Cass Tech High Sch, 1987; Detroit Award of Merit, Nat Coun Negro Women, 1987; Susan B Anthony Award, Nat Orgn Women, 1987; Founders Award, Black Am Law Stud Asn, 1988; Augustus Straker Award, Wolverine Bar Asn, 1989, 1997; Presidents Award, Nat Bar Asn, 1991, 2000; Anita Hill Award, Detroit Human Rights Comn, 1992; Fannie Lou Hammer Award, 1995; Women in Leadership Award, Oakgrove AME, 1997; Damon J. Keith Community Spirit Award, Wolverine Bar Asn, 2001. **Special Achievements:** Published "Judicial Selection & Diversity," Michigan Bar Journal Vol 64 No 6 1985; contributor and Michigan Non-Standard Jury Instructor for West Group, 1999, 2001. **Business Addr:** Adjunct Professor, University of Detroit Mercy School of Law, 651 E Jefferson, Detroit, MI 48226, **Business Phone:** (313)596-0200.

### STEPHENS, DAVID L.

Executive. **Personal:** children: 5. **Educ:** Southern Univ, BS, bus admin. **Career:** Ford Motor Co, sales mgt; Pavilion Lincoln Mercury, Austin, dealer cand, 1990-93; Falls Lincoln Mercury, dealer prin & pres; Stephens Automotive Group, pres & chief exec officer, plano, currently. **Orgs:** Jaguar N Am Dealer Opers Coun; Ford Motor Minority Dealers Asn; Tex Automobile Dealers' Asn; Legis Comt; Nat Asn Minority Automobile Dealers; United Negro Col Fund; Am Cancer Soc; Crystal Charity Ball; Dallas Mus Art; Tex Animal Control Asn; African Am Mus; Jesuit Found; regent, Midwestern State Univ; bd mem, Pkwy Bank NA; dir, Greater Dallas Chamber; Credit Policy Comt; Compensation Comt; bd mem, Baylor Health Care Syst Found; bd trustee, Paul Quinn Col; bd mem, Sleep Develop Group; bd mem, Sp Bancorp Inc; CRA Int Inc. **Special Achievements:** Stephens is Jaguar's first African-American dealer and is also Audi's first African-American dealer. **Business Addr:** Chief Executive Officer, President, Stephens Automotive Group Inc, 4618 Columbus Rd, Macon, GA 31206, **Business Phone:** (478)477-5123.

### STEPHENS, DOREEN Y.

Marketing executive. **Personal:** Born Sep 10, 1963; daughter of Lolita. **Educ:** Univ Pa, BSE, chem engineering, 1985; Columbia Bus Sch, MBA, mkt & int bus, 1990. **Career:** Gen Foods, Battle Creek, Mich, asst engr & assoc chem engr, 1985-88, asst prod mgr, sr brand mgr, 1990-95; Kraft Gen Foods, Post Pebbles, White Plains, New York, assoc prod mgr, 1990-95, New Prod Develop, sr brand mgr, 1995-97, Maxwell House Coffee Div, sr brand mgr, 1997; Krafts Foods Int, coffee mkt mgr, 1997-98; Kraft Gen Foods, Post Pebbles, sr category bus dir, 1998-2002, vpres, post div & desserts div, 2002-03, vpres, strategy

& new prods, post div, 2003; Sch Bridge League, chief operating officer & vpres prog & mkt, 2007-10; Nonprofit Sector, consult, 2010-; Simply Seafood Restaurant & Fish Mkt, managing partner, 2011-. **Orgs:** Nat Black MBA Asn, 1990-; mentor, Black Scholars Mentor Prog, 1991-; alumni admis ambassador, Columbia Bus Sch, 1992; adv bd, Soaring Words; bd dir, In Roads Inc, Westchester, Fairfield County; bd dir, Girl Scouts Inc, Southwestern, Conn; treas, MEECO Inst, 2016-. **Honors/Awds:** Dean's List, Columbia Business School, spring, 1990; Outstanding Women in Marketing & Communications, Ebony Mag, 2000. **Special Achievements:** US patent 317372, 1992. **Home Addr:** 26 Village Grn, Port Chester, NY 10573-2655, **Home Phone:** (914)934-0937. **Business Addr:** Managing Partner, Simply Seafood Restaurant & Fish Market, 2542B White Plains Rd, Bronx, NY 10467, **Business Phone:** (718)231-0403.

### STEPHENS, E. DELORES B

Educator. **Personal:** Born Nov 30, 1938, Danville, VA; daughter of Henrietta H Betts and G A Betts Sr; married Charles R; children: Chandra R & Charlita R. **Educ:** Univ Exeter, Testamur; Spelman Col, BA, eng, 1961; Atlanta Univ, MA, eng, 1962; Emory Univ, PhD, eng, 1976; Univ London, cert; Univ Exeter, cert. **Career:** Educator, author; Atlanta Sch Bus, instr, 1962-63; Norfolk State Univ, instr, 1963; Morehouse Col, Eng Fundamentals Prog & var departmental comts, dir, 1964-76, prof, 1979, Dept Eng, chair, prof, 1995-; Freshman Eng Prog, dir, 1984-94; Dillard Univ, assoc prof & dir, gov rel, 1976-79; USY, FORSCOM, edu spt, 1980-83; St Leo Col, adj, 1987-95; Spelman Col, vis prof, 1991-94; Ind Purdue Univ, Indianapolis, vis prof, 1994-95. **Orgs:** Col Lang Assn, 1975-; Int Eng Hon Soc, 1976-; charter mem, Sigma Tau Delta Int Eng Hon Soc, 1976; Natl Coun Teachers Eng, 1984-; Upsilon Nu Chap sponsor, 1985-; Natl Hons Coun, 1988-, teaching & learning comt, 1990-93, planning comt; Morehouse Bd trustee; pres, Links Inc, Magnolia Chap, 1991; Langston Hughes Socs; charter mem, Charles Chesnutt Socs; charter mem, Alice Childress Soc; S Atlantic Mod Lang Assn, 1994-; Assn Study Afro-Am Life & Hist, 1994-; Ga Assn Women Educ, 1995-; Assn Depts Eng; reader, Educ Testing Serv; mentor, Duke Univ; mentor, Morehouse stud UNCF-Mellon Fels Program; Nat Asn Teachers Eng (NCTE); Am Shakespeare Asn; Nat Hons Prog; Col Lang Asn(CLA); vice chmn, Atlanta-Fulton Pub Libr Syst Bd trustee; alumna, United Way Metro Atlanta V.I.P. prog; Johnnetta B. Cole Soc; assoc ed, J Negro Hist; vol, Cascade United Methodist Church; Scholar Awards Comt, currently. **Home Addr:** 1369 Cascade Falls Dr SW, Atlanta, GA 30311, **Home Phone:** (404)505-1190. **Business Addr:** Professor, Morehouse College, 830 Westview Dr SW Brawley Hall 110, Atlanta, GA 30314, **Business Phone:** (404)681-2800.

### STEPHENS, JAMAIN

Football player. **Personal:** Born Jan 9, 1974, Lumberton, NC; son of Joseph and Dollie; children: Jayla, Jamain & DaRon. **Educ:** NC Agr & Tech State Univ, commun broadcast news. **Career:** Football player (retired); Pittsburgh Steelers, tackle, 1997, right tackle, 1998; Cincinnati Bengals, right tackle, 1999, 2000, tight end, 2003. **Honors/Awds:** Most Resilient Award, random voters of the University, 1993.

### STEPHENS, JOSEPH (JOE STEPHENS)

Basketball player, real estate agent, president (government). **Personal:** Born Jan 28, 1973, Riverside, CA; son of Joseph and Cheryl. **Educ:** Univ Ark, BS, 1996; Univ Phoenix, MBA, 2010. **Career:** Basketball player (retired), exec, pres; Houston Rockets, forward, 1996-98; Utah Jazz, 1999; Vancouver Grizzlies, 1999-2000; comnr, Tex Dept Transp; SDI Mortgage, pres; B4 Develop & Serv LLC, prin; Joe Stephens Ins Agency, owner, currently; Galena Pk ISD, pres, 2009-. **Orgs:** Founder, Joe Stephens Found, 1999; bd dir, N Channel Area Chamber Com; Nat Basketball Retired Players Asn. **Business Addr:** President, Galena Park I.S.D., 14705 Woodforest Blvd, Houston, TX 77015, **Business Phone:** (832)386-1000.

### STEPHENS, REV. SHAHEERAH

Religious educator. **Educ:** Wayne State Univ, BA, mass commun, 1981; Unity Sch Christianity, ThD, theol studies, 1997. **Career:** Transforming Love Community, founding pastor, minister, auth & trainer, 1997-. **Business Addr:** Founding Pastor, Transforming Love Community, 15400 Plymouth Rd, Detroit, MI 48227-2006, **Business Phone:** (313)270-2325.

### STEPHENS, SLOANE

Tennis player. **Personal:** Born Mar 20, 1993, Plantation, FL; daughter of John (deceased) and Sybil Smith. **Educ:** Evert Tennis Acad, Fla; Nick Saviano High Performance Tennis Acad; Us Tennis Asn. **Career:** Junior tennis player, 2009-10; professional tennis player, 2011-. **Honors/Awds:** Tournament results include: U.S. Open Junior, Runner-Up, 2008, Winner, 2010; French Open Junior, Winner, 2010; Wimbledon Junior, Winner, 2010; Grand Slam Tournaments: Australian Open, semifinals, 2013; Wimbledon, quarterfinals, 2013; French Open, fourth round, 2013; U.S. Open, fourth round, 2013. **Special Achievements:** As of January 2014, ranked number 12 in the world; featured in various publications, including "Vogue," "Teen Vogue," "ESPN: The Magazine," "USA Today," and "Sports Illustrated".

### STEPHENS, TREMAYNE RAPHAEL

Executive, football player. **Personal:** Born Apr 16, 1976, Greenville, SC. **Educ:** NC State Univ, BS, parks, recreation & tourism mgt, 1997. **Career:** Football player (retired), executive; San Diego Chargers, running back, 1998-99; Indianapolis Colts, running back, 1999-2001; Nat Football League, nfl running back, 2000-; Athletic Develop Systs, chief exec officer & speed develop trainer, 2003-; Parks & Recreation, City Gastonia, recreation ctr supvr, 2004-; Philips Recreation Ctr, dir, 2006-; Christian Athletes, fel. **Honors/Awds:** Doak Walker Award, 1997. **Business Addr:** Recreation Center Supervisor, Parks & Recreation, Memorial Hall, Gastonia, NC 28052, **Business Phone:** (704)866-6839.

### STEPHENS, WILLIAM HAYNES

Judge. **Personal:** Born Mar 2, 1935, New Orleans, LA; son of William and Myrtle; children: Michael (deceased), Stuart & Patrick. **Educ:** San Jose State Univ, San Jose, Calif, BA, 1956; Univ Calif, Hastings Col Law, JD, 1967. **Career:** Judge (retired); Nat Labor Rels Bd, atty, 1968; Contra & Costa County, dep pub defender, 1968-69; Bagley/Bianchi & Sheeks, assoc atty, 1969-72; Marin County Bar Asn, dir, 1970-73; law off, William H Stephens, atty law, 1972-79; Marin County Human Rights Comn, chmn, 1977-79; Marin County Dist, dist coun, 1977-79; Marin County Super Ct, arbitrator, 1977-79; Calif Agr Labor Rels Bd, admin law officer, 1978-79; Munic Ct County Marin, Calif, judge, 1979; Supr Ct County Marin, Calif, judge, 1988. **Orgs:** Amer Heart Asn, 1985-; Calif Judges Asn; Nat Bar Asn; Am Bar Asn. **Home Addr:** 904 Vernal Way, Mill Valley, CA 94941-4422, **Home Phone:** (415)388-1741.

### STEPHENSON, ALLAN ANTHONY

Executive director, executive, government official. **Personal:** Born Oct 27, 1937, New York, NY; married Deloris; children: Diane & Allan Jr. **Educ:** Morgan St Col, BA, 1960; NY City Univ, John Jay Sch, Crim Just, post grad. **Career:** Bus Educ Training, Intgerracial Coun Bus Opport, assoc dir, 1965-66; Urban League Westchester Co, dir econ develop & employ, 1966-67, assoc exec dir, 1967-68; Assist Negro Bus, exec dir, 1968-69; US Dept Com, Off Minor Bus Enterprise, actg dir & dep dir opers, br chief, 1970-73, reg dir, 1973-77; US Small Bus Admin, Baltimore Dist Off, dist dir, currently. **Orgs:** Bd mem, exec comt, NY St Coun Urban Leagues, 1967-68; secy, bd dir, Asn Assist Negro Bus, 1967-70; bd dir, Oakland Mills Youth Conf, 1975-76; adv comt, Comp Statewide Plan Vocation Rehab Serv, 1967-69; bd dir, Sr Personnel Employ Comt, 1967-69; Statewide Manpower Panel Job Train Employ, 1967-69; US Dept Com, Incent Awards Comt, 1975-77; Judo & Karate Club Baltimore; Roots Assoc Adv Comt, Comp Statewide Plan Vocat Rehab Serv, 1965; chairperson, Md Awards Breakfast Prog, 2007. **Honors/Awds:** Outstanding Performance Award, US Dept Com, 1974-75; Presidential Citation, 1975. **Home Addr:** PO Box 560, Suitland, MD 20752-0560. **Business Addr:** District Director, US Small Business Administration, 10 S Howard St Suite 6220, Baltimore, MD 21201, **Business Phone:** (410)962-6195.

### STEPHENSON, CHARLES E., III

Executive. **Career:** Stepco SC Inc, pres, secy & dir, currently. **Home Addr:** PO Box 23406, Columbia, SC 29224-3406. **Business Addr:** President, Stepco of South Carolina Inc, 1242 Aruba Cir, Charleston, SC 29412, **Business Phone:** (843)762-3009.

### STEPHENSON, DAMA F.

Banker, executive. **Personal:** Born Oct 23, 1955, Kansas City, MO; daughter of Clarence R Sr and Patricia M. **Educ:** Howard Univ, BA, 1977; George Washington Univ, MBA, int bus & finance, 1981. **Career:** US Dept State, Agency Int Develop, foreign affairs specialist, 1979-80; US Dept Com, Int Trade ADM, trade asst, 1980; CoreStates Financial Corp, asst vpres trade serv, 1981-90; Com Bank Kans City NA, vpres, 1990; State St Corp, vpres southern regional sales, 1993-2005; Wachovia Corp & Instnl Trust, managing dir sales, vpres southeastern regional sales, 2005-06; Com Bancshares, relationship mgr; Wells Fargo, sr relationship mgr & vpres, 2007-. **Orgs:** Adv bd mem, Nat Black MBA Asn, 1990-; treas, Kans City 100 Most Influential Charitable Orgs, 1991-92; bd mem, Kans City Area March Dimes, 1992-; bd mem, Are You Committed Kans City Inc, 1992-; Promethean Kappa Tau; Wolcott Fel. **Honors/Awds:** Chapter Member of the Year, Nat Black MBA Asn, 1989; Outstanding Business & Professional Award, Dollars & Sense Mag, 1991. **Home Addr:** 399 Pond St Apt E-1, Braintree, MA 02184. **Business Addr:** Vice President, Senior Relationship Manager, Wells Fargo, 420 Montgomery St, San Francisco, CA 94103, **Business Phone:** (415)979-0775.

### STEPHENSON, DWIGHT EUGENE

Football player. **Personal:** Born Nov 20, 1957, Murfreesboro, NC; married Dinah; children: Dwight Jr. **Educ:** Univ Ala. **Career:** Football player (retired); Miami Dolphins, ctr, 1980-87; Dwight Stephenson Found, founder, 2007; D. Stephenson Construct Inc, owner. Films: "Ace Ventura: Pet Detective", 1994; "NFL Monday Night Football ", 1970; Super Bowl XVII, 1983. **Orgs:** Charity work, Baby House & Boy Scouts, S Fla. **Honors/Awds:** Man of the Year; Champion, Asian Football Confederation, 1982, 1984; Offensive Lineman of the Year, Natl Football League Players Asn, 1983-87; USA Today NFL Offensive Lineman of the Year; Silver Medal Valor, Miami-Dade Police Dept, 1984; Walter Payton Man of the Year Award, 1985; Miami Dolphin's Honor Roll, 1994; Pro Football Hall of Fame, 1998; Virginia Sports Hall of fame, 1999; Walter Camp Man of the Year, 2005; Hampton Roads Sports Hall of Fame, 2011. **Business Addr:** Founder, The Dwight Stephenson Foundation, 6241 N Dixie Hwy Suite A, Fort Lauderdale, FL 33334-3620, **Business Phone:** (954)315-7020.

### STEPP, MARC (MARCELLUS STEPP)

Association executive, vice president (organization). **Personal:** Born Jan 31, 1923, Versailles, KY; married Elanor. **Educ:** Wolverine Trade Sch, 1949; Lewis Bus Sch, 1951; Univ Detroit, BBA, 1963. **Career:** Association executive (retired); Chrysler, Highland Pk, shop committeeman, chief steward, Chrysler-UAW Nat Negotiating Comt, vpres; Int Union, vpres; UAW Int, Region 1b, asst dir, UAW Region 1b, int rep, 1967-73, asst regional dir, 1973-74, int vpres, 1974-88; Common Pleas Ct, clerk; Community Health Asn, asst dir; Univ Detroit-Mercy, Inst Urban Community Affairs, exec dir. **Orgs:** UAW Int; exec bd dir, UAW Soc Tech Educ Prog; dir, Job Develop Training Prog; chmn, UAW SE Mich Community Action Prog; Dexter Ave Baptist Church; Nat Asn Advan Colored People; Trade Union Leadership Coun; Coalition Black Trade Unionists; Dem Black Caucus Steering Comt. **Honors/Awds:** Hon PhD, Lewis Col Bus, 1986, Saginaw St Univ, 1990, Univ Detroit, 1990. **Special Achievements:** First African-American to lead bargaining for the union at a Detroit automaker. **Home Addr:** 17160 Faust Ave, Detroit, MI 48219-9355, **Home Phone:** (313)531-7978.

### STEPPE, CECIL H.

Executive, law enforcement officer. **Personal:** Born Jan 31, 1933, Versailles, KY; son of Grant and Esther; married Evelyn Lee Elliott; children: Gregory, Russell, Steven, Cecily & Annette. **Educ:** San Diego City Col, AA, sociol, 1961; Calif Western Univ, BA, sociol, 1964; Community Col, life time teaching credential, 1972. **Career:** Executive; Grossmont Col, chief probation officer, 1966-80; instr criminol dept, 1969-73; Camp W Fork, dir, 1976-77, dir adult inst, 1977-80; San Diego Co, CA, supvr probation officer, 1968-73, dir juv intake, 1973-75, asst supt juv hall, 1975, finalization due-process syst adult inst, 1975-76; San Diego Co, Dept Social Serv, dir, 1992-97, Comm Initiatives Health & Human Serv Agency, dir, Urban League, dir & chief exec officer, 1999, pres & chief exec officer, Urban League San Diego County, 2001-07. **Orgs:** Black Leadership Coun, 1980; co-covenor, Black Co Admin, 1980; vpres, Chief Probation Officers CA, 1983; Equal Opportunity San Diego Urban League, 1983; bd mem, Am Probation & Parole Asn, 1984; chmn, State Adv bd, Victim/Witness Prog, 1984; bd mem, St Youth Prog; Mayors Crime Comn, Criminal Justice Coun; adv com, Interagency Youth; Nat Forum Black Pub Admin; Calif Black Correction Coalition; Am Probation & Parole Asn; Chief Probation & Parole Asn; Chief Probation Officers CA; San Diego Co Exec Asn; San Diego Rotary; Calif Welfare dir Asn; Am Pub Welfare Asn; Child Welfare League Am; chmn bd dir, Gompers Prep Acad, 2005-. **Home Addr:** 5988 Wenrich Pl, San Diego, CA 92120-2935. **Business Addr:** Chairman, Gompers Preparatory Academy, 1005 47th St, San Diego, CA 92102, **Business Phone:** (619)263-2171.

### STEPTO, ROBERT BURNS

Writer, educator. **Personal:** Born Oct 28, 1945, Chicago, IL; son of Robert C and Anna Burns; married Michele A Leiss; children: Gabriel Burns & Rafael Hawkins. **Educ:** Trinity Col, Hartford Conn, BA (cum laude), eng, 1966; Stanford Univ, CA, MA, 1968, PhD, 1974. **Career:** Williams Col, Williams town, Mass, asst prof, 1971-74; Yale Univ, New Haven, Conn, dir undergrad studies, 1974-77, dir grad studies, 1978-81, 1985-89, Spring 1994, prof, 1984-, African Am Studies, chair, 2005-08; Callaloo, assoc ed, 1984-88. Books: From Behind TheVeil, auth, 1979; The Reconstruction of Instruction, ed, 1979; Blue Lake, auth, 1988. **Orgs:** Chair, Comn Lits & Lang Am, Mod Lang Asn Am, 1977-78; Conn HumanitiesCoun, 1980-82; trustee, Trinity Col, 1982-92; Yale-New Haven TeachersInst, advisor, 1985-; Anson Phelps Stokes Inst, advisor, 1985-; Am Lit bdeds, 1987-88; Southern Conn Lib Coun, advisor, 1987; Callaloo, 1988-; AmStudies Asn. **Home Addr:** 80 Rimmon Rd, Woodbridge, CT 06525, **Home Phone:** (203)397-3566. **Business Addr:** Professor, African American Studies, English & American Studies, Yale University, 149 Elm St, New Haven, CT 06520-3388, **Business Phone:** (203)432-2300.

### STEPTOE, JAVAKA

Artist, designer, illustrator. **Personal:** Born Apr 19, 1971, New York, NY; son of John and Stephanie Douglas. **Educ:** Cooper Union Advan Sci & Art, BA, fine arts, 1995. **Career:** Artist, currently; Book: Do You Know What I'll Do, 2000; A Pocket Full of Poems, 2001; Original Art Work Show, Soc Illustrators, 2001; Swan Lake Projects; Hot Day on Abbott Avenue, 2005; Scream; The Jones Family Express, 2003; My Sweet Baby, 2004; In Daddy's Arms I Am Tall; In Praise of Our Fathers & Mothers, Rain Play, 2008; All of the Above, 2008; Amiri & Odette: A Love Story, 2009; Sounds Like a Rainbow, 2010; designer, currently. **Orgs:** Am Libr Asn; Int Reading Asn; Reading Fundamental Inc. **Honors/Awds:** Coretta Scott King Award, Am Libr Asn, 1998; Image Award, Nat Asn Advan Colored People, 1998; Honor for "In Daddy's Arms I am Tall", Brooklyn Pub Libr, 1998; Excellence in Children's Books, Blue Bonnet, 1998; Printmaking, Drawing & Artist Fellow, New York Found Arts, 2001; Jane Addams Children's Book Award for Hot Day on Abbott Avenue, 2005; Humanities Washington Grant The Creative Process, 2007; The Coretta Scott King Illustrator Award, 2011; Bookbinder's Guild of New York, 2011. **Special Achievements:** Original Art Work show, Society of Illustrators, 1998, City Scape Mural, Helena Robinstein Literacy Center at Childrens Museum of Manhattan, 1989, Legends, Folklore & real Life Stories (group Art exhibit), Art Institute of Chicago, 2000, Children's book art from In Daddy's Arms I am Tall (exhibit), Memorial Art Gallery, 2000, Kuba Cloth design for Congo exhibit, Bronx Zoo; 1998 Bluebonnet Award for Excellence Finalist for In Daddy's Arms I Am Tall. **Home Addr:** 960 Sterling Pl, Brooklyn, NY 11213, **Home Phone:** (718)778-4189. **Business Addr:** Artist, Designer, PO Box 330170, Brooklyn, NY 11233-0170, **Business Phone:** (718)778-4189.

### STEPTOE, SONJA

Journalist. **Personal:** Born Jun 16, 1960, Lutcher, LA; daughter of Eldridge W Jr and Rosa Jane Jordan. **Educ:** Univ Mo, Columbia, MO, BJ, jour, 1982, AB, econs, 1982; Duke Univ Law Sch, Durham, NC, JD, 1985. **Career:** Dow Jones & Co, New York, NY, staff reporter, Wall St J, 1985-90; Time Inc, New York, NY, staff writer, Sports Illus, 1990-96, sr ed, 1996-97; CNN & Sports Illus, nat corresp, 1997; People mag, sr ed; Time Warner Inc, Corresp, 1995-2000, Corresp, CNNSI, 1998-2000; Time Mag, dep news dir, bur chief, sr corresp, 2002-07; US Dept Com, dep dir; O Melveny & Myers LLP, client develop mgr, 2007-, global commun mgr, 2007-; global commun dir, 2010-. **Orgs:** Bd dir, Assoc Black Charities, New York, 1989-94; Am Bar Asn, 1986-; Pa Bar Asn, 1986-; Nat Asn Black Journalists, 1987-; bd dir, Univ Mo Arts & Sci Alumni Asn, 1986-97. **Honors/Awds:** Harry S Truman Scholar; Truman Scholar Found, 1980; award-winning author, Journalist & Pub Affairs Leader; Emmy Award, 1991. **Business Addr:** Client Development Manager, O'Melveny & Myers LLP, 400 S Hope St, Los Angeles, CA 90071, **Business Phone:** (213)430-6000.

### STERLING, H. DWIGHT, SR.

Newspaper executive, executive, association executive. **Personal:** Born Jun 7, 1944, Waco, TX; son of Lawrence Sr and Susie Lucille; children: Sherilyn L Vaughn, H Dwight Jr, Keith Morris, Dana & Shantelle. **Educ:** Merritt Col, AA, social sci & bus, 1969; Calif State Univ, BA, sociol, 1972; Univ Calif, Berkeley, MA, pub health, 1973. **Career:** County Alameda, regional adminr, 1974-78; City Oakland, dist coordr, 1978-86; Oakland Cancer Control Prog, pub health educr, 1986-89; Dwight Sterling Assoc, mgt consult, 1986-; Nat Univ, Urban & Regional Planning, asst prof, 1990-91; Post Newspaper, exec asst; Sunday Morning News, owner & publ, currently. **Orgs:** Asn Black Health Educr, 1973-92; Bay Area Black Prof Health Network, 1974; Am Pub Health Asn, 1974; Black Pub ADR Asn, 1979; chair, Alpha Phi Alpha Fraternity, Gamma Phi Lambda Chap, 1984; exec dir, 1991-92, Seventh Step Found, 1987-90; Pan African Chamber Com, Planning Comt, 1991-92; Bethel Missionary Baptist Church, 1962; W Coast Black Publishers Asn, 1992; div leader, Assault Illiteracy Process, 1993; life mem, UC Berkeley Alumni Assn; bd, Ocho Rios Sister City; fel Bethel Missionary Baptist Church; fel Tex Sports Hall Fame. **Honors/Awds:** Superior Accomplishment, US Defense Dept, 1968; Scholarship, US Pub Health Serv, 1972; Certificate of Appreciation, Alameda County, 1975; City Oakland Mayor Dwight Sterling Day Proclamation, 1986. **Home Addr:** 5441 Ygnacio Ave, Oakland, CA 94601, **Home Phone:** (510)533-8094. **Business Addr:** Owner, Publisher, Sunday Morning News, 337 17th St Suite 210, Oakland, CA 94612, **Business Phone:** (510)268-1121.

### STERLING, DR. JEFFREY EMERY
Physician. **Personal:** Born Jan 15, 1964, Chicago, IL; son of John Estes Sr and Ollie Mae Emerson. **Educ:** Northwestern Univ, Evanston, IL, BA, psychol, 1985; Harvard Univ Sch Pub Health, Boston, MA, MPH, 1991; Univ Ill Col Med, Peoria, IL, MD, 1991. **Career:** Cook Co Hosp, resident; Boston City Hosp Corp, Boston, Mass, consult comn, 1990; Cook Co Hosp, Chicago, Ill, resident physician-transitional/emergency med; JPS Health Network, Dept Emergency Med, chmn & dir; US Asthma Care, pres, founder & chief exec officer; Sterling HealthCare Initiatives, owner, currently; DFW Urgent Care PC, pres & chief exec officer, currently. **Orgs:** Co-founder, pres, Jr Auxiliary Hyde Pk Neighborhood Club, 1981-82; pres, One Step Before Premedical Or, 1982-84; vpres, Black Stud Alliance, Northwestern Univ, 1983-84; chmn, bd dir, Stud Nat Med Asn Inc, 1988-91; proj mgr, Wellness Coun Greater Boston Appl Res Forum, 1989-90; chmn, Health Indust Group Dalls Ft Worth Minority Bus Coun; chmn, Stud Nat Med Asn; Allergy Found Am; Wis Asthma Coalition; Tex Lung Assocs. **Honors/Awds:** Ill Dept Pub Health, Scholarship, IDPH, 1986-91; President's Certificate of Appreciation, Lincoln Univ, 1990; Jeffrey E Sterling, MD, MPH Gen Endowment Fund established Stud Nat Med Asn, 1991; Elected Chmn Emer, Stud Nat Med Asn, 1991. **Home Addr:** , Milwaukee, WI 53221, **Home Phone:** (414)447-2750. **Business Addr:** President, Chief Executive Officer, DFW Urgent Care PC, 500 8th Ave Suite 110, Ft. Worth, TX 76104-2065, **Business Phone:** (817)938-0965.

### STERLING, JOHN D.
Chief executive officer. **Personal:** children: 2. **Educ:** Jackson State Univ, comput sci. **Career:** Kraft Foods; Sears Logistics Syst; Synch-Solutions Inc, founder & chief exec officer, 1998-. **Orgs:** Bd trustee, Teachers Acad Math Sci; Boy Scouts Am; Woodlawn Orgn; Chicago Pub Schs; Union League Boys & Girls Club; chief exec officer, Nat Urban League. **Business Addr:** Founder, Chief Executive Officer, Synch-Solutions Inc, 211 W Wacker Dr Suite 300, Chicago, IL 60606, **Business Phone:** (312)252-3700.

### STETSON, JEFFREY PAUL (JEFF STETSON)
Screenwriter, educator. **Personal:** Born Jun 5, 1948, New York, NY; son of Isabella and John; married Carmen Hayward. **Educ:** Framingham State Col, BA, 1973; Boston Univ, MEd, 1974, ABD, 1976. **Career:** Mass State Col Syst, dir affirmative action & alternatives individual develop, 1974-79; Boston Univ, jr fel, 1975; Univ Lovell, dir affirmative action, 1979; Robert Redfords Sundance Inst, writing mentor; Calif State Univ, Theater Arts & Dance Dept, prof; Calif State Univ, dean fac & staff affairs, 1979-87; Calif State Univ, actg dir pub affairs, 1986-87; Calif State Univ, dean fac, staff affairs, dir pub affairs & univ rels, 1986; Stage Plays: Keep the Faith: A musical on the life & times of Adam Clayton Powell Jr; Fathers & Other Strangers; Fraternity; And the Men Shall Also Gather; To Play a Black Man; Love You Better; The Apology; The Meeting. **Orgs:** Pres & bd dir, Black Alliance Scholar & Educ, 1981-84; pres & bd dir, Concerned Helpers Inner Comn Endeavors, 1984-; Nat Asn Advan Colored People; Urban League; Am Asn Affirmative Action; Dramatists Guild, Los Angeles Black Playwrights; Los Angeles Actors Theatre Playwrights Lab; Writers Guild Am W. **Home Addr:** 14069 Marquesas Way Apt 310-D, Marina Del Rey, CA 90292-6051.

### STEVENS, ALTHEA WILLIAMS
Educator. **Personal:** Born Oct 23, 1931, Norfolk, VA. **Educ:** Calif State Univ, Los Angeles, BS, 1969; Rutgers Univ, MEd, 1974. **Career:** Los Angeles Co Probation Dept, stat coordr, 1966-68; Camden High Sch, instr data processing, 1970-75; Montclair State Col, instr bus educ & offsys adm, 1975-78; Bergen Co Comm Col, prof bus admin, 1977-78; Western Wyo Col, div chmn, assoc prof. **Orgs:** Consult, Comp Sweet Water Co; WY Planning Bd, 1978-79; gen pub mem, Wyo Bd Cert Pub Accts, 1980-83; Asn Comput Mgt AVA; Nat Bus Educ Asn; Wood Buffalo Environ Asn.

### STEVENS, BARRINGTON P. (BARRY STEVENS)
Manager. **Personal:** Born Nov 16, 1961, Miami, FL; son of Barrington and Bertha; married Catherine P; children: Barrington III & Isaiah. **Educ:** Johnson C Smith Univ, BS, 1983. **Career:** The Kroger Co, store mgr, 1983-90; Brown & Williamson Tobacco Corp, nat accts mgr, 1990. **Orgs:** Pres, Phi Beta Sigma, 1982-83. **Home Addr:** 822 Kipling Dr, Allen, TX 75002, **Home Phone:** (972)396-9603.

### STEVENS, EARL. See E-40, E.

### STEVENS, DR. GEORGE EDWARD
Educator. **Personal:** Born Mar 7, 1942, Philadelphia, PA; son of George Edward and Marstella Smalls Harvey; married Pamela Ann Giffhorn; children: Kwanza B & Charlie E. **Educ:** Delaware State Univ, Dover, DE, BS, 1971; Wash Univ, St Louis, MO, MBA, 1973; Thomas A Edison Col, Princeton, NJ, BA, social sci, 1976; Kent State Univ, Kent, OH, DBA, 1979. **Career:** Xerox Corp, Rochester, NY, financial analyst, 1972; Rohm & Haas Co, Philadelphia, Pa, employee rels, 1973-75; Kent State Univ, Kent, Ohio, instr, 1978-79; Ariz State Univ, Tempe, AZ, from asst prof to assoc prof, 1979-83; Univ Cent Fla, Orlando, Fla, assoc prof, prof interim dean, 1983-90; Oakland Univ, Rochester, Mich, prof & dean, 1991-95; Kent State Univ, dean, prof, 1995-. **Orgs:** Acad Mgt; Decision Sci Inst; Rotary Club Kent, OH; bd mem, Soc Advan Mgt; pres & bd mem, Kent Regional Bus Alliance; bd mem, AARP Acad Adv Coun; US Small Bus Develop Coun; pres, Mid-Continent E AACSB Deans; ed bd mem, Advan Mgt J; peer review teams, AACSB; chair, adv, Pre-Candidacy Adv; Sigma Pi Phi Fraternity; Alpha Kappa Mu; Beta Gamma Sigma; Phi Kappa Phi; Pontiac Area Urban League; Soc Human Resource Mgt, pres, Beta Gamma Sigma, 2008-. **Home Addr:** 4031 Queensbury Cir, Stow, OH 44242, **Home Phone:** (330)672-3000. **Business Addr:** Dean, Kent State University, College Business Administration, Kent, OH 44242-0001, **Business Phone:** (330)672-2772.

### STEVENS, DR. JOYCE WEST
Social worker, educator. **Personal:** Born Mar 15, 1936, Clayton, MO; daughter of John Lawrence and Gertrude Mitchell; children: Janet Leslie & Melinda Stevens-Ademuyiwa. **Educ:** Loyola Univ Chicago, BS, 1960, MSW, 1964, PhD, 1993. **Career:** Cook County, Dept Pub Aid, social worker & counr, 1960-66; YWCA Chicago, HeadStart, dir, 1969-71; Lake Bluff Homes C, social work counr & consult, 1972-73; Univ Ill Chicago, counr & psychotherapist, 1973-74; Chicago State Univ, fac advisor, 1974-75; Michael Reese Hosp, prog coordr & counr, 1974-91; Univ Chicago Social Serv Admin, field work instr, 1979-82; Coun Social Work Educ, minority fel, 1987-89; St Philip Neri Parish, Chicago, clin consult, 1989-91; Loyola Univ Chicago, instr, 1990-92; Ill Consortium Educ Opportunity fel, 1990-93; DePaul Univ, Clin field work instr, 1990-91; Smith Col Sch Social Work, adj prof, 1991-92; Boston Univ, asst prof, 1993-2001, prof emer, currently; Child & Adolescent Social Work Jour, bk rev ed, 1993-. Author: Smart and Sassy, 2002. Editor: Child and Adolescent Social Work Journal, 1993, 2002; Social Work Journal, 1999, 2002; Families in Society, 1998, 2002. **Orgs:** Nat Asn Social Workers, 1986-; Mass Acad Clin Social Workers, 1993-; Coun Social Work Educ, 1993-; DSS, Commonwealth Boston, prof adv comm, 1994-; IRB-Family Serv Boston & Latino Health Inst, 1998-; bd mem, Boston C Servs, 1998-; bd mem, Arts Progress, 1998-; trustee, Family Serv Greater Boston, 2000-02. **Home Addr:** 9 Greenway Ct Suite 4, Brookline, MA 02446. **Business Addr:** Professor Emeritus, Graduate School of Arts & Sciences, 1 Silber Way, Boston, MA 02215, **Business Phone:** (617)353-2000.

### STEVENS, K KENDALL. See MATHEWS, MAJ. K. KENDALL.

### STEVENS, LISA MARIA
Zoo keeper, zoologist. **Personal:** Born Nov 20, 1955, Springfield, OH. **Educ:** Mich State Univ, BS, zool & pre-vet med, 1977; AZA Sch Prof Mgt Develop Zoo & Aquarium Personnel. **Career:** Zoo keeper (retired): Smithsonian Nat Zool Pk, animal keeper, 1978-81, asst cur, 1981-11, sr cur. **Orgs:** Potomac Valley Dressage Asn, 1981-; Am Zoo & Aquarium Asn, 1981-87, 1996-; Capital Dog Training Club, 1993-; Nat Capital Day Lilly Club, 1994-96. **Business Addr:** Associate Curator, Smithsonian, 3001 Connecticut Ave NW, Washington, DC 20008, **Business Phone:** (202)633-4800.

### STEVENS, DR. MAXWELL MCDEW. See Obituaries Section.

### STEVENS, MICHELLE
Journalist. **Personal:** Born Feb 20, 1951, Chicago, IL. **Educ:** Northwestern Univ, BS, jour, 1973; John Marshall Law Sch, JD, 1982. **Career:** Chicago Sun-Times, asst home ed, 1975, dep ed, ed pages, 1983-94, ed, ed pages, 1995-97, night news ed, 1997-98, staff reporter, Sunday Commentary ed, ed writer; lett ed. **Orgs:** Founding mem, Asn Women Journalists; bd dir, Chicago Headline Club. **Home Addr:** 3624 S King Dr, Chicago, IL 60653, **Home Phone:** (773)285-2127. **Business Addr:** Staff Reporter, Chicago Sun-Times, 350 N Orleans, Chicago, IL 60654, **Business Phone:** (312)321-3000.

### STEVENS, DR. PATRICIA ANN
School administrator, government official, manager. **Personal:** married Dwight; children: Kimberly & Kenneth. **Educ:** Monroe Community Col, AAS, lib arts, 1968; State Univ NY, Brockport, BS, hist & psychol, 1970, MS, 1972, MS, admin, 1979; Nat Bd Cert Counselors Inc, cert, 1984; Univ Buffalo, PhD, 1994. **Career:** Monroe Community Col, counr, 1970-76, asst dir, 1976-81, dir, 1981-89, Div Temp & Disability Assistance, dep comnr; EOC State Univ NY, Brockport, exec dir, 1989-92; Monroe County Gov, costr eduction, proj mgr, 1992; US Dept Housing & Urban Develop, Div Community Develop, mgr, currently. **Orgs:** Genesee Settlement House Inc, 1982-; vpres, United Neighborhood Ctrs GrRochester, 1982-; United Way, Bd, 1994; treasr, Joe Joe While Growth League, 1994; trustee, Monroe Community Col, trustee, State Univ New York Syst. **Honors/Awds:** Outstanding Service & Dedication Grant, Rochester Area Spec Progs, 1983; Outstanding Administration, Standing Comm Blacks Higher Educ, 1984; Distinguished Service Award, Coun EOP Dirs, 1989; Leadership Award, Educ Opportunity Ctrs Dirs Coun, 1994. **Home Addr:** 476 Wellington Ave, Rochester, NY 14619, **Home Phone:** (585)478-5003. **Business Addr:** Manager, US Department of Housing & Urban Development, 8100 City Pl, Rochester, NY 14614-1308, **Business Phone:** (585)428-5325.

### STEVENS, REATHA J.
Executive director, association executive. **Personal:** Born Jun 21, 1931, Quitman, GA; married Ernest; children: Elinda, Ronald & Lavon (Nancy). **Educ:** Savannah State Univ, BS; Univ Ga, MS. **Career:** Executive (retired); Family Coun Ctr, Savannah, community organizer social serv visitor, 1966-69; Dept Family & C Servs, caseworker, 1969-70, casework supvr, 1970-72; Wesley & Community Ctrs, Savannah, exec dir, 1972-96; New Zion Independent Methodist Church, chief financial officer. **Orgs:** Social Planning Steering Bd United Way Chatham Ctny, 1970-; Ga Asn Young C, 1974-75; Armstrong-Savannah State Col Social Work Adv Coun, 1974-75; den mother, 1964-65; bd dir, Frank Callen Boys Club, 1965-72; treas, 1970-71; consult, Savannah Asn Blind, 1968-69; bd dir, Chatham Counc Human Rels, 1973-74; hon mem, Barons Goodwill Rehab Club; Savannah Fed Colored Women's Club Inc; New Zion Independent Methodist Church. **Home Addr:** 105 Greenbriar Dr, Savannah, GA 31419, **Home Phone:** (912)925-6498. **Business Addr:** Member, New Zion Independent Methodist Church, 11826 Apache Ave, Savannah, GA 31419-1602, **Business Phone:** (912)961-0701.

### STEVENS, ROCHELLE
Track and field athlete, entrepreneur. **Personal:** Born Sep 8, 1966, Memphis, TN; daughter of John Holloway and Beatrice Davis. **Educ:** Morgan State Univ, BS telecom & sls, 1988; Columbus Univ, MS, pub rels. **Career:** Athlete (retired), executive; Olympic silver medalist, 1992; Olympic gold Medalist, 1996; Cherokee Elem Sch, behav specialist; Fortune 500 Co, spokeswoman & motivational speaker; Johnson Prod, spokesperson; Maybelline, spokesperson; Blue Cross & Blue Shield, spokesperson; Sara Lee, spokesperson; Nike, spokesperson; Bank Am, spokesperson; Rochelle's Health & Wellness Day Spa, founder & chief exec officer, 1998-. **Orgs:** Better Bus Bur; Black Bus Asn; Nat Speaker Bur; Word Life Ministry; Rochelle Stevens Scholar Fund; Rochelle Stevens Invitational Track Meet; Rochelle Stevens Sports Clin; Rochelle Stevens Fan Club. **Honors/Awds:** Three-time Female Athlete of the Yr, Morgan State Univ, 1985-88; received key to city of Memphis; NCAA Outdoor 400m champion, 1988; US Indoor 200m champion, 1991; Olympic Trials champion, 1992; 6th at Olympics, 1992; Olympic silver medalist, 1992; Four-time USA Track and Field National Champion; hon black belt in tae kwon do, 1992; World Champs gold medalist, 1995; Olympic gold medalist, 1996; Honorary Ambassador of MAR; Honorary Citizen of Parades; Eleven time NCAA All AMR; NCAA Division I 400 Meter Champion; Memphis Business Jnl Top 40 Under 40, 1997; Morgan State Univ "Varsity M" Club Hall of Fame, 1997; 2nd in 400m US Outdoor nationals, 1998; Olympian Rochelle Stevens Avenue; Tenn sports hall of fame, inductee, 2006. **Special Achievements:** Ranked Top Ten in the World six times in the 400 meters and in the top ten from 1987-98. **Home Addr:** 3107 Belgrave Dr Suite 200, Memphis, TN 38119-9143, **Home Phone:** (901)753-0661. **Business Addr:** Founder, Rochelle Health & Wellness, 319 Poplar View Lane W Suite 2, Collierville, TN 38017, **Business Phone:** (901)365-0505.

### STEVENS, SHARON A.
Journalist. **Personal:** Born Jun 14, 1949, Chicago, IL; daughter of Clarence B and Erma. **Educ:** Northern Ill Univ, BS, journ, 1971; Columbia Univ, NYC, Fel, 1972. **Career:** WBBM Radio Chicago IL, reporter/anchor, 1971-75; NBC Radio NYC, reporter/anchor, 1975-78; WGBH-TV, Boston, MA, news reporter, 1978-82; KTVI-TV St Louis MO, news reporter/anchorwoman, educ reporter; KSDK-TV, educ reporter, currently; Nc A&T State Univ, mentor. **Orgs:** Alpha Kappa Alpha Sor Inc, 1968-, Am Fed Radio & TV Artists, 1971-; Greater St Louis Asn Black Journalists, 1985; bd dir, Girls Inc, 1990-; bd dir, St Louis Journalism Rev, 1989-; vp-broadcast, Nat Asn Black Journalists; Mo Asn Sch Adminr. **Honors/Awds:** Plexiglass Award, YMCA Black Achievers Award, 1974; Recognition Cert Outstanding Young Women Am Inc, 1977; Emmy Nomination, Nat Acad TV Arts & Sci, Boston Chap, 1979, 1980; Spec Recognition Boston Mag, 1979; Black Excellence Award, Best Series TV, 1987, Political Coverage TV, 1987; Emmy Nomination, NATAS, 1989; "Yes I Can", outstanding journalist, St Louis Metro Sentinel Newspaper, 1990; Silver Circle Award, Nat Acad Tv Arts & Sci. **Home Addr:** . **Business Addr:** Education Reporter, KSDK-TV, 1000 Market St, St Louis, MO 63101, **Business Phone:** (314)444-5125.

### STEVENS, TIMOTHY S.
Association executive, executive director. **Educ:** Urban & Regional Planning; BA, polit sci. **Career:** Humble Oil Co, Wash, DC, dealer sales trainee, 1967-68; Juv Ct, probation officer, 1968; Nat Asn Advan Colored People, youth dir, 1969; Pittsburgh Br Nat Asn Advan Colored People, exec dir, 1970, pres, 1994; Mike Douglas Show, guest, 1972; Black Polit Empowerment Proj, founder & chmn, 1986-; Mayview State Hosp, dept dir, 1989-2008. **Orgs:** Am Soc Composers, Authors & Publishers; Am Fedn Tv & Radio Artists; Am Guild Variety Artists; secy-treas, Stebro Enter; vpres, Arkel Publ Co & Stebro Rec; bd mem, Hill Hse Asn; bd mem, Hill Dist YMCA; host radio shows, WAMO, WWSW 14k radio; Manpower Adv Coun, Allegheny Co; Mayor's Art Comt; chmn, Black Polit Empowerment Proj. **Honors/Awds:** Entertainment & Community Award, Black Community Pittsburgh Clubs United, 1970; He's a Black Man Award, 1973; Whitney Young Award, Poor People's Dinner, Pittsburgh, 1974. **Home Addr:** 6393 Stanton Ave, Pittsburgh, PA 15206-2289, **Home Phone:** (412)661-6711. **Business Addr:** Founder, Chairman, The Black Political Empowerment Project, c/o Freedom Unlimited, Pittsburgh, PA 15219, **Business Phone:** (412)758-7898.

### STEVENS, WARREN SHERWOOD
Engineer, automotive executive, association executive. **Personal:** Born Jul 8, 1941, Urbana, OH; married Audrey Doreen; children: Warren D & Shanee A. **Educ:** Ohio State Univ, BS, bus admin, 1978. **Career:** USAF, admin clerk, 1960-64; Juv Diag Ctr, mail clerk, 1964-65; Western Elec Co, cable former, 1965-68 & 1971-73, tester, 1968-71, Local IBEW union steward, 1970-71, chief union steward, 1971-73; Int Harvester, employee interviewer, 1973-74, indust engr, 1974-80; St Regis Co, staff indust engr, 1981-83; Urban Univ, dir admin; City Urbana, city councilman; Baumfolder Corp, time study & methods engr, 1984-85; Williams Hardware, salesman, clerk, cashier, 1986-; Exec Fund life Ins Co, ins agt, 1987-89; Hoffman Wood Prod, working supvr, 1989-; Honda Am, Assoc Rels, admin staff mem, 1989-; Urbana City Sch Dist, pres. **Orgs:** MTM Asn, 1974; coach, Urbana City Baseball Prog, 1978; co-chmn, Champaign Co Am Cancer Soc Bd, 1981; pres, Champaign Co Am Cancer Soc Bd, 1981, 1995-; Kiwanis Club, 1982; coach, Urbana City Baseball pony league, 1983; coach, Urbana Baseball Boosters, 1983; coach, Urbana City Baseball pony league, 1984; adv, Pub Educ Comm Am Cancer Soc Bd; former Urbana Local Outdoor Educ Bd; former sec, Urbana Mens Progressive Club; Dem Champaign Co Cent Comm & Exec Comm; ed, Urbana Lions Club Newsletter; Am Red Cross Champaign Unit bd; bd trustee, Am Cancer, trustee at-large, Ohio Div; bd trustee mem, Urbana Univ. **Honors/Awds:** Tape Line Project Standard Labor Cost System St Regis Co, 1981-83, Baumfolder, 1984-85; Standard Labor Cost Savings Baumfolder, 1984-85; Am Red Cross Special Citation for Exceptional Volunteer Service. **Special Achievements:** First Black Trainee & Industrial Engineer International Harvester, 1974; Held highest administrative position of any Black ever in Urban University. **Home Addr:** 4545 Woodland Dr, Urbana, OH 43078-8725, **Home Phone:** (937)653-3439. **Business Addr:** Production Associate, East Liberty Plant, Marysville, OH 43040.

**STEVENS, YVETTE MARIE. See KHAN, CHAKA.**

## STEVENSON, ALEXANDRA WINFIELD

Tennis player. **Personal:** Born Dec 15, 1980, La Jolla, CA; daughter of Julius Erving II and Samantha. **Educ:** La Jolla Country Day Sch, grad, 1999; Univ Colo, BLA, sociol, 2007. **Career:** Prof tennis player, currently; US Open, 1998-2004; Wimbledon, 1999-2001; Fr Open, 2000-03; Australian Open, 2000-04; Cincinnati Women's Open, 2006. **Orgs:** US Nat Team, 1994-96; US Prof Develop Prog, 1998-02; US Pan Am Games Team, 1999; US Hopman Cup Team, 2000. **Honors/Awds:** Breitbard Athlete of the Year Award, 1997; Rolex Rookie of the Year, 1999; Bronze Medal, Pan Am Games, 1999; La Jolla Country Day School Hall of Fame, 2009; Rookie of the Year, Tennis Mag. **Business Addr:** Professional Tennis Player, US Professional Tennis Association, 3535 Briarpark Dr Suite 1, Houston, TX 77042, **Business Phone:** (713)978-7782.

## STEVENSON, DR. BRYAN A.

Association executive, educator. **Personal:** Born Nov 14, 1959, Milton, DE; son of Howard Carlton Sr and Alice Gertrude Golden. **Educ:** Eastern Univ, BA, 1981; Harvard Law Sch, JD, 1985; Harvard Univ, Kennedy Sch Gov, MPP, 1985. **Career:** Southern Ctr Human Rights Atlanta, atty, 1985; Ala Capital Representation Resource Ctr, exec dir, 1989-95; NY Univ Sch Law, from asst prof clin law to assoc prof clin law, 1998-2002, prof clin law, 2003-. **Orgs:** Equal Justice Initiative Ala, founder & exec dir, 1989-. **Special Achievements:** Just Mercy: A Story of Justice and Redemption. **Business Addr:** Professor of Clinical Law, New York University School of Law, 245 Sullivan St Suite 628, New York, NY 10012, **Business Phone:** (212)998-6456.

## STEVENSON, GEORGE

Executive director. **Career:** Detroit Mfg Training Ctr & Tigers game, exec dir, currently. **Business Addr:** Executive Director, Detroit Manufacturing Training Center, 1110 Rosedale Ct Bing Group Campus, Detroit, MI 48211, **Business Phone:** (313)852-7100.

## STEVENSON, REV. DR. JEROME PRITCHARD, SR.

Clergy, educator, association executive. **Personal:** Born Mar 28, 1941, Birmingham, AL; son of Jimmie and Dorothy; married Ida; children: Melissa Ruth, Jerome Jr & Julia P. **Educ:** Highland Pk Col, AS, 1971; Wayne State Univ, BS, 1973, MS, 1986; William Tyndale Col, BRE, 1993; Ashland Theol Sem, MA, 1995, DMin, 1999. **Career:** Detroit Postal Serv, lett carrier, 1966-73; Detroit Pub Schs, sci teacher, 1975-77, lead teacher, 1980; Ford Motor Co, mgt trainee, 1977-80; Renaissance Baptist Church, pastor; Morning Star Baptist Church, sr pastor, currently; United Theol Sem, asst prof pract pastoral care & coun, currently. **Orgs:** Nat Asn Advan Colored People, 1964; Am Legion, 1995-; Am Asn Christian Counors, 1995; Baptist Coun, 1995; Am Coun Asn, 1996; Mich Progressive Conv, 1997; VFW, 1997; Am Baptist Conv, 1997; The Socs Pastoral theol. **Honors/Awds:** Junior Achievement, Distinguished Advisor Award, 1977-78; Distinguished Service Award, 1997; Vision Award, Life Choice, 1997; Distinguished Service Award, Nat Asn Advan Colored People, 1982. **Home Addr:** 6336 Cheri Lynne Dr, Dayton, OH 45415, **Home Phone:** (937)387-5392. **Business Addr:** Senior Pastor, Religious Leader, Morning Star Baptist Church, 307 Shaw Ave, Clairton, PA 15025, **Business Phone:** (937)529-2274.

## STEVENSON, LILLIAN

Nurse. **Personal:** Born Nov 27, 1922, Indianapolis, IN; daughter of George and Jane; children: John Austin Anthony & Phillip Kelly. **Educ:** Ind City Hosp, Sch Nursing, 1944; Mdme CJ Walker Col Cosmotol, 1958; Debbie's Sch Cosmetology. **Career:** Nursing Serv, City Ambulatory Health Ctr, Neighborhood Health Care Facil, charging nurse; supvr head nurse, staff nurse; foot care specialist, manicurist. **Orgs:** Founding mem, pres, Black Nurse Asn Indianapolis, 1974-77; Ind Black Bicentennial Comn, 1976; Ind Conf Women, 1976; bd mem, St Vincent dePaul Soc, 1984; co-mem, Sisters St Joseph-Trton Ind, CSJ, 1986; Nat Black Nurse Asn; instr nurse, Marion Co Gen Hosp; surg supvr nurse, St Monica's Hosp; Ladies Aux Knights, St Peter Claver Ct; #97 Ind Christ Leadershp Conf; bd mem, Indianapolis Chap Oper PUSH; Nat Coun Negro Women; bd mem, Sub Area Coun Health Syst Agency; bd mem, NE Unit Am Cancer Asn; past bd mem, Model Cities Fed Cred Union; bd mem, Hillside Cult Ctr; bd, Cath Charities; pres, Archdiocesan Black Catholics concerned. **Honors/Awds:** Certificate of Distinction, Ind Black Assembly, 1975; Gold medal winner, Nat Knights, St Peter, Claver, 1979; Drum Major Award, ICLC, 1983; Pro Ecclesia Et Pontifice Award, Long Serv Church, 1994. **Special Achievements:** Third black graduate nurse in Indianapolis, 1944; First president of Black Nurse Asn. **Home Addr:** 1818 Sheldon St, Indianapolis, IN 46218.

## STEWARD, DAVID L.

Businessperson. **Personal:** Born Jul 2, 1951, Chicago, IL; son of Harold and Dorothy; married Thelma; children: 2. **Educ:** Cent Mo Univ, BS, bus admin, 1973. **Career:** Wagner Elec, prod mgr, 1974-75; Mo Pac RR, sls rep, 1975-79; Fed Express, sr acct exec, 1979-84; Transp Bus Specialists, owner, 1984-93; Transp Admin Servs, owner, 1987-90; World Wide Technol, founder & chmn, 1990-; Telcobuy.com, founder & chmn, 1997-; First Banks, dir, 2000-; Centene Corp, dir, 2003-. **Orgs:** Campaign chair, United Way Greater St Louis, MO; bd, Webster Univ; St Louis Sci Ctr; bd mem, BJC Health Syst; St Louis Reg Com & Growth Asn; Union Memorial Outreach Ctr; Greater St Louis Area Coun Boy Scouts Am; bd mem, Mo Technol Corp; leadership coun, Harris-Stowe State Col African-Am Bus; bd curators, Univ Mo. **Honors/Awds:** Distinguished Executive, Am Mkt Asn, 1996; Technology Entrepreneur of the Year, Ernst & Young, 1998; Small Business Hall of Fame Inductee, SBA; Business Person of the Year, St Louis Sentinel; Entrepreneur of the Year, Nat Soc Black Engrs; Fast 50 Awards; Granville T Woods Award, 1997; Business Person of the Year for Missouri, Small Bus Admin, 1998; 14th Best American Entrepreneur, Success Magazine, 1998; Top Minority Entrepreneur, Small Business Administration, 1998; Company of the Year, Black Enterprise, 1999; Phoenix Award, St Louis Minority Business Council, 2000; Entrepreneur of the Year, Black Enterprise, 2000; Small Business Association Hall of Fame, 2001; Fast 50 Awards, Five time winner; Honorary doctorate in humane letters, Harris Stowe State Col; Honorary doctorate in humane letters, Lindenwood Univ; Top 100 List of St Louis Leaders, 2002. **Special Achievements:** Named 100 Most Influential Black Americans by Ebony; Named America's 14th-Best Entrepreneur by Success Magazine; Published a book - Doing Business by the Good Book, 2004; Top 100 List of St. Louis Leaders, 2002. **Home Addr:** 309 Wyndmoor Ter Ct, Saint Louis, MO 63141-8021. **Business Addr:** Founder, Chairman, World Wide Technology Inc, 60 Weldon Pkwy, St Louis, MO 63043, **Business Phone:** (314)569-7000.

## STEWARD, ELAINE WEDDINGTON

Executive. **Personal:** Born Jan 1, 1963, Flushing, NY. **Educ:** St John's Univ, St Vincent Col, BS, athletic admin, 1984, Sch Law, JD, 1987. **Career:** Boston Red Sox, Boston, MA, assoc coun, 1988-90, asst gen mgr, 1990, legal coun, 1995, vpres, 1998, club coun, 2002. **Orgs:** Ny Bar, 1988; St Vincent's Col Hon Soc; Am Bar Asn. **Honors/Awds:** One of the Ten Outstanding Young Leaders of Boston, Greater Boston Chamber of Commerce, 1999; YWCA Academy of Women Achievers; Outstanding Alumna Award, St. John's Univ Black Alumni Asn, 2001; President's Medal, St. John's Univ; National Baseball Hall of Fame Women in Baseball; Jackie Robinson Foundation Sports Management scholarship; Sam Lacy Pioneer Award, Nat Asn Black Journalists Sports Task Force's. **Special Achievements:** The First female African-American executive when the Red Sox. **Business Addr:** Vice President, Club Counsel, Boston Red Sox, 4 Yawkey Way, Boston, MA 02215-3496, **Business Phone:** (617)267-6000.

## STEWARD, LOWELL C., SR.

Real estate appraiser. **Personal:** Born Feb 25, 1919, Los Angeles, CA; married Helen Jane Ford; children: Pamela O, Lowell Jr & Shelley. **Educ:** Santa Barbara State Col, BA, 1942; Univ Calif Los Angeles, attended 1952. **Career:** Lowell Steward Assoc, real estate appraiser. **Orgs:** Sr mem, Soc Real Estate Appraisers, 1970; pres & founder, Los Angeles Chap Tuskegee Airmen, 1974 bd dir, Consol Realty Bd; mem bd dir, Univ Calif, Santa Barbara Alumni Asn; past pres, Tuskegee Airmen Western Region; Kappa Alpha Psi; life mem, Nat Asn Advan Colored People; nat chmn, Tuskegee Airman Scholar Fund. **Honors/Awds:** Distinguished Flying Cross Air Medal, WWII; Lifetime Achievement Award, Univ Calif Santa Barbara Alumni Asn, 2004; Congressional Gold Medal, Continental Congress, 2007. **Home Addr:** 2731 Wood Opal Way, Oxnard, CA 93030, **Home Phone:** (805)981-0486.

## STEWART, DR. ALBERT C.

Educator, college teacher. **Personal:** Born Nov 25, 1919, Detroit, MI; son of Albert Q and Jeanne B Kaiser; married Colleen M Hyland. **Educ:** Univ Chicago, BS, chem, 1942, MS, chem, 1948; St Louis Univ, PhD, 1951. **Career:** Sherwin-Williams Paint Co, 1943-44; St Louis Univ, instr chem, 1949-51; Knoxville Col, prof chem & physics, 1953-56; John Carroll Univ, Cleveland, Ohio, lectr chem, 1956-63; Union Carbide Corp, int bus mgr, 1973-77, dir sales, 1977-79, nat sales mgr, 1979-82, dir univ rels, 1982-84; Western Conn State Univ, assoc dean, prof emer, 1999-. **Orgs:** Oak Ridge, Tenn Town Coun, 1953-57; pres & chmn, Urban League, Cleveland/NY, 1959-69; Rotary, Cleveland/NY, 1962-69; trustee, NY Philharmonic Soc, 1975-80; Radiation Res Soc; Am Mkt Asn; emer mem, Am Chem Soc; advisor, consult & bd dir, US Dept Com; Nat Aeronaut & Space Admin; Urban League; fel Am Inst Chemists. **Honors/Awds:** Alumni Merit Award, St Louis Univ, 1958; Cert Merit, Soc Chem Prof, Cleveland, 1962; Alumni Citation Award, Univ Chicago, 1966; Am Acad Arts & Sci. **Home Addr:** 28 Hearthstone Dr, Brookfield, CT 06804, **Home Phone:** (203)775-4496. **Business Addr:** Professor Emeritus, Western Connecticut State University, 181 White St, Danbury, CT 06810, **Business Phone:** (203)837-8754.

## STEWART, ALISON

Journalist, television news anchorperson. **Personal:** Born Jul 4, 1966, Glen Ridge, NJ; daughter of Joseph T Jr and Carol; married Bill Wolff; children: 1. **Educ:** Brown Univ, BA, eng & Am lit, 1988. **Career:** Brown Univ radio sta, deejay, prog dir, 1984-88; MTV Networks, gofer, asst & floor producer, 1988-91, Viacom, reporter, 1991-95; CBS News, corresp, 1996-99; ABC News, anchor, 2000-02; MSNBC NEWS, day time anchor, reporter 2003-09, Most with Alison Stewart, host, 2006-07, guest anchor, currently; Nat Pub Radio, Bryant Pk Proj, host, 2007-09, TED Radio Hour, 2012; Pub Broadcasting Serv, anchor, 2010-11; NBC News, contribr, currently. CBS News, 2011-; Freelance Journalist, 2012-; FIRST CLASS, auth, 2013; Chicago Rev Press, JUNK-Due out Spring 2016, auth, 2013-; Travel Channel, Follow Your Past, host, 2014-. **Orgs:** Bd Trustee, Brown Univ; reader, Lighthouse Reading Serv Blind. **Business Addr:** Follow Your Past Host, Travel Channel, 5425 WIs Ave Suite 500, Chevy Chase, MD 20815.

## STEWART, BERNARD

Television producer. **Personal:** Born Jul 3, 1950, Birmingham, AL; married Alice Faye Carr; children: Anthony. **Educ:** Ball State Univ, Muncie, IN, BS, film & tv jour, 1974; S Conn State Univ, New Haven, CT, MS, Urban Studies, 1977, MS, media technol, 1979. **Career:** Self Employed, independent producer dir, 1977-80; WTNH-TV, New Haven, Conn, producer, 1977-80; Southern Conn State Univ, adjunt fac, 1979-81; ESPN Int Inc, coord producer, 1980-85, dir prog planning, 1987-91, coord producer, 1980-85, vpres programming & prod, 1991-99; WBZ-TV, Boston, Mass, exec news producer, 1985-87; ESPN STAR Sports Asia, bd dir, 1999-2008; auth & featured speaker, 1998-; ESPN Asia Pac, vpres & gen mgr, 1999-2008; Disney & ESPN Media Networks, vpres & gen mgr, 2008-13; Bart World Communcations Ltd, founder & managing partner, 2013-. **Orgs:** Chmn, Japan Sports Broadcasting, 1999-2008. **Honors/Awds:** Lapides Award, Ctr Urban Studies; Outstanding Young Man of America, US Jaycees. **Special Achievements:** Two Emmy Nominations, Nat TV Acad, 1978, 1979; Author: Legends of Cricket, 2002; Fifty50 A Guide to a successful Work Life Balance, 2010. **Business Addr:** Vice President, General Manager, Disney and ESPN Media Networks.

## STEWART, DR. BESS

Educator. **Personal:** Born Buffalo, NY; daughter of Curtis Boyd and Margaret Boyd; married Wilbert E; children: Kimberleyh. **Educ:** Incarnate Word Col, BSN, 1976; Univ Tex Health Sci Ctr, Sch Nursing, San Antonio, TX, MSN, 1978; Univ Tex, Austin, TX, PhD, 1986. **Career:** Baptist Hosp Sch Nursing, asst prof, 1976-78; Univ Tex Health Sci Ctr, San Antonio, Sch Nursing, assoc prof, 1979-; ANA Minority, fel, 1984-86; chair nursing educ, assoc dean stud, interim assoc dean, 2003-05. **Orgs:** Vice chair, Am Nurses Coun Cult Diversity, 1982-87; Am Cancer Soc, 1988-; Am Nurses Credentialing Ctr, 1991-; fel Am Acad Nursing, 1993; pres, Asn Black Nursing Fac, 1998-2000. **Home Addr:** 7219 Saddle Creek, San Antonio, TX 78238-3612, **Home Phone:** (210)256-0656. **Business Addr:** Associate Professor, University of Texas Health Science Center, 7703 Floyd Curl Dr, San Antonio, TX 78229-3900.

**STEWART, BILL J. See STEWART, WILLIAM.**

## STEWART, BONITA COLEMAN

Marketing executive. **Personal:** married Kevin. **Educ:** Howard Univ, BA, jour; Harvard Bus Sch, MBA, 1983. **Career:** Chrysler Corp, dir; Dodge Car, Mkt Plans DaimlerChrysler, dir; IBM Corp, exec mkt, 1979-91; One Moment Time Inc, founder, pres, 1989-93; DaimlerChrysler, Chrysler Brand Communs, mkt, dir, 1993-2000, Interactive Commun, dir, 2002-06; Nia Enterprises, co-founder, pres & chief operating officer, 2000-02; Chrysler Grp Interactive Communs, dir, 2005; Google Inc, nat indust dir, automotive, 2006-09, managing dir US sales, 2009-11, vpres US sales, 2011-12, vpres, americas, partner bus solutions, 2012-15, vpres, global partnerships, 2006-; BeautyBooked, advisor, 2015-16; Deckers Brands, bd dir, 2014-. **Orgs:** Bd Gov, Cranbrook Art Acad; Bd Trustee, Detroit Music Hall; Bd mem, Birmingham Bloomfield Art Ctr; bd dir, Harvard Bus Sch Club. **Honors/Awds:** Ebony Award, 2003; African American on Wheels, 2004; Interactive Marketer of the Year, Advertising Age, Chrysler Group, 2005; Google OC Award, 2010; Top African-American Executives, Black Enterprise, 2011; Professional Achievement Award, Harvard Bus Sch African Am Alumni Asn, 2012; W50 Celebration, Harvard Bus Sch African Am Alumni Asn, 2013; Global Visionary Leadership Award, Howard Univ Sch Commun, 2013; Women to Watch Tech, Crain's, 2014; Most Powerful Women, Crain's NYC, 2015. **Special Achievements:** Speaker, numerous mkt & interactive conf: iMedia, eTail, AD: TECH & Automotive CRM Roundtable; featured in various magazines including Automotive News, Brandweek, USA Today & Leaders Mag.In 2005 she co-authored The Fifth P of Marketing an article for CRM Magazine. **Business Addr:** Vice President, Google Inc, 2000 Town Ctr Dr, Southfield, MI 48075, **Business Phone:** (248)351-6220.

## STEWART, BRITTANICA

Business owner, beautician. **Personal:** Born Sep 16, 1950, Atlanta, GA; daughter of James and Bessie Gordon (deceased). **Educ:** Ophelia DeVore Sch Beauty & Charm, 1976; Int Mannequin Sch Models, 1978; Robert Fiance Sch Beauty, beauty salon hair stylist, 1983. **Career:** Ophelia DeVore Sch Beauty & Charm, teacher models, 1971-76; independent fashion model, 1975-82; Black Hair Is, asst mgr & fashion coordr, 1984-86; Brittanica & ASC, pres, 1986-; Bronner Bros Beauty & Brittanica Hair Studio, owner, producer, summer fashion show, 1989-. **Orgs:** NY Ker Club, 1990. **Honors/Awds:** Award of Appreciation for Outstanding Achievement, Hal Jackson's Talented Teens, 1987 & 1988; Certificate of appreciation, Friends Sr Citizens Springfield Gardens & St Albans, 1991; Award of Gratitude for Assistance, Arms Around Harlem Homeless, 1992. **Special Achievements:** Guest speaker on WBLS Radio for hair fashion, 1988-; Advisor to Vogue Magazine for hair fashion, 1989-; Guest advisor on hair fashion, Essence Mag, 1989-. **Home Addr:** 78 26 267th St, Floral Park, NY 11004. **Business Addr:** Owner, Producer, Brittanica Hair Salon Inc, 864 Lexington Ave, New York, NY 10021-6659, **Business Phone:** (212)717-2753.

**STEWART, BUBBA. See STEWART, JAMES, JR.**

## STEWART, CARL E.

Judge. **Personal:** Born Jan 1, 1950, Shreveport, LA; son of Richard and Corine; married Jo Ann Southall; children: 3; married Jo Ann Southall; children: 3. **Educ:** Dillard Univ, BA, 1971; Loyola Univ, JD, 1974. **Career:** Piper & Brown, atty, 1977-78; Off Atty Gen, State La, staff atty, 1978-79; Western Dist La, Dept Justice, asst US atty, 1979-83; La State Univ, adj prof, 1982-85; Stewart & Dixon, partner, 1983-85; Caddo Parish, State La, spec asst dist atty, 1983-85; City Shreveport, asst city prosecutor, 1983-85; La Dist Ct, First Judicial Dist, judge, 1985-91; La Ct Appeal, Second Circuit, judge, 1991-94; US Circuit, judge, 1994-2012, chief judge, 2012-. **Orgs:** Am Bar Asn; Black Lawyers Asn Shreveport-Bossier; Harry Booth Chap Am Inn Ct; La State Bar Asn; La Conf Ct Appeal Judges; Nat Bar Asn; Shreveport Bar Asn; Omega Psi Phi; Sigma Pi Phi; Fed Judges Asn; pres, Community Found Shreveport-Bossier; bd mem, KDAQ Pub Radio Adv Bd; bd mem, coun pres, Local Coun Rep, Boy Scouts of Am; active mem, St James United Methodist Church. **Honors/Awds:** Distinguished Alumnus of the year, Dillard Univ, 1998; Award of Excellence, Omega Psi Phi, 1998; Liberty Bell Award, Shreveport Bar Asn; Raymond Pace Alexander Award, Judge William H Hastie Award, Nat Bar Asn; The Silver Beaver Award; The Silver Antelope Award; The Silver Buffalo Award; Clyde E Fant Memorial Award for Outstanding Community Service; AP Tureaud Achievement Award, Loyola Univ Sch Law Black Law Students Asn, 2008; The Times Leadership Award, Shreveport Times & the Alliance Educ, 2008; Louisiana Outstanding Young Man of the Year, La Chap; Black Leader of the Year Award, Southern Univ Shreveport-Bossier Afro-Am Socs. **Special Achievements:** First African-American ever to serve on the Fifth Circuit. **Home Addr:** 6805 Snowmass St, Shreveport, LA 71119-7521, **Home Phone:** (318)636-4829. **Business Addr:** Chief Judge, US 5th Circuit Court Appeals, 300 Fannin St Suite 2299, Shreveport, LA 71101, **Business Phone:** (318)676-3765.

## STEWART, CAROLYN HOUSE

Lawyer, party leader. **Personal:** Born Nov 11, 1952, Columbia, SC; daughter of Mary Green Myers; married Delano S; children: Delsha

C. **Educ:** Univ S Fla, BA, hist & social sci, 1974; Univ SC Law Ctr, JD, 1977. **Career:** Law Stud Civil Rights Res Coun, legal intern, 1975-76; Law Inc Legal Servto Poor, legal intern, 1976; Univ SC Law Ctr, first black legal writing inst, 1976-77; Jim Walter Corp, assoc litigation coun, 1977-80; State Attorneys Off Hillsborough Co, asst state atty, 1980-81; Hillsborough County Atty, asst county atty, 1985-87; Butler & Burnette, atty, 1987-89; Travelers Ins Co, staff coun, 1989-94; MacFarlane Ferguson & McMullen, coun, partner & shareholder firm, 1994-. **Orgs:** Kappa Alpha Sorority, 1972-74, 1984-98; spec consult to pres, Nat Bar Asn; asst to pres, 1979, CLE, chmn, 1980, vpres, 1983-85, Fla Chap Nat Bar Asn; bd dir, Tampa Orgn Black Affairs, 1980; bd dir, Hillsborough County Ment Health Asn, 1980; bd dir, Tampa Philharmonic Soc, 1980; Greater Tampa Chap, Jack & Jill Am Inc, 1990-; legal adv, Gamma Theta Omega Chap; pres, Gamma Theta Omega Chap Alpha Kappa Alpha Sorority, 1992-95, int pres, 2010-; chmn, Int Prog Comt, 1998-2002; life mem, Greater Tampa Urban League; Citizens Adv Comtto Pres, Univ S Fla; Tampa Heights Neighborhood Revitalization Alliance; secy, Educ Advances Found, 2002-; trustee, Hillsborough County Bar Found; vpres, Zeta Upsilon Chap; Alpha int secy, 2002-; Fla Bd Bar Examiners; Am Inst Parliamentarians; Hillsborough Asn Women Lawyers; Nat Asn Advan Colored People; Fla Bar; Hillsborough County Bar Asn; George Edgecomb Bar Asn. **Honors/Awds:** Member of the Year, Fla Chap, Nat Bar Asn, 1983; Leadership Excellence Award, Tampa Chap, Epicureans Int, 1992; Sorority of the Year, Alpha Kappa Alpha Sorority Inc, 1995; Francisco A Rodriguez Award, Edgecomb Bar Asn, 2000; Achievement Award, Fla Comn on Status Women, 2006; Presidential Award, 2006; Gertrude E Rush Award, National Bar Association, 2012. **Special Achievements:** First president to serve a full term in the Sorority's second century. **Home Addr:** 11719 Tom Folsom Rd, Thonotosassa, FL 33592-2933, **Home Phone:** (813)986-2211. **Business Addr:** Attorney, Shareholder, MacFarlane Ferguson & McMullen, 1 Tampa City Ctr 201 N Franklin St Suite 2000, Tampa, FL 33602, **Business Phone:** (813)273-4200.

### STEWART, CHARLES J.

Government official, administrator. **Personal:** Born Nov 7, 1930, Montgomery, AL; son of Roy Clinton and Helen (deceased); married Annette Stokes; children: Malcolm Rogers, Valarie & Ellie Rose Williams. **Educ:** Richard J Daley Col, Chicago IL, AAS Fire Sci, 1976; Southern Ill Univ, Carbondale IL, BS, fire sci, 1978. **Career:** Chicago Fire Dept, Chicago, Ill, firefighter, 1962-67, Engr, 1967-78, lt, 1978-79, capt, 1979-88, dep dist chief, 1988-; consult, Citywide Detective Agency, 1987-; The Fireman Annuity & Benefits Fund Chicago, first dep fire comnr. **Orgs:** Past master, King David Lodge 100 F&AM, PHA, Ill, 1951; Oper PUSH, 1971; Chicago Urban League; Nat Asn Advan Colored People, 1987; Xi Lambda Chap, Alpha Phi Alpha Inc, 1988. **Honors/Awds:** Mason of the Year, MW Prince Hall Grand Lodge, Ill, 1965; Award Recognition, Ill Coun Delibration 33 degree, 1980; Certificateof Achievement, Chicago Fire Dept, 1981; Distinguished Serv Award, Oper PUSH, 1988; Afro-Am Symbol Excellence, Life Ctr Church, 1988. **Home Addr:** 1700 E 56th St Suite 901, Chicago, IL 60637-1970, **Home Phone:** (312)684-9347. **Business Addr:** Deputy District Chief of Records, Chicago Fire Department, 1338 S Clinton St Acad S Rm 300, Chicago, IL 60609, **Business Phone:** (773)746-6923.

### STEWART, DAVID KEITH (DAVE STEWART)

Baseball player, executive. **Personal:** Born Feb 19, 1957, Oakland, CA; son of David and Nathalie; married Amy Sue Besse; children: Symone Perris Besse. **Career:** Baseball player(retired), baseball coach, executive; Los Angeles Dodgers, pitcher, 1978, 1981-83; Tex Rangers, pitcher, 1983-85; Philadelphia Phillies, pitcher, 1985-86; Oakland Athletics, pitcher, 1986-92, 1995; Toronto Blue Jays, 1993-94, pitching coach & asst to gen mgr, 1996; San Diego Padres, pitching coach, 1998; Milwaukee Brewers, pitching coach, 2002; NBX, MLB analyst, currently; Sports Mgt Partners, founder & sports agt, currently; Ariz Diamondbacks, sr vice pres & gen mgr, currently. **Home Addr:** 17762 Vineyard Lane, Poway, CA 92064-1061. **Business Addr:** MLB Analyst, NBX Inc, 875A Island Dr Suite 334, Alameda, CA 94502, **Business Phone:** (408)872-0433.

### STEWART, DIANA BROWN

Association executive, executive director. **Educ:** BS, bus admin; Wayne State Univ, MEd, coun prog. **Career:** Jefferson E Bus Asn, exec dir, 2002-. **Orgs:** Bd Detroit Eastside Community Collab; Bd Eastside Community Policing Partnership. **Business Addr:** Executive Director, Jefferson East Business Association, 14628 E Jefferson Ave, Detroit, MI 48215, **Business Phone:** (313)331-7939.

### STEWART, DR. DONALD MITCHELL

Chief executive officer. **Personal:** Born Jul 8, 1938, Chicago, IL; son of Elmer and Ann; married Isabel Carter Johnston; children: Jay Ashton & Carter. **Educ:** Grinnell Col, BA, polit sci, 1959; Yale Univ, MA, polit sci, 1962; Grad Inst Int Studies, Geneva, Switz, studies int orgn & econ, 1962; Harvard Univ Kennedy Sch Govt, MPA, 1969, DPA, l975; Harvard Grad Sch Bus Admin, advan mgt prog, 1983. **Career:** Ford Found, asst rep W Africa, 1962-64, prog asst, Mid E Africa Prog, 1964-66, asst rep, Cairo, 1966-67, asst rep, N Africa, 1966-68, prog officer, Mid E Africa prog, 1968-69; Univ Pa, exec asst pres, 1970-72, dir, comn leadership sem prog, 1973-75, assoc dean fac arts & sci, dir, col gen studies, counr provost, asst prof, prof, res assoc, dir, continuing educ sch pub & urban policy, 1975-76; Spelman Col, pres, 1976-86, pres emer, currently; Col Bd, pres, 1987-99, chief exec officer; Kennedy Sch Govt, adj lectr, pres & chief exec officer; Carnegie Corp, spec adv pres & sr prog officer, 1999-2000; Chicago Community Trust, emrita pres & chief exec officer, 2000-05; Harris sch pub Policy Studies, visit prof, 2005-11; Zero Wait-State Inc, dir prod develop. **Orgs:** Nat Acad Pub Admin; bd dir, trustee, Grinnell Col; bd dir, Prin Ins Co Iowa; Coun Foreign Rel; dir, New York Times Co; Prin Life, 1979-2003; Prin Financial Group, 2001-03; trustee, Metrop Family Serv; bd dir, Campbell Soup Co, 2005; Deans Int Coun; Am Acad Arts & Sci; Comt Econ Develop; Coun Foreign Rels; trustee, Mayo Found Med Educ & Res. **Home Addr:** 5555 S Everett Ave Apt B1-2, Chicago, IL 60637-2271, **Home Phone:** (773)684-9044. **Business Addr:** Visiting professor, The Harris School of Public Policy Studies, 1155 E 60th St, Chicago, IL 60637, **Business Phone:** (773)702-8400.

### STEWART, DOROTHY NELL (DEE STEWART)

Government official. **Personal:** Born Sep 2, 1949, Centerville, TX; daughter of Murry B Fortson Jr and Artince Houston-Fortson; children: Aretha R Ferrell & Craig-Murry III. **Educ:** Tarrant Co Jr Col; Amber Univ. **Career:** Ft Worth Police Dept, Ft Worth, pub safety dispatcher, 1973-80; City Ft Worth Action Ctr, admin aide, 1980-82, admin asst, 1982-84, coordr, off city mgr, 1984-. **Orgs:** Am Soc Pub Adminrs; prog chairperson, 1982-83, 1984-85, secy, 1983, N Tex Conf Minority Pub Admins; vice chairperson, 1985-86, co-chairperson, 1986-87, Urban Mgt Assts N Tex; chap pub rel officer, 1986-, Nat Forum Black Admins, coun pres, 1991; Tex City Mgt Asn; pres, legacy mem, Nat Forum Black Pub Admin; N Tex Chap, 1991; Forum Ft Worth; bd mem, Sickle Cell Dis AsnAm/Tex Chap; Minority Leaders & Citizen's Coun, bd mem, nominations comt chair. **Business Addr:** Manager, Fort Worth City Action Center, 1000 Throckmorton St, Ft. Worth, TX 76102, **Business Phone:** (817)871-8888.

### STEWART, EDWARD L.

Airline executive, executive director. **Personal:** Born Sep 17, 1957, Milwaukee, WI; son of Claud and Lena; married Carolyn R Sexton; children: Cristin & Eric. **Educ:** Univ Wis, BA, commun, 1978. **Career:** Southwest Airlines, sr dir & chief spokesperson, 1990-2006; Network Affil Milwaukee & Okla, reporter; Southwestern Bell Tel, mgr; Am Airlines, media spokesperson; Ticketmaster Entertainment, vpres corp commun, 2006-07; Fleishman-Hillard Inc, sr vpres, 2007-09, 2010-; Delta Air Lines, External Corp Commun, managing dir, 2009-10. **Orgs:** Public Relations Soc Fame; Press Club of Dallas. **Home Addr:** 6137 San Villa Dr Apt C, Fort Worth, TX 76135-4107, **Home Phone:** (817)238-6765. **Business Addr:** Senior Vice President, Fleishman-Hillard Inc, 1999 Bryan St Suite 3400, Dallas, TX 75201, **Business Phone:** (214)665-1333.

### STEWART, DR. ELIZABETH PIERCE

Educator. **Personal:** Born Apr 18, 1947, Laurel, MS; married Valentine. **Educ:** Stillman Col, BS, 1970; Univ Ala, MSW, 1972; Univ Pittsburgh, PhD, social work, 1986. **Career:** EducatorHEW Wash, DC, mgt analyst, 1971; Crawford Co Bd Assistance Meadville PA, housing specialist, 1973; Edinboro St Col, asst prof social work, 1973, prof. **Orgs:** Pres & treas, Pa Asn Under Grad Social Work Educ, 1978-80; bd mem, Community Health Serv, 1978-82; bd mem, United Fund Crawford Co, 1979-80; pres, Martin Luther King Scholar Found, 1980-82; pres, Pa Asn Undergrad Social Work Educrs; bd mem, Erie County Ment Health Ment Retardation Adv Bd. **Home Addr:** 944 Liberty St, Meadville, PA 16335, **Home Phone:** (724)286-9802.

### STEWART, ELLA

Educator. **Personal:** Born Vicksburg, MS; daughter of Lee Andrew and Mary Elizabeth Young. **Educ:** Calif State Univ, Los Angeles, BA, speech, 1983, MA, speech, 1989. **Career:** Los Angeles Trade Tech Col, adj speech prof, 1992-97; Martin Luther King Dispute Resolution Ctr, Los Angeles, Calif, comm mediator, 1996-97; Compton Community Educ Ctr, asst prof of speech commun, club's advisor, 1996-. **Orgs:** Nat Commun Asn, 1987-; Am Asn Univ Women, 1996-; Los Angeles World Affairs Coun, 1996-; Black Women's Forum; KCET Community Serv TV, 2000-; Course Identification No Syst proj. **Home Addr:** 4823 W Slauson Ave Suite 8, Los Angeles, CA 90056, **Home Phone:** (323)299-0508. **Business Addr:** Assistant Professor of Speech, Compton Community Educational Center, Rm Modular P2, Compton, CA 90221, **Business Phone:** (310)900-1600.

### STEWART, DR. GREGORY

Counselor, school administrator. **Personal:** Born May 28, 1958, Cincinnati, OH; son of Margaret Marie Evans and Curtis. **Educ:** Salem Int Univ, cert, youth agency admin, 1978; Univ Cincinnati, BSW, social work, 1981, MSW, social work, 2012; Miami Univ, OH, MS, coun, 1982; Ohio Univ, PhD, educ leadership, 1993. **Career:** Denison Univ, asst dir admis, 1982-84, asst to dean, 1984-85, assoc dean studs, 1988-89; Univ Cincinnati, admis officer, 1985-86, dir ctr access & transition, 2004-06; Ohio Univ, Col osteop Med, asst dir admis, 1986-88; Northern Ky Univ, Highland Heights, KY, dir admis, 1989-94, assoc vpres enrollment mgt, 1999-2002; Talbert House Drug & Family Coun Ctr, therapist, 1990; United Way of Greater Cincinnati, Partic, Proj Blue Print, 1993-94; Univ Akron, dir admis, 1994-99, fac mem, 1997-; Amercian Col Testing Inc, vol, Ohio ACT, 1995-99; City Cincinnati, staff; Stewart & Assocs, pres, 2002-; Univ of Cincinnati, Dir, Ctr for Access and Transition, 2004-06; Eng Lang Learning Found, vpres develop & bd dir, 2004-12; Cent State Univ, vpres enrollment mgt & stud affairs, 2006-08; LULAC, vol, 2006; Union Inst & Univ, vpres enrollment mgt, 2008-10; Gateway Community & Tech Col, prog coordr, 2012-. **Orgs:** Nat Asn Col Admis Counr, 1982-; Human Serv Adv Comt; United Way Greater Cincinnati, Partic, 1993-94, vol, 2008-13; vol, Region VI Ohio Chap, Nat Asn Social Workers, 2001-10; vol fundraising, Santa Maria Community Serv Bienestar Prog, 2005-07; bd dir, Wesley Educ Ctr C & Families, 2008-2009; bd mem, Inner City Tennis Proj, 2008-10; Human Serv Adv Comn, City Cincinnati, 2010-; adv comt chair, Evanston Community Coun, 2010-13; specialist roster mem, Fulbright prog, 2014-; Nat Asn Advan Colored People; Greater Cincinnati World Affairs Coun. **Home Addr:** 549 Moreley Ave, Akron, OH 44320-2024, **Home Phone:** (330)865-7920. **Business Addr:** President, Stewart & Associates, Cincinnati, OH 45201.

### STEWART, BISHOP IMAGENE BIGHAM

Bishop, clergy. **Personal:** Born Sep 23, 1942, Dublin, GA; daughter of Rev J C Bigham and Mattie Watkins; married Lucius Johnson; children: Michael Tyrone & Jeffrey Lorenzo. **Educ:** Univ DC, AA, 1972. **Career:** US Govt Printing Off, inventory mgt specialist; Relig Coalition Reproductive Choice, chairwoman; The Greater Pearly Gates Baptist Church, pastor; African Am Women's Clergy Asn, nat chap, founder, chief exec officer & pres, 1972-; WOL radio, radio personality, 1992. **Orgs:** Founder, House Imagene; New Baptist Covenant; nat chaplain, Am Legion Auxiliary; dir, US Dept Veteran Affairs; chairwoman, Relig Coalition Reproductive Choice (RCRC). **Honors/Awds:** Living the Dream Award, 1992; Womens Leadership Awards, DC Chamber Com, 2000; Emma V Kelly Achievement Award, Grand Temple Improved Benevolent Protective Order; Social Activist of the Year Award. **Special Achievements:** House of Imagene is the First Washington, DC based shelter founded by an African American woman. **Home Addr:** 2314 Brooks Dr, Suitland, MD 20746, **Home Phone:** (301)420-2663. **Business Addr:** Founder, Chief Executive Officer & President, African-American Women's Clergy Association, 1110A 6th St NE Suite 4, Washington, DC 20002, **Business Phone:** (202)518-8488.

### STEWART, JACQUELINE NAJUMA

College teacher, writer. **Educ:** Univ Chicago, AM & PhD, eng, 1999; Stanford Univ, AB, eng interdisciplinary emphasis. **Career:** Univ Chicago, assoc prof; Northwestern Univ, Dept Radio, Tv, Film & African Am Studies, assoc prof, prof cinema studies, currently; Univ Chicago, Dept Cinema & Media Studies, prof, currently; South Side Home Movie Project, dir; Author: Migrating to the Movies: The Making of Black Urban Film Cult, 1893-1920, 2005; Migrating to the Movies: Cinema and Black Urban Modernity. **Orgs:** Appointee, Nat Film Preserv Bd. **Business Addr:** Professor of Cinema Studies, Northwestern University, 1920 Campus Dr 2nd Fl, Evanston, IL 60208, **Business Phone:** (847)491-4245.

### STEWART, JAMES, JR. (BUBBA STEWART)

Television show host, athlete. **Personal:** Born Dec 21, 1985, Bartow, FL; son of James Sr. **Career:** Motocross Bike Racing: 125 Supercross Lites West, second place 2002, first place 2003; 125 Motocross, first place 2002, third place 2003, first place 2004; 125 Supercross Lites East, first place 2004; Supercross, 10th place 2005, fourth place 2006, first place 2007, 23rd place 2008, first place 2009; Motocross, 12th place 2005, fourth place 2006, seventh place 2007, first place 2008; Motocross of Nations, first place 2006, first place 2008; FIM World Supercross GP, first place 2006, first place 2007; Paris-Bercy Supercross, first place 2008; X-Games MotoX Best Trick, Silver Award, 2009; AMA Supercross champion, 2009; AMA Supercross, 20th place 2010 (injured), fourth place 2011, seventh place 2012; AMA Motocross, 35th place 2010, 11th place 2012; Fuel TV reality show "Bubba's World", 2010-.

### STEWART, JAMES A., III

Insurance executive. **Career:** Peoples Funeral Home Inc, vpres; Peoples Assured Family Life Ins Co, co exec, currently. **Business Addr:** Company Executive, Peoples Assured Family Life Insurance Co, 886 N Farish St, Jackson, MS 39202, **Business Phone:** (601)969-3040.

### STEWART, DR. JAMES BENJAMIN

Consultant. **Personal:** Born Jul 18, 1947, Cleveland, OH; son of Reuben and Clora; married Caryl Sheffield; married Sharon; children: Talibah, Lorin & Jaliya. **Educ:** Rose-Hulman Inst Technol, BS, math, 1969; Cleveland State Univ, MA, econs, 1971; Univ Notre Dame, PhD, econs, 1976. **Career:** Cleveland & Elec Illum Co, asst & assoc tech studies engr, 1969-74; Dyke Col, part-time instr, 1972-73; Univ Notre Dame, asst prof econ & dir black studies prog, 1975-80; Pa State Univ, assoc prof econ, dir black studies prog, 1984-86, dir black studies prog, 1980-90, assoc prof labor & indust rels, 1989-90, vice provost educ equity, 1990-98, Ctr Study Higher Educ, adj prof, 1991-98, prof labor studies & indust rels & African & African Am studies, 1998-2004, prof labor studies & employ rels, 1998-2009, Univ Pk & Greater Allegheny, prof labor studies & employ rels & African & African Am studies, 2001-, prof labor studies & employ rels, African & African Am studies & mgt & orgn, 2004-, sr fac mentor, 2000-, prof emer, 2009-10; consult, diversity mgt & Africana studies prog develop, 1985-; Rev Black Polit Econ, ed, 1987-95; Temple Univ, vis adj prof, 1990-91; Defense Equal Oppurtunity Mgt Inst, Col Shirley J. Bach Vis Prof, 1998-99. **Orgs:** Nat Coun Black Studies, 1975-, vice chair, 1981-85, pres, 1998-2002; Delta Tau Kappa, 1979-; Omicron Delta Kappa, 1982-; Nat Econ Asn, 1984-; Phi Delta Kappa, 1988-; chairperson, Pa State Univ, Equal Opportunity Planning Comt, 1988-90; pres, Nat Econ Asn, 1994; pres, Asn Study African Am Life & Hist, 2009-12. **Honors/Awds:** Outstanding Volunteer Award, Rockview State Correctional Inst, 1987; Hon Outstanding Black Delawarean, Black Studies Prog & Student Government Asn, Delaware State Col, 1985; First Humanitarian Service Award, Forum on Black Affairs, 1985; Presidential Award, Nat Coun Black Studies, 1990; Award for Outstanding Contributions to Improving Equal Opportunity, Pa State Univ, 1992; Nguzo Saba Award, US, Los Angeles, Calif, 2000; African American Culture and Philosophy Award, Purdue Univ, 2004; Cheikh Anta Diop Award, ANKH, 2004; Anna Julia Cooper & CLR James Award, Nat Coun Black Studies, 2006; Award for Service, Asn Study African Am Life & Hist, 2006; Senior Scholar Award, Bros Acad, 2006. **Home Addr:** 8101 Palomino Dr, Bridgeville, PA 15017-1172, **Home Phone:** (412)221-2141.

### STEWART, JAMES OTTIS, III

Football player. **Personal:** Born Dec 27, 1971, Morristown, TN. **Educ:** Univ Tenn. **Career:** Football player (retired); Jacksonville Jaguars, running back, 1995-99; Detroit Lions, running back, 2000-03. **Honors/Awds:** Ed Block Courage Award, 1999. **Special Achievements:** Films: "1995 NFL Draft", 1995, "1996 AFC Championship Game", 1997, "1999 AFC Championship Game", 2000 Contingency, militia soldier, 2010.

### STEWART, JARVIS CHRISTOPHER

Executive, lobbyist. **Personal:** Born Jun 24, 1968, Houston, TX; son of Rayfield and Autrey Dunlap; married Stacey D; children: Madeleine & Savannah. **Educ:** Prairie View A&M Univ, BA, polit sci/geog, 1991. **Career:** Off Secy, Alexis Herman, Dept Labor, spec asst, 1997-99; Off Rep Harold E Ford, Jr, chief staff, 1998-2000; Capitol Coalitions, partner, 1999-2001; Stewart Partners LLC, chmn & mng partner, 2001-08; Ian Reid LLC, chmn & mng partner, 2007-; IR+-Media LLC, chmn & chief strategist, 2014-. **Orgs:** Art & Drama Ther Inst, 2000-01; adv bd, Ronald H Brown Found, 2001; Tavis Smiley Found, 2000-01; PAC trustee, DC Chamber Com, 2001; Dem Nat Comt, African Am Leadership Coun, 2001; Wash Nat Baseball Club LLC; Cong Black Caucus Found Corp Adv Coun; Nat Conf & Caucus Black Aged, MenzFit; YMCA Nat Capital Area. **Home Addr:** 2113 N St NW Suite 101, Washington, DC 20037, **Home Phone:** (202)785-2712. **Business Addr:** Chairman, Chief Strategist, 1900 L St NW Suite 611, Washington, DC 20036, **Business Phone:** (202)833-9400.

**STEWART, JOHN B., JR.**
Firefighter. **Personal:** Born May 16, 1930, Hartford, CT; son of John Sr and Mattie Baker; married Gladys Strong; children: Wendy, William, Donald, John, Jeffrey & Holly. **Educ:** Univ Mass, Amherst, MA, 1980; Univ Conn, Hartford, CT, BA, 1991. **Career:** City Hartford Fire Dept, Conn, firefighter, 1952-63, dep chief's aide, 1963-66, line lt, 1966-68, admin lt, 1968-74, admin fire capt, 1974-80; City Hartford, Conn, spec asst city mgr, 1971-76, actg dep city mgr, 1971-76; Hartford Ct Common Coun, majority leader, 1995-99; Collin Bennett Realty, broker, 1999; Stewart Assoc LLC, owner & founder, 2004-. **Orgs:** Founding chmn, Int Asn Black Prof Firefighters, 1969-70; consult, Int Asn Fire Chiefs, 1980-; chmn, Chief Officers Resource Comt, 1986-; chmn, Metrop Sect, IAFC, 1987-89; chmn, Conn Career Fire Chiefs, 1990-91. **Honors/Awds:** Outstanding Civic Employee Award, Greater Hartford Jaycees; American Society & Black Students Union Award, Barbados; Outstanding Community Service Award, Kiwanis; Connecticut Fire Marshal's Association Recognition Award; Roy Wilkins Award, Nat Asn Advan Colored People; Dr. John E. Rogers Sr. History Month Award; Black History Award, Urban League Greater Hartford; Crispus Attucks Award; Mildred Walton Layperson of the Year Award, Christian Activ Coun; Steward Community Center Award; Thomas Hooker Award, 2004. **Special Achievements:** Seventeenth recipient of the Thomas Hooker Award; First African-American to be trained as an Apprentice Machine Operater in the history of Company, 1948-50. **Home Addr:** 34 Canterbury St, Hartford, CT 06112, **Home Phone:** (860)522-8990. **Business Addr:** Owner, Founder, Stewart Associates LLC, 34 Canterbury St, Hartford, CT 06112, **Business Phone:** (860)522-8900.

**STEWART, JOHN OGDEN**
Lawyer. **Personal:** Born Dec 19, 1935, Springfield, IL; son of Arthur and Helen. **Educ:** Univ Calif, AB, 1959, Sch Law, JD, 1964. **Career:** US Atomic Energy Comn, contract adminr, 1965-66; Econ Opportunity Coun, gen coun, 1968-69; US Dept Housing & Urban Develop, Housing Opportunity Div, regional dir, 1969; San Francisco Legal Assistance Found, dir, 1970-74; Bechtel Corp, chief coun, corp atty, currently. **Orgs:** Comn Bar Examiners State Bar Calif; Charles Hoston Law Club; bd dir, San Francisco Gen Hosp; Comn Disadvantaged & Law State Bar Calif; Calif State Bar Asn, 1966; judiciary comn, San Francisco Bar Asn, 1970-73; treas, RENVC Ltd. **Home Addr:** 6290 Aspinwall Rd, Oakland, CA 94611.

**STEWART, DR. JOHN OTHNEIL**
Educator, writer. **Personal:** Born Jan 24, 1933; son of Ernest and Irene Holder; married Sandra McDonald; children: John Malcolm, Ernest Jabali & Ruth Laini. **Educ:** Calif State Univ, BA, 1960; Stanford Univ, MA, 1965; Univ Iowa, MFA, 1966; Univ Calif, PhD, anthrop/lit, 1973. **Career:** Univ Iowa, eng instr; Calif State Univ, prof; Univ Ill, prof, anthrop & writer; Ohio State Univ, prof, 1984-91; Univ Calif Davis, prof african am studies, prof emer, currently. **Orgs:** Inst Advan Study Princeton, 1979-80; Am Anthrop Asn. **Honors/Awds:** Winifred Holtby Prize for Novel Royal Soc Lit London, 1972; Hon Mem, Golden Key Int Honour Socs. **Special Achievements:** Author: Coolie and Creole, Ann Arbor Mich Univ Microfilms Int, 1973. **Home Addr:** 214 Avocet Ave, Davis, CA 95616-7514, **Home Phone:** (530)756-4733. **Business Addr:** Professor Emeritus, University of California Davis, 2205 Hart Hall, Davis, CA 95616, **Business Phone:** (530)752-1548.

**STEWART, JOSEPH M.**
Executive, chief executive officer, founder (originator). **Personal:** Born Dec 23, 1942, Maringouin, LA; son of Willie Sr and Stella M (Patterson); married Clara J; children: Erick J & Kendra L. **Educ:** Southern Univ, Baton Rouge, LA, BA, foods & nutrit, 1965. **Career:** Howard Univ, Wash, DC, dir food serv, 1969-71; Wash DC Pub Schs, Wash, DC, dir food serv; Dc, state dir, child nutrit prog; Kellogg Co, Battle Creek, Mich, dir child nutrit progs, food serv mkt dept, 1980, dir, corp commun pub affairs div, 1981, dir corp commun, 1981-85, vpres, pub affairs, 1985, sr vpres, corp affairs & chief ethics officer; Stewart Industs LLC, co founder & chief exec off, currently. **Orgs:** Past bd dir, Am Sch Food Serv Asn, 1971-; IFMA, Int Gold & Silver Plate Soc, 1971-; bd dir, Battle Creek Area Urban League, 1983-88; bd mem, Battle Creek Area United Way, 1985-; bd dir, PRIDE Inc, 1986-88; bd gov, Pub Affairs Coun Am, 1987-; bd mem, Nat Agr-Users Adv, 1988-, State Mich Food & Nutrit Adv, 1988-; bd trustee, Battle Creek Health Syst, 1988-; regional bd dir, Mich Nat Bank, 1990; bd trustee, Second Harvest Nat Network Food Banks, 1990; bd dir, Med Educ SAfrican Blacks, 1990; Exec Leadership Coun, 1990; chair bd, Battle Creek Health Syst, 1991; bd trustee, Grand Valley State Univ, 1991; Sigma Pi Phi Frat, 1992; trustee, WK Kellogg Found; secy, Agr Exten Users Adv Bd; bd mem, Nat Resource Ctr Healing Racism, currently; bd mem, Southern Univ Syst Found; bd mem, Med Educ S African Blacks; bd mem, Auto Club Mich; bd mem, Stewart Industs; bd mem, Pyper Prod; bd mem, Westbrook Hosp; bd mem, Stand Fed Bank Adv Regional; chmn gov bd, Calhoun County Health Improv Prog; adv bd mem, Johns Hopkins Sch Pub Health & Hyg; bd mem, Grand Valley State Univ Bd Control; bd mem, Found Am Commun. **Home Addr:** 231 Cent, Battle Creek, MI 49017, **Home Phone:** (616)962-4090. **Business Addr:** Chief Executive Officer, Co-Founder, Stewart Industries LLC, 150 McQuiston Dr, Battle Creek, MI 49015-1076, **Business Phone:** (269)660-9290.

**STEWART, KEBU OMAR**
Basketball player. **Personal:** Born Dec 19, 1973, Brooklyn, NY. **Educ:** Calif State Univ, Bakersfield, 1997; Univ Nev, Las Vegas. **Career:** Philadelphia 76ers, forward, 1997-88; Sioux Falls Skyforce, 1999-2000; Vaqueros de Bayamon, 1999; Atlanta Hawks, 1999; Atleticos de San Ger (Pr), 2000; Hapoel Jerusalem, 2000-01; Avtodor Saratov (Russia), 2001-02; UNICS (Russia), 2003; Prokom Trefl Sopot (Poland), 2003; Adecco Estudiantes (Spain), 2003; Vojvodina (Serbia & Montenegro), 2003-05; KK Vojvodina Novi Sad, 2003-05; Vertical Vision Cantu (Italy), 2005-06; Seoul SK Knights (S Korea), 2006-07; Crvena zvezda (Serbia), 2007; Barons/LMT Riga (Latvia), 2007; Red Star Belgrade, 2007; Real GM LLC, free agt, currently. **Business Addr:** Free Agent, RealGM LLC, 109 N Russell St Suite 2, Marion, IL 62959, **Business Phone:** (618)993-7592.

**STEWART, KENNETH C.**
Clergy, missionary. **Personal:** Born Sep 28, 1939, Washington, DC. **Educ:** St Joseph's Col, BA, 1964; Capuchin Sem St Anthony, attended 1968. **Career:** St Francis, St Elizabeth, Milwaukee, parish assoc, 1968-69; Francis Comm Sch, Milwaukee, adminstr pub rels, 1969-70; St Boniface Parish, Milwaukee, pastor, 1970-73; Queen Angels Retreat Ctr Saginaw, retreat tm, 1973-74; Nat Orgn Bar Coun Wash, DC, dir ch vocations, 1974-. **Orgs:** A solemnly professed friar, St Joseph Prov Capuchin Order, 1963; Nat Black Cath Clergy Caucus; ordained priest, 1967. **Business Addr:** Provost of St Joseph-Capuchin, Saint Bonaventure Monastery, 1740 Mt Elliott, Detroit, MI 48207, **Business Phone:** (313)579-2100.

**STEWART, KORDELL**
Broadcaster, football player. **Personal:** Born Oct 16, 1972, New Orleans, LA; children: Syre; married Porsha Williams. **Educ:** Univ Colo, attended. **Career:** Football player (retired), executive; Pittsburgh Steelers, quarterback, 1995-2002; Chicago Bears, 2003; Baltimore Ravens, quarterback, 2004-05; Entertainment & Sports Programming Network, Col Football Live, analyst, 2009, analyst, currently; United Football League, sideline reporter; Afternoon Dr Radio Sports Talk Show, co-host, 2012-. **Honors/Awds:** Rookie of the Year, Pittsburgh Steelers, 1995; Joe Greene Great Performance Award, 1995; Pro Bowl, alternate, 1996; All Madden Team, 1996-97; Louisiana's Most Valuable Player; New Orleans Player of the Year; Offensive Player of the Year, Am Football Club, 2001; Most Valuable Player, Pittsburgh Steelers, 2001.

**STEWART, LARRY A., JR.**
Basketball coach, basketball player. **Personal:** Born Sep 21, 1968, Philadelphia, PA; son of Larry Sr and Lois; married Toi; children: Lexis, Laryn & Tai. **Educ:** Coppin State Univ, BA, mgt sci & sociol, 1991. **Career:** Basketball player (retired), coach; Wash Bullets, Power forward, 1991, forward & small forward, 1992-95; Quad City Thunder, 1995; Zaragoza, Spain, 1995-96; Seattle SuperSonics, small forward, 1996-97; Galatasaray, Turkey, 1997-98; Girona, Spain, 1998-2001; Caceres, Spain, 2001-02; Peristeri, Greece, 2002-04; Maroussi, Greece, 2004-05; AEL 1964, Greece, 2005-06; Paris Basket Racing, France, 2006-07; Union Jeanne d'Arc Phalange Quimper, France, 2007-08; Bowie State Univ Athletics, assoc head coach, 2011-12. **Honors/Awds:** Player of the Year, Mid-Eastern Athletic Conf, 1990, 1991; Black College Player of the Year, 1991; John B. Wooden Award; Hall of Fame, Mid-Eastern Athletic Conf, 2005. **Home Addr:** 3135 Cambridge Dr, Windsor Mill, MD 21244-3417. **Business Addr:** Associate Head Coach, Bowie State University Athletics, 4000 Jericho Pk Rd, Bowie, MD 20715-9465, **Business Phone:** (301)860-3898.

**STEWART, LORETTA A.**
Secretary (office). **Personal:** Born Jul 30, 1930, Muskogee, OK; daughter of James A Taylor and Agnes Taylor Berry; children: Arrilinda Delgoda, Darryl Delgoda, Calvin, Kevin & Shelia Jordan. **Educ:** Detroit Bus Inst, attended 1974; Henry Ford Community Col, attended 1976; Wayne State Univ, attended 1981. **Career:** Massey Ferguson, 1965-75; Wayne State Univ, 1975-79; Owens Corning Fiberglass, 1979-83; Stewart's Secretarial Serv, own, 1981-82; Wendy's Franchise; Ford Elem Sch, 1984-87, ade secy; Southfield Sch Dist, substituting admin secy, currently. **Orgs:** MIC Cancer Found, bd mem; United Way; UNF; D'Accord Soc; Justice, Unity, Generosity, Serv. **Honors/Awds:** Heart of Gold Award, United Way, MIC Cancer Found, 1991; Citizen of the Week Award, WWJ News Radio 95, 1992. **Home Addr:** 29520 Sharon Lane, Southfield, MI 48076-5213. **Business Addr:** Substituting Administrative Secretary, Southfield School District, Southfield, MN 48034, **Business Phone:** (248)746-8588.

**STEWART, DR. MAC A.**
Educator. **Personal:** Born Jul 7, 1942, Forsyth, GA; son of Zillia and Alonzo; married Ernestine Clemons; children: Bruce Kifle & Justin Che. **Educ:** Morehouse Col, BA, sociol, 1963; Atlanta Univ, MA, coun, 1965; Ohio State Univ, PhD, higher educ admin, 1973. **Career:** Jasper County Training Sch, teacher/counr, 1963-64; Crispus Attucks HS, teacher, 1965-66; Morehouse Col, dir stud financial aid, 1966-70; Ohio State Univ, from asst dean to assoc dean, 1973-90, actg dean, 1990-91, dean, 1991-2000, vice provost, monority affairs, spec asst diversity; Acad Search, sr consult, currently. **Orgs:** Consult, KY State Univ, 1978; mem bd dir, Buckeye Boys Ranch, 1979-85; mem bd dir, Bethune Ctr Unwed Mothers, 1980-83; consult, Wilberforce Univ, 1980; fac mem, Ohio Staters Inc, 1982-91; bd mem, Negro Educ Rev, 1983-, ed-in-chief, 1999-2007, pres, 2007-, ed bd chair; consult, Ohio Bd Regents, 1986; consult, Univ Nebr; consult, US Dept Educ, 1990; consult, Temple Univ, 1991; bd trustee, Columbus Acad, 1991-; consult, VA Common wealth Univ, 1992; conslt, Tex A&M Univ; Am Personnel Guid Asn; Am Col Personnel Asn; Nat Asn Stud Personnel Adminr; Mid-Western Asn Stud Fin Aid Adminr; Alpha Kappa Delta Nat Hon Sociol Soc; Phi Delta Kappa; Nat Hon Educ Fraternity; Phi Kappa Phi; Nat Hon Soc; Am Asn Higher Educ; bd mem, Human Subj Res Comt C's Hosp; vice chair, Int Found Educ Self-Help; founder & bd mem, Nat Asn Diversity Officers Higher Educ; consult, Acad Search Inc; bd trustee, Ohio Hist Soc; bd trustee, Mt Carmel Sch Nursing; bd trustee, Columbus Urban League; bd trustee, Boys & Girls Clubs Columbus;Mary McCleod Bethune Ctr. **Honors/Awds:** Distinguished Affirmative Action Award, The Ohio State Univ, 1984; Outstanding Alumni Award, Hubbard Sch, 1986; Distinguished Service Award, Negro Educ Rev, 1992; Frederick D Patterson Award, United Negro Col Fund, 1992; Josephine Sitterle Failer Award, 2009. **Home Addr:** 930 Notchbrook Dr, Delaware, OH 43015-8996, **Home Phone:** (740)548-2486. **Business Addr:** Senior Consultant, Academic Search Inc, 1825 K St NW Suite 705, Washington, DC 20006, **Business Phone:** (202)332-4049.

**STEWART, MAE E.**
City commissioner. **Personal:** Born Jun 4, 1926, Memphis, TN; daughter of John and Lilian (deceased); married Robert Leonard; children: Jacqueline, Robert Jr, Saundra & Ernest. **Career:** Cuyahan Metro Housing Authority, comnr, 1999-; Plain Talk Mae E Stewart, TV show, host; Govt Off, Activist; E Cleveland City Comn, city comnr, pres; E Cleveland Police Dept, E Cleveland K9 Unit, founder, 1998. **Orgs:** Co-founder, Rozelle Super Civic Asn, 1963; co-founder, E Cleveland Scholar Fund; Huron Road Hosp Asn; vpres, E Cleveland Second Ward Dem Club; bd trustee, Ohio Munic League; exec bd, 21st Cong Dist; Nat League Cities, Human Resources Polit Comn; bd dir, E Cleveland Police Athletic League; Nat Asn Advan Colored People; Urban League; former dir, chair, Friends E Cleveland; House Com A M McGregor Retirement; NE OH Jazz Soc Inc; E Cleveland Comn Task Force; E Cleveland City Coun; Seam Builders Asn; Regional Transit Authority, Redevelop Comn; Community Based Prosecution; citizens adv coun. **Honors/Awds:** East Cleveland Citizen of the Year, 1971. **Special Achievements:** First Black president, East Cleveland School District PTA, 1962; First Black woman elected to East Cleveland City Commission. **Home Addr:** 1252 Melbourne Rd, East Cleveland, OH 44112-4137, **Home Phone:** (216)761-2358.

**STEWART, MICHAEL CURTIS (YOGI STEWART)**
Basketball player. **Personal:** Born Apr 24, 1975, Cucq; son of Michael and Carolyn. **Educ:** Univ Calif, attended 1997. **Career:** Basketball player (retired); Sacramento Kings, ctr, 1997-98; Toronto Raptors, ctr, 1998-2002; Cleveland Cavaliers, ctr, 2002-03; Boston Celtics, ctr, 2003-04; Atlanta Hawks, 2004-05.

**STEWART, PAUL ALLEN**
Baseball player. **Personal:** Born Oct 21, 1978, Alexandria, VA. **Career:** Milwaukee Brewers, player, 1996-2002 & 2004; Red Sox, player, 2002-03; Tampa Bay Devil Rays, player, 2003-04; Pittsburgh Pirates, player, 2004.

**STEWART, PAUL WILBUR**
Curator, founder (originator). **Personal:** Born Dec 18, 1925, Clinton, IA; son of Eugene Joseph and Martha L Moore; married Johnnie Mae Davis; children: Mark, Tracy, Linda & Earl. **Educ:** Hampton Inst; Roosevelt Univ; Moler Barber Col, cert, 1947. **Career:** Post Off, mail sorter; Black Am W Found, cur; lic barber, Ill, Wis, NY, Colo; Black Am W Mus & Heritage Ctr, founder, cur & dir, currently. **Orgs:** Musician, Consult Co; Hist Rec Adv Bd Colo; estab Afro-Am Bicentennial Corp Colo; App Gov's Comn Highways, Bi-Ways Comt, 1989-; adv bd, Metrop State Col. **Honors/Awds:** Interviewed by Denver TV & radio stations; Featured in several magazines; Barney Ford Award, 1977; Black Educators United Award, 1977; George Washington Honor Medal Achievement, Valley Forge, 1985; Featured in Smithsonian Mag, (front cover), 1989. **Special Achievements:** Co-producer, documentary, "Blacks Here & Now", Educ TV, Ch 6, Denver, 1972; Black Educators United Award, 1977. **Home Addr:** 17954 E Linvale Dr, Aurora, CO 80013, **Home Phone:** (303)369-5032. **Business Addr:** Museum Founder, Curator, Black American West Museum, 3091 Calif St, Denver, CO 80205, **Business Phone:** (303)292-2566.

**STEWART, PEARL**
Journalist, educator. **Educ:** Howard Univ, BA, Afro-Am studies; Am Univ, MA, commun. **Career:** Campus Newspaper, Hilltop, ed; Oakland Tribune, reporter & features ed, ed, 1992-93; Howard Univ, ed stud newspaper, jour-in-residence, 1994; La State Univ, jour instr; Xavier Univ, jour instr; Tribune, San Francisco Chronicle, reporter, staff writer, ed; Harvard Univ Shorenstein Ctr Press, Polit & Pub Policy fel, 1995; Univ Southern Miss, vis prof, 1995, adj prof, currently; Fla A&M Univ, dir career serv, jour instr, 2002; Barry Bingham Sr fel, 2006; Stewart Media Consult Inc, media consult, currently; Dillard & Xavier Univs, New Orleans, fac; Howard Univ, Wash, DC, fac; La State, Baton Rouge, fac; East Bay Express; Black Enterprise; Essence.com; The Fort Worth Star-Telegram; Diverse Issues Higher Educ, corresp, currently. **Orgs:** Nat Asn Black Journalists; founder, chair, Black Col Commun Asn; resident fel, Harvard Univ's Shorenstein Ctr. **Home Addr:** , MS. **Business Addr:** Adjunct Professor, University of Southern Mississippi, S Hall 216 118 Col Dr Suite 5121-0001, Hattiesburg, MS 39406-5121, **Business Phone:** (601)266-4258.

**STEWART, RAYMOND C.**
Executive. **Educ:** Cornell Univ, BS, econ & pub policy, 1976; Columbia Univ, Columbia Bus Sch, MBA, money, fin markets & fin, 1980. **Career:** Salomon Bros Inc, banking analyst, 1979-83; New York Kendo Club, asst instr, godan, 1981-; Warren Marcus Assocs Inc, exec vpres, 1983-2007; RASARA Strategies Inc, portfolio mgr, founder & chief invest officer, 1997-2011; Conquest Strategies LLC, sr managing dir, 2008-. **Orgs:** Cornell Black Alumni Asn; Columbia Bus Sch Alumni Club New York. **Special Achievements:** Publications: 2013 Conquest Performance, 2013; 2Q2014 Conquest Performance, 2014; 1Q2014 Conquest Performance, 2014; Conquest Business Cycle Investing ("BCI") - MidCap Portfolio, Q4 2015 Report, 2016. **Business Addr:** Senior Managing Director, Conquest Strategies LLC, 199 Main St Suite 300, White Plains, NY 10601-3206, **Business Phone:** (914)681-8777.

**STEWART, RAYNA COTTRELL, II**
Football player, football coach. **Personal:** Born Jun 18, 1973, Oklahoma City, OK; married Sonia; children: ShaRae, Tre, Mycah & Jadyn. **Educ:** Northern Ariz, BS, advert & bus admin, 1995; Tenn State Univ, MS, educ, admin & supvr, 2006. **Career:** Football player (retired), football executive & coach; Houston Oilers, defensive back, 1996; Tenn Oilers, strong safety, 1997; Miami Dolphins, 1998; Jacksonville Jaguars, 1999, free safety, 2000; Arena Football League, Austin Wranglers, 2003-04; Northwestern Univ, Dept Athletics, defensive grad asst, 2007-08; Tenn Titans, qual control, defensive asst, currently; Whites Creek High Sch, Nashville, Tenn, football coach, currently. **Honors/Awds:** All-America honors, Northern Ariz. **Home Addr:** , Nashville, CA. **Business Addr:** Defensive Assistant-Quality Control, Tennessee Titans, 460 Great Circle Rd, Nashville, TN 37228, **Business Phone:** (615)565-4000.

**STEWART, RENEIRHA**
College teacher. **Career:** Detroit Bd Edu, teacher. **Business Addr:** Teacher, Detroit Board of Education, 17181 Greenview St, Detroit, MI 48219, **Business Phone:** (313)533-0042.

**STEWART, RONALD PATRICK**
Educator. **Personal:** Born Nov 14, 1942, Birmingham, AL. **Educ:** Drake Univ, BFA, 1966; Ohio Univ, MEd, 1968; Univ Cincinnati, MA, 1970. **Career:** Nat Teacher Corps, teacher, 1966-68; Hammond Sch City, 1968-69; Englewood Community Theatre, dir, 1969; Univ Cincinnati, instr, 1969-71, asst prof, 1971; Contemporary Arts Ctr, consult dir, 1974. **Orgs:** Bd dir, Arts Coun Ohio River Valley; exec dir, Arts Consortium; coconvenor, Cult Task Force Cincinnati; consult, Bicentennial Progs Queen City Met; adv comt, Beamon Hough Art Fund, Links Inc Steering Comt; Individual Artist, Arts Coun Ohio River Valley; Nat Art Educ Asn; City Core Activ Comn; Ohio Art Educ Asn; Phi Delta Kappa.

**STEWART, RUTH ANN. See Obituaries Section.**

**STEWART, RYAN EVAN**
Football player, radio host. **Personal:** Born Sep 30, 1973, Moncks Corner, SC. **Educ:** Ga Inst Technol. **Career:** Football player (retired), radio host; Detroit Lions, defensive back, 1996, 1997-2000; ESPN's First Take, contribr; WQXI AM, Atlanta Broadcasting Studio, host, currently. **Business Addr:** Host, WQXI AM, 3350 Peachtree Rd Suite 1610, Atlanta, GA 30326, **Business Phone:** (404)237-0079.

**STEWART, SHANNON HAROLD**
Baseball player. **Personal:** Born Feb 25, 1974, Cincinnati, OH. **Career:** Baseball player (retired); Toronto Blue Jays, outfielder, 1995-2003, 2008, free agt, 2008; Minn Twins, outfielder, 2003-06; Oakland Athletics, outfielder, 2007.

**STEWART, SHELLEY, JR.**
Executive, vice president (organization). **Educ:** Northeastern Univ, BS, MS, criminal justice; Univ New Haven, MBA. **Career:** United Technologies Corp, 1982-00; Raytheon Co, vpres supply chain mgt, 2000-02; Invensys, sr vpres, 2002-03; Tyco, sr vpres oper excellence & chief procurement officer, 2003-12; DuPont, vpres sourcing & logistics & chief procurement officer, 2012-. **Orgs:** Bd mem, Inst Supply Mgt; bd dir, Cleco Corp; appointee, U.S. Dept Com Nat Adv Coun Minority Bus Enterprise; bd chair, Howard Univ, Sch Bus; vice chair, Nat Minority Supplier Develop Coun (NMSDC); Northeastern Univ Corp; pres bd, Boys & Girls Club Trenton/Mercer County. **Business Addr:** Board of Director, Cleco Corporation, 2030 Donahue Ferry Rd, Pineville, LA 71361-5000, **Business Phone:** (1-8)00622-65.

**STEWART, STACEY D.**
Chief executive officer, president (organization). **Personal:** married Jarvis C; children: Madeleine & Savannah. **Educ:** Georgetown Univ, BA, econs, 1985; Univ Mich, MBA, finance, 1987. **Career:** Merrill Lynch, pub finance div, invest banker; Pryor McClendon & Counts Co, Atlanta, Ga, vpres; Fannie Mae Found, dir regional pub affairs Southeastern region, 1992-95, vpres Housing & Community Develop Southeastern region, 1995-99, pres & chief exec officer, 1999-2007, chief diversity officer & sr vpres, 2007-09; United Way Worldwide, exec vpres community impact, 2009-12, pres, 2012-. **Business Addr:** US President, United Way Worldwide, 701 N Fairfax St, Alexandria, VA 22314, **Business Phone:** (703)836-7112.

**STEWART, STACEY DAVIS. See DAVIS, STACEY H.**

**STEWART, TYLITHA HELEN**
Government official. **Personal:** Born Jul 9, 1981, Detroit, MI; daughter of Joe and Belvayona. **Educ:** Univ Mich, BA, polit sci, 2001, MBA, 2006; Univ Mich Col Eng. **Career:** State Mich, policy anal, 2000-01; Papyrus Group, ambassador emer, currently; City Detroit, Mayors Off & Strategic Mgt Ctr, proj mgr, 2002-04, strategy lead, 2005-; City Detroit Exec Off, strategic bus develop & int rels mgr, 2004-06; Home Depot, assoc, internal leadership develop prog, 2006-08; Target, sr financial analyst, 2008-10, supply chain finance mgr, 2010-11; Tony Howard Basketball Camp, acad prog dir; Microsoft, sr mgr, 2012-15, sr opers mgr, 2015-. **Orgs:** Bd mem, Detroit SNAP, 2002-; founder, Detroit Area Mentors Prog; Nat Black MBA Asn, 2004; Jack & Jill Seattle, 2013. **Home Addr:** 7803 Watford Dr, PO Box 252662, West Bloomfield, MI 48322-2881, **Home Phone:** (248)592-9240. **Business Addr:** Senior Operation Manager, Microsoft, 1 Microsoft Way, Redmond, WA 98052.

**STEWART, W. DOUGLAS**
Government official. **Personal:** Born Apr 8, 1938, Paterson, NJ; son of Irene; married Norma S; children: Giselle. **Educ:** Fairleigh Dickinson Univ, BS, 1970. **Career:** Wend Realty, pres; Nj Bank NA, asst treas; City Paterson, dir div real estate & assessment; City Orange Twp, tax assessor, dir finance dept; Atlantic City, tax assessor, currently. **Orgs:** Rotary Club; Jersey Ski; Int Asn Assessing Officers, NE Region Asn Assessing Officers; Soc Prof Assessors. **Honors/Awds:** Past Officers Award, Passaic Co Child Care Coordr Agency, 1978; Distinguished Service Award, Passaic Co Planned Parenthood, 1984. **Home Addr:** 2242 Murray Ave, Atlantic City, NJ 08401-1529, **Home Phone:** (609)344-2962. **Business Addr:** Tax Assessor, Atlantic City, 1301 Bacharach Blvd Rm 606, Atlantic City, NJ 08401, **Business Phone:** (609)347-5380.

**STEWART, DR. WARREN HAMPTON, SR.**
Clergy. **Personal:** Born Dec 11, 1951, Independence, KS; son of Jesse Jared and Jessie Elizabeth Jenkins; married Karen E; children: Warren Hampton Jr, Matthew Christian, Jared Chamberlain, Justin Mitchell, Aaron Frederick Taylor, Jessica Elizabeth Curry & Jamila Imani. **Educ:** Coffeyville Community Jr Col, AA, 1971; Bishop Col, Dallas TX, BA, relig & philos, 1973; Union Theol Sem, New York, NY, MDiv, 1976, STM, 1977; Am Baptist Sem W, Berkeley, CA, DM, 1982; Ottawa Univ, DDiv, 1994. **Career:** Cornerstone Baptist Church, Brooklyn, NY, assoc minister, 1973-78; First Instnl Baptist Church, Phoenix, Ariz, pastro, sr pastor, 1977-; Ottawa Univ, Phoenix Campus, adj prof; Fuller Theol Sem, Doctor Ministry Prog. **Orgs:** Life mem, Nat Advan Asn Colored People; Nat Baptist Conv USA Inc, evangel bd, exec secy, 1994-2005, chmn, currently; pres, Am Baptist Churches; Am Baptist Churches Ariz; bd mem, pres, Am Baptist Churches Pac Southwest; chairperson, Ariz a Martin Luther King Jr. State Holiday; pres, Paradise Missionary Baptist State Conv Ariz Inc; Bd Nat Immigration Forum. **Honors/Awds:** Image Award, Nat Advan Asn Colored People; Award of Excellence in Black Church Studies, Ecumenical Ctr Black Church Studies, 1982; American Muslim Mission Award; Reverend William Hardison Memorial Award; Roy Wilkins Memorial Award, Nat Advan Asn Colored People, Maricopa County chap; Humanitarian Award, Cent Dist Congress Christian Educ; Martin Luther King Jr Justice Award, First Int Baptist Church, 1988; Distinguished Service Award, United Nations Asn, Greater Phoenix chapter; Living Legend, Arizona Daily Star, 2002; hon Doctor of Divinity, Ottawa Univ. **Special Achievements:** One of the ten most influential religious leaders in the Valley Phoenix, The Arizona Republic Newspaper, 1985; Attended the First African/African-American Summit held in West Africa, 1991; Led statewide campaign to win Martin Luther King Jr-Civil Rights Day, Arizona, 1992; Appointed Executive Secretary of the Home Mission Board of the Nat Baptist Convention, USA Inc; Author: Interpreting God's Word in Black Preaching, Judson, 1984; established Samaritan House, emer shelter for homeless; First General Chairperson for ARIZONANS FOR A MARTIN LUTHER KING, JR. STATE HOLIDAY; One of ten people whose achievements had the most notable effect on Arizona, Arizona Daily Star, 2002. **Home Addr:** 2407 W Mineral Rd, Phoenix, AZ 85041-9559, **Home Phone:** (602)841-6090. **Business Addr:** Senior Pastor, First Institutional Baptist Church, 1141 E Jefferson St, Phoenix, AZ 85034, **Business Phone:** (602)258-1998.

**STEWART, WILLIAM (BILL J STEWART)**
Executive. **Personal:** Born Wilmington, TN. **Educ:** Tenn State Univ, BS, physics. **Career:** Apollo Programming Industs, pres & chief exec officer, currently. **Orgs:** Bd dir, Glaucoma Res Found; founding mem, Leadership Coun, Black Col & Univs (HBCU). **Business Addr:** President, Chief Executive Officer, Apollo Programming Industries, 4546 El Camino Real Suite 215, Los Altos, CA 94022, **Business Phone:** (650)941-8027.

**STEWART, DR. WILLIAM H.**
Educator, clergy, executive director. **Personal:** Born Apr 18, 1935, Greensboro, NC; son of Harold W and Mildred Hancock; children: Candida. **Educ:** NC Agr & Tech State Univ, BS, 1960; Cent Mich Univ, MA, 1973; Blackstone Sch Law, JD, 1977; Western CO Univ, DB Adm, 1980. **Career:** Coop League USA, dir demonstration prog, 1966-69; Gen Elect Co Chic Blackstone Sch Law, Jdago, training dir, 1969-70; City Ann Arbor, dir model cities prog, 1970-71; US Dept Housing Urban Dev, div dir, 1971-75; Exec Sem Ctr US Civil Serv Comn, assoc dir, 1975-78; TN Valley Authority Div Energy, mgr, 1978-86; Mutual Housing Corp, exec dir, 1987-90; Knoxville Col, Div Bus & Social Sci, dir, 1987-91; Mother Love Baptist Church, pastor, 1987-92; US Dept Energy, Southeastern Power Mkt Div, prog mgr, 1991-94; Macedonia Outreach Ministries, pres, 1994-96; Rochdale Inst, chief exec officer, 1996-. **Orgs:** Alpha Phi Alpha Fraternity, 1959-; pres & bd dir, Stewart-Candida Co, 1978-85; dean, Chattanooga Baptist Bible Col, 1981-84; pres & bd dir, Chattanooga Area Minority Investment Forum, 1981-87; chmn & bd dir, Sun Belt Allied Industs, 1985-86; pres, Oper PUSH, Chattanooga, TN, 1986-88; chmn, Seville-Benz Corp, 1986-93. **Honors/Awds:** Doctorate of Divinity, Laurence Univ, 1968; Doctor of Laws, Buckner Univ, 1970; Youth & Commun Serv Frederick Douglass Chapter Hamilton Co, 1981; Service Award, Lane Col, Jackson, TN, 1981; Distinguished Citizen, City of Chattanooga, TN, 1981; Outstanding Mem Alpha Iota Alpha, 1983; Distinguished Serv Sun Belt Asn Ind, 1984; Humanitarian Award, Jas B Dudley High School Alumni Asn, 1988; Distinguished Service Award, Southeastern Power Admin, 1994. **Home Addr:** PO Box 6245, Chattanooga, TN 37401, **Home Phone:** (423)756-8897. **Business Addr:** Pastor, New Monumental Baptist Church, 901 Woodmore Lane, Chattanooga, TN 37411-2312, **Business Phone:** (423)267-6106.

**STEWART, YOGI. See STEWART, MICHAEL CURTIS.**

**STEWART-COPES, MICHELE LYNN**
Consultant, social worker. **Personal:** Born Feb 9, 1954, New Britain, CT; daughter of Charles Stewart and Bessie; married Aelix; children: Tonya Wrice-Smith & Rashida. **Educ:** Cent Conn State Univ, BS, Eng, 1976, MS, counr educ/sch coun & guid serv, 1980; State Conn, teacher cert, 1976; Univ Conn, MSW, 1988. **Career:** Urban League Greater Hartford, remedial teacher, 1976-78; YMCA, recruitment, placement specialist, 1978-80; Dept C & Families, social worker, 1980-83; Cath Family Servs, prog consult, 1983-87; St Francis Hosp, Teen Parent Prog, dir, 1987-94; SEET Consult, pres, 1992-, chief exec officer, 2005-; Conn State Dept Educ, educ consult, 1999-2000; Wraparound Pract Model, nat consult, currently; Vroon VanDenBerg LLP, skilled trainer, consult, therapist, currently; POWER, founder & co chair; Vroon VanDenBerg, trainer, lectr & sr coach; Southern Conn State Univ, adj prof. **Orgs:** Vpres, Coalition 100 Black Women, 1992-; Black Dem Club, 1992-; Conn Cross Cult Training Comt; Women League Voters, 1997-; chair, Nat Asn Advan Colored People, 1997-; Multicultural Health Adv Comn; bd mem, United Way, 1998-2000; bd mem, New Brit Found Pub Giving, 1999-2000; African Am neighborhoods, Hartford; fel Faith Based Community Develop Leadership Inst; New Eng Regional Health Equity Coun; Community Develop Comn New Brit; chair, Workforce Develop Comt Conn Multicultural Health Partnership. **Honors/Awds:** Outstanding Young Women of America, 1991; Women in Leadership Award, YWCA, 1995; Community Service Award, NAACP, 1995; Community Relations Award, US Dept Justice, 1995. **Special Achievements:** Congressional District 6 Advisory Council Permanent Commission on the Status of Women, 1996; Governor's Educational Improvement Panel Advisory Review Committee, 1997; Co-Author: Sexuality and Parenting Curriculum For Young Minority Fathers; Recognized consultant in adolescent sexuality and the wraparound process, appearing on local television talk shows and speaking at statewide & national conferences; First African American to be elected to the Board of Educ in New Britain, 1992-95. **Home Addr:** 281 Rocky Hill Ave, New Britain, CT 06051, **Home Phone:** (860)225-9349. **Business Addr:** Trainer, Coach, Vroon VanDenBerg LLP, 10822 Quail Creek Dr E, Parker, CO 80138, **Business Phone:** (303)790-4099.

**STICKNEY, JANICE L.**
Consultant, pharmacologist, president (organization). **Personal:** Born Jul 21, 1941, Tallahassee, FL; daughter of William H (deceased) and Nerissa Lee (deceased). **Educ:** Oberlin Col, BA, zool, 1962; Univ Mich, PhD, pharamacol, 1967. **Career:** UCSF, postdoctoral fel, 1967-68, instr, 1968-69, asst prof, 1969-72; Mich State Univ, asst prof, 1972-75, assoc prof, 1975-81, prof, 1981; GD Searle & Co, sr sci, 1981-83, assoc dir off sci affairs, 1983-87, dir dept med & sci info, 1987-88; Brokenburr Stickney Assoc, pres, 1988-; J.L. Stickney, pres, prin, 1988-; Steritech Inc, dir regulatory affairs & clin pharamacol, actg dir toxicol, 1992-95; Baxter, consult, 2004-05; Kyowa Pharmaceut, consult, 2006-08. **Orgs:** Consult, FDA, 1971-80; adv coun, NIEHS, 1979-83; elected nominating comn, 1978, 1989, mem comn, 1981-84, counr, 1984-87; Am Asn Advan Sci; Sigma Xi; Am Soc pharamacol & Exper therapeut; Am Heart Asn; Int Soc cardiovasc Pharmacotherapy; Am Med Writers Asn; AAAS; Asn Women Sci; Am Soc Clin Pharmacol & Therapeut; Drug Info Asn; Regulatory Affairs Profs Soc. **Special Achievements:** Author of many books. **Business Addr:** President, JL Stickney Biopharmaceutical Consulting Services, 2227 US Hwy 1 Suite 232, North Brunswick, NJ 08902, **Business Phone:** (732)422-8856.

**STICKNEY, PHYLLIS YVONNE**
Actor. **Personal:** Born Little Rock, AR; daughter of Felix and Belle. **Educ:** Univ Calif, Los Angeles. **Career:** Streets of Fire, 1984; Beat Street, 1984; Frederick Douglass: An Am, 1986; House Party, 1990; Jungle Fever, 1991; Talkin ' Dirty After Dark, 1991; Malcolm X, 1992; What's Love Got to Do With It, 1993; The Inkwell, 1994; Die Hard: With A Vengeance, 1995; Tendrils, 1996; How Stella Got Her Groove Back, 1998; Big Ain't Bad, 2002; See Dick Run, 2009; Trapped: Haitian Nights, 2010; Dolls of Voodoo, 2013; Pound of Flesh, 2014. TV series: "The Women of Brewster Place", 1989; "New Attitude", 1990; "Clippers", 1991; "The Colored Museum", 1991; "A Different World"; "The Cosby Show"; "The Late Show"; "Show time at the Apollo"; "Daddy's Girl", 1996; "Linc's", 1999-2000; "Sex Chronicles", 2008; "Glenn Martin DDS", 2009; "Gun Hill", 2011. Stage credits include: Death & the King's Horseman; Striver's Row; The Contract, Know Your History, 2008. **Honors/Awds:** AUDEL CO Awards for Excellence in Black Theater. 1983, 1984; Arkansas Black Hall of Fame, 1998; Custodian of the Cultural Consciousness Award, Chicago's ETA Creative Arts Ctr; Ellie Charles Artists Award, African Voices Mag; African Jewel Award, African Focus Inc, 2006. **Special Achievements:** One of the first comedians of color to perform at the Juste Pour Rire Comedy Festival in Montreal; writer/Creative Consultant on the ABC short lived series New Attitude a Castle Rock production. **Home Addr:** 853 Broadway Suite 1516, New York, NY 10003, **Home Phone:** (212)300-7086. **Business Addr:** Actress, Carson-Adler Agency Inc, 250 W 57 St Suite 2030, New York, NY 10107, **Business Phone:** (212)307-1882.

**STICKNEY, WILLIAM HOMER**
Writer. **Personal:** Born Apr 2, 1945, Nashville, TN; son of William Homer Sr and Nerissa Lee Brokenburr; children: William Homer III. **Educ:** Prairie View A&M Univ, BS, 1968. **Career:** Baylor Col Med, Houston, lab tech, 1968-69; US Dept Agri, Houston, livestock inspector, 1969; Prairie View A&M Univ, Prairie View, lab technician, 1969-70; Houston Chronicle, Houston, sportswriter (retired). **Orgs:** Tex Sportswriters Asn, 1974-; US Basketball Writers Asn, 1978-; US Track & Field Writers Asn, 1989-; US Boxing Writers Asn, 1988-; Heisman Trophy Award, Selection Com, 1992-. **Honors/Awds:** Asod Press Managing Ed Asn Tex, Honorable Mention Spot Sports Reporting, 1994. **Home Addr:** 2916 Meadowgrass Lane, Houston, TX 77082, **Home Phone:** (713)597-0494.

**STIELL, ESQ. PHELICIA D.**
Lawyer, government official. **Personal:** Born Jul 21, 1959, Chancellor, AL; daughter of Elnor Sconyers Hornsby; children: Justin & Brooke. **Educ:** Ala A&M Univ, BS, 1981; Miss State Univ, attended 1983; Univ W Fla, MPA, 1985; Fla State Univ Col Law, JD, 2000. **Career:** Thad Green Enterprises, career counr, 1981-82; Community Coun Serv, social worker, 1982-83; Air Force Systs Command, financial mgt specialist, 1985-91; Air Force Spec Opers Command, prog mgt analyst, 1991-; Fla Supreme Ct, legal intern, 1999; Parks & Crump LLC, assoc atty, 2000-01; Steill law firm, atty & counr law, 2001-. **Orgs:** Alpha Kappa Mu, Nat Hon Soc, 1979; secy, Delta Sigma Theta Serv Sorority, 1980-; Acad fel Miss State Univ, 1983; Am Soc Pub Adminr, 1984-86; Nat Coalition 100 Black Women, 1994-; chmn, Dem Black Caucus Fla conv, 1994-; DOD Exec Leadership Develop, 1995; Fla Bar Asn; Nat Bar Asn; Capital City justice Asn; Nat Congres Negro Women; Tallahassee Urban League; Sickle Cell Found; 100 Black Women Pesnacola Fla Chap. **Home Addr:** 2660 Old Bainbridge Rd Suite 507, Tallahassee, FL 32303, **Home Phone:** (850)536-1921. **Business Addr:** Attorney, Counselor at Law, The Steill Law Firm, 2920 Capital Med Blvd, Tallahassee, FL 32308, **Business Phone:** (850)877-3529.

**STILL, ARTHUR BARRY**
Football player. **Personal:** Born Dec 5, 1955, Camden, NJ; son of Gwendolyn; children: Luka. **Educ:** Univ Ky, BA, 1978. **Career:** Football player (retired); Kans City Chiefs, left defensive end, 1978-87; Buffalo Bills, left defensive end, 1988-89. **Honors/Awds:** All-America, 1977; All-Rookie, NFL, 1978; Second-team All-American Football Conference, 1979, 1982, 1984; First-team All-AFC, 1980, 1986; AP Second-team All-Pro selection, 1980, 1984; NEA, All-Pro selection, 1980; Professional Football Writers of America, All-Pro selection, 1980; Pro Football Weekly, All-Pro selection, 1980; Pro Bowl selection, 1980-82, 1984; Kans City Chiefs's Most Valuable Player, 1980, 1984; South Eastern Conference Player of the Year, Univ Ky.

**STILL, BRYAN ANDREI**
Football player, teacher. **Personal:** Born Jun 3, 1974, Newport News, VA. **Educ:** Va Polytech Inst & State Univ, BS, commun. **Career:** Football player (retied), teacher, gym coach; San Diego Chargers, wide receiver, 1996-99; Atlanta Falcons, wide receiver, 1999; Dallas Cowboys, 1999; Cosby High Sch, gym class, coach, teacher, currently. **Honors/Awds:** Most Valuable Person, Sugar Bowl, 1995. **Special Achievements:** TV Series: "ESPN Sunday Night Football" 1987; "NFL Monday Night Football" 1970. **Business Addr:** Teacher, Cosby

High School, 14300 Fox Club Pkwy, Midlothian, VA 23112, **Business Phone:** (804)639-8340.

### STILL, VALERIE
Basketball player, basketball coach, musician. **Personal:** Born May 14, 1961, Camden, NJ; daughter of Gwendolyn; married Robert Lock; children: Aaron. **Educ:** Univ Ky, BS, animal sci, 1979; Ohio State Univ, MS, African Am studies, 2007, PhD, sports humanities, 2010. **Career:** Basketball player, basketball coach (retired); Wash Mystics, Womens Nat Basketball Asn, player & asst coach; Prof caliber jazz, pop & concert pianist; Jones Cup competition, 1982; Columbus Quest, forward, 1996; Orlando Miracle, asst coach; Int Basketball Player Ital Prof League. Book: Still Alive on the Underground Railroad, 2012. **Orgs:** Founder & adv comt, Valerie Still Found; WNBA Player's Adv Coun, 2000; founder, Valerie Still Kids Improv Prog; charter mem, Am Basketball League Women; All-ABL Team; fel Women Nat Basketball Asn; fel Nat Socs Arts & Lett. **Home Addr:** , Powell, OH 43065. **Business Addr:** Founder, Valerie Still Foundation, PO Box 452, Powell, OH 43065, **Business Phone:** (614)675-1311.

### STINSON, ANDREA MARIA
Basketball player. **Personal:** Born Nov 25, 1967, Cornelius, NC. **Educ:** NC State Univ, attended 1991. **Career:** Basketball player (retired), basketball coach; Tarbes GB, france, 1992-94; Lavezzini Parma, Italy, 1994-95; Ahena Cesena, Italy, 1995-96; Thiene, Italy, 1996-97; Charlotte Sting, guard, 1997-2004; Galatasaray Cafe Crown Istanbul, Turkey, 1998-2001; Botassport Adana, Turkey, 2001-02; Detroit shock, guard, 2005; Cent Cabarrus High Sch, Concord, Nc, coach, 2007-09; Harding Univ High Sch, security assoc, currently; Newton-Conover High Sch, Lady Red Devils, head coach, 2013-. **Business Addr:** Security Associate, Harding University High School, 2001 Alleghany St, Charlotte, NC 28208, **Business Phone:** (980)343-6007.

### STINSON, CONSTANCE ROBINSON
Teacher, real estate agent. **Personal:** Born Windsor, ON; daughter of Theodore R Robinson and Eliza Smith Robinson; married Harold N Sr; children: Dr Harold N Jr. **Educ:** Barber Scotia Col, BS, 1949; Teachers Col, Columbia Univ, MA, 1962. **Career:** Burke County, Ga Sch Sys, teacher, 1940-67; Pearl High Sch, Nashville, Tenn, teacher, 1964-65; Eng Workshop, Southern Univ, Baton Rouge, La, dir NDEA, 1966; Elon Miller Realty, Tuscaloosa, Ala, realtor, 1971-94; Hamner Real Estate Inc, realtor, 1996-. **Orgs:** Ala Asn Realtors; Nat Asn Realtors; Womens Coun Realtors, 1972-; elder, Brown Mem Presbyt Church, Tuscaloosa, AL, 1972-; charter mem, life mem, Million Dollar Roundtable, Tuscaloosa, AL, 1979-; assembly mission bd, Presby Chrch, 1982-85; mem bd dir, Presbyt Apts Northport, AL, 1982-85; Church Vocations Ministry Unit, Presby Church, 1985-92; Tuscaloosa Asn Realtors. **Honors/Awds:** Salesperson of the Year, Tuscaloosa Bd Realtors, 1979; Salesperson of the Year, Tuscaloosa Asn Realtors, 1996. **Special Achievements:** First Afro-American Realtor in Tuscaloosa. **Home Addr:** 1313 Wakefield Dr, Tuscaloosa, AL 35405, **Home Phone:** (205)345-4717. **Business Addr:** Realtor, Hamner Real Estate Inc, 1412 Univ Blvd, Tuscaloosa, AL 35401-0636, **Business Phone:** (205)345-0654.

### STINSON, DONALD R., JR.
Artist, vice president (organization). **Personal:** Born Jan 29, 1929, Detroit, MI; married Clara Key. **Educ:** E La Jr Col, attended 1949; Wayne Univ, attended 1951; Compton Jr Col, attended 1962. **Career:** Golden St Life Ins Co, field rep, 1956-71; Vetinary Hosp Long Beach, practnurse, 1955-56; City Berkeley CA, rec dir, 1949-50; Nat Conf Artists, Nat Exec Bd, second vpres, currently. **Orgs:** Bd dir, Adv Med Diag Labs La; prog dir, bd mem, Willing Worker Ment Retarded La; exec bd, Simon Rodias Towers Watts La; bd mem, Stewart Grant AME Ch La; Out Home Care Tech Adv Comt La; bd mem, Hub City Optimist Club Compton; Art W Asn Inc; Black Art Coun; Calif Caretakers Org; owner, Billees Liquor; Nat Conf Artist; Watts Fest Art Show; Calif Black Craftsman Show; Black Artisits Am Calif Artist Coalition Los Angeles. **Honors/Awds:** Master Enamelist Award, MaDonna Fest; Barnsdall all City Show La; wonserval awards & hon, selling for Golden St Life Inst. **Home Addr:** 630 W 118th St, Los Angeles, CA 90044-4004, **Home Phone:** (323)757-6004. **Business Addr:** Vice President, National Conference of Artists, 361 W 125th St, New York, NY 10027, **Business Phone:** (212)410-7892.

### STINSON, DR. JOSEPH MCLESTER
Physician, educator. **Personal:** Born Jul 27, 1939, Hartwell, GA; son of James Isham and Julia Mae; married Elizabeth; children: Joseph Jr, Jeffrey & Julia. **Educ:** Paine Col, BS, 1960; Meharry Med Col, MD, 1964. **Career:** Hubbard Hosp, intern, 1965-66; Harvard Med Sch, res fel physiol, 1966-68; Meharry Med Col, Nashville, instr physiology, 1965-72, assoc prof to prof, 1972-76, pulmonary disease, dir, 1976-81, Dept Physiol, chmn, 1981-84, assoc prof med & physiol, 1984-; Vanderbilt Univ, fel pulmonary dis, 1974-76; Macy Fac, fel, 1974-77; Va hosp, consult pulmonary dis, 1976-. **Orgs:** Bd dir, Tenn Lung Asn, 1976-; Tenn Thoracic Soc, secy & treas, 1977-; pres, Tenn Thoracic Soc, 1985-87; bd dir, Paine Col Nat Alumni Asn, 1985-; Am Physiol Soc; Thoracic Soc Sec, St Luke Geriat Ctr; Tenn Heart Asn; Nashville Soc Internal Med. **Honors/Awds:** Pulmonary Academy Award, Nat Heart, Lung & Blood Inst, 1977-82; Alpha Omega Alpha; Memorial Award Excellence in Teaching, Meharry Medical College, 1999. **Special Achievements:** Numerous (24) Science Publications, 1969-76. **Home Addr:** 104 Amherst Way, Nashville, TN 37221, **Home Phone:** (615)373-8869. **Business Addr:** Pulmonologists, 2500 N State St, Jackson, MS 39216, **Business Phone:** (601)984-6603.

### STINSON, LINDA
Librarian. **Personal:** Born Sep 1, 1965, Boston, MA; daughter of James and Frances Laverne Johnston. **Educ:** Emmanuel Col, BA, 1987; Simmons Col, MLS, 1989. **Career:** Emmanuel Col, lib asst, 1983-86; Boston Pub Libr, librn, 1987-89; Rogers & Wells, New York, NY, ref librn, 1989-90; Forbes Mag, New York, info specialist, ref librn, 1991-98; GE Capital, corp librn, 1998-2000; LifeCare, mgr, info serv, 2000-02; Northrop Grumman Info Systs, mgr, strategic res & anal, 2006-11; Hewlett-Packard, mgr bus planning, 2011-. **Orgs:** Black Librarians Asn, 1989; Spec Libr Asn, 1989-. **Special Achievements:** Author: What Is This Sadness, American Poetry Anthology, 1987. **Home Addr:** 66-34 108 St Suite 6G, Forest Hills, NY 11375. **Business Addr:** Manager of Business Planning, Hewlett-Packard, 1331 Pa Ave NW, Washington, DC 20004, **Business Phone:** (202)637-6700.

### STITH, ANTOINETTE FREEMAN
Marketing executive. **Personal:** Born Aug 10, 1958, Atlanta, GA; daughter of William Anthony Freeman and Eva Mae Cobb Freman; children: Larkin Antonio & Skeeter. **Educ:** Newport News Shipbuilding Apprentice Sch, cert, 1981; Thomas Nelson Community Col, Hampton, VA, indust mgt trainee cert, 1982, AA, bus mgt, 1990. **Career:** Capitol Bankers Life, Norfolk, VA, mkt rep, 1990-; Reliance Standard Life, Norfolk, VA, mkt rep, 1990-; Financial Security Corp Am, Maitland, FL, mkt rep, 1991-; Newport News Shipbuilding, supvr. **Orgs:** Apprentice Alumni Asn, 1981-; pub rels officer, Coalition 100 Black Women, 1985-86; lic real estate agt, 1985-; pub rels officer, charter mem, Peninsula Chap Newport News, Hampton, VA; vpres, Assure Choices. **Honors/Awds:** Real Estate Sales Assoc of the Month, 5-Star Real Estate, 1987; Outstanding Am Award, Outstanding Young Am. **Home Addr:** 812 Seminole Dr, Suffolk, VA 23434-4131.

### STITH, BRYANT LAMONICA
Basketball coach, basketball player, executive. **Personal:** Born Dec 10, 1970, Emporia, VA; married Barbara; children: Brandan & B J. **Educ:** Univ Va, BA, sociol, 1992. **Career:** Basketball player (retired), coach, business owner; US Nat team, FIBA World Championship, 1990; Denver Nuggets, shooting guard, 1992-2000; Boston Celtics, shooting guard, 2000-01; Cleveland Cavaliers, shooting guard, 2001-02; Los Angeles Clippers, guard, 2002; Brunswick High Sch Bulldogs, athletic dir, head coach, 2006-13; Nat Asn Stock Car Auto Racing, mgr, currently; SCORE Inc, founder, currently; Old Dom Univ, men's asst basketball coach, 2013-. **Orgs:** Bd trustee, St Paul Col. **Honors/Awds:** Atlantic Coast Conference Men's Basketball Rookie of the Year, 1989; Bronze Medal, FIBA World Championship, US National team, bronze medal, 1990; Silver medal, Goodwill Games, 1990; Most Valuable Player Award, Nat Invitation Tournament, 1992; NIT champion, 1992; Virginia Sports Hall of Fame, 2007. **Home Phone:** (434)634-5856. **Business Addr:** Founder, SCORE Inc, 20927 Christanna Hwy, Lawrenceville, VA 23868-2533, **Business Phone:** (434)848-9449.

### STITH, DR. CHARLES RICHARD
Clergy, ambassador. **Personal:** Born Aug 26, 1949, St. Louis, MO; married Deborah; children: Percy & Mary. **Educ:** Baker Univ, BA, 1973; Interdenominational Theol Ctr, MDiv, 1975; Harvard Univ, ThM, 1977. **Career:** Wesley United Methodist Church, Boston, MA, minister, 1977-79; Boston Col, Dept Theol, lectr, 1979-87; Union United Methodist Church, sr minister, 1979-94; Orgn New Equality, pres, 1985-98; Int Rels, adj prof; Us Am United Repub Tanzania, ambassador, 1998-01; Harvard Univ Divinity Sch, vis lectr, 1992-94; Boston Univ, African presial Arch Res Ctr, dir, 2001-, Int Rels, vis prof, 2006-. **Orgs:** Lena Park Community Develop Corp, 1982-92; Incorporator, Boston Bank Com, 1984; bd mem, WCVB TV Ed Bd, 1984-98; Martin Luther King Ctr Nonviolent Social Chg, 1985-94; trustee, MLK Ctr Nonviolent Social Chg; dir, African Presidential Arch & Res Ctr; dir, United Way Mass Bay, 1986; Wang Ctr Performing Arts, 1992-98; Orgn a New Equality, founded, pres; People Am Way, 1992-98; adv bd, Fannie Mae, 1994-96; Fleet InCity Adv Coun, 1994-98; W Ins Co Inc, 1996-98; Boston Col & Harvard Divinity Sch; sr minister, hist Union United Methodist Church; bd mem, Fleet Incity Bank, 1995-98; Coun Am Ambassadors, 2001; Alliance Commonwealth, 2003; Int Finance Corps Global Bus Sch Network, 2005; The Un Asn Greater Boston, 2005. **Honors/Awds:** Outstanding Leadership Civil Rights, Anti-Defamation League, 1983; Racial Harmony Award, Black Educr Alliance Mass, 1984; Frederick Douglass Award, YMCA, 1985; Ingram Memorial Award, Boston Urban Bankers Forum, 1985; Paul Revere Bowl, City Boston, 1989; Hon Ddiv, Baker Univ, 1991; City of Boston, Paul Revere Bowl, 1994; Nat Adv Bd, FannieMae & Fleet InCity Bank; ed bd, WCVB-TV; bd, W Ins Inc; Community Service Award, Quincy Geneva Housing Develop Corp, 1995; hon doctorates from the University of South Carolina; Distinguished Alumni, Interdenominational Theol Ctr, 1999; Outstanding Leadership, Boston City Coun, 2000; Outstanding Leadership, House of Representatives Commonwealth Massachusetts, 2000; Citation Outstanding Leadership, State Senate Commonwealth Massachusetts, 2000; The Medal of Hope, Orgn New Equality, 2001; Leadership Citation, Minority Bus Develop Agency, 2001; Lee F Jackson Achievement Award, Urban League of Eastern Massachusetts, 2002; Int Citizen Award, World Boston, 2003; Morehouse Col, Inductee MLK Collegium Scholars, 2004; Doctor Humane Lett, Clark Atlanta Univ, 2006; Doctor Humane Lett, Univ Sc, 2006. **Special Achievements:** Author, Polical Religion, Abingdon Press, 1995. **Business Addr:** Director, Visiting Professor, Boston University, 141 Bay State Rd, Boston, MA 02215, **Business Phone:** (617)353-5452.

### STITH, HANA L.
Educator. **Personal:** Born Aug 25, 1928, Ft. Wayne, IN; daughter of Miles Bryant and Viola; married Harold; children: Robin S. **Educ:** Wilberforce Univ, attended 1947; St Francis Col, BS, 1960, MS, 1965; Purdue Univ, guid & coun. **Career:** Educator (retired), Executive; Ft Wayne Community Schs, teacher, 1960-96; African/African-Am Hist Soc, pres, 1999-; African/African-Am Hist Mus, cur & founder, 2001-. **Orgs:** Secy, Ft Wayne Redevelop Comn, 1974-86; Ft Wayne Metropolitan Human Rels, 1986-90; secy, Ft Wayne Bd Safety, 1990-96; chairperson, Afro-Am Entrepreneurs, 1990-98; Nat Asn Advan Colored People, 1998; co-founder, African/African Am Hist Soc, 1998; Fair Housing Group; Panel Am Women; Turner Chapel AME Church; dir, Comn Christian Educ. **Home Addr:** 5620 Gaywood Dr, Ft. Wayne, IN 46806, **Home Phone:** (219)744-9351. **Business Addr:** Curator, African/African-American Historical Museum, 436 E Douglas Ave, Ft. Wayne, IN 46802, **Business Phone:** (260)420-0765.

### STITH, DR. MELVIN THOMAS
Educator, school administrator. **Personal:** Born Aug 11, 1946, Jarratt, VA; married Patricia Lynch; children: Melvin Jr, Lori & William. **Educ:** Norfolk State Univ, BA, sociol, 1968; Syracuse Univ, Sch Martin J Whitman Mgt, MBA, 1973, PhD, mkt, 1978. **Career:** Syracuse Univ, dir, MBA prog, 1976-77, Martin J Whitman Sch Mgt, dean, 2005, dean emeritus, currently; Univ S Fla, Col Bus, asst dean & asst prof, 1977-82, assoc dean & assoc prof, 1982; Fla A&M Univ, Sch Bus & Indust, vis prof, 1982-85; Anheuser-Busch Inc, consult, 1982-83; Drackett Co, consult, 1984; Fla State Univ, assoc prof & chmn dept mkt, 1985-91, Col Bus, dean, 1991-2004, Jim Moran prof bus admin; Synovous Financial Corp, 1998-; Fireman's Fund Ins Co, consut; Kent Publ Co, consut; Flowers Foods Inc, independent dir, 2004; JM Family Enterprises, consult; Univ Wis, lectr; Grad Mgt Admis Coun, chair; Am Hosp Supply, consut; Glembys, consult. **Orgs:** Polemarch, Syracuse Alumni Kappa Alpha Psi Fraternity, 1976-77; polemarch, Tampa Alumni Kappa Alpha Psi Fraternity, 1981; bd dir, Tampa Br Urban League, 1981; consult, Mgt Horizons, 1984, Am Hosp Supply, 1985; Fla Coun Educ Mgt, 1988-; social environ comm, 21st Century Coun, Tallahassee; bd dir, Chamber Com, Tallahassee; Fla Black Bus Investment Bd; dir, Tallahassee State Bank, Tallahassee; dir, JM Enterprises Youth Automotive Prog, Deerfield Beach, FL; dir, Sprint & United Tel Fla, Altamonte Springs, FL; dir, chmn, Palmetto Hosp Trust Serv Ltd, Columbia, SC; Asn Advan Col Sch Bus; dir, Grad Mgt Admis Coun; dir, Fla Endowment Fund; dir, Beta Gamma Sigma Int Hon Soc; Sigma Rho Sigma Hon Soc; Phi Kappa Phi Hon Soc; bd dir, Esmor Corp, New York; dir, Correctional Serv Corp, 1994-; dir, Corp & Estate Anal Inc; dir, Rexall Sundown Inc, 1997-; dir, Keebler Foods Co, 1999-; dir, trustee, Synovus Financial Corp Leadership Inst; dir, Synovus Mem Audit Comt; bd dir, Flowers Food Corp; dir, Pathways Comn; dir, Everson Mus Art & Crouse Hosp boards; vpres, Crouse Hosp Found; Syracuse Stage bd. **Home Addr:** 2588 Noble Dr, Tallahassee, FL 32312-2818, **Home Phone:** (904)385-4701. **Business Addr:** Dean Emeritus, Syracuse University, 721 Univ Ave, Syracuse, NY 13244-2450, **Business Phone:** (315)443-3751.

### STITH-PROTHROW, DEBORAH
Public health official, physician, writer. **Personal:** Born Feb 6, 1954, Marshall, TX; daughter of Percy; married Charles Richard Stith; children: 2. **Educ:** Spelman Col, mathematics, 1975; Harvard Univ Med Sch, MD, 1979. **Career:** Boston Univ Sch Med, teacher; Boston City Hosp, staff physician; Adolescent Clin Harvard St Neighborhood Health Ctr, physician, 1982-87, 1990-96; Commonwealth Mass (Mass Dept Pub Health, app by Gov. Michael Dukakis), comnr pub health, 1987-; Harvard Univ Sch Pub Health, assoc dean fac develop & dir div pub health pract; Nat speaker media & pub forums violence prev. **Honors/Awds:** Secretary of Health and Human Services Exceptional Achievement in Public Service Award, 1989; American Psychiatric Association's Solomon Carter Fuller Award, 1998; World Health Day Award, 1993; ten honorary doctorates. **Special Achievements:** First female and youngest Commissioner of Public Health for the Commonwealth of Massachusetts; her "Violence Prevention Curriculum for Adolescents" is used throughout the United States; author of "Deadly Consequences: How Violence is Destroying Our Teenage Population and a Plan to Begin Solving the Problem" (1991); National Commission on Crime Control and Prevention (appointed by President Bill Clinton), 1995; co-author of "Murder is No Accident: Understanding and Preventing Youth Violence in America" (2003), "Sugar and Spice and No Longer Nice: How We Can Stop Girls' Violence" (2006), "Peacezone: A Program for Teaching Social Literacy, Grades 4-5: Student Manual" (2005), "Peacezon: A Program for Teaching Social Literacy, Grades 2-3: Student Manual" (2005), "Peacezon: A Program for Teaching Social Literacy, Grades K-1: Student Manual" (2005).

### STOCKARD, BETSY
Government official. **Personal:** children: 6. **Educ:** Ill State Univ, BS, spec educ, 1989; Richland Community Col, assoc degree, sociol, 1986. **Career:** Decatur Area Tech Acad, ged classroom instr, instr, coun mem; Decatur City Coun, councilwoman, 1997. **Orgs:** Founder, Cent Ill first violence-gang prev Agency, 1993; bd mem, Women Munic Govt; Crime & Pub Safety Comt Nat League Cities; N Jasper St Church Christ. **Honors/Awds:** Bronze Level Award for Leadership Training Skills, Nat League Cities, 2003; Woman of Excellence (Leona Bowman) Government & Politics Award, YMCA-YWCA, 2002; Illinois Woman of Achievement Award, Lt Governor Corrine Wood, 2002. **Special Achievements:** First African American woman to serve on council; Serves as one of 41 planners from across the United States for the 79th Congress of Cities & Exposition in Salt Lake City, Utah, 2002. **Home Addr:** 881 S Jefferson Dr, Decatur, IL 62521-4243. **Business Addr:** Councilwoman, Decatur City Council, 1 Gary K Anderson Plz, Decatur, IL 62523, **Business Phone:** (217)424-2804.

### STOCKMAN, DR. IDA J.
Educator. **Personal:** Born Sep 6, 1942, Sumner, MS; daughter of Samuel Jones and Angie Burton; married George; children: Demress Elise & Farah Nisa. **Educ:** Jackson State Univ, Jackson, MS, BS, 1962; Univ Iowa, Iowa City, IA, MA, 1965; Pa State Univ, State Col, PA, PhD, 1971. **Career:** Jackson State Univ, Jackson, Miss, instr, 1965-66; Rehab Ctr, Binghamton, NY, speech & lang pathologist, 1966-67; Howard Univ, Wash, DC, from asst prof to assoc prof, 1971-79; Kantonsspital St Gallen, St Gallen, Switz, res assoc, 1972-76; Ctr Appl Ling, Wash, DC, res assoc, 1980-82; Mich State Univ, E Lansing, Mich, assoc prof, 1983, Col Commun Arts & Sci, Dept Audiol & Speech Sci, prof, 2007, prof emer, currently; J Ling & Educ, ed bd, 1988-; Howard J Commun, Howard Univ, Wash, DC, ed bd, 1988-. **Orgs:** Phi Delta Kappa Prof Hon Soc, 1981; bd dir, Nat Asn Black Speech, Lang & Hearing, 1989-; bd dir, Mich Asn-Deaf, Speech & Hearing Serv, 1989-; educ stand bd & fel, Am Speech, Lang, Hearing Asn, 1990-; adv bd, Prompt Inst. **Home Addr:** 326 Northlawn, East Lansing, MI 48823, **Home Phone:** (517)351-2134. **Business Addr:** Professor Emeritus, Michigan State University, Dept Audiol & Speech Sci, East Lansing, MI 48824-1220, **Business Phone:** (517)353-6764.

### STOCKMAN, SHAWN PATRICK
Singer. **Personal:** Born Sep 26, 1972, Philadelphia, PA; son of Thurman Sanders and JoAnn; married Sharonda Jones; children: 2. **Career:** Boys II Men, founding member, currently; "Visions of a Sunset", singer; Albums with Boys II Men: Cooley highharmony, 1991; II, 1994; Evolution, 1997; Full Cir, 2002; Throwback Vol1, 2004; The Remedy, 2007; MoTown, 2007; Love, 2009; Soul Chem Proj, rec label, owner; recording studio, Ohio. TV series: "The Jacksons: An American Dream", 1992. Films: Blood and Bone, 2009; Getting Back to Zero, 2013. **Honors/Awds:** Grammy Award, 1992, 1995; 9 American Music Awards; 9 Soul Train Awards; 3 Billboard Awards; MOBO Award, 2011. **Business Addr:** Recording Artist, c/o J Records LLC, 745 5th Ave, New York, NY 10151, **Business Phone:** (646)840-5600.

**STOCKS, ELEANOR LOUISE**
Association executive, chief executive officer. **Personal:** Born May 10, 1943, Talladega, AL; daughter of Walter Locust and Cora Locust; married James A Jr; children: Kevin & Kim. **Educ:** Cent State Univ, BS, educ, 1965; Ohio Univ, MEd, 1971; Miami Univ, attended 1978. **Career:** Dayton Pub Sch, educr, 1966-69; Ohio Univ, adminr, 1970-72; Sinclair Comm Col, assoc prof, 1973-84; Ee & Jj Enterprises, pres, 1987-; DBA Cora's Inc, pres, 1987-; Govrs Minority Bus Coun, pres, chief exec officer, currently. **Orgs:** Vpres, Dayton Chap Jack & Jill Am, 1984; bd mem, Human Serv Adv Bd, 1985-; pres, Ohio Coun Urban League Exec, 1986-; Nat Urban League Educ Initiative Comm, 1986; Nat Asn Advan Colored People, 1986-87; pres, charter mem Black Women Prof Develop; vpres, Nat Bus League, Dayton Chap, 1988-; pres, chief exec officer, Springfield Urban League, 1985-. **Home Addr:** 4755 Fawnwood Rd, Dayton, OH 45429-1866, **Home Phone:** (937)293-6949. **Business Addr:** President, Chief Executive Officer, Gr Dayton African-Amerian Chamber Of Commerce, 184 Salem Ave, Dayton, OH 45406.

**STOCKTON, CARLTON A.**
Executive. **Personal:** Born Oct 19, 1940, Martinsville, VA; son of Alonza and Willie Sue; married Margaret C; children: Khary Alonza. **Educ:** St Paul's Col, BS, sociol, 1962; Atlanta Univ, MA, 1969; Harvard Univ, MPA, 1977. **Career:** Executive (retired); City Highland Pk, Mich, dir model cities, 1969-72; Health Cares Financing Admin, Div Qual Control, dir, 1972-81; Berkeley Dist, Supvr; MCI Worldcom, vpres external affairs, 1980-98. **Orgs:** Chmn bd, Black Human Resource Network, 1991-92; chmn bd, Northern Va Urban League, 1992-95; James City County Bd Supvrs; Immanuel Church Hill, warden, 1996-98; chair develop comm, CLG William & Mary Endowment Asn, 1997-98; life mem, Omega Psi Phi fraternity; chair & bd trustee, St Paul's Col; pres & bd dir, Two Rivers Country Club; chair, Nominating W&M Muscarelle Mus Art; bd dir, TowneBank Williamsburg. **Home Addr:** 3201 Fowler, PO Box 5332, Williamsburg, VA 23185-7506, **Home Phone:** (757)258-8727.

**STOCKTON, CLIFFORD, SR.** **See Obituaries Section.**

**STOCKTON, DMITRI**
Vice president (organization), president (organization), chief executive officer. **Educ:** NC Agr & Tech State Univ, BS, acct, 1986. **Career:** GE Capital, leadership assignments, 1987-2001; GE Capital Bank, chief exec officer, 2001-05; GE Consumer Finance, vpres, 2005-08; GE Capitals Global Banking unit, sr vpres, 2008-11; GE Asset Mgt, pres & chief exec officer, 2011-16; GE Co, spec advisor chmn & sr vpres, 2016-. **Orgs:** Bd GE Found; GE's Corp Exec Coun; Exec Leadership Coun; exec adv bd, NC A&T State Univ Sch Bus & Econs; bd drs, John Deere, 2015-. **Honors/Awds:** "Black Enterprise", 75 Most Powerful Blacks on Wall Street, 2011. **Business Addr:** GE Asset Management Inc, 1600 Summer St Suite 3, Stamford, CT 06905, **Business Phone:** (203)326-2300.

**STODGHILL, DR. RONALD**
School administrator. **Personal:** Born Dec 21, 1939, White Plains, NY; son of Joseph and Marian; children: Kimberly Denise Minter & Ronald III. **Educ:** Western Mich Univ, MA, 1961; Wayne State Univ, EdD, 1981. **Career:** City Detroit Dept Parks & Recreation, instr, 1961; Detroit Bd Educ, sci & eng teacher, 1963, biol teacher, 1963-65; Western Mich Univ Custer Job Corps, team leader, 1965-67; US Ind Custer Job Corp, maintenance sch adv adminr, 1967-68; MI-OH Regional Educ Lab, prog assoc, 1968-68; St Louis Pub Sch, assoc supt, 1976-79, dep supt, 1979-82, interim supt, 1982-83, dep supt instr, 1983-84. **Orgs:** Coordr comt, Mich-OH Regional Educ Lab, 1968-69; dir educ, New Detroit Inc, 1973-76, assoc dir, 1970-73, bd dir, 1977-79, chmn, 1977, exec coun mem, 1979; Am Asn Sch Adminr; Asn Supv & Curric Develop; Int Reading Asn; Nat Alliance Black Sch Educrs. **Honors/Awds:** Special Achiever, 1979; Commission Recognition Award, Coca-Cola Bottling Co, 1982. **Home Addr:** 25 Calverton Rd, St Louis, MO 63135, **Home Phone:** (660)238-7215.

**STOKES, BUNNY, JR.**
Banker. **Career:** Banker (retired); Citizen's Fed Savings Bank, Birmingham, Ala, chief exec officer, 2003; Citizens Trust Bank, pres, 2004; RealtySouth Relocation Serv Inc, sales assoc, jr realtor, currently. **Orgs:** Birmingham Asn Realtors; Ala Asn Realtors; Nat Asn Realtors. **Special Achievements:** Bank listed at 19 on Black Enterprise's list of top African American-owned banks, 1998. **Home Phone:** (205)244-0268. **Business Addr:** Sales Associate, RealtySouth, 2501 20th Pl S Suite 400, Birmingham, AL 35223-1744, **Business Phone:** (205)991-6565.

**STOKES, CAROLYN ASHE**
Educator. **Personal:** Born Nov 18, 1925, Philadelphia, PA; daughter of Charles Malcolm Ashe and Louisa Burrell; married Joseph H; children: Michael, Monica & Craig. **Educ:** Howard Univ, BA, lang & sociol, 1947; Univ Calif, Berkeley, grad educ, 1970; John F Kennedy Univ, BA, lang & sociol, MA, consciuosness & arts, 1983, leadership, 1987. **Career:** Scott Air Force Thrift Shop, WW II bookkeeper; Joseph H Stokes DDS, dental asst & off mgr; Citizen's Eisenhower Cong Comm, Wash, DC, dir pub rel res dept; Dept Com Immigration & Naturalization Serv/Office Price Admin Wash, officer; Media Group, script writer; Class Enterprises Art Consciousness & Well-Being Workshops, dir & founder; Conflict Resolution Panel, Contra Costa County, sr peer counr; Calif Sr Legis, org leadership consult, sr senator; CLAS Choices-Hologramatic Planning Consult, dir & founder; Mentoring Partners Alliance, pres, dir & consult; Nfld Herald, entertainment ed; Gibbs Mag, publ poet & weekly columnist. **Orgs:** Pres, Annual meeting chair, Ment Health Asn Contra Costa Co; mem-at-large, planning chair, Adv Coun Aging; bd mem, Ctr New Am; pub rels comm, Family Serv East Bay; trustee, Health Career assistance comm Alta Bates Hosp Asn; bd mem, Howard Thurman Educ Trust; life mem, Nat Coun Negro Women; vol AAUW Diablo Int Resource Ctr; consult, Coun Civic Unity Orinda Lafayette Moraga; leadership comm, United Way Opportunity West; West Co Women's Forum, diversity chair, Am Asn Univ Women; Entrepreneurial Skills Ctr; Inst Arts & Disabilities; bd mem, Helping Other People Evolve Inc; founder & dir, Diversity Dialogue Group, Mentoring Partners Alliance; Int Soc Poets; dir & founder, Bay Area Youth-On-The-Move; Women Vision Alliance; Am Postal Workers Union; Am Soc Indust Security. **Home Addr:** 90 Estates Dr, Orinda, CA 94563, **Home Phone:** (925)254-5191. **Business Addr:** Director, Manager & Teacher, Family Management education/ Mentoring Partners Alliance, 90 Estates Dr, Orinda, CA 94563, **Business Phone:** (925)253-9233.

**STOKES, CHRIS (CHRISTOPHER B STOKES)**
Movie director, manager, chief executive officer. **Personal:** Born Jan 1, 1966; son of Irene. **Career:** Franchise Boys, founder; Ultimate Group, chief exec officer, currently; mgr var artists incl IMX, B2k, Jhene, TG4, Gyrl, Tilt, Monteco, Sec NSol, Quindon & Mq3; Films: House Party 4: Down to Last Minute, 2001; Now That's What I Call Music, 2003; You Got Served, writer & dir, 2004; Somebody Help Me, producer, writer & dir, 2007; Cloning Made Easy, ed, cinematographer, 2007; Somebody Help Me 2, producer, writer & dir, 2010; Battlefield Am, producer, dir, 2012; 9mm, dir, 2012. **Business Addr:** Owner, Chief Executive Officer, The Ultimate Group, 848 N La Cienega Blvd, West Hollywood, CA 90069.

**STOKES, ERIC**
Executive, football player, scout. **Personal:** Born Dec 18, 1973, Hebron, NE; married Tisa; children: Erisa, Payton & Madison. **Educ:** Univ Nebr, BA, sociol. **Career:** Football player (retired), scout, executive; Seattle Sea hawks, defensive back, 1997-98, area scout, 2000-01, 2005-09, asst pro personnel, 2002-04, asst dir col scouting, 2010-11; Tampa Bay Buccaneers, dir col scouting, 2012-13; Miami Dolphins, asst gen mgr, 2014-; Carolina Panthers, area scout, currently. **Orgs:** KAP; Fitz Pollard Alliance; Nat Football League Players Asn. **Business Addr:** Assistant General Manager, Miami Dolphins, 7500 SW 30th St, Davie, WA 33314, **Business Phone:** (954)452-7000.

**STOKES, DR. GERALD VIRGIL**
Scientist, educator, research scientist. **Personal:** Born Mar 25, 1943, Chicago, IL; son of Henry and Louise Shelman; married Charlotte M Eubanks; children: Gordon K & Garrett K. **Educ:** Wilson Jr Col, AA, chem, 1965; Southern Ill Univ, BA, chem & microbiol, 1967; Univ Chicago, PhD, microbiol, 1973. **Career:** Univ Chicago Hosp, lab technician & researcher; Rabida C's Hosp Chicago; Univ Colo, 1973-76; Meharry Med Col, asst prof, 1976-78; George Wash Univ, Sch Med, asst prof, assoc prof, microbiol & trop med, 1976-. **Orgs:** Postdoctoral fel, Nat Insts Health, 1976; Asn Am Med Col, 1977-87; CSMM-chmn Am Soc Microbiol, 1984-; pres elect, Wash DC Br Am Soc Microbiol, 1986-87; rev comm, Minority Biomed Res Support, 1986-90; Am Soc Microbiol; bd scientific counsrs, Nat Ctr Infections Dis, CDC, Atlanta, 1993-96; Sigma Xi; Health & safety comt. **Home Addr:** 7222 Devereux Ct, Alexandria, VA 22310-4229, **Home Phone:** (703)922-6448. **Business Addr:** Associate Professor, George Washington University, 2300 Eye St NW, Washington, DC 20037, **Business Phone:** (202)994-2850.

**STOKES, HERB**
Executive. **Personal:** Born Newark, NJ; married Valeria. **Educ:** Rutgers State Univ NJ, Newark. **Career:** Affluencegroup LLC, founder & chief exec officer, 2000-; Aero Space Mgt Systs, officer strategic develop, 2002-; Promet Energy Partners LLC, vicepresident bus develop, 2008-; Enterprise Content Solutions, sr vpres enterprise mkt develop, 2013-; Burchell Upholstery, chief mkt officer, 2015-; Allied Van Lines, laborer, exec vpres qual mgt; Alliance Relocation Serv LLC, pres & chief exec officer, owner, currently. **Orgs:** Vice chair, Northwest Minority Bus Coun, 2002. **Business Addr:** Chief Executive Officer, Alliance Relocation Services LLC, 1327 W Wash Suite 106, Chicago, IL 60607, **Business Phone:** (312)491-9970.

**STOKES, JEREL JAMAL**
Football player, broadcaster. **Personal:** Born Oct 6, 1972, San Diego, CA; married Jill; children: Jayla. **Educ:** Univ Calif, Los Angeles, BS, sociol. **Career:** Football (retired), analyst; San Francisco 49ers, wide receiver, 1995-2002; Jacksonville Jaguars, wide receiver, 2003; New Eng Patriots, 2003; Espn, "J.J., Josh and Mouth", co-host; Fox Sports, analyst, currently. **Honors/Awds:** All-American, 1993; Pac-10 Offensive Player of the Year, 1993; Super Bowl champion, 2003. **Special Achievements:** Films: 1995 NFL Draft, 1995; 1997 NFC Championship Game, 1998; The Superstars, 1998; The Superstars, 1999. **Business Addr:** Analyst, Fox Sports Interactive Media LLC, 10201 W Pico Blvd, Los Angeles, CA 90035, **Business Phone:** (310)369-7069.

**STOKES, JOHNNIE MAE**
Educator, nutritionist. **Personal:** Born Oct 15, 1941, Tuscaloosa, AL; son of Lathan and Minnie Langford; married Julius; children: Salvatore & Zachary. **Educ:** Ohio State Univ, BS, educ, 1962; Portland State Univ, MS, educ, 1974. **Career:** Va Hosp Hines IL, clin dietitian, 1963-65; Bronx VA Hosp, dietetic intrnshp, 1963; Chicago Bd Health, mem & nutritionist, 1966-67; Va Hosp Vancouver WA, clin dietitian, 1967-69; Good Samrtn Hosp & Med Ctr, clin dietitian, 1971-75; Mt Hood Community Col, coun instr. **Orgs:** Vpres, Portland Chap Links Inc, 1979-81; Adv bd mem, E Multnomah Co Leag Women Voters; Am & OR Dietetic Asn; Ore Asn Sch Couns; Alpha Kappa Alpha Sor. **Honors/Awds:** Outstanding Young Women of America, 1975; Home ec hon Phi Upsilon Omericon; educ hon Phi Lambda Theta. **Home Addr:** 14219 NE Beech St, Portland, OR 97230-3636, **Home Phone:** (503)255-1957.

**STOKES, JULIE ELENA**
Educator. **Educ:** Chaffey Community Col, AA, correctional sci, 1989; Calif State Univ, BA, psychol, 1991; Univ Calif, Riverside, MA, psychol, 1993, PhD, psychol, 1994. **Career:** Univ Calif, Riverside, res asst, 1990 & 1991; Orange County, grad fel, 1991-92, Dept Educ ACCESS Prog Safe Schs Evaluator, 2000-; Univ Calif, grad fel, 1991-92, Riverside, lectr African-Am Families Child Develop, 1993-94, African-Am Family Res Coordr, site supvr, 1993-94, lectr, Study African Am Women, 1995; Univ Calif, Riverside, res asst, 1993; Calif State Dept Educ, Reader Talent Search Res Proposals, 1993; Calif State Graduation Equivalency Dipl, Adult Literacy Prog, part-time vol fac, 1993; Calif State Univ, Long Beach, Taught Black Family, part-time fac, 1994; Calif State Univ, Taught Race & Racism, Social Sci, Taught Introd to Psychol, Taught Study African Am Women & Taught Life Span Develop, Psychol, 1995; San Bernardino, lectr, Life Span Develop, part-time fac, 1933, 1994 & 1995; Calif State Univ, Long Beach, lectr African-Am Families Child Develop, 1994; Calif State Univ, Long Beach, lectr African-Am Families Child Develop, 1994; San Bernardino, lectr, Life Span Develop, 1994 & 1995; CA State Univ, Fullerton, lect, Dept Psychol, asst prof psychol, 1995-2003, asst prof, taught intro to afro-ethnic studies, hist racism, intracultural socialization, psychol african americans, study black family, learning & memory, 1997-, assoc prof psychol, 2003-, Dept Afro-Ethnic studies, chair, currently; Partnership Responsible Parenting Teen Preg Prog, proj dir, 1996-97, African An Family Res Proj, res dir, 1993-95; Social Sci Res Ctr, Fullerton, res assoc, 1997-; Bel Community Outreach & Human Develop, proj evaluator, 1997-; 100 Black Men, Passport to Future, proj evaluator, 1997-; San Bernardino County Ment Health, comnr, 1998-; Charles Drew Med Ctr OASIS Clin, Spec Projs Nat Significance Proj Evaluator, 2000-03. **Orgs:** Western Psychol Asn, 1991-; Asn Black Psychologists, 1992-; comt mem, Univ Calif, Riverside, Affirmative Action Educ Comt, 1993; comt mem, Univ Calif, Riverside, Grad Coun, 1993; comt mem, Univ Calif, Riverside, Sexual Harassment Comt, 1993; comt mem, Univ Calif, Riverside, Campus Bd Rev, 1993; Chair, Grad Stud Asn Affirmative Action, 1993; comt mem, Univ Calif, Riverside, Chancellor's Adv Acquired Immune Deficiency Syndrome Policy Comt, 1993; Am Evaluators Asn; Am Psychol Asn, 1995-; Am Psychol Soc, 1995-; dir coun, church adminr, exec comt mem, Eccelesia Christian Fel Church; adv bd mem, Sci Journals Int; exec bd mem, Calif State Univ; comt mem, Human Rels Tasks Force, 1996; comt mem, African Am Town Hall, 1997. **Business Addr:** Professor, University of California, H-324F 800 N State Col Blvd KHS 115B, Fullerton, CA 92831, **Business Phone:** (657)278-3485.

**STOKES, DR. LILLIAN GATLIN**
Educator, nurse. **Personal:** Born Feb 18, 1942, Greenville, NC; married Robert; children: Everett & Robyn. **Educ:** Kate Bitting Reynolds Sch Nursing, dipl, 1963; NC Cent Univ, BS, 1966; Ind Univ, MSc, 1969, PhD, RN, FAAN, educ psychol, 1998. **Career:** Norfolk Comm Hosp, staff nurse, 1963-64; Silver Cross Hosp, staff nurse, 1966-67; Purdue Univ, asst prof nursing, 1969-72; Nat Inst Health, peer rev spec proj grants, 1977; Ind Univ, Sch Nursing, assoc prof nusing, assoc prof emer, 1972-, dir diversity & enrichment, 1996-. **Orgs:** Am Nurs Asn; Ind St Nurse Asn; Nat Leag Nurs; chairperson, Aud Nurs Com Home Care Agency Gr Indianapolis, 1974-76; bd dir, Ind Univ Sch Nurs Alumni Asn, 1973-; pres, Chi Eta Phi Sor; Sigma Theta Tau; Alpha Kappa Alpha Sor; Women's Aux Indianapolis Dist Dent Soc; Jack & Jill Am Inc, Coalition 100 Black Women; Links Inc; exec coun, Ind Univ Alumni Assoc; bd dir, Girls Clubs Greater Indianapolis; fel Am Acad Nursing, 2001; vpres, 2003-05, pres, Chi Eta Phi Sorority, 2005-; Ind Citizens League Nurs; Midwest Nurs Res Soc. **Honors/Awds:** Lucille Petry Leone Award, Nat League Nurse, 1975; Special Achievement Award, Chi Eta Phi Sor, 1975; Lillian G Stokes Award, Ind Univ Sch Nursing Alumni Assoc, 1980; Outstanding Service Award, Jack & Jill Am Inc; Distinguished Service Award, Girls Clubs Greater Indianapolis Inc; Madame C J Walker Award, 1996; Distinguished Hoosier, Governor Ind, 1998; Mary Mahoney Award, Am Nurses Asn, 2000; Distinguished Alumni Award, NC State Univ, 2001; fel Am Acad Nurs, 2001; Joseph T Taylor Award for Excellence in Diversity, 2002; Distinguished Service Award, Annual Black Chamber of Commerce, 2006. **Special Achievements:** Co-author "Adult & Child Care a Client Approach to Nursing" CV Mosby Co, 1973, 2nd ed 1977; co-author "Medical-Surgical Nursing, Common Problems of Adults and Children Across the Life Span," 1983, second edition, 1987. **Home Addr:** 5310 Olympia Dr, Indianapolis, IN 46228-2241, **Home Phone:** (317)257-2607. **Business Addr:** Associate Professor Emerita, Director of Diversity & Enrichment, Indiana University, 600 Barnhill Dr, Indianapolis, IN 46202-5107, **Business Phone:** (317)274-2806.

**STOKES, PATRICK**
Association executive. **Educ:** Western Md Col, BA, biol, 1991; Univ Pa, MBA, entrepreneurial & strategic mgt, 2000. **Career:** McEnroe Voice & Data, sr acct mgr, 1992-96; McEnroe Voice & Data, nat acct mgr, 1996-98; Sprint, intern, broadband local networks, 1999, sr mgr, broadband wireless group, 2000-01, dir, PCS, Indirect Sales Philadelphia, 2001-02, dir sales & distrib, 2002; Verizon Wireless, dir indirect retail distrib, 2002-04, dir strategic alliances, 2004-06, vpres bus distrib, 2006-08. vpres mkt & distrib, 2008-09; Brightstar Corp, US, pres & chief operating officer, 2009-11; Sage Bros Holdings, pres, 2011-14; Tech Data, US, head, mobile solutions, sr vpres, mobile solutions & retail, 2015-.

**STOKES, RUEBEN MARTINE**
Executive. **Personal:** Born Mar 27, 1957, Los Angeles, CA; son of Bailey L (deceased) and Alma M; married Alana Maria Fullove; children: Rueben Martine II & Blair Elizabeth. **Educ:** Dartmouth Col, BA, 1979; Nat Univ, attended 1987; Univ NC, Exec Educ Cert, advan mkt; Univ Pa, Exec Educ, Cert Sales Force Mgt. **Career:** Airborne Express, sales rep, 1981-82; N Am Van Lines Inc, territory sales mgr, 1982-85; Advan Traffic Serv Inc, mkt mgr, 1985-87; Mayflower Transit Inc, dist sales vpres, 1987-91; Allied Van Lines, nat sales dir, 1991-94; Ryder Move Mgt, nat sales dir, 1994-96; ADT Security Serv Inc, dir diversity & community affairs, 1999, dir multicultural mkt, 2003-04, exec dir diversity, 2004-07; Tyco Int, global dir diversity, 1999-2003; Terex Corp, dir, global diversity & inclusion, 2007-10; Ryder Syst Inc, group dir, 2010-13, advan fuels-dir bus develop, 2013-. **Orgs:** Dartmouth Col Alumni Asn; Theta Delta Chi Frat Inc; bd dir, Nat Asn Hisp Real Estate Professionals; 100 Black Men Am. **Home Addr:** 811 Heritage Dr, Weston, FL 33326-4540, **Home Phone:** (305)389-9166. **Business Addr:** Group Director, Ryder System Inc, 11690 NW 105th St, Miami, FL 33178, **Business Phone:** (305)500-3726.

**STOKES, SHEREITTE CHARLES, III**
Vice president (organization), school administrator. **Personal:** Born Apr 9, 1953, Philadelphia, PA; son of Eleanor Hasben and Shereitte C. **Educ:** Wilberforce Univ, BA, polit sci & econs, 1974; Univ Phoenix, MEd, adult educ & distance learning, 2004. **Career:** Omega Psi Phi Fraternity Inc, staff, 1971; AT&T, acct exec & indust consult, 1981-87; New Covenant Church Philadelphia, dir stewardship, 1987-90; Mac Intyre Assoc, campaign dir, 1989-92; Philadelphia Opportunities Industrialization Ctr, develop dir, 1993-94; Univ Toledo, develop officer, 1995-96; Rutgers Univ, assoc dir corp & found rels, 1996-99; Spelman Col, assoc vpres, 1999-2003; Tuskegee Univ, vpres, univ advan, 2004-06; Tenn State Univ, vpres, univ rels & develop, 2006-11; SC Stokes

Consults, prin, 2011-; St Xavier Univ, vpres, 2014-. **Orgs:** Coun Advan & Support Educ, 1995-; bd trustee, NJ Ctr Outreach & Serv Autistic Community, 1997-99; NJ chap bd mem, Nat Soc Fund Raising Execs, 1998-99; dir, consult, Advan Cert Fundraising Exec Bd, 2010-14; exec dir, Cradleboard Found, 2012-13; Omega Psi Phi Fraternity. **Home Addr:** 327 2nd Ave, Decatur, GA 30030. **Business Addr:** Vice President for University Advancement, Saint Xavier University, 3700 W 103rd St, Chicago, IL 60655, **Business Phone:** (773)298-3315.

### STONE, ANGIE (ANGELA LAVERNE BROWN)
Songwriter, singer, lyricist. **Personal:** Born Dec 18, 1961, Columbia, SC; married D Angelo; children: Michael; married Lil Rodney Cee; children: Michael & Diamond. **Career:** Com rec artist, 1980; songwriter, 1990; Albums of Sequence: The Sequence, 1982; Vertical Hold, 1992; solo album: Just A Pimp; Black Diamond, 1999; Mahogany Soul, 2001; Stone Love, 2004; Stone Hits: The Very Best Of Angie Stone, 2005; The Art of Love & War, 2007; Unexpected, 2009. Films: The Hot Chick, 2002; The Fighting Temptations, 2003; Caught on Tape, 2008; Pastor Brown, 2009. TV: "Moesha", 2000; "Girlfriends", 2002; One on One, 2004; Ellen: The Ellen DeGeneres Show, 2007; Jimmy Kimmel Live, 2007; Later with Jools Holland, 2007; Lincoln Heights, 2008. Writer: Bamboozled, 2000; Dr Dolittle 2, 2001; Blue Crush, 2002; Brown Sugar, 2002; The Fighting Temptations, 2003. **Business Addr:** Singer, Arista Recs, 888 7th Ave, New York, NY 10106, **Business Phone:** (212)489-7400.

### STONE, AUBRY L.
President (organization), chief executive officer, teacher. **Personal:** married Evelyn; children: 4. **Career:** Capitol Area Develop Authority, state comnr econ develop, currently; Calif Black Chamber Com, pres & chief exec officer, currently; Calif Black Chamber Found, dir, currently. **Orgs:** Bd mem, Nat Asn Advan Colored People; bd dir, US Black Chamber Com, bd chair & co-founder, currently; bd mem, Metro Chamber Com; bd mem, Cal Trans Small Bus Roundtable; Mayors Econ Develop Coun; City Sacramentos Community Serv Comt; Dist Attorneys Citizen Cabinet; bd mem, Sacramento Black Chamber Com; bd mem, Channel 10 Community Serv Comt; bd dir, Calif Black Chamber Com, currently. **Special Achievements:** African American owned and operated low powered radio station (97.7 KDEE FM), Sacramento Region. **Business Addr:** President, Chief Executvte Officer, California Black Chamber of Commerce, 1600 Sacramento Inn Way Suite 232, Sacramento, CA 95815, **Business Phone:** (916)463-0177.

### STONE, DWIGHT
Football player, police officer. **Personal:** Born Jan 28, 1964, Florala, AL; married Jennifer; children: Ciara, Cailin & Celena. **Educ:** Marion Mil Inst, social work, 1984; Mid Tenn State Univ, BS, social psychol, 1987. **Career:** Football player (retired), police officer; Pittsburgh Steelers, wide receiver, 1987-95; Carolina Panthers, 1995-98; New York Jets, 1999-2001; Charlotte Mecklenburg Police Dept, police officer, 2002-. **Home Addr:** 1128 Deep Hollow Ct, Waxhaw, NC 28173-6759. **Business Addr:** Police Officer, Charlotte Mecklenburg Police Department, 3500 Latrobe Dr, Charlotte, NC 28211, **Business Phone:** (704)943-2400.

### STONE, HAROLD ANTHONY
Marketing executive. **Personal:** Born Aug 9, 1949, New Bedford, MA; married Elizabeth G Bates. **Educ:** Univ Mass, Amherst, BBA, 1973; Clark Atlanta Univ, MBA, mkt, 1978. **Career:** Maxwell House Div & Gen Foods, sales rep, 1973-76; Coca-Cola USA Cincinnati, control & Mid e area spl mkt mgr, 1976; UniWorld Group Inc, acct dir, 2003-09; H. Stone Consult, consult, 2009-. **Orgs:** Nat Asn Mkt Develop; Nat Asn Advan Colored People; Oper PUSH Inc. **Home Addr:** 7223 Autumn Hill Dr Apt 38, West Bloomfield, MI 48323, **Home Phone:** (248)709-6239.

### STONE, DR. JOHN S.
Obstetrician, gynecologist. **Personal:** Born Jul 16, 1930, Tampa, FL; son of Edward W; married Gertrude Jane Holliday; children: Faith, Enid Griner & John. **Educ:** Talladega Col, BS, 1951; Meharry Med Col, MD, 1956; Univ Tex St Joseph Hosp, attended 1972. **Career:** Houston Med Forum, pres, 1986-88; pvt pract obstetrician & gynecologist. **Orgs:** Bd mem, Cent Life Ins Co Fla, 1973-87; founder & pres, St Elizabeth Hosp Houston Found, 1974-78; United Fund Agency Opers Comm, 1975; Am Med Asn; Tex Med Asn; Harris County Med Soc; bd mem, Cath Charities, Cent Life Ins Co Fla, 1978-87; pres med staff, Riverside Gen Hosp, 1981-82; bd mem, Cath Charities, 1983-87; Houston Med Forum, 1986-87; Am Med Asn; Lone State State Med Asn; Harris County Med Soc; Houston Acad med, Nu Boule; dir, St Mary Purification Cath Church Found. **Home Addr:** 3402 Binz St, Houston, TX 77004. **Business Addr:** Physician, 5511 Austin St Suite B, Houston, TX 77004-7161, **Business Phone:** (713)529-4281.

### STONE, REESE J.
Executive, executive director. **Personal:** Born Feb 26, 1945, Dublin, GA; son of Reese J Sr and Mildred Andrews; married Brenda Yearwood; children: Meris E. **Educ:** Tenn State Univ, Nashville, TN, BS, polit sci, 1966; Howard Univ, Wash, DC, MPA, pub admin, 1971. **Career:** Howard Univ, assoc dir stud affairs, 1970-72; Nat Educ Asn, communs coord, 1972-79; Metrop Transit Authority, dir pub affairs, 1979-82; Planned Parenthood Fed Am, dir communs, 1985-87; Philip Morris Co Inc, mgr corp communs, 1989-93; Sandstone Assoc, 1991-; LLT Int Advert, vpres bus develop; Access LLC, pricipal, 2003-10; My Shuttle LLC, managing partner, 2010-. **Orgs:** Vpres, prin, Com Real Estate-Sandstone Assoc Inc, Newark NJ, 1981-; mentor, Columbia Univ Mentor Prog, 1987-89; bd mem, Hisp Media Ctr, 1988-; Pub Affairs Coun, 1988-; Nat Press Club; Overseas Press Club; Nat Med Asn, dir external affairs, 1999-2007; 100 Black Men. **Home Addr:** 57 Nishuane Rd, Montclair, NJ 07042. **Business Addr:** Managing Partner, My Shuttle LLC, Montclair, NJ, **Business Phone:** (973)744-8482.

### STONE, RONALD CHRISTOPHER
Football player, football coach. **Personal:** Born Jul 20, 1971, Boston, MA; married Roxane; children: Ronnie & Ronna. **Educ:** Boston Col. **Career:** Football player (retired), coach; Dallas Cowboys, 1994, guard, 1995; New York Giants, right guard, 1996-2001; San Francisco 49ers, right guard, 2002-03; Oakland Raiders, right guard, 2004-05; Calif Prep Power Valley Christian High Sch, offensive line coach, currently. **Honors/Awds:** Pro Bowl, 2000, 20001, 2002; Super Bowl Champion XXVIII, XXX. **Business Addr:** Offensive Line Coach, Valley Christian High School, 100 Skyway Dr Suite 110, San Jose, CA 95111, **Business Phone:** (408)513-2400.

### STONE, WILLIAM T.
Lawyer, executive, judge. **Personal:** Born Jan 8, 1931, Washington, DC; son of Thomas and Beulah; married Sara Cumber; children: William T Jr, Jacquelyn E, Michael R & Christopher D. **Educ:** Cent State Univ, BS, 1953; New Eng Inst Anat, attended 1956; Am Univ, JD, 1961. **Career:** Law Pract, 1962-2000; Williamsburg City & James City Co Cts, substitute judge, 1968-2000; Whiting's Funeral Home, owner; Stone & Assocs, mgr & atty, 2000-. **Orgs:** Old Dom, PA, Am, Williamsburg & Peninsula Bar Asns; Va Trial Lawyers Asn; Nat Funeral Dirs & Morticians Asn; Va Mortician's Asn; First Baptist Ch; Omega Psi Phi. **Home Addr:** 305 Pocahontas St, Williamsburg, VA 23185-4710, **Home Phone:** (757)229-3324. **Business Addr:** Attorney, Manager, Stone & Associates, PO Box HB, Williamsburg, VA 23187-3606, **Business Phone:** (757)877-3601.

### STOREY, ROBERT D.
Businessperson, chairperson. **Personal:** Born Mar 28, 1936, Tuskegee, AL; married Juanita Kendrick Cohen; children: Charles, Christopher & Rebecca. **Educ:** Harvard Univ, AB, 1958; Case Western Res Univ, JD, 1964; Tri-State Univ, LHD, 2000. **Career:** Partner (retired), director; E Ohio Gas Co, atty, 1964-66; Burke Haber & Berick, partner, 1967-90; GTE Corp, dir, 1985-2000; McDonald, Hopkins Burke & Haber Co, partner, 1990-92; Thompson, Hine & Flory, partner, 1993; May Dept Stores Co, St Louis Mo, dir; Verizon New Eng Inc, dir, 2000-; Verizon New York Inc. dir, 2000-; Procter & Gamble, Cincinnati, Ohio, chmn, dir, 1998-2006; Verizon Commun Inc, dir, 2000-08. **Orgs:** City Planning Comn Cleveland, 1966-74; asst dir, Legal Aid Soc, 1966-67; trustee, Phillips Exeter Acad, 1969-83-; trustee, Cleveland St Univ, 1971-80, chmn, 1979-80; trustee, Univ Sch, 1974-99; vpres, Asn Harvard Alumni, 1974-80; trustee, Great Lakes Sci Ctr; trustee, overseer, Harvard Univ, 1980-86; trustee, Univ Hosp Cleveland, 1982-90; trustee, Kresge Found, Troy Mich; trustee, George Gund Found, Cleveland Ohio; trustee, Spelman Col; trustee emer, Case Western Res Univ, currently; Pub Policy Comt, Verizon New Eng Inc; Corp Governance & Policy Comt, Verizon Commun Inc, 2000-; trustee, Cleveland State Univ; trustee, Overseer Harvard Univ. **Honors/Awds:** Top 10 Young Men of the Year, Cleveland Jr COC, 1967; Chief Marshal, 25th Reunion, Harvard Class, 1958; Charles Flint Kellogg Award, ASN Episcopal Col, 1984. **Home Addr:** 2385 Coventry Rd, Cleveland Heights, OH 44118-4074, **Home Phone:** (216)721-4391. **Business Addr:** Director, Verizon Communications Inc, 140 W St Fl 29, New York, NY 10007, **Business Phone:** (212)395-1000.

### STORM, QUIET. See HARRIS, RAYMONT LESHAWN.

### STORY, CHARLES IRVIN
Executive, president (organization). **Personal:** Born Aug 10, 1954, Richmond, VA; son of John R and Geraldine; married Deborah Ellis; children: Lachelle. **Educ:** Fisk Univ, BA, psychol & mgt, 1976; Univ Tenn, MPA, 1978. **Career:** Fisk Univ, mgt analyst, 1976-77, personnel dir, 1977-78; INROADS, managing dir, 1978-81, reg dir, 1982, vpres, 1983, exec vpres, 1983-87, pres & chief exec officer, 1993-2005; Dept Econ & Community Develop, State TN, asst comnr, 1987-88; First Am Nat Bank, vpres & dir community develop, 1989-91, vpres opers, 1991-92; Exec Coaching Solutions Group Inc, pres, 2005-. **Orgs:** Alumni trustee, Fisk Univ, 1976-79; Leadership Nashville, 1981-82; bd mem, Sch Bus TN State Univ, 1982-83; bd mem, Rochelle Training & Rehab Ctr, 1982-83; chmn, Strategic Planning Comn Child Guid Ctr, 1984-; United Way Disabled Serv Panel, 1984-; vice chmn, 1987, Allocation Comn, Way Mid Tenn, 1989-93; bd mem, Nashville Bus Incubation Ctr, 1989-; bd mem, Goodwill Mid Tenn, 1989-, vice chmn, 1992; secy, bd mem, Ctr Non-Profit Mgt, 1990-; bd mem, Nashville Area Red Cross, 1990-; bd mem, Watkins Inst, 1990-; adv bd, AmSouth Bank, 1993-; bd dir, Briggs & Stratton Corp, 1994-; adv bd, Hanigan Consult Group, 1996-; bd dirs, ChoicePoint Inc, 1997-08; adv bd dirs, Regions Bank. **Honors/Awds:** Ranked One, Col Grad Class, Fisk Univ, 1976; Outstanding Young Man of America, US Jaycees, 1978; Alumni Appreciation Award, INROADS, 1983; Distinguished Service Award, INROADS, 1984. **Home Addr:** 5505 Saddlewood Lane, Brentwood, TN 37027-4795, **Home Phone:** (615)370-8521. **Business Addr:** President, Executive Coaching Solutions Group Inc, 5543 Edmondson Pke Suite 206, Nashville, TN 37211, **Business Phone:** (615)781-4278.

### STORY, OTIS L., SR.
Executive director, hospital administrator. **Personal:** Born Nov 17, 1951, Anniston, AL; son of Tom Elbert and Martha Lou Wilson; married Ava D McNair; children: Jasmyn E, Avana Leigh & Prince James Elbert. **Educ:** Cornell Univ, Ithaca, NY, BA, social sci, 1976; Univ Chicago, Chicago, IL, MA, 1977; Univ Ala, Birmingham, AL, MA, HH, 1981. **Career:** Ochsner Found Hosp, New Orleans, La, admin asst dir, 1978-85; Univ Ala, Birmingham Hosp, admin, 1985-90; Univ Med & Dent NJ, adminr & chief operating officer, 1990-96; Health Alliance Greater Cincinnati, Cincinnati, Univ Hosp Inc, assoc exec officer, 1996-98; Quorum Health Resources, Mem Health Univ Med Ctr, Savannah, Ga, exec vpres & chief operating officer, 1998-2001; Shands Jacksonville Med Ctr, interim pres, chief exec officer, 2001; Cooper Health Syst, vpres opers, consult 2003-04; Huron Consult Serv LLC, exec dir, 2004; St Vincent Cath Med Ctr, St John's Queens Hosp, NY, exec dir, 2004-07; Grady Health Syst, pres & chief exec officer, 2007-08; W Penn Allegheny Health Syst, vpres, 2008-11; Cooper Green Mercy Health Serv, chief restructuring officer, 2012-13; Azul Health Group, prin, 2011-13. **Orgs:** Nat Asn Health Care Exec, 1982-; Am Col Health Care Execs, 1982-; bd dir, N Jersey Blood Ctr; sr fel Nat Pub Health & Hosp Inst, 1995; Savannah On-Stage; Coastal Empire Coun; Boy Scouts Am; Univ Ala, Grad prog Health Admin, Alumni Asn; bd dir, Shands Jacksonville; Azul Health Group, partner. **Home Addr:** 4 Wild Thistle Lane, Savannah, GA 31406, **Home Phone:** (912)354-8987. **Business Addr:** Principal, Azul Health Group, 13245 Atlantic Blvd Suite 4-263, Jacksonville, FL 32225.

### STORY, TIMOTHY KEVIN (TIM STORY)
Movie director, movie producer. **Personal:** Born Mar 13, 1970, Los Angeles, CA; married Vicky Mara; children: 3. **Educ:** Univ SC, Sch Cinematic Arts, cinema prod, 1991. **Career:** Univ Southern Calif; Dir, producer, ed & writer; Story Co, founder, 1996-. Films: One of Us Tripped, dir & ed, 1997; The Firing Squad, dir, writer & co-ed, 1999; Urban Menace, writer, 1999; Barbershop, dir, 2002; Taxi, dir, 2004; Fantastic Four, dir, 2005; Fantastic Four: Rise Silver Surfer, dir, 2007; First Sunday, producer, 2008; Hurricane Season, 2009; Think Like a Man, 2012; The Signal, 2013; Ride Along, 2014; Think Like a Man Too, 2014. TV Ser: "12th Man", exec producer, 2006; "Standoff", producer, 2006-07; "CSI: Miami", 2010; "Supah Ninjas", 2011. **Business Addr:** Director, William Morris Agency, 151 El Camino Dr, Beverly Hills, CA 90212, **Business Phone:** (310)274-7451.

### STOTTS, REV. DR. VALMON D., SR.
Clergy. **Personal:** Born Oct 24, 1925, Detroit, MI; married Ethel Jean; children: Valmon Jr, Angela & Valarie. **Educ:** Detroit Bible Col, attended 1957; Bible Sch Community Col, THB, 1958; William Tyndale Col, BA, theol; Wayne St Univ, MA, educ; Urban Bible Col, Hon DDiv; Int Minister Urban Soc, Hon DDiv; Birmingham Bible Col, Hon DDiv. **Career:** Unity Baptist Church, pastor, 1963-. **Orgs:** Counr Billy Graham Campaign, 1954; bd dir, Opportunity Ind Corp; Big Bros Am; pres, Sherrill Sch PTA; chaplain, Detroit Gen Hosp, 1969-70; second vpres, Coun Baptist Pastors; secy, St Cong Evangelism; youth leader, inst Abouts; Metrop Baptist Dist Asn; Unity Missionary Baptist Church; pres, Coun Baptist Pastors, 1984-86; bd mem, State Mich Marriage Bd, 1984. **Home Addr:** 22433 Outer Dr, Dearborn, MI 48124-4200, **Home Phone:** (313)722-4348. **Business Addr:** Pastor, Unity Baptist Church, 7500 Tireman Rev Valmon D Stotts Ave, Detroit, MI 48204, **Business Phone:** (313)933-9799.

### STOUDEMIRE, AMAR'E CARSARES
Basketball player. **Personal:** Born Nov 16, 1982, Lake Wales, FL; son of Hazell and Carrie; married Alexis Welch; children: 4. **Career:** Basketball player, actor, producer; Phoenix Suns, corner, 2002-10; New York Knicks, ctr & forward, 2010-15; Dallas Mavericks, 2015; Miami Heat, 2015-; Film: MacGruber, 2010; New Year's Eve, 2011; Beyond lights, 2014; Trainwreck, 2015; TV Series: "Entourage", 2011; "The Exes", 2012; Producer: Little Ballers, 2013; Village peace, 2014; Beyond lights, 2014. **Business Addr:** Professional Basketball Player, New York Knicks, Madison Sq Garden 2 Pa Plz, New York, NY 10121-0091, **Business Phone:** (212)465-6471.

### STOUDMAIRE, DAMON
Basketball coach, basketball player. **Personal:** Born Sep 3, 1973, Portland, OR; son of Willie and Liz; married Natasha Taylor; children: Damon & Brandon. **Educ:** Univ Ariz, attended 1995. **Career:** Basketball player (retired), coach; Toronto Raptors, guard, 1995-98; Portland Trail Blazers, 1998-2005; Memphis Grizzlies, guard, 2005-08; San Antonio Spurs, 2008; Rice Univ, dir player develop, coach, 2008-09; asst coach, Memphis Grizzlies, 2009-11; Memphis, asst coach, 2011-13, 2015; Ariz Wildcats men's basketball, asst coach, 2013-2015. **Home Addr:** PO Box 12007, Portland, OR 97212. **Business Addr:** Assistant Coach, Memphis Tigers men's basketball, Memphis, TN.

### STOUTE, STEVE
Executive, chief executive officer. **Personal:** Born Jan 1, 1971, New York, NY. **Educ:** Syracuse Univ. **Career:** Rd mgr, 1990; Interscope Rec, artists & repertoire exec, pres black music, 1998; Sony Music Entertainment, pres urban music; Interscope Geffin A&M Rec, pres urban music div, exec vpres; PASS, founder, 2001-02; Mary J Blige, mgr; Transl LLC, founder & chief exec officer, 2005-; Carols Daughter, chief exec officer, Managing Dir, 2005-. Author: The Tanning of America: How Hip-Hop Created a Culture That Rewrote the Rules of the New Economy, 2011; TV: "The Black List Project". **Orgs:** Co-chmn, NY Fresh Air Fund; co founder, Advan Women Now. **Business Addr:** Founder, Chief Executive Officer, Translation LLC, 145 W 45th St 12 Fl, New York, NY 10036, **Business Phone:** (212)299-5505.

### STOUTMIRE, OMAR ARRAY
Football player, football coach. **Personal:** Born Jul 9, 1974, Pensacola, FL. **Educ:** Fresno State Univ, bus mkt. **Career:** Football player (retired) football coach; Dallas Cowboys, defensive back, 1997, free safety, 1998; Cleveland Browns, 1999; New York Jets, right safety, 1999; New York Giants, 2000-01, 2004, free safety, 2002-03; Wash Redskins, defensive back, 2005, 2007; New Orleans Saints, strong safety & defensive back, 2006; Prestonwood Christian Acad, varsity track head coach, currently. **Honors/Awds:** All-WAC, 1996; Inducted into the Fresno Athletic Hall of Fame, 2013. **Business Addr:** Varsity Track Head Coach, Prestonwood Christian Academy, 6801 W Park Blvd, Plano, TX 75093, **Business Phone:** (972)820-5300.

### STOVALL, AUDREAN
Executive. **Personal:** Born Sep 18, 1933, Lexa, AR; daughter of John F Rice and Fredonia Little John Rice; married Williard; children: Darryl Byrd. **Educ:** Mercy Col, Detroit, BS, 1984; Wayne State Univ, attended 1986. **Career:** Mich Bell Tel Co, var positions, 1953-83; Electronic Data Syst, telecommunication specialist; US Sprint, acct consult; A B Stovall Consult, ITSI; MCI Customer Serv, supvr, 1985-86; Integrated Telecommunication Serv Inc, Detroit, Mich, entrepreneur, pres, owner, 1986-; AB Stovall Consult Inc, Detroit, Mich, owner, pres, 1986-. **Orgs:** Bus corp comn ABWA, 1963-; bus corp com, NBMBA, 1985-86; AFCEA; Am Bus Women's Asn; Urban League Guild;Nat Asn Advan Colored People; Jr Achievement, Pioneers Am; Founders Soc Detroit Inst Arts; admis & fund comn; telethon comn United Negro Col Fund; Univ Detroit Mercy Alumna Planning Comn; Northwest Area Bus Asn, 1988-; Greater Detroit Chamber Com, 1988-; Nat Asn Female Exec, 1989-; Nat Black MBA Asn; bus & corp, Oakland County Bus Consortium, 1990; Mich Minority Bus Devt Corp. **Home Addr:**

13131 Columbia, Redford, MI 48239-4600, **Home Phone:** (313)387-2045. **Business Addr:** AB Stovall Consulting Inc, MI.

### STOVALL, STANLEY V.
Television news anchorperson, journalist. **Personal:** Born Feb 24, 1953, Rochester, NY. **Educ:** Ariz State Univ, BS, 1975. **Career:** Reporter, producer, film photographer & film editor; KTVK-TV, anchorman, reporter & photographer, 1970-75; KTAR-TV, Phoenix, anchorman & reporter, 1975; KSDK-TV, St Louis, anchorman & reporter, 1975-78, anchorman, 1983-86; WBAL-TV, Baltimore, anchorman, 1978-83, co-anchor, 2003-; WCAV-TV, Philadelphia, news anchor & reporter, currently. **Orgs:** Greater & St Louis Asn Black Journalists, 1975-78; Asn Black Media Workers, Baltimore; Nat Asn Advan Colored People, Baltimore Br, 1980-83, St Louis Br, 1983-86; exec off, Living Legacy Found, currently. **Honors/Awds:** Mr Maryland Bodybuilding Champion, Baltimore, 1980; Mr South Atlantic Bodybuilding Champion, Baltimore, 1980; "Hard Hat" Award, Citizens Housing & Planning Asn, Baltimore, 1983; Baltimore City Council proclamation for Community Service, Baltimore, 1983; Journalist of the Year, Greater St Louis Asn Black Journalists, St Louis, 1986; Emmy Award for Best News Anchor, St Louis, 1985; Four-time State Powerlifting Champion; Holds titles of Junior Mr. Arizona, Mr. Maryland, Mr. South Atlantic & Mr. Delmarva in body building. **Special Achievements:** First Black TV Anchorman in Phoenix; First African-American news reporter in the state of Arizona; Became the youngest news anchor in the United States at the age of 18. **Business Addr:** Co-Anchor, WBAL-TV, 3800 Hooper Ave, Baltimore, MD 21211, **Business Phone:** (410)467-3000.

### STOVALL-TAPLEY, MARY KATE
Mayor, funeral director. **Personal:** Born Dec 13, 1921, Uniontown, AL; daughter of Tim Sanders Sr and Estella Billingsley Sanders; married Turner Stovall; children: Kathleen D Stovall Caldwell & Audrey Y Stovall Hayes. **Educ:** Ala State Univ, BS, 1949, MEd, 1955; Atlanta Univ, MLS, 1969. **Career:** Perry County Bd Educ AL, teacher, 1943-51; Russell Co Bd Educ AL, teacher & librn, 1951-76; Town Hurtsboro, AL, counwomen, 1976-84, mayor, 1984-; Stovall Funeral Home, exec funeral dir & chief operating officer, currently. **Orgs:** State democratic exec comt, Democratic Party, 1991-; pres, E Ala Ment Health Bd dir; treas, E Ala Funeral dir Asn; chairwoman, Hurtsboro Ladies Aux. **Special Achievements:** First black and woman to be mayor of Hurtsboro, Alabama, 1984. **Home Addr:** PO Box 154, Hurtsboro, AL 36860. **Business Addr:** Executive Funeral Director, Chief Operating Officer, Stovall Funeral Home, 605 Main St, Hurtsboro, AL 36860, **Business Phone:** (334)667-7679.

### STRACHAN, LLOYD CALVIN, JR.
Electrical engineer, manager. **Personal:** Born Apr 12, 1954, Greensboro, NC; son of Lloyd C Sr and Dorothy B Lane (deceased); married Carolyn Mintz; children: Camille. **Educ:** NC Agr & Tech State Univ, Greensboro, NC, BS, elec engineering, 1976. **Career:** Carolina Power & Light Co, Telecom Construct Unit, from engr to sr engr, 1977-85, supt, 1985-89, Telecom Support Unit, mgr, 1989-92, Telecom Servs Sec, proj analyst, 1992-. **Orgs:** Am Asn Blacks Energy, 1989-; Inst Elec & Electronics Engrs; steering comt mem, Black Achievers, Raleigh Chap, 1991; regist mem, Prof Engr NC. **Home Addr:** 3904 Lacy Ave, Greensboro, NC 27405, **Home Phone:** (910)272-3095. **Business Addr:** Senior Analyst, Carolina Power & Light Co, 410 S Wilmington St, Raleigh, NC 27601, **Business Phone:** (704)382-3853.

### STRACHAN, DR. RICHARD JAMES
School administrator. **Personal:** Born Jan 21, 1928, Miami, FL; married Lorraine M Farrington; children: Denia, Richard II, Reginald, Regina & Lori. **Educ:** Bethune-Cookman Col, BS, 1956; Ind Univ, MS, 1966; Barry Univ, MS, 1972; Atlanta Univ, PhD, 1978. **Career:** Educator (retired); N Dade Jr Sr HS, teacher & athletic dir, 1960-66; Miami Cent, dept head & band dir, 1966-72; Hialeah HS & Carol City & Norland, asst prin, 1972-81; COPE Sch N, prin; King Clubs, pres, currently. **Orgs:** Bd mem, Off Black Affairs, 1981-86; bd mem, Nat Asn Advan Colored People; bd mem, YMCA; bd mem, Inner City Sch Dance; bd mem, Dade Co Admin Asn; bd mem, Fla Alternative Admin Sch Educr; bd mem, Omega Psi Phi; bd mem, Youth Adv Coun. **Honors/Awds:** Rockefeller Grant, 1975; Outstanding Bethune-Cookman Col Exelloc Club, 1975; Service Award, Sigma Gamma Rho DLS-SA-NABSE-YMCA-NCAO Atlanta Univ, 1986. **Home Addr:** 8841 NW 14th Ave, Miami, FL 33147-3202, **Home Phone:** (305)691-3209.

### STRAHAN, MICHAEL ANTHONY
Football player, business owner, entertainer. **Personal:** Born Nov 21, 1971, Houston, TX; son of Louise and Gene; married Wanda Hutchins; children: Tanita & Michael Jr; married Jean Muggli; children: Sophia & Isabella. **Educ:** Tex Southern Univ, attended 1992. **Career:** Football player (retired), manager; New York Giants, defensive end & left defensive tackle & left defensive end & right defensive end, 1993-2007; Michael Strahan Enterprises, owner; Pros vs. Joes, host; Fox NFL Sunday, football analyst, currently. TV Series: "Chuck", 2008; "Brothers", 2009; "Are We There Yet?", 2011; "WWF Raw", 2013. **Orgs:** Am Cancer Soc; C Miracle Network; Housing Enterprises Less Privileged (H.E.L.P.); People Ethical Treat Animals (PETA); Starlight C Found. **Honors/Awds:** Super Bowl XLII champion; SWAC Defensive Player of the Year, 1991-92; Edd Hayes Black College Sports All-American, 1992; Pro Bowl, 1997-99, 2001-05; Defensive Player of the Year, Nat Football League, 2001 NFC Defensive Player of the Year, 2001 & 2003; NFL Alumni Pass Rusher of the Year, 2003; Pro Football Hall of Fame, 2014. **Special Achievements:** Playoffs and appeared on ABCs pregame show prior to Super Bowl XXXVII; contest Americas Craziest Sports Fan; Strahan has also served as the Giants United Way Spokesman; Worked for Fox network, 2001; One of the judge for December 7, 2004; FOXs Best Damn Sport Show during the 2004 and 2005 post seasons. **Business Addr:** SMAC Entertainment, 1100 Glendon Ave Suite 1220, Los Angeles, CA 90024-3521, **Business Phone:** (310)208-7622.

### STRAIGHT, CATHY A.
Journalist. **Personal:** Born Sep 20, 1963, Ocean Springs, MS; daughter of Turner Joseph Sr and June Rose Spears. **Educ:** Univ Southern Miss, BS, journ, 1985. **Career:** The Hattiesburg Am, Hattiesburg, Mich, reporter, copy ed, 1982-87; The Jackson Sun Jackson, Tenn, feature reporter, ed, 1987-89; The Brandenton Hearld, Brandenton, Fla, features reporter on aging, 1989-90; The Tennessean, Nashville, Tenn, gen assignment, features, 1990; The Tennessean, dep mng ed, editor, & reporter, 1999-2000; St Paul Pioneer Press, sr mgr & managing ed, 2000-06; USA Today, sr assignment ed, 2006-10; CNN Wire, sr ed, 2010-12, sr ed, content, 2012-. **Orgs:** Nat Asn Black Journalist, 1990-; Tenn Press Asn, 1990-; Miss Press Women Asn, 1985-87. **Home Addr:** 1199 Murfreesboro Rd, Nashville, TN 37217, **Home Phone:** (615)360-7825. **Business Addr:** National Editor, USA Today, 7950 Jones Br Dr, McLean, VA 22108-0605.

### STRAIT, GEORGE ALFRED, JR.
Journalist. **Personal:** Born Mar 24, 1945, Cambridge, MA; married Lisa Michelle McIver; children: Eric Mathew & Kevin Michael Angelo. **Educ:** Boston Univ, BA, biol, 1967; Atlanta Univ, MS, biochem genetics, 1969. **Career:** WQXI Atlanta, GA, anchor, 1969-72; WPVI Philadelphia, PA, anchor, 1972-76; ABC News, Wash corresp, 1976-77, gen assign corresp, 1977-78, White House corresp, 1978-82, spec proj corresp, 1982-84, chief med corresp, 1984-99; IssueSphere/Nelson Communications Inc, sr coun, 1999-2000; Dr Spock Co, sr vpres, content & media, 2000-01; pvt pract, Belmont, CA, Health & Media Consult, 2001-; Univ Calif, Berkeley, asst vchancellor pub affairs, 2003-; MedComm, chief exec officer; Nat Ctr Minority Health & Health Disparities, commun dir; Food & Drug Admin, asst comnr pub affairs. **Orgs:** Charter mem, Nat Asn Black Journalists; bd chair, Henry J Kaiser Family Foundation; lay reader, Episcopal Church Am, 1984-. **Home Addr:** 743 Crestview Dr, San Carlos, CA 94070. **Business Addr:** Assistant Vice Chancellor, University of California, Office of Public Affairs, Berkeley, CA 94720-4204, **Business Phone:** (510)643-6998.

### STRATHER, VIVIAN CARPENTER. See CARPENTER, DR. VIVIAN L.

### STRAUGHTER, EDGAR, SR.
School administrator, mayor. **Personal:** Born Feb 8, 1929, Willis, TX; son of K J and Annie Lee; married Betty Harvey; children: Edgar, Lewis, Ernest, Johnnie, Sherman & Betty, Debra. **Educ:** Tex Southern Univ. **Career:** Supervisor (retired), administrator; Willis Independent Pub Sch Dist, pres; La-Pac, qual control supvr; City Willis, Tex, mayor, 1989-93; Montomery Co, mediator; drill instr. **Orgs:** Vpres, Montgomery Co Voters League; Willis Fire Dept, 1965-; Willis City Planning Comn; Willis Bd Educ. **Special Achievements:** First African American to serve as a President in Willis Independent Public School District. **Home Addr:** 206 Straughter St, Willis, TX 77378, **Home Phone:** (409)856-9082.

### STRAUTMANIS, MICHAEL A.
Government official, lawyer. **Personal:** Born Mar 24, 1969, Chicago, IL; married Damona; children: Nia, Michael Damani & J Jori. **Educ:** Univ Ill, BS, 1991; Univ Ill Col Law, JD, 1994. **Career:** USAID, chief staff, 1998-2000; Rep Rod Blagojevich, legis dir, 1999-2001; Amer Assoc Justice, 2001-05; Obama's presidential team, jr sen, sen, chief coun & dir pub laison & Intergovernmental affairs, dep asst to Barack Obama; Coun to Barack Obama, 2005-08, counr, chief staff to valerie jarrett, 2008-; Paralegal Sidley Austin; Pres's Coun Jobs & Competitiveness, sr advisor. **Orgs:** Am Asn Justice. **Special Achievements:** Named to the 13-member Transition Senior Staff on the Obama-Biden Transition Project. **Business Addr:** Deputy Assistant, The White House, 1300 Pa Ave, Washington, DC 20004, **Business Phone:** (202)456-1111.

### STRAWBERRY, DARRYL EUGENE, SR.
Executive, baseball player. **Personal:** Born Mar 12, 1962, Los Angeles, CA; son of Henry and Ruby; married Lisa Watkins; children: Darryl Jr & Diamond; married Charisse Simons; children: Jewel Nicole, Jordan & Jade; married Tracy. **Career:** Baseball player (retired), association executive; New York Mets, outfielder, 1983-90; Los Angeles Dodgers, outfielder, 1991-93; San Francisco Giants, 1994; New York Yankees, 1995-99; New York Mets, instr, 2005, anchor, 2007-08; Strawberry's Sports Grill, owner, 2010-; Darryl Strawberry Recovery Ctr, co-founder, currently; Sports Net New York, analyst, currently. **Orgs:** Founder, Darryl Strawberry Found. **Honors/Awds:** Rookie of the Year, Nat League, 1983; Rookie Player of the Year, Sporting News; All-Star Team, 1984-91; Home Run Champion, Nat League, 1988; Silver Slugger Award, 1988, 1990; Gotta Have Heart Award, 1999; Hall of Fame, NY Mets, 2010; John Murphy Award; Doubleday Award. **Special Achievements:** Guest apperance: "The Simpsons"; featured, "Chocolate Strawberry". **Business Addr:** Co Founder, The Darryl Strawberry Recovery Center, 81 Beehive Circle Dr, Saint Cloud, FL 34769, **Business Phone:** (888)513-0317.

### STRAYHORN, LLOYD
Writer. **Personal:** Born Harlem, NY. **Career:** AstroNumerologist, Author; Tree of Life Bookstore, teacher numerology, 1976-83; Big Red Newspaper, "Numbers & You", weekly columnist, 1978-; NY Amsterdam News, weekly column "Numbersand You", 1979-; Proj ENTER, teacher numerology, 1979-; Arts & Cult, teacher numerology, 1980-81; BMI Syndication, weekly columnist, "Astro/Numerology & You", 1980-; WLIB-AM, "Numbers & You", AstroNumerologist, currently; Book: Numbers & You: A Numerology Guide for Everyday Living, 1980. **Home Addr:** 163 W 136th St Apt 2C, New York, NY 10030-2669. **Business Addr:** AstroNumerologist, Numbers & You, 2266 5th Ave Suite 136, New York, NY 10037, **Business Phone:** (800)581-4401.

### STREET, VIVIAN SUE
Administrator. **Personal:** Born Jun 21, 1954, Edgefield, SC; daughter of James Harry Bussey and Susie Bell Werts; married Ronnie; children: Jermaine Toriano. **Educ:** State Univ NY Col, Brockport, NY, BS, 1976; Col New Rochelle, MS, 1981. **Career:** Westchester Devel Ctr, Orangeburg, NY, spec educ teacher, 1971-76; Westchester Devel Serv, White Plains, NY, community residence supvr, 1977-78, placement coord, 1978-82; Letchworth Village Devel Serv, team leader, placement team, 1982-86; Black Caucus PS&T Workers PEF, vpres, 1983-; Westchester Devel Disabilities Serv, Tarrytown, NY, prog develop specialist, fiscal liaison, 1986-90, treat team leader, 1990-92; Letchworth DDSO, develop disabilities prog specialist & steward 1992-95; Hudson Valley Develop Disabilities Serv Off, Develop Disabilities Prog, specialist & coordr, 1995-; PEF Div 276, steward. **Orgs:** Conv deleg, Pub Employees Fed, 1985-; steering comt, Black Tennis & Sports Found, 1986-; treas, Nat Asn Advan Colored People, Spring Valley, NY, 1988-98, pres, 1999; Tops Tot s Nursery Sch, 1989-; CNL leader, Pub Employees Fed Div 336, 1992; United Way; bd trustee appointee, First Baptist Church; pres, Spring Valley Br, Nat Asn Adv Colored People; PEF Exec Coun; PEF Polit Action Comt; Joint Labor-Mgt Comt; PEF Spec Elections Comt. **Home Addr:** 55 Creekside Cir, Spring Valley, NY 10977-3906, **Home Phone:** (845)426-6569. **Business Addr:** Developmental Disabilities Program Specialist, Hudson Valley Development Disabilities Services Office, 9 Wilbur Rd, Thiells, NY 10984, **Business Phone:** (845)947-6333.

### STREETER, DEBRA BRISTER
Executive. **Personal:** Born May 23, 1956, Birmingham, AL; daughter of Edward and Ella Scott; married Otis Jr; children: Otis & Sheeba L. **Educ:** Univ Ala, Birmingham, AL, cert acct, 1981; Booker T Wash Bus Col, Birmingham, AL, cert secretarial & sci, 1984. **Career:** Turning Point Prod, Birmingham, Ala, admin secy, 1976-84, comptroller, 1988-; Zegarelli & Assoc, Birmingham, Ala, secy, 1984-86; Beverly Health Care Ctr W, Fairfield, Ala, secy & bookkeeper, 1986-87; Univ Ala, Birmingham, Ala, secy, 1987-88. **Home Addr:** 2448 Tempest Dr, Birmingham, AL 35211, **Home Phone:** (256)362-2928.

### STREETER, DENISE WILLIAMS
Educator, executive, chief financial officer. **Personal:** Born Apr 27, 1962, Washington, DC; daughter of Michael G and Patricia A Dorn; married Christipher M; children: Mikala P, C Christipher K & Ronald M. **Educ:** Howard Univ, Wash, DC, BBA, 1984; Johns Hopkins Univ, Carey Bus Sch, MS, finance, 2005; Old Dom Univ, Col Bus & Pub Admin, cert, investments, 2004, MA, econs, 2012, PhD, finance, 2013. **Career:** Coopers & Ly brand, Wash, DC, auditor, sr acct, 1984-86; ICMA Retirement Corp, Wash, DC, sr trust acct, 1986-87, mgr trust acounting, 1987-89; F S Taylor & Assts, Wash, DC, mgr, 1989-92; Nat 4-H Coun, dir, acct & financial admin, 1992-97; chief financial officer, 1997-2000, sr vpres, chief financial & admin officer, 2000-06; Old Dom Univ, adj instr & res asst, fin, 2007-10; Am Finance Asn Conf, grant, 2009; Johns Hopkins Univ, Carey Bus Sch, adj instr finance, 2011-13; Univ Md Univ Col, adj assoc prof finance, 2011-14; Penn State Univ, instr bus, 2014-15; Howard Univ, asst prof finance, 2015-. **Orgs:** Chap pres, Int Fraternity Delta Sigma Pi, 1982-; chap pres, Nat Asn Black Accts Inc, 1982-; Beta Gamma Sigma Nat Hon Soc, 1983-; Dist Columbia Inst CPAs, 1986-; Am Inst CPAs, 1990-; asst treas, Mt Pleasant Baptist Church, 1991-96; Am Soc Asn Execs, 1992-; sr vpres, Nat 4-H Coun, Acct & Financial Admin, dir, 1992-97, chief financial officer & asst corp treas, 1997-2000, chief operating officer, chief financial & sr vpres, 2000-06; Planning Comm, 1993; Eastern Region NABA Stud Conf, 1993-; officer, Ken moor Elem PTA, 1996-; leader, PG County 4-H Teen Coun, 1997; lead teacher, 10-12 Girls Cs Ministry, First Bapt Church Glenarden, 1997-; adv coun, Howard Univ Acct, 1999-2007; treas, Md 4-H Found, 2002-06; Am Inst Cert Pub Accountants; Am Socs Asn Execs; Financial Mgt Asn Int, 2008-; Am Finance Asn, 2008-; Acad Int Bus, 2008-; founding mem, vpres, & pres, Old Dom Univ Bus Admin Doctoral, 2009-10; Omicron Delta Epsilon, Int Hon Soc Econs, 2010; grad fel, Old Dom Univ; City Franklin, Va Econ Develop Team, 2010-; pres, KPMG Liaison, 2010-; Eastern Finance Asn, 2010-. **Home Addr:** 2004 Parkside Dr, Mitchellville, MD 20721-4233, **Home Phone:** (301)758-2729. **Business Addr:** Assistant Professor of Finance, Howard University, 2400 6th St NW, Washington, DC 20059, **Business Phone:** (202)806-6100.

### STREETER, DR. ELWOOD JAMES
Dentist. **Personal:** Born Jun 14, 1930, Greenville, NC; son of William and Hattie Forbes; married Martha; children: Agnes & Nicole. **Educ:** NC Col, BS, 1952; Howard Univ, DDS, 1956; Univ Calif, Los Angeles, cert, 1969. **Career:** Perez & Streeter Dent Corp, dentist, 1958-; La Co USC Med Ctr, dent attend staff; Hollywood Presby Med Ctr, attend staff; pvt pract, currently. **Orgs:** Am Dent Asn; Calif Dent Asn; Sothern Calif Stomatognathic & Res Sem; YMCA; Nat Asn Advan Colored People; NC Col Alumni Asn; La Dent Soc Dent Care, mem, 1958-; Angel City Dent Soc, 1956-; partner, Amalgamated Devel Asn; fel Acad Gen Dent, 1972; pres, Southern Calif, Acad Gen Denist, 1978, pres adv coun, 1979-; treas, Amada Enterprises Inc; treas, Allied Diversified Asn; bd dir, Delta Dent Calif, 1994-. **Honors/Awds:** Fel, Am Col Dentists, 1985; Fel, Intl Col Dentists, 1983; Fel, Pierre Fuchard Acad, 1988. **Home Addr:** 665 E Mendocino St, Altadena, CA 91001-2336. **Business Addr:** Dentist, Streeter & Perez Dental Corporation, 3701 Stocker St Suite 405, Los Angeles, CA 90008, **Business Phone:** (323)291-1024.

### STREETS, FRAN A.
Association executive, chief executive officer. **Career:** Bank San Francisco, from vpres to sr vpres, 1985-91; sr vpres mkt & investor rels, 1991-92; Wells Fargo Bank, City Dir Pvt Banking Div, vpres, 1992; Int Women's Forum, pres, 1997-99; Pac Bank, dir; Heald Col, chmn bd, 2001-, interim pres & chief exec officer. **Orgs:** Adv bd, City Nat Corp; dir, Audit & Fin Comt, Loan Comt, Nominating &Compensation Comt, Pac Bank; comnr, City San Francisco's Libr Comn, chair, Fin Comt; pres, bd dir, Int Women's Forum; co-chmn bd, San Francisco Ballet; trustee emer, Univ San Francisco; bd dir, New Resource Bank. **Business Addr:** Board of Director, New Resource Bank, 405 Howard St Suite 110, San Francisco, CA 94105, **Business Phone:** (415)995-8100.

### STREETS, TAI LAMARR
Football player. **Personal:** Born Apr 20, 1977, Matteson, IL; son of Clayton and Karen. **Educ:** Univ Mich. **Career:** Football player (retired); San Francisco 49ers, 1999, wide receiver, 2000-03; Detroit Lions, wide receiver, 2004; Meanstreets, founder; Thornton's Football team, asst coach. **Honors/Awds:** Bo Schembechler Award; Athletic Academic Achievement Award.

## STRICKLAND, CLINTON VERNAL, JR.

School administrator. **Personal:** Born Dec 19, 1950, Elmira, NY; son of Clinton V Sr and Grace Brooks; married Holly E Williams; children: Crystal V, Cicely V, Clinton III, Christopher V & Caitlyn V. **Educ:** Univ Rochester, BA, 1974, MA, 1975; State Univ NY, Brockport, cert study educ admin, 1977; State Univ NY, Buffalo, NY, doctoral prog. **Career:** Rochester City Sch Dist, teacher, 1974-79, counr, 1979, dean stud, 1980-82, jr high admin, 1982-84, proj mgr Sch environ prog, 1984-85; Nathaniel Rochester Community Sch, vice prin; Adlai E. Stevenson Sch No.29, prin, currently. **Orgs:** Vol, Urban League Rochester NY Inc 1979-; bd dir, Off Black Ministries Cath Diocese Rochester, 1982-83; chmn, Eureka Lodge 36 Educ & Charitable Trust; life mem, Theta Omicron Chap Omega Psi Phi Frat; trainer, facilitator, NYSCCT United Teachers; mem Phi Delta Kappa; pres & founder, Black Educ Asn Rochester. **Home Addr:** 25 Wild Berry Lane, Pittsford, NY 14534-9524, **Home Phone:** (585)248-2621. **Business Addr:** Principal, Adlai E Stevenson School No 29, 88 Kirkland Rd, Rochester, NY 14611, **Business Phone:** (585)328-8228.

## STRICKLAND, DEMERICK MONTAE. See STRICKLAND, ERICK.

## STRICKLAND, DOROTHY S.

Educator. **Personal:** Born Sep 29, 1933, Newark, NJ; daughter of Leroy Salley Sr and Evelyn Daniels; married Maurice R; children: Mark, M Randall & Michael. **Educ:** Kean Col, BS, 1955; NY Univ, MA, 1958, PhD, 1971. **Career:** Learning Disability Spec E Orange, teacher, reading consult, 1961-66; Jersey City State Col, Reading Dept, asst prof, 1966-70; Kean Col, from assoc prof to prof, 1970-80; New York Univ, adj prof; Teachers Col Columbia Univ, prof, 1980-85, Arthur I Gates prof educ, 1985-90; Ctr Effective Sch Practices, sr adv coun; Rutgers Univ, prof reading, 1990-2002, Samuel De Witt Proctor chair & prof educ, 2002, prof emer, currently. **Orgs:** Bd dir, Nat Coun Teachers Eng; educ adv bd, Early Yrs Mag; chmn, Early Childhood Educ; j reading instr, Websters New World Dict, comnr, Sprint Mag; pres, Int Reading Asn, 1978-79; pres, Reading Hall Fame; Nat Comm Ed Migrant C; trustee, Res Found, Nat Coun Teachers Eng, 1983-86; Kappa Delta Pi; Pi Lamda Theta; Phi Delta Kappa; Am Educ Res Asn; Nat Asn Educ Young C; distinguished res fel NIEER, Rutgers Univ Grad Sch Educ; distinguished fel, Nat Inst Early Educ Res, Rutgers Univ; NJ State Bd Educ. **Honors/Awds:** Founders Day Recognition, NY Univ, 1971; National Research Award, Nat Coun Teachers Eng, 1972; Woman of the Year, Zeta Phi Beta, 1980; Outstanding Teacher of Education Reading, Int Reading Asn, 1985; Award Outstanding Contribution for Education, Nat Asn Univ Women, 1987; Emerging Literacy Award, Int Reading asn, 1989; Elected Reading Hall of Fame, Int Reading Asn, 1990; Distinguished Alumni Award, New York Univ, 1990; Outstanding Alumni Award, Kean Col NJ, 1990; DHL, Bank Street Col Educ, 1991; Nat Council Teachers English Award for Research; Rewey Bell Inglis Award as Outstanding Woman in the Teaching of English, Nat Coun Teachers Eng, 1994; Jubilee Medal, Archdiocese of Newark, 1997; Outstanding Educator in the Language of Arts, Nat Coun Teachers Eng, 1998; Ferguson Award for Outstanding Contributions to the field of Early Childhood Education, Nat-Louis Univ, 2005. **Special Achievements:** Author, editor, or co-editor, Language Arts: Learning and Teaching; Language Literacy and the Child, Process Reading and Writing; A Literature Based Approach, Emerging Literacy; Young Children Learn to Read and Write, The Administration and Supervision of Reading Programs, Educating Black Children; America's Challenge, Family Storybook Reading, Listen Children; An Anthology of Black Literature, Familie; An Anthology of Poetry for Young Children; Publications: Literacy Instruction in Half Day and Full Day Kindergartens, Newark, DE Intl Reading Asn, Morrow LM, Strickland, DS & Woo, D, 1998; Teaching Phonics Today, 1988; Literacy Leaders in Early Childhood; Learning About Print in Preschool Settings; Bridging the Literacy Achievement Gap; Improving Reading and Achievement Through Professional Development. **Home Addr:** 131 Coccio Dr, West Orange, NJ 07052-4121, **Home Phone:** (973)243-2795. **Business Addr:** Samuel DeWitt Proctor Chair in Education, Professor Emeritus, Rutgers University, 10 Seminary Pl Suite 229, New Brunswick, NJ 08901-1183, **Business Phone:** (848)932-7496.

## STRICKLAND, ERICK (DEMERICK MONTAE STRICKLAND)

Executive, basketball coach, basketball player. **Personal:** Born Nov 25, 1973, Opelika, AL. **Educ:** Univ Nebr, BS, sociol, 1996; Bellevue Univ, MBA, 2013-. **Career:** Basketball player (retired), executive, coach; Dallas Mavericks, guard & shooting guard, 1996-2000; NY Knicks, 2000-01; Vancouver Grizzlies, 2000-01; Boston Celtics, point guard, 2001-02; Ind Pacers, shooting guard, 2002-03; Milwaukee Bucks, guard & point guard, 2003-04, shooting guard, 2005; Dallas Mavericks, mgr bus rels, 2006-09; Potters House Sch Ministry; Goodson Acura, sales prof, 2010-12; Bellevue W High, asst coach, 2012-13; NMex Highlands Univ, asst coach, 2013-. **Honors/Awds:** University of Nebraska-Lincoln Hall of Fame; All-Big Eight Defensive Hons, 1994-96; Most Valuable Player, 1996; Bellevue West High Hall of Fame; Omaha Metro Hall of Fame. **Business Addr:** Assistant Basketball Coach, New Mexico Highlands University, 1005 Diamond St, Las Vegas, NM 87701, **Business Phone:** (505)425-7511.

## STRICKLAND, FREDRICK WILLIAM, JR.

Football player. **Personal:** Born Aug 15, 1966, Buffalo, NJ; married Shay. **Educ:** Purdue Univ. **Career:** Football player (retired); Los Angeles Rams, 1988, 1992, right inside linebacker, 1989, left inside linebacker, 1990, right linebacker, 1991; Minn Vikings, right linebacker, 1993; Green Bay Packers, mid linebacker, 1994-95; Dallas Cowboys, mid linebacker, 1996-98; Wash Redskins, linebacker, 1999.

## STRICKLAND, HERMAN WILLIAM, JR.

Vice president (organization), banker. **Personal:** Born Sep 10, 1959, Blytheville, AR; son of Herman W Sr; married Rhonda; children: Ashlee & Aryn. **Educ:** Ark State Univ, BS, mgt, 1980; Univ Memphis, MBA, finance, 1991. **Career:** First Tenn Bank, corp relationship mgr, sr credit officer, mgt training prog, 1981-83, acct officer, 1983-84, vpres, jr lender med serv, 1984-87, vpres, sr lender metro, 1987-93, sr vpres, mgr diversity banking, 1993-; Pinnacle Financial Partners, financial advisor, sr credit officer, 2015-. **Orgs:** Jr Achievement, loaned exec, 1984-85; steering comn mem, Rozelle Elem Adopt-a-Sch, 1987-; bd mem, Synergy Found, 1992-; bd mem, Dixie Homes Boys Club, 1994-; Leadership Memphis, 1997; bd dir, Alt consult; Memphis Urban League; Ark State Univ found; Community Lift; Communities Unlimited; Seedco; Rise Found. **Home Addr:** 9804 Woodland Run Lane, Cordova, TN 38018, **Home Phone:** (901)751-2887. **Business Addr:** Senior Vice President, Manager, First Tennessee Bank, 315 Poplar Ave, Memphis, TN 38103, **Business Phone:** (901)543-3220.

## STRICKLAND, MARK

Basketball player, basketball coach. **Personal:** Born Jul 14, 1970, Atlanta, GA. **Educ:** Temple Univ, attended 1992. **Career:** Basketball player (retired), basketball coach; Philadelphia Spirit, 1992; Atlanta Eagles, 1993; EBBC Den Bosch, 1993-94; Ft Wayne Fury, 1994-95; Atleticos de San Ger, 1994-95; Atlanta Trojans, 1994; Ind Pacers, pt forward, 1995; Yakima Sun Kings, 1995-96, 2005-06; Atlantic City Seagulls, 1996; Miami Heat, pt forward, 1997-2000; NJ Nets, shooting forward, 2000-01; Denver Nuggets, 2000-01; Atlanta Hawks, 2001-02; Gigantes de Carolina, 2002; Strasbourg IG, 2002; Zhejiang Wanma Cyclones, 2002-03; Jamhour Blue Stars, 2003-05; Dallas Mavericks, shooting forward, 2003; Rockford Lightning, 2005-06; Deportivo San Jose Asuncion, 2007; Arena Amman, 2007; Bakersfield Jam, asst coach, 2009-; Nat Basketball League Can, Oshawa Power, head coach, currently. **Business Addr:** Assistant Coach, Bakersfield Jam, 1400 Norris Rd, Bakersfield, CA 93308, **Business Phone:** (661)716-4526.

## STRICKLAND, R. JAMES

Executive, business owner, president (organization). **Personal:** Born Feb 24, 1930, Kansas City, KS; son of Roosevelt Joseph and Mable Yvonne Roberts; married Deanna Cartman; children: James, Jay, Jeffrey, Deanna & Dori. **Educ:** Kans Univ, BS, pharm, 1954. **Career:** Joslyn Clinic, mgr, 1954-68; Strickland Drugs Inc, pres & owner 1968-; boxing trainer, mgr. **Orgs:** Pres, Alpha Phi, Alpha Upsilon Chapter, 1953-54; housing chmn W Sub Nat Asn Advan Colored People, 1965; vpres, Nat Asn Advan Colored People West Sub Chap, 1966; vpres, MetImprov Asn, 1971; bd chmn, Met Improvement Ass, 1972-73; bd chmn, Chatham Bus Asn, 1976-77; vpres, ChicagoConf Brother hood, 1977; bd mem, Chicago Retail Druggist Asn, 1977; dir, Maywood Comt Spec Events, 1989-. **Home Addr:** 150 N Elmwood Ave Frnt A, Oak Park, IL 60302-2670, **Home Phone:** (708)386-5955. **Business Addr:** President, Strickland Drugs Inc, 316 Pecan St, Blanco, TX 78606, **Business Phone:** (830)833-4815.

## STRICKLAND, RODNEY (ROD STRICKLAND)

Basketball player, basketball executive. **Personal:** Born Jul 11, 1966, Bronx, NY; married Cheryl; children: Torin, Tai, Terell & Tanner. **Educ:** DePaul Univ, Chicago, IL, 1988. **Career:** Basketball player (retired), basketball exec; New York Knicks, guard, 1988-90, San Antonio Spurs, 1990-92, Portland Trail Blazers, 1992-96, 2000-01; Wash Wizards, 1996-2001; Miami Heat, 2001-02; Minn Timberwolves, 2002-03; Orlando Magic, 2003-04; Toronto Raptors, 2004; Houston Rockets, 2005; Memphis Tigers, dir stud athlete develop mgr, 2006-08, dir basketball opers, 2008-; Ky Wildcats, asst coach; Univ Ky, exec. **Business Addr:** Executive, University of Kentucky, 100 WD Funkhouser Bldg, Lexington, KY 40506-0054, **Business Phone:** (859)257-2000.

## STRICKLAND-HILL, DR. MARVA YVONNE

Educator. **Personal:** Born Jun 18, 1952, Savannah, GA; daughter of W S Strickland; married Larry Hill. **Educ:** Clark Col, BA, polit sci, 1974; Atlanta Univ, MA, polit sci, 1976, PhD, polit sci, 1988. **Career:** Clark Col, intern congressman, polit sci, 1973-74, cum laude grad, 1974; Grambling State Univ, polit sci instr, 1979; Morehouse Col, polit sci instr, 1984; NC A&T State Univ, polit sci instr, 1985; Bethune-Cookman Col, asst prof, polit sci, 1986; GA Southern Col, asst prof, polit sci, 1988; DeKalb Col, asst prof, polit sci, 1989-91; KY St Univ, asst prof, polit sci, 1992-. **Orgs:** Fel Ford Found, 1974-76; Zeta Phi Beta Sorority; Nat Conf Black Polit Scientists. **Home Addr:** 215 Capital Ave Apt G-4, Frankfort, KY 40601, **Home Phone:** (502)875-1315. **Business Addr:** Assistant Professor of Political Science, Kentucky State University, 400 E Main St Hathaway Hall, Frankfort, KY 40601, **Business Phone:** (502)597-6000.

## STRICKLIN, JAMES

Cinematographer, photographer. **Personal:** Born Mar 27, 1934, Chicago, IL; son of Phillip and Harriet; married Manita Joyce; children: Nicholas. **Educ:** Ill Inst Technol, BS, 1958; Art Inst Chicago. **Career:** Univ Chicago, lectr film cinematography; Can Broadcasting Corp, cameraman, 1964-67; NBC-News, chicago, cinematographer & cameraman, 1967-75, videographer & tech dir, 1975-; Stricklin Productions, cinematographer & dir. **Orgs:** Ill Arts Coun, 1976-77; US Yacht Racing Union, 1982-; Int Penguin Class Dinghy Asn, 1985-; Jackson Pank Yacht Club, 1985-; race comt, Columbia Yacht Club, 1993; Nat Acad TV Art & Sci; Chicago Asn Black Journalists. **Honors/Awds:** Univ Ill photos exhibited Smithsonian Inst, 1962; co-auth, "With Grief Acquainted", 1963; Emmy Outstanding Cinematographer, 1971-72. **Special Achievements:** Numerous doc films. **Home Addr:** 1364 E 48th St, Chicago, IL 60615-2028, **Home Phone:** (773)285-3270. **Business Addr:** Cinematographer, Cameraman, NBC-News TV, NBC-Tower, Chicago, IL 60611, **Business Phone:** (312)222-9611.

## STRINGER, CHARLAINE VIVIAN

Basketball coach. **Personal:** Born Mar 16, 1948, Edenborn, PA; married William D; children: David, Janine & Justin. **Educ:** Slippery Rock State Col, BA, 1970. **Career:** Cheyney State Univ, women's basketball coach, 1971-83; Univ IA, women's basketball coach, 1983-95; Rutgers State Univ, Louis Brown Athletic Ctr, women's basketball head coach, 1995-. **Orgs:** Hon mem, Alpha Kappa Alpha sorority, 2008; Co-founder, Women's Basketball Coaches Asn; Voting Bd, Amateur Basketball Asn US; adv bd, Nike Coaches; ALL-AM Selection Comt, Kodak; adv bd, Women's Sports Found; Alumni Hall Fame; Women's Basketball Hall Fame; Women's Sports Found Adv Bd. **Honors/Awds:** Bronze Medal, William Jones Cup, 1980; Nat Coach of the Year, 1982, 1988, 1993; District V Coach of the Year, 1985, 1988, 1993; Silver Medal, World University Games, 1985; Communiplex Hall of Fame, 1987; Time National Coach of the Year, Russell Athletic/WBCA National, 1988; Bronze Medal, Pan Am Games, coach, 1991; Big Ten Coach of the Year, 1991, 1993; Carol Eckman Award, 1993; Coach of the Year, Sports Illustrated, USA Today, 1993; Naismith College Coach of the Year, Black Coaches Asn,1993; Big East Coach of the Year, 1998, 2005; Coach of the Year, Metrop Basketball Writers Asn, 1998-2000, 2005; District I Coach of the Year, 1998; Women's Basketball Hall of Fame, 2001; Lifetime Achievement Award, Black Coaches Asn, 2004; Gold, Olympic Games, 2004; Sports Hall of Fame, NJ, 2005; DHL, Howard Univ, 2008; Basketball Hall of Fame, 2009. **Special Achievements:** NCAA Final Four, Cheyney State, 1982, Univ IA, 1993; World Championship Zone Qualification Tournament, coach, 1989; World University Games, coach, 1979, 1985; US Select Team, head coach, 1981; One of the youngest Women's Basketball Coaches to reach 500 Victories; one of the top Five Winningest active division I Women's Basketball Coaches; First female African American coach to win 600 games in Women's Basketball; Featured in many national media outlets and publications including HBO, ESPN, O Magazine & Sports Illustrated for Women. Film: This Is a Game, Ladies, 2000-01. **Business Addr:** Head Coach Women, Rutgers University, Louis Brown Athletic Center, Livingston Campus, Piscataway, NJ 08854, **Business Phone:** (908)445-4251.

## STRINGER, THOMAS EDWARD

Circuit court judge. **Personal:** Born Jul 8, 1944, Peekskill, NY; son of Theodore and Fannie; married Lillian Jean Cooper; children: Thomas E Jr, Daryl Q, Rhonda E & Roderick E. **Educ:** New York Univ, Wash Sq Col, BA, math, 1967; Stetson Univ Col Law, JD, 1974. **Career:** Hillsborough Co State Atty's Off, staff atty, asst state atty, 1974-76; Rosello & Stringer, Pa, staff atty, 1976-84; Hillsborough Co Ct, co judge, 1984-87; Hillsborough Co, admin judge, circuit judge, 1988-99; Second Dist Ct Appeals, judge, 1999-2009; Tampa Housing Authority, dir. **Orgs:** Nat Bar Asn, 1974-; Hillsborough Co Bar Asn, 1974-; bd dir, Boys & Girls Clubs Greater Tampa Inc, 1976-; Omega Psi Phi Fraternity, 1980-; bd dir, Bay Area Legal Serv, 1984-; bd overseers, Stetson Univ Col Law, 1986-; Bay Area Chamber Comn, 1986-. **Honors/Awds:** Citizen of the Year, Pi Iota Chap, Omega Psi Phi Frat, 1984; George E Edgecomb Award, Tampa Urban League, 1984.

## STRINGFELLOW, ERIC DEVAUGHN

Journalist, educator. **Personal:** Born Aug 31, 1960, Meridian, MS; son of Clintorice Sr and Delores Tartt; married Rachel Jones; children: Courtney DeVon. **Educ:** Jackson State Univ, Jackson, BS, mass commun, 1982, MS, urban commun, 1987. **Career:** Com News, gen assignment reporter, 1982; The Clarion Ledger, reporter, 1982-86; Plain Dealer, reporter, 1986-91; Jackson Clarion Ledger, polit ed, 1991-94; Jackson St Univ, adj prof, 1991-94, prof residence, journalism prof, 1991-99; Clarion Ledger, metro columnist; Tougaloo Col, journalism prof & chmn mass commun dept, 2003-; Jackson St Univ commun, exec dir, 2012-. **Orgs:** Pres, Jackson Asn Black Journalists, 1985-86, 1992-; parliamentarian, Cleveland Asn Black Journalists, 1987-89; pres, Cleveland Asn Black Journalists, 1989-91; pres, JSU Cleveland Alumni Chap, 1989-91; BlackMedia Workers, 1990-91; bd mem, Voice Calvary Ministries. **Honors/Awds:** John Hancock Award, John Hancock Co, 1985; Second Place Interpretive Reporting, Miss & La Asniated Press Contest, 1986. **Special Achievements:** Hundred Black Men of Jackson. **Home Addr:** 117 Kilkenny Blvd, Jackson, MS 39209-3743, **Home Phone:** (601)346-0540. **Business Addr:** Professor, Chairman of the Mass Communication, Tougaloo College, 500 W County Line Rd, Tougaloo, MS 39174, **Business Phone:** (601)977-7700.

## STRIPLING, DR. LUTHER

Educator, musician. **Personal:** Born Aug 25, 1935, Tingnall, GA; son of Luther and Catherine; married Myrtice Jones; children: Cedric Ravel & Lloyd Byron. **Educ:** Clark Col, AB, 1957; Atlanta Univ, attended 1965; Univ Ky, MMus, 1968; Univ Colo, DMus, 1971. **Career:** Hamilton High Sch, teacher, 1957-66, chmn music dept, 1960-66; Ga Interscholastic Asn, chmn vocal div, 1964-66; Univ Ky, instr, 1966-68; Univ Colo, 1970-71; Macalester Col, coordr vocal activ, 1971-78; S Ill Univ, Edwardsville, assoc prof, dir, opera workshop, 1978-83; Tarrant County Jr Col, NE Campus, 1983-91; Bel Canto Singles, prof, vocal music & dir, currently; Clark Atlanta Univ, Dept Music, prof, currently. **Orgs:** Nat Opera Asn Inc; Macalester Col Opera Workshop; Asn Col Twin Cities Opera Workshop; Pilgrim Baptist Church; Nat Asn Teachers Singing, St Louis Dist Chap, 1980-82; numerous performances orchestral appearances directing papersfield; bd gov, NE Trinity Arts Coun, 1989-91; life mem, Alumni Asn Univ Colo Boulder. **Honors/Awds:** Contributor Burkhart Charles Anthology for Musical Analysis third Ed, NY Holt Rinehart & Winston, 1978. **Home Addr:** 4105 Steeplechase Dr, Colleyville, TX 76034-3753, **Home Phone:** (817)577-7108. **Business Addr:** Professor, Clark Atlanta University, 223 James P Brawley Dr, Atlanta, GA 30314-4391, **Business Phone:** (404)880-8000.

## STRONG, AMANDA L.

Administrator, president (organization), nurse. **Personal:** Born Nov 22, 1935, Marvell, AR; daughter of Early Mae and Percy Watson; children: Cheryl Beard, Pamela Tender & Jerilyn S. **Educ:** St Vincents Hosp Sch Nursing, dipl, 1957; Ind Univ, BSN, 1973; ANA, cert, 1980, MSN, 1983; Family Nurse Practitioner, cert. **Career:** Nurse practitioner (retired); Ind Univ Med Ctr, asst head nurse, 1959-64; Vis Nurse Asn, supvr, 1964-72; Dept Corr, family nurse practr, 1974-80; Roudebush Vets Admin Med Ctr Home Based Primary Care Prog, nurse practr, 1980-, prog dir, HBPC, 1988-97; "Stuck on Wellness", Nikken Independent Distribr; Ind Sr Citizens' Ctr, audlt practrl NIKKEN health & wellness prod, distribr, currently. **Orgs:** Bd mem, Capitol Improv Bd, 1978-85; pres, Holy Angels Parish Coun, 1979-83; comm ch & bd mem, Coalition 100 Black Women, 1980-; black & minority health task force Ind State Bd Health; stand comn Chronic Health Ind State Bd Health; bd mem, Ind State Bd Nurses & Nurse Practr Coun; pres, Ind Univ Sch Nursing, 1988-91; secy, Dist 5 Alumni Asn Bd Nursing, Ind State Nurses Asn, 1987-89; facilitator, Hosp Based Home Care Support Group, 1989-; vice chmn, Archdiocesan Pastoral Coun, Indianapolis, Ind; elected pres, Cath Found Bd, Archdiocese Indianapolis, Multi-Cult Ministry Adv Comn; Frontline Vol, Indpls Mus Art; secy bd dir, Cath Community Found Archdiocese Indianapolis, currently Am Cancer Soc. **Honors/Awds:** Those Special People Sigma Phi Communications Award; Cert Am Nurses Asn Adult Practr, 1995-2000; Martin Luther King Leadership Award, SCLC; Citizen of Day, WTLC Radio; Chosen Hospital Based Home Care Nurse, 1985; Special Contribution Nursing Veterans Admin Nursing, 1989; Minority Nurse Role Model, Indianapolis Star, 1989; Sigma Theta Tau Nursing Hon Soc, 1989-; nominee, Federal Employee of the Year, Federal Government, 1991; Am Vets, Distinguished Nurse Award; Vol Service Award, Am Cancer Soc, 1995; Salute from WFMY Volunteerism. **Home Addr:** 402 E 46th St, Indianapolis, IN

46205-1758, **Home Phone:** (317)379-2219. **Business Addr:** 1424 E 91st St, Indianapolis, IN 46240, **Business Phone:** (317)709-3365.

**STRONG, HON. CRAIG STEPHEN**
Judge, lawyer, association executive. **Personal:** Born Sep 5, 1947, Detroit, MI; son of Erman and Manila Geraldine Powers. **Educ:** Howard Univ, BS, 1969; Detroit Col Law, JD, 1973. **Career:** Wayne Co Neighborhood Legal Serv, law intern & staff atty, 1970-73; Terry Ahmad & Bradfield, assoc atty, 1973; Elliard Crenshaw & Strong PC, partner, 1974-77; Recorder's Ct City Detroit Traffic & Ordinance Div, referee, 1978; City Detroit Recorder's Ct, judge; Wayne Co 3rd Dist Circuit Ct, judge, 2001-. **Orgs:** Pres, Wolverine Bar Asn; regional dir, Nat Bar Asn; former recorder's ct com chmn, Detroit Bar Asn; vice chmn bd dir, Wayne Co Neighborhood Legal Serv; rep, assembly State Bar Mich; Prince Hall Masons 32nd Degree; bd dir, Karmanos Cancer Inst; founding mem, former pres, Asn Black Judges Mich; life mem, mason, Nat Asn Advan Colored People; Alpha Phi Alpha Fraternity; 33 degree Masons; chair elect, judicial chair, Nat Bar Asn; Supreme Ct Safrica; Black United Fund Mich. **Honors/Awds:** Man of the Year Award, Detroit Urban Ctr, 1979; Howardite of the Year Award, Howard Univ Detroit Chap, 1979; Distinguished Service Award, Nat Coun Negro Women, 1980; Renaissance Award, 13th Dist Dem Party, 1982; Outstanding Museum Service Award, Afro-Am Mus Detroit, 1983; Humanitarian Award Excellence, Mother Waddles Perpetual Mission, 1983; Man Of The Year, North End youth Improv Coun, 1986; Award Of Appreciation, Boy Scouts Am Renaissance Dist, 1988; Civic & Community Contrib Award, Native Detroiter Mag, 1989; Legal Accomplishments Recognition, Wolverine Stud Bar Asn, 1990; Ron Brown Award Merit, Wolverine Stud Bar Asn, 1997; Spec Appreciation Award, SCLC, 1999; Charles H Wright Awar, 1999; Community Activism Award, Wolverine Bar Asn, 1999; Distinguished Service Award, Wolverine Bar Asn & Asn Black Judges, 2000. **Special Achievements:** Youngest president at age twenty-nine, Wolverine Bar Association. **Home Addr:** 1441 Saint Antoine St Suite 803, Detroit, MI 48226-2347. **Business Addr:** Judge, Wayne Co 3rd Circuit Ct, Frank Murphy Hall of Justice, Detroit, MI 48226, **Business Phone:** (313)224-5260.

**STRONG, DEREK LAMAR**
Basketball player, race car driver, businessperson. **Personal:** Born Feb 9, 1968, Los Angeles, CA. **Educ:** Xavier Univ, commun arts, 1990. **Career:** Basketball player (retired), race driver; Huesca La Magia (Spain), 1990-91; Miami Tropics, 1991; Wash Bullets, 1992; Quad City Thunder, 1992-93; Milwaukee Bucks, 1993-94; Boston Celtics, 1994-95; Los Angeles Lakers, 1995-96; Orlando Magic, 1997-2000; Los Angeles Clippers, 2000-01; Columbus Riverdragons, 2002-03; ASA Late Model Ser, race car driver, 2006; Strong Racing, co-owner. **Orgs:** Motor Sports Inst. **Business Addr:** Race Driver, ASA Late Model Series, 7360 Elm, Lexington, MI 48450, **Business Phone:** (810)650-6617.

**STRONG, MACK CARLINGTON**
Football player, executive, broadcaster. **Personal:** Born Sep 11, 1971, Ft. Benning, GA; married Zoe. **Educ:** Univ Ga, grad. **Career:** Football player (retired); Seattle Seahawks, fullback, 1994-2007, wide receiver, 2006; HOPE worldwide, Wash chap; Mack Strong TEAM-WORKS Acad, founder; FoxSports Northwest, sportscaster, 2008-. **Honors/Awds:** NFL Pro Bowl, 2005; Assoc Press All-Pro, 2005; Pro-Bowl, 2005, 2006. **Special Achievements:** Film: 2005 NFC Championship Game, 2006. **Business Addr:** Sportscaster, Fox Sports Northwest, 156th Ave SE Suite 3626, Bellevue, WA 98006, **Business Phone:** (425)641-0104.

**STRONG, OTIS REGINALD, III**
Executive, airline executive. **Personal:** Born Sep 26, 1954, Norfolk, VA; son of Mallie Swinson Smith and Otis; married Gloria W; children: Cayce J & Candace L. **Educ:** Elizabeth City State Univ, BS, health phys ed, recreation, 1976. **Career:** Delta Air Lines Inc, customer serv support agt, 1976-77, sr customer serv agt, 1978-83, sr passenger serv agt, 1983-84, consumer affairs rep, 1984, systs baggage coordr, 1988, elite serv, supvr, 2008. **Orgs:** Nat Asn Advan Colored People, 1976-, JOHER-AAHPR, 1976-; vpres, Uni-Time Inc, 1984-; pres, Alumni Chap ECSU, 1985-, Atlanta Alumni Chap ECSU, 1985-, atlanta metro; coach/head, Fayette Co Rec Asn, 1987-; coach, Fayette Co AAU Basketball-GA, 1988-; Alpha Phi Alpha Frat, 1990-. **Honors/Awds:** Distinguished Alumni Award, 1986. **Home Addr:** 140 Neola Lane, College Park, GA 30349-4922, **Home Phone:** (770)756-9325. **Business Addr:** Consumer Affairs Representative, Supervisor, Delta Air Lines Inc, 1030 Delta Blvd, Atlanta, GA 30320, **Business Phone:** (404)715-2600.

**STRONG-KIMBROUGH, DR. BLONDELL M.**
Management consultant, real estate agent. **Personal:** Born Jan 11, 1943, Ft. Pierce, FL; daughter of Jeff McDonald (deceased) and Bertha McDonald; married Charles E; children: Stanford II & Jeff Bertram. **Educ:** Tenn State Univ, BS, 1964; Geo Peabody Col, Vanderbilt Univ, MLS, 1967; Univ Mich, PhD, 1983, post-doctorate, 1985. **Career:** Lincoln Jr Col, librn & music instr, 1964-65; Indian River Jr Col, librn & asst cataloger, 1965-67; Meharry Med Col, libr dir, 1967-77; Fisk-Meharry Credit Union, gen mgr & treas, 1976-77; Univ Mich, post-doctorate fel, 1984-85, mgt consult; Bond Realty Inc, mgt exec, 1986-88; Bordeaux Realty Plus, pres & co-owner, currently. **Orgs:** Life mem, Nat Asn Advan Colored People, Nashville Br, 1991, treas, 1991, 1995-96; Alpha Kappa Alpha Sorority; Kappa Delta Pi Hon Soc; Beta Phi Mu Int Libr Sci Hon Soc. **Home Addr:** 3852 Augusta Dr, Nashville, TN 37207, **Home Phone:** (615)876-4863. **Business Addr:** President, Bordeaux Realty Plus, 3250 Dickerson Pke Suite 4, Nashville, TN 37207-2969, **Business Phone:** (615)227-3898.

**STROTHER, DR. GERMAINE D.**
Physician, educator. **Personal:** Born Oct 5, 1954, Enid, OK; daughter of Earl L and Ruth B; married Joseph Banks. **Educ:** Ohio State Univ Col Med, attended 1979. **Career:** Pvt pract, currently; Univ Southern Calif, Sch Med, clin asst prof, currently; Ohio State Univ Col Med, pres-elect, 2000-. **Orgs:** Pres, OH State Univ Col Med & Pub Health Med Alumni bd govs, 2000-. **Home Addr:** 7197 Brockton Ave Suite 1, Riverside, CA 92506-2637, **Home Phone:** (951)682-4560. **Business Addr:** Clinical Assistant Professor, University Southern California, PO Box 51358, Riverside, CA 92517-2358, **Business Phone:** (951)827-1012.

**STROUD, LOUIS WINSTON**
Executive, management consultant, manager. **Personal:** Born Nov 21, 1946, Cincinnati, OH. **Educ:** Canisius Col, AB, hist, 1968; Harvard Grad Sch Bus Admin, MBA, fin, 1970; Univ San Francisco Sch Law, JD, 1976. **Career:** Mfrs Hanover Trust, corp planner, 1973, prod mgr disbursements, 1974-76; Kaiser Aluminum & Chem Corp, merger acquisition specialist, sr strategic planner, 1976-82; Kuwait Petrol Corp, mgr, sr financial person, 1982-85; Coop Joint Venture Prog, 1986-96; HEDGE IQ, finance proj specialist, 1997-98; Bickel & Brewer, sr consult, 1998-99; independent financial analyst & consult, 1999-2005; US Small Bus Admin, 2005-07; Fidelity Investments, retirement investment specialist, 2007-08; independent financial consult, 2008-09; US Small Bus Admin, 2008-11; Statewide Remodeling Inc, sales lead generation, 2010-11. **Orgs:** Harvard Bus Sch Club; Harvard Club. **Business Addr:** Manager, Kuwait Petroleum Corp, PO Box 26565, Safat13126.

**STRUDWICK, LINDSEY H., SR.**
Executive, manager. **Personal:** Born Aug 8, 1946, Durham, NC; son of London L Sr and Christine Alston; married Gladys B; children: Lindsey Howard Jr & Casandra Michelle. **Educ:** Durham Bus Col, Durham NC, assoc degree sci & bus admin; Shaw Univ, Raleigh NC, BA; Southeastern Univ, Greenville SC, MBA. **Career:** Int Fertil Res, Chapel Hill NC, purchasing mgr, 1974-76; Northrop Corp, Res Triangle Pk NC, mgr purchasing & facil, 1976-78; Gen Tel Co, Durham NC, personnel asst, 1978-79; Northern Telecom Inc, Res Triangle Pk NC, group leader purchasing, 1979-81; Sci-Atlanta Inc, Atlanta GA, mgr purchasing & contracts, 1982-86; Adolph Coors Co, Golden, CO, dir purchasing & mat mgt, 1986-, dir proj purchasing & contracts. **Orgs:** Nat Asn Advan Colored People, 1978-; Nat Asn Purchasing Mgt, 1978-; Am Prod & Inventory Control Soc, 1980-; Am Purchasing Soc, 1985-; bd dir, Rocky Mountain Regional Minority Supplier Develop Coun, 1986-, chmn, 1986-88; bd dir, Nat Minority Supplier Develop Coun, 1987-; bd dir, Nat Minorities Bus Dirs, 1988-. **Honors/Awds:** Named Man of the Year, Nat Urban League, 1986; Corporate Citizenship Award, United Indian Develop Asn, 1988. **Home Addr:** 4908 N Granby St, Denver, CO 80239-4267, **Home Phone:** (303)371-0811. **Business Addr:** Director Purchasing, Adolph Coors Co, 3777 MC Intyre St, Golden, CO 80401, **Business Phone:** (303)277-5760.

**STUART, IVAN I.**
Military leader. **Personal:** married Dorthey M; children: Ivan jr, Connie, Selwyn, JoAnn & Desire. **Career:** AUS. **Orgs:** Bd gov's, New River Comt Action & Prog; delegate, Dem Comt; Va Deacon Little River Bapt Ch Floyd; Masonic Lodge 146; pres, Floyd Co Branch Nat Asn Advan Colred People.

**STUART, REGINALD A.**
Journalist, writer. **Personal:** Born Nov 26, 1948, Nashville, TN; son of William and Maxie Allen; married Daryl Thomas. **Educ:** Tenn State Univ, BS, 1968; Columbia Univ, MJour, 1971. **Career:** Nashville Tennessean, reporter, 1968-69; WSIX-AM-FM-TV, 1969-70; John Hay Whitney Found, New York, NY, consult, 1972-74; New York Times, bus & fin news reporter, 1974-76; Times, nat corresp, bur chief, 1976-87; Philadelphia Daily News, 1987-90; Knight-Ridder Newspapers, Wash Bur, asst ed, 1990-96, recruiter; Emerge Mag, contrib ed, 1995-2000; McClatchy Co, recruiter, 2006-. **Orgs:** Nat Asn Advan Colored People; CME; fel, Soc Prof Journalists; pres, Sigma Delta Chi Found. **Honors/Awds:** Carter G Woodson Nat Educ Asn Award, 1969; Nat Headliners Award, Best Team News Reporting, 1970; Serv Award, Nat Asn Advan Colored People, 1974; Wells Memorial Key, Soc Prof Journalists, 1992; Ida B Wells Award, Nat Asn Black Journalists. **Home Addr:** 13102 Tamarack Rd, Silver Spring, MD 20904. **Business Addr:** Recruiter, Knight Ridder, 50 W San Fernando St Suite 1500, San Jose, CA 95113, **Business Phone:** (408)938-7700.

**STUBBLEFIELD, DANA WILLIAM**
Actor, football player, football coach. **Personal:** Born Nov 14, 1970, Cleves, OH; children: Kayla. **Educ:** Univ Kans. **Career:** Football player (retired); San Francisco 49ers, defensive tackle, 1993-97; Wash Redskins, 1998-2000; San Francisco 49ers, 2001-02; Oakland Raiders, 2003; New Eng Patriots, 2004; Valley Christian High Sch, defensive line coach; Films: Reindeer Games, 2000.

**STUBBLEFIELD, JENNYE LEE WASHINGTON**
Educator, nutritionist. **Personal:** Born Mar 6, 1925, Jacksonville, FL; daughter of Marion Washington and Ira Johnson Washington; married Charles. **Educ:** Tuskegee Inst, BS, 1946; Rutgers State Univ, MS, 1966. **Career:** Educator, nutritionist (retired); Dietitian Lincoln Hosp, Durham, N Carolina, 1946-48, instr, veterans cooking & baking schs, 1948-50; William Jason High Sch, cafe mgr & voc foods teacher, 1950-56; St Francis Hosp Sch, nutrit, 1957-64; Helene Fuld Hosp Sch, 1964-70; Middlesex County NJ Head Start Prog, dir food serv, 1966-67; Home Econ Hamilton Twp NJ, teacher, 1967-71; Dept Health Recreation & Welfare Trenton, dir, 1971-74; dir, 1974-76; Trenton Pub Sch Bd Educ, supvr home econ & family life educ progs, 1976-92; City Trenton, coun woman, 1976-90. **Orgs:** Am Dietetic Asn, 1964-; Am Home Econ Asn, 1967-89; bd dir, Trenton chap Am Red Cross, 1972-77; Black Women Dem Action, 1978; Carver Youth & Family Ctr, 1983; vice chmn, Mercer County Dem Comt, 1981-83; Bilalian African Am Conf, 1983; Fairless Steel Black Caucus, 1984; Mercer Co NW Ward Dem Club, 1984; chmn, County Dem Comm Mercer County, NJ, 1984-85; LIFT, Comt Social Prog, Trenton Asn Pub Schs, 1990; Nat Asn Advan Colored People; Am Voc Asn; Women's Polit Caucus; Nj Asn Sec Sch Principals & Supervisors; Voc Educ Asn; Home Econs Educ Asn; Am Home Econs Asn. **Home Addr:** 21 Alden Ave, Trenton, NJ 08618-3001, **Home Phone:** (609)396-1014. **Business Addr:** 301 Prospect St, Trenton, NJ 08618, **Business Phone:** (609)989-3463.

**STUBBLEFIELD, MICHAEL JEROME, JR.**
Fashion designer, business owner. **Personal:** Born Feb 14, 1962, Detroit, MI; son of Wytche and Georgia. **Educ:** Univ Calif, Los Angeles, BA, politial sci & int rels, 1986. **Career:** Michael J Stubblefield Collection, chief exec officer & designer, 1992-. **Business Addr:** Chief Executive Officer, Designer, Stubblefield Collection, 1033 S Basset St, Detroit, MI 48217-1668, **Business Phone:** (313)841-2951.

**STUBBLEFIELD, RAYMOND M.**
Association executive, executive director. **Personal:** Born Aug 3, 1945, Abilene, TX; married Pat. **Educ:** NM Highland Col; Taft Col; San Diego State, BS & BA, 1969. **Career:** United Food & Com Workers Union, asst dir; Comm Rel Dept Retail Clks Int Asn, co-dir; Big Brothers, works correction officers. **Honors/Awds:** Commercial Service Award, San Diego Youth Leg, 1970. **Home Addr:** 1134 Reitz Dr, Cedar Hill, TX 75104. **Business Addr:** Assistant to Director, UFCW, 4552 Valley View Lane, Irving, TX 75038.

**STUBBS, DR. GEORGE WINSTON**
Physician, ophthalmologist. **Personal:** Born Sep 13, 1942, Brooklyn, NY; son of Cornelius A and Beryl Hinds; married Joyce Kennedy; children: George W II & C David L. **Educ:** Hunter Col, AB, 1964; Howard Univ Col Med, MD, 1968. **Career:** Bronx-Lebanon Hosp Ctr, resident Ophthal; Harlem Hosp Ctr, fel, 1975; Wills Eye Inst, fel, 1976; Wills Eye Hosp, resident, asst surgeon, 1977, assoc surgeon, 1993, ophthalmologist, currently; Med Col Pa, asst prof surg, 1979; Usphs Hosp, resident; G Winston Stubbs MD Ltd, pres, 1982; Ger town Hosp, attend opthalmologist; Chestnut Hill Hosp, attend ophthalmologist, Grad Hosp Country, staff; pvt pract, currently. **Orgs:** Fel Int Col Surg, 1979; fel Pa Col Physicians, 1980; fel Am Col Surgeon, 1981; Am Acad Ophthal, 1977; pres, Med Soc Pa, 1995; fel Am Col Surgeons; fel Heed opthalmic found. **Honors/Awds:** Physician Recognition Award, 1981, 1983, 1987. **Home Addr:** 530 E Mt Airy Ave, Philadelphia, PA 19119, **Home Phone:** (215)242-5532. **Business Addr:** Ophthalmologist, Wills Eye Hospital, 840 Walnut St, Philadelphia, PA 19107, **Business Phone:** (877)289-4557.

**STUCKEY, SHEILA ARNETTA**
Library administrator. **Personal:** Born Aug 12, 1964, Anderson, SC; daughter of Eugene J Sr and Early D. **Educ:** SC State Univ, BS, gen home econ libr sci, 1987; Univ Pittsburgh, MLS, 1989. **Career:** SC State Univ, coordr info retrieval serv ref librn, 1989-94; KY State Univ, collection develop librn, 1994-96, acq unit head, 1996-2001, from asst dir to assoc, 2001-05, dir, 2005-. **Orgs:** Am Libr Asn, 1988-; Black Caucus ALA, 1994-; KY Libr Asn, 1994-; cluster coordr, AKA Cent Region, 2001-02; pres, Alpha Kappa Alpha, Beta Upsilon Omega Chap, 2002-03. **Special Achievements:** Contributor, Notable Black American Men, Gale, 1999, 2006; Contributor, Notable Black American Women, 2003; Contributor, Encyclopedia of African American Business, 2006. **Home Addr:** 104 Palmer Dr, Frankfort, KY 40601, **Home Phone:** (502)226-1727. **Business Addr:** Director of Libraries, Kentucky State University, 400 E Main St, Frankfort, KY 40601, **Business Phone:** (502)597-6852.

**STUDDARD, CHRISTOPHER RUBEN.** **See STUDDARD, RUBEN.**

**STUDDARD, RUBEN (CHRISTOPHER RUBEN STUDDARD)**
Singer, actor. **Personal:** Born Sep 12, 1978, Birmingham, AL; married Surata Zuri McCants. **Educ:** Ala A&M Univ. **Career:** TV series: Christmas in Rockefeller Center, 2003; "8 Simple Rules for Dating My Teenage Daughter", 2005; "Life on a Stick", 2005; "All of Us", 2005; Eve, 2006; Real Husbands of Hollywood, 2013. Albums: Soulful, 2003; American Idol Season 2: All-Time Classic American Love Songs, 2003; American Idol: The Great Holiday Classics, 2003; Ain't Misbehavin', 2009; I Need an Angel, 2004; The Return, 2006; Love Is, 2009; Letters from Birmingham, 2012; Unconditional Love, 2014. Playlist: The Very Best of Ruben Studdard, 2010; Singles: "Flying Without Wings", 2003; "Superstar", 2003; "Sorry 2004", 2004; "What If", 2004; "I Need an Angel", 2004; "Change Me", 2006; "Make Ya Feel Beautiful", 2007; "Celebrate Me Home", 2008; "Together", 2009; "Don't Make 'Em Like U No More", 2009; "June 28th", 2009; "Meant to Be", 2014. J Records, singer, currently; Flim Musics: Scooby Doo 2: Monsters Unleashed, 2004; Natural Born Komics, 2006. Films: Lifted, 2010; The Perfect Gift, 2011. **Orgs:** Owner, Ruben Studdard Found Advan Children Music Arts. **Honors/Awds:** Am Idol Winner, 2003; Teen Choice Award, 2003; Best New Artist Award, Nat Asn Advan Colored People, 2004; Soul Train Award, 2004; Two Billboard Music Awards; Billboard R&B/Hip Hop Award; American Music Award, 2004; BET Awards, 2004 & 2005; Grammy Awards, 2004; Image Awards, 2004. **Home Addr:** PO Box 900, Beverly Hills, CA 90213-0900. **Business Addr:** Recording Artist, J Records, 745 5th Ave, New York, NY 10151, **Business Phone:** (646)840-5600.

**STULL, DONALD L.**
Executive, architect. **Personal:** Born May 16, 1937, Springfield, OH; son of Robert and Ruth Callahan Branson; married Patricia Ryder; children: Cydney Lynn, Robert Branson & Gia Virginia. **Educ:** Ohio State Univ, BS, 1961; Harvard Grad Sch Design, 1962. **Career:** George Mason Clark, architect designer, 1958-62; Boston Fed Off Bldg Architects, designer, 1961-62; Samuel Glaser & Partners, proj dir, 1962-66; Stull Assoc Inc, pres, 1966-83; Stull & Lee Assocs Inc, founding partner, owner, pres, 1984-. **Orgs:** Fel Am inst Architects; Boston Archit Ctr, 1972-; Resource Panel, Nat Endowment Arts, 1978-; adv bd mem, Mus Afro-Am Hist, Boston, 1979-; adv comn, Ohio State Univ, Sch Archit, 1980-; City Cambridge, Design Adv Group, 1980-90, 1994-; adv bd mem, Mus Nat Ctr Afro-Am Hist, 1982-; Boston Civic Design Community, 1987-98; vis comn, Harvard Grad Sch Design, 1988-94; adv comn, Suffolk Sch Bus Mgt, 1989-; Hist Boston, 1990-; trustee, Boston Found Archit, 1992-; vis design studio prof, Rice Univ Sch Archit, 1993; GSA's Pub Bldg Serv, Nat Regist Peer Professionals, 1994-96; bd overseers, Inst Contemp Art, 1996, 1997; Nat Accreditation Bd Col Sch Archit. **Home Addr:** 431 Marlborough St, Boston, MA 02115, **Home Phone:** (617)267-1137. **Business Addr:** President, Founding Partner, Stull and Lee Inc, 103 Ter St, Roxbury Crossing, MA 02120, **Business Phone:** (617)426-0406.

**STULL, EVERETT JAMES**
Baseball player. **Personal:** Born Aug 24, 1971, Ft. Riley, KS. **Educ:** Tenn State Univ. **Career:** Baseball player (retired); Montreal Expos, relief pitcher, 1997; Atlanta Braves, 1999; Milwaukee Brewers, 2000,

2002; Minn Twins, pitcher, 2003; Reno Silver Sox, 2006; Laredo Broncos, 2006; Grays, 2007.

## STULL, DR. VIRGINIA ELIZABETH

Physician. **Personal:** Born May 7, 1939, Springfield, OH. **Educ:** Tex S Univ, BS, attended 1960; Am Univ, attended attended 1961; Univ Tex Med Br, Galveston, MD, 1966; Capital Univ, 1972. **Career:** Pvt pract physician, 1967-; Bur Voc Rehab, field med; ER phy, 1967-71; Univ Calif Irvine Med Ctr, resident phys med & rehab; consult, 1968-75; Columbus Bd Educ, sch phy, 1968-73; Med Diag Serv Inc, pres & owner, 1975-; Ohio State Univ Med Sch, Dept Phys Med & Rehab, , clin prof; St Anthony Hosp. **Orgs:** Am Med Women's Asn; AMA; Acad Med Columbus & Franklin County; Alpha Kappa Alpha Sor; Sigma Xi Am Sci Soc. **Honors/Awds:** Lambda Chi Outstanding Black Woman in Ohio, 1975; Flowers for Living Award, 1975; Award, Columbus Chap, Nat Epicureans Inc. **Home Addr:** 3680 Waldo Pl, Columbus, OH 43220. **Business Addr:** Clinical professor, Ohio State University of Medical School, 3100 Needmore Rd, Dayton, OH 45414, **Business Phone:** (937)455-5240.

## STURDIVANT, COL. TADARIAL J.

Police chief, government official. **Career:** Mich State Police, dep dir, uniform serv bur, dir, currently. **Special Achievements:** First African American to direct the State Police. **Business Addr:** Director, Michigan State Police, 714 S Harrison Rd, East Lansing, MI 48823, **Business Phone:** (517)336-6157.

## STYLES, FREDDIE L.

Artist. **Personal:** Born May 12, 1944, Madison, GA. **Educ:** Morris Brown Col, attended 1965; Atlanta Sch Art. **Career:** Clark Atlanta Univ, artist-in-residence; Clayton State Univ, artist-in-residence; Spelman Col, artist-in-residence; Morris Brown Col Drama Guild, costume set designer, 1963-65; Black Artist, Carnegie Inst, lectr, 1969; Abbr Arts Proj Black Artists, co-dir; Nat Urban League, organizer art exhib, 1975; City Gallery E Atlanta, GA, dir, 2003-08. **Orgs:** La Watercolor Soc, 1973-74; Cooperstown Art Asn, 1974-75; High Mus Art; Black Artists; Clarence White Contemp Art Gallery. **Honors/Awds:** A third place-award in graphics; King Baudouin Foundation Cultural Exchange Program Grant, Community Found Greater Atlanta, 2001. **Home Addr:** 98 Candler Rd SE, Atlanta, GA 30317-3051, **Home Phone:** (404)371-0420. **Business Addr:** Artist, The Museum of Contemporary Art of Georgia, 75 Bennett St NW Suite A2, Atlanta, GA 30309, **Business Phone:** (404)367-8700.

## STYLES, KATHLEEN ANN

School administrator, association executive, educator. **Personal:** Born Aug 6, 1949, Baltimore, MD; daughter of Calvin P and Minnie V Brown. **Educ:** Coppin State Col, BS, elem educ, 1971, MS, spec educ, 1972; Univ Md, 1983. **Career:** CETA Prog, instr, 1971-72; Baltimore City Community Col, employ counr, 1974-76, col counr, 1976-79, actg dir stud act, 1979-80, prof develop specialist, 1981-, actg dir off campus & ext centers, asst exec dir enrollment mgt & registr, currently, Div Stud Affairs, exec dir, currently. **Orgs:** Housing adv, US Dept Housing & Urban Develop, 1972-73; Nat Task Force Career Educ, 1978-80; bd, SSD Inc, 1982-84; founder, Learning Intellectual Skills Advan, 1988-94; dir stud affairs, harbor campus, 1994-. **Home Addr:** 5709 Gwynn Oak Ave, Baltimore, MD 21207, **Home Phone:** (410)367-2793. **Business Addr:** Executive Director, Assistant Executive Director, Baltimore City Community College, 2901 Liberty Heights Ave, Baltimore, MD 21215-7893, **Business Phone:** (410)462-8365.

## STYLES, LORENZO

Football coach, football player. **Personal:** Born Jan 31, 1974, Columbus, OH. **Educ:** Ohio State Univ. **Career:** Football player (retired), coach; Atlanta Falcons, linebacker, 1995-96; St Louis Rams, 1997, 1999, linebacker, 1998, 2000; Marion Mayhem, defensive line coach, 2010; Ohio Dominican Univ, asst linebackers coach, 2010-11; Dayton Silverbacks, defensive coordr & defensive backs coach, 2011; Marion Blue Racers, head coach, 2011-12. **Orgs:** Founder, Lorenzo Styles & Friends found. **Honors/Awds:** Mercer County Hall of Fame, 1990, 1991. **Business Addr:** Founder, The Lorenzo Styles & Friends Foundation, 1376 E Livingston Ave, Columbus, OH 43205, **Business Phone:** (614)268-7800.

## STYLES, REV. DR. RICHARD WAYNE, SR.

Clergy. **Personal:** Born Jun 22, 1939, Waterbury, CT; son of James Lawrence Sr and Helene Marie Copeland; married Helen Penelope Horton; children: Richard Wayne Jr & Helene Rishae. **Educ:** Shaw Univ, BA, 1965; Southeastern Baptist Theol Sem, MDiv, 1969. **Career:** Tupper Memorial Baptist Church, pastor, 1965-68; Star Bethel Baptist Church, pastor, 1968-73; First Baptist Church Apple St, sr pastor, 1973-2010; Ministerial Fel Alliance Alamanee County; Shaw Univ Cape Fezr Ctr, prog bible, currently. **Orgs:** Bd dir, Burlington Housing Authority, 1977-; Recruiter, Crop Walk, 1977-; vol coun, Alamance County Ct Syst, 1979-83; dean inst, United Bible Inst, 1980-; exec comn, N State Legal Aid, 1980-; bd dir, Burlington Christ Acad, 1980-83; bd dir, Access, 1980-84; vicechmn bd dir, Allied Church Alamance County, 1983-; chmn relig activ, Broad view Mid Sch, 1984-; exec dir, lamance County Head start, 1984-; bd dir, Hospice Alamanee County; chair trustees bd, Gen Baptist Conv Inc, NC; bd dir, Home care Providers; bd dir, Care Ministry; bd dir, United Way; bd dir, Family Abuse Serv; bd dir, Fair Housing Comt; bd dir, Christian Coun Serv; bd dir, Alamance Coalition Against Drug Abuse, Alamanee City Dept Social Servs; chmn, Alamance County Bd Social Serv; Alamance-Burlington Schs Closing Gap Comt; Dropout Prev Task Force; Burlington Housing Authority. **Honors/Awds:** Good Shepherd Award for Distinguished Service, Boy Scouts Am, 1979; Volunteer Counselor Award, Gov James Hunt NC, 1983; Hon Doctorate, United Bible Inst; North Carolina Volunteer Award; Service Award for Meritorious Service, Nat Asn Advan Colored People, Alamance County Br; Outstanding Volunteer Award, United Way Alamance County Community Coun. **Home Addr:** 612 Crestview Dr, Burlington, NC 27217-1711, **Home Phone:** (336)226-8016. **Business Addr:** Senior Pastor, First Baptist Church of Apple Street, 508 Apple St, Burlington, NC 27217-2450, **Business Phone:** (336)227-2542.

## SUBER, DIANNE BOARDLEY

College administrator. **Personal:** children: Nichole Reshan Lewis & Raegan LaTrese Thomas (Farah). **Educ:** Hampton Univ, BS, early childhood educ, 1971; Univ Ill, Urbana Champaign, MEd, curric & supv, 1973; Va Polytech Inst & State Univ, Blacksburg, VA, PhD, educ admin, 1995. **Career:** Newport News Pub Schs, Va, Elem & Mid Sch, prin, 1976-92; Matthew Whaley Primary Sch, prin, 1983-86; Hampton Univ, dean admin servs, assoc provost acad affairs, 1992-96, vpres admin serv, 1996-99; St Augustines Col, pres, 1999-2014. **Orgs:** Am Coun Edu; bd dir, Cent Region Wachovia Bank; United Negro Col Fund; Nat Asn Independent Cols & Univs; Bus & Technol Ctr; Triangle Family Servs; Asn Episcopal Cols; Consortium Doctors LTD; S E Raleigh Improv Assembly; Livable St Comm; secy, Educ Historically Black Cols & Univs Capital Financing Adv Bd; comnr, Am Coun Educ Comn Women Higher Educ; pres, Coop Raleigh Cols; bd dir, Cent Region Wachovia Bank; Cent Intercollegiate Athletic Asn; United Negro Col Fund; Nat Asn Independent Cols; Univs (NAICU); Bus & Technol Ctr; Greater Raleigh Chamber Com; Communities Schs Wake County; Marbles Kids Mus; United Negro Col Fund's Exec; Asn Episcopal Cols; exec & nominating Comts, Nc Independent Cols & Univs; grants Comt, Women's Network Wake County; Consortium Doctors, LTD; Southeast Raleigh Improv Assembly; Blue Ribbon Comt Future Wake County; Rotary Club, Delta Sigma Theta Sorority; Pres bd advisors, White House Initiative Historically Black Cols & Univs, currently. **Business Addr:** Board of Advisors, Historically Black Colleges and Universities, 400 Md Ave SW Suite 4C128, Washington, DC 20202, **Business Phone:** (202)453-5634.

## SUBER, TORA

Basketball player. **Personal:** Born Nov 23, 1974, Coatesville, PA; daughter of Geraldine. **Educ:** Va Univ, attended 1997. **Career:** Basketball player (retired); Charlotte Sting, guard, 1997-98; Orlando Miracle, 1999; Houston Comets, guard, 2004. **Home Addr:** 83 S 6th Ave, Coatesville, PA 19320-3655, **Home Phone:** (484)786-9759.

## SUBRYAN, CARMEN BARCLAY

Writer, educator. **Personal:** Born Dec 30, 1944, McKenzie; daughter of Lawrence and Sybil Allicock; children: Nicole & Natasha. **Educ:** Howard Univ, Wash, DC, BA, 1971, MA, 1973, PhD, eng, 1983. **Career:** Univ DC, acad support, 1973-74; Howard Univ, Wash, DC, prog coordr, instr, 1974-2008, Ctr Acad Reinforcement, writing instr, currently; Montgomery Col, adj fac, 2004-06. **Orgs:** Phi Beta Kappa, Howard Univ, 1971; Nat Coun Teachers Eng, 1980-84; Col Lang Asn, 1981-86; Nat Asn Develop Educ, 1985-87; GUYAID, 1985-. **Special Achievements:** Reprise, a book of poetry, 1984; "Walter Dean Myers", Article in Dictionary of Literary Biography, 1984; "A B Spellman", article in Dictionary of Literary Biography, 1985; Woman's Survival, booklet, 1989; Black-Water Women, a novel, 1997; Rachel's Tears, poetry, 2000; Black-Water People, a novel, 2003; Black-Water Children, a novel, 2006. **Home Addr:** 11400 Pitsea Dr, Beltsville, MD 20705-1763, **Home Phone:** (301)937-3428. **Business Addr:** Writing Instructor, Howard University, Acad Support Bldg B 2400 6th St NW Suite 102, Washington, DC 20059, **Business Phone:** (202)806-7787.

## SUDARKASA, DR. MICHAEL ERIC MABOGUNJE

Lawyer, chief executive officer, founder (originator). **Personal:** Born Aug 5, 1964, New York, NY; son of Akin Mabogunje and Niara; married Joyce Ann Johnson; children: Jasmine Ayana Yetunde, Jonathan Michael Toure, Maya Elizabeth Sade & Marielle Iman. **Educ:** Univ Mich, BA, hist, 1985; Howard Univ, vis stud, 1983; Harvard Law Sch, JD, 1988; Univ San Diego, inst int & comparative law, 1990. **Career:** African Develop Bank, tech asst, pvt sector develop unit, 1988-89; Citibank-Abidjan, banking int, 1988-89; 21st Century Africa Inc, founder & consult, 1989; Steel, Hector & Davis PC, assoc, 1990; 21st Century Africa Inc, pres, 1990-97; Trade & Investment Prom Serv, dir, 1997-99; Georgetown Univ, Grad Sch bus, adj lectr; Africa Bus Direct, co-founder & chief exec officer, 2000-; Mchunu Koikanyang, SAfrica, atty, currently; Africa Bus Group, cheif exec officer, 2005-. **Orgs:** Overseas Develop Counc, Africa Round table; Am Bar Asn; Calvert New World Fund; Soc Int Developt. **Home Addr:** 1418 Woodman Ave, Silver Spring, MD 20902. **Business Addr:** Chief Executive Officer, President, Africa Business Group, Agence France Presse Bldg Keyes Ave, Johannesburg, VA 02196.

## SUDARKASA, NIARA (GLORIA A MARSHALL)

School administrator, scholar. **Personal:** Born Aug 14, 1938, Ft. Lauderdale, FL; married John L Clark; children: Michael Eric. **Educ:** Fisk Univ, attended 1956; Oberlin Col, BA, 1957; Columbia Univ, MA, 1959, PhD, anthrop, 1964. **Career:** School administrator (retired); Early Admis Col, Ford Found scholar, 1953-57; John Hay Whitney Oppty fel, 1959-60; John Hay Whitney Opportunity fel, 1959-60; Ford Found Foreign Area Training fel, 1960-63; Ford Found Foreign Area Training fel, 1960-63; Comn Comparative Study New Nations, Univ Chicago, fel, 1963-64; Carnegie Found Study of New Nation fel, 1963-64; Carnegie Found Study New Nation fel, 1963-64; NY Univ, asst prof, 1964-67; Univ Mich, from asst prof to prof, anthrop, 1967-76, Ctr Afro-Am & African Studies, dir, 1981-84, acad affairs, assoc vpres, 1986; Social Sci Res Coun fel, 1973-74; Soc sci Res Coun fel, 1973-74; Sr Fulbright Res Schol, 1982-83; Lincoln Univ, pres, 1987-98; Fla Atlantic Univ, distinguished vis scholar; African-Am Res Libr & Cult Ctr, Ft Lauderdale, FA, scholar in residence, currently. **Orgs:** African Studies Asn, 1959-69, 1982-; fel Am Anthrop Asn, 1964-; fel Am Anthrop Asn Exec Bd, 1972-75; bd dir, Ann Arbor Comn Ctr, 1983-; chmn, State Mich Comn Minorities Women & Handicappers Higher Educ, 1984-; Am Asn Higher Educ, 1986; Coun Foreign Rels; Nat Asn Adv Colored People; Nat Coun Negro Women; Asn Black Anthropologists; Acad Educ Develop; USIA Trilateral Task Force N Am Edu; Peace Corps Nat Adv Coun; White House Comn Presidential Scholars; bd dir, Acad Educ Develop. **Honors/Awds:** Senior Fulbright research scholarship, 1982-83; Achievement Award, Alpha Kappa Alpha; Achievement Award, Zeta Phi Beta; Achievement Award, Elks, City Ft Lauderdale. **Special Achievements:** Author Where Women Work, University of Michigan Press, 1973; Building a partnership in education, NAFEO Excellence Inc, 1992; The Barnes Bond Connection, Exploring the African- American experience, Lincoln University Press, 1995; The Strength of Our Mothers, Africa World Press, 1996; Education Is Still the Key, Africa World Press, 1998; The first woman to serve as president of Lincoln University; Received 13 honorary degrees from U.S. and African universities; She is one of 75 women included in Brian Lanker's book, "I Dream a World: Portraits of Black Women Who Changed America"; First Black woman to be appointed assistant professor of anthropology at New York University in 1964; First African America woman to teach at the university; First African American to be appointed to the Department of Anthropology at the University of Michigan in 1969; First female to serve as president of Lincoln University in Pennsylvania; First African American to be installed as a Chief in the historic life Kingdom of the Yoruba of Nigeria, 2001. **Business Addr:** Scholar in Residence, The African-American Research Library and Cultural Center, 2650 Sistrunk Blvd, Ft. Lauderdale, FL 33311-8658, **Business Phone:** (954)357-6282.

## SUDBURY, LESLIE G.

Chemist. **Personal:** Born May 11, 1939, Meridian, MS; son of James and Mamie; married Audrey Faulkens; children: Leslie D, Pamela M, David G & Gloria M. **Educ:** Xavier Univ, BSc, chem, 1961; Notre Dame Grad Sch, chem. **Career:** Whitehall Labs, pharm control chemist, 1961-65; Miles Labs Inc, res chemist, 1966-73, supvr control chemist, 1973-78, mgr div control, 1978-82, mgr biol eval, 1982-85; IYHL Soccer, coach, 1980-82; ICN Immuno, oper mgr, 1985-89, dir lab opers, 1989-. **Orgs:** Am Chem Soc, 1966-; bd mem, NBLCC, 1976-85; bd dir, treas, NOBC, 1977-85; secy & ed newsletter, Am Chem Soc, St Joseph Valley Sec, 1979-83; co-chmn, BAC Inter Community Comn, 1980-82; Am Soc Qual Control, 1982-86; Knights Peter Claver, 1984-85; Sec Coun 251 KPC; St Augustine Parish, S Bend, IN. **Honors/Awds:** Outstanding Service, Am Chem Soc, St Joe Valley Sec, 1981; Outstanding Service, NBLCC Midwest Regional. **Home Addr:** 431 E 20th St, Costa Mesa, CA 92627-2315.

## SUDLER, PEGGY

Association executive, administrator. **Career:** Ministry Caring Inc, prog dir; City Wilmington, Del, resource ctr coordr, currently. **Business Addr:** Program Director, City of Wilmington Resource Center, 100 W 18th St Shortlidge Acad Rm 110, Wilmington, DE 19802, **Business Phone:** (302)651-2758.

## SUGGS, DENIS

Media executive, vice president (organization). **Educ:** NC State Univ, BS, elec engineering, 1989; Duke Univ, MBA, 1998. **Career:** IBM, var, 1990-2001; PS OrangeCo, a Pub Storage Co, sr. vpres, opers,, 2001-02; Danaher, Portescap-A Danaher Co, pres, 2003-07; Miranda Technologies Inc, chief exec officer; Danaher Corp; Pub Storage Inc, sr vpres opers, 2003-07; Belden Inc, vpres Americas opers, 2007-09, exec vpres Americas div, 2009-13; Strategic Mat Inc, pres & chief exec officer, 2014-. **Business Addr:** Chief Executiv Officer, President, Strategic Materials Inc, 16365 Pk Ten Pl Suite 200, Houston, TX 77084.

## SUGGS, DR. ROBERT CHINELO

Educator, colonial administrator, photographer. **Personal:** Born Dec 23, 1943, Newport, RI; son of Lewis and Beatrice; married Mary Louise Morrison; children: Lawrence, Sarah, Elizabeth & James. **Educ:** Barrington Col, BA, 1967; State Univ NY, MS, 1971, EdD, coun & psychol, 1979. **Career:** Educator, (retired), photographer; State Univ New York, fel, 1971-73; State Univ NY, Dept Counr Educ, Brockport State Univ, asst prof, 1972-78; Community Bible Church, pastor, 1974-80; Ed Millersville Univ, Dept Counr, asst prof, 1982-85; Univ Md, Psycho physiol Clin, clin asst prof, 1983-85; Crossroads Coun Asns, therapist, 1983-; Christian Asn Psychiat Studies, newsletter ed, 1983-; Daystar Univ, vis prof, 1985-86; Messiah Col, assoc prof psycho, prof psychol, 1980-90, chair, 1984-85, dir personnel, 1990-92; Cornerstone Col, vpres acad affairs & dean, 1992-95; Malone Col, provost, 1995; Ashland Univ, provost, 2002-07; Aperture Fine Art Photog, photogr, 2010-. **Orgs:** Kappa Delta Pi, Rho Tau Chap; bd trustee, Judson Col, 1993-99; bd trustee, Pathway Inc, 1996-99; vpres, Canton Urban League, 1998-2001. **Honors/Awds:** Named to Top 500 High School Basketball Players, US Dell Mag, 1963; Outstanding Teacher, Messiah Col, 1981. **Special Achievements:** Messiah College Faculty Research Grant recipient, 1987; Listed in Who's Who in America 59th Edition, 2005. **Home Addr:** 5204 Discovery Dr, Kentwood, MI 49508.

## SUGGS, TERRELL RAYMONN

**Personal:** Born Oct 11, 1982, Minneapolis, MN; son of Donald Sr and Lavern. **Educ:** Ariz State Univ, grad. **Career:** Baltimore Ravens, defensive end, 2003-. **Honors/Awds:** Parade All-Am, 2000; Gatorade Arizona Player of the Year; Arizona Player of the Year, USA Today; Nagurski Award, 2002; Defensive Rookie of the Year, Pro Football Writers Asn, 2003; Defensive Rookie of the Year, AP Nat Football League, 2003; Pro Bowl, Nat Football League, 2004, 2006, 2008, 2010, 2011, 2013; Sacks leader, Am Football Conf, 2011; Defensive Player of the Year, AP Nat Football League, 2011; AFC Defensive Player of the Year, 2011; Champion, Am Football Conf, 2012. **Special Achievements:** Best player Ranking 60th in the nation, The Sporting News; No. 1 Jumbo Athlete in the Nation by SuperPrep Magazine; Top 100 Ranking in Nat Football League, 2012. **Business Addr:** Professional Football Player, Baltimore Ravens, 1 Winning Dr, Owings Mills, MD 21117, **Business Phone:** (410)701-4000.

## SUITE, DR. DEREK H.

Physician. **Personal:** married Darcel Dillard. **Educ:** Columbia Univ, BS, MS; Hahnemann Med Univ, MD; Albert Einstein Col Med, postgrad study. **Career:** Albert Einstein Col Med, chief resident psychiat; Emergency room doctor; US Dept Treas, sr consult; Dept Juv Justice, sr consult; Instnl Rev Bd, sr consult; Ny Off C & Family Serv, sr consult; Ny Housing Authority, sr consult; Ny Off Alcoholism & Substance Abuse Serv, evaluator; Full Circle Health, co-founder, chief exec officer, 1999-; Full Circle Health PLLC, Marriage & Family Enrichment Ctr, chmn & founder, 1999-. **Orgs:** Northeast & Mid-Atlantic Regional rep, Black Psychiatrists Am, currently; Acad Occup & Orgn Psychiat; Intl Soc Sport Psychiat; Bronx Family Ct; Ctr Ct Innovation Juv Accountability Prog; Jewish Child Care Asn; Mott Haven Community Serv; sr mem, Nat All Hazards Ment Health Asn; Inwood House; Leake & Watts; Am Psychiat Asn; Am Acad Sleep Med. **Honors/Awds:** Lighthouse Humanitarian Award, 2004. **Special Achievements:** Published in numerous periodicals. **Business Addr:** Chairman, Founder, Full Circle Health PLLC, 2429 E Tremont Ave, Bronx, NY 10461, **Business Phone:** (718)518-7600.

**SULIEMAN, DR. JAMIL**
Consultant. **Career:** Dallas Mavericks, team med consult, currently. **Business Addr:** Team Medical Consultant, Dallas Mavericks, 777 Sports St Reunion Arena, Dallas, TX 75207-4499, **Business Phone:** (214)988-0117.

**SULLIVAN, DR. ALLEN R.**
School administrator, consultant, association executive. **Personal:** Born Jul 15, 1941, Cambridge, MA; son of Fernando Cortez and Dorothy E; married Deborah M Haywood; children: Raylene & Reginald. **Educ:** Northeastern Univ, BS, 1965; Syracuse Univ, MS, 1966, PhD, 1970. **Career:** New Eng Home Little Wanders, asst supvr res, 1962-65; Syracuse Pub Sch, spec educ teacher, 1966-68; Univ Minn, dir training teachers, 1971-75, assoc prof psychol educ studies, 1970-75; Dallas Independent Sch Dist, asst supt stud develop, exec dir stud develop & advocacy serv, asst supt emer; Strategic Partnerships Inc, sr consult, currently; Sullivan Collab Group, owner, Currently. **Orgs:** Adv bd, Ft Worth State Sch, 1978-; bd dir, Conn Gen N Am Cigna, 1984-; min adv comn coun, Except C, 1984-; bd chmn, Jr Black Acad Arts & Lett, 1984-; bd, Friends Art Dist, 1984-86; bd dir, Dallas Co Ment Health & Ment Retardation; Omega Psi Phi Fraternity; bd dir, Dallas Challenge; bd dir, Dallas Youth Serv Corp; Coun Elders, Our Bros Keeper. **Honors/Awds:** Coach of the Year Award, Henniger High Sch; Outstanding Alumni Award, Northeastern Univ, 1982; Second Place for Color Photography, State Fair Texas; Psychology Honorary, Psi Chi. **Home Addr:** 3920 Deep Valley Dr, Dallas, TX 75234, **Home Phone:** (972)620-2916. **Business Addr:** Consultant, Strategic Partnerships Inc, Barton Oaks Plz 1 Suite 100, Austin, TX 78746, **Business Phone:** (512)531-3900.

**SULLIVAN, DR. ANDREA D.**
Writer, physician. **Educ:** Bastyr Univ, Seattle, PhD, ND, 1986; Homeop Acad Naturopathic Physicians, dipl; Univ Pa, PhD, sociol & criminol. **Career:** Am Univ, instr; Howard Univ, instr; Univ Md, instr; Nat Urban League, Admin Justice Dept, New York, asst dir, 1976-78; US Dept Housing & Urban Develop, Carter Admin, spec asst to secy, 1978-80; Prev Mag Health Bks, contrib ed, currently; Essence, contrib ed, currently; Heart & Soul & Health Quest Mag, contrib ed, currently; Ctr Natural healing Inc, naturopathic physician, pres, currently; Book: A Path to Healing: A Guide To Wellness for Body, Mind & Soul, 1998. **Orgs:** Founding mem, Am Asn Naturopathic Physicians; pres, DC Asn Naturopathic Physicians; Homeop Acad Naturopathic Physicians; Nat Ctr Homeop; chairperson, Naturopathic Med Bd DC. **Business Addr:** Naturopathic Physician, President, Center for Natural Healing Inc, 4601 Conn Ave NW Suite 6, Washington, DC 20008-5718, **Business Phone:** (202)244-4545.

**SULLIVAN, DR. EDWARD JAMES**
Pharmacist, dentist, educator. **Personal:** Born May 7, 1932, Cleveland, OH; son of Ann Lee Ervin; married Janet Grant; children: Kathi Ann, Steven & Alicia. **Educ:** Ohio State Univ, BS, pharm, 1956, DDS, 1969. **Career:** Univ Hosps Ohio State, pharmacist, 1957-64; Columbus Health Dept, dentist, 1969-73; dentist, pvt pract, 1969-; Columbus State Inst, dentist, 1973-79; OH State Univ, Dept Pedodontics, clin instr, 1981-, pediat dent, currently. **Orgs:** Bd mem, S State Health Ctr, 1975-77; bd dir, Hilltop Health Ctr, 1977; deleg, Nat Asn Neighborhood Health Ctrs, 1977-80; mem bd, Columbus Area Community Health Ctr, 1978-81; vpres, Buckeye State Dent Asn; pres, Columbus Asn Physicians & Dentists; pres, Columbus Dent Asn, 1994-96. **Home Addr:** 2755 Mitzi St, Columbus, OH 43207, **Home Phone:** (614)443-6966. **Business Addr:** Clinical Instructor, Pediatric Dentistry, The Ohio State University, 342 McCampbell Hall 1581 Dodd Dr, Columbus, OH 43210, **Business Phone:** (614)292-3160.

**SULLIVAN, EMMET G.**
Judge. **Personal:** Born Jan 1, 1947, Washington, DC. **Educ:** Howard Univ, BA, polit sci, 1968, Sch Law, JD, 1971. **Career:** Neighborhood Legal Serv Prog Wash, 1972; Super Ct Judge James A Wash Jr, law clerk, 1973; Houston & Gardner, atty, 1973, partner; Houston, Sullivan& Gardner, partner, 1980; Howard Univ Sch Law, adj prof, prof, actg dean; DC Super Ct, 1984-91; DC Ct Appeals, assoc judge, 1991-94, US dist judge, Wash, DC, 1994-. **Orgs:** Nat Bar Asn; Wash Bar Asn; DC Bar Asn; Bar Ass DC; dir, Frederick Abramson Mem Found, currently; Chair, Dist Columbia Judicial Nomination Comn, currently. **Business Addr:** Judge, US District Court, 333 Constitution Ave NW, Washington, DC 20001, **Business Phone:** (202)354-3260.

**SULLIVAN, ERNEST LEE**
Banker, executive. **Personal:** Born Dec 17, 1952, Columbus, OH; son of Robert Lee and Emma Jane. **Educ:** Capital Univ, BA, bus, 1980; Univ Va, Darden Sch, exec educ prog, 1993; Career Architect, cert, 1996; employee rel law, cert, 1996; PHR Accreditation, 1997; Kellogg Sch Mgt, dir develop cert, 2004. **Career:** Bank One Columbus, mgmt trainee, 1971-73, fraud investr, 1973-76, personnel generalist, 1976-77, prof recruiter, 1977-79, employ mgr, 1979-81; Rockwell Int, prof staff mgr, 1981-82, employ mgr, 1982-85, mgr, staffing, employee rel, 1985-88; Bank One Ohio Chicago, IL, asst vpres, exec selection, 1988-91, mgr, exec selection & employ, 1991-96, regional human res mgr, 1996-97, sr vpres, mgr, exec recruiting & nat staffing, 1997-2003; Sullivan Staffing Strategies, pres & chief exec officer, 2003-; Who's Who Publ Co., LLC, sr partner, 2004-. **Orgs:** Employ Mgr Asn, 1988-; adv bd, Cent State Univ, 1988-; personnel adv, Columbus Urban League, 1991-; adv bd, Columbus Bd Educ, 1991-; bd mem, Westerville Chamber Com, 1992-; pres, Jobs Columbus Prog, 1992-; bd pres, St Stephen's Community House, 1998-99; app Gov Policy Bd, 1999-2000; bd mem, Leadership Columbus, 2000-; chmn, Urban Adv Bd Boy Scouts Am, 2000-11; bd mem, Columbus Works, 2000-; bd mem, COTA; Personnel Soc Human Res Mgmt; Columbus Ohio Transit Authority Bd; adv bd, Capital Univ; vpres, Cent State Adv Bd; pres, St Stephen's Community House Bd; United Way Employ Vision Coun; bd mem, Siemon Kenton Coun, Boy Scouts Am; chair, Worker Qual Comt, Gov's Workforce Policy Bd; Adv Bd Capital Univ; Columbus Works Bd; Personnel Soc Human Resources Mgt; bus advisor, United Negro Col Fund. **Honors/Awds:** Hall of Fame, Columbus Metrop Housing, 1991; America's Best & Brightest, Dollars & Sense Mag, 1992; Pinnacle Award, 1993; African American Hall of Fame, 1994; Eagle Award, 1995; Outstanding Board Partner Award, 1995; Lazarus Award, 1997; Rosevelt Thomas Award, 2000; Ohio State Univ Diversity Leaders Award, 2002; Silver Beaver Award, Boy Scouts Am, 2002; Honorary Distinguished Alumni Award, Cent State Univ, 2003; Human Resources Excellence Award, Nat Asn African Americans, 2007; Champion Award, Nat Black MBA Asn, 2008; Diversity First Award, Nat Diversity Coun, 2010; Columbus Public Schools Hall of Fame; Dollars & Sense Hall of Fame; Roosevelt Carter Award. **Special Achievements:** He was selected by Dollars and Sense Magazine as One of America's Best and Brightest in 1992. **Home Addr:** 2258 Delavan Dr, Columbus, OH 43219, **Home Phone:** (614)258-7815. **Business Addr:** President, Chief Executive Officer, Sullivan Staffing Strategies, 2258 Dellavan Dr, Columbus, OH 43219, **Business Phone:** (614)537-7506.

**SULLIVAN, DR. J. CHRISTOPHER**
Actor, entertainer. **Personal:** Born Sep 15, 1932, Greenville, TX; son of Jack and Veola; married Eloise Hicks; children: Jerome. **Educ:** Prairie View A&M Univ, BA, 1953; Univ Tex, MA, 1958, PhD, 1964. **Career:** Abilene City Sch, teacher, 1955-58; Dallas Ind Sch, teacher, 1961-62; Prairie View A&M Univ, dir stud acts, 1962-63; Univ Tex, teacher, 1963-64; Screen Actors Guild, prof actor, currently. Films: DC Cab, 1983; Critters2: The Main Course, 1988; Arthur 2: On the Rocks, 1988; LA Bounty, 1989; Ghost, 1990; Caged in Paradise, 1990; Noises Off, 1992. TV series: "Starsky & Hutch", 1977; "Good Times", 1977; "Requiem for a Wino", 1977; "One Day at a Time", 1978; "Florence's Cousin", 1980; "The Jeffersons", 1980; "Hill Street Blues", 1986; "Elvis and Me", 1988; "Roots: The Gift", 1988; "Murder, She Wrote", 1989; "Night of the Tarantula", 1989; "L.A.Law", 1991; "As God is my Co-Defendant", 1991. **Orgs:** Screen Actors Guild; Am Fedn TV & Radio Artists; Acad TV Arts & Scis; Los Angeles Olympics Org Comt; vpres, Beverly Hills/Hollywood Nat Asn Advan Colored People, 1984-87. **Honors/Awds:** Distinguished Alumni, Prairie View A&M Phi Beta Sigma Inc, 1980; Phi Beta Kappa; Merit of Achievement Drama, Univ Tex, 1984; Image Award/Best Actor Natl Asn Advan Colored People Beverly Hills, 1986. **Home Addr:** 6326 Lexington Ave, Los Angeles, CA 90038, **Home Phone:** (213)462-5338. **Business Addr:** Actor, Screen Actors Guild, 8755 Melrose Ave, West Hollywood, CA 90069, **Business Phone:** (310)657-4630.

**SULLIVAN, JACK, JR.**
Clergy. **Personal:** Born Jun 1, 1959, Cleveland, OH; son of Jack Sr and Gloria Mae Connor McCoy; married Sekinah Hamlin; children: Nia, Imani & Jacquelyn. **Educ:** Ohio Univ, BS, commun, 1983; Lexington Theol Sem, Mdiv, 1986; United Theol Sem, DMin, 1993. **Career:** Mid-Am Region, Christian Church, Disciples Christ, assoc regional minister, 1986-89; Second Christian Church, pastor, 1986-89; Homeland Ministries Christian Church, Disciples Christ, US & Can, assoc, racial/ethnic & multicultural ministries, 1989-98; Christian Church Disciples Christ, NW regional minister, 1998-06; Pa Region Christian Church, Regional Minister & Pres, 2011-; Clevelands Fifth Christian Church, Disciples Christ, sr pastor, currently. **Orgs:** Nat Asn Advan Colored People, 1978-; Alpha Phi Alpha Fraternity Inc, 1984-; elder, youth dir, Faith United Christian Church, 1990-; big bro, Big Bros, Indianapolis, 1990-; Asn Christian Church Educr, 1988-; Urban League Greater Indianapolis; vol, Am Heart Asn; Boy Scouts Am; fel Lions Int; bd mem African Am Mus; fel Balm Gilead; pres, Black Ministers Fel; fel Outreach Transformation Regional Assembly Teams Christian Church; fel Alumni Coun of Lexington Theol Sem; bd trustee, Nat Convocation; trustee, Northwest Christian Col; bd, Wash State Asn Churches. **Honors/Awds:** George V Moore Award, Outstanding Field Ministry, Lexington Theological Seminary, 1986; Melvin Jones Award, Seattles Capital Hill Lions club. **Special Achievements:** Author: Out of Mighty Waters: Sermons of African American Disciples, 1994; Black Religion after the Million Man March, 1998; What Black Churches Can Teach White Churches, 2006. **Home Addr:** 3310 Carly Lane, Indianapolis, IN 46236, **Home Phone:** (317)894-8465. **Business Addr:** Senior Pastor, Fifth Christian Church, 14109 Benwood Ave, Cleveland, OH 44128, **Business Phone:** (216)752-5996.

**SULLIVAN, JONATHON LAMAR**
**Personal:** Born Jan 21, 1981, Griffin, GA. **Educ:** Univ Ga, grad. **Career:** Football player (retired); New Orleans Saints, defensive tackle, 2003-05; New Eng Patriots, defensive tackle, 2006. **Honors/Awds:** NFC All-Rookie, Pro Football, 2003. **Business Addr:** MA.

**SULLIVAN, LENCOLA**
Public speaker. **Personal:** Born Morrilton, AR; married Roel Verseveldt. **Educ:** Univ Cent Ark, BS, speech & theatre arts. **Career:** KARK-TV, news reporter, weathercaster; KTTV-TV, Austin, TX, weathercaster; Lionel Hampton Orchestra, vocalist; Neth Am Community Trust, managing dir, int speaker; A Soldier's Story, prod secy, 1984; TV Series: "The American Experience", 2002. **Orgs:** Bd mem, NY Nat Speakers Asn; USO; bd mem, Conextions. **Honors/Awds:** Inductee, Ark Black Hall of Fame. **Special Achievements:** First African American Miss UCA and Miss Arkansas, 1980; Miss Am, 4th runner-up, 1981; Sang at the Inaugural Ball Celebrations for President Clinton in 1992 and 1996; First African-American woman to win preliminary awards in the pageant; Guest appearances on the soap opera "All My Children," and many appearances in commercials and industrial films. **Business Addr:** International Speaker, OLS & Associates, 792 Columbus Ave 17B, New York, NY 10025.

**SULLIVAN, DR. LOUIS WADE**
Physician, school administrator, educator. **Personal:** Born Nov 3, 1933, Atlanta, GA; son of Walter Wade and Lubirda Elizabeth Priester; married Eva Williamson; children: Paul, Shanta & Halsted. **Educ:** Morehouse Col, BS, biol, 1954; Boston Univ, Sch Med, MD, 1958. **Career:** NY Hosp-Cornell Med Ctr, internship; Harvard Med Sch, instr, 1963-64; NJ Col Med, asst prof, 1964-66; Boston Univ, asst prof, 1966-68, assoc prof, 1968-74, prof med & physiol, 1974-75; Boston City Hosp, Boston, MA, dirhemat, 1973-75; Morehouse Col, prof biol & med, Med Educ Prog, dean, dir, 1975-81, Sch Med, dean, 1981-83, pres, 1987-89, 1993-2001; US Dept Health & Human Servs, Wash, DC, secy, 1989-93; Boy Scouts Am, bd mem, currently. **Orgs:** Ad hoc panel blood dis, Nat Heart Lung Blood Dis Bur, 1973; Sickle Cell Anemia Adv Comn, NIH, 1974-75; Nat Adv Res Coun, 1977; chmn, Med Educ S African Blacks, 1997-; Am Soc Hemat, Am Soc Clin Invest; Inst Med; Phi Beta Kappa; Alpha Omega Alpha; co-founder, Nat Asn Minority Med Educrs; founding pres, Asn Minority Health Professions; Alpha Phi Alpha fraternity. **Home Addr:** 5325 Crossroads Manor Rd NW, Atlanta, GA 30327. **Business Addr:** Board Member, Boy Scouts of America, PO Box 152079, Irving, TX 75015-2079.

**SULLIVAN, DR. ZOLA JILES**
Educator, elementary school teacher. **Personal:** Born Nov 5, 1921, Tallahassee, FL; daughter of Willis James and Susie Baker; married William David; children: Yolanda Sullivan Shelton, William D II, Shirley & Dexter Shelton. **Educ:** Fla A&M Univ, BS, MS; Fisk Univ; Univ Mich, Ann Arbor; Univ Miami, FL, post masters work, 1961; Oxford Univ, Eng, 1965; Univ Ill, Urbana-Champaign, PhD, 1970; Consult Ministry Educ, Nassau, BS, 1971. **Career:** Educator (retired); Broward Co Pub Sch Syst, Ft Lauderdale, teacher, 1942-43; Palm Beach Co Elem Sch, teacher, 1943-50; Fla A&M Univ, instr, 1950-53; Dade Co Pub Syst, prin elem teacher, 1953-71; Fla Int Univ, Miami, from asst prof to assoc prof educ, 1971-90, founding prof, 1971; Fla Memorial Col, adj prof, 1990-91. **Orgs:** Chmn, Num Childhood Educ Comn; consult, Num Educ Asn; speaker lectr, Num Elem Schs; coodr, Num Educ Workshops; Num Educ Asn; speaker Num Ch Grps; Richmond Heights Women's Club Fla; Alpha Phi Alpha Frat; Iota Pi Lambda Chap Miami; Fla Int Task Force Needs Assessment to Improve Educ Opportunities, Guinea; founding mem, Second Baptist Church, Miami, Fla, 1963; adv bd, Black Heritage Mus Dade Count, 1989-; Primary Readers & Evaluators First Ed Eric Early Childhood. **Honors/Awds:** Recip num sch & career opport cert; pub num papers educ; NDEA Fel UnivIll, 1969-70; Fla Governor's Award, 1986; Outstanding Serv to African Educrs Political Leaders & Stud, recognized by FL Chap of the Natl Coun Int Visitor. **Special Achievements:** First African American Female to receive a PhD in Miami, Fl, Univ of IL, 1970. **Home Addr:** 11601 SW 141st St, Miami, FL 33176, **Home Phone:** (305)233-8515.

**SULTON, DR. ANNE THOMAS**
Lawyer, educator. **Personal:** Born Oct 24, 1952, Racine, WI; daughter of William Thomas and Esther Phillips; married James E Jr; children: James III, William & Patrice. **Educ:** Wash State Univ, Pullman, BS, 1973; State Univ NY, Albany, MA, 1975; Univ Md, College Park, PhD, criminol & criminal justice, 1984; Univ Wis, Madison, JD, 1985. **Career:** Spelman Col, criminol instr, 1976-78; Howard Univ, criminol instr, 1980-84; pvt pract atty, 1985-; NJ City Univ, assoc prof; Sulton Law Offices, atty, currently; Jackson Advocate Newspaper, sr int corresp, currently. **Orgs:** Legal coun, Denver chap, Nat Asn Advan Colored People, 1993-99. **Honors/Awds:** William Robert Ming Advocacy Award, Nat Asn Advan Colored People, 2007; Smithsonian's National Air & Space Museum's Wall of Honor, 2012. **Special Achievements:** First African American female in Atlanta to earn a private pilot's license; First Certified Black Female Pilot by Atlanta Negro Airmen Intl Flying Club Organization, in Atlanta, 1977; Edited book entitled "African American Perspectives on Crime", 1996; wrote book entitled "Inner City Crime Control", 1990. **Home Addr:** PO Box 2763, Olympia, WA 98507. **Business Addr:** Attorney, Sulton Law Offices, PO Box 371335, Milwaukee, WI 53237, **Business Phone:** (360)870-6000.

**SULTON, DR. JACQUELINE RHODA**
Pediatrician, physician. **Personal:** Born Mar 27, 1957, Detroit, MI; daughter of Nathaniel O Holloway and Dorothy G Johnson; married Francis Arnold; children: Carmen Denease & Jonathan Francis. **Educ:** Spelman Col, BS, 1978; Meharry Med Col, MD, 1982. **Career:** Tulane Univ, Sch Med, intern, residency, 1982-85; Robinson-Gouri Pediat Group, New Orleans, LA, pediatrician, 1984-85; Morehouse Sch Med, stud preceptor, 1992-; Oakhurst Community Health Ctr, staff pediatrician, 1985-88; pvt group pract, Pediat & Adolescent Med, Lithonia, Ga, 1989-; Emory Univ, Sch Nursing, stud preceptor, 1990-; DeKalb Med Ctr, Dept Pediat, chief, 1998-2000, pediat, currently; Dekalb Med Dept, co-chief, 2000-02; C's Healthcare Atlanta; Sulton Pediat Group PC, Lithonia, Ga, prin pediatrician & owner, currently. **Orgs:** Alpha Kappa Alpha Sor; Atlanta Med Asn Inc; Am Acad Pediat, 1996. **Honors/Awds:** Ctr Biol Honor Soc, Atlanta Univ, 1976; Outstanding Acad Performance Biol, 1977; Nat Asn Advan Colored People; Certificate of Merit, Stud Res, 1980; Am Acad Pediatrics, Board Certified, 1989, fel, 1990, Recertified, 1997; Tiffany Award, Spelman Col; AOA Teaching Award, Morehouse Col Med. **Home Addr:** 5910 Hillandale Dr, Lithonia, GA 30058, **Home Phone:** (678)418-3990. **Business Addr:** Pediatrician, Owner, Sulton Pediatric Group PC, 5700 Hillandale Dr, Lithonia, GA 30058, **Business Phone:** (770)670-6100.

**SUMMER, CREE.** **See FRANKS, CREE SUMMER.**

**SUMMEROUR-PERRY, LISA**
Fashion model. **Personal:** Born Sep 5, 1962, Somers Point, NJ. **Educ:** Howard Univ, attended 1982. **Career:** Prudential Realty Group, legal secy, 1983-84; Sughrue Mion Zinn Macpeak & Seas, legal secy, 1984; Lenox China & Crystal, secy, 1985; Sands Hotel Casino, exec secy, 1985-86; TV series: "Mercury Rising", 1998; "Third Watch", 1999; "Law & Order: Special Victims Unit", 1999, 2001. **Orgs:** Nat Quill & Scroll. **Honors/Awds:** Southern Univ Acad Achievement Award; Miss Congeniality, Miss USA Pageant, 1986. **Home Addr:** 507 Grand St Apt 2D, Trenton, NJ 08611-2642.

**SUMMERS, KEVIN V.**
Executive, vice president (organization). **Personal:** children: 2. **Educ:** Col Charleston, BA, comput sci; Duke Univ, MBA. **Career:** Gen Elec; BellSouth, vpres info technol customer care & financial solutions; Coca-Cola Co, info technol regional leader concentrate prod supply bus & exec dir global supply chain; Whirlpool Corp, sr vpres & global chief info officer, 2007-12; Lowe's, chief info officer, 2012-. **Orgs:** Kappa Alpha Psi Fraternity; Info Technol Sr Mgt Forum. **Business Addr:** Chief Information Officer, Lowe's Companies , Inc, 1000 Lowe's Blvd, Mooresville, NC 28117, **Business Phone:** (704)758-1000.

**SUMMERS, LORETTA M.**
Consultant, president (organization). **Personal:** Born Oct 14, 1952, Cincinnati, OH; daughter of Stoughton and Lorena. **Educ:** Ind State Univ, BS, bus admin, 1974; Memphis State Univ, MBA, 1987; Cert SPHR. **Career:** Dial Corp, employee rels mgr, 1985-86, human resources mgr, 1986-90; Sprint, from human resources mgr to dir human resources, 1990-93, exec asst, 1993-95, dir human resources, 1995-96, asst vpres human resources, 1996-99; Summers Adv Group, pres, 1999-; CRK Interactive Inc, affil; Right Mgt Consults, adj consult; Avila Univ, adj prof; Baker Univ, adj prof; ProGroup Inc, strategic

partner; Johnson County Community Col, adj prof; Ottawa Univ, adj prof; Lee Hecht Harrison LLC, cert assoc. **Orgs:** Asst chap rep, Gospel Music Workshop, 1997-; Soc HR Mgt; Nat BMBA; Youth Opportunities Unlimited; Nat Asn African Am HR; Inst Mgt Consults; Am Soc Training & Dev; Prof Woman Network Speakers Bur. **Home Addr:** 12843 Bluejacket St, Overland Park, KS 66213, **Home Phone:** (913)681-2420. **Business Addr:** President, The Summers Advisory Group Inc, PO Box 26523, Overland Park, KS 66225-6523, **Business Phone:** (913)402-0400.

## SUMMERS, RETHA

Consultant. **Personal:** Born May 4, 1953, Goldsboro, NC; daughter of Harvey (deceased) and Aletha. **Educ:** NC Agr & Tech State Univ, BS, bus admin, 1975; Campbell Univ, MEd, coun & guid. **Career:** Employ Security Comn, employ interviewer, 1976-77; Carolina Tel, tel co rep, eng clerk; Bethesda Ministries, counr, currently. **Orgs:** Pres, Am Bus Womens Asn, 1984; Am Asn Coun & Develop, 1987; dir, Future Christian Leaders Am. **Honors/Awds:** Most Outstanding Business Student Award, N Lenoir High & Future Bus Leaders Am, 1971; Banner Award, Am Bus Womens Asn, 1984; Woman of the Year Award, Ram Neuse Chap, 1984. **Home Addr:** PO Box 366, La Grange, NC 28551, **Home Phone:** (919)823-4100. **Business Addr:** Counselor, Bethesda Ministries, PO Box 207, Tarboro, NC 27886, **Business Phone:** (252)937-4257.

## SUMMERS, DR. RODGER

School administrator, association executive, writer. **Personal:** Born Jan 10, 1945, Philadelphia, PA; son of Bennie and Viola Kemerlin; married Pamela F; children: Megan KF & Jordon F. **Educ:** Cheyney Univ, BS, educ, eng, 1968; Univ Vt, MA, eng, 1972; Ind Univ, EdD, higher educ, 1980. **Career:** Univ Vt, assoc dean stud affairs, asst dean stud affairs, 1974-81; N Adams State Col, vpres stud affairs, 1981-84; W Chester Univ, vpres stud affairs, 1991-2006; Binghamton Univ, vpres stud affairs, instr, Dean's Prof Pract, currently. **Orgs:** Salvation Army Bd, 1981; bd dir, Nat Asn Stud Personnel Adminr, 1983; bd mem, YMCA, 1985. **Special Achievements:** Co-author: "Commuter Marriages", Vt Jour, 1981; first faculty member to hold the distinctive title of Dean's Professor of Practice in the College of Community and Public Affairs. **Home Addr:** 701 Stonehedge Dr, Vestal, NY 13850-2919. **Business Addr:** Vice President, Binghamton University, Couper Admin Bldg AD-310, Binghamton, NY 13902-6000, **Business Phone:** (607)777-4788.

## SUMMERS, WILLIAM E., IV

Government official. **Personal:** Born Mar 11, 1943, Louisville, KY; son of William E III and Sallie Sellers; married Paulette Sweatt; children: Kimberly, William & Anthony. **Educ:** Cent State Univ, Wilberforce, OH, attended 1962; Univ Md, Far E Exten, MIL, 1965; Univ Louisville, Louisville, KY, attended 1971; Ky State Univ, Frankfort, KY, polit sci & commun, 1976. **Career:** Metrop Life Ins Co, ins consult, 1966-67; City Louisville, Louisville, KY, admin asst to Mayor, 1968-74; State Ky, Frankfort, KY, civil rights compliance officer & minority recruitment coordr, 1974-76; City Louisville, Louisville, KY, Dept Sanit, dir, 1976-79; Summers Broadcasting, WLOU, opers mgr & talk show host, 1979-82; Mr Klean's Janitor & Maintenance Serv, Louisville KY, vpres, 1979-82; Property Maintenance & Mgt Inc, Louisville KY, owner & pres, 1982-86; Greater Louisville Inc, exec vpres pub affairs & human resources, 1999-2003; City Louisville, Louisville, KY, Internal Opers, chief staff, 1985-99, dep mayor opers, 2003-11. **Orgs:** Bd dir, Nat Asn Advan Colored People, Louisville Urban League, Big Bros & Big Sisters, Kentuckiana Girl Scout Coun; bd overseers, Bellermine Col; Urban Affairs Asn, 1986; Soc Pub Admin, 1986; Conf Minority Pub Admin, 1987; bd dir, Humana Hosp Audubon, 1988; Nat Forum Black Pub Admin, 1989; Coun Higher Educ & Community Equal Opportunities; bd dir, Jefferson Community Col& Watterson Col, 1990; chair, Youth Alive Bd; chair, Kentuckiana Minority Supplier Develop Coun Bd; chair, Ky Derby Festival Found Bd; Greater Louisville Merger Transition Task Force; Merger Comt; Housing Partnership Bd; Greater Louisville Proj Steering Comt; Lewis & Clark Bicentennial Comt; Bridges Coalition; Greater Louisville Sports Comn Bd; Jewish Hosp Healthcare Serv Bd; bd, Ky Derby Festival; MWBE Adv Coun; Healing Pl Bd; Louisville Econ Develop Corp Bd; W Louisville Jaycees; Sertoma Club; Civil Liberties Union Bd; Salvation Army Boys & Girls Club Bd; Bellarmine Col Bd Overseers; Actors Theatre Bd; Neighborhood Housing Serv Bd; Jefferson Community Col Bd; Delta Dent Adv Coun; Clothe-A-Child Bd; Metro United Way Bd; Hospice Louisville Bd; Presby Community Ctr Bd; chair, Ky Southern Leadership Bd; co-chair, Nat Conf Community & Justice Dinner Comt; Jr Achievement Bus Hall Fame Selection Comt; bd trustee, Univ Louisville, 2015-. **Home Addr:** 3025 Bunker Hill Dr, Louisville, KY 40205-2771, **Home Phone:** (502)473-1564. **Business Addr:** Board of Trustee, University of Louisville, 2301 S 3rd St, Louisville, KY 40292, **Business Phone:** (502)852-5555.

## SUMMERVILLE, WILLIE T.

Educator. **Personal:** Born Aug 17, 1944, Sunshine, AR; son of Moses and Lenora; married Valerian A; children: Derrick, Shandra & William Moses. **Educ:** Ark AM&N Col, BS, music educ, 1966; Univ Ill, Champaign, Urbana, MS, music educ, 1967; Univ Utah; Ohio State Univ; Youngstown State Univ; E Stroudburg State Univ; Westminister Choir Col; Univ Mich; Mich State Univ; Jackson State Univ. **Career:** St Luke CME Church, choir dir, organist, 1966-; Champaign Unit Four Schs, elem music specialist, 1967-70; self-employed music consult, clinician, teacher, dir, 1970-; Urbana Sch Dist No 116, choral music teacher, 1970-2005; Canaan Baptist Church, minister music, 1977-; Univ Ill, Champaign, Ill, from adj prof to affairs specialist, 1992-2009; Parkland Col, Champaign, Ill, adj prof music, 2002-09; Canaan Acad, Urbana, Ill, music specialist, 2005-08; Millikin Univ, Decatur, Ill, adj prof, 2007-09; Canaan Acad-Urbana, IL, 2005-08. **Orgs:** Phi Beta Sigma Fraternity, 1963-; life mem, Music Educr Nat Conf; life mem, Nat Educ Asn; life mem, Univ Ill Alumni Asn, 1970-; Urbana Educ Asn, 1970-; bd mem, treas, Canaan Found, 1995-; Rotary Int, Urbana Rotary Club, 1995-; Ill Educ Asn; Phi Delta Kappa; Alpha Kappa Mu Nat Hon Socs; charter mem, Univ Ill Alumni Band; Ill Music Educr Asn; Ill Music Adjudicators Asn; Canaan Baptist Church Bd Deacons. **Home Addr:** 809 Ayrshire Cir, Champaign, IL 61820-7307, **Home Phone:** (217)359-7403. **Business Addr:** Affairs Specialist, Lecturer & Coordinator of Student Advising & Outreach, University of Illinois, IUB Suite 320E, Urbana, IL 61801, **Business Phone:** (217)244-8182.

## SUMMITT, GAZELLA ANN

Administrator. **Personal:** Born Feb 27, 1941, Wheatland, IN; daughter of John Ferrell Granger and Rhoda Gazella Howard Granger; married Paul O; children: Krista & Dana. **Educ:** Vincennes Univ, AS, 1964; Ind Univ, St Mary, Woods Col, BS, 1983; Ind State Univ, MS, 1993. **Career:** Vincennes Univ, secy pres, 1960-63, admin asst pres, 1963-80, asst pres admin & affirmative action officer, 1980-91, dir human resources & Am Acad Ophthal, 1991-2005, Vincennes Univ Found, rels asst, 2006-. **Orgs:** Dir & secy, Vincennes Univ Found, 1980-; state coord, Am Asn Women Community & Jr Cols, 1984-94; co chmn, Womens Div Knox County United Fund, 1985-91; secy, Region V Am Assoc Affirmative Action, 1986-88; co chmn, Ind Coalition Blacks Higher Educ, 1986; Hist Rev Bd City Vincennes, 1986; Steering Comt, March Dimes Walk Am, 1986-92; Steering Comt, Riley Childrens Hosp Campaign 1986-92; secy, Am Asn Affirmative Action, 1988-92, bd dir, 1988-96, pres, 1992-94; Steering Comt, FCA, 1991; Vincennes Housing Authority, counr, 1992-96, chmn, 1993-95; chmn, Am Asn Affirmative Action Found Bd, 1996-2000; Ind Comn Women, comnr, 1997-2005; Vincennes Educ Found; by-laws comt & elder, First Church God, 2005-13; Soc Human Resources Mgrs; Col & Univ Personal Asn; founding mem, Red Hot Poppies chap, Red Hat Soc; Red Skelton Gala Comt, 2005-08. **Home Addr:** 507 Grouseland Dr, Vincennes, IN 47591, **Home Phone:** (812)890-3369. **Business Addr:** Foundation Relations Assistant, Vincennes University Foundation & Alumni, 1002 N 1st St, Vincennes, IN 47591, **Business Phone:** (812)888-6944.

## SUMMITT, KRISTA E.

Association executive, executive. **Educ:** Vincennes Univ, attended 1985; Purdue Univ, attended 1987; George Washington Univ, masters cert, proj mgt; Wva Univ, 2011. **Career:** IBM, Res Triangle Pk, Raleigh-Durham, NC, sales rep, acct mkt rep, 1989-93, prod mkt mgr, 1993-94, pc sales mgr, 1994-96, mkt commun prog mgr N Am, 1996-98, e-com proj mgr, 1998-2001; Lenovo Int, global web strategist, 2006-09; SoulBounce.com, contrib ed, 2010-12; Comput Task Group, bus develop mgr, 2012-13, Lenovo Developer Prog, content mgr & community mgr, 2013-; BrainCurrency Co, brand humanizer, 2013-; Christian Athletes Stud Coun, fel; Old Post Sentinel, fel. **Orgs:** Chair, assoc minister & dir, Orange Grove Missionary Baptist Church, Durham, NC, co-chair, Hurricane Floyd Relief Task Force. **Honors/Awds:** Golden Circle Award, IBM; Outstanding Recent Graduate Award, Vincennes Univ; Excellence Awards, IBM; Academic Award; Lenovo Global Web Marketing Performance Award; WW IBM PC General Manager's Excellence Award for Deployment of e-Commerce Capabilities; e-Commerce Excellence Award, IBM; Hundred percent Club Sales Awards, IBM; Regional Vice-President's Sales Awards, IBM. **Business Addr:** Business Development Manager, Computer Task Group, 5565 Ctrview Dr, Raleigh, NC 27606-3562, **Business Phone:** (919)851-9248.

## SUMNER, THOMAS ROBERT

Lawyer, circuit court judge. **Personal:** Born Dec 4, 1949, Louisville, KY; married Sherry Ann Beene; children: Nyshana, Rahman & Kamilah. **Educ:** Univ Ill, Chicago, BA, sociol, 1971; John Marshall Law Sch, JD, 1977. **Career:** Judge (retierd); Cook County, Pub Defender Off, trial atty, 1978-82; Sumner & Smith, Partner, 1982-88; Univ Ill, Chicago, acad coun, 1971-77; Chicago Title Ins, title examr, 1977; Cook State Ill, Circuit Ct, Cook County Judicial Circuit, Criminal Div, assoc Judge, 1988-2008; Ill Supreme Ct Comn, prog coordr, 2010-12; Adult Redeploy Ill, tech assistance provider, 2010-. **Orgs:** US Ct Appeals 7th Circuit, 1977; US Dist Ct Northern Dist Ill, 1977; pres, Cook Co Bar Asn, 1985-86; Am & Trial Lawyers Asn; Ill State Bar Asn; Am Bar Asn; bd mgr, Chicago Bar Asn, 1986-88; bd dir, Nat Bar Asn, 1986-87; Ill Judges Asn; treas, Ill Judicial Coun, 2007-08; Nat Asn Securities Professionals; treas, Ill Judicial Coun Found. **Home Addr:** 10142 S Beverly Ave, Chicago, IL 60643, **Home Phone:** (773)230-3026. **Business Addr:** Technical Assistance Provider, Adult Redeploy Illinois, 300 W Adams St Suite 200, Chicago, IL 60606, **Business Phone:** (312)793-8550.

## SUMPTER, TIKA

Singer, actor. **Personal:** Born Jun 20, 1980, Queens, NY; daughter of Arthur Curtis and Janice Acquista; married Hoseas Chanchez; children: Ella-Loren. **Educ:** Marymount Manhattan Col, BA. **Career:** Model; actress, 2004-; Twise, an R&B/hip hop duo, co-founder. Television: Best Friend's Date, 2004; One Life to Live, 2005-10, 2011; Gossip Girl, 2011; The Game, 2011-12; The Haves and the Have Nots, 2013-. Film: Stomp the Yard 2: Homecoming, 2010; Salt, 2010; Whisper Me a Lullaby, 2011; What's Your Number?, 2011; Think Like a Man, 2012; Sparkle, 2012; A Madea Christmas, 2013; Being Mary Jane, 2013; Ride Along, 2014; My Man Is a Loser, 2014; Get On Up, 2014; Bessie, 2015; Ride Along 2, 2016; Southside with You, 2016. **Special Achievements:** Album contributor, One Life, Many Voices For Hurricane Relief. **Business Addr:** Brookside Artist Management, 250 West 57th St Suite 1820, New York, NY 10107.

## SUNDAY, DELENA MARIE

Manager, executive, vice president (organization). **Personal:** Born Jan 1, 1961; married Manuel; children: 2. **Career:** Executive (retired); Nordstrom Inc, salesperson, Tacoma, Wash, 1980-81, dept mgr role, 1981-90, human resource mgr, 1990-91, regional human resource dir diversity affairs, 1991-93, store mgr, 1993-96, dir corp diversity affairs, 1996-2000, from vpres to exec vpres, 1998-2002, exec vpres diversity affairs, 2000-02, exec vpres human resource, 2002-14. **Home Addr:** 13957 SE 159th, Renton, WA 98058-7832, **Home Phone:** (425)430-0717. **Business Addr:** Executive Vice President-Human Resources, Nordstrom Inc, 1617 6th Ave, Seattle, WA 98101, **Business Phone:** (800)282-6060.

## SUNEJA, DR. SIDNEY KUMAR

Radiologist. **Personal:** Born Jul 13, 1954, Chandigarh; married Kathleen. **Educ:** Howard Univ Col Med, MD, 1976; PhD, 1982, radiol, 1983. **Career:** Case Western Res Univ, intern, 1977; Howard Univ Hosp, Family Pract, resident, 1977-80, diag radiol, 1980-83; Johns Hopkins Hosp, nuclear med fel, 1983-85; Charity Hosp, New Orleans, assoc dir nuclear med, 1985-87; La State Univ Med Ctr, asst prof radiol, 1985-87; Howard Univ Hosp, asst prof radiol, 1987-97; Georgetown Univ Med Ctr, Viking radiol; Musculoskeletal MRI & imaging fel, 1998-99; Walter Reed Army Med Ctr, staff civilian radiologist, 1999; John Hopkins Med Inst, Breast Imaging fel, 2000-01; pvt pract, currently. **Orgs:** Asn Univ Radiologists; Am Ruentgen Roy Soc; Med Soc DC; Am Col Radiol; Soc Nuclear Med; Radiol Soc N Am; Am Med Asn; Southern Med Asn; bd mem, Am Bd Radiol, 1985; bd mem, Am Bd Nuclear Med, 1986; bd mem, Am Bd Family Pract, 1982; radiation safety comn, LA State Univ Med Ctr; NOLA; HUH; Am Bd certifications, Radiol & Nuclear Radiol; Am Bd Nuclear Med; Am Bd Family Practice. **Honors/Awds:** Physicians Recognition Award, Am Med Asn; Am Bd of Family Practice, Recertification, 1989. **Special Achievements:** Author of numerous peer-reviewed medical/scientific publications; lecturer: "Neuroreceptor Imaging with Positron Emission Tomography," "Nuclear Cardiology," New Orleans Fall Radiology CNF; "Nuclear Medicine, Breast Imaging, Magnetic Resorarce Imaging," Annual Review Course, Howard Univ CME; AMA category 1 lectures; ABD in Medical Physiology, PRD curriculum, 1997-81. **Business Addr:** Nuclear Medicine, Private Practition, 8215 Osage Lane, Bethesda, MD 20817, **Business Phone:** (301)229-3562.

## SUPERNAW, KYWIN

Football player. **Personal:** Born Jun 2, 1975, Claremore, OK. **Educ:** Univ Ind, grad. **Career:** Football player (retired); Detroit Lions, defensive back, 1998-99, free safety, safety, 2000.

## SURE, AL B. (ALBERT JOSEPH BROWN, III)

Songwriter, singer, chief executive officer. **Personal:** Born Jun 4, 1968, Boston, MA; son of Cassandra and Al Brown; children: Quincy Brown, Albert IV & Devin. **Educ:** Manhattan Ctr Media Arts. **Career:** Albums: In Effect Mode, 1988; Private Times & the Whole 9!, 1990; Sexy Versus, 1992; The Very Best of Al B Sure!, 2003; The Hit, actor, 2007; Honey I'm Home, 2009; TV series: "The Fresh Prince of Bel-Air", 1990; "Private Times", composer, 1991; "David Bowie: Black Tie White Noise", 1993; "VH-1 Where Are They Now?", 2000; "Rock the Cradle", 2008; Singles: "Nite & Day", "Off On Your Own Girl", "Rescue Me", 1988; "If I'm Not Your Lover", "Somebody for Me", 1989; "Secret Garden", "Misunderstanding", 1990; "No Matter What You Do", "Had Enuf", 1991; "Right Now", "Natalie", "U & I", 1992; "I Don't Wanna Cry", 1993; "Black Tie/White Noise", 1993; "I'm Still In Love", 1994; "I Love It, 2009; Warner Bros Rec, rec artist, 1988-94; Motown Rec, vpres a&r, 1994-96; ABC Radio Networks, syndicated radio host, 2002-06; Lyrical State Mind, vpres bus affairs, 2007-09; Clear Channel Radio, air personality, 2006-10; Notes & Numbers Co LLC, pres, 2007-; ABS Entertainment.net Inc, chief exec officer, currently. **Orgs:** Bd mem, B.R.A.I.N, 2008-. **Honors/Awds:** Received numerous awards including Grammy nominations, American Music Award, Soul Train Awards, New York Music Awards & over 30 ASCAP Awards. **Business Addr:** Recording Artist, c/o Warner Bros Records Inc, 3300 Warner Blvd, Burbank, CA 91505, **Business Phone:** (818)846-9090.

## SURTAIN, PATRICK FRANK

Football player. **Personal:** Born Jun 19, 1976, New Orleans, LA; son of Alced; married Michelle Weber; children: Patrick Jr & Paris. **Educ:** Univ Southern Miss, attended 1997. **Career:** Football player (retired); Miami Dolphins, 1998, defensive back, left defensive back, corner back, 1999, left defensive back, 2000-05; Kans City Chiefs, cornerback, 2005-08. **Orgs:** Founder, Patrick Surtain Found. **Honors/Awds:** Dolphins Community Service Award, 1999; Pro Bowl, 2002, 2003, 2004; All-Pro, 2002, 2003; Alumni Defensive Back of the Year, Nat Football League, 2002.

## SUTHERLAND, DR. FRANKIE

Educator. **Personal:** Born Apr 15, 1949, Greenville, MS; daughter of Mullen and Frankie; married Albert; children: Steven Craig. **Educ:** Tougaloo Col, BA, sociol, 1971; Chicago State Univ, MS, sch guid coun, 1991, MA, educ admin, 1996; Loyola Univ, PhD. **Career:** Chicago Pub Sch, Dist 299, teacher, 1984-92, Dist 147, counr, 1992-96, Dist 133, asst supt, prin, 1996-; Gen George Patton Sch Dist, Riverdale, Ill, from interim supt to supt, 2004-. **Orgs:** Exec comm, 1990, co-chair, 2015, Tougaloo Col Alumni; UNCF rep, Chicago Inter-Alumni Coun, 1996-; Ill Prins Asn, 1996; Asn Supvn & Curric Develop, 1997; Nat Asn Black Sch Educrs, 1997; Riverdale Redevelop Corp, Ad Hoc Comm, 1998; gen chairperson, Ebony Fashion Fair, 1998-. **Home Addr:** 914 E 193rd Pl, Glenwood, IL 60425-2182, **Home Phone:** (708)757-3146. **Business Addr:** Superintendent, General George Patton School District, 150 W 137th St, Riverdale, IL 60827, **Business Phone:** (708)841-2420.

## SUTHERLAND, DR. LYNNE

Dentist. **Educ:** DDS. **Career:** Pvt pract, dentist & periodontist, currently. **Business Addr:** Dentist, Periodontist, 2204 S Taylor Rd, Cleveland Heights, OH 44118-3007, **Business Phone:** (216)371-2510.

## SUTPHEN, MONA K.

Government official. **Personal:** Born Nov 10, 1967; daughter of Cecil; married Clyde E Williams; children: Sydney & Davis. **Educ:** Mount Holyoke Col, BA, 1989; London Sch Econ, MS, int polit econ. **Career:** Stonebridge Int, managing dir; Us Foreign Serv, officer, 1991-2000; Nat Security Coun, staff, 1998-2000; US Mission Un; High Rep, State Dept human rights bur, US Embassy Bangkok; White House Dep chief staff, 2009-11; US Nat Security Adv, spec asst. **Orgs:** Clinton Admin; Coun Foreign Rels; Women's Foreign Policy Group. **Special Achievements:** Co-author of The Next American Century: How the US Can Thrive as Other Powers Rise (Simon & Schuster 2008). **Business Addr:** Chief Staff, The White House, 1600 Pennsylvania Ave NW, Washington, DC 20500, **Business Phone:** (202)456-1414.

## SUTTLE, RHONDA KIMBERLY

Association executive, executive director. **Career:** Nat Asn Advan Colored People, Afro-Acad, Cult, Technol & Sci Olympics Prog, chair, 2001, nat dir, currently. **Business Addr:** National Director, National Association for the Advancement of Colored People, 4805 Mt Hope Dr, Baltimore, MD 21215-3297, **Business Phone:** (410)486-9160.

**SUTTON, CHARLES W.**
Automotive executive. **Career:** McKinney Dodge Inc, owner, chief exec officer & gen mgr, 1998. **Home Addr:** . **Business Addr:** Chief Executive Officer, General Manager, McKinney Dodge Inc, 700 S Cent Expressway, McKinney, TX 75070, **Business Phone:** (214)544-4500.

**SUTTON, CLYDE AVERY, SR.**
Executive. **Personal:** Born Oct 21, 1927, Atlanta, GA; married Evelyn Cook; children: Roswell, Cheryl, Francis, Clyde Jr (Deceased) & Terri Vinson. **Career:** Atlanta Newspaper Inc, 1962-; Sutton's ACE HArdware, owner, 1996-2003. **Orgs:** Am Numismatic Asn, 1956-. **Home Addr:** 3345 Benjamin E Mays Dr SW, Atlanta, GA 30311, **Home Phone:** (404)696-6013. **Business Addr:** Owner, Sutton's Cascade Heights Hardware, 2329 Cascade Rd SW, Atlanta, GA 30311, **Business Phone:** (404)346-1552.

**SUTTON, DIANNE FLOYD**
Management consultant, writer, educator. **Personal:** Born Dec 6, 1948, Houston, TX; daughter of Osborne English and Dorothy Woods; married Ronald N Jr; children: Ronald Jr; married Thomas Jones Jr; children: Anthony Specer Jones. **Educ:** Harris Stowe State Col, BA, educ & sociol, 1970; Wash Univ, St Louis, MO, MA, educ, curric develop, 1974. **Career:** St Louis Pub Sch Syst, math instr, 1970-76; Wash Univ St Louis, MO, Experienced Teachers Grad fel, 1971; US Equal Employ Opportunity Comn, St Louis Dist Off, investr & conciliator, 1976-78, trainer & course design, 1978-85; Creations Dyan, design silk flowers & floral arrangements, 1979-87; independent mgt consult, 1982; US Dept Agr, employee develop specialist, 1985-87; Sutton Enterprises, pres & sr trainer, 1987-; Montgomery Col, Diversity Mgt Inst, fac mem; Grad Sch USA, Ctr Leadership & Mgt, fac mem, 1995-12; GS New Leader Prog, fac, 1995-10; Am Univ, Sch Commun, Wash, DC, adj prof, 1990-2002; Wash, DC, adv neighborhood comnr, 2002-; Books: Workplace Savvy; Workplace Etiquette. **Orgs:** Nat Asn Female Execs, 1976-; life mem, exec bd, Training Officers Conf, 1980-; Policy Bd Nat Rural Health Asn; exec bd mem, Training Officers Conf Wash, DC, 1980-; comnr, Adv Neighborhood Comn. **Home Addr:** 9817 Campbell Dr, Kensington, MD 20895. **Business Addr:** President, Senior Trainer, Sutton Enterprises, 3032 Sanctuary Lane, Frederick, MD 21701-6804, **Business Phone:** (301)696-9898.

**SUTTON, GLORIA W.**
Librarian. **Personal:** Born Feb 17, 1952, Kinston, NC; children: Dimitri. **Educ:** Lenoir Community Col, AA, 1972; E Carolina Univ, BS, 1974; NC Cent Univ, MLS, 1987. **Career:** Librarian (retired); Lenoir Community Col, eve librn, 1974-75; Wayne Co Pub Libr, cataloguer, 1975-76; Sampson Tech Col, librn, 1976-81; Wake Tech Community Col, librn, 1981-03. **Orgs:** NC Community Col Learning Resources Assoc; Young Mens Christian Asn; youth minister, Wake Baptist Grove Church; Shaw Div Sch Libr; Wake Baptist Grove Church Libr, 1985-86; Capital Area Libr Asn 1985-86; Prof Develop Comm Wake Tech Col; Young Women's Christian Asn; ReHI Consortium. **Home Addr:** 206 Creekchannel Ct, Garner, NC 27529, **Home Phone:** (919)661-7198. **Business Addr:** Librarian, Bridges II Manual Editor, Wake Technical Community College, 9101 Fayetteville Rd, Raleigh, NC 27529, **Business Phone:** (919)212-3837.

**SUTTON, JAMES CARTER**
Purchasing agent, manager. **Personal:** Born Jan 6, 1945, Lynville, TN; son of Felton Eugene and Nannie Readus (deceased); married Joyce Roach; children: Kyra. **Educ:** Wayne State Univ, BS, bus admin, 1975; Univ Detroit, bus, MBA. **Career:** Ford Motor Co, finance; USaF, Intelligence Serv Opers; Eastman Kodak Co, staff, 1981, supv buyer, 1984, admin asst to vpres, 1984-85, proj mgr bus ed, 1985-86, corp diversity dir, 1995, pub affairs planning dir, Worldwide Corp Sourcing, mgr & dir minority supplier progs, sr mgr, engine components purchasing; Chrysler Corp, purchasing agt. **Orgs:** Fredrick Douglas African Hist Mus Adv Comt; Bus Policy Rev Coun, 1988-; bd mem, Otetiana Coun Boy Scouts Am Inc, 1988-; chmn bd, Urban League Rochester, Nat Minority Supplier Develop Coun, 1990; Corp Dir Supplier Progs Kodak; bd mem, Inst Am Bus, 1992; secy, Chase Manhattan-Rochester Metro Adv Bd; Sigma Phi Pi; bd, Geva Theatre Co; Bus Policy Rev Coun & Sigma Pi Phi Fraternity; mem adv comt, Frederick Douglass Mus; Bus Policy Rev Coun; chair, White House's nat celebration, Minority Enterprise Develop Week (MED WEEK). **Special Achievements:** Citation for involvement with Big Brother Prog; Served as advisor to South African Black Bus Develop; Recognized by Minority Business USA as one of the most effective supplier program managers in the country; Named regional minority supplier coordinator by the US Small Business Administration. **Home Addr:** 2927 Portage Trail Dr, Rochester Hills, MI 48309-3209, **Home Phone:** (248)375-5463.

**SUTTON, MARY A.**
Software developer. **Personal:** Born Oct 12, 1945, Los Angeles, CA. **Educ:** Prairie View A&M Col, BS, 1966; Univ Santa Clara, MS, 1973. **Career:** Ford Aerospace & Commun, sr software engr; Martin-marietta, assoc engr, 1966-67; Lockheed, assoc engr, 1967-69; TRW Systs, proj mgr, 1969-76. **Orgs:** Sunnyvale's TRW Affirmative Action Prog; pres, Sunnyvale Employees Asn TRW, 1973-74; Univ Santa Clara, Alumni Orgn, 1973-. **Honors/Awds:** First African American manager at TRW, Sunnyvale. **Home Addr:** 1205 Pembroke Dr, San Jose, CA 95131.

**SUTTON, NATHANIEL K.**
Automotive executive. **Educ:** Mich State Univ, BS, packaging engineering. **Career:** Owens Corning Fiberglas, staff; IBM, staff; Olympia Fields Ford Sls Inc, chief exec officer, 1989-; Sutton Ford, chief exec officer, pres & owner, 1989-. **Business Addr:** Owner, General Manager & Chief Executive Officer, Sutton Ford Inc, 21315 S Cent Ave, Matteson, IL 60443-2893, **Business Phone:** (708)720-8000.

**SUTTON, NORMA J.**
Lawyer, manager, executive. **Personal:** Born Jun 11, 1952, Chicago, IL; daughter of Harry Sams and Beatrice Ross; children: Edward M. **Educ:** Loyola Univ, BA, 1974; Govs St Univ, MA, 1976; Loyola Univ Chicago Sch Law, JD, 1980. **Career:** Cemrel Inc, off mgr, 1975-77; N Am Co Inst, legal asst, 1977-80; Appellate Ct, judicial clerk, 1980-82; Soft Sheen Prod, corp coun, 1982-85; Digital Equip Corp, managing atty, 1985; ebix.com & Delphi Info Systs Inc, corp coun, 1999-2001; Global Compliance Solutions, Zurich NA, dir bus serv & atty, 2000-02; Community Econ Develop Law Proj, atty, 2001-05; JPC, dir corp serv, 2005-07; State Ill, agency procurement officer, 2007-; Cent Reg Law Group, mgr, currently. **Orgs:** Secy, 1986-87, vice chair, 1987-88, Ill State Bar Asn YLD; Am Bar As, Cook County Bar Asn; Digital Equip Corp Comn Relns Coun. **Honors/Awds:** Leadership & Serv, Loyola Univ Sch Law Chicago, 1980. **Home Addr:** 825 S Oakley Blvd, Chicago, IL 60612-4227, **Home Phone:** (312)342-9476. **Business Addr:** Manager, Central Region Law Group, 100 NW Pt, Elk Grove Village, IL 60007-1018, **Business Phone:** (708)806-2530.

**SUTTON, DR. OZELL. See Obituaries Section.**

**SUTTON, PIERRE MONTE**
Executive, president (organization). **Personal:** Born Feb 1, 1947, New York, NY; son of Percy E and Leatrice; children: Keisha; married Karen Bunche Pierce; children: Maximillian & Danielle. **Educ:** Univ Toledo, BA, 1968; Tex Christian Univ, BS, polit sci, 1967; NY Univ; Harvard Univ Bus Sch, OPM Prog, grad; Univ Ky. **Career:** NY Courier Newspaper, exec ed, 1971-72; Inner City Broadcasting Corp, Res & Anal Corp, vpres, 1971, chm; WLIB Radio, gen mgr, 1972-75, vpres, 1975-77; Inner City Broadcasting Corp, pres, 1977; chmn & chief exec officer, currently; Gray Commun, Bussiness Ref. **Orgs:** Chmn, Harlem Boy Scouts, 1975-; Bd mem, Minority Investment Fund, 1979-; first vpres, Nat Asn Black Owned Broadcasters, 1979-; bd mem, exec, com New York City Marathon, 1979-; bd trustee, Alvin Ailey Dance Found, 1980-; bd mem, Better Bus Bur Harlem, 1972-77; bd mem, Hayden Planetarium, 1979-; Radio Advert Bureau. **Home Addr:** 45 Sunnybrook Rd, Bronxville, NY 10708-5716, **Home Phone:** (914)337-7401. **Business Addr:** Chairman, Chief Executive Officer, Inner City Broadcasting Corp, 601 Ashby Ave, Berkeley, CA 94710, **Business Phone:** (510)848-7713.

**SUTTON, DR. SHARON EGRETTA**
Architect, artist, educator. **Personal:** Born Feb 18, 1941, Cincinnati, OH; daughter of Booker Johnson and Egretta Johnson. **Educ:** Univ Hartford, BMus, 1963; Columbia Univ, MArch, 1973; City Univ NY, MPhil, 1981, MA & PhD, psychol, 1982. **Career:** Orchestras: "Fiddler on the Roof" "Man of La Mancha" the Bolshoi, Moiseiyev & Leningrad Ballet Co, 1963-68; Kouzmanoff & Assocs Architects New York, Studio di Architettura Forte Florence & Bond Ryder & Assocs Architects Architect, 1970-76; Pratt Inst, vis asst prof, 1975-81; SE Sutton Architect, pvt pract, 1976-97; Columbia Univ, adj asst prof, 1981-82; Univ Cincinnati, asst prof, 1982-84; Sims Varner & Assocs, proj mgr & consult, 1984-90; Univ Mich, assoc prof, 1984-94, prof archit & urban planning, 1994-97; Univ Wash, prof archit urban design & planning dir Ctr Environ, Educ & Design Studies, 1998-; Univ Mich, Vis Prof & Ohio State Univ, scholar, 2003. **Orgs:** Fel Am Inst Archit; Am Psychol Asn; Group VII Nat Fel W K Kellogg Found, 1986-89; fel, UM Sch Bus Admin, 1989; fel, Am Inst Architects, 1995; Danforth fel; pres, Nat Archit Accrediting Bd, 1996-97; mayoral appointee, Seattle Design Comn, 2000-04; prin investr, Constructing a Social Justice Framework Youth & Community Serv, Ford Found, 2004-06; city coun appointee, Seattle Design Rev Bd, 2007-11; founding dir, Urban Network: An Urban Design Prog Youth; dir, Ctr Environ Educ & Design Studies; Sev Shoon Printmaking Studio; mem, Local 802 Am Fedn Musicians. **Home Addr:** 1017 Minor Ave Gainsborough Apt 504, Seattle, WA 98104. **Business Addr:** Professor of Architecture & Urban Design, University Washington, 208 P Gould Hall, Seattle, WA 98195-5720, **Business Phone:** (206)383-6052.

**SUTTON, WILLIAM W., JR.**
Journalist, editor. **Personal:** Born Jun 12, 1955, New Orleans, LA. **Educ:** Hampton Univ, BA, mass media arts, 1977; Rutgers Univ-Camden Law Sch. **Career:** Boy Scouts Am, eagle scout & asst scoutmaster, 1968-; Hampton Script, ed & reporter, 1973-76; Times Picayune, mailer, 1974; Times-Picayune, New Orleans, La, reporter, 1975; Providence J, reporter, 1976; Virginian Pilot, Norfolk, reporter, 1976-77; Gannett Co, Courier-Post, Cherry Hill, NJ, 1977-80; Philadelphia Inquirer, reporter, 1980-87, 1988-91; Journalists of Color, co-founder, 1986-; UNITY Journalists Color, Co founder, 1986-2012; Harvard Univ, Nieman fel, 1987-88; Post-Tribune, Gary, managing ed, 1991-93, newsroom mgr, 1992, ed & vpres, 1993-96; McClatchy Co Inc, News & Observer, asst managing ed, 1996, dep managing ed, 1996-2005; Sutton Solutions, ed, 2005-; Scripps Howard Sch Journalism & Commun, Vis Prof, 2005-06; Daily Press, Multimedia Activist, 2006; Scripps Howard Sch Journalism & Commun, Hampton Univ, Endowed Prof & Vis Prof, 2005-08; Acad Writing Excellence, dir, 2005-08; AEJMC-ASJMC, JLID Fel, 2008-09; Achieving Dream, dir, Commun & Strategic Mkt, 2008-09; Nc Wildlife Resources comn, conserv educ div chief, 2010; Grambling State Univ, Reynolds Vis Prof Bus Journalism, 2012, Dir Pub Rels & Commun, 2012-; Dow Jones News Fund, dir, 2012-. **Orgs:** Pres & chief exec officer, Nat Asn Black Journalists, 1977-, pres, 1999-01; Omega Psi Phi Fraternity, 1982-. **Honors/Awds:** Educ Diversity Award, Maynard Ist Journ, 1996. **Special Achievements:** NABJ's first president back, 1977. **Business Addr:** co-founder, UNITY Journalists of Color Inc, 7950 Jones Br Dr, McLean, VA 22107, **Business Phone:** (703)854-3585.

**SUTTON, DR. WILLIAM WALLACE**
School administrator. **Personal:** Born Dec 15, 1930, Monticello, MS; son of Talmon L and Bessie Lewis; married Leatrice Eva Hubbard; children: William W Jr, Averell H, Sheryl Smith, Alan D, Allison M & Gavin J. **Educ:** Dillard Univ, BA, 1953; Howard Univ, MS, 1959, PhD, 1965; Harvard Univ, IST Educ mgt, 1991. **Career:** School administrator (retired); DC Gen Hosp Wash, med Tech, 1955-59; Dillard Univ, instr prof biol, 1959-79, chmn div nat sci, 1969-79; Chicago State Univ, vpres & acad affairs & provost, 1979-85, prof biol sci, 1982-85; Kans State Univ, vpres educ & stud servs, prof biol, 1985-88; Miss Valley State Univ, pres, 1988-98. **Orgs:** Sigma XiRes Soc Am, 1955; bd dir, Nat Conf Christians & Jews, 1968-79; bd dir, Urban League New Orleans, 1970-78; bd trustee, WYES TV New Orleans, 1973-79; bd dir, Methodist Hosp New Orleans, 1975-79; Am Coun Educ; past pres, Nat Inst Sci; Soc Sigma Xi; reg liaison off, Danforth Assoc Prog Danforth Found, 1975-79; consult, US Dept Educ, 1977-81, 1983-84; bd dir, Am Heart Assoc LA, 1977-79; consult, Nat Res Coun Nat Acad Sci, 1980, 1982-83; consult, Inst Health Sci Consortium; deacon Chicago United, 1980-82; bd dir, Greenwood-Leflore Chamber Com, 1989-91; Greenwood, Miss Rotary Club; adv bd, Deposit Guaranty Nat Bank Greenwood, Miss. **Honors/Awds:** Beta Kappa Chi Sci Hon Soc, 1955; Man of the Mid S, Changing Mid S Mag, 1973; Silver Beaver Award, Boy Scouts Am, 1976; Distinguish Alumni Award, Dillard Univ, 1978; Presidential Citation, Nat Asn Equal Opportunity, 1979, 1980; Distinguish Award, Dillard Univ, 1982; Alpha Kappa Mu Hon Soc, 1990; Dillard Univ LLD, 1991. **Home Addr:** 14000 Hwy 82 W Suite 7272, Itta Bena, MS 38941-1400, **Home Phone:** (662)254-3425.

**SUTTON, WILMA JEAN**
Executive. **Personal:** Born Nov 11, 1933, Murphysboro, IL; married Clarence E. **Educ:** Univ Ill, Urbana, cert mgt, 1969; Univ Conn Storrs, cert, 1970; Univ Ind, Bloomington, cert, 1976; Roosevelt Univ, Chicago, IL, BA, 1978, MA, 1979. **Career:** Chicago Title Ins Co Chicago IL, preliminary & examr, 1951-64; Hyde Pk Fed Savings & Loan Asn Chicago, exec vpres, 1964; Community Outreach Savages Am, VPres & Regional Supvr; Home Savings Am, vpres; Northeastern Il Univ, exec asst, 1996. **Orgs:** Bd dir, Hyde Pk Fed Savings & Loan Asn Chicago; bd dir Hyde Pk Nieghborhood Club; bd dir Loretto Adult Educ Ctr; mem Lambda Alpha Ely Chpt; mem UNICEF; mem US Savings & Loan League; mem Chicago Urban League; memNat Asn Advan Colored People; Ill Commn Status Women; mem Mus Sci & Indust; mem St Thaddeus Ch Appointment; mem Savings & Loan Adv Bd Gov Daniel Walker State IL; chmn, bd gov univs, Northeastern Il Univ, 1995; chmn, Black Creativity Adv Comt, 2002. **Home Addr:** 4800 Chicago Beach Dr, Chicago, IL 60615. **Business Addr:** Executive Assistant to President, Northeastern Illinois University, 5500 N St Louis Ave, Chicago, IL 60625-4625.

**SWAIN, HAMPTON J., JR. (HAMP KING BEE SWAIN)**
Consultant, radio host. **Personal:** Born Dec 3, 1929, Macon, GA; son of Hamp Sr (deceased) and Susie McIntosh; married Zenola Hardeman; children: Ronald Leo, Ouida Louise, Natalie Valencia & Jarvis Osmond. **Career:** Little Richard & Hamptones, band leader, sax player, 1949-56; pioneer broadcaster, 1954-81; WIBB-AM, radio broadcaster, announcer, 1957-81, disc jockey, currently; Huckabee Auto Co, sales consult, 1981-. **Orgs:** Nat Asn Advan Colored People; Wendell Mcintosh Bowl. **Honors/Awds:** Golden Voice Award, Jack Gibson Orgn, 1980; Georgia Music Hall of Fame, 2008. **Home Addr:** 3171 Stratford Dr, Macon, GA 31211-2642, **Home Phone:** (478)743-1688. **Business Addr:** Disc Jockey, WIBB-AM, 7080 Industrial Hwy, Macon, GA 31216-7538, **Business Phone:** (478)781-1063.

**SWAIN, JAMES H.**
Legal consultant, lawyer. **Personal:** Born Philadelphia, PA; married Sharon Matthews. **Educ:** Univ Bridgeport, BA, polit sci, 1975; Temple Univ Sch Law, JD, 1978; Univ Pa Law Sch, LLM, labor & indust rels, 1986. **Career:** US Atty So Dist NY, summer intern, 1977; Third Circuit Ct Appeals, clerkship intern Hon A Leon Higginbotham, 1978; US Dept Labor, trial atty off reg solicitor, 1978-89; US Dept Justice, Eastern Pa, asst US atty, 1989-94, Southern Dist Fla, asst US atty, 1994-2012; Asset Forfeiture Div US Atty, dep chief, 1994-2000, chief, 2000-03; Southern Dist Fla, US Atty's Off, exec asst US atty, 2003-. **Orgs:** Exec comt, Barristers Asn Philadelphia, 1979-80, 1986-89, legis rev com, 1978-82; bd dir, Community Legal Serv, 1988-94; bd dir, Wynnfield Residents Asn, 1988-94, exec vpres, 1992-93; Fed Bar Asn Philadelphia Chap, 1988-94; Philadelphia Bar Asn, 1989-94; Fed Bar Asn, Miami Chap, 1994-; Dade Co Black Lawyers Asn, 1994-; trustee, Mt Pleasant Baptist Church; Fed Bar Asn, Miami Chap, 1996-; Inns Ct Univ Miami's Chap, 1996-; Nat Bar Asn, Fla State Chap, 1996-. **Honors/Awds:** Scholar of the Year Award, Rho Upsilon Chap, Omega Psi Phi Fraternity Inc, 1975-76; Distinguished Service Award, Black Am Law Stud Asn, 1977-78; Certificate of Appreciation, Barristers Asn Philadelphia, 1978-79, 1979-80; John Marshall Award, Omega Psi Phi Fraternity Inc, US Dept Justice, 1992. **Special Achievements:** Author: "Protecting Individual Employers: Is it Safe to Complain About Safety?," Univ Bridgeport Law Review, 1988. **Business Addr:** Attorney, Counselor at Law, Southern District of Florida, 99 NE 4th St, Miami Beach, FL 33132-2131, **Business Phone:** (305)961-9001.

**SWAIN, MICHAEL B.**
Consultant, programmer analyst, association executive. **Personal:** Born Nov 5, 1965, Springfield, OH; son of Melvin and Charlene Freeman. **Educ:** Ohio Univ, BA, comput systs bus, 1987. **Career:** Mont Lawn Camp, counr, 1987-96, Data Image, comput programmer, analyst, 1987-89; Systs Engineering & Mgt Co, comput programmer, analyst, trainer, 1989-90; Decision Systs Technologies Inc, proj mgr, 1995-98; Andersen Consult LLP, sr consult, 1998-2000; iXL, proj mgr, 2000; EDS, proj mgr, 2000-03; State Ga, Div Pub Health, proj mgr, 2003-05, 2007-09, Prof Serv Comn, IT proj mgr, 2011-; Keane, proj mgr, 2005-07; Int Bus Mach Corp, proj mgr, 2009-10; Ga Prof Stand Comn, lead IT proj mgr & IT dir, 2010-14; StreetLight Pub Rels & Mgt, bus mgr & partner, 2010-. **Orgs:** Pres, Alpha Phi Omega Nat Serv Fraternity, 1986-87; treas, Springfield Metrop N Hill Housing Bd, 1988; bd chmn, develop chair, Springfield Urban League & Community Ctr, 1990-94; pres & vpres, Alpha Phi Alpha, 1991-96 & 2008; educ chair, Nat Asn Advan Colored People, 1991-93; gen chair, Ebony Fashion Fair, 1992-93; pres, Mountain Oaks Homeowners Assoc, 1999; pres, Ohio Univ, 2003; pres, Gateway Partnership LLC, 2013; pres, Lakes Stonebridge Master Asn, 2014; vpres, DeShong-Rockbridge Community Coalition, 2014. **Honors/Awds:** John Newton Templeton Award, Outstanding Sr Leader, Ohio Univ, 1987; Community Serv Vol of the Year, Wright-Patterson AFB, 1993. **Home Addr:** 1103 Lakeside Village Dr, Atlanta, GA 30317, **Home Phone:** (404)373-9930. **Business Addr:** Partner, Business Manager, Streetlight PR & Management LLC, 679 Mountain Oaks Pkwy, Stone Mountain, GA 30087-4737, **Business Phone:** (770)465-5301.

**SWAIN, DR. RONALD L.**
Educator, association executive. **Personal:** Born Oct 9, 1948, Macon, GA; son of Evelyn Denton and Hampton; married Chrystle A Bull-

ock; children: Ronald. **Educ:** Duquesne Univ, Pittsburgh, Pa, BA, hist, 1970, MEd, counr educ, 1972; Shaw Divinity Sch, NC, MDiv, 1975; Univ NC, Chapel Hill, MEd, orgn develop, 1983; George Washington Univ, DC, EdD, higher educ admin, 1987; Harvard Univ, Grad Sch Educ, IEM, 1994; Soc Col & Univ Planning Inst, cert planning, 2007. **Career:** Duquesne Univ, residence dir, 1970-72; NC State Univ, area coord, 1972-74; Shaw Univ, stud activ counr, 1974-75, dir coun, 1974-78, vpres instnl advan & planning, 1980-94, 1988-94, assoc dean stud, 1980-81, spec asst pres, 1981-85, dir church rel, 1984-85, dir develop, 1987-88, vpres instnl advan & planning, 1988-94; Univ NC, Grad Stud Ctr, dir, 1978-80; Woodrow Wilson Nat fel, Princeton, NJ, 1981-84; United Negro Col Fund, fel doctoral study, 1985-87; United Negro Col Fund, nat develop dir, 1995-97; Wiley Col, pres, 1998-2000; Southwestern Univ, sr adv to pres strategic planning & assessment, 2000-; Swain Consulting Services Inc, pres, currently. **Orgs:** Am Asn Higher Educ, 1985-87; Asn Study Higher Educ, 1985-87; Phi Delta Kappa Prof Educ Fraternity, 1985-87; Soc Col & Univ Planning, 1987-94, 2002-; Tex Ann Conf United Methodist Church, 1998; Dist supt, United Methodist Church Undergrad Educ Adv Comt; Comn Planning & Action; Asn Am Cols & Univs, 2000-; chair, Diversity Enrichment Comt, 2011-; First United Methodist Church, 2014; Proposal Planning Comt; Univ Coun; Provost Search Comt; Integrated Mkt Task Force; chair, Lifelong Learning Task Force; chair, Core Values Coun; chair, DEC subcomt Fac & Staff Recruitment & Retention; chair, Articulation Agreement Task Force. **Honors/Awds:** Outstanding Young Men in America, 1980; Charles A. Dana Faculty Improvement Award,, United Negro Col Fund Inc, 1985-87; Century Club Distinguished Duquesne Alumni, Duquesne Univ, 2000; Career Achievement Award, Mt de Sales Acad, 2004; Roll of Fame, Dist 5870 Rotary Int Inc, 2010; Owen W. Sherrill Lifetime Achievement Award, Georgetown Chamber Com, 2010. **Special Achievements:** Numerous publications Published. **Home Addr:** 103 Diamond Trail, Georgetown, TX 78628-1955, **Home Phone:** (512)868-9298. **Business Addr:** Senior Advisor to the President, Southwestern University, 1001 E Univ Ave, Georgetown, TX 78626, **Business Phone:** (512)863-1940.

### SWAINSON, SHARON C.

Executive, baseball executive. **Personal:** Born Powhatan, VA. **Educ:** George Mason Univ, BA, eng, 1988; Drexel Univ, MBA, 2001. **Career:** Independent sports producer, on-air talent, 1986-94; TV Reporter & Host, Freelance, 1990-94; Sharon PrattKelly Comt, mayoral campaign pres sec, 1994; Walt Disney World, sports event mgr, 1994-95, sr baseball opers mgr, events, 1995-97; sr prog mgr, TV events, 1997-98; Philadelphia Phillies, spec asst to pres, 1998-2001, chief communs officer & spokesperson, 1998-2003; Actress, 2003-13; Chg Agents LLC, pres, 2003-; MySupportPal.com, pres, 2013-. **Orgs:** SAG-AFTRA, 1989-; bd mem, Am Heart Asn, Eastern Region, 1999-; bd mem, Police Athletic League, Media Rels & Communs Comt, 1999; assoc dir, bd mem, Fla Citrus Sports & Citrus Bowls Org, 1995-99; Bd mem, Philadelphia Bus Leadership Group, 2002-. **Business Addr:** President, MySupportPal com, 6230 Wilshire Blvd Suite 188, Los Angeles, CA 90048, **Business Phone:** (800)218-1058.

### SWAN, DR. GEORGE W., III

Educator. **Personal:** Born Apr 4, 1957, Detroit, MI; son of George W Jr and Henrene W; married Deborah D Harris; children: George IV, Trevor Justin & Blake Aaron. **Educ:** Wayne State Univ, BA, speech commun & theatre, 1979, MEd, educ sociol, 1991, EdD, PhD, higher educ, 1999. **Career:** Satori Theatre Co Detroit, producer, dir & writer, 1971-77; Mayflower Congregational UCC, youth dir, 1975-80; Workshop Ensemble Co, dir & playwright, 1977-82; Lewis Co Bus, asst vipers, acad affairs, assoc dir, Upward Bound, 1981-82; Proj Job Club, dir, 1982, dir col rel & title III, 1982-86; Wayne State Univ, exten ctr prog coordr, 1986-87, dist vice chancellor external affairs adrian phillips, dist assoc vice chancellor enrollment mgt; Wayne County Community Col, dir community rel, 1987-91, dir pub affairs, 1991-98, asst dean, Humanities & Social Sci, 1998-2001, interim provost, downriver campus, 2001, regional dean, 2001-, pres, Eastern Campus, 2001-07, vice chancellor, 2007-10, exec vice chancellor, 2010-, interim vice chancellor educ affairs, 2015; WPXD-TV, Direct Impact Show, producer, host, 1996-99; peer-evaluator, Higher Learning Comn, 2009-. **Orgs:** James C Crump Family Club, 1972-2010; Wayne State Univ, Theatre Dept, 1974-77; pres, Nataki Talibah Schoolhouse Taupe & Tan Parents Club, 1986-95; Bd mem, pres, Lula Belle Stewart Ctr Inc, 1987-; Nat Coun Mktg & Pub Rel, 1989-98; bd mem, chmn, Evergreen C's Serv, 1989-99; bd secy, DCC & Monroe County Pvt Indust Coun, 1990-96; bd mem, 1993-, pres, bd chair, 1989-2007, Child Welfare League Am; bd mem, Southern Wayne County Chamber Com, 1988-99-; vice chmn, Detroit Educ Cable Consortium, 1993-97; New Detroit Inc, youth & young adults comn, 1994-99; bd mem, Am Heart Asn, S Wayne, 1995-96; bd mem, Coun Accreditation Serv Families & C, 1997-; secy, Detroit Chap, Nat Coun Black Am Affairs; vice chmn, Mich Inst Nonviolence Educ, 1999-; trustee, Coun Accreditation, 1999-2005; bd mem, George Crockett Acad, 2000-; Detroit City Coun, Keep Detroit Beautiful Taskforce, 2000-; bd mem, Warren Conner Develop Corp, 2003-07; bd mem, Northeast Guid Ctr, 2003-09; bd mem, treas & finance comt chair, Child Care Coord Coun Detroit & Wayne 4C, 2003-09; bd pres, Detroit Literacy Coalition, 2003-11; policy & prog comt mem, 2003-12, adv comt, 2004-10, standing comt, Episcopal Diocese Mich, 2007-12 & 2013-; Youth Develop Comn; Detroit Regional Chamber, 2009-10; dir, 2009-, bd dir, 2009-15, Detroit Workforce Investment Bd; coun mem, United Way Southeast Mich Financial Stability Impact Coun, 2009-11; adv bd mem, Detroit Col Promise, 2009-; Southeast Mich Coun Governments Educ Adv Group, 2009-11; steering comt mem, Mich Ctr Effective IT Adoption, 2010-11; workforce task group mem, New Econ Initiative, 2010-11; metrop affairs coalition & semcog talent task force mem, Southeast Mich Coun Governments, 2010-12; bd dir, City Detroit Local Develop Finance Authority, 2010-; bd dir, Detroit Workforce Develop Bd Corp, 2011-12; steering comt mem, Detroit Works Long Term Planning Steering Comt, 2011-13; Policy Link & PERE Community Adv Comt; bd mem, Workforce Intelligence Network, 2011-; bd vice chair & chair strategic planning, Detroit Employ Solutions Corp: A Mich Works! Agency, 2012-15; steering comt, Detroit Future City, 2013-15; coun mem, Southeast Mich Coun Governments Transp Coord Coun, 2014-; bd chair, Detroit Strategic Framework, 2015-; bd mem, ARISE Detroit, 2015-. **Home Addr:** 18690 Birchcrest Dr, Detroit, MI 48221, **Home Phone:** (313)341-3076. **Business Addr:** Executive Vice Chancellor, Dean, Wayne County Community College District, 5901 Connor, Detroit, MI 48213, **Business Phone:** (313)922-3311.

### SWAN, JOHN WILLIAM DAVID

Justice of the peace, executive, politician. **Personal:** Born Jul 3, 1935; son of John N (deceased) and Margaret E; married Jacqueline A D Roberts; children: 3. **Educ:** WVa Wesleyan Col, BA; Bermuda Col, BA; Atlantic Union Col, MA, 1991. **Career:** Rego Ltd, real estate salesman, 1960-62; John W Swan Ltd, founder, chmn, chief exec officer, 1962-; Bermuda Parliament, 1972, minister home affairs, 1978-82; Premier Bermuda, 1982-95; Swan Group Co, chmn, 1995-. **Orgs:** Trustee, Bermuda Biol Sta Res; Young PRSs' Orgn, 1974-86; World Bus Coun, 1986; Chief Execs Orgn; Hamilton Rotary Club; sen, Jun Chamber Int, 1992. **Honors/Awds:** Poor Richard Club Philadelphia, 1987; International Medal of Excellence, 1987; Outstanding Learning Disabled Achiever Award, Lab Sch Wash, 1992; Hon Doctorate, Wva Wesleyan Col; Hon LLD, Atlantic Union Col; Hon DHL, Morris Brown Col. **Special Achievements:** Minister: Marine and Air Services; Labour and Immigration, 1977-78; Home Affairs, 1978-82. **Home Addr:** 11 Grape Bay Dr, Paget ParishPG 06, **Home Phone:** (809)236-1303. **Business Addr:** Chairman, Swan Group of Co, 26 Victoria St, HamiltonHM 12, **Business Phone:** (441)295-1785.

### SWAN, DR. LLEWELLYN ALEX

Educator. **Personal:** Born Jan 17, 1938, Grand Turk; married Karla K. **Educ:** Wis Col, AS, 1964; Leg Aspects Bus, assoc cert, 1964; Blackstone Law Sch, LLB, 1966; Oakwood Col, BS, 1967; Atlanta Univ, MA, 1969; Univ Calif, Berkeley, MS, 1971, PhD, 1972. **Career:** Hampton Inst, commun skills instr, 1967; Columbia Univ, publ asst, 1967; Atlanta Univ, grad asst, 1967-68; Atlanta Univ, grad asst, 1967-68; Miami-Dade Jr Col, instr, 1968-70; sonoma State Col, lectr sociol, 1970-72; Univ Calif, Sch Criminol, teaching asst, tutor, managing ed, 1970-71; Fisk Univ, Dept Sociol & anthrop, chair & assoc prof, dept sociol & anthrop, 1972-78; Vanderbilt Univ, Afro-Am Studies Prog, vis prof, 1973; Tenn State Univ, vis prof, 1973-76; Scarritt Col, Dept Church & Community, vis prof, 1976; Tex Southern Univ, Houston, Sociol Col Arts, dean, 1978-89, prof, 1978-, vice chmn, 1989-; Rice Univ, vis prof sociol, 1988; Univ Houston, vis prof, 1991-92; Ranch, Trinity Life Ctr, clinician, 1994-96; GETS, pres, 1983; CATS, dir, 1999. **Orgs:** Nat coun family rels; taxes coun family rels; bd, southwest conf SDA; southern sociol socs; Asn Social & Behav Scientists; Am Sociol Asn; Coun Crime & Delinq; Phi Beta Lambda Nat Bus Hon Socs; AKD Nat Sociol Hon Socs; trustee, Human Res & Develop Serv; Black World Found; Nat Asn Advan Colored People, chmn, Leg Redress Comn, 1973-74; Sigma Rho Sigma Hon Socs Outstanding Acad Achievement Social & Behav Sci, 1977; Southwest CtrUrban Res, 1979-82; chair, fac assembly & senate, Tex southern Univ. **Special Achievements:** Published numerous Books & articles. **Home Addr:** 101 Burwell Cove Dr, Harvest, AL 35749, **Home Phone:** (256)539-4507. **Business Addr:** Professor of Sociology, Vice Chairman, Texas Southern University, 302AD Pub Affairs 3100 Cleburne St, Houston, TX 77004, **Business Phone:** (713)313-7249.

### SWANIGAN, JESSE CALVIN

Auditor, educator. **Personal:** Born Nov 18, 1933, Widener, AR. **Educ:** Wash Univ, St Louis, BS, acct, 1966; St Louis Univ, MBA, finance, 1977. **Career:** EB Koonce Mortuary Inc, supvr trainee, 1961; Johnson Publ Co, staff rep, 1962; McDonnell Douglas Aircraft Corp, sr specialist auditing, 1963-97; Univ Mo, St Louis, adj prof & sr lectr finance, currently. **Orgs:** Ordained elder United Presby Church USA, 1976; life mem, Nat Asn Advan Colored People, 1976; Nat Asn Black Acct, 1977; consult, United Negro Col Fund Comn, 1979; Black Presby United, 1980; bd mem, Nat Black MBA Asn; treas, 100 Black Men Am Inc; bd mem, Carver House; founder, pres, St Louis Black MBA Asn, 1988; pres, Nat Black Presby Caucus, 1993; vpres, 100 Black Men Metrop St Louis. **Honors/Awds:** Black Leader 1980, United Presby Church USA, 1979; Honor of Appreciation, Am Bus Women's Asn, 1989. **Home Addr:** 1519 Lyndale Ave, St Louis, MO 63130-1211, **Home Phone:** (314)862-7158. **Business Addr:** Faculty, Adjunct Professor & Senior Lecturer in Finance, University of Missouri - St Louis, 1 Univ Blvd 1102 SSB Tower, St Louis, MO 63121, **Business Phone:** (314)516-5896.

### SWANN, ERIC JERROD

Football player. **Personal:** Born Aug 16, 1970, Pinehurst, NC; married Celeste; children: Tevin, Austin & Eric Jr. **Educ:** Wake Tech Community Col, grad. **Career:** Football player (retired); Phoenix Cardinals, defensive tackle & left defensive tackle & left defensive end, 1991-93; Ariz Cardinals, left defensive tackle, 1994-98, 99; Carolina Panthers & defensive tackle & left defensive tackle, 2000; Hudson Valley Saints, 2007; Electric co, currently. **Honors/Awds:** Two tiime All-Pro selection, 1995, 1996; American Football Association's Semi Pro Football Hall of Fame, 1998.

**SWANN, EUGENE MERWYN. See Obituaries Section.**

### SWANN, LYNN CURTIS

Broadcaster, football player, politician. **Personal:** Born Mar 7, 1952, Alcoa, TN; married Bernadette Robi; married Charena; children: Braxton & Shafer. **Educ:** Univ Southern Calif, BA, pub rels. **Career:** Football player (retired), broadcaster, polititician; Pittsburgh Steelers, Punt returner, 1976, wide receiver, 1975-82; Ct TV, spec guest commentator, 2000; US Pres Coun Phys Fitness & Sports, chmn, 2002-05; ABC Sports, sports announcer, sports analyst & broadcaster, 1976-2006; Hershey Entertainment & Resorts Co Bd, dir; H J Heinz Co, dir; NBC, panelist, 1990-91; Diamond Edge Capital Partners LLC, manging dir, currently; Swann Inc, pres, currently; Wyndham Int, bd dir; Univ Southern Calif, Athletic dir, 2016, currently. **Orgs:** Screen Actors Guild; Am Fedn TV & Radio Artists; Augusta Nat Golf Club, 2009. **Honors/Awds:** Most Valuable Player, Super Bowl X, 1975; Pro Bowl, 1977-79; Nat Football Found, Col Hall of Fame, inducted, 1993; Man of the Year, Walter Camp Football Found, 1997; Pro-Football Hall of Fame, 2001. **Special Achievements:** movie: The Last Boy Scout 1991; The Waterboy, 1998; NFL Monday Night Football, 1970. **Business Addr:** President, Swann Inc, 506 Hegner Way, Sewickley, PA 15143, **Business Phone:** (412)749-4988.

### SWANSON, CHARLES

Educator, lawyer. **Personal:** Born Aug 16, 1949, Camp Hill, AL; married Anne Elizabeth Fox; children: Tesfaye C, Tonya D, Tamara A & Charles Joseph. **Educ:** Univ Wis, Madison, BA, 1971; Univ Wis Law Sch, JD, 1973. **Career:** Univ Wis-Madison, teaching asst afro-am hist, 1970-73; Racine Co Pub Defenders Off, asst pub defender, 1974-75; Nat Asn Advan Colored People, legal redress, 1978-; pvt pract atty, currently. **Orgs:** Am Bar Asn, Racine Co; Nat Asn Criminal Defense Lawyers; bd dir, Racine Nat Asn Advan Colored People; Racine Optimist Club. **Honors/Awds:** Racine County Circuit Court Commissioner, 1980; Outstanding Young Man of America, 1984; Outstanding Director, Racine Jaycees. **Home Addr:** 3908 Valley Rd, Racine, WI 53405-1116, **Home Phone:** (262)637-9781. **Business Addr:** Attorney, 101 Atlantic Ave, New Orleans, LA 70114-1210, **Business Phone:** (504)561-8833.

### SWANSON, O'NEIL D., SR.

Funeral director. **Personal:** Born Birmingham, AL; children: O'Neil II, Linda E & Kimberly E. **Educ:** Cent State Univ, BS, 1953; Cincinnati Col Embalming Mortuary Sci, cum laude, 1956. **Career:** Swanson Funeral Home Inc, founder, pres, dir & chief exec officer, 1958-. **Orgs:** Exec bd dir, life mem, Nat Advan Asn Colored People; dir, First Independence Nat Bank Detroit, 1970-80; dir, Nat Alumni Assoc Cent State Univ, 1978, Nat Funeral dir & Morticians Assoc, 1979; Nat Conf Funeral Serv Examiners Bd. **Business Addr:** President, Chief Executing Officer & Director, Swanson Funeral Home Inc, 2210 Martin Luther King Ave, Flint, MI 48503-1098, **Business Phone:** (810)232-7469.

### SWANSON, DR. O'NEIL D., II

Funeral director. **Personal:** Born Birmingham, AL. **Career:** Swanson Funeral Home Inc, founder, pres, dir & owner, 1958-. **Orgs:** Fight Freedom Fund Dinner, chair, 1994. **Business Addr:** Owner, Director, Swanson Funeral Homes Inc, 2210 Martin Luther King Ave, Flint, MI 48503-1030, **Business Phone:** (810)232-7469.

### SWAYNE, HARRY VONRAY

Football player, athletic director. **Personal:** Born Feb 2, 1965, Philadelphia, PA; married Dawn; children: Tosca, Sher, Nina, Chris & Rod. **Educ:** Rutgers Univ, BS, sports mgt, 1990; Liberty Univ, MS, social sci, 2011-. **Career:** Football player (retired), athletic director; Tampa Bay Buccaneers, tackle, 1987-90; San Diego Chargers, 1991-96; Denver Broncos, 1997-98; Baltimore Ravens, 1999-2000; Miami Dolphins, tackle, 2001; Chicago Bears, chaplain, 2003-07; Baltimore Ravens, asst dir player prog, 2008-.

### SWEAT, KEITH

Singer, songwriter, actor. **Personal:** Born Jul 22, 1963, Harlem, NY; son of Charles Crier (deceased) and Juanita; married Lisa Wu Hartwell; children: Keisha, Keia, Justin, Jordan & Joshua Welch; children: 2. **Educ:** City Col NY, BA, commun. **Career:** Singer, songwriter, actor, currently; Wall St, fl supvr; Jamilah, singer, 1975-84; New Jack City film soundtrack, contribr, 1991. Albums: Make It Last Forever, co-producer, 1987; I'll Give All My Love to You, 1990; Mississippi Masala, 1991; The Taking of Beverly Hills, 1991; Keep It Comin', 1991; New Jack City, 1991; Made in America, 1993; Merry Go Round; Get Up On It, 1994; Keith Sweat, 1996; Just a Touch, 1997; Still in the Game, 1998; Blue Streak, 1999; Didn't See Me Coming, 2000; Rebirth, 2002; Keith Sweat Live, 2003; The Best of Keith Sweat: Make You Sweat, 2004; Roll Bounce, 2005; Sweat Hotel Live, 2007; Just Me, 2008; The Magnificent, 2009. Films: Forbidden Fruits, 2006; Pastor Brown, 2009; Ridin' Solo, 2010; Open Invitation, 2011. TV series: "New Jack City", 1991; "Rhapsody", 2000. **Honors/Awds:** Make It Last Forever, double-platinum album; Number one new male artist, Black Radio Exclusive, 1988; Favorite Male R&B/Soul Artist, 1997; 16th Annual Trumpet Awards, 2008; BET Awards, 2009; Soultrain Lifetime Achievement Award, 2013. **Special Achievements:** Concert with Bell Biv Devoe, Johnny Gill, Ricky Harris. **Business Addr:** Singer, Atlantic Records, 1290 Avenue of the Americas, New York, NY 10104, **Business Phone:** (212)707-2000.

### SWEAT, SHEILA DIANE

Financial manager. **Personal:** Born May 8, 1961, New York, NY. **Educ:** Hampton Inst, BS, 1983. **Career:** Moody's Investors Serv, credit analyst, 1984-86; Irving Trust Co, invest analyst, 1986-. **Orgs:** Hampton Alumni Asn, 1984-; Long Island Chap. **Home Addr:** 178 39 137th Ave, Jamaica, NY 11434, **Home Phone:** (718)276-9148. **Business Addr:** Investment Analyst, Irving Trust Co, 1 Wall St, New York, NY 10015, **Business Phone:** (212)635-8740.

### SWEATT, DR. JAMES L., III

Surgeon. **Personal:** Born Jul 13, 1937, Ft. Worth, TX; son of James L Jr and Jewell Juanita; married Mary Lois; children: James IV, William, Alisa & Mary Elizabeth. **Educ:** Middlebury Col, BS, chem; Wash Univ Sch Med, St Louis, MD, 1962. **Career:** Colo Med Ctr, resident; Univ Tex Southwestern Med Ctr, resident; Metro Gen Hosp, intership; St Luke Presby Church, church elder; St James L Sweatt III MD & Assocs, thoracic surgeon, currently; pvt pract, surgeon, currently. **Orgs:** Pres, Dallas County Med Soc, 1995; alt deleg, Am med Asn, 1997; Tex Med Asn, Am col Surgeons; Soc Thoracic Surgeons; Am Med Asn; C V RomanMed Soc; trustee, Southwestern Med Fed; bd regents, Tex State Univ Syst; Grace Presby Village. **Special Achievements:** Become first African American member appointed to the board of directors of Parkland Memorial Hospital in Dallas, 1976; First African American president of the Dallas County Medical society, 1995; First African American Ever Admitted to the Washington University School of Medicine. **Home Addr:** 2745 Blackstone Dr, Dallas, TX 75237-2307, **Home Phone:** (214)331-2847. **Business Addr:** Thoracic Surgeon, James L Sweatt III MD & Associates, 2727 Bolton Boone Dr Suite 102, DeSoto, TX 75115, **Business Phone:** (972)780-1850.

### SWEET, LOLITA

Business owner. **Educ:** Calif St Univ, bus mgt. **Career:** Corp Am, acct; Bay Limousines, owner & pres, Currently. **Orgs:** Brisbane Chamber Com. **Business Addr:** Owner, President, Bay Limousines, 114 Colby St, San Francisco, CA 94134, **Business Phone:** (415)334-4224.

### SWEETNAM, JAMES E.

President (organization), chief executive officer. **Educ:** US Mil Acad, BS, appl sci & engineering, 1974; Harvard Univ, MBA, bus admin, 1987. **Career:** Olko Engineering New York, civil engr, 1974-75; Air Prod & Chem Allentown, Pa & Sao Paulo, Brazil, construct engr &

prod & opers engr, 1975-77; Can Liquid Air Ltd, Montreal, Que & Calgary, prog mgr, 1977-81, gas applications mgr, 1981-83, regional gas sales mgr, 1977-85, gas sales mgr, 1983-85; Cummins Engine, exec dir, 1988-89; Cummins Electronics, pres, 1989-93; Cummins Engine Co, exec dir, 1988-89, pres, 1989-93, vpres cummins & group managing dir, 1993-97; Holset Engineering Co Ltd, managing dir; Eaton Corp, Heavy-Duty Transmission Div, vpres & gen mgr, 1997, Heavy-Duty Transmission Clutch & Aftermarket Truck, vpres, chief exec officer, 1997-2009, Global Truck Group, sr vpres, pres, 2001-08; Dana Holding, pres & chief exec officer, 2009-10. **Orgs:** bd trustees, Ideastream, 2005-10; Bd mem, Lubrizol Corp, 2007-11; bd dir, LMI, 2011-; bd dir, SunCoke Energy, 2012-. **Honors/Awds:** "Black Enterprise," The 100 Most Powerful Executives in Corporate America, 2010.

### SWEETS, ELLEN ADRIENNE

Editor, journalist, food writer. **Personal:** Born Feb 1, 1941, St. Louis, MO; daughter of Nathaniel Allen and Melba Adrienne Ficklin; married Eric Dunning; children: Hannah Adrienne. **Educ:** Fairleigh Dickinson Univ, Madison, NJ; Wash Univ, St Louis, Mo; Antioch Col, Yellow Springs, OH, 1961. **Career:** Food writer (retired); The St Louis Post Dispatch, St Louis, Mo, reporter, 1969-78; The St Louis Civil Rights Enforcement Agency, St Louis, Mo, exec dir, 1977-81; AT&T, Short Hills, NJ, ed & sr copywriter, 1981-89; The Dallas Morning News, Dallas, Tex, food reporter, 1989-2000; Neiman Marcus Online, sr copywriter, 2000-02; The Denver Post, reporter, 2002-07; The Dallas Morning News, ed; The Dallas Morning News, spec contribr. **Orgs:** Bd mem, Journalism & Women's Symposium; bd mem, Press Club of Dallas; The Writer's Garret; founding mem, colo chap of les dames d'escoffier. **Honors/Awds:** James beard award, 2006; Lifetime achievement award, colo asn black journalists, 2007; Lifetime achievement award, st louis asn black journalists. **Home Addr:** 5612 Tremont St, Dallas, TX 75214, **Home Phone:** (303)595-3565. **Business Addr:** Special Contributor, The Dallas Morning News, PO Box 655237, Dallas, TX 75265, **Business Phone:** (214)977-8497.

### SWIFT, KAREN A.

Administrator, labor relations manager. **Personal:** Born Mar 15, 1940, Kansas City, MO; daughter of William Reece Jr and Velma M Bass; married Leroy; children: Andrea R Ingram & Lisa J Ingram; married Walter Ingram. **Educ:** Univ Miss, BA, sec educ, MA, coun guid, educ spec. **Career:** Westport High Sch, prin, 1980-88, eve sch prin, currently; KCMO Sch Dist, asst prin, Cent High Sch, 1986-87; Harrision Jr High Sch, prin, 1987-88; Hickman Mills Sch Dist, KCMO, dir personnel, 1988-95; Paseo Acad Visual Arts, vice prin. **Home Addr:** 7412 Larson Ave, Kansas City, MO 64133-7026, **Home Phone:** (816)353-0431. **Business Addr:** Principal Evening School, West Port High School, 3733 SW 80th Ave, Ocala, FL 34481.

### SWIFT, LINDA DENISE

Librarian. **Personal:** Born May 27, 1965, Detroit, MI; daughter of James (deceased) and Juliet Stanfield. **Educ:** Wayne State Univ, Detroit, MI, BA, commun, jour, & related progs, 1987, MSLS, libr & info sci, 1990. **Career:** Mich Opera Theatre, Detroit, Mich, audience develop intern, 1987; WJBK-TV Channel 2, Southfield, Mich, pub serv intern, 1987; BAC & K Advert, Birmingham, Mich, pub rels intern, 1987; Campbell Ewald Adv, Detroit, Mich, telemarketing mfg, 1988-89; Mich Bell, Detroit, Mich, res asst, 1989-90; Comerica Inc, Detroit, Mich, res librn, 1990-93; UAW Chrysler, librn; ich Humane Soc, spec events vol, 2009-; Gen Motors Corp, Info Scientist, 1999-2009, librn, currently; Borders Bks & Music, bookseller/keyholder, 2010-11; Newton Int, on-site recruiter, 2013; ManpowerGroup, on-site staffing specialist, 2013-14; LaJoy Group, acct serv mgr, 2014; Performance Driven Workforce, recuiting & retention specialist, 2015. **Orgs:** Am Libr Asn, 1989-; vpres, Asn African Am Librarians, 1990-; Spec Libr Asn, 1990-. **Home Addr:** 19356 Fenelon St, Detroit, MI 48234-2202, **Home Phone:** (313)368-1136. **Business Addr:** Librarian, General Motors Corp, 300 Renaissance Ctr, Detroit, MI 48265-3000, **Business Phone:** (313)556-5000.

### SWIFT, MICHAEL AARON

Executive, football player. **Personal:** Born Feb 28, 1974, Dyersburg, TN; married Jeanette; children: Janae & Michael Jr. **Educ:** Austin Peay St, grad. **Career:** Football player (retired); Rhein Fire, 1997; San Diego Chargers, defensive back, 1997; Carolina Panthers, defensive back, 1998-99; Jacksonville Jaguars, corner back, 2000; Protein Technologies, analyst, 2000-01; Uniform People, sales rep, 2001-02.

### SWINDELL, DR. WARREN C.

Educator, executive. **Personal:** Born Aug 22, 1934, Kansas City, MO; son of John Truman Jr and Estella Jaunita (McKittrick); married Monica Streetman; children: Warna Celia & Lillian Ann. **Educ:** Lincoln Univ MO, BS, music educ, 1956; Univ Mich Ann Arbor, MM, 1964; Univ IA, PhD, music educ, 1970. **Career:** Educator (retired); Cent High Sch, Haiti, MO, band & chair dir, 1956-57, dir musical act, 1959-60; Hubbard High Sch, dir music act, 1960-61; Flint MI Pub Schs, inst mus specialist, 1961-67; KY State Univ, chair & prof music, 1970-79, prof music, 1979-80; Ind State Univ, chair, dir & Dept African & African Am Studies, prof, 1980-96, prof emer, 1996-. **Orgs:** Evaluator, Nat Asn Sch Music Accred, 1977-78; screening panel, KY Arts Comn Proj, 1977-79; chaired State, Div & Nat MENC meetings, 1979-80; pres, Region V, Nat Coun Black Studies, 1989-91; worshipful master, Prince Hall Lodge 16, 1991-92; secy, IND Coalition BLKs Higher EDUC, 1992-93; first vpres, Ind Coalition Blacks Higher Educ, 1994-95; chair, Sch Instr, Prince Hall Masons, 1994-99; Terre Haute, Ind Br Nat Asn Advan Colored People, first vpres, 1995-96, pres, 1997-99; pres, Ind Coalition, 1996-99; Prince Hall Grand Lodge Jurisdiction Ind, chmn masonic hist & educ; elevated 33 Degree Grand Inspector Gen, United Supreme coun Ancient & Accepted Scottish Rite Free Masonry. **Honors/Awds:** Numerous Service Awards, NAACP, 1978-94; NEH Summer Seminar Col Teachers Grant, 1984; Faculty Res Grant Ind State Univ, 1985; IN State Univ Res Grant, 1987-88; Am Philos Soc Res Grant, 1988; Lilly Endowment Faculty Open Fel, 1993-94; Caleb Mills Distinguished Teaching Award, Univ Ind, 1996; Helm Fel Res Grant, The Lilly Librarian, Ind Univ, 1999. **Home Addr:** 10755 Hillshire Ave, Baton Rouge, LA 70810, **Home Phone:** (225)761-4902. **Business Addr:** Professor Emeritus, Indiana State University, 200 N Seventh St, Terre Haute, IN 47809-1902, **Business Phone:** (812)237-6311.

### SWINER, DR. CONNIE C., III

Physician. **Personal:** Born Sep 8, 1959, Washington, DC; son of Connie and Esther Wallace. **Educ:** Col William & Mary, BS, biol, 1980; Howard Univ Col Med, MD, 1985. **Career:** Michael Reese Hosp, Chicago, Ill, resident, 1987-90; Univ Ill, Col Med, Chicago, Ill, asst prof, 1990-; Provident Hosp, anesthesiol, currently; pvt pract, currently. **Orgs:** Am Med Asn, 1982-; Black Physicians Asn, Cook County Hosp, 1986-; Alpha Phi Alpha Frat Inc, 1978-; Howard Univ Med Alumni Asn, 1985-; Am Soc Anesthesiologists, 1987-. **Honors/Awds:** Alpha Omega Alpha Hon Med Soc, Howard Univ, 1985. **Home Addr:** 1501, Chicago, IL 60605-2846. **Business Addr:** Physician, Providence Hospital GNSouth, 500 E 51st St, Chicago, IL 60615-2494, **Business Phone:** (312)572-1200.

### SWINGER, RASHOD ALEXANDER

Executive, football player. **Personal:** Born Nov 27, 1974, Paterson, NJ. **Educ:** Rutgers Univ, BA, commun, 1997. **Career:** Football player (retired), executive; Ariz Cardinals Football Club, 1997, left defensive tackle, 1998-99, defensive tackle, 1999; T-Mobile, corp acct exec, 2004-06; Supercoups Inc, franchise licensing rep, 2006-09; Staples Advantage, bus develop & acct exec, 2009-10; Med Sales Mgt, regional acct mgr, 2010-11; Augusta Med Systs, clin educr & territory mgr, 2012-. **Business Addr:** Territory Manager, Augusta Medical Systems LLC, 1027 Broad St, Augusta, GA 30901, **Business Phone:** (706)821-3600.

### SWINNEY, DR. T. LEWIS

Physician. **Personal:** Born Jun 3, 1946, Nashville, TN. **Educ:** Benedict Col, BS, 1970; Meharry Med Col, MD, 1975. **Career:** Staten Island Hosp, internship, residency internal med, 1975-78; USN, chief pulmonary med, chief alcohol rehab unit, staff physician internal med, 1978-81; pvt pract physician, currently. **Honors/Awds:** Physician of the Year, Queens-Corona, 1984. **Home Addr:** 33 Front St Suite 306, Hempstead, NY 11550.

### SWINTON, DR. DAVID HOLMES

Chief executive officer, executive, president (organization). **Personal:** Born Mar 18, 1943, New Haven, CT; son of Morris and Pearl; married Patricia Lewis; children: Olaniyan, Ayanna, Aisha, Malika, Omari & Akilah. **Educ:** NY Univ, BA, 1968; Harvard Univ, MA, 1971, PhD, econs, 1975. **Career:** Harvard Univ, teaching fel, 1970-71, Grad Prize Fel; City Col NY, lectr, 1971-72; Black Econ Res Ctr, asst dir res, 1971-73; Wash Harriman Col Urban & Policy Sci, Undergrad Prog, assoc prof & dir, 1973-78; Urban Inst, dir, Minorities & Social Policy Prog, sr res assoc, 1973-78; Clark Col, Southern Ctr Studies Pub Policy Prog, dir, prof econ, 1981-87; Jackson State Univ Sch Bus, prof econ & dean, 1987-94; Benedict Col, pres & chief exec officer, 1994-; Clark Atlanta Univ, prof econs. **Orgs:** Ed adv bd, Rev Black Polit Econ, 1974-; econ adv, Nat Urban League, 1980-94; res coun mem, Econ Policy Inst, 1986-; bd trustee, Hinds City Econ Develop Dist, 1987-; adv bd, Jackson Enterprise Ctr, 1987-; bd economist, Black Enterprise Mag, 1990-; consult, Tenn Valley Authority, 1991-94; secy, SC Tuition Grants Higher Educ Comn, 1994-99; bd dir, SC Philharmonic; Capital City Club, 1994-; Rotary Club Columbia, 1994-; bd dir, Greater Columbia Chamber Comn, 1994-99; bd dir, Jr Achievement Greater Columbia Inc, 1994-; bd dir, United Way Midlands, 1995-2000; Columbia Econ Club; Cult Coun Richland & Lexington Cos; 100 Black Men SC Inc; Sigma Xi; Ford Found Fel; Phi Beta Kappa; Coat Arms Socs.chmn, Greater Columbia Chamber Com Bd; dean, Jackson State Univ; Southern Asn Cols & Schs. **Home Addr:** 6 Marrob Ct, Columbia, SC 29203-9104. **Business Addr:** President, Chief Executive Officer, Benedict College, Admin Bldg Suite 306, Columbia, SC 29204, **Business Phone:** (803)705-4681.

### SWITZER, LOU

Executive, founder (originator), chief executive officer. **Personal:** Born Oct 12, 1948, Orangeburg, SC; married Gina; children: Gregory & Rhonda. **Educ:** Pratt Inst Brooklyn, NY, attended 1973. **Career:** Sherburne Assoc Inc NYC, draftsman & designer, 1966-70; Off Design Assoc Inc & NYC, draftsman & designer, 1970-71; WE Htton & Co NYC, asstdir facil, 1971-73; LCL Desing Assoc Inc NYC, partner, 1973-75; Switzer Group Inc, chmn, pres, founder, 1975-; Switzer Group Inc, chmn, chief exec officer, 1975-. **Orgs:** Young Pres's Orgn, 1989-; Peat Marwick Mid Mkt Adv Bd; New York Bldg Cong; Real Estate Bd NY; bd trustee, Design Industs Found Fighting AIDS; bd dir, Bedford Stuyvesant Restoration Corp; trustee, Ace Mentor Foundation; bd mem, Metro New York Make-A-Wish. **Home Addr:** 233 E 69th St, New York, NY 10021. **Business Addr:** Chairman, Chief Executive Officer, The Switzer Group Inc, 3 E 535 5th Ave 7th Fl, New York, NY 10017-3620, **Business Phone:** (212)922-1313.

### SWITZER, VERYL A., SR.

Educator. **Personal:** Born Aug 6, 1932, Nicodemus, KS; son of Fred and Ora; married Fern N Stalnaker; children: Teresa, Veryl Jr & Calvin. **Educ:** Kans State Univ, attended 1954; DePaul Univ, grad work, 1969; KS State Univ, MS, 1974. **Career:** Green Bay Packers, punt returner, 1954, kick returner, punt returner, 1955; Calgary Stampeders, 1958; Can, prof & football player, 1958-60; Montreal Alouettes, 1959-60; Chicago Pub Schs, teacher, 1959-69; Minority & Cult Progs KS St Univ, dir, 1969-73; univ minority affairs, 1973-88; KS St Univ, dean minority affairs spec progs, 1973-; Earl Woods Nat Youth Golf Acad & Assoc Athletic Dir Academics, co-dir, 1988-. **Orgs:** Fac, Senate Univ Loan Comn; Univ Fair Pract & Housing Comn; Phi Delta Kappa; Nat Asn Stud Personel Adminrs; bd Educ USD 383 Manhattan KS; chmn, KS Univ Athletic Coun; Kans High Sch Activ Asn. **Honors/Awds:** Recipient, Numerous awards including Kappa Alpha Psi Achievement Award; all-armed forces football team; all-am first team NFL, 1953; all-am second team, 1951-52; NEA & AP; K-State Sports Hall of Fame; Big Eight Sports writers Hall of Fame; KSHSAA Hall of Fame, 1995. **Home Addr:** 1412 Wreath Ave, Manhattan, KS 66503-2402, **Home Phone:** (785)537-7098.

### SWOOPES, SHERYL DENISE. See SWOOPES-JACKSON, SHERYL.

### SWOOPES-JACKSON, SHERYL (SHERYL DENISE SWOOPES)

Basketball player. **Personal:** Born Mar 25, 1971, Brownfield, TX; daughter of Louise; married Eric; children: Jordan Eric. **Educ:** S Plain Col, 1991; Tex Tech Univ, 1993. **Career:** Basketball player (retired); Houston Comets, forward, 1997-2007; Seattle Storm, forward & out, 2008; Tulsa Shock, 2011; TV apppearances: "ESPNU Town-hall Meeting", 2005; Loyola Univ Chicago, head coach, 2013-. **Business Addr:** Professional Basketball Player, Tulsa Shock, 1 W 3rd St Suite 1100, Tulsa, OK 74103, **Business Phone:** (918)949-9700.

### SWYGERT, PROF. H. PATRICK

School administrator. **Personal:** Born Mar 17, 1943, Philadelphia, PA; son of Leroy Huzzy and Gustina; married Sonja E; children: Haywood Patrick Jr & Michael Branson. **Educ:** Howard Univ, BA, hist, 1965; Howard Univ Law Sch, JD, 1968. **Career:** Chap Judge William H Hastie, Fed Ct Appeals, law clerk, 1968-69; Temple Univ Sch Law, asst prof law, 1972-77; US Civil Serv Comn, gen coun, 1977-79; Merit Systs Protection Bd, spec coun, 1979; Temple Univ Sch Law, coun, 1980, prof law, 1982, exec vpres admin; Debevoise, Plimpton, New York, assoc, 1969-71; Cong Charles BRangel, admin asst, 1971-72; Temple Univ, exec vpres, 1987; State Univ NY, Albany, pres, 1990-95; Howard Univ, pres, 1995-2008, prof, law emer, 2008-; US Dept Educ, Historically Black Cols & Univs Capital Financing Prog Adv Bd, chmn, 2002-06; Cheyney Univ Pa, Adv Bd. **Orgs:** Mem bd dir, Wynnefield Residents Asn, 1973-75; exec comt, Pub Interest Law Ctr Philadelphia, 1973-77, 1980-; exec comt, Legal Careers Proj Am Fed Negro Affairs 1974-77, Minority Affairs Asn Am Law Schs, 1974-77; vice chmn, Pub Serv Comm Philadelphia Bar Asn, 1975-76; consult, Univ Wide Affirm Action, 1980; mem nominating comt, United Way SE PA, 1981; state rep, Bd Southeastern PA Transp Authority; bd dir, WHYY-TV WHYY-FM; vice chmn, Philadelphia City Charter Rev Comn; Mid States Comn Higher Educ; chair, NY State Spec Comn Educ Struct, Policies & Practices, 1993-94; chair, Summer Games Organizing Comt, Spec Olympics, NY, 1995, bd dir, Fannie Mae Found, 1999-; DC Emancipation Commemoration Comn, 2004-; Comn Presidential Debates; US Nat Comn UNESCO; hon mem, Golden Key Nat Hon Socs; Victory Funds, Cleveland, Ohio; Hartford Financial Serv Group Inc, Hartford, Conn; Hartford Life Ins Co, Hartford, Conn; chmn, Community Bus Partnership, Wash Bd Trade; Alpha Phi Omega Nat Serv Fraternity; Zeta Phi Chap; Omega Psi Phi; Alpha Chap. **Home Addr:** 3119 Arizona Ave, Washington, DC 20017. **Business Addr:** Professor of Law Emeritus, Howard University, 2900 Van Ness St NW, Washington,, DC 20008, **Business Phone:** (202)806-8000.

### SYKES, RAY A., III

Advertising executive, chief executive officer. **Personal:** Born Le-Compte, LA; children: Tracey, Raymonda & Ray Anthony. **Educ:** Santa Monica City Col. **Career:** Douglass Aircraft, machinist; Jack Box Restaurant, Los Angeles, owner; Super Ford Minneapolis, pres & owner; Ray Sykes Buick Kingwood, Tex, pres & owner; Sykes Commun, chmn, pres & chief exec officer, currently. **Orgs:** Civil serv comnr, City Houston; exec bd dir, Boy Scouts Am; bd dir, UNCF; vpres, Houston Buick Dealers Asn; adv bd, Sch Bus Tex Southern Univ. **Honors/Awds:** Houston Area Urban League Small Business Award. **Business Addr:** Chief Executive Officer, Sykes Communications, 1800 W Loop S Suite 1130, Houston, TX 77002-3290, **Business Phone:** (713)223-0333.

### SYKES, PROF. RICK

Educator, television news anchorperson. **Personal:** Born Saginaw, MI; married Marguerite Irene Cain; children: James William. **Educ:** Delta Community Col, Bay County, 1971; Cent Mich Univ, Mt Pleasant, BS, 1973, MA, broadcast & cinematic arts, 1980. **Career:** WNEM-TV, Saginaw, prod cameraman, 1973-75, reporter anchor, 1975-81, news mgr, 1981-82; WDIV-TV, Detroit, sr assignment ed, 1982-90; Herman off & Assoc, Farmington Hills, vpres, 1990-; Cent Mich Univ, full prof, broadcast & cinematic arts, currently. **Orgs:** Broadcast Educ Asn; Soc Prof Journalist; Radio Tv Digital News Asn. **Home Addr:** , Linden, MI. **Business Addr:** Professor, Central Michigan University, Mount Pleasant, MI 48859, **Business Phone:** (989)774-3851.

### SYKES, ROBERT A.

Executive, vice president (organization). **Personal:** Born Dec 25, 1947, Gary, IN; son of Jasper and Mary. **Educ:** Fisk Univ, Nashville, TN, BA, philos, 1969. **Career:** Natural Gas Pipeline Co Am, Chicago, Ill, employ compliance adminr, 1970-75; Fermi Nat Accelerator Lab, Batavia, Ill, mgr eeo & community rels, 1975-78; Gen Mills, W Chicago, Ill, asst personnel mgr, 1978-79; Wash Gas Light Co, Springfield, Va, vpres human resources, 1979-. **Orgs:** Am Gas Asn; Am Asn Blacks Energy; vice chair, Melwood Hort Training Ctr; founder, Black Human Resources Network; Sr Human Resource Exec Forum. **Home Addr:** 6723 Bock Rd, Fort Washington, MD 20744. **Business Addr:** Vice President, Human Resources, Washington Gas Light Co, 6801 Indust Rd, Springfield, VA 22151, **Business Phone:** (703)750-4440.

### SYKES, DR. VERNON LEE

Economist, state government official, educator. **Personal:** Born Oct 2, 1951, Forrest City, AR; son of Walter Jr and Valley Louise Walker; married Barbara Ann; children: Stancy & Emilia. **Educ:** Ohio Univ Col Bus Admin, BBA, mgt, 1974; Wright State Univ, Dayton, MS, social & appl econs, 1980; Kent State Univ, MPA, 1978; Harvard Univ, Cambridge, MPA, 1986; Univ Akron, PhD, pub admin, 2001. **Career:** Akron Bd Ed, sub teacher, 1974-75; UNCI-Econ Develop Prog, sr mgt specialist, 1975-76; Summit City Criminal Justice Comn, planner res & eval, 1976-79; Akron City Coun, chmn, vice chmn, mem, 1980-83; Wayne Col, Dept Polit Sci, adj fac, 1981-98; Univ Akron, part time instr; Clarence Allen Realty, salesman; Harvard Group; OH House Rep, 44th house dist, state rep, 1983-2000; Univ Akron, Community & Tech Col, Assoc Studies Dept, asst prof social Sci, 1998-2001; Kent State Univ, Polit Sci Dept, asst prof, 2001-, dir columbus prog, 2001-. **Orgs:** Pres, Akron/Summit Community Action Agency, 1977-; Ohio Job Training Coord Coun, 1982-83; human serv adv bd, County Summit, 1985-97; dir, Harvard Group, 1987-; pres's minority adv coun, Univ Akron, 1988-chair, presidents blue ribbon task force, black cult ctr, 1991-92, msw vis comt, social work dept, 1995-, Advancing Up Prog, 1996-, Ctr Conflict Mgt Adv Comt, 1999-; Presidential Rank Rev Bd, US Off Personnel, 1993; minority affairs adv coun, Ohio State Univ, 1997-; Hiram Col Bd Visitors, 1999-; Interstate Coop, Energy & Environ, Ways & Means Ref, State Govt, Pay Equity Adv Comn, Travel & Tourism, High Speed Rail Task Force, Job Training Coord Coun; chmn, Audit Comt, Recycle Energy Comn, Health &

Social Serv; vice chmn, Housing & Urban Develop, Downtown Redevelop Parks & Recreation Comn, Fin Comn, Annexation Comn, Akron Summit/Medina Pvt Ind Coun, Summit Cty Human Serv Adv Comn, Mayor RoyRay's Citizen's Financial Adv Comn, Western Econ Int, Alpha Homes; vpres, Alpha Libr Comn Inc, chmn Ed & Scholar Comn Alpha Phi Alpha. **Honors/Awds:** Emerging Leadership Award, Akron Frontiers Club Int, 1979; Grateful Emerging Leadership Award, Akron Frontiers Club Int, 1979; Outstanding Alumnus, Black Alumni, Ohio Univ, 1981; Councilman of the Year, Nat Asn Real Estate Brokers, Akron Chap, 1982; Community Service Award, Akron Summit Community Action Agency, 1984; Outstanding Alumni Award, Upward Bound Prog, Kent State Univ, 1985; Outstanding Service Award, Black Cult Ctr, Univ Akron, 1986; Legislator of the Year Award, Nat Asn Social Workers, Ohio Chap, 1987; Fair Housing Award, Ohio Fair Housing Cong, 1988; Fair Housing Award, US Dept Housing & Urban Develop, 1988; Outstanding Legislator, Ohio Caucus Black Sch Bd Members, 1990; Public Service Award, Fair Housing Contact Serv, Akron, Ohio, 1990; Resolution of Appreciation, Ohio Civil Rights Comn, 1992; State Independent Living Council Award, Ohio Rehab Serv Comn, 1992; Equal Opportunity/Affirmative Action Exemplary Practices Award, Am Soc Pub Admin, 1993; Special Achievement Award, US Dept Housing & Urban Develop, 1993; Legislator of the Year Award, Ohio Hunger Task Force, 1994; Legislator of the Year Award, Ohio Nurses Asn, 1995; Special Recognition, Ohio Asn Second Harvest Foodbanks, 1998; Community Service Award, Off Inst Diversity, Kent State Univ, 1999; Rising Star, Akron Summit Community Action Agency, 1999; Special Recognition, Ohio Legis Black Caucus, 2000; Hon & Recognition, Columbus City Coun, 2000; Jack Wolf Memorial Award, Secy State & Ohio Asn Election Officials, 2000. **Special Achievements:** Publication include: The Efficacy of Extra-Jurisdictional Facilitation of Electoral Participation: A Study of Public Administration. **Home Addr:** 615 Diagonal Rd, Akron, OH 44320, **Home Phone:** (330)434-0202. **Business Addr:** Assistant Professor, Director of the Columbus Program, Kent State University, 302 Bowman Hall, Kent, OH 44240, **Business Phone:** (330)672-8948.

### SYKES, WANDA Y'VETTE (ADRIANA BEDOYA)

Comedian, actor. **Personal:** Born Mar 7, 1964, Portsmouth, VA; daughter of Harry Ellsworth and Marion Louise; married David Hall; married Alex; children: Lucas Claude & Olivia Lou. **Educ:** Hampton Univ, BS, mkt, 1986. **Career:** Nat Security Agency, contracting specialist, procurement officer; Films: Tomorrow Night, 1998; Nutty Professor II: The Klumps, 2000; Down to Earth, 2001; Pootie Tang, 2001; Monster-in-Law, 2005; Clerks II, 2006; MySuper Ex-Girlfriend, 2006; Condom Nation, 2006; Evan Almighty, 2007; Licence to Wed, 2007; Rio, 2011; The Muppets, 2011; The Hot Flashes, 2013. TV series: "The Chris Rock Show", producer, 1997-2000; Best of the Chris Rock Show, 1999; "Curb Your Enthusiasm", 2000-11; "The Drew Carey Show", 2001; "Curb Your Enthusiasm", 2001-11; "Crank Yankers", 2002-03; "Wanda At Large", producer, 2003; "MTV: Reloaded", 2003; "Wanda Does It", exec producer, 2004; "Will & Grace", 2006; "Wanda Sykes: Sick & Tied", exec producer, 2006; "The New Adventures of Old Christine", sound track, 2006-10; "Back at the Barnyard", 2007-11; "Wanda Sykes: I'ma Be Me", exec producer, 2009; "Drop Dead Diva", 2011; "Bubble Puppy's Fin-tastic Fairytale Adventure", 2012; "Bubble Guppies", 2012; "Futurama", 2012; NewNowNext Vote with Wanda Sykes, exec producer, 2012; "Wanda Sykes Presents Herlarious", exec producer, 2013-14; "The Simpsons", 2013; "Real Husbands of Hollywood", 2013; "Alpha House", 2013-14. Writer: "The Keenen Ivory Wayans Show", 1997-98; "Comedy Central Presents", 1998; "The Chris Rock Show", writer & producer, 1997-2000; "Best of the Chris Rock Show: Volume 2", 2001; "The Downer Channel", 2001; "The 74th Annual Academy Awards", 2002; "Premium Blend", 2002-03; "Wanda Sykes: Tongue Untied", writer & producer, 2003; "Wanda at Large", writer & producer, 2003; "Wanda Does It", writer & producer, 2004; "Wanda Sykes: Sick and Tired", writer & exec producer, 2006; "The Wanda Sykes Show", writer & exec producer, 2009-10; "Last Comic Standing", writer & exec producer, 2014. **Orgs:** Alpha Kappa Alpha Sorority Inc. **Honors/Awds:** MTV Video Music Awards, 1997; MTV Movie Awards, 1998; MTV Video Music Awards, 1999; Primetime Emmy Award, 1999; American Comedy Award, 2001; Emmy Awards, 2002, 2004 & 2005; BET Comedy Award, 2005; Stephen F. Kolzak Award, 2010; Gracie Allen Award, 2014. **Special Achievements:** Ranks among Entertainment Weekly's 25 Funniest People in America. **Business Addr:** Actress, Endeavor Talent Agency, 9601 Wilshire Blvd Fl 3, Beverly Hills, CA 90210, **Business Phone:** (310)248-2000.

### SYLER, M. RENE

Television news anchorperson, founder (originator), chief executive officer. **Personal:** Born Feb 17, 1963, Belleville, IL; daughter of William Henry and F Anne McDonald; married Buff Parham; children: Casey, Cole & Olivia. **Educ:** Am River Col, Sacramento, CA, attended 1981; Azusa Pac Univ, Azusa, CA, attended 1984; Calif State Univ, Sacramento, CA, BA, psychol, 1987. **Career:** KTVN-TV, Reno, Nev, news reporter, 1987-89; KOLO-TV, Reno, Nev, news anchor, 1989-90; WVTM-TV, Birmingham, Ala, news anchor, 1990-92; WFAA-TV, Dallas, Tex, news anchor, 1992-96; KTVT-TV, Dallas, Tex, news anchor, 1997-2002; "The Early Show", CBS News, news anchor, 2002-06; Simon & Schuster, auth, 2005-07; Susan G Komen Cure, ambassador, 2007; Bill Cunningham Show, guest expert, 2012-14; Live Well Network, host, 2012-15; ASPiRE TV, co-host, 2012-; Good Enough Mother Media, founder, chief exec officer, currently; Circle Promise, co-chair, currently; Author: Good Enough Mother: The Perfectly Imperfect Book of Parenting. **Orgs:** Nat Asn Advan Colored People, 1988-; Nat Black Journalists Asn, 1988-; Northern Nev Black Cult Awareness Soc, 1989-; publicity comt, jr bd, YWCA, 1990-; life mem, Nat Asn Black Journalists. **Home Addr:** 304-9 Beacon Crest Lane, Birmingham, AL 35209, **Home Phone:** (205)942-7603. **Business Addr:** Founder, Chief Executive Officer, Good Enough Mother, 850 7th Ave, New York, NY 10019, **Business Phone:** (212)977-6990.

### SYLVAS, DR. LIONEL B.

School administrator, college administrator, consultant. **Personal:** Born May 10, 1940, New Orleans, LA; son of Iona and Junius; married Kathrine; children: Angela & Antoine. **Educ:** Southern Univ, BS, 1963; Univ Detroit, MA, 1971; Nova Univ, EdD, 1975. **Career:** College administrator (retired); Ford Motor Co, indust res anal, 1967-69, ed training spec, 1969-71; Miami Dade Community Col, assoc acad dean, 1971-74, asst to pres, 1974-77; Southern Asn Col & Schs Eval Team, consult, 1974; Northern Va Comm Col, admin coun, 1978-, Woodbridge campus provost, 2001-04; Va Power Co, consult adv group, 1983-87. **Orgs:** Adv Bd Black Am Affairs, Nat Sch Vol Prog, 1974-78; pres, Southern Reg Couns, 1977-88; field reader, Titles III & IV Off Educ, 1979; mem adv bd, Am Red Cross, 1982; panelist, Va ComnArts; Const Bicentennial Comn Va. **Honors/Awds:** Outstanding Educator, Miami Dade Community Col, 1975. **Home Addr:** 6666 Old Blasksmith Dr, Burke, VA 22015, **Home Phone:** (703)455-5793.

### SYLVESTER, MELVIN R.

Educator, association executive. **Personal:** Born Mar 25, 1939, New Orleans, LA; son of John and Myrtle Howard; married Frances Modica; children: Lori Alaine & Kyle Eugene. **Educ:** Dillard Univ, BA, 1961; Long Island Univ, MSLS, 1966, MEd, 1973. **Career:** Dillard Univ, circulation lib, 1961-62; CW Post Lib, head circulation dept, 1962-64; Long Island Univ, B Davis Schwartz Lib, head serials rec, 1964-, lectr african Am hist, 1995-, prof, prof emer, currently. **Orgs:** Fac & chap adv Tau Kappa Epsilon, 1965-; secy, Col & Univ Div Nassau Co Lib Asn, 1973-75; rep, CW Post Ctr Fac Coun, 1974-78; Martin Luther King Higher Educ Oppor Prog Adv Bd, 1974-78; Lib Fac Personnel Comn, 1974-78; Melvil Dui Marching & Chowder Asn, 1975-; adv bd, Friendship House Glen Core NY, 1975-78; Space Utilization Comn, CW Post Ctr, 1975-78; chmn, Space Utilization Comn, 1977-78; Comn Handicapped Glen Cove Sch, 1978-80; bd dir, Boy's Club Lincoln House Glen Cove NY, 1978-85; Day Care Head Start Ctr Glen Cove NY, 1979-89; mem stud affairs appeal comn, CW Post Ctr, 1979-82; Greater NY Metro Area Chap ACRL, 1983-; 100 Black Men Nassau Sulk Inc, 1983-; Lions Int, 1983-; chairperson, Affirmative Action Task Force, CW Post Ctr, 1984-86; Pre-Med Comn CW Post, 1984-; libr bd trust, Glen Cove Pub Libr, 1984-93; New York Libr Asn; Nassau Co Lib Asn; chairperson, Instr Comt, CW Post, 1986-88; bd dir, Alliance Coun Ctr, 1986-89; Career Adv Group, CW Post, 1986-; N Am Serials Group Libr, 1987-; Freshman Mentor Prog, CW Post, 1987-; bd trustee, Nassau Libr Syst, 1988-92; Campaign Comt & Youth & Family Serv Panel United Way Long Island, 1988-89; Legis Comt Long Island Resources Coun Inc, 1988-93; Univ Study Group V Long Island Univ LIU Plan, 1988; adv bd, Nassau County Dept Ment Health, 1988-92; LILRC Lobbyist Libr, 1990-92; GRASP-Comt CW Post, 1991-95; Univ Sect Comt Assoc Provost Enrollment Serv, 1996; Univ Outcomes Assessment Comn, 1997-; chair, Univ Ad Hoc Libr Comn Serials, Periodicals Long Island Univ. **Honors/Awds:** Faculty Recognition Award, Alpha Phi Alpha, 1979; Service Award, Glen Cove Public Schs Comn Handicapped, 1980; Public Service Award, Malik Sigma Psi, 1981; Twenty-Year Metal, Service & Recognition, LIU, 1984; Service Award, African Student Convocation, 1986; Student Government Association Award for Service to Students, CW Post Campus, 1986; Nassau Library System Award of Merit as Trustee, 1992; Nassau County Executive Citation as retired trustee, 1992; HEOP 25th Anniversary Service Recognition Award, 1994. **Special Achievements:** Printed publications, "Negro Periodicals in the US 1826-1960" an annotated bibliography; "A Library Handbook to Basic Source Materials in Guidance & Counseling" 1973; author: Content Consultant & revisionist, book on Martin Luther King Jr, 2000. **Home Addr:** 3718 Eagles Beek Cir, Lithonia, GA 30038-3549, **Home Phone:** (770)593-0619. **Business Addr:** Professor Emeritus, Long Island University, CW Post Campus, Brookville, NY 11548-1300, **Business Phone:** (516)299-2900.

### SYLVESTER, DR. PATRICK JOSEPH

Educator. **Personal:** Born Mar 1, 1932. **Educ:** St Francis Xavier Univ, Can, BA, 1960; Univ NB, Can, MA, 1962; Univ PA, MA, 1967; Bryn Mawr Col, PhD, 1973. **Career:** W Chester Univ, assoc prof econ, 1968, prof econ & finance. **Home Addr:** 160 E 38th St Apt 24C, New York, NY 10016-2613, **Home Phone:** (212)986-5769. **Business Addr:** Professor of Economics & Finance, West Chester University, 700 S High St, West Chester, PA 19380, **Business Phone:** (610)436-1000.

### SYMONE, RAVEN (RAVEN-SYMONE CHRISTINA PEARMAN)

Entertainer, actor. **Personal:** Born Dec 10, 1985, Atlanta, GA; daughter of Christopher Barnard and Lydia Gaulden. **Career:** Actress, currently; TV series: "A Different World", 1989; "The Cosby Show", 1989-92; "Hangin With Mr Cooper", 1993-97; "Kim Possible", animated, 2002-; "That's So Raven", 2003-07; "The Dress Is Always Greener", 2006; "The Way They Were", 2007; "Total Drama Island", 2007-08; "State of Georgia", 2011; "See Dad Run", 2013. TV movies: Queen, 1993; guest appearance: The Cheetah Girls 2, 2002; The Cheetah Girls, 2003; Fresh Prince of Bel-Air; For One Night, 2006; Revenge of the Bridesmaids, 2010; films: Dr Doolittle, 1998; Dr Doolittle 2, 2001; "That's So Raven", 2003-06; Dr Dolittle 3, 2006; Kim Possible, 2007; Col Rd Trip, 2008; Tinker Bell, 2008; Tinker Bell and the Lost Treasure, 2009; Good Hair, 2009; Tinker Bell and the Great Fairy Rescue, 2010; Pixie Hollow Games, 2011; Tinker Bell and the Mysterious Winter Woods, 2012; Secret of the Wings, 2012; The Pirate Fairy, 2014; Tinker Bell and the Legend of the NeverBeast, 2015; A Girl Like Grace, 2015; Animal Crackers, 2017. **Orgs:** Am Fed TV & Radio Artists, 1989-; Screen Actors Guild, 1989-. **Honors/Awds:** Youth in Film Award, Outstanding Young Actress, 1990-91; Outstanding Young TV Performer, 1991; Young Artist Award, 1991, 2005; The Peoples Choice Awards; Image Award, Nat Asn for the Advan of Colored People, 2004-08; Blimp Award, 2004; Kids' Choice Award, 2004-05; Michael Landon Award, 2005; Radio Disney Music Awards, 2005; Impact Award, 2011; SCLC, Junior Achievement Award for Excellence in TV Series; New York Music Awards, Inter Nat Emmy Awards. **Special Achievements:** Signed solo artist rec contract with MCA Recs at the age of 5 years old. **Home Addr:** 17 Beechwood Way, Briarcliff Manor, NY 10510, **Home Phone:** (914)792-6630.

# T

### TABB, ROOSEVELT

Business owner. **Personal:** Born AL. **Educ:** State Univ Col New York, Buffalo, BS, indust mgt & technol, 1967, MBA, mkt & finance, 1973. **Career:** Ford Motor Co, indust engr, 1967-69; Marine Midland Banks, loan officer, 1969-73; Fisher-Price Toys, mgr spec proj, 1973-78; Union Carbide Corp, mkt planning, acct mgr, 1976-90; Tabb & Assocs, owner, pres, 1990-. **Orgs:** Nat vpres, 1978, Nat Black MBA Asn, pres, 1978-81; bd pres, Nat Minority Col Golf Scholar Fund; Quote Wall St J. **Business Addr:** President, Tabb & Associates, 665 E Dublin Granville Rd, Columbus, OH 43234, **Business Phone:** (614)880-0000.

### TABOR, LILLIE MONTAGUE

Government official. **Personal:** Born May 13, 1933, Marianna, AR; married Norman. **Educ:** Univ Mich, MSW, 1961; Western Mich Univ, BA; Tuskegee Inst. **Career:** Detroit, nursery sch teacher, 1951-53; Bur Soc Aid, Detroit, social worker, 1954-57; Oak County C's Serv, child welfare worker, 1957-60; Mich, psyciat social worker, 1960-62; Dept Social Serv, admin, 1965-69; Mich Civil Serv Lansing, dir new careers, 1969-72; Social Serv Region 9 Wayne County, Consult Serv; State Mich, dep dir, 1963-65; Family Life Educ Merrill Palmer Inst, Detroit, assoc prof, 1968-71; Univ Mich, field instr soc, 1972-74. **Orgs:** Child Welfare League Am, 1964-68; bd mem, Neighborhood Serv Orgn, 1969-; adv comt, Vista Marie Sch, 1970-; NASW; Nat Asn Advan Colored People; Nat Coun Alcoholism Deleg, 1970, White House Conf C; Spec Review Successful Prog, 1970; Nat Inst New Careers Free press Frank Angelo Interesting Action People, 1971. **Home Addr:** 3774 Fullerton St, Detroit, MI 48238, **Home Phone:** (313)834-8468. **Business Addr:** Social Worker, Michigan State Plaza, 1200 6 St, Detroit, MI 48226.

### TADEMY, LALITA

Writer. **Personal:** Born Jan 1, 1948?, Berkeley, CA; daughter of Nathan Green Jr and Willie Dee Billes. **Educ:** Univ Calif, Los Angeles, BS, 1970, MBA, 1972. **Career:** Sun Microsystems, vp & gen mgr, 1992-95; Author: Cane River, 2001, Red Rivers, 2007. **Home Addr:** 45 Overlook Circle, Berwyn, PA 19312.

### TALBERT, MELVIN GEORGE

Clergy, bishop. **Personal:** Born Jun 14, 1934, Clinton, LA; son of Nettles and Florence George; married Ethelou Douglas; children: Evangeline Violet; married Marilyn W Magee. **Educ:** Southern Univ, Baton Rouge, La, BA, 1959; Gammon Theol Sem, Atlanta Ga, Md, 1962; Huston-Tillston Col, DDiv, 1972; Univ Pugent Sound, LLD, 1987. **Career:** Pastor, Dist Supt, Clergy (retired); Boyd Chapel, United Methodist Church, Jefferson, Tenn, pastor, 1960-61; Wesley United Methodist Church, Los Angeles, Calif, assoc pastor, 1961-64; Hamilton United Methodist Church, Los Angeles, Calif, pastor, 1964-67; Southern Calif-Ariz Conf, Long Beach, Calif, dist supt, 1968-73; Gen Bd Discipleship, Nashville Tenn, gen secy, 1973-80; Vis prof Evangelism at Claremont, 1978; United Methodist Church, Seattle Wash, bishop, 1980-88; United Methodist Church, San Francisco, Calif, bishop, 1988-2000; Coun of Bishop, Chief Ecumenical Officer & secy. **Orgs:** Pres, Nat Coun Churches, 1996-99; Nat Asn Advan Colored People; adv comt, Seattle Mayor; bd mem, Seattle United Way; exec comt, cent Comn, Finance Comn World Coun Churches; chair, Missional Priority Coord Comt, 1976-84; Gen Coun Ministries; pres, Gen Comn Relig & Race, 1983-88; Ecumenical Officer, Coun Bishops, 2000-04. **Honors/Awds:** National Achievement Award, Nat Asn Black Women, 1965; Bible Transl & Utilization Awards, Nat Coun Churches, 2000; Melvin George Talbert fund, Calif-Nev United Methodist Found, named in honor. **Special Achievements:** One of forty Presidential Guests to accompany US President Bill Clinton. **Home Addr:** 13816 Campus Dr, Oakland, CA 94605, **Home Phone:** (510)632-2965.

### TALBOT, GERALD EDGERTON

State government official. **Personal:** Born Oct 28, 1931, Bangor, ME; son of W Edgerton and Arvella McIntyre; married Anita J Cummings; children: Sharon Renee Verloo, Regina L Phillips, Rachel Ross & Robin M. **Educ:** Dipl lessons printing, 1970; ME State Apprenticeship Coun, cert apprenticeship printing, 1972. **Career:** State government official (retired); Portland Press Herald, printer; Maine State Legis, mem, 1972, 1974, 1976, 1978; Portland Savings Bank, corporator, beginning 1975; Guy Gannett Publ Co, state rep. **Orgs:** Co-sponsor, Sexual or Affectional Preference Amendment, 1977; City Mgrs Policy Adv Comn, 1979; adv coun, State Maine, Dept Manpower Affairs, 1979; State Bd Educ, 1980; founder, Black Educ & Cult Hist Inc, 1980; State Bd Educ, 1980, v chmn, 1981, chmn, 1983-84; Nat Asn State Bds Educ (GAC), 1981; Educ Comn Task Force Sex Equality, 1982; Congressman McKernan's Task Force C Youth &Families, 1983; Maine Cong Citizens Educ Adv Comnn, 1983; corporator, ME Med Ctr, 1984; Gr Portland Federated Labor Coun, Portland Typographical Union Local 66; Nat Asn Advan Colored People; Dem City Comn; Maine Asn Black Prog, ME Conf Human Serv; Southern Maine Area Agency Aging, 1986; bd, trust Maine Voc Tech Inst, 1986; bd dir, Portland United Way Inc, 1986; ME Proj Southern Africa, 1985; bd mem, US Selive Serv Syst, Maine, 1987; VeteransPeace, 1988; Community Task Force Bias Crime, 1989; bd visitor, Edmund SMuskie Inst Pub Policy, Univ Southern Maine, 1990; AARP, nat minority spokesperson, 1992; Nat Black Leadership Initiative Cancer, 1992; ALANA Conf Bd; US Comn Civil Rights, Maine; Tribute to Black Women Maine Awards Banquet, sponsor, 1992; Univ Southern Maine, African Am Arch Maine adv comt; Amistad Am, Maine Adv Coun. **Honors/Awds:** Golden Pin Award, 1967, Leadership Award, 1984, Twenty Years, 1964-84, NAACP, Portland Br; Hall of Fame Cert Laurel MS Nat Asn Advan Colored People, 1970-73; Outstanding Ser Comn & State Bangor, NAACP, 1974; Viva Cert Recog & Appreciation, 1974; Cert of Appreciation, Nat Asn Human Rights Workers, 1979; Right-On Brother of the Year Award; Certificate of Appreciation Maine Chap Multiple Sclerosis; Jefferson Award, Am Inst Pub Serv, WCSH-

TV, 1980; Black History Maker of Maine Award, 1984; Maine State Board Education Award, 1984; Martin Luther King Award, Maine Martin Luther King Comn, 1988; first Place Certificate of Excellence, Maine Multicultural Festival, 1987; Friendship Award, Portland West Neighborhood Planning Coun, 1989; Certificate of Achievement, People Regional Opportunity Program, 1990; DHL, Univ Southern Maine, 1995; Matlovich Award, 1990; Honorary Doctor of Humane Letters, Univ Southern Maine, 1995; John B Truslow, Md Area Agency on Aging Advocacy Award, 1995; Holocaust Human Rights Ctr, ME, 1995; Maine Channel Am Soc Pub Awards, 1995; Equity Inst Leadership Award, ME, 1995; Larry Connolly Award, ME Lesbian/Gay Political Alliance, 1995; Ctr for Visions & Policy, 50 Years Improving the Lives of Black Ams, 1997. **Special Achievements:** First African American elected to the Maine State Legislature in 1972; Author, Visible Black History of Maine; Underground Railroad in Maine; first African American member of the Maine House of Representatives; 240 seat auditorium at the University of Southern Maine was named in honor. **Home Addr:** 132 Glenwood Ave, Portland, ME 04103, **Home Phone:** (207)772-6098.

### TALIAFERRO, GEORGE
School administrator, football player, business owner. **Personal:** Born Jan 8, 1927, Gates, TN; married Viola Virginia Jones; children: Linda T, Renee, Donna & Terri. **Educ:** Ind Univ, Bloomington, BS, 1951; Howard Univ, Wash, DC, MSW, 1960. **Career:** Football player, sch adminr (retired); Los Angeles Dons, player, 1949; New York Yanks, kick returner, left halfback, punt returner, 1950-51; Dallas Texans, left halfback, 1952; Baltimore Colts, kick returner, left halfback, punt returner, 1953-54; Philadelphia Eagles, 1955; Lafayette Sq Community Ctr, Baltimore, dir, 1957-59; Prisoners Aid Asn, Shaw Residence, DC, caseworker, 1959-66; United Planning Org DC, dir com action progs, 1966-68; Univ Md, Dept Social Work, asst prof, 1966-68; Dico CorpMartin-Marietta Corp, Wash, DC, vpres & gen mgr, 1968-70; Univ, spec asst to pres, 1972; Morgan State Col, asst football coach, dean students, 1970-72; Couns Ctr & Drug Abuse Authority MD, exec dir, 1970; Big Ten Athletic Conf Spec Adv Comt, chmn, 1974; Taliaferro Appraisal Serv Inc, owner, currently. **Orgs:** Kappa Alpha Psi, 1948-; bd dir, Baltimore Big Bros & Druid Hill YMCA, 1962-68; pres & found, Monroe Co Big Bros & Big Sisters, 1973-; chmn bd, C's Organ Transplant Asn. **Honors/Awds:** Recipient All-Am All Big Ten & All State Awards Col Football Writers & Coaches, 1945-48; Col Football Hall of Fame, 1981; Ind Univ Hall of Fame, 1992; Volunteer of the Year Award, Children's Organ Transplant Asn, 2002; Pro-Bowl, 1950, 1951, 1952, 1953. **Special Achievements:** First African American to be drafted by an National Football League team in 1949; First African American to play quarterback in the history of professional football. **Home Addr:** 2708 Olcott Blvd, Bloomington, IN 47401, **Home Phone:** (812)339-4671. **Business Addr:** Owner, Taliaferro Appraisal Service Inc, PO Box 1691, Salem, VA 24153, **Business Phone:** (540)793-2597.

### TALIAFERRO, VIOLA J.
Judge. **Personal:** Born Sep 13, 1928, Evington, VA; daughter of Richard H Jones Sr and Mary Elizabeth Claiborne Jones; married George; children: Linda T Harvey, Renee A Buckner, Donna T Rutherford & Terri T Pendleton. **Educ:** Va State Col, BS, bus admin, 1947; Morgan State Univ, attended 1965; Johns Hopkins Univ, MLA, polit sci, 1969; Ind Univ, JD, 1977. **Career:** Judge (retired); Baltimore Dept Welfare, social worker, 1957-63; Baltimore Pub Sch, teacher, dept head, 1965-72; Sr Citizens Ctr, dir; Reading & Study Skills Ctr, counr; Sch law, Ind Univ, Bloomingotn, Ind, assoc instr; ICLEF Publ; pvt pratice, 1977-89; Monroe Circuit Ct, magistrate, 1989-95, judge. **Orgs:** Monroe County Bar Asn, 1977-; Am Bar Asn, 1977-; Del, lawyer discipline cms; bylaws comn chap; Ind State Bar Asn; del, Am Bar Asn; Rotary Int; bd mem, Boy Scouts Am; comnr, Bloomington Pks & Recreation; chair, Ind State Bar Asn House Del, 1989-90; Ky Col, 1989; fac, Ind Continuing Legal Educ Forum, 1992; Youth Serv Bur; Community Serv Coun; Bloomington Symphony Orchestra; Camerata Chamber Orchestra; Vital Adv Bd Mem; bd mem, Youth Serv Asn; Community Found Bloomington & Monroe County; Salvation Army; fel, Ind Bar Found; fel, Am Bar Found; Nat Coun Juv & Family Law Judges; Am Law Inst; former chair, Juv Justice Improv Comt; Ind Human Resource Investment Coun; Nat Res Coun juv crime. **Special Achievements:** Publ Delinquency; Detention, Waiver, Disposition, from IND Continuing Educ Forum, 1992; First African-American Judge in Monroe County; Viola J Taliaferro Family and Children Mediation Clinic, Indiana University's School of Law. **Home Addr:** 3103 Stratford Dr, Bloomington, IN 47401, **Home Phone:** (812)339-4671.

### TALLEY, BENJAMIN JERMAINE (BEN TALLEY)
Football player. **Personal:** Born Jul 14, 1972, Griffin, GA. **Educ:** Tenn Univ, grad. **Career:** Football player (retired); New York Giants, 1995, linebacker, 1996; Atlanta Falcons, 1998. **Honors/Awds:** All-Southeastern Conference second team.

### TALLEY, REV. DR. CLARENCE, SR.
Educator, clergy. **Personal:** Born Jun 12, 1951, Pineville, LA; son of Albert and Susie Edmond Newman; married Carolyn Westley; children: Clarence Jr & Crystal Ann. **Educ:** Southern Univ, Baton Rouge, BA, lib studies, 1973; La State Univ, Baton Rouge, MFA, 1975; Houston Grad Sch Theol, MA, theol, 1991; Master's Grad Sch Divinity, Evansville, IN, DBS, theol, 2004. **Career:** Southern Univ, Baton Rouge, La, instr, 1974; Prairie View Agr & Mech Univ, Prairie View, Tex, prof art & archit, 1975-; Mt Corinth Missionary Baptist Church, minister; N Harris County Community Col, 2002-03. **Orgs:** Nat Conf Artist; Tex Sculpture Asn; Tex Asn Sch Arts; Nat Artist Alliance. **Home Addr:** 21119 Briarmeadow, PO Box 2134, Prairie View, TX 77446-2134, **Home Phone:** (936)857-3414. **Business Addr:** Professor, Director of Art, Prairie View A&M University, Nathelyn Kennedy Sch Archit & Art Bldg Rm 213, Prairie View, TX 77446-0519, **Business Phone:** (936)261-3311.

### TALLEY, CURTISS J.
Administrator. **Personal:** Born Jul 16, 1939, Holly Springs, MS; son of Curtis and Jessie Mae Rucker Draper; married Corene Davidson; children: Chrystal DaNise, Curtiss Carlos & Chemberly D. **Educ:** Kilroe Col Sacred Heart, Honesdale, PA, BA, 1964; Memphis State Univ, Memphis, TN, 1982; Loyola Univ, New Orleans, LA, MPS, 1988; Shelby State Community Col, Memphis, TN, 1990. **Career:** Administrator (retired); Cadet Sch, Holly Springs, Miss, teacher & coach, 1966-72; Prudential Ins Co, Memphis, TN, dist agent, 1972-75; Thomas J Lipton Co Inc, Memphis, TN, sales rep, 1975-77; Wohl Shoe Co, Memphis, TN, supvr, 1977-78; St Joseph Church, Holly Springs, Miss, christian socialworker, 1978-81, deacon; Cath Diocese, Memphis, TN, dir multicultural ministries, 1981-2003; St Joseph Sch, teacher, 1985; African Am Cath Ministry, dir. **Orgs:** Fourth deg, Knights St Peter Claver, 1984-; vol, Prison Ministry, Shelby County Correctional Ctr, 1986-89; Serra Club, 1987-; Nat Black Cath Clergy Caucus, 1987; adv bd, Baptist Hosp, 1988; Nat Asn Black Cath Admin, 1990-; adv bd, Midtown Ment Health Asn, 1990; Aloysius Home Inc, AIDS Hospice, 1992; inter-religious affairs prof comt, St Peter Home C, 1992; vol chaplain, UT Med Ctr, 1992; Sacred Heart Southern Mission; Facing Hist & Ourselve; Vanderhaar Symp; Pastors Consortium HIV/AIDS; Multicultural Ministry City Memphi; Nat Alcohol Beverage Control Asn; KPC; IAACEC. **Home Addr:** 1515 Waverly, Memphis, TN 38106, **Home Phone:** (901)278-3761.

### TALLEY, DARRYL VICTOR
Football player, business owner. **Personal:** Born Jul 10, 1960, Cleveland, OH; married Janine; children: Alexandra & Gabrielle. **Educ:** WVa Univ, phys educ. **Career:** Football player (retired), business owner; Buffalo Bills, linebacker, 1983, left outside linebacker, 1984-86, right outside linebacker, 1986-94; Atlanta Falcons, right linebacker, 1995; Minn Vikings, left linebacker, 1996; Sentry Barricades Inc, pres, owner, currenlty. **Orgs:** W Va Univ Sports Hall Fame. **Honors/Awds:** Linebacker, Sporting News Col All-Am Team, 1982; Consensus first-team All-American, 1983; Played in AFC Championship Game, post-1988 season; All-Pro, 1990, 1993; Pro Bowl, 1990-91; Ed Block Courage Award, 1990; Ralph C Wilson Jr Distinguished Service Award, 2000; inducted, Buffalo Bills Wall of Fame, 2003; College Football Hall of Fame, 2008. **Home Addr:** 6607 Bittersweet Lane, Orlando, FL 32819-4635. **Business Addr:** Owner, President, Sentry Barricades Inc, 820 Creative Dr Suite 16, Lakeland, FL 33813-4957, **Business Phone:** (863)647-3688.

### TALLEY, DIANNE W.
Educator. **Personal:** Born Sep 14, 1955, Union, SC; daughter of Waddy and Lizzie Wright; married Michael F; children: Michanna & Michael F Jr. **Educ:** SC State Univ, BS; Univ SC, MEd; Clemson Univ, cert, supv, admin, 1997. **Career:** Jonesville Elementary, librn asst, 1977-79; Rutledge Col, adj instr, 1984-85; Greenville Tech Col, adjunct instr, 1984-87; Hillcrest High Sch, teacher, 1991-96; Bryson Middle Sch, admin asst, 1996-98; Green High Sch, asst prin, 1998-99; Berea High Sch, asst prin, 1999; Carolina High Sch & Acad, asst prin. **Orgs:** Asn Supervision & Curriculum, 1997-; Diversity Admin Leadership, 1999-; Nat Middle School Asn, 1996-; SC Alliance Black Educators, 1997-; SC Asn Sch Admin, 1997-; Greenville Children's Hosp, vol, 1995-; Greenville Literacy Asn, instr, 1996-; Jack & Jill Am Inc, 1999-; Prevent Child Abuse Carolina, 1995-. **Home Addr:** 208 Boling Rd, Greenville, SC 29611, **Home Phone:** (864)295-0011. **Business Addr:** Assistant Principal, Greenville County Schools, 301 E Camperdown Way, Greenville, SC 29601, **Business Phone:** (864)355-3100.

### TALLEY, JAMES EDWARD
Educator, mayor, radio host. **Personal:** Born Aug 22, 1940, Spartanburg, SC; son of Charles and Lula (deceased); married Barbara J Goins; children: James Carlton & Deidra Sharee. **Educ:** Livingstone Col, BS, math & sci, 1963; Converse Col, attended 1968; SC State Univ, attended 1972. **Career:** Educator (retired), mayor, radio host; Bryson High Sch, teacher & coach, 1967-68; Carver High Sch, teacher & coach, 1968-70; WSPA-TV, TV show host, 1973-75; WKDY Spartanburg, radio show host, 1975-78; City Spartanburg, councilman, 1981-85; Wofford Col, football coach & tutor math & sci, 1981-94; City Spartanburg, SC, mayor, 1993-; Spartanburg High Sch, teacher math, 1993 (retired). **Orgs:** LD Barksdale Sickle Cell Found, 1975-85; chmn, Bethlehem Ctr Trustees, 1978-81; chmn, Cammie F Clagget Scholar, 1979-85; basileus, Epsilon NuChap Omega, 1980-82; exec comt, Spartanburg Develop Coun; pres, SC Munic Asn; Uptown Optimist Club; Comn Minority Affairs SC. **Honors/Awds:** Man of the Year, Mt Moriah Baptist Church, 1979; Omega Man of the Year, Epsilon Nu Chap Omega, 1980; Human Relation Award, Spartanburg City Educ Asn, 1983; Algernon Sydney Sullivan Award, Wofford Col; Nat Alumni Distinguished Citizen Award, Wofford Col; Toast of the Town, Salvation Army; Neville Holcombe Citizen of the Year Award, Spartanburg Area Chamber Com; Kiwanis Club Citizen of the Year Award. **Home Addr:** 482 S Irwin Ave, Spartanburg, SC 29306-3333, **Home Phone:** (864)542-1323. **Business Addr:** Mayor, City of Spartanburg, 145 W Broad St, Spartanburg, SC 29306, **Business Phone:** (864)596-2000.

### TALLEY, JOHN STEPHEN
Educator, college teacher. **Personal:** Born Dec 12, 1930, Sterlington, LA; married Furman; children: Kimberly & Stephen. **Educ:** Grambling Col, BS, 1954; Columbia Univ, MA, 1958; prof dipl, 1964. **Career:** Grambling Col, Nursery Sch, teacher, 1954-56, dir teacher, 1956-63, col teacher, 1964-66, coordr head start staff training progs, 1966; Queens Col, Early Childhood Educ Ctr Flushing, head teacher, supv teacher, 1963-64; State La, Off Econ Opportunity Grambling, regulations training officer, 1966-67; Lincoln Parish, Kindergarten Progs, supvr; S Cent Regional Educ Lab, Little Rock, consult; SW Region Off Child Develop Int. **Orgs:** La Educ Asn; Asn Childhood Educ; Int Asn C Under Six; Nat Asn Educ Young C; Am Asn Univ Profs; Am Home Econs Asn; Day Care & Child Develop Coun Am; Alpha Kappa Alpha. **Home Addr:** 4355 Hidden Orch Lane, Indianapolis, IN 46228. **Business Addr:** 360 W 13th St, Indianapolis, IN 46204.

### TALLEY, MICHAEL FRANK, SR.
Lawyer, educator. **Personal:** Born Aug 14, 1945, Chesterfield, SC; son of Frank Sr (deceased) and Rosena A; married Dianne Wright; children: Michanna & Michael F Jr. **Educ:** SC State Col, BA, 1966; Howard Univ, MA, 1971, JD, 1976; Columbia Univ, graduate studies, 1973. **Career:** Wilson High Sch, Fr teacher, 1966-69; Howard Univ, Fr lab instr, 1969-70 & 1973-76; SC State Col, Fr instr, 1970-71; Tenn State Univ, Fr instr, 1971-73; Nationalist Cong Party Legal Defense Fund, Earl Warren Legal fel, 1973-76; Pres Clemency Bd, White House, staff atty, 1975; pvt pract atty, 1977-; Greenville Tech Col, bus law instr, 1984-90. **Orgs:** Kappa Alpha Psi, 1965-92; SC State Col, Gamma Mu Hon Soc, 1966; Howard Univ Alumni Asn, 1971-2003; SC Bar Asn, 1976-2001; SC Black Lawyers Asn, 1977-2001; mem bd dir, Legal Serv Western Carolina, 1978-82; US Ct Appeals, 4th Circuit; US Ct Appeals, 11th Circuit; Nat Bar Asn, 1985-2001. **Honors/Awds:** Certificate of Appreciation, SC Bar Pro Bono Prog, 1991; Plaque of Appreciation, Legal Serv Western Carolina, 1981. **Home Addr:** 208 Boling Rd, Greenville, SC 29611-7604, **Home Phone:** (864)295-0011. **Business Addr:** Attorney, 206 Green Ave, Greenville, SC 29601-3436, **Business Phone:** (864)233-6229.

### TALLEY, SARAH
Public relations executive, association executive. **Career:** Metrop Detroit, Social Security Off, pub affairs specialist, currently. **Orgs:** Inst Continuing Legal Educ; chairperson, Black Affairs Adv Coun, currently. **Special Achievements:** Featured in "Essence Magazine," serves as a columnist for the weekly "Michigan Chronicle" newspaper and has had a number of column features in the Detroit Free Press, including the "Money Report," "Financial Forum," and "Other Voices" sections. Ms. Talley has been a guest on several Detroit network and cable television programs, as well as on a number of local AM and FM radio stations. **Business Addr:** Public Affairs Specialist, Social Security Office, Rm 1500 477 Mich Ave, Detroit, MI 48226, **Business Phone:** (800)772-1213.

### TALLEY, WILLIAM B.
Educator. **Personal:** Born Sep 22, 1955, Sumter, SC; son of Charles Winslow and Louise Bultmon; married Tselate Betre; children: Massie Winslow. **Educ:** SC State, BA, psychol, 1976, MA, rehab coun, 1978; Southern Ill Univ, PhD, rehab, 1987. **Career:** State SC, counsr, trainee, 1976-78, voc rehab counr, 1978-80, disability examr, 1980-82; State La, LSU, educr, 1986-88; PSI Inc, counr, 1988-90; Univ MD, Eastern Shore, educr & chair, actg asst dean, health professions, dir rehab servs, dean, currently; Coppin State Col, asst prof. **Orgs:** Nat Rehab Asn, 1978-; Am Asn Coun & Devt, 1982-; Nat Asn Advan Colored People, 1973-; vpres, Alpha Phi Alpha; Delta Omicron Lambda Chap, 1994-; chair, Univ MD-Eastern Shore Fac Assembly, 1993-; chair & mem comt, MD Rehab Coun Asn, 1994-; Asn Black Psychologists, 1988-; Am Personnel & Guid Asn, 1984-; Nat Asn Cert Hypnotherapists, 1988-; MD Rehab Asn, 1990-; gov bd mem, Intercultural Cancer Coun. **Home Addr:** 1128 Buchanan St NW, Washington, DC 20011-4429. **Business Addr:** Educator, Chair, University of Maryland Eastern Shore, 934-5 Backbone Rd Hazel Hall Rm 1113, Princess Anne, MD 21853-1299, **Business Phone:** (410)651-6262.

### TANDY, DR. MARY B.
Publisher. **Personal:** Born Louise, MS; daughter of Florence Coleman (deceased); married O L; children: Bernice, Betty, Mary Ann, Alice M & Leroy Bryant. **Educ:** Ind Univ, attended 1966; Ivy Tech Col, AA, 1982. **Career:** Ind Herald, owner, ed & publ, currently. **Orgs:** IDEA Ind Demo Eds, 1975; Spec prog chmn, Am Bus Women Asn, 1980-82; noble gov Household Ruth, 1980-82; Democratic precinct comn; publicity comn, Nat Asn Advan Colored People. **Home Addr:** 1914 Bellefontaine St, Indianapolis, IN 46202, **Home Phone:** (317)925-4184. **Business Addr:** Editor, Publisher, Indiana Herald, 2170 N Illinois St, Indianapolis, IN 46202, **Business Phone:** (317)923-8291.

### TANKSLEY, ANN GRAVES
Artist, educator. **Personal:** Born Jan 25, 1934, Homewood, PA; married John B; children: 2. **Educ:** Carnegie Mellon Univ, BFA, 1956; Art Stud League, Parsons Sch Design; New Sch Social Res. **Career:** Queens Youth Ctr Arts, New York, art instr, 1959-62; Art Ctr Northern Nj, Instr art, 1963; Malvern Pub Schs, substitute Instr art, 1971-; Suffolk Co Community Col, adj art instr, 1973-75; artist: Time Capsule: A Concise Encyclopedia of of Women Artists by Robin Kahn; The Art of Black American Women: Works of Twenty Four Artists of the Twentieth Century by Robert Henkes; Forever Free: Art by African-American Women 1862-1980, currently. **Home Addr:** 18 Carlton Rd, Great Neck, NY 11021, **Home Phone:** (516)466-9639. **Business Addr:** Artist, 18 Carleton Rd, Great Neck, NY 10021, **Business Phone:** (516)466-9639.

### TANN, ESQ. DANIEL J.
Lawyer. **Personal:** Born Nov 23, 1960, Philadelphia, PA; son of Gladys L and Fee Otis; married Kimberly A Smith. **Educ:** La Salle Univ, BS, acct & orgn behav mgt, 1982; Drake Univ, JD, 1985. **Career:** Spear, Wilderman, Borish, Endy, Browning & Spear, Gen Pract Dept, assoc, dept mgr, managing atty, 1986-89; Gordon & Weinberg, PC, sr litigation atty, 1989-2001; Community Col Philadelphia, Dept Mgt Teaching Courses Bus Law, adj prof, 2000-; Law Off Daniel J Tann, pres, chief exec officer & atty, 2002-. **Orgs:** Nationalist Cong Party, 1980-; eastern Penn area dir, Nat Univ Sigma Chap, 1981-82, pres, 1988-90; bd dir, La Salle Univ Alumni, 1981-2005; Am Bar Asn, 1985-; Nat Bar Asn, 1985-; eastern regional legal coun, 1989-94, Phi Beta Sigma Fraternity Inc, eastern regional dir, 1997-2000; advisor & legal coun, Delta Theta Phi, Nu Sigma Youth Serv, 1990-; Pres Coun Assoc, 1991-2000; St. Joseph's Prep - A4 Mentor Prog, 1994-; Fair Housing Coun Southern Nj, 1997-2000; pres, LaSalle Univ African Am Alumni Asn, 2002-04; Spectrum Health Serv Inc, 2012-; Philadelphia Bar Asn; Penn Bar Asn; Am Trial Lawyers Am; Com Law League Am; Lawyers Club Philadelphia; Barristers Asn Philadelphia; Alumni Bd Dirs; First Baptist Church Jericho; Philadelphia Lawyers Club; Delta Theta Phi Int Law Fraternity; Asn Trial Lawyers Am; Com Law League Am; Dennis White Memorial Scholar Fund Inc; Waynesboro Area Learning Tree Inc; diversity fel GP/Solo Div Am Bar Associaition. **Honors/Awds:** Joseph Drogan Scholarship, Drake Univ, 1982-85; Memorial Development Award, Phi Beta Sigma Fraternity, 1990; Appreciation Award, Boy Scouts Am, 1992; Warren E Smith Award, Outstanding Alumnus, LaSalle Univ, 1996; Listed, Who's Who in American Law.; Liberty Bell Award, City Philadelphia. **Home Addr:** 1420 Walnut St Suite 1012, Philadelphia, PA 19102-4010, **Home Phone:** (215)670-0066. **Business Addr:** Attorney, Law Offices of Daniel J Tann, 100 S Broad St Suite 1355, Philadelphia, PA 19110, **Business Phone:** (215)670-0066.

## TANNER, CRAIG

Executive, founder (originator), president (organization). **Personal:** Born Jan 1, 1962. **Educ:** San Jose State Univ, finance & econs. **Career:** Urban Golf Gear, chief erban officer & pres, founder, 1997-2005; Fuzzy Bunny Films, bus dev, 2006-09; FlickLaunch, cofounder, 2010-12; Anshar Labs Inc, vpres bus develop, 2012-. **Special Achievements:** Prod line has been featured on var shows incl: The Steve Harvey Show; The Hughley's; MTV Lyricist Lounge; The Bernie Mac Show; Malcolm & Eddy; Moesha; Soul Food; HBO The Wire; BET 106 & Park; Girlfriends; Prod were also placed in the silver screen incl: Two Can Play that Game; SWAT. **Business Addr:** Vice President, Business Development, Anshar Labs Inc, 655 W Irving Park Rd Suite 2010, Chicago, IL 60613, **Business Phone:** (312)213-9459.

## TANNER, HON. GLORIA TRAVIS

State government official. **Personal:** Born Jul 16, 1935, Atlanta, GA; daughter of Marcellus Travis and Blanche Arnold Travis; children: Terrance Ralph, Tanvis Renee & Tracey Lynne. **Educ:** Met State Col, BA, polit sci, magna cum laude, 1974; Univ Colo, MA, urban affairs, 1976; Harvard Univ, J F Kennedy Sch Govt, Women Leadership Prog. **Career:** Executive retired; Great Western Mfg Co, off mgr, 1965-67; Off Hearings & Appeals US Dept Interior, admin asst, 1967-72; Denver Weekly News, reporter, feature writer, 1972-76; 888 Real Estate Off, real estate salesperson, 1976; Colo Lt Gov George L Brown, exec asst, 1976-78; Sen Regis Groff Comt Off, exec dir commun, 1978, pub admin, 1978-; House Minority Caucus, leader, 1987-90; State Colo, state sen, 1994-2000; Future Black Women Leaders Colo, natl exec dir, 2001-. **Orgs:** Colo State Treas, 1952-55; Colo Black Media Asn, 1972; Dist capt Denver Dem Comt, Colo, 1973-75; Pub chmn, Delta Sigma Theta, 1974; admin aide, Colo State Sen Regis Groff, Denver, 1974-82; chair, Sen Dist 3 Dem Party, 1974-80; Am Soc Pub Admin, 1976; Dem Nat Conv, 1976; comnr Colo Status Women, 1977; chmn, Colo Black Women Polit Action, 1977; CO Black Women Polit Action CBWPA, 1976-80; exec bd, CO Comm Women, 1976-79; chmn, Minority caucus, 1987-90; Colo State House Representatives Dist 7, 1985-94; Nat Assoc Real Estate Brokers; nat exec dir, Nat leadership Inst; Dist 33 Colo Senate, 1994; founder, Sen Gloria Tanner Leadership & Training Inst, 2001; alt deleg, United Negro Col Fund. **Special Achievements:** First African American woman to serve as a Colorado State Senator, 2000. **Home Addr:** 2150 Monaco Pkwy, Denver, CO 80207, **Home Phone:** (303)355-7288. **Business Addr:** National Executive Director, Senator Gloria Tanner Leadership & Training Institute, 2150 Monaco Pkwy, Denver, CO 80207-1217, **Business Phone:** (303)355-7288.

## TANNER, JAMES W., JR.

School administrator. **Personal:** Born Mar 18, 1936, Spartanburg, SC; married Priscilla; children: Tonya, Angela & James III. **Educ:** SC State Col, BSA, 1958; SC State Col, MEd, 1969; Univ SC, attended 1974. **Career:** School administrator (retired); Johnsonville Sch Dist No 5 Bd, teacher coordr dept head vo educ, 1973-74; Williamsburg Tech Col, dean stud servs. **Orgs:** Am Vocation Asn, 1962; SC Vo Agr Teacher Asn, 1962; Nat Vo Agr Teacher Asn, 1962; SC Voc Asn, 1962; Nat Vacation Agr Teacher Asn, 1963; Nat Educ Asn, 1964; Boy Scout Master, 1970-74; pres, Florence Co Voters League, 1970-; Masonic Blue Lodge Master, 1970; dist rep, 1970, Florence Co Educ Asn, vpres, 1971, pres, 1973; bd educ Florence Co, 1973-74; treas, Cong Dist 6 Voters Educ Proj, 1973-74; bd dir, SC Educ Asn, 1974-; S eastern Regional Educ Bd, 1978-81; Florence Co Dept Social Serv Bd, 1989-93; SC Voc & Tech Coun, 1989-93; SC State Election Comt, 1993-96; trustee bd, SC State Univ, 1996-; bd dir, Tri-Co Health Clin; Johnsonville-Hemingway Drug Community; recreation dir, Hickory Hill Comt; Johnsonville Devel Bd; Boy Scout post adv; chmn, Local Nat Asn Advan Colored People. **Honors/Awds:** Sears Roebuck Scholarship, Agr Ed, 1953; Recipient Distinguished Service Award, Agr Educ, 1969; Outstanding Secondary Educ Am, 1973; James W Tanner Jr Scholarship, named in honor, Williamsburg Tech Col. **Home Addr:** 263 Azalea St, PO Box 85, Johnsonville, SC 29555-4016, **Home Phone:** (843)386-4076.

## TANNER, DR. TYRONE

School administrator, educator, consultant. **Personal:** Born Apr 14, 1971, Los Angeles, CA; son of Albert Watson and Lucy Mae; married Keisha W. **Educ:** Newberry Col, BA, hist, 1994; Southern Univ, MEd, sch admin & supv, 1998; Univ Houston, EdD, educ leadership & cult studies, 1999. **Career:** New Orleans Marine Inst, GED coordr, 1995-96; JM Tate High Sch, Am hist teacher, 1997-98; Fontainebleau Jr High Sch, Am hist teacher, 1998-99; Houston Independent Sch Dist, human resource genist, 1999-2001, human resource recruiter, 2001; Ft Bend Independent Sch Dist, 6th grade prin, 2001; Tex Southern Univ, asst prof, Col Educ, currently; Prairie View A & M Univ, prof, 2011-. **Orgs:** Hundred Black Men Am, 1997-; Nat Asn Advan Colored People, 1999-; Houston Area Alliance Black Sch Educr, 2000-; Nat Asn Sec Sch Principals, 2001-. **Home Addr:** 2855 Lakeview Dr, Missouri City, TX 77459, **Home Phone:** (281)416-0352. **Business Addr:** Professor, Prairie View A & M University, FM 1098 Rd & Univ Dr Delco Bldg Rm 230, Prairie View, TX 77446, **Business Phone:** (936)261-3618.

## TANTER, RAYMOND

Educator. **Personal:** Born Sep 19, 1938. **Educ:** Roosevelt Univ, BA, 1961; Ind Univ, MA, PhD, polit sci, 1964. **Career:** Sch Foreign Serv Georgetown, fac; Gov Dept, vis researcher; Northwestern Univ, asst prof, 1964-67, assoc prof, 1967-72; US Dept Defense, Advan Res Proj Agency, dep dir behav sci, 1967; Univ Mich, assoc prof, prof, 1972, polit sci prof emer, Mid E Ctr, res assoc; Hebrew Univ Jerusalem, vis prof int rels, 1973-78; Civilian Exec Panel, chief naval opers, mem, 1980-81; Reagan-Bush Nat Security Coun, staff, 1981-82; Security Defense, personal rep, 1983-84; Nat Security Coun & Nat Republican Comn; Georgetown Univ, vis researcher, vis prof & adj prof, 2003-; Stanford, Hebrew Univ Jerusalem, vis prof; Tel Aviv Univ, vis prof. **Orgs:** Found, pres & co-chmn, Iran Policy Comt; Wash Ins Near E Policy; Middle E Inst; Coun Foreign Rels; vis fel Wash Inst Near E Policy, 2001. **Special Achievements:** Editor: Theory and Policy in International Relations, 1972. Author: Modelling and Managing International Conflicts: The Berlin Crises, 1974; Who's at the Helm? Lessons of Lebanon, 1990; Rogue Regimes: Terrorism & Proliferation, "In a forest of world politics, the West slew a dying Soviet bear, & Washington sees additional beasts hiding in the woods'; Co-author, Rational Decision making: Israel's Choices, 1980; Balancing in the Balkans, 1999;Appeasing the Ayatollahs and Suppressing Democracy, 2006; What Makes Tehran Tick, 2006; Baghdad Ablaze, 2007; President Obama and Iraq, 2009; President Obama and Iran, 2010; Terror Tagging of an Iranian Dissident Organization, 2011; Arab Rebels and Iranian Dissidents, 2013; Islamist Movements, Protegees of the Ayatollahs, 2016. He wrote Classifying Evil: Bush Administration Rhetoric and Policy toward Rogue Regimes and Rogue Regimes: Terrorism and Proliferation, which includes chapters on Iran, Iraq, and freelance terrorists who operate in a border less world of failed states like Afghanistan. **Business Addr:** Visiting Professor, Adjunct Professor, Georgetown University, 681 ICC 37th & O St NW, Washington, DC 20057, **Business Phone:** (202)687-6130.

## TARPLEY, NATASHA ANASTASIA

Writer. **Personal:** Born Jan 6, 1971, Chicago, IL; daughter of Herman and Marlene. **Educ:** Howard UNV, vis stud, 1992; Harvard Univ, BA, 1993; Georgetown Univ Law Ctr, attended 1994; Northwestern Univ, Sch Law, JD, 1998. **Career:** Beacon Press, auth, currently; Books: I Love My Hair, 1997; The Princess & the Frog; Bippity Bop Barbershop, 2002; Joe-Joes First Flight, 2003; Destinys Gift, 2004; Black Girls Write About Their World, 2007; Princess Tiana & the Royal Ball, 2009; What I Know is Me. **Orgs:** Black Law Stud Asn, 1993-. **Honors/Awds:** Award for Poetry, Howard Univ, 1992; Award for Poetry, Wash, Cms Arts, Larry Neal, 1992, 1994; Award for Poetry, Radcliffe Col, Joan Gray Undermeyer, 1993; Fellowship for Poetry, Nat Endowment for the Arts, 1994-95; Fellowship for Poetry, Mass Cult Coun, 1994-95. **Special Achievements:** Written articles for Essence Magazine, Cover Story on Black CLG Students, Oct, 1993; Inventions Piece, Nov, 1994; Testimony: Young AFA on Self-Discovery & Black Identity, Beacon Press, 1995; Girl in the Mirror & A Present Day Migration, for Minority from Beacon, 1997; I Love My Hair! Childrens Book, Little Brook & CPN, 1998; Book Reviews for the WAS Post, Los Angeles Times, The Quarterly Black Review and Chicago Tribune. **Home Addr:** 7339 Drexel Ave, Chicago, IL 60619-2027, **Home Phone:** (773)224-4905. **Business Addr:** Editor, Beacon Press, 25 Beacon St, Boston, MA 02108, **Business Phone:** (617)742-2110.

## TARTER, JAMES H., III

Executive. **Personal:** Born Mar 6, 1927, New York, NY; married Marion; children: Krishna, Yasmin, Karim, James & Gamal. **Educ:** NY Univ; St Johns Univ; Inst Advan Mkt Studies; Advert Club NY, Hon DD. **Career:** NAACP Spl Contrib Fund, fund raising & pub rels nat dir develop, 1967-76; Home Prods Corp, prod mgr; F&M Schaefer Co, adv supvr; Fuller Brush Co, br mgr; So Delicious Bakeries, pres, gen mgr; NAACP Nat Dept Tours, dir; NAACP Emergency Relief Fund, dir; Tarter & Wetzel Co Inc, pres. **Orgs:** Nat Soc Fund Raisers; NY Soc Fund Raising dir; Advert Club NY; Knights Columbus. **Home Addr:** 37 Adams St, Mt Vernon, NY 10550.

## TARTER, ROGER POWELL

Educator, physician. **Personal:** Born Aug 27, 1930, New York, NY; son of James H and Elizabeth; married Ana Maria Hernandez; children: Roger Jr, Richard, Diana-Maria, Peter, Marcia-Elizabeth & Patricia. **Educ:** Iona Col, BS, 1953; Long Island Univ, MS, biol, 1959; Univ Bologna, Fac Med, MD, med & surg, 1964; Bernadean Univ Col Law, JD, 1994. **Career:** Educator (retired), physician; Sloan Kettering Inst, Nat Inst Health, predoctoral res fel, 1960; Westchester County, NY, asst pathologist-med examr, 1967-69; Montefiore Hosp & Med Ctr-MMTP, med dir, 1971-74; Spec Action Off Drug Abuse Prev, Mem US, expert, 1971-73; Albert Einstein MedCol, asst clin prof, Comm Health Social Med, 1972-76; Coney Island Hosp, Comprehensive Drug Abuse Treat Prog, prog dir, 1974-78; Maimonedes Hosp, Coney Island Hosp Affil, asst clin prof & attend pathol & med, 1974-78; NYC Bur Prison Health Serv, Health Dept, med dir, 1978-81; pvt pract, 1981-90; Charles R Drew, Martin Luther King Jr Med Sch Found, sci & med adv, 1986-90; Mercy Col, Dept Psychol, Natural Sci & Criminal Justice, assoc prof; pvt pract, currently. **Orgs:** Alpha Phi Alpha Fraternity, ETA Chap, New York, 1951; Nat Asn Med Examr, 1969; Kiwanis Club, 1969; Nat Registry Specialist Microbiologist, Am Acad Microbiologists, 1970; Knights Columbus, 1970; adv bd trustee, Iona Col, 1972-; staff physician, NY Athletic Comn, 1984; New York Acad Sci, 1985; Am Col Physician Exec, 1994; Am Col Med Adminr, 1994. **Home Addr:** 37 Adams St, Mount Vernon, NY 10550, **Home Phone:** (914)376-2210.

## TARVER, AUSTRALIA

Educator. **Personal:** Born Feb 8, 1942, Ft. Worth, TX; married Duane. **Educ:** Fisk Univ, BA, 1964; Ohio Univ, MA, 1965; Univ Iowa, PhD, 1978. **Career:** Miami Valley St Col, staff, 1965-66; Pontiac N High Sch, teacher, 1966-69; AWAKE, teacher & dir, 1969; Fla A&M Univ, instr, 1968-71, asst prof, 1973-74; Univ Iowa, teaching res fel, 1971-74; Tex Christian Univ, Col Humanities & Social Sci, Eng Dept, assoc prof african-am lit, 1995-2014. **Orgs:** Fla A&M Univ Midwest Mod Lang Asn; S Atlantic Mod Lang Asn; Col Lang Asn. **Business Addr:** Associate Professor Emerita, Texas Christian University, 2800 S Univ Dr Reed Hall 121, Ft. Worth, TX 76129, **Business Phone:** (817)257-7240.

## TARVER, ELKING, JR.

Government official, manager. **Personal:** Born Nov 28, 1953, East Liverpool, OH; son of Elking Sr and Elsie Tarver-Byers. **Educ:** Gannon Univ, BS, acct, 1976; Univ Md Grad Sch, MS, financial mgt, 1998. **Career:** US State Dept, acct, 1976-78; US Agr dept, asst regional inspector genl, 1978-93, dir, qual assurance, 1993-98; pvt pract certified pub acct, 1994-; US Dept Housing & Urban Develop, audit mgr, prj mgr, currently; Cert Pub Accountants, assessment mgr. **Orgs:** Asn Black Accountants; Asn Govt Accountants, 1982-; Shiloh Baptist Church, 1983-; certified fraud examiner, Inst Certified Fraud Examiners, 1989; Certified Pub Acct, Am Inst Certified Pub Accountants, 1994. **Home Addr:** PO Box 4554, Capitol Heights, MD 20791, **Home Phone:** (301)686-9292. **Business Addr:** Project Manager, US Department of Housing & Urban Development, 1280 Maryland Ave SW Suite 800, Washington, DC 20024-2635, **Business Phone:** (202)708-4932.

## TARVER, GREGORY WILLIAMS, SR. (GREG TARVER)

Politician. **Personal:** Born Mar 30, 1946, Shreveport, LA; married Velma Jean Kirksey; children: Gregory Jr, Ballestine, Lauren, Rebekah & Caroline. **Educ:** Grambling State Univ; Centenary Col. **Career:** Charity Hosp, bd dir, 1973-75; Caddo Parish Police Jury, dist 5 seat, 1975-78; Shreveport City Coun, 1975-84; La State, sen, 1989-2004, 2012-; JS Williams Fun Home, pres, currently; Royal Life LA Ins Co, pres; lic fun dir; J S Williams Inc Co, pres. **Orgs:** Shreveport Fun Dir Caddo Parish Police Juror; bd dir, LA Men Health Asn; Zion Baptist Church; chmn bd, Caddo Barber Col; Thirty Third Degree Mason; Universal Grand Lodge; Shriner; United Dem Campaign Com; Shreveport Jr C of C; Nat Asn Advan Colored People; Shreveport Negro C of C; Adv Coun YWCA. **Honors/Awds:** Outstanding Young Men of America, 1978; Black Leader of the Year, 1983-84. **Home Addr:** 1135 Pierre Ave, Shreveport, LA 71103. **Business Addr:** Senator, Louisiana Secretary of State, 1104 Pierre Ave, Shreveport, LA 71103, **Business Phone:** (318)227-1499.

## TARVER, DR. LEON R., II

School administrator. **Personal:** married Cynthia Loeb; children: 3. **Educ:** Southern Univ, Baton Rouge, LA, BA, polit sci; Harvard Univ, John F Kennedy Sch Govt, Cambridge, MA, pub admin; Union Inst, PhD, pub admin. **Career:** Southern Univ Syst, Baton rouge, LA, vice-chancellor admin, prof pub admin, prof pub policy & urban affairs, 1992, pres, 1997-2005, Nelson Mandela Sch Pub Policy & Urban Affairs, pres emer, distinguished prof, currently; Southern Univ & A & M Col, Baton Rouge, Ctr Cult Heritage & Int Progs, exec adminr, 2005-10; La Dept Revenue & Taxation, secy, 1989-92; La Dept Educ, asst supt; La Dept Urban & Community Affairs, secy; John F. Kennedy Sch Govt, Harvard Univ, asst dean & dir; La Comn Intergovernmental Rels, exec dir; United Gen Financial Corp, Tricorp Develop Inc, pres/chief exec officer; Nat Compensation Control Systs Inc, exec vpres; J.S. Williams & Son Inc, pres/vpres; Southern Univ Mus Art-Baton Rouge & Southern Univ Mus Art-Shreveport, founder. **Orgs:** Chmn, Southern Univ Syst; dir, La Casino Cruises Inc, 1994; fel, Nat Acad Pub Admin Wash, 2004. **Business Addr:** President, Distinguished Professor, Southern University, 410 Higgins Hall, Baton Rouge, LA 70813, **Business Phone:** (225)771-3092.

## TARVER, MARIE NERO (MARIE ELOISE NERO)

Teacher, government official, educator. **Personal:** Born Aug 29, 1925, New Orleans, LA; daughter of Charles L Nero Sr (deceased) and Daisy Lee Blackmore Nero; married Rupert J Jr; children: Rupert J III, Charles L N, Stanley J, Gregory T, Bernard J & Cornelius A. **Educ:** Southern Univ Baton Rouge, BA, educ, 1945; Univ Wis Madison Sch Jour, MA, 1947. **Career:** New Orleans InNewspaper, women's ed, 1945-46; Southern Univ Baton Rouge, eng instr, 1947-49; Galesburg High Sch, Galesburg, IL, eng teacher, 1954-56; Dutchess Comm Col Pough keepsie, eng instr, 1961-62; Marist Col Pough keepsie, eng instr, 1963-68; Model City Agency, asst dir planning, 1968-70, dep dir, 1970-71, exec dir, 1971-77; City Pough keepsie, NY, dir social develop, 1977-90. **Orgs:** Nat Antapokritis Zeta Phi Beta Sorority Inc, 1948-52; Pres & bd educ, Poughkeepsie City Sch Dist, 1964-70; vpres, Nat Model Cities Comt Develop Asn, 1975-77; bd dirs, Dutchess Co NY, YMCA, 1970-74; chairperson bd dirs, United Way Dutchess Co NY Inc, 1979; chaiperson, United Way Campaign, 1982; comnr & chmn, Poughkeepsie Housing Authority; exec comm, Dutchess-Putnam Pvt Indust Coun; bd dir, Youth Resources Develop Corp; Mid-Hudson Reg Econ Develop Coun; Dutchess Co Arts Coun; trustee bd, Vassar Bros Hosp; New York St Asn Renewal & Housing Officials Inc; bd dirs, Dutchess County Child Develop Coun, Hudson River Housing Inc; Dutchess Dominica Partners Ams; Family Servs Inc; assoc bd mem, C Home Poughkeepsie; sororitys local chap, founder, pres, secy, parliamentarian; Grace Smith House; Community Found Dutchess County; Northern Dutchess Nat Asn Advan Colored People. **Honors/Awds:** First Recipient Sepia Award for Community Service, Alpha Phi Alpha Fraternity Inc Mid-Hudson Chap, 1976; Merit Award, Black Women's Caucus Polk, NY, 1979; Am Asn Univ Women, 1982; Alexis De Tocqueville Award, United Way Dutchess County, 1989; Gold Medal Humanitarian Award, St Cabrini, 1998; Women of Distinction, NY, 2005; President's Award, Marist Col; Eleanor Roosevelt Medal of Honor; Woman of the Year, Poughkeepsie Br Am Asn Univ Women, 1982; Service Above Self Award. **Special Achievements:** First African-American member of the Poughkeepsie Board of Education, 1965, 1970; first African-American to gain city-wide election; First African-American Chairperson on the Board of Dutchess County United Way; first woman in 39 years to head the United Ways annual campaign; First African American School Board President, 1970; First African American to teach at Marist College; First African-American teacher at Galesburg High School; First African American to become responsible for the distribution of federal funding. **Home Addr:** 313 Mansion St, Poughkeepsie, NY 12601-2716, **Home Phone:** (845)454-9715. **Business Addr:** Associate Board Member, The Childrens Home of Poughkeepsie, 10 Childrens Way, Poughkeepsie, NY 12601, **Business Phone:** (845)452-1420.

## TASCO, HON. MARIAN B.

Government official, city council member. **Personal:** Born Greensboro, NC; daughter of Tom Benton and Alice; married Thomas Earle Williams; children: Charles III. **Educ:** Bennett Col, attended 1958; Temple Univ, BS, bus educ, 1965. **Career:** City Philadelphia, city comnr, 1983-87, city coun woman, 1987-, ward leader, currently. **Orgs:** Deleg, Dem Conv, 1984, 1988, 1992; bd mem, Philadelphia Aiport Adv, 1988-; bd mem, Philadelphia Cult Fund; bd mem, Philadelphia Drama Guild, 1990-; Philadelphia Gas Comn; trustee, Bennett Col; nat pres, Women Munic Govt; hon chair & co-founder, Mayor's Telecom Policy & Adv Comn; bd mem, Elizabeth Blackwell Ctr; Dist Sorority; adv bd, Nat Polit Cong Black Women; Women's Way, Family Plng Coun Southeastern Pa; trainer, YWCA Leadership Inst; bd dir, Nat League Cities; Recreation Fund; ward leader, Mighty-Mighty 50th Ward Dem Exec Comt; chair, Philadelphia Gas Comn; Philadelphia City Coun; chair, City Coun Pub Health; chair, Human Serv Comt; vice chair, Coun Finance & Ethics Comts; Bd dir Bd City Trusts; Pa Conv Ctr Authority Bd. **Home Addr:** 1000 E Vernon Rd, Philadelphia, PA 19150, **Home Phone:** (215)924-0555. **Business Addr:** City Council Woman, City of Philadelphia District 9, City Hall Rm 577, Philadelphia, PA 19107-3290, **Business Phone:** (215)686-3454.

**TASSIE, ROBERT V.**
Marketing executive, business owner. **Personal:** children: James & Jonathan. **Educ:** St John's Univ; New Sch Social Res; Foreign Inst, Wash, DC. **Career:** CBS TV Network, acct exec network sales, vpres sports sales; CBS Sports Div, vpres commun; Denver Nuggets, vpres mkt; Unity Media Inc, owner & pres, chief exec officer, 1991-. **Orgs:** Int Soc TV Arts & Sci; bd mem, Ariz Sickle Cell Comn; Nat Minority Bus Coun. **Business Addr:** President & Owner, Chief Executive Officer, Unity Media Inc, 501 5th Ave 15th Fl, New York, NY 10017, **Business Phone:** (212)687-3100.

**TATE, ADOLPHUS, JR.**
Insurance executive, manager. **Personal:** Born Aug 18, 1942, Turrel, AR; son of Adolphus Sr and Ruth Lee Johnson; married Patricia Dawson; children: Adolphus III, Cherie Levelle & Faith Elizabeth Ann. **Educ:** La City Col, Ariz, attended 1964. **Career:** Western & Southern Life Ins Co, assoc sales mgr, 1968-75, dist sales mgr, 1975-85, sales mgr, 1988. **Orgs:** Bowen Un Meth, 1969-; pres, Gardena Interest Neighbor, 1990-97, vpres, 1971-73; vpres, Un Meth, 1976-86; Million Dollar Club Western & Southern Life Ins Co; Hollypary Comm Asn; co-chairperson, Bolden United Meth; 32nd-degree Prince Hall Mason; chairperson, Finance Comm Bowen Church, 1983-85; secy, United Methodist Men, 1987; chairperson, Trustee Bd Bowen Un-Meth Church, 1989-93; Bowen United Methodist Church, chairperson, adv coun, 1994-97; pres, Knight W Club, 1996; elected Worshipful Master, Western Knights 56, 1998. **Honors/Awds:** Policyholders Merit Award, 1971, 1976-79. **Special Achievements:** LUTCF, 1992. **Home Addr:** 13204 S Wilkie Ave, Gardena, CA 90249, **Home Phone:** (310)947-6649.

**TATE, BRETT ANDRE**
Executive. **Personal:** Born Apr 13, 1963, Seattle, WA; son of Margaret and Willis. **Educ:** Howard Univ, BA, bus mgt admin, 1986; Wash Univ, MS, criminal law, 1988. **Career:** Congressman John Conyers, intern, 1986-88; Primerica Financial Serv, sr vpres, pres; Eastern Airlines, supvr & labor disputes mediator; B&G Bldg Maintenance Inc, founder, pres & chief exec officer, 1989-; Network J, contribr. **Orgs:** Usher bd, Metrop Baptist Church, 1991-92. **Business Addr:** President, Chief Executive Officer, B&G Building Maintenance Inc, 1002 Queen St Suite 300, Alexandria, VA 22314-2449, **Business Phone:** (703)299-1781.

**TATE, DAVID FITZGERALD**
Football player. **Personal:** Born Nov 22, 1964, Denver, CO. **Educ:** Univ Colo. **Career:** Football player (retired); Chicago Bears, defensive back, 1988-92; New York Giants, defensive back, 1993; Indianapolis Colts, strong safety & defensive back, 1994-97.

**TATE, DAVID KIRK**
Association executive, army officer, lawyer. **Personal:** Born Apr 20, 1939, Detroit, MI; son of Andrew G and Izona Kirk; children: DeMarcus David Holland & Lisa Arlayne. **Educ:** Mich State Univ, East Lansing, BS, mathematics, 1963; Univ Detroit Sch Law, Detroit, MI, JD, 1973. **Career:** Patmon, Young & Kirk, Detroit, MI, assoc, 1973-76; Detroit Edison Co, Detroit, MI, staff atty, 1976-77; R J Reynolds Tobacco Co, Winston-Salem, NC, from asst to assoc coun, 1977-82, coun corp & com, 1982-86, sr coun, 1986-, asst secy, 1986-2007. **Orgs:** Am Bar Asn; NC Bar Asn; Wolverine Bar Asn; Alpha Phi Alpha Fraternity; bd mem, Exp; bd comnr, Housing Authority Winston-Salem. **Home Addr:** 2736 Woodlore Trl, Winston Salem, NC 27103-6546, **Home Phone:** (336)201-6836. **Business Addr:** Senior Counsel, R J Reynolds Tobacco Co, 401 N Main St, Winston Salem, NC 27101, **Business Phone:** (336)741-5000.

**TATE, EARNEST L.**
Law enforcement officer. **Personal:** married Norma Jean; children: Ricky & Terry. **Career:** Police officer (retired); City Selma, AL, asst police chief, police chief. **Orgs:** Ala Peace Officers Asn; bd mem, ARSEA. **Special Achievements:** First black police chief, Selma. **Home Addr:** 1415 Cole St, Selma, AL 36703, **Home Phone:** (334)874-4073.

**TATE, ELEANORA ELAINE**
Journalist, writer. **Personal:** Born Apr 16, 1948, Canton, MO; daughter of Clifford and Lillie; married Zack E Hamlett III; children: Gretchen. **Educ:** Drake Univ, Des Moines, IA, BA, jour, 1973. **Career:** Iowa Bystander, Des Moines, IA, news ed, 1966-68; Des Moines Regist & Tribune, reporter, 1969-76; Jackson Sun, Jackson, Tenn, staff writer, 1976-77; Memphis Tri-State Defender, free-lance writer, 1977; Kreative Koncepts Inc, Myrtle Beach, SC, writer, 1979-81; free-lance writer, 1982-; Postive Images Inc, Myrtle Beach, SC, pres & owner, 1983-93; Tate & Assocs, media consult, 1993-; Auth: "I'm Life, " C Longing, Holt, Rinehart & Winston, 1970; "An Ounce Sand, Impossible", Houghton-Mifflin, 1972; "Bobby Griffin, " Off-Beat, Macmillan, 1974; Just an Overnight Guest, Dial Press, 1980; Secret Gumbo Grove, Franklin Watts, 1987; Thank You, Dr Martin Luther King, Jr!, Franklin Watts, 1990; "Ethel's Story, " Storyworks Mag, 1992; Front Porch Stories at One-Room Sch, Bantam Bks, 1992; Retold African Myths, Perfection Learning Corp, 1992; "Secret Gumbo Grove, " play adaption, Scholastic Action Mag, 1993; "Hawkeye Hatty Rides Again, " Am Girl Mag, 1993; A Blessing Disguise, Delacorte, 1995; Don't Split Pole: Tales Down-home Folk Wisdom, Delacorte, 1997; "Momma's Kitchen Table, " essay publ in "Praise Our Fathers & Our Mothers, " Just Us Bks Publishers Inc, 1997; Just Overnight Guest, re-issued, Just Us Bks Publs Inc, 1997; Recorded Bks Inc, produced audio cassette tapes Secret Gumbo Grove & Thank You, Dr Martin Luther King, Jr; "Tracing Trilogy, " pub African Am Rev, Spring, 1998; "Novels With Deep Roots, " pub Bk Links mag, 2000; Afr Amer Musicians, John Wiley & Sons, 2000; "Tell Me Who You Hang Out With & I'll Tell You What You Are, " pub Lost & Found, 2000; Minstrels Melody, Pleasant Co, 2001; "Raggedy Pants & Dinosaur Wall, " Scholastic Story Works, 2001; partic, Langston Hughes Libr C's Bk Roundtable, 2000, 2001; Also, article "With DiSsector-Eds, Even C's Bk, Authors Have to Take a Stand, " pub, Obsidian III J, spring, 2001; "Don't Split Pole, " pub Big City Cool, 2002; co-auth: Black Start Harlem Renaissance, 2002; "Langston Hughes, Peoples Poet, " pub Dream & Girl Mag, Nov-Dec, 2002; Abram's Way, 2003; "To Be Free, Steck-Vaughn", 2004. **Orgs:** Iowa Arts Coun Artists Schs & Community, 1970-89; fel children's fiction, Breadloaf Writers Conf, 1981; SC Arts Comn Artists Educ, 1982-92; Nat Asn Advan Colored People, Georgetown chap, Georgetown, SC, 1984-89; Concerned Citizens Operation Reach-Out Horry County, 1985-; bd govs, SC Acad Authors, 1986-90; pres, secy, vpres, Horry Cult Arts Coun, 1986-92; Pee Dee Reading Coun, Myrtle Beach, SC, 1987-90; Arts Basic Currriculum Steering Comt, 1988-90; bd mem, Nat Asn Black Storytellers Inc, 1988-92, pres, 1991-92; NC Writers Network, 1993-; Twin Rivers Reading Coun IRA, 1993-99. **Honors/Awds:** Unity Award, Lincoln Univ, 1974; Community Lifestyle award, Tenn Press Asn, 1977; Parents Choice Gold Seal Award, 1987; Presidential Award, Nat Asn Negro Bus & Prof Womens Clubs, Georgetown SC chap, 1988; Grand Strand Press Asn Award, Social Responsibilities & Minority Affairs, 1988; Coastal Advert Fed, Addy Award, Positive Images Inc, 1988; Grace Brooks Memorial Humanitarian Award, SC Action Counc Cross-Cult Mental Health & Human Servs, 1991; Board of Director Award, Horry Cult Arts Coun, 1991; Distinguished Woman of the Year, Arts, Carteret County NC Coun Women, 1993; Excellent Communicator Award, Dept Pupil Servs, Horry County SC Sch Dist, 1990; American Booksellers Association Pick of the Lists for Front Porch Stories from the One-Room School Broad Leaf Fellow; Zora Neale Hurston Award, Nat Asn Black Storytellers, 1999; Dr Annette Lewis Phinazee Award, NC Cent Univ Sch Libr Info Sci, 2000; Parents Choice Recommended Award for African American Musicians, 2000; The Minstrels Melody named CBS & NCSS Noteable Children's Trade Book in Social Studies.

**TATE, GRADY BERNARD**
Entertainer, college teacher, singer. **Personal:** Born Jan 14, 1932, Durham, NC; married Vivian Tapp. **Educ:** NC Cent Univ, BA, 1959; Am Acad Dramatic Arts, NY. **Career:** Studio musician, asst conductor; NBC Tonight Show, musician; performed numerous night clubs prisons TV commercials; Johnny Carson's Tonight Show, drummer; singer: "I Got Six"; "Naughty No Nine", "Fireworks"; Howard Univ, jazz studies lectr, 1989-2009. Albums: Windmills of My Mind, 1968; After the Long Drive Home, 1970; Feeling Life, 1971; She Is My Lady, 1972; By Special Request, 1975; Master Grady Tate, 1977; TNT, 1991; Body & Soul, 1992; From the Heart: Songs Sung Live at the Blue Note, 2006. **Orgs:** New York Jazz Quartet. **Honors/Awds:** Special Award, Daytop Village Festival Music, New York, 1968; Record World All Star Band New Artist New York, 1968; Outstanding Achievement Award, Entertainment Hillside High Sch, Durham, NC, 1971; Humanitarian Award, NC Cent Univ, 1970-71; Overseas Jazz Club Award, 1971; Jazz Achievement Award, Jazz Home Club Am, 1971. **Business Addr:** Lecturer, Howard University, 525 Bryant St NW Suite 108 Rm B36, Washington, DC 20059, **Business Phone:** (202)806-7093.

**TATE, GREG**
Educator, journalist, writer. **Personal:** Born Dayton, OH. **Educ:** Howard Univ, jour & film; US Artists fel, 2010. **Career:** Village Voive, journalist, staff writer, 1987-2005; Brown Univ, vis prof Africana studies; Columbia Univ's Ctr, Louis Armstrong vis prof Jazz studies; auth: "Flyboy in the Buttermilk: Essays on Contemporary Am", 1992, "Everything But the Burden: What White People Are Taking from Black Culture", 2003, "Midnight Lightning: Jimi Hendrix and the Black Experience", 2003, "Flyboy 2: The Greg Tate Reader", 2016, "Brooklyn Kings", 2000, "11 Years 9 Months, and 5 Days: Burger Store Episodes and Frustrations", 2000, "The Fiction of Leroi Jones/Amiri Baraka", 2000 "Shopping Store Moments", 2002, "Black Light White Noise: Light and Sound in Contemporary Art", 2007, "Total Chaos: The Art and Aesthetics of Hip-Hop", 2007. **Orgs:** Founding mem, Black Rock Coalition, 1985; leader, Burnt Sugar Arkestra Chamber, 1999. **Honors/Awds:** United States Artists Fellow Award, 2010. **Special Achievements:** Conductor and music dir of Burnt Sugar. **Business Addr:** Visiting Professor of Africana Studies, Brown University, 155 Angell St, Providence, RI 02912, **Business Phone:** (401)863-3137.

**TATE, DR. HERBERT HOLMES, JR.**
Lawyer, executive, government official. **Personal:** Born Feb 22, 1953, Karachi; son of Herbert H Sr (deceased) and Ethel Harris. **Educ:** Wesleyan Univ, BA, hist, 1975; Rutgers Univ Sch Law, JD, 1978. **Career:** Essex Co Prosecutors Off Appellate Sect, law clerk, 1977-78; Hon Van YClinton, judicial clerk, 1978-79; Essex Co Prosecutor's Off, asst pros, 1979-83, trial sect dir juv trial sect, 1982-83; Carella Byrne Bain Gilfillan, assoc, 1983-85; pvt pract atty, 1985-86; Urban Enterprise Zone Authority, pub mem, 1985-86; Environ Protection Agency Asst Adminr Enforcement; Bloomfield Col, adj prof, 1985; Essex Co Prosecutor's Off, prosecutor; State NJ Bd Pub Utilities, pres, 1994-2001; NJ Inst Technol, res prof energy policy studies, 2001-02; Cent Vt Pub Serv Corp, dir, 2001-04; Environ Law Inst, bd dir, 2002-; Wolff & Samson, coun, 2002-04; NRG Energy Inc, independent dir, 2003-12; NiSource Inc, corp vpres regulatory strategy, 2004-06; Winstar, dir; IDT Capital Inc, dir; IDT Solutions, dir; IDT Spectrum, dir; U.S. Environ Protection Agency, asst adminr enforcement. **Orgs:** Kiwanis Int Newark Chap; NJ Bar, Fed Bar NJ Dist, Pa Bar; NJ State Bar Asn Criminal Law Comn, Exec Comn Criminal Law Sect; Essex Co Bar Asn; Nat Bar Asn; Nat Dist Atty Asn; Nat Black Prosecutors Asn; Nat Orgn Black Law Enforcement Execs; Int Narcotic Enforcement Officers Asn; State Youth ServComn, State NJ; Supreme Ct Task Force Minority Concerns; Co Prosecutors Asn; trustee, Boys & Girls Club Newark; trustee, Montclair Kimberley Acad; NJ State Bar Asn, 1978; mem bd, NRG Energy, 2003-; Pa Bar Asn; mem bd, Cent Vt Pub Serv, 2001-04; mem bd, IDT Capital; pres, Nj Bd Pub Utilities, 1994-2001; pres, State Utilities Bd. **Honors/Awds:** Commendation, City Newark Munic Coun; East Orange Optomist International Law Enforcement Award, 1987; Law Enforcement Award, Bronze Shields Inc, 1987; Law Enforcement Award, Nat Black Police Officers Asn, 1990. **Home Addr:** 169 Mt Pleasant Ave, West Orange, NJ 07052. **Business Addr:** NJ.

**TATE, DR. JAMES A.** See Obituaries Section.

**TATE, LARENZ**
Actor, movie producer. **Personal:** Born Sep 8, 1975, Chicago, IL; son of Larry and Peggy; married Tomasina Parrott; children: 3. **Career:** Actor, Singer, Rapper, Producer, Director. Film appearances: Menace II Soc, 1993; The Inkwell, 1994; Dead Presidents, 1995; Love Jones, 1997; The Postman, 1997; Why Do Fools Fall in Love, 1998; Love Come Down, 2000; Biker Boyz, 2003; A Man Apart, 2003; Crash, 2004; Ray, 2004; Waist Deep, 2006; Gun Hill, 2011; Sacks West, 2011; Gun Hill, 2014; Rush, 2014; White Water, 2015; Beta Test, 2015; Game of Silence, 2016; Girl Trip, 2017. TV series: "The New Twilight Zone", 1985; "Hunter", 1987; "Amen", 1988; "Television Movie The Women of Brewster Place", 1989; "21 Jump Street", 1989; "Matlock", 1989; "The Wonder Years", 1989; "New Attitude", 1990; "Family Matters", 1990-91; "Clippers", 1991; "Seeds Of Tragedy", 1991; "The Royal Family", 1991-92; "The Fresh Prince of Bel-Air", 1992; "S Cent", 1994; "187 Ride or Die", 2005; "Water Front", 2006; "Love Monkey", 2006; "Waist Deep", 2006, "Blue Blood", 2008; "Rescue Me", 2007-11; "Justified"; "House of Lies", 2013. Director: The Hot Spot, 2005; Producer: Love Come Down, 2000. **Orgs:** Founder, The Tate Bros. **Honors/Awds:** Black Film Award, 1999; Screen Actors Guild Award, 2005; Hollywood Film Award, 2005; Black Reel Award, 2006; Screen Actors Guild Award, 2006; Critics Choice Award, 2006. **Home Addr:** , Calabasas, CA. **Business Addr:** Actor, 1990 Bundy Dr, Los Angeles, CA 90025, **Business Phone:** (310)820-6666.

**TATE, DR. LENORE ARTIE**
Consultant, psychologist, government official. **Personal:** Born Apr 8, 1952, Los Angeles, CA; daughter of Earline Hopkins and Wilbur B. **Educ:** Mills Col, BA, 1974; Howard Univ, MS, psychol, 1977; Calif Sch Prof Psychol, PhD, psychol, 1980. **Career:** Prairie View A & M Univ, Child Psychol Prog, fac, 1982-84; Ariz State Univ, asst prof, 1984-86; Calif State Senate, prin consult, 1986-98; Senate Off Res, prin consult, 1986-2012; Calif WrapAround, prog dir, 1992-2012; Allilant Int Univ, interim prog dir, 2005-12; pvt pract, currently. **Orgs:** Minority Concerns Commity, 1984-87; Arizs Govs Conf Aging, 1984; bd mem, Am Soc Aging, 1985-87; co-chair, Arizs Govs Conf Aging, 1985; bd dir, Maricopa County Nat Asn Advan Colored People, 1985-87; Alpha Kappa Alpha Sorority Inc, 1986-; Sacramento County, Self-esteem Taskforce, 1988-90; Sacramento County, Ment Health Adv Bd, 1988-90; vice chair, Sacramento County, 1989; chair, Sacramento County, 1989-92; adv bd, expert emer, County Sacramento Health Servs Cabinet, 1992; Asn Black Psychologists, 1992-. **Honors/Awds:** Geriatric Psychology Post-Doctoral Fellowship, Nat Inst Ment Health, Tex Res Inst Ment Scis, 1980-82; Dean's Award, Calif Sch Prof Psychol-Fresno, 1980; Outstanding County Service Award, Sacramento County, 1991. **Special Achievements:** Author, "Life Satisfaction & Death Anxiety in Aged Women", International Journal of Aging & Human Development, 1982; "Employment Opportunities for Geropsychologists", AMR Psychologist; "Adult Day Care: A Practical Guidebook & Manual", Activities, Adaptation & Aging, special issue, 1988; Calif Mental-Health System: The History of Neglect, Senate Office of Research, 1991; "Adult Day Care", 1989, Not In My Backyard, 1996. **Home Addr:** 3060 Azevedo Dr, Sacramento, CA 95833, **Home Phone:** (916)646-3960. **Business Addr:** Psychologist, Private Practice, 2377 Gold Meadow Way Suite 100, Gold River, CA 95670, **Business Phone:** (916)428-0400.

**TATE, MATTHEW**
School administrator, administrator. **Personal:** Born Sep 16, 1940, McComb, MS; married Rosemary Brymfield; children: Mathis Melone. **Educ:** Southern Univ, BS, 1963; La State Univ, attended 1964; Southern Univ, MEd, admin, 1969; Southeastern La Univ, Educ Specialist, 1974. **Career:** Principal (retired), administrator; W S Young Constr Co, field coordr; Fed Summer Nutrit Prog, bookkeeper; La Asn Educr, rep, 1978-82; Wash Parish Police Juror, juror, 1984, bd mem; Franklinton High Sch, asst prin to prin; Mother Hen's Nursery/Preschool, adminr, owner, currently; Tate's Tax Serv, chief exec officer, currently. **Orgs:** Pres, Wash Parish Ed Asn, 1967; pres, Phi Delta Kappa, 1974; chair person, Supvry Comt Wash Parish Ed Fed Credit Union, 1980; sec, Franklinton Area Polit League; Comt Person Local Ment Health Asn; pres, Rural Franklinton Water Dist; bd mem, Rev Bd Capitol Region Planning Comn, La; Cong Contact Team LAE/NEA; pres, Good Samaritan Living Ctr. **Honors/Awds:** Police Juror Washington Parrish Police Jury, Franklinton, La. **Home Addr:** PO Box 368, Franklinton, LA 70438, **Home Phone:** (504)839-2693. **Business Addr:** Chief Executive Officer, Tate's Tax Service, 4500 Beech Rd, Temple Hills, MD 20748, **Business Phone:** (301)423-8249.

**TATE, ROBERT LEE**
Executive, football player, football coach. **Personal:** Born Oct 19, 1973, Harrisburg, PA. **Educ:** Univ Cincinnati. **Career:** Football player (retired), coach; Minn Vikings, wide receiver, defensive back, right corner back, 1997-2002; Baltimore Ravens, wide receiver, left corner back, 2002-03; Ariz Cardinals, wide receiver, left corner back, 2005-07; ACES, behavior coach. **Orgs:** Founder, pres & chief exec officer, Robert Tate Found, 2005-. **Honors/Awds:** Author: Former NFL Veteran Robert Tate Reveals How He Made It From Little League to the NFL: Overcoming His Secret Battle With Dyslexia, 2011. **Business Addr:** Founder & President, Chief Executive Officer, Robert Tate Foundation, 1535 Creek Bed Dr, Harrisburg, PA 17110-2905, **Business Phone:** (612)306-8668.

**TATE, SHERMAN E.**
Executive. **Personal:** Born Oct 5, 1945, Marvell, AR; son of Rufus Jr and Annie B Tucker; married Janet Davis; children: Amber Nicole DePries; married Marylene Williams. **Educ:** Philander Smith Col, Little Rock, AR, BA, 1970, DHL, 1988. **Career:** City Little Rock, Ark, consult, 1970; Ark State Personnel Div, Dept Finance & Admin, Little Rock, Ark, personnel analyst, 1970-73; Ark Legis Coun, Little Rock, Ark, personnel & budget specialist, 1973-75; Univ Ark Little Rock, dir personnel, 1975-77; Ark State Off Personnel Mgt, Little Rock, Ark, admin, 1977-80; Ark La Gas Co, Little Rock, Ark, asst vpres employee rels, 1980-83, vpres community & consumer rels, 1983-90, vpres, customer rels; ARKLAs, vpres & distrib opers, 1991-97; Alltel Corp, vpres external affairs & gen mgr, 1998-; Fletcher-Tate Ford, co-owner, 1996; First Choice Chevrolet, GMC, Pontiac & Buick, co-owner; Verizon, vpres & state affairs; Hamilton Tate & Assocs, managing dir, currently. **Orgs:** Chmn, Greater Little Rock Chamber Com, 1989; treas, Am Asn Blacks Energy; Nat energy comt; Nat Asn Advan Colored People; Nat adv coun; Nat Alliance Bus; bd dir, One Nat Bank; chmn, Ark State Police Comn; bd dir, Ctrs Youth & Families; chmn & bd trustee, Philander Smith Col; 100 Black Men Am; bd mem, Reynolds Inst Aging; bd dir, Ark Blue Cross. **Home Addr:** 4008 Longview Rd,

Little Rock, AR 72212-1925, **Home Phone:** (501)224-3873. **Business Addr:** Managing Director, Alltel Corp, 8924 Kanis Rd, Little Rock, AR 72204-2318, **Business Phone:** (501)350-4141.

### TATE, SONJA PATRICE

Basketball coach, basketball player. **Personal:** Born Sep 7, 1971, Hughes, AR; daughter of Robert Lee Sr and Artry Lee. **Educ:** Ark State Univ, BS, phys educ & health, 1996, MEd, 2005. **Career:** Basketball player (retired), basketball coach; Columbus Quest, guard, 1996-98; Minn Lynx, guard, 1999-2000; William A. Hough High Sch, head coach; Ark State Univ, asst womens basketball coach, 2012-. **Business Addr:** Assistant Women's Basketball Coach, Arkansas State University, 2105 Aggie Rd, Jonesboro, AR 72401, **Business Phone:** (870)972-2100.

### TATE, VALENCIA FAYE

Executive, vice president (organization). **Personal:** Born Sep 20, 1956, Petersburg, VA; daughter of Henry G (deceased) and Irene E; married Penfield W III; children: Elleana Elizabeth Wilson. **Educ:** Antioch Sch Law, JD, 1981; James Madison Univ, BA, eng lit, 1978. **Career:** Denver Juv Crt, clerk, 1982-84; Colo Nat Bank, acct adr, corp trust supvr, Mastercard & Visa, acct adminr, 1984-86; Denver Water, mgr eeo & minority bus, supvr real estate contracts, supvr tap sales & rec, 1986-95; CH2M Hill, vpres & dir diversity, currently; Western Union Co, co-chair. **Orgs:** Mile High Coun; bd mem, Girl Scouts Am; bd mem, Denver Dist Ct Child Care Ctr; bd mem, Metro Denver Chamber Found; bd mem, Rocky Mountain Minority Supplier Develop Coun; bd mem, Colo Bright Beginnings; bd mem, Denver Athletic Club; bd mem, Colo Asn Black Prof Engrs & Scientists Adv Bd; Jack & Jill Am; Nat Fedn Blind; pres, Links Inc; pres, Delta Sigma Theta, 1976-; Jr League Denver, 1987-; Leadership Denver Alumni Asn, 1992; bd mem, Hist Paramount Theatre Found, 1992; bd dir, Colo Bright Beginnings, 2008; pres's adv circle, co-chair, Urban League Metrop Denver. **Home Addr:** 2253 N Valentia St, Denver, CO 80238-3330, **Home Phone:** (303)320-4665. **Business Addr:** Vice President, Director of Diversity, Ch2m Hill, 6161 S Syracuse Way Suite 100, Greenwood Village, CO 80111, **Business Phone:** (303)706-0990.

### TATEM, DR. PATRICIA ANN

Physical chemist. **Personal:** Born Aug 21, 1946, Wilmington, NC; daughter of Ozie T Faison Sr and Martha Louise Smith Faison; children: Paul Hadley. **Educ:** Bennett Col, BS, 1967; George Washington Univ, MS, 1970, PhD, 1984. **Career:** Naval Res Lab, tech ed, 1967-72, res chemist, 1972-94, supvry res chemist, 1994-. **Orgs:** Wash Chromatography Discussion Group; Am Chem Soc; Combustion Inst; Sigma Xi. **Honors/Awds:** Summa Cum Laude Bennett Col, 1967; Research Publication Award for Applied Research, co-recipient, Nat Res Lab, 1973; Recipient Edison Memorial Grad National Research Lab, 1978-81; Publication Award for Applied Research, Co-recipient, National Research Lab, 1983; Black Engineer Award, Professional Achievement, Morgan State Univ/US Black Engr Mag, 1987; Council for Excellence in Government Fellow, 1994-95; Women of Color Technology Award for Lifetime Achievement, 2001. **Home Addr:** 3862 Florence Ave Apt 2, Alexandria, VA 22305. **Business Addr:** Research Chemist, Naval Research Laboratory, 4555 Overlook Ave SW Code 6180, Washington, DC 20375-5342, **Business Phone:** (202)767-3200.

### TATUM, DR. BEVERLY DANIEL

Educator, school administrator, president (organization). **Personal:** Born Sep 27, 1954, Tallahassee, FL; daughter of Robert Alphonse and Catherine Faith Maxwell; married Travis James; children: Travis Jonathan & David Alexander. **Educ:** Wesleyan Univ, Middletown, CT, BA, psychol, 1975; Univ Mich, MA, clin psychol, 1976, PhD, clin psychol, 1984; Hartford Sem, MA, relig study, 2000; Bates Col, LHD, 2000. **Career:** Coun psychologist, 1979-83; Univ Calif, Santa Barbara, dissertation fel, 1980-81, lectr, dept black studies, 1982-83; Westfield State Col, asst prof psychol, 1983-86, assoc prof, 1986-89; pvt pract psycholgist, 1989; Mt Holyoke Col, assoc prof, 1989-96, prof, 1996-2002, psychol & educ dept chair, 1997-98, dean & vpres, stud affairs, 1998-2001, actg pres, 2002; Wesleyan Col, Stone Ctr, vis scholar, 1991-92; Ford Found, postdoctoral fel, 1991-92; Spelman Col, pres, 2002-15, pres emerita, 2015-; Books: Why Are All The Black Kids Sitting Together in the Cafeteria? And Other Conversations About Race, 1997; Assimilation Blues: Black Families in a White Community, 2000; Can We Talk About Race?: And Other Conversations in an Era of School Resegregation, 2007. **Orgs:** Fel Am Psychol Asn Minority, 1976-79; bd dir, Equity Inst, 1985-90, chair, 1988-90; bd trustee, Williston N hampton Sch, 1999-; Hartford Sem, bd incorporators, 2000-; Am Psycho lAsn; Am Educ Res Asn; Am Col Personnel Asn; Am Asn Univ Women; Nat Asn Multicultural Educ; bd mem, Ga Power, 2007-; bd mem, Educ Testing Serv, 2013-. **Home Addr:** 2795 Peachtree Rd NE Suite 706, Atlanta, GA 30305-3790. **Business Addr:** President, Spelman College, 350 Spelman Lane SW 1st Fl Rockefeller Hall, Atlanta, GA 30314-4399, **Business Phone:** (404)270-5001.

### TATUM, ELINOR RUTH (E R TATUM)

Publisher. **Personal:** Born Jan 29, 1971, New York, NY; daughter of Wilbert and Susan; married Curtis R Simmons. **Educ:** St Lawrence Univ, Canton, NY, BA, govt, 1993; Stockholm Univ, Int Grad Sch, MA, 1994; New York Univ, Grad Sch Arts & Sci, MA, jour, 1997. **Career:** New York Amsterdam News, from asst publ to assoc publ, 1994-97, chief operating officer, 1996-97, publ, ed chief, 1997-; Manhattan Media, 1994-2008. **Orgs:** Wallenberg Comt US, 1994; chairwoman bd, Learning Tree Western Mass, 1997; US Comt UNIFEM, 1997; Greater NY Chap Links Inc, 1998; bd mem, New York Urban League, 1998-; Neighborhood Defender Serv; Creative Vision Found; bd mem, Chinatown YMCA, 2005-12; S St Seaport Museumand New York Press Asn; former secy, S St Seaport Museumand New York Press Asn; bd mem, Creative Visions, 2005-; trustee, St Lawrence Univ, 2006-; Keep-in it real, segment co-host, 2006-; Community Bd 3, 2008-. **Honors/Awds:** Good Scout Award, Greater NY Coun Boy Scouts Am, 1997; Woman of the Year, NY Championship Block Rodeo, 1998; Manhattan Borough Presidents Women Hist Month Award; Public Advocates Award; Outstanding Business Empowerment, New York Chap Black Bus Prof Women; Standing On their Shoulders Award, Nat Action Network. **Home Addr:** 41 2nd Ave, New York, NY 10001, **Home Phone:** (212)529-9902. **Business Addr:** Publisher, Editor-in-Chief, New York Amsterdam News, 2340 8th Ave, New York, NY 10027, **Business Phone:** (212)932-7400.

### TATUM, JAMES

Educator, lecturer, pianist. **Personal:** Born Jul 29, 1931, Mineola, TX; married Cleatrice. **Educ:** Prairie View A&M Univ, BA, 1951; Univ Mich, MM, 1953. **Career:** Butler Col, music dir, 1956; Murray Wright HS, fine arts dept head, 1957; Contemp Jazz Mass, composed, 1980; Spiritulotta Jazz Suite, recorded & publ, composed, 1983; Oakl Univ, jazz piano instr, 1993; Wayne County Community Col, music instr, 1990-2013. Recordings: Contemporary Jazz Mass, composer; Return of Joshua, composer; Back to the Roots, composer. **Orgs:** Dir, Ceciliaville Cult Ctr, 1968; dir, Prog Alternative Creative Ed, 1975; music dir, Upward Bound Prog-Wayne State Univ, 1979; Act-So Nat Asn Advan Colored People, 1982; pres, founder, James Tatum Found Arts, 1987-; Int Asn Jazz Educrs; Nat Comt Black Jazz Caucus; Am Fedn Musicians. **Business Addr:** Founder, President, James Tatum Foundation for the Arts, 20235 Alderton St, Detroit, MI 48232, **Business Phone:** (313)255-9015.

### TATUM, KINNON RAY, II

Executive, football coach, football player. **Personal:** Born Jul 19, 1975, Fayetteville, NC. **Educ:** Univ Notre Dame, BA, sociol, 1997. **Career:** Football player (retired), coach, executive; Carolina Panthers, linebacker, 1997-99; Tampa Bay Buccaneers, 2000; Sam Johnson's Cross Creek Lincoln Mercury Subaru, sales consult, 2003-04; Allstate, sr claims adjuster-bodily injury, 2004-06, field auto claims technician, 2013-14, agency process specialist, 2014-; Burt Diehl Henson Wallace & Assocs, sr field investr, 2006-07; Providence Sr High Sch, asst football coach, 2006-08; Univ Notre Dame, grad asst, 2008-10; Seton Hill Univ, asst football linebacker coach, 2010-12. **Business Addr:** Agency Process Specialist, Allstate, 2775 Sanders Rd, Northbrook, IL 60062, **Business Phone:** (847)402-5175.

### TATUM, MARK A.

Basketball executive, advertising executive, vice president (organization). **Educ:** Cornell Univ, BS, bus mgt & mkt, 1991; Harvard Bus Sch, MBA, 1998. **Career:** Procter & Gamble, 1991-95; Clorox Co, regional sales mgr, 1995-96; Pepsi-Cola Co, Sports Mkt Dept, 1997; Maj League Baseball, Corp Sponsorship & Mkt Dept, 1998-99; Nat Basketball Asn, sr vpres, vpres bus develop, sr dir & group mgr mkt properties, dir mkt partnerships, exec vpres global mkt partnerships, 2009-. **Orgs:** Cornell Col Agr & Life Sci Adv Coun & Athletic Alumni Adv Bd; bd trustee, Naismith Memorial Basketball Hall Fame; alumni bd, Harvard Bus Sch; trustee, Princeton Day Sch. **Business Addr:** Deputy Commissioner, Chief Operating Officer, National Basketball Association, 645 5th Ave, New York, NY 10022, **Business Phone:** (212)407-8000.

### TATUM, MILDRED CARTHAN

Government official, school administrator. **Personal:** Born Mar 26, 1940, Grady, AR; married Charles Leon Sr; children: Carl, Sharon, Charles Jr, Gerald, Terrance & Edwin. **Educ:** Voca Sewing Class, 1959; Sharter Col, NLR, spec educ, 1979. **Career:** PTA, pres, 1969; 145 St Liquors, owner, 1969; Fed Prog, pres, 1980; Grocery Store, owner, 1981; Regional 6 Chap 1 Prog, treas, 1981; State Dept PAC, treas, 1982; Judge Wood appointee to internal bd, 1985; owner rental houses. **Orgs:** Bd dir, Metroplan, 1984; nat bd, AAS bd, 1984; bd pres, Pulaski Co Spec Sch Dist; bd mem, Col Sta Elem Sch. **Honors/Awds:** Nat Honor Soc, 1974; Key to City of La Chapter PAC, 1976; Outstanding Leader Sch Dist, 1983. **Special Achievements:** First African American President School Bd, 1984. **Home Addr:** 11406 Hwy 365 S, Little Rock, AR 72206-4844, **Home Phone:** (501)897-1105. **Business Addr:** Board President, Pulaski County Special School District, 925 E Dixon Rd, Little Rock, AR 72206, **Business Phone:** (501)490-2000.

### TATY, TY. See ALI, TATYANA MARISOL.

### TAULBERT, CLIFTON LEMOURE

Business owner, writer, marketing executive. **Personal:** Born Feb 19, 1945, Glen Allen, MS; son of Morgan and Mary; married Barbara Ann; children: Marshall Danzy & Anne Kathryn. **Educ:** Oral Roberts Univ, BS, 1971; Southern Methodist Univ, Southwest Grad Sch Banking, grad. **Career:** Bank Okla, Tulsa, Okla, Investment Mkt, 1979-85, mkt vpres; Univ Village Inc, Tulsa, Okla, adminr, beginning 1972; Spike USA Inc, pres & chief exec officer; Freemount Corp, Tulsa, Okla, pres, chief exec officer & owner, 1985-; Thrive, content prof, 2013; Bldg Community Inst, pres & founder, currently; staff, Oral Roberts Univ; Roots Java Coffee, pres, chief exec officer. **Orgs:** Bd mem, Tulsa United Way; bd mem, Thomas Gilcrease Mus; bd mem, Tulsa Goodwill Indust; exec bd mem, Tulsa Metrop Chamber Com; bd mem, Bus Indust Develop Corp; trustee, Univ Tulsa; Nat Character Educ Partnership; Tulsa Area Salvation Army; Tulsa Hist Soc; Natchez Lit & Cinema Celebration; Okla Found Excellence; Eudora Welty Found; bd ref, Oral Roberts Univ; founding mem, Anne Kathryn Taulbert Sickle Cell Fund. **Honors/Awds:** National Volunteer, Natl Arthritis Fedn, 1985; Manager of the Year, Oklahoma Chapter Natl Mgt Asn, 1989; Mississippi Arts & Letters Award for Nonfiction, Image Award Lit, Nat Asn Advan Colored People. **Special Achievements:** Author, Once Upon a Time When We Were Colored, 1989; The Last Train North, 1992; Watching the crops come in, 1996; Eight Habits of the Heart: The Timeless Qualities That Build Strong Communities, Within Our Homes and Our Lives, 1997; Little Cliff and the Porch People, 1999; Little Cliffs First Day of School, 2001; Little Cliff and the Cold Place, 2002; The Journey Home: A Fathers Gift to His Son, 2002; But Equal: The Mississippi Photographs of Henry Clay Anderson, 2002; One of Americas outstanding black entrepreneurs, Time magazine. Harvard Univ Principals Ctr, lectured; UsaF Acad, lectured. **Home Addr:** 7802 S Louisville Ave, Tulsa, OK 74136-8001, **Home Phone:** (918)481-0264. **Business Addr:** President, Chief Executive Officer, Owner, The Building Community Institute, 4870 S Lewis Ave Suite 203, Tulsa, OK 74105, **Business Phone:** (888)388-6348.

### TAYARI, KABILI

Manager, mayor. **Personal:** Born Jun 26, 1950, Wilson, NC. **Educ:** Jersey City State Col, BA, media & health sci, 1974; Seton Hall Univ, grad study, 1976. **Career:** Hudson Co Welfare, analyst, 1974-78; Vornado Inc, mgr, 1974-79; Conrail Passenger Div, opers mgr, 1978-80; freelance lect, 1980-; Jersey City Bd Educ, chmn, 1996, dep mayor. **Orgs:** Pres, Jersey City NAACP chap, 1968; African Heritage Studies Asn, 1970-; exec mem, NJ Asn Black Educ, 1972-; Am Fedn State Co & Munic Employs, 1974-76; Coalition Black Trade Unionists, 1974-75; producer & critic Intl TV Asn, 1978-; Am Mgt Asn, 1978-; nat presiding officer, Nat Black Independent Polit Party, 1980-; prog coordr & tutor, Title 20 Aftersch Recreation & Tutorial Prog Eastern Co, YMCA, 1980-84; Nat Title I & Chap I Adv Coun; rep, Nat Black Leadership Roundtable; secy, Greenville Nat Little League; pres, Jersey City City Wide Parents Coun May, 1985-; NJ Black Issues Conv; bd mem, Econ Opportunity. **Honors/Awds:** Community Service Award, Black Asn Alumni Faculty Staff & Students Organ Jersey City State Col, 1981; Community Service Award, Title I & Chapter I Dist Wide Parents Adv Coun, 1985. **Home Addr:** 500A Ocean Ave, Jersey City, NJ 07305.

### TAYLOR, AARON MATTHEW

Radio host, football player, executive. **Personal:** Born Nov 14, 1972, San Francisco, CA; son of Curfman; married Lina Yanchulova; children: 2. **Educ:** Univ Notre Dame, BA, sociol. **Career:** Football player (retired), TV game show host; Green Bay Packers, left guard, 1994-97; San Diego Chargers, left guard, 1998-99; ABC Sports, analyst; CBS Col Sports Network, col football analyst, 2003-, co-host; TV sportscaster. **Orgs:** Impact Endowment Fund. **Honors/Awds:** Consensus All-American, 1992, 1993; Lombardi Award, 1993; Jim Parker Award, 1993; Notre Dame Lineman of the Year Award, Nat Football Found, 1993; Rookie of the Year, 1995; Champion, Super Bowl, XXXI. **Business Addr:** College Football Analyst, CBS College Sports Network, 51 W 52 St, New York, NY 10019-6188, **Business Phone:** (212)975-5100.

### TAYLOR, ALMINA ROBERTS

Musician, educator. **Personal:** Born Mar 24, 1933, Shelby, NC; daughter of Goald R and Willie Mae; married Charles H Jr; children: Angela T Bunch, Charles III, Barbara Spruill & Robert Owens III. **Educ:** Va State Univ, BS, vocal music educ, 1954, MS, music educ, 1971; Norfolk State Col, attended 1967; Univ Va, attended 1977; Univ Richmond, attended 1980; Shenandoah Conserv, attended 1983; Westchester Univ, attended 1985; Old Dom Univ, attended 1986. **Career:** Mt Pleasant Baptist Church, organist, choir directress, 1952-62; Person County High Sch, choral directress, 1954-55; Portsmouth Pub Schs, elem grades, music teacher & choral directress, 1955-62, jr high schchoral directress, 1962-79; Fel United Church Christ, organist, choir directress, 1978; Norcom High Sch, music career teacher, choir directress, 1979-91. **Orgs:** Nat Educ Asn; Nat Music Educr Conf; Va Music Educr Asn; Portsmouth Educ Asn; Alpha Kappa Alpha Sorority; Portsmouth Chap Delicados Inc; Portsmouth Chap Pinochle Bugs; Portsmouth Alpha Wires. **Home Addr:** 1409 Carson Cres W, Portsmouth, VA 23701-3157, **Home Phone:** (757)405-9508.

### TAYLOR, ANDERSON

Real estate agent, teacher. **Personal:** Born Autaugaville, AL; married Virginia Burgohoy. **Educ:** Tuskegee Inst AL, BS, 1956; Bradley Univ Peoria IL, MS, 1963; Atlanta Univ GA, attended 1965; GA Tech, attended 1968; Univ GA. **Career:** Real estate agent (retired); Miss Voc Col Itta Bena, teacher, 1957-59; Douglass Sch, teacher, 1959-65; Carver Voc HS Atlanta, teacher, 1965-74; Walter F George HS, dct coord, teacher; self-employed, real estate. **Orgs:** Deacon Bethel AME Ch, 1960-65; master Boy Scouts KeyW, 1962-64; Ed Lowndes City Christian Movement, 1966, Overseas Teacher Aid Prog Ethiopia NEA, 1967, Are Ind Arts Addis Tech TTI Univ, 1970; dir, Anti-Pov Prog Haynesville AL; fac rep, Carver Voc Sch, 1971-74; chmn, Ind Arts Dept. **Honors/Awds:** Award, Spec Summer Prog Univ Ga NEA, 1967; Teacher of the Year, 1974-75; Certification of Ind Arts, Self-Study Career Ed Prog Univ Ga. **Home Addr:** 1432 Martin Luther King D, Atlanta, GA 30314, **Home Phone:** (404)755-2688.

### TAYLOR, ANDRE JEROME

Public utility executive. **Personal:** Born Sep 10, 1946, Mobile, AL; son of Doris Collins and Willie; married Vivian Buffis; children: Tara, Marla, Andre & Gordon. **Educ:** Tuskegee Univ, Ala, attended 1967; Univ Ala, Tuscaloosa, Ala, BS, jour, 1973. **Career:** Public utility executive (retired); WBRC-TV, Birmingham, Ala, pub affairs dir, 1973-75; WACD Radio, Alexander City, Ala, asst gen mgr, 1975; WBLX-FM, Mobile, Ala, acct exec, 1975-77; Ala Ed TV Commis, Birmingham, Ala, asst dir prog eval, 1977-79; Birmingham Cable Commun, Birmingham, Ala, community rels dir, 1979-84; Ala Gas Corp, pub info, coordr, 1984-86, mgr, commun, 1986-88, asst vpres, commun, 1988-90, asst vpres, community affairs, 1990-95, vpres commun. **Orgs:** Pres, Ala Nat Alumni Asn, 2003-04; exec comt, Jefferson Co Chap, Univ Ala Nat Alumni Asn; pres cabinet, bd visitors, Col Commun & Info Serv, Univ Ala; exec comt, Birmingham Area Boy Scouts Coun; bd, Birmingham Chap, Am Red Cross; bd dir, Nat Mult Sclerosis Soc; Kappa Alpha Psi; AABE; Birmingham Asn Black Journalists; past chmn, Ala Veterans Leadership Prog; bd mem, Baptist Health Syst; adv bd, Plank Ctr Leadership Pub Rels; ROTC Rifle Team; chmn, Exec Comt Afro Am Asn; bd dir, Am Asn Blacks Energy; Pub rel Socs Am; Am Gas Asn Commun Comt; Southern Gas Asn Commun Comt; bd dir, Ala Veterans Memorial Found; Literacy Coun; Magic Moments; Mus Art; Ala Sch Math & Sci Found; bd mem, Capstone Found, bd Mem; Lawson State Adv Comt; Econ Develop Partnership Ala Found; Lakeshore Found; Press's Cabinet; bd trustee, Ala A&M Univ. **Honors/Awds:** Outstanding Alumni Public Relations, Univ Ala Sch Communs, 1989; Entrepreneur of the Year Award, Birmingham Black MBA Asn. **Special Achievements:** First black president of the Alabama's National Alumni Association. **Home Addr:** 3056 Nixon Rd, Bessemer, AL 35022-4956, **Home Phone:** (205)426-5004. **Business Addr:** Board of Trustees, Alabama A&M University, 4900 Meridian St N, Huntsville, AL 35810-1015, **Business Phone:** (256)372-5000.

### TAYLOR, ANNA DIGGS (ANNA KATHERINE JOHNSTON)

Judge. **Personal:** Born Dec 9, 1932, Washington, DC; daughter of Hazel B Johnston and V D Johnston; married Charles C Diggs Jr; children: Douglass Johnston Diggs & Carla Cecilia Diggs; married S Martin. **Educ:** Barnard Col, BA, 1954; Yale Univ, LLB, 1957. **Career:** US Dept Labor, atty off solicitor, 1957-60; Wayne Co MI, asst prosecutor, 1961-62; Eastern Dist MI, asst US atty, 1966; Detroit off mgr, legis assist to US Rep Charles C Diggs Jr, 1967-70; Zwerdling, Maurer, Diggs & Papp, partner, 1970-75; City Detroit, asst corp coun, 1975-79; Wayne State Univ Sch Labor & Indust Rels, prof, 1972-75, 1976-77; City Detroit, Law Dept, supvr asst corp coun, 1975-79; Wayne State Univ Law Sch, adj prof, 1972-75; MI, Eastern Dist Detroit, US Dist Ct, judge, 1979-99, chief judge, 1997-98, sr judge, 1998-. **Orgs:** Trustee, Henry Ford Health Syst; Founders Soc, DIA; Community Found SEMI; Fed Bar Asn, State Bar Mich, Wolverine Bar Asn, Women Lawyers Asn Mich; trustee, Community Found S Eastern Mich; vpres, Yale Law Alumni asn; Fed Bar; Wolverine Bar; Black Judges Asn; Women Judges Asn; Nat Lawyer's Guild; United Way; bd mem, Sinai Hosp; Mich Cancer Found. **Honors/Awds:** NBA Women Lawyer's Division Award, 1981; Michigan SCLC Award, 1984; Calvary Church Bridge Bladders Award, 1984; Absalom Jones Award Michigan Black Episcopalians, 1986; Detroit-Wolverine Bar Asn Bench Bar Award, 1990; Michigan Bell Living the Dream Award, 1991; Detroit Urban League Achievement Award, 1991; Histadrut Menorah Award, 1991; Women's Economic Club Dynamic Women Award, 1992; Steaker Bar Asn Trailblazers Award, 1995; Int Institute Hall of Fame, 1998; Marygrove Col, hon Doctor laws, 2000; Bleede Women Lawyers of MI Award, 2003. **Special Achievements:** First African American woman judge to be appointed to the United States District Court for the Eastern District of Michigan & First black woman Chief Judge; First federal judge to rule on the legal and constitutional issues of the NSA warrantless surveillance controversy. **Home Addr:** 43 Beacon Hill Rd, Grosse Pointe Farms, MI 48236-3001. **Business Addr:** Judge, United States District Court, Rm 1031 231 W Lafayette Blvd, Detroit, MI 48226, **Business Phone:** (313)234-5105.

### TAYLOR, DR. ARNOLD H.

Educator. **Personal:** Born Nov 29, 1929, Regina, VA. **Educ:** Va Union Univ, AB, 1951; Howard Univ, MA, 1952; Cath Univ Am, PhD, 1963. **Career:** Social Univ, New Benedict Col, from instr to prof hist, 1955-64; Orleans, prof hist, chmn div soc sci, 1964-65; NC Cent Univ, prof hist, chair, 1965-70; Ford Found fel, 1969-70; Univ Conn, Sterrs, prof hist, 1970-72; Howard Univ, prof hist & dept chmn, 1972-02, emer prof, 2002. Author: Travail & Triumph; Am Diplomacy & Narcotics Traffic, 1969; Black Life & Cult S Since Civil War, 1976. **Orgs:** Asn Study Afro Am Life & Hist; Social Hist Asn; Am Hist Asn; Orgn Am Historians; Am Hist Jadavpur Univ, Calcutta, India, 1967-68; Va Union Univ. **Home Addr:** 3133 Chestnut St NE, Washington, DC 20018. **Business Addr:** Professor Emeritus, Howard University, 2400 6th St NW, Washington, DC 20059, **Business Phone:** (202)806-6100.

### TAYLOR, BENJAMIN GARLAND

Law enforcement officer. **Personal:** Born Feb 27, 1950, Detroit, MI; son of Douglas A (deceased) and Evelyn N; married Madonna Darlene; children: Angelena R. **Educ:** Wayne County Community Col, AS, 1976; Wayne State Univ, attended 1979. **Career:** Detroit Police Dept, eastern oper enforcement, 1975-82, criminal investbur, gang squad, 1982-92, hq bur, clerical opers, 1992-, narcotics bur, 1997-, sgt, 1999-. **Orgs:** Wayne County Col Alumni Asn; Lieutenants & Sergeants Asn. **Home Addr:** 18645 Robson St, Detroit, MI 48235, **Home Phone:** (313)273-8209. **Business Addr:** 6840 McGraw, Detroit, MI 48210, **Business Phone:** (313)237-2555.

### TAYLOR, BOBBY, III (ROBERT TAYLOR, III)

Radio host, football player. **Personal:** Born Dec 28, 1973, Houston, TX; son of Robert; children: 2. **Educ:** Univ Notre Dame. **Career:** Football player (retired), radio host; Philadelphia Eagles, right corner back & corner back & left corner back, 1995-2003; Seattle Seahawks, corner back, 2004; 99.3 Talk FM, football analyst & host, 2011-. **Honors/Awds:** Eagles Ed Block Courage Award, 1998; Pro Bowl, 2002; All-Pro, 2002. **Business Addr:** Football Analyst, 99.3 Talk FM, 212 Grande Blvd Suite B100, Tyler, TX 75703, **Business Phone:** (903)581-5259.

### TAYLOR, CARL L.

Chief executive officer. **Career:** First Impressions Group, chief exec officer, 2002-. **Business Addr:** Chief Executive Officer, First Impressions Group, 20600 Tireman, Detroit, MI 48228, **Business Phone:** (313)963-9836.

### TAYLOR, CAROL (RUTH CAROL TAYLOR)

Association executive, journalist, activist. **Personal:** Born Dec 27, 1931, Boston, MA; daughter of William Edison and Ruth Irene Powell; married Rex Norman Legall; children: Cindy & Laurence. **Educ:** Elmira Col, attended 1951; Bellevue Sch Nursing, RN, 1955; NY Univ, attended 1956. **Career:** Mohawk Airlines, flight attend, 1958; Pearl & Edric Conners Theatrical Agency, mgr, 1961-63; Flamingo Mag, London, Eng, journalist, 1962-63; islands first prof nursing sch, founder, 1963; exec secy, Barbados, 1964-68; pvt duty nurse, 1977-86; Inst Interracial Harmony Inc, pres & co-founder, 1982-; freelance journalist; TV show presenter. **Orgs:** Bd dir, Inst for "Interracial" Harmony Inc, 1982-; founder, Negro Women March. **Special Achievements:** First African American airline flight attendant in the United States, 1958. Writer, The Little Black Book: Black Male Survival in America, 1985. **Home Addr:** , NY. **Business Addr:** President, Institute for Interracial Harmony Inc, 590 Flatbush Ave Suite 11A, Brooklyn, NY 11225-4935, **Business Phone:** (718)856-1271.

### TAYLOR, DR. CAROL ANN

Lawyer. **Personal:** Born Jan 17, 1956, Toledo, OH; children: Stephanie Travis & Jeremy Travis. **Educ:** Carleton Col, BA, polit sci, 1978; Univ Minn Law Sch, JD, 1981. **Career:** Western Life, contract analyst, 1982-85; Northwestern Nat Life, prod develop analyst, compliance anaylst, 1984-87; Amerisure Life, claims/compliance mgr, 1987-88; Mich Mutual, assoc coun, 1988-89, coun, 1989-93, asst vpres, coun; Amerisure Mutual Ins Co, asst vpres, vpres coun, compliance officer, 1987-. **Orgs:** Minn Bar Asn, 1985-; Am Bar Asn, 1988-; Mich Bar Asn, 1988-; coun, Magnolia Neighborhood Bd, 1990-. **Honors/Awds:** Minority Achievers Award, YWCA, 1989; Parent Volunteer, Girls Scouts Am, 1992; Volunteer Tutor, Detroit Tutorial Ctr, 1993; Outstanding Board Leadership, Vista Maria, 2016. **Home Addr:** 18155 Magnolia Ave, Southfield, MI 48075-4107, **Home Phone:** (810)559-0858. **Business Addr:** Vice President Counsel, Compliance Officer, Amerisure Mutual Insurance Co, 26777 Halsted Rd, Farmington Hills, MI 48333-2060, **Business Phone:** (248)426-7938.

### TAYLOR, CAROLE LILLIAN

Educator. **Personal:** Born Pittsburgh, PA; children: Colette & Yvette. **Educ:** BS, 1971; MEd, 1972; PhD, 1973; spec dipl, 1975. **Career:** EPIC Inc, exec dir; Akronite Mag, fashion ed, 1967-68; Tolatr Highland Pk Prep Acad, exec dir, currently; EPIC Pitts Bd Educ, exec, 1973-77, teacher, 1972-77; Tolafr Acad Elem Sch, 1978; Univ Pitts, Am Asn Univ Profs, model instr; Tolatr Highland Pk Prep Acad, exec dir. **Orgs:** Int Platform Asn; Doctorate Asn Univ Pitts; Am Asn Univ Profs. **Home Addr:** 5062 Rosecrest Pl, Pittsburgh, PA 15201. **Business Addr:** Executive Director, Tolatr Highland Park Preparatory Academy, 1112 N Negley Ave, Pittsburgh, PA 15206, **Business Phone:** (412)361-7733.

### TAYLOR, DR. CHARLES E.

College president, educator, businessperson. **Personal:** Born Jun 5, 1944, Columbus, OH; son of Robert and Catherine; married Judy; children: Enid, Antjuan & Jerome. **Educ:** Ohio State Univ, BA, 1967, MA, 1969, PhD, educ, 1971. **Career:** S Side Settlement House, prog dir, 1967-68; Ohio State Univ, Columbus OH, teaching res assoc, 1968-69; Columbus Metrop Area Community Action Org, dir, 1969-70; VISTA, prog officer, 1969; Urban Resources, consult, 1970; Battelle Memorial Inst, consult, 1970; Wash Internships Educ, intern, 1970-71; Inst Educ Leadership, staff assoc, 1971-72; Acad Contemp Probs, vpres opers, 1972-76; Wilberforce Univ, pres, 1976-84; Stand Oil Co, dir contrib & comm affairs, 1984-86; Stand Oil Co Marine Transp, gen mgr, 1986-89; Brand Implementation & Control, USA, mgr, 1989, mgr, Pub Affairs, 1991; Lamadie Amrop Int, partner, 1991-93, managing partner, 1993; Brit Petrol Shipping, pres; Morris Brown Col, pres, 2002-03; Hollins Group Inc, exec vpres, managing dir & consult, currently. **Orgs:** Steering community Develop Comn Greater Columbus, 1974-76; bd dir, chmn, Govt Rels Comm Berwick Civic Asn, 1974; bd dir, treas Columbus Area Leadership Prog, 1974-75; bd dir, CARE Regional Resources Bd, 1974-76; exec comt, Franklin County Dem Party, 1974-76; bd dir, chmn, personnel comm Neighborhood Develop Corp, 1974-76; Full Employ Action Coun; fel, adv bd, Joint Ctr Polit Studies; bd trustee, Franklin Univ, 1975-76; bd educ, Shaker Heights OH, 1985-89; bd dir, Ameritrust Develop Bank, 1988-; bd trustee, Univ Akron 1988-; fac, Inst Pract Polit; exec dir, Columbus Area Leadership Prog; dir, Ohio Educ Sem Am Educ Res Asn; Am Asn Sch Admin; Am Mgt Asn; Am Acad Polit & Social Sci; auth producer Color LineWVKO radio; bd dir, chmn, prog com Columbus Urban League; bd dir, Blacks Against Drugs Uhuru Drug Treat Facil; chmn, Manpower Adv Coun forColumbus, Franklin Col. **Business Addr:** Executive Vice President, Managing Director, The Hollins Group Inc, 225 W Wacker Dr Suite 1575, Chicago, IL 60606-1274, **Business Phone:** (312)606-8000.

### TAYLOR, CHARLEY ROBERT

Football coach, consultant, football player. **Personal:** Born Sep 28, 1941, Grand Prairie, TX; son of James Stevenson and Myrtle; married Patricia Grant; children: Charley Jr, Elizabeth Erin & Erica. **Educ:** Ariz State Univ, attended. **Career:** Football player, football coach (retired), consult; Wash Redskins, running back, wide receiver, halfback, split end, 1964-77, Front Off Dept, scout, 1978-81, receivers coach, 1981-94, consult, currently; Game & Inland Fisheries Community, Va, consult, 1983; Dept Conserv & Recreation, Va, 1999; Jerry's Ford, staff. **Orgs:** Northern Greater Love; Spec Olympics, Ment Retarded Bowls, 1963; app mem, Va Gov Charles Robb, Game & Inland Fisheries Community, 1983. **Honors/Awds:** UPI NFL Rookie of the Year, 1964; Pro Bowl, 1964, 1965, 1967, 1967, 1972, 1973, 1974, 1975; Rookie of the Year, Nat Football League, 1964; All Pro, 1967, 1969, 1974; Offensive Player of the Year, Wash Redskins, 1974; Arizona State Sports Hall of Fame, 1975; Pro Football Hall Fame, 1984; Tex Hall Fame, 1985; Redskins Ring Fame; Wash Touchdown Club Hall Fame, 1992. **Special Achievements:** NFL's 4th all-time leading receiver, 649 catches for 9130 yards; Washington Redskins, first round draft pick, 1964, all-time leader in touchdowns; Outstanding Citizen, City Grand Prairie, Tx, 1964; First rookie in 20 years to finish in the NFL's top 10 in both rushing (sixth with 755 yards) and receiving (eight with 53 catches for 814 yards). **Home Addr:** 12023 Canter Lane, Reston, VA 20191-2129, **Home Phone:** (703)264-0934. **Business Addr:** Consultant, Washington Redskins, Redskin Pk, Washington, DC 20041, **Business Phone:** (703)478-8900.

### TAYLOR, DR. CLEDIE COLLINS

Art museum director, educator. **Personal:** Born Mar 8, 1926, Bolivar, AR; daughter of Osie Gaines and Dallas; children: Paul Dallas (deceased). **Educ:** Wayne State Univ, BS, 1948, MA, 1957; Univ Per Stranieri, certetruscology, 1968; Wayne State Univ, SP cert humanities art & hist, 1970; Union Grad Sch, PhD, art hist, 1978. **Career:** Detroit Pub Sch, art teacher, 1979; Detroit Pub Sch, supvr art, 1980-; Wayne State Univ, instr fashion design, 1981; Pri Jewelry Design, practicing metal crafts person; C's Mus, asst dir, 1987-91; Arts Extended Gallery Inc, founder & dir, currently. **Orgs:** Chmn, Detroit Coun Arts, 1977-81; chmn, Minority Arts Adv Panel, Mich Coun Arts, 1982-; trustee, Haystack Mountain Sch Crafts, 1982-; Detroit Scarab Club, 1983-; adv & liason, Detroit Art Teachers Asn, 1983-; art adv, Nat Asn African Diaspora, 1980-; dir, Art Symp Surinam NAAD Conf, 1982; Berea Lutheran Church; Alpha Kappa Alpha Sorority; dir, Art Symp Barbados; Mich Coun Arts, 1987-; bd, Mich Arts Found, 1988-. **Honors/Awds:** Spirit of Detroit Award, City Detroit, 1983; Award, Spirit of Detroit, City Detroit Small Bus, 1988; Gov's Award for Contrib to Art Education, 1989. **Special Achievements:** Book publication: "Journey to Odiamola", 1978; Cur "African Tales in Words And Wood", 1984; "Words in a Sketch Bk", 1985; Cur - "Tribute to Ernest Hardman" Exhib Scarab Club, 1985; One Hundred Black Women for Art and Lit, 1989; First guest cur, Charles Wright Mus African Hist, Clear story, 2000. **Home Addr:** 5359 Vancouver St, Detroit, MI 48204-5041, **Home Phone:** (313)832-4534. **Business Addr:** Director, Founder, Arts Extended Gallery Inc, David Whitney Bldg 1553 Woodward Suite 2121, Detroit, MI 48226, **Business Phone:** (313)831-0321.

### TAYLOR, COLLEEN

Vice president (organization). **Educ:** Spelman Col, Econs, 1990; Univ Pa, Wharton Sch Bus, MBA, 1996. **Career:** Chase Manhattan Bank, vpres, 1990-2000; JP Morgan Chase, sr vpres 1990-05; Wachovia Bank, sr vpres, Global Payments & Liquidity Serv, 2005-09; Capital One, exec vpres, treas mgt & merchant serv, 2009-. **Orgs:** Bd mem, Veritas Therapeutic Community. **Honors/Awds:** "Black Enterprise", 75 Most Powerful Women in Business, 2010.

### TAYLOR, DAISY CURRY

Government official. **Personal:** Born Jul 24, 1948, Ft. Lauderdale, FL; married Theodore D; children: Tamila Annay & Tiffany Patrice. **Educ:** Bethune-Cookman, lib arts, attended 1970; Nova Univ, MPA, 1975; Cong Prof Devel Cert Cong Asst, 1984. **Career:** Fla Memorial Col, res analyst, 1970-71; City Ft Lauderdale, admin aide, 1971-74; City Oakland Pk, dir community affairs, 1974-84; Exquisito Serv Ft Lauderdale Mgt Consult Firm, chmn bd & pres; Congressman E Clay Shaw, cong aide, 1984-. **Orgs:** Bd dir, Area Agency Aging, 1974-; Early Childhood Develop; Community Action Agency; Urban League; Nat Asn Advan Colored People; Task Force Black Aged Women Bus; Am Soc Pub Admin; Forum Black Pub Admin; Urban League Guild; E Broward Med Asn Found; bd mem, Black Coalition Broward; bd mem, Coun African Am Econ Devel; Alzheimers Asn. **Home Addr:** 3860 NW 6th Pl, Ft. Lauderdale, FL 33311. **Business Addr:** Congressional Aide, E Clay Shaw, 299 E Broward Blvd, Ft. Lauderdale, FL 33301.

### TAYLOR, DR. DALE B.

Musician, publisher, educational consultant. **Personal:** Born Jun 13, 1939, Topeka, KS; son of Wesley E and Cassie L Moten; married Marguerite Davis; children: Shannon Michelle Davis & Shawn Jeffery. **Educ:** Col Emporia, KS, 1959; Univ Kans, BMusEd, 1963, MmusEd, 1971, PhD, 1984. **Career:** Milwaukee County Ment Health Ctr, music therapist, 1963; Mendota State Hosp, dir music ther, 1964-67; Univ Wis Eau Claire, dir music ther, 1969-2004; Mt Senario Col, 1975; Dept Allied Health Professions, chair, prof & chair emer, 1992-2004; Alverno Col, vis prof, 1998, 2010; Augsburg Col Music Ther, dir, 2008-09; Carroll Univ Music Ther, consult, 2014; Author: Biomedical Foundations of Music as Therapy, 1st ed, 2nd ed, 2010. **Orgs:** Co-founder, Wis Chap Music Ther, 1973; vis clinician, Univ Mo, Kans City, 1975; vis clinician, assembly delegates & int rels comt, Nat Asn Music Ther Inc, 1976-83, 1985-97; pres & vpres, Great Lakes Region NAMT, 1976-78; vice commodore, Lake Wissota Yacht Club, 1978-80, commodore, 1985-87, racing chmn, 1981-83; grants rev panelist, Wis Arts Bd, 1984-90; Eau Claire Affirmative Action Rev Comt, 1984-90; Pi Kappa Lambda Music Hon Soc; bd dir, Int Asn Music Handicapped Inc, 1986-91; conductor, accompanist, Eau Claire Gospel Choir, 1987-; adv comt, Univ Wis, Syst Inst Race & Ethnicity, 1988-90; planning comn, Univ Wis Syst Design Diversity Conf, 1989; Inst Arts Med Asn, 1990-; ed, bk & media rev, 1990-97, int adv com, 1990-, ed, 1997-; vpres, Valley Gospel Choir, soloist, 1992-, pres; pres, WI Bd Aging & Long Term Care, 2005-; pres, WI Dept Health Serv Music & Memory Adv Bd, 2014-; pres, Ohio Dept Aging, 2015-. **Special Achievements:** 2016 World Conference Keynote Speaker, Online Conference for Music Therapy; In 1985, First to use "plasticity" to describe brain functioning; "Best Actor" Jan 2, 2015 Children's Dyslexia Center Murder Mystery Co Fund Raiser Dinner. **Home Addr:** 1613 Sunrise Lane, Eau Claire, WI 54703-2574, **Home Phone:** (715)836-9029. **Business Addr:** Publisher, Barton Publications, 1613 Sunrise Lane, Eau Claire, WI 54703-2574, **Business Phone:** (715)836-9029.

### TAYLOR, DAVID RICHARD, III

Lawyer. **Personal:** Born Dec 17, 1949, Toledo, OH; son of David Richard Jr and Shirley L Swan; married Mary J Carrigan; children: Stacee L, Courtnee D, Davon R, Renesa Y, Evan K & Antoine L. **Educ:** Univ Toledo, BA, 1971; Col Law, JD, 1974. **Career:** Lucas County Juv Ct, referee, 1976-78; Lucas County Domestic Rels Ct, referee, 1978-80, chief referee, 1980-84; McConnell & Taylor Assocs, atty & partner, 1984-; State OH, atty gen, spec coun, 1989-90; Lucas County Ment Health Bd, atty & coun, 1990. **Orgs:** Life mem, pres, Nat Asn Advan Colored People, Toledo Br, 1997-98; life mem, Univ Toledo Alumni Asn; life mem, Kappa Alpha Psi Fraternity; McConnell & Taylor Assocs. **Home Addr:** 351 Sentry Hill Rd, Toledo, OH 43615, **Home Phone:** (419)531-5638. **Business Addr:** Attorney, Partner, McConnell & Taylor Associates, 316 N Mich St Suite 700, Toledo, OH 43604-1627, **Business Phone:** (419)244-1000.

### TAYLOR, DR. DAVID VASSAR

School administrator, educator. **Personal:** Born Jul 13, 1945, St. Paul, MN; son of Eula Vassar Murphy and Clarence; married Josephine Reed; children: Tyrone & Kenneth. **Educ:** Univ Minn, BA, 1967; Univ Nebr, MA, 1971, PhD, 1977; Harvard Univ, IEM Prog, 1985. **Career:** St Olaf Col, Northfield Minn, dir, Am minority studies prog, 1974-76; State Univ New York New Paltz Campus, chairperson, black studies dept, 1977-78; Hubert Humphrey Collection Minn Hist Soc, cur, 1978-79; Macalester Col, dir minority, spec serv prog, 1979-83; Col Charleston, dean undergrad studies, 1983-86; Minn State Univ Syst Off, assoc vice chancellor, acad affairs, 1986-89; Univ Minn, Gen Col, assoc prof, dean, 1989-2005; Morehouse Col, provost & sr vpres acad affairs, 2005-; Health E Care Sys, dir. **Orgs:** Bd dir, Hallie Q Brown Comm Ctr, St Paul, 1978-79; bd adv, Perrie Jones Libr Fund, St Paul, 1979-80; Minn Qual Life Study, 1979-80; vestry St Phillip's Episcopal Church, 1978-81; bd trustee, Seabury Western Theol Sem, 1985-90; chair, bd, Penumbra Theatre Co; bd, Friends St Paul Pub Libr; treas, Jean Covington Fund; adv bd, Moore House Res Inst; HealthEast Corp; dir, Minn Black Hist Proj Minn Hist Soc; bd dir, A Commitment Excellence; bd dir, Page Educ Found; bd dir, Jean Covington Found; bd dir, HOPE Community. **Honors/Awds:** Josie R Johnson Human Rights & Social Justice Award, Univ Minn, 1999; Whitney Young Lifetime Achievement Award, Viking Coun Boy Scouts Am, 2002; David Gebhard Award, Minn Chap Soc Archit Historians, 2003; Minnesota Book Award, 2003. **Special Achievements:** Author bibliography & 3 articles. **Home Addr:** 4710 Xene Lane N, Plymouth, MN 55446-2193. **Business Addr:** Provost, Senior Vice President for Academic Affairs, Morehouse College, 830 Westview Dr SW, Atlanta, GA 30314-3773, **Business Phone:** (404)681-2800.

### TAYLOR, DR. DONALD FULTON, SR.

College administrator. **Personal:** Born Jul 10, 1932, Charlestown, WV; married Phyllis Shirley Jackson; children: Donald Jr, Keith C, Pamela Jackson, Mark J & Christy A Butts. **Educ:** Shepherd Col, AB, 1957; Johns Hopkins Univ, PhD, 1971; Va Union Univ, Mdiv, 1982; Villanova Univ, MS. **Career:** Darby Township High Sch, head, dept sci, 1958-65; Cheyney State Col, coordr health sci, 1970-75; Norfolk State Univ, Sch Health Related Professions & Nat Sci, prof, dean, 1975-95, dean emer, 1995-. **Orgs:** Pastor, Greater Mt Zion Baptist Church, 1985; chairperson, Eastern Va Health Educ Consort, 1985; bd dir, Soc Aid Sickle Cell Anemia, 1985; bd dir, Nat Soc Allied Health, 1985; task force Med Aid, Orgn Transplant, 1985; bd dir, Norfolk Area Health Educ Ctr, 1985; Prince Hall Masons, Norfolk Rotary Club; bd dir & treas, Norfolk Area Health Ed Ctr, 1985; Am Pub Health Asn, 1985; Va Asn Allied Health Prof, 1985; Va Pub Health Asn, 1985, Tidewater Metro Ministers Asn, 1985; bd dir, Chesapeake Hosp Authority, 1986-90; vpres, Norfolk Area Health Educ Ctr, 1986; adv bd, Juvenile Court Conf Comn, 1986-. **Home Addr:** 431 Ivy Cres, Chesapeake, VA 23325-4356, **Home Phone:** (757)962-3408. **Business Addr:** Dean Emeritus, Norfolk State University, 700 Pk Ave, Norfolk, VA 23504, **Business Phone:** (757)823-8600.

### TAYLOR, DOROTHY SMALLS. See SMALLS, DOROTHY M.

### TAYLOR, EARTHA LYNN

Lawyer. **Personal:** Born Oct 28, 1957, Gary, IN; daughter of Silas and Mirtha; children: Barrett Alexander Boone. **Educ:** Ind Univ, BS, 1979; Valparaiso Univ Sch Law, JD, 1985. **Career:** Steven Rolle & Madden, law clerk, 1986-87; Law Off Frank Hernandez, 1987-88; Law Offices Eartha Taylor, atty, 1988-. **Orgs:** J L Turner Legal Asn, 1988-; Dallas Asn Black Women Attys, 1987-; Dallas Bar Asn, 1989-; Nat Bar Asn, 1988-; State Bar Tex. **Home Addr:** 6430 Los Altos Dr, Mesquite, TX 75150, **Home Phone:** (214)613-4265. **Business Addr:** Attorney, Law Office of Eartha L Taylor, 2501 Oak Lawn Ave Suite 360, Dallas, TX 75219-4044, **Business Phone:** (214)943-8801.

### TAYLOR, EDGAR R.

Marketing executive, executive director. **Personal:** Born Sep 7, 1953, Cheyenne, WY; son of Edgar N and Jeanette; married Cheryl S; children: Carly S, Scott A & Allison A. **Educ:** Adelphi Univ, BA, 1975; Imede Univ, Lausanne, Switz, exec develop, 1990. **Career:** Carnation Co, acct exec, 1978-80, dist mgr, 1980-82, region mgr, 1982-84, prom mgr, 1984-86, merchandising dir, 1986-90, category dir, 1990-91; Nestle USA, mkt dir, 1991-, Banking Div, dir; Taylor & Assocs, owner, dir, currently. **Orgs:** Bd dir, Prom Mkt Asn Am, 1989-; bd dir, Los Angeles Regional Food Bank, 1990-. **Home Addr:** 2287 Birchfield St, Simi Valley, CA 93065, **Home Phone:** (805)583-4631. **Business Addr:** Director, Taylor & Associates, 433 N Camden Dr, Beverly Hills, CA 90210, **Business Phone:** (310)285-1559.

### TAYLOR, EDWARD WALTER (ED TAYLOR)

Executive. **Personal:** Born Jul 17, 1926, Baltimore, MD; son of Elbert and Rebecca; married Alene Lassiter. **Educ:** Hampton Inst, 1950; Johns Hopkins Univ, Univ Md, 1974. **Career:** US Govt, chief drafting, 1950-59; Henry L Lives Balt, architect mgr, 1958-63; Westinghouse Elec, mech designer, 1960-73; Edward Q Rogers Balt, architect, 1964-67; Sultor Campbell Architects Balt, architect mgr, 1968-73; Atti Consult Ltd, owner, 1973-90; Morgan State Univ, architect. **Orgs:** Nat Tech Assoc; Comt Develop Adv Comn; Howard Pk Civic Assoc; AIA; NW Outer Urban Coaltion; Nat Asn Advan Colored People; tech adv Pan African Cong; dir, Model Cities Housing Corp; chmn, Md Comn Develop Comt, 1973; tech consult, E Baltimore Comt Corp; graphics adv, Voc Ed Baltimore Construct Specif IST; Construct Specif Inst; vice chairperson, EDUC COMT Concord Baptist Church; Concord Baptist Church, vice chair, Christian educ, 1991, church sch supt, 1992. **Home Addr:** 5507 Belleville Ave, Baltimore, MD 21207, **Home Phone:** (410)448-0610.

### TAYLOR, ELLIS CLARENCE, SR.

Engineer. **Personal:** Born Feb 4, 1931, New Hebron, MS; married Marva Manning Whitney. **Educ:** Universal TV & Electronics Systs, dipl, 1953; Cleveland Inst Electronics, dipl, 1956, dipl, 1988; Univ Kans, attended 1962; Cent Tech Inst, attended 1968; Univ Miss, Kansas City, video prod studies, 1982. **Career:** Engineer (retired); KPRS Radio, part-time engr, 1957-58; Taylor's TV Serv & Sls, 1957-63; AM-FM sta KPRS, chief engr; Forte Rec Co, founder, 1966-83; Freelance Music Producer & Contractor, 1967; KMBC TV, staff engr, 1968-98. **Orgs:** Licensing exam bd mem, KC Radio & TV, 1961-84; Nat Asn Advan Colored People; founding bd mem, United Minority Media Asn Miss, 1974-77; Rec Indust Am, 1976-83; exec bd dr, IBEW Exec Coun, 1977-79; Black Music Asn, 1980; Soc of Brdcst Engrs, 1980-; life mem, Univ Miss, Kans City, Alumni Asn; Audio Engrg Soc Inc, 1986-, Nat Rep Sen Inner Circle, 1991-; Heritage Found; Pres's Men Club, 2001-. **Honors/Awds:** Senatorial Medal of Freedom, 1994. **Home Addr:** 1859 E 76th St, PO Box 320541, Kansas City, MO 64132-2150, **Home Phone:** (816)444-2399.

### TAYLOR, HON. ERIC CHARLES

Lawyer. **Personal:** Born Jun 25, 1962, Sacramento, CA; son of John C Jr and Joan E. **Educ:** Dartmouth Col, BA, 1984; Univ Calif, 1985; Univ Va Sch Law, JD, 1988; Univs Granada & Salamanca, Spain, span lit. **Career:** Pettit & Martin, atty, assoc, 1988-90; Mr Ct, 1985-; Sonnenshein, Nat & Rosenthal, atty, assoc, 1990-92; Calif Judges Asn, pres, 2003; County Coun, County Los Angeles, supv judge, dep county counr, currently. **Orgs:** Pres, Career Ambitions Inc, 1989-;trustee, Cate Sch, Westside Neighborhood Sch; bd, At Risk Youth and Dartmouth Alumni Coun. **Home Addr:** 8712-J Chessington Dr, Inglewood, CA 90305, **Home Phone:** (310)412-0390. **Business Addr:** Deputy County Counsel, Supervising Judge, County of Los Angeles, Rm 358 Kenneth Hahn Hall Admin 500 W Temple St, Los Angeles, CA 90012, **Business Phone:** (213)974-2101.

### TAYLOR, DR. ESTELLE WORMLEY

College teacher. **Personal:** Born Jan 12, 1924, Washington, DC; daughter of Luther Charles and Wilhelmina Jordan; married Ivan Earle. **Educ:** Miner Teachers Col, BS, 1945; Howard Univ, MA, 1947; Cath Univ, PhD, 1969. **Career:** Howard Univ, instr eng & humanities, 1947-52; Langley Jr High, eng teacher, 1952-55; Eastern Sr High, eng teacher, 1955-63; Dist Columbia Teachers Col, eng instr, prof, 1963-76; Fed City Col, assoc provost, 1974-75; Dist Columbia Teachers Col, actg acad dean, 1975-76; Howard Univ, eng prof, chmn dept, 1976-85, assoc dean Col Lib Arts, 1985-86, dir, Grad Expository Writing, 1988-91, prof emer, currently. **Orgs:** Nat Coun Teachers Eng, 1955-80; Mod Lang Asn Am, 1963-; life mem, Col Lang Asn, 1963-; Shakespeare Asn Am, 1965, 1979-, vpres, 1979-81, corresp sec, 1989-91, rec sect, 1991-92, Capital City Links Inc; vice chmn, 1983, Univ Dist Columbia bd trustee; exec mem comt, Folger Inst, 1982-91; pub mem, US Dept State Foreign Serv Selection Bd, 1983; Comn Higher Educ, 1984-91; pub mem, Sr Threshold Foreign Serv Appointments Selections Bd, Agency Int Develop, 1984; res bd advis, Am Bibliog Inst Inc, 1985-; Women's Nat Dem Club, 1987-90; Malone Soc, 1987-90; life mem, Nat Coun Negro Women; Dist Columbia Urban League; life mem, Nat Asn Advan Colored People; life mem, Asn Study Afro-Am Life & Hist; assoc ed, Jour Afro-Am & Geneal Soc, 1990-93; Delta Sigma Theta Sorority; bd adv, Col Arts & Scis, Howard Univ, 2002-. **Business Addr:** Professor Emerita, Howard University, 3221 20th St NE, Washington, DC 20018.

### TAYLOR, FELICIA MICHELLE

Government official, educator, association executive. **Personal:** Born Feb 14, 1960, Concord, NC; daughter of Milton Lee and Shirley Alsbrooks. **Educ:** Cabarrus Community Col, pvt pilot ground sch, 1982; Univ NC, Chapel Hill, BA, sociol, 1982, Charlotte, MS, criminal justice, 1984; Fla State Univ, PhD, criminol, 1987. **Career:** Univ NC, Charlotte, admis counr, 1983-84; Barber-Scotia Col, asst financial planning & develop, 1984-85; Shaw Univ, Raleigh, prof, 1985-87, CAPE Ctr, Wilmington, adj prof, 1992; Fla State Univ, instr, 1988-91, Acad Support Servs, tutor, 1989-91; Fla Agr & Mech Univ, adj prof, 1990-91; Fla Dept Health & Rehabilitative Servs, abuse registry counr, 1991; Univ NC, Wilmington, guest lectr, 1992; Fed Bur Prisons, res analyst, 1992-; Shaw Univ, Raleigh, NC, prof criminal justice, 1993-. **Orgs:** Sweet Carolines, 1980-82; Young Dem, 1982-83, Cloud Cappers Ltd Asn, 1982-; Dist Inc, 1984-; CVAN, Vol Asn Battered Women, 1985; intake counr, Probation & Parole, 1983-84; counr, Mecklenburg Co, Charlotte; chmn, UNICEF; Hall Rep, 1980-81; UNC-Ch sec dorm, 1981-82; co-chmn, Univ NC, Chapel Hill, first UNCF Tennis Tourn Cabarrus Co; adv, Soc Criminal Justice, 1985-87; Coop Col Task Force, 1986; Am Criminal Justice Soc, 1987-; Criminol Asn, 1987-; Acad Criminal Justice Sci, 1989-90; Guardian Ad Litem, 1988-; Supreme Ct Hist Soc, 1994-; mediator, Durham County Mediation Servs, 1996-. **Honors/Awds:** Honor Court, Univ NC, Chapel Hill, 1980-82; Patricia Roberts Harris Fellowship, 1987. **Special Achievements:** Author, works presented: "Gender Bias Amongst State Institutional Drug Treatment Programs," April 1990; "Effects of Pornography on Women," April 1988; Assn of Criminal Justice Professionals, "History of Women's Prisons in the State of Florida"; Southern conf, "Role Play," 1987; Univ NC, Charlotte, First graduate of Masters of Science Degree in Criminal Justice Management Program, 1984. **Home Addr:** 1460 Flat Rock Rd, China Grove, NC 28023, **Home Phone:** (704)857-8327.

### TAYLOR, FRANK

Restaurateur, executive. **Personal:** Born Jun 4, 1965; married Carolyn Clifford. **Career:** Troy Marriott, dir food & beverage; Sheraton Imp Hotel, dir food & beverage; Doubletree Hotel; Pkwy Grille, Pontiac, MI, head develop & dir food & beverage; Detroit Sweet Ga Brown, co-owner; Pittsburgh Fish Mkt; Detroit Lions, partner; Seldom Blues, pres & chief exec officer, currently; Henry Ford Health Syst; minority partner, Aramark; Frank Taylor Mgt Group, pres. **Orgs:** Mich Tour & Travel Comn; Detroit Regional Chamber; Mich Restaurant Asn, bd dir, currently. **Honors/Awds:** Award of Excellence, Wine Spectator mag. **Business Addr:** President, Chief Executive Officer, Seldom Blues, 400 Renaissance Ctr, Detroit, MI 48243, **Business Phone:** (313)567-7301.

### TAYLOR, FRANK ANTHONY

Manager, business owner. **Personal:** Born Jun 4, 1965, Galveston, TX; son of Essie L; married Carolyn A; children: Courtney L, Airielle V & James V. **Educ:** Alvin Sr Col, attended 1986; Am Hotel & Motel, 1988. **Career:** Marriott Brookhollow, food, beverage dir, 1990-92; Holiday Inn San Antonio, resident mgr, 1992-94; Seldom Blues Inc, vpres, 1994-96; Sheraton Hotel Imp, dir food & beverage, 1996; Chamber, pres; Salvation Army, residential dir; Doubletree Hotel Corp, dir food & beverage; Marriotts Pkwy Grille Pontiac, head develop, dir food & beverage; Troy Marriott, dir food & beverage; Southern hospitality Restaurant Group, chmn, pres & chief exec officer, currently; Seldom Blues, co-owner, partner, pres & chief exec officer; Detroit's Breakfast House & Grill Merchants Row, pres & chief exec officer, currently; Sweet Ga Brown, co-owner, pres, mgr & operating partner, managing partner; Motown Soul Food Cafe, co-owner. **Orgs:** Detroit Med Ctr; Detroit Econ Growth Corp; bd dir, Mich Restaurant Asn; Black Enterprise Entrepreneurs Conf. **Honors/Awds:** Cert Food & Beverage Exec, Am Hotel & Motel Asn, 1988. **Home Addr:** 1613 King James Dr, Pittsburgh, PA 15237, **Home Phone:** (412)635-0701. **Business Addr:** President, Chief Executive Officer, Southern Hospitality Restaurant Group LLC, 243 W Cong Suite 1060, Detroit, MI 48226, **Business Phone:** (313)963-1940.

### TAYLOR, FRED (FREDERICK ANTWON TAYLOR)

Football player. **Personal:** Born Jan 27, 1976, Pahokee, FL; married Andrea; children: Kelvin, Nataajah & Inari. **Educ:** Univ Fla, sociol. **Career:** Football player (retired); Jacksonville Jaguars, running back, 1998-2008 & 2011; New Eng Patriots, running back, 2009-10. **Orgs:** Spokesperson, Leukemia Soc Am & Lymphoma Soc Am; spokesman, Glades Asthma Proj. **Honors/Awds:** SEC Championship, Nat Col Athletic Asn, 1994, 1995, 1996; Bowl Alliance National Championship, 1996; Citrus Bowl Most Valuable Player, 1998; Ed Block Courage Award, Nat Football League, 2002; Pro Bowl, 2007; Ground Player of the Year, FedEx, 2007; Florida-Georgia Hall of Fame, 2008; Athletic Hall of Fame "Gator Great", Univ Fla, 2010. **Special Achievements:** Florida High School Athletic Association recognized "100 Greatest Players of the First 100 Years" Florida high school football. **Home Addr:** , Jacksonville, FL. **Business Addr:** Football Player, Jacksonville Jaguars, 1 Stadium Pl, Jacksonville, FL 32202, **Business Phone:** (904)633-6000.

### TAYLOR, GAYLAND WAYNE

Civil engineer. **Personal:** Born Aug 12, 1958, Midland, TX; son of Samuel Lee and Ardis Faye Padgitt. **Educ:** Prairie View A&M Univ, BA, civil engineering, 1981. **Career:** EG & G Idaho Inc, Idaho Falls, ID, field inspector, mat lab tech, 1977-78; Arco, Arp, Tex, corrosion engr, 1979; Ariz Pub Serv Co, Phoenix, Ariz, civil engr, 1982-90; FAA, proj engr, civil engr, 1992-. **Orgs:** Chmn, KPNX Minority Adv Bd, 1982-86; pub rels chair & ed, Ariz Coun Black Engrs & Scientists, 1982-86; nat sect, Nat fundraiser, Nat Coun Black Engrs & Scientist, 1985-91; auditor, Fair Housing, 1987; bus owner, Minority Bus Enterprise City Phoenix, 1988; bus owner mem, Phoenix City Club, 1989-91; chair, Nat Black Coalition Fed Aviation Employees. **Honors/Awds:** Cert Achievement, Transmissions & Distribution Expo, 1982; Adult Develop Units, Univ Boy Scouting, 1982; Outstanding Leadership, Valley Christian Ctrs, 1983; Nominee Candidate Volunteer, The Ariz Democratic Party, 1988; Idealine, Ariz Pub Serv, 1990. **Home Addr:** PO Box 610449, DFW Airport, TX 75261-0449. **Business Addr:** Civil Engineer, Federal Aviation Administration, 10101 Hillwood Pkwy, Fort Worth, TX 76177, **Business Phone:** (817)222-4214.

### TAYLOR, GERREN (ASHLEIGH TAYLOR GERREN)

Fashion model, actor. **Personal:** Born Jul 6, 1990, Los Angeles, CA. **Career:** Actress & fashion model, currently; Films: America the Beautiful, 2007; TV series: Ripley's Believe It or Not!, 2003, Baldwin Hills, 2007. Documentary: America the Beautiful, 2007. **Business Addr:** Fashion Model, Elite Model Management, 345 N Maple Dr Suite 397, Los Angeles, CA 90210, **Business Phone:** (310)274-9395.

### TAYLOR, GILBERT LEON. See Obituaries Section.

### TAYLOR, GOLDIE

Columnist, talk show host, journalist. **Personal:** Born Jul 18, 1968, University City, MO; daughter of Mary. **Educ:** Emory Univ, Atlanta, BA, polit sci & int affairs, 1994. **Career:** Michael Lomax's mayoral campaign, unpaid deputy press secretary, 1993; Sara Lee Corp, dir; Writer for various publications Including "The Atlanta Journal-Constitution", "Creative Loafing", "Marie Claire", "TheGrio", CNN.com", "Americablog" and "MSNBC.com"; GCI Group San Francisco, External Affairs Executive; Edelman Atlanta Public Relations, External Affairs Executive, sr vpres, 2004-06; Goldie Taylor Brand Commun, chief exec officer, managing dir, 2005-15; MSNBC, CNN and HLN, Contributor; NBCUniversal News, exec consult, 2010-12; CNN Worldwide, exec consult, 2007-10; CNN documentary, "Black in America", exec consultant; Proctor & Gamble's marketing campaign, "My Black is Beautiful", chief architect; "The Goldie Taylor Project", managing ed & host, 2008-; Faithful Moon Productions, chief exec officer; DailyBeast, ed, 2015-; Blue Nation Rev, sr ed.

### TAYLOR, HENRY F.

Automotive executive. **Career:** Smokey Point Sales & Serv Inc, chief exec officer; Smokey Point Buick Pontiac GMC Inc, owner & chief exec officer, currently; Taylor Co, chief exec officer. **Business Addr:** Chief Executive Officer, Owner, Smokey Point Buick Pontiac GMC Inc, 16632 Smokey Pt Blvd, Arlington, WA 98223-8409, **Business Phone:** (360)659-0886.

### TAYLOR, DR. HENRY LOUIS, JR.

Consultant, educator. **Personal:** Born Sep 13, 1943, Nashville, TN; married Carol Dozier; children: Jean-Jacques, Keeanga & Chad-Cinque. **Educ:** Tenn State Univ, Nashville, TN, BS, speech path, 1965; Univ Tenn, Knoxville, TN, MS, audiol, 1966; State Univ NY, Buffalo, NY, MA, urban hist, 1973, PhD, urban hist, 1979. **Career:** Hampton Inst, Hampton, Va, assoc dir hearing clin, 1968-70; State Univ New York Buffalo, Buffalo, NY, coordr, independent study, learning ctr, 1972-74, assoc prof Am studies, founder, dir, Ctr Appl Pub Affairs Studies, 1987, prof, currently, dir, Ctr Urban Studies, currently; Univ Cincinnati, Cincinnati, Ohio, dir, employee's develop educ prog, 1974-76; Univ Cincinnati Med Sch, Cincinnati, Ohio, 1976-79; Ohio State Univ, Columbus, Ohio, asst prof, 1980-87; Perry Choice Neighborhood Hist Proj, coordr, founder. **Orgs:** Chair & chief consult, Buffalo Common Coun-Comn Urban Initiatives, 1988; Greater Buffalo Econ Develop Coord Comt, 1990-; Buffalo Pvt Indust Coun's Econ Develop Coord Comt, 1990-; Greater Buffalo Develop Found's Working Group Minority Econ, 1990; Urban League Adv Bd, 1991; Neighborhood Planning & Community Develop; Steering Comt Anchor Insts Task Force; bd, Overseers Nelson A. Rockefeller Inst Govt State Univ New York; bd, Urban Affairs Asn & Urban Hist Asn; bd ed, Univs & Community Schs; coordr, Buffalo Munic Housing Authority's Perry Choice Neighborhood Initiative. **Home Addr:** 360 Linwood Ave, Buffalo, NY 14209-1608, **Home Phone:** (716)883-5717. **Business Addr:** Director, Professor, State University of New York at Buffalo, 201G Hayes Hall, Buffalo, NY 14214-3087, **Business Phone:** (716)829-5458.

### TAYLOR, HERBERT CHARLES

Executive. **Personal:** Born Feb 2, 1948, Red Jacket, WV; children: Herbert Jr & Holly. **Educ:** Detroit Col Bus, BA, 1977; Cent Mich Univ, MA, 1981. **Career:** Gen Motor Corp, purchasing mgr, 1966-84; Bing Steel Inc, exec vpres, 1984-85; Superb Mfg Inc, pres. **Orgs:** Nat Black MBA Asn, 1985-; bd mem, Nat Asn Black Auto Suppliers, 1986-. **Home Addr:** 24520 Oneida Blvd, Oak Park, MI 48237, **Home Phone:** (313)933-6088. **Business Addr:** President, Superb Manufacturing Inc, 6100 15 Mile Rd, Sterling Heights, MI 48312, **Business Phone:** (313)268-2640.

### TAYLOR, HOWARD FRANCIS

Educator, association executive. **Personal:** Born Jul 7, 1939, Cleveland, OH; married Patricia A Epps. **Educ:** Hiram Col, AB, 1961; Yale Univ, MA, 1964; Yale Univ, PhD, 1966. **Career:** Ill Inst Tech, 1966-68; Nat Acad Sci, consult; Syracuse Univ, 1968-73; Princeton Univ, African Am Studies Prog, chair, 1973-88, Dept Sociol, prof, prof emer, currently. **Orgs:** NAAS; Am Sociol Asn; pres, E Sociol Soc; Am Asn Univ Profs; Asn Black Sociol. **Honors/Awds:** Various grants; published two books; numerous articles; Du Bois-Johnson-Fraizer Award, Am Sociol Asn, 1998; President's Award, Princeton Univ, 2000. **Special Achievements:** Books: "The IQ Game: A Methodological Inquiry into the Heredity Environment Controversy", 1980; "Sociology: Understanding A Diverse Society", First Edition, 2000, Second Edition, 2002, Third Edition, 2004. **Home Addr:** 165 Bull Run Rd, Pennington, NJ 08534-1248, **Home Phone:** (609)737-0980. **Business Addr:** Professor Emeritus of Sociology, Princeton University, Rm 21 201 Nassau, Princeton, NJ 08544, **Business Phone:** (609)258-4547.

### TAYLOR, IRIS

Journalist. **Personal:** Born Powhatan, VA; children: Tamarra & Christian. **Educ:** Rutgers Univ, Livingston Col, BA, jour, 1983; Columbia Univ, Sch Gen Studies, eng, 1980. **Career:** Essence Mag, New York, NY, contrib writer, 1974-86; Working Woman; Black Enterprise mag; Johnson & Johnson, Chicopee Div, ed; Horizons Mag, 1980-83; Star-Ledger, Newark, NJ, bus reporter, 1983-98; syndicated columnist, 1998-2000; Richmond Times Dispatch, bus & consumer columnist, 2000-. **Orgs:** Nat Asn Black Journalists, 1989-. **Honors/Awds:** Journalism Award, Lincoln Univ, 1979; Outstanding Journalism Award, White House Conf Small Bus, Minority Delegates Caucus, 1988; Small Bus Media Advocate of the Year, State NJ, US Small Bus Admin, 1989; Distinguished Service Award, NJ Press Women, 1989; Journalism Award, NJ Chap, Soc Prof Journalists, 1994; The Roses Scroll Woman of Achievement Award, NJ Asn Women Business Owners Inc, 1994; Salute to Women Leaders Award, NJ Asn of Women Business Owners, 1995. **Business Addr:** Consumer Columnist, Richmond Times-Dispatch, PO Box 85333, Richmond, VA 23293, **Business Phone:** (804)649-6349.

### TAYLOR, DR. JACK ALVIN

Educator, school administrator. **Personal:** Born Jul 15, 1949, Pittsburgh, PA; son of Jack and Jean; married Janet Victoria Bivins; children: Marcus, Matthew & Jack III. **Educ:** Calif Univ Pa, BA, psychol, 1971, MEd, elem guid, 1975; Bowling Green State Univ, PhD, 1985. **Career:** Calif Univ Penn, dir coun & spec serv, 1972-75; Frostburg State Col, asst dir minority affairs, 1975-78; Bowling Green State Univ, stud develop & spec serv, 1978-85, asst vpres multicultural affairs, 1985-95, asst vpres stud affairs, 1995, interim asst dir, Athletics Acad Advising, assoc prof emer ethnic studies, currently. **Orgs:** PA Intercollegiate Athletic Asn Championship Team, 1970; Consult Minority Affairs; Consult Educ Develop Progs; Nat Asn Stud Personnel Adminr; Kappa Alpha Psi Fraternity Inc; Wood County Pub Defenders Comn; Carter Pk Exec Bd. **Home Addr:** 16201 Haskins Rd, Bowling Green, OH 43402. **Business Addr:** Interim Assistant Director, Associate Professor Emeritus, Bowling Green State University, 132 Shatzel Hall, Bowling Green, OH 43403-0001, **Business Phone:** (419)372-9627.

### TAYLOR, HON. JANICE A.

Lawyer, president (organization), judge. **Personal:** Born May 23, 1954, Brooklyn, NY; daughter of Walter Earl and Avis Griffin. **Educ:** Col William & Mary, Williamsburg, Va, BA, Eng & polit sci, 1975; State Univ NY, Buffalo Sch Law, JD, 1978. **Career:** NY City Transit Authority, atty, 1978-81, assoc atty, 1981-86; Dist Coun 37 AFSCME AFL-CIO, asst gen coun, 1986-87; Civil Ct City NY, small claims arbitrator, 1987; Law Off Janice A. Taylor, atty, 1987-94; Supreme Ct, Appellate Div, referee, 1988-94; Queens County, legal counsel, 1990-92, Civil Ct, judge, 1995-97, Supreme Ct, judge, 1998-.; Staten Island Rapid Transit Oper Authority, secy; St John's Univ Col Bus Admin, adj assoc prof law, 1994. **Orgs:** Parliamentarian, Delta Sigma Theta Sorority, Inc, Queens Alumnae Chap, 1982; legal redress chairperson, Nat Asn Advan Colored People, Jamaica Br, 1983-85, 1987-88; regional coun mem, Nat Bar Asn, 1983-87; deaconette, Concord Baptist Church Christ, 1984-; bd mem, Black Women Transit, 1985-86; pres, Macon B Allen Black Bar Asn, 1985-88; secy, Network Bar Leaders, 1986-89; Guy R Brewer United Dem Club, 1989-94; Legal coun, Concerned Citizens S Queens, 1990-92; secy & bd mem, Jamaica Serv Prog Older Adults, 1990-94; Queens County Women's Bar Asn, 1991-95; United Progress Dem Club, 1992-94; officer, Black Law Stud Asn; anti-bias rep, Off Ct Admin; Asn Black Women Attorneys; NYS Bar Found; bd trustee, pres & chair, bd dir, Macon B. Allen Black Bar Asn, currently; Pemphigoid Found; secy, Network Bar Leaders; vpres, Bd Asn Civil Ct Judges NY, currently; deaconess, Links Inc. **Special Achievements:** Second African American Female to be elected to the Civil Court in Queens County; First Female Referee in Conservatorship in Queens County. **Home Addr:** 111 26 198th St, Jamaica, NY 11412, **Home Phone:** (718)523-6753. **Business Addr:** Judge, Queens County Supreme Court, 88 11 Sutphin Blvd, Jamaica, NY 11435, **Business Phone:** (718)298-1194.

### TAYLOR, JASON PAUL

Football player. **Personal:** Born Sep 1, 1974, Pittsburgh, PA; married Katina Thomas; children: Isaiah Paul, Mason Paul & Zoey Grace. **Educ:** Univ Akron. **Career:** Football player (retired); Miami Dolphins, right defensive end, 1997-98, defensive end, 1999-2007, linebacker, 2009, defensive end & linebacker, 2011; Wash Redskins, defensive end & linebacker, 2008; New York Jets, linebacker & tackle, 2010-11. **Orgs:** Miami Proj Cure Paralysis; Cystic Fibrosis Found; Dan Marino Found; founder, Jason Taylor Found, 2004-. **Honors/Awds:** All-MAC, 1995-96; NFL Alumni Pass Rusher of the Year, 2000; Honorable mention All-American, 1996; Pro Bowl selection, 2000, 2002, 2004-07; NFL All-Decade Team, 2000; AFC Defensive Player of the Year, 2002, 2006; AFC Defensive Player of the Week, 2003; Dan Marino Most Valuable Player Award, 2004; NFL Alumni Defensive Lineman Player of the Year, 2005-06; Defensive Player of the Year, Nat Football League, 2006; PFWA Defensive Player of the Year, 2006; Walter Payton Man of the Year Award, 2007; 100 Sacks Club; NFL Time Leader; Miami Dolphin Newcomer of the Year; Pro Football All Rookie-Team. **Special Achievements:** TV Series: "Pardon the Interruption", 2001; "Dancing with the Stars", 2005; "Jackass Number Two", 2006; "Holby City", 2006; "Ballers", 2016. Ten Sexiest Athletes, Sports Illustrated, 2001. **Business Addr:** Defensive End, Miami Dolphins, 7500 SW 30 St, Davie, FL 33314, **Business Phone:** (954)452-7100.

### TAYLOR, JEANINE Y. COOPER

Chief executive officer, public relations executive, president (organization). **Personal:** Born Washington, DC. **Educ:** Hampton Univ, BA, mass media, 1991; Univ DC, MBA, mkt, 1994; N Western Univ, IAMC. **Career:** Jeanine Cooper Entertainment & Commun, pres & chief exec officer, pub rels, currently; Jenesse Ctr Inc, pub rels rep. **Orgs:** Pub Rels Soc Am. **Business Addr:** President, Chief Executive Officer, JCEC Public Relations, 5482 Wilshire Blvd Suite 1541, Los Angeles, CA 90036, **Business Phone:** (213)399-5301.

### TAYLOR, ATTY. JEFFERY CHARLES

Lawyer. **Personal:** Born Nov 15, 1957, Staten Island, NY; son of Robert D and Pauline D. **Educ:** Pace Univ, BS, cum laude, 1984; Hofstra Univ, Sch Law, JD, 1988. **Career:** Community Legal Servs Corp, intern, 1987-88; Paralegal Support Servs Inc, legal asst, 1988-89; Am Civil Liberties Union, law clerk, 1989-90; MD Legal Aid Bur Inc, staff, atty, 1990-. **Orgs:** Mar Prison Renewal Comt, 1991; Proj Raise Mar, 1991-; Proj 2000 Mar, 1992-93; fin dir, Renaissance Econ Develop Proj Pk Heights Inc, 1993. **Home Addr:** 2912 W Coldspring Lane Suite C, Baltimore, MD 21215, **Home Phone:** (410)664-1563. **Business Addr:** Attorney, Legal Aid Bureau Inc, 500 E Lexington St, Baltimore, MD 21202-3559, **Business Phone:** (410)539-5340.

### TAYLOR, DR. JEROME

Educator, executive director. **Personal:** Born Jan 26, 1940, Waukegan, IL; son of George Washington and Willie Mae; married Tommie Nell; children: Kim, Lisa, Jacques & Zwehla. **Educ:** Univ Denver, BA, 1961; Ind Univ, PhD, clin psychol, 1965. **Career:** Menninger Found, fel, 1965-67; Ment Health Unit Topeka, dir, 1968-69; Univ Pittsburgh, Clin Psychol Ctr, dir, 1969-71, Psychol Educ, Sch Educ & African Studies, chair & assoc prof, currently, dir, Inst Black Family, currently; Ctr Family Excellence, exec dir, currently; Allegheny County, exec dir, pres & founder. **Orgs:** Am Psychol Soc; Asn Black Psychologists; Omicron Delta Kappa; Sigma Xi; Psi Chi; Nat Black Child Develop Inst; Nat Coun Family Rel; convener, Racial Justice Comt. **Honors/Awds:** Chancellor's Distinguished Public Service Award, Univ Pittsburgh; Black Alumni Pioneer in Civil Rights Award, Univ Pittsburgh; Kujichagulia Award, Sankofa Inst Pittsburgh; Distinguished Research Award, Int Asn Black Psychologists; Norman Dixon Award; Listed in Whos Who in Black America & Whos Who in American Education; Alfred W. Wishart Jr. Award, Ctr Family Excellence Inc. **Special Achievements:** Publications namely: Achievement gap between black and white students: Theoretical analysis with recommendations for remedy, 2003; Achieving excellence in urban schools: pitfalls, pratfalls, and evolving opportunities, 2005. **Business Addr:** Associate Professor, Chair, University of Pittsburgh, 4148 Wesley W Posvar Hall 230 S Bouquet St, Pittsburgh, PA 15260, **Business Phone:** (412)648-7540.

### TAYLOR, JOHN L.

Educator. **Personal:** Born May 7, 1947, Holly Springs, MS; son of Charlie E Sr and Cinderella Sims; married Naomi Ruth Thomas; children: Tony, Jonathan & Chere. **Educ:** Rust Col, BS, 1969; Univ Miss. **Career:** Educator, coach(retired); Marshall Co Dist 4, elected offical & election comnr; Independence High Sch, teacher, asst prin, coach, 2008; Northwest Community Col, Gen Educ Dipl Instr; Independent Ability-to-Benefit Tester. **Orgs:** Deacon & clerk, Baptist Church; mason, Waterford Lodge No 450; sunday sch eacher, Mt Moriah Baptist Church; deacon, clerk & adult sunday sch teacher, Chulahoma Missionary Baptist Church. **Honors/Awds:** Teacher of the Day, Radio Sta, 1984; Acad Career Day, Univ Miss, 1985; Achievement Award. **Home Addr:** 608 N Mullins Rd, PO Box 107, Byhalia, MS 38611-8716, **Home Phone:** (662)564-2189. **Business Addr:** Assistant Principal, Tate County School System, Independence High School, Independence, MS 38638, **Business Phone:** (662)233-9966.

### TAYLOR, JOHNNY ANTONIO

Basketball player. **Personal:** Born Jun 4, 1974, Chattanooga, TN; married Latwoin; children: Sherria, Jori, Jiselle & Johnny Jr. **Educ:** Univ Tenn, Chattanooga, attended 1997. **Career:** Orlando Magic, forward, 1997-98; Denver Nuggets, forward, 1999-2000; Toronto Raptors, forward, 2000; Chicago Bulls, forward, 2000; Adecco Milano, 2000-01; Portland Trail Blazers, forward, 2001; Philadelphia 76ers, forward, 2002; Santa Lucia Realty, 2002; Roanoke Dazzle, forward, 2002; Detroit Pistons, forward, 2003; Etosa Alicante, forward, 2005; Dexia Mons Hainaut, belg, 2006-07; Mitsubishi Diamond Dolphins, 2007-08; Al-Ahli, Bahrain, 2008-10, 2012; Al-Ahli, United Arab Emirates, 2010-11; Chattanooga Mocs Men's Basketball, stud asst, 2013-14.

### TAYLOR, JOHNNY C., JR.

Lawyer, executive director, association executive. **Personal:** Born Jun 20, 1968, Ft. Lauderdale, FL; son of Johnny C Sr and Deborah Mizell; married Charlotte Smith; children: 1. **Educ:** Univ Miami, BS, commun, 1989; Drake Univ, MA, mass commun, 1991; Drake Law Sch, JD, 1992. **Career:** Steel Hector & Davis, lawyer, 1992-93; Blockbuster Entertainment Corp, assoc gen coun, 1993-96, vp human resources, 1996-97; Alamo Rent-A-Car Inc, vp legal affairs, 1997-98; Compass Group USA Inc, Charlotte, NC, exec vpres, gen coun & secy, 2002-04; Paramont Parks & VIACOM, gen coun & sr vpres, human resources; McGuireWoods HR Strategies LLC, pres & sr consult; LendingTree.com, sr vpres human resources; InterActiveCorp, sr vpres human resources, 2005-07; RushmoreDrive.com, pres, chief exec officer, 2007-09; Thurgood Marshall Col Fund, pres & chief exec officer, 2010-. **Orgs:** Amr Corp Coun Asn, 1994-; bd counrs, Drake Law Sch, 1994-99; pres, Broward County Urban League, 1995-98; pres coun, Univ Miami, 1997-; bd mem, Urban League Cent Carolinas, 1998-99; bd mem, Dell Curry Found, 2000-; bd dir, Soc Human Resource Mgt, 2000-, chair; mem bd dir, YMCA; Kappa Alpha Psi Fraternity Inc. **Honors/Awds:** Young Alumni Award; Orange Award, Univ Miami, 1994; Price Waterhouse; Up & Comers Award, 1996; Achiever Award, Am Family Asn, JM Family & Southeast Toyota, 1998. **Special Achievements:** Author: "The Trouble with HR: An Insider's Guide to Finding and Keeping the Best People", 2009. **Home Addr:** 15600 Woodland Ridge Lane, Charlotte, NC 28278, **Home Phone:** (704)504-3773. **Business Addr:** President, Chief Executive Officer, Thurgood Marshall College Fund, 901 F St NW Suite 300, Washington, DC 20004, **Business Phone:** (202)507-4851.

### TAYLOR, JOSEPH (JOE TAYLOR)

Athletic coach, executive, football coach. **Personal:** Born May 7, 1950, Washington, DC; son of Choncie and Elnorma M; married Beverly Richardson; children: Aaron Joseph & Dennis Anthony. **Educ:** Western Ill Univ, BS, phys educ & health, 1972; Eastern Ill Univ, MS, educ admin, 1979. **Career:** Football coach (retired), coach, executive; Coach Joe Taylor, author, coach, motivational speaker, 1972-; HDC Sch, phys educ instr; Howard D Woodson High Sch, asst football coach, 1972-77; Eastern Ill Univ, offensive line coach, 1978-79; Va Union Univ, offensive coordr, 1980-81; Howard Univ, defensive coordr, 1982; Howard Univ, head football coach, 1983; Va Union, head coach, 1984-91; Hampton Univ, head football coach, 1992-2007; Fla A&M Univ, head football coach, 2008-12. **Orgs:** Kappa Alpha Psi Fraternity, 1971-; bd trustee & vpres, Am Football Coaches Asn, 1978-; adv bd, Wilson Sporting Goods, 1994-; football exec bd, vpres, Div 1-AA, 1997-; Citizens Unity Comn, 1998-; Black Coaches Asn; adv bd, Am Football Quarterly, 1997-; pres, Am Football Coaches Asn; bd dir, Am Football Coaches Found. **Honors/Awds:** Coach of the Year, Sports Club Wash, DC, Richmond, Va, Norfolk, Va, Atlanta, Ga, 1986, 1988, 1992-94, 1997-98; American Football Coach of the Year, 1986, 1992-94, 1997-98; CIAA Coach of the Year, 1986, 1992-94; HBCU Nat Champship, 1994, 1997; SBN Coach of the Year, 1994, 1997; MEAC Coach of the Year, 1997-98, 2004-06, 2010; Eddie Robinson Coach of Distinction Award; Johnny Vaught Lifetime Achievement Award, Am Football Found, 2000; Western Illinois University Hall of Fame, 2001. **Special Achievements:** Published articles on professional development in American Football Quarterly, 1994, AFCA summer manual, 1995; elected to Citizens Unity Commission, City of Hampton, 1998, The Making of a Champion-Success Is An Inconvenience, author. **Home Addr:** 427 E Queen St, Hampton, VA 23669, **Home Phone:** (757)723-3483. **Business Addr:** Head Football Coach, Division of Continuing Education, 635 Gamble St, Tallahassee, FL 32307.

### TAYLOR, KARIN KATHERINE

Entrepreneur, fashion model, interior designer. **Personal:** Born Nov 28, 1971, Kingston; married Bill Weinberg; children: 3. **Career:** Orlando water park Wet N'Wild, lifeguard; Walt Disney's Elec Light Parade, dancer; Ford Modeling Agency, model; Michele Pommier, Miami, Fla, model; Wilhelmenia, New York, model; David & Lee, Chicago, Ill, model; Agence Unique, Greece, model; ICE, Cape Town, Safrica, model; Miss June, Playboy, 1996; actress, appeared in Baywatch, Malcolm & Eddie & The Weird Al Show; host/spokesmodel, Keenen Ivory Wayans Show; Horace Brown's music video; Things we do for loveE! Gossip show & Playboy TV; Style House, Haverford, Pa, owner, interior designer & event planner, 2000-. **Orgs:** Spokeswoman, Pet Owners with AIDS Resource Service; supporter, AIDS Projects, Los Angeles. **Special Achievements:** The First African-American actress to don the infamous red Baywatch. **Business Addr:** Owner, Style House, 20 Haverford Sta Rd, Haverford, PA 19041-1507, **Business Phone:** (610)254-0902.

### TAYLOR, DR. KENNETH DOYLE

Engineer, scientist. **Personal:** Born Nov 5, 1949, Hartford, CT; son of Frank K and Adelaide P Tweedy Jordan; married Mattie Jane Dolphy; children: Jerome Daniel. **Educ:** Univ Conn, BS, elec engineering, 1971, MS, biomed engineering, 1974, PhD, biomed engineering, 1981; Rensselaer Polytech Inst, Hartford CT, MBA, technol mgt, 1988. **Career:** Picker Corp, design engr, 1973-74; St Francis Hosp & Med Ctr, mgr res lab, 1974-79; Univ CT, Dept Elec Engr, lectr, 1977-83; Hartford Grad Ctr, adj lect, 1982-; Nat Inst Health, asst dir, 1985-86; United Technol Res Ctr, sr proj engr, 1979-90; Pfizer Hosp Prods Group, dir, tech assessment, 1990-93; Valleylab, vpres res & develop, 1993-98; Medlogic Global Corp, vpres prod develop, 1998-99; Taylor Med Technol & Consult Inc, pres, 1999-; CO MEDtech Inc, Colo Opers, pres, 2000-02; ConMed Electrosurgery, vpres, res & develop, 2004-15; United Technologies Res Ctr, staff; Nat Heart, Lung & Blood Inst, staff. **Orgs:** Chmn & treas, Family Fed Credit Union, 1978-80, 1983-85; sr mem, Inst Elec & Electronics Engineering, 1983-; vpres Beta Sigma Lambda, Alpha Phi Alpha Frat, 1983-85; Sigma Pi Phi Fratm, 1984-; bd dir, Conn Pre-Engineering Prog, 1989-91; bd dir, Channel 3 Country Camp, 1989-91; treas, Hist Denver Inc, 1999-; treas, Beckworth Mountain Club, 1999; Am Col clin Engr, 1995-; Assoc Advan Med Instrumentation, 1993-; Sigma Xi; Tau Beta Pi; Delta Eta Boule; Sigma Pi Phi Fraternity; Alpha Phi Alpha Fraternity; Asn Advan Med Instrumentation; Am Col Clin Engineering; Inst Elec & Electronics Engrs; Alpha Phi Alpha Fraternity Inc, Delta Psi Lambda Chap; George E. Hailey Scholar Endowment Fund; Rose Biomed Found. **Honors/Awds:** United Technologies Award, 1981; Distinguished Gradugate Award, Univ Conn, 1982; AIAA Contribution to Society Award, 1985; President's Commn on Exec Exchange Class XVI, 1985-86; Registered Professional Engineer, State Connecticut, 1977. **Home Addr:** 375 Golden Eagle Dr, Broomfield, CO 80020, **Home Phone:** (303)460-7416. **Business Addr:** President, Taylor Medical Technology & Consulting Inc, 375 Golden Eagle Dr, Broomfield, CO 80020, **Business Phone:** (303)466-8718.

### TAYLOR, KENNETH MATTHEW

Auditor. **Personal:** Born Jersey City, NJ. **Educ:** BS; MBA. **Career:** Witco Chem Corp, sr auditor & financial analyst; Allied Chem Corp, sr auditor; Colgate-Palmolive Corp, sr acct; Philip Morris Inc, sr analyst & auditor; Bache & Co Inc, sr brokerage acct; Omega Psi Phi Fraternity Inc, dist auditor, currently; Omega Credit Union, founder. **Orgs:** Am Mgt Asn; Ins Internal Auditors; Nat Asn Black Acct; Nat Asn Acct NJ Chpt; Omega Psi Phi Fraternity Inc; chmn, 2nd Dist Budget & Finance Com Newark, 1972-74; Nat Budget & Financo Com, 1973-74; keeper finance, Upsilon Phi Chap, 1970-74; bd dir, Omega

Psi Phi Fraternity Fed Credit Union. **Honors/Awds:** Distinguished Award Chmn Finance Com, 1974. **Home Addr:** 811 Carnegie St, Linden, NJ 07036. **Business Addr:** District Auditor, The Omega Psi Phi Fraternity Inc, 3951 Snapfinger Pkwy, Decatur, GA 30035, **Business Phone:** (404)284-5533.

### TAYLOR, KIMBERLY HAYES

Journalist. **Personal:** Born Jul 9, 1962, Louisville, KY; daughter of James E Hayes and Loraine S Hayes; married Keith L. **Educ:** Morehead State Univ, Morehead, KY, BA, commun, 1984. **Career:** Courier-J, Louisville, Ky, clerk/writer, 1986-88; Com-News, Danville, Ill, police reporter, 1987-88; Observer-Dispatch, Utica, NY, ct criminal justice reporter, 1988; Peace Our Minds, W Edmeston, NY, ed chief, 1990; Hartford (CT) Courant, reporter; USA Today, reporter; Star Tribune, reporter, 1993-; Detroit News, health & features writer, currently; fruition factory, founder & chief exec officer. **Orgs:** Nat Asn Black Journalists, 1986-; dist comt, Boy Scouts Am, 1989-; exec bd mem, Young & Teen Peacemakers Inc, 1990-; exec bd, Oneida Co Chap Nat Asn Advan Colored People, 1990-; Greater Utica Multiculturalism Coalition, 1990-. **Honors/Awds:** Top Well Done Award for "Street Under Siege" series, Gannett Inc, 1991. **Special Achievements:** Books: "Black Civil Rights Champions"; "Black Abolitionists", "Freedom Fighters" and "Fish Lips". **Home Addr:** 15 Noyes St, Utica, NY 13502, **Home Phone:** (315)733-2639. **Business Addr:** Reporter, Star Tribune, 425 Portland Ave, Minneapolis, MN 55488, **Business Phone:** (612)673-4000.

### TAYLOR, LAWRENCE JULIUS

Actor, football player. **Personal:** Born Feb 4, 1959, Williamsburg, VA; son of Clarence and Iris; married Deborah Belinda, Jan 1, 1981, (divorced 1996); children: 3; married Maritza Cruz, Nov 28, 2000, (divorced 2005); children: Lawrence Jr; married Lynette, Jan 1, 2007. **Educ:** Univ NC. **Career:** Football player (retired), actor; New York Giants, linebacker & right outside linebacker & left inside linebacker, 1981-93; Films: Water boy, 1998; Any Given Sunday, 1999; Shaft, 2000; Mercy Streets, 2000; Savage, 2003; In Hell, 2003; The Comebacks, 2007. TV series: "1st & Ten: The Championship", 1988-91; "Sweating Bullets", 1992-93; "Arli$$", 2000; "Body & Soul", 2002. **Honors/Awds:** All-Am, NC; Atlantic Coast Conf Player of the Year, 1980; Defensive Rookie of the Year, NFL, 1981; Defensive Player of the Year, NFL, 1981-82; Defensive Player of the Year, NFC, 1983 & 1986; NFL Most Valuable Player, 1986; Bert Bell Award, 1986; played in East-West Shrine Game and Japan Bowl; unanimous All-NFL selection for 3yrs; top linebacker in NFL, NFL PA for 3 yrs; 2 time defensive MVP, Asniated Press; Seagram's Computer Awards Prog; Pro Bowl, 1981-1990; NFL Hall of Fame, inducted, 1999. **Special Achievements:** Author: Living on the Edge, 1987; Over the Edge, 2004.

### TAYLOR, LINDA SUZANNA. See TAYLOR, MARIE DE PORRES, SR.

### TAYLOR, LORENZO JAMES, JR.

School administrator. **Personal:** Born Sep 1, 1925, Detroit, MI; son of Lorenzo Sr and Rosa Ephriam; children: James, Lamar, Ronnie, Amino Mohamed, Denise & Paul Dallas (deceased). **Educ:** Wayne State Univ, attended 1967. **Career:** School administrator (retired); Detroit Bd Educ, transp mgr-Regional; Mich Liquor Comn. **Orgs:** Dexter Ave Baptist Church; Metro Detroit Sr Dance Group; founding mem, Arts Extended Gallery Inc. **Home Addr:** 2323 Waverly St, Detroit, MI 48238-3558, **Home Phone:** (313)883-3769.

### TAYLOR, MARIE DE PORRES, SR. (LINDA SUZANNA TAYLOR)

Association executive, nun, government official. **Personal:** Born May 27, 1947, Los Angeles, CA; daughter of James Sam and Isabel McCoy Clarke. **Educ:** Marylhurst Col, Marylhurst, OR, BA, 1970; Calif State Univ, San Francisco, CA, MA, 1976; Pac Lutheran Sem, Berkeley, CA, 1982; Calif State Univ, Hayward, CA, attended 1986. **Career:** Holy Names High Sch, Oakland, Calif, chair home econs dept, 1970-79; St Benedict Church, Oakland, Calif, assoc pastor, 1979-83; Roman Cath Bishop, Oakland, Calif, dir Black Catholics, 1982-89; Marquette Univ, Nat Black Sisters Conf, Oakland, Calif, exec dir, 1982-; Oakland Pvt Indust Coun, Oakland, Calif, prog coordr, 1989-91; City Oakland, asst mayor, job training & employ. **Orgs:** Chmn & bd dir, Bay Area Black United Fund; pres & bd dir, Oakland Citizens Comt Urban Renewal; pres, United E Oakland Clergy; bd dir, Holy Names Col; vice chmn & bd dir, Oakland Police Activ League; Mayor's Comt Homeless; bd mem, Patrons Arts & Humanities, 1990-; chmn, Patrons Arts & Humanities, 1993-; Mary'sPence; Bd Voc Nursing & Psychiat Technician; bd mem, Alameda County; pres, Bd Voc Nursing & Psychiat Technicians; bd dir, Occur. **Home Addr:** 5022 Camden St, Oakland, CA 94619, **Home Phone:** (510)261-7672. **Business Addr:** Executive Director, Marquette University, Office of Administration, 707 N 11th St Rm 422, Milwaukee, WI 53201-1881, **Business Phone:** (414)288-1463.

### TAYLOR, REV. DR. MARTHA C.

Police officer, clergy. **Personal:** Born Jul 26, 1941, Shreveport, LA; daughter of Henry and Viola Harris; married Royal Odell; children: Valerie L Thompson & Debra L Benton. **Educ:** Univ Calif, Berkeley, cert, human resources & training; Merritt Col, Oakland, CA, AA, 1977; Univ San Francisco, BS, orgn behav; Univ San Francisco, BA, 1979, MPA, 1981; Am Baptist Sem W, Masters Divinity; San Francisco Theol Sem, Doctorate Ministry. **Career:** Police officer (retired), clergy; Bay Area Rapid Transit Dist, Oakland, Calif, police officer, 1973-77, police sergeant, 1977-81, police lt, 1981-83, support & anal mgr, 1983-90, dept mgr, sta opers, 1990-92, asst chief transp officer, 1992-2000; Bethel Missionary Baptist Church, bible instr, 1987-; ordained minister; Allen Temple Baptist Church, adminr, asst to pastor; Allen Temple Leadership Training Inst, adj fac mem; San Francisco Theol Sem, adj prof. **Orgs:** Pres, Black Managers & Professionals Asn, 1981-; Conf Minority Transit Officials, 1985-; mem bd dir, E Oakland Youth Develop Ctr, CA, 1986-87; vpres, Nat Forum Black Pub Adminr, Oakland chap, CA, 1986-88; mem exec bd, Black Women Organized Polit Action, 1986-; Youth Mentor Prog, Oakland Pub Schs, CA, 1986-; chair comt training, Women Transit Am Pub Transit Asn, 1987-; Nat Negro Coun Women; owner, Ministry Christian Training; facilitator & trainer, Bd Christian Educ & Publ, Progressive Nat Baptist Conv; Delta Sigma Theta Sorority; Nat Asn Adv Coloured People; Women's Ministry 5th Episcopal Dist. **Honors/Awds:** MDiv, Am Baptist Sem W, Berkeley, Calif; DMin, San Francisco Theol Sem; Certificate of Recognition, Am Pub Transit Asn, Western Conf, 1985; Certificate for Outstanding Contributions, Am Pub Transit Asn, 1987; Meritorious Award, Nat Forum Black Public Adminr, 1991; Christian Woman of the Year, Hon Mayor Heather Fargo, Sacramento, Calif, 2006. **Special Achievements:** Author: The Challenge of Climbing the Organizational Ladder: A Matter Of Perspective, California Law Enforcement Association Police Recorder, 1988; First woman to Assistant Chief Transportation Officer, Department Head for all BART Stations, Police Lieutenant, Manager, Support & Analysis, where her budget was over $69 million dollars annually. **Home Addr:** 444 28th St Apt 11, Oakland, CA 94609-3617, **Home Phone:** (510)986-1348. **Business Addr:** Assistant to the Pastor, Administrator, Allen Temple Baptist Church, 8501 Int Blvd, Oakland, CA 94521, **Business Phone:** (510)544-8910.

### TAYLOR, MARY QUIVERS

School administrator. **Personal:** Born Mobile, AL; daughter of Stephen Quivers and Elizabeth; children: Roderick Maurice & Pamela Bonita. **Educ:** Univ Ala; Univ W Fla, BA, 1973; Univ S Ala, MEd, 1977. **Career:** Bishop State Community Col, coord & counr, 1985-92, admis counr, 1992-. **Orgs:** Vpres, Mobile Asn Black Social Workers, 1980-85, 1997-; Ala Couns Asn, 1993; City Mobile, Keep Mobile Beautiful Exec Bd, 1993; Southern Asn Admis Counrs, 1995-; Nat Asn Black Social Workers, 1997-; Stone Street Baptist Church. **Home Addr:** 1452 Basil St, Mobile, AL 36603, **Home Phone:** (251)432-5197. **Business Addr:** Admission Counselor, Bishop State Community College, 414 Stanton St, Mobile, AL 36617-2399, **Business Phone:** (251)662-5400.

### TAYLOR, MAURICE DE SHAWN

Basketball player. **Personal:** Born Oct 30, 1976, Detroit, MI. **Educ:** Univ Mich, attended 1997. **Career:** Basketball player (retired); Los Angeles Clippers, forward, 1997-2000; Houston Rockets, 2000-05; New York Knicks, 2005-06; Sacramento Kings, 2006-07; Olimpia Milano, 2009; Shanxi Zhongyu, 2009-10; Benetton Treviso, 2010; Enel Brindisi, 2011.

### TAYLOR, MICHAEL LOEB

Educator, arts administrator, painter (artist). **Personal:** Born Jan 11, 1947, Houston, TX; children: Christopher Kirrinkai Parrish & Jennifer Nichol Parrish. **Educ:** Univ Calif, Los Angeles, BA, 1970, MA, 1972, MFA, 1974. **Career:** Univ Nairobi, Kenya, lectr, 1972-73, 1975-77; Western KY Univ, asst prof, 1977-81; Exhibition: Pulliam Deffenbaugh Gallery, Portland; Lewis & Clark Col, assoc prof, assoc prof emer, currently. **Orgs:** Design consult, African Heritage Ltd, 1972-73, 1975-77; Mems Gallery, 1982-83; artist, Blackfish Gallery, 1984; Comn Wash State Arts Comn, 1989. **Business Addr:** Associate Professor Emeritus of Art, Lewis & Clark College, 0615 SW Palatine Hill Rd, Portland, OR 97219, **Business Phone:** (503)768-7000.

### TAYLOR, MILDRED D.

Writer. **Personal:** Born Sep 13, 1943, Jackson, MS; daughter of Wilbert Lee and Deletha Marie; married Errol Zea Daly. **Educ:** Univ Toledo, BA, 1965; Univ Colo Sch Jour, MBA. **Career:** Peace Corps, Ethiopia, taught Eng & hist, recruiter in the US, 1967-68, instr maine, 1968; Univ Colo, organizer black studies prog & study skills coordr; Novels: Song of the Trees, Dial, 1975; Roll of Thunder, Hear My Cry, Dial, 1976; Let the Circle Be Unbroken, Dial, 1981; The Gold Cadillac, 1987; The Friendship, 1987; Mississippi Bridge, 1990; The Road to Memphis, 1990; The Well, 1995; The Land, 2001; Logan, 2004. **Orgs:** Univ Colo, Black Students Alumni Grp. **Honors/Awds:** Award from the Council on Interracial Books for Children, 1975; New York Times Outstanding Book Award, 1975; Children's Book Showcase Award, 1976; Newbery Award, 1977; Horn Book Honor Award from Boston Globe; Coretta Scott King Award; Am Library Asn, honors, 1981; Coretta Scott King Award for Let the Circle Be Unbroken, 1982; Coretta Scott King Award for The Friendship, 1988; Christopher Award for The Gold Cadillac, 1988; Coretta Scott King Award for The Road to Memphis, 1990; Nat Coun Teachers Eng, ALAN Award for Significant Contribution to Young Adult Lit, 1997; Jason Award for The Well, 1997; Newbery Medal winner; Coretta Scott King Award for The Land, 2002. **Business Addr:** Author, c/o Dial Books, 2 Pk Ave, New York, NY 10016.

### TAYLOR, MILDRED E. CROSBY

Labor relations manager. **Personal:** Born Dec 18, 1919, Centralia, IL; married David P. **Educ:** LaSalle Ext Univ, attended 1941; US Dept Agr Grad Sch, cert; Exec Inst, exec develop training; US Dept Labor, leadership devel courses; Cath Univ, Wash, DC. **Career:** Women's Bur US Dept Labor, conv planner ret social sci advisor; Surgeon Gen's Off Dept Army, personnel asst; keynote speaker panelist moderator meetings & seminars. **Orgs:** Women's Bur liaison black women's orngs employ; Secy Labors Vol Day Com; bd dir, Dept Labor Recreation Asn; charter mem, Toast masters Int; vpres, Air & Cruise Travel Adminr, Wash, DC; charter mem, DC Women's Comn Crime Prev; charter mem, bd dir, Trinity AME Zion Ch Housing Corp; past pres, Century Club Nat Asn Negor Bus & Prof Women Inc; past loyal lady, ruler Order Golden Circle; past matron, Order Eastern Star; Urban League NAACP; past commandress, Mecca Ct Daughters; imp conv directness Imp Ct Daughters Isis; vol worker many charitable orgns. **Honors/Awds:** Recipient Outstanding Service Award, Prentiss Inst Hon Ky Col Gov Nunn, 1971; Distinguished Service Award, Mecca Temple Ancient Egyptian Arabic Order Nobles Mystic Shrine; Hon Dr Humanities, Ministerial InstCol W Point Miss, 1977.

### TAYLOR, MILES EDWARD

Technician, engineer, business owner. **Personal:** Born Apr 25, 1964, Nyack, NY; son of Aubrey and Lillian Murray. **Educ:** C W Post Col, Long Island Univ, Brookville, NY, BA, commun, 1986. **Career:** Fire Works Grucci, Brookhaven, NY, pyrotechnician, 1983-; Nyack High Sch, Nyack, NY, head cross country coach, 1987; Black Magic Video Prod, Nyack, NY, owner, 1987-; CNN New York, New York, NY, engr, 1987-; network video engr. **Orgs:** Vpres, Nyack Fire Dept, Jackson Fire Eng Co No 3, 1980; Tau Kappa Epsilon, 1983-. **Home Addr:** 54 Marion St, Nyack, NY 10960, **Home Phone:** (914)358-8769. **Business Addr:** Engineer, Control Room, CNN New York, 5 Penn Pl 22nd Fl, New York, NY 10001, **Business Phone:** (212)714-7858.

### TAYLOR, NATALIE MANNS

Manager, executive. **Personal:** Born Jul 14, 1959, Columbus, OH; daughter of Betty Manns Casey; married Timothy; children: Timothy Ryan. **Educ:** Radford Univ, Radford, VA, BS, bus mgt, 1982. **Career:** Food Lion Inc, cashier, 1982-83, customer serv mgr, 1983-84, asst mgr, 1984-85, store mgr, 1985-86, mgt develop admin, 1986-88, front end training supvr, 1988-91, employee develop supvr, 1991-93, dir community affairs, employ develop, 1993-95, dir diversity planning, 1995-97, Diversity, vpres, 1997-2003; Capture Commun Resource Group LLC, founder, owner & pres, 2004-. **Orgs:** Bd dir, Carolinas Minority Supplier Develop Coun, 1991; bd visitor, Livingstone Col Adv Bd, 1996-98; bd dir, Metrolina Minority Supplier Develop Coun, 1996-; co-chair & chair, Community Livingstone Col, 1996-98; Community Col Bus Admin Adv Bd, 1996-97; Nat Asn Female Exec, 1998-; bd dir, Winston-Salem Urban League, 1998-; Soc Human Resource Mgt, 1999-; chair, Equal Opportunity Day Gala Comm, 1999; Nat Asn Advan Colored People; United Negro Col Fund; Rowan Cabarrus; bd secy, Triangle Urban League; Network Exec Women. **Honors/Awds:** Positive Image Award, Minority Recruiter, 1992; Community Service Award, VA NAACP, Area II Branches, Martin Luther King, Jr. 1998; Black Achiever, Winston Lake Family YMCA, 1999. **Special Achievements:** Under her leadership in the Diversity area, Food Lion, Inc. has received: Natl Assn for the Advancement of Colored People, Fair Share Award, 1995, 1997; NC NAACP, Corp Supporter Award, 1996; The Charlotte Post, Corp of the Yr Award, 1998; Carolinas Minority Supplier Develop Coun, Inc., Corp of the Yr Award, 1999. **Home Addr:** 5202 Hayward Dr, Greensboro, NC 27407-8856, **Home Phone:** (336)218-8198. **Business Addr:** President, Founder, Capture Communications Resource Group, 2100 Fairfax Rd, Greensboro, NC 27407, **Business Phone:** (336)852-7500.

### TAYLOR, NORMAN EUGENE

Government official. **Personal:** Born Nov 12, 1948, Newark, NJ; son of Edwin Alfred and Martha Small; married Theresa LaVerne Singleton; children: Norman Assaf, Todd Farrell, Norman Amman, Joy Jamillah & Autier Dawn. **Educ:** Bethune-Cookman Col, Dayton Beach, FL, BA, social & polit sci, 1970; Fla Atlantic Univ, Boca Raton, FL, MPA, 1976; Univ Miami Sch Law, attended 1992. **Career:** October Ctr Inc, Ft Lauderdale FL, dir, 1973-80; Norman E Taylor & Assoc Inc, Miami FL, pres & chief exec officer, 1979-83, managing partner, founder, 2012-; Broward County Govt, Ft Lauderdale, Fla, pub rel mgr, 1983-84, OEO dir, 1984-96, Off Econ Develop, dir, 1996-12; Radio host, WRBD/WCKO/WMBM, 1978-82. **Orgs:** Omega Psi Phi Fraternity, 1967-; Minority Bus Affairs, dir, 1984; Broward Sr Exec, 1987-; Fla Asn Minority Bus Enterprise Officials, 1987-; chmn, Black Econ Develop, 1985-87; chair, Metro-Broward Capital, 1987-; Airport Minority Adv Coun, 1988-; Am Econ Develop Coun, 1996-; Urban Land IST, 1996-; Nat Forum Black Pub Adminr; Coun Black Econ Develop; bd mem, Greater Ft Lauderdale Alliance, 2000-12. **Home Addr:** 1966 SW 94th Ave, Miramar, FL 33025, **Home Phone:** (305)987-0911. **Business Addr:** Managing Partner, Founder, Norman E Taylor & Associates LLC, 2160 NW 72nd Way, Hollywood, FL 33024, **Business Phone:** (954)826-2827.

### TAYLOR, ORLANDO L.

Dean (education), president (organization), college administrator. **Personal:** Born Aug 9, 1936, Chattanooga, TN; son of Leroy and Carrie Lee Sanders; married Loretta M; children: Orlando II & Ingrid Boone. **Educ:** Hampton Inst, Hampton, VA, BS, 1957; Ind Univ, Bloomington, IN, MA, 1960; Univ Mich, Ann Arbor, MI, PhD, commun dis, 1966. **Career:** Ind Univ, Bloomington IN, fac mem, 1964-69; Ctr Appl Ling, Wash, DC, sr res fel, 1969-75; Univ DC, Wash, DC, prof, 1970-73; Stanford Univ, vis prof; Univ Pitts, adj prof; Carnegie Found Advan Teaching, vis scholar; Howard Univ, Wash, DC, prof commun, 1973, dean comun, 1985-, vice provost res, 2009; Chicago Sch Prof Psychol, pres, 2009-. **Business Addr:** President, The Chicago School of Professional Psychology, 901 15th St NW, Washington, DC 20005, **Business Phone:** (202)706-5052.

### TAYLOR, DR. PATRICIA E.

Lawyer, educator, manager. **Personal:** Born Feb 17, 1942, New Haven, CT; married Howard F; children: Carla Y. **Educ:** Ill Inst Tech, BS, 1967; Yale Law Sch, JD, 1971. **Career:** Commun Prog Inc, commun worker, 1963-65; Onondaga Legal Serv, law clerk, 1971-73; Princeton Univ, vis lectr, 1974-; Educ Testing Serv, asn gen coun, mgr. **Orgs:** Fel Reginald Herber Smith, 1971-73; NJ Bar Asn; US Supreme Ct Bar; assoc, Gen Coun Educ Testing Serv, Princeton, NJ; bd dir, ARC, 1972-73; bd dir, Allan Guttmacher Inst, 1986-89. **Honors/Awds:** Outstanding Young Women of America, 1974. **Home Addr:** 165 Bull Run Rd, Trenton, NJ 08638, **Home Phone:** (609)737-0980. **Business Addr:** Manager, Association General Counsel, Education Testing Service, Rosedale Rd, Princeton, NJ 08541.

### TAYLOR, PROF. PAUL DAVID

Health services administrator, consultant. **Personal:** Born May 1, 1937, Lexington, TN; son of Ray Otis (deceased) and Jessie Mae Williams (deceased); children: Paul David Jr & Bentley Christopher. **Educ:** Garden City Community Col, AS, 1957; Univ Kans, 1958. **Career:** Univ Colo Health Sci Ctr, biol lab tech, 1962-65, coordr organ transplant prog, 1962-92, res assoc, 1965-67, sr instr, 1969-92, prof, prof emer, 1992-; Univ Pittsburgh, Presby Univ Hosp, transplant admin, 1989-98; Veterans Admin Hosp, Pittsburgh, Pa, health tech, 1990-97. **Orgs:** Task Force Minority Org Donation Western PA; Minority Affairs Comt, Nat Kidney Fed Western PA; ed bd, J Transplant Coord; Dept Health & Human Servs, Bur Health Resources Develop; master, Prince Hall Masons, Denver, 1967; chmn, jurisp, Grand Lodge Co & Jurisdiction, 1970-90; founding mem, N Am Transplant Coordrs Orgn, 1975-98; bd dir, Colo Soc Prevent Blindness, 1977-80; treas, Am Soc Health & Transplant Profs, 1998-99. **Home Addr:** 507

S Magnolia Lane, Denver, CO 80224-1524, **Home Phone:** (303)333-2153. **Business Addr:** Professor Emeritus, University of Colorado Health Sciences Center, 13120 E 19th Ave, Aurora, CO 80045, **Business Phone:** (303)724-1812.

### TAYLOR, DR. QUINTARD, JR.

Educator. **Personal:** Born Dec 11, 1948, Brownsville, TN; son of Quintard and Grace (Brown); married Carolyn Fain; children: Quintard, Jamila & William. **Educ:** St Augustine's Col, BA, Am hist, 1969; Univ Minn, MA, Am urban hist, 1971, PhD, hist African people, 1977. **Career:** Univ Minn, instr, 1969-71; Gustavus Adolphus Col, instr, 1971; Wa State Univ, Black Studies Program, asst prof, 1971-75; Calif Polytech State Univ, prof, hist, 1977-90; Univ Lagos, Akoka Nigeria, vis fulbright prof, 1987-88; Univ Ore, prof, 1990-99, adj prof, 1990-94, actg dir, 1992-93, dept head, 1997-99, Knight distinguished prof, 1998-99, Benjamin H & Louise L Carroll vis endowed prof, 2006; Univ Wash, vis prof, 1995, Scott & Dorothy Bullitt prof Amer hist, 1999-; Pepperdine Univ, vis prof, 1997, 2000; BlackPast.org, developer & dir. **Orgs:** Great Plains Black Mus, 1980-85; Afro-Am Cult Arts Ctr, 1977-78; adv bd, Southern Conf Afro-Am Studies, 1981; Nat EndowmentHumanities, 1979-83; Martin Luther Fund, 1983-85, mem, 1979-; Endowment Comm "J Negro Hist" 1983-; Calif Black Fac Staff asn, 1985-, Golden Key Nat Hon Soc, 1987-, Phi Beta Delta SocsInter Nat Scholars, 1989-; Martin Luther King Voc-Tech Col, Owerri Nigeria, 1989-, African-Amer Voc Inst, Aba Nigeria, 1989-; Pac Northwest Quart, 1993-2000; Western Hist Quart, 1993-96; fel Nat Res Coun, 1996; chair, Am Hist Asn, Pac Coast Br, 1999-2000; Asn Study Afro Am Life & Hist; Asn Asian Am Studies; Black Heritage Soc Wash State; Am Hist Asn, 2003-06; Urban Hist Asn, 1998-2000; bd dir, Northwest African Am Mus, 2009-; James & Janie Rogella Wash Found Adv Group, 2005-; bd dir, Idaho Black Hist Mus, 2006-; Comt Chair, 1995-96, Western Hist Asn, 2006-09, pres-elect, 2009-11, pres, 2010-11. **Honors/Awds:** ASALH, Carter G Woodson Award, 1980; The Danforth Found, Kent Fel, 1974-77; Univ Minn, Bush Fel, 1971-77; NEH Travel & Collections Grant, Nat Endowment for the Humanities, 1988; The Emergence Afro-American Communities in the Pacific Northwest, 1865-1910; Carter G Woodson Award for best article published in the Journal of Negro History, 1978-79; Ore Humanities Ctr Res Fel; Meritorious Performance & Professional Promise Award, Calif Polytech State Univ, 1986; Vivian A Paladin Award, Montana Historical Soc, 1997; hon life mem, Western Hist Asn, 2005. **Special Achievements:** Has listed in Who's Who in American Education, 1991, 1992; Written: In Search of the Racial Frontier: African Americans in the American West, 1528-1990; The Forging of A Black Community Seattle's Central District from 1870 Through the Civil Rights Era; The Making of the Modern World: A Reader in 20th Century Global History, Kendall-Hunt Publishing Company, 1990; ed, Seeking El Dorado, 2001; ed, African American Women Confront the West, 1600-2000, 2003; From Timbuktu to Katrina: Readings in African American History, Vol. 1, Thomson Wadsworth, 2008; America-I-Am Black Facts: The Story of a People Through TImelines, Tavis Smiley Books, 2009; Dr. Sam, Soldier, Educator, Advocate, Friend; Website publication: Schomburg Studies in the Black Experience, 2005; has written numerous articles, chapters. **Home Addr:** 4545 Sand Point Way NE Suite 504, Seattle, WA 98105. **Business Addr:** Professor of American History, University of Washington, Rm 316-A Smith Hall, Seattle, WA 98195, **Business Phone:** (206)543-5698.

### TAYLOR, REGGIE (REGINALD TREMAIN TAYLOR)

Baseball player. **Personal:** Born Jan 12, 1977, Newberry, SC. **Career:** Baseball player (retired); Philadelphia Phillies, 2000-01; Cincinnati Reds, outfielder, 2002-03; Colo Rockies, outfielder, 2004; Tampa Bay Ray Devils, outfielder, 2005; Detroit Tigers, ctr field & left field, 2005; St Louis Cardinals, 2005; Lancaster Barnstormers, 2006; Long Island Ducks, 2007; Atlanta Braves; Richmond Braves; Olmecas de Tabasco, 2008; Dorados de Chihuahua, Sioux Falls Canaries, 2009; Kans City Royals, 2009; Olmecas de Tabasco, 2010; free agt, currently.

### TAYLOR, DR. REGINA

Actor, playwright. **Personal:** Born Aug 22, 1960, Dallas, TX. **Educ:** Southern Methodist Univ, attended 1981. **Career:** Actress & Playwright; Goodman Theater, distinguished artistic assoc, currently; Alliance Theatre, Atlanta, Ga, writer-in-residence, currently; TV films: "Nurse", 1980; "Crisis at Central High", 1981; "Concealed Enemies", 1984; "Lean on Me", 1989; "Howard Beach: Making a Case for Murder", 1989; "I'll FlyAway", 1991; "Law & Order: Mushrooms", 1991; "Jersey Girl", 1992; "I'll Fly Away: Then and Now", 1993; "Law & Order: Virtue", 1994; "Children of the Dust", 1995; "Losing Isaiah", 1995; "Clockers", 1995; "The Keeper", 1995; "Spirit Lost", 1996; "A Family Thing", 1996; "Courage Under Fire", 1996; "Feds", 1997; "Hostile Waters", 1997; "The Third Twin", 1997; "The Negotiator", 1998; "Strange Justice", 1999; "Cora Unashamed", 2000; TV Series: "The Education of Max Bickford", 2001; "In From the Night", 2005; "The Unit", 2006; "Grey's Anatomy", 2008; "Who Is Clark Rockefeller?", 2010; Stage: "Romeo & Juliet"; "As You like it"; "Macbeth"; "Machinal"; "A Map of The World"; "The Illusion"; "Jar the Floor"; "Tempest"; Playwright: "Oo-Bla-Dee, 2000; "Drowning Crow", 2003; "The Dreams of Sarah Breed love", 2004; "A Night in Tunisia"; "Escape from Paradise"; "Watermelon Rinds"; "Inside the Belly of the Beast"; "Crowns", 2004; "Magnolia", 2009; Goodman Theatre, artistic assoc, currently; Signature Theatre, writer, currently. **Honors/Awds:** Pea Body award, Gracy Award; L.A Dramalogue Award; Q Award for Best Actress in a Quality Drama Series, 1992, 1993; Golden Globe Award for Best Performance by an Actress in a TV-Series, Drama, 1993; Image Award for Outstanding Lead Actress in a Drama Series, 1995; New play Award, Am Critics Assn; NAACP Image Award For the Best actress in a Drama, 2008; Honorary Doc from DePaul univ. **Special Achievements:** Nominated twice for Emmy Award in Drama Series; first Black woman to play William Shakespeare's Juliet. **Business Addr:** Artistic Associate, Goodman Theatre, 170 N Dearborn St, Chicago, IL 60601, **Business Phone:** (312)443-3800.

### TAYLOR, REGINALD REDALL, JR.

Educator, school administrator. **Personal:** Born Jun 30, 1939, Waycross, GA; son of Reginald R Sr and Ellen Butler; married Laurine Williams; children: Robyn Michelle. **Educ:** Fla A&M Univ, BS, 1961; Ft Valley State Col, MS, 1973; Valdosta State Col, Valdosta, GA, 1990. **Career:** Educator (retired); Pierce Co Bd Educ, Blackshear, Ga; Lee St High Sch, social studies teacher & band dir, 1961-69; Blackshear High Sch, social studies teacher & counr, 1969-72, Pierce Co High Sch, counr, asst prin, 1973-90; City Blackshear, councilman, 1979-; Ware St Elem Sch, prin, 1990-. **Orgs:** Composite Lodge #40, Fla A&M Univ, 1960; pres, Pierce Co Assoc Educrs, 1964, 1967, 1968; pres, Consol Mens Club Inc, 1973; bd dir, Pierce Co Chamber Com, 1980-82; dir, Waycross Chorale Ensemble, 1988-90. **Home Addr:** 913 Cherry St, Blackshear, GA 31516-2028, **Home Phone:** (912)449-6630. **Business Addr:** Principal, Ware Street Elementary School, 623 Sycamore St, Blackshear, GA 31516, **Business Phone:** (912)449-2078.

### TAYLOR, DR. ROBERT, III

Dentist, educator. **Personal:** Born Apr 12, 1946, Ashburn, GA; son of Robert Jr and Susie Bell Hudson; married JoAnne Davis; children: Robert IV, Quentin, Sonya & Bridget. **Educ:** Albany State Col, BS, 1966; Atlanta Univ, MS, 1970; Med Col Ga, DMD, 1975; USN, cert, 1976. **Career:** Telfair Co GA, chem instr, 1966-69; Henry Co GA, biol instr, 1969-70; USn, asst sr dent officer, 1975-78; Turner Job Corps GA, head dentist, 1978-82; gen dent, self-employed; dent terminoly instr; Taylor Dent Clins, dentist, currently. **Orgs:** Am Dent Asn; Nat Dent Asn; Am Acad Gen Dentists; Res Officers League; GA Acad Gen Dentists; Phi Bet Sigma Frat Inc; chmn bd, Nat Asn Advan Colored People; vpres, Cong Black Orgns; Jack & Jill Am; Albany State Col Found; Title Twenty Found; Prince Hall Mason Lodge 360; Knights Columbus 4thDegree 3607; Post 512 Am Legion; VFW Post 7491; AL Ranken 142; Dougherty Co Bd Health; Sowega Health Care Providers; Educ Proj 2000. **Home Addr:** 512 S Monroe St, Albany, GA 31701, **Home Phone:** (229)435-4954. **Business Addr:** Dentist, Taylor Dental Clinics, 512 S Monroe St, Albany, GA 31701, **Business Phone:** (229)435-4954.

### TAYLOR, ROBERT, III. See TAYLOR, BOBBY, III.

### TAYLOR, ROBERT DEREK

Financial manager, chief executive officer. **Personal:** Born Jul 2, 1961, Los Angeles, CA; son of Robert M and Geneva Williams; married Joy L Johnson. **Educ:** Calif State Univ, Northridge, BS, engineering, 1982; Stanford Law Sch, JD, 1986; Stanford Grad Sch Bus, MBA, 1986. **Career:** McKinsey & Co, partner, 1986-97; Blue Capital Mgt, partner & co-founder, 1997-2007; Centinela Captial Partners LLC, founding partner & chief exec officer, 2006-. **Orgs:** Chair bd dir, Decorative Concepts Inc, chair; bd dir, M2 Automotive Inc; bd dir, Rebuild LA; bd trustee, sr vice chmn, Nat Urban League, 1995-2007; bd trustee, LA Urban League, 1995-2012; bd visitor, Stanford Law Sch; bd dir, Frontier Airlines; bd trustee, Aspiriant Global Equity Trust, 2012-; Calif Sci Ctr; Stanford Grad Sch Bus Mgt Bd; Stanford Law Sch Bd Visitor. **Business Addr:** Founding Partner, Chief Executive Officer, Centinela Capital Partners LLC, 777 S Figueroa St Suite 390, Los Angeles, CA 90017, **Business Phone:** (213)542-1800.

### TAYLOR, DR. RONALD LEWIS

Dean (education), college teacher, sociologist. **Personal:** Born Feb 27, 1942, St. Petersburg, FL; son of David and Lillian Bell Miller; married Bernice Chavis; children: Kevin & Darryl. **Educ:** Bethune-Cookman Col, Daytona Beach, FL, BA, 1963; Howard Univ, Washington, DC, MA, 1965; Boston Univ, Boston, MA, PhD, 1972. **Career:** Professor (retired), professor emeritus; US Dept Labor, res assoc & prog evaluator, 1963-64; Bethune-Cookman Col, dean, 1964-65, dir, financial aid, 1965-67; Boston Univ, instr, lectr, 1967-72; Univ Conn, from asst prof to prof, 1972, chair, sociol dept, 1981-86, die Inst African-Am Studies, 1993-99, vice provost Multi cult & Int Affairs, 1999-2009, prof emer, currently. **Orgs:** Ed bd, Am Jour Ortho Psychiat, 1978-85; ed bd, Contemp Sociol, 1980-84, 2000-02; ed bd, Univ Press New Eng, 1984-90; chair, DuBois-Johnson-Frazier Awards, Am Sociol Asn, 1987-90; exec comt, Am Asn Univ Profs, 1988-; ed bd, Jour African-Am Male Studies, 1991-; ed bd, Jour Mens Studies, 1992-; ed bd, Jour Res Adolescence, 1994-; pres, Am Asn Univ Profs, Univ Conn Chap; ed bd, Race & Soc, 1997-2002. **Home Addr:** 18 Partridge Lane, Tolland, CT 06084, **Home Phone:** (860)872-0596. **Business Addr:** Professor Emeritus, University of Connecticut, 344 Mansfield Rd, Storrs, CT 06269, **Business Phone:** (860)486-4422.

### TAYLOR, RUTH CAROL. See TAYLOR, CAROL.

### TAYLOR, RUTH SLOAN. See Obituaries Section.

### TAYLOR, S. MARTIN

Government official, executive. **Personal:** Born Bangor, ME; married Anna Diggs. **Educ:** Western Mich Univ, BS, polit sci & econs, 1964; Detroit Col Law, JD, 1967; Marygrove Col, hon doctor laws degree. **Career:** New Detroit Inc, pres; Mich Dept Labor & Mich Employ Security Comn, dir; Detroit Edison, Detroit, Mich, vpres govt rels, 1989, sr vpres, corp & pub affairs, DTE Energy Corp, Human Resources & Corp Affairs, exec vpres, retired, sr vpres; Detroit Renaissance, interim pres. **Orgs:** Chair, Univ Mich, 1996, 2004-, bd regent, currently; chair, Arts League Mich; chair, Detroit Econ Growth Corp; bd trustee & exec comt mem, Mich Econ Develop Corp, currently; dir, Blue Cross Blue Shield Mich; chair, Citizens Res Coun Mich; chair, Coun Mich Founds, currently; chair, Detroit Urban League; pres, Detroit Zool Inst; pres, New Detroit Inc; dir, State Mich Dept Labor; dir, Mich Employ Security Comn. **Business Addr:** Chairman, Board of Regent, University of Michigan, 43 Beacon Hill Rd, Grosse Pointe Farms, MI 48236, **Business Phone:** (313)235-4000.

### TAYLOR, DR. SANDRA ELAINE

Psychologist. **Personal:** Born Aug 8, 1946, New York, NY; daughter of Floyd Lee and Berthenia T; married Alvin; children: Kwam; married Walter C Bailey. **Educ:** Bronx Comm Col, Univ NY, AAS, 1965, AA, 1969; City Col NY, BA, 1970; City Univ NY, PhD, 1976. **Career:** Bronx Psychiat Ctr, head nurse, 1965-73; Albert Einstein Clin Internship Prog Psychol, intern psychologist, 1973-74; City Col, City Univ, New York, adj lectr, 1974-75; Bronx Psychiat Ctr, staff psychologist, 1974-76; St Joseph's Col, adj asst prof, 1976-77; Marymount Col, adj asst prof, 1976-79, coun psychologist, 1976-77; City Col & Harlem Hosp Ctr, Physician Asst Prog, educ coord, 1977-80; Brooklyn Develop Ctr, prin psychologist & exec asst dir, 1980-81; Bronx Develop Ctr, dep dir treat svcs, 1981-90; Kwam SET Publ Co Inc, pres, 1989-. **Orgs:** Nat Asn Female Execs, 1983-. **Honors/Awds:** First Pamela Galiber Memorial Scholarship Award, City Univ NY, 1976; "The Meaning of Scholarship", "Ethnic Self-Hatred in Black Psychotics, A Preliminary Report", Journal of the Bronx State Hosp Vol 1 No 2 Spring, 1973; "Racism and Psychiatry", Bronx Psychiatric Ctr guest lecturer for visiting medical residents, 1973. **Special Achievements:** Publications such as "The New York Urban League Presents", WBLS radio station guest speaker, 1976. **Home Addr:** PO Box 523, Bronx, NY 10472-0523. **Business Addr:** President, Kwam SET Publishing Co Inc, 1000 Grand Concourse, Bronx, NY 10451.

### TAYLOR, SANDYE R.

Vice president (organization), manager. **Educ:** Univ Md, College Park, BA, 1984; Univ Md Sch Law, JD, 1987. **Career:** Brown & Wood, assoc, 1988-89; Legal Serv Union 32B-J, staff atty, Civil Litigation Div, 1989-97; Taylor Law Off, solo practr, 1997-2000; Telcordia Technologies, software licensing, mgr, 2000-03; Merrill Lynch, Global Sourcing & Procurement Serv, vpres, 2003-06, dir, Head Global Supplier Develop, 2006-08; Bank Am Merrill Lynch, sr vpres, Global Supply Chain Mgt, 2008-10, sr vpres, Diversity & Inclusion, 2010-15; Bank Am Corp, global supply chain mgt, sr vpres; RBC Capital Markets, head diversity & inclusion, 2015-. **Orgs:** Dir, Merril Lynch. **Home Addr:** 103 S Grove St, East Orange, NJ 07018-4101, **Home Phone:** (973)675-0323. **Business Addr:** Vice President, Merrill Lynch & Co Inc, 4 World Financial Ctr, New York, NY 10080.

### TAYLOR, DR. SCOTT MORRIS

Physician. **Personal:** Born Oct 10, 1957, Berkeley, CA; son of Robert L (desceased). **Educ:** Morehouse Col, BS, 1980; Meharry Med Sch, MD, 1984. **Career:** Highland Hosp, surg resident, 1984-86; Los Angeles County Hosp, Los Angeles, Calif, resident; Martin Luther King Hosp, ortho pres, 1987-91; pvt pract, 1991-; C Hosp Med Ctr, Oakland, Calif, staff, 1992-99; Healthsouth Indust Clin, Oakland, Calif, consult, 1995-2001; Alta Bates Med Group, physician, currently, Alta Bates-Summit Med Ctr, chmn dept surg, chief orthopaedic surg; Summit Campus, Oakland, Calif, vice chmn dept orthopaedic surg, 2003-08. **Home Addr:** 400 29th St Suite 400, Oakland, CA 94609, **Home Phone:** (510)238-9600. **Business Addr:** Physician, 400-29th St Suite 400, Oakland, CA 94609-3549, **Business Phone:** (510)238-9600.

### TAYLOR, SID E.

Chief executive officer, president (organization). **Career:** Gen Motors, mgr, 1966-88; SET Steel Inc, founder, 1989; founder, Group Co: SET Enterprises Inc, SBF Automotive & T&B Conveyor Prod, currently; SET Enterprises Inc, owner, 1989-, chmn, pres & ceo, 2002-. **Orgs:** Founder, Intervale Cloverdale Lyndon Livernois Indust Pk Asn, 1997; pres, Nat Asn Black Automotive Suppliers, 2003; Mich Minority Bus Develop Coun; Nat Asn Advan Colored People; Econ Club Detroit; Detroit Golf Club; adv bd mem, Jackson St Univ; bd mem, YMCA, Warren, MI; Mich Minority Supplier Develop Coun; Corp Plus Prog, Nat Minority Supplier Develop Coun; adv bd mem, Jackson State Univ. **Business Addr:** President, Chief Executive Officer, SET Enterprises Inc, 30500 Van Dyke Ave Suite 701, Warren, MI 48093, **Business Phone:** (586)573-3600.

### TAYLOR, STACEY LORENZO

Military leader, marine corps officer. **Personal:** Born Sep 3, 1971, Sandersville, GA; son of Herbert and Annie; married Marsha; children: Nastacia D. **Educ:** Morris Brown Col, BS, acct, 1993; Fla State Univ, MBA, 2002. **Career:** USmC, air traffic controller, 1993-; Hq & Support Battalion, Sch Inf-E, comndg officer, 2011-12. **Orgs:** Kappa Alpha Psi Fraternity Inc, 1991-; Alpha Kappa Mu Hon Soc, 1992; Free & Accepted Mason, PHA, 1993-. **Honors/Awds:** Community Service Award, City New Orleans, LA, 1998. **Home Addr:** 2750 Old St Augustine Rd, Tallahassee, FL 32307, **Home Phone:** (850)878-5770. **Business Addr:** Air Traffic Controller, US Marine Corps, 2121 W Pensacola St Suite C, Tallahassee, FL 32304-3170, **Business Phone:** (850)574-4377.

### TAYLOR, STERLING R. See Obituaries Section.

### TAYLOR, STUART A.

Educator, consultant. **Personal:** Born Jul 2, 1936, Providence, RI; married Ella Marie; children: Sandre, Stuart, Sabrina & Scott. **Educ:** Oakwood Col, BS, acct bus, 1960; Univ RI, MBA, 1963; Ind Univ, PhD, indust mgt & psychol, 1967. **Career:** Harvard Bus Sch Prof, Elon Univ, Charles Stuart Mott distinguished prof; Illinova Univ, prof, dean & pres; Booz Allen Hamilton, dir; Textron Inc, dir; Eli Lilly, consult; Merck, consult; Glaxo Smith Kline, consult; Johnson & Johnson, consult; Coca Cola Co, consult; Investco Co, consult. **Orgs:** Acad Mgt; bd adv, Nat Urban League; founder, RI Com Advan Negro Ed; White House Fel Prog; Harvard Bus Sch African-Am Alumni Asn; bd mem, Grerater Greensboro Community Found; bd mem, Atlantic Union Col; bd mem, Oakwood Col; bd mem, Spears YMCA.

### TAYLOR, DR. SUSAN CHARLENE

Dermatologist. **Personal:** Born Oct 7, 1957, Philadelphia, PA; daughter of Charles and Ethel; married Kemel W Dawkins; children: Morgan Elizabeth & Madison Lauren. **Educ:** Univ Pa, BA, biol, 1979; Harvard Med Sch, MD, 1983. **Career:** Pa Hosp, Philadelphia, Pa, intern med, 1983-84; Pa Hosp, Philadelphia, Pa, resident med, 1984-86; Columbia Presby Med Ctr, resident dermat, 1986-89; Soc Hill Dermat, physician, dermatologist, 1989-; Univ Pa, Sch Med, Dept Dermat, clin instr, 1989-95; Thomas Jefferson Univ, Jefferson Med Col, instr med, 1994-96; Univ Pa, assoc fac sch med, clin asst prof dermat, 1995-; Columbia Univ, Col Physicians & Surgeons, asst clin prof dermat, 1998-; St Luke's Roosevelt Hosp Ctr, Skin Color Ctr, physician, 1998-2006, founding dir, 1998-2007, sr physician, 2007-. **Orgs:** AMA; bd dir, Am Acad Dermat; Pa Med Soc; Med Soc Eastern Pa; Philadelphia County Med Soc; Philadelphia Dermat Soc; trustee, Baldwin Sch; trustee, Univ Pa; Healthcare Delivery Comt; Minority Stud Mentors Prog;

founding pres, Skin Color Soc, 2004; bd trustee, United Way Eastern Pa; dipl, Am Bd Internal Med, 1986; dipl, Am Bd Dermat, 1989; Nat Med Asn; Pa Acad Dermat; Philadelphia Dermat Soc; Am Dermat Asn. **Honors/Awds:** Alumni Award of Merit, Univ Pa. **Special Achievements:** Auth, Brown Skin Dr Susan Taylor's Prescription for Flawless Skin, Hairand Nails. She was selected for the cover of Philadelphia Mag's, 1999 issue of the Top Doctors & has been included in the Essence Mag's list of top women physicians. **Business Addr:** Dermatologist, Society Hill Dermatology, 932 Pine St, Philadelphia, PA 19107, **Business Phone:** (215)829-6861.

### TAYLOR, SUSAN L.
Editor, publishing executive, executive. **Personal:** Born Jan 23, 1946, New York, NY; daughter of Lawrence and Violet Weekes; married Khephra Burns; married William Bowles; children: Shana Nequai. **Educ:** Fordham Univ, BA, social sci, 1991. **Career:** Negro Ensemble Com, actress; lic cosmetologist, 1970; Nequai Cosmetics, founder & pres, 1970-72; Essence mag, freelance writer, beauty ed, 1970-71, fashion & beauty ed, 1971-81, ed-in-chief, 1981-2000, vpres, sr vpres, 1993, ed dir, ed-in-chief emer, currently; Essense Commun Inc, tv host, exec coordr, pres, 1986, sr vpres, 1993; Nequai Cosmetics, founder; Nat CARES Mentoring Movement, founder & chief exec officer, currently. **Orgs:** Am Soc Mag Eds; Women Communs; Nat Asn Black Journalists; Black Women Publ; avid supporter, Comn Res Black Educ; adv bd, Black Adminrs Child Welfare; founder, Future PAC; hon mem, Delta Sigma Theta. **Honors/Awds:** Fifth Annual Kizzy Image & Achievement Award, 1981; Excellence in Media Award, Howard Univ, 1982; Women Communs Matirx Award, 1982; Nat Asn Negro Bus & Prof Womens Clubs, Bus Awards, 1983; inducted, Hall of Fame, Am Society Mag Eds, 2002; Matrix Award, New York Women Commun, 1987; Honorary degree, Lincoln Univ, 1988; Honorary degree, Univ Delaware, 1993; Henry Johnson Fisher Award, 1998; Honorary degree, Spelman Col; Honorary degree, Dillard Univ; Honorary degree, Bennett Col Women; Honorary degree, Fordham Univ; Most influential black woman in journalism, Am Libr; President's Award, Nat Asn Advan Colored People, 2006. **Special Achievements:** First African American woman to receive The Henry Johnson Fisher Award; Author: In the Spirit: The Inspirational Writings of Susan L Taylor, 1993; Lessons in Living, Anchor Books, 1995; Co-author: Confirmations: The Spiritual Wisdom That Has Shaped Our Lives, 1997. **Business Addr:** Chief Editor, Essence Magazine, 1500 Broadway, New York, NY 10036.

### TAYLOR, SYLVIA
Manager, vice president (organization), media executive. **Educ:** Howard Univ, BA, sociol, MBA, bus-labor mgt rels. **Career:** Gen Motors, labor rels rep, 1985-87; PepsiCo-Frito Lay Operating Div, human resources mgr, 1987-88; Mobil Oil, human resources mgr, 1988-99; ExxonMobil Corp, human resources mgr Singapore refineries, 1998-2000, mgr staffing & develop-Asia Pac, 2000-01; Target Corp, SE region human resources mgr, 2003; Cox Enterprises-AutoTrader.com, vpres human resources, 2004-10; Weather Channel, exec vpres human resources, 2010-13; Safe-Guard Prod Int LLC, sr vpres human resources, 2013-. **Orgs:** Human Resources Leadership Summit; Cable & Telecommunications Human Resources Asn; Human Resources Leadership Forum; Nat Asn Multi-Ethnicity Commun. **Home Addr:** 3319 Asbury Sq, Atlanta, GA 30346-2414. **Business Addr:** senior vice president, Safe-Guard Products International, LLC, 2 Concourse Pkwy Suite 500, Atlanta, GA 30328, **Business Phone:** (800)742-7896.

### TAYLOR, T. SHAWN
Journalist. **Personal:** Born Aug 23, 1966, Alton, IL; daughter of Robert and Armelia Jefferson. **Educ:** Univ Mo-Columbia, BA, jour, 1988. **Career:** St. Louis Post-Dispatch; Detroit Free Press, copy ed, 1988-89; Kans City Star, copy ed, 1989-90; Chicago Tribune, copy ed, 1990-96, reporter, 1990-2005, freelance writer, currently; Chicago Mfg Renaissance Coun, commun dir, 2006-08; Beaman Inc, writer, 2006-09; Treetop Consult, owner, 2006-, media consult, media rels, 2012-; Chicago Urban League, writer & media consult, 2006-; Level-1 Global Solutions, dir Commun & Media, New Equity Bus, writer, 2009-11; C's Neuroblastoma Cancer Found, writer & media consult, 2010-; AAR Corp, writer, researcher & media consult, 2011-; Family Defense Ctr, writer, media consult, 2012-. **Orgs:** Alpha Kappa Alpha Sorority Inc, 1986-; Nat Asn Black Journalists, 1987-; consult, Chicago Urban League, 2006-10; Fel League Black Women. **Business Addr:** Freelance Writer, Chicago Tribune, 435 N Mich Ave, Chicago, IL 60611, **Business Phone:** (312)222-3232.

### TAYLOR, TAMARA
Actor. **Personal:** Born Sep 27, 1970, Toronto, ON; married Miles Cooley. **Career:** TV series: "A Different World", 1991; "Freshman Dorm", 1992; "Party of Five", 1996-97; Senseless, 1998; "Alternative Lifestyles", 1998; "Dawson's Creek", 1998; Graham's Diner, 1999; "Early Edition", 1999; Introducing Dorothy Dandridge, 1999; "Providence", 1999; "City of Angels", 2000; "OneSpecial Moment", 2001; "Hidden Hills", 2002; "Miracles", 2003; "Everwood", 2003; "Becker", 2003; "Without a Trace", 2003; "Six Feet Under", 2004; "CSI: Miami", 2004; "One on One", 2004; Diary of a Mad Black Woman, 2005; "SWAK", 2005; "Navy NCIS: Naval Criminal Investigative Service"; Serenity, 2005; "Sex, Love & Secrets", 2005; "Special", 2005; "Lost", 2005; "Numb3rs", 2006; "Bones", 2006-14; "Bones: Access All Areas", 2008; "The Double Death of the Dearly Departed", 2009; "The Girl in the Mask", 2009; "The Beaver in the Otter", 2009; "The Critic in the Cabernet", 2009; "The End in the Beginning", 2009. Films: Senseless, 1998; Graham's Diner, 1999; Diary of a Mad Black Woman, 2005; Serenity, 2005; Gordon Glass, 2007; Shuffle, 2011. **Business Addr:** Actress, c/o NBC, 30 Rockefeller Plz, New York, NY 10112.

### TAYLOR, TENISHA NICOLE (TENISHA ABERNATHY)
President (organization), television producer. **Educ:** Clark Atlanta Univ, BA, mass media arts, commun, radio, tv, film; Kennesaw State Univ, MPA, pub admin, 2007. **Career:** WLWT, Cincinnati, OH, producer, 2000-02; WDSI, producer, Chattanooga, TN; WUSA, producer, 2002-03; CBS, producer; NBC, producer; ABC, producer; FOX, producer; CNN, Atlanta, news producer, 2003-, exec producer, 2005-; Clark Atlanta Univ, adj prof, 2009; Kennesaw State Univ, adj prof, 2010-15; Perfect Pitch Media Group LLC, pres, 2010-. **Orgs:** Nat Asn Black Journalists; Am Women Radio & TV; Nat Asn Multi-Ethnicity Commun; Delta Sigma Theta Sorority; pres, Atlanta Asn Black Journalists, 2010-14. **Business Addr:** News Producer, Executive Producer, CNN, Atlanta, GA 30303, **Business Phone:** (404)827-5332.

### TAYLOR, DR. TOMMIE W.
Public relations executive. **Personal:** Born Mar 4, 1929, Blytheville, AR; married Aubrey Sr; children: Aubrey Jr (deceased), Darryl E, Roderic K & Cabot O. **Educ:** Philander Smith Col, BA, 1955; Univ Ark, Little Rock. **Career:** Pub rel exec (retired); lic cosmetologist, 1948; Johnson Publ Co, stringer, 1954-65; Radio Sta KOKY-AM, prog asst, 1957-59; AR Baptist Col, registr psych instr, 1959-61; Teletype Corp, civil rel assoc, 1962-75; AT&T Info Systs, pub rels rep, 1982-87. **Orgs:** Pres, Urban League Greater Little Rock, 1971-75; tammateous, 1984-85, 2nd anti basileus, 1985-86, 1st anti basileus, 1986-87, Sigma Gamma Rho Sor; dir, Young Peoples Bapt Trng Union Dept NH Zion Baptist Church; bd trustee, Ark Baptist Col, 2001-. **Home Addr:** 806 S Miss St, Little Rock, AR 72205, **Home Phone:** (501)227-4565.

### TAYLOR, TYRONE CURTIS
Executive. **Personal:** Born Jul 20, 1953, Washington, DC; son of Arthur and Bernice; married Carolyn; children: Donovan & Briana. **Educ:** Wilmington Col, AB, bus admin & econs, 1975; Southeastern Univ, MBA, 1978. **Career:** NASA HQS, dir, Nat Serv, 1973-95; Fed Lab Conserv, Wash, DC, rep, 1995-98; Unisphere Inc, sr vpres, Mkt & Bus Develop, 1998-2003; Capitol Advisors Technol LLC, founder & pres, 2003-; Wva High Technol Consortium Found, dir, Wash Rels, currently. **Orgs:** Minority Bus Technol Transfer Conserv, 1999-; NASA Minority Res Comt, 1999-2001; bd dir, Pediat AIDS/HIV Care, 2002-; chair, small bus div, Nat Defense Indust Assoc, 2002-; comt visitors, NSF, 2003-; Nat Defense Indust Asn; Nat Res Steering Comt, 2003-. **Home Addr:** 8224 Crest Rd, Laurel, MD 20723-1032, **Home Phone:** (301)498-5683. **Business Addr:** Director, West Virginia High Technology Consortium Foundation, 1000 Technol Dr Suite 1000, Fairmont, WV 26554, **Business Phone:** (304)366-2577.

### TAYLOR, VALERIE CHARMAYNE
Advertising executive. **Personal:** Born Jan 19, 1962, Chattanooga, TN; daughter of Harvey E and Geneva Williams. **Educ:** Austin Peay State Univ, 1982; Mich State Univ, BA, telecommunications, 1985; Inst Educ Leadership, cert, 1988. **Career:** Mich Dept Nat Resources, community rels rep, 1983-85; Fed Social Security Dept, claims rep & asst spec emphasis coordr, 1985-86; Fed Dept Health & Human Serv LCC; Lansing Community Col, community rels mgr & proj co-ordinator, 1986-88; State Bar Mich, commun mgr, 1988-89; Mich Travel Bur, mkt mgr, 1989-91; Jamestown-Yorktown Found, Commonwealth Va, dir pub affairs & mkt, 1991-94; Siddall Matus & Coushter, Advert & Pub Rel, acct supvr, 1994-. **Orgs:** Nat pr chair, Delta Sigma Theta Sorority Inc, 1987-91; Nat Asn Mkt Developers; African Am Pub Rels Soc; charter mem, Mich Black Media Asn, vpres, 1987-89; bd dir, Lansing Food Bank, 1987-90; secy, Lansing Martin Luther King Comn, 1989-90; co-chair citywide radiothon, Lansing Br Nat Asn Advan Colored People, 1988; bd dir, Williamsburg Hotel Motel Asn, 1991-; ad-hoc Econs Bd Pub Rels Soc Am; Asn Travel Mkt Exec, 1991-. **Honors/Awds:** Outstanding Serv Award, US Dept Health & Human Serv, 1986; Serv Appreciation Recognition, Delta Sigma Theta Sorority Inc, 1987; Serv Appreciation Cert, Lansing United Negro Col Fund, 1988. **Special Achievements:** Implemented Mich segmented marketing prog focusing on Chicago, increased visitation by 18% first year, 1991; Instituted museums first-time co-op ticket program, generating more than $200, 000 in sales revenue & increasing visitation by 29% for record high levels; Implemented national media relations campaign for Virginia museums, resulting in first time feature coverage by CNN Headline News, Time Life Books, Americana Mag, Los Angeles Time & Walt Disney Prod, 1992; Developed Mich co-op travel marketing prog, increased travel budget by $4.5 million generated 190, 000 additional travel inquiry. **Home Addr:** 1334 Lake Dr, Newport News, VA 23602, **Home Phone:** (804)249-8568. **Business Addr:** Account Supervisor, Siddall Matus & Coushter Inc, Advert & Pub Rels 801 E Main St Ross Bldg, Richmond, VA 23219, **Business Phone:** (804)253-4138.

### TAYLOR, VANESSA GAIL
Law enforcement officer, educator, basketball coach. **Personal:** Born Sep 15, 1960, Lafayette, LA; daughter of Dalton Belson Jr; married John F; children: Tiffany & Timothy. **Educ:** Univ Southwestern La, AS, 1982, BS, 1994; Acadiana Law Enforcement Trng Acad, attended 1985; Drug Abuse Resistance Educ Trng, 1991. **Career:** Law enforcement officer (retired), educator, basketball coach; Lafayette Parish Juv Detention Ctr, 1981-82; Lafayette Police Dept, clerk II, 1982-85, corporal, 1985-97; St Landry Parish Sch Bd, N Cent High Sch, teacher, spec educr & basketball coach, currently. **Orgs:** La Peace Officers Asn, 1987-; Munic Police Officers Asn, 1987-; Magnolia Peace Officers Asn, 1988-; Police Assn Lafayette, 1989-; Lafayette Youth Conf Comn, 1991-; Black Adoption & Foster Care Advocacy Bd, 1991-. **Honors/Awds:** Officer of the Month, Lafayette Police Dept, 1992; Officer of the Year, Knights of Columbus 3202, 1992; Officer of the Year, Nat Assn Blacks Criminal Justice, 1993; Officer of the Year, Crime Prev Adv Comn Nominee, 1993; Officer of the Year, Kiwanis Club, 1994; Trio Achievers Award, 1994; District Coach of the Year; Parish Coach of the Year; St Coach of the Year. **Special Achievements:** First female to become a motorcycle officer in the state of Louisiana. **Home Addr:** 191 Thelma Dr, Sunset, LA 70584, **Home Phone:** (337)942-5872. **Business Addr:** Basketball Coach, Saint Landry Parish School Board, PO Box 10, Lebeau, LA 71345, **Business Phone:** (337)623-4966.

### TAYLOR, VERNON ANTHONY
Army officer. **Personal:** Born Jul 31, 1946, Easton, MD; son of Wayman W Sr and Evelyn S; married Judith Woodson; children: Anne Marie. **Educ:** Morgan State Univ, BS, 1969; Del Law Sch, Widener Univ, JD, 1980. **Career:** Justice Peace Ct, Ct 13, magistrate, dep chief magistrate, currently. **Orgs:** Rotary Int. **Home Addr:** 4613 Big Rock Dr, Wilmington, DE 19802-1001, **Home Phone:** (302)762-8488. **Business Addr:** Deputy Chief Magistrate, Judge, Justice of the Peace Court 20, 300 N Walnut St, Wilmington, DE 19801, **Business Phone:** (302)577-7234.

### TAYLOR, VERONICA C. See Obituaries Section.

### TAYLOR, VIVIAN A.
Government official. **Personal:** Born Oct 27, 1924, MD; married Lula M; children: Lavon E & Myron A. **Educ:** Stillman Col, attended 1943; Fisk Univ, attended 1948; State Univ NY, BA, 1973; Col Fredonia. **Career:** Jamestown Parks Dept, parks comnr, 1976-85; Black Awareness Studies, dir, 1984-85; TRW, bearings div; City Jamestown, city councilman. **Orgs:** Bd dir, Jamestown Better Living; Environ Coun; original appointee Jamestown Human Rights Comm; bd dir, Jamestown Family Serv; chmn bd trustee, Blackwell Chapel AME Zion Church; Boy Scout Comm; chmn, Jamestown Inter racial Forum, 1962-65; City Charter Adv Comm, 1977; gov bd, Chautauqua Oppors Inc Anti-Poverty Agency, 1977-79; bd dir, Crystal Ballroom Sr Citizens Ctr, 1981-84; United Auto Aerospace & Implement Workers Am, 1985; comtman Chautauqua Co Dem Comm, 1985; comtman Jamestown City Dem Comm, 1985. **Honors/Awds:** Certificate Honor, AME Zion Church, 1978; Martin Luther King Junior Peace Award, Southern Tier Peace Ctr, 1982. **Home Addr:** 31 W 18th St, Jamestown, NY 14701-3007, **Home Phone:** (716)484-8505. **Business Addr:** City Councilman, City of Jamestown, Municipal Bldg, Jamestown, NY 14701.

### TAYLOR, WILFORD, JR.
District court judge. **Personal:** Born Jan 15, 1950, Newport News, VA; son of Wilford Sr and Zenobia Miller; married Linda Holmes; children: Patrice D & Derek H. **Educ:** Hampton Univ, Hampton, Va, BS, bus mgt, 1972; Univ Richmond, Richmond, Va, MA, com, 1975; Marshall-Wythe Sch Law, Col William & Mary, Williamsburg, Va, JD, 1978. **Career:** Scott, Coles, Brown, Taylor & Melvin, PC, Newport News, Va, atty, 1979-82; City Hampton, Hampton, Va, dep city atty, 1983-85; Col William & Mary Sch Law, adj prof; Alma mater, adj prof; Commonwealth Via, Hampton, Va, gen dist ct judge, 1985-95, circuit ct judge, currently. **Orgs:** Va State Bar Asn; Peninsula Bar Asn; Old Dom Bar Asn; Asn Dist Ct Judges Va; Hampton Bar Asn; Nat Asn Advan Colored People, Hampton Chap; adv bd mem, Metrop YMCA; affirmative action comt mem, Marshall-Wythe Sch Law, Col William & Mary; Hampton Rotary Club; pres, Langley, PTA, 1990-; Am Judges Asn; Lawyers Helping Lawyers Comt. **Honors/Awds:** Man of the Year, Alpha Kappa Alpha Sorority, Hampton Chap, 1986; Man of the Year, Mega Psi Phi, Newport News Chap, 1990; St George Tucker Adjunct Professor Award, Col William & Mary Sch Law. **Special Achievements:** First full time African American judge; Taylor was part of the first group of African Americans to integrate Hampton High Sch. **Home Addr:** 12 Sugarberry Run, Hampton, VA 23669, **Home Phone:** (804)850-3928. **Business Addr:** Circuit Court Judge, Hampton City Circuit Court, 101 King's Way Mall, Hampton, VA 23669-0040, **Business Phone:** (757)727-6105.

### TAYLOR, WILLIAM GLENN
Executive, banker. **Personal:** Born Oct 17, 1942, Loma Linda, CA; son of Lucille and W G; married Gwendolyn A Mayeaux. **Educ:** Riverside City Col, attended 1963; Univ San Francisco, BS, 1979. **Career:** Banker, Executive (retired); First Interstate Bank, bus serv supvr, 1965-72; Union Bank Calif, admin officer, 1972-76; Bank Calif, operations supvr, 1976-77; Home Savings Am, br mgr, 1977-83; Saving Admin Specialists, 1983-99; AT&T Broadband, regional dir, 1999-2002. **Orgs:** Pasadena Jr Chamber Com, 1965-67; Oakland Chamber Com, 1977-82; San Francisco Chamber Com, 1982-83; Optimist Int, 1982-83. **Home Addr:** 5967 Contra Costa Rd, Oakland, CA 94618-2136.

### TAYLOR, WILLIAM HENRY, SR.
Labor activist. **Personal:** Born Aug 28, 1931, Ethel, LA; married Thelma Watkins; children: Daryl, William Jr, Dawn & Diane. **Educ:** Univ IL, Chicago, 1956; Roosevelt Univ, attended 1969. **Career:** Oil, Chem & Atomic Workers Union, Corp Coun, pres, 1971, Minority Affairs, chmn, 1975-79, 1983; Inter-Union Wet Corn Milling US & Can Coun, chmn, 1979. **Orgs:** Adv coun, Am Arbit Assoc, 1971-75, 1982-84; pres, Bowen HS PTA, 1973-75; instr, Roosevelt Univ Labor Ed Prog, 1975; adv coun Comm Fund, 1975-79; pres, Community & Econ Develop Asn Southwest Develop Assocs, 1977-80, 1983; bd dir, Cook County Community & Econ Develop Asn, 1978-81; exec comn, Labor Coalition Pub Utility, 1981. **Honors/Awds:** Humanitarian Award, St Matthew AM Church, 1974; Special Citation Crusade Mercy, 1977. **Home Addr:** 9608 S Yates Blvd, Chicago, IL 60617-4970, **Home Phone:** (773)731-3863.

### TAYLOR-ARCHER, DR. MORDEAN
Educator. **Personal:** Born Jul 13, 1950, North Little Rock, AR; daughter of John L Taylor and Louella Henry; married Dwain E. **Educ:** Univ Ozarks, BS, social sci; Univ Ark, MA, social, 1972; Brandeis Univ, MA, PhD, social policy, planning & admin, 1979; Harvard Univ, mgt prog, 1993. **Career:** Univ Ark, instr, 1970-74; Ford Found Fe, 1974-77; Boston Col, asst prof & coordr field work, 1975-78; Va Commonwealth Univ, asst dean & asst prof, 1978-90; Kans State Univ, asst provost, multicultural affairs, 1990-96, Diversity & Dual Career Develop, assoc provost, 1996-2001; Univ Louisville, Diversity & Equal Opportunity, vice provost, contribr, 2001-. **Orgs:** Founding mem, Nat Assoc Diversity Officers Higher Ed, 2007; bd mem, bd dir, Louisville Urban League Inc, 2002: bd dir, Nat Asn Advan Colored People, 2005; bd dir, W Louisville Perf Arts Acad, 2005; Nat Asn Black Social Workers, 1978-90; fel Human Rights, Herr Found, 1978; Nat Asn Social Workers, 1987-90; Nat Asn Stud Personnel Adminr, 1988-90; Asn Black Women Higher Educ, 1990; Am Asn Higher Educ, 1990; founder & mem, Kans Asn African Am Higher Educ, 1992-; Manhattan Retory Clubs, 1993-; League Women Voters, 1996-. **Home Addr:** 7906 Sutherland Farm Rd, Prospect, KY 40059. **Business Addr:** Vice Provost for Diversity & Equal Opportunity, University of Louisville, 209 Grawemeyer Hall 2nd Fl, Louisville, KY 40292, **Business Phone:** (502)852-5719.

**TAYLOR-THOMPSON, DR. BETTY E.**
School administrator, educator. **Personal:** Born Feb 6, 1943, Houston, TX; daughter of John Charles Taylor and Johnnie Mae Hart Brooks; married Oliver B Thompson Jr; children: Amnon James Ashe II & Ida Elizabeth. **Educ:** Fisk Univ, Nashville, TN, BA, 1963; Atlanta Univ, Atlanta, GA, MLS, 1964; Howard Univ, Wash, DC, MA, 1972, PhD, 1979. **Career:** Wash, DC, pub libr, technol librn, 1969-72; Tex Southern Univ, prof eng, 1979-2008; Houston Tex, instr eng, 1974-75; Houston Independent Schs, Houston, Tex, eng teacher & librn, 1965-68, 1982-84; Dept Eng & Foreign Lang, chair, 1989-91, assoc prof eng, 1991-98, prof, 1999-2008; dept eng, chair, 2008; Univ Phoenix, Devry Univ, adj prof eng, 2000-; Univ Md Eastern Shore, interim chair dept eng & mod lang, 2008-10. **Orgs:** Col Lang Asn, co-chair, Black Studies Comt; Nat Coun Teachers Eng; pres, Southern Conf Afro-Am Studies, 1990-92; Conf Col Teachers Eng; Am Lit Asn; pres, Southern Conf Afro-Am Studies; Nat Col Teachers Eng; Am Asn Univ Women. **Home Addr:** 3618 Glenhill Dr, Pearland, TX 77584-9173, **Home Phone:** (281)692-9504. **Business Addr:** Chair, Texas Southern University, 3100 Cleburne St, Houston, TX 77004, **Business Phone:** (713)313-7616.

**TEAGLE, TERRY MICHAEL**
Basketball player. **Personal:** Born Apr 10, 1960, Broaddus, TX. **Educ:** Baylor Univ, BS, phys educ, 1982. **Career:** Basketball player (retired); Houston Rockets, 1982-84; Detroit Pistons, 1984-85; Golden State Warriors, 1985-90; Los Angeles Lakers, 1990-92; Benetton Treviso, Italy, 1992-93; Houston Rockets, 1993; Goccia di Carnia Udine, Italy, 1993-94; Atenas de Cordoba, Arg, 1994-95.

**TEAGUE, GEORGE THEO**
Football player, football coach. **Personal:** Born Feb 18, 1971, Lansing, MI; married Consuela; children: James II & Jada. **Educ:** Univ Ala, elec engineering, 1993. **Career:** Football player (retired), football coach; Crimson tide Football team, starter, 1989-93; Green Bay Packers, def back, 1993-95; GeorgeTeague.com, pub speaker, 1993-2014; Dallas Cowboys, 1996, 1998-2001; Miami Dolphins, 1997; Harvest Christian Acad, athletic dir & head football coach, 2003-07; Carrollton Christian Acad, athletic dir, head football coach/dir phys educ, 2007-11; Shelton Sch, athletic dir & head football coach, dir phys educ, 2011-. **Orgs:** Pres, George Teague & Friends Found, 2002. **Home Addr:** 1000 Del Dr, Carrollton, TX 75010-1135. **Business Addr:** Athletic Director, Head Football Coach, Shelton School, 15720 Hillcrest Rd, Dallas, TX 75248, **Business Phone:** (972)774-1772.

**TEAGUE, ROBERT**
Executive. **Personal:** Born Oct 26, 1929, Durant, MS; married Tresa Marie Smith. **Educ:** Tougaloo Col, BA, 1955; Univ Ill, MSW, 1961; Univ SC, 1966. **Career:** Ed Oakley Trng Sch, dir playground, 1958-59; IL Pub Aid Comt, 1959-60; Danville VA Neuropsychiat Hosp, psychiat team, 1960-61; Sepulveda VA Hosp, sr psychiat soc worker, 1961-64; Pvt Marital Coun Clin, assoc dir, 1962-64; CA Dept Ment Hyg, sr psychiat soc worker, 1964-65, pgm consult, 1965-67; Harbor View House, dir part owner, pres, 1966-; Whitney M Young, Jr Psychiat Hosp, dir owner prof placement serv pres exec dir, 1971-74; Psychiat Pgms S Bay Ment Health Ctr, dir, 1974. **Orgs:** Chmn, Soc Work Res Comt VA Hosp Sepulveda, 1961-64; consult, Westminister Neighbhourhood Assoc Ment Health Clin, 1964-65; pres, Col Alumni, 1965-67; bd dir, S Cen Welfare Plng Coun, 1969-; bd dir, STEP Job Trng Proj; co founder, Pvt Marital Guid Clin; bd dir, W Reg Conf Ment Health Pgm Mgt, 1974-76; Ad HocCom Ment Health Ctrs, 1974; Greater LA Ment Health Assoc; bd dir, Nat Asn Soc Workers; LA Welfare Plng Coun; elder Westminister Presb Ch; Calif Regis Soc Workers; Am Psy Asn; Calif Welfare Conf; Acad Cert Soc Workers; Col Nursing Home Admin; Univ Ill, 2010-. **Honors/Awds:** LA men of tomorrow, YMCA; Community Service Award, LA Sentinel, 1972; Author of Various articles & resolutions. **Home Addr:** 515 Bain St, PO Box 282, Durant, MS 39063. **Business Addr:** President, Director Part Owner, Harbor View House, 921 S Beacon St, San Pedro, CA 90731, **Business Phone:** (310)547-3341.

**TEAMER, DR. CHARLES C., SR.**
School administrator. **Personal:** Born May 20, 1933, Shelby, NC; son of Mary; married Mary Alice Dixon; children: Charles Carl, Roderic F & Cheryl R. **Educ:** Clark Col, BA, 1954; Univ Omaha, post grad, 1963; Univ Nebr, MA; Tulane Univ, PhD, 1966. **Career:** SC State Col Orangeburg, acct, 1955-56; Tenn State Univ Nashville, asst bus mgr, 1958-62; Wiley Col Marshall, Tex, bus mgr, 1962-65; Dillard Univ, New Orleans, vpres fiscal affairs, 1965-2002; World Trade Ctr, pres, New Orleans, 2003; Enterprise Resource Planning Syst, mgr; Us Dept Educ, consult; Amistad Res Ctr, exec dir; Dryades Savings Bank, New Orleans, La, chmn, 1993-; chmn, Dock Bd. **Orgs:** Dir, New Orleans Pub Serv Comn; bd dir, Common Fund; vpres, United Way New Orleans; past dir, pres, Nat Asn Col & Univ Bus Officers; vpres, bd dir, New Orleans Area Coun; treas, M & T Area Com Lafon Protestant Home; bd dir, Ochner Med Found C's Hosp; New Orleans Chamber Com; Alpha Phi Alpha; life mem, Nat Comptroller Methodist Clubs; Masons; Shriners; pres, Southern Asn Col; Dirs Southern Educ Found. **Honors/Awds:** Silver Beaver Award, Boy Scouts Am, 1968. **Special Achievements:** One of 10 Outstanding Citizens of New Orleans', 1979; First African Am Bd Commissioners Port New Orleans. **Home Addr:** 4619 Owens Blvd, New Orleans, LA 70122-1224, **Home Phone:** (504)283-5807. **Business Addr:** Chairman, Dryades Savings Bank, 233 Carondelet St Suite 200, New Orleans, LA 70130, **Business Phone:** (504)598-7214.

**TEASLEY, LARKIN (LARKIN A TEASLEY)**
President (organization), executive, executive director. **Personal:** Born Sep 23, 1936, Cleveland, OH; married Violet M Williams; children: Lisa, Erica & Laura. **Educ:** Fisk Univ, BA, mathematics, 1957; Occidental Col, grad work actuarial sci, 1958; Univ Calif, Los Angeles, Calif, grad sch bus exec prog, 1972. **Career:** Golden State Mutual Life Ins Co, Los Angeles, Calif, asst actuary, 1958-63; NC Mutual Life Ins Co, actuary, 1963-69; Golden State Mutual Life Ins Co, dir, 1971-, pres & chief operating officer, 1980-90, chief exec officer, 1991-, chmn, 2001-. **Orgs:** Dir, Golden State Minority Found; dir, Broadway Fed Saving & Loan Asn; dir, Calif Chamber Com; dir, Los Angeles City Retirement Asn; fel Soc Actuaries; Am Acad Actuaries; Nat Asn Bus Economists; Alpha Phi Alpha; Phi Beta Kappa; Beta Kappa Chi Sci Hon Soc; bd mem, LACERA; bd dir, Fed Bank; Boy Scouts Am. **Home Addr:** 4581 Don Milagro Dr, Los Angeles, CA 90008. **Business Addr:** Chief Executive Officer, Chairman & President, Golden State Mutual Life Insurance Co, 1999 W Adams Blvd, Los Angeles, CA 90018-3595, **Business Phone:** (213)731-1131.

**TEASLEY, MARIE R.**
Newspaper editor, president (organization). **Personal:** Born Hannibal, MO; daughter of George Hannibal Wright (deceased) and Rose Venetia Trott (deceased); married Ronald; children: Ronald Jr, Timothy & Lydia. **Educ:** Wayne State Univ; Univ Detroit. **Career:** Newspaper editor (retired); Black Publ, writer, Aged 14; Fame Mag, writer; Pittsburgh Courier, writer; WSU campus paper; Philip Morris Co; NW Papers; Food & Music Radio, host; Regular TV Show Guest; Mich Chronicle, club & soc writer, 1966, women's ed, 1991, cruise rep, 1991-98, ed press assignment to Brazil, 1992, Los Angeles, Chicago & Dallas, 1993-94; Moscow, 1999. **Orgs:** Women Communications; adv bd, WXYZ; adv bd, Highland Park YWCA; Northwestern High School Alumni Asn; Detroit Chap Nat Asn Media Women; Cancer Soc; numerous Civic Orgs; chmn, founder, Detroit Sci Ctr Bus Fund, 1983; pres, Madonna Women on Action; Coalition of 100 Black Women; Urban League Guild; Nat Asn Travel Eds; Gamma Phi Delta Sorority, Delta Nu Chapter; life mem, Nat Asn Advan Colored People. **Honors/Awds:** Employee of the Year, MI Chronicle, 1972; SCLC Award, Top Communicator, 1973; Named Nat Media Woman of Year, 1974-75; Bridal Book edited Nat Asn Advan Colored People Award, 1974; Woman of Year, Catholic Archidose of Detroit, 1974; Detroit Chap Negro Bus & Prof Women Top Serv Award, 1974; Woman of Year, Detroit Chapter Media, 1974; NNAPA Best Women's Pages San Francisco, 1975; profiles in black CORE NY Publication, 1977; Top Jour Award, Bus & Prof Women, Nat Negro B&P Detroit Chap, 1977; Turner Broadcasting, Goodwill Ambassador to Moscow, 1986; Coalition of 100 Black Women; Outstanding Journ & Reporting, 1987; Community Serv Award, WC Exec William Lucas, 1986; NY Black Fashion Mus Reporting Award; Educ and Civics Awards, 1994-96; Serv Award, AA Sports Hall of Fame, 1996; Recog & Servs Award, Detroit City Coun. **Special Achievements:** Named one of the 17 Women of Action, State of MI, 1999. **Home Addr:** 19317 Coyle St, Detroit, MI 48235-2039, **Home Phone:** (313)863-0185.

**TEASLEY, MICHELLE NICOLE (NIKKI TEASLEY)**
Basketball player, basketball coach. **Personal:** Born Mar 22, 1979, Washington, DC; daughter of Ernestine; married Joshua Houston; children: 2. **Educ:** Univ NC, Chapel Hill, attended 2002. **Career:** Youth Summer Basketball Season, head coach, 2001; Los Angeles Sparks, guard, 2002-05; Wash Mystics, guard, 2006-07; Atlanta Dream, 2008-09; Detroit Shock, 2009; Tulsa Shock, 2010. **Orgs:** USA Basketball Women's Sr Nat Team, 2004; founder, Team Assist Hoops. **Business Addr:** Professional Basketball Player, WNBA LA Sparks, 865 S Figueroa St Suite 104, Los Angeles, CA 90017, **Business Phone:** (213)929-1300.

**TEASLEY, NIKKI. See TEASLEY, MICHELLE NICOLE.**

**TEASLEY, RONALD (ROOMIE TEASLEY)**
Educator, photographer, athletic coach. **Personal:** Born Jan 26, 1927, Detroit, MI; son of Ezra and Mattie; married Marie; children: Ronald Jr, Timothy & Lydia Vassal. **Educ:** Wayne State Univ, BS, 1955, MS, educ, 1958. **Career:** Baseball player (retired); Detroit Bd Educ, teacher, coach, suprv teacher, actg counsr, asst athletic dir; Mich Chronicle, columnist & photogr; Toledo Cubs, 1945; Minor Leagues, 1948-51; New York Cubans, 1948. **Orgs:** Kappa Alpha Psi Fraternity; Mich High Sch Baseball Coaches Asn; Afro-Am Sports Hall Fame & Gallery; Negro League Baseball Players Asn; Yesterday's Negro League Found; Adv Bd, Masters Sr Sports Prog; dir, Sr Golf Prog; Negro League Baseball Players Mus; Meals On Wheels Golf Hall Fame Comt; Ill-fated US League. **Home Addr:** 19317 Coyle St, Detroit, MI 48235-2039, **Home Phone:** (313)863-0185.

**TEEKAH, DR. GEORGE ANTHONY**
Physician. **Personal:** Born Mar 29, 1948; son of George D and Lottie Wason; married Theresa R Riley. **Educ:** Howard Univ, Col Med, BS, 1971, MD, 1975. **Career:** Greater SE Community Hosp, med dir ICU, respiratory ther, 1980-83; Richmond Community Hosp, med dir, respiratory ther, 1984-; Dc Gen Hosp, Int Med, resident; Hav Univ Hosp, Int Med, resident; Our Lady Mercy Med Ctr, Int Med, resident; pvt pract, currently. **Honors/Awds:** Beta Kappa Chi Scientific Hon Soc, 1972. **Home Addr:** 2721 Wicklow Lane, Richmond, VA 23236-1341, **Home Phone:** (804)276-6865. **Business Addr:** Physician, Private Practitioner, 505 W Leigh St Suite 207, Richmond, VA 23220, **Business Phone:** (804)788-0556.

**TEER, DEEN. See TEER, WARDEEN T.**

**TEER, WARDEEN T. (DEEN TEER)**
Government official, businessperson. **Personal:** Born Jul 8, 1945, Marvell, AR; daughter of Walter and Lillie M Townes; married Michael C Sr; children: Michael Jr & Monte. **Educ:** Southern Ill Univ, BA, econs, 1970. **Career:** Council member (retired), business executive; City E St Louis, sr planner, 1970-74; Nat Urban League, regional res dir, 1974-76; City Riverside, admin analyst, 1982-86, coun rels admin, 1986; Teer One Properties Inc, vpres, 2005-; Style Junkie Antiques, owner, 2005-14. **Orgs:** Bd mem, UCR Bot Gardens; Alpha Kappa Alpha Sorority; exec mgt prog, Univ Calif Riverside, 1992; comt chair, Orange Blossom Festival. **Home Addr:** 3978 Brockton Ave, Riverside, CA 92501-3203. **Business Addr:** Vice President, Teer One Properties Inc, 4051 10Th St, Riverside, CA 92501-3509, **Business Phone:** (951)683-5339.

**TEEUWISSEN, PIETER**
Lawyer. **Personal:** Born Sep 26, 1966, Ann Arbor, MI; son of John and Charlotte E; married Lisa M. **Educ:** Princeton Univ, attended 1986; Tougaloo Col, BA, hist, polit sci & pre med, 1987; Univ Minn, Law Sch, JD, 1990. **Career:** Miss Dept Human Servs, atty, spec assignments, 1990-91; Cherry Given Lockett Peters & Diaz, assoc, 1992-93; Byrd & Assoc, sr assoc, 1993-97; Danks, Simon & Teeuwissen Assocs, managing partner, 1997-98; Danks, Teeuwissen & Assocs, atty, 1998-2004; Pieter Teeuwissen, Esq, PLLC, pvt pract, 2004-; Law Off Pieter Teeuwissen; Jackson City, Miss, litigation & appellate cases, sr dep, spec asst city atty, 2004-09, interim city atty, city atty, 2009-13; Hinds County, bd coun, 2013-. **Orgs:** Sloan Found fel, 1986; Vice-Chair, Miss Bd Bar Admis; Am Bar Asn; Nat Bar Asn; Miss State Bar; life mem, Magnolia Bar Asn; Omega Psi Phi; alumini mem, Am Inns Ct; Fifth Circuit Bar Asn; Hinds County Bar Asn. **Home Addr:** 5920 Dabney Dr, Jackson, MS 39206-2025, **Home Phone:** (601)982-3370. **Business Addr:** Interim City Attorney, City Attorney, City of Jackson, 455 E Capitol St, Jackson, MS 39207-2779, **Business Phone:** (601)960-1799.

**TEI, DR. EBO**
Educator. **Educ:** Univ Ark, PhD. **Career:** Univ Ark, Planning Comn, Psychol Prog, dir, Dept Social & Behav Sci, Sch Arts & Sci, Div Acad Affairs, dept chair, 1999, prof, currently. **Orgs:** Authority EPSCoR Advisory Committee; Ark Health Ins State Planning Grant Initiative; Ark Sci & Technol Authority; UAPB admin; mem, Psychol Prog. **Home Addr:** , Pine Bluff, AR. **Business Addr:** Professor, University of Arkansas, 1200 N Univ Dr, Pine Bluff, AR 71601, **Business Phone:** (870)575-8175.

**TELFAIR, ESQ. BRIAN KRAIG**
Lawyer. **Personal:** Born Aug 11, 1961, Jacksonville, FL; son of Kenneth L and Roberta E. **Educ:** Va State Univ, BS, chem, 1983; Univ Mass, Amherst, MEd, 1985; Col William & Mary, Marshall-Wythe Sch Law, JD, 1990. **Career:** Adult Career Devt Ctr, teacher, 1985-87; Sands Anderson Marks & Miller, legal intern, 1988-89; Commonwealth Va, Off Atty Gen, legal intern, 1989; Dow Chem Co, corp coun, 1990-92; Miller, Canfield, Paddock & Stone, PLC, assoc, 1992-95; Wilder & Gregory, assoc, 1995-99; US Dist Ct, Eastern & Western Districts Va, atty, 1996; Bowman & Brooke, partner, 1999-2006; US Dist Ct, Eastern Dist Mich, atty, 2005; Womble Carlyle Sandridge & Rice PLLC, partner, 2005-06; LeClairRyan, atty, 2007-09; Telfair Law Firm LLC, managing partner, owner, atty, 2009-10; City Richmond, dep city atty litigation & pub safety, 2010-12; City Petersburg, city atty, 2012-16; Spencer Shuford LLP, atty, 2016-; US Ct Appeals, Fourth Circuit, atty. **Orgs:** Omega Psi Phi Fraternity, 1987-; State Bar Mich, 1990-; exec comt secy, Am Bar Asn, 1990-; Wolverine Bar Asn, 1992-; regional dir, Va Asn Defense Attorneys; bd mem, William & Mary Law Sch Asn; bd mem, Greater Richmond Urban League, 1996-01; Advisor, nat bar asn; bd dir, Gracious Smiles Inc. **Honors/Awds:** The Order of Barristers, Col William & Mary, Marshall-Wythe Sch Law, 1990. **Business Addr:** Attorney, Spencer Shuford LLP, 6806 Paragon Pl Suite 200, Richmond, VA 23230, **Business Phone:** (804)285-5200.

**TEMPLE, ESQ. DONALD MELVIN**
Lawyer. **Personal:** Born May 27, 1953, Philadelphia, PA; son of Joseph and Ursula; married Vonterris Hagan; children: Caira Suki & Imani Korina. **Educ:** Howard Univ, BA, 1975; Univ Santa Clara Law Sch, JD, 1978; Georgetown Univ Law Ctr, LLM, int & const law, 1982. **Career:** US Dept Housing, atty adv, 1978-80; US House Rep, sr staff coun, 1980-90; US House Rep, DC deleg, 1990; Donald M Temple PC, owner, prin, 1991-. **Orgs:** Pres, Stud Bar Asn, Univ Santa Clara Sch Law, 1977-78; pres, Nat Conf Black Lawyers DC, 1980-81; Nat Bar Asn, 1980-97; pres, DC Chap, Concerned Black Men Inc, 1982-83; nat chmn, 21st Century PAC, 1983-87; Bd mem, Wash Bar Asn, 1984-97; Chmn, Charles Hamilton Houston Legal Educ Inst, 1984-97; Kappa Alpha Psi Fraternity, 1985-; Prince Hall Masonic Lodge, 1985-; chmn, Adam Clayton Powell Soc, 1987; chmn, DC Civilian Complaint Rev Bd, 1991-94; Pa Bar Asn; pres, co-founder, Cong Black Assocs; bd dir, Archbishop Carroll High Sch; pres, Charlotte E. Ray Inn Ct. **Honors/Awds:** Role Model of Year, Legal Educ Nat Black Law Stud Asn, 1985; Best of Washington Hall of Fame, 1986; Harriet Tubman Award, Cong Black Asn, 1987; Outstanding Black Professional Business Exchange Network, 1987; Alumni of the Year, Geortown Law Ctr Black Stud Asn, 1988; Gertrude E Rush Award, Nat Bar Asn, 1990; Cora T. Walker Award, Nat Bar Asn; Gertrude E. Rush Award, Nat bar asn; Community Service Award, Howard Univ; Ollie Mae Cooper Award, Washington Bar Asn; "one of Thurgood Marshall Center Trust's Phenomenal Men", 2009. **Business Addr:** Attorney at Law, Donald M Temple PC, 1200 G St NW Suite 370, Washington, DC 20005-3814, **Business Phone:** (202)628-1101.

**TEMPLE, EDWARD STANLEY**
Educator, athletic coach. **Personal:** Born Sep 20, 1927, Harrisburg, PA; son of Christopher R and Ruth N; married Charlie B Law; children: Lloyd Bernard & Edwina R. **Educ:** Tenn State Univ, BS, health & phys educ, sociol, 1950, MS, health & phys educ, sociol, 1953; Pa State Univ, PhD, 1954. **Career:** Athletic coach, educr (retired); Tenn State Univ, head women's track coach, 1953-94, asst coach, 1980, assoc prof, sociol, 1950-94; US Women's Track Team, track coach, 1958-94, asst coach, 1980; U. S. Pan Am team, coach, 1959, 1975; Jr Nat Pan Am team, head coach, 1982. **Orgs:** Kappa Delta Pi Educ Fraternity; Golden Key Hon Soc; Int Track & Field Coun; exec comt, Nashville Sports Coun; life mem, Tenn State Univ Alumni Asn; Us Olympic Comt, 1960, 1964, 1968, 1972, 1976, 1980, 1984; Nashville YMCA; Omega Psi Phi Fraternity; Clark Memorial United Methodist Church; Nat Col Athletic Asn; Track & Field Coaches Asn; U.S. Olympic Comt; Int Women's Track & Field Comt, currently; chmn, Nashville's 200-plus mem Amateur Sports Comt. **Home Addr:** 2628 Delk Ave, Nashville, TN 37208-1919, **Home Phone:** (615)244-5711.

**TEMPLE, DR. JACQUELINE B. (JACKIE TEMPLE)**
Educator. **Personal:** Born Nov 4, 1946, New Orleans, LA; daughter of David L Bartholomew Sr; children: Elisa Harvey & Elena M. **Educ:** Spelman Col, BA, 1968; Univ New Orleans, MEd, 1985; Univ Wis-Madison, PhD, 1997. **Career:** Real Estate Ctr New Orleans, sales & listing agt, 1979-82; Orleans Parish Sch Dist, Area II Spec Edu Off,

spec educr, work adjust coord, 1977-89; Atlanta City Schs, spec educr, 1977-89; job developer, spec educr, 1990-93; Portland State Univ, assoc prof, currently, prof emer, 1997-2013. **Orgs:** Spelman Col Alumna Asn, 1968-; Coun Except C, Asn Supv & Curric Develop, 1997-2003; Nat Asn Multicultural Educrs, 2002-03; Fulbright Scholars Alumna Asn, 2002. **Home Addr:** 31 NE 179th Ave, Portland, OR 97230-6625, **Home Phone:** (503)667-9414. **Business Addr:** Associate Professor, Director, Portland State University, 615 SW Harrison St Rm 608D, Portland, OR 97207-0751, **Business Phone:** (503)725-5858.

### TEMPLE, ONEY D.

Executive, government official. **Educ:** Webster Col, MO, BA, MA; Ohio State Univ, Emerging Leaders Inst, 2002. **Career:** McDonalds; IBM; Xerox; Univ Akron, adj fac, 1991-93; Ohio Dept Develop, Econ Develop Div, dep dir, 1991-97; Off Governer, Akron reg liason; State & Local Govt Comn Ohio, mem bd, 1997-2001; Am Elec Power Energy Serv Inc, dir community serv, dir community serv & econ develop, mgr energy mktg, pres, 1997-2003; Cent State Univ Ohio, vice chair bd trustee, 2001-06; Moen Inc, dir target markets, 2003-06; El Paso Corp, 2006-12; ODT Consult, lead partner, 2012-. **Orgs:** Ohio State Bar Asn; trustee, Ohio Hist Soc, 1991-97; State & Local Govt Comn Ohio, 2000-03; Legal Ethics & Prof Conduct Comt, Ohio State Bar Asn, 2000-01; Fla Natural Gas Asn. **Business Addr:** Vice Chairperson of the Board of Trustees, Central State University, 1400 Brush Row Rd, Wilberforce, OH 45384, **Business Phone:** (937)376-6011.

### TEMPLETON, GARRY LEWIS

Baseball player, baseball manager. **Personal:** Born Mar 24, 1956, Lockney, TX; son of Spiavia and Otella Williams; married Glenda M Glenn; children: Garry Jr, Gerome & Genae Nicole. **Career:** Baseball player (retired), baseball coach, manager; St Louis Cardinals, shortstop, 1976-81; San Diego Padres, infielder, 1982-91; New York Mets, 1991; Calif Angels Baseball Orgn, Cedar Rapid Kernals, mgr, 1998; Erie Sea Wolves, mgr, 1999; Edmonton Trappers, 2000; Salt Lake Stingers, mgr, 2001; Gary Rail cats, field mgr, 2003-04; Gary South-Shore RailCats, mgr, 2003-04; Golden Baseball League's Fullerton Flyers, mgr, 2005-06; Palm Springs Chill, mgr, 2008; Long Beach Armada, mgr, 2009; Chico Outlaws, mgr, 2010; Maui Na Koa Ikaika, mgr, 2011; Newark Bears, mgr, 2013. **Home Addr:** 13552 Del Poniente Rd, Poway, CA 92064. **Business Addr:** Manager, Golden Baseball League, 2900 Orange Ave Suite 203, Signal Hill, CA 90755, **Business Phone:** (562)856-5551.

### TENNANT, MELVIN, II

Manager. **Personal:** Born Jul 2, 1959, Bryan, TX; son of Melvin and Cora; married Julie; children: Carla, Caroline, Brian, Matthew & Melanie. **Educ:** Rice Univ, BA, managerial studies, 1982; Liberty Univ, MA, christian leadership studies, 2011; Am Soc Asn Execs, cert asn exec. **Career:** Houston Conv & Visitors Bur, assoc dir sales, 1980-87; Corpus Christi Conv & Visitors Bur, conv div dir, 1987-88; Irving, Tex, Conv & Visitors Bur, assoc dir, 1988-90; Okla Conv & Visitors Bur, pres & chief exec officer, 1990-92; Charlotte Conv & Visitors Bur, pres & chief exec officer, 1992-2003; San Antonio Conv & Visitors Bur, exec dir, 2003-05; Innovative Mgt Resources, chief innovation officer, 2005-07; Internet Destination Sales Syst, chief exec officer, 2007-14; Meet Minneapolis, pres, chief exec officer, 2007-. **Orgs:** Houston Area Urban League, 1984-, Nat Coalition Black Meeting Planners, 1985-, Am Soc Asn Execs; bd mem, Patrons Humanities; bd mem, United Negro Col Fund, E Bay Chap; chmn, Int Asn Conv & Visitors Bureaus; bd mem, Western Asn Conv & Visitors Bureaus; Nat Tour Asn; Meet Minneapolis, 2007-08, ceo & pres, 2008-. Houston Area Urban League, 1984-, Nat Coalition Black Meeting Planners, 1985-, Am Soc Asn Execs; bd mem, Patrons Humanities; bd mem, United Negro Col Fund, E Bay Chap; chmn, Int Asn Conv & Visitors Bureaus; bd mem, Western Asn Conv & Visitors Bureaus; Nat Tour Asn; chmn, Destination Mkt Asn Int; Travel Indust Asn Am; Ctr Asn Leadership; Meet Minneapolis, 2007-08, ceo & pres, 2008-; chmn, Relig Conf Mgt Asn, currently; Minneapolis Regional Chamber Com; Minneapolis Downtown Coun & YouthLink. **Honors/Awds:** Certificate of Appreciation, Nat Tour Asn, 1984; President Award, RMCA; Chapter Legacy Award, MPI. **Business Addr:** Chief Executive Officer, Meet Minneapolis, 250 Marquette Ave S Suite 1330, Minneapolis, MN 55104, **Business Phone:** (612)767-7800.

### TERBORG-PENN, DR. ROSALYN M.

Educator, historian. **Personal:** Born Oct 22, 1941, Brooklyn, NY; daughter of Jacques Sr and Jeanne Van Horn; children: Jeanna C. **Educ:** City Univ NY, Queens Col, BA, hist, 1963; George Washington Univ, MA, hist & diplomatic hist, 1969; Howard Univ, PhD, US hist concentration Afro-Am hist, 1978. **Career:** Morgan State Univ, instr, 1969-, assoc prof hist, African Am Studies Prog, coordr, 1978-95, Oral Hist Proj Dir, 1978-89, PhD Hist prog, proj dir, 1989-92, Cornell-Morgan Distance Learning, campus coordr, 1996-, Grad Prog, grad coordr, 1995-2006, prof emer, 2006-; Howard Community Col, adj fac, 1970-74; Univ Md, fac, 1977-78; Baltimore County, Am Studies & Hist, instr; Ford Found, fel minorities, 1980-81; Alexander St Press LLC, 2010-. **Orgs:** Charter mem, Nat Asn Advan Colored People chap; campus coordr, Cornell-Morgan Distance Learning Proj, 1966; Iota Lambda Omega Chap, 1972-2015; dir, Morgan State Univ Oral Hist Proj, 1978-89; co-founder, Asn Black Women Historians, nat dir, 1979-83; comnr, Howard Cty Md Comn Women, 1980-82; Hist ed Feminist Studies, 1984-89; Res & Pubations Comn, Md Hist Soc, 1989-96; exec comt mem, Asn Caribben Historians, 1989-2013; chair, Am Hist Asn Comm Women Historians, 1991-93; Alpha Kappa Alpha Sorority Inc, Int Arch & Heritage Comn, 1994-96; comnr, Mary McLeod Bethune Coun House, Nat Hist Site, Fed Comn, 1996-; Asn Study Worldwide African Diaspora, founding mem, exec bd, 2001-07. **Honors/Awds:** Grad History Essay Award, Rayford Logan, Howard Univ, 1973; Graduate Fellow of History, Howard Univ, 1973-74; Visiting Scholar Grant, Smithsonian Inst, 1982, 1994; Travel Colcitions Grant, Nat Endowment Humanities, 1984; Letitia Woods Brown Award, 1987-88, Award for Best Anthology, 1995; Anna Julia Cooper Award, Sage Women's Educ Press, 1995; Award for Best Book, Asn Black Women Historians, 1998; Lorraine A Williams Leadership Award, 1998; Distinguished Black Marylander Award, Towson Univ, 2003; Carter G. Woodson Scholar's Medallion, Asn Study African Am Life & Hist, 2008; Outstanding Woman Award, Morgan State Univ, 2008; John Blassingame Prize, Southern Hist Asn, 2010; Letitia Woods Brown Memorial Prize, 2012; Received scores of awards and honors for her accomplishments. **Special Achievements:** First Woman Of Color To Become Chair Of The American Historical Associations Committee On Womens History; Author: Afro-American Woman-Struggles & Images, 1978, 1981 & 1997; Womenin Africa & the African Dispora, 1987 & 1996; Black Women in America: An Historical Encyclo, 1993; Women in Africa & the African Diaspora: AReader, 1996; African-American Women in the Struggle for the Vote, 1998; The Columbia Guide to African American History Since 1939. **Home Addr:** 5484 Sleeping Dog Lane, Columbia, MD 21045-2249, **Home Phone:** (301)596-4338. **Business Addr:** Emeritus Professor, Morgan State University, Rm 326-B Holmes Hall, Baltimore, MD 21251, **Business Phone:** (443)885-3333.

**TERRELL, BOB. See TERRELL, ROBERT E.**

### TERRELL, DR. CATHERINE MILLIGAN

Educator. **Personal:** Born Oct 28, 1944, St. Croix; daughter of Hugh and Exira; children: Natalie & Omar E. **Educ:** Temple Univ, Philadelphia, PA, BS, 1973; Antioch Univ, Yellow Springs, OH, MEd, 1974; Columbia Univ, New York, NY, PhD, 1991. **Career:** Sch Dist Philadelphia, Philadelphia, Pa, asst prin, 1980-86; St Dunstan's Episcopal High Sch, St Croix, VI, head, 1986. **Orgs:** Phi Delta Kappa, 1987-. **Home Addr:** Frederiksted, PO Box 3354, St. Croix00841, **Home Phone:** (809)772-3088.

### TERRELL, DONNA

Television news anchorperson. **Educ:** Cent Mich Univ, BA, brdcst & cinematic arts. **Career:** Kellogg Community Col, instr tv; WOTV, reporter & anchor; WKYC-TV, from med reporter, anchor & reporter; WKBD-TV, anchor; KLRT; FOX16 News; the "Family Health"; WWJ-TV, anchor; UPN Nightside News, anchor; "Arkansas Now", host; FOX16 sports; KLRT Fox 16, co-anchor, 2004-. **Orgs:** Susan G Komen Breast Cancer Found; Make A Wish Found; Ctrs C & Family Serv; Achievement Ctrs for C; Nat Asn TV Arts & Sci; Nat Asn Black Journalists; Easter Seals Ark; Ronald McDonald House; ambassador, Am Cancer Socs; Muscular Dystrophy Asn; Little Rock Chap Links. **Honors/Awds:** Two Emmy Awards; Associated Press Award; Best of Detroit, Detroit Free Press, 2002. **Special Achievements:** Cover several major events including Nelson Mandela's tour of the United States after his release from a South African prison. **Business Addr:** Co-Anchor, KLRT Fox 16, 10800 Col Glenn Rd, Little Rock, AR 72204, **Business Phone:** (501)225-0016.

### TERRELL, DOROTHY A.

President (organization), computer executive, chief executive officer. **Personal:** Born Jun 12, 1945, Hallandale, FL; daughter of Charles Walter Sr and Pearlie Weeks; married Albert H Brown; children: Dorian. **Educ:** A&M Univ, Fla, BA, Eng, 1966. **Career:** Job Corps, coun; Reverend Leon Sullivans Opportunities Indust Corp (OIC), from counr to asst dir, 1967; Commonwealth Mass Off C, assoc dir, 1975; Digital Equip Corp (DEC), training mgr, 1976, plant human rels mgr, 1978-80, group human rels mgr, 1980-83, group mgr, 1983-84, plant mgr, 1984, group mgr, 1987-91; Sun Microsystems, corp officer, 1991-97; Gen Mills Incorporation, dir, 1994, managing Partner, currently; Herman Miller Inc, dir, 1997-; NMS Commun, Platform Serv Group, sr vpres worldwide sales, Platform & Serv Group, pres, 1998-2002; First Light Capital, partner, 2003-10; FirstCap Advisors, managing partner, founder, 2010-. **Orgs:** Delta Sigma Theta, 1965-; adv comt, OIC, 1984-87; comn mem, Boston C C, 1984-88; trustee, Social Policy Res, 1985-89; bd mem, Boston YWCA, 1985-89; bd mem, Lera Pk Community Develop, 1985-89; bd mem, BostonClub, 1986-89; bd dir, Gen Mills, 1994-, chairperson, Pub Responsibility Comt; Sears Roebuck, 1995-2005; Lightbridge, 2003-; Corp Governance Comt; pres, chief exec officer, Competitive Inner City (ICIC), 2005-07; bd dir, Mass Gen Hosp; trustee, Boston Comput Mus. **Honors/Awds:** Achievement Award, Snowden Asn, 1984; Film Choosing to Lead AMA, 1986; Achievement Award, YWCA, 1986; Black Achievers, YMCA, 1987; Hecht-ShawAward, 1987; Mus of Afro-Am Hist Award, 1988; Leadership Pioneer Award, 1988; Edges Group Award, 1992; Women of Courage & Conviction Award, National Coun of Negro Women, 1993; Distinguished Alumni Award, FL A & M Univ, 1995; Named one of 20 Women of Power & Influence in Corp Am, Black Enterprise mag, 1997; Choice Leadership Award, Natl Women's Econ Alliance Found, 1997; Named one of Top 50 Women Line Mgrs in Am, Exec Female mag. **Special Achievements:** First African American woman to hold the plant manager of the DEC plant, Roxbury, Massachusetts. **Home Addr:** 15 Garland Rd, Lincoln, MA 01773-1816. **Business Addr:** Managing Partner, Director, General Mills Inc, No 1 Gen Mills Blvd, Minneapolis, MN 55426, **Business Phone:** (763)764-7600.

**TERRELL, DR. FRANCIS. See Obituaries Section.**

### TERRELL, FRANCIS D'ARCY

Educator, lawyer. **Personal:** Born May 13, 1940, Caledonia, OH; married Mary Jane Hawthorne; children: Derek M & Randall D. **Educ:** Univ Toledo, BS, 1970; Columbia Law Sch, JD, 1973. **Career:** Shearman & Sterling, assoc atty, 1973-75; pvt pract atty, 1975-77; Jones & Terrell, partner, 1977-82; Bronx Community Col, dep chmn & prof; City Col, Greenberg Legal Studies Prog, prof & dir. **Orgs:** Am Bus Law Asn, 1984-; Ny Bar. **Home Addr:** 50 Main St Suite 1000, White Plains, NY 10606. **Business Addr:** Attorney, 15 Stacey Ct, Peekskill, NY 10566-2502, **Business Phone:** (914)734-8085.

### TERRELL, FREDERICK O.

Chairperson, founder (originator), chief executive officer. **Personal:** Born Jan 1, 1952?, Chicago, IL; married Jonelle Procope; children: 2. **Educ:** Laverne Col, BA, 1976; Occidental Col, MA; Yale Sch Mgt, MBA, 1982. **Career:** Coro Found, post-grad fel; Credit Suisse First Boston Corp, sr banker, managing dir & partner, 1983-96; Provender Capital Group LLC, co-founder, managing partner & chief exec officer, 1998-2010; Credit Suisse, gen partner, 1997-, vice chmn investment banking, 2010-. **Orgs:** Mem bd advisor, Coro Found New York, 1977; dir, New York Investment Fund Mgr Inc; dir, New York Life Ins Co, 2003-; dir, Empire Blue Cross Blue Shield; dir, Nat Asn Investment Co; dir, PacPizza L.L.C; dir, Diversity Channel Inc; partner, New York Partnership, 2003; Univ Coun Yale Univ; chmn, Carver Bancorp Inc; mem bd, Vanguarde Media Inc; mem bd, WellChoice Inc; Fin adv, US Dept Veterans Affairs. **Honors/Awds:** Deal of the Year, 1985, 1993; "Black Enterprise", 75 Most Powerful Blacks on Wall Street, 2011. **Special Achievements:** One of 25 "Hottest Blacks on Wall Street", Black Enterprise, 1992. **Business Addr:** Managing Partner, Chief Executive Officer, Provender Capital Group LLC, 17 State St Suite 23, New York, NY 10004, **Business Phone:** (212)271-8888.

### TERRELL, HENRY MATTHEW

Manager, government official, lawyer. **Personal:** Born Dec 6, 1940, Caroline County, VA. **Educ:** Va State Col, BA, 1963; Howard Univ Sch Law, JD, 1971. **Career:** Prudential Life Ins Co, mkt & sales rep, 1965-71; EGS Fin Mgt Cons, pres, 1971-; Am Security & Trust Co, estate & pension admin, 1971-72; Aetna Ins Co, brokerage mgr, 1973-75; CT Hellmuth & Assoc, mgr, 1975-; Henry M Terrell & Assoc, owner, atty, currently. **Orgs:** Pres, Va State Col Alumni Asn, 1966-68; bd trustee, Va State Col Found, 1974; regional dir, Va State Col Alumni Asn, 1974; Recorder Deeds, DC, 1990-2000; bd dir, Va St Col Alumni Asn; past pres, Howard Univ Law Sch Alumni Asn; Alpha Phi Alpha; Delta Theta Phi Law Fraternity; bus mgr, Nubian Enterprises; dir, DC Chap Int Asn Fin Planners; Nat Patent Asn Dist Columbia Bar. **Home Addr:** 1128 16th St NW Suite 100, Washington, DC 20036, **Home Phone:** (202)584-1391. **Business Addr:** Owner, Henry M Terrell Associates, 1625 Mass Ave NW Suite 400, Washington, DC 20036, **Business Phone:** (202)628-3242.

### TERRELL, JOHN L.

School administrator. **Personal:** Born May 19, 1930, Forrest City, AR; son of Willie L and Velma Mclemore (deceased); married Betty R Phillips; children: Debra, Lanette, John & DeAnna. **Educ:** Muskegon Bus Col, Bus Admin, 1956. **Career:** School administrator (retired); Howmet Corp, x-ray tech, 1956-88; UAW Local 1243, sec-treas, 1958; Howmet Employee Credit Union, pres, 1962; Muskegon Heights Sch Bd, treas, 1969-79, vpres, 1979-85. **Orgs:** Pres, Muskegon Co Sch Bd Asn, 1987-91; pres, Muskegon Intermediate Sch Dist, 1989 & 1991; VFW. **Home Addr:** 2336 Maffett St, Muskegon Heights, MI 49444-1528, **Home Phone:** (231)737-4236.

### TERRELL, MARY ANN GOODEN

Judge. **Personal:** Born Jun 3, 1944, Jacksonville, FL; daughter of Quincy Gooden and Minnie Armstrong Gooden; married James Edward; children: Angela Rani, Mariessa Rebecca & James Stephen. **Educ:** Howard Univ, BA, 1966; Antioch Univ, MAT, 1969; Georgetown Univ Law Ctr, JD, 1980. **Career:** Judge (retired); Peace Corps & India, vol, 1966-68; Antioch Col, dir admin asst prof hist, 1969-73; Dix St Acad, dir & founder, 1974-80; Nat St Law Inst, consult, 1979-80; Ment Health Law Proj, lawyer, 1980-81; Coun Dc, Exec Asst to Chmn, 1980-83; Dist Columbia City Coun, exec asst to coun chmn, 1981-82; DC Dept Pub Works, hearing examr, 1983-84; Antioch Sch Law, adj prof, 1987-; Off US Atty, asst US atty, 1984-89; Fed, Home Loan Bank Bd, Wa, DC, sr atty, 1989; FDIC & RTC, Wa, DC, coun litigation, 1989-90, coun, corp affairs, 1990-92; Outside Coun Mgt Sect, Resolution Trust Corp Div, Sr Coun & Dir, 1992-95; Dept Legal Progs, RTC, sr coun dir, 1993-95; FDIC, assoc dir, 1995; Legal Progs Br, Off Equal Opportunity & Fed Deposit Ins Corp, Assoc Dir, 1996-97; Super Ct DC, assoc judge, 1997-2008. **Orgs:** App, Mayors Intl Adv Coun, 1983-; treas, Nat Polit Cong Black Women, 1985-91; Nat Asn Black Women Attys, 1985-, Women's Div NBA, 1986-; DC State Adv Comt Hands Across Am, 1986; Womens Bar Asn DC, 1987, Fed Bar Asn, 1987, Wa Bar; bd dir, Women Bar Asn, Wa, DC, 1990-92; co-chmn, comt exec & judicial appts, GWAC-NBA, 1990-91; co-chmn, person to person comt, THIS Meridan House Intl, 1990-; bd dir, DC Chap, Fed Bar Asn, 1988-; Dist Columbia Bar, 1983; vice chmn, Wa Lawyers Against Drugs Community, 1987; Bar Asn Dist Columbia, comt chmn, 1988-89; Fed Bar, DC Chap, bd dir; Wa Bar, NBA Conv Steering Comt, 1988, Law Day Dinner Comt, 1993; Nat Bar Asn, GWAC, judicial exec nomination community, 1990-91; Nat Asn Black Women Attys, Conf Steering Community, 1990; Womens Bar Asn, bd dir; vice chmn, Wa Lawyers Against Drugs; Black Asst US Atty Asn; Asst US Atty Asn; Exec Women Govt; adv comt mem, US Intl Cult & Trade Ctr; vpres, Young People Communicating Inc; Temp Panel Employees Appeal, app, 1992; Mayors Citizen Budget Adv & Rev Comt, app, 1992; Howard Univ Alumni Asn, Ad Hoc Exec; Comt Exec Bd; voting deleg, Dist Columbia Judicial Conf, 1985-87; secy, DC Bar, 1994; High Tea Soc Inc; founding mem, Nat Cong Black Women; co chair, Rotary Club Wash; bd dir, Int Judicial Acad & Continentals Inc; bd dir, Ctr Int Pvt Enterprise; cochair, Embassy Rels Comt Rotary Club. **Home Addr:** 3118 Westover Dr SE, Washington, DC 20020, **Home Phone:** (202)584-1524. **Business Addr:** Board of Director, Center for International Private Enterprise, 1155 15th St NW Suite 700, Washington, DC 20005, **Business Phone:** (202)721-9200.

### TERRELL, DR. MELVIN CLEVELAND

School administrator, educator. **Personal:** Born Oct 5, 1949, Chicago, IL; son of Cleveland and Ethel Lee McNeal. **Educ:** Chicago State Univ, BSEd, hist, 1971; Loyola Univ, Chicago, MEd, stud personnel, 1974; Southern Ill Univ, Carbondale, PhD, higher educ admin & black studies, 1978. **Career:** Kennedy-King Col, Chicago, stud devel specialist & coun instr, 1973-75; Eastern N Mex Univ, coordr, counr black affairs & asst prof ethnic studies, 1977-78; Chicago State Univ, proj dir & asst prof educ, 1978-79; Univ Ark, Monticello, Learning Develop Ctr, dir, 1979-80; Univ Wis-Oshkosh, dir multicultural educ ctr, 1981-85; Univ Toledo, dir minority affairs & adj asst prof, 1985-88; Northeastern Ill Univ, prof counr educ, 1988-, vpres stud affairs, 1988-2009, vpres emer, 2009-; Ill State Univ, vis prof, 1991; Fla State Univ, fel, 1993-94. **Orgs:** Vice chmn educ comt, Nat AsnAdvan Colored People Toledo Br, 1985-88; chmn, Am Asn Higher Educ, Black Caucus Exec, 1985-91; Educ Bd, Nat Asn Stud Personnel Admin J, 1986-89; Educ Bd, Leadership Educ, 1986-; chair educ comt, Alpha Phi Alpha, 1986-88; nat chmn, Ethnic Minority Network, Nat Asn Stud Personnel Asn, 1988-90; consult evaluator, N Cent Asn Cols & Univs, 1988-; vice chmn, Am Asn Higher Educ, 1989; Scott Goodnight Award Outstanding Performance a Dean, 1990; life mem, Alpha Phi Alphi Fraternity Inc; eval team mem, Mid States Asn Cols & Univs; Nat Asn Stud Personnel Adminr; nat coordr, Minority Undergrad Fel

Prog, Nat Asn Stud Personnel Admin, 1994-98, pres 2000-01, 2005-07; chair, Exec Comt, Ill Comt Black Concerns Higher Educ, 1995-; Am Col Personnel Asn. **Home Addr:** 4033 W Cullerton St, Chicago, IL 60623, **Home Phone:** (312)521-0733. **Business Addr:** Vice President Emeritus, Northeastern Illinois University, 5500 N St Louis Ave PE 1121, Chicago, IL 60625, **Business Phone:** (773)442-4608.

**TERRELL, REGINALD V.**
Lawyer. **Personal:** Born Mar 23, 1959, Vallejo, CA; son of Harold D and Codessa M. **Educ:** St Marys Col Calif, Moraga, CA, BA, 1981; Univ Calif, JD, 1984. **Career:** Univ Calif, Davis, Law Rev, staff, 1984; John L Burris Law Off, law clerk, lawyer; Terrell Law Group, owner, atty, currently. **Orgs:** Charles Houston Bar Asn, 1984-; Nat Bar Asn, 1984-; Calif State Bar, 1987-; Calif Consumer Attys 1988-; bd mem, St Marys Col, CA, 1992-97; trustee, St Marys Col, CA, 1997-99; regent bd mem, St Mary's Col; CA, 1999-; Am Trial Lawyers Asn, 1999-. **Home Addr:** 4808 Calderwood Ct, Oakland, CA 94605, **Home Phone:** (510)633-0549. **Business Addr:** Trustee, Saint Mary's College of California, 1928 St Marys Rd, Moraga, CA 94575, **Business Phone:** (925)631-4000.

**TERRELL, RICHARD WARREN**
Educator, executive. **Personal:** Born Nov 16, 1946, Ft. Riley, KS; son of Warren and Mary; married Phyllis Eileen Hargrove; children: Wesley & Rodney. **Educ:** CA Polytech State Univ, BSEL, 1968; San Jose State, MSEE, 1974. **Career:** IBM, engr, Large Scale Integration Packaging & Component Engineering, mgr, 1968-90; Prairie View A&M, adj prof, 1976-77; Compaq Comput Corp, storage & printer systs staff, 1990, mgr, gen mgr & vpres, nonstop hardware develop; SE Lab Inc, sr vpres, gen mgr, 2005-; Hewlett Packard Co, vpres, hardware develop enterprise div & mgr, storage prod group. **Orgs:** Alpha Phi Alpha; Nat Asn Advan Colored People; Antioch Baptist Church; Jack & Jill Am; bd mem, United Way Silicon Valley. **Home Addr:** 4959 Massachusetts Dr, San Jose, CA 95136-2927, **Home Phone:** (408)972-0220. **Business Addr:** General Manager, SE Laboratories Inc, 1065 Comstock St, Santa Clara, CA 95054, **Business Phone:** (408)727-3286.

**TERRELL, ROBERT E. (BOB TERRELL)**
Government official. **Personal:** Born Oct 4, 1943, Terry, MS; son of Rosie McNeil and Lonnie; married Karen K; children: Kelley L Carson. **Educ:** KS Univ, BS, social studies/educ, 1966, MPA, pub admin, 1975. **Career:** Government official (retired); Turner House Inc, exec dir, 1971-74; City Ft Worth, budget analyst, 1974-77; Ft Worth Econ Develop Corp, exec dir, 1977-79; City Ft Worth, asst to city mgr, 1979-85, asst city mgr, 1985-92, city mgr, 1992-2001; CH2M HILL, ft worth area mgr, emer employee, 2000-. **Orgs:** Officer, Kappa Alpha Psi Frat, 1962-; bd mem, Multicultural Alliance; fel, NASPAA, 1974-75; Nat Bd Conf Minority Pub Admin, 1979-81; Am Soc Pub Admin, 1979-; Asst Steering Com Intl City Mgt Asn, 1979-81; pres, Nat Forum Black Pub Adminrs, N Tex Chap, 1987-89; life mem, Nat Asn Advan Colored People, 1989-; Task Force mgr, ICMA Coun, 1993-95; Pub Tech Inc, steering comt, 1992-; Tex City Mgt Asn; Nat Conf Community & Justice; Ft Worth Exec Roundtable; Rotary Club Ft Worth; United Way Tarrant County; Am Diabetes Asn Tarrant County; Metrop YMCA; chair, Steering Comt Pub Technol. **Home Addr:** 7629 Nutwood Pl, Ft. Worth, TX 76133, **Home Phone:** (817)294-1821. **Business Addr:** Fort Worth Area Manager, CH2M HILL, 9191 S Jamaica St, Englewood, CO 80112.

**TERRELL, ROBERT L.**
Educator. **Personal:** Born Jul 19, 1943. **Educ:** Morehouse Col, Atlanta, BA, sociol, 1969; Univ Calif, Berkeley, MA, jour, 1974, PhD, educ, 1978. **Career:** NY Post, reporter, 1966-68; Pub poems short stories bks, 1967-; So Reg Coun Atlanta, res writer, 1968-69; Newsweek Mag, stringer, 1968-69; Southern Regional Coun, researcher & writer, 1968-69; Univ CA, teaching asst, 1969-70; Golden Gate Col, instr, 1969-71; fel, CA State, 1969-72, Grad Minority, 1969-72; San Francisco Chronicle, copy ed, 1970; fel, Fund Peace, 1970-71, NDEA, 1971-74; Deans fel Univ CA, 1974-75; CA Jour Teacher Ed, asst prof, 1971-76, ed, 1972-73; Off Res & Planning, coordr, 1974-75; St Mary's Col, Moraga, CA, Dept Educ, asst prof, 1971-76, off exp progs, 1975-76; Mid-Mo Asn Cols & Univs, consult, 1976-80; Stanford Univ, asst prof, 1976-88; Univ Mo, Sch Journalism, assoc prof, 1976-88; Sch Jour Univ CA Berkeley, vis prof, 1979; Columbia Missourian, city ed, 1980-88; Beijing Rev Mag, Beijing China, copy ed, 1981-82, ed consult, 1995-96; Share Int, corresp, 1984-; NY Univ, Dept Jour & Mass Commun, vis prof, 1995-96; Univ Nairobi Sch Journ, Full bright prof, sr lectr, 1994-95; N S News Serv, sr ed, 1985-86; Univ Colo, assoc prof, 1988-91, dir, Sch Journalism & Mass Commun, 1989, Off Int Educ, 1990-91; Univ Colo, Silver & Gold Rec, columnist, 1990-91; Calif St Univ, prin investr, Campus Climate Assessment Proj, 1993-95, Interim Chair, coordr internships, 1999-2006, chair, prof, 2014(retired); Calif State Univ, Hayward, Dept Mass Commun, Chair, 1991-94, African Am Fac & Staff Asn, pres, 1994-95, prof; Oakland Unified Sch Dist, Castlemont Arts & Entertainment Acad Oakland, consult, 1997-99; St Spirit, contrib writer & photogr, 2003-; Nat Res Coun Nat Academies Sci, Wa, fel, 2004-. **Orgs:** Bd dir, Calif Coun Teacher Educ, 1971-76; Am Asn Col Teacher Ed, 1973-76; Am Assoc Higher Ed, 1973-76; Am Ed Res Asn; Soc Col & Univ; managing ed Calif Jour Teacher Ed, 1973; Am Educ Res Asn, 1973-76; ed referee, Calif Jour Teacher Ed, 1974-; Kappa Tau Alpha, 1977-; adv, screening comt comn Coun Int Exchange Scholars Fulbright Prog, 1980-83; fel Univ Colo, 1990-91; Speech Commun Asn, 1985-86; pres-elec, Boulder Fac Assembly, 1991; bd adv, Ohlone Col, 1992-93; Asn Educ Jour; Int Commun Asn, 1992-96; Media Alliance, 1992-93; Mayors Coun Eliminate Chronic Homeless City San Francisco, 2004-06. **Honors/Awds:** Outstanding Professor of the Year, Calif State Univ, 1992; Outstanding Prof of the Year, Calif State Univ, 1991-92. Lecture: Problematic Aspects of Mass Mediated Realities, sponsored by the Univ of Calif Comt for Arts and Lect, Univ of Calif, Berkeley, July, 1979; Critical Issues Sem four maj lect on China and the World, Foreign Lang Publ Co, Beijing, China, spring, 1996; The Greening of the Peoples Repub of China: Current Econ and Social Reforms in the Worlds Next Dominant Superpower, sponsored by the Sch of Arts, Lett and Social Sci, Calif State Univ Hayward, October, 1996; Bldg a Successful Career as a Writer, N Coast Writers Group, Half Moon Bay, CA, May, 1999; Racial Apartheid, Class Discrimination and Lib Arts Ideology, sponsored by the Sch of Arts, Lett and Social Sci, Calif State Univ, Hayward, February, 1999; Nat Res Coun Panelist, 2004. **Home Addr:** 340 Ritch St Suite 2, San Francisco, CA 94107-1749, **Home Phone:** (415)243-8570.

**TERRELL, STANLEY E.**
Journalist. **Personal:** Born Feb 16, 1949, Newark, NJ; son of Millard E and Wilda M Johnson; children: Salimu Amini. **Educ:** Hampton Inst, 1968; Essex County Col, attended 1970. **Career:** Star-Ledger, gen assignment news reporter, 1968-88, ed writer & columnist, ed, 1988-2006. **Orgs:** Lectr, worked closely with National Association for the Advancement of Colored People; Urban League; Cong African People; Human Rights Comn; var tenant groups, juv progs, prison reform groups, drug rehab proj; founding mem, Black Heritage Day Parade Comn, 1979-. **Honors/Awds:** Merit Award, Newark Tenants Couns, 1974; Outstanding Achievement Award, Newark Human Rights Comn, 1974; 'Award from Newark Title I ESEA Prog for Outstanding Service to Newark Commission', 1975; Star-Ledger Bonus, 1971; New Jersey Black Achievers Award, 1989; Distinguished Service Award, Black Heritage Day Parade Comn, 1990. **Special Achievements:** Contributed articles to numerous magazines. **Home Addr:** 10 Hill St, Newark, NJ 07102. **Business Addr:** Columnist, The Star-Ledger, 1 Star Ledger Pl, Newark, NJ 07102, **Business Phone:** (973)297-5204.

**TERRY, ADELINE HELEN**
Lawyer, executive. **Personal:** Born Apr 17, 1931, Wichita, KS; daughter of Clifford Johnson and Narcissus O; children: Catherine. **Educ:** Calif State Col, BA, sociol, 1960; Southwestern Univ Law, LLB, 1969. **Career:** Lawyer (retired); Los Angeles County Dist Atty, investr, 1960-62, dep dist atty; Los Angeles County Supe Ct, domestic rel investr, 1962-65; Los Angeles County Probation Dept, 1965-69. **Orgs:** Asn Dept Dist Atty Los Angeles; Calif Dist Atty's Asn; Black Women's Lawyers Los Angeles; Langston Law Club; Women Lawyers Los Angeles; State Bar CA. **Honors/Awds:** Honor Roll of Donors, 2008-09. **Home Addr:** 4620 Angeles Vista Blvd, Los Angeles, CA 90043-1155, **Home Phone:** (323)294-0583.

**TERRY, DR. ANGELA OWEN**
School administrator. **Personal:** Born Feb 13, 1941, Memphis, TN; daughter of William Franklin Owen Sr and Addie Griffin Owen; married Elbert A; children: Angela Daphne & Warren Marshall. **Educ:** Spelman Col, BA, 1962; Univ Vienna, cert, 1963; Fisk Univ, MA, 1964; Univ Conn, PhD, 1973; Harvard Univ, Cambridge, Mass, cert, 1987, Mgt Develop Prog Col & Univ Adminr Inst Educ Mgt. **Career:** Sch adminr (retired); Albany State Col, asst prof psychol, 1964-69; Prospect Psychol Serv Ctr, psychol serv worker, 1969-71; Harvard Univ, fel, 1969; Univ Conn, assoc vpres stud affairs (retired), Storrs, Conn, 1969-93; Univ Conn, fel, 1971-73; Conn State Dept Educ, educ consult psychol serv, 1973-77; Univ Conn, asst dir, dept coun serv, 1978-83, asst vpres prog eval & res, 1983-89, asst vpres stud affairs, 1989-93, assoc vpres stud affairs, 1994-97; NASPA Jour, ed bd, 1988-91, 1993-96; vice chancellor stud affairs (retired), Durham, NC, 1993-2002; NC Cent Univ, Durham, NC, vice chancellor stud affairs, 1993-94; Asn Retired NCCU Personnel, pres; Genesis Home, bd mem; Nasher Mus Art, friends bd mem, 2004-11, 2013-, pres bd, 2009-11. **Orgs:** Am Asn Coun & Develop; Am Col Personnel Asn; Assoc Instnl Res; Dist Sorority Inc; Nat Asn Stud Personnel Adminr; Am Asn Higher Educ; Coalition 100 Black Women; hon mem, Golden Key Nat Honor Soc, 1990; Phi Delta Kappa; Nat Educ Honor Soc; Pi Lambda Theta Nat Educ Honor Soc; state coordr, Nat ID Prog Advan Women, 1992-93; adv bd, NASPA Region I, 1996-98; chair, Enrollment Mgmt Network, 1996-; Bd pres, Nasher Mus Art, Duke Univ, 2008-09; Two Thousand Women Achievement. **Honors/Awds:** Scholar, Univ Vienna, 1963; Leadership, NC Central Univ, 1994; Service Award, African Cult Ctr, Univ Conn; Recognition Award, The Women's Ctr, Univ Conn; Outstanding Educator Award, Windham-Willimantic Chap, NCP. **Home Addr:** 36 Patriot Rd, Windham, CT 06280.

**TERRY, CLARK**
Musician. **Personal:** Born Dec 14, 1920, St. Louis, MO; married Pauline Reddon; children: 2; married Gwendolyn Paris. **Career:** Pastel Music, pres, 1958; Etoile Music Prodns Inc, pres, 1955; Creative Jazz Composers Inc, vpres, 1972; itinerant jazz clinician & educr. Albums: Clark Terry, 1955; Duke With A Difference, 1957; Serenade to a Bus Seat, 1957; In Orbit, 1958; Out on a Limb with Clark Terry, 1958; Top and Bottom Brass feat, 1959; Color Changes, 1960; Everything's Mellow, 1961; Mellow Moods, 1961; All American, 1962; The Night Life, 1962; Oscar Peterson Trio with Clark Terry, 1964; Yes, the Blues, 1981; To Duke & Basie, 1986; Portraits, 1988; The Clark Terry Spacemen, 1989; What a Wonderful World: For Louis, 1993; One on One, 2000; A Jazz Symphony, 2000; Herr Ober: Live at Birdland Neuburg, 2001; Live on QE2, 2001; Jazz Matinee, 2001; The Hymn, 2001; Clark Terry & His Orchestra Featuring Paul, 2002; Live in Concert, 2002; Flutin' & Fluglin, 2002; Friendship, 2002; Live! At Buddy's Place, 2003; Live at Montmarte June 1975, 2003; George Gershwin's Porgy & Bess, 2004; Live at Marian's with the Terry's Young Titan's of Jazz, 2005; Clark Terry Big Bad Band. **Orgs:** Exec dir, Int Art Jazz. **Honors/Awds:** Received numerous awards including: The National Endowment for the Arts Jazz Master Award, 1991; NEA Hall of Fame, 1991; Beacon in Jazz Award, New Sch Music, 1991; Inducted, St. Louis Walk of Fame, 1996; Inducted, Down Beat Hall of Fame, 2000; The French Order of Arts and Letters, 2000; Honorary Doctorates, Teikyo Westmar Univ; Honorary Doctorates, Berklee Sch Music, Honorary Doctorates, Univ New Hampshire; wax figure, Black World History Museum in St. Louis; two Grammy certificates; lifetime achievements & halls of fame awards; Merit Award, NARAS, 2005; Trumpeter of the Year, Jazz Journalists Association, 2005; Grammy Lifetime Achievement Award, 2010. **Special Achievements:** Performed for seven U.S. Presidents, and was a Jazz Ambassador for State Department tours in the Middle East and Africa, author of Let's Talk Trumpet: From Legit to Jazz Interpretation of the Jazz Language, Clark Terry's System of Circular Breathing for Woodwind and Brass Instruments; autobiography, Clark: The Autobiography of Clark Terry, 2011. **Business Addr:** Musician, c/o Chesky Records, 355 W 52nd St 6th Fl, New York, NY 10019-6239, **Business Phone:** (212)586-7799.

**TERRY, HILLIARD C., III**
Chief financial officer, vice president (organization). **Educ:** Univ Calif, Berkeley, CA, BA, econs, 1991; Golden Gate Univ, MBA, 1997. **Career:** Kenetech Corp; VeriFone Inc; Goldman Sachs & Co; VeriFone Inc, 1995; Agilent Technologies Inc, head investor rels, 1999-2006, vpres & treas, 2006-12; Textainer Group Holdings Ltd, exec vpres & chief financial officer, 2012-. **Orgs:** Bd trustee, Oakland Mus Calif; bd dir, Umpqua Bank, Oakland Mus Calif; bd mem, bd dir, Umpqua Holdings Corp, 2010-. **Home Addr:** , Hamilton, **Home Phone:** (441)296-2500. **Business Addr:** Executive Vice President, Chief Financial Officer, Textainer Group Holdings Limited, Hamilton, **Business Phone:** (415)658-8227.

**TERRY, PATRICIA S.**
Educator, librarian. **Personal:** Born Aug 11, 1937, Brooklyn, NY; daughter of Philip Smith and Naomi McKeever Smith; married Namond; children: Naomi Brown, Mabel Mcleod, Derek Brown, Latrice Kendall, Arnold II & Edward Brown. **Educ:** Col New Rochelle, New Rochelle, NY, BA, lib arts, 1979, MA, geront, 1988; Pratt Inst, Brooklyn, NY, MS, libr & info sci, 1980. **Career:** Brooklyn Pub Libr, Brooklyn, NY, supvr clerk & librn, 1969-81; Col New Rochelle, New Rochelle, NY, br librn, 1981-, adj fac, 1982-, coordr libr servs, 1992-, Gill Libr, ref librn, currently; NY Tech Col, Brooklyn, NY, adj fac, 1988-89; Intervention Asst Off, Calif Dept Educ, educ progs consult. **Orgs:** Pilgrim Church Brooklyn, NY, 1959-; Linden Plaza Polit Action Comt, 1979; pres, NY Black Librns Caucus Inc, tenure, 1984-86; exec bd mem, Am Libr Asn Black Caucus, 1985-87; Am Libr Asn; NY Lib Asn; NY Black Librns'Caucus; Black Women Higher Educ; Alumni Asn Col New Rochelle & Pratt Inst. **Home Addr:** 1823 Dellwood Dr, Orangeburg, SC 29115-3911, **Home Phone:** (803)536-6553. **Business Addr:** Associate Professor & Coordinator of Library Services, College of New Rochelle, 1368 Fulton St, Brooklyn, NY 11216, **Business Phone:** (718)638-2500.

**TERRY, RICK, JR. (RICHARD ROSS TERRY)**
Football player. **Personal:** Born Apr 5, 1974, Lexington, NC; children: Jasmine. **Educ:** Univ NC. **Career:** Football player (retired); New York Jets, defensive tackle, 1997-98; Carolina Panthers, defensive tackle, 1998, 1999.

**TERRY, ROY**
Chief executive officer, executive. **Personal:** Born Dec 27, 1944, Dayton, OH; son of Velma G and Jesse A; married Willo; children: Corey & Cotina. **Educ:** Morehouse Col, BA, 1966. **Career:** Terry Mfg Co Inc, owner, pres & chief exec officer, 1972-. **Orgs:** Am Apparel Mfr Asn, 1969-; life mem, Nat Asn Advan Colored People, 1970-; founding mem, Many Bus Enterprise Legal Def & Educ Fund, 1980-; Ala Demc Conf, voting rights cordr, 1980-; Fed Res Bank, Birmingham Br, cbd, 1985-92; Oper PUSH, World Trade Coun, 1986-. **Honors/Awds:** Manufacturer of the Year, Black Enterprise Mag, 1974; AG Gaston Award, Ala Democratic Conf, 1980; Manufacturer of the Year, US Dept Commerce, 1989; Initial Shared Production Award, US Dept Defense, 1992; Bennie Award, Morehouse Col, 1993; National Minority Manufacturer of the Year, United States Small Bus Admin & Minority Bus Develop Agency. **Special Achievements:** Author: Shared Production Concept, adopted as model, $3.5 billion Defense Agency, 1992; company ranked #59 on Black Enterprise's list of top 100 industrial/service companies, 1998. **Business Addr:** President, Chief Executive Officer, Terry Manufacturing Company Inc, PO Box 2926, Birmingham, AL 35202-3804.

**TERUEL, LAUREN (LAUREN TERUEL RIDLOFF)**
Fashion model, educator. **Personal:** Born Chicago, IL; daughter of Joanne Scott and Hugo. **Educ:** Calif State Univ, Northridge, BA, eng, 2000; Hunter Col, MA, educ, 2002. **Career:** Miss Deaf America, 1998-2000; Calif State Univ Northridge, Nat Ctr Deafness, assoc proj coordr, currently. **Orgs:** Staff mem, Calif State Univ Northridge. **Business Addr:** Associate Project Coordinator, California State University, Chisholm Hall 18111 Nordhoff St, Northridge, CA 91330-8267, **Business Phone:** (818)677-1200.

**TESSEMA, TESFAYE**
Artist, muralist, painter (artist). **Personal:** Born May 5, 1951, Addis Ababa. **Educ:** Fine Arts Sch, Addia Ababa, dipl, 1970; Howard Univ, MFA, 1976. **Career:** African Am community, fel; City Wash, muralist & prog coordr, 1976-77; Harvest, graphics artist, 1976; Mus African Art, Wash, DC, designer & graphic artist, 1977-78; Arts DC, Wash, DC, mural prog coordr, 1978-80. **Home Addr:** 2480 16th St NW Suite 324, Washington, DC 20009. **Business Addr:** Painter, Harlem Open Artsit Studio, 115 E 34th St, New York, NY 10156, **Business Phone:** (212)795-7283.

**THACKERAY, ANJETTA MCQUEEN**
Public relations executive, administrator. **Personal:** Born Sep 12, 1966, Brooklyn, NY. **Educ:** Univ NC, Chapel Hill, NC, BA, jour, polit sci, 1988; Am Univ, Wash Col Law, JD, law, 2007. **Career:** News & Observer, Raleigh, NC, part-time copy ed, 1986-88; Philadelphia Inquirer, Philadelphia, Pa, copy ed, 1988-91; Ft Worth Star Telegram, reporter, 1991-93; The Plain Dealer, reporter, 1993-96; Congressional Quarterly, reporter, 2001-02; Brookings Inst, sr commun adv, 2005-07; Bush Gottlieb Singer Lopez Kohanski Adelstein & Dickinson, assoc, 2007-09. **Orgs:** Fleisher Art Memorial, 1988-; Int Soc Gen Semantics, 1989-; Nat Asn Black Journalists, 1989-; Urban League, 1990-; Carolina Alumni Asn; sen, Wash Col Law Stud Bar Asn; newswoman, Assoc Press, 1997-2000; sr press officer, Nat Educ Asn, 2002-05; commun consult, 2009-; sr commun consult, 2010-; Kaiser Permanente; nat coordr, Coalition Kaiser Permanente Unions, 2014-. **Home Addr:** 2011 Green St, Philadelphia, PA 19130. **Business Addr:** Senator, American University Washington College of Law, 4801 Massachusetts Ave NW, Washington, DC 20016, **Business Phone:** (202)274-4000.

**THARPE, LARRY JAMES**
Football player. **Personal:** Born Nov 19, 1970, Macon, GA. **Educ:** Tenn State Univ. **Career:** Football player (retired); Detroit Lions, tackle, 1992-94, right tackle, 1997-98; Ariz Cardinals, right & left tackle, 1995; New Eng Patriots, 1996; Pittsburgh Steelers, right tackle, 2000. **Home Addr:** 3665 Greenbriar Rd E, Macon, GA 31204, **Home Phone:** (478)746-0394.

### THAXTON, JUNE E. (JUNE T HOLMES)
Electrical engineer. **Personal:** Born May 28, 1961, Baltimore, MD; daughter of Fred (deceased) and Mildred. **Educ:** Howard Univ, BS, EE, 1984. **Career:** Potomac Electric Power Co, engr elect syst, 1985-. **Orgs:** Am Asn Blacks Energy, 1991-; Inst Elec & Electronics Engrs, 1986. **Special Achievements:** Biographical article, US Black Engineer Magazine, 1986; Ebony Magazine, 1987. **Home Addr:** 1722 Lakeside Ave, Baltimore, MD 21218, **Home Phone:** (410)467-3122. **Business Addr:** Engineer of Electric System, Potomac Electric Power Co, 1900 Pa Ave NW, Washington, DC 20068, **Business Phone:** (202)872-2859.

### THE ROCK. See JOHNSON, DWAYNE.

### THELWELL, MICHAEL M. EKWUEME
Writer, educator. **Personal:** Born Jul 25, 1939; children: Chinua & Mikiko. **Educ:** Howard Univ, BA, eng lit, 1964; Univ Mass, Amherst, MFA, 1969. **Career:** Jamaica Indust Develop, pub rels asst, 1958-59; Stud Nonviolent Coord Comn, dir wash off, 1963-64; Miss Freedom Dem Party, dir Wash off, 1964-65; Howard Univ, Soc Humanities, Cornell Univ, ed chief, 1968; Univ Mass, Amherst, W E B DuBois, Dept Afro-Am Studies, counr, 1969-75, founding chmn, 1970, assoc prof lit, 1972, prof, 1980-, fac; Nat Endowment Arts, adv & consult, 1970; Nat Endowment Arts, Writers Fel, 1980-81; WGBH TV, PBS, sr adv, 1989; Wash Incident, screenplay, 1972; The Harder They Come, novel; Girl Beneath Lion, screenplay, 1978; Short Stories: Duties, Pleasures, Conflicts & Essays Struggle, 1987. **Home Addr:** 5 Gulf Rd, Pelham, MA 01002-9763, **Home Phone:** (413)256-0218. **Business Addr:** Professor of Literature & Writing, University of Massachusetts, Afro-Am Studies 639 N Pleasant St, Amherst, MA 01003, **Business Phone:** (413)545-5169.

### THEODORE, YVONNE M.
School administrator. **Personal:** Born Mar 16, 1939, Prince George's County, MD; children: Pierre. **Educ:** Mt St Agnes Col, BA, 1961; Makerere Univ, Uganda, E Africa, MA, 1962; Fisk Univ, Spec Courses Race Relig, 1964; Johns Hopkins Univ, Cand M Lib Arts, 1976. **Career:** School administrator (retired); Mt St Mary's Namagunga, Uganda, E Africa, grad stud, teacher, 1961-64; Baltimore City Comm Relig Community, intergroup relig specialist, 1965-68; Provident Comp Neighborhood Health Ctr, from asst dir to dir, 1968-69; Johns Hopkins Univ, dir affirmative action, 1971-99, affirmative action officer, vol & consult, 1980-. **Orgs:** Nat Coun Negro Women; Col & Univ Personnel Asn; Kampala Singers, Interracial, Intercultural Class Singing Group, Uganda, E Africa; Black Professionals Int Affairs; Am Asn Univ Women; Phi Delta Kappa Fraternity; Am Coun Alcoholism; Md Tech Asst Prog; programmer, Good Taste, Manford Radio Reading Sta; Am Asn Higher Educ, Black Caucus; Int Duke Ellington Soc; Md Asn Affirmative Action Officers; coordr, Nation's Capital Area Disabled Stud Serv; Baltimore Metro Area Job Serv Employer Community. **Honors/Awds:** Recipient Recognition for Youth Motivation, Nat Alliance Businessmen, 1973-74; Academic Scholarship, Mt St Agnes Col; Recognition for Employee Recruitment, Am Indians. **Special Achievements:** Named illustrious Women Baltimore Afro-Am Newspaper, 1971. **Home Addr:** 2901 Boston, Baltimore, MD 21224. **Business Addr:** Affirmative Action Officer, Johns Hopkins University, Rm 205 Garland Hall 3400 N Charles St Suite 130, Baltimore, MD 21218-2696, **Business Phone:** (410)516-8075.

### THERMILUS, JACQUES EVENS
Executive, chief executive officer, president (organization). **Career:** Urban Constructors Inc, pres; Urban Orgn Inc, chief exec officer, owner. **Business Addr:** President, Urban Constructors Inc, 3800 N W 22nd Ave, Miami, FL 33142.

### THEUS, REGGIE WAYNE (REGGIE THEUS)
Basketball player, basketball coach. **Personal:** Born Oct 13, 1957, Inglewood, CA; married Elaine; children: Raquel, Ryan & Reggie Jr. **Educ:** Univ Nev, Las Vegas, attended 1978. **Career:** Basketball player (retired), basketball coach; Chicago Bulls, 1978-83; Kans City Kings, 1984-85; Sacramento Kings, 1985-88; Atlanta Hawks, 1988-89; Orlando Magic, 1989-90; NJ Nets, 1990-91; Ranger Varese, Ital League, 1991-92; Aris, Greece, 1993; TNT, TBS, studio analyst; Las Vegas Slam, 2002; Univ Louisville, asst coach, 2003-05; NMex State Univ, head basketball coach, 2005-07; Sacramento Kings, head coach, 2007-08; Minn Timberwolves, asst coach, 2009-11; Los Angeles D-Fenders, 2012-13; Cal State Northridge, 2013-.Film : Forget Paris, 1995; Light it up, 1999; Like Mike, 2002. **Orgs:** Little City Prog; AthletesBetter Educ, 1979; Nat Comm Against Child Abuse. **Business Addr:** Head Coach, Cal State Northridge, 18111 Nordhoff St, Northridge, CA 91330, **Business Phone:** (818)677-1200.

### THIBODEAUX, SYLVIA MARIE, SR.
Educator, clergy, religious leader. **Personal:** Born Nov 26, 1937, Breaux Bridge, LA. **Educ:** BA, 1967; MA, 1973; DHL. **Career:** Cath Sch, Tulsa, elem teacher, 1960-62; Opelousa, teacher, 1962-63; Tulsa, teacher, 1963-65; Witness Prog Educ Component, New Orleans, dir, 1967-68; Proj Commitment & Asn Urban Sisters, Boston, 1968-69; St Joseph Community Sch, Boston, prin, 1970-74; Holy Family Congregation, New Orleans, unity leader & congregational leader, head sisters, 1998-2006; Archdiocese New Orleans, Dept Relig, exec dir, currently. **Orgs:** Bd mem, Campaign Human Develop, Nat Off Black Cath; Nat Black Sisters Conf; DESIGN; Minority Evaluators Ginn & Co; bd trustee, Educ Develop Ctr; consult, AFRAM Asn; Planning Comt, Black Educ Conf; Teacher Training Col & Relig Formation, Benin City, Nigeria, W Africa; SCLC Most Creative Educ Prog; co-founder, Sisters of the Sacred Heart, Benin City, Nigeria. **Honors/Awds:** NIA Award, Innovative Educ Prog; Outstanding Contrib Black Community Award, Roxbury Action Prog; Outstanding Educr Am Award. **Home Addr:** Bishops House, PO Box 35, Benin City23401. **Business Addr:** Executive Director, Archdiocese of New Orleans, 7887 Walmsley Ave, New Orleans, LA 70125, **Business Phone:** (504)861-6300.

### THIERRY, JOHN FITZGERALD
Football player. **Personal:** Born Sep 4, 1971, Houston, TX. **Educ:** Alcorn State Univ. **Career:** Football player (retired); Chicago Bears, defensive end, 1994, 1996, 1999, right defensive end, 1995, left defensive end, 1997-98, linebacker & right outside linebacker, 1999; Cleveland Browns, 1999; Green BayPackers, defensive end, 2000-01; Atlanta Falcons, linebacker, 2002. **Business Addr:** Linebacker, Atlanta Falcons, 4400 Falcon Pkwy, Flowery Branch, GA 30542.

### THIGPEN, DR. CALVIN HERRITAGE
Teacher, physician, lawyer. **Personal:** Born Jan 7, 1924, Greenville, SC; married Vera Belle Crawford; children: Calvin Jr & Karen. **Educ:** Va State Col, BS, chem, 1953; Univ Va Health Syst, Sch Med, MD, 1962, JD, 1974. **Career:** Hopewell, Va, teacher, 1953-58; Stuart Prod Co, cosmetics & chem plant mgr, 1957-58; Med Col Va, intern, 1962-63; Petersburg Gen Hosp, staff mem, 1963, Chief Staff; pvt pract, 1963; Va State Col, assoc & physician, 1964-71; Petersburg Gen Hosp, vice chief, gen pract sect, 1969-70; Off Atty Gen, Va, intern, 1972-73; Univ Va, res asst legal adv, 1973-74; pvt pract atty, 1975-. **Orgs:** Sigma Pi Sigma Nat Physics Hon Soc; Beta Kappa Chi Nat Sci Hon Soc; Phi Delta Phi Legal Fraternity; Dem Com Hopewell, 1965-75; bd dir, Salvation Army; Hopewell Chamber Com; Old Dom Med Soc; exec comt, Old Dom Med Soc, 1965; pres, Nat Guardsmen Inc, 1967-70; Libr Human Resources, Am Bicentennial Res Inst, 1973; fel Am Col Legal Med, 1976; mem bd visitors, Va State Univ, 1978-82; Va Deleg toWhite House Conf Libr & Info Serv, 1979; Chief Staff Petersburg Gen Hosp, 1980; Dipl Am Bd Legal Med, 1982. **Honors/Awds:** Meritorious Service Award, lifetime achievement, Richmond Medical Society. **Home Addr:** 19801 Oakland Ave, Colonial Heights, VA 23834, **Home Phone:** (804)520-1883. **Business Addr:** Attorney, Physician, 734 S Sycamore St, Petersburg, VA 23803-5817, **Business Phone:** (804)733-0111.

### THIGPEN, ESQ. DONALD A., JR.
Lawyer. **Personal:** Born Aug 22, 1946, Jersey City, NJ; son of Donald A and Dorothy E. **Educ:** Kent State Univ, BA, polit sci, 1968; Howard Univ Sch Law, JD, 1974. **Career:** Kent State Univ, Human Rels Dept & Dept African-Am Studies, coordr Minority Affairs, 1968-71; Bur Nat Affair, ed, Family Law reporter, 1974-79; DC Off Corp Coun, prosecutor, 1979-81, Civil Litigation, trial atty, 1981-85, DC Ment Health Systs Reorganization, coun, 1985-87, Govt Contracts, legis atty, 1987-93, DC Redevelop Land Agency, gen coun, Land Use & Econ Develop, chief, 1993, sr coun; pvt pract, currently; Int Coalition Econ Unity Inc, co-founder & gen coun. **Orgs:** Co-founder & vpres, Waring-Mitchell Law Soc Howard County Md, 1992-93; co-founder & gen coun, Int Coalition Econ Unity Inc, 1992-99; asst treas, Nat Bar Asn, 1993-95, gen coun, 1995-96, 1996-99, exec comt, 1997-98, bd gov, regional dir, 1996-98; assoc grand chief justice, Sigma Delta Tau Legal Fraternity, 1995-99; bd chair, vpres, Wash Bar Asn, 1997-99, pres, 199-2001; nat pres, Howard Univ Law Alumni Assoc, 1996-98, vpres, Locust Grove Homeowners Assoc, 1998-99; pres, Greater Wash Area Chap, Univ Law Alumni Asn; chair, Howard Law Alumni Comn; co-founder & vpres, Waring-Mitchell Law Soc, Howard County Md; assoc grand chief justice, Sigma Delta Tau Legal Fraternity; sr class pres & pres, Delta Theta Phi Law Fraternity; pres, Locust Grove Homeowners Asn; gen coun, Allen & Partners; charter mem, Charlotte E Ray Inn Am Inns Ct; Retrospective Rev Adv Comt, DC Ct Appeals; chief judge, Charles Hamilton Houston Inst, Moot Ct Competition; mem comt, DC Bar; Leadership Montgomery Sr Class, 2009; African Am Dem Club Montgomery County; altimore Host Comt Thurgood Marshall Col Fund Awards Excellence. **Honors/Awds:** Mayoral Commendation, Mayor DC, 1994; Dedicated Alumni Service, Howard Univ, Stud Bar Asn, 1994; Presidential Outstanding Service Award, Nat Bar Asn, 1996; Outstanding Achievement Award, Wash Bar Asn, 1997; Grande Award Community Serv, Prince Hall Masons & Evening Stars, 1998; Leadership & Service Award, 2001; Alpha Alpha Chapter Outstanding Service, 2008; Presidential Service Award, Wash Bar Asn, 2009. **Special Achievements:** First African-American legal editor on the staff of the Family Law Reporter at the Bureau of National Affairs. **Home Addr:** 1820 Locust Grove Rd, Silver Spring, MD 20910-1379, **Home Phone:** (301)587-4780.

### THIGPEN, YANCEY DIRK
Football player. **Personal:** Born Aug 15, 1969, Tarboro, NC; married Maria Dunbar; children: Jasmine. **Educ:** Winston-Salem State Univ, grad. **Career:** Football player (retired); San Diego Chargers, wide receiver, 1991; Pittsburgh Steelers, 1992-93, wide receiver, 1994-97; Tenn Oilers, wide receiver, 1998; Tenn Titans, 1999-2000. **Honors/Awds:** Pro Bowl selection, 1995; 1997; Super Bowl. **Special Achievements:** Films: 1994 AFC Championship Game, 1995; 1995 AFC Championship Game, 1996; Super Bowl XXX, 1996; 1997 AFC Championship Game, 1998; 1999 AFC Championship Game, 2000. TV Series: "The Daily Show with Jon Stewart", 2000.

### THOMAS, ALTHEA SHANNON LAWSON
Educator, counselor. **Personal:** Born Jan 16, 1953, Ft. Gaines, GA; daughter of Wilson Robert and Arra Lightner; married Eddie Walden; children: Shadrin Vandell & Jasil Conrad. **Educ:** Hampton Univ, BA, 1973; Univ Tenn, MS, 1975; Troy State Univ, attended 1984. **Career:** Wallace Community Col, counr, 1975-82, instr, 1982-2000, inst coordr, 2000, coordr acad progs, currently, Acad Progs, Title III, activ dir, currently. **Orgs:** Ala Personnel & Guid Asn, 1975-82; pres, Young Women's Serv Club, 1977-79; chair, Henry County Bd Educ Bi-racial Comt, 1978-80; Nat Coun Negro Women, 1979-; secy, Wallace Col Educ Asn, 1986-88; pres, Delta Sigma Theta Sor Inc, Dothan Alumnae Chap, 1992-96; vpres, Delta Sigma Theta Sor Inc, 2002-. **Home Addr:** 900 Clearmont Dr, Dothan, AL 36301, **Home Phone:** (334)793-7325. **Business Addr:** Coordinator Academic Programs, Director, Wallace Community College, 1141 Wallace Dr Admin 116 E, Dothan, AL 36303-0943, **Business Phone:** (334)556-2269.

### THOMAS, ANTHONY J.
Football player, football coach. **Personal:** Born Nov 7, 1977, Winnfield, LA. **Educ:** Univ Mich, BA, edu, 2001. **Career:** American football player (retired), coach; Chicago Bears, running back, forward back,, 2001-04; Dallas Cowboys, 2005; New Orleans Saints, running back, 2005-06; Buffalo Bills, running back, 2006-07; Wva Wesleyan, running backs coach, 2011; Wva Wesleyan Col, Bobcat, spec teams coordr & asst head coach, 2012-. **Honors/Awds:** All-Big Ten, second & third-team All-Am hons; Football News Player of the Year, Semi-finalist; Doak Walker Award; Breakout Player of the Year, Sporting News; Michigan football MVP, 2000; NFL Rookie of the Year, Sports Illustrated, 2001; NFL Offensive Rookie of Year, 2002; Louisiana Sports Hall of Fame, 2015. **Business Addr:** Assistant Head Coach, Special Teams Coordinator, West Virginia Wesleyan College, 59 College Ave, Buckhannon, WV 26201, **Business Phone:** (304)473-8495.

### THOMAS, DR. ARTHUR E.
College president, executive, civil rights activist. **Personal:** son of Janie R Bradleymarried Dawn. **Educ:** Cent State Univ, Wilberforce, OH, attended 1962; Miami Univ, MEd; Univ Mass, EdD. **Career:** Cent State Univ, Wilberforce, OH, vpres acad affairs, 1977-85, pres, 1985-95; pres emer, 1985-95; Dayton Pub Sch Syst, fac; Wright State Univ, fac; Don King Productions Inc, dir community affairs; NAFEO, Prog Mgr, 2003-08; Morgan State Univ, currently. **Orgs:** Am Coun Educ; Nat Asn Equal Opportunity Higher Educ. **Special Achievements:** US Presidential Delegation to observe the first all-race election in South Africa. **Business Addr:** Program Manager, Morgan State University, 1700 E Cold Spring Lane, Baltimore, MD 21251, **Business Phone:** (443)885-3333.

### THOMAS, ARTHUR LAFAYETTE, III
Video producer, editor. **Personal:** Born Jan 14, 1960, Trenton, NJ; son of Arthur and Hermione Smith; married Robin M Golden; children: Sydney Golden, Paige Leigh & Arthur IV. **Educ:** Rutgers Univ, BA, 1982; Am Univ, attended 1987. **Career:** Powell Bros Inc, tech serv mgr; Black Entertainment Tv, videographer, currently. **Orgs:** Nat Asn Black Journalists; US Sen & House Rep News Galleries, 1987-. **Special Achievements:** Cable Ace Award, nomination, 1998; Attended President Clinton historical journey to Africa; One of the only two Black videographers chosen for the first sitting Presidents visit to the African continent. **Home Addr:** 2913 Gracefield Rd, Silver Spring, MD 20904-1668. **Business Addr:** Videographer, Black Entertainment Television, 1900 W Pl NE, Washington, DC 20018-1230.

### THOMAS, ARTHUR RAY
President (organization), executive. **Personal:** Born Aug 17, 1951, Ville Platte, LA; son of Ernestine and Artellus Jr. **Educ:** Southern Univ, Baton Rouge, BA, polit sci, 1972; Southern Univ Law Ctr, JD, 1976. **Career:** La State Legis Health & Welfare Comt, clerk; La state health Legis & welfare Comt, clerk; La House Rep, comt clerk, 1978-79, staff mem, 1980-81; Johnson Taylor & Thomas Law Firm, partner, 1980-90; La Dept Justice, staff atty; Arthur R Thomas & Assocs, pres, owner, 1990-; Renaissance Develop Corp, pres, 1993-; Phi Beta Sigma Fraternity Inc, Wash, DC, 31st int pres, 2001-05. **Orgs:** Int pres, Phi Beta Sigma Fraternity Inc, 2001-05; fel mem, Black Stone Socs; US Congressman Gillis Long; pres, Southern Univ Law Ctr Alumni Asn; Louis A Martinet Legal Socs; Capital Area Legal Serv Corp; La Capital Fund Inc; Louis A Martinet Legal Soc; Nat Pan-Hellenic Coun. **Business Addr:** President, Arthur R Thomas & Associates LLC, 3313 Govt St, Baton Rouge, LA 70806, **Business Phone:** (225)344-7370.

### THOMAS, DR. AUDRIA ACTY
Immunologist. **Personal:** Born Jun 6, 1954, Washington, DC; married Robert A Leycock; children: Shaunta Lindsey & Shavon. **Educ:** Meharry Med Col, MD, 1980. **Career:** Howard Univ Hosp, resident, 1980-83, fel, 1983-86; HUH fel, 1983-86; St Thomas, St John Med Soc, chief allergy dept; Roy L Schneider Hosp, med staff, 1986; VI Dept Health, dir, currently. **Orgs:** Soloist VI Chriistian Ministries, 1959-86; Nat Med Asn, 1980-86; pediat consult, 15-24 Free Clin Teenagers, 1980-86; consult, Virgin Island Lung Asn, 1986; Am Acad Pediat; Am Acad Allergy & Immunol. **Honors/Awds:** Howard Univ Fel, Allergy Immunol, 1983-86. **Special Achievements:** Published paper, "Cystic Fibrosis in Black", Layman's Journal update in allergy, 1985. **Home Addr:** PO Box 595, St. Thomas00804, **Home Phone:** (809)776-7782. **Business Addr:** Physician, Paragon Med Bldg 9149 Estate Thomas Suite 202, St Thomas, VA 00802, **Business Phone:** (340)776-5507.

### THOMAS, BARBARA LOUISE
Association executive, president (organization), chief executive officer. **Personal:** Born Dec 5, 1947, Dublin, GA; daughter of Horace Sanders and Jerrie Lee Tart; children: 2. **Educ:** Bernard Baruch Col, BA, 1970; Columbia Univ, MBA, 1973. **Career:** Columbia Broadcasting Syst, Radio Div, clerk, 1973, TV Div, network cutins, dir finance & admin, sr vpres, 1989; Mattapan Community Health Ctr, chief financial officer, 1989-99; The Young Women Christian Association Boston, sr vpres & chief financial officer, 1999-2001; Nat Black Master of Business Administration Asn, sr vpres finance & admin, chief financial officer, 2001-03, pres & ceo, 2003-09; Nat Black Bus Found, exec dir, 2010-; B Thomas & Assocs, pres & chief exec officer, 2010-. **Orgs:** Life mem, Nat Black MBA Asn; Univ Illinios. **Special Achievements:** First African American woman to attend CBS School of Management. **Business Addr:** President, Chief Executive Officer, B Thomas & Associates LLC, 1650 Pinehurst Lane Suite 100, Flossmoor, IL 60422, **Business Phone:** (708)960-0428.

### THOMAS, BETTE
Association executive. **Career:** Dept Housing & Urban Develop; City N Chicago, mayor; Community Action Partnership Lake County, dir. **Orgs:** Black Chamber Com Lake County. **Special Achievements:** First African American female mayor of North Chicago and Lake County; Bette Thomas Ave, Honorary Street Sign. **Business Addr:** Member, Black Chamber of Commerce of Lake County, 1020 W Glen Flora Ave Suite 104, Waukegan, IL 60085, **Business Phone:** (847)599-9510.

### THOMAS, BLAIR
Football player, football coach. **Personal:** Born Oct 7, 1967, Philadelphia, PA; married Lisa; children: 3. **Educ:** Pa State Univ, BS, recreation & parks mgt, 1989. **Career:** Football player, coach (retired); New York Jets, running back, 1990-93; New Eng Patriots, running back, 1994; Dallas Cowboys, running back, 1994; Atlanta Falcons,

1995; Carolina Panthers, running back, 1995; Temple Univ, running back coach, 1998-2005; Football Univ, instr, 2008; Kokomo's Sports Bar & Grill, partner. **Honors/Awds:** Most Valuable Player of the 1989 Holiday Bowl; Leading rookie rusher (326 yards), Am Football Conf, 1990; Pennsylvania Sports Hall of Fame, 2011. **Special Achievements:** Films: 1989 Holiday Bowl, 1989; 1990 NFL Draft, 1990. **Home Addr:** , King of Prussia, PA.

## THOMAS, BRANDY M.

Chief executive officer. **Educ:** Duke Univ Sch Engineering, BSE, biomed engineering, elec engineering & comput sci; Stanford Univ Grad Sch Bus, MBA. **Career:** Cyveillance Inc, founder, chmn & chief exec officer, 2000; Mercer Mgt Consult, sr assoc; Apple Comput a systs engr; New Ventures Group Nat Asn Securities Dealers, managing dir. **Orgs:** Bd mem, Northern Va Technol Coun; vpres, Nat Soc Black Engrs; vpres Omega Psi Phi Fraternity.

## THOMAS, BRODERICK LEE

Football player. **Personal:** Born Feb 20, 1967, Houston, TX; son of William and Linda; children: Broderick Jr & Elijah. **Educ:** Univ Nebr. **Career:** Football player (retired); Tampa Bay Buccaneers, linebacker, 1989, left outside linebacker, 1990, right linebacker, 1991-92, left linebacker, 1993; Detroit Lions, left outside linebacker, 1994; Minn Vikings, left linebacker, 1995; Dallas Cowboys, left linebacker, 1996, 1997-98. **Honors/Awds:** Big 8 Defensive Player of the Year, 1988; The 36th Greatest Buccaneer Player of all-time, Bucpower.com, 2003. **Special Achievements:** Film: 1989 NFL Draft, 1989.

## THOMAS, BYRON E.

Religious leader, minister (clergy). **Personal:** married DuWanna; children: Ntchwaidumela & Mustafa. **Educ:** Va Union Univ, BA, 1985; Southern Methodist Univ, Perkins Sch Theol, MDiv, 1988; McCormick Theol Sem, DMin, 2016. **Career:** Cent Methodist Church, Atlanta, pastor; Off Connectional Ministries N Ga Conf United Methodist Church, assoc dir; Ft St United Methodist Church, Atlanta, GA; Ben Hill United Methodist Church, Atlanta, GA, sr pastor, 2013-. **Orgs:** Bd mem, Hinton Rural Life Ctr; N Ga Black Methodist Church Renewal, pres, 2015-, comts N Ga Conf & Southeastern Jurisdiction United Methodist Church. Southeastern Jurisdiction Black Methodist Church Renewal, coordr, 2015-; Gen & Jurisdictional Conferences, clergy deleg, 2016. **Honors/Awds:** Malone Dodson Award, 2015. **Home Phone:** (404)626-9957. **Business Addr:** Ben Hill United Methodist Church, 2099 Fairborn Rd SW, Atlanta, GA 30331, **Business Phone:** (404)344-0618.

## THOMAS, CALVIN LEWIS

Football player. **Personal:** Born Jan 7, 1960, St. Louis, MO; married Bernadine; children: Nikkita, Bernadine & Thomas Jr. **Educ:** Univ Ill, BA, 1984. **Career:** Football player (retired); Chicago Bears, 1982-88; Denver Broncos, 1988. **Orgs:** Red Cloud Athletic Fund; Jr Variety Club; Big Brothers. **Home Addr:** 908 Manchester Ave, Westchester, IL 60154-2719.

## THOMAS, CARL

Singer. **Personal:** Born Jun 15, 1970, Aurora, IL. **Career:** Albums: Emotional, 2000; Let's Talk About It, 2004; So Much Better, 2007; Conquer, 2011. Singles: "Summer Rain", "I Wish", 2000; "Emotional", 2000; "She Is", 2004; "Make It Alright", 2004; "My First Love", 2004; "Another You", 2006; "2 Pieces", 2007; "Late Night Rendezvous", 2008; "Trey Songz", 2009; "Don't Kiss Me", 2011. **Honors/Awds:** Nominee, Grammy Award, 2006. **Business Addr:** Recording Artist, c/o Bungalo Records, 1755 Broadway, New York, NY 10019, **Business Phone:** (212)841-8000.

## THOMAS, CARL ALAN

Educator, clergy. **Personal:** Born Mar 21, 1924, Jersey City, NJ; children: Edward, Algynan, Elaine & Stanley. **Educ:** Rutgers Univ, BA, 1946; Union Sem, BD, 1949; NY Univ, MA, 1950; Univ KS, DD, 1970. **Career:** Fla A&M Univ, prof, 1960-64; Expert Int Living, dir, 1960; Wilberforce Univ, dean, 1964-66; Lincoln Univ, PA, dean, 1968, Stud Activ & Int Stud Affairs, dir; African Methodist Episcopal Zion Church, pastor; Lincoln Univ Oxford, prof Black studies; Training Inst Lincoln Univ, teacher; Community Col Philadelphia, dir & dean. **Orgs:** Alpha Psi Omega Frat; Kappa Alpha Psi Frat Swords & Shields Wilberforce, OH; Sons Wilberforce OH. **Home Addr:** 5215 Overbrook Ave, Philadelphia, PA 19131.

## THOMAS, CAROL M.

Government official, secretary (office). **Personal:** Born Dec 23, 1930, Washington, DC; married Laura Pedro; children: Kevin, Marla & Paul. **Educ:** Yale Univ, BA, 1953; John Hopkins Univ, MA, 1961. **Career:** Navy Dept, mgt internship, 1961; Navy Dept Wash, contract negotiator, 1961-64; Off Econ Opportunity Wash, br, 1964-65; Job Corps, proj mgr, 1965-67; Contracts Div Peace Corp Wash, dep dir, 1967-69; Am Soc Pub Adminrs, 1972-; Manasas Educ Found; Am Acad Polit & Social Scis, 1973-; Off Civil Rights US EPA Wash, 1974-77; Fed Trade Comn, secy, 1977-. **Orgs:** Dir, Peace Corps Sierraieone, 1969-71; Reston Golf & Country Club, 1971-; exec, Comn Bd Dir, 1972-; Alpha Phi Alpha Frat; Fed City Club Wash, 1972-; dir, Off Civil Rights & Urban Affairs US Environ Protection Agency, 1972-74.

## THOMAS, CHARLES

Television journalist. **Personal:** Born May 3, 1951, Webster Groves, MO; son of Clarence and Oneida; married Maria; children: 3. **Educ:** Univ Mo, Sch Jour, BA, 1973. **Career:** Reporter in Kansas City, MO; KGO-TV, San Francisco, CA, reporter, 1978-82; WCAU-TV, Philadelphia, reporter, 1982-86; WTAF-TV, general assignment reporter, 1986-88; ABC News bureau, St. Louis, MO and Chicago, reporter, 1988-91; ABC 7 News, Chicago, IL, general assignment reporter, 1991-2009, political reporter, 2009-. **Orgs:** Alpha Phi Alpha, 1969-. **Business Addr:** WLS-TV, 190 N State St, Chicago, IL 60601.

## THOMAS, CHARLES COLUMBUS

Educator. **Personal:** Born Sep 10, 1940, McAlester, OK. **Educ:** Langston Univ, BA, 1962; Brooklyn Col, MFA, 1972; City Univ NY, attended 1977. **Career:** Afro-Am Folkloric Troupe, artistic dir, 1963-70; Lefferst Jr High Sch, chmn, 1966-69; Egbe Omo Nago Folklorio Ensemble, dir, 1967-69; OEO Proj, dir, 1968; NY Community Col, asst prof, 1971-74; Afro-Am Inst Richmond Col, dir, 1972-73; Univ Ghana, vis prof, 1972; Ebony Success Libr, staff, 1972; Screen Actors Guild; Say Yes to Jesus, Gospel Musical, lead actor, 1992-99; "Life During War Time", Nuyorican Poets Cafe, NY, costume designer, 1993; Nat Black Theatre Festival, actor, 1999; KWANZAA Festival with Ossie Davis & Ruby Dee, dir, 2001; Opera, "Gethsemane Park", NY, lead actor, 2001; "Light in the Cellar", 2002; City Univ NY, Col Staten Island, asst prof, assoc prof performing & creative arts, dance coordr, 2003-; Staten & Island Repertory Ensemble, dir; vocalist with Roy Haynes Jazz Ensemble, Jimmy Owens Quartet, Bob Cunningham Trio, Marjorie Eliot's Jazz Parker Dwight Dickerson. **Orgs:** New York Coun Arts, 1968-70; Mayor's Coun Youth & Phys Fitness, 1969; African Heritage Studies Asn; Epsilon Chap Omega Psi Phi; Nat Acad Rec Arts & Sci; Nat Acad TV Arts & Sci; Grammy Awards Rec Acad. **Honors/Awds:** Research Award, City Univ NY, 1972; AUDELCO Theatre Award, 1991; Outstanding Alumni Award, Langston Univ, OK, 1995; President Citation, Nat Asn Equal Opportunity Higher Educ, Wash, 1995; Twentieth Century Achievement Award, Am Biog Inst, 1997; Xi Phi Chap Opportunity Achievement Award, 2000; Barber Scotia Col Achievement Award, 2001; Outstanding Faculty Award, Staten Island Col Stud Govt; Asn Black Educators of New York Award; Listed, Who's Who of Musicians. **Special Achievements:** Contributing author of We Speak as Liberators, 1971, Rinds for Revolution 1971, Probes an introduction to & poetry 1973, Yarbird Reader 1977. **Home Addr:** 1245 Pk Ave Suite 11K, New York, NY 10028. **Business Addr:** Associate Professor, The City University of New York, Rm 224A Bldg 1P 2800 Victory Blvd, Staten Island, NY 10314, **Business Phone:** (718)982-2525.

## THOMAS, CHARLES RICHARD

Educator, army officer. **Personal:** Born Jun 6, 1933, Evanston, IL; children: Charles Jr & Markham. **Educ:** Univ Wis-Madison Sch Educ, BS, 1957; Northwestern Univ, MA, 1966; NW Univ, attended 1970; Columbia Univ, Teachers Col, PhD, 1978. **Career:** Evanston HS, athletic coach, 1957-68, asst prin, 1964-67; Evanston Pub Sch, prin, 1968-71; Ill Off Educ, asst supt, 1971-73; N Chicago Sch Dist 64, supt, 1973; Nat Louis Univ, asst prof educ, prof educ, currently. **Orgs:** Ill Asn Sch Adminr; Am Asn Sch Adminr; Nat Alliance Black Sch Educr; Lake Co Asn Sch Adminr; Ill Asn Sch Bd Asn; Am Asn Sch Personnel Adminr; Asn Sup & Curric Develop; pres, Phi Delta Kappa, N Chicago Rotary Club; bd dir, Lake Co Urban Leg. **Honors/Awds:** Nat Asn Advan Colored People N Chicago Branch Award, Citizen Participation Sch Desegregation, Ill J Educ, 1972; Distinguished Service Award, Am Asn Sch Adminr; Hall of Fame, Nat Alliance Black Sch Educr; Distinguished Alumni Award, Wis Alumni Asn. **Special Achievements:** Published "Unique Problems Confronting the Black Sch Administrator", 1972; "The Purpose & Value of HS Athletics", Univ Mich, 1976; "Sch Desegregation what makes it work?", Ill School Board Journal, 1977; Top 100 School Executives in North America, Executive Educator. **Business Addr:** Professor of Education, National Louis University, 122 S Mich Ave, Chicago, IL 60603, **Business Phone:** (608)262-4847.

## THOMAS, CHARLES W. (CHUCK THOMAS)

Executive, manager. **Personal:** Born Mar 9, 1940, Boston, MA; son of Charles Edward and Pauline Delores Walker; married Ellen V Bell; children: Kevin Charles & Tracey Ann. **Educ:** Northeastern Univ, Boston, AS, 1963, BS, 1967; Univ Redlands, Redlands, CA, MA, 1983. **Career:** Raytheon Co, Bedford, MA, draftsman, 1961-64, engr, 1964-67; RCA, Chelmsford, MA, engineering mgr, 1967-70; Regional Transit, Sacramento, Calif, from asst gen mgr to gen mgr, 1970-81; SEPTA, Philadelphia, Pa, chief transp officer, 1981-85, from dep asst gen mgr opers to asst gen mgr opers, 1985-96, asst gen mgr, safety & risk mgt; Wash Metrop Area Transit Authority, Wash, DC, dep gen mgr opers, 1996-. **Orgs:** Alpha Phi Alpha Frat Inc. **Home Addr:** 8139 Wash Lane, Wyncote, PA 19095, **Home Phone:** (215)887-4958. **Business Addr:** Deputy General Manager Operations, Washington Metropolitan Area Transit Authority, 600 5th St NW, Washington, DC 20001, **Business Phone:** (202)637-7000.

## THOMAS, CHERYL T.

Association executive, chief executive officer. **Personal:** Born Oct 31, 1946. **Educ:** Marquette Univ, BS, biol & chem; Univ Ill, Chicago, MS, physiol. **Career:** Dept Aviation, dir, mgt serv, 1983-89; Dept Water, dir, personnel policy & utilization, 1989-92; Mayor Richard M Daley, City Chicago, dep chief staff, 1992-94; City Chicago, Dept Bldgs, comnr, 1994-98; US Rr Retirement Bd, City Chicago, bd chmn, 1998-2003; Ardmore Assocs, pres & chief exec officer, currently. **Orgs:** US Rr Retirement Bd, Comt Labor & Human Resources. **Honors/Awds:** Professional Achievement Award, Bd Trustees Marquette Univ Alumni Asn, 2015. **Home Addr:** 5020 S Lake Shore Dr Apt 2716N, Chicago, IL 60615-3220. **Business Addr:** President, Chief Executive Officer, Ardmore Associates LLC, 33 N Dearborn Suite 1720, Chicago, IL 60602, **Business Phone:** (312)795-1400.

## THOMAS, CHRIS ERIC

Manager, football player. **Personal:** Born Jul 16, 1971, Los Angeles, CA; children: Rylan. **Educ:** Calif Polytech State Univ, BA, Eng. **Career:** Football player (retired), manager; San Diego Chargers, wide receiver, 1993-94; San Francisco 49ers, wide receiver, 1995; Wash Redskins, wide receiver, 1997-99; St Louis Rams, wide receiver, 1999-2000; Kansas City Chiefs, wide receiver, 2001; Bank Am, Merrill Lynch, wealth mgr, currently. **Honors/Awds:** California Polytechnic Hall of Fame, 2007. **Business Addr:** Wealth Manager, Bank of America Merrill Lynch, 4 World Financial Ctr 250 Vesey St, New York, NY 10080.

## THOMAS, HON. CLARENCE

Supreme court justice, lawyer, government official. **Personal:** Born Jun 23, 1948, Pin Point, GA; son of M C and Leola Anderson Williams; married Kathy Grace Ambush; children: Jamal Adeen; married Virginia Lamp. **Educ:** Immaculate Conception Sem, attended 1968; Holy Cross Col, BA, 1971; Yale Univ Law Sch, JD, 1974. **Career:** Hill Jones & Farrington, legal aid, 1971-74; Atty Gen John Danforth, State Mo, staff mem, 1974-77; State Mo, asst atty gen, 1974-77; Monsanto Corp, legal coun, 1977-79; Sen John Danforth, leg asst, 1979-81; US Fed Govt, Dept Educ, asst secy civil rights, 1981-82; Equal Employ Opportunity Comn, chmn, 1982-90; US Ct Appeals Dist Columbia Circuit, app circuit judge, 1990-91; Monsanto Co, atty; US Supreme Ct, assoc justice, 1991-. **Orgs:** Founder, Black Stud Union, Holy Cross Col, 1971; adv bd, Lincoln Rev; Episcopal Church. **Special Achievements:** Second African American to serve on the nation's highest court; First black student to attend St John Vianneys Minor Seminary; Writings: Why Federalism Matters, My Grandfather's Son: A Memoir. **Home Addr:** 7542 Cross Gate Lane, Alexandria, VA 22310, **Home Phone:** (703)922-0148. **Business Addr:** Associate Justice, Supreme Court of the United States, 1 First St NE, Washington, DC 20543-0001, **Business Phone:** (202)479-3415.

## THOMAS, DAVE GARFIELD

Football player. **Personal:** Born Aug 25, 1968, Miami, FL; children: Zachary. **Educ:** Univ Tenn, grad. **Career:** Football player (retired); Dallas Cowboys, defensive back, 1993-94; Jacksonville Jaguars, defensive back, 1995, left cornerback, 1996, left & right cornerback, 1997, right cornerback, 1998, 1999; New York Giants, cornerback & left cornerback, 2000, left cornerback, 2001. **Honors/Awds:** Super Bowl Champion, 1993; Ed Block Courage Award, 1997; Beach High Hall of Fame plaque. **Special Achievements:** Films: 1993 NFL Draft, 1993; 1994 NFC Championship Game, 1995; Super Bowl XXXV, 2001.

## THOMAS, DAVID

Executive. **Career:** Bishop State Community Col, hist instr, 1993, dir SW campus, 2000-, dir div adult educ & econ develop, 2003-. **Business Addr:** Director, Bishop State Community College, 351 N Broad St, Mobile, AL 36603-5898, **Business Phone:** (251)690-6836.

## THOMAS, DAVID ANTHONY

Educator, dean (education). **Personal:** Born Sep 26, 1956, Kansas City, MO; son of Jewell Williams and Jesse; married Willetta Lewis; children: Sommer Iman, David Jr & Nelson Dubois. **Educ:** Yale Univ, BA, admin sci, 1978, MS, philos, 1984, PhD, orgn behav, 1986; Columbia Univ, MA, orgn sci, 1981. **Career:** Columbia Univ, grad fel, 1980-81; Yale Univ, grad fel, 1981-85; Wharton Sch Univ Pa, asst prof mgt & bus admin, 1986-90; Harvard Bus Sch, from asst prof to assoc prof, 1990-99, tenured prof, 1998-, Exec Educ Prog, sr assoc dean & dir, fac recruitment, 2005-08, unit head, org behav, currently, H Naylor Fitzhugh prof, bus admin & dir fac recruiting; J African Am Polit, Harvard Univ, ed bd, 1992; Georgetown Univ McDonough Sch Bus, dean, 2011-. Books: Breaking Through: The Making of Minority Executives in America, Harvard Bus Press, 1999; Leading for Equity: The Pursuit of Excellence in Montgomery County, Harvard Educ Press, 2009. **Orgs:** Wharton Sch, Atlantic Richfield Found, 1986-90; bd mem, WGBH Community Adv, 1993-96; trustee, Shady Hill Sch, 1996-; bd mem, Partnership, 1997-; fac chair, HBS Exec Educ prog; bd mem, Cambridge Trust Co; bd mem, Posse Found; Acad Mgt; Int Socs Psychoanal Study Orgn; Nat Training Labs. **Home Addr:** , Cambridge, MA. **Business Addr:** Dean, Georgetown University, 37th & O St NW, Washington, DC 20057, **Business Phone:** (202)687-0100.

## THOMAS, DEBI (DEBRA JANINE THOMAS)

Figure skater, physician. **Personal:** Born Mar 25, 1967, Poughkeepsie, NY; married Brian Vanden Hogen; children: Christopher Jules Bequette II; married Chris Bequette; children: Christopher Jules; married Jamie Looney; children: Ethan & Austin. **Educ:** Stanford Univ, BE, 1991; Northwestern Univ Feinberg Sch Med, 1997; Univ Ark Med Sci Hosp, surg residency; Martin Luther King Jr/Charles Drew Univ Med Ctr S Cent Los Angeles, orthop surg residency; Charles R Drew Univ, Orthop Residency Prog, 2005. **Career:** Figure skater (retired), orthop surgeon, skater; King-Drew Med Ctr, attend jr physician specialist, 2001-05; Carle Clin Asn, Champaign-Urbana, sub-specialist surg, 2007-; pvt pract, ortho xcellence, 2010-. **Orgs:** Fel Centinela Hosp, Dorr Arthritis Inst, 2006-07; Alpha Kappa Alpha sorority. **Honors/Awds:** Gold Medal, Skate Am Int Minneapolis & St Ivel Int Great Britain; US Ladies Figure Skating Champion, 1986; US Championships, 1985, 1986, 1987, 1988; World Championship, 1986, 1987, 1988; World Figure Skating Championships, Bronze Medalist, 1988; US Nat title, 1988; Winter Olympics, 1988; San Jose Sports Hall of Fame, 1998; US Figure Skating Hall Fame, 2000; Athletic Hall of Fame, San Mateo High Sch, 2010. **Special Achievements:** First African American to win the US Figure Skating & World Figure Skating Championship Senior Titles, 1986; First African American to win an Olympic figure skating medal, 1988; Jock-Docs. **Business Addr:** Physician, Carle Clin, 602 W Univ Ave, Urbana, IL 61801, **Business Phone:** (217)326-1894.

## THOMAS, DR. DENNIS E.

Athletic director, association executive, teacher. **Personal:** Born Sep 5, 1953, Heidelberg, MS; son of Russell and Marjorie. **Educ:** Alcorn State Univ, BS, 1974; Northeast La Univ, MEd, 1975; State Univ NY, Buffalo, NY, EdD, 1984. **Career:** Carroll High, Monroe, LA, teacher, 1976; Alcorn State Univ, instr, HPER, 1976-81; State Univ Buffalo, grad teaching asst, 1984; Alcorn State Univ, asst prof, HPER, 1984-86; S Carolina State Univ, head football coach, 1986-88; Hampton Univ, tenured asst prof, 1989, chair, HPER, 1989-95, dir athletics, 1990-2003. **Orgs:** Am Alliance Health, Phys educ, Recreation & Dance; N Am Soc Sport Mgt; Nat Asn Col dir Athletics; Va Asn Health, Phys Educ, Recreation & Dance; Nat Asn Supv & Curric Develop; NLI Policy & Rev Comt; NCAA Div I Leadership Coun; chmn, NCAA Div I-AA Football Comt; chair, NCAA Div I-AA (FCS) Comnr Asn; bd dir, Walter Byers Scholar Comt; bd dir, Advocates Athletic Equity; bd dir, Nat Football Found; bd dir, Col Hall Fame; exec comt, mem, Football Champion Subdivision Dir Athletics Asn; comnr & pres, Mid-Eastern Athletic Conf, 2002-; lifetime mem, Kappa Alpha Psi Fraternity Inc; bd dir, Black Coaches & Adminr. **Special Achievements:** State legislative of Mississippi proclaimed April 8 as the Dennis and Johnny (brother) Day in the state for their achievements in scholarship, athletics, and leadership, 1978. **Home Addr:** 130 Pine Creek Dr, Hampton, VA 23669-1244, **Home Phone:** (757)851-1683.

**Business Addr:** Commissioner, President, Mid-Eastern Athletic Conference, 222 Cent Pk Ave Suite 1150, Virginia Beach, VA 23466-2547, **Business Phone:** (757)416-7100.

### THOMAS, DEON LA VELLE
Basketball player, executive. **Personal:** Born Feb 24, 1971, Chicago, IL; married Daphna. **Educ:** Univ Ill, attended 1994. **Career:** Basketball player (retired), coach; Dallas Mavericks, ctr, 1994; Manresa, ctr, 1994-95; Girona, ctr, 1995-96; Unicaja, ctr, 1996-97; Sevilla, ctr, 1997-98; Maccabi RL, ctr, 1998-99; Gran Canaria, ctr, 1999-2001; Caceres, ctr, 2001-03; Turk Telekom, ctr, 2002-03; Maccabi Tel Aviv, ctr, 2003-04; A.E.L. 1964, 2005-06; Bulgarian CSKA Sofia, 2006; Maccabi Givat Shmuel, 2006-07; Maccabi Haifa BasketBall, ctr, 2007-08; Lewis & Clark Community Col, athletic dir, men's basketball head coach, 2009-. **Honors/Awds:** Illinois Mr. Basketball, 1989; McDonalds All-American, 1989; Maccabi Tel Aviv NBA Draft, 1994; European Champion, Euroleague, 2003, 2004, 2005; Illini All-Century Team, 2004. **Business Addr:** Head Coach, Athletic Director, Lewis & Clark Community College, 5800 Godfrey Rd, Godfrey, IL 62035, **Business Phone:** (618)468-7000.

### THOMAS, DERMOND EDWIN
Advocate, administrator. **Personal:** married Kimberly Lynn Johnson; children: Olivia & Cole. **Educ:** Wayne State Univ, grad; Amherst Col, BA, econs, 1998; Columbia Univ Sch Law, JD, 2001. **Career:** Talented Youth Develop Inc, exec dir & founder; Fried, Frank, Harris, Shriver & Jacobson LLP, atty; MSC Indust Supply, dir, corp coun; Arnold & Porter LLP, lawyer; Nassau County Interim Finance Authority, dir, currently. **Orgs:** Trustee, Village Valley Stream; bd mem, Nassau County Interim Finance Authority. **Business Addr:** Director, Nassau County Interim Finance Authority, 170 Old Country Rd Suite 205, Mineola, NY 11501, **Business Phone:** (516)248-2828.

### THOMAS, DORIS
Executive. **Personal:** married Henry; children: Chandra. **Educ:** Mott Community Col, Flint, MI. **Career:** Executive (retired); Bank One Corp, pres, community investment officer, vpres community develop & mkt officer. **Orgs:** Vpres, 2004, pres, adv bd chair & ex officio, Urban Financial Serv Coalition Found. **Home Addr:** 5165 N Jennings Rd, Flint, MI 48504, **Home Phone:** (810)785-8343. **Business Addr:** Vice President, Urban Financial Serv Coalition Found Inc, 2121 K St NW Suite 800, Washington, DC 20037, **Business Phone:** (202)261-3569.

### THOMAS, DUANE
Writer. **Educ:** Fashion Inst Technol, advert & commun, 1989. **Career:** Books: Truth About Handguns: Exploding The Myths, Hype, & Misinformation, 1998; Body & Soul: The Black Male Book, 1998; Duane Thomas & the Fall of America's Team, 1998; Soul Style: Black Women Redefining the Color of Fashion, ed, 2000; More Body, More Soul: Beautiful Black Men 2005; Conde Nast, assoc art dir. **Special Achievements:** Has contributed to Vogue, Elle, Harper's Bazaar, Talk, InStyle, Essence, O:The Oprah Magazine, and Esquire magazines. **Business Addr:** Author, c/o Rizzoli & Universe International Publications, 300 Pk Ave S 4th Fl, New York, NY 10010, **Business Phone:** (212)387-3400.

### THOMAS, EARL LEWIS
Executive, football player. **Personal:** Born Oct 4, 1948, Greenville, TX. **Educ:** Univ Houston, BS. **Career:** Chicago Bears, tight end, wide receiver, 1971-73; St Louis Cardinals, tight end, wide receiver, 1974-75; Houston Oilers, tight end, wide receiver, 1976; home bldg co, proj mgr; Oil Equip co, sales trainee, 1980; Gold Line Supply, founder, 1980; Gold Line Refining Ltd, founder, pres & chief exec officer, managing gen partner, 1990-2001. **Orgs:** Quail Valley Country Club. **Home Addr:** 11 Greenway Plz Suite 2602, Houston, TX 77046, **Home Phone:** (713)271-3550. **Business Addr:** General Partner, 9301 Southwest Fwy Suite 250, Houston, TX 77074, **Business Phone:** (713)271-3550.

**THOMAS, EARLE FREDERICK, SR. See Obituaries Section.**

### THOMAS, EDITH PEETE
Government official, nutritionist. **Personal:** Born Jul 30, 1940, Memphis, TN; daughter of James Walter and Carrie Bell; married Charles L; children: Stephanie Lynne & Charles Stephen. **Educ:** Fontbonne Col, BA, dietetics, 1960; St Louis Univ, MS, nutrit, 1966; Columbia Univ, EdM, nutrit educ, 1971; Ind Univ, PhD, nutrit & adult educ, 1977; Univ Iowa, postdoctoral studies, pediat nutrit, 1980. **Career:** Johns Hopkins Hosp, asst dir, dietetics & chief proj nutritionist, 1966-68; Ind Univ, lectr, adult educ, 1973-76; Univ NC, Chapel Hill, Dept Nutrit, asst prof, 1977-78; Nutrit Consult Assocs, dir, 1978-80; US Dept Agr Exten Serv, nat prog leader, Expanded Food & Nutrit Educ Prog, 1980-86; March Dimes Fel, 1984; George Mason Univ, vis res prof, 1986-88; Nat Training Labs, Org Develop Prog, postdoctoral prog, 1987-89; US Dept Agr Coop State Res, Educ & Exten Serv, nat prog leader org develop, 1988. **Orgs:** Alpha Kappa Alpha Sorority, 1959-; Am Dietetic Asn, 1960-; Nat Hon & Prof Asn Educ, 1975; Am Educ Res Asn, 1978-; prog chairperson, DC Dietetic Asn, 1980-81, mem, 1980-; Am Home Econ Asn, prog planning comn, 1982-88; DC Home Econ Asn, 1982-88, pres, 1984-85; Am Eval Asn, Topical Interest Group, Minority Issues, 1989-, chair, 1992. **Home Addr:** 63 E 130th St Suite 1, New York, NY 10037, **Home Phone:** (646)360-3213. **Business Addr:** AC.

### THOMAS, EDWARD ARTHUR
Insurance executive. **Personal:** Born Dec 30, 1952, Georgetown; son of Andrew and Eunice; married Cecelia; children: Erklin, Arthur, Carla & Mahala. **Educ:** City Univ NY, York Col, BA, 1977; Polytech Inst NY, MS, 1982; Univ Toledo Col Law, JD, 1988. **Career:** Blue Cross, Blue Shield of Greater NY, internal auditor, 1977-80; Metropolitan Life Ins Co, sls rep, 1980-81; Ins Serv Off, actuarial asst, 1982-85; Blue Cross, Blue Shield Ohio, actuarial analyst, 1985-88; Penn Dept Ins, chief HMO/PPO, 1988-91; Keystone Health Plan East, vpres & gen coun rev div, 1991-92; Lomax Health Syst, vpres managed care serv, 1992-94; New Century Consult Inc, pres & chief exec officer, 1994-; Symmetry Group Inc, prin, pres. **Orgs:** Penn Bar Asn, 1989-. **Home Addr:** 5141 S Deerfield Ave, Mechanicsburg, PA 17050-2496, **Home Phone:** (717)763-7610. **Business Addr:** President, Chief Executive Officer, New Century Consultants Inc, 900 E 8th Ave Suite 300, King of Prussia, PA 19406, **Business Phone:** (610)768-8078.

**THOMAS, EDWARD S. See Obituaries Section.**

**THOMAS, ELEANOR M. See CLARK-THOMAS, ELEANOR M.**

### THOMAS, ERIC JASON
Football player. **Personal:** Born Sep 11, 1964, Tucson, AZ. **Educ:** Pasadena City Col; Tulane Univ. **Career:** Football player (retired), motivational speaker; Cincinnati Bengals, defensive back, 1987, 1990, right cornerback, 1988-89, 1991-92; New York Jets, left cornerback, 1993-94; Denver Broncos, cornerback, 1995; motivational speaker. **Honors/Awds:** Post-season play, 1988: Pro Bowl, 1988; Championship Game, Am Football Club; Championship Game, Nat Football League.

### THOMAS, EULA WILEY
Educator, association executive. **Personal:** Born Apr 30, 1948, Arkadelphia, AR; daughter of Elmore Sr and Pernella Weaver; married Herman L; children: Traci A & Tiffani A. **Educ:** Ouachita Baptist Univ, BA, speech & drama, 1970; Henderson State Univ, MASAC Soc Agency Coun, 1976; Univ Colo Training Inst, attended 1980; Marquette Univ Training Inst Spec Prog, attended 1981; Wichita State Training Inst, attended 1984; Univ Ark, ABD. **Career:** AR Human Dev Ctr, recreation leader, 1970, speech pathologist, 1971-76; Henderson State Univ, coord handicapped serv, 1984, counr, instr, 1976, instr, 2006; Thomas Enterprises, owner, 2006-. **Orgs:** Clerk, secy, deaconess Greater Pleasant Hill Baptist Church; co-sponsor, Henderson State Univ Minority Stud Org, 1979-; pres, Arkadelphia Women's Develop Coun, 1980-; bd dir, Arkadelphia Chamber Com, 1983; chairperson, Arkadelphia Christmas Parade, 1983, 1984-; Ark Coun Asn, Ark Asn Stud Asn Prog, Nat Asn Advan Colored People; exec bd, Arkadelphia Housing Authority, 1989-; United Way Allocation Comt, 1991; instr/counr, Commun/Minority Affairs Coordr, 1993; trainer, Delta Sigma Theta Sorority Inc, 2003; Advisor Advising Ctr, 2009. **Honors/Awds:** WP Sturgis Found Grant Continuing Educ, 1966; Arkansas Handicapped Award for Special Educ, 1971; Outstanding Advisor of the Year, Ark Black Stud Asn, 1991; Outstanding Community Service Award African American, 2003. **Home Addr:** 4 Friendship Dr, Arkadelphia, AR 71923-2609, **Home Phone:** (870)246-2937. **Business Addr:** Coordinator, Henderson State University, 1100 Henderson St, Arkadelphia, AR 71999-0001, **Business Phone:** (870)230-5000.

### THOMAS, FRANK EDWARD, JR.
Executive, baseball player. **Personal:** Born May 27, 1968, Columbus, GA; son of Frank and Charlie Mae; married Elise Silver; children: Sterling Edward, Sloan Alexandra & Sydney Blake; married Megan; children: 1. **Educ:** Auburn Univ, attended 1989. **Career:** Baseball player (retired), executive; Chicago White Sox, infielder, 1990-2005; Big Hurt Enterprises, founder, 1994-99; Oakland Athletics, infielder, 2006, 2008; Un-D-Nyable Rec, founder; Toronto Blue Jays, 2007-08; Comcast SportsNet Chicago, Studio analyst, 2010-; Fox Sports, studio analyst, 2014-; W2W Rec, founder, chief exec officer, currently. **Orgs:** Pres, Frank Thomas Charitable Found, 1993; Am League Western Div Champion Chicago White Sox team; Am League Cent Div Champion Chicago White Sox teams, 1994-2000; Am League All-Star Team, 1994-95; Birmingham Barons. **Honors/Awds:** Players Choice Award, Major League Baseball Players Asn, 1993; Most Valuable Player, Am League, 1993, 1994; Home Run Derby Champion, 1995; AL All Star Team, 1993-97; Alabama Batting Champion, 1997; Silver Slugger Award, 1991, 1993, 1994, 2000; Comeback Player of the Year Award, Am League, 2000; Southeastern Conference Most Valuable Player; Alabama Sports Hall of Fame, 2011; Life-size Bronze Statue, US Cellular Field, 2011; National Baseball Hall of Fame, 2014. **Special Achievements:** First player in Major League history to win two silver slugger awards each at two different positions; Flim: Mr. Baseball, 1992. **Business Addr:** ON.

### THOMAS, FRANKLIN A. (FRANK AUGUSTINE)
Lawyer, executive, association executive. **Personal:** Born May 27, 1934, Brooklyn, NY; son of James and Viola; married Dawn Conrada; children: Keith, Hillary, Kerrie & Kevin. **Educ:** Columbia Col, BA, 1956; Columbia Law Sch, LLB, 1963. **Career:** Fed Housing & Home Finance Agency, atty, 1963; Southern Dist NY, asst US atty, 1964-65; NY Police Dept, dep police comnr charge legal matters, 1965-66; Bedford-Stuyvesant Restoration Corp, pres & chief exec officer, 1967-77; Citi bank, dir, 1970-98; pvt pract atty, 1977-79; Pepsi Co Inc, dir; Citi group, dir, pres; ALCOA, lead dir, 1977-; Ford Found, pres & chief exec officer, 1979-96; Warburg Pincus, sr advisor, 1995, 1998-2000; TFF Study Group, head, consult, 1996-2005, chmn, 2001-05; Study Group, consult, 2005-; Hillary Clinton Pres, atty; Nat Leadership Polit Action Comt, atty; Obama Am, atty; Obama Ill, atty; Women's Action Alliance, atty. **Orgs:** Trustee, Columbia Univ, 1969-75; bd mem, Cummins Inc; adv comm, Sec State S Africa, 1985-87; bd mem, Lucent Technologies, 1996-; chmn, September 11th Fund, 2001-05; dir, Conoco Inc, 1998; trustee, Friends Nelson Mandela C's Fund USA; Friends Const Ct S Africa USA; trustee, Green tree Found; UN Fund Int Partnerships; Obama Victory Fund, 2012; dir, Avaya Inc; dir, CBS Broadcasting Inc. **Honors/Awds:** LLD, Yale Univ, 1970; LLD, Fordham Univ, 1972; LLD, Pratt Inst, 1974; Award for Contribution to the Betterment of Urban Life, Lyndon B Johnson Found, 1974; Medal of Excellence, Columbia Univ, 1976; LLD, Pace Univ, 1977; LLD, Columbia Univ, 1979; Alexander Hamilton Award, Columbia Col, 1983; Columbia Law School's James Kent Award, 1992. **Special Achievements:** First African American president of the Ford Foundation; First black captain of an Ivy League basketball team. **Business Addr:** Lead Director, Alcoa Inc, 390 Park Ave, New York, NY 10022, **Business Phone:** (212)836-2600.

### THOMAS, FRED
Law enforcement officer. **Career:** Police (retired); Metrop Police Dept, 1965, dep chief, 1982; Metrop Police Boys and Girls Clubs of Wash, exec vpres, 1985-92; DC Police Dept, police off, 1985; Metrop Police Dept, DC, dep chief police, chief police, 1992-95; Homeland Security for Systs Applications & Technologies Inc, vpres, currently. **Orgs:** Head, exec vpres Metrop Police Boys & Girls Club, 1985-92.

### THOMAS, FRED L.
Football player. **Personal:** Born Sep 11, 1973, Bruce, MS. **Educ:** Univ Tenn, Martin, grad. **Career:** Football player (retired); Seattle Seahawks, 1996, 1999, defensive back, 1997-98; New Orleans Saints, 2000, 2007, right corner back & corner back & left corner back, 2001-07.

### THOMAS, DR. GERALD EUSTIS
Military leader, government official. **Personal:** Born Jun 23, 1929, Natick, MA; son of Walter W and Leila L Jacobs; married Rhoda Holmes Henderson; children: Kenneth A, Steven E & Lisa D Jacobs. **Educ:** Harvard Univ, BS, 1951; George Washington Univ, MA, 1966; Yale Univ, PhD, 1973. **Career:** Military leader (retired); govt off; USN, USS Newman K Perry, 1951-54, USS Worcester, 1954-56, Naval Acad, 1956-57, Nat Security Agency, 1957-60, USS Lowe, exec officer, 1960-62, asst head col training progs sect, Bur Naval Personnel, 1963-65, Naval War Col, 1965-66, Prairie View A&M's NROTC Units, exec officer, 1966-67, prof naval sci, 1967-69, Yale Univ, NROTC Unit, 1970-73, Comdr Destroyer Squadron Nine, 1973-74, Cruiser Destroyer Group Five, 1974-76, Near E & S Asia Region Off Asst Secy Defence, dir, 1976-78, Training Command Pac Fleet, comdr, 1978-81; State Dept, US ambassador Guyana, 1981-83, US ambassador Kenya, 1983-89. **Orgs:** Overseer, bd overseers, Harvard Univ, 1981-88; bd trustee, Univ San Diego, 1981-86; Orgn Am Historians; Alpha Phi Alpha fraternity Inc; Greek-lett fraternity. **Home Addr:** 10 Tucker Meadow Rd, Woodbridge, CT 06525-1943, **Home Phone:** (203)387-3166.

### THOMAS, GLORIA V.
Educator. **Personal:** Born Brenham, TX; children: Dino, Paul & Edwin. **Educ:** Tex Southern Univ, BS, 1953, MS, 1965, admin cert, 1968; Sorbonne, France, cert Fr; Baylor Univ; Univ Southern Miss, cert. **Career:** Phillis Wheatley Sr High Sch, chem teacher, 1959-72; Phillis Wheatley High Sch Houston Independent Sch Dist, regist. **Orgs:** Big Bros Houston, 1965; cancer found, 1970-74; Basileus Gamma Omega Zeta Zeta Phi Beta Sorority, 1971-72; Officer Houston Teachers Asn, 1971-72; vol Multi Schlerosis, 1972; sickle cell anemia, 1973-74; Civil Rights Comn, 1973-; United Fund Budget Panel, 1973; Human Rels Comn & Sexism Comn Huston Ind Sch Dist; Houston Teachers Asn; Tex State teachers Asn; Tex Classroom Teachers Asn; Nat Sci Teachers Asn; MacGregor Pk Civic Club; E Bethel Bapt Chap; Tex Atomic Energy Comn; Black Caucus Nat Educ Asn. **Honors/Awds:** Scholar Sorbonne, 1954-56; 15 Awards NSF, 1961-74; res particip grant, 1961; National Education Award, 1968; Outstanding leadership Award, Zeta Phi Beta Sor, 1971; Dr IGE Outcomes Achievement, 1974; Tex Aec Univ Tex.

### THOMAS, DR. HARRY LEE
Physician, surgeon. **Personal:** Born Apr 5, 1919, Richmond, VA; married Betty; children: Harriet & Harry. **Educ:** Lincoln Univ, AB, 1939; Howard Univ, MD, 1946. **Career:** Howard Univ, internship, 1946-47, surg res, 1947-52, instr, 1952-53; USAF Hosp, chief surg, 1953-56; Va Outpatient Facil, consult, 1956-60; Freedmen Hosp, internship, resident; Mercy Douglass Hosp, sr attend surgeon; Med Col Pa, clin prof surg, currently. **Orgs:** Dir, Mercy Douglass Hosp, Cancer Detection Proj, 1958-63; bd dir, Am Cancer Soc, 1977; N Med Asn; AMA. **Honors/Awds:** Distinguished Service Award, Med Col Pa; Golden Apple Teaching Award. **Home Addr:** 7042 Lincoln Dr, Philadelphia, PA 19119. **Business Addr:** Clinical Professor of Surgery, Medical College of Pennsylvania, 5555 Wissahickon Ave, Philadelphia, PA 19144, **Business Phone:** (215)843-9050.

### THOMAS, HENRY LEE, JR.
Football player. **Personal:** Born Jan 12, 1965, Houston, TX; married Eyvonne; children: Natasha & Sydney. **Educ:** La State Univ. **Career:** Football player (retired); Minn Vikings, left defensive tackle, 1987-94; Detroit Lions, left defensive tackle, 1995-96; New Eng Patriots, right defensive line, 1997-99, nose tackle, 2000. **Honors/Awds:** Pro Bowl, 1991-92; Second-team All-Pro, 1993.

### THOMAS, DR. HERMAN EDWARD
Educator. **Personal:** Born Dec 12, 1941, Bryson City, NC; married Mary Knox; children: Terence, Maurice & Katrina. **Educ:** NC Agr & Tech State Univ, BS, 1963; Duke Univ Divinity Sch, BD, sacred theol, 1966, ThM, 1969; Hartford Theol Sem Sch, PhD, 1978. **Career:** Berkley High Sch, Aberdeen, NC, teacher, 1966-67; Morris Col, Stud Affairs, 1968-69; Springfield Col, Relig & Philos, instr, 1969-74, Black Studies, coordr, 1971-74; AAA Studies Univ NC Charlotte, asst dir, 1974-86; Univ Transitional Opportunities Prog, dir, founder, 1986-; Shaw Univ, vpres acad affairs, 2004-, prof emer civil rights activist & stud advocate, currently. **Orgs:** Am Acad Relig, 1973-; chair, Steer Comt NC Coun Black Studies, 1975-76; assoc minister, Christian Educ, First Baptist Church-W, currently; chmn emer, bd mem, bd dir, chair, 1979-84, Afro-Am Cult Ctr, 1999-2001; pres, Charlotte Chap, Southern Christian Leadership Conf; bd mem, Charlotte-Mecklenburg Arts & Sci Coun; coordr, Humanist Afro-Am Hist Proj Charlotte, NC Humanities Comn, 1983-83; Interim pastor, First Baptist Church-W, 1993-95. **Home Addr:** 5913 Craftsbury Dr, Charlotte, NC 28215, **Home Phone:** (704)568-0949. **Business Addr:** Vice President Academic Affairs, Emeritus Professor Civil Rights Activist, Shaw University, 118 E S St, Raleigh, NC 27601, **Business Phone:** (919)546-8330.

### THOMAS, HERMAN L.
School superintendent, educator. **Educ:** Grambling State Univ, BA, Fr lang teacher educ, 1968; Henderson State Univ, MA, Eng lang arts teacher educ. **Career:** Arkadelphia Pub Schs, asst supt, supt curric & instr, 1968-2009; Arkadelphia High Sch, fr teacher, prin. **Honors/**

**Awds:** Milken Educator Award, 1991. **Business Addr:** Superintendent, Assistant Superintendent, Arkadelphia Public Schools, 235 N 11th St, Arkadelphia, AR 71923, **Business Phone:** (870)246-5564.

**THOMAS, HOLLIS, JR.**
Football player, football coach, television show host. **Personal:** Born Jan 10, 1974, Abilene, TX; children: Hydeia & Hallie. **Educ:** Northern Ill Univ, grad. **Career:** Philadelphia Eagles, defensive tackle & left defensive tackle & right defensive tackle, 1996-2005; New Orleans Saints, defensive tackle & nose tackle, 2006-08; St Louis Rams, 2009; Carolina Panthers, 2009; Arena Football League, defensive line coach, 2013; 94 WIP Philadelphia, sports talk show host, currently. **Orgs:** Partner, Asthma & Allergy Found Am, Southeast Pa Chap; Hollis Thomas Found. **Honors/Awds:** First-team All-Big West, 1995; Bert Bell Hero Award; Northern Illinois Athletic Hall of Fame, 2006. **Business Addr:** Sports Talk Show Host, 94 WIP Philadelphia, 400 Mkt St 9th Fl, Philadelphia, LA 19106, **Business Phone:** (215)625-9460.

**THOMAS, IRMA (IRMA LEE)**
Singer, musician, songwriter. **Personal:** Born Feb 18, 1941, Ponchatoula, LA; married Emile Jackson; married Andrew Thomas; children: 2. **Career:** Albums: Wish Someone Would Care, 1964; New Orleans Jazz & Heritage Festival, 1976; Irma Thomas Live, 1977; Soul Queen of New Orleans, 1978; Safe with Me, 1979; In Between Tears, 1981; Hip Shakin Mama, 1981; The New Rules, 1986; Down by Law, 1986; The Way I Feel, 1988; Simply the Best, 1991; True Believer, 1992; Walk Around Heaven: New Orleans Gospel Soul, 1994; The Story of My Life, 1997; Sing It!, 1998; My Heart's in Memphis: The Songs of Dan Penn, 2000; If You Want It, Come & Get It, 2001; Straight From The Soul, 2005; After the Rain, 2006; Wish Someone Would Care & Take a Look, 2006; A Women's Viewpoint, 2006; Wish Someone Would Care & Take A Look, 2006; Simply Grand, 2008; guest appearances: Blues Summit Duet on "We're Gonna Make It", MCA Recs, 1993; Various Artists & I Believe To My Soul, Rhino Recs, 2005; Various Artists & Our New Orleans, Elektra & Nonesuch Recs, 2005; The New Orleans Social Club & Sing Me Back Home, Burgundy Recs, 2006; Various Artists, Goin' Home: A Tribute to Fats Domino, 2007; Galactic, Ya-Ka-May (Anti) Vocals on "Heart Of Steel", 2010; Hugh Laurie, Let Them Talk, 2011; Film: New Orleans Music in Exile, 2006, Treme, 2010; Minit Rec, rec artist, 1963; Imp Rec, rec artist, 1963; Chess Rec, rec artist, 1967; Rounder Rec, rec artist, 1991. **Home Addr:** PO Box 26126, New Orleans, LA 70126, **Home Phone:** (504)245-1719. **Business Addr:** Recording Artist, c/o Emile Jackson, PO Box 104, Gonzales, LA 70737, **Business Phone:** (225)647-8121.

**THOMAS, ISAAC DANIEL, JR.**
Association executive, insurance executive, executive. **Personal:** Born Jan 31, 1939, Birmingham, AL; married Mary E Ellison; children: Peter Neil & Isaac Daniel III. **Educ:** Eastern Mich Univ; Wayne State Univ, BA, 1960; LA City Col, attended 1966; Pasadena City Col, attended 1968. **Career:** Wayne City Boys Detention Home, boys group leader, 1960; All state Ins Co, casualty claims supv, 1966, div personnel mgr, 1969, western zone human resources mgr, 1971, urban affairs dir, 1976, asst vpres employee rels. **Orgs:** Bd mem, Oper Snowball Ment Health Assoc Greater Chicago; bd dir, Southern Christian Leadership Coun; Du Sable Mus Chicago; SAFER Found Chicago; Kappa Alpha Psi. **Honors/Awds:** Motivator of Youth Award, YMCA Met Chicago Black & Hispanic Achievers Indust Recognition, 1978. **Business Addr:** Assistant Vice President Employee Relations, Allstate Insurance Co, Allstate Plz, Northbrook, IL 60062, **Business Phone:** (847)402-5000.

**THOMAS, ISIAH LORD, III**
Sports manager, executive, basketball player. **Personal:** Born Apr 30, 1961, Chicago, IL; son of Mary; married Lynn Kendall; children: Joshua & Lauren. **Educ:** Ind Univ, attended 1981, BA, 1987; Univ Calif, attended 2013. **Career:** Basketball player (retired), basketball coach, executive; Detroit Pistons, prof basketball player, guard, 1981-94; Toronto Raptors, gen mgr, part-owner, exec vpres basketball opers, 1994-98; Am Speedy Printing Ctrs Inc, co-chmn, 1994-; Marquis Jet Partners Inc, adv bd mem; NBC, NBA analyst, 1999; Continental Basketball Asn, owner, chief exec officer, 1999-2001; Ind Pacers, coach, 2000-03; New York Knicks, gen mgr, pres basketball opers, 2003-08, head coach, 2006-08; Fla Int Univ, head basketball coach, 2009-12; NBA TV, studio analyst, 2012-; WNBA New York Liberty, team pres, 2015-; San Antonio Spurs, asst coach, currently; Dale & Thomas Popcorn, partner, currently; Isiah Investments LLC, chmn & chief exec officer, currently; Sacramento Kings, guard, currently. **Orgs:** Founder, Isiah Thomas Found; bd mem, Chicago Stock Exchange; pres, NBA Players Asn, 1994-98; Am's Second Harvest; Easter Seals; Asn Help Retarded C; Isiah Thomas Scholar Fund, Ind Univ. **Business Addr:** NBA Assistant Coach, San Antonio Spurs, 1 AT&T Ctr, San Antonio, TX 78219, **Business Phone:** (210)444-5000.

**THOMAS, J. T. (JOHNNY LE'MON THOMAS)**
Football player. **Personal:** Born Dec 15, 1971, San Bernardino, CA. **Educ:** Ariz State Univ. **Career:** Football player (retired); St Louis Rams, wide receiver, 1995, 1998, kick returner, 1996. **Special Achievements:** Film: 1995 NFL Draft, 1995.

**THOMAS, JACQUELINE MARIE**
Journalist, college teacher. **Personal:** Born Aug 31, 1952, Nashville, TN; daughter of John James Jr and Dorothy Phillips. **Educ:** Briarcliff Col, AA, 1970, BA, 1972; Columbia Univ, Sch Int Affairs, MA, 1974. **Career:** Chicago Sun Times, reporter, 1974-85; Harvard Univ, Nieman Fel, 1983-84. Courier J & Louisville Times, assoc ed, 1985-86; Detroit Free Press, assoc ed, 1986-92; Detroit News, news ed, 1992-94, Wash bur chief, 1992-97; Baltimore sun, ed page ed, 1997-2001; New York Times, Vis Fel Ed bd, 2002; Kennedy Sch Govt, Harvard Univ, inst polit fel, 2003; Indianapolis Star, sr ed; freelance writer & ed; Univ Kans, William Allen White Sch Journalism & Mass Commun, Lacy C Haynes, vis prof, 2010-11; Ind Univ Sch Journalism, adj instr, currently; Univ Alaska Fairbanks, snedden guest lectr. **Orgs:** Bd mem, Nat Press Found, pres; Nat Asn Black Journalists; Am Soc Newspaper Eds; Nat Conf Ed Writers; Nat Asn Minority Media Execs. **Honors/Awds:** Pulitzer Prize Juror; Chairman's Award for Innovation, Times Mirror Co, 1997. **Business Addr:** Adjunct lecturer, Indiana University School of Journalism, 535 W Mich St, Indianapolis, IN 46202, **Business Phone:** (317)278-5320.

**THOMAS, JACQUELYN SMALL**
School administrator, educator. **Personal:** Born Oct 25, 1938, Jacksonville, FL; daughter of James Purcell and Lillian Louise Graham; married Willie; children: Nicole Jacquelyn. **Educ:** Hampton Univ, Hampton, VA, BS, 1959; Columbia Univ, New York, NY, MA, 1963. **Career:** Richmond Pub Schs, Richmond, Va, teacher, 1959-65, guid counr, 1965-67, asst prin, 1967-72; J Sargeant Reynolds Community Col, Richmond, Va, adj teacher, 1979-82; C's Ctr Richmond Inc, Richmond, Va, dir, 1983; Etiquette & Protocol Sch LLC, owner & dir, currently. **Orgs:** Pres, Richmond Chap, Delta Sigma Theta Sorority, 1960-72; vpres, Old Dom Vol League, 1979-80; pres, Richmond Chap, Jack & Jill Am, 1983-85; bd mem, Va Day Care Coun, Va Dept C, 1987-89; adv bd mem, Mayors Comn Young C, 1989-91; Coalition 100 Black Women, 1989-91; financial secy, James River Valley, Links Inc, 1991-93; Va Mus Fine Arts; bd optom, Commonwealth Va. **Home Addr:** 313 Burnwick Rd, Richmond, VA 23227-1632, **Home Phone:** (804)264-8211. **Business Addr:** Owner, Director, The Etiquette & Protocol School LLC, 313 Burnwick Rd, Richmond, VA 23227, **Business Phone:** (804)264-8211.

**THOMAS, JAMES ALBERT**
School administrator. **Personal:** Born Mar 15, 1939, Des Moines, IA; married Deborah G; children: Michael A & Karin R Minter. **Educ:** Wesleyan Univ, BA, 1961; Yale Law Sch, JD, 1964. **Career:** US Dept Justice, Civil Rights Div, atty, 1964-66; Iowa Civil Rights Comn, exec dir, 1966-67; US Senate Subcomm Admin Pract & Procedures, gen atty, 1967-68; Yale Law Sch, assoc dean, lectr, Jack B Tate sr fel & Decanal adv, currently; Yale Univ, Master Saybrook Col, 1990-96; UIL Holdings Corp, dir, 1992-2011. **Orgs:** Am Bar Asn, 1964-; Law Sch Admis Coun, 1969-90; Sigma Pi Phi, 1986-; dir, Peoples United Financial Inc, 1997; dir, Imagistics Int, 2001-05; dir, United Illum Co, currently; trustee, Yale New Haven Hosp; dir, Yale New Haven Health Syst; dir, Yale New Haven Health Serv Corp. **Home Addr:** 173 McKinley Ave, New Haven, CT 06515, **Home Phone:** (203)397-1792. **Business Addr:** Jack B Tate Senior Fellow, Decanal Adviser & Associate Dean, Yale Law School, 127 Wall St, New Haven, CT 06520-8215, **Business Phone:** (203)432-4992.

**THOMAS, JAMES L.**
Educator, state government official, teacher. **Personal:** Born Jun 29, 1943, White Hall, AL; son of James McKinley and Rebecca Gregory; married Evelyn Juanita Hatcher; children: Angela Carter. **Educ:** Ala State Univ, BS, 1965, MA, 1975. **Career:** Camden Acad High Sch, teacher, 1965-84; Wilcox Co High Sch, teacher, 1974-82, voc dir, 1982-89; State Ala, house rep, Dist 69, state rep, 2010; Wilcox Cent High Sch, prin dir, 1989; Thomas Construct Co, owner, currently. **Orgs:** Treas, pres, Nat Black Caucus State Legislators, 1990-; vpres, pres, Nat Asn Sec Sch Prin; Wilcox Co Admins Asn; Nat Educ Asn; Ala Educ Asn; Wilcox Co Educ Asn; Ala Dem Conf; New S Coalition; First Missionary Baptist Church. **Honors/Awds:** Teacher of the Year, Western Catholic Educ Asn, 1972; Outstanding Leadership Award, CAPA, 1986. **Home Addr:** 2713 Hwy 14 E, Selma, AL 36701, **Home Phone:** (334)872-6853. **Business Addr:** Principal, Wilcox Central High, 1310 TL Threadgill Rd, Camden, AL 36726, **Business Phone:** (334)682-9239.

**THOMAS, JAMES O.**
Government official. **Personal:** Born Feb 12, 1930, Screven County, GA; married Jacqueline Seward; children: Toniae & James O III. **Educ:** Savannah State Col, BS, chem, 1956; George Wash Law, attended 1957. **Career:** Government official (retired); US Patent Off, primary examr, 1967; US Patent Off, supvr patent exr 1975; US Patent Off, group direction, 1979, Patent Process Servs, dep asst comnr. **Orgs:** Pres Assoc Investors Inc, 1957; pres, Savannah St Col Alumni, 1973; pres, Far NE-SE Cnon, 1974; chmn bd, Capitol View Develop Inc, 1978; vpres, HELP Inc, 1981; chmn, Savannah St Fedn, 1983; pres, 3847 Corp Inc, 1984. **Honors/Awds:** President's Club Savannah State Col, 1973-81; Cynus Wiley Savannah State Col, 1979; NAFEO Distinguished Alumni, Savannah State Col, 1981; Alumnus Of Year, Savannah State Col, 1982; Gold Medal US Patent Off, 1983; Medallion of Excellence, Savannah State Col, 1986; EEO Supervisory Achievement Award, Patent & Trademark Off, 1986. **Home Addr:** 4339 H St SE, Washington, DC 20019, **Home Phone:** (202)584-5342.

**THOMAS, JANE ROSCOE**
College administrator, psychologist, dean (education). **Personal:** Born Dec 3, 1934, Brooklyn, NY; daughter of Herman Clinton Roscoe and Gladys Pelham; married Edward St Clair; children: Rebecca Pelham Thomas-Melbye. **Educ:** Rockford Col, BA, 1956; Univ Mich, MA, 1957; Wayne State Univ, PhD, 1976. **Career:** Teacher (retired); Detroit Pub Schs, teacher, 1957-67; Wayne State Univ, Col Nursing, acad adv, 1968-73, Sch Med, Office Stud Affairs, counr, 1974-91, adj instr, 1977-86, adj asst prof, 1986-; Office Stud Affairs, dir Coun Servs, 1991-92, asst dean, stud affairs, 1992-, asst dean, spec progs, currently; Liaison Comt Med Educ coordr, asst dean. **Orgs:** Co-Ette Club, 1957-; Detroit Study Club, 1958-; Detroit Inst Arts Founders Soc, 1961-; Wayne State Univ, Hilberry atre, Understudies Women's Comn, 1970-; Am Asn Univ Profs, 1972-; Asn Am Med Cols; Am Red Cross; bd dir, United Way SE MI, 1981; exec comt, Skillman Found, 1990-; Wayne County Med Soc, comn, Physician Health & Well Being, 1986-; bd dir, Mich Women's Found, 1991-; bd dir, MI's Children, 1992-, vice chair, 1999-, chair, 2001-; bd trustee, St John Sr Community, 2000-; trustee, Rockford Col; Sch Med Admis Comt; bd dir, Barbara Ann Karmanos Cancer Ctr. **Home Addr:** 838 Whittier Rd, Grosse Point Park, MI 48230, **Home Phone:** (313)821-5887. **Business Addr:** Assistant Dean for Special Programs, Wayne State University, School of Medicine, 540 E Canfield 1369 Scott Hall, Detroit, MI 48201, **Business Phone:** (313)577-1463.

**THOMAS, JANICE MORRELL**
Educator. **Personal:** Born Oct 6, 1946, Elizabeth, NJ; married Aaron D. **Educ:** Rutgers Univ, AB, 1968, EdM, 1975. **Career:** Rutgers Univ, from asst dir to actg dir admis, 1969-73, sr admis officer, Newark Campus, 1985. **Orgs:** Am Asn Col Registr & Admis Officers; Mid States Asn Col Registr & Admis Officers; Nat Asn Col Admis Counrs; Am Col Personal Asn; Asn Non-White Counrs; Rutgers Univ Black Org Fac; NJ Unit Nat Asn Negro Bus & Pro Womens Clubs; Nat Asn Advan Colored People; Urban League Union Co; NJ Asn Col Admis Counrs; NJ Asn Black & Puerto Rican Admis Counrs; Am Personal & Guid Asn.

**THOMAS, DR. JEWEL M.**
Consultant, educator. **Educ:** Miles Col, BA, 1960; Univ Ala, EdS, 1976; CP Univ, EdD, 1984. **Career:** Lawson State Community Col, grad adv, sophomore class adv, 1980; Twentieth Century Club, pres, 1982; Lawson Community Col, prof; City Brighton, mayor; A&M Univ, part-time instr; Independent Mary Kay Consult, currently; Miles Col, assoc prof eng & speech, dir stud activ. **Orgs:** Nat Baptist Conv USA, 1980; Ala Women's Nat Conv, 1980; Ala Jr Col Asn, 1980; pres, Kappa Delta Epsilon, 1981-84; Ala Educ Asn, 1984; Ala League Munic Exec Comt, 6th Dist, 1990, 1992; Nat League Cities Comt & Adv Human Develop; bd dir, ARC, 1991; bd dir & vpres, Jefferson Co Comt Econ Opportunity, 1991; Silver Haired Legis, 1997; regional dir, Alpha Kappa Alpha Sorority. **Home Addr:** 4900 Letson St, Brighton, AL 35020-1049, **Home Phone:** (205)424-0433.

**THOMAS, JIM (JAMES EDWARD THOMAS)**
Basketball player, basketball coach. **Personal:** Born Oct 19, 1960, Lakeland, FL. **Educ:** Ind Univ, BS, forensic studies, 1983. **Career:** Basketball player (retired), basketball coach; US Nat Team, FIBA World Championship, 1982; Minn Timberwolves, 1983-90; Ind Pacers, 1984-85; Evansville Thunder, 1985; Los Angeles Clippers, 1985; Kans City Sizzlers, 1985-86; Timber wolves; World Basketball League, Calgary 88s, 1987-88; Rapid City Thrillers, 1988-90; Nat Basketball League, Calgary Outlaws; CBA, Omaha Racers, player & asst coach, 1990-93; Minn Vikings, 1991; Span League, Murcia, pro player, 1993-94; Toronto Raptors, asst coach, 1996-99, scout, 2000-01; Butch Carter, asst coach; Ind Univ, asst coach, 2001-04; Atlanta Hawks, asst coach, 2013-. **Business Addr:** Assistant Coach, Atlanta Hawks, 1 CNN Ctr S Tower, Atlanta, GA 30303, **Business Phone:** (404)827-4229.

**THOMAS, JOAN MCHENRY BATES**
Executive, government official. **Personal:** Born Jun 26, 1928, Atlanta, GA; daughter of Henry McHenry and Pearl Bonnett McHenry; married Lee E; children: Edwin T Bates & Judith Z Stratton. **Educ:** USDA, attended 1960; Temple Bus Sch, attended 1963. **Career:** Catering Bus, pres; Dept Human Resources, social worker; Community serv worker, currently. **Orgs:** Chair, US Mil Wid, 1980; vpres, treas & comt mem, Ward 4 Dem; N W Boundary Civic Asn, 1980-; pres, Am War Mothers, 1984-87; chair, Adv Neighborhood Comt, 1984; treas, DC Dem Comn, 1988-92; nat carnation chmn, Nat Am War Mothers, 1989-92; chair, Adv Neighborhood Comn, 1989-90; conv chmn, Am War Mothers, 1989-. **Home Addr:** 715 Varnum St NW, Washington, DC 20011. **Business Addr:** Committee Member, Ward 4 Democrats, Washington, DC 20011.

**THOMAS, JOHN**
Basketball coach, basketball player. **Personal:** Born Sep 8, 1975, Minneapolis, MN. **Educ:** Univ Minn, attended 1997. **Career:** Minn Golden Gophers, cap, 1997; New York Knicks, 1997; Boston Celtics, forward, 1997-98; Toronto Raptors, 1998-2000; Xinjiang Flying Tigers, 2001-02; Dakota Wizards, 2002-03; Casademont Girona, 2003-04; Minn Timberwolves, forward, 2004-05; Memphis Grizzlies, forward & ctr, 2005; Atlanta Hawks, ctr, 2005-06; NJ Nets, 2006; Colorado 14ers, 2007-08; Hapoel Holon, 2009-10; Aris, Greece, 2011; Hapoel Jerusalem, Israel, 2011-12; Jeonju KCC Egis, 2012-13; Nat Mgr of Training; 2014-. **Business Addr:** National Manager of Training, Ultimate Hoops Corporate Office, 600 N 1 Ave, Minneapolis, MN 55403.

**THOMAS, JOHN CHARLES**
Judge. **Educ:** Univ Va, BA, 1972; Univ Va Sch Law, JD, 1975. **Career:** Supreme Ct Va, judge; Hunton & Williams, partner, currently. **Orgs:** Mem bd trustee, Thomas Jefferson Found; Va Bar Asn; Richmond Bar Asn; Old Dom Bar Asn; Nat Bar Asn; Am Bar Asn; Int Bar Asn; Am Arbit Asn; Ct Arbit Sport; mem bd visitors, Col William & Mary; Appellate Rules Adv Comt, Commonwealth Va, London Ct Int Arbit; Mem Coun Appellate Lawyers, ABA Judicial Div; Fel, Am Acad Appellate Lawyers. **Honors/Awds:** Lifetime Image Award, Nat Asn Advan Colored People, 1995; Fellow, Am Acad Appellate Lawyers. **Special Achievements:** First Black at the Hunton & Williams; First Black lawyer in the history of the American South; First African American and the youngest person of any race to be appointed to the Supreme Court of Virginia. **Business Addr:** Senior Partner, Litigation & Intellectual Property Practice, Hunton & Williams LLP, 951 E Byrd St, Richmond, VA 23219-4074, **Business Phone:** (804)788-8200.

**THOMAS, DR. JOHN HENDERSON, III**
Psychologist. **Personal:** Born Sep 7, 1950, Washington, DC; married Leslie F. **Educ:** Univ Detroit, AB, 1972; Univ Cincinnati, MA, 1976, DEd, 1982. **Career:** Mott Adults High Sch, consult, 1972; Univ Cincinnati, minority group coun ctr, 1973, Consult Serv, psychologist, 1975; Mott Adult High Sch, instr psych, soc engr, 1973; Univ Cincinnati Walk-In-Clin, psych; Ctr Develop Dis, psych, 1976; Ct Domestic Rel Ct Common Prac, psychol, 1976, control clin, 1976; Sonlight Lectr Inc, founder, pres; pvt pract, psychologist, 1998-. **Orgs:** Urban League; Nat Asn Advan Colored People; Black Stud; grad stud Psychol Asn, Kappa Alpha Psi; Zion Temple First Pentecostal Church; bd dir, Zion Temple Christian Acad; pres, Cincinnati Asn Prof Psychologists; treas, Asn Black Psychologists. **Honors/Awds:** Voc Rehab Scholar, 1968-72; Achievement Ed Award, Urban League, 1968; Scholar Graduate Studies, Univ Cincinnati, 1973-76; Leadership Award, Miss Black Am, 1973. **Home Addr:** 7525 Fernwood Dr, Cincinnati, OH 45237, **Home Phone:** (513)396-7699. **Business Addr:** Psychologist, Private Practice, 1420 E Mcmillan St Suite 1, Cincinnati, OH 45206-2225, **Business Phone:** (513)961-5682.

## THOMAS, JOHNNY B.

Government official. **Personal:** Born Nov 30, 1953, Glendora, MS; son of Henry Lee Loggins and Adeline Hill; married Shirley Ann Taylor; children: Loretta McGee, Leslie Johnson, Tyrus Davis, Ebony Taylor, Latasha Nicole Suggs, Pamela Williams, Prentiss Williams & Marsheka Smith; married Ella Rean Johnson; children: Leslie. **Educ:** Miss Valley State Univ, criminal justice, 1978. **Career:** Tallahatchie City, constable, 1976-80; Dept Corrections, correctional officer; Town Glendora, alderman, 1980-82, mayor, 1984-88, currently; Town Glendora, munic judge. **Orgs:** Chmn, Anti Crime Comn, 1976-80, Voters League, 1978-81; Criminal Justice Planning Comn, 1980-85; pres, Nat Asn Advan Colored People; Juv Justice Adv Comn; founding mem, Glendora Econ & Community Develop Corp, exec dir. **Honors/Awds:** Kirskey Found Equity & Justice; Who's Who among Black Americans. **Special Achievements:** Tallahatchie County's First African American County Supervisor; First African American Constable, 1975. **Home Addr:** PO Box 51, Glendora, MS 38928-0051. **Business Addr:** Mayor, Town of Glendora, 132 Main St, Glendora, MS 38928.

## THOMAS, DR. JOHNNY D.

Sports manager, educator. **Personal:** Born Heidelberg, MS. **Educ:** Alcorn State Univ, attended 1978; Univ Tenn, Health & Physic Educ, 1979; Univ Mo, Columbia. **Career:** Univ Ark, asst head football coach, defensive spec teams, recruiting coordr, 1987-89; UAPB, asst prof health & physic educ; Alcorn State Univ, head football coach, 1998, chairperson, assoc prof, currently, Athletic Admin & Coaching, grad acad advisor, currently. **Honors/Awds:** SWAC Announces 2007 Hall of Fame Inductees, 2007. **Business Addr:** Graduate Academic Advisors, Alcorn State University, 1000 ASU Dr Suite 1380, Lorman, MS 39096-7500, **Business Phone:** (601)877-6506.

## THOMAS, DR. JOSEPH EDWARD, JR.

Law enforcement officer. **Personal:** Born Jun 22, 1950, Mattson, MS; son of Joseph E Sr and Clara R; married Carol Wynne Carmody; children: Shayla Y, Joseph III & Daniel Wesley. **Educ:** Alcorn State Univ, BS, math, 1972; Jackson Community Col, AS, law enforcement, 1984; Mich State Police Sch Mgt, grad, 1985; AMR Mgt Asn, grad, 1986; Mich Criminal Justice Inst, grad, 1989; FBI Nat Acad, attended 1989; Univ Va, addn studies, pub admis, 1989; Western Mich Univ, MS, pub admis, 1989; Nat Fire Acad, attended 1989, 1992; Mich State Sch Traffic Engr, attended 1990; US Secret Serv Exec Sch, attended 1992; Oakland Community Col, addn studies, 1992; Eastern Mich Univ, educ leadership, doctorate, 2002. **Career:** Goodyear Tire & Rubber, supv, 1972-73; Montgomery Wards, salesperson, 1973-74; City Jackson, detective, lt, 1974-88; City Albion, dir, pub safety, 1988-91; Eastern Mich Univ, adj prof, currently; Oakland Community Col, adj prof, currently; Muskegon Community Col, adj prof, currently; City Southfield, chief, police dept, 1991-; Oakland Police Acad, fac basic & advan training; Schoolcraft Police Acad, fac basic & advan training; FBI Acad, fac; Nat Fire Acad, fac. **Orgs:** Nat Pub Safety Dir Asn, 1988-; Int Fire Chiefs Asn, 1988-; exec fire officer, Nat Fire Acad Asn, 1988-; Int Police Chiefs Asn, 1988-; bd dir, Mich Asn Chief Police, 1988-; FBI Nat Acad Asn, 1989-; Oakland County Sheriff Asn, 1991-; Police Exec Res Forum, 1991-; alt dist rep, Oakland County Police Chiefs Asn, 1991-; bd dir, Oakland County Narcotics Enforcement Team, 1991-; Kappa Alpha Psi Fraternity Inc; Nat Orgn Black Law Enforcemnet Exec; co chmn, Fight Crime, Invest Kids, currently; AUs Res orgn; Int Asn Chiefs Police; Int Fire Chief Asn; Mich Fire Chiefs Asn; Am Soc Indust Security; Nat Orgn Black Law Enforcement Execs. **Home Addr:** 21275 Va St, Southfield, MI 48076, **Home Phone:** (248)352-5181. **Business Addr:** Chief of Police, Southfield Polic Department, 26000 Evergreen Rd, Southfield, MI 48076, **Business Phone:** (248)796-5300.

## THOMAS, JOSEPH LEWIS

Singer. **Personal:** Born Jul 5, 1973, Columbus, GA. **Career:** Albums: Everything, 1993; All That I Am, 1997; My Name is Joe, 2000; Better Days, 2001; Love Joe, 2002; And Then, 2003; Joe Who?, 2006; Aint Nothin Like Me, 2007; New Man, 2008; Signature, 2009; Make Sure You're Home for Christmas, 2009; Home Is the Essence of Christmas, 2009; The Good, The Bad, The Sexy, 2011; Doubleback: Evolution of R&B, 2013; Bridges, 2014. Singles: "I'm In Love", "All Or Nothing", "The One For Me", 1993; "All the Things (Your Man Wont Do)", 1996; "Don't Wanna Be a Player", 1997; "The Love Scene", "Good Girls", "Still Not a Player", 1998; "Thank God I Found You", 1999; "I Wanna Know", "Treat Her Like a Lady", "Stutter", 2000; "Let's Stay Home Tonight", "It Won't End", 2001; "What If a Woman", 2002; More & More", 2003; "Ride Wit U", "Priceless", "I Wanna Get to Know Ya", 2004; Curious, 2005; "Where You At?", 2006; "If I Was Your Man", My Love", 2007; "We Are Family", "E.R. (Emergency Room)", "Why Just Be Friends", 2008. **Business Addr:** Singer, c/o Jive Records, 11 W 19th St 3rd Fl, New York, NY 10011, **Business Phone:** (212)727-0016.

## THOMAS, JOSEPHINE

Executive. **Personal:** married James II. **Career:** Thomas Foods Inc, founder, vpres sales & mkt, currently. **Business Addr:** Vice President Sales & Marketing, Founder, Thomas Foods Inc, 450 Clay Ave, Piscataway, NJ 08854, **Business Phone:** (732)968-0439.

## THOMAS, JOYCE CAROL

Writer, educator. **Personal:** Born May 25, 1938, Ponca City, OK; daughter of Floyd Haynes and Leona Thompson Haynes; children: Monica Pecot, Gregory, Michael & Roy. **Educ:** Col San Mateo, AA, 1964; San Jose State Univ, BA, span, 1966; Stanford Univ, MA, 1967. **Career:** Sec Sch teacher, 1967-69; San Jose State Col, asst prof, 1969-72, reading prog dir, 1979-82, prof, 1982-83; Contra Costa Col, teacher, 1973-75; St. Mary's Col, prof, 1975-77; Univ Tenn, Knoxville, Dept Eng, assoc prof, 1989-92, prof Eng, 1992-95; full-time writer, 1995-; Scovil Chichak Galen Literary Agency Inc, auth, currently. Author: Bittersweet, 1973; Crystal Breezes, 1974; Blessing, 1975; Black Child, 1981; Inside Rainbow, 1982; Marked by Fire, 1982; Bright Shadow, 1983; Water Girl, 1986; Golden Pasture, 1986; Journey, 1988; A Gathering Flowers: Stories about Being Young Am, 1990; When Nightingale Sings, 1992; Brown Honey Broom wheat Tea, 1993; Gingerbread Days, 1995; Blacker Berry, 1997; I Have Heard a Land, 1998; Cherish Me, 1998; You Are My Perfect Baby, 1999; Gospel Cinderella, 2000; Bowlegged Rooster & Other Tales That Signify, 2000; Hush Songs: African Am Lullabies, 2000; Joy, 2001; Angel's Lullaby, 2001; A Mother's Heart, a Daughter's Love, 2001; House Light, 2001; Abide with Me, 2001; Crowning Glory, 2002; Linda Brown, You Are Not Alone: Brown v. Bd Educ Decision, 2003. **Orgs:** Dramatist Guild; Authors Guild; YWCA, 1993; New York Pub Libr, 1993; Nat Coun Teachers Eng, 1994; Nat Conf Christians & Jews, 1994; Am Lib Asn, 1994. **Home Addr:** 2422 Cedar St, Berkeley, CA 94708-1823, **Home Phone:** (510)848-8105. **Business Addr:** Author, Scovil Chichak Galen Literary Agency Inc, 276 5th Ave Suite 708, New York, NY 10001, **Business Phone:** (212)679-8686.

## THOMAS, JUANITA WARE. See Obituaries Section.

## THOMAS, JUDITH A.

Executive director, chairperson. **Educ:** Southern Ill Univ, BS, commun, 1980; MoreSteam Univ, Six Sigma Green Belt Cert, 2010; Md Univ Col, MBA, bus admin, mgt & opers, 2012, MS, Prog Mgt, 2014, cert, acquisition & supply chain mgt, 2015. **Career:** Mutual Broadcasting Syst, assoc producer, 1983-97; Larry King Cardiac Found, co-chairperson & exec dir, 1995-2000; cable news network, assoc producer, 1997-98; Global Mgt Consults Inc, pres, owner & chief exec officer, 1998-; Allen Media Strategy, AMS Consult, 2007-09. **Orgs:** DC Habitat for Humanity. **Business Addr:** President, Chief Executive Officer, Global Management Consultants Inc, 8752 Lincon St Savage, Savage, MD 20763.

## THOMAS, KENDALL

Educator. **Personal:** Born Feb 22, 1957, East Chicago, IN. **Educ:** Yale Col, New Haven, CT, BA, 1978; Yale Law Sch, New Haven, CT, JD, 1982. **Career:** Columbia Univ City New York, New York, NY, from asst prof to assoc prof, 1984-92, prof, 1992-, Nash prof Law & codir Ctr Study Law & Culture, currently; Stanford Law Sch, vis prof; Princeton Univ, Am Studies & Afro-American Studies, vis prof. **Orgs:** Berlin Prize fel, Am Acad, Berlin, Ger; mem spl comt, Am Ctr, Paris; chair, Jurisprudence & Law & Humanities sect, Asn Am Law Sch; founding mem, Majority Action Caucus AIDS Coalition, AIDS Prevention Action League; vice chair, vice chair, bd dir, Gay Men's Health Crisis; Spec Comt Am Ctr. **Home Addr:** , NY. **Business Addr:** Nash Professor of law, Co-Founder & Director, Center for the Study of Law, Columbia University, Rm 608 Jerome Greene Hall 435 W 116th St, New York, NY 10027, **Business Phone:** (212)854-2288.

## THOMAS, KIMBERLY L. See JOHNSON, KIMBERLY LYNN.

## THOMAS, KURT VINCENT

Basketball player. **Personal:** Born Oct 4, 1972, Dallas, TX; son of John and Angela; children: Gabriella, Abigayl, Isabella & Kurt Jr. **Educ:** Tex Christian Univ, BS, psychol, 1995. **Career:** Basketball player (retired); Miami Heat, forward, 1995-97; Dallas Mavericks, 1997-98; New York Knicks, 1998-2005; Phoenix Suns, 2005-07; Seattle SuperSonics, 2007-08; San Antonio Spurs, 2008-09; Milwaukee Bucks, 2009-10; Nat Neurofi Bromatosis Found, spokesman; Chicago Bulls, 2010-11; Portland Trail Blazers, 2011-12; New York Knicks, 2012-13. **Business Addr:** Basketball Player, New York Knicks, Madison Sq Garden 2 Pa Plz, New York, NY 10121, **Business Phone:** (212)465-6471.

## THOMAS, LACY L.

Executive. **Educ:** Chicago State Univ, BS, acct. **Career:** City Col Chicago, chief financial officer; L Thomas Consult Serv, prin; ESI Healthcare Bus Solutions, sr vpres; United Microelectronics Corp, chief exec officer; John H Stroger Jr Hosp Cook Co, hosp dir, 2003; Univ Med Ctr Southern Nev, chief exec officer; Univ Nev, Off Protection Res Subj, fac, currently. **Orgs:** Metrop Chicago Healthcare Coun; Urban Chamber Com; Nev Hosp Asn; bd dir, Univ Southern Nev; Beta Alpha Psi; Las Vegas Urban Chamber Com; bd mem, Las Vegas Clark Co Urban League; Alpha Phi Alpha Fraternities Inc. **Business Addr:** Faculty, University of Nevada, 4505 S Md Pkwy, Las Vegas, NV 89154-1047, **Business Phone:** (702)895-3011.

## THOMAS, REV. DR. LATTA ROOSEVELT, SR.

Clergy, educator, association executive. **Personal:** Born Oct 12, 1927, Union, SC; son of Pickett R (deceased) and Alsie Creshaw (deceased); married Bessie Lowery; children: Latta Jr & Ronald. **Educ:** Friendship union Col, Rock Hill, SC, AA, 1949; Benedict Col, BA, 1951; Colgate Rochester Divinity Sch, BD, 1955; Andover Newton Theol Sem, MS, sacred theol, 1966, DMin, 1973. **Career:** Monumental Baptist Church, pastor, 1952-63, Elmira, NY, minister, 1955; Mt Olive Baptist Church, pastor, 1963-65; Benedict Col, chaplain, 1965-85, Dept Relig & Philos, from assoc prof to prof, 1968-95, actg dean stud affairs, 1974-75, head dept; Second Calvary Baptist Church, pastor, 1975-96; Morris Col, prof relig. **Orgs:** Pres, Elmira Br, Nat Asn Advan Colored People, 1957-62; Am Asn Univ Prof, 1970-95; chmn, SC Acad Relig; Kappa Alpha Psi; fac rep, bd trustee, Benedict Col, 1973-75; exec bd, Friendship Ctr, 1978-82; Richland-Lexington Coun Aging, 1980-84; Progressive Nat Baptist Conv; Clin Pastoral Educ Adv Coun, 1984-90; Kiwanis; SC Dem Party; exec bd, Greater Columbia Comm Rels Coun; Martin Luther King Jr Memorial Found Inc, 1984-96; SC Coun Holocaust, 1990-96; Fighting Back Anti-Drug Abuse Coun, 1990-96; Columbia Alumni Club. **Honors/Awds:** Outstanding Achievement Award, 2008. **Special Achievements:** Cited for civic service by Elmira Civic Improvement Club in 1960; Elmira Neighborhood House 1961; Elmira Br NAACP 1972; published numerous articles and two books Biblical Faith and the Black American in 1976 and the Biblical God and Human Suffering in 1987. **Home Addr:** 711 Isaac St, Columbia, SC 29203-5023, **Home Phone:** (803)786-4612. **Business Addr:** Professor of Religion, Morris College, 100 W Col St, Sumter, SC 29150-3599, **Business Phone:** (803)934-3200.

## THOMAS, PROF. LAURITA

Vice president (organization), administrator. **Personal:** children: Lemar & Wesley. **Educ:** Univ Mich, BA, polit sci & econs, 1970. **Career:** Off Reg, dipl clerk; Univ Mich Health Syst, human resources, admin, allied health educ, dir, 1998-; Univ Mich Hosp & Health Ctr, staff; Off Allied Health Educ; Univ Mich, staff, 1972-, assoc vpres & chief human resource officer, assoc vpres human resources, 2004-; Bethel A M E Church, supt. Books: Inside the Minds, The Role of Human Resources. **Orgs:** Med Ctr Employee Rels Asn; Soc Human Resources Mgt; Human Resources Planning Soc; Am Soc Healthcare Human Resources Admin; exec comt, Washtenaw County Work force Develop Bd; dir emer, SOS Community Serv Bd; Delta Sigma ta Sorority; pres, Ann Arbor Chap Links; chair, Univ Health Syst Consortium (UHC) Human Resources Officers Coun; AAU Human Resource Inst; adv coun, TIAACREF; CUPAHR; CIC Human Resources Officers. **Home Addr:** , MI. **Business Addr:** Associate Vice President, Chief Human Resource Officer, University of Michigan, 4021 Wolverine Towers, Ann Arbor, MI 48109-1281, **Business Phone:** (734)763-1284.

## THOMAS, LILLIE

Executive, radiologist, technologist. **Personal:** Born Oct 20, 1950, St. Louis, MO. **Educ:** Forest Pk Comm Col, AAS, 1970. **Career:** MO Baptist Hosp, rad tech, 1970-74, spec procedure tech; Peralta Hosp, spec procedure tech, 1975-79; SSM St. Joseph Health Ctr St Charles, chief technologist, 1993, admin dir, dir oncol serv. **Orgs:** Am Registry Radiol Tech; Am Soc Radiol Tech; Bd, Christian Educ; asst financial secy, bd trustee, chairperson, youth dir New Sunny Mt Bapt Ch. **Honors/Awds:** Excellence in Health Care Award. **Special Achievements:** First woman elected as chairperson of the trustee board for the New Sunny Mount Missionary Baptist Church. **Home Addr:** 22 St Gabriel Ct, St. Louis, MO 63114. **Business Addr:** Director Oncology Service, SSM St Joseph Health Center, 300 1st Capitol Dr, St. Charles, MO 63301, **Business Phone:** (314)355-7500.

## THOMAS, LINDA

Executive. **Educ:** Kent State Univ, BBA, bus admin. **Career:** Colgate Palmolive, sales rep, 1981-86; Nabisco, dir bus develop, 1996-98; Kraft Foods, regional mkt dir, 2000-03, region vpres, retail sales, 2011-; Taco Bell Express, gen mgr fast-food chain, northeast zone. **Orgs:** Delta Sigma Theta. **Special Achievements:** First African American to be named general manager of the northeast zone. **Business Addr:** Region Vice President, Kraft Foods Inc, 3 Lakes Dr, Northfield, IL 60093-2753, **Business Phone:** (847)646-2000.

## THOMAS, LIZ A.

Secretary (office), consultant. **Personal:** Born Apr 13, 1946, Portland, OR; daughter of Walter C Reynolds and Mildred E Squires Reynolds; married David A; children: Ife-Airegin V E. **Educ:** Mills Col, Oakland, CA, BA, sociol & anthropol, 1968; Univ Calif, Berkeley, MSW, 1970; Univ Wash, Seattle, health & social behav, 1975, quant methods, 1979. **Career:** Emanuel Hosp, Portland, OR, emergency med staff, 1964-66; Comm Act Prog, Portland, OR, community asst, 1966; Health Testing Serv, Berkeley, CA, med intake, 1967; People Pledged Community Progress, Richmond, CA, planner & evaluator, 1968-69; Nat Comn Against Discrimination Housing, San Francisco, CA, res asst, coordr, 1969; Berkeley Unified Sch Dist, Berkeley, CA, prog asst, 1969-70; Col San Mateo, CA, acad counr, 1970-73, instr, 1970-73; Univ Wash, Seattle, WA, asst dir career planning & placement off, 1973-85; Better Prepared, career consult, 1984-; King County Councilman, Seattle, WA, legis asst, 1985. **Orgs:** Vpres, Seattle Chap, LINKS, 1989-91; vpres, bd dirs, Int Res Ctr, 1989-91; vpres, 1989-91, co-chair, 1990-91, Long Range Planning Comn, Seattle C's Theatre; Nominating Comn, Seattle King Cuntyo Camp fire Coun. **Honors/Awds:** Leadership Tomorrow, 1985; Finalist, Fel in Cable Mgt, The Walter Kaitz Found, 1985; Commissioner at Large, The Goodwill Games, 1988-90; Leadership America, The Found for Women's Res, 1989; Participant, The ALKI Found, 1988; guest speaker, lectr, presenter. **Home Addr:** 924 17th Ave Suite 4, Seattle, WA 98122.

## THOMAS, LORNA E.

Movie producer. **Educ:** McGill Univ, Bronx HS Sci, BS, film & commun studies. **Career:** New York Ctr for Visual Hist, producer, 1992-95; Naked Eye Productions, co-producer, 1997-98; "The Digital Divide", producer & dir, 1998-99; Swing Pictures LLC, owner, 1998-2008; Mad Dog Films Inc, partner, 2000-; Granada, producer, 2004-05; Original Media, post producer, producer, 2005-06; Black Entertainment Tv, supv prod, currently; TLC, dir & producer; MTV ser, dir & producer, 2006-07; BET, supv producer, 2007-08; Granada Am, ser producer & showrunner, 2008-09; PSYCHIC KIDS, supv producer & showrunner, 2009; Engel Entertainment, supv producer & showrunner, 2009-10; Showrunner, Freelance, 2007-; Al Roker Entertainment, exec producer, 2010; Atlas Media Corp, co exec producer & showrunner, 2011; ITV, co executice producer, 2011-13; Discovery Commun, exec producer, 2013-. **Orgs:** Bd mem, Global Action Proj, 1998-2006. **Business Addr:** Partner, Mad Dog Films Inc, 131 Varick St Suite 917, New York, NY 10013.

## THOMAS, DR. LUCILLE COLE

Librarian, educator, chairperson. **Personal:** Born Oct 1, 1921, Dunn, NC; daughter of Collie Cole and Minnie Lee Cole; married George Browne; children: Ronald C & Beverly G. **Educ:** Bennett Col, BA, 1941; NY Univ, MA, Eng, 1955, DHL, 1996; Columbia Univ Sch, Lib Serv, MLS, libr sci, 1957. **Career:** Educator, librarian (retired); Bibb Co Bd Educ, teacher, 1947-55; Brooklyn Pub Libr, librn, 1955-56; New York Pub Sch, librn, 1956-68; New York Bd Educ, supvr libr, 1968-77, asst dir; New York Bd Educ, dir elem sch libr, 1978-83; Weston Woods Inst, consult, 1983-86, prog dir, 1994-94; New York Bd Examrs, exam specialist, 1985-90; Grad Sch Libr & Info Studies Queens Col, City Univ New York, vis prof, 1987-90. **Orgs:** Pres, NY Black Librns Caucus, 1974-75; bd dir, Am Reading Coun, 1976-89; pres, New York Libr Asn, 1977-78; pres, New York Libr Club, 1977-78; coordr, UNESCO & IASL Bk Prog, 1980-89; pres, Columbia Univ, Schl Libr Serv Alumni Asn, 1980-81, sec, 1985-, chair, 1988-93; NYS Regents Adv Coun Learning Technol, 1982-89; exec bd, Am Libr Asn, 1985-91; chmn, usher, vestry mem, St Johns Episcopal Church Brooklyn, Stewardship Comm, 1986-88; chair, Women's City Club, Educ Comm, 1988-90, pres, int Asn Sch Librarianship, 1989-95, vpres, 1992; chair, educ comm, Women's City Club, 1989-92; vice chair, Nat Alumnae Leadership Comt, Bennett Col Capital Campaign; vpres prog, 1990-92, vpres, Region II Trustees Div ALA, 1993-94; first vpres, pres, Alpha Kappa Alpha Sorority, 1991-94, 1992-98; AIA coun, 1992-2001; Brooklyn Pub Libr, trustee, New York mayor, 1993-, secy bd trustee,

1997-99, vpres, bd trustee, 1999-2003; chair, Legis Comm Trustees Div ALA, 1994; ALA Legis Assembly, 1995-; hon chair, Twenty-First Century Fund, Women's City Club New York, 1996-97; chair, Diversity Comn, 1999-2000; Intrels comm; Sch Librs Sect int Fed Libr Asns; Schomburg Corp & Schomburg Commn Preserv Black Cult; Centennial Comm Columbia Univ Sch Libr Serv; parliamentarian, Pi Phi Omega Chap; Ny Educ Comm, Eng lang arts assessment comm; int rels comm, Am Asn Schs Librn; rep, Int Fed Libr Asn, UN & UNICEF; dir, US Bd Bks Young People, 1995; co-coord Cluster II-IAKA Sorority, N Atlantic Region; pres & bd trustee, St Mark's Day Sch; Am Libr Asn Hon mem, 2003; pres & bd trustee, Brooklyn Pub Libr, 2003-; Freedom to Read Found; Kappa Delta Pi. **Honors/Awds:** Medal of Excellence, NY State Bd, 1984; Programs of Service Award, Eta Omega Omega Chap Alpha Kappa Alpha Sor; Grolier Award, Am Libr Asn, 1988; Service Award & Trail Blazers Award, Am Libr Asn, Black Caucus, 1992, 1995; Distinguished Service Award, Am Asn Sch Librarians, 1994; Humphrey Award, Am Libr Asn, 1995; Silver Award, US Natl Comn Libr & Info Sci, 1996; Awarded Honorary Doctorate, Bennett Col, 1996; Outstanding Service Award, Pi Phi Omega; Outstanding Service Award, Alpha Kappa Alpha Basilei Coun, 1998; Phenomenal Woman Achievement, Bennett Col, 2000; Literacy Award, ALTA Am Libr Asn, 2001; Phenomenal Woman Award, Public Sch 241, NYC Bd Edu, 2002; selected hon mem, ALA, 2003; Outstanding Service Award, St Mark's Episcopal Church, 2003; Freedom to Read Foundation Roll of Honor Award, 2007. **Special Achievements:** First African president of the New York City School Librarian's Association; First African-American elected president of the New York Library Club. **Home Addr:** 1184 Union St, Brooklyn, NY 11225-1512, **Home Phone:** (718)756-0729.

### THOMAS, DR. LYDIA WATERS

Executive. **Personal:** Born Oct 13, 1944, Norfolk, VA; daughter of William Emerson and Lillie Ruth Roberts; married James Carter; children: Denee Marrielle. **Educ:** Howard Univ, Wash, DC, BS, zool, 1965; Am Univ, Wash, DC, MS, microbiol, 1971; Howard Univ, Wash, DC, PhD, cytol, 1973. **Career:** Am Univ, Wash, DC, grad teaching asst, 1969-71; Howard Univ, Wash, DC, grad teaching asst, 1971-73; Mitre Corp, 1973-96; Mitretek's Ctr Environ, Resources & Space, sr vpres & gen mgr; MITRE Corp-Ctr, tech dir, 1982-89, vpres, 1989-92, sr vpres, gen mgr, 1992-96; Mitretek Systs Inc, sr vpres, gen mgr, pres, chief exec officer, bd trustees, 1996-; Bristol Group, pres, chief exec officer; Inova Health Systs Inc, treas; Noblis Inc, pres & chief exec officer, 1996-2007, consult, 2007-08. **Orgs:** Dir, Mueller Water Prod; Va Gov Higher Educ Summit Steering Comt; bd dir, Cabot Corp, 1994-; Environ Adv Bd, US Corp Engrs; chmn, Chems Regulation Sub-Group USEA; dir, Cabot Corp, 1994; Environ Res Develop Sci Adv Bd; Am Soc Toxicol; Nat Defense Indust Asn; Am Mgt Asn; dir, Wash Mutual Investors Fund Inc; trustee, George Wash Univ; Soc Macro Eng; dir, US Energy Asn; Supts Bus Indust Adv Coun Fairfax Co Pub Schs; trustee, Inova Health Systs; mem bd trustee, Bristol Group, 1996; trustee, Noblis Healthcare. 1996; assoc fel Am Inst Aeronaut & Astronaut; Defense Sci Bd at Us Dept; corp mem, Charles Stark Draper Lab Inc; dir, GAM Technol Co Ltd; bd mem, Northern Va Technol Coun; Va Res Tech Adv Comn, 2001-; secy's, Homeland Security Adv Coun, 2002; sr adv bd, Northern Va Technol Coun, 2003-; adv bd, AUs Corps Engr; Coun Foreign Rels; ITProfessional mag Ed Adv Bd; dir, Us Energy Asn; Am Soc Toxicol; adv bd, US Defense Dept's Strategic Environ Res & Develop Prog; Am Defense Preparedness Asn/Nat Defense Indust Asn; Am Inst Aeronaut & Astronaut; Conf Bd, & Teratology Soc; Northern Va Healthcare Workforce Alliance with Northern Va Community Col; co-chair, Govt Univ Indust Res Roundtable; Supt's Bus & Indust Adv Coun Fairfax County Pub Schs; Int Women's Forum Wash Chap; co-chair, R&D Investment Panel a Defense Sci Bd; Charles Stark Draper Lab Inc; Us Energy Asn; Supt's Bus/Indus Adv Coun, Fairfax Co Pub Sch; Int Women's Forum; Am Defense Preparedness Asn; Nat Defense Indust Asn; Teratology Soc; Conf Bd; mem pres, Homeland Security Adv Coun; Alpha Kappa Alpha.

### THOMAS, MABLE

Government official. **Personal:** Born Nov 8, 1957, Atlanta, GA; daughter of Bernard and Madie Broughton. **Educ:** GA State Univ, BS, pub admin, 1982, MA, pub admin; Atlanta Sch Real Estate, Atlanta GA, salesperson license, 1987. **Career:** GA Dept Natural Resources, personnel asst, 1978-79; City Atlanta Parks & Recreation, recreation super, 1980-81; GA State Univ Educ Talent Search, res asst, 1981-82; City Atlanta Comm Develop, worksite monitor, 1983; Univ Black Life & Cult Comm, GA State, chairperson, 1982-83; GA Gen Assembly, senate intern, 1984; Dist 31, state rep, 1985-86, 1987-88, 1989-90, 1991-92, Educ, Spec Judiciary & Indust Rels Standing Comts, GA Housing Needs Study Comn, adminr; Master Commun Inc, Pres, 1992; Ga House Rep, 55th dist, rep, 2012-. **Orgs:** vol worker, S Christian Leadership Conf, 1981-; vol, Martin Luther King CtrNonviolent Social Chg, 1981-; vol, United Way Metro Atlanta, 1982-; Vpres, Ga State Univ Stud Govt Asn, 1983-84; consult, Ga Dem Party, 1984; adv coun, Salvation Army Bellwood Boys & Girls Club, 1984-85; bd dir, GA Legis Black Caucus, 1985; mem chair, Black women Health Proj, 1985; hon mem chair, Nat Asn Advan Colored People Ann Mem Dr, 1985; Nat bd mem, Nat Polit Congr Black Women, 1985; founder Vine City Community improv Asn, Atlanta, 1985; Am Cancer Soc, 1988; bd mem, W End Med Ctr; bd dir, Econ Opportunities Atlanta; bd mem, Ga Housing Coalition, 1988-89; bd dirs, Ga Coalition Black Women, 1996; founder & pres, Greater Vine City Opportunities Prog Inc, 1990; city councilwoman, chair, comt coun Post 1 CityWide, 1998-2001; Conf Minority Pub Admin. **Honors/Awds:** GA State Univ Mortar Bd Leadership Award, 1982; Salvation Army Bellwood Girls Club Community Service Award, 1983; GA State University Women Excellence Award, 1983; Top Jesse Jackson Delegate, Democratic Nat Convention, 1984; City Atlanta Cultural Affairs Bronze Jubilee Award, 1984; Royal Arkansas Worshipful Masters Legion Honor Award for Social Justice, 1985; Ebony Magazine 30 Leaders Future, 1985; Outstanding Service Award, Tony Garden Civic Asn, 1985; NAACP Civic Award, 1985; Essence Women, Essence magazine, 1986; National Association Black Social Workers Human Service Award, 1986; Featured in Wash Post "New Black Women-Mold Breakers in Main Stream", 1986; Outstanding Freshman Legislator, GA Legis Black Caucus, 1986; Voted one of 20 Atlantans to Watch, Atlanta Trib newspaper, 1987; featured, India's Nat newspaper, India Times, 1988; Outstanding Georgia State University Alumni, GA State Univ, 1989; Front Page Coverage for Fast Forward Magazine, 1989; Outstanding Service Award, Conf Minority Pub Admin. **Home Addr:** 765 Jones Ave NW, Atlanta, GA 30314-3824, **Home Phone:** (404)525-7251. **Business Addr:** Representative, Georgia House Representatives, Rm 611 Legislative Off Bldg, Atlanta, GA 30334, **Business Phone:** (404)656-0314.

### THOMAS, DR. MARVETTE JERALDINE

School administrator. **Personal:** Born Jan 27, 1953, Montgomery, AL; daughter of Marvin and Bernice Morgan; married Richard E Cobb; children: Janel Bernice Cobb; married Charlie M Smith. **Educ:** Austin Peay State Univ, BS, 1977; Murray State Univ, MS, 1980; George Peabody Col Vanderbilt Univ, EdD, 1984. **Career:** Northwest High Sch, spec educ teacher, Vanderbilt Univ, teaching, grad asst, 1981; Nat Cert Counr, 1983; Women Non-traditional Careers Womens Initiative Network & Connection, dir proj, 1986-; La State Univ Eunice, counr, 1984, actg dir spec serv & develop educ, dir spec serv, 1985-89, dir acad asst progs, 1989-; spec asst to chancellor, affirmative action & equal opportunity, 1989. **Orgs:** Nat Asn Univ Women; Am Asn Coun & Develop; Nat Asn Female Execs; Nat Coun Negro Women; Am Col Personnel Asn; La Black Festivals Network; La Asn Develop Educ; Southwest Asn Stud Asst Prog; Opelousas Alumnae Chap Delta Sigma Theta Inc; pres, Clarksville Tenn Alumnae Chapt Delta Sigma Theta; bd dir, Eunice C C; bd dir, Bayou Girl Scout Coun, 1987-; bd dir, Moosa Memorial Hosp, 1988-; pres, La Asn Stud Assistance Prog, 1988-90; bd dir, Southwest Asn Stud Assistance Prog, 1988-90; Pres's Coun, Nat Coun Educ Opportunity Asn, 1988; pres, Socialite Club Eunice, 1989-; pres, Socialite Soc & Civic Club; secy, 1990-; Delta Sigma Theta Sorority; Phi Delta Kappa; Chi Sigma Iota; chmn, Black Cult Prog. **Honors/Awds:** Inductee Phi Delta Kappa, 1979; Chi Sigma Iota, 1985; Outstanding Woman of Eunice, The Eunice News, 1987. **Home Addr:** 301 Mae St, Eunice, LA 70535, **Home Phone:** (337)457-2012. **Business Addr:** Director of Academic Assistance Programs, Assistant Professor of Education, Louisiana State University, PO Box 1129, Eunice, LA 70535, **Business Phone:** (337)550-1206.

### THOMAS, MARY A.

Nurse. **Personal:** Born Jul 22, 1933, Gary, IN. **Educ:** Homer G Phillips Hosp Sch Nursing, St Louis, 1956; Univ, BS, 1968; Valparaiso Univ, MLa, Sociol; Univ IL Med Ctr. **Career:** Retired; Cook Hosp Chicago, head nurse Obstet, 1957-63; Chicago Osteop Hosp Chicago, head nurse Med Unit, 1963-64; Vis Nurse Assoc E Chicago Ind, staff nurse, 1964-68; Gary Ind, sch nurse, 1968-71; Gary Health Dept, asst dir nurses, 1972-74; Gary Health Dept, dir nurses, 1974-95; Purdue Univ Calumet Hammond Ind, asst prof nursing, 1995. **Orgs:** Consult Sr Cit Prog Gary Ind, 1972-; counr, Sickle Anemia Proj, 1975; scholar chmn Midtown Reg Nurses Club, 1971-; alumni Univ & Valparaiso Univ; bd mem, Fed Credit Union St Monica Ch, 1973; parish coun mem, 1974. **Home Addr:** 1304 Marshall Pl, Gary, IN 46404-2030, **Home Phone:** (219)949-1403.

### THOMAS, HON. MARY MAXWELL

Circuit court judge. **Personal:** Born Mar 18, 1943, Waukegan, IL; daughter of Isaiah Williams Jr and Mary Etta Jordan; married James A Cooper; children: Stacy L Mosley & Owen L II. **Educ:** Mich State Univ, attended 1963; NMex State Univ, BA, 1966; Univ Chicago Law Sch, JD, 1973; Univ Nev-Reno, judicial studies, 1996. **Career:** USN, comput programmer, 1967-70; Chicago Title Ins Co, atty title examr, 1973-74; City Evanston, Ill, asst city atty, 1974-77; US Attys Off, asst US atty, 1977-87; Sulzer & Shapiro Ltd, partner, 1987; Circuit Ct Cook Co, judge, 1987-. **Orgs:** Silver star mem, Alpha Kappa Alpha Sorority, 1962-; former bd mem, Cook Co Bar Asn, 1983-; Nat Bar Asn, 1983-; chmn, secy, bd mem, Ill Judicial Coun, 1987-; Womens Bar Asn Ill, 1987-; Nat Judicial Coun, 1987-; life mem, Nat Asn Advan Colored People, 1993-; Phi Kappa Phi Hon Soc, 1996; chmn, Youth Outreach Comn, 2001. **Honors/Awds:** Honoree, Black Women Lawyers Chicago, 1991; Woman of Distinction, Ebony Man Mag, 1992, 1992; Chairperson's Award & Meritorious Service, Ill Judicial Coun, 1992-94; Kentucky Colonel Award Commonwealth KY, 1994; Pacesetter Award, Nat Coun Negro Women, 1994. **Home Addr:** 3633 Liberty Lane, Glenview, IL 60025. **Business Addr:** Judge, Circuit of Cook County Illinois, 5600 Old Orchard Rd Suite 231-2, Skokie, IL 60077, **Business Phone:** (847)470-5961.

### THOMAS, MATTHEW W., JR.

Artist, educator. **Personal:** Born Jun 12, 1943, San Antonio, TX; son of Matthew and Ella; married Bee; children: Illah & Hashim. **Educ:** San Fernando Valley Col, Van Nuys, CA, attended 1963; Honolulu Acad Arts, Honolulu, HI, attended 1964; Chouinard Sch Fine Arts, Los Angeles, CA, attended 1967. **Career:** Visual artist, Ruth Bachofner Gallery, 1975-; Temecula Calif, artist resident; Pyong, TAEK Int, Korea, artist resident; TacikawaInt, Japan, Taiwan, artist resident; Angels Gate Cult Ctr, artist, currently. **Orgs:** Visual Artist & Chmn Visual Arts Dept, PS Arts Cross Roads, Conn; founder & vpres, Arts Org, Los Angeles. **Home Addr:** 609 W 40th St, San Pedro, CA 90731-7107, **Home Phone:** (310)831-1888. **Business Addr:** Artist, Angels Gate Cultural Center, 3601 S Gaffey St, San Pedro, CA 90731, **Business Phone:** (310)519-0936.

### THOMAS, MAUREEN A.

Police chief, government official. **Career:** New York Dept Invest, dep inspector gen, currently. **Business Addr:** Deputy Inspector General, The City of New York, 80 Maiden Lane, New York, NY 10038, **Business Phone:** (212)825-5900.

### THOMAS, MAURICE MCKENZIE

Librarian. **Personal:** Born May 1, 1943, St. Croix, VI; son of Maurice and Florence Bovell; married Monica Primas; children: Charles Randall & Onika Michelle. **Educ:** Long Island Univ, BA, hist, 1973; Atlanta Univ, attended 1982; Ball State Univ, MLS, libr & info sci, 1983. **Career:** Librarian (retired); Abraham & Strauss NY, sales person, 1969-73; Dept Educ The VI, social studies teacher, 1973-82, librn, info spec, coordr, social studies, 1987. **Orgs:** Courtyard Players Community Theatre, 1973-, Friends Petersen Pub Libr, 1983-; Sch Libr Asn, 1983-; Am Libr Asn, 1983-; bd mem, Theatre Dance Inc, 1983-84; Phi Delta Kappa. **Home Addr:** PO Box 7475 Sunny Isle Christiansted, St. Croix00820.

### THOMAS, DR. MAXINE SUZANNE

Administrator, educator. **Personal:** Born Jan 23, 1948, Junction City, KS; daughter of Morris Daniels; married Larry; children: Lauryn & Noel. **Educ:** Univ Wash, BA, 1970, JD, 1973. **Career:** Wash, asst atty gen, 1973-76; Univ Ore Sch Law, asst prof, 1976-89; Univ Ore, fac, 1973-76, asst dean, 1976-79; Kellogg Nat fel, 1985-88; Univ Ga, assoc, assoc dean & assoc prof, 1989-91; Kettering Found, Dayton, OH, vpres, secy & gen coun, currently. **Orgs:** Nat Asn Col & Univ Attys, 1974-76; standing comn environ law Am Bar Asn, 1979-; Kettering Found Task Force, 1993-; hon mem, Phi Delta Phi, 1977-; OR Am Coun Educ Comn Promote Women Higher Educ Admin, 1978-; exec dir, Law & Leadership Summer Inst. **Honors/Awds:** Nominated Oregon Outstanding Young Women, 1978. **Home Addr:** 5060 Donald, Eugene, OR 97405. **Business Addr:** Vice President, Secretary, Kettering Foundation, 200 Commons Rd, Dayton, OH 45459, **Business Phone:** (937)434-7300.

### THOMAS, DR. N. CHARLES (NATHANIEL CHARLES THOMAS)

Clergy, administrator. **Personal:** Born Jun 24, 1929, Jonesboro, AR; son of Willie James and Linnie; married Juanita Fanny Jefferson; children: Gina Charlise, Nathaniel Charles & Keith Antony; married Mary Elizabeth. **Educ:** Miss Indsl Col, BA, 1951; Lincoln Univ Theol Sem, BD, 1954; Lancaster Theol Sem, MDiv, 1974; Tex Col, DDiv, 1981. **Career:** CME Chs Water ford MS, pastor, 1949-51; Roanoke Va, 1954; Wrights ville Ark, 1954-57; Hot Springs Ark, 1957-60; Little Rock Ark, 1960-62; Memphis Tenn, 1966-67; CME Church, gen secy; pastor, Greenwood CME Church, 1980-81; Feather stone Temple, pastor, 1994; Christian Methodist Episcopal Church, dept personnel serv, gen secy. **Orgs:** Dir Christian educ, admin asst pres idingbi shop, 1954-74, first Dist CME Ch, 1958-74; Gen Bd Christian Educ CME Ch, 1958-; World Coun Churches, 1968; bd trustee, Smith-Keys Housing Proj, Texarkana Ark, 1969-; bd dir, Haygood-Neal Housing Proj Eldorado Ark, 1970-; bd dir, E Gate Vlge Union City Tenn, 1970-; secy, Gen Conf CME Ch, 1970-; presiding elder, SM emphis Dist, 1971-74; secy, Gen Correctional Bd, CME Ch, 1971-; bd dir, Memphis OIC, 1972-73; Gen Bd Pensions CME Ch, 1974-78, admin, Ministerial Salary, Suppl Prog CME Ch, 1974-90; bd trustee, Collins Chapel Hosp Memphis Tenn, 1974-; CME MinistersAlliance Memphis; Interdenom Ministers Alliance Memphis; chmn, Memphis Opportunities indust, 1976-78; gen secy, Gen Bd Personnel Serv, 1978; bd mem, Metrop Interfaith Asn, 1989-; Shelby County Inter faith Asn, 1990-; exec dir, New Day Coop, 1992. **Honors/Awds:** Dr Humanities, Tex Col Tyler, 1980; Golden Heritage Mem, Nat Asn Advan Colored People. **Home Addr:** PO Box 9, Memphis, TN 38107. **Business Addr:** .

### THOMAS, PROF. NATE

College teacher, movie producer. **Personal:** Born May 22, 1957, Warren, OH; son of Ace and Rose. **Educ:** St Edwards Univ, BA, theatre arts, 1979; Univ Tex, grad study film, 1980; Univ SC, MFA, cinema prod, 1984. **Career:** Petrified Forest, stage prod actor, 1975; TV commercials, Coca-Cola & New York Life Ins, actor, 1978; Warner Brothers, USC Cinema fel, 1982; PBS film The Last One Night Stands, producer, 1982-83; Walt Disney Prods & Disney Channel, asst to prod exec, 1984; anti-alcohol pub serv announcement geared black women, The Zone, dir & producer, 1987; Under the Rainbow: Jesse Jackson '88 for Pres, dir & producer, 1988; featurette Universal Pictures Ghost Dad, dir & producer, 1989; It chin' In My Heart, line producer; The Good Girls, music video; feature film East of Hope St, writer, dir & producer, 1998; Nate Thomas & Assocs, film producer various proj; PSA, dir & producer, 2004-; Feature Film Stompin', producer & dir, 2007; "Family Dinner", 2010; FBI intellectual property theft television PSA campaign, 2011-12; FBI cyber crime television PSA campaign, 2016; Calif State Univ. Northridge, Dept Cinema & TV Arts, Prof, Film Prod Option, head, currently. **Orgs:** Spec Youth Citation Urban League, 1975; pres, Jr Class St Edwards Univ, 1977-78; Screen Actors Guild, 1979-; Am Fedn Tv & Radio Artists, 1979-. **Honors/Awds:** Scholar Morning Star, Grand Chap Order Eastern Star, 1976; Dean's List, 1977-79, Student Activities Award of Excellence, 1978-79, nominee Man of the Year, St Edwards Univ, 1979; Nat Dean's List, 1979; Scholarship, USC Ebonics Support Group, 1981; USC Tommy Award for Outstanding Achievement in Cinema TV, 1984; Honorable Mention, Wellington Film Festival, New Zealand, 1984; Cine Golden Eagle & Honors, San Francisco Int Film Festival, 1984; Black Am Cinema Soc; Sony Innovator Award, Sony Corp, 1991; recognition & resolution, Warren, Ohio City Coun, 1992; inductee, Trumbull County Afro-American Hall of Fame, 1992; Outstanding Teaching Award, Calif State Univ, 1993; Distinguished Alumni Hall of Fame, Warren High Schs, 1994; Faculty Creativity Award, 1998; Jury Award, Hlwd Black Film Festival, 1999; First American in the Arts Award, 2000; Nominee Imagen Award (Spanish Image Awards), 2000; Special Commendation from FBI Director Robert Mueller, 2010; Emmy Award, 2014. **Special Achievements:** Director & producer of various 35 mm TV commercials, music videos, 1987-, feature film "East of Hope St", won Best Urban Drama at NY Int lIndependent Film Festival 1998; Best Feature Film at New Orleans Urban Film Festival, 1998; First Place, Cross Cultural at Black Filmmakers Hall of Fame Festival 1998; Has been featured in a variety of newspaper articles including the LA Times and The LA Daily News, has also been featured on E! Entertainment Television, Starz Movie News & numerous other television entities nationally. **Home Addr:** 616 Masselin Ave Apt 429, Los Angeles, CA 90036. **Business Addr:** Head, Film Production Option, Professor, California State University, Northridge, 18111 Nordhoff St, Northridge, CA 91330-8317, **Business Phone:** (818)677-3162.

### THOMAS, PROF. NINA M.

Law enforcement officer, educator. **Personal:** Born Bridgeport, CT; daughter of Eleanor McGarah and Livingston. **Educ:** John Jay Col Criminal Justice, BA, MA; Univ Conn, Storrs, CT, attended 1978; Univ New Haven, New Haven, CT; Housatonic Community Col, attended 1997; Criminal Justice Command Inst, Farmington, CT; Tunix Com Tech Col, 1997; Charter Oak State Col, 1997; Teikyo Post Univ, 1998. **Career:** Lieutenant (retired), educator; Mech & Farmers Savings Bank, Bridgeport Conn, mortgage rep, 1978-83; Bridgeport Police Dept, Bridgeport Conn, police officer, lt, 1983, patrol & commun div, supvr, undercover detective; Monroe Col, Dept Criminal Justice, adj fac, currently; Conn Community Col, minority fel. **Orgs:** Nat Black Police Asn; Bridgeport Guardians Inc; First Baptist

Stratford; Nat Black Women's Polit Cong; Nat Ctr Women Policing; Phi Theta Kappa; Waterbury Dem Club; vol, Olympics, 1996; Swing Phi Swing; Social Fel Inc; bd mem, E Orange Police Athletic League. **Home Addr:** 72 Hamden Ave, Waterbury, CT 06704, **Home Phone:** (860)260-5675. **Business Addr:** Adjunct Faculty, Monroe College, 434 Main St, New Rochelle, NY 10801, **Business Phone:** (914)632-5400.

**THOMAS, ORLANDO PAUL. See Obituaries Section.**

**THOMAS, PAMELA A. See THOMAS-GRAHAM, PAMELA.**

### THOMAS, DR. PAMELLA D.

Physician, health services administrator, educator. **Personal:** Born May 11, 1947, Westmoreland; daughter of Wellesley Johnston and Hyacinth Muir; married Earl A; children: Ramogi O & Monifa J. **Educ:** Univ Wis, Jamaica, MD, 1974; Univ Wis, Med Col, MPH, 1989. **Career:** Brookdale Hosp, emergency room attend, 1979-83; NYC Transit, asst med dir, staff physician, 1983-89; Lockheed Martin Aeronaut Systs Co, med dir, 1989-2002, dir, Wellness & Health Prom, 2002-; Emory Univ, Rollins Sch Pub Health, asst adj prof, 1991, adj assoc prof, currently; Emory Univ, Rollins Sch Pub health, Dept Environ & Occup Health, adj prof, 1992, assoc, 2002; IHPM's WorkPlace Ctr, chief med officer and exec dir; asst med dir & police surge, actg med dir, managing med serv. **Orgs:** Am Col Occup & Environ Med, 1983-; Am Pub Health Asn, 1986-; Am Col Prev Med, 1989-; Cobb County Med Soc, chair, pub rels, 1989-95; Aerospace Med Asn, 1989-; Med Asn Ga, 1990-; AMA, 1990-; bd dir, Cancer Soc, N Cobb Unit, 1990-; fac adv bd, Sch Pub Health, Emory Univ, 1991-, Environ & Occup Health Div, acad adv coun, 1992; chair, Occup & Environ Med Residency Prog Adv Bd, 1995-2001; Inst Health &Productivity Mgt, 1997; chair, Nat diabetes educ prog; Health and Productivity Mgt, 2002; boards dir, County Health Departments; Health & Productivity Mgt, 2002; preceptor, U.S. Occup Med Progs; Physician Exec, fel, Am Col Prev Med; Fel, Am Col Occup & Environ Med & Diplomat Am Bd Managed Care Med; exec, Am Col Physician; chair, GA ACOEM; chair, Lockheed GA Employees Community Credit Union; bd mem, chair, Nat Diabetes Educ Prog's Bus Strategies Work Group; founding mem, Heart Menders Asn; Bus Leadership Coun. **Home Addr:** 4058 Sandy Lake Dr, Lithonia, GA 30038-3800, **Home Phone:** (770)593-8042. **Business Addr:** Director, Lockheed Martin Aeronautical Systems Co, 86 S Cobb Dr, Marietta, GA 30063-0328, **Business Phone:** (770)494-4131.

### THOMAS, PATRICK ARNOLD

Executive, president (organization), business owner. **Personal:** Born Oct 6, 1956, Columbus, OH; son of Benjamin and Lucille W; married Shirley A Henry; children: Michelle, Kenneth & Nicholas. **Educ:** Kent State Univ, BA, bus admin, 1979; Nashville Tech Inst, AS, elec engineering; ICS cert elec & electronic engineering, 1980; Karras Sem, cert effective negotiating skills, 1981. **Career:** Johnson & Johnson Permacel Tape Div, reg rep, 1979-80; Ownes-Ill Forest Prod Div, reg rep, 1980-82; Nat Search Firm, sr tech recruiter, 1983-85; Eng & Exec Search Inc, pres, owner, 1985-. **Orgs:** Kentuckiana Minority Supplier Develop Coun; Nat Asn Personnel Consult; First Int Personnel Consults; Inst Elec & Electronic Engrs; Louisville Chap, Urban League; Louisville Chap, Nat Asn Advan Colored People; Gerald Neal State senate Campaign, asst dir, speakers bur; Louisville PTA; Little League Basketball Coach Newburg Community CTR, div champion, 1989, runner-up 1990, 1991. **Home Addr:** 3020 Meadowview Cir, Louisville, KY 40220-1406, **Home Phone:** (502)690-2347. **Business Addr:** President, Owner, Engineering & Executive Search Inc, 141 N Sherrin Ave Suite 221, Louisville, KY 40207, **Business Phone:** (502)895-3055.

### THOMAS, PHILIP MICHAEL

Actor. **Personal:** Born May 26, 1949, Columbus, OH; son of Louis Diggs and Lulu McMorris; married Dhaima Matthews; children: 2; married Kassandra; children: Noble, Kharisma, Sovereign, Sacred & Imaj. **Educ:** Oakwood Col, relig & philos; Univ Calif, Riverside; Univ Calif, Berkeley; DA, 1997. **Career:** Plays: Hair; No Place to Be Somebody, 1971; The Selling of the President, 1972; Reggae, 1980; Films: Come Back, Charleston Blue, 1972; Book of Numbers, 1973; Coonskin, 1975; Sparkle, 1975; Mr Ricco, 1974; Book of Numbers, lead role, 1973; Death Drug, 1978; The Dark, 1979; The Mushroom Eater, 1980; Of Stigma, 1982; Wizard of Speed & Time, 1988; Miami Shakedown, actor & exec producer, 1993; River of Stone, 1994; Vampirates, 2001; Fate, 2003. TV series: "Medical Center"; "Police Woman"; "Toma", 1973; 'Good Times'; "Society's Child"; "Lawman Without a Gun", 1979; "Valentine", 1979; "Roots: The Next Generation; Miami Vice", 1984-89; "Fight for Jennie", 1986; "False Witness", 1989; "A Little Piece of Sunshine", 1990; "Detective Extralarge: Moving Target", 1990; "Detective Extralarge: Miami Killer", 1991; "Detective Extralarge: Magic Power", 1991; "Detective Extralarge: Jo-Jo", 1991; "Detective Extralarge: Cannonball", 1991; "Detective Extralarge: Black Magic", 1991; "Extra large: Moving Target", 1990; "Extralarge: Black and White", 1991; "Perry Mason: The Case of the Ruthless Reporter", 1991; "Extralarge", 1991; "Fortune Hunter", 1994; "Noi siamo angeli", 1997; "We Are Angels", 1997; "Nash Bridges", 1997-2001. Albums: Living The Book of My Life; Singles: "Just the Way I Planned It", 1985; Videos: Grand Theft Auto: Vice City Stories, 2006; Nextones, spokesperson; Movie: Fate, 2003. **Orgs:** Screen Actors Guild; Actors' Equity; Am Fed TV & Radio Artists. **Honors/Awds:** Golden Globe Nominee for Best Performance by an Actor in a TV-Series-Drama, 1986; Image Award, Nat Asn Advan Colored People, 1987. **Special Achievements:** Promoted PMT women's clothing line, 1985. **Home Addr:** 2501 W Burbank Blvd Suite 304, Burbank, CA 91505. **Business Addr:** Actor, Kaye Porter, 2253 Loma Rica Dr, Prescott, AZ 86303.

### THOMAS, PHILIP S.

Administrator. **Personal:** Born May 24, 1946, Accomac, VA; children: Terrance Seegers. **Educ:** Montclair State Univ, BA, theater, 1977. **Career:** Greater Paterson Arts Coun, founder, exec dir, 1977-80; Montclair State Univ, BA Theater, 1977; Nat Endowment Arts, consult, 1977-87; NJ State Coun Arts, arts develop coordr, founder, 1980-82, consult, 1983-89; Newark Symphony Hall, dir mkt, 1982-84; Newark Pub Schs, Grants Develop Specialist, 1984-85; Carter G Woodson Found, artistic dir, pres, 1985-92; Pa Coun Arts, consult, 1986-90; Ohio Arts Coun, consult, 1990-90; Nj Performing Arts Ctr, vpres arts edu, founding dir, 1992-2004, pres, arts edu, 2004-. **Orgs:** Bd dir, founder, Carter G Woodson Found, 1974-99; evaluator, Nat Endowment Arts, 1981-; bd dir, NJ Black Issues Conv, 1984-99; bd dir, Educ Law Ctr, Nj, 1997-; Inst Sch Innovation, 1997-; Newark Boys Chorus Sch, 1993-99. **Home Addr:** PO Box 22075, Newark, NJ 07101, **Home Phone:** (973)477-1388. **Business Addr:** President, New Jersey Performing Arts Center, 1 Ctr St, Newark, NJ 07102, **Business Phone:** (973)642-8989.

### THOMAS, DR. PRISCILLA D.

County commissioner. **Personal:** Born Oct 26, 1934, Savannah, GA; daughter of Henry Robinson and Marie Edwards Baker; married Nathaniel; children: Deborah. **Educ:** Savannah State Col, Savannah, GA, BS, 1955; Bradley Univ, Peoria, IL, MS, 1960; Univ N Am, St Louis, MO, PhD, 1988; Atlanta Univ, cert, admin; Univ Ga, cert, admin. **Career:** Teacher, county commissioner (retired); Savannah Bd Pub Educ, Savannah, GA, elem teacher, 1956-67; Am Broadcasting Co, Savannah, GA, producer & hostess, TV pub serv programming, 1976-83, prin, 1968-86; Iota Phi Lambda Sorority Div, Savannah, GA, int pres, 1987-89; Thomas & Assocs, Savannah, GA, pres & chief exec officer, 1988; County Comn Chatham, Savannah, GA, county comnr, 1990-, vice chair, 1997; Conv & Visitors Bur, vpres mkt, 1995; Summer Bonanza Partnership, founder & pres; State Bd Educ, 11th Cong Dist, Atlanta, GA, rep; Savannah Ga Gen Assembly, sen. **Orgs:** Pub rel dir, Savannah Urban Dropout Collab, 1986-90; comnr, Citizens Crime Comn, 1986; nat liaison mem, Nat Legis Network, CBC, 1987; steering comt, Nat Coun Negro Women, 1989-91; local coordr, Nat Asn Counties Health & Human Serv, 1990; int pres, Iota Phi Lambda Sorority Inc; FairLawn Baptist Church; First Bryan Baptist Church; Coalition Black Meeting Planners; bd dir, vice chmn, Chatham Area Transist; founder, Chatham County Youth Comn. **Honors/Awds:** Mrs Black Heritage, Afro Am Life & Hist, 1976-77; On Air Personality Pioneer, Gospel Music Awards, 1983; Producer of the Year, Gospel Music Awards, 1983; 100 Top Black Business & Professional Woman, Dollars & Sense Mag, 1987; Kool Achiever Finalist, Kool Achievers, 1988; Woman Against the Odds, Polit Action Coun, 1988; Outstanding Woman of the Year, Savannah Bus & Prof Women Inc, 1991; Hometown Hero, WTOC-TV, 1994; Outstanding Citizen of the Year, Masons Int, Savannah Chap, 1994; MLK Day Celebration in Savannah, Parade Marshall; Hall of Fame, Dollars & Sense Mag, 1994; Nat Community Leader of the Year, Aunt Jemima Brands Quaker Oats Co, 1996. **Home Addr:** 1727 Chester St, Savannah, GA 31415-1707, **Home Phone:** (912)236-0459.

### THOMAS, RALPH ALBERT

Banker. **Personal:** Born Aug 5, 1954, Washington, DC; son of Joseph Samuel and Lucille Wade; married Valerie Thornton. **Educ:** Lehigh Univ, Bethlehem, BS, acct, 1976, MBA, finance, 1977. **Career:** Price Waterhouse & Co, Wash, intern, 1974, 1975, 1976, audit sr, 1976-80; Potomac Elec Power Co, Wash, proj syst acct, 1980-82; AT&T Info Syst, Murray Hill, NJ, mgr, cost & gov acct, 1982-84, mgr, corp acct policy & res, Murray Hill, 1984-85, mgr, financial anal, large bus syst, Morristown, 1985-87; Citicorp, NA, New York, vpres, region audit head, exec dir. **Orgs:** DC Inst CPA's, 1982-; Am Inst CPA's, 1983-; Lehigh Univ Black Alumni Asn, 1983-; chmn, by-laws comt, Northern Nj Chap Nat Asn Black Acct, 1985-; Urban Bankers Coalition, 1988-; exec coun, bd dir, 1980-, pres, 1990, Nat Asn Black Acct; chief exec officer, exec dir, Nj Socs Cert Pub Acct, 1999-. **Honors/Awds:** Professional Achievement Award, Nat Asn Black Accts, Northern New Jersey Chapter, 1990; Outstanding Member Award, Nat Asn Black Accts, 1988; Alumni Award, Lehigh University Black Alumni Coun, 1989. **Home Addr:** 21 Ireland Brook Dr, North Brunswick, NJ 08902-4762. **Business Addr:** Executive Director, New Jersey Society Certified Public Accountant, 425 Eagle Rock Ave Suite 100, Roseland, NJ 07068.

### THOMAS, RALPH CHARLES, III

Lawyer. **Personal:** Born Apr 10, 1949, Roanoke, VA. **Educ:** US Int Univ, AA, 1973; Univ Calif, BA, 1975; Harvard Law Sch, JD, 1978. **Career:** Bergson, Borkland, Margolis & Alder, atty assoc, 1978-80; George Washington Univ Nat Law Ctr, clin law inst, 1982-83; Law Off Ralph C Thomas III, chief coun, 1980-85; Nat Asn Minority Contractors, exec dir, 1985-92; Nat Aeronaut & Space Admin, asst adminr, assoc adminr, 1992-2005; Buchanan Ingersoll PC, spec coun, 2005-, dir, 2007-; Barton, Baker, Thomas & Tolle, LLP, founding partner, currently. **Orgs:** Nat Contract Mgt Asn; Sr Exec Asn; chmn, Fed Bar Asn, 2002-03; chmn, Sect's Comt; exec dir, Nat Bus Trade Asn. **Honors/Awds:** Federal Advocate Award, US Small Bus Admin, 1994; Advocate of the Year Award, Nat Asn Small Disadvantaged Bus, 1994; Exceptional Service Medal, NASA, 1994; Outstanding Leadership Award, Federal Small Bus Dir Interagency Coun, 1996; Federal Small Bus Advocate Award, Asian Am Bus Roundtable, 1996; Exceptional Achievement Medal, NASA, 1997; Ronald A Brown Award, Govt Excellence, Nat Coalition MNY Bus, 1999; Special Honor Award, World Asn Small & Medium Enterprises, Mumbai, India, 1999; Man of the Year, MNY Bus & Prof Network, 2000; Presidential Rank of Meritorious Exec, Exec Off Pres, 2000; Best of the Decade, MNY BUS News, 2000; Outstanding Leadership Medal, NASA, 2000; Pres Rank of Distinguished Executive, Exec Off Pres, 2001; Received Numerous Hons & Awards. **Special Achievements:** Author, African Americans in the Business of Space, Minorities in Business, vol III No 1, 1997; Lead Ed: "International Best Practices Manual for the Maximized Utilizatio of Small and Medium Enterprises". **Business Addr:** Partner, Barton, Baker, Thomas & Tolle LLP, 1320 Old Chain Bridge Rd Suite 400, McLean, VA 22101, **Business Phone:** (703)448-1810.

### THOMAS, RAYMOND A.

Artistic director. **Personal:** Born St. Louis, MO. **Educ:** Sch Art Inst Chicago, attended 1988. **Career:** Johnson Publ Co Inc, creative mgr, 1988-2011; Ebony Mag, creative art dir, currently. **Business Addr:** Creative Art Director, Ebony Magazine, 800 S Mich Ave, Chicago, IL 60605, **Business Phone:** (312)322-9200.

### THOMAS, REGINALD MAURICE

First lady, beautician, business owner. **Personal:** Born Jan 4, 1964, San Angelo, TX; son of Claude Leon Jr and Devada Roberts; married Lynn Regina Scott; children: Brittney Regina & Reginald III. **Educ:** Morehouse Col, Atlanta, Ga, attended 1983; Wayne State Univ, Detroit, Mich, attended 1984. **Career:** GAP, Southfield, Mich, salesman, 1981-83; Metric Med Lab, Southfield, Mich, supvr, motor pool, 1983-87; City Detroit Parks & Rec, Detroit, Mich, landscaper, laborer, 1987-88, Detroit Fire Dept, Detroit, Mich, emergency med tech, 1988, fire fighter; Ultimate Barber Shop, owner, barber, currently. **Honors/Awds:** Lifesaver of the Year, E Detroit Med Authority, 1990. **Home Addr:** 18375 Grayfield St, Detroit, MI 48219, **Home Phone:** (313)535-1006. **Business Addr:** Owner, Ultimate Barber Shop, 19310 Grand River Ave, Detroit, MI 48223-1202, **Business Phone:** (313)387-0376.

### THOMAS, ROBERT LEE, IV

Football coach, football player. **Personal:** Born Dec 1, 1974, Little Rock, AR. **Educ:** Henderson State Univ. **Career:** Football player (retired), football coach; Dallas Cowboys, running back, 1998, fullback, 1999-2002; Fifth Ann Dallas Cowboys Let Us Play! Sports Camp, football coach, 2001; Kans City Brigade, 2004; Ga Force, 2004-06; Colo Crush, linebacker, 2007-08; Ark Twisters, asst coach, 2009. **Honors/Awds:** Gulf South Conference Defensive Player of Year, 1995; Hall of Honor, Henderson State Univ, 2004; Jacksonville High School Hall of Fame, 2006.

### THOMAS, ROBERT LEWIS, JR.

Administrator, educator. **Personal:** Born Sep 25, 1944, Brewton, AL; son of Robert Lewis Sr and Earnestine Lane; married Wyvonnia Thompson; children: Michelle & Tiffani. **Educ:** Stillman Col, BA, 1967; Troy State Univ, MS, 1975. **Career:** Escambia Co Bd Educ, teacher, 1967-83; Brewton Police Dept, patrolman, 1969-; Faulkner State Jr Col, prof hist, 1983-; Faulkner State Community Col, Div Soc Sci, chairperson, currently. **Orgs:** Lifetime mem, Kappa Alpha Psi Fraternity, 1969-; Nat Asn Advan Colored People, 1983-; deleg, Conf Black Am Affairs, 1984-86; vpres, AEA Faulkner State, 1986-87, pres, 1987-88; deleg, AEA Conv, 1987-88; Ala Peace Officers Asn; Ala High Sch Athletic Asn; bd trustee, Zion Fountain AME Church; Ala Asn Historians, Nat Asn Advan Colored People. **Home Addr:** 612 Liles Blvd, Brewton, AL 36426, **Home Phone:** (205)867-9294. **Business Addr:** Chairperson, Faulkner State Community College, 1900 Hwy 31 S, Bay Minette, AL 36507, **Business Phone:** (251)580-2100.

### THOMAS, RODERICK

Consultant, association executive, association executive. **Personal:** Born Jan 12, 1939, Philadelphia, PA; son of Wiliam A and Virginia B Mosley; children: Jeffri Pierre, Roderick Jr & Shelley McGill. **Educ:** Temple Univ, BS, 1970; Drexel Univ, MBA, org dev, 1973. **Career:** DuPont CPN, org develop consult, 1973-78; Rod Thomas Assocs, prin, 1978; Rod Thomas Consult, owner; New Ventures W, coach. **Orgs:** Dir, Fed Comt Encour. **Special Achievements:** Produced a video, Diversity: Making It Work for You, 1992. **Business Addr:** Principal, Rod Thomas Consulting, 3064 Beechaven Rd, Columbia, SC 29204, **Business Phone:** (803)787-4587.

### THOMAS, RODNEY LAMAR

Football player. **Personal:** Born Dec 21, 1965, Los Angeles, CA. **Educ:** Brigham Young Univ. **Career:** Football player (retired); Miami Dolphins, 1990, cornerback & defensive back, 1988-89; Los Angeles Rams, 1991; San Francisco 49ers, 1992. **Business Addr:** Player, San Francisco 49ers, 4949 Centennial Blvd, Santa Clara, CA 95054.

### THOMAS, RODOLFO RUDY

Law enforcement officer. **Personal:** Born Feb 19, 1949, Highland Park, IL; son of Porter and Consuela; married Anna; children: Kimberly Stewart, Malia, Lattimer & Matthew Rodriguez. **Educ:** Highland Park Col, AA; Eastern Mich Univ, BS, police admin, MS, inter disciplinary technol. **Career:** Detroit Police Dept, police officer, 1974-83; sgt, 1983-85; lt, 1985-87, inspector, 1987-89, comdr/narcotics div, 1989-94, dep chief police, 1994, asst chief, 1997; Eastern Mich Univ, adj prof. **Orgs:** Optimist Club; Golden Key Hons Soc; Chamber Com Law Enforcement Consult; Drug Educ Adv; Community Policing Adv; City Heroin Task Force; Detroit Pub Sch Mentor; exec dir, Ariz State Bd Funeral dir & Embalmers. **Home Addr:** 8032 3rd Ave, Detroit, MI 48202. **Business Addr:** Executive Director, Arizona State Board of Funeral Directors & Embalmers, 1400 W Wash Suite 230, Phoenix, AZ 85007, **Business Phone:** (602)542-3095.

### THOMAS, RON

Writer, educator. **Personal:** Born Sep 13, 1949, Buffalo, NY; son of Laughton F and Ormah Dennis; married Iris T Crossley; children: Kali C. **Educ:** Univ Rochester, BA, polit sci, 1971; Northwestern Univ, MA, jour, 1973. **Career:** Rochester Times-Union, prep sports reporter, 1973-75; Chicago Daily News, col basketball, football reporter, 1975-78; San Francisco Chronicle, pro basketball reporter, 1978-82, sportswriter, 1984-93, news copy ed, 1993; USA Today, pro basketball ed/reporter, 1982-84; Home Box Off, doc researcher/feature producer, 1995; Marin Independent J, sportswriter, 1995-2000; San Francisco, examr, sports writer, columnist, 2000-03, freelance, currently; Black Am Web.com, sports & news reporter, 2003-06; More house Col, Journ & Sports Prog, Dept Eng, dir, currently, fac, 2007-; Author: "They Cleared the Lane: The NBA's BLK Pioneers", 2002; "Black Faces Still Rare in the Press Box"; "Sport in Socs: Equal Opportunity or BUS as Usual?"; "Col of Marin Star Fought Beyond Basketball Ct"; "The Black Coach Barrier"; "They Cleared the Lane". **Orgs:** Nat Asn Black Journalists, 1978-; Bay Area Black Journalists Asn, 1980-; Pro Basketball Writers Asn, 1984-94; Pro Football Writers Asn, 1987-91; N Am Soc Sports Hist, 1992-; Atlanta Asn Black Journalists; Trotter Group African-Am columnists. **Special Achievements:** First director of Morehouse Colleges Journalism and Sports Program. **Home Addr:** 2726 Rawson St, Oakland, CA 94619-3259. **Business Addr:** Director Journalism & Sports Program, Faculty, Morehouse College, Brawley Hall Rm 106 830 Westview Dr, Atlanta, GA 30314, **Business Phone:** (404)681-2800.

### THOMAS, DR. RONALD F.
Educator. **Personal:** Born Jul 2, 1944, Wilmington, DE; married Marva Wyche; children: Ronald LeRoy & Olivia Necole. **Educ:** Del State Col, BS, 1967; Cent Mich Univ, master, 1979, postgrad studies, 1987; Hamilton Univ, PhD, 2000. **Career:** Educator (retired); teacher, math, 1977; Capital Sch Dist, Dover, Del, math instr, 1970-74, reading & math ctr, oper, Title VII, Title I; Tel Rd Learning Ctr, comput lab supvr, teacher, math & sci; Red Clay Sch Dist, Wilmington, Del, teacher, math & sci, 1988, math & reading lab, instr. **Orgs:** Fel Groove Phi Groove Soc, 1963, VFW, 1974-, DOIC, GED, ABE Teacher, 1963; Va, 1967-; Del State Educ Asn, 1970-; Nat Educ Asn, 1970-; Capital Educ Asn, 1970-; Church Laymens Asn, 1970-; Probs & Rels Comt, 1971-73, 32nd Degree Mason & Shriner, 1972-; Human Rels Conf Rep Capital Sch Dist, 1972, 1973; bldg rep, 1972-74, lab del, assembly deleg, 1973, State Educ Asn; negotiation team schs, 1974; chmn, nom comn, Del State Educ Assembly, 1974; pres, DE State Minority Ed Asn, 1974-76; Del Disadvantaged Found Inc, 1974-; adv, Col Gospel Youth Group, 1974; vpres, De Front ierInt Club; Omega Psi Phi. **Home Addr:** 899 Woodcrest Dr, Dover, DE 19904-2440, **Home Phone:** (302)674-4490.

### THOMAS, ROY L.
Executive director, executive, government official. **Personal:** Born Jul 27, 1938, Forest, MS; married Altemese Woods; children: Micheal, Sandra & Mark. **Educ:** Univ Md. **Career:** Hercules Inc, prod foreman; Minority Bus Opportunities, enforcement officer; City Glen Falls, dir community develop. **Orgs:** Bd chmn, Local Housing Corp; Warren Co NY Sewer Dist 1; chmn, New York St Conf, Nat Asn Advan Colored People, Prisons Affrs Comt, New York Br, pres; exec dir, Vol Housing Surv; chmn, bd mem, E A dir ondack Econ Develop Auth; bd mem, Warren Co Alcoholic Bev Con Bd; Warren Co Rep Comn; New York Ancillary Manpower Planning Bd; Senate Lodge 456 F&AM Glens Falls. **Home Addr:** 11 Darwin Ave, Glens Falls, NY 12801-3416, **Home Phone:** (518)793-1947. **Business Addr:** President, Glens Falls NAACP, 35 Hudson Ave, Glens Falls, NY 12801, **Business Phone:** (518)793-1947.

### THOMAS, ROZONDA
Actor, singer. **Personal:** Born Feb 27, 1971, Atlanta, GA; daughter of Abdul Ali and Ava Thomas; married Dallas Austin; children: Tron; married Usher Raymond. **Educ:** Ga Southern Univ, fashion design. **Career:** Albums: Ooooooohhh....On the TLC Tip, 1992; Crazy Sexy Cool, 1994; Fan mail, 1999; 3D, 2002; Now & Forever: The Hits, 2005; Singles: "Ain't 2 Proud 2 Beg", 1992; "What About Your Friends", 1992; "Baby-Baby-Baby", 1992; Sleigh Ride", 1992; "Hat 2 Da Back", 1993; "Get It Up", 1993; "Creep", 1994; "Red Light Special", 1995; "Switch", 1995; "Waterfalls", 1995; "Kick Your Game", 1995; "Diggin' On You", 1995; "This Is How It Works", 1995; "Silly Ho", 1998; "No Scrubs", 1999; "I'm Good At Being Bad", 1999; "Unpretty", 1999; "Dear Lie", 1999; "What It Ain't (Ghetto Enuff)", 2000; "Girl Talk", 2002; "Hands Up", 2002; "Damaged", 2003; "Turnbtable", 2003; "Come Get Some", 2004; "Bi-Polar", 2009; Films: House Party 3, 1994; Hav Plenty, 1997; Snow Day, 2000; Ticker, 2001; TV series: "Love Song", 2000; Snow Day, 2000; "A Diva's Christmas Carol", 2000; "That '70s Show", 2003; "The Parkers", 2004; "Strong Medicine", 2004; "R U the Girl?", exec producer, 2005; "What Chilli Wants", exec producer & writer, 2010-11; "Single Ladies", 2011; CrazySexyCool: The TLC Story, exec producer, 2013. **Honors/Awds:** Four MTV Music Awards: Best R&B Video, Best Group Video, Best Video of the Year, Viewers Choice, "Waterfalls", 1995. **Business Addr:** Singer, Actress, c/o LaFace Records, One Capitol City Plz Suite 1500, Atlanta, GA 30326, **Business Phone:** (404)848-8050.

### THOMAS, HON. SAMUEL BUZZ, III
Government official. **Personal:** Born Jan 28, 1969. **Educ:** Univ Pa, BA. **Career:** Avis Tech Pk Partners, adminr, mgr; Bob Carr US Senate, Detroit Campaign dir, mgr; Parkside Bldg Co, construct mgr; US Congresswoman Barbara Rose Collins, sr legis asst; Mich State Legis, state rep, 1996-2002, 4th Senate Dist-Detroit, state sen, 2003-11. **Orgs:** Diabetes Asn Mich; founding mem, Independent Policy Group; bd dir, Matthew NcNeely Neighborhood Found; adv comt, Plowshares Theater Co; bd dir, 1000 Friends Metrop Detroit, 2003-; Alpha Phi Alpha Fraternity Inc; Chaldean-Americans Reaching & Encouraging; Detroit Inst Art Founder's Socs; Nat Asn Advan Colored People; Trade Union Leadership Coun; Travelers Aid Socs; vice chair, Econ Develop & Regulatory Reform; Energy Policy & Pub Utilities; Homeland Security & Emerging Technologies; Sigma Pi Phi Fraternity; fel Nat Boule Found; Pub Arts Comt mem; bd dir, Mich Humane Socs; Am Diabetes Asn; Nat Asn Advan Colored People. **Home Addr:** , Detroit, MI. **Business Addr:** State Senator, 4th Senate District Detroit, Capitol Bldg Rm S-9, Lansing, MI 48909-7536, **Business Phone:** (517)373-7918.

### THOMAS, SAMUEL C., SR.
Manager, accountant, executive. **Personal:** Born Aug 21, 1943, Malvern, AR; son of Robert and Altora Burks Boles; married Lura D Shannon; children: Samuel II & Jason Anthony. **Educ:** Monterey Peninsula Col, Monterey, CA, AA, 1974; Golden Gate Univ, San Francisco, CA, BA, 1977, MBA, 1984. **Career:** Pac Gas & Elec, pump test engr, 1977-78, mkt rep, 1978-80, local mgr, 1980-83, area mgr, 1983-86, employee participation adminr, 1986-90, continuing educ adminr, 1990; Am Protective Serv, acct mgr; Thomas & Assoc, pres, currently. **Orgs:** Pacifica Lions Club, 1980-91; Am Legion, 1982-91; Am Asn Blacks Energy, 1983-91; pres, Healdsburg Chamber Com, 1985-86; subscribing life mem, Nat Asn Advan Colored People, 1989-91; life mem, Nat Black MBA, 1989. **Honors/Awds:** Service Award, Am Legion, Pacifica Post, 1984; Service Award, Healdsburg Chamber Com, 1985; Community Service Award, Pac Gas & Elec, 1989; Dedicated Service Award, Math Engr & Sci Achievement, 1990. **Home Addr:** 10220 Singing View Ct, Las Vegas, NV 89129-8132, **Home Phone:** (702)869-3379. **Business Addr:** President, Thomas & Associates, 5155 Myrtlewood Ave, Las Vegas, NV 89122-6835, **Business Phone:** (702)456-3575.

### THOMAS, SAMUEL HAYNES, JR.
Lawyer, real estate executive. **Personal:** Born Oct 2, 1941, Detroit, MI; son of Samuel Sr and Margaret; children: Samuel III. **Educ:** Lafayette Col, AB, 1964; Harvard Law Sch, LLB, 1967. **Career:** Ford Motor Co, off gen coun, 1967-69; Jaffe, Snider, Raitt, Garratt & Heuer PC, 1970-77; Thomas & Pomeroy Inc, pres, 1977-80; Burlington Investments Inc, owner, 1980-; Thomas & Mancinelli Pizza Inc, pres, 1987-94; Metrop Realty Co LLC, dir, 1988-, vice chmn, 1989-; Phoenix Mgt, vpres, 1994-; Detroit Inst Arts, trustee. **Orgs:** Sigma Pi Phi Fraternity, 1993-95; State Bar Mich; Nat Bar Asn; Detroit Bar Asn; vice chair, State Mich Bldg Authority. **Home Addr:** PO Box 130020, Ann Arbor, MI 48113-0020, **Home Phone:** (313)920-0557. **Business Addr:** Vice Chairman, Director, Metropolitan Realty Company LLC, 535 Griswold Suite 748, Detroit, MI 48226, **Business Phone:** (313)961-5552.

### THOMAS, SHERRI
Executive, executive director. **Personal:** Born Richmond, VA; married Norman. **Educ:** Va State Univ, BS, geol & earth sci, gen, 1980; Univ SC, MS, geol & earth sci, gen, 1982. **Career:** Amoco, sr explor tech, 1978-79; Nat Assoc Black Geol & Geophysicists, secy, 1983-84; ConocoPhillips Co, geol, 1980-92, adv, 1993-2004, sr adv talent mgt, 2004-06, dir com campus staffing, 2006-11; Phillips 66, Early Career Facilitation Com, dir, 2012-14; Univ Tex Dallas, career advisor, 2014-. **Orgs:** Nat Assoc Black Geol & Geophys, 1982; secy, Ella Bouldin Missionary Soc 5 1983-; Am Assoc Petrol Geol, 1984, Geol Soc Am, 1985; Celestrial Choir Payne Chapel AME Church. **Special Achievements:** Article "Quartz Sand Provirence Changes" S Booker, R Ehrlich, 1981. **Home Addr:** 17047 Carbridge Dr, Houston, TX 77084. **Business Addr:** Senior Advisor Human Resource, Commercial Campus Staffing, ConocoPhillips Co, 600 N Dairy Ashford, Houston, TX 77079-1175, **Business Phone:** (281)293-1000.

### THOMAS, DR. SHERYL ANN BENNING
School administrator. **Personal:** Born Jan 1, 1947, Columbus, GA; daughter of Calvin and Emma; married Lee M; children: Khalia M & Shaura A. **Educ:** Fisk Univ, BA; Tex Southern Univ, masters; Wayne State Univ, ed spec, PhD, 1969; La Salle Univ. **Career:** Detroit Pub Schs, teacher, counr & adminr; Go lightly Educ Ctr, prin & exec dir schs, currently. **Orgs:** Nat pres, Jack & Jill Am, 1996-98; Links Inc, Detroit chap; Delta Sigma Theta Sorority; Phi Delta Kappa. **Home Addr:** 3515 Sherbourne, Detroit, MI 48221. **Business Addr:** Executive Director of Schools, Detroit Public Schools, 8770 W Chicago, Detroit, MI 48204.

### THOMAS, SHUNDRAWN A.
Executive, vice president (organization), writer. **Educ:** Fla Agr & Mech Univ, BS, acct, 1995; Univ Chicago Booth Sch Bus, MBA, acct & finance, 1999, exec educ progs corp strategy; Univ Notre Dame Mendoza Sch Bus, corp governance. **Career:** Morgan Stanley, analyst, fixed income div, 1994-97; Goldman Sachs, vpres, equities div, 1999-2003; Northern Trust-Chicago, vpres, alternative solutions group, 2004-05, sr vpres, head corp strategy, 2005-08, pres & chief exec officer, 2008-10, managing exec, head exchange-traded funds group, 2010-14, exec vpres, head funds & managed accounts group, 2014-. **Orgs:** Econ Club Chicago; Trustee, Wheaton Col; bd dir, Fla A&M Univ Found; Alpha Phi Alpha Fraternity Inc. **Honors/Awds:** "Crain's Chicago Business," 40 Under 40, 2007; Arthur N. Turbull Young Alumnus Achievement Award, Chicago GSB, 2008; Chicago United Business Leaders of Color, 2009; "Black Enterprise," 75 Most Powerful Blacks on Wall Street, 2011. **Special Achievements:** Published "Start Planting! A Spiritual Guide to Wealth Creation and Successful Investing," Adelphos Publishing, 2003; "Ridiculous Faith: Ordinary People Living Extraordinary Lives," Destiny Image Publishers, 2006; "Driving Under the Influence: Finding Your Way on the Road of Life," Tree of Life Resources, 2010. **Business Addr:** Executive Vice President, Head of Funds and Managed Accounts Group, The Northern Trust Co, 50 S La Salle St, Chicago, IL 60603, **Business Phone:** (312)630-6000.

### THOMAS, SPENCER
Physician, columnist. **Personal:** Born Gadsden, AL; married Lela; children: Spencer Jr. **Educ:** Ala St Univ, BS, 1952; Howard Univ, MD, 1959. **Career:** Mercy Douglas Hosp Philadelphia, intern, house physician, 1959-61; Philadelphia Gen Hosp, urol spec training, 1972-76, asst attend physician, 1976-77; Holy Name of Jesus Hosp, now Riverview & Baptist Mem (now Gadsden Regional) Hosp, Gadsden, staff physician; pvt pract, Gadsden Ala, physician; Gadsden Times Daily, weekly columnist. **Orgs:** Bd dir, Gadsden Progress Coun; sponsor, Proj Headstart, 1964-72 & 1980-; Indus Develop Bd Gadsden, 1968-72, 1978-80; med dir, Proj Head Start, 1968-72; pres, Community League Adv Social Socs Gadsden, 1969; pres, Gadsden Alumni Asn Ala St Univ, 1979-; chmn, admin bd, trustee, Sweethome United Methodist Ch, 1979-81; pres, Ala St Alumni Asn, Gadsden Chap, 1979-; Gadsden City Bd Educ, 1980-90, vpres, 1984; bd trustees, Ala A&M Univ, 1980-87, chmn, 1982-84; ch lay leader, 1981-84; pres, Gadsden-Etowah Ala Br, Nat Asn Advan Colored People, 1982-94; founder & mem gov bd, Colley Child Care Ctr, Gadsden; Nat Asn Advan Colored People; Alpha Phi Alpha Fraternity Inc, Ala St med Asn, Nat Med Asn, AMA, SCLC, Howard Univ Med Alumni Asn; Chamber Cerce, Gadsden Ala. **Honors/Awds:** Recipient Service Award, Gadsden Progress Coun, 1972. **Home Addr:** PO Box 835, Gadsden, AL 35902-0835. **Business Addr:** Physician, Private Practitioner, 1010 S 12th St, Gadsden, AL 35901-3811, **Business Phone:** (256)547-2293.

### THOMAS, STEPHEN
Executive. **Educ:** Ohio State Univ, BS, health educ; Ill State Univ, Carbondale, MA, health educ; Southern Ill Univ, community health educ, PhD. **Career:** Rollins Sch Pub Health, dir; Univ Md, dir, prof health serv admin; Minority Health Res Lab, cofounder; Emory Univ, assoc prof, 1992-2000; Nat Ctr HIV AIDS, vis scientist, 1996-98; Univ Pittsburgh, Ctr Minority Health, dir, prof community health & social Justice, currently; Southern Ill Univ, prof; Univ of Nc, prof; Health Prom Pract, assoc ed. **Orgs:** Consult, Nat Res Coun, 1995; Inst Med Comt, 1998; fel Am Acad Health Behav; Amas Ethical Force; bd, Rails Trails Conservancy; Robert Wood Johnson Found; bd dir, United Way; NIH State Sci Comt, Tobacco Cessation, Prev & Control; adv bd, Mayo Clin's Cancer Ctr & Mayo's Ctr Translational Sci Activ; dir, tranning site, Kellogg Health Scholars Post-Doctoral Prog; adv bd, Ctr on Ethics in Pub Policy; Int Union for Health Prom and Educ; Am Pub Health Asn; ed bd, Socs for Pub Health Educ. **Business Addr:** Director, Professor, University Pittsburgh, 125 Parran Hall, Pittsburgh, PA 15261, **Business Phone:** (412)624-5665.

### THOMAS, TERENCE
Disc jockey, television producer, radio engineer. **Personal:** Born Nov 15, 1966, Brooklyn, NY; son of Tijuana G. **Educ:** Audio Rec Tech Inst, 1989. **Career:** TBTA, 1985-89; Master Lab Prod Studio, pres & ceo, currently; First Priority Music, E W Rec, currently; TV appearances: "Arsenio Hall Show", 1990; "Show time at Apollo", 1990; "Living Color", 1992; "Soul Train", 1992; "NBA All-Star Game", 1992; "Phil Donahue Show"; "Geraldo Show"; "MTV"; "Yo MTV Raps"; "Party Mach"; Films: Boomerang & Mo Money; Moesha; Joan Rivers; BET; Video Soul; No Pl To Hide; Cabeza de Vaca. **Orgs:** SAG; AFTRA. **Home Addr:** 134-11 111th Ave, South Ozone Park, NY 11420, **Home Phone:** (718)322-2258. **Business Addr:** President, Chief Executive Officer, Master Lab Productions Studios, 134-11 111th Ave, South Ozone Park, NY 11420, **Business Phone:** (718)322-2258.

### THOMAS, ESQ. TERENCE A., SR.
Lawyer. **Educ:** Miss Valley State Univ, Hons Col, 1987; Albion Col, BA, hist, 1990; Univ Wis Law Sch, JD, 1993. **Career:** Raymond & Prokop PC, assoc, 1994-95; Miller, Canfield, Paddock & Stone PLC, assoc, 1995-2002, prin, 2002-03, atty; St John Health, sr vpres external affairs, 2003-05, sr vpres advocacy & corp responsibility, 2005-08; Mich Ministries Ascension Health, chief advocacy officer, 2008-10; Clairmount Group, PLC, gen coun, 2010-; Thomas Group Consult, partner, 2011-; Mich Supreme Ct Justice Conrad L Mallet Jr, judicial clerk. **Orgs:** Am Bar Asn; State Bar Mich; Wis Bar Asn; Detroit Metrop Bar Asn; Wolverine Bar Asn; Leadership Detroit Class XXI; Audit Comt, Detroit Econ Growth Corp; trustee, Music Hall Ctr; Detroit Regional Chamber Com; Mich Fitness Found; Detroit Wayne County Health Authorithy; adv bd, Univ Detroit Jesuit High Sch & Acad. **Business Addr:** Partner, Thomas Group Partners, 28 W Adams Ave Grand Pk Ctr Suite 1300, Detroit, MI 48226, **Business Phone:** (313)334-3488.

### THOMAS, THURMAN LEE
Football player, executive. **Personal:** Born May 16, 1966, Houston, TX; married Patti; children: Olivia, Angelica Annika Lee & Thurman III. **Educ:** Okla State Univ, attended 1989. **Career:** Football player (retired), exec; Buffalo Bills, running back, 1988-99; Miami Dolphins, running back, 2000; Thurman Thomas Enterprises, Niagara Falls, NY, owner, 2002-; Legends Energy Group, founder, 2010-; Energy Curtailment Specialists, prog rep, 2011-; BidURenergy Inc, prog rep, 2011-. **Honors/Awds:** Pro Bowl, 1989, 1990, 1991, 1992, 1993; Most Valuable Player, Nat Football League, 1991; Most Valuable Player, NFL Newspaper Ent, 1991; Offensive Player of the Year, NFL AP, 1991; Assoc Tex High Sch Hall of Fame, 1992; Buffalo Bills & Edge, Man of the Year, 1993; Buffalo Bills Wall of Fame; Pro Football Hall of Fame, 2007; College Football Hall of Fame, 2008. **Special Achievements:** First player ever to score a touchdown in 4 consecutive Super Bowls. **Business Addr:** Owner, Thurman Thomas Enterprises, Niagara Falls, NY 14301.

### THOMAS, TIMOTHY MARK (TIM THOMAS)
Basketball coach, basketball player. **Personal:** Born Feb 26, 1977, Paterson, NJ. **Educ:** Villanova Univ, attended 1997. **Career:** Basketball player (retired); Philadelphia 76ers, forward, 1997-99; Milwaukee Bucks, forward, 1999-2004; NY Knicks, forward, 2004-05, 2008-09, coach, 2006; Chicago Bulls, 2005-06, 2009; Phoenix Suns, 2006; Los Angeles clippers, forward, 2006-08; Dallas Mavericks, free agt, 2009-10.

### THOMAS, TRA (WILLIAM THOMAS, III)
Executive, football player. **Personal:** Born Nov 20, 1974, DeLand, FL; son of William; married Rosa Chanea; children: 3. **Educ:** Fla State Univ, BS, criminol. **Career:** Football player (retired), exec; Philadelphia Eagles, left tackle, 1998-2008, tackle, 1999, coaching intern, 2013, offensive asst coach, 2013-14; Jacksonville Jaguars, left tackle, 2009-10; San Diego Chargers, 2010; 7 Deuce Sports, owner, operator & trainer, 2011-; Comcast SportsNet Philadelphia, Eagles Post, analyst. **Honors/Awds:** NFC Pro Bowl, 2001, 2002, 2004; All Pro Slection, Once, 2002. **Business Addr:** Owner, 7 Deuce Sports, 175 Rte 70, Medford, NJ 08055, **Business Phone:** (877)727-2348.

### THOMAS, HON. W. CURTIS
State government official, educator. **Personal:** Born Apr 11, 1948, Philadelphia, PA; son of Hattie M and Curtis; children: Salim & Kareem. **Educ:** Temple Univ, BS, educ, 1975, educ admin, 1977; Antioch Sch Law, JD, 1980. **Career:** Legislator & teacher; Antioch Sch Law, Wash, DC, stud teacher, 1978-79, instr, property law and civil pract, 1998; Const and property law, instr, 1978-79; US Dept Health, Educ and Welfare, Wash, DC, law clerk, 1979-80; Commonwealth Pa, Harrisburg, Pa, law clerk, 1980-82; EPNAC Inc, Philadelphia, exec dir, 1982-87; Pa House Representatives, 181st Legis Dist, Philadelphia County, dem, state rep, 1989-, 14th consecutive term, currently; Pa Comn on Crime and Delinq, 1991-92. **Orgs:** 20th Ward Dem Comt, 11th Div, 1982; 14th Ward Dem Exec Comt; Co-chmn, Info Technol Subcomt House Intergovernmental Affairs Comt, 1995; co founder, Philadelphia Comt Serv Youth; chmn, Black Am Law Students Asn; founder & chmn, N Philadelphia br, E Poplar Community Econ Develop Corp Consumers Educ Protection Asn; vpres, Philadelphia Nat Asn Adv Colored People; United Supreme Coun, Northern Jurisdiction, 32nd Degree & 33rd Degree; Scottish Rite Mason; DeMolay Consistory #1; St Phillips Baptist Church; chmn, Pa Legis Black Caucus; chmn, Health & Welfare Comt; State Gov & Labor Rels Comt; brd dir, Penn Higher Educ Assistance Agency; coun, State Govt's Eastern Regional Conf Comt Health & Human Serv; founding mem, Dem Study Group; Philadelphia Welfare Pride & Blacks Educating Blacks About Sexual Health Issues; co-founder; dem chair, C First; Senate Pub Health & Welfare Comn; Appropriations, Educ & Policy; Am Fed State Co & Munic Employees Union; Prince Hall Grand Lodge Free & Accepted Masons; Philadelphia Int Airport Adv Brd; Father's Day Rally Comn; trustee, Mt Carmel Baptist Church; Speaker's Bipartisan Reform Comn; Joint State Govt Comn Real Property; Joint State Govt Comn Stroke Prev; bd trustee, Lincoln Univ; bd dir, Philadelphia

High Sch Academies; minority chmn, House Intergovernmental Affairs Comt, 2006-08; chmn, House Urban Affairs Comt, 2009. **Home Addr:** 530 W Girard Ave, Philadelphia, PA 19123, **Home Phone:** (215)560-3261. **Business Addr:** State Representative, Pennsylvania House of Representatives, 214 K Leroy Irvis Office Bldg, Harrisburg, PA 17120-2181, **Business Phone:** (717)787-9471.

## THOMAS, BISHOP WALTER SCOTT, SR.

Clergy. **Personal:** Born Apr 2, 1950, Balto, MD; son of Calvin and Elizabeth; married Patricia G; children: Joi, Walter Jr & Joshua. **Educ:** Univ Md, College Park, BS, econs, 1971; Howard Univ Divinity Sch, MDiv, 1976; St Marys Univ & Sem, DMin, 1985. **Career:** New Psalmist Baptist Church, pastor, 1975-. **Orgs:** Pres, Baptist Minister's Conf Balto, 1986-88; pres, Millenium Pastor's Conf, 1998-2001; pres, Hampton Univ Minister's Conf, 1999-2002; bd dir, Harbor Bank, 2000-; Sigma Pi Phi, 2001. **Honors/Awds:** Dean's Award, Howard Univ Divinity Sch, 2000; Hon Doctor Divinity, Va Sem; Hon Doctor Divinity, Bethune Cookman Col. **Special Achievements:** Author: Spiritual Navigation for 21st Century, 2000; Good Men Makes Its Own Gravy, 2000; Editor: Outstanding Black Sermons Vol 4, 2001; Articles: Afr Amer Pulpit. **Home Addr:** 8305 Gov Thomas Lane, Ellicott City, MD 21043, **Home Phone:** (410)465-3940. **Business Addr:** Pastor, New Psalmist Baptist Church, 6020 Marion Dr, Baltimore, MD 21215, **Business Phone:** (410)945-3000.

## THOMAS, WILBON

Government official, business owner, farmer. **Personal:** Born Mar 6, 1921, Midway, AL; son of Wilbon and Ada Brown; married Mary E Warren; children: 3. **Career:** Bullock County Schs, bus driver; farmer & serv sta operator, 1957-; Macon Co Racing Comn. **Orgs:** Vpres, pres, 1964, Nat Asn Advan Colored People, 1954-56-; pres, Midway Improvement Club, 1956-64; First Baptist Church Bullock Co ESPO, Deacon; jury comm, Bullock City, Bullock City Dist Adv Coun Title I, BTU & Sunday Sch Teacher; state bd mem, ESPO; supt, Sunday Sch; pres, First Baptist Usher Bd; organizer, Sunday Sch Prog; Bullock Co Dem Exec Comm. **Honors/Awds:** Bullock City PTA Award; Service Award, ASCAARV; Ala NAACP; Youth Coun & Col; 2 Leadership Awards, Ala Baptist State Conv; Certificate, Personal & Family Survival; Proclamation of Achievement, Gov Guy Hunt 50th Wedding Anniversary March, 1991; Proclamation of Service, 43 Years Bus Driver Bullock Co Pub Sch Gov Hunt, 1991. **Home Addr:** Rt 1 PO Box 170, Midway, AL 36053, **Home Phone:** (205)529-3600.

## THOMAS, DR. WILLIAM

School administrator. **Personal:** Born Jan 1, 1935, Cairo, IL; son of William H and Claudia Mae Campbell; married Majoice Lewis; children: Joyce D, Sharon S, William E, Anjanette & Marcus K. **Educ:** Southern Ill Univ, BS, elem educ & teaching, 1967; Purdue Univ, MS, 1969, PhD, educ leadership & admin, 1972. **Career:** City Gary Schs, head teacher, 1967-70; Purdue Univ, admin asst, 1970-72, David Ross fel, 1972, dir spec acad servcs & asst prof, 1973-75; Woodrow Wilson Found, Martin Luther King Jr fel, 1970-72; DePauw Univ, dir black studies & asst prof, 1972-73; Joliet Area Schs, educ consult, 1973-74; Off Educ Region V, 1974-75; Ind Dept Pub Instr, 1975-77; CIC Midwest Prog Minorities Engr, exec dir, 1975-77; Thomas Distrib, vpres, 1977-79; Cairo Sch Dist, from admin asst to supt, 1979-83; Carbondale Elem Sch, supt, 1983-87; New Orleans Pub Schs, assoc supt, 1987-91; Greenville Pub Schs, supt, 1991-94; Thomas Assocs, pres, 1994-; Philander Smith Col, dean instr, 1995-2000; educ consult, 2000-; Altheimer Unified Sch Dist, chief acad officer, 2002-04, Supt, 2004-06; G4S Justice Serv LLC, prin, 2008-13. **Orgs:** Vpres, secy & treas, Kiwanis Club Cairo, 1979-83; corp dir, Southern Med Ctr, 1980-84; Western Reg chmn, Egyptian Coun Boy Scouts Am, 1983-85; Carbondale Rotary Club, 1984-87; treas, Egyptian Coun Boy Scouts Am, 1985-87; educ consult, Ill State Bd Educ, 1986-87; educ consult, James Nighswander Assocs, 1987-; educ consult, Nat Sch Servs, 1988-; Partnership Educ Steering Comt, 1989. **Home Addr:** 4521 Valley Brook Dr, North Little Rock, AR 72116-7011, **Home Phone:** (501)771-2906.

**THOMAS, WILLIAM, III.** See THOMAS, TRA.

## THOMAS, WILLIAM HARRISON, JR.

Football player, football coach. **Personal:** Born Aug 13, 1968, Amarillo, TX; married Susan; children: Zion, Noah & Jonah. **Educ:** Tex A&M Univ. **Career:** Football player (retired), football coach; Philadelphia Eagles, right linebacker, 1991-98, linebacker, 1999; Oakland Raiders, linebacker, 2000-01; La Salle Univ, vol asst, 2007. **Orgs:** 20/20 Club. **Business Addr:** Volunteer Assistant, La Salle University, 1900 W Olney Ave, Philadelphia, PA 19141, **Business Phone:** (215)951-1398.

## THOMAS, WILLIAM L.

Executive. **Personal:** Born Apr 3, 1938, Cleveland, OH; married Joyce; children: Menelik & Malaka. **Educ:** OH Drug Studies Inst, 1974; Ohio Univ; Univ Madrid; Ghetto Univ; Univ Md. **Career:** City Cleveland, engr inspector, 1968-69; Black Unity House Inc, founder, exec dir. **Orgs:** Exec com, Ohio Black Polit Assembly, 1974; Cleveland Black Polit Assembly, 1974; trustee, Community Action Against Addiction, 1971-75; African Liberation Support Com, 1969-75; Community Coalition Construct, 1971-75. **Home Addr:** 3610 Tullamore Rd, University Heights, OH 44118.

## THOMAS-GRAHAM, PAMELA (PAMELA A THOMAS)

Executive, writer. **Personal:** Born Jun 24, 1963, Detroit, MI; daughter of Albert and Marian; married Lawrence Otis; children: Gordon Julian, Harrison & Lindsey. **Educ:** Harvard-Radcliffe Col, BA, econ; Harvard Bus Sch, MBA, 1988; Harvard Law Sch, JD, 1989. **Career:** Harvard Law Rev, ed; McKinsey & Co, consult, partner, 1989-99; NBC, vpres, 1999-2001, pres, 2001; CNBC, pres & chief exec officer, 2001-05; Liz Claiborne, pres; Clorox, bd dir, currently; New York Opera, Parsons Sch of Design, mem; Indenix, managing dir, currently; Author: A Darker Shade of Crimson, 1998; BlueBlood, 1999; Orange Crushed, 2004; Dunkelrot ist der Tod. **Orgs:** Phi Beta Kappa; bd dir, NY City Opera; bd dir, Am Red Cross Greater NY; bd dir, Girls Inc. **Business Addr:** Chief Executive Officer, Idenix Pharmaceuticals Inc, 60 Hampshire St, Cambridge, MA 02139, **Business Phone:** (617)995-9800.

## THOMAS-RICHARDS, JOSE RODOLFO

Surgeon. **Personal:** Born Jul 28, 1944; married Lynette; children: Jose & Raoul. **Educ:** Andrews Univ, BA, 1966; Kans City Col Osteo Med, DO, 1970. **Career:** Orthop surgeon, self; Martin Luther King Hosp, dir emergency med, chmn, Dept Orthop & Hand Surg, dir rehab med; St Luke's Hosp, Truman Med Ctr-W, resident; Lakeview Orthop & Hand Ctr, orthop surgeon. **Orgs:** Kans City Med Soc, 1973; SW Clin Soc, 1974; Med Sec Cent State ConfSeventh Day Adventists; AMA, 1975; Mo State Med Asn, 1975; Jackson Co Med Soc, 1975; Col Emergency Med, 1975; Nat Asn Advan Colored People, 1975; bd dir, Jackson Co Med Soc, 1977; Mo State Med Asn, 1977; Surg Hand, 1977-78; Golden Heritage Nat Asn Advan Colored People; bd trustee, PUSH; Wyandotte Co Jail & Dept Sheriff Kans City; bd dir, Martin Luther King Hosp; Nat Med Asn; Fla Osteo Med Asn; Am Acad Neurol & Orthopaedic Surg; Am Bd Clin Orthopaedic Surg. **Honors/Awds:** Mead-Johnson Award, 1971. **Home Addr:** 6564 W 49, Mission, KS 66202. **Business Addr:** Orthopaedic Surgeon, Lakeview Orthopaedic & Hand Center, 3750 Emergency Lane Suite 1, Sebring, FL 33870-5500, **Business Phone:** (863)471-1511.

## THOMAS-RICHARDSON, DR. VALERIE JEAN

Consultant. **Personal:** Born Apr 21, 1947, Akron, OH; daughter of Rev Charles Jr and Mary Carson. **Educ:** Akron Sch Piratical Nursing, LPN, 1969; Thomas A Edison Col, BA, soc sci, 1973; Univ Pittsburgh, MSW, 1976; Union Grad Sch, PhD, 1978; Int Apostolic Col Grace & Truth, PhD, christian educ, 1994; Medina Hosp, Cardiopulmonary Tech Training Prog. **Career:** NEOCROSS Inc, interim exec dir, 1978-79; Gilliam Family Serv Ctr, exec dir, 1979-82; Cleveland Adult Tutorial Serv, exec dir, 1983-86; Int Apostolic Col Grace & Truth, Richmond, site coordr, 1994; Georgian Allied Health Educ Serv, assoc dir; Greater Cleveland Tutorial & Training Serv Inc, exec dir, currently. **Orgs:** Zonta Club, 1969; bd mem, agency rep, Ohio Legal Serv Comns Consumer & Housing Task Force Comm Columbus, 1977-78; First aid & personal safety instr, cpr instr, Am Red Cross, 1975-87; former med newsletter ed "Heartbeat" Am Heart Asn Pub, 1976; nat pres appointment exec comm, Fed Coun Aging, Wash DC, 1978-; Am Asn Univ Women, 1984-86; Altrusa Greater Cleveland, 1985-86; bd mem, Greater Cleveland Blood Pressure Coalition, 1985-87; dir, Ohio Entrepreneur Women, 1986-87; hon mem res comn, Am Biog Inst; bd trustee, Int Apostolic Col Grace & Truth, Richmond, 1994; fel Int Bio Asn. **Honors/Awds:** Nat spec cardiovasc tech testing site for credentialing exam admin, 1986; "Off-campus" site for Cuyahoga Community Col's med courses; Silver Medal of Hon, Am Bio Inst. **Business Addr:** Executive Director, The Greater Cleveland Tutorial & Training Services Inc, 16000 Ter Rd Suite 2502, East Cleveland, OH 44112-0676, **Business Phone:** (216)249-2711.

## THOMAS-SAMUEL, KALIN NORMOET

Television producer, television journalist. **Personal:** Born Nov 20, 1961, Baltimore, MD; daughter of Louis N Thomas and Katherine Foote Thomas. **Educ:** Howard Univ, Wash, DC, BA, broadcast jour, 1983. **Career:** Cable News Network, Atlanta, Ga; Cable News Network Travel Now Prog, corresp; Tourism Peace, media producer, currently. **Orgs:** Women Communs, 1980-83, 1990-96; Sigma Delta Chi, Soc Prof Journalists, 1980-83, 1990-93; Alpha Kappa Alpha Sorority Inc, 1981-; Nat Asn Black Journalists, 1983-; vice chair, Atlanta Asn Black Journalists, 1991-93; Int Asn Black Travel Writers; fel N Am Travel Journalists Asn; Travel Professionals Color; Atlanta Press Club. **Honors/Awds:** Media Access Awards, Nat Easter Seals, 1989; Michigan Outdoor Writers Award, Michigan Outdoor Writers Association, 1990; Emory O Jackson Journalism Award, AK Sorority Inc, 1992; Nat Easter Seals EDI Award, 1993; Atlanta Asn Black Journalist Award, Feature Series, 1997; Md Off Tourism Develop Award, 1997. **Home Addr:** 829 Omaha Dr, Norcross, GA 30093. **Business Addr:** Media Producer, Tourism For Peace, 366 Oakland Ave SE, Atlanta, GA 30312-2233, **Business Phone:** (404)222-9595.

## THOMAS-WILLIAMS, ELAINE

Executive director. **Educ:** Fisk Univ, BA, educ. **Career:** Univ Hartford, Bus Advisor, 2008-. **Orgs:** Exec dir, Conn Minority Develop Ctr, 1990-93; Conn Minority Supplier Develop Coun, exec dir, 1993-2001; State Conn, Statewide Youth Entrepreneuship Coordr, 2001-06; Nat Found Teaching Entrepreneurship; New Haven Bd Educ, Youth Entrepreneuership Coordr, 2003-11. **Business Addr:** Business Adviser, University of Hartford, 200 Bloomfield Ave, West Hartford, CT 06117, **Business Phone:** (860)768-4100.

## THOMAS-WILLIAMS, GLORIA M.

Administrator, executive director. **Personal:** Born Jul 5, 1938, New York, NY; married Evrard; children: Michelle. **Educ:** NY Univ, Brooklyn Col. **Career:** Gloria Thomas Modeling Sch, prop; Schaefer Brewing Co, mgr pub rels; WCBS-TV, dir community affairs; Network Serv Inc, chief exec officer. **Orgs:** Prof Commentator; Mistress Ceremonies. **Honors/Awds:** Outstanding Achievement Award, Bottle & Cork Sales, 1970; Best Fashion Commentator, Cabaret Prods, 1971; Woman of the Year, 1972; Awards, Black Found Educ Sickle Cell, 1973; Community Service Award, 1973; Police File Commendation, 1974; Outstanding Performance of Community Service Strivers Award, The Guardians Asn, 1976; Community Service Award, Mt Calvary Methodist Church, 1976; Alma John Community Service Award, 1984; Cert ofAppreciation, Nat United Licensees Beverage Asn Inc, 1972; Certificate of Commendation, Nat Asn Visually Handicapped, 1979; Good Sportsmanship & Outstanding Service, WCBS-TV; Award of Merit, WCBS-TV, 1982; Mothers of Freedom Reward, 1984; Dr. Leo B. Marsh Memorial Award. **Home Addr:** 5900 Arlington Ave, Riverdale, NY 10471.

## THOMAS-WILLIAMS, JOVITA

Vice president (organization). **Personal:** Born Detroit, MI. **Educ:** Tuskegee Inst, BS; Cornell Univ, MBA & MILR. **Career:** Ford Motor Co, Supvr, Training/Supvr & Labor Rels, 1987-90; Allied Signal Automotive, dir corp human resource, 1996-97; Jovita Thomas-Williams Affil LLC, pres; Pepsi-Colas Mich Bus Unit, dir human resource, 1990-95; Textron Automotive Co, Textron Trim Div & Resources-Shared Servs, vpres human resources, 1998-2001; MGM Resorts Int, Corp HR vpres, 2002-07; MGM Grand Detroit Casino, vpres human resource, 2003-; C&S Wholesale Grocers, sr vpres human resource, 2008-09; Fed-Mogul Corp, dir, human resource, 2012-13; JTW Affil LLC, pres, 2007-14; Univ Toledo, vpres & chief human resources officer, 2014-. **Orgs:** Bd dir, chair nominating & governance comt, Pact, An Adoption Alliance, 2011-14. **Home Addr:** , Detroit, MI 48242. **Business Addr:** Vice President, Chief Human Resources Officer, The University of Toledo, 2801 W Bancroft St, Toledo, OH 43606, **Business Phone:** (800)586-5336.

## THOMASON, MARSHA

Actor. **Personal:** Born Jan 19, 1976; daughter of Peter and Phyllis; married Craig Sykes; children: Tallulah Anais. **Educ:** Manchester Metrop Univ, BA, Eng. **Career:** Oldham Theatre Workshop, actor, 1988; Plays: Our Day Out; Peace; BBC, "The8:15 from Manchester", 1990; BBC, "Pie in the Sky", 1994; TV Series: "Prime Suspect 5: Errors of Judgment", 1996; "Brazen Hussies", 1996; "Playing the Field", 1998; "Love in the 21st Century", 1999; "Table 12", 2001; Swallow, 2001; Burn It, 2003; Las Vegas", 2003-05; Cane, 2007; Messiah: The Rapture, 2008; "Lost", 2007-08; "Make It or Break It", 2009; "Easy Money", 2008-09; "General Hospital", 2009; "Make It or Break It", 2009-10; "White Collar", 2009-14; "2 Broke Girls", 2011; "Men at Work", 2014. Films: Black Knight, 2001; Long Time Dead, 2002; Pure, 2002; The Haunted Mansion, 2003; My Baby's Daddy, 2004; The Nickel C, 2005; The Package, 2006; Caffeine, 2006; The Fast One, 2006; The Tripper, 2006; Tug of War, 2006; LA Blues, 2007; Into the Blues 2-Reef, 2009. **Honors/Awds:** BFM Award, 2002. **Business Addr:** Actress, c/o Melanie Greene Management, 425 N Robertson Blvd, Los Angeles, CA 90048, **Business Phone:** (310)858-3200.

## THOMASON, WILLIAM, III

Entrepreneur. **Career:** Griffon Capital Mgt, vpres & portfolio mgr, 1992-95; Parnassus Investments, dir portfolio mgt, 1995-99; JP Morgan Bay Area Equity Fund, consult; Thomason Capital Mgt LLC, pres, chief investment officer & managing partner, 2000-; Taurum Capital Partners LLC, founder, chief investment officer & managing partner. **Orgs:** Bd mem & chair audit comt, Mitchell Kapor Found; Nat Asn Securities Profs; founder, Wall St W Financial Literacy Fund; founder & instr, Wall St Wizards; bd advisors, Urban Econ. **Special Achievements:** One of the Nations Fifty Leaders of the Future, Ebony Magazine; Author of Make Money Work for You - Money Lessons from a Portfolio Manager, 2005. **Business Addr:** President, Chief Investment Officer, Thomason Capital Management LLC, 300 Frank H Ogawa Plz Suite 210, Oakland, CA 94612, **Business Phone:** (510)763-7300.

## THOMPSON, AARON A.

Mayor, government official, technician. **Personal:** Born Jul 23, 1930, Philadelphia, PA; son of Alonzo A and Helen M Montier Blythe; children: Aaron G, Brion R, Shelley L, Lillian E, Marsha L & Eugene. **Career:** Bell Tel Penn, syst technician, 1986; City Camden, councilman, 1989-90, mayor, 1990-93. **Orgs:** Chmn, City Camden Parking Authority, 1988-89; bd mem, Cooper's Ferry Develop Asn; life mem, Tel Pioneers; Camden Co Nat Asn Advan Colored People; pres, Parkside Little League; pres, Parkside PTA. **Special Achievements:** Second Black mayor of City Camden. **Home Addr:** 2406 Denfield St, Camden, NJ 08104-2620, **Home Phone:** (609)365-7133.

**THOMPSON, AHMIR KHALIB.** See QUESTLOVE.

## THOMPSON, ALBERT N.

Chief executive officer, president (organization). **Career:** Vending Mach, owner, 1965; Pabst Blue Ribbon, wholesaler, 1975; Falstaff, wholesaler, 1975; Abelsons, retail beverage outlet owner; Pabst Blue Ribbon Prod, New York, master wholesaler; Pabst Brewing Co, New York Opers, dir, currently; Housing Authority Police Force, lt; Off Dist Atty, Invests Div, lt; Consol Beverage Corp, chief exec officer & pres, currently. **Orgs:** Founder, Bernice Riley Thompson Scholar Fund, 1985; Urban Resource Inst; Culinary Inst Am; Regional Plan Asn; New York City Partnership; New York Urban League; Harlem Dowling Soc; Serv Acad Review Bd Comn; ToysTots; Marine Corps Jr Cadets Scholar. **Home Addr:** 255 W 138th St, New York, NY 10030-2102, **Home Phone:** (212)862-6333. **Business Addr:** Chief Executive Officer, President, Consolidated Beverage Corp, 235 W 154th St, New York, NY 10039-1725, **Business Phone:** (212)926-5865.

## THOMPSON, ALICIA RACHELLE

Basketball player. **Personal:** Born Jun 30, 1976, Big Lake, TX. **Educ:** Tex Tech, attended 1998. **Career:** Basketball player (retired), basketball player coach; New York Liberty, forward, 1998; Ind Fever, forward, 2000-02; NWBL, 2002; Seattle Storm, forward, 2004-05; Wylie E Girls Varsity players, coach; Wylie E High Sch, head coach, 2012-. **Orgs:** Children's Miracle Network; ambassador, StorminSound off-season Community Prog. **Home Addr:** , Dallas, TX. **Business Addr:** Head Coach, Wylie East High School, 3000 Wylie E Dr, Wylie, TX 75098, **Business Phone:** (972)429-3150.

## THOMPSON, ANITA FAVORS

Government official. **Personal:** Born Feb 8, 1951, Kansas City, KS; daughter of Abraham and Barbara Franklin Neal; married Larry; children: Jocelyn, Wayman Jr & Ahmad Khalil. **Educ:** Pk Col, Parkville, MO, BA, 1977; Cent Mich Univ, MA, pub admin, 1981. **Career:** Area Agency Aging, Kans City, KS, exec dir, 1973-82; City Kans City, asst city adminr, 1982-83; Kans Comn Civil Rights by Kans Gov John Carlin, 1982-1985; Kans State Dept Soc & Rehab Serv, Adult Serv, comnr, 1983, govt accountability, People Comn by late Fla Gov Lawton Chiles, 1992-94; City Tallahassee, dep city mgr, 1990-95, sr asst city mgr, 1995-97, city mgr, 1997-; Kans City, Kans, asst to finance comnr; co-chair, Tallahassee Heart Walk, 2007. **Orgs:** Nat Asn Advan Colored People; NFBPA; ASPA; Tallahassee Urban League; Alpha Kappa Alpha; ICMA; Nat Women Achievement Inc; PTI; NAPA; Tallahassee Chap Links Inc; ICMA; bd mem, Leon County Tallahassee

Econ Develop Coun; bd dir, Int City County Mgt Asn, 1991-93; vpres & mem, Fla City County Mgt Asn; bd mem, 2008 regional chair, United Way serv; mem Alumnae chap, Alpha Kappa Alpha Sorority Inc; Bethel AME Church; bd dir, Pub Technol Inc; bd mem, vol, Tallahassee Habitat Humanity; nat bd dir, nat pres, Nat Forum Black Pub Adminr. **Honors/Awds:** Presidential Scholar, Park Col, 1977; Black Woman of Distinction, YWCA, Yates Branch, 1982; In Service to Kansas City Award, Panhellenic Coun, Kans City, 1983. **Special Achievements:** First African Am & first woman to become city manager in Tallahassee, FL. **Home Addr:** 7056 Standing Pines Lane, Tallahassee, FL 32312-9668, **Home Phone:** (850)668-9742. **Business Addr:** City Manager, City of Tallahassee, City Hall 300 S Adams St, Tallahassee, FL 32301-1731, **Business Phone:** (850)891-8576.

### THOMPSON, HON. ANNE ELISE
Lawyer, association executive, judge. **Personal:** Born Jul 8, 1934, Philadelphia, PA; daughter of Leroy Henry and Mary Elise Jackson Jenkins; married William H; children: William H Jr & Sharon A. **Educ:** Howard Univ, BA, 1955; Temple Univ, MA, 1957; Howard Univ Sch Law, LLB, 1964. **Career:** Off Solicitor US Labor Dept Chicago, staff atty, 1964-65; Legal Aid Soc Mercer Co, staff atty, 1966-67; Trenton, asst dep pub defender, 1967-70; Twp Lawrence, munic prosecutor, 1970-72; Dem Nat Conv, McGovern deleg, 1972; City Trenton, muni ct judge, 1972-75; Mercer Co Trenton NJ, prosecutor, 1975-79; US Dist Ct, NJ, fed judge, 1979, chief judge, 1994-2001, sr dist judge, 2001-. **Orgs:** Am Bar Asn; NJ St Bar Asn; Fed Bar asn; Mercer County Bar Asn; Comt Munic Cts, 1972-75; deleg, Dem Nat Conv, 1972; vice chmn, Mercer County Criminal Justice Planning Comt, 1972; NJ Supreme Ct, 1975-79; v pres, NJ County Prosecutors Asn, 1978-79; chmn juv justice comt, Nat Dist Atts Asn, 1978-79. **Honors/Awds:** Asn Black Women Lawyers Award, 1976; Distinguished Service Award, Nat Dist Atty Asn, 1979; Outstanding Leadership Award, NJ Co Prosecutors Asn, 1980; Gene Carte Memorial Award, Am Criminal Justice Asn, 1980; John Mercer Langston Outstanding Alumnus Award, Howard Univ Law Sch, 1981. **Special Achievements:** Notes ed, Howard Law Rev; first Woman & African-American Co prosecutor in NJ; First African-American to be appointed a judge of the US Dist Ct for the Dist NJ. **Home Addr:** 35 Foxcroft Dr, Princeton, NJ 08540, **Home Phone:** (609)921-2375. **Business Addr:** Senior District Judge, United States District Court, Clarkson S Fisher Fed Bldg, Trenton, NJ 08608, **Business Phone:** (609)989-2065.

### THOMPSON, ANTHONY
Entrepreneur. **Personal:** married Kim; children: Kristin & Michael. **Educ:** Univ Kans, BS, engineering, 1983; Webster Univ, MBA, finance, 1988; Wash Univ, St Louis, MS, construct mgt, 1999. **Career:** Monsanto Chem Co, mech engr; Anheuser-Busch Co Inc, proj engr, 1985-93; Kwame Bldg Group Inc, pres & chief exec officer, 1991-, chmn. **Orgs:** Construct Mgt Asn of Am; Int Facil Mgt Asn; Asn of Gen Contractors; Nat Socs of Archit Engrs; St Louis Coun of Construct Consumers; Socs of Am Value Engrs; Airport Consults Coun; Nat Asn of Minority Contractors; bd, Barnes-Jewish Hosp; bd, Gateway Classic Found; bd, United Way; bd, Annie Malone C's Home; bd, Black Leadership Roundtable; bd, Regional Bus Coun; bd, Wyman Ctr; bd, Family Support Network; bd, FOCUS, St Louis; bd, Regional Com Growth Asn; bd, William L. Clay Scholar Fund; mem adv bd, Sch of Archit & Sch of Archit Engineering, Univ Kans; mem adv bd, Sch of Bus, Webster Univ. **Honors/Awds:** Business of the Year Award, Mayor Francis Slay, 2002; Entrepreneur of the Year Award, St Louis Am Salute to Excellence, 2002; Spirit of St. Louis Award, Mayor Francis Slay, 2003; Distinguished Alumni Award, Webster Univ, 2003; Distinguished Alumni Award, Wash Univ, 2004; MBE of the Year Award, St Louis Coun Construct Consumers, 2004. **Home Addr:** . **Business Addr:** President, Chief Executive Officer, KWAME Building Group Inc, 1204 Wash Ave Suite 200, St Louis, MO 63103, **Business Phone:** (314)862-5344.

### THOMPSON, ART
Journalist. **Personal:** Born May 29, 1955, San Francisco, CA; son of Arthur Jr and Ocie Mae Matson; children: Arthur IV & Ania Rashida. **Educ:** W Los Angeles Col, Culver City, CA, AA, gen studies, 1975; Calif State Univ, Chicago, CA, BA, info & commun, 1978; Valley Electronics Sch, Van Nuys, CA, first class broadcasters lic, 1980; Univ Ariz, Inst J Educ, Tucson, AZ, 1982; Calif State Univ, Dominguez Hills, attended 2011. **Career:** Wave Newspapers, Los Angeles, Calif, sports ed, 1978-81; Modesto Bee, Modesto, Calif, sportswriter, 1981-84; St Louis Post-Dispatch, St Louis, Mo, sportswriter, 1984-88; Orange Co Regist, Santa Ana, Calif, sportswriter, 1988-2009; Nat Prep Power Long Beach Poly, asst girls basketball coach; UCLA, beat writer; Self Employed, freelance writer, 2009-; Compton Unified Sch Dist, 2011-. **Orgs:** Comt mem, Los Angeles Chap, Jack Yates Sr High Alumni; Baseball Writers Am Asn; Nat Asn Black Journalists; Pro Football Writers Am; Southern Calif Asn Black Journalists; US Basketball Writers Asn; Football Writers Asn Am; nat secy, w coast corresp, NABJ Sports Task Force. **Honors/Awds:** Excellence Award, Greater St Louis Asn Black Journalists, 1988; Writing Award in News, Asn Press Sports Eds, 1990, 1992-; Writing Award, Asn Pub Serv Excellence, 1992; Orion Hall of Fame, 2008. **Special Achievements:** Only African American staff writer in the Sports; Award-winning sports writer. **Home Addr:** 4146 E Mendez St, Long Beach, CA 90815. **Business Addr:** CA.

### THOMPSON, DR. BEATRICE R.
Psychologist. **Personal:** Born May 5, 1934, Townville, SC; daughter of Elliott Rice and Canary Rice; married Harry S; children: Randy, Stephen & Darryl A. **Educ:** SC State Univ, BA; Atlanta Univ, MA, Eng, 1973; Univ GA, PhD, 1978. **Career:** Anderson, SC, High Sch Eng teacher, 1954-65, High Sch guid counr, 1967-71, sch psychologist, 1972; Tri-Co Tech Col, psychol instr, 1972-74; Westside Community Ctr, exec dir, 2006-; City Anderson, coun mem. **Orgs:** Anderson United Way Bd; SC Nat Bank Bd; Crippled C Bd; Family Coun Bd; SC Dem Nat Com Woman, 1980; APGA; SCPGA; SC Pupil Personal Asn; SC Asn Sch Psychologists; NEA; Nat Coun Excep C; Nat Asn Black Psychologists; sec, Human Rels Coun; den mother; vol Cancer Soc; chmn, Sch Dist Five, Counr Orgn; SC Pers & Guid Asn; pres, Zonta Int Bus & Prof Womens Club; Delta Sigma Theta Sor; Phi Kappa Phi Hon Soc; Phi Delta Kappa Hon Soc; sec-treas, SC AMEG; sec-treas, Anderson Family Coun Ctr; pres, SC Munic Asn, 1987-88; bd dir, Good Neighbor Cupboard; bd dir, Wachovia. **Honors/Awds:** NDEA Guid & Counseling Fel; Gen Elec Guid Fel; South Carolina Headstart Association Award; The Omega Fraternity Citizen of the Year; South Carolina Party Service Award; The Beatrice Thompson Municipal Park. **Special Achievements:** First African-American elected to the Anderson City Council. **Home Addr:** 1111 Southwood St, Anderson, SC 29625, **Home Phone:** (864)224-1990. **Business Addr:** Executive Director, Westside Community Center, 1100 W Franklin St, Anderson, SC 29622, **Business Phone:** (864)260-1093.

### THOMPSON, BENJAMIN FRANKLIN
Administrator. **Personal:** Born Aug 29, 1947, Philadelphia, PA; married JoAnne Snow; children: Kaif. **Educ:** Boston State Col, attended 1974; Cambridge Col, MEd, 1979; Kennedy Sch Govt Harvard Univ, MPA, 1982. **Career:** MA Halfway Houses Inc, prog dir, 1975-78; MA Dept Corrections, dir prog, 1978-80; MA Dept Soc Servs, area dir, 1980-82; Dept Soc Servs, consult, 1983-84; Suffolk Cty Penal Dept, comnr, 1984-; City Boston, sr policy adv equal & humans rights, dep mayor, 1984; Zurriyat Transp Inc, co-owner & pres, 1991-2001. **Orgs:** Intl Halfway Houses Inc, 1976-84, Am Correctional Assoc, 1977-84; chmn Mayors Coordr Coun drug Abuse, 1984-85; candidate Boston Cty Coun, 1984; exec dir, Boston/STRIVE, currently; exec dir, Boston Univ, Criminal Justice Policy Coalition, currently. **Home Addr:** 11 Tremlett, Dorchester, MA 02124. **Business Addr:** Executive Director, Boston University, 143 Bay State Rd, Boston, MA 02215, **Business Phone:** (617)358-5930.

### THOMPSON, BENNIE
Football coach, football player. **Personal:** Born Feb 10, 1963, New Orleans, LA. **Educ:** Grambling State Univ. **Career:** Football player (retired), coach; Winnipeg Blue Bombers, Can Football League, 1986-88; New Orleans Saints, defensive back, 1989, 1991, defensive back, 1990; Kans City Chiefs, 1992-93; Cleveland Browns, 1994-95; Baltimore Ravens, 1996-99, sec coach. **Honors/Awds:** CFL All-Star, 1988; Pro Bowls, 1991, 1998; Ed Block Courage Award, 1995; Unsung Hero Award, Playoff Corp, 1996; Super Bowl Champion XXXV as coach.

### THOMPSON, BENNIE G.
Government official, mayor, politician. **Personal:** Born Jan 28, 1948, Bolton, MS; married London Johnson; children: BendaLonne. **Educ:** Tougaloo Col, BA, 1968; Jackson State Univ, MS, 1972. **Career:** Meadville, Miss, teacher, 1968-70; Town Bolton, alderman, 1968-72, mayor, 1973-80; Tri-Co Community Ctr, proj dir, 1970-74; Hinds Co, supvr, 1980-93; US House Reps, Miss Second Dist, dem congressman, 1993-. **Orgs:** Asst dir, Teacher Corps, 1974-; chmn, bd, Farish St YMCA; Mt Beulah Develop Found; vchmn, bd, Delta & Ministry; bd dir, S Regional Coun; Am Civil Libs Union; Asbury United Methodist Church; Kappa Alpha Psi Fraternity; chmn, U.S. House Comt Homeland Security, 2005; pres, Miss Asn Black Mayors; pres, state Asn Black Supervisors, 1980-93; pres, Nat Coun Health Planning & Develop; Stud Nonviolent Coord Comt; dem, Miss Cong Deleg; Nat Ctr Minority Health & Health Care Disparities; Agr, Budget & Small Bus Comts. **Honors/Awds:** Outstanding Young Men of Miss Award, NAACP; Outstanding Personalities of South, 1971; Politician of the Year, Jackson State Col, 1973; 'Alumnus of the Year Award', Utica Jr Col, 1974; ranking mem, Homeland Security Comn, 2005. **Special Achievements:** The longest-serving African-American elected official in the state of Mississippi; The first African American to chair the Homeland Security Committee in the House. **Home Addr:** PO Box 146, Bolton, MS 39041. **Business Addr:** Democratic Congressman, Mississippi Second District, 107 W Madison St, Bolton, MS 39041, **Business Phone:** (601)866-9003.

### THOMPSON, BETTE MAE
Librarian. **Personal:** Born Nov 12, 1939, Washington, DC; daughter of Louis Merritt and Dorothy Louise Hunter; married Jerry Ward O. **Educ:** Antioch Col, Yellow Springs, OH, BA, 1962; Univ Mich, Ann Arbor, Mich, AMLS, 1968. **Career:** Librarian (retired); Perry Nursery Sch, Ann Arbor, Mich, teacher, 1962-67; Detroit Pub Libr, Detroit, Mich, c's librn, 1969; Ann Arbor Dist Libr, Ann Arbor, Mich, ref libr, 1970-2004. **Orgs:** Am Libr Asn; Black Caucus Am Libr Asn; Pub Libr Asn; Mich Libr Asn; Asn African Am Librarians Mich. **Honors/Awds:** Beta Phi Mu. **Home Addr:** 648 Cloverdale St, Ann Arbor, MI 48105-1113, **Home Phone:** (734)662-9682.

### THOMPSON, REP. BETTY LOU
Government official, association executive, executive. **Personal:** Born Dec 3, 1939, Helm, MS; daughter of William Sam Bolden and Lubirtha Lacy; married Jack; children: Anthony, Tyrone, Sonja & Kwame. **Educ:** Harris Teachers Col, BA, 1962; Hubbard Bus Col, cert, 1965; Wash Univ, cert, 1972. **Career:** Human Develop Corp, area coordr, 1964-90; Daniel Boone PTO Univ City, pres, 1977-78; Women Munic Govt, past pres, 1983-84; St Louis Co Govt, spec asst, 1991-97; St Louis County, dist 72 rep, 1997-; MLK Mo Support Group, pres; K&M Delivery Serv, owner, currently; Kwame Found Inc, dir, currently; Univ City Coun. **Orgs:** Pres, Black Women Unity, 1975-79; Camp Fire Girls, 1982; pres, Dr MLK, 1988-89; Nat Asn Advan Colored People; Nat League Cities; Nat Asn Media Women; Better Family Life; pres, Dr Martin Luther King Jr St Louis Support Group; Banks & Fin Inst; vice chair, Tourism, Recreation & Cult Affairs appropriations social serv comm & econ develop; Dr Martin Luther King Jr Comn. **Honors/Awds:** Community Service Award, Zeta Phi Beta Sorority, 1973; George Washington Carver Award, 1977; Employee of the Year, Human Develop Corp, 1978; Martin Luther King Leadership Award, 1985 & 1999; Best Speaker of the Year Award, 1986-87; Dr MLK Award, 1987-88; Employee of the Year Award, 1989; Gwen Giles Award; Drum Major Peace Award, Clergy Coalition; St Louis Caring Communities Humanitarian Award; Outstanding Legislative Mother of the Year Award; KMOX & Suburban Journal Women of Achievement Award; Ernest & DeVerne Lee Calloway Award. **Special Achievements:** First African American female elected to the City Council of University City; First African American elected to Women in Government - an arm of the prestigious Nations League of Cities; First African American female arrested in Washington, DC for protesting Apartheid in South Africa; First African American to serve on the cabinet of St Louis County Executive, Democrat Buzz Westfall. **Home Addr:** 8315 Seville Ave, St Louis, MO 63132, **Home Phone:** (314)994-0434. **Business Addr:** Director, The Kwame Foundation Inc, 1204 Washington Ave Suite 400, St. Louis, MO 63103, **Business Phone:** (314)754-5619.

### THOMPSON, DR. BETTY TAYLOR
Educator. **Personal:** Born Feb 6, 1943, Houston, TX; daughter of John Charles Taylor and Johnnie Mae Hart Brooks; married Oliver B Jr; children: Amnon James Ashe II & Ida Elizabeth. **Educ:** Fisk Univ, BA, eng, 1979; Atlanta Univ, MLS; Howard Univ, MA, eng, PhD, eng. **Career:** Tex Southern Univ, prof Eng, 1979-2008; Univ Phoenix, Devry Univ, adj prof Eng, 2000-; Univ Md Eastern Shore, Princess Ann, md, 2008-10, fac, staff & adminr. **Orgs:** Pres, Southern Conf African Am Studies Inc; Grace Praise Dance Ministry Wheeler Ave Baptist Church; mem recruiting & retaining adv bd, HBCU. **Business Addr:** Adjunct Professor of English, University of Phoenix, Devry University, 2149 W Dunlap Ave, Phoenix, AZ 85021, **Business Phone:** (602)749-4500.

### THOMPSON, BOBBIE FAY
Nurse. **Personal:** Born Dec 26, 1952, Moddy, TX; daughter of Leonard and Vera Henderson; married Chester Odell; children: Torey Ann Moore. **Career:** Tex Instruments, assembly worker, 1972-79; Am Dist Teleraph, dispatch oper, 1979-80; Leisure Lodge Nursing Home, CNA, 1981-82; Camlu-Care-Ctr, CNA, 1984-94; Heartland, CNA, 1994-97; Manor Care W, Cert Nurses Aide, 1997-02. **Orgs:** Secy, Jeff Hamilton Homemaker Exten Club, 1996-00; vpres, Exclusive Golden Girls Club, 2001-02; pres, Eastside Neighborhood Watch Asn, 2000-02. **Honors/Awds:** Employee of the Month, Leisure Lodge Nursing Home, 1982; Employee of the Month, Camlu Care Center, 1992; Employee of the Month, Heartland, 1995; Humanitarian, Ebony Cultural Society, 2001; Employee of the Month, HCR Manor Care West, 2001. **Home Addr:** 607 S 16th St, Temple, TX 76501, **Home Phone:** (254)773-3506.

### THOMPSON, HON. BOBBY E.
Mayor, executive, association executive. **Personal:** Born Aug 15, 1937, Florence, AL; son of William and Althea Thompson Lovelace; married Vera L Pride; children: Cheryl L & Karen E Thompson-Sprewer. **Career:** Mayor (retired); Uptown Meat Mkt, owner, 1972-75; United Ins Co, agent, 1977-83; City N Chicago, mayor, 1983-97. **Orgs:** Lake Co Econ Develop Comn, Community Action Bd; potentate, Prince Hall Shriners; 33rd Degree Mason, Rufus Mitchell Lodge No 107 Prince Hall; Nat Asn Advan Colored People, 1976-; blue ribbon comt mem, Nat Prince Hall Shriners, 1988. **Honors/Awds:** Distinguished Service Award, We Do Care, 1981; Trend-Setter Award, LeMoyne-Owen Col Alumni Asn, 1989; Top Black Elected Off, Ill Black Elected Off, 1990; Expressway was named as Bobby E. Thompson Expressway. **Special Achievements:** First African-American mayor in Lake County. **Home Addr:** 1915 Dugdale Rd, North Chicago, IL 60064, **Home Phone:** (847)689-4805.

### THOMPSON, REV. CARL EUGENE, SR.
Insurance executive, clergy, real estate executive. **Personal:** Born Aug 9, 1953, Siler City, NC; son of Robert L and Minnie L; married Karen Mechelle McClain; children: Carla Michelle, Karen Nicole & Carl E Jr. **Educ:** NC Cent Univ, BA, philos, 1976; Univ Mass, Amherst, MA reg planning, 1984, Duke Univ, Divinity Sch, theol, 1992. **Career:** Pittsboro Police Dept, patrolman, 1976-78; Home Security Life Ins Co, sales rep, 1978-80; N State Legal Servs, legal asst, 1980-84; lic realtor, 1982-; Capital Develop Inc, chief exec officer, 1982-; Charlotte Liberty Mutual Ins Co, sales rep, 1984-; Chatham Co, co comnr; Atty Law, legal asst, 1986-92; Monumental Life Ins Co, sales rep, 1986-; Thompson Insu & Realty, owner, 1992-96; Beulah United Church Christ, pastor, 1992-95; Cent Carolina Community Col, life long learning coordr, 1997-99, Gen Educ Develop, basic educ instr, 1999-2006, dir continuing educ, 2006-; Word Life Christian Outreach Ctr, founder & co-pastor, currently. **Orgs:** Bd dir, Capital Health Syst Agency, 1978; bd dir, Joint Orange Chatham Comn Action, 1980; bd dir, Coun Aging Chatham Co, 1983; NC Woodcutters Asn, 1984-; Rural Econ Develop consult, 1984-; consult, Soc Security, 1984-; assoc minister, Wesley Chapel United Church Christ, 1986-; bd trustee, Cent Caroline Tech Col, 1986-; chairs, County Minority Exec Comt; Adult Care & Nursing Homes Comt; Human Rels Comn; Work First Planning Comt; Orange Chatham Leadership Coun; State Criminal Justice Partnership Adv Bd. **Honors/Awds:** Nat Rural Fel, Nat Rural Fellows Inc NY, 1983-84; Distinguished Civic Service Award, 2009. **Special Achievements:** In 1978, Mr. Thompson ran for the Chatham County Board of Commissioners and became the First African-American elected to the board. **Home Addr:** 67 Robert Thompson Rd, Bear Creek, NC 27207-8528, **Home Phone:** (919)837-2407. **Business Addr:** Pastor, Word of Life Christian Outreach Center, PO Box 1068, Liberty, NC 27298, **Business Phone:** (919)837-2407.

### THOMPSON, CAROL BELITA (CAROL THOMPSON COLE)
Government official. **Personal:** Born Aug 5, 1951, Washington, DC. **Educ:** Smith Col, BA, 1973; NY Univ, MPA, 1975. **Career:** Govt Dist Columbia, spec asst housing, 1979-81, dep mayor oper, act dir licenses, inv, 1981-83, dir consumer & reg affairs, 1983-86, mayor's chief staff, 1986-87, dep mayor econ develop, 1987-91; RJR Nabisco Inc, vpres govt & environ affairs; Pres Clinton, spec adv; Brookings Greater Wash Res Ctr, leadership coun mem; Curtex Group, adv; Venture Philanthropy Partners, pres & chief exec officer, currently. **Orgs:** Bd mem, Nat Conf Christians & Jews 1983-; bd mem, Ronald McDonald House, 1985-; bd pres, Asbury Dwellings Home Sr, 1985-; fel Nat Asn Schs Pub Affairs & Admin Urban Admin; co-chairperson, DC Downtown Partnership, 1987-; vpres proj planning, Fed City Coun; Lifetime Trustee, Urban Inst; trustee, Smith Col; bd dir, DC Agenda Support Corp; Trustee, Wesley Theol Sem & Summit Fund; adv bd mem, Sun Trust; Nat Capital Regions; exec dir, DC Inter Agency Task Force; vpres, RJR Nabisco; city adminr, Govt DC; Wash Regional Asn Grantmakers Bd dir; adv bd, Kaiser Permanente Regional; bd Hager Sharp; Fed City Coun; bd trustee, Friendship Pub Charter Sch; Wesley Theol Sem & Summit Fund; vice chair Community Found Nat Capital Region, lifetime trustee, Urban Inst. **Home Addr:** 2032 Belmont Rd Suite 207, Washington, DC 20009, **Home Phone:** (202)232-0232.

**Business Addr:** President, Chief Executive Officer, Venture Philanthropy Partners, 1201 15th St NW, Washington, DC 20005, **Business Phone:** (202)955-8085.

### THOMPSON, DR. CHARLES
Educator. **Personal:** Born Jan 15, 1954, Tachikawa; son of Charles and Eiko; married Tita; children: Danielle, Lara & Charles. **Educ:** NY Univ, BE, 1976; Polytechnic Univ, MSE, 1978; Mass Inst Technol, PhD, 1982. **Career:** Mass Inst Technol, teaching asst, 1978-81; Va Polytech Inst, asst prof, 1982-86; dir, Lab Comput Studies; Univ Mas, Lowell, dir, Lab Adv Comput; assoc prof, 1987-93, prof elec eng, 1993-, assoc dean, 1994-96; Ctr Adv Comput & Telecommunications, co-dir, 1992-; Massachusetts Inst Technol, dir, 2000-. **Orgs:** Acoust Soc Am, fel, 1982-; Am Phys Soc, 1984-; NSBE, advisor, 1987-90, 1992-; Lucent Tech Bell Labs, fel bd, 1991-99; Soc Mfg Eng, sr mem & fac adv, 1996-99; Inst Elec & Electronic Engrs, sr mem, 1996-; AT & TLabs, fel bd, 1996-; SWE, advisor, 1995-97; fac adv, Soc Women Eng, 1995-96; Tau Beta Pi; fel Acoust Soc Am. **Home Addr:** 1 Monza Rd, Nashua, NH 03060, **Home Phone:** (603)595-7307. **Business Addr:** Professor, Director, University of Massachusetts, 1 Univ Ave, Lowell, MA 01854, **Business Phone:** (978)934-3361.

### THOMPSON, DR. CHARLES H.
Business owner, swimmer. **Personal:** Born May 24, 1945, Kimball, WV; son of Herbert and Ardella Richardson; married Harriet Jones; children: Charles Jr, Kellye, Eric & NaShawn. **Educ:** Fisk Univ, BS, 1967; Tenn State Univ, MA, 1968; La State Univ, PhD, 1989. **Career:** Southern Univ, swimming coach, 1968-70; Dillard Univ, swimming coach, 1970-74; Tuskegee Univ, assoc prof, phys educ, 1975, head basketball coach, 1975-88; Charlie Tees Screen Printing, owner, 1982-. **Orgs:** Kappa Alpha Psi, 1966; aquatics dir, YMCA; Am Swmng Coaches Assoc; Am Alliance Health Phys Educ & Rec ARC; aquatics adv, Rec Dept, 1973-74; Nat Assoc Basketball Coaches; pres, SIAC Basketball Coaches Assoc; info dir, SIAC, 1981-85. **Honors/Awds:** First Black Swimming Champion So AAU Coached, 1973; SIAC Coach of the Year, 1979; SIAC Championships, 1979, 1980, 1982. **Home Addr:** 1204 Johnson St, Tuskegee, AL 36088-2324, **Home Phone:** (334)727-6957. **Business Addr:** Owner, The Great Tuskegee Trading Co, 1311 Old Montgomery Rd, Tuskegee, AL 36086, **Business Phone:** (334)724-0308.

### THOMPSON, DR. CLEON FRANKLYN, JR.
School administrator. **Personal:** Born Nov 1, 1931, New York, NY; son of Cleon F Sr and Maggie Eady; married Edwina White; children: Cleondra Jones. **Educ:** NC Cent Univ, BS, biol, 1954, MS, biol, 1956; Duke Univ, PhD, educ admin, 1977. **Career:** UNC-Chapel Hill Med Sch, sr res asst, 1956-60; NC A&T State Univ, asst prof, 1960-61; Tuskegee Univ, asst prof & actg chmn, dept biol, 1961-65; Shaw Univ, vpres acad affairs, 1970, sr vpres, 1971-73; Univ NC, actg vpres, 1975-76, vpres stud serv & spec prog; Shaw Univ, Raleigh, interim vpres instnl advan, currently, prof biol, chmn Div Natural Sci; Winston-Salem State Univ, chancellor emer, 1985-95. **Orgs:** Adv coun NC Comn Col Syst, 1978-81; bd dir, Shakespeare Festival, 1978-81; pres, Leadership Winston-Salem; bd dir, Winston-Salem Bus. **Home Addr:** 631 Banner Ave, Winston-Salem, NC 27107, **Home Phone:** (919)750-2057. **Business Addr:** Interim Vice President for Institutional Advancement, Shaw University, 118 E S St, Raleigh, NC 27601, **Business Phone:** (919)546-8260.

### THOMPSON, CLIFFORD
Editor, college teacher, writer. **Personal:** children: 2. **Educ:** Oberlin Col, BA, 1985. **Career:** Freelance writer/ed, 1995-; H.W. Wilson Co, asst ed, 1993, assoc ed, 1994-96, sr ed, 1997-98, ed chief biographies, 1998-2011; Inst C, Poverty & Homelessness, managing ed, 2012-14; taught writing at Columbia Univ, New York Univ, Queens Col & Gotham Writers. **Honors/Awds:** Autumn House Nonfiction Prize, 2012; Whiting Writers' Award for nonfiction, 2013. **Special Achievements:** Author, "Signifying Nothing", 2009; "Love for Sale and Other Essays", 2013; "Twin of Blackness", 2015. Contributor, The Iowa Review, The Los Angeles Review of Books, The Threepenny Review, Commonweal, Film Quarterly, and Black Issues Book Review. **Business Addr:** Autumn House Press, 5530 Penn Ave, Pittsburgh, PA 15206.

### THOMPSON, DANIEL JOSEPH, JR.
Lawyer. **Educ:** Tuskegee Inst, attended 1948; Brown Univ, BA, 1970; Harvard Law Sch, JD, 1973. **Career:** St Ala, asst atty gen, 1973-74; Auburn Univ, instr, 1974; Long Aldridge Hon Stevens & Summer, Ga, atty, 1974-77; S Cent Bell Tel Co, atty, 1978-79; AT&T Co, Wash, DC, atty, 1979-. **Orgs:** Vpres, Ala Black Lawyers Asn, 1974; Am Bar Asn, 1975-80; bd dir, Atlanta Urban League, 1975-77; exec comt mem, Gate City Bar Asn, 1977; Atlanta Judicial Comn, 1977; Nat Bar Asn; KY State Bar Asn. **Home Addr:** 2150 Wrights Mill Cir, Atlanta, GA 30324. **Business Addr:** Attorney, American Telephone & Telegraph Co, 1120 20th St NW 1000, Washington, DC 20036.

### THOMPSON, DAVID FARROD
Football player. **Personal:** Born Jan 13, 1975, Okmulgee, OK. **Educ:** Okla State Univ, speech commun. **Career:** Football player (retired); St Louis Rams, running back & kick returner, 1997-98; Nat Football League Europe, Amsterdam Admirals, 1999. **Honors/Awds:** Carroll Rosen bloom Memorial Award, St Louis Rams, 1997.

### THOMPSON, DAVID O'NEIL
Executive, basketball player, basketball coach. **Personal:** Born Jul 13, 1954, Shelby, NC; son of Vellie and Ida; married Cathy; children: Erika & Brooke. **Educ:** NC State Univ, BS, sociol, 1975. **Career:** Basketball player (retired), motivational speaker; Denver Nuggets, guard, 1975-82; Seattle Supersonics, guard, 1982-84; Charlotte Hornets, youth progs coordr, 1988. **Orgs:** FCA; X NBA Players Asn; YMCA. **Home Addr:** 445 Courtney Lane Suite A, Matthews, NC 28105.

### THOMPSON, DR. DEBORAH MARIA
Physician. **Personal:** Born May 4, 1958, Philadelphia, PA; daughter of William C and Hazel Logan; married Omer Abadir; children: Adam Omer Abadir, Alia Marie Abadir & Amira A Abadir. **Educ:** Howard Univ, BS, 1980; Howard Univ, Col Med, MD, 1982; Univ Md, Post Grad, 1985. **Career:** Univ Md, residency family pract, 1982-85, chief resident, 1984-85; Community Health Ctr, med dir, 1985-89; Kaiser Permanent Med Group, Wash, DC, physician, 1989-. **Orgs:** Am Acad Family Physicians; Md Acad Family Physicians, 1989-; fel Am Acad Family Physicians. **Honors/Awds:** Alpha Omega Alpha Medical Honor Soc, 1982-; Best Doctor, Prince George's County Gazette, 2013. **Home Addr:** 10741 Willow Oaks Dr, Mitchellville, MD 20721, **Home Phone:** (301)808-9682. **Business Addr:** Physician, Kaiser Permanente Medical Group, 5100 Auth Way, Suitland, MD 20746, **Business Phone:** (301)702-5000.

### THOMPSON, DEHAVEN LESLIE
Television broadcaster, journalist. **Personal:** Born Aug 22, 1939, Philadelphia, PA; married Patricia Marlene Eberhardt; children: Shannon Leslie & Tara Neile. **Educ:** Geneva Col, BA, 1968. **Career:** Beaver Falls News Trib, 1st blk sports reporter, 1959-64, 1st blk asst sports ed, 1964-66; WTAE-TV & WTAE, RADIO AM Pittsburgh, ed-reporter, 1966-70; Black Chronicle TV Show, 1968; WTAE-TV Pittsburgh, producer, assginment ed, 1970-75; WIIC-TV Pittsburgh, news & sports, reporter. **Orgs:** Pittsburgh Press Club; bd mem, Pittsburgh Pastoral Inst; Sigma Delta Chi; Pittsburgh Youth Motivation Task Force; Bob Moose Memorial Fund Comn. **Honors/Awds:** Penn Asso Press Award, Top Sports & News Story Yr, 1973; Golden Quill Award Ser, Handicapped Athletics, 1977; Meritous Serv Award, Penn Hills NAACP, 1977. **Home Addr:** 150 Old Eng Rd, Pittsburgh, PA 15237-1762.

### THOMPSON, DERRICK
Music publisher. **Personal:** Born May 3, 1963, East St. Louis, IL; son of John and Stevonne Gulley. **Educ:** Columbia Univ, BA, 1985. **Career:** EMI Music, dir sales, 1991-92; BMG Music Pub sr dir artist & repertoire, 1993-97, vpres, artist & repertoire, 1998-01, sr vpres, urban music, currently. **Honors/Awds:** Network Journal, 40 under 40 Award, 2000. **Home Addr:** 162 W 56th St, New York, NY 10019. **Business Addr:** Vice President, BMG Music Publishing, 1540 Broadway 28th Fl, New York, NY 10036, **Business Phone:** (212)930-3930.

### THOMPSON, DONALD
President (organization), chief executive officer. **Personal:** Born Mar 30, 1963, Chicago, IL; married Elizabeth. **Educ:** Purdue Univ, BS, elec engineering, 1984. **Career:** Northrop Corp, Rolling Meadows, IL, engr specialist defense systs; McDonald's Corp, restaurant systs engr, 1990-91, proj mgr, 1991-93, dir opers Denver Region, regional vpres San Diego Region, sr vpres, restaurant support officer Midwest Div, pres Midwest Div, pres W Div, exec vpres & innovation orchestration leader; McDonald's USA, exec vpres & chief operating officer, 2005-06, pres, 2006-10; McDonald's Corp, pres & chief operating officer, 2010-12, pres & chief exec officer, 2012-15. **Orgs:** Bd dir, McDonald's Corp; bd dir, Exelon Corp; bd dir, Northwestern Memorial Hosp; bd dir, Purdue Univ; Civic Comt Com Club; Econ Club; dir, World Bus Chicago; Brazier Found; independent dir, Northern Trust Corp, 2015-; dir, Royal Caribbean Cruises Ltd, 2015-; dir, Beyond Meat Inc, 2015-. **Business Addr:** President, Chief Executive Officer, McDonald's Corp, 1 McDonald's Plz, Oak Brook, IL 60523, **Business Phone:** (630)623-3000.

### THOMPSON, DR. EDWIN A.
College president. **Career:** Atlanta Metrop Col, GA, pres, 1974-93, pres emer, currently. **Special Achievements:** First president of AMC in student ctr. **Business Addr:** President Emeritus, Atlanta Metropolitan College, 1630 Metrop Pkwy SW, Atlanta, GA 30310, **Business Phone:** (404)756-4000.

### THOMPSON, EVELYN MARIA
College president. **Educ:** Tenn State Univ, BS, 1983; Ohio State Univ, MS, 1985; Univ Tenn, Knoxville, PhD, 1994. **Career:** State Univ New York, Oneta, instr, 1989-90; Univ Ky, Lexington, asst prof, 1992-97; Tenn State Univ, prog develop specialist, 1999-2003, interim dir Res & Sponsored Progs, 2003-04, dir Res & Sponsored Progs, 2006, assoc vpres Res Admin, 2006-08, interim vpres Res & Sponsored Progs, 2008-09, vpres Res & Sponsored Progs, 2009-11; Capital City Res Consortium, founder; State Univ New York at Oneonta, 2011-15; Coppin State Univ, pres, 2015-. **Orgs:** Cumberland Emerging Technologies Life Sci Ctr, adv bd; mem, Aaas, Nat Coun Univ Res Adminr, Nat Sponsored Progs Administors Alliance, Soc Res Adminr Int, Women Higher Educ Tenn. **Special Achievements:** First female president of Coppin State University National Science Foundation, grant proposal panel reviewer; author of conference papers, Writing Effective Grant Proposals for ARRA Funds, Women in Higher Education in Tennessee, Annual Conference, Nashville, TN (2009), Building Your Career in Higher Education Through Grant Writing, Women in Higher Education in Tennessee, Annual Conference, Nashville, TN (2010), Engaging Historically Black Colleges & Universities and Minority Institutes in Research Collaborations, National Council of University Research Administrators, Region III Spring Conference, Charleston, SC (2011); contributor, Partnerships for Emerging Research Institutions, The National Academies, National Research Council, Washington, D.C. **Business Addr:** Coppin State University, 2500 W North Ave, Baltimore, MD 21216-3698, **Business Phone:** (401)951-3838.

### THOMPSON, FRANCESCA
School administrator, nun, religious leader. **Personal:** Born Apr 29, 1932, Los Angeles, CA; daughter of Edward (deceased) and Evelyn Preer (deceased). **Educ:** Marian Col, BA, 1960; Xavier Univ, MA, educ, 1963; Univ Mich, PhD, speech & drama, 1972. **Career:** Marian Col, Indianapolis IN, Dept Dram & Speech, fac, chmn, 1966-82; Fordham Univ, asst dean, Multicultural Prog, dir, currently, assoc prof african am studies, 1982-. **Orgs:** Fac, Martin Luther King Fels, 1973-; Broadway Tony Bd; Martin Luther King Jr fel; adv bd, Push; Am Acad Theatre Fellows, 1998-. **Honors/Awds:** Key to the City, Clarksdale, Miss, 1978, Cincinatti; Brotherhood Award, Nat Conf Christians & Jews; Jan 12 1981 declared by Mayor of Oakland Calif to be Sister Francesca Thompson Day in appreciation for being "Scholar in Residence" for Oakland Public Sch System; Dr Martin Luther King Human Rights Award Indianapolis Educ Asn; NY State English Council Award Teacher Excellence Drama; Distinguish Alumnus Award Marian Col; Outstanding Teacher of the Year, Fordham Univ, 1986; Pierre Toussaint Award, Outstanding Service to the Black Catholic Community; Koob Award; NCEA Award, Outstanding Educator; Honorary Degrees: LeMoyne Col, Syracuse, NY, St Michael Col, Winooski, Vt, Marian Col, Indianapolis, Ind; Outstanding Alumnus Award, Dept of Theatre, Univ of Mich, Ann Arbor, Mich; American Theatre Asn Col of Distinguished Theatre Fellows; Appreciation for Research; Film Festival, 2001; Honorary Doctorate of Fine Arts, Fordham Univ, 2002. **Special Achievements:** Sagamore of the Wabash Awd, IN gov; Commendation of Achievement, OH IN & TX senators. **Home Addr:** 2511 Wilson Ave, Bronx, NY 10469, **Home Phone:** (718)798-5067. **Business Addr:** Assistant Dean, Director of Multicultural Affairs / Assistant Prof, Fordham University, McGinley Ctr Suite 211, Bronx, NY 10458, **Business Phone:** (718)817-4738.

### THOMPSON, GAIL L.
Manager, consultant, executive. **Personal:** Born Brooklyn, NY. **Educ:** Pratt Inst, BA, archit, 1980; Rutgers Univ, Grad Sch Mgt, MBA, 1988. **Career:** RDC Bedford Stuyvesant, planner, 1978-81; Am Stock Exchange, asst vpres, 1981-90; NJ Performing Arts Ctr, vpres, 1990-99; Performing Arts Ctr Greater Miami, proj dir, 1999-2004; Capital Proj Mgt LLC, consult, 2004-08; Sama Dubai, consult, 2008-09; Sama-ECH LLC, proj dir, 2008-09; AECOM, proj dir & proj mgt, 2009-11; Parsons Int, design dir, 2012; Parsons, sr proj mgr-archit, 2012-, lead Proj Mgr, 2013-14; Parsons Transp Group, Proj Dir, 2014; WSP & Parsons Brinckerhoff, Sr Proj Dir, 2014-15; WSP Group, Sr Proj Dir, 2014-. **Orgs:** Bd chair, Newark Emergency Serv Families Inc, 1993-98; bd mem, ACSF, 2006-08. **Business Addr:** Senior Project Manager - Architecture, Parsons, Doha, **Business Phone:** (974)4405-844.

### THOMPSON, GARLAND LEE
Journalist, college teacher, executive director. **Personal:** Born May 2, 1943, Chester, PA; children: Consuella Alicia & Grace Lynn. **Educ:** Temple Univ, BA, journ, 1975, JD, 1983. **Career:** Bell Tel, PA, switchman, 1963-73; Philadelphia Community Col, instr GED prep course, 1975-76; Philadelphia Inquirer, copy ed, 1975-78, ed writer, 1978-81, reporter, 1981-84; Philadelphia Tribune, exec ed; Sun, ed writer, 1992; Career Commun Group Inc, dir; Univ Baltimore Law Sch, prof; Hampton Univ, prof; US Black Engr & Info Technol & Hisp Eng & Info Technol, ed dir; Crisis, Nat Asn Advan Colored People, ed; Clark Atlanta Univ, co dir. **Orgs:** Joint Comt Minority Editorialists, Broadcast Ed Asn, 1979-81; Nat Asn Black Journalists; Nat Conf Ed Writers, 1979-81; fac ed, Inst Jorrn Ed-Editing Prog Minority Journalists, 1980, 1981, 1985; Pa Bar Asn, 1984-. **Honors/Awds:** Barrister's Award, Temple Univ, 1982; Univ Kans, Freedom Forum Prof-In-Residence, 1992-93. **Special Achievements:** First African-American member, Inquirer Ed Bd, 1978-81; ed of nation's oldest African-American newspaper, Philadelphia Tribune; Put together largest single editorial in the Tribunes history, 100 pages, 1984. **Home Addr:** , Baltimore, MD 21278, **Home Phone:** (301)332-6300.

### THOMPSON, GAYLE ANN-SPENCER
School administrator. **Personal:** Born Aug 17, 1956, Detroit, MI; daughter of Edward Spencer Sr (deceased) and Annie R Spencer (deceased). **Educ:** Marygrove Col, BA, 1979, MA, 1989. **Career:** Marygrove Col, dir residence, 1978-79, coordr stud servs, 1980-91, dir talent search, 1991-94, Marygrove Col, Job Placement & Developer, coordr, 1994-, pres. **Orgs:** Marygrove Alumni Asn, pres, 1990-, mem at large, 1989-90; Midwest Asn Stud Fin Aid ADM, 1992-; Because Christ, tutor, 1992-; Marygrove Col Alumni Asn, pres, 1993-. **Home Addr:** 3307 Whitney, Detroit, MI 48206, **Home Phone:** (313)897-9308. **Business Addr:** Director, Marygrove College, 8425 W McNichols Rd Rm 027, Detroit, MI 48221, **Business Phone:** (313)862-8000.

### THOMPSON, GERALDINE
Educator, nurse, consultant. **Personal:** Born Dunkirk, NY; daughter of George T and Hattie Dickey; married John W Sr; children: John Jr, Brian & Dennis. **Educ:** Jamestown Sch Practical Nursing, 1954; Jamestown Comn Col, attended 1968. **Career:** Jamestown Gen Hosp, staff nurse, 1954-75, psych nursing, 1975-85; Southern Chautauga Co, strategic planning consul, human serv agencies, currently. **Orgs:** Bd dirs, 1972-75, Jamestown YWCA, bd pres, 1990-92; bd dirs, Ebony Task Force, 1984-; vice chair, Selective Serv Bd, 1985-; bd dirs, Chautauqua Co Sch Bds Asn, 1987-90; bd dirs, Jamestown Community Schs Coun, 1988-95; Nat Caucus Black Sch Bd Mems; vpres, Jamestown Dem Women's Club, 1990-92; Jamestown Bd Pub Utilities, 1991-96; Links Inc, Jamestown Chap, 1995-. **Honors/Awds:** Adv Comn Minority Issues New York State Sch Bds Assoc, 1987-90; Jamestown Woman of the Year, 1991; New York State's Governors Award for African American of Distinction, 1993. **Special Achievements:** First Woman Pres Jamestown Sch Bd, 1983-85; First black on Selective Serv Bd. **Home Addr:** 95 Liberty St, Jamestown, NY 14701, **Home Phone:** (716)664-5526.

### THOMPSON, GLENDA M.
Executive, theater manager. **Personal:** Born Jun 20, 1954, Ft. Worth, TX; daughter of Willie E Murray; married Tyron; children: Glenn Murray. **Educ:** Tex Christian Univ, BFA, commun, 1988. **Career:** Wash Conv & Vistors Asn, conv sales exec, 1989-92; Aoni Shoreham Hotel, corp sales exec, 1992-94; Paul Quinn Col, dir alumni affairs, 1994-97; Ft Worth Transp Authority, mkt/community outreach adminr, 1997-2003; Nat Asn Women Construct, dir mkt & pub rels, 2000-03; Gestures Mkt Commun, prin, founder & pres, 2003-; Tex Christian Univ, teacher, 2009-10. **Orgs:** Bd mem, YMCA, E Br, 1996-; Pub Rels Soc Am, 1998-; bd mem, Ft Worth Metrop Black Chamber Comn, 1998-; Am Pub Transp Asn, 1998-; bd mem, Prevent Blindness, 1999-; vpres & secy, Neighborhood Link. **Home Addr:** 7413 Arbor Hill Dr, Ft. Worth, TX 76120, **Home Phone:** (817)496-0723. **Business Addr:** Founder, President, Gestures Marketing Communications, PO Box 8702, Ft. Worth, TX 76124, **Business Phone:** (817)907-5934.

**THOMPSON, GLORIA CRAWFORD**
Lobbyist, government official. **Personal:** Born Aug 12, 1942, Philadelphia, PA. **Educ:** Cheyney State Univ, PA, BS, 1968, real estate, 1973, MS, gov admin, 1990; St Joseph Col, PA, MBA, 1978. **Career:** SmithKline Beckman Corp, adv & sales promo, 1968-72, news rels assoc, 1973-75, pub affairs asn, 1975-87, Pa govt, assoc mgr, 1987-; Opportunities Industrialization Ctr Am, ed, OIC Keynens, 1970-72; Nat Alliance Businessmen, dir, col rels, 1974-76; Ross Assocs, Philadelphia, Pa, corp rels consult, 1989-. **Orgs:** Former nat secy, Nat Asn Mkt Developers; pres, Philadelphia Chap; Pub Affairs Comn PA, Chamber Com; State Govt Comn, Philadelphia Chamber Com; bd dir, Art Matters Inc; vice chmn & bd dir, Cheyney Univ Found, 1988-; adv bd, Mayor's Off Community Serv; Minority Retention Task Force, Hahnemann Hosp Univ. **Honors/Awds:** Marketer of the Year, Nat Asn Mkt Developers, 1974; Pres Gerald Ford, 1975; Recognition, Nat Alliance Businessmen, 1975; Honorable Professor, Prairie View State Univ, 1975; Outstanding Young Women in America, 1979-80; District Award, Dr Charles Drew Awards Comn, 1980. **Home Addr:** 2114 N 50th St, Philadelphia, PA 19131. **Business Addr:** Public Affairs, Pennsylvania Federation of CDCs, 523 E Vernon Rd, Philadelphia, PA 19119, **Business Phone:** (215)848-9843.

**THOMPSON, HERMAN G.**
Lawyer. **Personal:** Born Cincinnati, OH; son of Roscoe and Thelma; married Roberta Brown; children: Collette Hill & Janice Marva. **Educ:** Ludwig Col Music, BME, 1952; Harris Teacher's Col, BA, 1957; Howard Univ, Sch Law, JD, 1968. **Career:** Charlotte, NC, asst dist atty, 1972; Wash, DC, 1975-77; Southern Pines, NC, 1980-; US House Reps Post Off & Civil Serv Comn, atty, 1977-80; Pvt pract, atty. **Orgs:** Atty Com Dept, Off Minority Bus Enterprise, Wash, DC, 1972; pres, Moore County Chap, Nat Asn Advan Colored People, 1985-; chmn, Minority Affairs, Moore County Republican Party, 1985; NC State Bd Transp, 1987-91; NC Asn Community Col Trustees; Nc State Bar Asn. **Honors/Awds:** Freedom & Justice Award, Moore Co NC, Nat Asn Advan Colored People, 1983; Community Service Award, NC Black Lawyers Asn, 1994. **Home Addr:** 510 NW Broad St, PO Box 1181, Southern Pines, NC 28387-4805, **Home Phone:** (910)266-0206. **Business Addr:** Attorney, 225 N Bennett St, Southern Pines, NC 28387-4810, **Business Phone:** (910)692-1115.

**THOMPSON, JEFFREY EARL**
Certified public accountant, executive. **Personal:** Born Apr 13, 1955, Mandeville. **Educ:** Univ DC, BBA, 1980. **Career:** Nat Rifle Asn, asst comptroller, 1978-80; Mitchell Titus & Co, sr acct, 1980-81; Leeny Redcross & Co, mgr, 1981-83; Thompson, Cobb, Bazilio & Assocs, PC, founder, 1983-, chief exec officer & pres, 1998-. **Orgs:** Am Inst Cert Pub Accts, 1978-; Alumni Asn Col Bus & Pub Admin, Univ DC, 1980-; Nat Asn Black Accts, 1980-; chair tax issues sub-comt, DC Chamber Com, 1985-; bd dir, Metrop Wash Airports Authority, 1998; treas, Lincoln Theater Found; finance chair, 100 Black Men Greater Wash; chair budget comt, 100 Black Men Am Inc. **Honors/Awds:** Most Outstanding Accounting Graduate, Univ DC, 1980; Most Outstanding Alumni, Univ DC, 1986; Honorary Doctor of Laws, 1997; National Black College Alumni Hall of Fame, 2004. **Home Addr:** 322 Peabody St NW, Washington, DC 20011, **Home Phone:** (202)545-8646. **Business Addr:** Founder, Chief Executive Officer, Thompson Cobb Bazilio & Associates PC, 1101 15th St NW Suite 400, Washington, DC 20005, **Business Phone:** (202)737-3300.

**THOMPSON, JESSE M.**
Vice president (organization), school administrator. **Personal:** Born Nov 3, 1946, Oxford, MS; son of Irma and Jesse; children: Stacey L & Latoya S Taylor. **Educ:** Mott Community Col, AA, 1968; Eastern Mich Univ, BA, 1970; Univ Mich, MA, educ, 1975; Cent Mich Univ, MS, human resources & labor rels admin, 1980. **Career:** Intake, Assessment & Referral Ctr, exec dir, 1973-88; Detroit Col Bus, mgt instr, 1976-; Mich St Univ, Sch Criminal Justice, staff specialist, 1980-85; CS Mott Community Col, treas, bd trustee, 1980-87, dir human resources, 1990; City Flint, dir personnel & labor rels, 1988-90; JM Thompson & Associates Inc, resident agt; Bunker Hill Community Col, exec vpres & chief financial officer, currently; RH Perry & Assocs, sr consult. **Orgs:** Chmn, Genessee County Criminal Justice Staff Adv, 1981-84; Flint Asn Black Adminr, 1981-84; Paul Harris Fel Rotary Int, 1983-; Gov's Substance Abuse Adv Comn, 1989-91; bd mem, Eastern Asn Col & Univ Bus Officers. **Honors/Awds:** Humanitarian of the Year, Flint Inner-City Lions Club, 1980; Social Worker of the Year, Mich Asn Black Social Workers, 1981. **Home Addr:** 1810 Montclair Ave, Flint, MI 48503. **Business Addr:** Executive Vice President, Chief Financial Officer, Bunker Hill Community College, 250 New Rutherford Ave, Boston, MA 02129-2995, **Business Phone:** (617)228-2000.

**THOMPSON, JOHN, III**
Basketball player, basketball coach. **Personal:** Born Mar 11, 1966, Washington, DC; son of John Jr; married Monica; children: Morgan, John Wallacem & Matthew. **Educ:** Princeton Univ, attended 1988. **Career:** Basketball player (retired), basketball coach; Gonzaga Col High Sch, player, 1984; Princeton Univ, asst coach, 1995-2000, head coach, 2000-04; Georgetown Univ, head coach, 2004-. **Business Addr:** Head Basketball Coach, Georgetown University, Basketball Off 3700 O St NW, Washington, DC 20057, **Business Phone:** (202)687-2374.

**THOMPSON, JOHN R.**
Executive. **Educ:** Mercy Col, BS, bus mgt. **Career:** Goodys Family Clothing Inc, chief info officer, exec vpres merchandise planning & logistics, 1993-95; Liz Claiborne Inc, chief info officer, sr vpres, 1995-2001; BestBuy.com, Supply Chain & Bus Syst, sr vpres, 2001, sr vpres, gen mgr, 2002-12; Gen Elec Co, mkt, finance & oper position, Info Serv Div, mem; HP Compaq, direct sales & ecommerce logistics position; DHL, Customer Logistics Solutions, mgr; Am Bus Develop Support & Prog Mgt Group, mgr; Lee Apparel Co, vpres info syst & dist; Retail Syst Alert Group Inc, survr; Wendy's Int Inc, dir, 2004-; Belk Inc, dir, pres, chief operating officer, independent dir, 2006-; Norfolk Southern Corp, independent dir, 2013-. **Orgs:** Nat Retail Fedn, Info Technol Coun; bd dir, Vol Inter Indust Com Stand; bd dir, Best Buy C Found; Wendys Int Inc; ed bd, Black Retail Action Group Inc; bd dir, Belk Dept Store; trustee, Walker Art Ctr; mem audit comt, Wendy's Int Inc; Cristo Rey Jesuit Sch Network; Urban Ventures Leadership Found; bd dir, Vol Inter-Indust Com Stand; Vikings Coun Boy Scouts Am. **Special Achievements:** Named one of the 75 Most Powerful Blacks in Corporate America by Black Enterprise, 2005. **Home Addr:** 6912 Queen Ave S, Richfield, MN 55423, **Home Phone:** (612)824-3790. **Business Addr:** Director, Belk Inc, 2801 W Tyvola Rd, Charlotte, NC 28217-4525, **Business Phone:** (704)357-1000.

**THOMPSON, JOHN ROBERT, JR.**
Basketball coach, basketball player. **Personal:** Born Sep 2, 1941, Washington, DC; son of Robert Sr and Anna; married Gwendolyn; children: John III, Ronald & Tiffany. **Educ:** Providence Col, BA, econ, 1964, MA, guid & coun, UDC, 1971. **Career:** Basketball player, basketball coach (retired); Boston Celtics, 1964-66; St Anthony's High Sch, Wash, DC, head basketball coach, 1966-72; Georgetown Univ, Wash, DC, head basketball coach, 1972-99; US Olympic Basketball Team, asst basketball coach, 1976, head basketball coach, 1988; Commentator, TNT, Clear Channel Radio & Sports Talk 980, currently. **Orgs:** Past pres, bd dir, Nat Asn Basketball Coaches, 1976-; trustee, Basketball Hall Fame, 1999; Selection comt several int & natcompetitions; Nike, bd dir, 1991-. **Home Addr:** 3767 Jay St NE, Washington, DC 20019. **Business Addr:** Board of Directors, Nike, 1 Bowerman Dr, Beaverton, OR 97005, **Business Phone:** (503)629-3354.

**THOMPSON, JOHN W.**
Chief executive officer, executive, chairperson. **Personal:** Born Apr 24, 1949, Ft. Dix, NJ; son of John H and Eunice; married Sandi; children: John E & Ayanna. **Educ:** Fla A&M Univ, BBA, 1971; Mass Inst Technol, Sloan Sch Mgt, MBA, 1983. **Career:** IBM, sales rep, 1971-75, br off mgr, 1975-79, regional admin asst, regional mkt dir, 1980-84, asst to chief exec officer, 1984, dir mid-westopers, 1990-93, head mkt US opers, 1993, gen mgr personal software prods, 1994-98; IBM Americas, gen mgr, 1997-99; Symantec Corp, chief exec officer, 1999-2009, chmn bd dirs, 1999-2011; Nat Infrastructure Adv Comt, 2002; bd dir, Fortune Brands Inc; UPS, bd dir; Seagate Technol, bd dir; JovianDATA, bd dir; Virtual Instruments, chief exec officer, 2010-. **Orgs:** Bd dir, Northern Pub Serv Co; bd dir, Teach Am; chair, Silicon Valley Blue Ribbon Task Force Aviation Security & Technol; Microsoft; Ill Gov's Human Resource Adv Coun; Nat Infrastructure Adv Comt, 2002-; Financial Crisis Inquiry Comn, 2009. **Business Addr:** Chief Executive Officer, Virtual Instruments, 25 Metro Dr, San Jose, CA 95110, **Business Phone:** (408)579-4000.

**THOMPSON, JOHNNIE**
Government official, army officer. **Personal:** Born Jan 10, 1930, Walterboro, SC; married Thelma; children: Anita, Glen Ronald & Rochelle; married Thelma Clemmons. **Educ:** Palmer Col, AD, pub serv, criminal justice maj, 1976; Rice Bus Col, Charleston, SC. **Career:** Army officer (retired), council member; AUS, 1948-78; Armored Tank Platoon sgt; Army Commendation; CIB; Colleton County Polit Action, pres & founder, 1969; City Walterboro, Teledyne Inc, prod supvr, 1971-83; Big-O Chrysler, new car salesman; City Walterboro, city councilman, coun mem, 1979-2009, mayor pro-tem, 1991-95, dem, currently. **Orgs:** First exalted ruler, Colleton City Elk Lodge, 1975; 32nd Degree Mason; Nat AsnAdvan Colored People; Am Legion; Mt Olive Baptist Church; Tuskegee Airmen Inc; chartermem, TAI, Hiram E Mann, chap; Retired Enlisted Asn; SC Aviation Asn; George Wash Carver Consistory 162; Mystic Shrine Arabian Temple 139; Walterboro-Colleton Airport Commission. **Honors/Awds:** Noble of the Mystic, Shrine Arabion Temple 139; Bronze Level of Professional Sales Chrysler, 1984; Salesman of the Year, Big-O Chrysler Plymouth Dodge; Recognition for COT Service, APA, Beta Kappa Lambda chap, 2001; Humanitarian Award, Walterboro-Colleton Chamber of Comm, 2002. **Home Addr:** 502 Padgett Loop, Walterboro, SC 29488-4148, **Home Phone:** (843)549-2740.

**THOMPSON, DR. JOSEPH EARL, SR.**
School administrator, executive director. **Personal:** Born Columbia, SC; son of Hale B and Margaret Elizabeth Kennedy; married Shirley Williams; children: Shirley Elizabeth, Joseph Earl Jr & Amber Gale. **Educ:** Union Theol Sem, MDiv; NY Univ, MA, MEd, EdD. **Career:** School administrator (retired); Johnson C Smith Uni, Charlotte, NC, dir freshman sophomore studies, 1970-72; Southern Asn Cols & Sch, Atlanta, Ga, assoc exec dir, 1972-84; Talladega Col, Talladega, Ala, acad dean, 1984-88, interim pres, 1988-91; Atlanta Univ Ctr Inc, Woodruff Libr, exec dir. **Orgs:** Life mem, Nat Asn Advan Colored People; Kappa Delta Pi; Nat Asn Col & Univ Chaplains, 1960-72. **Honors/Awds:** Hon DHL, Talladega Col, 1990. **Home Addr:** 3161 Weslock Cir, Decatur, GA 30034, **Home Phone:** (404)242-4723.

**THOMPSON, JOSEPH ISAAC**
Postmaster general. **Personal:** Born Aug 21, 1922, Amelia County, VA; married Mabel K; children: Sina Joann. **Educ:** Va Union Univ, attended 1942. **Career:** US Post Serv, postmaster; Postal Workers Union Wis, pres; Madison, Wis, alderman, 5 yrs. **Orgs:** Grand lect Prince Masonic Lodge; Wis Dept Health & Soc Serv Oral Exam Bd; pres, City Madison Water Comn, 1970-75; Nat Asn Postmasters US. **Honors/Awds:** Sup Accomplish Award, Postal Serv, 1968. **Home Addr:** 419 N Ingersoll St, Madison, WI 53703.

**THOMPSON, KAREN ANN (KAREN ANN THOMPSON-NICKERSON)**
Financial manager. **Personal:** Born Jun 12, 1955, Fairborn, OH; daughter of Jack Long and Marlien Vaughn. **Educ:** Univ Mich, BS, 1977; Ind Univ, MBA, 1984. **Career:** Coopers & Lybrand, auditor, 1977-79; Cummins Engine Co, int collections mgr, 1979-82; Daimler Chrysler Corp, finance mgr; Automation Alley, mgr info security; Leverage Inc, dir community affairs & charitable outreach. **Orgs:** Alexis De Tocqueville, Univ Mich; dir, Am heart Asn Eastern Mich; treas, Port Huron Mus Arts & Sci; dir, Blue Water Area Am Heart Asn. bd dir, Nat Alumni Asn, Univ Dayton, 2001-. **Honors/Awds:** Certified Public Accountant State of IN 1980; Fellowship Consortium for Grad Study in Mgt, 1982-84; Library Certificate, OH Hist Soc. **Home Addr:** 17576 Glenwood Blvd, Lathrup Village, MI 48076-2707, **Home Phone:** (248)559-7255. **Business Addr:** Manager, Information Security, Automation Alley, 2675 Bellingham Dr, Troy, MI 48083-2044, **Business Phone:** (248)457-3205.

**THOMPSON, KEVIN LAMONT**
Basketball player. **Personal:** Born Feb 7, 1971, Winston-Salem, NC. **Educ:** NC State Univ, attended 1993. **Career:** Basketball player (retired); Portland Trail Blazers, 1993-94; Illycaffe Trieste, Italy, 1994-95; Scavolini Pesaro, 1995-97; Besiktas, Turkey, 1997-99; Wash Congressionals, 1999; Viola Reggio Calabria, Italy, 1999-2000; Lineltex Imola, Italy, 2000-01; Oyak Renault, Turkey, 2001-02; Caceres CB, Spain, 2003; Forum Filatelico, Spain, 2003-04; Casademont/Akasvayu Girona, Spain, 2004-06; Polaris World Murcia, Spain, 2006-07; Grupo Begar Leon, Spain, 2007-08; Plus Pujol Lleida, Spain, 2008. **Business Addr:** Professional Basketball Player, Plus Pujol Lleida, Pavello Barris Nord, Lleida25005.

**THOMPSON, DR. LANCELOT C. A, SR. See Obituaries Section.**

**THOMPSON, ESQ. LARRY D.**
Business owner, lawyer. **Personal:** Born Nov 15, 1945, Hannibal, MO; son of Ezra and Ruth Robinson Baker; married Brenda Anne Taggart; children: Larry Jr & Gary. **Educ:** Culver-Stockton Col, Canton, MO, BA, 1967; Mich State Univ, MA, 1969; Univ Mich, Ann Arbor, JD, 1974. **Career:** Ford Motor Co, ind rels rep, 1969-71; Monsanto Corp, staff atty, 1974-77; King & Spalding, assoc, 1977-82, partner, 1986-2001; US Dept Justice, Northern Dist Ga, US atty, 1982-86; Providian Fin Corp, dir; Dept Housing & Develop Investn, independent coun, 1995-98; US Dept Justice, dep atty gen, 2001-03; Pepsico, sr vice-pres govt affairs & gen coun, corp secy, 2004-14; Univ Ga law sch, John A. Sibley Prof Corp & Bus Law, 2011-; Ga State Univ Col Law, prof; Finch McCranie, coun, 2015-. **Orgs:** Am Bar Asn; Gate City Bar Asn; State Bar Ga; Mo Bar Asn; Nat Bar Asn; Ga Community Bicentennial US Const; bd dir, Atlanta Urban League; bd dir, Woodward Acad, Col Park, Ga; chmn, Ga Lawyers Bush, 1988; bd dir, Ga Republican Found, 1989; chmn, Press Nat Security Coord Coun, 2001; Nat Asian Pac Am Bar Asn; trustee, Arch Found, 2005; bd dir, Wash Post Co's; trustee, Franklin, Templeton & Mutual Series; dir, Southern Company; dir, The Brookings Institution; dir, National Center for State Courts; dir, Cbeyond. **Honors/Awds:** District Alumni Award, Culver-Stockton Col, 1983; AT Walden Award, Gate City Bar Asn, 1984; Outstanding Achievement Award, Fed Bar Asn, 1992; sr fel, Brookings Institution, 2004; Edmund Jennings Randolph Award, Dept Justice; Honorary Doctor of Laws degree, Pace Univ, NY; hall of fame, Atlanta Gate City Bar Asn. **Home Addr:** 2015 Wallace Rd, Atlanta, GA 30331, **Home Phone:** (404)349-5297. **Business Addr:** Executive Vice President, General Counsel and Corporate Secretary, PepsiCo, 1 Pepsi Way, Somers, NY 10589, **Business Phone:** (800)433-2652.

**THOMPSON, LASALLE, III**
Basketball player, business owner, basketball coach. **Personal:** Born Jun 23, 1961, Cincinnati, OH; children: Nickolas & Ruby. **Educ:** Univ Tex, Austin, attended 1982. **Career:** Basketball player (retired), basketball coach, bus person; Kans City Kings, 1982-85; Sacramento Kings, 1986-89; Ind Pacers, 1989-95, 1997; Philadelphia 76ers, 1996; Denver Nuggets, 1996-97; San Diego Wildfire, gen mgr & head coach, 2000-01; Charlotte Bobcats, asst coach, 2008-, strength & conditioning coach; Prime Time Motors, co-owner, currently. **Home Addr:** 111 W Main St Suite 2A, Carmel, IN 46032. **Business Addr:** Co-Owner, Prime Time Motors, 2557 Albatross Way, Sacramento, CA 95815, **Business Phone:** (916)929-6651.

**THOMPSON, LINDA JO**
Consultant, manager, business owner. **Personal:** Born Aug 29, 1953, Oklahoma City, OK; daughter of Moses E Paulden Jr (deceased) and Emma Lucille Jones Paulden; married French F Jr; children: Emerald Michelle & French F III. **Educ:** Lincoln Univ, Jefferson City, Mo, BA, 1975; Strayer Col, MS, bus admin. **Career:** Mid-Am TV, Jefferson City, Mo, off mgr, 1978-84; Zeta Phi Beta Sorority Inc, Wash, DC, exec dir, 1984-95, chap mem; LJT & Assocs, Clinton, Md, owner & consult, 1995-. **Orgs:** Nat Coalition Black Meeting Planners; bd mem, Nat Pan Hellenic Coun; bd mem, Black Women's Polit Action Forum; Am Soc Asn Exec, 1989-91; Int Soc Meeting Planners, 1990-91. **Honors/Awds:** Grantsman Training Prog, Grantsmanship Ctr, 1990. **Business Addr:** Consultant, Owner, LJT & Associates Inc, 9601 Hale Dr, Clinton, MD 20735-3324, **Business Phone:** (301)868-2942.

**THOMPSON, DR. LITCHFIELD O.**
Educator, administrator. **Personal:** Born Apr 15, 1937; married Bernadette Pearl Francis; children: Gennet & Hailu. **Educ:** Univ London, BS, sociol, 1969; Univ Ore, Eugene, MA, sociol, 1972, PhD, sociol, 1975. **Career:** Barbados Advocate Barbados WI, advert clerk, 1955-59, advert layout spec, 1959-61; Ford Found fel, 1972-73; WV St Col, prof, sociol, 1974-, Dept Sociol & Phil, chair emer, currently. **Orgs:** Am Sociol Asn; N Cent Sociol Asn; Asn Black Sociologists, WV Sociol Asn; Pac Sociol Asn. **Home Addr:** 326 Scenic Dr, St Albans, WV 25177, **Home Phone:** (304)727-9344. **Business Addr:** Professor, Chair Emeritus, West Virginia State College, PO Box 1000, Institute, WV 25112-1000, **Business Phone:** (800)987-2112.

**THOMPSON, DR. LLOYD EARL**
Physician, otolaryngologist. **Personal:** Born Apr 10, 1934, Kingston; married Mercedee Ball; children: Damon & Arie. **Educ:** Union Col, Lincoln, NE, BA, 1960; Howard Univ, DC, MD, 1964. **Career:** Sinai Samaritan Med Ctr, internship, 1964-65; Homer G Phillips Hosp, resident otolaryngol, 1965-69, supt; Christian Welfare Hosp, chief staff, 1977-79; Wash Univ Med Sch, clin instr; pvt pract physician; Provena St Marys Hosp, consult. **Orgs:** Dipl, Am Bd Otolarynology, 1970, fel, 1972; pres, St Clair Med Soc, 1979; pres, Community Hosp, bd dir, 1979; St Louis Ear Nose & Throat Club, Roman-Barnes Soc Ophthalmol & Otolaryngol; bd mem, So Ill Med Utilization Rev Org. **Home Addr:** 21 S Graeser Rd, St Louis, MO 63141. **Business Addr:** Physician, 129 N 8th St, East St. Louis, IL 62201, **Business Phone:** (618)482-7242.

**THOMPSON, LOWELL DENNIS**
Advertising executive, artist. **Personal:** Born Oct 8, 1947, Chicago, IL; children: Tanya Natasha. **Educ:** Art Inst Chicago, 1966. **Career:** Leo Burnett Co, art dir; J Walter Thompson Co, art dir, prod & creative group head; McLann Erickson Adv, art dir, 1968-71; Young & Rubi cam Adv, art dir, 1971-72; Greenwich Vlg NY, portrait art, 1971; Needham Harper & Steers Adv, art dir & producer, 1972-74; Am Assoc Adv Agencies, teacher, 1974; BBDO Chicago. **Honors/Awds:** Two Awards Rep In Creativity 77 Show, Art Dir Mag; 1st Prize, Lk Meadows Art Fair, 1966; represented in Commun Arts Magazine, 1976; Honorable Mention Adv Club of NY, 1971; numerous Gold Keys & Scholarships in Scholastic Magazine Annual Art Competition; Clio Award. **Special Achievements:** Book: "White Folks", 1996; First African Americans Hired In Advertising When American companies. **Home Addr:** 9722 S Ellis, Chicago, IL 60628. **Business Addr:** Prudential Bldg, Chicago, IL 60601.

**THOMPSON, HON. M. T., JR.**
Judge. **Personal:** Born Apr 15, 1951, Saginaw, MI; son of M T Sr and Pecola Matsey; married Ivory C Triplet; children: Felica L & Monica R. **Educ:** Oakland Univ, BA, 1973; Northeastern Univ Sch Law, JD, 1977. **Career:** MI Supreme Ct, atty, 1977; Mich Bell Tel Co, mgr, 1973-74; Nat Labor Rels Bd, atty, 1977-79; Lewis White & Clay PC, atty, 1979-83; US Sixth Circuit Ct Appeals, atty, 1980; MT Thompson Jr PC, atty, 1983-97; Supreme Ct, atty, 1984; State Mich Dist Ct, 70th District Court, Saginaw, MI, judge, 1997-. **Orgs:** Saginaw County Chamber Com; US Attys Off. **Home Addr:** 2207 Peale Dr, Saginaw, MI 48602, **Home Phone:** (517)790-8033. **Business Addr:** Judge, State of Michigan District Court, 111 S Mich Ave, Saginaw, MI 48602, **Business Phone:** (517)790-5368.

**THOMPSON, MARCUS AURELIUS**
Musician, educator. **Personal:** Born May 4, 1946, South Bronx, NY; son of Hattie Louise Stewart and Wilmore. **Educ:** Juilliard Sch Lincoln Ctr NYC, BM, violin, 1967, MS, violin, 1968, DMA, violin, 1973. **Career:** Recitalist, Carnegie Hall, 1968; Juilliard Sch Lincoln Ctr, viola fac, 1969-70; Oakwood Col, Ala, asst prof music, 1970-71; Wesleyan Univ, Middletown Conn, viola fac, 1971-73; Mt Holyoke Col, S Hadley Mass, lectr, 1971-73; Mass Inst Technol, prof music, 1973-94, Robert R Taylor prof music, 1995-, inst prof, 2015-; Eastman Sch Music, vis prof, 1983-; New Eng Conserv, viola fac, 1983-; NEA Solo Recitalist fel viola soloist, currently; soloist: Nat Symphony, Boston Pops, Czech Nat Symphony Prague, W Coast Premiere Harbison Viola Concerto, Chicago Premiere with Chicago Sinfonietta, Boston Premiere with New Eng Conserv Hons Orchestra; recitalist: Carnegie Hall, Young Concert Artists Ser, Metrop Mus Art New York, Isabella Stewart Gardener Mus Boston, Orchestra Hall Minneapolis, Terr Theater at Kennedy Ctr Wash, D.C, Herbst Theater San Francisco. **Orgs:** Viola dAmore Socs; Am Viola Socs; founder, MIT Chamber Music Socs way; host dir, Am Viola Socs Cong XIII, 1985; Chamber Music Am; Am String Teachers Asn; artistic dir, Boston Chamber Music Soc. **Honors/Awds:** First Prize, Hudson Valley Philharmonic Young Artists Comp, 1967; Winner Young Concert Artist Inc, Auditions NY, 1967; Winner String Prize, Nat Black Colloquim Compet Kennedy Ctr Performing Arts, Wash DC, 1980. **Special Achievements:** First person to hold the Robert P Taylor Professorship at MIT. **Home Addr:** 11 Waverley Ave, Newton, MA 02458-2103, **Home Phone:** (617)969-4311. **Business Addr:** Professor of Music, Massachusetts Institute of Technology, 77 Mass Ave, Cambridge, MA 02139-4307, **Business Phone:** (617)253-1000.

**THOMPSON, DR. MARK K.**
Neurosurgeon. **Personal:** Born Jul 29, 1961, West Islip, NY; son of Charles and Eiko. **Educ:** Harvard Univ, BA, 1983; Tufts Univ Med Sch, MD, 1990. **Career:** Temple Univ Hosp, Surg internship, 1990-91, Temple Univ Hosp Neurosurg resident, 1991-96; Univ Toronto, Med Staff, Neurosurg Spine fel, 1996-97; Brady Traumatic Brain Inst, neurosurg dir, 1997-99; Aitken Neuroscience Ctr, res consult, 1997-99; Jamaica Hosp, attend neurosurgeon, 1997-99; Lincoln Hosp, chief neurosurgeon, 2000-01; Columbia Univ, clin asst prof neurosurg, 2000-01; Kings County Hosp, spine dir, 2000-, chief neurosurgeon, 2000-; State Univ NY Downstate Med Ctr, asst prof, 2000-03, interim neurosurg prog dir, 2000-01, vice chmn, dept neurosurg, 2003; Police Surgeon, New York Police Dept, 2003; New York Methodist Hosp, physician; Brooklyn Univ Hosp, physician; Metrop Hosp Ctr, physician. **Orgs:** Am Asn Neurol Surgeons, 1993-; Cong Neurologic Surgeons, 1993-; Harvard Club NY, 1986-; Cong Neurol Surgeons; Am Col Surgeons; Am Bd Neurol Surg. **Honors/Awds:** Outstanding Young Men of America, US Jaycees, 1984, 1987 & 1998; Ruth Marguerite Easterling Community Service Award, Tufts Med Sch, 1990. **Special Achievements:** Public Health Dept Western Australia, Royal Flying Doctors of Australia, Aboriginal Health Liaison, 1990; Publ: Postenor Cervical Plate Fixation, 1996; Segmental Reconstruction of the Thoracic Spine with Pedicle Screw Fixation: A Safe and Effective Technique, 1996; Isolated Intramedillary Cervical Sarcoidosis: A Case Report and Review of the Literature, 1997; The Effects of Pentoxifylline on Spinal Cord Blood Flow After Experimental Spinal Cord Injury, 1999. **Home Phone:** (212)327-1958. **Business Addr:** Vice-Chairman, SUNY Downstate Medical Center, 400 E 71st St Unit 11E, Brooklyn, NY 10021, **Business Phone:** (718)270-4335.

**THOMPSON, DR. MAVIS SARAH (MAVIS BLAIZE)**
Physician. **Personal:** Born Jun 22, 1927, Newark, NJ; daughter of Nathaniel Albert and Mavis Carolyn; married James Blaize; children: Clayton, Marcia Adele Callender, Sidney, Ronald & Kevin. **Educ:** Hunter Col, NYC, BA, 1947; Howard Univ Med Sch, MD, 1953. **Career:** Physician (retired); Kings County Hosp, internship, 1953-54; Kings Co Hosp, resident internal med, 1954-57; Brooklyn, NY, pvt pract, 1957-76; Lyndon B Johnson Health Complex Inc, med dir, 1970-71, 1974-76; New York Bd Educ, sch med instr, 1962-85; Medgar Evans Col, teacher, dept nursing, 1975-76; Kingsboro Med Group, family physician, 1976-95. **Orgs:** Bd dir, Camp Minisink New York City, 1973-; adv comn, Geront Serv Ad New SchSoc Res, 1983-; bd, Episcopal Health Servs; Am Pub Health Asn, Nat Med Asn, Am Geront Asn; den mother BSA; pres, Black Caucus Health Workers Am Pub Health Asn, 1976-77; lic lay St Georges Episcopal Church, Brooklyn; pres, Nat bar asn; med dir, Neighborhood Health Ctr; bd dirs, Brooklyn Plaza Med Ctr. **Honors/Awds:** Community Service Award, St Mark's United Methodist Church, 1973; past pres, Award Black Caucus of Health Workers, 1977; Alberta T Kline Service Award, Camp Minisink, 1980; lectr med, Care & Geriatrics, 1984-; Bishop's Cross, Episcopal Church, 1990. **Home Addr:** 2600 Netherland Ave, Bronx, NY 10463, **Home Phone:** (718)601-3652.

**THOMPSON, MAVIS T.**
President (organization), lawyer. **Educ:** Univ Mo, BS, nursing, 1979, JD, 1990; Harvard Univ, attended 1995. **Career:** Mo State Pub Defender's trial off, assoc pub defender; St. Louis Metrop Police Dept, hearing officer; Medicaid Fraud Control Unit, asst atty gen; Sandberg, Phoenix PC, Health Law Pract Group, sr assoc atty; Berkeley, Mo, prosecuting atty; Wellston City, atty; 22nd Judicial Ct, St. Louis, Mo, circuit clerk; St. Louis City, lic collector, currently; Law Off Mildred Motley & Mavis Thompson, lawyer, currently. **Orgs:** Women Lawyer's Asn Greater St. Louis; Legal Serv Eastern Mo; pres, Mound City Bar Asn, 1999-2000; Women Lawyer's Asn Greater St. Louis; Legal Serv Eastern Mo; pres, Mound City Bar Asn, 1999-2000; bd trustee, Mt. Herald Missionary Baptist Church; pres, Nat Bar Asn, Wash, DC, 2009; Am Bar Asn; Mound City Bar Asn; Delta Sigma Theta Sorority; bd dir, Legal Serv Eastern Mo; bd dir, Human Develop Corp; Mo Div Employ Security Appeals Tribunal; St. Louis Urban League. **Special Achievements:** First African American female serve City in two different citywide elected offices. **Home Addr:** 3510 Dodier St, St. Louis, MO 63107-2624. **Business Addr:** License Collector, City of St. Louis, City Hall Rm 102-104 1200 Market St, St. Louis, MO 63103, **Business Phone:** (314)622-4528.

**THOMPSON, MILT (MILTON BERNARD THOMPSON)**
Baseball player, athletic coach. **Personal:** Born Jan 5, 1959, Washington, DC; married Rhonda Scott; children: Torri, Jennifer Brooke, Courtney & Alyssa. **Educ:** Howard Univ. **Career:** Baseball player (retired), athletic coach; Atlanta Braves, 1984-85; Philadelphia Phillies, player, 1986-88, 1993-94, coach, 1998-2000, outfield & base running coordr, 2001-02, hitting coach, 2003-10; St Louis Cardinals, outfielder, 1989-92; Houston Astros, 1994-95, coach, outfield/baserunning coordr, 2010-; Los Angeles Dodgers, 1996; Colo Rockies, baseball player, 1996; Devil Rays, outfield & base running coordr, 1997. **Orgs:** Bd mem, Indianapolis Indians Baseball Club; bd dir, Wittenberg's. **Home Addr:** , Washington, NJ. **Business Addr:** Outfield/Baserunning Coordinator, Houston Astros, 501 Crawford St, Houston, TX 77002, **Business Phone:** (713)259-8000.

**THOMPSON, MOZELLE W.**
Federal government official. **Personal:** Born Dec 11, 1954; son of Charles and Eiko Suzaki. **Educ:** Columbia Univ, AB, hist & urban studies, 1976, JD, 1981; Princeton Univ, MPA, pub & int affairs, 1980. **Career:** US Dist Ct, clerk, 1981-82; Skadden Arps, sr assoc, 1982-90; Slate, Meagher & Flom, assoc, 1982-90; Town Babylon, New York, spec coun to supr, 1988-90; New York State Housing Financial Agency, actg exec dir, exec vpres & gen coun, 1990-93; New York State Med Care Facil Financial Agency, actg exec dir, exec vpres & gen coun, 1990-93; New York State Affordable Housing Corp, New York State Munic Bond Bank Agency, New York State Proj Financial Agency, coun, secy, actg exec dir, exec vpres & gen coun, 1990-93; Fordham Univ, Sch Law, adj prof, 1992-93; State New York Mortgage Agency, sr vpres, gen coun, 1993; US Treas Dept, dept asst sec, 1993-96, prin dep asst secy, 1996-97; Fed Trade Comn, comnr, 1997-2004; Am Bar Asn Sect Antitrust Law, sect leadership, 1998-2012; Princeton Univ, vis lectr, 1999; Stanford Law Sch, vis scholar, 2001; Thompson Strategic Consult, chief exceuitve officer, 2005-; Facebook, adv bd, 2006-; Obama Biden Transition Team, team leader, 2007-08; ABA Bus Law Sect, bus law advisor, 2009-12; Am Bar Asn, bus law advisor, 2010-12. **Orgs:** Vice chair, 1998-2001, chair, 2000-, Consumer Policy Community; pres, Int Mkt Supv Network, 1999-2000; Facebook, 2006-; bd dir, Media Access Proj, 2007-12; bd mem, chmn, alumni serv & outreach comt, Columbia Alumni Asn, 2010-; bd dir, Atigeo, 2010-; adv bd mem, Samsung, 2013-; vpres, Columbia Col Alumni Asn; Asn Black Princeton Alumni; exec bd, Practicing Atty Law Studs; Am Bar Asn; Nat Bar Asn; Asn Bar City New York; Columbia Law Sch Alumni Asn; Orgn Econ Develop & Cooper; law clerk, Dist Ct Judge. **Business Addr:** Board Director, Media Access Project, 1625 K St NW, Washington, DC 20006, **Business Phone:** (202)232-4300.

**THOMPSON, HON. MYRON HERBERT**
Judge. **Personal:** Born Jan 7, 1947, Tuskegee, AL; married Ann. **Educ:** Yale Univ, BA, polit sci, 1969; Yale Law Sch, JD, 1972. **Career:** Ala Atty Gen Off, asst atty gen, AL, 1972-74; pvt pract law, 1974-80; Thompson & Faulk, partner, 1979-80; US Dist Ct, Mid Dist Ala, judge, 1980-91, 98, chief judge, 1991-98, sr judge, 2013. **Orgs:** Ala Bar Asn; State Bar Examrs, 1975-79; Am Bar Asn; Nat Bar Asn; Ala Lawyers Asn. **Special Achievements:** First African-American appointed to the US District Court, Mid District, AL; first African-American assistant attorney general of Alabama. **Business Addr:** District Judge, United States District Court, 1 Church St Suite B 100, Montgomery, AL 36101-0711, **Business Phone:** (334)954-3650.

**THOMPSON, PORTIA WILSON**
Government official. **Personal:** Born Oct 23, 1944, Washington, DC; children: Lisa-Marie, Joseph M & Jared M. **Educ:** Howard Univ, BA, 1968. **Career:** Bd Gov Fed Res Syst, res asst, 1968-71, programmer 1971-74, econ syst analyst, 1974-80, asst equal employ opportunity dir, 1980-81, mgr, equal employ opportunity, bd progs, 1982-84, equal employ opportunity progs adv, 1984-. **Orgs:** Consult, Soul Journey Enterprises, 1979-; life mem, Nat Asn Advan Colored People, 1980-; Am Asn Affirmative Action, 1980-; secy, Nat Black Hist Observance Comn, 1982-83; treas, Nat Black Heritage Observance Comt, 1983-; Friends Bethune Mus Arch Inc, 1984-; Nat Asn Banking Affirmative Action Dir, 1985-; Friends Dusable Mus, 1985-; secy, Wash Metro Am Asn Affirmative Action, 1985-; Friends Armistad, 1986. **Home Addr:** 1610-B Beekman Pl NW, Washington, DC 20009, **Home Phone:** (202)332-3465. **Business Addr:** EEO Programs Adviser, Board of Governors, 20th & C Sts Ave NW, Washington, DC 20551, **Business Phone:** (202)452-3693.

**THOMPSON, REGINA**
Nurse, educator, executive director. **Personal:** Born Beckley, WV; daughter of Elder L and Gracie M Allen. **Educ:** Bluefield St Col, WV, BS; Lincoln Sch Nurses, NY, dipl; Columbia Univ, MA. **Career:** Sea View Hosp, Staten Island, NY, clin instr & actg asst educ dir; WalterReed Gen Hosp, Wash, staff nurse & actg head nurse; USPHS Hosp, NY, staff nurse; Wagner Col Sch Nursing, NY, instr & asst prof nursing; Clemson Univ, Col Nursing, SC, asst prof nursing, prof emer nursing. **Orgs:** Nat Asn Black Nurses; Nat Asn Advan Colored People; Nat League Nursing; SC League Nursing; Am Nurses Asn; SC Nurses Asn; charter mem, Gamma Mu Chap Sigma Theta Int Hon Soc Nurses; SC League Nurses; bd dir, Oconee Chap, Am Red Cross; secy, SC Coun Human Rels; organizer, Oconee Co Chap MADD; SC Joint Pract Comn; chair, Publicity & Pub Rels Comt, Oconee Cancer Trust. **Honors/Awds:** New York Regents fel; Citizen of the Day, Local Radio Station; Woman of Achievement, Lambda Chap, Lambda Kappa Mu Sorority; Certificate of Appreciation, Oconne Co United Way Budget Review. **Special Achievements:** Research: E Colleaque, Hypertension, "Blood Pressure Patterns, Knowledge Level and Health Behaviors in Children and Adolescents," presented in Nairobi, Kenya and the University of South Alabama, 1989; Poetry: entries accepted for publication as follows: Great Poems of our times, National Library of Poetry, 1993, Library of Congress; Named an outstanding poet of 1994 by the National Library of Poetry, Library of Congress; Treasured Poems of America, any sparrow grass poetry, Forum Inc, Library of Congress. **Home Addr:** PO Box 565, Walhalla, SC 29691-0563. **Business Addr:** Professor Emerita of Nursing, Clemson University, 714 Strode Tower, Clemson, SC 29631, **Business Phone:** (864)656-3393.

**THOMPSON, RHONDA DENISE**
School administrator, athletic coach. **Personal:** Born Dec 21, 1969, Bartow, FL; daughter of Linda. **Educ:** Fla A&M Univ, BS, broadcast jour, 1992; Savannah State Univ, MPA, pub admin, 2000; Nova Univ, PhD, higher educ leadership, 2007. **Career:** Savannah State Univ, asst track coach, 1995, judicial affairs coordr, 2000-03; Cheyney Univ Penn, head coach, 2004-05, coordr athletic acad advising, 2004-07; Del State Univ, asst dir acad advisement, 2008-10, Col Arts, Humanities & Social Sci, dir acad advisement, 2012-; Univ Tenn, Chattanooga, Acad Support Serv, dir, 2010-11. **Orgs:** USA Track & Field Officials Asn & Coaches Asn, 1998-; Grad Asn Publ Admin, 1999-; adv, Savannah State Univ, Stud Govt Asn, 1999-, judiciary adv, 2000, Southern Asn Cols & Schs Intercol Athletics Steering Comt, 2000; Nat Asn Stud Affairs Profs, 2000. **Honors/Awds:** Junior Woman of Excellence, Savannah State Univ Ctr Coun, 1999. **Special Achievements:** Editor, Savannah State Univ Student Affairs Newsletter, 1999. **Home Addr:** 103 W Quail Forest Ct, Savannah, GA 31419, **Home Phone:** (912)921-7702. **Business Addr:** Director of Academic Support Services, University of Tennessee, 615 McCallie Ave Dept 3503, Chattanooga, TN 37403, **Business Phone:** (423)425-5562.

**THOMPSON, RICHARD ELLIS.** **See Obituaries Section.**

**THOMPSON, DR. ROBERT FARRIS**
Educator, college teacher. **Personal:** Born Dec 30, 1932, El Paso, TX; married Nancy Gaylord; children: Alicia & Clark. **Educ:** Yale Univ, BA, 1955, MA, 1961, PhD, 1965. **Career:** Yale Univ, fac, 1961-; African & Afro-Am Art Hist, prof, 1964-; Ford Found, res grant, 1962-64; Yale ConciliumInt & Area Studies grant, 1965; Univ Calif Mus Ethnic Arts, vis cur, 1970; Nat Gallery Art, vis cur, 1974; Nat Inst Med & Sci, 1975; Nat Inst MusZaire grant, 1976; Nat Gallery Art grant, 1977, 1979-80; Col John Trumbull Prof, currently. **Orgs:** Chmn, Humanities Comt African Studies Asn, 1966-70; Am Coun Learned Socs, 1966-73; African Studies Social Sci Res Coun Joint Comt. **Honors/Awds:** "Outstanding Contribution to Dance Research" Award, Cong Res Dance, 2007. **Special Achievements:** Author: African Influence on the Art of the United States, 1969; Black Gods & Kings, 1971; African Art in Motion, 1974; Four Moments of the Sun, 1981; Flash of the Spirit, 1983; Tango: The Art History of Love, 2005; organized exhibitions: The Four Moments of the Sun, 1981; The Face of the Gods: Shrines and Altars of the Black Atlantic World, 1985. **Home Addr:** 63 Wall St, New Haven, CT 06511. **Business Addr:** Col John Trumbull Professor, Yale University, Department Historical Art, New Haven, CT 06511, **Business Phone:** (203)432-2683.

**THOMPSON, RONALD ANTHONY (RONNY THOMPSON)**
Basketball coach, broadcaster. **Personal:** Born Apr 7, 1969, Washington, DC; son of John R Jr and Gwendolyn; married Erica G; children: Dylan & Devin. **Educ:** Georgetown Univ, BA, sociol, 1992. **Career:** Basketball coach (retired), broadcaster; Prudential, bond trader, 1992-93; Univ Ore, asst basketball coach, 1993-94; Loyola Col, asst basketball coach, 1994-96; Philadelphia 76ers, scout coordr, 1996-98; Georgetown Univ, asst basketball coach, 1998; Ball St Univ, head basketball coach, 2006; Comcast Sports Net, 2007; NBA TV, contribr; Univ Ark, asst coach; ESPN Radio, broadcaster. **Orgs:** Black Coaches Asn. **Home Addr:** 6641 Wakefield Dr, Alexandria, VA 22307, **Home Phone:** (703)768-6224.

**THOMPSON, ROSIE L. (ROSIE PRIDGEN)**
Educator. **Personal:** Born Aug 16, 1950, Macon, MS; daughter of Willie Lee Little Sr and Lula B Little; children: Cornelius Jr & Reginald Cornell. **Educ:** Jackson State Univ, BS, 1970, MS, 1976 & PhD, 1997; Phillips Col, AS; Univ Ark, MEd, 1985. **Career:** Canton Pub Sch, sci teacher, 1970-71; Tougaloo Col, data operator, 1971, teacher, 1983; S Cent Bell, data operator, 1972; Miss Sch Blind, teacher, 1972-79, orientation & mobility specialist, low vision clinician, 1985-92, asst prin, 1992-96, sec prin, 1996-98, supt, 1998-. **Orgs:** Bd mem, Asn Educ Blind; Asn Educ & Rehab Blind & Visually Impaired; bd mem, Miss Asn Educ & Rehab Blind & Visually Impaired; Black Women's Polit Action Forum; life mem, Zeta Phi Beta Sorority Inc, 1968-, regional dir, 1994-96; state coord, Miss Black Women's Polit Action Forum, 1987-89; City Coun, Jackson, MS, 1999; Beta Club, Phi Beta Sigma Fraternity, 1999; adv comt, Miss Sch Blind, 2003. **Home Addr:** 1254 Eastover Dr, Jackson, MS 39211-6314, **Home Phone:** (601)982-7787. **Business Addr:** Superintendent, Mississippi School for the

Blind, 1252 Eastover Dr, Jackson, MS 39211-6399, **Business Phone:** (601)984-8203.

**THOMPSON, RYAN ORLANDO**
Baseball player. **Personal:** Born Nov 4, 1967, Chestertown, MD; son of Earl and Arrie Lee; married Melody Blackstone; children: Ryan O Jr, Camren D & Taylor A. **Educ:** Univ Conn. **Career:** Baseball player (retired); Toronto Blue Jays, prof baseball player, 1987-92; New York Mets, prof baseball player, 1992-95; Cleveland Indians, 1996; Fukuoka Daiei Hawks, 1998; Houston Astros, 1999; New York Yankees, 2000; Fla Marlins, 2001; Milwaukee Brewers, 2002. **Orgs:** Md Prof Baseball Asn; Prof Baseball Asn. **Honors/Awds:** Most Valuable Player, basketball, baseball & football, Kent County High Sch, 1986-87; Labatts Player of the Year, Toronto Blue Jays, 1989; Maryland Star of Future, Md Prof Baseball Asn, 1993. **Home Addr:** 514 Charington Ct, Severna Park, MD 21146-1749, **Home Phone:** (410)544-4253.

**THOMPSON, HON. SANDRA ANN**
Superior court judge. **Personal:** Born Hawkins, TX; daughter of L R and Maye. **Educ:** Univ Southern Calif, BA, 1969; Univ Mich Law Sch, JD, 1972. **Career:** Assembly Health Comt, State Calif, legis intern, 1972-73; Assembly Judiciary Comt, State Calif, analyst, 1973-75; Dept Consumer Affairs, State Calif, legis coordr, 1975-77; City Atty's Off, Inglewood, CA, dep city atty, 1977-81; Los Angeles County Dist Atty's Off, dep dist atty, 1981-83; S Bay Judicial Dist, comnr, 1983-84, judge, 1984-86, presiding judge, 1986-87, judge, 1987-; S Bay Munic Ct, 1984-2000; Los Angeles Super Ct, super ct judge, 2000-. **Orgs:** Torrance League Women Voters, 1985-; bd trustee, Casa Colina Found S Bay, 1987-; Am Asn Univ Women, Torrance Br, 1988-; bd dir, Southern Calif Youth & Family Ctr, 1988-94; chair, Los Angeles County Munic Ct Judges Asn, 1991-93; chair, Munic Ct Judges Asn, 1991-92; Calif Asn Black Lawyers; Calif Ct Comnrs Asn; Calif Judges Asn; life mem, Calif Women Lawyers; Langston & Minority Bar Asn; pres, Nat Asn Women Judges; life mem, Nat Bar Asn; Phi Alpha Delta; Presiding Judges Asn; S Bay Bar Asn, S Bay Women Lawyers Asn; Los Angeles Urban League, Nat Am Advan Colored People Los Angeles Chap; bd dir, Nat Ctr State Courts. **Honors/Awds:** Woman of the Year, Torrance YWCA, 1992; Dr Martin Luther King Jr Human Dignity Award, 1994; Distinguished Service Award, Remraw Commanders Rite, 1995; Humanitarian Award, YMCA, 1995; Judge of the Year Award, Calif Asn Black Lawyers, 1999; Woman of the Year Award, Switzer Ctr, 2003; Joan Dempsey Klein Distinguished Jurist Award, Calif Women Lawyers, 2005. **Business Addr:** Superior Court Judge, Los Angeles Superior Court of California, 825 Maple Ave, Torrance, CA 90503, **Business Phone:** (310)787-3702.

**THOMPSON, SHARON**
Basketball player, basketball coach. **Personal:** Born Jan 21, 1976, Geiger, AL. **Educ:** Miss State Univ, BA, educ psychol, 1998; Univ W Ala, MA, phys educ, 2003. **Career:** Basketball player (retired), basketball coach; Lady Bulldogs, starter, 1994-98; San Jose Lasers, forward, 1997; ABLs San Jose Lasers, 1998-99; Ital Basketball League, 1999-2000; Lady Lion prog, asst basketball coach, 2001-; E miss Community Col, Scooba Campus, asst coach, stud activ dir, 2004, head womens basketball coach, 2005-, freshman-laden EMCC club, 2009-10. **Orgs:** Bd mem, Sumter County Bd Educ, 2004-; E Miss Community Col coaching family. **Home Addr:** Rt 1, PO Box 113, Emelle, AL 35459. **Business Addr:** Head Women's Basketball Coach, East Mississippi Community College, Scooba Campus 1512 Kemper St, Scooba, MS 39358, **Business Phone:** (662)476-5140.

**THOMPSON, DR. SIDNEY A.**
Teacher, school administrator. **Educ:** Calif State Univ, Los Angeles, MS, educ; Pepperdine Univ, LLD. **Career:** Los Angeles Unified Sch Dist, teacher, prin, supt, 1956-1997; Univ Calif Los Angeles, Educ Leadership Prog, sr fel, 1997-, prof, PLI, Ctr X, advisor, currently. **Orgs:** PDK; bd dir, Nat Ctr Educ & Econ; bd mem, Valley VOTE Inc; gov bd mem, Los Angeles Maritime Inst; adv Bd, US Merchant Marine Acad. **Home Addr:** 1538 Roscomare Rd, Los Angeles, CA 90077. **Business Addr:** Senior Fellow, University of California, 405 Hilgard Ave, Los Angeles, CA 90095, **Business Phone:** (310)794-9290.

**THOMPSON, SYLVIA MOORE**
Educator. **Personal:** Born Nov 4, 1937, Cincinnati, OH; daughter of Clinton and Edna; children: Yvette. **Educ:** Univ Cincinnati, BS, educ, 1960; Ohio State Univ, MA, educ, 1973, post grad work. **Career:** Midwest Inst Equal Educ Oppors, consult, 1973; Ohio State Univ, Off Minority Affairs, consult, 1974; Columbus City Sch, prog coordr, 1975-77; Otterbein Col Reading Ctr, tutor, 1979-84; Chap I, reading instr, 1991; Acad & Financial Assistance Serv, owner; Univ Cincinnati, adj prof; Coun Prof Recognition, field rep. **Orgs:** Pres, Columbus Alumnae Chap Delta Sigma Theta Inc, 1970-72; pres, Youth Serv Guild Inc, 1983-85, 1989-91; bus mgr, Columbus Girl choir, 1987-91; consult, Macedonia Baptist Church Educ Facil; treas, Bethune Serv Bd; bd dir, Learning Juncture. **Honors/Awds:** Outstanding Leadership Award, Delta Sigma Theta Inc, 1975-76; Meritorious Service Award, United Negro Col Fund, 1985-86; Dedicated Service Award, Univ Cincinnati, 2000. **Home Addr:** 1806 Andina Ave, Cincinnati, OH 45237, **Home Phone:** (513)641-5289.

**THOMPSON, TAWANA SADIELA**
Government official, editor. **Personal:** Born May 24, 1957, Tallahassee, FL. **Educ:** Fla A&M Univ, BS, jour/PR, 1976; St Thomas Univ, MS, mgt. **Career:** Fla A&M Univ Col Educ, ed educr, 1976-78; Ocala Star Banner, staff reporter, 1978-79; Capitol Outlook Newspaper, ed chief, 1979; Fla Occup Info Coord Comn, clearinghouse coordr, 1979-80; Dade Co Partners Youth, admin officer, 1981-82; Metro Dade Co, pub info officer; Miami Dade County, dir resident serv, 1996-98, dir affordable housing, 1998-2006; Fla Senate, legis asst, 2007; Fla Dem Party, dir opers senate, 2008-12; Tallahassee Housing Authority, dir resident initiatives, 2012, dir housing choice voucher, 2012-. **Orgs:** Exec bd mem, Dade Co Alumnae Delta Sigma Theta, 1983-; Nat Forum for Black Pub Admin, 1984-85, 1987-88; consult, Fla Inst Educ & Precollegiate Prog, 1984-85; Urban League Greater Miami, 1984-; Coconut Grove Jaycees, 1984-; dep polit dir, Statewide Campaign, 1986; exec bd mem, Greater Miami Chap Nat Asn Media Women; consult, S Fla Bus League. **Home Addr:** 8901 NW 14 Ave, Miami, FL 33147. **Business Addr:** Director of Housing Choice Voucher, Tallahassee Housing Authority, 2940 Grady Rd, Tallahassee, FL 32312, **Business Phone:** (850)385-6126.

**THOMPSON, DR. THEODIS E.**
Executive. **Personal:** Born Aug 10, 1944, Palestine, AR; son of Percy and Grozellia M Weaver; married Patricia Holley; children: Gwendolyn L Ware, Theodis E II & Omari Percy. **Educ:** Tuskegee Inst, AL, BS, 1968; Univ Mich, Ann Arbor, MPA, 1969, PhD, 1972; Harvard Univ, Cambridge, MA, PHSM, 1977. **Career:** Executive (retired); John T Stanley Co, New York, NY, sr chem tech, 1964-66; Inst Soc Res Univ Mich, Ann Arbor, Mich, res assoc, 1969-71; Howard Univ, Health Serv Adminr, Sch Bus Pub Admin, Wash, DC, asst prof, assoc dir & chmn, 1973-77, actg asst dean, 1977-78; Univ Southern Calif, Los Angeles, assoc prof, 1978-79; Memphis Health Ctr Inc, Memphis, Tenn, dir plng mkt res, 1979-85, chief admin officer, 1985-87, pres & chief exec officer, 1987-88; Brooklyn Plaza Med Ctr Inc, Brooklyn, NY, chief exec officer, 1988-; Florence, SC, Portsmouth, Va, St Louis, Mo, disc jockey & news reporter. **Orgs:** APHA, 1970-; Alpha Phi Alpha Fraternity Inc, 1962-; pres, Metro Wash Pub Health Asn, 1970-72; Black Caucus Health Workers, 1974-75; Nat Asn Community Health Ctrs, 1979-; Community Health Asn NY State Inc, 1989; bd dir, Community Assoc Develop Corp, 1989; host comt, Nat Asn People With AIDS; pres, MGNAA Inc. **Home Addr:** 4038 Glenroy Dr, PO Box 751344, Memphis, TN 38125, **Home Phone:** (901)624-3369.

**THOMPSON, TINA MARIE**
Basketball coach, basketball player. **Personal:** Born Feb 10, 1975, Los Angeles, CA; married Damon Jones; children: 1. **Educ:** Univ Southern Calif, sociol, 1997. **Career:** Basketball player (retired), Houston Comets, forward, 1997-2008; Rovereto Basket, Women's Nat Basketball League, 2001-02; Kumho Falcons, Women's Korea Basketball League, 2003; Houston Stealth, Women's Nat Basketball League, 2003; Spartak Moscow Region, Russia, 2006-07; Los Angeles Sparks, 2009-11; Seattle Storm, 2012-13; Longhorn Women's basketball, asst coach, 2015-. **Business Addr:** Assistant Coach, Texas Longhorns women's basketball, 403 E 23rd St, Austin, TX 78712.

**THOMPSON, WARREN M.**
Executive, chairperson, president (organization). **Educ:** Hampden-Sydney Col, BA, managerial econ, 1981; Univ Va, Colgate Darden Grad Sch Bus Admin, MBA, 1983. **Career:** Roy Rogers, asst mgr, 1983, regional mgr; NJ Turnpike, travel plazas; Thompson Hospitality LP, founder, pres, chmn, 1992-, Thompson Hospitality Serv LLC, chief exec officer, 1997-; Willis HRH, dir, 2004-08. **Orgs:** Bd vis, Univ Va; Compass Group N Am; Pepsi-Cola African Am Adv Bd; dir, Hilb Rogal & Hobbs, 2004-; Nat Black MBA Asn; bd dir, Darden Sch Bus; trustee, Fed Realty Investment Trust, 2007-; Wash Pvt Indust Coun; Ronald H Brown Found. **Business Addr:** President, Chairman, Thompson Hospitality LP, 1741 Bus Ctr Dr Suite 200, Reston, VA 20190, **Business Phone:** (703)757-5500.

**THOMPSON, WESTLEY V.**
Chief executive officer, president (organization), insurance executive. **Educ:** Brown Univ, BS. **Career:** Aetna, exec mgt prog, 1979-, regional sales mgr field mgt, dir technol strategy, asst vpres field opers & vpres aetna sales centers; Cigna, exec, 1994-98; Lincoln Financial Group, sr vpres, 1998-2002, pres & chief exec officer, 2000-06, pres employer markets, 2006-08; Hartford Hosp Inc, dir; LIMRA Inc, pres, dir, chief exec officer; Sun Life Financial Inc, pres, 2008-14; Sun Life Assurance Co, chmn bd, prin exec officer; Phoenix Co Inc, dir, 2014-. **Orgs:** Bd mem, Boys & Girls Club Greater Hartford; bd mem, Wadsworth Atheneum-Amistad Found. **Business Addr:** Director, The Phoenix Companies Inc, 1 American Row, Hartford, CT 06102-5056, **Business Phone:** (860)403-5000.

**THOMPSON, HON. WILLIAM COLERIDGE, SR.**
Judge, lawyer. **Personal:** Born Oct 26, 1924, New York, NY; son of William W and Louise; married Elaine; children: William Jr & Gail. **Educ:** Brooklyn Col, BA, 1948; Brooklyn Law Sch, LLB, 1954. **Career:** Judge (retired); State New York Supreme Ct, Appellate Div, Judge; NY State, sen, 1965-68; City NY, councilman, 1969-73; Supreme Ct State NY, admin judge, 1974-76, assoc judge, 1976-78; Supreme Ct Brooklyn & Staten Island, asst admin judge, 1978-80, appellate div, assoc justice, 1980-01; Ross & Hill, atty pvt pract, 2001-. **Orgs:** Founder, Restoration Corp; dir, Bed-Stuy Youth Action; reg dir, Nat Asn Advan Colored People; dir, Bed-Stuy Restoration Corp; Am Bar Asn; pres, Brooklyn Law Sch Alumni Asn, 1997; Metro Black Bar Asn; chmn, Angel Guardian Home; Daytop Village Inc; Brookwood Child Care; Navy Yard Boy's Club; pres, Ny Senate Club, 1980-81; co-pres, Blacks & Jews Conversation; treas, Judges& Lawyers Breast Cancer Alert; Comt Judicial Conduct; co-chair, Community Promote Pub Trust & ConfidenceLegal Syst; chmn, Joint Legis Comt. **Home Addr:** 228 Henry St Apt 2, Brooklyn, NY 11201. **Business Addr:** Attorney, Ross & Hill, 16 Ct St 35th Fl, Brooklyn, NY 11241, **Business Phone:** (718)855-2324.

**THOMPSON, WILLIAM COLRIDGE, JR.**
Government official, politician. **Personal:** Born Jul 10, 1953, Brooklyn, NY; son of William C Sr and Elaine; married Elsie McCabe; children: Erin, Eugene & Jennifer. **Educ:** Tufts Univ, attended 1974. **Career:** Off Congressman Fred Richmond, aide, chief staff & spec asst; Brooklyn, dep boroughpres, 1983-94; George K Baum & Co, sr vpres, 1993-96; NY City Bd Educ, Brooklyn rep, 1994-96, pres, 1994-2001; NY City, comptroller, 2002-09, chief financial officer; Siebert Brandford Shank & Co, chief admin officer & sr managing dir, 2010-. **Orgs:** Chmn, Battery Pk City Authority; bd trustee, Tufts Univ. **Business Addr:** Chief Administrative Officer, Senior Managing Director, Siebert Brandford Shank & Co, 100 Wall St 18th Fl, New York, NY 10005, **Business Phone:** (646)775-4850.

**THOMPSON, WILLIAM E.**
Government official. **Personal:** Born Dec 26, 1924, New York, NY; married Elaine Allen; children: 2. **Educ:** Brooklyn Col, BA; LLB. **Career:** NY City Coun, bd pres, Brooklyn rep. **Orgs:** NY State Senate, 1964-66; Am Bar Asn; Bedford Stuyvesant Lawyers Asn; exec bd regional dir chmn legal redress com Brooklyn Br; NY City Coun. **Home Addr:** 140 Cabrini Blvd, New York, NY 10033, **Home Phone:** (212)568-0131. **Business Addr:** Board President, Brooklyn Representative, 768 Putnam Ave, Brooklyn, NY 11221, **Business Phone:** (718)574-1125.

**THOMPSON, WILLIAM L.**
Lawyer, airplane pilot, executive. **Personal:** Born Jun 14, 1951, Orangeburg, SC; son of Willie J and Pearl Richburg; married Kathie Taylor; children: Taylor M & Sydney E. **Educ:** USAF Acad, BS, commandant's list, 1973; Calif State Univ, Sacramento, Calif, MA, deans list, 1977; McGeorge Sch Law, UOP, Sacramento, Calif, JD, 1980; Suffolk Univ Law Sch, Boston, Mass, 1992, dean's list. **Career:** USAF, minority adv supt, 1973-74, Sacramento, Calif, instr pilot, chief, life support, 1974-80, pres & chief exec officer; Delta Air Lines, Boston, MA, pilot, 1980-2005; Jr Officers Coun, pres; Air Force Instr Pilot Sch, air force instr, dep flight comdr, chief wing life support; UsaF Acad, pres & chief exec officer, currently; Summit Group Co, Boston, MA, founder & pres, 1982-2000, chief exec officer; Mass Aeronaut Comn, Boston, MA, comnr, 1983-2000; Regency Pk Assoc, Boston, MA, managing partner, 1986-2000; DC, atty-. **Orgs:** Sugar Bowl Team, 1971; Cadet Wing Staff; Comnr, Boy Scouts Am, 1982-89; chmn bd, Am Cancer Soc, 1983; bd mem, Finance Comt, Northeast Health Systs, 1983-2000; bd mem, Security Nat Bank, 1984-86; bd mem, Bank New Eng, 1986-90; trustee, Bridgton Acad, 1994-96; bd mem, Eastern Bank & Trust Co, 1996; pres, Boston Chap, Nat Asn Guardsmen, 1998-2000, Atlanta Chap, 2000-; found bd dir, Atlanta Tech Col, 2000-; 100 Black Men of Atlanta, 2001; supvry comt, Ent Fed Credit Union; Colo Thirty Group; Colo Springs Chamber Com; Pikes Peak Roundtable; bd dir, Winter Night Club; nat bd dir, Am Cancer Soc; Boeing, Boy Scouts Am; trustee, Bridgeton Acad; trustee, Air Force Acad Falcon Found; chmn, Air Line Pilots Asn; comt chmn, Black Airline Pilots (OBAP); comt chmn, Tuskegee Airmen; Massachusetts Bar; Wash, DC Bar; Colo Aeronaut Bd, 2013; pres, Delta Upsilon Boule, Sigma Pi Phi Fraternity; pres & chief exec officer, Asn Graduates, currently; trustee, Eastern Bank Corp, currently. **Honors/Awds:** Outstanding Service, 1986; Distinguish Achievement, Boy Scouts Am, 1986; Volunteer of the Year by Am Cancer Soc, 1992; Century Award from Boy Scouts of America; Distinguished Contribution, Mass Airport Mgrs Asn, 1995; Distinguished Service, Am Cancer Soc, 1996; Spirit of Aviation Award from Massachusetts Aviation Task Force; Bell South, African Am Hist Calendar, 1998; Guardsman of the Year, Am Cancer Soc; He was selected as an Outstanding Entrepreneur by Bank of Boston; Outstanding Achievement by Organization of Black Airline Pilots; 2000 Service Award by U.S. Security and Exchange Commission; Outstanding Service Award, Air Line Pilots Asn; Outstanding Contribution, Cadet Way Life Commitee by USAF Academy; Air Force Outstanding Unit Award; National Defense Service Medal; Air Force Longevity Service Award; Small Arms Expert Marksmanship Ribbon. **Special Achievements:** He is the first African American from South Carolina to receive an appointment to the U.S. Air Force Academy in Colorado. **Business Addr:** Chief Executive Officer, President, United States Air Force Academy, 2304 Cadet Dr Suite 2300, Colorado Springs, CO 80840, **Business Phone:** (719)333-2025.

**THOMPSON, DR. WINSTON EDNA. See Obituaries Section.**

**THOMPSON-MOORE, ANN**
Consultant. **Personal:** Born Oct 13, 1949, Edwards, MS; children: DeAnna. **Educ:** Jackson State Univ, BA, 1972, MS, educ, 1974. **Career:** Jackson-Hinds Co Youth Ct, counr, 1972-74; Miss Gulf Coast Jr Col, dir spec serv prog, 1974-82; Northern Ill Univ, counr, 1983-84; Miss Gov's Off Fed & State Prog, spec proj officer IV, 1984-87; The Kelwynn Group, sr consult. **Orgs:** MS State Dem Party, 1980; Phi Delta Kappa Frat E MS Chap, 1981; fund raising chair, Hinds County Dem Exec Comn, 1984; pres, United Black Fund Miss, 1984; bd mem, Hospice Friends Inc, 1985; coordr, United Negro Col Fund, 1985-86, 1986-87; peer panelist, Miss Arts Comn, 1986; Farish St Bapt Church; Delta Sigma Theta Sor. **Honors/Awds:** Outstanding Young Woman in America, 1979. **Home Phone:** (601)957-1561. **Business Addr:** Senior Consultant, The Kelwynn Group, PO Box 1526, Jackson, MS 39215-1526.

**THOMPSON-NICKERSON, KAREN ANN. See THOMPSON, KAREN ANN.**

**THOMPSON-WRIGHT, DR. BRENDA SMITH**
School administrator, lecturer, association executive. **Personal:** Born Jun 17, 1948, Richmond, VA; married Hugo Harrison Thompson; children: Rodney. **Educ:** Va Union Univ, BS, 1970; Va Commonwealth Univ, MS, 1977; Va Polytech Inst & State Univ, EdD, 1983. **Career:** Medical Col VA, lab specialist, 1970-75; J Sargeant Reynolds Community Col, instr, 1977-80; Doctoral Fellowship, State Coun Higher Educ Va, 1980, 81; State Coun Higher Educ VA, asst coordr, 1984-85; Va Union Univ, dir enrollment mgt, 1985; Fla A & M Univ, asst dean stud personnel servs, dir stud teaching, prof sec educ & found, asst dir, Collection Mgt, currently. **Orgs:** Pres, Nat Asn Univ Women Richmond Br, 1984-85; Richmond Prof Women's Network, VASFAA, SASFAA, NASFAA, VACRAO, SACRAO, NACDRAO; Nat Asn Advan Colored People; Alpha Kappa Alpha Sor. **Honors/Awds:** Distinguished Volunteer, Parent John B Gary Elem Sch, 1981, 83; Distinguished Alumni Award, Nat Asn Equal Oppor Higher Educ, 1986. **Home Addr:** 4004 Poplar Grove Rd, Midlothian, VA 23113. **Business Addr:** Assistant Director for Collection Management, Florida A&M University, 307 Coleman Library, Tallahassee, FL 32307-4700, **Business Phone:** (850)599-8675.

**THOMS, DONALD H.**
Television director, journalist, executive. **Personal:** Born Feb 28, 1948, Baltimore, MD; son of McKinley and Henrietta Austin; married Mariana Davis; children: Tracie Nicole & Austin Curtis. **Educ:** Morgan State Univ, BA, sociol & anthology, 1971. **Career:** WBAL-TV, Baltimore, opers dir, 1967-73; Md Pub TV, Owings Mills, stage

mgr, 1973-75, TV dir, 1975-80, producer, 1980-85, exec producer, 1985-90, sr exec producer, 1990-91, dir regional prods, 1991-93, dir prog mgt, 1993-96, air talent, 1995-, vpres programming; Pub Broadcasting Serv, vpres prog mgt, 1993-99, vpres gen audience programming, 2011-; Discovery Commun LLC., vpres, 1999-2007, Discovery Health Channel, head, prod, 1999, vpres prod, 1999-2007, interim gen mgr, vpres talent develop & diversity, 2007-08; ThomsMediaGroup, pres & owner, 2016-. **Orgs:** Bd govs, Nat Capital & Chesapeake Bay Chap Nat Acad TV Arts & Sci; adv bd & pres, CINE, 2001-; bd trustee, Centerstage, 2008-; WHUT. **Honors/Awds:** Best Entertainment Program Television Director, 1988; NATPE InterNat-Iris Award Winner, Best Entertainment Prog, 1988; CPB Public Television Local Program Award-Silver Award, Corp pub TV, 1990; Bronze Award, Producer, Film & TV Festival New York, 1989; Emmy Awards; Emmy Award Exec Producer, 1992, 1993; Telly Award, 1993. **Home Addr:** 4118 Balmoral Cr, Baltimore, MD 21208, **Home Phone:** (301)521-0514. **Business Addr:** Vice President, General Audience Programming, PBS, 2100 Crystal Dr, Arlington, VA 22202, **Business Phone:** (703)739-5000.

## THOMSON, ALICE G.
Chief executive officer, association executive. **Career:** Black Family Develop Inc (BFDI), chief exec officer, 1978-. **Business Addr:** Chief Executive Officer, Black Family Development Inc (BFDI), 2995 E Grand Blvd, Detroit, MI 48202, **Business Phone:** (313)758-0150.

## THOMSON, CYNTHIA BRAMLETT
Executive. **Personal:** Born May 18, 1949, Highland Park, MI; daughter of Cosby Jr and Carrie Frances; married Ronald L; children: Sela & Mance. **Educ:** Univ Mich, BA, lit, sci & arts, 1970; Mich State Univ, MS, nutrit, 1973, East Lansing, MA, PhD, agr econs; Wash Univ, St Louis, MBA. **Career:** GR Group, St Louis, co-owner & human resources exec, 1981-93, bd mem, 1981-; Midwest Stamping & Mfg Inc, co-founder & vpres human resources, 1993; Girl Scouts USA, nat pres, nat bd dir, chair, 2002-05. **Orgs:** Chair prog comt, bd mem & vpres corp planning, Girl Scout Coun Greater St Louis, 1989-93; bd dir, Girl Scout Nat, 1996; bd chair, Deke Welles, 2012-15; bd dir, Toledo Mus Art, bd chair, 2016-; St Louis Sci Ctr; cur emer, Univ MO Syst; Women's Forum MO; Links Inc; Alpha Kappa Alpha Sorority; Girl Scout Seven Lakes Coun Inc; bd mem, St Louis Sci Ctr; bd mem, Int Women's Forum, MO Chap; Mo State Bd Educ; Finance Human Resources & Fund Develop Comts; emer nat bd mem, Girls Inc; bd trustee, Med Univ Ohio. **Business Addr:** Board Chair, Board Director, Toledo Museum of Art, 2445 Monroe St, Toledo, OH 43620, **Business Phone:** (419)255-8000.

## THOMSON, GERALD EDMUND
Educator, physician, college administrator. **Personal:** Born Jan 1, 1932, New York, NY; son of Lloyd Thomas and Sybil Gilbourne; married Carolyn Webber; children: Gregory & Karen. **Educ:** Howard Univ, MD, 1959. **Career:** State Univ NY, Kings Co Hosp Ctr, intern, 1959-60, chief resident, 1962-63, Med Brooklyn Hosp, attend physician, 1966-70; resident med, 1960-62; chief resident, 1962-63; Univ NY, instr, 1963-68; clin dir, dialysis unit, 1965-67; Coney Island Hosp, assoc chief med, 1967-70; Columbia Univ, Harlem Hosp Ctr, dir med, prof, Presby Hosp, attend physician, clin asst prof med, 1968-70, dir nephrol, 1970-71, dir med, 1971-85, pres, 1976-78, Columbia Presby Med Ctr, exec vpres, chief staff, 1985-91, Col Physicians & Surg, assoc dean, 1990-91, sr assoc dean emer, 1991-, Lambert & Sonneburn prof emer med, 1997-; Columbia Col, assoc prof med, Phys & Surg, 1970-72; State Univ NY; Samuel Lambert, prof med, 1980-; Inwood Ambulatory Care Network, Wash Heights, pres, 1985-90. **Orgs:** Fel nephrol, NY Heart Asn, 1965-65; adv bd, NY Kidney Found, 1971-72; Health Res Coun City, NY, 1972-81; hypertension adv comt, NY City Health Serv Admin, 1972-75; Am Fedn Clin Res Soc Urban Physicians, 1972-73; bd dir NY Heart Asn, 1973-81; NIH, 1973-74; adv bd, Nat Asn Patients Hemodialysis & Transplantation, 1973-83; bd dir, NY Heart Asn, 1973-81; adv bd, Nat Asn Patient Hemodialysis & Transplantation, 1973-; AAAS, 1973-74; chmn, Com Hypertension NY Met Reg Med Prog, 1974-76; adv bd, Jour Urban Health, 1974-80; Health Res Coun City, NY, 1975-; Presby Med Bd, 1976-; chmn, Comn High Blood Press, 1976-81; Com Mild Hypertension Nat Heart & Lung Inst, 1976; NY State Adv Com Hypertension, 1977-80; adv bd, Sch Bio med Educ, CityUniv New York, 1979-83; clin trials rev com, 1980-85; com non-pharm treat hypertension, Inst Med Nat Acad Sci, 1980; clin & trials rev com, 1980-85; Am Soc Artificial Organs; NY Acad Med; Alpha Omega Alpha; NY Govs Health Adv Coun, 1981-84; pub Health Coun, NY, 1983-95; Joint Nat Com High Blood Pressure, NIH, 1983-84, 1987-88; rev panel hypertension detection & monitoring bd study cardiovasc risk factors young, Nat Heart, Lung & Blood Inst, 1984-90; adv com Heart & Hypertension Inst NY State, 1984; Grad Med Educ Comn, State NY, 1984-86; pres, WAHeights-Inwood Ambulatory Care Network Corp, 1986-91; pres, WAHeights-Inwood Ambulatory Care Network Corp, 1986-91; Comm End-State Renal Disease, 1985, 1989-90; pres, Asn Acad Minority Physicians, 1989-91; chmn, Am Bd Internal Med, 1990-92; Med News Network, 1993-95; bd dir, Primary Care Develop Corp, 1993-; Med News Network, 1993-94; Mayor's Commn Health& Hosp Corp; dir, Harlem Ctr Health Prom & DisPrev; bd dir, Primary Care Develop Corp; pres, Am Col Physicians, 1995-96; chmn, Federated Coun Internal Med, 1995-96; founder & pres, New York Soc Nephrol; chmn, Am Bd Internal Med; fel Am Col Physicians; fel Col Physicians Safrica, 1996; Bds Inst Profm Med, Columbia; Inst Med Nat Academies, 2015; dir, bd dir, Physicians Human Rights. **Special Achievements:** First African American president in the 85-year history of the organization. **Home Addr:** 85 Premium Pt, New Rochelle, NY 10801-5327, **Home Phone:** (914)633-5547. **Business Addr:** Professor Emeritus of Medicine, Senior Associate Dean, Columbia University, 630 W 168th St Rm 3-413, New York, NY 10032, **Business Phone:** (212)305-4158.

## THOMSON, J. PETER
Executive. **Educ:** Hampton Univ, BA; Wharton Sch Bus, MBA. **Career:** Bay Area Small Bus Develop Corp, dir; Black Adoption Placement & Res Ctr, dir; Nat Asn Investment Cos; Access 1 Commun, dir, currently; Bustos Media, dir, currently; Opportunity Capital Partners, managing partner, pres, currently; Tower Babel LLC, dir; Info Network Radio Inc, dir. **Orgs:** Bay Area Small Bus Develop Corp; Black Adoption Placement & Res Ctr; Nat Asn Investment Cos; charter mem, Marathon Club; trustee, Entrepreneurial Growth & Investment Inst. **Business Addr:** President, Opportunity Capital Partners, 2201 Walnut Ave Suite 210, Fremont, CA 94538, **Business Phone:** (510)795-7000.

## THOMSON, DR. THELMA B.
College president. **Personal:** Born Jul 22, 1940, Jamaica. **Educ:** Howard Univ, BA, 1970, MA, Eng, 1972, PhD, Eng lit, 1978; Bethlehem Teachers Col, dipl, teacher educ. **Career:** May Day Primary Sch, teacher, 1960-65; Wash Post Newspaper, Part-time proof reader, 1966-72; Franklin Adult Educ Ctr, Eng instr, 1966-72; Howard Univ, DC, grad asst Eng, 1970-72; Upward Mobility Col, teacher, 1971-72; City Univ new York, Herbert H Lehman Col, lectr Eng, 1974-82; Bowie State Col, asst prof & reading co-odr, 1974-76; Univ DC, Dept Eng, asst prof eng, 1976-79, dir freshman Eng, 1979-81, Grad Expository Writing Prog, dir, 1981-90, asst chair, 1982-88, dir dept activ & teaching duties, 1984-86, Col lib & Fine Arts, assoc dean, 1988-90; Norfolk State Univ, Sch Arts & Lett, dean, 1990-98, vpres acad affairs, 1998-2002; Univ Md, Eastern Shore, pres, 2002-11. **Orgs:** Historian & bd mem, Mid Atlantic Writers Asn, 1984-2000; comnr, Am Coun Educ (Women), 2003-; exec bd, Community Found, 2003-; Modem Lang Asn; Nat Coun Teachers Eng; Phi Beta Kappa; African-Am Writers' Guild; nat pres, Col Lang Asn; co-founder, Caribbean Studies Asn; co-chair, Southern Asn Schs & Cols. **Honors/Awds:** Outstanding Alumni of Year, Bethlehem Col, 2001; Administrator of the Year, Norfolk State Univ, 2002; Md Govr & Legis Citations, 2002; Service Award, Southern Asn Cols & Schs, 2002-03; Award, Langston Hughes Socs, 2002; Maryland's Top 100 Women. **Special Achievements:** Author, Seventeenth Century English Hymn: A Mode for Sacred and Secular Concerns, 1988.

## THORBURN, DR. CAROLYN COLES
Educator. **Personal:** Born Dec 20, 1941, Newark, NJ; daughter of Charles Edward and Dorothy Walker Coles. **Educ:** Douglass Col, BA, span, 1962; Rutgers Univ, MA, span, 1964, PhD, span, 1972; PhD, nutrit, 1987. **Career:** Barringer HS, Span teacher, 1964-66; Rutgers Univ, teaching asst Span, 1966-67; Upsala Col, prof Span & coordr black studies, 1967-95; Union County Col, adj prof Span, 1992-98; Seton Hall Univ, E Orange Sch Dist, educ consult, 1995-, adj Span prof, currently; Founder, Educ Res Lang Sch, pres, 1980-09. **Orgs:** Mod Lang Asn; Nat Coun Black Studies; Am Asn Univ Profs; Am Asn Teachers Span & Port. **Home Addr:** 77 Cent Ave, East Orange, NJ 07018, **Home Phone:** (973)677-9504. **Business Addr:** Professor of Spanish, Seton Hall University, 400 S Orange Ave, South Orange, NJ 07079, **Business Phone:** (973)761-9000.

## THORNE, DR. CECIL MICHAEL
Physician, pathologist. **Personal:** Born May 13, 1929, Georgetown; married Sandra; children: Timothy, Christine, Christopher, Jonathan & Victor. **Educ:** Queens Col; Lincoln Univ, AB, 1952; Mainz Univ, MD, 1957. **Career:** Springfield Hosp, intern res, 1958-62; Western Mass Hosp, demonstr res, 1962-63; Ohio State Univ, asst prof pathol, 1964-65, clin asn prof path, 1980. **Orgs:** Am Col Patho; Am Soc Clin Patho; pres, elect Ohio Soc Pathologists; pres, Ohio Asn Blood Banks; pres, Cent Ohio Soc Patho; bd gov, Ohio Soc Pathol; lab com, Ohio St Med Asn; AMA; Ohio State Med Asn; Licking Co Med Soc; Am Asn Blood Banks; Acad Clin Lab Physicians & Sci; chmn, bd dir, Licking Co Chap Heart Asn; Licking Co ARG; chmn, Cent Ohio Blood Prog Com; chmn, Med Adv Com Cent Ohio Blood Prog; dir, Newark Area C C; chmn, Licking Co Metro Pk Dist; Rotary Club; pres, Newark Pathologists Inc; pres, Licking Meml Hosp. **Home Addr:** 7301 Landon Lane, New Albany, OH 43054, **Home Phone:** (614)939-7301. **Business Addr:** Physician, 1320 W Main St, Newark, OH 43055, **Business Phone:** (740)348-4161.

## THORNELL, PAUL NOLAN DIALLO
Secretary (office). **Personal:** Born May 6, 1972, New York, NY; son of Richard Paul and Carolyn Atkinson. **Educ:** Univ PA, BA, 1994. **Career:** People Am Way, sr legis rep, 1994-96; Sen Dem Steering & Coordr Comt, assoc dir, 1996-98; Vpres Al Gore, dep dir; Hill & Knowltons, managing dir Pub Affairs; Citigroup Mgt Corp, Fed Govt Affairs Global Govt Affairs, lobbyist & group mem, managing dir; Senate Dem Leader Tom Daschle. **Orgs:** Bd mem, Ctr Lobbying Pub Interest; bd mem, DC Habitat Humanity; bd dir & trasurer, Generations United; sr vpres pub policy & field relationship, United Way Am, 2003-06, dir pub policy. **Home Addr:** 1111 Noyes Dr, Silver Spring, MD 20910, **Home Phone:** (301)565-2953. **Business Addr:** Director, Center for Lobbying in the Public Interest, 1612 K St NW Suite 505, Washington, DC 20006, **Business Phone:** (202)387-5048.

## THORNELL, RICHARD PAUL
Educator. **Personal:** Born Oct 19, 1936, New York, NY; son of Joseph and Elizabeth; married Joan Talbert; children: David; married Carolyn O Atkinson; children: Paul Nolan Diallo & Douglass Vashon. **Educ:** Pomona Col, attended 1955; Fisk Univ, hist, 1956; Woodrow Wilson Sch, MPA, econs & int affairs, 1958; Yale Law Sch, JD, 1971. **Career:** Grad fel Princeton Univ, 1958, Grant Yale Law Sch, 1956-58; US Dept State Agency Intl Develop, econ & intl relofcr, 1958-61; US Comm Rels Serv Dept Justice, chief fed progms staff, 1965-66; Univ Fac Senate, chair; Rosenman Colin Freund Lewis & Cohen NYC, assoc litigation dept, 1975-76; Africa Reg Officer US Peace Corps, chief prog staff; Howard Univ Sch Law, fac, 1976-2004, vpres & gen coun, 1984-88, prof law, currently. **Orgs:** Phi Beta Kappa, Delta Chap, Fisk Univ, 1956-; Bars NY/DC/Fed Cts/US Supreme Ct; exec com & gen coun, Fisk Univ Gen Alumni Asn, 1977-79; bd adv, Smithonian Environ Res Ctr; bd dir, YMCA Wash DC, 1977-83; bd dir Africare, 1977-83; trustee, Phelps Stoke Fund, 1980-85; lay leader Int Comt, Nat Bd YMCA'S USA; elected coun, Foreign Rels; exec comt, Howard Univ Repub SA Proj; vice chair & coun, Bd Dirs Africare, African Am develop assistance orgn. CLL, 2009; Nat Asn Advan Colored People; Ctr Lifelong Learning, 2009-; chair, Exchange Progs Comt Int Div YMCA US Am. **Honors/Awds:** Fisk Univ, Africare Distinguished Service Award; Fisk Univ Gen Alumni Asn, 1978; Int Achievement Award Willilam S Thompson Int Law Soc dir com Nat Bd YMCA'S USA; exec com, 1980. **Special Achievements:** Journal: The Future of Affirmative Action in Higher Education, 1986. **Home Addr:** 2901 S Leisure World Blvd Unit 126, Silver Spring, MD 20906-8363, **Home Phone:** (301)438-0185. **Business Addr:** Professor of Law, Howard University, 2400 6th St NW, Washington, DC 20059, **Business Phone:** (202)806-6100.

## THORNHILL, DR. HERBERT LOUIS, JR.
Physician. **Educ:** Univ Pittsburgh, BS, 1951; Howard Univ Col Med, Wash, DC, MD, 1955; Am Bd Phys Med & Rehab, dipl, 1964. **Career:** Freedmens Hosp, internship; Bronx Va Med Ctr, internship; Howard Univ Hosp, resident internal med; Montefiore Hosp & Med Ctr, asst attend, 1963-66, adj attend, 1966-67; Vet Affairs Med Ctr, resident Phys Med & Rehab; Yeshiva Univ, Albert Einstein Col Med, instr, 1963-65, asst clin prof rehab med, 1965-67; Harlem Hosp Ctr, asst dir rehab med, 1967-69, attend physician, 1969-, chief, amputee serv, 1969-, assoc dir, rehab med, 1969-78, actg dir rehab med, 1979-80, dir, rehab med, 1980-; Presby Hosp, asst physician, 1968-84; Columbia Univ, Col Physicians & Surgeons, asst clin prof rehab med, 1968-73, assoc prof clin rehab med, 1973-85, prof clin rehab med, 1985-; pvt pract physician, currently. **Orgs:** Am Acad Phys Med & Rehab, 1965-; Nat Med Asn, 1967-; New York Acad Med, 1968-; Bronx Co Med Soc; Pub Comm, 1970; Med Soc State New York; fel New York Soc Phys Med & Rehab, 1963-, prog chmn, 1970-71, vpres, 1971-72, pres, 1973-74; Conf Rehab Med; sec, Phys Med & Rehab, 1975-76, chair, 1976-77, adv coun, 1977-80; Howard Univ Res & Training Ctr Access Rehab & Econ Opportunity, 1988-; survr, Comn Accreditation Rehab Facil, 1982-89 Med Adv Comn, Greater Harlem Nursing Home, 1974-87, chmn, 1981-82; Adv Comn Disab, Bor Manhattan, 1989-92; NY Asn, Independent Living Ctrs, 1990-. **Honors/Awds:** New York City Independent Living Centers Award, 1991; Certificate of Appreciation, Harlem Hospital Auxiliary, 1994; Balm in Gilead Award, 1995; Legacy Award, Daughters Rizpah, 1998; Lifetime Achievement Award, Nat Med Asn, Manhattan Cent Med Soc, 1998. **Special Achievements:** Author of numerous publications and abstracts. **Home Addr:** 2 Aberdeen Ave, Spring Valley, NY 10977-7225. **Business Addr:** Physician, 506 Lenox Ave Wp-522, New York, NY 10037, **Business Phone:** (212)939-2740.

## THORNS, ODAIL, JR.
Automotive executive, manager. **Personal:** Born Jan 3, 1943, Pine Bluff, AR; married Mamie T; children: Michelle, Camille & Octavia. **Educ:** BS, chem, 1964; Kans State Univ, grad study, 1965; Harvard Grad Sch Bus Admin, PMD, 1984. **Career:** Exec (retired); Delco-remy Div GMC, chemist, 1965, asst supt mfg, process engr, res engr, mfg foreman, labor rel supvr, gen supvr mfg, plant supt, plant mgr, mfg mgr, oper mgr, dival dir personnel & dir; Qual Network & Synchronous Automotive Components Group, dir engine dr bus unit, Saginaw Div; Delphi Automotive Syst, Worldwide, gen dir mfg, global dir driveline, aftermkt & serv; Saginaw, dir develop. **Orgs:** Indust Mgt Club; bd dir, St Manpower Training Comn; bd dir, pres, Ind Forum; chmn, Region III Nat Asn Advan Colored People, 1974-75; chmn bd, United Way, 1979; Nat Bd Nat Asn Advan Colored People, 1980-84; chmn bd, Comn Hosp, 1983-85; trustee, Peerless Lodge F & AM; dir, Madison Co Br Nat Asn Advan Colored People; state adv, Nat Asn Advan Colored People Womens Aux; pres emer, Ind State Nat Asn Advan Colored People; chmn, Martin Luther King Memorial Comn; fel Golden Heritage; NCP; Saginaw Vision, 2000. **Home Addr:** 3678 White Trillum Dr W, Saginaw, MI 48603-5804, **Home Phone:** (989)793-2685. **Business Addr:** Director of Development.

## THORNTON, ANDRE
Baseball player, executive. **Personal:** Born Aug 13, 1949, Tuskegee, AL; son of Harold; married Gertrude; children: Andre Jr & Theresa (deceased); married Gail Jones; children: Jonathan & Dean. **Educ:** Capital Univ, BA; Cheyney State Col; Nyack Col. **Career:** Baseball player (retired), executive; Chicago Cubs, infielder, 1973-76; Montreal Expos, infielder, 1976; Cleveland Indians, infielder, 1977-87; Global Procurement Mgt Co, owner; Global Promotions Inc, pres & chief exec officer, 2002-06; Kent State Univ, pres ambassador, 2010-11; ASW Global LLC, pres & chief exec officer, 2011-. **Orgs:** Bd mem, Cleveland Coun World Affairs; Cleveland Zool Soc; Cuyahoga Comm Col; Leadership Cleveland; bd trustee, Nyack Col; Greater Cleveland Partnership; Greater Akron Chamber; chair, Int Warehouse Logistics Asn. **Special Achievements:** Co-Author: "Triumph Born of Tragedy", 1983. **Home Addr:** PO Box 395, Chagrin Falls, OH 44022. **Business Addr:** President, Chief Executive Officer, ASW Global LLC, 3375 Gilchrist Rd, Mogadore, OH 44260, **Business Phone:** (330)733-6291.

## THORNTON, CORA ANN BARRINGER
Chief executive officer, president (organization), executive. **Personal:** Born Jun 13, 1941, Washington, DC; daughter of George F Barringer and Pearl G; children: Johnnie R, Joseph T, Jerome F & Jenese E. **Educ:** DC Teachers Col, BS, 1964; Howard Univ, post grad, 1966; George Washington Univ, post grad, 1970; Trinity Col, MA, 1982. **Career:** Taft Jr High Sch, instr math, 1964-73; St Marys Sch, instr math, 1976-79; Eastern High Sch, instr math, 1979-85; Univ DIS, Dept Math, assoc prof, 1980-86; Barr-Thorn Enterprises, pres & chief exec officer, 1981; Trinity col, Dept Math, assoc prof, 1984; Lady K Corp, pres & chief exec officer, 1989-. **Orgs:** Nat coun Teacher Math; Delta Sigma Theta Sorority. **Home Addr:** 3968 Blaine St NE, Washington, DC 20019, **Home Phone:** (202)758-2689. **Business Addr:** President, Chief Executive Officer, Lady K Corp, 11160 Veirs Mill Rd L15143, Wheaton, MD 20902, **Business Phone:** (301)565-2395.

## THORNTON, CORNELIUS
Executive, vice president (organization). **Educ:** Univ Iowa; Univ Chicago Grad Sch Bus, attended 1973. **Career:** Aetna Life & Casualty Ins Co, common stock analyst; Morgan Stanley, instnl equity res area; First Boston Corp, vpres, sr securities analyst; Goldman, Sachs & Co, vpres, sr res analyst, 1992-. **Business Addr:** Senior Research Analyst, Goldman Sachs & Co, 85 Broad St, New York, NY 10282, **Business Phone:** (212)357-6641.

## THORNTON, DOZIER W.
Psychotherapist, educator. **Personal:** Born Aliquippa, PA; son of Myrtle and Dozier; married Kazuko Otaki; children: Monica, Lisa & Hugh Heslep. **Educ:** Univ Pittsburgh, MS, PhD, 1966. **Career:** Acting dean (retired); Mich State Univ, Dept Psychol, prof, 1965-2004, from

asst dean grad sch to assoc dean grad sch, 1991-94, actg dean urban aff prog, 2004, prof emer, 2004-, Univ Outreach & Engagement, mem, currently; psychotherapist. **Orgs:** Community Ment Health & Educ Consult; Am Psychol Asn; Mich Psychol Asn; founder, Listening Ear, 1969-. **Home Addr:** 1467 Stonegate Lane, East Lansing, MI 48823, **Home Phone:** (517)332-2853. **Business Addr:** Professor Emeritus, Michigan State University, 231 Psychol Bldg, East Lansing, MI 48824-1022, **Business Phone:** (517)355-9562.

### THORNTON, IVAN TYRONE, SR.

Financial manager. **Personal:** Born Aug 8, 1961, Brooklyn, NY; son of Paul A and Esther; married Thomasina Toles; children: Ivana, Alyse & Lee-Joy. **Educ:** Howard Univ, BBA, finance, 1983; NY Univ, MBA. **Career:** Midas Investment Corp, mgr, financial adminr, 1983-86; Merrill Lynch Pierce Fenner & Smith, sr financial consult, 1986-89; Salomon Smith Barney, vpres regist investment adv, 1989-96; Morgan Stanley, vpres financial consult, Pvt Client Serv, vpres, 1989-96; Regist Investment Advisor; Credit Suisse First Boston, vpres pvt equity sales, financial adv, 1996-2005; Fiduciary Mgt Group LLC, founder, sr managing partner, chief exec officier, 2005-. **Orgs:** Alpha Phi Alpha Fraternity, 1981-; Am Mgt Asn, 1991; pres, Howard Univ Alumni Asn, 1993-95; econ develop com, One Hundred Black Men Inc; Nat Asn Securities Profs; pub policy com, Black Exec Exchange Prog; Nat Urban League; chmn coun, Credit Suisse First Boston; Morgan Stanley, Pres's Coun. **Honors/Awds:** Executives Club, Merrill Lynch Pierce Fenner & Smith, 1989; Division Leader, New Bus Develop, Salamon Smith Barney, 1990; Presidents Club, Salamon, Smith, Barney, 1993-96. **Home Addr:** 183 Northwoods Dr, South Orange, NJ 07079-1122, **Home Phone:** (973)275-5053. **Business Addr:** Founder, Chief Executive Officer, Fiduciary Management Group LLC, 304 Pk Ave S 11th Fl, New York, NY 10010-4305, **Business Phone:** (212)590-2359.

### THORNTON, JACKIE C.

Executive. **Personal:** Born Apr 26, 1960, Pine Bluff, AR; daughter of Laudell and Beatrice. **Educ:** Univ Ark, Pine Bluff, BS, 1981; Kennesaw State Univ; Univ Wis Madison Sch Bus, MS, mkt, 1983. **Career:** Phillips Petrol, acct, 1981-82; IBM Corp, mkt sales asst, 1983; NCR Corp, educ analyst, 1984-88; Pitney Bowes, prod mkt mgr, 1988-91; United Am Healthcare Corp, New Prod Develop, 1992-94; Global Mkt & PR Inc, pres & owner, 1995-, integrated mkt consult, 1998; Monarch Marking; Ga Dept Indust, Trade & Tourism; Coca-Cola Co; BellSouth Mobility. **Orgs:** Dayton Chap Nat Black MBA Asn; Am Mkt Asn; Ga Minority Supplier Develop Coun. **Home Addr:** 3232 Cobb Pkwy, PO Box 260, Atlanta, GA 30337, **Home Phone:** (770)438-6882. **Business Addr:** President, Owner, Integrated Marketing Consultant, Global Marketing & PR Inc, 3330 Cumberland Blvd Suite 500, Atlanta, GA 30339-5995, **Business Phone:** (678)638-6610.

### THORNTON, JERRY SUE OWENS. See OWENS, DR. JERRY SUE.

### THORNTON, DR. JOHN C.

Executive, teacher, educator. **Personal:** Born May 22, 1940, Louisville, KY; son of William and Alberta; married Rochelle A Ray; children: Ardell N & Timothy. **Educ:** Ky State Univ, BS, 1963; Northeastern Univ, MA, 1975; Union Grad Sch, PhD, criminal justice, 1976. **Career:** Chicago Bd Educ, teacher, 1963-66; City Chicago, comt organizer, res analyst, criminal justice, dir, 1966-81; Columbia Col, prof, 1977-84; McDonald's Franchise, owner, 1996. **Orgs:** Nat Black McDonald's Owners' Asn, 1981. **Home Addr:** 10110 S Paxton, Chicago, IL 60617.

### THORNTON, LESLIE

Lawyer, government official, vice president (organization). **Personal:** Born May 2, 1958, Philadelphia, PA; daughter of Henry H and Ernestine L. **Educ:** Univ Pa, BA, polit sci & govt, 1980; Georgetown Univ Law Ctr, JD, 1983. **Career:** DC pub defender, 1983-87; Brand, Lowell & Ryan, assoc, 1987-89; Shea & Gardner, sr assoc, 1989-92; Clinton Admin, sr exec, chief staff, 1993-2000; US Secy Educ, dep chief staff, 1993-96, chief staff, 1996; Pres's White House Budget Working Group, 1995; Pres Clinton's presidential debate team, 1996; Patton Boggs LLP, partner, 2000-04; Dickstein Shapiro LLP, partner, 2004-11; Career Educ Corp, bd dir, 2005-; WGL Holdings & Wash Gas Light Co, vice pres & gen coun, 2012-14, sr vpres, gen coun & corp secy, 2014-. **Orgs:** DC Bar Asn; Greater Wash Area chap; Womens Law Div Outreach Community; Young Lawyers Div; Nat Bar Asn; Am Bar Asn; Georgetown Univ Law Ctr; Georgetown Law Corp Coun Inst; DuPont Women Lawyers' Network; founder, Educ Equity Inst; founder, Capitol Educ Fund. **Home Addr:** 3921 Courtland Cir, Alexandria, VA 22305, **Home Phone:** (703)684-9285. **Business Addr:** Senior Vice President, General Counsel & Corporate Secretary, Washington Gas Light Co, 101 Constitution Ave NW, Washington, DC 20080, **Business Phone:** (202)624-6677.

### THORNTON, MATTHEW, III

Vice president (organization). **Personal:** children: 2. **Educ:** Univ Memphis, BS; Univ Tenn, Knoxville, TN, MBA. **Career:** FedEx Corp, package handler, managing dir dist opers, vpres nat hub opers, vpres regional opers Cent region, sr vpres air, ground & freight serv, sr vpres US opers div. **Orgs:** Chair, FedEx Express United Way Campaign; hon co-chair, March Dimes, 2007; bd dir, Metrop Inter-Faith Asn (MIFA), 2007; Sherwin-Williams Co. **Business Addr:** Senior Vice President, FedEx Corporation, 942 S Shady Grove Rd, Memphis, TN 38120, **Business Phone:** (901)369-3600.

### THORNTON, DR. MAURICE M.

School administrator. **Personal:** Born Dec 31, 1930, Birmingham, AL; son of William and Alberta; married Elizabeth McDonald; children: Karen E, Susan & Christopher. **Educ:** Ala State Univ, BS, 1952; Cleveland State Univ, MEd, 1975; Nova Southeastern Univ, EdD, 1981. **Career:** Cuyahoga Co Welfare Dept Cleveland, investigative caseworker, supvr title V, coord neighborhood youth corps & asst dir personnel dept, 1958-67, equal employ opportunity officer, minority recruiter & dir equal opportunity, 1967-82; State Univ New York Cent Admin, dir affirmative action compliance & affirmative action officer, 1982-90; State Univ New York Cent Admin, affirmative action progs dir, 1990-97, adj prof, 1998, lectr, dept Africana Studies, currently. **Orgs:** Capital Dist Black & Puerto Rican Caucus; Am Asn Affirmative Action Officers; partic, Loaned Exec Prog; Leadership Develop Prog; consult training fund raising, Cleveland Found; chmn, Lee/Harvard Br, Nat Asn Advan Colored People Urban League; fund raiser, United Negro Col Fund; Omega Psi Phi Frat Inc; pres, Ala State Univ Alumni Asn; sire archon, Sigma Pi Phi Frat Beta Psi Chap; treas, 369th Veterans Asn; deacon, United Presby Church; vpres, Nova Univ Alumni Asn, New Eng, New York, 1989-90, pres; secy bd, Camp Opportunity, Albany, NY, 1989-90; Am Math Asn; Am Mgt Asn; Capital Dist Human Rights Adv Comt; Adv Comt Restoration & Display New York States Mil Battle Flags; bd dir, Nat Contact Points. **Home Addr:** 7 Keith Rd, Delmar, NY 12054-4006, **Home Phone:** (518)439-3583. **Business Addr:** Lecturer, State University of New York Albany, 1400 Washington Ave, Albany, NY 12222, **Business Phone:** (518)442-4730.

### THORNTON, OSIE M.

Association executive. **Personal:** Born Oct 6, 1939, Tuscaloosa, AL. **Educ:** Wayne State Univ, BA, 1961, MA, 1963. **Career:** Wayne Co Bur Soc Welfare; soc worker; Calif Dept Rehab Nat Rehab Assoc, vocrehab counr; Am Personnel & Guid Assoc; Big Bro Greater Los Angeles; lic child family marriage counr. **Orgs:** United High Blood Pressure Found; Nat Non-white Coun Assoc & Crenshaw Ctr Optimist Club. **Home Addr:** 8263 Pk Cir, Inglewood, CA 90305.

### THORNTON, OTIS J.

Entrepreneur, car dealer. **Personal:** Born Jan 1, 1952, Pocomoke City, MD; married Rosemary; children: 2. **Educ:** Lea Col, Minn, bus admin. **Career:** Gen Motors acceptance Corp, credit supvr, 1974; Joe Heidt Buick, Ramsey, NJ & Rea Buick Port Jervis, NY, salesman, sales consult & bus mgr, 1987-92; Coult Buick, Cherry Hill, NJ, owner, 1993; Ford dealership, 1995-96; E Brunswick, 1996; Chevrolet & Saturn franchises, Harlem Auto Mall, owner & operator, pres; Gen Motors Corp, chmn & chief exec officer, credit supvr; Gen Motors Acceptance Corp Platinum, dealer, 1974; Gen Motors Cert Used Vehicle, dealer, currently; Gen motors Goodwrench Lifetime Serv Facil, dealer, currently; E Breunswick Buick-Pontiac-GMC, currently; Automatic Data Processing Inc, Mgt Syst, suite dealer. **Orgs:** Gen Motors Minority Dealers Asn; Nat Asn Minority Dealers; Nat Asn Advan Colored People. **Special Achievements:** Black Enterprise Top 100 Auto Dealer, 1994, 2001, 2002; Entrepreneur of the Year, Baptist Ministries Conf of Greater NY & Vicinity, 2001. **Business Addr:** Chairman & Chief Executive Officer, Credit Supervisor, General Motors Corp, 300 Renaissance Ctr, Detroit, MI 48265, **Business Phone:** (313)556-5000.

### THORNTON, TRACEY E.

Government official. **Career:** White House, spec asst, pres legis affairs, 1994-98, dep asst, pres legis affairs & senate liaison, 1998-2000; US House Representatives, chief staff. **Orgs:** Electronic Frontier Found. **Business Addr:** Chief Staff, US House of Representatives, 2429 Rayburn HOB, Washington, DC 20515-0550, **Business Phone:** (202)225-3631.

### THORNTON, WAYNE T.

Banker, chief executive officer. **Personal:** Born Aug 13, 1958, Harrisburg, PA. **Educ:** Morgan State Univ, BS, finance, 1981. **Career:** US Off Comptroller Currency, nat bank examr, assoc bank examr, 1979-85; Indust Bank Wash & FinanCorp, asst vpres, 1985-87; Corvus Group Inc, founding prin, chief exec officer & owner, 1997-. **Orgs:** Realtor assoc, ERA Nyman Realty, 1985-; Resolution Trust Corp; bd dir, Univ Legal Serv, 1986-; founder, Corvus Group Inc. **Home Addr:** 2714 Matapeake Dr, Upper Marlboro, MD 20774-9475, **Home Phone:** (301)627-0898. **Business Addr:** Chief Executive Officer, Owner, The Corvus Group Inc, 9500 Arena Dr Suite 105, Largo, MD 20774, **Business Phone:** (301)322-8040.

### THORNTON, WILLIE

Businessperson, president (organization), business owner. **Personal:** Born Jan 22, 1954, Nettleton, MS; son of Willie and Birdie; married L Kay Collins; children: Willie III, Timothy, Jessica & Monica. **Educ:** Univ Nebr, BS, bus admin, 1976; MSP Col, MBA, 1983. **Career:** Ravelers, supvr data processing, 1976-83; Xerox Corp, acct mgr mkt, 1983-86; Cleaning Solutions Inc, pres & dir; Thorntons World Child Care, owner, 1998-; Summus Indust Inc, regional mgr, 2003. **Orgs:** T Charter mem, Amberton Univ, 1983; Garland Chamber Com, 1986-; Dallas Ft Worth Minority Bus Develop Coun, 1986-; Independent Small Bus Asn, 1989-; Houston Bus Coun, 1990-; OKL Minority Supplier Develop Coun, 1990-; Ark Regional Minority Purchasing Coun, 1990-; Dallas Black Chamber Com, 1992; mentor, entrepreneur prog, Dallas Ft Worth Minority Bus Develop Coun, 1996. **Home Addr:** 2221 Randi Rd, Rowlett, TX 75088, **Home Phone:** (972)412-2504. **Business Addr:** President, Director, Cleaning Solutions Inc, 4620 Industrial St Suite B, Rowlett, TX 75088, **Business Phone:** (972)412-2949.

### THORPE, EARL HOWARD

Computer executive, chief executive officer. **Personal:** Born Oct 15, 1936, Raleigh, NC; son of Marvin W and Lucille B; married Michelle N; children: Eric E, Wendy M, Zoe F, Alexia M & Scarlett V. **Educ:** NC Agr & Tech State Univ, BS, 1958. **Career:** US Dept Labor, asst dir dept acct opers, 1972-79; Dis Off Employ Security, dir, off budget & finance, 1979-80; US Dept Labor, dir, offfinancial mgt serv, 1980-86; Thorpe Int Inc, pres, chair, chief exec officer, 1986-. **Orgs:** Alpha Phi Alpha Fraternity, 1956-. **Home Addr:** 13312 Dove St, Silver Spring, MD 20904, **Home Phone:** (301)384-8035. **Business Addr:** Chairman, Chief Executive Officer, Thorpe International Inc, 2100 M St NW Suite 606, Washington, DC 20037, **Business Phone:** (202)857-7835.

### THORPE, HERBERT CLIFTON

Aircraft pilot, engineer, president (organization). **Personal:** Born Jan 9, 1923, New York, NY; married Jessie M Shorts; children: Jessica & R Clifton. **Educ:** NY Univ, BEE. **Career:** Aircraft pilot, engineer (retired); Rome Air Develop Ctr, elec engr. Tuskegee airman. **Orgs:** Pres, Rome Br, Nat Asn Advan Colored People; Mohawk Valley Frontiersmen; pres, Cosmopolitan Ctr; Heritage Asn, Rome, NY. **Special Achievements:** June 7th is declared as Herbert C Thorpe Day in Rome, NY. **Home Addr:** 6086 Shed Rd, Rome, NY 13440-8056, **Home Phone:** (315)337-5018.

### THORPE, JOSEPHINE HORSLEY

Lawyer. **Personal:** Born Jun 3, 1943, Elizabeth, NJ. **Educ:** Montclair St Univ, BA, 1964; Seaton Hall Univ, Sch Law & Rutgers Sch Law, JD, 1969. **Career:** Newark Legal Serv Proj, staff atty, 1969-70; Murphy Thorpe & Lewis, law partner, 1970-73; gen pract law, Newark, 1973-74; Educ Law, atty, 1974-75; Gen Attys Orgn, Western Elec Co Inc, atty, 1975. **Orgs:** Bar NJ; Bar NY; US Dist Ct, Dist NJ; vpres, Educ Law Ctr Inc, 1974-75; Garden St Bar Asn; Nat Bar Asn, 100 Women Integrity Govt. **Honors/Awds:** First place in oralpresentation of Appellants brief in Rutgers Moot Ct Competition, 1968; Recipient Regional Heber Smith Fellowship, 1969. **Home Addr:** 31 Kingman Rd, South Orange, NJ 07079-2718, **Home Phone:** (973)762-2885. **Business Addr:** 195 Broadway, New York, NY 12227.

### THORPE, OTIS HENRY

Basketball player. **Personal:** Born Aug 5, 1962, Boynton Beach, FL; married Donella; children: 2. **Educ:** Providence Col, RI, attended 1984. **Career:** Basketball player (retired); Kans City Kings, forward, 1984-85; Sacramento Kings, forward, 1985-88, 1998; Houston Rockets, forward, 1988-95; Portland Trail Blazers, forward, 1995; Detroit Pistons, forward, 1995-97; Vancouver Grizzlies, forward, 1997-98; Wash Wizards, forward, 1998-99; Miami Heat, forward, 1999-2000; Charlotte Hornets, forward, 2000-01. **Home Addr:** , Austin, TX.

### THORPE, WESLEY LEE, SR.

Executive director. **Personal:** Born Nov 20, 1926, Durham, NC; married Louise; children: Angela A & Wesley L Jr. **Educ:** A&T Univ, Greensboro, NC, grad, 1949. **Career:** Olin Matheson, scrap control mgr, 1952-56; Siskorsky Aircraft, inspector, 1956; Newhallville Cleaners, owner, 1965; Greaster New Haven Bus & Prof Mens Asn, exec dir; Delaney Cleaners Raleigh NC, asst mgr & tailor; Emergency Shelter Mgt Serv homeless shelter, chief exec officer, 1998-2013. **Orgs:** Widows Son Lodge 1 PH Mason NH; trustee, Immanuel Bapt Ch; sec Club 30 Inc; asst secy, Widows Son Lodge, 1955-56; bd dir, Community Progress Inc; bd Dir, BBB; bd Dir, JC New Haven; exec dir, Homeless To Independence Inc, currently. **Home Addr:** 75 Pembroke Rd, Hamden, CT 06514. **Business Addr:** Executive Director, Homeless To Independence Inc, 929 NJ-36, Union Beach, NJ 07735, **Business Phone:** (732)264-7500.

### THRASH, JAMES RAY

Executive, football player. **Personal:** Born Apr 28, 1975, Denver, CO. **Educ:** Mo Southern State Univ, BS, criminal justice, 2001. **Career:** Football player (retired), development staff; Wash Redskins, 1997, 1999, 2006, wide receiver, 1998, 2000, 2004-05, 2007-08, running back, 2005, fullback, 2008; Philadelphia Eagles, wide receiver, 1997, 2001-03; Christian evangelism; Wash Redskins, Redskins' player develop staff, currently. **Orgs:** Cert conditioning specialist, Nat Strength Prof Asn, 2003. **Honors/Awds:** Ed Block Courage Award, 2000; Unsung Hero Award, 2000; All-Am hons. **Business Addr:** Player Development Staff, Wash Redskins, 21300 Redskin Pk Dr, Ashburn, VA 20147, **Business Phone:** (703)726-7000.

### THREATT, SEDALE EUGENE

Basketball player, basketball coach. **Personal:** Born Sep 10, 1961, Atlanta, GA; married Nicole. **Educ:** WVa Univ Inst Technol, attended 1983. **Career:** Basketball player (retired), basketball coach; Philadelphia 76ers, guard, 1983-87; Chicago Bulls, guard, 1987-88; Seattle SuperSonics, guard, 1988-91; Los Angeles Lakers, guard, 1991-96; Paris Basket Racing, guard, 1996; Houston Rockets, guard, 1997; Larissa, Greece, guard, 1997-98; Olympique Lausanne, guard, 2001-02; Australian SEABL Team, Nunawading Spectres, head coach, 2008-09. **Business Addr:** Head Coach, Australian SEABL Team, PO Box 98, Nunawading3131, **Business Phone:** (610)39802-67.

### THROWER, JULIUS B.

Administrator, executive director. **Personal:** Born Mar 26, 1938, Mobile, AL; married Louise Green; children: Julian & Jason. **Educ:** Ala State Col Mobile Ctr, AS, 1962; Ala State Univ, BS, 1964; Univ Akron, cert, Phys Plant Admin, 1967; Auburn Univ, cert, jr col leader ship prog, 1969, MEd, 1971. **Career:** Mobile Co Pub Sch, high sch instr, 1964-66; SD Bishop State Jr Col, plant supvr, 1966-70, coordr spec serv & develop, 1971-73, dir veterans affairs, 1973-77, dir admin, veterans coord, 1977-. **Orgs:** Jr Col Leadership Conf Auburn Univ, 1969; VCIP adv bd, US Dept HEW, 1975-76; former sr warden, F & AM Onyx Ldg 676, 1975-76; asst recorder, Shriner Palestine Temple, 1975-76; bd mgt, Metro YMCA Mobile Deaborn St Br; adv bd, Mobile Consortium CETA; past vice chmn, Am Asn Minority Prog Admin, 1977-78; comr Nat Comns Employ Policy, 1979; vice chmn Am Asn Minority Veterans Prog Adminr. **Honors/Awds:** SGA Award, student govt asn SD Bishop State Jr Col, 1976; Good Conduct Medal. **Home Addr:** 1228 Dunaway Dr, Mobile, AL 36605, **Home Phone:** (205)473-4511.

### THURMAN, ALFONZO

Educator. **Personal:** Born Oct 24, 1946, Mayfield, KY; son of Togo and Georgia May Jones; married Brazilian Burnette; children: Alfonzo II. **Educ:** Univ Wis-LaCrosse, BS, eng lang & lit, 1970; Univ Wis-Madison, MA, educ policy studies & educ admin, 1973, PhD, educ policy studies & educ admin, 1979. **Career:** Univ Wisc-Whitewater, Minority Affairs, coordr, 1971-75; Univ Wisc-Oshkosh, Acad Develop Prog, dir, 1975-80; Northern Ill Univ, Spec Proj, dir, 1980-84, asst provost, 1984-87, Col Educ, prof, assoc dean, 1987-95, dean, 1995-2001; Univ Wisc-Milwaukee, Sch Educ, dean, prof, 2001-11, Res Ctr Urban Educ Leadership, prof & dir, 2011-, Urban Educ Doctoral Progs, dir, 2014-, Dept Admin Leadership, prof, currently. **Orgs:** Pres, Ill Asn Educ Opportunity Prog, 1983-84; chmn, DeKalb Human Rels Comn, 1983-86; parliamentarian, Mid-Am Asn Educ Opportunity Prog, 1989-90; bd dir, Ill Asn Col Teacher Educ; pres, Holmes Partnership; bd trustee Great Milwaukee Boys & Girls Clubs; Educare Gov Bd; bd dir, Coun Acad Deans from Res Educ Insts; bd dir, Am Asn Cols Teacher Educ. **Home Addr:** 527 Ridge Rd, DeKalb, IL 60115. **Business Addr:** Dean, University of Wisconsin-Milwaukee, Enderis Hall 513 2400 E Hartford Ave, Milwaukee, WI 53211, **Business Phone:** (414)416-2729.

### THURMAN, CEDRIC DOUGLAS

Banker, vice president (organization). **Personal:** Born May 5, 1964, Chicago, IL; son of Walter and Cleola Jr; married Michelle Speller. **Educ:** Univ Ill-Urbana, BS, finance, 1987; Northwestern Univ, J L Kellogg Grad Sch Mgt, MBA, mgt strategy & mkt, 1996. **Career:** Harris Trust & Savings Bank, com banking trainee, 1987-89, int banking rep, Trade Finance, 1989-91, asst vpres community develop, 1991-93, vpres br mgt, 1993-94, proj mgr, Personal Financial Serv Dept, 1994-2000; Jones Lang LaSalle, chief diversity officer & sr vpres, 2000-14. **Orgs:** Nat INROADS Alumni Asn, 1987-; Urban Bankers Forum Chicago, 1987-2000; bd mem, Univ Ill Com Alumni Asn, 1994-; area bd mem, Jr Achievement Chicago, 1995-; Nat Asn African Americans Human Resources, 2008-10; chair, Mus Sci & Indust, 2003-; bd mem, Diversity Exec Mag, 2008-. **Home Addr:** 4628 S Woodlawn Ave, Chicago, IL 60653-4410. **Business Addr:** US Head of Diversity & Inclusion, BMO Harris Bank, Chicago, IL 60601, **Business Phone:** (312)782-5800.

### THURMAN, MARJORIE ELLEN

Educator. **Personal:** Born Whiteville, NC. **Educ:** Fayetteville State Univ, BS, 1969; Seton Hall Univ, MA, 1977; Montclair State Univ, Thistle prog & admin cert, 1990. **Career:** Newark Bd Educ, teacher, (retired); Essex Col Bus, instr, 1975-85; Sawyer Bus Sch, eve dean, 1979-80; Sen Wynona Lipman, part-time clerical, 1985-; SCS Bus & Tech Inst, part-time instr, 1986-; Malcolm X Shabazz High Sch, bus teacher. **Orgs:** YWCA, 1972-83; sunday sch teacher, St Paul's Church, 1978-80; adv, Sr Class MX Shabazz, 1985-87; Minority Bus Orgn, 1985-; Nat Bus Educ Asn; NJ Bus Educ Asn; Newark Teacher's Union; Alpha Kappa Alpha Sorority. **Home Addr:** 222 Davey St Apt D, Bloomfield, NJ 07003. **Business Addr:** Business Teacher, Malcolm X Shabazz High School, Newark, NJ 07108.

### THURMOND, NATE (NATHANIEL THURMOND)

Sports manager, business owner, basketball player. **Personal:** Born Jul 25, 1941, Akron, OH; married Marci; children: Adam. **Educ:** Bowling Green State Univ, BS, 1963. **Career:** Basketball player (retired), sports manager, business owner; San Francisco Warriors, player, 1963-71; Golden State Warriors, player, 1963-74, dir community rels, 1981-95; NBA All-Star, player, 1965-68, 1970, 1973-74; Chicago Bulls, player, 1974-76; Cleveland Cavaliers, player, 1976-77; Big Nate's BBQ Restaurant, owner, 1990-2011. **Orgs:** Bd mem, SCARE. **Special Achievements:** Acted in a film Troika, 1969. **Home Addr:** 5094 Diamond Hts Blvd Suite B, San Francisco, CA 94131.

### THURSTON, DR. CHARLES SPARKS

Dermatologist, physician. **Personal:** Born Mar 13, 1934, King and Queen County, VA; married Marie; children: Renee, Cynthia, Patti & Carmen. **Educ:** Va State Col, BS, 1953; Meharry Med Col, MD, 1958. **Career:** Univ Mich Med Ctr, researcher, 1965-66; Howard Univ, asst clin prof, 1968-70; Georgetown Univ, 1968-70; G Wash Univ, 1968-70; Univ Tex, 1974-; Santa Rosa Hosp, chief dermatologist, 1978; Downtown Dermat Clin, dermatologist. **Orgs:** Pres local chap, Alpha Omega Alpha, 1957-58; fel Am Acad Dermat, 1967-; AMA, 1968-; Mass Med Asn, 1968-; pres, Asn Mil Dermat, 1975; San Antonio Dermat Soc, 1975-; Am Col Physiol, 1975-; pres, Calif Whittier Med Soc, 1977-78; vpres, Lone Star St Med Soc, 1977; chmn, Nat Dermat Sect, Nat Med Asn, 1977-79; Gamma Phi. **Honors/Awds:** R Braun Award, Outstanding Sr & Med Std Surg, 1958; cert, Achievement Surg Gen, 1970; V Marchbanks Award, Outstanding Air Force Physician, 1974. **Business Addr:** Dermatologist, Downtown Dermat Clinic, 343 W Houston St Suite 909, San Antonio, TX 78205, **Business Phone:** (210)222-0376.

### THURSTON, DR. PAUL E.

Educator, college teacher. **Personal:** Born Jul 13, 1938, Williamsport, PA; son of Helen Louise. **Educ:** Lafayette Col, BS, 1960; Cornell Univ, PhD, 1964. **Career:** Educator (retired); Tex Southern Univ, asst prof, 1966-73, assoc prof, 1974-81, prof emer chem. **Orgs:** Am Chem Soc; Am Asn Univ Prof; Phi Beta Kappa. **Honors/Awds:** Recipient of Dan forth fel & Woodrow Wilson fel. **Home Addr:** 4114 Belle Pk Dr, Houston, TX 77072-1304, **Home Phone:** (281)933-8767. **Business Addr:** Professor Emeritus of Chemistry, Texas Southern University, 3100 Cleburne St, Houston, TX 77004, **Business Phone:** (713)313-7011.

### THURSTON, WILLIAM A.

Clergy, architect, human rights activist. **Personal:** Born Jun 6, 1944, Chicago, IL; married Silvia M Petty; children: William A, Peter O, Omyia N & Pauline A. **Educ:** Graham Found Scholar, 1966; Univ Ill, BA, 1967; Moody Bible Inst, 1979; Candler Sch Theol, 1980; Emory Univ, Master Divinity, doctor philos ethics & soc. **Career:** Oper PUSH, nat dir; Seymour S Goldstein Assoc Chicago, arch, 1965-67; Dubin Dubin Black Moutoussamy Chicago, arch, 1967-69; Environ Seven Ltd, Chicago, pntr dir planning, 1969-74; ReMax Pacesetters, Realtor; Shaw Univ, dept relig & philos, chair, ethics & leadership develop, dir; Servants & Kingdom Advancing Ministries, co-founder; KAP Internet TravelPlus Ctr, Mkt Div, co-owner; Your Total Biz Network, founder, chief exec officer & Head Coach. **Orgs:** Assoc minister Fel, Missionary Baptist Church; bd mem, Comprehensive Res, Develop Chicago Arch Assis Ctr; Nat Asn Housing Owners & Mgr. **Business Addr:** Founder, Chief Executive Officer, 5232 Calverton Dr, Raleigh, NC 27613-5619, **Business Phone:** (919)523-7456.

### TIBBS, EDWARD A.

Lawyer, government official. **Personal:** Born Apr 12, 1940, Pittsburgh, PA; son of Mayme Yager and Otis H; married Sheila Christian, May 10, 1988; children: Darryl Wright & Leslie Wright (Deceased). **Educ:** Univ Pittsburgh; Wilson Col, attended 1980. **Career:** E Liberty-Garfield CAP, bd mem, 1968-74; Allegheny County, dem comt man, 1970-81, paymaster, 1980-81; Wilson Col, cert instr, 1980; IBPOE W Elks, asst grand exalted ruler, 1982-; Allegheny County, dist magistrate, 1982-; Spec Ct Judges Allegheny County, first vpres, 1995; Lincoln, Larimer, Lemington, Belmar, Citizens Revitalization Develop Corp, exec dir, 1993-97; Commonwealth Pa, Dist Justice Ct Allegheny County, Judge, currently. **Orgs:** Exec bd mem, Local 2596 CWA, 1973-80; chmn, Allegheny County Black Polit Assembly, 1976-77; exalted ruler, Greater Pittsburgh Elks, 1979-82; Comt Ethics Commun Workers Am, 1973-76; vpres, Pittsburgh Job Corps, Community Rels Coun, 1992-; life mem, Nat Asn Advan Colored People; life mem, Sixth Mt Zion Baptist Church. **Honors/Awds:** Community Service Award, Community Action Pittsburgh, 1975; Mr Elk, IBPOEW Pittsburgh, 1979; Meritorious Service Award, Pa Chaplains, Dept IBPOE WPa, 1981; Distinguished Achievement Award, Steel City Coun 8 IBPOE W Pa, 1981; Leadership with Excellence Award, Faith Tabernacle Church, 1986; Hall of Fame, Westinghouse High Sch, 1996; Wall of Fame The Westinghouse High Sch, 2007. **Home Addr:** 6399 Olivant St, Pittsburgh, PA 15206, **Home Phone:** (412)404-7686. **Business Addr:** Judge, Commonwealth of Pennsylvania, 1013 Lincoln Ave, Pittsburgh, PA 15206-2767, **Business Phone:** (412)661-8829.

### TIDWELL, ISAIAH

Banker. **Personal:** Born Feb 13, 1945, Charlotte, NC; son of William and Anna D; married Hellena O Huntley; children: William DeVane & Damion Lamar. **Educ:** NC Cent Univ, BS, accounting, 1967; Wake Forest Univ, MBA, 1980. **Career:** Banker (retired); NC Cent Univ, pres, 1965-67; Celanese Fibers Co, acct, 1967-70, cost acct, 1970-71, supvr, cost anal, 1971-72; Wachovia Bank & Trust Co, 1972-96, regional exec vpres, 1995-99, Ga Banking, pres, 1999-2001, exec vpres & dir wealth mgt opers, 2001-05; Lance Inc, bd dir, 1995-; Ruddick Corp, bd dir, 1999-; Lincoln Nat Corp, bd dir, 2006-. **Orgs:** Comn Fin, NC Cent Univ Alumni Asn, life mem, 1967-76, pres, Charlotte Chap, 1974-76; Omega Psi Phi, 1969-76; Charlotte Chamber Com, 1973-76; chmn bd, Charlotte Bus Devel Orgn, 1974-76; bd mem, Charlotte Bus Resource Ctr, 1975-76; bd trustee, fin secy, Friendship Baptist Church-E Winston; pres, PTA Moore Alt Sch; life mem, Omega Psi Phi Fraternity Inc, Basileus; Statement Studies Comn Robert Morris Asn; Region IV Charlotte Adv Coun US Small Bus Admin; bd dir, chmn Bus II Div, Campaign United Way Forsyth Co, 1982; pres, bd dir, Winston-Salem Neighborhood Housing Serv; bd dir, Fin Comm YMCA-Metro Bd, City/Co Utility Comn Winston-Salem & Forsyth Co, 1984; W/S Chamber Com, W/S Rotary; Bachelor Benedict's Club; Sigma Pi Phi Fraternity; founder, Piedmont Club, 1985-; 100 Black Men Atlanta; Atlanta Rotary Club; bd dir, Southern Educ Found; trustee, Woodruff Arts Ctr & Proj Grad; Cent Piedmont Community Col Found; Boy Scouts Am Atlanta Chap. **Honors/Awds:** Boss of the Year Award, Winston-Salem Chap, Am Bus Women's Asn, 1980; Omega Man of the Year Award, Winston Salem Chap, Omega Psi Phi Fraternity, 1983; Man Year, Winston-Salem Chronicle, 1988; Distinguished Service Award, Bachelor Benedict's Club, 1990; Charlotte NAACP Hall of Fame, 1996; Black Political Caucus Hall of Distinction Award, 1999; The Distinguished Alumnus Award, Nc Cent Univ. 2001. **Home Addr:** 1059 Hunters Brook Ct NE, Atlanta, GA 30319-4714, **Home Phone:** (404)760-9518. **Business Addr:** Board of Director, Lincoln National Corp, 150 North Radnor Chester Rd, Radnor, PA 19087, **Business Phone:** (877)275-5462.

### TIDWELL, JOHN EDGAR

Educator, administrator. **Personal:** Born Dec 13, 1945, Independence, KS; son of Harry Sr and Verlean; children: Levert, Trudy & Tuere. **Educ:** Washburn Univ, BA, Eng, 1969; Creighton Univ, MA, Eng, 1971; Univ Minn, PhD, Eng, 1981. **Career:** Maur Hill Cath Col Prep Sch, Atchison, KS, instr, 1968-70; Atchison Neighborhood Ctr, Atchison, KS, dir, 1969-70; Creighton Univ, Upward Bound Prog, instr, 1970 & 1971; Creighton Univ, New Careers Prog, instr, 1970-71; Univ Nebr, Omaha, instr, 1971-73; Univ Nebr, Omaha, Black Studies Dept, actg chmn, 1972-73; St Olaf Col, Am Minority Studies, dir, 1973-74; St Olaf Col, instr, 1973-75; Univ Minn, teaching assoc II, 1975-78; Am Lutheran Church Future Fac, fel, 1975-77; Carleton Col, vis instr, 1977, 1979; Univ Minn, Putnam Dana Mc Millan fel, 1979; Univ Ky, Eng Dept, asst prof, 1981-87; Nat Endowment Humanities, fel independent study & res, 1985-86; Miami Univ, asst prof, 1987-92; Miami Univ, asst prof, 1987-92, assoc prof, 1993-99; Kan State Univ, vis scholar eng & ethnic minority studies, 1993; Univ Kans, Langston Hughes vis prof eng, african & am studies, 1994, assoc prof, 1999, prof eng, currently. **Orgs:** Mod Lang Asn; Midwest Mod Lang Asn; Col Lang Asn; Langston Hughes Soc; vis fel Afro-Am Studies, Yale Univ, 1985-86; Non-resident Fel W E B Du Bois InstAfro-Am Res, Harvard Univ, 2003-04; fel Humanities Res Fel Hall CtrHumanities, Univ Kans, 2006. **Honors/Awds:** National Fellowships Fund Award, 1978-81; Jessamine Allen Dissertation Fund Award, Univ Minn, 1980; NEH Travel to Collections Grant, 1992; Grant for Research Graduate Assistant, Miami Univ, 1993-94. **Home Addr:** 2115 N 26th St, Laurence, KS 66046-5624, **Home Phone:** (785)331-4201. **Business Addr:** Professor, University of Kansas, 3027 Wescoe Hall, Lawrence, KS 66045-2115, **Business Phone:** (785)864-2583.

### TIGGER, BIG (DARIAN MORGAN)

Radio host. **Personal:** Born Dec 22, 1972, Bronx, NY. **Educ:** Univ Md. **Career:** WERQ FM; FM92 Q, Baltimore, dj; Detroit FM98 WJLB, Miami's new 103.5 FM & New York Power 105.1 FM, host; Black Entertainment Tv, 1996-; video jockey, 1999-2005; WPGC 95.5, Live in the Den, host, 2007-; Wash Wizards games, resident DJ, currently; Album: Snake; The Senior; TV Series: "Live in the Den with Big Tigger"; "Rap City: Tha Bassment"; "Tha Booth"; "BET Style", 2003; "Blueprint: Lil Wayne", 2008; "Where's the Love?", 2014; "Drumline: A New Beat", 2014; TV Show: DC50-TV/WDCW; WPHL-TV. **Orgs:** Street Corner found. **Special Achievements:** Six-year undefeated nighttime radio champion. **Business Addr:** Host, Live in the Den, 1270 Avenue of the Americas 14th Fl, New York, NY 10020.

### TILLERY, DWIGHT

Government official, president (organization). **Personal:** Born Mar 10, 1948, Cincinnati, OH; son of Wesley and Doris Mae. **Educ:** Univ Cincinnati, BA, polit sci, 1970; Univ Mich, JD, 1972. **Career:** City Cincinnati, asst solicitor, 1973-74; Univ Cincinnati, vpres, 1974-77; adj asst prof law, 1975-77; Univ Cincinnati Law Sch, consult, 1977-78; Tillery & Assocs, partner, 1977-83; City Cincinnati, consult, 1980-82; State Ohio, Columbus, sr asst atty gen, 1983-85; Off Atty Gen, Columbus, consult, 1985; Miami Univ, asst prof bus law, 1985; Cincinnati, mayor, 1991-93; City Cincinnati, coun mem, 1997-98; Ctr Closing Health Gap Greater Cincinnati, founder, 2004, pres & chief exec officer, currently. **Orgs:** Fel Am Nar Asn; Nat Bar Asn; Cincinnati Bar Asn; Asn Trial Lawyers Am; Black Lawyers Asn Cincinnati; bd dir, W. Montague Cobb/NMA Health Inst, Nat Med Asn, 2012; Ohio State Personnel Bd Rev. **Special Achievements:** First African American popularly elected Mayor of Cincinnati. **Home Addr:** 3462 Trimble Ave, Cincinnati, OH 45207-1626. **Business Addr:** President, Chief Executive Officer, The Center For Closing The Health Gap In Greater Cincinnati, 3120 Burnet Ave Suite 201, Cincinnati, OH 45229, **Business Phone:** (513)585-9872.

### TILLEY, DR. FRANK NEWTON

Physician. **Personal:** Born Jul 17, 1933, New York, NY; married Frances A Payne. **Educ:** Columbia Col, BA, 1955; State Univ NY Sch Med Downstate Med Ctr, MD, 1959; Columbia Univ Sch Pub Health & Admin Med, MPH, 1964. **Career:** New York Health Dept, 1965; Jewish Hosp & Med Ctr Brooklyn Green pt Affil, emer serv attend physician, 1965-67, 1969, Emer Dept, asst dir, 1971, coordr ambulatory care, 1971-73; United Mutual Life Ins Co, med dir, 1972; State Univ NY Downstate Med Ctr, Dept Environ Med & Community Health, lectr, 1972-74, Dept Family Prac, clin asst, 1974; Jewish Hosp & Med Ctr Brooklyn Green pt Affil, Dept Ambulatory Care, chief, 1973; United Mutual Life Ins Co, bd dir, 1974; Mt Vernon, NY, pvt pract, currently. **Orgs:** Fel Am Col Prev Med; Am Col Emer Physicians; Med Soc State NY; Med Soc Co Kings; Provident Clin Soc; Am Geriatrics Soc; Am Pub Health Asn; New York Pub Health Asn; Am Soc Trop Med & Hyg; New York Soc Topical Med; 100 Black Men. **Honors/Awds:** Commendation Medal, 1969; Certificate of Achievement, AUS, 1969. **Home Addr:** 102 Seton Dr, New Rochelle, NY 10804. **Business Addr:** Physician, 290 Bedford Ave, Mount Vernon, NY 10553-1548.

### TILLIS, BABY. See TILLIS, DR. FREDERICK CHARLES.

### TILLIS, DR. FREDERICK CHARLES (BABY TILLIS)

Educator, composer, writer. **Personal:** Born Jan 5, 1930, Galveston, TX; son of General and Zelma Bernice; married Edna Louise; children: Patricia & Pamela C. **Educ:** Wiley Col, BA, music, 1949; Univ Iowa, MA, music compos, 1952, PhD, music compos, 1963. **Career:** Educator (retired); Wiley Col, instr & dir, instrumental music, 1949-51, asst prof & chmn, dept music, 1956-61, 1963-64; Grambling Col, prof music & head theory dept, 1964-67; Ky State Univ, prof & head music dept, 1967-69; Univ Mass, assoc prof music, 1970-73, prof, music theory & compos & dir Afro Am music & jazz prog, 1973-97, U Mass jazz workshop, dir, 1974-80, dir fine arts ctr, 1978-97, assoc chancellor affirmative action & equal opportunity, 1990-97, Dept Music & Dance, prof emer, currently, Univ Fine Arts Ctr, dir emer, 1998-; Univ Fine Arts Ctr, prof emer dept music & dance; Univ Mass, Amherst, dir jazz, currently; P & P Publ, owner, currently; Cent Side High Sch, band dir; Poetry: In the Spirit & the Flesh, 1989; Images Mind & Heart, 1991; In Celebration, 1992; Of Moons, Moods, Myths & the Muse, P & P Publ, 1993; "Free as a Feather", Jazz Educr J, 1994; Harlem Echoes, 1995; C's Corner: From A to Z, 1997; Seasons, Symbols & Stones, 1999; Akiyoshidai Dairy, 2000; Bittersweet Harvests, 2001; Shattered Ghosts & Southern Walls, 2002; Breaking Dawn & Healing, 2005; The Nature of Things, 2006. Albums: "Freedom", 1970; "Fantasy on a Theme by Julian Adderley", 1975; "Music Frederick Tillis", Vol I, 1979; "Quintet for Brass", 1980; "Kcor Variations", 1980; "Elegy", 1983; "Swing Low, Deep River", 1984; "Contrasts & Diversions: The Tillis-Holmes Jazz Duo", 1987; "Voices Color", 1989; "Crucification", 1990; "Paintings in Sound", 1990; "The Second Time Around: The Tillis-Holmes Jazz Duo", 1991; "Among Friends, The Billy Taylor Trio & Fred Tillis", 1992; "Freedom: The Music Frederick Tillis", 1996; "Festival Journey Concerto", 1998; "Portraits from Gershwin's Porgy & Bess", 1999; "A Tribute to Duke Ellington", 1999. **Orgs:** Fac Senate Coun Status Minorities, 1984-; Chancellor's Exec Adv Coun, 1994-; ALANA Hon Soc Bd, 1994-; Music or DA bd dir, 1995; Musicorda, 1995-; Mass Cult Coun, 1997-; adv comm, Fac & Staff Capital Campaign, Univ Mass, 1998-; chair, edu adv comm, Nat Music Found, 1998-; Acad Am Poets; Am Composers Alliance; Am Fedn Musicians; Broadcast Music Indust; Ctr Black Music Res; Int Assoc Jazz Educr; Music Educr Nat Conf; Trans Africa Forum; Am Music Ctr; Mass Music Educr Assoc; bd dir, United Negro Col Fund. **Honors/Awds:** Recip United Negro Col Fund Fel, 1961-63; Rockefeller Fund Grant for Develop Compstn, 1978; Nat Endowment for the Arts, Composers Grant, 1979; Chancellor, Univ Mass, Distinguished Lecturer, 1980; Mass Cultural Coun, Commonwealth Award org leadership, 1997; Distinguished Achievement Award Black Musicians CNF, 1998; Recognition Award for 30 Years Serv Com for the Collegiate Edu Black and Other Minority Students (CCEBMS) 1998. **Special Achievements:** Published seven books of poetry. **Home Phone:** (413)549-6939. **Business Addr:** Owner, P & P Publications, 55 Grantwood Dr, Amherst, MA 01002-1537, **Business Phone:** (413)549-3632.

### TILLMAN, CEDRIC CORNELL

Football player, journalist. **Personal:** Born Jul 22, 1970, Natchez, MS. **Educ:** Alcorn State Univ, BA, mass commun, 1993. **Career:** Football player (retired), journalist; Denver Broncos, wide receiver, 1992-94; WDAM, prod asst, 1994-96; Jacksonville Jaguars, wide receiver, 1995; Ariz Rattlers, wide receiver, 1997-99; Alcorn State Univ, cable oper mgr, 1997-2001; WPRL-FM, sideline reporter, 2000-, host; Las Vegas Outlaws, 2001; City Vicksburg, videographer & photojournalist, 2001-06; Vicksburg Warren Sch Dist, videographer & photojournalist, 2006-. **Business Addr:** Videographer, Photojournalist, Vicksburg Warren School District, 1500 Mission 66, Vicksburg, MS 39180, **Business Phone:** (601)638-5122.

### TILLMAN, CHRISTINE L.

Government official, social worker. **Personal:** Born Dec 14, 1952, Richmond, VA. **Educ:** Radford Col, BA, 1975; Va Commonwealth Univ, 1976; J Seargeant Reynolds Community Col, attended 1984.

**Career:** Richmond Opport Indust Ctr, youth counr, 1975. **Orgs:** Basileus, 1972-75; Alpha Kappa Alpha; mem bd dir, Dawn Progressive Asn Inc, 1978-; Caroline County Bd Supvrs, 1983-, vice chmn, 1985, chmn, 1987-; Caroline Co Rec Adv Comn, 1984-; Caroline Co Ext Serv Adv Coun; Va Politech Inst & State Univ, 1984-; Caroline Co Local Welfare Bd, 1985; Nat Asn Advan Colored People Caroline Chapt; bd mem, Tri-County Med Corp, 1985-; Foster Care; County Recreation Comt; bd dir, Dawn Progressive Asn; Hanover County Dept Social Serv. **Honors/Awds:** Honoree Negro Achievers Award, Caroline County Chap, Nat Asn Advan Colored People, 1984. **Special Achievements:** First African American Female Member in the Caroline County Board of Supervisor. **Home Addr:** 30372 Sadie Lane Rd, Doswell, VA 23047, **Home Phone:** (804)994-5262. **Business Addr:** Social Worker, Hanover County, PO Box 507, Bowling Green, VA 22427.

### TILLMAN, GEORGE, JR.

Movie director, movie producer. **Personal:** Born Jan 26, 1969, Milwaukee, WI; son of George; married Marcia Wright; children: 1. **Educ:** Columbia Col, Chicago, IL, film & video, 1991. **Career:** Director, writer & producer; State St Pictures, owner; Films: Paula, 1992; Scenes for the Soul, 1995; Soul Food, 1997; Men of Honor, 2000; Barbershop, producer, 2002; Barbershop 2: Back in Business, producer, 2004; Beauty Shop, producer, 2005; Roll Bounce, producer, 2005; Nothing Like the Holidays, producer, 2008; Notorious, dir, 2009; Faster, dir, 2010; The Inevitable Defeat of Mister & Pete, dir, 2013; TV series: HBO First Look, 2000; Soul Food, exec producer, 2002; Barbershop, exec producer, 2005; The Brandon T Jackson Show, exec producer, 2006; Made in Hollywood, 2013. **Honors/Awds:** Midwestern Student Academy Award, 1990; Oscar Micheaux Excellence in Film Award, Nat Asn Black-Owned Broadcasters; Image Award, Nat Asn Advan Colored People; Academy of Motion Pictures Arts & Sciences Student Academy Award; The Black Filmmakers Hall of Fame Award. **Home Addr:** 2660 Hollyridge Dr, Los Angeles, CA 90068-3037. **Business Addr:** Director, Producer, 20th Century Fox, 10201 W Pico Blvd Bldg 50, Los Angeles, CA 90035, **Business Phone:** (310)369-5099.

### TILLMAN, DR. JOSEPH NATHANIEL

Executive, association executive, army officer. **Personal:** Born Aug 1, 1926, Augusta, GA; son of Leroy and Canarie; married Areerat; children: Alice Tillman Thornton & Robert Bertram; married Alice Lavonia Walton. **Educ:** Paine Col, BA, 1948; Northrop Univ, MS, 1975, MBA, 1976; Nova Univ, DBA, 1989. **Career:** Executive (retired); Rockwell Int, dir, 1958-84; Tillman Enterprises, staff, 1985-2005. **Orgs:** vpres, Paine Col Alumni Asn, 1976-2004; Pres, Nat Asn Advan Colored People, San Gabriel Chap, 1984; pres, Soc Logistics Engrs, Orange County Chap, 1984-88; chmn, Orgn Behav, Acad Mgt, 1985; Mem Acad Mgt, 1985-86; consult, Nat Univ, 1986. **Honors/Awds:** Presidential Citation, Nat Asn Equal Opportunity Higher Educ, 1986. **Special Achievements:** Numerous publications including "Computer Algorithm for OptimizingTestability" 1976; "Testability Optimizing at all Levels of Maintenance", 1984; "An Evaluation of Middle Managers Coping Strategies in AerospaceIndustries as a Predictor of their Success", 1986; "Job Stressors andCoping Strategies of Aerospace Managers: Their Influence on Healthy LifeStyles and Job Performance", 1989. **Home Addr:** 1550 S Rimpau Ave Suite 45, Corona, CA 92881-3206, **Home Phone:** (951)371-8179.

### TILLMAN, DR. MARY ANNE

Physician. **Personal:** Born Sep 4, 1935, Bristow, OK; daughter of Thomas Tuggle and Ruthie English Tuggle; married Daniel Thomas; children: Dana Tillman Chee & Daniel T Jr. **Educ:** Howard Univ, Wash, DC, BS, 1956, MD, 1960. **Career:** Physician (retired); Homer G Phillips Hosp, internship, transitional yr, 1960-61, residency, pediat, 1961-64; Self-employed, physician pediatrician, 1963; City St Louis Dept Health & Hosps, physician & supvr, 1963-85. **Orgs:** Nat grammateus, Zeta Phi Beta Sorority, 1965-70; pres, Mound City Med Forum, 1980-82; comt adoptions, Am Acad Pediat, 1970-76; pres, Homer G Phillips Internes Alumni Asn, 1980-82; pres, bd dir, Annie Malone C Home, 1991-94; Nat Med Asn; AMA. **Honors/Awds:** Woman of Achievement in Medicine, St Louis Globe Democrat, 1982; Outstanding Alumni Award, Howard Univ Sch Med, 1985; YWCA, Leader Award, YWCA, 1987; Feature article, Making Mama's Dream Come True, Good Housekeeping Mag, 1986; Outstanding Nat Service Award, Zeta Phi Beta Sorority, 1986; Laymen's Award, Cote Brilliante Presby Church, 1988; Distinguished Service Award, Pediat Sect Nat Med Asn, 1991; 25 Years of Excellence Award, Barnes Hosp, 1994; Women in Medicine Award, Nat Med Asn, 2002. **Home Addr:** 26 Washington Terr, St. Louis, MO 63112-1914, **Home Phone:** (314)355-7690. **Business Addr:** Pediatrician, Private Practioner, 330 Northland Med Bu, St. Louis, MO 63136-1412, **Business Phone:** (314)385-5522.

### TILLMAN, PAULA SELLARS

Lawyer, government official, association executive. **Personal:** Born Jun 21, 1949, Chicago, IL; daughter of Herschel L (deceased) and Sylvia L Cookman (deceased); married James Sr; children: Lisa & James III. **Educ:** Loyola Univ, Chicago, BA, magna cum laude, 1974; DePaul Col Law, JD, 1979. **Career:** Chicago Police Dept, youth officer, 1974-79, financial crimes invest, 1979-81, legal officer II, 1981-89, sgt, 1988-; liaison mayor's comn women, 1984-, EEO officer, 1984-; Labor Rels Coun Cook County Pub, Defender, currently; BT Express Trucking Inc, chief pres, currently. **Orgs:** Cook County Bar Asn, 1979-; comnr, Ill Atty Regist & Disciplinary Comn, 1981-; chairperson, personnel comn Chicago Coalition Against Abused Women, 1984-85; sec bd dir, Providence St Mel High Sch, 1984-85; Leadership Greater Chicago, 1985-86; Campfire Inc, 1986-97; legis chairperson, Nat Hook-Up Black Women Chicago Chap, 1986-90; vpres, legis affairs, Sojourner's United Polit Action Comn, 1990-; pres & co-chair, Ill Women's Comn Elect Carol Moseley Brown; pres/bd dir, Campfire Metrop Chicago, 1994; pres & co-founder, Women's Res Ctr, 1997; comnr, Ill Supreme Ct. **Home Addr:** 9139 May, Chicago, IL 60620. **Business Addr:** Chief President, Chief Executive Officer, BT Express Trucking, 744 Swallow Tail Ct, Valparaiso, IN 46385, **Business Phone:** (219)764-2100.

### TILLMAN, DR. TALMADGE CALVIN, JR.

Accountant, educator, certified public accountant. **Personal:** Born Nov 26, 1925, Brunswick, GA; son of Talmadge and Lavonn; married Leola Bennings; children: Timothy & Philip. **Educ:** Ind Univ, BS, 1948; Syracuse Univ, MBA, 1949; Univ Southern Calif, CA, CPA, 1965, DBA, 1967. **Career:** Howard Univ, Wash, 1949-50; Tex Southern Univ, chmn acct, 1950-51; Joseph S Herbert & Co, jr acct, 1951-52; Gilbert Drummont, cert pub acct, 1952-53; Sidney Spiegel cert pub acct, auditor-acct, 1953-54; Rec Merchandising Co, acct, 1954-55; Fremont High Sch, teacher & dept chmn, 1956-62; E Los Angeles Col, assoc prof accountancy, 1962-68; Price Waterhouse, fel & fac, 1969; Calif State Univ Long Beach, prof accountancy, 1968-91, prof emer accountancy, 1991-. **Orgs:** Treas, Syracuse Univ Alumni Asn, 1953; pres, Ind Univ Alumni Asn, 1978-79; Basileus Omega Psi Phi, Lambda Omicron Chap, 1978-80; pres, Ind Univ Club, 1978-80; pres, Big Ten Club Southern Calif, 1990-91; pres, Syracuse Univ Club, 1992-93; Syracuse Univ Alumni Asn Southern Calif, 1992; pres, Univ Southern Calif Alumni Club, 1998; Am Acct Asn; Calif Socs cert pub accountants; Am Inst cert pub accountants; Nat Acct Asn; Phi Delta Kappa; Alpha Kappa Psi; Beta Gamma Sigma; Beta Alpha Psi. **Home Addr:** 4578 Don Miguel Dr, Los Angeles, CA 90008, **Home Phone:** (323)292-7953. **Business Addr:** Professor Emeritus of Accounting, California State University Long Beach, 1250 Bellflower Blvd, Long Beach, CA 90840, **Business Phone:** (562)985-4111.

### TILLMAN-DEWITT, LILLIAN G.

Educator, school principal, elementary school teacher. **Personal:** Born Jan 27, 1934, Jamaica, NY; children: Kay Lynn & James Edward; married Kenneth. **Educ:** Hunter Col, attended 1952, 1961; NY Univ, attended 1954; Roosevelt Univ, BA, 1955; Northwestern Univ, attended 1956; Queens Col, attended 1961; Russell Sage Col, attended 1973; State Univ NY, MS, 1975. **Career:** Educator (retired); Albany, teacher, 1955-57, elem sch teacher, 1966, reading specialist, 1973; Arbor Hill Sch, teacher, 1956; Carousel Nursery Sch, teacher, 1960-61; first grade teacher, Copiague Pub Schs; Scudder Ave Sch, resource teacher, 1962-66; Arbor Hill Elem Sch, resource teacher, 1966-; NY State PTA, teacher fel, 1975; St Acad, Clinton Ave Sch, prin, 1979-91. **Orgs:** Inst Study Educ Probs Occasioned Desegration, State Univ NY, 1967-68; Nat Staff Develop Ctr, Sem Open Classroom, 1971; hon life mem, PTA, 1972; Continuous Progress Learning Inst, 1972; first pres, Urban League Guild Albany Area, 1973-76; Int Conf & Symp Trans-Cult Adaptation, Port-au-Prince, 1973; consult, Conf Concern Absenteeism Schs, 1974-75; pres, Albany Interracial Coun, 1978-80; City Club Albany; Phi Delta Kappa Fraternity; pres, vpres, chairperson, Spec Proj Comt, Albany Alumnae Chap, Delta Sigma Theta Sorority; vpres, chair person, Personnel Comt, Albany Interracial Coun; bd dir, Albany County, Div Youth; chairperson, Twin Proj, Albany Dist PTA; consult, Nat PTA; bd dir, Albany Urban League; Albany Pub Sch Teachers Asn; NY State United Teachers; NEA; Urban League Guild; Nat Asn Adv Colored People. **Honors/Awds:** Hall of Fame, 2016. **Special Achievements:** Co-hostess, TV prog "Talking With the Tillmans" 1972-75. **Home Addr:** 3 Stafford St, Loudonville, NY 12211.

### TILLMON, JOEY

Law enforcement officer. **Personal:** Born Mar 1, 1953, Victoria, TX; son of Lawrence Eugene and Florence Ann; married Jill; children: Logan, Haven & Brandy. **Educ:** Clark City Community Col, assoc degree, criminal justice; Tex A&M Univ, BA. **Career:** N Las Vegas Police Dept, interim dep chief, chief police, patrol officer, supvr & undercover narcotics officer. **Orgs:** Int Asn Chiefs Police; NOBLE; bd dir, Las Vegas "Vision 2003"; Southern NV Women's Prison Facil Community Rel bd; adv comn & Command Col Curric Comn & Strategic Planning, Community Col; Nat Orgn Black Law Enforcement Exec. **Business Addr:** Chief of Police, North Las Vegas Police Department, 1301 E Lake Mead Blvd, North Las Vegas, NV 89030, **Business Phone:** (702)649-9444.

### TIMBALAND (TIMOTHY ZACHERY MOSLEY)

Music producer, rap musician. **Personal:** Born Mar 10, 1972, Norfolk, VA; married Monique Idlett; children: 1. **Career:** Albums: Welcome to Our World, 1997; Tim's Bio, 1998; Indecent Proposal, 2001; Under Construction Pt II, 2003; Cop That Shit, 2003; Interscopeimprint label Beat Club, founder, 2000; "Steer" & "Put You on The Game", 2005; Music Composer: Doctor Do little, 1998; Can't Hardly Wait, 1998; Romeo Must Die, 2000; Nutty Professor II: The Klumps, 2000; G String Divas, 2000, 30 Years to Life, 2001; Lara Croft: Tomb Raider, 2001; Paidin Full, 2002; Hollywood Homicide, 2003; Timbaland Presents Shock Value, 2007; Wave of the Music, 2008; Shock Value II, 2009; Writer: Justified, 2002; Deliverance, 2003; The Hunger for More, 2004; Exodus, 2004; PCD, 2005; Loose, 2006; Good Girl Gone Bad, 2007; Hard Candy, 2008; In a Perfect World, 2008; Doll Domination, 2008; The Blueprint 3, 2009. **Business Addr:** Rap musician, Universal Music Group, 825 8th Ave, New York, NY 10019, **Business Phone:** (212)586-2656.

### TIMBERLAKE, DR. CONSTANCE HECTOR

Educator, executive director. **Personal:** Born St. John, NB; daughter of Gordon and Thelma; married Charles; children: Christian & Curtis. **Educ:** Syracuse Univ, Doctorate Educ Admin, 1979; MS; BA, cum laude; NYS, cert. **Career:** Syracuse Univ, Col Human Develop, assoc prof, Chair Child Family Community Study, fac, currently; Syracuse Sch Dist, ABE prog, chief counr & admin; Neighborhood Ctr, exec dir; Syracuse Pub Sch Dist, comnr educ; Adolescent Pregnancy Prev Prog, proj dir, 1987-. **Orgs:** NY Sch Bd Asn; Prog Comn; mem planning comn, Cent NY Sch Bd Inst; AERA; AAUP; Syracuse Prof Women; HEW Task Force Social Justice Nat Literacy Vol Am; Human Rights Comn Syracuse & Onondaga Co; vpres, Syracuse Nat Asn Advan Colored People; vice chmn, Coalition Qual Educ; vice chmn, Onondaga Urban League Guild; Nat Orgn Women; adv bd, Onondaga Community Col; adv coun, Neighborhood Health Ctr; Metr Ch Bd Human Serv Comn; Fair-Employ Rev Bd Onondaga Co; PEACE Head Start Self-Eval & Performance Stand Improv Plan; exec mem, Black Polit Caucus; Trust Pi Lambda Theta Inc; pres, NYS Coun Family Rel Coun; SUNY Oswego Adv Coun Oswego NY; vice chmn, Syracuse Univ Black & Latino Fac Orgn, 1986-89; hon adv bd mem, KidsSake, 1987; pres, NY Coun Family Rel, 1988-89; mem & prog dir, SyracuseBoys Club Syracuse; dir, Grants Develop Res. **Honors/Awds:** Jefferson Award, WTVH-TV/Am Inst Pub Serv, 1989. **Home Addr:** 8 Tallowood Dr, Voorhees, NJ 13214, **Home Phone:** (856)753-1598. **Business Addr:** Faculty, Syracuse University, 201 Slocum Hall CFCS Dept, Syracuse, NY 13244-5300, **Business Phone:** (315)443-5555.

### TIMBERLAKE, JOHN PAUL

Executive. **Personal:** Born Nov 12, 1950, Fackler, AL. **Educ:** Ala A&M Univ, BS, comput sci, 1975. **Career:** Chattanooga Bd Educ, sub teacher, 1975-77; Tenn Valley Auth, engr asst, 1976-77; Jackson Co Nat Asn Advan Colored People, pres, 1977-; Dept Ind Rel, programmer & analyst, 1977-. **Orgs:** Del, Jackson Co Voter's League; del, Ala Dem Conf; Jackson Co Nat Asn Advan Colored People; sr warden, Red Rose Lodge No 352; Jackson Co Chamber Com, 1980. **Home Addr:** PO Box 371, Fackler, AL 35746.

### TIMMONS, BONITA TERRY

Physicist. **Personal:** Born May 6, 1963, Norfolk, VA; daughter of Earl Nathanial and Laura Mae Hines; married Disoungh Lee. **Educ:** Purdue Univ, W Lafayette, IN, BS, 1986. **Career:** Nat Insts Health, Bethesda, Md, health physicist, 1987-89; Thomas Jefferson Univ, Philadelphia, Pa, health physicist, 1990-. **Orgs:** Health Physics Soc; Appalachian Compact Users Radioactive Isotopes. **Honors/Awds:** Scholar, Lions Club, 1981-82; Scholar, Disabled Am Veterans, 1981-82. **Home Addr:** 9200 Bustleton Ave Suite 1603, Philadelphia, PA 19115, **Home Phone:** (215)969-6115. **Business Addr:** Assistant Health Physicist of Radiation Safety, Thomas Jefferson University, 19 Walnut St Nevil Bldg Suite 820, Philadelphia, PA 19107, **Business Phone:** (215)955-7813.

### TIMMONS, OZZIE (OSBORNE LLEWELLYN TIMMONS)

Baseball player, baseball executive. **Personal:** Born Sep 18, 1970, Tampa, FL. **Educ:** Univ Tampa, attended 1991. **Career:** Baseball player (retired), baseball coach; Chicago Cubs, outfielder, 1995-96; Cincinnati Reds, outfielder, 1997; Seattle Mariners, outfielder, 1999; Tampa Bay Rays, outfielder, 2000, baseball coach, 2006-; Chunichi Dragons, outfielder, 2001; New York Mets, outfielder, 2004, Columbus Catfish, hitting coach, currently; Montgomery Biscuits, coach, currently. **Business Addr:** Baseball Coach, Tampa Bay Rays, Tropicana Field 1 Tropicana Dr, St. Petersburg, FL 33705, **Business Phone:** (727)825-3137.

### TIMMONS, QUACY. See BARNES, QUACY.

### TIMMONS-TONEY, REV. DEBORAH DENISE

Clergy, chaplain. **Personal:** Born Jan 8, 1961, Huntsville, AL; daughter of Emmett Timmons and Lela D Timmons; married Vincent Doyle. **Educ:** J F Drake Tech Col, attended 1981; Ala Agr & Mech Univ, BS, 1987; Gammon Theol Sem, MDiv, 1990. **Career:** Redstone Arsenal, Facil Engineering, procurement clerk, 1980-85, Prog Budget Analyst Br, budget asst, 1985-87; Gammon Theol Sem, admin asst, 1987-89; United Way, intern, 1990-91; Emory Univ Hosp, clin chaplain, 1990-91; Mt Mariah United Methodist Church, pastor, 1991-92; St Peter United Methodist Church, pastor, 1991-92; St Luke United Methodist Church, pastor, 1992-94; Asbury United Methodist Church, assoc pastor, 1994-96; Douglasville United Methodist Church, pastor, 1996-98; Lowe's UMC, pastor, 1998-2000; Ala Agr & Mech Univ, Campus Ministry asn, chaplain, 1999-; Spring Hill UMC, pastor, 2000-. **Orgs:** Secy, United Methodist Church, Bd Higher Educ; chairperson, nominations & personnel comt, Seminole Serv Ctr Bd Dir, 1992; bd trustee, stud rep, Gammon Theol Sem, 1988; Asn Clin Pastoral Educ Inc, 1990; Chaplain Asn, 1988; Nat Coun Negro Women; affil mem, Nat Fedn Blind; corresp secy, Greater Huntsville Ministerial Fel; Alpha Kappa Alpha Sorority Inc, Kappa Phi Omega Chap, 1993; Dixon Found Res & Develop, Women & Spirituality; founder, pres, Eagle Wing Ministries Int, 1999-. **Honors/Awds:** Outstanding Employee Award, Program Analyst Branch, 1986; Crusade Scholar, General Bd Global Ministries, 1988; Ministrial Scholarship, United Methodist Church Southeastern Jurisdiction, 1988; Outstanding Employee Award, Redstone Arsenal Engineering & Resources Management, 1988; Ford Foundation Fellow, Black Women in Church & Society, 1989. **Special Achievements:** First African-American woman ordained in the North Alabama Conference, UMC, 1992; First African-American woman to pastor in major denomination in Northwest Alabama; First female pastor, St Peter United Methodist Church, 1992, St Luke United Methodist Church, 1992, Asbury UMC, Douglasville UMC, Lowe's UMC; First African-American woman to be on radio program, "United Methodist Men's Hour," 1992; published numerous articles on Christian Literature; author, Stepping Out: Step Out of Your Comfort Zone, Step in Your Destiny, 2000; author, Be a Risk-Taker and Watch God Move, 2001. **Home Addr:** 6012 Belgrade Dr NW, Huntsville, AL 35810-1504. **Business Addr:** Pastor, United Methodist Church of Spring Hill, 7051 Mooresville Rd, Tanner, AL 35671, **Business Phone:** (256)353-9009.

### TIMPSON, MICHAEL DWAIN

Football player, football coach, television sportscaster. **Personal:** Born Jun 6, 1967, Baxley, GA; married Edwena; children: 2. **Educ:** Pa State Univ, BA, commun, 1990; Univ Phoenix, MBA, bus admin & mgt gen. **Career:** Football player (retired), football coach; New Eng Patriots, 1989-90, wide receiver, 1991-95; WRX Radio, news reporter, 1992; Chicago Bears, 1995, wide receiver, 1996; SportsChannel Chicago, football analyst, 1995-97; Philadelphia Eagles, wide receiver, 1997; WQAM Radio, football analyst, 1998-99; Good Shepherd Christian Bookstore, owner & operator, 1999-2002; Miami Dolphins, 1999; FOX Sports Radio, sports analyst, 2000-07; 1400 ESPN Radio, radio talent, 2004-05; Velocity Sports Performance, owner & operator, 2006-08; Morgan Stanley, serv assoc, 2014-15; Westminster Acad, head football coach; Poinciana High Sch, head football coach. **Honors/Awds:** US Olympic Trials 200 meters, 1992; Timed 33.01 in the indoor 300 Meters, NCAA record. **Home Addr:** 3020 Crested Cir, Orlando, FL 32837-6956.

## TINSLEY, HON. DWANE L.

Judge, lawyer. **Personal:** Born Aug 12, 1953, Fayetteville, WV; son of Elizabeth. **Educ:** Howard Univ Sch Social Work, Davis & Elkins Col, BA, sociol, 1975, MSW, 1978; WVa Univ Col Law, JD, 1981; Harvard Law Sch, Nat Inst Trial Advocacy's, teaching advocacy skills, 1995. **Career:** Pvt, partnership, assoc law pract & instr, 1979-91; US Atty's Off, asst US atty, 1987-91; WVa Univ Col Law, Trial Advocacy Prog, instr, 1989-2001; Nationwide Ins Co, Trial Div, trial atty, 1992-95, spec prosecuting atty, 1995-96, admin trial atty, 1995-96, managing trail atty, 1996-97, spec invest unit officer, 1997; Wva Ethics Comn, hearing examr, 1993-; Wva Bd Med, post-hearing adv, 1993-; Nat Football League Contract Adv, consult, 2000-; Hendrickson & Long PLLC, partner & atty, 2001-; US Postal Serv, mediator, currently; US Dist Ct Southern Dist Wva, fed magistrate judge, 2013-; US Dist Ct Southern Dist, pract atty; US Ct Appeals Fourth Circuit, pract atty. **Orgs:** Brown W Bayne fel 1980; treas, Fayette County, 1982-94; secy & treas, Fin Comt, Mountain State Bar Asn, 1987-92, pres, 1992-94; ethics comt, WVa State Bar Asn, 1988-94; minority lawyers comt, WVa State Bar Asn, 1990-92; Wva Supreme Ct Appeals; Am Bar Asn; Fayette Co Bar Asn; Int Asn Spec Invest Unit; Nat Bar Asn; Am Corp Coun Asn; Am Bd Trial Advocates; WVa Prosecuting Attys Asn; WVa Bar Asn; Nat Football Players Asn. **Honors/Awds:** West Virginia Honorary Scholar, 1971-75; Outstanding Black Attorney, Black Law Studs Asn, 1987; Special Achievement Award, US Dept Justice, 1990. **Home Addr:** 10 Carriage Rd, Charleston, WV 25314-2159, **Home Phone:** (304)343-1523. **Business Addr:** Federal Magistrate Judge, United States District Court, 5408 Robert C Byrd Us Courthouse 300 Va St E, Charleston, WV 25301, **Business Phone:** (304)347-3279.

## TINSLEY, HON. FRED LELAND, JR.

Lawyer. **Personal:** Born Aug 30, 1944, Detroit, MI; married Ollie M Brock, Oct 25, 1974. **Educ:** Southern Univ Law Ctr, BA, 1969, JD, 1972. **Career:** Reginald Heber Smith Fel Legal Serv, 1972; LA Const Conv, res asst, 1973; US Security & Exchange Comn, trial atty, 1973-75; Lone Star Gas Co, regulatory atty, 1975-76; Dallas Munic Ct, assoc judge, 1974-84; pvt prac, 1986; Tex State, dist 195th judge, 1986; Champman Tinsley & Reese, partner; Robinson & Hoskins LLP, atty, currently. **Orgs:** Bd dir, Ment Health Asn, Dallas, 1976-78; adv coun mem, Tex Employ Comn, 1977-79; bd dir, Dallas Legal Serv Found Inc, 1979-; exec comt, Dallas County Dem Party, 1980-; bd dir, Jr Black Acad Arts & Lett Inc, 1980-; Am Bankers Asn; Nat Asn Criminal Defense Lawyers; Dallas Bar Asn; Delta Theta Phi. **Honors/Awds:** Selected to Tx Super Lawyers, 2003, 2004, 2004. **Home Addr:** 770 Keswick Dr, Dallas, TX 75232. **Business Addr:** Attorney, 195th Judicial Dist Ct, 133 N Riverfront Blvd Frank Crowley Courts Bldg, Dallas, TX 75208, **Business Phone:** (214)653-5812.

## TINSLEY-TALABI, ALBERTA

Government official. **Personal:** Born Aug 14, 1954; daughter of Willie Tinsley and Mary Louise Tinsley; married Bamidele A; children: Carla, David & Charles. **Educ:** Eastern Mich Univ, Ypsilanti, MI, BS, social work & criminal justice, 1976; Wayne State Univ, Detroit. **Career:** Detroit Police Dept, Detroit, MI, rape counr, 1976-78; United Auto Workers, Detroit, MI, grp worker, 1978-80; Comprehensive Youth Trng & Community Involvement Prog, Detroit, MI, job develop counr, 1980-85; New Ctr Ment Health, Detroit, MI, stress mgt instr, 1985-87; Wayne County Comn, Detroit, MI, county comnr, 1987-90; Job Connection, proj specialist; Detroit City Coun, coun woman, 1993-2009. **Orgs:** Nat Orgn Black County Officials; Nat Asn Counties; Women NACO; Nat Asn Advan Colored People; Detroit Area Agency Aging; founder, Coalition Against Billboard Advert Alcohol & Tobacco; fel, Boston Univ; founder, Mack Alive; fel, Mich House Representatives, Dist 3, 2010. **Honors/Awds:** Outstanding Service Award, Govt Admin Asn, 1988; Shirley Chisholm Award, Nat Polit Cong Black Women, 1988; Spirit of Detroit Award, City Detroit City Coun, 1988; Public Citizen of the Year, 1992; White House Special Service Award Recipient. **Home Addr:** 12274 Rosemary, Detroit, MI 48213, **Home Phone:** (313)839-0601. **Business Addr:** Councilwoman, Detroit City Council, 1340 Coleman A Young Munic Ctr, Detroit, MI 48226, **Business Phone:** (313)224-1645.

## TIPPETT, ANDRE BERNARD

Sports manager, executive director, football player. **Personal:** Born Dec 27, 1959, Birmingham, AL; married Rhonda Kenney; children: Janea Lynn, Asia Barnes, Madison & Coby. **Educ:** Ellsworth Community Col, attended 1977; Univ Iowa, BA, 1982. **Career:** Football player (retired), executive director, sports manager; New Eng Patriots, linebacker & right outside linebacker & left outside linebacker, 1982-93, dir player resources, 1994-96, asst dir, pro-scouting, 1997-2003, dir, pro-scouting, 2003-04, dir, football develop & promotions, 2003-07, exec dir, community affairs, 2007-. **Honors/Awds:** NFL Defensive Player of the Week, Pro Football Weekly & ESPN, 1983; voted Best Linebacker & Defensive Back in AFC, 1984; Patriots Most Valuable Player, 1776 QB Club, 1984; Pro Bowl, 1984-88; AFC Defensive Player of Week, Sports Illustrated & League Office, 1985; AFL Defensive Player of the Year, United Press International, 1985; Co-Defensive Player of the Year, Newspaper Enterprise Association, 1985; Linebacker of the Year, NFL Players Association, 1985-87; Defensive Player of the Year Award, American Football Conference; Defensive Player of the Year Award, New York Daily News; Big Brothers & Big Sisters-Tums Neutralizer of the Year Award; NFL Alumni Assn, Linbacker of the Year, 1987; NFL Players Asn, Linbacker of the Year, 1985-87; Pro Football Hall of Fame, 2008; National Jewish Sports Hall of Fame, 2009; Alabama Sports Hall of Fame, 2012. **Business Addr:** Executive Director, New England Patriots, 1 Patriot Pl, Foxboro, MA 02035, **Business Phone:** (508)543-8200.

## TIPTON, DR. DALE LEO

Physician, otolaryngologist. **Personal:** Born Jul 8, 1930, Parsons, KS; son of Dale and Ruby; children: Jill & Jan. **Educ:** Univ Calif, Berkeley, AB, Physiol, 1952; Univ Calif, San Francisco, MS, pharamacol, 1959; Univ Calif, Sch Med, MD, otolaryngol-allergy, 1959. **Career:** Kaiser Found Hosp, intern, 1959-60; Univ Calif, San Francisco, resident gen surg, 1960-62; Moffitt Hosp Univ Ca, resident Otolaryngol, resident gen surg; Cancer Res Inst, Univ Calif, nat inst health fel, 1962-63; Univ Calif, San Francisco, resident otolaryngol, 1963-66; pvt Pract, physician, 1966-; Univ Calif Sch Med, Dept Otolaryngol, clin prof, 1976-; Sutter Med Network; Franklin Hosp, chief med staff, 1982-84. **Orgs:** Deleg, Calif Med Asn from San Francisco Med Soc, 1968-69; bd dirs, San Francisco Med Soc, 1972-75; med adv, Calif Blue Shield, 1977-; chmn, Dept Ear Nose & Throat San Francisco Gen Hosp, 1970-76; chmn, Dept Ear Nose & Throat Franklin Hosp San Fran, 1968-; bd dirs, San Francisco Peer Rev Org, 1983-86. **Honors/Awds:** Diplomat Am Bd Otolaryngolo, 1966; Am Acad Otolaryngol, Head & Neck Surg, 1967-. **Special Achievements:** Published: "Changes in Golgi Apparatus of Islets of Langerhans in the Rat following Glucose & Insulin Admins" Endocrinology 1959; "Effects of Chlorpromazine on Blood Level of Alcohol in Rabbits" Amer Journal of Physiology 1961; "Duration of Bronchial Squamous Metaplasia Produced by Dogs by Cigarette Smoke Condensate" Journal of the Natl Cancer Inst 1964; "The Experimental Effects of Cigarette Smoke Condensate on Laryngeal Mucosa", published in proceedings of Int Congress of Otolaryngology, 1965; "Osteochondroma of the tongue" Arch Path 1970; "Physiologic Assessment of Black People" Journal of Black Health 1975. **Home Addr:** 458 Briarwood Dr, South San Francisco, CA 94080, **Home Phone:** (415)952-7509. **Business Addr:** Physician, 45 Castro St Suite 220, San Francisco, CA 94114, **Business Phone:** (415)621-6191.

## TIPTON, DANELL

Athlete. **Personal:** Born Jul 22, 1973, Spencer, OK. **Career:** Int prof rodeo assoc, bull riding, 1995-; Event: Little Rock, 2003; Billing, 2003.

## TIPTON-MARTIN, TONI

Editor. **Personal:** Born Mar 6, 1959, Los Angeles, CA; daughter of Charles Hamilton and Beverly Dunbar; married Bruce Martin; children: 4. **Educ:** Univ Southern Calif, BA, 1981. **Career:** Waves Newspaper, Los Angeles, Calif, food ed, 1982-91; Los Angeles Times, staff writer, 1983-91; Plain Dealer, Cleveland, food ed, 1991-95; Heart & Soul Mag, food ed, 1997-; TTM Enterprises Inc, food & nutrit consult, 1999-; SANDE Youth Proj, founder & dir, 2008-; Whole Foods Culinary Ctr, guest instr; Austin Hist Ctr, speaker; Foodways Tex, co-founder & pres. **Orgs:** Black Journalists Asn, 1980-91; Nat Food Ed & Writers Asn, 1991; pres, Southern Foodways Alliance; Les Dames D'Escoffier Austin Chap. **Honors/Awds:** Media Award, Am Heart Asn, 1988; Nutrit Writing Award, Carnation County, 1988; Media Excellence Award, Am Heart Asn, 1989; Los Angeles Times Editorial Award, 1991; Outstanding Dedication & Service Award, 1995: Harry A. Bell Grants for Food Writers, 2003; James Beard Awards. **Special Achievements:** Coauthor of A Taste of Heritage: New African American Cuisine; First African American woman to hold the position of food editor at a major daily newspaper, 1991. **Business Addr:** Food Editor, The Plain Dealer, 1801 Super Ave, Cleveland, OH 44114, **Business Phone:** (216)999-4800.

## TISDALE, PROF. CELES

Educator, actor, poet. **Personal:** Born Jul 31, 1941, Salters, SC; son of Norman and Rachel; married Ann Parker; children: Yvette, Colette & Eric. **Educ:** State Univ Col Buffalo, BS, 1963, MS, 1969, PhD, 1991. **Career:** PS 31 Buffalo, eng teacher, 1963-68; Woodlawn Jr High, eng dept chmn, 1968-69; WBEN TV, writer, producer, 1969; WBFO-FM Radio, writer, announcer, 1969-70; State Univ NY, Col Buffalo, eng instr, 1969-72; Buffalo Pub Sch Syst, eng instr; WKBW TV, talk show host, 1979-83; WKBW Radio, talk show host, 1984-86; State Univ New York, Col Buffalo, emer prof englis, currently; Erie Community Col City, asst prof eng, currently. **Orgs:** Assoc dir, Buffalo Urban League, 1966-92; Young Audiences Inc, 1975-; bd dir, Artpark, 1981-84; dir, Adolescent Voc Explor, 1985-88; Career Educr Buffalo Urban League, 1987-91; NY African Studies Asn; exec dir, African Am Cult Ctr Buffalo. **Honors/Awds:** SUNY Chancellors Award for Teaching Excellence, State Univ NY, 1975; Man of the Year, Bus & Prof Women, 1977; Media Award, Sickle Cell Asn, 1978; Erie County Arts Council Artist of the Year; Outstanding Artist Award, WNY. **Special Achievements:** Published Anthology: Betcha Ain't: Poems from Attica as well as We Be Poetin, We the People. **Home Addr:** 47 Manchester Pl, Buffalo, NY 14213, **Home Phone:** (716)886-8259. **Business Addr:** Assistant Professor, Erie Community College, 2001 Main St, Buffalo, NY 14208-1098, **Business Phone:** (716)888-2629.

## TISDALE, DR. HENRY NEHEMIAH

School administrator, college president, association executive. **Personal:** Born Jan 13, 1944, Kingstree, SC; son of Walter; married Alice Rose Carson; children: Danica Camille & Brandon Keith. **Educ:** Claflin Col, BS, 1965; Temple Univ, EdM, 1967; Dartmouth Col, MA, 1975, PhD, 1978. **Career:** Philadelphia Sch Dist, math instr, 1965-69; Del State Univ, prof math, 1969-85, instr & summer eng inst, 1978-85, asst dir inst res, 1978-85, asst acad dean, planning & Info mgt, 1986-87, sr vpres & chief acad officer, 1987-94; Univ Del, spec asst pres, 1985-86; Claflin Col, pres, 1994-. **Orgs:** Bd mem, Holy Cross Sch Syst; State Del Task Force High Technol, 1986-87; bd dir, United Negro Col Fund; Nat Asn Sch & Col United Methodist Church; Educ & Inst Ins Adminr; fel Am Coun Educ Comn Leadership Develop; Claflin Col Nat Alumni Asn; Conf Finance & Admin Adv Comt SC; Conf United Methodist Church; Leadership SC; chmn, SC Tuition & Grants Comn; bd dir, Edisto United Way; bd gov, C Performing Arts Acad; Sigma Pi Phi Fraternity; Omega Psi Phi Fraternity; Trinity United Methodist Church; Nat Asn Schs & Cols United Methodist Church. **Honors/Awds:** Southern Fellowship Fund Award, 1976-78; Man of the Year, Omega Psi Phi, 1981; Distinguished Alumni Award, Nat Asn Equal Opportunity Higher Educ; Educator of the Year Award, Nat Assoc Advan Colored People. **Special Achievements:** Listed in Who's Who Among Black Americans. **Home Addr:** 674 Col St NE, Orangeburg, SC 29115-4476. **Business Addr:** President, Claflin College, 400 Magnolia St, Orangeburg, SC 29115-4476, **Business Phone:** (803)535-5412.

## TITUS, LEROY ROBERT

Chief executive officer, consultant, association executive. **Personal:** Born Dec 11, 1938, Pittsburgh, PA; married Anna Mary Adams; children: Shelley Meredyth, Sherre Mishel & Shelbi Melany. **Educ:** Lincoln Univ, AB, 1960. **Career:** Nat Insts Health, microbiologist, 1964-65; YMCA Pittsburgh, prog dir, 1965-69, Los Angeles, exec dir, chief exec officer; YMCA Ft Wayne/Allen Co, Kiwanis Westside Br, exec dir, 1969-72; Primerica Fin Servs, reg mgr, currently, reg vpres; Clothed Dignity, bus & prof training consult, vpres bus & prof training, currently. **Orgs:** Deleg nat coun, YMCA's USA, master trainer, 1981-; dist vpres, Asn Prof Dirs; pres, Nat Black & Non White YMCA's; pres, YMCA's Serv Disadvantaged Communities; pres, PANDA Productions; Alpha Phi Alpha Fraternity; prog dir, Centre Ave Br Pittsburgh Asn. **Honors/Awds:** Human Serv Award, Asn Prof Direct, 1982; Outstanding Service Award, CITIES Inc, 1984; Dr Martin Luther King Human Dignity Award, La Metro YMCA, 1985; VPI Award, Nat Asn Advan Colored People, Los Angeles Chap, 1987. **Home Addr:** 13282 Briarwood St, Cerritos, CA 90703-7323, **Home Phone:** (562)860-9607. **Business Addr:** Business & Professional Training Consultant, Vice President of Business & Professional Training, Clothed In Dignity, PO Box 14745, Long Beach, CA 90853, **Business Phone:** (562)961-9902.

## TITUS, ROBERT P.

Accountant, businessperson. **Personal:** Born Jan 1, 1941. **Educ:** Brooklyn Col. **Career:** Accountant, business person (retired); Nemiroff, Cosmas, Titus & Colchamiro, partner; Mitchell & Titus & Co, co-founder, managing partner, chief operating officer, 1973-95. **Orgs:** Pres, DC Chamber Com. **Special Achievements:** Co-founder of the largest minority-owned, certified public accounting firm in the United States. **Business Addr:** President, DC Chamber of Commerce, 506 9th St NW, Washington, DC 20004, **Business Phone:** (202)347-7201.

## TITUS-DILLON, DR. PAULINE Y.

Educator, physician, association executive. **Personal:** Born Jan 1, 1938; daughter of Ernest H Titus and Vera I Harvey; married Owen Christopher; children: Denyse & Paul. **Educ:** Howard Univ, BS, 1960, MD, 1964. **Career:** Freedmens Hosp, internship & resident; Medstar-Georgetown Univ Med Ctr, fel; Howard Univ Hosp, post grad trainee internal med, 1964-68, from asst prof to prof, 1971-2003, from assoc dean to sr assoc dean acad affairs, 1980-2003, dean, prof emer, 2003-; Georgetown Univ Hosp, Wash, DC, fel, endocrinol, 1968-69; Va Hosp Outpatient Clin Columbia SC, internist, 1969-71; DC Gen Hosp, chief, 1977. **Orgs:** DC Med Soc; fel Am Col Physicians; Prog Dirs Internal Med; Am Med Women's Asn Present; Alpha Omega Alpha Hon Med Soc Gamma Chap Present; Nat Med Asn, NY Acad Sci, AMA; dipl, Am Bd Internal Med, Philadelphia, 1972; fel NIH Bethesda, 1975-77 Med Stud Hon Soc. **Honors/Awds:** Daniel Hale Williams Award, Howard Univ, 1965, 1968; Inspirational Leadership Award, Student Coun, Howard Univ, Col Med, 1979; Superior Performance Award, Howard Univ, Dept Med, 1979; Excellence Award, Health Care Caribbean & Am Intercultural Org, 1996; Citation for Excellence, State Md, Delivery Health Care, 1996; Recipient, Mastership, 2004. **Home Addr:** 12601 Tribunal Lane, Potomac, MD 20854. **Business Addr:** Professor Emeritus, Howard University College of Medicine, Rm 527 520 W St NW, Washington, DC 20059, **Business Phone:** (202)806-6270.

## TOBIAS, RANDOLF A.

Educator, executive director. **Personal:** Born Jan 16, 1940, Bronx, NY; children: Meredith, Maurice & Tonya. **Educ:** BA, 1961; MA, 1968; Columbia Univ, Teachers Col, EdD, 1976. **Career:** New York Pub Schs, teacher, 1963-68; Mills Col Educ, instr, 1964-71; Bedford Stuyvesant Talent Search, proj dir, 1968-69; Martin Luther King Jr Scholar Prog, Long Island Univ, 1969-; Long Island Univ, Black Stud Cert Prog, dir, 1972-74; Shaw Univ, Div Educ, dir, chairperson & assoc prof, 1975-77; Winston-Salem State Univ, Div Educ, dir, chairperson & assoc prof, 1977-80; Queens Col, City Univ New York, Grad Dept Educ & Community Progs, assoc dean spec progs & dir seek prog, 1980-87, chair, 1988-94, assoc prof sch admin, 1994, Dept Educ & Community Progs, assoc prof educ leadership, prof, assoc prof emer, prof emer, currently; Teacher Educ, Long Island Univ, asst prof; Mellon fel, 1983; Black Family Found Inc, dir, 1987-. **Orgs:** Trustee, Deer Pk Bd Educ, Deer Pk, NY; Va Union Univ Alumni Asn; Alpha Phi Alpha Fraternity; Am Asn Univ Prof; African Heritage Students Asn. **Honors/Awds:** Nat Fraternity of Student Musicians-Performance Awards, 1956-57; Educational Honor Society Service Award, Kappa Delta Pi, 1996; Community Service Award, Suffolk County Black Caucus Democrats, 1997; Nnamdi Azikiwe Memorial Award for Youth Training, 1998. **Special Achievements:** Author of numerous books & articles. **Home Addr:** 89 Fillmore Ave, Deer Park, NY 11729-7003, **Home Phone:** (631)595-2632. **Business Addr:** Professor Emeritus, Queens College, City University of New York, Rm 033 Powdermaker Hall, Flushing, NY 11367, **Business Phone:** (718)997-5250.

## TOBIN, LAUREN

Publicist. **Personal:** daughter of Patricia (deceased)children: 1. **Educ:** Univ Southern Calif, BA, broadcast journalism, 1987. **Career:** CBS Entertainment, page asst; Steven Bochco Productions, 1989-95; Fox Network, coordr & jr publicist; Disney ABC Tv Group, ABC TV Network, from jr publicist to publicity dir, 1993-2006; Panther Pub Rels, founder & pres, 2006-; Tobin & Assocs, founder, 2006-, pres, 2008-, chief exec officer, currently. **Orgs:** Publicists Guild Am. **Honors/Awds:** Maxwell Weinberg Showmanship Award. **Business Addr:** Chief Executive Officer, Founder, Tobin & Associates Inc, 4929 Wilshire Blvd Suite 245, Los Angeles, CA 90010, **Business Phone:** (323)857-0869.

## TOBY, WILLIAM, JR.

Government official. **Personal:** Born Aug 12, 1934, Augusta, GA; son of William and Louise; married Diane Anderson; children: Michael & Kenneth. **Educ:** WVa State Col, BA, psychol & Span, 1961; Adelphi Univ, MSW, 1963; Harvard Univ John F Kennedy Sch Govt, MPA, 1986. **Career:** Government Official (retired); HEW, asst to regional dir, 1968; Natl Urban League; New York Off Mayor, inter-govt rels off, 1969-71; Health Edic Welfare Soc Rehab Serv, regional comnr, 1971-77; Health Care Fin Admin, Wash, DC, reg admin, 1977-96, actg HCFA adminr, 1992-93, regional dir; GNYHA Ventures Inc, consult. **Orgs:** Bd mem, Adelphi Univ Sch Social Work; Nat Conf Social Welfare; brd overseers, New York Univ Grad Sch Pub Admin; act admin, US Dept Health & Human Serv; bd mem, New York Univ's Wagner Grad Sch Pub Serv; bd mem, State Univ New York Col Optom; bd mem, Hosp Adv Coun; bd mem, Ny Senate; bd mem, Adelphi Univ Ctr Health Innovation; Century Club. **Honors/Awds:** HCFA Leadership Award, 1979; Exceptional Achievement, Sec Health Human Serv, 1982; Gubernatorial Citation, Gov NY, 1982; John W Davis

Meritorious Award, W Va State Col, 1984; Appreciation Award, Int Health Econ Mgt Inst, 1984; Meritorious Rank Award, 1988; Hon Doctor Humane Lett, New York Col Podiatric Med, 1992; National Role Model Award, 2004; Adelphi University Alumnus of Distinction Award; West Virginia State University Outstanding Alumnus Award. **Special Achievements:** First HCFA Leadership award in 1980. Honored by Adelphi Univ named Adelphi Alumni Of Distinction. **Home Addr:** 129 Willoughby Ave, Brooklyn, NY 11205, **Home Phone:** (718)834-8963.

### TODD, BEVERLY
Actor, television producer, administrator. **Personal:** Born Jul 11, 1946, Chicago, IL; daughter of Virena; married Kris Keiser; children: Malik Smith (deceased). **Career:** Films: The Lost Man, 1969; They Call Me MISTER Tibbs!, 1970; Brother John, 1971; A Piece of the Action, 1977; Vice Squad, 1982; Homework, 1982; The Ladies Club, 1986; Happy Hour, 1987; Baby Boom, 1987; Moving, 1988; Clara's Heart, 1988; Lean on Me, 1989; Exquisite Tenderness, 1995; Crash, 2004; Animal, 2005; Ascension Day, 2007; The Bucket List, 2007; The Lena Baker Story, 2008; I Will Follow, 2011; TV Series: "Deep Are the Roots", 1960; "Love of Life", 1968-70; Six Characters in Search of an Author, 1976; "The Write Channel", 1977; "Roots", 1977; "The Ghost of Flight 401", 1978; "Having Babies", 1978; "Having Babies III", 1978; "The Jericho Mile", 1979; "Lou Grant", 1 episode, 1980; "Quincy M.E.", 1 episode, 1981; "Don't Look Back: The Story of Leroy 'Satchel' Paige", 1981; "Please Don't Hit Me, Mom", 1981; "St. Elsewhere", 2 episodes, 1984; "A Touch of Scandal", 1984; Fraud Squad, 1985; "Magnum, P.I.", 1 episode, 1985; "The Redd Foxx Show", 6 episodes, 1986; "A Different Affair", 1987; "Hill Street Blues", 1 episode, 1987; Paramount Pictures: "Sliver"; Syndicate-It Pro, Los Angeles, Calif, co-producer: "A Laugh, A Tear", 1990-91; The Story of Black Humor In America."; tv guest star: "Equal Justice", ABC-TV, 1991, "Falcon Crest"; "A Different World", 1 episode, 1991; HBO, Los Angeles, Calif, co-producer: "The Don Jackson Story", 1991; dir: "I Need a Man", Embassey Theatre, La; "Six Feet Under", 4 episodes, 2002-03; "Ghost Whisperer", 1 episode, 2006; "House M.D", 1 episode, 2007; "The Closer", 1 episode, 2007; "Criminal Minds", 1 episode, 2010; "Taken from Me: The Tiffany Rubin Story", 2011; "Grey's Anatomy", 1 episode, 2011; "Days of Our Lives", 2012. **Orgs:** Pres, Kwanza Found, 1991; Delta Sigma Theta; vpres, Malik's Voice for Peace; Founder & Pres, Hollywood Sisters. **Honors/Awds:** Ben, Friends of Black Oscar Nominees, 1990; Woman of the Year, State of CA Legislature, 1990; 4 Time NAACP Image Award Nominee, 1978, 1984, 1988, 1989; Founder of the Malik Smith Scholar, 1989; Best Supporting Actress. **Special Achievements:** NAACP 4 Time Image Award Nominee, 1978, 1984, 1988, 1989; one of four women selected to write and produce "Tribute To The Black Woman" presented at the Shrine Auditorium in Los Angeles, California; A People's Choice Award. **Business Addr:** Actress, Producer, Screenwriter, William Morris Agency, 151 El Camino Dr, Beverly Hills, CA 90212.

### TODD, CHARLES O.
Educator, high school teacher. **Personal:** Born Nov 12, 1915, Lawrence, KS; son of Hazel Jr; married Geraldine Mann; children: Chrystal, Johnson & Karen Lang. **Educ:** Emporia State Univ, BS, 1940; Kans Univ, MS, 1948; Univ Southern Calif, MFA, 1957. **Career:** Educator (retired); Douglas Sch, Mayview, Mo, teacher, 1940; Western Univ High Sch, Quindaro, Kans, teacher, 1941-42; Douglas Elem Sch, Manhattan, Kans, prin, 1943; Dunbar Jr High Sch, Tucson, Ariz, teacher, 1947-51; Manfield Jr High Sch, teacher, 1951-67; Tucson Sr High Sch, teacher, 1967-82. **Orgs:** Kans Teachers & Admin, 1943; Phi Delta Kappa, 1946; Alpha Phi Alpha, 1950; treas, Tucson Fine Arts Asn, 1950; pres, Nat Asn Advan Colored People; Tucson Credit Union, 1964; pres, bd dir, Tucson Civic Chorus, 1965; Tucson Civic Chorus, 1966-67; mentor, Tucson Big Bros, 1966-67; treas, Tucson Br Nat Asn Advan Colored People, 1968-74; mentor, Acad Prep Excellence, 1987-89; Foster Care Rev Bd, 1988-96; pres, Eta Psi Lambda Chap, Alpha Phi Alpha, 1989; life mem, Dima Co Retired Teachers Asn. **Home Addr:** 848 E Grant Rd, Tucson, AZ 85719, **Home Phone:** (520)622-8710.

### TODD, CYNTHIA JEAN
Journalist. **Personal:** Born Jan 12, 1951, Peoria, IL; children: Wendy. **Educ:** Northern Ill Univ, DeKalb, BS, jour, 1972. **Career:** Journalist (retired), executive: Peoria J Star, reporter, 1969-73; WMBD-AM-FM TV Peoria, reporter, anchor, 1974-77; KSDK-TV St Louis, reporter, anchor, 1977-79; Harris Stowe State Coll, dir publ; St Louis Post-Dispatch, St Louis, reporter & dir, Newsroom Recruitment, 1983-2007; Pounce Online, staff mem; CJ Todd Commun LLC, owner, 2009-. **Orgs:** Ill Newsbroadcasters Asn, 1975-77; Greater St Louis Black Journalist Asn, 1977-; AFTRA, 1977; adv comn, Univ City HS, Univ City MO, 1978; Alpha Kappa Alpha Sor; bd dir, New City Sch, St Louis, 1980. **Honors/Awds:** Broadcast History Award, McLean County, Ill Hist Soc, 1976; Achiever in Industry Award, St Louis Metro Sentinel Newspaper, 1978; Nat Am Advan Colored People Media Roole Model Award, 1989; Missouri Asn Social Welfare Media Award, 1992. **Special Achievements:** Listed in Names & Faces Nat Publ, 1978.

### TODD, MELVIN R.
Administrator. **Personal:** Born Apr 24, 1933, Oklahoma City, OK; married Menzola Anderson; children: Sharon, Myra & David. **Educ:** Langston Univ, BA, hist, 1954; Univ Okla, MEd, sec, 1960; Univ Okla, EdD, soc admin & gen admin, 1973. **Career:** Neb High Sch Okla City, asst prin, 1967-69, prin, 1969-71; Consultative Ctr Equal Educ Opport Univ Okla, field consult, 1971-73; Okla City Pub Sch, dir curric, 1973-75; Okla State Regents Higher Educ, spec asst chancellor & stud & officer, 1975-80, vice chancellor acad admin, 1980; Langston Univ, Spec Asst to Pres, 1991-; Okla City Pub Schs, prin, asst supt. **Orgs:** Bd dir, E&C Trades Ltd, 1980; Okla Educ Asn; corp mem, Am Col Testing Prog Corp; Phi Delta Kappa; Urban League; Nat Asn Advan Colored People; Ok Higher Educ Heritage Soc. **Honors/Awds:** Outstanding Educator's Award, Okla Educ Asn, 1975; Distinguished Alumnus Award, Langston Univ, 1976; Presidential Citizen, Nat Asn Equal Educ Opport Highter Educ, 1980, Hall of Fame, Oklahoma Higher Education, 2002. **Special Achievements:** First Afro-American to serve on the Oklahoma State Regents staff. **Home Addr:** 1301 NE 52nd St, Oklahoma City, OK 73111-6605, **Home Phone:** (405)427-1881. **Business Addr:** Special Assistant to the President, Langston University, PO Box 667, Langston, OK 73050, **Business Phone:** (405)466-3453.

### TODD, THOMAS N.
College teacher, lawyer. **Personal:** Born Aug 24, 2016, Demopolis, AL; son of Cleveland and Alberta; married Janis Roberts; children: Traci Neuborne & Tamarla Nicole. **Educ:** Southern Univ, BA, polit sci, 1959, JD, 1963. **Career:** Lawyer (retired); US Dept Labor, off solicitor, 1963-64; US Atty Chicago, officer, 1967-70; Comn Inquiry into Black Panthers & Law Enforcement NY, consult, 1970-72; Northwestern Univ, law prof, 1970-74; Chicago Capt Social CLC, pres, 1971; Oper PUSH, exec vpres, 1971-73, pres, 1983-84; Midwest Task Force Comn Report "Search & Destroy", dir; Northwestern Univ Sch Law Chicago, asst prof law, asst dir ctr urban affairs; pvt pract atty. **Orgs:** Supreme Ct LA, 1963, US Ct Mil Appeals, 1965, Supreme Ct Ill, 1967, US Ct Appeals Seventh Circuit, 1968, US Dist Ct, No Dist Ill, US Supreme Ct, 1971, Chicago Community United Negro Col Fund, bd dir, Legal Opportunity Scholar Prog; adv bd, Ill Black Legis Clearinghouse Chicago; adv bd, Afro-Am Patrolmans League Chicago; pres oper, PUSH, 1983-84. **Honors/Awds:** Ammer Jurisprudence Award; Law Week Award; JS Clark Memorial Award; Criminal Law Award, Soc Univ Sch Law; 1 of 10 Outstanding Young Men, Chicago Jaycees, 1970; Leadership Council, Met Open Comn, 1970; Certificate Achievement, Kappa Alpha Phi Northwestern Univ, 1971; Certificate Achievement, Afro-Am Policemens League, 1971; Lawndale Peoples Planning & Action Comn, 1971; SCLC Operation Breadbaskets Activist Award, 1971; Ind Dem Org, 1971; Achievement Award, Mens Fed Soc Univ, 1972; Student Govt Award, Soc Univ, 1972; Power Inc Harambee Award, 1972; ListedOne Thousand Success Stories, 1973; Biog pub Chicago Negro Almanac, 1973; Outstanding Achievement Award, The Nat Consumer Info Ctr, 1974; BlackExcellence Award, Community Action PUSH Espo, 1974; National Education Award, Phi Beta Sigma, 1975; Meritorious Service Award, Nat Asn Black Political Sci, 1976; Appreciation Award, June tenth Comt, 1976; Appreciation Award, Nat Consumer Info Ctr host Tom Todd Show WLS Radio Chicago; "Voice Ebony" Radio Commercial Ebony Mag; hon doctorate Laws, Grambling State Univ, 1987; hon doctorate Laws, Syracuse Univ, 1990; hon doctorate, Wilberforce Univ, 1993; hon doctorate Talladega Col, 1998; hon doctorate, Southern Univ A&M Col, 1999; hon doctorate, Univ Maryland Eastern Shore, 2000; hon degree, Bethuna-Cookman Col; History Maker, 2002. **Special Achievements:** First Full time African American law professor at Northwestern University's School of Law, 1970-74. **Home Addr:** 1 N LaSalle St, Suite 3901, Chicago, IL 60602-4013.

### TODD, WILLIAM S.
Airplane pilot. **Personal:** Born Mar 10, 1940, Portsmouth, VA; son of William S and Martha E Muckle; children: David M, Kelly Yvette & William S IV. **Educ:** Va Union Univ, BS, 1962. **Career:** USAF, Comdr C-135 Aircraft, lt col; USAF Acad, liaison officer, dep comdr; Western Airlines, airline pilot Boeing 727, 1969-87, Boeing 737 capt, 1987-93; Delta 727 Airlines, 1993-96; Los Angeles, CA, Boeing 767, 757, capt, 1996-; City Bradbury, Bradbury, CA, chmn planning comn, 1990-99; Delta Airlines, check pilot, instr pilot, 1991-; City Bradbury, CA, mayor, 2001-02, coun mem. **Orgs:** Airline Pilots Asn, Alpha Phi Alpha Fraternity, US Jaycees; advert ed, mgr US Jaycees Publ, Accident Investr, Engineering & Air Safety Community Airline Pilots Asn; chmn, Comt Select City Slogan City Cerritos, CA; Youth Motivation Task Force, 1969-; Westside Fair Housing Coun, 1969-; campaign mgr, City Coun Cand, 1974; owner, Spectral Illuminations; bd dir, La County Sanit Districts; bd dir, Mid-San Gabriel Valley Consortium; bd dir, League Calif cities. **Honors/Awds:** Awards, Youth Motivation Task Force, 1970, 1972; Jaycee Sound Citizen Award, 1974. **Home Addr:** 43 Woodlyn Lane, Bradbury, CA 91010. **Business Addr:** Airline Pilot, Delta Airlines, Hartsfield Atlanta Airport, 6000 N Terminal Pkwy Suite 4000, Atlanta, GA 30320, **Business Phone:** (800)897-1910.

### TOKLEY, JOANNA NUTTER
Social worker. **Personal:** Born Nanticoke, MD; daughter of Clifton Nutter and Iolia Williams; married E James; children: Tyrone, Charles & Michael. **Educ:** Morgan State Univ, BS, 1962; Univ S Fla. **Career:** Hillsborough City Pub Sch, teacher, 1962-70, human rels spec, 1970-74; Tampa Urban Hillsborough League Inc, dep dir, econ develop, employ dir, 1974-82, exec dir, pres & chief exec officer, currently; Tampa Develop Consortium Inc, dir & secy; Tampa-Hillsborough Urban League Community Housing Inc, dir; Tampa Pvt Indust Coun Inc, pres. **Orgs:** Alpha Kappa Alpha, 1958-, pres, 1966-69, 1975; Toastmasters Chap 1810, 1980-; Gov Constituency Against Child Abuse, 1984-; Tampa Chamber Comn, 1985; Leadership Tampa, 1989-; vpres, Nat Coalition 100 Black Women, 1989-; Comn 100, 1990-; Regional Workforce Develop Bd. **Honors/Awds:** S Atlantic Region Ruby J Gainer Human Relations Award, AKA, 1975; Outstanding Community Service, The Charmettes Inc, Mt Calvary Day Adventist Church, 1979, 1985; Eddie Mitchell Mem Community Service Award, City Tampa Off Comm Rels, 1980; Dist Dramatic Speech Toastmasters FL, 1981; Woman of the Year, The Orchid Club, 1983; Leadership Tampa, Greater Tampa Chamber Comn, 1988; Martin Luther King Jr Bust Award, Tampa Orgn Black Affairs; Nat Conf Medallion. **Home Addr:** 2118 Carmen St, Tampa, FL 33606. **Business Addr:** President, Chief Executive Officer, Tampa Urban Hillsborough League Inc, 1405 Tampa Pk Plz, Tampa, FL 33605-4821, **Business Phone:** (813)229-8117.

### TOLBERT, ANTHONY LEWIS. See TOLBERT, TONY.

### TOLBERT, DR. HERMAN ANDRE
Psychiatrist, physician. **Personal:** Born May 29, 1948, Birmingham, AL; son of John and Ruth. **Educ:** Stillman Col, BS, 1969; Univ Calif, San Diego, MD, 1973; Am Bd Psychiatry Neurol, dipl, 1982. **Career:** Ohio State Univ, res, 1973-77, child flw, 1977-78, asst prof, 1978-89, assoc prof, 1989-2001, prof, 2001-03, prof emer, 2003-; Insight Matters, ed, 1994-. **Orgs:** Fel Am Psychiat Asn, 1977; Minister flw, Am Psychiat Asn, 1977; Am Psychiat Asn, 1978-; Am Acad Child Pschiatry, 1979-; Asn Acad Psychiat, 1980-; ed, Spectrm Newsletter, APA NIMH Flws, 1981-83; fel Am Acad Child & Adolescent Psychiat, 1982; secy, Psychiat Soc Cent Ohio, 1985-88; fel Am Psychiat Asn, 1989; pres-elect, Psychiat Soc Cent Ohio, 1989-90, pres, 1990-91; dir, Div Child & Adolescent Psychiat, Dept Psychiat, Ohio State Univ. **Honors/Awds:** Bk chaps, Behavioral Problem Childhood & Adolescence. **Home Addr:** 8231 Windsong Ct, Columbus, OH 43235-1491, **Home Phone:** (614)436-8201. **Business Addr:** Professor Emeritus, Ohio State University Medical centre, 1670 Upham Dr, Columbus, OH 43210, **Business Phone:** (614)293-8283.

### TOLBERT, JACQUELYN C. (JACKIE TOLBERT)
School administrator. **Personal:** Born Dec 20, 1947, Kilgore, TX; married Melvin Eugene; children: Alexis N. **Educ:** Kilgore Col, AA, scholastic hon, 1968; Stephen F Austin State Univ, BA, 1970, MA, 1975, mid mgt adminr cert, 1980; E Tex State Univ. **Career:** Longview Independent Sch Dist, teacher, 1970-71; Kilgore Independent Sch Dist, teacher, 1971-79, pub info coordr, 1979; Tidwell Elem Sch, asst supt; N Forest Independent Sch Dist, asst supt community rels, spokeswoman, dir pub rels. **Orgs:** Bd dirs, Longview Fine Arts Asn; Pub Rels Comn Jr Achievement E Tex; Delta Sigma Theta Sorority Longview Alumnae Chap, 1973-79; vpres, Tex Sch PR Asn, 1983-85; Nat Sch PR Asn Impact Comn, 1984-85; Nat Sch PR Asn J Coun, 1984-85; Tex Sch Admin Asn, 1984-; Prof Journalists Inc, 1985; Kilgore Kiwanis; bd dir, Gregg County Am Heart Asn; bd dir, Jr Achievement E Tex. **Honors/Awds:** Rookie of the Year, 1981; Bright Idea Award, Tex Sch Pub Relations Asn, 1982-83; Outstanding Woman Sigma Gamma Rho, 1985; Best of Contest, 1989, Professional Achievement, 1991, Tex Sch PR Asn, 1991; Auth: "How to Build a School Community Program", Tex Educ Agency, Tex Sch PR Asn, 1984. **Home Addr:** 2309 Pam St, Longview, TX 75602, **Home Phone:** (903)757-9392. **Business Addr:** Director of Public Relations, North Forest Independent School District, 7201 Langley Rd 77016, Houston, TX 77228, **Business Phone:** (713)491-1035.

### TOLBERT, TONY (ANTHONY LEWIS TOLBERT)
Football player. **Personal:** Born Dec 29, 1967, Tuskegee, AL; married Satasha C; children: Anthony Lewis. **Educ:** Univ Tex-El Paso, BA, criminal justice, 1991. **Career:** Football player (retired); Dallas Cowboys, defensive end, 1990, left defensive end, 1989, 1991-97. **Honors/Awds:** All-Western Athletic Conf, 1988; Pro Bowl, 1996; All-Pro selection, 1996; Super Bowl champion (XXVII, XXVIII, XXX). **Home Addr:** 475 S White Chapel Blvd, Southlake, TX 76092-7314, **Home Phone:** (817)329-8430.

### TOLDSON, IVORY A.
Periodical editor, teacher, government official. **Educ:** Louisiana State University, B.S. in Psychology, 1995; Pennsylvania State University, M.Ed. in Counselor Education, 1997; The U.S. Department of Justice, Federal Bureau of Prisons, Forensic and Correctional Psychology, 2001; Temple University, Ph.D. in Counseling Psychology, 2002; National Institute of Justice, WEB duBois, Predoctoral Psychology Internship, 2004. **Career:** The Consortium, Psychological Consultant and Evaluator, 1998-00; Mobile Therapist (Warren), Clinical Practicum, Psychological Consultant, and Behavior Specialist, 1998-00; Practicum (Group), Health Therapist, 1999-00; Clayton Center, Group Leader Psychology Intern, 2000-01; U.S. Penitentiary, Predoctoral Psychology Intern, 2000-01; Manhood Training Village, Clinical Director, 2001-05; Southern University Psychology Department, Asst. Professor, 2002-05; Office of the Public Defender, Forensic Examiner and Jury Consultant, 2005; American Psychological Association, COSIG Trainer, 2005; Howard University, Assoc. Professor, 2005-; Congressional Black Caucus Foundation, Senior Research Analyst, 2006-; "The Journal of Negro Education," Editor-in-Chief, 2008-; White House Initiative on Historically Black Colleges and Universities (HBCUs), Deputy Director, 2013-. **Orgs:** CratenFire Foundation, Board Member, 2009-10. **Honors/Awds:** "The Root" Magazine, The Root 100 Honorees, 2013. **Special Achievements:** Appointed to White House Initiative on HBCUs by President Barack Obama.

### TOLER, PENNY
Basketball player, sports manager. **Personal:** Born Mar 24, 1966, VA. **Educ:** Long Beach State Univ, attended 1989. **Career:** Basketball player (retired), general manager, vice president; Montecchio, Italy, guard, 1989-91; Pescara, Italy, 1991-94; Sporting Flash, Greece, 1994-96; Ramat HaSharon, Israel, 1996-97; Los Angeles Sparks, guard, 1997-99, gen mgr, 1999-, vpres, 2009-. **Business Addr:** General Manager, Vice President, Los Angeles Sparks, 555 N Nash St, El Segundo, CA 90245, **Business Phone:** (310)426-6000.

### TOLIVER, GEORGE
Manager, basketball executive. **Educ:** James Madison Univ, BS, social sci, MS, high educ. **Career:** Nat Basketball Asn D League, dir & supvr off; Nat Basketball Asn, referee, currently, Dept Basketball Opers, staff, 2004-; Toliver Basketball Officiating Sch, guest clinician, currently; James Madison Univ, instr & asst baseball coach, 1973-74, asst basketball coach, 1973-75; FIBA Int, off, 1985-. **Orgs:** Dir, Youth Basketball Camps, FIBA; founder & gen mgr, Harrisonburg HEAT Girls Basketball Club, 1995. **Home Addr:** 850 Parkwood Dr, 22801, VA 22801, **Home Phone:** (540)434-6037. **Business Addr:** Founder, General Manager, Harrisonburg HEAT Girls Basketball Club, 1001 Garbers Church Rd, Harrisonburg, VA 22801.

### TOLIVER, PAUL ALLEN
Vice president (organization), manager, executive. **Personal:** Born Sep 14, 1946, Baltimore, MD; son of Paul Arthur and Ruth Allen; married Jane D; children: Jill Arlene & Paul Russell. **Educ:** Univ Cincinnati, BBA, 1968, MBA, mgt & opers res, 1973. **Career:** ATE Mgt & Serv Comp, sr vpres, 1973-84; San Francisco Munic Rwy, chief transp officer, dep gen mgr, 1984-88; New Orleans Regional Transp Authority, asst gen mgr opers; Seattle Metro, dir transit, 1988-96; King County dept transp, dir, 1996-2002; Comput Intelligence Squared, vpres, transp, 2002-; New Age Industs, owner, 2002-13; Streetline Inc, adv bd, 2007-; New Orleans Regional Transp Authority, asst gen mgr; Wash Metrop Area Transit Authority, tech advisor, 2009-10; Detroit Dept Transp, chief operating officer, 2013-. **Orgs:** Nat pres, Conf Minority Transp Officials, 1986-88; Transp Res Bd, 1988-; chmn, Norman Y Mineta Intl Inst Surface Trans Policy Studies, bd dir; chmn, bd dir, Urban League Metro Seattle, 1992-97; vpres mgt & fin, Am Pub Transit asn, 1992-94; bd dir, Nat Urban League, 1994-97, exec comm; African Am Agenda; chmn, Seattle Art Mus's African Arts Coun,

1993-; bd trustee, Seattle Art Mus, 1998-; bd dir, Intelligent Transp Soc Am, 1999-2002; bd dir, Cent Dist Forum Arts & Ideas, 1999-2007; chmn, TCRP Proj J-9; bd chair, Earshot Jazz, 2009-11. **Home Addr:** 2320 W Viewmont Way W, Seattle, WA 98199, **Home Phone:** (206)284-8385. **Business Addr:** Chief Operating Officer, Detroit Department of Transportation, 1301 E Warren Ave, Detroit, MI 48207, **Business Phone:** (313)833-1017.

## TOLIVER, VIRGINIA F. DOWSING

Library administrator. **Personal:** Born Nov 1, 1948, Tupelo, MS; daughter of Frank D Sr and Jessie Spearman; children: Wilmetta J Diallo. **Educ:** Jackson State Univ, Jackson, Miss, BA, eng lit, 1969; Univ Ill, Urbana, Ill, MSLS, 1973. **Career:** Alcorn State Univ, Lorman, Miss, serials librn, 1973-77, actg libr dir, 1974-77; Lawrence Livermore Lab, summer intern tech info dept, 1977; Univ Southern Miss, Hattiesburg, Miss, coordr, info retrieval, 1977-81; Coun Libr Resources, acad libr mgt intern, 1981; Wash Univ, St Louis, Mo, dir, admin & planning, 1982-99, assoc dean admin, 1982-. **Orgs:** Am Libr Asn, 1982-87, 1989-; Ala Black Caucus, 1988-; Charmanine Chapman Soc, United Way, 1999-; moderator, Presbytery Giddings Lovejoy, 2004; bd dir, Eden Theol Sem; Libr Admin & Mgt Div; Asn Col & Res Libr; exec bd mem, Black Caucus Am Libr Asn; ACRL Budget Finance Comt, 2003-07; BCALA Lit Awards Comt, 2001-06, 2008-10; Human Resources Adv Comt, Wash Univ; bd dir, Eden Theol Sem; United Ways Charmaine Chapman Socs; Delta Sigma Theta Sorority; Benefits Comt; chaired, Presby Church USA Nat Comt. **Honors/Awds:** Inst Info Retrieval, Lawrence Livermore Lab, 1977; Acad Libr Mgmt Intern, Coun Libr Resources, 1981-82; Bob & Gerry Virgil Ethic of Service Award, 2012. **Special Achievements:** First Woman and the First African American to chair the Board of Trustees for Eden Theological Seminary in the Seminary 160 year history. **Home Addr:** 1029 Raritan Dr, St Louis, MO 63119, **Home Phone:** (314)961-0187. **Business Addr:** Associate Dean, Washington University Library, 1 Brookings Dr, St Louis, MO 63130, **Business Phone:** (314)935-5400.

## TOLLETT, DR. CHARLES ALBERT, JR.

Educator, association executive, surgeon. **Personal:** Born Muskogee, OK; son of Harrel E Sr and Hattie Mae Scruggs; married Katherine; children: Lynn, Charles Jr, Frank & Jeffery. **Educ:** Howard Univ, BS, 1950; Temple Univ Med Sch, MD, 1952; Am Bd Surg, cert, 1958; Temple Univ, DSc, 1957. **Career:** Temple Univ Hosp, intern, 1952-53, gen surg resident, 1953-57; jr instr surg, 1956-57; sr surg resident, 1957; gen surg, currently; St Anthony Hosp, chief surg, 1991-93; Huntingburg Surg Clin, physician; pvt pract, currently. **Orgs:** Phi Beta Kappa Med, AOA; Babcock Surg Soc; Howard Univ Alumni; Kappa Alpha Psi; Sigma Pi Phi; Philadelphia Co Med Soc; AMA; Okla State Med Dent& Pharm Asn; OK Co & State Med Soc; OK Surg Asn; Am Col Surgeons; YMCA; Control Chap Okla Howard Alumni Asn; bd, Okla Am Ins Co; pres, Okla Health Sci Ctr Fac House, 1974; Areawide Health Planning Org; assoc clin prof surg, Univ Okla Health Sci Ctr; Nat Med Asn, Pan Pac Surg Asn; pres, bd, City County Health Dept, 1984-89; Gov's Comn Okla Health Care, 1992-93; Allen Chapel AME Church, trustee bd; NCP, life mem. **Honors/Awds:** Volunteer of the Year Award in Recognition of Outstanding Serv to the East side Br YMCA, 1984; Fel, Am Col Surgeons, 1960. **Special Achievements:** Contributing author, A Century of Black Surgeons: The USA Experience. **Home Addr:** 407 E 22nd St, Huntingburg, IN 47542, **Home Phone:** (812)683-6339. **Business Addr:** Physician, Huntingburg Surgery Clinic, 214 E 17th St, Huntingburg, IN 47542, **Business Phone:** (812)683-6339.

## TOLLIVER, CHARLES

Trumpet player, educator, music producer. **Personal:** Born Mar 6, 1942, Jacksonville, FL; son of Samuel and Ruth Lavatt; children: Charles Edward. **Educ:** Howard Univ, Col Pharm, attended 1963. **Career:** Strata-E Rec, co-founder, pres, chief exec officer, 1970-; New Sch Jazz & Contemp Music, adj prof, jazz orchestra, dir, 1992-. **Orgs:** Broadcast Music Inc, 1964-; Am Fed Musicians, 1964-. **Business Addr:** President, Chief Executive Officer, Strata-East Records, Grand Central Sta, New York, NY 10163.

## TOLLIVER, REV. DR. JOEL

Clergy, educator, administrator. **Personal:** Born Feb 26, 1946, Philadelphia, PA; married Sharon; children: Joel Jr & Paul. **Educ:** Lincoln Univ, BA, 1969; Yale Univ, MPH, 1971; Colgate Bexler Crozer Theol Sem, MDiv, 1985; State Univ NY, Buffalo, PhD, educ admin, 1995. **Career:** Univ Rochester, health educr, 1971; Radio Sta WAXI, talk show host, 1973-77; Empire State Col, asst prof, 1973; City Rochester, asst city mgr, 1974-82; Brockport State Col, consult, 1974, chaplain, admin & instr, 1987; Genessee Community Col, consult, 1974; Haven Rest Missionary Baptist Church, pastor, 2004-; Monroe Community Col, chaplain & adminr; DeVry Inst Technol, dean. **Orgs:** Bd mem, United Church Ministry Inc, 1979; bd mem, Bridge Vol Inc, 1979; Urban League, 1979; Phi Delta Kappa Educ Soc, 1989; Alpha Phi Alpha Frat Inc; Alpha Phi Omega Nat Serv Frat; Benevolent Order Elks; Nat Sickle Cell Org; Martin Luther King Health Ctr. **Honors/Awds:** Young Man of American Commission Service, US Jaycees, 1977; Commission Service Award, Black Church & Comn, United Church Ministry, 1978 & 79; Commission Service, Nat Asn Advan Colored People Elmira State Prison, 1980; Church & Community Service Award, United Church Ministry, 1983; Editorial Excel Award, Black Stud Union Monroe Community Col, 1984; Outstanding Adult & Student Award, Rochester Area Col, 1985; Leadership Development Institute Award, State Univ NY, Brockport, 1986; Organization of Students of African Descent Award, Serv Afro-Am Stud, 1985-89; Award of Community Service, Nat Asn Negro Women, 1986; United Church Ministry Award, Serv Black Family & Community, 1986; Community Mediator, Hudson Valley Mohawk Asn, 1986; Certificate of Achievement, Martin Luther King Ctr Social Change, 1989-90; Conflict & Management Medicator, Ctr Dispute Settlement, 1990; New York State Assembly Award for Community Service, 1995; Phi Beta Delta Int Scholar, 1995. **Home Addr:** 1130 S Mich Ave Apt 2304, Chicago, IL 60605-2331. **Business Addr:** Pastor, Haven of Rest Missionary Baptist Church, 7925 S S Chicago Ave, Chicago, IL 60617-1016, **Business Phone:** (773)375-4489.

## TOLLIVER, NED, JR.

Educator, executive, association executive. **Personal:** Born May 2, 1943, Woodville, MS; son of Charlotte Bonney and Ned Sr; married Dorothy Bickham; children: Tony L & Daphne A. **Educ:** Miss Valley State Univ, BS, 1967; Western Mich Univ, cert, 1969; Jackson State Univ, cert, 1973; Delta State Univ, MA, 1983. **Career:** Negro Civic Club, corresp secy, 1973; E Side High Sch, team leader, Social Studies Dept, 1973-94; Summer Youth Prog, coordr, 1973-94; Cleveland Area Civic Club, vpres, 1978-; Selective Serv Bd, mem, Bolivar City, 1982-; Cleveland Bd Alderman, vpres, 1991; W Tallahatchie High Sch, prin, 1994-; Drew High Sch, prin, currently. **Orgs:** Cleveland Asn Educ, 1967-; Miss Asn Educr, 1967-; Nat Educ Asn, 1967-; sponsor, Citizenship Club, E Side High, 1968-; Dem Party Miss, 1977-; Notary Pub Bolivar Co MS, 1977-; bd trustee, United Baptist Church, 1980-; Nat Asn Advan Colored People, Cleveland Chap, 1982-; pres, Cleveland Area Civic Club, 1986; asst treas, Roar Found Inc. **Honors/Awds:** Star Teacher, 1987-90, 1992-93. **Home Addr:** 1819 Cowan Dr, PO Box 814, Cleveland, MS 38732-4419, **Home Phone:** (662)843-3176. **Business Addr:** Principal, Drew High School, 288 Green Ave, Drew, MS 38737, **Business Phone:** (662)745-8586.

## TOLLIVER, DR. RICHARD LAMAR

Clergy, housing developer. **Personal:** Born Jun 26, 1945, Springfield, OH; married Ann Cecile Jackson. **Educ:** Miami Univ, Oxford, OH, BA, relig, 1967; Boston Univ, Afro-Am studies, 1971, MA, polit sci, 1986; Episcopal Divinity Sch, Cambridge, MA, Mdiv, 1971; Howard Univ, Wash, DC, PhD, polit sci, 1982; Advan Mgt Develop Prog Real Estate Harvard Univ Grad Sch Design, 2015. **Career:** St Cyprian's Church, Boston, Mass, rector, 1972-77; St Timothy's Church, Wash, DC, rector, 1977-84; NSF fel, 1979-82; US Peace Corps, Kenya, assoc country dir, 1984-86; US Peace Corps, Mauritania, country dir, 1986-88; Howard Univ, Wash, DC, prof, 1988-89; St Edmund's Episcopal Church, Chicago, Ill, rector, 1989-; St Edmund's Redevelop Corp, rector, 1990-. **Orgs:** Omega Psi Phi Fraternity, 1968-; pres, St Edmund's Redevt Corp, 1989-; bd dir, Beverly Bank & Trust Co, Chicago; Beta Boule, Sigma Pi Phi Fraternity, 1991-; nat bd dir, Union Black Episcopalians; vip bd, St Edmund's Acad; bd trustee, three Historically Black Cols & Univs; trustee ravinia, Summer Residence Chicago Symphony Orchester. **Home Addr:** 4729 S Drexel Blvd, Chicago, IL 60615-1701, **Home Phone:** (773)924-0405. **Business Addr:** Rector, St Edmund's Episcopal Church, 6105 S Mich Ave, Chicago, IL 60637, **Business Phone:** (773)288-0038.

## TOLLIVER, THOMAS C., JR.

Government official. **Personal:** Born Oct 16, 1950, Woodville, MS; son of Tom C and Sarah; children: Tommie C. **Educ:** Jackson State Univ, BS, biol, 1972, MS, 1979; Univ Southern Miss, MS, 1978; Southern Univ A&M Col, MS, pub admin, 1995; Walden Univ, human serv, 2002. **Career:** Wilkinson County High Sch, teacher, 1972-79; Wilkinson County, chancery clerk, 1979-. **Orgs:** Asst state dir, Alpha Phi Alpha Frat, 1970-75; bd dir, Miss ChanceryClerk's Asn, 1979-85; bd dir, chmn, Chatwell Club Inc, 1982-88; bd dir, Friends Armisted, 1984-; worshipful master, F & AM Prince Hall Masons, 1985; 32nd degree mason, 33rd degree mason, Shriner. **Honors/Awds:** Man of the Year, Alpha Phi Alpha Frat, 1972-73. **Home Addr:** PO Box 1376, Woodville, MS 39669-1376, **Home Phone:** (601)888-3372. **Business Addr:** Chancery Clerk, Wilkinson County 17th Chancery Court District, 525 Main St, Woodville, MS 39669, **Business Phone:** (601)888-4381.

## TOMLIN, JOSEPHINE D.

Banker. **Personal:** Born Jul 5, 1952, Pittsburgh, PA; daughter of Charles C and Hattie Holmes; married Mark Washington. **Educ:** Allegheny Col, BA, 1974; Univ Pgh, MEd, 1975. **Career:** Univ Pgh, prog coun, 1975-76; La Roche Col, upward bound dir, 1976-81; Mellon Bank, Pittsburgh, corp demand des poit mgr, 1983-84, support serv sect mgr, 1984-85, retail systs mgr, 1985-88, loan serv mgr, 1988-90, proj consult, vpres, 1990-. **Orgs:** Bd dir, Women's Ctr Pgh, 1978-80; bus & fin acad consut, Urban League, 1985-86; career oppurtunity comm adv, Allegheny Col, 1987; Perry Traditional Acad Partnership Tutor Mellon Bank/Bd Educ, 1987; steering comm, Women's Forum, 1990-. **Honors/Awds:** Premier Achievement Award, Mellon Bank, 1985; Outstanding Trio Student, MAEOPP, 1986. **Home Addr:** 1205 Crucible St, Pittsburgh, PA 15220. **Business Addr:** Vice President, Mellon Bank, 4 E Sta Sq Dr, Pittsburgh, PA 15219, **Business Phone:** (412)434-6638.

## TOMLINSON, DR. MEL ALEXANDER

Dancer, educator, clergy. **Personal:** Born Jan 3, 1954, Raleigh, NC; son of Tommy Willie Amos and Marjoriline Henry. **Educ:** NC Sch Arts, Winston Salem, NC, BFA, 1974. **Career:** Coach, teacher, speaker, choreographer & dancewear designer; Agnes De Mille's Heritage Dance Theatre, Winston-Salem, prin dancer, 1972-74; Dance Theatre Harlem, dancer, 1974-77, 1978-81; Alvin Ailey Dance Theatre, NY, dancer & prin, 1977-78; New York City Ballet, dancer, 1981-87; NC Dance Theatre, dir educ servs, 1988-89, dancer, 1988-; Boston Ballet, prin dancer, 1991-92, City Dance Outreach Prog, master teacher, 1991; Boston Conserv Music & the Harvard summer prog, prof dance ed, 1991-93; Univ NC, prof dance & theatre arts, 1993-96; Choreographer: "No Right on Red", 1987; "Carnival of the Animals", 1988; "Karenda", 1990; "Sonata 5", 1991; "Alas!", 1992; "In the Beginning", 1993; "Pedipieds", 1993; DTSW Studio, guest fac, currently; pastor, currently. **Orgs:** Independent Film & TV Alliance; Int Platform Asn; Am Fedn TV & Radio Artists; Am Guild Musical Artists. **Honors/Awds:** North Carolina Prize, NY Times, 1983; Elliot Award, 1993. **Special Achievements:** Filmed documentary, "With A Clear Voice", NBC TV, 1993. **Home Addr:** 147 Maple Cir, Belmont, NC 28012. **Business Addr:** Guest Faculty, DTSW Studio, 4200 Wyo NE Suite B 2, Albuquerque, NM 87111-3161, **Business Phone:** (505)296-9465.

## TOMLINSON, DR. ROBERT

Educator, painter (artist), artist. **Personal:** Born Jun 26, 1938, Brooklyn, NY; son of Sydney and Julia Espeut. **Educ:** Pratt Inst, Brooklyn, BFA, 1961; Columbia Univ, Teachers Col, NY, attended 1963; City Univ NY Grad Ctr, NY, PhD, Fr lit, 1977. **Career:** This Week Mag, asst art dir, 1961-63; Ministere de l'Educ Nationale Paris, eng instr, 1963-68; HS Art & Design, NY, fr instr, 1968-72; Hunter Col NY, adj asst prof, 1972-78; Ford Found, Advan Study fel, 1972-76; City Univ NY, fel, 1975-77; Emory Univ Atlanta, asst prof, 1978-84, assoc prof, 1984-93, prof fr & int dir, 1990-91, prof, 1994-99; Emory Univ, Dept Fr & Ital Studies, prof emer, currently; Exhibits: Contemporary Black Artists in America, Great Neck NY, 1997, 1999, 2000, 2002 (group), Viridian Artists Inc, New York, 2005 (solo), Farleigh Dickinson Univ, Hackensack, NJ, 2006 (solo). **Orgs:** Am Soc Eighteenth Cent Stud Mod Lang Asn; chmn, Emory Univ Comn Status Minorities, 1980-81, 1984-85. **Honors/Awds:** Number 1 man exhibit of Painting Paris, London, NY, WA, 1968, 1971, 1979 & 1984; Am Coun Learned Societies Grant, 1979. **Special Achievements:** Author: La Fete Galante: Watteau et Marivaux, 1981. **Home Addr:** 413 8th St, Atlanta, GA 30309. **Business Addr:** Emeritus Professor, Emory University, 201 Dowman Dr, Atlanta, GA 30322, **Business Phone:** (404)727-6123.

## TONEY, ANTHONY

Football player, executive. **Personal:** Born Sep 23, 1962, Salinas, CA; married Mary Ann; children: Derrick. **Educ:** Hartnell Community Col; Tex A&M Univ. **Career:** Football player (retired), executive; Philadelphia Eagles, fullback, 1986-90; Household Credit Serv, collector & facilitator; Boys & Girls Clubs Monterey County, wellness coordr, sea side unit dir, 1994-. **Orgs:** Monterey County Safe Kids Coaliton. **Home Addr:** , Salinas, CA. **Business Addr:** Seaside Unit Director, Wellness Coordinator, Boys & Girls Clubs of Monterey County, 85 Maryal Dr, Seaside, CA 93906, **Business Phone:** (831)394-5171.

## TONEY, FREDERIEK

President (organization), vice president (organization), automotive executive. **Personal:** Born Dec 1, 1955?; married Cynthia; children: Frederiek Jr, Camille, Simone & Danielle. **Educ:** Univ Ala, BS, bus; Univ La Verne, La Verne, CA, MBA. **Career:** Caterpillar Inc, Peoria, Ill; Am Honda Motor Co, asst vpres procurement & distrib; Ford Motor Co, dir N Am logistics, 2000-03, dir N Am opers & mfg, 2003-04, dir global parts supply & logistics, 2004-05, exec dir mat planning & logistics, 2005-09, vpres & pres global ford customer serv div, corp officer, 2009-. **Orgs:** Bd trustee & Sch Bus Adv Coun, Univ Ala; Sch Bus Adv Coun, Cent State Univ. **Home Addr:** 18125 Peninsula Wy, Northville, MI 48168-8496. **Business Addr:** President of Global Ford Customer Service Division, Vice president, Ford Motor Company, PO Box 6248, Dearborn, MI 48126.

## TONGUE, REGINALD CLINTON (REGGIE TONGUE)

Football player. **Personal:** Born Apr 11, 1973, Baltimore, MD. **Educ:** Ore State Univ, grad. **Career:** Football player (retired); Kans City Chiefs, 1996, strong safety, 1997-99; Seattle Seahawks, strong safety, 2000-03, free safety, 2001; New York Jets, strong safety, 2004; Oakland Raiders, defensive back, 2005. **Honors/Awds:** Mack Lee Hill Award, 1996.

## TOO SHORT (TODD ANTHONY SHAW)

Rap musician. **Personal:** Born Apr 28, 1966, Los Angeles, CA. **Career:** Albums: Players, 1985; Born to Mack, 1987; Don't Stop Rappin, 1985; LifeI s.Too Short, 1988; Short Dog's in the House, 1990; Shorty the Pimp, 1992; Get in Where You Fit In, 1993; Cocktails, 1995; Gettin' It, 1996; Can't Stay Away, 1999; You Nasty, 2000; Uncensored, 2000; Chase the Cat, 2001; What's My Favorite Word?, 2002; It's About Time, 2003; Married to the Game, 2003; Pimpin' Incorporated, 2006; Gangsters & Strippers, 2006; Blow the Whistle, 2006; Mack of the Century, Greatest Hits, 2006; Bible of aPimp, 2007; I Love the Bay, 2007; Get Off the Stage, 2007; Still Blowin', 2010; No Trespassing, 2012; History: Mob Music, 2012; History: Function Music, 2012; Dangerous Music Rec Label, founder; Up All Nite Recs, owner, currently. **Business Addr:** Recording Artist, Jive Records, 137-139 W 25th St, New York, NY 10001, **Business Phone:** (212)727-0016.

## TOOMER, AMANI ASKARI

Football player, broadcaster. **Personal:** Born Sep 8, 1974, Berkeley, CA; son of Donald Sr; married Yola Dabrowski. **Educ:** Univ Mich. **Career:** Football player (retired), commentator; New York Giants, wide receiver, 1996-2008; Kans City Chiefs, 2009; Mich Wolverines, wide receiver; DeLaSalle Spartans, wide receiver; Richmond Steelers, receiver, punter, kicker, linebacker, running back; Berkeley Cougars, lineman; NBC Sports Radio, co-host, 2012-; Nat Football League, sports commentator, currently. **Orgs:** Founder, Amani Toomer Found; Breast Cancer Res Found; Newark YMCA; Autism Coalition; Big BAM! Found. **Honors/Awds:** Champion, Nat Football Conf, 2000, 2007; Man of the Year, 2003; Champion, Super Bowl, XLII; Ring of Honor, New York Giants; Neighborhood Most Valuable Player, Ameriquest, 2004; United Way Hometown Hero, United Way New York, 2004. **Special Achievements:** Films: Gift of New York, producer, 2006. **Business Addr:** Sports Commentator, National Football League, 345 Pk Ave, New York, NJ 10154, **Business Phone:** (212)450-2000.

## TOOMER, DR. CLARENCE

Librarian, administrator. **Personal:** Born Jun 12, 1952, Asbury Park, NJ; son of Hazel Markham and Willie. **Educ:** Livingstone Col, Salisbury, NC, BA, 1974; NC State Univ, MLS, 1976, EdD, 1993. **Career:** NC A&T State Univ, Greensboro, NC, librn, 1975-77; Johnson C Smith Univ, Charlotte, NC, asst librn, 1977-80; Shaw Univ, Raleigh, NC, dir libr serv, 1980-88; Greensboro Col, Greensboro, NC, libr dir, 1988-93; Univ NC, Pembroke, dir libr serv, 1993-; Ala A&M Univ, J F Drake Learning Resources Ctr, libr dir, dean, currently. **Orgs:** NC Libr Asn, 1977-; Am Libr Asn, 1984-; Guildford Libr Club, 1988-; Asn Col & Res Libr, 1988-; Nat Agr Libr; bd mem, Solas Technologies Group Inc; Nat Asn Advan Colored People. **Home Addr:** 5303 N Oaks Dr, Greensboro, NC 27455, **Home Phone:** (919)545-1463. **Business Addr:** Dean of Libraries, Alabama A&M University, 4900 Meridian St N, Normal, AL 35762, **Business Phone:** (256)372-5000.

## TOON, ALBERT LEE, JR. (AL TOON)

Football player, executive, real estate agent. **Personal:** Born Apr 30, 1963, Newport News, VA; married Jane; children: Kirby, Molly, Sydney & Nick. **Educ:** Univ Wis, BS, family resources, 1984. **Career:** Football player (retired), executive; New York Jets, wide receiver, 1985-92; Investor residential & com real estate, owner & mgr; Burger King Franchise; Taco Bell franchisee, dir & organizer; Capitol Bank Corp, co-founder, vpres; Olson Toon Landscaping Inc, sr vpres, co-onwer, 2011-. **Orgs:** Bd dir, Nat Guardian Life Ins Co; bd dir, Green Bay Packers; bd dir, Capitol Bank; pres, Univ Wis's Nat W Club. **Honors/Awds:** First team All Big 10 NFL All-Rookie by Football Digest; Player of the Year, Am Football Club, 1986; Most Valuable Player, New York Jets, 1986-88; Pro Bowl, 1986-88; Univ Wisc Hall of Fame, 1998; Ring of Honor, New York Jets. **Home Addr:** PO Box 628245, Middleton, WI 53562. **Business Addr:** Senior Vice President, Co-owner, Olson Toon Landscaping Inc, 4387 Schwartz Rd, Middleton, WI 53562, **Business Phone:** (608)827-9401.

### TOOTE, GLORIA E. A

Lawyer, administrator, real estate developer. **Personal:** Born Nov 8, 1931, New York, NY; daughter of Frederick A & Lillie M. **Educ:** Howard Univ Sch Law, BA, 1952, JD, 1954; Columbia Univ Grad Sch Law, MA, 1956, LLM. **Career:** Real Estate Entrepreneur; New York City, prac law, 1954-71, pvt prac; Time Magazine, Nat Affairs Section, editorial staff, 1957-58; Toote Town Publ Co & Town Recording Studios, pres, 1966-70; Action Agency Off Volunteer Action Liaison, asst dir, 1971-73; Dept Housing & Urban Develop, asst secy, 1973-75; auth & lecturer; New York State, deleg, 1976; US Off Pvt Sector Initiatives, vice chmn; Trea Estates & Enterprices Inc, pres, currently. **Orgs:** Bd mem, Arbitrator Asn; Consumer Alert; founding mem, Coun Econ Affairs Republic & Nat Black United Fund; Nat Bus League; Alpha Kappa Alpha Sorority; US Chamber Com; Nat Newspaper Publ Asn; Hoover Inst War; Revolution & Peace; bd dir, Fannie Mae; mem bd governors, Nat Black United Fund; steering comt Citizens Republic; Am Arbit Asn, chair, Nat Cong Black Women Inc, 1984-92; Nat Asn Real Estate Brokers; bd dir, Fed Nat Mortgage Asn, 1992-94; Delta Sigma Theta. **Honors/Awds:** News makers Award, Nat Asn Black Women Atty; YMCA World Service Award, Women's Nat Rep Club; Pol Leadership Award, Nat Newspaper Publ Asn; Special Achievement Awards, Asn Black Women Attys; Nat Asn Black Women Attys; Special Achievement Awards, Nat Polit Cong Black Women, 1992. **Business Addr:** President, Trea Estates & Enterprises Inc, 282 W 137th St, New York, NY 10030-2407, **Business Phone:** (212)926-5388.

### TORAIN, REV. DR. TONY WILLIAM

Clergy, school administrator. **Personal:** Born Jun 27, 1954, Mebane, NC; son of William and Myrtle Juanita Woody; married Celestine Best; children: Tony William II (Nnamdi) & James Best (Jay). **Educ:** Univ NC, Chapel Hill, BA, eng lit, 1975; Gordon-Conwell Theol Sem, MATS, new testament, 1979; Boston Univ, MA, African Am lit, 1980; Univ Md, Baltimore, JD, law, 1984, MSW, social work policy & admin, 1985; Princeton Theol Sem, ministry, 2010; Regent Univ, DMin, 2013. **Career:** Boston State Col, campus minister, 1978-80; Twelfth Baptist Church, assoc minister, 1978-80; Joint Orange-Chatham Comm Action, dir elderly serv, 1980-81; Off Atty Gen MD, clerk, 1982-83; Baltimore Asn Retarded Citizens, counr, 1983-85; Hwy Church Christ, assoc minister, 1982-85; Hwy Training Inst, dean, 1984-85; C H Mason Memorial COGIC, assoc minister, 1985-88; US Dept Health & Human Servs, employee coun serv asst, 1984-85, prog legal analyst, 1985-87; Towson Univ, African Am Cult Ctr, dir, 1987; Good Shepherd Church COGIC, Baltimore, MD, pastor & founder, 1989-; Univ Md, Sch Social Work, asst dean Stud Sers & Minority Affairs, 1991-93; Univ Baltimore, Sch Law, dean stud, 1994-2008; Good Shepherd Church God Christ, founding pastor, 1989-; Circuit Ct Baltimore City, asst chief dep clerk admin, 2010-; Md State Bd Dent Examiners, exec dir, 2015-. **Orgs:** Black & Jewish Forum Baltimore; dir, African-Am Cult Ctr, Towson State Univ; bd mem, Univ Md Sch Social Work, 1986-; Am Bar Asn, Comt Law Sch Admin; Comn Educ Church God Christ Inc. **Home Addr:** 9 Hard Spring Ct, Owings Mills, MD 21117, **Home Phone:** (410)363-4183. **Business Addr:** Pastor, Founder, The Good Shepherd Church of God, 8301 Liberty Rd, Baltimore, MD 21244, **Business Phone:** (410)922-1637.

### TORAN, KAY DEAN

Educator, president (organization), association executive. **Personal:** Born Nov 21, 1942, Birmingham, AL; daughter of Benjamin and Mary Rose Dean; married John; children: Traci Rossi & John Dean. **Educ:** Univ Portland, BA, 1964; Portland State Univ, MSW, 1970. **Career:** Portland State Univ, asst prof coun, 1970-71, Grad Sch Soc Work, asst prof, 1971-76; Adult & Family Serv Publ Welfare, asst mgr field opers, 1976-79; State Ore, asst & dir affirmative action; Ore State Off Serv C & Families, dir affirm action, 1979-87; Dept Gen Serv,, adminr purchasing div, 1987-90; CS Serv Div, regional adminr, 1991-94; C & Families, dir state off serv, 1995; Walker Inst, pres, 1990-94; Portland chap links inc, pres, 1990-92. Vols Am, pres & chief exec officer, 1999-. **Orgs:** Delta Sigma Theta Soc Serv Sor, 1964-; Girl Scouts Summer Camp, 1968; Girl Scouts, prog consult, 1969-70; Campfire Girls Inc, 1975-77; Met Fam Serv, 1976-82; Portland State Univ Found, 1980-; Catlin Gable Sch, 1980-84; bd, Ore Community Found, currently; bd, Providence Health & Serv, currently; bd, Univ Portland Bd Regents, currently. **Honors/Awds:** Research Grant for Curriculum Development Western Interstate Comm for Higher Education, 1973; Leader 80's Award, NW Conf Black Publication Officials, 1979; Outstanding Young Woman America, 1980; White Rose Award, March Dimes; Woman Excellence Delta Sigma Theta, 1982; Astra Award for Excellence, Int Astra Soc; Alumna of the Year, Portland State Univ, Urban Pioneer Award; Non profit CEO of the Year Award, Portland Business Journal, 2008; Governor Victor Atiyeh Leadership in Education Award, Concordia Univ; Nohad Toulan Urban Pioneer Award, Portland State Univ; CEO of the Year Award, Portland Bus J; Equal Opportunity Award, Urban League Portland; Honorary Doctorate, Univ Portland, 2012. **Special Achievements:** Publication: "Curriculum Development" 1974. **Home Addr:** 4008 NE 30th St, Portland, OR 97212-1702, **Home Phone:** (503)954-2252. **Business Addr:** President, Chief Executive Officer, Volunteers of America, 3910 SE Stark St, Portland, OR 97214, **Business Phone:** (503)235-8655.

### TORIAN, EDWARD TORRENCE

Executive. **Personal:** Born Dec 20, 1933, New Rochelle, NY; son of Edward (deceased) and Julia; married Pearl Cromartie; children: Curtis & Darlene. **Educ:** Westchester Bus Inst, cert acct, 1956; Iona Col, BBA, 1968, MBA, finance. **Career:** Perkin-Elmer Corp, sr contract acct, 1966-90; Hal-Tor Enterprises Co, partner & treas, 1970-; Danbury Common Coun, legislative leader, 1983, councilman-at-large, 1979-87; Hughes Danbury Optical Syst, sr admin, 1990. **Orgs:** Nat Asn Acct, 1967-; Iona Col Alumni Asn, 1968-;Nat Asn Advan Colored People, 1980-; treas, Black Dem Asn Danbury, 1981-; sec Men's Coun, 1981-84, treas, 1990-, New Hope Baptist Church; bd trustee, bd, United Way Northern Fairfield County, Conn; City Danbury, Charter Rev Comn, currently. **Home Addr:** 18 Indian Head Rd, Danbury, CT 06811-2919, **Home Phone:** (203)746-4140.

### TORRENCE, GWEN. See TORRENCE-WALLER, GWENDOLYN LENNA.

### TORRENCE-THOMPSON, JUANITA LEE

Poet, writer, public relations executive. **Personal:** Born Brockton, MA; daughter of James Lee Torrence and Dr Zylpha Mapp-Robinson (deceased); married Hugh; children: Derek Rush. **Educ:** New Sch; State Univ NY Empire State Col, BS, bus commun, 1983; Fordham Univ, MA, commun, 1989; Fine Arts Work Ctr, Provincetown, MA, poetry fiction, 2000; Bank St Col Educ, Writing C, 2002; Univ Wis, cert, poetry. **Career:** UN Int Sch, Newsletter, ed, 1976-77; Nat Asn Theatre Owners, Pub Rel, ed asst, 1979-80; freelance writer, 1983-; State Univ New York, Empire State Col, newsletter, ed, 1985-87; Dorf & Stanton Comms, ed, 1987-88; Mutual New York, pr consult, 1988-90; Torrence-Thompson Pub Rels, pres, 1988-; poet/writer, 1995-; Col New Rochelle, adj prof, 1997; Torderwarz Publ Co, currently; Mobius, Poetry Mag, owner, ed-in-chief, ed & publ, currently; Poems: Wings Span to Eternity, 1995; Spanning Yrs, 1996; Breath-Life, Scopcraeft Press, 2009; New York & African Tapestries; Talking With Stanley Kunitz; Black Enterprise articles; Celebrating a Tapestry Life, 2003; Kantonsschule Rychenberg, Winterthur, Switz, 1998, Bahai, Singapore, 1995; Pedestal Mag online poem & essays spec 9/11 issue, 2001; An Eye An Eye Makes World Blind: Poets 9/11 Anthology, 2002; Poetry Among Flowers: Queens Meets Asia. **Orgs:** Nat Asn Black Journalists, 1989-; Poetry Soc Am, 1995-; Poets House, 1995-; Poets & Writers, 1996-; Am Asn Univ Women, 1992-; Fresh Meadows Poets, 2000-; Black Am Pub; Acad Am Poets; PRSA; Am Asn Univ Women; 100 Black Women Long Island New York; Queens Coun Arts; Acad Am Poets; Fresh Meadows Poets; Socs C's Bk Writers & Illustrators; Native Am Journalists Asn; Black Americans Publ & Am Asn Univ Women; Nat Fedn State Poetry Socs. **Honors/Awds:** Feature Article Award, Writers Digest Mag, 1985; Meritorious Service Award, United Negro Col Fund, 1994; Nashville Newsletter, 1994; First Prize, New York Pub Lib Poetry Contest, 1996; Robins Nest Mag, 1996; Outstanding Achievement Award, SUNY, Empire State Col, 1996; Margaret A Walker Short Story Award, 1999, 2000; Editor's Choice Poetry Awards; Children's Fiction Award, Writer's Digest, 2000; Paul Laurence Dunbar Poetry Award, 2000; Dr Zylpha Mapp Robinson International Poetry Award, 2009. **Special Achievements:** Nominated Woman of the Year, Am Biographical Institute Bd International Research, 2009; One of 10 women who Made a difference, American Association University Women, New York City Branch; Fifth prize in the national Writer's Digest Poetry Award; Second prize in the Spoken Word Poetry Contest by New York Association of Black Journalists; second prize in the Poetry Society of Michigan International Poetry Contest. **Home Addr:** 144-53 77th Ave, PO Box 670158, Flushing, NY 11367-1058. **Business Addr:** Juanita Torrence-Thompson, Torderwarz Publishing Co, PO Box 671058, Flushing, NY 11367-1058.

### TORRENCE-WALLER, GWENDOLYN LENNA (GWEN TORRENCE)

Athlete, barber. **Personal:** Born Jun 12, 1965, Atlanta, GA; daughter of Dorothy; married Jody Smith; children: Manley & E'mon. **Educ:** Univ Ga, attended 1987. **Career:** Athlete (retired), hair dresser; US Olympic Team, track & field, 1984-97; Bangz & Tanglez LLC, hairdresser, currently. **Honors/Awds:** Gold Medal, World Univ Games, 1985, 1987; Bronze Medal, Nat Championships, 1986; Gold Medal, Pan Am Games, 1987; Gold Medal, Nat Championships, 1988; Gold Medal, Nat Indoor Championships, 1988, 1989, 1997; Silver medal, World Indoor Championships, 1989; Two Silver Medals, World Championships Games, Tokyo, Japan, 1991; Two Silver Medals, World Championships Games, Stuttgart, Ger, 1993; Bronze Medal, World Championships Games, Stuttgart, Ger, 1993; Two Gold Medals, Summer Olympics, Barcelona, Spain, 1992; Gold Medal, Summer Olympics, Atlanta, GA, 1996; Gold Medal, Goodwill Games, 1994; Georgia Sports Hall of Fame, 2000; Silver Medal, Summer Olympics, Barcelona, Spain, 1992; Bronze Medal, Summer Olympics, Atlanta, GA, 1996; Gold Medal, World Championships Games, Stuttgart, Ger, 1993; Two Gold Medals, World Championships Games, Gothenburg, Sweden, 1995. **Business Addr:** Hairdresser, Bangz & Tanglez LLC, 2617 Panola Rd Suite 105, Lithonia, GA 30058, **Business Phone:** (770)322-0322.

### TORRES, GINA

Actor. **Personal:** Born Apr 25, 1969, New York, NY; married Laurence Fishburne; children: Delilah. **Career:** Lincoln Ctr Theater Co; Films: Bed of Roses, 1996; The Substance of Fire, 1996; The Underworld, 1997; The Matrix Reloaded, 2003; The Matrix Revolutions, 2003; Hair Show, 2004; Fair Game, 2005; Serenity, 2005; Standoff, 2006; Five Fingers, 2006; Jam, 2006; I Think I Love My Wife, 2007; South of Pico, 2007; Standoff, 2007; Don't Let Me Drown, 2008; Criminal Minds, 2008; Pushing Daisies, 2009; Mr. Sophistication, 2010. TV appearances: One Life to Live, 1989-93; Unnatural Pursuits, 1991; "Law & Order", 1992-95; "MANTIS", 1994; "NYPD Blue", 1995; "Dark Angel", 1996; The Underworld, 1997; "Hercules: The Legendary Journeys", 1997-99; "Xena Warrior Princess", 1997; Profiler, 1997; La Femme Nikita, 1998; Encore!, Encore!, 1998; "Cleopatra 2525", 2000-01; "Alias", 2001-06; "Any Day Now", 2001-02; "Firefly", 2002-03; The Law & Mr. Lee, 2003; The Guardian, 2003; "The Agency", 2003; "The Henry Lee Project", 2003; "Angel", 2003; "24", 2004; "Gramercy Park", 2004; "Justice League", 2004-06; "A Man of His Word", 2005; "Soccer Moms", 2005; "The Shield", 2006; "Without a Trace", 2006; "Borderline", 2006; "Standoff", 2006-07; "Dirty Sexy Money", 2007; "Boston Legal", 2008; "Water & Power", 2009; "Gossip Girl:, 2009; "Pushing Daisies", 2009; "Best Laid Plans", 2009; "The Unit", 2009; "Applause for Miss E", 2009; "Washington Field", 2009; "Tailspin", 2009; "Eli Stone", 2009; "The Vampire Diaries", 2010; "Boondocks", 2010; "Huge", 2010; "Transformers: Prime", 2011-13; "DC Universe Online", 2011; "Open Season 3", 2011; "Hannibal", 2013-14; "Suits", 2011-14. **Honors/Awds:** ALMA Award, 2001; nominee, International Press Academy's Golden Satellite Award, 2004. **Business Addr:** Actress, c/o Badgley Connor King Talent Agency, 9229 Sunset Blvd Suite 311, Los Angeles, CA 90069, **Business Phone:** (310)278-9313.

### TORRES, SHERICE

Vice president (organization). **Educ:** Harvard Univ, BA; Stanford Univ, MBA. **Career:** Deloitte & Touche, sr consult, 1995-98; MTV Networks, sr vpres, Global Home Entertainment & Adult-Brand Licensing, 2000-; Nickelodeon Networks, Inc, dir Licensing Interactive, Home Entertainment, & Consumer Electronics, sr vpres Hard Goods Nickelodeon & Viacom Consumer Prod, 2006-. **Orgs:** Pres, New York chap Nat Asn. **Honors/Awds:** "The Network Journal: Black Professionals & Small Business Magazine: 25 Influential Black Women", 2006; "Black Enterprise", 100 Most Powerful Executives in Corporate America, 2009; "Black Enterprise", 75 Most Powerful Women in Business, 2010. **Business Addr:** Senior Vice President, Nickelodeon Networks Inc, 1515 Broadway, New York, NY 10036, **Business Phone:** (212)258-7500.

### TORRY, GUY (ROBERT TORRY)

Actor, comedian. **Personal:** Born Jan 5, 1969, St. Louis, MO; son of Robert and Rebecca; married Monica Renae Askew. **Educ:** Southeast Mo State Univ, BS. **Career:** TV appearances: "Family Matters", 1993; "Martin", 1995; "Sparks", 1996; "As Told By Ginger", 2000-02; "The X Files", 2000; "NYPD Blue", 2001; "The Shield", 2002; "One on One", 2002; "Blind Justice", 2005; "NFL Total Access", 2007; "Last Comic Standing", 2010. Films: Sunset Park, 1996; Dont Be a Menace to South Cent While Drinking Your Juice in the Hood, 1996; The Good News, 1997-98; One Eight Seven, 1997; Back in Bus, 1997; Am History X, 1998; Ride, 1998; The Strip, 1999-2000; Trippin', 1999; Life, 1999; The '70s, 2000; Pearl Harbor, 2001; The Animal, 2001; Don't Say a Word, 2001; Tara, 2001; With or Without You, 2003; The Runaway Jury, 2003; Jonah, 2003; Midnight Clear, 2005; Slow Burn, 2005; Funny Money, 2006; Flirt, 2006; The Last Stand, 2006; Dead & Deader, 2006; Writer: Def Comedy Jam, HBO; Minor Adjustments; Moesha; Slow Burn, 2005; Funny Money, 2006; "1st Amendment Stand Up", 2009. MO Films, actor, writer & producer. **Orgs:** Giving Back Love Found. **Business Addr:** Comedian, Actor, William Morris Agency, 1325 Avenue of the Americas Fl 15, New York, NY 10019, **Business Phone:** (212)586-5100.

### TORRY, ROBERT. See TORRY, GUY.

### TOSE, MAURICE B.

Chief executive officer. **Personal:** Born Jan 1, 1957, Ft. Bragg, NC; married Teresa; children: 7. **Educ:** US Naval Acad, BS, opers anal, 1978. **Career:** Dept Defense Progs Techmatics Inc, dir, 1986-87; Telecommun Systs Inc, founder, chief exec officer & pres, 1987-. **Orgs:** Bd chmn, Telecommun Systs Inc, 1987-; Wireless Data Forum; AT&T's Diversity Round table; Intl Engg Consortium; Intelligent Network Forum; treas & vpres, U.S. Naval Acad Class, 1978; Annapolis Jaycees & Annapolis Kiwanis; treas, vpres, dir, Arundel Bay Homeowners Asn; Budget & Fin Coun, Antioch Apostolic Church; co-found, chmn bd, United Stated Naval Acad Samuel P Massie Educ Endowment; Annapolis Neck Small Area Planning Comn; bd dir, First Night Annapolis; bd dir, Ginger Cove Retirement Community; bd dir, US Naval Acad Found; Fed Commun Comn; Commun Security, Reliability, & Interoperability Coun; Md Gov's Int Adv Coun; CTIA Wireless Asn, 2011; Trustee, U.S. Naval Acad Athletic Scholar Prog; bd dir, U.S. Naval Acad; dir, CTIA Wireless Internet Caucus. **Business Addr:** Chairman, Chief Executive Officer, Telecommunication Systems Inc, 275 W St, Annapolis, MD 21401, **Business Phone:** (410)263-7616.

### TOTTEN, DR. HERMAN LAVON

Educator. **Personal:** Born Apr 10, 1938, Van Alstyne, TX; son of Derrall Scott and Dulvi Sims. **Educ:** Wiley Col, Marshall, TX, BA, 1961; Univ Okla, MLS, 1964, PhD, 1966. **Career:** Wiley Col, dir libr & prof libr sci, 1966-70, prof & acad dean, 1970-71; Univ Ky, Col Libr Sci, assoc prof & dean, 1971-74; Univ Ore, Sch Librarianship, dean & prof, 1974-77; Univ N Tex, Sch Libr & Info Sci, prof & assoc dean, 1977-83, prof & actg dean, 1987, regents prof & assoc dean, 1991-97, exec fac asst to pres, 2002-05, dean, Col Info, 2005-; Univ Wash, Seattle, Wash, vis prof, 1987, 1989, 1991, vis regents prof, 1992-93, 1995, 1997, 1999, 2000-03; Univ Okla, vis regents prof, 1992; US Nat Comn Libr & Info Sci, comnr, 2005-. **Orgs:** Beta Phi Mu Int Libr Sci Hon Fraternity, 1964-; pres, Tex Libr Asn, 1966-71, 1978-; Asn Educ Commun & Technol, 1966-; Southwestern Libr Asn, 1966-71, 1978-82; life mem, Am Libr Asn, 1967-; Phi Delta Kappa Nat Hon Soc; Ky Libr Asn, 1971-74; Alpha Phi Omega Nat Serv Fraternity; Southeastern Libr Asn, 1971-74; Asn Libr & Info Sci Educ, 1971-; Ore Educ Media Asn, 1974-77; Pac Northwest Libr Asn, 1974-77; Ore Libr Asn, 1974-77; Tex Coun Libr Educr, 1978-90; trustee, Am Recs Mgt Asn; chmn, Tex State Libr Joint Comt, 1993-95; chmn, Am Libr Asn Comt Accreditation; chmn, Am Libr Asn Comt Minority Concerns. **Home Addr:** 2100 Pembrooke Pl, Denton, TX 76205-8208, **Home Phone:** (940)383-1902. **Business Addr:** Regents Professor, University of North Texas, 1155 Union Cir Suite 311277, Denton, TX 76203-5017, **Business Phone:** (940)565-2000.

### TOTTRESS, DR. RICHARD EDWARD

Clergy, president (organization), chaplain. **Personal:** Born Nov 25, 1917, Newby Creek, OK; son of Rev M (deceased) and Louisa Headspoth (deceased); married Margarreau Fluorine Norton; children: 1 (deceased). **Educ:** Pac Union Col, BA, 1943; Oakwood Col, BA, 1969; Univ Beverly Hills, MA & PhD, 1981. **Career:** Clergy (retired); Texaco Conf Tex SDA, minister, 1943; SW Region Conf, pastor, evangelist, 1947-52; S Atlanta Conf SDA, dist pastor, youth assoc, 1952-63; Your Bible Speaks radio show, pres, producer, speaker, 1953; Oakwood Acad & Col, dean, 1963-66, col pastor, chaplain, 1965-69, 1972-73; Oakwood Col Ch, co-pastor, 1973-79; W End SDA Church, assoc pastor, 1993-95. **Orgs:** Civilian chaplain, 1944; bd dir, CrusadeVoters Bibb County, GA, 1959-60; bd dir, Bibb County March Dimes, 1961; fel Int Biog Asn, 1970-80; broadcast prog, WEUP Radio, 1971-73; Bk Hon Am Biogr Inst, 1979; coordr, Metro-Atlanta Area SDA Pastors,

1982-84. **Honors/Awds:** Special Plaques, Oakwood Col Fac & Stud Ch Bld, 1977; Spec Plaques, S CentSDA, 1978; Plaque Notable Am Bicentennial Era, 1976; Cert Outstanding Sec Educr Am, 1975. **Home Addr:** 2871 Lakeshore Dr, Atlanta, GA 30337-4419, **Home Phone:** (404)766-7751.

## TOUSSAINT, LORRAINE

Actor. **Personal:** Born Apr 4, 1960, Trinidad; daughter of Janet Beane (deceased). **Educ:** Juilliard Sch, drama. **Career:** Films: Breaking In, 1989; Hudson Hawk, 1991; Point of No Return, 1993; Bleeding Hearts, 1994; Mother's Boys, 1994; Dangerous Minds, 1995; Psalms from the Underground, 1996; The Spittin' Image, 1997; BlackDog, 1998; Jaded, 1998; The Sky is Falling, 2000; Rwanda Rising, 2007; The Gold Lunch, 2008; The Soloist, 2009; Ask Me Anything, 2014; Selma, 2014. TV series: "The Face of Rage", 1983; "A Case of Deadly Force", 1986; "One Life to Live", 1988; "A Man Called Hawk", 1989; "Common Ground", 1990; "Law & Order", 1990-2003; "227", 1990; "Daddy", 1991; "Tequila & Bonetti", 1992; "Trial: The Price of Passion", 1992; "Bodies of Evidence", 1992; Red Dwarf, 1992; Class of '61, 1993; Love, Lies & Lullabies, 1993; "Where I Live", 1993; "Queen", 1993; "Where Ilive", 1993; "The Sinbad Show", 1993; "Queen", 1993; "A Time to Heal", 1994; "M.A.N.T.I.S.", 1994; "Amazing Grace", 1995; "It Was Him or Us", 1995; "Murder One", 1995; "Bless This House", 1995; "Dark Skies", 1996; "Nightjohn", 1996; "Mr. & Mrs. Smith", 1996; If These Walls Could Talk, 1996; Nightjohn, 1996; America's Dream?, 1996; "The Cherokee Kid", 1996; "Leaving L.A.", 1997; Promise Land, 1997; C-16: FBI, 1998; "BlackoutEffect", 1998; "Cracker", 1998; "Nothing Sacred", 1998; "Any Day Now", 1998-2002; "Crossing Jordan", 2002-03; "Threat Matrix", 2003-04; Frasier, 2004; Their Eyes Were Watching God, 2005; "Judging Amy", 2005; "The Closer", 2005; "Numb3rs", 2005; "CSI: Crime Scene Investigation", 2006-07; UglyBetty, 2007; Saving Grace, 2007-09; "Believe the Unseen", 2008; "ER", 2008; "Cover Me", 2009; "Am I Going to Lose Her?", 2009; "That Was No First Kiss", 2009; "Popcorn", 2009; "Looks Like a Lesbian Attack to Me", 2009; "Am I Gonna Die Today?", 2009. **Business Addr:** Actress, c/o Warren Cowan & Associates, 8899 Beverly Blvd Suite 919, Los Angeles, CA 90048, **Business Phone:** (310)275-0777.

## TOUSSAINT, DR. ROSE-MARIE

Health services administrator, physician. **Personal:** Born Jun 15, 1956, Port-au-Prince. **Educ:** Loyola Univ, BS, 1979; Howard Univ Col Med, MD, 1983. **Career:** Univ Pittsburgh, surg departments, resident; Univ Wis, resident; NIH, res assoc; Howard Univ Hosp, Col Med, asst prof surg, gen surg resident, Transplant Ctr, asst prof surg & assoc dir, 1971-77; Am Bd Surg, diplomat; Howard Univ Horus Corp, med dir, 1995-; holistic physician, 1995-; Master Mantak Chia, assoc instr; Holisticdoctor.org, dir; pvt pract, currently; Book: Never Question the Miracle A Surgeon's Story, author. **Orgs:** Delta Sigma Theta Sor, 1978; vpres, All African Physicians N Am, 1984; vpres, Cheasepeake 1988; chairperson. Liver Med Adv Comn; Wash Regional Transplant Consortium, 1993; Am Soc Transplant Surgeons; Transplant Soc; fel Transplantation TEStarzl Transplantation Inst, Transplant Soc; fel Am Col Surgeon; S Eastern Ore Procurement Org, 1996; bd trustee, Loyola Univ, Acad Achievement Comn, 1999; founding mem, Nat Transplant Found, 1999; dipl, Am Bd Surg; Int Transplantation Soc. **Home Phone:** (561)309-5511. **Business Addr:** Holistic Physician, 777 E Atlantic Ave Suite Z306, Delray Beach, FL 33483, **Business Phone:** (301)498-1353.

## TOVAR, STEVEN ERIC

Executive director, football player, athletic coach. **Personal:** Born Apr 25, 1970, Elyria, OH. **Educ:** Ohio State Univ, BS; Am Pub Univ Syst, MS, 2012. **Career:** Football player, football coach (retired); Ohio State Univ Buckeyes, 1989-92; Cincinnati Bengals, linebacker, 1992-97; San Diego Chargers, 1998-2000; Carolina Panthers, 1998-99; Ohio State Athletic Compliance Off, consult, 2003-04; Army Black Knights, linebackers coach, 2004-05; Upper Arlington High Sch, Columbus, OH, defensive coordr; Miami Dolphins, football opers staff, asst coach, 2006-07; Univ Kans Jayhawks, linebackers coach, 2007-09; Northern Ill Univ, asst dir, 2011-12, mkt asst career serv, 2012-13.

## TOWNES, CLARENCE LEE, JR.

Executive, activist, association executive. **Personal:** Born Jan 21, 1928, Richmond, VA; son of Clarence L Sr and Alice Smith; married Grace Elizabeth Harris; children: Clarence III, Michael S, Lisa F & June E. **Educ:** VA Union Univ, BS, com, 1951. **Career:** Va Mutual Benefit Life Ins Co, from asst mgr to dir training, 1964-66; Republican Nat Comm, asst to chmn, dir minority affairs, 1966-70; Joint Ctr Polit Studies, dir, govt affairs, 1970-74; Metrop Coach Corp, pres, chief exec officer, 1974-86; Richmond Renaissance Inc, dep dir, 1982-91, exec dir. **Orgs:** Alt deleg Republican Nat Conv, 1964; comm Rich Redev & Housing Auth, 1964-66; chmn, Electoral Bd Richmond VA, 1979-84; bd dirs, VA Mutual Benefit Life Ins Co, 1985-88; Phi Beta Sigma Frat, 1945-; Republican Party polit, 1965-66; treas, Nat Negro Republican Assembley, 1965-66; bd mem, Richmond City Republican Comt, 1958-61; comnr, Richmond Redevelop & Housing Authority, 1963-66; pres, Jefferson Townhouse Corp, 1964; bd dir, Consol Bank & Trust Co, 1970; bd dir, Am Bus Asn, 1976-82; pres, Arts Coun Richmond, 1986-88, Richmond Pub Sch Bd, chair, 1992; bd mem, Va Commonwealth Univ, 1993-97. **Honors/Awds:** Hon Discharge, 1953; Citizenship Award, Astoria Benefical Club Richmond, 1968; Man of the Year, Iota Sigma Chap Phi Beta Sigma, 1969; Good Government Award, Richmond First Club, 1987; Brotherhood Citation Award, Richmond Chapter, Nat Conf of Christians Jews, 1987. **Special Achievements:** first Black member of a Virginia delegation in modern times. **Home Addr:** 3103 Hawthorne Ave, Richmond, VA 23222-2516, **Home Phone:** (804)329-6923. **Business Addr:** VA.

## TOWNES, EMILIE M.

Dean (education), president (organization), clergy. **Personal:** Born Durham, NC. **Educ:** University of Chicago, A.B.; University of Chicago Divinity School, A.M. and D.Min., 1982; Northwestern University, Ph.D., 1989; Garrett-Evangelical Theological Seminary, Doctor of Human Letters, 2010. **Career:** Yale Divinity School, Andrew W. Mellon Professor of African American Religion and Theology, Associate Dean of Academic Affairs; Vanderbilt University, Divinity School and Graduate Department of Religion, Dean, 2013-, and E. Rhodes and Leona B. Carpenter Professor of Womanist Ethics and Society; "Huffington Post," Blogger; Feminism in Religion Forum, Blogger. **Orgs:** Society for the Study of Black Religion, President, 2012-16 term; Yale University, African Diaspora Initiative, Middle Passage Conversations on Black Religion, Founder. **Honors/Awds:** American Academy of Arts and Sciences, inducted as fellow, 2009; Black Religious Scholars Group, Distinguished Religious Scholar, 2010. **Special Achievements:** First African American woman elected to the American Academy of Religion's presidential line, 2008; first African American and first woman Associate Dean for Academic Affairs in the Divinity School, July 2008; author of "Womanist Ethics and the Cultural Production of Evil," Palgrave Macmillan Press (2006); "Breaking the Fine Rain of Death: African American Health Care and A Womanist Ethic of Care," Continuum (1998); "In a Blaze of Glory: Womanist Spirituality as Social Witness," Abingdon Press (1995); "Womanist Justice, Womanist Hope," Scholars Press (1993); co-edited "Womanist Theological Ethics: A Reader," Westminster John Knox Press (2011) with Katie Geneva Cannon and Angela D. Simms; co-edited "Religion, Health, and Healing in African American Life," Praeger (2008) by Townes with Stephanie Y. Mitchem.

## TOWNES, JEFFREY ALLAN. See JEFF, D J JAZZY.

## TOWNES, HON. SANDRA L.

Judge, lawyer. **Personal:** Born Jan 1, 1944, Spartanburg, SC. **Educ:** Johnson C Smith Univ, BA, 1966; Syracuse Univ Col Law, JD, 1976. **Career:** Onondaga County Dist Atty Off, from asst dist atty to chief asst dist atty, 1977-87, Career Criminal Sexual Crimes Unit, dir, Felony Trial Unit, chief asst dist atty, 1986-87; Syracuse Univ Col Law, adj prof, 1987-95; City Ct, judge, 1988-99; Onondaga Community Col, adj prof, 1992-2001; Fifth Judicial Dist, NY State Supreme Ct, Justice, 2000-04; Appellate Div, Second Judicial Depart, NY State Supreme Ct, assoc justice, 2001-04; US Dist Ct, Eastern Dist New York, dist judge, 2004-15, sr judge, 2015-. **Orgs:** Anti-Discrimination Panel Fifth Judicial Dist; Legis Comt Judiciary State New York; Ny Bar Asn; Ny Women's Bar Asn; Onondaga County Bar Asn. **Business Addr:** District Judge, United States District Court, 225 Cadman Plz E, Brooklyn, NY 11201-1818, **Business Phone:** (718)797-7425.

## TOWNS, EDOLPHUS, JR.

Government official, social worker, association executive. **Personal:** Born Jul 21, 1934, Chadbourn, NC; son of Dolphus and Vergie; married Gwendolyn Forbes; children: Darryl & Deidra. **Educ:** NC Agr & Tech State Univ, Greensboro, BS, 1956; Adelphi Univ Garden City NY, MSW, 1973. **Career:** New York Medgar Evers Col, Brooklyn, prof, dep hosp admin, 1965-71; Bor Brooklyn, dep pres, 1976-82; Beth Israel Med Ctr, adminr; Fordham Univ, pub sch teacher; US House Reps, rep, 1983-2013. **Orgs:** Adv coun, Boy Scouts Am, Salvation Army, Phi Beta Sigma, Kiwanis; Nat Asn Advan Colored People; Am Red Cross; Guardsmen; Boule; chmn, Cong Black Caucus, 1991-; Energy & Com Comt; Telecommunications &Internet Subcomt; chmn, House Oversight & Govt Reform Comt, 2009-11. **Honors/Awds:** Hon degrees: LLD, Va Sem Lynchburg, 1982; LLD, Shaw Univ, 1984; DSC, NC A&T Univ, 1985; LLD, Aldelphi Univ, 1988; Recognized by the American Cancer Society; Recognized for "Efforts to Fight Mortality", Healthy Start; Named "Friend of the Nat Parks", Nat Parks & Conserv Asn; Legislator of the Year, Nat Coalition Poison Control Ctr; Legislator of the Year, Am Asn Community Health Ctrs; Legislator of the Year, Am Acad Physician Assts; Legislator of the Year, Am Acad Nurse Practitioners; Home Care Hero, Nat Asn Home Care; Education All-Star Team, Nat Educ Asn; Congressional Leadership Award, Am Col Nurse-Midwives. **Special Achievements:** First African American to serve as Deputy Brooklyn Borough President. **Business Addr:** Representative, US House of Representatives, 2232 Rayburn House Off Bldg, Washington, DC 20515, **Business Phone:** (202)225-5936.

## TOWNS, DR. MYRON B., II

Physician, pathologist. **Personal:** Born Dec 18, 1943, Greensboro, NC; son of Myron B Sr and Miriam Gould. **Educ:** Fisk Univ, BA, foreign langs, 1970; Meharry Med Col, MD, 1978. **Career:** Tennesseean, copy ed, 1967-70; Waverly-Belmont Lab, co-organizer, 1972-74; Univ Ga, electron microscopist, 1974-75, pathol residency, 1978-83; G W Hubbard Hosp, Meharry Col, resident, 1978-83; Vanderbilt Univ Clin, pharm fel, 1982; Hebbronville Lab, owner, pathologist, 1984-86; Community Clin, physician, 1985-86; Doctor's Clin, 1986-87; Towns Clin, primary & indigent care, 1987-93; JJ Clark Mkt, med dir, 1996-98; adolescent med generalist; Meharry Med Col Sch Med, resident, 1998-2001; pvt pract, currently. **Orgs:** Mem, Col Am Pathologists; mem, Am Soc Clin Path; Am Col Forensic Examiners; med IS; bds: Wildlife Rehab Ctr, 1987-92; ICS Sch Bd, 1990-92; cert foster parent; life mem, Nat Asn Advan Colored People. **Honors/Awds:** Carter Woodson Award in jour, 1969; Hons biochem & pathol res, Meharry Med Col, 1972-83; Invited lectr drug abuse, tobacco & med ethics. **Home Addr:** 6324 Jackson St, Pittsburgh, PA 15206. **Business Addr:** Physician, Private Practitioner, 971 16th Ave N, Nashville, TN 37208-3368, **Business Phone:** (615)975-5482.

## TOWNS, ROSE MARY

Librarian. **Personal:** Born Jan 7, 1934, Houston, TX; married George Elbert; children: Gordon C. **Educ:** San Francisco State Col, BA, Social Sci 1955; Univ Calif, Berkeley, MLS, 1956. **Career:** Librn (retired); Oakland Pub Lib Oakland CA, jr, sr & supv librn, 1956-60; Oakland Pub Lib Oakland CA, sr libr, 1960-62; Oakland Pub Lib, Oakland CA, supvr libr, 1962-66; Richmond Pub Lib Richmond CA, asst city libr, city librn, 1966-70; Ref Referral Proj N Bay Coop Lib Sys, coord, 1975-79; N Bay Coop Libr Syst, syst prog coord, 1979-82; Laney Col Libr, 1983-87; Bay Area Libr & Info Syst, proj coord, 1982-83; City Col San Francisco, ref Librn & instr, 1987. **Orgs:** Intellectual Freedom Comt CA Lib Asn, 1966-69, 1980-; secy, Calif Libr Black Caucus N, 1972-73; secy, Calif Soc Libr; secy, Calif Libr Asn, 1979; Black Women Orgn for Polit Action; Calif Libr Black Caucus N; Long Range Planning Comt Calif Lib Asn; Am Libr Asn; Am Libr Asn Black Caucus; Calif Libr Asn. **Honors/Awds:** Delegate, Calif Govt Conf Lib & Info Serv, 1979. **Home Addr:** 2903 Oxford Ave, Richmond, CA 94806.

## TOWNS, DR. SANNA NIMTZ

Consultant, educator. **Personal:** Born Oct 12, 1943, Hawthorne, NV; daughter of August H Nimtz Sr and Margeurite Malarcher Nimtz; children: Joseph IV & Jawad. **Educ:** Southern Univ, BA, 1964; Teachers Col Columbia Univ, MA, teaching eng, 1967; Univ Southern Miss, PhD, 1985. **Career:** Educator (retired), consultant; Am Lang Prog Columbia Univ, Eng lang instr, 1969-71; Off Urban Affairs, State Univ NY, Buffalo, prog coord, 1973-75; Kuwait Univ, instr & admin, 1975-79; Eng Dept Univ New Orleans, lang coord & instr, 1980-82, 1985-86; Delgado Community Col, asst prof, asst chair, 1986-87, chair, commun div, 1987-92, assoc prof, Eng, 1992; Univ Minn, instr & admin; Metrop State Univ, St Paul, Minn, acad writing instr & consult, currently. **Orgs:** Delta Sigma Theta Sorority, 1962-; Conf Col Compos & Communs, 1980-; Mem Nat Coun Teachers Eng 1980-; LA Assoc Develop Educ, 1981-; Phi Delta Kappa 1984-; S Cent Mod Lang Assoc, 1986-; speaker, New Orleans Mus Art Speakers Bur, 1987. **Home Addr:** 3883 Pauger St, New Orleans, LA 70122, **Home Phone:** (504)949-1002. **Business Addr:** Academic writing instructor, Consultant, Metropolitan State University, 700 E 7th St, St Paul, MN 55106, **Business Phone:** (651)793-1300.

## TOWNSEL, RONALD P.

Educator, law enforcement officer, army officer. **Personal:** Born Nov 25, 1934, Chicago, IL; children: 3. **Educ:** George Williams Col, BS, 1957; Gov State Univ, MA, 1975. **Career:** Law enforcement officer, educator (retired); Chicago Bd Educ, teacher, 1957-58; Chicago Fed Settlements, youth gang worker, 1958-60; IL Youth Comn, area parole supr juv parole agt, 1960-70; IL Dept Corrections, Adult Div, supt parole, 1970. **Orgs:** ACA Compact St Gov; NICO; IPPCA. **Special Achievements:** The First Superintendent of Adult Parole in Illions. **Home Addr:** 566 Coolidge Ave, Glen Ellyn, IL 60137-6305, **Home Phone:** (630)858-7474.

## TOWNSEND, ANDRE S.

Executive, football player. **Personal:** Born Oct 8, 1962, Chicago, IL. **Educ:** Univ Miss. **Career:** Football player (retired), executive; Denver Broncos, 1984-90, left defensive end, 1986-87, right defensive end, 1988-89, defensive end, 1995; Wolf Creek Nuclear Operating Corp. **Orgs:** Kappa Alpha Psi Fraternity Inc. **Honors/Awds:** Clower-Walters Scholarship Award, 1983. **Home Addr:** 6206 Providence Club Dr, Mableton, GA 30126-3697, **Home Phone:** (770)732-3177.

## TOWNSEND, MURRAY LUKE, JR. See Obituaries Section.

## TOWNSEND, DR. NKECHIT FLORENCE O.

Association executive, executive. **Career:** Prof psychol; Asn Black Psychologists, mem comt chair, currently, regional rep, Midwestern Region, currently. **Orgs:** Midwest reg rep, bd dir, Asn Black Psychol, 2003-04, pres, lifetime mem. **Honors/Awds:** Awarded, Association of Black Psychologists, 2007. **Home Addr:** 8515 S Constance Ave, Chicago, IL 60617-2220, **Home Phone:** (773)721-8334. **Business Addr:** Lifetime Member, The Association of Black Psychologists, 7119 Allentown Rd Suite 203, Ft. Washington, MD 20744, **Business Phone:** (301)449-3082.

## TOWNSEND, BR. PRENTICE A.

Lawyer. **Personal:** Born Nov 29, 1914, Poplar Bluff, MO; son of Sol and Ava Porter; married Evelyn M; children: Prentice & Edward. **Educ:** Univ Kans, AB, 1934, LLB, 1937. **Career:** Lawyer (retired); State Kans, spec asst atty gen, 1937-41; Gen pract law, 1937-65; State Tax Comn, asst atty, 1947-52; State Corp Comn, asst atty, 1947-52; Missionary Bapt State Conv Kans, gen coun, 1948-62; Interstate Assoc Church God, gen coun, 1948-69; Prince Hall Grand Lodge Kans F&AM, grand atty, 1956-77, past grand master, 1979-81; State Kans, pardon atty, 1965-67; State Corp Comn, asst gen coun, 1967-70; Dept Housing & Urban Develop, atty, reg coun, 1970-82; Kans Conf, African Methodist Episcopal Church, atty; Munic Ct Topeka, judge pro-tem, 1983-90. **Orgs:** Founder, Bro Delta Eta Lamda Chapter, 1948-; Del at large Rep, Nat Conv, 1960; comn, Topeka Housing Auth, 1963-70; Gen Conf Comn, 1964; exec bd, Salvation Army, 1965; adv comm, Red Cross, 1966; pres, Judicial Coun, 1968-92; vice chmn, Rep State Comn, Two Terms; vice chmn, Shawnee Cty Cent Comn; 33 Degree Mason; Nat Asn Advan Colored People; Alpha Phi Alpha; Legal Redress Comn; bd trustee, Douglass Hosp; pres, judicial coun, St John African Methodist Episcopal Church; Kans Bar Asn; bond dr, Stormont-Vail Hosp; Legal Redress Comn, Nat Asn Advan Colored People; fund dr, Washburn Univ; comdr, Jordan-Patterson Post 319, Am Legion. **Home Addr:** 1010 Macvicar Ave, Topeka, KS 66604.

## TOWNSEND, ROBERT

Television producer, administrator, actor. **Personal:** Born Feb 6, 1957, Chicago, IL; son of Robert and Shirley; married Cheri Jones; children: Sierra, Skylar & Isaiah. **Educ:** Ill State Univ; William Paterson Col, NJ; Hunter Col, NY; Beverly Hills Playhouse. **Career:** Experimental Black Actors Guild & Second City, Chicago, 1970; Ensemble Co, Off-Broadway productions & performed at local comedy clubs, 1970-80; Films: 1985; Hollywood Shuffle, dir & producer, 1987; Eddie Murphy Raw, dir, 1987; The Five Heartbeats, writer, dir, 1991; Fraternity Boys, dir, 1999; Actor: Cooley High, 1975; Streets of Fire, 1984; A Soldier's Story, 1984; American Flyers, Hollywood Shuffle, 1987; The Mighty Quinn, 1989; The Five Heartbeats, 1991, The Meteor Man, 1993; The Taxman, 1999; Book of Love, 2000; Undercover Brother, 2002; Black Listed, 2003, Phantom Punch, 2009; TV Series: "Robert Townsend & His Partners in Crime", HBO, writer, actor, dir & producer, 1987-88; "Secrets", exec producer; "Lead Us Not Unto Temptation", exec producer; "The Truth Hurts", exec producer; "The Legacy", exec producer; "Happy Birthday", exec producer; "Fish and House Guests", exec producer; "The Parent Hood", Warner Bros, 1995; "Love Songs", dir, 1999; "Up Up & Away", dir, 2000; "Livin for Love: The Natalie Cole Story", 2000; "Holiday Heart", 2000; "Carmen: AHip Hopera", M TV, 2001; "10, 000 Black Men Named George", 2002; "Spoken", 2005, 2006; "Gory Stories", 2005; "The World According to Kids", 2005; "Pilot Central", 2005; "Lisa Knight & the Round Table", 2005-07; "Souled Out", 2005; "Thousand Dollar Bee", 2005-07; "The B5 Christmas Special", 2006; "Rising", 2006; "Playhouse 22", 2006; "The Envy Life", 2006;

"Pilot Central", 2006; "The Envy Life", 2007; "Partners in Crime", 2007; "Of Boys & Men", actor & producer, 2008; "Going to Mexico", exec producer, 2011; "In the Hive", 2012; "Scooby-Doo! Music of the Vampire", 2012; "Playin for Love", 2014; Townsend Entertainment Corp, owner & chief exec officer, currently; Black Family Channel, pres & chief exec officer, 2004-; The Tonight Show Starring Johnny Carson, appearances. **Orgs:** Founder, Robert Townsend Found. **Business Addr:** President of Production, Chief Executive Officer, Black Family Channel, 800 Forrest St NW, Atlanta, GA 30318, **Business Phone:** (404)350-2509.

### TOWNSEND, RONALD

Executive, association executive. **Personal:** Born Sep 23, 1941, Jacksonville, FL; married Dorothy; children: Michelle Townsend-Smith, Ronnie Jr & Gina. **Educ:** City Univ NY, Baruch Col, bus. **Career:** CBS-TV, staff, 1960-64, dir bus affairs & programming, 1964-69; C's TV Workshop, dir field serv, 1969; WTOP-TV, sta mgr, 1974-82; WTOP-TV, gen mgr; Gannett TV Group, pres, 1989-96; Alltel Corp, dir, mem exec comt & mem audit comt, 1992-2007; Bank Am Corp, dir, 1993-2004, mem audit comt, currently; Jacksonville, Fla, commun consult, 1997-; Nielsen Media Res Inc, bd dir, 1999; Rayonier Advan Mat Inc, dir, currently; Winn-Dixie Stores Inc, dir, 2000-; Rayonier Inc, dir, 2001-14. **Orgs:** Augusta Nat Golf Club; dir & trustee, Univ N Fla; Jacksonville Symphony Orchestra; Jacksonville Port Authority; United Way Northeast Fla; Freedom Forum Newseum; Nat Jewish Ctr Immunol & Respiratory Med. **Honors/Awds:** Honored by United Negro Col Fund, 1986; Trumpet Award, 1996. **Special Achievements:** First African American member of the Augusta National Golf Club. **Business Addr:** Director, Rayonier Inc, 50 N Laura St Suite 19, Jacksonville, FL 32202, **Business Phone:** (904)357-9100.

### TOWNSEND, HON. WARDELL C.

Consultant, president (organization), government official. **Personal:** Born Oct 16, 1952, Baltimore, MD; son of Wardell Clinton Sr and Toyoko Yonamine; married Diane Martin; children: Sarah Sachiko, Claire Keiko, Jordan Hideto & Aaron Masao. **Educ:** Western Carolina Univ, BS, psychol & social welfare, 1975; WVa Univ, MSW, 1979; acad cert social workers, 1982; S Calif Univ, post grad studies, orgn psychol. **Career:** Boys Club Asheville, group counr, 1975-76; Asn Sickle Cell Disease, health educr/outreach coordr, 1976-77; Human Resource Develop Found, planning & develop mgr, 1979-80; Henderson County, dir, Community Develop Dept, 1980-82; Cherokee Minority Bus Develop Ctr, bus develop mgr, 1982-83; US Rep, Jamie Clarke, proj dir, 1983; US Rep, Mike Espy, legis dir, assoc staff Budget Comt, admin asst/chief staff; US Rep, Doug Applegate, proj dir, 1985; Clinton Presial Transition Team, 1992-93; US Dept Agricul, asst secy admin, 1993; Exec Coach & Consult, sr assoc, currently; Compubahn Inc, sr vpres; Enterprise informational technol policy, USDA designated sr IRM off; U.S Rep Mike Espy, chief staff; Townsend Dantai, pres, currently; Uman Res Assocs Inc, assoc, currently. **Orgs:** Nat Asn Social Workers, 1974-; Acad Cert Social Workers, 1982-; Diocesan Investment Comt, Episcopal Diocese Wash, 1991-; bd dir, Admin Assts Asn, 1991-92, vpres, 1992; Coun African Admin Assts; Ascension Church; numerous mem; Japanese Am Citizens League, 1993-; House Admin Assts Alumni Asn, 1993-; NC Dem Club Wash, 1993-; coordr, Pres's Coun Mgt Improv, 1993-96; asst secy, USdA, 1993-97; Fed CIO Coun; chief staff, legis dir & proj dir, cong, 1983-93; Indust Adv Coun; Nat Asn Social Workers; Asian Am Govt Exec Network, 1996-; bd chmn & vice chmn, Faith & Polit Inst; treas, Univ DC, bd dir; bd dir, Western Carolina Univ Found. **Home Addr:** 8908 Ellsworth Ct, Silver Spring, MD 20910-4356. **Business Addr:** Senior Associate, Executive Coaching & Consulting Associates, 513 Capitol Ct NE Suite 300, Washington, DC 20002, **Business Phone:** (202)544-0097.

### TRAINER, JAMES E.

Automotive executive. **Personal:** Born Birmingham, AL; married Mattie; children: Eric, Marcus & Jameta. **Career:** Trainer Oldsmobile-Cadillac-Pontiac-GMC Truck Inc, pres, chief exec officer, 1991-. **Special Achievements:** Trainer was first African American salesman to work for Edwards Chevroletin Birmingham, AL, the oldest Chevrolet dealership in the US, 1971; company led all US black-owned auto dealerships with sales of $254.6million, 1992; Company is ranked No one on Black Enterprises list of Top100 Auto Dealers, 1994. **Business Addr:** Chief Executive Officer, President, Oldsmobile-Cadillac-Pontiac-GMC Truck Inc, Warner Robins, GA.

### TRAMIEL, KENNETH RAY, SR.

Counselor. **Personal:** Born May 31, 1946, Shreveport, LA; married Sandra Mackel; children: Kenneth Jr, Kendra & Kai. **Educ:** Univ Calif Berkel, social sci, 1965; Merrit Community Col, Univ Calif, Berkeley, BS, social sci african am studies, 1974; Calif State Univ, MS, coun, 1975. **Career:** E Oakland Youth Develop, head counr, 1979-80; Fed Govt Vietnam Outreach prog, asst team leader, counr, 1980-82; Oakland Unified Sch Dist, head counr, col & scholar counr, 1982-, afrocentric curric & coun tech, post traumatic stress disorder, currently; consult, currently; Contra Costa Col, San Pablo, Calif, adjunt prof psychol, 2009-. **Orgs:** Pres, Berkeley Youth Alternative, 1981-82; Oakland Personnel & Guid Asn, 1982-; Calif Asn Gifted, 1984; vpres, Oakland Pub Sch Affirmative Action Comn, 1985-86; bd mem, Berkeley Juneteenth Asn Inc; bd mem, Racial & Ethnic Ministry Comt, Presby Church USA, Synod Northern Calif; pres, Calif Sch Counr Asn. **Home Addr:** 2923 Jo Ann Dr, San Pablo, CA 94806-2718, **Home Phone:** (510)223-3397. **Business Addr:** Adjunt Professor, Contra Costa College, 2600 Mission Bell Dr, San Pablo, CA 94806, **Business Phone:** (510)235-7800.

### TRAMMEL, KIMBERLY ELISE (KIMBERLY ELISE OLDHAM)

Actor. **Personal:** Born Apr 17, 1967, Minneapolis, MN; daughter of Marvin and Erna Jean Johnson; married Maurice Oldham; children: Aja Arial & Jaela Rose. **Educ:** Minneapolis Community Col; Univ Minnesota, BA, mass commun; Am Film Inst. **Career:** Films: Set It Off, 1996; Beloved, 1998; Bait, 2000; John Q, 2002; The Manchurian Candidate, 2004; Diary of a Mad Black Woman, 2005; Pride, The Great Debaters, 2007; For Colored Girls, 2010; Ties That Bind, 2011; Highland Park, 2012; Event 15, 2013. TV movies:"The Ditchdigger's Daughters", 1997; "The Loretta Claiborne Story", 2000; "Bojangles", 2001; "The Twilight Zone", 2003; "Girlfriends", 2003; "Close to Home", 2005-07; "Private Practice", 2007; "Masters of Science Fiction", 2007; Gifted Hands: The Ben Carson Story, 2009; "Grey's Anatomy", 2009; "Hannah's Law", 2012. **Orgs:** Northern Warehouse Artists' Coop. **Honors/Awds:** Cable Ace Award, Best Supporting Actress in Movie or Mini Series, 1997; Chicago Film Critics Association Awards, 1998; Golden Satellite Award for Best Actress in a Supporting Role in a Motion Picture-Drama, 1999; Black Reel Award, 2002, 2005, 2006 & 2011; NAACP Image Awards, Image Award Outstanding Actress in a Motion Picture for Diary of a Mad Black Woman, 2006; NAACP Image Awards, Outstanding Actress in a Drama Series for "Close to Home", 2007; NAACP Image Awards, Outstanding Actress in a Television Movie, Mini-Series or Dramatic Special for "Gifted Hands: The Ben Carson Story", 2010; AAFCA, Best Supporting Actress for For Colored Girls, 2010; NAACP Image Awards, Image Award Outstanding Actress in a Motion Picture for "For Colored Girls", 2011. **Business Addr:** Actress, Writers & Artists Group, 8383 Wilshire Blvd Suite 550, Beverly Hills, CA 90211, **Business Phone:** (212)391-1112.

### TRAMMER, MONTE IRVIN

President (organization), newspaper publisher. **Personal:** Born Nov 11, 1951, Birmingham, AL; son of Jimmie and Edwenia Wilson; married Hilda Hudson. **Educ:** Ind Univ, Purdue Univ, IN, BS, polit sci, 1974; Kaplan Univ, Concord Law Sch, Exec JD, 2006. **Career:** Indianapolis Star, Indianapolis, IN, reporter, 1970-76; Baltimore Sun, Baltimore, MD, reporter, 1977-80; Detroit Free Press, Detroit, MI, bus writer, 1980-81, asst city ed, 1981-82; USA Today, Wash, DC, dep managing ed, 1982-86; Poughkeepsie J, Poughkeepsie, NY, asst to publ, 1986; Saratogian, Saratoga Springs, NY, publ, 1986-98; Star-Gazette, Elmira NY, pres & publ, 1999-; Ithaca Jour, publ, 2007-. **Orgs:** Past chair, New York Newpapers Found; New York Newspaper Publ Asn; Chemung County Nat Asn Advan Colored People; life mem, Nat Asn Advan Colored People; Elmira Rotary; trustee, Empire State Col Found; bd mem, Southern Tier Econ Growth Inc; dir, Empire State Col Found; J W Prostate Cancer Found; Fla Orchestra; past chair, United Way Northeastern New York; Chemung County Chamber Com; former dir, United Way NY; former regional adv bd mem, Lifetime Healthcare Co; Excellus Blue Cross & Blue Shield; Paul Harris Fel; Rotary Int; dir, Tampa Bay Black Bus Investment Corp, 2013-. **Home Addr:** 308 Chelsea Ct, Horseheads, NY 14845-2283, **Home Phone:** (607)739-3326. **Business Addr:** President, Publisher, Star Gazette, PO Box 285, Elmira, NY 14902, **Business Phone:** (607)271-8210.

### TRAPP, DONALD W.

Financial manager. **Personal:** Born Sep 28, 1946, Hampton, VA; son of Chester A and Ida Holt; married Shirley Ann Stokes; children: Rashaad, Brandon & Yvonne. **Educ:** Va State Univ, BS, bus admin, 1968; Ind Univ, MBA, finance, 1973. **Career:** Irwin Mgt Co Inc, mgr treas reporting, 1973-76; Cummins Engine Co Inc, dir pricing, 1978-82, asst treas, 1977-78, finan spec, 1976-77, dir components strategy, 1982-83, dir int logistics, 1983-84; Remote Equip Corp, pres, 1985-88, dir strategic planning, 1991-92, dir bus develop, 1992-94, dir, electronics bus strategy, 1994-96, exec dir, electronics, 1996-97, vpres & treas, 1997-2003, vp bus devel, 2003-, vpres, polit action comm; UNC Ventures Inc, vpres & treas, 1988-90. **Orgs:** C C, 1975; Kappa Alpha Psi Frat Inc, 1967-; bd dir, William R Laws Found, 1975-84; bd dir, Columbus United Way Am, 1976-79; bd dir, Accent Hair Salons, 1988-90; bd dir, Xinix Corp, 1989-90; Nat Black Mba Asn. 1991-; bd, Columbus Enterprise Develop Corp, 1994-97; bd, Bartholomew County Big Bros/Big Sisters, 1995-99; bd, Ind Univ Bus Sch Alumni Asn, 1996-99; bod, United Way Bartholomew County, 1996-2002, Columbus Regional Hosp Found, 2005-; bd dir, Community Educ Coalition. **Honors/Awds:** Achievement Award, Wall St Jour, 1968; Distinguished Service Citation, United Negro Fund, 1977. **Home Addr:** 3241 Beechnut Ct, Columbus, IN 47203, **Home Phone:** (812)376-6484. **Business Addr:** Vice President Business Development, Cummins Inc, PO Box 3005, Columbus, IN 47202-3005, **Business Phone:** (812)377-8889.

### TRAPP, JAMES HAROLD

Football coach, football player. **Personal:** Born Dec 28, 1969, Greenville, SC. **Educ:** Clemson Univ. **Career:** Football player (retired), football coach, producer; Los Angeles Raiders, defensive back, 1993-94; Oakland Raiders, defensive back, 1995-98, strong safety, 1997; Baltimore Ravens, 1999, cornerback, 2000-01, defensive back & left cornerback, 2001, defensive back, 2002; Jacksonville Jaguars, safety, 2003; NFL Europe, Sea Devils, coaching staff, currently; D1 Sports Training, co-owner & facil coordr, currently. **Honors/Awds:** Super Bowl ring champion, 2000. **Special Achievements:** TV series: The NFL on NBC, producer, 1965; Liberate Your Spirit, executive producer, 2012. Film: "Super Bowl XXXV", producer, 2001. **Business Addr:** Coaching Staff, NFL Europe, 73-75 ArenA Blvd, Amsterdam1101 DL, **Business Phone:** (310)20465-05.

### TRAUGHBER, CHARLES M.

Government official. **Personal:** Born Feb 13, 1943. **Educ:** Tenn State Univ, BS, hist & polit sci, 1968, Grad Sch, 1970. **Career:** Tenn State Penitentiary, counr I, adult prison instnl counr, 1969, sr instnl counr, 1971; spec asst to Warden, Tenn Main Prison, 1972; Tenn Dept Correction, consult; Nat Parole Resource Ctr, Joint Comt Dept Correction, exec mgt. **Orgs:** Am Correctional Asn; Nat Asn Advan Colored People; Tenn Correctional Asn; Am Paroling Asn; dir, Adult Coun Serv Adult Inst State Tenn, 1972; chmn, Tenn Paroles Bd, 1972, 1978, 1988; chmn, Tenn Bd Probation & Parole, 1999; bd mem, Statewide Criminal Justice Coord Coun; exec bd, Memphis-Shelby County Crime Comn; bd mem, Steering Comt Tenn Dept Correction; bd mem, Tenn Bd Probation & Parole Joint Offender Mgt Plan; Nat Comt Regarding Offenders Ment Health; Tenn's Gov's Statewide Comt Training Law Enforcement Officers; Tenn Sentencing Comn; Tenn Juv Justice Comn; Sentence Enhancement Comn; Tenn Legis Black Caucus criminal justice; Statewide Comn Homeless; pres, Asn Paroling Authorities Int. **Honors/Awds:** Outstanding Black Citizen Award; Chattanooga Civitan Club Award; Appreciation Award, Tenn Legis Black Caucus; Appreciation Award, Memphis Chap, Kappa Alpha Psi Fraternity, Appreciation Awards, Am Correctional Asn; Ben Baer Award, Asn Paroling Authorities Int, 1999. **Home Addr:** Apt A 2122 14 Ave N, Nashville, TN 37208. **Business Addr:** Chairman, Tennessee Board of Probation & Parole, 404 James Robertson Pkwy Suite 1300, Nashville, TN 37243-0850, **Business Phone:** (615)741-1150.

### TRAVIS, REP. GERALDINE W.

Legislator. **Personal:** Born Sep 3, 1931, Albany, GA; daughter of Joseph T and Dorothy Marshall; married William Alexander Sr; children: William, Michael, Ann, Gerald & Gwendolyn. **Educ:** Xavier Univ, attended 1949. **Career:** Dem Nat Conv Miami, deleg, 1972; Dem Mini-Conv Kans, deleg, 1974; Dem Nat Conv NY, deleg, 1976; State Mont, legislator, 1975-77. **Orgs:** Pres, Cascade County Women's Polit Caucus, 1968; foundind mem, Nat Asn Advan Colored People, 1968; co-chmn, Dem Party Minorities Comn, 1972-74; Nat Steering Comn, 1973-74; State Coord Comn Int Womens Year, 1977; Off Observer Nat Womens Conf, 1977; bd dir, YWCA Great Falls, 1979; co-chmn, Dem Women's Club; St Peter & Paul Cath Church; Nat Womens Polit Caucus; Nat Order Women Legislators; YWCA; founder, Nat Coun Negro Women; Mont Women's Polit Caucus; Nat Urban League; Am Civil Liberties Union; Sierra Club; MT Womens Pol Caucus; MT Crime Control Bd, Human Resources Comn; Criminal Justice Info Comn; Precinct Comn Woman Precinct 42 Cascade City; MT Adv Comn US Comn Civil Rights; chmn, Cascade City Detoxification Adv Bd; Am Indian Action Coun; chmn, Sub-Comm Admin Justice; Ariz Precinct Comn Women; Dem Dist No 12; Ariz Dem State Comn. **Special Achievements:** Only African American ever to serve in the Montana Legislature. **Home Addr:** 7421 W Denton Lane, Glendale, AZ 85303-5753, **Home Phone:** (623)848-9319.

### TRAVIS, JACK

Architect, interior designer. **Personal:** Born Mar 2, 1952, Newellton, LA; son of Sam L and Mary L Brown. **Educ:** Ariz State Univ, BA, 1977; Univ Ill, Champaign Urbana, 1978. **Career:** Whisler-Patri, designer, archit, 1978; Pac Gas & Elec, draughtsman, archit, 1978-79; Eyes Group Design, designer, draughtsman, archit, 1979-80; Skidmore Owings & Merrill, designer, interior archit, 1980-82; Switzer Group Inc, designer, interior archit, 1982-84; Sydney Philip Gilbert Assoc, designer, interior archit, 1984; Sidney Philip Gilbert Assocs, sr designer, 1984; NBC Broadcasting Co, designer, interior archit, 1985; Charter High Sch Archit, mentor; Univ Cincinnati, vis prof, 2008; Howard Univ, silcott chair recipient, 2009-10; Fashion Inst Technol, adjunct prof; Pratt Ist Sch Interior Design, adjunct prof, currently; Parsons Sch Design, adjunct prof, currently; Jack Travis archit, prin, owner, 1985-. **Orgs:** Am Inst Archits, Nat AIA Task Force on Civil Rights & Cultural Diversity, 1992; NOMA; Nat Coun Archit Regist Bds; Nat Coun Interior Design Qualification; Harlem Comt Bd 10 mem, 2001; fel Am Inst Architects. **Honors/Awds:** Forty Under Forty, Crain's NY bUS, 1992; Certif of Appreciation, Lanier High Sch, 2000; Certif of Appreciation, Jackie Robinson Middle Sch, 320, 2002. **Special Achievements:** Publications: "African American Architecture: From Idea to Published Design," JAE, 1993; "Cultural Differences & Their Manifestations," Blacklines, 2000; "Minor Architects: What You Don't Know," Natl Associates Committee Quarterly, 2003. **Business Addr:** Owner, Jack Travis Architect, 416 E 176th St Fl 2, Bronx, NY 10457-6025, **Business Phone:** (917)701-0870.

### TRAVIS, TRACEY T.

Businessperson, executive. **Personal:** Born Jan 1, 1962. **Educ:** Univ Pittsburgh, BS, indust engineering, 1983; Columbia Univ, MBA, finance & opers mgt, 1986. **Career:** Pepsi Bottling Group, mkt unit gen mgr & bus unit chief financial officer, 1989-99; PepsiCo Inc, gen mgr, 1995-99; Am Natl Can, Beverage Can Americas Group, chief financial officer, 1999-2001; Ltd Brands Inc, chief financial officer, 2001-02, sr vpres finance, 2001-04; Intimate Brands Inc, chief financial officer, 2001-04; Polo Ralph Lauren, sr vpres finance & chief financial officer, 2005-12; Gen Motors, sr financial exec; Estee Lauder Co Inc, exec vpres & chief financial officer, 2012-. **Orgs:** Bd dir, Jo-Ann Stores Inc; trustee, Lincoln Ctr Theater; Exec Leadership Coun Found; Ralph Lauren Ctr Cancer Care & Prev; dir, chmn, Audit Comt & Mem Corp Governance Comt; treas, Ralph Lauren Found; Financial Execs Int; Nat Assoc Corp, dir; NY Women's Forum; Nat Asn Corp Dirs; bd mem, Campbells Soup Co. **Honors/Awds:** Best CFO Award, Institutional Investor, 2008; Distinguished Alumni Award, Univ Pittsburgh, 2009. **Special Achievements:** Awarded a GM Fellowship to pursue her MBA; recognized by Treasury and Risk Management as on of the Top 25 Women in Finance, 2005; named one of the top 50 Women in Business by Black Enterprise magazine, 2006. **Business Addr:** Chief Financial Officer, Executive Vice President, The Estee Lauder Companies Inc, 767 Fifth Ave, New York, NY 10153, **Business Phone:** (212)572-4200.

### TRAYLOR, BYRON KEITH. See TRAYLOR, KEITH.

### TRAYLOR, PROF. ELEANOR W.

Educator. **Personal:** Born Dec 12, 1933, Thomasville, GA; daughter of Phillip Williams and Esther M G Williams Smith. **Educ:** Spelman Col, BA; Atlanta Univ, MA; Cath Univ, PhD. **Career:** Montgomery Col, eng, prof, 1965-90; Dept Agri, Grad Sch, eng dept, chair, 1966-67; Howard Univ, Col Fine Arts, adj prof, drama, 1968-75; Hobart & William Smith Col, vis humanist; Cornell Univ, vis prof, lit, 1979-80; Tougaloo Col, vis humanist, 1982; Cath Univ Am, adj prof; Howard Univ, prof, eng & chair, eng dept, 1990-, From Text to Stage to Text, proj dir; Humanities Dept, chair, 1990-93, dept eng, chair, 1993-; Books: College Reading Skills, 1966; The Dream Awake: A Spoken Arts Production, 1968; The Humanities and Afro-American Literary Tradition, 1988; Broad Sympathy: The Howard University Oral Traditions Reader, 1996. **Orgs:** Proj dir, Larry Neal Cult Ser, 1984; founder, Elders Advan Am LitPub Sch, 1984; Col Lang Asn; Mod Lang Asn; evaluator, African Mus Asn; script writer, Smithsonian Inst; script writer, Prog Black Am Cult; Nat CounTeachers Eng; panelist, Nat Endowment Humanities; lit consult, Nat Blacks Arts Festival, 1994-; bd mem, DC Reperatory Theater Co; bd mem, Duke Ellington High Sch Performing Arts; Am Asn Univ Professors. **Home Addr:** 1624 Riggs Pl NW, Washington, DC 20009, **Home Phone:** (202)232-2269. **Business Addr:** Professor of English, Graduate Faculty, Howard University, 216 Locke Hall, Washington, DC 20059, **Business Phone:** (202)806-7754.

**TRAYLOR, DR. HORACE JEROME**
Association executive, educator. **Personal:** Born Mar 15, 1931, La-Grange, GA; married Theola Dennis; children: Sheryl Lynn, Linda Gail, Yohanna Faye, Chequeta Renee & Tonya Yvonne. **Educ:** Zion Col, AB, 1953; Gammon Theolo Sem, BD, 1958; Univ Tenn, Chattanooga, MEd, 1965; Univ Miami, PhD, 1978. **Career:** Chattanooga City Col, pres, 1964-69; Univ Tenn, spec asst chancellor, 1969-71; Miami-Dade Comm Col, Open Col, dean, 1971-74, pres develop, 1974-79, dist vpres, inst advan, 1980-. **Orgs:** Pres, Zion Col, 1959-64; Adv comm, Inst Study Educ Policy Howard Univ, 1967-; treas, Leadership Inst Comm Develop Wash DC, 1969-73; founder & bd dir, United Bank Chattanooga, 1971-; adv bd, United Bank Chattanooga, 1971; treas, Coun Black Am Affairs-Am Asn Comm & Jr Col, 1974-; pres, Miami-Dade Comm Col Fund Inc, 1985-. **Honors/Awds:** VSmith-Taylor Award for Excellence in Journalism, 1958; Outstanding Young Man of the Year Award, Nat Jaycees, 1965; Ambassador Good Will, Human Relations Counc Chattanooga, 1969; Named honor: Horace J. Traylor Minority Leadership Award; Lifetime Achievement Award, Univ Tenn Chattanooga, 2011. **Special Achievements:** First African American graduate from The University of Tennessee in 1965; First African American to earn a bachelorss degree in Chattanooga. **Home Addr:** 8940 SW 96th St, Miami, FL 33176. **Business Addr:** District Vice President, Institutional Advancement, MDC Kendall Campus 11011 SW 104 St, Miami, FL 33176-3393, **Business Phone:** (305)237-2000.

**TRAYLOR, KEITH (BYRON KEITH TRAYLOR)**
Football player. **Personal:** Born Sep 3, 1969, Little Rock, AR; married Krista; children: Brandon. **Educ:** Cent Okla Univ, indust safety, 1991. **Career:** Football player (retired); Denver Broncos, linebacker, 1991-92, left defensive tackle, 1997-2000, defensive tackle, 1999; Los Angeles Raiders, 1993; Green Bay Packers, 1993; Kans City Chiefs, defensive tackle, 1993-96; Chicago Bears, right defensive tackle, 2001-03, left defensive tackle, 2003; New Eng Patriots, left defensive tackle & nose tackle, 2004; Miami Dolphins, nose tackle, 2005-07, left defensive tackle, 2007. **Honors/Awds:** All-Lone Star Conference, 1990; All-Rookie, Pro Football Weekly & Football Digest, 1991; Super Bowl Champion, XXXII, XXXIII, XXXIX. **Home Addr:** 508 E Shreveport St, Broken Arrow, OK 74011-8866, **Home Phone:** (501)332-2984.

**TRAYNHAM, ROBERT LEE, II**
Government official. **Personal:** Born Aug 9, 1974, Philadelphia, PA; son of Robert and Debra; married Brent. **Educ:** Cheyney Univ, BA, polit sci, 1996; George Mason Univ, MA, polit commun, 2000. **Career:** Republican Nat Conv, intern, 1995-96; Black Am's Polit Action Comt, Polit dir, 1996-97; Am's Voice, Polit contrib panelist, 1996-; George Mason Univ, 1997-2001; US Sen Rick Santorum, dep saff dir, 1997, dep chief staff & dir comn, 1996-2001; US Senate Leadership, dep chief staff & commun dir, 2001-06; Walmart, dir fed govt media, 2006-07; CNN/MSNBC/FOX/NPR, nat polit anaylst, 2006-11; US Presidential Campaign, sr polit adv; George Wash bush, sr advisor & campaign mgr; George Wash Univ, prof, 2007-12; Comcast Network, CN8, bur chief, corresp, 2007-15, network host & columnist; MSNBC, polit analyst, 2009-; NBC Universal Inc, bur chief; CQ Roll Call, ed; Philadelphia Tribune, columnist, corresp & polit analyst; Georgetown Univ, asst dean, 2012-13; Sirius XM Radio Inc, polit analyst, 2012-; Bipartisan Policy Ctr, vpres commun 2015-. **Orgs:** Nat Ctr Pub Policy Res, Proj 21; Republican Comns Asn; vice chair Republican Nat Comt, New Majority coun; Ctr Study Presidency; Nat Press Club; bd trustee & coun trustee, Cheyney Univ; pres, US Senate Press Secretaries Asn; bd mem, AIDS Responsibility Proj; bd mem, ARP; dir, Thomas Jefferson Univ. **Home Addr:** 2001 12th St NW, Washington, WA 20009, **Home Phone:** (202)249-9954. **Business Addr:** Vice President of Communications, Bipartisan Policy Center, 1225 Eye St NW, Washington, DC 20005.

**TREADWELL, DAVID MERRILL**
Journalist. **Personal:** Born Feb 21, 1940, Dayton, OH; son of Euretta Moore Boyce and Timothy D Sr. **Educ:** Ohio State Univ, BA, eng, 1964, MA, Jour, 1974. **Career:** US Bur Land Mgt, pub rels spec, 1969-70; Ohio State Univ, asst dir intl progs, 1970-73; Assoc Press, reporter, 1974-80; LA Times, Wash corresp, 1980-85, Atlanta bur chief, 1985-89; NY Bur corresp, 1989-93; Kean Univ, asst prof, asst chair, secy, treas & cea Liaison, 1994-. **Orgs:** Kappa Alpha Psi; Nat Asn Black Journalists; Asn Educ Journ & Mass Communs; Nat Coun Teachers Eng; NJ Col Eng Asn. **Honors/Awds:** Sloan Found Fellowship, Econ Jour Princeton Univ, 1979-80. **Home Addr:** 147 W Jersey St Suite 303, Elizabeth, NJ 07202, **Home Phone:** (908)820-8764. **Business Addr:** Assistant Professor, Secretary, Kean University, 1000 Morris Ave, Union, NJ 07083, **Business Phone:** (908)629-7172.

**TREADWELL, TINA MCKINLEY**
Music director, casting director, executive. **Personal:** Born Mar 21, 1958, New York, NY; daughter of George McKinnley and Fayrene Johnson. **Educ:** Princeton Univ, BA, eng lit, 1980. **Career:** Merrill & Assoc, partner, casting dir, 1986-90; Treadwell & Assoc, pres, casting dir, 1990-96; Treadwell Prods, dir, producer, 1990-96; Blind Pig Prods, co-producer, 1996; Disney Channel, exec dir talent develop & music specialist, 1997, music specialist, vpres talent develop & alternative programming, 1997-2001; Sweet Lorraine Productions, consult, producer, 2002-03; Walt Disney Co, music supvr, casting dir, 2002-03; Treadwell Entertainment, pres & chief exec officer, 2004-; Film: Northern Lights, exec in-chg casting, 1997; Smart House, exec in-chg casting, 1999; Model Behavior, exec in-chg casting, 2000; The Luck of the Irish, exec in-chg casting, 2001; Hounded, exec in-chg casting, 2001; Scream Team, casting dir, 2002; You Wish!, casting dir, 2003; The Even Stevens Movie, exec in-chg casting, 2003; The Cheetah Girls, exec in-chg casting, 2003; The Guardian, exec in-chg casting, 2006; ELLE: A Mod Cinderella Tale, exec producer, producer & casting dir, 2010. TV Series: True Colors, casting associate, 1990-91; The Famous Jett Jackson, exec in-chg casting, 1998-2002; So Weird, exec in-chg casting, 1999-2001; Even Stevens, exec in-chg casting, 2000-01; Lizzie McGuire, exec in-chg casting, 2001-02. **Orgs:** Bd mem, fundraising co-chair, Educating Young Minds, 1998-; Women in Film; Women in Cable; Namic. **Business Addr:** President, Chief Executive Officer, Treadwell Entertainment, 1321 Garden St, Glendale, CA 91201-2715, **Business Phone:** (818)243-2446.

**TREES, CANDICE D.**
Government official. **Personal:** Born Jul 18, 1953, Springfield, IL; daughter of Peggie D Neal Senor and Clarence L Senor; married John F; children: Peggi, Jessi & Johanna. **Educ:** Sangamon State Univ, BA, 1981. **Career:** Town & Co Bank, teller, 1976-77; State Ill Off Govt, exec corresp, 1977-79; City Springfield, city clerk, 1979-86; Circuit Ct Sangamon Co, clerk, 1986-92. **Orgs:** United Way Sangamon County; Jr League Springfield; prog vpres Spring field Area Arts Coun; treas Munic Clerks Ill; vpres Lincoln fest; Spring field Area Labor Mgt Comm; admin vpres Springfield Area Arts Coun; Jr League Springfield; chmn bd, HAT Construct, 1986; bd dir Kennerer Village C's Home; sec adv bd, Salvation Army, 1987-; Greater Springfield Chamber Com, 1987-88; Ill Asn Ct Clerks; bd mem, Ment Health Ctr Cent Ill, 1987; Nat Asn Ct Mgrs; Asn Rec Mgr & Admin. **Home Addr:** 1106 N 32nd St, Springfield, IL 62702, **Home Phone:** (217)522-5886. **Business Addr:** IL.

**TREMITIERE, CHANTEL RUTH**
Basketball player, football player, basketball coach. **Personal:** Born Oct 20, 1969, Williamsport, PA; daughter of William and Barbara. **Educ:** Auburn Univ, BA, pub rels, 1991. **Career:** Basketball player (retired), basketball coach (retired), football player; Auburn Tigers, 1991; Auburn Univ, asst coach, 1991-92; Texas Univ, asst coach, 1992-93; Univ Mass, asst coach, 1993-96; Sacramento Monarchs, guard, 1997; Utah Starzz, 1998-99; Indiana Fever, 2000; YorkCity Noise, 2002; Independent Women's Football League, Shreveport Aftershock, quarterback; 2007. Film: "Double Teamed", 2002. **Orgs:** Assist One; N Am Coun Adoptable C (NACAC)'s, 2005.

**TRENT, DR. CALVIN R.**
Manager, administrator, executive director. **Educ:** Howard Univ, biol, 1964; Wayne State Univ, MI, BS, psychol, 1992, MEd, educ, 1993; Univ Detroit, Mercy, MA, clin psychol, PhD, clin psychol, 1997. **Career:** Detroit Dept Health & Wellness Prom, City Detroit, Mich, Bur Substance Abuse Prev, Treat & Recovery, dir, Spec Pop Health Serv Div, gen mgr, currently; Veterans Adminr Hosp, therapist, currently; Highland Park Community Col; pvt practr, currently; etroit Recovery Proj, vpres, 2013-. **Orgs:** Co-chair, Partnership Drug Free Detroit & Recovery Community; pub policy advocate, dept head bur substance abuse, Detroit Health Dept; dir, Bur Substance Abuse Prev; prin investr, Substance Abuse & Ment Health Serv Admin-Targeted Capacity Abbr; prin investr, Detroit Recovery Proj, Detroit Youth-Bldg Communities Support Prog, Youth Develop Inst; Exec Dir, R.E.A.L. Mich, 2011-. **Home Addr:** 2230 Hyde Pk Rd, Detroit, MI 48207. **Business Addr:** General Manager, Director, Detroit Department of Health & Wellness Promotion, Rm 317 B Wing 1151 Taylor Main Bldg, Detroit, MI 48202, **Business Phone:** (313)876-4566.

**TRENT, GARY DAJAUN**
Basketball coach, consultant, basketball player. **Personal:** Born Sep 22, 1974, Columbus, OH; married Natalia; children: Gary Jr, Garyson, Grayson & Graydon. **Educ:** Ohio Univ, attended 1995; Univ Phoenix, BA, bus mgt, 2010. **Career:** Basketball player (retired), basketball coach, consultant; Portland Trail Blazers, forward, 1995-98; Toronto Raptors, 1998; Dallas Mavericks, 1998-2001; Minn Timber wolves, 2001-04; Panellinios, Greece, 2004-05, 2006-07; Lottomatica Roma, Rome, 2005-06; Pallacanestro Virtus Roma, 2005; Uneek Inc LLC, basketball coach, trainer & consult, 2007-; St. Paul Pub Schs, intervention specialist, 2011-. **Business Addr:** Intervention Specialist, Saint Paul Public School, 360 Colborne St, St Paul, MN 55102, **Business Phone:** (651)767-8100.

**TRENT, JAMES EUGENE**
Executive, educational consultant. **Personal:** Born Jan 14, 1936, Uniontown, PA; son of James Robert and Lyda Mae (Reed) T; married Rosalie L Mahaley; children: Jamie Toi, Kelly Rose & Jill Roslyn. **Educ:** Wayne State Univ, BS, bus admin, 1957; Univ Detroit, MBA, 1965. **Career:** Chrysler Corp, indust engr, 1968-70; Chrysler Realty Corp, vpres, community oper, property mgr, 1970-79; City Detroit Mayor's Off, exec asst productivity, 1979-80; Chrysler Learning Inc, vpres, govt training, 1980-85; Chrysler Motors, educ consult, 1985-87, staff exec, 1987. **Orgs:** Life mem, Pole March Kappa Alpha Psi Detroit Alumni, 1977-83; dir & secy, Metro Detroit Youth Found, 1978-95; Detroit Pvt Indust Coun, 1983; pres, Univ Detroit Titan Club, 1984-86; pres, Detroit Asn Black Orgn, 1985-; pres, Detroit Pan-Hellenic Coun, 1985-88; pres, Detroit Black Inter-Greek Coun, 1985-88; dir, Univ Detroit Black Alumni, 1986-90; Metro Detroit NPHC Liason; Mich Asn Black Orgns. **Honors/Awds:** Roy Wilkins Award, Detroit Asn Black Orgn, 1985. **Home Addr:** 5366 W Briarcliff Knoll Dr, West Bloomfield, MI 48322-4119, **Home Phone:** (248)851-0266.

**TRESCOTT, JACQUELINE ELAINE**
Journalist. **Personal:** Born Jan 2, 1947, Jersey City, NJ; daughter of Alfred P and Adelaide C; married Edward M Darden; children: Douglass. **Educ:** St Bonaventure Univ, BS, 1968; New York Univ. **Career:** Wash Star, reporter, 1970-75; Wash Post, reporter, 1975-2012, staff writer, currently. **Orgs:** Nat Asn Black Journalists; fac Summer Prog Minority Journalists, 1978-. **Home Addr:** 2224 First St NW, Washington, DC 20001, **Home Phone:** (202)387-6820. **Business Addr:** Reporter, Washington Post, 1150 15th St NW, Washington, DC 20071, **Business Phone:** (202)334-7544.

**TRESVANT, RALPH EDWARD, JR.**
Singer, actor. **Personal:** Born May 16, 1968, Boston, MA; son of Ralph Sr and Patricia; married Amber Serrano. **Career:** New Edition, musical group mem; singer & actor; Albums: Ralph Tresvant, 1990; It's Goin' Down, 1993; Rizz-Wa-Faire, 2006; Singles: "Sensitivity", 1990; "Stone Cold Gentleman", 1991; "Do What I Gotta Do", 1991; "Rated R", 1991; "Yo Baby Yo", 1991; "Money Can't Buy You Love", 1992; "Who's the Mack", 1993; "When I Need Somebody", 1994; "My Home girl", 2006; "Magic Underwear", 2008; "Never Noticed", 2008; "It Must Be You", 2009; Films: Paper Soldiers, 2002; Brown Sugar, 2002; Barbershop Blues, (voice), 2004; Triple Cross, (voice), 2005; Motives 2, 2007; Behind RizzWaFaire, 2008; Mama, I Want to Sing!, 2009; Get On Up as Sam Cooke, 2014. TV series: "Krush Groove", 1985; "Knight Rider", 1985; "Top of the Pops", 1996; "New York Undercover", 1996; "Soul Train", 1994-2004; "R U the Girl", 2005; owner, Rated R records. **Business Addr:** Singer, Actor, c/o Xzault Media Group, 2242 Washington Ave, San Leandro, CA 94577, **Business Phone:** (510)895-9002.

**TRIBBETT, CHARLES A., III**
Executive, chief executive officer. **Personal:** Born Oct 25, 1955, LA; son of Charles Jr and Dorris Morris; married Lisa; children: Jason, Charles & Jillian. **Educ:** Marquette Univ, BA, 1977; Univ Va Law Sch, JD, 1980. **Career:** Reid & Priest, assoc, 1980-82; Mayer Brown, assoc, 1982-84; Skadden, Arps, Slate, Meagher & Flom, Chicago, assoc, 1984-87; coop securities atty; Abraham & Sons, partner, managing dir, 1987-89; Russell Reynolds Assocs Inc, managing dir, pres, exec vpres, co-leader & chief exec officer bd serves pract, 1989-; Skadden, Arps Corp, Securities Atty; Meir Brown & Platt; Reid & Priest, Corp Securities Atty. **Orgs:** Dir, Northern Trust Corp; Dean, NW Univ J L Kellogg Sch Mgt; bd mem, Northern Trust Bank; bd mem, Chicago Symphony Orchestra; Chicago Coun Global Affairs; Rush Univ Med Ctr; Global Exec Comt; chair, LEAP Comt; Northwestern Kellogg Sch Mgt's Adv Bd; bd mem, Abbott Labs, Amoco, Northern Trust, 2005-; trustee, Chicago Symphony Orchestra; Com Club Chicago; Obama Am; Obama Victory Fund, 2012; Urban League Chicago; Chmn, Firm's Leadership Assessment & Promotions Bd, 2006. **Home Addr:** 741 W Gordon Ter, Chicago, IL 60613-2224, **Home Phone:** (239)261-6446. **Business Addr:** Co-Leader, Chief Executive Officer of Board Services Practice, Russell Reynolds Associates Inc, 200 S Wacker Dr Suite 2900, Chicago, IL 60606-5802, **Business Phone:** (312)993-9696.

**TRIBBLE, HUERTA CASSIUS**
Business owner, engineer, government official. **Personal:** Born Sep 15, 1939, Terre Haute, IN; children: Huerta Lee, Steven Harold & Kevin in Eugene. **Educ:** Ind State Univ, AB, 1962. **Career:** PR Mallory, pr ma eng, 1966-69; Ind Urban League Inc, proj dir to asst dist, 1969-81; US Small Bus Admn, asst dist dir minority small bus & capital ownership develop, 1983-91; Huerta C Tribble & Assocs, owner, currently. **Orgs:** Ind Minority Splr Dev Coun, 1983-85; coordr, Ind Minority Bus OppurtunityCoun, 1983-85; trustee, Martin Ctr Col, 1984-85. **Business Addr:** Owner, Huerta C Tribble & Associates, 3710 N Meridian St Apt 6, Indianapolis, IN 46208-4336, **Business Phone:** (317)924-2746.

**TRIBBLE, KEITH**
Athletic director. **Personal:** Born Jan 1, 1955, Miami, FL; married Michelle Ann Leporati; children: 2. **Educ:** Univ Fla, BA, journalism, 1977. **Career:** Univ Nev, Las Vegas, assoc athletic dir, 1981-89; Sunshine festival football inc, exec dir, 1990-92; Univ Fla, athletic dir, 1992-93; Orange Bowl Comt, chief exec officer, 1993-2006; Univ cent Fla, dir athletics, 2006-11. **Orgs:** Orange Bowl comt; managing dir, Blockbuster Bowl; chmn, football bowl Asn. **Honors/Awds:** Hall of Fame, Univ Fla, 2011. **Special Achievements:** First African American executive director of a major bowl game (OrangeBowl), 1993. **Business Addr:** Director of Athletics, University of Central Florida, Wayne Densch Sports Ctr Suite 38, Orlando, FL 32816-3555, **Business Phone:** (407)823-2261.

**TRICE, DR. JUNIPER YATES.** **See Obituaries Section.**

**TRICE, TRENA (TRENA TRICE HILL)**
Basketball player, basketball coach. **Personal:** Born Aug 4, 1965, Norfolk, VA; married Derrick A Hill; children: Kiana. **Educ:** NC State Univ, BS, speech commun, 1987. **Career:** Basketball player (retired), basketball coach; NY Liberty, forward ctr, 1997-98; Fed Intl Basketball Asn; Hampton Univ, asst coach, 2002-04; NC State Univ, asst coach, 2004-09; Va Commonwealth Univ, asst coach, 2010-12; Norfolk State Univ, asst coach, 2012-15; Columbia Univ, asst coach, 2015-. **Business Addr:** Assistant Coach, NC State University, PO Box 8502, Raleigh, NC 27695-8501, **Business Phone:** (919)515-2101.

**TRICE, DR. WILLIAM BENJAMIN**
Educator, dentist. **Personal:** Born Jan 28, 1924, Newton, GA; married Mildred Moore; children: Sheila T Bell & Angela M. **Educ:** Univ Pittsburgh, BS, 1951, DMD, 1953. **Career:** Pvt pract, dentist; Hamot Hosp, staff; Erie Univ Pittsburgh Sch Dent, coordr continuing educ; Univ Pittsburgh Sch Dent Med, lectr, Dept Pub Health, adj instr, 1974-75. **Orgs:** Past pres, Univ Pittsburgh Sch Dent Med, 1974-75; Am & Nat Dent Asns; Pierre Fauchard Acad; Fedn Dentaire Inte; Int Asn Dent Res; Am Asn Dent Res; Acad Gen Dent; Am Acad Dent Electrosurg; Alpha Phi Alpha; Rotary Club; pres, Am Heart Asn; Knights Columbus; trustee, Stoneleigh Burnham Sch Fel Am Col Dentists; Int Dent Asn. **Honors/Awds:** Distinguished Alumnus of the Year Award, Univ Pittsburgh Sch Dent Med, 1953. **Home Addr:** 5501 Fulda Dr, Erie, PA 16505-1219, **Home Phone:** (814)833-7297. **Business Addr:** Dentist, 1611 Peach St Suite 275, Erie, PA 16501, **Business Phone:** (814)455-5116.

**TRICHE, ARTHUR**
Public relations executive. **Personal:** Born Aug 16, 1961, Mound Bayou, MS; son of Arthur Sr and Beatrice Anderson; married Velma Slack; children: Brandon Arthur. **Educ:** Tulane Univ, New Orleans, LA, BGS, lib arts & commun, 1983. **Career:** Tulane Univ, New Orleans, La, Athletic Dept, asst sports info dir, 1983-86; La State Univ, Baton Rouge, La, asst sports info dir, 1986-88; Detroit Lions, Pontiac, Mich, asst dir, pub rels, 1988-89; Atlanta Hawks, Atlanta, Ga, vpres media rels & commun, 1989-2012; spokesman, currently; SportsRadio 929 Game, exec producer, 2012-. **Orgs:** NBA Pub Rels Dirs Asn, 1989-. **Special Achievements:** First black public relations director for an NBA team. **Home Addr:** 2095 Kolb Ridge Ct SW, Marietta, GA 30008-4480. **Business Addr:** Executive Producer, SportsRadio 929 The Game, 1201 Peachtree St Suite 800, Atlanta, GA 30361, **Business Phone:** (404)898-8900.

**TRIM, JOHN H.** **See Obituaries Section.**

**TRIMIAR, JIMMIE SINCLAIR.** **See TRIMIAR, DR. SINCLAIR J.**

**TRIMIAR, DR. SINCLAIR J. (JIMMIE SINCLAIR TRIMIAR)**
Surgeon, educator, physician. **Personal:** Born Dec 17, 1933, Lynchburg, VA; married Anna H; children: Stefanie & Jay. **Educ:** Howard Univ, BS, 1960, DDS, 1964; NY Univ, oral surg cert, 1968. **Career:** Harlem Hosp Ctr, oral surg intern, 1964-65, anethesia res, 1965-67, oral surg res, 1968-69, Dept Oral Surg, asst vis att, Respiratory Ther Serv, chief, 1969, ambulatory anethesia chief, 1970, Infections Com Harlem Hosp Ctr, co-chmn, 1971-74, dir, 1974; Columbia Univ Col Physicians & Surgeons, asst prof clin anesthesiol; pvt pract, gen & family pract, currently. **Orgs:** Pres, Harlem Dent Soc Greater NY; pres, Harlem Hosp Soc Oral Surgeons; Am Dent Asn; Nat Dent Asn; First Dist Dent Soc; NY State Soc Oral Surgeons; Am Asn Respiratory Ther; Am Soc Oral Surgeons; Am Soc Dent Anesthesiol; One Hundred Black Men Inc; Omega Psi Phi Frat; Am Acad Pediat Dent. **Special Achievements:** First vice president of Black Caucus of Harlem Health Workers. **Business Addr:** Physician, Harlem Hospital Center, 506 Malcolm X Blvd, New York, NY 10037, **Business Phone:** (212)939-2882.

**TRIPP, DR. LUKE SAMUEL**
Educator. **Personal:** Born Feb 6, 1941, Atoka, TN; son of Luke Sr and Dorothy; married Hedy Bruyns; children: Ruth Sherman, Azania & Comrade. **Educ:** Wayne State Univ, BS, 1966; Univ Mich, MA, 1974, PhD, 1980. **Career:** Community Skills Ctr, math & sci teacher, 1972-73; Univ Mich, grad res dir, 1977-80; Univ Ill, asst prof African Am studies, 1981-82; Southern Ill Univ, asst prof Black Am studies, 1982-89; St Cloud State Univ, asst prof, 1989-92, prof, 1992-, Dept Community Studies, chair, 2003-11, Dept Ethnic & Women's Studies, prof, 2011-. **Orgs:** Co-founder, League Revolutionary Black Workers, 1969; dir, polit educ Nat Black Independent Polit Party, 1980-81; Nat Coun Black Studies, 1983; Ill Coun Black Studies, 1983; Soc Ethnic & Spec Studies, 1983; coord, Southern Ill Anti-Apartheid Alliance, 1985-89; Minority Concerns Comt, St Cloud State Univ, 1989-; founding mem, Fac & Staff Color Caucus, 1989-; founder, Human Rights Coalition, 1990. **Home Addr:** 804 Wash Memorial Dr, St. Cloud, MN 56301-4018. **Business Addr:** Professor, St Cloud State University, 200 51B, St. Cloud, MN 56301-4498, **Business Phone:** (320)255-3913.

**TRIPPLETT, LARRY**
Executive, educator. **Educ:** Calif State Univ, Long Beach, BS, MS. **Career:** Asst prin; McDonalds restaurants, owner, 1986; Stanford Univ Sch Educ, E Palo Alto Acad, mentor, currently; Tripplett Mgt Corp, pres, currently. **Orgs:** Pres & bd dir, Menlo Pk-based Boys & Girls Clubs; pres, at-large officer, Nat Black McDonalds Operators Asn, vice chmn & pres, chmn & chief exec officer, Western Div; Adv Coun, Stanford Univ Sch Educ. **Business Addr:** Mentor, Stanford University School of Education, 485 Lasuen Mall, Stanford, CA 94305-3096, **Business Phone:** (650)723-2109.

**TROPEZ-SIMS, DR. SUSANNE**
Physician, educator, dean (education). **Personal:** Born Apr 13, 1949, New Orleans, LA; daughter of Maxwell Sterling and Ethel Ross; married Michael Milroy Sims; children: Lisa L Arceneaux, Janifer S Martin & James C White Jr. **Educ:** Bennett Col, BS, pre-med & pre-med studies, 1971; Univ NC, Chapel Hill, MD, 1975, MPH, 1981. **Career:** Univ NC, Chapel Hill, instr, 1979-82, asst prof, 1982-88, postdoctoral fel; LSU Health Sci Ctr, assoc prof, div chief, 1988-97; Meharry Med Col, Sch Med, prof & chairperson pediat, 1997-2005, Acad Support Servs, assoc dean acad affiliations & prof, 2005-, prog dir, clerkship dir, currently; Vanderbilt Univ, adj prof, 2000-. **Orgs:** Am Pediat Asn, 1979-; Am Acad Pediat, 1979-; Am Acad Pediat Sch Health Comt, 1993-99; AMSPDC, 1997-2005; co-chair, Tenn Am Acad Pediat, Sch Health Comt, 1998-2000; Nat Med Asn; Am Bd Pediat; Alpha Omega Alpha Med Hon Soc. **Home Addr:** 509 Banshire Ct, Brentwood, TN 37027, **Home Phone:** (615)445-3176. **Business Addr:** Professor & Associate Dean of Academic Affiliations, Clerkship Director, Meharry Medical College, 1005 Dr D B Todd Jr Blvd Suite 2, Nashville, TN 37208, **Business Phone:** (615)327-6925.

**TROTMAN, RICHARD EDWARD**
Educator. **Personal:** Born Jun 22, 1942, East Orange, NJ; married Cordell Jones; children: Richard Jr & Raheem. **Educ:** Shaw Univ, BA, 1964; Kean Col, MA, 1971; Rutgers Univ, attended 1978; Waldon Univ, PhD, 1998. **Career:** Educator (retired); NJ Dept Educ, supvr, 1973-76; Kean Col NJ, assoc dir, 1976-79; Bergen Community Col, dir, 1979-82; Somerset County Col, Spec Educ Serv, dir, 1982; Raritan Valley Community Col, dir, 1982-03, chief examr, dean col advan, 2002-03; dean emer col advan. **Orgs:** Passaic County Manpower Prog, Mayors Planning Coun, Paterson, NJ, 1971-73; NJ Educ Opportunity Funding dir, 1976-86; NJ Asn Black Educators, 1984-86; Nat Asn Advan Colored People, 1985-86; Nat Urban League, 1985-86; mem adv bd, Cent NJ Col, LD prog, 1989; Reach Prog Adv Bd, NJ Social Serv, 1989. **Home Addr:** 141 Clark Pl, Piscataway, NJ 08854, **Home Phone:** (732)752-6414.

**TROTTER, ANDREW LEON**
Government official. **Personal:** Born Sep 7, 1949, San Antonio, TX. **Educ:** NMex State Univ, BA, 1972. **Career:** Human Serv Dept, caseworker, 1972-79, supvr, 1979-. **Orgs:** Secy, Mt Olive Baptist State Con Laymen Aux, 1974-; christian educ dir BSBC, 1983-; treas, New Hope Baptist Dist Laymen's Asn, 1985-; Dona Ana Br Community Col, 1985-95; supt, church sch BSBC, 1990-; vpres, New Hope Dist Cong Christian Ed, 1997; treas, Human Serv Consortium; Am Pub Welfare Asn; musician, BSBC Mt Olive Baptist State Cong; El Paso-Chap Gospel Music Workshop Am; Nat Asn Advan Colored People; treas, Asn Prof Supvr NM; coordr, Mt Olive State Music Workshop; Nat Baptist Conv USA Inc, Laymens Depart, Corinth Baptist Church, Bethel Second Baptist Church; bd mem, Adult Basic Educ; bd mem, RSVP Dona Ana City; Mesilla Valley Civitan. **Honors/Awds:** Cert Achievement State NMex, 1982; Advanced Cert Nat Congress Christ Educ NBC, USA Inc, 1983. **Home Addr:** 1440 N Paxton, Las Cruces, NM 88001, **Home Phone:** (505)524-0780. **Business Addr:** Member, National Baptist Convention USA Inc, 400 Del, Alamogordo, NM 88310, **Business Phone:** (575)312-3886.

**TROTTER, CORTEZ**
Executive, firefighter, commissioner. **Personal:** Born Jan 1, 1955. **Career:** Fire commissioner (retired), vpres, dir; Chicago Fire Dept, paramedic, 1976, Emergency Med Serv, paramedic-in-charge, area supvr, dep fire comnr, first dep fire comnr, 2000; Chicago Off Emergency Mgt & Commun, head, 2001-04, fire comnr, 2004-06, exec dir; Chicago Dept Pub Health; City Chicago, chief emergency officer, 2006-08; James Lee Witt Assocs, vpres & dir midwest region, currently. **Honors/Awds:** Fireslayer of the Year, 2005. **Special Achievements:** First Black fire commissioner of Chicago City. **Business Addr:** Vice President, Director of the Midwest Region, James Lee Witt Associates, 1501 M St NW Suite 500, Washington, DC 20005, **Business Phone:** (202)585-0780.

**TROTTER, DONNE E.**
State government official. **Personal:** Born Jan 30, 1950, Cairo, IL; son of James and Carita; married Rose Zuniga; children: 4. **Educ:** Chicago State Univ, BA, hist & polit sci, 1976; Loyola Univ Law Sch, MJ, health & policy jurisp. **Career:** Ill State House, mem, 1988-93; Ill State Senate, leader Black Caucus, sen, 1993-. **Orgs:** Chmn, Senate Appropriations I Comn; Com & Econ Develop; vice chairperson, Senate Comt Whole Environ & Energy; Senate Comt Appropriations II; Senate Comt Appropriations III; Senate Comt Exec Appointments. **Home Addr:** , Chicago, IL 60617. **Business Addr:** State Senator, Illinois State Senate, 8704 S Constance Ave Suite 324, Chicago, IL 60617-2746, **Business Phone:** (773)933-7715.

**TROTTER, JAMES**
Entrepreneur, executive, business owner. **Career:** ACME Muscle Scooters, founder, pres, 1995-. **Business Addr:** President, ACME Muscle Scooters, 2821 N 4th St, Milwaukee, WI 53212, **Business Phone:** (414)263-7595.

**TROTTER, JEREMIAH**
Executive, radio host, football player. **Personal:** Born Jan 20, 1977, Hooks, TX; married Tammi; children: TreMil & Jeremiah Jr. **Educ:** Stephen F Austin Univ, BS, bus mgt. **Career:** Football player (retired), exec, radio host; Philadelphia Eagles, 1998, mid linebacker, 1999-2001, 2004-06, 2009; T&I Unisex Salon, owner, 2000; Wash Redskins, 2002-03; Trott's Spot Car Wash, owner, 2003; Tampa Bay Buccaneers, mid linebacker, 2007; Radio Sta 97.5, Philadelphia, radio host, currently. **Orgs:** Founder, Jeremiah Trotter Found. **Honors/Awds:** All Pro Bowl Selection Twice, 2000-01; Pro Bowler, 2000, 2001, 2004, 2005. **Special Achievements:** Films: "The North Star", 2016.

**TROTTER, DR. LLOYD G.**
Executive, association executive. **Personal:** Born Jan 1, 1945?, Cleveland, OH; married Teri; children: 3. **Educ:** Cleveland State Univ, BBA, 1972, PhD, bus admin, 2001. **Career:** GE Lighting, field serv engr, 1970; GE Elec Distrib & Control, vpres & gen mgr, 1990-92, pres & chief exec officer, 1992-98; GE Consumer & Indust, pres & chief exec officer, 2004-06; GE Indust Systs, vice chmn, pres & chief exec officer, 2006-08; Gen Nx360, managing partner, 2008-; PepsiCo Inc, independent dir, 2008-; Daimler AG, dir, 2009; syncreon Int Group, dir, 2009-; syncreon Holdings plc, independent dir; Syncreon US Holdings Inc, dir; Meritor Inc, dir, 2015. **Orgs:** Bd dir, Conn Pre-Engineering Prog; Americas Promise; chmn bd govs, Nat Elec Mfrs Asn; bd mem, Nat Asn Mfrs; bd, Pepsi Co;dir, Genpact Ltd, 2007-08; bd dir, Textron Inc, 2008-; chmn, Horsburgh & Scott Co Inc. **Honors/Awds:** Black Achievers in Industry Award, Harlem YMCA; Benjamin Mays Award. **Home Addr:** , Plainville, CT. **Business Addr:** Director, Textron Inc, 40 Westminster St, Providence, RI 02903, **Business Phone:** (401)421-2800.

**TROTTER, LLOYD G.**
Founder (originator), executive. **Personal:** Born Jan 1, 1945, Cleveland, OH; married Terri; children: 3. **Educ:** Cleveland State Univ, BBA, 1972. **Career:** Gen Elec, exec, 1970-2008; GE Lighting, field serv engr, 1970, vpres & gen mgr mfg ED&C, 1990, pres & chief exec officer, 1992; GE Elec Distrib & Control, pres & chief exec officer, 1992-98; GE Consumer & Indust Systs, pres, sr vpres & chief exec officer, 1998-2005; Gen Elec Co, sr opers officer, 2004-06, exec vpres oper, 2005-06, exec vice chmn, 2006-; Gen Elec Indust, vice chmn, pres, chief exec officer, 2006-08; Genpact Ltd, dir, 2007-08; Gen Elec Capital Serv Inc, dir; Gen Elec Capital Corp, dir; GenNx360, vice chmn, 2006-; GenNx360 Capital Partners, founder & managing partner, 2008-; PepsiCo Inc, dir, 2008-; Textron Inc, dir, 2008-. **Orgs:** Bd mem, Nat Asn Manufacturers; bd mem, Nat Action Coun Minorities Engineering (NACME); be mem, GE Found; dir, Daimler AG, supvry bd mem, 2009-; bd mem, Syncreon Holdings Ltd; bd mem, Syncreon US Holdings Inc; bd mem, Syncreon US Inc; Nat Soc Black Engrs. **Honors/Awds:** Cleveland State Univ, Hon Doctorate, 2001; NC A&T Sch Bus, Hon Doctorate; "Black Enterprise," 75 Most Powerful Blacks on Wall Street, 2011; Lifetime Achievement Award; GE Chmn Awards 2003, 2004, 2005; Black Achievers Indust Award. **Business Addr:** Director, Textron Inc, 40 Westminster St, Providence, RI 02903, **Business Phone:** (401)421-2800.

**TROTTMAN, CHARLES HENRY**
Educator, historian, scientist. **Personal:** Born Jul 29, 1934, Pine Bluff, AR; married Evelyn Marie Royal; children: Rodney, Jeniffer, Phyliss, Calliette & Charlette. **Educ:** Ark AM&N Col, BS, 1957; Tuskegee Inst, 1959; Syracuse Univ, MS, 1961; Univ NC, 1969; Univ Wis, PhD, 1972. **Career:** Coleman HS, instr, 1959; So Univ, asst prof chem, 1961-67; Ark AM&N Col, assoc prof chem, 1967-69; Univ Wis, res asst, 1969-72; Jackson St Univ, assoc prof chem, 1972-. **Orgs:** Fac, Sen Jackson St Univ 1974-76; consult, Argonne Nat Lab, 1974-76; dir, Nat Sci Found, 1977-78; Sigma Xi; Am Chem Soc; MS Acad Sci; Hist Sci Soc; MS Asn Educr; AAAS; Nat Asn Advan Colored People; AAUP; Omega Psi Phi Frat; Nat Orgn Prof Adv Black Chem & Chem Eng; Nat Inst Sci. **Home Addr:** 8713 W Broune Dr, Jonesboro, GA 30238. **Business Addr:** Associate Professor, Jackson State University, 1400 J R Lynch St, Jackson, MS 39217.

**TROUP, DR. ELLIOTT VANBRUGH, SR.**
President (organization), ophthalmologist, physician. **Personal:** Born Feb 28, 1938, Brunswick, GA; married Linda E; children: Elliott Jr, Traci & Patrick. **Educ:** Fisk Univ, BA, 1959; Meharry Med Col, MD, 1963; Am Bd Ophthal, cert, Ophthal, 1971. **Career:** Univ Minn, residency ophthal, 1969; Hurley Hosp, internship; ophthalmologist, pvt practr. **Orgs:** Pres, St Paul Ophthal Soc, 1977-78; Acad Ophthal & Otolaryn; Nat Med Asn; AMA; Med Prod Div 3m Co; Alpha Phi Alpha Fraternity; bd pres & pres, Mn Bd Med pract. **Home Addr:** 3410 Chandler Ave St, St Paul, MN 55126-3914. **Business Addr:** President, Minneosota Board of Medical Practice, 2829 Univ Avn SE Suite 400, Minneapolis, MN 55414-3246, **Business Phone:** (612)617-2130.

**TROUPE, REP. CHARLES QUINCY**
State government official. **Personal:** Born May 12, 1936, St. Louis, MO. **Educ:** Wash Tech Sch; Denver Univ. **Career:** Dem First Ward St Louis, committeeman; Amalgamated Transit Union, vpres; MO House Representatives, Dist 62, state rep, 1978-; City St Louis, ward 1 aldermen, currently, elec contractor, currently. **Orgs:** Com & econ develop; chmn, subcomt tobacco settlement; chmn, joint interim comt dept social serv. **Home Addr:** 5353 Union St, St. Louis, MO 63120, **Home Phone:** (314)383-3814. **Business Addr:** State Representative, MO House of Representatives, 201 W Capitol Ave Rm 113, Jefferson City, MO 65101, **Business Phone:** (573)751-2851.

**TROUPE, DR. MARILYN KAY**
Educator. **Personal:** Born Sep 30, 1945, Tulsa, OK; daughter of Ernest Robinson and Lucille Andrew. **Educ:** Okla State Univ, BA, hist, 1967, MA, hist, 1976, EdD, occupational & adult educ, 1993. **Career:** Tulsa Pub Sch, teacher, 1969-81; McLain-Tulsa Pub Schs, instr cosmetology, 1982-94; CETA City Tulsa, summer youth counr, 1980-; Okla State Univ, hist instr, 1981-82; Okla State Voc & Tech Educ, curric support & instrnl develop specialist, 1987-94; Lane Col, TCR Educ Prog, asst prof & coordr, Div Lib Studies & Educ, chair, 1995-97; Ky Dept Edu, Teacher Edu & Cert, dir, 1997-99; Ky State Univ, Educ Prof Stand Bd, div dir educr prep, 1999-. **Orgs:** Pres, Okla State Beauty Culturalists League, 1979-85; Zeta Phi Beta Sor, 1985; bd dir, Stillwater Co, 1988-94; Nat Asn Minority Polit Women, 1988-89; bd dir, Adult Day Care Ctr, 1990-94; bd mem, Cot Rels City Stillwater, 1991-94; bd mem, Pk & Recreation City Stillwater, 1991-94; bd mem, Life Ctr Elderly, 1991-94; bd examiner, Nat Coun Accreditation Teacher Educ, 1997-; post sec task force, KY Ctr Sch Safety, 2000-; Prof Develop Early Childhood Coun, 2001; KY Lit Partnership, 2001; Cath Daughters Am Tulsa Ct; bd mem, Links Inc; Iota Lambda Sigma; Phi Delta Kappa; Theta Nu Sigma; Phi Alpha Theta; Langston Alumni, Nat Asn Advan Colored People; Nat State Local Bus & Prof Womens Club; Nat State Local Beauty Culturists League Inc; Am & Okla Voc Asn; Voc & Ideal Clubs Am; Am Voc Asn; charter mem, State & Nat Asn Advan Black Am Voc Educ; grad adv, Okla State Univ, Theta Beta Chap; chair, Womens Adv Coun; vol, Frankfort Soup Kitchen; Okla Task Force, Goals Tomorrow, Adv Comt; Am Asn Univ Women; bd mem, Unit Accreditation Bd; Asn Supv & Curric Develop; Nat Coun Accredition Teacher Educ; Spec Olympics State Games; Meals Wheels; Frankfort-Lexington Links. **Home Addr:** 1004 Excell Ct, Frankfort, KY 40601. **Business Addr:** Director, Education Professional Standards Board, 100 Airport Rd 3 Fl, Frankfort, KY 40601, **Business Phone:** (502)573-4606.

**TROUPE, QUINCY THOMAS, JR.**
Poet, educator. **Personal:** Born Jul 22, 1939, St. Louis, MO; son of Quincy Sr and Dorothy Marshall Smith; married Margaret Porter; children: Antoinette, Tymme, Quincy & Porter. **Educ:** Grambling Col, BA, 1963; Los Angeles City Col, AA, 1967. **Career:** Watts Writers Movement, Los Angeles CA, creative writing teacher, 1966-68; Shrewd Mag, Los Angeles, assoc ed, 1968; Univ Calif, Los Angeles, instr creative writing & black lit, 1968; Ohio Univ, Athens, instr creative writing & third world lit, 1969-72; Richmond Col, Staten Island NY, instr third world lit, assoc prof Am & third world lit & dir poetry ctr, 1971-90; Columbia Univ, NY, fac grad writing Prog, 1985-; New York Found Arts fel, 1987; Styx River Mag, ed; Univ Calif, San Diego, prof, 1990-2002; emer prof, currently; Bks: Giant Talk: An Anthology Third World Writing, 1972; Inside Story TV's Roots, 1978; Snake-Back Solos:Selected Poems 1969-77, 1979; James Baldwin: Legacy, 1989; Miles: Autobiography Miles Davis, 1989; Weather Reports: New & Selected Poems, 1991; Univ Calif, San Diego, instr creative writing, Caribbean lit, 1991-2002; Code mag, ed dir, 2000; Take it to hoop Magic Johnson, 2001; Little Stevie Wonder, 2005; Archit Lang, poems, 2006; Nat Found Arts; New York Found Art; Ny Coun Arts. **Orgs:** Poetry Soc Am; dir, Malcolm X Ctr, 1969-70. **Home Addr:** 1925 7th Ave Apt 7L, New York, NY 10026. **Business Addr:** Professor Emeritus, University of California, 9500 Gilman Dr, La Jolla, CA 92093.

**TROUPE-FRYE, BETTY JEAN**
Government official, nurse. **Personal:** Born Mar 8, 1935, St. Louis, MO; daughter of Phillip Jeffery and Ruth Townsend; children: Armont, Mona Long Roberts & Evette Boykins. **Educ:** State Community Col, attended 1974; Tariko Col, BS, mgt, 1988; Webster Univ, MA, 1991. **Career:** Wellston Sch Bd, pres, 1981-84; Wellston City Coun, councilperson, 1982-84; Wellston First Ward, pres; C's Home Soc, nurse, currently. **Orgs:** Nurse Olsten Health Serv; chmn, ANSCA, 1982-; Campaign Human Dignity, 1984; St Louis Chap 46 OES Prince Hall Affil; ACORN; bd mem, BCDI, 2000-. **Honors/Awds:** Appreciation, Noble, 1982; Appreciation, Women Munic Govt, 1983; Appreciation, St Louis Head Start, 1983; Appreciation, Enforcers Amateur Athletic Asn. **Home Addr:** 1538 Ogden Ave, St Louis, MO 63133-2413. **Business Addr:** Nurse, Children's Home Society, 9445 Litzsinger Rd, St Louis, MO 63144-2113, **Business Phone:** (314)918-0492.

**TROUTMAN, DR. ADEWALE**
Physician, administrator, educator. **Personal:** Born Mar 17, 1946, New York, NY; married Denise; children: Anasa & Nandi. **Educ:** Lehman Col, BA, 1969; State Univ NY, Albany, MA, 1972; Univ Med & Dent NJ, MD, 1979; Columbia Univ Sch Pub Health, MPH, 1992; Nat Bd Pub Health Examiners, bd cert pub health, 2009. **Career:** St Michaels Med Ctr, med dir, 1982-84; United Hosp Med Ctr, dir emergency serv, 1984-97; City Newark, med dir, 1987-90; Rutgers Univ, Dept Africana Studies, Lectr, 1992-97; Univ Med & Dent, asst clin

prof, 1995-97; Fulton County, dir, Dept Health & Wellness, 1997; Morehouse Sch Med, clin assoc prof, 2001-; Ft Valley State Univ, Dept Pub Health, adj fac, 2002-03; Emory Univ, adj fac, 2002-03; Univ Louisville Sch Pub Health, assoc prof, 2004-10; Louisville Metro Health Dept, dir, 2004-10; Univ S Fla, Pub Health Leadership & Pract, dir, 2010-. **Orgs:** Am Soc Clin Hypn, 1982-; Nat Med Asn, 1990-; Am Pub Health Asn, 1994-; 100 Black Men Am, 2000-; pres, Black Centers Health Workers, 2000-; bd mem, Soc Advan African Am Pub Health Issues; chair, Health & Social Justice Adv Comt, Nat Asn County & City Health; bd dir, Jomandi Theatre Co; Greater Louisville Med Soc; Am Heart Asn; Acad Health Equity; Am Cancer Asn. **Home Addr:** 1208 Clearbrook Dr, Atlanta, GA 30311, **Home Phone:** (404)691-9608. **Business Addr:** Director, Louisville Metro Health Department, 400 E Gray St, Louisville, KY 40202, **Business Phone:** (502)574-6520.

## TROUTMAN, DR. PORTER LEE, JR.

Educator, association executive. **Personal:** Born Apr 4, 1943, Newellton, LA; married Bobbie Jean Martin; children: Gregory & Portia. **Educ:** Univ Nev, educ spec; Southern Univ, Baton Rouge, LA, BS; Northern Ariz Univ, MA, educ, EdD, 1977; Univ Nev, educ. **Career:** Rec Ctr, dir, 1965-66; Clark Co Sch Dist, teacher, 1966-71; SELD Prog Title I, current spec, 1968; Clark Co Teacher Asn, staff rep, 1970-71; Univ Nev, Las Vegas, Teacher Corps, lectr, assoc dir, dir, 1971-74, dir, 1974-75, Dis Off Prof Studies, chair, prof educ, 1974; Nat Asn Multicult Educ, dir, founder, state pres, prof emer, 1990-; Nev Nat Asn Multicult Educ, pres, currently; dir, Nat Youth Sports Prog. **Orgs:** CCSD Task Force; Actg Pring; Clark Co Teacher Asn; Clark Co Sch Dist Adv Facil Com; chmn, Jo Mackey Elem Sch Adv Bd; Clark Co Teacher Asn; Human Rels Comn; Alt Sen Jo Mackey Elem Sch; Nev State Ed Resolution Comt; Adv Stud Nat Ed Asn Univ; deleg, Nat Ed Asn Detroit deleg First Nat Cong Black Prof Higher Ed Univ Tex; Nat Educ Asn; Knights Columbus; Am Asn Sch Admin; Am Asn Col Teacher Ed, AACTE Comn Perf Based Educ; Kappa Delta Pi; Phi Delta Kappa Hon Soc; NCATE; Asn Teacher Educr, Am Asn Col Teacher Educr Nat Asn Multicultural Educ, Nat Coun Social Studies, Am Educ Res Asn, Nat Coun Educating Black C, Nat Rural Educ Asn; life mem, Nat Asn Black Sch Educr. **Honors/Awds:** William G Anderson Award, Am Alliance Health, Phys Educ, Recreation & Dance, 2002; Higher Education WEB Dubois Award, Nat Alliance Black Sch Educr, 2003. **Special Achievements:** Journals: Field Experiences Strategies for Exploring Diversity in Schools, 1996; Research in Middle Level Education Quarterly for Winter, 1997; Peace Education Influencing International Education, 1997; Beyond Instructional Racism: The Integrative Curriculum of Brown Barge Middle School, 1998; Action in Teacher Education, Beyond Instructional Racism, 1999; Looking for Artifacts and Agency: A Basic to Diversity for Preservice Teachers, Pre-service Teacher Construct a View on Multicultural Education: Using Banks Levels of Integration of Ethnic Content to Measure Change, LEA Associates, 2001; Milkin Monograph, Julian, A Case Study, 2002; Publications: Hong, Eunsook, Troutman, Porter, Hartzell, Stephanie & Kyles, Carli, Development and Validation of a Self Assessment Questionnaire on Multicultural Teaching Competencies, Physical Activity Patterns of Students From Low Social Economic Households, Signs, Symbols, and Perceptions in Grant Theft Auto, Vice City, 2005. **Home Addr:** 6333 Stonegate Way, Las Vegas, NV 89146-3012. **Business Addr:** Founder, National Association for Multicultural Education, 5272 River Rd Suite 430, Bethesda, MD 20816, **Business Phone:** (301)951-0022.

## TROWELL-HARRIS, IRENE

Military leader, executive director. **Educ:** Columbia Hosp Sch Nursing, attended 1959; Squadron Officer Sch, 1968; Air Command & Staff Col, 1971; Jersey City State, NJ, BA, health educ, 1971; Yale Univ, MA, pub health, 1973; Nat Security Mgt Course, distinguished grad, 1981; Columbia Univ, doctorate health educ, 1983; Air War Col, attended 1990. **Career:** Military leader (retired), executive; NY Air Nat Guard Bur, first lt, 1963, capt, 1964, maj, 1973, lt col, 1980, col, 1988, brig gen, 1993, maj gen, 1998-2001; Uniformed Serv Univ Health Serv, asst prof; Dept Veterans Affairs, Ctr Women Veterans, dir, patient care inspections & eval div, currently. **Orgs:** Aerospace Med Asn; Am Nurses Asn; Am Pub Health Asn; Ny Nurses Asn; Sigma Theta Tau; Asn Mil Surgeons Us; Nat Guard Asn Us; Kappa Delta Pi Hon Soc. **Home Addr:** 2582 S Arlington Mill Dr, Arlington, VA 22206-3352, **Home Phone:** (703)671-1833. **Business Addr:** Director, US Department of Veterans Affairs, 810 Vermont Ave NW, Washington, DC 20420, **Business Phone:** (202)273-6193.

## TROY, ADAM K.

Entrepreneur, chief executive officer. **Educ:** Morehouse Col, BA, banking & finance; Ohio State Univ. **Career:** Omni Mgt Group Ltd, managing partner & founder, 1996-; Mahogany Ventures, prin & managing partner; M Retail Ventures, managing partner; TROY Enterprises, pres & chief exec officer, 2004-. **Orgs:** Bd trustee, Mansion Day Sch; co-founder, Cent Ohio United Way Key Club. **Business Addr:** Chief Executive Officer, TROY Enterprises, Easton Town Ctr, Columbus, OH 43219, **Business Phone:** (614)509-0001.

## TROY-BROOKS, PATRICIA

Chief executive officer, administrator. **Career:** Advan Staffing Inc, pres & chief exec officer, 1996-10; Workforce Consult & Auth, 2010-12; PeopleShare, br mgr, 2012-13; Life Reimagined/AARP, Lead Vol, 2009-2005. **Orgs:** Co-chair, Nat Coalition 100 Black Women Signature Scholar. **Business Addr:** DE.

## TRUE, RACHEL INDIA

Actor. **Personal:** Born Nov 15, 1966, New York, NY; daughter of Richard true and Verona Barnes. **Career:** Films: CB4, 1993; Embrace of the Vampire, 1994; The Craft, 1996; Nowhere, 1997; Half Baked, 1998; With or Without You, 1998; The Big Split, 1999; The Auteur Theory, 1999; Groove, 2000; Who Is AB?, 2001; New Best Friend, 2002; The Pink eye, 2006; The Perfect Holiday, 2007; Killing of Wendy, 2009; Noah's Ark: The New Beginning, 2009; Noah, 2012. TV Series: "The Cosby Show", 1991-92; "Moment of Truth: Stalking Back", 1993; " A Girls' Guide to Sex", 1993; "Beverly Hills, 90210", 1993; "Dream On", 1994-95; "A Walton Wedding", 1995; "The Drew Carey Show", 1997-98; "The Apartment Complex", 1999; "Once& Again", 1999-2000; "Love Song", 2000; "Half & Half", 2002-06; "Noah's Arc", 2006; "Sugar Mommas", 2012; "Social Nightmare", 2013; "Blood Lake: Attack of the Killer Lampreys", 2014; "Sharknado 2: The Second One, 2014. **Business Addr:** Actress, c/o Lorrie Bartlett Gersh Agency, 232 North Canon Dr Beverly Hills CA 90210, Beverly Hills, CA 90210.

## TRUEBLOOD, VERA J.

Engineer. **Personal:** Born Dec 10, 1962, Minneapolis, MN; daughter of Wiley Jr and Maurine Alexander. **Educ:** Univ Minn, Minneapolis, Minn, BS, mech engineering, 1985; Univ Mich, Ann Arbor, Mich. **Career:** Donaldson Mfg Co, Minneapolis, Minn, prod test engr, 1983-85; Chrysler Corp, Highland Pk, Mich, prod qual engr, design develop engr, 1985-. **Orgs:** Explorer Scout Develop Community Develop, STRIVE, 1985-; Ind Ambassadors, Engrg Soc Detroit, 1986-; bd dir, Youth Develop Comt, Detroit Urban League, 1987-; bd mem, scholar comt, Nat Alumni, Inroads/Metrop Detroit, Inroads, 1989-; community action comt, scholar comt, Black MBA Asn, 1989-; ann dinner chair, Single Minded Inc; bd mem, Detroit Urban League. **Honors/Awds:** Outstanding Young Woman of Year, 1987; Directors Award, Chrysler Corp, 1988; Chairmans Award, Chrysler Corp, 1989; Ebony Magazine, "10 Young Achievers", Johnson Publishing, August 1989. **Home Addr:** 8214 Santa Clara, Detroit, MI 48221, **Home Phone:** (313)563-1903. **Business Addr:** Design Engineer, Interior Trim Engineering, Chrysler Motors, PO Box 214468, Auburn Hills, MI 48326, **Business Phone:** (313)589-5369.

## TRUEHEART, DR. WILLIAM E.

Association executive, president (organization), executive director. **Personal:** Born Jul 10, 1942, New York, NY; son of Louise Elnora Harris and Junious Elton; married Carol Ann Word. **Educ:** Univ Conn, Storrs, BA, polit sci & econs, 1966; Harvard Univ-Kennedy Sch Govt, Cambridge, Mass, MPA, 1973; Harvard Univ, Grad Sch Educ, Cambridge, Mass, EdD, 1979; Bridgewater State Col, PhD, educ; Johnson & Wales Univ, DBA. **Career:** Univ CT, Storrs, CT, asst dir & asst to pres, 1966-68 & 1969-70; Univ Conn-Col Lib Arts & Sci, Storrs, CT, asst to dean & dir acad adv ctr, 1970-72; Harvard Univ-John F Kennedy Sch Govt, Cambridge, MA, asst dean & dir master pub admin prog, 1979-83; Harvard Univ-Off Gov Boards, Cambridge, MA, assoc sec to univ, 1983-86; Bryant Col, Smithfield, RI, exec vpres, 1986-89, pres, 1989-96; Harvard Univ, Grad Sch Educ, vis scholar, 1996-97; Reading Fundamental Inc, pres & chief exec officer; PNC Financial Corp, vpres; Nat Flag Found, founder & vpres; St. Clair Memorial Hosp, dir emer; Fleet Nat Bank, bd dir; Fleet Nat Bank Southern New Eng Banking Group, bd dir; Narragansett Elec Co, bd dir; New Eng Educ Loan Mkt Corp, bd dir; RI Pub Educ Fund, bd dir; Nat Educ Fund Network, bd dir; Woods Hole Oceanog Inst, bd dir; RI C's Crusade, bd dir; Am Inst Cert Pub Accountants, bd dir; Pittsburgh Found, pres & chief exec officer, 2001-; Independent Sector, chmn emer, currently; Univ Pittsburgh, bd dir; Allegheny Conf Community Develop, bd dir, currently; Nellie Mae Educ Found, bd dir, currently; NTL Inst, Practising Social Chg, pres & chief exec officer, currently. **Orgs:** Bd dir, Nellie Mae Inc, 1988-; bd dir, Pub Educ Fund Network, 1990-; bd dir, Providence Chamber Com, 1990-; bd dir, Fleet Nat Bank, 1990-; bd dir, Narragansett Elec, 1990-; Am Inst Cert Pub Accts; treas, Life span Inc; Narragansett Elec Co; New Eng Educ Loan Mkt Corp; chmn, RI Independent Higher Educ Asn; RI Pub Expenditure Coun; Woods Hole Oceanog Inst; pres & ceo, Pittsburgh Found; Ford Found; bd, trustee, Commonfund Inc, currently; Johnson & Wales Univ; Pittsburgh Cult Trust; Highmark Blue Cross/Blue Shield. **Honors/Awds:** ACE fel, Am Coun Educ, 1968-69; Littauer fel, Harvard Univ, 1973; Travelli fel, Charles I Travelli Found, 1973-79; Ford Found fel, Ford Found, 1974-79; Black Alumni Asn Award Excellence, Univ CT, 1989; hon doctorate, Bryant Col, 1996, Johnson & Wales Univ, 1996; Man of the Year in Finance, Vectors/Pittsburgh, 2004; Distinguished Alumni Award, Univ Conn. **Special Achievements:** First African American to head a four year, private college in New England; co-author: "Production Function Analysis in Higher Education: General Methodology & Applications to Four Year Black Colleges, Government Printing Office", 1977; author: "The Underside of Federal Involvement with Higher Education"; "The Federal Purse and the Rule of Law, University of Notre Dame", 1983. **Business Addr:** President, Chief Executive Officer, The Pittsburgh Foundation, 1 PPG Pl, Pittsburgh, PA 15222.

## TRUESDALE, DR. CARLTON MAURICE

Scientist. **Personal:** Born May 25, 1954, High Point, NC; son of Emma and Gonzalee; married Linda; children: Wytheria, Tiffiany, Arthur, Carl & Emmanuel (deceased). **Educ:** Morehouse Col, BS, chem, 1976; Univ Calif, Berkeley, PhD, phys chem, 1983. **Career:** Corning Inc, sr scientist, 1983-86, sr res scientist, 1987-89, assoc, 1990-97, sr res assoc, 1998-2000, mgr, specialty fiber, appl res, 2001-02, res fel, 2005-. **Orgs:** Nat Asn Advan Colored People, 1983-2008; Corning Chmn's Diversity Coun, 2001-03; Citizens Revitalizing Communities, 2003-04. **Honors/Awds:** Golden Torch Award, Nat Soc Black Engs, 1998; Corning Professional Women's Forum Diversity & Development Award, 2002; Distinguished Citizen Award, Economic Opportunity Program, 2005; Jefferson Award Community Serv, 2006; Most Important Black in Technology, 2008, 2009. **Special Achievements:** Authored 22 publications in referred journs, 1976-2005; author, book chapter in Electro-Optics Handbook, 1993; author, award-winning packet for NSBE Exec Dir's Advancing Diversity, 2000; 22 patents granted, 7 additional filed; USBE & IT Mazagine's One of 100 most important Blacks in Technology, 2006-08. **Home Addr:** 11948 River Rd, Corning, NY 14830, **Home Phone:** (607)562-8264. **Business Addr:** Research Fellow, Inorganic & Integration Technology, Corning Inc, Sullivan Pk SPAR02-2, Corning, NY 14831, **Business Phone:** (607)974-3003.

## TRUITT, KEVIN

Government official. **Personal:** Born Jan 2, 1953, Chicago, IL; son of Alfred Henry and Ethel Henry; married Karen McDowell; children: Marissa. **Educ:** Loyola Univ, BBA, acct & econs, 1975; DePaul Univ, MBA, corp finance & managerial acct, 1977. **Career:** Arthur Young & Co, staff auditor, 1977-79; Baxter-Travenol, sr financial analyst, 1979-80; First Chicago Corp, corp banking officer, 1980-87; Bank Hapoalim, com banking officer, 1987-88; Harris Trust & Savings Bank, asst, vpres, 1988-90; City Chicago Dept Revenue, dep dir revenue, 1991-; Mid Am Bank Fsb, exec, currently. **Orgs:** Loyola Univ alumni associations; DePaul Univ alumni asn; bd dir, Chicago Chap Am Asn Individual Investors. **Business Addr:** Executive, Mid America Bank Fsb, 3844 W Belmont Ave, Chicago, IL 60618-5245, **Business Phone:** (773)282-3131.

## TRUMBO, GEORGE WILLIAM

Judge. **Personal:** Born Sep 24, 1926, Newark, OH; son of George Frank and Beatrice; married Sara J Harper; children: Constance, James, Kimberlee, Karen & Adam. **Educ:** Ohio State Univ, BS & BA; Case Western Res Law Sch, LLB. **Career:** Judge (retired); Sunday Sch teacher; Ct Common Pleas, referee, 1977-82; Cleveland Munic Ct, judge, 1982. **Orgs:** Dir, Jr Church Mt Olive Baptist Church; Nat Bar Asn; Greater Cleveland Bar Asn; Ohio Bar Asn; Cuyahoga Co Bar Asn; Elks Lodge IBPOE W; Kappa Alpha Psi; Nat Asn Advan Colored People; bd dir, Judicial Coun Nat Bar Asn; pres, Shaker Sq Kiwanis Club; pres, trustee bd, Cleveland Pub Libr, 1984; chmn, Task Force House Corrections; pres, Northern Ohio Munic Judges Asn; El Hasa Temple No 28; United Supreme Coun Ancient & Accepted Scottish Rite Freemasonry. **Honors/Awds:** Cuyahoga County Criminal Court Bar Association Award, 1973; Superior Judicial Service, 1982, 1984, 1985; Hall of Fame, Nat Bar Asn, 1993. **Home Addr:** 13807 Drexmore Rd, Cleveland, OH 44120, **Home Phone:** (216)991-6068.

## TRUVILLION, VANESSA

Choreographer, executive. **Educ:** Northwestern Univ, Kellogg Sch Mgt, attended 2009. **Career:** Soul Food, choreographer, 1997; Flim: Hoodlum, 1997; Joel Hall Dancers & Ctr, dancer & asst artistic dir, 2004, chief opers officer, currently; Mayfair Acad Fine Arts, dance instr; Hyde Pk Sch Dance, dance instr. **Orgs:** Bd mem, JHD II; co mem, Joel Hall Dancers & Ctr. **Home Addr:** 820 E 101st St, Chicago, IL 60628, **Home Phone:** (312)587-1122. **Business Addr:** Chief Operations Officer, Joel Hall Dancers & Center, 5965 N Clark St, Chicago, IL 60660, **Business Phone:** (773)293-0900.

## TRUVILLION, WENDY

Athletic coach. **Personal:** Born Detroit, MI. **Educ:** La State Univ, attended 1987; Argosy Univ Atlanta, PhD, 2008; Ga State, sports admin; Lincoln Memorial Univ, educ specialist. **Career:** Ga Tech Univ, asst track coach, 1988-93, head track coach, 1993; Phoenix Union HS Dist, asst prin athletics & activ, 2007-; IAAF World Jr Championship, staff, 2008; Detroit Cheetah Track Club, co-founder; Penn State Univ, track coach; McEachern High Sch, varsity asst, track coach; Cobb County Sch Dist, acad discipline specialist; Grand Canyon Univ, adj prof; US-ATF, coordr coaches educ, vpres admin, Athletics & Activ Alhambra HS, asst prin, currently; Women's Jr Develop, co-comnr, currently, sch dir, currently. **Orgs:** USA Track & Field. **Home Addr:** 149 Barrington Lane, Hiram, GA 30141, **Home Phone:** (770)364-3643. **Business Addr:** Assistant Principal, Phoenix Union High School District, 4502 N Cent Ave, Phoenix, AZ 85012, **Business Phone:** (602)764-6017.

## TSHOMBE, DAWN. See ROBINSON, DAWN SHERRESE.

## TUBBS, WINFRED O'NEAL

Football player. **Personal:** Born Sep 24, 1970, Fairfield, TX. **Educ:** Univ Tex, psychol. **Career:** Football player (retired); New Orleans Saints, right inside linebacker, 1994, middle linebacker, 1995-97; San Francisco 49ers, middle linebacker, 1998, linebacker, 1999-2000, left inside linebacker, 1999, right inside linebacker, 2000; TW Oil Field Serv, pres & founder, currently. **Honors/Awds:** Rookie of the Year, 1994; Pro Bowl, 1998; President's Award, Ford Motor Co, 2010. **Business Addr:** President, Founder, TW Oil Field Services, 10814 Crooked Creek Dr, Dallas, TX 75229, **Business Phone:** (972)880-0918.

## TUCKER, CHRISTOPHER

Comedian, actor. **Personal:** Born Aug 31, 1971, Atlanta, GA; son of Norris and Mary; children: Destin Christopher. **Career:** Actor, 1994-; Films: House Party 3, 1994; Friday, 1995; Panther, 1995; Dead Presidents, 1995; The Fifth Element, 1997; Money Talks, actor & exec producer, 1997; Jackie Brown, 1997; Rush Hour, 1998; Rush Hour 2, 2001; Rush Hour 3, 2007; Silver Linings Playbook, 2012. TV series: "Hangin' with Mr Cooper", 1992; "Def Comedy Jam", 1994; "The Roseanne Show", 1998, "Diary", 2001; "African American Lives", 2006; Comedy Cafe, owner, currently. **Orgs:** Founder, Chris Tucker Found. **Honors/Awds:** Blockbuster Entertainment Award, 1999; MTV Movie Award, 1999, 2008; Blimp Award, Kids' Choice Awards, 2002; Teen Choice Award, 2002. **Business Addr:** Actor, c/o Samantha Mast, 8687 Melrose Ave 7th Fl, Los Angeles, CA 90069, **Business Phone:** (310)854-8100.

## TUCKER, CLARENCE T.

Manager, teacher, chairperson. **Personal:** Born Feb 22, 1940, Elba, AL; son of Samuel T and Josephine; married Delores B; children: Reginald & Ryan. **Educ:** Ala A&M Univ, BS; Atlanta Univ, MS. **Career:** Chattanooga Pub Sch, teacher & dept chair, 1962-65, 1966-68; Clark Col, lab instr, 1968-69; Polaroid Corp, process eng to prod mgr, 1969-, small bus liaison officer, currently. **Orgs:** Exec bd chmn, NOBCCUE. **Honors/Awds:** Outstanding Teacher Award, Chatanooga Science Fair Group, 1966; Outstanding Service Award, Atlanta Univ, 1984; Meritorious Service Award, NOBCCUE, 1985. **Home Addr:** 8 Longmeadow Rd, Westborough, MA 01581-2406, **Home Phone:** (508)366-9374. **Business Addr:** Small Business Liaison Officer, Polaroid Corp, 300 Baker Ave Suite 330, Concord, MA 01742-2131, **Business Phone:** (781)386-2000.

## TUCKER, CYNTHIA ANNE

Journalist. **Personal:** Born Mar 13, 1955, Monroeville, AL; daughter of John Abney and Mary Louise Marshall. **Educ:** Auburn Univ, BA, 1976. **Career:** Atlanta Jour, reporter, 1976-80, ed writer, columnist, 1983-86; Philadelphia Inquirer, reporter, 1980-82; Atlanta Const, assoc ed page ed, 1986-91, ed page ed, 1992-, columnist, 2009-; Harvard Univ, Nieman fel, 1988-89. **Orgs:** Am Soc Newspaper Ed; bd dir, Int Media Women's Found; Am Socs Newspaper Ed; Nat Asn Black Journalists; Nat Asn Minority Media Execs; adv bd, Poynter Inst; African Am Planning Comn Inc; adv bd, Poynter Inst. **Honors/Awds:** Exceptional Merit Media Award, Nat Womens Polit Caucus, 1993; Pulitzer

Prize winner; Distinguished Writing Award for Commentary/Column Writing, Am Soc Newspaper Ed, 2000. **Special Achievements:** First black woman to edit the editorial page of a major daily newspaper, the Atlanta Constitution. **Home Addr:** 807 Dixie Ave, Atlanta, GA 30307-2409, **Home Phone:** (678)705-1319. **Business Addr:** Editorial Page Editor, The Atlanta Constitution, 75 Marietta St, Atlanta, GA 30303-2804, **Business Phone:** (404)526-5084.

### TUCKER, DR. DOROTHY M.
Psychologist, educator, executive director. **Personal:** Born Aug 22, 1942, Spartanburg, SC; daughter of James Anderson and Cleo Christine Fant. **Educ:** Bowling Green State Univ, BS, educ; Univ Toledo, MA, coun; Ohio State Univ, PhD, 1972; Calif Sch Prof Psychol, PhD, 1976. **Career:** Brentwood Pub Schs & Ford Found, demonstration teacher & curric writer, 1963-65; Dept Defense, Spangdahlem, Ger, educr, 1965-67; Wright Inst Los Angeles, dir clin teaching; Calif State Univ, Los Angeles, asst prof, 1968-69; Ohio State Univ, res assoc, 1969-71; Bur Drug Abuse, Columbus, Ohio, consult psychol, 1971; Fla Int Univ, asst & assoc prof, 1971-74; Charles Drew Med Sch, assoc prof, 1977-78; Cranston Senate Com, fld dir, 1980; Off Speaker, Calif Assembly, Willie Brown Jr, spec asst, 1981-84; Nat Training Labs Inst, dir; Crenshaw Consortium, Los Angeles, Calif, pres, 1984-; Saybrook Grad Sch & Res Ctr, San Francisco, Calif, consult fac, 1989-; Los Angeles Police Dept, Calif Comn Post, consult org psychol. **Orgs:** Western Psychol Asn; Am Psychol Asn; Asn Black Psychologists; S Calif Asn Black Psychologists; Asn Soc & Behvrl Scientists; chmn exec com Forum, 1979; commnr, CA Jud Nominees Evaluation Comn, 1979; commnr, Inglewood Housing Comn, 1980; pres, United Negro Col Fund So CA Adv Bd, 1980; gov, Calif State Bar Bd Gov, 1990-; pres, Los Angeles Bldg & Safety Comn, 1990-; past chair, Calif Bd Psychol; treas, Asn Black Psychologist, Southern Calif; bd gov, State Bar Calif; Nat Conf Bar Found; pres, Convenor Alliance AFA Psychol; vpres, Found State Bar Calif; judicial coun, Access Fairness, Calif; past chair, Calif Psychol Asn, Pub Interest Div, exec comt, pres-elect, 1998-99; chair-elect, AMR Psychol Asn, Urban Initiatives Comn, 1999; Black Womens Forum; One Hundred Black Women; Effective Influence Conf. **Honors/Awds:** First chair, Fac Senate, Fla Int Univ, 1972-74; First Chair, Fla State Univ Fac Senate, 1972-74; Pi Lambda Theta Educ Hon; Natl Women's Polit Caucus; Natl Orgn Women, 1975; Black's Women's Forum, 1977; Outstanding Woman, Calif Legislature, 1985; Women In Public Service Award, W side Women's Clinic, 1987; Helen Mehr Public Interest Award, Calif Psychol Asn, 1994; Silver Psy Award, 1995; Distinguished Alumni Award, Bowling Green State Univ, 1998; Mentor Award, Los Angeles Womens Found, 2001. **Business Addr:** Consulting Faculty, Saybrook Graduate School & Research Center, 747 Front St 3rd Fl, San Francisco, CA 94111-1920, **Business Phone:** (800)825-4480.

### TUCKER, GERALDINE COLEMAN
Journalist. **Personal:** Born Mar 23, 1952, Cincinnati, OH; daughter of Robert A (deceased) and Marian Annamae Taylor; married Michael Anthony; children: Christopher. **Educ:** Kenyon Col, Gambier, OH, AB, 1974; Wayne State Univ, Detroit, MI, 1979; George Mason Univ, Fairfax, VA, 1986. **Career:** Beacon J, Akron, OH, reporter, 1975-79; Detroit Free Press, Detroit, Mich, copy ed, 1979-82; USA Today, Arlington, Va, front page ed, spec sects ed, 1982-87, dep managing ed, currently; Gannett News Serv, Arlington, Va, managing ed/Midwest, 1987-. **Orgs:** Nat Asn of Black Journalists, 1976-; Wash Asn Black Journalists, 1982-. **Honors/Awds:** Fel, US Dept Educ/African Studies, 1981; Fel, Am Newspaper Publs Asn, 1987; Fel, Gannett Mgmt Seminar, 1989. **Home Addr:** 8613 James Creek Dr, Springfield, VA 22152-1518, **Home Phone:** (703)569-6471. **Business Addr:** Deputy Managing Editor, USA Today, 7950 Jones Br Dr, McLean, VA 22108, **Business Phone:** (703)854-3400.

### TUCKER, GERALDINE JENKINS
Lawyer. **Personal:** Born May 3, 1948, Newark, NJ; daughter of Richard Sr and Helen; children: Carmen Alicia. **Educ:** Fisk Univ, BA, Eng, 1970; Howard Univ, MS, stud personnel admin, 1973; Univ Tex, JD, 1986. **Career:** Howard Univ, Wash, DC, asst dir admis, 1970-73; Ford Found, Ford fel grad study, 1970; Calif Sch Prof Psychol, dean stud affairs, 1973-75; Hughes Aircraft Co La, sr personnel rep, 1975-77; ARA Food Servs La, training mgr 15 states, 1977-78; Tex Rehab Comn Austin, civil rights specialist, 1978-80; NuScope Cons, pres, 1980-85, consult, 1986-95; Lower Co River Authority, dir human resources, 1986-91; Pvt Pract, atty law, 1986-2008; Austin Community Col, Off Human Resources, vpres human resrouces, 1998-; Austin Am Statesman, Austin, TX, freelance writer. **Orgs:** Chair, Austin First Step Inc; Leadership Austin; Leadership Tex; secy, Austin Community Found; Top Ladies Distinction; Links Inc; Sinai Missionary Baptist Church; bd trustee, Fisk Univ, Nashville, 1970-74; columnist, Village Newspaper, Austin, 1970-; western bd adv, United Negro Col Fund, 1975-77; bd dir, Austin Women's Ctr, 1979-; Austin Area Urban League; Austin Nat Asn Advan Colored People; Austin C C; Austin C's Mus; pres, Howard Univ Alumni Asn, 1989; bd dir, Austin Area Urban League, 1990; Jack & Jill, 1989; founder, Black Mgr's Network, 1990; bd mem, Communities Schs. **Honors/Awds:** Alumni Leadership Award, Fisk Univ, 1970; YWCA Woman of Achievement, 2013; First Tees Integrity Award, 2014; Women of Distinction, Fisk Univ, 2015. **Special Achievements:** Author: Bedside Chat. **Home Addr:** 3302 Hyclimb Cir, Austin, TX 78723. **Business Addr:** Vice President, Austin Community College, 5930 Mid Fiskville Rd, Austin, TX 78752-4390, **Business Phone:** (512)223-7572.

**TUCKER, JAMES F. See Obituaries Section.**

### TUCKER, KAREN
Editor. **Personal:** Born Jul 18, 1952, Washington, DC; daughter of Willie Jr and Marie Roberson. **Educ:** Trinity Col, Hartford, BA, 1974; Univ Hartford, Grad Study Cert, bus admin, 1979, orgn behav, 1979; Antioch Sch Law, paralegal cert, 1983, MA, legal studies, 1984. **Career:** CT Gen, supvr admin, 1974-80; AT&T Long Lines, NJ, operations supvr, 1980-81; New York cost support, admin mgr, 1981-82; Pepper, Hamilton & Scheetz, legal ed, 1984-89; Steptoe & Johnson, legal ed & sr legal ed, partner, 1989-; Publications: Spec Task Force ABA Sect Int Law Pract, Report on the Proposed Rules of Procedure & Evidence, Int Tribunal Adjudicate War Crimes Comn, Yugoslavia, chief ed, 1995; articles: "Organizing Basics, ", Wash Living, 1985; "Be Your Own Best Legal Editor, ", The Docket, 1986; "Getting the Word Out", The Docket, 1988; "A Positive Life Step", Woman Engineer, spring 1992; Res & Writing, Practising Law Institute & Laurie Beth Zimet, Chapter 9; Basic Research & Writing for Legal Assistants; A Satellite Progr, 1994. **Orgs:** Affil mem & regist paralegal, Nat Fedn Paralegal Asn Inc, 1990-; Trinity Club Wash; vpres & bd mem, Nat Capital Area Paralegal Asn, 1991-93; Nat Capital Area Paralegal Asn, 1993-; facilitator, Citechecking & Legal Res Sem, Univ Md, Alumni Paralegal Asn, 1993; fac mem, Legal Res & Writing Paralegals, Practising Law Inst, Nat Brdcst Simulcast, 1994; founding bd mem, vpres, Pub Rels, Nat Black Am Paralegal Asn; exec comt, Nat Black Am Paralegal Asn, 1994-96; ed, NBAPA Rev, 1994-96; speaker & facilitator, Latham & Watkins, 1996-01. **Home Addr:** 9200 Edwards Way, Adelphi, MD 20783-3439, **Home Phone:** (301)608-0035. **Business Addr:** Senior Legal Editor, Steptoe & Johnson LLP, 1330 Connecticut Ave NW, Washington, DC 20036-1795, **Business Phone:** (202)429-3000.

### TUCKER, DR. LEOTA MARIE
Administrator. **Personal:** Born Aug 1, 1944, New Haven, CT; daughter of Curtis Saulsbury and Viola Kittrell Goodman; married Robert Clifton; children: Ronald. **Educ:** Southern Conn State Col, BA, 1968; Univ New Haven, MA, 1975; Union Grad Sch, PhD, psychol, 1977. **Career:** Dixwell Crisis Prevnt Serv, proj dir, 1973; Yale & Univ Conn Ment Health Ctr, ment health adminr, 1973-75, dir prevent & commun educ proj, 1975-78; City New Haven, dir welfare, 1978-80; Karonee Inc, Ctr Appl Behav Sci, pres, 1980-89; Tucker Assocs, New Haven, Conn, sr assoc, 1989; Katherine Brennan Sch, Family Resource Ctr Initiative, dir, currently. **Orgs:** Bd dir, United Way Greater New Haven, 1978-; bd dir, ARC New Haven Chap, 1979-; bd dir, St Raphaels Hosp, 1980; Theta Epsilon Omega Chap; New Haven Chap Girl Friends Inc. **Home Addr:** 280 Ray Rd, New Haven, CT 06515-2326, **Home Phone:** (203)389-2210. **Business Addr:** Project Director, Early Childhood learning Center-Head Star Program, 495 Blake St, New Haven, CT 06515, **Business Phone:** (203)946-5300.

### TUCKER, DR. M. BELINDA
Psychologist, educator. **Personal:** Born May 19, 1949, Washington, PA; daughter of Robert Benjamin and Margaret Louise Jones Chandler; married Russell L Stockard; children: Desmond Mosi & Daren Blake. **Educ:** Univ Chicago, AB, psychol, 1971; Univ Mich, MA, PhD, social psychol, 1975. **Career:** Univ Mich, Inst Social Res, study dir, 1975-81; Univ Calif Los Angeles, Afro-Am Studies, asst dir, 1978-89, psychiat & bio behav Sci Dept, asst res psychiat, 1983-, psychiat Dept, asst res psychiat, 1987, Afro-Am Studies, actg dir, 1989, prof psychiat & bio behav sci, 1990-, assoc prof psychiat, 1991, Family Res Consortium IV, dir, 2004-09, assoc dean grad div, 2007-11, Inst Am Cultures, vice provost, 2011-. **Home Addr:** 460 N Pk Springs Ct, Oak Park, CA 91377-3816, **Home Phone:** (818)991-0723. **Business Addr:** Vice Provost, Professor of Psychiatry & Behavioral Sciences, University of California Los Angeles, 1237 Murphy Hall, Los Angeles, CA 90095-1419, **Business Phone:** (310)206-3411.

### TUCKER, MICHAEL ANTHONY
Baseball player. **Personal:** Born Jun 25, 1971, South Boston, VA; married Azurre; children: Aspen Chardanay. **Educ:** Longwood Col, attended 1992. **Career:** Baseball player (retired); Wilmington Blue Rocks, 1993; Omaha Royals, 1994; Kans City Royals, outfielder, 1995-96, 2002-03; Atlanta Braves, 1997-98; Cincinnati Reds, 1999-2001; Chicago Cubs, 2001; San Francisco Giants, 2004-05; Philadelphia Phillies, 2005; New York Mets, 2006; Wash Nationals, 2006; Boston Red Sox, 2007; Southern Md Blue Crabs, currently; Newark Bears Alantic League, 2009-. **Business Addr:** Player, Southern Maryland Blue Crabs, 11765 St Linus Dr, Waldorf, MD 20602, **Business Phone:** (301)638-9788.

### TUCKER, MICHAEL KEVIN
Executive, lawyer. **Personal:** Born Sep 16, 1957, Albany, NY; son of Carroll B and Norma G Foulkes; married Judith C Henry. **Educ:** Cornell Univ, BS, 1979; Boston Univ Sch Law, JD, bus law, 1983. **Career:** Int Bus Mach, recruiting specialist, 1979-80; Csaplar & Bok, assoc, 1983-88; Top 100 Law Firms, assoc, 1983-92; Bingham, Dana & Gould, assoc, 1988-90; Ballard, Spahr, Andrews & Ingersoll, sr assoc, 1990; Gen Elec Capital Serv, Transp Int Pool & Modular Space, atty, 1992-2005; Tyco Int, vpres & TEPS div gen coun, 2005-07; Tucker Assocs, managing partner, 2007-10; Avis Budget Group Inc, exec vpres & gen coun, 2010-; Zipcar (UK) Ltd, exec vpres, gen coun & chief compliance, 2013-. **Orgs:** Alpha Phi Alpha Fraternity, 1976-; Am Bar Asn, 1983-; Philadelphia Bar Asn, 1990-; Boston Bar Asn. **Home Addr:** 501 N Hortter St B 7, Philadelphia, PA 19119. **Business Addr:** Executive Vice President, General Counsel, Avis Budget Group Inc, 6 Sylvan Way, Parsippany, NJ 07054.

### TUCKER, NORMA JEAN
Educator, association executive. **Personal:** Born Jan 28, 1932, Muskogee, OK; children: Kumigawa & Keith Aaron Vann. **Educ:** Langston Univ, OK, BS, 1953; Univ Okla, Med, 1966; Univ Calif, Berkeley; Calif State Univ. **Career:** Douglass High Sch, teacher, 1953-56; Oakland Tech High Sch, teacher, 1962-68; Merritt Col, Grove St, instr, 1968-72, Oakland, Calif, dean instr, 1975, actg pres, pres, 1982-88; N Peralta Col, coordr instr, 1972, actg dean instr, 1972, dean instr, 1973, dean col, 1974-75; Col Alameda, instr secretarial sci & bus, Bus & Transp Dept, prof. **Orgs:** Sr vpres, bd dirs, United WayBay Area; life mem, Alpha Kappa Alpha Sor; past pres, Alpha Nu Omega Chap Alpha Kappa Alpha Sor Inc; E Bay Area Club Bus & Prof Women; vpres, bd dirs, Am Red Cross, Bay Area Chap, 1994-95, 1996-98; chmn, Alameda County; Kappa Delta Pi; Coun Black Am Affairs; former mem, Christian Educ Bd Pk Blvd Pres Church; western areavice dir, Links Inc; life mem, Nat Asn Advan Colored People; Nat Hon Soc; Alpha Zeta Chap; fel Am Coun Educ, Wash, DC; Am Red Cross-Bay Area Chap; Rayfield Baptist Church, sunday sch secy. **Honors/Awds:** Award Alpha Kappa Alpha Sor; Ida L Jackson Award, Alpha Kappa Alpha Sor; Outstanding Women of the E Bay, Allen Temple Bapt Ch; Honour Outstanding Women in an Unusual Prof, St Paul AME Church; featured February, 1986; Ebony magazine Black Women College Presidents, 1986; Charter Day speakerfor alma mater Langston Univ Langston, OK; several other hon & achievements. **Home Addr:** 1516 Holman Rd, Oakland, CA 94610.

### TUCKER, ROBERT L.
Administrator, lawyer. **Personal:** Born Feb 14, 1929, Chattanooga, TN; married Shirley Cross; children: Terri E & Arnold. **Educ:** Tenn St Univ, BS, 1951; NW Univ Sch Law, JD, 1955. **Career:** Atty, pvt prac, 1955-68; Metro Inter-Ins Exchange, gen counr, 1963-65; McCoy Ming & Leighton Chicago, mem firm, 1963-65; NW Univ Sch Law, mem facil; US Dept Housing & Urban Develop, US asst reg adminr, 1968-71; McCarty Watson & Tucker, partner, 1971-73; Gen Couns, Metro Casualty Co Chicago, vpres, 1971-72; Tucker Watson Butler & Todd Attys Couns Law Chicago, partner, 1973-. **Orgs:** Gen couns & mem bd, People United Save Hum, 1971-; gen counr & trustee, MERIT Real Estate Invest Trust, 1972-; Am Bar Asn; Chicago Bar Asn; Cook Co Bar Asn; Comn Cand Chicago Bar Asn; Spec Com Civil Dis; Phi Alpha Delta; Spl couns St Ill Comn Human Rel, 1974-; Alpha Phi Alpha; Am Judicature Soc; PUSH; Chicago Urban League; Nat Asn Advan Colored People; bd dir, Ill Div Am Civil Liberties Union; Roger Baldwin Found; Am Civil Liberties Union; Nat Asn Comn Legal Coun. **Honors/Awds:** Richard E Westbrook Memorial Award & Plaque Outstanding Contribution to Legal Profession, 1968; Citation, Cook Co Bar Asn, 1969; Hall of Fame, Nat Bar Asn, 1997. **Home Addr:** 6901 S Oglesby Ave Apt 11D, Chicago, IL 60649-1805, **Home Phone:** (773)363-4691.

### TUCKER, DR. SAMUEL JOSEPH
Psychologist. **Personal:** Born Nov 5, 1930, Birmingham, AL; son of Daniel and Lucille McGhee; married Arlene Kelly; children: Samuel Jr, Sabrina, Sharon & Sterling. **Educ:** Morehouse Col, Atlanta, BS, 1952; Columbia Univ NYC, MA, 1956; Atlanta Univ, PhD, 1969. **Career:** Psychologist (retired); Morehouse Col, dean studs, 1963-71; Univ Fla, Gainesville, asst prof, 1971-73; Harvard Univ, post doctoral, 1973; Edward Waters Col, Jacksonville, pres, 1973-76; Ala State Univ, Montgomery, dean, prof, 1976-78; Langston Univ, Okla, pres, 1978; Atlanta Human Develop Ctr, psychologist, pres, 1978. **Orgs:** Am Psychol Asn, 1958-; Consult Stanford Res Inst, Menlo Pk, CA, 1965-70; consult, Princeton Univ, 1965-70; consult, Univ Mich, Ann Arbor, 1965-70; chap pres, AlphaPhi Alpha Frat Inc, 1971-73; Jacksonville Area Planning Bd, 1973-76; bd gov, Jacksonville Area Chamber Com, 1973-76; Nat Acad Neuropsychologists, 1988-. **Honors/Awds:** Travel Grant Ford Found, 1967; Res Grant Danforth Found, 1968; Res Grant, Univ Fla, 1972. **Special Achievements:** Publications: 'The Baby Boomers Survival Handbook For The 21st Century: Essential Strategies for Mental, Physical, Financial, Social, and Spiritual Success', 1999; 40 Articles on mental health issues. **Home Addr:** 735 Peyton Rd SW, Atlanta, GA 30311-2306, **Home Phone:** (404)755-4244.

### TUCKER, SHERYL HILLIARD
Editor, journalist. **Personal:** Born Jul 13, 1956, Passaic, NJ; daughter of Arthur and Audrey; married Roger C III; children: Ara & Alexis. **Educ:** Cornell Univ, BA, psychol, 1978; Columbia Univ, Grad Sch Jour, MS, jour prog, 1982; NY Univ, cert, 2013. **Career:** CBS Spec Interest Publ, ed, 1978-81; Tucker Hilliard Mkt Commun, exec vpres, 1987-91; Black Enterprise Mag, personal finance assoc ed, managing ed, ed-in-chief, 1982-95, vpres, 1991-95; Your Co Mag, ed, 1995-98; Money Mag, asst managing ed, exec ed, 1995-2006; Time Inc, exec ed, 2006-10; Essence Mag, actg ed chief, 2010-11; Time Warner, spec proj mgr, 2011-13; Planned Parenthood, Essence Commun, strategic planning consult, exec coaching, conf develop, 2010-; AFS Intercultural Progs Inc, dir mkt & commun, 2014-; Hilliard Tucker Mkt Commun. Editor: Prime Time: African American Women's Guide to Midlife Health and Wellness; The New Money Book of Personal Finance. Co-author: Tomorrow Begins Today: African-American Women as We Age. **Orgs:** Bd mem, Am Soc Mag Ed, 1993-95; Nat Asn Black Journalist, 1982-, chair, Bus Writers Task Force, 1994; March Dimes Nat Commun Coun, 1985-; Pub Serv Elec & Gas Co, Tech Adv, 1990-92; Press Coun Carnell Women, 1991-; vice chair, Carnell Mag, bd dir, 1992-99; bd mem, St James Prep Sch, 1992-; bd trustee, Cornell Univ, vice chair, founding mem; chairwomen, Cornell MOSAIC; chairwomen, Gaston & Porter Health Improv Ctr; chair, Time Warner Women's Network; bd mem, Am Soc Mag Ed; adv bd mem, New York Univ Ctr Publ; nat adv bd mem, Poynter Inst; Time Warner Found. **Home Addr:** 1 Ashley Rd, West Orange, NJ 07052, **Home Phone:** (201)731-5144. **Business Addr:** Director of Marketing & Communications, AFS Intercultural Programs Inc, 71 W 23rd St 6th Fl, New York, NY 10010-4102, **Business Phone:** (212)807-8686.

### TUCKER, DR. WALTER RAYFORD, III
Government official, lawyer, clergy. **Personal:** Born May 28, 1957, Compton, CA; son of Walter R Jr (deceased) and Martha; married Robin Marie; children: Walter Rayford IV & Autumn Monet. **Educ:** Princeton Univ, attended; Univ Southern Calif, BA, polit sci, 1976; Georgetown Univ Sch Law, JD, 1981. **Career:** Los Angeles Co, dep dist atty, 1984-86; State Bar Calif, 1984; City Compton, mayor, 1991-93; House of Representatives, dem, 1992; US Congressman, 37th Cong Dist, Calif, dem, 1993-95; Heart Church Chicago, pastor, currently; Crenshaw Christian Ctr, helps ministry mgr; Fel Ministry, area dir; Truth & Love Christian Church, pastor. **Orgs:** Nat Asn Advan Colored People; Kiwanis Club Compton; Los Angeles Co Bar Asn; S Cent Bar Asn; Langston Bar Asn; Pub Works & Transp Comt; House Small Bus Comt. **Business Addr:** Pastor, The Heart Church Chicago, 3742 Forest Ave, Brookfield, IL 60513, **Business Phone:** (708)387-1487.

### TUCKER, DR. WILBUR CAREY
Gynecologist, obstetrician, physician. **Personal:** Born Apr 3, 1943, Philadelphia, PA; son of Wilbur and Rose; married Faye; children: Maria & Caren. **Educ:** Temple Univ, AB, 1965, Sch Med, MD, 1972; Howard Univ, MS, 1968; Am Bd Obstet & Gynec, dipl, 1977. **Career:** Nat Aeronaut & Space Admin, biochem, 1965-68; Off Naval Res, physiol, 1968; Temple Univ Hosp, resident Obstet & Gynec, 1972-75, clin instr, 1975-80; Univ Penn, clin assoc prof, 1975-; Presby Hosp, Dept Obstet & Gynec, actg chmn, 1990-91; pvt pract, physician, currently. **Orgs:** Phi Rho Sigma Med Frat; Omega Psi Phi Fraternity, 1966; Sigma Pi Phio Fraternity, 1991-; fel Am Col Obstet & Gynec. **Home Addr:** 46 Eagle Rd, Phoenixville, PA 19460-1065, **Home**

**Phone:** (239)390-0310. **Business Addr:** Physician, Private Practice, 3819 Chestnut St Suite 210, Philadelphia, PA 19104, **Business Phone:** (215)387-8776.

## TUCKER-ALLEN, DR. SALLIE

Educator, publisher, founder (originator). **Educ:** Hampton Univ, BS, nursing; Hunter Col, MS; Benedictine Col, MBA; PhD, admin, policy studies. **Career:** Univ Ill, instr & lectr; Col DuPage, instr & lectr; Lewis Univ, asst prof; Valparaiso Univ, asst prof; Bradley Univ, grad coordr; Univ Wis-Green Bay, dept chair; Del State Col, dept chair; Methodist Med Ctr, Sch Nursing, dir; Chicago State Univ, Col Health Sci, interim dean, asst dean & prof; Tucker Publ, founder, 1987-. **Orgs:** Asn Black Nursing Fac (ABNF), founder, 1987-; US Dept Health & Human Serv, Div Nursing, Minority Nurse Leadership Coun, former mem; Nat League Nursing, Task Force Cult, Ethnic & Racial Diversity, past chair; Am Acad Nursing, fel; Charles R Drew Univ Med & Sci, Mervyn M Dymally Sch Nursing, cult diversity endowed chair. **Honors/Awds:** Sigma Theta Tau International Nursing Honor Society, Inductee; Hampton University Hall of Fame, Inductee; Recipient Of Numerous Awards. **Special Achievements:** Author of "Directory of Black Nursing Faculty" (1990, 1994, 1996); publisher of "The ABNF Journal," "The Journal of Cultural Diversity: An Interdisciplinary Journal," and "The Journal of Theory Construction and Testing"; speaker at numerous national and international forums and symposiums.

## TUCKETT, LEROY E.

Architect. **Personal:** Born May 21, 1932, New York, NY; son of Issac and Helen; children: Amy, Lori, Lee & Lise. **Educ:** Columbia Col, attended 1952; Pratt Inst, BArch, 1960. **Career:** LaPierre Litchfield & Partners, 1961-64; Charles Luckman & Assoc, proj architect, 1964-67; Petroff & Jones Architects, assoc partner, 1967-69; LE Tuckett Architect PC, owner, prin, 1969-; State Univ NY, archit design instr, 1983-86; LE Cadd Corp, pres, 1986-. **Orgs:** Am Inst Architects, 1965-; charter mem, Nat Orgn Minority Architects, 1972-; vpres, NY Coalition Black Architects, 1973-; bd higher educ, rev comt, City Univ New York, 1973-78; panelist, Am Arbit Asn, 1978-; archit judge, mentor prog, ACTSO, 1992; NCP; Durham Comn Affairs Black People; Durham Chamber Com; chair, Durham Bus & Prof Chain, Econ Develop Comt. **Honors/Awds:** Charter Member Recognition, Nat Orgn Minority Architects, 1972; Founding Mem honor, NY Coalition Black Architects, 1992; Community Service recognition, First Calvary Baptist Church, 1998. **Business Addr:** Owner, Principal, L E Tuckett Architect, 2107 Stuart Dr, Durham, NC 27707-2263, **Business Phone:** (919)419-1715.

## TUCKSON, REED V.

Vice president (organization), school administrator. **Educ:** Georgetown Univ Sch Med; Howard Univ; Wharton Sch Bus, health care admin & policy. **Career:** DC, comnr pub health, 1986-90; Hosp Univ Pa, intern, resident, fel, Gen Internal Med; Prog March Dimes Birth Defects Found, sr vpres, 1990-91; Charles R Drew Univ Med & Sci, pres, 1991-97; United Health Group, sr vpres, exec vpres & chief med affairs, 2006-; Tuckson Health Connections, managing dir, pres. **Orgs:** Sr vpres, prof stand, Am Med Asn; Nat Patient Safety Found; Accreditation Coun Grad Med Educ; Accreditation Coun Continuing Med Educ; Inst Med Nat Acad Sci; chairperson, Qual Chasm Summit Comt; Bd's Audit & Compliance Comt; Compensation Comt & Corp Governance & Nominating Comt; bd dir, Cell Therapeut, Am Telemedicine Asn, Howard Univ, Alliance Health Reform, Arnold P. Gold Found Humanism Med; adv comt, Nat Insts Health; adv comt, Health reform, infant mortality, c's health, violence & radiation testing; chair, Secy Health & Human Serv Adv Comt Genetics, Health & Socs, Comnr, Comn Health Info Technol, Performance Measurement Workgroup, Ambulatory Care Qual Alliance, Qual Workgroup, Am Health Info Community, currently. **Business Addr:** Executive Vice President, Chief of Medical Affairs, UnitedHealth Group, PO Box 1459, Minneapolis, MN 55440-1459, **Business Phone:** (952)992-5450.

## TUFFIN, ESQ. PAUL JONATHAN

Magistrate. **Personal:** Born Sep 9, 1927, Charleston, WV; son of Gerald D and Nellie Carter; married Virginia L Hamilton; children: Paula A & J Brian. **Educ:** Bluefield State Col, BS, 1951; Cleveland Marshall Law Sch, LLB, 1956, JD, 1968. **Career:** Magistrate (retired); US Post Off, clerk, 1952-55; Cleveland Bd Educ, sub teacher, 1952-54; IRS, revenue officer, 1955-59; US Veterans Admin, adjudicator sect ch, 1959-84; Cleveland Press, lawyer & pres, 1964; Cleveland Munic Ct, referee, 1984-95, magistrate, 1990-95. **Orgs:** Asst supt, Sunday sch & atty trustee bd St John AME Ch, 1957-; nat parliamentarian Bluefield State Col Nat Alumni Bd, 1986-87; Pi Omega Pi; Nat Asn Advan Colored People, Kappa Alpha Psi. **Honors/Awds:** Meritorious & Conspicuous Service Military Order of the Purple Heart, 1984; Citation, Appreciation The Am Legion, 1984; Outstanding Service Award, Disabled Am Veterans, 1984; Disting Service Award, VFW Cleveland, 1984. **Home Addr:** 3637 Sutherland Rd, Shaker Heights, OH 44122-5134, **Home Phone:** (216)664-4760.

## TUFON, CHRIS

Public utility executive, educator. **Personal:** Born Sep 18, 1959; son of Elias and Scolastica Ngong; married Bernadette Ahlijah. **Educ:** Brigham Young Univ, Provo, UT, BS, mech engineering, 1984, MS, chem, 1986; Calif State Univ, Fresno, CA, MS, 1988. **Career:** Calif State Univ, Fresno, CA, lectr, 1988-89; Pac Gas & Elec Co, Hayward, CA, mkt assoc, Corp Opers Regulatory Strategy, prin, 1989-, tariff specialist, sr tariff analyst, currently. **Honors/Awds:** Student of the Year, Brigham Young Univ, 1985. **Home Addr:** 5813 Dresslar Cir, Livermore, CA 94550-7195, **Home Phone:** (925)454-1189. **Business Addr:** Senior Tariff Analyst, Pacific Gas & Electric Co, Rm 2541 123 Mission St, San Francisco, CA 94105, **Business Phone:** (415)973-4212.

## TUGGLE, DORIE C.

Manager. **Personal:** Born Mar 31, 1944, Detroit, MI; daughter of Frank (deceased) and Pearl (deceased). **Educ:** Detroit Inst Com, AS, 1963; Univ Mich, attended 1965; Pa State Univ, attended 1978; Univ Calif, Los Angeles, exec mgt, 1980; Emory Univ, attended. **Career:** IBM Corp, mkt mgr, 1977-79, equal opportunity prog mgr, 1979-80, regional personnel mgr, 1980-82, mgt develop mgr, 1982-85, employee rels mgr, 1985-87, div prog mgr, 1987-88; Lockheed Martin Aeronaut Systs, equal opportunity mgr, 1989-2000, Diversity & Equal Employ Opportunity, sr mgr; independent mgt consult. **Orgs:** Vpres, bd, Atlanta Indust Liaison Group, 1989-; bd vice chair, secy, S Eastern Consortium Minorities Eng, 1989-; Alanta Merit Employ Asn, chp, 1990-; adv bd, Cobb County Urban League, 1991-; Girls Inc, com of 100, 1992-; Nat Asn Advan Colored People, life mem; Tuskegee Airmen, Alanta chap, com chp, 1992-; pres's coun, Kennesaw State Col, 1992-; Ga State Rehab Coun; vice chairperson, Civil Serv Bd Cobb County. **Honors/Awds:** Hearts for Youth Award, City of Atlanta, 1991; AFA Woman Achievement Award, Dollars & Sense Magazine, 1992; US Dept of Labor, Affirmative Action Achievements, 1990; Gift of Time Volunteer, Cobb County Girls Inc, 1992; MNY Recruiter Newspaper Positive Image Award, Pee Dee Newspaper Group, 1992. **Special Achievements:** Guest columnist, MIC Chronicle, Detroit News, 1980, 1982; Visiting lecturer, human resources mgt, labor relations, general mgt, 1980-; Elected, Union Baptist Church BRD of Trustees, 1986; Consultant, trainer, human resources; Speaker, motivational techniques. **Home Addr:** 2693 Twigg Cir, Marietta, GA 30067, **Home Phone:** (404)850-9842.

## TUGGLE, JESSICA LLOYD, JR.

Executive, football player. **Personal:** Born Apr 4, 1965, Griffin, GA; son of Jesse Sr and Ada; married Dujuan; children: Justin & Jessica. **Educ:** Valdosta State Univ. **Career:** Football player (retired), executive; Atlanta Falcons, linebacker, 1987, 1999-2000, right inside linebacker, 1988-89, 1991-92, left inside linebacker, 1990, mid linebacker, 1993-2000; Real Estate Bus, currently; Fatherhood Campaign, spokesperson. **Orgs:** Bd dir, Atlanta Falcons Youth Found. **Honors/Awds:** GSC Defensive Player of the Year, 1986; Pro Bowl, 1992, 1994-95, 1997-98; Named to Sports Illustrated's All-Pro team in 1991, 1994, 1998; Awarded NFC Defensive Player, Month December, 1991; Man of the Year, Atlanta Falcons, 1993; Peach of an Athlete Award, 1996; Jersey retired, Georgia Dome in Atlanta, 2003; College Football Hall of Fame, 2007; Ring of Honor, Atlanta Falcons. **Special Achievements:** Most career tackles in Falcons' hist; at 5, NFL record for most touch downs by recovery of opponents' fumbles.

## TUGGLE, REV. REGINALD

Vice president (organization), publishing executive, clergy. **Personal:** Born Apr 9, 1947, Denver, CO; son of Mertis Jean Marie Hawkins and Otis; married Evette Beckett; children: Karleenam, Regine Marie & Regine Perry; married Marie R Peoples. **Educ:** Cent Phillippine Univ, attended 1968; Bishop Col, BA, philos & psychol, 1969; Univ Ghana, cert econs, 1971; Union Theol Sem, Mdiv, 1972; Yale Univ, master, corp ethics, 1975; Commonwealth Univ, hon DD, 1985. **Career:** Memorial Presbyterian Church, pastor, 1973-; Urban League Long Island NY, exec dir, 1975-79, chief exec officer; Town Hempstead, from exec asst to presiding supvr, 1979-81; Newsday Newspaper, community rels dir; Nassau Community Col, from exec asst to pres, dir col & community rels, currently, vpres mkt & commun, currently. **Orgs:** Vice chmn, Community Develop Corp; bd mem, Long Island United Way; trustee, Dowling Col; chmn, Black Leadership Comn AIDS Nassau County; chmn, Nassau County Health Systs Agency, 1979; chmn, Nassau County Dept Social Servs, 1980-81; vpres, Roosevelt Youth Bd 1983-; pres, Memorial Econ Develop Corp; moderator, Long Island, NY Presbytery; keynote speaker, N Atlantic Treaty Orgn; guest speaker, Am Press Inst; bd dir, Justice Initiatives, currently. **Home Addr:** 2 Danas Hwy, Glen Cove, NY 11542-1220, **Home Phone:** (516)671-6377. **Business Addr:** Director, Vice President, Nassau Community College, 1 Education Dr, Garden City, NY 11530-6793, **Business Phone:** (516)572-7501.

## TUKUFU, DR. DARRYL S.

Association executive, educator. **Personal:** Born Jul 27, 1949, Cleveland, OH; married Myra C; children: Ricky & Khari Ture. **Educ:** Youngstown State Univ, AB, social studies, 1976; Univ Akron, MA, 1977, PhD, sociol, 1984; Jacksonville Theol Sem, DMin, 2006. **Career:** Youngstown Urban League, dep dir, 1971-75; Youngstown Hometown Plan, actg dir & equal employ opportunity officer, 1975-76; Univ Akron, grad res asst, 1976-77; City Akron, equal employ opportunity officer & labor stand enforcement officer, 1977-79; Akron-Summit Community Action Agency, mgr, 1979-80; Fair Housing Contact Serv, exec, 1980-82; Univ Akron, grad teaching asst, 1982-84; Kent State Univ, vis asst prof, 1984-85; Vol & Emp Proj, proj dir, 1985; Northeastern Univ, asst prof, 1985-86; Univ Memphis, asst prof sociol, 1986-90; LeMoyne-Owen Col, asst prof, 1990; Urban League Portland, pres & chief exec officer, 1990-93; Pub Servs Inst, exec dir; Corain Co Community Col, Pub Servs Div, div dir, 1993-96; Tukufu Group, pres, 1999-; Urban League Mid Tenn, pres & chief exec officer, 2001-03; Memphis Urban League, pres & chief exec officer, 2003-06; Crichton Col, Dept Lib Arts & Humanities, assoc prof, vpres acad affairs, 2006-09, vpres strategic rels, external affairs & chief diversity officer, 2009-13; Victory Univ, exec dir pre-col progs & corp rels, assoc prof, 2013-14; Belhaven Univ, adj fac, 2014; Memphis Ctr Urban Theol Studies, adj fac, 2014; Cambridge Col, adj fac, 2014; Bethel Univ, asst prof sociol, 2014-. **Orgs:** Comnr, Port Portland, 1991-93; exec comt mem, Leaders Roundtable, 1991-93; fel Ore Chap, Am Leadership Forum, 1991-; Minority Affairs Rev Bd, NIKE Inc, 1991-93; Emanuel Med Ctr Found Bd, 1991-93; Northeast Econ Develop Alliance Bd, 1991-93; pres & exec dir, Greater Cleveland Roundtable, 1996-99; life mem, Nat Asn Advan Colored People; life mem, Kappa Alpha Psi Fraternity; Nat Speakers Asn; ordained minister, Miss Blvd Christian Church, 2005-; bd mem, Memphis Challenge; bd mem, Nat Civil Rights Mus; bd mem, Am Leadership Forum, Ore Chap; bd mem, Leadership Memphis; bd mem, Cleveland Leadership Ctr. **Home Addr:** 341 Wallingford Glen, Richmond Heights, OH 44143, **Home Phone:** (216)731-8451. **Business Addr:** Assistant Professor of Sociology, Bethel University, Campbell Hall 325 Cherry Ave 2nd Fl Rm 209D, McKenzie, TN 38201, **Business Phone:** (731)352-4226.

## TUNIE, TAMARA RENEE (TAMARA TUNIE BOUQUETT)

Actor, television director. **Personal:** Born Mar 14, 1959, McKeesport, PA; daughter of James W and Evelyn Hawkins; married Gregory Bouquett; married Gregory Generet. **Educ:** Carnegie Mellon Univ, BFA, 1981. **Career:** Films: Sweet Lorraine, 1987; Wall Street, 1987; Bloodhounds of Broadway, 1989; Rising Sun, 1993; City Hall, 1996; The Money Shot, 1996; Spirit Lost, 1996; Quentin Carr, 1996; Rescuing Desire, 1996; Eve's Bayou, 1997; The Peacemaker, 1997; The Devil's Advocate, 1997; Snake Eyes, 1998; The Caveman's Valentine, 2001; Broadway: Lena Horne; Oh Kay; Sweet Lorraine; Dreamgirls, 2001; AfterLife, 2007; See You in September, exec producer & dir, 2010; Missed Connections, 2012; Flight, 2012; Fall to Rise, 2014. TV series: "Spenser: For Hire", 1986; "As the World Turns", 1987-2009; "Tribeca", 1993; " Up On the Roof", 1994-97; "Good Time Charlie'; "New York Undercover", 1995-98; "Sea Quest DSV", 1995; "Bad Girls", 1995; "Dead Beat", 1996; "Caulkmanship", 1996; "Rebound: The Legend of Earl 'The Goat' Manigault", 1996; "Swift Justice". 1996; "Feds", 1997; "Chicago Hope", 1997; "Prince Street", 1997; "Taillight's Last Gleaming, ", 1997; "Missing Pieces", 1997; "Leggo My Ego, "1997; "I Love Lucy", 1997; "Sign o' the Times", 1998; "Sex & the City", 1999; "Law & Order: Special Victims Unit", 2000-14; "24", 2002; "Law & Order: Trial by Jury", 2005; "Days of Our Lives:, 2011; "Captain Blackout", 2013; "The Good Wife", 2013; "Golden Boy", 2013; "The Red Road", 2014; "Alpha House", 2014; "The Science cool", dir, currently. Stage: "Loose Knit", 1993; "Troilus and Cressida", 1995; "Sheba", 1996; "Antony and Cleopatra", 2000; "Cat on a Hot Tin Roof"; "Lena Horne, Oh, Kay". **Honors/Awds:** Antoinette Perry Award, co-producer, 2007. **Special Achievements:** She Sang "We Should Be Together For Christmas" for the A Soap Opera Christmas album. **Home Addr:** 457 W 148th St, New York, NY 10031, **Home Phone:** (212)283-5754. **Business Addr:** Actress, c/o William Morris Agency, 151 El Camino Dr, Beverly Hills, CA 90212, **Business Phone:** (310)859-4000.

## TUNLEY, NAOMI LOUISE

Nurse. **Personal:** Born Jan 10, 1936, Henryetta, OK; daughter of Alexander (deceased) and Ludia B Franklin (deceased). **Educ:** Dillard Univ, BS, nurs educ, 1958; Univ Iowa, 1967; Univ Mo, KC, MA, sociol, 1974. **Career:** Nurse (retired); Va Hosp, staff nurse serv Ed; Okla City Va Hosp, assoc cheif nurs serv 1958-65; Iowa Luth Hosp, Des Moines, med & Surg instr, 1965-66; Mercy Hosp Iowa City, IA, emerg rm chrg nurs, 1966; Va Hosp, KC, assoc cheif nurs serv, charge Nurs, psychiatric unit, staff nurs, ins instr 1967-77, head nurs; patient care surgical coordr, 1977; Va Medical Ctr, Kansas City, Mo, nurse mgr, 1977-94. **Orgs:** Trustee, Nat Coun Alcoholism & Drug Abuse, 1985; Nat Honor Soc Nurse; Am Red Cross; Am Sociol Asn; Big Sisters Org Am; Iowa Nurse Asn Instr Home Nurse; Am Red Cross; March Dimes; Muscular Dystrophy Asn; Mo Teacher Religious Ed, Faith Mission Chap. **Honors/Awds:** KC, Mo Nat Honor Soc, 1953-54; State Honor Soc, 1953-54; Scholar, EK Gaylor Philanthropist. **Special Achievements:** First Black to hold position as Associate Chief of Nurse Service, Oklahoma City First Black to hold position as Medical-surgical Instr, Des Moines. **Home Addr:** 3120 Poplar Ave, Kansas City, MO 64128, **Home Phone:** (816)861-6545.

## TUNSIL, NECOLE MONIQUE (NIQUE TUNSIL)

Basketball coach, basketball player. **Personal:** Born Aug 22, 1970, New York, NY; daughter of Chester and Estella. **Educ:** Univ Iowa, BCS, jour & mass commun. **Career:** Basketball player (retired), basketball coach; Long Beach Stingrays, forward, 1997; Lakewood High Sch, coach & reading teacher, currently. **Home Addr:** 1174 54TH AVE S, St Petersburg, FL 33705. **Business Addr:** Coach, Reading Teacher, Lakewood High School, 1400 54th Ave S, St. Petersburg, FL 33705, **Business Phone:** (727)893-2955.

## TUNSTALL, DR. JUNE REBECCA

Educator, physician, association executive. **Personal:** Born Jun 20, 1947, Baltimore, MD. **Educ:** Bennett Col, BS, 1969; Meharry Col Sch Med, MD, 1974. **Career:** Worcester City Hosp, intern, 1974-77; Univ MA, resident family med, 1975-77, fam physician & educ coordr fam pract dept, 1977; Surry County HURA Proj, staff physician, 1978; Surry Co Fam Health Group Inc VA, staff physician, med dir, 1979-80, med exmr; John Randolph Hosp Hopewell VA, staff physician, 1979-; Hopewell Med Group, group pract; Commonwealth Univ Med Col, VA Dept Fam Pract, Richmond, instr, 1979-80; Columbia John Randolph Med Ctr, assoc prof; family pract, currently. **Orgs:** Chair person, bd dir, Surry Co Fam Health Group Inc, 1979-80; pres, Old Dom Med Soc; vpres, Surry Co Unit Am Heart Asn, 1979-80; pres, Surry Co Unit Am Heart Asn, 1980-81; VA Acad Family Physicians; Med Soc Southside VA; bd dir, Southern Chirstian Leadership Conf; Am Acad Family Physcians; MA Acad Family Physicians; New Eng Med Soc Bd; dir, Family Planning Serv Gr Worcester; bd dir, United Way Cent MA; bd dir & chmn, VHQC, 2000-; NMA. **Home Addr:** PO Box 42, Spring Grove, VA 23881. **Business Addr:** Hopewell Medical Group, 401 Hopewell St, Hopewell, VA 23860, **Business Phone:** (804)458-6396.

## TUNSTALL, RICHARD CLAYTON

Executive, manager. **Personal:** Born May 6, 1953, Warrenton, NC; son of Melvin D and Edna S; married Phyllis Fogg; children: Ashlyn Nikole & Richard Jr. **Educ:** NC State Univ, BS, indust engineering, 1975. **Career:** Corning Int, engineering, prod planning, prod mgt, 1973-87; Konica Mfg USA, prod control mgr, 1988-92, sr mgr planning & logistics, 1992; Konica Minolta Mfg USA Inc, vpres planning & logistics, 1988-2007; ZINK Imaging Inc, sr mgr planning & logistics, vpres planning & logistics, 2007-10; Bonset Am Corp, plant mgr, 2010-. **Orgs:** Am Prod & Inventory Control Soc, 1992-; trustee, Mt Zion Baptist Church Inc, 1992-; NC World Trade Orgn, 1994-; bd mem, Greensboro Educ & Develop Coun, 1996-; Bennett Col Bus Adv Coun, 1999-. **Home Addr:** 6104 Westwind Dr, Greensboro, NC 27410-4908, **Home Phone:** (336)299-6233. **Business Addr:** Plant Manager, Bonset America Corporation, 6107 Corp Pk Dr, Browns Summit, NC 27214, **Business Phone:** (336)375-0234.

## TUNSTEL, DR. EDWARD, JR.

Astronaut. **Personal:** Born Harlem, NY; son of Edward Sr and Agnes. **Educ:** Howard Univ, Wash, DC, BS, mech eng, 1986, ME, mech eng, 1989; Univ Nmex, PhD, elec & comput eng, 1996. **Career:** Nat

Aeronaut & Space Admin, Robotic Intelligence Group, 1989; Nanorover Technol Task, cognizant engr, 1998-2000, MER Surface Mission Phase Team, Autonomous Navig, flight systs engr, 2001-03; FIDO Rover, lead syst engr, 2000-02, Univ Robotics Software Study, task mgr, 2002-03, Task Field Integrated Design & Opers, lead systs engr, 2003, Mobility & Robotic Arm Subsyst: MER Spacecraft & Rover Eng Team, surface ops lead, 2003-, Distrib Spectrometer Mobility & Surv, task mgr, 2004-, group leader & sr robotics engr, currently. **Orgs:** Inst Elec & Electronics Engrs; Asn Advan Artificial Intelligence; Sigma Xi Sci Res Soc; NY Acad Sci; Am Soc Mech Engrs. **Honors/Awds:** NASA Group Achievement Award, Robotic Intelligence Team, 1991; JPL Minority fel, 1992; NASA Group Achievement Award, TOPEX S/C GDS Sci Data S/S, 1993; NASA/US Dept of Interior WT Pecora Group Award, TOPEX/Poseidon, 1998; JPL Notable Org Value Added Award, Improv & Innovation, 2001; NASA Group Achievement Award, Safe Rover Navigation Team, 2002; NASA Space Act Award, Cognitive Sensor Technol, 2003; NASA Group Achievement Award, MER Flt Syst Eng Team, 2004; NASA Group Achievement Award, MER Avionics Team, 2004; NASA Group Achievement Award, MER Project Opers Team, 2004; JPL SPOT Award, NASA SBIR Subtopic Mgt, 2005; NASA Group Achievement Award, MER 1st/2nd Ext Mission Teams, 2005. **Special Achievements:** Authored over 75 journal, book chapter & conference publications. **Business Addr:** Senior Robotics Engineer, NASA Jet Propulsion Laboratory, 4800 Oak Grove Dr, Pasadena, CA 91109, **Business Phone:** (818)393-2666.

### TUPPER, LEON E.

Automotive executive, founder (originator). **Career:** Southfield, Mich, sales & admin offices; Boyne City, Mich, prod facil; N Am automotive mfrs, dir sales & mkt; Gilreath Mfg Inc, pres, owner & chief exec officer, 1991-2004; Arete Indust, chief exec officer, 2000-, founder & chmn bd dir, 2006-. **Orgs:** Bd dir, Mich Roundtable; bd mem, InterFaith Leadership Coun; bd mem, HighScope Educ Res Found; Trustee, Cleary Univ, 2006-. **Home Phone:** (248)240-9016. **Business Addr:** Chairman, Founder, Arete Industries Inc, 24400 Northwestern Hwy Suite 204, Southfield, MI 48075-2413, **Business Phone:** (248)352-7205.

### TUREAUD, LAWRENCE

Actor, social worker, wrestler. **Personal:** Born May 21, 1952, Chicago, IL; son of Nathaniel Tureaud Sr; married Phillys Clark; children: Lesa; children: Erika & T Jr. **Educ:** Prairie View A&M Univ, attended 1971. **Career:** Gym teacher; bouncer; wrestler; actor, currently; Illinois Army National Guard, 1975; Bodyguard Muhammed Ali, Leon Spinks, Donna Summer, Diana Ross, Rev Jesse Jackson, Michael Jackson; Films: Rocky III, 1982; Young Doctors in Love, 1982; The A Team, 1983-97; Mister T, animated, 1983; DC Cab, 1983; Straight Line, 1989; Freaked, 1993; The Magic of the Golden Bear: Goldy III, 1994; Spy Hard, 1996; Inspector Gadget, 1999; Not Another Teen Movie, 2001; Judgment, 2001; Undercover Brother, 2002; Cloudy with a Chance of Meatballs, 2009; TV series: "The A-Team", 1983-87; "Different Strokes", 1983; "The Toughest Man in the World", 1984; "T. & T.", 1988-90; "Eek the Cat", animated, 1988-90; "Eek! the Cat", 1992; "Blossom", 1994; "Martin", 1996; "Suddenly Susan", 1996; "Howard Stern", 1996-2002; "Sabrina the Animated Series", 1999; "Malcolm & Eddie", 1999; "Pecola", 2001-03; "WWF Raw Is War", 2001; "Praise the Lord", 2002-04; "Teamo Supremo", 2002; "The Simpsons", 2003; "The Contender", 2005; "Late Night with Conan O'Brien", 2005-08; "The 100 Greatest TV Quotes & Catch phrases", 2006; "I Pity the Fool", 2006; "Bring Back"; "The A-Team", 2006; "Guys Choice", 2007; "Taurus World Stunt Awards", 2007; "Behind the Taurus", 2008; "Xpose", 2009; "The One Show", 2009; "Finders Keepers", 2010; "World's Craziest Fools", 2011. **Honors/Awds:** Football Scholarship. **Special Achievements:** Author: Mr. T: the Man with the Gold, 1984; Albums: Mr. T's Commandments, 1984; Be Somebody or Be Somebody's Fool!, 1984; People's Choice Award, 1984. **Business Addr:** Actor, William Morris Agency, 1 William Morris Pl, Los Angeles, CA 90212, **Business Phone:** (310)859-4000.

### TURLEY, LOUIS EDWARD, JR.

Executive, educator. **Personal:** Born Mar 11, 1952, South Bend, IN; son of Louis and Carrie Bell; married Phillis Mae; children: Michael Landon. **Educ:** Ball State Univ, BS, 1975; Ind Univ, MS, 1981. **Career:** S Bend Community Schs, instr & educr, 1978-86; ABJ Community Servs Inc, prog dir, 1990-98; Zeigler Habilitation Homes, asst admin, 1998-, prog dir. **Orgs:** Nat Rehab Asn, 1990-94; Alpha Phi Omega; Nat Serv Fraternity; Kiwanis Club Am. **Honors/Awds:** Outstanding Young Man of America, 1986. **Special Achievements:** Study: 18 wks, Zimbabwe & Malawi Africa Comparison Education, 1986. **Home Addr:** 4404 Airport Hwy Suite 5, Toledo, OH 43615, **Home Phone:** (419)389-6865. **Business Addr:** Assistant Administrator, Program Director, Zeigler Habilitation Homes Inc, 715 Spencer Ave Suite H, Toledo, OH 43609, **Business Phone:** (419)382-9040.

### TURMAN, GLYNN (GLYNN RUSSELL TURMAN)

Actor. **Personal:** Born Jan 31, 1947, New York, NY; married Aretha Franklin, Apr 11, 1978, (divorced 1984); children: Glynn Jr (deceased); married Jo-Ann Allen, Jan 1, 1992; children: Delena Joy; married Ula M Walker, Jan 1, 1965, (divorced 1971); children: 3. **Career:** Films: Five on the Black Hand Side, 1973; Thomasine & Bushrod, 1974; The Nine Lives of Fritz the Cat, 1974; Together Brothers, 1974; Cooley High, 1975; The River Niger, 1976; Minstreal Man; JD's Revenge, 1976; Attica, 1980; Penitentiary II, 1982; Secrets of a Married Man, 1984; Out of Bounds, 1986; A Different World, 1988-93; Deep Cover, 1992; Buffalo Soldiers, 1997; How Stella Got Her Groove Back, 1998; Light It Up, 1999; The Visit, 2000; Freedom Song, 2000; Men of Honor, 2000; Air Rage, 2001; The Seat Filler, 2004; Sahara, 2005; City Teacher, 2007; Kings of the Evening, 2008; Preaching to the Pastor, 2009; Takers, 2010; Burlesque, 2010; Super 8, 2011; John Dies at the End, 2012; Act Like You Love Me, 2013; Cowgirls n' Angels 2: Dakota's Summer, 2014. Rescue at Pine Ridge, currently; Race, 2016. TV series: "Peyton Place", writer, 1964; "The Parent Hood", dir, 1995; "The Wayans Bros", dir, 1995; "Resurrection Blvd", 2000-02; "Big Apple", 2001; "Fire & Ice", 2001; "The Wire", 2004-08; "Law & Order: Special Victims Unit", 2005; "The Bernie Mac Show", 2005; "All of Us", 2006; "Law & Order: Special Victims Unit", 2006; Murder 101: New Age, 2008; Night Life, 2008; "Cold Case", 2008; "ER", 2008; "Scrubs", 2009; "In Treatment", 2008-09; "Southland", 2009; "FlashForward", 2009; One-man Show, Movin Man, currently. **Honors/Awds:** Nat Asn Advan Colored People Image Award; Dramalogue Award, 1974; Nat Asn Advan Colored People Image Award; Primetime Emmy Award, 2008. **Special Achievements:** Album: co-author "I'm Your Speed which appeared on her "Almighty Fire". **Business Addr:** Actor, Stone Manners Agency, 8436 W 3rd St Suite740, Los Angeles, CA 90048, **Business Phone:** (323)655-1313.

### TURMAN, REV. DR. KEVIN

Clergy, president (organization). **Personal:** married Denise Thomas; children: Theodore & Benjamin. **Educ:** Harvard Univ, BA, govt; Yale Divinity Sch, MDiv; United Theol Sem, Dayton, OH, DMin. **Career:** Bethany Baptist Church, Brooklyn, assoc pastor; Ebenezer Baptist Church, Boston, pastor; co-pastor, Black Church; Second Baptist Church Detroit, sr pastor, currently. **Orgs:** Pres, Mich Progressive Baptist Conv; pres, Metrop Organizing Strategy Enabling Strength; bd dir, Metrop Detroit Jail Ministry; Detroit Ministers Coun; Alpha Phi Alpha Fraternity. **Honors/Awds:** National Achivement Scholar, Benjamin E Mays Fel. **Special Achievements:** Outstanding Young Men of American by the National Jaycees, 1982. **Business Addr:** Senior Pastor, Second Baptist Church, 441 Monroe St, Detroit, MI 48226, **Business Phone:** (313)961-0920.

### TURNBULL, DR. CHARLES WESLEY

Educator, governor. **Personal:** Born Feb 5, 1935, Charlotte Amalie; son of John Wesley and Ruth Ann Eliza Skelton. **Educ:** Hampton Univ, Hampton, VA, BS, 1958, MA, 1959; Univ Minn, Minneapolis, MN, PhD, educ admin, 1976. **Career:** Virgin Island Dept Educ, St Thomas, VI, social studies teacher, 1959-61, asst prin, 1961-65, prin, 1965-67, asst comnr educ, 1967-79, comnr edu, 1979-87; Univ Vi, St Thomas, VI, prof hist, 1988-99, prof emer, currently; US Vi, gov, 1999-2007. **Orgs:** Alpha Phi Alpha Fraternity Inc, 1958-; Asn Caribbean Historians; Orgn Amn Historians; Coun Chief State Sch Offrs, 1979-87; bd trustee, Univ Vi, 1979-87; Vi Bd Elections, 1974-76; pres, Vi Hist Soc, 1976-; Vi Bd Educ, 1988-; Vi Humanities Coun, 1989-; Am Hist Asn; Nat Gov Asn; Southern Govs' Asn; Democratic Govs Asn; Vi Fifth Const Conv; chmn, Pub Finance Authority; W Indian Co Ltd; chmn, Virgina Isalnds Bd Educ . **Home Addr:** Charlotte Amalie, PO Box 2265, St. Thomas00803, **Home Phone:** (809)774-7994. **Business Addr:** Professor Emeritus, University of the Virgin Islands, John Brewers Bay Suite 2, St. Thomas00802-9990, **Business Phone:** (340)693-1160.

### TURNBULL, HORACE HOLLINS

Administrator. **Personal:** Born Mar 26, 1949, Greenville, SC; married Eunice Carter; children: LaChandrea, Tamari & Courtney. **Educ:** Tougaloo Col, BS, sociol & psychol, 1971; Columbia Univ, MA, 1975; Long Island Univ, MBA, 1978. **Career:** Leake & Watts Childrens Agency, soc worker, 1971-72; Planned Parenthood NYC, dir, coord, 1974-76; Lakeside Sch, exec dir, 1983-86; St. Christopher's Inc, chief operating officer, 2010-; St Peters Sch, coord; St Mary's in-the-Field, res dir; The Equitable Financial Serv, regist rep; Childrens Village, grp home parent; Abbott House Childrens Home, cons. **Orgs:** Vpres, Harlem Boys Choir Bd Dir; Interest Health & Human Serv Admin. **Home Addr:** 17 Valley Dr, Spring Valley, NY 10977, **Home Phone:** (914)425-4452.

### TURNBULL, RENALDO ANTONIO

Football player. **Personal:** Born Jan 5, 1966, St. Thomas; son of George and Ellina; married Thea Lynn Winick; children: Royce Alexander. **Educ:** Wva Univ, BA, commun, 1990. **Career:** Football player (retired); New Orleans Saints, linebacker, 1990-96, right defensive end, 1990, 1995-96, right outside linebacker, 1993-94; W Va Univ, linebacker-defensive, 1990-97; Carolina Panthers, defensive end, 1997. **Honors/Awds:** NFL draft, 1990; Pro Bowl, 1993. **Home Addr:** 9507 Chanson Pl, Matthews, NC 28105-7661.

### TURNER, BOBBY. See TURNER, ROBERT, JR.

### TURNER, DR. CASTELLANO BLANCHET

Educator. **Personal:** Born Jun 14, 1938, Chicago, IL; son of James Julius and Loretta Ganier; married Barbara Formaniak; children: Adam Justin & Shomari Megan. **Educ:** DePaul Univ, BA, 1962, MA, 1963; Univ Chicago, PhD, 1966. **Career:** Chicago State Hosp, clin internship psychol, 1962-63, psychologist, 1963; Univ Chicago, Exten Div, lectr psychol, 1965-68; Manteno State Hosp, Prog Psychologist, prog dir, Woodlawn-Hyde Pk-Kenwood Prog, 1966-68; Univ Chicago Med Sch, clin instr, 1966-68; Univ Chicago, Sch Social Serv Admin, sr res assoc; Univ Mass, Col Ed Black Stud, Coun & Tutoring Prog, dir, 1969-70, Amherst, Boston, prof psychol, prof & dir clin psychol prog, 1989-96, inst actg dir, William Monroe Trotter Inst, interim dir, prof emer, psychol, currently. **Orgs:** Am Psychol Asn. **Home Addr:** 95 Wood End Rd, Newton Highlands, MA 02461-1402, **Home Phone:** (617)965-6636. **Business Addr:** Professor Emeritus, University of Massachusetts Boston, 100 Morrissey Blvd, Boston, MA 02125-3393.

### TURNER, DIANE YOUNG

Library administrator, librarian. **Personal:** Born Jan 2, 1950, New Orleans, LA; daughter of William Young and Mary Montana Young; married John; children: Kyra Denita, Jayna Ymon & John Kenneth. **Educ:** Grambling Col, BA, 1972; State Univ NY, MA, 1974. **Career:** Renselaer Polytech Inst, Troy, NY, asst dir, admis; Roxbury Community Col, Roxbury, MA, dir, financial aid; Yale Univ, New Haven, CT, asst dir, financial aid, sr human resource specialist, dir, libr human resources, assoc univ librn, human resource & orgn develop, training & security, New Haven Community Hiring Initiatives, dir, currently. **Orgs:** Alpha Kappa Alpha Sorority, 1970-; Jr League Greater New Haven, 1985-89; bd mem, Greater New Haven Community Action Agency, 1988-99; pres, New Haven Chap Jack & Jill, 1989-94; pres, Hamden PTA Coun, 1989-91; bd mem, Greater New Haven Arts Coun, 1990-99; bd mem, YWCA Greater New Haven, 1990-92; pres, Hamden High Sch PTSA, 1993-96; vpres, Hamden Mid Sch PTA, 1998; vpres, New Haven Chap, Girlfriends, 1998-; vpres, 1999-2001, pres, 2001-, Hamden High Sch PTSO; pres-elect, Quota Int; bd dir, Creative Arts Workshop, 2002-; lifetime mem, Nat Asn Advan Colored People; bd chair, United Way Greater New Haven campaign, 2009; bd dir, Success by Six Adv Coun, 2007-09; Fel Pierson Col; Nat mem, Am Libr Asn; Nat mem, Black Caucus Am Libr Asn; bd dir, AIDS Interfaith Network; bd dir, Sister Cities/Freetown; active mem, Christian Tabernacle Baptist Church. **Honors/Awds:** Distinguished Mother Award, Jack & Jill, 1993; Elm Ivy Award, 1994; Hamden Notables Award, 1995; Secretary of State's Public Service Award, 2002; Hamden Black Notables Award, 2003; Advancing the Common Good Award, 2007. **Special Achievements:** Special Olympics World Games, dir of volunteers at Yale Univ; Participated in Leadership Greater New Haven, Institution and Volunteer Action Agency, 1989-; First African Am to serve as Campaign Chair, 2009. **Home Addr:** 55 Chatterton Woods, Hamden, CT 06518, **Home Phone:** (203)432-1806. **Business Addr:** Director of New Haven Community Hiring Initiatives, Yale University, 221 Whitney Ave, New Haven, CT 06511-3760, **Business Phone:** (203)436-5812.

### TURNER, DORIS (DORIS TURNER KEYS)

Secretary (organization), association executive. **Personal:** Born Jun 20, 1930, Pensacola, FL; married Willie D Keys; children: 2. **Career:** Lenox Hill Hosp, dietary clerk, 1956; Dist 1199 Nat Union Hosp & Health Care Employees, pres, secy. **Orgs:** App mem, NY State Hosp Rev & Planning Coun, 1978-81; pres, Local 1199 Drug Hosp & Health Care Employees Union, 1982-86; Sec Nat Union Hosp & Health Care Employees; union trustee Hosp League & Dist 1199 Trng & Upgrading; union trustee Nat Benefit & Pension Fund Hosp & Health Care Employees; Exec Comt Nat Benefit & Pension Funds; bd mem, Am Dem Action; bd mem, Martin L King Ctr Soc Chg; State NY Comn Health Educ & Illness Prev; Coalition Labor Union Women; founding mem, prin organizer, secy, State AFL CIO. **Honors/Awds:** District Services Award, NY City Cent Labor Coun AFL CIO, 1969; Award of Merit, The Black Trade Unionist Leadership Comt NY Cent Labor Coun, 1974; Hispanic Labor Committee Award, 1978; Eugene V Debs & Norman Thomas Award, 1978; Bessie & Sarah Delaney Award. **Home Addr:** 460 E Prospect Ave, Mount Vernon, NY 10553-1120, **Home Phone:** (914)699-0400.

### TURNER, DR. DORIS J.

Educator, executive director. **Personal:** Born St. Louis, MO; daughter of Julius Adams and Adeline Herndon. **Educ:** Stowe Col, St Louis, BA, 1953; Universidade da Bahia Salvador BahiaBrazil, attended 1963; St Louis Univ, PhD, 1967. **Career:** Ind Univ, vis scholar, 1987-88; Kent State Univ, Dept Romance Lang, assoc prof & lit, currently, Latin Am Studies, dir, currently. **Orgs:** Elected mem, chmn, Nat Off Steering & Comt, Consortium Latin Am Studies Prog, 1973-76; field reader, US Off Educ, 1979; Danforth Asn, 1976. **Honors/Awds:** Fulbright fel, Brazil, 1962-64; res grant, Brazil, Kent State Univ, 1976; NEH Summer fel, Brown Univ, 1979; Outstanding Teaching Award, Col Arts & Sci, Kent State Univ, 1986; Postdoctoral fel, Ford Found, 1987-88. **Home Addr:** 475 Dansel St, Kent, OH 44240-2626, **Home Phone:** (330)678-6529. **Business Addr:** Associate Professor, Kent State University, 101 Satterfield Hall 800 E Summit St, Kent, OH 44242, **Business Phone:** (330)672-3000.

### TURNER, ELMYRA G.

Teacher, educator. **Personal:** Born Nov 27, 1928, Longview, TX; married James M; children: 3. **Educ:** BS, 1952; MEd, 1959; MEd, 1969; Tex southern Univ, admin cert, 1973. **Career:** Tex Southern Univ, secy, 1952; Crawford Elem Sch, 1953; Elmore High Sch, secy & teacher, 1954; Langston Elem Sch, teacher, 1959; Lockett Jr High, 1964; Lincoln Jr-Sr High, 1968; Sam Houston Sr High, counr, 1970; Deady Jr High, asst prin, 1970. **Orgs:** Houston Principals Asn, 1970-; Houston Coun Educ, 1972; supt com Community Rels Area, 1972-74; Nat Coun Negro Women, 1973; Nat Asn Advan Colored People, 1973-74; Eval Panel Interviewers-Area V PTA Deady Jr High Sch; vpres, Lockhart Elem Tex State Teachers Asn; Top Ladiel Distinction Inc; pres, Beta Pi Chap Iota Phi Lambda Sor Inc; organizer, Houston Chap Nat Tots & Teens Inc; Houston League Bus & prof Women; Home Improv & Protec Asn; chmn, Youth Comn; Delta Sigma Theta Sor Inc; Am Asn Univ Women. **Honors/Awds:** President's Award, 1971; Iota Phi Lambda Sor Inc; Outstanding Woman the Year, 1974-75; Iota Phi Lambda Sor Inc; Beta Pi Chap, Houston, TX; Human Rel Educ Award, outstanding achievement in human rels, 1977. **Home Addr:** 3530 Rosedale Ave, Houston, TX 77004-6406, **Home Phone:** (713)249-1725.

### TURNER, ERIC SCOTT

Football player, politician. **Personal:** Born Feb 26, 1972, Richardson, TX; married Robin. **Educ:** Univ Ill, MBA, human resource develop. **Career:** Football player (retired), politician; Wash Redskins, 1995-97; San Diego Chargers, defensive back, 1998, 1999, cornerback, 2000-01; Denver Broncos, 2003; Turner Cong, politician, currently; Morning star Christian Church, asst pastor, currently; San Diego, assist pastor, currently; Prestonwood Baptist, bible fel leader, currently; Bus Develop Systemware Inc, dir, currently. **Orgs:** Prestonwood Baptist Church. **Special Achievements:** Involved with the national political process when he secured a position as an intern in California and Washington with Congressman Duncan Hunter, chairman of the House Armed Services Committee. **Business Addr:** Politician, Turner for Congress, 11232 El Camino Real Suite 150, San Diego, CA 92130, **Business Phone:** (858)350-9192.

### TURNER, ERNESTINE. See BROWN, ERNESTINE.

### TURNER, ERVIN (PETER TURNER)

Executive. **Personal:** Born Mar 20, 1948, Monroe, LA; married Kathleen Lindsey; children: Christopher Earl & Roanita. **Educ:** Ne La Univ, 1972; Boys' Clubs Am, cert, 1974. **Career:** Ouachita Parish Police Jury, police juror; EPT Enterprise AAA LTD, pres & owner; Tri-Dist Boys' Club, exec dir, currently; Ervin Peter Turner Found, dir, 2003-. **Orgs:** NAACP; NE LA Sickle Cell Anemia; NLU Booster Club Bus Action Assoc; Amer Entrepreneurs Asn; zool Soc LA Purchase Gardens & Zoo; bd mem, Northeast La Indus Develop Bd; bd mem, NE LA Indus Bd; bd mem, La Minority Bus Develop Auth Bd; BCA Prof; coord, Vol Job Corps; secy, Luminous Civic Club; bd mem, Youth House Quachita; bd mem, Bus Action Asn; bd mem, Better Bus Bur; exec secy, La Area Coun BCA, 1974; vpres, N Delta Regional

Planning; Tri-Dist Boys & Girls Ctr & Family Develop Inc, exec dir, 1971-. **Home Addr:** 185 Ross Rd, Monroe, LA 71202-8012, **Home Phone:** (318)325-0964. **Business Addr:** Executive Director, Tri-District Boys' Club, 2920 Louberta St, Monroe, LA 71201, **Business Phone:** (318)387-0903.

### TURNER, DR. EUGENE A., SR.
Clergy. **Personal:** Born Apr 17, 1934, Macon, GA; married Sylvia Baskerville; children: Peter, Paul & Lennie Elis. **Educ:** Knoxville Col, BA; Pittsburgh Theol Sem, MDiv; Harvard Univ. **Career:** Clergy (retired); Pittsburgh, asst pastor; Patterson NJ, pastor; Philadelphia, organising pastor; Gen Assembly, staff; Presbeytery Philadelphia, asst leadership develop, coord Met Mission; Synod Golden Gate San Francisco, assoc exec; United Presby Church Syracuse NY, exec Synod Northeast; Johnson C Smith Theol Sem, pres. **Orgs:** Bd mem, No Calif Coun Church; bd mem, Nat Planned Parenthood, 1964-66; bd mem; Coun Black Clergy; bd mem, Black Presby United; steering comt, Nat Black Conf, 1968; bd mem, Model Cities Phila; bd chair, bd trustee, Johnson C Smith Theol Sem. **Home Addr:** 12 Bovington Lane, Fayetteville, NY 13066-9750, **Home Phone:** (315)446-6952.

### TURNER, FRANKLIN JAMES
Engineer. **Personal:** Born Aug 16, 1960, Birmingham, AL. **Educ:** Ala A&M Univ, BS, 1983. **Career:** Rockwell Int, software engr, 1984-86; Northrop, software qual engr, 1986-. **Honors/Awds:** Pride Award for Engineering Outstanding Achievement, Rockwell Int, 1986. **Home Addr:** 19101 Pricetown Ave, Carson, CA 90746, **Home Phone:** (213)329-2896.

### TURNER, GENEVA
Business owner, educator, nurse. **Personal:** Born Jul 6, 1949, Columbus, GA; daughter of George Robert (deceased) and Mollie Bell; children: Gennyce Ashley Nelson. **Educ:** Columbus Col, ADN, 1971; Ga Southwestern Univ, BSN, 1979; Univ Ala, MSN, 1982; Tex Woman's Univ, PhD, nursing sci, 1987; Luther Rice Sem & Univ, MA, bibl coun, 2011. **Career:** Nurse (retired) business owner; Med Ctr, staff nurse, 1971, staff nurse, 1978-79; Talmadge Mem Hosp, staff nurse, 1971-73; R E Thomason Gen Hosp, charge nurse, 1973-74; Convalescent Ctr, charge nurse, 1974; Aus Hosp, actg head nurse, 1975-77; Columbus Col, assoc prof nursing, 1979-93; Turner & ASC Consult, owner, 1989-; Muscogee County Sch Dist, bd dir, 1989; FamilyProjs Publs, owner, 1992-. **Orgs:** Scholar, fel Am Nurses Asn, 1979-, 1986; Sigma Theta Tau, 1983-; Nat Coun Marriage & Family Rels, 1986-; secy, scholar, Res Officers Asn, 1986; Phi Kappa Phi, 1987-; Asn Mil Surgeons US, 1988-; Asn Black Nursing Fac, 1989-93; Nat League Nursing Higher Educ, 1990-93; Nat Asn Nurses Bus, 1991-93; Publishers Mkt Asn, 1992-; Network Profs & Execs Inc, 1994-; Alliance Homelessness, 1994-; deleg, bd dir, Third Dist Nurses Asn. **Honors/Awds:** Outstanding Sophomore Teacher in Nursing, Columbus Col, 1981; Dr John Townsend Award for Outstanding Service to the Community in Medicine, 1983; Certificate of Appreciation, Combined Communities Southeast Columbus, 1989; Outstanding Service to the City of Columbus, Mayor's Off, 1990; Service Award, Greater Columbus Chap Alzheimer's Dis, 1991. **Special Achievements:** Disseminating Intravascular Coagulation, Nursing Interventions, 1991; Preceptorship Program: A Public Relations Tool, 1991; Dealing with Polychronic or Monochronic Individuals in the Work Place, 1992; Black Am Folk Medicine Health Care Beliefs: Implications for Nursing, 1992; "Theory of Homelessness Using Gibb's Paradigm", 1992; How to Plan a Spectacular Family Reunion, Family Proj Pub Mission Sq, 1993; Fathers Cry, Too, Family Proj Pub Mission Sq, 1995.; What if Our Father Were Not a Man, WestBowPress 2012. **Home Addr:** 4815 Velpoe Dr, Columbus, GA 31907-6516, **Home Phone:** (706)687-0997. **Business Addr:** Owner, Family Projects Publishers, 3009 Hamilton Rd, Columbus, GA 31907, **Business Phone:** (706)687-4296.

### TURNER, GEORGE CORDELL, II
Executive, educator. **Personal:** Born Jun 3, 1937, McGehee, AR; son of George C Sr and Mary L; married Nancy C; children: Melissa & George III. **Educ:** Univ Ark, Pine Bluff, hist & govt, attended 1959; Univ Ark; Univ Fla; Univ Ill. **Career:** Educator (retired); Helena-W Helena Pub Schs, instr, 1959-64; Conway Pub Schs, instr admin, 1964-69; Consumers Power, human resources, dir, 1969. **Orgs:** Mich Chap AABE, treas, 1987-; Am Asn Blacks Energy, 1988-; Charter Mem Jackson Serv Club, held all offices, 1974-. **Home Addr:** 3280 Chrysler Cove, Conway, AR 72034, **Home Phone:** (501)327-5513.

### TURNER, GEORGE R.
Podiatrist. **Personal:** Born Jun 14, 1944, Bryn Mawr, PA; married Betty M; children: Gayle R, Garrett & Avis. **Educ:** Lincoln Univ, AB, 1967; Temple Univ, EdM, 1969; Pa Col Podiatric Med, DPM, 1976. **Career:** Philadelphia Bd Educ, teacher, 1967-69; IBM, mkt rep, 1969-72; Pa Col Podiatric Med, 1972-76; Hardy's Orthop Appl Inc, consult; Lawndale Community Hosp, podiatrist. **Orgs:** Am Podiatry Asn; bd mem, Nat Podiatry Asn; Pa Podiatry Asn; Metro Podiatry Asn; Philadelphia County Podiatry Asn; Omega Psi Phi Fraternity. **Honors/Awds:** Morris prize, 1967; Outstanding Young Man in Am, 1976; Achievement Award, Metrop Podiatry Asn, 1976. **Home Addr:** 192 Hearthstone Dr, Berlin, NJ 08009-9550. **Business Addr:** 74 Ave, Philadelphia, PA 19138.

### TURNER, GEORGE TIMOTHY
Automotive executive. **Career:** Plain field Lincoln Mercury Merkur Inc, Grand Rapids, Mich, chief exec officer, 1986-. **Business Addr:** Chief Executive Officer, Plainfield Lincoln Mercury Merkur Inc, 2424 28th St SE, Grand Rapids, MI 49512-1687, **Business Phone:** (616)363-5551.

### TURNER, HARRY GLENN
Automotive executive. **Personal:** Born Jul 23, 1951, Chicago, IL; son of William and Ruby; married Elizabeth; children: John & Laura. **Educ:** Univ Ill, Sch Engineering, BME, 1976; Oakland Univ, Grad Sch Bus Admin, MBA, mkt, 1979; Kettering Univ. **Career:** Chevrolet Sporty Car, engr, 1971-83, engineering mgr, 1983-85, exec engineering mgr, 1985-86, chief engr, export group, 1986, chief engr, body systs, 1987, large car prod planning, 1988-90, Corvette & Camaro prod planning & sporty car segment mgr, 1990-2005; Gen Motors, motor sports strategic planning, 1996-, exec mgr, 1971-2005, GM Racing, rd racing group mgr, 1971-2005; Sports Car Club Am, sr tech & race opers dir, 2005-06; Tom Hammonds Enterprises LLC, chief operating officer, 2007. **Orgs:** BLK BOD Proj; bd, Grand Canyon Coun Boy Scouts Am. **Home Addr:** PO Box 1452, Southgate, MI 48195-0452, **Home Phone:** (313)356-8923. **Business Addr:** Group Manager, General Motors Corp, PO Box 33170, Detroit, MI 48232-5170, **Business Phone:** (248)857-5000.

### TURNER, ISIAH
Government official. **Personal:** Born May 15, 1945, St. Joseph, LA; son of Isiah and Leona Johnson; married Carmen Cayne; children: Damon & Terrie Lynn. **Educ:** Evergreen State Col, Olympia, WA, BA, lib arts, 1986; John F Kennedy Sch Govt, sr execs state & local govt; Harvard Univ, 1987. **Career:** Government official (retired); Seattle Opportunities Industrialization Ctr, Seattle, WA, dir educ, 1971-79; Oper Improv Found, Seattle WA, dir indust rels, 1980-83; Wash State Employ Security, Olympia, WA, comnr, asst comnr, 1983-85; Richmond City, city mgr, 2004; Tom Butt, dep city mgr. **Orgs:** Nat Job Training Partnership; bd mem, pres, Nat Black Pub Adminr Forum; Blacks Govt; Interstate Conf Employ Security Agencies; Northwest Conf Black Pub Offs; Wash State Econ Develop Bd; bd mem, Richmond Police Dept; bd mem, Calif Workforce Investment; Contra Costa county Econ Coun; Gov Gray Davis' Workforce Investment Bd; bd dir, Calif Asn Local Econ Develop.

### TURNER, JEAN TAYLOR
Educator. **Personal:** Born Nov 13, 1943, Philadelphia, PA; daughter of Clarence William (deceased) and Roberta Hargrove; children: Christopher Francis & Sean Michael. **Educ:** Univ Calif, Los Angeles, BSN, 1973, MN, 1975; Med Col Va, Va Commonwealth Univ, PhD, health servs orgn & res, 1987. **Career:** Fox Hills County Hosps, Los Angeles, staff develop dir, 1974-75; Va Commonw wealth Univ, Sch Nursing, Med Col Va, Dept Psychiat Ment Health, intern, 1979-84, asst prof nursing admin, 1984-92; Nat Inst Ment Health, post doctoral fel, 1984-87; Univ Va, assoc prof nursing, 1992-98. **Orgs:** Am Nurses Asn, 1980-; Am Pub Health Asn, 1987-; Sigma Theta Tau Int Nursing Hon Soc, 1988-; ed rev bd, Asn Black Nursing Fac Higher Educ, 1989-; Asn Health Servs Res, 1993-. **Home Addr:** 22 Fairwood Dr, Richmond, VA 23235, **Home Phone:** (804)320-6429.

### TURNER, JESSE H., JR.
Banker, executive. **Personal:** Born May 6, 1950, Memphis, TN; son of Jesse H Sr (deceased) and Allegra W; married Joyce Hays; children: Jesse III, Michael, Christy & Brian. **Educ:** Univ Chicago, BS, maths, 1971, MBA, acct & finance, 1973; Memphis Sch Banking, attended 1979; ABA Stonier Grad Sch Banking, attended 1984; Christian Bros High Schs; St Augustine Grad Sch. **Career:** Tri-State Bank, Memphis, Tenn, exec vpres, cashier, vpres, auditor & trainee, 1973-83, bd dir, 1983-, pres & chief exec officer, 1990-, chmn, 1994-; Jesse H. Turner CPA, owner, 1989-. **Orgs:** Nat asst treas & nat bd mem, Nat Asn Adv Col People; treas & life mem, Nat Asn Adv Col People, Memphis br; mem finance coun, St. Augustine Cath Church; Am Inst CPAS; bd mem, Dept Redevelop Corp Memphis & Shelby County; Delta Boule; Sigma Pi Phi Fraternity; Black Bus Asn; pres & vpres, Memphis Nat Asn Advan Colored People Youth Coun; pres, Region V Youth; founder & pres, Univ Chicago Col Chap. **Honors/Awds:** Distinguished Service Award, Nat Asn Advan Colored People Memphis Branch, 1993; Hall of Fame, Christian Bros High Sch, 1995; Simply The Best CEO Award, 1996; Hon Doctorate, Lemoyne-Owen Col, 2004; B. Doyce Mitchell Award, Nat Bankers Asn, 2006; African American Legacy Award, N Memphis Dist, AME Church, 2009. **Special Achievements:** Listed at #18 of 25 top financial companies, Black Enterprise, 1992, ranked #18, 1998; First black to desegregate high school in Memphis. **Business Addr:** President, Chief Executive Officer, Tri-State Bank of Memphis, 180 S Main St, Memphis, TN 38103-3616, **Business Phone:** (901)525-0384.

### TURNER, JIM ALLEN
Football player. **Personal:** Born Nov 13, 1975, Jacksonville, FL. **Educ:** Syracuse Univ, psychol. **Career:** Football player (retired); Carolina Panthers, wide receiver, 1998-2001.

### TURNER, JOHNNIE RODGERS
School administrator. **Personal:** Born Jun 23, 1940, Hughes, AR; daughter of Charlie Mae Watson Rodgers and Clayton Rodgers; married Larry; children: Larry R. **Educ:** LeMoyne-Owen Col, BS, 1962; Memphis State Univ, MEd, 1971; Univ Tenn, Knoxville. **Career:** Educator (retired); Memphis City Schs, teacher, 1965-, supvr, dir, staff develop, 1986-90, co-dir, Prof Assessment Develop & Enhancement Ctr (PADEC), 1991-. **Orgs:** Pres, exec dir, Memphis Br Nat Asn Advan Colored People, 1977-78; pres, Memphis Alumnae Chap Delta Sigma Theta Sor, 1978-80; Leadership Memphis, 1979-; ASCD, 1980-; Nat Staff Dev Coun, 1980-; MABSE, 1981-; Phi Delta Kappa, 1982-; Nat Alliance Black Sch Educrs, 1982-; bd mem, Health Educ & Housing Facil Bd Shelby County, Tenn, 1982-; pres, asst secy & founding mem, Memphis Alliance Black Sch Educrs, 1988-90; exec comt mem, Nat Asn Advan Colored People, LeMoyne Owen Nat Alumni Asn, asst secy; Memphis Retired Teachers Asn; Memphis/Shelby County Anti-Predatory Lending Coalition; Westwood Neighborhood Asn, adv bd Memphis Juv Ct Syst; vice chmn, Health, Educ & Housing Facil Bd Shelby County; Memphis Alumnae Chap Delta Sigma Theta Sorority Inc, pres, Greater Mid Baptist Church, bd trustee; Dist 85 Shelby County; Dem Women Shelby County; United Teaching Profession; Westwood Neighborhood Asn; treas, Tenn Black Caucus State Legislators; 106th Gen Assembly. **Honors/Awds:** Merit Award for Outstanding Service Memphis Br, Nat Asn Advan Colored People, 1975; co-ed "Why Doesn't An Igloo Melt Inside?" handbook teachers gifted, 1978; Citizen of the Week, Gilliam Comt Station WLOK, 1978; Citizenship Award, Moolah Temple No 54 Shriner, 1979; Delta of the Year, 1983; Golden Apple Award, Nat Alliance Black Sch Educrs (NABSE), 1988; Living Legends Award, Northeast Region Nat Asn Advan Colored People; Living Legends Award, Memphis Griszzlies & Nat Civil Rights Mus; Addie G Owen Racial Justice Award, YWCA Greater Memphis; Legends of Memphis Award, Memphis Chap; Freedom Award, Univ Memphis Chap Nat Asn Advan Colored People, Women of Excellence Award, Tri-State Defender, Friend of Education Award, Memphis Educ Asn; Women Making a Difference Award, Delta Sigma Theta Sorority; Ruby R Wharton Award. **Home Addr:** 752 W Levi Rd, Memphis, TN 38109, **Home Phone:** (901)785-6750. **Business Addr:** Executive Committee Member, National Association for the Advancement of Colored People, 588 Vance Ave, Memphis, TN 38126, **Business Phone:** (901)521-1343.

### TURNER, JOSEPH ELLIS
Military leader, executive. **Personal:** Born Sep 2, 1939, Charleston, WV; son of Joseph (deceased) and Annetta Frances Malone (deceased); married Norma Jean Sims; children: Alan, Brian & Joseph Jr. **Educ:** WVa State Col, BS, math, 1961; Univ Southern Calif, aviation safety, 1968; Army Command & Gen Staff Col, grad; Indust Col Armed Forces, Air War Col; Sr Off Chem, CSE; Force Integration, CSE; Nat Orien, CSE; BG, Orien Conf. **Career:** AUS (retired); U3a U6a, 1963; CV2 1963; U8D, G, F, U21A, 1968; First Officer L1011 Delta Air Lines, LAX, 1970-; USAR, maj gen, 1970-, brig gen; Fixed wing OH58, 1975; UHIH, 1975; U3A, 1976; rotary wing; Master Army Aviator; vice dir, dirate; Off Info Systs Command Control Commun & Comput; 17th Aviation Co Vietnam, aviator & commun officer; HHC, 210th Combat Aviation Battalion, safety officer & comdr. **Orgs:** NAI, 1969-; Airline Pilots Asn, 1970-; ROA, 1970-; Am Soc Miltary Comptrollers, 1984-; Orgn Black Airline Pilots, 1984-; Sr Army Res Commanders Asn, 1988; Armed Forces Commun Electronics Asn, 1988-; Signal Corp Regimential Asn, 1988-; Black Mil Hist Inst Am Inc, 1989-; Caribon Asn, Army Otter. **Honors/Awds:** ROTC Hall of Fame, WVa State Col, 1984; General Officer Hall of Fame, Wva State UNiv, 1988; Distinguished Alumni Citation of the Year Award, NAFEO, 1989. **Home Addr:** 1630 Loch Lomond Trl SW, Atlanta, GA 30331.

### TURNER, KIM SMITH
School administrator. **Personal:** Born Apr 11, 1959, New York, NY; daughter of Solomon Smith and Bernice Alford Smith; married Ray Mills; children: Kory & Kortnie. **Educ:** Morgan State Univ, Baltimore, MD, bus admin & mgt, gen, 1978, bus, admin, 1979; State Univ Educ Opportunity Ctr, Albany, NY, cert, 1980; Emory Univ, Atlanta, GA, attended 1989. **Career:** State New York, Rochester Psychiat Ctr, Rochester, NY, 1981; US Gov Soc Security Admin, Atlanta Ga, secy, 1982-83; Am Rheumatism Asn, Atlanta, Ga, meetings coordr, 1983-86; Emory Univ Bus Sch, Atlanta, Ga, dept oper coordr, 1986-90, bus mgr, 1990-94, actg assoc, dir exec progs, 1995, assoc dir fin & admin, 1995-99, Goizueta Bus Sch, dir human resources, 1986-2006; D'VINE Connections Intl Inc, owner, consult, 2006-; Sacred Praise United Methodist Church, church adminr, 2010-14; DeKalb County Bd Commissioners, Dist 3, adminr, 2014-15. **Orgs:** Pres, Emory Univ Employee Coun, 1987-88; Emory Univ pres's Comn Status Women, 1988-89; Nat Asn Advan Colored People, Atlanta Chap, 1988, 1990-; Emory Univ, EEOC Task Force, 1989; Emory Univ pres's Comn Status Minorities, 1989-92; co-founder, Emory's Black Educ Network, 1990; MEECA Chap Nat Coalition 100 Black Women; 1999, chair, Parking & Transp Comn, 2000-; Nat Black Herstory Task Force Inc. **Home Addr:** 2247 Jones Rd NW, Atlanta, GA 30318. **Business Addr:** D'VINE Connections Intl, Inc, 20725 8th St E, Sonoma, CA 95476, **Business Phone:** (707)938-7494.

### TURNER, L. ROBERT
Chief executive officer, president (organization). **Career:** Toyota Town, 1983-84; Butts Oldsmobile, 1984-89; Reliable Chevrolet, 1989-98; Showcase Chevrolet, 1998-2000; Capital One, sr vpres, dir; Turner Chevrolet & Jk Chevrolet Subaru, gen mgr, owner, 2000-; Turner Chevrolet, owner, 2014-; JK Chevrolet Isuzu, pres & chief exec officer, currently. **Orgs:** Bd mem, chmn, Greater Beaumont Chamber Com; bd mem, Greater Richmond Technol Coun. **Business Addr:** President, Owner, JK Chevrolet, 1451 Hwy 69, Nederland, TX 77627, **Business Phone:** (409)722-0443.

### TURNER, LANA
Real estate agent. **Personal:** Born Feb 8, 1950, New York, NY; daughter of Lee Arthur and Ida Ford; children: Eric M Fane. **Educ:** City Col NY, attended 1976; Sarah Lawrence Col, Bronxville, NY, attended 1989. **Career:** Men Who Cook, NY, pres, 1982; Denise Shaw Esq & Assocs, real estate agt, 1999-. **Orgs:** Adv bd, Manhattan Bor Historian Comn, 1986; chairperson, Lit Soc, 1982; adv bd, Breast Exam Ctr, 1982. **Honors/Awds:** Pictures of Fathers, NY, Sarah Lawrence Col, 1988. **Special Achievements:** Author, Travelling Light. **Home Addr:** 270 Convent Ave, New York, NY 10031-9104, **Home Phone:** (212)368-9099. **Business Addr:** Licensed Real Estate Salesperson, Denise Shaw Esq & Assocs, 185 E 85th St, New York, NY 10028.

### TURNER, LESLIE FORD
School principal, teacher. **Career:** Robert C Hatch High Sch, Eng teacher, 1996-2002, prin, 2002-. **Business Addr:** Principal, English Teacher, Robert C Hatch High School, 470 W Ave, Uniontown, AL 36786, **Business Phone:** (334)628-4061.

### TURNER, LESLIE MARIE
Government official. **Personal:** Born Oct 2, 1957, Neptune, NJ; daughter of Robert and Jeanette. **Educ:** NY Univ, BS, 1980; George Town Univ Law Ctr, JD, 1985; Am Univ, MLL. **Career:** DC Ct Appeals, judicial law clerk, 1985-86; Akin Gump Strauss Hauer & Feld, sr assoc, 1986-93, counr; US Dept Interior, asst secy territorial & int affairs, 1993-95, counr secy & dir off inter govenmental affairs, 1995-; Coca-Cola N Am, chief legal officer, assoc gen coun, 2006-; Hershey Co, sr vpres, gen coun & secy, 2012-. **Orgs:** DC Coalition Environ Justice, 1995-; vice chair comn environ justice, Am Bar Asn, 1996-; comt pub understanding law, DC Bar, 1996-; bd dir, Ga Appleseed; bd visitor, Georgetown Univ Law Ctr; trustee, Wash Lawyers Comt Civil Rights & Urban Affairs. **Home Addr:** 1333 New Hampshire Ave NW, Washington, DC 20036, **Home Phone:** (202)887-4438. **Business Addr:** Senior Vice President, Secretary, The Hershey Co, 100 Crystal A Dr, Hershey, PA 17033, **Business Phone:** (717)534-4200.

### TURNER, LINDA DARNELL

Vice president (organization), manager. **Personal:** Born Mar 29, 1947, River Rouge, MI; daughter of Beatreat and Alean Darnell; children: Akaia. **Educ:** Univ Detroit Mercy, BA, finance & mkt, 1981, MA, finance & mkt. **Career:** Independence Capital Formation, mgr, 1972-79; Detroit Econ Growth, mgr, 1979-81; Barton Malow Corp, dir & vpres, 1981-2003; W-3 Construct, client rels. **Honors/Awds:** Bus Develop, Gov State Ga, 1989; Major Corp Achievement, NAMC, 1989; Minority Achiever, Detroit Young Women's Christian Asn, 1987; MBE Corp Role Model, Chrysler Corp, 1996; Cert Contract ADR, 1998; Cert contract adminr, 1998. **Home Addr:** 40076 Bexley Way, Northville, MI 48167, **Home Phone:** (734)516-2325. **Business Addr:** Director, Vice President, Barton Malow Corp, 26500 Am Dr, Southfield, MI 48034, **Business Phone:** (248)436-5000.

### TURNER, M. ANNETTE (M ANNETTE MANDLEY-TURNER)

Administrator, president (organization), chief executive officer. **Personal:** Born Feb 17, 1953, Belhaven, NC; daughter of James W and Edna Mae Jones; married James Roderick. **Educ:** Univ Louisville, Louisville, KY, BS, sociol, 1980, MS, 1987, BS, ed psychol, 1991. **Career:** St Denis Sch, Louisville, KY, teacher, 1975-84; Regional Youth Prog, Louisville, KY, coordr, 1984-89; Human Resource Plus, Louisville, KY, diversity consult, 1988-97; Archdiocese Louisville, Off African-Am Catholics, KY, exec dir, 1989-; Turner & Assocs, chief exec officer, 1992-; Turner Mandley & Turner, pres & chief exec officer, currently. **Orgs:** Dir, Archdiocese Louisville's Off Multicultural Ministry, 1984; founder, Nat African Am Youth Ministry Network; chair, Nat Fedn Cath Youth Ministry Ethnic Concern Comt, 1986-90; Grand lady, Knights Peter Claver Ladies Aux, 1989-90; exec bd mem, Nat Fed Cath Youth Ministry, 1990-; Nat Coun Negro Women, 1990-; bd, One Church One Child, 1992-; bd trustee, Nat Black Cath Cong, 1992; pres, region rep, Nat Asn Black Cath Admins; founding mem, IAACEC; exec bd, NAACYMN; bd dir, W Louisville Community Ministry; bd dir, Healing Pl; exec dir, Ky Interfaith Community; Int Cult Coun; NCNW; Jack & Jill Am;bd, Overseers St Meinrad Sem & Sch Theol St. Meinrad; regional coordr, Nat Black Cath Cong; Interregional African Am Cath Evangelization Conf; founder, Regional African Am Cath Young Adult Network; Archdiocesan Priorities Educ. **Home Addr:** 8506 Image Way, Louisville, KY 40299, **Home Phone:** (502)491-0375. **Business Addr:** Executive Director, Archdiocese of Louisville, 1200 S Shelby St, Louisville, KY 40203, **Business Phone:** (502)636-0296.

### TURNER, MARGARET DODSON

Museum director, fund raising consultant, vice president (organization). **Educ:** Howard Univ, BFA; Harvard Univ, MEd. **Career:** Nat Law Enforcement Officers Memorial Fund Inc, chief develop officer; Corcoran Gallery Art, vpres instnl advan; Meharry Med Col, assoc vpres instnl advan; Higher Horizons, develop comt chair; Smithsonian Inst, Nat Mus African-Am Hist & Cult, dir planned giving, cent develop officer. **Orgs:** New Col Inst, bd trustees mem. **Business Addr:** Central Development Officer, Smithsonian Institute, 4210 Silver Hill Rd, Suitland, MD 20746.

### TURNER, MARK ANTHONY

School administrator, accountant. **Personal:** Born Feb 23, 1951, Lynch, KY; son of William Earl and Naomi Miller Randolph; children: Andrea Kamille & Brittany E Nelson. **Educ:** Univ Ky Southeast Community Col, AA, 1972; Western Ky Univ, BS, 1974. **Career:** Deloitte Haskins & Sells, sr asst, 1974-78; Bus Resource Ctr, sr consult, 1978-79; Ohio River Co, financial analyst, 1979-80; Arthur Young & Co, sr consult auditor, 1980; Univ Col, Univ Cincinnati, asst dean, 1982-95; MarkA Turner & Assoc, sr partner, 1988-; Taxx Express, cpa & owner 1996-. **Orgs:** Treas, NABA Cincinnati Chap, 1980-84; founding mem, Cincinnati Chap Nat Asn Black Acct, 1980; treas, Bond Hill Community Coun, 1980-84; consult, Sickle Cell Awareness Group Greater Cincinnati, 1982-84; co treas, Cincinnatians Yates Coun, 1984-86; treas, Cent Community Ment Health Bd, 1990-91, bd trustee, 1989-91; Univ Col Minority Scholar Bd, 1988-91; pres, bd trustee, CCUB; founding treas, 4 Sq Found. **Home Addr:** 5411 Carrahen Ct, Cincinnati, OH 45237, **Home Phone:** (513)242-1152. **Business Addr:** Certified Public Accountant, Owner, Taxx Express, 2248 Losantiville Ave, Cincinnati, OH 45237-4206, **Business Phone:** (513)351-8299.

### TURNER, MARVIN WENTZ

Federal government official, president (organization), consultant. **Personal:** Born Oct 17, 1959, Philadelphia, PA; son of Gilbert Jr and Frances B McAlister. **Educ:** Howard Univ, BBA, ins, 1981; Temple Univ, MBA, opers mgt, 1986; George Washington Univ, MBA, finance/info systs mgt, 1988; Univ Pa, Wharton Sch, exec training finance, intensive prog financial leadership, 1989; Georgetown Univ Law Ctr, JD, 1998; Harvard Univ, John F Kennedy Sch Govt, exec educ fed govt execs, 1999. **Career:** Prudential Ins, Ft Wash, Pa, external rels adv, 1982-86; Mgt Enterprise, Philadelphia, Pa, bus adv, 1984-86; CNA Financial Group, Wash, DC, claim adjuster, policy analyst, 1986-88; Bell Atlantic-Network Sers Inc, Arlington, Va, mgr creative financial planning & anal, 1988-93; Local Gov Insu Trust, chief financial officer, 1993-95; Hopkins Turner Wharton Inc, Bethesda, Md, managing dir, 1995-97; Fin Assets Capital LLC, managing dir, 1995-2000; Univ Md Univ Col, adj prof, 1997-; Law Off Larson-Jackson PC, atty, 1997-99; L William Teweles, managing dir, 1997-2000; Baytree Investors Inc, managing dir, 1998-2000; Am Intercontinental Univ, adj prof, 1998-2001; NASD, securities arbitrator, 1999-2006; US Dept Housing & Urban Develop, Nat Capitol Region, dir, 1999-; Black Arrow Advisors Inc, founder & pres, 2006-10. **Orgs:** Life mem, Alpha Phi Alpha Fraternity Inc; Bus & Econ Develop Comn, Nat Black MBA Asn, 1986-; George Wash Univ, fel; treas, 1986-, exec bd mem, 1988-93, Nat Black MBA Asn, DC Chap; Asn MBA Execs; Delta Sigma Pi Prof Bus Fraternity; Asn Individual Investors; Howard Univ Sch Bus & Pub Admin Alumni Asn; Telecommunications Network Exchange; bd mem, United Way Nat Capital Area Mem & Allocations Bd; trustee, Nat Black MBA Asn Scholar Fund; life mem, Wash Urban League; life mem, Nat Asn Advan Colored People; bd dir, COT Hope; supvr comt mem, Wash Area Tel Fed Credit Union; Wash Soc Investment Analysts; Financial Execs Int; US Small Bus Admin; builder fel US Dept Housing & Urban Develop Community; sr fel Coun Excellence Govt; vpres, Howard Univ Stud Asn; Howard Univ Sch Bus & Pub Admin Stud Asn; Asa T Spaulding Ins Soc; Iota Rho Chap; Beta Gamma Sigma Bus Hon Soc; pres, Gamma Iota Sigma Ins Hon Soc; Club Philadelphia; Pvt Equity Network; Phi Delta Phi Int Legal Fraternity; City Club Wash; ConnectorsNet; Citizens Democracy Corps; bd mem, HUD Fed Credit Union; chair, Supvry Comt, Wash Tel Fed Credit Union; treas & exec comt mem, Community Hope Inc; Develop Roundtable Upward Mobility (DRUM); 100 Black Men Greater Wash, DC, Educ Comt; Several Wright Hand Groups. **Home Addr:** P O Box 3911, Capitol Heights, MD 20791. **Business Addr:** Director, US Department of Housing & Urban Development, 820 1st St NE Suite 300, Washington, DC 20002.

### TURNER, MELVIN E.

Law enforcement officer. **Personal:** Born Nov 5, 1947, Detroit, MI; son of M E and Martha; children: Naetta Williams, Tramale & Dorian. **Educ:** Madonna Col, Livonia, AA, police admin, 1976, BS, 1977; Univ Detroit, Detroit, MA, criminal justice, 1979; FBI Nat Acad, master, 1986. **Career:** Wayne County, police officer, 1969, investr, 1973, sgt, 1976, lt, 1980, inspector, 1983, capt, 1987, police cmdr, 1988, exec dep chief, 1990, under sheriff & chief dep, 1991-99, expert witness law enforcement, 1999-; FBI Nat Acad, 1986; BNDD Acad, 1973; City Hamtramck, dir pub safety & police comnr, 2001-03; City Highland Pk, dir pub safety, 2001-03; Sumpter Twp Police, chief, 2004-07; police consult, currently. **Orgs:** Nat Asn Chief Police; FBI Nat Acad Asn, 1986-; Int Narcotic Enforcement Officers Asn; Mich Sheriffs' Asn; bd dir, Woodward Acad, bd pres, 2001. **Home Addr:** 4711 W Outer Dr, Detroit, MI 48235, **Home Phone:** (313)861-2359.

### TURNER, MIKOEL

Manager, association executive. **Personal:** Born Aug 22, 1950, New York, NY; son of Richard and Enid Gordon; children: Mekell Mia. **Educ:** Cobleskill A & T Col, New York, NY, AAS, 1971; Cornell Univ, Ithaca, NY, BS, 1974; Univ Phoenix, MA, orgn mgt, 1999; Columbus Phoenix City Inventors, pres. **Career:** Marriott Corp, dept mgr, 1975-81, gen mgr, 1981-84; Fletcher Consult Serv, partner, 1982-; Bd Ed, NJ, supvr, 1984-88; Turner & Assoc, owner; Chelsea Catering, NJ, dept mgr, 1988; New York Bd Educ, culinary arts coordr, 1990; Guest Serv Health care Co, pres, 1994; Nat Asn Black Hospitality, founder, prof, pres. **Orgs:** Bd mem, Union County Psychol Clin; bd mem, Plainfield Econ Develop Corp. **Honors/Awds:** Food MGT Prof, certified; certified teacher; certified hospitality prof. **Home Addr:** 50 Lee Rd 68, Smiths Station, AL 36877-4910, **Home Phone:** (334)298-4802.

### TURNER, DR. MOSES

Educator. **Personal:** Born Mar 28, 1938, Athens, GA; son of Audly and Roberta; married Joan; children: Shaul, Lisa & Chris. **Educ:** Albany State Col, BA, 1962; Cent Wash State Col, MA, 1969; Wash State Univ, PhD, 1974; Harvard Univ, Inst Educ Mgt, 1982. **Career:** Pub sch teacher; Columbia Basin Community Col, chair & dir music prog, 1969-72; Wash State Univ, asst dean students, 1972-77; Tex Tech Univ, dean & dir stud life, 1977-79; Mich State Univ, vpres stud affairs, 1979-204, prof educ admin; Peace Corps, Safrica, dir, currently. **Orgs:** Bd mem, Opera Co Mid-Mich, Oakes Sports Prog, Boy Scouts Am; Gov's Prayer Breakfast Comn; Mich Black Caucus Found; bd mem, Himan Found Awarding Scholar Deserving High Sch Students; spokesperson, Youth Motivation Mich; bd mem, Lansing Symphony Bd dir; Subcomt Fed Stud Fin Assistance, Nat Asn State Univs & Land-Grant Cols; bd mem, Golden Key Nat Hon Soc; Lansing Asn Black Org; Lansing Chap Alpha Chi Boule; Ed Bd, Nat Asn Stud Personnel Adminr Inc; Nat Cong Black Fac. **Home Addr:** 1335 Cove Ct, Okemos, MI 48864, **Home Phone:** (517)349-1532.

### TURNER, NINA

State government official. **Personal:** Born Dec 7, 1967, Cleveland, OH; married Jeffery Turner Sr.; children: Jeffery Turner Jr.. **Educ:** Cuyahoga Community College, Associates of Art; Cleveland State University, B.A. and M.A., 1997. **Career:** State Senator Rhine McLin, Legislative Aide; Mayor Michael White, Executive Asst. of Legislative Affairs; City of Cleveland, City Council Member, 2006-08; Ohio Senate, Senator (Democrat), 2008-, Minority Whip, 2011-. **Orgs:** Insurance & Financial Institutions Committee, Ranking Member; Finance Subcommittee on Education, Ranking Member; Commerce and Labor Committee, Member; Education Committee, Member; Rules Committee, Member; Transportation Committee, Member; Ohio Ballot Board, Member; United Way of Greater Cleveland, Board Member; Cleveland Police Foundation, Board Member; Great Lakes Science Center, Board Member. **Honors/Awds:** "The Root" Magazine, The Root 100 Honorees, 2013. **Business Addr:** Senate Building 1 Capitol Sq., 2nd Fl., Columbus, OH 43215, **Business Phone:** ((61)4)466-45.

**TURNER, PETER. See TURNER, ERVIN.**

### TURNER, REGINALD M., JR.

Lawyer. **Personal:** Born Feb 25, 1960, Detroit, MI; son of Reginald M Sr and Anne L; married Marcia Holland. **Educ:** Wayne State Univ, BS, 1982; Univ Mich, Law Sch, JD, 1987. **Career:** Mich Supreme Ct, law clerk to Justice Dennis Archer, 1987-89; Sachs, Waldman, O'Hare, partner, 1989-2000; Clark Hill PLC, 2000-; Comerica Inc, dir, 2005-; Masco Corp, dir. **Orgs:** Labor & Employ Sect; life fel Am Bar Found; Blue Ribbon Comn Mich Gaming; chmn, City Detroit Bd Ethics; City Detroit Brownfield Redevelop Adv Comt; dir, Comerica Inc; Detroit Bd Educ; vchmn, Detroit Inst Arts; mem labor & employ sect, Detroit Metrop BarAsn; vchmn, Detroit Police Found; Fed Mediation & Conciliation Serv; bdmd, Hudson-Webber Found; chmn, United Way Southeastern Mich; secy, Wayne County Econ Develop Corp; Wayne County Aero tropolis Task Force; bd mem, Mich State Bd Educ; mem Labor & Employ Sect; Gov John Engler's Blue Ribbon Comn Mich Gaming & City Detroit Brownfield Redevelop Adv Comt; vichmn, Detroit Inst Arts; vchmn, Detroit Police Found; Mich State Deleg, Am Bar Asn House Delegates; past chair, ABA House Delegates Rules & Calendar Comt, Comt Issues Concern to Profession, Comt Credentials & Admis; past chair ABA Comn Racial & Ethnic Diversity Profession; Life Patron Fel, Am Bar Found; chmn, Detroit Pub Safety Found, vice chmn, Detroit Inst Arts, vice chmn, Community Found Southeast Mich, trustee, Hudson-Webber Found' past chair, United Way Southeastern Mich; Secy Wayne County Airport Authority; Mich Employ Adv Coun, Am Arbit Asn; pres, State Bar Mich, 1987-; pres, Wolverine Bar Asn, 1987-; pres, Barristers Detroit Metro Bar Asn, 1987-97; chmn, Mem Labor & Employ Sect United Way Southeastern Mich; pres, Nat Bar Asn, 1994-, bd govr exec comm, 1995-, gen coun, 1999-; comnr, State Bar Mich fel, 1995-, vpres, 2000-01, pres, 2002-03; White House fel, 1996-97; Detroit Bd Educ, 1999-2003; Detroit Bd Educ, 2000-; Am Bar Fed Fel, 2002; pres, State Bar Mich 2002-03; Best Lawyers Am, 2003-; Mich State Bd Educ, 2003-09; bd dir, Am Soc Employers, 2004-08; Super Lawyers, 2005-; pres, Nat Bar Asn, 2005-06; house del, Am Bar Asn, mich state deleg, 2009-, Comn Racial & Ethnic Diversity Profession, chair, 2011-13. **Business Addr:** Attorney, Clark Hill PLC, 500 Woodward Ave Suite 3500, Detroit, MI 48226-3435, **Business Phone:** (313)965-8318.

### TURNER, RICHARD M., III

School administrator, educator. **Personal:** Born Charleston, SC; married Dolores Walker; children: 2. **Educ:** Fisk Univ, BA, 1956; Ind Univ-Bloomington, MME, 1961, DME, 1972. **Career:** Baltimore City Community Col, Dean Stud Activ, 1971-74, Dean Fac & Provost, 1974-79, interim pres, 2004-06, prof emer, 2006-; S Cent Community Col, pres, 1979-85; Lane Community Col, pres, 1985-88; Nashville State Tech Inst, pres, 1988-91; Fisk Univ, assoc prof music, Dept Music, chmn, Fisk Jubilee Singers, dir; Wayne Co Community Col Northwest Campus, dean; Am Asn Community Cols, spec consult to pres, 1991-92; Wayne Co Community Col, interim pres, 1994-95. **Orgs:** Int Educ Comn Am Coun Educ; bd trustee, Nat Comn Coop Educ; bd mem, Nat Coun Black Am Affairs; United Way; Am Red Cross; Nat Conf Christians & Jews; Am Asn Univ Profs, 1963-, vpres, Ala Conf, 1967-68; Am Coun Edu, 1979-2006; bd trustee, Yale-New Haven Hosp, 1984-85; bd dir, League Innovation Community Col, 1985-88; pres, Turner Assocs & Mentors Inc, 1996-04. **Business Addr:** Professor Emeritus, Baltimore City Community College, 2901 Liberty Hts Ave, Baltimore, MD 21215-7807, **Business Phone:** (410)462-7600.

### TURNER, ROBERT, JR. (BOBBY TURNER)

Football coach. **Personal:** Born May 6, 1949, Midway, AL; son of Robert Sr and Julia Ann; married Kimberly Jean; children: Nacole, Krishana & Kiaana. **Educ:** Ind State Univ, Terre Haute, IN, BS, 1972, MS, 1976. **Career:** Haworth High Sch, Kokomo, Ind, asst football/basketball coach, admin asst, 1972-74; Ind State Univ, running backs & quarterbacks, 1975-82, defensive backs coach & conditioning coordr, 1976-77, spec team coordr, 1978-81, defensive backs & spec teams coordr, 1982; Fresno State Univ, running backs coach, 1983-88; Ohio State Univ, running backs coach, 1989-90; Purdue Univ, asst head football coach & offensive coordr, 1991-94; Denver, running backs coach, 1995-2009;Wash Redskins, running backs coach, 2010-14; Atlanta Falcons, running backs coach, 2015-. **Orgs:** Am Football Coaches Asn; Black Coaches Asn; Nat Asn Advan Colored People; Ind State Univ Alumni Asn; Kappa Alpha Psi Fraternity; Fel Christian Athletes.

### TURNER, REP. ROBERT LLOYD

Legislator, state government official. **Personal:** Born Sep 14, 1947, Columbus, MS; son of Roosevelt and Beatrice; married Gloria Harrell; children: Robert, Roosevelt & Ryan. **Educ:** Univ Wisc, Parkside, BS, bus admin, 1976. **Career:** Military personnel (rertired), publisher, personnel manager, restaurant owner; City Racine, City Coun Mem, 1976-2004; Wisc State Assembly, 61st Assembly Dist, state rep, 1991-. **Orgs:** Alderman, Racine City Coun, 1976-2004; chmn, City Racine Fin Comt, 1987-2003; chmn, State Wisc Elections Bd, 1990; State Wisc Bldg Comn, 1991-99; Gov Task Force Fed Clean Air Act Implementation, 1993-94; sgt arms, minority caucus, 1997; Dem Caucus, chmn, 2002, 2004; Community Develop Comt; chmn, Econ Develop Comt, City Racine; Assembly Comt Judiciary; Assembly Comt Criminal Justice & Homeland Security; Assembly Comt Veterans Affairs; Assembly Comt Rules; Assembly Comt Orgn; life mem, Vietnam Veterans Am; Nat Asn Advan Colored People; Urban League; Dem Party; Am Legion; S Gate Lodge 6 Prince Hall; Masonic Fraternity & Shriner Club; chair, Minority Caucus; Northside Revitalization Comt; Post 1391 Veterans Foreign Wars. **Honors/Awds:** The 33 Degree Mason, 1999. **Home Addr:** 36 McKinley Ave, Racine, WI 53404, **Home Phone:** (262)634-7371. **Business Addr:** State Representative, Legislator, Wisconsin State Assembly, Rm 223 N State Capitol, Madison, WI 53708-8953, **Business Phone:** (608)266-0731.

### TURNER, SHARON V.

Government official. **Personal:** Born Jul 8, 1945, Kansas City, MO; daughter of O E Douglass and Eunice Weaver Douglass Shellner; children: Sheri Lynette Duff & Paul Eugene Jr. **Educ:** Park Col, Kans City, MO, BS, Soc AC, psychol, 1993; Baker Univ, Overland Park, KS, MS, mgt, 1994. **Career:** Telecommunications mgr, 1966-93; Kans City Election Bd, Mo, dir, 1994. **Orgs:** Secy, Leon Jordan Scholar fund, 1984-95; trustee, Urban League, 1985-89; trustee, Rehab Loan Corp, 1987-89; chair, Scholar Comn, Southern Christian Leadership Conf, 1988-95; gen telethon chair, United Negro Col Fund, 1989; vpres, Black Achievers Soc, 1989-90; vpres, Black Chamber Com, 1989-90; pres, Urban League top Notch Team, 1991-93; bd dir, Kans City Visitors & Conv Bur, 1991-94; gala co-chair, Kans City Friends Alvin Ailey, 1992; first vpres, Southern Christian Leadership Conf, 1992-95; fund develop chair, Jackson County Links Inc, 1994-; Elections Ctr, 1995-; Int Asn Clerks Recorders; Exec comt Nationalist Cong Party, 2001-. **Home Addr:** 2525 Main St Apt 409, Kansas City, MO 64108, **Home Phone:** (816)221-5215. **Business Addr:** MO.

### TURNER, SHIRLEY A.

Educator, association executive. **Personal:** Born Mar 22, 1936, South Bend, IN; children: Dawn, Kimberly & Steven. **Educ:** Western Mich Univ, BS, 1972, MA, 1977. **Career:** Fiskal Univ, dean studs, dir career planning & placement; Western Mich Univ, Placement Serv, asst dir; Western Mich Univ, Para Sch Learning Ctr. **Orgs:** Dir educ, Urban Leg S Bend St Joseph County; Kalamazoo Pub Lib pub sch; bd dir, Planned Parenthood Asn; bd, Young Men's Christian Asn; Young Men's Christian Asn Community Outreach Adv; Youth Serv Syst Adv Bd; Cont Educ Young Women Adv Bd; consult, Upward Boun Univ Notre Dame; Planned Parenthood Teen Clinics; Delta Sigma Theta

Serv Sorority; Dulcet Club Kalamazoo; Mich Asn N White Concerns; Kalamazoo Personnel Asn; Midwest Cool Placement Asn. **Honors/Awds:** Teach Award, Laubaugh Lit Inst; Award, Mich Nat All Bus Career Guid Inst; Award of Excellence, Western Mich Univ; Certificate of Academic Appreciation; Certificate of Career Exploration Excel. **Special Achievements:** Produced, directed video tape, demo prof interview tech. **Business Addr:** Director of Career Placement, Rider College, 2083 Lawrenceville Rd, Lawrenceville, NJ 08648-3099, **Business Phone:** (609)896-5000.

### TURNER, TERESA ANN

School administrator, teacher. **Personal:** Born Aug 17, 1971, Columbus, OH; daughter of William and Bernice. **Educ:** Jackson State Univ, BS, 1993, MST, 1995; Univ Miss, Eds. **Career:** Jackson Pub Schs, teacher, 1993-96; Tupelo Pub Schs, asst prin, 1996-2003; Lawndale Elem Sch, princ, 2003-06. **Orgs:** MS Sci Teachers Asn, 1993-95; Nat Asn Sec Sch Principals, 1998-; Lee County Big Bro Big Sister, 1998-; Phi Delta Kappa, 2001; Kappa Delta Pi Int Hon Soc Educ; Delta Sigma Theta; Asn Supv & Curric Develop. **Home Addr:** 1107 Nixon Dr, Tupelo, MS 38801, **Home Phone:** (601)842-3041.

### TURNER, TINA (ANNA MAE BULLOCK)

Actor, dancer, singer. **Personal:** Born Nov 26, 1939, Nutbush, TN; daughter of Floyd Richard and Zelma Priscilla; married Ike; children: Raymond Craig, Ike Jr, Michael & Ronald; married Erwin Bach. **Career:** Ike & Tina Turner Revue, 1960-76; Tina Turns the Country On!, 1974; Acid Queen, 1975; Rough, 1978; Love Explosion, 1979; Solo Albums: Private Dancer, 1984, Break Every Rule, 1986; Tina Live in Europe, 1988; Foreign Affair, 1989; Look Mein the Heart, 1990; Simply the Best, 1991; What's Love Got to Do With It", 1993; The Collected Recordings, 1994; Wildest Dreams, 1996; Good Hearted Woman, 1998; Twenty Four Seven, 1999; Back to Back, 2003; Country My Way, 2003; All the Best, 2004; Tina Turner Sings Country, 2005; Country in My Soul, 2005; All the Best: The Hits, 2005; Film appearances: Mad Max Beyond Thunder dome, 1985: Last Action Hero, 1993; Brother Bear, 2003; All the Invisible C, 2005; "80s", 2005; All the Invisible Children, 2005; Flushed Away, 2006; "Atrapats pel cap d'any", 2007; "Memories de la tele", 2008; The Platinum Collection, 2009. Documentary Film: The Big T.N.T. Show, 1966; It's Your Thing, 1970; Soul to Soul, 1971; Ally McBeal, 2000; Care Bears, 2005. **Honors/Awds:** Grammy Award for Record Of The Year, 1984; Grammy Award for Pop Female Vocal, 1984; Grammy Award for Rock Female Vocal, 1984; Grammy Award for Rock Female Vocal, 1985; Grammy Award for Rock Female Vocal, 1986; Grammy Award for Rock Female Vocal, 1988; 2 American Music Awards; Triple Platinum Album "Private Dancer"; Gold Single "What's Love Got To Do With It?"; Silver Disk Award "Let's Stay Together"; Honoree, ABAA Music Award, 1985; Honored with a star on the Hollywood Walk of Fame and St. Louis Walk of Fame; MTV Video Award, 2005; Kennedy Center Honors, 2005; Grammy Hall of Fame. **Special Achievements:** Citation, Ms Magazine, 1984; author, I, Tina, My Life Story, 1986; Subject of the movie, What's Love Got to Do With It", 1993; Ranked 2 on VH1's Greatest Women of Rock N Roll; Ranked 6 on VH-1's 100 Sexiest Artists, 2002. **Business Addr:** Singer, Virgin Records, 150 5th Ave, New York, NY 10011.

### TURNER, VIVIAN LOVE

Executive, manager, president (organization). **Personal:** Born May 25, 1947, Concord, NC; daughter of F Haywood Love and Othella Spears Love; married William H; children: Kisha, Jomo & Hodari. **Educ:** Livingstone Col, Salisbury, NC, BS, math, 1968; Univ Notre Dame, S Bend, IN, MA, educ, 1971. **Career:** Fisk Univ, Nashville, Tenn, programmer & analyst, 1971-73; Univ Md, Princess Anne, Md, lectr, 1974-77; Digital Equip Corp, Lanham, Md, sr educ specialist, 1977-79; Lexington Community Col, Lexington, Ky, assoc prof, data processing tech, 1980-85; R J Reynolds Tobacco Co, Winston-Salem, NC, programmer & analyst II, 1985-90, mgr community prog, dir contrib & comm affairs, pres, currently. **Orgs:** Alpha Kappa Alpha Sorority, 1966-; Ky Acad Comput Users Group, 1980-85; stud chap sponsor, Data Processing Mgt Asn, 1981-85; dir Christian educ, Emmanuel Baptist Church, 1989-; bd mem, Winston Lake YMCA, 1990-91; bd mem, Forsyth County United Way, 1993-; bd, Winston-Salem State Univ, 1994-; Links, 1996-; life mem, Nat Asn Advan Colored People; bd mem, Nc Bus Comt Educ; bd mem, NC Bus Comt Educ, bd mem, N Carolina Pub Sch Forum, bd mem, Crosby Scholars Prog, bd mem, Livingstone Col Corp Adv Bd; bd mem, Leadership Winston-Salem found; bd mem, Collab Proj. **Home Addr:** 5821 Brookway Dr, Winston-Salem, NC 27105, **Home Phone:** (336)744-5611. **Business Addr:** Director Contributions and Community Affairs, President, RJ Reynolds Tobacco Co, PO Box 2959, Winston-Salem, NC 27102, **Business Phone:** (336)741-0049.

### TURNER, DR. WILLIAM HOBERT

Educator, consultant. **Personal:** Born Jul 20, 1946, Lynch, KY; married Vivian Love; children: Kisha, Jomo & Hodari. **Educ:** Southeast Community Col, UK, grad, 1966; Univ Ky, BS, sociol, 1968; Univ Notre Dame, MS, sociol, 1971, PhD, sociol & anthrop, 1974. **Career:** Howard Univ, sr res fel, 1977-79; Univ Ky, asst prof sociol, 1979-83; Nat Res Coun, Ford Found fel, 1983; Ky State Univ, dean arts & sci, 1983-84, interim pres, 2003-04, vpres univ engagement & assoc provost multicultural & acad affairs, currently; Winston Salem State Univ, chmn social sci, 1985; Winston-Salem State Univ, admin; Blacks Appalachia, Univ Press Ky, 1985; Berea Col, distinguished vis prof Black & Appalachian studies, 1988-89; Brandeis Univ, vis res prof, 1990-91; B&C Int Inc, sr vpres; Turner & Assoc, pres, currently; Univ Pa, fel; George Wash Univ, fel; Duke Univ, fel; Fisk Univ, admin; African Am Miners & Migrants: Eastern Ky Social Club, Univ Press Ill, 2004; Path My Pilgrimage: Autobiography Marshall B Bass; Black Cols: Essays Cult Legitimacy & Econ Efficiency; Appalachian Heritage. **Orgs:** Historian/archivist, Eastern Ky Social/Heritage Soc, 1977-; res assoc, Roots, 1979-91; consult, US AID, 1986; comnr, Comn Relig Appalachia, 1986-; ed/publ, EKSC; Black Mountain Improv Asn, 1988; Southern Regional Coun; Appalachian African Am Community Develop Ctr; Phi Beta Sigma Fraternity; trustee mem, Prince Hall Masons, Lees-McRae Col Bd; Trotter Group, Harvard Univ; Chair, Appalachian Studies, 2007-. **Home Addr:** 5821 Brookway Dr, Winston Salem, NC 27105, **Home Phone:** (336)744-5611. **Business Addr:** Vice President, Associate provost for Multicultural & Academic Affairs, University of Kentucky, 529 Patterson Off Twr, Lexington, KY 40506-0027, **Business Phone:** (859)257-3381.

### TURNER, WINSTON EDWIN. See Obituaries Section.

### TURNER, YVONNE WILLIAMS

Community activist, counselor. **Personal:** Born Apr 5, 1927, Birmingham, AL; daughter of John Harvey and Leitha W (deceased); married James L Sr; children: Philandus C, Roderick G, Keith H, Leitha B & Stanley M. **Educ:** Booker T Wash Jr Col Bus, Birmingham, AL, dipl, 1952; Rosetta Reifer's Sch Modeling, NY, cert, 1954; Anna Watson's Sch Millinery Designing, 1968; Dale Carnegie Sch, Birmingham, AL, cert, 1960. **Career:** Community activist (retired); Booker T Wash Ins Co, Birmingham, AL, clerk, 1946-64; Clyde Kirby Ins Agency, Birmingham, AL, secy, 1965-66; Dept Housing & Urban Devel, Birmingham, AL, clerk typist, 1966-77, comput technician, 1977-82, community resources specialist, 1982-86, prog asst single family div loan mgt, 1986-87; Birmingham Housing Authority, Birmingham, AL, housing counr, 1987-90. **Orgs:** Life mem, Ala Christian Movement Human Rights & Southern Christian Leadership Conf, 1956-; fund raiser, United Negro Col Fund, 1965-; Birmingham Design Rev Comt, Birmingham, Ala, 1979-85; Birmingham Arts Comn, Birmingham, Ala, 1985-; Jefferson-Blount-St Clair Ment Health/Ment Retardation Authority Bd, 1989-91; Birmingham's Image Comt, 1990-91; assoc mem, Ala State Univ Alumni, 1990-; band mother, Ala State Univ, 1979-; pres or bus mgr, Wilkerson Elem & A H Parker High Band Boosters, 1975-89; Red Cross Minority Involvement Comt, 1989-91; chartered mem, Magic City Chap Links Inc, 1993; dep registr, Ala Election Law Comnr. **Honors/Awds:** Certifictate of Recognition in Field of Business, Booker T Washington Jr Col Bus Alumni Asn, 1978; Iota Phi Lambda Sorority, 1981; Outstanding Serv, Nat Southern Christian Leadership Conf, 1982; alumni merit award, Booker T Washington Jr Col Bus, 1984; Alpha Phi Chi Sorority, 1985; Faithful Serv US Government Award, 1987; named in House of Rep Resolution 125, 1988; HR & auth column "Socially Speaking," Birmingham Times, 1988-92; Honored by Gov Guy Hunt, Arts, 1989; Zeta Phi Beta Sorority, Women of the Year, 1990; Civil Rights Honoree, 1991, Omisson Lambda Chpt; Alpha Phi Alpha Fraternity Inc; SCLS Women, Spec Award, 1991; WENN 107-WAGG 1320 and Anheuser's Citizen of the Week, 1991; Birmingham Comm Schs Appreciation, 1991-92; 21st Century Human Rights Movement, Appreciation for Dedicated Services to Mankind, 1991; HUD's Ladies of Distinction, Sixth Ave Bapt Church, 1992; Channel 42, WBMG/TV Jefferson Award, Bronze Medal, Documentation on Civil Rights, 1992; United to Serve Am Diamond Award, 1992; Certificate of Appreciation, Ala State Univ, Connection Day Comt, 1992; Curioso Club's Rose Award, 1992; Certificateof Appreciation, Birmingham City Coun, Dist 4; Meritorious Serv Award, United Negro Col Fund Inc, 1993; Honored for 14 years, Faithful and Dedicated Servs, Ala State Univ Marching Band of Montgomery AL, 1994; Community Serv Award, Birmingham Baptist Col, Black Catholic Ministries, Nat Islam; Invisible Giants of the Voting Rights Movement, Honored in Selma, Commendation of the Voting Rights March & Bloody Sunday, 1995; Plaque, Nat Asn Advan Colored People, Outstanding African Am, 1996; Acad Fine Arts Inc, Citizen Arts Award, 1996. **Special Achievements:** Lectured at the Birmingham Civil Rights Institute, "Yesterdays Voices of Women of the Movement", 1996. **Home Addr:** 504 10th Ct W, Birmingham, AL 35204-2924, **Home Phone:** (205)252-3659.

### TURNER-FORTE, DIANA

Educator, choreographer, dancer. **Personal:** Born Aug 24, 1951, Columbus, OH; daughter of Ethel S Turner and Everhart S Turner Sr; married Kenneth T. **Educ:** Capital Univ, BA, dance theory & anat, 1985; Antioch Univ, MA, dance, 1991; Royal Acad Dance, London, UK, cert, ballet teaching studies. **Career:** Des Moines Ballet Co, dancer, soloist, 1980-81; Ohio Arts Coun, minority arts asst, 1981-83; Balitmore Sch Arts, fac, 1983-86; BalletMet Dance Acad, fac, 1986-; Antioch Univ, adj fac, 1990-; Greater Columbus Arts Coun, founder & artistic dir, 1991-; Brian Gym, instr & consult; Choreographic Inst NC, artistic dir, 2012-. **Orgs:** Dance adv panelist, State Arts Coun, 1984-86; arts adv panel chair, Franklin County Edu Coun, 1991; adv bd, Ohio Dance, 1991; fundraising comt, Third Ave Performing Space, 1992; bd trustee, WOSU Radio, 1992; Nat Registry Dance Educr; Royal Acad Dance. **Special Achievements:** First book, Letters to Amelia was recently published by Vantage Press. **Home Addr:** 2693 Reynoldsburg-New Albany Rd, Blacklick, OH 43004, **Home Phone:** (614)855-2248. **Business Addr:** Artistic Director, Choreographic Institute of North Carolina, 1662 Richards St, Southern Pines, NC 28388, **Business Phone:** (910)725-0595.

### TURNER-GIVENS, ELLA MAE (ELLA MAE TURNER GIBBONS)

Educator, consultant, teacher. **Personal:** Born Jun 5, 1927, Los Angeles, CA; daughter of Ezekiel Moore and Ruth Dean; married Walter; children: Edward Samuel Turner. **Educ:** Univ Southern Calif, BMus, 1957; St Calif, Dept Educ, life dipl, spec sec teaching credent music, 1965; Univ Calif, Los Angeles, Grad Sch, attended 1966 & 1968; Calif Dept Educ, life dipl, stand sec teaching credent Eng, 1968. **Career:** Foshay Jr High Sch, teacher, 1957-58; Markham Jr High Sch, teacher, 1958-66; Manual Arts High Sch, teacher summer, 1962; Markham Jr High Sch Summer Opportunity Ctr Prog, teacher, 1965; Girls Social Adjust Sch, teacher, 1966-67; Los Angeles High Sch, teacher, 1967-71; Los Angeles Unified Sch Dist, teacher, 1971-. **Orgs:** Chmn, Nat Adv Coun, Environ Educ; HEW; adv coun, HUD; Urban Studies Fel Prog, Textbk Adoption Comm Los Angeles Unified Sch Dist; adjudicator Southern Calif Vocal Asn; host, chmn Southern Calif Vocal Asn Choral Festivals; pres, Sec Music Teacher Asn; chmn, bd dir, Do Re Me Child Develop Ctr; NEA, Calif Teacher Asn; Los Angeles Teacher Asn; Music Educ Nat Conf Life; Los Angeles County Music Educ Asn; Am Choral Dir Asn; Southern Calif Vocal Asn; Adv Health Coun; St Dept Health; Child Develop Adv Bd; consult, Gen St Dept Health; Calif St Dept Health, St Calif Personnel Bd, W Interstate Commn Higher Educ, Calif WorkIncentive Plan Prog, Neighborhood Adult Participation Proj, Delinq Prev Ctr; Atty Gen, Vol Adv Coun, Neumeyer Found; rep, St Control Comm; appointee, Calif Gov Comm Employ Handicapped; St wide Planning Proj Vocat Rehab, Adv Comm Voc Rehab; sec adv comm, Urban Affairs Inst; Dist Atty Adv Coun; dist atty, Legis Coun. **Honors/Awds:** Recipient 10th Dist PTA 4 year scholarship; Delta Sigma Theta Sor Scholar; E Star Scholarship Award, twice; Women's Polit Study Club Scholarship. **Special Achievements:** First African American woman in US history to chair a National Advisory Council. **Home Addr:** 2158 W 82nd St, Los Angeles, CA 90047-2620, **Home Phone:** (323)971-3830.

### TURNIPSEED, CARL WENDELL

Banker. **Personal:** Born Dec 21, 1947, Baltimore, MD; son of Willis and Alice Poyner; married Joyce Hill; children: Danielle. **Educ:** Morgan State Col, BS, 1969; NY Univ Grad Sch Bus, MBA, 1974; Columbia Univ, exec mgt prog. **Career:** Fed Res Bank NY, acct, govt bonds, check proc, elect funds transfers, personnel, foreign rels, vp, pres, personnel function, Buffalo Br, sr vpres & mgr, 1994-, NY Bus Develop Off, head, 1998-; Fed Res Bank NY, exec vpres, financial serv, currently. **Orgs:** Union Baptist Church, 1980-; Nat Asn Advan Colored People, 1982-; Asn MBA Execs, 1982-; Urban Bankers Asn, 1983-; Black MBA Asn 1983-; MBA Exec; 16th SEANZA Cent Banking Prog, 1986; Keeper Exchequer Brooklyn Long Island Alumni Kappa Alpha Psi Fraternity, l988-; vis prof, Nat Urban League BEEP; life mem, Kappa Alpha Psi Fraternity; founding mem, Classroom Inc; bd chair, INROADS/Western NY; bd mem, United Way Buffalo & Erie County & Niagara Inst Trade Coun; Sigma Pi Phi Fraternity; Morgan State Univ Alumni Asn; Nat Asn Urban Bankers; bank's mgt comt. **Home Addr:** 8199 Fernleaf Ct, Williamsville, NY 14221. **Business Addr:** Executive Vice President, Federal Reserve Bank New York, 33 Liberty St, New York, NY 10045, **Business Phone:** (212)720-5000.

### TURNQUEST, SANDRA CLOSE

Executive. **Personal:** Born Jul 19, 1954, Bainbridge, GA; daughter of Frank and Daisy. **Educ:** Fla A&M Univ, Tallahassee, FL, BS, polit sci, 1975; Fla Atlantic Univ, MPA, pub admin, Boca Raton, FL, 1977; Harvard Univ, exec mgt prog; Univ Mich Sch, bus exec mgt prog; Am Mgt Asn, cert. **Career:** S Fla Water Mgmt Dist (SFWMD), dist admin off I-III, 1977-2011, admin officer IV, 1980-84, asst to dir, 1984-87, exec asst, 1984-87, dir, admin serv, 1987, Dist W Palm Beach, human resource dir, 1987-94, Mgt Serv & Hr Dept, dir, 1999-2005, dep exec dir corp resources, 2011; Govt Admin & HR prof; Corp Resources, dep exec dir, 2005. **Orgs:** Pres, Sickle Cell Found PB County, 1991-92; fin secy, Delta Sigma Theta Sorority, 1989-91; second vpres, Bus & Prof Women's Club, 1987-; Exec Women Palm Beaches; Vital Progs Leadership Palm Beach County, 1987; chairperson, fund-raising, Fla A&M Univ Alumni Asn; Links Inc, W Palm Beach Chap, 1992-; pres, Delta Sigma Theta Sorority Inc, W Palm Beach Alumni Chap, 2003-; Soc Hr Mgt; Am Mgt Asn; Nat Forum Black Pub Adminr; Palm Beach HealthCare Found; Girls II Women; S Fla Hr Exec Roundtable; Socs Hr Mgt & Am Mgt Asn; Fla A&M Univ Alumni Asn; Trustee Tabernacle Missionary Baptist Church. **Home Addr:** 1429 6th St, West Palm Beach, FL 33401, **Home Phone:** (407)835-8055.

### TUSAN, HON. GAIL S.

Judge, lawyer. **Personal:** Born Aug 3, 1956, Los Angeles, CA; daughter of Willie Jr and Lois Carrington; married Carl V Washington Jr; children: 4. **Educ:** Univ Calif, Los Angeles, CA, BA, psychol, 1979; George Washington Univ, JD, 1981. **Career:** US Dept Justice, intern, 1980-81; Kilpatrick & Cody, assoc, 1981-84; Asbill, Porter, assoc, 1984-86; City Ct Atlanta, admin law judge, 1984-86, judge, 1990-92; Joyner & Joyner, partner, 1986-90; Magistrate Ct Fulton, judge, 1986-90; Univ Nev-Reno, Nat Judicial Col, fac, 1990-; City Ct Atlanta, judge, 1990-92; State Ct Fulton Co, judge, 1992-95; Inst Continuing Judicial Educ, fac mem; Ga State Univ Law Sch, fac mem; Super Ct Fulton Co, judge, 1995-. **Orgs:** Pres, Bd dir Camp Fire USA, Ga Coun; Ga State Bar, 1981-; vpres, Legal Clin Homeless; pres, Ga Asn Black Women Attys, 1983, exec comm; Gate City Bar Asn; Atlanta Bar Asn; Judicial Procedure & Admin Adv Comn; Comnon Profism. **Home Addr:** 602 McGill Pl, Atlanta, GA 30312, **Home Phone:** (404)584-2907. **Business Addr:** Judge, Superior Court of Fulton County, Justice Ctr Twr 185 Cent Ave SW Suite T8955 Ct Rm 8F, Atlanta, GA 30303, **Business Phone:** (404)612-8520.

### TUTT, DR. WALTER CORNELIUS

Dentist. **Personal:** Born Jan 29, 1918, Birmingham, AL; son of Walter Andrew and Corinne Flood; married Julia Smith; children: Lia. **Educ:** Livingstone Col, BS, 1939; Howard Univ, Grad Sch, attended 1943, DDS, 1957; Univ Florence, attended 1945. **Career:** Dentist (retired); NC Pub Sch, teacher, 1941-42; VA Pub Sch, teacher, 1947-48; pvt pract dent surgeon. **Orgs:** Robert T Freeman Dent Soc; Nat Dent Asn; Am Dent Asn; pres, Prince Williams County Teacher Asn, 1948; pres, WA Grad Chap Chi Delta Mu Nat Med Fraterntiy; grand exec comm, Grand Chap Chi Delta Mu; Kappa Alpha Psi; mem adv comm, WA Alumni Chap Kappa Alpha Psi; bd dir, WA Alumni Chap Kappa Alpha Psi; Rock Creek E Neighborhood League, Pigskin Club WA; Howard Univ, Gen & Dent Alumni Asn; treas, Hellians Inc. **Honors/Awds:** Conspicuous Service Award, Chi Delta Mu; Distinguished Alumni of Historically Black, Col Nat Asn Equal Opportunity in Higher Ed; Combat Infantry Badge, AUS; Three Battle Stars & Two Campaign Ribbons, AUS; Good Conduct Medal, AUS. **Home Addr:** USSAH-1037 3700 N Capitol St NW, Washington, DC 20317, **Home Phone:** (202)545-8149.

### TWIGG, DR. LEWIS HAROLD, JR.

Educator, gynecologist, physician. **Personal:** Born Oct 5, 1937, Muskogee, OK; son of Lewis Sr and Ann R; married Myrna; children: Lewis III & Karen. **Educ:** Morehouse Col, BS, 1958; Atlanta Univ, MS, 1960; Meharry Med Col, Sch Med, MD, 1967. **Career:** Hurley Med Ctr, internship, 1968, resident gen pract, 1973, vice chmn, dept obstet & gynec, resident, 1978-81; Mich State Col, assoc clin prof, dept obstet & gynec, reproductive biol human med; All Womens Clin, group pract; pvt practr, physician, currently. **Orgs:** Flint Acad Surg; Alpha Phi Alpha Frat; dipl, Am Bd obstet & gynec; fel Col obstet & gynec; Sigma Pi Phi Fraternity. **Honors/Awds:** Co-author, "Cutaneous Streptococcal Infections in Vietnam, " Archives of Dermatology, Sept, 1971. **Home Addr:** 6242 Covered Wagon Tr, Flint, MI 48532-2169, **Home Phone:** (810)733-1103. **Business Addr:** Physician, 4250 N Saginaw St, Flint, MI 48505, **Business Phone:** (810)787-2266.

**TWIGGS, DR. LEO FRANKLIN**
Artist, educator, vice president (organization). **Personal:** Born Feb 13, 1934, St. Stephen, SC; son of Frank and Bertha L Moultrie; married Rosa Johnson; children: Kenneth, Darryl & Keith. **Educ:** Claflin Col, BA, art & art studies, 1956; NY Univ, Art Inst Chicago, MA, 1964; Univ Ga, EdD, art & art studies, 1970. **Career:** Lincoln High Sch, Sumter, SC, art teacher, 1958-64; SC State Univ, art prof, exec dir, Stanback Mus, 1964-98, fine art dept developer, 1973-98, prof emer, 2000, dir emer, currently; Claflin Univ, distinguished artist residence, 2000-; White House Christmas, design ornaments, 2002-08; Ga Mus Art, 2004-06. **Orgs:** Mus comt, State Mus 1972-; bd, vpres, SC Art Found, 1985-; chair, African Am Mus Asn, long range planning comt, 1985-; trustee, New Mt Zion Baptist Church, 1987-; SC Gov Sch Arts & Humanities, 1992; SC Hall Fame, 1992; bd mem, Orangeburg County Fine Arts Ctr; bd mem, Sc Arts Comn. **Home Addr:** 420 Woodlawn Parlerdale Subdivision, Orangeburg, SC 29115, **Home Phone:** (803)534-9796. **Business Addr:** Distinguished Artist-in-Residence, Claflin University, 400 Magnolia St, Orangeburg, SC 29115, **Business Phone:** (803)535-5000.

**TYLER, B. J. (BRANDON JOEL TYLER)**
Basketball player. **Personal:** Born Apr 30, 1971, Galveston, TX. **Educ:** DePaul Univ, attended 1990; Univ Tex, attended 1994. **Career:** Basketball player (retired); Philadelphia 76ers, power guard, 1994-95; Toronto Raptors, 1995-2000; Essex CC, power guard, 1996-97. **Honors/Awds:** Player of the Year, S W Conf, 1994.

**TYLER, CHERYL LYNNETT**
Law enforcement officer. **Educ:** Spelman Col, BA, sociol; Atlanta Univ, MA, pub admin & criminal justice. **Career:** Special agent (retired); US Secret Serv, spec agt, 1984-99; Us Postal Serv Off Inspector Gen, criminal investr, 1999-2001; US Dept Homeland Security, Transp Security Admin, criminal investr, 2001-09; US Customs & Border Protection, Off Internal Affairs BIU, case mgr, 2008-09; CLT3 Security Consutling, founder & chief exec officer, 2010-. **Business Addr:** Chief Executive Officer, Founder, CLT3 Consulting LLC, 410 O St SW Suite 107, Washington, WA 20024, **Business Phone:** (240)481-7756.

**TYLER, DELORA HALL**
Business owner. **Educ:** Univ Detroit, BA, 1977. **Career:** Freelance media consult; Detroit News; WGPR; First Media Group, founder, pres, cheif exec officer, 1990-. **Orgs:** Pres, Rosa Parks Scholar Found. **Honors/Awds:** Best Small Bus, Mich Small Bus Develop Ctr, 1999. **Business Addr:** Chief Execuitve Officer, President, First Media Group, 29600 NW Hwy Suite 112, Southfield, MI 48034, **Business Phone:** (248)354-8705.

**TYLER, REV. GERALD DEFOREST**
School administrator. **Personal:** Born Feb 28, 1946, Louisa County, VA; son of John and Annie; children: Michael Jerone & Jerome Duvall. **Educ:** Norfolk State Univ, BS, 1977, MA, 1983; Old Dom Univ, PhD, 1983. **Career:** Dalmo Sales Co, salesman, 1964-66; USMC, adm orderly, 1966-69; Tidewater Regional Transit Syst, bus oper, 1969-77; Elizabeth City St Univ, spec asst to chancellor, 1977-84; Norfolk St Univ, dir univ rels, 1984-2000, mil prog coordr, 2000-, advisor, counr, Reclamation Proj, st. **Orgs:** Nat Asn Advan Colored People, 1979-; adv, ECSU Stud Chap Nat Asn Advan Colored People, 1980-84; NC St Employees Asn Inc, 1980-84; pres, Prof Bus Asn, 1980-81; alt deleg, Thirty Fifth Ann NCSEA Conv Comn, 1980-81; SHumanities Conf, 1980-82; chmn, NC St Employees Asn Inc, 1981-82; Greater Bibleway Temple 120 Club, 1981; vpres, Pasquotank Co Br, 1981-84; NCSEA Inc Area 24 Exec Bd, 1981-84; adv, ECSU Sr Class, 1981-84; vice chmn, Pasquotank Co Voting Precinct 3B, 1981-82; NCSEA Inc Bd Gov, 1981-82; chmn, NCSEA Inc Area 24, 1981-82; bd mem, Gov's FOTC Asn, 1982-84; bd mem, Albemarle Develop Auth, 1982-84; head adv, ECSU SrClass, 1982-84; NCSEA Inc State Organ Study Comt, 1982-83; Pasquotank CoVoting Precinct 3B, 1983-84; Pasquotank Co Improv Asn, 1983-84; NewTowne Civic League, 1984-86; Tidewater Media Prof Asn, 1984-89; bd mem, New Towne Civic League, 1984-86; Va Social Sci Asn, 1984-94; Va Asn Printing, Publ & Pub Rels, 1986-; bd mem, Miss Black Va Pageant, 1986-88; bd dir & adv, Pepper Bird Found, 1988; mem bd adv, Miss Col African Am Pageant, 1989-93; mem bd, Tidewater Charter, Am Red Cross, 1990-92; Hampton Roads Black Media Prof, 1990-; bd dir & nominating comt mem, CounAdvan & Support Educ Dist III, 1993-95. **Special Achievements:** Book: Three In One. **Home Addr:** 4305 Sonoma Ct, Virginia Beach, VA 23456. **Business Addr:** Millennium Program Coordinator, Norfolk State University, 700 Pk Ave, Norfolk, VA 23504, **Business Phone:** (757)823-8600.

**TYLER, KATHRYN BRADFORD. See PRIGMORE, KATHRYN TYLER.**

**TYLER, LAUREN M.**
Businessperson. **Personal:** children: 5. **Educ:** Yale Univ, BA; Harvard Bus Sch, MBA. **Career:** Morgan Stanley & Co Inc, Mergers & Acquisitions Dep, financial analyst, 1984-86; TSG Capital, partner; Allen & Co, dir, vpres, dir, 1995-; Quetzal JP Morgan Partners, partner, 2000-05, managing mem, currently; JP Morgan Partners, partner, 2005-; Capital Advisors LLC, managing dir; JPMorgan Chase & Co, vpres, 2011, gen audit, 2011-. **Orgs:** Fed Adv Comt mem, Fed Commun Comn; bd dir, Archway Broadcasting Group; bd dir, Col Sports TV; bd dir, Radiovisa Corp; Investment Comt, Quetzal JPMorgan Partners; Nat Asn Investment Co; bd mem, Archway Broadcasting Group LLC; bd mem, Radiovisa Corp; bd mem, CML Group Inc; bd mem, ICBC Broadcast Holdings Inc. **Special Achievements:** 75 Most Powerful Blacks on Wall Street. **Business Addr:** Partner, JP Morgan Partners, 1221 Ave of the Americas, New York, NY 10020, **Business Phone:** (212)270-8205.

**TYLER, MICHAEL LAWRENCE**
Rap musician. **Personal:** Born Sep 22, 1970, New Orleans, LA; children: 3. **Career:** Big Boy Records, 1994; No Limit Records, 1997-99; Jive Records, 1995-2000; Cash Money Records; Universal Republic Records; Big Truck Records, 2000. Albums: Mystikal, 1995; Mind of Mystikal, 1996; Unpredictable, 1997; Ghetto Fabulous, 1998; Let's Get Ready, 2000; Tarantula, 2001, Price of the South, 2004; Chopped & Screwed, 2004; Original, 2015; Monsta, 2015. Actor: Lil' Pimp, 2005; "We Are the Beginning", 2012; Mac & Devin Go to High School, 2012; Blues for Life, 2015; My Side Piece, 2015. **Home Addr:** 12th Ward, New Orleans, LA 70112.

**TYLER, ROBERT JAMES, SR.**
Real estate executive, government official, business owner. **Personal:** Born Dec 14, 1935, Darby, PA; son of Joseph and Katharine; married Phyllis E; children: Mary E & Robert J Jr. **Educ:** Univ Pa, ABA bus 1978; William Pa Sch, sch dir, 1998. **Career:** Philadelphia Svg Fund Soc, mortgage loan solicitor, 1967; Hope Develop Corp, mgt, 1971; First Pa Bank NA, appraisal dept, 1973; Tyler Realty Co, owner, 1978-; William Pa Sch Dist, sch dir, 1998. **Orgs:** Numerous memships incl trustee, First Baptist Church Darby, 1960-; Darby Bus Lianson, comt mem; Pa Notary Pub, pub safety, 1978-; Pa Real Estate Broker, 1978-; Nat Asn Advan Colored People, Darby Area Br, 1980-, exec comt, 1989-94, chair, housing comn, 1991-94; Darby Free Libr, bddirs, 1980-, treas, 1991-93; co-chair, Equal Opportunities & Govt Agencies, Pa State Realtor, 1983-84; Wm Pa Sch Authority, 1983-; pres, Darby-Lansdowne Rotary, 1984-85; treas, Del County Bd Realtors, 1985; Equal Opportunity co-chair, Bd Realtors, 1985; Darby Salvation Army Adv Coun, 1985; dir, Del County Red Cross, 1985-88; Darby Bobo Coun, chair, 1987-88; pres, Del County Bd Realtors, 1988; bd dir, Affordable Housing Opportunities Inc, 1990-; Grants, Recreation, Munic Serv, parking authority, Darby Boro Coun, chmn, 1991-95; Pa Certify Residential Appraiser, 1992-; Darby Bus Asn, 1992-; Del County Asn Realtors, co-chair, equal opportunity comn, 1993-; Darby Revitalization Task Force, 1994-; Del County Wm Pa Sch Dist, 1995; Task Force Sch Safety & Violence Prev; vice chmn, Del County Bd Assessment, 1995; Pa Asn Realtors, mult listing comn, equal opportunity comn; DeL County Bd Assessment Appeals, 1996; County Action Agency Del County, 1998; bd mem, William pa sch bd. **Honors/Awds:** Civic Award, Chapel Four Chaplains, 1970; Civic Award, Penguin Club Darby, 1972; Civic Award, First Baptist Church Darby, 1980; Community Service Award, Penguins Darby, 1988; Board Member of the Year, County Act Agency Del County, Pa, 2001. **Home Addr:** 759 Fern St, Darby, PA 19023, **Home Phone:** (610)237-6512. **Business Addr:** Owner, Tyler Realty Co, 850 Main St, Darby, PA 19023, **Business Phone:** (610)461-2225.

**TYLER, SELMA L. DODSON**
Consultant. **Personal:** Born May 21, 1955, Chicago, IL; daughter of Robert W and Juanita L; married Melvin Douglas Tyler. **Educ:** Northwestern Univ, BS, 1977; Clark Atlanta Univ. **Career:** WZGC Radio, promotions dir/pub affairs, 1979-82; KFMK Radio, acct exec, 1982-85; KO5HU TV, sales mgr, 1985-86; KMJQ-KBXX Radio-Houston, local sales mgr, 1989-93; Clear Channel Works, gen mgr, 1997-2000; Hands Experience Advert & Mkt, owner, 2001-09; Defender Media Group, sls & mkt dir, currently. **Orgs:** Am Women Radio/TV, historian, 1979-81; Am Women Radio/TV, 1981-83; Am Mkt Asn, 1984-85; Houston Nat Asn Advan Colored People, chap publicity/comm Ann Freedom Fund Banquet, 1989-92; Houston Coalition 100 Black Women, 1989. **Home Addr:** 43250 La Scala Way, Indio, CA 92203, **Home Phone:** (281)721-5137.

**TYLER, SHIRLEY NEIZER**
School administrator, association executive, educator. **Personal:** Born Jan 1, 1929, Philadelphia, PA; daughter of Raymond F Neizer and Frances Washington Neizer; children: Richard J Jr & Kathryn T Prigmore. **Educ:** Simmons Col, BS, MA; Univ Va. **Career:** School administrator (retired); NSA, exec secy, 1950-51; Nat Scholar Serv & Fund Negro Stud, staff assoc, 1953-54, assoc coun, prin; Arlington City Pub Sch Va, educr; Gilchrist Co, Boston, Va, personnel admin; US Nat Stud Asn, Madison, Wis, exec sec; Grace Episcopal Church, head sch. **Orgs:** Bd dir, Mid Atlantic Episcopal Sch Asn; Va Gov Ed Block Grant Comt; prin, Nat Asn Elem Sch; Nat Asn Ed Young C; chmn, vicechmn, Alexandria City Sch Bd, 1973-82; vice chmn, Alexandria Community Health Coun; INOVA Alexandria Hosp Corp; bd dir, Northern Va Family Serv; Nat Asn Advan Colored People; NOVA Urban League; Alexandria mem; Nat Coun Black Women; Alexandria City Community Partnerships Comt. **Honors/Awds:** Distinguished Service Citizens, Alexandria, Va; Outstanding Service in Education, Northern Va, Urban League; Outstanding Community Service, Nat Asn Advan Colored People, Alexandria Br; Community Activist, Hopkins HouseAsn; Alexandria Women's CMS, 1984; Alexandria Coun. **Home Addr:** 3703 Edison St, Alexandria, VA 22305, **Home Phone:** (703)548-8407.

**TYNER, ALFRED MCCOY (MCCOY TYNER)**
Jazz musician, music director, composer. **Personal:** Born Dec 11, 1938, Philadelphia, PA; married Aisha; children: 1. **Educ:** W Philadelphia Music Sch; Granoff Sch Music. **Career:** Benny Golson/Art Farmer Jazztet, 1959; John Coltrane Quartet, 1960-65; solo performer, 1960-; Recordings: "Inception", 1962; "Reaching Fourth", 1962; "Nights of Ballads & Blues", 1963; "Today and Tomorrow", 1963; "Live at Newport", 1964; "McCoy Tyner Plays Ellington", 1964; "The Real McCoy", 1967; "Tender Moments", 1967; "Time for Tyner", 1968; "Expansions", 1968; "Cosmos", 1968-70; "Extensions", 1970; "Asante", 1970; "Sahara", 1972; "Song for My Lady", 1972; "Echoes of a Friend", 1972; "Song of the New World", 1973; "Enlightenment", 1973; "Sama Layuca", 1974; "Atlantis", 1974; "Trident", 1975; "Fly with the Wind", 1976; "Focal Point", 1976; "Supertrios", 1977; "Inner Voices", 1977; "The Greeting", 1978; "Passion Dance", 1978; "Counterpoints", 1978; "Together", 1978; "Horizon", 1979; "Quartets 4 X 4", 1980; "13th House", 1981; "La Leyenda de La Hora", 1981; "Looking Out", 1982; "Love & Peace", 1982; "Dimensions", 1984; "It's About Time", 1985; "Just Feelin", 1985; "Double Trios", 1986; "Major Changes", 1985; "Bon Voyage", 1987; "Blues for Coltrane", 1987; "Live at the Musicians Exchange Cafe", 1987; "Revelations", 1988; "Uptown/Downtown", 1988; "Live at Sweet Basil", 1989; "Things Aint What They Used to Be", 1989; "Round Midnight", 1989; "One on One", 1990; "Blue Bossa", 1991; "Autumn Mood", 1991; "Soliloquy", 1991; "Remembering John", 1991; "New York Reunion", 1991; "44th Street Suite", 1991; "Key of Soul", 1991; "Solar: Live at Sweet Basil", 1991; "In New York", 1991; "Live in Warsaw", 1991; "The Turning Point", 1991; "Journey", 1993; "Manhattan Moods", 1993; "Prelude and Sonata", 1994; "Infinity", 1995; "What the World Needs Now", 1997; "McCoy Tyner Plays John Coltrane", 1997; "McCoy Tyner and the Latin All-Stars", 1999; "McCoy Tyner with Stanley Clarke and Al Foster", 2000; "Land of Giants", 2003; "Illuminations", 2004; "Quartet", 2007; "Guitars", 2008; "Solo: Live from San Francisco", 2009. **Honors/Awds:** Jazz Master, Nat Endowment Arts, 2002; "2003 Hero Award, 2003; GRAMMY Award for Best Jazz Instrumental Album, 2004; honorary doctor of music degrees, Berklee College of Music, 2005; Presidential Merit Award from the Grammy Foundation, 2008. **Home Addr:** 1755 Broadway 8th Fl, New York, NY 10019. **Business Addr:** Jazz Pianist, Blue Note Management Group, 131 W 3rd St, New York, NY 10012, **Business Phone:** (212)475-0049.

**TYNER, REV. CHARLES R., SR.**
Clergy, educator. **Personal:** Born Jun 23, 1950, Murfreesboro, NC; married Betty Ricks; children: Charles & Christopher. **Educ:** Shaw Univ, Raleigh, NC, BA, relig & philos & hist, 1972; NC Cent Univ, Durham, MS, admin, 1979; Southeastern Baptist Sem, Wake Forest Univ, NC; E Carolina Univ, Greenville; Univ Nc, Chapel Hill. **Career:** Mt Moriah Baptist Church, pastor, 1969; White Oak Baptist Church, pastor, 1972; Tarboro City Sch, admin asst supt; White Oak Missionary Baptist Church, pastor, currently. **Orgs:** Exec comt, W Roanoke Bapt Asn; Shaw Theol Alumni Asn; pres, Hertford Co Min Alliance; NC Asn Educ; Nat Asn Advan Colored People; Prince Hall Grand Lodge F & A Masons NC; vpres, New Hope Baptist Asn; vpres, Gen Baptist State Conv Inc; pres, White Oak Found Inc, exec dir, 1988. **Honors/Awds:** Merit Outstanding Leadership, Shaw Univ, 1969-72; Outstanding Work, Gen Baptist Conv NC, 1971-73; Great Leadership, Comn Murfreesboro, NC, 1973. **Home Addr:** 1206 Barrett Cabin Rd, Murfreesboro, NC 27855-9377, **Home Phone:** (252)398-4863. **Business Addr:** Pastor, White Oak Missionary Baptist Church, 1621 White Oak Church Rd, Apex, NC 27523, **Business Phone:** (919)362-6768.

**TYNER, MCCOY. See TYNER, ALFRED MCCOY.**

**TYNER, REGINA LISA**
Publishing executive. **Educ:** Univ Puget Sound, BS, bus admin, 1969, MA, bus admin, 1971; Harvard Univ, state & local exec prog, 1980. **Career:** City Tacoma, minority emply spec civil serv coord, 1971-72; City Tacoma Tech Transfer Ctr, dir, 1972-77; Off Inter govt Affairs City Tacoma, dir, 1977; Wash State Dept Retirement Systs, dep dir, 1977-79; City Seattle, dir, dept licenses & consumer affairs, 1979-86; Continental Tel NW, dir pub affairs, 1986-88; Am Commun Enterprises Inc, pres, 1988-; MWBE Dig, publ, currently. **Orgs:** Alpha Kappa Alpha Sorority Inc, 1975-; Vice chair found comn Int City Mgt Asn, 1975; bd dir, United Way King County, 1980-86; rep, City Seattle Pub Tech Inc, 1982; Am Soc Prof Admin, 1982; Leadership Tomorrow, 1983-87; instr, S Seattle Community Col, 1985; Ladies Auxiliary Veterans Foreign Wars, Post 2289, Seattle, WA, 1985-; bd dir, Wash Leadership Inst, 1988-, Munic League King County, 1988-, Medina C Servs, 1988-. **Honors/Awds:** Award of Excellence, Am Soc Pub Admin, 1986. **Home Addr:** 816 Fairway Lakes Dr, Redmond, WA 32578-3844, **Home Phone:** (850)897-0379. **Business Addr:** President, American Communications Enterprises Inc, 2819 1st Ave Suite 250 Vanderveer Bldg, Seattle, WA 98121-1113, **Business Phone:** (206)728-8911.

**TYREE, OMAR**
Writer, journalist, entrepreneur. **Personal:** Born Apr 15, 1969, Philadelphia, PA; married Karintha; children: 2. **Educ:** Howard Univ, BA, print jour, 1991. **Career:** Mar Productions, owner; The Capital Spotlight, reporter, asst ed, 1991; News Dimensions, chief reporter; Wash View Magazine, freelancer; MARS Productions, founder; Author, Colored, On White Campus (title later changed to Battlezone), 1992; participated in BET talk show pilot, For Black Men Only, 1992; Novels: Capital City, 1993; Flyy: Girl: Inside the Big City There's a Mad Obsession for Gold, Sex-n Money, 1993; Battlezone, 1994; A Do Right Man 1997; Single Mom, 1998; Sweet St. Louis, 1999; For the Love of Money, 2000; Just Say No!, 2001; Col Boy, 2002; Leslie, 2002; Diary of a Groupie, 2003; Cold Blooded, 2004; Boss Lady, 2005; What They Want, 2006; The Last Street Novel, 2007; Pecking Order, 2008; The Traveler: No Turning; The Traveler: Welcome to Dubai, 2013. **Honors/Awds:** Entrepreneurial Spirit & Leadership Plaque, Multicultural Youth Inc, DC; NAACP Image Award, 2001; Phillis Wheatley Literary Award, 2006. **Business Addr:** Author, c/o Simon & Schuster, New York, NY 10020, **Business Phone:** (800)223-2348.

**TYREE, PATRICIA GREY**
Teacher, executive, association executive. **Personal:** Born Nov 8, 1942; married Winston E. **Educ:** Carlow Col, BS, 1966; Antioch Col, MA, 1973; Univ Pittsburgh, PhD, 1974. **Career:** Holy Family Sch, teacher, 1966-67; St Mary's Sch, teacher, 1967-68; Carlow Col, Proj Upward Bound Mt Mercy, moderator, 1968; Diocesan Off Econ & Oppurtunity, Compensatory Educ Prog, assoc dir, 1968-69; Nat Black Sisters Conf, dir, 1969-72; Antioch Putnam Grad Sch Educ & Carlow Col, design training lab, 1972-73; Design Progs Inc, exec dir, 1972-74; Tyree Corp, corp vpres & bus dir, vpres finance; Wilkinsburg Sch Dist, dir curric, instr & assessment; Pittsburgh Found, sr prog officer; Norwalk Pub Schs, dir curric and assessment; Physicians Imaging Centers, chief exec officer; Chagrin Falls Exempted Village Schs, prin; Euclid Pub Schs, internship; John Carroll Univ, vis asst prof; NBSC, exec dir; Compensatory Educ Progs Diocesan Off Econ Opportunity, assoc dir. **Orgs:** Bd dir, Black Women's Community Develop Found; Pa Dept Educ; bd trustee, Pittsburgh Tech Inst; Americans Libr Coun; co-founder, bd dir, Norwalk Educ Found; co-founder, Norwalk C First; bd dir, Stepping Stones Mus C; Nat Asn Elem Sch Principals; bd dir, Nat Off Black Catholics; bd dir, Am Sickle Cell Anemia Asn. **Honors/Awds:** Religion in Action Award, Delta Sigma Theta. **Home Addr:** 329 Ferry St, Sewickley, PA 15143.

**TYREE-WALKER, IDA MAY**
Real estate agent. **Personal:** Born Mar 16, 1941, Philadelphia, PA; daughter of Albert and Sophie; children: Dawn Walker-Anderson & Mark Gregory Walker. **Educ:** Philadelphia Col Textile & Sci, BS, bus admin, 1975; Bowie State Univ, MSA, admin mgt, 1992. **Career:** Phil-

adelphia Nat Bank, sr financial analyst; Container Corp Am, controller, sales purchasing mgr; Bowie State Univ, asst internal auditor; Qual Care Dialysis Inc, opers mgr, 1992-2005; Weichert Realtors, realtor, 2011-; Century 21 Real Estate LLC, prin, currently. **Orgs:** Nat Asn Women Bus Owners, 1995-97; mentor, BEGIN Prog, 1995-97; Nat Asn Health Servs Execs, 1995-97; chair, bd dir, Hosanna Ministries, 1996-98; bd dir, YMCA Black Achievers, 1996-97. **Honors/Awds:** Certificate of Excellence, Meridian Bank, 1995; Business Owner of the Year Nominee, NAWBO, 1996; Outstanding Leader, Phi Delta Kappa, 1996. **Home Phone:** (267)475-4524. **Business Addr:** Principal, Century 21 Real Estate LLC, 630 Germantown Pke Sute 1, Philadelphia, PA 19444, **Business Phone:** (610)828-2700.

## TYSON, ANDRE

Choreographer, dancer, educator. **Personal:** Born Jan 1, 1960, Greenville, NC. **Educ:** Rutgers Univ, Newark, NJ, jour, 1980; Power Pilates, New York, NY, cert, 1999, teacher educ, 2007; Jacksonville Univ, MS, dance & choreography, 2014. **Career:** Westport Dance Ctr, Westport, Conn, dance teacher, 1983; Alvin Ailey Am Dance Ctr, New York, NY, prin, dance teacher, principle dancer, 1885-94; Premiere Dance Theatre, Montclair, NJ, artistic dir, 1993; Laban Ctr Transitions Dance Co, London, Eng, rehearsal dir, 1993; Victoria Arts Collab, Victoria, Can, dance teacher, 1994; Assoc iazione Italiana Danzatori Rome, Italy, dance teacher, 1995; Dance Pt Osaka, Japan, dance teacher, 1995-96; Prof Dance Ctr, Tokyo, Japan, dance teacher, 1995-96; NC Sch Arts, Winston-Salem, NC, dance teacher, 1995-97; Hungarian Dance Acad, Winston-Salem, NC, dance teacher, 1995; Universidade Fed do Bahia Salvador, Brazil, dance teacher, 1996; Austin Contemp Ballet, Austin, Tex, dance teacher, 1996; Internationale Tanz Wochen Vienna, Austria, dance teacher, 1996; Arena 225, Zurich, Switz, dance teacher, 1996; Internationale Sommerakademie des Tanzes Koln, Ger, dance teacher, 1997 & 1999; Jacob's Pillow Lee, dance teacher, 1997; Smith Col, N Hampton, Mass, dance teacher, 1998; Univ SC, Columbia, SC, dance teacher & asst dean, 1998; Univ Wis-Milwaukee, Peck Sch Arts, Dept Dance, assoc prof, 1998-2008; Anando Shankar Ctr Performing Arts, Calcutta, India, dance teacher, 1998; City Ballet Theatre, Milwaukee, Wis, dance teacher, 1998-2004; Milwaukee Ballet Sch, dance teacher, dir, 1999-2000, artistic coordr, 2002; Theater Sch Amsterdamse Hoge Sch voor de Kunsten, Neth, dance teacher, 2000; Ballet Tenn, Chattanooga, Tenn, dance teacher, 2001 & 2002; Ailey Camp Berkeley, artistic dir, 2001; Ko-Thi Dance Co, Milwaukee, Wis, artistic consult, 2001; Bucknell Univ, Lewisburg, Pa, dance teacher, 2002; Ballet Idaho, dance teacher, 2002; CAP/Lula Wash Contemp Dance Prog, supvr; Lake Shore Dance Studio, Milwaukee, Wis, dance teacher, 2003-05; Calif Inst Arts Sharon Disney Lund Sch of Dance, Dance Dept, asst dean & fac contemp tech, pilates & jazz, 2008-. **Orgs:** Compexions Dance Co, 1995-. **Home Addr:** 626 E State St Suite 1601, Milwaukee, WI 53202, **Home Phone:** (414)226-2374. **Business Addr:** Assistant Dean, Faculty, California Institute of Arts, Rm E123F 24700 McBean Pkwy, Valencia, CA 91355, **Business Phone:** (661)255-2416.

## TYSON, ASHA

Writer, president (organization). **Personal:** Born Jan 1, 1970, Detroit, MI. **Educ:** Suomi Col, assoc degree; Northern Mich Univ, BA, polit sci, MA, pub admin. **Career:** Northern Mich Univ, asst dean stud; Marygrove Col, dir personal finance; Asha Tyson Dynamics, pres, currently; ATD Publ, owner; motivationalspeaker; Author: How I Retired at 26!: A Step-by-Step Guide to Accessing Your Freedom & Wealth at Any Age, 2001. **Business Addr:** President, Asha Tyson Dynamics LLC, PO Box 442347, Detroit, MI 48244-2347, **Business Phone:** (313)393-5123.

## TYSON, BERNARD J., SR.

Chairperson, president (organization), executive. **Personal:** Born Vallejo, CA; married Carla J Robinson; children: Bernard J Jr, Alexander J & Charles J. **Educ:** Golden Gate Univ, BS, health serv mgt, MBA, health serv admin; Harvard Univ, advan leadership cert. **Career:** Kaiser Permanente, hosp adminr & div pres, 1997-2002, sr vpres, brand strategy & mgt, 2002-06, exec vpres, health plan & hosp opers, 2006-10, pres & chief operating officer, 2010-13, chmn & chief exec officer, 2013-. **Orgs:** Past chmn, Exec Leadership Coun; bd mem, Occidental Col; bd mem, chief exec officer roundtable mem, Am Heart Asn; bd dir, Int Fedn Health Plans; bd dir, Ams Health Ins Plans; co chair, World Econ Forums Health Gov Community. **Special Achievements:** First African American chief executive officer of Kaiser Permanente. **Business Addr:** Chairman, Chief Executive Officer, Kaiser Permanente, Kaiser Plz 19th Fl, Oakland, CA 94612.

## TYSON, EDWARD CHARLES

Manager. **Personal:** Born Jul 31, 1957, Brooklyn, NY; son of Dr Clarence and Cleo; married Diane K. **Educ:** Howard Univ, BA, 1979; Cent Univ, MBA, 1983. **Career:** Mfrs Nat Bank, asst br mgr, 1979-83; Life Va Ins Co, spec agt, 1983-85; COBO Conven Ctr, event mgr, 1985-90; Tampa Conven Ctr, mgr mkt & event serv, 1990-. **Orgs:** Omega Psi Phi Fraternity, 1977-; Nat Coalition Black Meeting Planners, 1990-; Int Asn Assembly Mgrs, 1990-; Int Asn Expos Mgrs, 1990-; Nat Forum Black Pub Admin, 1992-. **Honors/Awds:** Howardite of the Year, Howard Univ Alumni Asn, 1989. **Home Addr:** 8305 Lane Serena Dr, Tampa, FL 33614, **Home Phone:** (813)390-0871. **Business Addr:** Manager Marketing, Event Services, Tampa Convention Center, 333 S Franklin St, Tampa, FL 33602, **Business Phone:** (813)274-8422.

## TYSON, JESSE J.

Association executive, president (organization), businessperson. **Personal:** married Cheryl; children: Tamika, Cormisha & Christina. **Educ:** Lane Col, BS, bus & econs, 1974; Ohio State Univ, Fisher Col Bus, MBA, mkt, 1976; Brookings Inst, attended; Int Mgt Develop Sch Switz, attended. **Career:** ExxonMobil Inter-Am Inc, mkt dir & pres, spokesperson, global customer serv & logistics mgr, Exxon Mobil Sam Fuels Group, chief, Global Aviation Brussels, Belg, pres & sales dir; Nat Black MBA Asn, pres & chief exec officer, interim, 2013-14, 2014-. **Orgs:** Ensemble Theatre, 1991-95, 2012-; C's Mus Houston, past bd mem, 1993-95; treas, Jack & Jill Found Am, 1999-2006; FIU, Dean's Adv Bd, former mem; bd dir, Found Mgt Educ Cent Am, 2003-08; Nat Black MBA Asn, lifetime mem; Fisher Col Bus at Ohio State Univ, adv bd mem; Lane Col, Bd Trustees; Orange Bowl Comt; ELC; Alpha Phi Alpha Fraternity Inc; Exec Leadership Coun. **Honors/Awds:** Ronald McDonald House Charities, Twelve Good Men, Recipient; NAACP Achievement Award, 2001; UNCF Alum of the Year Award, 2004; "Black Enterprise," Most Influential Black Executive, 2009; Fisher College of Business, Pace Setters Award, 2014; Business School Global Diversity Award, Ohio State Univ Fisher Col;f 100 Black Men of America Lifetime Achievement Award for Service and Leadership, Recipient; Pacesetter Award. **Business Addr:** President, Chief Executive Officer, National Black MBA Association Inc, 400 W Peachtree St NW Suite 203, Atlanta, GA 30308, **Business Phone:** (404)260-5444.

## TYSON, LANCE C.

Lawyer, association executive. **Educ:** Lake Forest Col, BA, 1993; Univ Iowa Col Law, LLB, 1996. **Career:** Mayor's Off, chicago, Ill, 1997; Kutak Rock LLP, assoc, atty, coun, currently; Govt Regulatory Law Pract Group, partner, currently; Freeborn & Peters LLP, partner; Tyson Strong Hill LLC, managing mem, atty, currently. **Orgs:** Chicago Bar Asn; 2016 Olympic Comt; Mt Sinai Hosp Bd; Loretto Hosp Adv Bd; co-chair, Interfaith House Adv Bd; Nat Asn Bond Lawyers; Am Bar Asn; off pres, Cook County. **Business Addr:** Partner, Attorney, Kutak Rock LLP, 1 S Wacker Dr, Chicago, IL 60606-4614, **Business Phone:** (312)602-4133.

## TYSON, LORENA E.

Educator. **Personal:** Born Dec 1, 1933, Montclair, NJ; daughter of Alfred E and Clariee Love. **Educ:** Col St Elizabeth Convent Sta, BS, chem, 1955; Cath Univ Am, MS, chem, 1965; Seton Hall Univ, math cert, 1967; Rutgers Univ, attended 1975; NJ Inst Technol, attended 1978; Kean Col, supvr, cert, 1994. **Career:** Sacred Heart Acad, teacher, chem & math, 1956-59; St Joseph High Sch, teacher, physics, chem & math, 1959-62; Cath Univ Am, NSF Fel Chem, 1962-64; St Peter & Paul High St, Thomas VI, teacher, physics, chem & math, 1962-71; NSF Fel, Seton Hall, 1966-67; Essex County Col, adj math, 1971-78; Kean Col, adj math, 1971-83; Montclair High Sch, Montclair Bd Ed, chem teacher, 1971-97; Middlesex County Col, adj math teacher, 1989-93; Montclair High Sch, dept chair sci, 1994-97. **Orgs:** Nat Educ Asn, 1971-; NJ Educ Asn, 1971-; Montclair Educ Asn, 1971-95; treas, Essex County Educ Asn, 1971-98; ACS Teacher Affil, 1974-98; League Women Voters Montclair, 1974-90; NJ Sci Teachers, 1975-98; NJEA Except Child Comn, 1975-90; EOF Adv Bd, Col St Elizabeth, 1976-83, Centennial Comn, 1999-2000, bd dir, 1999-, secy, 2001-05; Nat Coun Negro Women, 1978-82; NJ Math Teachers, 1979-83; Phi Delta Kappa, 1981-; treas, Phi Delta Kappar, Montclair State Col, 1987-89; bd trustee, Montclair Vol Ambulance Unit, 1990-94; NJEA Human Rights Comn, 1997-; NJREA, 1997-; NJREA Prog Planning Comn, 1999-2003; bd dir, Alumnae Asn, vpres, 2005-09, pres, 2009-; NJREA Secy, 2005-09; NJREA Minority Rep on Exec Bd, 2009-11; Teachers Pension & Annuity Fund. **Honors/Awds:** Human Relations Award, Essex County Educ Asn, 1980; Contribution to Education Award, Montclair Educ Asn, 1980; Resolution of Commendation, Montclair Bd Educ, 1980; NJ Governor's Teachers Recognition Program, 1987; Montclair Teacher of the Year, Montclair Bd Educ, 1989; Eve Marchiony Outstanding Teacher Grant, Montclair Bd Educ, 1989; Edward J Merrill Award, Am Chem Soc, 1990; Middle Atlantic Regional Award, HS Chem Teaching, Am Chem Soc, 1992; Educator of the Year Award, Essex County Educ Asn, 1993; Princeton Distinguished Educator Award, 1994; Public School Teacher of the Year, 1995; Weston Award for Excellence, Knights Columbus Coun, 1996; Rev Edward M Farrell Distinguished Alumnus Award, Immaculate Conception HS, 1999; Hon LLD, Col St Elizabeth, 2000. **Home Addr:** 15 Montague Pl, Montclair, NJ 07042-2808, **Home Phone:** (973)509-0279.

## TYSON, MIKE (MICHAEL GERARD TYSON)

Boxer, actor. **Personal:** Born Jun 30, 1966, Brooklyn, NY; son of Jimmy Kirkpatrick and Lorna Smith; married Likha Spicer, Jun 9, 2009; children: Miguel; married Robin Givens, Feb 7, 1988, (divorced 1989); children: Milan, Morocco, Mikey, Milan, Morocco, Mikey, D'Amato, Exodus(deceased), D'Amato & Exodus (deceased); married Monica Turner, 1997, (divorced 2003); children: Reina & Amir. **Career:** Boxer (retired), actor; professional boxer, 1985-2005; World Wrestling fed, spec enforcer; Films: Play It to Bone, 1999; Crocodile Dundee Los Angeles, 2001; When Will I Be Loved, 2004; Rocky Balboa, 2006; Fool N Final, 2007; Tyson, exec producer, 2008; Hangover, 2009; Every Little Step, 2010; Herman Cain's Campaign Promises with Mike Tyson, 2011; Da Brick, exec producer, 2011; When Harry Met Sally 2 with Billy Crystal & Helen Mirren, 2011; Oscar Talk, 2011; Cookout 2, 2011; Hangover Part II, 2011; Hangover Part II, 2011; Yahoo! News/Funny or Die GOP Presidential Online Internet Cyber Debate, 2012; Cain Time Live, 2013; My Last Chance, launch dir, 2013; Scary MoVie, 2013; Undisputed Truth, exec producer, 2013; TV Ser: "Who's Boss?", 1989-90; "Webster", 1987; "I Love 1980's", 2001; "Den Lille of den store", 2001; "ESPN Sports Century", 2001; "Legendary Nights", 2003; "Beyond Glory", 2003; "Driven", 2004; "Otro rollo con: Adal Ramones", 2004; "ESPN 25: Who's #1?", 2004; "Festival di Sanremo", 2005; "Jimmy Kimmel Live!", 2005; "Mad TV", 2005; "Big Idea with Donny Deutsch", 2006; "Larry King Live", 2008; "Grand j de Canal+, Le", 2008; "High Chaparall", 2008; "Bros", 2009; "Ara", 2009; "Entourage", 2010; "Taking Tyson", exec producer, 2011; "Breaking In", 2011; "How I Met Your Mother", 2013; "Law & Order: Spec Victims Unit", 2013; "Mike Tyson Mysteries", 2013; "Being: Mike Tyson", exec producer, 2013. **Orgs:** Founder, Mike Tyson Cares Found, 2012. **Honors/Awds:** Junior Olympic Games, Gold Medals, 1981-82; Olympic super heavyweight, Gold Medal, 1984; Ring magazine Prospect of the Year, 1985; Heavy weight boxing champion, (WBC), 1986-90; Ring Magazine Fighter of the Year, 1986, 1988; Heavyweight boxing champion, (WBA), 1987-90; Heavyweight boxing champion, (IBF), 1987-90; BBC Sports Personality of the Year Overseas Personality, 1989; Heavyweight boxing champion, (WBC), 1996; Heavyweight boxing champion, (WBA), 1996; Boxer of the Year, WBC Quantas, US Boxing Writers & other organizations; Triple crown winner; DHL, Central State Univ, 1988, WBC Quantas, US Boxing Writers and other organizations; Featured athlete on fox sports net's beyond the Glory; Nominated for Teen Choice Award, 2009; inducted, International Boxing Hall of Fame, 2011; WWE Hall of Fame, 2012. **Special Achievements:** Junior Olympic quickest KO; Youngest Heavyweight Champion in Boxing History; featured in Guinness Book of World Records; featured in Guinness Book of World Records; triple crown winner. acted in various films, albums & tv serials. special enforcer for a World Wrestling Entertainment match at Wrestle Mania XIV on March 29, 1998, in which he pretended to be a member of D-Generation X and ended uppunching out Shawn Michaels after making the 3 count for Stone Cold Steve Austin to win the WWE Championship from Michaels; Received Doctorate in Humane Letters from Central State University. **Home Addr:** 6740 Tomiyasu, Las Vegas, NV 89120.

## TYSON, RON (RONALD TYSON PRESSON)

Singer, songwriter. **Personal:** Born Feb 8, 1948, Philadelphia, PA. **Educ:** Thomas Edison; Olney; Granoff Sch Music. **Career:** Singer/songwriter/producer: Albums: The Ethics Sing, 1967; Heaven Only Knows, 1973; The Magic of the Blue, 1974; Welcome Back, 1974; Thirteen Blue Magic Lane, 1975; Survival, 1975; The Very Best of South Shore Commission, 1975; Dance your troubles away, 1975; Love Committee, 1976; Locker Room, 1976; Break Away, 1980; All things happen in time, 1981; Hold your horses, 1983; Sal soul Classics Vol 1, 1990; Original Sal soul Classics: The 20th Anniversary, 1992; Love & Happiness, 1994; 25th Anniversary, 1994; This Is Where the Happy People Go: The Best of Trammps, 1994; Tightening it up, 1994; Give your body up, 1995; Passionate Breezes: The Best of the Dells 1975-91, 1995; Mazimim Classics Vol 2, 1995; Greatest Hits, 1996; People Get Ready: The Curtis May field Story, 1996; Best of Blue Magic: Soulful Spell, 1996; Smooth Grooves: A Sensual Collection Vol 6, 1996; Greatest Hits, 1996; Every body Dance, 1997; Super Rare Disco Vol 2, 1997; Keith Haring: A Retrospective The Music of His Era, 1997; Vol 1-Maximum Club Classics, 1997; Philly Sound: Kenny Gamble Leon Huff & the Story of Brotherly Love, 1997; Storm Warning: Philly Original Soul Classics Vol. 1, 1998; Maximum Club Classics Vol.2, 1998; Masters at work Masterworks: Essential Ken Lou House Mixes, 1998; Run away Best of Loleatta Holloway, 1999; Harris Machine/Here to Create Music, 1999; The best of Double Exposure, 1999; We Come In Peace/Take It To The Streets, 1999; Runaway Love: The Singles Anthology, 2000; Def com Vol. 2, 2001; Queen of the Night: The Ultimate Club Collection, 2001; Disco Heat, 2002; The Four Tops Anthology 50th anniversary, 2004; The Ethics, 1967-74; Love Committee; The Temptations, singer, master ceremonies, currently; Films: Happy New Year, 1987; Walk Hard: The Dewey Cox Story, 2007. **Honors/Awds:** Grammy Award. **Business Addr:** Singer, William Morris Agency, 1 William Morris Pl, Beverly Hills, CA 90212, **Business Phone:** (310)859-4000.

## TYUS, WYOMIA

Athlete, public relations executive. **Personal:** Born Aug 29, 1945, Griffin, GA; daughter of Willie and Maria; married Duane Tillman; children: Simone & Tyus. **Educ:** Tenn State Univ, BS, recreation, 1967. **Career:** Track athlete, 1962-75; Afro-Amer Ctr Univ Calif Los Angeles, pres asst, 1969-70, Black Studies Ctr; Bret Harte Jr HS LA, phys edt chr, 1970-72; Beverly Hills HS, track coach, 1972-73; Intl Track Asn, pub rel staff, 1973-76; ABC coverage Olympic Games Montreal, commentator, 1976; Councilman David Cunningham, community liason, 1978; US Dept Labors sponsored Sports Career Dev, instr, 1979-81; Coca-Cola USA, pub rels, 1981-84; Olympic Comt; Los Angeles Unified Sch Dist. **Home Addr:** 1102 Keniston Ave, Los Angeles, CA 90019, **Home Phone:** (323)934-6559.

# U

## UGGAMS, LESLIE (MARIAN UGGAMS)

Actor, singer. **Personal:** Born May 25, 1943, New York, NY; daughter of Harolde and Juanita; married Grahame Pratt; children: Danielle (Chambers) & Justice Pratt. **Educ:** NY Prof C's Sch; Juillard Sch Music, 1963. **Career:** TV series: "Beulah", 1949; "Your Show of Shows", 1953; "The Milton Berle Show"; "Name That Tune"; "Sing Along With Mitch", "The Ed Sullivan Show", 1960, 1961-64; "Roots", 1979; "The Muppet Show"; "The Book of Lists", 1982; "Backstairs at the White House", 1982; "Sizzle", 1981; "Magnum, P.I.", 1984; "Hotel", 1987; "The Cosby Show", 1991; "A Different World", 1993; "Under One Roof", 1995; "All My Children", 1996; "Broadway Beat", 2003; "Memphis Beat", 2011; "The Good Wife", 2011; "NYC 22", 2012; "Christmas at Radio City, Fantasy". Plays include: Hallelujah Baby, 1967, Her First Roman, 1968, Blues in the Night, 1982, Jerry's Girls, 1985, The Great Gershwin, 1987, Anything Goes, 1989; Films: Black Girl, 1972; Skyjacked, 1972; Poor Pretty Eddie, 1975; Sugar Hill, 1993; Toe to Toe, 2009. Albums: On My Way To You; numerous nightclub & musical variety show appearances; "A Different World", 1993; Sugar Hill, 1994; "All My Children", 1996; King Headley II, 2001, The Rink; movie: Deadpool, 2016. **Orgs:** Screen Actors Guild; Actor's Equity; Am Fedn TV & Radio Artists; founder, BRAVO Chap, City Hope; bd mem, Alvin Ailey Am Dance Theatre; bd mem, TADA; Delta Sigma Theta Sorority Inc; Am Guild Musical Artists. **Honors/Awds:** Best Singer on TV, 1962-63; Tony Award, Best Actress, Halleulajah Baby, 1967; Emmy Award, Fantasy; Drama Critics Award, 1968; Critics Award, Best Supporting Actress, Roots, 1979; Emmy Nomination, Roots, 1979; Daytime Emmy Award, 1983; Anniversary Award, 2007; honorary Doctor of Fine Arts, 2015. **Special Achievements:** Author of Leslie Uggams Beauty Book in 1962. **Home Addr:** 8899 Beverly Blvd, Los Angeles, CA 90048. **Business Addr:** Actress, William Morris Agency, 151 El Camino, Beverly Hills, CA 90212, **Business Phone:** (310)859-4000.

**UGGAMS, MARIAN. See UGGAMS, LESLIE.**

## UKABAM, INNOCENT O.

Executive. **Personal:** married Chidi; children: 4. **Educ:** Univ Nigeria, BS; Univ Wis, MS. **Career:** Protein Tech Int, Cent am & Caribbean divisions, area dir; DuPont Protein Technologies, St Louis, Mo, mkt dir foodservice distrib, 2002; biotechnologist. **Business Addr:** Marketing Director, DuPont Protein Technologies, 1034 Danforth Dr, St. Louis, MO 63188, **Business Phone:** (800)325-7108.

**UKU, EUSTACE ORIS**
Consultant, executive, lawyer. **Personal:** Born Jun 1, 1947, Ibadan; son of Augustine and Mabel; children: Eustace Jr & Austin. **Educ:** Univ Lagos, Lagos, Nigeria, LLB, 1970; Nigerian Law Sch, Lagos, Nigeria, BL, 1971; Long Island Univ, Brooklyn, NY, MBA, finance, 1974; Duquesne Univ Sch Law, Pittsburgh, PA, cert law, 1981. **Career:** Lawrence & Co, Lagos, Nigeria, atty, 1971; Garrick & Co, Benin, Nigeria, atty, 1976-79; Delstacy Mgmt Serv, Benin, Nigeria, managing dir, 1976-79; Greater Pittsburgh Bus Develop Corp, Pittsburgh, Pa, financial analyst, 1980-81; Equibank, Pittsburgh, Pa, mgr pricing & budgeting, 1981-82, asst vpres, 1982-84; Exico Inc, Pittsburgh, Pa, corp lawyer, chmn, pres & chief exec officer, 1984-; Exico Bus Ctr, owner. **Orgs:** Pa Bar Asn; dir, Functional Literacy Ministry; bd dir, Umoja African Arts Co; adv trustee, Bros Bro Found; bd mem, Environ Financial Adv Bd; dir emer, African Am Chamber Com; dir emer, NEED; dir emer, Am Heart Asn. **Home Addr:** 8260 Chaske St, Verona, PA 15147, **Home Phone:** (412)371-4390. **Business Addr:** Chairman, Chief Executive Officer, Exico Inc, 214 Farmington Rd, Pittsburgh, PA 15215-1633, **Business Phone:** (412)261-3073.

**ULMER, BISHOP KENNETH C.**
Bishop, college teacher. **Personal:** married Togetta; children: Kendan & RoShaun. **Educ:** Univ Ill, BA, broadcasting & music, 1969; Pepperdine Univ; Hebrew Union Col; Univ Judaism; Grace Grad Sch Theol, Long Beach, Calif, PhD, 1986; United Theol Sem, PhD, 1989, doctorate ministry, 1999; Oxford Univ, Magdalene Col, ecumenical liturgy & worship, 1994; Oxford Univ, Christ Church & Wadham Col. **Career:** Macedonia Bible Baptist Church, San Pedro, Calif, founder, 1979; Faithful Cent Missionary Baptist Church, pastor, 1982; Biola Univ, adj prof; Pepperdine Univ, adj prof; Grace Theol Sem, Pastoral Ministry & Homiletics, instr; Fuller Theol Sem, instr; United Theol Sem, mentor; King's Col & Sem, adj prof, currently, pres, 2008-; Faithful Cent Bible Church, sr pastor, bishop, 1982; Macedonia Int Bible, fel; Calif Atty Gen's Policy Coun Violence Prev; bd dirs, Rebuild Los Angeles Comn. **Orgs:** Bd dir, Gospel Music Workshop Am; bd trustee, Biola Univ; Bishop over Macedonia Int Bible; Pastors Adv Coun, City Inglewood; bishops coun, Gospel Baptist Church; bd trustee, Southern Calif Sch Ministry; founding bd mem, King's Col & Sem. **Honors/Awds:** The King's Apostelos Christou Award, 2007. **Special Achievements:** Author of five books: A New Thing; Spiritually Fit To Run The Race; The Anatomy Of God; In His Image; Making Your Money Count. **Business Addr:** Bishop, Faithful Cent Bible Church, 333 W Florence Ave, Inglewood, CA 90301-1103, **Business Phone:** (310)330-8000.

**UMBAYEMAKE-HAYES, LINDA**
Librarian. **Personal:** Born Feb 19, 1953, Cleveland, OH; daughter of C Morgan McDonald and Helen Loretta Ballard-McDonald; married Thomas Lee; children: Manu Rashad, Kumar Rashad, Bari Zaka, Mayi UmBayemake, Thurayya UmBayemake & Glenn Chinua Bayemake-Hurt. **Educ:** Cuyahoga Community Col, Cleveland, OH, AA, 1980; Kent State Univ, OH, BA, 1984; Tex Women's Univ, Denton, TX, MLS, 1989; Univ Ky, Lexington, MRC, 1998. **Career:** Denton City, Planning Dept, Denton, TX, planning asst, 1986-87; Tex Woman's Univ, Denton, TX, librn asst II, 1988-89; Univ N Tex, Denton, TX, librn asst II, 1988-89; Cuyahoga County Pub Libr, Warrensville Hts, OH, librn, 1989-90; Santa Fe Community Col, Grants, NM, librn, instr, 1990; Ga Dept Corrections, librn supvr, 1991-92; Ky State Univ, Frankfort, KY, ref librn, 1992-96; Owensboro Community Col, Owensboro, KY, asst librn, 1996; LUMBAY6 Intervention Journeys Inc, 1997-; Franklin City Pub Schs, substitute teacher, 1996-98; Ky Dept Ment Health, Offender Rehab Specist, 1998-2000; Bk Wholesalers, Inc, Colction Develop, 1999-2000; Univ Akron, STAR coordr, 2001; E Cleveland Pub Libr, Caledonia Br Libr, mgr, 2001-; Fair Housing Servs, Akron, OH, tester, 2002-03. **Orgs:** Am Libr Asn, 1988-; Black Caucus Am Libr Asn; Ky Blacks Higher Educ, 1993-96; vice chair, ADA Network Adv Coun, 1998; Ky Citizens Foster Care Rev bd, 1999-2000; Franklin County, Ky, Family Ct visitation, support comt, 1999-2000; bd dir, Kent City, OH Cable Comn, 2002-; Holden Parent Asn, 2000-04; secy, Roosevelt HS Parent-Teacher Org, Kent, OH, 2000-03; Kent State Univ Upward Bound Parent Adv Coun Secy, 2001-03; Longcoy Elem Parent Asn, 2004-. **Honors/Awds:** Hon Award of Service, Kent State Student Government, 1982-85; Hon Award of Service, COSO, 1982-85; Certificate of Service, Margaret Fain Elementary, 1990; Chi Sigma Iota, 1998; Elkhorn Middle School Site Base Council Award of Service, 1998; Foster Care review Committee Service Award, 2000, State Ky, 2000. **Home Addr:** 1056 Munroe Falls Rd, Kent, OH 44240, **Home Phone:** (330)554-9165. **Business Addr:** Branch Manager, East Cleveland Public Library Caledonia Branch, 960 Caledonia Ave, Cleveland Heights, OH 44112, **Business Phone:** (216)268-6280.

**UNAEZE, FELIX EME**
Librarian, educator. **Personal:** Born Apr 12, 1952, Owerri; son of James and Mary Mgbakwo Oguike; married Victoria Nwachukwu; children: Obi, Kenny & Laura. **Educ:** Lincoln Univ, BA, jour, 1980, MA, bus admin & polit sci, 1981, MBA, mgt, 1983; Univ Mo, Columbia, MALS, 1984. **Career:** Univ Lagos, Nigeria, libr asst three, 1971-73; Natl Libr Nigeria, Lagos, libr asst one, 1973-76; Lincoln Univ, Jefferson City, Mo, periodicals librn, adminr, ethnic studies, 1984-87; Northern Ill Univ, DeKalb, Ill, asst prof, bus econ librn, 1987-88; NMex State Univ, Las Cruces, NM, asst prof, bus ref librn, 1988-90; Ferris State Univ, Big Rapids, MI, head ref & instrnl servs, 1990-2001; Chicago State Univ, Douglas Libr, dir, LIS pub serv & assoc prof, 2002, actg dir media & instr serv, 2003-04; Univ Wis-Super, Jim Dan Hill Libr, dir, 2004-07, assoc prof libr sci; Grambling State Univ, dir libr serv & assoc prof, 2009-. **Orgs:** Asn MBA Execs, 1984-88; Alpha Phi Alpha Fraternity, 1985; Black Caucus Am Libr Asn, 1986-; Am Libr Asn, 1988-; NMex Libr Asn, 1988-90; bd regents, Univ Wis Syst; past chair, Africa Subcomt Int Rels Comt. **Home Addr:** 809 Willow Ave, Big Rapids, MI 49307-2552, **Home Phone:** (231)796-8157. **Business Addr:** Director, University of Wisconsin-Superior, Belknap & Catlin, Superior, WI 54880, **Business Phone:** (715)394-8346.

**UNDERWOOD, ANTHONY**
Automotive executive. **Personal:** Born Jan 23, 1957, Bessemer, AL; son of George Williams and Ruby; married Joyce Smith; children: Broderick Ryan & Roderick Bryan. **Educ:** Ford Dealer Training Prog, 1989. **Career:** Automotive Store, Talladega, owner, 1989; Ford Dealership, 1992-93; Dealers Trade Outlet, owner, 1995-2002; Used Car Mgr; Nat Independent Automobile Dealers Asn, pres, sr vpres; Anthony Underwood Automotive, pres & owner, currently. **Orgs:** Save Youth; Am Red Cross; bd dir, pres mem comt, Ala IADA. **Honors/Awds:** Nat Quality Dealer of the Year, Nat Independent Auto Dealer Asn, 2003; National Quality Dealer Award. **Home Addr:** 1436 Nocoseka Trl, Anniston, AL 36207-6719. **Business Addr:** President, Owner, Anthony Underwood Automotive, 4006 Bessemer Super Hwy, Bessemer, AL 35020, **Business Phone:** (205)424-4033.

**UNDERWOOD, ARTHUR C.**
Lawyer. **Educ:** Univ Wyo, BSBA, 1973, MBA, 1973; Univ Denver, JD; CPA, 1980. **Career:** Peat, Marwick, Mitchell & Co, CPA's, sr acct, 1973-75; Newman & Co, CPA's, independent consult, 1975; US Securities & Exchange Comn, legal intern, 1976, law clerk, 1977-78; Univ Wyo, acct, 1977; US State Dept officer, 1978; bus consult, 1979-80; Underwood & Assocs, owner & atty, 1981-; Securities Clearing Colo Inc, atty, acct exec, 1982-84. **Orgs:** Colo Soc Cert Pub Accts; Am Inst Cert Pub Accts; bd govs, Colo Bar Asn; Denver Bar Asn; Am Bar Asn; bd dir, Urban League Metrop Denver; treas, Urban League Metrop Denver; Joint Ctr Polit Studies. **Home Addr:** 4746 S Helena Way, Aurora, CO 80015, **Home Phone:** (303)693-4873. **Business Addr:** Attorney, Underwood & Associates, 1241 S Parker Rd Suite 103, Aurora, CO 80231-2160, **Business Phone:** (303)755-2002.

**UNDERWOOD, BLAIR ERWIN**
Actor. **Personal:** Born Aug 25, 1964, Tacoma, WA; son of Frank Eugene Sr and Marilyn Ann Scales; married Desiree; children: Paris, Brielle Nicole & Blake Ellis. **Educ:** Carnegie-Mellon Univ. **Career:** Films: Krush Groove, 1985; The Second Coming, dir, 1992; Posse, 1993; Just Cause, 1995; Set It Off, 1996; Gattaca, 1997; Deep Impact, 1998; Asunder, 1998; The Wishing Tree, 1999; Rules of Engagement, 2000; Free to Dance, 2001; Final Breakdown, 2002; G, 2002; Full Frontal, 2002; Truth Be Told, 2002; G, 2002; Malibus Most Wanted, 2003; Fronterz, 2004; Do Geese See God?, 2004; Hit Man; Straight Out of Compton 2, 2005; The Golden Blaze, 2005; Something New, 2006; Madeas Family Reunion, 2006; Operation Homecoming: Writing the Wartime Experience, 2007; The Hit, 2007; The Legend of Spyro: Dawn of the Dragon, voice, 2008, Weather Girl, 2009; The Art of Getting By, 2011; The Bridge to Nowhere, dir, 2009, guest star on various; The Bridge to Nowhere, dir, 2009; The Art of Getting By, 2011; I Will Follow, 2011; Woman Thou Art Loosed: On the 7th Day, 2012; The True Friendship or Not, 2012; The Trip to Bountiful, 2014. TV shows: The Cosby Show, 1984; recurring role in One Life to Live, 1985-86; A Different World, 1987; Scarecrow & Mrs King, 1987; Sex & the City, 2003-04. TV Series: "LA Law", 1987-94; "High Incident", 1996; "City of Angels", 2000; "Fatherhood", voice; LAX, 2005; "Covert One: The Hades Factor", 2006; "Madeas Family Reunion", 2006; "The Game", 2007; "The Wedding", 2007; "The Country House", 2007; "The Watch", 2007; "The Nutcracker", 2007; "Dirty Sexy Money", 2007; "The Real Thing", 2007; "Frasier", 2007; "The New Adventures of Old Christine", 2007; "Traffic", 2008; "The Big Bang", 2008; "Beauty Is Only Spanx Deep", 2008; "In Treatment", 2008; "The Organ Donor", 2008; "The Convertible", 2009; "The Unexpected Arrival", 2009; "The Bad Guy", 2009; "The Facts", 2009; "The Event", 2010-11; "Superman of Tokyo", 2012; "Thunder and Lightning", 2013; "Ironside", 2013; "Agents of S.H.I.E.L.D", 2015. Artists a New S Africa, co-founder, 1989. **Orgs:** Phi Beta Sigma Fraternity Inc; Trustee, Robey Theatre Company. **Honors/Awds:** Golden Globe Nominee, Best Performance by an Actor in a Supporting Role ina Series, Mini-Series or Motion Picture Made for TV, 1991; Humanitarian Award, Muscular Dystrophy Asn, 1993; Image Award, Nat Asn Advan Colored People, 1994; Image Award Outstanding Lead Actor in a Television Movie or Mini-Series, 1999; Image Award for Outstanding Actor in a Drama Series, 2001, 2011; Artist of the Year, Harvard Univ, Harvard Found, 2002. **Special Achievements:** Voted one of People magazine's "50 Most Beautiful People" in 2000 and one of TV Guide's most influential faces of the 90s; author: Your Child's Soul, Simon & Schuster, 2005. **Business Addr:** Actor, William Morris Agency LLC, 151 El Camino Dr, Beverly Hills, CA 90212, **Business Phone:** (310)274-7451.

**UNDERWOOD, JOSEPH M., JR.**
Sheriff. **Personal:** Born May 19, 1947, Dowagiac, MI; son of Joseph M Sr and Alma L; married Cindy L Glynn; children: Shannon & Sharon. **Educ:** Lake Mich Col, appl sci, attended 1978; Western Mich Univ, BS, criminal justice, 1982; FBI Nat Acad, grad, attended 1987. **Career:** Cass Co Sheriff's Dept, dep detective, 1973-79, lt, 1979-82, capt, 1982-85, under sheriff, 1985-88, sheriff, 1988, 1993-; Haggin-Wimberly Ford, asst bus mgr, fleet mgr, 1989-92. **Orgs:** Civitan Cass County; trustee, House Prayer Community Church, 1987-93, Hospice 1998-; bd mem, Westgate Ctr, 1988-; vpres, bd mem, Dowagiac Area Fed Credit Union; Vet Foreign Wars Post 10704; Dowagiac Rotary Club; Mich Sheriff's Asn. **Home Addr:** 26330 Beeson St, Cassopolis, MI 49031-9712, **Home Phone:** (269)782-4567. **Business Addr:** Sheriff, Sheriff Cass Co Sheriff, 321 M-62 Hwy, Cassopolis, MI 49031, **Business Phone:** (269)445-1201.

**UNDERWOOD, KING JAMES, SR.**
Bishop. **Personal:** Born Apr 24, 1938, Panther Burn, MS; son of Judge and Sarah Parson; married Evelyn Miller; children: Jeff, James L Burnett, Greg, Theodore, Timothy Burnett, Angela R Patterson, Janet, Herbert D Burnett, Judy Grant & King James Jr. **Educ:** Ill Inst Technol, cert; BA Theol; BA Rehab Coun; MA Relig Educ; Dr ministry; DDiv. **Career:** Univ Ill, Illini Union & Housing Div; Alloy Engineering & Casting Co; Gen Bishop, Gen Conf, Western Div, Free Will Baptist Inc, Ministers Conf, pres; Ken Ann Conf Western Div Free Will Baptist Inc, vice bishop, bishop, currently; Terre Haute Dist Ministers Conf, secy; St James Free Will Baptist Church, asst pastor; Emmanuel Free Will Baptist Church, pastor; New Free Will Baptist Church, pastor, gen contractor, builder, currently. **Orgs:** Hiram Lodge No 10, Blue Lodge, chaplain; St James No 3 Grand Consistory, AASR, Grand Hosp; Champaign County, Nat Asn Advan Colored People; spiritual counr & advisor, Danville Correctional Ctr; Champaign County Jail Bd; Univ Ill; Eastern Ill Univ; Ind Univ; Boy Scouts; tutorial progs; Urban league Champaign County; Citizens Concerned Qual Educ; ad bd, Rainbow Push Coalition, Champaign County; Empty Tomb; Ministerial Alliance Champaign-Urbana & Vicinity; justice comt, Dr Martin Luther King Jr Advocacy. **Honors/Awds:** Second Place Award, State Il, Industrial Arts, 1960; Outstanding Teacher Award, Terre Haute District Conf Educ Department; Honorary Doctor of Divinity; Susan Freiburg Award. **Special Achievements:** Mayoral proclamation of "Bishop King James Underwood Day" in Urbana, Illinois. **Home Addr:** 1309 Tremont, Urbana, IL 61801, **Home Phone:** (217)367-8215. **Business Addr:** General Bishop, New Free Will Baptist Church, 601 E Grove St, Champaign, IL 61820, **Business Phone:** (217)355-2385.

**UNDERWOOD, MAUDE ESTHER**
Executive. **Personal:** Born Jul 7, 1930, Cotton Valley, LA; married David C; children: Marcus, Sharon, Yvonne Holmes & James. **Educ:** Ruth Beauty Sch, dipl, 1958; Springhill HS, GED, 1979; Northwest La Vo-Tech Sch, dipl, 1982. **Career:** State La, LSU Ext agt, 1976; City Cullen, alderman, 1982, 87; Black Comn Broadcast, prod, 1983-. **Orgs:** Organizer treas, Springhill-Cullen Improv Asn, 1962; organizer treas, Cullen Ladies Club; chmn, Cystic Fibrosis; Order Eastern Star; orator, Clantha Pride La; N Webster Chamber Com. **Home Addr:** PO Box 336, Cullen, LA 71021, **Home Phone:** (318)994-2252.

**UNDERWOOD, DR. PAUL L., JR.**
Cardiologist. **Personal:** Born Mar 23, 1960, Knoxville, TN; married Hollis C; children: 3. **Educ:** Morehouse Col, BS, biol, 1980; Mayo Grad Sch Med, MD, 1984. **Career:** Henry Ford Hosp, resident, 1984-85; Cleveland Clin Found; Mayo Grad Sch Med, resident, 1985-87; St. Croix Hosp, Dept Intensive Care Unit, from physician to dir emergency dept & intensive care unit, 1987; Peer Rev Orgn, VI Med Inst, physician advisor; Cleveland Clin Educ Found, fel, 1990-93; Mercy Hosp, Iowa Heart Ctr, fel, 1993; MEDHELP, consult, 1997; N Phoenix Heart Ctr, cardiologist, 2006-; Advan Cardiac Specialists, mgr, currently. **Orgs:** Sigma Pi Phi Fraternity; Black Bd Dirs Proj; Soc Cardiac Angiography & Intervention; Nat Med Asn; community health advocacy, Am Heart Asn, 1994-2009; Nat Bd Med Examrs; pres, Asn Black Cardiologists Inc, 2004-06, bd dir; Improving Cardiovasc Educ & Screenings; Ctr Continuing Educ & Prof Develop; African Am Heart Failure Trial; black bd dir proj & use force disciplinary rev bd, Phoenix Police Dept. **Honors/Awds:** Lincoln J Ragsdale Sr Outstanding Director Award, 2006. **Special Achievements:** In 2004, he led the Association of Black Cardiologists to manage & unveil the results of the African American Heart Failure Trial (A-HeFT), the first study conducted in a heart failure population in which all of the participants identified themselves as black. **Home Addr:** 22264 N 51st St, Phoenix, AZ 85054-7129. **Business Addr:** Cardiologist, North Phoenix Heart Center, 9100 N 2nd St Suite 321, Phoenix, AZ 85020, **Business Phone:** (602)249-0212.

**UNION, GABRIELLE MONIQUE**
Actor. **Personal:** Born Oct 29, 1972, Omaha, NE; daughter of Sylvester and Haitian Mother Theresa; married Chris Howard; children: Zaire & Zion; married Dwyane Wade. **Educ:** Univ NE; Cuesta Col; Univ Calif, Los Angeles, BS, sociol. **Career:** Fashion model; actress, currently; Films: She's All That, 1999; 10 Things I Hate About You, 1999; Love & Basketball, 2000; Bring It On, 2000; The Brothers, 2001; Two Can Play That Game, 2001; Abandon, 2002; Welcome to Collinwood, 2002; Deliver Us From Eva, 2003; Cradle to the Grave, 2003; Bad Boys II, 2003; The Breakup Handbook, 2003; Constellation, 2004; Breakin' All the Rules, 2004; The Honeymooners, 2005; Say Uncle, 2005; Running with Scissors, 2006; Constellation, 2007; Daddy's Little Girls, 2007; The Box, 2007; The Perfect Holiday, 2007; Meet Dave, 2008; Cadillac Records, 2008; The Van Zandt Shakedown, 2010; Good Deeds, 2012; Think Like a Man, 2012; Miss Dial, 2013; Think Like a Man Too, 2014; Top Five, 2014; The Birth of a Nation, 2016; Almost Christmas, 2016; Sleepless, 2017. TV Film: "Body Politic", 2009; "The BET Honors", 2009; "Little in Common", 2011. TV Series: "Moesha", 1996; "7th Heaven", 1996; "Star Trek: Deep Space Nine", 1997; "ER", 2000; "Friends", 2001; "Pepsi Smash", 2003; "The Sharon Osbourne Show", 2003; "Family Guy", 2005; "Timeless", 2006; "Into Night", 2006; "The Sea", 2006; "Daddy's Little Girls", 2007; "The Box", 2007; "The Perfect Holiday", 2007; "A Thousand Words by Friday", 2008; "Ugly Betty", 2008; "Life", 2009; "FlashForward", 2009-10; "Army Wives", 2009-10; "NTSFSDSUV", 2011; Half the Sky, 2012; Being Mary Jane, 2012; "With This Ring", 2015; "The Lion Guard", 2015; "Sutton Barth & Vennari Inc", currently. **Honors/Awds:** Young Hollywood Award One to Watch, Female, 2001; Black Reel Award Theatrical, Best Supporting Actress, 2001; Ranked No 52 in 100 Sexiest Women, Maxim, 2002; ranked No 81 in 103 Sexiest Women, 2003; Am Black Film Festival Rising Star Award, 2003; BET Comedy Award, 2004; Best Actress, Palm Beach Int Film Festival, 2006; Image Award, Nat Asn Advan Colored People, 2014. **Business Addr:** Actress, Sutton Barth & Vennari Inc, 145 S Fairfax Ave Suite 310, Los Angeles, CA 90036, **Business Phone:** (323)938-6000.

**UNSELD, WES (WESTLEY SISSEL UNSELD)**
Sports manager, basketball player, basketball coach. **Personal:** Born Mar 14, 1946, Louisville, KY; married Connie; children: Kimberley & Westley Jr. **Educ:** Univ Louisville, BS, health, phys educ & hist, 1968. **Career:** Basketball player (retired), basketball coach, basketball executive; Baltimore Bullets, 1968-81; Capital Bullets, 1973-74; Wash Bullets, 1974-81, vpres, 1981-96, asst coach, 1987, head coach, 1988-94, exec vpres & gen mgr, 1996-; Wash Wizards, exec vpres & gen mgr, 1996-2003. **Orgs:** Head, Capital Ctr Charities; vol, Kernan Hosp; bd trustee, Mt St Marys Col; Alpha Phi Alpha; Am Basketball Asn, 1968.

**UPSHAW, REGAN CHARLES**
Football player, manager. **Personal:** Born Aug 12, 1975, Berrien Springs, MI. **Educ:** Univ Calif, Berkeley. **Career:** Football player (retired), executive; Tampa Bay Buccaneers, right defensive end, 1996-99; Jacksonville Jaguars, defensive end, 1999; Oakland Raiders, defensive end, 2000-02; Wash Redskins, defensive end, 2003; New York Giants, defensive end, 2004-05; Monarc Construct, asst proj mgr, currently. **Business Addr:** Assistant Project Manager, Monarc Construction Inc, 4532 Cimarron St, Los Angeles, CA 90062, **Business Phone:** (323)229-2086.

**UPSHAW, SAM, JR.**
Photojournalist. **Personal:** Born Jan 10, 1964, Louisville, KY; son of Samuel Sr and Mary Lou Parmer. **Educ:** Western Ky Univ, Bowling Green, KY, photo jour, 1987. **Career:** The Louisville Defender, Louisville, Ky, intern, 1985; Tennessean, Nashville, Tenn, intern, 1986; Los Angeles Times, Los Angeles, Calif, intern, 1987; Courier J, Louisville, Ky, staff photogr, 1987-. **Orgs:** Nat Press Photogrs Asn, 1985-; Nat Asn Black Journalists, 1986-; Ky News Photogrs Asn, 1987-; co-founder & vpres, Western Ky Univ's Asn Black Communicators. **Honors/Awds:** Best of Gannett, Gannett Co Inc, 1988-89; Pulitzer Prize, Team (Staff) Coverage Gen News, 1989; Best of Show first Place Feature Picture Story, Third Place Sports and Honorable Mention Pictorial Kentucky News Photographers Asn Contest, 1989; Honorable Mention (Photojournalism), Nat Asn Black Journalists, 1990. **Home Addr:** 521 Baxter Ave, Louisville, KY 40204, **Home Phone:** (502)584-2937. **Business Addr:** Staff Photographer, The Courier Journal, 525 W Broadway, Louisville, KY 40201-7431, **Business Phone:** (502)582-4604.

**UPSHAW, WILLIE CLAY**
Baseball player. **Personal:** Born Apr 27, 1957, Blanco, TX; married Cindy; children: Brock Anthony, Courtney & Chad. **Career:** Baseball player (retired); New York Yankees, 1975; Toronto Blue Jays, outfielder & infielder, 1978, 1980-87; Cleveland Indians, infielder, 1988; Fukuoka Daiei Hawks, 1989-90; Bridgeport Bluefish, mgr, 1998-2001, Currently; Akron Aeros, mgr; San Francisco Giants, base coach, 2006-07; Clubhouse, coach. **Home Addr:** 3250 Fairfield Ave Apt 211, Bridgeport, CT 06605-3271, **Home Phone:** (203)255-7932. **Business Addr:** Manager, Bridgeport Bluefish Professional Baseball Club, 500 Main St, Bridgeport, CT 06604, **Business Phone:** (203)345-4800.

**URDY, DR. CHARLES E.**
Educator. **Personal:** Born Dec 27, 1933, Georgetown, TX; son of William Braxton and Pearl Roberta Jackson; married Margaret Bright; children: Christopher Braxton Rodgers & Steven Eugene. **Educ:** Huston-Tillotson Col, BS, chem, 1954; Univ Tex, Austin, PhD, phys anal chem, 1962. **Career:** Professor (retired): Huston-Tillotson Col, prof chem, 1961-62; NC Cent Univ, prof Chem, 1962-63; Univ Tex Austin, post-doc Fel, 1962-63; Prairie View A&M Univ, prof chem, 1963-72; Dow Chem Co Freeport Tex, summer employee, 1970; MIT-Lincoln Lab Boston, Nat Urban League Fel, 1972; Huston-Tillotson Col, profchem, 1972-93; Lower Colo River Authority, Environ Sci & Technol Develop, mgr, 1993-; Nc Col, Durham, prof. **Orgs:** Hon Soc Phi Lambda Upsion Alpha Kappa Mu; Nat Sci Found Fel, 1959; Univ Tex Fel, 1960; Procter & Gamble Fel, 1960; Alpha Phi Alpha Frat; Am Chem Soc; Am Crystallog Asn; Sigma Xi; elected chmn, First Prairie View A & M Fac Coun, 1969; Fel Am Inst Chemists; numerous local civic orgn & comn; state sec-treas, Tex Asn Col Teachers, 1970; campaign mgr first Black Wilhelmina Delco elected Tex Legis Travis Co, 1974; Beta Kappa ChiHon Sci Soc; Cty Austin Charter Rev Comt; chmn, Black Voters Action ProjPol Com; elected coun mem, Austin City Coun, 1981-94; chmn, Austin Revitalization Authority. **Home Addr:** 7311 Hartnell Dr, Austin, TX 78723. **Business Addr:** Manager of Science & Technology, Lower Colorado River Authority, 3700 Lake Austin Blvd, Austin, TX 78703.

**USHER (USHER TERRY RAYMOND, IV)**
Actor, singer. **Personal:** Born Oct 14, 1978, Dallas, TX; son of Usher III and Johnetta Patton; married Tameka; children: Usher V & Naviyd Ely Raymond; married Rozonda Chilli Thomas. **Career:** LaFace Rec Label, rec artist, 1993-; Us Rec Label, co-founder, 2002-; Albums: Usher, 1994; My Way, 1997; All About U, 2000; 8701, 2001; Caught Up, 2005; Usher & Friends, 2005; TV guest appearances: "Moesha"; "The Parent Hood"; TV Movies: Geppeto, 2000; Films: The Fac, 1998; Light It Up, 1999; Tex Rangers, 2001; TV: "To Protect & Serve", 2002; "7th Heaven", 2002; "American Dreams", 2002; "The Twilight Zone", 2002; "Sabrina, the Teenage Witch", 2002; "Attracting Opposites", 2003; "Episode", 2004; "In the Mix", 2005; "Killers", 2010; "Justin Bieber: Never Say Never", 2011; "Scary Movie 5", 2013; "Justin Bieber's Believe", 2013; "Justin Bieber's Believe", 2013; "Muppets Most Wanted", 2014; "Hands of Stone", 2015. Usher: Evolution 8701: Live in Concert, 2002; In the Mix, 2005; One Night One Star: Usher Live, 2005; Rhythm City Volume One: Caught Up, 2005. **Business Addr:** Actor, Singer, LaFace Rec Label, 550 Madison Ave, New York, NY 10022, **Business Phone:** (212)833-8000.

**USHER, JESSIE T.**
Actor. **Personal:** Born Feb 29, 1992, MD; son of Jessie T Sr and Judith. **Career:** Actor, 2004-. Television: Without a Trace, 2005; Hannah Montana, 2007; Lincoln Heights, 2008; Numb3rs, 2008; The Mentalist, 2009; Criminal Minds, 2009; Summer Camp, 2010; G.I. Joe: Renegades, 2011; Level Up, 2011; Level Up, 2012-13; Survivor's Remorse, 2014-16. Film: Beautiful Boy, 2010; InAPPropriate Comedy, 2013; Teenage, 2013; When the Game Stands Tall, 2014; Independence Day: Resurgence, 2016; Almost Christmas, 2016. Appeared in print ads and commercials. **Orgs:** Alpha Gamma Sigma. **Honors/Awds:** Breakthrough Performer Award, Hamptons International Film Festival, 2015. **Business Addr:** Starz Entertainment, 9242 Beverly Blvd Suite 200, Beverly Hills, CA 90210.

**USSERY, ESQ. TERDEMA LAMAR, II**
President (organization), basketball executive. **Personal:** Born Dec 4, 1958, Los Angeles, CA; son of Terdema Sr and Jean Hendrick; married Debra Hubbard; children: Terdema L III & Elizabeth. **Educ:** Princeton Univ, Dept Hons, Princeton, NJ, BA, 1981; Harvard Univ, Cambridge, MA, MPA, hons, 1984; Univ Calif, Berkeley, CA, JD, 1987. **Career:** Morrison & Foerster, Los Angeles, Calif, assoc, atty, 1987-90; Continental Basketball Asn, dep comnr & gen legal coun, 1990-91, comnr, 1991-93; Univ Denver, grad sch bus, prof, 1991-; NIKE Sports Mgt, pres, 1993-96; Dallas Mavericks Found, pres & chief exec officer, 1997-2015; AXS TV LLC, chief exec officer, 2001-12; HD Net LLC, pres & chief exec officer, 2001-12; Calif Law Rev, exec ed; Treehouse Foods Inc, chief exec officer, 2001-12, lead independent dir, 2005-; Timberland Co, lead independent dir, 2005-11; Entrust Inc, dir & mem audit comt, 2006-09; Tex Higher, educ coord bd; Fantex Inc, dir, 2013-; Under Armour Inc, pres, 2015-. **Orgs:** Grad mem, Ivy Club, 1981-; Denver Games Comm, Fin Comm; Los Angeles Young Black Profs, 1984; Denver Games Comm, 1990; chair, Dallas Housing Authority Bd; bd gov, NBA; bd dir, WNBA; Coun Foreign Rels; Andre Agassi Charitable Found Bd; bd trustee, Princeton Univ's; trustee, Communities Found Tex; adv bd, Wingate Partners LLP; dir, Treehouse Foods Inc; dir, Dallas Symphony Orchestra; trustee, Princeton Univ, 2004; dir, Salvation Army; dep comnr & gen coun, Commonwealth Broadcasting Asn; dir, Tex Higher Educ Coord Bd; trustee, Communities Found Tex; mem adv bd, Wingate Partners. **Home Addr:** 2909 Taylor St, Dallas, TX 75226. **Business Addr:** President, Under Armour Inc, 1020 Hull St Suite 300, Baltimore, MD 21230, **Business Phone:** (888)727-6687.

**UTENDAHL, JOHN O.**
Chairperson, chief executive officer, founder (originator). **Personal:** Born Jan 1, 1956?, Queens, NY; married Phyllis Hollis; children: Madison & Sydney. **Educ:** Long Island Univ, BS, bus admin; Columbia Univ, MBA. **Career:** Salomon Bros, corp bond trader, 1982; Merrill Lynch, sr bond trader, corp bond trader, vpres, 1986-92; Utendahl Capital Partners, founder, res div, trading desk mgr, chmn, chief exec officer, 1992-2010; Deutsche Bank Americas, vice chmn, 2010; Bank Am, Global Corp & Investment Banking, exec vice chmn, 2016-; UCM Partners, chmn; Deutsche Bank Americas Holding Corp, vice chmn; Uni-World Capital LP, sponsor, partner; Praesidian Capital, partner. **Orgs:** Founding mem & chmn, Utendahl Orgn; bd, Family Promise; trustee, Buena Vista Univ; bd dir, Securities Indust Asn; bd dir, US Fund UNICEF; bd dir, Big Bros/Big Sisters. **Honors/Awds:** "Black Enterprise", 75 Most Powerful Blacks on Wall Street, 2011. **Special Achievements:** Utendahl Capital Partners was the largest African-American-owned investment bank in the United States. **Business Addr:** Executive Vice Chairman, Bank of America, 100 N Tryon St, Charlotte, NC 28255.

**UTLEY, RICHARD HENRY**
Public relations executive, chief executive officer, president (organization). **Personal:** Born Jan 2, 1949, Pittsburgh, PA; married Audrey L Ross. **Educ:** Univ Pittsburgh, BA, 1972, Law Sch, 1973. **Career:** Speaker, entrepreneur, auth, Artist & entertainment promoter; Penn Legal Serv, dir prog develop, 1980-82; City Harrisburg Dept Pub Safety, tech asst, 1982-83; Auditor Gen PA, asst dir, dep auditor gen admin, 2003-; Utley Assoc, pres, chief exec officer; Pub Affairs Consult Inc, vpres; State Penn, Bur Charitable Orgn, dir, currently. **Orgs:** Pres, Utley Assoc; Nat Asn Advan Colored People; vice chair, Harrisburg Housing Authority; sec bd Ctr; African Am Chamber Com Cent Pa. **Home Addr:** 122 Locust St, Harrisburg, PA 17101, **Home Phone:** (717)238-3677. **Business Addr:** President, Chief Executive Officer, Utley Associates, 600 N 2nd St Suite 305, Harrisburg, PA 17101, **Business Phone:** (717)238-3677.

**UZOIGWE, DR. GODFREY N.**
Educator, administrator. **Personal:** Born Sep 25, 1938; married Patricia Maria Cahill; children: Emeka Anthony, Amaechi Charles & Chinue Jaja. **Educ:** Univ Col Dublin, BA, hons, 1963; Trinity Col, Dublin, higher dipl educ, 1964; Christ Ch Oxford Univ, engineering, DPhil, hist, 1967. **Career:** Makerere Univ, Kampala Uganda, hist lectr, 1967-70; Mich Univ, from asst prof hist to prof hist, 1970-84, co-chair; Nig Nsukka Univ, vis prof hist, 1976-77; Univ Calabar Nigeria, Dept Hist, prof & head, 1981-87, dean, facarts, 1984-87, chmn, 1985-87; Hist Socs of Nigeria, fel, 1987; Imo State Univ, Okigwe Nigeria, prof hist, 1987-91, pioneer dir, Ctr Igbo Studies, 1987-91, dean, Col Humanities & Soc Sci, 1994-99; Cornell Univ, visting sr fel, 1989; Abia State Univ, Uturu, dean, Col humanities & soc sci, 1991-92, pioneer dir, 1991-93, prof hist, 1991-95, dean, Col Humanities & Social Sci, 1991-93, dean, Col post grad studies, 1993-95; The Presidency, Abuja, Nigeria, vis sr res prof hist, 1993-94; Lincoln Univ, Pa, Vis Dir & distinguished vis prof, 1997-98; Tulane Univ, vis prof, 1998-99; Miss State Univ, Dept Hist, Chair & prof, head, 1999-2005. **Orgs:** Life mem, Oxford Union Soc, Oxford, 1964-; Hist Asn, Ghana, 1967-; Royal African Soc, London, 1970-; Am Hist Asn, 1970; African Studies Asn, USA, 1970; Smithsonian Inst, 1974-; Intra Univ, Sem Armed Forces & Socs, 1974-; Imo State Libr, Owerri, Nigeria, 1984-87; Oxford & Cambridge Club, Nigeria, 1985-; pres, Hist Soc Nigeria, 1988-92; chair bd, Esr Thompson Publishers, 1991-; Rhodes Scholar New Panel, Nigeria, 1991-; chair, Ahiajoku Lecure Plng Comn, 1993-95; Imo State, Nigeria, 1993-95; consult, Danchimach Nigeria Am Lab Sch, 1993-; grp chair, Esr Thompson Consult, Owerri, Nigeria, 1995-; fel New York Acad Sci, 1995; chair, Imo St Coun Arts & Cult, 1995-97; pres gen, Mbaitoli Cult Union, Imo StateNigeria, 1996-; Fel Un Educ, Sci and Cult Orgn(UNESCO), 1997-; fel Aaas, 1997; fel Asn Third World Studies, 1999-; bd mem, W African Res Assn, 2001-; Phi Alpha ta, 2001-; Phi Kappa Ph, 2001-; ed bd, Lincoln J Social & Polit Thought; ed bd, Trans-African J Hist; ed bd, Kenya Hist Rev; ed bd, J African Studies; ed bd, Makerere Hist J; ed bd, J World Studies; ed consult, Calabar Hist J; ed bd, Nsukka J Humanities; consult ed, J Develop; ed advisor, J Prof Educr; ed bd, Bensu J Hist Studies; ed bd, Benin J Hist Studies. **Home Addr:** 203 Williamsburg Dr, Starkville, MS 39759-4231, **Home Phone:** (662)323-8475. **Business Addr:** Professor of History, Mississippi State University, 275 Allen Hall, Mississippi State, MS 39762, **Business Phone:** (662)325-7082.

# V

**VAAUGHTERS-JOHNSON, CECILIE A.**
Lawyer. **Personal:** Born Jul 29, 1953, Montclair, NJ; daughter of Vivian S and Alans H; married Robert W; children: Langston & Ciara. **Educ:** Ohio Univ, BBA, 1975; Georgetown Univ, Law Ctr, JD, 1978. **Career:** Gen Motors, Inland Div, comptroller's off intern, 1972-75; Clinton Chapman Law Off, assoc, 1978-82; Norwind & Vaughters Law Firm, chapman, 1982-86; Cecilie Vaughters-Johnson, Esq, prof consult, 1987-; Nat Legal Adv, Jack & Jill Am Inc, 2002-03; Kidz & Co Inc, legal coun & secy, 2002-04; pvt pract lawyer, atty at law, currently. **Orgs:** Pres, Greater Wash Area Chap Women Lawyers Div, Nat Bar Asn, 1983-84; vpres, Wash Bar Asn, 1983-85; reg dir, Nat Bar Asn, 1984-85; vpres, Palo Alto Chap, Nat Asn Advan Colored People, 1987-89; bd dir, Palo Alto Chap, Red Cross, 1989-96; chief fin officer, Johnson Tri-Dom Found, 1990-; reg dir, Georgetown Black Law Alumni Asn, 1991-94; treas, PTA, Montclaire Sch, 1992-94; bd dir, Los Altos Parent Presch Asn, 1992-94; treas, Jack & Jill Am, San Jose Chap, 1996-98, pres, 2002-04; Cupertino Jr High Sch, PTA bd, 1998-2000; Peninsula Bay Chap Links, pres. **Business Addr:** Lawyer, Attorney at Law, 1635 Candace Way, Los Altos, CA 94024-6243, **Business Phone:** (650)961-3312.

**VALDES, PEDRO H.**
Business owner, executive. **Personal:** Born Jan 20, 1945, Havana; son of Pedro H and Hesma; married Maria A Bermudez; children: Hesma, Pedro III & Xiomara. **Educ:** City Col NY, BA, romance lang, lit & ling, 1969; Middlebury Col, MA, romance lang, lit & ling, 1971; State Univ NY, Stony Brook, romance lang, lit, ling & philos, 1974; NY Univ, Sch Arts & Sci, Dept Hisp Lit & Lang, grad studies, 1978, romance lang, lit, ling & philos, 1980; Fairleigh Dickinson Univ-Metrop Campus, doctorate educ studies cand, 1980. **Career:** Sci Environ Ecol Knowledge Prog, tutor, 1963-65; NY Philantropic League, rehab counr, 1966-69; Alcur Tours Inc, tour guide & planner, 1968-72; Wm H Taft HS, span lang teacher, 1969-72; NY Col Podiatric Med, asst dean stud affairs, 1970-71, vpres stud affairs, 1972-75, exec vpres, 1975-80; State Univ NY Stony Brook, teaching asst dept hisp lang & lit, 1972-73; Premo Pharmaceut Labs Inc, export sales agt, 1980-81, exclusive export sales agt, int, 1981-82; Teaneck High Sch, teacher, span, 1985-2002; Protecom Inc, pres & dir, 1990-; Pedro's Wines, owner & pres, 1998-. **Orgs:** United Fedn Teachers, 1969-80; Am Asn Univ Prof, 1972-80; Am Asn Cols Podiatric Med, 1973-80; Am Pub Health Asn, 1973-; Nat League Nursing Policies & Procedures Comm, 1977-; Nat Health Coun Inc, 1980-; Nat Ctr's Adv Coun Res Voc Educ, 1981-84; adv comt, Nat Ctr Health Career Info Disadvantaged. **Business Addr:** President & Director, Owner, Protecom Inc, 3819 Penns Dr, Winfield, PA 17889, **Business Phone:** (201)836-6312.

**VALENTINE, DARNELL TERRELL**
Basketball player, basketball executive. **Personal:** Born Feb 3, 1959, Chicago, IL. **Educ:** Univ Kans, BS, polit sci, 1981. **Career:** Basketball player (retired), exec; Portland Trail Blazers, 1981-86; Los Angeles Clippers, 1986-88; Cleveland Cavaliers, 1988-91; Marr Rimini, 1991-92; Burghy Modena, 1992-93; Reggio Emilia, 1994; Nat Basketball Players Asn, regional rep, 1994-2004; Portland Trail Blazers, dir player progs, 2004-07; Precision Castparts Corp, currently. **Home Addr:** 7546 SW Ashford St, Portland, OR 97224-6629. **Business Addr:** Basketball Executive, Precision Castparts Corp, 4650 SW Macadam Ave Suite 400, Portland, OR 97239, **Business Phone:** (503)946-4800.

**VALENTINE, DIANN**
Entrepreneur, designer. **Personal:** Born Oakland, CA. **Educ:** Calif State Univ, BA, bus admin, 1994. **Career:** Warner Home Video. dir worldwide DVD prod; DR Valentine & Assoc Inc, pres & founder, creative dir, 1990-; Weddings Valentine Style, auth, 2006-; Wedding Day Tv Show TNT Network, Co-Host, 2009-. **Business Addr:** President & Founder, Creative Director, D R Valentine & Associates Inc, 650 S Raymond Ave, Pasadena, CA 91105, **Business Phone:** (626)395-0346.

**VALENTINE, HERMAN E., SR.**
Executive. **Personal:** Born Jun 26, 1937, Norfolk, VA; son of Frank (deceased) and Alice (deceased); married Dorothy Jones; children: Herman Edward Jr & Bryce Thomas. **Educ:** Norfolk State Col, BS, 1967; Am Univ, attended 1968; Col William & Mary, MBA, 1972. **Career:** USDA Grad Sch Dept Agr, exec admin officer, 1967-68; Syst Mgt Am Corp, founder, chmn & pres, 1970-94; Norfolk State Col, Norfolk, VA, bus mgr, 1969-70; Systs Mgt Am Corp, founder & chmn, 1970-94; SMA Microsystems Va LLC, chief exec officer, 1986-. **Orgs:** Am Mgt Asn; Armed Forces Commun Electronics Asn; bd dir exec comn, Greater Norfolk Corp; adv comm VA Chap St Jude C Res Hosp; adv coun, Va Stage Co; Air Traffic Cent Asn; Tidewater Reg Minority Purchasing Coun; Soc Logistics Engs; bd dir, Oper Smile; bd dir, PUSH Int Trade Bur Inc; Old Dom Univ; Hampton Roads Chamber Com; Downtown Norfolk Develop Corp; lifetime mem, Navy League US; Phi Bata Sigma Fraternity Inc. **Honors/Awds:** Presidential Citation, Nat Asn Equal Oppor in Higher Educ, 1981; Presidential Citation Entrepreneur of the Year, Dept Com Minority Bus Develop Agency, 1984; Delicados Inc Award Entrepreneurship, Blazing New Horizons, 1986; Citizen of the Year Award, Outstanding Leadership & Serv to the Comm, 1986; Regional Minority Manufacturing of the Year Award, MBDA, 1988; Certificate of Recognition, lt govr, Commonwealth Va, 1987; Outstanding Businessperson of the Year, State VA Award, black pres Round table Asn, 1987; Class III Supplier of the Year Award, Nat Minority Supplier Develop Coun, 1987; Ambassador of the City of Norfolk, Ca, 1986; Black Diamond Award, Rev Jesse Jackson, Operation PUSH, 1989; Patriotic Service Award, US Savings Bond Campaign, US Treas Dept, 1989; Community Service Award, Exemplary Blacks Bus, Int Am Bus, 1989; Certificate of Recognition, African American Entrepreneur, New York City Police Dept, 1990; named one of 100 Most Influential Black Americans, Upscale mag, 1994; Black United Press Award, 2000; inductee of National Black Press Hall of Fame, 2000; Colgate Darden Award. **Special Achievements:** First Alumni in History of Norfolk State University Invited Back to Present Norfolk State University Commencement Address. **Home Addr:** 917 Cranberry, Chesapeake, VA 23320, **Home Phone:** (757)479-1504. **Business Addr:** Chief Executive Officer, SMA MicroSystems LLC, 6104 Westgate Rd Suite 121, Raleigh, NC 27617, **Business Phone:** (919)510-5995.

**VALENTINE, J. T.**
Lawyer. **Personal:** Born Sep 21, 1918, Suffolk, VA; son of Miles E and Annie; married Rosetta Mozelle Cason (deceased). **Educ:** Howard Univ, BS, 1948, LLB, 1951. **Career:** Lawyer (retired); Fed Aviation Admin, Wash Contracts Off, supvr procurement officer, 1966, chief contract serv, 1970, supvr contracts specialist, 1970, Small Bus, Wash, officer, 1971, Law Div, indust rels officer. **Orgs:** Pres, Tuskegee Airmen, E Coast Chap; Israel Baptist Church; Nat Asn Advan Colored

People; Nat Camping & Hiking Asn. **Home Addr:** 3608 Carpenter St SE, Washington, DC 20020, **Home Phone:** (202)584-7574.

### VALMON, ANDREW ORLANDO
Athletic coach, track and field athlete, association executive. **Personal:** Born Jan 1, 1965, Brooklyn, NY; son of Oscar and Norma Haynes; married Meredith Rainey; children: Travis, Maya & Mallory. **Educ:** Seton Hall Univ, BA, mkt commun, 1987. **Career:** Athletic (retired), coach; Georgetown Univ, Mens Track & Field, assoc head coach, 1995-2003; Univ Md, Terrapins, head coach, 2003-. **Orgs:** Phi Beta Sigma Fraternity Inc; founder, Ave Prog; spokesman, US Olympic Comt. **Honors/Awds:** Inductee, NJ Sports Hall of Fame; Gold Medal, 4x400m relay, Olympic Games, 1988, 1992; Outstanding Performer, Big East Conference Championships, 1987; NJ Athlete of the Year, 1990, 1992; Gold Medal, 4x400m relay, Goodwill Games, 1990, 1994; Athlete of the Year, Metrop Athletics Cong, 1990; Silver Medal, TAC Nat Championship, 1991; 2nd Place, IAAF Mobil Grand Prix, 1991; World Record & Gold Medalist, World Championships, 4X400m relay, Best Relay Ever & New World Record, 1993; Hall of Fame, Track and Field, Seton Hall Univ, 1997; President Award, USA Track & Field, 2002. **Special Achievements:** World Record Holder, 4X400m Relay. **Home Addr:** 16403 Danforth Ct, Rockville, MD 20853, **Home Phone:** (301)774-7684. **Business Addr:** Head Coach, Terrapins, PO Box 295, College Park, MD 20742, **Business Phone:** (301)314-7070.

### VAN AMSON, GEORGE LOUIS
Banker, executive director, executive. **Personal:** Born Jan 30, 1952, New York, NY; son of Adolph and Willie-Mae (deceased); married Wendy Alicia Tempro; children: Alexandra Case, Victoria Taylor & G A Schuyler Van. **Educ:** Columbia Col, BA, econs, 1974; Harvard Bus Sch, MBA, 1982. **Career:** Revlon Inc, financial analyst, 1974-76; Citibank NA, asst controller, 1976-77; Goldman Sachs & Co, sr financial analyst, 1977-80, vpres, 1982-92; Morgan Stanley & Co Inc, vpres, Latin Am Trading, pres, 1992-94, prin, Intl Trading, co-head, 1995, prin, sr domestic trader, 1996, Inst Equities, managing dir, 2003; Rockefeller Bros Fund, Instnl Equity Div-Sales & Trading, managing dir, N Am Analyst & Assoc Advising & Develop Progs, mgt head, currently. **Orgs:** Dir, Alpha Phi Alpha Fraternity Inc, 1971-73; dir, Urban Leadership Forum, 1983-88; 21st Century PAC NY, 1984-87, Minisink Townhouse Inc, 1985-88; econ develop comt, 100 Black Men, 1985-; pres, HBS Black Alumni Asn, 1985-87; chmn, Int comt, Securities Traders Asn NY, 1987-89; trustee, Columbia Univ, 1994, trustee emer; trustee, Riverside Church, 1994; chair, Columbia Alumni Asn. **Honors/Awds:** Curtis Gold Medal, Columbia Col, 1974; Leadership Award, Harvard Bus Sch, 1982; Distinguished Service Award, United Negro Col Fund, 1989; Global Leader for Tomorrow, World Econ Forum, 1992; John Jay Award, 2000, Alumni of Color Heritage Award, 2003, Community Impact Making a Difference Award, 2004, Alumni Medal, Columbia Univ, 2009. **Home Addr:** 210 W 90th St Suite 4B, New York, NY 10024-1241, **Home Phone:** (212)362-6121. **Business Addr:** Managing Director, Rockefeller Brothers Fund, 475 Riverside Dr Suite 900, New York, NY 10115, **Business Phone:** (212)812-4200.

### VAN EMBRICQS, ALEXANDRA
Basketball player. **Personal:** Born Apr 14, 1968, Paramaribo. **Educ:** Univ Calif, Los Angeles, attended 1991. **Career:** Basketball player (retired); Holland, basketball player; Manresa, Spain, 1991-92; Texim Tonego, Holland, 1992-94; St Servais, Belg, 1995-97; Bourges, France, 1997-98; Los Angeles Sparks, forward, 1998-99.

### VAN EXEL, NICKEY MAXWELL
Basketball player, basketball coach. **Personal:** Born Nov 27, 1971, Kenosha, WI. **Educ:** Trinity Valley Community Col, attended 1991; Univ Cincinnati, attended 1993. **Career:** Basketball player (retired), basketball coach; Los Angeles Lakers, guard & pt guard, 1993-98; DenverNuggets, pt guard, 1998-2002; Dallas Mavericks, pt guard, 2002-03; Golden State Warriors, pt guard, 2003-04; Portland Trail Blazers, shooting guard, 2004-05; San Antonio Spurs, guard & pt guard, 2005-06; Tex Southern (NCAA I), asst coach, 2009-10; Atlanta Hawks, asst coach, 2010-12; Milwaukee Bucks, asst coach, 2013-14; Texas Legends, asst coach, 2014-16; Memphis Grizzlies, asst coach, 2016-. **Orgs:** Nat Benevolent Asn; All-Rookie Second Team. **Honors/Awds:** All-Rookie Second Team, Nat Basketball Asn, 1994; All-Rookie second team, Nat Basketball Asn, 1994; Chopper Travaglini Award; Victor Award; Comeback Player of the Year, 1998; All-Star, Nat Basketball Asn, 1998. **Business Addr:** Assistant Coach, Milwaukee Bucks, 191 Beale St, Memphis, TN 38103, **Business Phone:** (901)205-1234.

### VAN HICKS, DELPHUS, JR.
Executive, government official, sheriff. **Personal:** Born Feb 6, 1939, Ashland, MS; son of Delphus Van Sr and Gladys Woodson; married Frankie Marie Hamer; children: Early Hue, James Earl & Diane Lanell. **Educ:** Tenn Law Enforcement Acad, attended 1974; Donhue Barber Col, master barber lic, 1974. **Career:** Williams Candy Co, stockman, 1961-62; Reichold Chem Inc, inspector, mixer, lead man, 1967-72; Leadman Reichhold Chem Inc, mixer, insp, 1967-72; Hardeman Co, Sheriff Dept, chief, dep sheriff, 1968-72, 1974, 1978, sheriff, 1978-94, 2002-10. **Orgs:** Vpres, Tenn Sheriff's Asn, 1978-; W Tenn Criminal Invest Asn, 1980-; 25th Judicial Dist Drug Task Force, 1989-. **Honors/Awds:** Tennessee Outstanding Achievements Award, Gov Lamar Alexander, 1981; Outstanding Sheriff of the Year, Tenn Sheriff Asn, 1988-89. **Special Achievements:** First African-American Chief Dep Sheriff Hardeman County, 1974; First African-American sheriff in Tennessee, 1978. **Home Addr:** 503 Jackson St, Bolivar, LA 38008, **Home Phone:** (731)658-6237.

### VAN HOOK, GEORGE ELLIS, JR.
Judge, lawyer. **Personal:** Born Aug 27, 1948; married Margaret Ann Kendrix; children: Felecia Ann, Demetric, Alison Blossam & George Ellis III. **Educ:** Univ Ark, BSBA, bus com, gen, mkt, 1970; Univ Ark Sch Law, JD, 1973. **Career:** Walker, Kaplan & Mays, legal intern, 1971; Eugene Hunt, law clerk, 1973; Hunt & Van Hook, atty, 1973-74; Ark State Hwy Dept, staff atty, 1974-76; gen pract, law, atty, 1976-77; pvt prac, atty, 1977-79; pvt pract atty, 1979-; Union Co Child Support Enforcement Unit, contract atty, 1981-90; Union Co Munic Ct, magistrate, 1983-90; Union Co Dist Ct, judge, 1991-. **Orgs:** Bd advs, Union Co Bar Asn; Salvation Army; bd dir, Union Co United Way; Progressive Gentlemen Inc; El Dorado Chamber Com; Union Co Acad Found Inc; Boys & Girls Club El Dorado; Boy Scouts Union Dist; S Ark Arts Ctr; UALR Scholar Prog; Winthrop Rockefeller Scholar Prog; Ark Cost Judiciary Study Comn, 1986; Ark Munic Judges Coun; Ark Munic League; Bd, Independent Living Ctrs; Harold Flowers Law Soc; Union Co Community Found; Adv Bd, State Ark Community Punishment; Ark State Bar, currently. **Home Addr:** 307 S Hill Ave, El Dorado, AR 71730, **Home Phone:** (870)863-5119. **Business Addr:** Union County Municipal Judge, Union County District Court, 3801 Oleta Ave, El Dorado, AR 71730, **Business Phone:** (870)864-1950.

### VAN JOHNSON, RODNEY
Actor, business owner. **Personal:** Born Feb 20, 1961, Cincinnati, OH; married Carmen Obando; children: Quincy, Joshua & Alexis Antonio Benjamin Obando. **Educ:** Univ Cincinnati, BS, educ. **Career:** Actor, business owner; Koya Skin Care, pres & owner, currently; Film appearances: Dominic's Castle, 1994; Making the Rules, 1996; Tv guest appearances: Grace Under Fire, 1996; Jamie Foxx Show, 1996, 1997; Mad About You, 1998. Tv Episode: "Pensacola Wings of Gold", 1997; "The Young & the Restless", 1998; "Port Charles", 1999; "Passions", 1999-2007; "Girlfriends", 2000; "Hip-Ocracy", 2000; "The Eleventh Hour", 2002; Self: "The 28th Annual Daytime Emmy Awards", 2001; "Oh Drama!", 2002; "NBC's Funniest Outtakes", 2002; "Providence", 2002; "Soap Talk", 2004; "Starting Over", 2005; "Passion for the Game", 2005; "Without a Trace", 2008. **Orgs:** Bd mem, Pancreatic Cancer. **Honors/Awds:** Hall of Fame, Univ Cincinnati Track & Field, 2002. **Business Addr:** Owner, President, Koya Skin Care, 13430 N Valleyheart Dr N, Sherman Oaks, CA 91423-3122, **Business Phone:** (818)501-3371.

### VAN LEE, REGINALD
Consultant, association executive. **Personal:** Born May 8, 1957, Houston, TX; son of Tommie and Eva Elnora Jefferson. **Educ:** Mass Inst Technol, BS, civil engineering, MS, civil engineering; Harvard Bus Sch, MBA, 1984. **Career:** Exxon Prod Res Co, res engr; Booz Allen Hamilton iNC, partner, 1993, sr partner, 2003, exec vpres, currently. **Orgs:** Exec Leadership Coun; MIT Nat Selection Comm; bd dirs, Thurgood Marshall Col Fund; chmn emer, Evidence Dance Co; trustee, Studio Mus, Harlem, NY; treas, MAC AIDS Fund Bd; chmn, Wash Performing Arts Soceity; chmn bd trustee, Howard Theatre Restoration Proj; trustee, Mass Inst Technol Corp; Habitat Humanity; Am Cancer Soc; Am Heart Asn; founding mem, Clinton Global Initiative; chmn emer, Evidence Dance Co; cabinet mem, Habitat Humanity Int Cabinet; Press Comt Arts & Humanities, 2008. **Honors/Awds:** C. Walter Nichols Community Service Award, NY Univ; Spirit of Cabrini Award, Cabrini Mission Found; Joseph Papp Racial Harmony Award, Found for Ethnic Understanding; Black Engineer of the Year Award, 2008; Joseph Papp Racial Harmony Award, Found Ethnic Understanding; top 25 consultants in the world, Consult mag; Business Leader Award, Washington Business Journal, 2009; C. Walter Nichols Award; Renaissance Award, Abyssinian Develop Corp; Percy E. Sutton Civic Leadership Award, Apollo Theater Found; Frank C. Carr Award, InRoads Inc; International Leadership Award, Tex Women's Empowerment Found. **Special Achievements:** Co author of book - MEGACOMMUNITIES: How Leaders of Government, Busines sand Non-Profits Can Tackle Today's Global Challenges Together. Appeared numerous times on ABC's "World News This Morning" television program & CNBC speaking on the topics of CEO tenures, corporate values & enterprisere silience; One of the Top 25 Consultants in the world in "Consulting"magazine; One of NY's Finest Philanthropists; Black Engineer of the Year, 2008. **Business Addr:** Executive Vice President, Booz Allen Hamilton Inc, 8283 Greensboro Dr, McLean, VA 22102, **Business Phone:** (703)902-5000.

### VAN LIEROP, ROBERT F.
Lawyer, ambassador. **Personal:** Born Mar 17, 1939, New York, NY; son of Edward and Sylvia; married Toy; children: 1. **Educ:** Hofstra Univ, BA, econ, 1964; NY Univ Sch Law, JD, 1967. **Career:** Nat Asn Advan Colored People, asst legal coun, 1967-68; Fleisher, Dornbush, Mensch, Mandelstam, assoc atty, 1969-71; Self-employed, film prod photo journalist, 1971-; pvt pract atty, 1968-71; Van Lierop, Burns & Bassett law firm, partner & atty, 1978-81, 1994-; Repub Vanuatu, Ambassador to Un, 1981-94; NY City Community Bd No 9 Manhattan, chmn, 1985-87; Un, rep; Films: A Luta Continua, producer; O Povo Organizado, producer; Cowan, DeBaets, Abrahams & Sheppard LLP, atty, coun, currently; vpres, Ad Hoc Comt Whole during Sixteenth Spec Session Un Gen Assembly; WABC TV; Cohn Glickstein Lurie Ostrin Lubell & Lubell, coun; Lubell & Lubell, coun; Organisation African Unity, observer; NY law firm McLaughlin & Stern LLP, partner. **Orgs:** Bd mem, Lawyers ComnHuman Rights; Nat Asn Advan Colored People; bd mem, Arthur Ashe InstUrbanHealth; bd dir, Black Econ Res Ctr; mem exec comn, Am Comn Africa; founding mem, Nat Conf Black Lawyers; fel, Arthur Garfield Hays Civil Liberties; bd mem, Harlem C's atre; mem nat exec bd, Nat Lawyers Guild; chmn, Vanuatu deleg to 41 st, 42nd, 44th, 46th, & 48th Sessions Un Gen Assembly; chmn, Group Asian States Un; vpres, Conf Parties Un Framework Conv; vpes, Un Conf Environ & Develop; vpres, 43rd Session Un Gen Assembly; anuatu deleg to Non-Aligned Summit; int law activ Un; Exec Comt Asn Bar; chmn, Vanuatu deleg to Prep Comt; obsercer, Orgn African Unity; chmn, Fourth Comt 44th Session of Un Gen Assembly; bd mem, NY Civil Liberties Union; bd dir, Manhattan Bor Develop Corp, 1988-90; Am Bar Asn, African Law Comt; chair; AsnBarCity New York, African Affairs Comt; chmn, Coun Int Affairs & chmn exec comt; NY State Bar Asn; life mem, Black Entertainment & Sports Lawyers Asn; life fel Am Bar Found; Bar DC; Romare Bearden Found; Arthur Garfield Civic Liberties Fel, New York Univ; Phi Sigma Alpha, 1985. **Business Addr:** Attorney, Cowan, DeBaets, Abrahams & Sheppard LLP, 41 Madison Ave 34th Fl, New York, NY 10010, **Business Phone:** (212)974-7474.

### VAN PEEBLES, MARIO
Movie director, actor, writer. **Personal:** Born Jan 15, 1957, Mexico City; son of Melvin and Maria; married Chitra Sukhu; children: Makaylo, Mandela, Marley, Maya & Morgana; married Lisa Vitello. **Educ:** Columbia Univ, BA, econ, 1978. **Career:** NY City Mayor's Off Mgt, analyst, 1979; Films: Sweet Sweetback's Baadasssss Song, 1971; Exterminator 2, 1984; South Bronx Heroes, 1985; Rappin', 1985; Children of the Night, 1985; Heart break Ridge, 1986; Last Resort, 1986; Jaws: The Revenge, 1987; Identity Crisis, 1989; Blue Bayou, 1990; New Jack City, 1991; Full Eclipse, 1992; Stomping at the Savoy, 1992; Posse, dir, 1993; Highlander III: The Final Dimension, 1994; Gunmen, 1994; Solo, 1996; Gang in Blue, 1997; Los Locos, 1997; Mama Flora's Family, 1998; Love Kills, actor & writer, 1998; Standing Knockdown, writer, 1999; Ali, 2001; The Hebrew Hammer, 2003; BAADASSSSS!, dir, screenplay & producer, 2003; Carlito's Way: Rise to Power, 2005; Hard Luck, dir, 2006; Killers in the House; Kerosene Cowboys, 2009; Across the Line: The Exodus of Charlie Wright, 2010; Kerosene Cowboys; Redemption Road, dir, 2010; Black, White & Blues, dir, 2010; Lost, dir, 2010; All Things Fall Apart, dir, 2011; 5th & Alameda, 2011; Tied to a Chair, 2011; We the Party, actor, exec producer & dir, 2012; Red Sky, dir & screenplay, 2014. TV Series: "One Life to Live", 1982-83; "Sonny Spoon", 1988; "Rude Awakening, "2000-01; "44 Minutes", 2004; "LA Riots", 2004; "All My Children", 2008; "Damages", dir, 2009; "Mario's Green House", exec producer, 2009; "House houses ", 2009; "Hellcats", 2011; "The Game", 2011; "Boss", dir, 2011-12; "The Finder", 2012; "NCIS", dir, 2013; "Monday Mornings", dir, 2013; Zero Hour, dir, 2013; "Nashville", actor & dir, 2014; "Once Upon a Time", dir, 2014. **Orgs:** Screen Actors Guild; Actor's Equity; Am Fedn TV & Radio Artists; Dirs Guild Am. **Honors/Awds:** Emmy Award Nomination & Directors Guild Award, 1990; Bronze Halo Award; Pioneers of Excellence Award, World Inst Black Commun; Image Award, Nat Asn Advan Colored People, 1989; Silver Leopard, Locarno Int Film Festival, 1995; Copper Wing Tribute Award, Phoenix Film Festival, 2003; Audience Award, Philadelphia Film Festival, 2004; Black Reel Award, 2005. **Home Addr:** , Los Angeles, CA. **Business Addr:** Agent, Chris Black, 151 El Camino Dr, Beverly Hills, CA 90212.

### VAN PEEBLES, MELVIN
Actor, writer, composer. **Personal:** Born Aug 21, 1932, Chicago, IL; married Maria Marx; children: Mario, Megan & Melvin. **Educ:** Ohio Wesleyan Univ, BA, 1953; Univ Amsterdam. **Career:** Dutch Nat Theatre; Mabon Nugent & Co, consult, 1984; Music video: Whodini's song "Funky Beat", dir; TV Writing Projects: "Just an Old Sweet Song", 1976; "Sophisticated Gents", 1981; "American Stock Exchange", fl trader, 1984; Films: The Story of a Three Day Pass, writer & dir, 1967; Watermelon Man, actor, 1969; Slogan, writer, 1969; Don't Play Us Cheap, writer, 1973; Greased Lightning, writer, 1977; LA Law, actor, 1986; Jaws: The Revenge, actor, 1987; Vrooom Vroom Vrooom, writer, 1995; Gang in Blue, 1996; Love Kills, 1998; Time of Her Time, 1999; Smut, 1999; Antilles sur Seine, actor, 2000; Conte du ventre-plein, Le, writer, producer, composer & dir, 2000; How to Get the Man's Foot Outta Your Ass, writer, 2003; Baltimore, 2003; The Hebrew Hammer, 2003; Hard Luck, 2006; Blackout, 2007; Redemption Road, 2010; We the Party, 2010; Peeples, 2013. TV series: "Just an Old Sweet Song ", writer, 1976; "Living Single", 1996; "Calm at Sunset", 1996; "Homicide: Life on the Street", 1997; "The Shining", 1997; "Riot", 1997; "Classified X", writer, 1998; "Girlfriends", actor, 2005; "Unstoppable: Conversation with Melvin Van Peebles, Gordon Parks & Ossie Davis", composer, 2005; "Girlfriends", 2005; "The 2006 Black Movie Awards", 2006; Plays: Ain't Supposed to Die A Natural Death, writer & producer, 1971; Don't Play Us Cheap, writer & producer, 1972; Author: The Big Heart, 1957; Bold Money, A New Way to Play the Options Market, 1986; Bold Money: How to Get Rich in the Options Market, 1987; Director: Sunlight, 1957; Three Pickup Men for Herrick, 1957; Cinq cent balles, 1963; La permission, 1968; Sweet Sweetback's Baadasssss Song, 1971; Don't Play Us Cheap, 1973; Identity Crisis, 1989; Tales of Erotica, 1996; Gang in Blue, 1996; Le conte du ventre plein, 2000; The Real Deal, 2003; Confessionsofa Ex-Doofus-Itchy Footed Mutha, 2008; Documentary: How to Eat Your Watermelon in White Company, 2005. Others: Panther, 1995; All My Children, 2008; Us: A Love Story, 2009; Mario's Green House, 2009; Redemption Road, 2010; We the Peeples, 2011; Yale Univ; Harvard Univ; Columbia Univ. **Orgs:** Dirs Guild Am; French Directors Guild; Melvin Van Peebles Found. **Honors/Awds:** Tony Award, 1972; First Prize from Belgian Festival for Don't Play Us Cheap; Live-Action Humanitas Prize, 1987; honorary doctorate, Hofstra Univ, 1995; Lifetime Achievement Award, 1999; Best International Film Award, 2000; French Legion of Honor, 2001; Chevalier in the Legion D'Honneur, 2002; Critics Choice Award, San Francisco Film Festival; The Legion D'Honneur; Black Filmmakers Hall of Fame. **Business Addr:** Actor, Simon & Schuster, 1230 Avenue of the Americas, New York, NY 10020, **Business Phone:** (212)698-7000.

### VAN TRECE, JACKSON C.
Educator. **Personal:** Born Aug 31, 1928, Edwardsville, IL; married Dolores Wilson. **Educ:** Kans State Teacher Col, BS, 1952; Kans State Col, MS, 1960. **Career:** Educator (retired); Northeast Jr High Sch, teacher, 1952-56, counr, 1965-66; Sumner High Sch, Kans City, KS, asst prin, 1966-70; Univ Mo KC, asst vice chancellor, stud affairs, 1980-85. **Orgs:** Boy Scouts Am Troop Leader, 1952-58; admin & dir, Black Motivation Training Ctr, Kans, 1970; NEA; Region VII Trio Proj Dir, Oreg; Trio Progs UMKC; Kappa Alpha Psi Frat; Area Youth Groups; exec bd, YMCA, 1973. **Home Addr:** 1839 N 62 St, Kansas City, KS 66102, **Home Phone:** (913)334-4619.

### VANCE, COURTNEY BERNARD
Actor. **Personal:** Born Mar 12, 1960, Detroit, MI; son of Conroy and Leslie; married Angela Bassett; children: Bronwyn Golden & Josiah Slater. **Educ:** Harvard Univ, BA, 1978; Yale Sch Drama, MFA, 1986. **Career:** Stage: The Comedy of Errors, 1982; A Raisin in the Sun, 1983; Fences, Yale Repertory Theatre, 1985, Goodman Theatre, Chicago, 1986, Broadway, 1987; Romeo & Juliet, 1988; My C! My Africa!, 1989-90; Six Degrees of Separation, 1990-91. Films: Hamburger Hill, 1987; Hunt for Red October, 1990; The Adventures of Huckleberry Finn, 1993; Dangerous Minds, 1995; The Last Supper, 1995; Panther, 1995; The Preacher's Wife, 1996; Naked City, 1998; Cookie's Fortune, 1999; The Acting Class, 2000; Space Cowboys, 2000; D-Tox, 2002; HBO movie, Unchained Memories: Readings from the Slave Narratives; Whitewash: The Clarence Brandley Story, 2002; Nothing But the Truth, 2008; Hurricane Season, 2009; Extraordinary Measures, 2010; The Divide, 2011; Final Destination 5, 2011; Joyful Noise, 2012; Let It Shine, 2012; Book of the Year, producer. Tv Series: "thirtysomething", 1989; "Picket Fences", 1995; "Any Day Now", 1998; "The Wild Thornberrys", 1998; "Boston Public", 2000; "Law & Order: Criminal Intent",

2001-06; "The American Experience", 2001-04; "State of Mind", 2007; "ER", 2008-09; "The Spectacular Spider-Man", 2009; "FlashForward", ABC, 2009-10; "The Closer", 2010-11; "Revenge", 2012; "Graceland", 2013; "State of Affairs", 2014; "Masters of Sex", 2014; "Scandal", 2015; "American Crime Story", 2016. **Orgs:** Bd dir, Actors Ctr, currently. **Honors/Awds:** Clarence Derwent Award, 1987; Theatre World, Citation, 1987; Tony Award, 1987; Obie Award, 1990; Best Lead Actor, 1991; Video Premiere Award, 2001; Inductee, Alumni Hall of Fame, Boys & Girls Clubs Am; Black Reel Award, 2013. **Special Achievements:** Co-author: "Friends: A Love Story", 2006. **Business Addr:** Actor, Lighthouse Entertainment, 9701 Wilshire Blvd 10th Fl, West Hollywood, CA 90069, **Business Phone:** (310)246-0499.

## VANCE, ERIC DEVON

Football executive, football player. **Personal:** Born Jul 14, 1975, Tampa, FL; married Inika; children: Jalyn & Jordan. **Educ:** Vanderbilt Univ, BS, math & sec ed. **Career:** Football player (retired), dir; Carolina Panthers, 1997; Tampa Bay Buccaneers, defensive back & safety, 1998-2001, dir player develop; Indianapolis Colts, safety, 2002; New Eng Patriots, 2002; Univ Miami, asst dir football opers, 2013-. **Honors/Awds:** Rookie of the Year, 1998. **Home Addr:** PO Box 278202, Miramar, FL 33027-8202. **Business Addr:** Assistant Director of Football Operations, University of Miami, 5821 San Amaro Dr, Coral Gables, FL 33146, **Business Phone:** (305)284-3822.

## VANCE, DR. IRVIN ELMER

Educator. **Personal:** Born Apr 8, 1928, Mexico, MO; son of Virgil Lee and Dorothy Ayers; children: Barbara Ann Le Cesne, Velesha Ivy & Katrina Iris. **Educ:** Wayne State Univ, BS, 1957; Wash Univ, MA, 1959; Univ Mich, PhD, math, 1967. **Career:** Northeastern High Sch, math instr, 1957-59; Southeastern High Sch, math instr, 1959-62; Univ Mich, Math Dept, teaching fel, 1962-64, math instr, 1964-66; Mich State Univ, from asst prof to assoc prof math, 1966-71, prof math, 1989, Dept Math, prof emer, currently; NMex State Univ, dir black progs, 1971-72, from assoc prof math to prof math, 1971-89; Educ Develop Ctr, dir sch comt outreach proj one, 1973-75; Ley Col, lectr, 1974; Boston Univ, lectr, 1975. **Orgs:** Assoc dir, Grand Rapids Mich Mid Sch Math Lab Proj, 1967-68; Math Inst In-Serv Teachers, Mich State Univ, 1968, 1971; dir works oper, Col Teachers Math, Spelman Col, 1975; founder & dir, NMex State Univ Elem Teachers Math Proj, 1977-80; vpres, NMex Coun Teachers Math, 1978-81; reader advan placement exam math, Educ Testing Serv, 1979-84; pres, NMex Coun Teachers Math, 1984-85; prog chmn, Ann Conf NMex Coun Teachers Math, 1984-85; dir, Mich State Univ Math Proj Teachers Minority Youth, 1989-; bd dir, Nat Coun Teachers Math, 1992-95; chair, Coord Comt Alliance Involve Minorities Math, 1992; pres, Benjamin Banneker Asn, 1993-95, bd mem, exec dir; chmn & mem, Math Educ Comt, Planning Grant Comt, Adv Comt, Prom to Asn & Tenure Comt, Master Comt, Doctoral Comt, Comt Eval Ethnic Progs, NMex State Univ; External Affairs Comt & Nat Coun Teachers Math; chmn & bd dir, Develop Res & Human Resources; Nat Coun Accreditation Teacher Educ; bd dir, Nat Asn Advan Colored People; judge, Black Hist Knowledge Bowl; Rev Panel Minority Inst Sci Improv Prog, NSF; dir, Mich State Univ Math Proj Mich Minority Youth; chair, exec secy, Benjamin Banneker Asn Coord Comt; Math Asn Am; bd dir, Col Bound Kids Learning Ctr. **Honors/Awds:** Glenn Gilbert Leadership Award, 2004. **Special Achievements:** Published numerous books and articles. **Home Addr:** 1109 Bonanza Dr, Okemos, MI 48864-4069, **Home Phone:** (517)349-2383. **Business Addr:** Professor Emeritus, Michigan State University, 619 Red Cedar Rd C234 Wells Hall 220 Trowbridge Rd, East Lansing, MI 48824, **Business Phone:** (517)353-3833.

## VANCE, LAWRENCE N.

Journalist. **Personal:** Born Dec 20, 1949, Chicago, IL; children: 2. **Educ:** Roosevelt Univ, BS, 1973; Ill Inst Technol, Chicago Kent Law Sch, JD, 1977. **Career:** Cook County Pub Defender, investgr, 1973-79, atty, 1977-79; Pvt Pract, atty. **Orgs:** Nat Bar Assocs, Cook Cty, Ill, 1977-87. **Business Addr:** Attorney, Lawrence N Vance & Assoc, 53 W Jackson Blvd Suite 1334, Chicago, IL 60602, **Business Phone:** (312)236-5400.

## VANCE, VERA R.

Educator. **Personal:** Born Jul 11, 1908, Waskom, TX; children: James R. **Educ:** BA, 1939; MEd, 1962; Grad Stud, 1971. **Career:** Velie Elem, teacher, 1924; Galilee Elem Gilliam LA, teacher, 1929-31; Gainsville Elem, prin teacher, 1931-45; Beaver Pond Elem, prin teacher, 1945-47; Dixie Elem, prin teacher, 1948-81; Mooretown Elem Shreveport, teacher, 1951-56; Cent Jr HS, teacher, 1959-61; JS Clarke Jr HS, teacher & counr, 1961-72; Notre Dame High Sch, consult, 1973. **Orgs:** Secy, Inter Scholastic League; Tex & LA SS & BTU Cong, 1932-50; secy, Dist I SS Inst, 1932-47; basileus Sigma Gamma Rho; sec chap, 1974; YWCA; Caddo Ed; ASS; Teachers Asn Am Personnel-Guid; LA Guid Asn; Breezy Hill Comm Club; treas, Trinity Bapt Chap. **Honors/Awds:** Award Sigma Gamma, RI, 1962; Award in bus Sigma Gamma RI, 1974. **Home Addr:** 2803 Ashton St, Shreveport, LA 71103.

## VANCE, WILLIAM J., SR.

Teacher, clergy. **Personal:** Born Jan 14, 1923, Des Arc, AR; son of Ignatius D and Esther Butler; married Jacqueline G; children: Rene J Smith & William Jr (deceased). **Educ:** Roosevelt Univ, attended 1954; Moody Bible Inst, attended 1961; Gov State Univ, BA, 1974, MA, 1975; Parish Context Training, Pastoral Psysho-Ther Inst, 1984. **Career:** Chicago Post Off, 1948-69; Older Boys & Girls Conf, bible teacher, counr, summer camp, 1958-74; Berean Baptist Church, pastor, 1969-91, pastor emer, 1991-; Ctr African Bibl Studies, Trinity United Church Christ, bible teacher, 1980. **Orgs:** Ed, Berean News, 1969-75, bd mem, 1974; chmn, bd dir, Douglass Tubman Christian Ctr, 1976-78. **Honors/Awds:** Great Guy of Day, WVON, 1970; E Chicago Heights Comm Center Award, 1975; Great American Award, 1976. **Home Addr:** 6810 S Calumet Ave, Chicago, IL 60637-4005, **Home Phone:** (773)483-5914. **Business Addr:** Pastor Emeritus, Berean Baptist Church, 5147 S Dearborn St, Chicago, IL 60609, **Business Phone:** (773)924-4349.

## VANCE-COOKS, DAVITA

Publishing executive, federal government official. **Personal:** children: Chris & Chandra. **Educ:** Tufts Univ, BA, psychol, 1977; Columbia Univ, MBA, mkt & finance, 1979. **Career:** Blue Cross Blue Shield Plans, dir customer serv & claims, dir mem & billing, dir mkt res & prod develop, 1980-93; NYLCare Health Plans, mult positions, 1993-98; Aetna, site serv mgr, 1998-2000; U.S. Govt Printing Off (GPO), var sr mgt positions, 2004-11, dep managing dir customer serv, 2004-08, managing dir publ & info sales, 2008-11, chief staff, 2011, chief exec officer & agency dir, 2012-; Digital Ins, 2000-01; HTH Worldwide Ins Serv, gen mgr, 2001-04; Dep Pub Printer, 2011-13; NYL Care Mid Atlantic Health Plan, sr vpres opers; Pub Printer Us, August 2013-. **Orgs:** Delta Sigma Theta Sorority Inc; Northern Va Alumnae Chap. **Honors/Awds:** Outstanding Community Service Award, Kappa Scholar Endowment Fund, 2014. **Special Achievements:** First woman and first African America to lead the GPO.

## VANDERPOOL, ALEX. See MORRIS, NATHAN BARTHOLOMEW.

## VANN, ALBERT

Advocate, teacher. **Personal:** Born Nov 19, 1934, Brooklyn, NY; married Mildred E; children: Scott, Shannon, Fola & Binta. **Educ:** Univ Toledo, BBA, 1959; Yeshiva Univ, MS, educ, 1962; Long Island Univ, MS, guid & coun, 1973. **Career:** Asst prin, Bd Educ, 1964-67; New York Assemblyman, Dist 56, 1974-2002; Vassar Col, Urban Ctr Black Studies, instr; New York, Dist 36, coun mem, 2002-. **Orgs:** Dir, Talent Search Prog Dept HEW; Ny Assembly; founder & pres, African-Am Teachers Asn; bd dir, Bedford-Stuyvesant Restoration Corp; pres, Vannguard Civic Asn; chmn, Ny Blk & Puerto Rican Legis Caucus, 1977; bd mem, Nat Asn Advan Colored People; Blk Educs; founder, Medgar Evers Col Comn Coun; Alpha Phi Alpha Fraternity; co-founder & first chair, CoalitionComn Empowerment, 1982; chair, New Yorkers Jesse Jackson, 1984; chair, New York Asn Black & Puerto Rican Legislators Inc, 1990-94; chmn, Telecommunications & Energy Comn Nat Black Caucus State Legislators, 1994; founder & exec mem, Vaanguard Independent Dem Asn; Community Sch Bd 13; chair, Coun's Comt Community Develop; founder, 36th Coun Dist Katrina Relief Effort; founder, Black Brooklyn Empowerment Conv; founder, New York Works; Medgar Evers Col, City Univ New York, founder. **Honors/Awds:** Political Achievement Award, IDEA Inc; Community Service Award, Bus & Professional Negro Women Inc; Outstanding Educator Award, Bro & Sister Afro-Am Unity. **Home Addr:** 362 MacDonough St Suite 1, Brooklyn, NY 11233, **Home Phone:** (718)919-0740. **Business Addr:** Council Member, District 36 New York, 250 Broadway 17th Fl, New York, NY 10007, **Business Phone:** (212)788-7354.

## VANN, GREGORY ALVIN

President (organization). **Personal:** Born Apr 17, 1954, Washington, DC; married Joan A Simpson. **Educ:** Howard Univ, BArch, 1977; Univ Fla, MBC, construct mgt, 1978; Drexel Univ, MBA, finance, 1985. **Career:** Daniel Mann, Johnson & Mendenhall, draftsman, 1974-76; Bryant & Bryant Architects, designer & draftsman, 1976-77; Whiting Turner Contracting Co, proj engr, 1977; Catalytic Inc, sr planning engr, 1978-81; Burns & Roe Inc, sr planning engr, 1981-84; Vann Orgn, pres, 1984-. **Orgs:** Am Asn Cost Engrs, 1980-; Am Inst Architects, 1986-87; Philadelphia Chap, Nat Black MBA Asn, 1986-; Cherry Hill Minority Civic Asn, 1986-. **Home Addr:** 3026 W Chapel Ave, Cherry Hill, NJ 08002. **Business Addr:** President, The Vann Organization, 11 Sayer Ave Suite 102, Cherry Hill, NJ 08002, **Business Phone:** (856)486-4440.

## VANNAMAN, MADI T.

Administrator. **Personal:** Born Mar 18, 1957, Aberdeen, MD; daughter of Charles Robert Thornton and Nobuko Otsuki Thornton; married Robbie L. **Educ:** Univ Kans, BS, bus, 1979, JD, 1983. **Career:** E&E Specialties, personnel dir, 1983-85; State Kans, personnel mgt specialist, 1985-86, Dept Admin, mgt analyst, 1986-89, Dept Admin, actg benefits adminr, 1989; Univ Kans, assoc dir human resources, 1990-. **Orgs:** Nat TIAA-CREF Adv Coun; Kans State Employees Health Care Comn. **Honors/Awds:** Employee of the Month Award, Univ Kans, 1999. **Home Addr:** 1529 Burning Tree Ct, Lawrence, KS 66047-8937, **Home Phone:** (785)749-3517. **Business Addr:** Associate Director, Human Resources, University of Kansas, Rm 109 Carruth-O'Leary Hall 1246 W Campus Rd, Lawrence, KS 66045-7505, **Business Phone:** (785)864-4946.

## VANOVER, TAMARICK T.

Football player, football coach. **Personal:** Born Feb 25, 1974, Tallahassee, FL; married Deidra; children: Tamarick Jr & Dedrick. **Educ:** Fla State Univ. **Career:** Football player (retired), coach; Las Vegas Posse, 1994; Kans City Chiefs, wide receiver & Kick Returner & Punt returner, 1995-99; San Diego Chargers, wide receiver, 2002; Lake City Christian Acad, head coach & athletic dir, 2007-; asst wide receivers, 2009. **Honors/Awds:** Mack Lee Hill Award, 1995. **Business Addr:** Head Coach, Athletic Director, Lake City Christian Academy, 3035 SW Pinemount Rd, Lake City, FL 32024, **Business Phone:** (386)758-0055.

## VANZANT, REV. DR. IYANLA (RHONDA EVA HARRIS)

Association executive, writer, founder (originator). **Personal:** Born Sep 13, 1953, Brooklyn, NY; married Kirk, Jan 1, 1971, (divorced 1971); children: 1; married Charles, Jan 1, 1973, (divorced 1979); children: 1; married Adeyemi Bandele, Jan 1, 1997; children: 3. **Educ:** Medger Evers Col, BS, summa cum laude, 1983; City Univ NY, Sch Law, Queens Col, JD, law, 1988; Va Union Univ. **Career:** Cent Brooklyn Talent Search, counr & asst dir, 1970-76; Cent Brooklyn Talent Search, prog dir, 1980-83; City Univ New York, dir, alumni affairs & spec events, 1983-84; Medgar Evers Col, dir, mkt & planning, 1984-86; New York County Dist Atty, domestic violence unit, 1986; Law & Social Justice, ctr, 1986-87; Defender's Asn, criminal defense rep, 1988-90; Talk Show Host, Iylanla, exec dir, workshop facilitator, 1989-; Inner Visions Spiritual Life Maintenance Network, founder & chief exec officer, 1989-; KBT Commun, life skills, motivation mgt supvr, 1990-93; Paramount Publ, motivational lectr & human empowerment specialist, 1991-92; Auth, 1992-; TV: Bunim-Murray Productions/ Universal Productions, spiritual life coach & prog co-host, 2004-06; Bunim Murray Productions, co-host life coach, 2004-06. **Business Addr:** Chief Executive Director, Founder, Inner Visions Institute for Spiritual Development, PO Box 8517, Silver Spring, MD 20907, **Business Phone:** (301)419-8085.

## VARGUS, BILL (BILLY VARGUS)

Television news anchorperson. **Personal:** Born Jun 21, 1956, Chicago, IL; son of Bill and Ione D; married Sue Serio; children: Nia. **Educ:** Temple Univ, Philadelphia, PA, BA, Radio-TV-Film grad courses, 1980. **Career:** WHAT radio, news anchor; WDAS, anchor; Q102 radio, dir, anchor; KYW-TV, writer; WHYY TV, reporter, sports anchor, 1986-91; WCAU, sports reporter, 1989-91; WFIL, reporter; WWOR TV, sports anchor, 1992-93; WIVB TV, sports anchor, 1994-97; Fox TV Network 29, weekend sports anchor, 1997-09; WTXF TV, sports anchor & reporter, currently; Film: A Turn Blinds; Raising Heights. **Honors/Awds:** Emmy Winner, 2008, 2009. **Special Achievements:** Emmy awards, nominee, 5 times; Best Sports Anchor & Best Sports Reporter, nominee, 2005. **Business Addr:** Sports Anchor, Reporter, WTXF-TV, 330 Mkt St, Philadelphia, PA 19106, **Business Phone:** (215)925-2929.

## VARGUS, DR. IONE D.

Social worker. **Personal:** Born Jul 19, 1930, Medford, MA; daughter of Edward Dugger (deceased) and Madeline Kountze Dugger-Kelley; married William H Adams; children: Suzanne Holloman & William D. **Educ:** Tufts Univ, BA, sociol, 1952; Univ Chicago, MA, 1954; Brandeis Univ, PhD, 1971. **Career:** Social Work Pract Family Serv, Child Welfare Pub Housing Home Mgt Informal Educ, 1954-71; Brandeis Univ, asst prof, 1969-71; Univ Ill, asst prof, 1971-74; Temple Univ, Sch Social Admin, assoc dean, dean, 1974-91, Family Reunion Inst, Sch Social Admin, chmn, vol & founder, 1990-, actg vice provost undergrad educ, 1991-93, presidential fel, 1993-95, prof, prof emer, currently; Tufts Univ, Bd Trustees, trustee, 1981-91, trustees rmeriti, currently. **Orgs:** Trustee, Tufts Univ, 1981-91; bd mem, Tucker House II, 1990-96; founder, Family Reunion Inst at Temple Univ, 1990; bd mem, Multicultural Inst, 1990-; bd mem, Juv Law Ctr, 1991-99. **Honors/Awds:** Founders Award, Nat Asn Advan Colored People, 1991; Distinguished Service Award, Tufts Alumni Coun, 1993; Kwanzaa Holiday Expo Award, 1994: Academic Merit Award, 1997; Keeper of the Culture Award, 2002; History Maker's Education Maker, 2006. **Special Achievements:** Producer, radio doc on family reunions, WRTI; Author: Finding the Rest of Me: African American Family Reunions; Published numerous articles; First African American & first female academic dean, Temple Univ. **Home Addr:** 16115 SHannondell Dr, Audubon, PA 19403-5612, **Home Phone:** (610)382-6897. **Business Addr:** Founder, Professor Emeritus, Temple University, 1301 Cecil B Moore Ave, Philadelphia, PA 19122, **Business Phone:** (215)204-6244.

## VARNER, HAROLD R.

Executive, architect. **Educ:** Lawrence Technological Univ, BS, archit; Gen Servs Admin, eng cert. **Career:** Howard Sims & Assocs, 1973, prin, 1976-2000; New Detroit Inc; Varner & Assocs, co-founder, pres & chief exec officer, prin, 2001-; US Solar & Wind, partner, co founder, chief exec officer & chmn; City Detroit's Housing & Urban Redevelop, dir. **Orgs:** AIA Detroit, 1968; AIA Mich, 1968; Mich Bds Archit & Engrs; Detroit Pub Sch Voc & Tech Ctrs, task force; pres, Sims Varner & Assocs; founder, Varner & Assocs, bd mem, Founding Detroit LISC, 1990-2013. **Honors/Awds:** Hastings Award, 1996. **Special Achievements:** Formed MI requirements for Intern Development Program (IPP); Architect of the African American Museum, Detroit. **Business Addr:** Chairman, Chief Executive Officer, United States Solar & Wind, 14680 Jib St, Plymouth, MI 48170-6013, **Business Phone:** (888)733-8779.

## VARNER, JAMES, SR.

Executive, educator, president (organization). **Personal:** Born Nov 2, 1934, Jersey City, NJ; son of Charles and Mamie Dickerson; married Florence Johnson; children: 4. **Educ:** Univ Maine, BS, 1957; Rutgers Univ, MS, 1970, M City & Regional Planning, 1972. **Career:** Mt Sinai Hosp, chemist, 1957-58; Pub Sch, high sch teacher, 1960-66; Plainfield Comm Action, assoc dir, 1966; Morris Co Human Resources Agency, exec dir, 1966-82; Info Mgt Resources Inc, vpres, 1970-; WMTR Radio, Morristown, NJ, host & producer, 1970-2003; Drew Univ, counr & lectr part-time, 1972-82; Black Enterprise Mag, acct exec, 1982-85; Fallis Communs Inc, vpres, 1985-86; E Orange Bd Educ, E Orange, NJ, teacher, 1990-92; Univ Maine, asst dir admis minority recruitment, 1993-95, adv, lectr & consult, 1995-; State Maine Human Right Comm, comnr, pres. **Orgs:** Am Inst Planners; bd mem, Am Soc Planning Officials; Am Found Negro Affairs; Cong African Peoples; Rotary Club Morristown NJ; bd mem, Plainfield NJ Area YMCA; bd mem, Morris Co Nat Asn Advan Colored People; chmn emer, Nat Asn Planners, 1972; bd mem, Nat Asn Comm Develop; bd mem, Am Soc Planning Officials; pres, Greater Bangor Area Nat Asn Advan Colored People, 1994-; vice chmn, bd trustee, Memphis Univ Sch, 2003; Maine Human Rights Coalition Inc. **Honors/Awds:** First place, NJ Jaycees Area Speak Up Finals, 1967; Community Service Award, Morris County Urban League Inc, 1989. **Special Achievements:** Host of radio program, Community Update; First minority brother in the Phi Eta Kappa fraternity. **Home Addr:** 531 Brunswick St, Old Town, ME 04468, **Home Phone:** (207)827-4493. **Business Addr:** President, National Association for the Advancement of Colored People, 4805 Mt Hope Dr, Baltimore, MD 21215, **Business Phone:** (410)366-3300.

## VARNER, DR. NELLIE M.

Financial manager, educator. **Personal:** Born Aug 27, 1935, Lake Cormorant, IL; daughter of Tommie and Essie Davis; married Louis S Williams; children: Janniss LaTronia. **Educ:** Wayne State Univ, BS, polit sci, 1958, MA, polit sci, 1959; Univ Mich, PhD, russ & e europ polit, 1968. **Career:** Detroit Pub Sch, teacher, 1959-64; teaching fel, 1964; NDFL Fel, 1966-68; cong internship, US Cong, 1966; Univ Mich, Coll Lit Sci & Arts, spec asst dean, 1968-70, CIC grant Field Study USSR, 1968; Ctr Russ & Europ Studies, fac assoc, 1968-

78, asst prof polit sci, 1968-78; social Sci Res Coun Res Training Fel, 1970-71; res grant Univ MI, 1970-71; recip res travel grant to study Black Polit Elites Africa US & Caribbean Carnegie Endowment Int Peace, 1970-; Harvard Univ, res fel, 1970-71, res assoc, 1970-71; Univ Mich, Affirmative Action Progs, dir, 1972-75, Rackham Sch Grad Studies, assoc dean, 1976-79; Strather & Varner Inc Real Estate Invest Brokers, vpres, 1979-91; Primco Foods Inc, pres, 1988-93; N M Varner Co, pres, 1991-; At water Entertainment Assocs, vpres, 1994-98; Phoenix Entertainment LLC, chmn & chief exec officer, founder, currently. **Orgs:** Am Coun Educ Comt Women Higher Educ, 1976-; Nat Sci Found Adv Com Minority Progs Sci Educ, 1977-; chair, Real Estate Adv Bd State Mich, 1978-79; del, White House Conf Small Bus, 1980-; bd regents, 1980, regent emer, Univ Mich; bd dir, Highland Pk YMCA, 1980-83; exec bd, Detroit Chap Nat Asn AdvanColored People, 1985-86; bd dir, Am Inst Bus, 1986-92; Southern Oakland CoBd Realtors, Detroit Bd Realtors; chair, Equal Opportunity Com Nat AsnState Univ & Land Grant Col; Econ Action Com New Detroit Inc; Mich BdRealtors & Nat Bd Realtors; Equal Opportunity Task Force Am Coun Educ, Acad Affairs Fac Anal Proj Adv Com Univ Mich, Senate Assem Adv Com Real Estate, state Mich, exec bd, Wayne State Univ, Univ Mich; Inst Gerontol; execcom, Ctr Afro-Am African Studies, Univ Mich; HEW Title I State Adv Coun Bd Educ State Mich; consult Nat Sci Found Panel Awards Minority Col & Univ, Proj Acad Affirm Action Training Int Assoc Off Human Rights Agency, Dept HUD US Govt; dir, Inst Am Bus, 1986-94; trustee, New Detroit Inc, 1987-91; trustee, WTVS Channel 56, 1990-93; pres, At water Found, 1995; bd dir, Detroit Entertainment LLC, 1996-99; LSA Vis Comt, Univ Mich, 1997-2000; bd dir, Alumni Assoc, Univ Mich, 1998-; adv bd, Think Detroit Inc, 2000-. **Honors/Awds:** Florence Sweeney Scholarship, 1958; Detroit Women Principals ClubScholarship, 1959; Wilton Park Fellowship for Am participation Wilton ParkConf Steyning Sussex Eng, 1969; Distinguished Community Leadership AwardNat Asn Women Bus Owners, 1984; Delta Sigma Theta, Lillian Pierce BenbowAward, 1998. **Home Phone:** (313)368-9659. **Business Addr:** Chief Executive Officer, Phoenix Entertainment LLC, 1603 Balmoral Dr, Detroit, MI 48203, **Business Phone:** (313)962-5100.

### VASSER, REV. DELPHINE LYNETTA

Clergy. **Personal:** Born Dec 16, 1955, Flint, MI; daughter of Charles and Sister Ira L Williams. **Educ:** Emerson Col, BA, speech & commun, 1978; Suffork Univ, masters, pub admin, 1980; Oral Roberts Univ, Tulsa, OK, MDIV. **Career:** Greater Roxbury Corp, asst community rels dir, 1978-80; Mutual Omaha Ins Co, SW div off, off support, 1980-95; Bethel AME Church, pastor, 1988-90; Greater Johnson AME Church, pastor, 1991-; St James African Methodist Episcopal Church, Terrell, Tex, pastor; Greater Johnson African Methodist Episcopal Church, Ferris, Tex, sr pastor; St John African Methodist Episcopal Church, Mexia, Tex, pastor; St Paul African Methodist Episcopal Church, Mt Pleasant, Tex, 2006; Tenth Dist AME Church, asst property mgr, travel adm, currently. **Orgs:** Founder, Gainesville Community Interdenominational Ministerial Alliance, 1989-90; bd mem & secy, African Am Pastors Coalition; pres, Tenth Dist Women Ministry; bd mem, Cong Nat Black Churches; rec secy, Daughters Naomi Ministry, Dallas, TX; rec sec, African Am Pastor's Coalition, currently. **Honors/Awds:** Outstanding Leadership Award, Flint Central High, 1974; First Prize Oplehia Bonner Scholarship Award, Oplehia Bonner, 1974; Community Activist Award, Residence of Ferris; One of the Twenty Millenia Women, Tex Mag, 2005. **Special Achievements:** First Vice President of the African Methodist Episcopal Church/ Women in Ministry; Contributing writer, Sister to Sister Devotional. **Home Addr:** 5440 N Jim Miller Rd Apt 834, Dallas, TX 75227, **Home Phone:** (214)388-0601. **Business Addr:** Pastor, Saint James African Methodist Episcopal Church, 8401 Cedar Ave, Cleveland, OH 44103, **Business Phone:** (216)231-3562.

### VAUGHAN, GERALD R.

Financial manager, executive. **Personal:** Born Sep 9, 1957, Bronx, NY; son of Raymond and Juanita B Smith; married Ramona D Girtman. **Educ:** NC Agr & Tech State Univ, BS, 1980; Atlanta Univ, MBA, 1983; Adelphi Univ, CFP, 1985. **Career:** Liberty Mutual Ins Co, personal risk underwriter & indust regulator & tech analyst, 1976-80; Citizens & Southern Ga Corp, strategic planner & invest analyst, 1982-83; Entrepreneur, cert financial planner, 1985-; Grumman Corp, sr financial analyst, 1983-89; Ga Southern Univ, asst budget dir, 2003-; Grv Financial Group Inc, staff. **Orgs:** Asn MBA Execs, 1982-, Nat Black MBA Asn, 1982-; keeper finance, Omega Psi Phi Frat Inc, 1985-89. **Honors/Awds:** Fellowship Grants NC A&T St Univ & Atlanta Univ, 1975-83; Outstanding Young Americans, Int Biographical Inst, 1978-80. **Home Addr:** 3666 Cherry Ridge Blvd, Decatur, GA 30034, **Home Phone:** (404)244-0665. **Business Addr:** Assistant Budget Director, Georgia Southern University, PO Box 8033, Statesboro, GA 30460-8033, **Business Phone:** (912)681-5211.

### VAUGHAN, REV. DR. JAMES EDWARD

Minister (clergy), writer, journalist. **Personal:** Born Mar 7, 1943, Herdford, NC; son of John Henry and Jesse Mae Majette; married Renee J; children: Alvin, Patrinia & Meimii. **Educ:** NC Cent Univ, BA, art & eng, 1969; Southeastern Baptist Theol Sem, MDiv, seminarian, 2000, Apex Sch Theol. **Career:** NY Courier Newspaper, managing ed, 1969; NC Cent Univ lit mag, writer & ed; Capital Cities Comns Inc, promotions mgr, 1971-74; WYAH-TV, mgr promotion & producer, 1977-81; Christian TV Ministries Inc, founder, chmn & pres, 1980-; Small Bus Broadcasting Serv Co, founder, chmn & pres, 1982-; WJCB TV Tidewater Christian, founder, chmn & pres, 1983-; "Voices" TV Show, producer, 1998-; Christian Digital Media Ctr, founder, 1999; WTIK/WFTK Radio bd operator; Abundant Life Assembly Church, sr pastor, Christian TV Ministries-CTAB, Inc; cert res adminr Univ setting, currently. **Orgs:** Bd chmn, Durham City/County Cable Adv Bd; pres, DCTV 8 Access Asn; PR chairperson/Parlimentarian Interdenominational Ministerial Alliance Durham & Vicinity; bd dir, STOP Org; Am Mgt Assoc, InterdenomiNat Ministers Forum, AEH-RO Broadcast Frat; vpres, Southern Christian Leadership Conf, Va; chmn, media Tidewater Jesus Assoc; chmn, black broadcast ownership Nat Relig Broadcasters; Portsmouth Area Ministerial Asn, 1986-; adv bd, Inner-City Ministers Prayer Breakfast, 1989-; bd dir, Tidewater Chap Nat Conf Christians & Jews, 1991-; InterdenomiNat Ministerial Alliance, 1996-; Durham Ministers Asn, 1999. **Honors/Awds:** Citation of Merit, Nat Multiple Sclerosis Soc, 1984; Certificate of Service, Va State Adv Comm US Comn on Civil Rights, 1985; Oliver J Allen Award, WRAP Radio Gospel Music Awards, 1986; Excellence in Broadcast Pioneering, TCC Commun, 1986; Public Service Award, Portsmouth City Council, Portsmouth, Va, 1987; Media Service Award, Athletes Better Am, 1990; Appreciation Award Inspirational Columnist, New Journal & Guide Newspaper, 1996; IMA Meritorious Service Award, 2006. **Special Achievements:** Ex Umbra Radio/ TV Broadcasts and weekly column 1977-Developer, Christian Digital Media Applications. **Home Addr:** 3206 Cole Mill Rd, Durham, NC 27712-3240, **Home Phone:** (919)383-3488. **Business Addr:** Founder-President, Christian Television Ministries, PO Box 3195, Durham, NC 27715, **Business Phone:** (919)261-7635.

### VAUGHANS, KIRKLAND CORNELL

Clinical psychologist, psychoanalyst. **Personal:** Born Jan 8, 1944, Chicago, IL; son of Charles and Lillemae; married Renee Jones; children: Justine M & David. **Educ:** Univ IL-Chicago, Chicago, IL, BA, 1972; Adelphi Univ, NY, Inst Advan Psychol Studies, MA, clin psychol, 1979, PhD, clin psychol, 1985; NY Univ, postdoctoral prog psychother & psychoanalysis, cert, clin psychother & psychoanalysis, 1996; Adelphi Univ, Derner Inst, child & adolescent postdoctoral psychother prog, 1998. **Career:** New Hope Guild, regional dir, 1992-; City Univ NY, Brooklyn Col, Grad Prog Sch Psycol, clin supvr, 1995-, City Col, Psychol Ctr, Dept Psychol child Prog, adj clin assoc, 1997-; Adelphi Univ, Derner Inst Advan Psychol Studies, asst clin prof, assoc clin prof, 1999, adj fac, currently. **Orgs:** Am Psychol Asn, Div 29, 39, sect 20, 1989-; chmn, C Comt, Brooklyn Fedn Ment Health, 1987-89; NY Asn Black Psychologists; Int Soc Communicative Psychoanalysis & Psycholo-Ther; co-chair, NY State Psychol Asn, Comt Multicultural Concerns. **Honors/Awds:** Certificate of Appreciation, John F Kennedy Regular Dem Club, 1989. **Special Achievements:** Editor, Journal of Infant, Childs & Adolescent Psycho-Therapy; published & presented numerous articles. **Home Addr:** 66 Lincoln Ave, Wyandanch, NY 11798-4202, **Home Phone:** (631)491-6476. **Business Addr:** Adjunct Faculty, Adelphi University, 1 South Ave, Garden City, NY 11530-0701, **Business Phone:** (516)877-4828.

### VAUGHN, DR. ALVIN

Educator, teacher. **Personal:** Born Aug 30, 1939, Philadelphia, PA; son of Martha and Roger; married Eloise Stephens; children: Lois Jonneen & Edwards. **Educ:** Temple Univ, BS, 1963, MS, 1964; Int Grad Sch, EdD, 1984. **Career:** Educator (retired); Sch Dist Philadelphia, teacher, 1963-70; actg supvr, 1970-71, dept head, 1971-74, George Wash High Sch, asst prin, 1974-2002, eve sch prin, 1976-2000. **Orgs:** Bd dir, Drew Comm Ment Health Ctr, 1975-85; counr & admin, Negro Trade Union Leadership Coun, 1978-84; bd sch dir, Chelten Ham Twp Pa, 1978-87; bd dir, Philadelphia PUSH, 1982-87; Chelten Ham Art Ctr, 1982-86; Kappa Alpha Psi; Philadelphia Black Pub Rel Soc. **Home Addr:** 1376 Jasper Dr, Ambler, PA 19002-1010, **Home Phone:** (215)628-3221. **Business Addr:** Assisstant Principal, George Washington High School, 10175 Bustleton Ave, Philadelphia, PA 19116, **Business Phone:** (215)961-2001.

### VAUGHN, CLARENCE B.

Scientist. **Personal:** Born Dec 14, 1928, Philadelphia, PA; son of Albert and Aretha Johnson; married Sarah Campbell; children: Steven, Annette, Carl & Ronald. **Educ:** Benedict Col, BS, 1951; Howard Univ, MS, 1953, 1955, MD, 1957; Wayne State Univ, PhD, 1965. **Career:** DC Gen Hosp, intern, 1958; Freedmans Hosp, residency, 1959; Howard Univ Hosp, residency; Mich Cancer Found, fel; Wayne State Univ, fel; Res Physician, 1964-70; Milton A Darling Mem Ctr, clin dir, 1970-72; Providence Hosp, dir oncol, 1973-88; SW Oncolo Study Group, prin investor, 1978-94; Wayne State Univ, clin prof, 1988-; Southfield Oncol Inst Inc, dir oncol, pres, 1988-, founder; Oakland Univ, clin prof; Oncol Assocs PC. **Orgs:** Bd dir, Am Cancer Soc, Am Asn Univ Prof, AMA; nat chmn, Aerospace & Mil Sect NMA, Am Soc Clin Oncol, Nat Med Asn, Wayne County Med Soc, Oakland County med Asn, Res Officers Asn, US Asn Mil Surgeons, USAF Asn, Detroit Cancer Club, Detroit Physiol Soc; pres, Am Cancer Soc, Mich Div, 1986-; chmn adv comn, minority involvement field serv comn, Am Cancer Soc; educ rev comn, Nat Cancer Inst; Nat Surgeon Res Officers Asn; Metrop Detroit Steering CommCancer Prev Awareness; med dir, Oncol, Samaritan Health Ctr, 1986-; Southfield Oncol Inst; fel Am Inst Chemists. **Honors/Awds:** Outstanding Reserve Aerospace Medical Physician Award, 1974, 1979; 'Command Flight Surgeon of the Year', AFRES, 1974, 1979; Humanitarian of the Year, 1988. **Home Addr:** 20051 Kelly Rd, Detroit, MI 48225, **Home Phone:** (313)372-7679. **Business Addr:** President, Director, Southfield Oncology Institute Inc/Southfield Oncology Associates, 21751 W 11 Mile Rd Suite 114, Southfield, MI 48076, **Business Phone:** (248)356-2828.

### VAUGHN, COUNTESS DANIELLE

Actor, singer. **Personal:** Born Aug 8, 1978, Idabel, OK; daughter of Leo and Sandra; married Joseph James; children: Jaylen. **Career:** Films: Trippin, 1999; Max Keeble's Big Move, actor & off admin asst, 2001; More to Love, 2014. TV appearances: "227", 1985, 1988; The Lou Rawls Parade of Stars; "The Magical World of Disney", 1988; Orange Bowl Parade; Easter Seals Telethon; "Hangin' with Mr. Cooper", 1992; "Fievel's American Tails", 1992; "Thea", 1993; "Roc", 1993-94; "Minor Adjustments", 1996; "Moesha", 1996; "Goode Behavior", 1997; "The Martin Short Show", 1999; "The Parkers", 1999-2004; "Star Search", 2003; "Mad TV", 2003; "I Love the '90s: Part Deux", 2005; "I Love the 80's 3-D", 2005; "The Tyra Banks Show", 2006; "Cuts", 2006; "Thugaboo: Sneaker Madness", 2006; "Celebrity Rap Superstar", 2007; "Thugaboo: A Miracle on D-Roc's Street", 2006; "Let's Stay Together", 2011; "According to Him + Her", 2014. **Honors/Awds:** Image Award, Nat Asn Advan Colored People, 1998. **Business Addr:** Actress, c/o United Paramount Network, 11800 Wilshire Blvd, Los Angeles, CA 90025, **Business Phone:** (310)575-7000.

### VAUGHN, DAVID, III

Basketball player. **Personal:** Born Mar 23, 1973, Tulsa, OK; children: 2. **Educ:** Memphis State Univ. **Career:** Basketball player (retired); Orlando Magic, power forward, 1995-97; Golden State Warriors, 1997-98; Chicago Bulls, 1997-98; Near E, Greece, 1998-99, 2000-01; NJ Nets, power forward, 1998-99; Cantabria Lobos, 1999-2000; Viola Reggio Calabria, 2001; GS Olympia Larissa, 2002-03; Ittihad, 2003. **Home Addr:** 10565 Bastille Lane, Orlando, FL 32836, **Home Phone:** (407)239-4112.

### VAUGHN, ED (MWALIMU EDWARD VAUGHN)

Business owner, state government official. **Personal:** Born Jul 30, 1934, Abbeville, AL. **Educ:** Fisk Univ. **Career:** Mich House Reps, state rep, 1998-2000; Detroit Pub Schs, teacher; Citywide Citizens Action Comt, exec dir; Vaughn's Bk Store, co-founder & proprietor, currently. **Orgs:** Pres, Nat Asn Advan Colored People; Elks; Omega Psi Phi; Cent United Church Christ; head, Detroit chap Cong Racial Equality; coun mem & treas, Detroit City. **Business Addr:** Co-Founder, Proprietor, Vaughn Book Store, 12123 Dexter Ave, Monterey, CA 93940.

### VAUGHN, EUGENIA MARCHELLE WASHINGTON

Social worker. **Personal:** Born Oct 31, 1957, Columbus, OH; daughter of Eugene G and Lula Augusta Edwards; married Tannis Eugene; children: Shannon Eugene & Ieasha Michelle. **Educ:** Columbus State Community Col, assoc, social serv technol, 1977; Ohio Dominican Univ, BA, social welfare, 1982; Ohio State Univ, MSW, admin & clin, 1985. **Career:** Franklin County C Serv, social prog specialist & training coordr, 1977-2009, caseworker I, 1977-83, child welfare caseworker II, 1984; Columbus Area Ment Health Ctr, contract worker, 1985, child welfare caseworker II, III Foster Care, 1985-87, social worker III, 1987-89, treat mgr, 1989-91, child welfare supvr II, 1991; New Life Group Homes, dir opers, 2009-10; Jireh Serv Inc, independent contractor, 2011; United Methodist C's Home, adoption training coordr liaison, 2013-; Returns Inc, independent contractor, 2013-. **Orgs:** Nat Asn Social Workers, Nat Asn Black Social Workers; LSW Status Nat Asn Social Workers, 1986; initiator Scholar Alumni Asn; LISW, 1990. **Honors/Awds:** Minority Fellowship, 1983-84, Child Welfare Traineeship, 1984-85 OSU; Delta Epsilon Sigma Hon Soc, Alpha Delta Mu Social Work Honor Soc. **Home Addr:** 262 Eastcreek Dr, Galloway, OH 43119, **Home Phone:** (614)870-6656. **Business Addr:** Child Welfare Supervisor II, Franklin Co Children Services, 1951 Gantz Rd, Grove City, OH 43123, **Business Phone:** (614)278-5843.

### VAUGHN, GREGORY LAMONT (GREG VAUGHN)

Baseball player. **Personal:** Born Jul 3, 1965, Sacramento, CA; children: Cory. **Educ:** Sacramento City Col; Univ Miami. **Career:** Baseball player (retired); Milwaukee Brewers, outfielder, 1989-96; San Diego Padres, 1996-98; Cincinnati Reds, 1999; Tampa Bay Devil Rays, 2000-02; Colo Rockies, outfielder, 2003. **Home Addr:** 7482 Candlewood Way, Sacramento, CA 95822.

### VAUGHN, JACQUE

Basketball player, basketball coach. **Personal:** Born Feb 11, 1975, Los Angeles, CA; married Laura; children: Jalen & Jeremiah. **Educ:** Kans Univ, attended 1997. **Career:** Basketball player (retired), basketball coach; UT Jazz, guard, 1997-2001; Atlanta Hawks, guard, 2001-02, 2003-04; Orlando Magic, 2002-03; NJ Nets, guard, 2004-06; San Antonio Spurs, guard, 2006-09, asst coach, 2010-12; Orlando Magic, head coach, 2012-. **Business Addr:** Head Coach, Orlando Magic, RDV Sportsplex 8701 Maitland Summit Blvd, Orlando, FL 32810, **Business Phone:** (407)916-2400.

### VAUGHN, DR. JANICE S.

Health services administrator, educator, consultant. **Personal:** Born Jun 8, 1943, Augusta, GA; daughter of John Adam and Violet Allen Singleton; married Edward III; children: Kellye Baugh, Hope Brown, Enyce Thompson & Janna Harper. **Educ:** Talladega Col, BA, psychol, 1964; Atlanta Univ, MSW, 1971; Univ Pittsburgh, MPH, 1978, PhD, 1979. **Career:** Atlanta Un Chatam County Dept Family & C Servs, caseworker, 1968-71; Atlanta Univ, Sch Social Work, asst prof, 1971-87, assoc prof & chmn, 1979-81, assoc dean, 1982-86, dir doctoral prog, 1983-87; Ga Dept Human Resources, Div Family & C Servs, dep dir, 1987-93; Ga Southern Univ, prof & asst vpres acad affairs, Master Social Work Prog, dir, 1993-95; Links Inc, Magnolia Chap, vpres, 1997-99; More house Sch Med, Master Pub Health Prog, Dept Community Health & Prev, Family Health Track, track coord, 1998-, dir & prof, 1993-99; Edward Vaughn Supportive Serv, policy res consult, 1999-. **Orgs:** Nat Asn Black Social Workers, 1979-; comnr, Human Resources Res Rev, 1990; Jack & Jill Am, 1990-; chmn, Fulton County Bd Health, 1996-00; chair, Fulton County Community Serv Bd Ment Health, 1996-00; Ment Retardation & Substance Abuse, 1996; chairperson, Fulton County Health Dept, Community Serv Bd, 1997; Nat Adv Bd mem, Nat SIDS & Infant Death Prog, 1998; Self Study Steering Comt, More house Sch Med, 1999; Am Pub Health Asn; dep div dir, Ga Dept Human Resources, Atlanta & Div Family & C Serv; dir, Master Pub Health Prog, Morehouse Sch Med; chair, Fulton County Bd Health & Wellness & Community Serv Bd Ment Health. **Home Addr:** 111 Palm Grove Rd, Savannah, GA 31410, **Home Phone:** (912)898-1297. **Business Addr:** Policy Research Consultant, Edward Vaughn Supportive Services Inc, 111 Palm Grove, Savannah, GA 31410, **Business Phone:** (912)898-1297.

### VAUGHN, MARY KATHRYN

Government official. **Personal:** Born Sep 20, 1949, Kansas City, KS; daughter of Edward Parks and Kathryn Jones Parks; married Harvey L Jr. **Educ:** Col Wooster, Wooster, OH, BA, 1970; Rutgers Univ, NB, NJ, MSW, 1972; Harvard Univ Prog Sr Exec State & Local Govt, Cambridge, MA, 1985. **Career:** Jackson County Juv Ct, Kans City, Mo, residential servs admin, 1973-78; Univ Kans, minority affairs outreach counr, 1978-79; City Kans, Mo, dept head, 1979; City Wichita Housing Serv, Housing & Community Serv Dept, dir, 2004-, dept dir. **Orgs:** Prog coordr, Mayor's Christmas Tree Asn, 1980-; Full Employ Coun, 1986-; Pres, US Conf City Human Servs Offs, 1990-; Pvt Indust Coun, 1990-; Ad Hoc Task Force Homelessness, 2006-; dir, Wichita Police Dept. **Home Addr:** 6650 Paseo, Kansas City, MO 64132. **Business Addr:** Director, City of Wichita Housing Services, 455 N Main, Wichita, KS 67202, **Business Phone:** (316)462-3795.

### VAUGHN, MO (MAURICE SAMUEL VAUGHN)
Baseball player, business owner. **Personal:** Born Dec 15, 1967, Norwalk, CT. **Educ:** Seton Hall Univ. **Career:** Baseball player (retired), business owner; Boston Red Sox, designated hitter & first baseman, 1991-98; Anaheim Angels, first baseman, 1999-2001; New York Mets, first baseman, 2002-03; Mo Vaughn Hit Dog baseball clin, Tufts Univ, owner & operator, currently; Omni NewYork LLC, co-managing dir & co-founder, currently; Mo Vaughn Transp, pres & chief exec officer, currently. **Honors/Awds:** Bart Giamatti Award, Baseball Assistance Team, 1995; All-Star, Major League Baseball, 1995, 1996, 1998; Silver Slugger Award, 1995; American League Most Valuable Player, Baseball Writers Asn Am, 1995; RBI champion, American League, 1995; Trinity-Pawling's Hall of Fame, 2006; Boston Red Sox Hall of Fame, 2008. **Special Achievements:** Am League Eastern Div Champion Boston Red Sox team, 1995. **Business Addr:** Co-Founder, Managing Director, Omni New York LLC, 885 2nd Ave 31st Fl Suite C, New York, NY 10017, **Business Phone:** (646)502-7200.

### VAUGHN, MWALIMU EDWARD. See VAUGHN, ED.

### VAUGHN, DR. PERCY JOSEPH, JR.
College administrator, educator. **Personal:** Born Jan 11, 1932, New Orleans, LA; married Doris C; children: Percy Darrell, Rene, Denise & Tracy. **Educ:** Morris Brown Col, BS, 1957; Atlanta Univ, MBA, 1959; Tex Tech Univ, DBA, mkt, 1975, bus admin, 1975; Harvard Univ, attended 1978. **Career:** Dean & prof mkt (retired), 1972-; Jackson Brewing Co, sales & pub rels rep, 1960; Southern Univ, asst prof, 1968; Tex Tech Univ, instr, 1972, grad asst stud, 1972-75; Ala State Univ, dean & prof mkt, 1975-2009; Percy J Vaughn Jr & Assocs, dean, 1975-2010. **Orgs:** Fac coord, Nat Urban Leagues Black Exec Exchange Prog, 1976; Nat Adv Counc Fac Coord Career Awareness Prog, 1976; proj dir, Small Bus Inst US Small Bus Admin, 1978; chmn bd, Ala Consortium Deans Col Bus Admin estab ASBCD, 1978; Active Corp Execs Nat SCORE & Am Coun Exercise Coun, 1978; pres, Ala Coun Deans Ala Asn Higher Educ Bus, 1979. **Home Addr:** 5794 Carriage Barn Lane, Montgomery, AL 36116-1506, **Home Phone:** (334)277-1751.

### VAUGHT, LOY STEPHEN
Basketball player. **Personal:** Born Feb 27, 1968, Grand Rapids, MI; son of Loy Sr and Ozzie Friend Jager; married Yvette. **Educ:** Univ Mich, bus mgt, 1990. **Career:** Basketball player (retired); Los Angeles Clippers, forward-ctr, 1990-98; Detroit Pistons, 1998-2001; Wash Wizards, 2000-01; Dallas Mavericks, forward-ctr, 2000-01.

### VEAL, HOWARD RICHARD, SR.
Executive. **Personal:** Born Oct 24, 1942, Jackson, MS; married Elizabeth; children: Howard Jr & Jason. **Educ:** Utcc Jr Col, attended 1964; Alcorn A&M Col, BS, 1966; Ind Univ, attended 1969. **Career:** Elkhrt Urban League, dir housing community serv, 1968-70, act exec dir, 1970-71; Springfield Urban League, exec dir, pres & chief exec officer, 1972-2001. **Orgs:** Chmn, prog rev subcomt Gov Adv Coun Emp & Training, 1974; City Springfield Citz Adv Comn, 1974; pres, Ill Coun Urban League, 1975-; Bd Higher Educ Planning Comn, 1975; adv plan comn, White Hs Conf Libr, 1977; Omega Psi Phi Fraternity; First Bd Zion Baptist Church; secy, Urban League Coun; Cent Reg Civic Serv. **Honors/Awds:** Outstanding Citizen Award, Nat Asn Advan Colored People, 1970, 1975; Outstanding Service Award, Springfield Urban League, 1976; NYNEX Scholarship Award, 1996. **Home Addr:** 2016 Randall Ct, Springfield, IL 62703-3382, **Home Phone:** (217)528-5294.

### VEAL, DR. YVONNECRIS SMITH
Executive, physician, association executive. **Personal:** Born Dec 24, 1936, Ahoskie, NC; daughter of Dempsey Porter and Zeora Ida Lewis; married Henry Veal Jr; children: Michael E. **Educ:** Hampton Univ, BS, 1957; Med Col Va, MD, 1962. **Career:** Kings County Hosp, internship, residency, fel; Jamaica Hosp, Sickle Cell Clin, attend physician, 1967-69, Child Develop Clin, pediatrician, 1967-69; Windham, Child Care, med staff physician, 1967-71; pvt pract pediat, 1967-71; Carter Community Health Ctr, pediatrician, 1968-79, med dir, 1981-84; E NY Neighborhood Family Care Ctr, dir med affairs, 1975-81; US Postal Serv, contract physician, 1984-85, Long Island Div, field div med officer, 1985-93, NY Metro Area, sr med dir, 1993-. **Orgs:** Delta Sigma Theta Sorority, 1955-, Gamma Iota Chap, 1955-57, pres, 1956-57, Queens Alumnae Chap, 1966-, pres, 1980-84; Nat Asn Advan Colored People; YWCA; Nat Coun Negro Women, 1965-67, 1980-; Nat Med Asn, 1966-, 95th pres, 1995-96, chair bd trustees, 1989-91; Am Med Asn, 1968-; Med Soc, State NY, 1968-; Queens County Med Soc, 1968-; Dalton Sch PTA, 1970-81; Queens Pediat Soc, 1973-84; Nat Nominating Comt, 1976-78, chair, Regional Nominating Comt, 1979-83; Queens County Prof Stand Rev Org, 1977-88; Comtpres, 1980-84; Community Family Planning Coun, 1981-85; Health Systs Agency NYC, Queens Sub-Area Adv Comt, 1981-96; Pre-Kindergarten Educ; chair, ATLED, 1986-89, bd dirs, 1986-; Nat Mem Servs Comt, 1991-95, Eastern Region Sci Liasion, 2000-; Merck Y Day Care; Am Col Occup & Environ Med, 1992-; Am Heart Asn, 1992-; fel NY Acad Med, 1995-. **Honors/Awds:** New York State Senator Carol Berman, Community Service Certificate of Merit, 1979; East New York NFCC Community Bd Appreciation Award, 1981; Distinguished Leadership Award, United Negro Col Fund, 1984; Special Award for Outstanding Contribution to South east Queens Community, Saint Albans Congregational Church, 1984; Cert of Appreciation, Morris Brown Col, 1987-88; Special Award, Wives of Club 50, 1988; Special Achievement Award, US Postal Serv, 1989, Appreciation Award, 1990, Pride in Performance Award, 1991; Certificate of Achievement, Delta Sigma Theta, 1989; Associate Member of the Year Award, NY Chap, Morris Brown Alumni Asn, 1990; Susan Smith Mckinney Steward Medical Society Recognition Award, 1991; Ivan Allen Jr Award for Excellence in Public Relations, Morris Brown Col, 1993; Mary McLeod Bethune Award, Nat Coun Negro Women, 1996; Yvonnecris Smith Veal Achievement Award, 1997; US Postal Service National Medical Directors Award, E NY Diagnostic & Treatment Ctr, 1997, 2002, Spot Award, 1998, Human Resources Process Recognition Award, 1998; numerous others. **Special Achievements:** Fifth African American student enrolled at the Medical College of Virginia in Richmond, 1960; First woman to chair the Board of Trustees of the Nat Med Asn, 1989; spokesperson for more than 25, 000 African American physicians. **Home Addr:** 112-30 Farmers Blvd, Jamaica, NY 11412-2360, **Home Phone:** (718)740-9850. **Business Addr:** Senior Medical Director, US Postal Service, New York Metropolitan Area, 78-02 Liberty Ave, Ozone Park, NY 11417-9451, **Business Phone:** (718)529-7027.

### VEALS, CRAIG ELLIOTT
Judge. **Personal:** Born Jan 21, 1955, Los Angeles, CA; son of Charles Edward and Rhoda Maida; married Barbara Martha O; children: Aaron Elliott & Philip Seth. **Educ:** Occidental Col, BS, 1977; Univ Calif, Los Angeles, Sch Law, JD, 1980. **Career:** Calif State Atty Gen, dep atty gen, 1981-83; Los Angeles Dist Atty, dep dist atty, 1983-94; Los Angeles Munic Ct, judge, 1994-97; State Calif, Los Angeles Super Ct, judge, 1997-. **Orgs:** Phi Alpha Delta Law Fraternity, 1977-; Asn Dep Attys Gen, 1981-83; Calif State Dep Dist Attys Asn, 1986-94; Asn Dep Dist Atty's, 1986-94; Const Rights Found, 1989-; La County Bar Asn, vice chmn, Environ Law Air Qual Sub-Sect, 1992-93; Western Regionals Moot Ct Competition, judge, 1992; Los Angeles Municip Ct, temp judge, 1992; Langston Bar Asn, 1994-; Los Angeles County Bar Asn, exec comt mem, Criminal Law Sect, 1994-; Calif Judges Asn, Criminal Law & Procedure Subcomt, 1995-96; Municip Ct Judges Asn, 1994-; Am Judges Asn, 1994-; Atty Screening Comt, La Super Ct, 1994-; Const Rights Found, bd dir, 1997-. **Honors/Awds:** Scholarship, Occidental Col, 1973-77; Calif State Scholarship, State Calif, 1973-77; law scholarship, Univ Calif Los Angeles Law Sch, 1977; Attorney of the Year, Los Angeles County Bar Asn & Const Rights Found, 1993; Commendation for Los Angeles Police Dept, 1996; Service Award, Asn Dep Dist Attys, 1994; Service Award, La Dist Atty's Off, Environ Crimes Div, 1994; Judge of the Year, Const Rights Found, 1997. **Special Achievements:** Competition judge for Constitutional Rights Found, Mock Trial Competition, 1989-. **Home Addr:** 110 N Grand Ave, Los Angeles, CA 90012. **Business Addr:** Judge, Los Angeles Superior Court, Clara Shortridge Foltz Criminal Justice Ctr, Los Angeles, CA 90012, **Business Phone:** (213)974-5759.

### VELAND, TONY
Football coach, football player. **Personal:** Born Mar 11, 1973, Omaha, NE; married Brooke; children: T J & Arianna. **Educ:** Nebr Univ, attended. **Career:** Football player (retired), Football coach; Denver Broncos, defensive back, 1997; Carolina Panthers, 1998; Omaha Beef, def coordr, 2002-; Warren Acad, staff. **Orgs:** Nebr Nat championship team, 1994, & 1995. **Business Addr:** Defensive Coordinator, Omaha Beef Football, 1804 Capitol Ave Suite C, Omaha, NE 68102, **Business Phone:** (402)346-2333.

### VELEZ, LAUREN
Actor. **Personal:** Born Nov 2, 1964, Brooklyn, NY; married Mark Gordon. **Career:** Films: I Like It Like That, 1994; City Hall, 1996; I Think I Do, 1997; Buscando un sueno, 1997; The LaMastas, 1998; Taino, 1999; Prince of Central Park, 2000; Prison Song, 2001; Barely Buzzed, 2005; Dexter, 2006; Serial, 2007; Rosewood Lane, 2011. TV appearances: "New York Undercover", 1995-98; "Oz", 1997-2003; "Thicker Than Blood", 1998; "St Michael's Crossing", 1999; "Love & Treason", 2001; "Dragnet", 2003; "Law & Order: Special Victims Unit", 2004; "Numb3rs", 2006-07; "Dexter", 2006-11; "Law & Order: Criminal Intent", 2008; "Ugly Betty", 2009; "Breakout Kings", 2011; "Hawthorne", 2011; "Unforgettable", 2014. **Honors/Awds:** NYFCCA Award; NCLR Bravo Award, 1996; ALMA Award, 2001, 2009 & 2013; Best Supporting Actress Award, Long Island Film Expo Festival, 2006; Vision Award, Nat Asn Multi-Ethnicity Commun, 2007; HOLA Award, Hisp Orgn Latin Actors, 2010. **Business Addr:** Actress, c/o Home Box Office Inc, 1100 Avenue of the Americas, New York, NY 10036, **Business Phone:** (212)512-1000.

### VELJOHNSON, REGINALD
Actor, writer. **Personal:** Born Aug 16, 1952, New York, NY; son of Dan and Eve. **Educ:** Long Island Inst Music & Arts; NY Univ, BA, theater; studied under Lloyd Richards. **Career:** Films: But Never Jam Today, 1979; Wolfen, 1981; Inacent Black, 1981; The World of Ben Caldwell, 1982; Ghost Busters, 1984; Oh! Oh! Obesity!, 1984; Spell No 7, 1987-88; Film appearances: Wolfen, 1981; The Cotton Club, 1984; Ghost busters, 1984; Remo Williams: The Adventure Begins, 1985; Crocodile Dundee, 1986; Armed & Dangerous, 1986; Die Hard, 1988; Plain Clothes, 1988; Turner & Hooch, 1989; Die Hard 2, 1990; A Fond Little Memory, 1991; Posse, 1993; Ground Zero, 2000; Like Mike, 2002; The King, 2002; Waitin' To Love, 2002; Death to the Super models, 2005; Hidden Secrets, 2006; Three Days to Vegas, 2007; Out at the Wedding, 2007; Steppin, 2008; Jelly, 2010; You Again, 2010; Sex Tax: Based on a True Story, 2010; Marriage Retreat, 2011; Brother White, 2012; On Angel's Wings, 2014; The Formula, 2014; Strike One, 2014; 12 Dog Days Till Christmas, 2014. TV series: When Hell Freezes Over, I'll Skate, 1979; Kojak: The Belarus File, 1985; Doing Life, 1986; "Quiet Victory: The Charlie Wedemeyer Story", 1988; "The Bride in Black", 1990; "Jury Duty: The Comedy", 1990; "Perfect Strangers", 1988-89; "Family Matters", 1989; "The Joan Rivers Show", 1989; "Good Morning America", 1990; "The Byron Allen Show", 1991; "Regis & Kathy Lee", 1991; "The Arsenio Hall Show", 1991; "Grass Roots", 1992; "Yuletide in the 'hood (voice)", 1993; "One of Her Own", 1994; "Deadly Pursuits", 1996; "Ghost Whisperer", 2005; "Monk", 2006; "Nerve Endings", 2007; "On the Lot", 2007; "Out at the Wedding", 2007 "Bones"; "Chuck", 2008; "Sunday Evening Haircut", producer, 2005; "Three Gifts, TheThe Three Gifts", 2009; "I'm in the Band", 2009-10; "Funny or Die Presents", 2010; "The Bold and the Beautiful", 2010; "Meet the Browns", 2010; "Mike & Molly", 2011-13; "Hart of Dixie", 2011-14; "Upcoming, Tron: Uprising", 2012-13; "Real Husbands of Hollywood", 2013; "The Neighbors", 2013; "I Didn't Do It", 2014. **Orgs:** Joseph Papp's Black/Hispanic Shakespeare Co; nat spokesman, Big Brothers Am, Pass It On Prog. **Honors/Awds:** WRIFF Award, Wild Rose Independent Film Festival, 2013. **Home Addr:** c/o Jeralyn Bagdley, Bagdley Connor, Los Angeles, CA 90069. **Business Addr:** Actor, Lori DeWaal & Associates, 7080 Hollywood Blvd Suite 515, Los Angeles, CA 90028-6932, **Business Phone:** (323)462-4122.

### VENABLE, ANDREW ALEXANDER, JR.
Library administrator, president (organization). **Personal:** Born Nov 11, 1944, Staunton, VA; married Maxine Cockrell; children: Angela & Andrew III. **Educ:** Va State Univ, Petersburg, BS, bus admin, 1967; Case Western Res Univ, Cleveland, MSLS, 1978. **Career:** Stand Oil Co Mkt Dept Ohio, capital budget planning controls analyst, 1968-70; Cleveland Pub Libr, asst dir personnel serv, 1970-71; dir finance admin serv, 1972-78, dep clerk treas, 1975-76, clerk treas, 1976-78, head comm serv, 1978, dir, 1999-2008, dep dir, 1997; dir & bd trustee, currently; People's Univ, dir. **Orgs:** Pres, Pub Libr Employees Credit Union, 1978-; libr tech adv comt, Cuyahoga Community Col, 1978-; Ohio Libr Asn; Am Libr Asn, 1978-; trustee, Urban Leage Greater Cleveland Inc, 1979-82; trustee, Consumer Protection Asn, 1979-; Cleveland City Club; trustee, Harvard Community Serv Ctr; allocations pnl United Way Serv, 1979-81; Beta Phi Mu Int Libr Sci Hon Soc, 1979. **Honors/Awds:** Andrew A Venable Scholar, Va State Univ Alumini Asn, 1973; Serv Appreciation Award, Alpha Phi Alpha Frat Inc, Cleveland Grad Chap, 1977; Outstanding Young Men of Am, 1978; Outstanding Greek of the Year, Greater Cleveland Pan Hellenic Coun, 1979. **Special Achievements:** He was the first black director of the Cleveland Public Library; Ohio Library Council named him one of two librarians of the year. **Home Addr:** PO Box 50328, Washington, DC 20091-0328. **Business Addr:** Library Dir, Cleveland Public Library, 325 Super Ave NE, Cleveland, OH 44114, **Business Phone:** (216)623-2800.

### VENABLE, MAX (WILLIAM MCKINLEY VENABLE)
Baseball player, athletic coach. **Personal:** Born Jun 6, 1957, Phoenix, AZ; married Molly; children: William Dion & Winston. **Career:** Baseball player (retired), baseball coach; San Francisco Giants, outfielder, 1979-83; Montreal Expos, outfielder, 1984; Cincinnati Reds, outfielder, 1985-87; Calif Angels, outfielder, 1989-91; Chiba Lotte Marines, 1992-93; Dragons, hitting coach, 2004; Ft Wayne Wizards, hitting coach; Lake Elsinore Storm, hitting coach; Double-A San Antonio Missions, hitting coach; Triple A Portland Beavers, hitting coach, currently; SK Wyverns, hitting coach, 2013-. **Home Addr:** 2834 Azevedo Dr, Sacramento, CA 95833-1432, **Home Phone:** (916)922-7277. **Business Addr:** Hitting Coach, Triple A Portland Beavers, 1844 SW Morrison, Portland, OR 97205, **Business Phone:** (503)553-5400.

### VENABLE, REV. ROBERT CHARLES
Clergy. **Personal:** Born Jan 26, 1950, Camden, NJ; married Cherly A Pitts; children: Tisa L Mateo, Lovell V, Marc R, Alvin, Labree, Justin, Steven & Elijah David Mateo. **Educ:** Shaw Univ, Bible Col. **Career:** New Wesley AME Zion Church, assoc pastor, 1975-82; Harris Temple AME Zion Church, pastor 1982-. **Orgs:** Bd educ, Camden City, 1982-96; dir educ, Camden Ministerial Alliance; chairperson, Affirmative Action; chairperson, BSIP; chairperson, Finance Educ Bd; Camden Ministerial Alliance; Penn Ministerial Alliance; Camden Dist Ministerial Alliance AME Zion Church; Nat Asn Advan Colored People; S Christian League Conf; Urban League; Asn Sch Bus Officials US & Can; NJ Sch Bd Asn; PTA; Boy Scouts Am; Nat Black Caucus State Legislators; Nat Caucus Black Sch Bd Mem; Joint Ctr Polit Studies; Nat Black Elected Officials; NJ Pan Methodist Comn Liaison; Penn Pan Methodist Celebration Finance; Camden Co Dem Comn; Nat Parks & Conserv Wash, DC; Nat Trust Hist Preserv; Orient Lodge No 1 F&AM-PHA; faith work ministries. **Honors/Awds:** Youth Choir Christian Serv, New Wesley AME Zion Church, 1982; Christian Serv Award, Harris Temple AME Zion Church, 1983; Christian Serv Award, Elegant Charm Modeling Sch, 1985; Thirteenth Ward Whitman Park Little League, 1985-92; Community Serv Award, EL L Bonsall Sch, 1985; Community Serv Award, Camden Co Coun Econ Opportunities, Inc, 1985; Christian Serv Award, Harris Temple AME Zion Church, 1986; Bishops EL Huff Community Serv Award, Union Am ME Church, 1990; Community Serv Award, Camden City Youth Asn, Inc, 1991; Community Serv Award, Prida Camden Lodge No 83, 1993; The Castle Award, Camden High Sch Outstanding Achievements, 1994. **Home Addr:** 210 E Chapel Ave, Cherry Hill, NJ 08034-1205. **Business Addr:** Pastor, Harris Temple AME Zion Church, 926 Florence St, Camden, NJ 08104, **Business Phone:** (856)541-6608.

### VENABLE, WILLIAM MCKINLEY. See VENABLE, MAX.

### VENEY, MARGUERITE C.
Insurance executive. **Personal:** Born Mar 8, 1949, Melfa, VA; daughter of George and Maggie Chandler. **Educ:** Va State Univ, BS, 1971; Northeastern Univ, MBA, 1995. **Career:** John Hancock Mutual Life Ins Co, contract mgr, currently. **Honors/Awds:** Black Achievers Award, Boston YMCA, 1990. **Business Addr:** Contract Manager, John Hancock Mutual Life Insurance Co, 200 Berkley St B 9, Boston, MA 02117.

### VENSON, CLYDE R.
Association executive, executive director. **Personal:** Born May 8, 1936, Alexandria, LA; son of Samuel S and Effie Kellum; married Annette Broussard; children: Jane A & Lisa A. **Educ:** Southern Univ, Baton Rouge, La, BS, sociol & recreation, 1959; FBI Nat Acad, Wash, DC, FBI basic & agency network, 1971. **Career:** Shelby Co Sheriffs Dept, Memphis, TN, dep sheriff, 1960-65, dir traffic safety, 1985-88; TN state Dept Corrections, adult probation & parole officer, 1965-85, criminal investr, 1968-80; TN Dist Atty Gen, asst chief criminal invests, 1980-85; Shelby Co Corrections, Memphis, TN, dep admin security, 1988-91; VCI & Assoc Inc, security consult, pres, 1993-2000, pres, 2000-; Memphis Housing Authority, security chief, dir security & safety, 1993-2000; Venson's Criminal Invests & Assocs, pres, 1991-; Nat United Law Enforcement Officers Asn, exec dir, currently. **Orgs:** Alpha Phi Alpha Fraternity, 1958-; exalted ruler, IBP Order Elks W, 1965-69; nat gen chmn, Memphis Kemet Jubilee, 1985-; exec dir, Blacks Law Enforcement, 1986-; US/Japan Bilateral Session Legal Rels, Tokyo, Japan, 1988. **Honors/Awds:** Man of the Year, Nat United Law Enforcement Officers Asn, 1980; Memphian of the year, Moolah Shirine Temple 54, 2000-; Dr RQ Venson Pioneer Award, 2000. **Home Addr:** 135 Exped Pl, Memphis, TN 38103, **Home Phone:** (901)526-8271. **Business Addr:** President, Executive Director, National United Law Enforcement Officers Association Inc, 265 E McLemore Ave, Memphis, TN 38106-2833, **Business Phone:** (901)774-1118.

**VERBAL, CLAUDE A.**
Engineer, executive. **Personal:** Born Nov 12, 1942, Durham, NC; son of Sidney Sr and Mary Gladys; married Dorothy Simmons. **Educ:** NC St Univ, BSME, 1964. **Career:** Buick Motor Div GMC, engr res develop, 1964-66, exp lab test engr, 1966-69, chassis design engr, 1969-73, staff proj engr supv exp engr, 1974-75, asst supt qual control, 1976-77, supt qual control, 1977; Milford Proving Ground, engr supv, 1973-74; BOC Powertrain GMC, supt mfg, 1985-87; Serv Parts Oper GM, plant mgr, 1987-98; Wesley Indust, chief operating officer, 1999-. **Orgs:** Soc Automotive Engrs Int, 1966-; Mid-Mi Gov Bd Soc Auto Engr, 1970-; Soc Mech Engr; Nat Soc Prof Engr Regist, 1971; Bsls Omcrn Rho Chap Omega Psi Phi Frat Inc, 1971-; bd dir, Hurley med Ctr, 1984-; nat bd dir, Soc Automotive Engr, 1988; pres bd dir, Hurley Med Ctr, 1989; Flint Airport Authority, 1991; pres, Pontiac Vis Nurses Asn, 1991; bd campaign chair, N Oakland United Way, 1992; pres, Soc Automotive Engrs, 1996; bd control, Mich Technol Univ, 1997-, chmn, 2000-01; bd dir, Flint Urban League; pres, Flint Econ Develop Corp; Leadership Flint; FAM Masterr Mason Erk Lodge 32 Deg; Flnt Urban League Hrt City Adv Bd; first vpres, Flint Inner City Lion's Club; Water-ford Rotary Club; vpres, pres, Detroit Conf United Methodist Men; Omega Psi Phi Fraternity; Prof Engrs Soc. **Honors/Awds:** Young Engr of the Ur, Flint Chap Prof Engr, 1974; Omega Man of the Year, Omicron Rho Chap Omega Psi Phi, 1974; Nat Media Women Award, 1977; Distinguished Alumnus of North Carolina State Univ Award, 1997; Engineer of the Year Award, Flint chapter Nat Soc Prof Engr, 1997; Distinguished Engineering Alumnus Award Recipient, 1997. **Special Achievements:** First African-American to hold an executive position in the Buick Motor Division; First African-American to be elected president of the Society of Automotive Engineers International. **Home Addr:** 1800 Valley Lane, Flint, MI 48503, **Home Phone:** (810)837-9568. **Business Addr:** Chief Operating Officer, Wesley Industries Inc, 41000 N Woodward Ave Suite 395E, Bloomfield Hills, MI 48304.

**VEREEN, BEN (BENJAMIN AUGUSTUS MIDDLETON)**
Entertainer, actor. **Personal:** Born Oct 10, 1946, Miami, FL; son of Essie May Middelton (deceased); married Andrea Townsley; children: Ben Jr; married Nancy Brunner; children: Malaika, Naja (deceased), Kabara & Karon. **Educ:** Pentacostal Theol Sem, New York, NY. **Career:** Stage appearances: The Prodigal Son, 1965; Sweet Charity; Golden Boy; Hair; Jesus Christ Superstar; Pippin; Cabaret; Grind. TV appearances: "Roots", 1977; "Ben Vereen-His Roots", 1978; "Fosse", 2001; "Ten speed & Brown Shoe"; "Webster"; "Great Performances: Dance in America", 2001; "Feast of All Saints", 2001; "Oz", 2006; "Law & Order: Criminal Intent", 2007; "Grey's Anatomy", 2007; "Grey's Anatomy", 2007; "Your Mama Don't Dance", 2008; "Accidental Friendship", 2008; "How I Met Your Mother: Cleaning House, False Positive, Mom and Dad and The End of the Aisle", 2010-14; "NCIS as Lamar Addison", 2013. Films: Sweet Charity; Funny Lady; Louis Armstrong-Chicago Style; All That Jazz, 1979; Lost in London, 1985; Zoo Gang, The, 1985; Buy and Cell, 1989; Once Upon a Forest, 1993; Why Do Fools Fall in Love?, 1998; I'll Take You There, 1999, 2002; The Painting, actor, 2001; Idle wild, actor, 2006; Holiday in Bryant Park, 2007; & Then Came Love, 2007; Mama, I Want to Sing!, 2007; And Then Came Love, 2007; 21 and a Wake-Up, 2009; Broadway: The Next Generation, 2011; Khumba, 2013. **Orgs:** Celebrity spokesperson, Big Brothers; nat celebrity spokesperson, A Drug-Free Am. **Honors/Awds:** Theatre World Award, Jesus Christ Superstar, 1972; Tony Award; Drama Desk Award; CLIO Pippin Humanitarian Award, Israel, 1975; George M Cohen Award, AGVA; Best Song & Dance Star; Best Rising Star; Entertainer of the Year, 1976; TV Critics Award, Roots, 1977; Image Award, Roots NAACP, 1977, 1978; 7 Emmy Awards for Ben Vereen-His Roots; Cultural Award Roots, Israel, 1978; Humanitarian Award, State of Israel, 1979; Eleanor Roosevelt Humanitarian Award, 1983; Helping Enforcement Reach Our Streets Award, City of Miami, 2002; TV Land Awards, 2007; Prism Award, 2008. **Home Addr:** 301 W 53rd St Suite 10J, New York, NY 10019, **Home Phone:** (212)586-4978. **Business Addr:** Entertainer, Virtual Office & Website Management, 8256 Quail Meadow IBIS, Palm Beach Gardens, FL 33412, **Business Phone:** (561)254-8335.

**VEREEN, DIXIE DIANE**
Editor. **Personal:** Born Nov 6, 1957, Colorado Springs, CO; daughter of Willie C and Dixie Lee Dorsey. **Educ:** Randolph Tech Col, Asheboro, NC, AAS, photo, 1977; George Mason Univ. **Career:** Raleigh News & Observer, photogr, 1978-80; Newsday, photogr, 1980; Philadelphia Inquirer, photogr, 1981-82; USA Today, photogr & photo ed, 1982-85; USA Weekend, dir opers, 1986-90; Wilmington News J, asst managing ed, 1990; USA Today, design ed, 1991-. **Orgs:** Chmn, Minority Affairs Comt, Nat Press Photogr Asn, 1988; Nat Asn Black Journalists; White House Press Photogrs Asn. **Business Addr:** Design Editor, USA Today, 7950 Jones Br Dr, McLean, VA 22108-0605, **Business Phone:** (703)854-3400.

**VEREEN, MICHAEL L.**
Electrical engineer, business owner. **Personal:** Born Aug 15, 1965, Southport, NC; son of William B and Thelma L Hankins; married Erdyne L Yates. **Educ:** NC State Univ, Raleigh, NC, BS, elec engineering, 1989. **Career:** Carolina Power & Light, Raleigh, NC, engr, 1985-89; GLAXO Smith Kline Inc, Zebulon, NC, sr syst analyst, engr, end user comput specialist II, 1989-94, end user comput specialist III, 1994-97, sr syst analyst, 1998-2006, tech serv analyst, 2010-; V Tech Properties NC, co owner, 2003-08; ACS Xerox Co, infrastructure mgt sr unix analyst, 2006-10. **Orgs:** Bd dirs, Nat Soc Black Engrs, 1983-; Kappa Alpha Psi Fraternity, 1987-; Rotary Club Wendell, NC; bd dir, Eastern Wake Sr Citizen Ctr; steering comt, Wake County Communities schs Prog; bd dir, Zebulon Chamber Com; bd dir, Vereen sch Dance Arts; bd dir, Eastern Wake Boys & Girls Club; bd dir, NC Bus Comt Educ; pres, Rotary Club Wendell, 1996-97; Pleaseant Grove Baptist Church; supt, Wendell NC Sunday sch; pres, Rotary Club Wendell, 2000-01; NC Family Training & Conseling Ctr; GSK Employees & Alumni Network. **Special Achievements:** Copyright for Recloser Computer Program, Carolina Power & Light Co, 1989. **Home Addr:** 712 Moss Rd, PO Box 1194, Zebulon, NC 27597-8857, **Home Phone:** (919)269-6197. **Business Addr:** Technical Services Analyst, Glaxo Smith Kline Inc, 1011 N Arendell Ave, Zebulon, NC 27597, **Business Phone:** (919)269-1065.

**VERNON, EASTON DAVE**
Consultant, financial manager. **Personal:** Born Jan 14, 1934, Montego Bay; son of Walter (deceased) and Serina (deceased); children: Theresa Howe, Steve, Michelle Medine, Lisa Fassari & David. **Career:** IDS Financial Serv, financial planner, 1973-85, dist mgr, 1985-87, div vpres, 1987-92, diversity consult, financial planner, 1992-93; Vernon & Assocs, owner & consult, 1994-2009; Nathional Planning Corp, 2001-02; Nathan & Lewis Securities Inc, 2002-03; Walnut St Securities Inc, advisor, 2003-09; Gfa Securities LLC, advisor, 2009-; Gerstein Fisher & Assocs Inc, 2009-. **Orgs:** Vpres, Harlem Interfaith Counselling Serv, 1977-; found bd, Westchester Community Col, 1991-. **Home Addr:** 2871 Thompson Rd, Harleysville, PA 19438, **Home Phone:** (610)287-0706. **Business Addr:** Advisor, GFA Securities LLC, 565 5th Ave 27th Fl, New York, NY 10017, **Business Phone:** (212)968-0707.

**VERNON, FRANCINE M.**
Educator, executive director. **Personal:** Born Nov 14, 1939, New York, NY; married Bernard R; children: Richard, Carolyn-Michelle & Michael. **Educ:** Howard Univ, BS, 1961; Hunter Col, MS, 1973; Fordham Univ, dipl, prof admin, 1976. **Career:** Dept HEW, claims rep, 1962-67; New York Bd Educ, dir adult basic educ prog; Hunter Col, instr, 1973-75; Ossining Community Action Prog, exec dir; Elmsford Community Opportunity Prog, dir, currently. **Orgs:** NY Asn outstanding Comm Educ; Nat Asn Pub Adult Educ; Kappa Delta Pi; Nat Asn Teachers Eng Speakers; pres, Ossng Nat Asn Advan Colored People; trustee, Afro-Am Found; pres, trust Ossng Bd Educ; pres, Greenburgh Eleven Sch Bd; bd mem, Ossng Community Action Prog; trustee, The Children's Village, 2003; trustee, Mark & Phil llc. **Honors/Awds:** Achievement Award, Nat Asn Pub Continuing Adult Educ, 1975; Recognisation Award, Commrs Nat Conf on Career Educ, 1976; apprec Award Ossng Joycs, 1977. **Home Addr:** 65 Cedar Lane, Ossining, NY 10562, **Home Phone:** (914)941-2364. **Business Addr:** Director, Elmsford Community Opportunity Program, 2269 Saw Mill River Rd, Elmsford, NY 10523, **Business Phone:** (914)592-5600.

**VERNON-CHESLEY, MICHELE JOANNE (MICHELE VERNON-CHESLEY)**
Journalist. **Personal:** Born Aug 23, 1962, New York, NY; daughter of Hayden Arthur and Mae Sawyer; married Roger Thomas; children: Roger Thomas Jr, Christine & Maya. **Educ:** Long Island Univ, Brooklyn, NY, BA, jour, 1984. **Career:** Detroit Free Press, Detroit, Mich, copy ed, 1984-86, asst news ed, 1986-88; page designer, 1988-90; reporter, 1991-93; coordr, high sch jour, 1993-94; Wayne State Univ, Jour Inst Minorities, dir, 1994-97; McCormick fel; Virginian-Pilot, dep managing ed, sr ed; Health & Med Ed, features ed, currently, sr ed, currently. **Orgs:** Rep assembly, News Paper Guild, 1988-; Nat Asn Black Journalists, 1984-; Soc Newspaper Design, 1989-; dir, Journalism Inst Minorities; Detroit E Area Residents Asn, 1990-; secy, Detroit Chap Nat Asn Black Journalists, 1985-86; chmn human rights comt, Newspaper Guild, 1990-. **Honors/Awds:** Design Award & Merit, Soc Newspaper Design, 1990; Intern of the Year, Detroit Free Press, 1984. **Home Addr:** 5224 Breezewood Arch, Virginia Beach, VA 23464-8472, **Home Phone:** (757)495-2369. **Business Addr:** Senior Editor, The Virginian-Pilot, 150 W Brambleton Ave, Norfolk, VA 23510, **Business Phone:** (757)446-2000.

**VERRET, C. REYNOLD**
College president. **Educ:** Columbia Col, BA, biol chem, 1976; Mass Inst Technol, PhD, biol chem, 1982. **Career:** Yale University Howard Hughes Institute, research fellow, 1982-84; MIT Center for Cancer Research, research fellow, 1984-88; Morehouse School of Medicine, adjunct professor, 1994-2008; Clark Atlanta University, chemistry department chair, 1996-2002; University of the Sciences in Philadelphia, dean of the Misher College of Arts and Science, 2002-07; Wilkes University, professor, 2001-12, provost and vice president of academic affairs, 2007-12; Savannah State University, professor, 2012-15, provost, 2012-15; Xavier University of Louisiana, pres, 2015-. **Orgs:** Phi Beta Kappa, 1976; Pa Humanities Coun, bd mem, 2005-& mem exec comt; mem, Aaas, Nat Orgn Black Chemists & Chem Engrs, Am Asn Immunol, Am Soc Biochem & Molecular Biol, Fedn Am Socs Exp Biol, Am Chem Soc, Coun Undergrad Res, Coun Cols Arts & Sci. **Business Addr:** Xavier University of Louisiana, 1 Drexel Dr, New Orleans, LA 70125, **Business Phone:** (504)520-7541.

**VERRETT, JOYCE MCKEE**
Educator, administrator, dean (education). **Personal:** Born May 26, 1932, New Orleans, LA; married Wilbert; children: Lester McKee, Jeannine, Stanley & Rory. **Educ:** Dillard Univ, BA, 1957; NY Univ, MS, 1963; Tulane Univ, PhD, biol & biomed sci, 1971. **Career:** Educator, dean (retired); Orleans Parsih, LA, high sch teacher, 1958-63; Dillard Univ, Div Natural Sci, instr, prof biol, chmn; Gov State Univ, Col Arts & Sci, Chicago, dean. **Orgs:** Alpha Kappa Mu Nat Hon Soc, 1956; Beta Kappa Chi Nat Sci Hon Soc, 1956; Reg 9 Sci Fair, 1958-; fel NSF Adv Study, 1960-62; Nat Asn Adv Colored People, 1960-; La Heart Asn, 1973-; Beta Kappa Chi Sci Hon Soc, Cancer Asn Greater ND, 1974; Int Soc Am; Nat Inst Sci; Beta Bial & Hon Soc. **Honors/Awds:** Outstanding Educr Am, 1972. **Special Achievements:** First African American Women to receive PhD in Bio from Tulane Univ 1971; First Women Chairperson of Dillard University division of Natural Sciences. **Home Addr:** 4832 Ray Ave, New Orleans, LA 70126.

**VERTREACE, WALTER CHARLES**
Lawyer, executive. **Personal:** Born Sep 17, 1947, Washington, DC; son of Walter C and Modena K; married Peggy A; children: Bryan (deceased), Kelly & Erin. **Educ:** Howard Univ, BA, 1968, MS, 1970; Temple Univ, Sch Law, JD, 1982. **Career:** USAF Human Resources Lab, res psychologist, 1970-72; Info Sci Inc, human resources consult, 1972-75; Hertz Corp, mgr, EEO progs, 1975-76; INA Corp, mgr, eeo opers, 1976-80; Amerada Hess Corp, mgr, dir & corp eeo, 1980-2009, Equal Employ Opportunity, dir, 1980-; NIMH fel; Howard Univ fel. **Orgs:** Bd mem, Equal Employ Adv Coun; bd mem, Nat Indust Liaison Group; bd mem, Black Collegian Mag; past pres, United Way Cent Jersey, 1990-92; Am Bar Asn; Nat Bar Asn; NJ State Bar Asn; past vchmn, Manhattan Affil NY Urban League; past vicechmn, Philadelphia Urban League; past pres, EDGES Group Inc; Omega Psi Phi; past pres, NY State Adv Coun Employ Law; deacon, Grace Baptist Church, Germantown; chair, Tri-State Corp Campaign, UNCF; Lt Col, Chief Staff, PA Wing Civil Air Patrol. **Honors/Awds:** United Way Distinguished Volunteer, 1993; Civil Air Patrol Lampligter Award, 1996; CAP Commander's Commendation; Meritorious Service Award; Chuck Yeager Aerospace Education Achievement Award; Gill Robb Wilson Award. **Special Achievements:** Author, 'Congratulations, You Received A Job Offer! Now What? - How to Evaluate a Job Offer'. **Home Addr:** 609 E Gorgas Lane, Philadelphia, PA 19119-1325. **Business Addr:** Director, Amerada Hess Corp, 1185 Avenue of the Americas, New York, NY 10036, **Business Phone:** (212)977-8500.

**VERTREACE-DOODY, MARTHA MODENA**
Educator, teacher, writer. **Personal:** Born Nov 24, 1945, Washington, DC; daughter of Walter Charles Vertreace and Modena Kendrick Vertreace; married Timothy John. **Educ:** DIS Teachers Col, BA, 1967; Roosevelt Univ, MA, 1971, MPh, 1972; Mundelein Col, MS, 1981; Vermont Col, MFA, 1996. **Career:** Roosevelt High Sch, Eng instr, 1967-72; Rosary Col, assoc adj prof, 1981-82; Kennedy-King Col, resident poet, 1976-95, distinguished prof, 1995-96, prof commun, currently.Books: Under a cat's-eye moon : poems, 1991; Kelly in the Mirror, 1993; Second house from the corner; Light Caught Bending, 1995; Maafa: When Night Becomes a Lion, 1996; Glacier Fire, 2005. **Orgs:** Kappa Delta Pi Hon Soc, 1966-; Pi Lambda Theta Hon Soc, 1973-; Modern Language Asn, 1982-; Nat Coun Teachers Eng, 1982-; Midwest Modern Language Asn, 1982-; second vpres, Poets & Patrons, 1986-; Ill Asn Teachers Eng, 1986-; Soc Study Midwestern Lit, 1987-; fel Nat Endowment Arts; fel Hawthornden Int Writers Retreat; fel St Deiniol's Libr. **Home Addr:** 5232 S Greenwood Ave, Chicago, IL 60615-4316, **Home Phone:** (773)363-0766. **Business Addr:** Distinguished Professor, Communications, Poet-in-Residence, Kennedy-King College, Y177 6301 S Halsted, Chicago, IL 60621, **Business Phone:** (773)602-5182.

**VESSUP, DR. AARON ANTHONY**
Writer, educator, college teacher. **Personal:** Born Mar 28, 1947, Los Angeles, CA. **Educ:** N Eastern Wesleyan Univ, BS, 1970; Ill State Univ, MA, sci, 1972; Univ Pittsburgh, PhD, 1978; Univ Edinburgh, Scotland, media studies, 1984. **Career:** Ill State Univ, comt instr, 1971-72; City Bloomington, human rels coordr, 1972-75; Univ Pittsburgh, teaching fel, 1975-78; Rockwell Int, commun intern, 1977-78; Tex Southern Univ, asst prof commun, 1978-; Elgin Community Col, dir forensics, prof speech & drama, 1981-2002, prof emer, 2002-; Univ Edinburgh, media studies fel; Inter cult Commun, consult; Dialoque Masters, dir, 2005-; Huaqiao Foreign Lang Inst, foreign expert, 2007-11; Dialoque Masters2, founder, 2009-10, dir, 2009-11; Beijing Best Educ Consultancy, asst gen mgr, 2014-. Books: "Symbolic Communications: Understanding Stereotypes that Persist", 1983; "The Generic Speaker", 1984; "The Lead Softly Plows", 1987; "You Can Control Speech Anxiety", 1990; "Themes From Libido", 1990; "Mud Notes Singing", 1990; "Fires of Desire", 1994; "Selected Verses", 2002; "Two Swords, One Heart", 2002; "Beyond Cultural Anxieties: Ingredients of Fear", Tests of Character, 2004; "Making Cultural Adjustments: Dialogue to Harmony", 2009; "Easy Talk II: Guide to Western Slang", 2010; "Making Adjustments: Accused, Abused, or Unexcused--Issues In Cultural Mis-Education"; Poems: "The Myna Bird". **Orgs:** Ed, Interracial Comn Bloomington Press, 1977; dir, Grant Proj Tex Comn Humanities, 1979-80; Kellogg fel Speech-Commun; Soc Int Educ Asn; Tex Speech Comn Asn; US Tennis Asn; Int Comn Asn; Am Mgt Asn; Speech Commun Asn; Am Acad Poets; lifetime mem, Int Socs Poets; lifetime mem, World Cong Poets; ASTD; SIETAR; Int CtrPhotog; Chicago Artists Coalition; lifetime mem, Int Freelance Photogr Orgn. **Honors/Awds:** Australian Peace Medallion; Silver Bowl, Int Platform Asn, Acad Poets. **Special Achievements:** "Produced & hosted, Cultures in Focus; published text book in Urban Comm Winthrop Press", 1977; Co-author, Conflict Mgt Acad Mgmt Rev, 1979; author: "Symbolic Communication, Understanding Racial Stereotypes Brethren Press", 1983. **Home Addr:** 575 Adams St, Elgin, IL 60123-7429, **Home Phone:** (847)931-0490. **Business Addr:** Professor Emeritus, Elgin Community College, 1700 Spartan Dr, Elgin, IL 60123-7193, **Business Phone:** (847)697-1000.

**VEST, DONALD SEYMOUR. See Obituaries Section.**

**VEST, HILDA FREEMAN**
Publisher, editor. **Personal:** Born Jun 5, 1933, Griffin, GA; daughter of Pharr Cyral (deceased) and Blanche Heard (deceased); married Donald; children: Karen, Donald Jr & Carl. **Educ:** Wayne State Univ, Detroit, MI, BS, educ, 1958. **Career:** Editor, publisher (retired): Detroit Bd Educ, Detroit, Mich, teacher, 1959-88; Broadside Press, Detroit, Mich, publ, pres, secy & ed, 1985-98; Bks: Lyrics I, 1981; Sorrows End, 1993. **Honors/Awds:** Southeastern Michigan Regional Scholastic Award, Detroit News, 1950; Writing Award for Poetry, Detroit Women Writers, 1982. **Special Achievements:** Featured in Broadside Poets Theater, 1982; Featured in Detroit Sings Series, Broadside Press, 1982. **Home Addr:** 4734 Sturtevant St, Detroit, MI 48204-1464, **Home Phone:** (313)935-8396.

**VESTER, DR. TERARY Y. (TERRY Y VESTER)**
Physician. **Personal:** Born Sep 9, 1955, Houston, TX; son of Willie T Busby; married Alphonza; children: Jennifer, Alexandria & Geoffrey. **Educ:** Univ San Francisco, BS, 1978; Howard Col Med, MD, 1982. **Career:** Montgomery Residency Prog, family pract, 1982-85; Vester Health Ctr, pvt pract physician, currently. **Orgs:** Amer Acad Family Physicians, 1982-87; Nat Med Asn, 1986-87; Southern Med Asn, 1986-87; Med Asn State Ala, 1986-87; Chambers Co Med Asn, 1986-87. **Home Addr:** 501 Hospital St, Lafayette, AL 36862-2210, **Home Phone:** (334)864-7150. **Business Addr:** Physician, Vester Health Center, 140 First St SE, Lafayette, AL 36862, **Business Phone:** (334)864-7887.

**VIA, THOMAS HENRY**
Engineer, air force officer, executive. **Personal:** Born Sep 12, 1959, Martinsville, VA; son of Henry and Margaret Dandridge. **Educ:** Solano Community Col, AS, welding technician, 1980, AS, mach tool technician, 1982; Community Col Air Force, AAS, metals technol,

AAS, aircraft maintenance technol, 1982; Southern Ill Univ, BS, ind engineering technol, 1982; Golden Gate Univ, MBA, mgmt, 1984; Univ Calif, Berkeley Extenstion, cert voc educ & engineering, 1986. **Career:** Solano Community Col, Suisun, Calif, part-time welding, mach tool, bus instr, 1982; Viking Steel, Anaheim, Calif, ironworker, welder, 1983; Tegal Corp, Novato, Calif, electro mech technician, 1984; Southern Ill Univ, Carbondale, Ill, instr, mfg engr, 1985; United Airlines, San Francisco, Calif, jet mech, welder, 1985; Via Technols, Fairfield, Calif, prin, mfg engr, owner, 1985-. **Orgs:** D16 comt on robotics, C2 Thermal Spray Comm, Am Welding Soc, 1986; Robotic Inds Asn, R15.06, safety stand comm, 1986; tech forum, CASA/SME, 1986; A15.08 sensor interfaces comt, Automated Imaging Asn, 1986-; ASM Int thermal spray automation comt, 1988; Robotics Intl Soc Mfg Engrs, bd advs, 1993-94. **Honors/Awds:** Challenges & Opportunities for Manufacturing Engrs, Soc Mfg Engrs, Nuts & Bolts, 1989; Editor, Curricula 2000 Workshop Proceeding, Soc Mfg Engrs, 1990; Soc Mfg Engrs, 'Outstanding Young Manufacturing Engineer Award', 1994; Solano Community Col, Distinguished Adjunct Faculty, 1997-98; Outstanding American Award. **Business Addr:** Manufacturing Engineer/Principal/Welding Instructor, Owner, Via Technologies, 2123 Madrone Dr, Fairfield, CA 94533, **Business Phone:** (707)425-0365.

### VICKERS, ERIC K.
Lawyer. **Personal:** Born Feb 16, 1953, St. Louis, MO; son of Robert and Claire; married Judy Gladney; children: Erica & Aaron. **Educ:** Wash Univ, BA, polit sci, 1975; Occidental Col, MA, 1976; Univ Va Sch Law, JD, 1981. **Career:** Bryan Cave, assoc atty; Vickers & Assocs, atty, currently. **Orgs:** Bd mem, Minority Bank; chmn bd, Islamic Ctr St Louis, 1983-85, bd mem, Am Muslim Alliance, 1995; founder, pres, N St Louis Econ Develop Inc, 2000; exec dir, Am Muslim Coun, currently. **Home Addr:** 7436 Tulane Ave, St. Louis, MO 63130-2937, **Home Phone:** (314)863-3251. **Business Addr:** Attorney, Vickers & Associates, 7436 Tulane Ave, St. Louis, MO 63130-2937, **Business Phone:** (314)367-0120.

### VICKERS, KIPP EMMANUEL
Football player. **Personal:** Born Aug 27, 1969, Holiday, FL; married Tracy; children: Treme, Trinity & Tajay. **Educ:** Miami Univ. **Career:** Football player (retired); Indianapolis Colts, guard, 1993-97; Wash Redskins, guard, 1999, 2002, left tackle, 1996; Baltimore Ravens, right guard, 2000-01, left guard & right tackle, 2001. **Honors/Awds:** Rookie of the Year, 1993.

**VIEIRA, BOBBY. See VIEIRA, FRANKLIN.**

### VIEIRA, FRANKLIN (BOBBY VIEIRA)
Association executive, chief executive officer, president (organization). **Career:** One Caribbean Radio 97.9FM-HD2, vpres; We Are Caribbean Media Serv, exec dir; Caribbean Cargo & Package Serv, pres & chief exec officer, 1999-; One Caribbean Radio, gen mgr, currently. **Orgs:** House Radio-Tv Gallery. **Business Addr:** Chief Executive Officer, President, Carribbean Cargo & Package Services Inc, 147-46 176th St, Jamaica, NY 11430, **Business Phone:** (718)995-2055.

### VIERA, PAUL E.
Chief executive officer. **Educ:** Univ Mich, BA, econs; Harvard Bus Sch, MBA, 1985. **Career:** Bankers Trust, vpres; Invesco, fund mgr, global partner & sr mem; Harbor Small Cap Value Fund, fund mgr & portfolio mgr; Earnest Partners LLC, founder, chief exec officer & partner; Aetna. **Orgs:** Coun Foreign Rels; Atlanta Soc Financial Analysts; vice chmn, Nc Outward Bound Sch; bd mem, C's Mus Manhatta; bd mem, Nat Ctr Civil & Human Rights. **Business Addr:** Chief Executive Officer, Partner, Earnest Partners LLC, 1180 Peachtree St Suite 2300, Atlanta, GA 30309, **Business Phone:** (404)815-8772.

### VILLAROSA, CLARA
Bookseller, entrepreneur. **Personal:** children: Linda. **Educ:** Roosevelt Univ, BA, sociol & educ, 1952; Loyola Univ, MSW, Psychiat Social Work, 1954; Denver Univ, strum col law, SSW, 1982. **Career:** Owner(retired); Mt. Sinai Hosp, psychiat social worker, 1958-54; Cs Hosp, chief psychiat social worker, 1968-76, dir dept behav sci, 1976-78, asst hosp adminr, 1978-80; United Bank Denver, vpres human resources, 1982-84; Financier; psychologist; Hue-Man Experience, Denver, Colo, owner & pres, 1984-04; Hue-Man Bks, Harlem, NY City, co-owner, ed, 2002-, founder, 1985-2004; auth: Down to Bus: First 10 Steps to Entrepreneurship Women. **Special Achievements:** One of the nation's most noted Black booksellers as a owner. **Business Addr:** Owner, Hue-Man Bookstore & Cafe, 2319 Frederick Douglass Blvd, New York, NY 10027, **Business Phone:** (212)665-7400.

### VILTZ, DR. STANLEY
Executive. **Personal:** Born Oct 4, 1944, Berkeley, CA; daughter of LB and Renee Benson; children: Raven & Wren. **Educ:** Univ Southern Calif, BA, 1965, MPA, 1974; Univ Calif, Los Angeles, EDD, 1998. **Career:** La Community Col Dist, coordr Community Serv, 1976-79, assist dean, voc educ, 1979-90, exec asst chancellor, 1991-92, dean, instr, 1992-95; Compton Community Col, vpres, stud & acad Affairs, 1995-2001, vpres voc & econ develop, spec proj, 2001-, vpres voc technol, extended studies, assoc supt admin staff rep, currently; BWLC, co-founder, currently; Antelope Valley Col, dean, 2007-08; Bennett Col, assoc provost, 2008-13; Fullerton Col, interim dean. **Orgs:** Life mem, Delta Sigma Theta; charter mem, Century City Chap, 1964-; exec bd & vpres prog, Asn Pan African Doctoral Scholars, 1996; sch Bd mem, W Angeles Church God in Christ, 2001-; Mgmt Develop Comn; Nat Pub Serv Sorority; Los Angeles African Am polit action comt; interim vpres, Academic Affairs and Student Life. **Home Addr:** 1608 Va Rd, PO Box 19728, Los Angeles, CA 90019-5934, **Home Phone:** (323)737-0841. **Business Addr:** Vice President of Special Projects, Vice President of Vocational Technology, Compton Community College, 1111 E Artesia Blvd, Compton, CA 90221, **Business Phone:** (310)900-1600.

### VINCENT, ANTON
Vice president (organization), marketing executive. **Personal:** married Lindy; children: 3. **Educ:** Ind Univ, MBA; Kelley Sch Bus. **Career:** Gen Mills Inc, Minn, asst mkt mgr, 1993-95, mkt mgr, 1995-98; Delta Bluff, managing partner, 1998-2000, dir corp develop, 2000-02, Pillsbury Co, key mem, 2001, mkt mgr, 2002-04, vpres mkt baking, 2005-10, corp officer, 2006-, pres baking, 2010-12, vpres, frozen foods, 2012-, pres, Snacks div, 2014; Applebee's franchises, managing partner; Milestone Growth Fund Inc, vpres, dir & pres. **Orgs:** Founding mem, Gen Mills' Employee Black Champions Network; bd dir, Milestone Growth Fund; trustee, Breck Sch; bd mem & vice chmn, Gen Mills community.

### VINCENT, DANIEL PAUL
Executive. **Personal:** Born Jun 19, 1939, New Orleans, LA; son of Howard and Josephine; married Leatha; children: Dannette, Robin & Daryl. **Educ:** Southern Univ, BS; Loyola Univ, MBA; Univ Northern Colo, MA; United Educators Credit Union, PhD; Shrtr Col, Hon PhD. **Career:** Chrysler Corp, engr, 1966-68; Equity Funding Corp Am, rep, 1968-70; Total Community Action Inc, exec dir, 1969-; Mayor New Orleans, Mayor's Charter Rev Com, spec adv vice chmn, 1970-; EDU Inc, pres & chmn, 1975-; La State Univ Health Sci Ctr, consult lectr; TLN Univ, lectr; Xavier Univ, lectr; La Housing Assistance Corp, chmn; Human Serv Inst, founder; Archdiocese New Orleans, Off Black Cath Ministries, Black Cath Ministries Adv Bd, dir, currently. **Orgs:** Adv bd, NO Area Boy Scouts; pres, TCA Fed Credit Union; exec bd, Nat Asn Comn Develop; pres, LA Asn Comn Action Agencies; Nat Asn Housing & Redevelop; vice chmn, New Orleans Manpower Adv Planning Coun; bd dir, New Orleans Area Health Planning Coun; NY Stock Exchange; Addn Study Orleans Parish Sch Syst. **Home Addr:** 6911 Lake Willow Dr, New Orleans, LA 70126-3105. **Business Addr:** Director, Archdiocese of New Orleans, 7887 Walmsley Ave, New Orleans, LA 70125-3496, **Business Phone:** (504)861-6207.

### VINCENT, IRVING H.
Administrator, educator, actor. **Personal:** Born Nov 28, 1934, St. Louis, MO; married Delora Sherleen Sinclair; children: Terrel Lynn French, Mark, Paul & Samantha. **Educ:** St Louis Univ, BS, speech, 1957; HB Studios Lee Strasberg, prof actg, attended 1970; Brooklyn Col, 26 MFA credits, 1974; Third World Cinema, attended 1977. **Career:** Broadway, Off-Broadway, stage mgr, 1961-69, stage dir, 1966-; Downstate Med Ctr, personnel dir, 1966-69; Brooklyn Col, teacher, 1969-74; freelance video artist, 1977-81; DJR Inc, dir & producer, 1980; ABC-TV, unit mgr, 1981-2001; New York Univ, Opportunity Prog Video Lab, dir, multimedia, 1995-2011. **Orgs:** Pres, Seminole Group, 1979-81; bd dir, Media Other Arts, 1981-, admin & staff writer, 2000-04, eng writing & spanish tutor, 2004-. **Home Addr:** 155 Bank St Apt 913, New York, NY 10014-2049, **Home Phone:** (212)242-5947. **Business Addr:** Director, New York University, 8th Fl Greene St, New York, NY 10016, **Business Phone:** (212)998-5670.

### VINCENT, MARJORIE JUDITH
Television news anchorperson, journalist, fashion model. **Personal:** Born Nov 21, 1964, Chicago, IL; daughter of Lucien and Florence Bredy; married Wesley Tripp; children: 1. **Educ:** DePaul Univ, Chicago, IL, 1988; Duke Univ Law Sch, Durham, NC; Fla Coastal Sch Law, law, 2008. **Career:** Brooks, Pierce, McLendon Humphries, Greensboro, NC, law intern, 1989; Mudge, Rose, Guthrie, Alexander & Ferdon, New York, NY, law intern, 1990; Miss Am, 1991; WGBC-TV, anchor & reporter, 1993-94; Ohio News Network, anchor; news anchor, currently; WHOI, Peoria, Ill. **Orgs:** Alpha Kappa Alpha Sorority, 1987-. **Honors/Awds:** Hon chair, Coun Safe Families; Nat Ambassador, Childrens Miracle Network; Peace Begins at Home Award, Women Against Abuse; Law Scholar, Duke Univ Law Sch. **Special Achievements:** Miss Illinois, 1991; Miss America, 1991. **Business Addr:** News Anchor, Ohio News Network, 770 Twin Rivers Dr, Columbus, OH 43215, **Business Phone:** (614)280-6300.

**VINCENT, MARK SINCLAIR. See DIESEL, VIN.**

### VINCENT, TROY DARNELL
Football player, executive. **Personal:** Born Jun 8, 1971, Trenton, NJ; married Tommi; children: Desire, Troy Jr, Taron, Hadassah Grace & Tanner Abraham. **Educ:** Thomas Edison State Col, BA, lib arts, 2007. **Career:** Miami Dolphins, defensive back & left corner back, 1992-95; Philadelphia Eagles, left corner back & corner back, 1996-2003; Buffalo Bills, free safety & corner back, 2004-06; Wash Redskins, 2006; NFL Players Asn, Bd Player Rep & vpres, pres, 2004-08; NFL's Active Player Develop, vpres, 2010; NFL Player Engagement Orgn & vpres, 2011; nat football league, head Football Opers, 2014-currently. **Orgs:** Founder, Love Thy Neighbor; Prof Bus Financial Network; Christian Athletes United Spiritual Empowerment; Christian Bus Network; All Pro Dad; parter, FeedChildren, 2010; bd dirs, Univ Wis Found. **Honors/Awds:** Ed Block Courage Award, 1994, 2000-01; Pro Bowl, 1999-2003; All-Pro selection, 2000-02; Troy Vincent Day declared by NJ General Assembly, 2001; Walter Payton Man of the Year, 2002; "Whizzer" White NFL Man of the Year, 2002; Humanitarian of the Year Award, 2003; Bart Starr Award, 2004; NFL Man of the Year, Nj Sports Writers Asn, 2004; Ameriquest Mortgage Neighborhood MVP, 2004; Pennsbury High School Athletic Hall of Fame, 2004; Urban Education Leadership Award, 2007; Warner Award, 2008; University of Wisconsin Hall of Fame, 2008; Distinguished Alumnus Award, Thomas Edison State Col, 2008; All Time Roster, Univ of Wis Badgers, 2009; Pennsylvania Sports Hall of Fame, 2009; Best NFL Player by Jersey Number 23, 2010; Leadership in Sport Award, 2011; Eagles Hall of Fame, 2012. **Special Achievements:** TV & Film appearance: 1992 NFL Draft, 1992; 1992 AFC Championship Game, 1993; "NFL Monday Night Football", 1993-2003; "ESPN's Sunday Night Football", 1994-2005; "NFL NBC", 1995; "NFL FOX", 1996; "Wheel Fortune", 2003; "Katie", 2013; "60 Minutes Sports ", 2014. **Business Addr:** Head Football Operation, 345 Park Ave, New York, NY 10154, **Business Phone:** (212)450-2000.

### VINSON, ANTHONY CHO (TONY VINSON)
Football player. **Personal:** Born Mar 13, 1971, Frankfurt. **Educ:** Purdue Univ; Towson Univ. **Career:** Football player (retired); London Monarchs, running back, 1996; Baltimore Ravens, running back, 1997-99; Atlanta Falcons, running back, 1999. **Honors/Awds:** Towson Hall of Fame, 2005. **Home Phone:** (410)857-2569.

### VINSON, CHUCK RALLEN
Television director. **Personal:** Born Jul 14, 1956, Elkhart, IN; son of Ray and Charlotte Moxley; married Pamela; children: 2. **Educ:** Ball State, Muncie, Ind, attended 1975; Los Angeles Col, Los Angeles, Calif, attended 1980. **Career:** Director: Benson, stage mgr, 1980-84; Carsey/Werner Productions, 'Cosby Show', stage mgr, 1984-87, dir, 1986-92; HBO Spec, Sinbad, Atlanta, GA, dir, 1990; Films: Sinbad: Son of a Preacher Man, 1996; The Right Connections, 1997; Jamie Foxx: I Might Need Security, 2002; Latham Entertainment Presents, 2003; Tall, Dark, & Funny, 2005; A. **Honors/Awds:** The 19th Annual People's Choice Awards, 1993; The 12th Annual Stellar Gospel Music Awards, 1997; 29th NAACP Image Awards, 1998; The 13th Annual Stellar Gospel Music Awards, 1998; The 29th NAACP Image Awards, 1998; The 14th Annual Stellar Gospel Music Awards, 1999; 30th NAACP Image Awards, 1999; The 15th Annual Stellar Gospel Music Awards, 2000; 31st NAACP Image Awards, 2000; NAACP Music Image Awards, 2001; 17th Annual Stellar Gospel Music Awards, 2002; 18th Annual Stellar Gospel Music Awards, 2003. **Home Addr:** 4229 Fair Ave, Studio City, CA 91602, **Home Phone:** (818)753-8688. **Business Addr:** Director, c/o Latham Entertainment, Greensboro, NC 27408, **Business Phone:** (336)315-1440.

### VINSON, NATHAN
Association executive, executive. **Personal:** Born Aug 29, 1937, Detroit, MI; son of Adam and Annie; married Nora; children: Tyrone & Kimberly. **Educ:** Wayne State Univ, BS, bus admin, 1970; Henry Ford Community Col, Dearborn, 1973; Univ Wis-Madison, cert, personal mgt, 1974. **Career:** Owner & mgr, Vince Rec Shop, 1970-80; City Detroit; Gen Motors, 1975-96; Phoenix Job Develop Serv Inc, bd dir, pres, 1990-2007; Vince Mkt & Real Estate Mgt Inc, 1990-; Arbitrator Better Bus Bur, 2000; Motown First Fed Credit Union, bd dir, chmn, pres, 1999-2007; NRCC Bus Adv Coun, hon chmn, 2004-07; pres, Northwest Detroit Lions Club. **Orgs:** Pres, Holbrook Ave Fed Credit Union, 1984-88;pres, Dash Club Inc, 1986-95; bd dir, Phonix Job Develop Serv Inc; state coordr, community opers AARP, 1996-2000; liaison, labor & relig groups, 2000; pres bd dir, Motown First Fed Credit Union, 1999-2007; hon chmn, NRCC Bus Adv Coun, 2004-07; Nat Asn Advan Colored People; Nat Panel Consumer Arbitrators; Coalition Black Trades Unionists. **Honors/Awds:** Director of the Year, Nat Ctr Credit Unions. **Business Addr:** Board President, Chairman, Motown First Federal Credit Union, 2112 Holbrook St, Hamtramck, MI 48212, **Business Phone:** (313)872-1277.

**VINSON, ROSALIND ROWENA. See Obituaries Section.**

**VINSON, TONY. See VINSON, ANTHONY CHO.**

### VIOLENUS, DR. AGNES A.
Educator, executive. **Personal:** Born May 17, 1931, New York, NY; daughter of Antonio and Constance. **Educ:** Hunter Col, BA, 1952; Columbia Univ Teachers Col, MA, 1958; Bank St Col, prof cert comput educ, 1984; Nova Southeastern Univ, EdD, 1990. **Career:** New York State Educ Dept, head teacher day care ctr, 1952-53; NYC Bd Educ, teacher common br, 1953-66; New York, bd Educ, asst prin elem sch, 1966-91; City Col New York, adj adv, open educ prog, 1974-75, adj teacher mentor prog, 1990-91; York Col, Continuing Educ Div, adj instr comput, 1985-87; City Col New York, supvr stud teachers, 1997-; Hunter Col, adj lectr, 1998-; Hunter Col, Alumni Assoc, pres, 2005-. **Orgs:** Asst secy, Bank St Alumni Coun, 1991-93; New York Club Nat Asn Negro Bus & Prof Women, co-chair scholar comn, 1991-99; bd dir, New York Affilate Nat Black Child Develop Inst, 1992-; New York Acad Sci, partic scientist sch prog, 1994-; pres, Schomburg Corp, 1995-98; treas sec, bd dir, Hunter Col Alumni Asn, 1995-; vpres, treas, New York Pub Libr Vols, 1996-99; bd dir, Hunter Col Scholar & Welfare Fund, 1997-; pres, Manhattan Psychiat Ctr, bd visitor, 1999-. **Home Addr:** 626 Riverside Dr Suite 24P, New York, NY 10031, **Home Phone:** (212)862-3431. **Business Addr:** President, Hunter College, 695 Pk Ave 10th Fl Rm E1022, New York, NY 10065, **Business Phone:** (212)650-3850.

**VISHER, MARSHA WATTS. See WATTS, MARSHA.**

### VIVIAN, DR. CORDY TINDELL
Clergy, executive director, president (organization). **Personal:** Born Jul 30, 1924, Howard County, MO; son of Robert Cordy and Euzetta; married W Octavia Geans; children: Jo Anna, Denise, Cordy Jr, Kira, Mark, Charisse & Albert. **Educ:** Western Ill Univ, BA, 1948; Am Baptist Theol Sem, BD, 1958; Western Ill Univ, doctorate, 1987. **Career:** Nat Baptist Conv, USA Inc, nat dir, 1955-61; 1st Community Church, pastor, 1956-61; Cosmo Community Church, pastor, 1961-63; SCLC, nat dir, 1962-67; Shaw Univ, minister, 1972-73, nat dir sem without walls, 1974-; Black Action Strategies Info Ctr Inc, bd chmn, dir & pres, currently; Wartburg Theol Sem, vis prof. **Orgs:** Vpres, Nat Asn Advan Colored People, 1953; bd chmn, Nat Anti-Klan Network; Nat Black Leadership Roundtable; chmn, Southern Organizing Comn Educ Fund; bd mem, Inst Black World; bd mem, Int United Black Fund; co-dir, Southern Reg Twentieth Anniversary March Wash Jobs Peace Freedom; bd mem, Southern Christian Leadership Conf; Southern Organizing Comn; Nat Coun Black Churchmen; African Inst Study Human Values; bd mem, Capitol City Bank Trust Co; chair bd, Black Action Strategies & Info Ctr; Racial Justice Working Group; Southern Christian Leadership Conf; Nat Coun Churches; Int Lect & Consult Tours Africa, Tokyo, Isreal, Holland, Manila, Japan. **Honors/Awds:** Hon doctorate, New Sch Social Res, 1984; Editor the Baptist, Layman Mag for Baptist Men; Listed in 1000 Successful Blacks, The Ebony Success Library, Odyssey; A Journey Through Black Amer; From Montgomery to Memphis, Clergy in Action Training; Unearthing Seeds of Fire; The Idea of Highlander, The Trouble I've Seen; Trumpet Award, 2006. **Special Achievements:** Author Black Power & The American Myth, 1970; American Joseph Date & Fact Book of Black America. **Home Addr:** 1328 Cascade Falls Dr SW, Atlanta, GA 30311-3655, **Home Phone:** (404)505-0472. **Business Addr:** President, Southern

Christian Leadership Conference, 320 Auburn Ave NE, Atlanta, GA 30303, **Business Phone:** (404)52-21420.

### VIVIANS, NATHANIEL ROOSEVELT

Engineer, educator. **Personal:** Born Feb 6, 1937, Mobile, AL; son of Charlie and Ella Lett Sellers; married Dorothy C Willis; children: Venita Natalie & Mark Anthony. **Educ:** Tuskegee Inst, BSEE, elec & electronics engineering, 1961; Univ Dayton, MS, eng, 1975, MS, mgt sci, 1977. **Career:** Engineer (retired); Aeronaut Systs Div, elec eng, 1964-71, prog mgr, 1971-80, tech advr, 1980-85, techn dir, 1985-87, co-dep, 1987; Univ Wilberforce, asst prof, 1980-90. **Orgs:** Basileus Omega Psi Phi Fraternity, 1957-; EEO counr, Aeronaut Systs Div, 1969-; trustee, Holy Trinity Am Church, 1975-; chap pres, Nat Soc Prof Eng, 1970-; pres, WCPOVA, 1974-80; Sigma Pi Phi Fraternity; Lambda Epsilon Alumni. **Honors/Awds:** Outstanding Service, NSPE Greene Xenia, 1975; Commendation, ASD/AE WPAFB, 1978; Man of the year, Omega Psi Phi Fraternity, 1980; Outstanding performance, Aeronaut Syst Div, 1983-84, 1986-90; Parent of the Year, Tuskegee Univ, 1988; 100 Men of Distinction. **Home Addr:** 3479 Plantation Pl, Dayton, OH 45434-7330, **Home Phone:** (937)427-2717.

### VOGEL, DR. ROBERTA BURRAGE

Psychologist, educator. **Personal:** Born Jun 13, 1938, Georgetown, SC; daughter of Vivian Helen Bessellieu and Demosthenes Edwin Burrage Sr; children: Duane Stephen & Shoshana Lynn. **Educ:** Temple Univ, Philadelphia, PA, BA, 1960, MA, 1962; Mich State Univ, E Lansing, MI, PhD, 1967; Ackerman Inst Family Ther, New York, NY, post-doctoral cert, 1981. **Career:** Mich State Univ, E Lansing, Mich, instr, 1966-67, asst prof, 1967-68; Ctr Chg, New York, NY, co-leader & staff mem, 1970-72; N Richmond Comm Ment Health, Staten Island, NY, staff psychologist, 1971-72; City Univ NY, Col Staten Island, NY, asst prof & counr, 1972-74, assoc prof, 1974-78, SEEK Prog, dep dir & coordr coun, 1978-, Off Spec Prog, 1981-88, prof, currently; RH Clark Assocs, consult & eval res, 1978-83; Steinway Family & Child Develop Ctr, consult & psychologist, 1984-88; Harlem-Dowling Child & Family Servs, Consult & psychologist, 1989-. **Orgs:** Res fel, Nat Inst Health, 1964; dir clin serv, Black Psychol Inst, NY Asn Black Psychologists, 1978-81; adv bd mem, NY Urban League, Staten Island Br, 1980-; pres, NY Asn Black Psychologists, 1982-83; Staten Island Human Rights Adv Comm, 1986-; bd mem, Staten Island Ment Health Soc, 1987-; Staten Island Task Force AIDS, 1988-; comnr, NY Black Leadership Comn AIDS, 1988; Nat Asn Prof Women; fac advisor, XAE Hon Soc. **Home Addr:** 173 St Paul, Staten Island, NY 10301, **Home Phone:** (718)816-7272. **Business Addr:** Professor, Deputy Director & Coordinator of Counseling, City University of New York, Rm 1A Bldg 112 2800 Victory Blvd, Staten Island, NY 10314, **Business Phone:** (718)982-2410.

### VOLDASE, IVA SNEED

Aerospace engineer, manager. **Personal:** Born Nov 9, 1934, Frankston, TX; daughter of Mr Bynus Sneed; children: 2. **Educ:** Prairie View A&M Univ, BA, math, 1954; El Camino Col, AA, math, 1977; Univ San Francisco, BS, 1983; Calif State Univ, Dominguez Hills, comput sci, 1988. **Career:** Aerospace engineer (retired); N Am Aviation, math analyst, jr eng, 1954-59; STL, comput, math analyst, 1960-61; STL becomes TRW Inc, sr mem tech staff, Cost Estimation Off, mgr, 1961. **Orgs:** Pres, Carson Black Heritage Asn, 1969-; Harriet Tubman Sch Unwed Mothers, original charter bd mem, 1970-90; pres, Nat Coun Negro Women, 1976-90; pres, TRW SEA Bootstrap, 1976-78; affiliate, Int COCOMO Users group, 1989-; speaker, Soc of Cost Est & Analysis, 1989; Int Soc speaker, Parametic Analysts, 1990-; ast gen coord, United Christian Women, 1995-97. **Honors/Awds:** Women of Achievement Award, TRW DSSG Nat Women's Week, 1978; Community Serv Award, Vols of Am, 1983; Outstanding Software Parametic Tech Paper, Int Soc Parametic Analysts, 1997; Top Minority Women in Sci & Eng, Jour NTA, 1996; Black Engr of the Year, Community Serv, Coun Eng Deans of Historically Black Colleges & Career Communications Group, 1995. **Special Achievements:** Not All COCOMOs Are Alike, Technical Paper presented at a REVIC Conf, published, 1991; Parametic Modelling at TRW, SSCAG Symposium, published, 1997; The Use of Parametic Models for Historical Data, IConf, published, 1997; Software Modelling Risk Management, technical class, class book, 1996; Minority Women in the Aerospace Labor Market, Career Conf for Women, 1978; Speaks fluent Spanish; One among 25 black women in the US to enter into the Aerospace Engineering field in 1954 working on early US Satellites. **Home Addr:** 19419 Tajauta Ave, Carson, CA 90746, **Home Phone:** (323)636-9429.

### VOORHIES, LARK

Actor. **Personal:** Born Mar 25, 1974, Nashville, TN; daughter of Tricia; married Miguel Coleman; married Andy Prince; children: 1. **Career:** Third Degree, founder & lead singer; Lark Voorhies Productions & Voorhies Mgt Inc, co founder; Films: Saved by the Bell: Hawaiian Style, sound track, 1992; Saved by the Bell: Wedding in Las Vegas, 1994; The Last Don, 1997; Def Jam's How to Be a Player, 1997; Longshot, 2000; How High, 2001; Civil Brand, 2002; The Next Hit, associate producer, 2008; Mimi's Place, 2009; Redemption, 2010; Measure of Faith, 2011; Little Creeps, 2012; Closer to God: Jessica's Journey, 2012; The Comeback Kids, 2014. TV series: "It's OK to Be a Kid", 1987; "Small Wonder", 1988; "Good Morning, Miss Bliss", 1988-89; "Saved by the Bell", 1989-93; "The Fresh Prince of Bel-Air", 1992; Saved by the Bell: Hawaiian Style, 1992; "Martin", 1993; "Getting By", 1993; "Days of Our Lives", 1993-94; "Saved by the Bell: The College Years", 1994; Saved by the Bell: Wedding in Las Vegas, 1994; "Me & the Boys", 1994; "Saved by the Bell: The New Class", 1994; "CBS School break Special", 1995; "Star Trek: Deep Space Nine", 1995; "Family Matters", 1995; "What About Your Friends", 1995; "The Bold & The Beautiful", 1995-96; "In the House", 1997-99; "The Last Don", 1997; "Malcolm & Eddie", 1997; "In the House", 1997-98; "The Love Boat: The Next Wave", 1998; "Mutiny", 1999; "The Parkers", 1999; "Grown Ups", 2000; Fire & Ice", 2001; "Widows", 2002; Boo Cocky, 2008; "Robot Chicken", 2008; "Black to the Future", 2009. **Honors/Awds:** Young Artist Award, 1990 & 1993. **Business Addr:** Actress, c/o Gold Marshak Liedtke & Associates, 3500 W Olive Ave Suite 1400, Burbank, CA 91505, **Business Phone:** (818)972-4300.

# W

### WADDELL, RUCHADINA LADESIREE

Lawyer. **Personal:** Born Feb 21, 1965, Wilmington, NC; daughter of Charles R and Ruth Weaver. **Educ:** Univ NC, Greensboro, NC, BS, 1985; Univ Wis, Sch Law, JD, 1989. **Career:** Dept Indust Labor & Human Rels, admin law judge, 1990-91; Dept Health Social Servs, asst legal coun, 1992; Grant Co, corp coun, 1992-94; Walworth Co, asst corp coun, 1994-97; Law Off Ruchadina L Waddell, lawyer, 1997-; Guilford County Atty'S Off, lawyer, currently. **Orgs:** Wis State Bar Asn; Grant County Bar Asn; Dane County Bar Asn; Phi Delta Phi; Delta Sigma Theta Sorority; fel AOF, Univ Wis, Law Sch, 1987-89; Nc State Bar. **Home Addr:** 3844 Battleground Ave Apt 32, Greensboro, NC 27410, **Home Phone:** (336)282-4290. **Business Addr:** Lawyer, Guilford County Attorney'S Office, 301 W Market St, Greensboro, NC 27402, **Business Phone:** (336)641-4913.

### WADDY, JUDE MICHAEL

Football player, executive. **Personal:** Born Sep 12, 1975, Washington, DC. **Educ:** William & Mary Col, BS, kinesiology & biology, 1998. **Career:** Football player (retired), owner; Green Bay Packers, linebacker, 1998-99; Tampa Bay Buccaneers, 2001; Denver Broncos, 2002; Berlin Thunder, linebacker, 2002; Physipet LLC, founder; San Diego Chargers, linebacker, 2003; Gogo Inflight, Mkt Mgr, 2007-09; Mirrorball, Producer-Mirrorball Group, 2009-10; Am Express, Event Mgr, 2010-12; Smith & Nephew, Endoscopy Sales Rep, 2012-15; Stryker, Med Sales Rep, 2015-. **Orgs:** NFL Players Asn, pres, 2008. **Honors/Awds:** All-National Football League Europe, 2002; World Bowl champion (X). **Home Addr:** 139 Post Oak Rd, Yorktown, VA 23693. **Business Addr:** Founder, PhysiPet LLC, 100 S Eola Dr, Orlando, FL 32801.

### WADE, ACHILLE MELVIN

School administrator. **Personal:** Born Nov 5, 1943, Clarksville, TN; son of Bennie Albert and Electra M Freeman; married Angela Nash; children: Chaka L. **Educ:** Okla State Univ, BA, speech commun, 1966, MA, speech commun, 1969; Univ Tex, folklore & antropology. **Career:** Black Studies Ctr, Univ Calif Santa Barbara, acting dir, 1969-70; Black Studies Univ Omaha, Nebr, dir, 1970-71; Black Studies Vassar Col, dir, 1971-73; Black Studies Univ Austin Tex, lectr, 1973-86; Moorhead State Univ Minn, Minority Stud Affairs, coordr, 1988-89; Yale Univ, asst dean studs, dir, Afro-Am Cultural Ctr, 1989-92; Upward Bound, Univ Bridgeport, Conn, dir, 1993; Univ RI, Multicultural Ctr, dir, 1994-. **Orgs:** Arts Comn City Austin, 1981-; bd mem, Laguna Gloria Art Mus, 1982-84; pres, Tex Asn Study Afro-Am Life & Hist Inc, 1986-88; bd mem, CTA fro-Am Hist Soc, 1990-; first pres & secy, Northeast Multicultural Col Adminr Asn, 1995; bd mem, New Haven Ethnic Hist Ctr, 1990-92; chmn, RI Multicultural Dirs Group, 1998; coordr, New Eng Higher Educ Resource Ctr, 2003. **Honors/Awds:** Melvin Wade Day, Univ RI, 2002. **Home Addr:** 7305 Grand Canyon D, Austin, TX 78752, **Home Phone:** (401)273-8684. **Business Addr:** Director, University of Rhode Island, 74 Lower Col Rd, Kingston, RI 02881, **Business Phone:** (401)874-2851.

### WADE, BERYL ELAINE

Lawyer, government official. **Personal:** Born Jul 1, 1956, Wilmington, DE; daughter of Clarence W R and Geneva M S. **Educ:** Univ NC, Chapel Hill, CA, BA, 1977; Univ Mich, Sch Law, JD, 1980. **Career:** Cumberland Co Dist Attys Off, asst dist atty, 1980-82; NCA Sen Tony Rand, campaign coordr, 1982; NJ Justice Acad, legal instr, 1982-84; City Fayetteville Police Dept, asst city atty & police atty, 1984-93; State NC, dep legis coun, off gov, 1993-95; Coun Gov James B Hunt Jr, 1996-. **Orgs:** Cumberland Co Bar Asn, 1980-93, Cumberland Co Bd HTH, 1988-94; NC State Bar, 1980-; comnr, ADM Rules Rev CMS, 1985-90, 1992-; bd gov, NC Asn Black Lawyers, 1985-91, asst secy, 1991-; secy & treas, NCA Asn Police Attys, 1987, pres, 1988; bd gov, United Way, 1988, chair, Nominating Comt, 1991, chair, Proj Blueprint Comt, 1991-92, NCP, 1981-; trustee, Col Heights Presby Church, 1990; bd visitor, UNC-CH, 1996-. **Honors/Awds:** Partial Award, 7th Dist Black Leadership Caucus, 1984. **Home Addr:** 303 S King Charles Rd, Raleigh, NC 27610-2738, **Home Phone:** (919)250-0083. **Business Addr:** Counsel to the Governor, North Carolina State Government, 424 N Blount St, Raleigh, NC 27601-2817, **Business Phone:** (919)733-2698.

### WADE, BRENT JAMES

Manager, writer. **Personal:** Born Sep 19, 1959, Baltimore, MD; son of James Bennett and Sylvia; married Yvette Jackson; children: Wesley & Claymore Dotson. **Educ:** Univ Md, BA, Eng, 1981; George Washington Univ, Master's cert, proj mgt, 1996. **Career:** Westinghouse Elec Corp, mkt rep, 1981-87; LSI Logic Corp, mkt mgr, 1987-89; Alcatel-Lucent, acct mgr, 1989-94, AT&T Network Systs, sr progs & sales realization mgr, 1994-96, Global Com Markets, dir, proj mgt global com markets, 1996-98, sales dir emerging serv providers, 1998-2001, dir, acct mgt verizon wireline data acct, 2001-03, sales dir, lucent-juniper channel develop & sales, 2003-05, sales mgr, AT&T mobility md/dc/va/wva markets, 2005-13; Ciena Govt Solutions Inc, acct dir, civilian healthcare, sci, optical &virtual networking solutions sales, 2013-15; ExteNet Systs Inc, Sales AT&T Acct Team, exec dir, 2015-. **Special Achievements:** Author: Company Man, novel, 1992. **Home Addr:** 108 Bayview Dr, Chapel Hill, NC 27516-9232. **Business Addr:** Executive Director, ExteNet Systems Inc, 3030 E Warrenville Rd Suite 340, Lisle, IL 60532, **Business Phone:** (630)505-3800.

### WADE, HON. CASEY, JR.

Government official, mayor. **Personal:** Born Oct 7, 1930, Pickens, MS; son of Casey Sr and Kate; married Doris Taylor; children: Robert, Diane & Joycherie. **Career:** Northfield Sq mall, security guard; Ill Dept Ment Health, Kankakee, security officer, 1966; Village Sun River Terr, founder, mayor. **Orgs:** Minister, Pleasant Grove Baptist Church, 1980-; mayor, Village Sun River Terr, 1980-; Kankakee County Mayors Asn, 1988; Nat Asn Advan Colored People, 1982-; Teachers Union, 1987-; Leadership Inst Black Mayors Cert, 1990; Black Mayors Asn, 1990-. **Home Addr:** 123 N Riverwood Rd, St. Anne, IL 60964, **Home Phone:** (815)937-1219. **Business Addr:** Minister, Pleasant Grove Baptist Church, 908 Martin Luther King Jr Dr, Springfield, IL 62703, **Business Phone:** (217)522-2513.

### WADE, DAISY GRIFFIN HARRIS. See HARRIS, DAISY.

### WADE, DWYANE

Basketball player. **Personal:** Born Jan 17, 1982, Chicago, IL; son of Dwyane Sr and JoLinda; married Gabrielle Union; married Siohvaughn Funches; children: Zaire Blessing Dwyane & Zion Malachi Airamis; children: Xavier Zachariah. **Educ:** Marquette Univ, Wis, attended. **Career:** Marquette Univ Basketball Team, shooting guard, 2001-03; NBA Miami Heat, shooting guard, 2003-16; Chicago Bulls, 2016-. **Orgs:** Co-founder, Athletes Relief Fund Haiti, 2010. **Honors/Awds:** NBA All-Rookie Team, 2004; 2004 Summer Olympics, Team USA, Bronze Medal; Best Breakthrough Athlete ESPY Award, 2005; NBA All-Star, 2005-14; Best Breakthrough Athlete ESPY Award, 2005; NBA Finals, MVP, 2006; NBA champion with Miami Heat, 2006, 2012-13; Best NBA Player ESPY Award, 2006; "Sports Illustrated", Sportsman of the Year, 2006; "Sporting News", Sportsman of the Year, 2006; 2006 FIBA World Championship, Team USA, Bronze Medal; 2008 Summer Olympics, Team USA, Gold Medal; NBA All-Star MVP, 2010; NBA Community Assist Award, 2012-13. **Special Achievements:** Author "A Father First: How My Life Became Bigger than Basketball" ; selected as fifth overall selection in 2003 NBA draft; participated in 2008 Summer Olympics basketball team; has had top-selling jersey in 2013-14; Miami's all-time leading scorer in history; Movie: What to Expect When You're Expecting, 2012.

### WADE, DR. EUGENE HENRY-PETER

Physician. **Personal:** Born Nov 20, 1954, Washington, DC; son of Samuel and Dorothy Heyward Vallentine; married Portia Battle; children: Kim M, Eugene Henry-Peter II & Kara. **Educ:** Brown Univ, AB, ScB, 1978; Howard Univ, Col Med, MD, 1981; Univ Ala, Post-grad training. **Career:** Univ Ala Col Community Health Sci, resident, 1981-84; Alamance Regional Med Ctr, pvt pract; Memorial Hosp Alamance Co, pvt pract; Cornerstone Med Ctr, family physician. **Orgs:** Co-chmn, NC Acad Family Physicians, Minority Affair Comm; Indigent Care Task Force NC Med Soc; NC Gen Assembly Indigent Health Care Study Commr; diplo, Am Acad Family Physicians. **Home Addr:** 3218 Hiddenwood Lane, Burlington, NC 27215. **Business Addr:** Physician, Cornerstone Medical Centre, 1041 Kirkpatrick Rd Suite 100, Burlington, NC 27215, **Business Phone:** (336)538-0565.

### WADE, HAWATHA TERRELL. See WADE, TERRELL.

### WADE, JAMES NATHANIEL

Executive. **Personal:** Born Oct 2, 1933, Paterson, NJ; son of Edward and Eleanor; children: Valarie, JaJa & Atiba. **Educ:** Voorhees Col, AA, 1954; St Augustine Col, Raleigh, NC, BA, 1956; Howard Univ, MSW, community orgn, 1967; Univ Pittsburgh, PhD, higher educ admin, 1975. **Career:** Del County Juv Ct, juv probation officer, 1959-60; Philadelphia City Policeman, 1960-63; Erie Community Action Comt, dep opers, 1967-69; Erie Urban Coalition, exec dir, 1968-71; Dept Community Affairs & Commonwealth, dep secy, 1971-74, gov spec asst, 1974-75, secy admin, 1975-79; Wade Commun Inc, chmn bd. **Orgs:** Chmn, First & Second Philadelphia United Negro Col Fund; vpres, Basan Develop; exec comt, Crisis Intervention Network; bd mem, Philadelphia Dance Co; bd mem, Congreso De Latinos Unidos Inc; life mem, Nat Asn Advan Colored People; life mem, Kappa Alpha Psi; Nat Black MBA Asn; Bay City Masonic Lodge; bd chmn, Walt Disney Cancer Memorial Inst; trustee, Orlando Sci Ctr. **Home Addr:** 2280 Bryn Mawr, Philadelphia, PA 19131.

### WADE, DR. JOSEPH DOWNEY (JOE WADE)

School administrator, football coach. **Personal:** Born Jan 16, 1938, Beaumont, TX; son of Rufus and Lorene; married Judith Allen; children: Stacy & Joseph Jr. **Educ:** Ore State Univ, BS, 1959, MEd, 1961; Univ Ore, PhD, 1982. **Career:** Educator (retired); Compton Col, head football coach, 1969-71; Univ Ore, asst football coach, 1972-75, assoc dir admis, 1975-76, assoc dir, acad adv & stud serv, 1976-84, dir, acad adv & stud serv, adminr, dir, acad adv & stud serv. **Orgs:** Comnr, chair, Ore Comn Black Affairs; univ senate, Fac Adv Coun; exec coun, Nat Stud Exchange; bd trustee, Northwest Christian Col. **Home Addr:** 5260 Saratoga St, Eugene, OR 97405, **Home Phone:** (541)342-7318.

### WADE, JOYCE K.

Banker, vice president (organization). **Personal:** Born May 2, 1949, Chicago, IL; daughter of Ernest S Sr and Martha L Davis. **Educ:** Northwestern Univ, Evanston IL, BS, educ, 1970; Univ Chicago, IL, MBA, finance & gen, 1977. **Career:** US Dept Housing & Urban Develop, Chicago, Ill, housing rep, 1970-78; Ill Housing Develop Authority, Chicago develop off rep, 1978-79; Community Bank Lawndale, chicago loan off rep, 1979-87, chief exec officer, 1988-90, mem bd dir, 1988-, vpres, sr loan officer; CHAs Housing Mgt Opers Div, financial mgt adminr, 1990-92; Spertus Col, Chicago, adj fac, budgeting & financial mgt; Chicago Housing Authority, Sect 8 Housing Progs, dir, 1993-95; Habilitative Systs inc, vpres finance, 1998-; Women's Bus Develop Ctr, dir, 1995-98. **Orgs:** Treas, Carole Robertson Ctr Learning, 1980-; mem bd control, treas & chair Loan Comn, Neighborhood Network & Housing Serv; Marshall Sq & Douglas Pk, 1984-; Urban Renewal Bd City Chicago, 1987-; treas, Nat Asn Negro Bus & Prof Women, 1987-; dir, Am Civil Liberties Union Ill, 1988-; Urban Bankers Forum Chicago, 1988-. **Honors/Awds:** Marilyn V Singleton Award, US Dept HUD, 1975; Bank Operation Outstanding Student Award, Asn Bank Oper Mgt, 1980; Positive Self Image Award, Westside Ctr Truth, 1988; Outstanding Service Award, Carole Robertson Ctr, 1989. **Special Achievements:** Top 100 Business & Professional Women, Dollars & Sense Magazine, 1988. **Home Addr:** 1050 W Berwyn, Chicago, IL 60640, **Home Phone:** (312)561-3197. **Business Addr:** Vice President Finance, Habilitative Systems Inc, 415 S Kilpatrick, Chicago, IL 60644, **Business Phone:** (773)854-8300.

## WADE, KIM MACHE
Beautician, playwright. **Personal:** Born Sep 25, 1957, Manhattan, NY; daughter of Curtis L (deceased) and Rosa Jean; children: Rossi Jewel & Courtney Semaj. **Educ:** A&T State Univ, attended 1973; Univ NC, Greensboro, attended 1974; Shaw Univ, attended 1978; Sandhills Community Col, BA, lic cosmetology, 1986. **Career:** Moore County Arts Coun, playwright/producer, 1984; Innervision Theater Co, producer/playwright/dir, 1984-; Hometown News Mag, assoc ed, 1984-; Sandhills Community Col, instr; Mache Beauty Sta, owner. **Orgs:** Nat Asn Advan Colored People; Moore Co Chapter, 1975-; summer youth counr, Southern Pines Recreation Dept, 1984-85; missionary, Harrington Chapel Young Adult Missionary, 1986-; active coordr, Ebonette Cultural Club, 1986-. **Honors/Awds:** Young Black Achiever Award, Black History Month Observation, 1986. **Home Addr:** 240 S Stephens St, Southern Pines, NC 28387-4634, **Home Phone:** (910)692-4518. **Business Addr:** Owner, Mache Beauty Sta, 388 N Stephens St, Southern Pines, NC 28387.

## WADE, HON. LYNDON ANTHONY
Social worker, executive. **Personal:** Born Jun 30, 1934, Atlanta, GA; married Shirley M; children: Lisa, Nora, Jennifer & Stuart. **Educ:** Morehouse Col, AB, 1956; Atlanta Univ, MSW, 1958; Menninger Found Topeka Kans, adv cert psychol social work, 1963. **Career:** Social worker, executive (retired); Emory Univ, asst prof, 1963-68; Atlanta Urban League Inc, pres & chief exec officer, 1968. **Orgs:** bd dir, Metrop Atlanta Rapid Transit Authority, 1971-85; Acad Cert Social Workers; Atlanta Action Forum; Nations Bank Com Reinvestment Comn; Jr League Adv Comt; Vision 20/20 Task Force; Atlanta Comt Pub Educ; life mem, Cent United Methodist Church; Am Bar Asn. **Honors/Awds:** Distinguished Community Service Award, Atlanta Morehouse Alumni Club, 1965; Distinguished Service Award, Fulton City Medical Soc, 1971; Social Worker of the Year, N Ga Chap NASW, 1971; 10 Years Outstanding Service, Atlanta Urban League, 1978-10. **Home Addr:** 3529 Lynfield Dr SW, Atlanta, GA 30311, **Home Phone:** (404)696-5847.

## WADE, NORMA ADAMS
Journalist. **Educ:** Univ Tex, Austin, BJ, jour, 1966. **Career:** Collins Radio Co Dallas, ed, proofer tech equip manuals, 1966-68; Bloom Advert Agency, Dallas, advert copywriter, prod asst, 1968-72; Post Tribune, Dallas, Tex, staff writer & asst ed, 1972-74; Dallas Morning News, Tex, staff writer & columnist, 1974-2002, writer, currently. **Orgs:** Dallas-Ft Worth Asn Black Communicators; founding mem, Nat Asn Black Journalists, 1974. **Honors/Awds:** Juanita Craft Award, Nat Asn Advan Colored People, 1985; Bronze Heritage Award, 1989; Lifetime Achievement Award, Dallas & Ft Worth Asn Black Communicators, 1994; She Knows Where She's Going Award, Girls Inc Metropolitan Dalls, 1998. **Special Achievements:** First African American fulltime reporter, Dallas Morning News, 1970; Only texan represented. **Home Addr:** PO Box 655237, Dallas, TX 75265. **Business Addr:** Writer, The Dallas Morning News, 508 Young St, Dallas, TX 75202, **Business Phone:** (214)977-8222.

## WADE, TERRELL (HAWATHA TERRELL WADE)
Baseball player. **Personal:** Born Jan 25, 1973, Rembert, SC; married Nicky Stokes; children: 1. **Career:** Baseball player (retired); Atlanta Braves, pitcher, 1995-97; Tampa Bay Devil Rays, pitcher, 1998; Cincinnati Reds, 1999; Houston Astros, pitcher, 2004; plumber, Atlanta area, Currently. **Home Addr:** 840 Greebvine Trace, Roswell, GA 30076.

## WADE, UNAV OPAL
Beautician, college administrator, barber. **Personal:** Born Jan 1, 1930; married Ernest; children: Gwendolyn, Gary, Aaron, Mike, Gregory, Margena & Ann. **Educ:** Morristown Normal Col; Col Alameda. **Career:** Charmetts Beauty Salon, owner, 1962-74; Unav's Salon Clothes Hats Wigs, owner, 1977-; Gen & Masonry Contractors, secy. **Orgs:** Secy, Alameda Br Nat Asn Advan Colored People, 1966-67; treasurer, Alameda Br Nat Asn Advan Colored People, 1968-69; pres, Alameda Br Nat Asn Advan Colored People, 1970-75; Jasper Beauticians Club, 1984-2000; chairwoman, Pvt Indust Coun, 1989-97; bd mem, Jasper Chamber Com, 1998; bd dir, Complete Health Serv; pres, Evergreen Baptist Church. **Home Addr:** 4698 FM 1747, Jasper, TX 75951, **Home Phone:** (409)384-3607. **Business Addr:** Owner, Unav's Salon Clothes Hats Wigs, 400 S Main St, Jasper, TX 75951, **Business Phone:** (731)824-3152.

## WADE, WILLIAM CARL
Manager, educator. **Personal:** Born Aug 24, 1934, Rocky Mount, VA; son of William Taft and Della Fox; married Mary Frances Prunty; children: Pamela Renee Stockard, Marcus Sidney & Carl Tracy. **Educ:** Franklin Univ, BS, 1968; Univ Dayton, MBA, 1972. **Career:** Ross Lab, financial reporting surv, 1966-72, credit mgr, 1976-77, customer serv & credit dir, 1977-90, fiscal serv dir, 1990-; Xerox Inc, acct analyst, 1972-74, credit mgr, 1974-76; Gen Motors, payroll acct, 1976; Franklin Univ, fac, currently. **Orgs:** Am Legion, 1965-; Franklin Univ Alumni Asn, 1968-; Univ Dayton Alumni Asn, 1972-; Exec's Club, 1977-, pres, 1991-93; Cent Ohio Treas Mgt Asn, 1990-. **Home Addr:** 3680 Parker Knoll Lane, Columbus, OH 43219-6209, **Home Phone:** (614)337-2368. **Business Addr:** Faculty, Franklin University, 201 S Grant Ave, Columbus, OH 43215, **Business Phone:** (614)947-6540.

## WADE-GAYLES, DR. GLORIA JEAN
Poet, writer, editor. **Personal:** Born Memphis, TN; daughter of Robert and Bertha Reese Willett; married Joseph Nathan; children: Jonathan & Monica. **Educ:** LeMoyne Col, BA, 1959; Boston Univ, MA, 1962; George Washington Univ, PhD, 1967; Emory Univ, PhD, 1981. **Career:** Woodrow Wilson fel, 1959-62; Spelman Coll, instr Eng, 1963-64, from asst prof to prof, 1984-92, eminent scholar prof, currently; Howard Univ, instr Eng, 1965-67, DuBois fel Harvard Univ; Morehouse Col, asst prof, 1970-75; Danforth fel, 1974; Emory Univ, grad teaching fel, 1975-77, adj prof African Am studies; Talladega Col, asst prof, 1977-78; UNCF Mellon Res grant, 1987-88; George Wash Univ, adj fac; Dillard Univ, eminent scholar chair, prof; Howard Univ, teacher. **Orgs:** Fel Woodrow wilson, Boston Univ, 1962; Teacher COFO Freedom Sch & Valley View MS, 1964; bd dir, WETV 30-WABE-FM, 1976-77; sec, Guardians Qual Educ, 1976-78; exec bd, Col Lang Asn, 1977; ed bd Callaloo, 1977-80; exec bd, Coll Lang asn, 1977-80; Nat Asn Advan Colored People, ASNLC, CORE; Alpha Kappa Alpha Sorority; partner, Jon-Mon Consults; dubois res fel, Harvard Univ, 1990, founding dir, SIS Oral Hist Proj. **Home Addr:** 3970 Thaxton Rd SW, Atlanta, GA 30331. **Business Addr:** Professor, Founding Director, Spelman College, 350 Spelman Lane SW, Atlanta, GA 30314, **Business Phone:** (404)270-5565.

## WADEN, FLETCHER NATHANIEL, JR.
Executive. **Personal:** Born Jan 30, 1928, Greensboro, NC; son of Fletcher Sr and Rosa P; children: Betty. **Educ:** Am Bus Inst, attended 1948; Winston-Salem State Univ, attended 1974; NC Agr & Tech State Univ, attended 1976; Univ NC, attended 1987. **Career:** Ritz Loan, owner, gen mgr, 1951-57; Gnato's C Clothing Store, owner, 1960-70; Gnato's Construct cpn, pres, owner, 1979-; Nat Financial & Bus Consult Inc, pres; Waden Supply Co Inc, pres, currently. **Orgs:** DAV & VFW; Nat Suppliers Develop Coun Inc; NCP; Bus Enterprise Legal Defense & Educ Fund Inc; US Dept Defense, Defense Mfrs & Suppliers Asn; Pub Serv Comn SC. **Honors/Awds:** Honorary chair, bus Adv coun; National Leadership Award, Bus Adv coun, 2002; Republican Gold Medal, 2002. **Business Addr:** President, Waden Supply Co Inc, 1401 E 5th St Apt 4, Winston-Salem, NC 27101-3350, **Business Phone:** (336)721-0308.

## WADSWORTH, ANDRE L.
Executive, football player. **Personal:** Born Oct 19, 1974, St. Croix; son of Andrew and Lylith; married Subyn; children: Sophia, Sarah, Selah & Sahmone. **Educ:** Fla State Univ, BA; MBA. **Career:** Football player (retired), executive; Tampa Bay Buccaneers, defensive end, 1998; Ariz Cardinals, left defensive end, 1998, defensive end, 1999-2000; New York Jets, 2007; Impact Church, co-founder & exec pastor, currently; Desert Life Church, Scottsdale, AZ, co-founder & exec pastor; All Pro Imports Automotive Group, owner. **Orgs:** Adv bd mem, Cactus Athletic Camps; bd mem, Mothers Awareness Sch-Age Kids, currently. **Honors/Awds:** Player of the Year, Atlantic Coast Conf, 1997; Defensive Player of the Year, Atlantic Coast Conf, 1997; Rookie of the Year, 1997; Hall of Fame, Fla State Univ, 2004. **Special Achievements:** First African American picked in 1998 NFL draft. **Home Addr:** 14003 N 99th Way, Scottsdale, AZ 85260-8851. **Business Addr:** Board Member, Mothers Awareness on School-Age Kids, 8937 E Bell Rd Suite 202, Scottsdale, AZ 85260, **Business Phone:** (480)502-5337.

## WAFER, DEBORAH
Physician. **Educ:** Calif State Univ-Northridge, Los Angeles, CA, 1974. **Career:** Univ Calif Los Angeles Med Ctr, nurse practr, 1985-99; Agouron Pharmaceut Inc, mgr, 1999-2005; Pfizer Inc, brand mgr, 2002-06; Gilead Sci, sr mgr, 2006-10; Gilead Sci Inc, nat acct mgr, 2010-13, sr mgr mkt, 2013-. **Orgs:** Bd mem, NAPWA, 2009-11. **Honors/Awds:** Corporate Award. **Business Addr:** Senior Manager HCV Marketing, Gilead Sciences, 333 Lakeside Dr, Foster City, CA 94404, **Business Phone:** (650)574-3000.

## WAGNER, ANNICE M.
Judge, government official. **Personal:** Born Jan 1, 1937, Washington, DC. **Educ:** Wayne State Univ, BA, JD. **Career:** Government offical, judge (retired); Nat Capital Housing Authority, gencoun, 1973-74; People's Counsel DC, staff, 1975-77; Super Ct DC, assoc judge, 1977-90; DC Ct Appeals, assoc judge, 1990; DC Supreme Ct, chief judge, 1994-2005; Harvard Univ, instr. **Orgs:** Bd trustee, United Planning Orgn; vpres, UPO Bd, 988; bd dir, Conf Chief Justices; Chair, Joint Comt Judicial Admin; Am Bar Asn comt on mediation law; chairperson, Comt Selection Dc Judicial Syst; Super Ct Rules Comt; Sentencing Guidelines Comn; chairperson, Cts Adv Comt; chairperson, Task Force Gender Bias Courts; chairperson bd dir, Nat Ctr State Courts; interim pres, Orgns Bd trustee; Trial Advocacy Workshop Harvard Law Sch;. **Business Addr:** DC.

## WAGNER, DAVID H. See Obituaries Section.

## WAGONER, J. ROBERT (TOM RIVERS)
Television producer, executive, writer. **Personal:** Born Mar 27, 1938, Concord, NC; son of Elijah James and Virginia L. **Educ:** Manhattan Sch Music, 1963; NC Agr & Tech State Univ, BS, Eng drama, 1968; Univ NC, MA, film, tv & drama, 1974; Univ Southern Calif Grad Sch Cinema, attended 1984. **Career:** NC Agr & Tech State Univ, lectr, photog, 1964-67; Black Jour, writer, producer, dir, camera, 1968-71; "Black Roots", cinematographer, 1970; Fayetteville State Univ, commun ctr designer, 1971-72; "Black Fantasy", cinematographer, 1972; Cap Cities Community, promotions mgr, 1974-75; Transvue Films, writer, dir, 1975-79; "Disco Godfather", writer & dir, 1979; Calif State Univ, Long Beach, assoc prof, 1980-83; Televersity, pres, chief exec officer, 1985-; Col Cable Channel, chair bd, chief exec officer, currently. **Orgs:** Bushido Int, grand master, NC A&T Alumni Karate-do, 1967-; bd chmn, Greater African Am, All Am Univ Marching Band, 1993-. **Honors/Awds:** Sci, Special Jefferson Broadcast Fel, Univ NC, 1968; Movie Lab Fel, Int Film Seminars, 1969; White House Photographer's Asn Award, Univ F & V Prod Asn, 1972; WGBH Fel, WGBH Ed Found, 1992; CPB SC Educ TV, delegate, Int TV Screen Conf, 1992. **Special Achievements:** One of six producers, Nat Acad TV Arts & Emmy, 1969; City of Pasadena & The Ralph Parsons Co, special directing citation, 1978; Author, Pieces of My Heart. **Home Addr:** 1226 Brynn Marr Rd, Jacksonville, NC 28546. **Business Addr:** President, Televersity, 179 E Franklin, Chapel Hill, NC 27514, **Business Phone:** (919)968-9836.

## WAGSTAFF, JACQUELINE
City council member. **Career:** Northeast Cent Durham-Partners Against Crime; Durham City Council, Chairperson; Durham County NC, Mayor, 2005-. **Orgs:** Bd mem, Durham Pub Sch. **Business Addr:** Member, Durham City Hall, Durham, NC 27701, **Business Phone:** (919)949-3731.

## WAIGUCHU, DR. JULIUS MURUKU
College teacher, educator. **Personal:** Born Nov 29, 1937; son of Mugure and Waiguchu Sr; children: 3. **Educ:** Cent Col, BA, polit sci, econ & bus admin, 1965; Queens Col, MA, pub admin, 1967; Temple Univ, PhD, pub admin, 1971. **Career:** St John's Univ, African Studies Ctr, instr, 1968-69; Rutgers Univ, Urban Univ, asst prof, 1969-70; William Paterson Col, NJ, assoc prof & chairperson, 1973-78, Pub Admin, prof, 1980, Sch Mgt, Dept Acct & Law, prof, currently; Univ Md, Col Pk, Off Minority Stud Educ, dir, 1978-80; Columbia Univ, Teacher's Col, lectr; Kenyan Govt, advisor & consult. **Orgs:** AHSA; ASA; NCBPS; ABSW; NJABE; INCCA; Am Soc Pub Admin. **Special Achievements:** Edited a book: Management of Organizations in Africa, Greenwood Publication Group, 1999. Authored Several Books, Monographs & Articles. **Home Addr:** 353 38 St, Paterson, NJ 07504-1327, **Home Phone:** (973)742-3176. **Business Addr:** Professor, William Paterson University, 300 Pompton Rd, Wayne, NJ 07470, **Business Phone:** (973)720-2000.

## WAINWRIGHT, GLORIA BESSIE
Government official. **Personal:** Born Jul 13, 1950, Cleveland, OH; married Roy; children: Roy Jr & Jason. **Educ:** Case Western Res Univ, Cert, 1971; Jane Addams Sch Pract Nursing, Dipl, 1975; Cuyahoga Community Col, 1980. **Career:** Ward 5 Block Club, pres, 1980; New Bethel AME Church, steward bd, 1984-85; Bathsheba Order Eastern Star, chaplain, 1983. **Orgs:** Quater Century Club; Oakwood Vlg City Coun, Coun mem, 1984-. **Home Addr:** 7226 Wright Ave, Oakwood Village, OH 44146. **Business Addr:** Council Member, Oakwood Village City Council, 24800 Broadway Ave, Oakwood Village, OH 44146, **Business Phone:** (440)232-9988.

## WAINWRIGHT, HON. J. DALE
Judge. **Personal:** Born Jun 19, 1961, Nashville, TX; son of Mary; married Debbie; children: Jeremy, Phillip & Joshua. **Educ:** London Sch Econs, attended 1981; Howard Univ, BA, 1983; Univ Chicago Law Sch, JD, 1988. **Career:** Bass, Berry & Simms, atty, 1988-90; Andrews & Kurth, atty, 1990-95; Haynes & Boone, atty, 1996-99; Harris County Civil Dist Ct, 1999-2002; Temp Comn Supreme Ct, justice, 2001; Supreme Ct Tex, Republican justice, 2002, 2008-; coach, Little League baseball. **Orgs:** Vis comt, Univ Chicago Law Sch; vis comt, S Tex Col Law; Am Law Inst; bd dir, Houston Bar Asn; dir, Houston Vol Lawyers Prog; dir, Tex Young Lawyers Asn; pres, Houston Young Lawyers Asn; Second Baptist Church; co-founder, Aspiring Youth Prog; YMCA; Tex Young Lawyers Asn; pres, Houston Young Lawyers Asn. **Special Achievements:** First African Americans in history to be elected to the Texas Supreme Court. **Business Addr:** Republican Justice, Supreme Court of Texas, 201 W 14th St, Austin, TX 78711-2248, **Business Phone:** (512)463-1332.

## WAINWRIGHT, DR. OLIVER O., SR. (OLLIE WAINWRIGHT)
Manager, executive. **Personal:** Born May 6, 1936, Nanticoke, MD; son of Jesse and Victoria Nutter; married Dolores Moorman; children: Oliver Jr, Stephen C & Eric C. **Educ:** Hampton Inst, BS, 1959; William Paterson Col, MA, commun, 1972; Cent Mich Univ, MA, indust mgt, 1974; AUS Command & Gen Staff Col, attended 1975; Nova Univ, MPA, 1979, DPA, 1981; Rutgers Univ, advan mgt, resident, 1985. **Career:** SCM Corp, mgr corp security, 1979-85; Mobil Corp, Stamford, Conn, corp security mgr, 1985-87; Am Int Group, asst vpres, dir corp security, 1987-; Hoffman-LaRoche Inc, dir corp security, currently; Wainwright & Assocs, Piscataway, NJ, pres. **Orgs:** Kappa Alpha Psi; mayoral appintment, Human Resources Coun Piscataway, 1980; trustee, N Stelton AME Church, 1980-81; Am Soc Indust Security, 1981-; Asn Polit Risk Analysts, 1982; bd dir, Acad Security Ed & Trainers, 1982-85; cert bd, Acad Security Ed & Trainers, 1983-85; assoc mem, Int Asn Chiefs; bd dir, Am Soc Indust Sec, 1985-87; Int Security Mgt Asn, 1985-; Alliance Concern Citizens, Piscataway, NJ; bd educ, Piscataway, NJ, 1987-90; Oversea Security Coun, US Dept State, 1988-90. **Honors/Awds:** Nat Training Award, Defense Intelligence Sch, Nat Training Officers Conf, 1977; Polit Risk Assessment Article, Risk Planning Group, 1980; Cert Protection, Prof Am Soc Indust Sec Int, 1981; Cert Security Trainer Acad Security Security Ed & Trainers, 1981; Black Achievers Indust Award, Harlem, YMCA, 1982; Mgt Future Article Security Mgt Mag, 1984; Certificate of Appreciation, bd dirs, Am Soc Ind Sec, 1987; Distinguished Service Award, L I University, Sch Pub Admin, 1985; Certificate of Appreciation, Community Service Award, Piscataway Sportsmen, 1989; Hon Cert, New York City Police Dept, 1990. **Home Addr:** 63 Coventry Cir, Piscataway, NJ 08854-5249, **Home Phone:** (732)985-6618. **Business Addr:** Director Corporate Security, Hoffman-LaRoche Inc, 340 Kingsland St, Nutley, NJ 07110, **Business Phone:** (973)235-5000.

## WAITE, DR. NORMA LILLIA POLYN
Physician. **Personal:** Born Kingston; married Ainsley Blair; children: Craig, Duane & Andre Blair. **Educ:** Howard Univ, BS, obstet & gynec, 1972; Howard Univ Med Sch, MD, 1977; Webster Univ, MA, health servs mgt. **Career:** Brookdale Hosp Med Ctr, resident, 1977-81; Orlando Regional Hosp, Humana Hosp Lucerne, physician; Fla Hosp, physician, currently; pvt pract physician, currently. **Orgs:** Fel Am Col Obstet & Gynecol, 1982; fel Am Bd Obstet & Gynecol; Cent FL Med Asn; Phi Beta Kappa Soc. **Home Addr:** PO Box 1727, Windermere, FL 34786. **Business Addr:** Physician, Florida Hospital, 6000 Turkey Lake Rd Suite 112, Orlando, FL 32819, **Business Phone:** (407)363-9499.

## WAITERS, DR. ANN GILLIS
Educator, school principal, association executive. **Personal:** Born Dec 5, 1939, Philadelphia, PA. **Educ:** Cheyney State Col, BS; Temple Univ, elem & urban educ. **Career:** William Penn Sch Dist, supt; Philadelphia Sch Dist, regional supt; Bodine High Sch Intl Affairs, prin; Univ Sch Rels Temple Univ, Philadelphia, fel; Temple Univ Col Educ, adj prof; Sch Dist Philadelphia, coordr int stud exchange prog, performance appraisaladmin & suprs; Temple Univ, reading teacher; Maritime Acad Charter Sch, prin, chief admin officer, chief exec officer, chief exec officer emerita, currently. **Orgs:** Rev Com Educ; Educ & Human Rel Com Asn Field Serv Teacher Edn; Black Educ Forum; Educ Equality League; Nat Coun Admin Women Educ; Pa

Asn Supv & Cur Develop; Pa Cong Sch Adminr; charter mem, Cong Sch Adminr. **Honors/Awds:** Principal of the Year, Educr Round Table; Phil Delta Kappa Service Award; Bicentennial Award, Nat Asn Univ Women; Appreciation Award, Linpark Civic Asn Trevose. **Home Addr:** 3600 Conshohocken Ave Apt 102, Philadelphia, PA 19131-5301, **Home Phone:** (215)878-9453. **Business Addr:** Chief Executive Officer Emerita, Maritime Academy Charter School, 2275 Bridge St, Philadelphia, PA 19137, **Business Phone:** (215)535-4555.

### WAITES-HOWARD, SHIRLEY JEAN

Public relations executive. **Personal:** Born Dec 29, 1948, Philadelphia, PA; daughter of James Harvey Waites (deceased) and Bessie E Hill Waites; married Alfred Howard Jr; children: Demarcus Reginald. **Educ:** Pa State Univ, BA, psychol, 1971; Bryn Mawr Grad Sch Social Work, MSS, 1977; Eastern Baptist Theol Sem, Wynnewood, PA, currently. **Career:** Ment Health Consortium Inc, consult & educ specialist social worker therapist; W Philadelphia Community, consult & educ, 1971-77; Women's Network Consult, pub rels consult, 1974-; Baptist Childrens Serv, clin dir, 1978-80; LaSalle Univ, coordr & instr, social work dept, 1980-83; Villanova Univ, instr, 1980-85; Priosn Proj, coordr; WDAS-AM Talk Show, prog asst, 1982-84; Haverford State Hosp, psychiat social worker, 1983-85; Lincoln Univ, instr, 1984; MaGee Rehab Hosp, staff social worker, 1987-. **Orgs:** Adv team mem, Triple Jeopardy Third World Women's Support Network; Nat Asn Black Psychologists; Nat Asn Black Social Workers; Nat Asn Social Workers. **Home Addr:** 1708 N 55th St, Philadelphia, PA 19131, **Home Phone:** (215)878-6873. **Business Addr:** Staff Social Worker, MaGee Rehabilitation Hospital, 6 Franklin Plz, Philadelphia, PA 19102, **Business Phone:** (215)587-3000.

### WAITS, REV. VA LITA FRANCINE

Judge, lawyer, clergy. **Personal:** Born Jan 29, 1947, Tyler, TX; daughter of Melvin Jr and Sibbie Jones. **Educ:** Howard Univ, BA, 1969; Am Univ, MA, 1974; Tex Southern Univ, Thurgood Marshall Sch Law, JD, 1980; Southern Methodist Univ-Perkins Sch Theol, Mdiv, relig, 2003. **Career:** WRC-TV & NBC, producer, 1971-74; Southwestern Bell Tel Co, mgr, 1975; Tex Southern Univ, instr, KTSU-FM, mgr, 1975-76; US Dept Energy, regional atty, 1980-81; Nat Labor Rels Bd, field atty, 1981-82; Law Off Va Lita Waits, prin, 1982-; City Tyler, alt munic judge, 1984-94; Windsor Village United Methodist Church, 1995-2005; Wesley Found Kilgore Col, exec dir, campus minister, 2003-05; Tex Col, campus minister, 2005-06; Jenkins Memorial Christian Methodist Episcopal Church, pastor, 2006-10; Moving Spirit, spiritual dir, 2009-; . **Orgs:** Smith County Bar Asn, 1982-; Supreme Ct, State Tex, Bar Admis Comt, 1983-87; Nat Bar Asn, 1984-; Leadership Tex, 1987-; founding pres, Tyler Metrop Chamber Com, 1989-92; founding bd mem, Smith County Ct App Spec Advocates, 1989-; founder, Tyler Metro Chamber Com, 1990; pres, Delta Sigma Theta Sorority, Tyler Alumnae Chap, 1990-92; Nat Asn Black Women Lawyers, 1992-; secy, Tex Asn African Am Chambers Com, 1993-; founder, Ctr Non profit Develop, Houston, 1996; Leadership Tyler; asst prior, Order St Luke, Perkins Sch Theol chap; Exec Coun Hawk, Moore & Martin Halls, S Methodist Univ; pres, dir orgn develop, Ctr Non-Profit Orgn Develop Inc. **Home Addr:** 3410 Dyer, PO Box 751395, Dallas, TX 75275-1395, **Home Phone:** (214)768-5973. **Business Addr:** Principal, Waits Law Firm, 305 S Broadway Ave Suite 405, Tyler, TX 75702-7392, **Business Phone:** (903)533-8887.

### WAKEFIELD, J. ALVIN

Consultant, president (organization). **Personal:** Born Jul 25, 1938, New York, NY; son of James Alvin and Dorothy Nickerson Bradshaw; children: Shawna Michelle & Adam Malik. **Educ:** Syracuse Univ, attended 1957; NY Univ, BA, Eng lit, 1960; Pace Univ Grad Sch Bus, MBA, 1972. **Career:** Mobil Oil Corp, Boston, Mass, employee rels asst, 1966-68; Celanese Corp, New York, NY, supvr personnel, 1968-70; Singer Co, New York, NY, recruiting mgr, 1970-73; Avon Prod Inc, New York, NY, vpres admin, 1973-81; Korn/Ferry Int, New York, NY, vpres & partner, 1981-83; Wakefield Enterprises, Rutl, Vt, pres, 1983-86; Gilbert Tweed Assocs, Pitts ford, Vt, managing dir & partner, 1986-93; Wakefield Talabisco Int, pres, 1993-. **Orgs:** Chmn Coun Concerned Black Execs, 1970-73; bd mem, NY Urban League, 1980-83; exec comt, Vt Achievement Ctr, 1988-91; bd mem, Vt Bus Round table, 1988-; bd mem, New Eng Bd Higher Educ, 1990-91; Dem Party Exec Comt, 1993-95; Govs Coun Econ Advisors, 1994-; bd dir, Trinity Col, 1994-2000; vice chmn, bd dir, Vt Pub Radio, 1998-; founder, Wakefield Talabisco Int; bd chmn, Paramount Theatre; bd chmn, Crossroads Arts Coun; Green Mountain Col; SIAS Int Univ; Killington Music Festival; Direct Selling Asn; Vt Community Found. **Honors/Awds:** Academic Scholarship, Syracuse Univ, 1956; Outstanding Achievement Award, Black Retail Action Group, 1979; Partnership Award, Direct Selling Association Partnership Award, 2000. **Special Achievements:** America's Top 100 Executive Recruiters, Career Makers, 1991; North Americas Top 150 Executive Recruiters, Career Makers, 1992, 1995. **Home Addr:** 16 Cream Hill Rd, Mendon, VT 05701, **Home Phone:** (802)775-6899. **Business Addr:** President, Executive Recruiter, Wakefield Global, 534 Cream Hill Rd Suite 1, Mendon, VT 05701, **Business Phone:** (802)747-5901.

### WALBEY, THEODOSIA EMMA DRAHER (DODIE T DRAHER)

Actor, singer, writer. **Personal:** Born Apr 13, 1950, Bangor, ME; married Daniel A Draher; children: Timothy W Wright, Stephen S Wright & Daniel Jr. **Educ:** Univ Md; Univ Colo; Kinman Bus Univ. **Career:** Ritchie Family Album, co-writer; Films: Give Me A Break, Can't Stop the Music, 1980; La Borbichette; TV series: "The Ritchie Family", singer & actress, 1975; "Dinah Shore"; "Merv Griffin"; "Rock Concert"; "Midnight Special"; "Soul Train"; "Am Bandstand"; "Mike Douglas"; "Dance Fever"; "Soap Factory"; "Numerous countries around the world"; "Woman of Many Faces"; Can't Stop Prod, singer, dancer & actress. **Honors/Awds:** Gold & Platinum Records from around the world, 1976-77. **Home Addr:** 165 E 32nd St Apt 11d, New York, NY 10016-6014, **Home Phone:** (212)685-2797. **Business Addr:** Actor, Singer, Dancer, 330 West 38th Str Suite 309, New York, NY 10018, **Business Phone:** (212)904-1626.

### WALBURG, JUDITH ANN

Financial manager, educator. **Personal:** Born Feb 19, 1948, New York, NY; daughter of Charles A and Florence Perry. **Educ:** Fisk Univ, Nashville, TN, BA, 1969. **Career:** Olivetti Corp Am, New York, customer rels rep, 1970-72; United Negro Col Fund, New York, asst dir educ servs, 1972-75; Alumni Nat Org, dir, 1975. **Orgs:** New York Alumni Asn, 1975-79; Nat Urban Affairs Coun, 1984-89; Corp Women's Network, 1986-89; bd mem, Coun Environ, 1987-89. **Home Addr:** 284 Convent Ave, New York, NY 10031-6301, **Home Phone:** (212)281-5604. **Business Addr:** NY.

### WALCOTT, LOUIS EUGENE. See FARRAKHAN, LOUIS.

### WALDEN, BARBARA

Executive, business owner, movie actor. **Personal:** Born Sep 3, 1936, Camden, NJ. **Educ:** Eccles Bus Col. **Career:** Films: The Private Lives of Adam & Eve, 1960; Car Wash, 1976; Freaky Friday, 1976; Frohes Fest, 1981; Ten Commandments; What A Way to Go; Global Affair; Bob Hope; Night of the Quarter Moon; TV Shows: "Disneyland", "Freaky Friday: Part 1", "Freaky Friday: Part 1", 1982; Barbara Walden Cosmetics Inc, founder & pres, currently. **Orgs:** Bd mem, Am Civil Liberties Union, 1985-; United Way, 1986-; bd mem, May Co So Calif Women's Adv Coun, 1986-; Comt 200, Coalition 100 Black Women; co-sponsor, Self-Image workshop sem; lecr at cols, univs, women's groups, orgn, caucus, Los Angeles Unified Sch Dist yearly Career Day; keynote speaker New York's Dept States, Comn Econ Develop Prog, Syracuse, New york; guest lectr, Unic Calif Los Angeles, Women Mgt; guest lectr, Southern Calif, Bus Women's Caucus; bd dir, Love Feeding Everyone. **Business Addr:** Founder, President, Barbara Walden Cosmetics Inc, 13221 Adm Ave, Marina Del Rey, CA 90292, **Business Phone:** (310)823-4186.

### WALDEN, MARK E.

Health services administrator. **Career:** Physician, Self employed, currently. **Business Addr:** Physician, Self employed, 313 Stevenson Lane, Towson, MD 21204, **Business Phone:** (410)525-2522.

### WALDEN, NARADA MICHAEL

Singer, entertainer, musician. **Personal:** Born Apr 23, 1952, Kalamazoo, MI; married Anukampa. **Educ:** Western Mich Univ, attended 1972. **Career:** Music producer, drummer, singer & song writer; Warner Bros Recs, rec artist, writer & rec producer; songwriter Gratitude Sky, 1976-; various groups, drummer; various rec artists albums, pianist; Perfection Light Prod, pres, 1976-; Tarpan Studion Inc, owner, 1985-; Albums: Garden of Love Light, 1976; I Cry, I Smile, 1977; Awakening, 1979; The Dance of Life, 1979; Victory, 1980; Confidence, 1982; Looking At You, Looking At Me, 1983; The Nature of Things, 1985; Divine Emotions, 1988; Ricochet, 1991; Free Willy, 1993; Deliver Us from Eva, 2003; Zack and Miri Make a Porno, 2008; Thunder, 2012. Singles: "Delightful", 1977; "Give Your Love a Chance", 1979; "I Don't Want Nobody Else", 1979; "I Shoulda Loved Ya", 1980; "Tonight I'm Alright", 1980; "The Real Thang", 1980; "Summer Lady", 1982; "Reach Out (I'll Be There)", 1983; "Gimme, Gimme, Gimme", 1985; "Divine Emotions", 1988; "Top of the Pops", 1988; "Soul Train", 1988; "Can't Get You Outta My Head", 1988; "Whitney Houston: The True Story, 2002; Randy Jackson, 2005. **Orgs:** Founder, Narada Michael Walden Found. **Honors/Awds:** Numerous honors & awards including Honorary Citizen Award, Atlanta, 1979; Honorary Citizen, New Orleans, 1980; Outstanding Black Contemporary ArtistAward, Bay Area Music Awards, San Francisco, 1982; Grammy Award, Best R&B Song "Freeway of Love" Aretha Franklin, 1986; Producer of the Year, Billboard Mag, 1986 & 1992. **Special Achievements:** Spokesperson for "The Peace Run", 1987. **Business Addr:** Owner, Tarpan Studios Inc, 1925 E Francisco Blvd Suite L, San Rafael, CA 94901, **Business Phone:** (415)485-1999.

### WALDON, HON. ALTON RONALD, JR.

Lawyer, judge. **Personal:** Born Dec 21, 1936, Lakeland, FL; son of Alton R Sr and Rupert Juanita Wallace; married Barbara DeCosta; children: Alton III, Dana & Ian. **Educ:** City Univ NY, John Jay Col, BS, criminal justice, 1968; NY Law Sch, JD, 1973. **Career:** New York Housing Auth Police Dept, capt, 1962-75; NY Div Human Rights, dep comnr, 1975-81; County Serv Group NYS Off Ment Retardation & Develop Disabilities, asst coun, 1981-83; NY Assembly, assemblyman 33rd dist, 1982-86; US House Rep, congressman, 1986-87; NY State Invest Comn, comnr, 1987-90; NY Senate, sen, 10th S D, 1990-2000; NY Ct Claims, judge, 2000-; NY Law Sch, Thurgood Marshall fel; NY State Crime Victims bd, comnr. **Orgs:** United Black Men Queens Inc; K C; Am Bar Asn; Alumni Asn New York Law Sch; Macon B Allen Bar Asn; bd dir, USO Greater NY; Nat Asn Advan Colored People; F & M Prince Hall 33 degrees; Am Judges Asn; Alumni Asn; John Jay Col Criminal Justice; Asn Former Mems Cong Asn; Sigma Pi Phi Fraternity; Comus Club Brooklyn, NY; Nat Org Black Law Enforcement Execs; Housing Police Acad. **Special Achievements:** First African American Congressman elected from Queens, New York. **Home Addr:** 115103 222nd St, Cambria Heights, NY 11411-1230, **Home Phone:** (917)751-5711. **Business Addr:** Judge.

### WALKER, ADRIAN

Government official, columnist. **Personal:** Born Miami, FL. **Educ:** Fla Int Univ. **Career:** Gen assignment & police reporter, 1986; Globe, gen assignment reporter, 1989; papers dep polit ed, 1995-97; Boston Globe, metro columnist, 1998-. **Business Addr:** Columnist, Boston Globe, 135 Morrissey Blvd, Boston, MA 02205-5819, **Business Phone:** (617)929-2000.

### WALKER, ALICE MALSENIOR

Writer. **Personal:** Born Feb 9, 1944, Eatonton, GA; daughter of Willie Lee and Minnie Tallulah Grant; married Melvyn Roseman; children: Rebecca Grant. **Educ:** Spelman Col, attended 1963; Sarah Lawrence Col, BA, 1965; Russell Sage Col, PhD, 1972. **Career:** Voter regist worker, GA; Head Start, MS, staff mem; Welfare Dept New York, staff mem; writer-in-res & teacher black studies, Jackson State Col, 1968-69, Tougaloo Col, 1970-71; Wellesley Col & Univ MS-Boston, lectr lit, 1972-73; Univ CA-Berkeley, distinguished writer Afro-Am studies, 1982; Brandeis Univ, Fannie Hurst Prof Lit, 1982; Wild Trees Press, co-founder & publ, 1984-. Author: Once, 1968; Revolutionary Petunias & Other Poems, 1973; Good Night Willi Lee I'll See You In the Morning, 1979; Horses Make a Landscape Look More Beautiful, 1984; Absolute Trust in the Goodness of the Earth: New Poems, 2003; A Poem Traveled down My Arm: Poem & Drawings, 2002; Collected Poems, 2005. Novels: Five Poems, 1972; In Love & Trouble: Stories of Black Women, 1973; Langston Hughes: Am Poet, 1973; Meridian, 1976; Diary of an African Nun, 1977; I Love Myself When I am Laughing, 1979; You Can't Keep a Good Woman Down, 1981; The Color Purple, 1982; In Search of Our Mothers' Gardens, 1983; The Color Purple, 1985; To Hell W Dying, 1988; Living by the Word, 1988; The Temple of My Familiar, 1989; Her Blue Body Everything We Know: Earthling Poems, 1965-90 Complete, 1991; Possessing the Secret of Joy, 1992; Film: Warrior Marks, producer; Warrior Marks, 1993; The Same River Twice: Honoring the Difficult; Anything We Love Can Be Saved, Random, 1997; Pema Chodron and Alice Walker in Conversation, 1999; Sent By Earth: A Message from the Grandmother Spirit After the Bombing of the World Trade Center and Pentagon, 2001; Everyday Use, 2003; Now is the Time to Open Your Heart, 2004; We Are the Ones We Have Been Waiting For, 2006; Devil's My Enemy, 2008; Overcoming Speechlessness, 2010; Chicken Chronicles, 2011. **Orgs:** Consult black hist, Friends C Miss, 1967; bd trustees, Sarah Lawrence Col, 1971-73. **Honors/Awds:** Merrill Writing fellow, 1966; Mc Dowell Colony fellow, 1967 & 1977-78; National Endowment Arts grant, 1969 & 1977; Radcliffe Institute Fellowship, 1971-73; Merrill Fellowship; hon PhD, Russell Sage Univ, 1972; Lillian Smith Award, Southern Regional Coun, 1973; National Book Award nomination, 1973; Rosenthal Foundation Award, Am Acad & Inst Arts & Letters, 1974; Guggenheim Award, 1977-78; National Endowment Arts fellow, 1979; National Book Critics Circle Award nomination, 1982; American Book Award, 1983; DHL, Univ Mass, 1983; Pulitzer Prize, 1983; O Henry Award, 1986; Honorary degree, Calif Inst Arts, 1995; Sheila Award, Tubman African Am Mus, 1997; Humanist of the Year, Am Humanist Asn, 1997; Lillian Smith Award, Nat Endowment Arts; Rosenthal Award, Nat Inst Arts & Lett; Literary Ambassador Award, University of Oklahoma Center for Poets and Writers, 1998; Georgia Writers Hall of Fame, 2001; California Hall of Fame, Calif Mus Hist, Women & Arts, 2006; Domestic Human Rights Award, Global Exchange, 2007; LennonOno Grant for Peace, 2010. **Business Addr:** Author, Random House Inc, 1745 Broadway Suite 3, New York, NY 10019, **Business Phone:** (212)782-9000.

### WALKER, ALLENE MARSHA

Health services administrator. **Personal:** Born Mar 2, 1953, Chicago, IL; daughter of Major and Mabel H Thompson. **Educ:** Michael Reese Hosp Sch Med Tech, MT, 1973; Univ Ill, Chicago, IL, BS, 1974; Roosevelt Univ, MS, 1983. **Career:** Damon Clin Labs, lab supvr, 1974-85; Med Care HMO, provider rep, 1985-89; Jacqueline Inc, sec & treas, 1989; Med Care HMO, Maywood, Ill, dir & provserv, 1989-91, asst vp prov adm, 1991-92; HMO Ill, supvr Health Servs Progs, 1993-96; Blue Cross Blue Shield Ill, HMO training coordr, 1996, commun consult, ed staff, currently. **Orgs:** Oper PUSH Inc, 1972-; bd mem, Rainbow PUSH. **Home Addr:** 1417 W 73rd Pl, Chicago, IL 60636. **Business Addr:** Communications Consultant, Blue Cross & Blue Shield of Illinois, 300 E Randolph St 25th Fl, Chicago, IL 60601-5099, **Business Phone:** (312)653-4019.

### WALKER, ANGELINA

Government official. **Career:** The White House, exec asst to coun vpres, currently. **Business Addr:** Executive Assistant to the Council for the Vice President, The White House, 1600 Pennsylvania Ave NW, Washington, DC 20500, **Business Phone:** (202)456-1414.

### WALKER, ANTOINE DEVON

Basketball player. **Personal:** Born Aug 12, 1976, Chicago, IL; son of Diane; married Chad Johnson; children: Crystal & Alana. **Educ:** Univ Ky, attended 1996. **Career:** Basketball player (retired); Boston Celtics, power forward, 1996-2003, 2005; Dallas Mavericks, power forward, 2003-04; Atlanta Hawks, power forward, 2004-05; Miami Heat, power forward, 2005-07; Minn Timber wolves, power forward, 2007-08; Memphis Grizzlies, power forward, 2008; Guaynabo Mets, power forward, 2010; Idaho Stampede, power forward, 2010-12; 120 Sports, basketball analyst, currently. **Honors/Awds:** NBA All-Star, 1998, 2002-03; Player of the Week, Nat Basketball Asn, 2003; Champion, Nat Basketball Asn, 2006. **Business Addr:** Analyst, 120 Sports, 75 Ninth Ave, New York, NY 10011, **Business Phone:** (212)485-4500.

### WALKER, ARMAN KENNIS

Banker. **Personal:** Born Oct 15, 1957, Minneapolis, MN; son of Simon W and Anna M Gallo; married Gabrielle; children: 3. **Educ:** Univ Calif, Berkeley, CA, BA, econ, 1979. **Career:** Wells Fargo Bank, corp banking officer, 1979-83; Marine Midland Bank, asst vpres corp banking, 1983-84; Sanwa Bank Calif, vpres, sr mgr Proj & Corp Finance, 1985-93; Pine Cobble Partners, managing gen partner, 1990; Pine Cobble Funding Corp, founder, 1993-97; City Nat Bank, vpres mid mkt lending, 1997-99; KBK Financial, Inc, western regional mgr, 2000-01; One United Bank, chief lending officer & calif regional pres, 2004-07; Tarkus Capital Corp LLC, managing dir, 2007-; Cranbury Group, LLC, prin, 2012-; SBDavos, managing dir, 2013-. **Orgs:** Omicron Epislon Delta, 1979; co-chairperson, LAs Young Black Prof, 1989-; LA Urban Bankers Asn; bd dir, Watts Heath Found, 1992-; bd trustee, treas, Church Christian, 1992-; co-chair, Banking & Finance Conf, 1992; co-chair, Calif Money Mgr Networking Forum, 1992; co-chair, African-Am Women Distinction Mixer, 1993. **Honors/Awds:** City Attorney, Los Angeles, Commendation, 1992. **Special Achievements:** One of America's Best & Brightest, Dollars & Sense Mag, 1988. **Home Addr:** 530 S Rossmore Ave, Los Angeles, CA 90020-4744, **Home Phone:** (323)934-3253. **Business Addr:** Managing Director, Tarkus Capital Corp LLC, 66320 Canoga Ave Suite 1500, Woodland Hills, CA 91367, **Business Phone:** (310)405-2790.

### WALKER, BETTY STEVENS

Educator, lawyer. **Personal:** Born Feb 3, 1944, New York, NY; daughter of Anne Wood; married Paul T; children: Camarf, Tarik & Kumi. **Educ:** Spelman Col, Atlanta, BA, hist, 1964; Harvard Law Sch, JD, law, 1967. **Career:** Harvard Law Sch Scholar, fel; John Har Whitney, fel; Aaron Norman fel; Harvard Bus Sch, res asst, 1966; Wake Opportunities Inc, Raleigh, coordr youth prog, 1968; Shaw Univ, curric consult, 1968, asst prof, polit sci, 1968-70, fac fel; So Rwy Co Wash, DC, atty, 1974-77; Farmers Home Admin US Dept Agr, asst admin, 1977; Walker & Walker Assocs, atty, co-prin, currently. **Orgs:** DC Ct Appeals; US Dist Ct DC; US Ct Appeals DC Dist; Supreme Ct US Am; DC Bar Asn; Wash Bar Asn; Nat Bar Asn; Spel man Col & Harvard Law Alumni Asn; fel John Hay Whitney, 1964; fel Aaron Norman, 1964; Bethel AME Church, Baltimore; steward, Bethel AME Church, 1989; Southern sch co-ordinator, Nat Asn Advan Colored People, Legal Defence & Educ Fund. **Honors/Awds:** Outstanding Leadership Award, Nat Asn Equal Opportunity, 1990. **Special Achievements:** First African American woman to Ames Competition 2 consecutive semesters at Harvard Law. **Home Addr:** 5033 Rushlight Path, Columbia, MD 21044, **Home Phone:** (301)596-6630. **Business Addr:** Attorney, Co-Principal, Walker & Walker Associates, 2807 18th St NW, Washington, DC 20004, **Business Phone:** (202)842-4664.

## WALKER, BRACEY WORDELL

Football player. **Personal:** Born Oct 28, 1970, Portsmouth, VA; married Levoda; children: Bracy Jr. **Educ:** Univ NC. **Career:** Football player (retired); Kans City Chiefs, defensive back, 1994, 1998-2001, free safety, 1999; Cincinnati Bengals, strong safety, 1995-96; Miami Dolphins, 1997-98; Detroit Lions, safety, 2002, strong safety, 2003-04; free safety, 2005. **Honors/Awds:** NFC Special Teams Player of the week Award, 2004; First-team All-America honors, Football Writers Asn, Second-team All-America pick, Sporting News. **Special Achievements:** Film: 1994 NFL Draft, 1994; Walker's 92-yard jaunt is the longest recorded blocked-field-goal return for a touchdown in NFL history; first non-Lions kick-returner to be given the NFC special teams award, since its inception. **Home Addr:** 5683 Notting Hill Rd, Gurnee, IL 60031-1021, **Home Phone:** (847)623-2052.

## WALKER, BRIAN

Football player. **Personal:** Born May 31, 1972, Colorado Springs, CO. **Educ:** Wash State Univ. **Career:** Football player (retired); Wash Redskins, defensive back, 1996, 1997; Miami Dolphins, 1998, strong safety, 2000-01; Seattle Sea hawks, 1999; Detroit Lions, free safety, 2002-03, strong safety, 2002. **Orgs:** Prudential No Passing zone prog, 2000. **Honors/Awds:** NFLPA, Unsung Hero Award, 2000.

## WALKER, CAROLYN

State government official. **Personal:** Born Yuma, AZ; daughter of Clyde and Lenora Jones; children: 1. **Career:** Mountain Bell Tel Co, mkt mgt, 1976; Ariz State House Representatives, Phoenix, AZ, state rep, 1983-86; Ariz St, st sendist 23, 1986. **Orgs:** Sickle Cell Anemia Coun. **Honors/Awds:** Second African American female in Arizona State House of Representatives; First African American female in the Arizona State Senate.

## WALKER, CHARLES

Actor, educator. **Personal:** Born Jan 21, 1945, Chicago, IL; son of Charles and Robbie Edith Hutchinson; married Lillian Beatrice Lusk; children: Leah Cher & Chasen Lloyd; married Ilona Massey. **Educ:** Career Acad Sch Broadcasting, Milwaukee, WI, broadcasting degree, 1967; Wilson City Col, Chicago, IL, attended 1967; Calif State Univ, Los Angeles, CA, BA, theatre arts, 1980, MA, speech commun, 1982. **Career:** Writer: General Hospital, 1963; WXYZ TV, Detroit, Mich, tv news rep, 1967-68; prof actor, Los Angeles, Calif, TV, film & commercials, 1968-; Los Angeles Unified Sch Dist, Los Angeles, Calif, sub teach, 1980-; Calif State Univ, Los Angeles, Calif, instr speech comm, 1980-81; City Los Angeles, Calif, lectr work experience prog, 1981-83; Hollywood High Sch, Los Angeles, Calif, teacher, 1984; Los Angeles Southwest Col, Los Angeles, Calif, instr pub speaking, 1984-; Calif State Univ, Dominguez Hills, Calif, instr fund speech, actg & inter cult comm, 1984-; WVOL Radio, Nashville, Tenn, radio news reporter; Films: Set It Off, 1996; Liar, 1997; Why Do Fools Fall in Love, 1998; Trippin, 1999; Almost Famous, 2000; Nutty Prof II: The Klumps, 2000; Rennies Landing, 2001; First Watch, 2003; Wake Up, Ron Burgundy: The Lost Movie, 2004; Anchorman: The Legend of Ron Burgundy, 2004; Soul Plane, 2004; Gridiron Gang, 2006; Always and Forever, 2009; TV Series: "Melrose Place", 1997; "The Practice"; "1998-2010"; "Once & Again", 2000; "Dead Last", 2001; "Power Rangers Time Force", 2001; "NYPD Blue", 2001; "Just ShootMe", 2003; "The Parkers", 2002; "The W Wing", 2002; "Navy NCIS: Naval Criminal Investigative Service", 2004; "Greys Anat", 2005; "Blind Justice", 2005; "Everybody Hates Chris", 2006; "Without a Trace", 2006; "What About Brian", 2006; "The Nine", 2007; "The Secret Life of the American Teenager", 2009; "Community", 2012. **Orgs:** Nat Asn Advan Colored People; Screen Actor's Guild; Am Fedn TV & Radio Artists; Mt Zion Missionary Baptist Church. **Home Addr:** PO Box 481315, Los Angeles, CA 90048, **Home Phone:** (213)935-2286. **Business Addr:** Professor, California State University Dominguez Hills, 1000 EVictoria St, Carson, CA 90747, **Business Phone:** (213)516-3588.

## WALKER, HON. CHARLES EALY, JR.

Executive, lawyer, educator. **Personal:** Born May 1, 1951, Anchorage, AK; son of Charles E Sr and Marguerite Lee; married Dorothy Sanders; children: Sydney & Courtney. **Educ:** Univ Calif, Santa Barbara, BA, polit sci, 1973; London Sch Econs, BS, 1977; Boston Col Law Sch, JD, 1978. **Career:** Executive; Oxnard Union High Sch Dist, teacher, 1974-75; USDA Off Gen Coun, atty, 1978-79; Boston Super Ct, law clerk, 1979-81; Suffolk Univ Law Sch Coun Legal Educ Opportunity, teaching fel, 1981-82, 1987-89; Univ Mass, instr, 1980-82; Mass Ct Appeals, law clerk, 1980-81; Commonwealth Mass, asst atty gen, 1981-87; New Eng Sch Law, asst prof, 1987-; Boston Col, adj prof; Exec Elder affairs, gen coun; Mass Comn Against Discrimination, chair;Chmn, Mass Comn Against Discrimination, 1994-2000; Commonwealth Mass Dept Indust Accidents, admin judge, 2000-04; Employ Discrimination Specialist, 2004-05; Gen Coun, 2007-14; Roxbury Community Col, chief human resources officer, 2014-15. **Orgs:** Pres & co-founder, Boston Col Law Sch Black Alumni Network, 1981-; chair, Mass Bar Asn Comt Bar Admin; pres, Roxbury Defenders Comt Inc, 1982-; Cambridge Econ Opportunity Comn, 1982-86; Nat Asn Advan Colored People Nat Urban League, 1985-; trustee bd & chmn, Good Shepherd Church God Christ, 1985-; ed bd, Mass Law Rev, 1990-; pres, Mass Black Lawyers Asn Exec Bd, 1993-95; bd dir, Wheelock Col Family Theatre; chair, Mass Comn Against Discrimination; exec dir, Lawyers' Comt Civil Rights Under Law Boston Bar Asn, currently. **Home Addr:** 80 Maskwonicut St, Sharon, PA 02067-1216, **Home Phone:** (617)784-6061. **Business Addr:** Executive Director, Under Law of the Boston Bar Association, 294 Washington St Suite 443, Boston, MA 02108, **Business Phone:** (617)482-1145.

## WALKER, CHARLES H.

Lawyer. **Personal:** Born Nov 11, 1951, Columbus, OH; son of Watson H and Juanita Webb; married Amanda T Herndon; children: Katrina Della, Allison Lyles & Carlton Wesley. **Educ:** Tufts Univ, BA, 1973; Emory Univ Sch Law, JD, 1976. **Career:** Lawyer (retired); Bricker & Eckler LLP, assoc, 1976-81, partner, sr coun; I-670 Corridor Develop Corp, mem & pres, 1992-99; Thomas D Lambros Dispute Mgt Ctr LLC, exec dir, 1996-98. **Orgs:** Pres & mem, Columbus Acad Alumni Asn, 1979-83, 1993-95; Planned Parenthood Cent OH, 1984; chairperson, Battelle Youth Scholars Prog, 1988-94; Prof & Legal Ethics Comn, 1988-96; City Columbus Sports Arena Comn, 1989; Columbus Light Opera, 1990-94; Columbus Neighborhood Housing Serv, 1990-94 vpres, pres, trustee, Life Care Alliance bd; Ohio State Bar Asn; chmn, Tufts Univ Alumni Admis Prog, Cent, OH; pres, Am Bar Asn. **Honors/Awds:** Service Award, Columbus Bar Asn, 1998; Distinguished Alumnus Award, 2014; Listed in Who's Who in American Law, Who's Who Among Black Americans, Who's Who in the Midwest, and Men of Achievement; Charles H. Walker Minority Scholarship named in honor of him. **Special Achievements:** First African American partner in Bricker & Eckler LLP, 1982. **Home Addr:** 40 E Frankfort St, Columbus, OH 43206, **Home Phone:** (614)444-1919.

## WALKER, CHARLES W., SR.

State government official. **Personal:** Born Nov 8, 1947, Burke County, GA; married Shelia; children: Monique W. **Educ:** Augusta Col, BA, bus admin. **Career:** Walker Group, founder & pres; BLs Restaurant & Dining; Ga Senate, senate majority leader, 1996. **Orgs:** State senator (retired) Chmn, Ga Asn Human Rels Comn; Sickle Cell Adv Bd; founder & sponsor, CSRA Classic Football Game; Senate Budget Conf; State Comn Ment Health, Ment Restoration & Substance Abuse Serv Delivery; Govs Comn Health Care Reform; Southern Conf Legislators; Nat Conf State Legis; Alpha Phi Alpha Fraternity Inc; bd trustee, Mt Vernon Baptist Church; trustee, Morris Brown Col; trustee, Paine Col; trustee, Morehouse Sch Med; Interstate Coop, 2005; State Insts & Property, 2005; Veterans & Mil Affairs, 2005.

## WALKER, CHESTER (CHET WALKER)

Basketball player, movie producer. **Personal:** Born Feb 22, 1940, Benton Harbor, MI. **Educ:** Bradley Univ, Peoria, IL, attended 1962. **Career:** Basketball player (retired), film producer; Syracuse Nationals, forward, 1962-69, Philadelphia 76ers, 1962-69; Chicago Bulls, forward, 1969-75; "Long Time Coming: A Black Athlete's Coming-Of-Age in America ", 1995; independent film producer.

**WALKER, CRYSTAL. See KEYMAH, CRYSTAL T.**

## WALKER, CYNTHIA BUSH

Educator. **Personal:** Born Dec 8, 1956, Ft. Benning, GA; children: Christa S. **Educ:** Morehead State Univ, BA, 1977, MHE, 1978. **Career:** Kent Metroversity, counr, 1978-80; Jefferson Comm Col, counr, 1980-, prof, currently. **Orgs:** Kent Asn Blacks Higher Educ; Col Student Personnel Asn Kent. **Home Addr:** 5511 McDeane Rd, Louisville, KY 40216-2742, **Home Phone:** (502)448-8058. **Business Addr:** Faculty, Jefferson Community & Technical College, 109 E Broadway, Louisville, KY 40202, **Business Phone:** (502)213-5333.

## WALKER, DARNELL ROBERT

Football coach, football player. **Personal:** Born Jan 17, 1970, St. Louis, MO; married D Elbie; children: Darnell Robert Jr & Derra Lynn. **Educ:** Coffeyville Community Col; Univ Okla. **Career:** Football player (retired), football coach; Atlanta Falcons, defensive back, 1993-96; San Francisco 49ers, 1997-99; Detroit Lions, 2000; Bacone Col, asst coach, 2009; Southwest Baptist Univ, defensive backs coach, 2009-; TV Series: "Call 911", 2008. **Business Addr:** Defensive Backs Coach, Southwest Baptist University, 1600 Univ Ave, Bolivar, MO 65613, **Business Phone:** (417)328-5281.

## WALKER, DARRELL

Basketball coach, basketball player. **Personal:** Born Mar 9, 1961, Chicago, IL; married Lisa; children: Darrell, Jerrell, Jarrett, Jarren & Felicia. **Educ:** Westark Community Col; Ark Ft Smith, 1980. **Career:** Basketball player (retired), basketball coach; New York Knicks, 1983-86, asst coach, 2012-14; Denver Nuggets, 1986-87; Wash Bullets, 1988-91; Detroit Pistons, 1992, asst coach, 2008-11; Chicago Bulls, 1993; NBA Players Asn, field rep, 1993-95; Toronto Raptors, asst coach, 1995-96, interim head coach, 1996-98; Wash Wizards, interim head coach, 1999-2000, dir player personnel, 2000-01, head coach, 2000, scout, 2002-04; Rockford Lightning, 1999-2000; Wash Mystics, interim head coach, 2000; New Orleans Hornets, asst coach, 2004-08. **Orgs:** Kappa Alpha Psi Fraternity. **Business Addr:** Assistant Coach, New York Knicks, Madison Sq Garden 4 Pa Plz, New York, NY 10001, **Business Phone:** (212)465-6741.

## WALKER, DENARD ANTUAN

Football player. **Personal:** Born Aug 9, 1973, Dallas, TX. **Educ:** La State Univ, grad. **Career:** Football player (retired); Tenn Oilers, left cornerback, 1997-98; Tenn Titans, left cornerback, 1999-2000, right cornerback, 2000; Denver Broncos, right cornerback, 2001-02, cornerback, 2001; Minn Vikings, left defensive back, 2003; Oakland Raiders, defensive back, linebacker, cornerback, strong safety, 2004-05. **Special Achievements:** Films: 1999 AFC Championship Game, 2000; Super Bowl XXXIV, 2000. **Business Addr:** Defensive Back, The Oakland Raiders, 1220 Harbor Bay Pkwy, Alameda, CA 94502, **Business Phone:** (510)864-5000.

## WALKER, DERRICK NORVAL

Broadcaster, football player. **Personal:** Born Jun 23, 1967, Glenwood, IL; married Rhonda. **Educ:** Univ Mich, educ. **Career:** Football player (retired), commentator; San Diego Chargers, tight end, 1990-93; Kans City Chiefs, tight end, 1994-97; Oakland Raiders, tight end & wide receiver, 1999; Big Ten Network, commentator, currently. **Honors/Awds:** All-Am hon mention, Sporting News; All Big-Ten Conf first team. **Home Addr:** 4661 Stoneview, West Bloomfield, MI 48322-3499, **Home Phone:** (248)737-1726. **Business Addr:** Commentator, Big Ten Network, 600 W Chicago Ave Suite 875, Chicago, IL 60654, **Business Phone:** (312)665-0700.

## WALKER, DOUGLAS F.

Editor. **Personal:** Born Dec 28, 1937, Detroit, MI; married Mattie Ruth. **Educ:** LaSalle Univ, BA; Wayne State Univ. **Career:** Transition Newspaper, ed; Model Neighborhood Health Prog; Libr Cong, Braille transcriber; Sound Off Newspaper, ed; auth numerous articles var publ. **Orgs:** New Bethel Bapt Chap; Mayor's Com Human Resources. **Home Addr:** 10250 Woodland Dr, Jerome, MI 49249-9560.

## WALKER, DWAYNE M.

Executive. **Personal:** Born Jul 11, 1961, Jena, LA; son of Arthur and Elnora. **Educ:** Calif State Univ, AA. **Career:** Hughes Aircraft, comput operator & programmer, 1983; TRW, programmer & systs analyst, 1983; Ashton Tate, database prod & software appln develop mgr, 1986; DMR technol & mgt consult, 1989; Microsoft Corp, dir Windows NT & networking prod, dir sales & mkt, 1989-96; Network Com Inc, chmn & chief exec officer, 1996-2002; Micro Gen Inc, dir, 1999-2002; Fidelity Nat Info Solutions, pres & chief operating officer, 2002-05; Pvt Equity Investor, investor, dir, 2005-10; RealEC Technol, pres; Rightside Group, Ltd., sr vice pres bus & mkt develop, currently; Oversee.net, sr vpres, 2010-. **Orgs:** Chmn bd, US Connect, 1995-96; bd mem, Micro Gen Corp; bd mem, dir, investor, escrow.com, 1999-2002; bd mem, Proznet; bd mem, Beyond Ventures, 1999-2001. **Special Achievements:** Book, Micro to Mainframe: Creating an Integrated Environ, 1985. **Business Addr:** Senior Vice President, Oversee.net, 515 S Flower St Suite 4400, Los Angeles, CA 90071, **Business Phone:** (213)408-0080.

## WALKER, DR. EDWIN L.

State government official. **Personal:** Born Aug 29, 1956, Richmond, VA; son of Thomas Job and Mary Ella Christopher; married Marcia Kay Alexander; children: Jennifer Elaine. **Educ:** Hampton Univ, Hampton, VA, BA, mass media arts, 1978; Univ Mo, Columbia Sch Law, JD, 1983. **Career:** Daily Press Inc, Newport News, Va, dist mgr, 1978-80; MO Dept Social Serv, Jefferson City, Mo, aging prog specialist, 1984-85, mgt analyst specialist, 1985-87, exec asst dir, 1987-88, prin asst dir, 1988, dir, divageing, 1988; Mo Div Aging, dir; Fed Agency, chief career off; Admin Aging, US Dept Health & Human Serv, dep asst secy prog opers, currently. **Orgs:** Columbia Human Rights Comn; MO Bd Nursing Home Adminr; exec adv comt mem, Nat Leadership Inst Aging, 1990; adv comt mem, Nat Resource Ctr Minority Aging Pop, 1990; nat adv comt mem, Health Ways Found, 1990; dep asst secy, U.S. Dept Health & Human serv, 1992-. **Home Addr:** 714 Bonnie Meadow Lane, Ft. Washington, MD 20744, **Home Phone:** (301)567-1309. **Business Addr:** Deputy Assistant Secretary, Administration on Aging, 1 Mass Ave NW Suite 4100, Washington, DC 20001, **Business Phone:** (202)401-4634.

## WALKER, DR. ETHEL PITTS

Educator. **Personal:** Born Feb 4, 1943, Tulsa, OK; daughter of Wilhelmina Teresa Miller and Opie Donnell Pitts; married Phillip E; children: Travis Donnell; married Angela DiPiano. **Educ:** Lincoln Univ, BS, educ, 1964; Univ Colo, MA, speech & drama, 1965; Univ Mo, PhD, theatre, 1975. **Career:** Southern Univ, instr, 1965-68; Lincoln Univ, asst prof, 1968-77; Univ Ill, asst prof, 1977-79; Laney Col, instr, 1979-80; African Am Drama Co, exec dir, 1980; Univ Calif, asst prof, 1988; Wayne State Univ, vis asst prof, 1988-89; San Jose State Univ, teacher scholar, 1999-2000, interim dept chmn, Dept TV Radio, Film & Theatre, prof, 1989-. **Orgs:** Am Theatre Asn, 1984-85, chmn, 1985-; Nat Asn Dramatic & Speech Arts; Theta Alpha Phi Dramatic Fraternity; Speech Community Am; Zeta Phi Beta; chmn bd, Christian Educ, Third Baptist Church; pres, Adv Coun IC'sPerformance Ctr; pres, Black Theatre Network, 1985-88; Asn Theatre Higher Educ; pres, Calif Educ Theatre Asn; pres, Legis Action Coalition Arts Educ. **Home Addr:** 9200 Milliken Ave Suite 7102, Ranho Cucamonga, CA 97130. **Business Addr:** Professor Emeritus (retired), San Jose State University, Hugh Gillis Hall 213 1 Wash Sq, San Jose, CA 95192-0098.

## WALKER, EUGENE KEVIN (GENE WALKER)

Executive, manager. **Personal:** Born Aug 12, 1951, St. Louis, MO; son of Willie and Nadine; children: Kristen V. **Educ:** Cornell Univ, BS, hotel admin & hotel & restaurant Mgt, 1975. **Career:** New York Hilton Hotel, conv serv mgr, 1975-76, acct exec, 1976-78, supt front serv, 1978-79; Hilton Hotel Philadelphia, exec asst mgr, 1979-81; Wash Hilton & Tower, exec asst mgr, 1981-85; Logan Airport Hilton, resident mgr, 1985-91; Greater Boston Conv & Visitors Bur, dir conv & customer serv, nat sales mgr, 1991-2002; DoubleTree OHare Rosemont, bus travel sales mgr, 2004-08; Hyatt Regency OHare, sr sales mgr; Hilton Chicago Magnificent Mile Suites, asst dir sales, 2008, sr sales mgr, 2008-; Roosevelt Univ, Hospitality Sales & Serv Course, adj prof, 2010-. **Orgs:** Cornell Soc Hotelmen, 1975-; Cornell Club, 1975-; Coalition Black Meeting Planners, 1991-; chair internship comt, Acad Travel & Tourism, 1992-; chmn, Asn Conv Opers Mgrs; Prof Conv Mgt Asn, chair, currently; Diversity Comt Asn Forum; Comt & Col Stud Mentor Coalition Black Meeting Planners; chair, Awards Comt Asn Conv Oper Managers. **Home Addr:** 105 Flagg St, Clinton, MA 01510-1535, **Home Phone:** (978)368-4393. **Business Addr:** Adjunct Professor, Roosevelt University, 430 S Mich Ave, Chicago, IL 60605, **Business Phone:** (312)341-3500.

## WALKER, DR. EUGENE P., SR. (GENE WALKER)

Teacher, government official. **Personal:** Born Thomaston, GA; married Patricia Carter; children: 2. **Educ:** Clark Col, BA, social sci, 1958; Johns Hopkins Univ, cert, southern hist, 1968; Atlanta Univ, MA, hist, 1969; Duke Univ, PhD, hist, 1978. **Career:** Teacher, government official (retired); Drake High Sch, teacher, 1958-67; basketball & football teams, coach; Clark Col, prof, asst football & basketball coach; DeKalb Col, vpres, Personnel & Community Rels, 1981-85; DeKalb Tech Inst, exec vpres, 1985-89; 43rd Ga Sen Dist, sen, 1984-92; Dept Juv Justice, comnr, 1995-99; State Bd Pardons & Paroles, 1999-2006; Develop Authority DeKalb County, chmn, 2001-09; Duke Univ Rockfeller Found fel; Johns Hopkins Univ, fel. **Orgs:** Nat Asn Blacks Criminal Justice; Am Correctional Asn; Parole Asn Ga; chmn, bd dir, DeKalb County Develop Authority; chmn, W Care-Ga C's Ctr Bd dir; life mem, Nat Asn Advan Colored People; Green forest Community Baptist Church; chmn, Senate Reapportionment Comt; chmn, GA Chap Westcare; chmn, Develop Authority DeKalb; Ga Correctional Asn; Am Probation & Parole Asn; DeKalb Bd Educ, Dist 9, bd mem, 2008-; Senate Dem Policy Comt; Statewide JTPA Comt; Ga Endowment Humanities; Ga Partnership Excellence Educ; Metrop Atlanta Rapid Transit Authority Overview Comt; bd trustee, Lit Action Inc; bd dir, United Cerebral Palsy; bd dir, Shop 'n Check; bd trustee, John Marshall Sch Law; bd trustee, DeKalb County Chap 100 Black Men Am Inc; bd trustee, Butler St YMCA; bd trustee, DeKalb County Adminr Asn; bd trustee, DeKalb Chap Am Red Cross.

### WALKER, FELIX CARR, JR.

Advertising executive, business owner, chief executive officer. **Personal:** Born Sep 1, 1949, Memphis, TN; son of Felix (deceased) and Estelle. **Educ:** Memphis Col Arts, BFA, 1977. **Career:** Felix Way Advert, pres, chief exec officer & owner, currently. **Orgs:** Pres, Onyx. **Business Addr:** Owner, Chief Executive Officer, Felix Way Advertising, 937 Peabody Ave, Memphis, TN 38104-6227, **Business Phone:** (815)932-4666.

### WALKER, FREEMAN, III

Executive. **Personal:** Born Jul 18, 1965, Roxboro, NC; son of Freeman Jr and Phyllis Umstead; married Kimberle Wathall. **Educ:** Univ Ga, BA, polit sci, 1987; NCA Cent Univ, MPA, 1992. **Career:** Nations Bank, fin banking intern, 1984-87; Int Bus Mach, personnel intern, 1988; Orange Co dept Aging, asst dir, 1990; Durham Reg Hosp Corp, media specialist, 1991; Family Health Int, asst int crd, 1992; We-Saw Inc, dir. **Orgs:** Rotary Club N High Pt, 1985; opp, 1988; Alpha Kappa Psi Prof Bus Fraternity, 1983-; Durham Companions, 1993-. **Home Addr:** 1800 Grande Oaks Rd, Durham, NC 27712-2046, **Home Phone:** (919)620-9488.

### WALKER, GARY LAMAR

Football player. **Personal:** Born Feb 28, 1973, Royston, GA; children: Gary Jr. **Educ:** Auburn Univ, grad. **Career:** Football player (retired); Houston Oilers, left defensive tackle, 1995-96; Tenn Oilers, left defensive tackle, 1997-98; Jacksonville Jaguars, left defensive tackle, 1999-2001, defensive tackle, 2000; Houston Texans, defensive tackle, 2002-05, left defensive tackle, 2004. **Honors/Awds:** Rookie of the Year, 1995; Pro Bowl Selection, 2001, 2002; All-Pro Selection, 2002. **Special Achievements:** Film: 1999 AFC Championship Game, 2000. **Home Addr:** , Franklin County, GA. **Business Addr:** Defensive Tackle, The Houston Texans, 2 NRG Pk, Houston, TX 77054, **Business Phone:** (832)667-2002.

**WALKER, GENE.** See WALKER, EUGENE KEVIN.

**WALKER, GENE.** See WALKER, DR. EUGENE P, SR.

### WALKER, GEORGE EDWARD

Artist. **Personal:** Born May 16, 1940, Memphis, TN; married Delores Prince; children: Genene. **Educ:** Memphis State Univ, BFA, MA. **Career:** Freelance designer & artist, 1969-71; artist, 1977-; Graphic Arts Memphis, owner & artist, 1978; Shelby State Comm Col, dir publ. **Orgs:** Alpha Phi Alpha, 1977. **Honors/Awds:** Pyramid Award, Advert Fedn Memphis, 1972 & 1977. **Special Achievements:** Designed & Published "Our Precious Baby" (first complete black baby book), 1971. **Home Addr:** 1574 Pinecrest Dr, Memphis, TN 38111. **Business Addr:** Artist, 1574 Pinecrest Dr, Memphis, TN 38111.

### WALKER, GEORGE RAYMOND

Educator. **Personal:** Born Oct 13, 1936, Little Rock, AR. **Educ:** San Francisco State Univ, BA, 1959; Univ Southern Calif, MS, 1967, EdD, 1972. **Career:** San Francisco City Schs, teacher, 1959-62; US Dependent Schs Germany, teacher, 1962-67; US Dependent Schs Spain, dir curriculum, 1967-69; Compton Col, Compton CA, instr, 1970; Calif Comn Teacher Prep & Licensing, consult, 1971-72; Calif St Univ, Pomona, prof educ, 1972-76; Calif St Univ, Dominguez Hills, dean Sch Educ & prof grad educ, 1976-94. **Orgs:** Pres, Calif State Univ, Dominguez Hills Chap Phi Delta Kappa, 1977-78; profs sec educ Nat Asn Sec Sch Prin, 1979-80; Alpha Phi Alpha Frat. **Home Addr:** 5131 Chesley Ave, Los Angeles, CA 90043, **Home Phone:** (323)651-2652.

### WALKER, DR. GEORGE T., JR.

Composer, pianist, educator. **Personal:** Born Jun 27, 1922, Washington, DC; son of George T and Rosa King; children: Gregory & Ian. **Educ:** Oberlin Col, Mus B, 1941; Curtis Inst Music, artist dipl, 1945; Univ Rochester, DMA, 1956. **Career:** Dalcroze Sch Music, teacher, 1960-61; Smith Col, prof, 1961-68; Univ Colo, vis prof, 1968-69; Rutgers Univ, Music Dept, chmn, prof, 1969-92, prof emer, 1992-; Univ DE, prof, 1975-76; Johns Hopkins Univ, Peabody Inst, prof, 1975-78. **Orgs:** Fulbright fel, 1957; John Hay Whitney fel, 1958; Frederic Chopin Soc; Guggenheim fel, 1969, 1988; Rockefeller fel, 1972, 1975; New York; Am Socs Composers Authors & Publishers; Am Symphony League; Am Acad Arts & Lett. **Honors/Awds:** Am Acad & Inst Arts & Letters Award, 1981; Hon Dr Fine Arts, Lafayette Col, 1982; Hon Dr Music, Oberlin Col, 1983; Harvey Gaul Prize; MacDowell Colony; American Academy of Arts & Letters Award; Mary Flagler Cary Charitable Trust Award; Koussevitsky Prize, 1988, 1998; Pulitzer Prize, Columbia Univ, 1996; Alumni Award, Eastman Sch Music; Whitney Award; Hon Dr Letters, Montclair State Univ; Hon Dr Fine Arts, Bloomfield Col; Univ Scholar, Univ Rochester, 1996; Hon Dr Music, Curtis Inst Music, 1997; Composers Award, Lancaster Symphony, 1998; Letter Distinction, Am Music Ctr, 1998; Am ACA Arts & Letters, 1999; Am Classical Music Hall of Fame, 2000; Dorothy Maynor Outstanding Arts Citizen Award, Harlem Sch, Sch Arts, 2000; Hon Dr Music, Spelman Col, 2001, 2005; First annual Classical Roots Award, Detroit Symphony, 2001; AI Dupont Award, 2002; Washington Music Hall of Fame, 2003; Annual Legacy Award, Nat Opera Asn, 2007; Mason Gross Memorial Award; Aaron Copland Award, ASCAP. **Special Achievements:** First Black Pianist to play with the Philadelphia Orchestra, first Black Pianist to play in Town Hall, NY, first black tenured faculty member, Smith College, first Black DMA recipient from the Eastman School of Music, first Black Composer to receive a John First Black Pianist to play with the Philadelphia Orchestra, First Black Pianist to Play in Town Hall, NY, First Black Composer to receive a John Hay Whitney Fellowship, First Black Graduate to receive a DMA from the Eastman School of Music, First Black to receive a John Hay Whitney Fellowship, first Black winner of the Pulitzer Prize In Music: Commissions from NY Philharmonic, Boston Symphony, Cleveland Orchestra, NJ Symphony, Kennedy Center Performing Arts, Las Vegas Philharmonic, National Endowment, Kindler Foundation, Fromm Foundation, NJ Youth Orchestra, Network for New Music: published over 90 works for orchestra, chamber orchestra, piano, strings, voice, organ, clarinet, guitar, brass, woodwinds & chorus; Scarecrow Press released Reminiscences an Am Composer & Pianist; George Walker: Great Am Orchestral Works, Vol. 2 One Five Most Outstanding Cds Contemp Am Music 2010. **Home Addr:** 323 Grove St, Montclair, NJ 07042-4223, **Home Phone:** (973)746-2794. **Business Addr:** Professor Emeritus, Rutgers University, Newark, NJ 07102, **Business Phone:** (973)353-1731.

**WALKER, GIBBS.** See WALKER-GIBBS, SHIRLEY ANN.

### WALKER, DR. GREGORY T. S.

Musician, educator. **Personal:** Born Oct 19, 1961, Northampton, MA; son of George and Helen Hill; married Lori Wolf; children: Grayson Wolf. **Educ:** Ind Univ, BS, music, eng, 1983; Univ Calif, San Diego, MA, comput music, 1985; Mills Col, MA, musical compos, 1987; Univ Colo, DMA, musical compos, 1992. **Career:** Composer & Violinist; Boulder Philharmonic Orchestra, concert master, 1987; Fort Collins Symphony Orchestra, concertmaster, 1988-90; Univ Colo, Denver, assoc prof, 1991-; Dream N Hood Rapper & Orchestra, Colo Symphony, composer, 1993; Performances: Kaleidoscope: Music by African-Am Women, Leonarda CD, with Helen Walker-Hill, 1995; Hsing-I, multimedia concert tour, 1998; Microphone Amplified Orchestra, Detroit Symphony Orchestra, composer, 1998; Am Acad Arts & Lett, charles ives fel, 2000; Song of the Untouchable, 2012; McCoy Artists Group LLC, soloist, 2012; CyberGuitar & Symphony Orchestra, 2013; Kawanakajima Video Guitar & Chamber Orchestra, 2016; Colo NeXt Music Festival, artistic dir, currently; George Walker Poem Violin & Orchestra, Albany CD, Cleveland Chamber Symphony; Breckenridge Festival Orchestra; Ft. Collins Symphony; Yaquina Chamber Orchestra; Colo Music Festival Orchestra. **Honors/Awds:** Special Award, Am Soc Composers, Authors & Publ, 1997-00; UNISYS Competition winner, Detroit Symphony Orchestra, 1998. **Special Achievements:** First African American to win the Pulitzer Prize in Music during his lifetime, 1996. **Home Addr:** 28620 Hwy 72, Golden, CO 80403, **Home Phone:** (303)642-0605. **Business Addr:** Associate Professor, University of Colorado, Arts 288, Denver, CO 80217-3364, **Business Phone:** (303)556-4009.

### WALKER, GROVER PULLIAM

Entrepreneur, lawyer, chief executive officer. **Personal:** Born Jan 14, 1941, Chicago, IL; son of Vernell Crawford and Rice; children: Jasmine. **Educ:** Univ Mont, AB, 1963; Univ Calif, Los Angeles, JD, 1967; Harvard Bus Sch, MBA, 1971. **Career:** Calif State, atty gen, dep atty gen, 1968-69; Rand Corp, consult, 1969; McKinsey & Co, int consult, 1970; Exxon Corp, corp atty, 1971-73; Johnson Prod Co, gen corp coun, 1973-75; Los Angeles State Univ, asst prof law & bus admin, 1973; Chicago State Univ, asst prof law & bus, 1974; pvt law pract, financial planning, 1975-87; Calif Non-Ambulatory Med Servs Inc, pres & chief exec officer, 1987-. **Orgs:** Calif Bar Asn, 1968; co chmn, Afro Am Stud Union Harvard Bus Sch, 1969; Ill Bar Asn, 1974; Fla State Bar Asn, 1976; bd mem, New Wash Heights Community Develop Corp, 1976-77; Total Care Home Health Agency Fla, 1976-77; City Miami Fla Zoning Brd, 1977-79; exec dir, Black Agenda, 1982-84; Cook Co & Chicago Bar Asn; Harvard Bus Sch Century Club; Harvard Club Chicago; PAD Legal Frat; bd mem, Afro-Am Family Community Serv. **Honors/Awds:** Victor Wilson Scholar, Univ Mont, 1959-63; Harvard Leadership Award, 1970. **Business Addr:** President, Chief Executive Officer, California Non-Ambulatory Center, 2012 S Rimpau Blvd, Los Angeles, CA 90016-1514, **Business Phone:** (323)936-0923.

### WALKER, HERSCHEL (HERSCHEL JUNIOR WALKER)

Football player, business owner, actor. **Personal:** Born Mar 3, 1962, Augusta, GA; son of John Willis and Christine; married Cindy DeAngelis Grossman; children: Christian. **Educ:** Univ Ga, BS, criminal justice, 1984. **Career:** Football player (retired), martial artist, actor, business owner; US Football League, NJ Gen, running back, 1983-85; Dallas Cowboys, 1986-89, 1996-97; Minn Vikings, 1989-91; Philadelphia Eagles, 1992-94; NY Giants, 1995; Renaissance Man Food Serv LLC, owner & chief exec officer, 1999; H Walker Enterprises, chief exec officer & owner, currently; Actor: Necessary Roughness, 1991; TV Series: "1981 Sugar Bowl", 1981; "ESPN's Sunday Night Football", 1987-93; "NFL Monday Night Football", 1986-97; "The Superstars", 1998; "Damn Good Dog", 2004; "The Apprentice", 2004; "Pros vs. Joes", 2006; "ESPN 25: Who's #1?", 2006; "Inside MMA", 2007; "Rome Is Burning", 2008; "2009 World Series of Poker", 2009; "Pardon the Interruption", 2010; "Strikeforce", 2010; "Rachael vs. Guy: Celebrity Cook-Off", 2012. **Orgs:** US Olympic Bobsled Team; Nat Minority Supplier Develop Coun. **Honors/Awds:** All-American, 1980-82; UPI Player of the Year, 1982; TSN College Player of the Year, 1982; Harley Award, 1982; Heisman Trophy, 1982; Maxwell Award, 1982; Walter Camp Award, 1982; 3 time All Am; USFL Outstanding Running Back, 1983, league leading rusher, 1983, 1985, Most Valuable Player, 1985; Pro Bowl, 1987, 1988; All-Pro, 1987, 1988; Collegiate Football Hall of Fame, 1999; Florida-Georgia Hall of Fame; USFL All-Time Team. **Special Achievements:** Guest appearance, TV show, "The Hour of Power", "Inside MMA", 2007; Fifth degree black belt inTae Kwon Do; performed with the Fort Worth Ballet. **Business Addr:** Owner, Chief Executive Officer, Renaissance Man Food Services LLC, 22 E Montgomery Crossroads, Savannah, GA 31406, **Business Phone:** (912)961-0002.

### WALKER, BISHOP HEZEKIAH XZAVIER, JR.

Writer, gospel singer, clergy. **Personal:** Born Dec 24, 1962, Brooklyn, NY; married Monique; children: KyAsia Monet. **Educ:** Long Island Univ, sociol; Hugee Theol Sem; New York Sch Bible; Philadelphia Bible Univ, Bensalem. **Career:** Gospel vocalist; Church Our Lord Jesus Christ Apostolic Faith Inc, chief apostle; Greater Refuge Temple COOLJC, sr pastor; Pentecostal Church Jesus Christ, youth pastor; Love Fel Tabernacle Church, pastor, currently; Albums: I'll Make It, 1987; Crusade Choir, 1990; Oh Lord We Praise You, 1990; Focus Glory, 1992; Live Toronto, 1993; Live Atlanta At Morehouse Col, 1994; Live New York By Any Means Necessary, 1995; Live London, 1997; Presents LFT Mass Choir, 1998; Family Affair, 1999; Hezekiah Walker Presents LFT Church Choir: Love Live, 2001; Family Affair, II: Live at Radio City Music Hall, 2002; 20/85 Experience, 2005; Compilations: Gospel Greats, 1995; Hooked Hits, 2003; Gospel Soundtrack, 2005; Essential Hezekiah Walker, 2007; Souled Out, 2008; Azusa: Next Generation, 2013; Labels: Sweet Rain Rec; Benson Music Group; Verity Rec Hezekiah Walker & Love Fel Crusade Choir; Hezekiah Walker & Love Fel Choir; Hezekiah Walker & LFC, 2005. **Orgs:** Pres & founder, Love Fel Bible Inst; founder & overseer, Covenant Keepers Int Fel. **Honors/Awds:** Vision Award, 1994; Stellar Award, Best Music Video, 1994; Excellence Award, Gospel Music Workshop Am, 1994; Contemporary Choir of the Year, Gospel Music Workshop Am, 1994; Grammy nominee, Best Album by a Choir or Chorus, 1996, 1997, 1998; Best Gospel Album Award by a Choir or Chorus, 1995; Grammy Award, Love Fellowship Crusade Choir. **Special Achievements:** Books published: Destiny: Dream It, Declare It, Do It, 2003. **Business Addr:** Pastor, Gospel Vocalist, Love Fellowship Tabernacle Church, 464 Liberty Ave, Brooklyn, NY 11207, **Business Phone:** (718)235-2266.

### WALKER, DR. HOWARD KENT

Ambassador, government official, educator. **Personal:** Born Dec 3, 1935, Newport News, VA; son of William R Jr and Jean K; married Terry B Taylor; children: Gregory & Wendy. **Educ:** Univ Mich, AB, high hons, 1957, MA, conley scholar govt, 1958; Boston Univ, PhD, 1968. **Career:** Boston Univ, African Studies fel, 1958-60; Boston Univ, teaching asst, 1960-62; US Dept State, res analyst, 1965-68; George Washington Univ, from asst to assoc prof, 1966-70; Bur African Affairs, un adv, 1968-69; Off Inter-African Affairs, int rels officer; Kaduna, prin officer, 1971-73; Am Consulate Kaduna, consult, 1970-73; Dept State, desk officer, 1973-75; Am Embassy Amman, polit counr, 1975-77; Am Embassy Dares Salaam, dep chief mission, 1977-79; Am Embassy Pretoria, dep chief mission, 1979-81, charged affiaries, a/i; Am Embassy Lome, ambassador Togo, 1982-84; Foreign Serv IST, Foreign Affairs fel, 1984-85; Ctr Study Foreign Affairs Foreign Serv Inst, Foreign Affairs fel, 1984-85; Dept State, Off W Africa, dir, 1985-87; Off Inspector Gen, Dept State, sr inspector, 1987-89, Am Embassy Antananarivo, ambassador Madagascar, ambassador Islamic Repub Comoros, 1989-92; Nat Defense Univ, vpres; NATO Defense Col, Rome, dep commandant, 1993; US Dept State, foreign serv officer. **Home Addr:** 1310 Pennsylvania Ave, Cape May, NJ 08204. **Business Addr:** Foreign Service Officer, United States Department of State, Washington, DC 20520, **Business Phone:** (202)663-1123.

### WALKER, IAN ROBIN

Playwright. **Personal:** Born Feb 13, 1964, North Hampton, MA; son of George and Helen Hill; married Andrea C Trindle. **Educ:** Univ Colo, Boulder, CO, BA, 1985. **Career:** Musician & playwright; Second Wind Prod Inc, co-founder, 1984-, playwright-in-residence, currently; Boulder Valley Sch Dist, theatre trainer, consult, 1989-91; E Bay Community Proj, Improv Theatre Proj. coordr, 1994-; Actor's Collective, co-founder, 1996-2000; Plays: Killing Time, 1998; Meadowland; Black Lies; Vigilance; Under a White Paradise; Erins Hope; Ghost in the Light; The Stone Trilogy; A Beautiful Home for the Incurable; The Gravediggers Tango; The History of Stone. **Honors/Awds:** Numerous awards including Drama Logue Award, 1996; Best of San Francisco Fringe Festival, 1998; John Golden Prize, 2000; Best of San Francisco Fringe Festival, 2001; Best of San Francisco Fringe Festival, 2003; Larry Corse International Playwriting Prize, 2006; Best Play: Bay One Act Festival, 2006. **Home Addr:** 231 Sadowa St, San Francisco, CA 94112, **Home Phone:** (415)239-4928. **Business Addr:** Playwright-in-Residence, Co-Founder, Second Wind Productions Inc, 505 Faxon Ave Suite 6, San Francisco, CA 94112, **Business Phone:** (415)508-5614.

### WALKER, JAMES, JR.

Executive. **Career:** Aptakisic Tripp Elem Sch Dist, asst supt, admin serv, currently. **Orgs:** Adv coun, exec dir, A Safe Place, Lake County Crisis Ctr. **Business Addr:** Assistant Superintendent, Aptakisic-Tripp Elementary School District, 1231 Weiland Rd, Buffalo Grove, IL 60089, **Business Phone:** (847)353-5650.

### WALKER, JAMES ZELL, II

Hostage, editor, executive. **Personal:** Born Mar 23, 1932, Birmingham, AL; married Jeanette Adams; children: Jimmy Zellbig, Debra Leartine, Ronnetta Marie, Freda Michetta & James III. **Educ:** San Francisco Jr Col, attended 1955. **Career:** Clarion Defender Newspaper, ed; Knockout Indstrs Inc, pres, 1971; KGAR Radio, weekend disk jockey, 1968-76; KPAM-FM, radoi host, 1971; KNEY Radio, talk show host, 1977; Org & Bio Degradable Cleanser, mfr. **Orgs:** Trustee & chmn, Billy Webb IBPOE of W, 1962-70; co-founder, Miss Tan Am Pageant, 1965; bd mem, Portland Br Nat Asn Advan Colored People, 1967; Nat Bus Leg, 1968; Nebr Portland YMCA; Freedom Black Fin, 1968; founder, Jimmy Bang Bang Youth Found, 1969; Portland City Club, 1970; charter Mem Albina Lions Club, 1970; sponsored, OR & WA, Black Am Contest, 1970-75; OR Black Caucus, 1972; mason Odd Fellws Pact Inc, 1972; C of C 69 Fed Title 1, 1973; pres, Jefferson PTA, 1974-75, 1977-78; Nat Black Mfg, 1977; Am Cancer Soc Neighborhood Chap, 1978-80; voting mem, Portland Local 8 & ILWU, 1980; sponser, Campfire Bonnie Blue Birds; co-chmn, Pub Sch Career Educ; Jefferson Cluster Study Com; adv bd, Beach Sch; adv comt, Jefferson

High Portland Pub Sch Cold Card Mem Billy Webb Elks Bldg; Fisk Univ Boosters Club 9; Jesuit HS Parents Group. **Honors/Awds:** Diamond Belt, 1950; Golden Gloves, 1953-54; AAU Western Boxing Champ, 1954; San Francisco Pacif NW Pro Boxing Champ, 1958-63; Rose Fest Parade, 1968-71; Albina Women Leg Achievement Award, 1972; Spec Portland PMSC Award, 1973. **Special Achievements:** First Black nominated for major Political Party in OR Group, 1970. **Home Addr:** 0320 SW Lane St, Portland, OR 97239, **Home Phone:** (503)220-0330.

## WALKER, JAY
Politician, business owner, president (organization). **Personal:** Born Jan 24, 1972, Los Angeles, CA; married Monique; children: 3. **Educ:** Howard Univ, BA. **Career:** Football player, business owner (retired); New Eng Patriots, 1994; Barcelona Dragons, 1995; Minn Vikings, quarterback, 1996-97; Sky Walker Flight Sch Football Camp, founder & chmn, 1998-; Walker Financial Serv, pres & chief exec officer, currently; ESPN, sports analyst; Dem, Dist 26, Prince George's County, 2007-. **Orgs:** House Delegates in Md, 1997; Prince George's County Dem Cent Comt, 2002-; Prince George's Black Chamber Com; Coalition Concerned Black Christian Men; House Del, 2007-; Legis Black Caucus Md, 2007-; Treas, Legis Black Caucus Md, 2010-; Task Force Estab Voc & Tech Educ High Sch Academies, Prince George's County, 2007-; Tantallon N Area Civic Asn; Task Force Stud Phys Fitness, Md Pub Sch, 2008-; Task Force Study Thoroughbred Horse Racing, Rose croft Raceway, 2008-. **Honors/Awds:** Hall of Fame, Howard Univ Athletics, 2005. **Business Addr:** President, Chief Executive Officer, Walker Financial Services, 6009 Oxon Hill Rd Suite 412, Oxon Hill, MD 20745, **Business Phone:** (301)749-5524.

## WALKER, JIMMIE (JAMES CARTER WALKER)
Actor, comedian. **Personal:** Born Jun 25, 1947, Bronx, NY; married Jerelyn Fields. **Educ:** RCA Tech Inst, art announcing & trade radio eng. **Career:** WRBR, part time engr; WMCA radio, 1967; Films: Let's Do It Again, 1975; Rabbit Test, 1978; The Concorde-Airport 79, 1979; Airplane!, 1980; Stiffs, 1985; Doing Time, 1985; Kidnapped, 1986; My African Adventure, 1987; Water, 1985; Going Bananas, 1987; Guyver, 1991; Home Alone 2: Lost in New York, 1992; Monster Mash: The Movie, 1995; Open Season, 1995; Ripper, 1996; Plump Fiction, 1997; Sweet Lorraine, 2010; Big Money Rustlas, 2010; Super Shark, 2011; TV series: "Good Times", 1974-79; "The Love Boat", 1977-85; The Greatest Thing That Almost Happened, 1977; "B A D Cats", 1980; Murder Can Hurt You, 1980; "Today's F.B.I.", 1982; "Fantasy Island", 1980; "At Ease", 1983; "Cagney & Lacey", 1983; "The Jerk Too", 1984; "The Fall Guy", 1984; "Bustin Loose", 1987; "Matchmaker host", 1987; "Bustin' Loose", 1987; "An Evening of Comedy with Jimmie Walker & Friends", 1988; "Jimmie Walker & Friends II", 1989; "In the House", 1995; "Deadly Games", 1995; "Chienne de vie", 1996; "The John Larroquette Show", 1996; "Late Show with David Letterman", 1996-2007; "Hollywood Squares", 1999-2002; "Shriek If You Know What I Did Last Friday the Thirteenth", 2000; "Son of the Beach", 2002; "George Lopez", 2003; "A Very Elimidate Christmas", 2005; "Everybody Hates Chris", 2006-08; "The 100 Greatest TV Quotes & Catchphrases", 2006; "The Real Match Game Story: Behind the Blanks", 2006; "Chelsea Lately", 2007; "Back to the Grind", 2007; "TV Land Confidential", 2007; "Entertainment Tonight", 2008; "Funny or Die Presents", 2010-11; "Traffic Light", 2011; "Mr. Box Office", 2012. Record album: Dyn-o-mite, Buddah Records; Video Games: Voice-Soap Betty, Ripper, 1996. **Honors/Awds:** Most Popular TV Performer, Family Circle Mag, 1975; Comedian of the Decade, Time Mag; various awards from civic groups in regard to role as JJ Evans; Impact Award, 2006. **Home Addr:** 9000 Sunset Blvd Suite 400, Los Angeles, CA 90069. **Business Addr:** Actor, Comedian, International Creative Management Inc, 8942 Wilshire Blvd, Beverly Hills, CA 90211, **Business Phone:** (310)550-4000.

## WALKER, JIMMIE
Administrator. **Personal:** Born Nov 4, 1945, Mendenhall, MS; married Virginia Finley; children: Baron, Lorria & Erica. **Educ:** Prentiss Jr Col, Prentiss, AA, MS, 1967; La Bapt Col, BA, 1969. **Career:** Sec Asn Prof Dir Cluster, 1974. **Orgs:** Sec Asn Prof Dir Cluster, 1974; bd mem, Youth Christ, 1975; bd mem, S Cent Rural Health Asn, 1979; bd mem, Farish St Hist Dist Revitalizatn Asn, 1980; Noon Optimist Club Jackson, 1980; bd mem, Voice Calvary Ministeries, 1980. **Honors/Awds:** Outstanding Basketball Player, Sports Writers Association Southern California, 1969; Sports Ambassador S Pacific, 1970; inductee, Los Angeles Bapt Collab Hall of Fame, 1971. **Home Addr:** 306 Millsaps Ave, Jackson, MS 39202-1414.

## WALKER, JIMMY L.
Automotive executive, business owner. **Career:** ULW Broadcasting Inc, owner; Laurel Ford Lincoln-Mercury Inc, chief exec officer, owner, pres. **Honors/Awds:** Co is ranked No 83 on Black Enterprise's list of top 100 auto dealers, 1994, ranked No 86, 1998. **Business Addr:** Owner, President, Laurel Ford Lincoln-Mercury Inc, 2018 Hwy 15 N, Laurel, MS 39440-1837, **Business Phone:** (601)425-3069.

## WALKER, JOHN LESLIE
Banker, vice president (organization). **Personal:** Born May 4, 1933, York, SC; son of Walter and Neely; married Mary Alberta Carlton; children: John L Jr & Karen F Walker-Spencer. **Educ:** Wilberforce Univ, BS, 1956; Rutgers Univ, Stonier Grad Sch Banking, attended 1972; Harvard Exec Sem, attended 1978. **Career:** France Chem Bank, vpres, 1978-80; Egypt Chem Bank, vpres, 1980-83; Repub Nat Bank New York, int pvt banking officer Mid E & Africa, 1988-91; US Dept Com, dept asst secy, 1994-96; Merrill Lynch, vpres, financial consult, 1996-. **Orgs:** Nat Bankers Asn, 1973-78; finance secy, United Black Men Queens Co, 1976-78; treas, Urban Bankers Coalition, 1977-78; African Develop Found, 1991-94; Kappa Alpha Psi Fraternity; Prince Hall Masons; Nat Asn Advan Colored People; Urban League; chmn bd trustee, Wilberforce Univ; bd mem, Jamaica Serv Prog Older Adults. **Home Addr:** 85-03 Wareham Pl, Jamaica, NY 11432. **Business Addr:** Vice President, Merrill Lynch & Co, 2 World Financial Ctr, New York, NY 10080, **Business Phone:** (212)236-5500.

## WALKER, HON. JOSEPH M., III
Judge. **Educ:** Harvard Col, AB, 1973; Harvard Grad Sch Educ, EdM, 1974; Univ Calif, JD, 1978. **Career:** Alameda County, asst dist atty, 1978-83; Suffolk County, asst dist atty, 1984-89; US, criminal bur & crime drug enforcement task force, asst atty, 1989-94; Dist Ct, 1994-2000; Suffolk Superior Ct, assoc justice, 2000, judge, 2004-. **Orgs:** Massachusetts Black Judges Conf, 2008. **Business Addr:** Associate Justice, Suffolk Superior Court, 90 Devonshire St Rm 1509, Boston, MA 02109, **Business Phone:** (617)788-8130.

## WALKER, JOSEPH W., III
Clergy. **Personal:** Born Jan 1, 1968?, Shreveport, LA; son of Deacon Joseph and Rosa; married Diane Greer; married Stephaine Hale; children: Jovanni Willow. **Educ:** Southern Univ, BA; Vanderbilt Univ, MDiv; Princeton Theol Sem, DMin. **Career:** Mt. Zion Baptist Church, Nashville, TN, pastor, 1992-; New Level Community Develop, founder, 2001; Nashville Unites, founder, 2014-; Full Gospel Baptist Church Fel, bishop, 2015-. **Orgs:** Omega Psi Phi; Kappa Kappa Psi Band; mem bd dir, Meharry Med Col **Honors/Awds:** Honorary doctorates from Meharry Medical College and Southern University. Named one of the top 20 black preachers in the United States by Root. com, 2013. **Special Achievements:** Drs. Joseph & Stephaine Walker Scholarship Fund, founder. Author, Life and Intimacy; Life Between Sundays; RESET: Make a New Start; monthly op-ed piece in the Reset. **Business Addr:** Bishop Joseph Walker Ministries, PO Box 330374, Nashville, TN 37203, **Business Phone:** (615)254-7296.

## WALKER, KARA
Artist. **Personal:** Born Nov 26, 1969, Stockton, CA; married Klaus Burgel; children: 1. **Educ:** Atlanta Col Art, BFA, 1991; RI Sch Design, MFA, 1994. **Career:** Columbia Univ, MFA prog, fac mem, currently. **Home Addr:** 606 W 116th St Apt 73, New York, NY 10027-7024. **Business Addr:** Faculty Member, Columbia University, 310 Dodge Hall, New York, NY 10027, **Business Phone:** (212)854-4065.

## WALKER, KAROL CORBIN
Lawyer, executive. **Educ:** NJ City Univ, BA, polit sci & govt, 1980; Seton Hall Univ Sch Law, JD, 1986. **Career:** Super Ct NJ, Appellate Div, 1986-87; Day Pitney, 1987-89; Seiden Wayne LLC, parter, 1989-2007; LeClairRyan, shareholder, partner, 2007-; US Dist Ct, Dist NJ, arbitrator & mediator; St John & Wayne Law Firm, partner, NJ. **Orgs:** NJ State Bar Asn, chair, 1998, pres, 2003-04; pres, Garden State Bar Asn; trustee, Essex County Bar Asn; chair, Morris County Bar Asn; house delegates mem, Am Bar Asn; chair, Nat Bar Asn, Com Law Sect, 2003-07; pres, Nat Conf Bar Pres, 2012-13; chair, Am Bar Asns Standing Comt Fed Judiciary, 2015; trustee, pres, 2015-16, Asn Fed Bar State NJ; fel Am Bar Found; bd dir, Nj Inst Continuing Legal Educ; Nj State Ethics Comn. **Honors/Awds:** Professional Lawyer of the Year Award, NJ Commission, 2007. **Special Achievements:** First African American woman to attain Partner status at any major New Jersey law firm; One of New Jersey's Top 20 African American Business People, Bus News, 1999; One of New Jersey's top 25 Women of Influence, NJBIZ, 2003; co-author, How to Establish & Maintain a Professional Relationship, Garden State Woman Mag, 2003; co-author, Privileges Chapter of New Jersey Trial & Evidence Treatise, Inst Continuing Legal Educ, 2003; first African American President in the then 105-year history of the New Jersey State Bar Association; recognized her as one of New Jersey's "Super Lawyers" by New Jersey Monthly Magazine in 2005-10; First African American appointed as Chair of the NJSBAs most prestigious Judicial and Prosecutorial Appointments Committee; Listed in Best Lawyers in America in 2006; First African American female President of the National Conference of Bar Presidents, 2012; Top 50 Women Attorneys in New Jersey, Law & Polit Mag, 2013; Gertrude E. Rush Award, Nat Bar Asn, 2013; First African American President of the Association of the Federal Bar of New Jersey, 2015. **Business Addr:** Partner, Shareholder, LeClairRyan, One Riverfront Plz 1037 Raymond Blvd 16th Fl, Newark, NJ 07102, **Business Phone:** (973)491-3522.

## WALKER, KENNETH R.
Executive, journalist, association executive. **Personal:** Born Aug 17, 1951, Washington, DC. **Educ:** Cath Univ Am. **Career:** Wash Star Newspaper, foreign corresp, nat affairs journalist & staff reporter, 1968-81; WJZ-TV Baltimore MD, prog moderator & asst producer, 1978-79; ABC News, polit corresp & news anchor, 1981-85; Nat Pub Radio, African bur chief, 1999-2003; Independent TV producer, corresp; USA Today, Good Morning Am, anchor: Tv Show, Night watch; Lion House Strategic Commun, pres, chief exec officer, 2000-. **Orgs:** Exec vpres, Nat Media Syst Inc, 1970-74; mem bd dir, Townsend Reading CtrInc, 1976; bd dir, Thurgood Marshall Meml Scholar Fund. **Honors/Awds:** Recipient, Washington Star Univ Scholarship, 1969; First Place, Washington-Baltimore Newspaper Guild Award, 1977; Emmy Award, Nat Acad TV Arts & Scientists, 1981; Dupont Gold Baton Award, Columbia Univ Sch Jour, 1981; Journalist of the Year Award, Nat Asn Black Journalists, 1985; Image Award, NAACP, 1985; Media Award for Excellence, Africa Am Inst, 2001; Top Award for radio journalism, Nat Asn Black Journalists, 2001. **Business Addr:** Owner, Lion House Publishing, 1119 Staples St NE, Washington, DC 20002, **Business Phone:** (202)388-5532.

## WALKER, DR. KENNETH R., SR.
Basketball executive, educator. **Personal:** Born Dec 19, 1930, East Providence, RI; son of Frank and Lillian; married Gail Beverly Smith; children: Kenneth Jr, Michele & Leanne. **Educ:** Providence Col, BA, 1957; RI Col, MEd, 1962; Boston Univ, EdD, 1977. **Career:** E Providence RI Sch Dept, teacher, eng & social studies, 1957-68, asst prin, 1968-70; Proj Upward Bound, asst dir, 1967-69; RI Col, assoc prof educ, 1970-93, prof, 1989, dir urban educ; Big E all-stars, basketball referee, 1982; Johnson & Wales Univ, adj prof, 1998; Early Enrollment Prog; Cent Jr High Sch, asst prin, dir. **Orgs:** Omega Psi Phi Fraternity Gov's Task Force, 1991; Consult HEW Title IV; mem Guid & Personnel Asn; Int Asn Approved Basketball Officials; Col Basketball Officials Asn; Asn Curric Devel Specialist; Amer Fedn Teachers; Ri State Parole Bd; consult, Ri State Dept Educ; Report Educ Ri; Big Bros RI; chairperson, State RI, Parole Bd Sex Offender Community Notification Unit; pres, Big Bros RI. **Honors/Awds:** RI Big Brother of the Year Award, 1963; IBA Man of the Year Award, 1967; Serv to Youth Award No Kingston Jr HS, 1969; Recip Afro-Am Award EPHS, 1971; Exemplary Citizenship Award, 1974; NAACP Freedom Fund Award in Education, 1980; Providence Col, HonSocD, 1983; East Providence High School Hall of Fame, 1987; Vincent O' Leary Award, 2004. **Home Addr:** 399 Brown St, East Providence, RI 02914, **Home Phone:** (401)434-5569.

## WALKER, KURT. See BLOW, KURTIS.

## WALKER, LANEUVILLE V.
Insurance executive, vice president (organization). **Personal:** Born Oct 13, 1947, Prospect, VA; daughter of Moses E Scott (deceased) and Sophia V; married Ernest L II; children: Ernest L III & Steven S. **Educ:** Cortez Peters Bus Col, attended 1966; Univ Ala, attended 1968; Va Common wealth Univ, BS, 1975. **Career:** Southern Aid Life Ins Co, ade asst, 1981-82, corp secy, 1982-88; Atlanta Life Ins Co, asst vpres, 1988. **Orgs:** Asst secy, Friends Club Beulah Baptist Church, 1981-; mem prog comt, Delver Woman's Club, 1982-, vpres; trustee, bd mem, Third St Bethel AME Church, Missionary Soc, 1981, 1990; bd mem, Jackson Ward Bus Asn, 1990. **Honors/Awds:** Leadership Award, Third St Bethel AME Church, Women's Day Chap, 1992.

## WALKER, LARRY MOORE
Artist, educator, association executive. **Personal:** Born Oct 22, 1935, Franklin, GA; son of Willie B and Cassandra; married Gwendolyn Elaine Howell; children: Dana, Larry & Kara. **Educ:** Wayne State Univ, BS, art educ, 1958, MA, drawing & painting, 1963. **Career:** Col Pac, Univ Pac, prof, Dept Art, prof drawing, painting & art educ, 1964-83, chmn, 1973-80; Detroit Pub Sch Syst, art instr, 1958-64; 30 one-man exhib; 60 group exhib; Ga State Univ, Dept Art, prof, chmn, 1983-85; Ga State Univ, Sch Art & Design, dir, 1983-94, chmn, prof drawing & painting, 1983-2000, prof emer, art & design, 2000-. **Orgs:** Stockton Arts Comn, 1976-77; Nat Asn Sch Art & Design, 1983-; Marta Arts Coun, 1983-; bd dir, Nat Coun Art Admin, secy, 1985, chmn, 1986, 1987; bd dir, Atlanta Arts Festival, 1986-89; adv coun, Binney & Smith Co, 1986-90; pres, Dekalb Coun Arts, 1987, 1989-90. **Honors/Awds:** Pacific Family Award, 1968; Distinguished Faculty Award, 1975; Award for Leadership & Appreciation of Service to the Stockton Arts Commission, Ann Recognition Awards Prog, 1981; Plaque for Service to the Arts Community, Stockton City Coun, 1981; Certificate of Appreciation, Univ Pac, 1982; Founders Wall Plaque, La Guardia HS of the Arts NYC; Certificare of Appreciation, Nat Coun Art Admin, 1988; Purchase Award, African Am Mus, 1997; Distinguished Faculty Award, Ga State Univ, 2000; Purchase Award, LaGrange Nat XXII Biennial, LaGrange, Georgia, 2002; Honorable Mention Award, The Red Clay Survey, 2005; Distinguished Alumni Award, Wayne State Univ, 2007; Wayne State University Arts Achievement Award, Wayne State Univ, 2007; ARTADIA Award, 2009. **Home Addr:** 5271 Walker Rd, Stone Mountain, GA 30088-2228, **Home Phone:** (404)498-7441. **Business Addr:** Professor Emeritus, Georgia State University, PO Box 3965, Atlanta, GA 30302-3965, **Business Phone:** (404)413-2000.

## WALKER, DR. LARRY VAUGHN, SR.
School administrator. **Personal:** Born Aug 8, 1939, Meridian, MS; son of Edd Sanders and Jessie Mae; children: Derrick B & Terri L. **Educ:** Jackson State Col, BS, 1960; Fisk Univ, MA, 1964; Roosevelt Univ, MST, 1974; Northern Ill Univ, EdD, educ admin, 1983. **Career:** Sch adminr (retired); Wayne County Schs, teacher, 1961-63; Jackson Pub Schs, teacher, 1964-65; Proviso Twp High Sch, teacher, 1965-74, dean, asst prin, 1974-82; Oak Pk & River Forest High Sch, assoc prin, from asst supt to assoc supt, 1982-93. **Orgs:** Bd mem, Family Serv & Ment Health Oak Pk, 1982-; presenter, Nat Assoc Sec Sch Principals, 1985; bd mem, Oak Pk YMCA, 1985-; pres, Nat Coun Meridianites/ Jacquelyn Sweetner Caffey Found, 1996-. **Home Addr:** 1764 Quiver Pt Ave, Henderson, NV 89012-3481, **Home Phone:** (702)263-9906.

## WALKER, LEE H.
Executive. **Personal:** Born Oct 6, 1938, Troy, AL; married Audrey Davis; children: 4. **Educ:** Fordham Univ, New York, NY, BS, econ & bus mgt, 1975; Univ Chicago; Ala State Univ; Brooklyn Col, NY Univ. **Career:** Am Prog New York, instr, 1960-61; Winston-Muss Corp New York, dir employee rel, 1961-70; Sears Roebuck & Co Chicago, Ill, grp dist mgr, 1970-93; New Coalition Econ & Social Chg, founder, dir & pres, 1980-; Heartland Inst, bus exec & vpres; Am Progressive Ins, ins salesman. **Orgs:** Am Mgt Asn; sr fel Heartland Inst; chmn, Ill State Adv Comt; dir, Black United Fund Ill; Urban Probs Community, 1968-69; chmn bd Am Fund; Local Draft bd, 1969-72; pres, Polit Club Rep; bd dir, AIM, 1970, chmn, 1970-72; vpres, New York chap, Nat Asn Advan Colored People; Univ Chicago's Off Spec Progs, 1981-; Ill Bd Higher Educ; dir, Chicago State Univ Found; trustee, Ill State Community Col Syst; comnr, Midwestern Higher Educ Comn; trustee & chmn, Found Bd Univ Orange Free State; Nat Urban League Guild NY; black rep, Westchester Co; Chicago Chap Nat Black Journalists; Sigma Pi Phi, Delta Alpha Boule; Chicago Chap Nat Guardsmen Inc; chmn, merit Adv Bd, Off Secy State Ill, Dept Personnel, 1990-92; nat pres, Nat Guardsmen Inc, 2002; dir, Coaliation, currently; Asn Integration Mgt. **Home Addr:** 8086 Garfield Ave Apt 7-1, Burr Ridge, IL 60527-7912, **Home Phone:** (630)655-1571. **Business Addr:** President, The New Coalition for Economic and Social Change, 19 S LaSalle St Suite 903, Chicago, IL 60603, **Business Phone:** (312)377-4000.

## WALKER, DR. LEWIS
Sociologist. **Personal:** Born Oct 22, 1936, Selma, AL; son of Joseph (deceased) and Thelma Watts Freeman; married Georgia Doles. **Educ:** BA, 1959; MA, 1961; Ohio State Univ, PhD, 1964. **Career:** Wilberforce Univ, stud instr, 1958-59; Ohio Higher Educ Asst Commn, admin specialist, 1962; Ohio State Univ, lectr, 1964; Ohio Hosp Asn, res specialist, 1964; Western Mich Univ, asst prof, assoc prof, 1964-71, prof, 1971, chmn, sociol, 1989-99, interim dir, chair emer & prof emer, currently, chair, Lewis Walker Inst Study Race & Ethnic Rels. **Orgs:** Douglass Comm Asn, 1965-69; Sr Citizens Inc, 1967; founder & dir, Kalamazoo Resources Develop Coun, 1967-68; consult & prog develop, Ford Motor Co, 1968-69, Police-Comm Rels Progs, 1968-70; ARC Bd, 1969-70; adv bd, Learning Village, 1970; Am Soc Asn, 1974-; Mich Soc Asn, 1974-; Miami Valley Soc Asn, 1974-; Kalamazoo Co Crime Comn, 1984-; pres, Walker-Taylor Thermics Inc, 1984-; bd,

Goodwill Indus, 1986-; Differential Flow Systs Inc, 1986-; Spare Time Pursuits Inc, 1986-. **Honors/Awds:** Distinguished Servervice Award, Jaycees, 1967; One of Five Outstanding Young Men of Mich Jaycees, 1967; Award for Teaching Excellence, Western Mich Univ Alumni Asn, 1971; inventor, US patent on low pressure boiler heating syst, 1984; invention, US patent on furnace syst, 1986; Distinguished Service Award, Western Mich Univ, 1989; Ujuma Liberator Award, 2003; Western Mich Univ W Club's Man of the Year Aware, 2007; Iichigan Career and Tech Inst Multi-Cult Coalition Award, 2009; Humanitarian Award, Nat Asn Advan Colored People, 2012. **Home Addr:** 3080 S 6th St, Kalamazoo, MI 49009-6478, **Home Phone:** (616)387-5270. **Business Addr:** Professor Emeritus, Chair Emeritus, Western Michigan University, 1903 W Michigan Ave, Kalamazoo, MI 49008, **Business Phone:** (269)387-8400.

### WALKER, LINDA T. (LINDA THOMPSON WALKER)

District court judge. **Personal:** Born Jan 1, 1960?. **Educ:** Southern Univ, BS, 1983; Atlanta Univ, MS, 1987; Univ Ga Sch Law, JD, 1989. **Career:** US Dist Ct, Northern Dist Ga, law clerk, 1989-90, magistrate judge, 2000-; law firm Webb & Daniel Atlanta, Ga, litigation assoc, 1990-92; Fulton Co, dep county atty, 1992-97, atty, 1997-99, Reg & Elections Off, dir, 1999. **Business Addr:** Magistrate Judge, United States District Court, 1856 Richard B Russell Fed Bldg & Us Courthouse, Atlanta, GA 30303-3309, **Business Phone:** (404)215-1370.

### WALKER, LISA

Executive director, manager. **Career:** Bridal registry, mgr; Macys Inc, dir reg & coordr spec events, currently. **Business Addr:** Regional Director of Special Events, Macy's, 22 4Th St, San Francisco, CA 94103-3131, **Business Phone:** (415)422-1000.

### WALKER, LORETTA YOUNG

Vice president (organization), media executive. **Educ:** Auburn Univ, Montgomery, BBA, comput info systs, 1985; Samford Univ, MBA, 1988; Nat Asn Multi-Ethnicity Cable (NAMIC), Exec Leadership Develop Prog, grad. **Career:** BellSouth Serv, dir human resources, analyst, 1985-88, staff mgr, 1988-91, mgr, 1991-93; BellSouth Cellular, corp human resources mgr, 1993-95, corp human resources dir, 1995-97; BellSouth Long Distance, dir human resources, 1997-99; Turner Broadcasting Syst Inc, Entertainment Div, vpres human resources, 1992-2002, recruiting, 1999-2007, sr vpres, 2002-07, chief human resources officer, 2007-13; Grainger, head human resources-Americas, 2015-; Diversity Best Practices, sr vice pres & chief human resources officer. **Orgs:** Fel Betsy Magness Leadership Inst; pres bd dir, Warren/Holyfield Boys & Girls Club; Emma Bowen Found; Nat Asn Multi-Ethnicity Cable (NAMIC); bd dir, Cancer Treat Centers Am, 2012-; at-large mem, Atlanta Housing Authority's Bd Commissioners, 2012-; Alpha Kappa Alpha Sorority; AUM Cheerleader.

### WALKER, LULA AQUILLIA

Government official, executive, secretary (office). **Personal:** Born Mar 1, 1955, Derby, CT; married William E Zimmerman; children: William Zimmerman Jr (deceased), Tyron & Garrett. **Educ:** Shaw Col Detroit, ded asst cert, 1974; US Acad Health & Sci, med spec cert, 1977. **Career:** Olson Dr Tenants Assoc, pres, 1979; Housing Authority City Ansonia, asst treas, 1980; City Ansonia, co chmn printing & signs, 1982, chmn, claims comn, 1984; Ansonia Bd Alderman, fourth ward alderman; St CT, menthealth worker II. **Orgs:** Adv bd, Valley legal Asst, 1980; asst rec secy, A Philip Randolph Lower Naaugatuck Valley Chap, 1982; bd Lower Naugatuck Valley Chap Nat Asn Advan Colored People, 1983; seargent arms Lower Naugatuck Valley Chap Black Democratics, 1983; vice dgt, ruler Lily Valley Temple H406 IBPOE World, 1984-; chmn, ClaimsComn, 1986; serve olice Comn bd aldermen. **Honors/Awds:** Woman of the Month, Women's Ctr Ansonia, 1979; 3 Awards, Dedicated ServCommunity Friends Lulu Ansonia, 1984; Dedicated Service Plaque, Community Magicians AC, 1984. **Home Addr:** 68 Jackson St, Ansonia, CT 06401-1210.

### WALKER, DR. M. LUCIUS, JR. See Obituaries Section.

### WALKER, DR. MANUEL LORENZO

Executive, physician. **Personal:** Born Mar 22, 1930, Battle Creek, MI; son of Charles S and Manuella Beck; married Joan Lucille Carter Parks; children: Gregory Parks; married Romaine Yvonne Smith; children: Linda Lee & Lorenzo Giles. **Educ:** Howard Univ Col, BS, 1951, Med Col, MD, 1955. **Career:** Philadelphia Gen Hosp, Intern, 1955-56; Mercy-Douglass Hosp, staff, 1958-73; pvt pract, 1958-; Mercy Cath Med Ctr, staff mem, 1968-; Lankenau Hosp, staff, 1979-; St Joseph's Hosp, staff, 1987-95; St Ignatius Nursing Home, med dir, 1972-; Univ Pa Health Syst, staff, 1995-2006. **Orgs:** Alumni pres, Class, 1955-, Howard Univ Med Asn; pres, Med Soc Eastern Pa, 1968-70; bd sch dir, Yeadon (PA), 1968-71; ed, MSE Pulse Newsletter Med Soc Eastern Pa, 1969-; AMA; Nat Med Asn, Pa Med Soc & Philadelphia County Med Soc; vpres, Howard Univ, Med Alumni Asn, 1970-75; bd dir, Philadelphia Acad Family Physicians, 1970, pres, 1980-84; pres, Keystone State Med Soc, 1971-73; Am Geriatrics Soc. **Honors/Awds:** Practitioner of the Year, Philadelphia County Med Soc, 1979; alumni pres, Class of 1955 Howard Univ Med Sch, 1955-; legion, Honor Chapel of Four Chaplains, 1978-; med honor soc, Kappa Pi & Alpha Omega Alpha; Practitioner of the Year, Nat Med Asn, 1986; President's Award, N Philadelphia, Nat Asn Advan Colored People, 1990; Mercy-Douglass Lecturship Award, Med Soc Eastern Pa, 1989. **Home Addr:** 425 Jamaica Dr, Cherry Hill, NJ 08002-1920, **Home Phone:** (856)779-0597. **Business Addr:** Family Physician, Medical Director, St Ignatius Nursing Home, 4401 Haverford Ave, Philadelphia, PA 19104, **Business Phone:** (215)349-8800.

### WALKER, MARGIE

Educator, writer, editor. **Personal:** Born Sep 23, 1952, Houston, TX; daughter of Elius and Lucy Rose; married Sherman; children: Sherman Leo II & Shomari Lukata. **Educ:** Tex Southern Univ, BA, speech commun, MA, speech commun; Colo State Univ, post-grad studies, 1976; Univ Houston, anthrop. **Career:** Writer, 1988-; KTSU FM, prog & pub affairs dirs; KMJQ-Magic 102, Programming Dept; Houston Defender Newspaper, ed & reporter; Bks: Harvest the Fruits, Spirit of the Season, 1994; Sweet Refrain, 1994; Breathless, 1995; Indiscretions, 1996; Conspiracy, 1997; Pub Affair, 1998; Season's Greetings, 1998; Kwanzaa Kupendi; Remember Me, 1999; Tex Southern Univ, Dept Commun, adj prof, vis prof, 2000-05; Where There's a Will, 2004; Writers In The Schs, writer-in-residence; Col Watch, editor, 2009-14, essay develop ed, 2009-; Images & Expressions, creative dir, 2010-; Univ Houston, Downtown, Tex, adj prof, 2012-; Books: A Slice of Reparations, 2011; In Blood Only, 2012; Stolen Moments, 2013. **Orgs:** Houston chap Mystery Writers Am; Arthurs Guild; Houston Writers Guild. **Home Addr:** 11615 Jutland Rd, Houston, TX 77048-2635, **Home Phone:** (713)738-6092. **Business Addr:** Creative Director, Images & Expressions, Houston, TX.

### WALKER, DR. MARIA LATANYA

Physician. **Personal:** Born Jul 3, 1957, Greenwood, SC; daughter of H W Jr and Leola Grant; married Albert L Thompson; children: Albert IV. **Educ:** Furman Univ, Greenville, SC, BS, 1978; Harvard Med Sch, Boston, MD, 1982. **Career:** Grady Memorial Hosp, internship; Ga Baptist Med Ctr, resident; Emory Univ Sch Med, fac, clin physician; pvt pract, 1990-; Piedmont Minor Travel Clin, med dir, currently; Piedmont Minor Emergency Clin PC, clin physician, pres, owner, currently. **Orgs:** Delta Sigma Theta, 1976; Med Asn Ga; Peabody Acad Soc/Harvard Med Sch, Am Med Asn; Phi Beta Kappa Beta Chap, Furman Univ, 1978. **Home Addr:** 1287 Beechwood Hills Ct NW, Atlanta, GA 30327-3126, **Home Phone:** (404)264-0973. **Business Addr:** Medical Doctor, President, Piedmont Minor Travel Clinic, 3108 Piedmont Rd NE Suite 100, Atlanta, GA 30305, **Business Phone:** (404)237-1755.

### WALKER, DR. MARK LAMONT

Educator, surgeon. **Personal:** Born Jan 5, 1952, Brooklyn, NY; son of Philip David and Ann Boston. **Educ:** City Col NY, BS, 1973; Meharry Med Col, MD, 1977; Howard Univ, hosp surg residency training prog, 1982. **Career:** Traumatology fel, Md Inst Emergency Med Serv Systs, 1982-83; Howard Univ Hosp, surg residency training prog, 1982, instr dept surg, 1983-85; Morehouse Sch Med, asst prof surg, 1985-90, assoc prof & chmn, 1990-94, Surg Residency, prog dir, 1990-96; Surg Health Collective, surgeon, med dir & owner, 1996-. **Orgs:** Alpha Omega Alpha Hon Med Soc, 1976-; fel Intl Col Surgeons, 1984; Asn Acad Surg, 1984; Atlanta Med Asn, 1985; Nat Med Asn, 1986; Cert Surg Critical Care, 1987; fel Am Col Surgeons, 1988. **Home Addr:** 4267 Palm Springs Dr, East Point, GA 30344, **Home Phone:** (404)768-1274. **Business Addr:** Surgeon & Medical Director, Owner, Surgical Health Collective, 777 Cleveland Ave SW Suite 305, Atlanta, GA 30315, **Business Phone:** (404)761-7482.

### WALKER, MARQUIS ROSHE

Football player, executive, football coach. **Personal:** Born Jul 6, 1972, St. Louis, MO. **Educ:** Southeast Mo State Univ, attended 1996. **Career:** Football player (retired), coach, executive; Wash Redskins, defensive back, 1996; St Louis Rams, defensive back, 1996-97; Oakland Raiders, right cornerback, 1998-99; Detroit Lions, linebacker, 2000; St Louis Warriors, dir sports prog; Wohls Recreational Ctr, St Louis, MO, vol, currently; Olivet Col, asst football coach, 2013-. **Business Addr:** Assistant Coach, Olivet College, 320 S Main St, Olivet, MI 63113, **Business Phone:** (269)749-7000.

### WALKER, MARY L.

Television journalist. **Personal:** Born Nov 17, 1951, Shreveport, LA; daughter of Sam and Jennie V Johnson Wilson. **Educ:** La State Univ, Baton Rouge, LA, BA, 1973. **Career:** KJOY Radio, Stockton, Calif, advert rep, 1974; KTBS-TV, Shreveport, La, gen assignments reporter, 1974-76; KSAT-TV, San Antonio, Tex, police beat reporter, 1976; Child Protective Serv, pub info dir & spokeswoman, currently; Tex Dept Family & Protective Serv, spokeswomen. **Orgs:** Nat Asn Black Journalists, 1986-; Soc Prof Journalists, 1988-; comt mem, Martin Luther King Comt, City San Antonio, 1988-. **Honors/Awds:** Outstanding Achievement in News Media, Beta Omega Sigma, 1975; Nomination for Best Television Documentary, Nat Acad TV Arts & Scis, 1976; Media Award, Tex Pub Health Asn, 1977; Media Awards for Excellence in Reporting Concerns of Children, Best TV Documentary, Odyssey Inst, 1980; Communications Award, Iota Phi Lambda Soc, 1980; Best Television News Story: Film & Script, Sigma Delta Chi, 1980; Best Television News Documentary, Sigma Delta Chi, 1982; Best Documentary, Tex Associated Press, 1982; Best Public Affairs Documentary, Tex United Press Int, 1983, Civilian Service Award, TV Documentary, Dept Army, 1984; Best Spot News Story (Team Report), 1986. **Home Addr:** 3223 Howard Suite 57, San Antonio, TX 78212, **Home Phone:** (210)822-3976. **Business Addr:** Spokeswoman, Public Information Director, Child Protective Services, 3635 SE Mil Dr, San Antonio, TX 78223, **Business Phone:** (210)333-2004.

### WALKER, MAY E.

Law enforcement officer, police officer. **Personal:** Born Dec 18, 1943, New Orleans, LA; daughter of Thomas J Jackson and Beatrice Ball; married Thomas Jr; children: Jemal R. **Educ:** Tex Southern Univ, BA, 1969; Univ Houston, MA, 1975, JD; Tex A & M Univ, MIS, 1990; United Way Tex Gulf Coast, attended 1990. **Career:** Police officer (retired); Lockwood, Andrews & Newman Inc, Houston, Tex, specif writer & librn, 1964-72; Houston Independent Sch Dist, instr, 1970-72; Light House Blind, Houston, Tex, admin asst, 1972-74; Houston Police Dept, community liaison police officer, 1974. **Orgs:** AKA Sorority; NOBLE; Nat Coun Negro Women Inc; Nat Black Police Asn; Coalition 100 Black Women; League Women Voters & Women Community Serv. **Home Addr:** 3922 Belgrade Dr, Houston, TX 77045-3404, **Home Phone:** (713)721-1646.

### WALKER, DR. MELVIN E., JR.

Educator, college administrator. **Personal:** Born Oct 23, 1946, Shivers, MS; son of Melvin E Sr and Rosie; married Jeraldine Wooden; children: Angela, Daphne Melinda, Melvin III (deceased) & Melanie Latrice. **Educ:** Prentiss Jr Col, AS, 1967; Alcorn A&M Col, BS, gen agr, 1969; Univ Ill, Urbana-Champaign, MS, agr econs, 1971, PhD, agr econs, 1973. **Career:** Ft Valley State Univ, from asst prof to assoc prof, 1973-84, coordr rural develop res, 1974-78, res dir, 1978-88, prof agri econ, 1984-, dean, 1987-88, 1990-98, actg pres, 1988-90, dean & res dir, 1990-98, prof, agr econs, 1998-2007, prof, econs, 2007-12. **Orgs:** Chmn, Asn Res dir, 1982-86; chair, Asn 1890 Agri Adminrs, 1984-85; chmn, Asn Res dir, 1986-; vpres, Camp John Hope NFA Alumni Asn, 1986-; Am Agri Econ Asn; Camp John Hope NFA Asn; Optimist Club; bd dir & treas, Asn Social & Behav Sci; bd dir, Ga Agr Econs Asn; Joint Coun Food & Agr Sci, Us Dept Agr; Am Asn Univ Professors; Southern Agr Econs Asn; Nat Econs Asn; Am Rural Sociol Soc; pres, Alumni Chap Future Farmers Am; Us Dept Agr; Southern Rural Develop Ctr's Impact Govt Transfer Payments Human Resource Develop Network; Am Rural Sociol Soc's Comt Develop Rural Sociol S; Adv Comt Western Rural Develop Ctr; Exp Sta Comt Orgn & Policy; pres & bd mem, Ft Valley Kiwanis; pres & bd mem Ft Valley Eve Optimists; Leadership Ga; pres, Leadership Peach; bd trustee, Peach Pub Libr; bd dir, Cent Ga Coun, Boy Scouts Am; chmn, Peach County Water & Sewage Authority; chmn, Peach County Bd Commissioners; bd dir, treas, Asn Social & Behav Scientists; bd dir, Nat Asn State Univs & Land Grant Cols; bd dir, Citizens Bank, Columbus Bank & trust; Warner Robins; Gamma Sigma Delta; Hon Soc Agr; Beta Chi Boule. **Home Addr:** 19 Duncan St, Ft Valley, GA 31030-4592.

### WALKER, MONICA L.

President (organization). **Educ:** Univ Tex, Arlington, BBA, acct, 1980. **Career:** Tex Utilities, supvr, 1981-91; Holland Capital Mgt LLC, founding partner, pres, finance, mgr, chief exec officer, chief investment officer, chief financial officer, 1991-. **Orgs:** Bd mem, YWCA Metrop Chicago; bd mem, Chicago Cs Choir; bd mem, Chicago United; chief exec officer, Coun Chicago United; Int Found Employee Benefit Plans Investment Mgt Comt; Chartered Financial Analyst Soc Chicago; Ill Cert Pub Accountants Soc; Tex Soc Cert Pub Accountants; Am Inst Cert Pub Accountants; Investment Policy Comt; Nat Asn Securities Professionals (NASP); Execs Club Chicago; Women Investment Professionals; Alliance Bus Leaders & Entrepreneurs; Econ Club Chicago. **Honors/Awds:** National Association of Securities Professionals (NASP), Chicago Chapter, Chicago Women Blazing the Path to Power, 2008; "Black Enterprise", 75 Most Powerful Women in Business, 2010. **Business Addr:** Chief Executive Office, Holland Capital Management LLC, 1 N Wacker Dr Suite 700, Chicago, IL 60606, **Business Phone:** (312)553-4830.

### WALKER, MOSES L.

Executive, health services administrator, association executive. **Personal:** Born Oct 21, 1940, Kalamazoo, MI; son of Arthur Sr and Erie Smith; married Ruthie; children: Tari, Mark & Stacy. **Educ:** Western Mich Univ, BS, 1966, MBA, 1990; Wayne State Univ, MSW, 1968. **Career:** Douglass Comm Asn, outreach worker, 1966; Kalamazoo Co Comm Action Prog, team capt, 1966; Comm Serv Coun, adminr asst, 1966; Archdiocese Detroit, Comm Affairs Dept, 1967; Douglass Comm Asn, dir, assoc dir, 1968-78; Borgess Ment Health Ctr, exec dir, 1978-83; DeLano Clin Inc, pres, 1983-91; Borgess Med Ctr, Behav Med Serv, vpres; Borgess Health Alliance, Community Rels, exec dir & chief diversity officer; Family Health Ctr Inc, interim pres & Treas; Federally Qualified Health Ctr, chief exec officer, 2007; Kalamazoo Comm Ment Health & Substance Abuse Serv, vice chiar, Currently. **Orgs:** Chmn, Educ Advan Scholar Comn, 1973; chmn, United Negro Col Fund, 1973; dir, First Am Bank, 1978-; pres, Asn Ment Health Adminr, 1987-89; chair, Mich Hosp Asn, 1988-; Kalamazoo City Comn; N side Asn; Nat Asn Social Workers; steering comt, Nat Asn Black Social Workers; bd dir, Kalamazoo Communities Schs; treas, Family Health Ctr. **Honors/Awds:** Outstanding Young Men of MI, Jaycees, MI Chap, 1969; Distinguished Service Award, Kalamazoo Chap, 1969; Outstanding Service Award, Northside Asn Educ Advan, 1972; Community Service Award, Southwestern MI Chap Nat Asn Social Workers, 1974; Distinguished Alumni Award, Wayne State Univ Sch Social Work, 1981. **Home Addr:** 1725 Cobb Ave, Kalamazoo, MI 49007-1707, **Home Phone:** (269)345-9968. **Business Addr:** Vice Chair, Kalamazoo Community Mental Health and Substance Abuse Services, 3299 Gull Rd, Kalamazoo, MI 49048, **Business Phone:** (269)553-8000.

### WALKER, PHILLIP EUGENE

Actor, artistic director. **Personal:** married Ethel Pitts; children: 1. **Educ:** Loyola Univ Chicago, BA, theatre; Univ Ill-Urbana, MA, theatre hist; Univ Calif-Davis, MFA. **Career:** Am Conserv Theatre; San Jose St Univ, Yuba Col; Santa Clara Univ; Lincoln Univ Miss; Univ Ill-Urbana; Oakland Ensemble Theatre, pres; African Am Drama Co, artistic dir, currently; Third Baptist Church, youth prog developer, 2003-09.TV Series: "The Evidence", 2006; "Trauma", 2009, "Welcome Space Brothers", 2010; "Hit the Floor", 2013; "Did You Watch", 2014; "Black-ish", 2015; "College Humor Originals", 2015; "Murder in the First", 2015. Films: Three Tutus and a Gun, 2014; America Is Still the Place, 2015; Hollywood Adventures, 2015; The Nostalgia Inn, 205; Steve Jobs, 2015; Stage Presence, Hickey, Casey and the Death Pool, forthcoming, Cardinal X, forthcoming, 2015; Dead Island 2, La La Land, Impetus, Longshot, forthcoming, 2016. **Orgs:** Touring arts Coordr, Calif Arts Coun; founding asst treas, Black Theatre Network. **Business Addr:** Artistic Director, African American Drama Co, 30 E Julian Suite 218, San Francisco, CA 95112-4076, **Business Phone:** (415)378-0064.

### WALKER, RHONDA

Founder (originator), television news anchorperson. **Personal:** married Derrick. **Educ:** Mich State Univ, BA, commun. **Career:** WJBK Fox 2 News, Detroit, 1998-2002; WDIV-TV Local 4, news anchor, 2003-07, noon news anchor, eve co anchor & health reporter, 2007-; spec prog: Thanksgiving Parade, Arts Beats& Eats, 35th Ryder Cup Matches, 2004, Maj League Baseball's All-Star Game, 2005, Super Bowl XL, 2006 & N Am Int Auto Show Charity Preview Spec; Rhonda Walker Found, Founder & pres, currently; Cornerstone Schs, partner. **Orgs:** Nat Asn Breast Cancer Orgns; Detroit Med Ctr; Mich Minority Bus Develop Coun; Nat Asn Black Auto Suppliers; Nat Asn Black Acctants; Hope United Methodist Church, Southfield, MI; active mem, Renaissance Chapter Links Inc; Fel Winning Futures Mentor Collaboration; bd trustee, Detroit Receiving Hosp. **Business Addr:** Founder, President, Rhonda Walker Foundation, PO Box 251746, West Bloomfield, MI 48325, **Business Phone:** (800)652-2989.

### WALKER, RONALD PLEZZ

School administrator. **Personal:** Born Oct 16, 1953, Boley, OK; married Glenda Gay; children: Terrance Scott. **Educ:** Langston Univ, BS, 1974; Cent State Univ, MEd, 1988; Okla State Univ. **Career:** Okla City Sch, sci teacher, 1973-76, bio-med prog dir, 1976-77, sci & eng ctr dir, 1977-80; Boley Pub Sch, supt, 1981-91; Jackson Mid Sch, prin, 1996-2001; IUSD 475, supt, 2003-13; Geary County Sch, KS, supt, 2004-14. **Orgs:** Pres, Nat Young Adult Coun, CME Church; vpres, Langston Univ, Alumni Asn; vpres, Orgn Rural Okla Schs; pub rels dir, Zeta Gamma Lambda Chap Alpha Phi Alpha; bd mem, Geary Community Hosp; bd dir, Geary County Sch, currently; bd dir, Nat Asn Federally Impacted Sch, currently; Mil Impacted Schs Asn; Mil Impacted Schs Asn; Nat Sch Boards Asn; Coun for Pub Sch Improv; Supt Leadership Inst. **Business Addr:** Superintendent, Geary County Schools USD 475, 123 N Eisenhower, Junction City, KS 66441-0370, **Business Phone:** (785)717-4000.

### WALKER, RONALD WAYNE (WAYNE WALKER)

Football player. **Personal:** Born Dec 27, 1966, Waco, TX. **Educ:** Tex Tech Univ. **Career:** Football player (retired); San Diego Chargers, wide receiver, 1989; San Antonio Riders, 1992; Ottawa Rough Riders, 1992-93, 1996; Shreveport Pirates, 1994-95; Sask Roughriders, 1996; Tampa Bay Storm, 1997-2000.

### WALKER, ROSLYN ADELE

Museum director. **Personal:** Born Memphis, TN. **Educ:** Hampton Univ, BS; Indiana Univ, MA, PhD, hist. **Career:** Museum director (retired); Univ Mus, Ill State Univ, dir; Nat Museum African Art, Smithsonian Inst, cur, sr cur, dir, 1997-2002; Dallas Mus of Art, cur, 2003-. Book: Olowe of Ise: a Yoruba Sculptor to Kings, 1998. **Orgs:** Arts Coun African Studies Asn; Col Art Asn; bd mem, African Am Muss Asn; bd mem, Midwest Art Hist Socs Online; adv bd mem, PCNAF Inc.

### WALKER, RUSSELL DEWITT

Safety engineer, government official. **Personal:** Born Aug 30, 1946, New York, NY; son of Elizier Amos and Armstead; married Mary Ann; children: Lisa, Danielle & Lael. **Educ:** Mt San Antonio Col, AA, 1967; Ventura Col, attended 1977; Calif State Univ, Northridge, attended 1979; Univ LaVerne, BS, 1980, MS, 1981. **Career:** Safety engineer (retired); Los Angeles County Dept Beaches, ocean lifeguard, 1965-72, sr ocean lifeguard, 1972-78, seasonal lt lifeguard, 1979-82, lt ocean lifeguard, 1982-92; Los Angeles County Fire Dept, capt lifeguards, 1992-98, asst chief lifeguard. **Orgs:** Pres, Sickle Cell DisServs Ventura County, 1976-96; Omega Psi Phi Fraternity, 1983-; int trng officer, World Lifesaving Asn, 1985-; stand comt mem, So Calif Pub Pool Oper Asn, 1989-90; Asn Chiefs, 1994-; bd dir, pres, Aquatic Found Metro Los Angeles, 1994; bd dir, Pat McCormick Educ Found, 1996-. **Honors/Awds:** Letter of Commendation, Los Angeles County Sheriff, 1977; Letter of Appreciation, Romper Room Show, 1979; Service Award, Sickle Cell Anemia Disease Services of Ventura County, 1979; Certificate of Appreciation, Burke Aquatic Found, 1995; Certificate of Appreciation, Zenith Youth Homes, 1996. **Special Achievements:** Author of Emergency Medical Section of Ocean Lifeguard Manual, 1973; Designed & Developed Beach Lifeguard Training Program, 1977; Created, Developed & Planned Water Awareness Training Education, Recruitment Program, 1985; Initiated Planning & Implementation of Lifeguard 911 Emergency System, 1986; Established Emergency Response Guidelines Book for Central Section Ocean Lifeguards, 1993. **Home Addr:** 694 Pac Cove Dr, Port Hueneme, CA 93041, **Home Phone:** (805)984-1221. **Business Addr:** Board of Director, Pat McCormick Education Foundation, 915 Elec Ave, Seal Beach, CA 90740, **Business Phone:** (562)493-0388.

### WALKER, SAMAKI IJUMA

Basketball player, entrepreneur. **Personal:** Born Feb 25, 1976, Columbus, OH; children: Dabaji & Sakima. **Educ:** Univ Louisville, commun, 1996. **Career:** Dallas Mavericks, forward, 1996-99; San Antonio Spurs, 1999-2001; Lady's & Gent's, owner, 2000-; Los Angeles Lakers, 2001-03; Miami Heat, 2003-04; Wash Wizards, forward, 2004-05; Ind Pacers, forward, 2005-06; Unics Kazan, forward, 2006; Al Jalaa Aleppo, 2007, 2010-11; Club Sagesse, 2008-09; Shandong Lions, 2009; Seoul SK Knights, 2009-10. **Orgs:** Founder, Life Choices Found, 2007. **Business Addr:** Owner, Lady's & Gent's, Columbus, OH 43222.

### WALKER, DR. SANDRA VENEZIA

Dean (education), dean (education), educator. **Personal:** Born Nov 1, 1949, Little Rock, AR; daughter of Otis L and Ardelia H Thomas; children: Brandon. **Educ:** Univ Mo, Kans City, MO, BA, 1970, MA, 1972; Wash Univ, St Louis, MO, PhD, sociol, 1976. **Career:** Wash Univ, St Louis, Mo, adj asst prof, 1976-77; St.Louis Community Col; Southern Ill Univ; City Kans City, Mo, dir pub serv & com support prog, dept housing & com develop, 1977-81; Univ Mo, Kans City, Mo, dir affirmative action & acad personnel, 1981-85, asst dean, col arts & scis, 1985-; Kans City, Region VIII, Secys regional rep. **Orgs:** Sec & treas, Asn Black Sociologists, 1983-86; vpres, Kans City, Mo Sch Bd, 1986-90; bd mem, Mo Sch Bds Asn, 1988-90; pres, Asn Black Sociologists, 1989-90. **Business Addr:** Associate Dean, University of Missouri-Kansas City, 5100 Rockhill Rd, Kansas City, MO 64110, **Business Phone:** (816)235-1000.

### WALKER, SEAN N.

Vice president (organization). **Educ:** York Univ. **Career:** Hershey Co; Gen Mills Can, vpres finance, 1989; Gen Mills, vpres mkt green giant bus, 2003-, Betty Crocker Div, dir financial opers, Meals Div, vpres financial opers, regional vpres, sr vpres & pres, Latin Am, 2007-. **Business Addr:** President, General Mills Latin America, 8400 NW 36 St Suite 310, Miami, FL 33166, **Business Phone:** (786)336-8900.

### WALKER, DR. SHEILA SUZANNE

Writer, video producer, anthropologist. **Personal:** Born Nov 5, 1944, Jersey City, NJ; daughter of James O and Susan Robinson Walker Snell. **Educ:** Sorbonne & Inst d'Etudes Politiques, 1965; Bryn Mawr Col, BA, polit sci, 1966; Univ Chicago, MA, 1969, PhD, anthrop, 1976. **Career:** Elmhurst Col, lectr, 1969; Chicago Model Cities Health Proj, res analyst, 1970; Chicago Urban League, res specialist, 1970; World Bank, Abidjan, Ivory Coast, translr, 1972; Harvard Univ Divinity Sch, res asst, 1972-73; Univ Calif, Berkeley, Calif, from asst prof to assoc prof, 1973-86, Dept Afro-Am Studies, assoc prof, 1986-89; City Univ New York, City Col, vis assoc prof, 1987; Schomburg Ctr Res Black Cult, scholar-in-residence, 1987; Col William & Mary, prof anthrop, 1989-91; Tex Univ, Austin, Tex, Ctr African & African Am Studies, dir, 1991-2001, Col Lib Arts, Dept Anthrop, Annabel Irion Worsham Centennial Prof, 1991-; Spelman Col, Atlanta, Ga, William & Camille Cosby Endowed Prof Humanities, 2002-04, fac social serv, 2003-04, prof, currently; Auth: Ceremonial Spirit Possession in Africa & Afro-Am, 1972; The Relig Revolution in the Ivory Coast: The Prophet Harris & the Harrist Church, 1983; African Roots/Am Cultures; Africa in the Creation of the Americas, 2001; Doc Video, Scattered Africa: Faces & Voices of the African Diaspora, 2002; African Christianity: Patterns Relig Continuity, co-ed, 1979; Global African Dispora, leading officer; Afrodiaspora Inc, pres & exec dir. Films: Slave Routes: Scattered Africa: Faces and Voices of the African Diaspora, 2008; A Global Vision, 2010; Africa on the Pacific: Esmeraldas, Ecuador, 2011. Books:, Conocimiento desde adentro: Los Afrosudamericanos hablan de sus pueblos y su historia; African Roots/American Cultures: Africa in the Creation of the Americas and produced the documentary Scattered Africa. **Orgs:** Int Exec Comt; Inst des Peuples Noirs, Ouagadougou, Burkina Faso, 1986-91; jury mem, Tenth Festival Panafricain de Cinema de; Ouagadougou, 1987-; Slave Rte Proj, Inst Sci & Tech Comt, Un Educ, Sci & Cult Orgn, 1991-; ed bd, Alpha Kappa Alpha. **Home Addr:** 540 N St SW Apt 5904, Washington, DC 20024, **Home Phone:** (202)863-1128. **Business Addr:** President, Executive Director, Afrodiaspora Inc, 540 N St SW Suite S904, Washington, DC 20024.

### WALKER, REV. SONIA

Publicist, executive, teacher. **Personal:** Born Apr 10, 1937, Columbus, OH; married Walter. **Educ:** Wilbur Force Univ, undergrad, 1956; Bennett Col, Greensboro, NC, BA, 1958; Howard Univ Sch Soc Work, MSW, 1963. **Career:** Elem teacher, 1958-61; Social Work Priv & Pub Agency, 1963-74; Univ Chicago, housing staff, 1970-74; WHBQ-TV RKO-GEN, dir comn rel, 1975; First Congregational Church, Midtown, assoc pastor, 2008-. **Orgs:** Memphis Asn Black Comt; bd dir, Memphis Orch Soc Memphis Urban Leag Nat Conf Christ & Jews Beale St Reprtory Co Memphis Art & Sci Comt; prog coordr, TN Womens Mtg; supt, adv coun, Memphis Pub Sch; PUSH; Nat Asn Advan Colored People; trustee bd & chair, Miss Blvd Christian Church; founding bd mem & former chair, Leadership Memphis. **Honors/Awds:** Honorary Doctorate in Humane Letters, Tennessee School of Religion; Women of Achievement's Award for Initiative, 2010; Outstanding Alumnae Award. **Home Addr:** 5050 Cole Rd, Memphis, TN 38117-4345, **Home Phone:** (901)683-7042. **Business Addr:** Associate Pastor, First Congregational Church, 1000 S Cooper, Memphis, TN 38104, **Business Phone:** (901)278-6786.

### WALKER, STANLEY MICHAEL

Educator, lawyer. **Personal:** Born Jul 15, 1942, Chicago, IL; son of Alfred and Georgia; married Elizabeth Mary Pearson; children: Darryl & Edana. **Educ:** Harvard Col, AB, 1964; Yale Univ Law Sch, New Haven, CT, JD, 1967. **Career:** Judge A Leon Higginbotham US Dist Ct, law clerk, 1967-69; Dechert Price & Rhoads, assoc, 1969-70; Pepper, Hamilton & Scheetz, assoc, 1970-71; Penn State Bd Law Exams, examr, 1971-74; Comm Legal Serv, staff & mng atty, 1971-72; Greater Philadelphia Comm Develop Corp, exec vpres, 1972-73; Rouse Co, sr atty, 1973-79; Univ Tex Sch Law, assoc prof, 1979-89; Exxon Co, USA, atty; Friendswood Develop Co, gen coun, 1995. **Orgs:** Am Bar Asn & Nat Bar Asn; Bars US Supreme Ct, DA, Pa, Md & TX; Austin Econ Develop Comm, 1985-89; alt mem, City Austin Bd Adjust, 1985-86; Action Metrop Govt Comm, 1988-89. **Home Addr:** 2714 Laurel Garden Dr, Kingwood, TX 77339-2505, **Home Phone:** (281)358-6310.

### WALKER, TANYA ROSETTA

Mayor, administrator. **Personal:** Born Apr 2, 1953, Philadelphia, PA; daughter of James and Lucille; children: Al Qadir R. **Educ:** Stenotype Inst NY, cert, 1970; Rutgers State Univ, BA, 1974; Essex Col Bus, cert legal & admin asst, 1977. **Career:** Lofton & Lester Esqs, paralegal, 1979-83; Gov Brendan T Byrne, exec asst, 1983-85; Althear A Lester Esq, legal asst, 1985-92; Essex Cty Prosecutors Off, exec adv, 1992; Twp irvington off mayor, off mgr. **Orgs:** Nat & Essex Cos Legal Secretaries & Paralegals Asn, 1979-89; Notary Pub NJ, 1982-; vol, Big Brothers & Big Sisters Am, 1983-88; bd mem, Boy Scouts Am, 1983-; bd dir & vpres, Make-A-Wish Found NJ, 1983-86; Union County CC, 1986-87. **Home Addr:** 555 Mansfield Vlg, Hackettstown, NJ 07840-3515, **Home Phone:** (908)269-8653.

### WALKER, PASTOR TERRY

General, manager, clergy. **Career:** ABC TV, music supvr, 2004-; 1988 Summer Olympic Games; All My C, music supvr; Tribe Judah Christian Motorcycle Ministry, Brisbane, owner. **Special Achievements:** Outstanding Original Song, nominee; Outstanding Drama Series Directing Team, Assoc Dir nominee; Outstanding Achievement in Music Direction & Composition for a Drama Series, nominee. **Home Addr:** 50 King St Apt 5C, New York, NY 10014, **Home Phone:** (212)989-3702. **Business Addr:** Music Supervisor, ABC TV, 500 S Buena Vista St, Burbank, CA 91521-4551, **Business Phone:** (818)460-7477.

### WALKER, TRACY A.

Manager. **Personal:** Born Jun 12, 1969, Detroit, MI; daughter of Charles N and Delma L. **Educ:** Univ Mich, Ann Arbor, BA, commun & Eng, 1991; Wayne State Univ, MA, pub rels & orgn commun, 1997; MA, libr & info sci, 2017. **Career:** Dow Corning, chem engineering intern, 1988; Palace Sports & Entertainment, community rels asst, 1991-92, educ progs coordr, community rels supvr, 1992-95, dir community rels/prog officer, 1995-2000, PK prog dir commun, 1997-99, dir community rels & prog officer, 1995-2000; Univ Mich Ann Arbor, Housing Dept, minority peer adv, 1988-90, resident dir, 1990-91, spring, summer coord, 1991; Detroit Pistons, admin asst, 1991, county rels asst, 1992, educ prog coord, 1992, county rels supvr, 1992-95, asst dir community rels, 1995-97, dir community rels, 1997-; Contact Sports, partner, 2000-03; Ntouch Commun Group, pub rels exec, 2004-06; Univ Phoenix, cert advan facilitator, 2003-14, area chair, commun, 2004-07; Affiniti Commun, prin, 2003-07; US House Representatives, commun dir, 2006-11; Wayne State Univ, Mich Area Health Educ Ctr, web content adminr & info officer II, 2011-14, assoc dir mkt & commun, 2016-. **Orgs:** DST Sorority Inc, 1989-, Detroit Alumnae Chap, 1993-; Blacks Advert, Radio & TV; lifetime mem, NCP; Univ Mich Alumni Asn; Nat Asn Female Exec; vpres admin, Women Community Detroit, 1996-97; prog officer, Pistons-Palace Found; Delta Sigma Theta Sorority Inc. **Honors/Awds:** Employee of the Year, Community Rels Dept, Detroit Pistons, 1991, 1992, 1994. **Home Addr:** 16750 Westmoreland Rd, Detroit, MI 48219, **Home Phone:** (313)538-7130. **Business Addr:** Associate Director Marketing and Communications, Michigan Area Health Education Center, 4201 St Antoine UHC Suite 9A, Detroit, MI 48201, **Business Phone:** (313)577-9802.

### WALKER, TRISTAN

Chief executive officer, founder (originator), entrepreneur. **Personal:** Born Jul 5, 1984. **Educ:** State Univ NY, Stony Brook, BA, econs, 2005; Stanford Univ Grad Sch Bus, MBA, bus admin & mgt, gen, 2010. **Career:** Foursquare, Dir Bus Develop, 2009-12; Andreessen Horowitz, Entrepreneur-in-Residence, 2012-; Chronos Mobile Technologies, Advisor, 2012; Main St Hub, Advisor; Walker & Co Brands Inc, Founder & chief exec officer, 2013-. **Orgs:** Founder & chmn, CODE2040, 2012-. **Business Addr:** Entrepreneur-in-Residence, Andreessen Horowitz, 2865 Sand Hill Rd Suite 101, Menlo Park, CA 94025.

### WALKER, DR. VALAIDA SMITH

School administrator, educator. **Personal:** Born Darby, PA; daughter of Samuel and Rosa Lee. **Educ:** Howard Univ, WA, BS, 1954; Temple Univ, Philadelphia, MED, 1970, EdD, 1973. **Career:** Temple Univ, Philadelphia, prof, 1974-, chairperson, dept spec educ, 1980-83, assoc dean, 1983-84, assoc vice provost, 1984-90, vice provost, 1987-90, vpres, studs affairs, 1990-2002, prof emer; Ment Retardation, Southern Pa, comnr. **Orgs:** Pres, Am Asn Ment Retardation; PA Adv Bd Spl Educ; bd mem, William Penn Adult Community, 1976; exec advsr, Caribbean Asn Ment Retardation; chmn, bd dir, Elwyn Inc, Elwyn, Pa; pres, Alumni Asn Bd, Temple Univ. **Special Achievements:** First woman to chair the board of directors of Elwyn Inc; Only African-American president of the American Association of Mental Retardation; First commissioner of Mental Retardation for Southern Pennsylvania; First vice president for student affairs at Temple University. **Home Addr:** 19 Elder Ave, Yeadon, PA 19050-2819, **Home Phone:** (610)623-8676. **Business Addr:** Chairman, Elwyn Inc, 111 Elwyn Rd, Elwyn, PA 19063.

### WALKER, VERNON DAVID

Computer executive. **Personal:** Born Jun 16, 1950, New Rochelle, NY; son of Edward and Veronica; married Sabrina Highsmith; children: Aminah & Aliyah. **Educ:** Univ Md, BS, bus admin & mgt, 1976. **Career:** Bendix Field Eng Corp, sr buyer, 1972-77; Satellite Bus Syst, sr procurement admin, 1977-82; MCI Telecommunication Corp, sr staff mem, sr mgr info systs, 1993-2000, sr consult, 2001-02; Synnap, opers mgr, 2000-01; Commun Networks Corp, IT serv delivery consult, vpres, 2001-; Radware, consult, 2002-04; IMTAS, IT consult, 2006-09; New Hope Baptist Church, sr technol consulant, 2006-11. **Orgs:** One Hundred Black Men NY, 1993-; Nat Black MBA Asn, 1993-. **Honors/Awds:** Cert Purchasing Mgr, Nat Asn Purchasing Mgt, 1986; Cert Netware Engr, Novell, 1996. **Home Addr:** 13 Hill St Suite 2, Norwalk, CT 06850-3007, **Home Phone:** (203)847-1471. **Business Addr:** Vice President, Communication Networks Corp, 13 Hill St, Norwalk, CT 06850, **Business Phone:** (203)847-3000.

### WALKER, W. VIRGINA

Entrepreneur. **Educ:** San Jose State Univ, BS, bus admin; Stanford Univ, exec mgt prog. **Career:** Enea Embedded Technol, gen mgr, corp strategy & mkt, sr vpres; CFO OSE Systs, exec vpres; JTS Corp, exec vpres, finance & admin, chief financial officer, secy; Jamison Group LLC, gen mgr; CFO Sagent Technol, exec vpres; Jamison Group Consult, gen mgr, currently; Scios Inc, vpres finance, admin, chief financial officer, 1985-95; Intersil Inc, controller; P&L responsibilities, gen mgr. **Orgs:** Founder, Asn Bioscience Financial Officers; Tri Counties Bank & TriCo Bancshares. **Honors/Awds:** Recognized as a "Guru" for her leadership among CFO's in the Biotech Industry, CFO magazine, San Francisco Chronicle's business section. **Business Addr:** General Manager, Jamison Group Consulting, 800 High St Suite 119, Palo Alto, CA 94301, **Business Phone:** (408)569-3005.

**WALKER, WAYNE. See WALKER, RONALD WAYNE.**

### WALKER, WENDELL P.

Administrator, association executive, executive. **Personal:** Born Jun 6, 1930, Painesville, OH; son of Robert M and Evelyn Wieker; married Doris Thomas; children: Kevin, Andrea & Brian. **Educ:** Defiance Col, BA, 1951; Western Res Univ, attended 1956; Univ Kans, attended 1971; Lake Erie Col, teaching cert, 1972; John Carroll Univ. **Career:** Teacher, administrator (retired); Poly Clin Hosp, 1955-60; Northeastern Ohio Gen Hosp, Med Lab dir, 1960; City Painesville, Councilman; City Painesville, activist & leader; Painesville City Improv Corp, trustee & pres; Harvey High Sch, African-Am History Adult Educ Prog, teacher. **Orgs:** Bd, Lake County YMCA, 1970; pres, Ohio State soc Am Med Technol, 1972-75; nat scientific comt; Am Med Technol, 1972, nominating comt, 1973, state bd, 1971-74, 1975-78; pres, Lake County health & Welfare coun, 1973-74; chmn, vchmn, Lake County Metropolitan Housing Authority, 1973-74; bd, United Way Lake County, 1974-76; vice chmn, Cent Br YMCA, 1973-74, chmn, 1975-76, bd, 1976; bd, pres, Free Clinic, 1975; Nat bd Am Med Technol, 1976-81; NEO Hop, bd; cub pack chmn, Boy Scouts Am, Dan Beard Dist; bd pres, Catholic Serv Bur Lake County; bd pres, Lifeline Economically Disadvantaged Consumers; Lake Metro Housing; Coalition Homeless Task Force; Lake County Jail Comn; Soc Bank; Metrop Health Planning Corp Cleveland. **Honors/Awds:** AMT National Presidents Award, 1973; Journal Award, OSSAMT, 1973; Painesville Area Chamber Comm Outstanding Citizen, 1994; Lake County Senior Citizen Hall of Fame; Alumni of the Year, Defiance

Col, 1995. **Special Achievements:** Area Chamber of Commerce; fdr Free Clinic; Lake County Grand Jury Foreman, 1973; Painesville City council man, 1986-95, Last 4 years as council president; represented Painesville School Systems for State of Ohio Consensus for education, KEDS Program; study for Lakeland col, need for education and vocation project projection for future; involved in first Project Testing for Sickle Cell Anemia (county-wide); social science inr for Painesville Night School; publication of numerous articles; Radio Personality-WBKC Radio, Fainesville, OH; First African American student admitted to John Carroll University. **Home Addr:** 26 Orchard Grove, Painesville, OH 44077, **Home Phone:** (216)354-8954.

### WALKER, WESLEY DARCEL

High school teacher, football player. **Personal:** Born May 26, 1955, San Bernardino, CA; children: John, Taylor & Austin. **Educ:** Univ Calif; Mercy Col; Fordham Col, MEd. **Career:** Football player (retired); NY Jets, wide receiver, 1977-89; Sports Radio Show, commentator, currently; Pk View Elem Sch, Kings Park, NY, phys educ teacher. **Honors/Awds:** Two Pro Bowls, 1978, 1982; All Pro, 1978; New York Jets Ring of Honor, 1978. **Home Addr:** PO Box 20438, Huntington Station, NY 11746-0857, **Home Phone:** (631)667-7160. **Business Addr:** Teacher, Park View Elementary School, 23 Roundtree Dr, Kings Park, NY 11754, **Business Phone:** (631)269-3770.

### WALKER, WILBUR P.

Educator, teacher. **Personal:** Born May 6, 1936, Okmulgee, OK; son of Hugh and Mae Ella Hill; married Tomycine Lewis; children: Wilbur Jr & Natalie. **Educ:** Langston Univ, BA, 1958; Cent State Univ, MT, 1968; Univ Okla, EdD, 1974. **Career:** Educator (retired); Okla City Pub Schs, teacher, 1967-69; Urban League Okla City, dir comm org, 1969; Univ Okla, spec asst to pres, 1970-73; Okla Univ, dir spec stud prog, 1973-75; Benedict Col, dean acad affairs, 1975-78; Okla St Regents Higher Educ, dir stud info serv, 1979-95. **Orgs:** Life mem, Phi Delta Kappa; Urban League Okla City, Black Inc; Nat Asn Stud Personnel Admin; Okla Col Personnel Asn. **Home Addr:** 12840 Burlingame Ave, Oklahoma City, OK 73120-8705, **Home Phone:** (405)748-4904.

### WALKER, WILLIAM B.

Automotive executive. **Educ:** Oakland Univ, BS, commun & bus, 1979. **Career:** Ford Motor Co, bus mgt mgr, 1984-90; New Castle Ford Lincoln-Mercury Inc, pres, owner, 1990-; New Castle Reinsurance Ltd, pres, 1991-. **Business Addr:** President, New Castle Ford Lincoln-Mercury Inc, 221 N Memorial Dr, New Castle, IN 47362, **Business Phone:** (765)827-8585.

### WALKER, DR. WILLIAM SONNY

Government official. **Personal:** Born Dec 13, 1933, Pine Bluff, AR; son of James D and Mary V Coleman Bell; children: Cheryl D, James D II, Lesli W Williams & William L Jr. **Educ:** Univ Ariz Pine Bluff, BA, 1955; AZ State Univ, cert, 1962; Univ Oklahoma, cert, 1968; Fed Exec Inst, cert, 1979. **Career:** Ark pub sch, teacher, athletic coach & adminr; State AR & Governer Winthrop Rockefeller, agency dir & asst to governer, 1969-71; US Dept Housing & Urban Develop, div dir, 1971-72; US Off Econ Opportunity, southeast regional dir, 1972-75; US Community Serv Admin, regional dir, 1975-81; Nat Alliance Bus, vpres; Nat Alliance Black Sch Educr, lectr; Sonny Walker Group, founder & chief exec officer, currently; Leap Frog Sch House, consult, currently; Morris Brown Col, bd trustees/exec comt & chair strategic planning. **Orgs:** Bd dir, United Way Metro Atlanta, 1977-87; bd dir, exec dir & chief operating officer, Martin Luther King Jr Ctr, Nonviolent Social Chg, 1979-; bd dir, Southern Christian Leadership Conf, 1980-87; bd dir, Metro Atlanta Community Design Ctr, 1981-; bd dir, Metro Atlanta Black & Jewish Coalition, 1981-87; vice chair, GA Asn Black Elected Officials & Corp Round table, 1982-87; bd trustee, Metro Atlanta Youth Women's Christian Asn, 1982-89; chmn, Econ Develop Task Force Nat Conf Black Mayors, 1983-87; vice chair, bd trustee, Metro Atlanta Crime Comn, 1983-; pres, Re surgens Atlanta, 1984-85; chmn, Collections Life &Heritage, 1984-87; bd dir, Consumer Credit CounAsn, 1984-, bd dirs emer; bd dir & chr, Pub Broadcasting Asn Atlanta, 1988-90; prin Ctr Excellence Govt, 1988; Metro Atlanta Rapid Transit Authority Bd dir, 1990-; chmn, Sustaining memship Enrollment Boy Scouts Am, 1990-92; life mem, Kappa Alpha PsiFrat, Nat Asn Advan Colored People (Nat Asn Advan Colored People); bd trustees chair, Bennett Col, 1991-; pres, 100 Black Men Altanta, GA, 1991-; GEO Partnership Excellence Educ, 1991-; pres, Nat Alliance Bus; pres, Little Rock & Ark Associations Teachers; bd dir, Atlanta Educ Telecommunications Collab; Friendship Baptist Church; Leadership Atlanta Alumni; chmn emer, UAPB Ann Fund Nat Campaign; chmn & pres, UAPB Nat Alumni Asn; bd dir & exec committe, UAPB Metro Atlanta Alumni Chap; vice chair, bd dirs & exec comt, Univ Ark Pine Bluff Found; exec comt, Atlanta Black Agenda; Atlanta Sch Bd; chair, bd dir, Metro Atlanta Chamber Com Polit Action Comt; treas, Margarethia Inc; chair, bd dir, Butler St YMCA; Nat Heritage Task Force YMCA; Y-USA Nat Assembly, chair, Y-USA Southeast Asn Assembly Steering Comt. **Honors/Awds:** Outstanding Public Service, State of GA House & Senate Resolutions, 1979; Achievement, Kappa Alpha Psi Frat, 1980; Community Service, Atlanta Bus League, 1984; Dr Laws, Shorter Col, Allen Univ, Edward Waters Col, Morris Booker Col; Distinguished Service Award, Atlanta Urban League, 1986; Roy Wilkins Award, Ga Nat Asn Advan Colored People (NAACP), 1986; President's Award, Nat Conf Black Mayors Econ Develop Task Force, 1986; Leadership Award, Metro-Atlanta United Way, 1987; President's Award, Nat Alliance Bus, 1988; Inspiring Self-Sufficiency Award, Southeast Asn Community Action Agencies; Southwestern Prov Achievement Award; Lyndon B Johnson Award, Nat Asn Community Action Agencies; Lifetime Achievement Award, Nat Head Start Asn; Outstanding Performance Award, US Dept Health & Human Serv; Hall Fame Inductee, Univ Ark Pine Bluff; Chairperson's Award, Martin Luther King Ctr; Hon doctorate, Humane Lett, Allen Univ; Hon doctorate, Humanities, BL Lee Theol Sem; Hon doctorate Law, Morris Booker Memorial Baptist Col; Hon doctorate Law, Shorter Col; Hon doctorate Law, Univ Ark Pine Bluff. **Home Addr:** 710 Peachtree St NE Suite 624, Atlanta, GA 30308, **Home Phone:** (404)885-1617. **Business Addr:** Chief Executive Officer, The Sonny Walker Group, 710 Peachtree St Suite 624, Atlanta, GA 30308-1221, **Business Phone:** (404)881-0857.

### WALKER, WILLIE F.

Association executive, president (organization). **Personal:** Born Feb 6, 1942, Vernon, AL; son of Naomi Ford and Willie B; married Frizal Glasper; children: Shannon, Willie Jr, Alex & Teresa. **Educ:** Southern Ill Univ, BS, 1965; Univ Wis, MS, 1971. **Career:** President & chief executive officer (retired); Venice Sch Syst, teacher, 1965-69; Venice-Lincoln Educ Ctr, dir placement, 1971-73; Madison/St Clair County, dir manpower, 1973-76; Nat Urban League Regional Off, regional coordr, 1976-77; Madison County Urban League, exec dir, 1977-85; Dayton Urban League, Dayton, Ohio, pres & chief exec officer, 1988-08. **Orgs:** Co-chair, Black Leadership Develop, 1986-; bd treas, Dayton Free Clin, 1987-; co-chair, Ohio Black Family Coalition, 1987-; bd mem, Ohio Elected Pub Officials, 1987-; bd secy, Ohio Coun Urban League, 1987-; Black Managers Asn, 1987-; pres, United Way Agency Exec, 1989; acct chair, United Way Campaign, 1989; co-chair, Dayton Urban League; bd trustee, Victoria Theatre Asn, 2002. **Home Addr:** 4758 Kentfield Dr, Trotwood, OH 45426, **Home Phone:** (513)837-4111. **Business Addr:** OH.

### WALKER, WILLIE LEROY

Government official. **Personal:** Born Dec 26, 1945, Detroit, MI; son of Stanley and Leila; married Edna; children: Dwayne & Takesha. **Educ:** Wayne State Univ, BS, bus admin, 1971, MBA, mgt, 1974; Walsh Col, MBA, acct, 1990. **Career:** City Detroit, proj mgr, prod div, Mayor's off, 1975-78, div head, prog mgt Employ & Training, 1978-91, coordr, admin serv, Employ & Training, 1991-93, dep dir, Employ & Training, 1993, Detroit Employ & Training, 1994-. **Orgs:** Adv bd, Multi Media Partnership, 1995; adv bd, Mich Jobs Comn, 1994-, work first, finance comt chair, 1994-; adv bd mem, Mich Dept Ed, 1984-; Booker T Wash Bus Asn, bd mem, 1995; audit comt mem, Ebenezer AME Credit Union, 1989-90, vice chair, 1991; Detroit Police Athletic League, mgr/asst coach, 1978-88; Mich Dept Ed, Mich Family Resource Coalition, 1995; Mercy Col, acct tutor acct club, 1987. **Home Addr:** 15754 Ashton, Detroit, MI 48223, **Home Phone:** (313)836-5930. **Business Addr:** Director, City Detroit, 707 W Milwaukee 1st Fl, Detroit, MI 48202, **Business Phone:** (313)876-0674.

### WALKER, WOODSON DUBOIS

Secretary general, lawyer. **Personal:** Born Apr 6, 1950, Springfield, AR; married Hope Labarriteau King; children: Yedea H, Ajamu K, Fwatula, Ajani & Chike. **Educ:** Univ Ark Pine Bluff, BA, hist & philos, 1971; Univ Minn Sch Law, JD, 1974. **Career:** Walker Kaplan & Mays Pa Little Rock, assoc atty, 1976-77; Cent Minn Legl Serv Corp, Minneapolis, assoc atty, 1974-76; Walker Co, exec secy, 1975-2011; City Menifee Ark, city atty, 1977; City Menifee Ark, city atty, 1977; Cinula & Walker Pa, Little Rock, partner, 1978; City Allport Ark, legal consult, 1980; Wealth I Walker Co, property mgr, property rehabilitator & real estate investment consult, 2000-; Walker & Dunklin, Little Rock, sr partner & pres, currently. **Orgs:** Nat Bar Asn, 1974; secy, Ebony Plz Corp, Little Rock Ark, 1976; Little Rock Wastewater Utility Comn, 1979; Ark St Bd Corrections, 1980; Ark Bar Asn; Minn Bar Asn; Am Bar Asn; bd mem, Boatmen's Nat Bank; bd mem, AP& L Utility Co; Pulaski Bar Asn; W Harold Flowers Law Soc. **Honors/Awds:** Outstanding Student Leader, Zeta Phi Beta Sorority, Univ Ark Pine Bluff, 1971; Higher Achievements Award, Phi Beta Omega Fraternity Inc Chi Psi Rho Chap Pine Bluff Ark, 1971; Lawyer-Citizen Award, Pulaski County Bar Asn, 1981; Act of Kindness Service Award. **Home Addr:** 6805 Talmage Dr, Little Rock, AR 72204-4746, **Home Phone:** (501)568-2817. **Business Addr:** Senior Partner, Walker & Dunklin, 2020 Broadway St, Little Rock, AR 72201, **Business Phone:** (501)372-4623.

### WALKER, REV. WYATT TEE

Clergy. **Personal:** Born Aug 16, 1929, Brockton, MA; son of John Wise and Maude Pinn; married Theresa Ann Edwards; children: Wyatt Tee Jr, Ann Patrice, Robert Charles & Earl Maurice. **Educ:** Va Union Univ, BS, chem, physics, 1950, MDiv, 1953, LHD, 1967, Hon Doctorate; Rochester Theol Ctr, Dmin, 1975; Edward Waters Col, Hon DD, 1985; Gettys burg Col, LittD, 1988; Princeton Univ, Hon Doctorate. **Career:** Clergy (retired); Hist Gillfield Baptist Church, minister, 1953-60, pastor; Dr Martin Luther King Jr, chief staff; Southern Christian Leadership Conf, Atlanta, vpres, exec dir, 1960-64; Canaan Baptist Church Christ, sr pastor, pastor emer; Abyssinian Baptist Church, NYC, pulpit minister, 1965-66; Cannan Baptist Church Christ NYC, pastor, 1967-2004, sr pastor, pastor emer, 2004-; New York Gov Nelson Rockefeller, specialist, 1970-80; Church Housing Develop Fund Inc, pres, chief exec officer, 1975. **Orgs:** World Peace Coun, 1971-; pres, Nat AsnAdvan Colored People; world comnr, Programme Combat Racism World Coun Churches; chair, Consortium Cent Harlem Develop secy gen; bd mem, Southern Christian Leadership Conf; pres, co-founder Relig Action Network, Am Comt Africa, 1980; chair bd dir, Nat Action Network; pres, Nat Asn Advan Colored People; dir, Cong Racial Equality; founder, Petersburg Improv Asn; Montgomery Improv Asn; Alpha Phi Alpha fraternity. **Honors/Awds:** Received numerous human rights awards incl Elks Human Rights Award, 1963; Nat Alpha Awards Civil Rights, 1965; Shrine's Nat Civil Rights Award, 1974; Civil Rights Award, ADA, 1975; Sisulu-Walker Charter School of Harlem, named in honor, 2005; Inducted, Civil Rights Walk of Fame, Atlanta, 2008; Keepers of the Flame, African-Am Church Inaugural Ball, Wash, 2009. **Special Achievements:** Wyatt was the first African-Am to meet with Chmn Yasir Arafat; Author: Black Church Looks at the Bicentennial, Somebody's Calling My Name, 1979, The Soul of Black Worship, 1984, Road to Damascus, 1985, Common Thieves, 1986, Gospel in the Land of the Rising Sun, New York, 1991, The Harvard paper, 1994, A Prophet from Harlem Speaks, 1997, Soweto Diary, Del World Conf on Relig and Peace, Japan, China Diary, Common Thieves, The Harvard Paper, Soweto Diary, Occas Papers of a Revolutionary, Spirits that Dwell in Deep Woods; Top Fifteen Greatest African Am Preacher In the US, Ebony Magazine, 1993; Films: "Mama, I Wanna Sing", "Malcolm X", 1992, "4 Little Girls", 1997, "Adam Clayton Powell", 1989, "Committee on UnAmerican Activities", 1962. **Business Addr:** Pastor Emeritus, Canaan Baptist Church of Christ, 132 W 116th St, New York, NY 10026, **Business Phone:** (212)866-0301.

### WALKER-GIBBS, SHIRLEY ANN (GIBBS WALKER)

Advocate, basketball coach, basketball coach. **Personal:** Born Nov 19, 1945, Bude, MS; daughter of James Bruno Sr and Curlee Smith; married Lonnie R Walker; children: Lonnie R Jr & Marino L. **Educ:** Alcorn State Univ, BS, health & phys rec, MS, athletic admin, health & phys. **Career:** Basketball coach (retired), educator, lawyer; Los Angeles Sch Dist, Health, Phys Educ & Recreation & Sci, teacher, coach, 1968-69; HISD, HPER & Sci, teacher, 1969-72; Alcorn State Univ, senior women's adminr, head women's basketball coach, 1977-2008; SWAC, advocate, currently-. **Orgs:** Delta Sigma Theta Sorority, 1970-; Nat Col Athletic Asn Women's Basketball, 1982-86; Nat Col Athletic Asn Coun Comt, 1990-95; Nat Col Athletic Asn Minority Opportunity & Interest, 1990-95; Nat Col Athletic Asn Midwest Reg Adv, 1990-93; Nat Col Athletic Asn Basketball Officiating, 1992-94; Nat Col Athletic Asn Spec Event, 1992-94; Black Coaches Asn.

### WALKER-KUHNE, DONNA

President (organization). **Educ:** Loyola Univ, BA; Howard Univ Sch Law, JD, 1980. **Career:** State New York, asst corp coun; Thelma Hill Performing Arts Ctr, managing dir; Dance Theater Harlem, dir, 1984-93; Walker Int Commun Group, pres, 1984-, chief exec officer, 2010-; Pub Theater, dir mkt & audience develop, 1993-2002, nat coordr; Ford Found, Changing World fel, 2001; Brooklyn Col, adj prof; Columbia Univ, adj prof; New York Univ, adj prof; Univ Berlin, lect; Impact Broadway, co-founder; Apollo Theater, George C. Wolfe's Harlem Song, assoc producer. Book: Invitation to the Party, 2005. **Orgs:** Brooklyn Arts Coun; vice chair, Greater Harlem Chamber Com Arts Cult & Entertainment Comt; co-chair, Spence Chapin African Am Parents Adv Comt; Broadway League; vdir, New York & a lic Minister Ceremonies NY; bd mem, Theater Riverside Church; bd mem, New Fed Theater; Int Theater. **Business Addr:** President, Chief Executive Officer, Walker International Communications Group, 293 E 18th St, Brooklyn, NY 11226, **Business Phone:** (718)703-2260.

### WALKER-SLOCUM, FRANCES

Educator, pianist. **Personal:** Born Mar 6, 1924, Washington, DC; daughter of George Theophilus (deceased) and Rosa King (deceased); married Henry Chester; children: George Jeffrey. **Educ:** Dunbar High Sch, attended 1941; Oberlin Conserv, BMus, 1945; Curtis Inst, Philadelphia, attended 1946; Columbia Univ Teachers Col, MA, 1952, prof dipl, 1971. **Career:** Pianist, educator (retired); Barber-Scotia Col, Concord, NC, 1947-48; Tougaloo Col, Miss, 1948-49; Third St Settlement Sch, New York, piano instr, 1957-64; Lincoln Univ, Pa, pianist-in-residence, 1968-72; Univ DE, 1968-69; Rutgers Univ, Nb, NJ, asst prof, 1972-76; Oberlin Conser Music, vis assoc prof piano forte, 1976-77, assoc prof, 1979, prof, 1981-85, chmn dept, 1985-86, prof emer, 1991-. **Orgs:** Pres, Pi Kappa Lambda, 1983-85; Spec Educ Opportunities Prog, 1985-88. **Honors/Awds:** Achievement Award, Nat Asn Negro Musicians, 1979, 1985; Lorain County Women of Achievement Award, Oberlin Col, 1985; Black Heritage Award, Langston Univ, 1986; Appreciation Award, Nat Bus & Prof Womens Club, 1995; Award of Distinction, Oberlin Col, 1998; Alumni Medal, Oberlin Col, 2004. **Special Achievements:** Completed 'Albums of music' by Samuel Coleridge Taylor, William Grant Still, Wendell Logan, and many lesser know minority composers; First African American tenured professor at the Oberlin Conservatory. **Home Addr:** 26 Shipherd Cir, Oberlin, OH 44074, **Home Phone:** (440)775-0274. **Business Addr:** Professor Emeritus, Oberlin Conservatory of Music, 39 W College St, Oberlin, OH 44074-1588, **Business Phone:** (440)775-8121.

### WALKER-SMITH, REV. DR. ANGELIQUE KETURAH

Clergy. **Personal:** Born Aug 18, 1958, Cleveland, OH; daughter of Roosevelt V Walker and Geneva Willis; married R Drew. **Educ:** Kent State Univ, Kent, OH, BA, telecommunications & dance, 1980; Yale Univ, Divinity Sch, New Haven, CT, MDiv, 1983; Princeton Theol Sem, Princeton, NJ, DMin, 1995. **Career:** WFSB-CBS TV, Hartford, Conn, prod asst, 1982-83; Oper Crossroads Africa, New York, NY, develop dir, leader, 1983-85; Cent Baptist Church, Hartford, Conn, assoc pastor, 1983-86; TEAM, Trenton, NJ, exec minister, dir, 1986-90; Lilly Endowment, Indianapolis, Ind, consult, 1990-; The Church Fedn Greater Indianapolis, Ind, project dir, 1991, interim exec dir, 1993-94, exec dir, 1995-; WKIV-Channel 6/AB, Faces Faith, TV host, 1992-; Keturah Productions, founder, chief exec officer; Odyssey Big Screen, co-host, currently. **Orgs:** Off int affairs, Partners Ecumenism, Nat Coun Churches USA, 1986-88; secy, bd dir, Nat Asn Ecumenical Staff, 1986-89; Ecumenical Liaison, Nat Baptist Conv USA Inc, 1989-94; co-chair, Yale Divinity Sch (YDS) first alumni color reunion & convocation, 2003; pres, Global Exchange Study Assocs, 1990-; prison chaplain, Ind Women's Prison; cent comt, World Coun Churches, 1991-. **Honors/Awds:** State of New Jersey Commendation Proclamation, New Jersey State Legislature, 1990; Mayoral Commendation Proclamation, Trenton, 1990; Valiant Christian Womans Award, Church Women United, 1990; YDS Alumnal Award for Community Service; Kent State University 's Special Achievement Award. **Special Achievements:** The First African American executive director-minister of The Church Federation of Greater Indianapolis; One of the youngest people ever elected to the Central Committee, the top governing body of the World Council of Churches. **Business Addr:** Executive Director, Vice Chair, The Church Federation of Greater Indianapolis, 1100 W 42nd St Suite 345, Indianapolis, IN 46208, **Business Phone:** (317)926-5371.

### WALKER-THOTH, DAPHNE LAVERA

Executive director. **Personal:** Born Sep 16, 1954, St. Louis, MO; daughter of Sidney J Carson Jr and Zelma J McNeil Carson; children: Aaron Walker & Candace Thoth. **Educ:** Truman State Univ, Kirksville, MO, BA, mass commun, 1977; Univ Mo, St Louis, MEd, 1990. **Career:** St Louis Globe Dem Newspaper, secy & calendar events ed, 1977-78; St Louis Argus Newspaper, reporter, 1978; St Louis Am Newspaper, Assoc Ed, 1978-80; Spectrum Emergency Care Inc, Mo, commun asst, 1980-82; CV Mosby Publ Co, manuscript ed, 1982-83; St Louis Area Coun Boy Scouts Am, exploring exec, 1983-85; Vol Interdistrict Coord Coun, asst to dir, 1985-89; Anti-Defamation Leauge B'nai B'rith, community coordr, 1989-91; Community Partnership Prev Substance Abuse Inc, dir, 1991-94; Mo Dept Ment Health Div Alcohol & Drug Abuse, proj dir, 1994-99, fac res assoc, 1999-2010;

Committed Caring Faith Communities Inc, exec dir, 2004-10; Balm Gilead Inc, dir, 2010; St. Louis County Kathy J Weinman Domestic Violence Shelter, grants adminr, 2011-13; St. Louis Community Col, acad grant writer, 2013-. **Orgs:** Chmn, bd dir, Committed Caring Faith Communities, 1999; chmn, United Methodist Gateway Bd Mission & Growth, 2014; Grant Prof Asn, 2014; adv bd, Mo Inst Ment Health at UMSL, 2015; adv coun, Nothing Wasted Inc, 2015. **Home Addr:** , MO 63139. **Business Addr:** Academic Grant Writer, St. Louis Community College, 300 S Broadway, St. Louis, MO 63102.

## WALL, TARA

Politician, association executive. **Educ:** Eastern Mich Univ, BS, telecommun & film. **Career:** Journalist & media entrepreneur; Mich Gov John Engler Off, asst dir, 1999-2000; PTP Found for Media Arts, founder, pres; video commentary segment, 2003; Repub Nat Comt, spokeswoman, press secy outreach, 2004-05, Minority Outreach Prog, sr adv, dir commun, 2005-07; Off Pub Affairs, dir, 2007-; WWJ & WKBD-TV, "St Beat", creator, pub affairs dir, host & exec prod; "The Washington Times", columnist, dep ed page ed & news anchor; CNN polit contribr, 2008. **Orgs:** Vol team leader, Bush Cheney Campaign, 2000; Faith Int Christian Ctr; PTP Found Media Arts; commun dir & spokesperson, Off Fed Coordr Gulf Coast Rebuilding, Dept Homeland Security; sr adv, Republican Nat Comt; dir, Off Pub Affairs, Admin C Families & U.S. Dept Health & Human Serv, 200-08. **Business Addr:** Director of Public Affairs, Administration for Children & Families, 370 L'Enfant Promenade SW, Washington, DC 20201, **Business Phone:** (202)401-9215.

## WALLACE, ADRIAN L.

President (organization). **Educ:** Tex Southern Univ, BS, chem, 1977; McNeese State Univ, MBA, 1990. **Career:** Vista Chem, chief chemist, 1978-95; Alpha Phi Alpha Fraternity Inc, gen pres, 1997-2000; Nat Pan-Hellenic Coun Presidents, nat pres, 2000; Univ Phoenix Online, cert advan facilitator, 2002-; Lake Charles City, econ & bus develop dir, 2003-08, asst city adminr, 2010-13; Cruise Planners, owner, 2001-; Martin Luther King Jr Nat Memorial Proj Found Inc, Wash, DC, dir & pres, 2001; Univ Phoenix Online, fac facilitator, 2002-; Southwest La Econ Develop Alliance, SEED Ctr, prog dir, 2011, Lake Charles N Redevelop Authority, dir, 2013-. **Orgs:** Gen pres, Alpha Phi Alpha, 1997-2000; nat pres, Nat Pan-Hellenic Coun Pres, 2000; prog dir SEED Ctr, Nat Incubator Asn, 2006-11; bd mem, St. Patrick's Hosp, 2007-10; life mem, Nat Speakers Asn, 2008-2009; bd mem, CHRISTUS Health, 2008-11; bd mem, March Dimes, 2009-10. **Business Addr:** Owner, Cruise Planners, 281 Debra Lane, Lake Charles, LA 70611, **Business Phone:** (337)217-9558.

## WALLACE, AL (ALONZO DWIGHT WALLACE)

Executive, football player. **Personal:** Born Mar 25, 1974, Delray Beach, FL; son of Andrew; married Shelley. **Educ:** Univ Md, BS, health & phys educ, 1997. **Career:** Jacksonville Jaguars, Off season/pract mem, 1997; Philadelphia Eagles, defensive end, 1997-99; Chicago Bears, 2000; Miami Dolphins, pract/squad mem, 2002; Carolina Panthers, 2004, defensive end, 2002-03, 2005, defensive end, left defensive tackle, 2006; Buffalo Bills, defensive end, 2007; free agt, currently; Marvin Ridge High Sch, defensive coordr, 2008-11; ESPN 730 Radio, sports analyst, 2012-13; Am Prod Distribr Inc, prod & data analyst, acct mgr, 2013-. **Business Addr:** Account Manager, American Product Distributors Inc, 8350 Arrowridge Blvd Suite E, Charlotte, NC 28273, **Business Phone:** (704)522-9411.

## WALLACE, ARTHUR, JR.

School administrator, executive. **Personal:** Born Jun 12, 1939, Muskogee, OK; son of Arthur and Edna Collins; married Claudina Young; children: Dwayne, Jon & Charles. **Educ:** Langston Univ, Langston, Okla, BS, 1960; Okla State Univ, Stillwater, Okla, MS, 1962, PhD, 1964. **Career:** Gen Foods Corp, White Plains, NY, dir commodity res, 1964-67; Merrill Lynch, New York, NY, vpres & sr economist, 1967-71; Group IV Econ, New York, NY, sr partner, 1971-76; Int Paper, Purchase, NY, vpres & corp secy, 1976-; San Francisco State Univ, Sch Bus, dean, 1993-98. **Orgs:** Nat Adv Bd, US Dept Com, 1973-74; trustee, Am Mgt Asn, 1982-84 & 1987-90; Adv Bd, Columbia Univ Workplace Ctr, 1985-89; Adv Bd, Scarsdale Day Care Ctr, 1985-88; Am Econ Asn; Nat Asn Bus Economists; dir, San Franciso Conv & Vishes Bur; Romberg Tibron Res Ctr. **Honors/Awds:** Arthur Wallace Diversity Scholarship, named in honor. **Special Achievements:** Arthur Wallace was the first African American dean of the College of Business at SF State. **Home Addr:** 1085 Greenwich Suite 1, San Francisco, CA 94133, **Home Phone:** (415)922-6971. **Business Addr:** Corporate Secretary, International Paper Co, 6400 Poplar Ave, Memphis, TN 38197.

## WALLACE, BARRON STEVEN. See WALLACE, STEVE.

## WALLACE, BEN CAMEY

Basketball player. **Personal:** Born Sep 10, 1974, White Hall, AL; married Chanda; children: Ben Jr, Bryce & Bailey. **Educ:** Va Union Univ, attended 1996. **Career:** Basketball player (retired); Wash Wizards, forward & power forward, 1996, ctr, 1997-99; Orlando Magic, power forward, 1999-2000; Detroit Pistons, ctr, 2000-06, 2009-12; Chicago Bulls, ctr, 2006-08; Cleveland Cavaliers, ctr, 2008-09; Detroit Pistons, ctr, 2009-12. **Honors/Awds:** Defensive Player of the Year Award, Nat Basketball Asn, 2002, 2003, 2005, 2006; All-Star, Nat Basketball Asn, 2003, 2004, 2005, 2006; All-Nat Basketball Asn Second Team, 2003, 2004, 2006; All-Nat Basketball Asn Third Team, 2002, 2005; Rebounding Champion, Nat Basketball Asn, 2002, 2003; Blocks leader, Nat Basketball Asn, 2002; All-Defensive First Team, Nat Basketball Asn, 2002, 2003, 2003, 2004, 2005, 2006; Champion, Nat Basketball Asn, 2004; All-Defensive Second Team, Nat Basketball Asn, 2007. **Special Achievements:** Only player in NBA history to record 1, 000 rebounds, 100 blocks, & 100steals in 4 Consecutive Seasons, 2001-04.

## WALLACE, BUBBA. See WALLACE, DARRELL, JR.

## WALLACE, C. EVERETT. See Obituaries Section.

## WALLACE, CHARLES LESLIE

Real estate executive, chief financial officer, vice president (organization). **Personal:** Born Dec 26, 1945, Monmouth, IL; son of Harriet and Leslie; married Marie Elizabeth Lancaster; children: Allison & Bryan. **Educ:** Northern Ill Univ, BS, acct, 1967; Univ Chicago, MBA, finance, 1973, CPA, 1973. **Career:** Arthur Andersen & Co, auditor, 1967-74; Jos Schultz Brewing Co, financial analyst, 1974-76; Univ Foods Corp, treas, 1976-81; Pabst Brewing Co, treas, 1981-85; Norrell Corp, treas, 1985-87; N Milwaukee State Bank, pres, 1987-89; Ameritech Mobile Commun Inc, vpres finance & admin, 1989-94; Grucon Corp, vpres, chief financial officer, 1991-94; Steel tech Mfg Inc, chmn & chief exec officer, 1994-2000; Baird & Warner, sr vpres & chief financial officer, 2001. **Orgs:** Finance Execs Inst, Chicago Chap; Am Inst CPA's; Kappa Alpha Psi; Sigma Pi Phi. **Honors/Awds:** Black Excellence Award, The Milwaukee Times, 1989; Outstanding Accounting Alumnus, Northern Ill Univ, 1991; Outstanding College of Business Alumnus, Northern Ill Univ, 1995. **Home Addr:** 800 S Wells St, Chicago, IL 60607, **Home Phone:** (312)896-8817.

## WALLACE, DARRELL, JR. (BUBBA WALLACE)

Race car driver. **Personal:** Born Oct 8, 1993, Mobile, AL; son of Darrell Sr and Desiree. **Educ:** NASCAR's Dr Diversity Prog, cert. **Career:** Stock car racing driver, 2010-. **Honors/Awds:** K&N Pro Series East, Rookie of the Year, 2010. **Special Achievements:** Youngest driver to win at the Franklin County Speedway in Virginia; first African American driver to win in a NASCAR national series since 1963; first African American to win Rookie of the Year in a NASCAR series; by the end of the 2014 season, he had a career five wins, 26 top ten finishes, and three poles.

## WALLACE, DERRICK D.

Executive, business owner, president (organization). **Personal:** Born Nov 4, 1953, Orlando, FL; son of Theressa Williams; children: Daunte & Deja. **Educ:** Fla A&M Univ, BS, acct, 1975. **Career:** Price Waterhouse & Co, CPA, staff acct, 1975-77; Tuttle/White Constructors Inc, chief acct, 1977-80; Construct Two Group, owner, pres & chief exec officer, chm, 1980-; Granduer Corp, Pres, 2002-. **Orgs:** Bd mem, Cent State Asn Minority Contr; Greater Orlando Chamber Com, 1984; class mem, Leadership Orlando, 1988; bd mem, Greater Orlando Chamber Com, 1989; chmn, Pvt Indust Coun Cent Fla; comnr, Mayor's Comn Arts; sub comt chair, Mayor's Youth Comn; Greater Fla Minority Purchasing Coun; partner, Partners Educ-Wash Shores Elem; partner, Partners Educ-Rock Lake Elem; pvt indust coun chmn, sponsored minority (Black) Role Model Proj Orange County Schs; pres, Orange County Br Nat Asn Advan Colored People; bd mem, Orlando/Ore County Compact, 1990-91; bd mem, Addn, 1990-91; bd dir, Econ Develo CMS Mid-Fla; bd dir, Nat Asn Minority Contractors; founder, 100 Black Men Orlando Inc; bd mem, African Am Chamber Com Cent Fla; bd mem, Cent Fla Jobs Educ Partnership; bd dir, Goodwill Industs; bd dir, Cent Fla Fair; chair, Mayor's Martin Luther King Comn; founding trustee, Minority/Women Bus Enterprise Alliance Inc; founding trustee, Bus Better Educ. **Home Addr:** 1456 Kozart Ct, Orlando, FL 32811-4013, **Home Phone:** (407)730-5336. **Business Addr:** Owner, Chief Executive Officer, Construct Two Group, 30 S Ivey Lane, Orlando, FL 32811-4222, **Business Phone:** (407)295-9812.

## WALLACE, GEORGE E.

Government official, executive director, mayor. **Educ:** NC Cent Univ, Durham, NC, BS, acct; Golden Gate Univ, San Francisco, CA, MPA. **Career:** Off Human Affairs, City Newport News, dep dir, 1965-72; Southeast Tidewater Area Manpower Plng Authority, City Norfolk, exec dir, 1972-75; Community Serv, City Hampton, asst city mgr, 1975-90; Strategic Plng & Econ Develop, City Hampt, asst city mgr, 1990-97, city mgr, 1997-2005, vice mayor, 2010-. **Orgs:** Int City/County Mgt Asn (ICMA); pres, Am Socs Pub Admin (ASPA); Nat Asn Advan Colored People; Omega Psi Phi Fraternity; Sigma Pi Phi Fraternity; Pi Alpha Alpha Hon Fraternity Pub Admin; Va Econ Develop Asn; Nat Urban Econ Develop Coun; trustee, First Baptist Church; Beau Brummell Civic & Social Club; fel Hampton Rotary; Pres, Boys & Girls Clubs Greater Hampton Roads; Treas, & Pres, Va First Cities Coalition, Founder; Local Pres, & Nat Treas, Conf Minority Pub Adminr, Local Chap Founder; Nat Forum Black Pub Adminr; dir & vpres, 100 Black Men Va Peninsula; Hampton City Coun, 2008-; pres, Am Soc Pub Admin; Va Munic League. **Home Addr:** 3 Colonnade Ct, Hampton, VA 23666, **Home Phone:** (757)826-9078. **Business Addr:** Vice Mayor, City of Hampton, 22 Lincoln St, Hampton, VA 23669-3522, **Business Phone:** (757)727-6392.

## WALLACE, REV. HAROLD GENE

School administrator. **Personal:** Born Aug 13, 1945, Gaffney, SC; son of Charles T Sr and Melinda Goudelock; married Cindy; children: Toya Bonita, Shonda Lee, Harold Gene Jr & Charles Marion. **Educ:** Claflin Col, Orangeburg, SC, BS, 1967; Duke Univ Div Sch, Durham, NC, Mdiv, 1971. **Career:** School administrator (retired); Bethesda Presby Church, Gaffney, SC, pastor & youth counr, 1968; Durham Comm House, counr, 1968-69; Duke Univ, Summer Transitional Prog, asst dir, 1969, asst dean undergrad educ, stud adv, 1969-72, assoc dir, 1970, co-dir, 1971, dir, 1972, asst provost, dean black stud affairs, interim dir comm & field work Afro-Am majors & sem instr Afro-Am studies, 1972-73, prof; Univ NC, Chapel Hill, assoc dean stud affairs & dir dept spec progs, 1973-79, asst vice chancellor stud affairs, 1979-80, vice chancellor univ affairs, 1980-96, spec asst minority affairs, 1996-99, prof. **Orgs:** Pres, Alpha Kappa Mu Nat & Hon Soc Claflin Col, 1966-67; Rockefeller fel Duke Univ, 1967; group moderator, Regional Educ Bd Conf Black Stud & Univ, 1971; Nat Comn United Ministers Higher Educ, 1971-75; consult, Minority Stud Progs, Univ SC Furman & Wake Forest, 1971-78; secy & treas, Black Fac Staff Caucus, Univ NC Chapel Hill, 1974-80, chair person, 1987-90; bd dir, Wesley Found Campus Ministry, Univ NC, 1976-80; Inst Study Minority Issues, NC Cent Univ, 1977-; chairperson, Upward Bound Adv Bd, Univ NC, 1980-; chairperson, Black Cult Ctr Adv Bd Univ NC, 1990-; chair emer, Sonja Haynes Stone Black Cult Ctr, UNC-Chapel Hill; bd dir, Found End Life Care; former chmn & bd trustees, Claflin Univ; bd dir, Caring Foundation. **Honors/Awds:** Faculty Awards, Black Stud Movement, Univ NC Chapel Hill, 1981, Univ NC Black Alumni Asn, 1982; Martin Luther King Jr Award, South Orange Black Caucus, Chapel Hill, NC, 1988; Award of Commitment to Justice and Equality, Butner NC Nat Asn Advan Colored People, 1989. **Special Achievements:** Published "Studies in Black" 1969, "Three Years of the Duke Summer Transitional Program" 1973; First African American vice chancellor of UNC. **Home Addr:** 2601 Cammie St, Durham, NC 27705, **Home Phone:** (919)477-6142. **Business Addr:** Board of Director, The Foundation for End-of-Life Care, 5430 NW 33rd Ave Suite 106, Ft. Lauderdale, FL 33309, **Business Phone:** (954)777-2447.

## WALLACE, HELEN WINFREE-PEYTON

School administrator, elementary school teacher. **Personal:** Born Dec 19, 1927, New York, NY; daughter of Hugh and Agnes; married Walter; children: Walter S Peyton IV. **Educ:** Va Union Univ, BA, 1949, 1959; Northwestern Univ, MA, 1955; Univ Calif; Va State Univ; Va Commonwealth Univ; Univ Caltolica, Di Milano Italy, 1968. **Career:** School administrator (retired); Richmond Pub Sch, teacher, 1949-69, langarts consult, 1969-71, diag & prescriptive reading, coordr, 1971-75; Richmond Pub Sch, Chap I reading coordr, 1975. **Orgs:** Crusade Voters, 1949; Nat Educ Asn, 1950; vpres, Richmond Educ Asn, 1950; consult, Comm Groups, 1975-83; pres, Elem Teachers Asn, 1967; vpres, Asn Classroom Teachers, 1973; Exec Bd Nat Asn Advan Colored People, IRA-RARC-VSRA; historian, Continental Soc, 1976-91; reading supvr, Chap I, 1979-93; pres, Richmond Chap, Continentals Inc, 2000-03. **Home Addr:** 8222 Whistler Rd, Richmond, VA 23227, **Home Phone:** (804)266-9443.

## WALLACE, DR. JEFFREY J.

School administrator. **Personal:** Born Apr 7, 1946, Mobile, AL; married Patricia A Henderson; children: Jeffrey, Jennifer, Justin & Jawaan. **Educ:** State Univ Col, Fredonia, BA, hist, 1968; State Univ NY, Buffalo, MEd, 1973, PhD, hist & philos educ, 1980. **Career:** State Univ NY, Fredonia, admin asst admis & rec, 1969-72, dir educ opportunity prog, educ develop prog 1972-81, asst vpres acad affairs, 1977-81; State Univ Col, Buffalo, dir educ opportunity prog, educ develop prog, 1981-86, asst vpres acad affairs, 1986-. **Orgs:** State Univ NY Chancellors Taskforce Minority Grad Opportunity, 1983; Nat Asn Acad Adv, 1984; bd chairperson, Buffalo Post-Sec Consortium Spec Progs, 1985; pres, Spec Prog Personnel Asn, 1984-; evaluator/edconsult, PNJ Consult. **Business Addr:** Assistant Vice President Academic Affairs, State University of New York, 1300 Elmwood Ave CA 306, Buffalo, NY 14222.

## WALLACE, JOHN A.

Executive, executive director. **Educ:** Univ Pac, polit sci & statist, BA, 1977. **Career:** Delta Air Lines, mgr mkt planning, 1977-88; Aeronomics Inc, vpres consult, 1988-95; Talus Solutions Inc, vpres consult, 1995-2001; Axicom Digital/Kefta, travel & hosp prac; Manugistics, vpres, 2001-03; Acxiom Corp, client rep, 2003-07; Acxiom Digital / Kefta, dir sales, 2007-08; Rainmaker Inc, vpres bus consult, 2008-11, managing dir gaming/hospitality, 2011-13, pres gaming/hospitality, 2013-. **Business Addr:** President, Gaming/Hospitality, The Rainmaker Group, 4550 N Pt Pkwy Suite 400, Alpharetta, GA 30022, **Business Phone:** (678)578-5700.

## WALLACE, JOHN GILBERT

Basketball player, television show host. **Personal:** Born Feb 9, 1974, Rochester, NY; children: John Jr & Joseph. **Educ:** Syracuse Univ, social, 1996. **Career:** Basketball player (retired); New York Knicks, forward, 1996-97, 1999-2000; Toronto Raptors, 1997-99; Detroit Pistons, 2000-01; Phoenix Suns, 2001-02; Panionios, 2002-03; Miami Heat, forward, 2003-04; Snaidero Udine, Italy, forward, 2005; Knicks C's Aid Soc Christmas, co-host; Rochester AAU Basketball, Pres & Gen Mgr; Winning Because I Tried, Vice Pres; New York Knicks, alumni rels & fan develop rep; Hotaling Ins Group, Ins Agt; Petro River Oil Corp, Dir, 2013-. **Orgs:** Exec bd mem, Heavenly Productions Found.

## WALLACE, JOHN M., JR.

Clergy, educator. **Educ:** Univ Chicago, BA, sociol, 1987; Univ Mich, MA, sociol, 1988, PhD, sociol, 1991, post doctoral, 1993. **Career:** Univ Chicago Metrop Opportunity Proj, res asst, 1986-87; Univ Mich, Ctr Afro-Am & African Studies, res asst, 1987-88, assoc prof, 1991-2003; Comt Instnl Coop fel, 1987-90, teaching asst, 1988-; Inst Social Res Pilot Study White Racial Attitudes, res asst, 1988; Inst Social Res Monitoring Future, res asst, 1989-91; Ford Found Dissertation fel, 1990-91; Nsf post doctoral fel, 1991-94, res investr, 1992-94; Inst Labor & Indust Rels, Dept Sociol, adj asst prof to assoc prof, instr, 1991-92, 1994-2004, Inst Social Res Prog Youth & Social Issues, fac assoc, 1994-; Poverty, Risk & Ment Health Res Ctr, fac assoc, 1994-99; Sch Social Work, asst to assoc prof 1994-2003, fac assoc, 1995-2004, 1996-2004, vis assoc prof, 2004-, assoc prof, 2004-; Univ Pa, Ctr Res Relig Urban Civil Soc, non-resident fel, Univ Pittsburgh, assoc prof, 2004-, Sch Social Work, Philip Hallen prof community health & social justice, 2004-; Baylor Univ, Ctr Relig Inquiry Across Disciplines, non-resident fel, 2006-; Search Inst, Ctr Spiritual Develop Childhood & Adolescence, sci advisor, 2006-; Skillman Found grant, prin investr, currently. **Orgs:** Philip Hallen Endowed Chair in Community Health & Social Justice, 2009-; Soc Social Work Res; vice-chair bd, Washtenaw County Community Ment Health Bd, 1994-96; bd dir, Nat Asn Leadership Stud Assistance Progs, 1995; Nat Coun Alcoholism & Drug Dependence, 1996-97; Nat Inst Healthcare Res/Templeton Found, Addictions Group, 1996-; prog evaluator, Detroit Urban League/Empowerment Zone Community Prev Coalition, 1996-98; prog evaluator, Empowerment Zone Coalition, 1999-2000; prog evaluator, Mich Neighborhood Partnership, 2000; Homewood-Brushton Community Ministries, 2004-; vice-chair bd, Washtenaw County Community Ment Health Bd; sr pastor, Bible Ctr Church, 2004-; Homewood-Brushton Community Coalition Orgn, 2006-09; Pittsburgh Theol Sem, Metro Urban Inst, 2006-10; pres, Oper Better Block, 2006-; Youth Futures Comn, Co-Founder ad Bd Pres, Homewood C's Village, 2009-. **Business Addr:** Associate Professor, University of Pittsburgh, Sch Social Work, Pittsburgh, PA 15260, **Business Phone:** (412)624-6349.

**WALLACE, LINDA SKYE**
Chief executive officer, executive. **Personal:** Born Nov 14, 1958, Akron, OH; daughter of William and Helen M Bell (deceased); children: Tamika Rachelle Dryden. **Educ:** Southern Ohio Col, assoc, 1985; Ohio Sch Broadcasting, dipl, 1987; Oglethorpe Univ. **Career:** Rick Angelo Commun, pres, 1989-98; Tamika Rachelle Life Enhancement Ctr Women, founder, 1997; Markara Lachelle Sch Performing Arts, founder, 1998. **Orgs:** Ohio Black Women Leadership Caucus, 1988; Vol coord, New Birth Inner City Life Ctr, 1999. **Home Addr:** 1682 Grace Ave, Atlanta, GA 30316, **Home Phone:** (404)635-1804.

**WALLACE, MILTON DE**
Chief executive officer, school administrator, school principal. **Personal:** Born Jul 7, 1957, Tyler, TX; son of John and Thelma Jackson; married Gwendolyn A. **Educ:** Tex A&M Univ, BS, com, 1978, MEd, 1979; Univ N Tex, Denton, TX, 1988. **Career:** Educator (retired), exec; Com ISD, teacher, 1978-83, asst prin, 1983-84; Union Hill ISD, prin, 1984-87; Denton Independent Sch Dist, Denton, prin, 1987-2003, head prin, 1990-2007; Longview High Sch, prin, 2007-08; Dreams Come True Travel, owner & chief exec officer, 2007-; YTB, travel agt & bus owner, 2007-; M & L Educ Scholar Serv, owner; All Nations TV, co-owner, 2012-. **Orgs:** Pres, RAWSCO Inc, 1983; vpres, Prof Mens Serv Club, 1983-84; Tex Asn Elem Sch Prins, 1983; Tex Asn Sec Sch Prin, 1984-95; Denton Adminrs Asn, 1987-95; Tex Asn Black Sch Educrs, 1989-; Dir Summer Workshop, Tex Asn Stud Coun, 1989-90; vpres, Denton Adminrs Asn, 1991-93, pres, Denton Adminrs Asn, 1994-95; Nat Asn Sec Sch Prin, 1991-95. **Home Addr:** 300 Pear Tree Pl, Denton, TX 76202. **Business Addr:** Principal, Longview High School, 201 E Tomlinson Pkwy, Longview, TX 75605, **Business Phone:** (903)663-1301.

**WALLACE, PEGGY MASON**
Government official. **Personal:** Born Sep 5, 1948, Salisbury, MD; daughter of Rayfield J Sr (deceased) and Hattie A (deceased); married Joseph R; children: Shawn. **Educ:** Morgan State Univ, BS, math, 1970; Univ Ill, MA, math, 1971. **Career:** Bell Lab, tech staff, 1972-75; Calculon Consult Firm, syst analyst, trainer, 1975-81; Strategic Systs Progs US Dept Navy, mgt info systs, mgr, 1981-96, dir, Mgt Info & Support Serv, head, 1996-. **Orgs:** Pres, Alpha Kappa Mu Hon Soc, 1967-70; charter mem, pres, Math Club, 1970; Fed Women's Prog, 1982-83; Dept Navy's Tutoring Prog, 1985-. **Home Addr:** 8412 Grandhaven Ave, Upper Marlboro, MD 20772, **Home Phone:** (301)627-8157. **Business Addr:** Director, Strategic Systems Programs of US Department of Navy, 3801 Nebraska Ave NW, Washington, DC 20393-5446.

**WALLACE, RASHEED ABDUL**
Basketball coach, basketball player. **Personal:** Born Sep 17, 1974, Philadelphia, PA; son of Jackie and Sam Tabb; married Fatima Sanders; children: Ishmiel Shaeed, Malik, Nazir & Rashiyah. **Educ:** Univ NC, attended 1995. **Career:** Basket player (retired), basketball coach; Wash Bullets, ctr-forward, 1995-96; Portland Trail Blazers, ctr-forward, 1996-2004; Atlanta Hawks, ctr-forward, 2003-04; Detroit Pistons, power forward, 2004-09, asst coach, 2013-14; Boston Celtics, 2009-10; New York Knicks, 2012-13. **Orgs:** Founder, Rasheed Wallace Found, 1997. **Home Addr:** 1979 Arthurs Way, Rochester Hills, MI 48306-3363.

**WALLACE, DR. RENEE C.**
Psychologist, educator. **Personal:** Born New Britain, CT; daughter of Elmo Sr and Chaudette J; children: Love & Lovely. **Educ:** Cent Conn State Univ, BA, 1974; Univ Iowa, MA, 1975, PhD, 1977. **Career:** Univ Iowa, admin asst, 1974-77; Morgan State Univ, admin asst prof, 1977-79; Clayton Univ, adj fac, 1979-; James Madison Univ, coun psychologist, 1980-84; Wallace & Wallace Assocs, dir, 1980-; State Univ of New York, Potsdam, dir coun, 1984; Dept Corrections, adminr, 1986, prin, 1986-89; Cent Conn State Univ, New Brit, asst prof, 1989-; Fla A&M Univ, assoc prof, dept sec educ & foundations, currently. **Orgs:** Secy, Phi Delta Kappa, 1979; consult, Southern Asn Col & Sch, 1981-84; educ consult, Black Educ Res & Inf Ctr, 1984; bd dir, Nat Comm Educ Youth Energy. **Home Addr:** 3308 Forest Ridge Dr, Albany, GA 31721-1508, **Home Phone:** (229)430-9769. **Business Addr:** Associate Professor, Florida Agricultural & Mechanical University, Bldg 8 444 Gamble St GEC-C Suite 319, Tallahassee, FL 32307, **Business Phone:** (850)599-3846.

**WALLACE, RICHARD WARNER**
Engineer. **Personal:** Born Nov 6, 1929, Gary, IN; son of Othello and Ruth; married Lillian Mozel. **Educ:** Purdue Univ, BS, 1951; George Washington Univ, Am Univ, Wash, DC, post grad studies. **Career:** Engineer (retired); USN Naval Sea Systs Command, designer devel & testing elec, electronic systs ships & submarines, 1951, mgt tech & logistics support navy's deep submergence vehicle progs & nuclear powered submarine NR 1, 1951-85; TRW Systs Integration Grp, asst proj mgr, 1985-94. **Orgs:** Life mem, Nat Soc Prof Engrs; bd dir, Potomac Chap, Md Soc Prof Engrs; Am Soc Naval Engrs; Naval Submarine League; Marine Tech Soc; Amateur Radio; Astron; Photog; life mem, Alpha Phi Alpha; charter mem, Beta Mu Boule, Sigma Pi Phi; Guardsmen, Wash DC Chap; regist prof engr, Wash, DC, 1958-. **Honors/Awds:** Navy Group Achievment Award, 1972; Navy Meritorious Civilian Serv Award, 1974; Superior Civilian Serv Award, Dept Navy, 1985. **Home Addr:** 30 Norwood Rd, Silver Spring, MD 20905-3874, **Home Phone:** (301)384-6366.

**WALLACE, RITCHIE RAY (RICK WALLACE)**
Executive, entrepreneur. **Personal:** Born Mar 9, 1955, Hastings, NE; son of Andrew and Laura E; married Kenetta Brown; children: Joshua, Eboni & Ritchie II. **Educ:** Kearney State Col, BA, 1979. **Career:** Wallace Consult Inc, pres, 1979-; Antelope Valley Proj, pub involvement consult, 1996-; Antelope Valley Investment Study, pub process consult; Pac Inst, nxlevel instr & facilitator. **Orgs:** Bd, Cot Bus Asn Neb, 1989-; life-time mem, NCP, 1989-; bd, Cornhusker Bank, 1991-94; Asn Gen Contractors, 1991-92; Self Employ Loan Fund; treas, Newman United Methodist Church, 1992; Newman United Methodist Church, Ethnic Local Church Comt, 1992-; econ develop consult, City Lincoln Mayor's Off; pres, Nat Am Advan Colored People, Lincoln Br, 1992-97; partner, Chambers Com; vpres, Nat Asn Advan Colored People, 1994-; bd dir, Heritage Nebr; Cornhusker Banks Bd dir; bd mem, United Way& Jr Achievement; exec dir, Community Develop Resources. **Home Addr:** 3737 Mohawk St, Lincoln, NE 68510, **Home Phone:** (402)484-5019. **Business Addr:** Executive Director, Community Development Resources, 285 S 68th St Pl Suite 520, Lincoln, NE 68510-2572, **Business Phone:** (402)436-2387.

**WALLACE, STEVE (BARRON STEVEN WALLACE)**
Football player, executive, spokesperson. **Personal:** Born Dec 27, 1964, Atlanta, GA; married Vassar; children: Elle, Xaia, Steven Jr & Keely. **Educ:** Auburn Univ, BA, sec educ math & psychol, 1992. **Career:** Football player (retired), motivational speaker; Birmingham Stallions, 1986; San Francisco 49ers, 1986, tackle, 1987, 1989, left tackle, 1988, 1991-96, right tackle, 1990; B & V Enterprises LLC., owner, 1992-; Kans City Chiefs, 1997; 3Rings Construct Co., co-owner, 1999-2008; Pro Speakers Bur, motivational speaker, currently. **Orgs:** Founder, Steve Wallace Found. **Honors/Awds:** Pro Bowl, 1992; "Community Player of the Year" Extra Award, 1992; Bobb Mckittrick Award, 1988; Super Bowl Champion, (XXIII, XXIV, XXIX); All pro selection, 1992 & 1994; Alabama Sports Hall of Fame, 2012.

**WALLACE, THOMAS ALBERT**
Counselor. **Personal:** Born Jan 31, 1954, Williamsburg, VA; son of William and Virginia; married Bettie L; children: Thomas Jr, Melissa & Christina. **Educ:** George Mason Univ, BS, 1980; Bowie State Univ, MA, 1991. **Career:** Lutheran Ministries Ga, prog mgr, 1997-98; Savannah State Univ, stud affairs counr, 1998-. **Orgs:** Nat Orgn Stud Affairs Profs, 1998; ACPA, 1998; Nat Orgn Am Disability Coordrs, 1998; GCPA, 1999. **Honors/Awds:** Emmy nominee: 1995, 1996, 1998. **Home Addr:** 4 Watermill Ct, Savannah, GA 31419-8951, **Home Phone:** (912)920-7927. **Business Addr:** Student Affairs Counselor, Savannah State University, 3219 Col St King Frazier Stud Complex Rm 233, Savannah, GA 31404, **Business Phone:** (912)356-2202.

**WALLACE-BENJAMIN, JOAN**
Consultant, chief executive officer. **Educ:** Wellesley Col, BA, psychol, 1975; Brandeis Univ, Heller Sch, PhD, social policy & mgt, 1980. **Career:** ABCD head start dep dir, 1985; Boys & Girls Clubs Boston, dir oper, 1989; ABT Assocs, res analyst; Urban League Mass, pres & chief exec officer, 1989-2000; Whitehead Mann, consult, 2000-02; Off Gov Deval Patrick, chief staff, 2006-07. **Orgs:** Pres & ceo, Home Little Wanderers, 2003-. **Business Addr:** President, Chief Execuitng Officer, The Home for Little Wanderers, 271 Huntington Ave, Boston, MA 02115, **Business Phone:** (617)267-3700.

**WALLER, REV. DR. ALYN ERRICK**
Clergy. **Personal:** Born Aug 8, 1964, Cleveland, OH; son of Alfred M and Belva J; married Ellyn Jo; children: Ellynn Morgan & ErKya Lynn. **Educ:** Ohio Univ, BMus, 1987; Southern Baptist Theol Sem, MDiv, 1990; Eastern Baptist Theol Sem, PhD, 1998. **Career:** Army Nat Guard, chaplain asst, 1982-98; Simmons Bible Col, instr, psychol music, 1989-90; Canaan Missionary Baptist Church, music minister; First Baptist Church, pastor, 1990-94; Enon Tabernacle Baptist Church, Philadelphia, PA, pastor, 1994, sr pastor, currently; Christian Urban Theol, sem teacher, 1999; Alyn Waller Ministries; Commando Krav Maga-Del Valley, instr, currently; Albums: Holy Is Your Name; Seasons; This Must Be The Place; I Know the Lord Will Make A Way; Love Somebody; My Father's Name; Hymn Medley; I Trust You Lord; Heart Of God; Send Me Your Word; What A Friend We Have In Jesus; I Won't Complain. **Orgs:** Penn Conv, 1987-; Nat Baptist Conv USA Inc, 1987-; Lott Carey Foreign Mission Conv, 1987-; Allegheny Union Baptist Asn, 1987-90; Pittsburgh Minister's Conf, 1987-90; vpres, Monongahela Balley Nat Asn Advan Colored People, 1988-90; Monoghela Valley Drug & Alcohol Task Force, 1988-90; bd dir, Philadelphia Baptist Asn, 1999-. **Honors/Awds:** Men of the Year, Penn State Baptist Conv, 1996; Outstanding Young Men of America, 1988; Distinguished Leadership Award, Men Making a Difference, 2000; GEGI Music Award, 2000. **Business Addr:** Senior Pastor, Enon Tabernacle Baptist Church, 2800 W Cheltenham Ave, Philadelphia, PA 19150, **Business Phone:** (215)276-7200.

**WALLER, KATHY N.**
Vice president (organization), controller. **Educ:** Univ Rochester, New York, BA; Univ Rochester, New York, William E Simon Sch Bus Admin, MBA. **Career:** Deloitte Touche Tohmatsu, sr acct; Coca-Cola Co, sr acct acct res dept, 1987-90, prin acct, Northeast Europe/Africa Group, 1990-91, mkt controller McDonald's Group, 1991-96, financial serv mgr Africa Group & Minute Maid Co, 1996-98, dir financial reporting, 1998-04, chief internal audits, 2004-05, vpres, 2005-, controller, 2009-. **Orgs:** Bd trustee, Spelman Col; chair, Coca-Cola Co's Women's Leadership Coun; Bd Trustees Mem & Catalyst Bd Advisors, Univ Rochester; Univ Rochester's William E Sch Bus Exec Adv Coun. **Honors/Awds:** University of Rochester Career Achievement Award, 2005; "Treasury & Risk Magazine", 100 Most Influential People in Finance, 2007; University of Rochester William E Simon School Distinguished Alumna Award, 2007; "Black Enterprise", 75 Most Powerful Women in Business, 2010. **Business Addr:** The Coca-Cola Co, 1 Coca-Cola Plz, Atlanta, GA 30313, **Business Phone:** (404)676-2121.

**WALLER, RUBY LARRY**
Entrepreneur, contractor. **Personal:** Born Jun 9, 1947, Chicago, IL; son of Willis and Hulena Hubbard; married Ruby L; children: Kelly D. **Educ:** Malcolm X Col, Chicago, IL, AA 1974; Gov State Univ, Pk Forest S, IL, BS, 1978, MBA, 1979. **Career:** Assoc with Fullerton Mech Contractors, Elk Grove Village, Ill, 1969-76; Dyd Construction, Phoenix, Ill, supt, 1977-79; Pyramid Industs Inc, Riverdale, Ill, pres, 1979-; L. Waller Enterprises. **Orgs:** Dir, Black Contractors United, 1979-; Nat Asn Independent Bus, 1979-, Asn Energy Engrs, 1984-, Builders Asn Chicago, 1984-; founder & dir, Black Mech Contractors Asn, 1983-; original founding comn, Ben Wilson Found, 1985-; comt mem, Black Musicians Hall of Fame, 1986-87; Little Ciy Found, 1986-. **Honors/Awds:** Copyright on seminar material, "Wisdom ", 1989. **Special Achievements:** Became first black company to install elevators in the US, 1987. **Home Addr:** 2909 Embassy Row, Flossmoor, IL 60422, **Home Phone:** (708)799-3111. **Business Addr:** L Waller Enterprises, 2818 Chayes Pk Dr, Flossmoor, IL 60422, **Business Phone:** (708)206-0699.

**WALLICK, ERNEST HERRON**
State government official. **Personal:** Born Jan 15, 1928, Huntingdon, TN; married Jean Ellen Allen; children: Claudia Marie Barkley & John Herron. **Educ:** Tenn A&I State Univ, BS, 1950; Mich State Univ, MS, 1955. **Career:** Carroll County Bd Educ, high sch voc educ instr, 1950-51; Mich Wayne County, Dept Soc Servs, pub welfare worker, 1955-58, spec investr, 1958-64, asst supv personnel, 1964-65, supv off mgt, 1965-66, supv mgt planning, 1966-67; Mich Dept Civil Servs, dir spec progs, 1967-72, dir spec & regional serv div, 1972-75, dir bur selection, 1975-82, chief dep dir, 1982-96. **Orgs:** Lansing Community Col Social Work Curric Adv Comt, 1970-75; State Voc Rehab Adv Coun, 1973-80; Gov's Mich Equal Employ Opportunity Coun, 1975-82; Trinity AME Bd trustee, 1978-; treas, Alpha Chi Boule Sigma Pi Phi Frat, 1982-; Mich Correctional Officer's Training Coun, 1982-, Gov's Mich Equal Employ & Bus Opportunity Coun, 1983-; bd trustee, Alpha Phi Alpha Frat, 1985-; pres, Nat Inst Employ Equity, 1985-; Nat Urban League; Nat Asn Advan Colored People; Phi Beta Kappa Honor Soc. **Home Addr:** 1400 Wellington Rd, Lansing, MI 48910, **Home Phone:** (517)371-3098.

**WALLS, REV. FREDRIC T.**
Clergy. **Personal:** Born Oct 28, 1935, Denver, CO; married Delorez M Louise; children: Fredric T II, Agu Odinga-Ivan & Malaika Annina-Emma Delorez Louisa. **Educ:** Los Angeles City Col, AA, 1957; Knoxville Col, BA, 1963; Princeton Theol Sem, MDiv, 1963; Union Grad Sch, PhD, 1979; Urban Training Inst, Chicago, cert; Univ Tenn. **Career:** Clergy (retired); Westminister Neighborhood Asn, organiser, 1960; Good Shepherd-Faith, Broadway & Sound View Presby Church, stud asst pastor, 1960-63; Bel-Vue Presby Church, supply asst pastor, 1964-65; Knoxville Col, assoc dean students, 1965-68, dir Upward Bound, 1967-68; Univ Presby Church, minister, 1968-69; Houston Urban Univ, pastor, 1969-80; Univ Houston, chmn dept relig activ, 1974-; Danforth-Underwood fel, 1976-77; Self-Develop People Presby Church, dir, 1980-2002. **Orgs:** Pres sr class, JC Fremont Sr High Sch, 1953-54; pres sr class, Knoxville Col, 1959-60; treas sr class, Princeton Theol Sem, 1962-63; Gulf Coast Presby Com, 1969-; bd dir, Cit Good Sch, 1969; Presby Housing Comn, 1969-74; Human Rels Training Houston Police Cadets, 1970-72; bd dir, Ministries Blacks Higher Educ; bd dir, Houston Met Ministries, vpres, 1971-74, pres, 1975-76; SW Steering Com, United Presby HEW, 1971-74; Nat Commun Comt, United Ministries Higher Educ, 1972-75; exec comt, Tex United Campus Christian Life Comn, 1973-75; Houston Jail Chaplaincy Exec Comt, 1973-75; Bi-Racial Com HISD, 1973-75; policy bd, United Ministries Higher Educ; exec dir, FundSelf-Develop People United Presby Church. **Honors/Awds:** Outstanding Young Men Am, 1966. **Home Addr:** 6108 Orion Rd, Louisville, KY 40222-5941, **Home Phone:** (502)426-7341.

**WALLS, GEN. GEORGE HILTON, JR.**
School administrator, military leader, executive director. **Personal:** Born Nov 30, 1942, Coatesville, PA; son of Philip Robert and Elizabeth Gibson; married Portia D Hall; children: George III, Steven & Kevin. **Educ:** W Chester State Univ, Pa, BS, educ, 1964; NC Cent Univ, Durham, NC, MA, educ, 1975; U S Marine Corps Command & Staff Col, 1976; Nat War Col, Wash, DC, attended 1983. **Career:** NC State Univ, chmn Naval Sci dept, 1989-91; NC Cent Univ, spec asst chancellor, asst secy to Bd Trustees, 1993-2000; Mercantile Bankshares Corp, pres, chief exec officer, dir, chief dep auditor, 2000-04; State NC, chief dep auditor, 2001-04; State Auditor, chief dep NC off; Lincoln Elec Holdings Inc, dir, 2003-, currently; USmC, Engr Systs, prog mgr; Pub univ campuses, chmn, sr adminr; Univ NC, Chapel Hill, chmn Naval sci dept; Thomas Industs Inc, dir, 2003-05; PNC Financial Serv Group Inc, dir, 2006; PNC Bank Nat Asn, dir, 2006. **Orgs:** Marine Corps League, 1991; Montford Pt Marine Asn, 1991; Sigma Pi Phi; Rotary Int; Carolina Sem; bd mem, Thomas Industs Inc; bd mem, PNC; bd mem, PNC Fin Serv Group Inc, Lincoln Elec Holdings Inc, bd mem-currently; Res Triangle Pk Chap; Nat Asn Corp Dirs. **Honors/Awds:** Inductee, Chapel Four Chaplains, Valley Forge, Pa, 1986; Honorary doctor of humane letters, Va Union Univ, 1993; Roy Williams Meritorious Service Award, NAACP, 1993; Humanitarian Service Award, Chapel Four Chaplains, 1993. **Home Addr:** 100 Canberra Ct, Cary, NC 27513-2923. **Business Addr:** Board Member, Lincoln Electric Holdings Inc, 22800 St Clair Ave, Cleveland, OH 44117, **Business Phone:** (888)935-3876.

**WALLS, MELVIN**
Educator, government official, football coach. **Personal:** Born Nov 9, 1948, St. Louis, MO; married Veronica Estella Robinson; children: Farrell LaPez (Deceased) & Delvin L. **Educ:** St Louis Community Col, Florissant Valley, AA, 1973; Harris Teachers Col, BA, 1976. **Career:** St Louis City Sch, wrestling coach, 1977-83, tennis coach, 1979-80; Blue Jays, baseball coach, 1981, football coach, phys educ teacher; City Northwoods, city collector; Gateway Tech Jaguars, football head coach. **Orgs:** Treas, Boy Scouts Am, 1981-; coord, Normandy Baseball, 1981-. **Honors/Awds:** All Conf Player, St Louis City Sch, 1965-67; All Star Player, St Louis City Sch, 1965-67; Proj MEE Award, 1983; NMC Human Service Award, 1987. **Home Addr:** 2417 Riverwoods Trails Dr, Florissant, MO 63031. **Business Addr:** Football Coach, Gateway Tech Jaguars, 5101 McRee Ave, St. Louis, MO 63110-2082, **Business Phone:** (314)776-3300.

**WALSH, EVERALD J.**
Health services administrator. **Personal:** Born May 6, 1938, New York, NY; children: Evette Michelle & Eric Michael. **Educ:** City Col NY, BA, 1963; Adel phi Univ, MSW, 1970, CSW, 1980. **Career:** Cath Youth Org, group worker, 1963-66; Little Flower C Serv, group Supr, Soc Worker, 1966-71; Fed Addiction Agency, exec dir, 1971-74; Manhattan C Psychiat Ctr, team leader, 1974-77; Colony S Brooklyn Houses, dir ment retardation staff training prog, 1978-; Brooklyn Develop Ctr. **Orgs:** Nat Fed Concerned Drug Abuse Workers, 1972. **Home Addr:** 195 Willoughby Ave, Brooklyn, NY 11205.

**WALTER, DR. JOHN C.**
Educator. **Personal:** Born May 5, 1933. **Educ:** Ark AM&N Col, BS, mech engineering & hist; Univ Bridgeport, MA, Am hist; Univ Marine, Orono, PhD, Afro-Am & US hist, 1972. **Career:** Professor (retired), Purdue Univ, instr hist, 1970-72, asst prof hist, 1972-73; Univ Kokomo, vis asst prof black polit, 1971-73; John Jay Col Criminal Justice CUNY, assoc prof hist, chmn black studies, 1973-76; Bowdoin Col, dir, asst prof hist Afro-Am Studies Prog, 1976-80; Smith Col, assoc prof Afro-Am Studies; John F. Kennedy Inst N Am Studies, lectr; Free Univ of Berlin, lectr; John Moores Liverpool Univ, lectr; Manchester Metrop Univ, lectr; US Embassy, lectr; Univ Wash, adj prof, Dept Hist, prof, Dept Am Ethnic Studies, prof emer, currently. **Orgs:** Contrib ed Jour, Afro-Am New York Life & Hist State Univ Col NY, 1976-; Rev Afro-Am Issues & Cult Syracuse Univ, 1976-; org, chmn, 1976-80; UMOJA A Scholarly Jour Afro-Am Affairs Univ CO, 1976-; exec bd mem, 1978-; Wesleyan Univ, 1978; consultnison Univ, 1979; bridge comt & instr Smith Col, 1980-; New Eng Jour Black Studies Hampshire Col, 1981-; New Eng Conf Nat Coun Black Studies; exec comt, Five Coll Black Studies, 1982-; develop & org Bridges Pluralism, 1983-; Am Hist Asn; Assoc Caribbean Historians; Asn Study African-Am Life & Hist; Col Lang Asn; New Eng Hist Asn; Nat Asn Interdisciplinary Ethnic Studies; Org am Historians; Soc Hist Asn; reader Nat Endowment Humanities, Univ Press Am; Black Stud Comn. **Business Addr:** Adjunct Professor, University of Washington, Padelford Hall B-504, Seattle, WA 98195-4380, **Business Phone:** (206)543-5401.

**WALTER, MILDRED PITTS**
Writer. **Personal:** Born Sep 9, 1922, Sweetville, LA; daughter of Paul Pitts and Mary Ward; married Earl Lloyd; children: Earl Lloyd & Craig Allen. **Educ:** Southern Univ, Baton Rouge, La, BA, Eng, 1944; Calif State Univ, elem teaching cert, 1954; Antioch Col, Yellow Springs, OH, MEd. **Career:** Los Angeles City Schs Dist, teacher, 1955-70; Houghton Mifflin Co, writer, 1969-; Fiction: Lillie of Watts: A Birthday Surprise, 1969; Western Interstate Higher Educ, consult, 1970-73; Lily of Watts-A Birthday Discovery, 1969; Lily of Watts Takes a Giant Step, 1971; The Liquid Trap, 1975; Ty's One-Man Band, 1980; The Girl on the Outside, 1982; Because We Are, 1983; My Mama Needs Me, 1983; Have a Happy, 1984; Brother to the Wind, 1985; Trouble's Child, 1985; Justin & the Best Biscuits in the World, 1986; Mariah Loves Rock, 1988; Two & Too Much, 1990; Mariah Keeps Cool, 1990; Tiger Ride, Macmillan, 1994; Darkness, 1995; Second Daughter, 1996; Suitcase, 1999; Ray & the Best Family Reunion Ever, 2001; Non Fiction: The Mississippi Challenge, 1992; Kawanzaa: A Family Affair, 1995. **Orgs:** Soc C's Bk Writers & Illustrators; Auth's Guild; Cong Racial Equality. **Honors/Awds:** Irma Simonton, Black Honor Book, 1981; Christian Sci Monitor, Best Book: Writing, 1982; Public TV, Reading Rainbow, 1983, 1985; Parent's Choice Award, Literature, 1983-85; ALA Social Resp Round Table, Coretta Scott King Honorable Mmention, 1984; Corretta Scott King Award, 1987; Christopher Award, 1993; Colorado Women's Hall of Fame, inducted, 1996. **Business Addr:** Author, Houghton Mifflin Co, 222 Berkeley St, Boston, MA 02116, **Business Phone:** (617)351-5000.

**WALTERS, CURLA SYBIL**
Educator. **Personal:** Born Jun 3, 1929, Jamaica. **Educ:** Andrews Univ, BA, biol, 1961; Howard Univ, MS, microbiol, 1964; Georgetown Univ, PhD, microbiol & immunol, 1969; Univ Colo, postdoctoral tenure. **Career:** Howard Univ, res, asso, 1964-65, assoc prof, 1975, Dept Med, adjunt asso prof, prof emer, 2005-, ly dir Immunol; Am Asn Univ Women, fel, 1969, Departments Microbiol & Dermat, assoc prof; Co Univ, instr, asst prof, 1971-74; Univ Colo, Div Clin Immunol, from instr to asst prof. **Orgs:** Am Asn Immunologist, 1972-; founding mem, Jamaica Vols Asn; bd mem, George E Peters Elem Sch; First Seventh-day Adventist Church, Wash, DC; Col Med, Admis Comt; Col Med, Nominating Comt; Col Med, Grievance Comt; Col Med, Sabbatical Leave Comt. **Home Addr:** 8404 11th Ave, Silver Spring, MD 20903-3001, **Home Phone:** (301)439-3021. **Business Addr:** Adjunct Associate Professor, Professor Emeritus, Howard University, 2041 Ga Ave NW, Washington, DC 20060, **Business Phone:** (202)865-6100.

**WALTERS, FRANK E.**
Athletic trainer. **Personal:** Born Aug 26, 1954, Munich; son of Ulysses and Alma; married Anne Marie; children: Jason & Tiffany. **Educ:** Brooklyn Col, BS, phys educ, 1976; Ind State Univ, MS, phys educ, 1977; Tex A&M Univ, PhD, kinesiology, 1988. **Career:** Pharr San Juan, Alamo HS, Pharr, Tex, teacher & athletic trainer, 1977-78; MB Smiley HS, Houston, Tex, teacher & athletic trainer, 1978-81; Prairie View A&M Univ, hd athletic trainer, 1981-83; Tex A&M Univ, asst prof, 1983-90; DC Pub Schs, Athletic Health Care Serv, coordr, asst dir athletics, 1991-2006; Broward Health, dir sports med & wellness, 2006-07, dir Gen Med Ctr's Wellness Ctr, 2007, athletic trainer dir, 2009-. **Orgs:** Ed bd, J Nat Athletic Trainers Asn, 1990-96; ed bd, Athletic Trng Sports Health care Perspectives, 1991-96; Nat Athletic Trainers Asn; chmn, Ethnic Minority Adv Coun, 1991-94; Univ Wash; guest fac, Nat Leadership Inst, 1991-92, 1994-95; res awards comt, Mid Atlantic, 1992-95; Educ Task Force, Nat Athletic Trainers Asn, 1995-96; sports med adv com, Nat Fed State High Sch Asn, 1996-97; Educ Coun Exec Comt, 1997-; BOC Partners Inc. **Honors/Awds:** Certificate of Merit, Univ Tex Dent Sch, Continuing Educ, 1983; Sports Medicine Alumnus Award, Dept Phys Educ, Brooklyn Col, 1986; First Outstanding Alumnus Award, Athletic Training Dept, Ind State Univ, 1994; Outstanding Service Award, Nat Athletic Trainers Asn, Ethnic Minority Adv Coun, 1995, Outstanding Service Award, Educ Task Force, 1997; Most Distinguished Athletic Trainer, Nat Athletic Trainers Asn, 2003. **Special Achievements:** Published Microfilm Your Student Emergency Cards, The Physician & Sports Medicine, 1981; JC Sterling & MC Meyers, Tennis Elbow A Brief Review of Treatment, 1988; Quarterback Mouth guards & Speech Intelligibility, The Physician & Sports Medicine, with RM Morrow, WA Kuebker, M Golde, 1984, 1988. **Home Addr:** 5860 NW 99th Ave, Parkland, FL 33076-2565, **Home Phone:** (954)345-7475. **Business Addr:** Athletic Trainer Director, Broward Health, 303 SE 17th St, Ft. Lauderdale, FL 33316, **Business Phone:** (954)759-7400.

**WALTERS, GEORGE W., JR.**
Insurance agent. **Personal:** Born Sep 3, 1950, Bridgeport, CT; married Elizabeth Kramer. **Educ:** S Cent Community Col; Huebner Sch Col Studies, Am Col. **Career:** GW Walters Ins, pres & owner, currently; gen agt, broker, currently; Life Underwriters Training Coun, fel. **Orgs:** Million Dollar Round Table; Life Underwriters Polit Action Comn; Provident Mutual Leader's Asn; Nat Asn Ins & Financial Advs; Conn AFA Hist Soc; First Blk Stud Union, New Haven, CT; Greater New Haven Asn Afr Am; Universal Life Church, ordained minister, doctor motivation; NCP. **Honors/Awds:** Nat Quality Award; Nat Sales Achievement; Cert Life Pres's Club; Wall Fame; Grand Award; Balance Performance Award, Provident Mutual; Milestone Club; Scholar, Urban League Greater New Haven; Premier Gen Agt, Bankers Life NY. **Business Addr:** Owner, President, GW Walters Insurance Agency, 200 Hilton Ave Suite 53, Hempstead, NY 11550-8178, **Business Phone:** (516)489-4422.

**WALTERS, REV. HUBERT EVERETT**
Educator. **Personal:** Born Apr 27, 1933, Greenville, NC; children: Sonya Yvette, Hubert Sharif, Narda Rebecca & Julian Herman. **Educ:** NC Cent Univ, BA, music hist, lit, & theory, 1955; Va State Univ, attended 1959; E Carolina Univ, MM, 1965; Boston Univ, Sch Theol, PhD, Mdiv, pursing. **Career:** Tex Col Tyler, Tex, chmn dept Music, 1965-66; Shaw Univ Raleigh, NC, asst prof Music, 1966-69; Harvard Univ, lectr Black Music, 1970-73; Goddard Col Vt, lectr Black Music, instr, 1971-73; Boston St Col, asst proj Music, 1971-82; Boston Col/Harvard Univ, asst prof, 1975-2010; Boston Col, African & African Diaspora Studies, lect, 1982-, prof, currently, Voices Imani, music dir, currently; Simmons Col, prof, 1982-85; Univ Mass Boston, asst prof Music, 1982-2004. **Orgs:** Vpres, NC State Music Teachers, 1963; Music Educr Nat Conf; Am Choral Dir Asn; Omega Psi Phi Frat; deacon, Emmanuel Bapt Church; minister, Worship Peoples Baptist Church, Boston Mass; charter mem, Black Studies Dept Harvard Univ. **Home Addr:** 208 Bishop Dr, Framingham, MA 01702-6522, **Home Phone:** (508)879-5836. **Business Addr:** Professor, Music Director, Boston College, 301 Lyons Hall 140 Commonwealth Ave, Chestnut Hill, MA 02467, **Business Phone:** (617)552-3300.

**WALTERS, DR. MARC ANTON**
Educator. **Personal:** Born Jul 18, 1952, New York, NY. **Educ:** City Col NY, BS, 1976; Princeton Univ, PhD, 1981; Mass Inst Technol, postdoctoral res. **Career:** Mass Inst Technol, res, NIH, Postdoctoral fel, 1982-84; Epply Found, fel, 1982; New York Univ, assoc prof chem, 1985-; NYU Whitehead, fel, 1988; Exxon, fel, 1991. **Orgs:** Am Chem Soc; AAAS; Nat Asn Advan Colored People; Nat Orgn Prof Advan Black Chemists & Chem Eng; New York Acad Sci; chair, Indicator Mag, 2008. **Home Addr:** 1 Wash Sq Village Suite 8-L, New York, NY 10012, **Home Phone:** (212)673-7539. **Business Addr:** Associate Professor of Chemistry, New York University, Brown Bldg 29 Wash Pl Rm 556, New York, NY 10003, **Business Phone:** (212)998-8477.

**WALTERS, RONALD L., JR.**
Music director. **Personal:** Born Sep 16, 1970, Chicago, IL; son of Ronald and Sandra. **Educ:** Columbia Col, BA, music, 1995. **Career:** Elias Music, composer & producer; Steve Ford Music, composer & producer; Slang Music, composer & producer; Music On The Move, music teacher; Am Idol, guest music dir, 2004. TV: Barry Manilow: Songs from the Seventies, 2007. **Orgs:** BMI; Am Fedn Musicians; All Nations Mission Church; pres, Anointed Ones. **Honors/Awds:** Jazz Student of the Year, Chicago State Univ, 1993; Teacher of the Year, St. John de La Salle, 1996. **Special Achievements:** Producer of three commercially released recordings, 1994, 1995, 1996. **Home Addr:** 203 E 113th St, Chicago, IL 60628, **Home Phone:** (312)568-1695. **Business Addr:** Principal, Ronald Walters & Associates PC, 53 W Jackson Blvd Suite 1250, Chicago, IL 60604, **Business Phone:** (312)341-0801.

**WALTON, ANTHONY SCOTT**
Writer. **Personal:** Born Mar 8, 1965, South Bend, IN; son of Cullen Jr and Judith Elaine Tidwell. **Educ:** Vanderbilt Univ, Nashville, Tenn, BA, commun, 1987. **Career:** Nashville Tennessean, sports intern, 1985-87; Detroit Free Press, Detroit, Mich, sports statistician, writer, 1987-88, sports writer, 1988-91, columnist, 1991-93; Atlanta J-Const, fashion reporter, 1993-94, daily ed, 1994-96, olympic boxing reporter, 1996, writer, columnist, 1996-99, fashion ed, 1999-2001, fashion columnist, 2001-06, online entertainment producer, 2006-08; EyeSeeStyle, ed, 2008-; Mod Luxury, sr managing ed; WordPlayInk, writer, ed, mkt consult, 2008-; Digistrive inc, nat daily deal writer, 2012-; Atlanta Voice, managing ed, digital content dir, exec ed, 2013-. **Orgs:** Alpha Phi Alpha Fraternity Inc, 1984-; Atlanta Asn Black Journalists; mentor, Proj Male Responsibility, 1988-. **Honors/Awds:** Honorable Mention, Best Enterprise Story, Associated Press, 1991. **Home Addr:** 3421 Rohns St, Detroit, MI 48214, **Home Phone:** (313)579-1202. **Business Addr:** Managing Editor, Atlanta Voice, 633 Pryor St, Atlanta, GA 30312, **Business Phone:** (404)524-6426.

**WALTON, CAROL ANN (KARA WALTON)**
Social scientist, educator. **Personal:** Born Mar 17, 1935, Niagara Falls, NY; daughter of Wilker and Carol Smitherman Dozier; married Ortiz Montaigne; children: Omar Kwame. **Educ:** NY State Univ Col, Buffalo, NY, BS, 1957; Suffolk Univ, MA, 1963; Univ Calif, Berkeley, CA, PhD, 1975; Howard Univ, PhD, 1977. **Career:** Univ Calif, Berkeley, Urban educ fel, 1970, prog analyst & eval consult, 1975-76; Berkeley Unified Sch Dist, sr res assoc, 1972-73; W Lab, dir admin servs, 1974; Multi Ethnic Inst Res & Eval, vpres, 1975-; Howard Univ, fel NIE, 1977; Archidiocese New York Head Start, eval dir, 1986-92. **Orgs:** Alpha Kappa Alpha, 1955-60; adv mem, Berkeley Unified Sch Dis, supt desegregation comt, 1967-68; Am Edu Res Asn, 1969-86; Pi Lambda Theta, 1971-83; Kappa Delta Pi, Gamma Mu chap, 1975-84; vpres, E Bay Ment Health, 1978-82; Community Coun W Harlem, 1988-89, 1998-2000. **Home Addr:** 1129 Bancroft Way, Berkeley, CA 94702-1849, **Home Phone:** (510)649-0504. **Business Addr:** Vice President, Multi Ethnic Institute for Research & Education, 1129 Bancroft Way, Berkeley, CA 94702, **Business Phone:** (810)376-9615.

**WALTON, DR. EDWARD D.**
Educator. **Personal:** Born Montgomery, AL. **Educ:** Howard Univ, WA, BS, 1969; Univ Md, College Park, PhD, chem, 1979. **Career:** US Naval Acad, Md, prof, chem, 1979-87; Lawrence Hall Sci, Univ Calif, prog coordr, 1985-86; Calif State Poly tech Univ, Pomona, chem, fac, 1987-, prof, 1997-, co-dir, prof emer, currently. **Orgs:** Fel Towson State Univ, Md, 1978-79; pres, Nat Orgn Prof Advan Black Chemists & Chem Eng; rev comt, Nat Assessment Educ Progress Sci; Educ Testing Serv's Comt SAT II Chem Exam; Nat Acad Sci. **Home Addr:** PO Box 517, Mount Baldy, CA 91759. **Business Addr:** Professor Emeritus, California State Polytechnic University, 3801 W Temple Ave 4/1-426, Pomona, CA 91768-2557, **Business Phone:** (909)869-3661.

**WALTON, ELBERT ARTHUR, JR.**
Government official, lawyer. **Personal:** Born Feb 21, 1942, St. Louis, MO; son of Elbert A Sr and Luretta B Ray Hawkins; married Juanita Alberta Head; children: Rochelle, Rhonda, Angela, Elbert III & Johnathan. **Educ:** Harris-Stowe State Col, AA, com & finance, 1963; Univ Mo, St Louis, BA, acct, 1968; Wash Univ, MBA, acct, 1970; St Louis Univ, JD, law, 1974. **Career:** Homer G Phillips Hosp, comptroller; Continental Oil Corp, fin analyst, 1969; Univ Mo, St Louis, instr, bus law & acct, 1971-78; atty, 1974; St Louis Munic Ct, judge, 1977-78; Mo House Rep, state rep 61st dist, 1979-93; Ala State Univ, asst prof mgt; Metro Law Firm LLC, owner, atty & Counr, 2004-. **Orgs:** Beta Alpha Psi Nat Acct Fraternity, 1971; Phi Delta Phi Int Legal Frat, 1973; nat vpres, Nat Asn Black Accountants, 1976-77, chap pres; parliamentarian, Mound City Bar Asn, 1979; parliamentarian, Mo Legis Black Caucus, 1979-85; grand counr, Omega Psi Phi Frat, 1980-83; Mo Bar; Am Acct Asn; Midwestern Bus Admin Asn; William's Community Sch; Halls Ferry Twp Dem Club; Omicron Sigma Chap; Track & Cross Country; Stud Coun. **Business Addr:** Attorney, Counselor, Metro Law Firm LLC, 2320 Chambers Rd, St. Louis, MO 63136, **Business Phone:** (314)388-3400.

**WALTON, DR. HARRIETT J.**
Educator. **Personal:** Born Sep 19, 1933, Claxton, GA; daughter of Ester James Jr and Mable Rose Myrick Jr; married James; children: Renee Yvonne, Anthony Alex, Jennifer Denise & Cyrus Bernard. **Educ:** Clark Col, AB, math, 1952; Howard Univ, MS, math, 1954; Syracuse Univ, MA, math, 1957; Ga State Univ, PhD, 1979; Atlanta Univ, MS, comput sci, 1989. **Career:** Educator (retired); Hampton Inst, instr math, 1954-55, asst prof mathm, 1957-58; Morehouse Col, instr math, asst prof math, assoc prof math, prof math, 1958-2000. **Orgs:** Bd trustee, Morehouse Col; Clerk Providence Baptist Church, 1968-84; secy & treas, Nat Asn Math, 1982-; treas, Phi Delta Kappa, 1984-85; deacon, Providence Baptist Church, 1984-; adv bd, Benjamin E Mays Acad; Beta Kappa Chi; treas & pres, Delta Sigma Theta; YWCA; Nat Asn Advan Colored People; consult, Atlanta Pub Sch; Math Asn Am; speaker/presider, Nat Coun Teachers Math; Pi Mu Epsilon; Phi Beta Kappa; Am Math Soc; secy-treas, Nat Asn Math. **Home Addr:** 860 Venetta Pl NW, Atlanta, GA 30318-6030, **Home Phone:** (404)799-6347.

**WALTON, JAMES DONALD**
Executive. **Personal:** Born Jan 31, 1952, Albany, NY; son of Zymora Louise Burrell (deceased) and Allen (deceased); married Nadine Renee; children: 3. **Educ:** Univ Vt, BS, educ, 1975; Northwestern Univ, Kellogg Sch Mgt, advan exec prog, 1998. **Career:** Xerox Corp, sales rep, 1976-79; Abbott Lab, chem syst specialist, 1978-82, nat acct mgr, 1982-83, dist sales mgr, 1984-87, regional mkt mgr, 1987-90, sr recruitment mgr, 1990-91, nat sales mgr, regional mgr, 1991-95, hemat syst, nat sales mgr, 1995-98, diagnostics div, div vpres, worldwide mkt, 1998-2000, vpres worldwide mkt, vpres US sales, 2000-03; Thermo Electron, vpres global sales, 2003-04; Allen & Burrell Consult, vpres, US sales. chief exec officer & pres; Black Bus, owner, currently; Corp Express Inc, div sales vpres, 2005-06; Global Recruiters Oak Pk, founder, chief exec officer & pres, managing partner, 2007-. **Orgs:** Bd dir, Clara Abbott Found, 1997-2005. **Honors/Awds:** First Black Dist Mgr, 1983; First Black Regional Mkt Mgr, 1987; Regional Mkt Mgr of the Year, 1988; First Black Regional Mgr, 1990; First Black Nat Sales Mgr, 1995; First Black Vpres Mkt & Sales. **Home Addr:** 949 Fair Oaks Ave, Oak Park, IL 60302-1335. **Business Addr:** President, Managing Partner, Global Recruiters of Oak Park, 1135 Schneider St, Oak Park, IL 60301, **Business Phone:** (708)665-8004.

**WALTON, JERRY**
Executive. **Educ:** Hampton Univ, BS, bus admin & mgt, gen, 1983; Mich State Univ, MBA, 1993. **Career:** Gen Motors, area sales mgr, 1983-89; BMW Hudson Valley, pres, 1999-2013. **Orgs:** Bd mem, Miles Hope Breast Cancer Found; Omega Psi Phi Fraternity; bd dir, Marist Col, 2008.

**WALTON, KARA. See WALTON, CAROL ANN.**

**WALTON, LINDA G COOPER. See KEE, LINDA COOPER.**

**WALTON, R. KEITH**
College administrator, vice president (organization). **Personal:** Born Birmingham, AL; married Aubria D Corbitt; children: Rachel, Alexander & Gabrielle. **Educ:** Yale Col, BA, hist & biol, 1986; Harvard Law Sch, JD, 1990. **Career:** US Dist Ct, Northern Dist AL, law clerk, 1990-91; US Dept Treas, chief staff, enforcement, 1993-96; King & Spalding, assoc, 1991-93; White House Security Rev, dep dir, 1994-95; Columbia Univ, exec vpres & secy, 1996-2007, sr mem, 2007; Global Infrastructure Partners, prin & chief admin officer; dir, Zweig Total Return Fund Inc & Zweig Fund Inc, 2004-; Alcoa Inc, vpres govt affairs, 2011-. **Orgs:** Adv bd, Enterprise Found, 1996-; Coun Foreign Rels, New York, NY, 1996-, co-chair, 2000-; dir, secy, Apollo Theatre found, 2002; dir, Orchestra St Luke's; Asn Better New York, 2001-; vpres, Riverside Church, 2002-; Alpha Phi Alpha; Century Asn; Am Law inst; Coun US & Italy; trustee, Sanctuary Families; Adv Bd N Gen Hosp, 2002; Henry Crown Fel Aspen Inst, 2005. **Business Addr:** Vice President, Alcoa Inc, 201 Isabella St, Pittsburgh, PA 15212-5858, **Business Phone:** (412)553-4545.

### WALTON, REGGIE BARNETT
Educator, government official, judge. **Personal:** Born Feb 8, 1949, Donora, PA; son of Theodore and Ruth; married Debra; children: Danon. **Educ:** WVa State Col, BA, 1971; Am Univ Wash Col Law, JD, 1974. **Career:** Defender Asn PA, staff atty, 1974-76; US Atty Off DC, asst US atty, 1976-81, Career Criminal Unit, chief, 1979-80, exec asst, 1980-81; Super Ct DC, 1981-89, assoc judge, 1991-2001, Criminal Div, dep presiding judge, 1986-89; US Off Nat Drug Control Policy, assoc dir, 1989-91; US fed bench, 2001; US Dist Ct, DC, judge, 2001-15, sr judge, 2015; Us Foreign Intelligence Surveillance Ct, Judge, 2007-14; Harvard Univ Law Sch Advocacy Workshop, instr; Ky Col. **Orgs:** Am Bar Asn; Wash Bar Asn; Dist Columbia Bar Asn, 1975-; Judicial Conf DC, 1980-; Nat Inst Trial Advocacy Advocates Asn, 1985-; Big Bros Am, 1987-; bd dirs, Nat Ctr Missing & Exploited C, 1990-; Big Bros Big Sisters Am; Alpha Phi Alpha Fraternity; Chairperson, Nat Prison Rape Reduction Comn, 2004; fed judiciary's Criminal Law Comt, 2005; fac mem, Nat Judicial Col Reno, Nev. **Honors/Awds:** Distinguished Service Award, Bar Asn DC Young Lawyer's Sect, 1989; Community Service Award, Alpha Phi Alpha Inc, Iota Upsilon Lambda Chap, 1990; President's Image Award, Madison County Indiana Urban League, 1990; The Distinguished Service Award, NJ State Asn Chiefs of Police, 1990; James R Waddy Meritorious Service Award, The W Va State Col Nat Alumni Asn, 1990; one of 14 judges profiled in a 1994 book entitled Black Judges On Justice: Perspectives From The Bench; Marquis Who's Who in America, 2001; numerous honors and awards, including Distinguished Alumni Award, County Spotlight Award, James R. Waddy Meritorious Service Award. **Business Addr:** Judge, United States District Judge, 333 Constitution Ave NW, Washington, DC 20001, **Business Phone:** (202)354-3290.

### WALTON, DR. TRACY MATTHEW, JR.
Radiologist. **Personal:** Born Nov 12, 1930, Columbia, SC; married Mae Yvonne Squires; children: Adrienne, Tracy III, Terri & Brien. **Educ:** Morgan State Col, BS, 1953; Howard Univ Col Med, MD, 1961. **Career:** Freedman's Hosp, asst radiol, 1965-66; Howard Univ, asst radiol, 1965-66; Georgetown Univ Sch Med, clin instr, 1968; DC Gen Hosp, med officer, 1967-71, actg chief med officer, 1971, chief med officer, 1971-80; Univ DC, med dir sch radiol tech, med radiography prog, dept health sci, 1994-. **Orgs:** Pres, Nat Med Asn, 1961, treas, Region II; Rgnl radiotherapy comt, Met Wash Regnl Med Prog, 1968-; Cancer Aid Plan Com DC Chap ACS, 1968-81; chmn, Am Cancer Soc, 1968-, pres, DC div, 1984; adv bd, United Nat Bank Wash, 1974-; licensure, SC Bd Med Examr, 1981; vpres, DC Div Am Cancer Soc, 1983-; bd trustees, chmn, 1990-91, pres, 1994-95, Nat chmn, Radiol Sect Nat Med Asn, 1983-; Med Soc DC, provisional speaker house delegs, 1992; Nat Med Asn; Am Col Radiol; So Med Asn; licensure, Md Bd Med Exam; DC Bd Med Exam; Medico Chirurgical Soc DC, Morgan State Col. **Home Addr:** 7506 9th St NW, Washington, DC 20012-1602, **Home Phone:** (202)882-5038. **Business Addr:** Radiologist, General Practitioner, 4118 Grant St NE, Washington, DC 20019-3550, **Business Phone:** (202)396-8600.

### WAMBLE, CARL DEELLIS
Administrator, naval officer, real estate agent. **Personal:** Born Apr 11, 1952, Kansas City, KS; son of Amos Sylvester Sr (deceased) and Geraldine Phillips (deceased); married Naomi Jean Cannon; children: Christopher DeEllis & Christina Rochelle. **Educ:** Philander Smith Col, BS, biol, 1975; Webster Univ, MA, health serv mgt, 1983. **Career:** Navy official (retired), real estate agent; Vr Med Clin, Fallon, operating room technician, 1977-78; USS McKean, DD784, commun officer, electronic platerial officer, 1979-81; USS NJS, BB62, weapons, 2nd battery officer, 1981-84; Orgal Effectiveness Ctr, Yokosuka, OE consult, 1984-86; Naval Hosp, Yokosuka, Japan, opers mgt officer, 1986-87; Naval Sch Health Sci, master training specialist, 1987-90; Br Med Clin, Treasure Island, officer-in-charge, 1990-93; NATO Allied Forces Southern Europe, Naples, Italy, 1993-96; Uniform Serv Univ Med Sch, co comdr, asst commandant, 1997. **Orgs:** APA Frat, 1971-; Alpha Phi Omega Frat, 1971-; Nat Naval Officers Asn, 1982-; Surface Warfare Officers Asn, 1990-; Am Acad Med Adminr, 1991; Am Mil Evangelizing Nations; Alpha Phi Alpha Fraternity Inc.

### WAMBU, MUTHONI
Founder (originator), administrator, political consultant. **Educ:** Howard Univ, BS, jour, 1997. **Career:** Am Fedn Labor Cong Indust Orgns, Comt Polit Educ Polit Contrib Comt, coordr; Baker Wambu & Assocs, partner & owner, 2000-. **Orgs:** Delta Sigma Theta Sorority; regional polit opportunity prog dir, EMILYs List; bd mem, Dem GAIN. **Business Addr:** Owner, Partner, Baker Wambu & Assocs, 611 Pennsylvania Ave SE, Washington, DC 20003, **Business Phone:** (202)546-2227.

### WAMUTOMBO, DIKEMBE MUTOMBO MPOLONDO MUKAMBA JEAN JACQUE. See MUTOMBO, DIKEMBE.

### WANSEL, DEXTER GILMAN
Composer, singer. **Personal:** Born Aug 22, 1950, Bryn Mawr, PA; married Lorna Millicent Hall. **Career:** Philadelphia Int Rec, dir artist, repertoire, musician & rec artist, 1980; Wansel Enterprises, independent rec producer, 1973-75; Various Rec Co, musician, arranger, orchestral dir, synthesizer & programmer, 1973-75; Albums: Life on Mars, 1976; What the World Is Coming To, 1977; Voyager, 1978; Time is Slipping Away, 1979; Captured, 1986; Digital Groove World, 2004; Voyager & Time Is Slipping Away, 2005; Jazz In The City, 2007; Disco, 2008. Singles: "One Million Miles From The Ground", 1976; "Together Once Again", 1976; "Life On Mars", 1976; "Disco Lights", 1977; "Holdin' On / Dance With Me Tonight ", 1977; "All Night Long", 1978; "I'm In Love / Solutions", 1978; "Solutions", 1978; "It's Been Cool / I'll Never Forget", 1979; "The Sweetest Pain/Funk Attack", 1979; "I'll Never Forget 3 versions", 1979; "Beginning/Time Is Slipping Away", 1979; "Peter Royer Featuring Dexter Wansel - Love Is In Season", 1985; "Dexter Wansel / Willie Bobo - Life On Mars/Always There", 1985; "Captured", 1986. **Orgs:** Wissahickan Civic Asn, 1978. **Honors/Awds:** Twenty Eight Gold & Platinum Records; Grammy Award, Am Asn Rec Artists, 1978. **Home Addr:** 1050 Livezey Lane, Philadelphia, PA 19119, **Home Phone:** (215)224-6893. **Business Addr:** Singer, Philadelphia International Records, 309 S Broad St, Philadelphia, PA 19107, **Business Phone:** (215)985-0900.

### WANSLEY, LISA PAYNE
Publicist. **Personal:** Born Apr 2, 1962, Bronx, NY; daughter of Harold Sr and Florence Grant; married Terrance A. **Educ:** Univ Dayton, Dayton, Ohio, BA, 1984; Fordham Univ, Bronx, NY, MA, 1989. **Career:** Girls Club NY, Bronx, NY, dir, youth employ servs, 1984-86; Monroe Bus Col, Bronx, NY, community liaison, 1986-87; Union Theol Sem, New York, NY, dir, housing, 1987-89; Bronx Mus Arts, Bronx, NY, dir, pub affairs, 1989-92; Gov Mario Cuomo, regional rep, 1992-95; Off NYS Gov Mario Cuomo, bronx regional rep, 1992-94, dir, community affairs, 1995-2005; Col New Rochelle, adj prof, commun, 1999-2004; Off Bronx Dist Atty, dir, community affairs, admin chief, 2005-. **Orgs:** Network dir, Nat Asn Female Execs, 1983-; founder, NIA, network dir: A Minority Women's Prof Network Inc, 1984-; 100 Blacks Law Enforcement Who Care; pres, founder, Bronx Asn African Am Profs; bd trustees, Bronx Mus Arts, 1994-95; bd dir, Edenwald Community Ctr. **Honors/Awds:** Humanitarian Award, NIA: A Minority Women's Prof Network, 1988; Woman Year, All Saints Roman Cath Church Harlem, 1990; COT Serv Award, Bronx Ctr Progressive Servs, 1992; Outstanding Serv, Bronx Democratic Party, 1994; Achievement Award, Nat Coun Negro Women, 1995; Outstanding Role Model for Women in NYC Government, Women's Advisors New York, 2002; COT Serv, East Laconia Asn, 1997; Women of theYear, Bronx YMCA, 1998. **Home Addr:** 17 Woodfield Rd, Pomona, NY 10970, **Home Phone:** (718)655-6691. **Business Addr:** Administrative Chief, Office of the Bronx District Attorney, 198 E 161st St, Bronx, NY 10451, **Business Phone:** (718)590-2405.

### WARD, HON. ANNA ELIZABETH
Government official, consultant, mayor. **Personal:** Born Dec 20, 1952, Miami, FL; married Sterling Andrew; children: Johnathan Travis & Rochelle Marie. **Educ:** Miami Dade Com Col, AA, 1978; Fla Int Univ, BS, crim justice, 1980, MPA, 1980, PhD, 1980. **Career:** Fla Int Univ, 1971-80; Village El Portal, mayor; Sangamon State Univ, circulation dept admin, 1980-81; City Dallas, asst to asst city mgr, 1981-83; Miami Dade Col, adj prof & adminr; Dallas Cty Com Col Dist, asst internal auditor, 1984-85; City Emporia, VA, asst to city mgr; City Hallandale Beach, spec proj coordr; Martin Luther King Econ Develop Corp, pres & chief exec officer; Miami Dade Econ Advocacy Trust, exec dir, vice chair community & econ develop; Miami-Dade County, Citizens' Independent Transp Trust, District, mem, currently. **Orgs:** Pres, N Cent Tex COMPA, 1982-83; prog moderator, Int City Mgt Asn, 1982; mediator, Dispute Mediation Dallas Inc, 1982-85; Better Bus Bur Dallas, 1982-85; teen counr, Women Community Serv, 1983; co-chairperson, prog comUrban Mgt Asst N Tex, 1983; bd mem, N Cent Tex ASPA, 1983-85. **Honors/Awds:** Nominee Outstanding Young Am, 1981; Service Award, N Tex Conf Minority Pub Admin, 1983. **Special Achievements:** Author: Public Management ICMA, 1982-84; First Vice Chairperson of the Transportation Trust. **Home Addr:** 5737 Valley Mills Dr, Garland, TX 75043. **Business Addr:** Chair Person, Member, Miami-Dade County, 111 NW 1 St, Miami, FL 33128, **Business Phone:** (305)375-4466.

### WARD, ARNETTE SCOTT
School administrator, educator, association executive. **Personal:** Born Dec 2, 1937, Jacksonville, FL; daughter of Isiah and Albertha E; married John W; children: Elra Douglas. **Educ:** Edward Jr Col, AA; Fla A&M Univ, BS, 1962; Ariz State Univ, MA, 1972. **Career:** Lincoln High Sch, teacher, 1963; Fla A & M Univ, asst prof, 1964; Fall Recreation Dept, dir recruitment, 1964; Roosevelt Sch Dist, elem sch teacher, 1968; Mesa Comm Col, counr, 1971, div chmn, dean stud serv, 1979; Chandler-Gilbert Community Col, provost, 1985-92, pres, 1992-2002, pres emer, 2002-. **Orgs:** Comn on Trail Court Appt, 1985; nominating comn, Ariz Cactus Pine Girl Scout; Black WomenHigh Educ, 1986; Am Asn Comm & Jr County, 1986; Nat Coun Black Am; Affairs Coun AACJS; Am Asn Women Jr Col, 1986; pres, Delta Sigma Theta, 1986; Nat Coun Instrnl Adminr; Accrediting Comn Community & Jr Cols. **Honors/Awds:** Music Scholar, Edward Water Jr Col, 1957; hon mention as singer, Alex Haley "Author of Roots, " 1974; Outstanding Participation, Tempe Sch Dist, Black Culture Week, 1976; Women of the Year, Mesa Soroptomist & Delta Sigma Theta, 1977 & 1984; Merit Award, Black Youth Recognition Conf, 1982. **Special Achievements:** First African American Female college president in Arizona. **Home Addr:** 3015 Hawks Landing Dr, Tallahassee, FL 32309, **Home Phone:** (850)877-0574. **Business Addr:** President Emeritus, Chandler-Gilbert Community College, 2626 E Pecos Rd, Chandler, AZ 85225-2499, **Business Phone:** (602)732-7000.

### WARD, BILL
Association executive. **Career:** Grand Lodge Mkt Comt, chmn, currently; Habitat Humanity Int, affil serv mgr, midwest regional dir, currently. **Business Addr:** Midwest Regional Director, Habitat for Humanity Intl, 1920 S Laflin St, Chicago, IL 60608, **Business Phone:** (800)643-7845.

### WARD, CALVIN
Banker. **Personal:** Born Dec 10, 1955, Chicago, IL; son of Thomas (deceased) and Annie M (deceased). **Educ:** Ill State Univ, BS, bus mgt, 1977; DePaul Univ, Charles H Kellstadt Grad Sch Bus, MBA, 1990. **Career:** OSCO Drugs Inc, asst gen mgr, 1977-83; Northern Trust Co, asst vpres, recruiting team leader, 1984-91, vpres, bus develop officer, 1991-99, vpres, actg managing dir/ southside financial ctr, 1998-99, vpres, corp banking relationship mgr, 1999-2004; Wells Fargo Bank, sr vpres, sr relationship mgr, 2004-. **Orgs:** Pres, Chicago Chap, Nat Black MBA Asn, 1985; Urban Bankers Forum Chicago, 1986; Nat Asn Urban Bankers, 1986; United Negro Col Fund, telethon, 1987; chmn, local sch adv coun, Fulton County Schs, 2008-12; chmn, bd trustee, 2009-10, church coun chmn, 2011-12, Cascade United Methodist Church. **Honors/Awds:** Certificate of Recognition, 1990; Member of the Year, Chicago Chap, Nat Black MBA Asn, 1991; Brother of the Year, Alpha Phi Alpha Fraternity Inc, 1992. **Home Addr:** 2821 W Seipp, Chicago, IL 60652, **Home Phone:** (773)471-6461. **Business Addr:** Vice President, The Northern Trust Co, 50 S LaSalle St, Chicago, IL 60675, **Business Phone:** (312)444-2388.

### WARD, DR. CALVIN EDOUARD
Musician, educator. **Personal:** Born Apr 19, 1925, Atlanta, GA; son of Jefferson Sigman and Effie Elizabeth Crawford; married Adriana Wilhelmina deGraaf. **Educ:** Northwestern Univ, Evanston, IL, BMus, 1949, MmusEd, 1950; Staats Akademie fuer Musik, Vienna, Austria; Univ Vienna, Austria, PhD, 1955. **Career:** Educator (retired); Fla A&M Univ, Tallahassee, Fla, inr, music, Univ organist, 1950-51; Southern Univ, Baton Rouge, LA, assoc prof, music, Univ organist, 1957-58; SCA State Col, Orangeburg, SC, prof, chair, Dept Music& Fine Arts, 1959-61; Kingsborough Cot Col, City Univ NY, 1964-66; Tuskegee Univ, Tuskegee Inst, AL, assoc prof, chm, Dept Music, conductor, Tuskegee Concert Choir, 1968-72; Johns Hopkins Univ, Peabody Inst, Baltimore, Md, fac, theory, Afa class music, 1972-73, appl music, organ, 1973-77; Univ Md, Baltimore County, Md, fac, AFA studies, 1976-77; Coppin State Col, Baltimore, Md, prof, music, 1973-83; Trenton Pub Schs, Trenton, NJ, music spt; prof music edr & spt, Afa class music; freelance consult, choralonductor & elem sch resource person; Calvin Edouard Ward Educ Fund Minority Studs, chief adv. **Orgs:** Am Choral dir Asn; Am Guild Organists; Am Humanities Forum; African Am Music Opportunities Asn; Nat Educ Asn; NJ Educ Asn; Trenton Educ Asn; Phi Mu Alpha Sinfonia. **Home Addr:** 4 Terrell Lane, Willingboro, NJ 08046-3605, **Home Phone:** (609)877-3020.

### WARD, CARLA MOSBY. See MOSBY, DR. CARLA MANE.

### WARD, CHARLIE
Basketball player, basketball coach, football coach. **Personal:** Born Oct 12, 1970, Thomasville, GA; son of Charlie Sr and Willard; married Tonja F Harding; children: Caleb, Hope & Joshua. **Educ:** Tallahassee Community Col; Fla State Univ, therapeut recreation, 1994. **Career:** Basketball player (retired), basketball coach, football coach, executive; Milwaukee Brewers, pitcher, 1993; NY Knicks, guard & point guard, 1994-2004; San Antonio Spurs, 2003-04; Houston Rockets, 2004-05, asst coach; Westbury Christian Sch, Houston, Tex, asst coach, 2007-08, head football coach, 2008-; aWard Found, founder; Booker T. Wash High Sch Pensacola, Fla, head coach, 2014-. **Orgs:** mem, Omega Psi Phi Fraternity Inc. **Honors/Awds:** Heisman Trophy, 1993; Johnny Unitas Award, 1993; James E. Sullivan Award, Amateur Athletic Union, 1993; Walter Camp Award, 1993; NCAA Top QB of the Year, 1993; Maxwell Award, 1993; Davey O'Brien Award, 1993; ACC Athlete of the Year, 1993, 1994; All-American, 1993; Bowl Coalition National Championship, 1993; Sporting News College Football Player of the Year, 1994; Chic Harley Award, 1994; NBA Draft, 1994; College Football Hall of Fame, 2006; Florida Sports Hall of Fame. **Business Addr:** Head Coach, Booker T Washington High School, 6000 Col Pkwy, Pensacola, TX 32504, **Business Phone:** (850)475-5257.

### WARD, HON. CHRISTOPHER EVAN
Lawyer, judge. **Personal:** Born Jul 8, 1971, Atlanta, GA; son of Leila Bates and Evan Jr; married Meka Brumfield; children: Linda Christina & Evann Marie. **Educ:** Morehouse Col, BA, int studies & polit sci, 1993; Univ Miami, Sch Law, JD, 1997; Univ Ga. **Career:** Attorney (retired), judge; Fulton County Pub Defender, staff atty, 1998-2000; Fulton County Dist Atty, sr asst dist atty, 2000-07, chief sr asst dist atty, 2000-07, chief sr asst dist atty, 2012; Maj Narcotics Unit, sr asst dist atty, 2001-02; Illegal Firearms Unit, dir, 2002-05; Ga Power Co, sr staff atty, 2007-12; Fulton County Juv Ct, assoc judge, 2008-09; Munic Ct Atlanta, judge, 2012, presiding judge DUI div, 2013-, chief judge, 2015-16; Dekalb county, atty; Vaughan & Evans LLC, atty. **Orgs:** Ga Asn Criminal Defense Lawyers, 1998-2000; Gate City Bar Asn, 2004-; Scholar Comts & Found Bd, 2005-07; exec bd, Hall Fame selection & scholar comt, chair, 2007-11; external adv group mem, Justice Reinvestment Initiative Fulton County, 2016; bd dir, John Harlan Boys; bd dir, Girls Club & Grow Kids Inc; State Bar Ga; Cascade United Methodist Church; Kappa Alpha Psi Fraternity Inc; Kappa Boule Sigma Pi Phi Fraternity. **Home Addr:** 4365 Pk Ctr Dr SW, Atlanta, GA 30331-2067, **Home Phone:** (404)696-5389. **Business Addr:** Presiding Judge, Municipal Court of Atlanta, 150 Garnett St SW, Atlanta, GA 30303, **Business Phone:** (404)658-6940.

### WARD, DANIEL
School administrator, school superintendent. **Personal:** Born Mar 15, 1934, Memphis, TN; son of Gus; married Margie Marie Brittmon; children: Muriel Dawn, Maria Diane & Marcus Daniel. **Educ:** Tenn State Univ, BS, music educ, 1956; USAF, Multi-Engine Pilot Training Sch, cert, 1957; USAF Radar Controller Training, cert, 1958; USAF Air Force Instr Course, cert, 1960; USAF Air Command & Staff Sch, cert, 1976; Drug & Alcohol Abuse Workshop, cert, 1975. **Career:** School administrator (retired); USAF, pilot & radar contr, 1956-59; Tenn State Univ, sec sch instr, 1960; Douglass HS, teacher vocal music, 1960-62, prog coordr, 1962-65; Hyde Park Elem Sch, asst prin, 1965-67; Grant Elem Sch, prin, 1967-68; Porter Jr HS, prin, 1968-70; Vance Jr HS, prin, 1970-81; Fairley HS, prin, 1981-83; Memphis City Sch, dist IV supt, 1983, asst supt, sec dept, 1987-94, actg dep supt, 2003, consult, interim supt, head, dist's interim supt. **Orgs:** Asn Supv & Curric Devel; Omega Psi Phi Frat; AASA; TN State Univ Alumni Asn; Nat Guard Asn TN; bd trustee, Metropolitan Baptist Ch; vchmn emer, pres, Memphis-Shelby County Airport Authority, 1967-99; Nat Asn Advan Colored People. **Honors/Awds:** Four-year scholarships to: Tenn State Univ, Ark State Univ, Howard Univ, LeMoyne Col, Stillman Col; Omega Man of the Year, Epsilon Phi Chap, 1976, nominated, 1980; Omega Citizen of the Year, 1992; Awarded Meritorious Service Medal by Pres of the US, 1981; Danforth Admin Fellow, 1983-84; First Oak Leaf Cluster, 1984; Minute-Man Award for Outstanding Service to the Tenn Air Natl Guard. **Home Addr:** 6746 Briarmeadows Dr, Memphis, TN 38120, **Home Phone:** (901)751-3626.

### WARD, REV. DR. DARYL
College president, clergy. **Personal:** Born Sep 12, 1957, Cincinnati, OH; son of Maudie and Lester; married Vanessa Oliver; children: Joshua (Barbara), Rachel & Bethany. **Educ:** Col Wooster, BA, 1979; Georgetown Univ, Law Ctr, JD, 1985; Colgate Rochester Divinity Sch, Mdiv, 1986. **Career:** Fed Energy Regulatory Comn, legal intern, 1982; Rochester Soc Prev Cruelty to C, legal intern, 1984-85; United Theol Sem, dir admis, 1986-89, dean African Am ministries, 1986-96; Ome-

ga Baptist Church, pastor, 1988, sr pastor, currently; United Theol Sem, Dayton, Ohio, exec vpres & COO, 1989-93, pres & COO, 1993-96, pres emer, 2000. **Orgs:** Benjamin E Mays Fel, Fund Theol Educ, 1984, 1985; bd trustee, Good Samaritan Hosp, 1989-98; Tony Halls Cong Adv Coun, Dayton, 1991-; Ohio State Bar Asn; Victoria Theatre Bd, 1993-; Hospice Dayton, 1993-96; pres& Chief Exec Officer Urban Outreach Found, 1996-98; pres emer, United Theol Sem; Parents Advancing Choice Educ. **Home Addr:** 313 Cheryl Ct, Dayton, OH 45415, **Home Phone:** (513)890-8033. **Business Addr:** Senior Pastor, Omega Baptist Church, 1821 Emerson Ave, Dayton, OH 45406-5803, **Business Phone:** (937)278-1006.

### WARD, DEDRIC LAMAR

Football player, football coach. **Personal:** Born Sep 29, 1974, Cedar Rapids, IA; children: Mason. **Educ:** Northern Iowa Univ, BA, psychol. **Career:** Football player (retired), football coach; New York Jets, wide receiver, 1997-2000; Miami Dolphins, 2001-02; Baltimore Ravens, 2003; New Eng Patriots, 2003; Dallas Cowboys, 2004; Mo State Univ, coach, 2006; Ariz Cardinals, offensive qual control, 2007-08; Kans City Chiefs, coaching staff, 2009; Northern Iowa, coach, 2010. junior warriors, coach, 2010-; Travling Team, coach, 2014-. **Honors/Awds:** Super Bowl champion XXXVIII. **Home Addr:** , Cedar Rapids, IA.

### WARD, HON. DORIS MARGARET

Consultant, government official, commissioner. **Personal:** Born Jan 27, 1932, Chicago, IL; daughter of Robbie Floyd and Jesse Keys. **Educ:** Ind Univ, BA, 1953, MS, 1964; San Francisco State Univ, MA, 1974; Univ Calif, PhD. **Career:** Government official, commissioner (retired); Indianapolis Pub Sch, teacher, 1959-67; Ind State Teacher Corps, team leader, 1967-68; San Francisco State Univ, adj lectr, 1969-70, 1972; San Francisco Bd Supervisors, pres, 1990-96; San Francisco, City & County, assessor, 1995-2006; Asian Art Mus, San Francisco, comnr, 2005-; Mateo County Off Educ, coordr; Waterloo Iowa Sch, consult. **Orgs:** Trustee, vpres, trustee, San Francisco Community Col Dist, 1972-79, county supvr, 1979-90; San Francisco County Assessor Recorder, 1996; deleg, Dem Nat Conv, 2000-06; Minority Affairs Assembly Asn Community Col; exec coun, Asn Study African-Am Life & Hist; nat bd, western reg bd coun, Black Am Affairs Asn Am Community & Jr Col; Nat Asn Advan Colored People; SF Div Nat Women's Polit Caucus; Alpha Kappa Alpha; Betty J Olive Memorial Found; vpres, San Francisco Black Leadership Forum; Black Women Orgn Action; Dayton Police Dept Conflict & Violence; bd dir, Asian Art Museum; bd dir, Am Cancer Asn; bd mem, Former Community Col; former pres San Francisco Bd Supervisors. **Honors/Awds:** NDEA grant, Ind State Univ, 1966; Lilly Found grant, Ind State Univ, 1967; NDEA, Univ Calif, 1968; Special Merit Award, Sup Reporter, 1973; Rockefeller Found Grant, 1974; Community Service Award, Kappa Alpha Psi, 1975; Living Legend Award, Black Women Orgn Action, 1975; Distinguished Women Award, Girls' Club, Med-Peninsula & Lockheed Missilies & Space Co Inc, 1975; Bicentennial Award, Trinity Baptist Church, 1976; Recognition Exemplary Community Leadership Award, Black Student Psychol Asn, 1976; publ Indianapolis Comm Ctr Proj, 1968-69; Education Honorary, Pi Lambda Theta; Govt Honorary, Pi Sigma Alpha. **Business Addr:** Commissioner, Asian Art Museum, 200 Larkin St, San Francisco, CA 94102, **Business Phone:** (415)581-3500.

### WARD, DOUGLAS TURNER

Actor, playwright. **Personal:** Born May 5, 1930, Burnside, LA; son of Roosevelt and Dorothy Short; married Diana Hoyt Powell; children: 2. **Educ:** Wilberforce Univ; Univ Mich; Paul Mann's Actors Workshop, actor training. **Career:** Theater appearances: Lost in the Stars, 1958; A Raisin in the Sun, 1959; The Blacks, 1961-62; One Flew Over the Cuckoo's Nest, 1963; Day Absence, actor & writer, 1965; Daddy Goodness, dir, 1968; Kongi's Harvest, 1968; Ceremonies in Dark Old Men, 1969; The Reckoning, actor & writer, 1969; Perry's Mission, dir, 1971; Frederick Douglass Through His Own Words, 1972; The River Niger, actor & writer, 1972; The First Breeze of Summer, 1975; The Offering, 1977; Old Phantoms, 1979; Ride a Black Horse, dir, 1971; A Ballet Behind the Bridge, dir, 1972; Waiting for Mongo, dir, 1975; Livin' Fat, dir, 1976; Home, dir, 1979; A Season to Unravel, dir, 1979; Zooman and the Sign, dir, 1980; A Soldier's Play, dir, 1982; The Redeemer, writer, 1983; Negro Ensemble Co, co-founder & artistic dir, 1967-; Films: Man & Boy, 1972; Tigus, 1983; Go Tell It on the Mountain, 1984; Black Eros, 2014. TV series: "East Side/West Side", 1963; "Ceremonies in Dark Old Men", 1975; "The Women of Brewster Place", 1989; "Law & Order", 1993; "Cosby", 2000; "For Love of Olivia", 2001. **Honors/Awds:** Obie Award, Happy Ending, 1966; Creative Arts Award, Happy Ending, Brandeis Univ, 1969; Vernon Rice Drama Desk Award, Best Play, Day Absence, Happy Ending, 1966-69; Obie Award, The River Niger, 1973; Tony Award nomination, Best Supporting Actor, 1974; Boston Theatre Critics Circle Award, 1986. **Home Addr:** 222 East 11th St, New York, NY 10003.

### WARD, EVERETT BLAIR

Administrator, association executive. **Personal:** Born Nov 6, 1958, Raleigh, NC; son of William H and Dorothy Williams; married Cassandra Lloyd. **Educ:** St Augustine Col, BA, eng & commun, 1981; NC State Univ, MA, African-Am/black studies, 2003; NC A&T State Univ, PhD, leadership studies, 2013. **Career:** Westinghouse Elec Corp, Raleigh, mkt asst, 1980-82; NC Dem Party, Raleigh, NC, polit dir, 1983-89, african am exec dir, 1989-93, spec asst chmn; NC Dept Transp, adminr local & community affairs, Prog Minority Serv Inst, dir, Hist Black Col Univ Prog, dir, sect head, currently. **Orgs:** Life mem, asst vpres, chmn, regional vpres, southern region vpres, Alpha Phi Alpha Fraternity Inc, Phi Lambda Chap; Raleigh Hist Properties; comn chmn, elder, Davie St Presby Church USA; NC Black Leadership Caucus; Raleigh-Wake Citizens Asn; adv bd, Mech & Farmers Bank; cochmn credentials comt & vice chmn, Dem Nat Comt; Wake Co Dem Men; NC Lit & Hist Asn; Golden Key Hon Soc; bd mem, Nc State Capital Found; chair, Sigma Pi Phi Fraternity; bd trustee, St Augustine's Col; treas, 100 Black Men; bd mem, Clarence E. Lightner Found. **Home Addr:** 3112 Falconhurst Dr, Wake Forest, NC 27587, **Home Phone:** (919)554-2318. **Business Addr:** Director, North Carolina Department of Transportation, 1511 Mail Service Ctr, Raleigh, NC 27699-1511, **Business Phone:** (919)508-1810.

### WARD, FRANCES MARIE (FRANCES WARD-JOHNSON)

Journalist. **Personal:** Born Mar 23, 1964, Goldsboro, NC; daughter of Joe and Occie Whitfield. **Educ:** NC Agr & Tech State Univ, Greensboro, NC, BA, jour, eng, 1986, MA, african am lit; Univ NC, PhD, mass commun res. **Career:** Assoc Press, Raliegh, NC, bur news reporter broadcast writer, 1986; Wilson Daily Times, Wilson NC, feature writer, 1988-89; Greensboro News & Rec, Greensboro, NC, feature writer, 1989; NC A&T, coordr pub rels; Elon Univ, adj prof, 1995-99; Ctr Creative Leadership, pub rels mgr, 1995-99; Elon Univ, Sch Commun, assoc prof, interim dept chair, 2003-. **Orgs:** Triad Black Media Profs, Greensboro, NC, 1990-; Nat Asn Advan Colored People, Reidsville, NC, 1991; Nat Asn Black Journalists, 1990-; NC Press Women's Asn, 1990-; Pub Rels Socs Am; St's Delight Church, Goldsboro, NC, 1981-; Sigma Tau Delta, Nat Hon Soc Eng Majrs, 1983-; Orgn Universal Accreditation Bd. **Honors/Awds:** Second Place Award Winner For Profiles, NC Press Women's Asn, 1990; Most Promising Journalism Student Award, NC A&T State Univ, 1985; English Dept Award, NC A&T State Univ, 1986; Excellence in Teaching Award in the School of Communications, 2009; Faculty of the Year Award for teaching and scholarship, African-American Studies program, 2010. **Home Addr:** 268 N Oakland Ave Suite 6B, Eden, NC 27288, **Home Phone:** (919)627-1781. **Business Addr:** Associate Professor, Elon University, McEwen 101-B, Elon, NC 27244, **Business Phone:** (336)278-5738.

### WARD, GARY LAMELL

Baseball player. **Personal:** Born Dec 6, 1953, Los Angeles, CA; children: Daryle & Agee. **Career:** Baseball player (retired); Minn Twins, outfielder, 1979-83; Tex Rangers, outfielder, 1984-86; New York Yankees, outfielder & infielder, 1987-89; Detroit Tigers, outfielder, 1989-90; Int League, Charlotte Knights, hitting coach, 1999-2001; Chicago White Sox, hitting coach, 2001-08; Charlotte Knights, Batting coach, 1999-2001; Winston-Salem Dash, hitting coach, 2011-12; Birmingham Barons, 2013. **Home Addr:** 318 W Raymond St, Compton, CA 90220.

### WARD, HASKELL G. (HASKEL SEARS WARD)

Consultant, administrator. **Personal:** Born Mar 13, 1940, Griffin, GA; son of George Allen Ward Dumas and Margaret Poe Dumas; married Kathryn Lecube; children: Alexandra & Michelle. **Educ:** Clark Col, BA, 1963; Univ Calif, Los Angeles, MA, 1967. **Career:** Haile Selassie Univ, Vol Us Peace Corps, Instr, 1963-65; Opers Crossroads Africa, Dir recruitment & selection, 1967-69; Ford Found, asst prog officer, 1969-72; Mid E & Africa Lagos, asst rep, 1975-77; Specialist Africa, Us Dept State, mem policy planning staff, 1977-78; Comnr, Community Develop Agency, 1978; dep asst secy; City New York, dep mayor, 1979; Health & hosps Corp, New York, chmn bd, 1979-; Haskell G. Ward Assocs, pres, 1980; Ward Assocs, consult, currently; Global Alumina Corp, sr vpres gov rel, 2000-; Seacom, vpres, currently. **Orgs:** mem, Trilateral Comn, 1980-87Mid-Atlantic Club; bd dir, New York Partnership, 1982-86; bd dir, African Med Res Found; bd dir, Am Coun Ger; mem adv comn, Gov Mario Coumo World Trade Coun, 1984; Bd dir, Am Coun Ger, 1985. **Honors/Awds:** Woodrow Wilson Hon Fel; John Hay Whitney Fel; Several awards for citizenship, community service & achievement. **Special Achievements:** First African American on the policy planning staff of the State Department during the Carter Administration. **Business Addr:** Senior Vice President Government Relations, Global Alumina Corp, 245 Pk Ave 38th Fl, New York, NY 10167, **Business Phone:** (212)351-0000.

### WARD, HORACE TALIAFERRO. See Obituaries Section.

### WARD, DR. JAMES DALE

Educator. **Personal:** Born Feb 3, 1959, Nettleton, MS; son of J L and Alice Harper Marion. **Educ:** Univ Miss, BA, jour & sociol, 1980; Univ Cincinnati, MPA, pub affairs, 1983, PhD, polit sci, 1988. **Career:** Knoxville News-Sentinel, staff writer, 1980; WCBI-TV Columbus, TV reporter, 1980-86; Univ New Orleans, asst prof, 1990-94; Univ NMex, vis asst prof, 1995-98, assoc prof, 1998-2005; Miss Univ Women, Col Arts & Sci, Dept Hist, Polit Sci, Geog & Paralegal Studies, assoc prof polit sci, coordr pub admin cert prog, 2005-, prof polit sci, currently. **Orgs:** Am Soc Pub Admin; Am Polit Sci Asn; Conf Minority Pub Add; Am Polit Sci Asn. **Home Addr:** PO Box 8601, Columbus, MS 39705, **Home Phone:** (662)329-7173. **Business Addr:** Professor of Political Science, Coordinator of Public Administration Certificate Program, Mississippi University for Women, Dept Hist Polit Sci Geography, Columbus, MS 39701, **Business Phone:** (662)329-4750.

### WARD, JEFF T.

Accountant. **Career:** PFA Entertainment Inc, pres. **Business Addr:** President, PFA Entertainment Inc, 4201 Neshaniny Blvd, Bensalem, PA 19020.

### WARD, DR. JERRY WASHINGTON, JR.

Writer. **Personal:** Born Jul 31, 1943, Washington, DC; son of Jerry Washington Sr and Mary Theriot. **Educ:** Tougaloo Col, BS, 1964; Ill Inst Technol, Chicago, IL, MS, 1966; Univ Va, Charlottesville, VA, PhD, 1978. **Career:** Ill Inst Technol, teaching asst, 1965-66; State Univ New York, Albany, NY, teaching fel, 1966-68; Upward Bound Prog, coordr Eng, 1970-71; Tougaloo Col, Tougaloo, Miss, asst prof & prof Eng, 1970-2002, chmn dept Eng, 1979-86, 2001-02, Lawrence Durgin Prof Lit, 1988-2002; United Negro Col Fund fac grant, 1974-75; Univ Va, instr transition prog, 1974; Kent fel, 1975-77; Univ Va, fac, 1976-77; NEH Inst Southern Black Cult, fac, 1981; Spelman Col, fac, 1982; Miss Comm Humanities, fac, 1983; Tougaloo Col, NEH Summer Sem Col Teachers, dir, 1984; Nat Endowment Humanities, Wash, DC, prog officer, 1984; Univ Miss, Eng Dept, vis prof, 1987; Talladega Col, UNCF Resident scholar, 1987-88; Univ Va, Common wealth Ctr, Charlottesville, Va, prog dir & prof, 1990-91; New York Univ, Fac Resource Network Sem, 1993; Univ Memphis, Moss chair excellence Eng, 1996; Nat Humanities Ctr, fel, 1999-2000; Dillard Univ, distinguished prof Eng & African world studies, 2002-12. **Orgs:** Alpha Phi Alpha Fraternity Inc, 1961-; exec comt, Col Lang Asn, 1974-76, black studies comt, 1977-91; chmn, Div Black Am Lit, Mod Lang Asn, 1986-87; Miss Adv Comt, US Civil Rights Comn, 1988-98; Authors Guild, 1988-; adv bd, George Moses Horton Soc, Study African Am Poetry, 1997-; exec coun, Soc Study Southern Lit, 1997-99; African Am Lit & Cult Soc; Am Lit Asn. **Home Addr:** 1928 Gentilly Blvd, New Orleans, LA 70119, **Home Phone:** (504)940-6368. **Business Addr:** Independent Scholar, 1928 Gentilly Blvd, New Orleans, LA 70119-2002, **Business Phone:** (504)940-6368.

### WARD, JOEL (JOEL RANDAL WARD)

Hockey player. **Personal:** Born Dec 2, 1980, North York, ON; son of Randall and Cecilia. **Educ:** Univ PEI, BA, 2005. **Career:** Junior hockey player, Owen Sound Attack, 1997-2001; professional hockey player, Houston Aeros (AHL), 2005-08; Minnesota Wild, 2006-08, Nashville Predators, 2009-11, Washington Capitals, 2011-15, San Jose Sharks, 2015-. **Honors/Awds:** Rookie of the Year, University of Prince Edward Island, 2001; three time team MVP University of Prince Edward Island. **Business Addr:** SAP Center, 525 W Santa Clara St, San Jose, CA 95113.

### WARD, KEITH LAMONT

Lawyer, consultant. **Personal:** Born Nov 12, 1955, Bridgeport, CT; son of Willie and Vera S; married Jacqueline B; children: Alexandra. **Educ:** Southern Univ, BA, polit sci, 1978; Southern Univ Law Ctr, JD, 1982. **Career:** Keith L Ward PLC, atty, 1982-99; EXCEL Telecommunications, sr dir, 1996-2004; 5LINX Enterprises, sr vpres, 2005-09; Youngevity, Essential Health Sci, 2010-; Soul Purpose, 2010-; Financial Destination Inc, mkt consult, 2010-; CLR Roasters, mkt consult, 2010-; YGY Mineral Makeup Collection, mkt consult, 2012-; YGY JavaFit, mkt consult, 2012-; Wor(l)d Global Network Pvt Ltd, dir gold, 2014-; OneCoin, pro trader, 2016-. **Orgs:** Omega Psi Phi Fraternity Inc; Prince Hall Mason; life mem, Nat Asn Advan Colored People; Southern U. Alumni-Life; Nat Urban League. **Business Addr:** Director Gold, Wor(l)d Global Network Pvt Ltd, 600 Brickell World Plz Suite 1775, Miami, FL 33132, **Business Phone:** (985)377-8959.

### WARD, LENWOOD E.

Executive. **Educ:** NC Cent Univ, Durham, BS, 1963. **Career:** Arco, Calif, org & co adv, 1973-74, sr employee rels adv, 1974-78, employee rels mgr, 1978-, org & co mgr, 1978-80, corp employee rels mgr, 1980-89, human resources servs mgr, 1989-. **Business Addr:** Manager of Human Resources Services, ARCO, 515 S Flower St AP 4265, Los Angeles, CA 90071, **Business Phone:** (213)486-1670.

### WARD, LLOYD DAVID

Executive. **Personal:** Born Jan 22, 1949, Detroit, MI; married Estralita; children: Lloyd II & Lance. **Educ:** Mich State Univ, BS, mech engineering, 1970; Xavier Univ, MBA, 1984. **Career:** Procter & Gamble, mgr, 1970-85, Div Mfg, mgr, 1985-86, adv mgr, pkg soap & det, 1986-87, vpres & gen mgr, dishcare, 1987-88; Ford Motor, mgr, 1977-78; Pepsi Co Inc, Pepsi-Cola E, vpres opers, 1988-91; Frito-Lay, W Div, pres, 1991-92, Cent Div, pres, 1992-96; Maytag Corp, Maytag Appliances, exec vpres, 1996-98, pres & chief operating officer, 1998-99, chmn & chief exec officer, 1999-2000; iMotors, chmn & chief exec officer, 2001; US Olympic Comt, chief exec officer & secy gen, 2001-03; BodyBlocks Worldwide LLC, bd dir, chmn, 2003-; JP Morgan Chase Co, bd dir; Cent & Southwest Corp, bd dir; Yuanzhen Org Dairy Co Ltd, chief exec officer & gen mgr, 2006-; CleanTech Solutions Worldwide LLC, chmn & chief exec officer, 2010-. **Orgs:** Exec Leadership Coun; bd dir, Presidents Coun Phys Fitness & Sports; bd dir, Ronald McDonald House; bd dir, Dallas YMCA; bd dir, Paul Quinn Col; bd dir, Jimmy Johnson Found; bd dir, Inroads Southwest Ohio; bd dir, Gen Motors Corp, 2000-; bd dir, JP Morgan Chase Co, 1999-2003; bd dir, Cent & Southwest Utilities Corp; bd dir, Belo Corp, 2001-; Ymca. **Honors/Awds:** American Best & Brightest Business & Professional Men and Women, Dollars & Sense Mag, 1995; Executive of the Year, Black Enterprises Mag, 1995; Jack Breslin Life Time Achievement Award, Mich State Univ, 1996; Alumni of the Year Award, Mich State Univ; Marketer of the Year, BrandWeek Mag; Outstanding Leadership Award, Ctr Creative Leadership. **Special Achievements:** Black Belt, Karate; First African American CEO of US Olympic Comm; First African American CEO of a Fortune 500 Company. **Home Addr:** 1281 Gulf Mex Dr APT 1001, Longboat Key, FL 34228. **Business Addr:** Chairman, BodyBlocks Worldwide LLC, 3340 Peachtree Rd NE Suite 100, Atlanta, GA 30326, **Business Phone:** (404)364-1997.

### WARD, MELISSA

Airplane pilot. **Educ:** Univ Southern Calif, BS, bus admin, 1986. **Career:** Tex Air Force, flight instr, 1988-91, aircraft comdr, co-pilot, capt, beginning, 1997; Tenn Air Nat Guard, capt; United Airlines, flight officer, 1992, capt, 1998-. **Honors/Awds:** Women's Basketball NCAA Champions, 1983, 1984; Alumni Merit Award, Univ Southern Calif, 2009. **Special Achievements:** First female African American capt for commercial airline; First female African-American stud in pilot training, fighter pilot rating & instr pilot, Tex Air Force. **Business Addr:** Captain, United Airlines, 1200 E Algonquin Rd, Elk Grove Township, IL 60007, **Business Phone:** (847)700-4000.

### WARD, REV. MELVIN FITZGERALD, SR.

Clergy. **Personal:** Born Jul 2, 1918, New Bern, NC; son of Dolphin and Nancy Forbes; married Lessie Pratt; children: Dorothy Buckner, Mary Francis Martin, Nancy Bullet & Melvin F Jr. **Educ:** Nat Bible Inst, DDiv, 1944; Lawson Bible Inst, BTh, 1945; Teamers Bible Inst, DDiv, 1972; Union Christian Bible Inst, DDiv, 1974; Livingston Col, Salesbury, NC, DDiv, 1976; Clinton Jr Col, Rork Hill, SC, DDiv, 1975; Union Christian Bible Inst, MDiv, 1984. **Career:** African Methodist Episcopal Zion Church, minister, 1943-, pastor, 1940-91; TWIU, pres, 1950-68; Tobacco Works Int Union, rep, 1977; Bakery Confectionery & Tobacco Workers, Union AFL-CIO-CLC, Kensington, Md, rep. **Orgs:** Bd mem, home mission bd, AME Zion Ch; bd trustee, Christian Bible Inst; dir, Pub Rel VI & S Am Conf; Human Rel Comn, 1960-65. **Honors/Awds:** Award Pres of Local 256 TWIU 25 yrs; Dedicated Service Appreciation Award & Unselfish Service, Hood Theological Seminary, 1989. **Home Addr:** PO Box 2035, Durham, NC 27702, **Home Phone:** (919)682-8773. **Business Addr:** Pastor, African Methodist Episcopal Zion Church, PO Box 1634, Wilson, NC 27893.

**WARD, NOLAN F.**
Lawyer, executive director. **Personal:** Born Jan 14, 1945, Columbus, OH; son of Clifforn Loudin and Ethel Shaffer (deceased); married Hazel Williams; children: Penelope Kaye. **Educ:** Prairie View A&M Univ, BA, MA, 1968; Univ Nebr, 1967; S Univ, attended 1969; Univ Tex, JD, 1973. **Career:** State Tex, chmn exec dir, Tex Employ Comn; Gov Dolph Briscoe, legal staff, 1976-; pvt pract, 1975; Co Judge Bill Elliott, clerk, 1975; St Rep Anthony Hall, admin aid, 1973-74; EEOC, case analyst, 1970-73; Waller ISD, instr, 1967-69; Job Corps, advr, 1966-67; Austin, Tex, atty gen, 1983-. **Orgs:** Nat Asn Advan Colored People; Tex Bar Asn; Omega Psi Phi; Omicron Kappa Delta; Delta Theta Phi; Thurgood Marshall Legislative Sec; Dist & Co Atty Asn, Urban League. **Special Achievements:** First African American to serve on the three-member Texas Employment Commission. **Home Addr:** 12900 Trailwood Rd, Austin, TX 78727-3041, **Home Phone:** (512)458-0264. **Business Addr:** Attorney, Private Practice, 6421 Camp Bowie Blvd Suite 312, Ft. Worth, TX 76116, **Business Phone:** (512)239-5803.

**WARD, DR. PERRY W.**
College president, educator. **Educ:** Miles Col, BS; Univ Ala, MSW, PhD. **Career:** Miles Col, instr, adult educ prog, 1969-71, assoc dir emergency sch asst prog, 1972-73, dir emergency sch aid act prog, 1973-75; Birmingham Pub Schs, dir fed progs admin, 1975-79; Univ Ala, Grad Sch Social Work, adj prof, 1977-82; Univ Ala, dir basic educ, 1979-87; Lawson State Community Col, Birmingham, AL, pres, 1987-. **Orgs:** Pres, Ala Col Asn; vpres, Cent Ala Athletic Asn; Mercedes Benz Pride Comn; nat bd mem, Am Asn Community Cols; bd mem, Compass Bank; bd mem, Univ Ala Health Servs Found; pres, Birmingham Urban League; Nat Alternative Fuels Training Consortium; Ala Region 4 Workforce Develop Comt; Jefferson County Workforce Develop Bd. **Honors/Awds:** Outstanding Service Award; Boy Scouts of America Appreciation Award, Nat Asn Advan Colored People; Academy of Fellows Distinguished Educators Award, I-D-E-A; Kermit Mathison Outstanding Community Col Administrator Award. **Business Addr:** President, Lawson State Community College, 3060 Wilson Rd SW, Birmingham, AL 35221, **Business Phone:** (205)925-2515.

**WARD, RONALD R.**
Lawyer. **Personal:** Born Jun 12, 1947, Sacramento, CA; son of Robert L and Audrey; married Willetta L; children: Sara A. **Educ:** Calif State Univ, BA, 1973; Univ Calif, Hastings Col Law, JD, 1976. **Career:** State Wash, Off Atty Gen, state asst atty gen, 1979-82; Levinson, Friedman Law Firm, atty law, partner, 1982-; Jones & Ward PLLC, partner & atty, 1986-; Ward Smith PLLC, atty law, owner, 2005-. **Orgs:** Loren Miller Bar Asn, 1979-; bd gov, Wash State Trial Lawyers Asn, 1989-95; pres, Wash State Bar Asn, 2004-05; King Co Bar Asn; Nat Bar Asn; Am Bar Asn House Deleg; pres, Am Bd Trial Advocates; Justice Advocacy Africa. **Honors/Awds:** Special President's Recognition Award, Wash State Trial Lawyers Asn, 1995; Super Lawyer, Wash Law & Polit Mag, 2003; American Bar Association Partnership Award, WLI, 2005; Ron R Ward President's Award, named in honor, 2006; Outstanding Plaintiff Trial Lawyer Award, Wash Defense Trial Lawyers, 2006; Distinguished Service Award, Anheuser-Busch Co, Nat Bar Asn; Washington State Trial Lawyers President's Award, 2006; Washington State Bar Foundation Award of Merit; Excellence Diversity Award, Wash State Bar Found; Justice Carl Maxey Award, Wash State Bar Found; Lifetime Achievement Award, Loren Miller Bar Asn, 2014; Philanthropy Award, Wash State Bar Found, 2014. **Special Achievements:** First African-American to serve as president of the Washington State Bar Association. **Business Addr:** Attorney, Partner, Jones & Ward PLLLC, 1000 2nd Ave Suite 4050, Seattle, WA 98104-1023, **Business Phone:** (206)866-2832.

**WARD, RONNIE V. (RODNEY GLEN)**
Football player. **Personal:** Born Feb 11, 1974, St. Louis, MO. **Educ:** Univ Kans. **Career:** Football player (retired); Miami Dolphins, linebacker, 1997.

**WARD, SANDRA L.**
Executive. **Personal:** Born May 23, 1963, Atlanta, GA; daughter of Aston Roy and Betty Jean. **Educ:** Howard Univ, BA, 1985; John Marshall Law Sch, attended 1995. **Career:** EPIC Radio Network, sr acct exec; Chief Justice Robert Benham, chief staff; Supreme Ct Ga, Off Comn & Progs, dir; Ga Merit Syst Legal Serv Off, sr lobbyist; Global Govt Strategies, Govt Affairs & New Bus Develop, vpres, currently. **Orgs:** Black Entertainment & Sports Lawyers Asn; Nat Urban League; Nat Asn Media Women; Howard Univ Alumni Asn; bd mem, Queen Hearts Found. **Home Addr:** 275 Dix-Lee On Dr, Fairburn, GA 30213. **Business Addr:** Board of Member, Queen of Hearts Foundation, 500 Claudel Ct SW, Atlanta, GA 30331, **Business Phone:** (404)661-2411.

**WARD, VELMA LEWIS**
Scientist. **Personal:** Born Columbus, OH; daughter of John F and Anna C; children: Broderick Lewis. **Educ:** Univ Mich, attended 1949; Wayne State Univ, BS, MT, 1953, Col Med, MS, biochem, 1961, Inst Geront, grad cert, 1986, PhD, 1996. **Career:** Lafayette Clin, Detroit, Mich, res assoc, Clin Lab, asst dir, biochem, 1956-84; Prudentia Worth, dir; Drake Inst Sci Consult, 1971-73; Detroit Area Pre-Col Engineering Prog, asst dir, 1985-91; Philadelphia Geriat Ctr, res prof mgr, 1992-94; Wayne State Univ, vis asst prof, 1996-98, adj prof, 1998-. **Orgs:** New York Acad Scis; Asn Women Sci, AWIS-DAC, exec bd, vp; Geront Soc Am; Am Anthrop Asn; Asn Anthropol & Geront; Am Asn Univ Women; Res Rev Bd, Southfield Oncol Inst; Mich USn Scholar Info Team, NAVSIT, Detroit; USn Off Educrs Vis Team, Pensacola, Fla; Alpha Delta Theta, Med Tech; Alpha Kappa Alpha Sorority; Navy League US; Reg Am Soc Clin Path; Am Chem Soc. **Honors/Awds:** Distinguished Alumna Award, Northville High Sch, 1992; Minority Graduate Research Training Award, Nat Inst Aging, 1992; Am Inst Chemists, Fellow; Sigma Xi, Fel; Royal Soc Chem, 1996; 'Top Fifty Minority Women Scientists', Nat Tech Asn Scientists & Engrs, NTA, 1996; Diversity Award Honoree, Wayne St Univ Eugene Applebaum Col Pharm & Health Sci. **Special Achievements:** Has authored several papers and has presented papers widely. **Home Addr:** 16500 N Pk Dr Apt 1210, Southfield, MI 48075. **Business Addr:** Adjunct Faculty, Wayne State University, 42 W Warren Ave, Detroit, MI 48202, **Business Phone:** (877)978-4636.

**WARD, WALTER L., JR.**
Executive, state government official, association executive. **Personal:** Born Oct 28, 1943, Camp Forest, TN; son of Walter and Kathryn; children: Dionne & Walter L III. **Educ:** Univ Wis-Milwaukee, BS, 1969; Univ Wis Law Sch; Milwaukee Area Tech Col; Marquette Univ, grad work. **Career:** State Wis, Dist 17, state rep, 1972-. **Orgs:** Coun work; chmn, bd mem, OIC Indust Adv Bd; Martin Luther King Orgn; chmn, Jr Chamber Com; vice chmn, Opportunities Industrialization Ctr Greater Milwaukee Indust Adv Bd; bd dir, Milw Girls Club; Wis State Assembly, 1972-; Biennial comt assignments, 1979-. **Home Addr:** 3124 N 13th St, Milwaukee, WI 53206, **Home Phone:** (414)372-8681. **Business Addr:** Rm 325 W State Capitol, Madison, WI 53702, **Business Phone:** (608)266-0960.

**WARDEN, GEORGE W.**
Insurance agent. **Personal:** Born May 18, 1944, Richmond, VA; son of George Sr and Hilda Y; married Sylvia Washington; children: Monica, Nicholas & Cecilia. **Educ:** Va Union Univ, BS, bus, 1966. **Career:** State Farm Ins Co, mgr, ins agt, currently. **Orgs:** Vpres, Rosa Pk Scholar Found; Nat Asn Life Underwriters; Oakland Co Life Underwriters; Detroit Property & Casualty Agents Asn, Kiwanis Club; Pres Coun; Greater Detroit Asn Life Underwriters; Pres, Va Union Univ Detroit Alumni Chap; fel Sanctuary Choir. **Honors/Awds:** National Achievement Sales Award, Nat Asn Life Underwriters, 1992-98; Legion of Honor, 1998-2002; Life Honor Agent; Leading Health Producer, 2001; Business Leading Sales Achievement Award, Nat Asn Ins & Financial Advisors; Leading Sales Achievement Award, Nat Asn Ins & Financial Advisors; Michigan Health Hall of Fame; Nat Asn Ins & Financial Advisors. **Special Achievements:** Insurance Experience of 25 years. **Business Addr:** Agent, State Farm Insurance Co, 24361 Greenfield Suite 201, Southfield, MI 48075-3165, **Business Phone:** (248)569-8555.

**WARDER, JOHN MORGAN**
Banker, businessperson, president (organization). **Personal:** Born Jan 7, 1927, Ellsworth, KS; son of Beulah and Warner; married Margie; children: Linda, Kent & David; married Benola Foster. **Educ:** Univ Kans, BA, 1952. **Career:** Businessperson (retired), president; Litho Supply Depot Inc, Minneapolis, Minn, off mgr, 1952-62, vpres, 1962-68; Plymouth Nat Bank, pres, 1969-82; First Plymouth Nat Bank, cbd, 1982-84; First Bank Minneapolis, vpres urban develop, 1984-86; First Bank Syst Inc, vpres urban develop, 1987-88; Relax Back Store Franchise, pres, owner, 1992-. **Orgs:** Chmn, Zion Baptist Church Bldg Coun, 1962-64; trustee, Macalester Col, 1970-81; bd mem, Minneapolis Found, 1972-81; Helen Harrington Trust, 1972-; Bush Found Panel Judge, 1973-; treas, Minneapolis UNCF Campaign, 1975-; Alpha Phi Alpha Frat; co-chmn, Alpha Phi Alpha, 1978; Nat Conf Com; Minneapolis Club; Prince Hall Masons; Dunkers Club; vice chmn, 1980-85, bd mem, 1985-, Nat Med Flwsps Inc; treas, Delta Dent Minn, 1984; trustee, Univ Minn Med Found, 1985-; bd mem, Minn News Coun; treas, W Harry Davis Found, 1986-; bd mem, Minn Bus League, 1985-; Nat Asn Advan Colored People; Minneapolis Urban League; Zion Bapt Ch Cty Mpls. **Honors/Awds:** Disting Service Award, 1964; Outstanding Service Award, Afro Am Edu Asn, 1968; Gtr Mpls C C Award, 1973; Miss Black Minn Outstanding Achievement Award, 1975; Minneapolis Urban League's Cecil E Newman Humantarian Award, 1976; Man of the Year Award, Insight Publ, 1977; Outstanding Service Award, Alpha Phi Alpha, 1978; Man of the Year Award, Alpha Phi Alpha, 1979; Outstanding Service Award, Minn Black Chemical Abuse, 1982; Minn Urban League Volunteer Service Award, 1986; Nat Conf Christian & Jews Brotherhood & Sisterhood Humanataria, 1991. **Home Addr:** 1201 Yale Pl Suite 1210, Minneapolis, MN 55403-1958. **Business Addr:** President, Owner, Relax The Back Store, 7533 France Ave S, Edina, MN 55435, **Business Phone:** (612)831-3205.

**WARDLAW, ALVIN HOLMES**
Executive, educator. **Personal:** Born Jan 3, 1925, Atlanta, GA; married Virginia Cage; children: Alvia W Shore & Joy Elaine. **Educ:** Morehouse Col, BS, 1948; Atlanta Univ, MS, 1950; Univ Mich, attended 1954; Univ Wis, attended 1966. **Career:** Educator (retired); Tenn State Univ, asst prof, 1950-65, actg dept head, 1969-72; Tex Southern Univ, prof, Coop Ctr Minn Math & Sci Teaching Proj, dir, 1963-64; Upward Bound Proj, dir, 1970-73; EPDA Inst Tenn State Univ, assoc dir, 1970-73; Tex Southern Univ, asst vpres acad affairs; Tex Tech Univ, dir fin reporting. **Orgs:** Rockefeller Found Fel, 1952-54; NSF Fac Fel, 1959-60; consult, Adminr Conf Houston Indep Sch Dist, 1960; Carnegie Found Fel, 1965-66; Nat Sic Inst Southern Univ; fac rep, Athletics Tenn State Univ, 1969-72; NAIA Dist eligibility com, 1971-73; pres, Tex Asn Stud Assist Progs, 1973; Athletic Adv Coun, 1974-75. **Home Addr:** 3307 Rosedale St, Houston, TX 77004-6310, **Home Phone:** (713)523-8601.

**WARE, ALBERT M.**
Automotive executive, manager. **Personal:** Born Oct 13, 1952, Detroit, MI; son of Albert and Bessie; married Wendy R; children: Christina M & Albert B. **Educ:** Wayne State Univ, BS, mech engineering, 1977; Univ Mich, exec bus prog, 1994. **Career:** Ford Motor Co, suspension systs engr, 1977-81; Gen Motors, chassis syst engr, 1981-94, supvr, chassis syst, 1991-92, vehicle syst integration mgr, 1993-95, asst chief engr, 1995-96, truck plant integration eng, dir, 1996-98, Qual Engineering, dir, 1996-2003, plant support team eng, dir, 1998, dir design & math process, 2002-04, Vehicle Safety & Crashworthiness Lab, dir, 2004-09, Vehicle Safety & Crashworthiness Lab, sr mgr, 2009-. **Orgs:** Dir, Pre Eng Educ Prog, Detroit Sec, Soc Automotive Engineering, 1987-; chmn bd, finance & develop comt, Detroit Area Pre Col Eng Prog, 1992-; bd trustee, SAE fed, 1996; treas, Gen Motors Corp; Detroit Area Pre-Col Engineering Prog. **Honors/Awds:** US Black Eng Mag & Several Corp Sponsors, 1988-89; Spec Recognition Award, SAE, 1989; Black Engineer of the Year President's Award, Eng Deans Historically Black Col & Univ, 1994. **Special Achievements:** Sixth Annual Alumi Asn, Design & Fabrication Seminar Award, for developing a new innovative forged aluminum design for use in a high volume automotive application, 1985. **Home Addr:** 6761 Maple Creek Blvd, West Bloomfield, MI 48322-4556, **Home Phone:** (248)539-0975. **Business Addr:** Senior Manager, General Motors Co, 300 Renaissance Ctr, Detroit, MI 48265, **Business Phone:** (313)556-5000.

**WARE, ANDRE**
Radio host, football player. **Personal:** Born Jul 31, 1968, Dickinson, TX; son of Robert and Joyce. **Educ:** Univ Houston, BS, mkt. **Career:** Football player (retired), radio host, analyst; Detroit Lions, 1991, quarterback, 1990, 1992-93; Minn Vikings, 1994; Los Angeles Raiders, 1994; Jacksonville Jaguars, 1995; Can Football League: Ottawa Rough Riders, 1995; BC Lions, 1996; Toronto Argonauts, 1997; Europ NFL: Berlin Thunder, 1999; Houston Cougar Radio Network, color commentator; CBS, sports commentator; Houston Texans Radio Network, game analyst; ESPN SEC Network, Analyst, currently. **Honors/Awds:** Heisman Trophy, 1989; Davey O'Brien Award, 1989; College Football Hall of Fame, 2004; Named UPI National Player of the Year; Chevrolet Offensive Player of the Year; Southwest Conference Player of the Year; Texas Sports Hall of Fame, 2012. **Business Addr:** Game Analyst, ESPN Regional, 11001 Rushmore Dr, Charlotte, NC 28277, **Business Phone:** (704)973-5000.

**WARE, CARL H.**
Executive, executive director. **Personal:** Born Sep 30, 1943, Newnan, GA; son of U B and Lois Wimberly; married Mary Clark; children: Timothy Alexander. **Educ:** Clark Atlanta Univ, BS, 1965; Carnegie Mellon Univ, attended 1966; Univ Pittsburgh, MPA, 1968; Harvard Bus Sch, int sr mgt prog, 1991. **Career:** Urban League Pittsburgh, dir housing, 1968-70; Atlanta Housing Authority, dir, 1970-74; Atlanta City, pres city coun, 1974-79; Coca-Cola Co, Atlanta, GA, urban & govt affairs specialist, 1974-79, USA spec markets vpres, 1979-82, vpres urban affairs, 1982-86, sr vpres, 1986-91, Northeast Europe & Africa, dep pres, 1991-93, Africa Group, pres, 1993-2000, Global Pub Affairs & Admin Div, exec vpres, 2000-03, sr advisor, 2003-05; Chevron Corp, dir, 2001-. **Orgs:** Policy Com Nat League Cities; GA Munic Asn; Comn Develop Comt; bd dir, Metro Atlanta Coun Alcohol & Drugs; elected to Atlanta City Coun, 1973; bd dir, US Civil Rights Comn, 1983; Nat Coun Black Agencies, 1983-; United Way Metro Atlanta, 1983-; trustee, Clark Col Gammon Theol Sem; GA State Univ Found; Sigma Pi Phi; bd trustee, Clark Atlanta Univ; bd dir, Ga Power Co; bd dir, PGA TOUR Golf Course Properties Inc; bd dir, Southern Africa Enterprise Develop Fund; bd dir, Med Educ S African Blacks; bd dir, Africa-Am Inst; Coun Foreign Rels; bd mem, Chevron Texaco, 2001-05; bd mem, Cummins, 2004-; bd mem, Chevron, 2005-; bd mem, Coca-Cola Bottling Consol; chair & bd trustees, Clark Univ. **Honors/Awds:** Numerous Civic Awards. **Home Addr:** 1596 Willis Mill Rd SW, Atlanta, GA 30311. **Business Addr:** Director, Chevron Corp, 6001 Bollinger Canyon Rd, San Ramon, CA 94583-2324, **Business Phone:** (925)842-1000.

**WARE, CHARLES JEROME**
Association executive, lawyer. **Personal:** Born Apr 22, 1948, Anniston, AL; son of John Edward and Vonnie Marie; married Lucinda Frances Hubbard; children: Lucinda-Marie. **Educ:** Univ Ala Sch Med, attended 1971; Talladega Col Ala, BA, 1970; Howard Univ Law Sch, JD, trial advocacy/antitrust & corp, 1975; Boston Univ Sch Bus MA, MBA, 1976. **Career:** Inst Study Educ Policy, legal legis & econ asst, 1974-75; Boston Col Law Sch, atty writer, consult, asst dir & lectr, 1975-77; Boston Univ Martin Luther King Ctr, atty, 1976; Middlesex Co MA Dist Attys Off, asst dist atty, criminal list mgr, 1975-77; Arent Fox Kintner Plotkin & Kahn, anti-trust atty, 1977; Criminal Div US Dept Justice, sr trl atty & appellate atty, asst US atty, 1977-83; US Dept Justice, anti-trust atty, 1979-82; US Immigration, judge, 1980-81; US Fed Trade Comn, first asst to dir bur competition, 1982-83, spec coun chmn, 1983-87; St Paul's Col Lawrenceville, Va, exec vpres & genl coun, 1987-88; Charles Jerome Ware, Pa, atty & counr, sr partner & pres, 1988-. **Orgs:** Fel Univ Fla Gainesville, Med & Sci, 1969 &1971; MBA fel Boston Univ; life mem, Nat Asn Advan Colored People, 1966-; SCLC, 1966-; dir & ed, Am Bar Asn; Asn Trl Lawyers Am; Nat Bar Asn; DC Bar Asn; Pa Bar Asn, 1975; Md Bar Asn; Va Bar Asn; founder & pres, William Monroe Trotter Polit Res Inst, 1978; nat legal adv, Nat Tots & Teens Inc, 1986-; Gen Coun, Md State Conf Nat Asn Advan Colored People. **Home Addr:** 5032 Rushlight Path, Columbia, MD 21044, **Home Phone:** (410)720-4254. **Business Addr:** Attorney, President & Senior Partner, Charles Jerome Ware Attorney & Counselor, 10630 Little Patuxent Pkwy Suite 113, Columbia, MD 21044-3273, **Business Phone:** (410)720-6129.

**WARE, DYAHANNE**
Lawyer. **Personal:** Born Jul 26, 1958, Chicago, IL; daughter of Freddie Mae and Clinton; children: Sherry Goldman & Tracey Love. **Educ:** Univ IL, BA, criminal justice, 1980; John Marshall Law Sch, JD, law, 1984; Univ Chicago, Grad Sch Bus, MBA, 1990. **Career:** Encycl Britannica USA, atty, FTC compliance audit staff, 1984-85, staff atty, 1985-86, atty gen coun & dir legal compliance staff; Ware Group, atty, 1984-2012; Encyclopaedia Britannica, asst gen coun, 1984-94; Lexis-Nexis, corp coun consult, 1994-95; Com Clearing House, int sr atty, 1995-96, assoc gen coun; Wolters Kluwer, assoc coun, 1995-2007; Hudson Global, prin consult, 2008-09; Walmart Corp, mkt human resource mgr, 2010-12; DeVry Univ, adj prof, 2011-; State Ill, Dept Financial & Prof Regulations, chief gen prosecutions, 2012-14, Div Family & Community Serv, dir, 2014-15; SOS C's Villages Ill, proj recruiter, 2015-16; specforeign asst, Guadeloupe, FWI; pvt pract, atty, currently. **Orgs:** Chicago Bar Asn, 1985-; Nat Black MBA Asn, 1989-90; Cook County Bar Asn, 1990; Rotary Int, 2014; Am Bar Asn; Chicago Vol Legal Servs; nat bd realtor, Urban League, Nat Conf Black Lawyers; Nortcenter Chamber Com; League Black Women; Int Alliance Wome; Nat Asn African Am HR Professionalsn. **Honors/Awds:** Honoree YWCA Leadership Award, 1985; Honoree YMCA Black & Hispanic Leaders of Indust, 1987. **Home Addr:** 3651 N Mozart, Chicago, IL 60618, **Home Phone:** (312)539-0916. **Business Addr:** Director, State of Illinois, 401 S Clinton St, Chicago, IL 60607, **Business Phone:** (312)793-2354.

**WARE, HENRY A., JR.**
Chief executive officer. **Educ:** Tenn State Univ, BA, polit sci & eng. **Career:** Southaven Chamber Com, pres; DeSoto County Econ Develop Coun, pres; Southaven Pontiac Buick GMC Inc, owner & chief

exec officer, pres, currently. **Orgs:** Bd secy, Gen Motors Minority Dealers Asn; Nat Asn Minority Automobile Dealers; DeSoto County Econ Develop Coun; bd dir, Nat Automobile Dealers Asn; chmn, Nat Athena Found. **Business Addr:** Owner, Chief Executive Officer, Southaven Pontiac Buick GMC Inc, 78 Goodman Rd E, Southaven, MS 38671, **Business Phone:** (662)349-5600.

## WARE, IRENE JOHNSON

Radio broadcaster. **Personal:** Born Apr 24, 1935, Blacksher, AL; married Fred E; children: Darryl & Ronald. **Educ:** Allen Inst, 1953; Besteda's Sch Cosmetology, 1961. **Career:** Gospel Serv ABC & Dunhill Rec, dir; The Mandy Show, host & gen mgr; WGOK Radio, announcer & gen mgr, 1962-; Rec World Mag NYC, gospel ed, 1967-; WDLT-AM, midday Gospel prog, host, currently. **Orgs:** NATRA; BAMA; GMWA; exec dir, Nat Asn Gospel Announcers & Affil; gospel ed, Black Radio Exclusive Mag; vpres, bd dir Gospel Music Asn, 1980; bd dir, OIC Mobile Area; Oper PUSH Chicago; pres, Nat Black Programmers Coalition, 1992; bd mem, Living Legends Found, currently. **Honors/Awds:** Named 1 Top 10 Gospel Announcers, Open Mike Mag, 1965; Gospel Personality of The Year, Open Mike Mag, 1966; Top 10 Gospel Personality, Record World Mag, 1967; Humanitarian Award, NATRA, 1971; Woman of the Yr, Black Radio Conf, 1977; Hamilton Award, Jack The Rapper's Roy, 1977; Gospel Announcer of Year, Gospel Music Workshop Am, 1979; Black Gospel Announcer of Year Award, SESAC, 1978; Outstanding Citizen of the Year, Stewart Memorial CME Ch, 1980; Jack Walker Award for Excellence in Broadcasting, NATRA, 1973; Excellence in Broadcasting, Utterbach Concert Choir Carnegie Hall, 1969; First Heritage Award, NBPC, 1990; Gospel Announcer of The Year Award, NBPC, 1990; Urban network's Living Legend Award, 1992; PUSH Excellence Award, 1997; Thomas Dorsey Award, Midwest Radio & Music Asn; General Manager of The Year, BRE Mag. **Home Addr:** 755 Donald St, Mobile, AL 36651, **Home Phone:** (334)457-5581. **Business Addr:** Board Member, The Living Legends Foundation, Los Angeles, CA.

## WARE, JANIS L.

Newspaper publisher. **Personal:** daughter of J Lowell (deceased). **Educ:** Univ Ga, Bus Sch, BS, bus admin. **Career:** Atlanta Voice, Black Press USA Network, publ & owner, 1991-; Voice News Network, pres; Essence Unlimited, pres & chief exec officer. **Orgs:** Exec dir, Summech Community Develop Corp, 1989-; chair, Southside Med Ctr; City Atlanta, Beltway Steering Comt; Atlanta Zoning Task Force; chair, vice chair, Atlanta Housing Authority; Habitat Humanity; Empire Real Estate Bd; Atlanta Bus League; City Atlanta's Beltway Steering Comt; Atlanta's Zoning Task Force; bd dir, Nat Newspaper Publishers Asn, nat secy & treas. **Honors/Awds:** One of the 100 Most Influential Women in Atlanta, Atlanta Bus League; Who's Who of Black Atlanta; Women Making the Mark Award recipients, Atlanta Mag. **Business Addr:** Publisher, Owner, The Atlanta Voice Newspaper/Voices News Network Inc, 633 Pryor St SW, Atlanta, GA 30312, **Business Phone:** (404)524-6426.

## WARE, HON. JEWEL C.

Government official. **Personal:** daughter of Mattie. **Educ:** Univ Detroit, BA, guid & coun, MA, guid & coun. **Career:** Wayne County Bd Comnrs, comnr, 1995-, chair, 2003; Wayne County Comn, comnr & chairwomen, currently. **Orgs:** Chair, Wayne County Comn, 2003-; vice chair, Comt Audit; vice chair, Subcomt Sr Citizen Affairs; Health & Human Serv Comt; Pub Safety & Judiciary Comt; Legis Res comt; Genesis Lutheran Church; Nat Black Caucus Aging Coalition Labor Union; Mack Alive; Pittman Memorial Housing Develop; found, Seniors Networking Inc; Mattie Ware Found; bd mem, Boysville Mich; bd mem, Friends Tri-County; bd mem, Mack Alive; Detroit Health Adv Comn; bd mem, chmn, Detroit RiverFront Conservancy; Helping Our Prisoners Elevate (HOPE); Develop Corp Wayne County; HealthChoice; Mich Universal Health Care Access Network; Warren-Conner Develop Coalition; Elks, Nettie Carter Jackson Temple;Nat Asn Advan Colored People; Charles H. Wright Mus African Am Hist; bd mem, Detroit Super Bowl XL Host Comt; bd mem, Mich Asn Counties. **Business Addr:** Commissioner, Chairwoman, Wayne County Commission, Wayne County Bldg 600 Randolph Suite 449, Detroit, MI 48226, **Business Phone:** (313)224-0900.

## WARE, DR. JOHN E.

Educator. **Educ:** Xavier Univ La, BA, music lib arts minor educ & philos, 1977; Eastern Mich Univ, MA, voice & theatre, 1980; Mich State Univ, DMA, choral conducting, master music-voice, 1991. **Career:** New Orleans Black Chorale, dir; Xavier Univ, Dept Music, prof & dir choirs, currently, chair, Rosa Keller Endowed Chair Music. **Orgs:** Nat Asn Teachers Singing; Am Choral Dir's Asn; Phi Mu Alpha Sinfonia Nat Music Fraternity; Alpha Phi Alpha Fraternity Inc. **Business Addr:** Professor, Director, Xavier University, 1 Drexel Dr, New Orleans, LA 70125, **Business Phone:** (504)520-7597.

## WARE, LELAND

Lawyer, college teacher. **Personal:** married Melva; children: Leland Jr. **Educ:** Fisk Univ, BA, 1970; Boston Col Law Sch, JD, 1973. **Career:** Pvt pract, Atlanta, Ga prior to 1979; U S Dept Justice, Civil Div, trial atty, 1979-84; Howard Univ, univ coun, 1984-87; Boston Col Law Sch, vis prof, 1992; Ruhr Univ, vis prof, 1997; St Louis Univ Sch Law, prof, 1987-2000; Univ Del, Sch Pub Policy & Admin, assoc dir, Louis L Redding Chair, prof study law & pub policy, 2000-. **Orgs:** Mem, Am Law Inst; bd dirs, Legal Defense Fund, Am Asn Univ Professors; Legal Steering Comt, Nat Off, Nat Asn Advan Colored People; Del Civil Liberties Union. **Special Achievements:** Served as first Louis L. Redding Chair, selected in 2000; author: "Thurgood Marshall: Freedom's Defender" (Time-Life Books, 1999); Co-author: "Brown v. Board of Education: Caste, Culture, and the Constitution" (University of Kansas Press, 2003); Co-editor: "Choosing Equality: Essays and Narratives on the Desegregation Experience" (Penn State Press, 2009); numerous articles and other writings in academic and other publications. **Business Addr:** Associate Director, Louis L. Redding Chair and Professor, University of Delaware, 180 Graham Hall, Newark, DE 19716-7380, **Business Phone:** (302)831-3930.

## WARE, LELAND BRETT

College teacher, lawyer. **Personal:** Born Jan 1, 1948?. **Educ:** Fisk Univ, BA, 1970; Boston Col Law Sch, JD, 1973. **Career:** Wyatt & Assocs, assoc atty, 1973-75; Hill, Jones & Farrington, assoc atty, 1975-76; U.S. Dept Health, Educ & Welfare, asst regional atty, 1976-79; U.S. Dept Justice, trial atty-civil div, 1979-84; Howard Univ, univ coun, 1984-98; St. Louis Univ Sch Law, asst prof, 1987-91, assoc prof, 1991-94, prof law, 1994-2000; Boston Col Law Sch, vis prof, 1992; Ruhr Univ, vis prof, 1997; Univ Del, Louis L. Redding chair & prof Study Law & Pub Policy, Sch Pub Policy & Admin, 2000-. **Orgs:** Bar State Ga, 1973-; Bar DC, 1985-; Am Law Inst, NAACP (legal steering comt nat off; mem bd dirs, Legal Defense Fund; mem bd dirs, Am Asn Univ Professors; mem bd dirs, Del Civil Liberties Union; trustee, Christina Hosp Corp; mem bd dirs, WHYY Inc.; mem bd dirs, Legal Defense Fund Am Asn Univ Professors; mem bd dirs, Metrop Wilmington Urban League; mem bd dirs, Del Civil Liberties Union. **Special Achievements:** Author: "Thurgood Marshall: Freedom's Defender", 1999; co-author, "Brown v. Board of Education: Castle, Culture, and the Constitution", 2003. contributor, "Delaware Law Review, Forum on Public Policy". **Business Addr:** Institute for Public Administration, 180 Graham Hall, Newark, DE 19716-7380, **Business Phone:** (302)831-3930.

## WARE, OMEGO JOHN CLINTON

Consultant, administrator. **Personal:** Born Mar 13, 1928, Washington, DC; son of Omego J C Sr and Bertha Shipp; married Elinor Gwen Smith; children: Karl R, Keith R & Karlene R. **Educ:** Georgetown Univ, BS, foreign com, 1960; AUS War Col, attended 1969. **Career:** CIA, SIS Off, Ombudsman, Dir Ctr Study Intelligence, dir, 1955-82; Univ Calif, Lawrence Livermore Nat Lab, adminr, 1982-93; Counter Terror Specialist US Dept Energy, Wash, Intelligence consult, adv, 1982-83; Ware Assoc Int, founder, 1993-, pres, currently. **Orgs:** BSA; SCIP; charter mem, Sr Intelligence Servs. **Honors/Awds:** CIA Awards, Senior Intelligence Servs; First "Trailblazer" Award, Cent Intelligence Agency, 1991; 50th Anniversary Trailblazer Award, CIA, 1997; Special DOE Awards. **Home Phone:** (202)584-0011. **Business Addr:** President, Founder, Ware Associates International, 3244 Pope St SE, Washington, DC 20020-2318, **Business Phone:** (202)584-9683.

## WARE, R. DAVID

Executive director, lawyer. **Personal:** Born May 20, 1954, Franklin, GA; son of Roosevelt Sr and Lorine Kelly; married Sharon Ward; children: Jerris, Candace & Breana. **Educ:** W Ga Col, BA, Eng, 1976; Univ Ga Sch Law, JD, law, 1979. **Career:** Coun Legal Educ Opportunities, teaching asst, 1977; Small Bus Develop Ctr, grad staff consult, 1978-79; PRO Larry E Blount, res asst; Kilpa trick & Cody, assoc, 1979-82; Vaughn, Phears & Murphy, assoc, 1982-83; Floyd, Jones & Ware, founder, 1982-89; Law Off R David Ware, pres, 1983-; Thomas, Kennedy, Sampson, Edwards & Patterson, partner, 1989-94; Ware & Assocs Related Sports Agencies, owner, exec vpres, 1994-2004; State Ct, magistrate judge; Supreme Ct, magistrate judge; Ware & Assocs PC, founder, managing partner, 1994-2000; Constangy, Brooks & Smith LLP, partner, 2000-04; CSMG Sports Inc, exec vpres sports, 2003; Fulton County Govt, County Atty, 2004-15; Fulton County Ga, interim fulton county chief exec offficer, 2013-14; Ichter Kresky & Assocs LLC, partner, 2015-16; Hall Booth Smith P.C, Coun, 2016-. **Orgs:** State Bar Ga; Gate City Bar Asn, exec comt, 1984, vice pres, 1985, pres, 1987-88; Atlanta Bar Asn; Nat Bar Asn; Am Bar Asn; Atlanta Vol Lawyers Found; Fulton County Bd Ethics, 1989-. **Honors/Awds:** Alumnus of the Year, Univ GA Sch Law, 1981-82; numerous college & law school honors. **Special Achievements:** How to Select a Sports Agent", 1983; "Why Are There So Few Black Sports Agents?" Sports, Inc, 1988; The Effects of Gender and Race on the Practice of Law, State Bar of Ga, 1992. First African American male to be named to the position Served as legal counsel to Fulton County; First African American member of the American Bar Association Moot Court Team; first African-American coach of a Moot Court team. **Business Addr:** County Attorney, Hall Booth Smith PC, 191 Peachtree St NE, Atlanta, GA 30303, **Business Phone:** (404)954-5000.

## WARE, WILLIAM J.

Insurance executive. **Personal:** married Carole M Wiggins. **Educ:** Goddard Col, BA, MA, environ risk mgt & ins. **Career:** William J Ware & Assoc, pres & chief exec officer, currently. **Orgs:** Chmn & exec dir, Ga Asn Ins Prof; chmn, Atlanta Exchange Found Inc; coordr, Prof Bus Proj, Role Models, Career Day Prog Stud; life mem, Disabled Am Veterans; Leadership COBB Class, 1994-95; COBB COC; numerous others. **Honors/Awds:** Certificate of Appreciation, Atlanta Olympic force; Certificate of Appreciation, Atlanta Asn Ins Prof. **Home Addr:** 2128 Caneridge Dr SW, Marietta, GA 30064-4357, **Home Phone:** (678)289-6188. **Business Addr:** President, Chief Executive Officer, William J Ware & Associates Inc, 3655 Cherokee St Nw Suite 21, Kennesaw, GA 30144, **Business Phone:** (770)420-8555.

## WARE, DR. WILLIAM LEVI

Educator, executive director. **Personal:** Born May 15, 1934, Greenwood, MS; son of Leslie (deceased) and Katherine Bowden; married Lottie Herger; children: Felicia Joyner, Trevor & Melvinia Abdullah. **Educ:** Miss Valley State Univ, Itta Bena, BS, MS, 1957; Calif State Univ, Los Angeles, CA, MA, 1969; Univ Southern Calif, Los Angeles, CA, PhD, 1978. **Career:** Educator (retired); Greenwood Pub Sch, health educ, coach, 1957-63; Bellflower Pub Sch, phys educ, coach, 1963-72; Calif State Univ, Northridge, CA, asst prof, 1964-78; Miss State Univ, Miss State, MS, assoc prof, 1979-90; Miss Valley State Univ, prof, educ dept chair, 1990, asst to pres, 1995-98; comt outreach specialist, exec dir serv learning, 1998. **Orgs:** Dir, United Way Oktibbeha City, 1982-85; Boy Scouts Am, Pushmatha Coun, 1983-85; Vols Youth, 1985; pres, Kiwanis Club, Starkville, 1986-87. **Honors/Awds:** Service Award, Calif Congress Parents & Teachers Inc, 1969; Leadership Starkville, Starkville Chamber Com, 1985; Kiwanian of the Year, 1985; Distinguished Educ Award, IDEA, 1987; Outstanding Service Award, Phi Delta Kappa, 1989; Pres Citation; Nat Asn Equal Opportunity Higher Educ, 1989; Fac Fel & Found Mid-South, 1994. **Home Addr:** 75 Choctaw Rd, Starkville, MS 39759, **Home Phone:** (662)323-5087.

## WAREHAM, DR. ROGER S.

Lawyer. **Educ:** Harvard Univ, BA, 1972; Columbia Univ Law Sch, JD, 1976. **Career:** John Jay Col Criminal Justice, fac; Col New Rochelle, Sch New Resources, fac; Fed Dist Courts, atty; Thomas, Wareham & Richards LLP, Brooklyn, NY, atty. **Orgs:** Int secy gen, Int Asn Against Torture; Nat Conf Black Lawyers; Bur US Non-Govt Orgn Comt Human Rights. **Special Achievements:** Numerous television appearances include Like it Is with Gil Noble and news programs on NBC, CBS, BET, ABC, CNN, Court TV, New York 1, Fox, BBC & PBS. **Business Addr:** Attorney, Thomas, Wareham & Richards LLP, 394 Putnam Ave, Brooklyn, NY 11216-1518, **Business Phone:** (718)230-5270.

## WARFIELD, ERIC ANDREW

Football executive, football player. **Personal:** Born Mar 3, 1976, Vicksburg, MS; son of Rose. **Educ:** Univ Nebr, grad. **Career:** Football player (retired); Kans City Chiefs, 1998, right cornerback, 1999, 2001, 2005, left cornerback, 2000, 2002-04, cornerback, 2001, 2004; New England Patriots, pract squad mem, 2006; community mentor, currently. **Orgs:** Love Fund Children. **Special Achievements:** TV Series: ESPN's Sunday Night Football, 2001-05; The NFL on CBS, 2002; NFL Monday Night Football, 2003-04.

## WARFIELD, MARSHA FRANCINE

Comedian, actor, writer. **Personal:** Born Mar 5, 1954, Chicago, IL. **Career:** Actress, 1974-; stand-up comic & comedienne in clubs throughout US & Canada, 1976-; Films: D C Cab, 1983; Mask, 1985; Gidget Goes to Harlem, Caddyshack II, 1988; TV series: "The Richard Pryor Show", 1977; "Riptide", 1983; "The Marva Collins Story", 1981; "Teddy Pendergrass in Concert", comic, 1982; "Family Ties", 1984; "Night Court", 1984, 1986-92; "Harry Anderson's Sideshow", comic, 1987; "Comic Relief", 1987; "Just for Laughs", 1987; "On Location", comic, 1987; "The Thirteenth Annual Circus of the Stars", 1988; "Marsha", hostess, 1990; "The Marsha Warfield Show", actress & co-exec producer, 1990-91; "Comic Relief", 1993; "Empty Nest", 1993-95; "The John Larroquette Show", 1994; "Living Single", 1997; "Dave's World", 1997; Doomsday Rock", 1997; "Mad About You", 1997; "Smart Guy", 1997; "Moesha", 1997; "Clueless", 1998; "The Joint", 1998; "The Love Boat: The Next Wave", 1999; guest appearance, "Veronica's Closet", 1999; Writer: "The Richard Pryor Show", 1977; "Uptown Comedy Express", 1987; Others: That Thing on ABC, 1978; They Call Me Bruce?, 1982; The Whoopee Boys, 1986; Truly Tasteless Jokes, 1987; Caddyshack 2, 1988; A Thanksgiving Story; Tommy Chong Roast. **Honors/Awds:** Winner, San Francisco Nat Stand-up Comedy Competition, 1979. **Business Addr:** Actress, c/o Fred Amsel & Associates, 6310 San Vicente Blvd Suite 407, Los Angeles, CA 90048.

## WARFIELD, ROBERT N.

Financial manager, executive. **Personal:** Born Nov 29, 1948, Guthrie, KY; married Gloria Jean. **Educ:** Eastern Ky Univ, BS, mass commun/media studies, 1970; Columbia Univ Grad Sch Jour, attended 1971; Stanford Univ, Grad Sch Bus; Wharton Bus Sch. **Career:** Orion Broadcasting, news reporter & photogr, 1971-72, prom & advert mgr, 1972-73; WAVE-TV, producer, 1973-75; KDKA-TV, exec producer, 1975-78; WTNH-TV, prod mgr; WDIV-TV, from asst news dir to news dir, 1979-84, vpres news, 1984-89, sta mgr, 1989-91; Alpha Capital Mgt Inc, co-founder & partner, 1991; Studio 600 Productions Inc, owner, 2001-; Bing Youth Inst, exec dir, 2014-; City Detroit, chief commun officer, 2011-13; Alpha Partners LLC, chair investment rev comt, owner, pres & chief exec officer, currently. **Orgs:** Co-founder, Alpha-Munder Found, 1991; chair, Investment Rev Comt; founding bro & pres, Omega Psi Phi Fraternity; vpres, EKU Stud Asn. **Business Addr:** President, Chief Executive Officer, Alpha Partners LLC, 600 W Lafayette Blvd Suite 100, Detroit, MI 48226, **Business Phone:** (313)963-4911.

## WARMACK, KEVIN LAVON

Executive. **Personal:** Born Dec 20, 1956, Chicago, IL; son of Kenneth Lowe and Jacqueline Elliott; married Delma LaSane; children: Delma, Kevin II, Nadia & Marcus. **Educ:** Ripon Col, BA, eng, 1979; Keller Grad Sch Mgt, Devry Univ, 1982; Concord Law Sch, Kaplan Univ, JD, 2011. **Career:** Lawyer'sWord Processing Ltd, mgr, 1979-81; Mayer Brown & Platt, asst super, 1981-83; Arnstein Gluck Lehr, legal asst, 1983-85; Hisaw & Schultz, legal asst, 1985-86; McSherry & Gray Ltd, legal asst, 1986-87, law resources, 1987-88; Financial Indust Regula; NASD, sr compliance examr, 1988-95; Rodman & Renshaw, assoc, regulatory acct, 1995-96; Warmack Consult Ltd, pres, 1996-97; Melvin Securities, sr assoc compliance, 1997-2000; Man Financial Inc, regulatory acct, 2001; CMG Instnl Brokerage, compliance officer, 2001-02; Nat Compliance Consults Inc, bd specialist, 2001-07; optionsXpress, compliance specialist, 2007-08; SBK Brooks Investment Corp, vpres & chief compliance officer, 2008-09; Blaylock Robert Van LLC, vpres compliance, 2009-10; Contract Compliance Assoc, Experis, 2013-14; Unlimited Freedom Compliance Consult, compliance specialist, 2010-. **Orgs:** Nat Black MBA Asn, 1989-; bd mem, Harvard Sch; Woodgate Fathers; Church St John Evangelist Episcopal Church; Nat Asn Black Accts; Securities Indust Asn; Nat Asn Securities Profs; pres, Chicago Chap; Federalist Soc Law & Justice. **Home Addr:** 50 Cloverleaf Rd, Matteson, IL 60443-1114, **Home Phone:** (773)933-0480. **Business Addr:** Compliance Specialist, Unlimited Freedom Compliance Consulting Inc, 6110 S Rhodes Ave, Chicago, IL 60637, **Business Phone:** (773)220-5360.

## WARMLY, LEON

Manager, radio journalist. **Personal:** Born Apr 28, 1941, Shreveport, LA; son of Joe Williams and Gertrude Williams. **Educ:** Bill Wade Sch Modern Radio, cert, 1966; San Diego City Col, AA, 1973; San Diego State Univ, San Diego, CA, BA, 1982, CA, comm col instr credentials, 1990. **Career:** Manager (retired); KDIG-FM Radio, announcer, 1966-67; KFMB Radio, San Diego, CA, new reporter, 1973-75; Toastmaster's Int, Dist 5, San Diego, CA, publicity dir, 1974-75; Monford Pt Marine Asn, publicity dir, 1975-79; DECA Commissary, store mgr, 1991-96. **Orgs:** Toastmasters Int Dist 5; San Diego Club Bi Centennial 2675, 1969-74; chmn bd dir, Bay Vista Methodist Heights Apts HUD, 2001. **Honors/Awds:** KFMB Radio News Scholarship, 1973. **Home Addr:** 4079 Euclid Ave, San Diego, CA 92105, **Home Phone:** (619)280-4836.

**WARNER, REV. EDWARD L.**
Clergy. **Personal:** Born Oct 20, 1939, Franklin Township, NJ. **Educ:** Rutgers Univ, AB, 1961; Mdiv, 1964. **Career:** St Albans, deacon, priest, vicar, 1964-67; St Augustine's Episcopal Church, rector. **Orgs:** Diocesan Coun & Steering Comt Coun; Standing Comt; chmn, Mayor's Comn Human Rights Nb NJ; past pres, Interdenominational Ministerial Alliance; bd educ, chmn, Community Rel Comn Presby. **Honors/Awds:** Interracial Award, 1969; Omega Si Phi Citizenship Award, 1973; Citizenship Award, Kansas City C C, 1974. **Home Addr:** 3229 E 28 St, Kansas City, MO 64128.

**WARNER, ISIAH MANUEL**
Scientist, educator. **Personal:** Born Jul 20, 1946, DeQuincy, LA; son of Humphrey and Irma; married Della Blount; children: Isiah M Jr, Chideha Charles & Edward. **Educ:** Southern Agr & Mech Univ, BS, chem, 1968; Univ WV, PhD, anal chem, 1977. **Career:** Battelle Northwest, Richland, WA, res chemist, 1968-73; Univ Wash, Chem Dept, teaching asst, 1973-75, res asst, 1975-77; Tex Agr & Mech, asst prof, 1977-82; Emory Univ, Dept Chem, assoc prof, 1982-86, prof, 1986, chair, 1987, Samuel Chandler Dobbs prof, 1987-92; NSF, prog officer anal & surface chem, 1988-89; La St Univ, Philip W W Prof anal chem, 1992-, chair, dept chem, 1994-97, Boyd prof, 2000-, Off Strat Initiatives, vice chancellor, 2001-, Howard Hughes med inst, prof, 2002-; Res/Teaching, Kenya, Fulbright Fel, 1998. **Orgs:** Advisor, Nat Acad Sci Adv Panel Ctr Anal Chem, 1983-86; Adv Coun, Nat Res Resources Div; Nat Insts Health, 1986-90; fel External Rev Comt Anal Chem Div, 1990-92; fel Pharamacol Sci Rev Comt Nat Inst Gen Med Sci, 1990-93; Prog Officer, NSF, 1988-89; RCMI External Adv Comt, 1992-; NY Acad Scis, 1995-; Am Chem Soc, Minority Taskforce, 1996-98; fel Vision, 2020 comt Chem Measurements, 1996-; fel Adv Comt Meyerhoff Scholar, 1996-; fel ACS Comt Minority Affairs, 1996-98; fel ACS Comt Pub rel, 1996-98; fel ACS Comt Comts, 1996-; fel MPS adv Comt NSF, 1996-99; Nat Acad Sci, Chem Sci Roundtable, 1997-98; Nat Academies Bd Chem Sci & Technol, 1997-2001; co-chair, FACSS Meeting Austin, TX, 1998; rep, Coun Undergrad Res, 1998; adv coun bd, Nat Inst Gen Med Sci, NIH, 1999-2002; Nat Orgn Black Chemists & Chem Engrs; fel, Soc Appl Spectros, 2010; Sigma Xi; Nam Chap Int Chemometrics Soc; Soc Fluorescence; fel, Am Asn Advan Sci, 2003; New York Acad Sci; Am Asn Univ Professors; Am Nano Soc. **Honors/Awds:** Presidential Award for Excellence in Sci, Mathematics, & Engrg Mentoring, 1977 &1997; 1984 Presidential Young Investr Awards; 1988 Percy Julian Award, ACS Task Force for Monitoring Anal Chem, 1989; Charles Herty Medal, Ga sect Am Chem Socs, 1992; Gold Medal, New York Sect Socs Appl Spectros, 1991; Outstanding Teacher Award, 1993; Bennedetti Pichler Award, Am Microchemical Socs, 1994; Distinguished Alumni Award, Nat Asn for Equal Opportunity in Higher Edu, 1995; Southern University Award, 1996; Eastern Anal Symp Award, 2000; Lifetime Mentor Award, AAAS, 2000; Distinguished Fac Award, La State Univ, 2000; La Prof of the Year, CarnegieFound CASE, 2000; LSU Distinguished Fac Award, 2000; Howard Hughes Medical Institute Professorship, 2002; American Chemical Society; Distinguished Lecturers, Sigma Xis College, 2003-04; Eminent Scientist Lectureship, 2003; ACS Award, 2003; Council for Chemical Research Diversity Award, 2003; Distinguished Alumnus Award, University of Washington, 2004; Quality Education for Minorities Networks Giant in Science Award, 2004; Carver Achievement Award, Tuskegee Univ, 2005; Southern Chemist Award, 2006; Association of Analytical Chemists Award, 2007, 2008, 2013; ACS Stanley C. Israel Regional Award, 2014; Outstanding Contributions to Professionalism, 2014; Iddles Lectureship, 2015; SEC Professor of the Year, 2016. **Special Achievements:** Author of numerous articles, book chapters and books; Who's Who in the S & Southwest in 1978-79 & 1980-81; Listed in Int Dir of Distinguished Leadership in 1985; Listed in Who's Who in Frontiers of Sci & Technol in 1985; Int Who's Who of Professionals, 1995; Listed in the 18th Ed of Who's Who in the World in 2000. **Home Addr:** 13020 Springview Ave, Baton Rouge, LA 70810, **Home Phone:** (225)769-3017. **Business Addr:** Boyd Professor, Louisiana State University, 436 Chpoin Hall, Baton Rouge, LA 70803-1804, **Business Phone:** (225)578-2829.

**WARNER, MALCOLM-JAMAL**
Singer, actor, musician. **Personal:** Born Aug 18, 1970, Jersey City, NJ; son of Robert and Pamela. **Career:** Actor, 1984-; dir, 1989-; musician, 1990. TV series: Matt Houston, 1982; Fame, 1983; Call to Glory, 1984; The Cosby Show, 1984-92; CBS Storybreak, host, 1985; Saturday Night Live, host, 1986; A Different World, 1988-89; Tour of Duty, 1989; Saturday Morning Videos, host, 1990; Here & Now, 1992-93; The Magic Sch Bus, animated, 1994-98; Malcolm & Eddie, 1996-2000; Jeremiah, 2002-04; Listen Up, 2005; Dexter, 2006. Films: The Father Clements Story, 1987; Mother's Day, 1989; Drop Zone, 1994; Tyson, 1995; The Tuskegee Airmen, 1995; Restaurant, 1998; A Fare to Remember, 1998; Sliders, 1999; author of Theo & Me, Growing Up Okay, Dutton, 1988; Reflections: A Story of Redemption, 2004; I am Perfect, 2005; Contradictions of the Heart, 2006; Fools Gold, 2008; HawthoRNe, 2009; Sherri, 2009; True Blue, 2010; Community, 2011-; Reed Between the Lines, 2011; Key & Peele, 2013; The Michael J. Fox Show, 2014; Major Crimes, 2014; Sons of Anarchy, 2014; American Horror Story: Freak Show, 2014. Malcolm Jamal Warners Miles Long, owner, currently. **Orgs:** Chair, Nat PTA; nat chmn, Miracle Network Telethon; co-chair, Black Family Reunion Celebration. **Honors/Awds:** Young Artist Award, 1985, 1989 & 1990; Impact Award, 2011; Image Award, Nat Asn Advan Colored People, 2012. **Special Achievements:** Young Artist Award, 1985, 1988, 1989, 1990; Nominee, Emmy Award, 1986; ranked 32 in VH1 list of the "100 Greatest Kid Stars"; nominee, BET Comedy Award, 2005. **Home Addr:** , Los Angeles, CA. **Business Addr:** Actor, Singer, Warner Management, 13547 Ventura Blvd, New York, NY 10010, **Business Phone:** (818)385-1641.

**WARNER, DR. NEARI FRANCOIS**
College administrator. **Personal:** Born Jul 20, 1945, New Orleans, LA; daughter of Enell Francois and Cornelius; children: Jimmie D Jr. **Educ:** Grambling State Univ, BS, 1967; Atlanta Univ, MA, 1968; La State Univ, Baton Rouge, LA, PhD, curric & instr, 1992. **Career:** Southern Univ New Orleans, assoc prof Eng, 1968-75, dir, Upward Bound, 1976-88, dean, jr div, 1989-94, co-ordinator, TRIO progs; Grambling State Univ, asst vpres acad affairs, 1994-96, vpres develop, 1997-98, provost & vpres acad affairs, 1998-2000, actg pres, 2001-04, pres, Interim vpres, Stud Affairs, currently. **Orgs:** Pres, vpres & secy, La Asn Stud Assistance Progs, 1974-88; grad adv & regional comt mem, Alpha Kappa Alpha Sorority, 1975-2002; bd mem, Southwest Asn Stud Assistance Progs, 1987-89; bd mem, Gov's Task Force Tech Prep, 1991-93; treas & facet chair, Links Inc, 1997-2002; exec bd secy, La Endowment Humanities, 1998-; secy, Conf La Cols & Univs, 1999-2000; pres, La Women Higher Educ, 2002-; Golden Key, Pi Gamma Mu & Alpha Gamma Delta Soc, Austerlitz St Baptist Church, New Orleans; New Rocky Valley Baptist Church, Grambling; Nissan/ETS fel; Cong HBCU Pres's Task Force; Sourn Assn Cols; La Endowment Humanities. **Home Addr:** PO Box 989, Grambling, LA 71245, **Home Phone:** (318)274-6370. **Business Addr:** President, Grambling State University, 1866 S Lane, Decatur, GA 30033-4097, **Business Phone:** (404)679-4500.

**WARREN, REV. ANNIKA LAURIN**
Clergy. **Personal:** Born Dec 8, 1959, Hartford, CT; daughter of Hubbard H I and Annie McLaurin; married Mozallen McFadden; children: Shomari & Catherine Alannie. **Educ:** St Augustine's Col, BA, urban affairs, 1981; Va Theol Sem, MDiv, 1984. **Career:** Greater Hartford Chamber Com, Weaver High Sch, drop-out prev counr, 1983-91; Christ Church Cathedral, staff priest, 1984-88; St Monica's Episcopal Church, rector; St. Martin's Church, rev. **Orgs:** Alpha Kappa Alpha, 1977-; Alpha Kappa Mu Hon Soc, 1981-; bd dir, Greater Hartford Urban League, 1989-90; Coalition 100 Black Women, 1990-; bd dir, Greater Hartford United Way, 1992-; bd dir, Hartford Action Plan Infant Health, 1992-. **Honors/Awds:** Harriett Tubman Book Award, 1983. **Special Achievements:** First African to be ordained to the Episcopal Priesthood in the Diocese, 1985. **Home Addr:** 31 Woodland St Apt 1K, Hartford, CT 06105-4301, **Home Phone:** (860)293-1076. **Business Addr:** The Reverend, St Martin's Church, 290 Cornwall St, Hartford, CT 06120, **Business Phone:** (860)242-0318.

**WARREN, CLARENCE F.**
Car dealer. **Personal:** Born Feb 15, 1941, Detroit, MI; son of Clarence R and Opal C; married Geraldine; children: 2. **Educ:** Wayne State Univ, BA, 1963; Univ Ga, advan studies. **Career:** Kroger Co, corp dir, labor rels, 1958-86; PS I Love Yogurt, chair, chief exec officer, 1986-89; Network Video, pres, chief exec officer, 1986-89; 32 Ford Mercury Inc, pres & chief exec officer, 1990-. **Orgs:** Dir, Nat Asn Minority Auto Dealer, 1990-; NCP; Urban League; Wayne State Univ Alumni; Ford Lincoln Mercury Minority Dealer Asn, 1994. **Honors/Awds:** Minority Supplier of the Year, Cincinnati Minority Supplier Develop Coun, 1992; Top Profit DD Dealer in US, Ford Motor Co, 1992; Top Profit Dealer Award, Ford Motor Co, 1994. **Special Achievements:** Opened New Store, Sidney Ford Lincoln Mercury, Sidney, Ohio; Company ranked 10 on Black Enterprise's list of top 100 auto dealerships, 1998. **Home Addr:** 8239 E Kemper Rd, Cincinnati, OH 45249-1627. **Business Addr:** President, Chief Executive Officer, 32 Ford Mercury Inc, 610 W Main St, Batavia, OH 45103, **Business Phone:** (866)912-3232.

**WARREN, DORIAN T.**
Activist, television journalist, college teacher. **Personal:** Born Chicago, IL. **Educ:** Univ Ill, Urbana-Champaign, BA, 1998; Yale Univ, PhD, 2005. **Career:** Univ Chicago, post-doc & vis fac mem, 2004-06; Roosevelt Inst, fel, 2011-; Nation, ed bd mem, 2012-; Columbia Univ, assoc prof, 2012-; MSNBC, contribr, 2014-; Nerding Out, host & exec producer. **Orgs:** Appl Res Ctr, 2005-; Ctr Community Chg, 2008-; Discount Found, 2011-; Race Forward, Alliance a Greater New York, Working Partnerships USA, Model Alliance, Workers Lab. Co-chair, AFL-CIO's Comn Racial Justice Adv Coun. **Honors/Awds:** Peters' Fellow, University of Notre Dame, 2003-04; fellowships and grants from the Ford Foundation, CUNY's Murphy Institute, the Public Welfare Foundation, Open Society Foundations, and the Russell Sage Foundation; listed in NBC's theGrio's 100 people making history today. **Special Achievements:** Worked with national and local organizations including the Leadership Conference on Civil and Human Rights, American Rights at Work/Jobs with Justice, AFL-CIO, CTW, UNITE-HERE, SEIU, UFCW, Steelworkers, and the NGLTF Policy Institute. Commentator on public affairs with NBC Nightly News, ABC, MSNBC, CNN, CNBC, BET, BBC, NPR, Bloomberg, and NY1. **Business Addr:** Roosevelt Institute, 570 Lexington Ave Fifth Fl, New York, NY 10022, **Business Phone:** (212)444-9130.

**WARREN, GERTRUDE FRANCOIS**
Educator. **Personal:** Born Jul 4, 1929, Detroit, MI; daughter of John Henry and Lela Long; married Minor; children: Lela Valsine Battle & Herbert W Francois Jr. **Educ:** Eastern Mich Univ, Ypsilanti, MI, BS, 1949, MS, spec educ, PhD. **Career:** Meisners, Detroit, Mich, personnel mgr, 1950-55; Ypsilanti Bd Educ, Ypsilanti, Mich, teacher; Detroit Bd Educ, Detroit, Mich, teacher eng, dept head; Payne Fund, New York, 1927. **Orgs:** Pres, Palm Leaf Club, 1955-; comnr, Pub Housing, 1965-70; comnr, Mental Health, Wash Co, 1970-79; parliamentarian, charter mem, Alpha Kappa Alpha Sorority, 1970-74; mem chair, Dorcas Soc, 1971-; comnr, Low Cost Housing, 1971-; Nat Asn Advan Colored People, 1981-; secy, Kings Daughters, 1985; Steering Comt, REACT, 1987-; L Esprit Club; pres, New Era Study Club, 1987-; pres, Mich State Asn Colored Women's Clubs, 1987; found, Metro Women's Civic Club, 1988-. **Home Addr:** 26842 Hopkins St, Inkster, MI 48141, **Home Phone:** (313)561-4694.

**WARREN, HERMAN LECIL**
Educator. **Personal:** Born Nov 13, 1933, Tyler, TX; son of Cicero and Leola Mosley; married Mary K; children: Michael J, Christopher L & Mark H. **Educ:** Prairie View A&M Univ, BS, 1953; Mich State Univ, MS, plant path, 1962; Univ Minn, PhD, 1970. **Career:** Professor (retired), professor emeritus; Olin Chem Corp, New Haven CT, res scientist, 1962-67; USDA, Beltsville, Md, plant pathologist, 1969-71; USDA, Purdue Univ, W Lafayette, Ind, from asst to assoc prof & plant pathologist, 1972-89; Va Polytech Inst & St Univ, prof, plant pathol, 1989-2003, prof emer, 2003-. Author: Some Factors Affecting the Pathogenicity of Cornyebacterium Sepedonicum (Spieck. and Kott.) Skapt. and Burk. **Orgs:** Am Phytopathological Soc; New York Acad Sci; fel African Sci Inst, 1993. **Home Addr:** 411 Floyd St, Blacksburg, VA 24060-5070, **Home Phone:** (540)552-8897. **Business Addr:** Professor Emeritus, Virginia Polytechnic Institute and State University, Special Collections, Blacksburg, VA 24061-0434, **Business Phone:** (540)231-6308.

**WARREN, JAMES KENNETH**
Sales manager, manager. **Personal:** Born Jan 1, 1947, Detroit, MI; son of Amos and Ocie Chapman; married Diedre Peterson; children: Jacqueline Carmila Plair. **Educ:** Howard Univ, Wash, BA, 1970. **Career:** BASF Corp, Dearborn, mgr planning, 1976-79, area sales mgr, 1979-88, spec prog developer, 1988-91, Automotive Refinish, training mgr, currently. **Orgs:** Howard Univ Alumni Asn, 1970-91; Automotive Serv Indust Asn, 1974-91; Automotive Training Mgr Coun, 1991. **Home Addr:** 20526 Basil, Detroit, MI 48235, **Home Phone:** (313)862-9244. **Business Addr:** Training Manager, US Automotive Refinish, 1609 Biddle Ave, Wyandotte, MI 48192, **Business Phone:** (734)324-6000.

**WARREN, HON. JOYCE WILLIAMS**
Judge, lawyer, association executive. **Personal:** Born Oct 25, 1949, Pine Bluff, AR; daughter of Albert Lewis Williams and Marian Williams Johnson; married James Medrick; children: Jonathan, Jamie & Justin M. **Educ:** Univ Ark, Little Rock, Ark, BA, 1971, JD, 1976; Nat Coun Juv & Family Ct Judges & Nat Col, attended 1983. **Career:** Gov Bill Clinton, Little Rock, Ark, admin asst, 1979-81; pvt law pract, Little Rock, Ark, atty-at-law, 1981-82; Cent Ark Legal Servs, Little Rock, Ark, staff atty, 1982; Pulaski Co, Ark, Little Rock, Ark, juv judge, 1983-87, paternity judge, 1987-89; State Ark, Little Rock, Ark, Sixth Judicial Circuit, Div 10, circuit judge, 1989-; Judicial Discipline & Disability Comn. **Orgs:** Sigma Gamma Rho Sorority Inc, 1968-; Am Nat Ark & Pulaski Co Bar Asn, 1971-; Nat Coun Juv & Family Ct Judges, 1983-; Ark State Bd Law Examr, 1986-93; Ark Judicial Coun, 1989-; Am Bar Asn; Nat Bar Asn; Ark Bar Asn; Pulaski Bar Asn; Nat Asn Women Judges; Ark Asn Women Lawyers; W Harold Flowers Law Soc; Nat Coun Juv & Family Ct Judges. **Honors/Awds:** Very Special Arkansas Women, Ark Sesquicentennial Off Event, 1986; Gold Medal for Excellence in Law, Sigma Gamma Rho Sorority Inc, 1986; Arkansas Professional Women of Distinction, Worthen Bank Women's Adv Bd, 1988; Resolution for Outstanding Services, Pulaski Co Quorum Ct, 1988; Top 100 Women in Arkansas, 1995, 1996 & 1997; Juvenile Judge of the Year, Ark Coalition Juv Justice, 2000. **Special Achievements:** First African American person elected to a state level trial court judgeship in the State of Arkansas. First African American female graduate of the University of Arkansas; first black female judge in the Pulaski County system and the first in Arkansas; First black chairperson of the board; First black president of the Arkansas Judicial Council. **Home Addr:** 1916 S Pine St, Little Rock, AR 72204-3930. **Business Addr:** Circuit Judge, State of Arkansas, Circuit Court, 6th Judicial Circuit, 3001 W Roosevelt, Little Rock, AR 72204, **Business Phone:** (501)340-6724.

**WARREN, KEVIN**
Chairperson, president (organization), chief executive officer. **Educ:** Georgetown Univ, BS, finance, 1984; Harvard Bus Sch Advan Mgt Prog, grad, 2007. **Career:** Xerox, chmn, chief exec officer, 1984-, chmn, pres & chief exec officer, Can, 2007-10, vpres, 2010, Global Growth Opportunities, pres, pres US client opers, 2010-13, pres strategic growth initiatives, 2014-, Indust, Retail & Hospitality Bus Group, pres, 2014-; Com Bus Group, Xerox Serv, pres, 2016-; US Solutions Group, US Eastern Sales, sr vpres, 2004-07; Acquisition Transition Off, sr vpres, 2007. **Orgs:** Bd dir, Ill Tool Works, 2010-; adv bd mem, Nat Black MBA Asn; nat bd mem, Big Bros Big Sisters Am; Exec Leadership Coun; Young Presidents' Orgn; bd mem, Conf Bd Can; bd dir, chmn, Georgetown Univ; bd dir, Community Anti-Drug Coalitions Am; bd dir, Rochester Bus Alliance; Exec Leadership Coun. **Honors/Awds:** International Association of Business Communicators (IABC), Excellence in Communication Leadership (EXCEL) Award, Recipient, 2010; "Black Enterprise," The 100 Most Powerful Executives in Corporate America, 2010; Humanitarian Award, Young Presidents Orgn; Humanitarian Award, Community Anti-Drug Coalitions Am. **Special Achievements:** Publications: "Jay Z is Right: You're Not a Businessman, You're a Business, Man", Real Bus Blog, 2013; "Changing Your Business Model? 3 Key Actions and 4 Critical Checkpoints", Forbes, 2013. **Business Addr:** President, Xerox Corp, 45 Glover Ave, Norwalk, CT 06856-4505, **Business Phone:** (800)275-9376.

**WARREN, LLOYD MICHAEL.** **See WARREN, MICHAEL.**

**WARREN, MICHAEL (LLOYD MICHAEL WARREN)**
Actor, television producer, basketball player. **Personal:** Born Mar 5, 1946, South Bend, IN; married Susie W; children: Koa, Cash (Jessica Alba), Grayson & Makayla; married Jenny Palacios; children: 1. **Educ:** Univ Calif, Los Angeles, BA, theatre arts. **Career:** TV series: "Hill St Blues", actor, 1981-87; "City of Angels", actor, 2000; "The District", actor, 2001; "The District", actor, 2001; "Girlfriends", actor, 2001-07; Normal Again, actor, 2002; "Buffy the Vampire Slayer", actor, 2002; "Soul Food", actor, 2002; Secret Agent Man, actor, 2003; "JAG", actor, 2003; "Lost & Found", actor, 2004; "The Division", actor, 2004; "American Dreams", actor, 2004; Kevin Hill, actor, 2005; "Night Stalker", actor, 2005; "Kevin Hill", actor, 2005; "Night Stalker", actor, 2006; "Lincoln Heights", actor, 2007; "Lincoln Heights", 2007-09; "Criminal Minds", 2010; "Single Ladies", 2011. Films: Drive, He Said, actor, 1971; Norman. Is That You", actor, 1976; Fast Break, actor, 1979; Dreamaniac, actor, 1987; Cold Steel, 1987; Heaven Is a Playground, 1991; "Storyville", 1992; "A Passion to Kill", 1994; "The Hunted", 1995; Trippin', 1999; Mother and Child, 2009; Anderson's Cross, 2010. TV movies: The Child Saver, actor, 1989; The Kid Who Loved Christmas, actor, 1990; Buffalo Soldiers, actor, 1997; The Wedding, actor, 1998; Family Matters, producer; Step By Step, producer; Hangin' With Mr Cooper, producer; TV pilot, Home Free, actor, producer, 1988. **Honors/Awds:** All-Am Basketball Player, Univ Calif, Los Angeles; Acad All Am NCAA, 1966; Emmy Award nomination (Hill Street Blues); UCLA Athletic Hall of Fame, 1990. **Business Addr:** Actor, Moore Creative Talent, 3130 Excelsior Blvd, Minneapolis, MN 55416, **Business Phone:** (612)827-3200.

**WARREN, NAGUEYALTI**
School administrator, educator. **Personal:** Born Oct 1, 1947, Atlanta, GA; daughter of Booker T Thompson and Frances Herrin (deceased);

married Rueben C; children: Alkamessa Dalton, Asha & Ali. **Educ:** Fisk Univ, BA, eng, 1972; Simmons Col, MA, eng, 1974; Boston Univ, MA, 1974; Univ Miss, PhD, higher educ admin, 1984; Goddard Col, MFA, 2005. **Career:** Elma Lewis Sch Fine Arts, teacher, 1973-74; Howard Univ, res asst, 1975, grad teaching asst, 1975-77; N eastern Univ, dept Eng, instr, 1977-78; Univ Calabar, lectr, 1979-80; Weaver High Sch, Eng Teacher, 1980-81; Fisk Univ, asst prof & chmn, Dept Eng, 1984-88; Emory Univ, asst dean, assoc prof, 1988-97, assoc dean Arts & Sci, 1997-2005, sr lectr & dir undergrad studies, 2005-. **Orgs:** Col Lang Asn; Mod Lang Asn; Southern Conf Afro-Am Studies; adv bd mem, William Edward Burghardt Du Bois Found; fel, Cave Canem Workshops African Am poets, 2003-06. **Home Addr:** 7469 Asbury Dr, Lithonia, GA 30058-5904, **Home Phone:** (770)482-6067. **Business Addr:** Senior Lecturer, Director Undergraduate Studies, Emory University, 550 Asbury Cir 207 Candler Library, Atlanta, GA 30322, **Business Phone:** (404)727-6847.

### WARREN, OTIS, JR.

Real estate executive. **Personal:** Born Aug 25, 1942, Baltimore, MD; son of Otis Sr and Rose; married Sharon; children: Otis III. **Educ:** Community Col, Baltimore, AA, bus. **Career:** Otis Warren & Co, chief exec officer & owner, 1970-. **Orgs:** Pres, Greater Baltimore Bd Realtors, 1983; dir, Med Mutual Liability Ins Soc Md, 1988-; Nations Bank, 1989-; Nat Asn Realtors, 1989-91; Higher Edu Comn, 1990; Fannie Mae Adv Bd, 1990-91; Baltimore City Chamber Com, 1992; NCP. **Honors/Awds:** Realtor of the Year, Greater Baltimore Bd Realtors, 1976; Realtor Fair Housing Service Award, 1990; Distinguished Service Award, Morgan State Univ, 1990; Ranked 23 among the Baltimore Business Journals List of largest minority-owned businesses in Greater Baltimore. **Special Achievements:** Obtained largest minority contract with the govt for the development of an office bldg in downtown Baltimore, 1990; Business Opportunity Fair Honoree, MDDC, 1991; MAR Asn Realtors, Equal Opportunity Housing, 1991. **Home Addr:** 1003 Bellemore Rd, Baltimore, MD 21207, **Home Phone:** (410)433-1996. **Business Addr:** Owner, Chief Executive Officer, Otis Warren & Co, 2223 Wheatley Dr, Baltimore, MD 21207, **Business Phone:** (410)539-1010.

### WARREN, RICKY

Businessperson, business owner. **Career:** Artco Syst Inc, chief financial officer, co-owner, currently. **Business Addr:** Co-owner, Artco Syst Inc, 1810 Forest Lakes Ave SE, Atlanta, GA 30317, **Business Phone:** (404)635-9001.

### WARREN, ROLAND C.

Executive, president (organization). **Personal:** Born Toledo, OH; married Yvette Lopez; children: Jamin & Justin. **Educ:** Princeton Univ, BA, psychol; Univ Pa, Wharton Sch Univ Pa, MBA. **Career:** PepsiCo; IBM; Princeton Univ, assoc dir develop; Goldman Sachs & Co, fin consult. **Orgs:** Bd, Southern Home Serv; Urban Family Coun; First Ladys Helping Americas Youth Initiative, Care Net; Nat Campaign Prevent Teen Pregnancy; Nat PTA; Parent TV Nat Adv Coun; Cong Black Caucus; African Am Healthy Marriage Initiative; Kiwanis Club; YMCA; 100 Black Men Am; Gallup Inst; Nat Head Start Asn; Heartbeat Int; Urban League; Nat Youth Summit; Philanthropy Roundtable; Ann Mich Fathers Conf; pres & bd dir, Nat Fatherhood Initiative, 2001-. **Home Addr:** 23143 Newcut Rd, Clarksburg, MD 20871, **Home Phone:** (301)540-5034. **Business Addr:** President, National Fatherhood Initiative, 12410 Milestone Ctr Dr Suite 600, Germantown, MD 20876, **Business Phone:** (301)948-0599.

### WARREN, DR. RUEBEN CLIFTON

Health services administrator, government official. **Personal:** Born Aug 16, 1945, San Antonio, TX; son of Bobbye Owens; married Nagueyalti; children: Alkamessa Dalton, Asha & Ali. **Educ:** San Francisco State Univ, BA, 1968; Meharry Med Col, DDS, 1972; Harvard Sch Pub Health, MPH, 1973, DrPH, 1975. **Career:** Univ Lagos, Nigeria, W Africa, 1975-76; Harvard Sch Dent Med, residency dent pub health, 1975, instr, 1976-77; Univ Conn Health Ctr, asst prof, 1977-80; State Miss, dent dir, 1981-83, Med Ctr, clin assoc prof, 1982-83; Meharry Med Col, assoc prof & dean, 1983-88, Sch Dent, adj prof, 1998-; Ctr DisControl & Prev, Atlanta, Ga, assoc dir minority health, 1988-97; Morehouse Sch Med, Dept Prev Med & Community Health, clin prof, 1989-; Emory Univ, Rollins Sch Pub Health, Dept Behav Sci & Health Educ, adj prof, 1996-; Agency Toxic Substances & Dis Registry, assoc adm, 1997-; Nat Ctr Bioethics Res & Health Care, prof & dir, currently; dir Inst Faith-Health Leadership; Dept Community Health/Prev Med, clin prof, currently; Centers DisControl & Prev, asst dir minority health. **Orgs:** Meharry Alumni Asn; Nat Dent Asn; chap, Nat Dent Asn Del CNF Africa, 1982; Nat Asn Advan Colored People; Am Pub Health Asn; Am Asn Pub Health Dent; chairperson, Caucus Pub Health & Faith Communities PHA, 1997; UNC's Fund. **Home Addr:** 7469 Ashbury Dr, Lithonia, GA 30058, **Home Phone:** (770)482-6067. **Business Addr:** Administrator for Urban Affairs, Agency for Toxic Substances & Disease Registry, 1600 Clifton Rd NE, Atlanta, GA 30333, **Business Phone:** (404)639-5060.

### WARREN, DR. STANLEY

Dean (education), educator. **Personal:** Born Dec 18, 1932, Indianapolis, IN; son of Stanley Johnson and Rachel. **Educ:** Ind Cent Col, BS, 1959; Ind Univ, MAT, 1964, EdS, 1971, EdD, 1973. **Career:** Educator (retired); Ind-Purdue Univ, acad counr, 1969-71; DePauw Univ, dir, 1973-79, prof educ & dean acad affairs, 1985, prof & dean emer; Purdue Univ, human rels consult, 1992-95; Marion Co Dept Pub Welfare, case worker; Ind polis Pub Sch, teacher admin, 1960; Ind Comn Humanities, assoc; proj: Ind Ave; Beyond Rainbow. **Orgs:** Asn Study Negro Life & Hist; Urban League; Am Asn Teacher Educr; Ind Coalition Blacks Higher Educ; Afro-Am Hist & Geneal Soc; Head Start Policy Coun; Univ Indianapolis Alumni Asn; Great Lakes Col Asn; Ind Hist Soc; Hist Landmarks Found Ind. **Special Achievements:** Written numerous books, articles & poetry. **Home Addr:** 3412 Maritime Dr, Indianapolis, IN 46214-4103, **Home Phone:** (317)297-9885. **Business Addr:** Professor & Dean Emeritus, DePauw University, PO Box 37, Greencastle, IN 46135-0037, **Business Phone:** (765)658-4800.

### WARREN-MERRICK, GERRI

President (organization). **Personal:** daughter of Mary Farr; married Leon Merrick. **Educ:** Pa State Univ, BA, journalism. **Career:** Time Warner Inc, vpres of Global Pub Policy, vpres corp social responsibility, 2000-08; WarrenMerrick Commun, pres, 2009-. **Orgs:** SUNY Bd Trustees, 2006-; bd mem, Abyssinian Develop Corp; bd mem, Big Bros, Big Sisters. **Honors/Awds:** National Ethnic Coalition of Organizations' Ellis Island Medal of Honor; The Penn State University College of Communications Alumni of the Year Award; New York Women's Agenda Star Award; Medgar Evers College Legacy Award for Outstanding Corporate Leadership; The Girl Scouts Woman of Distinction Award; Abyssinian Baptist Church Unsung Heroine Award; "The Network Journal: Black Professionals & Small Business Magazine", 25 Influential Black Women in Business, 2009. **Business Addr:** President, Warren-Merrick Communications, 260 W 139th St Suite 3, New York, NY 10030, **Business Phone:** (212)694-4933.

### WARRICK, DR. ALAN EVERETT

Lawyer. **Personal:** Born Jun 18, 1953, Hampton, VA; son of John H (deceased) and Geri; children: Alan Everett II, Whitney Blair & Everett Alan. **Educ:** Howard Univ, BA, polit sci, 1975; Ind Univ Sch Law, Indianapolis, JD, 1978; ITT Tech Inst Tempe, BS, construct mgt, 2011. **Career:** Joint Ctr Polit Studies, res asst, 1972-74; Ind Civil Rights Comn, civil rights specialist, 1975; US Sen R Vance Hartke, campaign aide, 1976; ITT Tech Inst, construct mgt stud, 1977-2011; Marion Co Prosecutors Off, intern, 1977-78; Ind Law Rev, assoc ed, 1977-78; Branton & Mendelsohn Inc, atty, 1978-82; City San Antonio, Judge, munic ct, 1982; Law Off Alan E Warrick, atty, 1989-2005; ITT Tech Inst, construct mgt stud, 2007-11; OneRoof Energy Inc, energy rep, 2013-; Immaculate Prod LLC, sr vpres, 2015-. **Orgs:** Sec, San Antonio Trial Lawyers Asn, 1979-80, vpres, 1980-81, bd dir, 1981-82; bd mem, San Antonio Festival Inc, 1982-, exec comt, 1992-; selection panel, Golden Rule Award JC Penney, 1984; exec bd gov, United Way San Antonio, 1985-; bd gov, Nat Bar Asn, 1990-; pres, San Antonio Black Lawyers Asn, 1990-; bd dir, State Bar Tex, 1991-93; Asn Trial Lawyers Am; TX Young Lawyers Asn; TX Trial Lawyers Asn; San Antonio Bar Asn; San Antonio Young Lawyers Asn; Ancient Free & Accepted Masons; Omega Psi Phi Fraternity; Van Ct land Social Club; chair, AFA Lawyers Sect, 1993-94; Delta Sigma Theta; Omega Psi Phi Network; Men Omega Psi Phi Fraternity; Am Bar Asn; Phi Alpha Delta. **Honors/Awds:** Scroll Honor for Outstanding Achievement Field Law, Psi Alpha Chap Omega Psi Phi Fraternity, 1982; Achievements Recognition, Van Court land Social Club, 1982; Man of the Year, Elks Mission Lodge 499; Citizen of the Year, Psi Alpha Chap Omega Psi Phi Fraternity, 1982; Appreciation Award, Alamo Br YMCA, 1983; Outstanding Leadership Award, Alpha Tau Omega Chap, Alpha Kappa Alpha Sorority, 1984; Recognition Award, Smart Set Social Club, 1984; Phi Beta Kappa, Howard Univ; Pi Sigma Alpha Political Science, Honor Soc; Iota Phi Lambda Honoree Law Enforcement, 1985; Outstanding Service Award, Judicial Coun, Nat Bar Asn, 1989. **Business Addr:** Energy Representative, OneRoof Energy Inc, 4445 Eastgate Mall Rd Suite 240, San Diego, CA 92121, **Business Phone:** (858)458-0533.

### WARRICK, BRYAN ANTHONY

Basketball player, basketball coach. **Personal:** Born Jul 22, 1959, Moses Lake, WA. **Educ:** St Josephs Univ, attended 1982. **Career:** Basketball player (retired), basketball coach; Wash Bullets, 1982-84; Los Angeles Clippers, 1984-85; Wis Flyers, 1985-86; Milwaukee Bucks, 1985; Ind Pacers, 1986; Rockford Lightning, 1986-87; BSC Saturn Koln, 1987-88; Rancocas Valley Regional High Sch, coach.

### WARRICK, MARIE DIONNE. See WARWICK, DIONNE.

### WARWICK, DIONNE (MARIE DIONNE WARRICK)

Singer. **Personal:** Born Dec 12, 1940, East Orange, NJ; daughter of Lee Drinkard and Mansel; married William Elliott; children: David & Damion. **Educ:** Ed Hartt Col Music, Hartford, CT. **Career:** Singer & Actress; Gospel singer & organist with the Gospel aires & Drinkard Singers, 1955-60; solo performer, 1960-; Dionne Warwick Design Group Inc, co-founder, 2002; Food & Agr Orgn, UN Global Ambassador; US Ambassador of Health; Singles: "Don't Make Me Over", 1962; "This Empty Place", 1963; "Anyone Who Had a Heart", 1963; "Make the Music Play", 1963; "Walk On By", 1964; "A House is Not a Home", 1964; "You'll Never Get to Heaven (If You Break My Heart)", 1964; "Reach Out For Me", 1964; "Who Can I Turn To", 1965; "You Can Have Him", 1965; "Here I Am", 1965; "Looking With My Eyes", 1965; "Are You There (with Another Girl)", 1966; "Message to Michael", 1966; "Trains Boats & Planes", 1966; "Another Night", 1966; "I Just Don't Know What to Do with Myself", 1966; "Alfie", 1967; "The Windows of the World", 1967; "I Say a Little Prayer", 1967; "(Theme from) Valley of the Dolls", 1967; "The April Fools", 1968; "Do You Know the Way to San Jose", 1968; "Always Something There to Remind Me", 1968; "Promises, Promises", 1968; "This Girl's in Love with You", 1969; "You've Lost That Lovin' Feelin'", 1969; "I'll Never Fall in Love Again", 1970; "Make it Easy on Yourself", 1970; "Paper Mache", 1970; "Let Me Go to Him", 1970; "Who Gets the Guy", 1971; "Then Came You", 1974; "Take it From Me", 1975; "Once You Hit the Road", 1975; "I'll Never Love This Way Again", 1978; "Deja Vu", 1979; "After You", 1980; "No Night So Long", 1980; "Some Changes Are For Good", 1981; "Friends in Love", 1982; "Heart breaker", 1982; "All the Love in the World", 1983; "How Many Times Can We Say Goodbye", 1983; "Take the Short Way Home", 1984; "Finder of Lost Loves", 1985; "Run to Me", 1985; "That's What Friends Are For", 1985; "Love Power", 1987; "Reservations for Two", 1987; "Another Chance to Love", 1988; Albums: Presenting Dionne Warwick, 1964; Anyone Who Had a Heart, 1964; Make Way for Dionne Warwick, 1964; The Sensitive Sound of Dionne Warwick, 1965; Here I Am, 1965; Dionne Warwick in Paris, 1966; Here Where There Is Love, 1967; On Stage & in the Movies, 1967; Windows of the World, 1967; The Magic of Believing, 1967; Valley of the Dolls & Others, 1968; Soulful, 1969; Greatest Motion Picture Hits, 1969; Dionne Warwick's Golden Hits, Vol 1, 1969; Dionne Warwick's Golden Hits, Vol 2, 1970; I'll Never Fall in Love Again, 1970; Very Dionne, 1971; Promises, Promises, 1971; From Within, Vol 1, 1972; Dionne, 1973; Just Being Myself, 1973; Then Came You, 1975; Track of the Cat, 1975; Love at First Sight, 1977; Dionne, 1979; No Night So Long, 1980; Hot! Live & Otherwise, 1981; Heart breaker, 1983; Finder of Lost Loves, 1985; Dionne & Friends, 1986; Anthology, 1962-71, 1986; Then Came You, 1986; Masterpieces, 1986; Reservations for Two, 1987; Sings Cole Porter, 1990; Friends Can Be Lovers, 1993; Celebration in Vienna, 1994; Aquarela Do Brazil, 1995; Dionne Sings Dionne, 1998; The Definitive Collection, 1999; Soulful Plus, 2004; Love Songs, 2005; My Favorite Time of the Year, 2004; Say a Little Prayer, 2004; Me & My Friends, 2006; Gospel Album "Why We Sing?", 2008; Carr, Torr & Warwick Productions Inc, co founder; Warwick Design Group, co founder, currently; series: "Slaves", 1969; "Rent-A-Cop", 1988; "The Bold & the Beautiful", 1998; "The Wayans Bros", 1998; "Johnny Bravo", 1999; "Walker, Texas Ranger", 2000. **Orgs:** Owner, BRAVO (Blood Revolves Around Victorious Optimism); spokeswoman, Am Sudden Infant Death Syndrome Inst; founder, Warwick Found; hon mem, Zeta Phi Beta Sorority Inc. **Business Addr:** Singer, c/o Red Entertainment Group, 16 Penn Plz Suite 824, New York, NY 10001, **Business Phone:** (212)563-7575.

### WASH, DR. DAVID K.

Physician. **Educ:** Wayne State Univ Sch Med, MD; Am Bd Med Sci, Bd Family Med, cert. **Career:** Flower Hosp, residency; Va Pk Med Ctr, physician; Barbara Ann Ctr Family Med, owner, physician, currently; Sinai & Grace Hosp, physician, currently; St John Macomb Hosp, physician, currently. **Business Addr:** Physician, Owner, Barbara Ann Center for Family Medicine, 15565 Northland Dr E Suite 108 E, Southfield, MI 48075-5357, **Business Phone:** (248)905-5470.

### WASH, DR. DAVID KEANE

Physician. **Personal:** married Ursula Kelley. **Educ:** Wayne State Univ Sch Med, MD, 1999. **Career:** Flower Hosp, resident; St. Elizabeth Family Pract, physician; Thea Bowman Health Ctr, Physician, currently; Barbara Ann Ctr Family Med, Physician, currently. **Home Addr:** 1837 Campau Farms Cir, Detroit, MI 48207, **Home Phone:** (248)905-5470. **Business Addr:** Physician, Barbara Ann Center for Family Medicine, 15565 Northland Dr Suite 108E, Southfield, MI 48075, **Business Phone:** (248)905-5470.

### WASH, GLENN EDWARD

Construction manager, founder (originator). **Personal:** Born Feb 26, 1931, Grand Rapids, MI; son of George and Ethel; children: Glennda Marie. **Educ:** Highland Park Col; Univ Detroit, engineering; Urban Land Inst. **Career:** AJ Etkin Construct Co, Oak Pk, MI, construct supt, 1957-61; Leonard Jarosz Construct Co, Oak Pk, MI, construct supt, 1954-57; Practical Homes Builders, Oak Pk, MI, construct supt, 1961-65; HL Vokes Co, Cleveland, OH, construct supt, 1965-67; G E Wash Construct, founder; Glenn E Wash & Assoc Inc, founder, pres, 1977-. **Orgs:** Asn Gen Contracts Am, Detroit Chap, 1977-2001; Eng Soc Detroit, 1977-2001; Better Bus Bur, 1979-2001; secy & chmn, Mich Minority Bus Develop Coun, 1979-85; bd trustee, New Detroit Inc, 1980-2001; Minority Input Comt, Wayne State Univ, 1984-85; Comt Soc Econ Policy, Am Concrete Inst, 1984-85; chmn, Gov Construct Safety Stand Comn, 1986-; Coun Better Bus Bur. **Home Addr:** 9000 E Jefferson Ave Apt 21-9, Detroit, MI 48214-5602, **Home Phone:** (313)822-2028. **Business Addr:** President, Founder, Glenn E Wash & Assoc Inc, 14541 Schaefer Hwy, Detroit, MI 48227, **Business Phone:** (313)838-0800.

### WASHINGTON, ADA CATHERINE

Educator, songwriter, composer. **Personal:** Born Sep 19, 1950, Shreveport, LA; daughter of Willie J Miller Sr and Elizabeth J; married Valdemar L; children: Valdemar L II & Christopher J. **Educ:** Grambling Col, BS, music educ, 1972; Eastern Mich Univ, MS, 1982. **Career:** Music teacher, 1972-, Flint Bd Educ, teacher, 1973-85; Citizens Com Savings bank, dir, 1993; Mott Community Col, consult, 1995; Album: Aunty K N'Em in Pigsburgh, 2006. **Orgs:** Bd mem, Cedar St Childrens Ctr, 1986-87; Delta Sigme Theta Sorority, 1984-; Jr League Flint, 1986-88; pres, Pierians Inc, Flint Chap, 1990-93; nat law day chairperson, Am Lawyers Auxiliary, 1994; state law day chairperson, Mich Lawyers Auxiliary, 1993; pres, Genesee Bar Auxiliary, 1989-90; bd mem, McLaren Regional Med Ctr Found, 1995-. **Honors/Awds:** Ike Award, Distinguished Service, Eisenhower Comt Sch, 1980; African American Women of Achievement Award, Dozier Mem CME Church, 1995. **Special Achievements:** composer:composed 18 songs. **Home Addr:** 1505 Arrow Lane, Flint, MI 48507-1882, **Home Phone:** (810)742-2441.

### WASHINGTON, ADRIENNE TERRELL

Educator, columnist, association executive. **Personal:** Born Mar 28, 1950, Washington, DC; daughter of Earl Anthony Randall and Gwendolyn W Johnson; married Milton Robert; children: Misti E & Mario E. **Educ:** Hampton Univ, attended 1969; Northern Va Comm Col, attended 1976; Howard Univ, attended 1982; Am Univ, attended 1986; Johns Hopkins Univ, MA, writing, non-fiction & fiction, 2008. **Career:** Alexandria Gazette, reporter, 1972-73; Folger Shakespeare Libr, ed & admin asst, 1973-75; Wash Star, reporter & ed asst, 1975-81; WRC TV, metro ed, futures ed, 1982-87; Wash Times, dep metro ed, asst metro ed & dist bur chief, 1987-91, columnist, citizen journalism ed, 1991-2010; Cath Univ, adj prof, 2010-; Potomac Col, adj prof, 2010-; AFRO.com, columnist, 2010-; Northern Va Community Col, adj prof, 2011-; Univ DC Community Col, adj prof, 2011-. **Orgs:** Wash Asn Black Journalists, 1975-86; Nat Asn Black Journalists, 1979-; Leadership Wash, 1993-; Sasha Brice Youthworks Anti-Violence Campaign, 1993-95; Capital Press Club, 1993-; Women Wash, 1994; Monroe E Trotter Group, 1994-; Nat Soc Newspaper Columnists, 1994-; Md/DC/Del Press Asn, 1996. **Honors/Awds:** The Washington Baltimore Newspaper Guild, 1979; Soc Prof Journalist, 1993, 1994, 1997; Nat Soc Newspaper Columist, 1994; Am Asn Univ Women, 1994. **Home Addr:** 3413 Woods Ave, Alexandria, VA 22302, **Home Phone:** (703)379-5253. **Business Addr:** Adjunct Professor, Potomac College, 4000 Chesapeake St NW, Washington, DC 20016, **Business Phone:** (202)686-0876.

### WASHINGTON, ALONZO LAVERT

Publisher, writer, activist. **Personal:** Born Jun 1, 1967, Kansas City, KS; son of Millie C; married Dana D; children: Antonio S Davis, Akeem Alonzo, Kamaal Malik, Malcolm, Khalid & Alona. **Educ:**

Kans City Community Col; Pioneer Community Col. **Career:** AD HOC Group Against Crime, gang & youth counr & intervention specialist, 1990-92; Swope Pkwy Health Ctr, outreach specialist & counr, 1992-94; Omega 7 Comics Inc, pres, publ, writer & designer, 1992-. **Orgs:** Pres, Black Nat Cong, 1990-; hon mem, Black United Front, 1990-; AD HOC Group Against Crime, 1990-; New Democracy Movement, 1993-; pres, Asn African Am Comic Bk Publ, 1994-. **Home Addr:** 1155 E 75th Ter, Kansas City, MO 64131, **Home Phone:** (816)444-4204. **Business Addr:** Owner, President, Omega 7 Comics Inc, 1925 N 83rd Ter, Kansas City, KS 66117-0046, **Business Phone:** (913)321-6764.

### WASHINGTON, ALTON J.

Government official. **Educ:** Ariz State Univ, BS, polit sci, MS, pub admin. **Career:** Phoenix City Hall, dep pub work dir, dir human resource servs, dep citymgr, 1998-2002, spec asst city mgr, 2002-. **Orgs:** Am Soc Pub Admin; Acad Polit Sci; bd dir, Valley Sun United Way; vice chmn, Blue Cross Blue Shield Ariz; chair, Deferred Compensation Plan Bd; Ariz Hispanic Chamber Com. **Business Addr:** Assistant City Manager, Phoenix City Hall, 200 W Wash St 12th Fl, Phoenix, AZ 85003, **Business Phone:** (602)262-6941.

### WASHINGTON, ANTHONY

Athlete. **Personal:** Born Jan 16, 1966, Glasgow, MT; married Lesley; children: Colemen & Turner. **Educ:** Univ Syracuse, attended 1990. **Career:** Athlete (retired); USA Track & Field Inc, track & field athlete. **Home Addr:** , Parker, CO.

### WASHINGTON, ARNIC J.

Government official. **Personal:** Born Nov 19, 1934, Ladson, SC; married Rosalee Williams; children: Myra & Raymond. **Educ:** Nielson Computer Col Charleston SC. **Career:** Lincolnville Sc, vice mayor, 1967-, councilman. **Orgs:** Chmn, St Dept; Health Dept; Pub Bldg Dept; SC Munic Asn, SC; Small Towns Asn, SC; Black Mayors Asn; Southern E Conf Black Elected Officials; Southern E Regional Coun Inc Nat League Cities; Berkeley Co Chap Nat Asn Advan Colored People; W Master Saxon Lodge #249 FAM Midland Park, SC; chmn trustee bd, Wesley Meth church Ladson SC; pres, Willing Workers; Admin Bd; Coun Ministries; Adult Class Teacher; vpres, Caration Gospel Singers. **Honors/Awds:** Certificate of Recognition, SC Legis House Rep Outstanding Contributions in Field of Com & Pub Affairs; For Civic & Polit Leadership & Accomplishments in Country Charleston; Outstanding Performance as Councilman, Historic Town of Lincolnville, SC. **Home Addr:** 758 E Randolph St, Summerville, SC 29485-7232, **Home Phone:** (843)873-2982. **Business Addr:** PO Box 536, Summerville, SC 29483.

### WASHINGTON, DR. ARTHUR CLOVER

Educator, dean (education). **Personal:** Born Aug 19, 1939, Tallulah, LA; married Almrta Hargest; children: Arthur, Angela & Anthony. **Educ:** Tex Col, BS, biol, 1961; Tuskegee Inst, MS, biol, 1963; Ill Inst Tech, PhD, biol, 1971. **Career:** Talladega Col, instr, 1965-67; City Col Chicago, assoc prof, 1967-71; Langston Univ, prof, 1972-74; Prairie View A&M Univ, dean grad sch, prof, 1974-91; Tenn State Univ, vpres, Acad Affairs, 1991-93, prof, 1993-97; Fla A & M Univ, prof biol sci, dean, Col Arts & Sci, 1997-. **Orgs:** Extramural assoc, NIH, 1979; pres, Woodedge Civic Asn, 1981; nat exec sec, Nat Inst Sci, 1983-. **Home Addr:** 456 Meadow Ridge Dr, Tallahassee, FL 32312, **Home Phone:** (850)906-9765. **Business Addr:** Dean, Professor, Florida A & M University, Col Arts & Sci, Tallahassee, FL 32307, **Business Phone:** (850)599-7767.

### WASHINGTON, BEN JAMES, JR.

Executive. **Personal:** Born Feb 10, 1946, Chicago, IL; son of Frances and Bennie; children: Stephanie & Bennie III. **Educ:** Wright Col, attended 1976; Harold Wash Col, cert, 1988. **Career:** Aldens Catalog Inc, exec mgr, 1968-76; Penn-Corp Financial Inc, mgr, 1977-81; Health Tech Indust Inc, pres & ceo, 1985; Whitestar Sportsgear Inc, pres & chief exec officer, currently. **Orgs:** Pres, Am Animal Asn Inc, 1977-86; pres, ed, Am Pet Asn Inc, 1981-86. **Home Addr:** 5745 Taft Pl, Merrillville, IN 46410, **Home Phone:** (219)981-1486. **Business Addr:** President, Chief Executive Officer, Whitestar Sportsgear Inc, 2533 Bernice Rd Suite D1, Lansing, IL 60438, **Business Phone:** (708)895-8858.

### WASHINGTON, BETTY LOIS (BARABARA L WASHINGTON)

Executive, lawyer. **Personal:** Born Apr 16, 1948, New Orleans, LA. **Educ:** Southern Univ New Orleans, BA, 1970; Mich State Univ, MA, 1971; Tulane Univ Sch Law, JD, 1983. **Career:** Southern Univ New Orleans, counr, 1972-73; N Urban League, prog dir, 1973-75; Desire Area Comm Coun, exec dir, 1975-79; Southern Univ Syst, bd supvr, 1978-80; Teach A Brother, exec dir, 1979-80; Ward Design Team, team chief, 1985; Images Corp, sec, 1985; Mgt Assoc, pres; Mgt Assoc New Orleans, pres, 1985; pvt pract atty, currently. **Orgs:** Phi Alpha Theta Hist Hon Soc; Zeta Phi Beta Sor; credit com, Southern Univ Alumni Asn. **Home Addr:** 8500 Fordham Ct, New Orleans, LA 70127, **Home Phone:** (504)466-6512. **Business Addr:** Attorney, 8500 Fordham Ct, New Orleans, LA 70127-2006, **Business Phone:** (504)945-4683.

### WASHINGTON, BILL. See WASHINGTON, WILLIAM MONTELL.

### WASHINGTON, CARL ROUCHE

Association executive, executive director, educator. **Educ:** Univ Southern Calif, BA, commun arts & sci, 1992. **Career:** UMCA Sports, founder & owner; HBO, consult; Urban Movie Corp Am, pres; Reebok, urban mkt & sales, 1991-99; Urban Mkt Corp Am, co-founder & pres, 1999-; Pre-Draft Camp, co-owner, 2012-; Elite Youth Invitational Basketball Tourney, co-owner, 2012-; Mad Crush Sports & Entertainment, managing partner, 2012-; Ideas United, bus develop advisor sports & entertainment, 2014-; Promotions Dept, vpres, 2014-; the raouche trading co, exec vpres-bus develop, 2015-. **Orgs:** Big Bros Big Sisters Am, 1995-2005; teacher, Last Mile, 2013-. **Business Addr:** Co-Founder, President, Urban Marketing Corp of America, 1450 S Fairfax Ave, Los Angeles, CA 90019, **Business Phone:** (323)934-8622.

### WASHINGTON, CONSUELA M.

Lawyer. **Personal:** Born Sep 30, 1948, Chicago, IL; daughter of Hilliard L and Conzoella Emanuelita Brulee. **Educ:** Upper Iowa Univ, Fayette, IA, BA, polit scici, 1970; Harvard Univ, Cambridge, MA, JD, 1973. **Career:** Senior minority counsel (retired); Kirkland & Ellis, Chicago, assoc, 1973-74; Allis-Chalmers Corp, Corp Law Dept, atty, 1975-76; Securities & Exchange Comn, off chief coun, div corp finance, atty advr, 1976-79, spec coun, 1979; US House Reps, Comn Energy & Com, cheif coun, 1979-94; minority coun, 1995-2000, sr minority coun, 2001, sr minority coun. **Orgs:** Ill Bar Asn; Harvard Law Sch Asn; Harvard Club Wash; Scholastic Hon Soc, Upper IA Univ, Hon Leadership Soc, 1968-70; Harvard Bd Overseers, 1987-93; US Bd dir, Med Educ S African Blacks, 1995. **Honors/Awds:** Bradley Invitation Speech Tournament Award for Excellence, 1969; Notable American, 1978-79; Equal Employment Opportunity Award, SEC, 1978; Alumni Achievement Award, Upper Iowa Univ, 1977. **Home Addr:** 2301 Jefferson Davis Hwy, Arlington, VA 22202, **Home Phone:** (703)418-6870.

### WASHINGTON, COQUESE MAKEBRA

Basketball player, basketball coach. **Personal:** Born Jan 17, 1971, Flint, MI; married Raynell Brown; children: Quenton & Rhaiyan Kamille. **Educ:** Univ Notre Dame, BA, 1992, JD, 1997. **Career:** Basketball player (retired), basketball coach; Flint Northwestern High Sch, teacher, basketball player; Hoosier All-Stars; Notre Dame Women's Basketball, basketball player, 1989-93, asst coach, 1999-2005, assoc head coach, 2005-07; New Eng All-Stars; Portland Power, guard, 1997-98; NY Liberty, 1998-99; Houston Comets, guard, 2000-02; Ind Fever, guard, 2002-03; Penn State women's basketball, head coach, 2007-. **Orgs:** Womens Nat Baseball Players Asn, founding pres, 1999-2001, exec vpres, 2001-03. **Business Addr:** Head Coach, Penn State Women's Basketball, 25 Yearsley Mill Rd, Media, PA 19063, **Business Phone:** (610)892-1200.

### WASHINGTON, CRAIG ANTHONY

Lawyer. **Personal:** Born Oct 12, 1941, Gregg County, TX; son of Roy and Azalia; married Karen Joyce Haller; children: Craig Anthony II, Chival Antoinette, Alexander Haller, Cydney Alexandra & Christopher Alfred. **Educ:** Prairie View A&M Univ, BS, biol, 1966; Tex Southern Univ Law Sch, JD, 1969. **Career:** Tex Southern Univ Law Sch, asst dean, 1969-70, asst prof law; Wash & Randle, Houston, founding partner, 1970; Tex House Rep, Dist 86, 1973-83; Tex Senate sen, Dist 13, 1983-89; US House Rep, Dist 18, mem, 1989-94; Distinguished Vis Prof, 2000-01; Craig Wash Law Firm, Houston, Tex, atty, currently. **Orgs:** Nat Bar Asn; Tex Bar Asn; pres, Houston Lawyers Asn; Houston Bar Asn; Harris Co Criminal Lawyers Asn; Tex Criminal Defense Lawyers Asn; Tex Trial Lawyers Asn; Galveston Co Criminal Lawyers Asn; Houston Chap Am Civil Liberties Union; Houston Bill Rights Found; Nat Conf Crime & Delinquincy; Nat Asn Advan Colored People; adv bd mem, Focus Mag; chmn, Houston Lawyers Asn Legis Comt; Houston Bar Asn Planning Comt; Houston Comt Humanities & Pub Policy; Citizens United Rehab Errants; Hope Ctr Youth; Const Rev Comt State Jr Bar; bd mem, Citizens Good Schs; Criminal Justice & Consumer Affairs Task Force Nat Conf State Legislatures; Martin Luther King Jr Community Ctr; Southern Regional Coun, Atlanta, Ga; St James Episcopal Church, Houston, Tex; pres, Stud Bar Asn, 1968-69; chmn, Legis Black Caucus. **Home Addr:** 1919 Smith St Suite 820, Houston, TX 77002. **Business Addr:** Attorney, Craig Washington Law Firm, 1000 The Houston Bldg, Houston, TX 77004, **Business Phone:** (713)659-9090.

### WASHINGTON, DANTE DENEEN

Soccer player, television broadcaster. **Personal:** Born Nov 21, 1970, Baltimore, MD; son of Yolanda Robinson and Don; married Holly Lynn; children: Nahla. **Educ:** Radford Univ, BA, hist & pol sci, 1992. **Career:** Soccer player (retired), television broadcaster, executive; Howard Co Libr, libr page, 1987; John Elicker, architect apprentice, 1987-88; Columbia Day Soccer Camp, coach, 1988-95; Joe Wyzkoski, resident mgr, 1990-92; World Cup Org Comm, admin asst, 1993-94; Wash Warthogs, 1994-95; NBC Olympics, logistics coordr, 1995-96; Columbus Crew, soccer player, 1996-97, 2000-03, 2004-05; Dallas Burn, soccer player, 1996-99; VA Beach Mariners, soccer player, 2003-04; Real Salt Lake, forward, 2005; Baltimore Blast, MISL, 2005-06; Columbus Crew's TV broadcasts, color commentator; Maj League Soccer, ambassador, 2007; TV soccer color analyst; FC Dallas, TV broadcaster, 2012-; Nationwide Ins. sr consult, strategic partnerships, 2013-. **Orgs:** Keeper, rec & exchequer, Kappa Alpha Psi Fraternity, 1990-92. **Honors/Awds:** Soccer All-Am, NSCAA, NCAA Div I, 1991; State Of Virginias Player of the Year, 1991; Acad All-Am, 1992; Alumni Minority Scholar, Radford Univ, 1991-92; MLS Player of the Month, 2000; MLS Player of the Week, 1997, 2000, 2001. **Special Achievements:** Met Pres Clinton as part of his work as the league's anti-drug spokesperson, 1998; First Afro American to score a goal for the US Natl Team. **Home Addr:** 341 Leestone Ct, Sunbury, OH 43074-8544. **Business Addr:** Tv Broadcaster, FC Dallas, 9200 World Cup Way Suite 202, Frisco, TX 75033, **Business Phone:** (214)705-6700.

### WASHINGTON, DARRYL MCKENZIE

Manager, association executive, engineer. **Personal:** Born Jan 29, 1948, New York, NY; son of McKenzie T and Leslie Taylor; married Barbara Gore; children: Monika, Matthew & Morgan. **Educ:** NC Agr & Tech State Univ, Greensboro, BSEE, elec engineering, 1974. **Career:** RJR Archer Inc, Winston-Salem, NC, engr, 1974-78; Miller Brewing, Eden, NC, tech servs mgr, plant engr, 1978-2001; Wash Group, principle inspector, 2001-. **Orgs:** Inst Elec & Electronics Engrs, 1967-; Soc Mech Engr, 1989-; Nat Food Processors Asn, 1989-; Am Inst Plant Engrs, 1989-; Soc Prof Real Estate Inspectors; NC Lic Home Inspectors Asn. **Home Addr:** PO Box 21242, Greensboro, NC 27420, **Home Phone:** (919)273-9582. **Business Addr:** Principle Inspector, The Washington Group, 1700 Martin Luther King Jr Dr, Greensboro, NC 27406, **Business Phone:** (336)280-0507.

### WASHINGTON, DAVID WARREN

Administrator. **Personal:** Born Jan 13, 1949, Mound Bayou, MS; married Clotee Woodruff; children: Rynetta Rochelle, Vernekia Bradley, Monique Caldwell, Rodney Brown & Vietta Leflore. **Educ:** Coahoma Jr Col, AA, 1970; Delta State Univ, BS, 1972, addn grad study, guid & coun, 1974. **Career:** Ford Found Leadership Develop Prog, 1974-75; Bolivar Co Community Action Agency, equal opportunity officer, 1977-79; serv third term asvice-mayor, Town Pace, Miss; Bolivar Co Head start Personnel & Training, dir human resources & adminr, currently; Delta Health Ctr, Mound Boyon, consult, currently. **Orgs:** Chmn bd, election Comn, 1984; Bolivar Co Dem exec comn, 1984-86; sch bd chmn, Bolivar Co Sch Dist I; election comnr, Bolivar County Dist I, 1984-88; Spangle Banner MB Church; chmn, Bolivar Co Election Comnr, 1988-92; chmn by-laws comn, Bolivar Co Asn Black Officials, 1989-92; dir, Bolivar Co Summer Food Serv Prog; former pres, Pace Voters League; chmn, Bolivar Co Election Comn; comt chair, Delta Health Ctr; human resource & training dir, Co Head Start. **Honors/Awds:** In Appreciation Outstanding Serv, Bolivar County Community Action Agency Bd Dir, 1980; Outstanding Serv, Miss Pace Community Asn, 1980; Concern & Dedication Shown, Staff Bolivar County Head start Training Ctr, 1982; Appreciation for Faithful Serv, St James Missionary Baptist Church, 1983; Most Outstanding Citizen Award, Pace Community Asn, 1983; Dedicated Service Award, Parents Bolivar County Head start Training Ctr, 1984. **Home Addr:** PO Box 245, Pace, MS 38764-0245, **Home Phone:** (601)723-6742. **Business Addr:** Director, Human Resources, Bolivar County Headstart Program, 810 E Sunflower Rd Suite 120, Cleveland, MS 33732, **Business Phone:** (662)846-1491.

### WASHINGTON, DR. DENZEL HAYES, JR.

Actor, video producer. **Personal:** Born Dec 28, 1954, Mt. Vernon, NY; son of Denzel and Lynn; married Pauletta Pearson; children: John David, Katia, Malcolm & Olivia. **Educ:** Fordham Univ, BA, drama & jour, 1977; Am Conserv Theatre, actg; Wynn Handman, actg. **Career:** Theater appearances: Coriolanus, 1979; One Tiger to a Hill, 1980; When the Chickens Come Home to Roost, 1981; A Soldier's Play, 1981-83; Every Goodbye Ain't Gone, 1984; Checkmates, 1988; Richard III, 1990. TV movies: "Wilma", 1977; "Flesh & Blood", 1979; "St Elsewhere", 1982-88; "In Harm's Way" video for BeBeWinans, dir, 1997; "Half Past Autumn: The Life & Works of Gordon Parks", 2000; "Cubed", 2010. Films: Carbon Copy, 1981; A Soldier's Story, 1984; The George McKenna Story, 1986; Power, 1986; Cry Freedom, 1987; For Queen & Country, 1989; The Mighty Quinn, 1989; Glory, 1989; Heart Condition, 1990; Mo' Better Blues, 1990; Ricochet, 1991; Mississippi Masala, 1992; MalcolmX, 1992; Much Ado about Nothing, 1993; Philadelphia, 1993; Crimson Tide, 1995; Virtuosity, 1995; Devil In A Blue Dress, 1995; The Preacher's Wife, 1996; Courage Under Fire, 1996; Fallen, 1997; He Got Game, 1998; The Siege, 1998; The Bone Collector, 1999; The Hurricane, 1999; Remember the Titans, 2000; Training Day, 2001; John Q, 2002; Antwone Fisher, dir & producer, 2002; Out of Time, 2003; Man on Fire, 2004; The Manchurian Candidate, 2004; Inside Man, 2006; Deja Vu, 2006; American Gangster, 2007; The Great Debaters, dir, 2007; The Taking of Pelham 1 2 3, actor, 2009; Unstoppable, 2010; The Book of Eli, 2010; Flight, 2012; Safe House, 2012; 2 Guns, 2013; The Equalizer, 2014. **Orgs:** Nat spokesperson, Boys & Girls Clubs Am, 1993-. **Honors/Awds:** Obie Award, 1982; Image Award, Nat Asn Advan Colored People, 1988; Best Performance by a Supporting Actor, 1990; Golden Globe Award, 1989; Academy Award, 1990; American Black Achievement Awards; Ebony Career Achievement Award, 1994; Audelco Award, When the Chickens Come Home to Roost; Best Actor Award, Nat Asn Advan Colored People, 1998; New York Film Critic's Circle Award; Critic's Award, Boston Society of Film; Dallas/Ft Worth Film Critic's Asnn Award; Washington D.C. Area Film Critics Association Award, 2001; Chicago Film Critic's Award; Golden Globe Award; Academy Award, 2001; Critics Asn Awards for Best Actor, Los Angeles Film, 2001; Black Entertainment Awards for Best Actor, 2001; Black Reel Award for Theatrical Best Actor, 2001; Boston Society of Film Critics Awards for Best Actor, 2001; Image Award for Outstanding Actor in a Motion Picture, 2001; AFI Film Award, Actor of the Year, 2002; MTV Movie Award for Best Villain, 2001; Oscar Award for Best Actor in a Leading Role, 2001 & 2002; Black Reel Award for Theatrical, Best Actor, 2002; Image Award for Outstanding Actor in a Motion Picture, 2002; Kansas City Film Critics Circle Awards for Best Actor, 2002; Black Reel Awards for Theatrical, 2003; Image Award for Outstanding Actor in a Motion Picture, 2003; Image Award for Outstanding Supporting Actor in a Motion Picture, 2003; Stanley Kramer Award, 2003; Tree of Life Award, 2003; Tony Award for Best Performance by a Leading Actor in a Play, 2010 & 2014; hon doctorate, Fordham Univ, 1991, hon doctorate, 2007; hon degree, Univ Pennsylvannia, 2011; African-American Film Critics Association Award, 2012; Received more than awards; Cecil B. DeMille Lifetime Achievement Award, 73rd Golden Globe Awards, 2016. **Special Achievements:** Golden Globe Nominee for Best Performance by an Actor in a Motion Picture Drama, 2002. **Business Addr:** Actor, c/o International Creative Management Inc, 10250 Constellation Blvd, Los Angeles, CA 90067, **Business Phone:** (310)550-4000.

### WASHINGTON, DEWAYNE NERON

Football player, manager. **Personal:** Born Dec 27, 1972, Durham, NC; married Adama; children: Dj, Demi & Delaney. **Educ:** NC State Univ, BA, mult disciplinary studies; Univ Pa, Wharton Bus Sch, NFL Bus Mgt & Entrepreneurial Prog, 2005. **Career:** Football player (retired), manager, coach; Minn Vikings, defensive back, 1994-97; Pittsburgh Steelers, corner back, 1998-2003; Jacksonville Jaguars, corner back, 2004; Kans City Chiefs, corner back, 2005; Green fire Devel, asset mgr, 2007-, Ravenscroft Sch, asst coach; Green Hope High Sch, head coach, Heritage High Sch, head football coach, currently. **Orgs:** Pres, Dewayne Wash Found, 1995-2004; bd trustee, Union Baptist Church; Durham YMCA Bd; NC St Alumni Bd. **Home Addr:** 6205 Rocky Creek Way, Wake Forest, NC 27587-6267. **Business Addr:** Asset Manager, Greenfire Development, 101 W Main St, Durham, NC 27701, **Business Phone:** (919)667-9770.

### WASHINGTON, DR. EARL MELVIN

Educator. **Personal:** Born Jun 22, 1939, Chicago, IL; son of Hester L and Henry W; married Dianne Elizabeth Taylor; children: Jason Todd & Tiffany Anne. **Educ:** Western Mich Univ, BA, eng & speech, 1963, MA, speech educ & teaching, 1968, EdD, educ leadership; Univ Mich,

1971; Grand Rapids Junior Col, assocs degree. **Career:** Cleveland Pub Schs, teacher, 1963-68; Kalamazoo Valley CC, instr, 1968-70; Western MI Univ, asst prof communs, 1975-82, assoc prof communs, dir black fac devel prog, 1982-01, asst dean, 1984-01, assoc prof, communs, trustee, assoc prof emer, currently; Col Arts & Sci, asst dean, 1986; IST Study Race Ethnic Rels, dir, consult & workshop presenter; Historically Black Cols, recruit fac; . **Orgs:** Vpres, Kalamazoo Phys Ther Asst; press & publ dir, Kalamazoo Metro Br Nat Asn Advan Colored People, 1984-84; vpres, 100 men Kalamazoo, 1983-85; papers presented incl Nat Asn Equal Opportunity; Phi Kappa Phi; dir, Black Col Prog; dir, Black Am Studies Prog. **Home Addr:** 2504 Cutty Sark Dr, Kalamazoo, MI 49009. **Business Addr:** Associate Professor Emeritus, Western Michigan University, 1903 W Michigan Ave, Kalamazoo, MI 49008, **Business Phone:** (269)387-1000.

## WASHINGTON, EARL S.

Executive, chairperson, executive director. **Personal:** Born Los Angeles, CA. **Educ:** Calif State Univ, Los Angeles, BS, bus. **Career:** Rockwell Int, Anaheim, CA, mkt analyst, vpres bus develop, vpres strategic mgt & int, Autonetics Marine Systs Div, vpres & gen mgr, Rockwell Corp Off, vpres advert & pub rels, sr vpres mkt & communs; Financial Partners Credit Union, chmn bd & dir, currently. **Orgs:** Exec Leadership Coun; bd trustee, Harvey Mudd Col. **Special Achievements:** First African-American vice president at Rockwell International. **Home Addr:** 323 S Snyder Pl, West Covina, CA 91791-2300, **Home Phone:** (626)966-2445. **Business Addr:** Chairman of the Board, Director, Financial Partners Credit Union, 7800 E Imp Hwy, Downey, CA 90242, **Business Phone:** (562)923-0311.

## WASHINGTON, EARLENE

Manager, statistician, accountant. **Personal:** Born Nov 15, 1951, Brookhaven, MS; daughter of Lonnie McLaurin and Geraldine Gaston McLaurin; married Ralph Campbell; children: Latonya, Kimberly & Jasmine. **Educ:** Alcorn State Univ, Lorman, Miss, BS, 1973; Jackson State Univ, Jackson, MS, 1973; Miss Col, Clinton, Miss, MBA, 1975. **Career:** Utica Jr Col, payroll clerk Utica, Miss, accts payable & inventory mgr, 1973-79; Miss Power & Light, Jackson, Miss, statistician, 1979-86, contract adminr, procurement spt, 1986-. **Honors/Awds:** Dean's List, Alcorn State Univ, 1969-73, National Honor, 1969-73, President Scholar, 1971-73. **Home Addr:** 201 Donald St Suite 7, Jackson, MS 39216, **Home Phone:** (601)368-9227. **Business Addr:** Procurement Specialist, Purchasing & Material Management, Mississippi Power & Light Co, 308 E Pearl St, Jackson, MS 39201, **Business Phone:** (601)949-9247.

## WASHINGTON, DR. EDITH MAY FAULKNER

Counselor, consultant, president (organization). **Personal:** Born Jul 28, 1933, Queens, NY; daughter of Henry Ozman Faulkner and Edalia Magdalene O; married George Clarence; children: Desiree Elaine Singletary, James Henry (Barbara) & Edahlia Magdalene Kelley Woods. **Educ:** NY State Univ Col, Buffalo, BS, HEc, Ed, 1968, MS, HEc, Ed, 1971; Ind Univ, Gas City, Ind, DHR, Human Rels Psych, 1973; Elmira Col, MSEd, behav sci, 1981. **Career:** SEEK Disadvantaged Students, coordr, 1969-71; NY Univ, Buffalo, instr, Afro-Amer studies, 1969-71; PEACE Inc, consult, 1971; NY Off Drug Abuse Serv Masten Pk Community Rehab Ctr, inst teacher, 1971-76; NY Off Drug Abuse Serv, Manhattan Rehab Ctr, inst teacher, 1976-77; Church God Christ, Cent Am W Indies, mission worker/teacher, 1980-; NY Dept Correction Serv, acad classification analyst, correction counr, 1991; WFHW Channel 58, co-host; Appl Christianity Inc, consult, counr, currently. **Orgs:** Co-founder, Afro-Am Cult Ctr, Buffalo, New York, 1960; state pres, Bus & Prof Women, Church God Christ; bd mem, Church God Christ Dept Missions; mem & workshop leader, Corrective Educ Asn, 1971; prod/dir, Benefits Missions Church God Christ Inc, Missions Benefit Breakfast; execdir, Anegada House Cult Inst; bd mem, Nat Asn Advan Colored People Elmira Corning Ctr, 1977; bd mem, Adv Coun Citizens Adv Coun Comnr Social Serv, 1978; Southern Tier Regional Planning Bd, 1976; Chemung Co Planning Bd, 1976, Appl Christianity Church God Christ, 1980-; ordained Evange list Independent Holiness Assembly Church Inc, 1986; vol nutritionist/coordr, Appl Christianity Inc, Food Pantry; admin, Appl Christianity Church God Christ. **Honors/Awds:** Ford Co Town Crier Award, Ford Motor Co; Outstanding Community Service Award, 1969; Outstanding Community Service Award, ACCEP Buffalo, New York, Frontier Citizens & Agng Comn, Cult Educ Prog Ctr, 1970; Outstanding Academic Achievement Award, Pentecostal Temple Church God Christ, 1971; Outstanding Community Servicve Award, Chemung Co, 1979; Humanitarian Award, Nat Asn Blacks Criminal Justice, 1985; Mt Nebo Ministries MLK Drum Major for Freedom Award, co-recipient w/spouse, Rev G C Washington, 1986; hon mem, Sigma Gamma Rho, 1988. **Home Addr:** 1341 South Ave, Niagara Falls, NY 14305-2844, **Home Phone:** (716)285-0513. **Business Addr:** Worker, Teacher, Church God Christ, 1063 W N Bend Rd, Cincinnati, OH 45224, **Business Phone:** (513)542-7643.

## WASHINGTON, EDITH STUBBLEFIELD

Executive, consultant. **Personal:** Born Jan 1, 1948, Almo, KY. **Career:** SSOE Inc, Toledo, OH, chief specif coordr; Univ Toledo Col Engrg, instr; Construct Specif Inst, pres; Stubblefield Grp Inc, pres, 1994-; archit & engrg firms, specif consult. **Orgs:** Fel Construct Specif Inst; pres, CSI Allentown Chap, currently. **Business Addr:** President, Stubblefield Group Inc, 1946 N 13th St Suite 482, Toledo, OH 43624, **Business Phone:** (419)255-3200.

## WASHINGTON, EDWARD, JR.

Manager. **Personal:** Born Nov 25, 1931, Logan County, KY; married Ruth Shorton; children: James, Phillip, Terry, Bobby, Francine Wynn, Cherri & Nancy. **Career:** Ky, councilman, 1970; Auburn Hosiery Mill, foreman; fireman; emer worker; ambulance svc. **Orgs:** Barroh River Health Syst; Adairville City Coun; S Hogan Cham Comn; Mason. **Special Achievements:** Kentucky first African American councilman, 1970.

## WASHINGTON, ELMER L.

Association executive, executive, educator. **Personal:** Born Oct 18, 1935; married Anna Ross; children: Lisa & Lee. **Educ:** Tex Southern Univ, BS, 1957, MS, 1958; Ill Inst Tech, PhD, 1965. **Career:** Univ Chicago, res asst, 1958-61; Pratt & Whitney Div United Aircraft, asst proj engr & res assoc, 1965-69; Chicago St Univ, dean natural sci & math, 1972-74, vpres Res & Develop, actg vpres stud affairs, dean Col Arts & Scis, dean Natural Scis & Math, prof emer; Univ Prof Ill, chief contract negotiator, 1992-2000. **Orgs:** AAAS; Am Chem Soc; Electro chem Soc; Am Asn Univ Prof; Am Asn Univ Adminsr; Alpha Kappa Mu Hon Soc, 1956; bd mem, Ill Bd Higher Educ. **Honors/Awds:** Welch Found Scholarship, 1957; Petroleum Research Fellowship, 1961-65; Phi Lambda Upsilon Scientific Honor Soc, 1964. **Home Addr:** 221 Grant St, Park Forest, IL 60466, **Home Phone:** (708)748-8256. **Business Addr:** Board Of Member, Illinois Board of Higher Education, 431 East Adams, Springfield, IL 62701-1404, **Business Phone:** (217)782-2551.

## WASHINGTON, REV. DR. EMERY, SR.

Clergy. **Personal:** Born Feb 27, 1935, Palestine, AR; son of Booker Taliferro and Fannie Mae Norrington; married Alice Marie Bogard; children: 4. **Educ:** Philander Smith Col, BA, philos & theol, 1957; Va Theol Sem, MDiv, 1961; Christ Church Col, Canterbury Eng, grad study, 1988; Ark State Univ, cert. **Career:** Clergy (retired); St Andrew's Episcopal Church, 1961-65; Christ Church Episcopal, 1961-71; Episcopal Diocese Ark, 1971-76; St Michael's Episcopal Church, 1973-76; Emmanuel Episcopal Church, 1976-83; All Saints' Episcopal Church, 1983-01; Episcopal Church Holy Communion, priest; Diocese Ark, educr, priest & chaplain; Eden Theol Sem, field educr. **Orgs:** Pres, Alpha Phi Alpha, 1954-; dep, Gen Conv Dep, 1969, 1970, 1973, 1991, 1994; reg dir mid w, Union Black Episcopalians, 1975-; chair, Racism Comn, 1985-86, 1991-93, Leadership, St Louis, 1988-89, diversity facilitator, 1997-99; develop chair, St Louis Clergy Coalition, 1985; Leadership St Louis Inc, 1988-89; Focus St Louis Inc, Valuing Our Diversity, 1989-; St Louis Black Leadership Roundtable, 1991-; dep gen conv, Cong Allied Community Improv, 2000, vpres, 2000-01, pres, 2002; Faith Beyond Walls, 2000-; Nat Comn Nat Concerns, 2000-; founding mem, Diocesan Comn Dismantling Racism; ecumenical & interreligious officer, Comn Dismantling Racism; Commun Ed bd, Diocese MO. **Honors/Awds:** Clergy of the Year, Diocese Arkansas, 1970; Literacy Promoter, Alpha Kappa Alpha, 1990; John D Buckner Award, 1990; Excellence in Religion, 1992; William M Alexander Service Award, Alpha Phi Alpha, 1999; Unsung Hero Award, Univ Montana / Columbia & Black Expo, 1999; Bishop's Award, 2001; Human Develop Corp of Metro STL, 2001; Hond DD, Eden Theological Seminary, 2002. **Special Achievements:** Designed the "Shield of All Saints", 1987; Author, copyright, 1987; Designed two stained glass windows: Baptism and Communion, 1988-; Guest speaker 80th Celebration of First African American Bishop E T Demby. **Home Addr:** 1267 Mojave Dr, Saint Louis, MO 63132-2148, **Home Phone:** (314)567-5308.

## WASHINGTON, ENRICO ALICENO. See WASHINGTON, RICO.

## WASHINGTON, ERIC MAURICE

Basketball player. **Personal:** Born Mar 23, 1974, Pearl, MS. **Educ:** Univ Ala, attended 1997. **Career:** Basketball player (retired); Idaho Stampede, USA D League; Zhejiang C, China; Jerusalem, Israel; Denver Nuggets, guard, 1997-99; Amyntas Dafnis BC, 1999-2000; Basket Rimini Crabs, 2000-02; Hapoel Jerusalem, 2003-04; Idaho Stampede, 2005-06; Tampereen Pyrinto, 2006-08; Kauhajoen Karhu, 2008-09; KTP-Basket, 2009-10; Nurnberger BC, 2010.

## WASHINGTON, GLADYS J. (GLADYS J CURRY)

Educator, president (organization). **Personal:** Born Mar 4, 1931, Houston, TX; daughter of Eddie Joseph and Anita Joseph. **Educ:** BA, attended 1952; MA, attended 1955; Univ So CA & Tulane Univ, addl study; Univ London, Eng, summer, 1981. **Career:** Educator (retired); So Univ Baton Rouge, Eng instr; So Univ New Orleans, assoc prof Eng; TX So Univ, assoc prof Eng. **Orgs:** Col Lang Asn, S Cent Mod Langs Asn; Nat Coun Teachers Eng; Tex Asn Col Teachers, Women Action; Church Women United; secy, S Cent Lang Asn (Women Color Sect), 1988-89; Mod Lang Asn & Southern Conf Afro-Am Studies, 1988-; pres, Churches Interested Premature Parentage, 1989; artistic dir, Cyrenian Prods (Drama Group) 1985; pres, Arts Collective Houston. **Honors/Awds:** Alpha Kappa Mu Nat Hon Soc; Lambda Iota Tau Lit Hon Soc; has done extensive work with sch & little theatre groups in New Orleans & Houston; pub "View points From Black Amer" 1970; ed "Cult Arts Rev"; A World Made Cunningly, A Closer Look at the Petry's Short Fiction, CLA Jour, 1986; Teacher of the Year, Tex Southern Univ, 1988; auth, A Core Curric Approach to Col Writing, Littleton, MA, Copley Publ Group, 1987. **Special Achievements:** Ann Petry, "The Narrows"; James Weldon Johnson, "Autobiography of an Ex-Coloured Man"; Lorraine Hansberry, "A Raisin in the Sun" in Master plots II: African-American Literature, 1993; Alice Childress, The African-American Encyclopedia, Supplement, 1996; Ann Petry "In Darkness and Confusion" and "Solo on the Drums" in Master plots II, Short Story, Supplement, 1996; "The Chambered Nautilus", Oliver Wendell Holmes, in Master plots II, Poetry Supplement, 1998; Paule Marshall in Critical Survey of Long Fiction, 2nd Revised Edition, 1999. **Home Addr:** 5875 Reed Rd, Houston, TX 77033-2236, **Home Phone:** (713)738-6080.

## WASHINGTON, REV. HENRY L.

Clergy. **Personal:** Born Nov 15, 1922, Earlington, KY; married Azlea; children: Argene, Lamar, Henry & Clyone. **Educ:** Ashland Theol Sem, OT-NT, 1976; Dyke Col, cert realtor, 1978. **Career:** Metro Ins Co, sales rep, 1969-76; Alpha & Omega COGIC, pastor, 1970-85; Mansfield City, OH, councilman, 1983. **Orgs:** Pres, Concerned Black Citizens, 1976-78; Real Estate Mgrs Asn, 1978-85; community, chmn, Nat Asn Advan Colored People, 1982-84; Richland Transit Bd, 1983-84; Affirmative Scholar Del State Univ, 1984-85. **Honors/Awds:** House of Representative, State Ohio, 1979; Mayors Award, City Mansfield Oh, 1982. **Home Addr:** 312 Second Ave, Mansfield, OH 44902-5007, **Home Phone:** (419)522-4988. **Business Addr:** Pastor, Alpha & Omega Church Of God In Christ, 530 Pearl St, Mansfield, OH 44905, **Business Phone:** (419)526-6353.

## WASHINGTON, HERBERT L.

Baseball player, president (organization). **Personal:** married Gisele. **Career:** Baseball player(retired); Syracuse Minority TV Inc, owner; McDonald's Restaurants, owner & oper, currently; HLW Fast Track Inc, founder, pres & owner, currently; Manufacturers & Traders Trust Co, dir, 1996-. **Orgs:** Community Reinvestment Act Comt; bd dir, Youngstown Chamber Com; bd mem, Strong Memorial Hosp; trustee, Rochester Inst Technol; audit & risk comt, M&T Bank Corp; community reinvestment act comt, T Bank Corp. **Business Addr:** President, HLW Fast Track Inc, 4900 Market St, Youngstown, OH 44512, **Business Phone:** (330)783-5659.

## WASHINGTON, HERMAN A., JR.

Educator. **Personal:** Born Jul 12, 1935, Norfolk, VA; son of Herman A and Naomi Hucles; married Daryl E Jordan; children: Keith, Lori, Michael, David, Tunja & Gina. **Educ:** Manhattan Col, BEE, 1958; NY Univ, MBA, 1973. **Career:** Prof (retired), prof emer; Western Elec, engr, 1958-59; G C Dewey CRP, consult, 1959-61; IBM, prog mgr & sys analyst, 1961-69; Systs Discipline Inc, vpres, sr proj mgr, 1969-71; City NY Addiction Servs Agency, dir, 1971-72; La Guardia Community Col, prof, 1972-06, prof emer, 2006-; GMLC Assocs Ltd, founder, 1982-; Model Cities Prog, vpres. **Orgs:** Pres, Brookhaven Lab Community Adv Coun; 100 Black Men Long Island, 1974-; Suny Col Optomerty, Col Coun, 1978-2000; Family & C's Asn, 1988-; bd, United Way Long Island, 1990-96; bd, Cath Charities, 1991-2000; trustee, S County Pub Libr, 1999-2002, pres, PTA; pres, Nat Asn Advan Colored People; pres, Civic Asn Setaukets, 1982-; Stony Brook Univ Community Adv Counc, 1997, chmn, 2005-. **Home Addr:** 261 Durkee Lane, East Patchogue, NY 11772-5820, **Home Phone:** (631)289-5828. **Business Addr:** Professor Emeritus, LaGuardia Community College, 31-10 Thomson Ave, Long Island City, NY 11101, **Business Phone:** (718)482-5499.

## WASHINGTON, ISAIAH, IV

Actor. **Personal:** Born Aug 3, 1963, Houston, TX; married Jenisa Marie; children: Isaiah V, Tyme & Iman. **Educ:** Howard Univ. **Career:** Films: The Color of Love, 1991; Land Where My Fathers Died, 1991; Strictly Business, 1991; Crooklyn, 1994; Alma's Rainbow, 1994; Clockers, 1995; Dead Presidents, 1995; Stonewall, 1995; Girl 6, 1996; Get on the Bus, 1996; Love Jones, 1997; Bulworth, 1998; Rituals, 1998; Mixing Nia, 1998; Out of Sight, 1998; True Crime, 1999; A Texas Funeral, 1999; Kin, 2000; Dancing in September, 2000; Veil, 2000; Romeo Must Die, 2000; Sacred Is the Flesh, 2001; Exit Wounds, 2001; Welcome to Collinwood, 2002; Ghost Ship, 2002; This Girl's Life, 2003; From the Outside Looking In, 2003; Hollywood Homicide, 2003; Trois 3: The Escort, 2004; Dead Birds, 2004; Wild Things 2 (voice), 2004; The Moguls, 2005; The Least of These, 2008; Hurricane Season, 2009; The Under Shepherd, 2012; Blue Caprice, 2012; Doctor Bello, 2013; Go for Sisters, 2013; The Trials of Cate McCall, 2013; Blackbird, 2014. TV series: Law & Order, 1991; "Strapped", 1993; "Lifestories: Families in Crisis", 1994; "Homicide: Life on the Street", 1994; "NYPD Blue", 1995; "New York Undercover", 1996; "Mr & MrsLoving", 1996; "Soul of the Game", 1996; "Living Single", 1996; Joe Torre: Curveballs Along the Way, 1997; "High Incident", 1997; "Ally McBeal", 1998; "Always Outnumbered", 1998; "Soul Food", 2000; "All My Children", 2001; "Touched by an Angel", 2001; "Grey's Anatomy", 2005-14; "Bionic Woman", 2007; "The Cleaner", 2008; "Single Ladies", 2011; "The 100", 2014. **Orgs:** Pan African Film Festival. **Honors/Awds:** Image Award, Nat Asn Advan Colored People, 2006 & 2007; Satellite Award, 2006; Screen Actors Guild Award, 2007. **Business Addr:** Actor, c/o Innovative Artists, 1505 10th St, Santa Monica, CA 90401, **Business Phone:** (310)656-0400.

## WASHINGTON, JACQUELIN EDWARDS

Association executive. **Personal:** Born May 20, 1931, St. Augustine, FL; daughter of Clarence Edwards and Grace Benson Albert; married Kenneth B; children: Saundra, Byron & Kristin. **Educ:** Fisk Univ, BA, 1951; Wayne St Univ, MSW, 1965. **Career:** Detroit Dept Pub Welfare, case worker & supvr, 1957-63; Detroit Pub Schs, sch social worker, 1965-75; New Options Personnel Inc, pres, 1975-80, co-founder; Bendix Corp, Southfield, Mich mgr, human resources, 1980-85; Vixen Motor Co, Pontiac, Mich dir, human resources, 1985-88; Pontiac Area Urban League, Pontiac, Mich pres, chief exec officer; Planned Parenthood SE MI, pres, chief exec officer, 1999; Wayne St Univ, chmn bd gov, 2001-08, gov emer. **Orgs:** Chair, Violence Against Women Comt NOW Detroit Chap, 1970; Nat Asn Soc Workers; St Mich Employ Agency Coun, 1978-80; trustee, Detroit Inst Arts, 1975-81; pres, Detroit Club Nat Asn Negro Bus & Prof Women, 1978-80; vpres, Girl Scouts Metro Detroit, 1979-80; pres, NOW Legal Defense & Educ Fund, 1979-91; bd mem, Mich Abortion Rights Action League, 1990-91; bd mem, St Joseph Mercy Hosp, Pontiac, Mich; exec, Mich Coun Urban League; exec dir, Planned Parenthood SE Mich; exec vpres, ACLU Fund Mich; Chmn, Cent UM Ch Community Develop Corp; treas, planned parenthood Affil Mich; treas, Alpha Kappa Alpha Found Detroit; chmn, Adminr Coun, Cent United Methodist Ch; Founders Soc; co-founding mother & pres, Sojourner Found; vice-chair, Eaton Acad; Womens Comn, City Detroit; Mich Metro Girl Scout Coun; NOW Minority Caucus. **Honors/Awds:** Female Pioneer Award, Women Lawyer Asn, 1975; Spirit of Detroit Award, Detroit Common Coun, 1978; Feminist of the Year Award, Detroit Chap Nat Orgn Women, 1978; Sojourner Truth Award, Nat Asn Negro Bus & Prof Women, 1985; Michigan Womens Hall of Fame; Hunger Advocate of the Year Award, 1990; Loretta Moore Award, 1991; Wonder Woman Community Service Award, 1992. **Special Achievements:** First African American elected to serve as President of the national NOW-Legal Defense and Education Fund; First African American to serve as LDEF's President; First African American woman to serve as executive director of the Planned Parenthood League of Southwest Michigan. **Home Addr:** 1315 Nicolet Pl, Detroit, MI 48207, **Home Phone:** (313)259-0425.

## WASHINGTON, JACQUELINE ANN

Executive. **Personal:** Born May 2, 1968, Highland Park, MI; daughter of William and Cora Johnson; married Kenneth B. **Educ:** Eastern Mich Univ, BS, 1990; Cent Mich Univ, MA, 1995. **Career:** City Ypsilanti, personnel asst, 1990-91; Wellness Plan, human resources rep, 1992-93; Huron Valley Ambulance, human resources coordr, 1993-.

**Orgs:** Treas & vpres, Alpha Kappa Alpha, 1989-; Human Resources Asn Greater Detroit, 1993-; Ann Arbor Area Personnel Asn, 1994-. **Home Addr:** 16510 Bramell St, Detroit, MI 48219, **Home Phone:** (313)541-4561. **Business Addr:** Human Resources Coordinator, Huron Valley Ambulance, 2215 Hogback Rd, Ann Arbor, MI 48105, **Business Phone:** (313)971-4211.

### WASHINGTON, JAMES A.

Newspaper publisher, newspaper editor. **Personal:** Born Apr 26, 1950, Chicago, IL; son of Frank S and Cecelia Burns Jones; married Victoria Meek; children: Patrick James & Elena Cecele. **Educ:** Southern Univ, Baton Rouge, La, BA, 1971; Univ Wis, Madison, WI, MA, 1973. **Career:** Tenn State Univ, Nashville, Tenn, worked develop off; Am Heart Asn, pub rels specialist; Dallas Ballet, pub rels mgr; Focus Commun Group, Dallas, Tex, founder & pres, 1980; Dallas Weekly, Dallas, Tex, owner & publ, 1985-; Ad-Mast Publ Co, Dallas, TX, chmn, currently. **Orgs:** Bd dir, Cotton Bowl; I Have a Dream Found; Sci Pl; Dallas Zool Soc; Family Guid Ctr; Adv coun small bus & agr; Fed Res Bank Dallas; chmn, minority bus adv comt, Dallas Independent Sch Dist; Dallas Together; exec comt, bd, Dallas Chamber Com; Am Heart Asn; Greater Dallas Planning Coun; Jr Achievement; admis comt, United Way, 1983; chmn pub rels comt; Nat Newspaper Publishers Asn. **Honors/Awds:** Danforth Fel, Univ Wis Madison; Woodrow Wilson Fel. **Business Addr:** Publisher, Owner, The Dallas Weekly Newspaper, 3101 Martin Luther King Blvd, Dallas, TX 75215, **Business Phone:** (214)428-8958.

### WASHINGTON, JAMES LEE, SR.

Basketball coach, teacher, mayor. **Personal:** Born Jun 14, 1948, Glendora, MS; son of Jessie James and Ella Wee Billingsley Johnson; married Zenolia Hayes; children: James Jr & Jessica Nicole. **Educ:** Coahoma Community Col, Clarksdale, MS, AA, 1970; Campbellsville Col, Campbellsville, KY, BS, 1972; Delta State Univ, Cleveland, MS, 1986. **Career:** Coahoma Agr HS, head basketball coach; Coahoma Jr Col, head men's basketball coach; Friars Pt NC, mayor; Coahoma Community Col, teacher, athletiv dir, head men basketball coach, currently. **Orgs:** Nat Conf Black Mayors; Nat Conf Coaches. **Honors/Awds:** Outstanding Service Award, N Atlantic Conf Boys Track, 1976; Class A State Championship Coahoma Agricultural HS (basketball), 1984; Coach of the Year, 1984-85; Won St Championship, Jr Col, 1986-87. **Home Addr:** 601 Broad St, Crenshaw, MS 38621, **Home Phone:** (662)383-2310. **Business Addr:** Head Coach, Coahoma Community College, 3240 Friars Point Rd, Clarksdale, MS 38614, **Business Phone:** (662)627-2571.

### WASHINGTON, JESSE

Writer, journalist, editor. **Personal:** Born Jun 3, 1969, New York, NY; son of Judith and McCleary. **Educ:** Yale Univ, BA, 1992. **Career:** Assoc Press, reporter, 1992-93, nat ed, 1993-95; New York, asst bur chief, 1995-96; Vibe Mag, chief & managing ed, 1996; Blaze, founding ed-in-chief; Assoc Press, entertainment ed, natl writer, Race & ethnicity, 2003-; Bks: Romare Bearden; Elizabeth Catlett; st basketball mag Bounce; Novel: Black Will Shoot. **Orgs:** Kappa Alpha Psi Fraternity Inc, 1987-. **Honors/Awds:** Race and ethnicity writer, news coop. **Business Addr:** Entertainment Editor, National Writer, Race & Ethnicity, The Associated Press, 450 W 33rd St, New York, NY 10001, **Business Phone:** (212)621-1500.

### WASHINGTON, JOHN CALVIN, III

Government official, vice president (organization). **Personal:** Born Dec 12, 1950, Coatesville, PA; son of John II and Mildred; children: Nathaniel, John IV & Tamara. **Educ:** Coatesville Sr HS, dipl, 1968; Col Prep. **Career:** S Coatesville Bor, pres, 1980-2013; ArcelorMittal, crane operator, 1969-, crane safety instr, 1995-; Chester County Planning Comt, 2000-; Western Chester County Appeals Bd, vpres, 2009-; Lilly Valley 59, Worshipful Master, 2009-13; Third Masonic Dist, pres, 2011-; United Steel Workers, pres, 2012-. **Orgs:** Elk Mt Vernon Lodge 151, 1975; Nat Asn Advan Colored People, 1975; vol, Va Med Ctr, 1978; Chester County Recreation Coun, 1981; master mason, Lily Valley 59, 1981; dir, S Coatesville Recreation, 1981; FOP, 1981; Hypertension Ctr, 1981; chmn, Grievance Comt Handicapped S Coatesville, 1984; chmn, Property Comn, 1984; Chester County Planning Comn Bd; bd mem, Coatesville Youth Initiative, 2009-. **Home Addr:** 34 1/2 Penn Ave, Coatesville, PA 19320. **Business Addr:** President, Borough of South Coatesville, 136 East Modena Rd Borough Hall, Coatesville, PA 19302, **Business Phone:** (610)384-1700.

### WASHINGTON, REV. JOHNNIE M.

Clergy, secretary (organization), president (organization). **Personal:** Born Sep 23, 1936, Paris, TX; married Naaman C; children: 8. **Educ:** Southern Evang Asn, LVN, 1970, DD, 1974; Roosevelt Univ, BS, 1979; Int Sem, BA, bible theol; Americus Univ, MDiv, ThD. **Career:** McGraw Concern, Munich, Ger, secy financial, 1964-68; Hotel Dieu Hosp, endoscopy supr, 1970; Nat Gastroenterol Tech, cert gi technician, 1973-80; NY Univ, Albany, ungrad nurse, 1977-80; El Paso Nat Asn Adv Colored People, pres, 1978-81, 1986-2004, bishop; Full Gospel Evangelistic Temple, pastor & found, 1985-; Church God Christ, Off Gen Secy, regional dir; Western Dist Christ Holy-Sanctified Churches Am, supt; C H Mason Syst Bible Col, sec, dean, pres; Jurisdictional Secretaries, reg dir, 2001; Church God Christ; Gospel Evangelistic Fel Int Inc, bishop, 2006. **Orgs:** Secy, El Paso Black Caucus, 1977-; Tex Western Jurisdiction, 1998; pres, Nat Asn Advan Colored People; chmn; Black Chamber Com; Atty Gen's Child Support Bd; El Paso Housing Authority Bd; Women's Auxillary El Paso Greater Chamber. **Honors/Awds:** Several Honorary DDiv, Southern Evangelistic Assoc, 1974; Cert of Appreciation, Black Hist Week, 1975; Outstanding Mother of the Year Award, 1976; Outstanding Black Citizen, White Sands Missile Range, 1978; World Church League of Bible Colleges, 1978; Outstanding Black Personality Award, White Sands, 1979; Cert of Appreciation, YMCA, El Paso, 1979; Outstanding Civil Rights Award, Nat Asn Adv Colored People, 6 Region Conf, 1980; cited, Who's Who Among Black America, 1980; Outstanding Woman of the Year, Deltas, 1988; Dr. Martin Luther King Jr. Award, MLK Comt, 1992; Public Service Award Afro-American Cult Asn UTEP, 1992; City of El Paso's Conquistador Award, 1992; inducted, El Paso Women's Hall of Fame, 1992; Grand Marshall, El Paso Black History Parade, 1993, 2000; Community Service Award, U. S. Justice Department, 1994; County of El Paso's Del Norte Award, 1998; Black History Parade Grand Marshall for Church, 2001; Jurisdictional Secretary of the Year Award, Churches of God in Christ. **Special Achievements:** First Woman in El Paso who pastored and built a church; Author of Gods Power For Gods Church, 2004. **Home Addr:** 5102 Danny Dr, El Paso, TX 79924, **Home Phone:** (915)751-3187. **Business Addr:** Pastor, Founder, Full Gospel Evangelistic Temple, 4631 Atlas Ave, El Paso, TX 79904-3313, **Business Phone:** (915)759-9259.

### WASHINGTON, JOSEPH R., JR.

Writer, educator. **Personal:** Born Oct 30, 1930, Iowa City, IA; married Sophia Holland; children: Bryan Reed & David Eugene. **Educ:** Iron Cross Univ, WI, BA, 1952; Univ Wis-Madison, BA, 1952; Andover Newton Theol Sch, BD, 1957; Boston Univ, PhD, 1961. **Career:** Dillard Univ, dean chapel asst prof philos relig, 1961-63; Dickinson Col, relig, chaplain asst prof, 1963-66; Albion Col, relig, dean chapel assoc prof, 1966-69; Beloit Col, relig, dean chapel prof, 1969-70; Univ Va, Relig Studies, fac, prof & chmn, Afro-Amer Studies, 1970-75; Univ Calif, Riverside, Relig Studies, prof, Black Studies, chmn; Univ Pa, Relig Studies, prof, Afro-Am Studies Prog, dir, prof emer relig studies. Books publication: "Black Relig", 1964; "Polit God", 1967; "Black & White Power Subreption", 1969; "Marriage Black & White", 1970; "Black Sects & Cults", 1972, "Anti-Blackness in English Religion 1500-1800", 1985, "Puritan Race Virtue, Vice and Values 1620-1820", 1987, "Black-Race Family Binds and White-Ethnic Kinship Ties", 1988, "Political Conflicts of True and Real Interests", 1988, "Race and Religion in Mid-Nineteenth Century America, 1850-1877", 1989, "Bk1-2: Race and Religion in Early Nineteenth Century America: 1800-1850", 1989, "The First Fugitive Foreign and Domestic Doctor of Divinity", 1990, "The First Afro-American Honorary Degree Recipient", 1990, "The Moral of Molliston Madison Clark", 1990. **Orgs:** Am Soc Chris Ethecis; Am Acad Relig. **Special Achievements:** Publ: "Rulers of Reality and the Ruler Races", 1990; "The First Afro-American Honorary Degree Recipient", 1990; "The Moral of Molliston Madison Clark", 1990; "The First Fugitive Foreign Doctor of Divinity", 1990. **Business Addr:** Professor of Social Ethics Emeritus, University of Pennsylvania, 647 Williams Hall 255 S 36th St, Philadelphia, PA 19104-6305, **Business Phone:** (215)898-6971.

### WASHINGTON, JOSIE B.

Educator. **Personal:** Born Mar 13, 1943, Leona, TX; daughter of Josephine Brooks and J B Brooks; married Eugene J; children: Eugenia J & Giovonna J. **Educ:** AA, BA, MS. **Career:** San Juan Sch Dist, 1968; Sacramento Co Welfare Dept Bur Invest, 1972; State Dept Rehab, 1974; Sacramento City Unified Sch Dist; Sacramento Urban League, site admin, head counr & chief examr, currently. **Orgs:** Sacramento Urban League; Youth Develop Delinq Proj Bd; Neighborhood Counc; adv, Youth Outreach; Vista Neuva Adv Comn; N Area Citizen Better Govt; Nat Rehab Asn; Calif Sch Bd Asn; San Juan Unified Sch Dist; adv comt, Bus Skills Handicapped; bd trustee, clerk, Grant High Sch Dist Bd Educ; Sacramento Area Regional Adult & Voc Educ; coun rep, Sacramento County Sch Bd; Sacramento County Cent Dem Comn; Sen SI Hayakawa Calif Constituency Coun; Comt elect Mayor Tom Bradley Govt Calif; Comt elec tv pres Mondale Pres; Comt Elect Pres Jimmy Carter; Nat Asn Advan Colored People; coun mem, Warren's High Sch Dipl. **Honors/Awds:** Written contributions Resource Directory Black Bus Sacramento area; invited hite House President Jimmy Carter, 1980. **Special Achievements:** The first African American Woman in Northern California to ever be elected a Grant Joint Union School District School. **Home Addr:** 1868 Alice Way, Sacramento, CA 95834-2806. **Business Addr:** Head Counselor, Chief Examiner, Sacramento Urban League, 2420 North St, Sacramento, CA 95816, **Business Phone:** (916)277-6620.

### WASHINGTON, KEITH

Singer. **Personal:** Born Nov 15, 1960, Detroit, MI; married Stephanie Grimes; married Marsha Jenkins. **Career:** Back-up singer; Albums: Make Time for Love, 1991; You Make It Easy, 1993; kw, 1998; Singles: "Are You Still in Love with Me", 1991; "Kissing You", 1991; "Make Time for Love", 1991; "When You Love Somebody", 1992; "Believe That", 1933-94; "Stay in My Corner", 1993-94; "Trippin", 1994; "Bring It On", 1998. TV guest appearance: "Martin", 1992; "Poetic Justice", 1993; "The Meteor Man", 1993; "Good Life", 1979-86, 2001; "General Hospital". **Honors/Awds:** Make Time for Love, nominated, Grammy Award, 1992. **Special Achievements:** Has worked with the Jacksons, George Clinton, Miki Howard, and Stevie Wonder. **Business Addr:** Vocalist, MCA Records, 2220 Colorado Ave Suite 1, Santa Monica, CA 90404, **Business Phone:** (310)865-4500.

### WASHINGTON, KERRY

Actor. **Personal:** Born Jan 31, 1977, Bronx, NY; daughter of Valerie and Earl; married Nnamdi Asomugha; children: Isabelle. **Educ:** George Wash Univ, theater prog, 1998; Michael Howard Studios. **Career:** Films: Magical Make-Over, 1994; Our Song, 2000; 3D, 2000; Save the Last Dance, 2001; Lift, 2001; Take the A Train, 2002; Bad Company, 2002; The United States of Leland, 2003; The Human Stain, 2003; Sin, 2003; Against the Ropes, 2004; She Hate Me, 2004; Ray, 2004; Strip search, 2004; Sexual Life, 2005; Mr & Mrs Smith, 2005; Fantastic Four, 2005; Wait, 2005; Little Man, 2006; The Last King of Scotland, 2006; The Dead Girl, 2006; Fantastic Four: Rise of the Silver Surfer, 2007; I Think I Love My Wife, 2007; Woman in Burka, 2008; Lake view Terrace, 2008; Miracle at St Anna, 2008; Life Is Hot in Cracktown, 2009; A Thousand Words, 2009; The People Speak, 2009; Night Catches Us, 2010; Mother and Child, 2010; For Colored Girls, 2010; The Details, 2011; A Thousand Words, 2012; Django Unchained, 2012; Peeples, 2013. TV Series: "ABC After school Specials", 1994; "Standard Deviants", 1996; "NYPD Blue", 2001; "Law & Order", 2001; "100Centre Street", 2001; "The Guardian", 2002; "Boston Legal", 2005-06; "Psych", 2008; "Black Panther", 2010; "Scandal", 2012-; "Jimmy Kimmel Live!", 2013; L'Oreal Group, Spokesperson, currently. **Honors/Awds:** Teen Choice Award, 2001; Future of Film Award, Urbanworld Film Festival MECCA, 2002; Breakthrough Award, 2004; Image Award, Nat Asn Advan Colored People, 2005, 2013 & 2014; Best Outstanding actress In a Motion Picture awd, 2005; Razzie Award, 2007; Black Reel Award, 2011, 2013; Outstanding Ensemble For Colored Girls, Black Reel Awards, 2011; BET Award, 2013; President's Award, Nat Asn Advan Colored People, 2013; TV Guide Award, 2013. **Business Addr:** Actress, c/o Abrams Artists Agency, 9200 Sunset Blvd Suite 1130, Hollywood, CA 90069, **Business Phone:** (310)859-0178.

### WASHINGTON, LEANNA M.

Government official. **Personal:** Born Jul 28, 1945, Philadelphia, PA; daughter of LeAnna M Brown; children: Tony, Edward & Tracey. **Educ:** Lincoln Univ, MHS, 1989. **Career:** Philadelphia Parking Authority Employee Assistance Prog, mgr; Pa State rep, 1993-2005; Pa state senate dist 4, sen, 2005-; Pa Senate, spec election, 2005; Commonwealth Pa Senate, sen, 2005-14. **Orgs:** Bd trustee, Lincoln Univ, 2004-05; Nat Org Women Legislators; bd mem, Pa Hospice Network; Women Legislator's Lobby; Teen shop Inc; exec comt, Nat Black Caucus, State Legislators; Nat Asn Advan Colored People; Alpha Kappa Alpha Sorority; Flemming FelsLeadership Inst; NW Action Polit Alliance; Women Govt; Lincoln Univ Alumni Asn; Pi Gamma Mu, Alpha lambda Chp; Wadsworth Area Bus Asn; Women Transition; Gaudenzia Eastern Region Adv Bd; chair, Pa Legis Black Caucus; JFK Sch Govt, Harvard Univ; Philadelphia Gas Works Adv Comt; Greater Philadelphia, Nat Asn Advan Colored People; bd fel col Lib arts, Templ Univ; bd, Pa Higher Educ Assistance Agency, 2009-10. **Business Addr:** State Senator, Pennsylvania House of Representatives, 182 Main Capitol Bldg, Harrisburg, PA 17120, **Business Phone:** (717)787-1427.

### WASHINGTON, LEONARD, JR.

Law enforcement officer. **Personal:** Born Nov 3, 1945, Pittsburgh, PA; son of Leonard Sr and Anniebelle; married Celestine; children: Leonard III, Maurice & Alonzo. **Educ:** Mercyhurst Col, Erie, PA, AA, 1978; Calif Univ Pa, BA, 1980. **Career:** N Am Rockwell, draftsman, 1968-73; PA State Police, trooper, 1973-78, corporal, 1978-80, sgt, 1980-82, lt, 1982-88, capt, 1988-98, maj, 1998, Bur Emergency & Spec Opers, dir, 2001. **Orgs:** Nat Asn Advan Colored People, 1987-; PA Chiefs Police Asn, 1988-; Nat Orgn Black Law Enforcement Exec, 1998-. **Home Addr:** 2138 Coral Point Dr, Cape Coral, FL 33990, **Home Phone:** (239)242-5252. **Business Addr:** Member, NOBLE, 4609-f pinecrest office pk dr, Alexandria, VA 22312-1442, **Business Phone:** (703)658-1529.

### WASHINGTON, LEROY

Teacher, educator, artist. **Personal:** Born May 1, 1925, Greenville, FL; married Edith; children: 4. **Educ:** FL A&M Univ, BA, 1950; Univ Miami, attended 1972. **Career:** Artist, educator (retired); Charlotte Jr Col, drama coach; Dade Pub Sch Miami, drama coach; Booker T Wash High Sch, speech & drama instr; Miami Sr High Sch; Miami Jackson Sr High Sch, drama coach & teacher; SW Miami Sr High Sch; sabbatical; Miami Northwestern Sr High Sch, teacher, 1976-83. **Orgs:** Pres, NC High Sch Drama Asn; Fla State Interscholastic Speech & Drama Asn; Dade County Speech Teacher Asn; UTD Prof Sect; Screen Actors Guild; Nat TV & Radio Broadcasters Union; Youth Emphasis Club Sponsor; NW Br YMCA; Model Cities; dir, vpres, CL Williams Memorial Scholar Found Inc; sponsor, Creative Dance & Interpretative Reading Training Classes; Comm Sch Vol Work Congregational Church Open Door. **Honors/Awds:** Man of the Year, 1975; Zeta Phi Beta Sorority; Miami Chap; Outstanding Citizen & Civic Leader, Charles L Williams Memorial Scholar Found; TV Personality of the Month, BTW Alumni Asn; coached drama group Booker T Washington HS; invited as one of top eight drama groups throughout city to perform at Univ of IN; 2nd place Rowe Peterson's annual drama photo contest; 2nd place Nat Thespian Soc annual printed prog contest. **Home Addr:** 1754 NW 56th St, Miami, FL 33142-3048, **Home Phone:** (305)836-2510.

### WASHINGTON, LESTER RENEZ

Government official. **Personal:** Born Feb 3, 1954, Kansas City, KS; son of Willie and Mable Watson; married Roberta Martin; children: Jennifer, Lesley, Lester Jr, Travis & Corey; married Luberta Brown. **Educ:** Univ Iowa, BBA, 1977; Univ Mo, attended 1980; Park Col, MPA, 1999. **Career:** Government official (retired); Lunam Corp, Kans City, Mo, mgr, 1979-81; Southland Corp, Kans City, Mo, dist mgr, 1981-85; Kans City, Mo, mgr MBE/WBE prog, 1985-95, prin asst dir Neighborhood Community Serv, 1996-2002, dir, Neighborhood Community Serv, 2002-09. Book: Bold Witness, 1989. **Orgs:** Nat Asn Advan Colored People, 1980-; Ad Hoc Group Against Crime, 1986-; Prince Hall Mason Lodge No 77; White House Deleg Minority Bus, 1989-; bd dir, Minority Network Asn, 1990-; bd dir, E Attucks Community Housing, 1990-. **Home Addr:** 1707 E 97th Ter, Kansas City, MO 64131-3226, **Home Phone:** (816)941-8408. **Business Addr:** MO.

### WASHINGTON, DR. LINDA PHAIRE

Scientist. **Personal:** Born Aug 11, 1948, New York, NY; married Joey; children: Kamau & Imani. **Educ:** Boston Univ, BS, biol, 1970; Mt Sinai Med Ctr, City Univ NY, PhD, 1975. **Career:** Laguardia Col, lectr, 1973-75; Rockefeller Univ, res fel, 1975-77; City Univ, asst prof, 1976-77; Howard Univ Col Med, asst prof, 1977-79; Tuskegee Inst, Dept Biol, prof, 1981-; Cell Cult Sci Ctr, dir, 1981-, prof immunol & cell biol, Nat Sci Res Div, dir, 1984-; Int Progs Tuskegee Inst Liberia Linkage, consult, 1982-83; Ctr Adv Training Cell & Molecular Biol, adv res training, 1983; Argonne Nat Lab, bioscientist & prog admin, Div Educ Prog, sr prog leader, 1995-. **Orgs:** Gen Res Support Rev Comt Sub comt Nat Inst Health DRR, 1983-87; Gen Res Support Rev Comt, NIH DRR, 1983-87; proposal reviewer, Nat Sci Found, 1985; panel reviewer, NIH DRR, 1986-87. **Home Addr:** 1001 Guy St, Tuskegee, AL 36083. **Business Addr:** Senior Program Leader, Argonne National Laboratory, 9700 S Cass Ave DEP 223, Argonne, IL 36088, **Business Phone:** (630)252-2000.

### WASHINGTON, LIONEL

Football executive, football player, football coach. **Personal:** Born Oct 21, 1960, New Orleans, LA; son of Deron; married Karen; children: Deron, Lakaia & Jordan. **Educ:** Tulane Univ, sports admin. **Career:** Football player (retired), football coach; St Louis Cardinals, left cornerback, 1983-84, 1986, defensive back, 1985; Los Angeles Raiders, left cornerback, 1987-88, right cornerback, 1989-94; Denver Broncos, right cornerback, 1995-96; Oakland Raiders, cornerback, 1997, defensive backs coach, 2009-10; Green Bay Packers, asst defensive backs coach, 1999-2004, defensive nickel package & cornerbacks coach, 2005-08; Va Destroyers, defensive backs coach, 2010; United Football League's Va Destroyers, defensive backs coach, 2011; Tulane Green Wave, co-defensive coordr, 2012-. **Honors/Awds:** Hall of Fame Bowl, 1980; Louisiana Sports Hall of Fame, 2014; Greater New Orleans Sports Hall of Fame. **Business Addr:** Co-Defensive Coordinator, Tulane Green Wave, James W Wilson Jr Ctr, New Orleans, LA 70118, **Business Phone:** (504)865-5000.

## WASHINGTON, LORENZA BENARD, JR.

Executive. **Personal:** Born Oct 16, 1972, Marshall, TX; son of Benard Sr and Lorenza. **Educ:** Univ N Tex, BA, 1996. **Career:** Consol Freightways, sales exec; McLane Foodservice Distrib, staff, currently. **Orgs:** Big Bros Big Sisters, 1991-94. **Honors/Awds:** Most Valuable Employee, Consolidated Freightways, 1997. **Home Addr:** 4127 Polaris Dr Suite 2021, Irving, TX 75038. **Business Addr:** Sales Executive, Consolidated Freightways, 8505 N Freeport Pkwy Suite 500, Irving, TX 75063, **Business Phone:** (972)929-1202.

## WASHINGTON, MALIVAI

Tennis player, president (organization). **Personal:** Born Jun 20, 1969, Glen Cove, NY; son of William and Christine; married Jennifer; children: Mashona, Mashiska & Michaela. **Educ:** Univ Mich, attended 1989; Univ N Fla, BBA, finance, 2010. **Career:** Professional tennis player (retired), president; tennis player, 1989-99; Pub Speaker, 1990-; US Davis Cup Team, 1993-94, 1996-97; US Olympic Team, 1996; Wash Properties LLC, owner & broker, currently; Diamond Life Realty LLC, founder & pres, 2000-; Voice Over Actor, 2012-13. **Orgs:** Founder, MaliVai Wash Youth Found, 1994-. **Business Addr:** Founder, President, MaliVai Washington Kids Foundation, 1096 W 6th St, Jacksonville, FL 32209, **Business Phone:** (904)359-5437.

## WASHINGTON, MARIAN E.

Basketball coach. **Personal:** Born Aug 26, 1946, West Chester, PA; children: Josie. **Educ:** W Chester State Col, BA, physics, 1970; Univ Kans, MS, 1976. **Career:** Basketball coach (retired); Martin Luther King Jr HS, teacher; Univ Kan, grad asst health phys educ & recreation, 1972; Univ of Kans, athletics dir, 1974-79; Women's Basketball Team, head coach, 1974-2004; USA Nat Team, asst coach, 1996. **Orgs:** Vpres, Black Coaches Asn, 1991, pres, 1993-94; dir, Women's Basketball Coaches Asn. **Special Achievements:** First African American woman to play on a United States national team; First African American woman to coach a United States international team.

## WASHINGTON, MARVIN ANDREW

Football player. **Personal:** Born Oct 22, 1965, Denver, CO; children: Evan. **Educ:** Univ Idaho, grad. **Career:** Football player (retired); New York Jets, defensive end & right defensive end & left defensive end & left defensive tackle, 1989-96; San Francisco 49ers, defensive end, 1997, 1999; Denver Broncos, 1998. **Honors/Awds:** Champion, Super Bowl XXXIII. **Special Achievements:** Film: Super Bowl XXXIII, 1999. TV Series: "The NFL on NBC", 1990-95; "ESPN's Sunday Night Football", 1992-94; "NFL Monday Night Football", 1992.

## WASHINGTON, MARY PARKS

Teacher, artist, educator. **Personal:** Born Jul 20, 1924, Atlanta, GA; daughter of Walter Parks; married Samuel; children: Eric (deceased) & Jan. **Educ:** Spelman Col, BA, 1946; Univ Mex, attended 1947; San Jose State Univ, San Jose, CA, MA, fine arts, 1978, painting grad; Black Mountain Col Nc, Summer Art Inst. **Career:** Howard Univ, 1948-51; Dartmouth Jr HS, teacher, 1961-80; San Jose Union Sch Dist, teacher, 1988 (reired); David T Howard High Sch, teacher. **Orgs:** Bd mem, Nat Asn Advan Colored People; chmn, 1958-; San Jose Art League, 1960, 1977; chmn, Human Rels, Union Sch Dist Teachers Asn, 1968-72; bd mem, Info Referral Santa Clara Co, 1974-75; Calif Teachers Asn; Nat Cong Artists; Nat Art Asn; coun mem, Calif Art Educ Asn; coun dir, Tutoring Prog Minority Stud; charter mem, San Jose Chap AKA Sorority; San Jose Chap Jack & Jill; Collector's Choice chmn fund raising, San Jose Art League; Am Cancer Soc; State Calif's Art Curric Criteria Comt; adv comt, Links, Fine Arts Mus San Francisco; Links Inc, Arts Comt, chair; Nat Conf Artist; San Jose Art League; Alpha Kappa Alpha. **Honors/Awds:** California Art Educator Association, 1995; Rosenwald Foundation Scholarship, Black Mountain College Summer Art Institute, 1946; Community Excellence Award Virginia Kiah; National Conference of Artists Award; Distinguished Art Educator of the Year, City of San Jose; Artist of the Year, Links Inc. **Special Achievements:** Publication: Black Artist on Art Vol 1; A Soul A Mirror by Sarah Webster Fabia; The Spelman Story; Black Soul, Ebony Mag; num one woman shows; Johnson Publishes Art Col; Author of numerous articles. **Home Addr:** 746 Emory Ave, Campbell, CA 95008-5348, **Home Phone:** (408)378-6701.

## WASHINGTON, DR. MICHAEL HARLAN

Educator. **Personal:** Born Sep 25, 1950, Cincinnati, OH; son of Herbert William and Willa Alice; children: Michael Jr, Milo Robeson & Chi'Kah Masaru. **Educ:** Raymond Walters Col, AA, 1971; Univ Cincinnati, BS, 1973, MEd, 1974, Educ Founds Dept, EdD, 1984; Am Univ, Cairo, Egypt, Arab hist, cult, polit & relig, 1991. **Career:** Fleischmanns Boy's Clubs Greater Cincinnati, Social educ dir, 1972-74; Univ Cincinnati, learning skills specialist, 1974-79; Northern Ky Univ, learning skills specialist, 1979-80, assoc prof hist, 1980-95, Afro-Am Studies prog, dir, 1986-, full prof hist, 1995-; Malone & Fulbright, fel; Tokyo Christian Women's Univ, Fulbright lectr; Kyoritsu Women's Univ, Tokyo, Japan, lectr, 2001. **Orgs:** Northern Ky Univ, Consults Off In-Serv Educ, 1980; Univ Cincinnati, United Christian Miniseries & Black Campus Ministries, 1980-81; Univ Cincinnati, Med Ctr, 1980; Northern Ky Univ, Div Continuing Educ, 1980-81; Ky Asn Teachers Hist, 1981; Inservice Teacher Training, SW Bus Col, 1982; Black Hist Arch Community, 1985-; Phi Alpha Theta, 1985-; Minority Students Retention Scholar, Northern Ky Univ, founder, 1986; Afro-Am Studies Prog, Northern Ky Univ, founder, 1986; Greater Cincinnati World Affairs Coun. **Home Addr:** 11043 Wood Ave, Blue Ash, OH 45242-1965, **Home Phone:** (513)469-1815. **Business Addr:** Professor of History, Director, Afro American Studies Program, Northern Kentucky University, 415 Landrum Acad Ctr, Highland Heights, KY 41099, **Business Phone:** (859)572-6483.

## WASHINGTON, MICKEY LIN

Lawyer, football player. **Personal:** Born Jul 8, 1968, Galveston, TX. **Educ:** Tex A&M Univ, BS, sociol, 1990. **Career:** Football player (retired), lawyer; New Eng Patriots, defensive back, 1990-91; Wash Redskins, 1992; Buffalo Bills, left corner back, 1993-94; Jackson ville Jaguars, right corner back, 1995-96; New Orleans Saints, defensive back, 1997; Ft Bend Dist Attorneys Off, clerk; Taylor & Ernster Law Firm, union rep; PC & Assoc, atty, 2002; Southern Dist Fed Ct, lawyer; Miss Cts, Fifth Circuit, lawyer; Tex State Ct, lawyer; VW Sports & Entertainment, LLC, dir; Wash Law Firm, Pllc, dir, Wash & Ernster LLC, atty, currently. **Orgs:** Union rep, Nat Football Players Asn; State Bar Col; Nat Employ Lawyers Asn; Wash & Assocs, Pllc; Achievement 4 All, L.L.C. **Honors/Awds:** Hold Several Honors Including: Unsung Hero, All American Honorable Mention, Texas A&M Team Captain, First Team All Southwest Conference and Texas A&M All Decade Team. Texas Rising Stars, 2007. **Business Addr:** Attorney, Director, Washington & Ernster PLLC, Great SW Bldg, Houston, TX 77002, **Business Phone:** (713)821-9433.

## WASHINGTON, NANCY ANN

Certified public accountant, auditor. **Personal:** Born Nov 30, 1938, Kansas City, KS; daughter of E B Owens and Essie Mae Williams Owens; children: Georgetta Grigsby, Bertram Grigsby & Charles III. **Educ:** KCK Community Col, Kans City, KS, AA, 1977; St Mary Col, BSBA, 1979; Univ Mo, Kans City, KS, MBA, 1989. **Career:** Internal Revenue Serv, Kans City, Mo, agt, 1979-80; Wash Acct Serv, Kans City, Kans, owner, 1980-83; Kans Corp Comt, Topeka, Kans, sr utility regulatory auditor, 1983-88; Bd Pub Utilities, Kans City, Kans, internal auditor, 1988-. **Orgs:** League Women Voters, 1985-, AICPA, 1987-, KS Cert Pub Accountants Soc, 1988-, Inst Internal Auditors, 1988-; treas, Am Asn Black Energy; owner, Untouchable Concepts Beauty Salon, Kans City, KS. **Honors/Awds:** Candlelight Service Award, KCK Community Col, 1976. **Home Addr:** 809 N 57th St, Kansas City, KS 66102, **Home Phone:** (913)287-4474. **Business Addr:** Internal Auditor, Board of Public Utilities, 700 Minn Ave, Kansas City, KS 66101, **Business Phone:** (913)573-9123.

## WASHINGTON, PATRICE CLARKE

Airplane pilot. **Personal:** Born Sep 11, 1961, Nassau; daughter of Peggy Ann and Nathaniel Clarke; married Ray; children: 2. **Educ:** Fla's Embry-Riddle Aeronaut Univ, BS, aeronaut sci, 1982. **Career:** Trans Island Airways, pilot, 1982-84; UPS Airlines, flight engr, 1988-90, first officer, 1990-94, captain, 1994-98. **Orgs:** Organization of Black Airline Pilots. **Honors/Awds:** Turner Broadcasting Trumpet Award. **Special Achievements:** First African American female to obtain rank of captain for a major airline; First female to fly for Trans Island Airways and Bahamasair; First African American female pilot UPS. **Business Addr:** Captain, United Parcel Service, 1400 N Hurstbourne Pkwy, Louisville, KY 40223, **Business Phone:** (502)327-7639.

## WASHINGTON, REGYNALD G.

Executive. **Personal:** Born Jan 1, 1954?, Marathon, FL. **Educ:** Miami Dade Community Col, AB, 1960; Fla Int Univ, BS, int hotel & restaurant admin, 1970; Grad, Exec Tech Chicago; Educ Inst Am Hotel & Motel Asn, cert food & beverage exec; Educ Found Nat Restaurant Asn, cert foodservice mgt prof. **Career:** Magic Pan Restaurant, gen mgr; Air Terminal Servs Inc, Wash Nat Airport, gen mgr food & beverage; Concessions Int Inc, corp sr vpres, corp exec vpres, W coast reg vpres & gen mgr; Epcot, gen mgr food; Walt Disney World Co, dir resort food & beverage opers, gen mgr food & beverage; Disney Regional Entertainment, vpres & gen mgr, 2004. **Orgs:** Educ Inst Am Hotel & Motel Asn; bd trustees, Educ Found Nat Restaurant Asn; Ga Hospitality & Travel Asn; adv bd mem, sch hotel & restaurant admin, Ga State Univ; adv bd mem, Sch Hospitality Mgt, Univ Del; past pres, Ga Restaurant Asn; past bd dir, Atlanta Symphony Orchestra; mem bd dir, Fla Restaurant Asn; chmn, Fla Restaurant & Lodging Asn; chmn, Restaurant & Hospitality Asn Ind; bd trustee, Nat Restaurant Asn, mem bd dir, treas, 2001-02, vchmn bd, 2001-02, chmn bd, 2003-. **Honors/Awds:** Industry Leader of the Year Award, Ga Hospitality & Travel Asn, 1994; Top-50 Tastemaker, 1999. **Special Achievements:** Keynote Speaker for the MultiCultural Foodservice & Hospitality Alliance and the Southern California Restaurant Association conference August 27, 2001 in Los Angeles, CA; Moderated Salute to Excellence Forum for the Educational Foundation of the National Restaurant Association, May 2001; Delivered Commencement address for the Chattanooga State Community College, May 12, 2001, Chattanooga, TN; Speaker for the Educational Foundation of the National Restaurant Association during the Chain Operators Exchange (COEX) conference February 29, 2000 in Las Vegas, NV; Delivered keynote address for the National Restaurant Association Education Foundation's Salute to Excellence for May, 1992, May, 1995 and May 1998; Named one of The NRN 50 The New Taste Makers, Nation's Restaurant News, Vol. 33, No. 4, January 1999; Lifetime Penn State Conti Professor for the School of Hospitality Management for Pennsylvania State University, 1999. **Business Addr:** Vice President, General Manager, Disney Regional Entertainment, 500 S Buena Vista St, Burbank, CA 91521-8392, **Business Phone:** (818)526-4462.

## WASHINGTON, RICO (ENRICO ALICENO WASHINGTON)

Baseball player. **Personal:** Born May 30, 1978, Milledgeville, GA. **Career:** Baseball player (retired); Pittsburgh Pirates, 1999-2002; San Diego Padres, 2002-04; Tampa Bay DevilRays, 2004; Minor League, Montgomery Biscuits, 2005; Springfield Cardinals, 2006; Minor League, Memphis Redbirds, 2006-09; St. Louis Cardinals, 2008; Uni-Pres 7-Eleven Lions, Chinese Prof Baseball League, 2009-10; Kans City T-Bones, 2010-11. **Business Addr:** Professional Baseball Player, Uni-Pres 7-Eleven Lions, 301 Chung Cheng Rd, Yungkang710.

## WASHINGTON, ROBERT BENJAMIN, JR.

Lawyer. **Personal:** Born Oct 11, 1942, Blakely, GA; married Nola Wallette, Dec 27, 1969; children: Todd & Kyle W. **Educ:** St Peters Col, BA, econ & polit sci, 1967; Howard Law Sch, JD, 1970; Harvard Univ Law Sch, LLM, 1972. **Career:** Howard Law Sch, cobb fel, 1969, teaching fels, 1970-72; US Senate Com Dist Columbia, atty, 1971-72; Howard Univ Law Sch, assoc prof law & dir commun skills, 1972-73; Christopher Columbus Col Law, lectr, 1972-73; US House Reps Com Dist Columbia, atty, 1973-75; George Washington Univ Law Ctr, lectr, 1975, assoc prof law, 1978; Danzansky, Dickey, Tydings, Quint & Gordon, sr partner, 1975-81; Georgetown Law Ctr, assoc prof, 1978-82; Finley, Kumble, Wagner, sr partner & mem nat mgt comt, 1981-87, managing partner, Wash off, 1986-88; Finley, Kumble, Wagner, Heine, Underberg, Manley, Myerson & Casey, Wash, DC, co-managing partner, 1986-88; Laxalt, Wash, Perito & Dubuc, managing partner, 1988-91; Wash & Christian, managing partner, 1997-99; Caribbean Cage LLC, chmn & chief exec officer, 2004-; Las Vegas Gaming Inc, dir, 2006-07; Leeward Islands Lottery Holding Co Inc, chmn & chief exec officer; Charlotte Bobcats & NBA Basketball Team, owner; Wash Strategic Consult Group Inc, chmn & chief exec officer, currently. **Orgs:** Bd mem, Nat Bank Wash, 1981-89; Dist Columbia Bar Asn; Am Bar Asn; Nat Bar Asn; Wash Bar Asn; Fed Bar Asn; Am Judicature Soc; Supreme Ct Hist Soc; Phi Alpha Delta Legal Fraternity; bd mem, Medlantic Healthcare Group; bd mem, Medlantic Mgt Corp; bd mem, Healthcare Partners; bd mem, AVW Electronic Systs Inc; bd mem, Home Group (Am Base); bd trustee, Corcoran Gallery Art; bd mem, Nat Symphony Orchestra Asn; Metrop AME Church; Pres's Export Coun. **Home Addr:** 4555 Dexter St NW, Washington, DC 20007-1116, **Home Phone:** (202)338-0535. **Business Addr:** Chairman, Chief Executive Officer, Caribbean Cage LLC, 1-9-7 Estate Peterborg, Saint Thomas, VI 00918, **Business Phone:** (340)777-9023.

## WASHINGTON, ROBERTA

Executive. **Educ:** Howard Univ, Wash, DC, BA, archit; Columbia Univ, NY, MS, archit. **Career:** New York, health facil planner; Mozambique, head, prov design off, 1977-81; Maputo Prov Off Pub Works, dir archit studio, 1977-81; Mason DeSilva Architects, health facil planner, 1982-83; Roberta Wash Architects PC, prin, owner & proj dir, 1983-; Univ sch archit, juror & lectr; NYC Landmarks Perservation Comn, Comnr, 2007-. **Orgs:** Bd mem, fel Am Inst Architects, 1986-; bd mem, Nat Org Minority Architects, 1989-, pres; bd mem, Former Land Use & Housing Comt Chairperson, 1991-2002; pres, NY State Bd Archit, 1994-2004; Am Inst Architects Col Fellows, 2006; bd mem, Ctr Archit Found, 2007-, pres; advisor, Beverly Willis Found, 2011-; james e. silcott endowed chair, Howard Univ Sch Archit & Design, 2011; co-chair, housing comt chairperson, Cent Harlem's Community Planning Bd; fel Am Inst Architects Col; LEED Accredited Prof; Nat Coun Archit Regist Bds. **Business Addr:** Principal, Owner, Roberta Washington Architects PC, 68 E 131st St Suite 605, New York, NY 10037, **Business Phone:** (212)281-5700.

## WASHINGTON, ROBIN

Journalist, editor. **Personal:** Born Dec 29, 1956, Chicago, IL; son of Atlee David and Jean Birkenstein; married Lynn Goldberg; children: Erin Jenica. **Educ:** Ill Inst Tech, engineering sci, attended 1977. **Career:** Loyola Univ Med Ctr, ed, 1977-78; Save Buying Guide, ed, 1978-83; Minn Engineer, founder, publ, 1983-86; Lake County, MN, News-Chronicle, publ, ed, 1986-87; WGBH-TV, producer, reporter, 1987-89; BET News, corresp, 1989-92; Northeastern Univ, adj prof, 1991; Fel Reconciliation, commun dir, 1991-92; Bay State Banner, managing ed, 1993-96; Emerson Col, adj prof, 1994; Wombat Media, pres, 1996-; Nat Pub Radio, commentator & guest; Roads Scholar & Sq Deal, columnist; Boston Herald, sports copy ed, 1996-98, columnist, 1996-04; Duluth News Tribune, ed page ed, 2004-, news dir, currently. **Orgs:** Bd mem, Two Harbors, Minn Chamber Com, 1986; pres, Boston Asn Black Journalists, 1990, 1999-; bd mem, Univ Mass, Boston, Summer Jour Prog, 1991-; Nat Endowment Arts, Radio Grants panelist, 1994; chair, co-founder, Alliance Black Jews, 1995; parliamentarian, exec bd mem, Nat Asn Black Journalists NABJ, 1997-2001; bd mem, New Eng Press Asn, 1997-99. **Honors/Awds:** Freedom of Info Award, Minn Newspaper Asn, Lake County News-Chronicle, 1986; fel, WGBH Educ Found, Sci Broadcast Journalism, 1987; Gold Award, NY Radio Festival, 1988; Grand Award, NY Radio Festival, 1988; NABJ Radio News Award, NPR Crossroads, 1988; New Eng Emmy for Vt: The Whitest State in the Union, WGBH_TV, 1989; Asniated Church Press Most Improved Publ Award, Fel mag, 1992; Silver Gavel Award, Am Bar Asn, 1996. **Special Achievements:** The Boston Globe, Los Angeles Times, op-ed contributor, 1995; Black & Jewish Like Jesus & Me, "Multi-America", essayist, Ishmael Reed, Viking, 1997. **Home Addr:** 293 Turnpike Rd, Westborough, MA 01581, **Home Phone:** (508)366-9862. **Business Addr:** Editorial Page Editor, Duluth News Tribune, 424 W 1st St, Duluth, MN 55802, **Business Phone:** (218)723-5301.

## WASHINGTON, ROBIN L.

Vice president (organization), chief financial officer, auditor. **Personal:** married Carl; children: Ennis & Kendyl. **Educ:** Univ Mich, BA; Pepperdine Univ, MBA. **Career:** Deloitte & Touche, sr auditor; Fed Res Bank of Chicago, acct analyst; Tandem Comput, dir finance; PeopleSoft, sr vpres & corp controller, 1996-2005; Hyperion Solutions, chief financial officer, 2006-07; Gilead Sci Inc, sr vpres & chief financial officer, 2008-. **Orgs:** Bd dir, Tektronix Inc, Danaher; bd dir, MIPS Technologies Inc (Imagination); bd dir, Honeywell Int; bd dir, Salesforce.com; bd dir, San Jose C Discovery Mus; bd visitor, Graziadio Sch bus & mgt, Pepperdine Univ; Exec Leadership Coun, several forums Chief Financial Officers, forum Women Execs & Entrepreneurs, & supporting mem, Blind Babies Found. **Honors/Awds:** "Black Enterprise", 75 Most Powerful Women in Business, 2010. **Home Addr:** , CA. **Business Addr:** Senior Vice President and Chief Financial Officer, 333 Lakeside Dr, Foster City, CA 94404, **Business Phone:** (650)574-3000.

## WASHINGTON, DR. ROMANUEL, JR.

Administrator. **Personal:** Born Sep 17, 1926; married Bertha Bibbs. **Career:** Chiropractic Arts & Sci Clin, owner, currently. **Home Addr:** 3300 Crawford St, Houston, TX 77004, **Home Phone:** (713)522-3878. **Business Addr:** Owner, Chiropractic Arts & Sci Clin, 3300 Crawford St, Houston, TX 77004-2927, **Business Phone:** (713)522-3878.

## WASHINGTON, DR. ROOSEVELT, JR.

Educator, naval officer. **Personal:** Born Feb 8, 1932, Swan Lake, MS; children: LuWanna, Ronald, Kenneth & Pamela. **Educ:** Roosevelt Univ, BA, 1960, MA, 1962; Marquette Univ, attended; Chicago State Univ; DePaul Univ, adv study; Northern Ill Univ, EdD, bus & mgt,

1971. **Career:** Educator (retired); Ctr St Sch & Fulton Jr HS, teacher & counr, 1960-61; Manley Upper Grade Ctr, teacher & dept chmn, 1961-68; McDade Elem Sch, asst prin, 1968-69; Noll Univ, 1969-71; Marquette Univ, asst prof, 1971-74; Harambee Independent Comn Sch Inc, chief admin, 1973-74; Univ N Tex, Denton Tex, Dept Teacher Educ & Admin, prof, 1974-96. **Orgs:** Nat Asn Sec Sch Prins; Am Educ Res Asn; Asn Supv & Curric Devel; Phi Delta Kappa; Am Asn Sch Admin; Nat Orgn Legal Probs Educ. **Special Achievements:** Published numerous articles. **Home Addr:** 2125 Woodbrook St, Denton, TX 76205, **Home Phone:** (940)382-2873.

### WASHINGTON, ROSE WILBURN

Executive director, association executive. **Personal:** Born Sep 4, 1940, Daphne, AL; daughter of Emory William and Emma L Chancley; married Regis G McDonald; children: Gerald, Carlos, Werhner Von & Tanya Monica. **Educ:** State Univ, Oneonta, BS, 1975; Marywood Col, MS Ed, 1979; City Col, NY, attended 1988. **Career:** Charles Loring Brace Youth Camp, dir, 1978-80; Tryon Sch Boys, dir, 1980-83; Spofford Juv Detention Ctr, NYC, exec dir, 1983-85; Dept Juv Justice, NYC, asst comnr, 1985-90, comnr, 1990-94; Dallas Co Juv Dept, dir & chief probation officer, 1994-95; Berkshire Farm Ctr & Serv Youth, chief exec officies, 2005, exec dir emer; Berkshire Farm Jr/Sr High Sch, pres. **Orgs:** Presidential appointee, Nat Juv Justice Coord Coun, 1994-; bd gov, Am Correctional Asn; chair, Juv Detention Comm; auditor, Comn Accreditation; Nat Asn Juv Correctional Agencies; New York Detention Asn; Nat Black Child Develop Inst; Westchester Co Black Women's Polit Caucus. **Honors/Awds:** Carter G Woodson Acad, Leadership & Support, 1988; Nelson Rohlilahla Mandela, NY Asn Black Psychologists, 1993; Outstanding Leadership, Det Juv Justice, New York, 1994; Devotion & Leadership, Spofford Juv Ctr, 1994; Kellogg's Child Development Award, World C Award. **Special Achievements:** Black Identity, Where We've Been Where We Are, 1981; Presented paper at Thistle town Regional Cte, Ontario, Canada, "Case management as a Crisis Intervention In a Secure Setting", 1987; presented paper at the Chapel Hill Workshop, "Accountability: Is There Light at the End of Tunnel?", 1989; featured in PBS Documentary, "In Search of Excellence", 1989; Kennedy Sch Govt Case Study, "Taking Charge: Rose Wash & Spofford Juvenile Detention Ctr", Harvard Univ, 1989. **Business Addr:** Executive Director Emeritus, Berkshire Farm Center & Services for Youth, 13640 Rte 22, Canaan, NY 12029-3500, **Business Phone:** (518)781-4567.

### WASHINGTON, RUDY

Association executive, basketball coach. **Personal:** Born Jul 14, 1951, Los Angeles, CA; married Gail Terry; children: Crystal Wilks, Corey Wilks, Raymond & Rudy Jr. **Educ:** Univ Redlands, Redlands, CA, grad, 1983. **Career:** Verbum Dei High Sch, basketball coach, 1976-77; Univ Southern Calif, asst basketball coach, 1977; Los Angeles Lakers, asst coach, 1982-83; Compton Jr col, head basketball coach, 1983-84; Clemson Univ, head basketball coach, 1984-85; Univ Iowa, coaching staff, 1986-90; Drake Univ, head basketball coach, 1990-96; Southwestern Athletic Conf, comnr, 2001; San Jose State Univ, asst coach; iSyndicate Inc, comnr; San Bernardino Valley Col, athletic dir; Locke High Sch, jr varsity basketball coach. **Orgs:** Exec dir head, & founder, Black Coaches Asn; former bd mem, Nat Col Athletic Asn; Nat Asn Basketball Coaches; Womens Basketball Coaches Asn; 100 Black Men Los Angeles. **Honors/Awds:** Coach of the Year, Nat Asn Basketball Coaches, 1993; 100 Most Powerful People in Sports, The Sporting News, 1996; Thirty Most Valuable Professionals in the Business of Sports, Black Enterprise mag; commissioner of the year, AAFF. **Special Achievements:** Author of two books on rebounding. **Business Addr:** Member, National Association of Basketball Coaches, 1111 Main St Suite 1000, Kansas, MO 64105-2136, **Business Phone:** (816)878-6222.

### WASHINGTON, DR. SANDRA BEATRICE

Educator, counselor. **Personal:** Born Mar 1, 1946, Nashville, TN; daughter of Henry F Tucker and Sadie Lewis; children: Howard LaMont. **Educ:** Loyola Univ, BA, 1968; Univ Nebr, MS, 1977; Vanderbilt Univ, EdD, 1990. **Career:** Sacred Heart Grade Sch, teacher, 1968-71; Omaha OIC, instr, 1972-73; Greater Omaha Community Action, counsr & supvr, 1972-75; PCC/Head Start, pi/soc serv coordr, 1976-78; Metro-Tech Community Col, counsr & career develop, 1978-81; Comput Inst Youth, educ coordr, 1984-85; Nashville Pub Sch, counr, 1986-99, chairperson, Guid Dept, 1994-; Univ Tenn, Stokley fel, 1992; Mid Tenn State Univ, psych dept, adj prof, 2000-01; Cohn Adult High Sch, Guid Counr, currently. **Orgs:** Career consult Girls Club Omaha, 1978-81; counsr-on-call, Planned Parenthood Nashville, 1985-; ed newsletter, Chi Sigma Iota, Coun/Acad & Prof Hon Soc Int, 1991; ed bd, Elem Sch Guid & Coun, 1991-94. **Home Addr:** 703 Davis Dr, Brentwood, TN 37027, **Home Phone:** (615)373-0696. **Business Addr:** Guidance Counselor, Cohn Adult High School, 4805 Pk Ave, Nashville, TN 37209, **Business Phone:** (615)298-8053.

### WASHINGTON, DR. SARAH M.

Educator. **Personal:** Born Aug 10, 1942, Holly Hill, SC; daughter of David Harry (deceased) and Sarah Harmon; children: Walter Dawit. **Educ:** Tuskegee Inst, Tuskegee, AL, BS, 1964; Univ Ill, Urbana, IL, MS, 1970, PhD, 1980. **Career:** Educator (retired); Spartanburg Dist, Inman, SC, Eng teacher, 1964-65; Anderson Pub Schs, Anderson, SC, Eng teacher, 1965-67; Sumter Schs, Sumter, SC, social studies teacher, 1967-68; Ala State Univ, Montgomery, AL, eng instr, 1971-74; Univ Ill, Urbana, Ill, teaching asst, 1974-80; SC State Col, Orangeburg, SC, assoc prof Eng & mod lang, 1979-2009. **Orgs:** Pres, Orangeburg Br, Asn Study Afro-Am Life & Hist, 1980-85; pres, 1991, chaplain, 1982-89, Phi Delta Kappa; SC State Dept Writing Adv Bd, 1983-89; Am Asn Univ Women; reader, Nat Teachers Exam, 1989; Nat Coun Teachers Eng; Nat Black Child Develop Inst; field coordr, Assessment Performance Teaching, 1988-90. **Home Addr:** 781 Whitman St, Orangeburg, SC 29115-6163, **Home Phone:** (803)533-1049. **Business Addr:** SC.

### WASHINGTON, SHAUNISE A.

Executive. **Personal:** Born Feb 29, 1964, Columbia, SC; daughter of Walter and Elizabeth Hammond; married Donald T; children: Michael & Chad. **Educ:** Univ SC, BS, math & psychol, humanities & social sci, 1985, Cognate, math. **Career:** Entrepreneur (retired): Twp Auditorium, SC, staff; Lt Gov off, staff; Phillip Morris USA, 1987-93, sr acct mgr, sales, 1993-94, dist mgr, sales, 1994-95, dir, trade mkt, 1995-96, dir, trade & bus rel, 1996-98, dist dir, state govt affairs, 1998-99; Altra Corp Serv, dir, Was rels, 1999-2000, vpres, external affairs, 2000-02, vpres, govt affairs policy & outreach, 2002-08; Wash Solutions LLC, founder & chief exec officer, 2008-13; Wash Rels Philip Morris Mgt Corp, dir; Cong Black Caucus Found, pres & chief exec officer, 2013-. **Orgs:** Bd dir, chair, Cong Black Caucus Found; White Rose Found Inc; Future PAC; Links Inc; Delta Res & Educ Found; asst dir, Sc Prog Assistance Line. **Business Addr:** President, Chief Executive Officer, Congressional Black Caucus Foundation Inc, 1720 Massachusetts Ave, NW Washington, DC 20036, **Business Phone:** (202)263-2800.

### WASHINGTON, SHERRY ANN

Administrator, painter (artist). **Personal:** Born Oct 28, 1956, Detroit, MI; daughter of William Taft (deceased) and Virginia Hall; married Floyd Haywood; children: Khalid R Haywood. **Educ:** Univ Mich, BA, gen studies, 1977. **Career:** Govt adminr, 1981-88; Sherry Wash Gallery, founder, owner, director, 1989-; BWW Group, founder; Wayne County Coun Arts, arts consult, 1989-93. **Orgs:** Delta Sigma Theta Sorority, 1974-; Nat Asn Advan Colored People, 1984-; bd mem, Detroit Inst Arts, Friends African Art, 1988-; bd mem, Detroit Cult Affairs Comt; bd mem, Metrop Growth & Develop Corp; Black Women Contracting Asn; bd mem, Black Women Contracting Asn; bd mem, Detroit Athletic Club; bd mem, Detroit Pub Schs; Nebr Libr Asn. **Home Addr:** 1300 E Lafayette St, Detroit, MI 48207-2905, **Home Phone:** (313)259-8807. **Business Addr:** Founder, Owner, Sherry Washington Gallery, 1274 Libr St Suite 1A, Detroit, MI 48226, **Business Phone:** (313)961-4500.

### WASHINGTON, STANLEY E.

Chief executive officer. **Career:** Am Express, Com Card, Western Region, vpres & gen mgr; LA Sports & Entertainment Comn, chmn, actor, regional vpres & gen mgr; Pantheon Lifestyle Services LLC, founder & chief exec officer, Currently. **Orgs:** Los Angeles Sports & Entertainment Comn; Los Angeles Metro YMCA; Bowers Mus Cult Art; Mus African Am Art; bd mem, Magic Johnson Found; bd dir, Znetix; chmn, Los Angeles Convention & Visitors Bur, 2006-; chmn, Nat Black Econ Develop Coalition; bd mem, Nat Coalition African Am Owned Media; bd mem & sr advisor, Los Angeles Nat Asn Advan Colored People; bd mem, City Hope Found & Hosp; adv bd, Mayor Los Angeles Econ Develop Coun; bd advisors mem, HollyRod Found. **Business Addr:** Founder & Chief Executive Officer, Pantheon Business Consulting, 9461 Charleville Blvd Suite 462, Beverly Hills, CA 90212, **Business Phone:** (310)300-1883.

### WASHINGTON, TAMIA MARILYN. See HILL, TAMIA MARILYN.

### WASHINGTON, TERI

Marketing executive, basketball executive. **Educ:** Howard Univ, BBA, mkt, 1987; Temple Univ, MA, sports admin, 1992. **Career:** Ga Tech, asst dir, sports info, 1991-93; Denver, spokeswoman; Nat Basketball Asn Commun, sr dir community rels, 1993-2004; Denver Nuggets, sr dir, commun, 2004-06; Dasuren Inc, managing partner, 2006-08; Events DC, dir mkt & commun, 2008-. **Orgs:** Nat Basketball Asn marijuana rehab prog, spokeswoman. **Business Addr:** Senior Director of Communication & Marketing, National Basketball Association, 645 5th Ave, New York, NY 10022, **Business Phone:** (212)407-8000.

### WASHINGTON, THEODORE, JR.

Football player. **Personal:** Born Apr 13, 1968, Tampa, FL; son of Ted Sr; married Verlisa; children: Ashley, Allison, Adrianne, Teddy & Thadeous. **Educ:** Univ Louisville, phys educ. **Career:** Football player (retired); San Francisco 49ers, defensive tackle, 1991, nose tackle, 1992, right defensive tackle, 1993; Denver Broncos, left defensive tackle, 1994; Buffalo Bills, nose tackle, 1995-2000, defensive tackle; Chicago Bears, left defensive tackle, 2001-02; New Eng Patriots, nose tackle, 2003; Oakland Raiders, defensive tackle, defensive end, nose tackle, 2004, nose tackle, 2005; Cleveland Browns, nose tackle, 2006-07. **Honors/Awds:** Pro Bowl selection, 1997, 1998, 2000, 2001; All-Pro selection, 1997, 1998, 2001; Super Bowl champion; Super Bowl XXXVIII. **Home Addr:** 1916 Iverson Lane, Waxhaw, NC 28173-6658.

### WASHINGTON, DR. THOMAS

Educator, litterateur. **Personal:** Born Dec 8, 1937, Rock Island, IL. **Educ:** Univ Ill, BA, 1961, MA, 1964; Univ Minn, PhD, 1982. **Career:** Champaign Centennial HS, teacher Eng, Span, 1968-70; Hamline Univ Minn, instr Span, 1970-73; Women's Self Defense Empowering Women, lectr, instr, 1972-; Univ Minn, instr Span, 1974-78, 1980-81. **Orgs:** Nodarse Lang Learning Method, 1978-; Women's Self Defense seminars & workshops, 1982; Sigma Delta Pi; Phi Kappa Phi Nat Hon Soc. **Home Addr:** 188 Haskell St E, St Paul, MN 55118, **Home Phone:** (651)291-2740. **Business Addr:** Director, Lecturer, Instructor, Women's Self Defense Empowering Women, 706 Imperial Dr Apt 109, Morris, MN 56267-1057.

### WASHINGTON, TODD PAGE

Football player, football coach. **Personal:** Born Jul 19, 1976, Nassawadox, VA; married Shannon; children: Cameron, Ava & Zane. **Educ:** Va Polytech Inst & State Univ, BS, phys educ, 1998. **Career:** Football player (retired), football coach; Tampa Bay Buccaneers, 1998-2000, ctr, 2001, 2004-05, guard, 2001-02, left guard, 2003; Houston Texans, ctr, 2003-05, left guard, 2003; E Tex Baptist Univ, coaching intern, 2006; Amsterdam Admirals, coaching intern, 2006; Univ San Diego, offensive line coach, 2007-08, offensive coordr & offensive line coach, 2009; St. Louis Rams, intern coach, 2010; Hartford Colonials, offensive line coach, 2010; Baltimore Ravens, asst offensive line coach, 2011-. **Honors/Awds:** Super Bowl champion (XXXVII). **Business Addr:** Assistant Offensive Line Coach, Baltimore Ravens, 1 Winning Dr, Owings Mill, MD 21117, **Business Phone:** (410)701-4000.

### WASHINGTON, TOM

Sports manager, basketball executive. **Personal:** Born Dec 25, 1957, Ft. Smith, AR. **Educ:** Norfolk State Univ, attended 1978. **Career:** Nat Basketball Asn, staff mem, referee, currently. **Orgs:** Amachi Big Bros Prog; Sharon Baptist Men's fel; C's Choice Adoption Agency; Mt Zion Baptist Youth Orgn; PGA Juniors Prog; exec bd mem, Nat Basketball Referee Asn. **Business Addr:** Referee, National Basketball Association, 645 5th Ave 15th Fl, New York, NY 10022-5910, **Business Phone:** (212)826-7000.

### WASHINGTON, UKEE (ULYSSES SAMUEL WASHINGTON, III)

Television news anchorperson, actor. **Personal:** Born Aug 20, 1958, Philadelphia, PA; son of Ulysses S. **Educ:** Dover High Sch; Univ Richmond. **Career:** Channel 3 news, sports anchor, 1986; WBBH-TV Ft Myers Fla & WSB-TV Atlanta, sports anchor; KYW-TV Sta, weekend sportscaster, 1986, co anchor, 1996, news anchor; CBS Broadcasting Inc, CBS 3, news anchor, currently; Tv: "Death of Innocence", 2002, "Bros in Arms", 2003, "Out of the Ashes", 2003; "The Squeeze", 2003; "Presumed Guilty", 2003; " As the World Turns ", 2009; Films: Unbreakable, 2000; Signs, 2002; The Manchurian Cand, 2004; Shooter, 2007; Live Free or Die Hard, 2007; The Happening, 2008; Booted, 2011. **Orgs:** Philadelphia Boys Choir. **Home Addr:** , Wilmington, DE. **Business Addr:** TV News Anchor, CBS Broadcasting Inc, 1555 Hamilton St, Philadelphia, PA 19130, **Business Phone:** (215)977-5300.

### WASHINGTON, VALDEMAR LUTHER

Lawyer, circuit court judge. **Personal:** Born Jun 21, 1952, Baltimore, MD; son of Vivian E and G Luther; married Ada C Miller; children: Valdemar L II & Christopher James. **Educ:** Baltimore Polytech Inst, BA, 1970; Mich State Univ, BA, 1974; Univ Mich Law Sch, JD, 1976. **Career:** Judge (retired); Baker Law Firm Bay City, assoc lawyer, 1977, 1981-86; Acct Aid Soc Flint, dir, 1978; Pvt Pract, atty, 1978-80; Robinson Wash Smith & Stanfield, partner, 1981; Circuit Ct Judge Genesee County, judge, 1986-96, chief ct circuit judge, 1990-92; Univ Mich, adj lecttr, 1989; Wayne State Sch Law, adj lectr, 1995; Seventh Circuit, circuit ct judge; SETTLEmate Inc, founder, pres, chief facilitator, prin, 1996-; Mich Ct Appeals, vis judge, 1988, 1995; Detroit Edison Co, 1998-2004; dep state treas, State Mich, 2007-10; interim chief judge, 22nd Dist Ct, 2011. **Orgs:** Mich State Bar Asn; Big Sisters Bd Dir; pres, McCree Theater Adv Bd, 1979-81; Flint Community Found, Mensa, 1980-; pres, Theatre Adv Bd, 1982-83; Legal Redress Comn, Nat Asn Advan Colored People, 1983-86; Am Judges Asn, 1986-87; Mich Trial Lawyers Asn, 1986-; Am Trial Lawyers Asn, 1986-; Am Col Civil Trail Mediators; life mem, MENSA, 1980-; bd mem, Homeless Empowerment Registry Orgn, 1994-95; pres, Genesee County Bar Asn, 1996-97; assoc mem, Ethics Comt, 1996-98; Establishing Law Pract Comt, 1996-98; Am Acad Civil Trial Mediators. **Honors/Awds:** University Rhodes Scholar, Mich State Univ, 1974; Argus Award, Genesee County Consortium Child Abuse & Neglect, 1989; Inductee Baltimore Polytechnic Alumni Hall of Fame. **Home Addr:** 1505 Arrow Lane, Flint, MI 48507-1882, **Home Phone:** (810)742-2441. **Business Addr:** President, Chief Facilitator, SETTLEmate Inc, 328 S Saginaw St Suite 9001, Flint, MI 48501-0187, **Business Phone:** (810)743-0101.

### WASHINGTON, DR. VON HUGO, SR.

Educator, actor. **Personal:** Born Mar 9, 1943, Albion, MI; son of Alice Coleman and Hugh; married Frances Mosee; children: Von Jr & Alicia Rene. **Educ:** Western Mich Univ, Kalamazoo, MI, BS, sociol, 1974, MA, theatre, 1975; Wayne State Univ, Detroit, MI, PhD, speech commun, 1979. **Career:** Actor, director, teacher; Univ Mich, Ann Arbor, MI, dir, black theatre, 1975-77; Wayne State Univ, Detroit, MI, dir, black theatre, 1979-88; Wash Productions Inc, artistic dir; Western Mich Univ, Kalamazoo, Mi, dir, multi-cult theatre, 1989-, prof, Theatre, Currently; Director: Native Son; Remnants From Senegal; Seven Stops To Freedom. **Orgs:** Artistic dir & co-founder, Afro-Am Studio Theatre, Detroit, 1983-86; Black Theatre Network, 1986-96; pres & co-founder, WAS Prod, 1992-. **Home Addr:** 1004 Cohasset Lane, Kalamazoo, MI 49008-2327, **Home Phone:** (269)657-8953. **Business Addr:** Professor, Director, Western Michigan University, 1903 W Mich Ave, Kalamazoo, MI 49008-5239, **Business Phone:** (269)387-3220.

### WASHINGTON, DR. WARREN MORTON

Scientist. **Personal:** Born Aug 28, 1936, Portland, OR; son of Edwin Sr and Dorothy Morton; married Joan A; children: Jocelyn Montgomery, Michelle Meney & Quentin Hunt; married Mary C; married LaRae Kemp; children: Teri Lyn Ciocco, Kim Ann Pierce & Tracy LaRae Cannon-Smith. **Educ:** Ore State Univ, Corvallis, OR, BS, physics, 1958, MS, meteorol, 1960; Penn State Univ, PhD, meteorol, 1964. **Career:** Stanford Res Inst, mathematician, 1959; Penn State Univ, res assoc, 1960-63; Nat Ctr Atmospheric Res, Boulder, CO, res scientist, 1963-, prog scientist, 1972-73, proj leader, 1973-74, sr scientist, 1975-87, dir, climate & global dynamics div, 1987-95, Climate Chg Res Sect, sect head, orgns climate chg res sect climate & global dynamics div, sr scientist, 1995-; Univ Mich, adj assoc prof meteorol, 1968-71. **Orgs:** Nat Acad Sci & NSF, 1969-; Govt Sci Adv Comt, 1975-78; Nat Adv Comt Oceans & Atmosphere, 1978-84; Fel Am Meteorol Soc, 1980, pres, 1995, hon mem, 2005; fel AAAS, 1981; fel Alumni Fel Prog, Penn State Univ, 1990; bd dir, Am Asn Advan Sci, 1991-95; fel Alumni Fel Prog, Ore State Univ, 1990; secy, Energy Adv Bd, 1990-93; fel African Sci Inst, 1993; Nat Sci Bd, 1995-2006; Am Geophys Union; Nat Sci Bd, 1994-2006, chair, 2002-04; Nat Acd Eng, 2002; Am Philos Soc, 2003; Am Geophys Union Sigma Xi; secy, Energys Biol & Environ Res Adv Comt; Modernization Transition Comt; Nat Centers Environ Prediction Adv Comt; Advan Sci Comput Adv Comt. **Honors/Awds:** Distinguished Alumni Award, Penn State Univ, 1991; President-Elect, Am Metrol Soc, 1993; Le Verrier Medal, Societe Meterologique die France, 1995; Distinguished Alumni Award, Ore State Univ, 1996; Exceptional Service Award, Dept Energy Biologican & Envir Research Program, 1997; Sigma Xi Distinguished Lecturer, 1998-99; Walter Orr Roberts Lecturer, 1998; Nat Weather Service Modernization Award, 1999; Dr Charles Anderson Award, Am Meteorol Soc, 2000; Celebrating 20th Century Pioneers Atmospheric Science Award, 2000, Howard Univ; Bonfils-Stanton Found Award, 2000; Reed Col Vollum Award, Distinguished Accomplishment in Sci & Technol, 2004; Science Spectrum Trailblazer, Sci Spectrum Mag, 2006; Honorary DSc, Oregon State Univ, 2006; Charles Franklin Brooks Award, Am Meteorol Soc, 2007; Honoray DSc, Bates Col, 2008; Le Vernier Medal. **Special Achievements:** One of 16 scientists featured in the Chicago Museum of Science and Industry "Black Achievers in Science" Exhibit. **Home Addr:** 8633 E Iliff Dr, Denver, CO 80231. **Business Addr:** Senior Scientist, Section Head, Climate Change Research Section, National Center for Atmospheric Research, PO Box 3000, Boulder, CO 80307-3000, **Business Phone:** (303)497-1321.

## WASHINGTON, WENDY

Executive. **Educ:** Vassar Col, BA, hist. **Career:** Arista Recs, mgr publicity, 1994; Universal Motown Recs, sr vpres media rels; Zomba Label Group, sr vpres media rels & spokeswoman, 2007-; Sony Music Entertainment Inc. **Business Addr:** Senior Vice President, Zomba Label Group, 137 139 W 25th St, New York, NY 10001, **Business Phone:** (212)824-1223.

## WASHINGTON, WILLIAM

Banker. **Personal:** Born Chicago, IL; son of Susie M. **Educ:** Ill Inst Technol, BS, sociol, bus econs, MS, mgt, finance. **Career:** LaSalle Home Mortgage Corp, mortgage collections, mortgage originations, home improvement loan coordr, sec mortgage mkt coordr, mortgage loan underwriting mgr, vpres, currently. **Orgs:** Christian educ dir, New Friendship Baptist Church Robbins, Ill; Teen Living Prog Chicago; Soc Mortgage Profs; NFBC Homeless Servs. **Business Addr:** Vice President, LaSalle Home Mortgage Corp, 4242 N Harlem Ave, Norridge, IL 60634-1283, **Business Phone:** (708)456-0400.

## WASHINGTON, WILLIAM MONTELL (BILL WASHINGTON)

Executive. **Personal:** Born Apr 2, 1939, Columbia, MO; son of William and Narcissia. **Educ:** Lincoln Univ Mo, BS, educ & math, 1962; Univ Mo, Kansas City, MA, educ, 1970. **Career:** KC Mo Sch Dist, high sch teacher & coach, 1963-67; Urban League Kans City, assoc dir econ develop, 1967-71; United Telecommunications Inc, affirmative action officer, 1971, exec; Swope Health Serv, dir, 1988-; Sprint Inc, dir, cre rel, exec, 1990-2001; Swope Community Enterprises, secy, dir, 2003-; Kans City Parks & Recreation Comn, comnr; Wash Consult Group, pres; Felton & Harley, sr consult. **Orgs:** Omega Psi Phi, 1959; bd dir, Metro YMCA, 1973; adv bd, United Negro Col Fund, 1976; chmn bd, Urban League Kans City, 1978; KC Harmony, 1996; chmn, Black COT Fund; HTH Midwest; INROADS Kans City; Bruce R Watkins Cult Heritage Ctr; Urban League, Kans City; YMCA Kans City; mem compensation comt, Swope Community Enterprises Inc. **Honors/Awds:** Outstanding Leadership Award, Minority Bus Awareness Prog, Black Econ Union, 1977. **Home Addr:** 7509 E 74th St, Kansas City, MO 64133. **Business Addr:** Director, Swope Health Services, 3801 Blue Pkwy, Kansas City, MO 64130, **Business Phone:** (816)923-5800.

## WASHINGTON, ZENOBIA

Artist. **Personal:** Born Nov 24, 1966, Newark, NJ; daughter of J H Grant and Susan Armstrong; married Willie Washington, Oct 5, 1991; children: Susan Alexis Washington. **Educ:** Art & Fashion Inst, AA, 1987. **Career:** Artist, 1987-; International Association of Special Education, art and culture editor for the newsletter; South Carolina Arts Commission, artist in residence. **Orgs:** Bd dir, Five Rivers Community Develop Corp. **Special Achievements:** Created handmade dolls of traditional African-American women, such as "The Healer" and "The Washer Woman", in her collection, "Women of Inspiration", 1998-; art featured in art galleries and private art collections. **Business Addr:** 122 Cleland St, Georgetown, SC 29440, **Business Phone:** (843)340-0936.

## WASOW, OMAR TOMAS

Executive. **Personal:** married Jennifer Michelle Brea. **Educ:** Stanford Univ, BA, 1992; Harvard Univ, MA, govt, 2008, MA, statist, 2011, PhD, African Am studies, 2013. **Career:** Stuyvesant Stud Union, Stuyvesant High Sch, New York, pres, 1987-88; Congressman William Gray III, House Rep, Majority Whip, DC, intern, 1990; Strictly Bus, Citizens Comt NYC, assoc dir, 1992-93; Stanford Univ, Calif, teacher, 1992; New York Online, Diaspora Inc, Brooklyn, NY, pres & founder, 1993-99; MSNBC, CNN, NBC, NPR, Oprah, PRI, Secaucus, NJ, technol analyst, 1996-2012; Next Generation Leadership Fel, Rockefeller Found, 1997-99; BlackPlanet.com, Community Connect Inc, co-founder, air technol analyst, exec dir, 1999-2005; Inst Humane Studies, Humane Studies Fel, Nsf, Grad Res Fel, 2007-10; Nsf, grad res fel, 2007-10; Aspen Insts Henry Crown, fel, 2008-10; Aspen Inst, Henry Crown Fel, 2008-10; W.E.B. Du Bois Inst, Sheila Biddle Ford Found Fel, Proj Justice, Welfare & Econs, 2010-11; Proj Justice, Welfare & Econs, Dissertation fel, 2011-12; Princeton Univ, postdoctoral res fel, 2012-13, Dept Polit, asst prof, polit, 2013-. **Orgs:** Brooklyn Excelsior Charter Sch, Brooklyn, NY, 2000; Am Soc Mag Ed, 2002-05; Stanford Sch Edu, 2004; YMCA, New York, 2005-06; fel Rockefeller Founds Next Generation Leadership prog. **Business Addr:** Assistant Professor, Princeton University, 231 Corwin Hall, Princeton, NJ 08544-1012, **Business Phone:** (609)258-2551.

## WATERMAN, JEFFREY TREVOR

Consultant. **Personal:** Born Sep 25, 1971, Rocky Mount, NC; son of Connie Walston Jr and Carolyn Walston. **Educ:** St Augustine Col, Raleigh, NC, BA, 1993; Univ Akron, Akron, OH, MA, commun, sales & mkt, 1996. **Career:** Innovex Inc, specialty pharmaceut rep, 1999-2004; Eisa, sales rep, 2004-07; Vitas Inc, sales rep, 2007-09; Amedisys, acct exec, 2009-10; Ohio Surg Solutions Lanx, territory mgr, spine rep, 2010-. **Orgs:** APA Fraternity Inc, 1991-. **Special Achievements:** Carnegie Hall performance, 1988; thesis: A Cluster Analysis of Martin Luther King's "I've Been to the Mountaintop". **Home Addr:** 1614A Treetop Trail, Akron, OH 44313. **Business Addr:** Territory Manager, Ohio Surgical Solutions, 10165 Brecksville Rd, Brecksville, OH 44141, **Business Phone:** (440)526-9440.

## WATERS, BRENDA JOYCE

Journalist, television news anchorperson. **Personal:** Born Jan 29, 1950, Goldsboro, NC; daughter of Dilliah and Levi. **Educ:** Univ Md, BS, 1973; Am Univ, MS, 1975. **Career:** WTVR-TV-6, reporter & anchor, 1975-76; WLOS-TV-13, reporter & anchor, 1977-79; WPXI-TV-11, reporter, 1979-85; KDKA-TV-2, weekend anchor & reporter, 1985-. **Orgs:** Nat Asn Advan Colored People; bd dir, Sickle Cell Socs; Small Seeds Bd; POWER Bd; Myriam's Women's Shelter; Lydia's Pl & Women Inc. Southwestern Pa. **Honors/Awds:** Certificate of Recognition, Jimmy Carter Fed Disaster Assist Admin, 1977; 1st Pl Associate Press Award, 1982, 1984; Cecile B Springer Womenpower Award; Emmy award; Woman of distinction, Girl Scouts Southwestern Pa; 50 Women of Excellence, Pittsburgh Courier, 2008. **Special Achievements:** Twice as one of 100 outstanding women in the community, Ebenezer Baptist Church. **Home Addr:** 5109 Riverfront Dr, Pittsburgh, PA 15238. **Business Addr:** Weekend Anchor, Reporter, KDKA-TV-2, 651 Holiday Dr, Pittsburgh, PA 15220, **Business Phone:** (412)920-9400.

## WATERS, CRYSTAL

Singer, songwriter. **Personal:** Born Oct 10, 1964, Philadelphia, PA; daughter of Junior and Betty; married Lamont Reese; children: Morgan & Lindsay. **Educ:** Howard Univ, BS, comput sci, 1985. **Career:** Albums: Surprise, 1991; Storyteller, 1994; Crystal Waters, 1997; The Best Of, 1998; Gypsy Woman - The Collection, 2001; 20th Century Masters - The Millennium Collection: The Best of Crystal Waters, 2001; Singles: "Makin' Happy", 1991; "Megamix", 1992; "You Turn Me On", 1993; "100% Pure Love", 1994; "What I Need", 1994; "Ghetto Day", 1994; "Relax", 1995; "In De Ghetto", 1996; "The Boy from Ipanema", 1996; "Say... If You Feel Alright", 1997; "Just a Freak", 1997; "Come On Down", 2001; "Enough", 2001; "Night in Egypt", 2001; "My Time", 2003; "Destination Unknown", "Lies", 2004; "Destination Calabria", 2006; "Dancefloor", 2008; Never Enough, 2009; "Say Yeah"; "When People Come Together", 2010; "Le Bump", 2011; "Oh Mama Hey", 2013; "Blow", 2013; "Be Kind", 2014. **Honors/Awds:** Billboard Music Award, 1994. **Business Addr:** Singer, c/o Troy Bronstein, 508 Honey Lake Ct, Danville, CA 94506, **Business Phone:** (925)736-1991.

## WATERS, DIANNE E.

Entrepreneur. **Personal:** Born Apr 28, 1954, Austin, TX; daughter of Billie Bacon Richards; married Clifton; children: Jamil. **Educ:** N Tex State Univ, BS, 1979. **Career:** Barretts Prod Co, regional dir, 1980-85; Concessions Unique Inc, pres, 1986-. **Orgs:** Alpha Kappa Alpha, 1974; founding mem, Airport Minority Adv Coun, 1988; Jack & Jill Am, 2001. **Honors/Awds:** Quest For Success, Dallas Black Chamber, 1992; Parent Teacher Asn Award, 1994. **Home Phone:** (214)707-5356. **Business Addr:** President, Concessions Unique Inc, 501 Wynnewood Village Suite 102B, Dallas, TX 75224, **Business Phone:** (214)946-1444.

## WATERS, JOHN W.

Executive, educator, clergy. **Personal:** Born Feb 5, 1936, Atlanta, GA; son of Henry (deceased) and Mary Annie Randall (deceased). **Educ:** Fisk Univ, BA, chem, 1957; Atlanta Univ Summer Sch, 1958; Univ Geneva Switz, cert pastoral care, 1962; GA State Univ; Boston Univ, STB, 1967, PhD, bibl studies hebrew bible, 1970; Univ Detroit, 1975; Harvard Univ Divinity Sch. **Career:** Educator (retired), clergy; Army Ed Ctr Ulm Western Ger, admin, 1960-63; Atlanta Bd Ed, instr, 1957-60, 1963-64; Ebenezer Baptist Church, minister relig educ & asst minister, 1965-69; Experiential Elem Sch, Boston, MA, teacher; Myrtle Baptist Church W Newton MA, minister, 1969; Ctr Black Studies Univ Detroit, adj prof, dir, assoc prof, 1970-76; Fund Theol Educ, interviewer, 1972-83; Inst Christian Thought, John Courtney Murray Newman Ctr, distinguished lectr, 1975; Interdenom Theol Ctr, prof, 1976-86; Shaw Univ, adj prof; Walden Univ; Morris Brown Col, adj prof; Interdenominational Theol Ctr, prof hebrew bible & chairperson, 1976-86; Boston Univ, instr; Greater Solid Rock Baptist Church, minister, 1981, sr minister, 1980-2005, sr vpres, 1984, sr minister emer, 2005-; Primerica Financial Serv, sr vpres, 1984-2001; Cong Christian Educ, Progressive Nat Baptist Conv, fac mem; Black Leadership Conf Southern Baptist Conv, fac mem. **Orgs:** Am Acad Relig, 1969; Soc Bibl Lit, 1969; Mich Black Studies Asn, 1974; rep, Nat Alliance Businessmen/ Atlanta Univ, 1978-81; bd trustee, Interdenom Theol Ctr, 1980-84; bd dir, Habitat Humanity Atlanta, 1983; vpres, Col Pk Ministers fel; chair, S Atlanta Joint Urban Ministry, 1984-94; treas, Prison Ministries Women Inc, 1988-96; pres, Coun Overseers, New Era Baptist Conv Ctr, 1996-2001; bd gov, Univ Detroit Fac Club; pres, Univ Detroit Chap AAUP; pres, Clayton County Ministers Conf, 2000; bd dir, Atlantic Col & Theol Sem; Fairburn Baptist Asn; Socs Bibl Lit; Am Asn Univ Professors; Int Socs Theta Phi; Nat Asn Colored People; treas, Prison Ministries with Women Inc; vpres, S Metro Ministers Fel; bd dir, Southeast Mich Ethnic Heritage Studies Ctr. **Honors/Awds:** First Faculty Lecturer, Interdenominational Theol Ctr, 1979; Distinguished Faculty Award, ITC, 1981; Religion Leader of the Year, Concerned Black Clergy Metropolitan Atlanta, 2000. **Home Addr:** 1516 Niskey Lake Trl SW, PO Box 310416, Atlanta, GA 30331-0416, **Home Phone:** (404)344-8104. **Business Addr:** Senior Minister-Emeritus, Greater Solid Rock Baptist Church, 6280 Camp Rd, Riverdale, GA 30296, **Business Phone:** (770)997-4666.

## WATERS, KATHRYN (KATHY WATERS)

Vice president (government), executive, government official. **Educ:** Univ Md, College Park, BA, sociol, 1971; Univ Md Baltimore, MCP, community planning, 1973. **Career:** Md Transit Admin, Dir, MARC Train Serv, 1996-2002; Dallas Area Rapid Transit, vpres, Commuter Rail & Rr Mgt, 2002-07; Md Transit Admin, sr dep adminr, 2007; Am Pub Transp Asn, vpres, mem serv, 2007-13; Am Pub Transp Asn, exec vpres, mem serv, 2013-. **Orgs:** Past chair, Commuter Rail Comm; Am Pub Transit Asn; Md Chap; Conf Minority Transp Offs; adv bd, Eno Transp Found; Rail Safety Adv Community, 1997-; Fed Railroad Admin; Transp Res Bd, 2004-; vpres, Am Pub Transp Asn, 2007-. **Honors/Awds:** Railway Age W Graham Claytor Jr Award, 2009; DHL, Eastern Theol Sem, 2003. **Special Achievements:** First African American & woman in MD to manage a commuter railway service. **Business Addr:** Vice President, Trinity Railway Express, Commuter Rails 1401 Pac Ave, Dallas, TX 75202, **Business Phone:** (214)979-1111.

## WATERS, MARY D.

Human services worker, government official. **Personal:** Born Aug 27, 1955, Greenville, AL; daughter of William and Willie M. **Educ:** Detroit Bus Inst, 1975; Univ Mich, BA, commun & behav sci, 1988. **Career:** McDonalds, 1973-75; Nat Bank Detroit, 1975-76; Blue Cross Blue Shield, benefit specialist; Mich House Rep, state rep, 2007; Childrens Ctr, develop coordr; Oper Dent Flush, founder. **Orgs:** Facilitator, Metrop Detroit Youth Found, 1988-89; Collections Pract Bd; bd mem, d Direction, 1990-92; vice chair, Detroit Charter Rev Comn; Mgt asn, Blue Cross/ Blue Shield; Int Asn Bus Communs; Univ Mich Alumni; Nat Asn Advan Colored People; Plymouth United Church Christ; Midwestern Legis Conf MidwestCanada Rels Comt, 2003-04; 13th Cong Dem Dist; Trade Union Leadership Coun; Nat Polit Cong Black Women; Nat Black Cong State Legislators; Women Govt; Women Legis Leadership; Women's Action New Directions; Span Speaking Dem. **Home Addr:** 2701 E Lafayette, Detroit, MI 48207. **Business Addr:** Legislator, Michigan House of Representatives, Capitol Bldg Rm 141, Lansing, MI 48909-7514, **Business Phone:** (517)373-1008.

## WATERS, MAXINE

Politician, government official, educator. **Personal:** Born Aug 15, 1938, St. Louis, MO; daughter of Remus Moore and Velma Moore Carr; married Sidney Williams; children: Edward & Karen; married Edward. **Educ:** Calif State Univ, Los Angeles, BA, sociol, 1970. **Career:** Head Start, asst teacher; Los Angeles City Councilman David Cunningham, chief dep, 1973; Calif State Assembly, 1976-91; Dem Party, chief dep; US House Rep, 29th dist, 1991-93, 35 Dist Columbia, rep, 1993-, congresswomen, currently. **Orgs:** Dem Nat Comt; del alt, Dem Conventions; Comn Status Women, Nat Women's Polit Caucus Adv Comt; Comt Black PACS; nat bd dir, Trans Africa; chief co-founder & pres, Black Women's Forum; House Comt Banking, Finance & Urban Affairs; Veterans Sub comt Educ, Employ, Training & Housing; Banking Sub comt Housing & Community Opportunities; co-chair, Cong Urban Caucus; nat co-chair, Clinton Pres Campaign; chair, Cong Black Caucus, 1997-98; Cong Progressive Caucus; founding mem & chair, Out Iraq Cong Caucus. **Honors/Awds:** Freedom & Justice Award, Detroit Nat Asn Advan Colored People, 2001; Hon doctorates, Spelman Col & NC Agri & Tech State Univ. **Special Achievements:** First woman to be ranked 4 on the leadership team; First African American female mem of Rules Comm; First non lawyer on the Judiciary Comm; One of the outstanding leaders at the Intl Women's Year Conf in Houston; sponsored legislation concerning tenant protection, small bus protection, the limiting of police strip-and-search authority. **Business Addr:** Congresswoman, United States House of Representatives, 2221 Rayburn House Off Bldg, Washington, DC 20515-0535, **Business Phone:** (202)225-2201.

## WATERS, NEVILLE R., III

Business owner, radio director. **Personal:** Born Feb 22, 1957, Washington, DC. **Educ:** Springfield Col, BS, 1978, MA, psychol serv, 1980; Georgetown Univ, MBA. **Career:** Nat Broadcasting Co, fel; WMAS Radio, announcer, 1980-81; A&M Rec, prom, merchandising, 1982-83; WQXQ Radio, traffic dir & music dir, 1983; WOL Radio, prog dir; Metro Talk, producer & dir; DC Today, producer; Waters Group, founder & owner, currently. **Orgs:** Bd mem, Young Mens Christian Asn Chap; bd mem, House Mercy Mission Shelter; bd mem, Sidwell Friends School. **Home Addr:** 2729 P St NW, Washington, DC 20007, **Home Phone:** (202)965-5309. **Business Addr:** Founder, The Waters Group, 222 Longfellow St NW, Washington, DC 20011, **Business Phone:** (202)291-2879.

## WATERS, PAUL EUGENE, JR.

Executive. **Personal:** Born Sep 9, 1959, Harrisburg, PA; son of Paul E Sr and Sylvia Byers; married Sonja Powell; children: Paul E III & Meredith Colleen. **Educ:** Lincoln Univ, attended 1980; Temple Univ, Philadelphia, PA, BA, radio, tv & film, 1984. **Career:** Cable AD Net, Acct Exec, 1984-85; NY Times Cable TV, Cherry Hill, NJ, acct exec, 1984-88; WHTM TV, Harrisburg, PA, acct exec, 1987-88; TCI Cable, gen sales mgr, 1988-91; CNBC, Ft Lee, NJ, dir local advert, 1991-95; Food Network, vpres, 1996-98; Meredith Farms, pres, 1998-2003; Black Family Channel, exec asst chmn, 2003-05; CoLours TV, sr vpres, 2005-08; AccuWeather, tv & digital ad sales, 2008-09; BBN, sr vpres sales & mkt, 2009-; SBGC, distrib & sponsorship sales exec, 2009-13; Gen Sentiment, social & digital media analytics, 2012-. **Orgs:** Nat Asn Advan Colored People, 1972-; Omega Psi Phi Fraternity, 1978-. **Home Addr:** 2105 Bradley Dr, Harrisburg, PA 17110-9514, **Home Phone:** (717)541-9775. **Business Addr:** Social and Digital Media Analytics, General Sentiment, 720 Northern Blvd, Brookville, NY 11548, **Business Phone:** (802)321-0361.

## WATERS, SYLVIA ANN

Journalist. **Personal:** Born Sep 29, 1949, Corsicana, TX; daughter of George and Gertrude (deceased). **Educ:** E Tex State Univ, BA, 1971. **Career:** Corsicana Daily Sun Newspaper, reporter, prog dir, Boys & Girls Clubs, 1972-. **Orgs:** Publicity chairwoman, Navarro Co United Fund, 1975-; Nat Fedr Press Women, Tex Press Women, 1982-; pres, Jackson Ex-Students Asn, 1983-; Nat Asn Advan Colored People, 1986; Nat Asn Black Journalists, 1986-; Am Bus Women Asn Golden Horizons Chap, 1986-; chairwoman, Navarro Co Coalition Black Demo, 1986-. **Home Addr:** 601 E 14th Ave, Corsicana, TX 75110-8139, **Home Phone:** (903)872-2736. **Business Addr:** Reporter, Program Director, Corsicana Daily Sun Newspaper, 405 E Collin, Corsicana, TX 75110, **Business Phone:** (903)872-9231.

## WATERS, WILLIAM DAVID

Government official, commissioner. **Personal:** Born Sep 14, 1924, Camden, NJ; son of William A and Rebecca Jones; married Viva Edwards. **Educ:** Temple Univ Philadelphia, BS, acct, 1947, MBA, acct, 1948. **Career:** Government Official (retired); IRS, Mid-Atlantic Region Philadelphia, fiscal mgt & officer, 1964-66, regional comnr, 1974-85; Albany, asst dist dir, 1966-67; Baltimore, asst dist dir, 1970-73, dist dir, 1973-74; NJ Casino Control Comn, comnr, 1986-91. **Orgs:** Vpres & dir, YMCA Camden County, 1980-; St John's United Methodist Church Columbia; Housing Task Force Columbia. **Home Addr:** 1011 Rymill Run, Cherry Hill, NJ 08003.

**WATERS, WILLIE ANTHONY**
Conductor (music). **Personal:** Born Oct 11, 1951, Goulds, FL; son of Lee Andrew and Valuda Hooks. **Educ:** Univ Miami, BMus, 1973; Memphis State Univ, MMus, 1975. **Career:** Memphis Opera Theatre, asst conductor, 1973-75; San Francisco Opera, artistic adminr, 1975-79; Greater Miami Opera, music dir, 1982-85, artistic dir, 1985-92, prin conductor, 1992-95; New World Sch Arts, actg dean, 1992-93; Conn Opera Co, music dir, 1996-99, gen & artistic dir, conductor, 1999-, artistic dir, 2007-; UConn Opera Theater, co dir; Guest conductor: Australian Opera; Arizona Opera; Boston Lyric Opera; Capetown, South Africa; Chautauqua Opera; Cincinnati Opera; Cologne Opera; Dayton Opera; Edmonton Opera; Fort Worth Opera; Kentucky Opera; Manitoba Opera; Michigan Opera; Montreal Opera; New York City Opera; Opera Memphis; Opera Carolina; Opera Colorado; Opera de Quebec; Orlando Opera; San Diego Opera; San Francisco Opera; Vancouver Opera; Cologne Opera; Opera de Montreal; Fla Grand Opera, artistic dir, prin conductor; Porgy & Bess, 1995& 2008. **Orgs:** Alpha Phi Alpha, 1972-73; Phi Mu Alpha, 1973-75. **Honors/Awds:** Distinguished Alumni, Univ Miami, 1985; Martell, Prix De Martell, 1991, Hon Doctorate, Univ Hartford, 2005. **Special Achievements:** First Black Artistic Director of Major American Opera Co, 1985; Conducted First Production of Porgy & Bess in South Africa, 1996. **Home Addr:** 1 Gold St Apt 19G, Hartford, CT 06103, **Home Phone:** (860)525-0111. **Business Addr:** Artistic Director, Conductor, Connecticut Opera, 226 Farmington Ave, Hartford, CT 06105, **Business Phone:** (860)486-3728.

**WATFORD-MCKINNEY, YVONNE V.**
Lawyer, government official. **Personal:** Born Jan 1, 1948, Brooklyn, NY. **Educ:** Mount Holyoke Col, S Hadley, BA, 1970; Wayne State Univ Law Sch, JD, 1980. **Career:** US Dept Justice, asst US atty, chief greenville, 1983-, asst US atty, eastern dist NC, 1995-. **Orgs:** Wake County Am Heart Asn, 1995-; State Bar Mich; State Bar NY; Fed Bar Asn; State Bar NC. **Business Addr:** Assistant US Attorney, US Attorneys Office, 310 New Bern Ave Suite 800, Raleigh, NC 27601-1461, **Business Phone:** (919)856-4530.

**WATKINS, DR. ANTHONY E.**
Cardiologist. **Educ:** Howard Univ, biol, 1962; Howard Univ Med Sch, MD, 1966. **Career:** Homewood Hosp Ctr, intern, 1966-67; Johns Hopkins Univ Sch Pub Health, internship, 1967; VA Med Ctr, fel cardiovasc disease, 1975-76; Greater Southeast Community Hosp, chief cardiol & dir coronary care unit; MedStar Wash Hosp Ctr, resident internal med, 1971-73, resident nuclear med, 1973-74, pres med & dent staff, vpres, Med Staff Develop, currently; pvt pract cardiologist, currently. **Orgs:** Wash Hosp Ctr, fel 1974; fel Veterans Admin Med Ctr, 1976; bd mem, VHA Inc; bd mem, ROW Sci Inc; Am Hosp Asn; Alpha Omega Alpha Med Hon Soc; fel Am Col Cardiol. **Business Addr:** Vice President of Medical Staff Development, MedStar Washington Hospital Center, 106 Irving St NW Suite 3200, Washington, DC 20010, **Business Phone:** (202)726-7474.

**WATKINS, ARETHA LA ANNA**
Journalist. **Personal:** Born Aug 23, 1930, Blairsville, PA; daughter of Clifford Fox Sr and Carrie Thompson; married Angelo Sr; children: Angelo Jr. **Educ:** Wayne State Univ, attended 1950; Wayne State Univ, Col Lifelong Learning; Marygrove Col. **Career:** Detroit Courier, staff writer, 1963-64, asst to ed, 1964-66; Mich Chronical, staff wirter, columnist, 1966; Mich Chronicle Publ Co, asst managing ed, 1968-81, managing ed, 1981-, copy ed, currently. **Orgs:** Sigma Delta Chi Prof Journ Soc Prog Comt Asn, 1968; adv bd mem, Sigma Delta Chi Prof Journ Soc; Nat Asn Advan Colored People. **Honors/Awds:** Best Ed Award, Nat Newspapers Publ Asn, 1972; Black Communicator Award, MI SCLC, 1972; Dist Comn Serv Award, Lafayette Allen Sr, 1974; Community Serv Award, Alpha Theta Chap Gamma Phi Delta, 1981; Corp Serv Award, African Am Mus Detroit, 1984; Sojourner Truth Award, Bus Woman of the Year, Detroit Chap Nat Asn Negro Bus & Prof Women's Clubs Inc, 1984; MI SCLC Martin Luther King Jr Award, 1986. **Home Addr:** 95 Elmhurst St, Highland Park, MI 48203-3527, **Home Phone:** (313)866-7675. **Business Addr:** Managing Editor, Michigan Chronicle, 479 Ledyard, Detroit, MI 48201, **Business Phone:** (313)963-5522.

**WATKINS, BARBARA LORD**
President (organization), foundation executive. **Educ:** Fisk Univ, BA, biol, 1955; Meharry Med Col, Med Technologist, 1957; Southern Methodist Univ, MPA, pub policy anal & admin, 1978. **Career:** Parkland Found, founding mem, 1985-95, pres & chief exec officer, 1995-2005; pres emerita, 2005-. **Orgs:** Parkland Found, bd dirs. **Honors/Awds:** North Central Texas Council of Governments, Linda Keighly Award for women in public management; United Way of Texas, Helen Farabee Award; Legal Aid of North West Texas, Women's Advocacy Award for Non-profit Leadership, June 2005. **Business Addr:** President Emerita, Parkland Foundation, 2777 N Stemmons Fwy Suite 1700, Dallas, TX 75207, **Business Phone:** (214)266-2000.

**WATKINS, DR. CHARLES B.**
Educator, school administrator. **Personal:** Born Nov 20, 1942, Petersburg, VA; son of Charles B Sr and Haseltine Thurston Clements. **Educ:** Howard Univ, BSME, 1964; Univ NMex, MS, mech engineering, 1966, PhD, mech engineering, 1970. **Career:** Sandia Nat Labs, staff mem, 1964-71; Howard Univ, asst prof, 1971-73, dept chmn & assoc prof, 1973-78, prof & chmn, 1978-84, 1985-86; Nat Gov Asn, srfel, 1984-85; City Col NY, dean, sch eng, 1986-00, Herbert G Kayser prof mech eng, 2000-, Ctr Mesoscopic Modeling & Simulation, dir, currently. **Orgs:** Consult, USN, 1975-82; Nat Sci Found, 1976-78; AUS, 1979; nat chair, dept heads comn, 1986-87, mem bd, engrg educ, 1986-88, vice chair, engrg & pub policy dir, 1987-88, assoc fel, Am Inst Aeronaut & Astronaut, 1993; Am Soc Engrg Educ; bd dir, Parsons Brinker hoff Inc, 1994-98; fel, Am Soc Mech Engrs, 1990; fel, AAAS, 2005; dean, African Sci Inst. **Home Addr:** 171 Sherman Ave, Teaneck, NJ 07666. **Business Addr:** Herbert G Kayser Professor, Director, The City College of New York, Steinman Hall ST-237 160 Convent Ave, New York, NY 10031, **Business Phone:** (212)650-5439.

**WATKINS, CHERYL L. (CHERYL WATKINS-SNEAD)**
Executive. **Educ:** Univ Mass, BS, mech engineering, 1981; Purdue Univ, MBA, bus admin & mgt, 1987. **Career:** Gen Elec Corp; Banneker Indust Inc, founder, owner, pres & chief exec officer, 1991-. **Orgs:** Bd dir, Bank Ri, 1995-2012; charter mem, pres, Greater Providence RI Chap Links Inc, 1995; bd dir, Amica Mutual Ins Co, 2000; bd trustee, Bryant Univ, 2007; bd dir, Waterfire Providence, 2008-12. **Business Addr:** President, Chief Executive Officer, Banneker Industries Inc, 582 Great Rd Suite 101, North Smithfield, RI 02896, **Business Phone:** (401)534-0027.

**WATKINS, HON. CRAIG**
Lawyer. **Personal:** Born Nov 16, 1967, Dallas, TX; married Tanya; children: Chad, Cale & Taryn. **Educ:** Prairie View A&M Univ, BA, polit sci, 1990; Tex Wesleyan Univ Sch Law, JD, 1994. **Career:** Munic prosecutor; Fair Pk Bail Bonds, defense atty & owner; Pvt pract defense atty, currently; Dallas County, criminal dist atty, 2007-. **Orgs:** Am Bar Asn; Nat Asn Criminal Defense Lawyers; Tex Criminal Defense Lawyers Asn; Dallas Criminal Defense Lawyers Asn; Friendship-W Baptist Church; Kappa Alpha Psi Fraternity; Prairie View A&M Univ Alumni Asn; Nat Asn Advan Colored People; Dallas Bd; bd dir, Circle 10 Boy Scouts Am. **Special Achievements:** First African American district attorney, 2007. **Home Addr:** 900 Frost Hollow Dr, Desoto, TX 75115-7411. **Business Addr:** Criminal District Attorney, Dallas County District Attorney's Office, Frank Crowley Crt Bldg 133 N Industrial Blvd LB 19, Dallas, TX 75207, **Business Phone:** (214)653-3600.

**WATKINS, DONALD V.**
Executive. **Personal:** Born Sep 8, 1948, Parsons, KS; son of Levi Sr (deceased) and Lillian (deceased); married DeAndra Johnson; children: Donald Jr, Drew, Derry & Dustin; children: Claudia Rose. **Educ:** S Ill Univ, attended 1970; Univ Ala, law, 1973; Howard Univ, attended 1970. **Career:** Donald V Watkins, PC Fund, pres & chief exec officer, 1973-; Law off Fred B Gray; own law off, Birmingham, Ala, 1979; Birmingham City Coun, city atty, 1979-83; spec coun to mayor Birmingham, 1985-99; AlAm Bank, founder & chmn bd, 1999-; Masada Oxynol, owner, currently; Voter News Network, founder, 2006-; Watkins-Pencor LLC, owner. **Orgs:** Trustee, Ala State Univ, 1994-01; life mem, Alpha Phi Alpha Fraternity Inc; bd, State Mutual Insurance Company, Rome, Ga. **Business Addr:** Chairman of the Board, Founder, Alamerica Bank, 2170 Highland Ave Suite 150, Birmingham, AL 35205, **Business Phone:** (205)558-4600.

**WATKINS, DURAND**
Basketball coach. **Career:** Baldwin High Sch, 1988-92; Mich Mayhem Roster, asst coach, currently. **Business Addr:** Assistant Coach, Michigan Mayhem Roster, 1050 W Western Ave Suite 310, Muskegon, MI 49441, **Business Phone:** (231)728-7526.

**WATKINS, FAYE**
Library administrator, dean (education), librarian. **Educ:** Univ Tex, Austin, BA, Eng lit, 1990; Univ SC, Columbia, MA, Eng lit, 1998, MLS, 1998. **Career:** Johnson C Smith Univ, collection develop librn, 1999-2004, assoc dir libr serv, 2004-05, actg dir libr, 2006; Hampton Univ, libr dir, 2007-13; Fla Agr & Mech Univ, dean univ libr, 2014-. **Orgs:** New Libr Dirs Mentor Prog, bd dirs.

**WATKINS, HAROLD D., SR.**
Firefighter. **Personal:** Born Feb 19, 1933, Detroit, MI; son of Clara B McClenic and Jesse; married Edna Jean Ridgeley; children: Harold D Jr, Kevin Duane & Keith Arnette. **Educ:** Macomb Community Col, Mt Clemens, MI, AA, 1976. **Career:** Firefighter (retired); City Detroit, fire fighter, 1955-76, sgt, 1976-78, lt, 1978-84, capt, 1984-88, battalion chief, 1988, chief fire opers, 1988-93, exec fire comnr, 1994-98. **Orgs:** Llife mem, Nat Asn Advan Colored People; 47-4900 Spokane Block Club, 1959-; pres, Lay Ministers, CME Church, 1965-; bd dir, Manhood Orgn, 1986-, pres, 1988-; Int Bd Fire Chiefs; Int Asn Black Firefighters Phoenix; Black Prof Fire Fighters Asn. **Special Achievements:** One of the First African American to serve in the City of Detroit Fire Department. **Home Addr:** 571 New Town St W, Detroit, MI 48215-3288, **Home Phone:** (313)821-0927.

**WATKINS, IRA DONNELL**
Educator. **Personal:** Born Feb 12, 1941, Waco, TX; son of Artist and Lois; children: Sina. **Career:** Family First Art Prog, art teacher; Tenderloin Self Help Ctr; Hosp House Art Prog, art teacher; Nat Inst Art & Disabilities, interim dir & instr, currently. **Orgs:** Artist, Pro Art; artist, AMES Art Gallery; artist, John Natsoulas Art Gallery; artist, SF Rental Gallery. **Home Addr:** 650 44th St Apt 1, Oakland, CA 94609, **Home Phone:** (510)420-1413. **Business Addr:** Interim Director, Instructor, National Institute of Art & Disabilities, 551 23rd St, Richmond, CA 94804, **Business Phone:** (510)620-0290.

**WATKINS, DR. JAMES DARNELL**
Dentist, vice president (organization). **Personal:** Born Aug 29, 1949, Reidsville, NC; son of James Granderson and Sadie Lamberth; married Hardenia Ruth Jefferson; children: Daryl Granderson & Deveda Camille. **Educ:** VA Polytech Inst, State Univ, Blacksburg VA, BS, biol, 1971; Med Col Va Sch Dent, Richmond, DDS, 1975. **Career:** Pvt pract dentist, 1977-; State Bd Dent, gov appointee, 1989; Watkins Dent Assocs, dentist, currently. **Orgs:** Am Dent Asn, 1975-; Acad Gen Dent, 1975-; sec, Old Dom Dent Soc, 1978-; vpres, Century Investment Club, 1979-; Nat Asn Advan Colored People; Grad Chap Groove Phi Groove Soc Fel Inc; Beau Brummels Social & Civic Club; fel Acad Gen Dent; pres, bd dir, Citizens Boys Club Hampton VA; Penninsula Dent Soc, VA Dent Asn; pres, VA Bd Dent, 1993-; fel Va Dent Asn; Am Dent Asn's Coun Dent Educ & Comn Dent Accreditation, 1995-98; fel Int Col Dentists; fel Am Col Dentists; ADA rep, Dent Asst Nat Bd; Nat Dent Asn; secy, Old Dom Dent Soc Inc, 1977-2007; Am Asn Dent Examiners; Norman Lassiter Dent Soc; pres, Peninsula Dent Soc, 2000. **Honors/Awds:** President's Award, Old Dom Dent Soc, 1986; Dentist of the Year, Old Dom Dent Soc, 1987, 1990, 2005; Laymen of the Year, Boys Club Bd Dirs, 1995; American College of Dentists, 1995; Most Influential Black Alumni Award, Va Tech, 2010; Harry Lyons Distinguished Alumnus award, Med Col Va, 2010. **Special Achievements:** First African-American president of the Virginia State Dental Board, 1992; First African-American commanding officer in US Naval Reserve Dental Unit, Little Creek Amphibious Base; First African-American dentist to serve on the board. **Home Addr:** 1635 Big Bethel Rd, Hampton, VA 23666-1412, **Home Phone:** (757)766-0216. **Business Addr:** Dentist, Watkins Dental Associates, 2207 Exec Dr Suite C, Hampton, VA 23666, **Business Phone:** (757)827-5225.

**WATKINS, REV. JOSEPH PHILIP**
Journalist. **Personal:** Born Aug 24, 1953, New York, NY; married Stephanie Taylor; children: Tiffany Ann & Courtney Andrea. **Educ:** Univ Pa, BA, hist, 1975; Princeton Theol Sem, MA, Christian educ, 1979. **Career:** Daily Pennsylvani, ed cartoonist; Talladega Col, chaplain relig instr, 1978-79; Ind Purdue Univ Ft Wayne, campus minister, 1979-8l; US Sen Dan Quayle, asst state dir, 1981-84; US Cong, Republican nominee 10th dist, 1984; Saturday Eve Post, vpres & dir missions, 1984-; Merchants Nat Bank, com accts rep, 1984; Univ of Pa, asst, 1986; Advent Capital Mgt Partners, 1995-; Christ Evangel Lutheran Church, pastor, 1998-; MDL Capital Mgt firm, managing dir, prin; Middlesex Sch Bd Trustees, Eastern Technol Coun; Youth Inc; Crossroads Christian Commun. **Orgs:** Bd dir, Big Bros Greater Indianapolis; bd dir, Arthritis Found Indianapolis; bd dir, Poison Control Ctr Ind; bd dir, Salvation Army Indianapolis; bd dir, Penrod Soc; bd dir, C's Bur; adv bd Training Inc; bd dir, Humane Soc; bd dir, Jameson Camp; life mem, Nat Asn Advan Colored People; Bd Main Line Health; Bd Lankenau Hosp; Bd Steppingstone; Hist Socs Pa; vpres, Dan Quayles; dir, Hill Solutions; pres, Advent Capital Mgt Partners; dir, White House Off Pub Liaison, 1991. **Home Addr:** 5306 N Kenwood Ave, Indianapolis, IN 46208. **Business Addr:** Vice President, Director of Missions, Saturday Evening Post, 1100 Waterway Blvd, Indianapolis, IN 46202, **Business Phone:** (317)634-1100.

**WATKINS, ESQ. KENNETH T.**
Executive. **Educ:** Detroit Col Law, JD, 1992; Northwestern Univ, BS. **Career:** Urban Solutions Inc, vpres, currently; Sommers Schwartz PC, atty, 1992-. **Orgs:** Co-pres, Bro Rice High Sch Dads Club; dir, Dads Club Bd; trustee, Motor City Optimist Club; pres, Wolverine Bar Asn; bd, Mich Asn Justice; Am Bar Asn; mem, Nat Bar Asn; Fed Bar Asn. **Business Addr:** Vice President, Urban Solutions Inc, 269 Walker St Suite 124, Detroit, MI 48207, **Business Phone:** (313)567-2251.

**WATKINS, LOTTIE HEYWOOD**
Executive, chief executive officer. **Personal:** Born Atlanta, GA; daughter of Eddie and Susie Wilson; children: Joyce Bacote & Judy Yvonne Barnett. **Educ:** Booker T Wash High Schs, 1935; Reids Sch Bus. **Career:** Clerk, exec (retired); Alexander-Calloway Realty Co, sec 1945-54; Mutual Fed S&L Asn, teller-clerk, 1954-60; Lottie Watkins Enterprises, pres, chief exec officer, 1960. **Orgs:** Sec So Christian Leadership Conf, 1967; vice chmn, Fulton Co Dem Party, 1968; Fulton Co Jury Comnr, 1972-; Gov's Comm Voluntarism, 1972; Fulton Co Bd Regist & Elections, 1973-; Citizens Exchange Brazil, 1973; partic White House Conf Civil Rights; Ga Residential Finance Auth, 1974; Ga House Representatives, 1977; chmn, Am Cancer Soc; chmn, Comm Chest; exec comm bd dir, Nat Asn Advan Colored People; chair, Christmas Cheer Fund Atlanta Inquirer; League Women Voters, Atlanta Women's C C; Innumerable civic & prof organs; co-chair, YMCA Mem Campaign. **Home Addr:** 107 Mathewson Pl SW, Atlanta, GA 30314, **Home Phone:** (404)752-9322.

**WATKINS, MELVIN LENZO**
Basketball player, basketball coach. **Personal:** Born Nov 15, 1954, Reidsville, NC; married Burrell Bryant; children: Keia, Marcus & Manuale. **Educ:** Univ NC, Charlotte, BA, econ, 1977. **Career:** Basketball player (retired), basketball coach; NBA, Buffalo Baves, 1977-78; Univ NC, Charlotte, asst coach, 1978-87, assoc head coach, 1987-96, head basketball coach, 1996-98; Tex A&M Univ, head basketball coach, 1998-2004; Univ Mo, assoc head coach, 2004-11; Univ Ark, assoc head coach, 2011-. **Orgs:** Co-chair, Battered Women's Shelter; 100 Black Men Charlotte. **Special Achievements:** First African-American head coach in the school's history, 1998. **Business Addr:** Associate Head Basketball Coach, University of Arkansas, 471 N Garland Ave, Fayetteville, AR 72701, **Business Phone:** (479)575-2000.

**WATKINS, DR. MICHAEL THOMAS**
Surgeon. **Personal:** Born Nov 17, 1954, Washington, DC; son of Harding Thomas and Muriel Knowles; married Paula Pinkston; children: Steven Thomas & Adrienne Elise. **Educ:** NY Univ, BS, biol, 1976; Harvard Med Sch, Boston, Mass, MD, 1980. **Career:** Johns Hopkins Hosp, Dept Surg, Baltimore, Md, intern, 1980-81, asst resident, 1981-82; Uniformed Servs Univ Health Scis Sch Med, Bethesda, Md, res fel, 1982-84, res instr, 1983-84; Strong Memorial Hosp, Dept Surg, Rochester, NY, Sr resident, 1984-85, chief resident, 1985-86; Univ Rochester Sch Med, instr surg, 1985-86; Harvard Med Sch, Boston, Mass, clinal fel surg, 1986-87, vis surgeon & assoc prof; Mass Gen Hosp, Boston, Mass, Vascular Surg Dept, chief resident, 1986-87, Vascular Surgeon Res, Mass, dir, 2002-, Wound Clin, co-dir, vis surgeon, currently; Boston Univ Sch Med, Dept Surg, Boston, Mass, res fel, 1987-88, asst prof Surg & path, 1988-; Boston City Hosp, Mallory Inst Pathol, Boston, Mass, res assoc. **Orgs:** Nat Med Asn; Am Heart Asn, Thrombosis Coun; fel Am Col Surgeons; Nat bd Med Examrs; Am Bd Surg; Soc Univ Surgeons; Soc Black Acad Surgeons; Soc Vascular Surg. **Honors/Awds:** Resident Teaching Award, Dept Surg, Univ Rochester, Rochester Gen Hosp, 1986; Minority Med Fac Develop Award for In Vitro Response Vascular Endothelium to Hypoxia & Reoxygenation, Robert Wood Johnson Found, 1987-91; Grant-in-Aid for Phospholipid & Free Fatty Acids in HypoxicVascular Cells, Am Heart Asn, 1990-93; author with C.C. Haudens child, H.Albadawi, "Synergistic Effect Hypoxia & Stasis on Endothelial Cell Lactate Production, Journal Cellular Biol, 1990; R29 Res Award, Endothelid CellResponses to Acute Hypoxia & Reoxygenation, NIH, 1993-97; VA Merit Review Res Award, Signal Transduction in Hypoxic Vascular Cells, 1994-97; Board certified in General Surgery, 1987, Vascular Surgery, 1998. **Special Achievements:** Author with M.R. Graff, C.C. Haudenschild, F. Velasques, R.W. Hobson, "Effect Hypoxia & Reoxgenation Perfused Bovine Aortic Endothelial Cells, Journal Cellular Biol, 1989; author

numerous other articles &presentations. **Home Addr:** 14 Buchanan Rd, Roslindale, MA 02131, **Home Phone:** (617)323-2403. **Business Addr:** Director, Visiting Surgeon, Massachusetts General Hospital, 15 Parkman St WAC 440, Boston, MA 02114-3117, **Business Phone:** (617)726-0908.

## WATKINS, MOZELLE ELLIS

Government official, commissioner. **Personal:** Born May 18, 1924, Crockett, TX; daughter of Leroy (deceased) and Sallie Elizabeth Fleeks (deceased); married Charles Philip; children: Phyllis Caselia Jones & Eunice Juaquina Cothran. **Educ:** Hughes Bus Col, dipl, 1945; Extended Sch Law, attended 1960; Famous Writers Sch, Hartford, cert, 1970; Cath Univ, cert pub speaking, 1970; Georgetown Univ, Sch Law, attended 1977; Montgomery Col, span cert, 1978. **Career:** Government official (retired); Fed Govt, statist clerk & secy, 1945-69; Anacostia Citizens & Merchants Asn, admin asst, 1969-70; Montgomery County Govt Human Rel Comn, investr, 1971-93; DC Adv Neighborhood, comnr, 1976-96. **Orgs:** St Baptist Church 19th, 1946-; comt mem, DC Gov ANC-5A Single Dist 14, 1976-92; Brookland Comn Corp, 1978-89; chairperson, ANC 5A, 1978, 1979, 1985; 12th St Neighborhood Corps, 1979-89; pres, Jarvis Mem Club, 1983-; bd dir, Christian Educ, 1985-89; deleg, DC Dem State Conv, 1986; Northeast News Publ, 1986; 19th St Baptist Church, deaconess, 1987-; Ward V Unity County Comn, 1988; vice chairperson, DC Adv Neighborhood Comn 5A, 1989; bd dir, Nat Found Deaf, 1989-96; Montgomery County, Comn Employ People Disabilities, 1989-93; Adv Neighborhood Comn 5A, 1989; Woodridge Orange Hat Team, 1992-; elected comt mem, ANC 5A Single Dist 11, 1992-96; vpres & pres, Chinese-Am Lions Club, 1994-96, 2002-03; Nat Asn Advan Colored People; Woodridge Civic Asn; Gateway Community Asn; TASSL Block Club; Upper Northeast Family Day Comn; Citizens Adv Comt Dist Bar; Anacostia Citizens & Merchants Asn; DC Coun; Dept Defense, Bur Supplies & Accounts; coun mem, Ward V William R Spaulding; DC Chap Howard Univ, Moorland-Spingarn Res Ctr. **Honors/Awds:** Outstanding Serv & Dedication, State Tex, 1991; Cert of Recognition, Am Soc, 1992-93; Cert of Election, 1993-95; Cert of Recognition, Fifth Dist DC Metrop Police Dept & Citizens Adv Coun, 1996; ANC-5A Resolution Dedicated Commitment & Serv to the Community, 1999; Cert of Appreciation, Am Red Cross. **Special Achievements:** Author: "Two Zodiac Calendars", 1975 & 1977; Author proposal entitled "Resolution for the Conservation of a Section of the Nation's Capital as a Tribute to ARO" published in the DC Register, 1977. **Home Addr:** 3225 Walnut St NE, Washington, DC 20018, **Home Phone:** (202)529-0927.

## WATKINS, ROLANDA ROWE

Entrepreneur. **Personal:** Born Feb 22, 1956, Detroit, MI; daughter of Carlos Rowe and Doris Louie Rowe; married James Abel. **Educ:** Wayne State Univ, Detroit, MI, exec secy, stenographer, certi, 1973; Detroit Bus Inst, Detroit, MI, exec secy, cert, 1976; Detroit Col Bus, Dearborn, MI, assoc, bus admin, 1981, bachelor bus admin, 1988, masters, bus admin, 1998. **Career:** Provident Mutual Life Ins, Southfield, Mich, secy, 1980; Chevrolet Cent Off, Warren, Mich, secy, 1981; Midwestern Assocs, Detroit, Mich, secy, 1982-; Downtown Fish & Seafood, Detroit, Mich, owner, 1987-97; Acad Oak Park, bus educ teacher, 1999-; Carring Kids, founder, currently. **Orgs:** Founder, coordr, Caring Kids Youth Ministry, 1983-; Washington Blvd Merchants Asn, 1987-. **Honors/Awds:** Go 4 It Award, WDIV-TV 4, 1985; Devoted & Invaluable Service to the Youth, 14th Precinct, Detroit Police Dept, 1985; Senator Carl Levin, 1985, 1986; Governor James Blanchard, 1986, Mayor Coleman Young, 1986-93; Devoted & Invaluable Service to the Commendations, 1987; Youth, 2nd Precinct, Detroit Police Dept, 1987; Dedicated Service to Community, New Detroit, Inc, 1989; Spirit of Detroit Award, 1989; Outstanding Entrepreneurial Achievements, 1989; Black Women in Business Award, Nat Asn Negro Bus & Prof Women's Club, Inc, 1989; Nat Sojourner Truth Award, Nat Asn Negro Bus & Prof Women's Club, Inc, 1990; Living the Dream Award, Blacks Govt, 1992-93; Key to the City of Detroit, Mayor Coleman Young, 1993; Jefferson Award, 1995; WDIV and Hardee's Hometown Heros Award, 1993; Jefferson Award Winner, 1995; Community Service Award, 1997. **Special Achievements:** Serving free Thanksgiving Dinner to over 9000 homeless people, 1986. **Home Addr:** 14236 Burt Rd, Detroit, MI 48223, **Home Phone:** (313)533-3037. **Business Addr:** Founder, Caring Kids, PO Box 23161, Detroit, MI 48223, **Business Phone:** (313)614-8675.

## WATKINS, ROSYLN

Law enforcement officer. **Personal:** Born Dec 20, 1956, Omaha, NV. **Career:** Zor Productions, owner, 1998-; Alameda County Sheriffs Off, dep sheriff investr, currently. **Orgs:** Vice chmn, Nat Black Police Asn, 1998-2000; officer, Drug Abuse Resistance Educ, 1996-; Crime Prev Officer, 1996-; secy, dir, Lovelife Found, 1998-; pres, W Region Nat Black Police Asn. **Home Addr:** 2558 99th Ave, Oakland, CA 94605. **Business Addr:** Deputy Sheriff Investigator, Alameda County Sheriff's Office, 1401 Lakeside Dr Fl 12, Oakland, CA 94612, **Business Phone:** (510)667-3622.

## WATKINS, SHIRLEY R.

Consultant, government official. **Personal:** Born Jan 7, 1938, Hope, AR; daughter of Robert Robinson; married George R; children: Robert T & Miriam Cecelia. **Educ:** Univ Ark Bluff, BS, home econs, 1960; Univ Memphis, MEd, 1970, post grad, 1991. **Career:** Univ Ark Exten Serv, asst negro home demonstration agt, 1960-62; Memphis City Schs, fourth grade teacher, 1962-63, home econs teacher, 1963-69, food serv supvr, 1969-75, dir nutrit serv, 1975-93; US Dept Agr, dep asst secy, FCS, 1993-95, dep under secy, FNCS, 1994-95, dep asst secy mkt & regional progs, 1995-97, under secy Food Nutrit & Consumer Serv, US Dept Agr, 1997-2001; Southern Educ Serv, consult, currently; Pa State Univ, prof; SR Watkins & Assocs LLC, pres & founder, currently. **Orgs:** Alpha Kappa Alpha, 1958-; life mem subscribing golden heritage, Nat Asn Advan Colored People, 1970-; vpres, sect chair, legisl comt, 1982-90; pres, Les Casuale, vpres, treas, hospitality, 1982-93; pres, Am Sch Food Serv Asn, 1988-89; chmn, Int Facil Mgt Asn Gold & Silver Plate Soc, secy, treas. **Business Addr:** President, Founder, SR Watkins & Associates, 16612 Sea Island Ct, Silver Spring, MD 20905, **Business Phone:** (301)476-7533.

## WATKINS, TIONNE TENESE

Singer, actor. **Personal:** Born Apr 26, 1970, Des Moines, IA; daughter of James and Gayle; married Dedrick Rolison; children: Chase Anela. **Career:** Singer & actress; TLC, group mem; Albums: Ooooooohhh.... On the TLC Tip, 1992; Crazy Sexy Cool, 1994; Fan Mail, 1999; 3D, 2002; Singles: "Touch Myself", 1996; "Ghetto Love", 1996; "My Getaway", 2000; "Tight To Def", 2000; "Someday", 2009; Films: House Party 3, 1994; Belly, 1998; TV series: "CBS School break Special", 1992; Living Single, 1997; "One World Music Beat", 1998; "TLC: Sold Out", 2000; "Class of 3000", 2006; The Apprentice, 2009. **Orgs:** Spokesperson, Sickle Cell DisAsn Am. **Special Achievements:** Book: "Thoughts", 1999; Named one of the 50 most beautiful people of the world by People Magazine twice for the year 1994 & 2000. **Business Addr:** Singer, Actress, c/o Sony BMG Music Entertainment, 550 Madison Ave, New York, NY 10022, **Business Phone:** (212)833-8000.

## WATKINS, DR. WALTER J.

School superintendent, teacher. **Educ:** Ind Univ Bloomington, BS, Eng, sec educ; Ind Univ-Purdue Univ Indianapolis, MS, sec educ; Purdue Univ, W Lafayette, IN, PhD. **Career:** Sch City Hammond, Eggers Mid Sch, teacher, asst prin, prin, dir sec curric & instr, supt, 2003. **Orgs:** Fel Ctr Leadership & Sch Reform; Hammond Educ Found; Hammond Woodmar Kiwanis; Northwest Ind Habitat Humanity. **Special Achievements:** District's first black superintendent. **Business Addr:** Superintendent, School City of Hammond, 41 Williams St, Hammond, IN 46320-1948, **Business Phone:** (219)933-2400.

## WATKINS, WILLIAM, JR.

Executive. **Personal:** Born Aug 12, 1932, Jersey City, NJ; son of William J and Willie Ree Blount; married Sylvia I Mulzac; children: Cheryl, Rene M & Linda M. **Educ:** Pace Univ, BBA, 1954; NY Univ, MBA, 1962. **Career:** Executive (retired); Consol Edison Co New York Inc, staff asst, 1957-65; Volkswagen Am Inc, syst mgr, 1965-71; Volkswagen, Nebr, Wilmington, MA, exec, 1971-72; New Eng Elect Sys, Westborough, MA, exec, 1972-82; Naragansett Elec Co, vpres, 1982-86, exec vpres, 1992-98, dir econ develop; New Eng Power Serv Co, vpres, 1986-92. **Orgs:** Bd dir, Bank Boston RI, 1987-99; Leadership RI, 1992-97; INROADS Cent New Eng, 1993-97; Nat Conf Christians & Jews, 1993-97; chmn, RI Indust Competitiveness Alliance, 1994-97; RI Hosp, 1994-97; Lifespan, 1997-2000; chair & bd trustee, RI Sch Design, 1998-2000. **Home Addr:** 5114 87th Ct E, Bradenton, FL 34211, **Home Phone:** (941)752-6376.

## WATKINS, WYNFRED C. (WYNN WATKINS)

Manager, association executive. **Personal:** Born Apr 15, 1946, Toledo, OH; son of Clifford G and Marie B Marr (deceased); married Brenda J Sparks; children: Suzan Marie & Tara Edwina. **Educ:** Bowling Green State Univ, Bowling Green, OH, 1966. **Career:** JC Penney Co Inc, Saginaw, Mich, dist mgr, 1990-93, Dallas, Tex, dir geog mkts, vpres & dir investor rels, 1998-2000, sr vpres pub rel, dir commun & pub affairs, 2000-05, sr vpres & dir diversity, 2005-06; Ergo-Voice Inc, chmn. **Orgs:** Chmn, JC Penney Northeastern Regional Affirmative Action Comt Southwest, Cleveland, OH, 1989, 1990; bd mem, Adv Bd Parma Gen Hosp, Cleveland, OH, 1989; spiritual aim chmn, Kiwanis Club Saginaw Westshields, currently; Zion Baptist Missionary Church, Saginaw, currently; life mem, Nat Asn Advan Colored People; bd dir, Dallas Black Dance Theatre; trustee bd dir, Jarvis Christian Col; chmn bd dir, Jr Achievement Metrop Dallas; Exec Leadership Coun & Found. **Honors/Awds:** Store Manager of the Year Award, JC Penney, Cleveland District, 1989; various company awards for beating sales/profit objectives. **Home Addr:** 3522 Haldeman Creek Dr, Naples, FL 34112, **Home Phone:** (941)774-0053. **Business Addr:** Chairman, Ergo-Voice Inc, 102001 S Padre Island Dr, Corpus Christi, TX 78418.

## WATKINS-SNEAD, CHERYL. See WATKINS, CHERYL L.

## WATLEY, JODY VANESSA

Singer, songwriter, founder (originator). **Personal:** Born Jan 30, 1959, Chicago, IL; married Andre Cymone; children: Lauren & Arie. **Career:** Singer, songwriter, record producer, pianist; model; Soul Train, dancer; Shalamar, vocalist, 1978-83; model, 1983-85; Avitone label, founder, 1995, rec artist, 1997; Ford Modeling Agency, model; Shanachie label, rec artist, 2002-; Avitone Recordings, chief exec officer, currently; Solo Albums: Jody Watley, 1987-88; Larger than Life, 1989, Affairs of the Heart, 1991-92. Intimacy, 1993-94; Affection, 1995; Greatest Hits, 1996; Flower, 1997-98; Saturday Night Experience, 1999; Midnight Lounge, 2001-05; Ocl Looking For a New Love Oco Remix EP, 2005; Borderline, 2006; Makeover, 2006-14; Live with Regis & Kathie Lee, 2006; Unsung, 2009; Paradise & Reloading Shalamar, 2014-; Live Albums: Super Hits Live, 2007; Eps: Paradise, 2014; Compilation albums: 20th Century Masters-The Millennium Collection: The Best of Jody Watley, 2000; Remix albums: You Wanna Dance with Me?, 1989; Remixes of Love, 1994; Singles: "Looking for a New Love", 2005; "Borderline", 2006; "I Want Your Love", 2007; "A Beautiful Life", 2008; "Candlelight", 2009; "Nightlife", 2013; performer & writer: "Forever Knight", 1989; "Doogie Howser, M.D.", 1989; Switch, 1991; White Men Can't Jump, 1992; "Melrose Pl", 1993; Doctor Dolittle, 1998; Lost & Found, 1999; "Live from Studio Five", 2010; self: "New Am Bandstand 1965", 1979; "Soul Train", 1980; 1987 Power Hits: New Yr's Eve Countdown, 1987; 20th NAACP Image Awards, 1988; The 15th Ann Am Music Awards, 1988; The 2nd Ann Soul Train Music Awards, 1988; Dance to Fitness, 1990; Red Hot & Blue, 1990; The 17th Ann Am Music Awards, 1990; The 4th Ann Soul Train Music Awards, 1990; The 19th Ann Am Music Awards, 1992; "Ebony/Jet Showcase", 1992; The 6th Ann Soul Train Music Awards, 1992, 1994; "ABC Afterschool Specials", 1994; "The Daily Show with Jon Stewart", m1998; "The Rosie O'Donnell Show", 1998; "Top Ten", 2001; Babyface: A Collection of Hit Videos, 2001; "Pyramid", 2003; "I Love the '80s Strikes Back", 2003; "Work Out", 2006; "VH1 Rock Docs", 2010. **Business Addr:** Artist, Shanachie Entertainment Corp, 37 E Clinton St, Newton, NJ 07860, **Business Phone:** (973)579-7763.

## WATLEY, MARGARET SEAY

Educator. **Personal:** Born Oct 19, 1925, Nashville, TN. **Educ:** Tenn A&I State Univ, BS, 1947; HM Nailor, Cleveland, MS, 1957; Columbia Univ, MA, 1965. **Career:** Educator (retired); Jasper Co, GA, teacher, 1950-53; Winchester Comm Sch, 1958; New Haven Pub Sch, teacher. **Orgs:** Nat Asn Negro Bus Prof Women's Clubs Inc, 1971-72; New Haven Educ Asn, 1972-76; Conn Del NEA Rep Assembly, 1972; NE Dist Org Nat Asn Negro Bus & Prof Women's Clubs Inc, 1976; founder, organizer, Elm City Sr Club & Elm City Youth Club, 1976; Elm City Young Adult Club, 1977; reappointed organizer, NE Dist Gov NANBPW Inc, 1979; pres, Elm City Sr Club New Haven & Vicinity, 1977-81; treas, African-Am Women's Agenda, 1992-2001; bd dir, New Haven Colony Hist Soc, 1995-2001; life mem, Nat Educ Asn; life mem, NANB BWC Inc; pres, New Haven Club; Conn Educ Asn; Christian Tabernacle Baptist Church; bd dir, League Women Voters New Haven, dir voters serv, New Haven Scholar Fund; Edgerton Garden Conservancy Bd; Libr Bd city New Haven; Friends Grove St Cemetery; bd dir, New Heaven Free Pub Libr; hon dir, New Haven Mus. **Honors/Awds:** Outstanding Elementary Teachers of America, 1972; Outstanding Participation Award, NANB & PW Clubs Inc, 1976-77; Nat So journer Truth Meritorious Service Award, Elm City Sr Club, 1978; Leadership Development Award, Conn Educ Asn; Mary B. Ives Award, New Haven Pub Libr; vol Extra ordinare Award, Greater New Haven Asn vol Administrators. **Home Addr:** 19 Read St, New Haven, CT 06511-1120, **Home Phone:** (203)624-8963. **Business Addr:** Board of Director, New Haven Free Public Library, 133 Elm St, New Haven, CT 06510, **Business Phone:** (203)946-8130.

## WATLINGTON, JANET BERECIA

Executive, government official. **Personal:** Born Dec 21, 1938, St. Thomas; married Michael F MacLeod; children: Gregory & Kafi. **Educ:** Pace Univ, attended 1957; George Washington Univ, attended 1977. **Career:** Action & Peace Corps, asst dir legis affairs, 1979-; Hon Ron deLugo US House ofReps, admin asst, 1968-78; Legis VI St Thomas, exec secy, 1965-68. **Orgs:** Co-chmn, Dem Nat Conv Rules Comn, 1976; appointee, Dem Party ComnPresidential Nomination & Party Struc, 1976; dem nominee cong, VI, 1978; vice chair, Dem Nat Comn, Eastern Region, 1972; steering com, Dem NatCom Black Caucus, 1974; exec com, Dem Party Chtr Comn, 1974; Cong Black-Caucus, 1974; charter mem, Sr Exec Serv Fed Govt, 1979; dir, VI Fed ProgsOff. **Home Addr:** 4324 Westover Pl NW, Washington, DC 20016. **Business Addr:** Assistant Director, Action & Peace Corps, 806 Connecticut Ave NW, Washington, DC 20525.

## WATSON, AARON

Government official, lawyer. **Personal:** married Sandra; children: Jennifer, Andrew & Jana. **Educ:** Univ Notre Dame, BS, acct, 1978; Duke Univ, JD, law, 1985. **Career:** Attache Pub Affairs, pres, 1982-; Atlanta Bd Educ, chmn, pres, 1994-2002; pvt pract atty & bus consul, currently; A-AB2, pres; Greenberg Traurig, atty; Merit Span Holdings Inc, pres; Deloitte & Touche, acct; Barnes & Thornburg LLP, coun, 2012-13; Thompson Hine LLP, sr coun, 2013-. **Orgs:** Atlanta Recycles Steering Comt; bd mem, Atlanta Develop Authority, 1990-2000; pres, Piedmont Park Conservancy, 1992-2000; bd comnr, Atlanta Housing Authority, 2005-09; City Atlanta Gen Employees' Pension Fund; coun mem, Atlanta City Coun Post 2 At-Large, 2010-13. **Home Addr:** , GA. **Business Addr:** Senior Counsel, Thompson Hine LLP, 2 Alliance Ctr 3560 Lenox Rd NE Suite 1600, Atlanta, GA 30326-4266, **Business Phone:** (404)407-3645.

## WATSON, ANNE

Consultant, executive, financial manager. **Personal:** Born Feb 19, 1945, Belzoni, MS; married John; children: Brianna. **Educ:** Western Mich Univ, BA, 1970; Univ Mich, attended 1976. **Career:** Western Mich Univ, tutor counr & asst dorm dir, 1967-70; Shaw Col Detroit, financial aid dir, 1971-76; Univ Detroit, financial aid dir; Wayne St Univ, financial aid counr, 1974-75; Dept HEW, consult, 1976, discussion leader, 1977-; MI Financial Aid Asn, presentor & panelist, 1980; Nelnet Inc, regional dir; Independent Cols, vpres; Univs Mich, vpres. **Orgs:** Nat Asn Advan Fin Aid Adminstr, 1975-80; chairperson, Comn Physically & Ment Handicap, 1978-79; bd dir, Black United Fund, 1979-80; elected off, app chair, co-chair, & vol mem, MSFAA & MASFAA. **Honors/Awds:** Cert, Moton Consortium Dept HEW, 1974-75; Cert Moton Consortium, Dept HEW, 1975, MSFAA Distinguished Service Award, 1999; President's Award, 2012-13; Lifetime Achievement Award, 2012. **Home Addr:** 16166 Rosemont Ave, Detroit, MI 48219.

## WATSON, ANNIE MAE

Association executive. **Orgs:** Exec comt mem, Nat Assoc Advan Colored People, currently. **Business Addr:** Executive Committee Member, National Association for the Advancement of Colored People, 1104 Broadway Ave Suite F, Seaside, CA 93955, **Business Phone:** (831)394-3727.

## WATSON, ANTHONY J. See WATSON, TONY J.

## WATSON, BARBARA M.

Business owner. **Career:** La Tienda Inn & Duran House, owner, 1994-. **Business Addr:** Owner, La Tienda Inn & Duran House, 138 W Manhattan Ave, Santa Fe, NM 87501, **Business Phone:** (505)984-8001.

## WATSON, BEN

Television journalist. **Personal:** Born Jan 28, 1955, Muskegon Heights, MI; son of Bennie Sr and Lionel Matthews. **Educ:** Cent Mich Univ, Mt Pleasant, MI, BS, jour, 1978; Poynter Inst; New York Univ. **Career:** WZZM TV, Grand Rapids, Mich, tv camera operator, 1978-79; WEYI TV, Flint, Mich, tv reporter, 1979-80; WOTV, Grand Rapids, Mich, tv reporter, 1980-83; WLMT TV, Grand Rapids, Mich, tv reporter, 1983-86; Grand Rapids Press, Grand Rapids, Mich, newspaper weekend reporter, 1983, 84; WMC TV, Memphis, Tenn, gen assignment reporter & corresp, 1986-. **Orgs:** National Association for the Advancement of Colored People, 1986-; Nat Asn Black Journalists, 1987-; Omega Psi Phi, 1975-; Manna Outreach, 1990-; Profiles Recent Develop. **Honors/Awds:** Communicator Award, Am Cancer

Soc, 1983; Journalism Award, Flint Urban League, 1979; Achievement Award, Interpreting Serv Deaf, 1989; Volunteer Award, Miss Blvd Chap Church, 1990; Gabriel Award, 1999; Nat Asn Black Journalist Award; The Hal Walton Journalism Award, Am Cancer Soc. **Home Addr:** PO Box 18216, Memphis, TN 38118-0216, **Home Phone:** (901)795-4830. **Business Addr:** TV Reporter, Anchor, WMC-TV, 1960 Union Ave, Memphis, TN 38104-4031, **Business Phone:** (901)726-0416.

### WATSON, DR. BERNARD C.

Educator. **Personal:** Born Mar 4, 1928, Gary, IN; son of Homer Bismarck and Fannie Mae Browne; married Lois Lathan; children: Barbra D & Bernard C Jr. **Educ:** Ind Univ, BS, 1951; Univ Ill, MEd, 1955; Univ Chicago, PhD, social sci, 1967; Harvard Univ, Cambridge, MA, postdoctoral advan admin, 1968. **Career:** Gary Pub Sch, Gary, Ind, teacher, counr, prin, 1955-65; Univ Chicago, Chicago, Ill, staff assoc, 1965-67; Philadelphia Sch Dist, 1967-70; Temple Univ, chmn & prof, dept urban educ, 1970-75, vpres, acad admin, 1976-81, presidential scholar, 1994, urban educ, endowed chair, anchor, currently; William Penn Found, pres, chief exec officer, 1982-93; HMA Found, chmn, 1994-97. **Orgs:** Bd dir, AAA Mid-Atlantic; vice chmn, Nat Adv Coun Educ Professions Develop, 1967-70; steering comt, exec comt, Nat Urban Coalition, 1973-89; mem vis comt, Harvard Col, Dept Afro-Am Studies, 1974-78; Nat Coun Educ Res, 1980-82; mem vis comt, Harvard Univ Grad Sch Educ, 1981-87; Pa fed judiciary nominating comn, 1981-89; sr vice chmn, bd dir, Nat Urban League, 1983-96; vice chmn, bd dir, Pa Conv Ctr Authority, 1986-; vice chmn, Pa Coun Arts, 1986-93; William T Grant Fedn Comn Work, Family & Citizenship, 1987-88; secy bd, Nj State Aquarium, 1988-93; chmn, Ave Arts Inc, 1992-97; Judicial Conduct Bd, Supreme Ct Pa, 1993-97; chmn, Health Mgt Alternatives Found, 1993-97; trustee, Thomas Jefferson Univ, 1993-94; Nat Adv Coun Historically Black Col & Univ, 1994-97; Am Philos Soc; Am Acad Polit & Social Sci; Phi Delta Kappa; Kappa Delta Pi; Adv Comn, Patterson Res Inst CLG Rund, UNCF, 1996-; pres, bd trustee, Barnes Found, 1999-. **Honors/Awds:** More than 100 major awards, including 23 honorary degrees; Dr Bernard C Watson Grad Sem Room and Award presented for best social sci dissertation, Temple Univ, Col of Educ; Philadelphia Award, 2001. **Special Achievements:** First endowed chair in honor of an African American in Temple University's history; Author: "In Spite of the System: The Individual & Educ Reform", 1974; "Plain Talk About Educ: Conversations with Myself", 1987; "Testing: Its Origin, Use and Misuse", 1996; "Colored, Negro, Black: Chasing the American Dream", 1997; 13 monographs; chapters in 28 books; 100 career folios; 35 articles in professional journals; A school was named in his honor by the Gary, Indiana Board of Education, 2005. **Home Addr:** 473 Copper Beech Cir, Elkins Park, PA 19144, **Home Phone:** (215)886-2048. **Business Addr:** Endowed Chair, Temple University, 1801 N Broad St, Philadelphia, PA 19122, **Business Phone:** (215)204-7000.

**WATSON, BOB.** See WATSON, ROBERT JOSE.

### WATSON, CAROLE M.

Social worker, chief financial officer. **Personal:** Born Aug 3, 1944, New Orleans, LA; daughter of Herman and Frances; children: Dionne T. **Educ:** Western Mich Univ, BS, 1965; Wayne State Univ, MSW, 1970. **Career:** Milwaukee Area Tech Col, instr, 1972-73; Tenn State Univ, Dept Social Welfare, instr, curric coordr, 1973-77; Univ Tenn, Sch Social Work, asst prof, 1977-79; WZTV Channel 17 Black Pulse, hostess, 1981-85; Nashville Urban League, exec dir, 1979-85; Bay Area Urban League, Oakland, Calif, vpres, pres, chief exec officer, 1985-90; United Way, San Francisco, Calif, sr vpres, chief investment officer, 1990, chief community investment officer, 2011. **Orgs:** United Way Am/Anne E. Casey Found fel, John F. Kennedy Sch Govt, Harvard Univ; Delta Sigma Theta Nashville Alumnae, 1963-; Acad Cert Social Workers, 1975-; adv coun, Brd Cert Master Soc Workers, 1980-81; dir, Tenn Chap Nat Assn Social Workers, 1980; vpres, natl coun execs, Nat Urban League; consumer adv comn, S Cent Bell; bd dir, Tenn Opp Prog Legal Serv Mid, TN; Nat Asn Advan Colored People; Bay Area Assn Black Social Workers, 1986-. **Honors/Awds:** Appreciation Award, Alpha Delta Mu, Nat Soc Worker Hon Soc Iota Chap, Tenn St Univ, 1978; Congressional Record Award, Bill Booner 5th Congressional Dist State Tenn, 1985; 'Wall of Distinction', Western Mich Univ, 1986; Employee of the Year, Bay Area Urban League, 1987; Appreciation Award, Calif Asn Black Social Worker, 1989; Citizen of the Year, Riverside Seventh-day Adventist Church. **Home Addr:** 6321 Outlook Ave, Oakland, CA 94605, **Home Phone:** (510)639-7770. **Business Addr:** Chief Investment Officer, United Way of the Bay Area, 1970 Broadway Suite 600, Oakland, CA 94612, **Business Phone:** (510)238-2421.

### WATSON, CHESTER N.

Auditor, vice president (organization). **Personal:** married Francine; children: Talik & Daren. **Educ:** Rochester Inst Technol, BS, acct, 1974; State NY, pub acct, cert. **Career:** Bell Atlantic Corp, exec officer & vpres internal auditing, 1992-2000; Lucent Technol Inc, vpres corp audit & security, 2000-03; Gen Motor Corp, gen auditor. **Orgs:** Bd trustee, Rochester Inst Technol, currently.

### WATSON, DR. CLYNIECE LOIS

Physician, pediatrician. **Personal:** Born Jan 27, 1948, Chicago, IL; married Sloan Timothy Letman III; children: Sloan Timothy Letman IV. **Educ:** Loyola Univ, BS, 1969; Meharry Med Col, MD, 1973; Univ Ill, MPH, 1977. **Career:** John H Stroger Hosp Cook County, resident, 1973-75; Columbus-Cuneo-Cabrini Med Ctr, Dept Pediat, resident, 1981-82; Provident Hosp, assoc med dir, 1977, assoc res integrity officer; pvt pract pediatrician, currently. **Orgs:** Am Med Womens Asn; Am Pub Health Asn; Black Caucus Health Workers; Am Col Prev Med; AMA; St Med Soc; Med Soc Ill; Pub Health Asn; Am Asn Univ Women; Nat Med Asn; bd dir, Komed Health Ctr; Phi Delta Kappa Hon Educ Fraternity; Womens Fel Congregation Church; bd, Religions Educ, Congregational Church; Meharry Alumni Asn; Univ Ill Alumni Asn; Asn Physicians Cook Co, 1971-73; Lambda Alpha Omega Chap, Alpha Kappa Alpha Sorority Inc. **Honors/Awds:** Merit Award, Womens Fel Congregational Church; Outstanding Young Citizen Chicago Jaycees, 1980; fel Martin Luther King Jr. **Business Addr:** Physician, Associate Research Integrity Officer, Provident Hospital of Cook County, 500 E 51st St, Chicago, IL 60615, **Business Phone:** (312)572-2696.

### WATSON, CONSTANCE A.

Public relations executive. **Personal:** Born Aug 17, 1951, Nashville, TN; children: Shannon. **Educ:** Tenn State Univ, MSSW, 1978. **Career:** Dede Wallace Ment Health Ctr, psychiat social worker, 1973-82; Neuville Indust, dir ocean pac div, 1982-86; W W & Assocs Pub Rels, pres & founder, 1985-. **Orgs:** Chairperson, Nat Hook Up Black Women, 1980-82; Exec Comt, Nat Asn Advan Colored People, 1984-86, vpres, 1986-; bd dir, Found Educ, 1984-. **Honors/Awds:** Achievement Award, Golden W Mag, 1987. **Special Achievements:** Public relations consultant for major Hollywood and Los Angeles celebrities and events, i.e. 19th NAACP Image Awdstelevised on NBC. **Home Addr:** 1115 W 42nd St, Los Angeles, CA 90037, **Home Phone:** (213)752-4770. **Business Addr:** President, Founder, W W & Associates, 1539 W 56th St, Los Angeles, CA 90062, **Business Phone:** (213)752-4770.

### WATSON, DANIEL

Business owner, investment banker, consultant. **Personal:** Born Apr 11, 1938, Hallettsville, TX; married Susan Smallwood; children: Pamela, Bradley, Stanley, Jodney & Narlan. **Educ:** Univ Wash, BS, 1959, MS, 1965. **Career:** Wash Nat Inst, agt, 1966-68, mgr, 1968-71, gen agt, 1971; Daniel Watson Agency Inc, owner & founder, investment advisor, currently. **Orgs:** Seattle Planning Redevel Coun, 1967-71; Nat Gen Agents & Mgrs Asn, 1971-; Chicago Asn Life Underwriters, 1979. **Honors/Awds:** Agency Builder Award Wash Nat, 1970-75, 1977. **Special Achievements:** Article published Psychological Reports, 1965. **Home Addr:** 28W251 Bellean Dr, Winfield, IL 60190, **Home Phone:** (800)888-0179. **Business Addr:** Founder, Owner, Daniel Watson Agency Inc, 2607 W 22nd St Suite 46, Oak Brook, IL 60523, **Business Phone:** (630)572-0260.

### WATSON, DENNIS RAHIIM

Lecturer, writer, educator. **Personal:** Born May 14, 1953, Hamilton; son of Eula Watson-Stewart and Arthur Daniels. **Educ:** Fordham Univ, attended 1976; Pace Univ, attended 1978; NY Univ. **Career:** Theater Everyday Life, exec dir, 1980-83; New York Coun, exec asst, 1983-84; Natl Black Youth Leadership Coun, founder, exec dir, pres & chief exec officer, 1984-. **Orgs:** UNCF, 1980-86; NY Urban League, 1980-86; vol, Bay view Correctional Facility Women, 1980-86; Nat Alliance Black Sch Educr, 1984-86; Coun Concerned Black Execs, 1980-86; Nat Asn Advan Colored People, 1984-86; Black Leadership Round Table, 1984-86. **Honors/Awds:** Performing Arts Award, Sigma Gamma Rho, 1984; Nat Black Leadership Round table Award, 1984; US Dept of Justice Drug Enforcement Admin Volunteer Award, 1984; Mayors Ethnic New Yorker Award, 1985; Presidential White House Citation, 1985; Pvt Sector Initiative Award, 1986; Bayview Correctional Facility for Women Male Performer of the Year, 1986; OIC Appreciation Award, 1988; Leadership Appreciation Award, Univ Calif Los Angeles, 1989; The Black Women Task Force Award, 1989; Nat Black Grad Student Award, Miss State Univ, 1990; Black Student Alliance Award, Univ Va; Human Res Admin Spec Award, City of New York; Delta Sigma Theta Youth Award, Apple P; Western Mich Univ Student Leadership Conf Award, 1991; Fla Int Univ Black Family Award; Youth Award, Aspira; Youth Award, Family Christian Asn Am; Black Historian Month Award, Burlington County Col; Received 250 Award for Black Youth Nationwide; Caribbean Impact Award. **Special Achievements:** Americas Best & Brightest Young Business & Professional Man, 1987; One of America's most powerful motivational speakers. **Business Addr:** President, Chief Executive Officer, Nat Black Youth Leadership Coun, 250 W 54th St Suite 800, New York, NY 10019, **Business Phone:** (212)541-7600.

### WATSON, PROF. DENTON L.

Writer, public relations executive, journalist. **Personal:** Born Dec 19, 1935, Kingston; son of Ivy L and Audley G; married Rosa Balfour; children: Victor C & Dawn M. **Educ:** Univ Hartford, BA, 1964; Columbia Univ, Grad Sch Jour, MS, 1965; Cath Univ Chile, Inter Am Press Asn scholar, 1967. **Career:** Hartford Courant, reporter, 1965-67; Time Mag, writer; NCP Dept Pub Rels, asst dir, 1971; Baltimore Sun, ed writer; auth; State Univ NY, Col Old Westbury, Am Studies, assoc prof, 1992-; State Univ NY Col, assoc prof, 1992-; Papers Clarence Mitchell Jr, proj dir, ed. **Orgs:** Am Hist Asn; Nat Asn BalckJournalists; Authors Guild Inc; dir pub rel, Nat Asn Advan Colored People. **Special Achievements:** Author: Lion in the Lobby, Clarence Mitchell Jr's Struggle for the Passage of Civil Rights Laws; The Papers of Clarence Mitchell, Jr, Confirm the 101st Senator's Unique Role In Seeking Passage of Civil Rights Laws, Volumes I & II, III, 2002. **Home Addr:** 137 W Seaman Ave, Freeport, NY 11520, **Home Phone:** (516)546-3754. **Business Addr:** Associate Professor, State University of New York, E215 223 Store Hill Rd, Old Westbury, NY 11568-0210, **Business Phone:** (516)876-2885.

### WATSON, DR. DIANE EDITH

College administrator, psychologist, congressperson (U.S. federal government). **Personal:** Born Nov 12, 1933, Los Angeles, CA; daughter of William Allen Louis and Dorothy Elizabeth O. **Educ:** Los Angeles City Col, AA, 1954; Univ Calif, BA, 1956; Calif State Univ, MS, psychol, 1967; Claremont Col, PhD, educ admin, 1986; Harvard Univ, Kennedy Sch Govt. **Career:** US Representative (retired); Los Angeles Unified Sch Dist, teacher, 1956-60, asst prin & teacher, 1963-68, asst supr, Child Welfare & Attendance, 1968-69, sch psychologist, 1969-70; AUS Okinawa & France, teacher, 1960-63; Calif State La Dept Guid, assoc prof, 1969-70; Univ Calif Sec Schs Allied Health Proj, depdir, 1969-71; Health Occup Los Angeles Unified Sch Dist, specialist, 1971-73; Bd Educ, 1975-78; Calif State Senate, Dist 26, sen, 1978-98, Health & Human Servs Comt, chairperson, 1981; Us Ambassador Micronesia, 1999-2000; US House Rep, congresswoman, 2001-03, California's 33rd congressional district, US rep, 2003-11; Calif State Univ, lectr; Los Angeles pub schs, advocate. **Orgs:** Dem Nat Comt; founder & pres, Nat Orgn Black Elected Legis Women; Calif Elected Women's Asn Educ & Res; Nat Adv Panel mem, Univ Calif Ctr Study Eval; Med Policy Comn; auth & adv com mem, McGraw Hill/Gregg Div; consult, Calif Comn Status Women; Nat Sch Bds Asn; Calif Sch Bds Asn Calif Asn Sch Psychologists & Psychometrists; LA Elem Coun & Guid Asn; United Teachers LA; Calif Teachers Asn; hon life mem, PTA; mem exec bd, Coun Great Cities Schs; bd mem, Stevens House; Friends Golden State Minority Found; Nat Black Womens Polit Caucus; Coun Black Admins; Calif Dem Cent Com Educ Comn; Nat Asn Advan Colored People; Media Women; Alpha Kappa Alpha Nat Sorority; chair, Cong Entertainment Industs Caucus; co chair, Cong Korea Caucus; co chair, US-UK Caucus; House Foreign Affairs Comt; House Oversight and Govt Reform Comt. **Home Addr:** 5331 Harcourt Ave, Los Angeles, CA 90043, **Home Phone:** (323)295-5555.

### WATSON, DR. ELIZABETH DARBY

Educator. **Personal:** Born Nov 18, 1945, Harlem, NY; daughter of Samuel Darby and Jayne Doswell Darby; children: Leslie Watson Bray, L Roger III & Ercell I II. **Educ:** Columbia Union Col, BA, 1967; Howard Univ, MSW, 1969; Andrews Univ, PhD, hist, 2001. **Career:** Tenn Christian Med Ctr, dir social servs, 1981-87; Rebound CHI Facil, prog coordr coun, 1987-89, community developer, 1989-90; Cumberland Hall, psychiat social worker, 1991; Orchard Grove, consult, 1991-98; Andrews Univ, assoc prof social work, 1991-, Genesis Single Parent Prog, dir, 1991-97, Ctr Inter cult Rels, assoc dir, 1993-95, dir admis, 1997-, BSW prog dir, 2003-. **Orgs:** Nat Asn Social Workers, 1981-; Coun Social Work Educ, 1991-; bd mem, Mich League Human Serv, 1991-2000; Lake Union Women's Ministries Comt, 1993-97; Lake Region Women's Comt, 1993-; vpres bd, United Way Berrien Co, 2002-; chair, Black Hist Celebration Comt, 2002-. **Home Addr:** 1652 Broadway, Niles, MI 49120, **Home Phone:** (269)683-4212. **Business Addr:** Associate Professor, Andrews University, 8833 Univ Blvd, Berrien Springs, MI 49103, **Business Phone:** (269)471-3156.

### WATSON, ERIC

Vice president (organization). **Educ:** Livingstone Col, Salisbury, NC, BS, eng lit. **Career:** St. Paul Co Inc, vpres global diversity; Williams Co Inc, exec dir diversity & workforce capability; Food Lion, vpres diversity & inclusion, 2003-07, exec comt & head talent acquisition, 2007-09, Delhaize Am, vpres off diversity & inclusion, 2010-. **Orgs:** Bd dir, Exec Leadership Coun; bd mem & bd dir, Urban League Cent Carolinas, Charlotte, NC; bd visitor, Johnson C. Smith Univ, Corp Alliance Prog; bd visitor, Livingstone Col; 100 Black Men Am-Greater Charlotte Chap; bd dir, Next Generation Network; Conf Bd Coun Work Force Diversity; bd dir, Univ Nc-Ctr Int Understanding; chair, Urban Youth Empowerment Prog (UYEP); Leadership Team Community Bldg Initiative (CBI); adv bd mem, Nc Nat Asn Advan Colored People Youth & Col Div; bd dir, Pk, Charlotte, NC; lead corp adv partner, E Carolina Univ-Equity, Diversity & Community Rels Corp Adv Partner Group; Charlotte Alumni Chap Kappa Alpha Psi Fraternity. **Business Addr:** Vice President of the Office of Diversity & Inclusion, Delhaize America, PO Box 1330 Suite 2110 Exec Dr, Salisbury, NC 28145-1330, **Business Phone:** (704)636-5024.

### WATSON, ESQ. GARY A.

Lawyer. **Educ:** Stanford Univ, Palo Alto, CA, AB, econs, 1980; Univ Calif, Berkeley, CA, JD, 1984. **Career:** Finley, Kumble, Wagner, Heine, Underberg, Manley, Myerson & Casey, assoc, 1984-86; Dern, Mason & Floum, assoc, 1986-88; Universal Pictures, atty, 1989-91; Greenberg, Glusker, Fields, Claman & Machtinger, assoc, 1992-93; Law Off Gary A. Watson, owner, 1993-2001; Huron Law Group LLP, coun, 2001-05; Gary A Watson & Assocs, owner & atty, 2005-; Pvt pract lawyer. **Orgs:** Los Angeles County Bar Asn, 1984-; Beverly Hills Bar Asn, 1984-; lect, Black Entertainment & Sports Lawyers Asn, 1992-99, 2001-06, treas, 1994-96; mem bd trustee, Am Cinematheque, 1993-94; int adv comt mem & celebration black cinema comt, Chicago Int Film Festival, 1997-98; chair, Am Bar Asn Forum Entertainment & Sports Industs, 2005-07; lect, 1999-2002, 2004; Asn Media & Entertainment Coun, 2006; Entertainment Dept Century City. **Honors/Awds:** Completion Award, Arts Inc, 1993; Hall of Fame, Black Entertainment & Sports Lawyers Asn, 2001. **Business Addr:** Lawyer, Law Offices Gary A Watson, 1800 Century Pk E Suite 600, Century City, CA 90067-2306, **Business Phone:** (310)203-8022.

### WATSON, GENEVIEVE

Educator, college administrator. **Personal:** Born Apr 2, 1950, Gilbert, LA; daughter of Joe Thomas Jr and Laura Gilbert Thomas; married Alvin Jr; children: Alvin L, Gene L & Thomas L. **Educ:** Grambling Col, Grambling, LA, BA, 1972; Drake Univ, Des Moines, IA, MAT, 1978. **Career:** Drake Univ, Des Moines, spec servs coordr, 1974-81, asst dir, financialaid, 1981-85, assoc dir financial aid, 1985-86; Univ Ariz, Tucson, asst dir financial aid, 1986-88, assoc dir, financial aid, 1988-95, actg assoc dean studs, 1989-90; Phoenix Col, dir, financial aid serv, 1995-, secy, currently. **Orgs:** Exec coun, Minority concerns comt, Mid-W Asn Stud Fin Aid Admn, 1983-86; Scholar serv governance Comn, Col Bd, 1984-86; pres, Iowa Asn Stud Fin Aid Admn, 1986; comn mem, IA Gov's Task Force Ed, 1985-86; exec coun, rep at large minority concerns chair, Western Asn Stud Fin Aid Admn, 1990-92; pres, pres, pres-elect, exec coun, Ariz Asn Stud Fin Aid Adminrs, 1990-93; Tucson United Way, Fund Distrib Steering Com, 1995; Col bd, Western Regional Planning Com; bd dir, Nat Asn Stud Financial Aid Adminrs; co-chair, Fund Develop Com, Western Asn Stud Fin Aid Admin, 1997-98; vpres mem, Nat Coun Black Am Affairs, 2009; vpres, Nat Coun Black Am Affairs, 2010-. **Home Addr:** 87 S Bonanza Ave, Tucson, AZ 85748-6789, **Home Phone:** (520)722-4911. **Business Addr:** Director of Financial Aid Services, Secretary, Phoenix College, 1202 W Thomas Rd, Phoenix, AZ 85013, **Business Phone:** (602)285-7410.

### WATSON, HON. J. WARREN

Judge, lawyer, army officer. **Personal:** Born Feb 20, 1923, Pittsburgh, PA; son of James Warren and Eula Henderson; married Carole A Whedbee; children: James Guy, Meredith Gay Young, Wrenna Leigh, Robert Craig, Sheila Tyler & Kevin McDowell. **Educ:** Duquesne Univ, BA, polit sci, Econ, 1949, LLB, 1953. **Career:** Judge (retired); Pvt pract, atty, 1954-66; City Pittsburgh, city solicitor, 1960-66; Commonwealth PA, judge; Ct Common Pleas Allegheny Co, Fifth Judicial Dist Pa, judge, 1966, sr judge. **Orgs:** Bd mem, Judicial Inquiry & Rev Bd, 1981-85; chmn, Media Rel Comt Bd Judges, 1984; bd mem, Estate Planning Comt St Trial Judges Conf, 1984; pres, coun Carlow Col; bd dir, Comt Action Pittsburgh; trustee, Community Serv PA; Nat Asn Advan Colored People; State Bar Asn; Nat Bar Asn; Allegheny County Bar Asn. **Honors/Awds:** Man of the Year, Disabled Am Veterans,

1969; Hon Mem Chiefs Police; Certificate of Merit, Nat Asn Negro Bus Prof Civic & Cult & Polit Endeavor, 1972. **Special Achievements:** First African-American recipient of Man of the Year award. **Home Addr:** 4305 Dakota St, Pittsburgh, PA 15213-1205, **Home Phone:** (412)687-3646.

## WATSON, JACKIE

Police officer, president (organization). **Personal:** Born Oct 29, 1968, Jackson, MS; daughter of Jerry and Laura. **Educ:** BS, criminal justice, 1994; GWP & Coun, MSEd, 1998. **Career:** Jackson Police Dept, police woman, 1992-; Eve's Fruit Inc, owner, pres, currently. **Orgs:** Nat Asn Advan Colored People; Police Union Asn. **Home Addr:** 340 Arbor Dr Suite 1275, Ridgeland, MS 39157, **Home Phone:** (601)957-5884. **Business Addr:** Police Officer, Jackson Police Department, 327 E Pascagoula St, Jackson, MS 39201, **Business Phone:** (601)960-1234.

## WATSON, DR. JANICE

Executive, educator. **Educ:** Andrews Univ, BA, 1981, MA, 1983; Univ Minn, PhD, 1997. **Career:** Andrews Univ, assoc prof commun, prof commun, currently; Oakwood Univ, assoc prof, 2008-. **Orgs:** Comt mem, Oakwood Univ; coordr, Int Stud Serv Off. **Business Addr:** Associate Professor, Oakwood University, 7000 Adventist Blvd NW, Huntsville, AL 35896, **Business Phone:** (256)726-7000.

## WATSON, REV. DR. JOANN NICHOLS

Civil rights activist. **Personal:** Born Apr 19, 1951, Detroit, MI; daughter of Jefferson Nichols Sr and Lestine Kent Nichols Franklin; children: Damon Gerard, Celeste Nicole, Stephen Bernard & Maya Kristi. **Educ:** Univ Mich-Ann Arbor, BA, jour, 1972; Mich State Univ, attended 1975; NY Univ, Inst Educ Leadership, educ policy fel prog, 1987. **Career:** Community Parents Child Care Ctr, exec dir, 1973-75; Lake Mich Col, instr, racism & sexism, 1975-76; Coalition Peaceful Integration, ed, social worker, 1976-77; Focus Hope, resource coordr, 1978; Daily Urban Announcer Talk Show Host, WGPR "Wake Up Detroit, Joann Watson Show", 1996-; Ed columnist Mich Citizen 50, 000 subscribers, 1996-; Jo Ann Watson Syst Inc, chief exec officer & pres; Equality Compliance Inc, chief exec officer & pres; Detroit City Coun, coun mem, 2003-; Wayne County Community Col, prof. **Orgs:** Nat Coun Negro Women, 1979-; Women's Conf Concerns, 1979-; Wayne State Univ, Upward Bound Alumni Asn, 1980-; Mich Women's Hall Fame Rev Panel, 1982-; vpres, Mich Nat Asn Advan Colored People, 1982-87; Racial Justice Working Group Nat Coun Churches, 1987-; Asn Black Women Higher Educ, 1987-; Black Child Develop Inst, 1987-; exec bd, Nat Proj Equality EEO, 1988-; pres, New York Alumni New York Inst Educ Leadership, 1988-; Nat Inter relig Civil Rights Comn, 1988-; co-founder, vice chair nat bd, Ctr Study Harassment African-Am, 1991-; bd mem & exec comt, United Way Community Serv, 1991-; bd mem, Nat Coun Alcoholism & Other Dependencies, 1991-; Pay Equity Network, Coalition Labor Union Women, mem, 1991-; bd dir, Am Red Cross, 1992; YWCA, Detroit; Ctr Dem Renewal; bd dir, Am Civil Liberties Union, 1992-; hon trustee, Cranbrook Peace Found, 1992-; nat bd mem, Nat Alliance Against Racist & Polit repression, 1992-; adv bd mem, Nat Lawyers Guild, 1993-; Women Bd, Coalition Women Corp Bds, Am Jewish Comt, founder & co-chair, 1994-; bd mem, Self Help Addiction Rehab, 1994-; bd dir, Detroit Women's Forum, 1995; Nat Asn Blacks Radio, 1995-; bd dir, New Detroit Inc, 1996-; assoc pastor, W Side Unity Church; chair, Detroit chap Nat Coalition Blacks Reparations Am. **Honors/Awds:** Thalheimer Awards, Newsletter Ed, Mich Mobilizer, Nat Asn Advan Colored People, 1978-88; State Mich Govr & Legis Proclamation, 1987; City Detroit, Spirit of Detroit Award, 1987; Life Achievement Award, Womens Equality Day, City Detroit, 1987; Hall of Fame Award, YWCA Detroit, 1987-88; organizer & co-sponsor, Martin Luther King first Ann Youth Conf, 1988; vice chair, 25th Commemorative March Wash, 1988; Minority Womens Network, "Civil Rights Activist of the Year", 1990; Annual Malcolm X Comm Ctr, African Heritage Award, 1993; Mich Civil Rights Commission, Distinguished Achievement Award, 1994; Woman of the Year Award, Zeta Phi Beta Sorority Inc, 1994; Natl Lawyers Guild, Detroit Chap, Anniversary Award, 1994; Nat Council of Negro Women, Nat Tribute to Women Award, 1994; Alternatives for Girls, Annual Award, 1994; Bennett Col, Greensboro, NC, Distinguished Achievement Award, 1994; Senate Star of MI, Tribute Award, 1994; City Council Resolution, Tribute Award, 1994; Wayne County Comm, Tribute Award, 1994; City of Detroit, Mayoral Proclamation, Tribute Award, 1994; United Comm Svcs, Tribute Award, 1994; Nat Political Congress of Black Women, Distinguished Svc Award, 1994; Wayne County Clerk, Tribute Award, 1994; Detroit City Clerk, Tribute Award, 1994; Inner City Sub Center, Distinguished Svc Award, 1994; Outstanding Comm Leader Award, Nat Coun Negro Women Detroit Sect, 1994; Detroit Urban League, Distinguished Comm Svc Award, 1995; Michigan Civil Rights Commission, Distinguished Service Commemoration Award, 1995; WXYZ-TV - Channel 7, Outstanding Women Award, 1995; Special Recognition Award, Nat Anti-Klan Network, 1996; Distinguished Alumnus of the Year & Leonard Sain Award, The African-American Alumni Univ Mich, 1996; Ameritech Black Advocacy Panel, Humanitarian of the Year Award, 1996; Detroit Col of Law, Humanitarian Award, 1996; Nigerian Foundation of Michigan, Special Recognition Award, 1996; East Side Slate, Outstanding Comm Svc Award, 1996; Malcolm X Academy, Ancestors Day Award, 1996; US Dept of Labor, Working Women Count Leadership Award, 1996; author, Should America Pay, 2003; Woman of Wonder Award, National Council of Negro Women; Political Activist of the Year Award, Fannie Lou Hamer; Peacemaker Award, West Side Unity Church; Most Valuable Local Official, Nation Mag, 2010. **Special Achievements:** First woman to serve as Executive Director of the Detroit Branch National Association for the Advancement of Colored People. **Home Addr:** 737 Sturtevant, Detroit, MI 48206, **Home Phone:** (313)934-1557. **Business Addr:** Council Member, Detroit City Council, Coleman A Young Municipal Ctr, Detroit, MI 48226, **Business Phone:** (313)224-3443.

## WATSON, JOE

Chief executive officer. **Educ:** Dickinson Col, BA, lib arts & sci, 1987. **Career:** Eastman Kodak Co, corp exec & staff; Gartner Group, dir, area Mgr, dist mgr, regional dir & corp exec; Robert Half Int, dir, area mgr, dist mgr, regional dir, position, mgt & corp exec; Va Gov Mark Warner's Transition Team, dir personnel, 2001; Exec Leadership Coun, strategic advisor; Strategic Hire & Without Excuses, pres & chief exec officer, 2000-. Books: Without Excuses: Unleash the Power Of Diversity to Build Your Business, 2006; Where The Jobs Are Now, 2010. **Orgs:** Co-founder, African Am Chief Exec Officer Coun; founder, Strategic Hire; chmn, Va High Tech Partnership; chmn, Greater Reston Chamber Com; bd mem, Nat Asn Investment Co; bd mem, Marathon Club; chmn, Marathon Club, 2008-; Co-founder, Exchange; sr advisor, Laurel Strategies Inc. **Business Addr:** President, Chief Executive Officer, Strategic Hire, 1851 Alexander Bell Dr Suite 301, Reston, VA 20191, **Business Phone:** (703)467-9093.

## WATSON, JOHN CLIFTON

Journalist, college teacher. **Personal:** Born Jan 22, 1954, Jersey City, NJ; son of John; married Laura St Martin. **Career:** Jersey City State Col, writing instr, 1992-94; Rutgers Col Newark, Jour instr, 1992-; Jersey Jour, news ed, reporter, 1975; Am Univ, Sch Commun, asst prof, currently. **Orgs:** Garden State Asn Black Journalists, 1992-. **Home Addr:** 31 Cottonwood St, Jersey City, NJ 07305, **Home Phone:** (201)433-9124. **Business Addr:** Assistant Professor, American University, 4400 Massachusetts Ave NW, Washington, DC 20016-8017, **Business Phone:** (202)885-2083.

## WATSON, JOSEPH W.

Educator, college teacher, chemist. **Personal:** Born Apr 16, 1940, New York, NY; married Mary Slater; children: Ruth, Jerome, Jennifer & Elizabeth. **Educ:** City Col NY, BS, 1961; Univ Calif, Los Angeles, PhD, org chem, 1966, postdoctoral; Harvard Univ Inst Educ Mgt, Exec Develop Prog, 1983. **Career:** Univ Calif San Diego, from asst prof to prof, 1966-88, Thurgood Marshall Col, provost, 1970-81, vice chancellor stud affairs, 1981-07, prof emer chem, 1981-2007. **Orgs:** Am Chem Soc; Nat Orgn Prof & Advan Black Chems & Chem Engrs; Calif Black Col Fac & Staff Asn; chmn, Calif Stud Aid Comn, 1990-, 92 & 1999-2001; chair, 1990-92; Nat Asn Advan Colored People; life mem, Urban League; Western Asn Schs & Cols, 1985-89; bd dir, Col Access Found Calif bd, 2005-. **Home Addr:** 8666 Cliffridge, La Jolla, CA 92037. **Business Addr:** Board of Director, College Access Foundation of California, 1 Front St Suite 1325, San Francisco, CA 94111, **Business Phone:** (415)287-1800.

## WATSON, JUSTIN SEAN

Football player, administrator. **Personal:** Born Jan 7, 1975, Bronx, NY. **Educ:** San Diego State Univ, BA, criminal justice, psychol, 1998. **Career:** Football player (retired), administrator; St Louis Rams, running back, 1999-2002; Studio Physique Athletic Club, owner, 2004-. **Orgs:** San Diego State Univ Alumni Asn. **Business Addr:** Owner, Studio Physique Athletic Club, 315 N San Marino Ave, San Gabriel, CA 91775, **Business Phone:** (626)576-9600.

## WATSON, KAREN ELIZABETH

Executive, vice president (organization). **Personal:** Born Sep 11, 1957, New York, NY; daughter of James L and D Jaris E Hinton; children: Erika Faith Allen & James Austin Allen. **Educ:** Bard Col, BA, Am studies, 1979. **Career:** Macneil/Lehrer Report, prod asst, 1979-81; Nat Pub Radio, asst producer / desk asst, Morning Ed, 1981-83; Select Comn Narcotics Abuse & Ctrl, US House Rep, press secy, 1983-85; Mondale Ferraro presial Campaign, pres advan, 1984; Capitol J, Wash, DC, reporter, res, 1985; Pub Broadcasting Serv, Alexandria, Va, assoc dir, news & pub affairs, 1985-92; WGBH Educ Found, Boston, MA, dep proj dir, Africans Am, 1992-94; Southern Ctr Intl Studies, Atlanta, Ga, tv & educ consult, 1993-94; Fed Commun Comn, Diector, Off Pub Affairs, 1994-96; Echostar Commun Corp, govt affairs dir & vpres, 1996-2005; chief commun officer, sr vpres, 2006-; Nielsen Co, sr vpres global commun & chief commun officer, currently; Nielsen Co, Govt, Pvt Sector Sales, managing dir, 2008-14. **Orgs:** Radio & TV News dir Asn; bd mem, Southern Ctr Int Studies. **Home Addr:** 1704 Kalmia Rd NW, Washington, DC 20012, **Home Phone:** (202)291-0839. **Business Addr:** Chief Communications Officer, Senior Vice President, The Nielsen Co, 770 Broadway, New York, NY 10003-9595.

## WATSON, LEIGHTON

Hotel executive, business owner. **Career:** La Tienda Inn, owner, 1994-, innkeeper. **Business Addr:** Owner, La Tienda Inn, 445 447 W San Francisco St, Santa Fe, NM 87501, **Business Phone:** (505)989-8259.

## WATSON, MARY ELAINE

Educator. **Personal:** Born Aug 24, 1942, Springfield, OH; daughter of Ferdinand Benjamin and Lillie Belle Quisenberry Clarke; children: Monyca Lynn Gordon & Aaron Marshall. **Educ:** Miami Univ, Oxford, OH, BS, educ, 1964. **Career:** Middletown Monroe City Sch, teacher, 1964-99; J&W Fashions & Designs, co-owner, currently; Mary Elaine Watson Arts, pres, currently. **Orgs:** Alpha Kappa Alpha Sorority, 1962; Girl Scouts Am, leader, 1969-95, bd dir, 1986-88; counr, OH 4-H, 1978-87, 1998-99; Nat Asn Advan Colored People; adv asst, Girls Assembly & Sojourner Truth No 13, 1985-99; deaconess, Mt Zion Missionary Baptist Church, Middletown, OH, 1994-; Nat Sorority Phi Delta Kappa, 1995; Order Eastern Star, Chap 55, 1995. **Home Addr:** 6194 Hamilton Middletown Rd, Middletown, OH 45044, **Home Phone:** (513)539-8955. **Business Addr:** President, Mary Elaine Watson Arts, 6194 Hamilton Middletown Rd, Middletown, OH 45044, **Business Phone:** (513)539-8955.

## WATSON, MICHAEL A.

Executive. **Personal:** Born Mobile, AL. **Educ:** Duke Univ, BA; Columbia Univ, BL. **Career:** New York off Hunton & Williams & Milbank, Tweed, assoc, proj finance; New York Life Ins Co, from asst gen coun to named vpres & assoc gen coun, 1996-2001, vpres & dep gen coun, 2001-. **Orgs:** Cong Black Caucus Found. **Home Addr:** , NY. **Business Addr:** Vice President, Deputy General Counsel, New York Life Insurance Co, 51 Madison Ave Suite 3200, New York, NY 10010, **Business Phone:** (212)576-7000.

## WATSON, MILTON H.

Executive, president (organization). **Personal:** Born Mar 12, 1927, Detroit, MI; son of Elzie L and Fannie M; married Mary Kathryn; children: Milton P & Kathryn M. **Educ:** Wayne State Univ, BA, 1949; Univ Mich, MSW, 1962. **Career:** Executive (retired); OMNI Care Health Plan, corp secy, bd trustee, 1971; Health Coun Inc, exec dir; Millar Agency Equitable Life Assurance Soc, asst agency mgr; State Mich, supvr c div dept soc serv; Harvard Univ JF Kennedy Sch Govt, lectr, 1971; Univ Mich Sch Pub Health, lectr, 1971; Cottillion Club, fin secy, 1971-84. **Orgs:** Am Pub Health Asn; Nat Asn Social Workers; vpres & vice chmn, Nat Healthcare Scholars Found. **Home Addr:** 3260 Waverly, Detroit, MI 48238. **Business Addr:** Vice Chairman, Vice President, National Healthcare Scholars Foundation, 300 River Pl Suite 4950, Detroit, MI 48207, **Business Phone:** (313)393-4549.

## WATSON, PERLE YVONNE. See BURKE, YVONNE WATSON BRATHWAITE.

## WATSON, PERRY, III

Automotive executive, association executive, executive director. **Personal:** Born Apr 16, 1951, Muskegon Heights, MI; son of Perry Jr and Roberta; married Ida Janice Reynolds; children: Perry, Robert, Anthony & Maya. **Educ:** Western Mich Univ, BBA, mkt, 1973, MBA, mkt, 1976. **Career:** Keene CRP, purchasing agt, 1974; County Muskegon, contract specialist, 1975; Xerox Corp, acct rep, 1977-83, mkt mgr, 1980-83, sales opers mgr, 1983-85, regional sales mgr, dist syst mgr, 1985-90; Brookdale Dodge Inc, pres, 1993-; Lexus Mishawaka, pres & chief exec officer, 2001-; Urban League, mentor; Boys & Girls Club, mentor; Jack & Jill Am, mentor. **Orgs:** Omega Psi Phi Fraternity; Jack & Jill Am; Exec Black Forum; Boy Scouts Am; Black Men Rise; Chrysler MNY Dealers Asn; Elkhart chambers com; Ind Auto Dealers Asn; Nat Asn Minority Dealers. **Home Addr:** 2067 Riverwood Dr, Okemos, MI 48864, **Home Phone:** (517)349-8124. **Business Addr:** President, Chief Executive Officer, Lexus of Mishawaka, 4325 Grape Rd, Mishawaka, IN 46545, **Business Phone:** (888)775-3987.

## WATSON, PERRY

Basketball player, basketball coach. **Personal:** Born May 1, 1950, Detroit, MI; married Deborah; children: Paris. **Educ:** Eastern Mich Univ, BA, 1972, MA, 1976. **Career:** Basketball Player, basketball coach (retired); Henry Ford CC, guard, 1968-70; Eastern Mich, guard, 1970-72; Southwestern High Sch, Detroit, boy's basketball coach, counr, 1979-91; Nike all-star camp, dir; Univ Mich, asst men's basketball coach, 1991-93; Univ Detroit-Mercy, Detroit Titans, head basketball coach, 1993-2008. **Home Addr:** 1242 Navarre Pl, Detroit, MI 48207, **Home Phone:** (313)763-5504. **Business Addr:** Head Basketball Coach, University Detroit-Mercy, 4001 W McNichols Rd, Detroit, MI 48221-3038, **Business Phone:** (313)993-1731.

## WATSON, ROBERT JOSE (BOB WATSON)

Baseball player, vice president (organization), baseball manager. **Personal:** Born Apr 10, 1946, Los Angeles, CA; married Carol; children: Keith & Kelley. **Educ:** La Harbor Col; Empire State Col, BS, bus, mgt & econ, 1997. **Career:** Baseball player (retired); executive, consultant; Houston Astros, baseball player, 1966-79, outfielder, gen mgr, 1993; Boston Red Sox, player, 1979; New York Yankees, prof baseball player, 1980-82, gen mgr, 1995-98; Atlanta Braves, 1982-84; Oakland A's, full-time batting coach; Maj League Baseball's, gen mgr, vpres rules on-field opers, 2001-10; baseball consult, currently. **Orgs:** Bd mem, Youth Men's Christian Asn & Metro, 1988-. **Special Achievements:** First African American GM to win a World Series championship. **Home Addr:** 13164 Memorial Dr Suite 121, Houston, TX 77079, **Home Phone:** (713)799-4500. **Business Addr:** Vice President, Major League Baseball, 350 Pk Ave, New York, NY 10022, **Business Phone:** (212)339-7800.

## WATSON, SOLOMON B., IV

Executive, lawyer. **Personal:** Born Apr 14, 1944, Salem, NJ; son of Denise A Jones and S Brown Jr; married Brenda J Hendricks; children: Katitti M & Kira P. **Educ:** Howard Univ, Wash, DC, BA, Eng, 1966; Harvard Law Sch, Cambridge, Mass, JD, 1971. **Career:** Bingham, Dana & Gould, Boston, Mass, assoc, 1971-74; New York Times Co, atty, 1974-76, asst secy, 1976-79, secy, 1979-89, asst gen coun, 1984, gen coun, 1989-2005, vpres, 1990-96, sr vpres & chief legal officer, 2006-15. **Orgs:** Mass Bar Asn; Ny Bar Asn; Am Bar Asn; Asn Bar City NY; Legal Affairs Comm Newspaper Asn Am; 100 Black Men Inc; dir, Am Corp Coun Asn; Nat Bar Asn; adv bd, Agt Orange Settlement Fund; Anglers Club NY. **Honors/Awds:** Nat Equal Justice Award, 2002; Pioneer of the Professional Award, Minority Corp Counsel Asn, 1998; Distinguished Service Award, Am Corp Coun Asn, Greater New York Chap, 1999; National Equal Justice Award, Nat Asn Advan Colored People, Legal Defense & Educ Fund Inc, 2002; America's Top Black Lawyers, Black Enterprise magazine, 2003; MLRC First Amendment Leadership Award, 2006. **Home Addr:** 341 W 87th St Apt G, New York, NY 10024-2635, **Home Phone:** (212)721-2834.

## WATSON, TIMOTHY S.

Auditor, entrepreneur. **Educ:** Fla A&M Univ, BS, acct, 1992. **Career:** Ernst & Young LLP, supv sr auditor, 1992-98; KPMG Peat Marwick LLP, supv sr auditor, 1995-98; Wash, Pittman & McKeever LLC, staff auditor; Deloitte & Touche LLP, staff auditor; Watson Rice LLP, staff auditor; Aon Corp, dept internal audit; Ill Tool Works Inc, dept internal audit; Benford Brown & Assocs LLC, partner, 1998-; Ameritech Corp, dept internal audit, 1999. **Orgs:** State Ill, lic Cert Pub Acct; Am Inst Cert Pub Acct; treas, Chicago chap, Nat Asn Black Accts; instr, Nonprofit Financial Ctr; adv bd, GA Doty Health Educ Fund; Nat Black MBA Asn; Am Poolplayers Asn; Inst Internal Auditors; Peer Rev Acceptance Comt, currently. **Business Addr:** Managing Partner, Benford Brown & Associates LLC, 8334 S Stony Island Ave, Chicago, IL 60617-1749, **Business Phone:** (773)731-1300.

## WATSON, TONY J. (ANTHONY J WATSON)

Military leader, president (organization). **Personal:** Born May 18, 1949, Chicago, IL; son of John and Virginia; married Sharon; children: Erica & Lindsay. **Educ:** US Naval Acad, BS, 1970; Golden Gate Univ, MBA, 1989. **Career:** Potomac Elec Power Co, mgr plant opers & opers coordr, 1981-83; USS Birmingham, SSN 695, weapons officer, 1983-84; USS Hammerhead, SSN 663, exec officer, 1984-86;

USS Jacksonville, SSN 699, comndg officer, 1987-89; US Naval Acad, dept commandant, 1989-93; Submarine Squadron 7, comdr, 1992-93; Ops, Nat Mil Command Ctr, dep dir, 1993, rear adm, 1997; Ctr Mil & Pvt Sector Initiatives, chief exec officer, 1997; US Alliance Leadership Group, founder & chief exec officer, 2000-; Qualx Serv Govt Solutions, chief exec officer; Alliance Leadership Group, chief exec officer, 2003-; TCE Global Energy Corp, chmn & chief exec officer, currently. **Orgs:** US Naval Inst, 1987-; Naval Submarine League, 1993-; partner, Chicago Youth Centers; chap pres, Nat Naval Officers Asn; co-chmn, Black Engr Yr Alumni Asn, currently; bd dir, Serv Disabled Veteran Enterprises Inc. **Home Addr:** 2335 S Rolfe St, Arlington, VA 22202-1544. **Business Addr:** Chief Executive Officer, Chairman, TCE Global Energy Corp, 3350 Riverwood Pkwy Suite 1900, Atlanta, GA 30339, **Business Phone:** (770)240-5303.

## WATT, GARLAND WEDDERICK

Judge. **Personal:** Born Feb 10, 1932, Elizabeth City, NC; married Gwendolyn LaNita Canada. **Educ:** Lab Sch, prep ed; Elizabeth City St Univ; NC Cent Univ, AB, 1952; Harvard Univ; DePaul Univ, JD, 1961. **Career:** DePaul Law Rev, assoc ed, 1960-61; Turner, Cousins, Gavin & Watt, partner, 1961: Gen Pract, atty, 1961-75; Circuit Ct Cook Co, judge, 1975-79; Indecorp Inc, dir & gen couns; Sonicraft Inc, dir & gen couns; Inner City Industs Inc, dir & gen couns; Watt W Garland & Assoc LLC, atty, 2001-. **Orgs:** Bd mem, Independence Bank; adv bd, Supreme Life Ins Co Am; Union League Club; Econ Club; Nat Asn Advan Colored People; vice chmn, Legal Redress Com, chmn, 1964-70; bd mem, Joint Negro Appeal; City Club Chicago, 1971-73; Chicago Hearing Soc, 1972-74; comn, Cook County, State Bar Asn; Am Bar Asn; bd mem, Am Red Cross, 1973; Supreme Ct Ill Hearing Bd, Atty Regist & Disciplinary Comn, 1973-75; mem comn, Character & Fitness, Ill Supreme Ct; Chicago Mortgage Attys Asn; Nat Asn Bond Lawyers & Govt Finance Officers Asn; Nat Asn Securities Prof; bd mem, Mus AFA Hist Inc; Ada S McKinley Community Serv Inc; S E Chicago Comn; Sigma Pi Phi; Beta Boule; Omega Psi Phi; Alpha Kappa Mu Hon Soc; Prince Hall Masons 33; Union League Club Chicago; Econ Club Chicago; Royal Coterie Snakes; Chicago Assembly. **Honors/Awds:** Richard E Westbrooks Award, Cook County Bar Asn, 1972; Judical Award, Cook County Bar Asn, 1975; PUSH Found Award, 1977; Judge of the Year Award, Cook County Bar Asn, 1979. **Home Addr:** 5201 S Cornell Ave Apt 10B, Chicago, IL 60615-4204, **Home Phone:** (773)667-0339. **Business Addr:** Attorney, Watt W Garland & Associates LLC, 53 W Jackson Blvd Suite 504, Chicago, IL 60604-3701, **Business Phone:** (312)663-1440.

## WATT, MELVIN LUTHER

**Personal:** Born Aug 26, 1945, Mecklenburg County, NC; married Eulada Paysour; children: Brian & Jason. **Educ:** Univ NC, Chapel Hill, BS, 1967; Yale Univ, JD, 1970. **Career:** Chambers, Stein, Ferguson & Becton, atty, 1971-72; Ferguson, Stein, Watt, Wallas & Atkins Law Firm, atty, partner, 1972-92; NC State Senate, 1985-87; US House Rep, congressman, 1992-2014; Fed Housing Finance Agency, dir, 2014-. **Orgs:** Life mem, Nat Asn Advan Colored People; Mt Olive Presby Church; Mecklenburg County Bar; chmn, Cong Black Caucus, 2005-06; pres, Mecklenburg County Bar; publ mem, Yale Law J; Cong Progressive Caucus; Int Conserv Caucus; House Judiciary Comt. **Home Addr:** 515 N Poplar St, Charlotte, NC 28202, **Home Phone:** (704)344-9950. **Business Addr:** Director, Federal Housing Finance Agency, 400 7th St SW, Washington, DC 20219, **Business Phone:** (202)649-3800.

## WATTERS, LINDA A.

Commissioner, executive. **Personal:** Born Aug 7, 1953, Dayton, OH; daughter of Arthur Davis and Arlessie Cooper Davis; married Ronald Edd. **Educ:** Bowling Green State Univ, BA, bus admin, econ, 1975; Univ Dayton, MBA, 1979; Harvard Univ Kennedy Sch Govt, exec educ, 2011. **Career:** Comerica Bank, loan analyst, corp banking officer, asst vpres, vpres, 1988-96; Detroit Com Bank, pres & chief exec officer, 1998-2003; State Mich, comnr off financial & ins serv, 2003-07; KPMG LLP, managing dir financial risk mgt, 2007-09; John Hancock Life Ins Co, vpres govt rels, 2009-, dir. 2014-; Mich Nat Bank, vpres & relationship mgr; Gen Motors Corp, Finance Staff, analyst; Stand Fed, vpres & relationship mgr; Conf State Bank Supvrs, Dist 2, bd dir & chmn, currently. **Orgs:** Dir, Found Nat Arch, 2014-; Detroit Chap, Nat Black MBA Asn; vol, Bd-MI Opera Theatre; Urban Bankers Forum; Delta Sigma Theta Sorority; bd dir, Detroit Regional Chamber Com; bd dir, Detroit Downtown Develop Authority; bd dir, Metro Growth & Develop Corp; bd dir pres & chmn, United Am Healthcare Corp; exec adv coun & bd visitor, Wayne State Univ, Sch Bus Admin; Finance Comm; dir, Metrop Growth & Develop Corp; bd trustee, Hutzel Women Hosp; dir, Detroit Regional Chamber Com, exec comm; Urban Fin Servs Coalition; bd visitors, Wayne State Univ, Sch Bus Admin; dir, Detroit Downtown Develop Authority; dir, New Eng Col Bus; dir, Life Ins Asn Mich; dir, Life Ins Guaranty Associations, Mich, New York & Nj; Asn Calif Life & Health Ins Co; Successful Women; Successful Families Task Force-State MA; Life Ins Coun New York Inc; Capital Campaign; Bowling Green State Univ, Boston Club; Middlesex County Chap Links Inc. **Honors/Awds:** Top 100 Black Bus & Prof Women, Dollars & Sense mag, 1986; 100 Most Influential Women in Metropolitan Detroit, 2005, 2007; Academy of Distinguished Alumni - Distinguished Alumni Award, Bowling Green State Univ, 2012. **Home Addr:** 3 Kylie Lane, Natick, MA 01760-4548, **Home Phone:** (617)487-8641. **Business Addr:** Vice President, Government Relations, John Hancock Life Insurance Co, 1 John Hancock Way Suite 1101, Boston, MA 02217-1099, **Business Phone:** (800)377-7311.

## WATTERS, RICKY (RICHARD JAMES WATTERS)

Football player, entrepreneur. **Personal:** Born Apr 7, 1969, Harrisburg, PA; son of Ulysses and Frances Marie; married Catherina Chang; children: Ricky Jr & Shane. **Educ:** Notre Dame, BA, graphic design. **Career:** Football player (retired), writer, host, chief exec officer; San Francisco 49ers, running back, 1991-94; Philadelphia Eagles, 1995-97; Seattle Seahawks, 1998-2001; Tigero Entertainment, rec artist, music producer, Pres, chief exec officer, currently; Albums: "Any Given Sunday"; Films: Any Given Sunday, 1999; Tv appearances: "In The House", 1997; Host: 49ers Playbook, San Francisco, 1994; Monday Night Live with Ricky Watters, Philadelphia, 1996; Guest appearances: The Tonight Show, 1995; Live performance: MTV Jams, 1996; "It's in the Game" with Method Man House of Blues, New Orleans, 1997; Book: "For Who For What, a Warriors Journey". **Orgs:** Hon spokesperson, Eagles Fly for Leukemia, 1995-98; Founder, Ricky Watters Found, 1998-2008; hon bd mem, Unity-One/Amer-I-Can, 2003-06; hon guest speaker, Morehouse Col, 2005; hon guest speaker, Wall St Proj, 2005; founder, Urban Youth League, 2008-; hon chmn, PA Big 33 Game, 2010. **Business Addr:** Owner, Tigero Inc, 8815 Conroy-Windermere Rd Suite 332, Orlando, FL 32835, **Business Phone:** (321)278-7237.

## WATTLETON, ALYCE FAYE (FAYE WATTLETON)

Television show host, president (organization), executive. **Personal:** Born Jul 8, 1943, St. Louis, MO; daughter of George and Ozie; married Franklin Gordon; children: 1. **Educ:** Ohio State Univ, BS, nursing, 1964; Columbia Univ, MS, nursing, midwifery, maternal & infant health, 1967. **Career:** Miami-Dade Hosp, instr; Miami Valley Sch Nursing, instr, 1964-66; Dayton Pub Health Nursing Asn, asst dir nursing, 1967-70; Dayton-Miami Valley chap Planned Parenthood, exec dir, 1970-78; Planned Parenthood Fedn Am Inc, pres, 1978-92; Tribune Entertainment, tv show hostess, currently; Alvarez & Marsal, managing dir, 2010. **Orgs:** Chairperson, Young Presidents Orgn, Metro Chap; bd dir, Ecofund, 1992; pres, Ctr Advan Women, 1995; bd dir, Nat Comt Responsible Philanthropy; adv coun, Woodrow Wilson Sch Pub & Int Affairs, Princeton Univ; adv comt, Nature Conservancy; nat adv bd, Inst Prof Excellence; adv coun mem, Young Sisters & Bros Mag, BET; Women's Forum; Am Pub Health Asn; bd trustee, Calif Wellness Found; bd trustees, Henry J Kaiser Family Found; pres, Ctr Advan Women; UN Asn US Am; Alpha Kappa Alpha Sorority Inc; bd dir, Columbia Univ, Sarient Pharmaceut; Lincoln Ctr Found. **Honors/Awds:** American Humanist Award; Congressional Black Caucus Foundation Humanitarian Award; Women's Honor in Public Service Jefferson Award; Claude Pepper Humanities Award, Int Platform Asn, 1990; Pioneer of Civil Rights & Human Rights Award, Nat Conf Black Lawyers, 1990; Florina Lasker Award, NY Civil Liberties Union Found, 1990; Whitney M Young Jr Service Award, Boy Scouts Am, 1990; Ministry of Women Award, Unitarian Universalist Women's Feation, 1990; Spirit of Achievement Award, Albert Einstein Col Med, Yeshiva Univ, 1991; GALA 10 Honoree, Birmingham Southern Col, 1991; 20th Anniversary Advocacy Award, Nat Family Planning & Reproductive Health Asn, 1991; Commencement Address, Antioch Univ, 1991; Women of Achievement Award, Women's Projs & Prod, 1991; Margaret Sanger Award, 1992; Jefferson Public Service Award, 1992; Dean's Distinguished Service Award, Columbia Sch Pub Health, 1992; Nat Women's Hall of Fame, 1993, 1996; Honorary degree: Hon doctorate, St. Pauls Col, 1985; Hon doctorate, Spellman Col, 1986; Hon doctorater, Northeastern Univ Law Sch, 1990; DHL, Long Island Univ, 1990; DHL, Univ Pa, 1990; LLD, N eastern Univ Law Sch, 1990; LHD, Bard Col, 1991; DHum, Oberlin Col, 1991; LLD, Wesleyan Univ, 1991; Hon doctorate, Bard Col, 1991; Hon doctorate, Wesleyan Univ, 1991; Hon doctorate, Oberlin Col, 1991; Hon doctorate, Wesleyan Univ, 1991; Hon doctorate, Univ Chicago, 1992; Hon doctorate, Haverford Col, 1992; Hon doctorate, Hofstra Univ, 1992; Hon doctorate, Simmons Col, 1993; Hon doctorate, Bates Col, 1994; Hon doctorate, Claremont Grad Univ, 2007. **Special Achievements:** First female to serve as president of the Planned Parenthood Federation of America; First African American woman honored by the Congressional Black Caucus; Published memoir, Life on the Line; Second woman president of the organization fought for women's reproductive rights. **Business Addr:** President, Center for the Advancement of Women, 25 W 43rd St Suite 1120, New York, NY 10036, **Business Phone:** (212)391-7718.

## WATTLETON, FAYE. See WATTLETON, ALYCE FAYE.

## WATTLEY, THOMAS JEFFERSON, JR.

Entrepreneur. **Personal:** Born Aug 28, 1953, Dallas, TX; son of Thomas and Johnnie Scott; married Cheryl Elizabeth Brown; children: Marissa, Scott, Elizabeth & Andrew. **Educ:** Amherst Col, BA, econs & black studies, 1975; Yale Sch Mgt, MPPM, finance & acct, 1980. **Career:** LTV Corp, corp planner, 1980-82; Grant Thornton, sr mgt proj dir, 1982-86; Stewart-Wattley Mat Handling Equip Co, pres & chief exec officer, 1987-92; TJW Enterprises Inc, pres, chief exec officer, 1992-2004; Wattley Consult Group, sr prin, 2009-. **Orgs:** Chmn bd dir, Creative Learning Ctr, 1981-86; bd dir, Dallas Black C C, 1983-; Dallas Assembly 1984-; Mayors Task Force Housing & Econ Develop Southern Dallas, 1985; mem bd dir, Child Care Partnership Inc, 1986-; Chief Exec Round Table, 1988; Dallas Planning & Zoning Comn, 1990; bd trustee, Paul Quinn Col, 1991; bd mem, Dallas Citizens Coun, 1991; bd mem, St Paul Med Ctr Found; bd mem, Soc Int Bus Fel. **Home Addr:** 1620 Kent St, Dallas, TX 75203, **Home Phone:** (214)943-5351. **Business Addr:** Senior Principal, The Wattley Consulting Group, 1620 Kent St, Dallas, TX 75203-4521, **Business Phone:** (214)300-1183.

## WATTS, ANDRE

Educator, pianist. **Personal:** Born Jun 20, 1946, Nuremberg; son of Sergeant Herman and Maria Alexandra Gusmits. **Educ:** Philadephia Acad Music, 1963; Peabody Inst, BM, 1972. **Career:** Philadelphia Orchestra C's Concert, pianist; New York Philharmonic Orchestra, pianist, 1963; Los Angeles Philharmonic, pianist; Philadelphia Orchestra; Chicago Symphony, pianist; Boston Symphony, pianist; Cleveland Orchestra, pianist; London Symphony, pianist, 1966; Lincoln Ctr, pianist, 1976, 1985; Un Day performance with Eugene Ormandy & Philadelphia Orchestra, pianist; BBC presentations London Symphony, pianist; PBS telecasts with Seiji Ozawa & Boston Symphony performances Liszt A Maj & St Saens G minor concertos; Lincoln Ctr New York Philharmonic & Zubin Mehta, pianist, 1987-88; Casals Festival, pianist; recordings, Chopin Recital, Schubert Recital; Univ Md, artist residence, 2000-; Ind Univ, Sch Music, Jack I & Dora B. Hamlin endowed chair music & prof music, 2004-. **Orgs:** Class Action, Performing Arts Against AIDS. **Honors/Awds:** Grammy Award, 1963; Order of the Zaire Congo, 1970; Musical America's Musician of the Month, 1973; Lincoln Center Medallion, 1974; Gold Medal of Merit Award, Nat Soc Arts & Letters, 1982; University of the Arts Medal, University Arts Philadelphia; Distinguished Alumni Award, Peabody Conserv Johns Hopkins Univ, 1984; Avery Fisher Prize, 1988; Univeristy Arts Of Medal, 1988; National Medal of Arts, 2011; Music Hall of Fame, 2013; MacDowell Medal, Cincinnati MacDowell Soc's, 2014; Honorary doctorates: Yale Univ, 1973, Albright Col, 1975, Univ PA, Miami Univ OH, Trinity Col, Julliard Sch Music. **Special Achievements:** Soloist for US State Dept; Toured Soviet Union with San Francisco Symphony, 1973; Copland's "A Lincoln Portrait" at Ford's Theatre, 1975; Ten years on series "Great Performers, " Lincoln Ctr; performed first full-length piano recital in the history of television, 1976; Performed the first full-length recital to be aired nationally in prime time, 1985; First Black concert pianist to achieve international super stardom. **Business Addr:** Professor, Jack I & Dora B Hamlin Endowed Chair in Music, Indiana University, Merrill Hall MU100, Bloomington, IN 47405-2200, **Business Phone:** (812)855-5105.

## WATTS, DR. ANNE WIMBUSH

Educator, school administrator. **Personal:** Born Jan 1, 1943?, Grambling, LA; daughter of V E Wimbush and R P Wimbush; married William; children: Michael Kevin & Christopher Nolan. **Educ:** Grambling State Univ, BS, 1962; Univ Wis, MA, 1964; Atlanta Univ, MA, 1966; Ga State Univ, PhD, 1982. **Career:** Grambling State Univ, instr, 1964-65; Jackson State Univ, instr, 1965-66; Atlanta Univ, instr, 1966-67; Spelman Col, vis prof, 1991; Morehouse Col, class dean, prof, dir, acad, 1991-, vice provost, assoc vpres, acad affairs. **Orgs:** Consult, Nat Black Polit Action Forum, 1987-89; chairperson curric comt, Nat Cancer Inst Adv Com, 1988-90; int pub ed, 100 Women Atlanta, 1988-; Nat Coun Negro Women, 1990-; int consult, AKA Sorority, 1991-; adv comt, Atlanta Job Corps Ctr, 1992-; founder, Kappa Omega Finishing Sch; liaison officer, Morehouse Col. **Home Addr:** 5245 Orange Dr, Atlanta, GA 30331, **Home Phone:** (404)349-4646. **Business Addr:** Associate Vice President, Director, Morehouse College, 830 Westview Dr, Atlanta, GA 30314, **Business Phone:** (404)681-2800.

## WATTS, BEVERLY L.

State government official. **Personal:** Born Feb 4, 1948, Nashville, TN; daughter of William E Lindsley and Evelyn L Lindsley; children: Lauren D. **Educ:** Tenn State Univ, BS, sociol, 1969; Southern Ill Univ, MS, 1973. **Career:** Chicago Model Cities Prog, activ coordr, 1972-74; US Dept Health, Educ & Welfare, equal opportunity specialist, 1974-78; US Dept Agr, Civil Rights/EEO, regional dir, 1978-87, 1989-91; Ill Minority Female Bus, exec dir, 1987-89; RGMA Inc, sr consult, 1991-92; Ky Commn Human Rights, exec dir, 1992-04, currently; US Dept Housing & Urban Develop, Nat Fair Housing Training Acad, exec dir, currently; Tenn Human Rights Comn, exec dir, currently. **Orgs:** Nat bd mem, Nat Urban Affairs Coun, 1981-93; bd dir, former pres, Affirmative Action Asn, 1982-92; IAOHRA, 1993; bd mem, Kentuckian Minority Purchasing Coun, 1993; Ky Coun Postsecondary Educ Equal Opportunity Comt, 1993; bd mem, Nat Asn Human Rights Workers; March Dimes Bd; agencies bd, Int Asn Human Rights; Leadership Louisville Bd; pres, Int Asn OfficialHuman Rights Agencies, 2000-; bd dir, Metro United Way; bd dir, KyWomen's Leadership Network; bd dir, ACLU; leadership adv comt, StennisCtr S Women Pub Serv; bd dir, 1997-2000, chair, 2001-, Women Execs StateGovt; pres, Int Asn Off Human Rights Agencies, 2001-03; fel Women Execs State Govt. **Honors/Awds:** OAE Partnership Award, US Dept Agr, 1990; Outstanding Contributor Award, RGMA, 1991; Nominee, Bus & Prof Women River City Woman Achievement, 1998; Individual Human Rights Award, Nat Asn Human Rights Workers, 1998; Kentucky Charles W Anderson Laureate Award, 1999; Pacesetter Award, Stennis Ctr S Women Pub Serv; Kentucky Hall of Fame, Kentucky Commission on Human Rights, 2005. **Special Achievements:** Graduate of Leadership Louisville; Leadership Kentucky; Kentucky Women's Leadership Network; Selected to attend as an observer the UN Fourth World Conference for Women, Beijing, China; Second term President of the International Association of Official Human Rights Agencies, 1999; recipient of Business and Professional Women River City "Women of Achievement" Award; Accorded an Anderson Laureate; Attended UN World Conf Against Racism, Racial Discrim, Zenophobia & Related Intolerance, Durban, S Africa, 2001. **Home Addr:** 1705 Fraser Dr, Louisville, KY 40205-2749, **Home Phone:** (502)451-8555. **Business Addr:** Executive Director, US Department of Housing and Urban Development, 451 7th St SW, Washington, DC 20410, **Business Phone:** (202)708-1112.

## WATTS, DAMON SHANEL

Dean (education), football player. **Personal:** Born Apr 8, 1972, Indianapolis, IN; married Veronica; children: Alisha. **Educ:** Ind Univ, Bloomington, IN, BA, criminal justice, 1994. **Career:** Football player (retired), dean; Indianapolis Colts, defensive back, 1994-98; Ace Mortgage Funding, loan officer, 1998-2003; Touchdown Appraisal Group LLC, lic residential, 2004-13; Indianapolis Pub Schs, asst dean discipline, 2008-12; TC Howe High Sch, dean students, 2012-14, athletic dir, 2013-14; Ind Univ, stud recruiter, 2015-. **Orgs:** Ind Football Coaches Asn, 2012; Black Coaches Asn, 2012-; Ind Interscholastic Athletic Adminr Asn, 2013-; NFL Legends Community, 2014-. **Home Addr:** 5352 Hawthorne Dr, Indianapolis, IN 46226-1616, **Home Phone:** (317)997-3327. **Business Addr:** Student Recruiter, Indiana University, 107 S Indiana Ave, Bloomington, IN 47405-7000, **Business Phone:** (812)855-4848.

## WATTS, JULIUS CAESAR, JR.

Football player, executive. **Personal:** Born Nov 18, 1957, Eufaula, OK; son of JC Sr and Helen; married Frankie Jones; children: LaKesha, Jerrell, Jennifer, Julia & JC III. **Educ:** Univ Okla, Norman, OK, BA, jour, 1981. **Career:** Football player (retired), political contributor, business owner; Can Football League, Ottawa, Can, quarterback, Ottawa Roughriders, 1981-85, Toronto Argonauts, 1986; Watts Energy Corp, Norman, OK, pres, owner, 1987-89, Sunnylane Baptist Church, Del City, OK, youth dir, 1987-94, assoc pastor, 1994-; Okla State Corp comn, baptist minister, comnr, 1990-95, chair, 1993-95; US House Reps, Okla, congressman, 1995-2003; House Repub Leadership, conf chmn, 1998-2003; CNN, Analyst; JC Watts Co, founder & chmn, currently; Oakcrest Capital Partners LLC, co-found, 2006-. **Orgs:** Bd mem, Fel Christian Athletes, OK, 1981-; Nat Drinking Water Adv Coun; OK Spec Olympics; JC & Frankie Watts Found; co-founder, Coalition AIDS Relief Africa; bd mem, Africare; bd mem, Boy Scouts Am; bd mem, U.S. Mil Acad, W Pt; bd mem, Restoring Am Dream; bd mem, Terex, 2003-; bd mem, Dillard's, 2003-;

bd mem, Clear Channel, 2003-; bd mem, Burlington Northern Santa Fe, 2003-; bd mem, Burlington Northern; technologies adv bd, ICx Technologies; columnist, Sporting News; bd dir, Boy Scouts Am; bd dir, Restoring Am Dream; House Armed Serv Comt; House Transp & Infrastructure Comt. **Special Achievements:** First African-American in Oklahoma to win statewide office. **Business Addr:** Chairman, Founder, JC Watts Companies, 600 13th St NW Suite 790, Washington, DC 20005, **Business Phone:** (202)207-2854.

## WATTS, HON. LUCILE A.

Judge. **Personal:** Born Alliance, OH; daughter of George and Doris; married James. **Educ:** Univ Detroit; Detroit Col Law, LLB, JD, 1962. **Career:** Judge (retired); Twp Royal Oak, gen coun; House Labor Comn, legal coun; Lucile A Watts PC, pres; City Detroit Common Pleas Ct, judge; Third Judicial Circuit Ct, judge, 1992; FACES Inc, bd dir, legal adv, 2004; ADR Systs Am LLC. **Orgs:** Am Bar Asn; Mich Bar Asn; Detroit Bar Asn; Women Lawyers Mich; Wolverine Bar Asn; pres, Womens Div Nat Bar Asn; pres, Metro Soc Crippled Child & Adults; chmn, bd dir, Focus Hope; vol capacities, Young Women Christian Asn; Detroit Golf Course Prop Own Asn; Delta Sigma Theta; Cath Inter-Racial Coun; Womens Econ Club; life mem, Nat Asn Advan Colored People; pres, Asn Black Judges Mich, chair, Asn Black Judges Mich; reg dir, Nat Asn Women Judges; bd trustee, Cent Mich Univ; chair, Mary McLeod Bethune Asn Mich; bd mem, Woodward Acad, 2003-. **Honors/Awds:** Award for Outstanding Service, Nat Bar Asn. **Special Achievements:** First African American woman in Michigan to be elected to the Circuit Court, 1980. **Home Addr:** 1180 W McNichols Rd, Detroit, MI 48203-4201, **Home Phone:** (313)861-0119. **Business Addr:** Board Member, Woodward Academy, 951 E Lafayette, Detroit, MI 48207, **Business Phone:** (313)961-2108.

## WATTS, MARSHA (MARSHA WATTS VISHER)

Association executive. **Educ:** Bowling Green State Univ, BA, psychol, sociol, 1976; Xavier Univ, MEd, guid & coun, 1981. **Career:** Right Mgt Consults, vpres, 1991-97; Cincinnati State Tech & Community Col, adj instr, 1991-2014, interim assoc dean, 2009; Urban League Greater Cincinnati, vpres workforce develop, 1997-2002, sr vpres, Youth, Health & Leadership, exec vpres, 1997-2008; Lee Hecht Harrison Career Mgt Consults, consult, 2008-10; Wilmington Col, dir, 2010-11; Mt St. Joseph Univ, dir mt st joseph univ upward bound, 2014-. **Orgs:** Uptown Transp Adv Comt, 2005; Sch Community Rel, Econ Ctr Educ & Res, 2008; Cincinnati USA Regional Chamber; Connect Execs & Bus Leaders; bd mem, Everybody Rides Metro; adv bd mem, ACF Enterprises; Pi Sigma Zeta Chap, OH; team mem, Partnership Greater Cinn; Zeta Phi Beta Sorority; Black Stud Union. **Home Addr:** 3458 Reading Rd, Cincinnati, OH 45231, **Home Phone:** (513)281-9955. **Business Addr:** Director, Mount St Joseph University, 5701 Delhi Rd, Cincinnati, OH 45233-1670, **Business Phone:** (513)244-4885.

## WATTS, PATRICIA L. (PAT WATTS)

Executive, consultant. **Personal:** Born Apr 26, 1949, Los Angeles, CA; daughter of James C and Marjorie A; children: Marshan L & Mondel E. **Educ:** Univ La Verne, bus mgt, 1994; Calif State Univ, Dominguez; Tuck Sch Bus, Dartmouth Col, advan minority bus exec prog. **Career:** Southern Calif Edison, clerk trainee, 1974-75, counter cashier, 1975-76, customer serv bookkeeper, 1978-79, supvrs coordr, 1979-80, energy servs rep, 1980-87, regional mgr, area mgr, 1987-97; Community Renewal, proj mgr; FCI Mgt Consults, pres & chief exec officer, 1998-. **Orgs:** Vpres, Am Blacks Energy, 1991-; pres, Soroptimist Inglewood & Hawthorne, 1991-93; bd dir, Black Women Achievement; Inglewood YMCA, 1991-; bd dir, Inglewood Chamber Com, 1991-; Nat Forum Black Pub Adminrs, 1991-; Black Womens Forum, 1991-93; bd dir, Hawthorne Chamber Com, 1991-93; bd dir, Calif Black Chamber Com; bd dir & treas, Goals Life; Southern Calif Minority Bus Develop Coun Inc; bd dir secy, Community Community Build; bd dirs vpres, Koreatown Youth & Community Ctr; Minority Bus Enterprise Input Comt (MBEIC); chair, Indust Am Asn Blacks Energy (AABE); bd dirs Asn Energy Serv Professionals (AESP); Asn Energy Engrs (AEE); Calif Pub Utilities Comn (CPUC). **Honors/Awds:** Honoree, YWCA Leader Luncheon XIV, 1989; Black Women of Achievement Award, 1991; Woman of the Year, Calif State Legislature 50th Assembly Dist; Team Kenyon Award, 1992; Inductee of Fremont HS Hall of Fame, 1992; Outstanding Entrepreneur Award, Black Bus Asn, 2006; Supplier of the Year Class III Award, Southern Calif Minority Supplier Develop Coun Inc, 2009; Small Business of the Year Award, Black Chamber's; Leadership Impact Award, Joseph Bus Sch's, 2009; President's Award, Long Beach 100 Black Men, 2011; NAWBO Hall of Fame, 2012; Entrepreneur of the Year, Am Asn Blacks Energy (AABE) Nat, 2013; Minority Contractor of the Year, Nat Minority Contractor Asn, 2014; Minority Energy Firm of the Year, Minority Bus Develop Agency, 2015; Ernst & Young Entrepreneur of the Year Award. **Home Addr:** 2032 W 109th St, Los Angeles, CA 90047-4607, **Home Phone:** (213)777-3256. **Business Addr:** President, Chief Executive Officer, FCI Management Inc, 3850 E Gilman St, Long Beach, CA 90815, **Business Phone:** (562)719-9300.

## WATTS, DR. ROBERTA OGLETREE

School administrator, association executive, executive. **Personal:** Born May 12, 1939, Lawrenceville, GA; daughter of Walter Ogletree and Jolly Jennie; married Roger William Sr; children: Roger Jr & Roderick Dewayne. **Educ:** Tuskegee Inst, BSN, 1961; Emory Univ, Minn, 1969; Univ Ala, EdD, 1983. **Career:** Va Hosp, staff nurse, 1961-62; Etowah County Health Dept, staff nurse, 1962-69; Jacksonville State Univ, asst prof, 1969-83; Jacksonville State Univ, dean & prof, dean emer, 1983; Excel Inst, headmistress. **Orgs:** Wisteria Club, 1964 & 1990; Colley Child Care Ctr Inc, 1970-; pres, Alpha Kappa Alpha, 1975 & 1982-84; chairperson, Etowah Qual Life Inc, 1978-85; Kappa Delta Pi; Deans Bacc & Higher Degree Prog, 1984, Human Rel Coun; Allocation chair United Way, 1989; co-chair, Ala New S Coalition, 1990; All Am City found, 1991 Gadsden Bd Educ, 1994-99. **Honors/Awds:** Achievement Award, Nat Asn Advan Colored People, 1982; Service Award, Alpha Kappa Alpha, 1983, Am Asn Univ Women, 1982; Etowah Quality Life. **Special Achievements:** First African American faculty member in Jacksonville State University. **Home Addr:** 415 Crawford Ave, PO Box 894, Gadsden, AL 35902-0894. **Business Addr:** Dean Emeritus, Jacksonville State University, 700 Pelham Rd N, Jacksonville, AL 36265-1602, **Business Phone:** (256)782-5425.

## WATTS, ROLANDA

Television talk show host, actor, chief executive officer. **Personal:** Born Jul 12, 1959, Winston-Salem, NC; daughter of Roland and Velma Gibson. **Educ:** Spelman Col, Atlanta, GA, BS & BA, Eng & theatre arts, 1980; Columbia Univ Grad Sch Jour, New York, MS, jour, 1981; Howard Fine Actg Workshop, Los Angeles, Calif, actg; Aaron Speiser Actg Workshop, Los Angeles, Calif, comedy. **Career:** Talk show host, journalist, actor, writer, producer, chief exec officer; WFMY-TV, Greensboro, NC, gen assignment reporter; NBC weekend anchor; WNBC-TV, anchor; WABC-TV, news anchor & reporter; Lifetime Television, Attitudes, host, 1987-88; Inside Edition, news mag, sr corresp, weekend anchor & producer, 1988; Watts Works Productions, chief exec officer & pres, 1991-; King World Prodcutions, Inside Ed, 1992-98; King World & Watts Works Productions, 1993-98; PAX-TV, "Lie Detector", host, 2005; Watts Works Productions, chief exec officer & pres, currently; Films: Girl 6, 1996; The Stupids, 1996; Meet Wally Sparks, 1997; Defying the Stars; Shackles, 2005; PAX-TV, Lie Detector, host; Green Stone Media, radio host, 2006-07; PBS Kids animated program Curious George, voice, 2006-; TV series: "Life Stories: Families in Crisis", 1992; "You Get No Respect", 1995; "Sister, Sister", 1997-98; "Smart Guy", 1998; "The Jamie Foxx Show", 1999; "The Steve Harvey Show", 2000; "The West Wing", 2000; "The Division", 2001; "Days of Our Lives", 2001-03; "7th Heaven", 2001; "Days of Our Lives", 2001-08; "The District", 2001; "For Your Love", 2002; "One on One", 2003; Maniac Magee, 2003; "Boston Public", 2003; "The Bold & the Beautiful", 2003; "The Proud Family", 2003; "Yes, Dear", 2004; "Ned's Declassified School Survival Guide", 2004; "My Wife & Kids", 2004; "JAG", 2004; "Judge Joe Brown Show", Announcer, 2004-; "Complete Savages", 2005; "Temptation", 2007; "Can You Teach My Alligator Manners", 2008; "A BraveHearTView"; Announcer, radio & TV promo voice courtroom show Judge Joe Brown; "Divorce Court", Announcer & Promo Voice, 2014-; "The Daily Hotline", Promotions Specialist, 2014; "Sundays with Rolonda", host, CBS Local, 2015-; "Dr. Drew", HLN. **Orgs:** Bd dirs, Literacy Vols New York; bd adv, New York Univ Dent Sch; bd adv, Rahway State Prison Lifers Grp; spokesperson, UNCF; vol tutor, Hollywood Educ & Literacy Proj; Sigma Delta Chi. **Honors/Awds:** Most Outstanding Girl Camper Award, 1971; DHL, Winston-Salem State Univ, Winston-Salem, NC, 1998; Soap Opera Digest Award, 2002; Broadcast Legend, McDonald's Corp, 2008; Rolonda Day, named in honor, New York, Honorary Doctorate in Humane Letters; I Dare You Award; Bebe Moore Campbell Award, Nat Bk Club Conf, 2016. **Special Achievements:** Annual Cable ACE Award nomination, National Cable Television Association; Emmy Award nomination; Author: Destiny Lingers, 2016. **Business Addr:** Chief Executive Officer, President, Watts Works Productions, 137 N Larchmont Blvd Suite 652, Los Angeles, CA 90004, **Business Phone:** (323)465-5100.

## WAUGH, JUDITH RITCHIE

Executive, broadcaster. **Personal:** Born Jun 5, 1939, Indianapolis, IN. **Educ:** Ind Univ, BA, 1961, MA, 1969. **Career:** Indianapolis Pub Schs, teacher eng & humanities, 1961-73; McGraw Hill Broadcasting WRTV 6, dir human resources & pub affairs, mgr; Eli Lilly Found, fel. **Orgs:** Pres, Indianapolis Chap Links, 1989-91; Nat Asn Advan Colored People; Cathedral Arts; Crossroads Rehab Ctr; Dance Kaleidoscope; Walker Theatre Ctr; chmn, Nat Women's Polit Caucus; fel N Western Univ. **Honors/Awds:** John Hay Fellowship, Northwestern Univ, 1964-65; NDEA Grant, Purdue Univ, 1966. **Home Addr:** 3965 N Meridian St, Indianapolis, IN 46208, **Home Phone:** (317)283-2877. **Business Addr:** Public Affairs Director, Human Resources Director, McGraw-Hill Broadcasting Company Inc, 1221 Avenue of the Americas, New York, NY 10020-1001, **Business Phone:** (212)512-2000.

## WAULS, INEZ LA MAR

Social worker, commissioner. **Personal:** Born Feb 11, 1924, Williamson, WV; children: Agatha Kenner, Rita, Luther J Jr & Ronald. **Educ:** Howard Univ, BA, 1951. **Career:** Foster Care Serv LA City, Dept Soc Svc, soc work consult, 1955-; Alpha Kappa Alpha Sor Theta Alpha Omega Chapt, gramma, 1976-; Howard Univ Alumni Assoc, west reg rep; LA Cty Symphony League, pres, 1977-79; Bel Vue UN Presbyterian Church, presiding elder, 1977-80, 1980-81; Nat Comn Women, nat dir, 1978-80; Compton Comm Stat Women, comnr. **Orgs:** Minority womens task force Calif, State Comm Stat Women, 1984-; re-elected to far west reg rep, Howard Univ, 1984-86. **Honors/Awds:** Consistent Service Award, Howard Univ Alumni Asn S Calif, 1962; Jill of the Year, Jack & Jill of American Inc, 1976; Sor of the Year, 1979; Exemplary Citizenship, 20 yrs of Civic & Cult Serv Mayor & City Coun, 1979. **Home Addr:** 2119 Kalsman Ave, Compton, CA 90222.

## WAY, CHARLES CHRISTOPHER

Football player, executive director. **Personal:** Born Dec 27, 1972, Philadelphia, PA; son of Cleveland and Jacqueline; married Tahesha; children: 3. **Educ:** Univ Va, BS, civil engineering, 1994. **Career:** Football player (retired), executive; New York Giants, halfback & fullback, 1995-99, dir player develop, currently. **Orgs:** Keynote speaker, Bergen County Academies. **Home Addr:** 12 N Jersey Lane, Wayne, NJ 07470-2004, **Home Phone:** (973)628-9705. **Business Addr:** Director of Player Development, New York Giants, Giants Stadium, East Rutherford, NJ 07073, **Business Phone:** (201)935-8111.

## WAY, DR. CURTIS J.

Publishing executive, chief executive officer. **Personal:** Born Jun 19, 1935, Columbia, SC. **Educ:** Benedict Col, BA, 1962; NU Univ, MPA 1970; Nova Univ, DPA, 1977; Fordham Univ, New Sch Soc Res, Grad Stud. **Career:** Newark City Neighborhood Youth Corps, dep dir, summer exec dir, 1965-67; Philadelphia County Juv County, prob off; Newark Title Proj dir, training & job develop; Nat Asn Advan Colored People & Multi-Purpose Ctr, dir, chmn bd; Newark Inst Urban Prog, chief exec officer; Sickle Cell Anemia Assoc, chief exec officer, currently; Spoon Bk Publ, chief exec officer, currently. **Orgs:** Proj housing consult, Neighborhood Youth Corp, 1967-69; consult, Nat Alliance Bus; dir, City Passaic NJ; planner & prog develop, Early Childhood Ed; planner & prog develop, NJUP Theater Arts Newark NJ, Sickle Cell Anemia Proj; fund raiser & alumni org, Am Inst Planners; Am Soc Planning Off; Am Soc Publ Admin, Am Acad Pol & Soc Sci; trustee Benedict Col; mem Reg Health Planning Coun, Newark Urban Coalition, Minority Econ Devel Corp; past pres, NJ Chap Benedict Alumni; life mem, Nat Asn Advan Colored People; founder, Hillcreek Commun Ctr Philadelphia, Nat Asn Advan Colored People Multi-Purpose Ctr & Cult Ctr; panelist Am Arbit Assoc; 32Degree Mason. **Honors/Awds:** Outstanding Service Award, Benedict Col, 1970; Outstanding Service Award, Dept HUD, 1971; Excellent Citation Service Award, L Miller Civic Assoc, 1972; Better Comm Newark Br NAACP, 1973; Outstanding Community Service Newark, 1973, 1979; Outstanding Leadership Award, NAACP MPC, 1974. **Special Achievements:** Author of Numerous Books. **Business Addr:** Chief Executive Officer, Spoon Book Publishing, 870 Langford Rd, Blythewood, SC 29016, **Business Phone:** (803)691-0146.

## WAY, DR. GARY DARRYL

Lawyer. **Personal:** Born Feb 25, 1958, Newark, NJ; son of Robert and Pearl Rosser Childs; married Jill Green, Nov 28, 1987. **Educ:** Rutgers Col, Nb, NJ, BA, 1980; NY Univ Sch Law, New York, JD, 1983. **Career:** Haight, Gardner, Poor & Havens, New York, assoc, 1983-86; Nat Basketball Asn, New York, staff atty, 1986-88; NBA Properties Inc, New York, asst gen coun, 1988; Nike Inc, sr asst gen coun, sr sports mkt coun, managing partner & head, managing atty, vpres & global coun sports mkt, 2009-. **Orgs:** Org State Bar Asn; Nat Sports Law Inst; sports indust rep, Marquette Univ; New York Univ Sch Law. **Special Achievements:** Author of "Japanese Employers and Title VII", 1983. **Home Addr:** 3234 SW Upper Dr, Portland, OR 97201-1771. **Business Addr:** Vice President, Global Counsel, Nike Inc, Rm DF 4 1 Bowerman Dr, Beaverton, OR 97005-6453, **Business Phone:** (503)671-6453.

## WAYANS, DAMON KYLE

Comedian, screenwriter, actor. **Personal:** Born Sep 4, 1960, New York, NY; son of Howell and Elvira; married Lisa Thorner; children: Damon Jr, Michael, Cara Mia & Kyla. **Career:** Actor; writer, currently. Films: Beverly Hills Cop, 1984; Hollywood Shuffle, 1987; Roxanne, 1987; Colors, 1988; I'm Gonna Git You Sucka, 1988; Punchline, 1988; Earth Girls Are Easy, 1989; Look Who's Talking Too; The Last Boy Scout, 1991; Mo' Money, 1992; Blankman, 1994; Major Payne, 1995; Celtic Pride, 1996; The Great White Hype, 1996; Bulletproof, 1996; Harlem Aria, 1999; Goosed, 1999; Bamboozled, 2000; Marci X, 2003; Behind the Smile, writer, actor, producer, dir, 2004; Farce of the Penguins, 2006. TV: "In Living Color", writer, actor, 1990-94; "413 Hope Street", creator, producer, 1997-98; "Damon", 1998; "Pilot", 2001; "My Wife & Kids", writer, actor, producer, 2001-05; "Failure to Communicate", 2002; "Calvin Goes to Work", 2004; "Rodney", 2004-08; "Premium Blend", 2005-06; "The Underground", writer, actor, producer, dir, 2006; "Never Better", 2008; "Eye Shat", 2009; "Giuseppe", 2009; "Happy Endings", 2011; "Herd Mentality", 2011; "Untitled Damon Wayans Project", currently. **Business Addr:** Actor, Comedian, Wife N Kids Productions, 10202 Wash Blvd, Culver City, CA 90232-3195, **Business Phone:** (310)280-8000.

## WAYANS, KEENEN IVORY, SR.

Actor, comedian, talk show host. **Personal:** Born Jun 8, 1958, New York, NY; son of Howell and Elvira; married Daphne; children: Jolie, Nala, Daphne Jr, Bella & Daphne Ivory. **Educ:** Tuskegee Univ, Ala. **Career:** Actor, currently; Films: Star 80, 1983; I'm Gonna Git You Sucka, 1989; The Five Heartbeats, producer, 1991; Soul Train Comedy Awards, 1993; A Low Down Dirty Shame, 1994; The Glimmer Man, dir, 1996, Most Wanted, exec producer, 1997; The Keenen Ivory Wayans Show, producer, 1997-98; Scary Movie, dir, 2000; Scary Movie, writer, 2000; My Wife & Kids, 2001; Scary Movie 2, dir, 2001; White Chicks, dir & producer, 2004; Little Man, producer, dir & writer, 2006; Littleman, producer; Thugaboo: A Miracle on D-Roc's Street, writer & producer, 2006; The Life & Times of Marcus Felony Brown, producer & writer, 2008. TV series: "CHiPs", 1977; "Cheers", 1982; "For Love & Honor", 1983; "In Living Color", exec producer & head writer & actor, 1990-94; "The Keenan Ivory Wayans Show", talk show host; "My Wife & Kids", 2001; Dance Flick, producer, writer & dir, 2009. **Orgs:** Alpha Phi Alpha Fraternity Inc. **Honors/Awds:** Emmy Awards, 1990; PGA Awards, 1992; BET Comedy Awards, 2004. **Special Achievements:** Primetime Emmy Award, 1991; Nominated for Emmy Awards, 1992, Emmy Awards, 1990 & 91, Razzie Awards, 2005 & 2007; Nova Award, 1992; BET Comedy Award, 2004; TV Land Award, 2012. **Home Addr:** 6959 Dume Dr, Malibu, CA 90265, **Home Phone:** (310)694-9658. **Business Addr:** Actor, The Keenen Ivory Wayans Show, 7095 Hollywood Blvd, Hollywood, CA 90028.

## WAYANS, MARLON

Actor. **Personal:** Born Jul 23, 1972, New York, NY; son of Howell and Elvira; married Angelica Zackary; children: Shawn Howell & Arnai Zackary. **Educ:** Howard Univ, Sch Performing Arts, New York, grad. **Career:** Films: I'm Gonna Git You Sucka, 1988; Mo' Money, 1992; Above the Rim, 1994; Don't Be a Menace to South Central While Drinking Your Juice in the Hood, actor, co-exec producer & writer, 1996; The Sixth Man, 1997; Senseless, 1998; Requiem for a Dream, 2000; Scary Movie, actor, producer & writer, 2000; Dungeons & Dragons, 2000; The Tangerine Bea, 2000; Scary Movie 2, actor, co-exec producer & writer, 2001; The Lady killers, 2004; Behind the Smile, 2004; White Chicks, actor, producer, screenplay & writer, 2004; Little Man, actor, producer & writer, 2006; Norbit, 2007; Dance Flick, actor, producer, & writer, 2009; G.I. Joe: The Rise of Cobra, 2009; Marmaduke, 2010; Scary Movie 5, 2012; A Haunted House, actor, producer & writer, 2013; The Heat, 2013; A Haunted House 2, actor, producer & writer, 2014; TV series: "In Living Color", 1990; The Best of Robert Townsend & His Partners in Crime, 1991; "In Living Color", 1992-93; "The Wayans Bros", 1995-99; "Wayne head", 1996-97; "Comics Come Home 4", writer, 1998; "Happily Ever After: Fairy Tales for Every Child", 1999; "Dream girl", 1999; "Summer Music Mania", 2001; "Six Degrees", 2006; "Thugaboo: Sneaker Madness", exec producer & writer, 2006; Thugaboo: A Miracle on D-Roc's Street, exec producer & writer, 2006; "The Life and Times of Marcus Felony Brown", exec producer & creator, 2008; "Childrens Hospital", 2011; "Second Generation Wayans", exec producer, 2013; "Legit", 2013; "Tom Green Live", 2014. **Honors/Awds:** BET Comedy Award, 2004; Razzie Award, 2007; TV Land Award, 2012. **Business Addr:** Actor, c/o United Talent

Agency, 9560 Wilshire Blvd Suite 500, Beverly Hills, CA 90212-2401, **Business Phone:** (310)273-6700.

### WAYANS, SHAWN MATHIS

Actor, movie producer, movie director. **Personal:** Born Jan 19, 1971, New York, NY; son of Howell and Elvira; married Ursula; children: Laila, Illia & Marlon. **Career:** Actor, producer, director & writer; Films: I'm Gonna Git You Sucka, 1988; Don't Be a Menace to South Central While Drinking Your Juice in the Hood, co-exec producer, actor & writer, 1996; New Blood, 1999; Scary Movie, producer, actor & writer, 2000; Open Mic, 2000; Scary Movie 2, co-exec producer & actor, 2001; Scary Movie 3, writer, 2003; White Chicks, producer, actor, screenplay & stoty, 2004; Little Man, writer & producer, 2006; Scary Movie 4, writer, 2006; Dance Flick, writer, 2009; White Chicks 2, 2011; Scary Movie 5, 2012; TV series: "In Living Color", 1990-94; The Best of Robert Townsend & His Partners in Crime?, 1991; "MacGyver", 1991; "Hangin' with Mr. Cooper", 1993; "The Wayans Bros", 1995-99; "Waynehead", 1996-97; "Happily Ever After: Fairy Tales for Every Child", 1999; Thugaboo: Sneaker Madness, dir, exec producer & writer, 2006; Thugaboo: A Miracle on D-Roc's Street, dir, exec producer & writer, 2006; The Life & Times of Marcus Felony Brown, exec producer & writer, 2008. **Honors/Awds:** BET Comedy Award, Black Entertainment Tv, 2004; Razzie Award, 2007; TV Land Award, 2012. **Business Addr:** Actor, c/o Montgomery Glick & Co, 5951 Variel Ave, Woodland Hills, CA 91367, **Business Phone:** (818)999-6967.

### WAYNE, GEORGE HOWARD, SR.

School administrator, educator. **Personal:** Born Mar 10, 1938, Meridian, MS; son of Jerry; married Juanita R Robinson; children: Lisa Monet, George Howard Jr & Kimberly Ann. **Educ:** Univ Nebr, MA, 1967; Univ Colo, MPA, 1971; Univ Denver, MA, EdD, 1979. **Career:** Asst prof hist, 1972-76, intelligence officer, 1967-71; Univ Colo, asst prof, 1974; USAF Acad; Colo Dept Educ; Calif St Univ, vpres stud affairs, fac emer & dean, currently; sr sch adminr, currently. **Orgs:** Pres, Kappa Alpha Psi Fratenity, 1978, bd dir, 1980; pres, Aspen Educ Consult; Phi Alpha Theta; Nat Asn Advan Colored People; Am Soc Pub Admin. **Honors/Awds:** Race Relations a time phase III Air Univ Rev, 1972; Industrial Use Disadvantaged Am, Air Univ Rev, 1974; Black Migration Colo Journal of the Week, 1976; Black Alcoholism: Myth vs Res, 1978; Outstanding Kappa AlphaPsi Frat, 1979. **Home Addr:** 1375 Wyo St, Golden, CO 80403, **Home Phone:** (303)215-1266. **Business Addr:** Faculty Emeritus, California State University, 6000 J St, Sacramento, CA 95819, **Business Phone:** (916)278-6011.

### WAYNE, NATE (NATHANIEL WAYNE, JR.)

Football player, executive. **Personal:** Born Jan 12, 1975, Chicago, IL; married Tamiko; children: Nata, Tamia & Nalen. **Educ:** Univ Miss, BS, criminal justice, 1997. **Career:** Football player (retired), executive; Denver Broncos, outside linebacker, 1998-99; Barcelona Dragons, 1999; Green Bay Packers, linebacker, 2000-02; Philadelphia Eagles, linebacker, 2003-04; Detroit Lions, 2005; Jacksonville Jaguars, 2005; Progistics US, co-founder & vpres, 2012-13. **Orgs:** Kappa Alpha Psi Fraternity Inc. **Honors/Awds:** Defensive Most Valuable Player Award, Rebel Club of Jackson, 1996; Super Bowl Champion XXXIII. **Special Achievements:** Being Named Mr. Monday Night by John Madden. **Home Addr:** 128 Slate Dr, Buford, GA 30518-1662.

### WAYNER, RICHARD A.

Chief executive officer, founder (originator), president (organization). **Personal:** children: 2. **Educ:** Harvard Col, AB, hist & econs; Stanford Univ Grad Sch Bus, MBA. **Career:** TRACE TV, founder, Alliance TRACE Media & TRUE Agency, chmn, pres, co-founder & chief exec officer, currently; Keffi Group, partner. **Orgs:** Bd mem, Sponsors Educ Opportunity; Fr Am Found. **Home Addr:** , NY. **Business Addr:** Chairman, Chief Executive Officer, Trace TV, 41 Great Jones St 3rd Fl, New York, NY 10012, **Business Phone:** (212)625-1192.

### WAYNEWOOD, DR. FREEMAN LEE

Administrator, dentist. **Personal:** Born Jun 30, 1942, Anson, TX; married Beverly; children: Tertia & Dorian. **Educ:** Univ Tex; Univ Wash, BAED, 1970, DDS, 1974. **Career:** Real Estate, salesman, 1968-71; Weyhauser, 1970-71; Richardson's Assoc, constr res, 1971-73; pvt pract dentist; FL Waynewood & Assocs, Pa, pres, cheif exec officer, currently. **Orgs:** Am Dent Asn; Minn Dent Asn; St Paul Dist Dent Soc; Am Soc Prev Dent; Am Soc Dent C; staff mem, United Hosp St Paul; bd mem, Model Cities Hallie Q Brown Comm Ctr; Alpha Phi Alpha; Flight Unlimited; bd mem, Webster Sch; St Paul Opera Workshop. **Home Addr:** 1148 Grand Ave, St Paul, MN 55105, **Home Phone:** (651)224-0001. **Business Addr:** President, Chief Executive Officer, Waynewood & Associates PA, 393 Dunlap St Suite 650, St. Paul, MN 55104, **Business Phone:** (651)647-9697.

### WEAD, DR. RODNEY SAM

Administrator. **Personal:** Born Jun 28, 1935, Omaha, NE; son of Sampson Lester and Daisy Shanks; children: Denise Michelle Rawles, Owen Eugene, Ann Lineve Kimbrough & Melissa Cheryl Rivas. **Educ:** Dana Col, Blair, NE, BS, educ, 1957; Roosevelt Univ, Chicago, IL, MA, urban studies, 1976; Union Inst, Cincinnati, OH, PhD, sociol, 1981. **Career:** Grace Hill Settlement House Inc, pres & chief exec officer, director (retired); United Methodist Centers Inc, exec dir, 1968-74; Community Renewal Soc, Chicago, Ill, assoc exec dir, 1974-83; United Methodist Community Centers Inc, Omaha, Nebr, exec dir, 1983-91; Creighton Univ, assoc prof, sociol, 1987-92; interim prof, Black Studies, Univ Omaha, 1991-92; exec dir, Neighborhood House Inc, 1992-97. **Orgs:** Kappa Alpha Psi Fraternity Inc, 1955-; Clair United Methodist Church, Omaha, NE, 1955-; life mem, Nat Asn Advan Colored People, 1967- Nat Asn Black Social Workers, 1981-; comnrn Metrop Area Transit, Omahan NE, 1985-; bd dir, N Side Villa, Omaha NE, 1986-; adv comt, Old N Neighborhood Partnership, Univ Miss Lincoln Univ; dir, United Methodist Community Ctr. **Honors/Awds:** Econ Democracy Low Income Neighborhoods, res publ, 1982; Outstanding Volunteer, Urban League Nebraska-Omaha, 1987; Dr Rodney S Wead Scholar, Dana Col, Blair NE, 1989; The African-Am Family in Nebraska, res publ, 1989; Malcolm X Award, 1991; Golden Rule Award, Columbus Pub Schs, 1993; Merit Award, United Neighborhood Centers, 2001; Old North Neighborhood Spec Distinguished Award, 2001; inducted, Omaha Single Hall Of Fame, 2007. **Special Achievements:** Publications include: Frederick Douglass, 1985; Juneteenth, 1996; Tribute to Martin Luther King, 1997 & 2000; Giving a Gift That Multiplies, 1998; MORE-A Viable Self-Help Option for Low Income Communities, 2002. **Home Addr:** 3000 Farnam St Apt 3N, Omaha, NE 68131, **Home Phone:** (402)345-7324. **Business Addr:** .

### WEARING, MELVIN H.

Law enforcement officer. **Educ:** Univ New Haven, AS, 1981, BS, 1984. **Career:** Police (retired); New Haven Police Dept, police officer, 1968-73, detective, 1973-84, sgt, 1984-88, lt, 1988-91, chief detectives, 1991-93, asst chief police, 1993-97, chief police, 1997-2003. **Orgs:** Nat Orgn Black Law Enforcement Execs; Police Exec Res Forum; New Haven City Silver Shields; New Haven City Detectives Asn; Conn State Police Asn; Nat Asn Advan Colored People; bd dir, Child Develop Inst Conn Inc; Int Asn Chiefs Police. **Home Addr:** 17 Kilborn St, West Haven, CT 06516.

### WEARY, REV. DOLPHUS

Clergy. **Personal:** Born Aug 7, 1946, Sandy Hook, MS; son of Albert and Lucille Granderson; married Rosie Marie Camper; children: Danita R, Reggie (deceased) & Ryan D. **Educ:** Piney Woods Jr Col, AA, 1967; Los Angeles Baptist Col, BA, 1969; Los Angeles Baptist Theol Sem, MRE, 1971; Univ So Miss, MEd, 1978. **Career:** Voice Calvary Ministries, dir summer leadership, 1968-71, dir, 1971-75; Los Angeles Baptist Col, coach freshmen team, 1969-71; Piney Woods Sch, coorde christian educ, 1975-84; Mendenhall Ministries Inc, pres, 1986; Inter-Varsity Christian Fel; REAL Christian Found, pres, 2009- . **Orgs:** Bd mem, World Vision, 1998-2009; exec dir, Mission Miss, 1998-, dir develop, pres, 2005-; bd dir, Voice Calvary Health Ctr; So Cent MS Rural Health Asn; Koinonia Farms Americus GA; Voice Hope Dallas TX; Nat Alumni Asn, Piney Woods Sch; Mendenhall Ministries bd; Nat Black Evangel Assoc bd; nat bd, Faith Work; bd dir, mem, Miss Relig Leadership Conf, MRLC; bd dir, mem, Miss C's Home Soc; Mendenhall Chamber Com; Nat Black Evangel Asn; Nat Asn Evangelicals; Evangel Coun Financial Accountability; Belhaven Col; Wheaton Col Bd Visitors; pres, Rural Educ & Leadership; Christ Community Develop Asn; Keep Miss Beautiful; Miss Leadership Conf; Worldvision; William Winter Inst Racial Reconciliation; bd mem, InterVarsity Christ Fel, 2004-10; dir devel, Mission Miss; bd mem, ECFA, 2005-09; Cath Charities; Christian Community Develop Asn Adv Bd. **Honors/Awds:** Alumnus of the Year, Los Angeles Baptist Col, 1979; Mississippi Religious Leadership Award, 1985; Humanitarian Award, Central Mississippi Legal Serv, 1985; Outstanding Citizen of the Year, Civic Circle Club Simpson County; Honorary doctorate: Belhaven Col, Waynesburg Col, 2006; Distinguished Meritorious Leadership Award, Tougaloo Col, 2004; Alumni Hall of Fame, Univ Southern Miss. **Special Achievements:** First African-American to earn a scholarship to Los Angeles Baptist College; Author, I Ain't Comin' Back, 1990; While President of Mendenhall Ministries, this organization was honored by former President George Bush in receiving the 541st Daily Point of Light Award; Renowned speaker for many organizations, including teams in the National Football League. **Home Addr:** 109 Southwind Dr, Richland, MS 39218-9595, **Home Phone:** (601)932-4837. **Business Addr:** President, REAL Christian Foundation, PO Box 180059, Richland, MS 39218, **Business Phone:** (601)932-1101.

### WEATHER, DR. LEONARD, JR.

Surgeon, gynecologist. **Personal:** Born Jul 6, 1944, Albany, GA; son of Leonard and Lucille; married Cynthia Montgomery; children: Marcus & Kirstin. **Educ:** Howard Univ, Col Pharm, BS, pharm, 1967; Rush Med Col, MD, 1974. **Career:** Johns Hopkins Univ, intern, resident, 1978; Tulane Univ, instr, 1978-86; Xavier Univ, assoc prof, 1984-; Omni Fertil & Laser Inst, dir, 1985; Univ Ethiopia, vis prof; pvt pract, currently. **Orgs:** Dir & vpres, Bayou Fed Svgs & Loan, 1983-; dir, YMCA, 1984-; mem Minority Inst Adv Coun, Xavier Univ Res Ctr; host radio talk show Doctor's Corner, WYLD AM 940, 1985-; Omega Psi Phi Frat, 1985; pres, Black Leadership Awareness Coun, 1985; nat pres, Chi Delta Mu Med Frat, 1986; pres, La Med Asn; Original Ill Club Reigned King, 1989; bd trustee, econ develop chair, Nat Med Assoc, 2003-; dir, pres, Omni Fertil & Laser Inst; past pres, Nat Med Asn; Omega Psi Phi Fraternity; bd mem, Howard Univ Bison Found Inc; Whos Who S & Southwest; Emerging Leaders Am Black Americans; former region v chmn, Howard Univ Alumni Asn; pres, New Orleans Med Asn. **Honors/Awds:** Distinguished Alumnus, Howard Univ Col Pharm, 1988; Best Doctors In The World, Chi Delta Mu Medical Fraternity, 2000. **Special Achievements:** Book: "Why We Can't Have a Baby", 1985; article "Carbon Dioxide Laser Myomectomy" Journal Natl Medical Assoc, 1986; "CO2 Laser Laproscopy-Treatment of Disorders of Pelvic Pain & Infertility" 1986; books of poetry, "Love Is", 1996; "God First", 2000. **Home Addr:** 6831 Lake Willow Dr, New Orleans, LA 70126, **Home Phone:** (504)242-1317. **Business Addr:** Physician, Private Prctice, 2120 Bert Kouns Loop, Shreveport, LA 71118, **Business Phone:** (318)671-5320.

### WEATHERS, ANDRE LE'MELLE

Football player, football coach. **Personal:** Born Aug 6, 1976, Flint, MI. **Educ:** Univ Mich, grad. **Career:** Football player (retired), football coach; New York Giants, defensive back, 1999-2000; Univ Michi, head coach defensive coordr, 2007; Genesee County Patriots, head coach; Flint Cent High Sch, coach, currently. **Honors/Awds:** All Big Ten as a Corner. **Business Addr:** Football Coach, Flint Cent High School, 601 Crapo St, Flint, MI 48503-2057, **Business Phone:** (810)760-1042.

### WEATHERS, CARL

Actor. **Personal:** Born Jan 14, 1948, New Orleans, LA; married Mary Ann Castle, Feb 17, 1973, (divorced 1983); children: Matthew & Jason; married Rhona Unsell, Feb 20, 1984; married Jennifer Peterson, Mar 15, 2007, (divorced 2009). **Educ:** San Diego State, BA, drama, 1974. **Career:** Football player (retired); Oakland Raiders, 1970-71; B.C. Lions Canadian Football League, 1971-73; stage appearance: Nevis Mountain Dew, 1981; TV series: "The Hostage Heart", 1977; "The Bermuda Depths", 1978; "Braker", 1985; "Fortune Dane", 1986; "The Defiant Ones", 1986; "Fortune Dane", 1986; "Tour of Duty", 1987; "In the Heat of the Night", 1988; "Dangerous Passion", 1990; "Street Justice", 1991; "In the Heat of the Night: Who Was Geli Bendl?", 1994; "OP Center", 1995; "Assault on Devil's Island", 1997; "Shadow Warriors II: Hunt for the Death Merchant", 1999; "Sheena", dir, 2000; "The Shield", 2002-; "For the People", dir, 2002; "Partners", 2003; "Arrested Development", 2004-13; "Allien Blood", 2005; "Spawn: The Animation", 2006; "The Comebacks", 2007; "Phoo Action", 2008; "ER", 2008; "Brothers", 2009; "Psych", 2010; "Regular Show", 2011-13. Films: Friday Foster, 1975; Bucktown, 1975; Rocky, 1976; Close Encounters of the Third Kind, 1977; Semi-Tough, 1977; Force 10 from Navarone, 1978; Rocky II, 1979; Death Hunt, 1981; Rocky III, 1982; Rocky IV, 1985; Predator, 1987; Action Jackson, 1988; Hurricane Smith, 1992; Happy Gilmore, 1996; Little Nicky, 2000; Eight Crazy Nights, voice, 2002; Balto III: Wings of Change, voice, 2004; Mercenaries, voice, 2005; The Sasquatch Dumpling Gang, 2006; The Comebacks, 2007; Sheriff Tom Vs. The Zombies, 2013; Think Like a Man Too, 2014; Stormy Weathers Prods, founder. **Honors/Awds:** Football Hall-of-Fame coach, Don "Air" Coryell. **Business Addr:** Actor, David Shapira & Associates, 15821 Ventura Blvd, Encino, CA 91436, **Business Phone:** (818)906-0322.

### WEATHERS, DIANE

Executive. **Personal:** married Ronald Smothers. **Educ:** Syracuse Univ, BS, mag jour. **Career:** Black Enterprise Mag; Newsweek Mag, writer & Wash bur corresp, assoc ed, 1978-86; World Food Programme, pub info officer, 1987-91; Consumer Reports Mag, assoc ed, 1994-98; Readers Dig, publ; Ebony, publ; Redbook mag, sr ed, news features; Essence mag, ed-in-chief, 2001-05; Univ Med & Dent NJ, sr vpres advan & commun, 2008-; Bronx Community Col City Univ New York, asst vp commun & mkt, 2012-. **Orgs:** Nat Pub Radio; pub info officer, UN World Food Prog, 1986-92. **Business Addr:** Assistant Vice President Communications and Marketing, Bronx Community College of the City University of New York, 2155 Univ Ave, New York, NY 10453, **Business Phone:** (718)289-5100.

### WEATHERS, REV. DR. J. LEROY

Clergy, army officer. **Personal:** Born May 21, 1936, Georgetown, SC. **Educ:** Allen Univ, AB, 1964; Dickerson Theol Sem, BD, 1965; Urban Training Ctr Christian Mission, attended 1970; Univ Miami, Drug Ed, 1973; Air Force Chaplain Sch, attended 1974. **Career:** Young Chapel AME Church, pastor, 1960; Mt Olive AME Church, pastor, 1961-; Myrtle Beach AFB, civilian aux chaplain, 1975; Greater Beard Chapel AME Church, prin. **Orgs:** Chmn, Mayor's Bi-racial Comn, 1964; Horry-Georgetown Ec Opport Bd, 1965-; Del Gen Conf AME Church, 1968; civilian adv, Relig Adv Comt Myrtle AFBSC, 1969; asst treas, SC Nat Asn Advan Colored People, 1969-73; Myrtle Beach C C, 1970; vchmn, Dem Party Myrtle Beach, 1970-72; chaplain, Myrtle Beach Jaycees, 1970-74, dir, 1971-72; Fed Prog Adv Coun, Horry Co Dept Educ, 1971; secy, Kiwanis Club Myrtle Beach, 1971; pres, Myrtle Beach Ministerial Asn, 1973-74; secy, Myrtle Beach Ministerial Asn, 1975-76; Mil Chaplains Asn; SC Comn Pastoral Care Alcohol & Drug Abuse, 1975-76; Masonic Lodge 423; life mem, Nat Asn Advan Colored People; fed, pres, Myrtle Beach Nat Asn Advan Colored People; trustee, Allen Univ; Horry Co Ambulance Serv Comn. **Honors/Awds:** Recipient Outstanding Leadership Award, Mt Olive AME Church, 1967; Certificate of Merit SC, Nat Asn Advan Colored People, 1967; Cert of Appreciation, Econ Opportunity Comn Act, 1971; Spkr-of-the-Month Award, US Jaycees, 1971-72; Jaycee-of-the-Month, Myrtle Beach Jaycees, 1972; Key Man Award, Myrtle Beach Jaycees, 1972; Kiwanian-of-the Year, 1972; Outstanding Young Man Award, Jaycees, 1972; Outstanding Young Man With Distinguished Service Award, SC Jaycees, 1972; named in hionor, JL Weathers Religious Education Building, 1973; Home Coming Award, Singleton AME Church SC, 1973; Citizen of the Year, Beta Tau Chap of Omega Psi Phi Frat; Distinguished Unit President & Unit Citation; AF Outstanding Unit Award. **Special Achievements:** First African American president of Myrtle Beach Ministerial Association. **Business Addr:** Chaplain, Myrtle Beach AFB SC, Route 1 Box 138, McClellanville, SC 29458.

### WEATHERS, MARGARET A.

Teacher, association executive. **Personal:** Born Feb 9, 1922, Forrest City, AR; daughter of Oscar Allman and Lillie Allman; married Ernest A; children: Margaret Kathryn. **Educ:** Lincoln Univ; Western Res Univ; Indust Col, MS; Tulane Univ, cert inner city training prog, 1971; Capital Univ, BA. **Career:** Association executive (retired); MO, teacher, 1940-50; GM Chevrolet Plant Cleveland, worker, 1951-55; Child Welfare Dept Cleveland, operated nursery, 1955-60; Head Start Comt Act Youth & Coun Churches, teacher, 1964-66; Cleveland Div Rec, 1966-70; Lk Erie Girl Scout Coun, field dir, 1985, mem specialist, 1993; Weathers Unique Cleaners, co-mgr; EA Weathers Realty; Weathers Travel Agency; Mags Kustard, co-owner; Multi-Serv Ctr, pres corp bd. **Orgs:** Pres, Hough Multi-Serv Ctr; Health Planning & Develop Comn, Welfare Fed; bd mem, Hough Area Develop Corp & Coun; pres, Church Women United Greater Cleveland, 1996-98; field dir, Lake Erie Girl Scout Coun. **Honors/Awds:** Plaques Hough Multi-Serv Ctr Bd, 1973; Parkwood CME Church, 1973; Cert Merit, Hough Comn Coun, 1973; plaque One Who Served with Dedication, The Hough Multi-Serv Ctr Bd Trustees; Cong Achievement Award; City Cleveland Congratulatory Award, 1977; Denominational Rep Church Women United for the CME Church; assoc dir scouting Ministries, Girl Scouts USA, CME Church. **Home Addr:** 1610 Ansel Rd, Cleveland, OH 44106, **Home Phone:** (216)795-7526.

### WEATHERSBEE, TONYAA JEANINE

Writer. **Personal:** Born Jun 7, 1959, Jacksonville, FL; daughter of William and Wallace. **Educ:** Univ Fla, BS, jour & commun, 1981. **Career:** Pensacola News Jour, reporter, 1981-85; Fla Times-Union, reporter, 1985-92, copy ed, 1992, reporter, 1993, interim Ga ed, 1994, zone ed, 1994-95, columnist, 1996-; journalist & speaker, 2003-, ed bd mem, 2008-11; Black Am Web, columnist, 2003-. **Orgs:** Jacksonville Asn Black Communicators, 1986-95; Nat Asn Black Journalists, 1986-; Nat Trust Hist Preserv, 1994-99; bd mem, Bridge Northeast Fla, 1996-2001; Leadership Jacksonville, 1994-95; First Coast Black Communicators Alliance, 1995-2001; William Monroe Trotter Group, 1997-; Jacksonville Asn Black Journalists, 2002-; Investigative Reporters & Eds, 2002-; managing ed, Inst Advan Journalism Studies, 2002-; Nat Press Club, 2003-; Soc Prof Journalists, 2003-; Univ Fla Alumni Asn, 2003-. **Honors/Awds:** Third Place for Columns, Fla Soc Newspaper Ed, 1999; First Place, Opinion Writing, Fla Press Club, 2000; Honorable Mention for Columns, Fla Soc Newspaper Ed, 2000; First Place Commentary Salute to Excellence, NABJ, 2000; Third Place, Commentary, S Fla Chap Soc Prof Journalists Sunshine State Awards, 2002; Second Place, Commentary, Fla Press Club, 2002; Sunshine State Awards, Honorable Mention, Commentary, 2003; NABJ Region V Hall of Fame, 2005. **Special Achievements:** Scriptwriter for Mayo Clinic Video Alzheimer's Disease: What Every African-American Needs to Know, 1998, managing editor and writer on Home Away from Home: Africans in the Americas, commentaries have also been published in the Houston Chronicle, Baltimore Sun and Kansas City Star. **Home Addr:** 428 W 7th St, Jacksonville, FL 32206, **Home Phone:** (904)356-8486. **Business Addr:** Columnist, Journalist & Speaker, The Florida Times-Union, 1 Riverside Ave, Jacksonville, FL 32231, **Business Phone:** (904)359-4251.

### WEATHERSBY, JOSEPH BREWSTER

Clergy. **Personal:** Born Nov 23, 1929, Cincinnati, OH; son of Albert and Gertrude; married Louberta. **Educ:** Berkeley, Divine Sch, STM, 1960; Salmon P Chase Col, BBA. **Career:** St Mary Episcopal Church, rector, 1960-68; Saginaw Urban Ministry, ombudsman, 1969-72; St Clement Episcopal Church, rector, 1972-74; Saginaw Off, Civil Rights Dept, exec, 1975-83; Mental Health Dept, civil rights exec, 1986-. **Orgs:** Alpha Phi Alpha Fraternity, 1979-. **Home Addr:** 48641 I-94 S Serv Dr Apt 310, Belleville, MI 48111, **Home Phone:** (313)699-9094.

### WEATHERSPOON, CLARENCE, SR.

Basketball player. **Personal:** Born Sep 8, 1970, Crawford, MS; married Hazel; children: 3. **Educ:** Univ Southern Miss, attended 1992. **Career:** Basketball player (retired), coach; Philadelphia 76ers, forward, 1992-98; Golden State Warriors, 1997-98; Miami Heat, 1998-2000; Cleveland Cavaliers, 2000-01; New York Knicks, 2001-03; Houston Rockets, 2004-05; Boston Celtics, 2005; free agt, currently; Southern Miss, asst coach, 2016-. **Honors/Awds:** Silver Medal, Goodwill Games, 1990; Metro Conference Player of the Year, 1990, 1991, 1992; Bronze Medal, Pan Am Games, 1991; Rookie of the Year, 1992; Hall of Fame, Southern Miss Alumni Asn, 2007. **Business Addr:** Assistant Coach, University of Southern Mississippi, 118 Col Dr, Hattiesburg, MS 39406, **Business Phone:** (601)266-1000.

### WEATHERSPOON, JIMMY LEE

Computer engineer. **Personal:** Born Mar 10, 1947, Ft. Lauderdale, FL; married Marian Wilson; children: Joy LaWest & Kendra LaVett. **Educ:** Automation Sch, cert, 1968; Fla Atlantic Univ. **Career:** Int Bus Mach, asst systs analyst, 1980-; Carver Cmmty Mid Schl PTA, adv bd, 1981-82, vpres, 1982-83; Delray Beach Voters League, vpres, 1982-84; Urban League Palm Beach County, housing counr, 1986-2008, housing dir, 2008-10, sr housing counr, 2010-; Delray Beach City, comnr. **Orgs:** Trustee bd chmn, Community Primitive Bapt Church Trustees, 1982-; rep, Dist 69 Palm Beach County Dem Exec Comm, 1984; Delray Beach Dem Club, 1984; pres, Nacirémas Club Inc, 1984; vice chmn, City Delray Beach WARC Bd; bd mem, Palm Beach housing Authority; vice mayor City Delray Beach; chmn Palm Beach County Fair Housing Bd; pres, Rotary Club Delray Beach; Dist Dep Grand Master Prince Masons; vice chair, W Atlantic Redevelop Coalition. **Special Achievements:** Vice mayor polled highest vote in 1984 Delray Beach, first African American so honored. **Home Addr:** 130 NW 8th Ave, Delray Beach, FL 33444, **Home Phone:** (561)278-8779. **Business Addr:** Associate Systems Analyst, International Business Machines, PO Box 1328, Boca Raton, FL 33432.

### WEATHERSPOON, TERESA GAYE

Basketball player, basketball coach. **Personal:** Born Dec 8, 1965, Pineland, TX; daughter of Charles Sr and Rowena. **Educ:** La Tech Univ, phys educ, 1988. **Career:** Basketball player (retired), basketball coach; La Tech Busto, 1984-88; Arsizio, 1988-92; Magenta, 1992-93; Como, 1993-94; CSKA Moscow, 1994-96; New York Liberty, guard, 1997-2003; Los Angeles Sparks, guard, 2004; Westchester Phantoms, head coach, 2007-08; La Tech Univ, assoc head coach, 2008-09, head coach, 2009-. **Orgs:** Women's Sports Found. **Home Addr:** 215 Youpon Ridge, Hemphill, TX 75948-5963. **Business Addr:** Head Coach, Louisiana Tech University, Thomas Assembly Ctr, Ruston, LA 71270, **Business Phone:** (318)257-4111.

### WEAVER, AFAA MICHAEL (MICHAEL S WEAVER)

Educator. **Personal:** Born Nov 26, 1951, Baltimore, MD; son of Otis and Elsie; married Ronetta I Barbee, Apr 1, 1978, (divorced 1985); married Eleanora Maddox, Dec 1, 1970, (divorced 1976); married Aissatou Mijiza, Sep 27, 1986; children: Kala Oboi. **Educ:** Univ Md, engineering & sociol, 1970; Excelsior Col, BA, lit eng, 1986; Brown Univ, MFA, 1987. **Career:** Bethlehem Steel Co, 1970-71; Nat Endownment Arts, fel, 1985; Essex County Col, lectr, 1987-88; Seton Hall Law Sch, writing specialist, 1988-90; City Univ New York, lectr, 1988-90; New York Univ, adj asst prof eng, 1988-90; Rutgers Univ, assoc prof eng, 1990-98; PEN Arts Concil, fel, 1994; Simmons Col, alumnae prof eng, 1998-; Penn Arts, fel, 1998; Nat Taiwan Univ, fulbright, fel, 2002. **Orgs:** Poetry Soc Am; Dramatists Guild; founder Seventh Son Press, 1980; Acad Am Poets; Nat Writers Union; exec bd, Pen New Eng, 2001. **Home Addr:** 88 Highland Ave Suite 7, Somerville, MA 02143, **Home Phone:** (617)312-7928. **Business Addr:** Alumnae Professor of English, Simmons College, 300 The Penway, Boston, MA 02115, **Business Phone:** (617)521-2220.

### WEAVER, AISSATOU MIJIZA

Artist, curator, arts administrator. **Personal:** Born Jul 31, 1954, Philadelphia, PA; daughter of Sallye A Warr; married Michael; children: Kala Oboi. **Educ:** Univ Arts, BFA, painting; Md Inst Col Art, MFA, painting. **Career:** Baltimore Sch Arts, instr, art hist & painting, 1983-84; Neighborhood Reinvestment Corp, field serv officer, 1985-87; Asian Am Art Ctr, develop coordr, 1988; The Printmaking Workshop, asst dir, 1989-90; St George Acad, art instr, 1990-91; The Painted Bride Art Ctr, dir visual & media arts, 1992-98; Samuel S Fleisher Art Memorial, fac, 1992-; Exihib: Philadelphia Mus Art, 2006. **Orgs:** City Philadelphia Off Arts & Cult, 1992-96; bd mem, Jane D Kent, St Nicholas Day Care Ctr, 1993-94; Prog comt, Contemp Mus, 1995-; bd mem, Nat Asn Arts Orgn, 1995-98; women's comt, Col Arts Asn, 1997-98. **Home Addr:** 5320 Haverford Ave, Philadelphia, PA 19139, **Home Phone:** (215)747-7953. **Business Addr:** Faculty, Samuel S Fleisher Art Memorial, 709-721 Catharine St, Philadelphia, PA 19147-2811, **Business Phone:** (215)922-3456.

### WEAVER, FRANK CORNELL

Marketing executive. **Personal:** Born Nov 15, 1951, Tarboro, NC; son of Frank B and Queen Lewis; married Kathryn Ann Hammond; children: Christina. **Educ:** Howard Univ, BSEE, 1972; Univ NC, Chapel Hill, MBA, mkt, 1976. **Career:** Westinghouse, asst sls engr, 1972-73; NC Cent Univ, asst prof, 1975; Mellon Bank, credit analyst, 1976-77; RCA Astro-Space Div, mgr commun satellites, 1977-88; Gen Dynamics Commun Launch Serv, dir, Wash off, 1988-90; UNET Commun Inc, Ft Wash, Md, pres & chief exec officer, 1990-93; Fed Aviation Admin, Off Com Space Transp, assoc adminr, 1993-97; Boeing Co, Telecom Policy, dir, 1998-2013; Howard Univ's Schs Bus & Engineering, Bd Visitors; Howard Univ sch bus, Dean's Adv Coun, mem. **Orgs:** Vis prof, Nat Urban League BEEP, 1978-; panelist, Cong Black Caucus Comm Braintrust, 1983; bd dir, Direct Brdcst Satellite Asn, 1990-91; RCA Minorities Engrg Prog; chmn emer, Wash Space Bus Roundtable; Soc Satellite Prof; fin secy, Nat Space Club; Tau Beta Pi Engr Hon Soc; bd dir, US Telecom Trng Inst; bd, KIN Found; Alpha Phi Omega nat serv Fraternity; Campus Pals; Tau Beta Pi; sr fel Am Inst Aeronaut & Astronaut. **Honors/Awds:** Hon ScD, St Augustine's Col, Raleigh, NC; Honoray DHL, Shaw Divinity Sch, Raleigh, NC; Distinguished Auth, RCA, 1984, 1985; Arlem YMCA Black Achiever Indust, 1986; McGraw Hill Yearbk Sci & Technol; Black Engr of the Yr Deans Award, 2003. **Special Achievements:** D-Sign Graphics, "UDI Supermkt" Case Studies Minority Venture Mgt, 1975; "Intro to Commun Satellites", RCA Engr, 1983; "RCA's Series 4000 Commun Satellites", Satellite Comm, 1984; "DBS Satellite Tech", IEEE Electro, 1985; "Atlas Family of Launch Vehicles", 1991; Via Satellite Mag, "Satellite 100" Top Exec, "A Communication Satellite Dedicated To Delivery of Educational Programming", 29th Space Cong Proceedings, 1992. **Home Addr:** 6311 Battlement Way, Alexandria, VA 22312-1900, **Home Phone:** (703)941-3568. **Business Addr:** Director of Telecommunications Policy, The Boeing Co, 1200 Wilson Blvd, Arlington, VA 22209, **Business Phone:** (703)465-3448.

### WEAVER, DR. GARLAND RAPHEAL, JR.

Dentist. **Personal:** Born Jun 8, 1932, Baltimore, MD; married Barbara C Gee; children: Garland III & Edward. **Educ:** Howard Univ, BS, 1958, DDS, 1966. **Career:** Pvt pract dentist, currently. **Orgs:** Med Dent Soc; Kappa Alpha Psi Fraternity. **Business Addr:** Dentist, 5441 Pk Heights Ave, Baltimore, MD 21215-4615, **Business Phone:** (410)542-1225.

### WEAVER, GARY W.

Executive, president (organization), real estate executive. **Personal:** Born Sep 3, 1952, Washington, DC; married BV Goodrich. **Educ:** Va Commonwealth Univ, BS, bus admin, 1974. **Career:** City Richmond, zoning officer, insp dept, 1974-75; Va Hsg Dev Auth Richmond, proj mgr, 1975-77; Trifam Sys Inc, owner, pres, 1977-; Asn Fed Appraisers, appraiser, 1978-; Soc Real Estate Appraisers, assoc, 1978-; N Va Bd Rltrs, rltr, 1978-; Merit Properties, prin & broker. **Orgs:** Adv bd, Horizon Bank Va. **Home Addr:** 9112 Ridge Lane, Vienna, VA 22180-2139, **Home Phone:** (540)898-8942. **Business Addr:** Owner, President, Trifam Systems Inc, PO Box 3490, McLean, VA 22103-3490, **Business Phone:** (703)281-4186.

### WEAVER, HERBERT C.

Manager, founder (originator), civil engineer. **Personal:** Born Pittsburgh, PA; son of Joseph G and Lucy Gardner; married Rayma Heywood; children: Carol & Jonathan H. **Educ:** Univ Pittsburgh, BS, 1961. **Career:** Commonwealth Pa, bridge designer, hydraul engr; Rust Engineering Co, civil engr; Pullman Swindell Co, proj engr, civil engr; Allegheny County Dept Engineering & Construct, proj mgr; Herbert C Weaver Assoc Inc, pres, founder, secy, treas; Allegheny County Sanit Authority, proj mgr, currently. **Orgs:** Trustee, Grace Presby Church, 1963-; ASCE, PSPE, NSPE; appt panel arbitrators, Am Arbit Asn, 1970; reg prof engr; reg land survr; vpres, Booster Club Wilkinsburg Christian Sch, 1971-72; E Hills Pitt Club, 1974-; cert off, USA-Track & Field, 1980; asst track coach, Churchill Area Track Club, 1980-85. **Home Addr:** 2104 Swissvale Ave, Pittsburgh, PA 15221-1569, **Home Phone:** (412)243-6881. **Business Addr:** Project Manager, Alcosan-Allegheny County Sanitary Authority, 3300 Preble Ave, Pittsburgh, PA 15233-1092.

### WEAVER, JEFFERY JEROME

Executive director, financial manager, vice president (organization). **Personal:** son of Lucius and Mildred; married Tracey Robin Forde. **Educ:** Cornell Univ, AB, econs & govt, 1986; Cornell Univ, Samuel Curtis Johnson Grad Sch Mgt, MBA, finance, 1990. **Career:** Citicorp Investment Bank, asst mgr, 1986-88; J.P. Morgan & Co, summer assoc, 1988-89; Bank New York, asst treas, 1990-92; TD Securities, managing dir & head trans, 1992-2002, managing dir & regional portfolio mgr USA, Europe & Australia, 2002-05; KeyCorp, exec vpres & group head, credit portfolio mgt, risk capital comt. **Orgs:** Treas & bd dir, Int Asn Credit Portfolio Managers; adv coun mem, Cornell Univ; adv coun mem, Johnson Sch; chmn investment comt & bd trustee, Community Serv Soc New York; dir, St. Vincent's Charity Hosp Community Bd; dir, Cleveland State Univ Found Bd; bd trustee, Union Club Cleveland; bd trustee, Musical Arts Asn; Exec Leadership Coun; bd trustee, Roxbury Latin Sch, W Roxbury, Mass, Finance Comt. **Business Addr:** Executive Vice President, Group Head, KeyCorp, 219 S Main St, Akron, OH 44308.

### WEAVER, DR. JOHN ARTHUR

Physician. **Personal:** Born Nov 23, 1940, Hemingway, SC; son of Arthur C and Winnie Mae Williams; married Yvonne Jackson; children: Jennifer & Jessica. **Educ:** Va Union Univ, BS, 1964; Howard Univ, MS, 1968, PhD, chem, 1970, MD, 1978. **Career:** NC State Univ, assoc prof, chem, Greensboro, NC, 1970-74, summer, 1975; Howard Univ, intern, 1978-79, resident, 1979-81; Johns Hopkins Insts, fel, nuclear med, 1981-83; Weaver Med Assocs, PC, pres, 1983-; Howard Univ Hosp, asst prof, radiol, 1991-93; Va Med Ctr, 2001-; pvt pract, currently; Wash Adventist Hosp, Silver Spring, Md, physician, currently; Bon Secours-Richmond Comm Hosp, Richmond, Va, physician, currently; Vet Affairs Med Ctr, Richmond, Va, physician, currently; Hunter Holmes McGuire Veterans Affairs Med Ctr, physician, currently. **Orgs:** AMA; past pres, Richmond Med Soc. **Honors/Awds:** NSF grantee, 1972; NIH grantee, 1972; Piedmont grantee, 1973. **Business Addr:** Physician, Hunter Holmes McGuire Veterans Affairs Medical Center, 1201 Broad Rock Blvd, Richmond, VA 23249, **Business Phone:** (804)675-5114.

### WEAVER, MARISSA

Executive director. **Educ:** Alverno Col, BA, bus admin, 1993. **Career:** Americas Black Holocaust Mus Inc, exec dir; Harley-Davidson Motor Co, dir diversity, 2002-05; Let's Party LLC, owner, 2005-. **Orgs:** Chairwoman, Milwaukee Mus bd.

### WEAVER, MICHAEL S. See WEAVER, AFAA MICHAEL.

### WEAVER, REGINALD LEE

Teacher, association executive, educator. **Personal:** Born Aug 13, 1939, Danville, IL; son of Carl and Mary Alice; married Betty Jo Moppin; children: Reginald Von & Rowan Anton. **Educ:** Ill State Univ, BA, spec educ physically challenged, 1961; Roosevelt Univ, MA, 1971. **Career:** Sch Dist 152, teacher, 1961-; Budget Comt, 1971-81; Ill Educ Asn, vpres, 1977-81, pres, 1981-87; PACE Comt Ill, vice chmn, 1977-81; Staff & Retirement Comt, chmn, 1979-81; Nat Educ Asn, vpres, 1996-2002; Nat Educ Asn, pres, 2002-08; Gen Elec. **Orgs:** Masons, 1965-; pres, Harvey Educ Asn, 1967-68; Harvey Educ Asn, Negotiatong Team, vpres, 1970; Teacher Cert Bd Ill Off Ed, 1972-83; Nat Educ Asn, Int Rels Comt, 1975-81; deleg, World Confederation Orgns Teaching Prof, 1976-80; Nat Educ Asn, Exec Comt, 1989; Nat Bd Prof Teaching Stand, 1989; vpres, bd mem, Educ Int, 2004-10; Dept Ed, Hall Fame, Ill State Univ; Nat Asn Advan Colored People; Nat Coun La Raza; pres, Harvey Ill; pres, Nat Educ Asn affil Ill. **Honors/Awds:** Outstanding Young Men of America, 1972; Human Relations Award, Ill Educ Asn, 1974; Spirit of Liberty Award, People Am Way, 2005; George Meany Latino Leadership Award, US Hispanic Leadership Inst, 2006; Honorary Doctor of Humane Letters to Weaver, Nc's Shaw Univ, 2006; DHL, NC Shaw Univ, 2006; Great Points of Light Award, Brain trust, 2006; Chairman's Award for Educational Leadership, 100 Black Men of Am, 2006; Doctor of Public, SC State Univ, 2007; Excellence in Leadership Award, MALDEF, 2007; Lincoln Univ, Honorary Doctor; Leadership Award, US Action Progressive; President's Award, Nat Conf Black Mayors; Influential Black Educators Award, Ebony; 100 Most Influential Black Am for his nat influence, Ebony magazine; world-class leadership in the efforts to educate children, Lincoln Univ.

### WEBB, ANTHONY JEROME. See WEBB, SPUD.

### WEBB, BRENDA EASLEY. See EASLEY, BRENDA VIETTA.

### WEBB, GEORGIA HOUSTON

School administrator. **Personal:** Born May 16, 1951, Moorseville, AL; daughter of George Houston and Annie Thatch Harris; married Harold; children: Ayinde Pendleton. **Educ:** Univ Iowa, Iowa City, Iowa, BA, philos, 1973; Univ Wis, White water, WI, MS, coun psychol, 1974. **Career:** Univ Wis, Eau Claire, Wis, career counr, 1974-76; Cornell Univ, Ithaca, New York, asst dir, minority affairs, 1976-80; Mt San Antonio Col, Walnut, Calif, instr, 1984-88; Calif Polytech Univ, lectr, 1988; Scripps Col, Claremont, Calif, sr asst dir admis, 1988-91; WEBB Connection, co-fed, pres, exec dir, 1990-; Univ Calif, Berkley, asst dir, 2001-05, assoc dir, undergrad admis, dir, southern area outreach, currently; Outreach & Mkt, asst dir; S Calif Outreach, co-ordr. **Orgs:** Pomona Valley-Nicaragua Friendship Proj, 1988-; deleg, State Cent Comt, Calif Dem Party, 1988-; bd mem, Community Friends Int Studs-Claremont Col, 1989-; Claremont League Women Voters, 1989-; Calif Rainbow Coalition; Los Angeles Dem Party; Upland Bus & Prof Women's Club; League Conserv Voters; nominee, Nat Asn Advan Colored People. **Home Addr:** 110 E Arrow Hwy, Claremont, CA 91711, **Home Phone:** (714)625-6495. **Business Addr:** Director of Undergraduate Admissions, University of California at Berkeley, 110 Sproul Hall Suite 5800, Berkeley, CA 94720-5800, **Business Phone:** (510)642-3175.

### WEBB, HAROLD H.

Government official. **Personal:** Born Apr 30, 1925, Greensboro, NC; son of Haywood Eugene Sr and Vina Wadlington; married Lucille Holcomb; children: Kaye. **Educ:** A&T State Univ, Greensboro, NC, BS, biol, 1949, MS, educ admin, 1952. **Career:** Univ NC, hillsborough, teacher, 1948-54, prin, 1954-62; State Sci Consult, Raleigh, 1962-66; Nat Def Educ Act, asst dir, 1966-69; Hum Rel, asst dir, 1969-70; Tit I ESEA, dir, 1970-73; Comp Educ, dep asst supt, 1973-77; Off State Personnel NC, state personnel dir, 1977-86; NC Gen Assembly, legis agt; Wake County, bd comnr, 2003-; New Millennium LLC, consult; Charlotte Hawkins Brown Hist Found Inc, exec dir. **Orgs:** Pub Welfare Outstanding Adminr Orgn Co Schs, 1960; deleg, Nat Conf Educ Poor Chicago, 1973; chmn, Wake County NC Planning Bd, 1988-; Univ NC Bd Govs, 1989-; NEA; NSTA; vice chmn NC Asn Adminr Comp Educ; Nat Comp Educ Mgt Proj; truste, Wake Tech Inst; bd dir, Raleigh Little Theatre; bd dir, New Bern Ave Day Care Cent; bd dir, Raleigh Coun Aging; exec comt, Raleigh Citizens Asn; bd trustee, Shaw Univ; vice chair, Wake Health Servs Inc; exec dir, Charlotte Hawkins Brown Hist Found Inc; bd advisors, UNC-Chapel Hill Sch Pub Health. **Honors/Awds:** Honorary Degree Doctor of Humanities, NC A&T State Univ, 1978; Tarheel of the Week, Raleigh News & Observer, 1980; Distinguished Service Award, St Augustine's Col & Shaw Univ; Nat Alumni Achievement Award, NC A&T State Univ; Cong Gold Medal, Tuskegee Airmen, 2007. **Home Addr:** 1509 Tierney Circle, Raleigh, NC 27610-1635, **Home Phone:** (919)834-8862. **Business Addr:** Commissioners, Wake County, 509 Tierney Circle, Raleigh, NC 27610, **Business Phone:** (919)856-5573.

**WEBB, DR. HARVEY, JR.**
Military leader, dentist. **Personal:** Born Jul 31, 1929, Washington, DC; married Z Ozella; children: Tomai, Harvey III & Hoyt. **Educ:** Howard Univ, BS, 1956, DDS, 1960; Howard Univ, MS, 1962; Johns Hopkins Univ, MPH, 1967. **Career:** Military official (retired), dentist; AUS, 2nd lt, 1948-52; USAR, maj, 1953-70; Howard Univ, intern, 1960, instr, 1962-63; pvt pract, 1960-77; Grp Health Asn Am, 1962-63; Johns Hopkins Univ, assoc dir, 1969-71; Constant Care Com Heallth Ctr, exec dir, 1971-87; Univ Md Sch Nur, treas, 1976-85. **Orgs:** Bd mem, Md Heart Asn, 1969-74; trustee, 1978-85, bd mem, 1979-82, Howard County Gen Hosp, 1978-85; pres, Health Resources Inc, 1978-80; Cent Md Health Sys Agen, 1980-81; Alpha Phi Alpha; Am Dent Asn; pres, Nat Dent Asn; Robert T Freeman Dent Soc; AAAS; Int Asn Dent Res; DC Dent Soc; Maimonides Dent Soc; DC Pub Health Asn; DC Health & Welfare Coun; Am Pub Health Asn; Polit Action Com RT Freeman Dent Soc; Am Asn Pub Health Dentists; Md State Pub Health Asn; coord Comm Vol Dent Serv; Dental Co-ord, Provident Hosp; Balt City Dent Soc; life mem, Nat AsnAdvan Colored People; Howard Univ Alumni; Neighbors Inc; Brightwood Civic Asn; WA Urban League; bd dir, WA, DC Home Rule Comm; Sarasota County rev bd, 1994-97; bd mem, S WHospice, 1995-97; bd mem, N Port Area Chamber Com, 1995-97; Tiger Bay Club, 1994-; Asolo Theatre, Angel, 1995-; Venice Found grant rev comt, 1995-97; bd mem, N County Ed, 1994-; chair, Sarasota County dem exec, 1992-, issues, 1994-95; pres, Holistic Health works Inc, 1995-97; bd mem, N Port Kiwanis, 1996-97; pres, N Port Utility Adv Comt, 1994-; Unity Church Sarasota; bd mem, N Port Dem Club, 1992; Friends Selby libr, 1994-; Venice Hosp Community Health Assessment Comm, 1992-95; bd mem, Hisp Am Alliance Inc, 1996-; Fla Acad African Am Cult, 1995-; Sigma Pi Phi-Boule, 1997; coord, Black Hist Month, N Port, Fla, 2002; Asn Study African Am Life & Hist, 2002; sec, Manasota Basin bd, SW Fla Water Mgmt Dist, 1997-2004; Manasota Basin Bd, 1999-2002. **Honors/Awds:** Outstanding Men of Decade, 1979; Com Service Award, Pi Eta Chi, 1979; NM Carroll Meth Home Award, 1980; numerous publs & presentations; Presidents Award, Md Primary Care Asn; Presidents Award, Nat Dent Asn; Outstanding Community Service Award, Urban Serv Agency. **Home Addr:** 5835 Covey Ct, Bradenton, FL 34203, **Home Phone:** (941)739-9400.

**WEBB, HORACE S.**
Executive, president (organization), chief executive officer. **Personal:** married Virginia; children: 2. **Educ:** Univ Southern Miss, BS, chem, 1985, Sch Law, JD, 1990. **Career:** US Dept Justice, dep dir pub affairs, dep dir pub info, spokesperson; Con Edison Inc, sr vpres pub affairs; Potomac Elec Co, vpres corp affairs; Hill & Knowlton, vpres; Hoechst Celanese Corp, vpres commun & pub affairs; Entergy Corp, sr vpres external affairs, 1999. **Orgs:** Chmn, Cong Black Caucus Found, currently; bd mem, Amistad Res Ctr; pres & chief exec officer, sr vpres external affairs, Entergy Charitable Found, currently. **Business Addr:** President, Chief Executive Officer, Entergy Corp, PO Box 61000, New Orleans, LA 70161, **Business Phone:** (504)576-4360.

**WEBB, JAMES EUGENE**
Executive. **Personal:** Born Aug 31, 1956, Cleveland, OH; children: Brian James, Richard Anthony, Khalam James-Kirsten, Elijah Kharmonee, Larry & Brandon. **Educ:** Cleveland Inst Banking, attended 1976; Cuyahoga Community Col, attended 1978. **Career:** Warrensville Ctr Ment Retarded, caseworker, 1975-78; Rep Steel, millwright, 1978-82; Webb Mfg Co/Webb World Inc, pres, 1983-95; Culligan Water Int, sales mgr, res sales Fla & Ill, 1985-89; Great Lakes Water, water qual analyst, sales rep, 1986-2008; Elizabeth Baptist Church, custodian, 2000-12. **Orgs:** Consult, Career Progs, Cleveland Pub Schs, 1985; vpres, Cleveland Bus League, 1985-86; speaker several groups; parent adv comn, Canterbury Sch. **Honors/Awds:** Business of the Year for City of Cleveland, Webb Mfg, 1984; Entrepreneur of the Year City of Cleveland, 1984; Man of the Year, Cleveland Sr Coun, 1985. **Business Addr:** President, Webb World Inc, 9200 Folsom Ave, Cleveland, OH 44104, **Business Phone:** (216)491-0103.

**WEBB, JAMES OKRUM, JR.**
Administrator, president (organization), mayor. **Personal:** Born Nov 25, 1931, Cleveland, OH; son of James O Sr and Bessie R; married Frankie L Lowe(deceased); children: Lisa S & Paula R Dixon. **Educ:** Morehouse Col, BA, 1953; Univ Mich, MBA, actuarial sci, 1957. **Career:** Mayor (retired); Mutual NY, actuarial asst, 1957-62; Supreme Life Ins co, vpres actuary, 1962-66; Blue Cross-Blue Shield Ill, asst actuary, asst vp prod develop, sr vpres, 1966-84; Dent Network Am, pres & chief exec officer, 1984-94, chm, bd dir, 1990-94; Harris Bank, dir; James O Webb & Assoc, pres & chief exec officer, currently; Managed Dent Care Can, pres, chmn, chief exec officer, 1986-94; Glencoe, Illinois, mayor, 2001; Village Glencoe, pres, 1993-2001; Baker-Eubanks, LLC, managing prin, 1995; Harris Bank, dir, 2001. **Orgs:** Founder & chmn, dir Home Investments Fund, 1968; pres, Glencoe Sch Bd, 1971-77; dir, S Shore Bank, 1975-89; dir, treas, exec comn Am Acad Actuaries, 1975-78; gov comm Health Ast Prog, 1979-83; Chicago Metro Housing & Planning Coun, 1980-85; planning exec inst, Midwest Planning Asn; exec comt, vpres, N Cook Cty Pvt Indust Coun, 1983-86; founder & convenor, Bus Develop Inst Blue Cross-Blue Shield, 1983-88; Security Sol Inc, chmn, 1995-; Ill Facilitates Fund, dir, 1996-2000; Evanston-Northwestern Healthcare, dir, 1999; Chicago Bot Garden, 1999-; bd trustee, NC Arts Coun, 2006. **Honors/Awds:** Outstanding Businessmen's Award, Young Blacks Polit, 1984. **Special Achievements:** First African American-owned and operated insurance company in the northern United States. **Home Addr:** 71012 Everard, Chapel Hill, IL 27517, **Home Phone:** (708)835-2921.

**WEBB, JOE, SR.**
Clergy, executive. **Personal:** Born Aug 18, 1935, San Antonio, TX; married Frances; children: Joe Jr, Linda Ray, Vincent & Daniel; married Barbara. **Educ:** San Antonio Col, assoc; St Marys Univ, Pre-Law Courses; HEB Mgt Sch, cert. **Career:** HEB Supermarket, store dir, 1969-80; Neighborhood Grocery Store, independent grocer, 1980-; Webb Way Supermarket, pres & owner 1983-; City San Antonio, city councilman, 1977-91; Handy Stop Convenience Store, secy, treas & owner, 1980-; Zion Star Baptist Church, assoc minister, 1982-; Pleasant Zion Baptist Church, pastor 1986-; independent grocer, 1980-93; Webway Supermarket, 1983-85; Guadalupe Theol Sem, assoc minister; Webbs Eastlawn Food Ctr, owner, currently. **Orgs:** YMCA, pub rels dir, 1957-69; Black Cong Caucus, 1977-; State grand sr warden Masonic Lodge, 1981-; steering comt mem, Nat League Cities 1983-85; chmn, Jesse Jackson Campaign, 1984; chmn, bd dir, Am Asn Oral & Maxillofacial Surgeons N & S Am Imp Grand Coun NBC LEO; treas, Reg Dir XVII, 1987-89; Alamo City Chamber Com; grand master, 1996, grand sr warden, 1981-96, pres, State Tex MW St Joseph Grand Lodge. **Business Addr:** Owner, Webbs Eastlawn Food Center, 1006 Grimes N, San Antonio, TX 78202-2614, **Business Phone:** (210)223-0787.

**WEBB, JOSEPH**
Executive. **Educ:** Northwestern Univ. **Career:** First Nat Bank Chicago, prof staffing, 1989-95, col rels mgr, mgr career coun, EEO compliance mgr, 1992-94; Motorola Mobility, mgr exec staffing, relocation & corp human resources, 1994-98; Stump LLC, chief exec officer, founder, 1998-2004; Gen Elec, strategic staffing initiative consult, 2004-06; Advan Consult Solutions, strategic human resource consult, 2006-; Advan Coating Solutions, chief exec officer, 2008-. **Business Addr:** Chief Executive Officer, Strategic Human Resource Consultant, Advance Coating Solutions, 748 E Sunnyside Ave, Libertyville, IL 60048, **Business Phone:** (847)812-4127.

**WEBB, DR. JOSEPH G.**
Police officer, lawyer. **Personal:** Born Dec 3, 1950, Chicago, IL; son of Wellington M and Mardina G Williams; married Marilyn L Bell; children: Alishea R, Ami R & Ciara M. **Educ:** Univ Colo, AA, 1971; Metrop State Col, BA, 1987; Univ Denver Col Law, JD, 1991. **Career:** Denver Gen Hosp, ment health worker, 1972-77; Denver Police Dept, sgt, 1988; Ireland, Stapleton, Pryor & Pascoe, PC, gen coun, partner, currently; pvt pract atty; Bayaud Industries Inc, bd dir; Webb & Schtul, LLC, co-founder; Webb Law Group LLC, owner, currently. **Orgs:** Nat Black Police Asn, 1983-; Colo Bus League, 1985-86; Colo Black Round table, 1985-; consult, Oasis Proj, 1986-87, NE Denver Task Force Drug Abuse, 1988-89; Phi Delta Phi; Skadden Fel; Colo Bar Asn, Bd Gov; Bd Trustee, Denver Bar Asn; Bd Dir, Denver Zoo; Bd Dir, Victim Witness Adv Bd. **Honors/Awds:** Citizens Appreciate Police Award; SCAT Appreciation Award; Peer Support Recognition Award; Black Officer of the Year; Officer of the Month; Optimist International Law Enforcement Recognition; Intelligence Bureau Appreciation Award; National Black Police Association Leadership Award. **Special Achievements:** Arapahoe Youth League Eagles Football Coach. **Home Addr:** 3694 S Poplar St, Denver, CO 80237-1330. **Business Addr:** Owner, Webb Law Group LLC, 925 S Niagara St, Denver, CO 80224-1682, **Business Phone:** (303)861-5500.

**WEBB, LINNETTE**
Executive. **Personal:** Born Charleston, SC; daughter of Carl and Naomi (deceased); married Albert Pershing Black Jr. **Educ:** Lehman Col; Baruch Col, MPA. **Career:** Renaissance Diag & Treat Ctr, staff; Harlem Hosp Ctr, exec dir; Health & Hosps Corp, New York, sr vpres, exec dir & chief. **Orgs:** Chairperson, bd dir, Greater Harlem Nursing Home; fel mem The New York Acad Med, New York. **Home Addr:** 4131 Presidential Dr, Lafayette Hill, PA 19444-1609.

**WEBB, MELVIN RICHARD**
Educator. **Personal:** Born Feb 9, 1940, Cuthbert, GA; married Brenda Janet Burton. **Educ:** Albany State Col, BS, 1992; Atlanta Univ, MS, 1968; Ohio State Univ, PhD, 1977. **Career:** Lee Co Bd Educ, sci teacher, 1962-63; Dougherty Co Bd Educ, biol & chem, 1963-66; Atlanta Bd Educ, biol teacher, 1967-69; Clark Col, prof biol & sci educ, 1972-, Resource Ctr Sci & Engineering, asst dir, prof biol, 1978-. **Orgs:** Nat Sci Teachers Asn; GA Sci Teachers Asn; Phi Delta Kappa; Nat Asn Advan Colored People; Soc Christian Leadership Conf; dir, Prog Res Integration & Support Matriculation; dir, Atlanta Comprehensive Regional Ctr Minorities. **Home Addr:** 2344 Springside Way, Decatur, GA 30032, **Home Phone:** (404)288-5855. **Business Addr:** Professor, Clark Atlanta University, 223 James P Brawley Dr Rm 3005A RCST, Atlanta, GA 30314, **Business Phone:** (404)880-6790.

**WEBB, REGINALD (REGGIE WEBB)**
President (organization), chairperson. **Personal:** Born Mar 25, 1948, South Bend, IN; children: 2. **Educ:** Calif State Univ, Los Angeles, polit sci. **Career:** Nat Black McDonald's Operators Asn, chmn & chief exec officer, 1994-97, pres, currently. **Orgs:** Chmn, Nat Leadership Coun McDonald's. **Honors/Awds:** McDonalds 365Black Award, McDonald's, 2004. **Business Addr:** President, National Black McDonald's Operators Association, 1 Kroc Dr, Oak Brook, IL 60523, **Business Phone:** (630)623-6988.

**WEBB, RICHMOND JEWEL, JR.**
Football player. **Personal:** Born Jan 11, 1967, Dallas, TX. **Educ:** Tex A&M Univ, BS, indust distrib, 1993. **Career:** Football player (retired); Miami Dolphins, left tackle, 1990-2000, tackle, 1999, 2005; Cincinnati Bengals, left tackle, 2001, tackle, 2002. **Honors/Awds:** Earned Many post season hons in 1990 included: Rookie of the Year, Nat Football League; Pro Bowl appearances; Rookie of the Year, United Press Intl AFC; SportsIllustrated Rookie of the Year, 1990; Sporting News Rookie of the Year; 2ndteam All-Pro from Col & Pro Football Newsweekly, 2nd team All-AFC, United Press Intl, 1990, 1993; All-Rookie teams; United Press Intl; Outstanding Offensive Lineman, Miami Dolphins, 1990-94; Outstanding Offensive Lineman, S Fla Media, 1990-95; Rookie of the Year, S Fla Media; Tommy Fitzgerald Award; first-team All-AFC hon, The Football News, 1992; first-team All-AFC hon, United Press, 1992; Dolphins Honor Roll, 2006. **Special Achievements:** First tackle in Dolphins hist to be selected to the Pro Bowl as a starter; the first Dolphins offensive lineman to win the hon since Dwight Stephenson in 1987.

**WEBB, SCHUYLER CLEVELAND**
Psychologist, military leader. **Personal:** Born Jun 28, 1951, Springfield, MA; son of Cleveland and Bettye Wright; children: Kayla Monique. **Educ:** Morehouse Col, BA, 1974; Am Inst Foreign Study, cert, 1975; Univ Mass, MS, 1978; Nat Univ, MBA, 1986; Pac Grad Sch Psychol, PhD, currently. **Career:** Univ Mass, asst trainer & alcoholism counr, 1974-77; Inst Studying Educ Policy Howard Univ, res asst, 1978; Lawrence Johnson & Assoc Inc, tech staff cont, 1978-81; Howard Univ, Ctr Sickle Cell Disease, Wash, DC, ed comm mem & consult, 1979-81; Higher Horizons Day Care Ctr, Crossroads, VA, consult, 1980-81; USN Med Serv Corps, res psychologist & hosp corpsman, 1981; Naval Health Res Ctr, San Diego, res psychologist, 1983-86; Diving & Salvage Sch, Panama Beach, Fla, instr & res psychologist, 1986-87; Naval Biodynamics Lab, New Orleans, res psychologist, admin & equal opportunity officer, 1987-91; Defense Equal Opportunity Mgt Inst, Patrick AFB, res intern, 1991; Naval Bur Personnel, dep dir res psychologist, 1994; Navy Inspector Gen Off, tech consult, 1994. **Orgs:** Asn Mil Surgeons; Human Factors Soc; Sleep Rsch Soc; Asn Black Psychologists; Am Psychol Asn; pub rels & scholar comn, Nat Naval Officer Asn, San Diego Chap, 1983-; co-chair, Cult Heritage & Black Hist Comn, San Diego, USN, 1984-86; advan open water diver, Prof Asn Diving Instrs, 1986-; Nat Asn Advan Colored People, Alpha Phi Alpha, Urban League; equal opportunity officer, combined fed campaign officer, Morehouse Alumni Asn; vpres mem, nat Naval officers Asn, 1988-89; Second Harvest Food Bank, 1987-; Asn Study Class African Civilizations, 1990-. **Special Achievements:** Certificate of Achievement in Community & Counseling Psychology, 1974; Horace Barr Fellowship, 1974-77; Collegiate Commission for the Education of Black Students Fellowship, 1974-75; Our Crowd Scholarship; Springfield Teachers Club Scholarship; Community Service Award, Springfield Col; Academic Scholarship 4 year tuition scholarship, Morehouse College, 1970-74; Psychology Department honors, Morehouse College, 1974; National University leadership Scholarship, Nat Univ, 1984; "Jet Lag in Military Operations", Naval Health Res Ctr, San Diego, CA 1986; publ:"Comparative Analysis of Decompression Sickness", Jour Hyperbaric Med, 2:55-62, 1987; Duty Under Instruction Scholar, USN, 1991-94. **Home Addr:** 8014 Ebbtide Dr, New Orleans, LA 70126-1972, **Home Phone:** (504)788-7409. **Business Addr:** Consultant, Bureau of Naval Personnel, 5720 Integrity Dr, Millington, TN 38054, **Business Phone:** (901)874-6615.

**WEBB, DR. SHELIA J.**
Health services administrator. **Personal:** Born New Orleans, LA. **Educ:** Dillard Univ, BS, nursing; Univ Southern Miss, MS, nursing; Southern Univ, A & M Col, PhD, nursing. **Career:** Clin nurse specialist, psychiat ment health nursing; New Orleans Health Dept, exec dir, dir health; City New Orleans, dir health dept; Ctr Empowered Decision Making, dir, 2003-. **Business Addr:** Director, Center for Empowered Decision Making, 1515 Poydras St Suite 1060 City Hall, New Orleans, LA 70112-3723, **Business Phone:** (504)620-0024.

**WEBB, SPUD (ANTHONY JEROME WEBB)**
Television show host, basketball player, businessperson. **Personal:** Born Jul 13, 1963, Dallas, TX. **Educ:** Midland Col, Midland, TX, attended 1983; NC State Univ, Raleigh, NC, attended 1985. **Career:** Basketball player (retired), business owner, executive, TV show host, business person; RI Gulls, 1985; Atlanta Hawks, guard, 1985-91, 1995-96; Sacramento Kings, guard, 1991-95; Minn Timberwolves, guard, 1996; Scaligera Verona, Italy, 1996-97; Mash J. Verona, Italy, 1996-97; Orlando Magic, guard, 1998; Idaho Stampede, 1998; Dallas Mavericks, Pre-game & Post-Game Shows, host; Spud Webb Enterprises, owner, currently; delivering keynote addresses, currently; D-League Franchise, Frisco, Tex, pres, basketball opers, currently. **Business Addr:** Owner, Keynote Speaker, NOPAC Talent -Sports Stars & Celebrities, 2247 Rickover Pl, Winter Garden, FL 34787, **Business Phone:** (888)883-7783.

**WEBB, STANFORD**
Executive. **Career:** R Stanford Webb Agency, founder, 1925-. **Business Addr:** Founder, R Stanford Webb Agency, 216 Asheland Ave, Asheville, NC 28801, **Business Phone:** (828)258-2663.

**WEBB, UMEKI**
Basketball player. **Personal:** Born Jun 26, 1975. **Educ:** NC State Univ, attended 1997. **Career:** Basketball player (retired); Phoenix Mercury, guard forward, 1997-98; Miami Sol, guard, 2000; Lubbock Hawks, 2005. **Home Addr:** 2057 W Hebron Pkwy Apt 1732, Carrollton, TX 75010-6369, **Home Phone:** (214)242-7112.

**WEBB, VERONICA LYNN**
Fashion model, journalist, actor. **Personal:** Born Feb 23, 1965, Detroit, MI; daughter of Doug and Marion; married George Robb; children: Leila Rose & Molly Blue. **Educ:** Parson's Sch Design; New Sch Social Res. **Career:** Ford Model Mgt, free-lance model, 1984; Interview, Andy Warhol, contrib ed, 1990; Spike Lee's Jungle Fever, supporting role, 1991; Revlon Consumer Prod Corp, color style spokesperson, 1992. Films: Jungle Fever, 1991; Malcolm X, 1992; Catwalk, 1996; Damon, 1998; 54, VIP patron, 1998; Holy Man, 1998; The Big Tease, 1999; In Too Deep, 1999; Becker, 2001, Dirty Laundry, 2006. **Orgs:** Steering comt head, Black Girls Coalition, 1989-; sustaining mem, Planned Parenthood, 1992-; 21st Century Party, 1992-; RPM Nautical Found; LIFEBeat; Product Red. **Home Addr:** 343 E 18th St, New York, NY 10003, **Home Phone:** (212)475-8718. **Business Addr:** Contract Model, Ford Models, 350 5th Ave, New York, NY 10118, **Business Phone:** (646)530-8333.

**WEBB, WELLINGTON E.**
Teacher, executive director, mayor. **Personal:** Born Feb 17, 1941, Chicago, IL; married Wilma J; children: Keith, Tony, Allen & Stephanie. **Educ:** Colo St Col, BA, sociol, 1964; Univ Northern Colo, Greeley, MA, sociol, 1971. **Career:** Denver pub schs, teacher; Colo St Univ Manpower Lab, dir, 1969-74; Colo House Rep, st rep, 1972-77; Colo Carter/Mondale Campaign, 1976; US Dept Health & Human Serv, regional dir, 1977-80; Dept Regulatory Agencies, exec dir, 1981-87; City Denver, auditor, 1987-91, mayor, 1991-2003; Nat Conf Black Mayors, pres; US Conf Mayors, pres; Harvard Univ's Kennedy Sch Govt, guest lectr; Nat Conf Dem Mayors, pres; Webb Group Int, founder, 2003-; Maximus Corp, bd dir; Ntional Conf Black Mayors, pres. **Orgs:** Chmn, Dem Caucus CO House Rep, 1975-; chmn, Health Welfare & Inst Com, 1975-76; del, Dem Nat Conv, 1976, 1992; trustee bd, Denver C's Hosp, 1975-; bd dir, Denver Oper PUSH, 1975-; bd dir, Denver Urban Coalition, 1975; chmn, United Negro Col Fund,

1973-75; vice pres, pres, Nat Conf Black Mayors. **Honors/Awds:** Barney Ford Award for Political Action, 1976; Leadership of the Year Award, Thomas Jefferson HS, 1976; Nat Wildlife Federation's 1999 Achievement Award; The Wellington E Webb Municipal Office Building, named in honor, 2002; Distinguished Public Service Award, 2003; US Conference of Mayors highest honor; Outstanding Achievement in Public Policy Award; Hon doctorate, Univ Colo, Denver; Hon doctorate, Metrop State Col. **Special Achievements:** First African American Mayor of Denver; Only African-American candidate for the DNC chairmanship. **Home Addr:** 2329 Gaylord St, Denver, CO 80205-5627, **Home Phone:** (303)321-4092. **Business Addr:** Founder, Webb Group International LLC, 1660 Lincoln St Suite2820, Denver, CO 80264, **Business Phone:** (303)893-9322.

### WEBB, REV. WILLIAM C.
Disciples of christ clergy. **Personal:** Born Fordyce, AR; married Violene C; children: Yolanda & Lafayette. **Educ:** Philander Smith Col, BA, pre ministry, 1956; Va Union Univ, MDiv, 1959. **Career:** Second Baptist Church, pastor, interim Pastor, 2006-08, pastor, currently. **Special Achievements:** William C Webb Circle, Wedekind Road, Clear Acre Lane, City of Reno, 2004. **Business Addr:** Pastor, Second Baptist Church, 1265 Montello St, Reno, NV 89512, **Business Phone:** (775)786-1017.

### WEBB, WILMA J. GERDINE
Labor activist, mayor. **Personal:** Born May 17, 1943, Denver, CO; daughter of Frank Wendell Gerdine (deceased) and Faye Elizabeth Wyatt Gerdine; married Wellington; children: Keith, Anthony, Stephanie & Allen. **Educ:** Univ Colo, Denver; Harvard Univ; John F Kennedy Sch Govt. **Career:** Mobil Corp, admin assoc; Bank Denver, admin assoc; City Denver, legislator, mayor, 1991; Colo House Rep, state rep; US Labor Dept, Region 8, secy's rep, 1997-; ed, Dem State Newsletter. **Orgs:** Denver Cs Home; chair, Martin Luther King Jr Colo Holiday Comn; founder, chair, Mayors Comn Art Cult & Film; Colo Joint Budget Comm; Zion Baptist Church; Delta Sigma Theta sorority; Links Inc; co-founder, Comt Greater Opportunity; Dem Party secy; Dem Committeewoman, 1973; chair, Dem Comt Housing; Colo Legis, 1980; founder, Denver Art, Cult, & Film Found, 1994. **Honors/Awds:** Martin Luther King Jr Humanitarian Award; hon doctorate, Colo Institute of Art; Carter G. Woodson Award, Nat Educ Asn; Legislator of the Year Award, Asn Retarded Citizens; Political Award, Colo Banking Asn. **Special Achievements:** First African American to serve Region 8; First woman to serve Region 8; First minority female mem of Colorado Joint Budget Comm; First African American mayor of Denver in 1991; First woman to serve in the US Department of Labor as the primary official for Colorado, Montana, North Dakota, South Dakota, Utah, and Wyoming. **Business Addr:** Secretarys Representative, US Labor Dept, 1999 Broadway Suite 600, Denver, CO 80202, **Business Phone:** (720)264-3000.

### WEBBER, CHRIS, III (MAYCE EDWARD CHRISTOPHER WEBBER)
Basketball executive, basketball player. **Personal:** Born Mar 1, 1973, Detroit, MI; son of Doris and Mayce; married Erika Dates. **Educ:** Univ Mich, BS, psychol, 1993. **Career:** Basketball player (retired); Golden State Warriors, forward, 1993-94, 2008; Wash Wizards, 1994-98; Sacramento Kings, 1998-2005; Philadelphia 76ers, forward, 2005-07; Detroit Pistons, 2007; NBA TV, NBA Gametime Live, analyst, currently; C-Webb Restaurant, Owner, 2009-. **Orgs:** Founder, Timeout Found, 1993-; charity, Bada Bling, 2007-. **Honors/Awds:** McDonald's All-American Most Valuable Player, 1991; Naismith Prep Player of the Year, 1991; Rookie of the Year, Nat Basketball Asn, 1994; Most Valuable Player, 2000-01; Western Conference Player of the Week, 2001-02; Western Conference Player of the Month, 2002-03; Sacramento Kings & Oscar Robertson Triple Double Award; Community Assist Award, Nat Basketball Asn, 2003; Wish Maker of the Year, Make a Wish Found, 2003; Ranked No. 64 in Top 75 NBA Players of all time, SLAM Magazine, 2003. **Special Achievements:** Album: Surviving the Times; Hip Hop Is Dead. **Business Addr:** Owner, C-Webb Restaurant, 3600 N Freeway Blvd, Sacramento, CA 95834-2904, **Business Phone:** (916)419-4667.

**WEBBER, MAYCE EDWARD CHRISTOPHER.** **See WEBBER, CHRIS, III.**

### WEBBER, HON. PAUL R., III
Judge. **Personal:** Born Jan 24, 1934, Gadsden, SC; son of Paul Jr and Clemmie Embley; married Fay DeShields; children: Paul IV, Stephen & Nikki. **Educ:** SC State Univ, BA, polit sci, 1955, Sch Law, JD, 1957. **Career:** Allen Univ, Columbia, SC, pvt pract & lect, 1958-59; UCLA, asst law lib, 1959-60; Golden State Mutual Life Ins Co LA, assoc coun, 1960-64; Antitrust Div US Dept Just, trial atty, 1964-67; Neighborhood Legal Serv Prog, Dist Columbia, managing atty, 1967-69; Dolphin Branton Stafford & Webber, atty, 1969-77; Howard Univ, lectr; George Wash Univ Law Sch, adj prof, summer, 1973; DC Super Ct, judge, 1977-98, sr judge, 1998-. **Orgs:** Am, Nat, Dist Columbia, Calif & Sc Bar Asns; Alpha Phi Alpha; gen coun, Sigma Pi Phi; Guardsmen; past chmn, Civil Pract & Family Law Sec Nat Bar Asn; Judicial Coun Wash Bar Asn; Nat Asn Parliamentarians, 2001; Joint Ctr Polit Econ Studies. **Honors/Awds:** Trial Judge of the Year, unanimous vote Trial Lawyers Asn Metro, Wash, DC, 1985-86. **Home Addr:** 1627 Myrtle St NW, Washington, DC 20012-1129, **Home Phone:** (202)829-1368. **Business Addr:** Senior Judge, DC Super Ct, 500 Ind Ave NW Rm 4242, Washington, DC 20001, **Business Phone:** (202)879-0157.

### WEBBER, WILLIAM STUART (BILL WEBBER)
Government official, commissioner. **Personal:** Born Oct 17, 1942, Hartshorne, OK; children: Natalie Jewell, Stuart Franklin & Timpi Armelia. **Educ:** Eastern Okla A&M Univ, attended 1962. **Career:** Rancher Santa Gertrudis Breeder, 1958-; Rockwell Int, electronic technician, 1964-83; Pittsburg County, county comnr, 1983-99; Bill webber Ranch, owner, currently. **Orgs:** Mason AF&M, Pittsburg County Cattleman's Asn, 1967-; real estate developer; prof coon hunter, Prof Coon Hunters Asn, 1981-85; Church God Christ; Am Cattle Breeder's Asn. **Honors/Awds:** Hall of Fame, Am Cattle Breeders Asn. **Home Addr:** HCR 74, PO Box 240, Hartshorne, OK 74547. **Business Addr:** Owner, Bill webber Ranch.

### WEBER, CARL
Writer, publisher. **Educ:** Va State Univ; Va State Univ, MBA, mkt, 1999. **Career:** Urban Bks, founder, publ & ed dir, 1996-; Author: Baby Momma Drama, Married Men, Lookin' for Luv, 2000, Married Men, 2001, Baby Momma Drama, 2003, Player Haters, 2004, The Preacher's Son, 2005, So You Call Yourself a Man, 2005, The First Lady, 2006. **Honors/Awds:** Blackboards 2005 publisher of the year; Blackboards Bookseller of the Year Award. **Business Addr:** Founder, Publisher, Editorial Director, Urban Books, Richmond, VA 23219.

### WEBER, DR. SHIRLEY NASH
School administrator, educator. **Personal:** Born Sep 20, 1948, Hope, AR; daughter of David and Mildred (deceased); married Daniel; children: Akilah Faizah & Akil Khalfani. **Educ:** Univ Calif, LA, BA, speech commun, 1970, MA, speech commun, 1971, PhD, speech commun, 1975. **Career:** Episcopal City Mission Soc, case worker, 1969-72; Calif State Col, instr, 1972; San Diego State Univ, asst prof, prof, 1972-, chairperson emer, currently; San Diego City Schs, pres bd educ, 1990-91; W.E.B. DuBois Leadership Inst Young Black Scholars, co-founder & dir, currently; Calif State Assembly, 79th dist, assembly mem, 2012-. **Orgs:** Bd mem, Calif Black Fac & Staff, 1976-80; regional ed, Western j Speech, 1979-; pres, Black Caucus Speech Comm Asn, 1980-82; adv bd; Battered Women's Serv YWCA, 1981-; pres, Nat Comm Asn, 1983-85; bd mem, Coun 21Southwestern Christian Col, 1983-; vpres, Nat Sorority Phi Delta KappaDelta Upsilon Chap; trustee, Bd Educ, San Diego Unified Sch Dist, 1988-96; dir, Acad Effectively Teaching African Am Stud; bd mem, Nat Coun Black Studies Inc, secy; vpres, chair, dir, Nat Asn Advan Colored People; Womens Int Ctr. **Honors/Awds:** Outstanding Young Woman in America, 1976, 1981; Outstanding Faculty Award, 1981, 1988 & 1990; Black Achievement Action Enterprise Development, 1981; Women of Distinction, Women, 1984; National Citation Award, Nat Sorority Phi Delta Kappa, 1989; Citizen of the Year, Omega Psi Phi Fraternity, 1989; Carter G Woodson Education Award, NAACP, San Diego, 1989; Local Hero Award, Ankh Maat Wedjau Honor Soc; NCBS Presidential Award, YMCA; Living Legacy Award, Women's Int Ctr, 1997. **Special Achievements:** Became one of seventeen Woodrow Wilson fellows out of a class of over 6, 000 from UCLA in 1970, also hosted her own talk show. She has authored numerous articles and chapters in books & referred journals on Black language Marcus Garvey, Gwendolyn Brooks, Black Nationalism, Black Studies and service learning. Work on black language also appears in a translated text in Polish; First African American to be elected to office South of Los Angeles and was selected Outstanding Young Woman in America twice; First African American From South of Los Angeles to be Elected to California State Legislature. **Home Addr:** 2498 Kathleen Pl, San Diego, CA 92105-5032, **Home Phone:** (619)972-1140. **Business Addr:** Professor, Chairperson Emeritus of Black Studies Department, San Diego State University, 5500 Campanile Dr AL 371, San Diego, CA 92182, **Business Phone:** (619)594-5200.

### WEBSTER, DR. CHARLES L.
Dentist, army officer. **Personal:** Born Dec 15, 1936, LeCompte, LA; son of Charles Sr and Carrie Hills. **Educ:** Southern Univ, BS, 1959; Howard Univ, MS, 1971, Col Dent, DDS, 1977. **Career:** Army national guard (retired), dentist; St Elizabeth Hosp, residency training, dent intern, 1977-78; Montgomery Co Detention Ctr, dent dir, 1978; GA Ave Kiwanis Club, bus mgr, 1984-85, Dept Human Servs, dent officer; pvt pract, dentist, currently. **Orgs:** Kappa Alpha Psi, 1957-; Am Soc Dent C, 1978; Am Dent Soc, 1981; Asn Mil Surgeons, 1981, Anethesiol Training Uniform Serv Med Sch, 1982-84; Robert T Freeman Dent Soc; Nat Dent Asn; Eta Chi Sigma Hon Biol Soc; Beta Beta Beta Hon Biol Soc. **Honors/Awds:** Certificate of Merit, Am Cancer Soc, 1977. **Home Addr:** 6713 14th St NW, Washington, DC 20012, **Home Phone:** (202)291-8596. **Business Addr:** Dentist, Private Practice, 7723 Alaska Ave NW, Washington, DC 20012, **Business Phone:** (202)829-0177.

### WEBSTER, JOHN W., III
Chief executive officer, foundation executive, software developer. **Personal:** Born Oct 19, 1961, Highland Park, MI; son of John W Jr and Melceina L Blackwell; married Michele S Peters. **Educ:** Mass Inst Technol, Cambridge, BS, comput sci, 1983, MS, comput sci, 1987; Duke Univ, Fuqua Sch Bus, MBA, mkt & entrepreneurship, 1997. **Career:** Int Bus Mach Corp, Cambridge, Mass, sci staff mem, 1983-87, sci proj mgr, 1987-88; Int Bus Mach Corp, Res Triangle Pk, NC, commun & syst mgt designer, 1988-89, develop mgr, 1989; GE, mgr, 1995-97; Spaceworks, vpres, 1997-2000; Permitsnow Inc, chief exec officer; Softcomp Inc, vice chmn & pres, chief exec officer; Odyssey Technologies Inc, chief exec officer, currently. **Orgs:** Pres, Greater Olney Civic Asn, 2014-15. **Business Addr:** Chief Executive Officer, Odyssey Technologies Inc, 14504 Greenview Dr, Laurel, MD 20708, **Business Phone:** (301)256-0000.

### WEBSTER, LARRY MELVIN, JR.
Football player. **Personal:** Born Jan 18, 1969, Elkton, MD. **Educ:** Univ Md, grad. **Career:** Football player (retired); Miami Dolphins, defensive tackle & left defensive tackle, 1992-94; Cleveland Browns, 1995; Baltimore Ravens, defensive tackle & left defensive tackle, 1996-2001; New York Jets, 2002; Baltimore Polytech Inst, asst coach, 2009-12; Baltimore Polytech Engrs, head coach, 2012-. **Honors/Awds:** Baltimore Ravens Super Bowl XXXV Champions. **Special Achievements:** Film: Super Bowl XXXV, 2001. **Business Addr:** Head Coach, Baltimore Polytech Engineers, 1400 W Cold Spring Lane, Baltimore, MD 21209, **Business Phone:** (410)396-7026.

### WEBSTER, LENNY (LEONARD IRELL WEBSTER)
Baseball player, actor. **Personal:** Born Feb 10, 1965, New Orleans, LA. **Educ:** Grambling State Univ. **Career:** Baseball player (retired); Minn Twins, platoon catcher, 1989-93; Montreal Expos, 1994, 1996, 2000; Philadelphia Phillies, 1995; Baltimore Orioles, 1997-99; Boston Red Sox, 1999. **Special Achievements:** Flim: Little Big League, 1994.

### WEBSTER, LESLEY DOUGLASS
Lawyer. **Personal:** Born Jun 9, 1949, New York, NY; son of Bernard; married Jules A; children: Jules S. **Educ:** Northeastern Univ, Boston, MA, BA, 1972; Georgetown Univ Law Ctr, JD, 1975; Wharton Col; Rutgers Univ. **Career:** Cambridge Redevel Authority Mass, comt organiser, 1970-72; Criminal Justice Clin, Georgetown Univ Law Ctr, prosecution coord, 1974-75; US Dept Energy, Region II, NY, atty, adv, 1975-77; Col Staten Island, NY, adj prof, 1977-78; US Dept Energy, Reg II, NY, dep regional coun, 1977-79; Northville Ind Corp, compliance coun, 1979-84; New York Dept Com, dep comnr, coun; City New York Parks & Recreation Dept, atty; legal asst comm, currently. **Orgs:** New York Bar, 1976-; chairwoman bd, Asn Energy Prof, 1980-84. **Honors/Awds:** Superior Service Award, US Dept Energy, 1976. **Home Addr:** 470 Lenox Ave Apt 14P, New York, NY 10037. **Business Addr:** Attorney, Legal Assistant Commissioner, City of New York Parks and Recreation Department, Arsenal Cent Pk, New York, NY 10021, **Business Phone:** (212)360-1312.

### WEBSTER, NIAMBI DYANNE
Educator. **Personal:** children: K Tyronne Colemon. **Educ:** Drake Univ, BA, Eng, 1973; Mankato State Col, MS, curriculum & instr, 1975; Univ Iowa, PhD, curriculum & instr, 1991; Jacksonville Theol Soc, ThD. **Career:** Des Moines Pub Schs, instr, 1975-78; Iowa Bystander, free lance writer, assoc ed, 1976-80; Univ Iowa, coordr minority prog, 1978-83; Iowa Arts Coun, touring music & theatre folk artist, 1978-; Univ Iowa, grad asst instr, 1980-83; Coe Col, instr dir spec servs; Skidmore Col, dir multicultural & int stud affairs, 1989-91; Sonoma State Univ, Dept Am Multicultural Studies, asst prof, prof, 1993-; Wooddale High Sch, instr, currently. **Orgs:** Outreach counr, YMCA Des Moines, 1974-78; instr, Gateway Oppor Pageant, 1975-78; pres & publicity chair, Nat Asn Advan Colored People Des Moines Chap, 1976-78; founder & dir, Langston Hughes Co Players, 1976-82; co-chair, Polk Co Rape/Sexual Assault Bd, 1977-80; artist-in-schs, IA Arts Coun, 1978-; 6th Judicial Dist Correctional Serv CSP & News Ed Vol, 1984-; chairperson, Mid-Amer Assoc Ed Opportunity Prog Personnel Cult Enrichment Comm, 1984-; Iowa City Comm Schs Equity Comm mem, 1985-87; Delta Sigma Theta Sor, Berkeley Alumnae. **Honors/Awds:** Community Service in the Fine Arts NAACP Presidential, 1978; Black Leadership Awd Univ of IA, 1979; Social Action Awd Phi Beta Sigma Frat, 1980; Outstanding Young Woman in the Arts NAACP Natl Women Cong, 1981; Women Equality & Dedication Comm on the Status of Women, 1981; Trio Achievers Awd Natl Cncl of Educ Oppor Assoc, 1985; Outstanding Woman of the Year Awd Linn Co Comm, 1986. **Home Addr:** 10 Meridian Cir, Rohnert Park, CA 94928-3657. **Business Addr:** Instructor, Wooddale High School, 5151 Scottsdale Ave, Memphis, TN 38118, **Business Phone:** (901)416-2440.

### WEBSTER, THEODORE E.
Executive. **Educ:** MBA. **Career:** Webster Eng Co Inc, Dorchester, MA, pres & chief exec officer, 1977-. **Orgs:** Pres, Mass Chap Nat Assn Minority Contractors; chmn, Mass Alliance Small Contractors; exec comt, Burroughs Group; Veterans Benefits Clearing house; US Dept Labor; New Eng Chap. **Home Addr:** 1241 Adams St Apt 612, Dorchester, MA 02124-5775, **Home Phone:** (617)298-1416. **Business Addr:** President, Chief Executive Officer, Webster Engineering Co Inc, 2300 Crown Colony Dr Suite 101, Quincy, MA 02169, **Business Phone:** (617)265-5500.

### WEBSTER, WILLIAM H.
Lawyer, executive. **Personal:** Born Oct 26, 1946, New York, NY; son of Eugene Burnett and Verna May Bailey; married Joan Leslie; children: Sydney. **Educ:** NY Univ, BA, 1972; Univ Calif Sch Law, JD, 1975. **Career:** Black Law J, Univ Calif, Berkeley, res assoc, 1973; Nat Econ Develop & Law Proj, post-grad, 1974-76; Nat Econ Develop & Law Ctr, Berkeley, Calif, atty, 1976-82; Hunter & Anderson, partner, 1983-; Webster & Anderson, managing partner, atty, 1993-; Martin Luther King fel. **Orgs:** Nat Training Inst Com Econ Develop, Artisans Coop Inc; Mayors Housing Task Force Berkeley; State Bar Calif; US Dist Ct No Dist Calif; US Tax Ct; Nat Asn Bond Lawyers; Nat Bar Asn; Charles Houston Bar Asn; City Berkeley Citizens Com Responsible Invests; Kappa Alpha Psi. **Honors/Awds:** NY State Regents Incentive Awards; Howard Mem Fund Scholar; Alpha Phi Alpha Scholar; pub, "Housing, Structuring Housing Develop, " Econ Develop Law Ctr Report, 1978, "Tax Savings through Inter corporate Billing, " Econ Develop Law Ctr Report, 1980; various other publications. **Home Addr:** 4520 Fallow Dr, Antioch, CA 94509. **Business Addr:** Attorney, Managing Partner, Webster & Anderson Law Office, 469 9th St Suite 240, Oakland, CA 94607-4047, **Business Phone:** (510)839-3245.

### WEBSTER, WINSTON ROOSEVELT
College teacher, lawyer. **Personal:** Born Apr 22, 1943, Nashville, TN. **Educ:** Fisk Univ, AB, 1965; Harvard Univ, LLB, 1968. **Career:** Neighberhood Legal Serv Prog, staff atty, 1968-69; Urban Inst, think tank researcher, 1969-70; Off Legal Servs WA, supvry gen atty, 1970-72; practicing atty, 1971-; Cable TV Info Ctr, regional dir, 1972-74; Tex Southern Univ, law prof, 1974-77, mem bd regents, 1979-. **Orgs:** US Dist Ct DC & TC; Super Ct DC; Supreme Ct TX; DC Bar Asn; Tex Bar Asn; Am Asn Trial Lawyers; Nat Conf Black Lawyers; bd dir, Nat Paralegal Inst, 1972-75; legal adv comt, Tex Asn Col Teachers, 1976-77; bd gov, Wash Athletic Club, 1974. **Honors/Awds:** Hon Citizen New Orleans, 1971; Duke of Paducah, 1972; Ky Col, 1973; Professor of the Year, Thurgood Marshall Sch of Law, 1976-77; Outstanding Young Men of Am, 1977; Numerous articles. **Business Addr:** Attorney, PO Box 710106, Houston, TX 77271-0106, **Business Phone:** (713)668-9097.

### WEDDERBURN, DR. RAYMOND
Hospital administrator, surgeon. **Personal:** Born May 1, 1961, Kingston. **Educ:** Brown Univ; Cornel Univ Med Col, attended 1986. **Career:** St Luke's-Roosevelt Hosp Ctr, Dept Surg, Chief-Trauma & Critical Care, intern, resident, surg, 1987-91, jr asst attend, 1992, asst dir critical care, 1992, assoc dir trauma & critical care, 1993, actg chief, 1994, chief surg critical care, 1995-99, assoc dir residency training prog, 1997-, chief, Trauma & Surg Critical Care, 1999-; Univ Miami, Jackson Mem Hosp-19Surgical Critical Care Fel, 1993; Columbia Col Physicians & Surgeons, instr surg, 1995-99, asst clin prof

surg, 1999-. **Orgs:** pres, Stud Nat Med Asn, Cornell Chap, 1983-84; Soc Sigma XI - Brown Univ Chap. **Honors/Awds:** CIBA Award for Outstanding Community Service, 1984; Charles L. Horn Prize, 1986; Resident' Award for Excellence in Teaching, Dept Surg, St Luke's-Roosevelt Hosp Ctr, 1993-94, 1996-97, 1999-2000; Distinguished Young Physician of the Year Award, 2004. **Special Achievements:** Publication: Management of Paroxysmal Atrioventricular Nodal Reentrant Tachycardia in the Critically Ill Surgical Patient. Kirton OC, Windson J, Civetta, JM, Cudson-Civetta J, Wedderurn R, Gomez DV, Shatz J, Hudson-Civetta S, Komanduri S. Critical Care Medicine: 25 (5):May 1997; 761-6; Failure of Splanchnic Resuscitation in the Acutely Injured Trauma Patient Correlates with Multiple Organ system Failure and Length of Stay in the ICU. Iirton O, Windsor HJ, Wedderburn R, Hudson-Civetta J, Shatz, D, Mataragas N, Civetta J. Chest:113(4): April 1998, 1064-9; Many presentations. **Home Addr:** 322 W 57th St Apt 27H, New York, NY 10019-3708, **Home Phone:** (212)974-2289. **Business Addr:** Chief, Trauma, Critical Care, St Luke-Roosevelt Hospital Center, 1000 10th Ave Suite 2B, New York, NY 10019, **Business Phone:** (212)523-7780.

### WEDDINGTON, BILL
Educator, counselor. **Educ:** Calif State Univ, Chico, BA, MA; Univ San Francisco, EdD. **Career:** Napa Valley Col, prof psychol, coun, currently. **Orgs:** Counr, Acad Stand & Practices Comt, Napa Valley Col. **Business Addr:** Professor of Psychology, Napa Valley College, 2277 Napa Vallejo Hwy, Napa, CA 94558-6236, **Business Phone:** (707)253-3000.

### WEDDINGTON, DR. WILBURN HAROLD, SR.
Physician, educator. **Personal:** Born Sep 21, 1924, Hiram, GA; son of Charlie Earl and Annie Mae Moore; married Rose Carline Howard; children: Wilburn H Jr, Cynthia D, Kimberly K, Marisia D & Wilburn C. **Educ:** Morehouse Col, Atlanta, GA, BS, 1945; Howard Univ, Wash, DC, MD, 1948; Univ Buffalo, Buffalo, NY, radiol; Harvard Univ, electrocardiography, 1962; Univ Mex, course obstet & pediat; Howard Univ, family med rev. **Career:** Mercy Hosp, staff physician, 1957-70; Grant Hosp, staff physician, 1957-; St Anthony Hosp, staff physician, 1958-; Ohio State Univ, Col Med, Columbus, Ohio, staff physician, 1970-88, clin assoc prof, 1980-85, Self Insurance Board, 2004-07, prof clin family med, assoc dean med, prof emer clin family med, currently. **Orgs:** Am Med Asn, 1952-; Nat Med Asn, 1954-; Ohio State Med Asn, 1958-; Columbus& Franklin Co Acad Med, 1958-; Am Soc Hypnosis, 1963; Ohio Acad Family Physicians, 1968-; Cent Ohio Acad Family Physicians, 1968-; 1968-, Am Acad Family Physicians, fel 1974-; co-founder, Columbus Asn Physicians & Dentistry, 1973-; Omega Psi Phi; Sigma Pi Phi. **Home Addr:** 4236 James River Rd, New Albany, OH 43054-8939. **Business Addr:** Professor Emeritus, Ohio State University, 2231 N High St, Columbus, OH 43201, **Business Phone:** (614)293-2653.

### WEDGEWORTH, ROBERT W., JR.
Librarian, school administrator. **Personal:** Born Jul 31, 1937, Ennis, TX; son of Robert Sr and Jimmie Johnson; married Chung Kyun; children: 1. **Educ:** Wabash Col, BA, 1959; Univ Ill, MS, libr & info sci, 1961. **Career:** KC Publ Libr, cataloger, 1961-62; Seattle Worlds Fair Libr 21, staff mem, 1962; Pk Col, asst librn, 1962-63, head librn, 1963-64; Meramec Community Col Kirkwood, head librn, 1964-66; Brown Univ Libr, asst chief order librn, 1966-69; Libr Resources & Tech Serv off, ALA Jour, ed; Rutgers Univ, asst prof, 1971-72; Univ Chicago, lectr; Columbia Univ, Sch Libr Serv, dean, 1985-92; Univ Ill, Urbana-Champaign, interim librn, 1992, univ librn, prof libr admin & prof libr & info sci, 1993-99; Laubach Literacy Int, pres, 2001-; Univ Ill, interim librn, 1992; Univ Librn & Prof Libr Admin, 1993-2001; ProLiteracy Worldwide, pres & chief exec officer, 2002-07. **Orgs:** Nat Asn Advan Colored People; Pub Serv Satellite Consortium Bd; adv coun mem, exec dir, Am Libr Asn, 1972-85; trustee, Newberry Libr; Grolier Soc; Adv Comt, US Bk & Libr; vpres, Wabash Col Alumni Bd; mem adv, Coun WBEZ Chicago; Am Antiqn Soc; exec bd mem, 1985-91, pres, 1997-97, Int Fed Libr Assoc & Insts; SYRACUSE 20/20's Educ Task Force; chair, Comt Accreditation, ALA, 2003-05; Nat Comn Adult Literacy. **Honors/Awds:** Most Distinguished Alumnus Award, Univ, Ill, 1996; Medal of Honor, Int Coun Archives; Lippincott & Melvil Dewey Awards, Am Libr Asn, 1977; Humphry/OCLC/Forest Press Award; DHL, Syracuse Univ, 2008; Joseph Lippincott Award. **Special Achievements:** Editor of two major reference works, ALA Yearbook, 1976-85 and the World Encyclopedia of Library and Information Services, 3d edition, 1993; Co-author of Starvation of Young Black Minds: The Effects of the Book Boycotts in South Africa, 1989. **Home Addr:** 2626 N Lakeview Ave Apt 3603, Chicago, IL 60614-1830, **Home Phone:** (773)525-6609. **Business Addr:** Library Emeritus, University of Illinois, 2626 N Lakeview Ave, Chicago, IL 60614-1830.

### WEEKS, DEBORAH REDD
Lawyer, executive director, commissioner. **Personal:** Born Dec 23, 1947, Brooklyn, CA; daughter of Warren Ellington and Edna Loretta Mayo; children: Monteil Dior & Kristienne Dior. **Educ:** Fisk Univ, Nashville, Tenn, BA, 1970; Univ Ky, Lexington, Ky, JD, 1978. **Career:** KY State Govt, dir contract compliance state KY, 1980-83; Urban League, dir adoption, 1983-85; WLEX TV, talk show host, 1984-86; State Univ NY, dir AA EEO, 1986-89; Monroe Co, coun dir AA EEO, 1989-90; Health & Hosp Corp, assoc legal, 1991; Dept Bus Serv, comnr, currently. **Orgs:** Coalition 100 Black Women, 1984-; Links, 1988-; chmn, EEO Comt, Harlem Bus Alliance, 1989-; RACOL Ctr Bd, 1990-; Negro Bus & Prof Women, 1990-. **Honors/Awds:** Kentucky Colonel, State Ky, 1986; Multiculturism, New York Asn Col Personnel Admin, summer, 1987. **Home Addr:** 475 Wash Ave, Brooklyn, NY 11238, **Home Phone:** (718)789-4794. **Business Addr:** Commissioner, Department of Business Services, 110 William St, New York, NY 10038, **Business Phone:** (212)513-6300.

### WEEKS, JUANITA BYNUM. See BYNUM, DR. JUANITA, II.

### WEEKS, HON. RENEE JONES
Lawyer, judge, association executive. **Personal:** Born Dec 28, 1948, Washington, DC. **Educ:** Ursuline Col, BA, 1970; Rutgers Law Sch, JD, 1973. **Career:** Judge (retired); State NJ, dep attorney gen, 1973-75; Prudential Ins Co Am, staff, 1975-89; Super Ct NJ, judge, 1989-2009. **Orgs:** Pres, Women's Div, Nat Bar Asn; Am Bar Asn; pres, Asn Black Women Lawyers NJ, 1975-; asst treas, Nat Asn Black Women Attys; Nat Asn Women Judges, 1986-; Alpha Kappa Alpha; Minority Interchange; vice pres, Nat Bar Asn, 1979-81; chair judicial coun, Nat Bar Asn, 1995-97; trustee, Essex Co Bar Asn; secy, Garden State Bar Asn; Nat Coun Juv & Family Ct Judges Nj Family Prac Comt & Domestic Violence Working Group NJ Supreme Ct, Minority Concerns Comt; secy, Judicial Coun, Nat Bar; Nat Bar Judicial Coun; Alpha Kappa Alpha Sorority; Rho Sorority. **Honors/Awds:** Young Lawyers Division Section Award, NJ State Bar, 1980; President's Award, Nat Bar Asn, 1984; Garden State Bar Award, 1998; Mem Distinction Award, Essex County, 2001; Rho Gamma Omega Chapter, 2002; Raymond Pace Alexander Award. **Special Achievements:** First African-American woman to preside New Jersey's general equity and probate court. First African-American woman appointed in Essex Co Court; first African-American woman assistant general counsel at Prudential Insurance. **Home Addr:** , Newark, NJ, **Home Phone:** (973)693-5891.

### WEEMS, LUTHER BENJAMIN, JR. See AKBAR, DR. NA'IM.

### WEEMS, DR. VERNON EUGENE, JR.
Association executive, lawyer, executive director. **Personal:** Born Apr 27, 1948, Waterloo, IA; son of Eugene and Anna Marie Hickey. **Educ:** Univ Iowa, BA, 1970; Univ Miami Sch Law, JD, 1974. **Career:** US Small Bus Admin, atty & advisor, 1977-81; Weems Law Off, atty, 1978-; Nation United Inc, pres, chief exec officer & chmn bd, 1982-85; Weems' Prod Enterprises, owner, chief exec officer & consult, 1987-. **Orgs:** Am Bar Asn, 1977-82, Iowa State Bar Asn, 1977-82; affil, St Johns Lodge Prince Hall, 1977-86, Fed Bar Asn, 1979-82; bd dir, Black Hawk County Iowa Br, Nat Asn Advan Colored People. **Honors/Awds:** Leadership Award OIC/Iowa, 1982; Service Appreciation Award Job Service of Iowa, 1985; Recognition of Excellence, 1986. **Special Achievements:** Publication "Tax Amnesty Blueprint for Economic Development", 1981. **Business Addr:** Owner, Chief Executive Officer, Weems Production Enterprises, 637 Independence Ave, Waterloo, IA 50703-4114, **Business Phone:** (319)233-6058.

### WEISS, ED, JR.
Automotive executive. **Career:** Allegan Ford-Mercury Sales Inc, Allegan, Mich, chief exec officer, 1984-. **Business Addr:** Chief Executive Officer, Allegan Ford-Mercury Sales Inc, 1250 Lincoln Rd Hwy 89, Allegan, MI 49010-9706, **Business Phone:** (616)673-5591.

### WEISS, DR. JOYCE LACEY
Educator. **Personal:** Born Jun 8, 1941, Chicago, IL; daughter of Lois Lacey Carter. **Educ:** Bennett Col, BA, 1963; Troy State Univ, MS, 1971; Univ Mich, Ann Arbor, MI, EdD, 1988. **Career:** Coweta County GA, elem class teacher, 1963-64; Montgomery AL, elem class teacher, 1964-69, Carver Elem Sch, elem sch prin, 1969-75; Troy State Univ, instr & supvr stud teachers, 1975-, asst prof & dept chmn, elem educ; Concordia Lutheran Col, fac; Ala State Univ, adj prof, currently; Huntingdon Col, adj prof, currently. **Orgs:** Delta Sigma Theta; Montgomery AL Chap Nat Asn Advan Colored People; Links Inc; Nat Educ Asn, 1963-; Zeta Gamma Chap Kappa Delta Pi, 1973-; Asn Teacher Educrs, 1975-; Troy Univ Chap Phi Delta Kappa, 1980-; Int Reading Asn; Ala Reading Asn; Am Educ Res Asn; Ala Educ Asn. **Home Addr:** 4947 Pk Towne Way Suite 46, Montgomery, AL 36116. **Business Addr:** Adjunct Professor, Huntingdon College, Cloverdale 121B 1500 E Fairview Ave, Montgomery, AL 36106, **Business Phone:** (334)833-4497.

### WEISS, LEVEN C.
Manager. **Personal:** children: Jourdan & Peyton. **Educ:** Univ Iowa, BBA, indust rels, 1980; Howard Univ Sch Law, JD, law, 1984; INSEAD, Fontainebleau, France, cert, 1999. **Career:** Dow Chem Co, atty, 1984-85; Fiat Chrysler Automobiles, Civic & Community Rels, sr mgr, 1985-; Chrysler Corp, personnel rep, 1985-87, shift opers personnel rep, 1987-89, personnel staff specialist, 1989-90, staff labor exec, 1990-92; Leven C Weiss Atty Law, atty, 1986-2009; Chrysler Corp & DaimlerChrysler Corp, sr mgr, 1992-2002; Chrysler LLC, dir community rels, civic & community rels sr mgr, 2002-. **Orgs:** Mich Bar Asn; Iowa's rep, chair, Big Ten Conf Adv Comn; Bd Southeastern Mich Girl Scout Coun; United Way Oakland County; Boys & Girls Clubs Southeastern Mich; Marygrove Col; SER Nat; Detroit Urban League; NAACP; Alpha Phi Alpha Fraternity Inc; Detroit Fire Dept Adv Comn, currently, Detroit Metro Conv & Visitors Bur, currently. **Business Addr:** Senior Manager, Chrysler LLC, 1000 Chrysler Dr, Auburn Hills, MI 48326-2766, **Business Phone:** (248)512-2950.

### WEISSINGER, THOMAS
Librarian. **Personal:** Born Jul 29, 1951, Silver Creek, NY; son of Tom and Hattie Bryant; married Maryann Hunter; children: Thomas Jr, Sandra & Eric. **Educ:** State Univ NY, Sch Arts & Sci, Buffalo, NY, BA, 1973; Univ Pittsburgh, Sch Arts Sci, Pittsburgh, PA, MA, 1978; Univ Pittsburgh, Sch Libr & Info Studies, Pittsburgh, PA, MLS, 1980. **Career:** Newark Pub Libr, NJ, city hall librn, 1980-82; Rutgers Univ, Kilmer Area Libr, ref librn, 1982-85; Cornell Univ Libr, Ithaca, NY, head, John Henrik Clarke Africana Librn, dir, 1985-01; Univ Ill Libr, Urbana-Champaign, Urbana, IL, African Am studies & philos bibliogr, 2001-, assoc prof african am studies, 2003-. **Orgs:** Am Libr Asn; chmn, Black Caucus Am Libr Asn Pub Comt, 1984-87; African Studies Asn; exec comt mem, Africana Librarians Coun, 1992-94; secy, Coop Africana Microfilming Proj, 1993-95; vice chmn, African Am Studies Librarians Sect, Asn Col & Res Libr, 2007-08; chmn, African Am Studies Librarians Sect, Asn Col & Res Libr, 2008-09. **Special Achievements:** Co-compiler, Black Labor Am: A Selected Annotated Bibliog, Westport, CT, Greenwood Press, 1986; Author: (2002) "Black Studies scholarly communication: A citation analysis of periodical literature. Collection Management 27, nos. 3/4: 45-56"; (2007) "Black Power Movement book publishing: Trends & issues. Collection Management 31, no. 4: 4: 5-18"; (2010) "The core journal concept in Black Studies. Journal of Academic Librarianship 36, no. 2: 119-24. **Home Addr:** 1921 David Dr, Champaign, IL 61821. **Business Addr:** African American Studies & Philosophy Bibliographer, University of Illinois, 1408 W Gregory Dr 246 Libr, Urbana, IL 61801, **Business Phone:** (217)333-3006.

### WELBORN, EDWARD THOMAS, JR.
Executive director. **Personal:** Born Dec 14, 1950, Philadelphia, PA; son of Edward Sr and Evelyn Welburn. **Educ:** Howard Univ, BFA, fine arts, 1972. **Career:** Gen Motors Corp, design studio intern, 1970, Buick div employee, 1972; GM Oldsmobile div employee, 1975; Oldsmobile Exterior II Studio, chief designer, 1989; GM Corp Brand Character Ctr, dir, 1998, exec dir, 2002-03, chief designer, 2003. **Orgs:** Bd dir, LeMay Mus; bd gov, Cranbrook Inst Sci; bd trustee, Col Creative Studies Detroit. **Special Achievements:** First African American to rise to what is considered one of the most prestigious jobs in the automotive industry. **Business Addr:** Executive Director, Chief Designer, General Motors Corp, 300 Renaissance Ctr, Detroit, MI 48265-3000, **Business Phone:** (313)556-5000.

### WELBURN, CRAIG B., JR.
Executive, chief executive officer. **Personal:** son of Craig T and Diane; married Eugenia; children: 3. **Educ:** James Madison Univ, BA, social sci, 1996. **Career:** McDonald's African Am Consumer Mkt Advert Comt, chmn; McDonald's Corp, Philadelphia, PA, restaurant owner, head, chmn & chief exec officer, 1998-2001, 2004-, Baltimore Wash Region, Owner & Operator, Welburn Mgt, vpres Opers; Owner-Operator Nat Advert Fund. **Orgs:** Bd dir, Ronald McDonald House; bd dir, Del Valley Friends Sch; Alpha Phi Alpha Fraternity Inc; pres, Nat Black McDonald's Operators Asn. **Home Addr:** 12805 Reserve Lane, Manassas, VA 20110-8853. **Business Addr:** Vice-President of Operations, Welburn Management, 2334 Georgia Ave, Washington, DC 20001, **Business Phone:** (202)387-2111.

### WELBURN, EDWARD THOMAS, JR.
Automotive executive. **Personal:** Born Dec 14, 1950, West Chester, PA; son of Edward Sr and Evelyn Thornton; married Rhonda Doby; children: Adrienne & Brian. **Educ:** Howard Univ, BA, sculpture & prod design, 1972. **Career:** Gen Motors Corp, design staff, assoc designer, 1972, creative designer, 1972-75, sr creative designer, 1976-81, asst chief designer, 1981-89, chief designer, 1989, exec opers comt, Advan Design Warren, Mich, dir, 1998, Design N Am, exec dir, 2002-03, chief designer, vpres, 2003-16; Buick Exterior Studio, 1973; Oldsmobile Exterior studio, chief designer, 1989; Chevrolet, vehicle chief designer, currently. **Orgs:** Cabinet, 1983-; Founders Soc Detroit Inst Art; bd gov, Cranbrook Inst Sci; bd dir, LeMay Mus; GM Found; bd trustees, Col Creative Studies Detroit, Mich. **Honors/Awds:** Alumni of the Year, Howard Univ Stud Asn, 2004; Man of Excellence Award, Mich Chronicle; Distinguished Service Citation, Automotive Hall of Fame; Nicola Bulgari Award; Trumpet Awards, 2013. **Special Achievements:** First African American to rise to what is considered one of the most prestigious jobs in the automotive industry; First African American to lead a global automotive Design organization. **Home Addr:** 1570 Balmoral Dr, Detroit, MI 48203-1445, **Home Phone:** (215)362-6175. **Business Addr:** Vice President, General Motors Corp, PO Box 33170, Detroit, MI 48232-5170, **Business Phone:** (817)608-2346.

### WELBURN, RONALD GARFIELD (RON WELBURN)
Writer, educator. **Personal:** Born Apr 30, 1944, Berwyn, PA; son of Howard Watson and Jessie W; married Cheryl T Donahue; children: Loren Beatty, Justin Beatty & Elliott. **Educ:** Lincoln Univ, PA, BA, psychol & eng, 1968; Univ Ariz, MA, creative writing, 1970; NY Univ, PhD, Am studies, 1983. **Career:** Syracuse Univ, Syracuse, NY, asst prof Afro-Am studies, 1970-75; Rutgers Univ, Nb, NJ, Inst Jazz Studies, asst prof Eng, 1983; Western Conn State Univ, Danbury, CT, asst prof eng; Univ Mass, Amherst, Dept Eng, prof, assoc prof, dir, 1992-; Author: Hartfords Ann Plato and the Native Borders of Identity; Roanoke and Wampum: Topics in Native American Heritage and Literatures; Peripheries: Selected Poems, 1966-68, Greenfield Review Press, 1972; Council Decisions: Poems, American Native Press Archives, 1991; A Most Secret Identity: Native American Assimilation & Identity Resistance in African America; Heartland: Selected Poems, Lotus Press, 1981; Brownup and other poems. **Orgs:** Bd mem, Eagle Wing Press, 1989-; co-founding mem, Ctr Interdisciplinary Study Am; chair, Native Am Studies Comt, 1994-98; Asn Study Am Indian Literatures. **Home Addr:** 52 Roosevelt St, Hadley, MA 01035-0420, **Home Phone:** (413)549-4518. **Business Addr:** Professor of English, University of Massachusetts Amherst, 460 Bartlett Hall, Amherst, MA 01003-0515, **Business Phone:** (413)545-3694.

### WELCH, D. MICHELLE FLOWERS
Business owner. **Personal:** Born Greensboro, NC; daughter of Thomas and Catherine; married Anthony M. **Educ:** Winston Salem State Univ, BS, Eng, 1976; Northwestern Univ, MS, advert, 1982. **Career:** Integon Ins Co, commun specialist, 1976-78; Chicago Urban League, internal & field commun specialist, commun spec & media rel mgr, 1978, dir pub rel, 1983; Golin & Harris Commun, acct supvr, pub rel, 1984; Burrell Pub Rel, asst vpres, 1986, vpres, 1987, sr vpres, 1989; Flowers Commun Group Inc, chmn & chief exec officer, 1991-. **Orgs:** Mus SCI & Indust, former adv bd chmn, adv comt, Black Creativity Adv com; Alpha Kappa Alpha Sorority; Publicity Club Chicago; Pub Rels soc ame; Black Pub Rels soc; Nat Black Pub Rels Socs; Chicago Urban League. **Honors/Awds:** More than 75 industry awards, including IABC Award, Cystic Fibrosis Found; Pub Rels Soc Am, Three Silver Anvils; Gold & Four Silver Trumpets from the Publicity Club Chicago; Founders Award, Nat Black Pub Rels, 2003; Society Platinum Trumpet Award, Publicity Club Chicago, 2006; 10 Spectra Awards, International Association of Business Communicators; Two CIPRA Awards, Inside PR magazine; Woman of the Year Award, National Council of Negro Women; Beautiful People Award, Chicago Urban League; Top 100 Black Business and Professional Women; Ten Outstanding Young Citizens; PRNews Hall of Fame; Hall of Fame, Northwestern Univ; PCC Lifetime Achievement Award. **Home Addr:** 5201 S Cornell Suite 22B, Chicago, IL 60615, **Home Phone:** (773)643-1914. **Business Addr:** Founder, Chairman, Flowers Communications

Group, 303E Wacker Dr Suite 1000, Chicago, IL 60601, **Business Phone:** (312)228-8800.

### WELCH, HARVEY

Basketball player, school administrator. **Personal:** Born Jun 5, 1932, Centralia, IL; married Patricia Kay; children: Harvey, Gordon, Karen & Brian. **Educ:** Southern Ill Univ, Carbondale, BS, 1955, MS, educ, 1958. **Career:** Southern Ill Univ, actg vpres stud affairs, dean & vice chancellor stud affairs, 1985-99, vice chancellor emer, 1999-. **Orgs:** Joint Serv Comt, 1973; Carbondale Planning Comn, 1976-78; Ill Guid& Personel Asn; Adv Bd Ill State Scholar Comt; Mid-W Equal Educ Opportunity; Southern Ill Univ, Am Asn Coun & Develop Asn; Nat Asn Advan Colored People; Nat Asn Stud Personal Admin; Nat Asn Stud Financial Aid Admin; Nat Asn Women Deans; Rotary Int; Southern Ill Regional Social Serv; chair, Epiphany Lutheran Church All Saints. **Home Addr:** 1003 W Sycamore St, PO Box 209, Carbondale, IL 62901-5100, **Home Phone:** (618)529-1661. **Business Addr:** Vice Chancellor Emeritus, Southern Illinois University, 1900 N Ill Ave, Carbondale, IL 62901-6899, **Business Phone:** (618)453-2121.

### WELCH, JESSE ROY

Executive director, educator. **Personal:** Born May 29, 1949, Jonesville, LA; married Vickie Ragsdale; children: Symia. **Educ:** Wash State Univ, BA, 1971, ED, 1977. **Career:** Big Bro-Big Sister Prog Benicia, dir, head counr, 1967-68; Pullman YMCA, prog adv, 1968-70; Wash State Univ, fin aid counr, 1970-71, assoc dir admis, transfer articulation specialist; Evergreen State Col, enrollment mgr, dir & dean enrollment serv; Bill & Melinda Gates Found, consult; Col Success Found, Col & Alumni Serv, dir col prog, 2005. **Orgs:** Partic Johnson Found Wingspread Conf Minority Groups Col Stud-Personnel Prog, 1971; Am Asn Col Registrs & Admis Officers, 1971-, WA State Univ Affirmative Action Coun, 1972-74; comt min affairs, WA Coun HS Col Rel, 1973-; consult, Spokane Nursing Sch Minority Affairs Comt Spokane, 1973-74; WICHE Fac Devel Meet Minority Group Needs, 1973-74; adv bd, 1974-, co-chmn, 1974-76, YMCA Pullman WA Wash Coun High Sch Col Rels; Wash State Univ Col Educ; bd mem, Northwest Leadership Found. **Special Achievements:** Numerous publications & papers Published. **Home Addr:** 1702 Sargent, Klamath Falls, OR 97601, **Home Phone:** (503)884-9851. **Business Addr:** Director of College Programs, The College Success Foundation, 1605 NW Sammamish Rd Suite 200, Issaquah, WA 98027-5388, **Business Phone:** (425)416-2024.

### WELCH, LOLITA

Health services administrator, administrator. **Personal:** Born Detroit, MI. **Educ:** Univ Detroit, BBA, 1989. **Career:** State MI, minority bus specialist, 1990-95, acct mgr, 1995-97; Detroit Med Ctr, mgr, 1997; MGM Grand Detroit Casino, dir purchasing, currently; MGM Grand Hotel & Casino, dir purch. **Orgs:** Coun Supplier Diversity Prof, Officer, 2001. **Home Addr:** , MI. **Business Addr:** Director Purchasing, MGM Grand Detroit Casino & Deb, 1300 John C Lodge, Detroit, MI 48226, **Business Phone:** (313)394-4423.

### WELCH, DR. OLGA MICHELE

Educator, school administrator, dean (education). **Personal:** Born Dec 30, 1948, Salisbury, NC; daughter of S E Barnes; married George E; children: Taja Michele & Stephani Amber. **Educ:** Howard Univ, BA, salutatorian, hist, eng, educ 1971; Univ Tenn, MS, deaf educ, 1972, EdD, educ admin & super, 1977. **Career:** Model Sec Sch Deaf, instr, 1972-73, Tenn Sch Deaf, instr, 1973-75, sup vprin, 1977-78; Univ Tenn, Dept Spec Educ & Rehab, asst prof, 1977-82, assoc prof & dir, 1982-93, dir deaf educ prog, Rehab & Deafness Unit, prof; Barbara Jackson Scholars Prog, mentor, 2005-; Duquesne Univ, Sch Educ, prof & dean, currently. **Orgs:** Interdenomi nat Concert Choir, 1975-; chmn, Girl Scout neighborhood, 1977-; Coun Except C; Alexander Graham Bell Asn; Conv Am Instr Deaf; Nat Educ Asn; Asn Supr & Curric Develop; vpres, Knoxville Chap Nat Black Women's Hook-Up, 1980-81; Proj HELP tutorial prog disadvantaged students, 1983; Am Educ Res Asn; co-dir, Proj Excel. reform bd, Pittsburgh Pub Schs High Sch; vice chair bd dir, YWCA; mem Hill House Asn Adv Bd; Am Asn Cols Teacher Educ; Orgn Instnl Affil, Am Educ Res Asn; Coun Acad Deans from Res Educ Insts; Univ Coun Educ Admin; chair, Nat Adv Group Nat Tech Inst Deaf, 1998-2001; founding bd mem, Entrepreneuring Youth, 2009-; elected secy, Pittsburgh Promise, 2008-. **Honors/Awds:** Phi Beta Kappa; Phi Delta Kappa; Phi Kappa Phi; Phi Alpha Theta; Appointed National Educ Adv Bd, 1983; E C Merrill Distinguished Research Award, 1990, 1992; Dept Award, "Most Creative Dissertation Topic", Chancellor's Award, Univ Tenn, 1998; Professor of the Year Award, Phi Delta Kappa-2002; Excellence in Educational Administration Award, Nat Asn Black Social Workers-2004; Women Leadership in Education Award, YWCA, 2009; Recipient of 50 Women of Excellence Award, The New Pittsburgh Courier, 2009. **Special Achievements:** Olga Welch is the first black woman to serve as a dean of Duquesne University's School of Education. **Business Addr:** Professor, Dean School of Education, Duquesne University, 600 Forbes Ave, Pittsburgh, PA 15282, **Business Phone:** (412)396-6000.

### WELDON, RAMON N.

Law enforcement officer. **Personal:** Born Jul 26, 1932, Keokuk, IA; son of Clarence and Virginia; married Betty Jean Watkins; children: Ramon N Jr. **Educ:** Keokuk Sr High Sch, dipl, 1951. **Career:** Law enforcement officer (retired); Keokuk Police Dept, patrolman, 1962-74, detective, 1974-80; capt, 1980-82; chief police, 1982-87. **Orgs:** Lee County Juv Restitution Bd, 1982; Keokuk Humane Soc, 1982; trustee, Keokuk Libr Bd 2nd six yr term; active mem, Iowa Chief's Assoc Nat Chief's Asn Int Chief's Asn, 1982-; chmn, United Way Bd; Hoerner Y Ctr Bd; chmn, Tri-State Coalition Against Family Violence; Lee County Compensation Bd, chmn. **Home Addr:** 2510 Decatur St, Keokuk, IA 52632-2411, **Home Phone:** (319)524-2238.

### WELLS, BILLY GENE

Mayor, executive, business owner. **Personal:** Born Bluff City, TN; son of Harley Boyd and Grace Isbella Black; married Irene Elizabeth Coleman; children: Cynthia Anita & Rebecca Jean. **Career:** Tenn Eastman Co, printer, 1964-; B&I Offset Printing, owner, 1971-; City Bluff City, mayor, 1985-91. **Orgs:** Bd mem, Sr Citizens, United Way & Teen World, Ill, 1985-; Martin Luther King Jr State Holiday Community, 1986-. **Honors/Awds:** First black mayor elected in Tennessee; First mayor elected 3 times in a row in Bluff City. **Home Addr:** 198 Holston Dr, Bluff City, TN 37618, **Home Phone:** (423)538-7414. **Business Addr:** Owner, B&I Offset Printing, 429 B & I Pvt Dr, Bluff City, TN 37618, **Business Phone:** (423)538-5877.

### WELLS, BONZI (GAWEN DEANGELO WELLS)

Basketball player. **Personal:** Born Sep 28, 1976, Muncie, IN; son of Gawen and Christine Scaife Coleman; children: Duane, Gawen & Christian. **Educ:** Ball State Univ, attended 1998. **Career:** Basketball player (retired); Detroit Pistons, 1998; Portland Trail Blazers, small forward, 1998-2001, shooting guard, 2001-03; Memphis Grizzlies, shooting guard, 2003-05; Sacramento Kings, shooting guard, 2005-06; Houston Rockets, small forward, 2006-07, shooting guard, 2007-08; New Orleans Hornets, shooting guard, 2008; Chinese Basketball Asn, Shanxi Zhongyu, China, 2008-09; Capitanes de Arecibo, Pr, 2009-10. **Honors/Awds:** Freshman Player of the Year, 1994-95; MAC Player of the Year, 1996, 1998; All-Am Hons.

### WELLS, DR. ELMER EUGENE

School administrator. **Personal:** Born Oct 6, 1939, Mt. Pleasant, IA; married Georgia Lee Gehringer; children: Monte, Debra, Christian & Kori. **Educ:** Univ Alaska, MA, 1970; Univ NMex, PhD, 1974. **Career:** Low Mt Boarding Sch Bur Indian Affairs Ariz, 1962-64; Mobil Oil Co Santa Fe Springs CA, explor worker, 1964-65; Off Econ Opportunity, teen post dir, 1965-66; Bur Indian Affairs Pt Barrow AK, teacher, asst prin, prin, 1966-71; Albuquerque Pub Sch, teacher, 1973-74; Univ Southern Colo, Teacher Corps Cycle 9 & 11 Pueblo, educ spec, 1974-78; Int Stud Serv Univ Southern Colo, dir, 1978; CSU-Pueblo, dir. **Orgs:** Pres & founder, Albuquerque Ethnic Communities Inc, 1973-74; pres & founder, CO Ethnic Communities Inc, 1975-80; exec bd, Pueblo Chap Nat Asn Advan Colored People, 1979-80. **Honors/Awds:** Speaker Annual Freedom Fund Banquet Colo Springs Chap, Nat Asn Advan Colored People, 1980. **Special Achievements:** Publications: "The Mythical Negative Black Self Concept" R & E Res Asn, 1978; "Destroying a Racial Myth "Social Studies Vol69 No 5, 1978; TV Debate Grand Wizard KKK Colo Springs Involvement Prog Channel 11, 1979; "Peace talks, Blacks and Jews. **Home Addr:** 32240 Kalorama Pl, PO Box 11473, Pueblo, CO 81006, **Home Phone:** (719)948-4254. **Business Addr:** Director, CSU-Pueblo, 2200 Bonforte Blvd, Pueblo, CO 81001-4901, **Business Phone:** (719)549-2462.

### WELLS, GAWEN DEANGELO. See WELLS, BONZI.

### WELLS, JAMES A.

Executive. **Personal:** Born Aug 13, 1933, Atlanta, GA; married Mary E; children: James A Jr & John F. **Educ:** BSEE, 1965; MSAT, 1976. **Career:** Process Equip Design IBM-Endicott, eng, 1965-67; Aerospace & Avionic Comput Syst Final Test IBM-Owego, systs test mgr, 1967-74; IBM-Owego, proj engr, 1974. **Orgs:** Assoc mem, Inst Elec Electronics Engrs Asn; vpres, Jaycees; den leader, WEBELOS; mem Amvets; Aircraft Owners & Pilots Asn. **Home Addr:** 1648 Rita Rd, Vestal, NY 13850, **Home Phone:** (607)748-8777.

### WELLS, FR. PATRICK ROLAND

Clergy, educator, administrator. **Personal:** Born Apr 1, 1931, Liberty, TX; son of Luther T Sr and Stella Wickliff. **Educ:** Tex Southern Univ, BS, pharm, 1957; Univ NE Lincoln, MS, pharamacol, 1959, PhD, pharmaceut sci, 1961; Sacred Heart Sch Theol, MDiv, 1993. **Career:** Educator, clergy (retired); Fordham Univ, asst prof pharamacol, 1961-63; Univ NE, asst prof pharamacol, 1963-65, assoc prof & dept chmn, 1965-70; Col Pharm & Health Sci, Tex Southern Univ, dean & prof, 1970-90, dean emer; Radio Show "Lifeline", KTSU-FM, host, 1969-70; St Francis Assisi Cath Church, pastor, 1993; Diocese Galveston Houston, ordained roman cath priest, 1993; Episcopal Vicar, Cent Vicariate, 2000-06. **Orgs:** TX Pharmaceut Asn, Am Pharmaceut Asn, Nat Pharmaceut Asn, Sigma Xi Sci Hon, Rho Chi Pharm Hon; St Philip Neri Parish; St Philip Neri Coun 222 Knights Peter Claver; lay oblate Order St Benedict; Asn Minority Health Prof Schs; Am Asn Cols Pharm; Grand regent Kappa Psi Pharmaceut, 1983-87; ed, Journ Nat Pharmaceut, Asn, 1987-90; Nat Black Cath Clergy Caucus; bd dir, Sacred Heart Sch Theol African-Am Bishops comt; bd trustee, Nat Black Cath Cong. **Honors/Awds:** Outstanding Educr, Tex Pharm Asn, 1990; Dean Emer, Tex Southern Univ, 1990; Dehon Distinguished Ministry Award, 1999; prelate hon, "Reverend Monsignor", granted Pope John Paul II, 2000. **Special Achievements:** Books: "The Effects of Hormones and X-Irradiation On the Survival Of Isografted Fetal Mouse Hearts", 1961. **Home Addr:** 5330 Fairgreen Lane, Houston, TX 77048-2718, **Home Phone:** (713)734-2304.

### WELLS, PAYTON R.

President (organization), business owner. **Personal:** Born Jun 24, 1933, Indianapolis, IN. **Educ:** Butler Univ, Indianapolis Ind, attended 1957. **Career:** Payton Wells Ford Inc, pres; GM & Ford Motor Co Automotive Sch; Payton Wells Chrysler, Dodge Jeep Eagle, pres; Payton Wells Automotive Group, pres, 2005-; Payton Wells Chevrolet, owner. **Orgs:** Bd mem, Jr Achievement; Nat Asn Advan Colored People; Urban League; vpres, Flanner House Inc; bd mem, Indianapolis Pvt Indust Coun Inc; bd mem, Anderson Symphony Orchestra. **Honors/Awds:** Junior Achievement of Central Indiana Business Hall of Fame, 2002. **Home Addr:** 6933 W 79th St, Indianapolis, IN 46278. **Business Addr:** President, Payton Wells Automotive Group, 1510 N Meridian St, Indianapolis, IN 46202, **Business Phone:** (317)638-4838.

### WELLS, ROBERT BENJAMIN, JR.

Administrator. **Personal:** Born May 21, 1947, Cleveland, OH; married Phillis Sharlette McCray; children: Michelle Renne. **Educ:** Miami Dade Comn Col, AA, 1974; Fla A&M Univ, BS, 1976; NC Cent Univ, Law Stud, 1985. **Career:** Gen Tel Southeast, serv cost admin, 1978-80, gen acct suprv, 1980-81, gentax suprv, 1981-. **Orgs:** Consult, Youth Motivation Task Force, 1979-82; pres, Employees Club, 1980-81; dept rep, United Way Campaign, 1982-84; chmn, Econ Develop Comn, NC Assoc Black Lawyers Land Loss Prev Proj; vpres mkt, Nat Assoc Accts; chmn, Nat Alliance Bus Youth Motivation Task Force; pres, Durham Area Chap, Nat Assoc Accts, 1986-88; GTE Loaned Exec, United Way Campaign, 1986; chmn, Greater Durham United Way Loaned Exec Alumni Comn, 1987. **Honors/Awds:** Distinguished Service Award, Miles Col Birmingham, Ala, 1982; Distinguished Service, Plaque Edward Waters Col, Jacksonville, Fla, 1984; Distinguished Service, Plaque Fla A & M Univ, Tallahassee, 1986. **Home Addr:** 2617 Glenbrook Dr, Durham, NC 27704-3317. **Business Addr:** General Tax Supervisor, General Telephone of the Southeast, 3632 Roxboro Rd, Durham, NC 27702.

### WELLS, RODERICK ARTHUR

Municipal government official, president (organization). **Personal:** Born Feb 10, 1952, New Orleans, LA; son of Thomas L Jr and Maggie L; married Betty Lewis; children: Rashaad Aneisha & Roderick Lewis. **Educ:** Southern Univ BR, BS, zool, 1975, MEd, counr educ, 1981. **Career:** Kaiser Aluminum, environ tech, 1980-81, production foreman, 1982-83; CityBR, Human Servs Division, prog planner, 1983-84; E Baton Rouge Mosquito Abatement, asst dir, 1984-, biologist, 1984-86, pres, currently; La Mosquito Control Asn, pres, 2006. **Orgs:** Naval Reserve Asn, 1982-; SU Fed Comm Officers, 1985-; LA Pesticide Applicators, 1988-; Am Mosquito Control Asn, 1988-; Naval Memorial Asn, 1989-; BR High Sch Football Offs, 1990-; bd dir, LA Mosquito Control Asn, 1991-, pres, 1994; chair, Recruiting Assist Coun, 1994-. **Home Addr:** 10717 Foster Rd, Baton Rouge, LA 70811, **Home Phone:** (225)775-1232. **Business Addr:** Assistant Director, President, East Baton Rouge Mosquito Abatement, 2829 Lt Gen Ben Davis Jr Ave, Baton Rouge, LA 70807, **Business Phone:** (225)356-3297.

### WELLS, THEODORE V., JR.

Lawyer. **Personal:** Born Apr 28, 1950, Washington, DC; married Nina Mitchell. **Educ:** Col Holy Cross, BA, 1972; Harvard Bus Sch, MBA, 1976; Harvard Law Sch, JD, 1976. **Career:** Lectr, Securities Regulation Inst; Lowenstein Sandler LLP, partner, 1982; Paul, Weiss, Rifkind, Wharton & Garrison LLP, atty & litigation partner, currently. **Orgs:** Co-chair, White-Collar Criminal Sect, Nat Asn Criminal Defense Lawyers; gen coun, NJ Nat Asn Advan Colored People; co-chairperson, United Negro Col Fund; gen coun, NJ Dem Party; fel Am Col Trial Lawyers, 1993; fac mem, Practising Law Inst Trial Advocacy Prog; teaching team mem, Harvard Law Sch Trial Advocacy Workshop; nat treas, Dem Bill Bradley's Presidential Campaign; bd dir, CIT Corp; trustee, NJ Performing Arts Ctr; trustee, Holy Cross Col, currently; trustee, Nat Asn Advan Colored People Legal Defense Fund bd dir, currently. **Honors/Awds:** Lawyer of the Year, Nat Law J, 2006. **Special Achievements:** One of America's best white-collar defense attorneys, Nat Law Journal. He has also has been recognized as one of the outstanding jury trial lawyers in the United States by numerous publications including Chambers USA 2006 which noted he is recognized by many as the greatest trial lawyer of our generation. **Home Addr:** 24 Canoe Brook Dr, Livingston, NJ 07039-6135. **Business Addr:** Attorney, Litigation Partner, Paul, Weiss, Rifkind, Wharton & Garrison LLP, 1285 Avenue of the Americas, New York, NY 10019-6064, **Business Phone:** (212)373-3089.

### WELLS, TINA

Entrepreneur, chief executive officer, consultant. **Educ:** Hood Col, BA commun arts, 2002; Univ Pa, Wharton Sch Bus, mkt mgt, 2010, post-baccalaureate prog; Mass Inst Technol, orgn leadership, 2012. **Career:** New Girl Times, writer, 1996; Buzz Mkt Group, founder & chief exec officer, 1996-; Wharton Sch, Leadership Bus World, acad dir, 2014-. **Orgs:** Adv bd, Christopher Reeve Found; Viral & Buzz Mkt Asn; adv bd, inducted the Friends Orphans Proj, FRIENDS; Kids for Kids Adv Bd; bd dir, Philadelphia Orchestra, 2008-; bd mem, Franklin Inst, 2010-; global entrepreneurs coun, Un Found, 2013-. **Honors/Awds:** Black Voices Black Female Entrepreneurs Award, AOL; Essence 40 Under 40 Award; Billboard's 30 Under 30 Award; 30 Under 30, Inc Mag; Black Voices Black Women Leaders in Business top ten list, AOL; Young Entrepreneur of the Year Award, Philadelphia Chamber Com, 2009. **Special Achievements:** The Voices Black Women Business Leaders Top Ten List; Author of upcoming tween series "Mackenzie Blue". **Business Addr:** Chief Executive Officer, Buzz Mkt Group, 1018 Laurel Oak Rd Suite 1, Voorhees, NJ 08043, **Business Phone:** (856)346-3456.

### WELLS, VERNON MICHAEL, III

Baseball player. **Personal:** Born Dec 8, 1978, Shreveport, LA; son of Vernon Jr; married Charlene Valenti; children: 2. **Career:** Toronto Blue Jays, 1999-2000; ESPN, analyst, 2006; Los Angeles Angels Anaheim, 2011-12; New York Yankees, 2013-. TV Series: "Sunday Night Baseball", 1990. "MLB All-Star Game", 2003, 2006. **Orgs:** Hon comnr, Toronto Rookie League, 2002. **Business Addr:** Professional Baseball Player, New York Yankees, Yankee Stadium 161st St & River Ave, Bronx, NY 10452, **Business Phone:** (718)293-4300.

### WELLS-DAVIS, DR. MARGIE ELAINE

Consultant, teacher, manager. **Personal:** Born Apr 27, 1944, Marshalltown, IA; daughter of Gladstone and Ida; married Allan C; children: Allana E. **Educ:** Simpson Col, AB, 1966; Syracuse Univ, MA, 1968; Univ Cincinnati, PhD, 1979. **Career:** St Louis Syracuse, NY, teacher, 1966-68; Univ Cincinnati, asst dean students, 1968-70; Syracuse Univ, actg dir, 1971; Cent Comn Health Bd, coordr consult educ, 1972; US Pub Health Serv DHEW, sociologist, 1973; Eharlem Ext Serv Jewish Hosp, consult, 1973-76; Cincinnati Health Dept, dir staff & org develop, 1974-77; Procter & Gamble, affirmative action coordr, 1977-, human resources mgr, consult, currently. **Orgs:** Am Soc Training & Develop, 1977-80; Original Develop Network, 1978-80; bd mem, New Life Girls, 1977-80; treasr & bd mem, Cincinnati Human Rels Comn, 1978-80; bd mem, Cincinnati Womens City Club, 1979-80; bd mem, Gen Protestant Orphan Home; Grassroots Leadership Acad. **Honors/Awds:** Hon Soc Epsilon Sigma, Gold Key Hon Soc, 1966; Resolution for Outstanding Service, City Cincinnati Bd Health, 1976; Alumni Achievement Award, Simpson Col, 1990. **Home Addr:** 3900 Rose Hill Ave Apt 401b, 565 Blair, Cincinnati, OH 45229-1481, **Home Phone:** (513)221-6869.

**WELLS-MERRICK, LORRAINE ROBERTA**
Educator. **Personal:** Born Jan 5, 1938, Syracuse, NY; daughter of Robert Wells and Dorothy Copes Wells; married James A Merrick Jr. **Educ:** Cheyney State Univ, Cheyney, PA, BS, 1959; Syracuse Univ, Syracuse, NY, MS, 1973, doctoral cand, currently. **Career:** City Sch Dist, Syracuse, New York, teacher, 1959-69, prin/adminr, 1970-79, dep supt, 1979-88; Ny Educ Dept, Albany, New York, asst comnr, 1988-; Univ State New York, asst comnr, gen & occup educ. **Orgs:** Syracuse chap, Links Inc, 1976-; Nat Coun Negro Women, 1960-; Syracuse Alumnae, Delta Sigma Theta Sorority Inc, 1973-; Nat Grand Basileus, Lambda Kappa MuSorority, 1985-90. **Home Addr:** 404 Kimber Rd, Syracuse, NY 13224, **Home Phone:** (315)446-6943. **Business Addr:** Assistant Commissioner, New York State Education Department, Washington Ave 979 EBA, Albany, NY 12234, **Business Phone:** (518)473-7155.

**WELMON, DR. VERNIS M.**
School administrator, educator. **Personal:** Born Mar 13, 1951, Philadelphia, PA; son of Vernis B and Sara H; married Pamela Blake; children: Ain. **Educ:** Temple Univ, BA, 1980; Columbia Univ, MA, 1982; Pa State Univ. **Career:** Univ Mass, grad asst, 1973-74; Bd Educ Springfield, MA, classroom instr, 1974-82; Pa State Schuylkill Campus, prog asst, 1981-84; Tertiary Educ Linkage Proj, consult; Penn State Univ Hazleton Campus, Instr, 1981-, dir continuing educ, 1984-, Dept African Am Studies, instr, currently; Penn State Univ, Instr, prof bus dept 2012-. **Orgs:** Advisor, Phi Chi Theta, 1991-; Acad Polit Sci; Am Acad Polit & Social Sci; Nat Coun Black Studies; Pa Conf Higher Educ; Black Resources CTR; Trans Africa; numerous other civic groups; Phi Beta Kappa, 1980; advisor, Minority MBA Asn. **Home Addr:** 929 Lilian Cir, State College, PA 16801, **Home Phone:** (814)238-2815. **Business Addr:** Assistant Dean for Diversity Enhancement, Clinical Professor of International Business, Pennsylvania State University, 366 Business Bldg, University Park, PA 16802, **Business Phone:** (814)863-1228.

**WELSH, DR. KARIAMU**
Educator, choreographer. **Personal:** Born Sep 22, 1949, Thomasville, NC; daughter of Harvey Farabee and Ruth Hoover; married Molefi K; children: Daahoud & Khumalo. **Educ:** State Univ NY, Buffalo, BA, 1972, MA, 1975; NY Univ, doctorate, arts, 1992. **Career:** Black Dance Workshop, choreographer, 1970-77; Ctr Positive Thought Buffalo, NY, artistic dir, 1971-81; Nat Endowment Arts Choreography, fel, 1973; Kariamu & Co, choreographer, 1977-84, artistic dir; Nat Dance Co Zimbabwe Harare, artistic dir, 1981-83; Univ Zimbabwe, Fulbright Scholars, fel, 1982-83, Fulbright scholar, 1990-92; Minority Choreographers, fel, NY State Coun Arts, 1984; co-ed, African Cult, Rhythms Unity, 1985; Temple Univ, prof & choreographer, 1987, prof dance, 2001-; Commonwealth Pa Cou Arts, dance hist fel, 1988; ed, African Aesthet: Keeper Traditions, Greenwood Press, 1989; ed, Jour African Dance, 1989; Pew & Simon Guggenheim, fel, 1997; Auth: zimbabwe Dance: Rhythmic Forces, Ancestral Voices; An Aesthet Anal & Umfundalai: An African Dance Tech; African Cult: Rhythms Unity, ed, 1985; African Aesthet: Keeper Traditions, 1994; African Dance: An Artistic, Hist & Philos Inquiry, 1996. **Orgs:** Dir, Mus African Am Art & Antiq, 1978-; ed bd, Jour Black Studies, 1982-; panel mem, Buffalo Arts Coun, 1983-85; panel mem, NYS Coun Arts Spec Arts Serv, 1984-85; consult, Nat Dance Co Zimbabwe, 1984-; dir, Inst African Dance Res & Performance, Temple Univ, 1985-; dance panel, Commonwealth Pa Coun Art, 1991-93; fel Pew, 1996. **Home Addr:** 8630 Trumbauer Dr, Philadelphia, PA 19038, **Home Phone:** (215)233-0692. **Business Addr:** Professor of Dance Studies, Temple University, 1700 Broad St 305A, Philadelphia, PA 19122, **Business Phone:** (215)204-6286.

**WELSING, DR. FRANCES CRESS**
Psychiatrist. **Personal:** Born Mar 18, 1935, Chicago, IL; daughter of Henry N and Ida Mae. **Educ:** Antioch Col, BS, 1957; Howard Univ, Sch Med, MD, 1962. **Career:** Cook Co Hosp, intern, 1962-63; St Elizabeth Hosp, res gen psychiat, 1963-66; C's Hosp, fel, child psychiat, 1966-68; Howard Univ, Col Med, asst prof pediat, 1968-75; Hillcrest C's Ctr, clin dir, 1975-76; pvt pract, currently. **Orgs:** Nat Med Asn; AMA; Am Psychiat Asn. **Honors/Awds:** Black Book Award, 2005. **Special Achievements:** Author: "The Cress Theory of Color Confrontation & Racism", "The Isis Papers", "The Keys to the Colors", 1991; Films: 500 Years Later, 2005, Motherland, 2010, Hidden Colors: The Untold History Of People Of Aboriginal, Moor and African Descent, 2011, Ink Spot on Canvas, 2011. **Home Addr:** 2526 Pennsylvania Ave SE, Washington, DC 20020, **Home Phone:** (202)581-6328. **Business Addr:** Physician, 7603 Georgia Ave NW Suite 402, Washington, DC 20012-1617, **Business Phone:** (202)829-0430.

**WESCOTT, ABRAHAM L., JR.**
Government official, administrator. **Educ:** Va State Univ, BS, pub admin, 1987; Akron Univ, MA, geog, 1989. **Career:** City Akron, Dept Planning & Urban Develop Land Mkt, Develop Serv Div, relocation officer, adminr, 1989-, develop mgr, 2010-. **Orgs:** Pre Law Socs; Pub Admin Club; Kappa Alpha Psi Fraternity. **Business Addr:** Development Manager, Administrator, City of Akron, 161 S High St Suite 201, Akron, OH 44308, **Business Phone:** (330)375-2696.

**WESLEY, BARBARA ANN**
School administrator, association executive. **Personal:** Born Jun 7, 1930, Wichita, KS; children: Ronald Frank & John Edgar. **Educ:** Univ Puget Sound, BA, 1963; Univ Puget Sound Tacoma, MEd, 1972; Univ Mass, EdD, 1977. **Career:** Clover Pk Sch Dist, elem teacher, 1960-64; Tacoma Pub Sch, classroom teacher, 1964-74; Westfield St Col, proj dir, 1974-75; Alternative Prog Tacoma Pub Sch, educ specialist, 1975-78; Ariz State Univ, Delta Kappa Gamma fel, 1978; Foss High Sch Tacoma Pub Sch, high sch admin, 1978-79; Wilson High Sch, Tacoma Pub Sch, admin, 1979-82; Magnet Prog, dist admin, 1982-. **Orgs:** Inst Elem Teachers Denver Univ, 1969; Adult Educ Inst Univ WI; NY State Univ Albany, 1972-73; NSF, 1972-73; bd trustee, Tacoma Comm Col, 1977-82; Delta Sigma Theta; bd dir, YWCA Tacoma, 1977-78; bd dir, Campfire Tacoma, 1979-83; State Voc Coun Voc Educ, 1982-; Wash Women Employ & Educ Bd dir, 1982-; Phi Delta Kappa, Delta Kappa Gamma. **Home Addr:** 1845 N Hawthorne Dr, Tacoma, WA 98406-1917, **Home Phone:** (253)752-5095. **Business Addr:** District Administrator, Tacoma Public School, Cent Admin Bldg, Tacoma, WA 98405, **Business Phone:** (253)571-1000.

**WESLEY, CLARENCE EUGENE**
Executive. **Personal:** Born Sep 24, 1940, Coffeyville, KS; married Peggy L; children: Keira & Marquel. **Educ:** Pittsburgh State Univ, BS, 1962; Wichita State Univ, MA, 1968. **Career:** Teacher & admin asst, 1962-70; Wichita State, Kans State, Sterling Col, lectr, 1968-75; Upward Bound Wichita State, asst dir, 1969-70; Wichita Area CC, mgr comm develop; Wichita Pub Sch Syst. **Orgs:** Pres, Wes & Berry Int; pres, Ctrl Syst Develop Corp; bd dir, Kans C Minority Bus; Nat Adv Coun Small Bus Admin; pres, Wichita Urban League; chmn & trustee coun, Black Heritage Pk, Kans; trustee & dir, Wichita Coun Ch; CETA Manpower Bd; bd dir, Vet Adv Coun. **Home Addr:** 4819 N Harding, Wichita, KS 67220-1437, **Home Phone:** (316)744-7873. **Business Addr:** 350 W Douglas, Wichita, KS 67202.

**WESLEY, DAVID BARAKAU**
Tailor, basketball player. **Personal:** Born Nov 14, 1970, San Antonio, TX; married Shannon Elliott; children: Brittany, Hallie Jazmyne, Jada & David. **Educ:** Temple JC Univ, 1989; Baylor Univ, PhD, 1992. **Career:** Basketball player (retired); Analyst; Continental Basketball Asn, Wichita Falls Texans, 1992-93; NJ Nets, free agt, 1993-94, 2007; Boston Celtics, 1994-97; Charlotte Hornets / New Orleans Hornets, guard, 1997-2004; Houston Rockets, guard, 2004-06; Cleveland Cavaliers, guard, 2006-07; Baylor Bears Men's Basketball Team, stud mgr; New Orleans Pelicans, tv color analyst, currently. **Home Addr:** 2506 Baywater Canyon Dr, Pearland, TX 77584-4310. **Business Addr:** Analyst, New Orleans Pelicans, 1501 Girod St, New Orleans, LA 70113, **Business Phone:** (504)301-4000.

**WESLEY, DR. HERMAN EUGENE, III**
Evangelist, publisher. **Personal:** Born Oct 17, 1961, Newark, NJ; son of Herman E Jr and Anne M; married Sonja McDade; children: Brandon JeMarcus & Christian Rischard. **Educ:** Southwestern Christian Col, AS, 1981; Okla Christian Univ, BS, bible & church growth, 1983, Nat Acad Christian Studies, MA, biblical studies & church growth, 2002. **Career:** Evangelist, 1986-; Revivalist Mag, publ, 1989-; Ebony News Jour Tex, publ, 1992-; Christian Square Co Tex, chief exec officer, 1992-; Southside Church Christ, minister; Wash Douglas Tribune, ed-in-chief, currently; Herman Wesley Co, publ, chief exec officer. **Orgs:** Comnr, Denton Housing Authority, 1989-92; chmn, Multicultural Adv CMS, 1989-92; chmn bd, Martin Luther King Jr Ctr Adv Bd, 1989-92; exe bd, NCP, Denton Br, 1990-; chair, Black Leadership Coord CNL, 1991-; founding chmn, Denton Black Chamber Com. **Home Addr:** 708 Morse St, Denton, TX 76205, **Home Phone:** (817)380-0840. **Business Addr:** Publishing Editor, Revivalist Newsmagazine, PO Box 240923, Montgomery, AL 36124-0923, **Business Phone:** (334)263-6098.

**WESLEY, HOWARD-JOHN**
Activist, college teacher, minister (clergy). **Personal:** son of Alvin J and Helen J; married Debbie McCain; children: Howard-John II & Cooper Reece. **Educ:** Duke Univ, BSE, 1994; Boston Univ Sch Theol, MDiv, 1997; Northern Baptist Theol Sem, DMin, 2003; Oxford Univ, postdoctoral studies. **Career:** Lic to preach, 1989; ordained, 1997; Boston Univ & Hartford Sem, adj prof; St. John's Congregational Church, pastor, 1997-2008; Alfred St Baptist Church, Alexandria, VA, sr pastor, 2008-; Sunday, Life App Moment with Pastor Wesley, host; regular guest var MSNBC talk shows. **Orgs:** Alexandria NAACP, Northern Va Urban League, Community Coalition Haiti; Kappa Alpha Psi; mem bd dirs, Hopkins House; mem bd dirs; mem bd dirs, Inst Responsible Citizenship; mem bd dirs, Lott Carey Conv; mem bd dirs, John Leland Ctr Theol Studies. **Honors/Awds:** The Root 100: A Who's Who of Black America Award, 2013; James Floyd Jenkins Pillar of Faith Award, 2014; Rev. Dr. Martin Luther King Jr. Board of Preachers of Morehouse College, inductee, 2015; NAACP Chairman's Image Award, 2016. **Business Addr:** Alfred Street Baptist Church, 301 South Alfred St, Alexandria, VA 22314, **Business Phone:** (703)683-2222.

**WESLEY, JOSEPH**
Football player, manager. **Personal:** Born Nov 10, 1976, Jackson, MS. **Educ:** La State Univ, BS, indust safety, 1998. **Career:** Football player (retired), manager; San Francisco 49ers, linebacker, 1999-2000; Jacksonville Jaguars, linebacker, 2001-03; Jacobs Engineering, HSE mgr, 2007, 2009, 2012-. **Orgs:** Bd Dirs, Tex Med Ctr Child Care, 2010; President, NFL Players Asn, 2010. **Honors/Awds:** Rookie of the Year, 1999. **Business Addr:** HSE Manager, HSE Engineering, 5995 Rogerdale Rd, Houston, TX 77072, **Business Phone:** (832)351-6000.

**WESLEY, NATHANIEL, JR.**
Executive. **Personal:** Born Jan 13, 1943, Jacksonville, FL; married Ruby L Williams; children: Nataniel III. **Educ:** Fla A&M Univ, BS, accountancy, 1965; BS, health care mgt; MS, health admin educ progs; Univ Mich, master hosp admin, 1971. **Career:** Albert Einstein Col Med, adminr, consult, 1971-72; NY City Health & Hosp Corp, spl asst to vpres, 1972-73; SW Community Hosp, dept dir, 1973-75; Sidney A Sumby Memorial Hosp, exec dir, 1975-76; Meharry Med Col, asst prof, 1977-79; DC Hosp Asn, asst exec dir; Ins Pub Health Col Pharm Pharmaceut Sci, dir; Fl A&M Univ, Div Health Care Mgt, Sch Allied Health Sci, dir, 2002-; Nat Black Health Leadership Dir, ed; Fla A&M Univ, prog dir. **Orgs:** Secy & exec, Nat Asn Health Serv, 1974-78; pres, Detroit & Nashville Chapters N Am Asn Synagogue Execs, 1975-79; pres & owner, NRW Assoc Inc; BCHW Alpha; Am Pub Health Asn; fel Am Col Healthcare Execs. **Special Achievements:** Nominee, American College of Hospital Administrators; Book: Black Hospitals in America: History, Contributions and Demise. **Home Addr:** 3118 Berry Rd NE, Washington, DC 20018. **Business Addr:** Director Health Care Management Division, Florida A&M University, Sch Allied Health Sci, Tallahassee, FL 32307, **Business Phone:** (850)561-2020.

**WESLEY, VALERIE WILSON**
Writer. **Personal:** Born Nov 22, 1947; married Richard; children: 2. **Educ:** Howard Univ, BA, philos, 1970; Banks St Col Educ, MS, early childhood educ; Columbia Univ Sch jour, MS, jour. **Career:** Scholastic News, asst ed; Essence Mag, exec ed; freelance writer; Ramapo Col, adj, currently; Tamara Hayle Ser: When Death Comes Stealing, 1994; Devil's Gonna Get Him, 1995; Where Evil Sleeps, 1996; No Hiding Pl, 1997; Easier to Kill, 1998; Devil Riding, 2000; Dying Dark, 2004; Blood & Sorrow, 2008; Willimena Rules Ser: How to Loose Your Cookie Money, 2004; How to Almost Ruin Your Class Play, 2005; 23 Ways to Mess Up Valentine's Day, 2006; How to Face Up to Class Bully, 2007; How to Have Best Kwanzaa Ever, 2007; Willimena & Cookie Money 2001; Novels: Where Do I Go from Here?, 1993; Freedom's Gifts, 1997; Ain't Nobody's Bus If I Do, 1999; Always True to You My Fashion, 2002; No Way Dying, 2004; Playing My Mother's Blues, 2005; Chapbooks: How to Lose Your Class Pet, 2003; Tales Willimena, 2004; How to Fish Trouble, 2004; How to Lose Your Cookie Money, 2004; 23 Ways to Mess up Valentine's Day, 2005; How to (almost) Ruin Your Sch Play, 2005; Non fiction:Afro-Bets Bk Black Heroes from A to Z: An Introd to Important Black Achievers Young Readers, 1988. **Orgs:** YWCA N Essex; bd mem, Sisters Crime; bd trustee, Montclair Art Mus, Montclair, NJ; bd dir, Newark Arts Coun, Newark, NJ. **Honors/Awds:** Griot Award, Nat Asn Black Jour, 1993; Excellence in Adult Fiction award, Am Lib Asn, 2000. **Business Addr:** Writer, c/o Celeste Bateman & Assocs, Newark, NJ 07112, **Business Phone:** (973)705-8253.

**WESSON, CLEO**
Government official. **Personal:** Born Aug 27, 1924, Ozan, AR; married Julia; children: Helayne. **Educ:** Gary Col. **Career:** City Gary Common Coun, councilman, 1959, vice committeeman. **Orgs:** John Will Anderson Boys Club; Lake City Lodge, 182; King Solomon Lodge 57; Magic City Consistory 62; Mohomet Temple 134; Rebecca Chap 39; Sallie Wyatt Stewart Guild; Urban League Northwest Ind Inc; life mem, Nat Asn Advan Colored People (Nat Asn Advan Colored People); Israel CME Church; bd dir, March Dimes; secy, Lake County Dem Cent Comt; deleg, State Dem Conv; founder, Gary Community Ment Health Facil; founder, Marina Comt & Hist & Cult Soc. **Honors/Awds:** Recipient, Certification of Merit, Gary Branch Nat Asn Advan Colored People (NAACP), 1965; Service Award, 3rd Episcopal Dist, CME Church, 1965; Distinguished Service & Outstanding Leadership, pres, Common Coun, City Gary, 1966; J Claude Allen, Presiding Bishop Seepa, 1967; Meritorious Service Award, Ind Asn Cities & Towns, 1997. **Home Addr:** 2456 Maryland St, Gary, IN 46407, **Home Phone:** (219)885-7090.

**WESSON, HERMAN JASON, JR. (HERB J WESSON)**
Government official. **Personal:** Born Nov 11, 1951, Cleveland, OH; son of Herman Sr (deceased) and Gladys Wesson-Strickland; married Fabian; children: Douglas, Ralph,P J Herb III & Justin. **Educ:** Lincoln Univ, BA, hist, 1999. **Career:** Councilman Nate Holden, chief staff, 1987-92; Supvr Yvonne B Burke, chief staff, 1992-98; State Calif, assembly rep, 1998-; Tenth Dist, Los Angeles, councilman, 2005-, pes, 2011-. **Orgs:** Mid-City Chamber Com, 1992-; Culver City Chamber Come, 1992-; bd dir, Martin Luther King Hosp Found, 1992-2002; bd mem, Second Dist Educ Found, 1996-; adv bd, African Community Resource Ctr, 1997-2002; ex-off trustee, Calif State Univ, 2002-; ex-officio regent, Univ Calif, 2002-. **Business Addr:** Assembly Rep, State Of California, 31770 Gonzaga Rd, Gustine, CA 95322, **Business Phone:** (209)827-5100.

**WEST, BENNETTA NELSON (BENNIE WEST)**
Administrator, founder (originator). **Personal:** Born Oct 19, 1944, Memphis, TN; daughter of Benjamin H Nelson and Jeannette Brown Nelson; married Leonard D West; children: Joshua Parks, Jacob Ford & Sarah June Parks. **Educ:** Tuskegee Inst, BS, 1962; Columbia Col, MPH, 1979; Univ Memphis, grad studies, 1988; New Sch Social Res. **Career:** Health educr; human serv advocate, planner & lobbyist; ClaySpirits Studio, potter & operator; Shelby State Community Col, mem continuing educ dept & adminr; Memphis Black Arts Alliance Inc, founder & exec dir, 1982-. **Special Achievements:** Participant, black arts movement, New York City, 1968-78; organized the First National African American Crafts Conference & Jubilee; conceived and organized the annual FireHouse Community Arts Festival, 1999. **Business Addr:** Memphis Black Arts Alliance, 985 S Bellevue Blvd, Memphis, TN 38106, **Business Phone:** (901)948-9522.

**WEST, BR. BRUCE ALAN**
Sales manager. **Personal:** Born Mar 31, 1957, Los Angeles, CA; son of Lenon and Betty; married Cathy; children: Chastin & Cheldon. **Educ:** Miss State Univ, BA, 1978. **Career:** Thrifty Drug Stores, asst mgr, 1980-85; Lindsey Prod Co, sales rep, 1985-86; Brown & Williamson Tobacco Corp, sect mgr trade mkt. **Orgs:** Univ Human Rels Comn, 1975-76; Phi Beta Sigma Fraternity, 1976-; Theta Iota Chap, 1976-. **Home Addr:** 4389 Timberdale Rd, Moorpark, CA 93021-3706, **Home Phone:** (805)523-3345.

**WEST, CHERYL L.**
Playwright, social worker. **Personal:** Born Jan 1, 1965, Chicago, IL. **Educ:** Univ Ill Champaign-Urbana. **Career:** Social worker; teacher; playwright, currently; Plays: Before It Hits Home, 1989; Jar the Floor, 1991; Puddin 'n Pete, 1993; Holiday Heart, 1994; Play On!, 1997; Birdie Blue, 2005; Addy: An American Girl Story; Librettist; Film: Glitter, story writer, 2001; TV series: Play On!, 2000; Holiday Heart, producer, 2000; Glitter, 2001; Life Raft, 2009; Diary of a Single Mom, 2009; Pullman Porter Blues, In the Hive, 2012. **Honors/Awds:** Susan Smith Blackburn Prize, co-winner, 1990; AUDELCO Award, 1991; Helen Hayes Charles McArthur Award, 1992; National Endowment for the Arts Playwrighting Award, 1995-96; Best Play Award, Beverly Hills/Hollywood Nat Asn Advan Colored People, 1995; Jeff Award for Best Musical. **Business Addr:** Playwright, c/o The Gersh Agency, 41 Madison Ave 33rd Fl, New York, NY 10010, **Business Phone:** (212)997-1818.

**WEST, CORNEL RONALD**
School administrator, educator. **Personal:** Born Jun 2, 1953, Tulsa, OK; son of Clifton Louis Jr and Irene; married Elleni; children: Clifton & Dilan Zeytun; married Hilda Holloman; children: 1. **Educ:** Harvard Univ, BA, eastern lang & lit, 1973; Princeton Univ, MA, 1975, PhD, philos, 1980. **Career:** Yale Univ Divinty Sch, prof, 1984; Le Monde Diplomatique, Am corresp; Yale Divinity Sch, educr; Univ Paris, educr; Harvard Univ, African Am studies fac; Harvard Univ, Du Bois fel; Union Theol Sem, prof, philos & christian pract; Princeton Univ, Dept Relig, prof, sr fac, 2002-, Dept Afro-Am Studies, dir. Film:The Matrix Reloaded, 2003; The Matrix Revolutions, 2003; Street Fight, 2005; Examined Life, 2008. TV Series: "What Will Happen to the Gang Next Year?", 2012. Albums: Sketches of My Culture, 2001; Street Knowledge, 2004; Never Forget: A Journey of Revelations, 2007. **Orgs:** Alpha Phi Alpha; World Policy Coun; Mod Lang Asn; Dem Socialists Am; co-chair, Tikkun Community; bd mem, Int Bridges to Justice. **Business Addr:** Professor of Religion & African American Studies, Princeton University, 1 Palmer Sq Suite 315, Princeton, NJ 08544, **Business Phone:** (609)258-0021.

**WEST, DENISE JOYNER**
Marketing executive. **Personal:** Born NJ; daughter of Carver and Olivia; married Alfred L; children: A Justin J. **Educ:** State Univ NJ; Douglass Col, BA, psychol; Rutger Bus Sch, MBA, mkt; Howard Univ, cert, advert lateral mover; SMMU, cert, social media mkt strategist, 2010. **Career:** Nabisco, assoc brand mgr, asst brand mgr, mkt asst, 1980-85; Revlon, mkt mgr, 1985-88; Advan Mkt, mkt coordr, 1988-90; Eastman Kodak, mkt develop mgr, 1990-92; Loews Corp, Lorillard Tobacco Co, sr brand mgr, 1992-97, brand mgr, 1997-2002; Essence Commun, dir corp mkt, 1997-2002, online mkt, 1997-2000; bus develop officer, 2000; Essence.com, mkt dir, 2000-02; Wychwood Profs Inc, mkt consult, prin, owner, 2002-11, bus develop consult, 2002-15; Footsteps Groups, freelance media & brand strategy res mgr, 2011-12; Redcom Design & Construct LLC, mkt assoc, 2013-; Technol Concepts Group Int, dir bus develop, 2015-. **Orgs:** Nat Black MBA Asn; fund raising co-chair, NY Chapt, 1985-86; Westfield YMCA Black Achievers, 1998-2001. **Honors/Awds:** Westfield Y Golden Volunteer, 2008. **Home Addr:** 809 E Broad St, Westfield, NJ 07090-2003, **Home Phone:** (908)789-0842. **Business Addr:** Director Business Development, Technology Concepts Group International, 67 Veronica Ave Suite 14, Somerset, NJ 08873, **Business Phone:** (732)659-6031.

**WEST, DOUG (JEFFERY DOUGLAS WEST)**
Basketball player, basketball coach. **Personal:** Born May 27, 1967, Altoona, PA; married Wuela; children: Tyson & Braedyn. **Educ:** Villanova Univ, Villanova, PA, BA, commun, 1989. **Career:** Basketball player (retired), coach; Minn Timberwolves, guard & forward, 1989-98; Vancouver Grizzlies, guard, 1998-2001; Canon-McMillan High Sch, boys' varsity & jr varsity asst coach, 2001-03; Mt de Chantal Visitation Acad, athletics dir & strength & conditioning coordr, 2004; Win by 2 LLC, founder & owner, currently; Duquesne Univ, asst women's basketball coach, 2006-07; Rio Grande Valley Vipers, coaching staff, 2012; Penn State Altoona, head coach, 2015; Altoona Area High Sch, coach, 2016; I Bleed Blue, asst coach; Villanova Wildcats, asst coach, currently. **Orgs:** Philadelphia Big Five; Retired Nat Basketball Players Asn. **Honors/Awds:** Blair County Sports Halls of Fame; Big Five Hall of Fame; Defensive Player of the Year, Timberwolves. **Business Addr:** Assistant Coach, Villanova Wildcats, 800 Lancaster Ave Kennedy Hall, Villanova, PA 19085-1603, **Business Phone:** (610)519-6000.

**WEST, EDWARD LEE, III**
Artist, journalist, football player. **Personal:** Born Aug 2, 1961, Colbert County, AL; married Kecia; children: Jennifer, Edward Lee IV & Whitley. **Educ:** Auburn Univ, grad. **Career:** Football player (retired), martial artist, journalist; Green Bay Packers, tight end, 1984-94; Philadelphia Eagles, tight end, 1995-96; Atlanta Falcons, tight end, 1997; martial artist; British journalist.

**WEST, GEORGE FERDINAND, JR.**
Lawyer, editor. **Personal:** Born Oct 25, 1940, Adams, CO; son of George Ferdinand Sr (deceased) and Artimese M; married Billie Guy; children: George III, Heath & Jarrod. **Educ:** Tougaloo Col, BA, 1962; S Univ, Sch Law, JD, 1966; Univ Miss, JD, 1968. **Career:** Natchez Adams Co Sch Bd, appt, co-atty, 1967-95; State Adv Bd Voc Educ, appt, 1968; Natchez-Adams Co C of C, appt, dir, 1974; Jeff Co Sch Sys, atty, 1974; Miss Sch Bd Asn, dir, atty; Radio Prog, "FACT-FINDING", moderator; Copiah-Lincoln Jr Col Natchez Br, bus law prof; Natchez News Leader, managing ed; Natchez, Miss, pvt pract, currently. **Orgs:** Miss Bar Asn, 1968; res, procter, Miss State Univ, 1973; Nat Asn Advan Colored People; Natchez Bus & Civic League; vpres, Gov Com Hire Handicap; trust, sunday sch teacher, Zion Chap AME Church; contrib ed, Bluff City Post, 1978-; chmn, Natchez-Adams Sch Bd, 1988-. **Honors/Awds:** Outstanding Young Men in America, 1967-; Community Leader of America, 1972; Lifetime Rosco Pound fel, 1972; Most Distinguished Black Attorney Travelers Coalition, 1988; Doctor of Humane Letters, Natchez Col, 1989; Man of the Year, Natchez, Miss, Nat Asn Advan Colored People, 1990; Man of the Year, Natchez Bus & Civic League, 1991; Most Outstanding Atty, Nat Asn Advan Colored People, 1992; Outstanding Attorney for the African Methodist Episcopal Southern Dist & Man of the Year, Zion Chapel AME Church, 1995; Pioneer and Leadership Award, 1998; Hall of Fame, Tougaloo Col Nat Alumni Asn, 2009. **Special Achievements:** Radio Prog, "FACT-FINDING"; Recorded first music album entitled, "Ole TimeWay", 1993. **Business Addr:** Attorney, 10 St Catherine St, Natchez, MS 39121-1202, **Business Phone:** (601)442-3641.

**WEST, DR. GERALD IVAN**
Psychologist, dean (education). **Personal:** Born Jun 3, 1937, St. Louis, MO; son of Frank and Effie; married Blondel B McKinnie; children: Gerald I Jr. **Educ:** Univ Denver, BA, 1958; Southern Ill Univ, MS, 1963; Purdue Univ, PhD, 1967. **Career:** San Francisco State Univ, Dept Coun, chair, Col Ethnic Studies, interim dean, Univ Dean Fac affairs & prof develop, Col Health & Human Serv, prof counselling, prof emer, 2005-. **Orgs:** Past pres, Western Asn Counr Educrs & Supvrs; Am Psychol Asn; SigmaPi Phi; Kappa Alpha Psi. **Honors/Awds:** Annual Memorial Award, Asn Black Psychologist, 1980; Annual Award, Pub Advocates, 1983; Certificate of Honor, City County, San Francisco, 1983; Professional Development Award, Am Asn Coun & Develop, Multicultural Coun, 1985; Award of Merit, San Francisco State Univ, 1985; Admin Fellow, Calif State Univ, 1987; H B McDaniel Award, Stanford Univ, 1992. **Special Achievements:** Elected as first Human Rights Comnr, Calif Personnel & Guid Asn, 1973; Lead case of Larry P vs State of California, first successfully litigated case disproving the theory of racial genetic intellectual inferiority according to IQ tests, which led to federal law prohibiting the use of IQ tests to place African American children in classes for the retarded in California. **Home Addr:** 1 Winged Foot Dr, Novato, CA 94949. **Business Addr:** Professor Emeritus, San Francisco State University, 1600 Holloway Ave, San Francisco, CA 94132, **Business Phone:** (415)338-1111.

**WEST, DR. HERBERT LEE, JR.**
Educator. **Personal:** Born May 4, 1947, Warrenton, NC; son of Wilhemenia Jones and Herbert Lee Sr; married Mary Bentley; children: Tamekah Denise & Marcus Delaney-Bentley. **Educ:** NC Cent Univ, BA, 1969; Univ Minn, MA, 1972, PhD, 1974. **Career:** Univ Minn, Teacher asst, 1972; Univ Md, Baltimore Co, asst prof, 1974-80; Howard Univ, asst prof, 1980-85; fac intern, House Urban Develop, 1980; adv, Summer Work Prog-Prince Georges Co, Md; educr/admin, Howard Co Bd Educ, 1985-; Villa Julie Col, assoc prof, 1993. **Orgs:** Nat Asn Advan Colored People; Triangle Geographers; Nat Coun Black Studies; Assoc Study Afro-Am Life; Black Stud Achievement Prog, Howard Co, Md. **Home Addr:** 6316 Loring Dr, Columbia, MD 21045, **Home Phone:** (301)596-5796. **Business Addr:** Educator, Howard County Board of Education, 10910 Clarksville Pke Rte 108, Ellicott City, MD 21042, **Business Phone:** (410)313-6600.

**WEST, JEFFERY DOUGLAS.** See WEST, DOUG.

**WEST, JOHN ANDREW**
Judge, lawyer. **Personal:** Born Sep 15, 1942, Cincinnati, OH; married Miriam Evonne Kennedy; children: Melissa Evonne. **Educ:** Univ Cincinnati, BA, BS, 1966; Salmon P Chase Law Sch, JD, 1971. **Career:** Pitzer W Cutcher & Gilday, atty; GE Co Large Jet Engine Div, buyer & contract admin, 1968-71; Hamilton Co Courthouse, judge, 2010-. **Orgs:** Nat Am & Ohio Bar Asn, 1972-; chmn, Hamilton Co Pub Defender Comn, 1976; Ohio State Bar Asn. **Home Addr:** 1000 Main St Ct Rm 595, Cincinnati, OH 45202-1286. **Business Addr:** Judge, Hamilton County Courthouse, 595 Hamilton County Courthouse 1000 Main St, Cincinnati, OH 45202, **Business Phone:** (513)946-5785.

**WEST, DR. JOHN RAYMOND**
College administrator, educator. **Personal:** Born Apr 9, 1931, Birmingham, AL; son of John H and Mignonette Mason; married Suzanne Marie Lancaster; children: Ronald, John Jr, Gerald, Reginald, Teresa, Semara, Tia & Joshua. **Educ:** Calif State Univ, Fullerton, BA, anthrop, 1969, MA, anthrop, 1970; Nova Univ Fla, EdD, admin, 1975. **Career:** S Counties Gas Co, sr scheduler, 1961-69; State Calif, employ serv officer, 1969-70; Santa Ana Col, anthrop, sociol, prof, 1970-, dir, assoc dean, dean stud serv, 1973-86; Nova Univ, cluster coordr, 1975-90; Saddleback Col Mission Viejo, instr, 1976-; Afro Ethnic Studies Calif State Univ Fullerton, lectr; Santiago Canyon Col, Humanities & Sci, div chair, currently, Dept Anthropol & Sociol, prof, currently. **Orgs:** Founding pres, Orange County Chap Sickle Cell Dis Res Found, 1972; 100 Black Men Orange County; bd dir & vpres, Legis Affairs Western Region Counc Black Am Affairs; bd dir, Assoc Calif Comn Col Admin, 1972; bd dir, Calif Comn Col Extended Oppty Prog & Serv, 1977-79. **Home Addr:** 26525 Sierra Vis, Mission Viejo, CA 92692-3333, **Home Phone:** (949)582-5748. **Business Addr:** Chairman, Professor of Sociology & Anthropology, Santiago Canyon College, D 116-6 8045 E Chapman Ave, Orange, CA 92869, **Business Phone:** (714)628-4870.

**WEST, JOSEPH KING**
Judge, lawyer, association executive. **Personal:** Born Sep 11, 1929, Yonkers, NY; son of Ralph and Nellie Brown; married Shirley Arvene Gray; children: Rebecca & Joseph Jr. **Educ:** Howard Univ, BS, 1952; Brooklyn Law Sch, JD, 1961. **Career:** City Yonkers, asst corp coun, 1964-65, city ct judge, 1983-84; County Westchester, dep dist atty, 1965-82; Elected County Ct Judge, 1984, re-elected, 1994; St New York, 9th Judicial Dist, supv judge, criminal ct, 1991-98; New York Supreme Ct, judge; Co Ct, judge, currently. **Orgs:** Alpha Phi Alpha Frat, 1948-; bd dir, Yonkers Big Bro-Big Sisters, 1982-, St Joseph's Hosp, 1983-; life mem, Alpha Phi Alpha Fraternity; life mem, Nat Asn Advan Colored People. **Honors/Awds:** Achievement Award Asn Black Lawyers of Westchester Co, 1981; Comn Serv Westchester Rockland Guardians Asn, 1984; Commission Service Award Yonkers Coun Churches, 1985; Civic Award Frederick D Patterson Alpha Phi Alpha, 1987. **Home Addr:** 2 Fairfield Pl, Yonkers, NY 10705, **Home Phone:** (914)964-6946. **Business Addr:** Judge, Westchester Co, 111 Grove St, White Plains, NY 10601, **Business Phone:** (914)285-4305.

**WEST, LENA L.**
Executive. **Personal:** Born White Plains, NY. **Career:** Freelance technol consult, 1994-97; xynoMedia Technol, founder & chief exec officer, chief strategist, owner, 1997-; Pitney Bowes, consult, 1998; Philips Magnavox, consult, 1999; Hyperion, consult, 1999; MasterCard Int, consult, 2000-04; BlogHer, co-chair, 2007. **Orgs:** Tech dir & bd mem, Sister to Sister Int, 1996-2002; Kindness Strangers, 2001-03; bd mem & secty, redIbis, 2003-04; CBLit, Technol Dir, 2003-04; Women in Power, 2003-04; Women Presidents Org; Technol Execs Networking Group; Downtown Women's Club; Ctr Women's Bus Res Adv Bd; BlogHer Bus Adv Bd; Women's Cong Nat Adv Bd. **Business Addr:** Founder, Chief Executive Officer, XynoMedia Technology, 1 Saw Mill River Rd Suite 190, Yonkers, NY 10701, **Business Phone:** (914)377-0600.

**WEST, MARILYN H.**
Chief executive officer, business owner. **Personal:** married Edward G; children: Meaghan & Brennan. **Educ:** Waynesburg Col, Waynesburg, PA, math; Univ Pittsburgh, Grad Sch Pub Health, MA. **Career:** Allegheny Health Dept, Pittsburgh, statistician, asst dir planning; Continuing Educ Proj Ment Health, dir; Va Commonwealth Univ, dir planning, ment retardation & substance abuse serv; Va Cert Pub Need Prog, dir; M H W & Co Inc, owner, chmn & chief exec officer, 1991-. **Orgs:** Parent delg, White House Conf Educ, 1992; cong appointee, White House Conf Small Bus, 1995; Delta Sigma Theta Sorority; Links Inc; Jack & Jill Am; Coalition 100 Black Women & Continental Socs; St Philips Episcopal Church; chmn, Bon Secours Joint Hosps Bd; exec comt, Richmond Renaissance; adv bd, Metrop Bus League; exec comt, C Home Soc; exec comt, Atlantic Rural Expos; chair, Richmond & Capital Area Workforce Invest Bd; exec comt, Richmond City Police Found, Am Red Cross; chair, Leadership Metro Richmond; Pres's Coun UNOS; bd trustee, Waynesburg Univ, 2009; dir, Richmond Va Metrop Authority, 2012-. **Business Addr:** Chairman, Chief Executive Officer, M H West & Co Inc, 919 E Main St Siute 1302, Richmond, VA 23219-2602, **Business Phone:** (804)782-1938.

**WEST, MARK ANDRE**
Basketball player, sports manager, vice president (organization). **Personal:** Born Nov 5, 1960, Petersburg, VA; married Elaina; children: Marcus & Markyle. **Educ:** Old Dom Univ, BS, bus admin, 1983; Univ Phoenix, MBA, 2010. **Career:** Basketball player (retired), basketball coach, exec; Dallas Mavericks, ctr, 1983-84; Milwaukee Bucks, 1984; Cleveland Cavaliers, 1984-88; Phoenix Suns, 1988-94, 1999-2000, asst gen mgr, 2001, vpres player prog, 2006-, asst coach, 2013; Detroit Pistons, 1994-96; Cleveland Cavaliers, 1996-97; Ind Pacers, 1997-98; Atlanta Hawks, 1999; Native Am Basketball Invitational, co-founder. **Business Addr:** Vice President of Player Relations, Assistant Coach, Phoenix Suns, 201 E Jefferson St, Phoenix, AZ 85004, **Business Phone:** (602)379-7867.

**WEST, MARY BETH**
Vice president (organization), marketing executive. **Educ:** Nazareth Col Rochester, BS, mgt, 1984; Columbia Univ, MBA, mkt, 1986. **Career:** Mondelez Int Inc, assoc prod mgr & mkt, 1986-98, vpres new bus develop, 1998-99, vpres mkt enhancers div, 1999-2001, Meals Div, 2001-04, group vpres, 2005-07, N Am Grocery Sector, pres, 2005-07, exec vpres & chief mkt officer, 2007; JC Penney Co Inc, mkt officer & exec vpres, 2015-. **Orgs:** Dir, JC Penney Co Inc; Exec Leadership Coun; dir, Advert Coun Inc, 2005-15. **Honors/Awds:** Minority MBA's Next Generation of Business Leaders, Honoree; "Crain's Chicago Business", 40 Under 40, Honoree; "Black Enterprise", 100 Most Powerful Executives in Corporate America, 2009; "Black Enterprise", 75 Most Powerful Women in Business, 2010. **Business Addr:** Chief Marketing Officer, Executive Vice President, Mondelez International Inc, 3 Pkwy N, Deerfield, IL 60015, **Business Phone:** (847)943-4000.

**WEST, PROF. PHEORIS**
Educator, artist. **Personal:** Born Aug 17, 1950, Albany, NY; son of James and Mary Wilson McDowell; married Michele Barbette Hoff; children: Jahlani, Adwin, Pheannah & Adji. **Educ:** Col Brockport State Univ NY, 1970; Pa Acad Fine Arts, prof cert, painting, 1974; Yale Univ, MFA, painting, 1976. **Career:** Artist, 1976-; Ohio State Univ, asst prof, assoc prof art, 1976, Dept Art, Painting & Drawing prog, assoc prof emer, currently; Hill house HS New Haven, Ct, resident artist, 1976; Educ Ctr Arts, dir, resident artist, 1976; Martin Luther King Ctr, curator, 1999. **Orgs:** Nat Conf Artists, 1970; Artist Equity, 1978-; bd mem, Columbus Metrop Area Community Action Orgn Cult Arts Ctr, 1979-; Bahia Bridge, 1988-; bd mem, Columbus Art League, 1988-; Nat Endowment Arts Abbr Arts Panel; Ohio Arts Coun; Int Juror Nat Exhib Zimbabwe. **Honors/Awds:** ICresson Award Travelling Fellowship to Europe PA Acad of Fine Arts, 1973; J Scheidt Award Travelling Fellowship to Ghana, 1974; Special Recognition, Ohio House Rep, 1988; International Juror, Zimbabwe Heritage, 1992; Individual Artists Grant, Ohio Arts Coun, 1988; Special Recognition from the City of Hartford, CT, 1996: Inducted into the Hall of Fame for the Educational System of the Capital District of Albany, NY, 2009. **Home Addr:** 1800 Hillandale Ave, Columbus, OH 43229-1414, **Home Phone:** (614)882-1969. **Business Addr:** Associate Professor Emeritus, Ohio State University, 258 Hopkins Hall 128 N Oval Mall, Columbus, OH 43210-1363, **Business Phone:** (614)292-5072.

**WEST, PHILLIP CURTIS**
Mayor. **Personal:** Born Nov 30, 1946, Natchez, MS; son of George F Sr and Elodie; married Carolyn Mosby; children: Dana, Danessa, Kareem & Samuel. **Educ:** Alcorn State Univ. **Career:** Adams County, supvr, 1980-97; Adams, Jefferson & Franklin Counties, Dist 94, state rep; City Natchez, mayor, 2004. **Orgs:** Chmn, Miss Legis Black Caucus; pres, Boys & Girls Club Miss-Lou; chmn emer, Sadie V Thompson Era Reunion; chmn, Miss Asn Supvrs Minority Caucus; pres, Natchez High PTA; chmn, Adams County Dem Party; little league coach, TM Jennings Baseball League; pres, Natchez Br, Nat Asn Advan Colored People; vpres, Miss State Nat Asn Advan Colored People; Rose Hill Missionary Baptist Church; Mason & Eastern Star Lodges; Omega Psi Phi Fraternity; Alcorn State Univ Alumni Asn; Nat Asn Wholesaler. **Honors/Awds:** Alcorn State University Sports Hall of Fame, 2004. **Special Achievements:** First African-American president of the Adams County Board of Supervisors; First African-American Mayor of Natchez. **Business Addr:** Mayor, City of Natchez, 124 S Pearl St, Natchez, MS 39120, **Business Phone:** (601)445-7500.

**WEST, RODERICK K.**
President (organization), chief executive officer, educator. **Educ:** Univ Notre Dame, BA, 1990; Tulane Univ Sch Law, JD, 1993; Tulane Univ, MBA, 2005. **Career:** New Orleans off Vial, Hamilton, atty; Koch & Knox, LLP, Com Litigation Dept, atty; Jones; Walker, atty, 1993-98; Waechter; Poitevent; Carrere & Denegre LLP; Tulane Univ, adj prof, 1993-2001; Regulatory Affairs Entergy New Orleans, dir, 2001-03; Entergy Serv Inc, Distrib Opers, region mgr, 2003-05; Metro Distrib Opers Entergy Serv Inc, dir, 2005-06; Entergy New Orleans, dir, 2005-, pres & chief exec officer, 2007-10; Entergy Corp, sr regulatory coun, 1999-2001, exec vpres & chief admin officer, 2010-. **Orgs:** Dir, First Bank & Trust (New Orleans, LA); dir, Greater New Orleans Inc; State Bar La; Am Bar Asn; chmn, La State Univ Syst Bd Supervisors; bd dir, 2006, 2007; trustee, Univ Notre Dame, 2009; First Trust; bd dir, Allstate Sugar Bowl; bd dir, Edison Elec Inst; Exec Leadership Coun, 2007-16; Sigma Pi Phi Fraternity; Smart Wires Inc. **Honors/Awds:** "Black Enterprise," The 100 Most Powerful Executives

in Corporate America, 2010. **Business Addr:** Chief Administrative Officer, Executive Vice President, Entergy Corp, 639 Loyola Ave, New Orleans, LA 70113, **Business Phone:** (504)576-4000.

### WEST, HON. ROYCE BARRY

Lawyer, politician. **Personal:** Born Sep 26, 1952, Annapolis, MD; son of Willis and Gloria Morris Ashford; married Carol Richard; children: Steve, Tara, Royce, Remarcus, Rolando, Roddrick & Brandon. **Educ:** Univ Tex, BA, sociol, 1975, MA, sociol, 1979; Univ Houston, JD, 1979. **Career:** Harris County Dist Attorneys Off, Houston, Tex, asst dist atty, 1979-80; Dallas County Dist Attorneys Off, Dallas, Tex, asst dist atty, 1979-84; Royce W & Assocs, Dallas, Tex, lawyer, 1984-88; Brown, Robinson & W, Dallas, Tex, lawyer, 1988-91; Robinson, W & Gooden, partner & atty, 1992-; Tex state sen, Dist 23, 1993-; W & Ass LLP, managing partner, 1994-. **Orgs:** Bd dir, Tex Turnpike Authority, 1983-90; deacon, Good St Baptist Church, 1984-; bd secy, Dallas County Dent Health, 1989-; co-chmn, United Negro Col Fund, 1990; pres, JL Turner Legal Asn, 1990-91; circleten exec comt, Boy Scouts Am; Dallas County Dem Party Fin Coun; life mem, Nat Asn Advan Colored People; Nat Bar Asn; chmn, Intergovernmental Rel Comt; Senate's Comt; Educ Comt; standing comt, NCSL; Educ Comn, 2005; Pres, Pro Tempore Tex Senate, 2006; Intergovernmental aff Comt, 2009-; adv mem, Southern Regional Educ Bd, 2009. **Special Achievements:** First African American to serve as president of the Student Congress. **Home Addr:** 7318 Oakmore, Dallas, TX 75249, **Home Phone:** (214)780-1500. **Business Addr:** Honorable Royce West, Texas State Senator, Capitol Sta, Austin, TX 78711, **Business Phone:** (512)463-0123.

### WEST, DR. TOGO DENNIS, JR.

President (organization), lawyer, chief executive officer. **Personal:** Born Jun 21, 1942, Winston-Salem, NC; son of Togo Dennis Sr and Evelyn Carter; married Gail Estelle Berry; children: Tiffany Berry & Hilary Carter. **Educ:** Howard Univ, BSEE, 1965, Sch Law, JD, 1968; Gannon Univ, D Law, 1968; Winston-Salem Univ, DLaw, 1996. **Career:** Duquense Light & Power Co, elec engr, 1965; Sughrue Rothwell Mion Zinn & McPeak, patent researcher, 1966-67; US Equal Employ Opportunity Comn, legal intern, 1967; Covington & Burling, law clerk, 1967-68, summer assoc, 1968, assoc, 1973-75, 1976-77; Hon Harold R Tyler Judge, US Dist Ct, Southern Dist, NY, law clerk, 1968-69; Howard Law J, managing ed, 1968; Dept Justice, assoc dep atty gen, 1975-76; Dept Navy, gen coun, 1977-79; Dept Defense, spec asst sec & dep sec, 1979-80, gen coun, 1980-81; Patterson Belknap Webb & Tyler, partner, 1981-90; pvt pract, 1981; Northrop Corp Inc, sr vpres, govt rels, 1990-93; Veterans Affairs secy, 1998-2000; Joint Ctr Polit & Econ Studies, pres & chief exec officer, 2004-06; Nat Capital Area Coun, pres, currently; TLI Leadership Group, chmn, 2006. **Orgs:** Dist Bar, 1968; NY Bar, 1969; US Mil Appeals, 1969; dir, Wash Coun Lawyers, 1973-75; US Supreme Ct, 1978; US Ct Claims, 1981; comnr & chair, Dist Law Rev CMS, 1982-89; trustee, Aerospace Corp, 1983-90; Nat Coun Friends Kennedy Ctr, 1984-91; bd dir, DC Law Stud Ct Prog, 1986-92; trustee, Ctr Strategic & Int Studies, 1987-90; chair, Legis Bur, 1987-89; bd dir, Greater Wash Bd Trade, 1987-93; chair, DC Comn Pub Educ, 1988-93; trustee, Inst Defense Anal, 1989-90; financial comt mem, Episcopal Diocese Wash, 1989-; Protestant Episcopal Cathedral Foun, 1989-; DC Ct Appeals Comn Admis, 1990-93; trustee, Shakespeare Theatre Folger, 1990-93; trustee, NC Sch Arts, 1990-; bd consult, Riggs Nat Bank, 1990-93; chair, Kennedy Ctr & Friends Bd, 1991-; Am Bar Asn; NBA; Eagle Scout Bronze Palm; sr warden & Vestry, St John's Church, Lafayette Sq; Alpha Phi Omega Fraternity; Phi Alpha Delta Fraternity; Sigma Pi Phi Fraternity; Omega Psi Phi Fraternity; Nat Exec Bd Boy Scouts Am; bd mem, Mt Vernon preserv soc. **Honors/Awds:** Eagle Scout Award with Bronze Palm, Boy Scouts Am, 1957; Howard Univ, ServAward, 1965; Distinguished Pub Serv Medal, Dept Defense, 1981, 1998; Distinguished Eagle Scout Award, Boy Scouts Am, 1995; Distinguished Civilian Serv, Dept Amry; Distinguished Pub Serv, Dept Navy, 1998; Except Civilian Serv, Dept Air Force, 1998; Silver Buffalo Award. **Business Addr:** Chief Executive Officer, President, Joint Center for Political and Economic Studies, 1090 Vt Ave NW Suite 1100, Washington, DC 20005-4928, **Business Phone:** (202)789-3500.

### WEST, VALERIE Y. (VALERIE WEST-HILL)

Educator, teacher, manager. **Personal:** Born Jul 8, 1965, Newport News, VA; daughter of Woodrow W Sr and Lula A. **Educ:** Hampton Univ, BA, eng & theatre educ, 1987; Va Commonwealth Univ, MFA, directing & theatrical prod, 1992. **Career:** Lindsay Mid Sch, 8th grade Eng teacher, 1989-90; VA Commonwealth Univ, adj instr, 1990-92; VA Union Univ, asst prof theatre, 1992-2006, chair, dept fine arts, 2000-06; Gilbane Bldg Co, swam coordr, 2006-15, proposal mgr, 2007-12, assoc bus develop mgr, 2012-15, bus develop coordr; Waller, Todd & Sadler, mkt coordr, 2015; W.M. Jordan Co, sr mkt coordr, 2015-. **Orgs:** Nat Conf African Am Theatre, 1992-; Black Theatre Network, 1992-94; VA Speech Commun Asn, 1994-; Am Alliance Theatre Educ, 2000-; Educ comt mem, SMPS Va, 2014; progs comt mem, HRACRE, 2014. **Home Addr:** 4340A Lakefield Mews Dr, Richmond, VA 23231, **Home Phone:** (804)222-9548. **Business Addr:** Associate Business Development Manager, Gilbane Building Co, 7 Jackson Walkway, Providence, RI 02903, **Business Phone:** (401)456-5800.

### WEST, WILLIAM LIONEL, II

Pharmacologist, college teacher. **Personal:** Born Nov 30, 1923, Charlotte, NC; son of Lionel Beresford and Cornelia T Hairston; married Edythe Kearns; children: William II & Edythe P. **Educ:** Johnson C Smith Univ, BS, 1947; State Univ Iowa, PhD, 1955. **Career:** St Univ Iowa, res asst zool, 1949-54; Radiation Res, Dept Col Med St Univ Iowa, res assoc, 1954-56; Howard Univ, Ctr Drug Abuse Res, prin investr; Howard Univ Col Med, asst prof pharmacol, instr pharmacol, 1956-69, prof dept pharmacol, 1969-72, prof, chmn dept pharmacol, 1972-92, prof, dept radiol, 1971-92, prof emer, currently. **Orgs:** Am Soc Pharmacol & Exp Therapeut; Int Soc Biochem; Am Nuclear Soc; Am Asn Clin Chem; Am Soc Zoologist; Soc Exp Biol & Med; Am Physiol Soc; Am Inst Chemist; Asn Cancer Res; fel Am Inst Chem; Int Acad Law & Sci; Sigma Xi Sci Soc; NY Acad Sci; fel AAAS; fel ASI. **Honors/Awds:** Outstanding Scholar, Howard Univ, Ctr Health & Sci, 1986. Published numerous articles. **Home Addr:** 10287 Paige Rd Ivy Hill Farm, PO Box 79, Woodford, VA 22580-2625, **Home Phone:** (804)448-2118. **Business Addr:** Professor Emeritus, Howard University College of Medicine, 520 W St, Washington, DC 20059, **Business Phone:** (202)806-6311.

### WEST-HILL, VALERIE. See WEST, VALERIE Y.

### WESTBROOK, BRYANT ANTOINE

Football player, football coach. **Personal:** Born Dec 19, 1974, Charlotte, NC. **Educ:** Univ Tex, Austin. **Career:** Football player (retired), coach; Detroit Lions, left cornerback, 1997-2001, cornerback, 1999; Dallas Cowboys, left cornerback, 2002; Green Bay Packers, 2002-03; Shadow Mountain High Sch, defensive back coach, 2011-12; Cactus High Sch, Glendale, defensive back coach, 2012-; Ariz powerhouse Saguaro High Sch, asst football coach, currently. **Honors/Awds:** Chuck Hughes, Most Improved Player Award, 2000. **Special Achievements:** First round pick, No 5, NFL Draft, 1997. **Business Addr:** Defensive Back Coach, Cactus High School, 6330 W Greenway Rd, Glendale, AZ 85306, **Business Phone:** (623)412-5000.

### WESTBROOK, DR. JOSEPH W, III. See Obituaries Section.

### WESTBROOK, MICHAEL DEANAILO

Football player, wrestler. **Personal:** Born Jul 7, 1972, Detroit, MI; son of Bobby Sledge and Mercy. **Educ:** Univ Colo, grad. **Career:** Football player (retired), wrestling trainer; Wash Redskins, wide receiver, 1995-2001; Cincinnati Bengals, wide receiver, 2002; Ariz Combat Sports, wrestling trainer, currently. **Honors/Awds:** Brown Belt, Int Brazilian Jiu-Jitsu Fedn, 2008; Black Belt in Brazilian Jiu-Jitsu, 2010. **Home Addr:** , Mesa, AZ. **Business Addr:** Wrestling Trainer, Arizona Combat Sports, 525 S McClintock Dr Suite 103, Tempe, AZ 85281.

### WESTBROOK, PETER JONATHAN

Executive. **Personal:** Born Apr 16, 1952, St. Louis, MO; son of Moriko; married Susan Miles; children: Dorian. **Educ:** NY Univ, NY, BS, 1975. **Career:** Speaker, Athlete & competitor; Peter Westbrook Found, pres, chief exec officer, founder & exec dir, 1991-. **Orgs:** Bd dir, Us Olympic Comn, 1992-; Abyssinian Bapt Church, 1992-; trustee, Arthur Ashe Athletic Asn, 1996-; Japanese Am Socs; Women Sports Found; bd mem, New York Sports Comn, 1996-. **Business Addr:** Founder, Executive Director, President, Chief Execuive Officer, Peter Westbrook Foundation, 229 W 28th St 2nd Fl, New York, NY 10116, **Business Phone:** (212)459-4538.

### WESTBROOKS, LOGAN H.

Executive, consultant, president (organization). **Personal:** Born Aug 28, 1937, Memphis, TN; married Geraldine Douthet; children: Babette. **Educ:** Lincoln Univ, BA, bus admin, 1975, MA, Bibl coun. **Career:** R&B Capitol Rec, mid-w prom mgr, 1965-67; Mkt Capitol Rec Inc, from admin asst to vpres, 1969-70; Spec Mkt Col Rec US, dir, 1970-71; R&B Mercury Rec, dir Nat prom, 1970; Spec Mkts CBS Rec Int, dir, 1971-76; Source Rec Co Inc, founder, owner, pres, 1977-; Int Mkt CBS Rec, int exec, vpres, 1977; Temple Faith, pastor; RCA Vic Dist Corp, from mgt trainee asst to mkt mgr; real estate entrepreneur; Rec co, exec, 2008-. **Orgs:** Co-founder, Cont Inst Tech, 1971; mem Omega Psi Phi; PUSH Chicago; FORENY; consult, Nat Med Asn, 1971; bd trust Merit Rl Est Invst Trust Chicago, 1973; Helping Hands Home Boys; pres, W brooks Artist mgt; vp mktg, Soul Train Productions & Rec Co; ambassador, Ann African Music FestivalEduc, 1977; Historically Black Cols & Univs; educr, lectr, African-Am music & cult; founding mem, City Azusa's Human Rels Comt; Booker T Wash Alumni Asn, currently. **Honors/Awds:** Recognition Commission Certificate, LA City Coun, 1970; Certificate of Merit, LA Urban League, 1970; Merit citation proj, 1975; Boston, 1973; spec pres, Mrs Martin Luther King, Atlanta, 1974; Distinguished Alumni, Lincoln Univ, 1983; National Black College Alumni Hall of Fame. **Special Achievements:** Author: The Anatomy of a Record Company; Appeared on numerous PBS specials. **Home Addr:** 15223 Rayneta Dr, Sherman Oaks, CA 91403-4431, **Home Phone:** (912)784-6912. **Business Addr:** 280 S Bev Dr Suite 206, Beverly Hills, CA 90212.

### WESTBROOKS, PHIL

Mayor, president (organization), chief executive officer. **Personal:** Born Chandler, AZ. **Educ:** Chandler-Gilbert Community Col, attended 1991; Mesa Community Col, AA; Ariz State Univ, BA, pub & urban recreation, MA, pub admin; Nova Southeastern Univ, PhD, higher educ. **Career:** Model, entrepreneur; Spectrum Solutions LLC, founder, pres & chief exec officer, 2002-; City Chandler, councilman, 1998, vice mayor, 2004-06. **Orgs:** Fel Ariz State Univ Community; exec adv, Improving Chandler Area Neighborhoods; advocacy chair, Am Heart Asn, Oper Heartbeat; YMCA; Chandler Boys & Girls Club; Maricopa Asn Govt Human Serv Comt; Harry Mitchell Cong; Ariz Asn Retarded Citizens; Desert Cancer Found Ariz; charter mem, Optimist Club Chandler; dir educ, Chandler Regional Hosp; bd mem, Chandler AARC. **Business Addr:** President, Chief Executive Officer, Spectrum Solutions LLC, 108 E 2nd Ave, Mesa, AZ 85210, **Business Phone:** (480)206-3999.

### WESTER, RICHARD CLARK

Firefighter, city council member. **Personal:** Born Sep 24, 1945, West Palm Beach, FL; son of Walter and Hazel Fisher; married LaDarn Hudson; children: Anita Michelle & Angela Monique. **Educ:** Fla State Fire Col, Ocala; Valencia Community Col, Orlando, FL, attended 1988. **Career:** Firefighter (retired); City Riviera Beach Fire Dept, Riviera Beach, Fla, chief, 1969. **Orgs:** Nat Forum Black Pub Adminr, 1981-; treas, Fire Chiefs Asn Palm Beach County, Fla, 1990-; Training Officers Asn Palm Beach County, Fla. **Honors/Awds:** Ricky Award, JFK High Sch Class of '65, 1990. **Special Achievements:** First Black Firefighter, Palm Beach County, FL; First Black Lieutenant of Fire, Palm Beach County, FL; First Black Captain of Fire, Palm Beach County, FL; First Black Fire Chief, Palm Beach County, FL; First Black Chief in the State of Florida of a major municipality. **Home Addr:** PO Box 9522, West Palm Beach, FL 33419, **Home Phone:** (407)844-8391.

### WESTFIELD-AVENT, LISA

Executive. **Educ:** Univ Ore, advert; San Jose State Univ, BA, advert & mkt, 1981. **Career:** 1984 Olympics, licensing, 1980-84; Mattel Toys, licensing mgr, Barbie & Hot Wheels, 1988-90; 20th Century Fox, dir, 1990-94; Sony Signatures, dir domestic sls; Nelvana Commun, vpres, domestic licensing; Metro-Goldwyn-Mayer Consumer Prods, vpres worldwide licensing retail develop, 1997-2004, vpres, domestic licensing, 1999-2002; Warner Bros Consumer Prod, vpres mkt, 2005-06; Disney Consumer Prod, vpres tv licensing, 2006-08; Walt Disney Co, vpres, gm franchise develop & mkt, 2006-; Disney Consumer Prod, Walt Disney Co, vpres & gen mgr, global franchise develop & mkt, 2008-10; Disney Consumer Prod, vpres & gen mgr, global tv franchise develop & mkt, 2010-12; Disney Consumer Prod, vp Strategic Mkt & Consumer Mkt, 2013-. **Orgs:** Delta Sigma Pi. **Business Addr:** Vice President, General Manager, The Walt Disney Co, 500 S Buena Vista St, Burbank, CA 91521-0644, **Business Phone:** (818)560-1000.

### WESTMORELAND, SAMUEL DOUGLAS

College teacher, educator. **Personal:** Born May 29, 1944, West Chester, PA; son of Nip Thorton Sr and Ella Dee (Ingram) W; married Mary Elizabeth Hampton; children: Lesia Annetra, Samara Elizabeth & Diana Haskins. **Educ:** Kutztown State Col, BS, 1966, MEd, 1971; Lehigh Univ, MA, 1978. **Career:** World Cultures, teacher, 1967-71; Kutztown Univ, assoc prof social & anthrop, fac, 1971-2007. **Orgs:** YMCA, Reading, Pa, 1966-67; consult, Black Cult Orgn, Kutztown State Col, 1970-71; Black Conf Higher Educ, 1972-74; Nat Asn Advan Colored People, 1972; Black Conf Basic Educ, 1972-73; lectr, Educ & Black Child, Downington Br, Nat Asn Advan Colored People, 1972; Nat Conf Black Family, 1976-87; chairperson, Pa Sociol Asn Conf, 1983-84; exec bd, Asn Sci & Behav Sci, 1984-87; chair, Nat Conf Black Family, 1989-92; chair, life mem comt, ASBS, 1990-97; Human Diversity Comt; Comt Status Minorities; cofounder & chair, Black Fac Caucus; Nat Coalition Bldg Inst; cofounder, Scoop; Asn Black Sociologists; Eastern Sociol Soc; Pa Sociol Soc; Lehigh Valley Black Admin; pres, Asn Social & Behav Scientist Inc; pres, Kutztown Univ Found Alumni Asn, bd dir. **Honors/Awds:** Life Membership Award, Penn Asn Student Financial Aid Administrators. **Home Addr:** 1 Bird Song Ct, Reading, PA 19607, **Home Phone:** (610)775-1015. **Business Addr:** Board Director, Kutztown University Foundation, PO Box 151, Kutztown, PA 19530, **Business Phone:** (610)683-1394.

### WESTON, LARRY CARLTON

Lawyer, manager. **Personal:** Born Jul 6, 1948, Sumter, SC. **Educ:** SC State Col, BA, 1970; Univ SC, JD, 1976. **Career:** BF Goodrich Footwear Co, asst personal mgr, 1970-72; Gray & Weston Attys Law, atty, 1976-. **Orgs:** Adv bd, YWCA, 1977-78; Dist coun SC Conf Br Nat Asn Advan Colored People, 1978-; bd dir, vice chmn, Sumter Co Pub Defender Corp, 1979-; Sumter Co Comn Higher Ed, 1979-; Sumter Co Election Comn, 1980-, chair. **Home Addr:** 15 Chappell Cir, Sumter, SC 29150, **Home Phone:** (803)775-5787. **Business Addr:** Owner, Larry C Weston Law Firm, 201 N Main St, Sumter, SC 29150-4958, **Business Phone:** (803)778-2421.

### WESTON, MARTIN V.

Journalist. **Personal:** Born Mar 14, 1947, Philadelphia, PA; son of Rubin and Cozetta Walker; married Brenda Catlin. **Career:** Philadelphia Bulletin, Philadelphia, Pa, ed writer, 1979-82; Channel 6-TV, Philadelphia, Pa, producer vision, 1982-83; W Wilson Goode, Mayor, Philadelphia, Pa, spec aide, 1983; Newsday, Melville, NY, ed writer, 1984-. **Orgs:** Nat Asn Black Journalists. **Honors/Awds:** Journal Award, Socs Motion Picture & Tv Engrs, 1979. **Special Achievements:** Author, "Prized Banister Found in One Quick Step". **Business Addr:** Editorial Writer, Newsday, 235 Pinelawn Rd, Melville, NY 11747, **Business Phone:** (516)454-2911.

### WESTRAY, REV. KENNETH MAURICE

Clergy. **Personal:** Born Jun 15, 1952, Washington, DC; son of Kenneth Maurice Sr and Jean Virginia Hughes. **Educ:** US Merchant Marine Acad, Kings Pt, NY, BS, 1974; Mt St Mary's Semi, Emmitsburg, Md, 1978; St Patrick's Sem, Menlo Pk, Calif, MDiv, 1979; Grad Theol Union, Berkeley, Calif, attended 1986. **Career:** Am Export Isbrandsten Lines, New York, NY, third mate, 1974-76; Nativity Grammar Sch, Wash, DC, teacher, 1979; Sacred Heart Parish, San Francisco, Calif, deacon, seminarian, 1980-83; St Elizabeth Parish, San Francisco, assoc pastor, 1983-85; Sacred Heart Parish, San Francisco, pastor, 1985-2000; St Vincent de Paul Church, San Francisco, Calif, pastor, 2000-. **Orgs:** Bd mem & pres, Archdiocese San Francisco Black Cath Apostolate Affairs, 1979-; former bd mem, Nat Black Cath Clergy Caucus, 1980-; counr, Archdiocese San Francisco Priests Coun, 1985-88; regent, St Ignatius High Sch, 1986-89; bd mem, Nat Fedn Priests Coun, 1988-; bd mem, Cath Charities San Francisco, 1988-92; bd mem, St Isabella Sch; regent mem, Marin Cath High Sch. **Special Achievements:** Rep to Int Federation of Priests Council, Ghana, 1988. **Business Addr:** Pastor, St Vincent de Paul Church, 2320 Green St, San Francisco, CA 94123, **Business Phone:** (415)922-1010.

### WETHERS, DR. DORIS LOUISE

Physician. **Personal:** Born Dec 14, 1927, Passaic, NJ; daughter of William A and Lilian Wilkinson; married Garvall H Booker; children: Garvall H Booker III, Clifford Booker & David Boyd. **Educ:** Queens Col, NY, BS, magna cum laude, 1948; Yale Univ, Sch Med, MD, 1952. **Career:** New York Presby Med Ctr, attend pediatrician, 1956-2000; St Luke's-Roosevelt Hosp Ctr, dir pediat, 1973-79, attend pediatrician, 1973, founder & dir, comprehensive Sickle Cell prog, 1978-2000; Columbia Univ Col Physicians & Surgeons, prof clin pediat, 1987-2000, spec lectr, currently. **Orgs:** Am Pediat Soc; fel Am Acad Pediat; NY County & State Med Socs; Susan Smith McKinney Steward Med Soc; Am Soc Pediat Hemat & Oncol; chair, NIH Consensus Develop Conf, Screening Sickle Cell Dis, 1987; adv coun, Nat Heart, Lung, & Blood Inst, 1991-94; med adv bd, Sickle Cell dis Asn Am, 1999-. **Honors/Awds:** Preceptor of the Year, NYC Health Res Training Prog, 1991; Recognition Award, Southern Regional Sickle Cell Asn, 1993; Community Service Award, St Luke's-Roosevelt Hosp Ctr, 1993; Recognition Award, Hearbeats Jamaica Inc, 1995; Lifetime Achievement Award, Manhattan Cent Med Soc, 1999; Honorary Doctor of Science Degree, Queens Col, 1999. **Special Achievements:** Introduction to the Sickle Cell Trait Conference, 11th Nat Neonatal Screening Symposium, Corpus Christi TX, 1995; Newborn Screening for Sickle Cell Disease, 2nd International African Symposium on Sickle Cell Disease, 1995; Missed Diagnosis of S Korle-bu in Prenatal Diagnosis and Newborn Screening, 16th Annual Mtg of the Nat Sickle Cell Disease Prog in Mobile, Alabama, 1991; numerous other publications in professional journals and contributions to medical texts; First African American appointed to head a New York City voluntary hospital department. **Home Addr:** 1201 Cabrini Blvd Apt Suite 57, New York, NY 10033, **Home Phone:** (212)928-2600. **Business Addr:** Director, Columbia University College of Physicians & Surgeons, 630 W 168th St P&S 3-401, New York, NY 10032, **Business Phone:** (212)305-3806.

## WHACK, RITA COBURN

Novelist, television producer. **Personal:** Born Jun 13, 1958, Harvey, IL; daughter of Charles G and Willie E; married Harold Lee; children: Christine & Harold Jr. **Educ:** Ill State Univ, attended 1976; Columbra Col, Chicago, IL, attended 1977; Northwestern Univ, BA, commun, 1980. **Career:** WBBM & WTTW, Chicago, doc producer, 1995-01; WYCC, Chicago, producer, currently; Chicago Pub Radio, WBEZ-FM, contribr; Author: Two Women and a Little Oliver Oil, 1997; Meant to Be, 2002. **Orgs:** Founding mem prayer ministry, New Faith Baptist Church, 1998-2002, youth ministry adult leader, 2000-03; Nat Asn Black Journalists, 2002-03. **Honors/Awds:** Emmy Award, African Soil, Afr Am Agr, 1995-96; Emmy Award, Remembering 47th Street, 2000-01. **Home Addr:** 1413 Heather Hill Crescent, PO Box 607, Flossmoor, IL 60422-1770, **Home Phone:** (708)957-9250. **Business Addr:** Contributor, Chicago Public Radio, 848 E Grand Ave, Chicago, IL 60611, **Business Phone:** (312)948-4600.

## WHALEY, BO. See WHALEY, EDWARD I.

## WHALEY, CHARLES H.

Executive. **Personal:** Born Jan 15, 1958, Elmhurst, NY; son of Charles III and Edna; married Jeanette Smith. **Educ:** Queensborough Community Col, AAS, 1979. **Career:** Gen Tel & Electronics, test engr, 1979-81; Gen Dynamics Communs Co, opers engr, 1981-83; United Technols Communs Co, proj mgr, 1983-86; Telex Comput Prod, proj mgr, 1986; Pertel Communs Corp, pres, 1986-91; Pertel Commun New Eng Inc, owner, pres, 1990-. **Orgs:** Minority bus roundtable, Hartford Chamber Com, 1990-91; bd dir, New York High Sch Telecommunications, 1991-; Minority Input Comt, Conn Minority Supplier Develop Coun. **Home Addr:** 867 Smith St, Uniondale, NY 11553, **Home Phone:** (516)565-4025. **Business Addr:** President, Pertel Communications of New England Inc, 750 Main St Suite 506, Hartford, CT 06103, **Business Phone:** (860)293-0019.

## WHALEY, EDWARD I. (BO WHALEY)

College administrator, counselor. **Educ:** State Univ NY Col, Oneonta, BS. **Career:** Educator (retired); State Univ NY, SUNY Col Oneonta, alumni prog coordr & counr. **Business Addr:** Counselor, SUNY College at Oneonta, 108 Ravine Pkwy, Oneonta, NY 13820, **Business Phone:** (607)436-3500.

## WHALEY, MARY H.

Chief executive officer, school administrator. **Personal:** Born Jan 1, 1937, Clarksville, TN; daughter of Adolphus David Harrison and Sadie Beatrice Allen Harrison; children: Brian Cedric & Kevin Allen. **Educ:** Fisk Univ, AB, 1959; Univ Tenn, Sch Social Work, MSW, 1968; Univ Tenn, Knoxville, TN, EdD, 1990. **Career:** Tenn Dept Human Serv, caseworker, 1961-63, casework supvr, 1966-72, staff consult E Tenn, 1972-74; Knoxville Col, vis instr, 1971-73, assoc dean students, 1974-78; Univ Tenn, prof asst, 1978; Knoxville Col, Morristown, Tenn, assoc acad dean, 1989-90; Knoxville Col, Knoxville, Tenn, head, Div Bus & Social Sci, asst acad dean, assoc prof, 1990; Dynamic Connections Inc, chief exec officer, currently. **Orgs:** Chmn, Various community Nat Asn Social Workers, 1968; chmn, various community Asn Black Social Workers, 1972; bd dir, Phyllis Wheatley, 1972-74; Community Improv Found Bd, 1972-74; bd dir, Planned Parenthood, 1973-77; UTSSW com Minority Admis & Retention, 1974-76; League Women Voters, 1976; bd dir, Helen Ross McNabb, 1977; bd dir, Tenn NASW Chap, 1985; Friends Black C, 1985; deacon, 1987-90, elder, 1990, Moderator Women's Asn First United Presbyterian Church, 1986; Community Youth Mentoring, 1989; Friends Black C State Adv comt & local affiliate; Social Serv Panel, Tenn Black Legis Caucus; adv comt Child & Family Serv; bd mem, Nat Resource Ctr Family Based Serv, Univ Iowa; Bijou Lime lighters; nominating community Girl Scout Coun; RAM House Bd; chairperson panel, United Way Greater Knoxville, 1990; laura Counr Br, 1991, prog chair, 1992-93, bd dir, Boys & Girls Club; Comnr-Presbytery E Tenn, 1993; Dynamic Connections, 1999-; Fourth United Presbyterian Church. **Home Addr:** 2449 Brooks Rd, Knoxville, TN 37914, **Home Phone:** (865)524-4680.

## WHALEY, WAYNE EDWARD

Educator. **Personal:** Born Oct 23, 1949, Lincoln, DE; married Janice Evans; children: Sean E & Dane M. **Educ:** Del State Col, BS, 1971; Univ Del, MA, 1977. **Career:** Red Clay Sch Dist, asst prin, 1978-86; Smyrna Sch Dist, teacher, 1971-75, asst prin, 1978-86, teacher, 1986-; Wilmington High Sch, assoc prin. **Orgs:** YMCA; Del Spec Olympics; Del Except C Coun, 1985; bd pres, Centennial United Methodist Church, 1985; Nat Assoc Equal Opportunity Higher Educ, 1986; bd mem, Wilmington Lions Club, 1986; Nat Sch Curric Asn, 1986. **Home Addr:** 3892 E Ravenswood Dr, Gilbert, AZ 85298-9135. **Business Addr:** Instructor, Smyrna School District, 82 Monrovia Ave, Smyrna, DE 19977, **Business Phone:** (302)653-8585.

## WHALUM, KIRK

Musician. **Personal:** Born Jul 11, 1958, Memphis, TN; married Ruby styne; children: 4. **Educ:** Tex Southern Univ, saxophone. **Career:** Saxophonist, 1985-; Albums: Floppy Disk, 1985; And You Know That!, 1988; The Promise, 1989; Cache, 1993; In This Life, 1995; Joined at the Hip, 1996; Colors, 1997; Gospel According to Jazz? Chapter 1, 1998; For You, 1998; Joy, 1999; Hymns In The Garden, 2000; Unconditional, 2001; The Christmas Message, 2001; BWB - Groovin', 2002; The Best of Kirk Whalum, 2002; Gospel According to Jazz: Chapter 2, 2002; Into My Soul, 2003; Kirk Whalum Performs the Baby Face Songbook, 2005; Ultimate Kirk Whalum, 2007; Round Trip, 2007, Promises Made: The Millennium Promise Jazz Project, 2008; Everything Is Everything: The Music of Donny Hathaway, 2010; The Gospel According To Jazz Chapter III, 2010; Romance Language, 2011; The Gospel According to Jazz Chapter IV, 2014. TV series: "Jean Michel Jarre Rendezvous Houston: A City in Concert", 1986; Film: The Prince of Tides, actor, 1991. **Orgs:** Boys & Girls Club; Houston Leukemia/Lymphoma Soc. **Honors/Awds:** Eight Grammy Nominations & 2 Stellar Awards; Grammy award, 2011. **Business Addr:** Saxophonist, c/o Variety Artists International, 793 Higuera St Suite 6, San Luis Obispo, CA 93401, **Business Phone:** (805)545-5550.

## WHARTON, A. C., JR.

Educator, lawyer, mayor. **Personal:** Born Aug 17, 1944, Lebanon, TN; married Ruby; children: 6. **Educ:** TSU, BA, polit sci, 1962; Univ Miss, JD, 1971. **Career:** EEOC, decision drafter, 1967-68; trial atty, 1971-73; Lawyers Comt Civil Rights Under Law, proj dir, 1973; Univ MS, adj prof; Shelby County TN, chief pub defender, 1980; Pvt Pract, Wharton & Wharton; Equal Employ Opportunity Comn, investr; Shelby County, mayor, 2002-09; Tenn, Memphis, mayor, 2009, 2012-. **Orgs:** Past exec dir, Memphis Area Leagul Serv Inc; Am Bar Asn; Nat Legal Aid & Defender Asn; Nat Bar Asn; TN Bar Asn; Nat Asn Advan Colored People; pres, Leadership Memphis Alumni Asn, 1979; Oper PUSH; Urban League; Alpha Phi Alpha. **Home Addr:** 1183 E Pkwy S, Memphis, TN 38114-6726, **Home Phone:** (901)726-6884. **Business Addr:** Mayor, City of Memphis, 65 Union Ave Suite 840, Memphis, TN 38103, **Business Phone:** (901)278-0881.

## WHARTON, DR. CLIFTON REGINALD, JR.

Association executive, executive. **Personal:** Born Sep 13, 1926, Boston, MA; son of Clifton R Sr and Harriette Banks; married Dolores Duncan; children: Clifton III (deceased) & Bruce. **Educ:** Harvard Univ, BA, hist, 1947; Johns Hopkins Univ, MA, int affairs, 1948; Univ Chicago, MA, econs, 1956, PhD, econs, 1958. **Career:** Am Int Asn Econ & Social Develop, exec trainee, 1948-49, prog analyst, 1949-51, head reports & anal dept, 1951-53; Univ Chicago, res assoc, 1953-57; Agr Develop Coun Inc, 1957-69; Agr Develop Coun Assoc, Southeast Asia, 1958-64; Univ Malaya, vis prof econs; Stanford Univ, prof econs, 1964-65; Agr Develop Coun Am Univ Res Prog, dir, 1964-66, actg dir coun, 1966-67, vpres, 1966-70; Mich State Univ, pres & prof econs, 1970-78; State Univ New York (Syst), chancellor, 1978-87; Comn World Hunger, 1978-80; TeachersIns & Annuity Asn & Col Retirement Equities Fund, chmn & chief exec officer, 1987-93; Dept State, Dep Sec State, 1993; Knight Found Comn, vice chmn, 2005; Knight Found Comn, co-chmn, 2006-; dir, Burroughs Corp; dir, Equitable Life Assurance Soc; dir, Fed Res Bank New York; dir, Federated Dept Stores; dir, Ford Motor Co; dir, Harcourt Gen; dir, NY Stock Exchange; Agr Develop Coun, economist & vpres; dir, Gannett Co Inc; dir, Kellogg Co; dir, Phillips Petrol Co; dir, Nat Pub Radio; dir, COMSAT; dir, Mich Bell; dir, NY Tel Co; dir, Capital Bank & Trust Co. **Orgs:** Bd overseers, Teachers Ins & Annuity Asn; bd mem, Tenneco; Time Inc; trustee, Ctr Strategic & Int Studies; trustee, Glimmer glass Opera; trustee, City Ctr; co chmn, Comn Security & Econ Assistance; chmn, Bd Int Food & Agr Develop, 1976-83; trustee, Am Assembly; bd mem, Time Warner; trustee, Aspen Inst; trustee, Asia Soc; trustee, Coun Foreign Rels; trustee, Rockefeller Found; trustee, Mus Mod Art. **Honors/Awds:** Awarded sixty one honorary degrees from various universities in US; Man of the Year, Boston Latin Sch, 1970; Amistad Award, Am Missionary Asn, 1970; Joseph E Wilson Award, 1977; Alumni Medal, Univ Chicago, 1980; Samuel Z Wester field Award, Nat Econ Asn, 1985; Benjamin E Mays Award, Boston Black Achievers, YMCA, 1986; Black History Makers Award, New York Asniated Black Charities, 1987; Frederick Douglass Award, NY Urban League, 1989; Rockefeller Public Service Award, 1993; Africare Legacy Award, 2005. **Special Achievements:** First African American Chairman & CEO of Fortune 500 company, TIAA-CREF, 1987; Named first African American chancellor of the State Univ of New York; First African American chairman Rockefeller Found; First Black admitted Johns Hopkins Univ Sch Adv Int Studies; First African American president of Michigan State University.

## WHARTON, DOLORES D.

Association executive. **Personal:** Born Jul 3, 1927, New York, NY; daughter of V Kenneth Duncan and Josephine Bradford Owens; married Clifton R Wharton Jr; children: Clifton III & Bruce. **Educ:** Chicago State Univ, BA, fine arts. **Career:** Phillips Petrol Co, bd mem; Kellogg Co, dir; Gannett Co, dir; Fund Corp Initiatives Inc, chief exec officer, chmn; Tulane Univ, bd vis. **Orgs:** Nat Coun Arts Nat Endowment Arts, 1974-80; China Med Bd, 1977-81; trustee, Mus Mod Art, 1977-87; dir, Albany Inst Hist & Art, 1977-87; Asia Soc, 1982-87; trustee, Mass Inst Tech, 1987-94; Albany Law Sch; bd mem, Nat Pub Radio; bd mem, Mich Bell Tel Co; bd dir, New York Tel Co; bd dir, Mich Nat Bank; bd dir, Key Bank, Albany; bd dir, Bank & Trust Co, Albany; trustee emer, Ctr Strategic & Int Studies; COMSAT Corp; trustee, New York Ctr; bd mem, Capital Bank & Trust Co; Ethics Resource Ctr; Aspen Inst; Fashion Inst Technol (SUNY); Women's Econ Round Table; Duke Ellington Memorial Fund Inc. **Honors/Awds:** Received hon degree from various univ. **Special Achievements:** Mrs. Wharton was elected the first woman and first black to the board of the Phillips Petroleum Company; author of "Contemporary Artists of Malaysia: A Biographic Survey"; First lady Mich State Univ, 1969. **Business Addr:** Trustee Emeritus, Center for Strategic and International Studies, 1800 K St NW, Washington, DC 20006, **Business Phone:** (202)887-0200.

## WHARTON, HON. MILTON S.

Judge. **Personal:** Born Sep 20, 1946, St. Louis, MO. **Educ:** Southern Ill Univ, Edwardsville, BS, 1969; DePaul Univ, Sch Law, JD, 1975. **Career:** St Clair Co Pub Defender, chief judge, atty, Ill Judiciary, judge, 1976, circuit judge, currently; 20th Judicial Circuit Ill, circuit judge, 1988; pvt pract atty, currently. **Orgs:** Vice chmn, Ill St Bar Asn, Standing Comt Juv Justice; vice chmn, St Louis Bi-state Chap, Am Red Cross; bd mem, YMCA S Ill; bd mem, St Marys Hosp, E St Louis; bd mem, Higher Educ Ctr St Louis; life mem, St Clair Co Bar Asn, pres, 2002-03; pres, SIUE Found Bd Dir. **Honors/Awds:** Alumnus of the Year, Southern Ill Univ, Edwardsville, 1977; Man of Year, Nat Coun Negro Women, E St Louis, 1982; Man Of Year, S Dist Ill Asn Club Women, 1982; District Service Award, Belleville Jaycees, 1983; Civic Service Award, Phi Beta Sigma-Zeta Phi Beta, 1985; Citizen of the Year Award, Omega Psi Phi Fraternity Inc, 2003; North Central Province Humanitarian Award, St Clair Co Bar Asn, 2003; Kimmel Community Service Award, St Clair Co Bar Asn; Martin Luther King Humanitarian Award; Whitney E. Young; Jr. Service Award of the Boy Scouts of America; Pro Ecclesia Et Pontifice, late Pope John Paul II. **Special Achievements:** named a "Legend in the Legal Community" by the St. Louis Argus Newspaper; named the SIUE Distinguished Alumnus of the Year, 1998. **Business Addr:** Circuit Judge, St Clair County Court, Suite 10 Pub Sq, Belleville, IL 62220, **Business Phone:** (618)398-0612.

## WHATLEY, ENNIS

Clergy, basketball player. **Personal:** Born Aug 11, 1962, Birmingham, AL; married Ritza. **Educ:** Univ Ala, attended 1983. **Career:** Basketball player (retired), clergy; Univ Ala, 1981-83; Chicago Bulls, 1983-85; Cleveland Cavaliers, 1986; Wash Bullets, 1986, 1987; San Antonio Spurs, 1986; Atlanta Hawks, 1988; Los Angeles Clippers, 1989; Wichita Falls Texans CBA, 1990; Portland Trail Blazers, 1991-92 & 1996-97; Israel DVAT, 1992-93; Atlanta Hawks, 1994-95; Kids in His Christian Daycare, minister, 1996-97; Lithuania Kalgiris Team, 1997-98; pastor, currently. **Orgs:** Pres & co-founder, Christian Outreach Orgn; Sapphire Ministries; founder, Ennis Whatley Enterprises; Philippine Basketball Asn, 1989. **Home Addr:** 42 Brinkwood Rd, Brookeville, MD 20833-2303, **Home Phone:** (301)260-1267. **Business Addr:** Founder, Ennis Whatley Enterprises, 9705 Wash Blvd N, Laurel, MD 20723, **Business Phone:** (301)604-9293.

## WHEAT, HON. ALAN DUPREE

Government official, consultant. **Personal:** Born Oct 16, 1951, San Antonio, TX; son of James and Jean; married Yolanda Townsend; children: Alynda, Christopher & Nicholas. **Educ:** Grinnell Col, BA, econs, 1972. **Career:** HUD Kans City, Mo, economist, 1972-73; Mid-Am Reg Coun, Kans City, econ, 1973-75; Co Exec Off KC, aide, 1975-76; Miss House Reps Jefferson City, rep, 1977-82; Cong 5th Dist, Mo, congressman, 1983-95; CARE Found, vpres pub policy & govt rels, 1995-97, bd dir, 2006-; SmithKline Beecham, vpres Fed Rels, 1996; Clinton 96 Campaign, dep campaign mgr, 1996; Wheat Govt Rels Inc, pres, founded, 1998-; Mo State Off Legis Aide to County Exec. **Orgs:** Rules Comt, Select Comn C Youth & Families; chmn, Sub comt Govt Opers & Metro Affairs Comn Dist Columbia; Select Comt Hunger, US House Reps, beginning 1990; comnr, Martin Luther King Jr, Fed Holiday Comn, beginning 1989; pres, Cong Black Caucus Found, beginning 1990; bd dir, CARE, currently; Dem Cong Campaign Comt. **Special Achievements:** Nation's First African-Americans to represent a district with a majority white population. **Business Addr:** President, Wheat Government Relations Inc, 1201 S Eads St Suite 2, Arlington, VA 22202, **Business Phone:** (703)271-8770.

## WHEAT, DEJUAN SHONTEZ

Basketball player. **Personal:** Born Oct 14, 1973, Louisville, KY. **Educ:** Univ Louisville, BA, sociol, 1997. **Career:** Basketball player (retired); Minn Timberwolves, guard, 1997-98; Los Angeles Lakers, 1997-98; Vancouver Grizzlies, free agt, 1998-2000; Idaho Stampede, 1999-2000; Panteras de Miranda, Venezuela, 2001-02; Buffalo City Thunder, 2002-03; Juarez Gallos de Pelea, Mex, 2003-04; Calgary Drillers, 2004-05; Soles de Mexicali, Mex, 2005-10.

## WHEAT, JAMES WELDON, JR.

Executive. **Personal:** Born Mar 16, 1948, Tuskegee, AL; son of James Weldon and Emogene Dupree; married Panchit Charanachit; children: Saranya J & Annalai B. **Educ:** Grinnell Col, Grinnell, Iowa, BA, 1969; Cornell Univ, Ithaca, NY, MBA, 1971; Univ Chicago, cert, advan mgt, 1982. **Career:** Bankers Trust Co, New York, NY, vpres, 1973-84; Corning Inc, asst treas; Corning Int Corp, treas, vpres & chief financial officer. **Orgs:** Soc Black Professionals, 1986-. **Home Addr:** 2868 Chequers Cir, Big Flats, NY 14814, **Home Phone:** (607)562-3468.

## WHEATLEY, TYRONE ANTHONY, SR.

Football player, football coach. **Personal:** Born Jan 19, 1972, Inkster, MI; married Kimberly; children: 5. **Educ:** Univ Mich, BS, kinesiology, 2005. **Career:** Football player (retired), football coach; New York Giants, running back, 1995-98; Miami Dolphins, 1998-99; Oakland Raiders, running back, 1999-2004; Tampa Bay Buccaneers, coaching intern, 2005; Univ Mich, Mich Wolverines, track coach, 2005-06; Dearborn Heights Robichaud High Sch, head football & track coach, 2006-07; John Fontes, asst coach, 2008; Ohio Northern Univ, running back coach, 2008; Eastern Mich Univ, asst coach, running back coach, 2009; Syracuse Orange, running backs coach, 2010-12; Buffalo Bills, running backs coach, 2013-14; Univ Mich, running back coach, 2015-. **Orgs:** Minority Fel Internship Prog, Nat Footbll League. **Honors/Awds:** MHSAA state champion, Mich High Sch Athletic Asn, 1990; Big Ten Offensive Player of the Year Award, 1992; Big Ten rushing champion, 1992; Big Ten scoring champion, 1992, 1993; Rose Bowl Player of the Game, 1993; Most Valuable Player, 1993; Michigan Sports Hall of Fame, 2012; Big Ten high hurdle champion. **Special Achievements:** First round, 17th overall NFL draft pick, 1995. **Business Addr:** Running Backs Coach, University of Michigan, 500 S State St, Ann Arbor, MI 48109.

## WHEATON, ESQ. FRANK KAHLIL

Movie producer, lawyer. **Personal:** Born Sep 27, 1951, Los Angeles, CA; son of James Lorenzo and Helen Ruth Alford; married Robin Louise Green; married Jean Carn; children: Jean, Joseph, Maryam, Marissko & Summer; married Jennifer Jones. **Educ:** Willamette Univ, attended 1971; CA State Univ, Northridge, BA, radio/tv & film, 1973; Univ W Los Angeles Sch Law, JD, 1986. **Career:** WHUR-FM, broadcast announcer, eng, producer, 1973-74; NBC, broadcast eng, 1975-78; freelance TV actor & producer, 1975-; 300 TV Coms Nat Employers Coun, legal rep, 1984; Mgt Group, chmn, 1984-; Law Offices Frank K. Wheaton, owner, chief exec officer, 1987-; Global Entertainment Properties LLC, atty bus consult, 1987-; Michael Jordan & UNCF Celebrity Golf Classic, creator & exec producer, 1988-89; Law Offices Bicker staff & McNair, off coun, 1993-; City Compton, off spokesperson, 1999-2001; James Worthy All-Star Basketball Clin, creator & exec producer, 1991-; Milton Berle Celebrity Golf Classic, producer, 1990-91; Films: Hair, 1979; The Seduction of Joe Tynan, 1979; Hammerlock, 2000. TV series: "The Greatest American Hero", 1983; "Flight 90: Disaster on the Potomac", 1984; "Dynasty", 1986; "Matlock", 1986-91. Producer: "World's Fastest Athlete", ABC, 1990-91; "Sports Greats: One On One with David Hartman", ESPN, 1994; Madans & Wheaton, partner, 2009-; Management Group, founder; Direct Selling Live, chief financial officer; Veterans Broadcasting Co, chief exec officer, currently; UWLA, Sch Law, adj fac mem, currently; Scolinos, Sheldon & Nevell, coun mem, currently. **Orgs:** Bd mem, Black Entertainment & Sports Lawyers Asn, 1993-; bd mem, Big Bros Greater Los Angeles, 1994-; bd mem, 28th St & Crenshaw, YMCA, 1994-; bd mem, Markham Theatre Proj, 1994-; Sports Lawyers Asn; Am Bar Asn; Nat Basketball Players Asn; Screen Actors Guild; Moot Ct Bd Gov; vpres, Sports Entertainment Law Soc; Ind State Bar; dean, Delta Theta Phi Law Soc; US Ct Appeals, Fifth Circuit. **Honors/Awds:** City of Compton, CA, Mayoral Resolution, 1986, Mayoral Proclamation, 1992. **Home Addr:** 225 S Lake Ave Suite 300, Pasadena, CA 91101, **Home Phone:** (310)505-3524. **Business Addr:** Owner, Chief Executive Officer, The Law Offices of Frank K Wheaton Esq, 201 N Ill St S Tower 16th Fl, Indianapolis, IN 46204, **Business Phone:** (317)610-3455.

**WHEATON, KENNY TYRON**
Football player. **Personal:** Born Mar 8, 1975, Phoenix, AZ; married Franchell; children: Kendall. **Educ:** Univ Ore, grad. **Career:** Football player (retired); Dallas Cowboys, defensive back & corner back & safety, 1997-99; Detroit Fury, 2002; Toronto Argonauts, defensive back, 2003-09. **Honors/Awds:** CFL All-Star, 2007; Oregon University Athletics Hall of Fame, 2011.

**WHEATON, WENDY E.**
Chief executive officer, radio host. **Personal:** Born May 5, 1965, Boston, MA; daughter of Ronald and Ruth. **Educ:** Emerson Col, BA, jour, 1988; Univ Calif, Los Angeles, grad cert, bus mgt & entrepreneurship, 1999. **Career:** WHSH-TV, news anchor, 1989; WHLL-TV, news anchor; Investigative Group Int, mkt dir; Extra, tv producer; var nat tv shows, commentator; Wheaton Entertainment Inc, agt, exec producer, pres & chief exec officer, currently; Hollywood Scoop, reporter, producer & host; Independent Pub Rels, Mkt, TV develop, 2008; R&B Radio Sta, entertainment reporter; film agt, exec producer; half hour music prog, exec producer. **Orgs:** Nat Asn Tv Prog Exec; Nat Asn Women Bus Owners. **Business Addr:** Chief Executive Officer, President, Wheaton Entertainment Inc, 330 N Screenland Dr, Burbank, CA 91505, **Business Phone:** (818)842-5011.

**WHEELAN, BELLE SMITH**
School administrator, educator. **Personal:** Born Oct 10, 1951, Chicago, IL; daughter of Frank (deceased) and Adelia (deceased); children: Reginald. **Educ:** Trinity Univ, BA, psychol & sociol, 1972; La State Univ, MA, develop educ psychol, 1974; Univ Tex, Austin, PhD, educ admin, 1984. **Career:** San Antonio Col, assoc prof psychol, 1974-84, dir develop educ, 1984-86, dir acad support serv, 1986-87; Thomas Nelson Community Col, dean stud serv, 1987-89; Tidewater Community Col, Portsmouth Campus, provost, 1989-91; Community Col, Portsmouth Campus, 1989-91; Cent VA Community Col, pres, 1992-98; Northern Va Community Col, pres, 1998-2001; Va Gov, commonwealth va, secy educ, 2002-05; Southern Asn Cols & Schs Comn Cols, pres, 2005-. **Orgs:** Aka Sorority Inc, 1969-; Am Asn Women Comm & Jr Cols, 1983-91; pres, Tex Asn Develop Educr, 1987; Portsmouth Col, 1990-91; Portsmouth Sch Bd, 1991; Ideal Develop Authority Lynchburg, 1992-; Lynchburg Rotary Club, 1992-, preselect, 1995, pres, 1996; Lynchburg Chamber Com Bd, 1993-97; Cent Health Bd, 1993-95; Nat Conf Christians & Jews, 1993-95; pres, YWCA Lynchburg, 1993-95; Rotary Int; Alpha Kappa Alpha Sorority Inc; Am Col Testing Inc; bd dir, Am Asn Community Cols; bd dir, Lumina Found Educ; pres, Nat Coun Black Am Affairs; pres, Cent Va Community Col; bd mem, Excelencia Educ, 2012. **Special Achievements:** First African American woman to serve as president of a two or four year public institution of higher education in the Commonwealth of Virginia. **Home Addr:** 917 Rothowood Rd, Lynchburg, VA 24503. **Business Addr:** President, The Southern Association of Colleges & Schools Commission on Colleges, 1866 S Lane, Decatur, GA 30033, **Business Phone:** (404)679-4500.

**WHEELER, BEVERLY**
College administrator. **Personal:** Born Palestine, TX; daughter of Ruth Henry. **Educ:** Univ Tex, BA, social work; Southwest Tex State Univ, MA, adult & develop educ. **Career:** Southwestern Univ, admis counr, assoc dir admis, 1996; Tex Asn Col Admis Coun, pres, 2001; Nat Asn Col Admis Coun, pres; Univ Tulsa, regional dir admis, 2003-. **Orgs:** Pres, Tex Asn Admis Coun; bd mem & pres, Nat Asn Col Admis Coun. **Business Addr:** Regional Director of Admission, University of Tulsa, Collins Hall, Tulsa, OK 74104, **Business Phone:** (918)631-2307.

**WHEELER, CHESTER A.**
Executive director. **Career:** City Macon, Dept Econ & Community Develop, dir, proj mgr, currently. **Business Addr:** Director, City of Macon, 200 Cherry St Suite 300, Macon, GA 31201, **Business Phone:** (478)751-7190.

**WHEELER, HEASTER**
Executive director. **Personal:** married Jennifer; children: Khari, Jeneva & Jeremiah. **Educ:** Wayne County Community Col, assoc degree, gen studies; Clark Atlanta Univ; Wayne State Univ, dipl, col prep, 1973. **Career:** City Detroit Fire Dept, firefighter, 1977-90; State Rep Carolyn Kilpatrick, legis asst; State Govt Affairs Ameritech, mgr & dep dir; Detroit Pub Schs, Off Govt Rels, lobbyist, 1999; Mich House Reps, Curtis Hertel, dep dir commun; Detroit Alliance Fair Banking, chmn, 2005-. **Orgs:** Dept Community Rels Speakers Bur; pres, Phoenix; co-convener, Mich Legis Black Caucus Summit; All Kids First, 2000; Fel Chapel Church; Univ Dist Community Asn; Booker T Wash Bus Asn; Advocates & Leaders Police & Community Trust; Citizens Alliance Prisons & Pub Safety; Mich Land Use Leadership Coun; exec dir, Nat Asn Advan Colored People Detroit Br, 1999-; co chmn, One United Mich; Cub Scouts; Detroit Hist Dist Commision. **Business Addr:** Executive Director, Detroit Branch NAACP, 8220 2nd Ave, Detroit, MI 48202, **Business Phone:** (313)871-2087.

**WHEELER, LEONARD TYRONE**
**Personal:** Born Jan 15, 1969, Taccoa, GA; married Chandra E; children: Lindsey. **Educ:** Troy State Univ, BS, bus admin. **Career:** Football player (retired), President; Cincinnati Bengals, defensive back, 1992-96; Minn Vikings, 1997; Carolina Panthers, 1998-2001; Athletes Health Inc, founder; Christian Athletes, fel; Savior Faire mag, columnist; Wheelers Enterprises Inc, founder, 2001. **Orgs:** Christian Athletes United Spiritual Empowerment; former pres & mem, Nat Football League Players Asn, 2008-; bd mem, 2XSalt ministriesCharlotte, NC; Nat Speaker, NFL Play 60; Nat speaker, Nat Col Scouting Asn; bd dir, Youth Comn Int. **Honors/Awds:** Hall of Fame, David Thompson and Bobby Jones. **Home Addr:** 10300 Otterdale Ct, Charlotte, NC 28277, **Home Phone:** (704)540-9860. **Business Addr:** Founder, President, Wheeler Enterprises Inc, 10300 Otterdale Court, Charlotte, NC 28277, **Business Phone:** (704)543-0559.

**WHEELER, MARK ANTHONY**
Football player. **Personal:** Born Apr 1, 1970, San Marcos, TX; son of Peggy Burleson; married Diona; children: Devin. **Educ:** Tex A&M Univ, grad. **Career:** Football player (retired); Tampa Bay Buccaneers, left defensive tackle, 1992-95; New England Patriots, left defensive tackle, 1996-97, Defensive tackle, 1998; Philadelphia Eagles, 1999. **Honors/Awds:** Athletics Hall of Fame, 1993. **Special Achievements:** Films: 1992 NFL Draft, 1992; 1996 AFC Championship Game, 1997; Super Bowl XXXI, 1997. **Home Addr:** , San Marcos, TX.

**WHEELER, DR. MAURICE B.**
Librarian. **Educ:** Shorter Col, BMus, 1980; Univ Mich, MMus, 1982, MILS, 1987; Univ Pittsburgh, PhD, libr sci, 1994. **Career:** Detroit Pub Libr, cur, 1987-90; Univ Mich Libr, staff develop & recruitment officer, 1990-93, asst dean, 1993-95; Detroit Pub Libr, dep dir, 1995-96, dir, 1996-2002; Univ Mich, Sch Info, guest lectr, 1998-2002; Wayne State Univ, Dept Libr Sci, vis fac, 1999; Univ N Tex, Dept Libr & Info Sci, assoc prof, 2002-, chair, 2008-09; Int J Humanities, assoc ed, 2004-; Int J Diversity, assoc ed, 2004-; Univ Ri, Sch Libr & Info Studies, vis fac, 2007. **Orgs:** Am Libr Asn, 1987-; bd dir, exec search comt, Friends Detroit Pub Libr; vchmn, bd dir, Detroit Area Libr Network; group facilitator & mentor, Snowbird Leadership Inst, 1998-2000; Humanities Ctr, steering comt, Wayne State Univ; bd dir, human resources comn, Literacy Vols Am; adv bd, Urban Libr J, 1999-; ed bd, J Bibliog Instr Electronic Resources, 1998-2002; ALA Council, 1998-2002; Press Events Comt, 1998; Black Caucus, ALA Rels Comt, 1987-2001; Libr Res Sem II, Res Inst Planning Comt, 1998-2001; bd dir, Univ Cult Ctr Asn, 1996-2002; bd dir, Literacy Vols Am, Human Resources Comt, 1998-2002; Urban Libr Coun, 2000-02; chair, Spectrum Scholar Jury, 2001-02 & 2007; Sch Libr & Info Sci Comt Comt, 2002-03; Stud Affairs Comt, 2002-03; Diversity Adv Rep, 2002-06; Tocker Found Comt, 2002-06; Curric Comt, 2002-03; Univ N Tex, 2002-; Personnel Affairs Comt, 2002-03 & 2005-08; comt chair, Orientation, Training, & Leadership Develop, 2003-04; Fedn N Tex Area Univs, 2003-05; Diversity Comt, 2004-07; Learning Technologies Dean's Cabinet; External Rels Comt, col info, 2008-09; Athletic Council, 2006-09. **Honors/Awds:** Scholastic Merit Fellowship, Univ Mich, Sch Music, 1980; Scholastic Merit Fellowship, Univ Mich, Rackham Grad Sch, 1986; Outstanding Young Men of America, 1988; Academic Fellowship, University of Pittsburgh, Sch Info Sci, 1993; Leadership Detroit, Detroit Regional Chamber Com, Detroit, Mich, 2000; Diversity Award, Univ Mich Libr, 2001. **Special Achievements:** Numerous publ. **Home Addr:** PO Box 2858, Detroit, MI 48202, **Home Phone:** (313)962-8079. **Business Addr:** Associate Professor, University of North Texas, 1155 Union Circle, Denton, TX 76203-5017, **Business Phone:** (940)565-2445.

**WHEELER, PRIMUS, JR.**
Hospital administrator. **Personal:** Born Mar 3, 1950, Webb, MS; son of Primus Sr; married Earlene Jordan; children: Primus III & Niki. **Educ:** Tougaloo Col, BS, biol, 1972; Hinds Jr Col, AD, respiratory ther, 1977; Jackson State Univ, MST, educ & admin, 1982. **Career:** Univ Miss, Med Ctr, respiratory ther tech, 1975-77, respiratory therapist, 1977-78, instr respiratory ther, 1978-80, instr & clin coordr, respiratory ther, 1980-81, chmn, asst prof, respiratory ther, 1981-86; Apria Health Care, region vp, 1986-96; UMC, dir ambulatory servs, 1997-; Jackson Med Mall Found, pres, exec dir, 2001-. **Orgs:** Miss Soc Respiratory Therapists, 1978-; Am Asn Respiratory Ther, 1978-; advr, UMC Med Explorers Post 306, 1983-; Nat Soc Allied Health, 1984-; bd dir, Northwest Jackson YMCA, 1984-; Miss Hosp Asn; Phi Kappa Phi Nat Scholastic Hon Soc; Alpha Eta Nat Scholastic Hon Soc; bd trustee, Cade Chapel M. B. Church; Am Pub Health Asn. **Home Addr:** 132 Azalea Cir, Jackson, MS 39206-4401, **Home Phone:** (601)982-2818. **Business Addr:** Executive Director, Jackson Medical Mall, 1st Fl 350 W Woodrow Wilson Ave Suite 107, Jackson, MS 39213, **Business Phone:** (601)982-8467.

**WHEELER, ROBYN ELAINE**
Presidential aide, administrator. **Personal:** Born Dec 7, 1963, Brooklyn, NY; daughter of Raleigh and Muriel. **Educ:** Hunter Col, BA, media studies, 1988. **Career:** CNN-NY, field producer & assignment ed, 1988-95; NBC-Chicago, assignment ed, 1995-98; US Rep Bobby L Rush, communs dir, 1998-; Chicago State Univ, dir univ rels & dean, currently, commun dir. **Orgs:** Black Rels Soc Chicago; Coun Advan & Support Educ; Chicago Asn Black Journalists, 1995-; vpres mem, Black Pub Rels Soc Am, 2001-. **Honors/Awds:** Features Award, New York Association of Black Journalists, 1993; Unity Award, Univ Mo's Journalism Sch, 1994; Midwest Emmy Award, 1996; Outstanding Spot News Coverage, Chicago. **Home Addr:** 1617 E 50th Pl 14B, Chicago, IL 60615, **Home Phone:** (773)955-8675. **Business Addr:** Director of University Relations, Dean, Chicago State University, 95th St King Dr ADM 322, Chicago, IL 60628, **Business Phone:** (773)995-2387.

**WHEELER, SHIRLEY Y.**
Nurse, educator. **Personal:** Born Feb 14, 1935, Pittsburgh, PA; married Bennie J Jr; children: Teresa Marie & Bryan Joseph. **Educ:** Univ Pittsburgh, BSN, 1957, MNEd, 1965, MEd, 1968. **Career:** Magee Woman's Hosp Pittsburgh, staff nurse, 1957-58; Montefiore Hosp Pittsburgh, staff nurse, 1958-59; Lillian S Kaufmann Sch Nursing, instr & maternity nursing, 1959-60; Univ Pittsburgh Sch Nursing, instr maternity nursing, 1963-67, asst prof maternity nursing, 1967-72; Duquesne Univ Sch Nursing, assoc prof, 1972-. **Orgs:** Org Childbirth Ed, 1967; test writer, Maternity Nurse Cert Exam; Master's Degree Rep Nursing Aluminee Assoc; Univ Pittsburgh; moderator, Nurses Assoc, Am Col Obstetricians & Gynecologists Conf, 1974; Clin Specailist Maternity & Infant Care, 1963; Sigma Theta Tau Prof Nurses Hon Soc; Univ Pittsburgh Sch Nursing; Dept Maternity Nursing, Univ Pittsburgh Sch Nursing; Black Stud Nurses Univ Pittsburg; vpres, Univ Pittsburgh Nurses Alumni Asn, 1976, pres, 1977; Resolutions Com Pa Nurses Asn; Minority Recruitment, Univ Pittsburgh Sch Nursing; nurse, Am Youth Chorus Eurpoean Tour, 1977; chmn, Duquesne Univ, curric develop, 1986-88; Nurse Recruitment Coalition, 1988-91; vchmn, African Am Alumnae, Univ Pittsburgh, 1989-90; chmn, African Am Alumna, Univ Pittsburgh, 1990-91. **Honors/Awds:** Achievement Award for Teaching Friends of Braddock, 1990. **Home Addr:** 129 Mayberry Dr, Monroeville, PA 15146, **Home Phone:** (412)373-1777. **Business Addr:** Associate Professor of Nursing, Duquesne University School of Nursing, 5th Fl Fisher Hall, Pittsburgh, PA 15282, **Business Phone:** (412)396-6550.

**WHEELER, THEODORE STANLEY (TED WHEELER)**
Athletic coach. **Personal:** Born Jan 30, 1931, Chattanooga, TN; children: Theodore Jr, Mary Frances & James. **Educ:** Univ Iowa, BS, polit sci, 1957. **Career:** Athletic coach (retired); Univ Iowa, asst track coach, 1972, head track coach, 1978-96. **Honors/Awds:** Four Times Big Ten Champion; Melbourne Australia Drake Hall of Fame, 1962; Athletics Hall of Fame, Univ Iowa, 2000. **Special Achievements:** First African American all-American cross-country runner, 1951; First Black American distance runner in Olympic Games, 1956. **Home Addr:** 904 Christopher Rd, Chapel Hill, NC 27514-4026.

**WHIGHAM, LARRY JEROME**
Football player, football coach. **Personal:** Born Jun 23, 1972, Hattiesburg, MS; married Twanna; children: D Aunte & Brandi. **Educ:** Northeast La Univ, criminal justice. **Career:** Football player (retired), football coach; New Eng Patriots, defensive back & free safety, 1994-2000; Chicago Bears, defensive back & linebacker, 2001-02; Excell Holding, LLC, pres & chief exec officer, 2003-07; Pearl River Community Col, defensive back coach & special teams defensive coach, 2006-08; Univ Southern Miss, Asst Football Coach, 2011; Patriot Printing Ink, Mkt & Sales Mgr, 2011-13. **Honors/Awds:** Mackey Award, 1996; Pro Bowl Selection, 1997. **Home Addr:** , Houston, TX.

**WHIPPER, HON. LUCILLE SIMMONS**
State government official, educator, executive director. **Personal:** Born Jun 6, 1928, Charleston, SC; daughter of Joseph Simmons and Sarah Marie Washington Simmons Stroud; married Rev Benjamin J Whipper Sr; children: Benjamin J Jr, Ogretta W Hawkins, Rosmond W Black, J Seth, Stanford Edley (deceased) & Cheryl D Hamilton. **Educ:** Talladega Col, BA, econ & sociol, 1948; Univ Chicago, MA, polit sci, 1955; SC State Col, cert, guidance & counseling, 1961. **Career:** State representative (retired); Charleston Co Sch, teacher & counr, 1949-65; Catch-Up, organizer & dir, 1960; Burke HS, counr & chmn dept, 1965-73; Charleston Co Off Econ Opportunity, admin & prog dir, 1966-68; Col Charleston, asst to pres & dir human rels, 1972-75, 1977-81; Charleston Co Sch, dir proj, ESAA, 1975-77; SC House Rep, state rep, 1986-96. **Orgs:** Ment Health Comt, 1969-71; Mayor's Adv Comn Human Rels, 1971; vice chmn, Dem Party Conv, 1972; Charleston Dist 20 Sch Bd; pres, Gamma Xi Omega Chap; Comn Minimal Competency SC Gen Assembly, 1977-78; Alpha Kappa Alpha, 1978-80; SC Adv Tech Educ, 1979-; SC Adv Coun Voc & Tech Educ, 1979-; Charleston Constituent Bd Twenty, 1980-84; Col Entrance Exam Bd; founder, pres, Avery Inst Afro-Am Hist & Cult, 1980-84, 1987-89; pres, Charleston, SC Chap Links Inc, 1984-86; Charleston County; pres, Woman's Educ & Missionary Conv S Carolina; Nat Cong Christian Educ; Morris St Baptist Church; bd trustee, Morris Col; bd trustee, Benedict Col; fac mem, Nat Cong Christian Educ; bd mem, Int African Am Mus. **Honors/Awds:** Fellow Grant for Graduate Study, Univ Chicago, 1954-55; Community Service Award, Charleston Chap Omega Psi Phi, 1968; DHL, Morris Col, 1989; DHL, Univ Charleston, 1992; SC Black Hall of Fame, 1995; The Order of The Palmetto, 1996; SC African Am Hist calendar, Bellsouth, 2003; Marjorie Amos-Frazier Pacesetter Award, 2013. **Special Achievements:** First African American administrator & developed its first affirmative action plan in College of Charleston; First African American female to serve as an elected state official from the Tri-County area. **Home Addr:** 2051 Hallahan Ct, Mount Pleasant, SC 29464-6250, **Home Phone:** (843)881-1337.

**WHISENTON, ANDRE C.**
Librarian, executive, government official. **Personal:** Born Feb 4, 1944, Durham, NC; son of Andrew C and Margret Y; married Vera Norman; children: Andre Christopher & Courtney Yvonne. **Educ:** Morehouse Col, BPS, 1965; Atlanta Univ, MLS, 1966. **Career:** Naval Sea Sys Command, lib dir, 1973-76; US Dept Labor, exec develop prog, 1979, librn, lib dir, 1978, 1980-82, chief, dir, Equal Employ Opportunity Complaints Off, 1987-. **Orgs:** Bd mem, Nat Asn Blacks Within Govt, 1985; Nat Asn Advan Colored People, 1988; Alpha Phi Alpha, 1988; Montgomery Co MLK Jr Commem Comn, 1988-89, bd mem, 1990-91. **Honors/Awds:** DOL ECO Award, 1978; Fed Womens Impact Award, 1979; Secy of Labor Rec Award, 1982; Board Service Award, 1986. **Home Addr:** 1204 Canyon Rd, Silver Spring, MD 20904-1404. **Business Addr:** Director, US Department of Labor, Equal Employment Opportunity Complaints Office, 200 Const Ave NW, Washington, DC 20210, **Business Phone:** (202)693-6000.

**WHITAKER, FOREST STEVEN, III**
Actor, movie director, administrator. **Personal:** Born Jul 15, 1961, Longview, TX; son of Forest Jr and Laura Francis Smith; married Keisha Nash; children: Sonnet & True. **Educ:** Calif State Polytech Univ; Univ Southern Calif, attended 1982. **Career:** Films: The Assassination Game, 1982; Fast Times at Ridge mont High, 1982; Vision

Quest, 1985; North & South, 1985; The Color of Money, 1986; Platoon, 1986; North & South, Book II, 1986; Good Morning Vietnam, 1987; Stakeout, 1987; Bird, 1988; Bloodsport, 1988; Johnny Handsome, 1989; Downtown, 1990; Diary of a Hitman, 1991; A Rage in Harlem, 1991; Hit man, 1992; Article 99, 1992; Dr Giggles, 1992; Consenting Adults, 1992; The Crying Game, 1992; Consenting Adults, 1992; Bank Robber, 1993; Strapped, dir, 1993; Body Snatchers, 1993; Blown Away, 1994; Pret a Porter, 1994; Jason's Lyric, 1994; Waiting to Exhale, dir, 1995; Species, 1995; Smoke, 1995; Phenomenon, 1996; Body Count, 1998; Hope Floats, dir, 1998; Ghost Dog: The Way of the Samuri, 1999; Light It Up, 1999; Witness Protection, 1999; Battlefield Earth, 2000; Four Dogs Playing Poker, 2000; Green Dragon, 2001; The Follow, 2001; The Fourth Angel, 2001; Feast of All Saints, dir, 2001; Panic Room, 2002; Phone Booth, 2002; Deacons for Defense, actor & dir, 2003; First Daughter, dir, 2004; Amercian Gun, 2005; Mary, 2005; A Little Trip to Heaven, 2005; The Last King of Scotland, 2006; The Shield, 2006-07; Even Money, 2006; The Marsh, 2006; Everyone's Hero, 2006; The Air I Breathe, 2007, Ripple Effect, 2007; The Great Debaters, 2007; Vantage Point, 2008; Street Kings, 2008; Dragon Hunters, 2008; Powder Blue, 2009; Hurricane Season, 2009; Winged Creatures, 2009; Where the Wild Things Are, 2009; Repo Men, 2010; Lullaby for Pi, 2010; My Own Love Song, 2010; The Experiment, 2010; Our Family Wedding, 2010; Catch 44, 2011; Freelancers, 2012; A Dark Truth, 2012; The Last Stand, 2013; Zulu, 2013; Pawn, 2013; The Butler, 2013; Black Nativity, 2013; Out of the Furnace, 2013; Two Men in Town, 2014; Taken 3, 2014; Dope, 2015; Southpaw, 2015; Story of Your Life, forthcoming, 2016; Rogue One: A Star Wars Story, forthcoming, 2016. TV prog: "Making The Grade", 1982; "Cagney & Lacey", 1983; "Trapper John, M.D.", 1984; "Hill Street Blues", 1984; "Diff'rent Strokes", 1985; "The Grand Baby", 1985; "The Fall Guy", 1985; "Amazing Stories", 1986; "Hands", 1987; "Criminal Justice", 1990; "Lush Life", 1993; "The Twilight Zone", host & Narrator, 2002-03; "Last Light", 1993; "The Enemy Within", 1994; "Rebound: The Legend of Earl "The Goat Manigault", 1996; "Body Snatchers", 1997; "Heart of the Matter", 2006; "Jigsaw", 2006; "ER", 2006-07; "Tell Me No Secrets", 2006; "Smoked", 2006; "Of Mice & Lem", 2006; "Postpartum", 2006; "A House Divided", 2007; "Murmurs of the Heart", 2007; "On the Jones", 2007; "Back to One", 2007; "Meter Made", 2007; "American Dad!", 2007-09; "Criminal Minds", 2010; "Criminal Minds: Suspect Behavior", 2011; "Africa", narrator, 2013; "Roots", forthcoming, 2016. **Home Addr:** 9200 Sunset Blvd Suite 428, Los Angeles, CA 90069. **Business Addr:** Actor, DGA, 7920 Sunset Blvd, Los Angeles, CA 90046.

### WHITAKER, LOUIS RODMAN, JR. (LOU WHITAKER)
Baseball player, baseball manager. **Personal:** Born May 12, 1957, Brooklyn, NY; son of Louis Sr and Marion Arlene Williams; married Crystal McCreary; children: Asia, Angela, Jessica & Sarah. **Career:** Baseball player (retired), baseball coach; Detroit Tigers, second baseman, 1977-95, spec coach, 2003-. **Home Addr:** 803 Pipe, Martinsville, VA 24112. **Business Addr:** Coach, Detroit Tigers, Comerica Pk 2100 Woodward Ave, Detroit, MI 48201-3470, **Business Phone:** (313)962-4000.

### WHITAKER, MICAL ROZIER
Theatrical director, educator. **Personal:** Born Feb 10, 1941, Metter, GA; son of Ellis and Alma Mical; married Georgenia; children: Mical Anthony. **Educ:** Howard Univ, attended 1961; Am Acad Dramatic Arts, New York, attended 1962; Circle-in-the-Sq, New York, attended 1966; NC Agr & Tech State Univ, BFA, 1989. **Career:** E River Players, founder, artistic dir, 1964-76; Union Settlement's Dept Perf Arts, founder, dir, 1972-76; Ossie Davis & Ruby Dee Story Hour, producer, dir, 1977-78; Richard Allen Ctr Cult & Art, artistic dir, 1978-81; Ga Southern Univ, theatre dir, Dept Commun Arts, asst prof, asst prof emer, currently. **Orgs:** Co-founder & coord, Lincoln Ctr St Theatre Fest, 1970-81; dir, Black Theatre Fest USA Lincoln Ctr, 1979; dir, Int Black Theatre Fest Lincoln Ctr, 1980; dir, Averitt Youth Theatre prog Averitt Ctr Arts, Statesboro; guest lectr & dir, Theatre & Performance Prog. **Honors/Awds:** AUDELCO Award, Dir Musical, 1979; Paul Robeson Theatre Award, NC A&T State Univ, 1989; Seattle Emmy Award; CEBA Award; Joseph Jefferson Award. **Special Achievements:** CEBA radio sta production "The Beauty of Things Black" 1978; Emmy Production & Set Design "Cellar George" Seattle Chap, 1979. **Home Addr:** 515 Wash St, Metter, GA 30439-3812, **Home Phone:** (912)685-6844. **Business Addr:** Assistant Professor Emeritus, Georgia Southern University, Rm 1116 Forest Dr Bldg, Statesboro, GA 30460, **Business Phone:** (912)478-0090.

### WHITAKER, PERNELL
Boxer, athletic trainer. **Personal:** Born Jan 2, 1964, Norfolk, VA; married Rovanda; children: Dominique, Pernell Jr, Dantavious & Devon. **Career:** Boxer (retired); prof boxer, 1984-2005; trainer, currently. **Orgs:** Retired boxers found. **Honors/Awds:** World Boxing Council, Welterweight Title Holder; World Championships, Lightweight, Silver Medal, 1982; Pan American Games, Lightweight, gold medal, 1983; Olympics, Lightweight, gold medal, 1984; Named Fighter of the Year, Ring Mag, 1989; IBF Lightweight Champion, 1989-92; WBC Lightweight Champion, 1989-92; WBA Lightweight Champion, 1990-92; IBF light Welterweight Boxing Champion, 1992-93; WBC Welterweight Champion, 1993-97; WBA Light Middleweight Boxing Champion, 1995-95; NABF Lightweight Champion; Hampton Roads Sports Hall of Fame, 2010.

### WHITAKER, VON BEST. See BEST-WHITAKER, DR. VAUGHN.

### WHITAKER, VON FRANCES
Nurse, educator, psychologist. **Personal:** Born New Bern, NC; daughter of Cleveland W Best and Lillie Best (deceased); married Roy Jr; children: Roy III. **Educ:** Columbia Union Col, BS; Univ Mar, Baltimore City Campus, MS; Univ NCChapel Hill, PhD. **Career:** Wash Adventist Hosp, staff nurse; Prince Georges County Mar Health Dept, pub health nurse; Howard Univ, instr nursing; Coppin State Col, instr nursing; Univ NC Chapel Hill, vis lectr nursing; Univ MSR-Columbia, asst prof; Boston Col, asst prof; NC Agr & Tech State Univ, Faan prof, asst dean nursing; Univ Tex Heath Sci Ctr, asst prof; Ga Southern Univ, assoc prof; Memorial Med Ctr Hosp, clin res coordr, currently. **Orgs:** Chair res comt, Am Soc Opthalmic Regist Nurses, 1988-; grant rev panel, Nat Ist Health, 1991-94; chair nominations comt, Am Pub Health Asn, Pub Health Nursing Sect, 1992-93; Tex Nurses Asn, Mem Comt D No8, 1992-94; Planned Parenthood San Antonio & S Tex, 1993-95; Eye Bank San Antonio, 1992-94; C A Whittier Med Auxilary, chairperson nursing Scholar, 1993. **Honors/Awds:** Fellow, Univ NC Chapel Hill, 1977-78; Sigma Theta Tau Inc, Nat Hon Soc Nursing, 1979; Bush Inst Child & Family Policy, Fel, 1979-81; Co-winner, Southeastern Psychol Asn, Comt on Equality Prof Opportunity Stud Res Competition, 1988 fellow Am Acad Nursing; Certificate of Apppreciation, Agency for Health Care Policy & Res, 1992. **Special Achievements:** Articles: Whitaker & Aldrich, a breast self exam prog for adolescent spec educ studs, 1993; Sexual Dysfunction, Nursing Diagnosis In Clinical Pract, 1992; Violence Risk, Nursing Diagnosis In Clinical Pract, 1992, Whitaker & Morris ORG, Key for a Successful Presentation, 1992. **Home Addr:** 5308 Bayberry Lane, Greensboro, NC 24755-1139, **Home Phone:** (336)286-8034. **Business Addr:** Clinical Research Coordinator, Memorial Medical Center Hospital-Georgia Eye Institute, Dept Res, Savannah, GA 31411, **Business Phone:** (912)351-3000.

### WHITAKER, WILLIAM THOMAS, JR.
Television journalist. **Personal:** Born Aug 26, 1951, Philadelphia, PA; son of William T and Marie Best; married Teresita Conley; children: William Thomas Jr & Lesley Rakiah. **Educ:** Hobart Col, BA, am hist, 1973; Boston Univ, Mass, african am studies, 1974; Univ Calif, Berkeley, Sch Jour, grad jour prog. **Career:** KQED, San Francisco, researcher & writer, 1977-78, assoc producer, news producer, 1979-81; WBTV, Charlotte, NC, reporter, corresp, 1981-84; CBS News, corresp, Atlanta, 1984-89, Tokyo corresp, 1989-92, Los Angeles, 1992-; Hobart & William Smith Col, bd trustees; CBS News, corresp, 1992-. **Orgs:** Nat Asn Black Journalists, 1985-89; Los Angeles Asn Black Journalists, 1993-; CBS Black Employees Asn, 1993-; Nat Asn Advan Colored People, 1993-; Ctr Early Educ. **Honors/Awds:** Emmy Award, Acad TV Arts & Sci, 1998; DHL, Hobart & William Smith Col, 1997; Striving for Excellence Award, Minorities Broadcasting, 2000. **Home Addr:** 3144 Nichols Canyon Rd, Los Angeles, CA 90046, **Home Phone:** (213)436-0639. **Business Addr:** Correspondent, Los Angeles Bureau, CBS News, Rm 23 7800 Beverly Blvd, Los Angeles, CA 90036, **Business Phone:** (213)852-2202.

### WHITAKER-BRAXTON, BEVERLY
School administrator, executive, executive director. **Career:** Baker Sch, prin, 1977-79; Va Union Univ, community taskforce coun mem; Richmond Pub Schs, prin, 1978-91, James River Valley Link, pres, 2007-09; exec dir Support Serv, currently. **Business Addr:** Executive Director, Richmond Public Schools, 301 N 9th St 13th Fl, Richmond, VA 23219, **Business Phone:** (804)780-7711.

### WHITBY, DR. LINDA J.
Physician. **Educ:** Howard Univ, MD, 1974. **Career:** Pvt pract physician, currently. **Business Addr:** Physician, Oasis Access Health, 3666 Muddy Creek Rd, Edgewater, MD 21037-3418, **Business Phone:** (443)203-0103.

### WHITE, ALAN SCOTT
Executive, association executive. **Educ:** Univ Mich, Ann Arbor. **Career:** Colliers Int, sr sales assoc, 1996-2003; WISE Com Real Estate, pres, chief exec officer, 2003-. **Orgs:** Bd pres, Jefferson E Bus Asn; treas, Detroit/Wayne County Inc; bd dir, LAND Inc. **Business Addr:** President, Chief Executive Officer, WISE Commercial Real Estate, 980 N Mich Ave Suite 1400, Chicago, MI 60611-7500.

### WHITE, DR. ALVIN, JR.
Clergy, executive, chief executive officer. **Personal:** Born Houston, TX; son of Alvin Sr (deceased) and Louis Renee; married Carolyn Joyce Smith; children: Alvin III, Daniel Lynn & Paul Christopher. **Educ:** Univ Tex, BBA, 1976, MBA, 1986; Faith Evangel Col & Sem, Doctorate Strategic Leadership, 2012. **Career:** Johnson & Johnson, mgr, personnel, 1968-71; Pepsi Co Inc, dir personnel admin, 1971-79, vpres, 1991-98; ABC Inc, dir, compensation, 1979-81; United Gas Pipeline, vpres, human resources, 1981-90; Ivex, vpres, human resources, 1990-91; Pizza Hut Int, vpres, human resources, 1991-95; Frito-Lay, group vpres, human resources, 1995-98; AEA Serv Solutions, founder, owner; Vistana Inc, sr vpres, 1998-2001; Green Leaf Develop Syst Inc, chmn & chief exec officer, currently; Shiloh Baptist Church, sr pastor, 2001-. **Orgs:** Alpha Phi Alpha Fraternity, 1970-; Mt Pleasant MBC; adv bd, KSU Sch Bus, 1992; Greater Trinity Baptist Fel, sr pastor, 2009-. **Honors/Awds:** Legend Award, Univ Tex. **Home Addr:** 3401 Lilas Ct, Windermere, FL 34786-7612, **Home Phone:** (407)909-0877. **Business Addr:** Chairman, Chief Executive Officer, Green Leaf Development System Inc, 8516 Old Wintergarden Rd Suite 101, Orlando, FL 32835, **Business Phone:** (407)822-9224.

### WHITE, ANTHONY CHARLES GUNN. See KAMAU, MOSI.

### WHITE, ARTHUR W., JR.
Executive. **Personal:** Born Oct 25, 1943, St. Louis, MO; son of Arthur W Sr and Julia Arnold; married Virginia A Green; children: Arthur W III. **Educ:** Lincoln Univ, BS, 1965; USAF Mgt Anal Sch, cert grad, 1967. **Career:** Equitable Life Assurance; Soc US, admin trainee, 1965-66, group sales rep, 1971-74, div group sales mgr, 1974-76, dir sales, 1976-77, vpres, 1977; United Mutual Life Ins, pres & chief exec officer, 1985; NYC Summer Jobs '90 Prog exd; Equitable Life Ins Co, vpres; Tex Health Choice LC, dir com sales, 1999-. **Orgs:** Vpres, Nat Asn Advan Colored People, 1961-62; Alpha Phi Alpha, 1962; chmn, social performance comm Equitable Life Assurance Soc, 1984; adv bd, Bronx Lebanon Hosp, 1986; adv bd, Salvation Army Greater NY, 1986; NJ State Investment Adv Coun, 1989; Leadership Dallas, Class 2000; Dallas 2012 Olympic Bid Comn. **Honors/Awds:** Outstanding Performance Award, Equitable Life Assurance Soc Group Oper, 1969; Man of the Year Award, Alpha Phi Alpha; Outstanding Achiever, Econ Develop New Era Demo Club, 1985; TOR Special Inspiration Award, Theatre Renewal, 1986; Notable Americans. **Home Addr:** 1105 Greenbrair Dr, Desoto, TX 75115-3248. **Business Addr:** Director of Commercial Sales, Texas Health Choice LC, 9330 Amberton Pkwy, Dallas, TX 75243, **Business Phone:** (972)479-5000.

### WHITE, DR. ARTIS ANDRE. See Obituaries Section.

### WHITE, DR. AUGUSTUS A., III (ELLIOTT WHITE)
Surgeon, educator, association executive. **Personal:** Born Jun 4, 1936, Memphis, TN; son of Augustus A (deceased) and Vivian Dandridge; married Anita Ottemo; children: Alissa Alexandra, Atina Andrea & Annica Akila. **Educ:** Brown Univ, BA, 1957; Stanford Univ, MD, 1961; Karolinska Inst Sweden, PhD, biomechanics spine, 1969; Univ Hosp, rotating intern, 1962; Presby Med Ctr, asst residential surgeon, 1963; Yale New Haven Hosp, asst residential orthop surgeon, 1965, chief resident 1965; Newington C Hosp, resident 1965; Va Hosp New Haven, Conn, chief resident 1966; NIH, orthop trainee, 1969; Harvard Bus Sch, advan mgt prog, 1984. **Career:** Va Hosp W Haven, Conn, consult orthopaedic surgeon, 1969-78; Hill Health Ctr, consult orthopaedic surgeon, 1969-78; Yale Univ Sch Med, orthopaedic surg, assoc prof, 1972-76, prof, 1976-78; Conn Health Care Plan, chief orthopaedics, 1976-78; Harvard Univ Sch Med, prof orthopaedic surg; Mass Gen Hosp, vis orthopaedic surgeon; C Hosp Med Ctr, sr assoc orthopaedic surg; Peter Bent Brigham Hosp, assoc orthopaedic surg, 1979-80; Sidney Farber Cancer Inst, consult div surgeon; Brigham & Woman's Hosp; Beth Israel Deaconess Med Ctr Boston, orthopaedic surgeon chief, 1978-90; Orthopadic Surgeon Chief, emer, currently; Harvard Med Sch, Oliver Wendell Holmes Soc, master, currently; Ortho Logic Corp Phoenix, Ari, chmn sci adv bd, 1990-91; Am Shared Hosp Servs, San Francisco, Calif, bd officers, 1990-91; Harvard Med Sch, Ellen & Melvin Gordon prof med educ, 2001, orthopaedic surgeon, currently; Tiova, vpres, prod mgt. **Orgs:** Brown Univ Community Dept Orthopaedic Surgeons, Yale Univ Sch Med, 1972-73; Brown Univ Community Med Educ; Med Conf Community Beth Israel Hosp; Fac Coun, Community Harvard Med Sch; area concent adv, Musculoskeletal Harvard-MIT Div Health Sci & Tech, 1978; sub-Comm prof, Harvard Med Sch, 1982; ed bd SPINE, reviewer, Harper & Row, 1976-82; ed bd, Annals Sports Med, 1983; reviewer, New Eng J Med; New Haven Chap Nat Advan Asn Colored People; Sigma Pi Phi Fraternity, 1979; visitng prof over 11 col & univs; vis comn, minority Life & Educ Brown Univ, 1985, 1986; pres, Cervical Spine Res Soc, 1988-89; chair, Diversity Comn Am Acad Orthop Surgeon; founding pres, J Robert Gladden Orthopaedic Soc, 1990-2000; dir, Capstone Therapeut Corp, 1993-2012; Health Policy Coun, Am Acad Orthopaedic Surgeons; Coun Acad Affairs, Am Acad Orthopaedic Surgeons, 2001; dir, Zimmer Holdings Inc, 2001-10; nat adv Coun, Nat Ctr Minority Health & Health Disparities, 2002. **Honors/Awds:** Ebony Magazine Black Achievement Awards, 1980; Eastern Orthopaedic Association Award, Spine Res, 1980; Distinguished Service Award, Northfield Mt Hermon Alumni Asn, 1983; William Rogers Award, Alumni Brown Univ & Delta Upsilon Fraternity, 1984; Delta Upsilon Frat Award Outstanding Achievement, 1986; Honorary, DHL Univ New Haven, 1987; Honorary Doctor Med Sci, Brown Univ, 1997; Honorary Doctor Sci, Southern Conn State Univ, 2000; Nix Ethics Award, Clinical Orthopaedic Soc, 2002; Brown Bear Award, Brown Alumni Asn, 2002; Athletic Hall of Fame, Northfield Mount Hermon, 1990; Outstanding Orthopaedic Scholar, Nat Med Asn, 1994; AAOS Diversity Aard; American Orthopaedic Association Distinguished Clinician Educator Award; Ten Outstanding Young Men Award; Martin Luther King Jr Medical Achievement Award; Kappa Delta/ Orthopaedic Research & Education Foundation Research Award; Tipton Award, 2010. **Special Achievements:** Clinical Biomechanics of the Cervical Spine, 2nd ed, Lippincott, co-author, 1990; Author: "Your Aching Back", Revised Edition, Simon & Schuster, translated and published in Germany, 1990; Co-Author Biomechanics in the Musculoskeletal System, Churchill Livingstone, 2001; Published over 150 Clinical & Scientific Articles; First African American to graduate from Stanford University School of Medicine; First African-American orthopaedic resident at Yale Medical Center. **Home Addr:** 20 Westerly Rd, Weston, MA 02493-1054, **Home Phone:** (781)891-9048. **Business Addr:** Orthopedic Surgeon, Harvard Medical School, 25 Shattuck St, Boston, MA 02115-0962, **Business Phone:** (617)432-1000.

### WHITE, DR. BARBARA WILLIAMS
School administrator, social worker, dean (education). **Personal:** Born Feb 26, 1943, Macon, GA; daughter of Ernestine Austin; married Julian E; children: Tonja & Phaedra. **Educ:** Fla State Univ, BS, 1964, BS, 1974, MSW, 1975, PhD, 1986. **Career:** Lake County Pub Sch, teacher, 1964-65; Duval County Pub Sch, teacher, 1965-73; Leon County 4-C Coun, dir, 1975-77; Fla A&M Univ, asst prof, 1977-79, assoc dean, 1979-92, Master Social Work prog dir; Univ Tex, Austin, Sch Social Work, dean, 1993-, Ctr African Am Studies, prof, currently. **Orgs:** Acad Cert Social Workers, 1978-; vpres, Nat Asn Social Workers, 1983-85, pres, 1991-93, chair; comnr accreditation & pres & chair, Coun Social Work Educ, 1984-87; Links Inc, Tallahassee Chap, Alpha Kappa Alpha Sor; vpres, United Way Leon County, 1988-91; bd dir, Int Asn Sch Social Work; Class Leadership Tex; Nat Selective Serv Appeal Bd; nat consult, social work curric; pres, Fla Chap Nat Asn Social Workers. **Special Achievements:** First black dean at the University of Texas. **Home Addr:** 5811 Mesa Dr Suite 1214, Austin, TX 78731. **Business Addr:** Dean, Centennial Professor, University of Texas, 1925 San Jacinto Blvd D3500, Austin, TX 78712-0358, **Business Phone:** (512)471-1937.

### WHITE, BEVERLY ANITA (BEVERLY WHITE)
Television journalist, television news anchorperson. **Personal:** Born Aug 4, 1960, Frankfurt; daughter of Modesta Brown and Freeman. **Educ:** Univ Tex, Austin, TX, jour, 1981. **Career:** KMOL-TV, San Antonio, Tex, news intern, 1980; KCEN-TV, Waco, Tex, reporter, 1981-84; KENS-TV, San Antonio, Tex, reporter & anchor, 1984-85; WKRC-TV, Cincinnati, OH, reporter & anchor, 1985-89; WTVJ-TV, Miami, Fla, reporter & anchor, 1989-92; Univ Southern Calif, adj prof; KNBC-TV, NBC4, reporter & co-anchor, 1992-, gen assignment reporter, currently; Univ Southern Calif, adj prof. **Orgs:** Nat Asn Black Journalists, 1985-; pres, Southern Calif Chap, Black Journalists Asn, 1995-96. **Honors/Awds:** Peabody Award, WTVJ-TV/NBC Miami, 1992; Best Local News Reporter, LA's New Times mag, 1997; Scholar Residence, Citrus Col; Leadership Award, California Legislative Black

Caucus; Scholar in Residence, Citrus Col; Distinguished Journalist Award, 2012; Distinguished Alumni Award, Killeen Independent School District; THE 50 Fabulous Women, 2013. **Home Addr:** 201 Highland Pl, Altadena, CA 91001. **Business Addr:** Reporter, Co-anchor, NBC4, 3000 W Alameda Ave, Burbank, CA 91523, **Business Phone:** (818)840-3469.

### WHITE, BILL (WILLIAM DE KOVA WHITE)
Broadcaster, baseball executive, baseball player. **Personal:** Born Jan 28, 1934, Lakewood, FL; children: 5. **Educ:** Hiram Col, attended 1953. **Career:** Baseball player (retired), baseball executive, broadcaster; New York Giants, infielder, 1956, San Francisco Giants, infielder, 1958, St Louis Cardinals, infielder, 1959-65, 1969; Philadelphia Phillies, infielder, 1966-68; WPVI-Radio, Philadelphia, Pa, sportscaster, 1967-68; WPIX-TV, New York, NY, broadcaster & baseball analyst, 1970-88; New York Yankees, broadcaster, 1971-88; WMCA, broadcaster, 1971-77; WABC; CBS Radio Network, sports report; ABC, pregame reports; Nat League Prof Baseball Clubs, New York, NY, pres, 1989-94. TV Series: "Monday Night Baseball", 1976; "1977 World Series", 1977; "It Don't Come Easy: The 1978 NY Yankees", 1978. **Orgs:** Comt baseball veterans, Nat Baseball Hall Fame, 1994-, bd dir, 2000-. **Home Addr:** 1750 Highview Lane, PO Box 199, Upper Black Eddy, PA 18972.

### WHITE, BILLY RAY
Consultant, government official, mayor. **Personal:** Born Jun 29, 1936, Center, TX; married Zerlene Victor; children: Elbert Ray, William Douglas, Jeanetta Marie, Johnetta Marie, CharlesVernon & Billy Ester. **Educ:** Prairie View A&M Univ Tex, attended 1957. **Career:** Meth Hosp Lubbock Tex, clerk, 1957-64; Varian Assoc Calif, mech, 1964-77; Ray Chem Corp Calif, buyer, 1977; Menlo Pk, mayor, 1981, 1983, 1986. **Orgs:** Consult, gr Menlo-Atherton Bd Raltors; plan bd State Calif E Palo Alto, 1971-72; chmn, plan comm City Menlo Pk, 1974-78; chmn, HCD bd Coof San Mateo, 1978-; bd dir, Ctr Independence Disabled Inc. **Honors/Awds:** First Black elected to Council City Menlo Park; Tulip L Jones Women's Club Inc, 1978; Man of the Year, Belle Haven Home Asn, 1980. **Special Achievements:** First African American mayor of Menlo Park. **Home Addr:** 1131 Menlo Oaks Dr, Menlo Park, CA 94025, **Home Phone:** (408)315-6127. **Business Addr:** Buyer, Ray Chemical Corp, 300 Constitution Dr, Menlo Park, CA 94025.

### WHITE, BRYAN
Automotive executive. **Career:** Mission Blvd Lincoln Mercury Inc, pres & chief exec officer, currently; NASA Midwest Inc, series dir. **Orgs:** Nat Auto Sport Asn. **Business Addr:** President, Mission Boulevard Lincoln Mercury Inc, 24644 Mission Blvd, Hayward, CA 94544-1636, **Business Phone:** (510)886-5052.

### WHITE, CAROLYN
Educator. **Personal:** married Jerry L; children: Christopher Lee. **Educ:** Wayne State Univ, BA, MA. **Career:** Highland Pk Community Sch, dir spec educ, currently. **Orgs:** Secy & treas, Greater Northeast Optimist Club. **Business Addr:** Director Special Education, Highland Park Community Schools, 15900 Woodward, Highland Park, MI 48203, **Business Phone:** (313)957-3000.

### WHITE, CHARLES E.
Executive. **Personal:** married Carolyn H; children: 4. **Educ:** Univ Detroit, BA, bus admin. **Career:** Ford Motor Co; Borg Warner; Lear Corp, mgr, supplier develop purchasing Div, 1991, dir, supplier diversity & develop, supplier diversity & develop, vpres, 2000-05, vpres minority supplier prog; Diversity Resource Assocs LLC, pres, 2007-. **Orgs:** Am Soc Qual Control; Soc Mfr Engrs. **Home Addr:** 561 Parkview Dr, Detroit, MI 48214-2967, **Home Phone:** (313)331-1682. **Business Addr:** President, Diversity Resource Associates LLC, 1326 Village Dr, Detroit, MI 48207-4025, **Business Phone:** (248)877-0980.

### WHITE, CHARLES R.
Civil engineer. **Personal:** Born Nov 25, 1937, New York, NY; son of Clarence R and Elise; married Dolores; children: Darryl & Sherryl. **Educ:** Howard Univ, BS, 1959; Univ S Calif, MS, 1963. **Career:** Civil engineer (retired); Civil engr planner, regist prof engr, Calif, 1965; State Calif, La Dept Water Resources Southern Dist, prog mgr geothermal resources; chief planning br, chief, southern dist. **Orgs:** Omega Psi Phi Frat, 1956; Am Soc Civil Engrs, 1957; Tau Beta Pi Town Hall of Calif, 1970; Toastmasters Int, 1970. **Honors/Awds:** Principal author Planned Utilization of Ground Water Basins San Gabriel Valley, 1969; Meeting Water Demands Chino-Riverside Area, 1971; Meeting Water Demands San Juan Area, 1972; Co-author, Water & Power from Geothermal Resources CA-An Overview, 1974; Publ paper on Lake Elsinore Flood Disaster of March, 1980; Nat Acad Press, 1982; Author, San Bernardino-San Gorgonio Water Resources Mgt Invest, 1986. **Home Addr:** 30433 Calle La Resolana, Rancho Palos Verdes, CA 90275-4530, **Home Phone:** (310)377-2062.

### WHITE, CHRISTINE LARKIN
Nurse, chief executive officer. **Personal:** Born Mar 12, 1946, Birmingham, AL; daughter of Robert and Catherine Mills; married Roger; children: Eugena & Karen. **Educ:** Tuskegee Inst, Tuskegee, Ala, BSN, 1968; Univ Ala, MSN, 1976; Univ Md, College Park, BA, bus, mgt, mkt & related support serv, 1989. **Career:** Univ Hosp, Birmingham, Ala, staff nurse, 1968-70, 1974-77, staff develop, 1977-80, dir psychiat nursing, 1980-; Manpower Training & Develop, Akron, OH, instr, 1970; Planned Parenthood, Akron, OH, clin nurse, 1971-73; BMC Software, engagement mgr, 1997-99; Teges Corp, co-founder, pres & chief exec officer, 2000-08; IBM, br mgr DCI recruiting, 2002-04; Swink LLC, co-founder, 2008-14; John Galt Ins Agency, com lines agt, 2012-13; DataCore Software; bus partner mgr, 2013-14; mPWR LLC, managing prin & owner, 2014-. **Orgs:** Epsilon Beta Chap Chi Eta Phi, 1966; Omicron Omega Chap, Alpha Kappa Alpha, 1979; Qual Assurance Community Med & Dent Staff, Univ Ala Hosp, 1985-88; Nursing Res Community Univ Hosp, 1986-87. **Honors/Awds:** Alpha Sigma Lambda, National Honor Society. **Home Addr:** 212 4th Ave S, Birmingham, AL 35205-3232, **Home Phone:** (205)252-8519. **Business Addr:** Managing Principal, Owner, mPWR LLC, 840 Malaga Dr, Boca Raton, FL 33432.

### WHITE, CLARENCE DEAN
Financial manager, artist, president (organization). **Personal:** Born Nov 27, 1946, Ellaville, GA; son of Charlie George and Tymy Hartage. **Educ:** Univ Paris, attended 1968; Morehouse Col, BA, 1969; Northwestern Univ, MBA, 1972. **Career:** First Nat Bank, trust officer, 1969-82; Clarence White Contemp Art, art dealer, 1974-95; Artist & Art Critic, freelance basis. **Orgs:** Dir, Film Symp, 1976-85; Mens Coun Mus Contemp Art; pres, Belmont Hills Homeowners Asn; Ebenezer Baptist Church. **Business Addr:** President, Belmont Hills Homeowners Association, 50 Belmont Circle SW, Atlanta, GA 30311, **Business Phone:** (404)758-8958.

### WHITE, CLAUDE ESLEY
Lawyer. **Personal:** Born Jan 2, 1949, Bridgeton, NJ; son of John Hosea (deceased) and Viola (Sumrell) W; married Jane Denise Rice; children: Claude Jr, Stephanie Edith, Christopher Michael & Alicia. **Educ:** Rutgers Col, BA, polit sci, 1971; Rutgers Law Sch, JD, law, 1974. **Career:** Pitney, Hardin, Kipp & Szuch, assoc atty, 1974-76; Liggett Group Inc, corp coun, 1976-83; Newark Community Sch Arts, vice chmn, 1980-85; GrandMet USA Inc, corp coun & vpres, 1976-87; Qual Care Inc, vpres, gen coun & secy, 1985-87; Staff Builders Inc, vpres, gen coun & secy, 1987-89; Burns Int Security Serv Inc, vpres & div coun, 1989-91; William A. Thomas & Assocs, atty, 1992-95; Paragon Enterprises Int, pres & chief exec officer, currently; IntegraMed Am Inc, bd secy & vpres & chief compliance officer & gen coun, 1995-2014, Sr Legal Advisor & Consult, 2015-; Rutgers Univ, community adv bd, chm. **Orgs:** Chmn, Rutgers Col Econ Opportunities Prog Adv Comt; Nat Study Regist, 1971; bd dir, Inmate-Self Help Com Inc, 1974-76; chmn, bd trustee & treas, St Paul Bapt Ch, 1974; Am Bar Asn, New York; adv bd, Sigma Delta; bd dir, Nat Asn Home Care, 1986-89; chmn, Home Health Serv & Staffing Asn, 1987-89; secy, Comt Nat Security Co, 1991-; 100 Black Men S Metro Atlanta, 1992-; Ben Hill United Methodist Church; Nat Bar Asn. **Business Addr:** Vice President, General Counsel, IntegraMed America Inc, 2 Manhattanville Rd, Purchase, NY 10577-2113, **Business Phone:** (914)253-8000.

### WHITE, DR. CLAYTON CECIL
Educator, special education teacher, founder (originator). **Personal:** Born Nov 4, 1942, New York, NY; married Le Tretta Jones; children: Shannon. **Educ:** Temple Univ Col Music, MusB, 1964, MusM, 1969; Westminster Choir Col, postgrad studies. **Career:** Sch Dist Philadelphia, music teacher, dept head, 1964-69; Westminster Choir Col, guest lectr african-am church music; Community Col Philadelphia, Music Dept, assoc prof, 1970-2003, prof music & dept chair; Nat Opera Ebony, choral dir, chorus master & conductor, 1976-; Clayton White Singers, music dir & founder, 1978-. **Orgs:** Dir, Cult & Educ Ctr, Heritage House, 1962-69; Minister Music Canaan Baptist Church, 1980; bd dir, Settlement Music Sch; bd dir, Penn Presents. **Home Addr:** 1139 E Phil Ellena St, Philadelphia, PA 19150-3118. **Business Addr:** Music Director, Founder, Clayton White Singers, 5732 Race St, Philadelphia, PA 19107, **Business Phone:** (215)476-5320.

### WHITE, CONSTANCE C. R.
Journalist. **Personal:** Born London; daughter of Randall and Hazel; married Denrick Cooper; children: Nefatari Cooper & Kimathi Cooper. **Educ:** NY Univ, BA, jour. **Career:** NY Mag, Writer; MS Mag, Numerous underground publs, assist ed, 1985-86; Freelance; Women's Wear Daily, assoc sportswear ed, 1988-93; Elle Mag, exec fashion ed, 1993-95; NY Times, fashion writer & reporter, 1995-2000; Full Frontal Fashion TV, news anchor & correpondent, 2000-02; Ebay Inc, style dir, 2003-. **Orgs:** Pres & founder, Fashion Outreach, 1992-; Fashion Group, 1993-95; bd mem, Women In Need, 1994-. **Special Achievements:** Interviewed the world's top designers including: Calvin Klein, Donna Karan, Ken Lagerfeld, etc; author, Style Noir: The First How-to Guide to Fashion Written With Black Women in Mind, Perigree, 1998. **Business Addr:** Style Director, eBay Inc, 2145 Hamilton Ave, San Jose, CA 95125, **Business Phone:** (408)376-7400.

### WHITE, COUNCILL, JR. See WHITE, JOSEPH COUNCILL.

### WHITE, D. RICHARD
Chief executive officer, executive, lawyer. **Personal:** Born Aug 5, 1947, Richmond, VA; children: Maleeka Renee. **Educ:** NY City Community Col, AAS, 1968; Bernard Baruch Col, BBA, mkt res, 1970; Kans Univ, JD, 1983. **Career:** Reliance Ins Co, personal injury claims rep, 1975-80; Liberty Mutual Ins Co, claims exam, 1972-83; Nationwide Inter-Co Arbit, arbitrator, 1977; D. Richard White Atty at Law, pvt pract, 1983-97; Farmers Ins Co, sr claims rep, 1997-2004; Shook, Hardy & Bacon LLD, litigation support, 2005; Rosie Quinn & Assocs, personal injury atty, 2006-08; MoKan Personal Injury Group, chief exec officer & head atty, 2007-. **Orgs:** Omega Psi Phi, Dem Club NY; founder, Coop Adventure, 1977; Nat Free Lance Photogr Asn, 1977; Com Better New York. **Honors/Awds:** Bedford-Stuyvesant Civic Award, 1974; Achievement Scroll, Omega Psi Phi, 1974; Bernard Baruch Act Collgian Award, 1974; Recognition of Achievement Reliance Ins Co, 1976. **Home Addr:** PO Box 42, Lawrence, KS 66044, **Home Phone:** (785)727-0510. **Business Addr:** Chief Executive Officer, Head Attorney, MoKan Personal Injury Group, 750 Ann Ave, Kansas City, KS 66101-3014, **Business Phone:** (877)463-4884.

### WHITE, DEBRA Y.
Government official. **Personal:** Born Sep 4, 1966, Portsmouth, VA; daughter of Preston Diggs and Mary; married Alan F; children: Tiffani V & Alexis D. **Educ:** Old Dom Univ, bus admin. **Career:** City Portsmouth, sr dep city clerk, 1991-96; City Portsmouth, chief dep city clerk, 1996-97, city clerk, 1997-. **Orgs:** Va Munic Clerks Asn, 1991-; Int Inst Munic Clerks, 1991-; co-leader, Girl Scout Colonial Coast Coun, 1997-. **Home Addr:** 8 Watch Water Close, Portsmouth, VA 23703, **Home Phone:** (757)638-1150. **Business Addr:** City Clerk, City of Portsmouth, 200 High St Suite 200, Portsmouth, VA 23704, **Business Phone:** (757)393-8639.

### WHITE, DEIDRE R.
Journalist. **Personal:** Born Jun 8, 1958, Chicago, IL; daughter of Thomas and Vivian. **Educ:** Univ Ill, Chicago, IL, BA commun, 1979. **Career:** CBS/WBBM-AM, Chicago, Ill, desk asst, 1979-83, news writer, 1983-87, afternoon producer, 1987-89, managing ed, 1980-90, asst news dir/exec ed, 1990-, planning ed, 1998-2000; CBS News, assignment mgr, news planning mgr, currently; WWJ-AM, dir news & programming. **Orgs:** Nat Asn Black Journalists; Radio Tv News Dirs Asn; Writers Guild Am; bd dir, Univ Ill, Alumni Asn; CBS Mentor vols, 2007. **Honors/Awds:** Kizzy Award, Kizzy Found, 1990; 100 Women to Watch, 1991, Today's Chicago Woman, 1991. **Business Addr:** Assistant News Director, Executive Editor, WBBM-AM/CBS News, 630 N McClurg Ct, Chicago, IL 60611-4495, **Business Phone:** (312)951-3313.

### WHITE, DEVON MARKES (DEVON MARKES WHYTE)
Baseball player, baseball executive. **Personal:** Born Dec 29, 1962, Kingston; married Colleen; children: Thaddeus, Davellyn Rae & Anaya Jade. **Career:** Baseball player (retired), baseball executive; Calif Angels, outfielder, 1985-90; Toronto Blue Jays, outfielder, 1991-95; Fla Marlins, outfielder, 1996-97; Ariz Diamondbacks, outfielder, 1998; Los Angeles Dodgers, outfielder, 1999-2000; Milwaukee Brewers, outfielder, 2001; Wash Nationals, outfield coordr, 2007-08, Player Dev, spec asst, 2008; Chicago White Sox, outfield coordr & baserunning instr, 2011-12. **Home Addr:** 474 W 158th St Suite 42, New York, NY 10032. **Business Addr:** Outfield Coordinator, Chicago White Sox, US Cellular Field 333 W 35th St, Chicago, IL 60616, **Business Phone:** (312)674-1000.

### WHITE, DR. DEZRA
Physician, obstetrician, gynecologist. **Personal:** Born Dec 11, 1941, Beaumont, TX; married Geraldine; children: Dezra Jr, Nicole & Darren. **Educ:** Morehouse Col, BS, 1963; Univ Tex, MD, 1968. **Career:** Christus St Joseph Hosp, internship, 1968-69, resident, 1970-72; Pk Plaza Hosp, physician; St Joseph Hosp, physician; Univ Tex Med Br Hosps, resident, 1969-70; Houston Med Forum, asst secty; Univ Tex, Med Sch, clin assoc; Dept Obstet & Gynec, St Elizabeth Hosp, chmn, 1980-84, 1984-85; Mid-Town Obstet-Gynec Assocs, physician, pvt prac, currently. **Orgs:** Am Asn GYN LSP, Harris Co Med Soc; Houston Obstet & Gynec Soc, Nat Med Asn; pres, Houston Morehouse Alumni Asn; Alpha Phi Alpha, Tots & Teens; fel Am Col Obstet & Gynec; cert Am Bd Obstet & Gynec; mem-at-large, Houston Med Forum; Brookhollow Baptist Church; United Negro Col; Ensemble Theater; predominantly black performing arts ctr; African Am Art Adv Asn; Morehouse Col Houston Alumni Asn; Mus Fine Arts; fel Am Cong Obstetricians & Gynecologists. **Special Achievements:** First African American graduate from University of Texas Medical Branch, Galveston. **Home Addr:** 2105 Jackson St Suite 100, Houston, TX 77003. **Business Addr:** Physician, 3624 Timberside Circle Dr, Houston, TX 77025, **Business Phone:** (713)492-2191.

### WHITE, DONALD R.
Government official. **Personal:** Born Oct 14, 1949, Oakland, CA; son of Louis R and Barbara A Morton; married Lillian P Green; children: 3. **Educ:** Calif State Univ, Hayward, CA, BS, bus admin. **Career:** Arthur Young & Co, San Francisco, CA, auditor, 1971-75; Agams, Grant, White & Co, Oakland, CA, auditor & partner, 1975-85; Ernst & Young, Pub Acct; Alameda County Deferred Compensation Plans, plan adminr; County Alameda, Oakland, CA, cfo, treas-tax collector, currently; Adams, Grant, White & Co, partner. **Orgs:** Active mem, Nat Asn Black Accountants, 1972-; ex-officio mem, Alameda County Employees Retirement Asn Bd Trustees; chairperson, Ad Hoc Audit; chairperson, GASB Community Investment Comt; Ad Hoc Eval Comt; bd dir, E Oakland Youth Develop Ctr Found; City Oaklands bd, adv comt, Budget Adv Comn; Active mem, Nat Asn Advan Colored People; Am Inst Cert Pub Accountants; Calif Soc Cert Pub Accountants; bd dir, Episcopal Diocese Calif; fin chair, USA/NSA Athletics Found; treas, Black Elected Officials E Bay. **Special Achievements:** First African American elected as County Treasurer-Tax Collector of Alameda County. **Home Addr:** 11351 Greenbrier St, Oakland, CA 94605-5537, **Home Phone:** (510)568-7386. **Business Addr:** Treasurer-Tax Collector, Alameda County, 1221 Oak St Rm 131, Oakland, CA 94612, **Business Phone:** (510)272-6800.

### WHITE, EDWARD CLARENCE, JR.
Financial manager, executive. **Personal:** Born Oct 9, 1956, Newark, NJ; son of Edward C Sr and Viola L Williams. **Educ:** Princeton Univ, BA, econ, 1977; NY Univ, MS, quant anal, 1981. **Career:** Merrill Lynch Pierce Fenner & Smith, indust anal, 1977-79; LF Rothschild Unterberg Towbin, vpres, 1979-83; E F Hutton & Co, analyst, vpres, 1983-86, first vpres, 1986-87; Tucker Anthony (John Hancock Fin Serv), New York, NY, first vpres, l988; Technol LBO Partners LP, mng gen partner, 1988-90; Lehman Bros, vpres, 1990-92, sr vpres, 1992-95, mng dir, 1995-; sr semiconductor equip anal, managing dir, Currently. **Orgs:** New York Soc Securities Anals, 1978-. **Honors/Awds:** CFA Designation, Asn Invest Mgt & Res, 1984; Ranked among top anal worldwide Euro Money Mag Global Res Surv, 1985; ranked runner up Inst Invstr Mag Anal Surv, 1986; Lehman Brothers Ten Uncommon Values Award, 1993, 1995 & 1999; Ranked 2 out of 633 anal Bloomberg Bus News, 1995; Surv US Stock Recommendations; Ranked 3 Inst Investor Mag, Anal Surv, 1995; Ranked Runner Up, Investor Mag, Anal Surv, 1996, 1998; Ranked Reuters Surv, 1997-99; Cited Instnl Investor, Mag Home Run Hitter, 1995, 1996; Wall St Journ All-Star Surv, 1999. **Home Addr:** 155 W 70th St Apt 14E, New York, NY 10023-4428.

### WHITE, ELLIOTT. See WHITE, DR. AUGUSTUS A, III.

### WHITE, EVELYN M.
Government official, secretary of health and human services (U.S. federal government). **Personal:** Born Kansas City, MO. **Educ:** Cent

Mo Univ. **Career:** US Dept Agr, dep dir personnel, dir personnel; US Dept Health & Human Servs, dep asst secy human resources, 1997, Off Secy, prin dep asst secy admin & mgt, 2001-, Prog Support Ctr, actg dir, 2003-, sr exec serv, currently. **Special Achievements:** First women to hold the position as dir of personnel for the U.S. Department of Agriculture. **Business Addr:** Senior Executive Service, United States Department Health & Human Service, 200 Independence Ave SW Rm 536E, Washington, DC 20201, **Business Phone:** (202)690-6191.

### WHITE, FRANKIE WALTON

Lawyer. **Personal:** Born Sep 8, 1945, Yazoo City, MS; daughter of William Howard and Serena Brown; children: Carlyle Creswell. **Educ:** Tougaloo Col, BA, Eng, 1966; Univ Calif, Los Angeles, CA, MA, Eng, 1967; Syracuse Univ, Syracuse, NY, attended 1973; Univ MS, JD, 1975. **Career:** Fisk Univ, instr eng, 1967-69; Wellesley Col, lectr eng, 1969-70; Tougaloo Col, asst prof eng, 1970-71; Syracuse Univ, asst dir financial aid, 1971-72; Cent Miss Legal Serv, staff atty, 1975-77; State Miss, spec asst atty gen, 1977, asst atty gen; Tex Southern Univ, stud legal counr, 1977-79; Univ NC Greensboro, SERVE Ctr, MS Dept Educ, sr policy res analyst, 2007-. **Orgs:** Alpha Kappa Alpha Sor Inc, 1964-; Magnolia, Miss Bar Asn, 1975-; Links Inc, 1977-; Comn Col Southern Asn Col & Sch, 1982-; bd trustees, SouthernAsn Col & Sch, 1988-91; Leadership Jackson, 1989-; chmn, Coun State Educ Atty, 1990-91; bd dir, Nat Asn State Bd Educ, 1991. **Honors/Awds:** Woodrow Wilson Fellow; Reginald Heber Smith Comm Lawyer Fellow; Women Achievement Award in Law & Government, Women Progress Mississippi Inc, 1981; Distinguished Alumni Citation, Nat Asn Equal Opportunity Higher Educ, 1986. **Special Achievements:** First african american female to be appointed special asst atty gen, 1977 & asst atty gen, 1986. **Home Addr:** 931 Rutherford Dr, Jackson, MS 39206-2033, **Home Phone:** (601)366-4110. **Business Addr:** Senior Policy Research Analyst, University of North Carolina at Greensboro, Cent High Bldg 359 NW St, Jackson, MS 39201, **Business Phone:** (336)574-8732.

### WHITE, FREDERIC PAUL, JR.

Educator. **Personal:** Born Feb 12, 1948, Cleveland, OH; son of Frederic Paul and Ella Johnson; children: Alfred Davis & Michael Lewis; married Phyllis; children: Jahru. **Educ:** Columbia Col, BA, 1970; Columbia Univ Sch Law, JD, 1973. **Career:** Squire, Sanders & Dempsey, assoc atty, 1973-78; Cleveland State Univ Marshall Col Law, from asst prof to assoc prof, 1978-86, assoc dean, 1994-99; Golden Gate Univ Sch Law, dean & prof law, 2004-08; Tex Wesleyan Univ Sch Law, prof law, dean, 2008-13, chief acad & admin officer; Tex A&M Univ Sch Law, prof law, 2013-. **Orgs:** Bd trustee, Cleveland Legal Aid Soc, 1981-84; Trinity Cathedral Comm Develop Fund, 1981-89; pres, Norman S Minor Bar Asn, 1984; actg judge & referee, Shaker Heights Munic Ct, 1984-90; Zeta Omega Chap; host, CSU City Focus Radio Show, 1981-85; bd advrs, African-Am Mus, 1986-90; charter mem, 100 Black Men Cleveland Inc, 1998-; Law Sch Admis Coun, 1999-2001; Asn Am Law Schs, chair; Am Bar Asn, Accreditation Comt; Law Sch Admis Test; Am Arbit Asn; Omega Psi Phi Fraternity Inc; US Dept State. **Special Achievements:** Books written are "Ohio Landlord Tenant Law, " West Publishing, Co, 1984, 2nd ed, 1990, annually; 2 law review articles, Cleveland Housing Ct, Ohio Open Meeting Law; Contrib Author Antieau's Local Govt Law; co-author chapts "Criminal Procedure Rules for Cleveland Housing Ct"; Frequent guest on local TV/radio landlord-tenant law subjects; contributing editor, Powell on Real Property; Thompson on Real Property; First African American dean of Golden Gate University School of Law. **Home Addr:** 16100 Van Aken Blvd Apt 306, Cleveland, OH 44120-5304. **Business Addr:** Professor of Law, Texas A&M University School of Law, 1515 Com St, Ft. Worth, TX 76102-6509, **Business Phone:** (817)212-4100.

### WHITE, GARY

Executive. **Personal:** married Linda; children: 2. **Educ:** Cuyahoga Col, bus admin, 1973; Harvard Univ, Sch Leadership Negotiation, 1993; Stanford Exec Educ, bd dirs consortium, 1997. **Career:** Savers Inc, chief exec officer; Gymboree Corp, chief exec officer, 1996-2000; Target Inc, vpres regional, Store Mgr & dist mgr, 1976-92, exec vpres, 1992-96; Wet Seal Inc, chief operating officer & exec vpres, 2004-08; United Retail Group Inc, chief exec officer, 2008-10; Redcats USA, exec team, 2008-10; GW Retail Consult, pres & chief exec officer, 2010-. **Orgs:** Bd March Dimes & K.I.D.S. (Kids Distressed Situations); Alumnus Henry Crown Fel prog at Aspen Inst. **Business Addr:** Chief Executive Officer, President, GW Retail Consulting, Orange County, CA.

### WHITE, GARY LEON

Manager, executive, association executive. **Personal:** Born Dec 17, 1932, Windsor, ON; son of George W and Anna Louella Talbot; married Inge Topper; children: Karen, Janet, Gary, Christopher & Steffanie. **Educ:** Univ Md; Wayne State Univ; Carnegie Mellen Univ, Pittsburgh Grad Sch Indust Admin, 1980. **Career:** Cobo Hall, conv, 1960-64; Jam Handy Org, assoc prod, 1964-64; Tom Thomas Orgn, exec vpres & gen mgr, 1965-70; White Assoc Inc, pres, 1970-75; Ford Motor Co, mgr, 1977-87; City Detroit, dir pub info, 1975-77; Jones Transfer Co, chmn, chief exec officer; Automotive Logistics Productivity Improve Syst, pres & chief exec officer. **Orgs:** Bd dir, Metro Affairs Corp; bd dir, United Way; bd dir, Monroe Mich; bd dir, Monroe High Sch Scholar Fund; Nat Minority Enterprise Legal Defense Fund; Greater Detroit Interfaith Round Table Nat Conf Christians & Jews, Boysville, Mich; Nat Asn Black Automotive Suppliers; Nat Asn Advan Colored People; adv bd, Liberty Mutual Ins Co; African Develop Found; regional adv coun, Small Bus Admin; bd gov, Mich Trucking Asn; Jobs & Econ Develop Task Force; Detroit Strategic Planning Proj; Commun Comn; Am Trucking Asn; vice chmn, Booker T Wash Asn, 1991-. **Honors/Awds:** Testimonial Resolution, Detroit City Coun; Outstanding Serv, Corp Coordr, NMSDC; Concurrent Resolution, Mich Legis, 1987; Cert of Spec Tribute, Gov, State Mich, 1987; Lett of Commendation, Pres Ronald Reagan, 1987; Black Enterprise Mag Top 100, 1988. **Home Addr:** 2600 Shagbark Lane, Milford, MI 48380. **Business Addr:** President, Chief Executive Officer, Automotive Logistics Productivity Improvement System Inc, 28510 Hildebrandt, Romulus, MI 48174, **Business Phone:** (734)947-3640.

### WHITE, GEORGE GREGORY (GEORGE WHITE)

Journalist. **Personal:** Born Dec 3, 1953, Detroit, MI; son of George Bernard and Edna. **Educ:** Mich State Univ, E Lansing, MI, BA, hist & Jour, 1975, MA, african hist, 1981. **Career:** Minneapolis Tribune, Minneapolis, Minn, reporter, 1975-79; US News & World Report, Detroit Bur, corresp, 1982-84; Detroit Free Press, Detroit, Mich, reporter & columnist, 1984-87; Ford found, res analyst & writer, 1999-2001, consult, 2002; Los Angeles Times, Los Angeles, Calif, reporter, ed, 1988-99; Univ Calif, Ctr Communs & Community, Los Angeles, asst dir & ed, currently; Ctr Commun & Community, asst dir, ed & develop dir, 2002-09; Un Develop Programme, media consult, 2002-09; Calif Wellness Found, consult, writer; Robert L Green & Assocs, commun dir, ed, mkt dir & res analyst, 2011-; New Am Media, pub progs coordr & corresp, 2013-. **Orgs:** Dir, bd mem, La Chap Nat Asn Black Journalists, 1990-; const affairs comt mem, Nat Asn Black Journalists, 1990-; former mem, bd trustee, diversity comt advisor, Kripalu Ctr Yoga & Health; World Affairs Coun, LA, currently; bd adv, Youth Radio; bd dir, Los Angeles Press Club; African Univ Col Commun, consult, 2009; vpres, Black Journalists Asn Southern Calif. **Honors/Awds:** Honors Col, Mich State Univ, 1971-75; Lilly Endowment Fel, 1979-81; Los Angeles Press Club Award for Outstanding Dedication, 1992; Pulitzer Prize, Los Angeles Times Riot Coverage Team; Los Angeles Times Team Awarded, 1994; Asniated Press Award, 1995. **Home Addr:** 5928 W Lindenhurst Ave, Los Angeles, CA 90036, **Home Phone:** (213)935-6330. **Business Addr:** Assistant Director, Editor, University of California, 4250 Pub Policy Bldg 405 Hilgard Ave, Los Angeles, CA 90024, **Business Phone:** (310)206-3109.

**WHITE, IDA MARGARET. See Obituaries Section.**

### WHITE, JACK E., JR.

Journalist. **Personal:** Born Jun 30, 1946, Washington, NC; son of Jack Sr; married Cassandra Clayton; children: 4. **Career:** Wash Post, reporter, staff writer, 1966-68; Race Rels Info Ctr, Nashville, TN, staff writer, reporter, 1969-72; Time Mag, staff writer, 1972-79, Nairobi Bur, chief, 1980-82 & 1985, Chicago Bur, chief, 1985-88, dep chief corresp, 1987-88, sr ed & nat ed, 1988-92; Nation, New York, corresp, 1982-84, nat corresp; ABC World News Tonight, sr producer, 1992-93; Time Inc, ed, 1995-2001; Atlanta, Ga & Boston, corresp; Va Commonwealth Univ, adjust prof journalism; Roberts vs Texaco: A True Story Race & Corp Am, co-auth, 1998; Howard Univ Sch Journalism, writer-in-residence, scripps howard endowed chair, 2005. **Orgs:** Nat Asn Black Journalists. **Business Addr:** National Correspondent, Time Magazine, 283 Genesee St Suite 3, Rochester, NY 14611-3496, **Business Phone:** (585)235-7150.

### WHITE, JAHIDI

Basketball player, actor. **Personal:** Born Feb 19, 1976, St. Louis, MO. **Educ:** Georgetown Univ, attended 1998. **Career:** Basketball player (retired); Wash Wizards, forward, 1998-2003; Phoenix Suns, 2003-04; Charlotte Bobcats, guard, 2004-05; Cleveland Cavaliers, 2006-07. **Orgs:** Jahidi White Charitable Found Kids Inc. **Special Achievements:** Film Appearances: Showdown at Area 51, 2007.

### WHITE, JALEEL AHMED

Actor. **Personal:** Born Nov 27, 1976, Pasadena, CA; son of Michael and Gail; married Bridget Hardy; children: Samaya. **Educ:** Univ Calif Film Sch, Los Angeles, attended 2001. **Career:** TV series: "The Jeffersons", 1984; "Silence of the Heart", 1984; "The Cosby Show", 1984; "Charlie & Company", 1985-86; "Kids Don't Tell", 1985; "The Leftovers", 1986; "Mr. Belvedere", 1987; "Good Morning, Miss Bliss", 1987; "Full House", 1987; "Family Matters", 1989-98; "Camp Cucamonga", 1990; "Step By Step", 1991-97; "The Adventures of Sonic the Hedgehog", 1993-96; "Sonic the Hedgehog", 1993-95; "ER", 1994; "The Fresh Prince of Bel-Air", 1995; "Sonic Christmas Blast", 1996; "Sonic Underground", 1998; "Grown Ups", 1999-2000; "111 Gramercy Park", 2003; "Inspector Gadget's Last Case", 2003; "Half & Half", 2005; "Boston Legal", 2007; "The Game", 2007; "Psych", 2009; "Race to the Altar", 2009; "Dancing with the Stars", 2012; Films: The Howard Stern Show, 1994; "Diagnosis Murder", 1997; Meego, 1997; Quest for Camelot, 1998; Big Fat Liar, 2002; Puff, Puff, Pass, 2006; Miracle Dogs Too, 2006; Who Made the Potatoe Salad, 2006; Dreamgirls, 2006; Kissing Cousins, 2008; Green Flash, 2008; The Call of the Wild, 2008; Road to the Altar, 2009; "Fake It Till You Make It", auth, producer & dir, 2010; Syfy channel, Total Blackout, host, 2012. **Honors/Awds:** Young Artist Award, 1991; Image Award, Best Child Actor TV Comedy, Nat Asn Advan Colored People, 1992, 1993; Sammy Davis Jr Award; Youth Achievement Award, 1993; Image Award, 1994, 1995; Image Award, Best Male Actor TV Comedy, Nat Asn Advan Colored People, 1997. **Special Achievements:** Ranked 37 in VH1s list of the 100 Greatest Kid Stars; Ranked 1 in Q Ratings, 1991. **Home Addr:** c/o Gail White, PO Box 580, Agoura Hills, CA 91376, **Home Phone:** (818)324-4074. **Business Addr:** Actor, Shuman Co, 3815 Hughes Ave 4th Fl, Culver City, CA 90232, **Business Phone:** (310)841-4344.

### WHITE, JAMES D.

President (organization), chief executive officer. **Personal:** married Lisa; children: Jasmine & Krista. **Educ:** Univ Mo, BS, mkt; Fontbonne Univ, MBA. **Career:** Coca-Cola Foods, 1980-86; Nestle Purina Petcare, exec positions, 1987-2005; Customer Develop E, vpres, 1997-1999; Customer Interface Group, 1999-2002; Gillette Co, sr vpres bus develop, 2002-05; Safeway Inc, sr vpres consumer brands, 2005-08; Jamba Inc, pres & chief exec officer, 2008-. **Orgs:** Nat Jr Tennis League; Matthews Dickey's Boys & Girls Club; dir, Keane Inc, 2004-; United Way; dir, bd, chmn, Jamba Inc, 2008-, chmn, 2010-; dir, Daymon Worldwide Inc, 2010-; dir, Hillshire Brands Co, 2012-; Org Ctr's Bd dir; PTA, Adv Bd.

### WHITE, JAMES LOUIS, JR.

Executive, vice president (organization). **Personal:** Born Jul 14, 1949, Charlottesville, VA; son of James Louis and Myrtle Virginia Garland; married Cynthia Phina Austin; children: James Louis III, Charles Marquas & Matthew David. **Educ:** St Paul's Col, Lawrenceville, VA, BS, 1973; Univ Kans, Lawrence, KS, cert, 1982; Univ Pa, Philadelphia, PA, cert, 1982; Fla State Univ, Tallahassee, FL. **Career:** Centel Tel, Charlottesville, VA, div & dist eng, 1973-74, Des Plaines IL, dist mgr & personnel mgr, 1974-75, Chicago IL, asst staff mgr, 1975-77, asst customer serv mgr fla state oper, 1977-79, Chicago, gen customer staff mgr, 1979-84, gen customer serv mgr fla state oper, 1984-88; Centel Cellular, FL, regional vpres, 1988-; 360 Degree Commun, regional pres, 1995-97; 360 Degree Long Distance, pres, 1997; Alltel Communs Inc, vpres govt ralations & external affairs, currently. **Orgs:** Chamber Com & Econ Club, 1985-89; pres, Big Ben Independent Tele Pioneer Asn, 1988; mem bd dir, Dick Howser Ctr Cerebral Palsy & Fla Spec Olympics, 1989. **Special Achievements:** Author of article "Centel Puts Prewiring Costs Where They Belong", Team magazine, August 15, 1980. **Home Addr:** 13031 Huntley Manor Dr, Jacksonville, FL 32224, **Home Phone:** (904)992-0058. **Business Addr:** Vice President External Affairs, Alltel Communication Inc, 6867 Southpoint Dr N Suite 103, Jacksonville, FL 32216-8005, **Business Phone:** (904)470-4769.

### WHITE, JAMES MATTHEW, JR.

President (organization), founder (originator), educator. **Personal:** Born Mar 13, 1958, Salisbury, MD; son of James and Irene; married Anna; children: 8. **Educ:** Univ Md Eastern Shore, BA, 1982; Wilmington Col, MA, 1990, EdD, 2000. **Career:** Univ Md Eastern Shore, residence counr, 1982-91, dir stud activ, 1991-2001, asst to vpres stud affairs, 2001, assoc vpres stud affairs, currently. **Orgs:** Life mem, APA Fraternity, 1978-; Asn Col Unions Int, 1991-; pres, Princess Anne Town Comnr, 1996-98, vpres, 1998-; founder, Princess Anne Youth Orgn, 1999-. **Business Addr:** Associate Vice President, University of Maryland Eastern Shore, Stud Serv Ctr Col Backbone Rd Suite 2169, Princess Anne, MD 21853-1299, **Business Phone:** (410)651-8440.

### WHITE, JANICE G.

School administrator. **Personal:** Born Aug 21, 1938, Cincinnati, OH; daughter of Murray C Gray and Odessa Parker Grey; married Amos J Jr; children: Janine, Amos III & David. **Educ:** Case Western Res Univ, BA, 1963; Capital Univ Law Sch, JD, 1977. **Career:** Legal Aid Soc Columbus, Reginald Heber Smith Community, Law fel, 1977-79; Franklin Co Pub Defender, juvenile unit, pub defender, 1979-80; Ohio StateLegal Servs Asn, legis coun, 1980-84; State Employment Rels Bd, labor relsspecialist, 1984, administrative law judge, 1984-88; Capital Univ Law & Grad Ctr, alumni rels & multi-cult affairs dir, 1988-. **Orgs:** Am Bar Asn; Ohio Bar Asn; Cent Community House; Links Inc; Nat Conf Black Lawyers; Women Lawyers Franklin Co Inc; Columbus Comn Community Rels; Delta Sigma Theta Sorority Inc; United Negro Col Fund. **Home Addr:** 665 S High St, Columbus, OH 43209, **Home Phone:** (614)237-0819. **Business Addr:** Director Alumni Rels & Minority Affairs, Capital University, 303 E Broad St, Columbus, OH 43215-3200, **Business Phone:** (614)445-8836.

### WHITE, JESSE C.

Government official. **Personal:** Born Jun 23, 1934, Alton, IL. **Educ:** Ala State Col, BS, 1957. **Career:** Isham Memorial YMCA, phys educ dir, 1955-74; Jenner Sch, teacher, 1959-63; Schiller Elem Sch, teacher, 1963-90; Ill Gen Assembly, state rep, 1975-77, 1979-92, Chicago Bd Ed Phy Ed, prog coordr, 1990-92; Cook County, recorder deeds, 1992-99; Dem committeeman; Chicago Cubs & orgn, prof baseball player; State Ill, 37th secy state, 1998-99, 2002-; re-elected again 2006. **Orgs:** Founder, coach, Jesse White Tumbling Team, 1959-; Chicago Cubs orgn, 1959-66; scoutmaster, Boy Scouts Am, 1967-; Ill Nat Guard; partner, Mothers Against Drunk Driving; Chicagos 27th Ward Dem Committeeman, 1996. **Home Addr:** 300 W Hill St, Chicago, IL 60610, **Home Phone:** (312)944-0949. **Business Addr:** Secretary, State of Illinois, 213 State Capitol, Springfield, IL 62756, **Business Phone:** (217)782-3000.

### WHITE, JO JO (JOSEPH HENRY WHITE)

Athletic director, basketball player, executive. **Personal:** Born Nov 16, 1946, St. Louis, MO; married Estelle Bowser; children: Brian J; married Deborah. **Educ:** Univ Kans, attended 1969. **Career:** Basketball player (retired); Boston Celtics, guard, 1969-79, dir spec proj, community rels rep, 2000-; Golden State Warriors, guard, 1979-80; Kans City Kings, guard, 1980-81; Jayhawks, asst coach, 1982-83; Continental Basketball Asn, guard, 1987-88; JoJo's West, owner, 2009-10; Jo Jo White Found, exec dir, 2012. **Orgs:** Nat Basketball Asn, 1974 & 1976; Gold-Medal-Winning US Olympic team, 1968. **Business Addr:** Director of Special Projects & Community Relations, Boston Celtics, 226 Causeway St 4th Fl, Boston, MA 02114, **Business Phone:** (866)423-5849.

### WHITE, JOHN CLINTON

Journalist. **Personal:** Born May 5, 1942, Baltimore, MD; married Elaine B; children: Anthony C & David E. **Educ:** Morgan State Univ, BS, polit sci & govt, 1970. **Career:** WJZ-TV, news producer & Writer, 1968-69; The Balt Afro-Am, reporter, 1969; The Evening Sun, reptr, 1969-72; The WA Star, staff writer; Wash Suburban Sanit Comn, pub affairs mgr, 2007-. **Orgs:** Managed ed, The Spokesman Morgan State Univ, 1969-70; treas, Asn Black Media Workers, 1975-77; dir commun, Nat Asn Advan Colored People, 1999-2006; founder, Nat Asn Black Journalists. **Honors/Awds:** Group W Award, completion of Westinghouse Broadcasting Int prog, 1968. **Home Addr:** 3414 Dennlyn Rd, Baltimore, MD 21215. **Business Addr:** Public Affairs Manager, Washington Suburban Sanitary Commission, 14501 Sweitzer Lane, Laurel, MD 20707, **Business Phone:** (301)206-9772.

### WHITE, JOHN H.

Photojournalist. **Personal:** Born Mar 18, 1945, Lexington, NC; son of Reid Ross and Ruby Mae; married Emily Lee Miller; children: Deborah, Angela, Ruby & John Henry. **Educ:** Cent Piedmont Community Col, AAS, com art & advert design, 1966. **Career:** Com Photo Studio, lab technicians; USMC, photogr; Chicago Daily News, photogr, 1969-78; Environ Protection Agency Documerica, photogr, 1973-74; Chicago Sun-Times, photojournalist, 1978-; Columbia Col, Chicago, artist residence, instr, 1978-, head photojournalism dept, 1988-; Northwestern Univ, instr; Northwestern Univ, Medill Sch Journalism, Adj Lectr, 2002-04; La Rabida C's Hosp Chicago, photogr. **Orgs:** Pres, Chicago Press Photogr Asn, 1977-78. **Honors/Awds:** Photographer of the Year Award, Ill Press Photogr Asn, 1971, 1979, 1982; Marshall Field Award, Chicago Sun-Times, 1976; National Headliner Award,

1979, 1990, 1999; Robert F Kennedy Journalism Award, 1979; World Press Photo Competition Award, 1979; Pulitzer Prize, Feature Photography, 1982; Illinois United Press International Awards, 1982; Outstanding Photojournalist Award, Chicago Asn Black Jour, 1981, 1982, 1984; Joseph A Sprague Memorial Award, Nat Press Photogrs Asn, 1989; Associated Press Award, 1991; Nat Press Award, Mandela Release, 1991; Inductee, Chicago Jour Hall of Fame, 1993; Award of Excellence in General News Photography, Nat Press Photogr's Asn, 1994; Chicago Medal of Merit, 1999; Studs Terkel Award, 1999; Inducted into Chicago State University Hall of Fame, 2002; Recipient of Lifetime Achievement Award, Chicago Headliners Club, 2003; The Nikon Award for years of service and friendship to photojournalism, 2006; The Chicago Journalists Association Lifetime Achievement Award, 2007; Associated Press Spot News Award, 2008; Teacher of the Year Award, 2008; The Southern Short Course in News Photography Lifetime Achievement Award, 2009; Peter Lisagor Award for Best News Photo, 2009. **Special Achievements:** Photo Exhibitions: "My People: A Portrait of Afro-American Culture," Rockefeller Ctr, New York City, 1991; "The Soul of Photojournalism," Comenius Univ, Slovakia, 1993; "John H. White: Portrait of Black Chicago," National Archives Exhibit, 1997; contributed to book and exhibit: "Songs of My People;" Published books: This Man Bernardin, 1996; The Final Journey of Joseph Cardinal Bernardin, 1997. **Business Addr:** Photo Editor/Staff Photographer, Chicago Sun-Times, 401 N Wabash Ave, Chicago, IL 60611, **Business Phone:** (312)321-3000.

### WHITE, JOSEPH COUNCILL (COUNCILL WHITE, JR.)

Executive, vice president (organization). **Personal:** Born May 12, 1942, Mobile, AL; son of Council and Estelle; married Theresa Lorraine Carraway; children: Shawn Lenard & Derrick Gerrard. **Educ:** Ala State Univ, BS, 1965; Atlanta Univ, MS, 1967; Wash State Univ, PhD, 1970. **Career:** Chevron Chem Co, tech coordr, regist, 1985-88; Abbott Labs, dir regulatory affairs, 1988-92, qual assurance & regulatory affairs, div vpres, 1992-99; Cardinal Health Inc, vpres qual mfg, 1999-2000, sr vpres qual, 2000-. **Orgs:** Vice chmn, Abbott Labs Employee Credit Union, 1989-99; pres, Big Brother/Big Sister Lake Co, 1991-99; adv coun, Nat Inst Environment Health Sci, 1996-99; Parental Drug Asn; Kappa Alpha; Fla A&M Univ Sch Pharmaco Bd Visitors. **Home Addr:** 13 Georgetown Ct, Basking Ridge, NJ 07920, **Home Phone:** (908)781-1551. **Business Addr:** Senior Vice President of Quality, Cardinal Health Inc, 7000 Cardinal Pl, Dublin, OH 43017, **Business Phone:** (614)757-5000.

### WHITE, JUNE JOYCE

Police officer. **Personal:** Born Feb 25, 1949, Flushing, NY; daughter of Jean Dolores DeVega Hampton and Marion Luther Hampton; married James R; children: Wenty Morris III, Ellie Morris, Mario St John, Lena, James, Clifton, Roxanne, Jasmine & Chamara. **Educ:** Queens Col, Flushing NY, attended 1971; NYC Health & Hosp, New York, NY, respiratory cert, 1973. **Career:** Police officer (retired); New York Hosp Police, police officer, 1973-74; Jamaica Hosp, Jamaica NY, respiratory therapist, 1975-76; Brunswick Hosp, Amity ville, NY, respiratory therapist, 1978-83; NMex State Corrections, Cent NMex Corrections Facil, Los Lunas NMex, officer, 1983, lt, 1984-88. **Orgs:** Nat Asn Advan Colored People, 1969-, chair, Educ Comm, 1988; NM Correctional Workers Asn, 1983-88; consult, NM Multi Investors, 1983-91; pres, Black Officers Asn NM, 1983-91; NM Spec Needs C, 1984-91; NM deleg, Nat Black Police Asn, 1985-; pres, Rio Rancho Human Rights Comn, 1988-90; host chair, Nat Black Police Southern Region Conf, 1988; Comn Defense Human Rights Workplace, 1988-91; Am Correctional Asn. **Honors/Awds:** Joseph "Tree Top" Turner Achievement Award, Nat Black Police Asn, 1987; Guardian of the Treasury, Govs Off, 1988; Award of Excellence, Black Officers Asn NM, 1989; Award of Excellence, Black Officers Asn NMex, 1990. **Special Achievements:** Ed, NM Law Enforcement Journal, 1983-91. **Home Addr:** 2379 Lema Rd, Rio Rancho, NM 87124, **Home Phone:** (505)891-8022.

### WHITE, KARYN LAYVONNE

Singer. **Personal:** Born Oct 14, 1965, Los Angeles, CA; daughter of Vivian and Clarence; married Terry Lewis; children: Tremain, Chloe, Brandon & Ashley Nicole; married Bobby G. **Career:** Flyte Time Prod, Minneapolis, vocalist; Warner Bros Rec, vocalist, 1986-99; Albums:Karyn White, 1988; Ritual of Love, 1991; Make Him Do Right, 1994; Sweet & Sensual, 1995; Rhino Hi-Five: Karyn White-EP, 2005; Sista Sista, 2006; Superwoman: The Best, 2007; Songs: "Facts Of Love", 1986; "Ritual of Love", 1991; "The Way I Feel About You", 1991; "Walkin' the Dog", 1992; "Hungah", 1994; "I'd Rather Be Alone", 1995; "Sista, Sista", "Carpe Diem", KW Entertainment, 2011-. **Business Addr:** Singer, c/o Warner Bros Recording, 3300 Warner Blvd, Burbank, CA 91505, **Business Phone:** (818)846-9090.

### WHITE, DR. KATIE KINNARD

Educator. **Personal:** Born Feb 28, 1932, Franklin, TN; daughter of Arthur and Era Smith; married Joseph; children: Joletta & Angela. **Educ:** Tenn State Univ, Nashville, BS, 1952, MS, 1959; Eastern Mich Univ, Ypsilanti, attended 1961; George Peabody Col, Nashville, TN, attended 1965; Walden Univ, Naples, FL, PhD, 1976. **Career:** Educator (retired); Bedford County Schs, Shelbyville TN, teacher, 1952-53; Shelbyville City Schs, Shelbyville TN, teacher 1953-59; Nashville CitySchs, Nashville TN, teacher, 1959-62; Tenn State Univ, Nashville TN, prof sci educ, 1962-70, prof biophys sci & coordr teacher educ biol, 1970-97. **Orgs:** Imp Club; Carondelet Civic Asn; Nat Asn Biol Teachers; Nat Coun Negro Women; Nat Asn Advan Colored People; Alumni Asn Tenn State Univ; Tenn AcadSci; hon adv bd mem, Am Biog Inst, 1982-89; pub educ co-chair, Assault Illiteracy Prog, 1988; nat pres (Grand Basileus), Sigma Gamma Rho, 1988-92; bd dir, Sigma Gamma Rho; fund fel, Nat Educ Fund, Sigma Gamma Rho. **Home Addr:** 9007 Oden Ct, Brentwood, TN 37027, **Home Phone:** (615)373-3850.

### WHITE, DR. KEITH L.

College administrator. **Personal:** Born Jul 30, 1948, Boston, MA; married Cheryl C. **Educ:** Morehouse Col, BA, 1972; Wayne State Univ, MEd, 1992, EdS, 1997, EdD, 1999. **Career:** Archdiocese Detroit, teacher & adminr, 1974-84; Thirty sixth Dist Ct, probation officer, 1985-87; Detroit Bd Educ, teacher, 1987-90; Wayne State Univ, admin, adj prof, 1991-, Wayne County, dir, currently. **Orgs:** APA Fraternity Inc, 1967-; chair, Doctors Inc Network & Support Group, 1996-; adv bd, Proj Soaring Retention Prog, 1999-; Asn Continuing Higher Educ, 1999-; chair, Wayne County Child Foster Care Rev Bd, 2000-03; UAW, Community Caring Scholar, 2000-; YMCA Minority Achievers, 2001-. **Business Addr:** Director, Wayne State University, 7800 W Outer Dr Suite 300, Detroit, MI 48235.

### WHITE, KENNETH EUGENE, SR.

Military leader, business owner. **Personal:** Born Mar 9, 1953, Columbus, OH; son of David and Helen; children: Kenneth E II & Malcolm J. **Educ:** Ohio State Univ, BS, 1977. **Career:** Military leader (retired), business owner; Investor Real Estate Services, broker, 1977-; USAR, sargent first class, recruiter, 1987; 4 Life Enterprises, owner, 1991-. **Orgs:** St Mark 76A Masons; pres, Central Ohio Young Republican, 1979; vol, I Know I Can, 1988-; Toastmaster, 1990-; 100 Black Men Cent Ohio; adv, Knights 100 Mentoring Prog. **Honors/Awds:** Recruiter Ring, AUS, 1993; Mentor of the Year Award, Columbus Army Recruiting Battalion, 1997; Blue Ribbon, Photography, OH State Fair, 1998. **Home Addr:** 1657 Franklin Pk S, Columbus, OH 43205-2104, **Home Phone:** (614)252-4845. **Business Addr:** Owner, Your Favorite Photographer, 2127 Leeonard Ave, Columbus, OH 43219, **Business Phone:** (614)252-4845.

### WHITE, LEO, JR.

Military leader. **Personal:** Born Nov 3, 1957, Monterey, CA; son of Leo and Winifred; married Jacqueline Murray; children: Leo Edward; married Jackie. **Educ:** Cumberland Col, BS, 1980; Distinguished Mil Grad; Who's Who Am Cols & Univs. **Career:** Athlete, judo player, military captain (retired); USY, Transp, capt, 1980; Waka Mu Sha Judo Club, coach, currently. **Orgs:** Bd dir, USS Olympic Comt, 1992-96, athlete adv coun, 1992-; Va Peninsula Chamber Cong; Nat Judo Coaching Staff; Athletes Adv Coun Rep, U.S. Olympic Festival, 1994, Pan Am Games, 1995, Olympic Games, 1996; Goodwill Games Team. **Honors/Awds:** Judoka of the Year, 1958; Pan American Games, Bronze Medal, 1979; Pan American Championships, Gold Medal, 1980; Olympia Award, 1983; Meritorious Service Medals; NCJA All American; Army Athlete of the Year Award, 1983; U.S. Olympic Training Center Judo Team, captain, 1985, 1987-89; U.S. Senior Judo Championships Outstanding Competitor, 1988; Pacific Rim Games Team, Gold Medal, 1991; Pan American Games Team, Silver Medal, 1991; Pacific Rim Championships, Gold Medal, 1993; U.S. Olympic Festival Champion, 1995; World Masters Champion, 1998; U.S. Judo Champion, Senior Nationals, 1998; 6 time U.S. Olympic Festival Championship; 4 time U.S. International Invitational Champion; 4 time World Military Champion; 2 time member of the U.S. Olympic Judo Team; 4 Time Pacific Rims Games, gold medal; 4 Time Collegiate Judo Champion; Most Improved Player of the year, U.S. Judo Association. **Special Achievements:** USS Olympic Team, Judo Athlete, 1984, 1992; Military Athlete of the Year, 1983; Timmie Award, Touchdown Club, 1983; Black Belt Hall of Fame, 1983; Only U.S. judo athlete to win a Senior National Championship in each of the last 3 decades; 18 Time U.S. Senior National Champion; Holds record for most medals won by a judo athlete in Pan American Games. **Home Addr:** 4371 Weston Dr SW, Lilburn, GA 30047-3168, **Home Phone:** (678)924-1161. **Business Addr:** Coach, Waka Mu Sha Judo Club, 790 Berne St SE, Atlanta, GA 30312, **Business Phone:** (770)337-8537.

### WHITE, LUTHER J. See Obituaries Section.

### WHITE, MARGARETTE PAULYNE MORGAN

Journalist. **Personal:** Born Sep 11, 1934, Tattnall County, GA; daughter of Riley Morgan; married Frank; children: Lairalaine. **Educ:** Reids Bus Col, dipl, 1952; Morris Brown Col, BA, 1957; Univ Toledo; Univ Tenn; Ga State Univ, cert. **Career:** Teacher, 1957-66; commun specialist, 1967-69; Morris Brown Col, dir Pub rels & dir spec events proj; Atlanta Enquirer, assoc ed & columnist, 1988; Atlanta Housing Authority, bd commissioners, currently; Mgt & Training Corp, community & pub rel specialist, Pub Rels, dir; Guys & Dolls Inc. **Orgs:** Nat pub rels dir, Bus & Prof Women's Asn, 1973; pub rels chmn, Delta Sigma Theta; Am Bus Women; Atlanta Club Bus & Prof Women; founder & pres, Sparklers Inc; founder, Atlanta Jr Club; pres, Gay G Club; Atlanta League Women Voters; Leadership Atlanta; Nat Urban League; 100 Women Int; life mem, Award J Educ Asn; nat treas, Nat Asn Media Women; life mem, Nat Asn Advan Colored People. **Honors/Awds:** Leading Lady Atlanta, Assoc Ed, Atlanta Inquirer, 1977; Delta Women Breaking New Ground Award; Appreciation Award, Journ Educ Asn; Best Youth Page Award, NRPA; National Media Woman of the Year; Alumna of the Year, Morris Brown Col; The Pres's Award, Founder's Cup, Media Women Inc; Black Women Achievers, Southern Bell, 1990; Bronze Woman of the Year, 1992. **Home Addr:** 3509 Rolling Green Rd SW, Atlanta, GA 30331-2323, **Home Phone:** (404)344-5609. **Business Addr:** Public Relations Specialist, Atlanta Housing Authority, 230 John Wesley Dobbs Ave, Atlanta, GA 30303, **Business Phone:** (404)685-4902.

### WHITE, DR. MARILYN ELAINE (MARILYN WILLIAMS WHITE)

Educator. **Personal:** Born Jul 30, 1954, Gary, IN; daughter of Herschel and Martha Williams; children: Chris, Kyle & Kory. **Educ:** Univ Mich, BA, jour, 1976; Oakland Univ, MAT, reading & instrnl technol, 1992, PhD, reading & instrnl technol, 1998. **Career:** Detroit Pub Sch, reading specialist, 1976-; Marygrove Col, prof educ, 1998; BWW Group Inc, co-founder. **Orgs:** Nat Coun Teachers Eng, 1985-; Mich Reading Asn, 1990-; Friends African & African Am Art, exec bd, 1993-; Metro Detroit Reading Coun, 1994-; Mich Asn Comput-related Users Educ, 1994-; Nat Alliance Black Sch Educ, 1995-; head educ agenda, Women's Leadership Inst, 2001; Int Reading Asn; adv bd, Nat Healthcare Scholars Found; Bethany Youth Group; Detroit Inst Arts; Oakland Univ Black Alumni Asn; Univ Mich Alumni Asn; Delta Sigma Theta Inc; exe dir, Black Women Contracting Asn, 2002-. **Home Addr:** 5229 Bishop, Detroit, MI 48224, **Home Phone:** (313)300-9354. **Business Addr:** Reading specialist, The Detroit Public Schools, 3031 W Grand Blvd, Detroit, MI 48202, **Business Phone:** (313)873-3111.

### WHITE, MAURICE

Songwriter, television producer, singer. **Personal:** Born Dec 19, 1941, Memphis, TN; son of Verdine Sr; children: 1. **Educ:** Chicago Conserv Music. **Career:** Singer; producer; composer; bandleader; Chess Rec, studio drummer, 1962-67; Earth, Wind & Fire, founder & mem, 1971-; albums: All 'n All, 1977; Kalimba Prod, 1983; Undercover-Paul Taylor, 2000; Gratitude 5.1 Surround Sound, 2001; "Get Over It", composer, 2001; The Essential Earth, Wind & Fire, 2002; "Austin Powers in Gold member", composer, 2002; That's The Way Of The World Live In '75, 2002; Live In Rio, 2002; The Promise, 2003; "Get Up!", composer, 2003; "Be Cool", composer, 2005; Now, Then & Forever, 2013.Series: "Late Night with Jimmy Fallon", writer, 2010; "Banda sonora", writer, 2011; "No me la puc treure del cap", writer, 2012; "The Tonight Show with Jay Leno", writer, 2012; Songs: "September", 1971; "Boogie wonderland", 1979; "Let's groove", 1981; "After the love has gone", 1979; "shining star", 1975. **Business Addr:** Singer, Magnet Vision Inc, 1358 5th St, Santa Monica, CA 90401, **Business Phone:** (310)576-6140.

### WHITE, MICHAEL JAI

Actor. **Personal:** Born Nov 10, 1967, Brooklyn, NY; married Courtenay Chatman; children: Morgan Michelle. **Career:** Films: The Toxic Avenger, Part II, 1989; The Toxic Avenger Part III: The Last Temptation of Toxie, 1989; Teenage Mutant Ninja Turtles II: The Secret of the Ooze, 1991; Ring of Fire, 1991; True Identity, 1991; Universal Soldier, 1992; Spawn, starring role, 1997; City of Industry, 1997; Ringmaster, 1998; The Bus Stop, 1998; Thick as Thieves, 1999; Breakfast of Champions, 1999; Universal Soldier: The Return, 1999; Exit Wounds, 2001; Pandora's Box, 2002; Honor Among Thieves, 2002; Justice, 2003; Kill Bill Vol 2, 2004; Getting Played, 2005; Undisputed II: Last Man Standing, 2006; Why Did I Get Married?, 2007; PVC-1, exec producer, 2007; The Dark Knight, 2008; The Slammin' Salmon, 2009; Black Dynamite, 2009; Blood and Bone, co-producer, 2009; Three Bullets, writer, producer & dir, 2009; Mortal Kombat: Rebirth, 2010; Mortal Kombat: Legacy, 2011; Tactical Force, 2011; Never Back Down 2, dir, 2011: The Beatdown, 2011; Shadow Vengeance, 2011; We the Party, 2012; Freaky Deaky, 2012; The Philly Kid, 2012; Android Cop, 2014; Falcon Rising, 2014; TV series: "Tyson", 1995; "Mutiny", 1999; "Freedom Song", 2000; "Wonderland", 2000; "Chapter Eighteen", 2001; "Hotel", 2003; "Chin Music", 2004; "The Doomsday Sanction", 2005; "Spawn: The Animation", 2006; "The Legend of Bruce Lee", 2008; "The Boondocks", 2010; "Batman: The Brave and the Bold", 2011; "For Better or Worse", 2011-12; "Black Dynamite", screenplay, 2012; "Somebody's Child", exec producer, 2012; "Metal Hurlant Chronicles", 2012-14; "Arrow", 2013-14. **Honors/Awds:** Nominee, Best Male New comer for the Blockbuster Entertainment Awards, 1997. **Special Achievements:** Is an accomplished martial artist, holding seven legitimate black belts indifferent martial arts styles with a specific focus in Kyokushin karate (although his style incorporates aspects of many different martial arts forms); First African American to portray a major comic book superhero in a major motion picture. **Business Addr:** Actor, Writers & Artists Agency, 8383 Wilshire Blvd Suite 550, Beverly Hills, CA 90211, **Business Phone:** (323)866-0900.

### WHITE, MICHAEL REED

Mayor, politician, government official. **Personal:** Born Aug 13, 1951, Cleveland, OH; married Tamera. **Educ:** Ohio State, BA, educ, 1973, MA, pub admin, 1974. **Career:** Cleveland City Coun, admin asst, 1976-77, councilman, 1978-84, mayor, 1990-2002; Burks Elec Co, sales mgr, 1982-85; Beehive & Doan Partnership, partner, 1983-84; Burks Develop Corp, assoc, 1984-85; OH Senate, 21st Dist sen; State Ohio, state sen, 1984-89. **Orgs:** Bd mem, Glenville Housing Found, 1978-; bd mem, Glenville Develop Corp, 1978-; bd mem, Cleveland Scholar Prog, 1981-85; Glenville Festival Found; United Black Fund; Greater Cleveland Dome Corp; Royal Ridge-Pierce Found; Waterfront Devel Corp; Am Const Freedom, Univ Circle Inc. **Honors/Awds:** Outstanding Young Leader, Cleveland Jaycees, 1979; Service Award, East Side Jaycees, 1979; Outstanding Service Award, Nat Asn Black Vet Cleveland Chap, 1985; Community Service Award, East Side Jaycees; Freedom Award, Cleveland Nat Asn Advan Colored People; Public Service Award, Cleveland State Univ's; Man-of-the-Year, Baptist Ministers Conf. **Special Achievements:** Cleveland's second African American mayor as well as the city's second youngest mayor. **Home Addr:** 1057 E Blvd, Cleveland, OH 44108-2984. **Business Addr:** 601 Lakeside Ave E, Cleveland, OH 44114-1012.

### WHITE, NAN ELIZABETH

Consultant. **Personal:** Born Mar 15, 1931, Jacksonville, IL; daughter of Mitchell Cook and Grace L; married Wilmer M; children: Michael Anthony. **Educ:** Bradley Univ, BS, 1952; George Warren Brown Sch Social Work, Wash Univ, MSW, 1955; Chicago Univ Sch Continuing Educ Summer Inst, attended 1964. **Career:** Consult (retired); Family & C Serv Greater St Louis, work-study stud, caseworker III, stud supvr, 1954-67; Lincoln HS, E St Louis, IL, sch social worker, 1967-68; Annie Malone C's Home, social work dir, therapist, 1968-69, exec dir, 1970-78; Satellite Group Home Girls, dir, 1971-73; Independent Child Welfare, consult, 1979-84. **Orgs:** Allocations Panel, United Way, 1978-88, admis comn, 1989-94, priorities comn, 1992-94; St Louis Div Family Serv, Permanency Planning Rev Teams, 1982-85; Sch Syst incl Counpregnant Teenagers, 1985-87; St Louis Pub Sch Syst, 1985-89; Southern Poverty Law Ctr, 1993-; Am Cancer Soc & St Louis Pub Y Read Tutoring Prog, 1996-97; vol servs, Storytime, Buena Pk Libr Dist, 1999-; Ladies Auxilary VFW, 2001-; Long Beach, CA, Veterans Hosp; NCP. **Honors/Awds:** Award for Civic Service, Zeta Phi Beta Sorority, 1976; Federal Award, Annie Malone Children's Home, 1991; Volunteer Recognition Award, Library, 2001; George Washington Carver Award for Service to Youth, Sigma Gamma Rho Sorority. **Home Addr:** 4902 St Andrews Cir, Buena Park, CA 90621, **Home Phone:** (714)522-2153.

### WHITE, PAUL EDWARD

Government official. **Personal:** Born Aug 19, 1941, Brazil, IN; son of William Clarence and Lillian Olivia Brackette; married Somphon. **Educ:** Valparaiso Univ, BA, 1964; Univ Hawaii, attended 1966; Stanford Univ, attended 1980. **Career:** Government official (retired); Foreign serv officer; int training & develop alliance bldg expert; US Agency Int Develop, minister coun develop coop & mission dir, 1991-97. **Orgs:** Int Hon Soc; vpres, Toastmasters Int Dist Gov, 2005; Soc

Am Magicians Int Brotherhood Magicians; Lions; Rotary Int; bd dir, Aid Artisans Inc. **Home Addr:** 3919 Moss Dr, Annandale, VA 22003.

## WHITE, PERSIA

Actor, singer. **Personal:** Born Oct 25, 1972, Miami, FL; married Saul Williams; children: Mecca; married Joseph Morgan. **Career:** Actress, musician, activist; Black White, band mem, currently; XEO3, band mem, currently; "Prob Child", 2009, Mecca, singer, 2010; Films: Blue Chips, 1994; Frankie D, 1996; Blood dolls, 1999; Red Letters, 2000; Stalled, 2000; Earthlings, producer, 2003; The Fall of Night, 2007; Everyday Joe, actress & co-producer, 2007; Spoken Word, 2009; Dysfunctional Friends, 2012; The Marriage Chronicles, 2012; Guardian of Eden, 2012; Black November, 2012; No More Games, 2012; Mafia, 2012; Revelation, 2013; Manifesto, 2014. TV series: "Another World", 1964; "Goode Behavior", 1996; Saved by the Bell: The New Class", 1996; "Malibu Shores", 1996; "Suddenly", 1996; "NYPD Blue", 1996; "Breaker High", 1997; "Buffy the Vampire Slayer", 1997-2004; "Another World", 1999; "Clueless", 1999; "Girlfriends", 2000-07; "Operation Sandman", 2000; "Angel", 2001; "Unscripted", 2005; "Kiss the Bride", 2011; "The Vampire Diaries", 2012-13. **Orgs:** Humane Soc US; Global Green; Farm Sanctuary; Citizens Comn Human Rights; People Ethical Treat Animals; Sea Shepherd Conserv Soc; bd dir, Sea Shepherd Conserv soc. **Honors/Awds:** Humanitarian of the Year, PETA, 2005; Grand Jury Prize, Am Black Film Festival, 2011. **Business Addr:** Board of Director, PO Box 2616, Friday Harbor, WV 25661, **Business Phone:** (360)370-5650.

## WHITE, RALPH L., JR.

Executive, businessperson, chief executive officer. **Personal:** Born Mar 13, 1930, Decatur, AL; son of Edmond and Bertha M; married Chrysanthemum Robinson; children: Rodney M, Lorrie C & Kimberly L. **Educ:** Ala A&M Col, Huntsville, BS, 1951; Air Force Inst Tech, hon grad, 1958; Tex Christian Univ, Ft Worth, MS, 1965; Webster Univ, St Louis, MO, MBA, 1983. **Career:** Herf Indust Inc, Little Rock, AR, pres & founder, 1972-75; Southwestern Bell Tel Co, AR, worked eng planning, switching syst eng, outside plant construct, dist personnel mgr, regional mgr external rels; MDI Inc, pres & chief exec officer, currently. **Orgs:** Nat Biol Hon Soc, 1964; consult, AR Bus Coun, 1988; trustee, Hendrix Col, 1988-; Govs Task Force Sch Dropouts, 1988-89; Little Rock Chamber Com Educ Comn, 1988-; bd dir, Ark Pvt Indust Counil, 1988-; AR Advocates C & families, 1989, Legis Planning Group C. **Special Achievements:** Author of Effect of Capacitor Discharge on Microorganisms, 1965. **Business Addr:** President, Chief Executive Officer, MDI Inc, 913 S Hughes St, Little Rock, AR 72204-1536, **Business Phone:** (501)661-9332.

## WHITE, RALPH LEE

Real estate agent, association executive, founder (originator). **Personal:** children: 1. **Career:** White Ralph Bail Bonds, owner, 2008-; real estate agt; Comn Status African Am Males, comn mem; Stockton City Coun, mem, vice mayor. **Orgs:** Pres, Stockton Nat Asn Advan Colored People; founder, Stockton Youth Found. **Special Achievements:** First African American to be elected vice-mayor of the city of Stockton, 1972. **Business Addr:** Owner, White Ralph Bail Bonds, 2230 S Airport Way, Stockton, CA 95206-2419, **Business Phone:** (209)464-8371.

## WHITE, RANDY

Basketball player. **Personal:** Born Nov 4, 1967, Shreveport, LA. **Educ:** La Tech Univ, attended 1989. **Career:** Basketball player (retired); Dallas Mavericks, forward, 1989-94; Peristeri Athens, 1994; Pfizer Reggio Calabria, Italy, 1994-95; Joventut Badalona, Spain, 1995-96; Okla City Cavalry, 1996; Maccabi Tel Aviv, 1996-98; CSKA Moscow, Russia, 1998-99; Aris Thessaloniki, Greece, 1999; Near E BC, Greece, 1999.

## WHITE, RAYMOND RODNEY, SR.

Government official. **Personal:** Born Feb 15, 1953, Newark, NJ; son of Henry W Sr and Lucille M Jackson Sr; married Karmen; children: Nia; married Linnie B Adams; children: Raymond Rodney Jr. **Educ:** Rutgers Univ, BA, community develop & econ develop, 1975; Ga Inst Tech, MA, city planning, housing & econ develop, 1977; Carl Vinson Inst Gov, cert pub mgt, 1988; Ga Tech Col Archit, PhD, city & regional planning, 2015. **Career:** Plainfield City, sr planner, 1977-78; Fulton Co Planning Dept, planner ii-long-range & zoning planner, 1978-81; Williams Russell & Johnson Inc, sr airport, transp & parks planner, 1981-82; Harrington George & Dunn PC, sr planner, 1982; Oglethorpe Power Co, land planner, land use analyst, 1982-83, econ develop mgr, prin planner, 1983-; Dekalb County Planning Dept, econ develop mgr, 1983-92, dir planning, 1992-2004; White Strategic Serv, principle consultan & owner, 2004-. **Orgs:** Am Planning Asn 1979-; planning task force chmn, Col Pk Neighborhood Voters League, 1980-; DeKalb County Chamber Com, 1983-; Develop Authority DeKalb County, 1983-94; bd mem, Foxhead Develop Corp, 1983-; vol, Habitat Humanity Atlanta, 1984-; pres, Develop Alliance Unlimited Inc, 1984-; Ga Indust Developers Asn, 1984-; Nat Forum Black Pub Admin, 1984-; bd mem, Ga Econ Developers Asn, 1984-93; Metro Atlanta Chamber Com; Corp Mkt Task Force, S Side Develop Task Force; local exhib comt chmn, Am Planning Asn, 1984-97 & 1998-2002; DeKalb County Econ Develop Team, 1988-2004; co-chair, UNCF Bus Community, 1989-91; bd chmn, Oakhurst Community Health Center, 1989-91; Am Inst Cert Planners, 1992-95; secy, 1990, dir, 1991-92, Ga Planning Asn; Decatur-Dekalb YMCA Bd, 1990-92; One Hundred Black Men Am Inc, 1991-2003; bd dir, Ga Indust Developers Asn; Dekalb comt mem, County Dist Boy Scouts Am, 1992; vice chair econ develop comt, 100 Black Men Am Inc, Dekalb County Chap, 2009-; Comn mem, Gov's Int Adv Coun, 1992-; Atlanta Regional Comn Alumni, 1992; historian, Male Acad, 1994-96; Decatur Rotary Club, 1994-2004; dev comt chair, Soccer St Inc, 1995-96; bd mem, Our House Inc, 1995-98; Ga Conservancy, 1998. **Home Addr:** 3972 Cheru Dr, Decatur, GA 30034, **Home Phone:** (404)987-4955.

## WHITE, RICHARD C.

Manager. **Personal:** Born Feb 22, 1941, New York, NY. **Educ:** NY Univ, BS, econ, 1962; Howard Univ, JD, law, 1967. **Career:** Boston Symphony Orch, asst; Peace Corp, staff; pvt consult & artist mgr. **Orgs:** Nat Asn Advan Colored People; ACLU; Phi Alpha Delta Legal Frat.

## WHITE, RICHARD H.

School administrator. **Personal:** Born Jun 1, 1950, Chicago, IL; son of Herman and Luvenia; married Valencia Peters. **Educ:** Cath Univ, Washington, DC, BA, 1973; Howard Univ, Washington, DC, MA, 1979. **Career:** Am Red Cross, Atlanta, Ga, dir develop, 1980-85; Civitan Int, Birmingham, Ala, dir develop, 1985-88; Riverside Community Col, Riverside, Calif, chief develop officer, 1988-90; Morris Brown Col, Atlanta, Ga, vpres develop, 1990-92; Emory Univ, Robert W Woodruff Lib, dir develop libr & info technol, 1992-97; Clark Atlanta Univ, vpres, instnl advan & univ rels, 1998-. **Orgs:** Ga Joint Bd Family Pract, Gov & State Ga, 1984; Child Abuse Prev Bd, Gov & State Ala, 1986; sr exec, Serv Rank Rev Bd, 1996; bd pres, Nat Soc Fund Raising Execs. **Home Addr:** 251 Highland Lake Trace, PO Box 50564, Atlanta, GA 30349. **Business Addr:** Vice President, Clark Atlanta University, 223 James P Brawley Dr, Atlanta, GA 30314, **Business Phone:** (404)880-8000.

## WHITE, RICHARD THOMAS

Lawyer. **Personal:** Born Jan 10, 1945, Detroit, MI; son of Raymond Wendell and Joyce Loraine Thomas; married Tanya; children: Richard T Jr, Devin A & Andrew S. **Educ:** Morehouse Col, BA, hon, 1967; Harvard Univ Law Sch, Cambridge, Mass, JD, 1970. **Career:** Dykema Gossett, assoc, 1970; Patmon, Young & Kirk PC, assoc, 1971-72; Lewis, White & Clay PC, founder & pres, currently; Auto Club Group, sr vpres, secy, gen coun, currently. **Orgs:** City Detroit Human Rights CMS, 1964-65; Corp & Health Law Sect, Am Bar Asn, 1970-; Nat Health Lawyers Asn, 1975-; compensation com bd dir, United Am Health Care Corp, 1983-; bd dir audit comt, Detroit Med Ctr, 1990-95; bd dir, Am Basic Indust Inc, 1991-; vice chair, MIC Transp CMS, 1991-; comnr, Foreign Claims Settlement Comn, 1995-; chmn bd, Asn Corp Coun, 2007-; chmn, Mich Transp Comn, 2007-; finance com bd, Detroit-Macomb Hosp; mem nat policy bd, InfiLaw Syst; dir, Am Corp Coun Asn. **Business Addr:** Senior Vice President & Secretary, General Counsel, Auto Club Group, 1 Auto Club Dr, Dearborn, MI 48126, **Business Phone:** (313)336-1284.

## WHITE, ROBERT C.

Police chief. **Personal:** Born May 6, 1952, Richmond, VA. **Educ:** George Wash Univ, contemp exec develop prog, 1991; Univ DC, BA, pub admin, 1993; Johns Hopkins Univ, MS, appl behav sci, 1996. **Career:** Metrop Police Dept Dc, policeman, 1972; Dc Housing Authority Off Pub Safety, dir, 1995-97; NC Police Dept, chief police, 1998; Louisville Metro Police Dept, chief police, 2003-11; Denver Police Dept, chief police, 2011-. **Special Achievements:** First Metro Louisville's Chief of Police; first Director of Public Safety for the District of Columbia Housing Authority; first African-American police chief. **Business Addr:** Chief of Police, Denver Police Department, Police Administration Bldg 1331 Cherokee St, Denver, CO 80204-4507, **Business Phone:** (720)913-2000.

## WHITE, RONDELL BERNARD

Consultant, baseball player. **Personal:** Born Feb 23, 1972, Milledgeville, GA; married Zanovia; children: Zaiya. **Career:** Baseball player (retired), free agent; Montreal Expos, outfielder, 1993-2000; Chicago Cubs, outfielder, 2000-01; New York Yankees, outfielder, 2002; San Diego Padres, outfielder, 2003; Kans City Royals, outfielder, 2003; Detroit Tigers, outfielder, 2004-05; Minn Twins, outfielder, 2006-07, free agt, currently. **Home Addr:** 11111 Pine Lodge Trail, Davie, FL 33328. **Business Addr:** Free Agent, Minnesota Twins, 34 Kirby Puckett Pl, Minneapolis, MN 55415, **Business Phone:** (612)375-1366.

## WHITE, RORY WILBUR

Basketball coach, basketball player. **Personal:** Born Aug 16, 1959, Tuskegee, AL; married Julie; children: Rory Jr, Josh & Jenna. **Educ:** Univ S Ala, phys educ, 1982. **Career:** Basketball player (retired), basketball coach; Phoenix Suns, 1982-83; Wyo Wildcatters, 1983-84; Milwaukee Bucks, 1984-87; Albuquerque Silvers, 1984; Los Angeles Clippers, head coach, 1984-87; Collado Villalba, 1987-88; Caripe Pescara, 1989; Maristas, 1989; Santa Barbara Islanders, 1989-90; Oostende, 1990-91; Rapid City Thrillers, 1991; Ferro Carril Oeste, 1991-92; Okla City Cavalry, 1992; Fargo-Moorhead Fever, 1992-94; Fargo-Moorhead Beez, coach, 1995-98, 2001-02; Fla Sharks, coach, 1997; Idaho Stampede, asst coach, 1999-2001, head coach, 2000, 2002-03; Marinos de Oriente, coach, 2001; Dakota Wizards, head coach, 2009-. **Home Addr:** 1609 Linden Ave B, Nashville, TN 37212, **Home Phone:** (615)631-0106.

## WHITE, DR. SANDRA LAVELLE

School administrator, educator. **Personal:** Born Aug 30, 1941, Columbia, SC; daughter of Christopher O and Rosena E Benson; married Kenneth Olden; children: Heather Alexis. **Educ:** Hampton Inst, BA, biol & chem, 1963; Univ Mich, MS, microbiol, 1971, PhD, microbiol, 1974. **Career:** Sloan Kettering Inst Cancer Res, res asst, 1963-69; AT&T, res asst, 1969; Univ Mich Dept Microbiol, teaching asst, 1969-71, Med Sch, asst lectr microbial, 1970, guest lectr immunol, 1973; Howard Univ Col Med, asst prof Microbiol, 1974-76, assoc prof microbiol & oncol, Cancer Ctr, 1979-92, Cancer Ctr, adj fac; NIH, staff fel, 1976-79; Duke Univ Med Ctr, assoc res prof, 1993-98; NC Cent Univ, Dept Biol, prof & chair, 1998-2003, Ctr Math, Sci & Technol Educ, dir, 2004-. **Orgs:** Nat Sci Found Traineeship, 1970-71; Pathol B Study Sect Nat Insts Health, 1980-84; Bd Sci Counselors, Div Cancer Biol & Diag, Nat Cancer Inst, NIH, 1985-89; Nat Bd Med Examrs, Microbiol Test Comt, 1989-93; Am Asn Cancer Res, 1990-; Am Asn Immunol, 1991-; bd dir, GLYCO Design Inc; bd dir, NC Mus Life & Sci; Am Soc Microbiologists; Am Asn Women Cancer Res; Delta Sigma Theta Sorority Inc; Am Soc Cell Biol; bd dir, NC Mus Life &Sci; bd dir, Women Action Prev Violence & Its Causes; Links Inc; Jack & Jill AME Inc; Smaty Set Inc. **Honors/Awds:** Ford Found Fellowship, 1970-74; Kaiser Permanente Award, Excellence in Teaching, 1982. **Home Addr:** 19 Quail Ridge Rd, Durham, NC 27705. **Business Addr:** Professor, Director, North Carolina Central University, 1801 Fayetteville St, Durham, NC 27707, **Business Phone:** (919)530-7060.

## WHITE, SHARON BROWN

School administrator. **Personal:** Born Sep 29, 1963, Pineville, LA; daughter of Eva M Brown; married Wilbur James. **Educ:** Grambling State Univ, Grambling, BS, 1985; Alcorn State Univ, Lorman, MS, 1988. **Career:** Alcorn State Univ, Lorman, sec, 1985-88, admin asst, 1988; Fisk Univ, Nashville, sec, 1989, dir, career planning & placement, 1989. **Home Addr:** 2801 Lincoya Dr, Nashville, TN 37214, **Home Phone:** (615)883-6579.

## WHITE, STEPHEN GREGORY

Writer, football player. **Personal:** Born Oct 25, 1973, Memphis, TN. **Educ:** Univ Tenn, BA, psychol. **Career:** Football player (retired), sports blogger; Tampa Bay Buccaneers, 1996, 1998, 2000, defensive end, 1997, 2001, right defensive end, 1999; New York Jets, 2002; Sports Blog Nation, sports blogger, contribr, currently. **Business Addr:** Contributor, SB Nation, c/o Vox Media Inc, Washington, DC 20036, **Business Phone:** (202)591-1140.

## WHITE, SYLVIA KAY

Fashion consultant. **Personal:** Born Dec 5, 1955, Washington, DC; daughter of James Odessa and George D Sr (deceased). **Educ:** Fashion Inst Tech, AA, 1975; State Univ NY, fashion buying. **Career:** Alexander Inc, buyer, mens, 1975-83; Montgomery Ward Inc, buyer, boys, 1983-87; Nordstroms, McClean, sales mens merchandise, 1988-. **Orgs:** Trustee, 1985-, First Union Baptist, Budget & Finance Comn, chair, 1986-88. **Honors/Awds:** Outstanding Young Women of America, 1985. **Home Addr:** 7912 Grant Dr, Lanham, MD 20706. **Business Addr:** Sales Men, Nordstroms, 8075 Tysons Cor Ctr, McLean, VA 22102, **Business Phone:** (703)761-1121.

## WHITE, THURMAN V., JR.

Chief executive officer, president (organization). **Educ:** Princeton Univ, Woodrow Wilson Sch, BA, pub & int affairs; Stanford Univ, MA, commun; Univ Calif, Berkley, JD. **Career:** Progress Investment Mgt Co LLC, prod mgr, chief operating officer, 1992-, managing dir, 1994-2001, chief exec officer & pres, 2001-; Fed Commun Comn (FCC), staff atty; Calif Legis's Assembly Utilities & Com Comt, legal coun; Pac Bell, dir. **Orgs:** Calif Bar, 1981; dir, Nat Asn Investment Co; dir, Philippe Investment Mgt Inc; bd dir, Silicon Valley Community Found; bd dir, Nat Asn Investment Co; dir, Fourpoints Asset Mgt Inc. **Honors/Awds:** "Black Enterprise," 75 Most Powerful Blacks on Wall Street, 2011. **Business Addr:** President, Chief Executive Officer, Progress Investment Management Company LLC, 33 New Montgomery St 19th Fl, San Francisco, CA 94105, **Business Phone:** (415)512-3480.

## WHITE, DR. TOMMIE LEE

Psychologist, counselor, college teacher. **Personal:** Born May 20, 1944, Dublin, GA; son of Mack F Sr and Daisy. **Educ:** Yankton, BA, 1966; Univ SD, MA, 1967; Univ Southern Calif, PhD, 1974, PhD, 1982; Bd Cert Dipl Pscyhopharmacol, Prescribing Psychol, Regist FPPR. **Career:** Horace Mann Jr H LA, teacher hist & phys educ, 1967-70; Univ SD, grad asst, 1966-67, asst res dir, 1967; US Olympic Team, Psychologist; Calif State Univ Northridge, Dept Kinesiol, fac, 1970-2005, chair & prof, prof emer, 2005; clin, coun psychologist, pvt pract; Samra Univ, Doctoral Adv Comt, bd mem. **Orgs:** Am Psychol Asn; Asn Black Psychologists; Calif Fac Asn; Calif Psychol Asn; Am Fedn Teachers; clin, coun Sport Psychologist, US Olympic Comm & USATF; AAASP; Phi Delta Kappa, Alpha Phi Alpha Fraternity Inc, APA-Exercise & Sport Psychol. **Honors/Awds:** SD Col Track Athlete of Decade, 1960-69; Alumni of the Year, 1976; All-Am TrackHon, 1965; SDak Athlete of the Year Award, 1965; Hall of Fame, Howard Wood, 1978; dean's list hon stud Yankton Col, 1965-66; Track & Field News All-American Award, 1971; World's best record 60 meter high hurdles 74 sec Moscow, 1972; Nat Amateur Athlete Rep to AAU, 1975-; West Region top assistant in womens hurdles, 2006. **Special Achievements:** Published: "Seven Keys to Hurdling Excellence" Coach and athletic dir, 2002; "the relationship between physical educ admin values & their attitudes toward education Innovations", 1974, "The Relationship Between Cognitive Style and Locus of Reinforcement", 1978, "Essentials of Hurdling "Athletic Journ, 1980, "Hurdling-Running Between The Hurdles" Athletic Journal 1980; Publications: "Reparenting Schizophrenic Youth in a Hospital Setting", 1985; Presentations: "African-American Athletes: Distorted Vision sand Shattered Dreams", "Standing Alone: The Spinal Injured", 1992; "Diversity in Sports: Are We Doing Enough", 1993. **Home Addr:** 6635 Kentwood Bluffs Dr, Los Angeles, CA 90045-1260, **Home Phone:** (310)410-1426. **Business Addr:** Professor Emeritus, California State University, 18111 Nordhoff St Redwood Hall, Northridge, CA 91330-8287, **Business Phone:** (818)677-4528.

## WHITE, TYTRAL T. (TY WHITE)

Basketball coach. **Educ:** Va State Univ, BS, phys & health educ, 2002. **Career:** Petersburg High Sch, asst basketball coach, 2002-10; John Marshall, head coach, 2010-. **Orgs:** Head, AAU prog, Cameron Found. **Business Addr:** Assistant Basketball Coach, Petersburg High School, 207 Jefferson Ave, Petersburg, VA 26847.

## WHITE, VALERIE D.

Executive director. **Personal:** children: Joslynn & Monica. **Educ:** Fordham Univ, BA, commun arts, 1983, JD, law, 1996; New Sch Univ, MS, mgt, 1986. **Career:** NYC Dept Personnel, dep dir mgt planning & anal, 1985-90; New York Housing Authority, dep dir asset mgt & pvt mkt opers, 1991-99; Stand & Poor's, dir, 1999-2009, US Pub Finance Housing, anal mgr & team leader, 2009-13, managing dir; lead anal mgr housing enterprises & structured securities, 2013-15; Valerie D White LLC, prin, 2015-. **Orgs:** Co-Chair, Brooklyn Alumnae Chap, Delta Sigma Theta Sorority Inc, 1993-, e kings county alumnae chap; bd mem, Brooklyn Arts Coun; exec comt mem, Women's Leadership Comt, United Way New York; alumni mentor, Fordham Univ, 2012-; bd advisor, exec leadership inst, Coun Urban Professionals, 2013-; bai Mentor, Harlem YMCA bai, 2014-. **Home Addr:** , Brooklyn, NY.

**WHITE, WENDELL F.**
Executive, executive director, association executive. **Personal:** Born Aug 20, 1939, Atlanta, GA. **Educ:** Morehouse Col, BA, 1962; Atlanta Univ, MBA, 1967; Univ Calif, Los Angeles, addn studies. **Career:** Williamson & Co Real Estate, 1961-65; Johnson Publ Co; Gen Motors Corp, 1965; Coca-Cola Co, mkt exec, 1965-70; US Dept Com, dir off minority bus enterprise, 1970-74; Empire Investment Enterprises Inc, pres; Empire Realty Co, chief exec officer, pres, currently. **Orgs:** Former pres, Empire Real Estate Bd; Atlanta Bus League; former mem, Citizens Trust Bank Adv Bd; former mem, Nat Asn Mkt Developers; former mem, bd dir, Travelers Aid Soc; Southern Christian Leadership Conf; Nat Asn Advan Colored People; Urban League, Butler St YMCA. **Honors/Awds:** Leadership Award, Butler St YMCA; Letter of Commendation, Pres US; Cert Merit, Nat Asn Advan Colored People. **Home Addr:** 1314 Wesley Oaks Ct NW, Atlanta, GA 30327. **Business Addr:** President, Chief Executive Officer, Empire Realty Co, 535 Joseph E Lowery Blvd SW, Atlanta, GA 30310-1400, **Business Phone:** (404)758-1462.

**WHITE, WILLIAM DE KOVA.** See WHITE, BILL.

**WHITE, WILLIAM JOSEPH**
Electrical engineer, association executive, military engineer. **Personal:** Born Aug 6, 1926, Philadelphia, PA; son of James Earle and Mary Valentine; married Althea de Freitas; children: Karen & William Jr. **Educ:** A&T Col, attended 1943; Syracuse Univ, attended 1950; NY City Univ, BS, physics & mathematics, 1960; AUS Command & Gen Staff Col, attended 1956. **Career:** Electrical engineer & army major (retired); Andrea Radio & TV, tech writer, 1955; NY Transit Authority, elec engr, 1958; US Appl Sci Lab & electronics engr & scientist; Fed Aviation Admin, elec engr, 1961-87, Systs & Equip Br, mgr; Cong Church Hempstead Monthly, ed, 1989-; Hempstead, ed; Hempstead Little League, monthly newsletter ed. **Orgs:** Chmn bd trustee, United Cong Church, 1970-72; pub rels, Hempstead Little League, 1970-78; Pres, Local 2791 Am Fed Govt Employ, 1972-80; pres, SE Civic Asn, 1972-; pres, Hempstead Bd Ed, 1973-78; Authors Guild, 1974-; Nat Writers Club, 1975-, Hempstead Planning Bd. **Honors/Awds:** Man of the Year, Hempstead Little League, 1972; Outstanding Community Serv, CRUSH, 1988; Martin L King Jr Mem Award, United Black Christians, 1990; Humanitarian Award, Hempstead NAACP, 1991; Hempstead Medal Honor. **Special Achievements:** Listed in, Community Leaders & Noteworthy Americans, Contemporary Authors vols 97-100, Men of Achievement; Free Lance Writer, Frequent Flyer, Newsday/Nat Rifleman Christian Herald; Published his first book Airships For the Future in 1972. **Home Addr:** 174 Lawson St, Hempstead, NY 11550-6947, **Home Phone:** (516)485-8726.

**WHITE, WILLIAM TURNER, III**
Executive. **Personal:** Born Nov 12, 1947, Jacksonville, FL; married Patricia E; children: William Thomas IV. **Educ:** Bethune-Cookman Col, attended 1966; TN State Univ, BS, polit sci, 1969; Dartmouth Col, BA; Emory Univ, MA, metrop govt, 1972. **Career:** Emory Univ, fel, 1970; Off Mayor, Model Cities Atlanta GA, res eval spec, 1973-75; Inst Sch Res, res assoc, 1975-78; Grassroots Inc, exec dir, 1978-80; DeKalb County Planning Dept, human serv facil coordr, 1980; Kirkwood & Edgewood Eastlake Econ Develop Corp, chief exec officer, 1982; Manufacturers Hanover, vpres corp banking; Equity Group Investments LLC, managing dir corp investments; Lurie Investment Fund LLC, exec vpres, 2000-; Cernium Corp, bd dir, currently; CytoPherx Inc, dir; NanoInk Inc, dir, currently; Kionix Inc, dir, currently; Impact Health Inc, dir, currently; Joint Juice Inc, dir, currently; Nephrion Inc, dir, currently; Viamet Pharmaceut Inc, dir, currently; Manufacturers Hanover, vpres corp banking; HealthpointCapital, dir, currently; Discera Inc, dir, 2010-; Nanosphere Inc, dir, 2012-13. **Orgs:** Worshipful Master Royal Ark Masonic Lodge F & AA York Rite Masons, 1978; past Grand Jr Warden Smooth Ashlar Grand Masonic Lodge, 1978-82; bd Community Rel Comn DeKalb Cty, 1979-82; DeKalb-Atlanta Voter's Coun, 1982; Nat Forum Black Pub Admin, 1983; SE Atlanta Intown Businessmen Asn, 1985; bd mem, SE Atlanta YMCA. **Honors/Awds:** Illus Inspector Gen Nat Supreme Coun Scottish Rite 33rd degree Mason, 1978; Outstanding Young men Am, 1979; Lt Col Aid de Camp Off Govt State GA, 1983; Spec Dep Sheriff DeKalb Cty; Worshipful Master of the Year Masons, 1980-81. **Home Addr:** 3411 Elgin Dr, Decatur, GA 30032. **Business Addr:** Executive Vice President, Lurie Investment Fund LLC, 2 N Riverside Plz St Suite 1500, Chicago, IL 60606, **Business Phone:** (312)466-3750.

**WHITE, WINIFRED VIARIA**
Broadcaster, executive. **Personal:** Born Mar 23, 1953, Indianapolis, IN; daughter of Walter H and Winifred Parker; married Kenneth Neisser; children: Alexis & Nick. **Educ:** Harvard Radcliffe Col, BA, ling, 1974; Lesley Col, MA, elem educ & teaching, 1975; Univ Wis Madison, commun arts. **Career:** Nat Broadcasting Co, mgr, proj peacock, 1981-82, c progs, 1982-84, dir, c progs, 1984-85, vpres, family progs, 1985-89, dir, motion pictures TV, 1989; Columbia TriStar Tv, vpres movies tv & miniseries; Sony Pictures Tv, sr vpres, movies & miniseries, currently. **Orgs:** Bd dir, Harvard-Radcliffe Club, 1983-; former mem, Harvard Bd Overseers; Adv Bd Radcliffe Inst; bd govrs, TV Acad, 1986-; bd dir, Planned Parenthood, 1986-; bd dir, Women Film, 1990-; bd trustee, Otis Col Design; bd trustee, Nat Guild Community Arts Schs. **Honors/Awds:** A Raisin Sun, ABC; Broken Trail, western AMC; The Best Miniseries; The Company; Having Our Say: Delaney Sisters First 100 Yrs; Crossing, Arts & Entertainment Channel; Beach Boys: An Am Family. **Home Addr:** 3267 Glendon Ave, Los Angeles, CA 90034. **Business Addr:** Director Motion Pictures for Television, Sony Pictures Entertainment Corporate Communications, 10202 W Wash Blvd, Culver City, CA 90232, **Business Phone:** (310)244-4000.

**WHITE, WOODIE W.**
Clergy. **Personal:** Born New York, NY; married Kim Tolson; children: Kimberly Yvette, Hope Angela, Valerie Elizabeth, Sharon Denise & Bryan Michael. **Educ:** Paine Col, BA; Boston Univ Sch Theol, MDiv. **Career:** St Andrews Methodist Church, Worcester, Mass, Pastor; E Grand Blvd Methodist Church, Detroit, Mich, from assoc pastor to pastor; United Methodist Church, gen secy, 1969-84, southern & cent Ill conf, bishop, head, 1984-92, Gen Bd Discipleship, 1988-92; Ind State United Methodist Church, bishop, head, 1992-2006; Christian Theol Sem, Indianapolis, Ind, adj fac; Howard Univ Sch Relig, Wash, DC, adj fac; Wesley Theol Sem, Wash, DC, adj fac; Emory Univ, Candler Sch Theol, bishop residence, currently. **Orgs:** Mem, Ill Great Rivers Area; Ind Conf; United Methodist Church; gen secy, Gen Comn Relig & Race United Methodist Church, 1969-84; rlected a bishop, 1984; pres, Gen Bd Discipleship, 1988-92; pres, Coun Bishops, 1996-97; elected mem, Martin Luther King, Jr Int Bd Preachers at Morehouse Col Atlanta, Ga. **Honors/Awds:** Distinguished Alumni Award, Boston Univ, Sch Theol, 1970; Distinguished Service Award, United Comm Negro Hist, 1974; Urban Award, US Off Econ Opportunity; Hon Degrees: Univ Evansville, Adrian Col, Rust Col, McKendree Col, Ill Wesleyan Col, MacMurray Col, Paine Coll, Univ Indianapolis, Martin Univ. **Special Achievements:** Racial Transition in the Church, co-author, 1980; Confessions of a Prairie Pilgrim, author, 1988; Conversations of the Heart, author, 1991; Our Time Under God Is Now: Reflections on Black Methodists for Church Renewal, author, 1993; First African-American named to lead the United Methodist Church in Ind, 1992. **Business Addr:** Bishop-in-Residence, Emory University, Bishops Hall 500 S Kilgo Circle, Atlanta, GA 30322, **Business Phone:** (404)727-0734.

**WHITE, DR. YOLANDA SIMMONS**
Educator. **Personal:** Born Apr 6, 1955, Baltimore, MD; daughter of Carlton and Edna Eva Johnson; married Edward Clarence. **Educ:** Princeton Univ, Princeton, NJ, BA, 1977; Yale Univ, New Haven, CT, MA, 1978, MA, philos, 1980, PhD, 1982. **Career:** World Without War Coun, NY, proj dir, 1980-81; Y S White & Co, pres, 1982-84; Queens borough Community Col, asst to dean, 1985-88; St Francis Col, assoc dean, 1988-91; Audrey Cohen Co; Wagner Col, Hofstra Univ, currently; "The new arms control-mindedness of the Chinese", auth. **Orgs:** Bd dir, Asn Black Women Higher Educ, 1989; bd dir, UNA-New York, 1989-91; head mem, Centre For Mgt And Tech Educ(CMTE). **Home Addr:** 155 W 70th St Apt 14E, New York, NY 10023-4428, **Home Phone:** (212)925-4957.

**WHITE-HUNT, DEBORAH JEAN**
Executive, educator. **Personal:** Born Jul 21, 1951, Detroit, MI; daughter of Sylvester White and Jean; married Bruce James; children: Alise Frances. **Educ:** Mich State Univ, BA, 1972; Wayne State Univ, MEd, 1975. **Career:** Detroit Pub Sch, dance & health teacher, 1973-95; Detroit-Windsor Dance Acad & Co, artistic dir & owner, 1984-; Martin Luther King Jr Sr High Sch, teacher, currently. **Orgs:** Golden life mem, Delta Sigma Theta Sorority Inc, 1970-; Detroit Inst Arts Founders Soc, 1994; Nat Asn Advan Colored People. **Home Addr:** 19541 Cranbrook Dr, Detroit, MI 48221, **Home Phone:** (313)861-8188. **Business Addr:** Teacher, Martin Luther King Jr Senior High School, 3200 E Lafayette St, Detroit, MI 48207, **Business Phone:** (313)494-7373.

**WHITE-PARSON, WILLAR F.**
Educator, nurse. **Personal:** Born Nov 11, 1945, Norfolk, VA; daughter of Joseph S White and Willar M White; married Wayman L; children: Davida Josette. **Educ:** Hampton Univ, BSN, 1974, MA, guid & coun, 1976, MSN, 1979; Old Dom Univ, PhD, urban serv curric develop, 1984. **Career:** Norfolk State Univ, assoc prof nursing, 1974, Dept Nursing, prof & chair, prof emerita, Emerging Nursing Scholars Enhancement Proj, proj dir; Norfolk Psychiat Ctr, nursing supvr, 1990-92; Sentara Norfolk Gen Hosp, psychiat nurse consult, 1991-; pvt pract nurse psychotherapist, 1991-. **Orgs:** Am Asn Univ Professors, 1976-; Minority fel, Old Dom Univ, 1984; Nat League Nursing, 1989-; Va League Nursing, 1989-; Asn Black Nursing Fac Higher Educ, 1990-; Am Nurses Asn, 1990-; VIR Nurses Asn, 1990-; Tidewater Acad Clin Nurse Specist, 1991-; Va Coun Clin Nurse Specist, 1991-; Va fel Am Acad Nursing, 1994; Secy Health & Human Resources; chmn, Develop LPN to RN curric; co chmn, develop RN to BSN curric; co chmn, develop second degree BSN curric; Gubernatorial & Mayoral adv boards. **Special Achievements:** She was the first NSU alumna (1963) from the Associates Degree Program to serve as the Nursing Department Head from 2000-03. **Home Addr:** 1101 Malcoms Way, Virginia Beach, VA 23464-5311, **Home Phone:** (757)420-1633. **Business Addr:** Nurse Psychotherapist, Private Practice, 1101 Malcoms Way, Virginia Beach, VA 23464-5311, **Business Phone:** (757)420-1633.

**WHITE-PERKINS, DENISE M.**
Health services administrator, physician. **Educ:** Univ Mich Med Sch, MD, 1994; Metro Health Med Ctr, OH, family med; Univ Mich, PhD, psychol. **Career:** MetroHealth Med Ctr, physician, 1994-97; Henry Ford Health Syst, family pract, currently, sr staff physician, fac, 1997-, Inst Multicultural Health, dir, 2003-; Wayne State Univ Sch Med, clin asst prof, 2009-; Afiya Group, consult, 2011-. **Orgs:** Dir, Inst Multicultural Health; Am Bd Family Med; bd mem, Hope Community Outreach Develop; Asn Community Health Improv; Health Ministry Asn; Am Pub Health Asn; Soc Teachers Family Med; Nat Soc Health Coaches, 2010-. **Business Addr:** Director of the Institute of Multicultural Health, Henry Ford Health System, Detroit NW, Detroit, MI 48235, **Business Phone:** (800)436-7936.

**WHITE-WARE, GRACE ELIZABETH**
Educator. **Personal:** Born Oct 5, 1921, St. Louis, MO; daughter of James Eathel White Sr and Madree Penn White; children: Oloye Adeyemon (James Otis Ware II). **Educ:** Harriet Beecher Stowe Teacher's Col, BA, 1943; Columbia Univ, NY, attended 1945; Scott Fores man Inst summer, attended 1951; Wayne State Univ, attended 1966; St John Col, John Carroll Univ, attended 1975; Kent State Univ, attended 1976; Ohio Univ, attended 1978. **Career:** Educator (retired); Super Press, mgr advert, 1935-39; Carolina Oil Corp, vpres, 1938-42; Bell Tel Labs Inc, acct supvr overtime payroll, 1943-46; Wentworth Rec Distribr, owner & mgr, 1947-51; St Louis, Chicago, NY, Cleveland, teacher, 1946-82; Cleveland Pub Sch, teacher elem, adult educ, 1954-82; secy bd dir, Hough Pub Co, Hough Area Develop Corp, Cleveland, 1968-69.Tutoring & Nutrit Proj, prog adminr, 1983-88; Delta Sigma Theta Sor Inc, mem founder. **Orgs:** Phi Delta Kappa Fraternal Group, 1979-; regional, nat treas, Eta Phi Beta Sor Inc, 1980-88; Delta Kappa Gamma Soc Int, Nat Mus WomenArts; Kiwanis Int, 1987; treas, Nat Asn Univ Women, 1987-; Greater Cleveland Neighborhood Ctr Asn; Food First Prog; co-chmn, Black Econ Union; Youth Understanding Teenage Prog; Cleveland Coun Human Rels; Cong Racial Equality; Tots & Teens; Jr Women's Civic League; Afro-Am Cult Hist Soc; Talbert Clin & Day Care Ctr; Langston Hughes Lib; Women's Allied Arts Asn; Nat Asn Advan Colored People; Phyllis Wheatley Asn; Nat Coun Negro Women; Nat Sor Phi Delta Kappa; Top Ladies Distinction Inc; Smithsonian Inst; Nat Asn Pub Sch Adult Educ; Cleveland Educ Associations. **Honors/Awds:** Outstanding Volunteer of the Year, NY, 1949; Outstanding Teacher Award, 1973; Certificate of Appreciation, Cleveland, 1973; Master Teacher Award-Martha Jennings, 1973; Pan-Hellenic Outstanding Greek Award, 1979, 1984; Educ Service Award Urban League of Greater Cleveland, 1986; Humanitarian Award Top Ladies of Distinction Inc, 1986. **Home Addr:** 3591 E 154th St Apt 154, Cleveland, OH 44120-4913, **Home Phone:** (216)991-2782.

**WHITEHEAD, ANDRE**
Executive, business owner, journalist. **Personal:** Born Feb 22, 1967, Portsmouth, VA; son of Richard and Bessie; children: Lake. **Educ:** Norfolk State Univ; Liberty Univ, BA, 1988. **Career:** Whitehead Media Ventures, owner, mgr & chief exec officer, 1989-. **Orgs:** Bd mem, Roanoke Community Rels Comn; bd mem, New Vistas Sch, 1999; exec bd mem, Nat Asn Advan Colored People, 1999, youth coun chairperson, Lynchburg, VA, 2001; chairperson, Omega Psi Phi, Gamma Omega, 2000. **Honors/Awds:** D-Day Memorial Award, D-Day Nat Mem, 1999; Award of Participation, 4thRegional Conf Community Rels, 2000; Image Award in Television Media, Nat Asn Advan Colored People, Roanoke, 2001. **Business Addr:** Chief Executive Officer, Owner, Whitehead Media Ventures, 306 Blue Ridge St, Lynchburg, VA 24505-0041, **Business Phone:** (434)528-9828.

**WHITEHEAD, ARCH COLSON CHIPP.** See WHITEHEAD, COLSON.

**WHITEHEAD, COLSON (ARCH COLSON CHIPP WHITEHEAD)**
Writer. **Personal:** Born Jan 1, 1969?, New York, NY; son of Arch and Mary Ann; married Natasha Stovall. **Educ:** Harvard Col, attended 1991. **Career:** Writer, currently; Village Voice, New York, NY, tv critic; Cullman Ctr Scholars Writers, fel; MacArthur Fel; A Guggenheim Fel. Books: The Intuitionist, 1999; John Henry Days, 2001; The Colossus of New York: A City in Thirteen Parts, 2003; Apex Hides the Hurt, 2006; Sag Harbor, 2009; Zone One, 2011; The Noble Hustle, 2014. **Business Addr:** Author, c/o Random House Inc, 1745 Broadway Suite 3, New York, NY 10019, **Business Phone:** (212)782-9000.

**WHITEHEAD, DAVID WILLIAM**
Executive, vice president (organization). **Personal:** Born Sep 7, 1946, Cleveland, OH; son of Mack Thomas and Leila Wall; married Ruvene Proa; children: Lisa & Lora. **Educ:** Cleveland State Univ, Cleveland, OH, BA, 1968, JD, 1973. **Career:** Executive, vice president (retired); Cleveland Bd Educ, Cleveland, OH, teacher, 1968-73; Howard, Watson & Whitehead, Cleveland, OH, self-employed atty, 1973-79; Cleveland Elec Illum Co, Cleveland, OH, atty, 1979; First Energy Corp, region vip, Chief Ethics Off, vpres & corp secy, 2007; Jersey Cent Power & Light Co, secy, vpres, 2007; FirstEnergy Serv, vpres, corp secy & chief ethics officer, 2007; Pa Power Co, secy; Toledo Edison Co, corp secy. **Orgs:** Bd dir, United Way Serv; pres emer, Neighborhood Ctr Asn; vpres, bd comnr, Cleveland Metroparks; bd trustee, Cleveland Scholar Prog Inc; bd dir, Cleveland State Univ Found; bd dir, First Tee; Adv Bd, ASW Global, LLC. **Home Addr:** 5245 Stonebridge Ct, Solon, OH 44139-1192, **Home Phone:** (407)876-8493.

**WHITEHEAD, DAWN MICHELE**
Administrator. **Educ:** Indiana Univ, Bloomington, BA, hist & Afro-Am studies, 1997, MS, int & comparative educ, 2003; PhD, educ policy studies/int & comparative educ, 2007. **Career:** Pike High Sch, social studies teacher, 1997-2001; Ind Univ Bloomington, stud teacher supvr, 2001-02; Improving Learning Through Partnerships, intern Ghana, 2003; Ind Univ Bloomington, assoc instr overseas stud teaching proj, 2003-05, site visitor & researcher, 2005-07, assoc instr Am Indian Reservation Proj, 2006-07; Global Inst Leadership & Civic Develop, instr, 2004-05; Ind Univ-Purdue Univ Indianapolis, dir curric internationalization, 2007-14; Asn Am Cols & Univs, sr dir global learning & curricular chg Off Integrative Lib Learning & Global Commons, 2015-. **Special Achievements:** Work focuses on advancing practices, strategies, and projects for integrative global learning across the undergraduate curriculum; areas of expertise include civic engagement, education abroad, global learning, international and comparative education, international service learning, and internationalization of the curriculum. **Business Addr:** Association of American Colleges and Universities, 1818 R St NW, Washington, DC 20009, **Business Phone:** (202)387-3760.

**WHITEHEAD, MAJOR GEN. JAMES T., JR.**
Pilot, flight engineer. **Personal:** Born Dec 10, 1934, Jersey City, NJ; children: Brent, Janet, Kenneth, Joel & Marie. **Educ:** Univ Ill, BS, sec edu, 1957; Monmouth Univ, MA, coun. **Career:** Pilot, flight engineer (retired); USAF, Univ Ill, commd 2nd lt, 1957-AFROTC; USAF, pilot training, 1958; KC-135, co-pilot, 1959-63; KC-135, aircraft comdr, 1963-65; Vietnam combat, 1965; U-2 Reconnaissance, aircraft comdr, 1966-67; TWA, flight engr, 1967, first officer, Boeing 707, 1968, flight engr/instr/check airman B-747. **Orgs:** Airlines Pilot Asn, 1967; ALPA activ; TWA co-chmn Hazardous Mat Comn, 1974-; TWA Master Exec Counc Fleet Security Comn, 1975; pres, Kiwanis Madison Twp, NJ, 1968; Jaycees Madison Twp, 1973-; served squadron comdr 103rd Tactical Air Support Squardon, 1977-83; app Hq, Pa Air Nat Guard dir opers, 1983-, promoted to Col, 1983, asst to dir, 1990-93; Kappa Alpha Psi Frat; chmn, 111th Tactical Air Support Group Minority Recruit com, 1972-74; NJ Bd Educ; pres, Fox Found; chmn, Minter Field Air Mus; chmn, Community Adv Bd; pres, Calif State Univ Bakersfield; mentor, Bakersfield Downtown Rotary. **Honors/Awds:** Outstanding Asn Mem, Madison Township Jaycees, 1974; Pres, Old Bridge Township Bd Educ, elected 3 years, 1975. **Special Achievements:** First African AmericanU2 pilot, 1966. **Home Addr:** 201 Throckmorton Lane, Old Bridge, NJ 08857.

### WHITEHEAD, JOE B., JR.

Chancellor (education), dean (education), physicist. **Educ:** Delta State Univ, BA, physics, 1983, MA, physics, 1985; Kent State Univ, PhD, physics, 1989. **Career:** Univ Southern Miss, asst prof physics & astron, 1990-91; John C. Stennis Space Ctr, NASA/ASEE Fac Fel, 1991; Univ Southern Miss, assoc prof, prof, Dept Physics & Astron, chair, 1998-04, Col Sci & Technol, assoc dean, 2004-09, interim dean, 2009-10, dean, 2010, Col Sci & Technol, dean, 2010-13; NC Agr & Tech State Univ, provost & vice chancellor acad affairs, 2013-. **Honors/Awds:** Kent State University, New Millennium Alumni Award; Delta State University, Alumni Association Hall of Fame, 2010.

### WHITEHURST, CHARLES BERNARD, SR.

Government official, president (organization), vice president (organization). **Personal:** Born Jun 4, 1938, Portsmouth, VA; son of John E Sr (deceased) and Bernice N (deceased); children: Lisa W Pretlow & Charles Jr. **Educ:** Norfolk State Univ, BS (magna cum laude), 1979; Univ Colo, Boulder, Grad Degree, bank mkt, 1981. **Career:** Cent Fidelity Bank, asst vpres & loan officer, 1977-85; Portsmouth City, treas, 1986-93, city coun, 1998-2006, 2008-, vice mayor, 2010-; Century Capital, dir, chief opetaing officer & chief financial officer; Century Capital Holdings Inc, chief opetaing officer; Century Capital Mortgage Inc, vice chmn & mktg dir; Va Bible Univ, dean; 5LINX Enterprises Inc, exec dir, 2010-; Home BanCorp, vpres; Century Capital Holdings Inc, chief operating officer;dir, Hampton Roads 200+ Men. **Orgs:** Portsmouth Sch Bd, 1977-81; pres, Portsmouth Chamber Com, 1982; chmn, Va Munic League; chmn, Solid Waste Asso N Am; pres, Worthington Sq Condominium BOD; chmn, Portsmouth Seawall Festival, 1984-85; bd dir, Old Dom Univ, 1984-88; Mary view Hosp, 1985-88; pres, Downtown Portsmouth Asn, 1987-89; pres, Retired Officers Asn, Portsmouth Area Chap, 1989; pres, Eureka Club Inc, 1991-93, 1996-97; golden heritage, life mem, Nat Asn Advan Colored People; Optimist Club; pres, Va Games Inc; pres, Sports Mgt & Promotions Inc; vpres, Port City Publ Inc; ROCKS Inc.; Star base Atlantic; staff writer, Port Cities Concerns; founder, pres, African Am Hist Soc, Portsmouth, VA; chmn, Urban Sec, VA; exec comt, Munic League, VML, 2003; chmn, Southeast Pub Serv Authority, 2002-03; dist chmn, Merrimal Dist, BSA, 2002; chmn, Portsmouth Schs found; chmn, Elected Mems Comt, Solid Waste Asn N Am, 2003; life mem, Vietnam Veterans Am; life mem, 3rd Marine Div Assoc; life mem, Mil Officers Assoc Am; Am Mus Nat Hist; chmn security comt, Old Town Portsmouth Asn; chair & bd dir, Va State Chap, March Dimes; chair, Hampton Roads Div, March Dimes; bd visitor, Providence Bible Col & Theol Sem; IC Norcom Alumni Asn; 3rd Marine Div Asn; Mil Officers Asn Am; Nat Asn Advan Colored People; pres, Safety Town Comt; Libr Adv Comt; Housing Develop Bd; Portsmouth Sch Bd; Educ Comt; Enterprise Zone Task Force; Gov Comt Small Bus; Educ Adv Comt; Tidewater Coun; Kiwanis Club Portsmouth; Am Socs Pub Adminr; Diversity Task Force; Enterprise Zone Comt; Diplomat Club; Small Bus Comt. **Home Addr:** 342 Worthington Sq, Portsmouth, VA 23704, **Home Phone:** (804)399-0998. **Business Addr:** Mayor, Portsmouth City Council, 801 Crawford St, Portsmouth, VA 23704, **Business Phone:** (757)393-8000.

### WHITEHURST, STEVEN LAROY

Writer, business owner, educator. **Personal:** Born Mar 3, 1967, Chicago, IL; son of Steven Fondren and Oneda Fondren; married Noreen Halbert; children: Bajani Anise. **Educ:** Thornton Community Col, AA, hist, 1987, AS, geog, 1988; Chicago State Univ, BA, hist, minor polit sci, 1990. **Career:** S Suburban Col, grad ambassador, 1988-90; Equal Employ Opportunity Comn, investr, 1990-91; S Suburban Col, acad skills, transition adv, 1991-94, dir stud develop, 1994-97; Steven White hurst Homepage, owner, 1998-; Wilberforce Univ. Auth: "WORDS FROM AN UNCHAINED MIND", "Rodney King & the L.A. Rebellion". **Orgs:** Thornton Community Col Affirm Action Adv Comt, 1988; Phi Theta Kappa, PsiPi Chap, 1989-; Cook County Bd Elections, elections judge & registr, 1990; Am Black Book Writers Asn, 1991-; Equal Employ Opportunity Comt, 1991; ILAEOPP, 1991-92; MAEOPP, 1991-92; Multicultural Publ Exchange, 1992-94; Proj Vision, head proj & task force, 1994-97; Phi Alpha Theta, 1997-. **Home Addr:** 240 Yates Ave Apt 1 S, Calumet City, IL 60409, **Home Phone:** (708)862-2950.

### WHITELY, DONALD HARRISON

Counselor, educator. **Personal:** Born Mar 4, 1955, Tarrytown, NJ; son of Henry Harrison and Helen Elizabeth Cardwell; married Angela Smith; children: Asha Elizabeth & Maya Nicole. **Educ:** State Univ NY, Albany, New York, BA, African-Am & black studies, 1977; John Jay Col Criminal Justice, New York, MA, human serv, 1982. **Career:** IBM, Harrison, New York, inventory control asst, 1980-82; Jewish Child Care Agency, Pleasantville, New York, diag unit counr, 1983-88; Malcolm-King Col, Harlem, New York, from asst dir HEOP to dir HEOP, 1988-89; Westchester Community Col, Valhalla, New York, admis counr & instr, 1989, asst prof & counr, assoc prof & counr, currently. **Orgs:** Higher Educ Opportunity Prog Prof Orgn, 1988-89; Westchester Educ Coalition, 1989-; Admis Adv Comt, W Chester Community Col, 1989-; Mid States Asn Col Registr & Officers Admis, 1989-; fac adv, African Cult Club, W Chester Community Col, 1990; State Univ New York, Multicultural Community. **Honors/Awds:** Distinguished Community Service Award, Tarrytown Community Opportunity Ctr, 1992; Community Service Award, Nat Asn Adv Coloured People, 1995; Adult Recognition Award for Community Service, Westchester City Youth Bd & Bur, 1998. **Special Achievements:** First African American elected in Board of Trustees, Village Tarrytown, 1992, Reelected to 3rd term, 1996; Coordr, Open Views Youth Group Tarrytowns; Asst hd coach, Tarrytown Pop Warner Football; Village Tarrytown Liaison; Tarrytown Sch Bd Munic Housing Authority. **Home Addr:** 16 Mech Ave, Tarrytown, NY 10591-3315, **Home Phone:** (914)631-0067. **Business Addr:** Associate Professor, Admissions Counselor, Westchester Community College, Rm 210 Admin Bldg 75 Grasslands Rd, Valhalla, NY 10595, **Business Phone:** (914)606-6741.

### WHITEMAN, RAYMOND A.

Executive. **Educ:** Williams Col, BA, polit sci; NY Univ Stern Sch Bus, MBA, finance & acct. **Career:** Carlyle Group LP, managing dir & co-head Carlyle Strategic Partners, 1996-; Carlyle's US Buyout Group, prin; Carlyle Mgt Group, founding prin, 2000-03; Citicorp; Chase Manhattan Bank; Credit Lyonnais, Leveraged Finance Group, vpres & group head; Frontier Group, sr advisor; Stellex Capital Mgt, managing partner, founder, currently. **Orgs:** Bd mem, Diversified Mach Inc; bd mem, RPK Capital Partners LLC; bd mem, MD Investors Corp; Prince George's Community Col Found; exec comt mem, Nat Symphony Orchestra; Lehman scholar, Williams Col; exec comt mem, John F. Kennedy Ctr; exec comt mem, Smithsonian's Nat Mus African Art; chmn, MHI Holdings Llc; chmn, Morbark Holdings Llc; Metaldyne Llc; Stellex Aerostructures Inc; Brintons Carpet Ltd; DPG Aerospace & Serv King; investment comt, RLJ Equity Partners; dir, BAE Systs Ship Repair Inc; Aerostructures Corp. **Honors/Awds:** "Black Enterprise," 75 Most Powerful Blacks on Wall Street, 2011. **Business Addr:** Founder, Managing Partner, Stellex Capital Management, 900 3rd Ave 22nd Fl, New York, NY 10022, **Business Phone:** (212)710-2323.

### WHITEN, MARK ANTHONY

Baseball executive, baseball player. **Personal:** Born Nov 25, 1966, Pensacola, FL. **Educ:** Pensacola Jr Col. **Career:** Baseball player (retired), athletic coach; Toronto Blue Jays, rightfielder, 1990-91; Cleveland Indians, rightfielder, 1991-92, 1998-2000; St Louis Cardinals, rightfielder, 1993-94; Boston Red Sox, rightfielder, 1995; Philadelphia Phillies, rightfielder, 1995-96; Atlanta Braves, rightfielder, 1996; Seattle Mariners, rightfielder, 1996; NY Yankees, rightfielder, 1997; Tex Rangers, hitting coach, 2005, Rangers Rookie League club, hitting coach, 2006.

### WHITESIDE, ERNESTYNE E.

Educator. **Personal:** Born Pine Bluff, AR. **Educ:** Mech & Norm Col, Pine Bluff, BA, agr; NY Univ, MA; Ouachita Univ, Arkadelphia; Okla Univ; Univ Ariz. **Career:** Dollarway Pub Sch Dist, eng instr. **Orgs:** Pres, Jeferson Co Reading Coun; Ariz Educ Asn; Asn Classrooms Teachers; Nat Ariz Coun Teachers Eng; Nat Reading Coun; Nat Asn Univ Women; Gov's Coun Aerospace Educ; St Orgn Minority Evolvement; Nat Alumni Asn AM&N Col; Eastern Star; Delta Sigma Theta; Am Woodman Asn. **Home Addr:** 2501 Whiteside Ave, PO Box 5823, Pine Bluff, AR 71601, **Home Phone:** (870)536-2478.

### WHITFIELD, ALPHONSO, III

Banker. **Educ:** Morehouse Col, BA, polit sci, 1977; Union Col, MA; Carnegie-Mellon Univ, MS. **Career:** Prudential Ins, vpres, 1972-85; SunTrust Bank, comput operator, 1979-80; Roe Martin & Neiman, investment mgr, 1980-87; Nat Minority Supplier Develop Coun, pres, 1985-88; Whitfield Scott Inc, owner, 1987-95; Fed Home Loan Bank New York, pres, 1988-94; Mutual Fed Savings bank Atlanta, pres & chief exec officer, 1994-98; City Atlanta, Housing & Econ Develop, dep dir, 1996-2002; AIT Atlanta LLC-Dealership, dealership partner, 2004-07; Advan Internet Technologies Inc, vpres mkt & bus develop, 2007-09; Vital Inc, owner, 2002-. **Orgs:** Co-founder, Regional Lender Consortia; pres, Nat Minority Supplier Develop coun; vpres, Social Investments Prudential Ins Am; vpres, Com Group Progress Investment Asn; consult, Fayetteville Cumberland County Chamber Com, 2009-10. **Business Addr:** Chairman, Owner, Vital Inc, 342 Marietta St Suite 2, Atlanta, GA 30313, **Business Phone:** (404)523-3435.

### WHITFIELD, DONDRE T.

Actor. **Personal:** Born May 27, 1969, Brooklyn, NY; married Salli Richardson; children: Parker Richardson & Dre Terrell. **Career:** Films: Bright Lights, Big City, 1988; Homeboy, 1988; Home boyz II: Crack City, 1989; White Man's Burden, 1995; Happy Birthday, 2001; Two Can Play That Game, 2001; Biker Boyz, 2003; Mr. 3000, 2004; The Salon, 2005; Pastor Brown, 2009; 35 and Ticking, 2011; Middle of Nowhere, 2012; TV series: "The Cosby Show", 1985-87; "Diff'rent Strokes", 1986; "Another World", 1989-90; "ABC After sch Specials", 1990; "All My C", 1991-94; "The Crew", 1995; "The Jamie Foxx Show", 1996; "Martin", 1997; "Between Bros", 1997; "Living in Captivity", 1998; Secret Agt Man, 2000; Alien Fury: Countdown to Invasion, 2000; "The X Files", 2000; "Nash Bridges", 2000; "NYPD Blue", 2001; On the Edge, 2001; "Girlfriends", 2001-02; "Inside Schwartz", 2001; "Hidden Hills", 2002; "The Partners", 2003; "Strong Med", 2004; "Second Time Around", 2004; "Half & Half", 2004; "Less Than Perfect", 2004; "Briar & Graves", 2005; "Jake in Progress", 2005; "Ghost Whisperer", 2005-06; Our Thirties, 2006; "CSI: Miami", 2006; Cold Case, 2008-10; "Samantha Who?", 2009; "Night and Day", 2010; "The Event", 2010-11; "Grey's Anatomy", 2011; "Make It or Break It", 2012; "Eureka", 2012; "Company Town", 2013; "Walk This Way", 2013; "Mistresses", 2013-14; "Hart of Dixie", 2014. **Business Addr:** Actor, c/o Writers & Artists Agency Inc, 8383 Wilshire Blvd Suite 550, Beverly Hills, CA 90211, **Business Phone:** (323)866-0900.

### WHITFIELD, JENENNE

Executive. **Personal:** Born Aug 29, 1961, Pontiac, MI; daughter of Dan and Delores; married Tyree Guyton; children: Chloe D Butler. **Educ:** Wayne State Univ, 1995. **Career:** Profit corp, exec dir, 1993-; Self-employed agent, 1994-; Heidelberg Proj, bd mem, 1993-, exec dir, currently. **Orgs:** Hon bd mem, Mona Mus, 2000-. **Home Addr:** 20000 Northrop St, Detroit, MI 48219, **Home Phone:** (313)532-6156. **Business Addr:** Executive Director, The Heidelberg Project, 3360 Heidelberg St, Detroit, MI 48219, **Business Phone:** (313)974-6894.

### WHITFIELD, KENNARD O.

Cartographer, mayor. **Personal:** Born May 28, 1933, St. Louis, MO; son of Ossie and Nettie; married Ettie Jean; children: Stacy Marie Ruff & Lorna Jean. **Educ:** Xavier Univ; St Louis Univ, BS, 1958, MPA, 1963; Yale Univ. **Career:** Ccartorapher, Mayor (retired); Defense Mapping Agency, cartorapher/div chief, 1958-93; City of Rock Hill, mayor, 1997-04. **Orgs:** United Way, loan exec, 1971-73; St Louis County Munic League, 1973-, pres, 1987-88; MO Munic League, 1973-, pres, 1990-91; Metro Sewer Dist Civil Srvice Comm, 1973-94; Community Adv Bd KSDK-TV, 1986-; Nat Conf Black Mayors, pres MO Chap; Nat League Cities, 1994-; MO Seismic Safety Comn, 1994-. **Honors/Awds:** East/West Gateway Coordinating Council, Government Achievement Award, 1998; MO Municipal League, Distinguished Service Award, 1999. **Home Addr:** 507 Hinsdale Ct, Rock Hill, MO 63119, **Home Phone:** (314)961-3910.

### WHITFIELD, LYNN C. (LYNN BUTLER-SMITH)

Actor. **Personal:** Born May 6, 1953, Baton Rouge, LA; daughter of Valerian Smith and Jean (nee) Butler; married Vantile; married Brian Gibson; children: Grace. **Educ:** Howard Univ, BFA. **Career:** TV series: Heartbeat, 1988; The Women of Brewster Place, 1989; Stomp in at the Savoy; The George McKenna Story; The Johnnie Mae Gibson Story; Cosby Mysteries, 1994; The Josephine Baker Story; The Wedding, 1998; The Color of Courage, 1999; Deep in My Heart, 1999; A Girl Thing, 2001; The Cheetah Girls, 2003; Redemption: The Stan Tookie Williams Story, 2004; Strong Medicine, 2004; The Cheetah Girls 2, 2006; Shark: Pilot, 2006; "FlashForward", 2009; "Prodigy Bully", 2012; "Somebody's Child", 2012; "Are We There Yet?", 2012; "Hit the Floor", 2014; "My Other Mother", 2014; "The Fright Night Files", 2014; "Family Time", 2014; "How to Get Away with Murder", 2014. Films: Dr Detroit, 1983; Silverado, 1985; Sluggers Wife, 1985; A Thin Line Between Love & Hate, 1996; Eves Bayou, 1997; Stepmom, 1998; A Time for Dancing, 2000; Head of State, 2003; Madeas Family Reunion, 2006; Confessions, 2006; The Cheetah Girls 2, 2006; Shark, 2006; Kings of the Evening, 2008; The Women, 2008; Mama, I Want to Sing, The Rebound, 2009; Mama I Want to Sing, 2011; All Things Fall Apart, 2011; Battlefield America, 2012; Redemption of a Dog, 2012; The Trace, 2012; Lonely Boy, 2013; 24 Hour Love, 2013; King's Faith, 2013; Act Like You Love Me, 2013; And Then There Was You, 2013; The Last Letter, 2013; The Dempsey Sisters, 2013; Take the Spotlight, 2014; 30 Days in Atlanta, 2014; Lap Dance, 2014; For All Eyes Always, 2015; Curve Ball, 2015; The North Star, 2015; Prayer Never Fails, 2016; Solace, 2017; Deaf Ghost. **Orgs:** Alpha Kappa Alpha Sorority Inc; Links Inc. **Honors/Awds:** Emmy Award, The Josephine Baker Story, 1991; Alumni Achievement Award, Howard Univ, 1992; Image Award, Nat Asn Advan Colored People, 1993, 1994, 1998, 2000 & 2005; Black Reel Award, 2005. **Home Addr:** 8942 Wilshire Blvd, Beverly Hills, CA 90211. **Business Addr:** Actress, William Morris Agency, 151 El Camino Dr, Beverly Hills, CA 90212.

### WHITFIELD, ROBERT LECTRESS, JR.

Chief executive officer, football player. **Personal:** Born Oct 18, 1971, Carson, CA; married Sheree Fuller; children: Laniece & Kodi. **Educ:** Stanford Univ, attended 1992, econs, 2012. **Career:** Football player (retired), chief exec officer; Atlanta Falcons, tackle, 1992-2003; Jacksonville Jaguars, 2004; New York Giants, 2005-06; Stanford Univ's Hall of Fame, 2011; pre game analyst, guest analyst, Sky Sports; Patch werk Recordings, founder, 1994-2009, chief exec officer, 1993-. **Business Addr:** Chief Executive officer, Patchwerk Recordings, 1094 Hemphill Ave NW, Atlanta, GA 30318-5431, **Business Phone:** (404)874-9880.

### WHITFIELD, VAN

Novelist. **Personal:** Born Jan 1, 1960?, Baltimore, MD. **Career:** Employed at Lorton Prison, Wash, DC; worked Mayor's Youth Initiative Off, Wash, DC, 1995; Whitfield Entertainment LLC, owner; Books: Beeperless Remote, 1997; signed contract with Doubleday Books; Something Wrong with Your Scale!, 1999; Guys in Suits, 2001; Dad Interrupted, 2004. **Orgs:** Founder, Educ Works. **Honors/Awds:** Nominated for six Ben Franklin awards for Beeperless Remote, 1997; Featured in a wide range of periodicals including Ebony, Essence, Publisher's Weekly, Black Issues Book Review, BET Weekend, Jane, MODE, The Washington Post, The Baltimore Sun, The La Times, The NY Daily News, The Miami Herald & a host of other publications around the world; California Book award, 2000; "Book Oscar", 2002. **Special Achievements:** Beeperless Remote, publ, 1997; 'There's Something Wrong with Your Scale!', 1999; wrote scripts for UPN TV series, Grown Ups, 2000; Guys in Suits, publ, 2001; Dad Interrupted, 2004. **Business Addr:** Author, Marie Brown & Associates, 625 Broadway Suite 902, New York, NY 10012, **Business Phone:** (212)939-9725.

### WHITING, DR. ALBERT NATHANIEL

School administrator, educator. **Personal:** Born Jul 3, 1917, Jersey City, NJ; son of Hezekiah Oliver and Hildegarde Freida; married Charlotte Luck; children: Brooke Elizabeth. **Educ:** Amherst Col, AB, 1938, LLD, 1968; Fisk Univ, MA, 1941, LDH, 1980; Am Univ, PhD, sociol, psychol, 1952; Western Mich Univ, LLD, 1974; Duke, LLD, 1974; Kyung Hee Univ, LLD, 1981; NC Cent Univ, LDH, 1983. **Career:** Educator (retired), administrator; Fisk Univ, teaching & res fel, 1939-41; Bennett Col, instr sociol, dir rural community study, 1941-43, 1946-47; Atlanta Univ, asst prof sociol, 1948-53; Morris Brown Col, dean Col & prof sociol, 1953-57; Morgan State Col, from asst dean to dean Col, 1957-67; NC Cent Univ, chancellor, 1967-72, chancellor, 1972-83, pres, 1983, chancellor emer. **Orgs:** MD Comn New York World's Fair; comn acad affairs, Am Coun Educ, 1968-70; mem bd trustee, Educ Testing Serv, 1968-72; mem bd dir, Nat League Nursing Inc, 1970-71; mem bd dir, Am Coun Educ, 1970-73, 1974-75; policies & purposes comn, bd dirs pres, Am Asn State Cols & Univs; Col Entrance Exam Bd; vpres, Int Asn Univ Pres, 1971-74, 1975-78; mem bd dir, NC Mem Hosp, 1974-77; treas, Int Asn Univ Pres, 1978-84; Joint Panel Grad Rec Exam Bd & Coun Grad Sch US; bd govs, exec comt & bd res, Triangle Inst Res Triange Park NC; mem bd dir, Greater Durham Chamber Com; US Civil Serv Comn Southern Region; mem bd dir, Gen Tel Co Southeast; mem bd dir, Rose'sres, Inc, 1981-88; mem bd regents, Univ MD Syst, 1988-92; nat Urban League fel Univ Pittsburgh; Alpha Kappa Delta Hon Sociol Fraternity. **Honors/Awds:** Fourth President & First chancellor, Nc Cent Univ, 1967-84; Six Hon Degrees LLD's & LHD's. **Special Achievements:** Numerous bks reviews & contrib prof journals. **Home Addr:** 11253B Slalom Lane Suite B, Columbia, MD 21044-2810, **Home Phone:** (410)992-9251. **Business Addr:** Chancellor Emeritus, North Carolina Central University, 1801 Fayetteville St, Durham, NC 27707-3129, **Business Phone:** (919)530-6100.

### WHITING, BRANDON RENEE

President (organization), football player. **Personal:** Born Jul 30, 1976, Santa Rosa, CA; son of Thomas. **Educ:** Univ Calif, grad, 1999. **Career:** Football player (retired); Philadelphia Eagles, left defensive tackle, 1998, right defensive tackle, 1999, defensive end, 1999-2003; San Francisco 49ers, defensive end, 2003-04; Speed Raceway, pres, 2012-. **Honors/Awds:** Joe Roth Award. **Business Addr:** President, Speed Raceway, 1103 US-130, Cinnaminson, NJ 08077, **Business Phone:** (877)757-7333.

**WHITING, LEROY**
Government official, executive director. **Personal:** Born May 17, 1938, Rodney, MS; son of Johnnie and Gertrude Jackson; married Annette Mattie Watkins; children: Oran. **Educ:** Alcorn A&M Col, BS, 1959; Mich State Univ, MAT, 1965; Univ Ill, Chicago, attended 1980. **Career:** Government official (retired); Meridian Bd Educ, Miss, sci teacher, 1959-60; Chicago Bd Educ, Ill, sci teacher, 1960-68; City Chicago, Ill, dir external affairs, asst to mayor, 1968, spec asst to plng & develop comnr, 1993, Intergovernmental Comn, exec dir, 2001. **Orgs:** Alpha Phi Alpha, 1957-; bd trustee, Francis Parker Sch, 1968-75; chair, User Requirement Pub Tech Inc, 1980; GaP Community Orgn, 1983-; Nat Forum Black Pub Admins, 1986-89; Dent Assisting Nat Bd, 1988-; chair church coun, Hartzell Memorial United Methodist Church, Chicago, 2003; Alpha Kappa Mu Hon Soc. **Home Addr:** 3344 S Calumet Ave, Chicago, IL 60616, **Home Phone:** (312)326-1493.

**WHITING, VAL (VAL RAYMOND)**
Basketball player, entrepreneur. **Personal:** Born Apr 9, 1972; married Jay Raymond; children: Joseph & Victor. **Educ:** Stanford Univ, BS, biol, 1993. **Career:** Basketball player (retired), executive; San Jose Lasers, 1996-97; Seattle Reign, ctr, 1997-99; Detroit Shock, ctr, 1999; Minn Lynx, ctr, 2001-02; Game shape Inc, founder, currently. **Orgs:** Bd dir, Rough Diamonds Athletic Found; Bd dir, InfluenceHer. **Business Addr:** Founder, Gameshape Inc, 455 Rte 9 S, Manalapan, NJ 07726, **Business Phone:** (732)617-8090.

**WHITING-WRIGHT, BARBARA E.**
Lawyer. **Personal:** Born Jul 28, 1936, Tabb, VA. **Educ:** Hampton Inst, Hampton, Calif, BS, 1963; Howard Univ Sch Law, JD, 1963. **Career:** Lawyer (retired); Howard Univ Dept Med, med secy, 1957-63; Howard Univ, librn, 1964; US Customs Serv Wash, customs law specialist, 1964-96. **Orgs:** Pres, Howard Law Alumni Asn, 1974-78; Nat Bar Asn, Greater Wash Chap, Women Lawyers Div, 1974-; vol, Oper Sue, 1974; bd dir, Greater Wash Area Chap, 2011. **Special Achievements:** First Black female appointed Customs Law Specialist, US Customs Service; First President of Greater Washington Area Chapter. **Home Addr:** 2831 Hillcrest Dr SE, Washington, DC 20020-7207, **Home Phone:** (757)868-9567.

**WHITLEY, JAMES**
Architect, executive. **Personal:** Born Apr 29, 1934, Rochester, NY; children: Kent. **Educ:** Kent State Univ, BS, archit, 1957. **Career:** Whitley/Whitley Architects & Planners LLC, co-founder, pres & designer, 1963-. **Special Achievements:** Firm focuses on urban areas, including public facilities; worked on projects for city and state public agencies, and city groups in Cleveland, OH, the State of Ohio, St. Louis, MO, Indianapolis, IN, Chicago, IL, Saginaw, MI, and New York City. **Business Addr:** Whitley/Whitley Architects and Planners LLC, 12806 Northwood Ave Suite 5, Cleveland, OH 44120, **Business Phone:** (216)370-7883.

**WHITLEY, WILLIAM N.**
Planner, executive, architect. **Personal:** Born Apr 29, 1934, Rochester, NY; married Kaysonia Forney; children: Kyle, Kym & Scott. **Educ:** Kent State Univ, BS, archit, 1957. **Career:** Whitley/Whitley Architects & Planners LLC, co-founder, partner & proj prin, 1963-, vpres arch; Regist, Ill, OH. **Orgs:** Am Inst Archs; Archs Soc OH; OH Prestressed Concert Assoc Design, 1973; Cleveland Eng Soc; Soc Arch Design, 1974; Women's Allied Arts Assoc, 1974. **Home Addr:** 19315 Shaker Blvd, Shaker Heights, OH 44122. **Business Addr:** Vice President, Project Principal, Whitley/Whitley Architects & Planners LLC, 12806 Northwood Ave Suite 5, Cleveland, OH 44120, **Business Phone:** (216)370-7883.

**WHITLOW, BARBARA WHEELER**
Executive. **Personal:** Born Jul 20, 1939, Sale City, GA; daughter of Benjamin Wheeler Sr and Luecilla Donaldson Wheeler; married Charles E; children: Charlene Gena & Darlene Denise. **Educ:** Albany State Col, attended 1961; Atlanta Jr Col, attended 1981. **Career:** Fed Bur Invest, res analyst, 1964-67; Defense Contract Admin, qual control specialist, 1967-85; Lows Enterprises Inc, pres, chief exec officer, chmn, 1985-. **Orgs:** Secy, Region IV 8a Contractors Asn, 1991-. **Honors/Awds:** Show Stoppers Award, Ga Minority Purchasing Coun, 1992; Salute to Black Bus Owners, Atlanta Tribune, 1992; Salute to Small Bus Suppliers, Lockheed Aeronaut Systs Co, 1992; Adminr Award Excellence, US Small Bus Adminr, 1996. **Special Achievements:** Founder of Lows Enterprises Inc, Minority Female-Owned Electronic Mfg Firm, 1985. **Home Addr:** 3450 Glenview Cir SW, Atlanta, GA 30331-2410, **Home Phone:** (404)349-9493. **Business Addr:** President, Chief Executive Officer, Lows Enterprises Inc, 3966 Shirley Dr, Atlanta, GA 31131-0032, **Business Phone:** (404)699-0582.

**WHITLOW, DR. WOODROW, JR.**
Research scientist. **Personal:** Born Dec 13, 1952, Inkster, MI; son of Woodrow and Willie Mae O; married Michele C Wimberly; children: Mary Annessa & Natalie Michele. **Educ:** Mass Inst Technol, Cambridge, BS, 1974, MS, 1975, PhD, phiosophy, aeronaut & astronaut, 1979. **Career:** NASA Langley Res Ctr, Hampton, Va, res scientist, 1979-86, res scientist/group leader, 1986-88, sr res scientist, 1988-89; adj prof, Old Dom Univ, 1987-; lectr, Cairo Univ Aeronaut Sem Ser, 1988; NASA, Wash, DC, prog mgr, astrophys, 1990, prog mgr, struct & dynamics, asst head, aero serv elasticity br, 1990-91, head, aero dynamics br, 1991-94, dep dir, Aeronaut Progs, 1995-97; chief, Struct Div, 1997-98, dir, Critical Technols Div, 1994-94; NASA Glenn Res Ctr, Cleveland, Ohio, dir, Res & Technol, 1998-2003, dep dir, 1995-98, dir, 2005-10; NASA Kennedy Space Ctr, dep dir, 2003-05; NASA HQ, Assoc Adminr Mission Support, 2010-. **Orgs:** Am Inst Aeronaut & Astronaut; coach, Phillips Athletic Asn Girls Softball, 1981-84; pres, Hampton Univ Lab Sch Adv Bd, 1982-83; Nat Tech Asn, 1983-; MIT Aeronaut & Astronaut Vis Comt, 1987-93; MIT Educ Coun, 1987-; Women Aerospace, 1991-. **Honors/Awds:** First place, Student Research Competition, AAIA New England Section, 1974; James Means Memorial Prize, MIT Aeronautics & Astronautics, 1974; Special achievement awards, NASA Langley Research Center, 1982, 1986, 1989; Black Engineer of the Year in Government, Career Communications Group, 1989; Outstanding Performance Award, NASA Langley, 1990; Associate fellow, American Institute of Aeronautics & Astronautics, 1993, 2010; NTA Engineer of the Year, 1996; MIT Martin Luther King Alumni Award, 2000; US Black Engineer of the Year in Government; NASA Exceptional Service Honor Medal; NASA Equal Opportunity Honor Medal; William Sweet Smith Prize, Institution of Mechanical Engineers; Presidential Rank of Meritorious Executive. **Home Addr:** 17141 Amber Dr, Cleveland, OH 44111-2901. **Business Addr:** Director, National Aeronautics and Space Administration, 21000 Brookpark Rd Mail Stop 3-5, Cleveland, OH 44135, **Business Phone:** (216)433-3193.

**WHITMORE, CHARLES**
Government official, conservationist. **Personal:** Born Jan 25, 1945, Mason, TN; son of Morris and Katherine; married Cynthia M Huff; children: Lashawn, Charles Marcus & Corey Demond. **Educ:** Tenn State Univ, BS, agron, 1969, MS, plant sci, 1970. **Career:** Natural Resources Conserv Serv, Midwest Region, Madison, WI, soil conservationist, 1970, dist conservationist, 1973-76, state res specialist, 1976-79, state res specialist, 1976-79, area conservationist, 1979-85; dep state conservationist, 1985-87, state conservationist, Maine, 1987-91, state conservationist Ill, 1991-94, Conserv Planning Div, dir, 1994, regional conservationist, Conserv Opers Div, actg dir, currently; USDA, SCS, state conservationist, currently; Great Lakes Info Network, natural resources conserv serv, assoc dep chief progs; Great Lakes Boating Fedn, natural resources conserv serv, assoc dep chief; Great Lakes Restoration, natural resources conserv serv, assoc dep chief; TEACH, natural resources conserv serv, assoc dep chief progs. **Orgs:** Asn Ill Soil & Water Conserv; Am Soc Agron; Prof Soc Black SCS Employees; Prince Hall Masonic Lodge; Bangor Lodge 22; Ill Gov, land & water task force. **Honors/Awds:** USDA Superior Service Award, 1976; Special achievement awards, 1976, 1984, 1991; Outstanding Performance Awards, 1980, 1981, 1990; Alumnus of the Year Award, Tenn State Univ, 1992. **Home Addr:** 285 Dickinson St 2, Springfield, MA 01108, **Home Phone:** (802)878-0390. **Business Addr:** State Conservationist, Acting Director, Natural Resources Conservation Service, 2820 Walton Commons W Suite 123, Madison, WI 53718, **Business Phone:** (608)224-3035.

**WHITMORE, DARRELL LAMONT**
Baseball player. **Personal:** Born Nov 18, 1968, Front Royal, VA. **Educ:** WVa Univ. **Career:** Baseball player (retired); Fla Marlins, 1993-95; Chiba Lotte Marines, 1996.

**WHITNER, DONNA K.**
Librarian. **Personal:** Born Jan 24, 1951, Champaign, IL; daughter of Lawrence and Gladys McMullen. **Educ:** Western Col, Oxford, OH, BA, 1973; Univ Ill, Urbana, IL, MLS, 1977; Univ Mo-Kans City, Kans City, MO, MBA, 1995. **Career:** Western Col, Oxford, OH, work grant stud, 1969-73; Urbana Sch Dist No 16, Urbana, IL, asst to dir libRs, 1973-76; Univ Ill, Champaign, IL, grad asst, 1976-77; Womens Employ Couns Ctr, Champaign, IL, researcher, 1977-78; Univ Ill, Champaign, IL, residence halls librn, 1978-86; Kans City Pub Libr, Kans City, MO, Tech Serv, dir, 1986-. **Orgs:** Am Libr Asn, 1980-; Pub Libr Asn, 1986-; Mo Libr Asn, 1986-; vchair, Tech Servs Coun, Mo Libr Asn, 1990-91; grad, centurions, Leadership Develop Prog, Greater Kans City Chamber Com. **Honors/Awds:** Woman of the Year, Western Col, Am Asn Univ Women, 1972-73. **Home Addr:** 2510 Grand Ave Suite 801, Kansas City, MO 64108, **Home Phone:** (816)221-2104. **Business Addr:** Director Technical Services, Kansas City Public Library, 311 E 12th St, Kansas City, MO 64106, **Business Phone:** (816)701-3480.

**WHITNEY, CHRISTOPHER ANTOINE**
Basketball player, founder (originator), basketball executive. **Personal:** Born Oct 5, 1971, Hopkinsville, KY. **Educ:** Lincoln Trail, attended 1991; Clemson Univ, attended 1993. **Career:** Basketball player (retired), basketball executive; San Antonio Spurs, pt guard, 1993-95; Continental Basketball Asn, Rapid City Thrillers, 1995-96; Continental Basketball Asn, Fla Beachdogs, 1995-96; Wash Bullets, pt guard, 1996-97; Wash Wizards, pt guard, 1996-2002, 2003-04; Denver Nuggets, pt guard, 2002-03; Orlando Magic, pt guard, 2003; Scavolini Pesaro, 2003-04; Charlotte Hornets, dir player develop, currently. **Orgs:** Founder, C-WHIT Found. **Business Addr:** Director of Player Development, Charlotte Hornets, 333 E Trade St, Charlotte, NC 28202, **Business Phone:** (704)688-8600.

**WHITNEY, ROSALYN L.**
School administrator. **Personal:** Born Jan 12, 1950, Detroit, MI; daughter of Robert L and Esther L DeCuir Hocker; children: Gina Michelle Lee. **Educ:** Oakland Univ, Meadow Brook, Mich, Sch Music, attended 1966; Eastern Mich Univ, Ypsilanti, Mich, BA, 1971. **Career:** Probe Inc, Detroit, Mich, vpres mkt, 1973-78; CBS Inc, Rec Div SD detroit, Mich, acct exec, 1978-82; Barden Communs, Detroit, Mich, dir mkt, 1984; New Detroit Inc, Detroit, Mich, dir media rels, 1984-91; Detroit Pub Schs, spokeswoman supt, asst supt communs, 1991-. **Orgs:** Vice chair bd, Creative Arts Collection, 1982-; Detroit Press Club, 1984-; bd mem, Int Visitors Coun Metro Detroit, 1985-92; St Dunstans Guild Cranbrook, 1989-92; bd mem, Non Profit Pub Rels Network, 1991-92; bd mem, Detroit Wayne Co Family Servs, 1992; Automotive Press Asn; NatSch Pub Rels; Nat Asn Tv Arts & Scis; NAB; Detroit Producers Asn; Am Soc Composers, Authors & Publs. **Honors/Awds:** Spirit Detroit, City Detroit, City Coun, 1979; CBS Detroit Branch of the Year, CBS Inc, 1980. **Home Addr:** 333 Keelson Dr, Detroit, MI 48215, **Home Phone:** (313)331-6418. **Business Addr:** Assistant Superintendent Communications, Detroit Public Schools, Rm 218 5057 Woodward Ave, Detroit, MI 48202, **Business Phone:** (313)494-2244.

**WHITNEY, DR. W. MONTY**
Educator, administrator. **Personal:** Born Sep 7, 1945, Philadelphia, PA; son of Wilbur M and Bessie M; married Bettye Roberts; children: Erica & Michelle. **Educ:** Lycoming Col, BA, 1967; Howard Univ, MA, psychol, 1969; Mich State Univ, PhD, psychol, 1974. **Career:** Southern Univ, instr, 1969-71; Univ Cincinnati, asst prof, 1974-76; Seven Hills Neighborhood Houses Inc, assoc dir, 1976-86; Cincinnati Human Rels Comn, exec dir 1986-92; Clark Atlanta Univ Head Start, dir, 1992-96; Morehouse Col, asst prof, dir off community serv, 1998-; Eval & Training Assocs, partner, 2001-09. **Orgs:** Pres, Social Tech Systs, 1978-92; nat pres, Asn Black Psychol, 1984-85; trans african, Nat Asn Advan Colored People; adv bd, Neighborhood Nexus. **Home Addr:** 2825 Spain Dr, Atlanta, GA 30344. **Business Addr:** Director of the Office of Community Service, Morehouse College, Rm 233 Dansby Hall 830 Westview Dr SW, Atlanta, GA 30314, **Business Phone:** (404)681-2282.

**WHITNEY, WILLIAM B.**
Executive, chief executive officer. **Educ:** Benedict Col, BS, biol, 1962; Univ SC, chem, attended 1968; Harvard Univ, JFK Sch Bus, exec mgt prog, 1981. **Career:** Ford Found Fel, 1970-71; Greenville Urban League Inc, exec dir, 1973-79, pres/chief exec officer, 1991; State SC Div Employ & Training, exec asst gov, 1979-86; State Bd Tech & Comprehensive Educ, spec asst employ & community affairs, 1986-91; Whitney Corp Columbia, pres, 1990-; Whitney Pl, chief exec officer & owner, 1990-; Whitney & Whitney Develop Corp, pres, brokerin charge, 1990-92. **Orgs:** Bd dir, Cities & Schs; Nat Asn Advan Colored People; bd dir, Greenville Area Nations Bank; bd chmn, SC Comn Poverty & Deprivation; bd dir, Greenville YMCA; bd dir, Clemson Univ Bd Visitors; Greenville Rotary Club; bd dir, Palmetto Proj. **Home Addr:** 11 Partridge Dr, Greenville, SC 29609-6626. **Business Addr:** 107 Cornwell St, Union, SC 29379-2404, **Business Phone:** (864)427-4275.

**WHITSETT, JAMES A., JR.**
Chief executive officer, executive. **Personal:** Born Feb 27, 1952, Greenfield, MA; son of James A Sr and Myrtle. **Educ:** Syracuse Univ, BS, jour, 1974. **Career:** Freelance TV, producer; CT Pub Broadcasting Inc, Conn Pub TV, vpres local programming, sr vpres local programming, 1995-2009; A Peaceful Planet Inc, pres & chief exec officer; Atlanta Pub Schs, dir broadcasting, 2010-13; Jwire Consult, chief exec officer, 2009-; jayw agency, owner, 2013-. **Orgs:** Big Bros; Nat Acad TV Arts & Sci. **Home Addr:** 342 Mercer Lane, Windsor, CT 06095. **Business Addr:** owner, Jayw Agency, 2347 Stanley St, New Britain, CT 06053, **Business Phone:** (860)558-9110.

**WHITT, DWIGHT REGINALD**
Clergy, priest, president (organization). **Personal:** Born Jul 17, 1949, Baltimore, MD. **Educ:** Loyola Col, AB, 1970; Pontif Fac Immaculate Conception, STB, 1974, STL; Duke Law Sch, JD, 1982; Cath Univ Am, JCL, 1993, JCD, 1995. **Career:** Ordained Roman Cath priest, 1976; Order Friars Preachers, mem; Spalding Col, chaplain; Villanova Univ, fac; Univ Ky, fac; Duke Univ, fac; Univ Notre Dame, fac; Univ St Thomas, Minn, fac; Dominican House Studies, pres, 2003-; Univ St.Thomas, prof law, 2007-. **Orgs:** Nat Black Cath Clergy Caucus; Canon Law Soc Am; Black Cath Theol Symp; Univ St.Thomas, founding mem law sch fac; bd dirs, Ctr Appl ResApostolate; Cath Common Ground Initiative Comt; founding mem, St.Thomas Sch Law fac. **Special Achievements:** Received first prize for article Not Rite Now: an African American Church? from Catholic press association in 1990. **Home Addr:** St Louis Bertrand Priory 1104 S 6th St, Louisville, KY 40203. **Business Addr:** Professor, University of St Thomas School of Law, 1000 LaSalle Ave, Minneapolis, MN 55403, **Business Phone:** (651)962-4921.

**WHITTAKER, TERRY MCKINLEY**
School administrator, association executive. **Personal:** Born Mar 14, 1950, Newport News, VA; son of Blanche Sutton and Julius; married Beverly. **Educ:** Univ Wis, BA, sociol, 1972; Univ Minn, MA, educ psychol, 1974; MA, educ psychol, 1981; Univ Del, EdD, educ leadership, admin & Policy. **Career:** Youth Coun Bur Brooklyn NY, juv delinq officer, 1973; Univ Minn, pre-maj advisor, 1974-76, bus sch coordr stud affairs, 1976-79; INROADS, dir, 1979-83; Univ Del, Resources Insure Successful Engrs Prog, dir, 1983-87, dir undergrad advisement & stud serv, 1987-92, Fortune dir, 1991-92, Lerner Col Bus & Econ, asst dean, Stud Spec Serv, Stud Prof Develop & Asst Dean Undergrad Affairs & Stud Support Serv, 1992-2003, asst provost stud diversity & success, 2003-. **Orgs:** Kappa Alpha Psi, 1969-; Am Soc Training & Develop, 1980-; Brandywine Prof Assoc, 1984-; Nat Acad Advising Asn, 1985-; chmn, Region A Nat Assoc Minority Eng Prog Adminrs, 1986-; Del Soc Prof Engrs; Nat Engrs Week Festivities Comn, 1986; Nat Assoc Acad Affairs Admins, 1986; bd dir, Forum Advan Minorities Eng, 1992-; chair, United Negro Col Fund Sch Campaign, 1995; chair, Educ Div Del United Way Campaign, 1996-2001; MBNA Educ Found, 1997-2006; bd dir, Metrop Wilmington Urban League Founding, 2000-; bd dir, Aberdeen Civic Asn, 2001-; trustee mem, Christiana Care Health Syst, 2002-; bd dir, United Way Del, 2003-; Nat Asn Stud Personnel Adminrs; Nat Asn Diversity Officers Higher Educ; Univ's Pillard Soc, Univ Del; DE State Bd Educ. **Honors/Awds:** Ivan Williamson Award, Univ Wis, 1972; Twin City Student Assembly Outstanding Contribution Award, Univ Minn, 1979; Commission Service Award, Kappa Alpha Psi, 1982; Minnesota Guidance Associate Award, 1983; Black Alumni Achievement Award, Univ Minn, 1983; Educator of the Year, INROADS Philadelphia Inc, 1985; Faculty Senate Excellence in Undergraduate Advising Award, Univ Del, 2000; Leon and Margaret Slocomb Professional Excellence Award; Outstanding Achiever in Education Award, Brandywine Prof Asn; Outstanding Community Service Award, Aberdeen Civic Asn. **Special Achievements:** First African American athlete to receive the University of Wisconsin's Ivy Williamson Award for outstanding academic and athletic achievements; First African American administrator to work in UD's College of Engineering Dean's Office as Director of Undergraduate Advisement and UD's Lerner College of Business and Economics as Assistant Dean. **Home Addr:** 33 Wenark Dr Suite 6, Newark, DE 19713, **Home Phone:** (302)368-7909. **Business Addr:** Assistant Provost for Student Diversity and Success, University of Delaware, 303 Alfred Lerner Hall, Newark, DE 19716, **Business Phone:** (302)831-2551.

**WHITTAKER, YOLANDA**
Actor, rap musician. **Personal:** Born Aug 4, 1971, Compton, CA; married DeAndre Windom; children: Tiffany & Sanai. **Career:** Rap musician & rec artist, actress, 1990-; Films: Boyz N The Hood, 1991; Menace II Society, 1993; Sister Act 2: Back in the Habit, 1993; Sprung, 1993; Panther, 1995; 3 Strikes, 2000; 3 Strikes, 2000; The Rev. DoW-

rong Ain't Right, 2000; Paper Soldiers, 2002. Tv: "Martin", 1993-95; "New York Undercover", 1995; "Trials of Life", 1997; "Da Jammies", 2015. Albums: Make Way for the Motherlode, 1991; Black Pearl, 1992; You Better Ask Somebody, 1993; Total Control, 1996; Ebony, 1998. Voice Work: Grand Theft Auto:San Andreas, 2004; Da Jammies, 2006; Waist Deep, 2006. **Orgs:** Founder, Intelligent Black Woman's Coalition. **Business Addr:** Rap Singer, c/o E W Rec Am, 75 Rockefeller Plz Frnt, New York, NY 10019, **Business Phone:** (212)275-2500.

### WHITTAKER-DAVIS, DR. SHARON ELAINE

Teacher, vice president (organization), college administrator. **Personal:** Born Sep 6, 1952, Gary, IN; daughter of Robert and Edith Elizabeth; married Frank Davis. **Educ:** Howard Univ, BA, 1974, MEd, 1976; Ill State Univ, PhD, 1983; Harvard Inst Educ Mgt, grad, 2001. **Career:** McKinley Tech High Sch, teacher, 1974-75; Cromwell Acad, teacher, counr, 1975-77; Howard Univ, residence hall counr, 1976-79; Ill State Univ, dir, 1979-84; Paine Col, dean students, 1984-90; Mary Holmes Col, vpres acad affairs, 1989-94; Stillman Col, vpres stud affairs, 1995-. **Orgs:** Nat Asn Stud Personnel Adminr; Nat Asn Stud Affairs, prof & pres, 1993; Phi Beta Kappa; Am Asn Univ Women; Bus Prof Women Inc; Alpha Kappa Alpha Sorority Inc; Campus Queen Asn. **Home Addr:** 241 Meadow Ridge Dr, Tuscaloosa, AL 35405, **Home Phone:** (205)758-6149. **Business Addr:** Vice President for Student Affairs, Miss Stillman Advisor, Stillman College, 3600 Stillman Blvd, Tuscaloosa, AL 35403, **Business Phone:** (205)366-8838.

### WHITTEN, ELOISE CULMER

Government official, association executive, executive. **Personal:** Born Apr 23, 1929, Philadelphia, PA; married Charles F; children: Lisa A & Wanda J Shurney. **Educ:** Temple Univ, BA, polit sci, 1950; Univ Pa, MA, polit, sci & pub admin, 1951; Wayne State Univ; Univ Mich. **Career:** Univ Pa Inst State & Local Govt, res asst, 1951-52; Detroit Urban League, dep dir housing dept, 1963-64, dep dir community affairs dept, 1970-71; Wayne State Univ, exec secy, 1966-67; Wayne County Community Col, instr, 1980; Shaw Col, instr, 1980. **Orgs:** Delta Sigma Theta, 1949-; Planned Parenthood League Detroit, 1959-; Mich County Social Serv Asn, 1963-; Detroit-Wayne County Community Ment Health Bd, 1973-; Wayne County Social Serv Bd, 1974-; bd dir, First Independence Nat Bank, 1983-97; Greater Wayne County Links, 1983-; mem multicultural adv comt, Mich Dept Ment Health, 1985-; mem western hemisphere region bd, Int Planned Parenthood Fed, 1990-; Family Preserv Commun Comt, 1990-; United Community Serv, 1990-; Am Pub Welfare Asn; Nat Conf Social Welfare; adv comt sch social work, Wayne State Univ, 1993-; Mich Asn Black Social Workers; Detroit Asn Black Human Serv Adminr; bd visitor, Sch Social Work, Wayne State Univ. **Honors/Awds:** Sojourner Truth Award, Nat Orgn Black Bus & Prof Women, Detroit Chap, 1980; Mich's Outstanding Black Women, Detroit Hist Soc, 1984; National Business and Professional Women's Award for Social Activism, Dollars & Sense Mag, 1986; Michigan Youth Conference & Youth Advocacy Award, 1993; Partners in Community Services Award, Black Caucus Found Mich, 1993; Michiganian of the Year, 2002. **Special Achievements:** Organized the first area-wide conference on the problems of unwed pregnancy and single parents; helped found Homes for Black Children and changed adoption agency requirements to ease adoption of black children, 1967; developed the Lula Belle Stewart Center, one of the first centers in the country established to provide services for single, African American, low-income women, 1969. **Home Addr:** 14540 Vassar Dr, Detroit, MI 48235, **Home Phone:** (313)864-0991.

### WHITTEN, JANET HUBERT. See HUBERT, JANET LOUISE.

### WHITTEN, THOMAS P.

Administrator, association executive, executive director. **Personal:** Born Sep 26, 1937, SC; son of Benjamin J and Hattie Brown; married Ruthann DeAtley; children: Karen, Alexander & Bryan. **Educ:** Lincoln Univ, Jefferson City, Mo, BA, 1963; Case Western Res Univ, Cleveland, OH, 1964. **Career:** Inner City Protestant Parish, Cleveland, Ohio, group unit leader, 1962; Chicago Renewal Soc, camp dir, 1963; League Park Ctr, Cleveland, Ohio, dir youth employ, 1963-64, dir spec interest groups, 1963-65; Int House RI, exec dir, 1965-67; Providence Human Rel Comn, field investr, 1966-67, exec dir, 1970-73; Harriet Tubman House, Boston, Mass, 1967-68; Hall Neighborhood House, Bridgeport, Conn, assoc exec dir, 1973-77; John Hope Settlement House, Providence, RI, exec dir, 1977-. **Orgs:** City Providence Affirmative Action Comn, 1975; Lippitt Hill Tutorial, Wiggin Village Housing, 1979; Providence Br Nat Asn Advan Colored People, W End Community Ctr, 1980; Minority Adv Comn; Cong woman Claudine Schneider; corp mem, Citizens Bank, Vol Action, Dep Reg State RI, First Unitarian Church Providence, RI; RI Comn Judicial Tenure & Discipline; bd dir, Decisions Inc, New Haven, Conn; Mt Hope Neighborhood Asn; United Neighborhood Ctrs Am; adv comt, Cent High Sch, Hope High Sch, WPRI-TV. **Honors/Awds:** Citizenship Award, City Providence, 1984; Agency Exec Year, Opportunities Industrialization Ctr, 1985; Joseph G Le Count Medal, Providence Branch, Nat Asn Advan Colored People, 1987; National Conference Community & Justice, Humanitarian Award, 1998. **Special Achievements:** Author: "John Hope Settlement House: 1929-2005", 2015. **Home Addr:** 50 Blackstone Blvd Suite 4, Providence, RI 02906, **Home Phone:** (401)273-9545. **Business Addr:** Executive Director, John Hope Settlement House, 7 Thomas P Whitten Way, Providence, RI 02903, **Business Phone:** (401)421-6993.

### WHITTINGTON, BERNARD MAURICE

Executive, football player. **Personal:** Born Aug 20, 1971, St. Louis, MO; married Dana. **Educ:** Ind Univ, sports mgt. **Career:** Football player (retired); Indianapolis Colts, defensive tackle & left defensive end & defensive tackle & defensive end, 1994-2000; Cincinnati Bengals, right defensive tackle & defensive end, 2001-02; Nat Football League Players Asn, pres, Currently. **Honors/Awds:** Rookie of the Year, 1994. **Business Addr:** President, National Football League Players Association, 1133 20th St NW Suite 600, Washington, DC 20036, **Business Phone:** (800)372-2000.

### WHITTLER, DR. TOMMY E.

Educator. **Personal:** Born Sep 27, 1955, Chicago Heights, IL; son of Thomas and Pearl. **Educ:** Bradley Univ, BA, psychol, 1977, MS, psychol, 1979; Purdue Univ, PhD, soc consumer psychol, 1985. **Career:** Univ Kent, asst prof, 1985-91, assoc prof, 1991; Univ Va, vis prof, 1997; DePaul Univ, assoc prof mkt, 2001-; Driehaus Col Bus, assoc prof. **Orgs:** Am Mkt Asn, 1985-; Asn Consumer Res, 1986-; co-chair, Soc Consumer Psychol; bd dir, Fessup Inc; ed rev bd, DePaul Univ. **Home Addr:** 25228 S O'Hare Ct, Monee, IL 60605, **Home Phone:** (708)534-3341. **Business Addr:** Associate Professor, DePaul University, 1 E Jackson Blvd DePaul Ctr 7521, Chicago, IL 60604, **Business Phone:** (312)362-5418.

### WHITWORTH, CLAUDIA ALEXANDER

Editor, publisher. **Personal:** Born Nov 7, 1927, Fayetteville, WV; daughter of Sedonia Rotan and Reverend Fleming; married Clifton B Jr; children: Robyn A Hale, Stanley R Hale, Eva J Crump & B Clifton. **Educ:** Bluefield State Col; Nat Bus Col. **Career:** Va Sem, teaching printing; Roanoke Tribune, linotype operator, 1945; New York Age; The Vinton Booster; Roanoke Tribune, ed, publ, owner, 1971-; Norfolk State Univ, pres rountable & bd visitors, 1989-95; NY City, Cleveland, Fayetteville Newspapers, linotype operator. **Orgs:** Bd mem, WBRA-TV; Am Red Cross; Roanoke Fine Arts Mus; Mill Mountain Playhouse; bd dir, Roanoke Voc Ed Found, Roanoke Pub Schs; adv bd, Salvation Army; Roanoke Col Constance J Hamlar Mem Fund Comt; League Older Am; Meals on Wheels; Baha'i Faith, Spiritual Assembly; National Association for the Advancement of Colored People; YWCA; chair, Employee Rels Comt; Welfare reform Comn; Agency Aging; Bradley Free Clin; Batterer Womens Shelter. **Honors/Awds:** Woman of the Year, Omega Zeta Chap, Zeta Phi Beta, 1982; Virginia Women's Hall of Fame, Va Coun, 1992; Nat Coun Criminal Justice BrotherhoodSisterhood Award, 1993; A Tribune to Women of Colour, US Postal Workers, 1997; Roanoke's Citizen of the Year, 2004. **Special Achievements:** Selected Leaders Pictorial Review Yesterday & Today, 1976; Outstanding Serv News Media, 1 of 20 Civic Leaders selected from throughout the State of VA to accompany Gov Linwood Holton to Strategic Air Comm Hdq Offutt NE Roanoke Valley Bus League & Ladies Aux VFW #1444. **Home Addr:** 3303 Olivet St NW, Roanoke, VA 24017-2931, **Home Phone:** (540)343-6343. **Business Addr:** Editor, Publisher, Roanoke Tribune, 2318 Melrose Ave NW, Roanoke, VA 24017, **Business Phone:** (540)343-0326.

### WHITWORTH, DR. E. LEO, JR.

Dentist. **Personal:** Born Kingston; son of Eabert and Violet; married Jennifer Ann Brown; children: Bianca, Lennox Valencia & Isaac. **Educ:** Northeastern Univ, BA, biol, 1971; Howard Univ, DDS, dent, 1976; Northeastern Univ, MBA, 1994. **Career:** St Anns Bay Hosp, dent surgeon, 1976-77; Comprehensive Clin Kingston Jamaica, dent surgeon, 1976-77; Whitworth Dent Assocs, dentist, pres & cheif exec officer, 1976-; Mattapan Health Clin, dent dir, 1977-79; Harvard Univ, clin instr oper dent, 1981; Tufts Univ Dent Sch, asst clin prof, 2008-. **Orgs:** Am & Nat Dent Asn, 1977-, Metrop Dist Dent Soc, 1977-, Mass Dent Soc, 1977-; pres, William B Price Unit Am Cancer Soc, 1978-80; Commonwealth Study Club, 1979-, Acad Gen Dent, 1979-; chairperson, Mass Div Am Socs Conf, "Meeting Challenge Cancer Black Am", 1980-81; completed post grad course, Mid-Amer Orthod Soc, 1983; Int Orthod Org, 1986; bd dir, William B Price Unit Am Cancer Soc; Cong Adv Bd; life mem, Nat Asn Advan Colored People; Northeastern Univ, corp bd, 1994; bd dir, Mattapan Community Develop Corp, 1996; Mattapan Family Serv Ctr; bd mem, United Methodist Urban serv. **Honors/Awds:** Martin Luther King Community Award, 1994; recipients of Community Awards, Action for Boston Community Development. **Home Addr:** 3 Loew Cir, Milton, MA 02186. **Business Addr:** Chief Executive Officer, President, Whitworth Dental Associates, 542 River St, Mattapan, MA 02126, **Business Phone:** (617)298-8200.

### WHYTE, AMELIOUS N., JR.

College administrator. **Personal:** Born Mar 15, 1968, Brooklyn, NY; son of Amelious N Sr and Dorothy. **Educ:** Univ Southern Calif, BS, pub admin, 1990; Univ Minn, MA, pub affairs, 1997, PhD, higher educ, 2013. **Career:** Univ Minn, Stud Develop, assoc to assoc vpres, 1993-2000, Boynton Health Serv, Chem Health Prog, coordr, 1995-2000, bd regents, asst to exec dir, 2000-03, asst to chief stud affairs officer, 2003-12, Off Stud Affairs, asst dean students & chief staff, 2012-14, interim vice provost stud affairs & dean students, 2013, sr assoc vice provost advocacy & support, 2014-, Col Lib Arts, dir, pub engagement, 2015-. **Orgs:** Counr, alumni adv, HOBY, 1996-99; acad advisr, bd mem, Phi Gamma Delta, 1998-2008; bd mem, Out Front Minn, 2000-; bd dir, Stud Today Leaders Forever, 2006-10. **Home Addr:** 330 Oak Grove St Suite 419, Minneapolis, MN 55403, **Home Phone:** (612)871-6834. **Business Addr:** Senior Associate Vice Provost, Director of Public Engagement, University of Minnesota, 109 Appleby Hall 128 Pleasant St SE, Minneapolis, MN 55455, **Business Phone:** (612)624-2678.

### WHYTE, DEVON MARKES. See WHITE, DEVON MARKES.

### WICKER, DR. HENRY SINDOS

Physician, ophthalmologist. **Personal:** Born Aug 8, 1928, New Orleans, LA; married Geralyn; children: Henry Jr & Stephen. **Educ:** Xavier Univ, BS, 1948; Howard Univ, MD, 1953. **Career:** Homer G Phillips Hosp, internship, 1953-54, resident ophthal, 1954-55; Howard Univ, resident ophthal, 1955-57; St Elizabeth's Hosp, dept Ophthal, chief; Am Bd Ophthal, diplomat; Am Acad Ophthal, fel; Howard Univ, asst prof; George Wash Univ, asst prof; pvt prac, currently. **Orgs:** Medico-chirurgical Soc; Med Soc DC; Nat Med Asn; AMA; bd regents, Ascension Acad, 1970-74; bd dir, Mater Dei Sch, 1970-74; bd dir, Nat Conference Christians & Jews, 1971-75; Alpha Phi Alpha frat; Sigma PiPhi Frat. **Home Addr:** 4239 Blagden Ave NW, Washington, DC 20011-4253. **Business Addr:** Physician, 5505 5th St NW Suite 303, Washington, DC 20011-6587, **Business Phone:** (202)829-6281.

### WICKER, LISA J. LINDSAY

Executive. **Personal:** Born Greenville, MS; children: 2. **Educ:** Mich State Univ, BS; Cent Mich Univ, MA. **Career:** LinWick & Assocs, pres & sr consult, currently; 101 Best Co to Work For in Metrop Detroit, founder & chmn, currently; Gen Motors Corp, mgr employee enthusiasm strategies; Wayne State Univ Sch Bus Admin, adj prof; MGM Grand Detroit Casino, vpres hr; DaimlerChrysler Corp, Diversity Strategies & Ops, sr mgr, 2001-04, Exec Mfg, grp hr exec, 2004-07; Chrysler Grp LLC, Global Diversity Off, dir, 2007-09, Talent Acquisition, Integrated Trng, Global Diversity & Compliance, dir, 2009-. **Orgs:** Historically Black Cols & Univs; Alpha Kappa Alpha Sorority Inc; White House Task Force on Historically Black Colleges & Universities (HBCUs). **Business Addr:** Director, Chrysler Group LLC, PO Box 21-8004, Auburn Hills, MI 48321-8004, **Business Phone:** (800)334-9200.

### WICKHAM, DEWAYNE

Journalist. **Personal:** Born Jul 22, 1946, Baltimore, MD; son of John Trevillion and DeSylvia Virginia Chase; married Ruth Ann Frederick; children: Vanessa Baker & Zenita; married Wanda Nadine Persons; children: Mikella Nicole. **Educ:** Community Col Baltimore, attended 1972; Univ Md, BSJ, 1974, cert, afro am studies, 1974; Univ Baltimore, MPA, 1982. **Career:** Baltimore Eve Sun, Md, reporter intern, 1972-73; Richmond Times-Dispatch, Va, copy editing intern, 1974; US News & World Report, Wash, DC, Capitol Hill corresp, 1974-75; Baltimore Sun, Md, reporter, 1975-78; WBAL-TV, Baltimore, Md, talk show host, 1976-89; Gannett News Serv, Arlington, Va, columnist, 1985-88; USA Today, columnist, 1988-; Black Enterprise mag, ed; Del State Univ, distinguished prof jour, 2001-; Inst Advan Journ Studies, dir, 2001-; Poynter Inst Journalism Ethics, fel, 2002; BlackAmericaWeb.com, exec ed; Book: Fire At Will, 1989; Woodholme: A Black Man's Story of Growing Up Alone, 1995; Thinking Black: Some of the Nation's Best Black Columnists Speak Their Mind, ed, 1996; Bill Clinton & Black Am, 2002. **Orgs:** Life mem, Nat Asn Advan Colored People; adv bd, Multicultural Mgt Prog Univ MO Jour Sch, 1986-92; pres, Nat Asn Black Journalists, 1987-89; Alumni Asn Bd, Univ Baltimore, 1989-90; bd visitors & chmn, Howard Univ Sch Jour, 1992-94. **Special Achievements:** Screenwriter of Judge Not, United Image Entertainment, 1992, author of Woodholme, Farrar, Straus & Giroux, 1995, Fire at Will, published by USA Today Books, 1989, editor of Thinking Black, Crown Books, 1996, author of Bill Clinton and Black American, Ballontine Books, 2002. **Home Addr:** 12118 Faulkner Dr, Owings Mills, MD 21117. **Business Addr:** Columnist, Gannett News Service & USA Today, 7950 Jones Br Dr 10th Fl, McLean, VA 22107, **Business Phone:** (703)276-5800.

### WICKWARE, DAMON

President (organization), automotive executive. **Educ:** Tex Tech Univ, BA, bus admin & mgt, gen, 1994; Cedar Valley Col, attended 2012. **Career:** Bayview Ford Lincoln-Mercury LLC, gen sales mgr opers, 1995-2006, chief exec officer, owner & pres, currently; MetLife Home Loans, Bus Procedures Analyst & Bus Continuity Coordr, 2007-12; Reynolds & Reynolds Co, bus consult, 2012-13; Berkshire Hathaway Automotive, sr bus consult, 2013-15; MarketSource Inc, bus analyst consult, 2015-. **Orgs:** Nat Asn Minority Automobiles Dealers; Mobile Area Chamber; Eastern Shore Chamber Com; Mobile Chamber Com; bd mem, S Baldwin United Way; Ruff Wilson Youth Orgn, Boys & Girls Club; oper mgt, Nat Automobile Dealers Asn Acad, 2005-06. **Business Addr:** Chief Executive officer, President, Bayview Ford Lincoln-Mercury LLC, 27180 Hwy 98, Daphne, AL 36526-4818, **Business Phone:** (251)626-7463.

### WIDEMAN, JAMILA

Lawyer, basketball player. **Personal:** Born Oct 16, 1975, Amherst, MA; daughter of John Edgar and Judith Ann. **Educ:** Stanford Univ, BA, polit sci, African Am studies, 1997; NY Univ Sch Law, JD. **Career:** Los Angeles Sparks, basketball player, 1997-98; Cleveland Rockers, 1999; Portland Fire, pt guard, 2000; Elitzur Ramla, Israel, 1999-2000. **Orgs:** staff atty, Legal Aid Soc. **Honors/Awds:** Named Most Caring Athlete of the Year, USA Today, 1998; New England High School Player of the Year; Massachusetts High School Player of the Year; Community Award, Nat Coun Crime & Delinq. **Special Achievements:** Poet: "Black", 1992. AP All-America, honorable mention, 1996. **Business Addr:** Staff Attorney, Legal Aid Society, 199 Water St, New York, NY 10038, **Business Phone:** (212)577-3300.

### WIDEMAN, JOHN EDGAR

Writer, educator. **Personal:** Born Jun 14, 1941, Washington, DC; son of Edgar and Betty French; married Judith Ann Goldman; children: Daniel, Jacob & Jamila Ann; married Catherine Nedonchelle. **Educ:** Univ Pa, BA, Eng, 1963; Oxford Univ, BA, 1966. **Career:** Writer, 1966-; Howard Univ, instr, 1965; Univ Pa, instr, prof, 1966-74, Afro-Am Studies Prog, dir, 1971-73, asst basketball coach, 1968-72; Univ Wyo, Laramie, WY, prof eng, 1974-85; Univ Mass, Amherst Campus, prof eng, 1986; Brown Univ, Asa Messer prof & prof africana studies & lit arts, asa messer prof emer & prof emer, currently. Author: A Glance Away, 1967; Hurry Home, 1970; The Lynchers, 1973; Hiding Place, 1981; Brothers & Keepers, 1984; Reuben, 1987; Sent For You Yesterday, 1983; Brothers and Keepers, 1984; The Homewood Trilogy, 1985; Reuben, 1987, Fever, 1989; Short Stories: Philadelphia Fire, novel, 1990; The Stories of John Edgar Wideman, stories, 1992; The HomewoodBooks, 1992; Fatheralong: A Meditation on Fathers & Sons, Race & Society, 1994; The Cattle Killing, Boston: Houghton Mifflin, 1996; Two Cities, 1998; Fanon, 2008; Conjunctions; writer, currently; Women's Nat Basketball Asn, player. **Orgs:** Tour-Europe Near E, 1976; Phi Beta Kappa, 1976; Am Acad Arts & Scis, 1992; bd dir, Am Asn Rhodes Scholars; state & nat selection comt, Rhodes Competition; Nat Humanities Fac; AgendaBlack Power. **Honors/Awds:** Rhodes Scholar, Oxford England, 1963-66; Philadelphia Big Five Basketball Hall of Fame, 1974; PEN/Faulkner Award for Fiction, 1984, 1991; National Book Award nomination for Brothers and Keepers, 1984; National Magazine Editors' Prize for Short Fiction, 1987; American Book Award, 1990; Benjamin Franklin Scholar Award, Univ Pa; O. Henry Award, 2000; MacArthur genius grant; Longwood College Medal; Langston Hughes Medal, City Col New York, 2004; Anisfield-Wolf Lifetime Achievement Book Award, 2011. **Special Achievements:** The only writer to have been awarded the PEN/

Faulkner Award for Fiction twice; first African American in more than a half-century to earn the important academic award; second African-American to win a Rhodes Scholarship; Rea Award for the Short Story, 1998. **Business Addr:** Professor Emeritus, Asa Messer Professor Emeritus, Brown University, 155 Angell St, Providence, RI 02912, **Business Phone:** (401)863-3137.

## WIGENTON, SUSAN DAVIS

Judge, lawyer. **Personal:** Born Oct 12, 1962, Neptune, NJ; married Kevin. **Educ:** Norfolk State Univ, BA, 1984; Col William & Mary, Marshall Wythe Sch Law, JD, 1987. **Career:** Judge Lawrence M Lawson, Monmouth Co Super Ct, law clerk, 1987-88; pvt pract, Middletown, NJ, 1988-00; Giordano, Halleran & Ciesla, PC, 1988-96, partner, 1996; City Asbury Pk, pub defender, 1989-93; US Dist Ct, Dist NJ, US magistrate judge, 2000-06, judge, 2006-. **Orgs:** Dist IX, Ethics Comt, 1991-94; chair, Dist IX, Ethics Comt, 1995; Supreme Ct, Adv Comt Prof Ethics. **Special Achievements:** Second African American woman of US District Federal Judge, NJ. **Home Addr:** , NJ. **Business Addr:** Judge, United States District Court, Martin Luther King Bldg & US Courthouse, Newark, NJ 07101, **Business Phone:** (973)477-9704.

## WIGFALL, SAMUEL E.

Manager, financial manager, accountant. **Personal:** Born May 4, 1946, Jacksonville, NC; married Mildred Z Jones; children: Tara & Darian. **Educ:** NC Agr & Tech State Univ, BS, acct, 1969; Univ Louisville, cost acct sys, 1973; Gov's State Univ IL, MBA, work, 1978; NY Univ, Capital Inv Acq Sem, 1982. **Career:** Brown & Williamson Tobacco Co, financial acct, 1969-73; Johnson & Johnson Corp, sr cost acct, 1973-77; Brunswick Corp, sr financial analyst, 1977-79; Sherwood Med Co, Monoject Div, financial analyst, budget mgr, 1979-83, nat dealer commun mgr, 1983-, sales admin mgr. **Orgs:** Scout master Broadway Temple Scout Troop, 1971-72; dir, B&W Employee's Credit Union, 1972; advisor Jr Achievement KY, 1972; pres, sr choir, Broadway Temple AME Zion Church, 1972, 1973; vpres, Richmond Pk ILJaycees, 1975; dir, Brunswick Employees Credit Union, 1976. **Honors/Awds:** Varsity football scholarship NC A&T State Univ, 1965-69; parts control procedure manual, Johnson & Johnson Corp, 1972; youth motivation prog, Chicago Asn Com & Ind, 1973-74; pub annual budget manual Brunswick Corp, 1978; Speaking of People, Ebony Magazine, 1984. **Home Addr:** 1446 Chandellay Dr, St Louis, MO 63146-4803, **Home Phone:** (314)872-3512. **Business Addr:** National Dealer Commission Manager, Tyco Health Care/Sherwood Medical Co, 1831 Olive St, St Louis, MO 63103, **Business Phone:** (386)734-3685.

## WIGGINS, CHARLIE RAY. See SAADIQ, RAPHAEL.

## WIGGINS, EDITH MAYFIELD

College administrator. **Personal:** Born Mar 18, 1942, Greensboro, NC; children: Balaam & David. **Educ:** Univ NC, Greensboro, BA, 1962, MSW, 1964. **Career:** College administrator (retired); NC Memorial Hosp, pediat clin social worker, 1964-67; Dept Defense Mid Sch, Clark AFB, Phillipines, guid counr, 1970-71; Int Church Coun Social Serv, social worker, 1971-72; Univ NC, dir campus, 1972-, asst vchancellor & assoc dean stud affairs, 1981-96, interim vchancellor. **Orgs:** Nat Asn Social Workers; mem, Chapel Hill Human Rel Comm Order Valkyries Univ NC, 1976; Order Golden Fleece, Univ NC, 1976; Acad Cert Social Workers; Nat Asn Social Workers, 1977-; bd educ mem, Chapel Hill, Carrboro, 1979; mem bd visitors, Univ NC, 2007-; chmn, Local Rels; vchancellor, Chapel Hill Town Coun. **Home Addr:** PO Box 16265, Chapel Hill, NC 27516-6265.

## WIGGINS, JOSEPH L.

Educator, administrator. **Personal:** Born Feb 13, 1944, Norfolk, VA. **Educ:** State Col, BA, 1966; Univ NC, attended 1967; Old Dom Univ, MS, 1970, cert adv study educ leadership serv & res. **Career:** Portsmouth City Sch Bd, asst elem sch prin, 1972-74, Admin Coordr Stand Qual & Prog, admin asst to supt, dir commun, currently; Shelton Pk Elem Sch, Va Beach, prin, 1974-; Norfolk City Pub Schs, dir commun, teacher; Norfolk State Col, asst instr govt. **Orgs:** Sigma Rho Sigma; life mem, Kappa Alpha Psi Fraternity; life mem, Nat Educ Asn; Va Asn Sch Execs; Va Educ Asn; trustee, St Thomas AME Zion Church Norfolk. **Home Addr:** 842 Benwood Rd, Norfolk, VA 23502, **Home Phone:** (757)466-7856. **Business Addr:** Director of Communications, Executive Administrator to the Superintendent, Portsmouth City School Board, 801 Crawford St, Portsmouth, VA 23704-3822, **Business Phone:** (757)393-8217.

## WIGGINS, LILLIAN COOPER

Business owner, government official, journalist. **Personal:** Born Jun 26, 1932, Cincinnati, OH; daughter of Ben Cooper (deceased) and Fannie Girdy Cooper; married Adolphus; children: Karen & Michael. **Educ:** Cortex Peters Bus Sch, attended 1953; Howard Univ, Berlitz Sch Lang Foreign Serv Inst & Serv Training Sch; USMC Pr Univ, attended 1957. **Career:** USMC, property & supply off, 1950; Wash, DC, Ghana Embassy, 1960-65; Ghana Govt, press & info officer; Wash Afro-Am Newspaper, journalist, past ed; Lil & Face Pl, co-owner; Adv Neighborhood Comn, comnr, currently. **Orgs:** Past pres, DC Tots & Teens; pub rels dir, Nat Tots & Teens; talk show hostess "FromDesk Lil" sta WHUR; former memship chmn, Capitol Press Club; former mem, State Dept Corres Asn; Women Jour; Media Women; app DC comn Women Status; roving chair, Orgn Black Activist Women; vpres, Cornelius Wiggins Int Black Owned Bus; app, polit action chairperson, DC Br, Nat Asn Advan Colored People; founder, DC Survival Conf; Eagles, Black Entrepreneurs; bd mem, United Black Fund; Sigma Delta Chi; vice chair, DC Charitable Games Control Bd; charter bd mem, DC Lottery, 1981-83; chmn, Indian Acres; secy, Bid Whist Club. **Honors/Awds:** Journalist of the Year, 1965; First Prize National Publishers Convention, 1974. **Home Addr:** 1501 Crittenden St NW, Washington, DC 20011, **Home Phone:** (202)291-5439. **Business Addr:** Chairman, Indian Acres Club, 6437 Morris Rd, Thornburg, VA 22565, **Business Phone:** (540)582-6314.

## WIGGINS, MITCHELL LEE

Basketball player, basketball coach. **Personal:** Born Sep 28, 1959, Kinston, NC; married Marita Payne; children: Andrew, Mitchell Jr, Taya, Angelica, Stephanie & Nick. **Educ:** Truett-McConnell Col, attended 1979; Clemson Univ, attended 1980; Fla State Univ, attended 1983. **Career:** Basketball player (retired), basketball coach; Chicago Bulls, 1983-84; Houston Rockets, 1984-87 & 1989-90; Tampa Bay Stars, 1987; Miss Jets, 1987-88; Quad City Thunder, 1987-88; CBA, 1988; Jacksonville Hooters, 1988; Philadelphia 76ers Rosters, 1991-92; Ft Wayne Fury, 1992; Okla City Cavalry, 1992-93; Aurora Desio, 1993; Milon BC, 1993-94; Tondena 65 Rhummasters, 1994; Sporting Athens, 1994-96 & 1997-98; Panionios BC, 1996-97; CSP Limoges, 1998-99; Spearfish XBA, head coach, 2002; Hickory Nutz, 2002; Spearfish Black Hills Heat, 2002-03; Europ Football League, Milon Nea Smirni Basketball Club; Europ Football League, Sporting Athens. **Home Addr:** , Vaughan, ON.

## WIGGINS, PAUL R.

Banker, vice president (organization), president (organization). **Personal:** Born May 19, 1955, Sarasota, FL; son of Paul and Adele; married Cassandra F Robinson; children: Paula R & Chelsea R. **Educ:** Fla Memorial Col, BS, bus adm, acct, 1981. **Career:** SunBank Tampa Bay, mgt assoc, vpres & credit dept mgr, currently; Bank Am, sr vpres mkt mgr; Mt Hermon Community Econ & Housing Develop corp, dir opers. **Orgs:** Omega Psi Phi, 1979-; bd mem, Tampa Bay Urban Bankers ASN, 1986-; Leadership Tampa Alumni, 1988-; Tampa Bay Male Club, chair, 1989-; bd trustee, finance comt, Fla Memorial Col, 1994-2005; pres, Nat Asn Urban Bankers, 1993-94; exec leadership, Collective Empowerment Group of South Florida, 100 Black Men for Greater Fort Lauderdale. **Home Addr:** 3413 E Knollwood, Tampa, FL 33610, **Home Phone:** (813)238-1747. **Business Addr:** Vice President, Credit Department Manager, SunBank of Tampa Bay, PO Box 3303, Tampa, FL 33601-3303, **Business Phone:** (813)224-2616.

## WIGGINS, WILLIAM H., JR.

Educator. **Personal:** Born May 30, 1934, Port Allen, LA; married Janice Louise Slaughter; children: Wesley Howard & Mary Ellyn. **Educ:** Ohio Wesleyan Univ, BA, pre-theol, 1956; Phillips' Sch Theol, BD, 1961; Louisville Prebyn Theol Sem, MTh, 1965; Univ, PhD, 1974. **Career:** Lane Col, prof, 1961-62; Freeman Chapel CME Church, pastor, 1962-65; TX Col, dir rel life, 1965-69; Ind Univ, Bloomington, grad teaching asst & lectr, 1969-73, asst prof, 1974-79, assoc prof, African Am & African Diaspora studies & folklore & ethnomusicology, prof emer, 1980-2004, Fac & Staff Stud Excellence Mentoring Prog, interim dir. **Orgs:** Fel Folklore Inst Univ; found, dir Afro-Am Folk ArchiveUniv; soc reg dir, Chap Asn Study Afro-Am Life & Hist; Smithsonian Inst African Diaspora Adv Gr Comt; exec bd, Hoosier Folklore Soc; ed bd J Folklore Inst; pres, Am Folk life Fest, 1975-76; field work Smithsonian Inst, 1975-76; pres, Asn African Am Folklorists Minister Christian Meth Epis Ch; Am Folklore Soc; Nat Coun Blk Studies; Asn Study Afro-Am Life & Hist; Asn African & African-Am Folklorists; Hoosier Folklore Soc; Pop Cult Asn; Num Grants; fel Guggenheim Found; fel Rockefeller Found; fel, Nat Endowment Arts; fel Ford Found. **Honors/Awds:** Numerous of Grants & Fellowships; Numerous Publications; Documentary Film: In the Rapture; Anthologized Weeks Appear Numerous publications & journals. **Special Achievements:** Author: O Freedom: Afro-American Emancipation Celebrations, 1990, Joe Louis: American Folk Hero. Editor: Jubilation! : African American celebrations in the Southeast. **Home Addr:** 604 Bayberry Ct W, Bloomington, IN 47401-4666, **Home Phone:** (812)339-7254. **Business Addr:** Professor Emeritus, Indiana University at Bloomington, 107 S Indiana Ave, Bloomington, IN 47405-7000, **Business Phone:** (812)856-1172.

## WIGGINS-OBIE, REV. DAPHNE CORDELIA

Clergy. **Personal:** Born Oct 21, 1960, Newark, NJ; daughter of Arthur Lee Sr and Thelma G. **Educ:** Eastern Col, St Davids, PA, BA, psychol & relig, 1982; Eastern Baptist Theol Sem, Philadelphia, PA, Mdiv, 1985; Emory Univ, Grad Inst Lib Arts, Atlanta, GA, PhD, lib arts/interdisciplinary studies, 1997. **Career:** Eastern Col, resident asst, 1981-82; Second Baptist Church, Wayne, PA, assoc minister, 1981-84; Yeadon Presby Church, pastoral asst, 1983; Saints Memorial Baptist Church, Bryn Mawr, PA, dir youth ministries, 1984-85; Brown Univ, assoc chaplain, 1985-91; Union Baptist Church, Pawtucket, RI, assoc minister, interim pastor, 1989-90, Tex Christian Univ, asst prof relig, 1996-99; Duke Univm Divinity Sch, assistsnt prof congregational studies, 1999-2003; Duke Youth Acad, instr, 2001-02; Union Baptist Church, assoc pastor & coordr congregational ministries, 2003-; Shaw Divinity Sch, adj prof, 2007. **Orgs:** Nat Asn Campus & Univ Chaplains, 1985-; univ rep, Soc Organized Against Racism, 1985-; bd mem, Dorcas Pl, 1986-88; bd adv, One Church One Child Adoption Prog, l987-; vpres, 1987-88, Ministers Alliance RI, treas 1990-; vpres, Soc Organized Against Racism New Eng, 1989-91; exec bd, Interfaith Call Racial Justice, 1990-; exec bd, Black United Methodists & Related Ministries Higher Educ, 1990-; bd mem, African-Am Ministers Leadership Coun. **Home Addr:** 212 Cottage St Apt 1, Pawtucket, RI 02860, **Home Phone:** (401)728-5668. **Business Addr:** Associate Pastor, Coordinator of Congregational Ministries, Union Baptist Church, 904 N Roxboro St, Durham, NC 27701, **Business Phone:** (919)688-1304.

## WIGGS, JONATHAN LOUIS

Photographer. **Personal:** Born Sep 20, 1952, New Haven, CT; son of Alma Varella and Louis. **Educ:** State Univ NY, Oswego, BA, 1980; Tsukuba Univ, Imbaraki, Japan, attended 1978. **Career:** Raleigh News & observer, staff photogr, 1983-87; St Petersburg Times, lab technician, staff photogr, 1987-90; Boston Globe, staff photogr, 1989-. **Orgs:** Nat Press Photogrs Asn, 1980-; Boston Press Photogrs Asn, 1982. **Honors/Awds:** Silver award for photographs on a train trip through Cuba; Regional Journalism Awards, Boston Press Photogr Asn, 2000 & 2005. **Home Addr:** 61 Brockton Ave, Scituate, MA 02066, **Home Phone:** (617)544-3138. **Business Addr:** News Photographer, Boston Globe, 135 Morrissey Blvd, Boston, MA 02107, **Business Phone:** (617)929-3173.

## WILBER, IDA BELINDA

Administrator, lawyer. **Personal:** Born Feb 8, 1956, Jonesboro, LA; daughter of Clayton Johnson and Rosie B Johnson. **Educ:** Northern Ariz Univ, BS, polit sci, 1978, MA, educ & coun, 1991; Univ Ariz, Col Law, JD, 1979. **Career:** Ariz Dept Corrections, New Down Ctr Girls, chief security, 1985-86, New Down Juv Inst, prog mgr, 1986-88, Desert Valley, prog adv, 1988-90; Ariz Dept Juv Corrections, transition adv, 1990, training mgr community serv, 1990-91; Catalina Juv Inst, supt, 1991-92; Ariz State Dept Youth Treat & Rehab, asst chief child care, 1992-; Salt River Pima-Maricopa Indian Community, atty, currently. **Orgs:** Nat Asn Blacks Criminal Justice, conf chair, 1987, pres, 1989-91, publicity chair, 1991-, nat chair, 1992; United Way, impact spending comn, 1991; bd dir, Ariz Black Town Hall, res & reports; Am Correctional Asn; bd dir, Planned Parenthood Southern Ariz; audience participation chair, UNF; state publicity chair & grad adv, ZPB, Omicron Zeta Zeta Chap; Phi Delta Phi. **Home Addr:** 17030 N 15th St 2007, Phoenix, AZ 85022. **Business Addr:** Attorney, Salt River Pima-Maricopa Indian Community, 10005 E Osborn Rd, Scottsdale, AZ 85256, **Business Phone:** (480)362-6315.

## WILBER, MARGIE ROBINSON

Founder (originator), government official, association executive. **Personal:** Born Florence, SC. **Educ:** SC State Univ, BA, 1942; Am Univ, grad study, 1955; George Washington Univ, attended 1958; Dept Agr Grad Sch, attended 1966. **Career:** Marion, SC, teacher, 1942-44; Wash State Dept, 1945-83, supvry ed publ div, 1962-83; Crime Stoppers Club Inc, founder & exec dir, 1967-; Neighbourhood Adv Comn, elec comnr, 1976. **Orgs:** Bd dir, DC Women's Comn Crime Prev; bd dir, Woman's Nat Dem Club, 2003; Wash Urban League; Nat Asn Advan Colored People; DC Fedn Bus Prof Women's Club; Delta Sigma Theta Sorority. **Honors/Awds:** Community Service Award, Boy's Club Greater Wash, 1968; Senate Citation, Cong Rec, 1969; US Presidential Citation, 1970; Community Service Award, Sigma Gamma Rho Sorority, 1971; DC-TRIBUTE, Nat Capital, 1971; Action of Federal Employee Distinguished Volume, 1973; Community Service Award, Iota Chi Lambda, 1973; Community Service Award, United Nation's Day, 1973; Outstanding Citizen Award, Capitol Hill Restoration Soc, 1974; Washington Volunteer Act Award, 1977; Children Kinder to Each Other, 1980; Hon PRS Reagan, Rose Garden, 1985; "Margie Wilber Day", Mayor, DC, 1987; Dedicated Community Service, DC Metrop Police Dept, 1988; Community Leader of the Year, Kiwanis Club, 1996; Woman of the Year, Shiloh Baptist Church, Wash, DC, 1997; Let's Get Together, Etiquette Zone, 2003; "From Whence We Came" Award, Allstate Insurance Co. **Special Achievements:** Appeared as contestant in the National television program "To Tell the Truth," " "The Real Margie Wilber," 1968. **Business Addr:** Founder, Executive Director, Crime Stoppers Club Inc, 1366 SC Ave SE, Washington, DC 20003-2371, **Business Phone:** (202)547-7867.

## WILBON, JOAN MARIE

Lawyer, executive, association executive. **Personal:** Born Aug 21, 1949, Washington, DC; daughter of Louise and Addison; children: 2. **Educ:** NY Univ, BA, 1971; George Washington Univ Law Sch, Wash, DC, JD, 1974. **Career:** Dept Labor Off Solicitor, law clerk, 1974; Equal Employ Opportunity Comm, trial atty, 1974-76; Howard Univ Sch Law, supv atty, 1976; Nat Bar Asn, EEO Div, dep dir, 1976-78; Dept Justice, trial atty, 1978-82; Joan M Wilbon & Assocs, founder, atty, 1981-; Bd Prof Responsibility, hearing examinar. **Orgs:** Am Dc Womens Wash Bar Asns; Pa Bar Asn; bd dir, Intergenerational Theater Co; bd dir, Coun Ct Excellence; trustee, DC Bar Client Security Fund. **Honors/Awds:** Presidential Scholar, Adelphi Univ, 1967; Martin Luther King Scholar, NY Univ, 1969-71; Federal Employee Litigation, Nat Bar Law J, 1978. **Business Addr:** Attorney, Joan M Wilbon & Associates, 1120 Conn Ave NW Suite 1020, Washington, DC 20036, **Business Phone:** (202)737-7458.

## WILBURN, VICTOR H.

Architect. **Personal:** Born Jan 23, 1931, Omaha, NE; son of Katherine and Victor; married Sally; children: Kim, Diane, Susan, Leslie, Victor & Jeff. **Educ:** Univ Chicago, attended 1954; Harvard Univ, attended 1959. **Career:** Victor Wilburn Assoc Architects & Mgrs, owner, 1962-; Urban Devel Group Inc, pres, 1970-; Univ Va, prof; Howard Univ, prof. **Orgs:** Am Inst Architect; Am Inst Planners. **Home Addr:** PO Box 5450, Washington, DC 20016, **Home Phone:** (202)244-0617. **Business Addr:** Owner, Victor Wilburn Architects PC, 3 Bethesda Metro Ctr 700, Bethesda, MD 20814-6300, **Business Phone:** (301)961-1582.

## WILCHER, DR. SHIRLEY JEAN

Government official. **Personal:** Born Jul 28, 1951, Erie, PA; daughter of James S and Jeanne (Evans) Cheatham. **Educ:** Mt Holyoke Col, BA, fr & philos, 1973; New Sch Soc Res, New York, NY, MA, urban affairs & policy anal, 1976; Harvard Law Sch, Cambridge, MA, JD, 1979. **Career:** Prudential Ins Co, auditing examr, 1973-73; Proskauer Rose Goetz & Mendelsohn, staff atty, 1979-80; Nat Women's Law Ctr, staff atty, 1980-85; US House Representatives Comt Educ & Labor, assoc coun, 1985-90; Nat Assn Independent Cols & Univs, gen coun & dir, state rels, 1990-94; US Dept Labor, dep asst secy, 1994-2001; Off Fed Contract Compliance Progs, dep asst secy, 1994, asst secy, 2000; Wilcher Global LLC, founder, Pres, 2001-; Wash Col Law, Am Univ, Wash, DC, adj assoc prof, 2001; Wilcher Global Diversity Mgt LLC, pres & chief exec officer, 2001-; Equal Employ Opportunity Comn, atty advisor, 2006; Am Asn Access, Equity & Diversity, exec dir, 2005-. **Orgs:** ABA; Nat Bar asn; Nat Conf Black Lawyers; exec dir, Am Asn Affirmative Action, currently; founding mem, Rec Secy, Nat Cong Black Women, currently. **Home Addr:** 15407 Blue Willow Lane, Accokeek, MD 20607-2717. **Business Addr:** Executive Director, American Association for Affirmative Action, 888 16th St NW Suite 800, Washington, DC 20006, **Business Phone:** (202)349-9855.

## WILCOX, THADDEUS

Banker, president (organization), chief executive officer. **Career:** Southeast Bank, exec, 1979-89; Peoples Nat Bank Com, dir, pres & chief exec officer, 1999.

## WILDER, CORA WHITE

Educator, lecturer. **Personal:** Born Jul 31, 1936, Columbia, SC; married Kenneth; children: Sharon Wilder Kornegay, Michelle Worthy, Maxine Sarjeant, Marilynn & Marlene. **Educ:** Howard Univ, BA,

1956, BSW, 1958. **Career:** Dept Pub Welfare, WA, DC, child welfare worker, 1958-61; VA Clin, Brooklyn, clin social worker, 1961-63; VA Neuro-Psychiat Hosp, Montrose, NY, 1963-64; Rockland & Co Ment Health Clin, Monsey, NY, psychiat social worker, 1964-67; St Agatha Home C, supvr; Fordham Univ, field work instr, 1967-69; Rockland Community Col, Human Serv Dept, asst prof & coord offield instr, 1969, assoc prof social sci dept, 1984, prof sociol, Dept Social Sci, chair, prof pluralism & diversity, currently, Inst Study & Advan Pluralism & Diversity, asst dir. **Orgs:** Secy, Am Fedn Teachers, 1973; dir, Comp Child Welfare Sem Scand; Delta Sigma Theta Sorority; life mem, Nat Asn Advan Colored People; Rockland Negro Scholar Fund; Day Care & Child Devel Coun Rockland Co; co-hosted radio prog, 1972-75; Rockland Co Cit adv comm, affirmative action comm; United Way, 1972-74, bd dir, 1974-; Rockland Co Bicentennial Comt, 1975; comy person, Rockland Co Dem Comt; gov's appointee bdvisitors, Letchworth Vlg Devel Ctr; co-partner Kenco Art Assoc Art Dist & Cons; consult, Staff Devel & Programming Day Care & Child Welfare; Nat Conf Artists; bd dir, Asn Community-Based Artists Westchester. **Honors/Awds:** Outstanding Leadership Award, Spring Valley Nat Asn Advan Colored People, 1972. **Home Addr:** 11 Brookside Ave, South Nyack, NY 10960-4407, **Home Phone:** (845)358-6236. **Business Addr:** Professor Pluralism & Diversity Department, Rockland Community College, 145 College Rd, Suffern, NY 10901, **Business Phone:** (845)574-4000.

## WILDER, JASON BARNARD

Interior designer, accountant, business owner. **Personal:** married Ceshia C. **Educ:** Fla A & M Univ, elem educ; Harrington Col, assocs residential design, interior design, 2003. **Career:** Fieldcrest Sch Performing Arts, instr, mode prog dir; Joffrey Ballet Chicago, staff acct; Room & Bd Classic Contemp Furniture Oak Brook, IL, interior design assoc, 1997-2000, distrib ctr acct mgr, 2000; Off Bolt Chicago, IL, showroom asst mgr, 2000-02; Robert Allen Group Beacon Hill, sales consult, 2003-04; Graystone Home Chicago, interior designer & showroom sales, 2004; Concepts Contrast, owner, currently; Wilder than imagination, owner & interior design, 2004-; RH Sch Performing Arts, dir modeling & creative dir, 2009-; 3 Day Blinds, design consult, 2011-. **Orgs:** Founder, Epiphany Modeling Troupe; pres, Jack & Jill Am Chicago Chap; vpres, creative dir, choreographer, Southland Scholar Found; New Life Covenant Church, Oakwood. **Business Addr:** Director of Modeling, RH School Of Performing Arts, 1014 E 47th St, Chicago, IL 60653, **Business Phone:** (773)850-1487.

## WILDER, KURT (HON. KURTIS T WILDER)

Judge. **Personal:** Born Apr 26, 1959, Cleveland, OH; married Cindy; children: Alycia & Klif. **Educ:** Univ Mich, AB, polit sci, 1981; Univ Mich, Law Sch, JD, 1984; Gen Jurisdiction, 1993; Financial Statements Courtroom, 1993. **Career:** City Cleveland Prosecutor's Off, litigation intern, 1983; First Dist Ct Appeals; Foster, Swift, Collins & Smith, PC & Butzel Long, PC, litigation atty, 1984-92; Washtenaw County Trial Ct, chief judge, 1992-98; State Mich, First Dist Ct Appeals, judge, 1998-. **Orgs:** Exec bd, Legis Comn, Mich Judges Asn; Am Judges Asn; State Bar Mich; fel Mich State Bar Found; Wolverine Bar Asn; Asn Black Judges Mich; Federalist Soc; pres, State Bar Mich Judicial Conf; pres, Mich Judges Asn; State Bar Mich Open Justice Comn; State Bar Mich Judicial Ethics Subcomt; Vanzetti Hamilton Bar Asn; Am Bar Asn; Am Red Cross, Washtenaw Co Chap, Strategic Planning Comn, bd dir, Fin Develop Comn, co-chair; bd trustee, Nat Kidney Found Mich; adv bd, Washtenaw Coun Arts; Nat Asn Advan Colored People; secy, Black Child & Family Inst, bd dir, 1986-89; bd dir, Ingham Co Bar Asn, 1989-91; human res coun, Ann Arbor Area Chamber Com, 1990-92; chmn, State Mich Community Corrections, vice chair, 1991; Ann Arbor Citizens Qual Serv Comn, 1992-93; Washtenaw County Bar Asn. **Business Addr:** Judge, State of Michigan, Cadillac Pl 3020 W Grand Blvd Suite 14-300, Detroit, MI 48202-6020, **Business Phone:** (313)972-5755.

## WILDER, LAWRENCE DOUGLAS

Government official, educator, mayor. **Personal:** Born Jan 17, 1931, Richmond, VA; son of Robert and Beulah; married Eunice Montgomery; children: Lynn Diana, Loren Deane & Lawrence Jr. **Educ:** VA Union Univ, BS, chem, 1951; Howard Univ Sch Law, JD, 1959. **Career:** Wilder, Gregory & Assoc, founder atty firm; Pvt Practices, atty, 1959; State Va, state sen, 1969-85; lt gov, 1986-90; Common Wealth VA, gov, 1990-94; Richmond, mayor, 2005-09; VA Common wealth Univ, adj prof, currently. **Orgs:** Am Bar Asn; Am Trial Lawyers Asn; Va Bar Asn; Am Judicature Soc; Old Dom Bar Asn; Richmond Trial Lawyers Asn; Richmond Chamber Com; Richmond Urban League; Red Shield Boys Club; CrusadeVoters, Nat Asn Advan Colored People; vice pres, Va Human Rels Coun; vice chmn, United Negro Col Fund; past mem, Nat Conf Lt Gov; co-chaired, Wilder-Bliley Charter Comn, 2002; chmn, Gov Mark Warner's Comn Efficiency & Effectiveness, 2002; Mayors Against Illegal Guns Coalition. **Honors/Awds:** Alumnus of the Year, 1970; Howard Univ Law Sch, 1970; Certificate of Merit, 1974; Certificate of Merit, Va State Col, 1974; Hon Doctor of Laws, 1979; Distinguished Alumni Award, VA Union Univ, 1979; Man of the Year Award, Omega Psi Phi; Astoria Benefit Asn Award, Delver Women's Club; Citizenship Award, 4th African Baptist Church; Civic Award, Omega Psi Phi Third Dist; Civitan Award, Red Shields Boys Club; Three dozen Hon degrees; Nat Asn Advan Colored People Spingarn Medal; Anna Eleanor Roosevelt Medallion of Hon; SCLC Drum Major for Justice Award; B'Nai B'rith's Gt American Traditions Award; Thurgood Marshall Award of Excellence; Honorary Doctorate, Ariz State Univ, 2004; Named its School Government Public Affairs in honor of L. Douglas Wilder, 2004. **Special Achievements:** First African-American state senator, Va, 1969; First mayor of the city of Richmond, Virginia; First African-American to be elected governor in the US, 1986. **Home Addr:** 2805 E Weyburn Rd, Richmond, VA 23235-3257, **Home Phone:** (804)320-7070. **Business Addr:** Adjunct Professor, Virginia Commonwealth University, 821 W Franklin St, Richmond, VA 23284, **Business Phone:** (804)828-0100.

## WILDERBRATHWAITE, DR. GLORIA

Physician, administrator. **Personal:** married Carlos; children: 3. **Educ:** Howard Univ, BS; Georgetown, MD, 1993; George Washington Univ, MPH, 1998. **Career:** Childrens Nat Med Ctr, Mobile Health Progs, dir. **Orgs:** Head, Cs Health Fund; founder, Core Health; bd dir, DC Primary Care Asn; bd dir, Cs Law Ctr; bd dir, Int Mobile Health Asn; bd dir, Meyers Found; bd dir, DC Action C; Prestigious; Nat Health Serv Corps; expert consult, Oprah Winfrey show; Todays Child Commun. **Business Addr:** Head, The Children's Health Fund, 317 E 64th St, New York, NY 10021, **Business Phone:** (800)535-7448.

## WILDERSON, DR. FRANK B., JR.

Psychologist, educator, teacher. **Personal:** Born Jan 17, 1931, Lutcher, LA; son of Frank and Valentean; married Ida Lorraine Jules; children: Frank III, Fawn, Amy, Wayne & Jules. **Educ:** Xavier Univ, BA, 1953; Univ Mich, MS, 1957, PhD, 1962. **Career:** Educator (retired); Orleans Parish Pub Schs, teacher, 1953-57; Univ Mich Child Psychiat Hosp Sch, teacher, 1957-58; Reading Clin Univ Mich, dir, 1958-61, Out Patient Educ Prog, dir, 1961-62; Univ Mich Sch Educ, lectr, 1960-62; Univ Minn, from asst prof to prof, asst dean, 1962-74, vpres stud affairs, 1975-90, prof psychol, 1990, prof emer, currently. **Orgs:** Classroom Mgt Withdrawn C, 1963; Minn Psychol Asn; Am Psychol Asn; Coun Execept C; Coun C Behav Dis; nat adv com, Handicapped C; adv com, US Pub Health Serv; nat adv com, Handicapped Childrens Early Ed; chmn, HEW/BEH Panel; Minn Asn Group Psychotherapist; Minn Asn Brain-Damaged C; Asn Black Psychologist; pub comn, Coun Except C; dir, Bush Found; trustee, Breck Col Prep Sch; Phi Delta Kappa; Black Coalition; chmn, Univ Com Develop BA Prog Area Afro-am Studies Pub. **Special Achievements:** Books published like: "A Concept of an Ideal Teacheral-Pupil Relationship in Classes for Emotionally Disturbed Children", 1967; "An Exploratory Study of Reading Skill Deficiencies & Psychiatric Symptoms in Emotally Disturbed Children", 1967. **Home Addr:** 1717 James Ave S, Minneapolis, MN 55403-2826, **Home Phone:** (612)377-0491. **Business Addr:** Professor Emeritus, University of Minnesota, 56 E River Rd, Minneapolis, MN 55455-0364, **Business Phone:** (612)624-5551.

## WILDERSON, THAD

School administrator, psychologist. **Personal:** Born Nov 13, 1935, New Orleans, LA; married Beverly; children: Troy, Dina, Lori & Marc. **Educ:** Southern Univ, BS, 1960, MA, 1968; Tulane Univ, addn psychol courses; Univ Minn, doctoral cand. **Career:** Tulane Univ, interviewer/analyst, 1959-69; St James Parish Sch, teacher, 1960-65; Orleans Parish Sch, teacher/counr, 1965-69; Juv Diag Ctr, counr, 1966; Upward Bound, counr, 1968; Macalester Col, assoc dean students/dir Minority Prog Psychologist, 1969, coordr community rels; psychologist pvt pract, 1970-; Carleton Col, counr/consult, 1971-75; Minn State Dept Educ, consult, 1973-; Thad Wilderson & Assoc, owner, psychologist, currently. **Orgs:** Am Personnel & Guid Asn; Minn Personnel & Guid Asn; Am Psychol Asn; Midwest Psychol Asn; Minn Psychol Asn; Monitors club; Minneapolis urban league; bd dir, Ramsey County cs ment health collab. **Home Addr:** 1015 Washburn Ave N, Minneapolis, MN 55411-3557, **Home Phone:** (612)529-7647. **Business Addr:** Psychologist, Thad Wilderson & Associates, 475 Univ Ave W Suite 103, St. Paul, MN 55103, **Business Phone:** (651)225-8997.

## WILDS, CONSTANCE T.

Educator. **Personal:** Born Jul 22, 1941, Stamford, CT; married Willie E; children: William Ernst. **Educ:** Wilberforce Univ, BA, 1969; Fairfield Univ, MA, 1972. **Career:** Western Conn State Col, Stud Affairs Off, dir comunity rels, dean stud affairs counr com, community coordr, 1971-73; Norwalk Community Col, adminr; Neighborhood Youth Corps, dir manpower; CTE Inc, actg dir, admn asst. **Orgs:** Conn Sch Counr Asn; Am Pub Gardens Asn; Am Personnel & Guid Asn; Asn Black Personal Higher Educ; vpres, Minority Higher Educ; Master Plan Higher Ed; Urban League; Ment Health Asn; Afro-Am Dem Club. **Honors/Awds:** Cert, Am Forum Int Study. **Home Addr:** 52 Winding Lane, Norwalk, CT 06851-1639, **Home Phone:** (203)847-0571.

## WILDS, TRISTAN PAUL MACK

Actor, singer. **Personal:** Born Jul 15, 1989, Staten Island, NY; son of Paul and Monique Moncion. **Career:** Actor, TV series, "Miracle Boys", 2005; "The Wire", 2006-08; "Cold Case", 2007; "Law & Order", 2008; "90210", 2008-13; "Black Actress", 2013. Films, "Half Nelson", 2006; "The Secret Life of Bees", 2008; "Red Tails", 2012. Stage: "Woo" Roundabout Theater Company; "Stockholm Brooklyn" Roundabout Theater Company. Music videos: Li'l Flip, "Ghetto Mindstate"; Jay Z, "Roc Boys"; Adele, "Hello", 2015. R&B/hip hop artist as Mack Wilds, 2010-; signed with Ten2One, 2010; albums, "Remember Remember", 2011; "New York: A Love Story", 2013. **Special Achievements:** Model for Rocawear's "I Will Not Lose" campaign, 2008.

## WILES, DR. LEON E.

Educator. **Personal:** Born May 28, 1947, Cincinnati, OH; married Maliaka Johnson; children: Tanzania & Saleda. **Educ:** Philander Smith Col, BA, psychol, 1970; Univ Pittsburg, educ, 1978; Univ SC-Columbia, PhD, educ admin; Baldwin-Wallace Col, cert; Harvard Univ, cert; Yale Univ, cert. **Career:** Slippery Rock St Col, chairperson, 1974-78; Penn State Univ, Develop Yr Prog, dir, 1978-82; Univ SC, dean stud, 1982, assoc chancellor stud affairs, vice chancellor stud & diversity affairs, 1981-2008; Clemson Univ, chief diversity officer, 2008-15. **Orgs:** Phi Delta Kappa; YMCA Black Achievers, Adv Comn; Personnel Asn Bd, SC Col; Progressive Men's Club Spartanburg; charter mem, Upstate Int. **Honors/Awds:** Davis Cup, 1994-95; Progressive Men's Outstanding Achievement Award, 1995; Omega Outstanding Educator, 1996; Piedmont Assembly Outstanding Citizen; Nat Asn Stud Personnel Admin; Spartanburg Repertory Theater Adv Comn; Upstate Diversity Leadership Award, Riley Inst, Furman Univ & Greenville Chamber Com, 2007. **Home Addr:** 109 Rock Cove Ct, Moore, SC 29369-9124, **Home Phone:** (864)574-7178. **Business Addr:** Chief Diversity Officer, Clemson University, 109 Daniel Dr 103 Sikes Hall, Clemson, SC 29634-5016, **Business Phone:** (864)656-3311.

## WILEY, AARON L.

Lawyer. **Educ:** Calif State Univ-Northridge, fine & studio arts, 1984; Calif State Univ-Dominguez Hills, eng lang & lit/lett, 1985; Univ Calif, Los Angeles, BA, Eng lang & lit/lett, 1988; Univ Mich Law Sch, JD, law, 1991. **Career:** Dern, Mason & Floum, summer assoc law clerk, 1989; Bickel & Brewer, summer assoc law clerk, 1990; Strasburger & Price LLP, summer assoc law clerk, 1990; Int Law Firm Fulbright & Jaworski, assoc, 1991-93; Dallas County Dist Atty's Off, asst dist atty, 1993-99; US Dept Justice, asst US atty, 2000-; St Ann Cath Church Kaufman, prosecutor & lectr; Northern Dist Tex, asst us atty, currently. **Orgs:** Tex State Bar, 1992-. **Business Addr:** Assistant United States Attorney, United States Department of Justice, 950 Pennsylvania Ave NW, Washington, TX 20530-0001, **Business Phone:** (202)514-2000.

## WILEY, CHUCK, JR. (SAMUEL CHARLES WILEY, JR.)

Consultant, football coach, football player. **Personal:** Born Mar 6, 1975, Baton Rouge, LA. **Educ:** La State Univ, BS, pre-phys ther, 1997, MS, sports mgt, 2005. **Career:** Football player (retired), coach, executive; Carolina Panthers, 1998, defensive end, 1999; Atlanta Falcons, 2000, defensive end, 2001; Bayou All-Stars Football & Cheerleader Camp, 2001-; Minn Vikings, defensive end, 2002-04; New York Giants, defensive end, 2004-05; Omega Football & Cheerleader Camp, 2004-; Morehouse Col, asst strength & conditioning, 2007; Stockbridge High Sch (GA), asst strength & conditioning, 2007; SPARQ, trainer, 2008-; Tucker High Sch(GA), boys basketball strength & conditioning, 2008-09; Nike Football Training Camps, defensive line coach, 2008-; Nike Football Combines, 2009-; Chattahoochee High Sch(GA), defensive line, 2010-; Chattahoochee High Sch(GA), 9th grade strength & conditioning, 2012-; Front 7, event coordr, 2009-; Ga Gwinnett Col, instr wellness, 2014-15; Southern Lab High Sch (LA), asst strength & conditioning consult, currently. **Orgs:** Twin Cities community; United Way; Epilepsy Found, Minn; ARC Hennepin-Carver; Omega Psi Phi fraternity; call 99 Wayz 2 Win. **Honors/Awds:** Defensive Most Valuable Player. **Special Achievements:** Film Appearance: Hood Rats, 2001. **Business Addr:** Event Coordinator, Front 7, PO Box 467004, Atlanta, GA 31146, **Business Phone:** (770)521-7640.

## WILEY, EDWARD, III

Journalist. **Personal:** Born Dec 23, 1959, Baltimore, MD; son of Edward Jr and B Maye Robinson. **Educ:** W Coast Christian Col, eng, 1983; Calif State Univ, Fresno, CA, BA, journ, 1985. **Career:** Fresno Bee, Calif, staff writer, 1982-87; Rep Tony Coelho, Calif, spec asst, 1986-87; House Majority Whip, media specialist, 1987-88; Educ Daily, Alexandria, Va, writer, ed, 1988; Black Issues Higher Educ, Fairfax, Va, asst managing ed, 1988-93; C's Defense Fund, ed, 1992-98, managing ed, 1994-97; Nat Wildlife Fedn, commun mgr, 1997-98; US Dist Ct, dep monitor, 1998-2002; BET.com, staff writer & managing ed, currently. **Orgs:** Nat Asn Black Journalists; Educ Writers Asn; life mem, Pi Eta Chi; Sigma Delta Chi. **Honors/Awds:** Educ Press Asn, Distinguished Achievement Award, series, 1989, feature writing, 1989; Young, Gifted & Black Award, Calif State Univ, 1990; Rosa Parks Meritorious Achievement Award, 1983. **Home Addr:** 3611 Cherryvale Dr, Beltsville, MD 20705-3841. **Business Addr:** Staff Writer, BET.Com, 1235 W St NE, Washington, DC 20018-1211, **Business Phone:** (202)608-2000.

## WILEY, ERLEIGH NORVILLE

Judge. **Personal:** daughter of Fern and Homer L; married Aaron L; children: Brad & Jacob. **Educ:** Tex Tech Univ, BBA, finance, 1984; Univ Tex Law Sch, JD, 1988; Col Judicial Studies, grad; Nat Drug Ct Inst, grad; DWI Col, grad. **Career:** Dallas County Dist Atty Off, asst dist atty, 1990-93, Juv Div, supv atty, 1993-2003; Kaufman County Ct Law, judge, 2003-; Kaufman County Indigent Defense Bd, mem; Kaufman County Juv Bd, pres; Univ N Tex, adj prof, 2011-. **Orgs:** Tex State Bar Asn; Amanda F Norville C's Shelter; Tex Health Resources-Presby Hosp; Kaufman County Bar Asn; bd trustee, Tex Health Resources Kaufman. **Business Addr:** Judge, Kaufman County, 100 W Mulberry St, Kaufman, TX 75142, **Business Phone:** (972)932-4331.

## WILEY, DR. FLETCHER HOUSTON

Lawyer. **Personal:** Born Nov 29, 1942, Chicago, IL; son of Fletcher and Mildred Berg; married Benaree Drew Pratt; children: Pratt Norton & Benaree Mildred. **Educ:** USAF Acad, BS, 1965; Univ Paris, L Inst Des Etudes Politiques, attended 1966; Georgetown Univ, MS, Am hist, 1968; Harvard Law Sch, JD, 1974; John F Kennedy Univ Sch Govt, MPP, pub policy, 1974. **Career:** ABT Assocs Inc, consult, 1972-75; Goldstein & Manello PC, sr partner to coun; Fine & Ambrogne, atty, 1975-78; Budd, Wiley & Richlin, PC, atty & managing partner, 1979-89; Econ Develop & Indust Corp, dir, 1980-83; Gov's Comn Minority Bus Develop, founder & chair, 1984-90; Wiley & Richlin, PC, atty & pres, 1989-91, dir econ develop & indust corp, 1980-93; PRWT Servs Inc, staff; Fitch, Wiley, Richlin & Tourse PC, pres, 1991-; PRWT Holdings, pres & chief operating officer; Bingham McCutchen LLP, coun, 2003; TJX Co Inc, dir, currently; PRWT Serv Inc, prin, exec vpres & gen coun, currently; PRWT Holdings, pres & chief operating officer, of counsel, 1999-. **Orgs:** Assoc comt mem, Mass Alcoholic Beverage Control Comn, 1977-81, 1983-84; bd mem, Dana-farber Cancer Inst, 1978-86; chmn, Boston Chamber Com, 1980-; Econ Devel & Indus Corp, 1981-; co-invstr, Unity Bank & Trust Co, 1982; New Eng Aquarium, 1982-86; chmn, Govt commr, Minority Bus Develop, 1985-; nat pres, Black Entertainment & Sports Lawyers Asn Inc, 1986-93, nat chmn; Coolidge Bank &Trust Co Am Bar; Asn Nat Bar; Asn Mass Bar Asn; Mass Black Lawyers Asn; founding mem, Harvard Law Sch Black Alumni Orgn; dir, New Eng Legal Found; trustee, US Nat Pk Found, African Am Experience Fund. **Honors/Awds:** Recipient of numerous civic and professional awards; Ten Outstanding Young Leaders, Boston Jaycees, 1978. **Special Achievements:** First African American from Indiana appointed to a military academy; Fifth African American graduate of the Air Force Academy and the Academy's first Fulbright Scholar. **Home Addr:** 27300 Alma Sch Pkwy, Scottsdale, AZ 85262, **Home Phone:** (617)731-0544. **Business Addr:** Of Counsel, Bingham McCutchen LLP, 1 Fed St, Boston, MA 02110-1726, **Business Phone:** (617)951-8978.

## WILEY, FORREST PARKS

Executive. **Personal:** Born Nov 1, 1937, Weldon, NC; married Gloria; children: Joseph, John & Linda. **Educ:** Tuskegee Inst, BS, 1966. **Career:** Executive (retired); WR Grace, res asst bio chem, 1967-70; New Ventures Inc, dir res, 1970-73; Letterflex Systs WR Grace, syst engr, 1970-73, reg mgr, 1973-75; Harris Corp Dilitho Syst, mgr sls mgr serv mgr. **Orgs:** Pres, Tuskegee Alumni Housing Found, 1977-; bd dir, WA Tuskegee Housing Found; Nat Geog Soc; Bot Soc Am; Am Soc Plant Physiologists; Am Inst Biol Sci; Tuskegee Alumni Asn; pres, Wa-Tuskegee Clb; Int Platform Asn. **Home Addr:** 299 Hedgewood Ct, Lexington, KY 40509-1106, **Home Phone:** (859)266-9085.

### WILEY, GERALD EDWARD
Executive. **Personal:** Born Jun 20, 1948, Belleville, IL; son of George and Mary; married Marquita Trenier; children: Raymond & Johanna. **Educ:** St Louis Univ, BS, sociol, 1970, MA, urban affairs, 1974. **Career:** Container Corp Am, personnel mgr, 1974-75; Gen Dynamics, employee rels dir, 1975-78; Wiley, Ette & Assoc, vpres, 1978-79; Monsanto Co, dir affirmative action & equal employ opportunity, 1979-. **Orgs:** Chmn, Howard Univ Cluster Exec Coun, Fla A&M; exec comt, St Louis Univ Billiken Club; bd dir, Franklin Neighborhood Asn; St Clair County Planning Comn. **Honors/Awds:** Illinois Basketball Hall of Fame, 1977; Metro Area Hall of Fame, 1987; St Louis University Hall of Fame, 1993. **Home Addr:** 13 Towne Hall Estates Lane, Belleville, IL 62223-7010, **Home Phone:** (618)616-1055. **Business Addr:** Director of Affirmative Action & Equal Employment Opportunity, Monsanto Co, 800 N Lindberg Blvd, St. Louis, MO 63167, **Business Phone:** (314)694-1000.

### WILEY, JOHN D., JR.
Educator. **Personal:** Born Sep 24, 1938, Fodice, TX; married Clara. **Educ:** BS, 1959; MS, 1960; Univ Houston. **Career:** Dillard Univ, instr, 1960-63; Inst Serv Educ & Advan Study, consult, 1967-70; Tex Southern Univ, asst prof, 1970-79, assoc prof, 1980-, Dept Math, 1989-. **Home Addr:** 7019 McCullum Rd, Missouri City, TX 77489, **Home Phone:** (281)437-2179. **Business Addr:** Professor, Texas Southern University, 3100 Cleburne Ave, Houston, TX 77004, **Business Phone:** (713)527-7580.

### WILEY, KEHINDE
Painter (artist). **Personal:** Born Jan 1, 1977?, Los Angeles, CA; son of Yoruba. **Educ:** San Francisco Art Inst, BFA, 1999; Yale Univ, Sch Art, MFA. **Career:** Portrait painter with works displayed at var insts incl Roberts & Tilton, Deitch Proj, Rhona Hoffman Gallery, Smithsonian Inst/Nat Portrait Gallery & Studio Mus in Harlem, New York; Minneapolis Inst Art; Brooklyn Mus; Columbus Mus Art; Kans City Mus; Oak Pk Pub Libr; Jewish Mus, New York; High Mus Art, Atlanta; Phoenix Art Mus, Phoenix; Los Angeles County Mus Art, Los Angeles; Hammer Mus, Los Angeles; Milwaukee Art Mus; Walker Art Ctr, Minneapolis; Detroit Inst Arts, Detroit. **Honors/Awds:** Artist of the Year Award, New York City Art Teachers Association/New York City Art Teachers Association/United Federation of Teachers; Canteen Magazine's Artist of the Year Award.

### WILEY, DR. KENNETH LEMOYNE, SR.
Physician. **Personal:** Born Jan 10, 1947, San Antonio, TX; son of Elmer and Dolores Shields (deceased); married Linda Diane Nixon; children: Kenneth Jr & Brian. **Educ:** Trinity Univ, BS, physics, 1968; OK State Univ, MS, biophysics, 1970; Meharry Med Col, MD, medicine, 1977. **Career:** George W Hubbard Hosp, resident internal med, 1977-80; Pvt pract, internal med, 1980-; Kenneth L. Wiley MD LLC, internal med physician, 2012-. **Orgs:** Alpha Phi Alpha; Alpha Omega Alpha; Soc Sigma Xi. **Home Addr:** 3840 St Bernard Ave, New Orleans, LA 70122, **Home Phone:** (504)283-4182. **Business Addr:** Physician, Private Practice, 105 St Rose Ave, St. Rose, LA 70087-3710, **Business Phone:** (504)466-6028.

### WILEY, LEROY SHERMAN
Government official, educator, executive. **Personal:** Born Oct 30, 1936, Sparta, GA. **Educ:** Ft Valley St Col, BS, 1960; Clark Col, attended 1968; Univ GA, attended 1969; GA Col, MS, 1977. **Career:** Ft Valley St Col, supv maintenance dept, 1958-60; Hancock Cent HS, instr dept chmn, 1960-61; Boddie HS, instr, 1963-64; Hancock Cent HS, instr, chmn sci dept, 1964-70; Hancock County, mgr, clerk Super ct, 1970-; Upward Bound Study Ctr, dir, 1973; Learning Ctr, couns asst field rep, 1975; Hancock County Emergency Mgt Agency, dir, coordr, 1984-. **Orgs:** Post comdr Am Legion #530, 1984-85; Kappa Alpha Psi; CB Radio Club Inc; Masonic Orders; Hancock County Dem Club; Hancock County Br Nat Asn Advan Colored People; GA Asn Black Elected Officials; Veterans Asn GA Col Milledgeville; GA Ed Assoc; GA Farm Bur Assoc; Nat Assoc Retarded C; County Officials Assoc GA; comt chmn, BSA trustee bd, St Mark AME Church. **Honors/Awds:** Outstanding Contrib Civil Rights Movement Hancock City, 1982. **Special Achievements:** First black since reconstr & only black serving as clerk of Superior Court. **Home Addr:** PO Box 642, Sparta, GA 31087-0642, **Home Phone:** (404)444-7434. **Business Addr:** Clerk Superior Court, Manger, Hancock County, 601 E Broad St, Sparta, GA 31087, **Business Phone:** (706)444-6644.

### WILEY, MARCELLUS VERNON
Football player, business owner. **Personal:** Born Nov 30, 1974, Compton, CA; son of Charles and Valerie Howard; children: Morocca Alise. **Educ:** Columbia Univ, BA, sociol, 1997. **Career:** Football player (retired), business owner; Buffalo Bills, defensive end, 1997-2000; San Diego Chargers, defensive end, 2001-03; Dallas Cowboys, defensive end, 2004; Jacksonville Jaguars, 2005-06; ESPN, NFL Live, substitute analyst, currently, SportsNation, co-host, 2013-; ESPN LA, Max & Marcellus, co-host; Prolebrity.com, co-founder; Dat Dude Entertainment, owner; Wiley enterprises, owner, chief exec officer, currently. **Honors/Awds:** National type-writing champion, 1988; National Defensive Player of Week, Sports Illustrated, 1994; Walter Payton Man of the Year Award, Nat Football League, 2002; selected, Pro Bowl, 2001; selected, all Pro, 2001; Phil Simms Ironman Award; Walter Payton Man of the Year; Sid Luckman Award; David W. Smyth Award; Invited to judge the Miss Universe Pageant in Panama, 2003. **Home Addr:** , CA. **Business Addr:** Chief Executive Officer, Wiley Enterprises, 416 Broadway, Santa Monica, CA 90401, **Business Phone:** (310)434-1010.

### WILEY, MARGARET Z. RICHARDSON
Executive. **Personal:** Born Jun 27, 1934, Jackson, NC; married Sampson; children: Brian & Judith. **Educ:** City Col NY, 1956; Scott's Col, cosmetology, 1965; Ind Univ, 1969. **Career:** Summit Labs Indianapolis, educ & mkt dir, 1965-72; Americana Salon, owner; Nat Develop Coun, exec dir, 1972-78; Devco Local Develop Corp, pres, 1973-78; Nat Minority Supplier Develop Coun, vpres, exec dir & chief oper officer, 1978-97; Liberty Bank, founder. **Orgs:** Adv Bd, Enterprising Women; Revenue Planning Bd, Montclair, NJ, 1978; exec dir, nat orgn, 1978; exec dir, New York & NJ Regional Br; Nat Asn Advancement Colored People. **Home Addr:** 26 Tuers Pl, Montclair, NJ 07043-2520, **Home Phone:** (973)744-0593.

### WILEY, MAURICE
Secretary (office). **Personal:** Born Jan 13, 1941, Pine Bluff, AR; son of Hosie. **Educ:** Univ Ark-Pine Bluff, BS, 1963; Calif State Univ Los Angeles, MA, 1972. **Career:** Pasadena Unified Sch Dist, math teacher, 1966-69; Inglewood Unified Sch Dist, math teacher, 1969-72, guid counr, 1972-82, coord col prep prog, 1982-88, admin asst supt, 1989-; Inglewood Unified Sch Dist, adminr, teacher, guid counr, career & col adv, coordr, currently. **Orgs:** Phi Delta Kappa Educ Frat, 1974-; pres, Inglewood Coun & Psychol Asn, 1986; partic, Nat Asn Equal Opportunity Conf Nations Black Col, 1986; partic, Univ Calif Los Angels Counr Inst Univ Calif, 1986; Inglewood Mgt Asn, Inglewood Centinela Valley Youth Coun Adv Comn; Inglewood Educ Found; Consult Col Prep Prog & H SCoun; Inglewood Chamber Com Educ Comn. **Honors/Awds:** Outstanding Young Men, Am Pasadena Chamber Com, 1970; Most Eligible Bachelor, Ebony Mag, 1971; Counr & Teacher of the Year, Inglewood High Sch, 1980; Award of Excellence, Inglewood Sch Dist, 1984; Comm Unity Commendation, City Inglewood Calif, 1986; Inglewood Chamber Com Commendation, 1989; Calif Lottery Millionaires Club, 1989-; Young Black Scholars Role Model of the Year, 1992; California Lottery's Hero in Education Award, 2003. **Home Addr:** 3823 Lorado Way, Los Angeles, CA 90043-1625. **Business Addr:** College Advisor, Coordinator, Inglewood Educational Foundation, 401 S Inglewood Ave, Inglewood, CA 90301, **Business Phone:** (310)680-5150.

### WILEY, MORLON DAVID
Basketball player, basketball coach. **Personal:** Born Sep 24, 1966, New Orleans, LA; married Stacey; children: Jeremiah. **Educ:** Calif State Univ, Long Beach, CA, attended 1988. **Career:** Basketball player (retired), basketball coach; Dallas Mavericks, 1988-89, 1992-93, 1994-95, player develop staff, 2000-04; Orlando Magic, asst coach, 1989-91, 2004-; Rapid City Thrillers, 1991; San Antonio Spurs, 1991; Atlanta Hawks, 1992-93, 1995; Grand Rapids Hoops, 1993, 1998-99; Quad City Thunder, 1993-94, 1995-98; Miami Heat, 1994. **Home Addr:** 2521 Fallview Lane, Carrollton, TX 75007-1934. **Business Addr:** Assistant Coach, National Basketball Association, RDV Sportsplex 8701 Maitland Summit Blvd, Orlando, FL 32810, **Business Phone:** (407)916-2400.

### WILEY, SAMUEL CHARLES, JR. See WILEY, CHUCK, JR.

### WILEY-PICKETT, GLORIA
Government official. **Personal:** Born Jul 5, 1937, Detroit, MI; daughter of Elmer and Fannie Smith; children: Michele Joy. **Educ:** Detroit Inst Tech, attended 1956; Wayne State Univ, attended 1982. **Career:** Government official (retired); US Dept Defense, acct tech, fed women prog coordr, 1971-73, supvr procurement asst, 1973-75; US Dept Labor & ESA/OFCCP, equal opportunity specialist, 1975-81, supvr equal opportunity specialist, 1981-89, asst dist dir, 1989-95. **Orgs:** Sub comn, SE Mich March Dimes Fashion Extravaganza, 1971; Nat Asn Human Rights Workers, 1981; Nat Asn Female Execs Inc, 1983-; treas, DGL Inc, 1984-86; chairperson, Prog Comt, Am Bus Womens Asn, Spirit Detroit Chap, 1985; bd dir, Mich Chap NAHRW, 1989; Founders Soc Detroit Inst Arts; Nat Asn Human Rights Workers; Nat Asn Female Execs Inc; Nat Asn Advan Colored People. **Home Addr:** 29065 Wellington Rd E Suite 8, Southfield, MI 48034-4535, **Home Phone:** (248)353-0269.

### WILFONG, HENRY T., JR.
Association executive, president (organization), accountant. **Personal:** Born Feb 22, 1933, Mt. Olive, AR; son of Henry T Sr and Geraldine; married Aline Jane Guidry; children: Bernetta & Brian. **Educ:** Univ Calif, Los Angeles, BA, 1958, MBA, 1960; CPA. **Career:** Nat Asn Minority CPA Firms, pres, 1971; city councilman, 1973; Wilfong & Co, sr partner; Minority Small Bus/Capital Ownership Develop, Small Bus Admin, assoc admin; Nat Asn Small Disadvantaged Bus, pres, currently. **Orgs:** Calif Coun Criminal Justice, 1974; bd dir, Nat Bus League; bd dir, Calif Soc CPA'S; Bush-Cheney Transition Team-SBA Adv Group; Dept Energy, Small Bus Adv Comt; Nat Coun Policy Rev-Black Capitalism; Presidential Task Force Int Pvt Enterprise; NASA Adv Coun; chair, NASA Minority Bus Resource Adv Comt; co-chair, Obama Unity Comt. **Home Addr:** 5520 Waters Dr, Savannah, GA 31406, **Home Phone:** (912)692-1168. **Business Addr:** President, National Association of Small Disadvantaged Businesses, 5520 Waters Dr, Savannah, GA 31406, **Business Phone:** (912)692-1168.

### WILFORD, GLORIA GANTT
Research scientist. **Personal:** Born May 23, 1945, Charleston, SC; daughter of Wilhelmenia Gordon Gantt (deceased). **Educ:** Hampton Inst, Va, BA, biol, 1965, Med Univ SC, Charleston, MS, 1972. **Career:** Scientist (retired); US Naval Res Lab, Wash, DC, tech librn, 1965-69; Burke High Sch, Charleston, teacher, 1969-70; Dept Med & Dept Basic Clin Immunol & Microbiol, res scientist, 1974-78; Med Univ SC, Dept Neurochem Med, Charleston, res scientist, 1978. **Orgs:** Am Soc Microbiol; Choraliers Music Club, Charleston; Hampton Alumni Asn, Charleston; YWCA; Morris St Baptist Church, Charleston; Alpha Kappa Alpha, 1963-. **Honors/Awds:** Pub sci paper on Immunologic Responses Assoc with Thoracic Duct Lymphocytes; Employee Service Awards, 2004. **Home Addr:** 3506 Rockville Ct, Charleston, SC 29414.

### WILFORK, ANDREW LOUIS
Government official. **Personal:** Born Apr 27, 1947, Quitman, GA; children: Jermaine. **Educ:** Fla Int Univ, BS, social work, 1974. **Career:** Metro-Dade County Waste Dept, serv rep, 1971-72, enforcement officer to coordr, 1972-74, area supvr, 1974-78; Miami Dade County Pub Works Dept, transfer sta, 1978-80, supvr transfer sta admin, 1980-86, supt, 1986-, Dept Solid Waste Mgt, dir, currently. **Orgs:** Fla Int Univ. **Home Addr:** 5264 SW 159th Ave, Miramar, FL 33027. **Business Addr:** Director, Miami Dade County, 8675 NW 53rd St Suite 201, Miami, FL 33166-4598, **Business Phone:** (305)594-1520.

### WILHOIT, CARL H.
Engineer, educator. **Personal:** Born Aug 15, 1935, Vandalia, MO; married Daisy Glascoe; children: Raquel & Marcus. **Educ:** Lincoln Univ, 1960; Howard Univ, BS, 1962; Cath Univ, 1973. **Career:** New Town Devel DC Dept Housing & Community Develop, engr coordr; DC Dept Highways & Traffic, civil engr, 1962-67; Col Wash, Dept Civil Engg Fed City, DC, lectr, 1975-76. **Orgs:** ASCE; Nat Asn Housing & Redevelop Officials, 1971; Nat Soc Prof Engrs, 1977. **Home Addr:** 3905 Kencrest Ct, Bowie, MD 20721, **Home Phone:** (301)262-4832.

### WILKENS, LENNY (LEONARD RANDOLPH WILKENS)
Basketball coach, basketball player, founder (originator). **Personal:** Born Oct 28, 1937, Brooklyn, NY; son of Henrietta Cross and Leonard R; married Marilyn J Reed; children: Leesha, Randy & Jamee. **Educ:** Providence Col, BA, econ, 1960. **Career:** Basketball player (retired), basketball coach, founder; St Louis Hawks, 1960-68; Seattle Super Sonics, player, 1968-72, coach, 1969-72, head coach, 1977-85, gen mgr, 1985-86, vchmn, 2006, pres basketball opers, 2007; Films: "1989 NBA All-Star Game", 1989, "1994 NBA All-Star Game", 1994, "Mania", 2008; Cleveland Cavaliers, 1972-74, head coach, 1986-93; Portland Trail Blazers, coach, 1974-75, coach, 1975-76; Atlanta Hawks, head coach, 1993-2000; Toronto Raptors, head coach, 2000-03; New York Knicks, head coach, 2004-05; Northwest FSN Studio, col hoops analyst, 2007; Lenny Wilkens Found, founder, currently; Nat Basketball Asn, coach, currently. **Orgs:** Hon chmn, Mary mt-Cavs RP Golf Classic, 1987-; chair, Make-a-Wish Golf Tournament, 1988; Boys & Girls Clubs, Greater Cleveland; Cath Diocese, Cleveland; Rainbow Babies; C's Hosp; Kidney Found; NBA Players Asn, vp, 1961-69; NBA Coaches Asn, pres; Lenny Wilkens Found, founder. **Honors/Awds:** National Invitation Tournament Most Valuable Player, 1960; Most Outstanding Player, 1960, 1961; Rhode Island Heritage Hall of Fame, 1961; NBA All-Star, 1963-65, 1967-71, 1973; NBA All-Star Game Most Valuable Player, 1971; Western Conference champion, 1978, 1979; NBA Championship, Seattle Super Sonics, 1979; City of Hope Sportsman of the Year, 1979; Congressional Black Caucus Coach of the Year, 1979; CBS Coach of the Year, 1979; Black Publisher of America Coach of the Year, 1979; hon doctor of humanities, Providence Col, 1980; Urban League-Witney Young Outstanding Citizen Award, 1980; Golden Shoe Award, Shoes for Kids, 1988; hon doctorates, Providence Univ, 1988; Digital NBA Coach of the Month, 1988; Naismith Memorial Basketball Hall of Fame, 1989; Basketball Weekly, Coach of the Year; Victor Award, City of Hope/Sport Magazine, 1994; IBM/NBA Coach of the Year, 1994; NIT-NIKE Hall of Fame; NYC Basketball Hall of Fame; Brooklyn Hall of Fame; Gold Medal, Olympic Games, 1996; Basketball Hall of Fame, coach, 1998. **Special Achievements:** United States Olympic Men's Basketball Team, asst, 1992, coach, 1996; Winningest coach in NBA history; participated in more games as player and/or head coach than anyone else in league history; winningest coach in Cleveland history, 1992-93; autobiography, Unguarded: My Forty Years Surviving in the NBA; One of the 50 Greatest Players & 10 Greatest Coaches in NBA History 1996. **Business Addr:** Founder, Lenny Wilkens Foundation, 5302 Lake Wash Blvd NE Suite G, Kirkland, WA 98033, **Business Phone:** (425)898-4592.

### WILKERSON, BRUCE ALAN
Football player. **Personal:** Born Jul 28, 1964, Loudon, TN; married Antionette; children: Starkicia & Jeremy. **Educ:** Univ Tenn, grad. **Career:** Football player (retired); Los Angeles Raiders, tackle & right guard & right tackle & left tackle, 1987-94; Jacksonville Jaguars, offensive tackle, 1995; GreenBay Packers, tackle & offensive tackle, 1996-97; Oakland Raiders, 1998; Aluminum Co Am, staff. **Orgs:** Integral mem, "Sugar Vols" squad, 1985. **Honors/Awds:** Champions, Super Bowl XXXI. **Special Achievements:** Films: 1987 NFL Draft, 1987; 1996 NFC Championship Game, 1997; Super Bowl XXXI, 1997. TV Series: "The NFL on NBC", 1989; "ESPN's Sunday Night Football", 1988-91; "NFL Monday Night Football", 1988-91. **Business Addr:** Machinist, Aluminum Company of America (ALCOA), 201 Isabella St, Pittsburgh, PA 15212-5858, **Business Phone:** (412)553-4545.

### WILKERSON, DANA
Basketball player, actor, teacher. **Personal:** Born Feb 27, 1969. **Educ:** Long Beach State Univ. **Career:** Basketball player (retired), actor, teacher; Film: Slam City with Scottie Pippen, 1994; Long Beach Stingrays, guard, 1997-98; Chicago Condors; Lynwood High Sch, phys educ teacher & girls athletic dir, currently. **Business Addr:** Physical Education Teacher, Girls Athletic Director, Lynwood High School, 11321 Bullis Rd, Lynwood, CA 90262, **Business Phone:** (310)886-1600.

### WILKERSON, HON. DIANNE
State government official. **Personal:** Born May 2, 1955, Pine Bluff, AR. **Educ:** Am Int Col, BS, public admin, 1978; Boston Col Law Sch, JD, 1981. **Career:** State Mass, state sen, 1992-2008. **Orgs:** Convener, Ann Twenty First Century Black Mass Conf; co-chair, Hynes Conv Ctr; Boston Common Parking Garage Legis Comn; Steering Comm Lawyers Comm Civil Rights under Law; trustee, Chinatown Trust Fund; hon mem, Capital Campaign Comt, Chinese Progressive Asn; Northeastern Univ Community Task Force; ex-officio mem, Action Boston Community Develop; Delta Sigma Theta Sorority Inc; Morning Star Baptist Church; Comn to Eliminate Racial & Ethnic Health Disparities; chair, State Admin & Regulatory Oversight; Co-Convener, Coalition Caring; Dudley St Neighborhood Initiative; vice chair, Joint Comm Financial Servs; Senate common Ways & Means; Bonding, Capital Expenditures & State Assets Educ; Ment Health & Substance Abuse; bd visitors, Fenway Community Health Ctr; adv bd mem, Asian Am Civic Assoc; ex-officio mem, Boston State Hosp Citizens Adv Comt; Caucus Women Legis, NE Univ Community Task

Force; Roxbury Strategic Master Plan Oversight Comt; trustee, trustee' FelsAthenaeum Trust Fund Adv Comt. **Home Addr:** 74 Howland St, Dorchester, MA 02121-1704, **Home Phone:** (617)506-0626.

### WILKERSON, ISABEL

Writer, educator, journalist. **Personal:** Born Jan 1, 1961?, Washington, DC; married Roderick Jeffrey Watts, Jan 1, 1989. **Educ:** Howard Univ, BA, jour, 1983. **Career:** New York Times, Chicago Bur Chief; Emory Univ, James M. Cox Prof Journalism; Princeton Univ, Ferris Prof Journalism; Northwestern Univ, Kreeger-Wolf Endowed Lectr; Boston Univ, Col Commun Prof Journalism & Dir Narrative Nonfiction; Author: "Minds Brains & People", 1974 "The Warmth of Other Suns", 2010, "The World Is Waiting for You", 2015, Gordon Parks, 2015. **Orgs:** Bd mem, Columbia Univ's Nat Arts Journalism Prog. **Honors/Awds:** George S. Polk Award, Regional Reporting, 1993; National Association of Black Journalists, Journalist of the Year, 1994; Pulitzer Prize in Journalism for Feature Writing, 1994; Guggenheim Fellowship for Creative Arts, U.S. and Canada; "Essence" Magazine, 40 Under 40; "The Warmth of Other Suns," winner of National Book Critics Circle Award (Nonfiction), 2010, Anisfield-Wolf Award for Nonfiction, 2011, Mark Lynton History Prize, 2011, Sidney Hillman Book Prize, 2011, Heartland Prize for Nonfiction, and NAACP Image Award for Outstanding Literary Work Debut Author (nominated), 2011. **Special Achievements:** First African American woman to win the Pulitzer Prize in Journalism for coverage of 1993 Midwestern floods (1994); author of nonfiction book "The Warmth of Other Suns: The Epic Story of America's Great Migration," Random House (2010); in 2012, the "New York Times" named her book as one of its All-Time Best Books of Nonfiction; several articles included in book "Pulitzer Prize Feature Stories: America's Best Writing, 1979-2003" (edited by David Garlock).

### WILKERSON, PROF. MARGARET BUFORD

Educator, executive. **Personal:** Born Apr 3, 1938, Los Angeles, CA; daughter of George and Gladys; married Stanley; children: Darren, Cullen & Gladys-Mari. **Educ:** Univ Redlands, BA, hist, 1959; Univ Calif, Los Angeles, Teachers Cred, 1961; Univ Calif, Berkeley, MA, dramatic art, 1967, PhD, dramatic art, 1972. **Career:** YWCA, Youngstown Ohio, adult prog, dir, 1959-60; YWCA, Los Angeles, dir, 1960-62; Jordan High Sch, Los Angeles, Calif, drama & eng teacher, 1962-66; Eng Dept Dramatic Art Dept, lectr, 1968-74; Univ Calif, Berkeley, Dept Afro-Am Studies, lectr, 1976-83, Ctr Study Educ & Adv Women, dir, 1975-83; Am Coun Educ, Kellogg lectr, 1980; Univ Calif, Berkeley, African Am Studies Dept, prof, chair, 1988-94, Dramatic Art Dept, Ctr Theater Arts, chair, dir, 1995-98, prof emer, currently; Ford Found, dir, media arts, Consult, prog officer, 1998; Watts High Sch, eng teacher; Arts & Cult at Ford Found, dir media, currently. **Orgs:** Ford Fel Dissertation Ford Found, 1970, Nat Res Coun, 1983-84; Kumoja Players Community Theater Group, 1971-75; Berkeley Black Alumni Club, Univ Calif, 1976; Am Theatre Asn, Black Theatre Prog, 1979-85; Am Coun Educ, Nat Identification Prog Women Admins, 1980; Bus & Prof Womens Found, 1983; Nat Res Coun humanities, Doct Comm, 1983; Calif Arts Coun, 1984; former first vpres, bd trustees, San Francisco Theol Sem, 1987-97; Asn Theatre Higher Educ, chair, Awards Comn, 1996-98; lifetime mem, Black Theatre Network, 1998; trustee, Mills Col Bd Trustees, 1999-2008, 2009-; adv coun mem, Raise Curtain Campaign, 2015-; Kennedy Ctr Felsof Am Theatre; Nat Asn Advan Colored People; Nat Coun Negro Women; Black Alumni Club, Univ Calif, Berkeley; dir, UC Berkeley Ctr Study, Educ & Advan Women; Bear Arts Found Bd; former trustee, Univ Redlands; Am Soc Theatre Res Exec Coun; Independent Tv Serv Exec Comt. **Honors/Awds:** DHL, Univ Redlands, 1980; Rockefeller Found, 1982-83; Honoree, Equal Rights Advocates, 1989; Award for Exemplary Educational Leadersip / BlackCaucus Am Asn Higher Educ, 1990; Profile Excellence, KGO-TV, San Francisco, 1990; Career Achievement Award for Outstanding Educator, Am Theatre Asn, 1996; Black Theatre Network Lifetime Memorial Award. **Special Achievements:** Co-author: Black Scholar theatre issue & other publs; author of "9 Playsby Black Women" New American Library 1986. **Home Addr:** 8 Highgate Rd, Kensington, CA 94707-1141, **Home Phone:** (510)647-9731. **Business Addr:** Professor Emeritus, University of California, 660 Barrows Hall Suite 2572, Berkeley, CA 94720, **Business Phone:** (510)642-7089.

### WILKES, JAMAAL (JACKSON KEITH WILKES)

Consultant, basketball player. **Personal:** Born May 2, 1953, Berkeley, CA; married Valerie; children: Sabreen, Omar & Jordan; married Joycelyn Bramlette. **Educ:** Univ Calif, Los Angeles, BS, econs, 1974. **Career:** Basketball player (retired), broker: Golden State Warriors, 1975-77, Los Angeles Lakers, 1978-85, Los Angeles Clippers, 1985-86; Am Basketball Asn, Los Angeles Stars, vpres, 2000; Prof Designation, Investment Real Estate; CAL Real Estate Broker; CAL Ins Agent & Broker; Jamaal Wilkes Financial Advisors LLC, founder, 2003-. **Orgs:** Bd dir, Los Angeles Urban League; bd dir, Western Region United Way; bd trustee, UCLA Found; bd governor, LA Athletic Club. **Honors/Awds:** NBA champion, 1975, 1980, 1982, 1985; NBA Rookie of the Year, 1975; All Star Team, 1976, 1981, 1983; 4 time NBA World Champion; 2 time NCAA Basketball & Scholastic All-Am; UCLA Athletic Hall of Fame; GTE Academic Hall of Fame, inductee, 1990; Boys & Girls Club America, Natl Hall Fame, Inducted; Award General BUS Studies; Naismith Memorial Basketball Hall of Fame. **Special Achievements:** Co-Author: Success Under Fire: Lessons For Being Your Best In Crunch Time, 2006. **Home Addr:** 433 N Camden Dr Suite 600, Beverly Hills, CA 90210, **Home Phone:** (310)288-1810. **Business Addr:** Founder, Jamaal Wilkes Financial Advisors LLC, 6601 Ctr Dr W Suite 500, Los Angeles, CA 90045, **Business Phone:** (310)209-8330.

### WILKES, REGGIE WAYMAN (REGINALD WAYMAN WILKES)

Football player, entrepreneur. **Personal:** Born May 27, 1956, Pine Bluff, AR. **Educ:** Ga Tech Univ, BS, biol, 1978; Morehouse Sch Med. **Career:** Football player (retired), executive; Philadelphia Eagles, Linebacker, 1978-85; Atlanta Falcons, 1986-87; GS Capital LP, founder, currently; Merrill Lynch adv group, staff, 1988; Pro-Cap LLC, sr vpres, 1999-; Merrill Lynch, 2007-; Mercantile Trust Bank, sr vpres sports banking div; Wilkes Group, broker. **Business Addr:** Vice President, Merrill Lynch & Co Inc, 4 World Financial Ctr, New York, NY 10080, **Business Phone:** (212)449-1000.

### WILKES, DR. SHELBY R.

Ophthalmologist. **Personal:** Born Jun 30, 1950, Crystal Springs, MS; married Jettie M Burnett; children: Martin & Andrew. **Educ:** Alcorn State Univ, BS, biol, 1971; Johns Hopkins Univ Sch Med, MD, 1975; Coles Col Bus, Kennesaw State Univ, Kennesaw, Ga, MBA, 1998. **Career:** Univ Rochester Sch med, Dept Surg, intern-resident, 1975-76; Univ Ill, Eye & Ear Infirmary, res fel, 1976; Mayo Clin, resident ophthal, 1977-79; Mass Eye & Ear Infirmary, fel retina serv, 1980-81; Harvard Univ, Sch Med, clin asst ophthal, 1982-83; Emory Univ, Sch Med, asst prof ophthal; Morehouse Sch Med, Atlanta, Ga, asst clin prof surg & ophthal; vitreoretinal surgeon, ophthalmologist; Atlanta Eye Consults, pres, currently, vitreoretinal surgeon, currently. **Orgs:** Alpha Phi Alpha, Nat Asn Advan Colored People, Atlanta Med Asn, Ga State Med Asn, Asn Res Vision & Ophthal, 1978-, Am Med Asn, 1978-; fel Am Acad Ophthal, 1981-; Nat Med Asn, 1981-; bd dir, Am Diabetes Asn, Ga Affil Inc, 1985; Beta Gamma Sigma Hon Soc; Phi Kappa Phi Hons Soc; deacon, Zion Hill Baptist Church; Coles Col Bus Adv Bd, Kennesaw State Univ; chmn audit comt & vice-chmn bd dir, Capitol City Bank; Dean's Coun; Rollins Sch Pub Health; Emory Univ; Alumni Coun Johns Hopkins Univ Alumni Asn; bd dir, Alcorn State Univ Found Inc. **Honors/Awds:** Hons Soc, Alcorn State Univ, 1970-71; Ophthalmic Alumni Award, Mayo Clin, 1979; Distinguished Alumni Citation, Nat Asn Equal Opportunity Higher Educ, 1985. **Special Achievements:** Wrote papers: with E S Gragoudas, "Regression patterns of uveal melanomas after proton beam irradiation" Ophthalmology, 1982 89, 7 p840; with MBeard, D M Robertson & L Kurland "Incidence of retinal detachment" Rochester MN Amer Journal of Ophthalmology, 1982; Listed in Marquis' of Who's Who in Finance and Industry. **Home Addr:** 6170 Old Nat Hwy, College Park, GA 30349-4367. **Business Addr:** Vitreoretinal Surgeon, Atlanta Eye Consultants, 830 W Peachtree St NW Suite 100, Atlanta, GA 30308, **Business Phone:** (404)881-6417.

### WILKINS, BETTY

Journalist, editor. **Personal:** Born Mar 31, 1922, Braddock, PA; children: Gloria, Raymond, Robert Jr, Donald, Margaret & Patricia. **Educ:** Wilberforce Univ; Denver Opportunity Sch Jour, attended 1957. **Career:** KFML Radio, 2 hr gospel show; KC Call, Denver ed; KDKO Radio, soc columnist with Honey Bee's show; Negro Weekly, assoc ed & soc ed; Denver Weekly News, socs ed. **Orgs:** Pres, Sophisticates & Soc & Civ Club; vpres, Astro Jets; secy, Pond Lily; Jane Jefferson Dem Club; Mayors coun human rels; Bronze Dau Am; founder, State Asn Colored Womens Clubs; Coun Negro Women; CO Spress Womens Club; black del Geo McGovern from Denver to Miami, 1972; comt woman, E Denver, 20 yrs; res, Delta Mothers Club; Zion Circle Seven; The Denver Beauty Guild; life mem & pub rel chmn, Nat Asn Advan Colored People; LaBelle Art; Lit club; Patrons Club; pres, Denver Fedn womens club; Denver Press Club. **Honors/Awds:** Originator of "Ten Best Dressed Black Women" Denver; Miss Bronze Dau Award, 1958; Robert L Vaden Award, 1972; Women of the Year, 1972; Harriet Tubman Dist Serv Award, 1973; Syl Morgan Smith Comt Award Trophy, 1976; Pub Relation Award, Astro Jets, 1977; Comt Award, Metro Club, 1979; Hall of Fame Award, May D & F, 1980. **Home Addr:** 7722 W Alder Dr, Littleton, CO 80123. **Business Addr:** Founder, Journalist, Denver Weekly News.

### WILKINS, CHARLES O.

Management consultant, business owner, vice president (organization). **Personal:** Born Jun 18, 1938, Louisville, KY; married Diane Blodgett; children: Nicole & Jennifer. **Educ:** Cent State Univ, Wilberforce, OH, BA, psychol, 1961; Univ Calif, Grad Sch, Los Angeles, CA, attended 1963. **Career:** Johnson & Johnson, Raritan, NJ, supvr, employ, 1965-72; Singer Co, New York, NY, mgr corp off personnel, 1972-80; NYS Urban Develop Corp, New York, NY, vpres hr, 1980-84; Performance Plus Human Resourses Mgmt Consult, E Brunswick, NJ, pres, owner, 1984-; YMCA, Greater New York, vpres human resources, 1991-. **Orgs:** Alpha Phi Alpha, 1958-; Sigma Pi Phi, 1987-; Am Soc Personnel Admin, 1991-; Urban League BEEP; bd mem, Health Watch; NJ Philharmonic Orchestra. **Home Addr:** 11 Pilgrim Run, East Brunswick, NJ 08816, **Home Phone:** (732)238-6896. **Business Addr:** Vice President of Human Resources, YMCA of Greater New York, 333 7th Ave 15th Fl, New York, NY 10001, **Business Phone:** (212)630-9615.

### WILKINS, DAVID BRIAN

College teacher, educator. **Personal:** Born Jan 22, 1956, Chicago, IL; son of Julian. **Educ:** Harvard Col, BA, govt, 1977; Harvard Law Sch, JD, 1980. **Career:** US Ct appeals Second Circuit Law, clerk to hon chief judge, 1980-81; US Supreme Ct, law clerk to hon Thurgood Marshall, 1981-82; Nussbaum, Owen & Webster, assoc specializing Civil Litigation, 1982-86; Harvard Law Sch, asst prof law, 1986-92, Prog Legal Prof, dir, 1991-, prof law, 1992-96, Global Initiatives Legal Profession, vice dean, Kirkland & Ellis Prof Law, 1996-2008, Ctr Lawyers & Prof Serv Indust, fac dir, 2004-, prin, leadership law firms, 2007-, Lester Kissel Prof Law, 2009-, prin, leadership corp coun, 2009-; Harvard Univ, fel, 1989-90, Ctr Ethics & Prof, fac assoc, 1990-; Univ Chicago Law Sch, vis prof, 1995; fel, Osgoode Hall Law Sch. **Orgs:** Judicial Conf US Ct Appeals DC Circuit, 1984; Judicial Conf US Ct Appeals Second Circuit, 1988; Am Asn Law Sch, 1991-93; bd dir, Law & Soc Asn, 1994-97; vis resr, Am Bar Found, 1995; sr resr fel, Am Bar Found, 1997-; Am Bar Asn; Open Soc Inst, 1998-2000; bar mem, DC; US Dist Ct DC; Harvard Civil Rights Civil Liberties Law Rev; Harvard Law Rev; Harvard Black Law Students Asn; fel, Harvard Univ Edmond J. Safra Found Ctr Ethics; mem, Am Acad Arts & Sci, 2012. **Home Addr:** 55 Appleton St, Cambridge, MA 02138, **Home Phone:** (617)354-2768. **Business Addr:** Professor, Harvard School of Law, 1563 Mass Ave, Cambridge, MA 02138, **Business Phone:** (617)495-0958.

### WILKINS, GERALD BERNARD

Broadcaster, basketball player. **Personal:** Born Sep 11, 1963, Atlanta, GA; married Vita; children: Damien, Jasmyn Alexandria & Holli Dai. **Educ:** Moberly Area Jr Col, attended 1982; Univ Tenn, Chattanooga, attended 1985. **Career:** Basketball player (retired), broadcaster; New York Knicks, guard, 1985-92; Cleveland Cavaliers, 1992-94; Vancouver Grizzlies, 1995-96; Orlando Magic, 1996-99. TV Series: "The NBA on CBS", 1985-87; "Ebony/Jet Showcase", 1998; "Dream Job", 2004.

### WILKINS, JACQUES DOMINIQUE

Basketball player, basketball executive. **Personal:** Born Jan 12, 1960, Paris; son of Gertrude Baker; married Nicole Berry; children: 4; married Robin Campbell; children: Jacob. **Educ:** Univ Ga, attended 1983. **Career:** Basketball player (retired), basketball executive; Atlanta Hawks, prof basketball player, 1982-94, spec asst exec vpres, 2004-, vpres basketball opers, 2004-; Los Angeles Clippers, 1994; Boston Celtics, 1994-95; Panathinaikos Athens, 1995-96; San Antonio Spurs, 1996-97; Team-Syst Bologna, 1997-98; Orlando Magic, 1999; Hawks games, color analyst. **Orgs:** United Negro Col Fund. **Business Addr:** Vice President of Basketball Operations, Atlanta Hawks, Centennial Tower 101 Marietta St NW Suite 1900, Atlanta, GA 30303, **Business Phone:** (404)878-3800.

### WILKINS, JANICE F.

Executive. **Personal:** married Alvin; children: 1. **Educ:** Xavier Univ, New Orleans, LA, BS, acct, 1967; Golden Gate Univ, San Francisco, MBA, acct, 1987. **Career:** Intel Corp, finance controller, 1980, dir internal audit & vpres finance & enterprise serv, 1995-2010; Am States Water Co, dir & bd mem, 2011-; Xavier Univ La, bd trustee, currently. **Orgs:** Bd trustee, Acad & Fac Affairs Comt, Xavier Univ; mem bd trustee, Sacred Heart Schs Atherton; Inst Internal Auditors; Financial Execs Int; bd mem, Peninsula Bridge; bd mem, Res Bank; Nat Asn Corp Dirs; bd trustee, Golden Gate Univ; Audit & Investment Comts; Finance Coun St. Pius Church Redwood City; Acad & Fac Affairs Comt Bd Trustees. **Honors/Awds:** Outstanding Businesswoman of the Year, Gamma Nu Chap Iota Lambda Sorority, 2004. **Special Achievements:** Recognized by Ebony Magazine as one of the top-ranking African American women in corporate America, 2001; First African American vice president of Intel Corp. **Business Addr:** Board Member, Director, American States Water Co, 630 E Foothill Blvd, San Dimas, CA 91773, **Business Phone:** (909)394-3600.

### WILKINS, DR. JOSETTA EDWARDS

Educator. **Personal:** Born Jul 17, 1932, Little Rock, AR; daughter of James Wesley Edwards and Laura Bridgette Freeman Edwards; married Henry III; children: Calvin Tyrone, Henry IV, Cassandra Felecia, Mark Reginald & Angela Juanita. **Educ:** AM&N Col, BS, educ & social sci, 1961; Univ Ark, MS, coun & guid, 1967; Okla State Univ, PhD, higher educ admin & adult educ, 1987. **Career:** Educator (retired); Ark Coun & Farmer Workers, dep dir, man-power training, 1967-73; Univ Ark, Pine Bluff, asst dir & coordr, coop educ, 1973-76, dir, coop educ, 1977-87, dir univ rels & develop, 1987-88, prof, trustee; Breast Cancer Res, chair; Pine Bluff State, rep. **Orgs:** Jefferson Co Juv Detention Comn; United Methodist Church; Episcopacy Comt; chair polit activ comt, Martin Luther King Jr, Holiday Comn; Am Asn Coun & Develop; Am Asn Adult & Continuing Educ; Ark Personnel &Guid Asn; Lit Coun Adv Bd; Joint Educ Comm. **Home Addr:** 1107 E 41st Ave, Pine Bluff, AR 71601-7434, **Home Phone:** (870)535-1985.

### WILKINS, DR. KENNETH C.

County government official, vice president (government). **Personal:** Born Sep 20, 1952, New York, NY; son of June I (Whitehead) and James A. **Educ:** Shaw Univ, Raleigh, NC, BA, 1974; Bowling Green State Univ, Bowling Green, OH, MA, 1975; Univ Ky, Lexington, JD, 1978. **Career:** NC Dept Correction, Raleigh, legal staff, 1978-79; Shaw Univ, Raleigh, NC, asst exec vpres, 1979-83; Wake County, Raleigh, NC, register deeds, 1983; NC Dept State Treas, admin, currently. **Orgs:** Mediation Serv Wake County, 1982-; exec comm, NC Leadership Forum, 1985-; bd mem, Haven House, 1986-; bd mem, Garner Rd Family YMCA, 1986-; chair, United Negro Col Fund Campaign, Raleigh, 1988-; Nat Asn Counties; NCAsn Registers Deeds; dep treas, dept state treas, Admin Serv Div. **Home Addr:** PO Box 2253, Raleigh, NC 27602, **Home Phone:** (919)755-6317. **Business Addr:** Administrator, North Carolina Department of State Treasurer, 325 N Salisbury St, Raleigh, NC 27603, **Business Phone:** (919)508-5176.

### WILKINS, RAY

Chief executive officer. **Personal:** Born Aug 9, 1951, Waco, TX; son of Rayford Sr and Loyce; married Lorena; children: Donovan Campbell. **Educ:** Univ Tex, Austin, BA, bus admin, 1974; Univ Pittsburgh, mgt prog execs, 1987. **Career:** Southwestern Bell, mgt trainee, 1974, var positions customer serv, mkt, Comptroller's off, 1970-90, regional pres, 1996-97; SBC Commun, pres, bus commun serv, 1997-99; Southwestern Bell, pres & chief exec officer, 1999; SBC Pac Bell/SBC Nev Bell, pres & chief exec officer, 2000-02, group pres sales & mkt; SBC Enterprise Bus Serv, group pres & chief exec officer; AT&T, diversified businesses chief exec officer, 2008-12. **Orgs:** Bd dir, H&R Block, 2000-; Tiger Woods Found; dir, Am Movil SAB de CV; dir, Valero Energy Corp; adv bd, McCombs Sch Bus Univ Tex Austin; adv bd, AT&T Found; bd mem, Nat Urban League; adv coun, Exec Leadership Coun; dr, Cingular Wireless Corp, 2002-; America Movil S.A.B. de C.V, 2005-; Valero Energy Corp, 2011-; dr, Telmex SA & YP Holdings LLC. **Honors/Awds:** CEO of the Year, Minority Supplier Coun, 1997; Eagle Award, Nat Eagle Leadership Inst, 1997; Distinguished Alumnus, Waco Independent Sch Dist, 2000; Nation's 50 Most Powerful Black Executives, Fortune mag; The 75 Most Powerful African Americans in Corporate America, Black Enterprise mag, 2005; The Top 100 Blacks in Corporate America, Black Professionals mag, 2006; The 100 Most Powerful Executives in Corporate America, Black Enterprise, 2010; Top 100 Most Influential Blacks in Corporate America, Savoy mag, 2010; The 100 Most Important Blacks in Technology, US Black Engr & Info Technol mag; The 50 Most Important African Americans in Technology, eAccess Corp.

### WILKINS, RAYFORD, JR.

Executive, chief executive officer, vice president (organization). **Personal:** Born Aug 9, 1951, Waco, TX; son of Rayford and Loyce; married Lorena; children: Donovan Campbell. **Educ:** Univ Tex, BA, 1974; Univ Pittsburgh, Mgt Prog, exec, 1987. **Career:** Southwestern Bell Tel, com asst, mgt trainee, 1974; Univ Pittsburgh, Mgt Prog Execs, 1987; Pac Bell Bus Communs Servs, pres, sales; SBC Commun,

Bus Commun Servs, pres, 1997-99; Southwestern Bell tel, pres & chief exec officer, 1999-2000; SBC Pac Bell & SBC Nev Bell, pres & chief exec officer, 2000-02, group pres, 2002-; Southwestern Bell, customer serv, mkt & comptroller's off; Diversified Businesses at AT&T, chief exec officer & group pres, currently. **Orgs:** Bd dir, Carver Avademy, 1999-2000; bd dir, H&R Block, 2000-; bd trustee, San Francisco Mus Mod Art, 2001-; bd mem, San Francisco Comn Jobs, 2001-; dir, Valero, 2011; bd mem, YMCA San Francisco; chmn bd, Cingular Wireless; mem bd, Valero Energy Corp; mem bd, Am Movil; mem bd, Tiger Woods Found; mem bd, Nat Urban League; bd, Morgan Stanley; adv coun, McCombs Sch Bus, Univ Tex, Austin. **Business Addr:** Group President International Operations, SBC Pacific Bell & SBC Nevada Bell, 2600 Camino Ramon Rm 4cS100, San Ramon, CA 94583, **Business Phone:** (925)866-2600.

### WILKINS, RILLASTINE ROBERTA

Chairperson, systems analyst, mayor. **Personal:** Born Jul 24, 1932, Taft, OK; daughter of Canzaty and Willie; married Clarence E; children: Nathlyn Barksdale & Clarence Henry. **Educ:** Muskegon Community Col; Muskegon Bus Col; Technol Instr Inst; Univ Wis, Eau Claire. **Career:** Mayor, system analyst (retired); Gen Tel Co, Mich tel oper, 1957-62, serv rep, 1962-67, div community instr, 1967-71, contact rec supvr bus accts, 1973-79, phone mart mgr, 1979-81, customer serv mgr, 1981-83, analyst customer rels, 1983-88; Muskegon Heights, Mich, mayor, 1999-2007. **Orgs:** Chairperson, Human Resources Comn, Muskegon County; chairperson, Community Develop Comn; bd mem, Econ Develop Comn, City Muskegon Heights; bd mem, Muskegon Area Transcript Syst, Muskegon County; chairperson, Zoning Bd Appeals City Muskegon Heights; chairperson, Community Serv Comn, Muskegon County; pres, Urban League; Nat Asn Advan Colored People; pres, Every Woman's Pl; pres, Tri-City Woman's Club; pres, Urban League Guild Greater Muskegon; bd mem, Heritage Hosp; bd mem, Greater Muskegon Chamber Com; bd mem, Black Women's Polit Caucus Greater Muskegon; St Bd Podiatric Med; pres, Women Municip Govt, State Mich, 1979; co-chairperson, Allocations & Rev Comt, United Way, 1980-81; bd mem & secy, Greater Musk Seaway Fest, 1980-82; vpres, Mondale Task Force Youth Employ, 1980; vice chmn, Reg Planning Comn, Muskegon County, 1981; chairperson, Community Emer Clrghs, 1983; reg convenor, Nat Urban League, 1983-84; Jr Achievement Advr, 1972; pres, NBC & LEO, Nat Black Caucus, 1988-90; bd mem, W Mich Shoreline Regional Develop Comn. **Honors/Awds:** Jr Achievement Adv, 1972; Speakers Bur, Gen Telephone, MI, 1973; Citizens Award, Residents Muskegon & Muskegon Heights, 1974; 'Certificate of Commendation', Muskegon Community Col, 1979; Boss of the Day WZZR, Grand Rapids, MI, 1980; 'Certificate of Merit', St Josephs Christian Community Ctr, 1980; Pace Award, Muskegon Community Col, 1980; Plaque of Congratulations, Black Women's Polit Caucus, 1980; Chosen Woman of the Year, Black Women's Polit Caucus, 1983; named Ambassador, Lagos Univ, Nigeria, 2002; named Woman of Accomplishment & Courage, 2003; Woman of Accomplishment, Mich Women's Found, Muskegon Community Col, 2001. **Special Achievements:** First Woman Post Advisor for Explorers Career Development, 1973; Muskegon Heights' first female city council member. **Home Addr:** 2305 5th St, Muskegon Heights, MI 49444-1404, **Home Phone:** (231)733-1581.

### WILKINS, ROGER WOOD

Publisher, educator. **Personal:** Born Mar 25, 1932, Kansas City, MO; son of Earl W and Helen Natalie Jackson Clayton; married Patricia A King; children: Amy T, David E & Elizabeth W C. **Educ:** Univ Mich, AB, 1953, JD & LLB, 1956. **Career:** Nat Asn Advan Colored People's Legal Defense Fund, intern; US Aid; Ohio Welfare Dept, caseworker; NY Atty, 1956-62; State Dept, foreign aid dir, spec asst, 1962-66; US Dept Justice, Wash, DC, asst atty gen, 1966-69; Ford Found, New York NY, prog dir, asst pres, 1969-72; Wash Post, Wash, DC, ed writer, 1972-74; New York Times, New York, NY, ed writer & columnist, 1974-79; Wash Star, Wash, DC, assoc ed, 1980-81, writer; Inst Policy Studies, Wash DC, sr fel, 1982-; CBS Radio, NY, radio commentator, 1982-85; Mutual Broadcasting, Alexandria, Va, radio commentator, 1985-87; George Mason Univ, Fairfax, Va, Clarence J Robinson Prof Hist & Am Cult, 1987-; Princeton Univ, Woodrow Wilson Sch lectr, 1987; Nat Pub Radio, Wash, DC, radio commentator, 1990-; Crisis, publ. **Orgs:** Bd mem, Nat Asn Advan Colored People, Legal Defense Fund, 1970-, bd chair, Pulitzer Prize Bd, 1980-89, Fund Investigative Jour, 1980-, Villers Found, 1987-, Nat Const Ctr, 1988-, PEN/Faulkner Found, 1989-, Univ DC, 1989-; vice chair bd, African-Am Inst, 1982-, bd trustee chair; Comn Racial Justice Policy, Joint Ctr Pol Studies, 1982-; mem comn overseers, Harvard Univ Afro-Am Studies, 1984-; Steering Comn, Free S Africa Movement, 1984-; chmn, Pulitzer Prize Bd, 1987-88; DC Bd Educ. **Special Achievements:** First African American on the editorial board for The New York Times; commentator and analyst for American public policy and social justice issues; First Black Chair of The National Pulitzer Prize Board, 1987-88. Author: A Man's Life, 1982, Jefferson's Pillow: The Founding Fathers and the Dilemma of Black Patriotism, 2001; co-author, Quiet Riots: Race and Poverty in the United States, 1988. **Home Addr:** 550 N St SW Apt 701, Washington, DC 20024-4603, **Home Phone:** (202)863-1198. **Business Addr:** Professor, Clarence J Robinson Professor of History & American Culture, George Mason University, 214 E Bldg 4400 Univ Dr, Fairfax, VA 22030-4444, **Business Phone:** (703)993-2162.

### WILKINSON, BRENDA SCOTT

Poet, writer, executive. **Personal:** Born Jan 1, 1946, Moultrie, GA; daughter of Malcolm Scott and Ethel Anderson Scott; children: Kim & Lori. **Educ:** City Univ, Hunter Col, New York. **Career:** United Methodist Church, Bd Global Ministries, Wilkinson, staff writer; Bks: African Am Women Writers; Civil Rights Movement; Jesse Jackson: Still Fighting Dream; Author: "Ludell", 1975; "Ludell and Willie", 1976; "Ludell s New York Time", 1980; "Not Separate, Not Equal", 1987; "Jesse Jackson: Still Fighting for the Dream", 1990; "Definitely Cool", 1993; "Angels In Art", 1994; "Civil Rights Movement: An Illustrated History", 1996; "African American Women Writers", 1999. **Orgs:** Authors Guild; Authors League Am. **Honors/Awds:** Best book for Young Adult Award, Am Libr Asn, 1977; Outstanding Children's books of the year Award, New York Times. **Special Achievements:** National Book Award nominee in 1976 for Ludel; Georgia writers Hall of Fame nominee. **Home Addr:** 210 W 230th St, Bronx, NY 10463.

### WILKINSON, DANIEL RAYMON

Football player. **Personal:** Born Mar 13, 1973, Dayton, OH; married Shawnda; children: Brooklyn, Daniel Jr, Taylor & Sydne; children: Kennedy & Klarke. **Educ:** Ohio State Univ. **Career:** Football player (retired); Cincinnati Bengals, right defensive tackle & left defensive tackle & right defensive end & defensive end, 1994-97; Wash Redskins, left defensive tackle & defensive tackle & right defensive tackle, 1998-2002; Detroit Lions, defensive tackle, 2003-05; Miami Dolphins, defensive tackle, 2006. **Honors/Awds:** First-team All-Big Ten, 1992, 1993; Bill Willis Trophy, 1993; Consensus All-American, 1993; Defensive Game Ball, 1997; All-Pro Team, Sports Illustrated, 2003. **Special Achievements:** Selected by Cincinnati Bengals as first pick overall in first round of NFL draft, 1994.

### WILKINSON, DONALD CHARLES

Educator. **Personal:** Born Feb 12, 1936, Madison, FL; children: Donald Clark. **Educ:** Wilbur Wright Tech, 1964; Detroit Inst Tech, 1965; Univ Mich, BA, 1968; Sonoma State Univ, MA, 1972. **Career:** Detroit Water Dept, engr, 1956-61; Detroit Courier, staff writer & repoter, 1961-62; WJ Maxey Boys Training Sch, boys supr, 1965-69; Educ Develop Ctr, Newton, MA, 1970-71; sculptr wood, 1970; Sonoma State Col, asst prof & counr Physiology, prof psychol, 1971-92, emer fac. **Orgs:** Alpha Phi Alpha; Freelance Civil Rights Activist, 1960-68; consult, Black Tutorial Proj, 1965; adv, Morgan Communty Sch, 1970-71; Ford Found Grantin Early Childhood Educ; res & teaching British Infant Sch Syst, Sherard Infant Sch Eng. **Home Addr:** 1838 Lawrence St, Eugene, OR 97401-3873.

### WILKINSON, DR. DORIS

Educator, college teacher, college administrator. **Personal:** Born Jun 13, 1936, Lexington, KY; daughter of Howard Thomas and Regina L. **Educ:** Univ Ky, BA, 1958; Case Western Univ, MA, sociol, 1960, PhD, med sociol, 1968; Johns Hopkins Univ, MPH, 1985; Harvard Univ, postdoctoral study, 1991. **Career:** Macalester Col, assoc prof & prof, 1970-77; Am Soc Asn, exec assoc, 1977-80; Howard Univ, prof, 1980-84; Univ Va, vis prof, 1984-85; Harvard Univ, Cambridge, Mass, vis scholar, 1989-90, vis prof, summers, 1992, 1993, 1994 & 1997; African Am Heritage, dir; Univ Ky, founder & dir African Am Studies & Res Prog, prof sociol, currently. Author: Alternative Health Maintenance and Healing Systems for Families. **Orgs:** Woodrow Wilson Fel, 1959-61; NIH Fel, 1963-66; pres, DC Sociol Soc, 1982-83; bd overseers, Case Western Res Univ, 1982-85; pub educ, Com Am Cancer Soc, 1982-85; exec officer, budget comn, Am Sociol Asn, 1985-88; pres, Soc Study Soc Prob, 1987-88; Ford Fel, Harvard Univ, 1989-90; vpres, Am Sociol Asn, 1991-92; Ky Comn Women, 1993-96; pres, Eastern Sociol Soc, 1993; Ky AFA Comn, 1994-; ASA coun, 1995-97. **Special Achievements:** First African-American student to graduate in 1957; First full-time African-American female faculty member at the University of Kentucky; Founder and first director of the African American Studies and Research Program at the University of Kentucky. **Home Addr:** 23211 Blue Grass Sta, Lexington, KY 40523-3211. **Business Addr:** Professor, Director Heritage Project, University of Kentucky, 1561 Patterson Off Tower, Lexington, KY 40506, **Business Phone:** (859)257-4415.

### WILKINSON, RAYMOND M., III

Automotive executive, chief executive officer, president (organization). **Personal:** Born Oct 28, 1943, St. Louis, MO; son of Raymond M Sr and Elizabeth; married Betty J Taylor; children: William, Ray III & Heather. **Educ:** Gen Motors Inst, Flint, MI, dealer-operator, 1981; Univ Pa, entrepreneurial mgt & mkt, 1988. **Career:** US Postal Serv, St Louis, Mo, carrier, 1961-75; Don Darr Pontiac, St Louis, Mo, salesperson, 1975-80, mgr, 1981-83; Ray Wilkinson Buick-Cadillac Inc, pres; Poughkeepsie Chevrolet Cadillac Inc, owner, pres & gen mgr, chief exec officer, 1997-2009; Gm Pontiac Motor Div, Dist Mgr, 1998-90; Wilkinson Allstate Agency, exec vpres, 2009-; Jeanette Heredia-Wilkinson Allstate Agency, exec vpres, 2009-12; Robert Alan Agency, independent ins broker, 2011-13; Jeanette Heredia-Wilkinson Nationwide Ins Agency, producer, 2013-. **Orgs:** Nat Asn Advan Colored People-Racine, 1984-, UNCF-Racine, 1985-; bd mem, Racine Wed Optimists, 1984-, W Racine Businessmen, 1985-, Racine Sickle Cell, 1986-; 100 Black Men Milwaukee, 2002. **Business Addr:** Producer, Jeanette Heredia-Wilkinson Nationwide Insurance Agency, 120 Bloomingdale Rd Suite 403, White Plains, NY 10605-1540, **Business Phone:** (914)263-7427.

### WILKINSON, RAYMOND M., III

Executive. **Personal:** Born May 22, 1966, St. Louis, MO; son of Raymond Jr and Betty J; married Jeanette Heredia; children: Wiliam, Wesley, Raymond IV & Jordan. **Educ:** Univ Pa, Wharton Sch Bus, entrepreneurial mgt & mkt, 1988. **Career:** Gen Motors, Pontiac Div, 1988-91; Ray Wilkinson, Buick Cadillac, gen sales mgr, 1991-95; Poughkeepsie Chevrolet Olds Cadillac, owner, pres & chief exec officer, 1997-2009; Jeanette Heredia-Wilkinson Allstate Agency, exec vpres, 2009-12; Robert Alan Agency, independent ins broker, 2011-13; Jeanette Heredia Wilkinson Nationwide Ins Agency, producer, 2013-. **Orgs:** Gen Motors Minority Dealers Asn, 1997-2003; bd mem, Poug Area Chamber Com, 1998-2003; bd mem, Rehab Progs Inc, 1998-2003; bd mem, United Way Dutchess County, 1999-2003; bd mem, Am Heart Asn, 2000-03; bd mem, Helen Hayes Hosp Found, 2001-03; Nat Automotive Dealer Asn Acad, 1995. **Home Addr:** 54 Creekside Rd, Hopewell Junction, NY 12533, **Home Phone:** (845)226-0855. **Business Addr:** Executive Vice President, Jeanette Heredia Wilkinson Allstate Agency, 2593 Rte 52 Suite 12, Hopewell Junction, NY 12533, **Business Phone:** (888)824-3158.

### WILKINSON, DR. ROBERT SHAW, JR.

Physician. **Personal:** Born Jul 11, 1928, Brooklyn, NY; son of Robert Shaw (deceased) and Melissa Ruth Royster (deceased); married Carolyn Elizabeth Cobb; children: Amy Elizabeth, Karin Lynn & Robert Montague. **Educ:** Dartmouth Col, BA, 1950; NY Univ, MD, 1955. **Career:** Southern Univ Health Sci Ctr, int med resident; Kings Co Hosp Ctr, int med resident; George Wash Univ, clin prof med; Am Bd Int Med, dipl; Group Health Asn Inc, staff physician, 1962-68; George Wash Univ Hosp, attend physician, 1962-; pvt pract physician, 1968-96, 2002-; med adv, Inter-Am Develop Bank, 1976-; Georgetown Univ Med Ctr Community Pract Network, 1996-2002; Georgetown Univ, Div Gen Med, asst prof med, 1996-98, assoc prof med, 1998-2002; Georgetown Univ Hosp, attend physician, 1996-; Sibly Memorial Hosp, attend physician, 2002-. **Orgs:** Med Soc DC, AMA, fel Am Col Physicians; SPP Fraternity, Espilon Boule, 1971-; Acad Med Wash, DC, 1975-, pres, 1998-2000. **Honors/Awds:** Distinguished Achievement Award, Am Heart Asn, nation's capitol affiliate, 1986; The Dartmouth Alumni Award, Dartmouth Col, 1987; Am Col Physicians, Wash DC Chap Laureate Award, 1999; recently named Professor Emeritus of Clinical Medicine, NY Univ; School Leadership Award, 2006; recipient, Am Col Physicians district of Columbia Chapter; Distinguished Acheivement Award, Washington Dc; Affiliate, American Heart Association; Master, American College of Physicians. **Home Addr:** 4827 16th St NW, Washington, DC 20011, **Home Phone:** (202)723-5956. **Business Addr:** Physician, Georgetown University Medical, 730 24th St NW Suite 7, Washington, DC 20037, **Business Phone:** (202)338-5050.

### WILKS, GERTRUDE (GERTRUDE DYER WILKS)

School administrator, association executive, founder (originator). **Personal:** Born Mar 9, 1927, Duboc, LA; daughter of Roosevelt and Eula; married Otis; children: Otis Jr, Danny & Patricia. **Career:** Mothers Equal Educ, dir, 1965, chmn, exec dir & founder, currently; Nairobi Day & High Sch, founder & dir, 1966-80; E Palo Alto Munic Coun, mayor, 1970; Gertrude Wilks Acad, founder & dir, 1981-. **Orgs:** Founder, MEE, 1955; founder, Res Corp, 1965; founder, Sat Tutorial Day Sch, 1966; org, Annette Latorre Nursery & Sch, 1967; founder, Mothers Home mkng Ind, 1968; org, Black & White Conf; org, MEE Educ Day Care, 1970; org, MEE Extended Day Care, 1976; consult, HEW; consult, Ravens wood Elem Dist; consult, Stanford Teacher Training; consult, San Jose Sch Dist; consult, Palo Alto Sch Dist; consult, Col San Mateo; consult, Foothill Col; consult, Wright Inst Coun; EPA Munic coun; mayor, 1976; United Way Plng; chmn bd trustee, Great Friendship Bapt Ch; commr & vice chmn Redevel E Palo Alto; charter mem, Nairobi Col Bd, 1963-72; comm coun, Ravens wood Elem Dist; bd dir, EPA Neigh Health Ctr; comnr, San Mateo Co Econ Opportunity Comn; ex-mem, Comt Action Coun; pres, Missionary Bapt Soc; dir & founder, Mothers Equal Educ. **Honors/Awds:** Outstanding community service, OICW, 1966; Black Child Development Institutional Award, 1973; Phoebe Hearst Award, 1974; Citizen Award, Kiwanis Club, 1976; Bicen Award, Trinity Baptist Church, 1976; Service Mankind Award, Los Altos Sertoma Club, 1977. **Special Achievements:** First city council, 1983. **Home Addr:** 1194 Saratoga Ave, East Palo Alto, CA 94303, **Home Phone:** (415)321-5160. **Business Addr:** Founder, Director, Gertrude Wilks Academy, 1194 Saratoga Ave, East Palo Alto, CA 94303.

### WILKS, JAMES LEE

Association executive. **Personal:** Born Feb 5, 1951, Chester, SC; son of James A and Ivry; married LaVon; children: Lega, Louia & Jordan. **Educ:** Bernard M Barnett, BBA, 1973. **Career:** Am Express, asst dir internal servs, 1980-85; Agency Child Develop & Head Start, fiscal coor dr, 1985-95, vpres finance, 1995-. **Orgs:** Pres, Fathers Rights Metro, 1990-, co-founding, 1991. **Honors/Awds:** Father of the Year, Fathers Rights Metro, 1994. **Home Addr:** 384 Greene Ave Suite 1, Brooklyn, NY 11216-1108, **Home Phone:** (678)472-6269. **Business Addr:** President, Fathers Rights Metro, PO Box 313143, Jamaica, NY 11431, **Business Phone:** (718)260-6915.

### WILLACY, HAZEL M.

Vice president (organization), lawyer. **Personal:** Born Apr 20, 1946, Jackson, MS; daughter of Willie Barnes Martin and Julious Martin; married Aubrey B; children: Austin Keith & Louis Samuel. **Educ:** Smith Col, BA, econs, 1967; Case Western Res Univ, JD, 1976. **Career:** Bur Labor Stats, libr economist, 1967-72; Baker Hostetler, atty, 1976-80; Sherwin Williams, labor rel atty, 1980-82, asst dir labor rels, 1983-87, dir labor rels, 1987-93, Employ Policies & Labor Rels, dir, 1993-2002, vpres, chair, 2002-09; Nat Dispute Resolution Serv LLC, arbitrator & mediator, 2010-. **Orgs:** Ohio Bar, 1976; bd trustee, Meridia Physician Network, 1995-; Am Bar Asn; Ohio State Bar Asn; Northeast Chap, Indust Rels Res Asn; bd trustee, Boy Scouts Am, Greater Cleveland Chap; Labor & Employ Rels Asn Oh Chap; vis comt, Case Western Res Univ Blue Ribbon Comn; Case Western Res Univ Soc Benchers; Palm Beach Co Bar Asn. **Honors/Awds:** Order of Coif, 1976. **Special Achievements:** Articles published 1970, 1976, 1980. **Home Addr:** 3337 Brainard Rd, Cleveland, OH 44124. **Business Addr:** Arbitrator, Mediator, National Dispute Resolution Service LLC, 14 Lexington Lane E Apt H, Palm Beach Gardens, FL 33418-7132.

### WILLIAMS, REV. A. CECIL

Clergy. **Personal:** Born Sep 22, 1929, San Angelo, TX; son of Earl Sr; married Evelyn Robinson; children: Kim & Albert; married Janice Mirikitani. **Educ:** Houston-Tillotson Col, BA, sociol, 1952; Southern Methodist Univ, Perkins Sch Theol, BD, 1955; Pac Sch Religon, grad work. **Career:** St Paul Methodist Church, asst minister, 1954; Methodist Church, minister, 1955; Houston-Tillotson Col, chaplain & teacher, 1956-59; St James Methodist Church, minister, 1961-64; Glide Memorial United Methodist Church, pastor, 1963, minister, 1964-2000, chief exec officer, currently. **Orgs:** Christian Soc Crisis; bd mem, Martin Luther King Ctr Soc Chg; host, KPIX-TV Vibrations New People; minister, Nat Int Ministries; GLIDE Found, founder, 1982-; chmn, Northern Calif Dr. Martin Luther King Jr Birthday Observance Comt, 1986. **Honors/Awds:** Man of the Year, Sun Reporter, 1967; Emmy Award, San Francisco National Acad TV Arts & Sci, 1972; featured, PBS-TV, 1992; National Caring Award, Caring Inst, Wash, 2008. **Special Achievements:** One of the first five African American graduates of the Perkins School of Theology, Southern Methodist University, 1955; Publ many magazines; created Glide Celebrations; One of the first to take a revolutionary stand for same sex couples by presiding over marriage. Author of I'm Alive, 1980; Beyond the Possible, 2013. **Business Addr:** Chief Executive Officer, Founder, Glide Memorial United Methodist Church, 330 Ellis St, San Francisco, CA 94102, **Business Phone:** (415)674-6000.

### WILLIAMS, AARON

Basketball player. **Personal:** Born Oct 2, 1971, Evanston, IL; married Heather; children: Danyelle, Cameron & Aaron Jr. **Educ:** Xavier

Univ, BA, criminal justice. **Career:** Basketball player (retired); Grand Rapids Hoops, 1993; Utah Jazz, power forward, 1993-94; Aresium Milan, 1993-94; Milwaukee Bucks, 1994-95; Denver Nuggets, 1996-97; Vancouver Grizzlies, 1996-97; Seattle Supersonics, power forward, 1997-99; Wash Wizards, power forward, 1999-2000; NJ Nets, power forward & ctr, 2000-04; Toronto Raptors, ctr, 2004-06; New Orleans Hornets, ctr & forward, 2005-06; Los Angeles Clippers, ctr forward, 2006-08. **Honors/Awds:** MCC Defensive Player of the Year; Eastern Conference Champion, 2002, 2003. **Business Addr:** Professional Basketball Player, Los Angeles Clippers, 1111 S Figueroa St Suite 1100, Los Angeles, CA 90015, **Business Phone:** (213)742-7500.

## WILLIAMS, ADA L.

School administrator, government official, association executive. **Personal:** Born Aug 22, 1933, Waxahachie, TX; daughter of Henry Lee and Lueada Gregory Lewis; married Clyde L; children: Adrian Dwight. **Educ:** Huston-Tillotson Col, BA, music, minor math, 1955; N Tex State Univ, MA, 1968, PhD. **Career:** School administrator (retired); Dallas Independent Sch Dist, dir, counr, emp rels, 1979-2002; Tex State Asn Parliamentarians, pres. **Orgs:** Life mem, NEA; TEA eval team, 1975; NE Univ Eval Team, 1975; Tex Asn Parlimentarians, Nat Asn Parlimentarians; pres, Classroom Teachers Dallas, 1975-79; mem coord bd, Nat Counc Accreditation Teacher Educ; St Paul AME Church; Nat Asn Advan Colored People; chair, Dallas Teachers Credit Union Bd, 1976-; Delta Sigma Theta Sor Inc; pres, Epsilon; Delta Kappa Gamma Soc Inc; Oak Cliff B & PW Club Inc; Nat Coun Accreditation Teacher Educ; vis team, Univ N Fla, Eastern Nmex Univ & Okla Christian Univ; parliamentarian, Tex PTA, 1984-86; appeals bd, NEA/NCATE, 1985-; Notary Pub; Nat Educ Asn; Dallas Chamber Com, Black; Tex State Teachers Asn; Nat Educ Asn; pres; Nat Asn Prof & Exec Women. **Honors/Awds:** Teacher of the Year, 1969-71; Trailblazer Award, S Dallas B&PW Club Inc, 1976; Achievement Award, Delta Kappa Gamma Soc, 1981-89; Outstanding Educator Tex Legislation, 1983-85; Obudswoman Award, S Dallas B&PW Club, 1984; Achievement Award, Nat Women Achievement Orgs, 1987; Honored Tex PTA Honorary Life Membership, 1987; Many educ, civic, religious, and club Awards; Honored by the Dallas Independent Sch Dist Bd Educ, 1997; Sojourner Truth Award. **Home Addr:** 1636 Indian Summer Trail, Dallas, TX 75241, **Home Phone:** (214)371-5077. **Business Addr:** President, National Association of Professional and Executive Women, 3280 Sunrise Hwy Suite 209, Wantagh, NY 11793, **Business Phone:** (516)933-4830.

## WILLIAMS, AENEAS DEMETRIUS

Executive, football player. **Personal:** Born Jan 29, 1968, New Orleans, LA; married Tracy; children: Saenea, Tirzah, Cheyenne & Lazarus. **Educ:** Southern Univ. **Career:** Football player (retired), executive; Phoenix Cardinals, defensive back, right cornerback, left cornerback, 1991, right cornerback, 1992, left corner back, 1993; Ariz Cardinals, left cornerback, 1994-98, left cornerback, cornerback, 1999, right cornerback, left cornerback, 2000; St Louis Rams, left cornerback, 2001-02, Free safety, safety, 2003, Free safety, left cornerback, safety, 2004; Spirit Lord Family Church, St Louis MO, founding pastor, currently. **Orgs:** Kappa Alpha Psi Fraternity Inc. **Honors/Awds:** Defensive Rookie of the Year, Nat Football Conf; Pro Bowl, 1994, 1995, 1996, 1997, 1998, 1999, 2001, 2003; Champion, Nat Football Conf; ; Super Bowl, XXXVI; Man of the Year Award, Bart Starr, 1999; Hall of Fame, San Francisco 49ers, 1999; Hall of Fame, Nat Football League; Ring of Honor, Ariz Cardinals, 2008; Hall of Fame, 2014. **Special Achievements:** Came in on a cornerback blitz from Youngs blindside, and came up with a clean hit. This occurred on national television, a Monday Night Football game. **Home Addr:** 12923 Conway Rd, St Louis, MO 63141-8508. **Business Addr:** Founding Pastor, Spirit of the Lord Family Church, 201 Brotherton Lane, St Louis, MO 63135, **Business Phone:** (314)260-7363.

## WILLIAMS, HON. ALEXANDER, JR.

Judge, lawyer. **Personal:** Born May 8, 1948, Washington, DC. **Educ:** Howard Univ, BA, govt, 1970; Howard Univ Sch Law, JD, cum laude, 1973, Sch Divinity, MA, relig studies & ethics, 1991; Temple Univ, MA, 1995. **Career:** Judge(retired), attorney, professor; Seventh Judicial Circuit Ct, Md, law clerk, 1973-74; Pvt Pract, Md, atty, 1974-86; Fairmount Heights, Md, munic atty, 1975-87; Prince George's County, Md Pub Defender's Off, asst pub defender, 1977-78, Md Bd Educ, Spec Coun & Hearing Examr, 1978-87, Md State Atty, 1987-94; Howard Univ Sch Law, prof, 1978-89; Glenarden, Md, munic atty, 1980-87; US Dist Ct, Dist Md, fed judge, 1994-2014. **Orgs:** Md Bar Asn, 1973; DC Bar Asn, 1974; founder, J Franklyn Bourne Bar Asn; Nat Prince George's County Bar Asns; Comn Med Discipline, 1980-85; Wash Suburban Sanit Comn, 1983-87; States Attys Coord Coun, 1987-89; Ct Appeals Standing Comt Rules Pract & Procedure, 1984-86; Handgun Roster Bd, 1992-94; Walker Mem Baptist Church, Wash, DC.

## WILLIAMS, ALFRED HAMILTON

Football player, radio host. **Personal:** Born Nov 6, 1968, Houston, TX; married Lena; children: Dominique, Justin & Christopher Alfred. **Educ:** Univ Colo. **Career:** Football player (retired), radio show host; Univ Colo, Boulder, linebacker, 1990; Colo Nat Championship Team, capt, 1990; Cincinnati Bengals, defensive end, 1991-94; San Francisco 49ers, 1995; Denver Broncos, 1996-99; KKFN 950 AM, sports talkshow host; Sports radio 950 FAN Studios, radio host, currently. **Business Addr:** Radio Host, Sportsradio 950 The FAN Studios, 7800 E Orchard Rd Suite 400, Greenwood Village, CO 80111, **Business Phone:** (303)321-0950.

## WILLIAMS, ALVIN LEON

Basketball player. **Personal:** Born Aug 6, 1974, Philadelphia, PA; son of Alvin Sr. **Educ:** Villanova Univ, BA, 1997. **Career:** Basketball player (retired), coach; Portland Trail Blazers, guard, 1997-98; Toronto Raptors, guard, 1998-2006, asst coach, 2009-10, Player Develop, dir, 2010-13; Los Angeles clippers, guard, 2007. **Business Addr:** Director, Toronto Raptors, 40 Bay St Suite 400, Toronto, ON M5J 2X2.

## WILLIAMS, ALYSON

Entertainer, actor, singer. **Personal:** Born May 11, 1962, New York, NY; daughter of Robert Lee Booker and Shirley M. **Educ:** City Col NY; Marymount Manhattan Col. **Career:** Singer & actress; Albums: Raw, 1989; Alyson Williams, 1992; It's About Time, 2004; Singles: "Yes We Can Can", 1986; "Less Than Zero", 1987; "Make You Mine Tonight", 1987; "Sleep Talk", 1989; "My Love is So Raw", 1989; "Just Call My Name", 1989; "I Second That Emotion", 1989; "I Need Your Lovin", 1990; "Not on the Outside", 1990; "Can't Have My Man", 1992; "Just My Luck", 1992; "Everybody Knew But Me", 1992; Plays: Wicked Way, I Need A Man. **Special Achievements:** First guest vocalist to perform with Branford Marsalis & the Tonight Show Band, 1992. **Home Addr:** 5358 Haras Pl, Ft Washington, MD 20744-3088. **Business Addr:** Actress, Singer, Def Jam Recordings, 825 Eighth Ave, New York, NY 10019, **Business Phone:** (212)491-4914.

## WILLIAMS, ANDREW B.

Engineer, founder (originator), college teacher. **Personal:** Born Junction City, KS; son of John M and Yuson Kim; married Anitra Williams; children: John, Adrianna & Rosa. **Educ:** Univ Kans, BS, elec engineering, 1988, PhD, elec engineering, 1999; Marquette Univ, MS, elec & comput engineering, 1995. **Career:** GE Healthcare, magnetic resonance systs engr & Edison engr, 1992-95; Univ Iowa, asst prof, 1999-2004; Apple, sr engineering diversity mgr, 2008-09; Spelman Col, assoc prof, 2004-12, comput sci dept chair, 2009-12; Marquette Univ, prof & distinguished chair, 2012-, dir, Co-Robots CompuGirls, 2014-, founding dir, Humanoid Engineering & Intelligent Robotics Lab, 2014-; AppRobo LLC, founder & chief creative officer, 2014- . **Special Achievements:** First African American to earn a PhD in electrical engineering from the University of Kansas, 1999; author, "Out of the Box: Building Robots, Transforming Lives" (2009). **Business Addr:** Marquette University, Engineering Hall 407, Madison, WI 53233, **Business Phone:** (414)288-7349.

## WILLIAMS, DR. ANITA SPENCER

Educator. **Personal:** Born Philadelphia, PA; daughter of Thomas and Julia Walker; married Willie G; children: Diane, Stephen & Karen. **Educ:** Cheyney Univ, Cheyney, PA, BS, 1967; Temple Univ, Philadelphia, PA, EdM, 1971, EdD, 1988. **Career:** Sch Dist Philadelphia, Pa, teacher, 1967-71, reading specialist, 1971-85, auxiliary vice prin, 1985-86, teacher trainer, 1986-87, admin asst, 1987-96; Simon Gratz Cluster, head; Philadelphia Educ Fund, proj dir, currently. **Orgs:** Alpha Phi Sigma Nat Hon Soc, 1966-; Int Reading Asn, 1972-; consult, Progress Educ Prog, 1977-80; Black Women's Educ Alliance, 1980-82; educ dir, Waters Community Ctr, 1980-88; Phi Delta Kappa Educ Fraternity, 1985-; bd trustee, Settlement Music Sch; Alleghany W Found; proj mgr, Philadelphia Sch Fund, currently. **Home Addr:** 7116 Mt Airy Terr, Philadelphia, PA 19119, **Home Phone:** (215)247-4841. **Business Addr:** Project Director, The Philadelphia Education Fund, 1709 Benjamin Franklin Pkwy Suite 700, Philadelphia, PA 19103, **Business Phone:** (215)665-1400.

## WILLIAMS, HON. ANN CLAIRE

Judge. **Personal:** Born Aug 16, 1949, Detroit, MI; daughter of Joshua and Dorothy; married David J Stewart; children: 2. **Educ:** Wayne State Univ, Detroit, Mich, BS, 1970; Univ Mich, MA, guid & coun 1972; Univ Notre Dame Law Sch, Ind, JD, 1975. **Career:** Judge Robert A Sprecher, law clerk, 1975-76; US Attys Off, Ill, asst atty, 1976-85; Northwestern Univ Law Sch, adj prof & lectr, 1979-; John Marshall Law Sch, adj prof & lectr, 1979-; Nat Inst Trial Advocacy, bd trustee, fac, 1979-; Criminal Receiving & Appellate Div, dep chief, 1980-83; US Attys Off, Organized Crime Drug Enforcement Task Force N Cent Region, chief, 1983-85; US Dist Ct, judge, 1985-99, 2001; Judicial Conf US, comt mem, 1990-93, Chair Ct, 1993-97; US Dist Ct Appeals 7th Circuit, judge, 1999-. **Orgs:** Bd trustee, Univ Chicago Lab Sch, 1988-; bd trustee, Univ Notre Dame, 1988-; bd trustee, Mus Sci & Indust, 1991-97; pres, Fed Judges Asn, 1999-2001; chair, Just Beginning Found, 1992; Supreme Ct Fels Prog Comn; chair, Ct Admin & Case Mgt Comt, 1993-97; founding mem, Black Women Lawyers Asn Chicago; co-founder, Minority Legal Educ Resources; bd, Equal Justice Works. **Honors/Awds:** Edith S Sampson Mem Award, Ill Judicial Coun, 1986; Thurgood Marshall Award, Chicago Kent Col Law, 1986; Headliner Award, Women of Wayne State Univ Alumni, 1987; Hon JD, Lake Forest Col, 1987; Hon DPS, Univ Portland, 1993; Hon JD, Univ of Notre Dame, 1997; Vanguard Award & Earl Burrus Dickerson Award, Chicago Bar Asn, 1997; Women with Vision Award, Women Bar Asn Ill, 1998; Chicago Lawyer Person of the Year award, 2000; Arabella Babb Mansfield Award, Nat Asn of Women Lawyers, 2005; Spirit of Excellence Award, Am Bar Asn Comn Racial & Ethnic Diversity; BWLA & MLE, 2007; Margaret Brent Women Lawyers of Achievement Award, Am Bar Asn, 2008; Gertrude E Rush Award, Nat Bar Asn, 2008; Cook Co Bar Asn Hall of Fame; William H Hastie Award, Nat Bar Asn; Illinois Judicial Council Special Achievement Award; Women Making History Award, Nat Coun Negro Women; Alumni Award, Nat Black Law Students Asn; Hon degree, Chicago Kent, William Mitchell Cols of Law & St Marys, Colby; Edward J Devitt Distinguished Service to Justice Award, 2010. **Special Achievements:** First African American ever appointed to the Seventh Circuit & third African American woman to serve on any United States Court of Appeals; First African American woman appointed to a district court in the Seventh Circuit; First woman & First African American to be Chair of the Court Administration and Case Management Committee; One of Chicago's 100 Most Influential and Powerful Women, Crain magazine and the Chicago Sun Times, 2004; One of the First two African American law clerks; First African American woman to serve as supervisor in that office; First Chief of the Organized Drug Enforcement Task Force. **Business Addr:** Judge, US District Ct Appeals 7th Circuit, Rm 2602 Dirksen Fed Bldg, Chicago, IL 60604, **Business Phone:** (312)435-5850.

## WILLIAMS, DR. ANN E. A.

Association executive, school administrator. **Personal:** Born Sep 21, 1946, Jacksonville, FL. **Educ:** Fla A&M Univ, BS, 1968. **Career:** Duval Co Juv Ct, coun, 1969; A Philliph Randoph Inst, exec coun; FLJr Col Jax Fla Adult Educ, instr; Minority Affairs Com Duval Teachers United; Duval Co Bd Pub Instr, instr, asst prin; Sisters Connection Int Network Inc, exec dir & founder, currently. **Orgs:** Jacksonville Jaycees; HOPE Chapel Christian Assembly Inc, Cub Scout Den Leader; pres, Dem Women's Fla Inc; Dem Exec Com; Nat Coun Negro Women Inc; exec com, Nat Asn Advan Colored People League Women Voters; vpres, Duval Teachers United; mem comt, YWCA; United Meth Women; vol, Jacksonville Inc, NABSE. **Home Addr:** 6479 San Juan Ave, Jacksonville, FL 32210, **Home Phone:** (904)695-2126. **Business Addr:** Founder, Executive Director, Sisters Connection International Network Inc, 5732 Normandy Blvd Suite 4, Jacksonville, FL 32205, **Business Phone:** (904)695-2126.

## WILLIAMS, ANNALISA STUBBS

Executive, judge. **Personal:** Born Sep 23, 1956, Youngstown, OH; daughter of Eula Grace Harris Stubbs and Julius Saffold Stubbs; married Michael D; children: Michael James (deceased), Alexandria Katherine-Grace & James Robert II. **Educ:** Kent State Univ, BA, polit sci, 1977; Univ Akron, MA, urban studies, 1980; Univ Akron Law Sch, JD, 1984. **Career:** Kent State Univ, pre-law adv, 1976-77, orientation instr, 1976-77, resident staff adv, 1976-77; Ohio Civil Rights Comn, investr, intake spec, 1977-79; Metro Regional Transit Auth, personnel equal employ minor bus dir, 1979-84, employ rels officer, 1984-85; City Akron, asst law dir, 1985-89; Roadway Serv Inc, Akron, Ohio, mgr, 1989-1992; Summit County Domestic Rels Ct referee, 1992-93; pvt pract law, 1992-2003; Akron Munic Ct, Judge, 2003-. **Orgs:** Delta Sigma Theta, 1980-; Urban Leagues Youth Comt; bd dir, Info Line; bd trustee, Prep Ohio; Delta Sigma Theta Sor Inc; Akron Barristers Club; Akron Bar Asn; Summit County Child Abuse & Neglect Adv Bd; Akron Urban League; W Side Neighbors; treas, Comn Re-elect Councilman Michael D Williams; United Way Summit County; Minerva Fund; trustee, Ohio Ballet, 1988-; life mem, Nat Asn Advan Colored People. **Home Addr:** 584 Avalon Ave, Akron, OH 44320, **Home Phone:** (330)375-2007. **Business Addr:** Judge, Akron Municipal Court, 217 S High St, Akron, OH 44308, **Business Phone:** (330)375-2007.

## WILLIAMS, ANNIE

School administrator. **Personal:** Born Jun 2, 1970, Springfield, IL; daughter of Rachel Brooks; children: Ashley Walton & Fletcher Jr. **Educ:** Lincoln Land Community Col, AS, bus admin; Univ Ill, Springfield, BA, mgt, 2002, MS, pub admin, 2004. **Career:** Touchette Reg Hosp, acct asst, 1996-97; Med Transp Mgt, com acct coordr, 1998; Mary Bell Transp, co owner, 1998; Ill Community Col Bd, acct asst, 1999-2002, asst dir adult educ & family lit & prog compliance, 2002-04. **Orgs:** Funding task force, Ill Community Col Bd, 2002-, adv coun, 2002-. **Home Addr:** 3205 Green St, Jacksonville, FL 32205-5709, **Home Phone:** (904)374-7495. **Business Addr:** Assistant Director for Adult Education & Family Literacy Program Compl, Illinois Community College Board, 401 E Capitol Ave, Springfield, IL 62701-1711, **Business Phone:** (217)785-0213.

## WILLIAMS, ANRE D.

President (organization). **Educ:** Stanford Univ, BA, 1986; Univ Pa, Wharton Sch, MBA, mkt, 1990. **Career:** Am Express Co, vpres acquisitions & advert, 1996-99, vpres & gen mgr large mkt Western region, 1999-2000, sr vpres US mid mkt, 2000-03; US Com Card, exec vpres, 2004-07, exec vpres & pres global com card bus, 2007-11; Global Corp Payments, pre, 2007-2011; Global Merchant Serv, pres, 2011-. **Orgs:** Trustee, Continuum Health Partners; dir, Ryerson; dir, Ill Tool Works Inc (ITW). **Business Addr:** President, American Express, 3 World Financial Ctr, New York, NY 10285.

## WILLIAMS, ANTHONY ALLEN (TONY WILLIAMS)

Mayor, executive. **Personal:** Born Jul 28, 1951, Los Angeles, CA; son of Lewis III and Virginia; married Diane Simmons; children: Asantewa Foster. **Educ:** Yale Col, BA, polit sci; Harvard Univ, Kennedy Sch Govt, MPP; Harvard Law Sch, JD. **Career:** Boston Redevelop Authority, head neighborhood housing & develop, 1988-90; St. Louis's Community Develop Agency, exec dir, 1990-91; Columbia Univ, adj prof; State Conn, dept controller, 1991-93; US Dept Agr, chief financial officer, 1993-95; State DC, chief financial officer, 1995-98; Govt DC, mayor, 1999-2007; Friedman Billings Ramsey Group Inc, partner, chief exec officer, 2007-, chief exec officer, 2009; DC law firm Arent Fox, dir state & local pract, 2009. **Orgs:** Sierra Club; Audubon Socs; Govt Fin Officers Asn; Asn Govt Accountants; Alfalfa Club, 2001; bd advisors, Close Up Found; hon mem, John Carroll Soc; Urban League Wash DC; mem, Debt Reduction Task Force, Bipartisan Policy Ctr; bd dir, Bank Georgetown, 2012. **Business Addr:** Partner, Chief Executive Officer, Friedman Billings Ramsey Group Inc, 1001 19th St N, Arlington, VA 22209, **Business Phone:** (703)312-9500.

**WILLIAMS, ANTHONY DEMETRIC.** See WILLIAMS, TONY.

## WILLIAMS, ARMON ABDULE

Football player, television broadcaster. **Personal:** Born Aug 13, 1973, Tempe, AZ. **Educ:** Univ Ariz, BA, polit sci, 1997. **Career:** Football player (retired), broadcaster, health & fitness trainer; Houston Oilers, 1997; Tenn Oilers, 1997; Minn Vikings; New Orleans Saints; Barcelona Dragons, 1998, health & fitness dir, health & fitness personal trainer, currently; COX A7 Sports, announcer, currently. **Orgs:** Col Football Track & Field. **Business Addr:** Announcer, COX A7 AZ Sports, 1550 W Deer Valley Rd, Phoenix, AZ 85027, **Business Phone:** (480)225-4357.

## WILLIAMS, ARMSTRONG

Public relations executive, columnist, talk show host. **Personal:** Born Feb 5, 1959, Marion, SC; son of James S (deceased) and Thelma Howard. **Educ:** SC State Col, BA, polit sci & eng, 1981. **Career:** Tv host, radio host, politcal activist, columnist & media exec; B & C Associations, vpres govt & int affairs; US Equal Employ Opportunity Comn, confidential asst to chmn; US Dept Agr, presidential appointee; US Rep Carrol Campbell, legis asst; US Sen Strom Thurmond, legis aide & advisor; WOL Radio 1450 AM, host, 1991; Syndicated shows, Talk Am Radio Network, host, 1995; Salem Radio Network, host, 1998; TV "Pt", host, 2002-05; Crisis mag, columnist; Guest commentator: CNN, MSNBC & NPR; Right Side Prod Inc, founder & chief exec officer, 2003-; XM Satellite Radio, host, 2008; Armstrong Williams Productions LLC, co owner, currently; Graham Williams Group, founder & chief exec officer, currently; Books: Beyond Blame-How We Can

Succeed by Breaking the Dependency Barrier, author, 1995; Letters to a young victim: Hope and Healing in America's Inner Cities, 1996; Reawakening Virtues: Restoring What Makes America Great, 2011. **Orgs:** Adv bd, Child-Help USA, 1982; life mem, Phi Beta Sigma Fraternity Inc; bd, Wash Afro-Am Newspaper; nat bd mem, Carson Scholars Fund; Pres Comm White House Fel; bd mem, Youth Leadership Found; bd dir, Independence Fed Bank; adv bd, NEWSMAX. **Business Addr:** Chief Executive Officer, Founder, The Graham Williams Group, 201 Mass Ave NE Suite C3, Washington, DC 20002-4957, **Business Phone:** (202)546-5400.

**WILLIAMS, ARNETTE L.**
Educator, chairperson. **Personal:** Born Logan, WV; married Clarence L; children: Cheryl & Reginald. **Educ:** BS, 1943. **Career:** Marion County WVa, teacher. **Orgs:** Chairwoman, bd co-founder, Reston Sect Nat Coun Negro Women, 1973; Reston Planned Parenthood Comm Estab Community Clin, 1974; Int Womens Org, 1975; Planned Parenthood Coun No, Va; Wolf Trap Asn Performing Arts; FISH; Former vol work, Girl Scouts Boy Scouts Little League PTA Grey Lady ARC Mil Hosps Overseas; United Fund; Social Club "Sagarities" Serv Oriented; Lions Aux. **Home Addr:** 11620 Sourwood Lane, Reston, VA 20191, **Home Phone:** (703)620-5093.

**WILLIAMS, DR. ARTHUR LOVE**
Educator, physician. **Personal:** Born Jun 4, 1940, Priscilla, MS; married Patricia A; children: Terri, Toni & Tara. **Educ:** Jackson State Col, BS, 1962; Meharry Med Col, MD, 1966. **Career:** GW Hubbard Hosp, intern, 1966-67, resident, 1970-73, Hosp, Dept Internal Med, instr, asst prof, chief resident, 1972-74; Med Prog Baylor Col Med, teacher comt, 1974-; Univ Tex, Med Educ Prog, teaching staff, 1976-; St Elizabeth Hosp, chief staff, pres med, 1977-; pvt pract physician, currently; Mcnairy Regional Hosp; Christus St. Joseph Hosp; internist, currently. **Orgs:** Houston Med Forum; Harris Co Med Soc; bd cert, Internal Med, 1973; Nat Med Asn; AMA; chmn, Educ Com, 1975-77; ann, GPA-Forde Mem Lectur & Banq, 1975-77; bd mem, Cypress Creek Emergency Med Serv, 1976-77; secy, Houston Med Forum, 1977; chmn, PPO Bd, chmn, Dept Med, 1992-94, St Joseph Hosp, 1994-95, gov bd, 1994-96. **Honors/Awds:** Flight Surgeon, 1967-70; Air Medal Commendation, 1969-70. **Home Addr:** 2101 Crawford St, Houston, TX 77002, **Home Phone:** (713)675-2651. **Business Addr:** Physician, Mullins & Williams Associates, 4315 Lockwood Dr Suite 5, Houston, TX 77026, **Business Phone:** (713)675-2651.

**WILLIAMS, AUBIN BERNARD**
Executive, construction engineer. **Personal:** Born Mar 27, 1964, Detroit, MI; son of Eddie C Sr and Sadie J Francis. **Educ:** Wayne State Univ, Detroit, MI, BS, 1987; Tuck Sch Bus, Dartmouth, exec bus mgt. **Career:** Williams & Gilliard, Detroit, Mich, field supt, 1978-82; A & S Construct, Detroit, Mich, mkt rep, 1982-85; Williams & Richardson Co Inc, Detroit, Mich, pres; Williams Corp, chmn, pres, 1990-2000; Ekklesia Bldg Corp, pres & chief exec officer, 2002-. **Orgs:** Mkt comt, Assoc Gen Contracts Am, 1988-; Detroit Econ Club, 1988-; secy, Asn Black Gen Contractors, 1989-; Nat Asn African Am Bus, 1991-. **Home Addr:** 8200 E Jefferson Suite 1410, Detroit, MI 48214. **Business Addr:** President, Chief Executive Officer, Ekklesia Building Corp, 3430 E Jefferson Ave Suite 533, Detroit, MI 48207, **Business Phone:** (313)427-3644.

**WILLIAMS, AUDREAN**
Entrepreneur. **Educ:** Wayne State Univ, BA, MA. **Career:** Detroit Pub Sch, teacher; Inst Design & Technol, col instr; Wayne Co Community Col, col instr; Blue Cross Blue Shield, Mich, trainer & curric developer; Precious Memories Wedding Chapel, owner, currently; Lula Belle Stewart Ctr, pres, currently; BCBSM Found, trainer & curric developer. **Orgs:** Prog dir, Youth Develop Comn; chair, Nat Asn Women Bus Owners; exec bd mem, Lula Belle Stewart Ctr Inc. **Business Addr:** Owner, Precious Memories Wedding Chapel, 19174 Livernois Ave, Detroit, MI 48221-1716, **Business Phone:** (313)864-9333.

**WILLIAMS, DR. AUDREY L. (AUDREY WILLIAMS MEYERS)**
Educator. **Personal:** Born Apr 11, 1939, Brooklyn, NY; daughter of Louis Hayworth and Gwendolyn Ashby; married Louis B; children: Alyson Kemba. **Educ:** City Univ NY, Queens Col, BA, 1959; CCNY, MA, 1965; Univ Conn, PhD, 1973. **Career:** NYC Bd Ed, teacher trainer, reading specialist, classroom teacher, 1959-70; Morgan State Univ, prog developer, Univ Without Walls, 1972-73; CUNY, Baruch Col, prof, chair, prog dir, actg dean, 1973-2001, prof emer, currently, Brooklyn Col, fac, currently. **Orgs:** NY African Am Techs Asn, 1966-74; Col Reading Asn, 1974-95; Am Col Personnel Asn, 1978-88; Int Reading Asn, 1980-91; Nat Asn Black Sch Educ, 1981-86; Asn Black Women Higher Educ, 1985-91; CUNY SEEK dir Coun. **Home Addr:** 9230 56th Ave Apt 5D, Elmhurst, NY 11373, **Home Phone:** (718)592-7538. **Business Addr:** Professor Emeritus, Baruch College, Academic Advisement Ctr, New York, NY 10010.

**WILLIAMS, BARBARA ANN**
Air traffic controller. **Personal:** Born Jun 12, 1945, Warrensville Heights, OH; daughter of Edward Jordan and Beatrice Hill (deceased); married Howard Louis; children: Nicole Yvonne. **Educ:** Cuyahoga Community Col, Cleveland, OH, 1965; Human resource mgt; Fed Aviation Admin, air traffic controller, mgt training progs; Embry-Riddle Aeronaut Univ, Daytona Beach, FL. **Career:** Fed Aviation Admin, Cleveland, OH, journeyman air traffic controller, 1970-77, training specialist, 1977-84, area supvr, 1984-88, sr mgr/area mgr, 1988-2006; Fed Aviation Admin, Des Plaines, Ill, qual assurance specialist, 1984. **Orgs:** Nat treas, Prof Women Controllers, 1978-81; pres, Negro Bus & Prof Women, Cleveland Club, 1985-89; Cleveland Chap, Jack & Jill Am, 1986-; gen chair, Ebony Fashion Fair, Negro Bus & Prof Women, Cleveland Club, 1986; Fed Mgrs Asn, 1986-; Links Inc, 1988-. **Honors/Awds:** Federal Woman of Achievement Award, Cleveland Fed Exec Bd, 1984 & 1986; Tribute, Congressman Louis Stokes, 1986; Professional of the Year, Negro Business & Professional Women, 1987; Admin Award of Excellence, Federal Aviation Admin, 1988; Professional Award, 1988. **Home Addr:** 25510 S Woodland Rd, Beachwood, OH 44122, **Home Phone:** (216)831-2990. **Business Addr:** Area Manager Air Traffic, Federal Aviation Administration-Cleveland ARTCC, 326 E Lorain St, Oberlin, OH 44074, **Business Phone:** (216)774-0022.

**WILLIAMS, BARRY LAWSON**
Executive. **Personal:** Born Jul 21, 1944, Manhattan, NY; son of Otis and Ilza; married Adrienne Maria Foster; children: Barry, Jaime & Andrew. **Educ:** Harvard Col, BA, 1966; Harvard Bus Sch, MBA, 1971; Harvard Law Sch, JD, 1971. **Career:** Mckinsey & Co, sr consult, 1971-79; Bechtel Group, mgr prin, 1979-86; Northwestern Mutual Life Ins Co, dir, 1986-; Williams Pac Ventures Inc, founder, pres, 1987-; C N Flagg Power Inc, pres, 1989-92; Pac Gas & Elec Co, dir, 1990-96; CH2M Hill Co Ltd, dir; Simpson Mfg Co Inc, dir, 1994-95; CompUSA, dir, 1995-2000; CH2M Hill, dir, 1995-; PG & E Corp, dir, 1996; RH Donnelly & Co, dir, 1998-; Corning fel; RH Donnellet Corp; Judicial Arbit & Mediation Serv Inc, sr mediator. **Orgs:** Pres, Harvard Alumni Asn, 1994-95; dir, SLM Corp, USA Group, 1995; Newhall Land & Farming, 1996-2003; Kaiser Health, 1999-2003; Am Mgt Asn, trustee, 1988-, interim pres & chief exec officer, 2000-01; Nat Pk Found; co-founder, African Am Experience Fund. **Home Addr:** 1737 Alhambra Lane, Oakland, CA 94611, **Home Phone:** (510)339-6364. **Business Addr:** President, Founder, Williams Pacific Ventures Inc, 4 Embarcadero Ctr Suite 3700, San Francisco, CA 94111, **Business Phone:** (415)896-2311.

**WILLIAMS, BART H.**
Lawyer. **Educ:** Yale Univ, BA, polit sci, 1984; Yale Law Sch, JD, 1987. **Career:** Cent Dist Calif, asst US atty, 1991-94; Munger, Tolles & Olson LLP, co-managing partner, African-Am partner, litigation assoc, 1987-91, atty, partner, 1995-2016, co-managing partner, 2005-07; Walt Disney Co, pres; lead trial coun, Sr Hyundai Motor Am exec; Brighton Collectibles Inc, trial atty, 2008; Proskauer Rose LLP, partner, 2016-; Loyola Law Sch, adj prof law; National Institute for Trial Advocacy, adjust prof; Univ Calif Los Angeles Sch Law, Lectr. **Orgs:** Am Bar Asn Litigation Sect; LA County Bar Asn Task Force; chair bd trustee, Charles R Drew Univ Med & Sci, 2004-10; founding co-chair, bd advisor, Los Angeles, Metrop Debate League, 2011-; chair bd dir, Alliance Childrens Rights, 2011-14; fel Am Col Trial Lawyers, 2014. **Honors/Awds:** Forty Under Forty-Five, The Rising Stars of the Private Bar; Top 20 lawyers in the State of California under 40 years of age, Calif Law Bus mag, 2002; Top 100 attorneys in the State of California, San Francisco Daily J legal newspaper; Top 45 Lawyers in America, Am Lawyer mag; One of the premier African-American attorneys in the United States, Black Enterprise mag. **Special Achievements:** Joe McReynolds Award as the team's Most Valuable Defensive Player in basketball, 1984. **Business Addr:** Partner, Proskauer Rose LLP, 2049 Century Pk E, Los Angeles, CA 90067-3206, **Business Phone:** (310)284-4520.

**WILLIAMS, BERNIE (BERNABE WILLIAMS FIGUEROA, JR.)**
Baseball player, musician. **Personal:** Born Sep 13, 1968, San Juan, PR; son of Bernabe Sr and Rufina; married Waleska; children: Bernie Jr, Beatriz & Bianca. **Educ:** Univ Pr, BS, biol. **Career:** Baseball player (retired), musician, author; New York Yankees, outfielder, 1991-92, ctr fielder, 1993-2006; Albums: The Journey Within, 2003; Moving Forward, 2009. Books: Rhythms of the Game, 2011. **Special Achievements:** Little Kids Rock honored Bernie with the 2010 "Big Man of the Year" award at the annual Right to Rock celebration, Hall of Fame, 2012.

**WILLIAMS, DR. BERTHA ALSTON**
Educator, psychologist. **Personal:** Born Jul 10, 1927, Brighton, TN; children: Kenneth M. **Educ:** Ariz State Univ, BA, 1964, MA, 1966, PhD, 1973; Mercy Ctr Spiritual Dir Inst, cert. **Career:** Luke Elem Sch Luke AFB, teacher, 1963-67, consult, 1967-71; Ariz State Univ Tempe, consult, 1971-73; Univ Tenn, Knoxville, asst prof & psychologist, 1973-76; Univ Calif Los Angeles, consult psychologist, 1976-; Univ Calif Berkeley, fac; San Damiano Retreat Ctr, counr & guide. **Orgs:** Bd dir, Desert Sch Fed Credit Union, 1968-71; consult, Sch Bd Louisville KY, 1975; bd mgt, YWCA, 1977-80; vpres bd mgt, YWCA, 1980-. **Home Addr:** 5950 Buckingham Pkwy 403, Culver City, CA 90230. **Business Addr:** Counselor, San Damiano Retreat Center, 710 Highland Dr, Danville, CA 94526.

**WILLIAMS, BETH. See WILLIAMS, ELIZABETH.**

**WILLIAMS, BETTY GRACE. See CURRIE, BETTY.**

**WILLIAMS, BETTY JEANE**
Manager. **Personal:** Born Aug 11, 1948; daughter of Charles and Jessie Mae. **Educ:** Los Angeles Harbor Jr Col, AA, 1970; Calif State Univ, BA, 1973. **Career:** Compton Urban Corps, counr, 1973-74, chief counr, 1974-75; City Compton Urban Corps, asst dir, 1975-76, urban corps dir, 1976-78; City Compton, manpower prog chief, 1978-80, manpower progs dir, 1980-; Compton Community Col, manpower consult chmn proj hope, 1979. **Orgs:** Employ Training Adv Comt, Nat Asn Female Execs; Veterans Comn, Compton Nat Asn Advan Colored People; Prime Agt Coun, Los Angeles Reg Coalition Serv Providers; Human Resources Develop Comn; United Way Southeast Agency Exec Comt; Nat Forum Black Publ Adminrs; Young Men's Christian Asn. **Home Addr:** 319 W 122nd St, Los Angeles, CA 90061, **Home Phone:** (323)779-4714. **Business Addr:** Manpower Program Director, City of Compton, 205 S Willowbrook Ave, Compton, CA 90220, **Business Phone:** (310)537-7650.

**WILLIAMS, DR. BETTY SMITH**
Nurse, educator. **Personal:** Born Jul 22, 1929, South Bend, IN; daughter of John Wesley and Nellie Mae Lindsay; married Harold Louis. **Educ:** Howard Univ, zool, BS; Western Res Univ, MN; Univ Calif, Sch Nursing, Los Angeles, MS, Sch Pub Health, DrPH. **Career:** Professor (retired); Vis Nurse Asn, Cleveland, staff nurse, 1954-55; Los Angeles City Health Dept, staff nurse, 1955-66; Mt St Mary's Col, Los Angeles, asst prof, 1956-69; Charles Drew Post Grad Med Sch, Los Angeles, pub health nurse consult, 1970-71; Univ Calif, Los Angeles, Sch Nursing, asst prof, 1969-, asst dean stud affairs, 1974-75, asst dean acad affairs, 1975-76; Sch Nursing, Colo Health Sci Ctr, Denver, dean & prof, 1979-84; fel, Am Acad Nursing, 1980; Calif State Univ, Long Beach, prof, 1988-96, prof emer, currently; Kaiser Permanente, consult; Delta Sigma Theta Ctr, Life Develop, exec dir. **Orgs:** Fel Am Pub Health Asn, 1969; pres, Coun Black Nurses Inc, 1969-74, founder; nat treas, DST Telecomm Inc, 1971-73, pres, 1975-79; bd dir, Blue Cross Southern Calif, 1976-80; dir, bd dir, Blue Cross Calif, 1986-95; founding charter mem, bd dir, exec comt, pres, Nat Black Nurses Asn, Wash, DC, 1995-99; nat hon mem, Iota Phi Lamda Sorority, 1997-; pres, Nat Coalition Ethnic Minority Nurse Asn, 1998-; Delta Sigma Theta Inc PublicServ Org; Op Womanpower Inc; Watts Towers Art Ctr; Com Simon Rodia's Towers Watts; Charles Drew Post-Grad Med Sch Continuing Educ Nurses Task Force; pres, Los Angeles Alumnae Chap, Delta Sigma Theta Inc; life mem, Nat Asn Advan Colored People; Nat Caucus Black Health Workers APHA; affirmative action task force, Am Nurses Asn; Calif Nurses Asn; fel Am Acad Nursing; hon mem, Chi Eta Phi. **Honors/Awds:** Nat Sojourner Truth Award, Nat Bus & Profl Womens Clubs Inc, 1972; Distinguished Alumna Award, Case Western Res Univ, Sch Nursing, 1998; Unsung Hero Award, Congressional Black Caucus Spouses, 1999; inducted in African American History Calender, 2003; Living Legend of the American Academy of Nursing, 2010. **Special Achievements:** First African American Nurse Hired As Faculty In Higher Education In California. **Home Addr:** 5630 Arch Crest Dr, Los Angeles, CA 90043-2043, **Home Phone:** (323)294-4676. **Business Addr:** Professor Emeritus, California State University, 1250 N Bellflower Blvd, Long Beach, CA 90840, **Business Phone:** (562)985-4111.

**WILLIAMS, BEVERLY JANICE**
Basketball coach, basketball player. **Personal:** Born Nov 9, 1965. **Educ:** Univ Tex, BA, kinesiology, 1992. **Career:** Basketball player (retired); Tex longhorns, guard, 1984-88; Univ Games gold medalist team, mem, 1987; Kodak All-Am, guard, 1988; PF Schio, guard, 1989-90, 1992-94; Trogylos Priolo, guard, 1991-92; Vicenza, guard, 1994-95, Long Beach Stingrays, guard, 1997-98; Ind Fever, 2000; Sacramento Monarchs, guard, 2002. **Home Addr:** , Del Valle, TX.

**WILLIAMS, BILLY DEE, JR. (WILLIAM DECEMBER WILLIAMS, JR.)**
Actor. **Personal:** Born Apr 6, 1937, New York, NY; married Teruko Nakagami, Dec 27, 1972; children: Hanako; married Audrey Sellers, Jan 1, 1959; children: Corey; married Marlene Clark, Jan 1, 1968, (divorced 1971). **Educ:** Nat Acad Fine Arts & Design. **Career:** Films: The Last Angry Man, 1959; The Cool World; A Taste of Honey; Hallelujah Baby; Firebrand of Florence; Lady Sings the Blues, 1972; Mahogany, 1975; Scott Joplin, 1977; The Empire Strikes Back, 1980; NightHawks, 1981; The Return of the Jedi, 1983; Marvin & Tige, 1983; Fear City, 1984; Deadly Illusion, 1987, Batman, 1989; Secret Agent OO Soul, 1990; Driving Me Crazy, 1991; Alien Intruder, 1993; The Prince, 1996; Steel Sharks, 1996; Moving Target, 1996; Mask of Death, 1996; The Contract, 1998; The Visit, 2000; The Ladies Man, 2000; The Last Place on Earth, 2000; Very Heavy Love, 2001; Good Neighbor, 2001; Undercover Brother, 2002; Constellation, 2005; Hood of Horror, 2006; Fanboys, 2008; Barry Munday, 2009; This Bitter Earth, 2009; The Perfect Age of Rock 'n' Roll, 2009; The Perfect Age of Rock 'n' Roll, 2009; Barry Munday, 2010; The Lego Movie, 2014. TV films: The Big Breakfast", 1992; "Carter's Army", 1970; "Mission Impossible", 1971; "Brian's Song", 1971; "The Glass House", 1972; "The Hostage Tower", 1980; "Children of Divorce", 1980; "Shooting Stars", 1983; "Chiefs", 1983; "The Jeffersons", 1978; "Christmas Lilies of the Field", 1979; "Time Bomb", 1984; The Impostor", 1984; "Dynasty", 1984-85; "The Right People", 1986; "Oceans of Fire", 1986; "Courage", 1986; "The Return of Desperado", 1988; "Dangerous Passion", 1990; "The Jacksons: An American Dream", 1992; "Marked for Murder", 1993; "Percy & Thunder", 1993; "Message from Nam", 1993; "Falling for You", 1995; "Triplecross", 1995; "Hard Time", 1998; "18 Wheels of Justice", 1998; "The Hughleys", 1999 & 2001; "Epoch: Evolution", 2000-01; "Gideon's Crossing", 2000; "Star Wars Rebels", 2014; "NCIS", 2014; "The Interns"; "The FBI"; "Mod Squad"; "Police Woman"; "Promised Land"; Broadway & off-Broadway appearances: Hallelujah Baby; Ceremonies in Dark Old Men; Fences. **Orgs:** Actors Workshop, Harlem. **Honors/Awds:** Emmy nomination for Brian's Song. **Home Addr:** 1240 Loma Vista Dr, Beverly Hills, CA 90210. **Business Addr:** Actor, The Artists Agency, 1180 S Beverly Dr Suite 400, Los Angeles, CA 90035, **Business Phone:** (310)277-7779.

**WILLIAMS, BILLY LEO**
Baseball player, athletic coach. **Personal:** Born Jun 15, 1938, Whistler, AL; son of Frank Levert and Jesse Moseley; married Shirley; children: Valarie, Nina, Julia & Sandra. **Career:** Baseball player, outfielder (retired), coach; Chicago Cubs, outfielder, 1959-74, minor league hitting instr, 1978-79, hitting instr, 1980-82, coach, 1986-87, 1992-, spec asst pres; Oakland Athletics, outfielder, 1975-76, coach, 1983-85; Cleveland Indians, coaching asst. **Home Addr:** 3227 Randolph Ave, Oakland, CA 94602.

**WILLIAMS, BILLY MYLES**
Executive, executive, manager. **Personal:** Born Sep 6, 1950, Kings Mountain, NC; son of Willis Frank and Mattie Ashley; married Rosemarie Delores Wesson. **Educ:** Univ NC, Chapel Hill, BS, chem, 1972; Cent Mich Univ, MS, org chem, 1980. **Career:** Martin Marietta Chem, 1972-74; Dow Chem Co, 1974-, lab dir, res & develop dir, 1994-2004; Alexandria Partners Inc, pres, 2004-06; Nat Acad Scis, sr prog officer, 2006-12; Am Geophys Union, dir sci, 2012-. **Orgs:** Mem Sigma Xi, 1982-; Sigma Iota Epsilon, 1984-; AAAS, 1985-; Big Bros; chmn, Midland Sect Am Chem Soc, 1988-89; Sci & Security; dir sci, Am Geophys Union, 2012-; Ctr Global Initiatives Alumni Network; Am Geophys Union Global Environ Chg Focus Group; Water Inst UNC; Dow Chem Alumni Group. **Special Achievements:** Publications: Using the Thriving Earth Exchange to Advance Community Science, Soc Explor Geophysicists, 2014. **Home Addr:** 8000 E Blvd Dr, Alexandria, VA 22308. **Business Addr:** Director of Science, American Geophysical Union, 2000 Fla Ave NW, Washington, DC 20009, **Business Phone:** (202)462-6900.

### WILLIAMS, BISA

Government official, diplomat. **Personal:** Born Trenton, NJ; daughter of Paul T and Eloise Owens; children: Michael. **Educ:** Yale Univ, BA, 1976; Univ Calif, Los Angeles, MA; Nat Defense Univ, MA. **Career:** Foreign Serv, 1984-; Conakry, Guinea, gen serv officer, 1984-86; Panama City, Panama, polit officer, 1986-88; Port Louis, Mauritius, dep chief mission, 2001-04; Nat Security Coun, dir int orgn, 2005-07; Bur Western Hemisphere Affairs, coordr cuban affairs, 2007-10, actg dep asst secy, 2010; Repub Niger, U.S. ambassador, 2010-13; U.S. Mission to Un, advisor; U.S. Dept State, Bur African Affairs, 2013-. **Honors/Awds:** Five Superior Honor and four Meritorious Honor Awards. **Special Achievements:** Speaks French, Spanish and Portuguese.

### WILLIAMS, BOBBY

Football coach. **Personal:** Born Nov 21, 1958, St. Louis, MO; married Sheila; children: Nataly & Nicholas. **Educ:** Purdue Univ, BS, gen mgt, 1982. **Career:** Ball State, running backs coach, defensive backs coach, 1983-84; Eastern Mich, offensive backfield coach, 1985-89; Kans, receivers coach, 1990; Mich State, running backs coach, 1990-99; Mich State Univ, head football coach, 1999-2002; Detroit Lions, coach, 2003; LSU Athletic Dept, wide receivers, 2003, assoc head coach, 2004; Miami Dolphins, running back coach, 2005-06; Univ Ala, tight ends coach & spec teams coordr, 2008-15, Off feild asst, 2016-. **Orgs:** Omega Psi Phi Fraternity Inc. **Business Addr:** Off Field Assistant, University of Alabama, 1201 Coliseum Dr, Tuscaloosa, AL 35401, **Business Phone:** (205)348-3600.

### WILLIAMS, BRAINARD

Automotive executive. **Career:** Hayward Pontiac Buick GMC Truck, pres, 1992-. **Business Addr:** President, Hayward Pontiac Buick Gmc, 21994 Mission Blvd, Hayward, CA 94541, **Business Phone:** (510)582-4436.

### WILLIAMS, BRANDON D.

Basketball player, basketball executive. **Personal:** Born Feb 27, 1975, Collinston, LA. **Educ:** Davidson Col, BA, sociol, 1996; Rutgers Univ Sch Law, JD, 2012. **Career:** Basketball player (retired), basketball executive; White House Proj, Domestic Policy Coun, intern, 1994; LE Haure, France, prof basketball player, 1996-97; Toronto Raptors, 1997; CBA, La Crosse Bobcats, 1997-98; Golden State Warriors, guard, 1997-98; San Antonio Spurs, forward, 1999; Milwaukee Bucks, 1999, 2004; New York Knicks, 2000; Seattle SuperSonics, 2000; Detroit Pistons, 2002-03; Atlanta Hawks, 2002-03; Ozone's Elevator Inc, pres, 2003-05; Sioux Falls Sky force, guard, 2005; Nat Basketball Asn, dir player develop, 2005-07, assoc vpres, basketball opers, 2008-12; MACU, guard, 2007; Philadelphia 76ers, basketball opers, 2013-; Delaware 87ers, gen mgr, 2013-. **Business Addr:** General Manager, Philadelphia 76ers, 3601 S Broad St, Philadelphia, PA 19148, **Business Phone:** (215)339-7676.

### WILLIAMS, BRIAN MARCEE

Football player. **Personal:** Born Dec 17, 1972, Dallas, TX. **Educ:** Univ SC, public admin, 1996. **Career:** Football player (retired); Green Bay Packers, 1995, right linebacker, 1996-98, right outside linebacker, 1999, linebacker, 2000; New Orleans Saints, 2001; Detroit Lions, 2003, right outside linebacker, 2001, linebacker, 2002. **Honors/Awds:** Super Bowl champion, XXXI. **Special Achievements:** Films: 1995 NFL Draft, 1995; Super Bowl XXXII, 1998.

### WILLIAMS, BRIAN O'NEAL

Entrepreneur, baseball player. **Personal:** Born Feb 15, 1969, Lancaster, SC; children: 3. **Educ:** Univ SC, attended 1990; Howard Univ, BBA, mkt, 1997. **Career:** Baseball player (retired), entrepreneur; Houston Astros, pitcher, 1991-94, 1999; San Diego Padres, 1995; Detroit Tigers, 1996; Baltimore Orioles, 1997; Fukuoka Daiei Hawks, 1998; Houston Astro, 1999; Chicago Cubs, reliever & baseball opers asst, 2000; Cleveland Indians, 2000; Columbus Clippers, 2001; Body Works LLC, owner, 2005-. **Special Achievements:** Omega Psi Phi Fraternity Inc, Alpha Chap. **Business Addr:** Owner, BodyWorks LLC, Washington, DC 20001, **Business Phone:** (202)365-4586.

### WILLIAMS, BUCK (CHARLES LINWOOD WILLIAMS)

Entrepreneur, basketball coach, basketball player. **Personal:** Born Mar 8, 1960, Rocky Mount, NC; married Mimi; children: Julien & Malek. **Educ:** Univ Md, gen studies, 1981. **Career:** Basketball player, basketball coach (retired), executive; US Olympic Team, 1980; NJ Nets, forward, 1981-89, Portland Trail Blazers, 1989-96, asst coach, 2010-12; NY Knicks, 1996-99; Century Technologies, partner, 2003-06; Md Madness, coach, 2006-10; Eagle Construct & Bldg Supplies, partner, 2007-11; Retired Players Asn, player progs, 2009-10; Portland Trail Blazers, asst coach, 2010; Glide Path Real Estate Investors, pres & chief exec officer, 2013-. **Orgs:** Pres, Nat Basketball Players Asn, 1992-96; hon chmn, March Dimes; Emanuel Hosp's C's Gala; Univ Marylands Athletic Hall Fame, 2001. **Home Addr:** 10716 Laurel Pl, Potomac, MD 20854-1770. **Business Addr:** President, Chief Executive Officer, Glide Path Real Estate Investors, 7945 MacArthur Blvd Suite 101 #62, Cabin John, MD 20818, **Business Phone:** (301)960-5204.

### WILLIAMS, BYRON

Clergy, radio host, journalist. **Educ:** Idaho State Univ, BA, polit sci, 1983; Pac Sch Relig, MA, liberation theol, 1997. **Career:** Resurrection Community Church, pastor, 2001; "The Huffington Post", contributor, 2005-; Kairos Moment, president and chief exec officer; "The Public Morality", National Public Radio, host. **Orgs:** People Am Way's African-Am Relig Affairs; Nat Black Justice Coalition Relig Affairs Comt, 2011-; bd mem, Death Penalty Focus. **Special Achievements:** Author of a twice-weekly column on politics and social issues for the Bay Area News Group; wrote articles and op-ed pieces for the Atlanta Journal Constitution, Baltimore Sun, Los Angeles Daily News, San Francisco Chronicle, Christianity Today, UK Guardian, Tikkun Magazine, and Public Theology; author, "Strip Mall Patriotism: Moral Reflections on the Iraq War"; "1963: Year of Hope and Hostility" (2013); lecturer; appearances on television and radio, including CNN, MSNBC, ABC Radio, Fox News, National Public Radio.

### WILLIAMS, CALVIN JOHN, JR.

Football player, executive, athletic director. **Personal:** Born Mar 3, 1967, Baltimore, MD; married Charese; children: Jonah, Sydney & Rachel. **Educ:** Purdue Univ, BA, hotel & instnl mgt, 1990. **Career:** Football player (retired), executive, coach; Philadelphia Eagles, wide receiver, 1990-96; Calese Inc, owner & pres, 1995-2009; Baltimore Ravens, 1996; Baltimore City Pub Sch Syst, phys educ & health educr, 1997-99; Morgan State Univ, asst football coach, 1999-2000; Bluford Drew Jemison STEM Acad, athletic dir, 2009-11, phys educ teacher; Purdue Univ, asst athletics dir, 2011-13, assoc athletics dir, 2013-. **Honors/Awds:** All-Rookie Team, NBA, 1990. **Home Addr:** 1110 Eton St, West Lafayette, IN 47906-1351. **Business Addr:** Associate Athletics Director, Purdue University, Rm 2200 Mackey Arena 900 John R Wooden Dr, West Lafayette, IN 47907, **Business Phone:** (765)494-3248.

### WILLIAMS, CARL. See KANI, KARL.

### WILLIAMS, CARLETTA CELESTE

Nurse. **Personal:** Born Mar 5, 1956, Steubenville, OH; daughter of Franklin T Platt Sr and Catherine B Scruggs Platt; married Calvin C Jr; children: Melissa M, Charles L, Peter J & Cecilia. **Educ:** WV Northern Community Col, AD, nursing, 1977; W Liberty State Col, BS, nursing, 1986; Duquesne Univ, MSN, nursing admin, 1992. **Career:** OH Valley Hosp, dietary aide, 1972-77; Weirton Med Ctr, Weirton, WV, reg nurse, 1977-79, CCU, 1980-, head nurse, critical care unit, 1986, dir critical care, 1992, cardiopulmonary adminr, 2001, dir cardiopulmonary serv, currently; Johns-Hopkins Hosp, reg nurse CCU, 1979-80. **Orgs:** AACN, 1986-; BPW, 1986-; church nurse Second Baptist Church, 1987; Golden Star Chorus, Second Baptist Church, 1988. **Honors/Awds:** CCRN, 1983-01; Woman of the Year in Health Care, Cameo-The Womens Ctr, Steubenville, OH, 1990; Sigma Theta Tau, 1992; Shero Award, Ohio Comn Minority Health, 2006. **Home Addr:** 522 Maxwell Ave, Steubenville, OH 43952-2518. **Business Addr:** Director Cardiopulmonary Services, Weirton Medical Center, 601 Colliers Way, Weirton, WV 26062, **Business Phone:** (304)797-6000.

### WILLIAMS, CAROL H.

President (organization), chief executive officer, vice president (organization). **Personal:** Born Chicago, IL; children: Carol Hood. **Educ:** Northwestern Univ. **Career:** Leo Burnett Co, Chicago, creative dir & vpres; Foote, Cone & Belding, San Francisco, sr vpres & creative dir; Carol H Williams Advert, pres, chief exec officer & chief creative officer, currently. **Orgs:** Cong Black Caucus; Nat Asn Advan Colored People; RainbowPUSH Coalition; US Dream Acad; Nat Newspaper Publishers Asn. **Special Achievements:** First female and African-American creative director and vice president in the field of advertising. **Business Addr:** President, Chief Executive Officer, Carol H Williams Advertising, 1625 Clay St Suite 800, Oakland, CA 94612, **Business Phone:** (510)763-5200.

### WILLIAMS, DR. CAROLYN GRUBBS

School administrator. **Personal:** married Houston; children: Stacy. **Educ:** Wayne State Univ, BS, sociol, MA, urban planning & social planning, PhD, higher educ. **Career:** Highland Pk Community Col, dean stud affair; Los Angeles Southwest Col, pres, 1992-96; Wayne County Community Col, vice provost, acad & stud affairs; Bronx Community Col, pres & pres emer, currently. **Orgs:** Chair, Am Asn Community Col, 1999-2000; Asn Am Cols & Univs; Nat Articulation & Transfer Network; bd mem, Res Found, City Univ NY; Comn on Global Educ; Am Coun on Educ; Comn on Int Initiatives; chair, Coun Adult & Experiential Learning; Higher Educ Develop; Nat Coun on Black Am Affairs; Coun Higher Educ Accreditation; Inst Community Col Develop; bd dir, Boy Scouts Am; bd dir, Bronx Coun Econ Develop; bd dir, S Bronx Overall Econ Develop Corp; bd dir, Asn a Better New York. **Business Addr:** President Emeritus, Bronx Community College, W 181st & Univ Ave, Bronx, NY 10453, **Business Phone:** (718)289-5100.

### WILLIAMS, HON. CAROLYN H.

Judge. **Personal:** Born Jan 1, 1943, Washington, DC. **Educ:** George Washington Univ Nat Law Ctr, BA, Polit Sci, 1964, JD, 1968. **Career:** Judge (retired); Mich Circuit Ct, Family Div, presiding judge; Kalamazoo Co Bar Asn, Kalamazoo Co Circuit Ct, Family Div, judge probate. **Orgs:** Pres, Mich Probate Judges Asn; Am Bar Asn; Mich Bar Asn; Kalamazoo Co Bar Asns; Delta Sigma Theta; Women Lawyers SW Mich; State Mich Child Support Coord Coun, 1997-; State Bar Mich, Open Justice Comn, 1998-. **Honors/Awds:** Women Aware Award, YWCA, 1987; William H Hastie Award Significant Contrib Law, Omega Psi Phi, Upsilon Pi Chap, 1987; Glass Ceiling Award, Kalamazoo Network, 1997; Red Rose Citation, Kalamazoo Rotary, 1997; Women Achievement, Kalamazoo YWCA, 1998. **Home Addr:** 2237 Lorraine Ave, Kalamazoo, MI 49008, **Home Phone:** (269)345-5113. **Business Addr:** Probate Judge, Kalamazoo County Probate Court, 1400 Gull Rd, Kalamazoo, MI 49007, **Business Phone:** (269)385-6001.

### WILLIAMS, DR. CAROLYN RUTH ARMSTRONG

Educator. **Personal:** Born Feb 17, 1944, Birmingham, AL; daughter of Lois Adel America Merriweather and Lonnie; married James Alvin Jr. **Educ:** Tenn State Univ, BS, 1966; Hawaii Univ, cert Asian studies, 1970; Northwestern Univ, MA, 1972; Cornell Univ, MA, 1978, PhD, 1978. **Career:** Barringer High Sch, hist teacher, 1967-69; Thomas Jefferson High Sch, hist teacher, 1969-70; Union Col, instr dept hist, 1970-73; Tompkins County Comm Col, adj prof, 1973-76; SUNY Cortland, lectr & instr, dept hist, 1973-76; Cornell Univ Career Ctr, fel, assoc dir, 1976-82; Harvard Univ, head proctor, 1983; US Sen Paul Tsongas, spec proj asst, 1983; NC Cent Univ, from asst to vice chancellor univ rels, 1983-87; Vanderbilt Univ, Minority Affairs & Women Engineering Prog, asst dean & assoc prof, 1987-97; biomed coordr, 1993-; Tenn State Univ, adj prof hist; NASA sec Navy Summer Res Residential Prog, consult, 1997; St Cloud State Univ Found, Col Social Sci, assoc dean, 1999-, Human Rels & Multicultural Educ, adj fac, currently. **Orgs:** Exec bd mem admin, counrs Nat Asn Women Deans Adminr & Counselors, 1980-82; Comm Blacks Higher Ed & Black Col & Univ, 1980-81; ed consult, LeMoyne Col Higher Ed Prep Prog, 1981-; ed consult & co-founder, Youth Data Inc, 1981-; exec bd mem, Phi Delta Kappa, Nat Asn Women Deans; Delta Sigma Theta Inc; counsrs jour bd, Nat Asn Women Admin, 1986-88; exec regional bd, Nat Soc Black Engrs, 1987-; proposal reader US Dept Educ, 1989-; Rotary Int; tech coordr Nat Soc Women Engrs, 1989-91; nat secy, Women Sci, 1992-94; bd chair, 1992-96, exec bd dir, 1992-, NAMEPA Region; nat adv comm, NIH, biomed res support, 1993-; Comm Nat Inst Environ, adv bd, 1993-; NSF Site Reviewer Gateway Coalition, 1994-; treas, NAMEPA Region B, 1996-98; founding officer, sec MIN chap, Black Women Higher Educ; Concerned Citizens Group; ed bd, St Cloud Times Newspaper; bd dir, YMCA, St Cloud, MN; Leadership Prog, St Cloud Chamber Comm; fel Woodrow Wilson Admin, 1983-86. **Home Addr:** 36 Morningside Dr, Cortland, NY 13045-1423, **Home Phone:** (607)753-1104. **Business Addr:** Adjunct Faculty, St Cloud State University, 720 4th Ave S, St. Cloud, MN 56301-4498, **Business Phone:** (320)308-3690.

### WILLIAMS, DR. CARROLL BURNS, JR.

Educator, scientist. **Personal:** Born Sep 24, 1929, St. Louis, MO; son of Carroll and Maxine Henderson; children: Robyn Claire, Margaret & Carroll Blake. **Educ:** Univ Mich, BS, 1955, insect ecol, MS, 1957, PhD, 1963. **Career:** US Forest Serv, res forester, 1961-65, res entomologist, 1965-68, proj leader, 1968-72 & 1984-88, forest insect ecologist, 1972-75, pioneer sci, 1975-84; Yale Sch Forestry, lectr, 1969-72; Univ Calif, Berkeley, adj prof, forest sci, 1988-. **Orgs:** Consult, Ecology & Ecosystems NSF, 1971-74; tech consult, USFS Insecticide Field Tests, 1973-; vis prof, Black Exchange Prog, Nat Urban League, 1975-84; Entomol Soc Am; Soc Am Foresters; dir, Berkeley Sch Bd Berkeley Unified Sch Dist, 1977-84; bd dir, Berkeley-Albany YMCA, 1979-; bd trustee, New Perspectives Inc, Alcohol & Drug Coun, 1985-87; bd dir, Berkeley Rotary, 1990-94; dir, E Bay Regional Park Dist, Ward 1, 1991-92; bd, Berkeley Pub Educ Found, 1993-95. **Special Achievements:** First black to be employed in the Branch of Research of the Forest Service in a professional capacity. **Home Addr:** 89 Arden Rd, Berkeley, CA 94704, **Home Phone:** (510)841-0612. **Business Addr:** Adjunct Professor, University of California, 108 Mulford Hall, Berkeley, CA 94720, **Business Phone:** (510)642-8092.

### WILLIAMS, CASSANDRA FAYE

Paleontologist. **Personal:** Born Aug 16, 1948, Sherrill, AR; daughter of Lewis and Millye L Dickerson-Beatty; children: Kyra Erica. **Educ:** Northeastern Ill State Univ, attended 1967; Univ Ark, Pine Bluff, AR, BS, 1970; Ky State Univ, S Dakota Sch Mines, attended 1978; Tulane Univ, New Orleans, LA, MS, 1979. **Career:** Univ Chicago Hosps & Clinics, Chicago, Ill, clinic biochemist, 1970-71; Orleans Parish Sch Bd, New Orleans, La, biol teacher, 1971-72; Chevron USA, New Orleans, La, exploration palaeontologist, 1972-. **Orgs:** Am Asn Stratigraphic Palynologists; Gulf Coast sect, Soc Econ Palaeontologists & Mineralogists; Int Comn Palynology; Am Asn BlacksEnergy; Tau Iota Mu; pres, New Orleans club, 1985-86, nat conventionco-chair, 1986, Nat Asn Negro Bus & Prof Women's Clubs; Delta Sigma Theta. **Honors/Awds:** Voluntary service awards, NAACP, 1984, Chevron USA, 1984; outstandingachievement awards, Nat Asn Negro Bus & Prof Women's Clubs, 1984, 1986; outstanding serv award, New Orleans chap, Nat Bus League, 1987; WorldService Award, & Volunteer Service Award, Girl Scouts Am, 1988. **Home Addr:** 7601 Briarwood Dr, New Orleans, LA 70128, **Home Phone:** (504)246-7604. **Business Addr:** Paleontologist, Chevron USA, 935 Gravier St Rm 748, New Orleans, LA 70112, **Business Phone:** (504)592-6325.

### WILLIAMS, CATHERINE GAYLE

Government official, executive, consultant. **Personal:** Born Nov 21, 1914, Des Moines, IA; daughter of Godfrey and Ethel Wells; married Charles Atkinson; married Richard Jr. **Educ:** Cortez Bus Col, grad, 1943; Drake Univ, soc & psychol, 1961; Univ Iowa, MA, soc work, 1965; Simpson Col, LHD, 1981. **Career:** Prof dancer; typist; Polk County Welfare Dept, secy to pub assistance worker II, 1955, social work supvr IV, 1965; pub welfare supvr, 1962; Div Comm Serv IA Dept Soc Serv, dir, 1973-75; Iowa Dept Social Serv, dep commr, 1975-81, actg comnr, 1979; Bur Family & Adult Serv Iowa Dept Assocs, dir; Bur Family & Adult Serv ID Soc Serv, assoc dir; IA Dept Social Serv, child welfare staff dev; Polk Co Iowa Dept Social Serv Com, child welfare supr, dep comnr; Johnson & Williams Assocs, consult, 1981. **Orgs:** Commr Planning & Zoning Commn Des Moines, 1980-; bd mem, Willkie Hosue; Health Facil Coun; City Des Moines Planning & Zoning Comt; Proj Helper Bd; Coun Human Serv; Simpson Col Task Force Minority Stud Concerns, United Way; Model Cities Allocation Comt; Community Rels Task Force; Nat Asn Advan Colored People; Jewish Fed. **Honors/Awds:** Social Worker of the Year, Nat Asn Soc Workers, Iowa Chap, 1980; Iowa Women's Hall of Fame, 1980; Black Women of Achievement Cult Develop Com, 1980; Mark Hall Lectr, Univ Iowa, Sch Social Work, 1980; Volunteer Award, State Iowa, 1984; Youth Women's Christian Asn/Mary Louise Smith Racial Justice Award, 1990; Sch Social Work Distinguished Alumnae Award, Univ Iowa, 1990; Iowa African-Americans Hall of Fame, 1999; PACE, 1999; Nat Black Child Develop Inst Award, 2000; Honorary degree, Simpson Col. **Special Achievements:** Highest-ranking African-American female in state government and one of the highest ranking in social services nationally. **Home Addr:** 4508 Wakonda Pkwy, Des Moines, IA 50315-3361, **Home Phone:** (515)244-1524.

### WILLIAMS, CHARLENE J.

Journalist. **Personal:** Born Jul 13, 1949, Atlantic City, NJ. **Educ:** Boston Univ, BS, 1971; Columbia Univ, MS, 1972. **Career:** Columbia Univ, adminr asst, 1971-72; WTOP Radio Post Newsweek Stas Inc, Wash DC, radio news ed, 1972-; Westinghouse Broadcasting Co NY, part-time rewriter; WBUR Boston Univ FM Radio Sta, disc-jockey, ed writer, prod dir; Boston Univ, Yr Bk Hub, gen assignment ed; WCRB Waltham Am Fed TV & Radio Artists. **Orgs:** Commun Asn; Sigma Delta Chi; Adams Morgan Orgn; vol, Heart Fund; ARC; DC Black Repetory; CRI Inst; pres, Stud Body Boston Univ, 1970-71; pres, Stud Body Columbia Univ, 1971-72. **Honors/Awds:** Nat Honor Soc Atlantic City High Sch, 1967; Scarlet Key Honor Soc Boston Univ, 1971. **Business Addr:** News Editor, WTOP-AM, 3400 Idaho Ave, Washington, DC 20016, **Business Phone:** (202)895-5149.

**WILLIAMS, CHARLES, JR.**
College teacher, anthropologist, founder (originator). **Educ:** Rust Col, BA, 1969; Univ Ill, Urbana, MS, 1971, PhD, anthrop, 1981. **Career:** Univ Memphis, Dept Anthrop, prof, 1979-2011, prof emer, 2011-, African & African Am Studies Prog, founder & dir, 1997-2001; Tenn Outcomes Alcohol & Drug Serv (TOADS), founder & dir, 1988-2000. **Orgs:** Tenn Alcohol & Drug Prev Outcomes Longitudinal Eval (TADPOLE) Proj, dir, 1992-; Tenn Dept Health, Community Coalition Adv Comt, 2002-; Tenn Black Caucus State Legislators, Tenn Black Health Care Comn, 2002-; Metrop Urban Demonstration Proj, LeMoyne-Owen Col, coalition mem, 2004-; Benjamin L Hooks Inst Social Chg, Univ Memphis, fac affil, 2004-; Meharry Med Col-Community Health Centers-Community Networks Prog (MMC-CHC-CNP) Initiative, Nat Cancer Inst & Ctr Res Cancer Health Disparities, Steering Comt, 2006-. **Honors/Awds:** The Martin Luther King Human Rights Award, The University of Memphis Human Rights Committee, 1997; Certificate of Appreciation, Douglas, Bungalow, and Crump Communities, 1997; The A.W. Willis, Jr. Award, Memphis Landmarks Commission Preservation Award, 1998; Area Health Education Centers (AHEC) Certificate of Appreciation, 2000; University of Tennessee McNair Scholars Faculty, the University of Tennessee, 2000; Alma Bucovaz Award for Urban Services, University College, The University of Memphis, 2003; The Summit Award, Bureau of Alcohol and Drug Abuse Services, Tennessee Department of Health, 2005; Igniting Excitement for Academic Excellence Award from the Black Scholars Unlimited, The University of Memphis, 2006. **Special Achievements:** Has written numerous articles, papers, and applied reports on substance abuse topics. **Business Addr:** Professor Emeritus, University of Memphis, 220 Browning Hall, Memphis, TN 38152, **Business Phone:** (901)678-0847.

**WILLIAMS, CHARLES C.**
Real estate developer, government official, commissioner. **Personal:** Born Oct 10, 1939, Pontiac, MI; children: Charles C III, Cassandra & Veronica. **Educ:** Fla Agr & Mech Univ, polit sci, 1962; NC Cent Univ Law Sch, 1963. **Career:** Atlanta Reg Comn, dir commun, 1974-78; Ga Power Co, manpower resources coordr, 1978-80; Amertelco Inc, exec vpres, 1980-84; Air Atlanta, spec consult chair bd, 1984-; Fulton City, Bd Comn, comnr, currently; Southwest Amusement Inc, chief exec officer. **Orgs:** Bd mgr, Asn City Commisioners Ga, 1978-; bd mem, W End Med Ctr, 1980-83; vpres, Nat Asn Counties, 1985-88; exec comt mem, Nat Dem City Officials, 1985-; dist mem, large Boy Scouts Am, 1985-86; bd mem, Neighborhood Justice Ctr, 1985-86; Mem Coalition 100 Black Men; Ga Asn Black Elected Officials; Nat Asn Advan Colored People; Kappa Alpha Phi; Nat Asn Black County Officials; W End Neighborhood Develop Inc; Workforce Investment Bd;United Negro Col fund. **Home Addr:** 731 Lawton St SW, Atlanta, GA 30310, **Home Phone:** (404)768-0465. **Business Addr:** Commissioner, Fulton County Commissioners, 165 Central Ave SW Suite 208, Atlanta, GA 30303, **Business Phone:** (404)572-2458.

**WILLIAMS, CHARLES E., III**
Lawyer, association executive, executive. **Personal:** Born May 10, 1946, New York, NY. **Educ:** Franklin & Marshall Col, AB, 1966; Columbia Univ Sch Law, JD, 1969. **Career:** US Ct Appeals Second Circuit, pract atty; US Dist Ct Eastern & Southern Districts New York, pract atty; Courts State New York, pract atty; Marshall Bratter Greene Allison & Tucker NYC, assoc, 1970-72; Nat Asn Advan Colored People Legal Defense & Ed Fund Inc, asst coun; Bur Labor Serv City New York, dir, 1978-79; Dep Sec State NY Dept, gen coun, 1979-82; State New York, actg secy state, 1982; New York Housing Authority, gen coun, 1983-86; New York Sch Construct Authority, vpres gen coun, 1989-93; Peckar & Abramson, partner & lawyer, currently. **Orgs:** NY City Bar Asn; Nat Basketball Asn; Nat Conf Black Lawyers; bd dir, Upper Manhatten Empowerment Zone; bd trustee, St Frances Col; Am Bar Asn; Construct Law Comt Asn Bar City New York; Am Bar Asn. **Honors/Awds:** Super Lawyer, White Collar Criminal Defense. **Home Addr:** 819 Riverside Dr, New York, NY 10032. **Business Addr:** Partner, Lawyer, Peckar & Abramson, 41 Madison Ave 20th Fl, New York, NY 10010, **Business Phone:** (212)382-0909.

**WILLIAMS, CHARLES EARL**
Government official, firefighter. **Personal:** Born Jul 29, 1955, Memphis, TN; son of Perry and Ardelia. **Educ:** Univ Mich, Fire Acad, advan fire fighting; Tustin Mich Sch Arson Investr. **Career:** River Rouge Fire Dept, sgt, 1987, lt engineer & line lt, 1991, capt engr, 1994, fire marshal, 1994-. **Orgs:** Downriver Mutual Aid Fire investigators, 1994-; Int Asn Fire Investigators, 1994-; pres, Union Local 517, River Rouge Firefighters Asn, 1994-; Demolition Comt & Renovation, City River Rouge, 1994-. **Business Addr:** Fire Marshal, River Rouge Fire Department, 10600 W Jefferson Ave, River Rouge, MI 48216, **Business Phone:** (313)842-2929.

**WILLIAMS, DR. CHARLES J., SR.**
Clergy, bishop. **Personal:** Born Apr 1, 1942, Wayne County, NC; married Linda Oates; children: Valerie, Charles Jr & Antraun. **Educ:** Christian Inst, attended 1966; Shaw Univ, AB, 1973; M Div, 1975; Ibis, DMin, 1975. **Career:** Cherry Hosp, Clin I Chaplain, ment health teacher, 1960-74; Western Assembly Disciples of Christ Churches, bishop, currently. **Orgs:** Chmn, Western Disciples Chs of Christ Coun Bd, 1969-72; pastor, White Oak Disciples Church, 1969-; Masons Founder, Western Assembly Disciples of Christ Ushers Conv, 1970; chmn, Evangelism Com of Wester Assy NC Asn of Chaplains, 1972-74; Disciples Churchs of Christ Coun; bd mem, Afro-ministers Alliance; Bishop, 1977; Alpha phi Alpha Fraternity; Free & Accepted Masons; CS Brown Masonic Lodge 782; Nat Asn Advan Colored People. **Honors/Awds:** Shepherd of Distinction, Christian Church Disciples of Christ; Jerusalem Pilgrims Award. **Special Achievements:** Youngest Presiding Bishop Western Assembly, 1977. **Home Addr:** 1406 S Slocumb St, Goldsboro, NC 27530, **Home Phone:** (919)735-5273. **Business Addr:** Council Member, Mayor Pro-Tem, 1406 S Slocumb St, Goldsboro, NC 27530, **Business Phone:** (919)735-5273.

**WILLIAMS, CHARLES LINWOOD.** **See WILLIAMS, BUCK.**

**WILLIAMS, CHARLES MASON, JR.**
School administrator. **Personal:** Born Nov 25, 1960, Newark, NJ; son of Charlie and Genetta; married Maritza Farnum Sharp; children: Aleida Mercedes. **Educ:** Rider Col, BA, 1984; Rutgers Univ, MPA, 1989. **Career:** Essex County Col, EOF officer, 1984-86; Rider Col, asst dir, admis, 1986-87; Trenton State Col, EOF acad advisor, 1989-2002; Col NJ, Equal Opportunity & Affirmative Action, dir, currently. **Orgs:** Corresp secy, NJS Educ Opportunity Fund Prof Asn, 1984-86, sector rep, 1993; Rider Col Inter-Cult Alumni Asn, 1990-; Comt Undergrad Progs, Practices & Stand, 1992-. **Honors/Awds:** NJEOFPA, Service Award, 1986; Outstanding Staff Award, Trenton State Col, Col Union Bd, 1990. **Home Addr:** 81 Lanning St, Trenton, NJ 08618. **Business Addr:** Director, The College of New Jersey, PO Box 7718, Ewing, NJ 08628-0718, **Business Phone:** (609)771-1855.

**WILLIAMS, DR. CHARLES THOMAS**
Executive, executive director, association executive. **Personal:** Born May 4, 1941, Charleston, MO; son of Melvin and Mary; married Janet E McLaughlin; children: Robin, Tracey, Justin, Drew & Douglass. **Educ:** Lake Mich Col, AA, 1962; Western Mich Univ, BS, 1965; Univ Mich, MA, 1970, PhD, 1971. **Career:** Detroit Sch, teacher, 1965-69; Mich Educ Asn, educ consult, 1971-73, educ adminr, assoc exec dir, 1973-84; Nat Educ Asn, assoc dir human & civil rights, 1984-. **Orgs:** Nat Alliance Black Sch Educrs, Am Soc Curric Develop, Phi Delta Kappa, Black Roundtable, Martin Luther King Jr Ctr Nonviolent Social Change; bd mem, Ctr Democratic Renewal. **Honors/Awds:** Alumni Service Award, Lake Mich Col, 1993. **Home Addr:** 12622 Thunderchase Dr, Herndon, VA 20191-5820, **Home Phone:** (703)437-5703. **Business Addr:** Associate Director Human & Civil Rights, National Education Association Building, 1201 16th St NW, Washington, DC 20036, **Business Phone:** (202)822-7700.

**WILLIAMS, CHARLIE J.**
Association executive. **Personal:** Born Jun 22, 1947, Camp Hill, AL; son of Jimmy D and Cora M; children: Renell & Darnella. **Educ:** Wayne State Univ, BS, recreation leadership, 1970, MPA, 1975; WSU Sch Law, JD, 1980; Walsh Inst Taxation Prog masters, 1982. **Career:** City Detroit, dep dir, Pub Works Dept, 1978-79; dir housing, 1979-80, exec asst mayor, 1980-82, dir, personnel, 1982-83, chief exec asst & chief staff, Mayors Off, 1992-93, dir, Water & Sewerage Dept, exec dir, 1993-94; New Detroit Inc, pres, 1994-96; MPS group, bd mem, 1999-, pres & chief exec officer, 2007-, chmn; Wayne County, dep county exec, 2004-05; Wayne Countys Airport Authority, bd mem, 2006-; City Highland Pk, Mich, Consult, 2006-; Magna Entertainment Corp, independent dir, 2007-09. **Orgs:** State Bar MI, 1980-; bd mem, Comprehensive Health Serv Detroit, 1982-; pres, Howard Baker Found, 1993-; Pvt Indust Coun, 1994-; bd mem, MI Cancer Found, 1994-; bd mem, Jr League, 1994-; Wolverine Bar Asn, 1994-; Booker T Wash Bus Asn, 1994-. **Honors/Awds:** Michigan Horseman of the Year, Mich United Thoroughbred Breeders & Owners Asn, 1991; President's Volunteer Action Award, Pres US, 1994. **Home Addr:** 4634 Three Mile Dr, Detroit, MI 48224. **Business Addr:** Chairman, MPS Group, 38755 Hills Tech Dr, Farmington Hills, MI 48331-3408, **Business Phone:** (313)841-7588.

**WILLIAMS, CHARLIE U.**
Football player. **Personal:** Born Feb 2, 1972, Detroit, MI. **Educ:** Bowling Green State Univ, BS, sociol. **Career:** Football player (retired); Dallas Cowboys, 1995-97, 2000, defensive back, 1998, cornerback, left cornerback & right cornerback, 1999. **Honors/Awds:** Champion, Super Bowl, XXX.

**WILLIAMS, CHARLOTTE LEOLA**
Health services administrator. **Personal:** Born May 28, 1928, Flint, MI; married Charles Clifford Williams Sr; children: Charlita Walker, Charles C Jr & Cathryn Sanders. **Educ:** Flint Sch Practical Nursing, cert, 1961. **Career:** Health service administrator (retired); St Joseph Hosp, recovery room nurse, 1961-65; Flint Bd Educ, counr, 1965-68; Genesee Co Govt, elected off, 1965-84; Flint Osteo Hosp, asst pres, 1980-83; Beecher Ballenger Health Syst, asst pres, 1983-90; City Flint, equal opp contract compliance officer, 1990; Mott Found & Flint Bd Educ, home-sch counr; Quinn Chapel AME Church, staff. **Orgs:** Co comn, Genesee Co Bd Comn, 1965-80; chair, Genesee Co Bd Health, Genesee Co Health Dept, 1968-85; pres, Nat Asn Counties, 1979-80; bd mem, YWCA Greater Flint, 1980-; aging comt, MichOff Serv Aging, 1983-; bd mem, United Way Genesee & Lapeer Counties, 1985; bd supvr, 1965, vpres, Nat Asn Counties. **Honors/Awds:** Political Achievement Award, Negro Bus & Prof Womens Club, 1975; Downtown Merchants Award, Flint Downtown Merchants, 1976; Public Service Award, Nat Asn Counties, 1980; AME Church Missionary Award, African Methodist Episcopal Church Missionary Women, 1983; Law Day Award, Genesee Co Bar Asn, 1984; Democracy Work Award, Flint's League Women Voters, 2008. **Special Achievements:** First African-American Female of Nat Asn Counties; First Female Elected of Genesee Co Bd Comn; First Democracy Work Award. **Home Addr:** 2030 Barks St, Flint, MI 48503-4306, **Home Phone:** (810)238-5475.

**WILLIAMS, CHERYL L.**
Executive. **Personal:** Born Dec 31, 1954, San Diego, CA; daughter of Joseph and Edna Payne; married Peavy; children: Derryl Jr & Cheryl. **Educ:** San Jose State Univ, BS, psychol, 1977; San Diego State Univ, summer prog, 1978; Univ Calif-San Diego, PPS, credential prog, 1981. **Career:** San Diego City Sch, hearing & placement officer, 1977-81; Nat Circuits, mkt dir, 1983-84; San Diego Circuit Bd Serv Inc, pres & chief exec officer, 1981-2000; Joe & Vi Jacob Ctr, consult, 2001-04; Mary Salas State Assembly, asst campaign field mgr, 2005-06; Calif State Assembly, constituent serv mgr, 2006-10; San Ysidro Health Ctr, community rels coordr, 2010-. **Orgs:** Webster Community Coun, 1986-; Delta Sigma Theta Sorority, 1976-; bd mem, San Diego Delta Found, 2012-; Osteop Med Bd Calif. **Honors/Awds:** Minority Small Business Person of the Year, US Small Bus, 1990; Sales Person of the Year. **Home Addr:** 1636 50th St, San Diego, CA 92102-2608, **Home Phone:** (619)263-4274. **Business Addr:** Community Relations Coordinator, San Ysidro Health Center, 4004 Beyer Blvd, San Ysidro, CA 92173, **Business Phone:** (619)428-4463.

**WILLIAMS, CHRISTOPHER J.**
Chief executive officer, chairperson, founder (originator). **Personal:** Born Jan 1, 1958?, New Milford, CT; married Janice Savin. **Educ:** Howard Univ, BA, 1979; Dartmouth Col, Amos Tuck Sch Bus, MBA, finance, 1981. **Career:** Cordova, Smart & Williams LLC, founding partner; Lehman Bros, sr vpres, 1992; Williams Capital Group LP, founder, chief exec officer & chmn, 1994-; Williams Capital Mgt LLC, chmn, founder & chief exec officer, 1994-; W Pierce Leahy Corp, sr vpres opers, 1995-2000; Telespectrum Worldwide Inc, exec vpres, 2000, dir, 2001, chief operating officer, 2001-; Caesars Entertainment Operating Co Inc, dir, 2008-; Cox Enterprises inc, dir, 2012-; Horseshoe Casino Hotel, dir. **Orgs:** Bd dir, Caesar's Entertainment Inc, 2003; Mt. Sinai Hosp; bd dir, SIA, 2003-06; bd dir, Wal-Mart Stores Inc, 2004-; bd dir, Brit Am Bus; bd dir, Lincoln Ctr Performing Arts; dir, Partnership New York Inc; bd mem, Teachers Col Columbia Univ; bd mem, Alvin Ailey Am Dance Theater; bd mem, Tuck Sch Bus Dartmouth Col; Young Pres's Orgn (YPO); Econ Club New York; trustee, Williams Capital Mgt Trust Mgt; bd dir, Harrah's Entertainment Inc; Gotham Chap Young Pres's Orgn; Century Asn; Nat Dance Inst; WNYC Radio; dir, Nat Asn Securities Professionals; dir, Securities Indust & Financial Markets Asn; Fresh Air Fund; dir & mem audit comt, The Clorox Company, 2015-; dr, Ameriprise Financial Inc, 2016-. **Honors/Awds:** "Crain's New York Business", 40 under 40, 1994; "Fortune", 50 Most Powerful African Americans in Corporate America; "Crain's New York Business", Top 100 Minority Business Leaders, 2003; "Black Enterprise", 75 Most Powerful Blacks on Wall Street, 2011; Executive Leadership Council Achievement Award, 2012. **Special Achievements:** The 50 most powerful African-American in corporate America, Fortune magazine, 2002; Top 100 minority business leaders, Crains New York Business, 2003. **Business Addr:** Chairman, Chief Executive Officer, The Williams Capital Group LP, 650 5th Ave 11th Fl, New York, NY 10019, **Business Phone:** (212)830-4500.

**WILLIAMS, CLARENCE**
Consultant, administrator. **Personal:** Born Oct 1, 1945, Shreveport, LA; son of Leonard Sr and Hearlean Willis; children: Kevin M, Makala O & Maleah R. **Educ:** Southern Univ, Baton Rouge; Seattle Community Col. **Career:** Seattle Black Fire Fighter Asn, pres, 1970; Int Assocs Black Prof Fire Fighters, nw region dir, 1975, exec vpres & a/a officer, 1980; Seattle Fire Dept, lt, 1981; Barden Cablevision Seattle, dir opers, 1982; IABPFF, pres, 1984-88; Pryor, McClendon & Counts Investment Bankers, consult, 1993; Southwest Mortuary, asst mgr & mgr; New Beginnings Christian Fel, deacon & dep chief security, Discipleship Ministry, dir, asst chief opers, currently. **Orgs:** Pres & bd dir, CACC, 1975; bd mem, NW Conf Black Pub Officials, 1980; co-chmn, Sea Urban League Scholar Fund Raising, 1981; trustee, Mt Zion Baptist Church, 1981; chmn publicity, Girls Club Puget Sound, 1984; regist lobbyist, State WA, 1993; bd mem, Seattle Urban League; rep, Nat Black Leadership Roundtable WA State MLK Jr Comn; Alumni Leadership Tomorrow Prog/Seattle Chamber Comm Southern Univ Alumni Seattle WA; pres, Int Asn Black Fire Fighters; pres & treas, Cent Area Motivation Prog; Christian Educ; chair Trustee bd; vice chair Finance Boards; Northwest Conf Black Pub Officials; exec comt, United Negro Col Fund. **Honors/Awds:** Hon Fire Fighter, Shreveport, La Fire Dept, 1976; Most Outstanding Young Man of America, US JayCees, 1978 & 1981; Furthering the Cause of Human Rights, Un Asn, 1979; Affirmative Action Award, Seattle Urban League, 1982; Community Service Award, Black Law Enforcement Officers Asn, 1984; Fire Fighter of the year, 1994; Men of Achievement, 1996; Who's Who in America, 1997; Strathmores Who's Who in America, 1998; Outstanding Fire Fighter, Wash State; International man of the year, Int Biog Centre, Cambridge, Eng. **Special Achievements:** Elected as Who's Who Among Black Americans. **Home Addr:** 10723 53 Ave S, Seattle, WA 98178-2104, **Home Phone:** (206)722-4314. **Business Addr:** Assistant Chief Operations, New Beginnings Christian Fellowships, PO Box 940, Renton, WA 98057, **Business Phone:** (425)282-6220.

**WILLIAMS, CLARENCE**
Football coach, football player. **Personal:** Born Jan 20, 1975, Crescent City, FL. **Educ:** Fla State Univ. **Career:** Football player (retired), coach; Buffalo Bills, running back, 1998; Crescent City High Sch, coach, currently. **Business Addr:** Coach, Crescent City High School, 2201 US 17, Crescent City, FL 32112, **Business Phone:** (386)698-1629.

**WILLIAMS, REV. DR. CLARENCE EARL, JR.**
Clergy. **Personal:** Born May 10, 1950, Tuscaloosa, AL. **Educ:** St Joseph Col, Rensselaer IN, BA, sociol & fr, 1973; Cath Theol Union Chicago, MDiv, 1978, MA, black cath hist, 1982; Union Inst, PhD, global educ & cult commun, 1998; Ecumenical Theol Sem, PhD, ecumenism & pastoral leadership. **Career:** Nat Black Seminarians Asn, bd chmn, 1970; Acad Afro-World Comm, founder & pres, 1977; St Anthony RC Ch, pastor, 1980-95; Black Cath Televangelization Network, pres, 1986; Bldg Bridges Black & Brown, co-convener, co-founder, 1992-96; Black Cath Ministries Archdiocese Detroit, dir, 1995-2007; Racial Equality & Diversity Initiatives Nat Off Cath Charities, Alexandria, Va, sr dir, currently; Inst Recovery Racisms, founder & dir, 1990-; Inst Social Sobriety, dir, 1992-; Cath Charities USA, sr dir racial equality & diversity, 2007-10. **Orgs:** Exec dir, This Far by Faith; bd trustee, Madonna Univ, 1997-; MissionariesPrecious Blood Roman Cath; vice chmn, Bread World. **Honors/Awds:** The Fr Clarence Williams Award, Nat Black Catholic Seminarians Asn, 1984; Keep the Dream Alive Award, St. Anthony Church, 1997; Dr Martin Luther King Award, 1998; The Archbishop Jame Lyke Award, Global Ministry Pan African Roman Cath Clergy Conf, 1999; Dr King Unity & Peace Award, St. Mary Cathedral, Miami, Fla, 1999; Teresa Maxis Award, 2008; Msgr. Phillip Murnion Award for Pastoral Excellence in Faith & Cuture, Nat Pastoral Life Ctr, New York, 2009. **Special Achievements:** Books: Recovery from Everyday Racisms, 1999; Racial Sobriety: A journey from hurts to healing, 2002; Spanish workbook, 2004; Portuguese workbook, 2005; The Black Cath Chapel Air national radio evangel prog; Created in 1983, "Come & Go" evangelization training prog cassettes & filmstrips; participant in int "Mass for Shut-Ins" TV prog from Detroit 1982-; producer of documentary series on TV "Search for a Black Christian Heritage"; producer & host of syndicated TV series "Black & Catholic" 1986; Editor of the Book, People of the Pyramids,

1998; First producer & dir of Black vocations filmstrips 1978; First black priestordained in Diocese of Cleveland 1978. **Business Addr:** Founder, Director, Racial Sobriety, 3015 Fourth St NE, Washington, DC 20017-1102, **Business Phone:** (202)269-2517.

### WILLIAMS, DR. CLARENCE G.

Educator. **Personal:** Born Dec 23, 1938, Goldsboro, NC; married Mildred Cogdell; children: Clarence Jr & Alton. **Educ:** NC Cent Univ, BA, 1961; Hampton Univ, MA, 1967; Univ Conn, PhD, higher educ admin & coun psychol, 1972; Cornell Univ, grad study, 1965; Harvard Univ, post doctoral study, 1975. **Career:** Williamsburg Pub Schs Va, teacher, 1961-64; Hampton Univ, asst dean, instr, 1964-68; Univ Conn, prof counsr, 1969-72, teaching asst, 1970-72; Mass Inst Technol, Grad Sch, asst dean, 1972, spec asst to pres & chancellor minority affairs, 1974, actg dir off minority educ, 1980-82, prof urban studies & planning, 1972-74, spec asst to pres, Off Minority Educ, actg dir, 1980-82, asst equal opportunity officer, 1984-97, actg dir off minority educ, 1984-97, adj prof urban studies & planning, adj prof urban studies & planning emer, currently; BankNew Eng, consult, 1986-92; Recipient Hampton Inst Summer Study fel; Ford Found fel Admin. Books: Technology and the Dream: Reflections on the Black Experience, auth, 2001; Reflections of the Dream: Twenty-One Years Celebrating the Life of Dr. Martin Jr. at the Massachusetts Institute of Technology, ed. **Orgs:** Phi Delta Kappan; NC CU Alumni Asn; Univ Conn Alumni Asn; Alpha Phi Alpha; Founder, co-chmn, Black Admin Conf Issues Facing Black Admin Predominantly White Inst, 1982-84; consult, founder, Greater Boston Inter Univ Coun, 1984-; bd dir, Buckingham Browne & Nichols Sch, 1985-91; bd dir, Freedom House, 1986-92; founder & bd dir, Concerned Black Men Mass, 1989; bd dir, New Repertory Theater. **Home Addr:** 14 Cottonwood Rd, Newton, MA 02459. **Business Addr:** Adjunct Professor of Urban Studies & Planning, Massachusetts Institute of Technology, 77 Mass Ave Bldg N52-405, Cambridge, MA 02139-4307, **Business Phone:** (617)253-5446.

### WILLIAMS, CLARENCE J., III

Photographer, photojournalist. **Personal:** Born Jan 22, 1967, Philadelphia, PA. **Educ:** Temple Univ, BA, mass commun, 1992. **Career:** Philadelphia Tribune, intern; York Daily Rec, intern; Times Community Newspapers, intern, staff; Los Angeles Times, staff photogr, 1995-2003; photogr, currently; Univ Southern Miss, vis lectr, 2003-08, photojournalist residence, currently. **Orgs:** Nat Asn Black Journalists; Nat Press Photogr Asn. **Special Achievements:** Fourth place, Photographer Forum & Nikon Contest, 1991; second place, sports feature category, California Press Photographers Association Gold Seal Contest, 1995. **Home Addr:** , CA. **Business Addr:** Photojournalist in Residence, University of Southern Mississippi, 118 College Dr S, Hattiesburg, MS 39406, **Business Phone:** (601)266-4918.

**WILLIAMS, CLYDE, JR. See Obituaries Section.**

### WILLIAMS, CODY

Government official. **Personal:** married Jeri; children: Alanna, Alan Travis & Cody Jerard. **Educ:** Univ Okla, BA; Ariz State Univ, MBA; Harvard Univ, John F Kennedy Sch Gov, grad. **Career:** Paine Webber, stock broker; MeriBank, com & consumer loan off; Minority & Women-owned bus prog, former coordr; Intel, human resources, diverse workforce specist & affirmative action counr; Security Pac Bank, human resources, vpres & affirmative action Officer; City Phoenix, Coordr Minority & Woman owned bus prog; Phoenix City Coun, mayor, councilman, 1994-02; Alms & Hosanna Consul, pres, currently; Univ Phoenix, Ariz State Univ, instr, currently; S Mountain Justice Ct, Maricopa County, justice peace, 2007-. **Orgs:** Nat League Cities, 1994-; Nat Black Caucus Local Elected Offs, 1995-; comm adv bd, Adult Probation Dept; Nat Asn Advan Colored People; pres, Greater Phoenix Black Chamber Com, chief exec officer; Gov's African Am Adv Coun. **Honors/Awds:** Rev Williams Hardison Memorial Service Award; Community Excellence Proj, Partner for Excellence Award; Maricopa County Adult Probation Dept & Garfield Organization Award; Man of the Year Make a Difference Found; Hall of Fame, State of Arizona's Democratic, 2003. **Special Achievements:** Only the Third African American ever elected to the Phoenix City Council; Only African American Justice in the 25 Justice Courts in Maricopa County. **Business Addr:** Judge, Maricopa County Justice Courts, 620 W Jackson St, Phoenix, AZ 85003, **Business Phone:** (602)372-6300.

### WILLIAMS, REV. DR. CURTIS CORTEZ

Clergy, funeral director. **Personal:** Born Dec 15, 1957, Detroit, MI; married Joyce; children: Jaclyn Denee, Curtis Cortez II & Janel Denise. **Educ:** Exten Sem Southern Baptist, 1978; Metro Jail Ministry Sem, 1980; AR Baptist Col, 1980; Detroit Col Bus, BA, 1987; Marygrove Col, MA, pastoral ministry, 1996. **Career:** Gen Motors, 1978-87; Trinity Chapel Funeral Home, admin & owner, 1989-; Aijalon Baptist Church, pastor, 1989-; Saturn Corp, 1990-92. **Orgs:** Fisher YMCA, instr, 1977-79; Detroit Recieving Hosp, chaplain, 1979-; alumnus, Marygrove Col; chair, Urban Banking Comt; pres, Mich Dist Cong Nat Baptist Conv, 1997-. **Honors/Awds:** Hon DDiv, Tenn Sch Relig; Cert of Appreciation, Mayor Coleman Young, 1989; Spirit Detroit Award, Detroit City Coun, 1984-85, 1989; Distinguished Service Award, Wayne County, 1989; Commeration, Mich State House Rep, 1992; Black United Fund Award. **Home Addr:** 19131 Berkeley Rd, Detroit, MI 48221-1801, **Home Phone:** (313)862-4639. **Business Addr:** Owner, Administrator, Trinity Chapel Funeral Home, 20226 W McNichols Rd, Detroit, MI 48219, **Business Phone:** (313)532-8182.

### WILLIAMS, CYNDA (CYNTHIA WILLIAMS)

Actor. **Personal:** Born May 17, 1966, Chicago, IL; married Roderick Plummer, Jan 1, 2001?; children: 1; married Arthur Louis Fuller, Jan 1, 1993, (divorced 1998); married Billy Bob Thornton, Jan 1, 1990, (divorced 1992). **Educ:** Ball State Univ. **Career:** Films: Mo Better Blues, 1990; One False Move, 1992; Grey Knight, 1993; Wet, 1995; The Tie That Binds, 1995; Condition Red, 1995; Gang in Blue, 1996; Tales of Erotica, 1996; Spirit Lost, 1996; The Sweeper, 1996; Black Rose of Harlem, 1996; The Last Call, 1998; Relax. It's Just Sex, 1998; Caught Up, 1998; The Courage to Love, 2000, Hidden Blessings, 2000; MacArthur Park, 2001; March, 2001; With or Without You, 2003; Shooter, 2004; When Do We Eat?, 2005; Frankie D, 2007; Divine Intervention, 2007; Beautiful Loser, 2008, Tru Loved, 2008; Turning Point, 2012. TV appearances: "Tales of the City", 1993; "New York Undercover", 1997; "The Wedding", 1998; "Introducing Dorothy Dand ridge", 1999; "Hidden Blessings", 2000; "The Courage to Love", 2000; "Violation", 2003; "Our House", 2006. **Special Achievements:** Nominee for Independent Spirit Award, 1993. **Business Addr:** Actress, Innovative Artists, 1999 Ave of the Stars Suite 2850, Los Angeles, CA 90067, **Business Phone:** (310)553-5200.

### WILLIAMS, DANIEL, II

Football player. **Personal:** Born Dec 15, 1969, Ypsilanti, MI. **Educ:** Univ Toledo. **Career:** Football player (retired); Denver Broncos, left defensive end & right defensive end, 1993-96; Kans City Chiefs, defensive end & right defensive end & right defensive tackle, 1997, 1999-2001.

### WILLIAMS, DR. DANIEL EDWIN

Clinical psychologist. **Personal:** Born Nov 24, 1933, Mobile, AL; son of Robert and Demaris Lewis Brown; married Mildred E Olney; children: Denise M, Michele & Melanie. **Educ:** Seton Hall US, Orange, NJ, BA, 1962; St Johns Univ, New York, MS, 1963, PhD, 1968. **Career:** Mt Carmel Guild, Newark, NJ, psychologist, 1963-65; E Orange, NJ, Pub Schs, sch psychologist, 1965-68; pvt pract clin psychologist, 1974-; J Pan African Studies, Ed Bd mem; Montclair State Univ, assoc prof, psychol, prof emer, 1998-. **Orgs:** Bd educrs, Plainfield, NJ, 1972-74; bd mem, Psychol Examiners, State Nj, 1973-75; pres, NJ chap, Asn Black Psychologists, 1973-75 & 1981-83; pres, Nat Asn Black Psychologists, 1980-81. **Honors/Awds:** ABPP dipl, clin psychol, Am Bd Prof Psychol, Am Psychological Asn, 1977. **Home Addr:** 1837 Rangewood Ct, Plainfield, NJ 07060-3441. **Business Addr:** Professor Emeritus, Montclair State University, Dickson Hall 4011 Normal Ave, Montclair, NJ 07043, **Business Phone:** (973)655-4000.

### WILLIAMS, DANIEL LOUIS

Executive, chairperson. **Personal:** Born Aug 15, 1926, Hardeeville, SC; son of Adbell Sr and Mattie Freeman; married Pauline Cave; children: Sharon, Daniel Jr, Brenda, Derrick, Devon, D Llewellyn & Dewitt. **Educ:** Savannah State Col, attended 1948. **Career:** Masons (Prince Hall), sr warden, 1950; Shriners, Ill potentate, 1968-70; St Phillips Baptist Church, decon, 1968; Beaufort-Jasper Career Educ Ctr, vchmn, 1974; Career Educ Ctr, chmn, 1986; Jasper County, sch bd mem. **Home Addr:** Williams Ave, PO Box 417, Hardeeville, SC 29927, **Home Phone:** (843)784-5925.

### WILLIAMS, PROF. DANIEL SALU (DAN WILLIAMS)

Educator. **Personal:** Born Feb 14, 1942, Brooklyn, NY; son of David D and Loriene H; married Sheila; children: Peter & Megan. **Educ:** Brooklyn Col, BA, gen, photog, fine & studio arts, 1965; Univ Ore, MA, gen, photog, fine & studio arts, 1969. **Career:** Ohio Univ, Col Fine Arts, assoc prof, art, 1969-88, photog, 1980-81, 1989-91, asst provost, 1987, prof, 1988, dir, Minority Grad Stud Recruitment, 1994, photog dept, 1995, asst vpres, minority grad affairs, 1997, prof emer, currently. **Orgs:** Images Gallery, Cincinnati, Ohio, 1987-91; Soc Photog Ed, 1970; Nat Conf Artists, 1972. **Honors/Awds:** Univ Oreg, 1967-69; OH Univ Res Grant, 1982, 1984; Individual Artist Fel, Ohio Arts coun, 1983-85, 1988, 1990; Langston Hughes Vis prof & African Am Studies, Univ Kans, 1992; Ohio Univ Res Grant, 1997; The Nat African Am Mus & Cult Ctr, Wilberforce, Ohio. **Special Achievements:** Photo-montage wall murals (12 panels), 22' high x 25' wide each & three simultaneous slide show projections depicting life 1950's era, "African Am Life from WW II to the Civil Rights Act of 1965," completed 1988; 1804 grant to develop a digital imaging component to the photography program, 1997; Art work in Permanent Collections: Studio Museum in Harlem, NY; Museum Modern Art, NY; Natl Museum Am Art, Smithsonian Institution, Wash DC; Univ Kans; Princeton Univ; Haver ford Col, Haver ford, Pa. **Home Addr:** 180 Main St, Andover, MA 01810, **Home Phone:** (718)467-2131. **Business Addr:** Professor Emeritus, Ohio University, 528 Seigfred Hall, Athens, OH 45701, **Business Phone:** (740)593-4288.

### WILLIAMS, DARRYL EDWIN

Football player. **Personal:** Born Jan 8, 1970, Miami, FL; married Marlina; children: Darryl Jr. **Educ:** Miami Univ, grad. **Career:** Football player (retired); Cincinnati Bengals, free safety, 1992-95, 2000-01; Seattle Seahawks, free safety, 1996-99. **Honors/Awds:** All-American, 1991; AP National Championship, 1991; Pro Bowl, 1997; All-Pro, 1997.

### WILLIAMS, DAVID, III

Lawyer, educator, athletic director. **Personal:** married Gail Carr; children: Erika, David III, Samantha & Nicholas. **Educ:** Northern Mich Univ, BS, social sci, 1969, MA, educ, 1970; Univ Detroit, MBA, 1979, JD, 1982; NY Univ, LLM, taxation, 1984. **Career:** Detroit Pub Schs, mid sch teacher & coach, 1970-80; Univ Detroit, Sch Law, vis asst prof law, 1985-86; Capital Univ, adj prof law, 1986-2000; Ohio State Univ, asst prof law, 1986-90, assoc prof law, 1990-95, vice provost off minority affairs, 1992-93, vpres stud & urban & community affairs off stud affairs, 1993-2000, prof law, 1995-2000; Univ Oxford, Ohio State Univ, Eng Law Prog, dir, 1993-95; Vanderbilt Univ, prof, 2000-, vice chancellor, univ affairs & athletics dir, law fac, 2013-. **Orgs:** Mich Bar Asn, 1982; Dc Bar Asn, 1989; Nat Asn State Univs & Land Grant Cols, 1996-2000; ed bd, Bus Lawyer, 1997-98; Tenn Bar Asn, 2000; chmn, Mid Tenn United Way, 2007-08; Am Corp Coun Asn; mem bar admis comt, mem sect legal educ, mem admis stand rev comt, & mem standing comt pub educ, Am Bar Asn; mem rev comt, Am Asn Law Schs; Nat Asn Col & Univ Atty; Atlanta Fed Res Bd, Nashville Br; gen adv bd & infractions appeals comt mem, Nat Col Athletic Asn; State Bars Mich, Tenn, & Dc; bd dir, Nashville Pub Tv; bd dir, Nashville Symphony; bd mem, Nashville Sports Coun; bd dir, Tenn Sports Hall Fame; bd mem, Adventure Sci Ctr; bd dir, 100 Black Men Mid Tenn; bd dir, Community Found; bd dir, Spec Olympics Tenn; bd dir, Ctr Nonprofit Mgt; bd dir, Rotary Club Nashville; Am Law Inst; bd dir, Mayor Karl Dean's Procurement Stand; Sports Lawyer Asn; bd dir, Mid Tenn YMCA; bd dir, OASIS Ctr; bd dir, Second Harvest Food Bank; bd dir, WO Smith Sch; Wellington Independent Sch Bd Dir; bd dir, Tuition Plan Inc; Ohio State Univ Athletic Coun. **Honors/Awds:** Most Outstanding Professor Award, Ohio State Univ, 1989-90; Most Outstanding Professor Award, Univ Detroit,. **Special Achievements:** Numerous publications. **Business Addr:** Vice Chancellor, University Affairs and Athletics, Vanderbilt Law School, Rm 305 131 21st Ave S, Nashville, TN 37203-1181, **Business Phone:** (615)322-8331.

### WILLIAMS, DR. DAVID GEORGE

Physician. **Personal:** Born Jan 5, 1939, Chicago, IL; married Judith; children: Sheryl, John & Jacqueline. **Educ:** Provident Hosp Chicago, RN, 1961; Trenton State Col, BA, 1972; Allegheny Univ Health Sci, HahneMann med Col, MD, 1976. **Career:** Philadelphia Gen Hosp, resident internal med, 1976-77; Univ Pa Health Syst, resident anesthesiol, 1977-79. **Orgs:** Vpres, Med Class, 1972; dir med, NJ Prison Syst, 1977; pres, Bell-Williams & Med Asn, PA, 1979; AMA. **Honors/Awds:** Hon soc, Trenton State Col, 1972. **Home Addr:** 430 Cinnaminson Ave, Palmyra, NJ 08065, **Home Phone:** (856)786-8181.

### WILLIAMS, DEBORAH A.

President (organization), chief executive officer, psychologist. **Personal:** Born Chicago, IL; married Herb. **Educ:** Tougaloo Col, BA, psychol, 1981; Univ Ga, MA, psychol & PhD, clin psychol, 1985. **Career:** Univ Ga, asst prof, 1985-87; Methodist Hosp, lic clin psychologist, 1987-89; Dept Social Security & Disability, regional off med consult, 1989-91; Nat Basketball Asn, family care psychologist, 1992-94; Harlem Hosp, retail mkt consult, 2009-10; Her Game 2 Inc, pres & chief operating officer, 1996-. **Orgs:** Founder & pres, Behind Bench: Nat Basketball Wives Asn, 1993-; bd dir, Child Welfare League Am; bd mem, Urban League Southern Conn; bd dir, Greenwich Found Women & Girls; bd dir, Miss Indianapolis Teen Scholar Found; Fairfield County Chap Links Inc. **Business Addr:** President, Chief Executive Officer, Her Game 2, Inc, 65 High Ridge Rd Suite 371, Stamford, CT 06905, **Business Phone:** (203)517-0535.

### WILLIAMS, DEBORAH ANN

School administrator. **Personal:** Born Nov 28, 1951, Washington, DC; daughter of Harold and Marguerite Stewart Hamilton. **Educ:** Ripon Col, AB, 1973. **Career:** Overlook Elem & Prince George's MD, teacher; C&P Tel Co, serv rep; US Dept Educ, sr educ prog specialist. **Orgs:** PRS Voices Corinthian Baptist Church; Northern Va Choral Guild. **Home Addr:** 3220 Sherman Ave NW, Washington, DC 20010. **Business Addr:** Senior Education Program Specialist, US Department of Education, OERI, 400 Maryland Ave SW, Washington, DC 20202-7241, **Business Phone:** (202)245-7770.

### WILLIAMS, DEBORAH BROWN

Clergy. **Personal:** Born Dec 15, 1957, Detroit, MI; daughter of Ellis Brown and Gloria Cole; married Gregory; children: Gregory C II & Gianna Charise. **Educ:** Wayne State Univ, Detroit, Mich, BS, educ, 1980; Garrett-Evangel Theol Sem, Evanston, Ill, Mdiv, 1983. **Career:** Ebenezer AME Church, Detroit, Mich, staff minister, 1977-80; Trinity AME Church, Waukegan, Ill, stud minister, 1982; Emmanuel Temple AME Church, Chicago, Ill, supply pastor, 1983; St Paul AME Church, Glencoe, Ill, sr pastor, 1983-; Hosanna Harvest Assembly, sr pastor. **Orgs:** Chicago Ministerial Alliance, 1983-; fourth dist coordr, African Methodist Episcopal Connectional Women Ministry, 1988-92; bd dir, chmn, minority task force, Ill Prairie Girl Scout Coun, 1989-; secy, Chicago Ann Conf, 1989-; nat minority recruiter, twelfth Nat Workshop Christians & Jews, 1989. **Honors/Awds:** Mediation Moments African Methodist, contribr, AME Publ, 1986. **Home Addr:** 336 Wash, Glencoe, IL 60022, **Home Phone:** (708)835-1655. **Business Addr:** Pastor, St Paul African Methodist Episcopal Church, 336 Wash St, Glencoe, IL 60022, **Business Phone:** (847)835-4421.

### WILLIAMS, DENIECE

Actor, songwriter, singer. **Personal:** Born Jun 3, 1950, Gary, IN; married Ken; children: Kenderick & Kevin; married Christipher Joy; married Brad Westering; children: 2. **Educ:** Purdue Univ, nursing. **Career:** Gospel & soul singer, Actress; mem, Wonder love, back-up singer, Stevie Wonder & Earth Wind & Fire. Albums: Too Much, Too Little, Too Late, duet with Johnny Mathis, 1978; You're All I Need to Get By, 1978; This Is Niecy, 1976; Free, 1976; Song Bird, 1977; I've Got the Next Dance, 1979; When Love Comes Calling, 1979; My Melody, 1981; Silly, 1981; Niecy, 1982; It's Gonna Take a Miracle, 1982; I'm So Proud, 1983; Let's Hear It for the Boy, 1984; Love Won't Let Me Wait, 1984; Next Love, 1984; Black Butterfly, 1984; Hot On the Trail, 1986; My Melody, 1981; Special Love; Let's Hear It for the Boy, 1984; So Glad I Know, 1986; Water Under the Bridge, 1987; I Can't Wait, 1988; As Good As It Gets, 1989; Love Solves It All, 1996; This Is My Song, 1998; This Is Niecy, bonus track, 2005; Love, Niecy Style, 2007; Christian Prod Co, founder. Tv series: "The Goodwill Industries Telethon", 1981; "Family Ties", 1983-89; "Noises Off", 1992; "VH-1 Where Are They Now?", 2000-02; "Oh Drama", 2002; "Celebrity Duets", 2006; "This is David Gest", 2007; One Kiss, 2008; "Dancing on Ice", 2009. Others: "Christmas Child", 2003; "Elimidate", 2005. **Honors/Awds:** Grammy Award, 1987-88 & 1999. **Special Achievements:** Presented her own BBC radio show in the UK, showcasing the best in new gospel and inspirational music. **Business Addr:** Singer, c/o Agency for Preferred Artists, 9000 Sunset Blvd, Los Angeles, CA 90069.

### WILLIAMS, DONALD

Executive, president (organization). **Personal:** son of Elmer and Jean. **Career:** Williams Graphics Inc, chief exec officer & pres, currently. **Business Addr:** President, Chief Executive Officer, Williams Graphics Inc, 2200 Spring Garden Ave, Pittsburgh, PA 15212-3146, **Business Phone:** (412)321-9250.

### WILLIAMS, DONALD H.

Educator, executive, association executive. **Personal:** Born Oct 29, 1936, Chicago, IL; son of Theresa P and Herbert G; married Sharon Rebecca Hobbs; children: David, Jonathan & Rebecca. **Educ:** Univ Ill, BA, 1957, MD, 1962. **Career:** Educator (retired), exec; Univ Chicago, instr, asst prof, 1967-71; Conn Ment Health Ctr, chief inpatient serv, 1971-73, Med Eval Unit, head, 1973-78, chief comm supp serv, 1973-79, asst chief clin aff, 1979-84; Yale Univ, asst prof, 1971-77, assoc prof psych, 1977-84; Mich State Univ, prof, chairperson psychiat, 1984-89, emer prof psychiat, 1990; Thurgood Marshall Inst, dir, 1998-. **Orgs:** Am Publ Health Asn, 1968; Am Ortho psychiat Asn, 1968; Nat Med Asn, 1968-; consult, Nat Inst Ment Health, 1971-81; consult, W Haven Veterans Admin Hosp, 1971-80; fel Am Psychiat Asn, 1974; treas, Black Psychiatrists Am, 1978-80; sec, Black Psychiatrists Am, 1996-98, vpres, 1998-; Soc Psychiat. **Honors/Awds:** IL Psychiatric Soc Research Award Referee, 1968. **Special Achievements:** Written 17 articles & numerous professional presentations. **Home Addr:** 236 E Fee Hall Suite A, East Lansing, MI 48823, **Home Phone:** (517)353-3888. **Business Addr:** Emeritus Professor of Psychiatry, Michigan State University, A222 E Fee Hall, East Lansing, MI 48824-1316, **Business Phone:** (517)353-3888.

### WILLIAMS, DOROTHY DANIEL

Educator. **Personal:** Born Aug 22, 1938, Kinston, NC; daughter of Willie Mae Wingate (deceased) and Fonie (deceased); children: William Daniel. **Educ:** Hampton Inst, BSN, 1960; NY Univ, grad courses, 1965; E Carolina Univ, MS, HEc, 1977, MSN, 1980. **Career:** New York & Los Angeles, CA, staff nurse, 1960-66; Einstein Hosp, Bronx, NY, head nurse, 1966-69; Baltimore City Sch, Voc Div, teacher, 1969-73; Lenoir Mem Hosp, Sch Nursing, instr, 1973-74; E Carolina Univ, Sch Nursing, asst prof maternal-child nursing, asst prof emer, currently. **Orgs:** Nat Nurse Hon Soc, Beta Chap, Sigma Theta Tau, 1978; Sch Nursing Curric Comn, 1980-, chmn, 1981-82, 1985, 1997-; law comn mem, NC Nurse Asn, 1983-85; secy, conv deleg Dist 32, NCNA, 1983-85; vpres, Delta Rho Zeta Chap, Zeta Phi Beta Sor Inc, 1983-85; adv, ECU Lambda Mu Chap Zeta Phi Beta, 1983-; ECU Greek Affairs Advisor Comn, 1984; laws comn, Asn Black Nursing Fac Higher Educ, 1986-; res bd advisor, Am Biog Inst Inc, 1987; bd rev, ABNFJ, 1991-; ECU Pre Med, Pre Dent Adv Coun, 1992-; chairperson, nominating Comn, ABNF, 1999; bd mem, Comn Health Ctr; Golden Lamp Soc, 2008; panelist, consult, developer, Adolescent Pregnancy/Parenting Sem; lectr, State Bd Nursing Rev Courses, AHEC; developer, Leadership Sem; mem task force, Infant Mortality & AIDS, Comn Task Force Comn Rels. **Honors/Awds:** HERA for Outstanding Sorority Advisor, Panhellenic Coun ECU, 1986; Zeta of the Year, Delta Rho Zeta Chap, Zeta Phi Beta Sorority, 1988, 1993. **Special Achievements:** Selected to participate in the minority health leadership workshop, ChapelHill, NC in 1985. **Home Addr:** 1384 Taylor Heath Rd, Kinston, NC 28501-7151, **Home Phone:** (252)527-0007. **Business Addr:** Assistant Professor Emerita, East Carolina University, 600 Moye Blvd, Greenville, NC 27834, **Business Phone:** (252)744-1020.

### WILLIAMS, DOROTHY PAYNE

School administrator. **Personal:** Born Nov 24, 1938, Tallahassee, FL; children: Gerald Herbert & Debra Michelle. **Educ:** Fla A&M Univ, BS, 1960; Syracuse Univ, MSLS, 1967; Univ N Fla, attended 1975. **Career:** Lincoln Mem HS, librn, 1960-61; JW Johnson Jr HS, head librn, 1962-68; Raines HS, head librn, 1968-71; Univ N Fla, asst dir libs, 1971-82, assoc prof; Fla A&M Univ, dir publ, 1983, asst vpres univ rels, 1999, asst corp sec, bd trustee, currently, exec dir, assoc vpres. **Orgs:** EEO/AA coord, Univ N Fla, 1976-82; staff coord, State Bd Educ Adv Comn Educ Blacks Fla, 1984-; bd mem, Jacksonville Comm Econ Dev Coun, 1981-83; pres, Jacksonville Nat Coun Negro Women, 1978-81; pres, Jacksonville Chap Links Inc, 1985-87; pres, Friends Fla A & M Univ Black Arch, 1985-88; bd dir, FAMU Found, exec dir, 1993-; secy & fundraising chair, Fla A & M Univ Nat Alumni Asn. **Honors/Awds:** Teacher of the Year, James Weldon Johnson Jr HS, 1966; Service Award, Alpha Kappa Alpha Sorority, 1978; Community Service Award, Grant Mem AME Church, 1979-88, 1990; Gallery Distinction, Fla A&M Univ, 1987; Distinguished Alumni Award, 1993; Rattler Pride Award. **Home Addr:** 748 E 9th Ave, Tallahassee, FL 32303, **Home Phone:** (850)224-4751. **Business Addr:** Secretary, Accountant, Florida A & M University, 1500 S Martin L King Jr Blvd, Tallahassee, FL 32307, **Business Phone:** (850)599-3376.

### WILLIAMS, DOUG LEE (DOUGLAS LEE WILLIAMS)

Football coach, executive, football player. **Personal:** Born Aug 9, 1955, Zachary, LA; son of Robert and Laura; married Raunda; children: Ashley, Adrian, Douglas Jr, Jasmine, Laura, Lee, Temessia & Carmaelta. **Educ:** Grambling State Univ, BS, health & phys educ, 1978. **Career:** Football player (retired), football coach, executive; Tampa Bay Buccaneers, quarterback, 1978-82, personnel exec, 2004-08, Coordr Pro Scouting, 2009-10; Okla Outlaws, quarterback, 1984; Ariz Wranglers, quarterback, 1985; Wash Redskins, quarterback, 1986-89; Pointe Coupee Cent, athletic dir & head coach, 1991; Northeast High Sch, head coach, 1993; US Naval Acad, Running Backs Coach, 1994; Scottish Claymores, offensive coordr, 1995; Jacksonville Jaguars, col scout, 1995-96; Morehouse Col, head coach, 1997; Grambling State Univ, head coach, 1998-2003; dir prof scouting, Tampa Bay Buccaneers, 2009-; UFL Norfolk, gen mgr, 2010-. **Business Addr:** Personnel Executive, Tampa Bay Buccaneers, 1 Buccaneer Pl, Tampa, FL 33607, **Business Phone:** (813)870-2700.

### WILLIAMS, DOUGLAS LEALLEN

Singer, administrator. **Personal:** Born Sep 3, 1956, Smithdale, MS; son of Leon (deceased) and Amanda (deceased). **Career:** Albums: Heart songs, 1995; Duets, 2001; When Mercy Found Me, 2003; Good Graces, 2005; Duet vol 2, 2008; Blackberry Rec, pres & ceo, 1991-; Blackberry Records, pres. **Business Addr:** President, Chief Executive Officer, Blackberry Records, PO Box 16469, Jackson, MS 39236, **Business Phone:** (601)206-4600.

### WILLIAMS, DR. DWIGHT

Nuclear engineer, educator. **Personal:** married Sonja. **Educ:** NC State Univ, BS, nuclear engineering, MS, nuclear eng; Univ Md, PhD, nuclear engineering, 2005. **Career:** US Dept Energy, asst prog mgr, 1994-95; Waste Policy Inst, assoc engr, 1995-96; Prototype Int Data Ctr, nuclear scientist, 1996-2000; US Dept Defense, sr nuclear engr, 2000-04, chief engr & prin nuclear physicist, 2004-05, prin nuclear physicist, 2005-; Mass Inst Technol, Dept Nuclear Sci & Engineering, Martin Luther King Vis Prof, 2006-; Brain Trust Technologies LLC, prin nuclear physicist; Mixed Greens Energy & Engineering Inc, pres & chief exec officer. **Orgs:** Am Nuclear Soc, 1997-; Nat Soc Prof Engrs, 1997-, pres chap; Soc Eng Educ, 1998-; Am Phys Soc, 2002-; prog evaluator, Accreditation Bd Eng Technol, 2003-; bd dir, Houston Acad, 2006-; bd dir, Mathcount, 2006-; vpres, Md Soc Prof Engrs, 2006-; Am Soc Engineering Educ. **Honors/Awds:** Southern Regional Education Board Doctoral Scholars Award, 1998, 2001; Honor Award, 2002; Young Engineer of the Year, Md Soc Prof Engrs, 2003, 2004; National Young Engineer of the Year, 2005, 2006; AEDC Humanitarian of the Year, Nat Soc Blach Engrs, 2006; Dominion Energy Excellence in Leadership Award, 2007; DNI Fellows Award, Off Assoc Dir Nat Intelligence Sci & Technol. **Special Achievements:** First African American to be named National Young Engineer of the Year by the National Society of Professional Engineers. **Business Addr:** Martin Luther King Visiting Professor, Massachusetts Institute of Technology, 77 Mass Ave NW14-2323, Cambridge, MA 02139-4307, **Business Phone:** (617)253-4244.

### WILLIAMS, DR. E. FAYE

Business owner, state government official, radio host. **Personal:** Born Dec 20, 1941, Melrose, LA; daughter of Frances Lacour and Vernon. **Educ:** Grambling State Univ, BS, 1962; Univ Southern Calif, MPA, pub admin, 1971; Howard Univ Sch Law, JD, 1985; City Univ Los Angeles, PhD, pub adminr, 1993. **Career:** Los Angeles City Schs, teacher & dept chairperson, 1964-71; Nat Educ Asn, dir Atlanta assoc educ, 1971-73, dir overseas ed assoc, 1973-75; Mich Educ Asn & NEA, dir orgn & pub rels, 1975-81, dir prof develop & human rights, 1981-82; George Wash Univ, DC, educ policy fel, 1981; DC Comt, Cong fel judiciary & ed; Off Gen Coun Nat Football League Players Asn Sports Law, intern; Larvadain & Scott Law Offices, atty-at-law; Southern Univ Law Ctr, Baton Rouge, La, prof int law; Natural Health Options, pres & chief exec officer, 2000-; Dc Coun mem, Legis Coun & Chief Staff. **Orgs:** Alpha Kappa Mu Nat Hon Soc, 1959; Unity Church; life mem, Delta Sigma Theta, 1959; life mem, Nat Asn Child Care Professionals; nat pres, Grambling State Univ Alumni Asn, 1981-90; bd dir, Partners Peace; bd dir, Coun Nat Interest; Women Mutual Security; bd dir, Grambling Univ Athletic Found; treas, Straight Talk Econ Roundtable; chairperson, Nat Black Fair; cand, US Cong; US House Representatives, Wash, DC, staff coun, 1990-; counr, Nat Cong Black Women; teacher, Col Kids; adv, Womans Health Network & Coun; steering comt, ChangeName. **Honors/Awds:** Numerous honors & awards including Outstanding Alumnus Award, Historically Black Col NAFEO, 1981; Joan of Arc Award, La Women Polit; Hall of Fame, Black Women Attorneys, 1986; Martin Luther King Jr Commemorative Award, 1988; They Dare to Speak Out Peace Award, 1993; Delta Legacy Award, 1994; Blessed Are the Peacemakers Award, 1995; Community Service Award, Asian Benevolent Soc, 1999; Iota Phi Lamda Sorority's Woman of the Year Award; Star Performer Award, Asian Benevolent Soc; African Hebrew Israelites, Humanitarian Award; Woman Entrepreneur of the Year Award, Indiana Black Expo; Distributor of the Year Award, Unither Pharma, 2003. **Special Achievements:** Numerous articles and books published; One of Ebony Magazine's "100 Most Influential Black Americans" and Ebony's Power 150"; First African American to run a viable congressional campaign in Louisiana. **Home Addr:** 1310 Saratoga Ave NE, Washington, DC 20018-1966, **Home Phone:** (202)526-3033. **Business Addr:** President, Chief Executive Officer, Natural Health Options Inc, 1251 4th St SW, Washington, DC 20024, **Business Phone:** (202)678-6788.

### WILLIAMS, E. THOMAS, JR.

Banker, teacher, chief executive officer. **Personal:** Born Oct 14, 1937, New York, NY; son of Edgar Thomas Sr and Elnora Bing Williams Morris; married Auldlyn Higgins; children: Brooke Higgins Bing & Eden Bradford Bing. **Educ:** Brooklyn Col, BA, econs, 1960. **Career:** Teacher, banker (retired); PS 35, Brooklyn, NY, teacher; Md Nat Bank, banker, 1968-71; Chase Manhattan Bank, vpres & sr loan officer int pvt banking, 1972-83; Fordham Hill Owners Corp, pres, 1983-89, chmn, 1990-92; Elnora Inc, pres & chief exec officer, 1993-98; Elliott Sch, pres; Peace Corps, vol; Johns Hopkins Sch Int Studies, teacher bus affairs; Chase Manhattan, lending officer. **Orgs:** Vol, Peace Corps, Ethiopia; trustee, Boys Harbor Inc; trustee, Cent Pk Conservancy Bd, Long Island Chap-E-Nature Conservancy; trustee, Atlanta Univ Ctr; bd mem, pres, Nat Am Asn Colored People Legal Defense Fund, Long Island Chap; pres, Brooklyn Col Chap, Nat Asn Advan Colored People; Sigma Pi Phi, Zeta Chap Boule; 100 Black Men Inc; Thomas Franklin Bing Trust; Nehemiah Housing Trust; dir chair audit comt, Fiduciary Trust Co Int; trustee, Vestry Trinity Church Wall St, Church Heavenly Rest Calvary/st. Georges Church; bd dir, Fiduciary Trust Co, New York, chair audit comt; trustee, Cadral Church St John Divine Treas; Schomburg Ctr Res Black Cult; chmn, Schomberg Soc; trustee, Grace Mansion Conservancy; trustee, Brooklyn Mus; trustee, Mus Mod Art, Aquisition Comt Studio Mus Harlem, Art Study Group, Naples, Fla; Univ Club, NY; River Club, NY; Knickerbocker Club, NY; Revielle Club, NY; Comus Club, Brooklyn; Omega Psi Phi; chmn, Romare Bearden Found; Trinity Church Wall St; Cent Pk Conservancy; Cathedral Church St. John Divine; Comus Club Brooklyn; Reveille Club New York; pres, Brooklyn-Staten Island Chap Jr Red Cross; chmn, bd & head, Fordham Hill Proj, New York; bd dir, Fiduciary Trust; chair, audit comt; bd, Brooklyn Mus & Mus Mod Art; bd, Nature Conservancy. **Home Addr:** 145 E 74 St, New York, NY 10021, **Home Phone:** (212)472-3111.

### WILLIAMS, EARL

Musician, educator, drummer. **Personal:** Born Oct 8, 1938, Detroit, MI; son of Paul and Evelyn Webb; married Ronda G Snowden; children: Earl Jr, Kevin, Damon, Lauren & Brandon. **Educ:** Detroit Conserv Music, attended 1951; Detroit Inst Musical Arts, attended 1953; Bor Manhattan Comm Col, attended 1975; Empire State Col, New York, NY, BA, 1988. **Career:** Paul Williams Orchestra, musician, drummer, 1957-59; Eddie Heywood Trio, musician, 1959-61; Rec & TV & Radio, studio drummer, 1961-73; Sam "The Man", Taylor Japan Tour, drummer, 1964-65, 1972; Music Matrix Publ Co, musician & pres; State Univ Old W bury, Old Westbury, NY, adj instr, 1991-92; Five Towns Col, Dix Hills, NY, adj instr, 1991-94; Long Island Univ, CW Post Campus, Brookville, NY, adj instr, 1994-, prof percussion studies, currently; Valerie Capers Trio, staff. **Orgs:** Broadcast Music Inc BMI, 1960; Nat Acad Recording Artists Arts & Sci, 1979. **Special Achievements:** Drummer with, Diahann Carroll-Cannes Film Festival 1965, WNET-TV "Soul Show" 1968-69; NBC-TV "Someone New Show" 1969-72, ABC-TV "Jack Parr Show", 1973-74, Lena Horne, 1973-74, A Chorus Line (Broadway), 1975-79, Alvin Ailey Dance Co 1979, Jean-Pierre Rampal 1980-81, JVC Jazz Festival, Nice, France, 1989, North Sea Jazz Festival, The Hague, The Netherland, 1993, Mary Lou Williams, Women in Jazz Festival Kennedy Center, 1997, Nassau County Jazz Legends in the African-American Community, 2001; Funny Girl, Hair, Don't Bother Me, I Can't Cope, & A Chorus Line. **Home Addr:** 17 Heather Lane, Jericho, NY 11753-1313, **Home Phone:** (516)942-3643. **Business Addr:** Professor of Percussion Studies, Long Island University, 720 Northern Blvd, Brookville, NY 11548, **Business Phone:** (516)299-2474.

### WILLIAMS, DR. REV. EARL, JR.

Clergy, school administrator, government official. **Personal:** Born Mar 27, 1935, Thomasville, GA; son of Earl Sr and Flossie Adams; married Faye Harris; children: Earl III, Jennifer, Angela, Thomas & Jeffrey. **Educ:** Ft Valley State Col, Ft Valley, Ga, BA, 1963; Valdosta State Col, Valdosta, Ga, MA, 1975. **Career:** Prof baseball, 1956, 1957, 1962; City Thomasville, Ga, mayor, 1985-89, city coun mem, 1980-91; Thomas Co Bd Educ, Thomasville, Ga, prin, 1963-91, trustee, currently; Presby Church, Thomasville, Ga, pastor, 1980-. **Honors/Awds:** Elected to the Hall of Fame, Fort Valley State Col, 1985; Doctor of Law, Faith Col Birmingham, Ala, 1986. **Special Achievements:** First Black City Council Person in Thomasville, GA, 1981-; First Black City Commissioner, 1982; First Black Mayor City of Thomasville, GA, 1985-89; first Black principal at Thomas County Central Middle School and is pastor of Second Presbyterian Church. **Home Addr:** 140 Felix St, PO Box 534, Thomasville, GA 31799, **Home Phone:** (229)226-6207. **Business Addr:** Trustee, Central Middle School, 200 N Pinetree Blvd, Thomasville, GA 31792, **Business Phone:** (229)225-4380.

### WILLIAMS, EARL WEST

Government official, executive director. **Personal:** Born Jul 20, 1928, Montgomery, AL; married Frances Jenkins; children: Earl Jr, Reginald & Eric. **Educ:** Morehouse Col, attended 1947; Ala State Univ, BS, 1950; Cleveland State Univ, attended 1973. **Career:** Cleveland Bd Educ, teacher, 1953-55; Beneficial Finance Co, asst mgr 1956-62; Cleveland City Community Develop, citizen participation adv 1962-64, proj dir 1964-70; Community Rels Bd, exec dir, 1971-; Cleveland Metrop Housing Authority, interim dir & chief exec officer. **Orgs:** Pres, 1986-87, Nat Asn Human Rights Workers; trustee, Kent State Univ OfficeGreater Cleveland Interchurch Coun, Off Sch Monitoring & Community Rels, St James AME Church; Leadership Cleveland, Omega Psi Phi Frat Inc, Beta Rho Boule-Sigma Psi Phi Frat; trustee, Kent State Univ Off. **Honors/Awds:** US Congressional Certificate of Achievement, US Congress, 1982; Distinguish Award, Cleveland, Community Rels Bd, 1986; Outstanding Citizen, Omega Psi Phi Frat, 1986; President's Certificate of Appreciation, Nat Assoc Human Rights Workers 1986. **Home Addr:** 18219 Van Aken Blvd, Shaker Heights, OH 44122, **Home Phone:** (216)921-9031.

### WILLIAMS, DR. EDDIE NATHAN

Research scientist. **Personal:** Born Aug 18, 1932, Memphis, TN; son of Ed and Georgia Lee Barr; married Jearline F Reddick; children: Traci Frink, Edward L & Terence Reddick. **Educ:** Univ Ill, Urbana, BS, 1954; Atlanta Univ, grad study, 1957; Howard Univ, grad study, 1958. **Career:** Atlanta Univ, Atlanta, postgrad study, 1957; Atlanta Daily World Newspaper, Atlanta, reporter, 1957-58; Howard Univ, Wash, DC, postgrad study, 1958; US Senate Comt Foreign Rels, Wash, DC, staff asst, 1959-60; US Dept State, Wash, DC, foreign serv res officer, 1961-68; Univ Chicago, dir ctr policy study, vpres, 1968-72; Chicago Sun Times newspaper, columnist; PBS, McNeil-Lehrer News, commentator; Joint Ctr Polit & Econ Studies, Wash, pres, 1972-04, pres emer, 2004-; Randall Hagner Real Estate Co, agt, currently. **Orgs:** Nat Coalition Black IVIC Participation, Riggs Nat Corp; vice chair, Black Leadership Forum; Coun Foreign Rels, Omega Psi Phi; Sigma Pi Phi; Resource Develop Bd, Univ Ill; Campaign Comm, Ernest N Morial Asthma & Respiratory DisCtr; AAAS; bd dir, Riggs Nat Corp; fel Am Acad Arts & Sci, 1998; Nat Acad Pub Adminrs; pres & chief exec officer, Eddie Williams & Assocs, currently; fel Howard Univ; chmn emer, Nat Coalition Black Civic Participation. **Honors/Awds:** Adam Clayton Powell Award, Cong Black Caucus, 1982; Keynote Address Award, Nat Conf Black Polit Scientists, 1988; Achievement Award, Black Alumni Asn, Univ Ill, 1988; Prize Fellows Award, MacArthur Found, 1988; Washingtonian of the Year Award, Washingtonian Mag, 1991; National Builder Award, Nat Black Caucus State Legislators, 1992; Alumni Hall of Fame, Memphis City Sch, 2000; Lamplighter Award Leadership, BLF, 2001; 100 Most Influential Organization Leaders, Ebony Mag, 2002. **Special Achievements:** Author of numerous newspaper, magazine, journal, and book articles. **Home Addr:** 3126 Ariz Ave NW, Washington, DC 20016. **Business Addr:** President Emeritus, Joint Center for Political and Economic Studies, 805 15th St NW 2nd Fl, Washington, DC 20005, **Business Phone:** (202)789-3500.

### WILLIAMS, DR. EDDIE ROBERT

School administrator, educator. **Personal:** Born Jan 6, 1945, Chicago, IL; son of E R and Anna Maude Jones; married Shirley King; children: Karen Lynn, Craig DeWitt & Evan Jonathan. **Educ:** Ottawa Univ, Ottawa, ON, BA, math, 1966; Columbia Univ, PhD, math, 1970. **Career:** Educator (retired); Northern Ill Univ, assoc prof mathematics, 1970-91, assoc dir, operating budgets, 1978-83, budget & planning, dep dir, 1983, dir, 1983-85, asst vpres acad affairs, Div Finance & Planning, vpres, 1985-96, sr vpres, finance & facil, 1996-2000, exec vpres, Bus & Finance, chief oper, 2000-13, assoc prof, 2013. **Orgs:** Asst pastor, dir, youth activ, S Pk Baptist Church, 1970-, sr pastor, 1997-; Univ Affirmative Action Comt, 1974-; Univ Resource Adv Comn; Presidential CMS Status Minorities; Am Math Soc; treas, Northern Ill Univ, 2009; bd mgr, Northern Ill Proton Treat & Res Ctr. **Home Addr:** 175 Buena Vista, DeKalb, IL 60115, **Home Phone:** (815)756-1752.

### WILLIAMS, EDWARD A.

Chief executive officer, founder (originator), association executive. **Educ:** Univ Md, BS; Harvard Bus Sch, MBA. **Career:** Black Enterprise/Greenwich St Corp Growth Partners LP, chief exec officer & co-founder. **Orgs:** Bd mem, Tama Broadcasting; bd mem, Nat Asn

Investment Co; bd mem, Access.1 Commun Corp; bd mem, Glory Foods; bd mem, Earl G Graves Ltd. **Honors/Awds:** "Black Enterprise," 75 Most Powerful Blacks on Wall Street, 2011. **Business Addr:** Chief Executive Officer, Greenwich Street Corporate Growth Partners L P, 399 Park Ave, New York, NY 10043.

## WILLIAMS, EDWARD ELLIS

Executive, vice president (organization), manager. **Personal:** Born Jun 23, 1938, Hazlehurst, MS; married Sarah Robertson; children: Karen & Edward Jr. **Educ:** Univ Ill, Col Pharm, attended 1963. **Career:** Walgreen, asst mgr, 1964-65, store mgr, 1965-68, dist mgr, 1968-79, dist mgr, 1979-91, regional vpres, 1991-. **Orgs:** Chicago S End Jaycees, 1966; Chicago Pharmacist Asn, 1967; dir events Miss State Traveling Club, 1976. **Honors/Awds:** Outstanding Young Man of the Year, Chicago S End Jaycees, 1966; Special Achiever Chicago, YMCA, 1978; Humanitarian Award, Miss State Traveling Club, 1979. **Home Addr:** 15806 Winding Moss Dr, Houston, TX 77068. **Business Addr:** Regional Vice President, Walgreen Co, 200 Wilmot Rd, Deerfield, IL 60015, **Business Phone:** (847)914-2500.

## WILLIAMS, EDWARD JOSEPH

Banker. **Personal:** Born May 5, 1942, Chicago, IL; son of Joseph and Lillian; married Ana Ortiz; children: Elaine & Paul. **Educ:** Roosevelt Univ, BBA, 1973. **Career:** Mut Home Delivery, Chicago, owner, 1961-63; Harris Trust & Savings Bank, Chicago, sr vpres, exec vpres, 1964-2004; NexGen Capital Partners LLC, sr advisor; Salford Primary Care Trust, commun mgr. **Orgs:** Pres, Harris Bank Found, community reinvestment act officer, 1977-2003; consumer Adv Coun, Wash, 1986-; chmn, Provident Med Ctr, 1986; dir, Chicago Capital Fund; dir, Chapin-May Found, 1988-; dir, Low Income Housing Trust Fund, 1989-; pres, Neighborhood Housing Serv, 1990-; trustee, treas, Adler Planetarium; adv comm chair, Art Inst Chicago; dir, Chicago Botanic Garden; dir, Chicago Coun Urban Affairs, vice chair; dir, Leadership Coun, Metro Open Communities; dir, Neighborhood Housing Servs Chicago, former pres; trustee, Provident Med Ctr, former chmn; trustee, Roosevelt Univ; Nat Bankers Asn; Urban Bankers Forum, Econ Club Chicago; chair, bd mem, Chinese Am Serv League. **Honors/Awds:** Distinguished Alumni Award, Clark Col, Atlanta, 1985; Pioneer Award, Urban Bankers Forum, 1986; Gale Cincotta Neighborhood Partnership Award, NHS. **Special Achievements:** First African American male employee of Harris Bank in 1964. **Home Addr:** 1336 S Plymouth 4W, Chicago, IL 60605. **Business Addr:** Senior Advisor, NexGen Capital Partners LLC, 2 First National Plaza, Chicago, IL 60603, **Business Phone:** (312)845-9055.

## WILLIAMS, DR. EDWARD M.

Oral surgeon. **Personal:** Born Dec 10, 1933, Augusta, GA; married Davide Bradley; children: Brent, Kurt & Scott. **Educ:** Morehouse Col, BS, 1954; Atlanta Univ, MS, 1963; Howard Univ, DDS, 1968. **Career:** Atlanta Pub Sch Sys, teacher, 1958-63; pvt pract oral surgeon, oral surg, maxillofacial surg, currently. **Orgs:** Am Dent Asn; Ga Dent Asn; Am Soc Oral Surg; Ga Soc Oral Surg; Internal Asn Oral Surg; fel Am Dent Soc Anethesiology; Nat Asn Advan Colored People; Am Cancer Soc; YMCA; Alpha Phi Alpha; Beta Kappa Chi. **Honors/Awds:** Award in Anesthesiology, Award in Periodontics, Howard Univ, 1968. **Home Addr:** 3377 Ardley Rd SW, Atlanta, GA 30311, **Home Phone:** (404)696-9675. **Business Addr:** Physician, 75 Piedmont Ave NE Suite 440, Atlanta, GA 30303, **Business Phone:** (404)659-3166.

## WILLIAMS, ELDREDGE M.

Insurance executive, executive. **Educ:** AM&N Col, BBA, 1956; Am Grad Sch Mgt, BBA, 1979. **Career:** Universal Life Ins Co, exec vpres & chief operating officer, 1956-2001. **Home Addr:** 5134 Dycus Cv, Memphis, TN 38116, **Home Phone:** (901)396-2623. **Business Addr:** Executive Vice President, Chief Operating Officer, Universal Life Insurance Co, 480 Linden Ave, Memphis, TN 38126, **Business Phone:** (901)525-3641.

## WILLIAMS, ELIZABETH (BETH WILLIAMS)

President (organization), chief executive officer. **Personal:** daughter of Archiechildren: Kameron Nobles. **Educ:** Brown Univ, BA, polit sci & urban develop, 1985. **Career:** Freedom Electronics, prod control mgr; Raytheon Corp, sub contract adminr; Blue Cross & Blue Shield, purchasing mgr, dir bus diversity, 1994-2003; Roxbury Technol Corp, owner, pres & chief exec officer, 2002-; Roxbury Lighting, pres & chief exec officer, 2016-. **Orgs:** Dir, Associated Industries of Massachusetts. **Honors/Awds:** "Boston Womens Business Journal", Hall of Fame, 2004; "Black Enterprise", Emerging Small Business of the Year, 2007; National Association of Black Professional & Business Women, "Business Woman of the Year"; "The Network Journal: Black Professionals & Small Business Magazine", 25 Influential Black Women in Business, 2009; Urban League of Eastern Ma Presidents Award, 2011; Shining Star Award, WBENC, 2011; Presidents Award, Greater New Eng Minority Develop Coun, 2011; Ernst and Young Social Entrepreneur of the Year, 2011; "Leading Woman", The Girl Scouts of America, The National Association of Black Professional & Business Women. **Business Addr:** President, Roxbury Technology Corp, 75 Sprague St, Hyde Park, MA 02136, **Business Phone:** (617)524-1020.

## WILLIAMS, DR. ELLA O.

Educator. **Personal:** Born Jun 21, 1931, Skippers, VA; daughter of Thomas and Mary Owens; married Charlie; children: Kalimah Matthews & Karl. **Educ:** St Paul's Col, BS, 1952; NY Univ, MA, 1957; Walden Univ, EdD, 1978; Clark Atlanta Univ, DA, 1987. **Career:** Pierce Col, Dept Eng, African Am Lit & Ethnic Humanities, instr, 1972-95; Wallace Community Coll, instr, 1995-96; Univ W Fla, coor, stud teacher, 1996-99; Pensacola Jr Col, instr, commun, 1999-2000; Okaloosa Walton Comm Coll, instr, 2001-. **Orgs:** Delta Sigma Theta Sorority, 1952-; Phi Beta Kappa, 1972-; Wash Hist Soc, 1985-89; AARP, 1985-89; Inst Africa, Hamlin Univ, 1986-87; Links, 1986-. **Home Addr:** 2551 Holley Pl, PO Box 5486, Navarre, FL 32566, **Home Phone:** (850)939-8027. **Business Addr:** Instructor, Okaloosa Walton Community College, 100 Col Blvd E, Niceville, FL 32578-1295, **Business Phone:** (850)678-5111.

## WILLIAMS, REV. ELLIS

Clergy. **Personal:** Born Oct 27, 1931, Raymond, MS; son of Currie and Elise Morrison McDowell; married Priscilla Norman; children: Debra Lucas, Rita Singleton, Claude, Lathan, Glenn & Zelia. **Educ:** Loyola Univ, New Orleans, LA, BA, 1972, MEd, guid & coun, 1974, MCJ, 1981. **Career:** Police lieutenant (retired), associate minister; New Orleans Police Dept, police officer, 1965, fingerprint tech, 1968, polygraphist, 1974, police comdr; Jefferson Voc & Tech Sch, lectr, 1981; Hist Second Baptist Church, New Orleans, La, assoc minister, currently. **Orgs:** Historian Kappa Delta Pi, 1973-74; vice chmn, La Polygraph Bd, 1981-82; La & Int Asn Ident; Freedmen Missionary Baptist Asn La; Nat Baptist Training Union; Sunday Sch Cong; Nat Missionary Baptist Conv; Nat Orgn Black Law Enforcement Exec; Imp Coun, Prince Hall Affil; Eureka Consistory 7 Prince Hall Affil; United Supreme Coun, Prince Hall Affil. **Special Achievements:** Author: From the Dust to Paradise; Out of Condemnation Into Glorification, 2005. **Home Addr:** 648 Aurora Oaks Dr, New Orleans, LA 70131, **Home Phone:** (504)393-9947. **Business Addr:** Associate Minister, Historic Second Baptist Church, 2505 Marengo St, New Orleans, LA 70115, **Business Phone:** (504)899-2107.

## WILLIAMS, ELVIRA FELTON

Health services administrator. **Personal:** Born May 13, 1937, Washington, DC; daughter of Edward P and Ocia A Felton; married Irving C; children: Andrea E, Donna R, Irving C II & Michael V. **Educ:** Howard Univ, BS, 1959; Univ Wis-Madison, MS, 1960; Southeastern Univ, MBPA, 1979. **Career:** Howard Univ, instr, 1960-64; Univ Wis-Milwaukee, asst prof, 1964-67; METCO, Mass State Dept Educ, coordr, 1971-74; Nyakohoja Pri Sch, educ specialist, 1974-77; Mont Co Pub sch, teacher specialist, 1980-86; Md State Dept Educ, proj specialist, 1983-85, dean studs, 1985-87; Adventures Health, Educ & Agr Develop Inc, exec dir, 1981-. **Orgs:** Gr Boston YWCA Comt Admin, 1969-73; US Comt Civil Rights, New Eng Chap, 1972-74; exec comt, Radcliff Col Prog Health Care, 1973-74; Co Exec Spec Proj Task Force, 1977-79; Am Friends Serv Comt, Mid Atlanta, 1979-81; vpres, Exec Comt, Mont Co, Nat Asn Advan Colored People, 1981-85; WETA-CH26 Community Adv Coun, 1983-85; Community Adv Comt, Holy Cross Hosp, 1985-87. **Home Addr:** 6324 Windermere Cir, Rockville, MD 20852, **Home Phone:** (301)530-8155. **Business Addr:** Executive Director, Adventures in Health, Education & Agricultural Development, 6324 Windermere Cir, Rockville, MD 20847, **Business Phone:** (301)530-3697.

## WILLIAMS, ELYNOR A.

Executive, president (organization). **Personal:** Born Oct 27, 1946, Baton Rouge, LA; daughter of Albert Berry and Naomi Theresa. **Educ:** Spelman Col, BA, home econs, 1966; Cornell Univ, MA, commun arts, 1973. **Career:** Eugene Butler Jr-Sr High Sch, home econs teacher, 1966-68; Genl Foods Corp, publicist, package ed & copy ed, 1968-71; Cornell Univ, comt spec educ proj tutor, 1972-73; NC Agr Exten Serv, comm specialist, 1973-77; Western Elec Co, sr pub rels specialist, 1977-83; Hanes Group, Winston-Salem, dir corp affairs, 1983-86; Sara Lee Corp, dir pub affairs, 1986-90, dir corp affairs, vpres, pub responsibility, exec secy employee, 1990-2002, Sara Lee Found, dir, Employee & Pub Responsibility Comt, exec secy bd dirs; Chestnut Pearson & Assocs, pres & managing dir, currently; Chicago Sinfonietta, dir, currently. **Orgs:** Bd dir, Univ NC Greensboro, 1981-91; bd dir, YWCA, 1984-86; adv bd, NC Womens Network, 1985; Nat Tech Adv Comm OICs Am Inc, 1985-92; exec, Comm Nat Womens Econ Alliance, 1985; vpres, publ affairs & comm bd dir Gr Winston-Salem Chamber Com, 1985-86; Bus Policy Rev Coun, 1988-; Women's Inst, 1988-; bd dir, Cosmopolitan Chamber Com, Chicago, IL, 1988-91; bd, Nat Coalition Hundred Black Women, 1991-; Nat Hisp Corp Coun; Nat corp adv bd Nat Orgn Women; corp adv bd, Nat Womens Polit Caucus; League Women Voters; Int Asn Bus Comm; Pub Rels Soc Am; Nat Asn Female Execs; founding bd mem & bd dir, Exec Leadership Coun; bd dir, Pub Responsibility Comt; founding bd mem & exec leadership coun, Spelman Col Corp Womens Roundtable; bd dir, Am Cancer Soc Found; bd mem, C's Memorial Hosp; Nat Coalition 100 Black Women Inc; Int Women's Forum; press coun, Cornell Univ Women; bd mem, Chicago Sinfonetta. **Special Achievements:** Founder of the Frontrunner Awards at Sara Lee; worked with National Women's Economic Alliance, National Coalition of 100 Black Women, Inc., International Women's Forum, and President's Council of Cornell University Women. **Home Addr:** 222 E Chestnut St Apt 9B, Chicago, IL 60611-2351, **Home Phone:** (312)587-7443. **Business Addr:** President, Managing Director, Chestnut Pearson & Associates, 222 E Chestnut St, Chicago, IL 60611, **Business Phone:** (312)587-3247.

## WILLIAMS, ERIC C.

Executive, consultant, basketball player. **Personal:** Born Jul 17, 1972, Newark, NJ; son of Clarence (deceased) and Patricia; children: Raquiesh; married Jennifer. **Educ:** Vincennes Univ, assoc degree, social sci, 1993; Providence Col, BS, western europ studies, 1995. **Career:** Basketball player (retired), executive, consultant; Boston Celtics, forward, 1995-97, 1999-2003; Denver Nuggets, 1997-99; Cleveland Cavaliers, 2003-04; NJ Nets, 2004; Toronto Raptors, 2004-06; San Antonio Spurs, 2006-07; Charlotte Bobcats, 2007; FarmOn! Found, NPO, 2010; Meridian Star Merchant Serv, spec consult, 2011-; GMI Holdings LLC, spec consult, 2012-. **Orgs:** BelieveMeEric Williams Found, 2003. **Special Achievements:** Film appearance: The Caribbean Heist, 2013. **Business Addr:** Special Consultant, GMI Holdings LLC, 21 Pond Hill Rd, Craryville, NY 12521, **Business Phone:** (518)325-9437.

## WILLIAMS, ERRICK LYNNE. See WILLIAMS, RICKY, JR.

## WILLIAMS, ETHEL LANGLEY

Librarian. **Personal:** Born Baltimore, MD; daughter of William H and Carrie A; married Louis J; children: Carole J Jones. **Educ:** Howard Univ, AB, 1930; Columbia Univ NYC, BS, 1933; Howard Univ, MA, 1950. **Career:** Bd Pub Welfare Wash DC, caseworker, 1933-35; Libr Congress, process filer & order searcher, 1936-40; Moorland Spingarn Collection, supvr project, 271 & 328, works progress admin, 1939; Howard Univ, reference librarian cataloger, 1941-47; Howard Univ Sch Religion Libr, librn, 1946-75; Writings, A Catalogue Books Moorland Found 1939, Af-Am Newspaper, 1945-46, Negro History Bulletin 110-16, 1945, Journal Negro Educ, 1945-46, Handbook Instr Use Sch Rel Libr, 1955, Revised, 1968; Biographical Dir Negro Ministers, Editor, 1965, 1970, 1975. **Orgs:** Co editor, Af-Am Rel Studies A Comprehensive Bibliography Locations Am Libraries, 1970, Howard Univ Bibliography & Af & Af-Am Religious Studies, 1977. **Special Achievements:** Author, Afro-American Religious Studies, Biographical Directory of Negro Ministers, Howard University Bibliography of African and Afro American Religious Studies: With Locations in American Libraries; Editor of several books. **Home Addr:** 1625 Primrose Rd NW, Washington, DC 20012, **Home Phone:** (202)723-6010.

## WILLIAMS, EUGENE, III (GENE WILLIAMS)

Football player. **Personal:** Born Oct 14, 1968, Blair, NE; married Melissa Denise; children: Maya Samantha. **Educ:** Iowa State Univ. **Career:** Football player (retired); Miami Dolphins, guard, 1991-92; Cleveland Browns, right tackle, 1993-94; Atlanta Falcons, guard, 1995-99, right guard, 1997-99. **Orgs:** Big Bros & Big Sisters. **Honors/Awds:** Doug Dieken Humanitarian Award, Cleveland Browns Touchdown Club, 1994.

## WILLIAMS, DR. EUGENE, SR.

Consultant, writer, educator. **Personal:** Born Nov 23, 1942, Orange, VA; son of Victor V Sr and Bertha M; married Mary H Johnson; married Helen M Barbary; children: Eugene Jr. **Educ:** St Paul's Col, BS, 1964; Univ Va, MS, admin & supv, 1968; Univ Miami, EdD, curric & Instr, 1972. **Career:** Jackson P Burley High Sch, Charlottesville, Va, eng teacher, 1964-72; Howard Univ, coordr sec educ, 1972-78; Lawrence Johnson & Assoc Inc, sr res scientist & curric designer, 1978-80; DC Pub Sch Systs, supvr, 1980-83, dir test imrpove, 1989-99; Soujourner Douglass Col, dean, 1981-82; Dunbar High Sch, Wash, DC, asst prin, 1983-89; Univ DC, voc trng prog coord; Prince George's County sch, eng teacher; Annapolis Road Acad Alternative High Sch, eng teacher, currently; Acad Resources Unlimited Inc, pres & founder, currently; Southeastern Univ, prof; Author: Getting the Job You Want with the Av Portfolio: A Practical Guide for Job Hunters & Career Changers, 1981; Keys to Quick Writing Skills:Sentence Combining & Text Reconstruction, 1982; Blueprint for Educ Chg: Improving Reasoning, Literacies & Sci Achievement with Coop Learning, 1992; It's A Reading Thing: Help Your Child Understand: A Parent's Guide to Improving Students' Verbal Performance on Standardized Exam Like the PSAT & SAT, 1992; Grounded In The Word: A Guide to Mastering Standardized Test Vocab & Bibl Comprehension, 1997; The Secret: His Word Impacting Our Lives, 2007; "Obama: Words Cross & Across", 2011; "Words Cross & Across: Word Search on Dr. Martin Luther King Jr", 2011; "Words Cross & Across: Word Search on Michelle Obama", 2013; "Keys to Quick Vocabulary", 2013; "Words Cross & Across Word Search on LeBron James", 2015; Invention: The Av Portfolio, 1979. **Orgs:** Nat Alliance Black Sch Educr; Alpha Phi Alpha. **Honors/Awds:** Compatriot in Education Award, Kappa Delta Pi, 1976. **Home Addr:** 9498 Nottingham Dr, Upper Marlboro, MD 20772, **Home Phone:** (301)599-8111. **Business Addr:** English Teacher, Annapolis Road Academy Alternative High School, 5150 Annapolis Rd, Bladensburg, MD 20710, **Business Phone:** (301)209-3580.

## WILLIAMS, DR. EUPHEMIA GOODLOW

Educator. **Personal:** Born Oct 17, 1938, Bagwell, TX; daughter of Blanche M Pouge Goodlow and Otis J Goodlow; married James A; children: Caren, Christopher, Curt & Catherine. **Educ:** Univ Okla, Norman, OK, BS, 1961; Univ Colo, Boulder, CO, MS, 1973, PhD, 1981. **Career:** Professor (retired), professor emeritus; Okla City-Co Health, Okla City, Okla, pub health nurse, 1966-70; Univ Colo, Boulder, Colo, campus nurse, 1973-74, Denver, Colo, asst prof, instr, 1974-81; Cameron Univ, Lawton, Okla, assoc prof & chair, nursing, 1981-82; Metrop St Col, Denver, Colo, dept chair & prof, assoc prof-nursing, 1982-88; Southwest Mo St Univ, Springfield, Mo, prof & depthead, nursing, 1988-; Colo State Univ, acad advisor, prof emer. **Orgs:** Am Nurses Asn; Am Pub Health Asn; fac counr, Alpha Kappa Chap, Sigma Theta Tau, Int Hon Soc Nursing, 1976-78; Human Rights Comn, Colo Nurses Asn, 1984-88; chairperson, Coun Deans & dir Nursing Progs Colo, 1986-87; Leadership Springfield, Springfield Chamber Com, 1989-90. **Home Addr:** 961 15th St, Springfield, MO 80302, **Home Phone:** (303)449-7134.

## WILLIAMS, DR. EVERETT BELVIN

Association executive, teacher, writer. **Personal:** Born Oct 26, 1932, Hennessey, OK; married Marianne Hansson; children: Karin Cecelia & Barbro Susanne. **Educ:** Denver Univ, BA, 1955; Columbia Univ, MA, 1957, PhD, 1962, MS, 1970. **Career:** Var NY & NJ VA Hosps, trainee, 1957-60; Hunter Col, lectr, counsr, 1960-62; Columbia Univ, Teachers Col, res assoc, 1961-62, counsr, 1963-64, dir, 1964-71, assoc prof, 1970-71, assoc dean, 1970-71, adj prof, 1971-75, vpres opers, 1972-75, vpres col prog, 1975-77; Barnard Col, lectr, 1962-63; Educ Testing Serv, sr vpres prog areas, 1982; Turrell Fund, exec dir, 1989; Williams & Weisbrodt, partner/pvt consult. **Orgs:** Cert Psychologist, NY, 1964; res fel Conf Learning & Educ Process, 1965; bd dir, Lisle Fel, 1964-67; bd trustee, Dalton Schs, 1967-74; NY State Comn C, 1971-74; Harvard Bd Overseers, 1973-74; dir, Index Fund Am Inc, 1974; Am Psychol Asn, AAAS, NY State Psychol Asn, Philos Sci Asn, Am Acad Polit & Soc Sci, Asn Educ Data Sys, Asn Comput Mach, Asn Symbolic Logic, Phi Delta Kappa, Kappa Delta Pi; adv com, Response NYSPA Social Issues; Inst Elec & Electronic Engrs; srconsult, Belmar Comput Serv Inc; chmn Asn Black Psychol; field assess mentofficer, field selection officer, Peace Corps; field selection officer, Teachers Corps; consult, psy chol, SEEK Prog; consult, Metro Ment Health Clin; consult, Fresh Air Fund; consult, Nat Ur League; chmn, Rev Com Testing Minorities; Inter coll Knights; Nat Sci Found; Omicron Delta Kappa; Psi Chi; Phi Beta Kappa; Dan forth fel Dan forth Teaching; fel Sigma Xi. **Special Achievements:** Author: Introduction to Psychology, 1963, Deductive Reasoning in Schizophrenia, 1964, Asn Between Smoking & Accidents, 1966, Driving & Connotative Meanings 1970. **Home Addr:** 12 S Mountain Ave 29, Montclair, NJ 07042-1711.

### WILLIAMS, DR. FELTON CARL
School administrator, president (organization). **Personal:** Born Mar 30, 1946, Los Angeles, CA; son of Abraham and Lula M; married Mary Etta Baldwin; children: Sonia Yvette & Felton Jr. **Educ:** Los Angeles Harbor Community Col, AA, 1970; Calif State Univ, Long Beach, BA, bus admin, 1972, MBA, bus admin, 1975; Claremont Grad Sch, PhD, educ admin, 1985. **Career:** Calif State Univ, Long Beach, jr staff analyst, 1972-73, admin asst, 1972-73, supvr, 1974-79; Learning Ctr Long Beach State, mgr; Calif State Univ, Dominguez Hills, affirmative action officer, asst to pres, 1985-86, assoc dir; Drew Physicians prog USC, consult; Learning Assistance Ctr, dir stud progs, 1991-; Scaramento City Col, dean coun serv, 1993-96; Long Beach City Col, dean, Sch Bus Trade & Indust, 1997-98, Sch Bus & Social Sci, dean, 1996-2007. **Orgs:** Pres, San Pedtro-Wilmington Nat Asn Advan Colored People, 1976-; pres, Region I Nat Asn Advan Colored People, 1979-80; bd mem, Selective Serv Syst, Region IV, 1981, Employee Readiness Support Ctr, 1986-87; CSULB Alumni Bd, 1991; Alpha Kappa Alpha Sorority Inc, 2001; Long Beach Unified Sch Dist, bd pres, 2004-. **Home Addr:** 2126 Daisy Ave, Long Beach, CA 90806, **Home Phone:** (213)591-4968. **Business Addr:** Board President, Long Beach Unified School District, 1515 Hughes Way, Long Beach, CA 90810, **Business Phone:** (562)997-8000.

### WILLIAMS, FITZROY E.
Computer executive, president (organization). **Personal:** Born Nov 6, 1953, St. James; son of Lester and Lurena; married Yvonne; children: Jhamel & Joshua. **Educ:** Col Arts Sci & Technol, asst electronic engineering, 1977. **Career:** Jamaica Int Telecommunication, sr tech, 1972-81; Sci Atlanta, sr engr, 1982-95; Dem Nat Conv, dir technol, 1995-96; Tri-Millennium Technologies, pres, 1996-. **Home Addr:** 1242 Overview Dr, Lawrenceville, GA 30044-6272, **Home Phone:** (770)676-0817. **Business Addr:** President, Tri-Millennium Technologies Inc, 225 W Washington St Suite 2200, Chicago, IL 60606.

### WILLIAMS, FRANK J.
President (organization), real estate agent, educator. **Personal:** Born Aug 29, 1938, AR; son of Ada Frye Jones and Seldon; married Joanne; children: Michael, Craig, Renee & Jannie. **Educ:** Bogan Jr Col; Kennedy-King Col; Real Est Inst Cent YMCA Community Col; cert, real estate brokerage mgr-CRB; cert, residential specialist-CRS. **Career:** US Post Off, mail carrier, 1961-66; Midwest Realty, salesman, 1966-68, sales mgr, 1968-70; Lic real estate broker, 1969-; EW Realty Co, prof, 1970-71; F J Williams Realty Co, founder, pres, 1971-, dir; Realtors Real Estate Sch, instr, currently; Univ Chicago, instr. **Orgs:** Pres, Nat Asn Real Estate Brokers; Lic Real Estate Lic Law Off Liaison Comn; Nat Asn Realtors-Area Prop; Mgmt Broker Va Admin; instr, Real Est Sales & Brokerage Real Est Inst Cent YMCA Community Col; chmn, Housing Comn, Nat Asn Advan Colored People, pres, Chicago Southside Br, 1978-85; asst chmn, Adv Comn Utilization Subsidies Increase Black Adoptions; chmn, SE Sect Luth Athletic Asn; Urban Homestead Coalition; Chicago Real Est Bd Admis Comn; Timothy Luth Church; Community Develop Adv Comt; chmn, Chicago Real Est Bd's Equal Opportunity Comn; chmn, New Horizons Task Force Gov James R Thompson; Recreanal Task Force Gov James R Thompson; adv bd, Black Black Love; bd mem, Black Hist Chicago Dusable Ft Dearborn Hist Comn Inc; Cancer Prev Soc; secy, Chicago Bd Realtors, 1987; bd mem, Community Investment Corp, 1988; bd mem, Ada S McKinley Serv, 1989; bd mem, Neighborhood Housing Serv, 1989; pres elect, Chicago Asn Realtor, 1989-90; Community Develop Adv Comt; Real Estate Serv Adv Coun; Ill Asn realtors; Affordable Housing Task Force. **Honors/Awds:** Education Development Award, Dearborn Real Estate Bd; Education Certificate of Appreciation, Phi Beta Lambda; Award of Achievement, Calif Asn Real Estate Brokers Inc; Black Businessman of the Month Award, Chicago South End Jaycees; Award of Recoginition, Chicago Real Est Bd, 1973; Elmore Baker Award, Dearborn Real Est Bd; Appreciation Award, Realtors Real Estate Sch; Outstanding Service Award, Nat Caucus & Ctr Black Aged Inc. **Special Achievements:** First Distinguished Member Award for Community Service, Ill Asn, 1991. **Home Addr:** 9428 S Damen Ave, Chicago, IL 60620. **Business Addr:** Real Estate Broker-Appraiser, F J Williams Realty, 7825 S Wern Ave, Chicago, IL 60620, **Business Phone:** (773)737-5600.

### WILLIAMS, FRANK JAMES
Artist, educator. **Personal:** Born Feb 17, 1959, Chicago, IL; son of Arthur Green and Barbara J; married Rebecca P Rubalcava; children: Rachel Elizabeth & Sarah Jean. **Educ:** Univ Okla, Norman, OK, BFA, painting & drawing, printmaking & design, 1984; Univ Calif, Los Angeles, CA, MFA, painting & drawing, 1988; Skowhegan Sch Art, ME, 1989. **Career:** Grad Opportunity fel, 1985; Univ Calif Los Angeles, teaching assoc, 1987-88; Skowhegan Art fel, Skowhegan Sch Painting & Sculpt, 1989; Daniel Weinberg Gallery, preparator, 1988-89; St Monica Col, art instr, 1990-91; Los Angeles Co Mus Arts, preparator, 1992; Bishop Mora Salesian High Sch, art chairperson & art teacher, 1992-94; Calif Afro-Am Mus, artist residence, 1995; Barnsdall Art Ctr, art instr, 1997; Univ Calif Los Angeles Exten, art instr, 1998; Riverside Community Col, instr, 2003; Los Angeles Trade Tech, instr, 2003-; Southwest Col, adj fac, 2008. **Home Addr:** 1709 Monte Vista St, Pasadena, CA 91106, **Home Phone:** (626)844-0142.

### WILLIAMS, FRED
Basketball coach, mayor. **Personal:** Born Feb 8, 1957, Lumberton, MS. **Educ:** Boise State Univ, attended 1979. **Career:** USCU, asst coach, 1983-91, head coach, 1995-97; Utah Starzz, scout, head coach, 1999-2001; Charlotte Sting, asst coach, 2003-04; San Diego Siege, head coach; City Kountze, mayor; Atlanta Dream, asst coach, 2009-12; Atlanta Dream, head coach & gen mgr; Seattle SuperSonics, scout; Sacramento Kings, scout; Utah Jazz, scout; Wash Mystics, scout. **Business Addr:** Assistant Coach, Atlanta Dream, 83 Walton St NW Suite 500, Atlanta, GA 30303, **Business Phone:** (404)604-2626.

### WILLIAMS, GAIL (GAIL CARR-WILLIAMS)
Association executive, lawyer, college administrator. **Personal:** married David Williams II; children: Erika, David III, Samantha & Nicholas. **Educ:** Univ Mich, BA, polit sci, 1979; Univ Detroit Col Law, JD, 1982. **Career:** Vanderbilt Univ, Community, Neighborhood & Govt Rels, assoc dir community engagement, 2001-. **Orgs:** Bd trustee & pres, Univ Sch Nashville; Metro Transit Authority, Bd Mem & Chair; Frist Ctr, Bd Mem; bd mem, Women's Fund Adv; Young Women Christian Asn, bd mem; Tenn Performing Arts Ctr, bd mem; Metrop Transit Authority; Our Kids Ctr; Arc Davidson County; Ladies' Hermitage Asn; Community IMPACT Nashville & Bd Prof Responsibility Supreme Ct Tenn. **Home Addr:** , Nashville. **Business Addr:** Vanderbilt University, 2007 Terrace Pl, Nashville, TN 37203, **Business Phone:** (615)343-0700.

### WILLIAMS, GARY C.
Attorney general (U.S. federal government), educator. **Personal:** Born Jan 7, 1952, Santa Monica, CA; son of James and Eva; married Melanie Reeves; children: Jennifer & Sara. **Educ:** Univ Calif, Los Angeles, BA, 1973; Stanford Law Sch, JD, 1976. **Career:** Calif Agr Labor Rel Brd, staff coun, 1976-79, staff atty; Am Civil Liberties Union Found Southern Calif, staff atty, 1979-85, asst legal dir, 1985-87; Loyola Univ Sch Law, vis prof, 1987-1989; Johnnie L. Cochran Jr, Civil Rights, prof law; 1989-2010, chair, 2010-. **Orgs:** Bd dir, Southern Christian Leadership Conf Los Angeles; bd dir, ACLU Southern Calif; chmn, Mt Hebron Baptist Church; Stanford Law Sch bd vpres; pres, bd dir Am Civil Liberties Union Southern Calif; prog dir, Nat Inst Trial Advocacy; pres, bd dir, Big Homies Found; mem, bd dir, Los Angeles Child Guid Clin; mem, Anti Discrimination Task Force Calif Dept Ins; mem, bd visitors, Stanford Law Sch, 1987-93. **Business Addr:** Professor of Law, Loyola University School of Law, 919 Albany St Burns 306, Los Angeles, CA 90015-1211, **Business Phone:** (213)736-1090.

### WILLIAMS, GAYLE TERESE TAYLOR
Journalist. **Personal:** Born Apr 5, 1964, Bronx, NY; daughter of Arthur James and Mararuth; married Terry Desmond; children: 2. **Educ:** Fordham Univ, Bronx, NY, BA, 1984; Columbia Univ, New York, NY, MSJ, 1986. **Career:** Newsday, Long Island, NY, reporter intern, 1984; New York Newsday, New York, NY, ed asst, 1984-85; New Haven Regist, New Haven, Conn, reporter, intern, 1985; Worcester Telegram & Gazette, Worcester, Mass, reporter, 1986-89; New Haven Regist, New Haven, Conn, reporter, 1990-91; Gannett Suburban Newspapers, reporter, 1991-94, reader serv ed, 1994-96; United Way Westchester & Putnam, vpres commun, 1996-99; J News, asst ed, 1999-03, asst Life & Style ed, 2003-. **Orgs:** Nat Asn Black Journalists, 1986-; bd mem, Conn Asn Black Journalists, 1990-91; Westchester Black Journalists Asn, pres, 1991; Westchester Black Journalists Asn, vpres, 1992-96; YWCA White Plains, 1996-. **Honors/Awds:** Volunteer Award, Bentley Gardens Nursing Home, 1990; Reporting Award, "Best of Gannett," 1992; Gannett Employee Merit, 1996; Several "Mighty Pen" Awards, Gannett Suburban Newspapers, 1994-96; Volunteer awards, YWCA White Plains, 1997-03. **Home Addr:** 333 Hillside Ave, White Plains, NY 10603-2807, **Home Phone:** (914)686-5224. **Business Addr:** Assistant Life & Style Editor, The Journal News, 1 Gannett Dr, White Plains, NY 10604, **Business Phone:** (914)694-5011.

### WILLIAMS, GENE. See WILLIAMS, EUGENE, III.

### WILLIAMS, GENEVA J.
Association executive, executive. **Personal:** Born Neptune, NJ; daughter of Ermon and Blanche Jones; married Otha; children: Monique, Otha & Devon. **Educ:** Morgan State Univ, Baltimore, MD, BA, Eng & speech, 1970; Bryn Mawr Col, MSW, community orgn, pub policy, 1973; Wayne State Univ, PhD, educ leadership, 2007; Harvard Bus Sch, attended. **Career:** Gov's Justice Comn, staff, 1973; United Community Serv Metrop Detroit, pres & chief exec officer, 1976-95; United Way Community Serv, chief operating officer & exec vpres, 1995-2001; City Connect Detroit, founding pres & chief exec officer, 2001-11; New Season Consults & Collaborators LLC, chief exec officer & co-founder, 2011-; United Way Am's Acad Volunteerism, fac; Detroit Workforce Develop, vice-chair; Pub Sch Academies Detroit, staff; Mich univ, guest lectr & adj fac. **Orgs:** Greater Detroit Vol Leadership Coalition, mbr; chair, United Way AmC & Families Nat Roundtable; Annie Casey-Harvard Fel Prog; chair, Detroit Compact Stakeholders Coun, 1987-95; Nat Asn Black Social Workers; co-founder & pres, Black Family Develop; chair & vice-chair, Western Mich Bd Trustees; Detroit Sch Bd; bd trustee, Music Hall; bd trustee, New Detroit inc; bd trustee, Detroit Econ Growth Corp; bd trustee, First Independence Bank; bd trustee, Detroit Pub Tv; consult, Kresge Found; chief exec officer, Detroit 9090. **Honors/Awds:** Heritage Award, Ford Motor Co; Dynamic Women Award, Woman's Econ Club; Women Achievement Award, Anti-Defamation League; Community Serv Award, Mich Bus & Prof Asn; "From Whence We Came" Award, All state Insurance Co;"People Helping People" Award, Traveler's Aid Soc; Silver Cup Award, Mich First Lady Michelle Engler; "Winning Ways" Award, Wayne County; Award Excellence, United Way Am. **Special Achievements:** One of Detroit's 100 Most Influential Women, Crain's Detroit Business; Michigan chronicle as one of the Most Influential Black Women in Metropolitan Detroit; First Female, President & CEO of United Community Services of Metropolitan Detroit (UCS). **Home Addr:** 19275 Burlington Dr, Detroit, MI 48203-1451. **Business Addr:** Chief Executive Officer, Co-Founder, New Season Consultants & Collaborators LLC, 8162 E Jefferson Suite 11A, Detroit, MI 48214, **Business Phone:** (313)550-6164.

### WILLIAMS, GEORGE
Athletic coach. **Personal:** married Olivia Hardy; children: Crystal Harrell. **Educ:** St Augustines Col, grad, 1965. **Career:** World Outdoor Championships, Seville, Spain, 1992-93; Olympic Games, asst coach, 1996; St Augustine's Col, dir alumni affairs, admis counr, dir stud activ, 1968, athletic dir, 1996-, mens head coach, 1999-; US Mens Olympic team, Athens, Greece, track & field coach, 2004. **Orgs:** Cent Intercollegiate Athletic Asn Hall Fame; Nc Sports Hall Fame; Fla Track & Field Hall Fame; St Augustine's Univ Athletic Hall Fame; Booker T. Wash High Sch Hall Fame; U.S. Track & Field & Cross Country Coaches Asn Hall Fame. **Honors/Awds:** The 90 Coach of the Year honor; The Order of the Long Leaf Pine, 1996 & 2004; CIAA indoor track and field coach of the year, 2005-06; CIAA Men's Cross Country Coach of the Year Award, 2006; Bighouse Gaines Unsung Hero Award, Winston-Salem State Univ Alumni Asn, 2008; Honoree, Booker T. Wash Alumni Asn, 2009; Lifetime Achievement Award, Raleigh Sports Coun, 2012; Raleigh Hall of Fame, inducted, 2013; National Outdoor and Indoor Mens Coach of the Year Award, Nat Col Athletic Asn, 2013, 2014, 2015 & 2016; Outdoor Mens Coach of the Year, US Track & Field & Cross Country Coaches Asn; Athletic Director of the Year, Cent Intercollegiate Athletic Asn, 2014. **Special Achievements:** Selected 13th among the CIAA 100 Greatest Athletes and Coaches during the year of the conference's 100th anniversary. **Business Addr:** Athletic Director, St Augustine College, 1315 Oakwood Ave, Raleigh, NC 27610, **Business Phone:** (919)516-4174.

### WILLIAMS, GEORGE L., SR.
Manager, teacher, school principal. **Personal:** Born Aug 6, 1929, Florence, SC; married Jean McKiever; children: Sandra, George Jr, Karen & Charles. **Educ:** SC State Col, BA, pre-law maj, 1953, MS, educ & pub sch admin, 1961; Cath Univ, attended. **Career:** School principal (retired); Pilgrim Ins, dist mgr, 1953-55; Pub Schs Horry County Chestnut High Sch, govt & econ teacher, 1956; Whittemore High Sch, govt & econ teacher, 1960; Conway High Sch, hist & geog teacher, 1968, asst prin, 1969, vice prin; Coastal Carolina Col, eve prof, 1969-74, minority stud rels dir, 1986-91; N Myrtle Beach High Sch, prin, 1974-86. **Orgs:** Nat Asn Sec Sch Principals; State Asn Sec Sch Principals; Horry County Asn Sch Admin, Omega Fraternity Inc; adv deleg, Nat Stud Coun Conv, 1965; pres, Horry County Asn Sch Admin, 1974; deleg, Nat Educ Conv, 1974 & 1975; pres, Horry County Educ Asn, 1975; chmn bd trustees, Horry Georgetown Tech Col, 1977-84; chmn, Conway Housing Authority, 1979; discussion chmn, Nat Asn Sec Sch Principals, 1982; app by Pres Ronald Reagan Local Selective Serv Bd; lic dir, McKievers Funeral Home Inc; bd trustees, First Citizen Bank; bd trustees, Conway Hosp Inc; bd trustees, Coastal Carolina Univ, 2000-03. **Honors/Awds:** Omega Man of the Year, Beta Tau Chap, 1975; Laverne H Creel Lifetime Achievement Award, Conway Area Chamber Com, 1992. **Special Achievements:** First African-American teacher; Only African-American high school principal in Horry County. **Home Addr:** 1803 Magnolia St, Conway, SC 29526, **Home Phone:** (803)248-2834. **Business Addr:** Licensed Director, McKiever Funeral Home Inc, 1408 Racepath Ave, Conway, SC 29526, **Business Phone:** (843)248-2706.

### WILLIAMS, GEORGE R.
Association executive, executive, writer. **Personal:** Born Apr 13, 1962, Ft. Riley, KS; son of John and Yuson; married Trudy; children: Timothy, Jeremy, Geordy & Sydney. **Educ:** Kans State Univ, AS, 1983, BS, comput sci, 1984; Friends Univ, MS, marriage & family ther, 2001; Kans State Univ, PhD, 2013. **Career:** Boeing Co, sr specialist info syst, 1986-98; Urban Youth Leadership, pres, 2000-01; Nat Ctr Fathering, exec dir, 1998-2007; Kauffman Scholars Inc, Mid-Am Head Start, Kans City Community Ctr, consult & dir, 2007-11; Kans Dept Social & Rehab Serv, dir addiction & prev serv, 2011-12; Kans Dept C & Families, secy, spec asst, 2012-; Am Independent Dist 79 Calif State Assembly, Assembly cand, 2014-. **Orgs:** Bd mem, Victory Temple Christian Life Ctr, 1998-02; Am Asn Marriage & Family Ther, 1999-02; Watch Dogs Across Am, 2001; Psi Chi, 2001; consult, dir Mid-Am Head Star |Kans City Community Ctr|Kauffman Scholars Inc, 2007-11; dir addiction & prev serv, Kans Dept Social & Rehab Serv, 2011-12; lifetime mem, Nat Hon Soc Psychol; Nat Coun Family Rels; Am Asn Marriage & Family Therapist. **Special Achievements:** Author: Quenching The Father-Thirst Curriculum, 2000; READ (Reconnecting Education and Dads) to Kids Curriculum, 2001; Developing A Dad Curriculum, 2002. **Home Addr:** 7617 Walmer St, Overland Park, KS 66204, **Home Phone:** (913)381-5659. **Business Addr:** Special Assistant, Kansas Department for Children & Families, 500 SW Van Buren St, Topeka, KS 66603, **Business Phone:** (785)296-2502.

### WILLIAMS, GEORGE ROGER, III
Football player. **Personal:** Born Dec 8, 1975, Roseboro, NC. **Educ:** NC State Univ. **Career:** Football player (retired); New York Giants, defensive tackle, 1998-2000. **Honors/Awds:** Rookie of the Year, 1998.

### WILLIAMS, GEORGE W., III
Educator. **Personal:** Born Dec 27, 1946, Chattanooga, TN; married A Virginia Davis; children: Darius. **Educ:** Lane Col, Jackson, TN, BS, 1968. **Career:** Beloit Mem High Sch Beloit, WI, math teacher, 1968-73, vpres, 1971; Rock Valley United Teachers, bd dir, 1972-73; Beloit Educ Asn, pres, 1973; Wis Educ Asn Coun, organizer, 1973-. **Orgs:** Wis Coun Math Teachers, 1968-73; del to rep assembly, Wis Educ Asn, 1968-74; Off Black Caucus, 1971-73; del, Nat Educ Asn Conv, 1971-73; del & chmn, Resolutions Comt, 1971-73; bd dir, Beloit Teen Ctr, 1971-73; Greater Beloit Kiwanis Club; Alpha Phi Alpha; bd dir, Black Resource Personnel; chmn, Martin Luther King Scholar Fund. **Honors/Awds:** Beloit Corp Scholarship Award, 1972; Outstanding Teacher of Beloit, 1972. **Home Addr:** 10455 W Goodrich Ave, PO Box 12868, Milwaukee, WI 53224-2654, **Home Phone:** (414)355-1508. **Business Addr:** Organizer, Wisconsin Education Association Council, 10201 W Lincoln Ave, West Allis, WI 53227.

### WILLIAMS, GEORGIANNA M.
Educator. **Personal:** Born Sep 23, 1938, Kansas City, KS; daughter of Walter George Carter Sr and Marguerite Buford Carter; married Wilbert B Sr; children: Candace R Cheatem & W Ben II. **Educ:** Univ Mo, Kans City, KS, BA, 1972, MPA, 1973; Ford Fel Prog, MPA, 1973; Drake Univ, educ admin, 1986; Iowa State Univ, Danforth Prog, 1992. **Career:** Kansas City, Mo Sch Dist, lang develop specialist, 1972-77; Des Moines Sch Dist, 20th century reading lab specialist, 1977-81, reading teacher, 1981-86, gifted/talented consult, 1986-; Univ Iowa Gifted Educ, Connie Belin fel, 1982; Drake Univ, Des Moines, IA, instr, 1987-89. **Orgs:** Bd dir, Young Women's Resource Ctr, 1985-; Young Women's Resource, 1985-90; Int Reading Asn; Iowa Women Educ Leadership, 1987-; Alpha Kappa Alpha; Drake Univ Grad Adv Coun; Asn Supv & Curric Develop, Iowa Women Educ Leadership, Nat Asn Gifted C, Iowa Talented & Gifted Asn, Des Moines Talented & Gifted Coun, Des Moines Pub Schs Staff Develop Adv Coun, Prof Growth Adv Comn, Nat Alliance Black Sch Educrs; Houghton Mifflin Teacher Adv Coun, 1989-; Phi Delta Kappa, 1989-; State Hist Soc Iowa, 1990-; bd dir, Edco Credit Union, 1992-; Delta Kappa Gamma Soc Int, 1992-; Nat Mid Sch Asn, 1991-; Phi Lambda Theta Hon Fraternity; Phi Theta Kappa Hon Fraternity. **Home Addr:** 4809 80th Pl, Des Moines, IA 50322-7344, **Home Phone:** (515)278-0756. **Business**

**Addr:** Consultant, Des Moines Independent School District, 1800 Grand Ave, Des Moines, IA 50307.

### WILLIAMS, GERALD
Football player, educator, football coach. **Personal:** Born Sep 8, 1963, Waycross, GA. **Educ:** Auburn Univ; Duquesne Univ, elem educ. **Career:** Football player (retired), teacher; Am football, defensive lineman; Pittsburgh Steelers, nose tackle, 1986-94; Carolina Panthers, 1995-97; Green Bay Packers, defensive end, 1997; Div II Catawba Indians, head coach, 2009; First Assembly Christian Sch, hist teacher.

### WILLIAMS, GERALD FLOYD
Baseball player. **Personal:** Born Aug 10, 1966, New Orleans, LA. **Educ:** Grambling State Univ, Grambling, La. **Career:** Baseball player (retired); New York Yankees, outfielder, 1992-96 & 2001-02; Milwaukee Brewers, 1996-97; Atlanta Braves, 1998-99; Tampa Bay Devil Rays, 2000-01; Florida Marlins, 2003; New York Mets, 2004-05.

### WILLIAMS, GREGORY HOWARD
Educator, school administrator. **Personal:** Born Nov 12, 1943, Muncie, IN; son of James Anthony and Mary; married Sara Catherine Whitney; children: Natalia Dora, Zachary Benjamin, Carlos Gregory & Anthony Bladimir. **Educ:** Ball State Univ, BA, social sci & educ, 1966, DHD, 1999; Univ Md, MA, polit sci & govt, 1969; George Washington Univ, JD, 1971, MPhil, polit sci, 1977, PhD, polit sci, 1982; Calif Western Sch Law, LLD, 1997; Col Wooster, DHD, 2000; NY Law Sch, LLD, 2009; Skidware Col, DL, 2010, Mercy Col, MBA, finance, 2014. **Career:** Del Co, Ind, dep sheriff, 1963-66; George Mason Jr-Sr High Sch, 1966-70; US Senate, legal aide, 1971-73; George Wash Univ, univ adminr, dir exptl progs, coordr, 1973-77, lectr, 1974-77; Univ Ia, assoc dean law prof, 1977-90, prof law, 1977-93, assoc vice-pres acad affairs, 1991-93; Durham Univ, vis prof, 1985-86; Univ Cambridge, vis scholar, 1986; Ohio State Univ, univ adminr, Col Law, dean, 1993-2000, Carter C Kissell prof law; City Col NY, pres, 2001-09; Univ Cincinnati, pres, 2009-12; univ adminr, Univ Iowa; Franklin Templeton Investments, independent trustee, 2008-. **Orgs:** Consult, Foreign Lawyer Training Prog, Wash, DC, 1975-77; consult, Nat Inst (Minority Ment Health Prog), 1975; Iowa Adv Comm US Civil Rights Commn, 1978-88; Iowa Law Enforcement Acad Coun, 1979-85; bd intercollegiate athletics, Univ Iowa, 1984-89; pres, Asn Am Law Sch, 1999; Kappa Alpha Psi fraternity, 2010-; Urban Am Fund II, LLC, 2006-15. **Business Addr:** President, The City College of New York, 138th St & Convent Ave, New York, NY 10031, **Business Phone:** (212)650-7000.

### WILLIAMS, GREGORY M.
Automotive executive. **Career:** Sentry Buick Inc, Omaha, NB, chief exec officer, 1988, pres; Pontiac-GMC Truck Inc, Tustin, Calif, chief exec officer, 1989, pres. **Business Addr:** Chief Executive Officer, President, Pontiac-GMC Truck Inc, 16 Auto Ctr Dr, Tustin, CA 92782.

### WILLIAMS, GUS
Basketball player. **Personal:** Born Oct 10, 1953, Mt. Vernon, NY; son of Rosanna. **Educ:** Univ Southern Calif, attended 1975. **Career:** Basketball player (retired); Golden State Warriors, guard, 1975-77; Seattle Super Sonics, guard, 1978-84; Wash Bullets, guard, 1984-86; Atlanta Hawks, guard, 1987. **Orgs:** Mentor, Boys & Girls' Club.

### WILLIAMS, H. JAMES
Dean (education), college president. **Personal:** married Carole Campbell Williams; children: Two children. **Educ:** North Carolina Central University, B.S. in Accounting, 1977; University of Wisconsin (Madison), M.B.A. in Accounting, 1979; University of Georgia (Athens), Ph.D. in Accounting, 1982; Georgetown University Law Center, J.D., 1989, LL.M. (Taxation), 1990. **Career:** Grand Valley State University, Seidman College of Business, Dean, 2004-13; Fisk University, President, 2013-. **Orgs:** Rotary Club of Nashville, Member; Leadership Nashville, Member; Nashville City Club, Member; University Club of Nashville, Member; Chi Boule Sigma Pi Phi Fraternity, Member; National Association for Equal Opportunity in Higher Education, Member; Association of Governing Boards (AGB), Member; American Institute of Certified Public Accountants, Member, 1980-; American Accounting Association, Member, 1983-; Virginia and Maryland State Bar Associations,, Member, 1988 and 1993-; Business Professionals of America, Honorary Lifetime Membership; Certified Public Accountant (North Carolina), 1979; Certified Management Accountant, Member; Kappa Alpha Psi Fraternity, Inc.; Baxter Community Center, Board Member; Civic Theatre, Board Member; Fifth Third Bank, Board Member; Forest Hills Public Schools Foundation, Board Member; Grand Rapids Arts Council, Board Member; St. Mary's Health Care, Board Member; The Washington Campus, Board Member. **Honors/Awds:** "Teacher of the Year," Florida A&M University and Texas Southern University. **Special Achievements:** Author of numerous articles, book chapters, and book reviews.

### WILLIAMS, HAL (HAROLD WILLIAMS)
Actor, business owner. **Personal:** Born Dec 14, 1938, Columbus, OH; son of Kenneth M Hairston; children: Halroy Jr & Terri; married Gay Anderson; children: 3; married Renee Himes. **Educ:** Ohio State Univ, Columbus, OH; Columbus Sch Art & Design, Columbus, OH. **Career:** TV: "That Girl", 1970-71; "Cannon", 1971-74; "Sandford & Son", 1972-76; "The Waltons", 1973-80; "The Magician", 1973; "Kung-Fu", 1973-75; "Police Story", 1973-77; "Good Times", 1974-78; "Police Woman", 1974; "Harry O", 1974-75; "Caribe", 1975; "SWAT", 1975; "Gunsmoke", 1975; "On the Rocks", 1975-76; "The Jeffersons", 1977-84; "Off the Wall", 1977; "Quincy, M E", 1977; "Whats Happening!!", 1979; "The White Shadow", 1979; "Root: The Next Generation", 1979; "Nobody's Perfect"; "Knots Landing", 1980; "Sanford", 1980-81; "Private Benjamin", 1981-83; "T J Hooker", 1982; "The Celebrity & the Arcade Kid", 1983; "Gimme a Break", 1984; "The Dukes of Hazzard", 1984; "227", 1985-90; "Hill Street Blues", 1986; "Magnum P I", 1988; "Night Court", 1991; "L A Law", 1992; "The Sinbad Show", 1993-94; "The West side Waltz", 1995; "Minor Adjustments", 1996; "Suddenly Susan", 1996; "Cherokee Kid", 1996; "Moesha", 1997; "Grandpa Roosevelt"; "The 10 Commandments"; "The Young Landlords"; "All the Money in the World"; "Skin Game"; "Moonlight", 2007; "Generation Gap", 2008; "Snow 2: Brain Freeze", 2008; "Snow 2: Brain Freeze", 2008; "Generation Gap", 2008; Films: Private Benjamin; Hard Core; On the Nickel; Cool Breeze; Escape Artist; The Rookie; Theater appearances: Spring Raining; Crossroads Hollywood Theatre; 1970; Right on Brother; Oxford Theatre, 1970; The Man Nobody Saw, 1970-74; Bakers Dream; LA Actors; Theatre, 1973; Midnight Moon at the Greasy Spoon; LA Actors Theatre, 1976; Marla Gibbs Cross roads Theatre, 1983-84; To Find A Man; Harman Art Theatre, 1988; Amen Corner, Cambridge Players, 1988; I Remember, Kennedy Ctr, 1993; Help Somebody, Baptist Temple, 1997; Guess Who, 2005; Halmarter Enterprises Inc, Los Angeles, Calif, owner, currently. **Orgs:** Am Fedn TV & Radio Artists, 1971-; Los Angeles, CA, 1975-; bd mem, LA Actors Theatre, 1976-; Watts Health Found; Nat Brotherhood Skiers Western Region Orgn; Nat Brotherhood Skiers; Us Ski Asn; Four Seasons W; bd mem, Challengers Boys/Girls Club, Screen Actors Guild; Actors Equity; host, Sickle Cell Anemia Found. **Business Addr:** Owner, Halmarter Enterprises Inc, 3870 Crenshaw Blvd, Los Angeles, CA 90008, **Business Phone:** (323)298-1013.

### WILLIAMS, HAROLD, JR. See PERRINEAU, HAROLD, JR.

### WILLIAMS, HAROLD DAVID
Executive. **Personal:** Born Jun 3, 1944, Fayetteville, NC; son of Willie Raymond and Willie Ann; married Sharon A; children: Markeith, Carmen & DeNai. **Educ:** Coppin State Col, MS, 1978; Johns Hopkins Univ, MAS, 1987; State Univ NJ, mgt cert, 1994. **Career:** Amtrak, buyer, 1980-82; Baltimore Gas & Elec, buyer, 1982-87, procurement admin, 1987-89, dir procurement opportunity program; Md Pub Serv Comn, comnr, 2002-. **Orgs:** Chmn, Minority Bus Develop Edison Elec Inst, 1993-96; Am Asn Blacks Energy, 1994-; chair, Md DC Minority Supplier Develop Coun, 1995-96, vice-chair, 1996-; Dept Energy Natural Gas Minority Bus Develop Roundtable, 1996-; bd dir, Jim Rouse Entrepreneurial Fund, 1997; bd dir, Alliance Inc, 1997; Purchasing Mgt Asn Md; Omega Psi Phi Fraternity; Comt Int Rels, Nat Asn Regulatory Utility Commissioners, 2002-; comt mem, Energy Resources & Environ Comt; chair, Utility Mkt Access Partnership bd; bd mem, Nat Minority Supplier Develop Coun. **Business Addr:** Commissioner, Maryland Public Service Commission, 6 St Paul St 12th Fl, Baltimore, MD 21202, **Business Phone:** (410)767-8116.

### WILLIAMS, HAROLD L., JR.
Consumer advocate. **Personal:** Born Jul 19, 1958, Louisville, KY; son of Harold and Frances; children: Harold III. **Educ:** Univ Louisville, BS, acct, 1981. **Career:** Brown & Williamson Tobacco Corp, consumer res analyst, currently. **Orgs:** Am Inst CPA's; Ky Soc CPA's. **Home Addr:** 1111 S Western Pky, Louisville, KY 40211, **Home Phone:** (502)774-4322. **Business Addr:** Consumer Research Analyst, Brown & Williamson Tobacco Corp, 401 S 4th St Suite 200, Louisville, KY 40202-3404, **Business Phone:** (502)568-7000.

### WILLIAMS, HAROLD LOUIS
Architect. **Personal:** Born Aug 4, 1924, Cincinnati, OH; son of Geneva C Timberlake and Leonard H; married Betty L Smith. **Educ:** Wilberforce Univ Acad, grad, 1943; Talladega Col, attended 1947; Miami Univ, Ohio, Barch, 1952; Univ Southern Calif, attended 1976. **Career:** Harold L Williams Assoc Archt & Urban Planners, owner, 1960-; Paul R Williams FAIA, proj arch, 1955-60; Fulton Krinsky & DelaMonte, arch draftsman, 1952-55. **Orgs:** Vpres bd dir Avalon Carver Comm Ctr, 1964; AIA; chmn, Comm Simon Rodia's Towers Watts, 1966-70; vpres, Nat Org Minority Arch, 1976-77, co-founder; LA Gen Plan Task Force, 1977; Soc Am Regist Arch; Constr Specs Inst; Nat Pres NOMA, 1982; pres, NOMA Found, 1995-; fdg 1st pres MNY Arch & Planners; Univ Southern Calif Arch Guild; LA C C; LA Town Hall Forum; Western Reg Urban League; life mem, Nat Asn Advan Colored People. **Honors/Awds:** Achievement Award Comm Simon Rodia's Towers in Watts, 1970; Award for Design Excell Compton City Hall; Award Design Excel LA Child Dev Ctr; Society Am Reg Arch, 1973; Onyx Award NOMA, 1975; Design Excellence, State Office Building, Van Nuys, CA, NOMA, 1985; Design Excellance, Compton Civic Center, NOMA, 1984; Advancement to Membership NOMA Counsel, 1993; Advancement to Col Fellows, AIA, 1994. **Home Addr:** 5630 Arch Crest Dr, Los Angeles, CA 90043, **Home Phone:** (323)294-4676. **Business Addr:** Co-Founder, National Organization of Minority Architects, 2366 6th St NW Rm 100, Washington, DC 20059, **Business Phone:** (202)686-2780.

### WILLIAMS, DR. HARRIETTE F.
School administrator. **Personal:** Born Jul 18, 1930, Los Angeles, CA; daughter of Orlando Flowers and Virginia C Flowers; married Irvin F; children: Lorin & Lori. **Educ:** Univ Calif, Los Angeles, CA, BA, 1952; Calif State Univ, LA, MBA, 1956, Gen Pupil Personnel Serv Credentials; Univ Calif, Los Angeles, Gen Admin Credential, Community Col Admin Credentials, Gen Elem Teaching Credential, 1973, PhD, urban educ policy & planning, 1973. **Career:** School administrator (retired); Dana JH; Mann JH, teacher & counr; Ramona High Sch, head counr & actg prin, 1960-63; Drew Jr High Sch, head counr, 1963-66; Div Sec Educ, proj coordr & asst admin coordr, 1966-68; Hollen beck Jr HS, vice prin, 1968; Bethune Jr HS, vice prin, 1968-70; Univ Calif Los Angeles, fel & asst dir, 1970-73; Palisades High Sch, asst prin, 1973-76; Pepper dine Univ, asst prof, 1975-80; Foshay Jr High Sch, prin, 1976-80; Manual Arts High Sch, prin, 1980-82; Sr High Sch Div, dir instr, 1982-85, admin opers, 1985-91; First 5 LA; educ consult; Univ La Verne, adj prof. **Orgs:** Wilfandel Club; Pi Lambda Theta, 1952, 1970-, pres, 1994-97, treas, 2000-03; Delta Sigma Theta Inc; Kappa Delta Pi, 1972; Delta Kappa Gamma, 1977; Nat Asn Second Sch Prin; adv bd, Hon Socs; Jr High Vice Prin Exec Comt; Sr High Asst Prin Exec Comt; Women Educ Leadership; Statewide Asn Calif Sch Adminr; state chairperson, Urban Affairs; resource person, Liaison Citizen Prog; chmn, Accreditation Teams Western Asn Schs & Cols; sponsor, GirlsWeek, 1981-84; citywide chmn, Girls Week; sponsor, Stud Week, 1984-91; exec bd mem, Univ Calif Los Angeles Doctoral Alumni Asn; vpres, exec bd, 1982-84, Coun Black Adminr; bd dir, 1982-84, vpres, 1992-94, 2000-; treas, Ingle woodPac Chap, Links Inc, 1987-89; pres, Lullaby Guild, 1987-89; Region16; pres, Asn Calif Sch Adminr Region XVI, 1989-90; Ralph Bunche Scholar Comt; bd dir, Univ Calif Los Angeles Gold Shield, pres, Gold Shield, 1998-2000; Univ Calif Los Angeles Educ Asn; Calif State Univ, Los Angeles Educ Support Group; rep, Los Angeles County Comnrs, C & Families, 1996-, chmn, 2003, UCLA Alumni Asn, Nat Asn Advan Colored People, Nat Coun Negro Women; chair, Rel Taskforce Comt, 1999; chair, Comns Rel Caregiver Comt, 2000. **Honors/Awds:** Hon Life Membership, PTA, 1975, 1981, 1990; Los Angeles Mayor's Golden Apple Award, 1980; Sojourner Truth Award, Los Angeles Chap Nat Asn Bus & Prof Women's Clubs; Minerva Award; Sentinel Community Award; Affiliated Teachers of Los Angeles Service Award; Univ Calif Los Angeles Award of Excellence, Black Alumni Univ Calif Los Angeles; Arthur Ashe Award. **Home Addr:** 6003 Wrightcrest Dr, Culver City, CA 90232, **Home Phone:** (310)839-6500. **Business Addr:** Member, Representative, Commission for Children Youth & Their Families, 200 N Spring St 22nd Fl, Los Angeles, CA 90012, **Business Phone:** (213)978-1840.

### WILLIAMS, DR. HARRY LEE
College president, educational consultant, executive. **Personal:** Born Greenville, NC; married Robin S; children: Austin & Gavin. **Educ:** Appalachian State Univ, BS, commun broadcasting, 1986, MA, educ media, 1988; E Tenn State Univ, PhD, educ leadership & policy anal. **Career:** Appalachian State Univ, assoc dir, 1998-2000; NC Agr & Tech State Univ, 2002-04; Appalachian State Univ, assoc vice chancellor, 2002-07; Noel-Levitz, nat mkt & recruitment assoc consult, 2002-08; Univ NC Gen Admin, interim assoc vpres acad affairs, 2007, interim sr assoc vpres acad & stud affairs, 2008; Del State Univ, provost & vpres acad affairs, 2008-10; Del State Univ, pres, 2010-. **Honors/Awds:** Appalachian State University, Distinguished Alumni Award, 2013. **Business Addr:** President, Delaware State University, 1200 N DuPont Hwy, Dover, DE 19901, **Business Phone:** (302)857-6060.

### WILLIAMS, HARVEY
Entertainer, teacher, school administrator. **Educ:** UAPB, BS; Univ Ariz, MS, educ, PhD, educ admin. **Career:** Teacher; Work Study Coordr; Sch Adminr; Entertainer; Promotor/Mgr Music Indust. **Orgs:** Nat Asn Advan Colored People; Nat Musician Union; Imperial Mystic Shrine; United Supreme Coun; 100 Black Men Am; Prinec Haal Masons; ELKS/VFW; pres, UAPB Alumn, Las Vegas Chap; IAM Youth. **Honors/Awds:** Urban League Man of the Year; Coach of the Year (Football and Track); Educator of the Year; Jefferson Award. **Special Achievements:** Started the Black College Tour for the State of Arizona. **Business Addr:** Member, President, UAPB/AM&N National Alumni Association Inc, 2201 Harbor Cliff Dr, Las Vegas, NV 89128, **Business Phone:** (702)219-0634.

### WILLIAMS, DR. HARVEY JOSEPH
Dentist. **Personal:** Born Sep 4, 1941, Houston, TX; married Beverly; children: Nichole, Natasha, Nitalya & Steven. **Educ:** San Fernando Valley St Col, BA, 1964; Univ Calif, attended 1965; Howard Univ Col Dent, DDS, 1969, cert ortho, 1971. **Career:** Gen pract, 1969-71; Nat Med Asn, asst regional dir, proj, 1971-74; Martin Luther King Jr County Hosp, staff orthodontist, 1972-80; Univ Calif, clin prof, 1972-84; pvt pract orthodontist, 1972-; Pvt Dent Pract, expanded, 1983, Renamed Tooth Spa Group Pract; Rec & Angel City Productions, chief exec officer & owner; Williams Enterprises, chief exec officer & owner; County Los Angeles, Contraction Pvt Dent Servs; H Claude Hudson Comprehensive Health Ctr, 1989-92; Hubert H Humphrey Comprehensive Health Ctr, 1990-; Edward R Royal Comprehensive Health Ctr, 1995-. **Orgs:** Western Dent Soc; Nat Dent Soc; Am Asn Ortho; Pac Coast Soc Ortho; Am Dent Asn; Angel City Dent Soc; Channels mayor City Los Angeles; Comm Ind & Com San Fernando Valley; Comm Econ Develop NE San Fernando Valley; bd trustee, Western Dent Soc; adv bd, Los Angeles Mission Col. **Honors/Awds:** Certificate of Appreciation, Pac Coast Soc Ortho; Commendation, City Inglewood, Los Angeles County. **Home Addr:** 5021 Topeka Dr, Tarzana, CA 91356-3909, **Home Phone:** (310)677-1152. **Business Addr:** Dentist, Private Practitioner, 8615 Crenshaw Blvd, Inglewood, CA 90305, **Business Phone:** (310)677-1152.

### WILLIAMS, DR. HEATHER ANDREA
Educator, writer. **Educ:** Harvard Univ, BA, 1978, JD, 1981; Yale Univ, MA, PhD, Am studies, 2002. **Career:** Author: Self-Taught: African American Education in Slavery & Freedom, 2005; US Dept Justice, asst atty gen & sect chief; Ny Atty Gen; Univ NC, Chapel Hill, asst prof hist, assoc prof, prof, currently; Nat Endowment Humanities Fel, 1995. **Orgs:** Fel, Ford Foundation; Nat Endowment Humanities Fel; Va Hist Soc. **Business Addr:** Professor, University North Carolina, Rm CB 3195 500 Hamilton Hall, Chapel Hill, NC 27599-3195, **Business Phone:** (919)962-2381.

### WILLIAMS, DR. HELEN ELIZABETH
Educator. **Personal:** Born Dec 13, 1933, Timmonsville, SC; daughter of Eugene Weldon and Hattie Pearl Sanders Baker; children: Broderick Kevin & Terrence Meredith. **Educ:** Morris Col, BA, 1954; Phoenix Col, cert, 1959; Atlanta Univ, MSLS, 1960; Queens Col, cert, 1966; Univ Ill, Urbana, CA, 1969; Univ Wis, Madison, WI, PhD, 1983. **Career:** Williams Mem High Sch, St George, SC, teacher & librn, 1955-57; Carver High Sch, Spindale, NC, teacher & librn, 1957-58; Percy Julian Elem Sch, librn, 1959-60; Brooklyn Pub Libr, librn, 1960-62; Mt Vernon Pub Libr, librn, 1963-64; Jenkins Hill High Sch, librn & teacher, 1964-66; Westchester Co Libr Syst, librn, 1966; White Plains City Pub Schs, librn, 1966-68, 1969-73; Bro-Dart Inc, libr consult, 1976-81; Univ Md, Col Pk, MD, lectr, 1981-83, prof; Univ S Pac, Suva, Fulbright prof, 1988-89. **Orgs:** Beta Phi Mu Int Libr Sci Hon Fraternity, 1960-; fel Higher Educ Act, 1966; fel Nat Defense Educ Act, 1967-68; fel Comn Instnl Coop, 1973-76; Libr Admin & Managerial Asn, 1977-80; Black Caucus Am Libr Asn, 1977-; Md Educ Media Org, 1981-; Am Libr Asn, 1977-; Am Asn Sch Librarians; Young Adults Serv Div; Asn Libr Serv C; Nat Coun Negro Women Inc, 1990-. **Home Addr:** 1921 Lyttonsville Rd, Silver Spring, MD 20910-2245.

### WILLIAMS, DR. HENRY R., JR.
Oral surgeon, dentist. **Personal:** Born Nov 3, 1937, Birmingham, AL; married Juanita; children: Leslie Alison, Mark & Matthew. **Educ:** Univ Cincinnati, BS, 1959; Meharry Med Col, DDS, 1967. **Career:** Albert B Sabin, res asst, 1959-61; Leon H Schmidt, res asst, 1961-63;

Christ Hosp, Inst Med Res, staff, 1963-67; Provident Hosp, intern, 1968-70; Univ Md, resident oral surg, 1970; pvt pract dentist & oral surgeon, currently. **Orgs:** Nat Dent Asn; treas, MC Dent Soc; bd, Oral Surg; Mid Atlantic Soc & Baltimore Soc Oral Surgeons. **Honors/Awds:** Winner Nat Elks oratorical contest, 1954. **Special Achievements:** First African American Oral Surgery Resident in University of Maryland. **Home Addr:** 4411 Old York Rd, Baltimore, MD 21212-4815. **Business Addr:** Dentist, East Baltimore Quality Dental - Sp, 308 Kerneway, Baltimore, MD 21205, **Business Phone:** (410)732-6720.

### WILLIAMS, HERB E.

Basketball coach, basketball player. **Personal:** Born Jun 26, 1946, Chicago, IL; son of Austin and Mary Poole; married Marilyn O; children: Allen, Mikki, Douglas & Mary. **Educ:** Univ Evansville, BA, 1967; Chicago State Univ, MA, admin, 1982. **Career:** Basketball player (retired), basketball coach; Centralia High Sch, Centralia, Ill, asst basketball coach, 1970-72; Rich SHigh Sch, Richton Pk, Ill, head track & asst basketball coach, 1972-74; Hillcrest High Sch, Country Club Hill, Ill, head basketball coach, 1974-75; Evanston High Sch, Evanston, Ill, head basketball coach, 1975-84; Mich State Univ, E Lansing, Mich, asst basketball coach, 1984-90; Idaho State Univ, Pocatello, ID, head basketball coach, 1990-99; Edison Schools, 2003-05. **Orgs:** Ill Basketball Coaches Asn, 1970-86; secy, Chessman Club, 1980-84; Nat Asn Basketball Coaches, 1983-; Rotary Club, 1990-; Idaho Coaches Asn, 1990.

### WILLIAMS, HERB L. (HERBERT L WILLIAMS)

Basketball player, basketball coach. **Personal:** Born Feb 16, 1958, Columbus, OH; married Deborah; children: Erica, Jabriele, Jacob & Jayda. **Educ:** Ohio State, attended 1981. **Career:** Basketball player (retired), basketball coach; Ind Pacers, 1981, forward-ctr, 1982-89; Dallas Mavericks, 1989-92; Toronto Raptors, 1996; New York Knicks, 1992-99, asst coach, 2003-05, 2006-, interim head coach, 2004-05, asst, 2005-06, New york Liberty, asst, 2015-. **Home Addr:** , Stamford, CT. **Business Addr:** Assistant Coach, New York Knicks, Madison Sq Garden 2 Pa Plz, New York, NY 10121-0091, **Business Phone:** (212)465-6471.

### WILLIAMS, DR. HERBERT LEE

Surgeon general. **Personal:** Born Dec 23, 1932, Citronelle, AL; children: Lezli & Candace. **Educ:** Talladega Col, BA, 1952; Atlanta Univ, MS, 1954; Meharry Med Col, Md, 1958. **Career:** Truman Med Ctr, prac; Herbert L Williams Inc, prac; pvt prac surgeon, 1965-. **Orgs:** Pres, Herbert Williams MD Inc; Alpha Omega Alpha Hon Med Soc; dipl, Am Bd Surg; fel Am Col Surgeons; Int Col Surgeons; Am Soc Abdominal Surgeons, chf surg serv, Williams AFB Hosp, 1963-65. **Home Addr:** 4508 Don Rodolfo Pl, Los Angeles, CA 90008. **Business Addr:** Physician, 644 E Regent St Suite 101, Inglewood, CA 90301, **Business Phone:** (310)674-3007.

### WILLIAMS, HERMAN

Administrator, government official, association executive. **Personal:** Born Dec 7, 1943, Washington, DC; children: Herman III, Daniel & James. **Educ:** Acad Health Sci, attended 1973; Baylor Univ, attended 1975; Montgomery Col, attended 1980. **Career:** City Takoma Pk, City Councilman, 1982-87; Comn Landlord Tenant Affairs, comnr, 1980-82; Metrop Coun Govts, comn mem, 1983. **Orgs:** Bd dirs, United Planning Asn, 1964-65; founder, Winchester Tenants Asn, 1978; vpres, Parkview Towers Tenant Asn, 1980; bd mem, Metrop Wash Planning & Housing Asn, 1980-82; liaison, Upper Maple Ave Citizens Asn, 1980, city-Counman, 1981; organizer, Takoma Parks Ceremony, honor Martin Luther King Jr, 1982-; instrumental redistricting, Takoma Park voting policy, 1982; establishing, Dept Housing, 1983; organized Takoma Park Youth Day. **Honors/Awds:** Elizabeth Skou Achievement Award, Winchester Tenants Asn, 1978; Second African American elected official in Takoma Park, Md, 1890-; Selected for Honorary Dinner Comn, Nat Asn Advan Colored People, 1984-85. **Special Achievements:** Only African American elected official in Montgomery County, MD. **Home Addr:** PO Box 11436, Takoma Park, MD 20913-1436.

### WILLIAMS, HERMAN, JR.

Executive, government official, commander in chief. **Personal:** Born Jan 1, 1931?, New York, NY; married Marjorie; children: Clolita, Herman, lll & Montel. **Educ:** Univ Md Sch Eng, Nat Fire Serv Staff, cert, fire serv instr & motor fleet supvr; Catonsville Community Col, fire mgt; Univ Baltimore, mgt & personnel admin. **Career:** Commander chief (retired), executive; Baltimore City fire dept, fire fighter, 1954, fire instr, 1967, capt, 1974, battalion chief fire prev bur, 1977, chief, 1992-2001, pump operator, Lt & fire acad, capt & fire safety officer & chief fire prev bur, 2001; Dept Pub Works, chief admin servs, 1980, exec asst dir pub works, 1984, commnr transp, 1988. **Orgs:** Phi Bets Sigma Fraternity Inc; Vulcan Blazer Inc; Int Asn Fire Chiefs; chmn bd dirs, Munic Employees Credit Union Baltimore City; bd mem, Munic Golf Corp; Living Class Rooms Found; Appeals Bd Baltimore City; chair bd, Munic Employees Credit Union Baltimore Inc; Knights Columbus; Prince Hall Masons. **Honors/Awds:** Firefighter of the Year Award, 1978; LOE Award, 2004. **Special Achievements:** First African American Chief of Fire Department, 1992. Book: "Firefighter". **Business Addr:** Board of Director, Municipal Employees Credit Union Baltimore Inc, 7 E Redwood St, Baltimore, MD 21202, **Business Phone:** (410)752-8313.

### WILLIAMS, HILDA YVONNE

Executive. **Personal:** Born Aug 17, 1946, Washington, NC; daughter of Willie Joseph and Martha Jane Blount. **Educ:** Hunter Col, New York, NY, attended 1980. **Career:** Teachers Col, exec sec, 1964-67; Bus Careers, exec, 1967-69; Esquire Mag, admin asst, 1969-73; RCA Corp, admin asst, 1973-75, regional prom mgr, 1975-87; RCA Rec, prom mgr, a&r admin mgr, 1982-87; Polygram Rec, northeast regional prom mgr, 1987-89; Capitol Rec, northeast regional prom mgr, 1989-90; Warner Bros Rec, nat dir, black music promoter, nat prom dir, 1990-96; Sony Music Epic Rec, northeast regional prom dir, 1997-98; Virgin Rec, staff, sr nat dir, 1998-2004; Weichert Realtors, realtor, 2005-08; RE MAX Advantage Plus, realtor, 2008-11; Keller Williams Village Sq Realty, realtor, 2011-14; Keller Williams Town Life, realtor, 2014; Coldwell Banker Residential Brokerage, sales assoc, 2015-. **Orgs:** Nat Asn Advan Colored People, 1976; Black Music Asn, New York Chap; bd dir, Nat Black Music Asn, 1986-88; Nj Realtor asn; Nat Asn Realtors Mem; Nj Asn Realtors Mem; RealSource Asn Realtors Mem; Nj Mult Listing Serv Mem; Garden State Mult Listing Serv Mem; Community Baptist Church Englewood. **Honors/Awds:** Black Achiever in Industry, YMCA of Greater New York, 1982; Jack the Rapper Black Music Award, 1990; Urban National Promotion Director of the Year; Griot Award, Midwest Radio & Music Association; Who's Who Among Black Americans; Outstanding Young Women in America. **Home Addr:** 356 E Ridgewood Ave Suite 3, Ridgewood, NJ 07450, **Home Phone:** (201)445-1259. **Business Addr:** Sales Associate, Coldwell Banker Residential Brokerage, 180 Main St, Madison, NY 07940, **Business Phone:** (973)377-4444.

### WILLIAMS, DR. HOMER LAVAUGHAN

Physician, orthopedist. **Personal:** Born Dec 10, 1925, Kalamazoo, MI; married Ruth; children: Aaron, Valerie & Andre. **Educ:** OH Col Chiropody, DSC, 1954; Western MI Univ, BS, 1962; Howard Univ Sch Med, MD, 1966. **Career:** Akron Gen Hosp, dr ortho surg, 1971; orthopaedist. **Orgs:** Charles Drew Soc; LA Co Med Asn; AMA; Chmn orthopaedic, Nat Med Asn; bd Morningside Hosp. **Honors/Awds:** W Adams Hosp Pub "Intraosseous Vertebral Venography in Comparison with Myelograph in Diagnosing Dis", 1969. **Home Addr:** 5331 Shenandoah Ave, Los Angeles, CA 90056, **Home Phone:** (310)670-8497. **Business Addr:** 110 S La Brea Ave Suite 540, Inglewood, CA 90301, **Business Phone:** (310)677-6161.

### WILLIAMS, HOPE DENISE WALKER

School administrator. **Personal:** Born Dec 24, 1952, Chicago, IL; daughter of Welmon Walker and Maryann Walker; children: Albert Lee & Ebony Emani Denise. **Educ:** Harvard Univ Grad Sch Design, cert, community develop finance, 1981; St Ambrose Univ, BA, psychol, 1985; Ashford Univ, MEd. **Career:** African Am Drama Co, midwest reg coord, 1982-83; Dramatic Mkt Asn, opers mgr, 1983-84; Scott County Davenport IA, admin intern, 1985-86; Marycrest Col Davenport, campus counr, 1986-87, asst dean & dir acad adv, 1987-90; Chancellors Diversity Cabinet; Northern Ill Univ, acad coordr; Augustana Col, asst dean stud servs, 1990-92, asst dean studs, 1991; Chicago Bears, intern, 1998; Univ Iowa, Hawkeye Football, asst dir & coordr, 2001-05; NC State Univ, bd dir, treas, currently; Univ New Orleans, dir stud athletic support serv; Univ Colo, assoc dir acad servs, 2006-, acad coordr football & acad coordr womens basketball & volleyball; Herbst Acad Ctr, coordr mentor & tutor prog; Southeastern La Univ, asst athletic dir acad affairs, 2008-11. **Orgs:** Treas, Quad Cities Career Womens Network, 1983; stud sen, MBA Senate StAmbrose Col, 1985; Nat Asn Black MBAs, 1986; bd mem, HELP Legal Aid, 1986; panelist, United Way Allocations, 1987; bd mem, NACADA, 1988-; mem comt, nat treas, NAWE, 1993-95; treas, Univ Iowa, African Am Staff Coun. **Honors/Awds:** Certificate of Appreciation, Conf Black Families, 1979 & 82; Certificate of Recognition, Church Women United, 1983; Yellow Belt Tae Kwon Do Karate, 1984; Junior Achievement, Recognition Personal Dedication, 1989-89, Hallof Fame Inductee, 1991; Award for New Professionals, ACAFAD, 1989; Award for New Professionals. **Home Addr:** 1217 Ripley St, Davenport, IA 52803. **Business Addr:** Associate Director of Academic Services, University of Colorado, 914 Broadway St, Boulder, CO 80302, **Business Phone:** (303)492-1411.

### WILLIAMS, HOTROD. See WILLIAMS, JOHN.

### WILLIAMS, DR. HOWARD COPELAND

Economist, educator, executive director. **Personal:** Born May 29, 1921, Quitman, GA; son of Edward and Janie; married Blanche; children: Stephanie & Howard. **Educ:** BS, MS; PhD, 1953. **Career:** Executive director, educator, economist (retired); NC Agr & Tech State Univ, assoc prof, 1947-51; OH State Univ, assoc prof, 1953-61, prof, 1964-7; NC State Univ, post doc fel, 1956; Soc Sci Coun, travel grant, 1964; Mershon Nat Security Prog, grant; Nommensen Univ, Medan, Indonesia, vis prof, 1961-63; Africa Reg Study Big Ten Univ's evaluate AID Univ Contracts Worldwide, home campus liaison, 1965-67; Off Spec Trade, Rep Exec Off Pres, sr agr adv, 1973-75; ASCS Off Admin, dir anal staff, 1976-81; ASCS, dir commodity anal div, 1981-87. **Honors/Awds:** Social Sci Res Coun. **Home Addr:** 12621 Prestwick Dr, Fort Washington, MD 20744-6427, **Home Phone:** (301)292-4623.

### WILLIAMS, DR. HUBERT

Police officer, law enforcement officer, executive director. **Personal:** Born Aug 19, 1939, Savannah, GA; married Annette; children: Alexis, Susan & Hubert Carl. **Educ:** Elec Engr Tech, cert, 1962; John Jay Col Criminal Justice, AS, 1968, BS, 1970; Harvard Law Sch, fel, 1971; Rutgers Univ Sch Law, JD, 1974; Fed Bur Invest Acad Nat Exec Inst, 1977. **Career:** Newark High-impact Anti-crime Prog, exec dir, 1973-74; Newark Police Dept, police officer, 1962-73, police dir, 1974-85; Rutgers Sch Criminal Justice, adj prof; Police Found, pres, currently. **Orgs:** Life mem, Int Asn Chiefs Police; Am Soc Criminol; adv com Nat Inst; founding pres, Nat Orgn Black Law Enforcement Officers; adv bd, Police Found Exec Training Sem, 1976-; selection com mem, City Stanford Conn Pol Ice Chief, 1977; Fed BurInvest Acad Nat Exec Inst, 1977; New Scotland Yard Eng, 1977; selection com mem, City LA Police Chief, 1978; pres, Nat Asn Police Com Rels Officers, 1971-73; Mayors Educ Task Force, 1971-76; bd dirs, Nat Asn Urban Criminal Justice Planners, 1972-74; Int Asn Chiefs Police, 1973-; trustee, Two Hundred Club, 1973-; bd dir, Police Exec & Res Forum, 1975-; camp mgmt com, UMCA, 1975-78; Am Bar Asn, 1976-; founding pres, Nat Orgn Black Law Enforcement Exec, 1976-79; Nj Bar, 1976-; Fed Bar Asn, 1977-; St & Com Educ Task Force, 1977-; adv bd, Esex Co Col Criminal Justice Prog, 1978-; consult to pub safety com, Nat League Cities, 1978-; edit adv bd mem, John Jay Col Jour Am Acad Prof Law Enforcement, 1978-; Acad Exp Criminol; mem bar, Supreme Ct US. **Honors/Awds:** Res fel, Harvard Law Sch for Criminal Justice; Bronze Shields & Merit Awards, 1965; honored Com for Incentive for Human Achievement, 1967; Humanitarian Award, Newark Businessmens Asn, 1968; Appreciation Award, SWard Little League, 1970; Leadership Award, Nat Asn Police Comn Rels Officer, 1973; Achievement Award Police Acad Asn, 1974; Man of the Year Award, 4H, 1974; Appreciation Award Spcl Police Asn, 1975; Achvmt Award Bronze Shields Orgn, 1975; Community Service Award Speedy Olympics, 1975; Recog Excel Award, Dr King Comn Ctr, 1976; spec Crime Recog Award, NJ Voice Newspaper, 1977; spec Narcotic Enforcement Award Drug Enforcement Admin, 1977; Appreciation Award Newark Intl Airports 50th Anniv, 1978; publ articles various magazines, 1978-79. **Special Achievements:** Youngest Chief Executive Officers of a Major Police Department in the US; Author of numerous Books namely Why we should establish a police code of ethics, in Criminal Justice Ethics, Volume 11, Number 2, 1993; New police for a new South Africa, Policing the Conflict in South Africa, 1993; The Abuse of Police Authority: A National Study of Police Officers Attitudes, 2001. **Home Addr:** 520 Highland Ave, Newark, NJ 07104. **Business Addr:** President, Police Foundation, 1201 Conn Ave NW Suite 200, Washington, DC 20036-2636, **Business Phone:** (202)833-1460.

### WILLIAMS, DR. HUGH HERMES

Educator, physician. **Personal:** Born Nov 11, 1945, Port-of-Spain; son of Hugh Lionel and Norma D Balcon Baird; married Leandra M; children: Kelly Victoria & Janelle Victoria. **Educ:** Univ W Indies, Kingston, Jamaica, attended 1972; Howard Univ, Wash, DC, 1976; McMaster Univ, Hamilton, ON, Can, attended 1978; Cleveland Clin Found, Cleveland, OH, attended 1980. **Career:** Univ Tenn, Memphis, instr, 1980-81, asst prof, med, 1981-90, assoc prof, 1990-91, clin assoc prof, 1991, pvt pract, currently. **Orgs:** Am Soc Nephrology; Nat Kidney Found; Int Soc Nephrology; Am Soc Internal Med; Am Heart Asn; fel, Am Col Physicians. **Home Addr:** 9469 Inglewood Cove, Germantown, TN 38139, **Home Phone:** (678)927-9686. **Business Addr:** Physician, 220 S Claybrook St Suite 314, Memphis, TN 38104, **Business Phone:** (901)276-6277.

### WILLIAMS, JAMAL

Football player. **Personal:** Born Apr 28, 1976, Washington, DC; son of Harriet; married Sureldie Rycha Davis; children: Joy Danielle & Jasmine D. **Educ:** Okla State Univ, attended 1997. **Career:** San Diego Chargers, left defensive tackle, left tackle & nose tackle, 1998, left defensive tackle, 1999, 2001-03, defensive tackle, left defensive tackle, 2000, defensive tackle, 2004-07, 2009, defensive tackle, nose tackle, 2008; Denver Broncos, defensive tackle & nose tackle, 2010. **Honors/Awds:** Ed Block Courage Award, 2002; Defensive Player of the Year, San Diego Chargers, 2004; Lineman of the Year, San Diego Chargers, 2004; Three Times All-Pro, 2004-06; Three Times Pro Bowl, 2005-07. **Special Achievements:** Named a first-alternate to the Pro Bowl, 2004. Film: 2007 AFC Championship Game, 2008. **Business Addr:** Defensive Tackle, San Diego Chargers, 4020 Murphy Canyon Rd, San Diego, CA 92123, **Business Phone:** (858)874-4500.

### WILLIAMS, JAMEL ISHMAEL

Football player. **Personal:** Born Dec 22, 1973, Gary, IN; married Sarah; children: Kaden, Jackson & Bryson. **Educ:** Univ Nebr, BS, commun. **Career:** Football player (retired); Wash Redskins, defensive back, 1997-99; Green Bay Packers, safety, 1999-2000; Las Vegas Outlaws, 2001; FedEx Kinkos, sales repr, 2007.

### WILLIAMS, JAMES

Public utility executive, air force officer, association executive. **Personal:** Born Dec 15, 1934, Huntsville, AL; son of William Clemons and Ovenia Smith; children: James E Jr, Gwendolyn A Iley & Regina L. **Educ:** Franklin Univ, assoc deg, bus admin, 1977; Southern Ill Univ, BS, occup educ, 1977; Mich State Univ, MBA prog, 1983. **Career:** Pub Utilities Comn Ohio, utilities examr II, 1975-83, utilities examr III, 1983-85, supvr, 1985-86, pub utilities adminr, 1986-; Williams Mkt, Self Employed, 2014-. **Orgs:** Veteran's comt chmn, Nat Asn Advan Colored People, Columbus Br, 1988-92; York Rite Masons (Colored) Columbus Ohio, Grand Secy State Ohio, 1978-89; nat grand secy, York Rite Masons, 1989-96-; co-chairperson adv bd, Am Cancer Soc, 1992-96; Franklin County Rehab Ctr, 1994-96. **Honors/Awds:** Spec recognition, CALP Grad, Ohio House of Rep, 1986; Outstanding Serv Award, Am Cancer Soc, 1991-92; Community Serv Award, Columbus Dispatch, 1992. **Business Addr:** Public Utilities Administrator, Public Utilities Commission of Ohio, 180 E Broad St Suite 9, Columbus, OH 43215-3707, **Business Phone:** (614)466-4687.

### WILLIAMS, JAMES ARTHUR

Musical group, educator. **Personal:** Born May 9, 1939, Columbia, SC; children: Angela, Melody & James II. **Educ:** Allen Univ, BA, 1960; Univ Ill, MS, music educ, 1964; Columbia Univ; Ohio State Univ. **Career:** Calif Johnson High Sch, educr, 1960-69; Morris Col, 1965 & 68; Stillman Col, Dept Music, chmn; Univ Ill, fac; Allen Univ, Columbia, fac; SC Pub Sch, staff; Sidney Pk CME Church SC, choir dir; Bethlehem Baptist Church SC, staff; Wilberforce Univ, prof, dir, 1994. **Orgs:** Bd dir, Columbia SC Choral Soc, 1967-69; adjudicator, Univ Ala, 1972; Tuscaloosa Co Jr Miss Pageant, 1972; music educr, Music Com Tuscaloosa Arts & Humanities Coun, 1992; Guest Cond All City High Sch Chorus SC; Columbia SC All City HS Chorus; Univ Ala, Tuscaloosa, AL; Tuscaloosa Comt Singers, AL; pres, Palmetto St Music Teachers Asn; Tuscaloosa Co Jr Miss Pageant; Music Educr Nat Conf; Alpha Phi Alpha Frat Inc; Steering Comt Mus Arts Dr; bd dir, Tuscaloosa Comt Singers. **Home Addr:** PO Box 4891, Tuscaloosa, AL 35401. **Business Addr:** Faculty, Allen University, 1530 Harden St, Columbia, SC 29204, **Business Phone:** (803)376-5700.

### WILLIAMS, JAMES EDWARD

Executive. **Personal:** Born Apr 29, 1943, Berkeley, CA; son of J Oscar Sr and Ruth E; children: Erin & Landin. **Educ:** San Francisco State Univ, BA, 1969; Golden Gate Univ, MBA, 1974. **Career:** ITEL Corp, int chief financial officer, 1971-81; Tektronix Corp, controller, 1982-84; Syntex Corp, treas & vpres, 1984-86; Masstor Syst, sr vpres & chief financial officer, 1987-89; Tegal Corp, chief financial officer, 1990-92; LePro Corp, pres, 1992-. **Orgs:** Bd, Nat Asn Cre Tres, 1985-; Fin Officers Northern Calif; Treas Club San Francisco; bd mem, Hubert Hoover Boys & Girls Club Menlo Pk. **Home Addr:** 3019 Calif Dr, Alameda, CA 94501, **Home Phone:** (510)814-9777.

### WILLIAMS, DR. JAMES H., JR.

Educator. **Personal:** Born Apr 4, 1941, Newport News, VA; son of James H and Margaret L Mitchell; children: James H III & Mariella L. **Educ:** Newport News Shipyard Apprentice Sch, mech designer, 1965; Mass Inst Technol, SB, 1967, SM, 1968; Trinity Col, Cambridge Univ, PhD, 1970. **Career:** Newport News Shipbuilding & Dry Dock Co, apprentice-sr design engr, 1960-70; Int consult, 1970-; Mass Inst Technol, Mech Engineering Dept, prof appl mech, prof writing & humanistic studies, 1970, prof teaching excellence, 1991, prof, currently. **Orgs:** NTA, 1975, ASME, 1978, ASNT, 1978; Diag Eng, 1983; Nat Sci Found, 1985-87. **Special Achievements:** Books: Fundamentals of Applied Dynamics, 1996; I Will Love You, Forever!-The Quantum Mechanics of Love, 2009. **Business Addr:** Professor, Massachusetts Institute of Technology, Rm 3-358 77 Mass Ave, Cambridge, MA 02139, **Business Phone:** (617)253-2221.

### WILLIAMS, DR. JAMES HIAWATHA

Chancellor (education), president (organization). **Personal:** Born Sep 10, 1945, Montgomery, AL; son of James Hiawatha and Johnnie Mae Robinson-Strother; married Jann A Fleming; children: James M, John V (deceased), Kasha G & Jameelah I. **Educ:** Los Angeles City Col, AA, 1967; Calif State Univ, Los Angeles, BA, 1973; Pepperdine Univ, Los Angeles, MS, 1974; Wash State Univ, Pullman, WA, PhD, 1983. **Career:** Chancellor (retired); Calif State Polytech Univ, Pomona, asst prof, 1977-81, assoc dean & assoc prof, 1980-85, dean col arts & prof; Spokane Community Col, pres, 1995-99; Arapahoe Community Col, pres; Yosemite Community Col Dist, interim chancellor, 2004-06, secy, bd trustee chancellor, 2004-07. **Orgs:** Phi Delta Kappa, 1977-; pres, Pomona Valley Nat Asn Advan Colored People, 1984-86; Phi Beta Delta, 1988-; exec bd mem, Nat Asn Ethnic Studies, 1988-95, pres, 1992-; Phi Kappa Phi, 1989-; pres-elect, Coun Cols Arts & Scis, 1994; Littleton Rotary Club. **Honors/Awds:** Prism of Excellence Award, Jerry Voorhis Claremont Dem Club, 1986; Martin Luther King Jr Humanitarian Award, Pomona Valley Nat Asn Advan Colored People, 1987; Services to Youth, Claremont Area Chapter Links Inc, 1988; Distinguished Alumnus Award, Calif State Univ, Los Angeles, 1994; Charles C. Irby Distinguished Service Award, Nat Asn Ethnic Studies. **Home Addr:** 2352 S Yukon Way, Lakewood, CO 80227.

### WILLIAMS, JAMES OTIS

Football coach, football player, executive. **Personal:** Born Mar 29, 1968, Pittsburgh, PA. **Educ:** Cheyney State Univ Pa, grad. **Career:** Football player (retired), football coach, radio colo analyst; Chicago Bears, 1991-93, right tackle, 1994-2002; Chicago Rush, rad color analyst; Concordia Univ, off line coach, currently. **Honors/Awds:** Brian Piccolo Award, Bears Asn, 2001; Pro Bowls, 2001; appeared, E-tv Wild Chicago episode. **Special Achievements:** TV Series: "NFL on FOX", 1994-2000; "NFL Monday Night Football", 1995-2002; "ESPN's Sunday Night Football", 1997-2002. **Business Addr:** Coach Off Line, Concordia University Chicago, 7400 Augusta St, River Forest, IL 60305-1499, **Business Phone:** (708)771-8300.

### WILLIAMS, JAMES R.

Lawyer, judge. **Personal:** Born Sep 16, 1936, Columbus, MS; married Catherine; children: Michael & Jacqueline. **Educ:** Univ Akron, BA, 1960, JD, 1965; Nat Judicial Col. **Career:** Judge, lawyer (retired); Parms Purnell, Stubbs & Williams, partner, 1969-78; Northern Dist Ohio, US atty, 1978-82; Guren, Merritt, Feibel, Sogg & Cohen, pvt pract; Akron Munic Ct, judge, 1983, 1985, 1987; City Akron, councilman-at-large, 1970-78; Summit Co Common Pleas Ct, admin judge, 1989, presiding judge, 1990, 1992, 1998, judge. **Orgs:** Treas, Akron Bar Asn; pres, Summit Co Legal Aid Soc; nat pres, prin founder & chmn emer, Alpha Phi Alpha Fraternity Inc, currently; Ohio Bar Asn; Am Bar Asn; pres, Common Pleas Judges Asn, Ohio; Nat Bar Asn; Supreme Courts Bd Comnr Grievances & Discipline. **Honors/Awds:** Outstanding Achievement Award, Alpha Phi Alpha, 1973; Liberian Humane Order of African Redemption Citation, Dr William R Tolbert Jr, Pres Rep Liberian, 1973; Top Hat Award, Pittsburgh Courier, 1977; Ebony's 100 Most Influential Black Ams, 1980; National Award of Merit, Alpha Phi Alpha Fraternity. **Home Addr:** 1014 Vine St Suite 2400, Cincinnati, OH 45202-1199, **Home Phone:** (330)867-7536. **Business Addr:** Principal Founder & Chairman Emeritus, Alpha Phi Alpha Homes Inc, 662 Wolf Ledges Pkwy, Akron, OH 44311-1511, **Business Phone:** (330)376-8787.

### WILLIAMS, DR. JAMES THOMAS

Educator, physician. **Personal:** Born Nov 10, 1933, Martinsville, VA; son of Ruth E and Harry Pemberton; married Jacqueline; children: Lawrence & Laurie. **Educ:** Howard Univ, BS, 1954, MD, 1958; Am Bd Internal Med, dipl, 1967, cert, 1974, 1980; Am Bd Endocrinol & Metab, dipl, 1972. **Career:** Philadelphia Gen Hosp, intern, 1958-59; DC Gen & Freedmens Hosp, resident, 1959-62, 1964-65; Howard Univ Col Med, fel endocrinol, 1965-67, physician, 1967-, from asst prof to assoc prof, 1967-85, prof, 1985-; DC Gen Hosp, physician, 1967-2000. **Orgs:** Med officer, Home Care Prog, DC Govt, 1968-89; Am Diabetes Asn; Medico-Chirurgical Soc DC; Nat Med Asn; Med Soc DC; Endocrine Soc; fel Am Col Physicians; Alpha Omega Alpha Hon Med Soc; Sigma Pi Phi Fraternity; fel Am Col Endocrinol. **Home Addr:** 13414 Tamarack Rd, Silver Spring, MD 20904-1469, **Home Phone:** (301)384-8495. **Business Addr:** Professor of Medicine, Howard University, 520 W St NW, Washington, DC 20059-1014, **Business Phone:** (202)806-6306.

### WILLIAMS, DR. JAMYE COLEMAN

Editor. **Personal:** Born Dec 15, 1918, Louisville, KY; daughter of Frederick Douglass Coleman Sr and Jamye Harris Coleman; married McDonald; children: Donna. **Educ:** Wilberforce Univ, BA, Eng, 1938; Fisk Univ, MA, Eng, 1939; Ohio State Univ, PhD, speech communication, 1959. **Career:** Educator (retired); Edward Waters Col, Jacksonville, Fla, educr, 1939-40; Shorter Col Little Rock, 1940-42; Wilberforce Univ Ohio, 1942-56; Morris Brown Col, 1956-58; Tenn State Univ, 1959-87, dept head commun, 1973-87; 13th Dist Lay Orgn, pres, 1977-85; African Methodist Episcopal Church Rev, ed, 1984-92. **Orgs:** Exec comm, Nashville Br Nat Asn Advan Colored People, 1960-; bd govs, Nat Coun Church, 1976-84; Nat Conf Community & Justice, 1988-; World Methodist Coun, 1981-91; Registry Election Fin TN, 1990-96; bd mem, Nashville Community Found, 1991-; Theta Alpha Phi; Pi Kappa Delta; Kappa Delta Pi; bd dir, John W Work III Found; Links Inc; Delta Sigma Theta; Nat Asn Adavan Colored People; trustee, Community Found. **Honors/Awds:** Teacher of the Year, Tenn State Univ, 1968; Outstanding Teacher Award, 1976; Woman of the Year, Nashville Davidson & Co Bus & Prof Women's Club, 1978; Citizen of the Year, Nashville Alumnae Chap Delta Sigma Theta, 1979; Salute to Black Women Award, Howard Univ, 1986; Distinguished Service Award, Tenn State Univ, 1988; Lifetime Achievement Award, Kappa Alpha Psi Fraternity, 1990; Recipient with McDonald Williams, Human Relations Award, The Nat Conf Christians & Jews, 1992; inductee, Acad Women of Achievement, 1996; Presidential Award, Nat Asn for the Advan of Colored People, 1999; recipient with McDnoald Williams, Joe Kraft Humanitarian Award, 2002; Honorary Degrees, The Inter denomi Nat Theol Ctr; Morris Brown Col; Payne Theol Sem. **Special Achievements:** Co-editor "The Negro Speaks: The Rhetoric of Contemporary Black Leaders". **Home Addr:** 125 Wynfield Way SW, Atlanta, GA 30331-6838, **Home Phone:** (404)346-8927.

### WILLIAMS, JAN

Financial manager. **Educ:** NC Agr & Tech State Univ, BS, finance & econs, 1976; Pepperdine Univ, MBA, finance, 1980; Naval Post Grad Sch, MS, info systs, 1985; Univ Pa, Wharton Sch, retirement planning cert, 2008. **Career:** Us Marine Corps, Marine Forces Pac, Camp Smith, Hawaii, controller, 1994-96; W End Med Ctr Bd Dir, treas; Nasd, mem; AXA Adv LLC, financial adv, retirement planning specialist, 1997-; Eagle Group Int, financial advisor & employee benefits consult, 2001-07. **Orgs:** Alliance Bersteins Elite Adv Team; AXA & Black Enterprise Ski Challenges; 100 Black Mens Pres Coun; Ga Dent Asn; Morehouse Sch Med Alumni Asn; Links Nat Assembly; instr, Good Choice Inc; 100 Black Men Am; Omega Psi Phi; life mem, Nat Black MBA Asn; Million Dollar Round Table; Buckhead Club, 2005-11; edu bd mem, Atlanta Bus League, 2007-12, co-chair, 2012-14; Am-Israel Chamber Com, 2013; Nat Asn Minority Auto Dealers. **Special Achievements:** Bicycles in 500+ mile events annually to raise money for AIDS vaccine research. **Business Addr:** Financial Advisor, Retirement Planning Specialist, AXA Advisors LLC, 3348 Peachtree Rd NE Suite 800, Atlanta, GA 30326-1443, **Business Phone:** (404)760-2400.

### WILLIAMS, JANICE L.

Manager, executive. **Personal:** Born Aug 23, 1938, Allentown, PA; daughter of William E Merritt and Cora L Merritt; children: Lisa & Jerome. **Educ:** Muhlenberg Col, BA, psychol, 1970; Lehigh Univ, MEd, educ admin, 1974. **Career:** Muhlenberg Col, asst dir admis, 1970-74; Pa Power & Light Co, mgrplacement & EEO prog, 1974-. **Orgs:** Bd mem, YWCA, 1975-77; pres, Negro Cult Ctr, 1975-77; bd mem, Head Start Lehigh Valley, 1975-77; Muhlenberg Col, Coun Continuing Educ, 1976; Educ Comn, Pa Chamber Com, 1976-77; bd mem, Allentown Police Civil Serv, 1979-, United Way Lehigh City, 1981-88; bd mem, Friends Comn, Muhlenberg Col Corp, 1987-89; dir, Allentown Sch Bd Educ, 1987-; Muhlenberg Col Bd Assocs, 1987-89; pres, Lehigh Valley Personnel Asn, 1989-90; Allentown Preserv Asn; Allentown Police Civil Serv Comn. **Honors/Awds:** Woman of the Year, Allentown Nat Asn Advan Colored People, 1987. **Special Achievements:** First Allentown School Board's only black member. **Business Addr:** Manager of Placement, EEO Program, Pennsylvania Power & Light Co, 2 N 9th St, Allentown, PA 18101, **Business Phone:** (610)774-3000.

### WILLIAMS, JASON HAROLD

Government official. **Personal:** Born Nov 11, 1944, Baltimore, MD; son of James Edward and Mary Boyd. **Educ:** Univ Md, College Park, Md, BS, 1966; Univ Calif, Los Angeles, Calif, attended 1973. **Career:** Bldg Servs, Los Angeles, Calif, exec asst, 1971-73, dep dir, 1973-75, chief dep dir, 1975-82, dir, 1982-85; Facil Mgmt, Los Angeles, Calif, asst dir, 1985-87; Los Angeles County, Dept Health Servs, Los Angeles, Calif, sr asst, hosps admin, 1987-, chair, currently. **Orgs:** Mem allocations comt, United Way Los Angeles, 1975-; United Way Bd, United Way Los Angeles, 1983-85; chmn, spec task force, United Way Los Angeles, 1988-; treas, Southern Calif Chap, Nat Forum Black Pub Adminrs, 1990-91; fin chair, Forum '91 Planning Comt, 1990-91. **Honors/Awds:** Silver & Gold Leadership, United Way, 1979-82, 1984-89; Outstanding Leadership, Brotherhood Crusade, 1980-82, 1985-87; Award of Appreciation, Los Angeles Olympic Org Comt, 1984; Award of Recognition, Los Angeles Olympic Org Comt, 1984; Distinguished Leadership, United Negro Col Fund, 1986; Award of Appreciation, USC Black Alumni Asn, Ebonics Support Group, 1990. **Home Addr:** 5273 1/2 Village Green, Los Angeles, CA 90016, **Home Phone:** (213)292-5854. **Business Addr:** Senior Assistant Hospitals Administration, County of Los Angeles, 313 N Figueroa St Suite 803, Los Angeles, CA 90012, **Business Phone:** (213)240-7785.

### WILLIAMS, JAY OMAR

Football player, businessperson. **Personal:** Born Oct 13, 1971, Washington, DC; married Erica T; children: Jamye, Jai & Roman. **Educ:** Wake Forest Univ, BS, sociol & criminal behav, 1994. **Career:** Football player (retired), exec; St Louis Rams, defensive end, 1995-99; Carolina Panthers, defensive end & defensive tackle, 2000-01; Miami Dolphins, defensive end, 2002-04; Jay's Tactical Gear & Accessories Inc, pres & chief exec officer. 2005-09; AlliedBarton Security Serv, spec police sgt, 2009-12; Eris Security Inc, capt, 2012-13; gun dealer, currently; Redfive Security, mobile security asst team leader, 2013-. **Honors/Awds:** Champion, Super Bowl, XXXIV. **Special Achievements:** TV appearance: Entertainment Tonight, 2014. **Home Addr:** 1306 Roxanna Rd NW, Washington, DC 20012-1321, **Home Phone:** (202)722-0623. **Business Addr:** Mobile Security Assistant Team Leader, Redfive Security, 1420 Beverly Rd Suite 330, McLean, VA 22101, **Business Phone:** (571)970-3526.

### WILLIAMS, JAYSON

Television broadcaster, basketball player, business owner. **Personal:** Born Feb 22, 1968, Ritter, SC; son of Elijah Joshua (deceased) and Barbara; married Kellie Batiste; married Tanya Young; children: Monique & Ejay. **Educ:** St John's Univ. **Career:** Basketball player (retired), analyst, business owner; Philadelphia 76ers, forward, 1990-92, NJ Nets, forward, 1992-99; Idaho Stampede, forward, 2005; NBC TV, analyst; T.R.Y. J's, co-owner, currently. Books: Loose Balls, 2001; Humbled, 2012. **Business Addr:** Owner, T R Y J's, 29 S Warren St, Trenton, NJ 08608, **Business Phone:** (609)392-4370.

### WILLIAMS, JEAN CAROLYN

Educator. **Personal:** Born Aug 30, 1956, Mullins, SC; daughter of Remel Graves Gause and Fred Gause Jr; married Vaugn McDonald Jr. **Educ:** Spelman Col, Atlanta, GA, BA, span, 1978; Univ Ibero Am, Mex, MAT, Span lit & span cult, cert, 1983; Univ Ga, Athens, cert, 1987; Ga State Univ, Atlanta, MAT, educ & Span, 1983, EdS, educ & span, EdD, educ & span; Nova Southeastern Univ, Ft Lauderdale, FL, EdS, educ leadership & sch improv, EdD, educ leadership & sch improv. **Career:** Douglas Co Schs Syst, Douglasville, Ga, Span teacher, 1978, teacher eng second lang, 1982-86, 1990-92, arts & lang dept, prin; Beulah Elem Sch, prin, currently; Ga Dept Educ, ambassador, speaker, consult, 1988; GovsTask Force Teachers Pay Performance, 1991. **Orgs:** Mem steering comt, Acad Alliances, 1986-; mem staff devel, Coun, Douglas Co Schs, 1986-; head, Instrnl & Prof Devel Comt, Douglas Co Asn Educrs, 1987-88 & 1989-90; chair challenge, Douglas Co High Sch, 1989-92; Foreign Lang Asn Ga; nat pres, Am Asn Teacher Span & Port, 1992-95; Ga Athletic Coaches Asn; adv bd, Southern Conf Lang Teaching, Am Asn Ga; Phi Delta Kappa; Alpha Kappa Alpha; Delta Kappa Gamma; Nat Educrs Asns Cong Contact Team; Prof Negotiation Task Force; Prof League Schs, Leadership Team; instr, Performance Learning Syst Inc. **Home Addr:** 6703 Sutton Pl, Douglasville, GA 30135, **Home Phone:** (404)489-7391. **Business Addr:** Principal, Beulah Elementary School, 4216 Beulah Rd, North Chesterfield, VA 23237, **Business Phone:** (804)743-3620.

### WILLIAMS, JEAN PERKINS

Labor relations manager. **Personal:** Born Sep 21, 1951, Mt. Olive, NC; daughter of Willie R; children: Sonja. **Educ:** Cornell Univ Sch Indust Rels, cert eeo spec, 1976; Pace Univ White, Plains, NY, BS, lib studies, 1981; NC Agr & Tech State Univ, Greensboro, NC, MA, adult educ, 1989. **Career:** Ciba-Geigy Corp, New York, corp eeo coordr, 1975-76, sr personnel admin, 1976-78; Am Cyanamid Lederle Labs, equal opportunity affairs mgr, 1978-80; Am Home Products Corp, personnel mgr, 1980-83; Goodyear Tire & Rubber Co, employ mgr; Guilford Tech Community Col, dir personnel, 1990. **Orgs:** Task force mem, Equal Employ Opportunity Comn, WA, 1975-76; bd dir, Union Child Day Care Ctr, White Plains, NY, 1976-77; Corp Womens Network, 1976-80; Nat Asn Advan Colored People, 1977-79; bd mem, Cent NC Sch Deaf, 1980-83; Am Bus Womens Asn, 1982-; search comt mem exec dir, YWCA-Greensboro, 1986; Personnel Mgrs Asn, Greensboro, NC. **Home Addr:** 925 New Garden Rd Apt 1410, Greensboro, NC 27410-3262, **Home Phone:** (336)315-2339.

### WILLIAMS, JEANETTE MARIE

Educator. **Personal:** Born Jul 11, 1942, Shaw, MS; daughter of Lonnie and Mary; children: Renee L Burwell, Howard S Jr, Karen A & Sharon A Gober. **Educ:** Wilson Jr Col, attended 1968; Chicago State Univ, BS, biol, 1969, MS, biol, 1977; Northern Ill Univ, EdS, 1995. **Career:** Haven Mid Sch, teacher, 1971-72; Chicago Pub Schs, teacher, 1972-74; Malcolm X Col, curric spec, 1974-77; Kennedy-King Col, asst prof biol, Title III, dir, 1983-86, asst dean stud servs, distinguished prof, 1998-99, prof biol sci, currently. Author: The Food & Mood Cookbook: Recipes for Eating Well and Feeling Your Best, 2004; Sins of the Wife, 2007; Out of Darkness Into His Marvelous Light by the Blood of Jesus; A daughter of the Seine; the life of Madame Roland; Learning to Write or Writing to Learn?; Lookin' in! and cookin' in! with the Jeanette MacDonald Raymonds (Gene) at Twin Gables; House of Pain-The Rayner Sisters' Story, 2002; How African Americans Reshaped the Curriculum and Purpose of Higher Education, 2012. **Orgs:** Nat Asn Biol Teachers, 1978-; Asn Supvr & Curric Develop, 1980; pres, Asn Study African Am Life & Hist, 1982-; consult, Educ Mgt Asn, 1982-83; advisor, Phi Theta Kappa, 1982-, pres Chicago Br; bd dir, Black Women's Hall Fame, 1983-; bd dir, Kennedy-King Col, Nat Youth Sports Prog, 1987-; Am Asn Univ Women, 1989-; Am Asn Women-Conn & Jr Cols; NCW Inc; AKA INT Sorority, Xi Nu Omega Chap. **Honors/Awds:** Scholar Chicago Chemical Co, 1971; Advisor's Hall of Honor Ill, Phi Theta Kappa, 1984, 1985, Outstanding Ill Advisor; Distinguished Teacher Award Local 1600, Kennedy King Chap, 1984; Ill Phi Theta Kappa Most Disting Advisor, 1985; Illinois Advisors Hall of Honor, Phi Theta Kappa, 1989, 1991; Women on the Move in the City Col, City Cols Chicago, 1990. **Home Addr:** 259 E 107 St, Chicago, IL 60628, **Home Phone:** (773)568-8951. **Business Addr:** Professor of Biology, Kennedy-King College, 3E18 6301 S Halsted St, Chicago, IL 60621, **Business Phone:** (773)602-5000.

### WILLIAMS, JEFFREY LEM

Editor, writer, journalist. **Personal:** Born Sep 21, 1959, Delhi, NY; son of Diane and Odell Sr; children: Alia. **Educ:** State Univ NY, New Paltz, BA, eng, 1981; Univ Md, MA, jour pub affairs reporting, 1985. **Career:** Frederick News-Post, copy ed, 1986; Lexington Herald-Leader, copy ed, 1987-88; Hartford Courant, copy ed, 1988-90; Chicago Tribune, asst metro copy ed, asst suburban ed, currently, SW Bur Chief, 2002-03, dep w bur chief, 2003-08; Consult Self employed, ed, writer, 2008-12; Newsday LI, dep long island ed, 2012-. **Orgs:** Nat Asn Black Journalists, 1987-; client exec, EquaTerra ERP Adv Pract. **Business Addr:** Assistant Suburban News Editor, The Chicago Tribune, 435 N Michigan Ave 4th Fl, Chicago, IL 60611, **Business Phone:** (312)222-3232.

### WILLIAMS, JENNIFER J. SCOTT

Engineer. **Personal:** Born Jan 31, 1978, Oklahoma City, OK; married Leon M. **Educ:** Ga Inst Technol, BEE, 2001; Spelman Col, BS, math, 2001. **Career:** Nat Aeronaut & Space Admin, Johnson Space Ctr, flight controller, currently. **Orgs:** Exec sec, Nat Soc Black Engrs, 1998-99, vpres, 1999-2000; exec bd mem, Nat Soc Black Engrs, 1998-99; vpres, Houston Space Chap, Nat Soc Black Engrs, Inst Elec & Electronics Engrs, 2012-13. **Honors/Awds:** Torchbearer, Nat Soc Black Engrs, 1996, 1997, 1998, 1999; Woman of Color Technology Award for Student Innovation, USBE, 1999. **Business Addr:** Flight Controller, National Aeronautics & Space Administration, Johnson Space Ctr, Houston, TX 77058, **Business Phone:** (281)483-8100.

**WILLIAMS, JEROME**
Basketball player, basketball executive, basketball coach. **Personal:** Born May 10, 1973, Washington, DC. **Educ:** Montgomery Col, BA, bus, 1994; Georgetown Univ, BA, sociol, 1996. **Career:** Basketball player (retired), coach, exec; Detroit Pistons, power forward, 1996-2001; Basketball Boot Camp, dir develop, 1997-; Toronto Raptors, power forward, 2000-04, community rep, 2006-07, legend ambassador, 2006-08, 2010-; Chicago Bulls, power forward, 2003-04; NY Knicks, small forward, 2004-05, consult/community rep, 2005-07; Nat Basketball Asn Entertainment, analyst & host, 2005-07; Romie Productions LLC, owner, 2005-14; Automotive St Style, founder, 2003-10, pres, 2006-08; Nat Basketball Asn, ambassador, 2006-07; Findlay Prep, dir player develop, develop coach, 2009-13, head coach, 2013-14; Nat Basketball Asn Summer League Player Develop, legend consult, 2009-; Sports Mgt World Wide, gen mgr, 2010-11; Basketball Channel, chief operating officer, 2014-. **Orgs:** Phoebe Found; MADD; Optimist Club Southfield; founder, Jerome Williams Rookie Camp & Mentor Prog; vpres/rep, Nat Basketball Asn Player Union, 1997-2004; founder, JYD Proj, 1998-. **Honors/Awds:** J Walter Kennedy Citizenship Award, 2000; National Award, Fannie Mae Home Team Partnership, 2000; Good Guys in Sports, Sporting News, 2002. **Special Achievements:** Film Appearances: Harold; Sue Thomas: F.B. Eye. **Business Addr:** Chief Operating Officer, The Basketball Channel, 2831 St Rose Pkwy Suite 231, Henderson, NV 89052.

**WILLIAMS, JEROME D.**
Educator. **Personal:** Born Jan 11, 1947, Philadelphia, PA; son of Jerome and Gloria; married Lillian Harrison; children: Denean, Derek, Daniel, Dante & Dachia. **Educ:** Univ Pa, BA, eng, 1969; Union Col, MS, indust admin, 1975; Univ Colo, MBA, 1980, PhD, bus admin, 1986. **Career:** Gen Elec Co, copy writer, sr publicist, supvr, energy systs info, 1969-78; Union Col, adj prof mkt, 1975-78; Solar Energy Res Inst, Golden CO, mgr, pub info, 1978-80; Univ Colo, Univ Denver, Metrop State Col, mkt instr, 1980-87; Pa State Univ, Univ Pk, PA, asst prof, 1987-1993; Univ WIndies, vis Summer Appointments, 1990-95; Pa State Univ, assoc prof, 1993-2001; Sierra Serv Inc, pres, 2002-; Howard univ, assoc prof, dir, ctr marketplace diversity, 2001-02, Anheuser-Busch/ John E.Jacob, prof, mkt, 2002-03; Univ Tex, Austin, Ctr African & African-Am Studies, prof, 2003-; F J Heyne Centennial, prof, commun, 2003-10; Rutgers Univ, prudential chiar bus & res dir, 2010-, PhD prog dir, 2011-, distinguished prof, 2012-, interim dir ctr Urban Enterpreneurship & Econ Develop, 2012-, prof, mkt dept, 2014-. **Orgs:** Am Mkt Asn, 1980-, bd dir, 2011-; Asn Consumer Res, 1982-; Acad Mkt Sci, 1984-; Am Psychol Asn, 1986-; exec bd, Co-chmn, Soc Consumer Psychol, 1989-; Nanyang Technol Univ, vis sr fel, 1995-96; Nat Univ Singapore, vis sr fel, 1997-98; Mkt Commun Spec Interest Group Am Mkt Asn, chmn; founding mem, Mkt Ethnic Fac Asn; founding mem, Mkt & Soc Spec Interest Group Am Mkt Asn; founding mem, Int Soc Qual Life Studies; Am Acad Advert; Sphinx Hon Soc, Univ Pa. **Home Addr:** 1003 Olympic Dr, Pflugerville, TX 78660, **Home Phone:** (512)272-2777. **Business Addr:** Distinguished Professor, Research Director, Rutgers Business School, 1 Wash Pk, Newark, NJ 07102-3122, **Business Phone:** (973)353-3682.

**WILLIAMS, JEWEL L.**
Social worker, executive. **Personal:** Born Feb 11, 1937, Canton, MS; married Frank; children: Anthony, Frank, Kerry, Debra Whitehead & Darcy Donaldson. **Educ:** Mary Holmes Jr Col, bus; Jackson State Univ, soc, 1971. **Career:** Government official (retired); Head Start, community organizer, 1966-73; Canton Pub Schs, social worker, 1974-84; Universal Life Ins Co, sales rep, 1984-86; City Canton, alderman, 1979-94; WMGO Radio Sta, dir pub affairs. **Orgs:** Asst secy, Woman Progress; secy, bd dir, MYL Family Health Ctr, 1973-79; bd mem, Cent Miss Legal Serv, 1976-83; bd mem, Nat Asn Advan Colored People, 1979-; pres, Madison County Women Progress, 1980-82; exec comt, MS Democ Party; pres, Lucy C Jefferson Federated Club Inc; bd dir, Rainbow Literacy; bd dir, Canton Chambers Com; bd dir, Save C Madison County; Madison County Hist Soc. **Honors/Awds:** Outstanding Service, Project Unity Inc, 1979; Outstanding in Community Women for Progress, 1983; Outstanding Sales Service, Universal Life Ins Co, 1985; Outstanding Award, Jackson Links Inc. **Home Addr:** 513 Cauthen St, Canton, MS 39046-4116, **Home Phone:** (601)667-3941.

**WILLIAMS, JOANNE LOUISE**
Journalist. **Personal:** Born Apr 10, 1949, Milwaukee, WI; daughter of John J and Vida Eugenia Smith; children: John Brooks & Christopher. **Educ:** Northwestern Univ, Evanston, IL, BS, 1971. **Career:** WTMJ-TV & Radio, Milwaukee, Wis, anchor, reporter, producer, 1971-77; WGN-TV & Radio, Chicago, Ill, reporter, producer, writer, 1976-78; WITI- FOX6, anchor & reporter, 1978-2008; Milwaukee Pub Tv, independent producer, 2011-12; MPTV Pub Tv Milwaukee, loaned exec united performing arts fund, 2012; United Way Greater Milwaukee, loaned exec, 2012; United Performing Arts Fund, loaned exec, 2013; Milwaukee Pub Tv, host & segment producer, 2012-. **Orgs:** Pres, Milwaukee Press Club, 1982; Milwaukee Forum, 1982-87; Future Milwaukee Grad, 1982; pres, NAB, 1983-99; pres, WIS Black Media Asn; bd dir, Wis Tennis Asn; bd, Milwaukee Tennis Educ Found. **Honors/Awds:** Woman of Color Award, Milwaukee Black Women's Network, 1983, 1999; First Television Fellowship, Case Western Res Sch Med, 1987. **Special Achievements:** Tv Show: "Black Nouveau", host & segment producer, 2012. **Home Addr:** 9524 N 60th St, Brown Deer, WI 53223-1217. **Business Addr:** Host, Segment Producer, Milwaukee Public Television, 1036 N 8th St, Milwaukee, WI 53233, **Business Phone:** (414)271-1036.

**WILLIAMS, JOE H.**
Government official, business owner. **Personal:** Born Oct 7, 1937, Tuskegee, AL; married Marilyn Bryant Hainesworth; children: Melani & Mario. **Educ:** Repub Indust Educ Inst, Elect Maint, 1978. **Career:** Gen Motors Corp, electrician, 1965-; Williams Elec Co, prin, 1973-; Precinct D Warren OH, prec inct comm head 1984-; Warren 7th Ward, councilman, 1977-, pres. **Orgs:** Bd mem, Nat Asn Advan Colored People, 1968-; pres, W Warren Improv Coun, 1968-; King Solomon Lodge 87; bd mem, Warren Electrician Bd, 1980-; elected pres, Warren City Coun, 1990-2000 Nat Steering Comt Clinton/Gore 1996 Campaign. **Honors/Awds:** Hon Mayor, Tuskegee, Ala, 1977; Gen Motors Award Excellence, GenMotors, Lordstown, 1984; Outstanding Community Serv Award, NAACP, 1984; Distinguished Serv Award, Black Elected Off City Warren, Nat AsnNegro Bus & Prof Women's Club, OH, 1985; Joe H Williams Day April 14, named hon, 1985; Outstanding Community Serv Award, Mayor Daniel JSferra Warren, OH; Gov's Spec Recognition, Richard Celeste, 1985; Hon Auditor State, Thomas E Ferguson, 1985; City Coun Citation, JerryCrispino; New York Assembly Citation, Larry Seebrook, 1991. **Home Addr:** 2855 Peerless Ave SW, Warren, OH 44485, **Home Phone:** (330)898-4477. **Business Addr:** Principal, Williams Electric Co, 695 Denton Blvd, Fort Walton Beach, FL 32547, **Business Phone:** (850)862-1171.

**WILLIAMS, JOHN (HOTROD WILLIAMS)**
Basketball player. **Personal:** Born Aug 9, 1962, Sorrento, LA; married Karen; children: John Jr, Johnfrancis, Johnpaul & Johnna. **Educ:** Tulane Univ, attended 1985. **Career:** Basketball player (retired); Ri Gulls, 1985; Staten Island Stallions, 1986; Cleveland Cavaliers, forward-ctr, 1986-95; Phoenix Suns, 1995-98; Dallas Mavericks, forward & ctr, 1998-99. **Orgs:** Alpha Phi Alpha.

**WILLIAMS, JOHN ALFRED. See Obituaries Section.**

**WILLIAMS, REV. JOHN HENRY**
Clergy. **Personal:** Born Feb 24, 1948, Venice, IL; married Emma Jean Johnson; children: Reginold, Dean, John Jr, Shelonda, Nicole & Milton. **Educ:** Southern Ill Univ, Edwardville, attended 1978; State Comm Col, E St Louis, attended 1981. **Career:** Venice Independent Baseball League, pres, 1970-81 New Salem MB Church, pastor 1982-; Venice City, Ill, alderman, 1989-. **Orgs:** Int Union Operating Engrs, 1971-; Free & Accepted Ancient York Rite Mason, 1972-; Nat Asn Advan Colored People, Madison Br, pres, 1976-80; Venice Citizen Community Develop, chmn, 1977-78; People Org Benefit C Venice, pres, 1981-83; former pres, Venice Park Bd Comn, 1982-83; Venice Local Utilities Bd, vice chmn, 1983-; Venice Neighborhood Crime Watch Prog, 1984; River Bluff Girl Scouts Coun, 1992. **Honors/Awds:** Two Local Awards, Madison Br Nat Asn Advan Colored People, 1980; Citation for Community Serv Tri-Cities Area United Way, 1982; Pastor of the Year Award, Spot Light Rev, 1983; Community Serv Award, Madison Progressive Women Orgn, 1984; Ark Travel Cert Award, Ark State Gov Bill Clinton, 1986; Achievement Award, Bethel AME Church, 1986; Proj Cleanup Drugs & Alcohol Cot Award, 1990; Kool Achiever Awards, Nominee, 1992; Martin Luther King Jr Cot Award, Venice Pub Sch, Jr Beta Club, 1992. **Home Addr:** 619 Wash, Venice, IL 62090. **Business Addr:** Pastor, New Salem MB Church, 1349 Klein St, Venice, IL 62090, **Business Phone:** (618)452-3157.

**WILLIAMS, JOHN L.**
Football player. **Personal:** Born Nov 23, 1964, Palatka, FL. **Educ:** Univ Fla. **Career:** Football player (retired); Seattle Seahawks, fullback, 1986-93; Pittsburgh Steelers, fullback, 1994-95. **Honors/Awds:** Second-team All-SEC, 1984, 1985; Honorable mention All-American, 1985; University of Florida Athletic Hall of Fame; Pro Bowl, 1990, 1991.

**WILLIAMS, DR. JOHNNY WAYNE, SR.**
School administrator. **Personal:** Born Dec 18, 1946, Lewisburg, TN; son of James A and Essie M; married Coralee L Henry; children: Kimberly M. **Educ:** Tenn State Univ, BS, 1968; Univ Northern Colo, MS, 1974; Troy State Univ, EDS, 1981; Univ Sarasota, EdD, 1993. **Career:** USAF, officer positions, 1968-88; NC A&T State Univ, chair, prof, Dept Aerospace Studies, 1985-88; Columbia State Community Col, exec dir job training progs, 1988-90, dean stud servs, 1990-94, vpres stud servs, 1994-98; Tenn Technol Ctr, Nashville, dir, 1998-. **Orgs:** Dir, Maury County Fed Credit Union, 1991-; Maury County Voc Prog, 1991-; Job Trainings Pvt Indust Coun, 1992-; Maury County Lit Coun, 1993-. **Home Addr:** 324 Alden Cove Dr, Smyrna, TN 37167-5742, **Home Phone:** (615)355-6047. **Business Addr:** Director, Tennessee Technology Center, 100 White Bridge Rd, Nashville, TN 37209-4515, **Business Phone:** (615)425-5500.

**WILLIAMS, JOSEPH BARBOUR**
Insurance executive, president (organization). **Personal:** Born Aug 20, 1945, New York, NY; son of Joseph Pins Barbour Jr and Mary Alice Porter; married Felicia Ann Thomas; children: Christie Dawn. **Educ:** Talladega Col, Talladega, Ala, BA, 1967. **Career:** Cent Life Ins Fla, Tampa, Fla, pres, chief exec officer, 1972; Cent Life Employees Credit Union, Tampa, Fla, pres, 1987-. **Orgs:** Asst treas, Greater Tampa Urban League, 1984-; Hillsborough Bd Consumer Affairs, 1986-90; Nat Asn Advan Colored People, Tampa Chap, 1990-. **Honors/Awds:** Service Award, Adv For Omega Psi Phi Fraternity, Univ S Fla, 1974; Certificate of Merit, Outstanding performance ins bur, National Ins Asn, 1982, 1976; Blount Trophy For Agency Offices, Exceptional Performance, National Ins Asn, 1985. **Home Addr:** PO Box 271501, Tampa, FL 33688, **Home Phone:** (813)968-4661.

**WILLIAMS, JOSEPH E.**
Executive, president (organization), chief executive officer. **Educ:** Boston Univ Sch Mgt, BA, finance; Univ Pa, Wharton Sch, MBA, multi nat enterprise & finance. **Career:** Salomon Bros; First Nat Bank Chicago, Hibernia Nat Bank; Bank Boston Global Capital Mkt, dir investor sales; Hibernia Southcoast Capital Inc, 1998, pres & chief exec officer, 2002-05; Beacon St Financial Group, pres; ValueSpark Capital LLC, co-founder, pres & chief exec officer, 2009-; Strategic Develop Partners LLC, Chmn, 2011-. **Orgs:** Exec dir, New Orleans Redevelop Authority, 2007-2008; Urban League Greater New Orleans. **Business Addr:** President, Chief Executive Officer, ValueSpark Capital LLC, 1750 St Charles Ave Lafayette Sq, New Orleans, LA 70130.

**WILLIAMS, DR. JOSEPH HENRY**
Physician. **Personal:** Born Jun 15, 1931, Columbia, SC; son of Carter Edmund and Ruby Catherine Winthrop; married C Patricia; children: Joseph Jr. **Educ:** Howard Univ, BS, 1950, MD, 1954; NY Univ, dipl, 1960. **Career:** Pk City Hosp, attend surgeon, 1962-. **Orgs:** Fel Am Soc Abdominal Surgeons, 1963; Am Bd Surg, 1967; Fairfield County Med Soc; fel Am Col Surgeons, 1982; Conn St Med Soc; Am Bd Psychiat & Neurol, 2004-. **Home Addr:** 601 Oak Lane Ave, Philadelphia, PA 19126-3041, **Home Phone:** (215)924-6624.

**WILLIAMS, JOSEPH LEE, JR.**
Mayor, executive. **Personal:** Born Mar 25, 1945, Madison, WV; son of Joseph Lee Sr and Loretta M Lawson; married Shirley Ann Johnson; children: Yvette, Yvonne, Mary & Joseph. **Educ:** Marshall Univ, BBA, fin, 1978; Mayors Leadership Inst, 1984. **Career:** Ebony Golf Classic, founder & dir, 1971-87; Basic Supply Co, chmn, pres & chief exec officer, 1977-; City Huntington, mem city coun, 1981-85, asst mayor, 1983-84, mayor, 1984-85; Abigail Adams Nat Bancorp, Wash, DC, dir, 1988-, bd mem, 1995-; Unlimited Future Inc, bd mem, dir, 1991-96; First Sentry Bank, bd dir & co-organizer, 1997-; Energy Serv Acquisition Corp, independent dir & mem audit comt, 2006-08; Consol Bank & Trust Co, chmn, pres & chief exec officer, 2007-09. **Orgs:** Community Huntington Urban Renewal Authority, 1983-85; Huntington Rotary Club, 1983-92; bd dir, Huntington Area Chamber Com, 1984-85; bd trustee, Cabell-Huntington Hosp, 1984-85; bd dir, United Way River Cities, 1984-90; City Huntington Interim Loan Comn, 1985-87; Huntington Area Chamber Com, WVa Partnership Progress Coun, 1989-93; exec bd mem, United Way River Cities Found; Marshall Univ, Col Bus, adv bd, 1994-2004; bd mem, Adams Nat Bank Inc, 1995-; US SBA Nat Adv Coun, 1997-2000; bd govs, Marshall Univ, 2001-05; fel Wva Workforce Investment bd, 2001-; Cabell-Huntington Hosp Found Bd, 2002-; bd mem, Energy Serv Am Corp, 2008-; fel instnl Bd Gov; bd dir, Huntington Ind Corp; Nat Asn Advan Colored People; bd mem, First Sentry Bancshares Inc; W Va Gov's Workforce Investment Coun. **Honors/Awds:** Outstanding Black Alumni, Marshall Univ, 1984; Outstanding Citizen Award, Huntington, WVa Negro Bus & Prof Women's Clubs, 1985; Subcontractor of The Year, WVa SBA, 1987; Minority Bus Person of the Year, WVa SBA, 1988; featured in Union-Carbide Corp's Nat News mag, 1989; featured in E I duPont de Nemours & Cos TEMPO Nat Newsletter, 1989; Huntington, VA, Med Ctrs Black Hist Month Award, 1990; Ernst & Young Inc, Merrill Lynch Entrepreneur of the Year, regional finalist, 1991; one of 50 most influential in Huntington Tri-State area, Huntington Herald, 1999; WVa Minority Bus Develop Ctr's Innovator Award, 2003. **Home Addr:** 3008 Stony Lake Ct, Richmond, VA 23235-6830. **Business Addr:** President, Chief Executive Officer, Basic Supply Co Inc, 628 8th Ave, Huntington, WV 25712-0936, **Business Phone:** (304)523-1587.

**WILLIAMS, JUAN**
Radio host, writer, journalist. **Personal:** Born Apr 10, 1954, Colon; son of Rogelio L and Alma Geraldine; married Susan Delise; children: Rae, Antonio & Raphael. **Educ:** Haverford Col, BA, philos, 1976. **Career:** Wash Post, reporter, ed writer & columnist, 1976-99; Am's Black Forum, host, 1996-; Fox News, anchor & contribr, 1997-, Fox News Sunday, panelist, currently; Nat Pub Radio, Talk Nation, radio show host, 2000-01, sr corresp, 1999-2010; Bks: Eyes Prize: Am's Civil Rights Years, 1954-65 & 1987; Enough: Phony Leaders, Dead-end Movements & Cult Failure That Are Undermining Black Am--& What We Can Do about It, 2006; (Auth essays) Black Farmers Am, 2006; Books: Eyes on the Prize, 1954-65; Thurgood Marshall: American Revolutionary; This Far by Faith: Stories from the African American Religious Experience; My Soul Looks Back in Wonder: Voices of the Civil Rights Experience and Enough: The Phony Leaders, Dead-End Movements and Culture of Failure That Are Undermining Black America--and What We Can Do About It, 2005. **Orgs:** No bds incl bd trustee, Haverford Col; bd managers, Aspen Inst Commun & Soc Prog; Wash Jour Ctr; NY Civil Rights Coalition; bd dir, New York Civil Rights Coalition. **Home Addr:** 607 Whittier St, Washington, DC 20012-2649, **Home Phone:** (202)829-6732. **Business Addr:** Senior Correspondent, National Public Radio, 635 Massachusetts Ave NW, Washington, DC 20001, **Business Phone:** (202)513-2300.

**WILLIAMS, JUDITH BYRD**
Artist, graphic artist. **Personal:** Born Jul 5, 1952, Philadelphia, PA; daughter of Henry and Frances. **Educ:** Cushing Col, AS, 1973; Cheyney State Col, BA, 1975; ITT Tech Inst, Info Technol Multimedia, 2005; Kutztown Univ Pa, MS, electronic media, 2007. **Career:** Media Ct House, intake worker; Del County Intermediate Unit, TA, artist, 1982-03; J Byrds Prods, chief exec officer, 2001-, owner, 2011-. **Orgs:** Pottstown Art Guild, 1995-2015; J Byrds Gospel Rev, 2002-03; black hist chair, YWCA Potts town, 2003. **Home Addr:** 715 Isabella St, Pottstown, PA 19464-4835, **Home Phone:** (610)718-8424. **Business Addr:** Chief Executive Officer, Owner, J Byrds Production, 715 Isabella St, Pottstown, PA 19464, **Business Phone:** (610)970-7501.

**WILLIAMS, ESQ. JUNIUS W.**
Lawyer. **Personal:** Born Dec 23, 1943, Suffolk, VA; son of Bernyce White and Maurice Lanxton; married Antoinette Ellis; children: Camille, Junea, Junius & Che. **Educ:** Amherst Col, BA, 1965; Yale Law Sch, JD, 1968. **Career:** Attorney, Musician, Educator & Independent Thinker; Newark Community Union Proj; SNCC, 1966; Newark Housing Coun, 1968, 1970, exec dir, 1969; Newark Community Develop Admin & Model Cities Prog, dir, 1970-72; pvt pract atty, 1973-82, 1984, 1994; Nat Bar Asn, Young Lawyers Div, pres, 1978-79; NJ Law J, assoc ed, 1978-81; City Newark, cand mayor, 1982; Essex Newark Legal Serv, exec dir, 1982-84; Return to Source, NJ, bus mgr, vocalist, instrumentalist, 1985-; real estate developer, Newark, NJ, 1987-; Univ Heights Develop Corp, dir, 1988-93; S African Nat Election, observer, 1994; Irvington, NJ, legis counr, 1990-94, atty, 1994-2002; Yale Univ, guest speaker & lectr; Harvard Law Sch, guest speaker & lectr; Cornell Univ, guest speaker & lectr; Univ NC, guest speaker & lectr; Harvard Col, fel; Rutgers Univ, guest speaker & lectr; Rutgers Univ, Abbott Leadership Inst, dir, currently. **Orgs:** Founder & dir, Newark Area Planning Asn, 1967-70; co-chmn, Comn Negotiating Team, NJ Col Med & Dent Controversey, 1967; fel MARC, 1967-68, 1973; Community Develop & Model Cities Prog City Newark, dir, 1970-72; bd dir, Nat Bar Asn, 1971, asst regional dir, vpres, pres, 1978-79; Equal Opportunities Fund Bd, 1980; Essex Co Ethics Comn, 1980; founder & pres, Leadership Develop Group, 1980-; bd trustee, Essex Co Col, 1980-84; fel Inst Pol Kennedy Sch, Gov Harvard Univ, 1980; pres, Yale Law Sch Asn, NJ, 1981-82; founder & chmn, Ad Hoc Comn, Univ Heights, 1984-86; consult & developer, Univ Heights Neighborhood Develent Corp, 1986-93; Univ Heights Develop Corp, dir, 1988-93; chmn bd trustee, Greater Abyssinia Baptist Church, 1990-2003;

chmn, Educ Law Ctr, 2000-05; bd dir, Agr Missions Inc; Essex Co Bar Asn; Critical Minorities Probs Comn; Nat Asn Housing & Redevel Officials; consult, Coun Higher Educ Newark; secy, Newark Collab Group; Stud Nonviolent Coord Comt; Abbott Leadership Inst, dir. **Honors/Awds:** Distinguished Service Award, Newark Jaycees, 1974; Concerned Citizens Award, Bd Concerned Citizens, Col Med & Dent, NJ. **Special Achievements:** Youngest person to be elected president of the National Bar Association. **Business Addr:** Director, Abbott Leadership Institute, Rm 179 Bradley Hall, Newark, NJ 07102, **Business Phone:** (973)353-3531.

### WILLIAMS, KAREN

Vice president (organization). **Personal:** daughter of Cornell. **Educ:** Univ Calif, Los Angeles, BA, econs, 1987, Anderson Sch Mgt, MBA, 1993. **Career:** ARCO Chem, internal auditor; Johnson & Johnson, mkt; Hearst Mag, mkt; Disney ABC Tv, vpres integrated mkt & promotions, 2000-06; Time Inc Essence Mag, vpres sales & mkt, 2007-12; Black Entertainment Tv, vice midwest pres sales, 2012. **Honors/Awds:** "The Network Journal: Black Professionals & Small Business Magazine", 25 Influential Black Women in Business, 2009.

### WILLIAMS, KAREN ELAINE

Airline executive, association executive. **Personal:** Born Apr 5, 1956, Louisa, VA; daughter of Marion Buckner and Curtis Jasper; children: Cossia & Yvette. **Educ:** Renton Voc Inst, cert, 1976; Lake Wash Voc Tech, cert, 1977; Griffin Bus Col, BA, 1980. **Career:** Ideal Realty Co, secy/receptionist, 1984-86; Deloitte Haskins & Sells, admin support, 1986-87; Boeing Co, data base controller, 1987-88, scheduler & planner, 1988-92, employee dev specialist, 1992-96; Eastern Star; cert trng adv, 1996-. **Orgs:** Electronettes Drill Team, tres; AIO Charter asn. **Honors/Awds:** Cert Training Proficiency, 1988; Cert Training Scheduler Briefing, 1989; Pride Excellence Award, 1987, 1990. **Home Addr:** 4212 S Juneau St, Seattle, WA 98118.

### WILLIAMS, KAREN HASTIE

Lawyer. **Personal:** Born Sep 30, 1944, Washington, DC; daughter of William H Jr and Beryl Lockhart; married Wesley S Jr; children: Amanda Pedersen Wesley Hastie, Bo & Bailey Lockhart. **Educ:** Bates Col, BA, 1966; Fletcher Sch Law & Diplcy Tufts Univ, MA, 1967; Columbus Law Sch Cath Univ Am, JD, 1973. **Career:** Fried Frank Harris Shriver & Kampelman, Asn atty, 1975-77; US Senate Comn Budget, chief coun, 1977-80; Off Fed Procurement Policy Off Mgt & Budget, adminr, 1980-81; Crowell & Moring, coun, 1982-2005, retired partner, currently; ABA Sect Pub Contract Law, chair, 1992-93; Supreme Ct, clerk. **Orgs:** Bd mem, Fannie Mae, 1988-99; bd mem, Continental Airlines, 1993-; bd dir, Gannett Co Inc, 1997-; life mem, Internal Revenue Oversight Bd, 2000-03; bd mem, WGL Holdings, 2000-; bd dir, Chubb Corp, 2000-; bd mem, SunTrust Banks, 2002-; chmn, Am Bar Asn Pub Contract Law Sect; bd dir, Sun Trust Bank; bd dir, Lawyers Comt Civil Rights Under Law; bd dir, Wash Gas Light Co; bd trustee, chair, Black Stud Fund; bd dir, bd trustee, Nat Asn Advan Colored People Legal Defense Fund; TrilateralComn; Nat Contract Mgt Asn; Black Women Lawyers Asn; Nat Bar Asn; bd dir, Sun Trust Bank; bd dir, Fed Nat Mortgage Asn Found; Women's Forum, Wash, DC; chair, Greater Wash Res Ctr; trustee, Amherst Col; bd dir, Wash Gas Holdings Co; bd dir, Continental Airlines Inc, currently; bd mem, SunAmerica; bd mem, Nat Cathedral Sch; bd mem, Crestar Financial Serv. **Honors/Awds:** Director's Choice Award, 1993; Breast Cancer Awareness Award, Columbia Hosp Women, 1994; Judge Learned Hand Award, Am Jewish Comt, 1995; Nat Women's Econ Alliance. **Special Achievements:** First African American to joined Crowell & Moring LLP. **Business Addr:** Retired Partner, Crowell & Moring, 1001 PA Ave NW, Washington, DC 20004-2595, **Business Phone:** (202)624-2680.

### WILLIAMS, DR. KAREN RENEE

Physician. **Personal:** Born Jan 27, 1954, Baton Rouge, LA; daughter of Alvin C and Eva Castain; married Cornelius A Lewis; children: Geoffrey P & Brittany E. **Educ:** Xavier Univ, BS, 1975; Howard Univ Col Med, MD, 1978. **Career:** Tulane Univ, inter, residency pediat, 1978-81, fel pediat infectious disease, 1993-94; La State Univ Sch Med & Earl K Long Hosp, instr & dir pediat emergency room, 1981-87, asst prof pediats, 1987-99, head pediat infectious dis, pediat dept, 1985-, assoc prof clin pediat, 1999-; pvt pract, currently. **Orgs:** E Baton Rouge Parish Med Assoc, 1981-87, E Baton Rouge Parish Med Soc, 1985-87; Alpha Omega Alpha Med Hon Soc; bd dir, Our Lady Lake Col. **Home Addr:** 5990 Stratford Ave, Baton Rouge, LA 70808-3528, **Home Phone:** (225)248-8012. **Business Addr:** Associate Professor of Clinical Pediatrics, LSU Mid-City Pediatric Clinic, 1401 N Foster Dr, Baton Rouge, LA 70808, **Business Phone:** (225)987-9040.

### WILLIAMS, KARL DANELL

Football player. **Personal:** Born Apr 10, 1971, Albion, MI. **Educ:** Tex A&M Univ, Kingsville. **Career:** Football player (retired); Tampa Bay Buccaneers, 1996, 2000, 2003, punt returner, wide receiver, 1997, tight end, wide receiver, 1999, wide receiver, 1998, 2001-02; Ariz Cardinals, wide receiver, tight end, 2004; Arena Football League. **Honors/Awds:** Super Bowl Champion, 2002; Super Bowl.

### WILLIAMS, KATHERINE S.

Artist, educational consultant. **Personal:** Born Sep 7, 1941; daughter of Hugh L and Norma D Baird; children: Garvin J. **Educ:** Harvard Univ, MEduc, 1984, EdD, 1987. **Career:** Workers Bank Trinidad & Tobago, opers officer & actg chief acct, 1971-75; Matouk Int, import officer, 1976; Consult Smithsonian Inst, Wash, 1977-83; Caribbean segment Festival Am Folklife Smithsonian Inst, coordr, 1979-80; Festivals Mag, ed & publ, 1979-83; Smithsonian Inst, Res Inst Immigration & Ethnic Studies, consult, 1979-83; Dept State Wash DC, consult, writer & software evaluator, 1985-86; NY Dept Social Serv, prog mgr, 1987-91; Instrnl Systs Inc, Hackensack, NJ, dir prog plng & implementation, consult, 1990-94; Consult Wash, 1992-; Educ Plng Consult, 1994-; US Dept State, Foreign Serv Promos Bds, 1999, 2003; US Dept Educ, reader, proposals, 2003. **Orgs:** Harvard Club Wash, DC, 1999-, secy, 2003-04; Pub Mem Asn Foreign Serv; Presidential Awards Boards. **Honors/Awds:** Women of Achievement, Montgomery Co, 1977; Fellowship grant, DC Comm Arts& Humanities, 1981. **Special Achievements:** Author of Computers, Our Road to the Future, used as text Washington DC Public Sch System 1982-, author of Where Else But America?; A 2-CD set of paintings and poems, photographic exhibit Museum of Modern Art of Latin America OAS Washington, DC 1981; Solo shows of water colours acrylics and oils: Sumner Museum & Archives, Washington DC, 1998; Touchstone Gallery, Washington DC 1998; Gutman Library, Harvard Univ, Cambridge, MA 1998-2000; National Center Gallery, US Geological Survey 1999; Space Telescope, Johns Hopkins Univ, Baltimore, MD, 1999; Fitting Them Together, Arts C, 2000; NASA, Goddard Space Flight Center, Greenbelt, MD 2001; Work shown incorporate offices and three embassies for in-house & public display, Group shows in Washington, DC, New York City, NY, Flint, MI, Stockholm, Sweden, University of Maryland, MD, Univ New England, ME, Tuscon Museum, AZ, & Mobile Museum of Art, AL.Author of Several Books. **Home Addr:** 1440 N St NW Suite 616, Washington, DC 20005-2819, **Home Phone:** (202)328-0652.

### WILLIAMS, KATHLEEN (KATHY WILLIAMS)

Executive, business owner. **Personal:** married Bobby; children: 4. **Educ:** Southern Nazarene Univ, BS, org leader; Okla City Univ, fin planner designation. **Career:** Regist Broker & Dealer; Regist Invest Adv; FSC Securities Corp, fin adv; Williams Fin Serv Group Inc, chief exec officer, owner & pres, currently; Jack & Jill Am Inc, 2008-. **Orgs:** Nat Asn Securities Dealers; Securities Investor Protection Corp; bd dir, Okla Coun Econc Educ; Co founder, bd dir, Shawna Nicole Williams Scholar Memorial Inc; State Chamber Com; Financial Planning Asn; Capitol Chamber Com; Leadership Okla City; Alpha Kappa Alpha Sorority Inc; Jack & Jill Am Inc; Chums Inc. **Honors/Awds:** Leadership Award, Leadership Oklahoma City; Outstanding Community Service Award, Alpha Kappa Alpha Sorority Inc; The Woman of the Year. **Special Achievements:** Featured in such publications as Journal Record, Daily Oklahoman, and Black Enterprise Magazine. **Business Addr:** President, Owner, Williams Financial Services Group Inc, 6901 N Robinson Ave, Oklahoma City, OK 73116, **Business Phone:** (405)843-2380.

### WILLIAMS, KATHRYN

Museum director, educator. **Personal:** Born Dec 25, 1949, Blytheville, AR; daughter of Clifton R and Eddie Bell Hunter-Yearby; children: Allan Wicker, Tonya LaNette & Toya Marie Wicker. **Educ:** Univ Mich-Flint, BTh, 1986; Mott Community Col, BA, social work, 1988. **Career:** Gen Motors-Buick, qual control, 1972-96; Foliage Decorations Kate, 1974-; Comm DoJo Martial Arts Sch Self-defense, founder & teacher, 1980-82; Mus Afrikan Am Hist, founder & pres, cur & researcher, currently; Agiza Histia Habari Newsletter, publ & ed, 1992-; Satora's Afrikan Dance & Drum Sch, founder, 1998-; Mus Black Am Hist Flint, founder & cur; Underground Rr, consult; Satora Black Hist Corner Internet Prog, historian/researcher, 2009-; Sloan Longway, guest serv rep, 2014-. **Orgs:** Asn Mus African Am Hist; Nat Coun Negro Women; Mich Underground Rr Network; MI Coalition Human Rights & Free Safric A; Greater Flint Arts Coun; Soc African Am Storytellers; Nat Asn Advan Colored People; Nat Million Women's March; Mich Humanities Coun. **Home Addr:** 6169 Eagle Ridge Lane Suite 104, Flint, MI 48505, **Home Phone:** (810)789-7324. **Business Addr:** Curator, Founder & Researcher, Museum of African American History, PO Box 660, Flint, MI 48501, **Business Phone:** (810)789-7324.

### WILLIAMS, KEITH DAVID

Actor, singer, comedian. **Personal:** Born Jun 4, 1956, Harlem, NY; son of Lester and Delores Tittley Dickinson; married Margit Edwards Williams; married Dionne Lea. **Educ:** Juilliard Sch, New York, NY, BFA, 1979. **Career:** Films: The Thing, 1982; Platoon, 1986; They Live, 1988; Road House, 1989; Men at Work, 1990; Marked for Death, 1990; Dead Presidents, 1995; The Quick and the Dead, 1995; Volcano, 1997; Armageddon, 1998; There's Something About Mary, 1998; Pitch Black, 2000; Requiem for a Dream, 2000; Barbershop, 2002; Agent Cody Banks, 2003; The Chronicles of Riddick, 2004; Crash, 2004; Mr & Mrs Smith, 2005; ATL, 2006; Delta Farce, 2007; Behind Enemy Lines: Colombia, 2009; Against the Dark, 2009; Don McKay, 2009; Coraline, 2009; The Butcher, 2009; The Princess and the Frog, 2009; Gamer, 2009; All About Steve, 2009; Pastor Brown, 2010; Death at a Funeral, 2010; Lottery Ticket, 2010; Stomp the Yard 2: Homecoming, 2010; Chain Letter, 2010; The Cape, 2010; Hawaii Five-0, 2010; Meeting Monica Velour, 2010; The Book of Matthew, 2011; The Inheritance, 2011.Behind Enemy Lines: Colombia, 2009; Against the Dark, 2009; Don McKay, 2009; Coraline, 2009; The Butcher, 2009; The Princess and the Frog, 2009; Gamer, 2009; All About Steve, 2009; Pastor Brown, 2010; Death at a Funeral, 2010; Lottery Ticket, 2010; Stomp the Yard 2: Homecoming, 2010; Chain Letter, 2010; The Cape, 2010; Hawaii Five-0, 2010; Meeting Monica Velour, 2010; The Book of Matthew, 2011; The Inheritance, 2011; Cloud Atlas, 2012; Smiley, 2012; Don't Pass Me By, 2012; Touch, 2013; Boiling Pot, 2013; Field of Lost Shoes, 2013; Assault on Wall Street, 2013; Enlisted, 2014; Union Furnace, 2014; The North Star, 2014; H4, 2014. voice work: Christmas In Tatter town, 1987; 3x3 Eyes, 1991; Fantastic Four, 1995; Yellowstone: Realm of the Coyote, 1995; Gargoyles, 1994-97; Hercules, 1997; Spawn: The Animation, 1997; Princess Mononoke, 1997; Fallout, 1997; Hercules The Animated Series, 1998; Spawn 3: Ultimate Battle, 1999; Plan escape: Torment, 1999; The Legend of Tarzan, 2001; Final Fantasy: The Spirits Within, 2001; House of Mouse, 2001-02; PBS Hollywood Presents, 2001; Tales From the Crypt: Fare Tonight, Followed by Increasing Clottiness!, 2002; Lords of Ever quest, 2003; Justice League, 2003; Spider-Man: The New Animated Series, 2003; Kaena: The Prophecy, 2003; BeefII, 2004; The Chronicles of Riddick: Dark Fury, 2004; Teen Titans, 2004; Halo 2, 2004; City Confidential, 2004; The Proud Family Movie, 2005; Saints Row, 2006; Walking the Bible, 2006; Halo 3, 2007; Primeval, 2007; Transformers: The Game, 2007; Mass Effect, 2007. Beautiful Loser, 2008; First Sunday, 2008; Superhero Movie, 2008; Chasing 3000, 2008; My Mom's New Boyfriend, 2008; The Sensei, 2008; Sid Meier's Civilization V, 2010; Mass Effect 2, 2010; The Avengers: Earth's Mightiest Heroes, 2010; Ken Burns' Baseball: The Tenth Inning, 2010; Ice Cube: I Am the West, 2010; Dissidia 012 Final Fantasy, 2011; WWE The True Story of WrestleMania, 2011; Transformers Universe, 2012; Mass Effect 3, 2012; WWE WrestleMania XXVIII, 2012; Community, 2012; Robot Chicken, 2012; Young Justice: Invasion, 2013; The Bible, 2013; Marvel Heroes, 2013; Saints Row IV, 2013; Free Birds, 2013; Halo: The Master Chief Collection, 2014; The Monday Night War: WWE vs. WCW, 2014-. **Honors/Awds:** Image Award Nomination, Nat Asn Advan Colored People, 1982; Sinclair Bay field Award Best Performance, Actors Equity, 1989; Emmy Award, 2005. Prime time Emmy Award for Outstanding Voice-Over Performance, 2008. **Business Addr:** Actor, Abrams Artists Agency, 9200 W Sunset Blvd Suite 1130, West Hollywood, CA 90069, **Business Phone:** (310)859-0625.

### WILLIAMS, KELVIN EDWIN

Educator. **Personal:** Born Aug 16, 1964, Detroit, MI; son of Mary; married Latrese; children: Kyrah. **Educ:** Fla Mem Col, BS. **Career:** Miami Dade Pub Sch, learning disabilities teacher, 1987-; Inst Black Family Life Inc, Prog Dir/chief financial officer; Nat Asn Intercollegiate Athletics Football Off; Broward Football Officials Assoc; Nat Fed Interscholastic Off Asn, referee, 1994-. **Orgs:** Kappa Alpha Psi Fraternity, 1983-; Miami-Dade Law Enforcement Task Force & Intergroup Rels, 1993; Miami Alliance Black Sch Educr, 1994-; 500 Role Model Excellence Prog, 1995-; vol, Off Comnr Barbara Carey, 1996-; environcbo adv bd, Miami-Dade Sports, 1997; bd mem, Arabian Nights Found, 1997-. **Home Addr:** 5001 SW 150th Ter, Miramar, FL 33027-3616, **Home Phone:** (954)430-0491. **Business Addr:** Program Director/Chief Financial Officer, Educator, Institute of Black Family Life Inc, 16405 NW 25th Ave, Opa-locka, FL 33054, **Business Phone:** (305)628-4354.

### WILLIAMS, DR. KENNETH HERBERT

Vice president (organization), government official. **Personal:** Born Feb 15, 1945, Orange, NJ; married Susan Marie Griffin; children: Kenneth H & Meryl E. **Educ:** Howard Univ Liberal Arts, BA, 1967; Howard Univ, Sch Law, JD, 1970. **Career:** US House Representatives, internship; US Capitol Police, patrolman, 1969-70; Newark Urban Coalition, exec dir; Model Cities Prog, asst to dir, 1970; City E Orange, judge munic, 1977-82, asst city coun, 1972-75, city councilman, 1984-85; Ernst & Ernst CPA Firm, tax atty, 1970-71; Nat Redevelop LLC, co-owner & partner, Broker Rec currently; US Capital Police Wash, officer; Newark Housing & Rehab Corp, atty & comptroller; Hopkins, Sampson & Brown Real Estate Adv Serv, sr vpres & sales assoc, currently. **Orgs:** Nat Asn Advan Colored People, 1970-, Am Bar Asn, 1971; coun E Orange Jaycees, 1972; chmn, City E Orange Juv Conf Comt, 1973-75; Nat Bar Asn; Judicial Comn, 1977-82, Am Judges Asn, 1978; Am Bar Asn; Garden State Bar Asn; bd trustee, Newark Regional Bus Partnership; Asn Minority Real Estate Professionals; Chair E Orange Juv Conf Comt; 100 Black Men NJ; NJ Asn Realtors; Each One Teach One. **Honors/Awds:** Outstanding Black Attorney, Black Women Lawyers NJ, 1979; White House Fellow Nomination, 1981; Outstanding Citizenship, NJ Fed Colored Womens Clubs Inc, 1984; Certificate of Appreciation, Seton Hall Univ, 1985; Who's Who in Black America, 1985. **Home Addr:** 98 Prospect St, East Orange, NJ 07017, **Home Phone:** (201)306-6195. **Business Addr:** Senior Vice President, Hopkins, Sampson & Brown Real Estate Advisory Services LLC, 89 Market St Suite 411, Newark, NJ 07102, **Business Phone:** (973)802-1504.

### WILLIAMS, KENNETH ROYAL

Baseball player, baseball executive. **Personal:** Born Apr 6, 1964, Berkeley, CA; married Jessica; children: Temeka, Dedrick, Ken Jr, Kyle & Tyler; married Zoraida Sambolin; children: Nicolas & Sofia. **Career:** Baseball player (retired), baseball executive; Chicago White Sox, outfielder & third baseman, 1986-89, dir minor league opers & spec asst to chmn, 1995-96, vpres player develop, 1997-2001, sr vpres & gen mgr, 2000-12, exec vpres, 2012-; Detroit Tigers, outfielder & third baseman, 1989-90; Toronto Blue Jays, outfielder & third baseman, 1990-91; Montreal Expos, prof baseball player, outfielder & third baseman, 1991; Sports Channel, studio analyst, 1995. **Orgs:** Bd mem, Athlete Against Drugs. **Special Achievements:** First African-American general manager in Chicago sports history and thethird in major-league history. **Home Addr:** , Naperville, IL. **Business Addr:** Executive Vice President, Chicago White Sox, 333 W 35th St, Chicago, IL 60616, **Business Phone:** (312)674-1000.

### WILLIAMS, KENNY RAY (KEN WILLIAMS)

Basketball player. **Personal:** Born Jun 9, 1969, Elizabeth City, NC. **Educ:** Barton County Community Col, attended 1989; Elizabeth City State Univ, attended 1990. **Career:** Basketball player (retired); Ind Pacers, forward & power forward, 1990, small forward, 1991-94; Olitalia Forli, Italy, 1994-95; ASVEL Villeurbane, France, 1995-96; Carne Mont Forli, Italy, 1995-97; Hapoel Jerusalem, 1997-2001; Boston Celtics, 2000-01; Troy Pilsener Izmir, 2000; Rocky Mountain Summer League, Denver Nuggets, 2001-02; Bnei Herzeliya, 2001-04; Ironi Ramat Gan, 2003-04; Maccabi Ironi Ramat Gan, 2004-05; Maccabi Givat Shmuel, 2005-06.

### WILLIAMS, KEVIN L.

Football player. **Personal:** Born Aug 4, 1975, Pine Bluff, AR. **Educ:** Okla State Univ, grad. **Career:** Football player (retired); New York Jets, free safety, 1998-2000, right striker, 2000; Miami Dolphins, 2000; Houston Texans, 2002.

### WILLIAMS, KEVIN RAY

Football player. **Personal:** Born Jan 25, 1971, Dallas, TX. **Educ:** Miami Univ, Fl, grad. **Career:** Football player (retired); Dallas Cowboys, kick returner, punt returner, 1993-94, kick returner, punt returner & wide receiver, 1994, wide receiver, 1996; Ariz Cardinals, kick returner, punt returner, 1997; Buffalo Bills, kick returner, punt returner, 1998, 1999; San Francisco 49ers, wide receiver, 2000. **Honors/Awds:** Super Bowl Champion (XXVIII, XXX).

### WILLIAMS, KIM

Basketball player. **Personal:** Born Oct 14, 1974. **Educ:** W Ark Community Col, attended 1995; DePaul Univ, attended 1997. **Career:** Utah Starzz, guard, 1997-98; Merit mgt & Group Inc, 1997-; Minn Lynx, guard, 1999; Chicago Blaze, guard, 2004-05; Maxpreps, 2008-. **Special Achievements:** First Lady Lion to be drafted in the WNBA. **Business Addr:** Basketball player, Merit Management Group Inc,

129 Surrey Dr, New Rochelle, NY 10804, **Business Phone:** (914)632-0927.

### WILLIAMS, LARRY
Educator. **Personal:** Born Nov 27, 1965, Washington, DC; son of Eddie N and Sallie E. **Educ:** Pa State Univ, music, 1985; Peabody Conservatory Music, BMus, 1988, grad performance dipl, 1990. **Career:** New World Symphony Orchestra, prin horn, 1990-92; Fla Int Univ, brass dept, chamber music dir & prof horn, 1991-94; Miami Brass Consort, hornist, 1992-94; Johns Hopkins Univ, Peabody Inst, Prep, Brass/Wind Dept, prof chamber music & horn minor, 1994-; Larry Williams Music Studio, prin owner, 1995-; Univ Md, Baltimore County; Centennial High Sch, coordr, Adult & Continuing Educ Prog, dir, currently; Univ Mich, distinguished vis prof, 2006, 2008; Am Studio Orchestra, artistic dir, 2007-; Music All Nat Festival, yamaha horn artist & clinician, 2009-; Morgan State Univ, adj prof horn; Black Pearl Chamber Orchestra, prin horn, 2011-; Ritz Chamber Players, hornist, 2013-; Howard Community Col, adj prof, 2014-. **Orgs:** Adv, Arts Talented Youth Prog, 1994-97; dir, Herald Brass Prog, 1994-; chair, Brass & Winds Dept, Peabody Prep, 1994-; Lyric Brass Quintet, 1998-; Morpheus Trio, 1998; Int Horn Soc. **Home Addr:** 1101 N Calvert St Apt 709, Baltimore, MD 21202, **Home Phone:** (410)539-6487. **Business Addr:** Chair, Director, Peabody Institute of the Johns Hopkins University, 1 E Mt Vernon Pl, Baltimore, MD 21202, **Business Phone:** (410)234-4500.

### WILLIAMS, LARRY C.
Lawyer, association executive. **Personal:** Born May 17, 1931, Seneca, SC; married Theresa; children: Margo, Larry Jr, Edward, John, David Lauren & Joseph. **Educ:** Howard Univ, BA, 1954, LLB, 1959. **Career:** Houston, Waddy, Bryant & Gardner; Variable Annuity Life Ins Corp; Corp Coun Off DC, asst corp coun; Larry C Wiliams & Asn, atty & owner, currently. **Orgs:** Regional Coun US & Brewers Asn; gen coun, Nat Bus League; Nat Funeral Dir & Morticians Asn; United Way Nat Capitol Area; pres, DC C C; Metro WA Bd Trade; bd mem, Metro YMCA; bd mem, Nat Coun Christians & Jews; life mem, Alpha Phi Alpha Frat Inc; 32nd Degree Mason; Shriner; Mecca Temple 10; Transition Comn Develop Orgn First City Coun under Home Rule. **Home Addr:** 1451 Jonquil St NW, Washington, DC 20012, **Home Phone:** (202)726-6048. **Business Addr:** Attorney, Owner, Larry C Williams & Associates, 7600 Ga Ave Nw, Washington, DC 20012-1616, **Business Phone:** (202)842-2222.

### WILLIAMS, LASHINA BRIGETTE
Administrator. **Personal:** Born Oct 22, 1957, Houston, TX; daughter of Chauncey K Morrow Jr and Myrtle Morrow. **Educ:** Prairie View A&M Univ, BS, 1980; Atlanta Univ, MBA, 1984. **Career:** Phillips Petrol, mech engr, 1980-82; Digital Equip, intern, 1983; IBM, Gaithersburg, Md, prod planning & prog mgt, 1985-, Fed Strategy & Technol Inst, sr proj mgr, currently. **Orgs:** Nat Black MBA Asn, 1983-; Delta Sigma Theta Sorority; Workshop Orgn Comt. **Home Addr:** 3819 Ridgeview, Missouri City, TX 77489. **Business Addr:** Senior Project Manager, IBM Corp, 800 N Frederick Ave, Gaithersburg, MD 20879, **Business Phone:** (301)240-0111.

### WILLIAMS, LAURYN
Athlete. **Personal:** Born Sep 11, 1983, Pittsburgh, PA; daughter of David and Donna. **Educ:** Univ Miami, BBA, 2004. **Career:** Track and field athlete, 2002-13; appeared in Summer Olympics, 2004, 2008, 2012; bobsledder, 2013-15; appeared in Winter Olympics, 2014. **Honors/Awds:** Big East Indoor Most Outstanding Track Athlete, 2002; World Junior Championships, gold medal 100m, 2002; Summer Olympics, silver medal 100m, 2004; World Outdoor Championships, gold medal 100m, 2005; World Indoor Championships, silver medal 100m, 2006; Visa Humanitarian of the Year Award, 2006; Summer Olympics, gold medal 4x100m, 2012; World Cup, silver medal two-woman bobsled, 2013; Winter Olympics, silver two-woman bobsled, 2014; University of Miami Sports Hall of Fame, inductee, 2015. **Special Achievements:** First American woman to win medals at both summer and winter Olympic games; volunteered with the USATF's Win with Integrity program. **Business Addr:** United States Olympic Committee, 1 Olympic Plz, Colorado Springs, CO 80909, **Business Phone:** (888)222-2313.

### WILLIAMS, DR. LEA E.
Vice president (organization), association executive, educator. **Personal:** Born Dec 21, 1947, Paducah, KY; daughter of Nathanial H and Mae Frances Terrell. **Educ:** Ky State Univ, Frankfort, KY, BA, elem educ, 1969; Univ Wis, Milwaukee, WI, MA, curric & instr, 1973; Teachers Col, Columbia Univ, New York, NY, MS, 1977, EdD, 1978. **Career:** Col New Rochelle's Sch New Resources-S Bronx campus, instr Eng; City Col New York, adj instr; Milwaukee Pub Sch, WI, sixth grade teacher, 1969-73; Milwaukee Area Tech Col, WI, ABE instr, 1973-74; United Negro Col Fund, New York, NY, prog evaluator, 1978-80, proposal writer, 1980-81, CAI res dir, 1981-82, Educ Serv, asst dir, 1982-86, Educ Serv, dir, 1982-86, Educ Serv, vpres, 1988-89; Nat Action Coun Minorities Engineering, exec vpres, 1989-2004; Bennett Col, exec dir, women's leadership inst, 1996-2003; Nat African-Am Women's Leadership Inst Inc, exec dir, 2000-06; NC A&T State Univ, interim assoc vice chancellor acad affairs univ planning & assessment, currently, interim dir, 2004-12. **Orgs:** Alpha Kappa Mu Hon Soc, 1969; Phi Delta Kappa, 1975; ed bd, Thrust employ jour, 1980-85; panelist, Nat Endowment Humanities, 1983-85; Nat Leadership Forum, Am Coun Educ, 1986; Am Educ Res Asn, 1986-; consult ed, NY Gov's Adv Comm Black Affairs, 1987-88; pres, Asn Black Women Higher Educ, 1987-89; adv comm, Asn Am Col, 1988; comnr, Nat Asn Independent Cols & Univs, 1988-91; exec bd, Am Asn Higher Educ, 1989-91; div chairperson, Nat Asn Women Educ, 1989-91, ed bd, Initiatives, 1989-; bd govs, Am Asn Engineering Socs, 1989-95; bd dir, Triangle Coalition Sci & Technol Educ, 1991-95, vpres & bd dir, 1993-95; bd trustee, Family Dynamics, 1993-; adv coun, Harlem Br YWCA, 1995-; exec dir, Nat African-Am Women's Leadership Inst; Greensboro Hist Mus, currently; Community Found Greater Greensboro, currently. **Home Addr:** 788 Riverside Dr Suite 8A, New York, NY 10032, **Home Phone:** (212)281-9012. **Business Addr:** Interim Associate Vice Chancellor, North Carolina Agricultural & Technical State University, 1601 E Market St, Greensboro, NC 27411, **Business Phone:** (336)334-7006.

### WILLIAMS, DR. LEON LAWSON
Government official. **Personal:** Born Jul 21, 1922, Weeletka, OK; son of Lloyd R and Elvira E Lott; married Margaret; children: Karen E, Leon L Jr, Susan P Rogers, Penny, Jeffery & Alisa O. **Educ:** San Diego State Univ, BA, psychol, 1950; Univ San Diego Sch Law, attended 1961; Nat Univ, doctorate, 1985. **Career:** Government official (retired); San Diego County Sheriff Dept, admin officer, 1957-66; Neighborhood Youth Corps, dir, 1966-70; San Diego Urban League, exec dir, 1968; City San Diego, councilman, 1969-82; Fed Mart Corp, consult, 1972-76; County San Diego, supv, 1983-95; San Diego Metrop Transit Develop Bd, chmn, 2005. **Orgs:** Alpha Pi Boule Sigma Pi Phi Frat, 1976-91; chair, bd supervisors, County San Diego, 1985 & 1990; dir, San Diego Col Retailing, 1986; life mem, Nat Asn Advan Colored People; chmn, Transit Syst's Bd dir; dir, Metro Transit Develop Bd; Nat Asn Counties; pres, Calif State Asn Counties; dir, San Diego Region Water Reclamation Bd; chmn, Serv Authority Freeway Emergencies; county supvr, Metrop Transit Develop Bd, 2005; Citizens Interracial Comt. **Special Achievements:** First African American elected to the San Diego City Council, 1969. **Home Addr:** 3024 E St, San Diego, CA 92102-2328, **Home Phone:** (619)234-5544.

### WILLIAMS, DR. LEONA CLARICE
Administrator, school superintendent. **Personal:** Born Dec 26, 1936, Los Angeles, CA; married Jarrod B; children: Jarrod Barrett II & Courtni Clarice. **Educ:** Calif State Univ, Los Angeles, BA, 1966; Calif State Polytech Univ, MA, 1974; Univ Nebr, Lincoln, PhD, 1978. **Career:** Los Angeles Unified Sch Dist, teacher, 1965-66; Ont-Montclair Sch Dist Ont, Calif, teacher, 1966-72; Fr Flanagan's Boys Town Sch Syst NE, reading specialist, reading coordr, asst prin, curric coordr, 1972-79; Riverside Unified Sch Dist, Monroe Elem, prin; Cent Mid Sch, prin, dist dir spec educ, 1979-82; Lucerne Valley Union Sch Dist Calif, dist supt, 1982; One Schwide Charter Sch Technol Inc, bd pres & chief exec officer, currently. **Orgs:** Phi Delta Kappa; Asn Calif Sch Adminr; Asn Supv & Curric Develop, Lucerne Valley Chamber Com. **Honors/Awds:** US Congressional Award, 1984. **Business Addr:** Board President, Chief Executive Officer, One Schoolwide Charter School of Technology Inc, 1790 Wash St, Riverside, CA 92506, **Business Phone:** (909)780-2590.

### WILLIAMS, LEROY JOSEPH
Auditor. **Personal:** Born Apr 13, 1937, New Orleans, LA; married Verna M Lewis; children: Linda M Thomes, Gregory C Lewis & Sandra Lewis. **Educ:** Olympic Col, AA, 1969; Univ WA, BA, 1972; Univ Puget Sound, attended 1974. **Career:** City Seattle, city coun legis auditor; USN Exchange Bremerton, buyer, 1960-61; Boeing Co, cost acct, 1972-73, mat controller, 1961-72; Seattle Model City Prg, fiscal consult, 1972-73; Municipality Metrop Seattle, audit mgr, 1972-. **Orgs:** Sch supt, 1965-70, mem trustee bd, 1965-, Sinclair Baptist Church, 1960-; Hamma Hamma #35 Masonic Lodge Prince Hall Grand Lodge Wash Jurisdiction, 1965-; Cascadian Consistory PHA AASR, 1970-; Bremerton Sch Bd, 1971-77; Williams Pvt Tax Consult, 1972-; charter mem, Cr Union Audit Comt, 1972-73; Olympic Col Asn Higher Educ, 1973-; Wash State Ferry Adv Comt, 1973-77; Wash State Educ TV Comn, 1974-77; legis rep, Wash State Sch Dir, 1974-; Aldephil Inst, 1975-; supreme Coun, 33 Deg Mason, 1977; Worshipful Master Hamma Hamma Lodge #35; African Am Affairs Comn, app by Gov Mike Lowery, 1995; Asn Govt Accountants. **Home Addr:** 3729 W E St, Bremerton, WA 98312-4644, **Home Phone:** (360)373-3091. **Business Addr:** Audit Manager, Municipality Metropolitan Seattle, 600 4th Ave Munic Bldg, Seattle, WA 98104, **Business Phone:** (206)684-5600.

### WILLIAMS, DR. LISA R.
Educator, management consultant. **Personal:** Born Feb 11, 1964, Toledo, OH. **Educ:** Wright State Univ, BS, bus, 1986, MBA, 1988; Ohio State Univ, MA, 1992, PhD, 1992. **Career:** Dayton Power & Light, mkt analyst, 1984-87; Gen Motors, mkt analyst, 1987; Cent State Univ, asst prof bus, 1988-89; Penn State Univ, asst prof bus logistics; William Res Inc, founder, pres & chief exec officer, currently; Univ Ark, Dept Mkt & Transp, prof, currently. Books: Evolution, Status and Future of the Corporate Transportation Function, co-auth; The electronic supply chain: Its impact on the current and future structure of strategic alliances, partnerships and logistics leadership, co-auth, 2002. **Orgs:** Alpha Kappa Alpha Sorority, 1990-; Coun Logistics Mgt, 1990-; Am Soc Transp & Logistics, 1992-; African Am Women Investment Group, treas, 1993-. **Home Addr:** 1691 Sheffield Ct, State College, PA 16801, **Home Phone:** (814)867-3955. **Business Addr:** Professor, University of Arkansas, Fayetteville, AR 72701, **Business Phone:** (479)575-2000.

### WILLIAMS, LLOYD A.
President (organization), chief executive officer. **Career:** LMR Productions Inc, Chmn & Co-Founder; HARLEM WEEK Inc, Chmn & Co-Founder; Greater Harlem Housing Develop Corp, pres; Harlem Arts Alliance, Vice Chmn; Urban Develop; Hunter Col; The City Col of New York; Rutgers Univ; Pratt Inst; Shaw Univ; Hostos Community Col; Univ Mich; Univ Massachusetts; Malcolm-King Col; Fordham Univ; New Sch Social Res & Cent State Col. **Orgs:** Mem Exec Bd, Dir, NYC & Co. **Business Addr:** President, Chief Executive Officer, Greater Harlem Chamber of Commerce, 200A W 136th St, Harlem, NY 10030, **Business Phone:** (212)427-7200.

### WILLIAMS, LLOYD L.
Legislator, executive. **Personal:** Born Jul 26, 1944, St. Thomas; married Irene Creque; children: Lisa Marie & Taya Ayanna. **Educ:** Moravian Col, BA, 1966; NY Univ, MA, cert orthodics & presthetics; VA Commonwealth Univ, MA; Am Univ, MA. **Career:** Youth Club Action, adv tutor; Wayhne Aspinall JHS, teacher, Dept Social Welfare, voc rehab counsr; VI Legis, from spec asst to legislator, 1972; VI 10th, 11th, 12th & 13th Legis, majority leader, 1976-78; Legis Vi, VI 14th Legis, sen, currently; Pub Safety Comn, chair; Commun Develop Corp, owner, pres & chief exec officer; Mgt Partnership Corp, bus partner; Lloyd's Gift & Jewelry Shop, owner, mgr. **Orgs:** Task Force Criminal Code Rev Proj; Bd Tri-Island Eco Devel Coun; Bd VI Montessori Sch Deleg Const Conv; Fifteenth Legis Vi. **Home Phone:** (340)775-5401. **Business Addr:** Senator, Legislature of the Virgin Islands, PO Box 1690, St. Thomas00801, **Business Phone:** (340)693-3701.

### WILLIAMS, DR. LOIS STOVALL
College administrator, chief executive officer, founder (originator). **Personal:** married Anderson J Jr; children: 8. **Educ:** Morgan State Univ, BS, natural sci; Loyola Col, MS, coun & psychol; Univ Conn, PhD, higher educ & sch psychol; Harvard Univ, Inst Educ Mgt, cert. **Career:** Education & training specialist, administrative project manager; Norfolk State Univ, prof psychol; educ advisor; Hampton Univ, Ctr Teaching Excellence, prof educ, dir; Am Testing Serv, sr vpres admin; Passaic Co Community Col, dean instr; Knoxville Col, pres, 1995; Va Beach City Pub Schs; Wiltex Inc, founder & chief exec officer, 1999-; Author: Wisdom Is Better Than Strength, 2008. **Orgs:** Comn educ reform; bd trustee, old dom univ; Sch Bd City Va Beach. **Home Addr:** 2532 Las Corrales Ct, Virginia Beach, VA 23456-4200. **Business Addr:** Chief Executive Officer, Wiltex Inc, 1012 Oaklawn Ave, Norfolk, VA 23504-3606, **Business Phone:** (757)304-7059.

### WILLIAMS, REV. LONDELL
Clergy, government official. **Personal:** Born Apr 23, 1939, Texarkana, AR; married Mary; children: Londell GeoAna John & Marian Londelon. **Educ:** Univ Ark, 1955; Los Angeles St Col, BA, 1958; Los Angeles Bible Inst, DD, 1960. **Career:** AUS Corps Engr, contract specl, 1955-58; US Treas Dept Bur Customs, acct tech, 1958-59; AUS, personnel specl, 1964-68; Ave Bapt Ch, pastor, 1969-; Dept HEW Soc Security Admn, claims Develr, 1969-; Pk Ave Bapt Church, pastor-tcr, asst mayor, 1969-; City Texarkana, Tex, ward three, asst mayor, 1977-2004; city councilman. **Orgs:** Texarkana Ministerial Alliance, 1971-77; grand master, Master Mason AF & AM Bronzeville Lodge 83, 1974-77; jury comnr Miller, Hempstead, Lafayette, Howard, 1975-76; Texarkana Ark & Texarkana Tex C C, 1976-; city bd dir, Texarkana Ark, 1977-; bd mem, Texarkana Human Develop Ctr, 1977. **Honors/Awds:** Outstanding Integrity & Character Displayed in City, 1973; Bert Lambert Award, 1974-75; High Quality Increase Award, HEW, 1976; Dr Martin Luther King Award, 1995; Earl Holmes Award, Outstanding Leadership & Excellence Serv Rendered All Texarkanians, 1996; Leadership Award, 2008; Wilbur Award Nominee; Sharp Shooter Award; Good Conduct Medal. **Special Achievements:** First ever elected Black City Councilman in Texarkana, Arkansas or Tex, 1976; First Black Mayor ever elected, 1992-95. **Home Addr:** 6 Preston Cir, Texarkana, AR 71854-5839, **Home Phone:** (870)773-1300. **Business Addr:** PO Box 2711, Texarkana, AR 75504.

### WILLIAMS, DR. LONNIE RAY
School administrator, manager, dean (education). **Personal:** Born Jan 21, 1954, Stephens, AR; son of Lonnie and Rosie M. **Educ:** Univ Ark, Fayetteville, BS, BA, finance & banking, 1977, MEd, higher educ admin & stud personnel serv, 1983, EdS, higher educ admin, 1991, EdD, adult educ, 2001. **Career:** Univ Ark-Fayetteville, police patrolman, 1976-78, night mgr, stud union, 1978-84, minority engineering, dir, 1983-86, asst dean students, 1986-91, asst vice chancellor stud serv, 1991-2003; Ark State Univ, Minority Engineering Progs Col Engineering, dir, 1984-86, Affairs Div Stud Serv, asst dean students & coordr, 1986-91, interim dir, 1998, career mgt ctr, staff Mem, assoc vice chancellor stud affairs, adj fac, 2003-, Ark Stud Union, night mgr; Univ Ark Police Dept, police sergeant; African Am Perspectives mag, Co-ed & Co-owner, 2007-13. **Orgs:** Adv bd mem, Region V, Nat Soc Black Engrs, 1984-87; Region B, chairperson, Nat Asn Multicultural Engineering Prog Advocates, 1985-86; chairperson, Ark Asn Multicultural Coun, 1986-87; Ark Asn Coun Guid & Develop, 1986-; bd mem, Wash County Equal Opportunity Agency, 1988-91; adminr, Ark Alumni Asn Black Alumni Socs, 1990-2003; Coordr, Ark Alumni Asn's Black Alumni Socs Reunions, 1990, 1993, 1995, 1990, 2000, 2003; bd dir, N Ark Girl Scouts Am, 1993-95; grant adminr, Youth Opportunities Unlimited; adminr, U. S. D. A. Food Grants, 1994-2000; pres, Ark Asn Multicultural Coun & Develop, 1995-97; exec bd mem, Ark Col Personnel Asn, 1992-96; Am Coun Asn, 1995-; Am Col Personnel Asn, 1995-; bd dir, Asn Black Cult Ctr, 1995-2003; adminr, Coca-Cola Found Scholarships, 1996-2003; Nat Asn Stud Personnel Adminr, 1997; adminr, Rodney E. Momon Memorial Scholar, 1998-2003; Daisy Gatson Bates Holiday Comt State Ark; Ark State Rep, Omega Psi Phi, 1999-; bd dir, onesboro Church Health Ctr, 2004-; bd trustee, Ark Baptist Col, 2005; coordr, Ark State Univ's Alumni Asn & Strong-Turner Black Alumni Chap Black Alumni Reunion, 2008; panel reviewer, Nsf; Omega Psi Phi Fraternity; Ark Laymen Asn; Nat Asn Stud Personnel Adminr; Ark Asn Multicultural Coun & Develop. **Home Addr:** P O Box 106, State University, AR 72467, **Home Phone:** (870)972-2048. **Business Addr:** Associate Vice Chancellor for Student Services, Arkansas State University, PO Box 106, Jonesboro, AR 72467-0106, **Business Phone:** (870)972-3025.

### WILLIAMS, LORECE P.
Educator. **Personal:** Born Jan 22, 1927, Luling, TX; married Nathan H; children: Nicholas & Natalie. **Educ:** Huston Tillotson Col, BS, 1947; Our Lady Lake Col, MSW, 1962. **Career:** Professor (retired); ARC Brooke Army Med Ctr, dir, 1969-; Our Lady Lake Col, prof social work, 1965-69; Incarnate Word Col, San Antonio, diagnostician, 1969; San Antonio Jr League Incarnate Word Clergy, lectr, group leader; Our Lady Lake Univ, prof, prof emer social work, currently. **Orgs:** Fac Welfare Coun; Alpha Kappa Alpha Sorority; Race & Rel Comn; Gov Comn Crime & Prev; Cath Family & Child; Child Serv Bur; Nat Asn Social Workers; Coun Social Work Educ; Theta Sigma Phi. **Honors/Awds:** Excellence in Writing Awards, Theta Sigma Phi. **Special Achievements:** Co-author Bientennial Book, Folklore Texas Cultures. **Home Addr:** 4627 Old Coach Lane, San Antonio, TX 78220-2518, **Home Phone:** (210)661-2144. **Business Addr:** Professor Emeritus, Our Lady of the Lake University, 411 SW 24 St, San Antonio, TX 78207, **Business Phone:** (210)434-6711.

### WILLIAMS, LORENZO
Basketball player, basketball coach. **Personal:** Born Jul 15, 1969, Ocala, FL; married Tracey. **Educ:** Polk Community Col, attended 1989; Stetson Univ, attended 1991. **Career:** Basketball player (retired), basketball coach; Fayetteville Flyers, 1991-92; Charlotte Hor-

nets, ctr, 1992-93, power forward, 1993-94; Orlando Magic, power forward, 1992-94; Boston Celtics, power forward, 1992-93; Dallas Mavericks, power forward, 1993-94, ctr, 1994-96; Wash Bullets, ctr, 1996-97; Wash Wizards, power forward, 1997-2000; Pine Ridge Educ Ctr, Ft Lauderdale; Univ Cent Fla, Five Star Basketball Camp, coach, currently. **Business Addr:** Coach, University of Central Florida, 500 Nepperhan Ave Suite 200, Yonkers, NY 10701, **Business Phone:** (914)964-6540.

### WILLIAMS, HON. LOUISE BERNICE

Association executive, government official. **Personal:** Born May 30, 1937, Abington, PA; daughter of Richard S Duncan and Mary Grasty Duncan; children: Cynthia Whitfield, Robert Whetts, Brian Whetts & Kimberly. **Educ:** Lancaster Sch Bus, attended 1964; Lincoln Univ; Shippenburg State Col, cert dist justices, 1973. **Career:** Dist Justice Off, admin clerk, 1970-73; City Lancaster 3rd & 7th Ward, dist justice, 1973-85; Girls Serv Lancaster Inc, pres, 1975-81; Consol Dist Justice Off, City Lancaster, admin dist justice, 1983-85; Pa State Bd Pardons, 2000; Community Cult Diversity, Millersville Univ; City Lancaster, Community Develop & Planning Personnel, vpres, pub safety chair, currently, pres, 2010-; Lancaster City Dem Comt, pres, currently. **Orgs:** Planned Parenthood Lancaster, 1978-81; Urban League Lancaster, 1979-84; pres, Nat Asn Advan Colored People, 1980-82; Lancaster County Dist Justice Asn; bd mem, Planned Parenthood Lancaster County, 1988-; bd pardons, Commonwealth Pa; Lancaster Independent Trash Haulers Asn; Boys & Girls Clubs Am; Lancaster Mediation Ctr; Crispus Attucks Community Ctr; pres, AARP Chap 530; bd dir, Community Action Prog Lancaster County, currently. **Honors/Awds:** Boss of the Year, Am Bus Women's Asn, 1976; Outstanding Citizen, City Lancaster, 1981; Past President Award, Girls Serv Lancaster Inc, 1981; CBK Breaking the Glass Ceiling Award, 2012; Catherine Baker Knoll Award, 2012. **Business Addr:** Chair Public Safety, President, City of Lancaster, 331 S Franklin St, Lancaster, PA 17602, **Business Phone:** (717)291-1374.

### WILLIAMS, LUCRETIA MURPHY

School administrator. **Personal:** Born Aug 16, 1941, Springfield, OH; daughter of Wilbur Otho and Lenore Dorsey Smith (deceased); married Robert; children: David Walter Bentley & Robin Lenore Goodwin. **Educ:** Cent State Univ, BS, elem educ, 1965, MEd, guid & coun, 1969; Ohio State Dept Educ, gen aptitude test battery training, voc guid training cert, 1974; Xavier Univ, admin cert elem & sec, 1976. **Career:** Onondago Co Welfare, social worker, 1966-67; Columbus Pub Schs, guid counr, 1969-77, asst prin, 1977-78, admin, 1979-99, asst supt, stud servs, 1994-98, Interim Acceleration & Extra Help coordr, currently; AT&T Technols, personnel counr, summer, 1970; Neptune Twp Pub Schs, princl, 1978-79. **Orgs:** Life mem, Nat Alliance Black Sch Employees; Nat Asn Sec Sch Prins; Ohio Alliance Black Sch Educ; Columbus Alliance Black Sch Educ; Columbus Admin Asn; Columbus Cent Off Admin Asn; Delta Sigma Theta; Mayor's Coun Youth. **Home Addr:** 5237 Garand Dr, Westerville, OH 43081-7822, **Home Phone:** (614)895-9497. **Business Addr:** Interim Acceleration & Extra Help Coordinator, Columbus Public Schools, 270 E State St, Columbus, OH 43215, **Business Phone:** (614)365-5000.

### WILLIAMS, LYNDA

Law enforcement officer. **Personal:** Born Jan 1, 1963?; children: Raelyn. **Educ:** Mid Tenn State Univ, attended 1985, 1993; Johns Hopkins Univ, MA. **Career:** Sheriff's dep, August, GA, 1985-88; Secret Serv, uniformed officer, spec agt, nat recruiter, U.S. attache to S Africa, spec agt in-chg cong affairs, head recruiting, head develop & training & dep asst dir off Human Resources, 1988-. **Special Achievements:** First African-American female manager of the Secret Service Washington field office. **Business Addr:** U.S. Secret Service, 245 Murray Lane, Washington, DC 20223, **Business Phone:** (202)406-5708.

### WILLIAMS, REV. DR. MACEO MERTON

Clergy, school administrator, association executive. **Personal:** Born Oct 27, 1939, Baltimore, MD; married Margaret D Moon. **Educ:** Morgan State Univ, AB, 1966; Univ Baltimore, MPA prog, 1976; Wesley Theol Sem, MDiv prog, 1985; Howard Univ, MDiv, 1986; Howard Univ Divinity Sch, DMin, 1991. **Career:** State Md, probation agt, 1965-66; Dept Housing, area coordr, 1966-71; US Dept Labor, Concentrated Employ Prog, coordr, 1971-74; Bay Col, Md, dean students, 1974-79; Md Parole Comn, comnr, 1983-88; Centreville-Cordova Charge United Methodist Church, pastor, 1986-90; Simpson United Methodist Church, pastor, 1991-95; Martin Luther King Jr Memorial United Methodist Church, pastor, 1995-, sr pastor, currently. **Orgs:** Bd mem, Dept Housing & Comn Develop UMC, 1970-; bd trustee, Keswick Nursing Home, 1973-76; pres, FiveFive Dem Club, 1974; Charter Rev Comn, 1974-76; Prince Hall Grand Lodge F & AM, MD Zion Lodge No 4; Nat Asn Stud Servs; Nat Asn Col Coun; Morgan State Univ Alumni; Howard Univ Alumni; life mem, Black Methodists Church Renewal; life mem, Nat Asn Advan Colored People; Pi Omega Chap; bd trustee, Baltimore City Col, 2002-. **Honors/Awds:** Hall of Fame, Baltimore City Col, 1997; Outstanding Alumni, Booker T Wash Jr High Sch, 2007. **Special Achievements:** Longest serving commissioner in state history. **Home Addr:** 3511 Lynchester Rd, Baltimore, MD 21215, **Home Phone:** (410)367-5365. **Business Addr:** Senior Pastor, Martin Luther King Jr Memorial United Methodist Church, 5114 Windsor Mill Rd, Baltimore, MD 21207-6657, **Business Phone:** (410)448-2312.

### WILLIAMS, MALINDA

Actor. **Personal:** Born Dec 3, 1975, Elizabeth, NJ; married Mekhi Phifer; children: Omikaye; married D-Nice. **Educ:** Union County Col; Actor's Conserv, New York. **Career:** Films: Laurel Avenue, 1993; High School High, 1996; Sunset Park, 1996; A Thin Line Between Love & Hate, 1997; Damn Whitey, 1997; An Invited Guest, 1999; The Wood, 1999; Dancing in September, 2000; Half & Half, 2003; The District, 2004; Exposure, 2005, Idlewild, 2006; A Day in the Life, 2007; Daddy's Little Girls, 2007; First Sunday, 2008; A Day in the life, 2009; Nailed; 2 Days in New York, 2011; The Under Shepherd, 2011; A Cross to Bear, 2011; Percentage, 2013. TV series: "The Cosby Show", 1987-90; "Miami Vice", 1990; "Roc", 1993; "South Central", 1994; "My So-Called Life", 1994; "Me and the Boys", 1994; "Captain Planet & the Planeteers", 1995; "Sister, Sister", 1994-95; "Moesha", 1996; "Outreach", 1999; "Soul Food", 2000-04; "The Big Much 'IDo' About Nothing Episode", 2003; The District, 2004; "Fear Eats the Soul", 2004; "The Getaway", 2006; "Windfall", 2006. **Honors/Awds:** Nominee, NAACP Image Award for Outstanding Actress, Drama Series SoulFood, 2003, 2004, 2005. Nominee, Black Reel Award, 2000. **Business Addr:** Actress, c/o West Entertainment, 6255 W Sunset Blvd Suite 923, Los Angeles, CA 90028, **Business Phone:** (323)468-9470.

### WILLIAMS, DR. MALVIN A., SR.

Educator. **Personal:** Born Apr 20, 1942, Mayersville, MS; son of Oscar and Catherine; married Delores G; children: Angela, Katrina, Tiffany & Malvin Jr. **Educ:** Alcorn State Univ, BS, math, 1962; Ariz State Univ, MNS, 1966; Univ La, Lafayette, PhD, 1975. **Career:** Greenville Pub Schs, educr, 1962-65; Alcorn State Univ, instr maths, 1966-71, comput programmer & analyst, registr & asst dean acad affairs, 1975-76, assoc prof stats & vpres acad affairs, 1976-05, pres, 2006-08, interim pres. **Orgs:** Bd dir, Watson Chapel AME Church, 1975-; mem planning & steering comt, Mgmt Info Syst Jackson MS, 1979-; bd dir, Claiborne Co Chamber Comt, 1982-; chmn, Coun Chief Acad Officers, 1984-86; Am Statist Asn; Am Maths Soc; Am Asn Higher Educ; Am Asn Acad Deans & VPres; Phi Delta Kappa; Miss Acad Scis; Nat Asn Cols, Deans, Registrs & Admis Officers; SACS Peer Evaluator; prin investr, Nsf. **Home Addr:** , Alcorn State, MS 39096-7500. **Business Addr:** Interim President, 1000 ASU Dr, Alcorn State, MS 39096-7500, **Business Phone:** (601)877-6143.

### WILLIAMS, HON. MARCUS DOYLE

Judge, lecturer. **Personal:** Born Oct 24, 1952, Nashville, TN; son of John F and Pansy D; married Carmen Myrie; children: Aaron Doyle & Adam Myrie. **Educ:** Fisk Univ, BA, 1973; Cath Univ Am, Sch Law, JD, 1977. **Career:** Off Commonwealth Atty, asst commonwealth atty, 1978-80; George Mason Univ, lectr bus legal studies, 1980-95; Off Co Atty, asst co atty, 1980-87; Gen Dist Ct, judge, 1987-90; Circuit Ct, judge, 1990-; Nat Judicial Col, fac, 1992. **Orgs:** Omega Psi Phi Fraternity, 1971; bd mem, Fairfax-Falls Church, Criminal Justice Adv Bd, 1980-81; freelance writer & reviewer, 1981-; Am Bus Law Asn, 1984-; bd assocs, St Paul's Col, 1986-87; vice chmn, Continuing Legal Educ Community, Fairfax Bar Asn, 1986-87; Va deleg, Nat Conf Spec Ct Judges, 1990; chmn, Victims Crime Community, Nat Conf Trial Judges, Am Bar Asn, 1996-; bd visitors, Cath Univ Am Sch Law, 1998-; Circuit Ct Jury Mgt Comt; Legis & Bd Supvr Rels Comt; Circuit Ct Rep Coun Govts. **Home Addr:** 9005 Stoneleigh Ct, Fairfax, VA 22031-3243, **Home Phone:** (703)849-9162. **Business Addr:** Judge, Circuit Court, 4110 Chain Bridge Rd, Fairfax, VA 22030, **Business Phone:** (703)246-4111.

### WILLIAMS, MARGARET ANN (MAGGIE WILLIAMS)

Government official, president (organization), manager. **Personal:** Born Dec 25, 1954, Kansas City, MO. **Educ:** Trinity Wash Univ, BA, polit sci, 1977; Univ Pa, Annenberg Sch Commun, MA, commun, 1990. **Career:** Dem of Ariz, aide, 1977-78; Press off D.N.C. conv, mgr, 1980; Ctr Budget & Policy Priorities, dir, 1983; Ctr Budget & Policy Priorities, dep dir, 1989-85; C's Defense Fund, dir commun, 1985-90; White House, Off Hilary Clinton, asst pres & chief staff first lady, 1993-97; Fenton Commun, pres, 2000-01; Griffin Williams Critical Pt, partner, 2005-; Hillary Rodham Clinton's presidential campaign, campaign mgr, 2008; Clinton campaign, sr adv; John F Kennedy Sch Govt, Cambridge, Mass, fel & trustee, currently. **Orgs:** Phi Beta Kappa Soc; Whitewater Scandal; bd dir, Delta Financial Corp; Clinton Global Initiative; press secy, Dem Nat Comt, 1979; campaign press secy, Dem Nj, 1982; conv staff D.N.C, 1984; commun dir, C's Defense Fund, 1984-90; dir, Scholastic Publ Corp, Clinton Health Access Initiative; trustee, Ri Sch Design, US Comnr Un Educ & Sci & Cult Orgn, 2007-2009; mortgage lender, bankruptcy, 2007; adv bd, Brandeis Univ & Kennedy Sch Govt, Harvard Univ. **Home Addr:** 3004 Benton Blvd, Kansas City, MO 64128-1553, **Home Phone:** (816)861-5960. **Business Addr:** Fellow, Trustee, John F Kennedy School of Government, 79 John F Kennedy St, Cambridge, MA 02138, **Business Phone:** (617)495-1100.

### WILLIAMS, MARGO E.

Journalist. **Personal:** Born Dec 30, 1947, St. Louis, MS; daughter of James R and Bertha. **Educ:** Harris Teachers Col, BA, educ, 1970; St Louis Univ, St Louis, MO, MA, counr educ, sch coun & guid serv, 1972, post grad; Southern Ill Univ, BA, 1975. **Career:** St Louis Bd Educ, teacher & counr, 1970-75; KMOX-TV, CBS, St Louis, TV teacher, 1973-75; Southern Ill Univ, acad advisor, 1975-76; WMAR-TV, Baltimore, MD, host & producer, 1976-77; WKBN-TV, CBS, Youngstown, OH, minority affairs dir, 1977-82; TV & radio producer & host, 1982-88; WKBD TV, Detroit, MI, News reporter/writer, producer/host; Black Hist segments, Detroit News, Detroit, MI, socs freelance writer; Barden Cablevision, sr producer, 1989-92; Margo E Williams & Assocs Inc, Pub Rels Firm, Detroit, MI, pres & chief exec officer, 1990-10, owner, 1990-; Crisis, Black Enterprise, freelance writer; White Castle, pub rels consult, 1998-; United Negro Col Telethon, Am Broadcasting Co, Youngstown, OH, host. **Orgs:** Alpha Kappa Alpha; Nat Asn Advan Colored People; Urban League; Soc Prof Journalists; vpres, Am Bus Women's Assoc, 1983-87; Altrusa Club Int; media-workshop coord, vpres, pres, Nat Asn Black Journalist, 1983-84; chmn, Ways & Means Comt, 1984; coord, Women's Career Workshops; Jim Dandy Ski Club; co-coord, Afro-Am Festival, Youngstown, OH; pres, Consumer Credit Adv Bd, Youngstown, OH; Your Heritage House Writers; Women's Econ Club; Nat Asn Women Bus Owners; bd mem, Booker T Wash Bus Asn; bd mem, Family Serv Detroit & Wayne County, 1995-. **Home Addr:** 615 Griswold Suite 820, Detroit, MI 48226, **Home Phone:** (313)961-6622. **Business Addr:** President, Chief Executive Officer, Margo E Williams & Associates Inc, 243 W Congress St Suite 350, Detroit, MI 48226-3262, **Business Phone:** (313)961-6622.

### WILLIAMS, MARSHA E.

President (organization), executive. **Educ:** Conn Col, BA, eng & psychol, 1981; Wash Univ, MA, psychol, 1982; Cornell Univ, ABD, develop psychol, 1991. **Career:** Psychol Corp, res asst, 1984-86; Sesame Workshop, res dir, 1991-96; Nickelodeon & MTV Networks' Kids & Family Group, sr vpres, Brand & Consumer Insights, 1996-2007; Harvest Res Group LLC, pres, 2007-. **Orgs:** Women C's Media. **Business Addr:** President, Harvest Research Group LLC, 3900 Rose Hill Ave Suite 402A, Cincinnati, OH 45229, **Business Phone:** (513)751-1600.

### WILLIAMS, MARTHA S.

Educator. **Personal:** Born Nov 30, 1921, Philadelphia, PA. **Educ:** State Col, BS, 1949; Wayne State Univ, MSLS, 1971. **Career:** Phil Tribune, newspaper exper, 1942-44; nursery sch, teacher, owner, 1949-64; Detroit Sch, librn, 1964-74; Gary Neigh House, dir nursery prog; Foch Sch, arts teacher, 1974-; Bristol Eng, exchange teacher, 1977. **Orgs:** Am Lib Asn; Asso Sch Libr; Mich Asn Media Educ; Rep Party; vchmn, Gary City Rep Comm; del, State Conv; del Rep, Nat Conv, 1976; Mich Rep State Comm Nat Black Rep Counc; Pct Police Community Coun; Greater Christ Bapt Ch; Sch Community Coun Nat Comn Libr & Inform Serv, 1977; Delta Sigma Theta Sor. **Home Addr:** 17420 Birwood St, Detroit, MI 48221, **Home Phone:** (313)372-7439.

### WILLIAMS, MAXINE

Executive director, lawyer. **Educ:** Yale Univ, BA, 1991; Oxford Univ, LLB, 1995. **Career:** Caribbean Human Rights Network, sr mgr, 1995-97; Univ W Indies, lectr, 1998-2000; on-air journalist, host, presenter & interviewer, 1999-2012; Chancery Chambers, Port Spain, Trinidad, atty-at-law, 2000-06; White & Case LLP, dir diversity progs, 2006-13; Facebook, global dir diversity, 2013-. **Orgs:** Mem bd dirs, Massy Group Co, 2015-. **Honors/Awds:** Rhodes Scholar, 1992-95. **Special Achievements:** Author: "Lean In Story", 2013; "Winner, Miss Junior Trinidad and Tobago". **Business Addr:** Facebook, 1 Hacker Way, Menlo Park, CA 94025.

### WILLIAMS, MAXINE BROYLES

Social worker. **Personal:** Born Pittsburgh, PA. **Educ:** Wilberforce Univ, BS; Univ Md, Advan Social Admn; WSU, Leadership Training & Publ; Wash County Solid Waste, In Training Prog, Cert Ed Soc Serv. **Career:** Wane Co Probate Ct Med Div, 1940-45; Wayne Co Dept Soc Welfare, 1949-66; Wayne Co Ment & Estates Div, 1966-73. **Orgs:** Dir, Publicity & Pub Rel Commun Comn; pres, gen chairperson & coord, Anniversary Celebrations, St Mattew's & St Jospeh's Episcopal Church, 1941-86; exec bd mem, African Art Gallery Comn, vestry-woman St Matthew's & St Joseph's Episcopal Church; pub rel AAGC; founder, Soc Detroit Inst Arts; consult, Santa Rosa Community Group; Women's Com United Negro Col Fund; Cathedral Church St Paul Chap; co-ord Coun Human Rels; Church Women United; League Women Voters; Detroit Asn Women's Clubs; Detroit Hist Soc; Int Inst; Metro YWCA; NW Voters Regist Group; Alpha Kappa Alpha Sorority; Alpha Rho Omega Detroit; Nat Asn Advan Colored People; Detroit Friends Pub Libr Inc; Detroit Urban League; Soc Workers Club Detroit; exec bd mem, Womens Coun United Negro Col fund; chmn, Ann Banquet UNGF; exec bd, Am Asn Univ Women; Tenn Wesleyan Col. **Honors/Awds:** Humanitarian Award, Wo-He-Lo Literary Soc; 30 Year Service Medallion, Alpha Kappa Alpha Sor, 1946-77; 15 Year Service Pin Detroit Urban League, 1953-68; numerous awards for Vol Work & Community Participation; Spirit Detroit Award in Recognition of Exceptional Achievement Outstanding Leadership and Dedication to Improving the Quality of Life; Award of Merit of many years of serv to Friends of African ArtFounders Soc Detroit Inst of Arts; Community Award, Vol Work Detroit Receiving Hosp; Nation-Wide Net Work Participant, Boston, MA, Conv, Amer Asn Univ Women; Citation Detroit Church Woman United; Induction Prestigious Quarter Century Club, Nat Urban league; Annual meeting Los Angeles Ca Detroit Citation AAUW 25 Year Service Pin Detroit Urban League. **Home Addr:** 9000 E Jefferson, Suite F4 Apt 7, Detroit, MI 48214, **Home Phone:** (313)822-8362.

### WILLIAMS, DR. MCDONALD

Educator, association executive, administrator. **Personal:** Born Nov 13, 1917, Pittsburgh, PA; son of Alexander and Margaret Bailey; married Jamye Harris Coleman; children: Donna M. **Educ:** Univ Pittsburgh, BA, 1939, LittM, 1942; Ohio State Univ, PhD, 1954. **Career:** Educator (retired); Wilberforce Univ Ohio, educr, 1942-56; Tuskegee Inst, vis prof eng, 1955; Morris Brown Col, Ga, educr, 1956-58; Atlanta Univ, 1957; Tenn State Univ, eng prof, educr, hons prog dir, 1966-88; African Methodist Episcopal Church Rev, assoc ed, 1984-92. **Orgs:** Mod Lang Asn; NW Nashville Civitan Club; exec comt, Northwest YMCA Ctr; exec comt, Nashville Br, Nat Asn Advan Colored People, 1968-; Alpha Phi Alpha; Sigma Pi Phi; Golden Key; vice chair, State Bd Prof Responsibility, 1998-2003. **Honors/Awds:** Teacher of the Year, Tenn State Univ, 1979; Corp sec, NW Nashville Civitan Club; Outstanding Service Award, Tenn State Univ, 1988; McDonald Williams Honors Center, named in honor, 1995; Joe Kraft Humanitarianism Award, Community Found, 2002. **Special Achievements:** Wellness Ctr, Northwest YMCA renamed 'McDonald Williams Wellness Center'; Honors Ctr, Tenn State Univ renamed 'McDonald Williams Honors Center', 1995; co-editor, "The Negro Speaks: The Rhetoric of Contempory Black Leaders". **Home Addr:** 125 Wynfield Way SW, Atlanta, GA 30331-6838, **Home Phone:** (404)346-8927.

### WILLIAMS, MCGHEE (MCGHEE WILLIAMS OSSE)

Executive. **Personal:** Born Columbus, GA; married Frantz Osse. **Educ:** Spelman Col, BA, eng; Univ SC, postgrad, advert. **Career:** Sears Atlanta Group Advertising, copywriter & layout artist; RTM Inc, mkt mgr; KFC, field-mkt mgr; Gen Mills Restaurant Group, mkt mgr; RTM Inc, mkt dir; Burrell Commun Group, managing dir mkt innovations, co-chief exec officer, 1986-, partner, 1994-. **Orgs:** Am Advert Fedn Mosaic Coun Exec Comt; Metrop Chicago Bd Cs Home & Aid Soc Ill; Asn Nat Advertisers; Nat Adv Bd Strive Media; Ctr Brand Res, Univ Tex, Austin, Adv Bd; Am Asn Advert Agencies, bd dir; Ad Coun Chicago Leadership Comt, bd dir; Strive Media, bd Advisor; Chicago Ad Coun; Partnership Drug Free Am; Women's Leadership Circle; Nat Asn Women Bus Owners; Found Sarcoidosis Res, Literacy Chicago; Clear Channel Radio-Chicago, Adv Bd; Med Wings Int. **Home Addr:** 1628 N Hermitage Ave, Chicago, IL 60622-1401, **Home Phone:** (773)235-4555. **Business Addr:** Co-Chief Executive Officer, Burrell Communications Group, 233 N Mich Ave Suite 2900, Chicago, IL 60601, **Business Phone:** (312)297-9600.

### WILLIAMS, MELTRIX GEROME
Football player. **Personal:** Born Jul 9, 1973, Houston, TX. **Educ:** Univ Houston, grad. **Career:** Football player (retired); San Diego Chargers, defensive back, 1997-98.

### WILLIAMS, MELVIN
Singer, guitarist. **Personal:** Born Jul 21, 1953, Smithdale, MS; son of Leon. **Career:** Albums: Holding On, 1973; Back to the Cross, 1988; In Living Color, 1992; So Good; Never Seen Your Face, 1998; WOW Gospel, 1999; This is Your Night; Crazy Like Love & Love Like Crazy, 2007; Cooling Water, co-write; Duets; Im Too Close; Stage Plays: Lord I am Coming Home; The William Brothers, lead guitarist; Blackberry Rec, secy, treas & rec artist, 1991-. **Orgs:** Crazy Like Love Found. **Honors/Awds:** Traditional Male Vocalist of the Year, 1998; Traditional Album of the Year; Stellar Award, 1991; Dove Award. **Special Achievements:** Was nominated in three categories at the 1998 Stellar Awards Ceremony for his album "Never Seen Your Face"; Three Grammy nominations; This is Your Night nominated for a Grammy Award in the category of Best Soul Gospel Album. **Business Addr:** Secretary, Treasurer, c/o Blackberry Records, PO Box 818, Summit, MS 39666, **Business Phone:** (601)684-0117.

### WILLIAMS, DR. MELVIN DONALD
Educator, school administrator. **Personal:** Born Feb 3, 1933, Pittsburgh, PA; son of Aaron and Gladys; married Faye W Strawder; children: Aaron E, Steven R & Craig H. **Educ:** Univ Pittsburgh, AB, econ, 1955, MA, anthrop, 1969, PhD, anthrop, 1973; Carlow Col, nat cert sec educ, 1973. **Career:** Wholesale Periodical Distrib Co, owner & operator, 1955-66; Johnson Publ Co, field rep, 1958-61; NDEA Title IV, fel anthrop, 1966-69; Carlow Col, fac instr, asst prof, dept sociol & anthrop, 1969-75; Colgate Univ, Olive B O'Connor Chair, 1976-77; Univ Pittsburgh, fac, assoc prof, anth rop, 1976-79, Int Jour Cult & Social Anthrop, assoc ed ethnol, 1976-79, adj res prof anthrop, 1979-82; Purdue Univ, Dept Sociol & Anthrop, fac, prof anthrop, 1979-83; Univ Md, Col Pk, Md, prof anthrop, 1983-88, affiliated prof urban studies, 1984-88, fac; Univ Mich, prof anthrop, 1988-, Comprehensive Studies Prog, fac assoc, 1988-91; Univ Mich, Ctr Afro-Am & African Studies, fac assoc, 1992-; Am Anthrop Asn, vis lectr. **Orgs:** Chmn, minority affairs comt, Colgate Univ, affirm action comm; dean grad rev bd, Fac Arts & Sci, rep fac assembly, Univ Pittsburgh; Univ Senate, Purdue Univ; chancellors commn ethnic minority issues, campus senate rep anthrop & Afro-Am studies, pres, Black Fac Staff Assoc, Univ Md; Ombudsman, 1991-93, senate assembly, 1993-96, Univ Mich; vis lectr, Am Anthrop Assoc; Am Assoc univ prof, Anthrop Soc Wash; Phi Delta Kappa; pres, Nat Asn Advan Colored People; Sigma XI; Soc Ethnic & Spec Studies; New York Acad Sci; fel Soc Appl Anthrop; Deans Coun, Univ Mich, African Studies Asn; fel Am Anthrop Asn; AAAS; Am Asn Univ Adminr; Am Asn univ prof; Am Ethnol Soc; Am Sociol Asn; Anthrop Soc Wash; Asn Sociol Relig; Asn Study Afro-Am Life & Hist; Asn Sociol Relig; Coun Anthropol & Educ; Dist Columbia Sociol Soc; Ethnic Planning Comt Pittsburgh Coun Higher Educ; Nat Coun Black Studies; Northeastern Anthrop Asn; Phi Delta Kappa; A Prof Educ Fraternity; Relig ResAsn; Sigma Xi: Sci Res Soci N Am; Univ Mich Chap; Soc Med Anthrop; Soc Psychol Anthrop; Soc Ethnic & Spec Studies; Econ Club Pittsburgh Inc. Soc Study Social Probs; Soc Sci Study Relig. **Home Addr:** 520 W Washington St, Ann Arbor, MI 48103, **Home Phone:** (734)665-9537. **Business Addr:** Professor, University of Michigan, 208W Hall 1085 S Univ Ave, Ann Arbor, MI 48109-1107, **Business Phone:** (734)764-7154.

### WILLIAMS, DR. MELVIN WALKER
Psychiatrist, physician. **Personal:** Born Jan 28, 1939, New York, NY; son of Wilhelmina Curtis and Shirley C; married Marilyann Thomas; children: Jennifer & Martin. **Educ:** Fordham Univ, BS, 1960; Howard Univ, Col Med, MD, 1967; Harvard Univ, Sch Pub Health, MPH, 1973. **Career:** US Pub Health Serv Hosp, internship, 1967-68; Mass Gen Hosp, Homewood Hosp Ctr-N Campus, resident Psychiat; US Pub Health Serv, command officer, 1967-77, 1980-2000; St Elizabeth's Hosp, 1968-70; NIMH-Staff Col, assoc dir, 1973-77; Job Corp Health Off, US Dept Labor, consult, 1973-; NIMH, teacher, 1973-77; Howard Univ, teacher, dept psychiat, 1974-75; Am Bd Psychiat & Neurol, cert, 1976; Howard Univ, asst clin prof, dept psychiat, 1976-93; Am Bd Psychiat & Neurol, examr, 1977-; Dist Columbia, interim comnr ment health, 1992-93; pvt practr, currently. **Orgs:** Black Psychiatrists Am; Nat Med Asn; AlliancePsychiat Prog; Am Psychiat Asn; AMA; Command Officers Asn US Pub Health Serv; WA Psychiat Soc Chi Delta Mu Frat; Customized Officers Asn US Pub Health Serv, 1967-; Kappa Alpha Psi Frat; fel Harvard Med Sch Dept Psychiat, 1970-73; assoc, NIMH Ment Health Career Develop Prog, 1970-75. **Special Achievements:** Co-author, Black Parent's Handbook, 1975. **Home Addr:** 9016 Alton Pkwy, Silver Spring, MD 20910. **Business Addr:** Psychiatrist, 1616 18th St NW Apt 101, Washington, DC 20009, **Business Phone:** (202)265-8708.

### WILLIAMS, MICHAEL DESHAUN
Football player. **Personal:** Born Jan 11, 1980, Dallas, TX; married Enisha. **Educ:** Univ Tex, Youth & comm studies. **Career:** Football player (retired); Buffalo Bills, offensive tackle, right tackle, 2002-04, right tackle, left guard, 2005; Jacksonville Jaguars, offensive tackle & guard, 2006; Wash Redskins, right tackle, right guard, 2009-10. **Honors/Awds:** Consensus All-American, 2001. **Business Addr:** Football Player, Washington RedSkins, 21300 Redskin Park Dr, Ashburn, VA 20147, **Business Phone:** (703)726-7000.

### WILLIAMS, MICHAEL DOUGLAS
Basketball player. **Personal:** Born Jul 23, 1966, Dallas, TX. **Educ:** Baylor Univ, attended 1988. **Career:** Basketball player (retired); Detroit Pistons, guard, 1988-89; Phoenix Suns, 1989-90, Charlotte Hornets, 1989-90; Ind Pacers, pt guard, 1990-92; Minn Timberwolves, guard, 1992-99; Toronto Raptors, 1998-99. **Orgs:** Founder, Assist-for-Life Found, 1992; developer, Paint Classic, Urban League.

### WILLIAMS, MICHAEL MICHELE
Actor. **Personal:** Born Aug 30, 1966, Evansville, IN; daughter of Jerry Thomas and Theresa; married Jimmy Rodriguez; children: J Brandon R. **Career:** Films: New Jack City, 1991; Private Times, 1991; The Sixth Man, 1997; Ali, 2001; Dark Blue, 2002; How to Lose a Guy in Ten Days, 2003; Kevin Hill, 2004; House M.D, 2007. TV series: "New York Undercover", 1994-98; "Homicide: Life on the Street", 1998-99; "ER", 1999-2002; TV movies: "The Substitute 2: Sch's Out", 1998; "Homicide: The Movie", 2000; "Judy's Got a Gun", 2007; "Relative Stranger", 2009; "Delirium", 2014. TV mini-series: "Trade Winds", 1993; "Peter Benchley's Creature", 1998; "Kevin Hill", 2004; "The Huntfor the BTK Killer", 2005; "Company Town", 2006; "Judy's Gota Gun", 2007; "Law & Order: Special Victims Unit", 2007; "Eden", 2007; "Gossip Girl", 2011; "Delirium", 2014; "The Following", 2015. fashion designer. **Business Addr:** Actress, The Gersh Agency, 232 N Canon Dr, Beverly Hills, CA 90210, **Business Phone:** (310)274-6611.

### WILLIAMS, MICHELLE (TENETRIA MICHELLE WILLIAMS)
Singer. **Personal:** Born Jul 23, 1980, Rockford, IL; daughter of Dennis and Anita. **Educ:** Ill State Univ, criminal justice. **Career:** R&B group, Destiny's Child, 2000-; Album: Survivor, 2001; Eight Days of Christmas, 2001; Heart to Yours, 2002; Do you Know, 2004; Unexpected, 2008; Singles: "Heard a Word", 2002; "Do You Know", 2004; "We Break the Dawn", 2008; "The Greatest", 2008; "Hello Heartbreak", 2008; Theatre Acting: "Aida", 2003; "The Color Purple", 2007; "Chicago", 2009-11; "What My Husband Doesn't Know", 2012; TV series: "Half & Half", 2006; "MTV's Top Pop Group", 2008; "RuPaul's Drag Race", 2009; "Gospel Dream", 2009; "You're Cut Off", 2010; "Strictly Come Dancing", 2014; Film: Blessed & Cursed, 2010. **Honors/Awds:** Grammy Award; Best New Artist, MOBO Awards, 2002; Lead Female Actress, 18th Annual NAACP Theatre Awards, 2008; Best R&B Vocal Performance By a Female Artist, New Now Next Awards, 2008. **Business Addr:** Recording Artist, Sony Music Entertainment, 550 Madison Ave, New York, NY 10022-3211, **Business Phone:** (212)833-8000.

### WILLIAMS, MILTON. See EL-KATI, MAHMOUD.

### WILLIAMS, MILTON LAWRENCE
Judge. **Personal:** Born Nov 14, 1932, Augusta, GA; son of William Richard and Helen Reilly; married Rose King; children: Milton Jr & Darrie T. **Educ:** NY Univ, BS, 1960; NY Law Sch, LLB, 1963. **Career:** Judge; All state Ins Co, staff atty; New York, police officer, 1957-63; Small Bus Admin, regional coun, 1966-68; Hunts Pt Legal Serv, gen coun & dir, 1968-70; Knapp Comn, assoc gen coun, 1970-71; McKay Comn Attica, exec dir, 1971-72; NYC Civil Serv Comn, spec prosecutor, 1971-74; John Jay Col, adj prof, 1973-77; Criminal Ct City NY, judge, 1977-78; NY County Criminal Ct, supv judge, actg justice supreme ct, 1978-83; Manhattan Community Col, adj prof, 1980-85; Supreme Ct, actg justice, 1981-84; NY Supreme Ct, admin judge first judicial dist, 1983-85; NY State Supreme Ct, justice, dep chief admin judge, 1985-93, Appellate Div, First Dept, assoc justice, 1993-2001, 2003-08, Appellate Div, presiding justice, 2002. **Orgs:** Asn Bar City NY; bd trustee, NY Law Sch; bd trustee, St Johns Univ; Am Asn Sovereign Mil Order Malta; bd trustee, St Patrick's Cathedral; bd trustee, Inner-City Scholar Fund; Pres Comn White House Fel; Sigma Pi Phi Fraternity; Zeta Boule. **Home Addr:** 511 E 20th St, New York, NY 10010, **Home Phone:** (212)475-5617. **Business Addr:** Associate Justice, Appellate Division First Department, 27 Madison Ave, New York, NY 10010, **Business Phone:** (212)340-0400.

### WILLIAMS, MOE (MAURECE JABARI WILLIAMS)
Football player, horse trainer. **Personal:** Born Jul 26, 1974, Columbus, GA; son of Marethia. **Educ:** Univ Ky. **Career:** Football player (retired), trainer; Minn Vikings, running back, 1996-2000, 2002-05; Baltimore Ravens, running back, 2001; St Louis Rams, running back, 2006; Calder Race Course, owner & horse race trainer, currently. **Orgs:** Twin Cities Community. **Honors/Awds:** All-Am hons, 1995. **Special Achievements:** Won his first horse race as a trainer at the Calder Race Course in Miami, Florida. **Business Addr:** Horse Race Trainer, Owner, Calder Race Course, 21001 Northwest 27th Ave, Miami Gardens, FL 33056, **Business Phone:** (305)625-1311.

### WILLIAMS, MONTEL (MONTEL BRIAN HANK WILLIAMS)
Talk show host, executive. **Personal:** Born Jul 3, 1956, Baltimore, MD; son of Herman Jr; married Rochele See, Jan 1, 1982, (divorced 1989); children: Ashley & Maressa; married Rochele See, Jun 6, 1992, (divorced 2000); children: Montel Brian Hank & Wyntergrace; married Tara Fowler, Oct 6, 2007. **Educ:** Naval Acad Prep Sch, 1975; US Naval Acad, BS, 1980; Defense Lang Inst, BA, russ, 1983. **Career:** Motivational speaker; Montel Williams Show, host & exec producer, 1991-2009; CBS, Matt Waters, actor, 1996; Film: The Peacekeeper, 1997; Noon Blue Apples, 2002; Am Dreams, 2003; Pauly Shore Is Dead, 2003; Am Cand, 2004; Second Time Around, 2004; Air Am Media, Montel Across Am, 2009-10; Golden Shoes, 2015. **Orgs:** MS Found, currently. **Honors/Awds:** Spec Serv Award, US Chamber Com, 1988; Man of the Year, Esquire Mag, 1988; Award for Meritous Work With Youth, Omaha Pub Sch, Omaha Pub Sch, 1991; NATAS Emmy Award, 1995-96; Silver Satellite Award, 1996; Silver Satellite Award, Am Women in Radio & Tv, 1996; Crystal Apple Award, 1996; Daytime Emmy Award, 1996; 2001, 2002; Man of Courage Award, Tommy Hilfiger Annual Race to Erase MS gala, 2001; Vanguard Award, Outstanding Man of the Year, Asn Black Harvard Women, 2003; Outstanding Actor in a Television Series, Nat Asn for the Advan of Colored People Image Award, 2009. **Special Achievements:** First African-Am male talk-show host on daytime tv; filmed introduction to motion picture Glory; first African Am enlisted marine selected to attend the Naval Acad Prep Sch and Annapolis; hosted a community affairs prog in Denveren titled "The Fourth R: Kids Rap About Racism", for which he won a local Emmy; Author: Mountain Get Out of My Way, 1997; Life Lessons and Reflections, 2000; Living Well Emotionally, 2009; Climbing Higher, auth; Mountain, auth. **Business Addr:** Host, Executive Producer, Air America Media, 641 6th Ave 4th Fl, New York, NY 10011, **Business Phone:** (212)871-8122.

### WILLIAMS, MONTY ELI, JR. (TAVARES MONTGOMERY WILLIAMS)
Basketball player, basketball coach. **Personal:** Born Oct 8, 1971, Fredericksburg, VA; married Ingrid; children: 5. **Educ:** Univ Notre Dame, commun & theatre, 1994. **Career:** Basketball player (retired), basketball coach; New York Knicks, forward, 1994-96; San Antonio Spurs, 1996-98; Denver Nuggets, 1999; Orlando Magic, 1999-2002; Philadelphia 76ers, forward, 2002-03; Portland Trail Blazers, asst coach, 2005-10; New Orleans Hornets, head coach, 2010-15; USA Basketball Men's Nat Team, asst coach, 2013-16; Okla City Thunder, assoc head coach, 2015-16; Christian Athletes, fel. **Orgs:** Vol, Youth Ministry Prog, San Antonio. **Business Addr:** Head Coach, New Orleans Hornets, 1450 Poydras St, New Orleans, LA 70113, **Business Phone:** (504)593-4700.

### WILLIAMS, MORRIS
Executive, accountant. **Personal:** Born Texarkana, AR; son of Edward and Izora; married Geraldine Copeland; children: Shawn Copeland. **Educ:** Wayne State Univ, BS & BA, 1940; Univ Detroit. **Career:** Detroit Housing Comn, jr acct, 1941-47; Morris O Williams & Co, owner, pres, 1948-. **Orgs:** Nat Soc Pub Acct; treasr, Ind Acct Asn Mich; bd dir, YMCA, Fisher Br; Omega Psi Phi Fraternity; African Methodist Episcopal Church; life mem, Nat Asn Advan Colored People; Detroit Idlewilders Inc; Nat Supreme Coun, A & ASR Masons; Nat Asn Enrolled Agts; Nat Soc Accts; Nat Rifle Asn. **Home Addr:** 1043 Trevor Pl, Detroit, MI 48207-3809. **Business Addr:** President, Morris O Williams & Co, 2101 W Grand Blvd, Detroit, MI 48208-1105, **Business Phone:** (313)894-3900.

### WILLIAMS, MOSES, SR.
Police officer. **Personal:** Born Aug 15, 1932, Franklin Parish, LA; married Matra; children: Rhonda, Matra, Lula, Otha, Brenda, James, Jessie, Moses Jr, Robert, Allen & Betty. **Career:** Police officer (retired); Tallulah Police Dept, 23 years. **Orgs:** Pres, Steering Comn, 1967-77; vpres, Madison Vote League Inc, 1964-84; pres, Delta Comn Action Colo Gov Treen Staff, 1979-83; bd dir, Develop Block Grant Wash DC; elected to state, HH Way from 5th Regional, 1980-; pres, vpres bd dir, Delta Comn Action, 1965-76; pres, Madison Parish Bd Econ Develop Loan Bd, 1971-77; Madison Parish Police Jury, vpres, 1972-77, serv 5th term, currently; HEW Police Jury Asn; Munic Police Off Asn; 5th Dist Black Caucus Comn; comnr, Madison Parish Port; adv coun bd, Title IV Sch Bd; Nat Asn Advan Colored People; RDA Rural Develop Asn; Magnolia St Peace Off Asn; BSA; McCall Sr High PTA; Marquis Who's Who Publ Bd, 1976-77; 5th Dist LA Educ Asn, 1972; Eve Star Lodge No 113 1972; La Police Officer Asn; City Tallulah, auxiliary police officer; Criminal & Juv Justice Comt; App to NACO Steering Comt, Justice & Pub Safety Steering Comt, WA DC; App to Drainage Pub Works & Water Resources Comt; elected pres, 5th Region Dist Police Jury Asn, LA; Elected, finance chmn, Madison Parish Police Jury; elected, chmn, All Black Election officerial Madison Parish. **Honors/Awds:** Colone Gov Staff, 1973, 1979-83; Reg VII Drug Training & Resource Ctr. **Special Achievements:** Only Black in the state of LA who was a Police officer & an Elected Police Juror at the same time; first blacks elected to the Madison Parish police jury. **Home Addr:** 601 W Green St, Tallulah, LA 71282, **Home Phone:** (318)574-2834.

### WILLIAMS, NAOMI B.
Educator, school administrator. **Personal:** Born Dec 4, 1942, New Smyrna, FL; married Mac James Sr; children: Pam, Mac Jr, Essie, Brenda Yolanda, Roderick & Wendell. **Educ:** Bethune-Cookman Col, BS, 1963; Fla A & M Univ, MEd, 1973; Stetson Univ, cert coun, 1974; Rollins Col, specialist educ, 1976; Nova Univ, EdD, 1980; Int Bible Inst & Sem Asn Relig Educ, ministers dipl. **Career:** Educator (retired); Volusia County Pub Schs, teacher, 1963-67, dean girls & counsr, 1967-73, asst high sch prin, 1973-74; Daytona Beach Jr Col, dir admis & recruiting, 1974-78; St Petersburg Jr Col, col registr, 1978, campus registr & dir admis, 1986; Volusia County Pub Sch, math & sci teacher, recruiter. **Orgs:** Am Asn Col Registr & Admis Officers; Fla Asn Col Registr & Admis Officers; Fla Asn Community Cols; Southern Asn Col Registr & Admis Officers; bd dir, United Way; Bethune-Cookman Col Alumni Asn; bd dir, Spirit; educ dir, Mt Carmel Baptist Church; Sunday sch teacher, Mt Carmel Baptist Church; Grad Chap Kappa Delta Pi; Grad Chap Delta Sigma Theta Sorority; Urban League; adult adv, Clear water Youth Coun; Nat Asn Advan Colored People; dir adult sunday sch dept, Mt Carmel Baptist Church; Top World Kiwanis Club. **Home Addr:** 1300 Ridge Ave, Clearwater, FL 33755-3659, **Home Phone:** (727)461-5827. **Business Addr:** FL.

### WILLIAMS, NATALIE JEAN
Basketball coach, basketball player, business owner. **Personal:** Born Nov 30, 1970, Long Beach, CA; daughter of Robyn Barker and Nate; children: Sydney & Turasi. **Educ:** Univ Calif, Los Angeles, BA, sociol, 1994. **Career:** Basketball player (retired), basketball coach; Am Basketball League, Portland Power, ctr, 1996-99; Jones cup, 1996; World cup, 1998, 2002; Utah Starzz, 1999-2002; Olympic games, 2000; Natalie's Restaurant, owner, 2002; Ind Fever, forward, 2003-05; UMMC Ekaterinburg Russia, 2003-04; Skyline High Sch, asst coach; Juan Diego Cath High Sch, head coach, currently; real estate agt, currently. **Special Achievements:** First woman to earn All-America honors in both basketball and volleyball in the same year. **Business Addr:** Head Coach, Juan Diego Catholic High School, 300 E 11800 S, Draper, UT 84020, **Business Phone:** (801)984-7656.

### WILLIAMS, NORMAN J.
Funeral director, chief executive officer, chairperson, funeral director. **Educ:** Amherst Col, AB, black studies, 1975; Worsham Col Mortuary Sci, 1976. **Career:** Unity Funeral Parlors Inc, pres funeral dir, 1975-; Ill Serv Fed S&L Asn, chief exec officer & chmn, 1997-; ABA Bus Solutions Inc, dir, currently. **Orgs:** Chmn, Ill League Fin Insts, 2007-2008; chmn bd trustee, Chicago Theol Sem, 2013-. **Business Addr:** Chief Executive officer, Board of Chairman, Illinois Service Federal S&L Association, 4619 S King Dr, Chicago, IL 60653-4199, **Business Phone:** (773)624-2000.

### WILLIAMS, NORRIS GERALD
School administrator, radio host. **Personal:** Born May 12, 1948, Oklahoma City, OK; son of Mattye and Norris; married Carolyn

Ann Moch; children: Diarra Koro, Ayanna Kai, Jawanza Jamaal & Norris Emanuel. **Educ:** Wiley Col, Tex, BS, hons, 1970; Cent State Univ Okla, MS, 1977. **Career:** Douglass High Sch, Okla City, all conf pitcher, 1966; Okla City Pub Schs, coach, 1970-75, teacher, 1970-77; Pk & Rec Dept Okla City, mgr, 1970-82; Images KFGL & KAEZ, radio talk show host, 1977-78; Univ Okla, black stud serv, coordr, 1977-, minority stud serv, dir, 1988-, Henderson Scholar Prog, dir, currently; Black Dispatch Pub Co, sports ed, 1979-82; R&B Prod, Jam Prod, Feyline Prod, C&F Prod, promotional consult, 1979-82. **Orgs:** Secy, treas, Kappa Alpha Psi, 1968-70; pres, KAZI Community Serv, 1972-73; pres, Images Community Serv, 1976-78; pres, Asn Black Personnel, Univ Okla, 1979-80; pres, Asn Black personnel, 1982-83; OKABSE, 1984-85; comn Okla Black Hist Soc, 1984-85; Alpha Chi Chap Kappa Alpha Psi; Polemarch Norman Alumni Chap, Kappa Alpha Psi, 1986-88. **Honors/Awds:** Outstanding Student, Kappa Alpha Psi Alpha Chi Wiley Col, 1969; Baseball Coach of the Year, Capitol Conf, OKla City, 1975; Staff Person of the Year, Black Peoples Union, Univ Okla, 1977-79; Community Service Award, 1983; Outstanding Achievement Award, Univ Okla, 1984; Comnr Higher Educ, Okla Assoc Black Sch Educr, 1985; The City of Norman Human Rights Award, 2001. **Home Addr:** 2708 Ashebrook Pl, Edmond, OK 73034-5848. **Business Addr:** Director, University of Oklahoma, Rm E-130 Couch Tower 1524 Asp Ave, Norman, OK 73019-2160, **Business Phone:** (405)325-0850.

**WILLIAMS, NOVELLA STEWART. See Obituaries Section.**

### WILLIAMS, DR. OLIVER J.

Educator, college administrator. **Educ:** Mich State Univ, BS, social work; Western Mich Univ, MSW, social work, 1980; Univ Pittsburgh, MPH, social work, 1984, PhD, social work, 1985. **Career:** Women's advocate; batterer intervention counr; trainer; Univ Minn, Inst Domestic Violence African Am Community, exec dir, 1994-2011, co-exec dir, 2011-; Univ Minn Sch Social Work, prof, currently. **Orgs:** Family Violence Prev Fund; Nat Coun Juv & Family Ct Judges; Nat Adv Comt, 2002-05; dir, Safe Return Initiative, 2003-14; Nat Family Justice Ctr Alliance Adv Bd, 2006-15. **Business Addr:** Executive Director, Institute on Domestic Violence in the African American Community, Rm 105 Peters Hall 1404 Gortner Ave, St. Paul, MN 55108-6142, **Business Phone:** (612)624-9217.

### WILLIAMS, PATRICIA ANNE

Judge. **Personal:** Born Dec 16, 1943, New York, NY; daughter of David Charles Jr and Kathleen Valerie Carrington. **Educ:** Cornell Univ, BA, 1965; African Inst, cert; Columbia Univ, MA, 1967; Yale Univ Law Sch, JD, 1972. **Career:** Phelps-Stokes Fund NYC, sec admin asst, 1967-69; New York Crim Justice Coord Coun, law clerk summer, 1970; New Haven Legal Asst Assoc, legal clerk, 1971-72; Willkie Farr & Gallagher, assoc atty, 1972-76; Southern Dist New York, asst US atty, 1977-86; Nat Inst Trial Advocacy, adj prof, 1978-; Supreme Ct New York, County Bronx, Criminal Div, judge, 1986, 2000 & 2009-, Supreme Ct, actg justice, 1989; New York Law Sch, adj prof, 1989-; fel, Aspen Inst Law & Soc Sem, 1997. **Orgs:** Asn Bar City New York; Fed Bar Coun; Am Judges Asn; Judicial Friends; New York County Lawyers Asn. **Honors/Awds:** Recognition Award, Criminal Justice Sect New York County Lawyers, 1996. **Special Achievements:** One of the most prominent African-American jurists. **Home Addr:** 392 Central Pk W Apt 7N, New York, NY 10025. **Business Addr:** Acting Justice of Criminal Division, Supreme Court of New York, 851 Grand Concourse, Bronx, NY 10451-3503, **Business Phone:** (718)590-3722.

### WILLIAMS, DR. PATRICIA HILL

School administrator, consultant. **Personal:** Born May 3, 1939, Richmond, VA; daughter of Marshall Jerome and Virginia (O'Brien) Hill; married Arthur Esterbrook; children: Tory Therese. **Educ:** State Univ NY, Old Westbury, BA, 1976; NY Inst Technol, MA, commun art, 1981; State Univ NY, Stony Brook, MA, lib studies, 1991; Harvard Grad Sch Educ, grad cert, mgt develop, 1992; Calif Coast Univ, EdD, 1996. **Career:** School administrator (retired), consultant; Babylon Beacon Newspaper, assoc ed, 1971-79; NY Amsterdam News, columnist, 1972-84; Am Cancer Soc, pub info officer, 1977-80; Suffolk County Human Rights, comnr, 1989-2009; Pres Bush's Bd Adv Hist Black Col & Univ, 1991; African Develop Found Bd Adv, adminr, 1993; Farmingdale State Col, Farmingdale, fac, from asst to pres, vpres, 1999-2000, vpres external affairs, 2000-05; Inter-Am Found, bd dir, 1994, vice chmn bd dir, 2001, Farmingdale State Col Coun, chmn, 2013-; develop consult pvt pract, currently. **Orgs:** Partners Am, 1980-; State Univ Confederation Alumni Asn, 1983-; Partners fel Kellogg Found, 1984-86; State Univ NY, Coun Univ Advan, 1985; pres, Reagan's appointee, Nat Adv Coun Women's Educ Prog, 1987-90; founding bd, Episcopal Charities Long Island, 1992; bd dir, Partners Am, 1992-94; vice chair, Inter-Am Found, 1995-2000; vpres, Long Island Women's Agenda, 1998; pres, 100 Black Women Long Island Found, 1998; chair pub policy, Nat Coalition 100 Black Women, 1998-2002; immediate past chmn bd (vol position), Partners Americas, 2012-; Links Int, Eastern Shore Chap; exec dir, Pres George W Bush Rep UN, DPI & NGO, exec comt; African Develop Found Adv Bd; charter mem, Alpha Kappa Alpha Theta Iota Omega; pres, Long Island Chap 100 Black Women; pres, Long Island & St. Vincent Partners; exec dir, Long Island & St. Vincent Partners; northeast region chairperson, Nat Black Repub Coun; life mem, Nat Asn Advan Colored People; life mem, Nat Coun Negro Women; former comnr, Babylon Hist Comm; adv coun, Women & Girls. **Honors/Awds:** Woman of the Year Media Award, Bethel AME Church, 1980; PR Award of Excellence, LI Flower Show, 1983; Woman of the Year, NY State Coun Black Republicans, 1986-88; Outstanding Alumna of the Year, State Univ NY Col Old Westbury, 1988; Newsday Community Service Award, 1990; Honoree in Education, Li Ctr Bus & Professional Women, 1992; Jr League of LI, Victims Info Bur Domestic Violence, 1996; Alumna Award, State Univ NY, 1999; NY State Senate Woman of Distinction, 1999; June Teacher Award in Education, Hecksher Mus, 2001; Top 50 Women on Long Island, Long Island Bus News, 2002; Cuad Hall of Fame, State Univ New York, 2003; Outstanding Alumni Supporter Award, Farmingdale State Col, 2009; Award For International Service, 2014; Woman of the Year, Zonta Suffolk. **Special Achievements:** L in Who's Who Among American Women. **Home Addr:** 15 Genoa St, West Babylon, NY 11704-1708. **Business Addr:** Chairman, Farmingdale State College, 2350 Broadhollow Rd, Farmingdale, NY 11735-1021, **Business Phone:** (631)420-2000.

### WILLIAMS, PATRICK

Football player, football coach. **Personal:** Born Oct 24, 1972, Monroe, LA; married Valarie; children: Crystal, Alesha & Pat. **Educ:** Northeastern Okla A&M Col, attended 1995. **Career:** Football player (retired), coach; Buffalo Bills, 1997-99, defensive end, 2000, right defensive tackle, 2001-04, defensive tackle, 2003; Minn Vikings, defensive tackle, left defensive tackle, nose tackle, right defensive tackle, 2005, nose tackle, 2006-10, left defensive tackle, 2008, defensive tackle, 2009, 2013; Sterlington High Sch, defensive line coach, currently. **Honors/Awds:** Ed Block Courage Award, 2003; Pro Bowls, 2006, 2007, 2008. **Business Addr:** Defensive Line Coach, Sterlington High School, 233 Keystone Rd, Monroe, LA 71203, **Business Phone:** (318)665-2725.

### WILLIAMS, PAUL

Federal government official. **Personal:** Born Aug 6, 1929, Jacksonville, IL; son of Russell and Bernice Wheeler; married Ora Mosby; children: Reva. **Educ:** Ill Col, BA, 1956; Fed Exec Inst, 1971; Brookings Inst, 1975; Harvard Univ, Kennedy Sch Govt, 1980; Am Univ, cert, Exec Develop Sem, 1984; Pac Inst, cert, Facilitator Investment Excellence, 1988. **Career:** Govt Off (retired); City Chicago, dir fin, 1956-63; Dept State, int admin officer, 1963-68; United Plng Orgn, assoc dir fin & admin, 1964; HUD, dir, Off Mgt Housing, FHA comnr, dir, 1968-90, Fair Housing, gen dep asst & secy, 1993-94, dep asst & secy, Mgt & Opportunity Fair Housing, 1994-96. **Orgs:** Treas, Housing & Urban Develop Chap Sr Exec Asn, 1989, pres, 1991-93. **Honors/Awds:** Citation for Outstanding Government Service, Md Govs, 1963-96; Commendation, US Comn Pac, 1967; Nominee, Presidential Award for Outstanding Civilian Service, 1973; Certificate of Merit, 1974; Superior Service Award, Housing & Urban Develop, 1975; Distinguished Citizens Award, 1976, honorary degree, Ill Col, 1979; Outstanding Performance Rating, 1982 & 1983; Senior Executive Service Performance Award, 1983; Certificate of Special Achievement, Comm Fraud Waste & Mismanagement, 1984; Certificate of Special Achievement, 1984; Outstanding Performance Rating, 1993-96; Distinguished Service Award, Housing & Urban Develop Sec, 1996; ALFA. **Home Addr:** 14009 Blazer Lane, Silver Spring, MD 20910.

### WILLIAMS, PAUL S.

Lawyer, executive. **Personal:** Born Oct 9, 1959, San Francisco, CA; son of Dr Henry S and Frances S; married Laura Coleman; children: Scott C & Ryan S. **Educ:** Harvard Col, AB, govt, 1981; Yale Law Sch, JD, law, 1984. **Career:** Gibson, Dunn & Crutcher, securities assoc, 1984-87; Vorys, Sater, Sermour & Pease, securities assoc, 1987-90; Borden Inc, coun, 1990-94; Info Dimensions Inc, vpres, gen coun, 1994-95; Cardinal Health Inc, dep gen coun, 1995-97, vpres, dep gen coun, 1997-99, sr vpres, dep gen coun, 1999-2001, exec vpres, chief legal officer & secy, 2005; State Auto Financial Corp, dir, 2003-; Maj, Lindsey & Africa, LLC, Chicago, Diversity Search, global pract leader & managing partner, 2005-; Allegis Partners, managing dir, 2015-; Bob Evans Farms, dir, currently; Compass Minerals Inc, dir, currently; Essendant Inc, dir, currently. **Orgs:** Calif Bar Asn, 1984-; Ohio Bar Asn, 1987-; Columbus Bar Asn, 1987-; Am Corp Coun Asn, 1996-; pres, bd trustee, Columbus Acad, 2001-; dir, State Auto Financial Corp, 2003-; bd mem, Leukemia & Lymphoma Soc; Cent Ohio Chap, Am Corp Coun Asn; Minority House Coun Group, Am Bar Asn; bd mem, Salesian Boys & Girls Club Columbus; Buckeye Ranch; Arthritis Found Cent Ohio; Ohio State Bar Asn; bd mem, Buckeye Boys Ranch; Black Law Students Asn. **Honors/Awds:** One of the 100 Leading Legal Consultants and Strategists for 2016, LawDragon. **Business Addr:** Managing Partner, Major Lindsey & Africa LLC, 1 S Wacker Dr Suite 1750, Chicago, IL 60606, **Business Phone:** (312)456-1848.

### WILLIAMS, PAUL T., JR.

Lawyer, association executive, executive. **Personal:** Born Mar 14, 1952, Trenton, NJ; son of Eloise and Paul D; married Ammie Felder; children: Marlowe, Paul III & Alexandra. **Educ:** Yale Univ, BA, 1974; Columbia Univ, Sch Law, JD, 1977. **Career:** Walker & Bailey, assoc, 1977-82; NY Assembly, Banking Comt, coun, 1980-84; Barnes, Wood, Williams & Rafalsky, partner, 1984-86; Wood, Williams, Rafalsky & Harris, partner, 1986-95; One Hundred Black Men Inc, asst coun & secy, 1986-2000, pres, 2000; Williams & Harris, partner, 1995-98; Earl G. Graves Ltd, mem, bd advisor, 1996-2008; Bryan Cave LLP, partner, 1998-2006; Toussaint Capital Partners LLC, pres & vice chair, 2004-07; Dormitory Authority State New York, pres & chief exec officer, 2008-15; Arent Fox LLP & Williams Strategy Advisors LLC, coun & chief exec officer, 2015-. **Orgs:** Metrop Black Bar Asn, 1986-; Sigma Pi Phi Fraternity, 1996-; Riverside Church, 1998-; Am Bar Asn, 1998-; Judiciary Comn, Asn Bar City NY, 1998-; interim bd mem, Hale House, 2000-03; 100 Black Men Am, 2000-06; bd mem, City Pk Dept Bd; 100 Black Men Inc; Eagle Acad Found, 2007-; City Parks Found; Greater Harlem Chamber Com; Asn a Better New York; Greater New York Hosp Asn; United Negro Col Fund; bd mem, Moynihan Sta Develop Corp, 2010-; vpres & bd mem, Nat Asn Health & Educ Facil Finance Authorities, 2012-. **Honors/Awds:** Ford Foundation Trustees Scholar to the American University in Cairo, 1972; Americas Top Black Lawyers, Black Enterprise Magazine, 2003; Trailblazer of the Year Award, Metrop Black Bar Asn, 2009; 10 Influential Black Leaders in Business Award, African-Am Chamber Com Westchester & Rockland Counties, 2009; Presidential Service Award, Empire Baptist Missionary Conv Ny, 2009; Public Partner Award, NY Chap Nat Asn Minority Contractors, 2009; Public Sector Leadership Award, Jamaica Bus Resource Ctr, 2009; Public Service Award, Munic Forum, 2011; Roy Wilkins Award, Nat Asn Advan Colored People Freedom Fund, 2011; Changemaker Award, NY Bar Asn, 2012; Pacesetter Award, Nat Asn Securities Professionals, 2013. **Business Addr:** Counsel, Arent Fox LLP, 1675 Broadway, New York, NY 10019, **Business Phone:** (212)492-3308.

**WILLIAMS, PAULETTE. See SHANGE, NTOZAKE.**

### WILLIAMS, PELHAM C.

Executive. **Personal:** married Mary Ellen; children: Tyrone C, Pelham L III & Pamela L. **Educ:** Morehouse Col, attended 1982. **Career:** Williams-Russell & Johnson Inc, vpres, chmn & chief exec officer, 1982-2007; Preferred Residential Real Estate Solutions, owner, currently. **Orgs:** Metro Atlanta Chamber Com; Metro Atlanta Regional Leadership Found. **Business Addr:** Owner, Preferred Residential Real Estate Solutions.

### WILLIAMS, DR. PEYTON, JR.

School administrator, association executive, association executive. **Personal:** Born Apr 10, 1942, Cochran, GA; son of Peyton and Georgia Reddick; married Sandra E Pryor; children: Rachelle Lenore & Tara Alyce. **Educ:** Ft Valley State Col, BS, 1964; Tuskegee Inst, MEd, 1968; Univ Ga, EDS, 1977; Ga State Univ, PhD, 1982. **Career:** Principal (retired); Screven County Schs, coordr & teacher, 1965-69; Cent High Sch, asst prin, 1964-68, prin, 1968-69; State Schs & Spec Activ, Ga Dept Educ, asst state supt, 1977, assoc state supt, 1978-95, sch supt external affairs, 1995, Ga P-16 Initiative, co facilitator, 1995; Cen Mid Sch, prin, 1970-77. **Orgs:** Bd dir, CSRA Off Econ Opportunity, 1971-77; Ga Asn Educrs, Gov Task Force; secy, Ga Mid Sch Prins Asn, 1973; Adv Com Gov Conf Educ, 1977; bd dir, Screen-Jenkins Regional Libr, 1973-77; bd dir, Screven Co, Dept Family & C Svcs; Citizens Adv Coun, Area 24 Ment Health, Ment Retardation; bd dir, Screven Co C C, 1974; chmn, First Dist Prof Develop Comn; Ga Teacher Educ Coun, 1974-77; Screven-Sylvania Arts Coun; adv bd, Screven Co Asn-Retarded C; choir dir, Omega Psi Phi Fraternity; Selective Serv Local Bd 128; Policy Com CSRA OEO; scoutmaster, Boy Scout Troop 348; organist choir dir, St Paul Bapt Church; Nat Dropout Prev Network, chmn exec bd, 1992-; grand grammateus/exec secy, Sigma Pi Phi Fraternity, Grand Grammateus, Exec Secy; pres & consult, Asn Supv & Curric Develop Int, 2002-; choir dir, Prince Hall Masons. **Honors/Awds:** Educator of the Year, Screven-Sylvania Optimist Club, 1976; Distinguished Service Award, Screven Co, Bd Educ; Most Valuable Mem Trophy, Ga Coun Deliberation 32 Degree Masons PHA; Outstanding Service Award, Screven CoChap, Nat Asn Advan Colored People; Plaque Appreciation, Screven Co, Chap Am Cancer Soc; Meritorious Service Award, St Paul Bapt Ch; 'Administrator of the Year Award, Phi Delt Kappa, 1980; Governor's Award for outstanding service instate government, State Ga; Distinguished Service Award, Southern Asn Col & Sch. **Special Achievements:** First African American to be appointed as Assistant Georgia State Superintendent of Schools, Office of Special Activities in 1977; Published the monograph, What It Means To Be A Professional Educator, 2001. **Home Addr:** 3380 Laren Lane SW, Atlanta, GA 30311-3642, **Home Phone:** (404)699-0730. **Business Addr:** Grand Grammateus, Executive Secretary, Sigma Pi Phi Fraternity of the Grand Boule, Philadelphia, PA 19131, **Business Phone:** (202)488-4948.

### WILLIAMS, PHARRELL

Singer, songwriter, music producer. **Personal:** Born Apr 5, 1973, Virginia Beach, VA; son of Pharoah and Carolyn; married Helen Lasichanh, Oct 12, 2013; children: Rocket. **Career:** Singer, songwriter, rec producer, fashion designer; NBC-TV Series "The Voice", coach, 2014. Recording production team with Chad Hugo as The Neptunes; Hip-hop band N.E.R.D., mem; Has clothing, footwear and jewelry lines. **Honors/Awds:** Grammy Awards, Producer of the Year for The Neptunes, 2004; "Esquire", Best Dressed Man in the World, 2005; Grammy Award, Album of the Year, "Money Maker" (with Ludacris), 2007; Academy Award nomination for Best Original Song, "Happy" ("Despicable Me 2") 2014; American Music Awards nomination for Single of the Year, "Happy", 2014; BET Awards, Video of the Year, "Happy", 2014; MTV Africa Music Awards, Best International Act, 2014. **Special Achievements:** Album, "In My Mind," 2006; album, "Girl," 2014; also a featured artist on numerous singles.

### WILLIAMS, PHILIP B.

Lawyer. **Personal:** Born Dec 30, 1922, Gonzales, TX; married Frances A. **Educ:** Roosevelt Univ, BS, 1952; DePaul Univ, LLB, 1963, JD, 1969. **Career:** Chicago, clerk, 1947-52; IRS, collection officer & revenue agt, 1952-64; Self Employed Atty, 1963-; Serv Fed Savings & Loan Assocs, mgr, 1964-66. **Orgs:** Bd coun mem, Pk Grove Real Estate Inc, 1967-; bd coun mem, Crestway Maint Corp, 1970-; Cook County, Ill State; Am Bar Asn; Tech Asst Adv Bd; United Builders Asn Chicago; Comt Adv Coun; Chicago Baptist Inst. **Home Addr:** 7739 S Prairie Ave, Chicago, IL 60619, **Home Phone:** (773)488-0699. **Business Addr:** Lawyer, Private Practice, 445 E 87th St, Chicago, IL 60619-6003, **Business Phone:** (773)994-1265.

### WILLIAMS, DR. PRESTON N.

Educator, minister (clergy). **Personal:** Born May 23, 1926, Alcolu, SC; son of Anderson James and Bertha Bell McRae; married Constance Marie; children: Mark Gordon & David Bruce. **Educ:** Washington & Jefferson Col, AB, 1947, MA, 1948; Johnson C Smith Univ, BD, 1950; Yale Univ Divinity Sch, STM, 1954; Harvard Univ, PhD, 1967. **Career:** Pa State Univ, asst chaplain, 1956-61, assoc chaplain; Boston Univ Sch Theol, prof, 1970-71; Brandeis Univ, protestant chaiplain; Johnson C Smith, fac; Knoxville Col, fac; NC Col Negroes, fac; Lincoln Univ, fac; Harvard Div Sch, Houghton prof, theol & contemp chg, 1971-2002, actg dean, 1974-75, Harvard's WEB Du Bois Inst, actg dir, 1975-77, res prof, dir emer, currently; Christian Century Mag, ed at large, 1972-; Nagoya Univ Japan, guest prof & speaker, 1996; Summer Leadership Inst, dir, 1998-2008. **Orgs:** Pres, Am Acad Relig, 1975-76; pres, Am Soc Christian Ethics, 1974-75; Phi Beta Kappa. **Home Addr:** 36 Fairmont St, Belmont, MA 02478-2919, **Home Phone:** (617)484-3857. **Business Addr:** Director Emeritus, Harvard Divinity School, 45 Francis Ave, Cambridge, MA 02138, **Business Phone:** (617)495-5761.

### WILLIAMS, RALEIGH R.

Real estate agent, football coach. **Personal:** married Vernell Johnson; children: Rudolph, Karen, Kevin & Kenneth. **Educ:** Univ Omaha, BGE, bus admin & econ; Univ Colo, grad work; Univ Puget Sound, grad work. **Career:** Real estate agent (retired); R R W Reality Construct & Income Tax Serv, rebroker, income tax consult, gen contractor & mgt consult. **Orgs:** Pres, Dulleton Ctr Nat Asn Advan Colored People; Boy Scout Master; Am Inst Indust Eng; pres, Young Men Bus

Assoc; treas, OEO; NCO Qtr. **Honors/Awds:** Spec Recognition, Nat Asn Advan Colored People Chap. **Special Achievements:** Baseball Champion, Colo Springs, 1965; mgr, Little League Baseball; coach, Little League Football. **Home Addr:** 1519 Rivers St, Walterboro, SC 29488-5352, **Home Phone:** (843)549-2756.

### WILLIAMS, RALPH O.
Executive, chief executive officer, chairperson. **Career:** ROW Sci Inc, Rockville, MD, founder, chmn & chief exec officer, 1992-98. **Business Addr:** Founder, Chief Executive Officer, ROW Sciences Inc, 1700 Research Blvd Suite 302, Rockville, MD 20850.

### WILLIAMS, RANDOLPH
Lawyer. **Personal:** Born Mar 29, 1944, Montgomery, AL; children: Randall. **Educ:** Bowie State Col, BA, 1969; Georgetown Univ Law Sch, JD, 1973. **Career:** City Philadelphia, Dist Atty's Off, asst dist atty, 1977-. **Orgs:** Nat Conf Black Laywers; Nat Bar Asn; Am Bar Asn; Nat Dist Atty Asn; Pa Bar Asn; Dist Columbia Bar Asn. **Home Addr:** 1504 N 26th St, Philadelphia, PA 19121, **Home Phone:** (215)763-0940. **Business Addr:** Assistant District Attorney, City of Philadelphia, 3 S Penn Sq, Philadelphia, PA 19107-3499, **Business Phone:** (215)686-8000.

### WILLIAMS, RASHEDA
Public relations executive. **Educ:** Wayne State Univ, BA, jour, 2001. **Career:** Nedd Worldwide Pub Rels, Ed Specialist, 1999-2002; Kumon N Am Inc, Midwest Pub Rels Coordr, 2002-10; Empowered Flower Girl LLC, chief empowering officer, 2010-; Wayne State Univ, pub info officer, 2010-. **Orgs:** Pub Rels Soc Am, 2012-; Soroptimist Int, 2011. **Business Addr:** Chief Empowering Officer, Empowered Flower Girl LLC.

### WILLIAMS, REBECCA
Vice president (organization). **Educ:** Scripps Col, BA, eng lang & lit, Gen. **Career:** UniWorld Group, Intern, copywriter, 1986-94; Lockhart & Pettus, assoc creative dir, 1994-95; Rush Media, creative dir, 1996-97; SpikeDDB, creative dir, 1997-98; Hot Sauce, Inc, co-founder, creative dir, 1998-2000; UniWorld Group, chief creative officer, 2000-11; Fame & Mkt, prin, 2011-; Burrell Commun, vpres, group creative dir, 2013-. **Orgs:** Advert Women New York (AWNY). **Honors/Awds:** Communications Excellence to Black Audiences (CEBA), Awards of Excellence & Distinction; 2008 NAMIC Award, Time Warner Cable; 2009 Silver Telly Award, 3 Musketeers Mani Pedi; 2009 Silver Addy Award, Marines Leap; 2009 Bronze Telly Award, Marines Leap; 2010 Gold Effie Award, Marines Real Talk.

### WILLIAMS, REGGIE
Basketball player, basketball executive, basketball coach. **Personal:** Born Mar 5, 1964, Baltimore, MD; married Kathy; children: 5. **Educ:** Georgetown Univ, attended 1997. **Career:** Basketball player (retired), basketball executive, basketball coach; Los Angeles Clippers, forward, 1987-89; Cleveland Cavaliers, forward, 1989-90; San Antonio Spurs, forward, 1990-91; Denver Nuggets, forward, 1990-95; Ind Pacers, forward, 1996; NJ Nets, forward, 1996-97; Jericho Christian Acad, boys basketball prog, head coach; Towson Cath High Sch, coach, 2009; Skipjacks Chesapeake Col, coach, 2009-; Archbishop Carroll High Sch, coach, 2010. **Orgs:** Nat Basketball Asn. **Business Addr:** Head Coach, Chesapeake College, PO Box 8, Wye Mills, MD 21679, **Business Phone:** (410)822-5400.

### WILLIAMS, REGINA VLOYN-KINCHEN
Government official. **Personal:** Born Nov 15, 1947, Detroit, MI; daughter of Nathaniel Kinchen (deceased) and Mary Lee (deceased); married Drew B; children: Traci A, Kristin L & Drew Michael. **Educ:** Eastern Mich Univ, BS, eng & sociol, 1971; Va Commonwealth Univ, MPA, 1987. **Career:** City Ypsilanti, dir personnel & labor rels, 1972-79; City Richmond, dir personnel, 1979-82; Commonwealth VA, state dir personnel & training, 1982-85; J Sargeant Reynolds Comm Col, adj prof, 1982-; City Richmond, VA, dep city mgr, chief staff, 1985-89; Nat Fire Training Acad, adj fac, 1989-; City SanJose, San Jose, CA, asst city Mgr, 1989-94, city mgr, 1994-99; San Jose State Univ, San Jose, CA, adj fac, 1991; City Norfolk, city mgr, chief exec officer, 1999-2011; cert MBTI facilitator; Harvard Univ, guest lectr; Stanford Univ, guest lectr; Nat Fire Training Acad; Norfolk State Univ, interim vpres finance & admin, chief fiscal officer, 2011. **Orgs:** Pres, exec dir, Nat Forum Black Pub Adminrs, 1991; vpres, Int City Mgt Asn; co-founder, Nat Acad Pub Admin; pres, Richmond Chap Conf Minority Pub Adminrs; workshop leader, guest lectr, Nat prof confs; Alpha Kappa Alpha Sor Inc; founding mem & vpres S Bay Chap 100 Black Women; bd mem, Cath Charities Eastern Va Inc; bd mem, Boys & Girls Clubs Southeast Va; fel Nat Acad Pub Admin, 1991; VA Tidewater Consortium Higher Educ, Security & Emergency Preparedness Comt; Gov. Tim Kaine's Econ Develop Adv Steering Comt. **Special Achievements:** First female and First African American to be Virginia State Director of Personnel and Training. First African American and woman to serve as city manager in Norfolk. **Home Addr:** 1451 Husted Ave, San Jose, CA 95125-4751.

### WILLIAMS, REGINALD CLARK (REGGIE WILLIAMS)
Chief executive officer, government official, clergy. **Personal:** Born Aug 22, 1950, DeLand, FL; son of Geraldine L Merrick; married Ella Mae Ashford; children: Deirdre LaFay & Andre Terrell. **Educ:** Seminole Jr Col, AA, gen studies, 1977; Univ Cent Fla, BS, bus admin, 1980. **Career:** E Cent FL Reg Plng Co, res analyst, 1971-77; C's Advocacy Ctr, chief exec officer; Volusia County, Volusia Plng Dept, prog coordr, 1977-80, community develop admin asst, 1980-81, actg dir, 1985-86, community develop, dir, 1981-86, community serv dir, 1986-12; Dept C & Families, Treas, currently. **Orgs:** Coach W Volusia Pop Warner Football Asn, 1976-84; Nat Assoc Housing & Redevelop Off, 1977-; sponsor Electrifying Gents, 1982-84; bd mem, FL Community Develop Asn, 1983-, chair, 1987, Community Housing Res Bd, 1984-88; nat Forum Black Pub Adminr, chmn, W Volusia Martin Luther King Plng Comt; bd mem, chair Alcohol, Drug Ment Health Plng Coun, 1992; Stewart Treat Ctr Adv Bd; deacon, Mt Calvary Free Will Baptist Church, 1988-92, minister, 1992-; bd mem, Volusia County; dir, advocacy ctr. **Home Addr:** 731 S Stone St, DeLand, FL 32720, **Home Phone:** (386)736-2943. **Business Addr:** Treasurer, Volusia County, 210 N Palmetto Ave, Daytona Beach, FL 32114, **Business Phone:** (386)238-4750.

### WILLIAMS, REGINALD T.
Executive, president (organization), chief executive officer. **Personal:** Born May 14, 1945, Newark, NJ; married Dorothy; children: Remington & Sunshine. **Educ:** Essex City Col, AAS, 1970; Rutgers Univ, NB, BA, 1972; Temple Univ, Philadelphia, MA, 1975. **Career:** Essex City Urban League, dir econ develop & employ, 1969-72; City Newark, NJ, dir consumer affairs, 1970-72; Bucks County Community Action Agency, asst exec dir, 1973-74; Var Corps & US Govt, consult minority affairs, var corps, 1973-; United Way Cent, Md, dir affirmative action, 1976-79; Urban League Lancaster City, exec dir; Procurement Resources Inc, chief exec officer & pres, currently; auth; facilitator; TV host. **Orgs:** Secy, Eastern Reg Coun Urban League; dept host, Eve Mag WJZ-TV Baltimore. **Home Addr:** 111 Petrol Pt Suite 204, Peachtree City, GA 30269, **Home Phone:** (404)631-3633. **Business Addr:** President, Chief Executive Officer, Procurement Resources Inc, PO Box 3489, Peachtree City, GA 30269, **Business Phone:** (770)631-4606.

### WILLIAMS, RICHARD LEE
Public relations executive. **Personal:** Born Sep 11, 1959, Edenton, NC; son of Luther L Sr and Annie M. **Educ:** NC A&T State Univ, BA, 1984; Wake Forest Univ, MBA, 1998. **Career:** Raleigh Times, reporter, 1984-87; Gannett Suburban Newspapers, asst city ed, 1987-92; Winston-Salem Chronicle, exec ed, 1993-94; RJ Reynolds Tobacco Co, pub rels rep, 1994-2000; Winston-Salem State Univ, adj prof mass commun, 2001-09; Black Bus Media LLC, pres & chief exec officer, 2000-; Black Bus Ink Mag, publ, 2003-. **Orgs:** Bd mem, Piedmont Opera, 1993; Steering comm chmn, Winston-Salem Urban League, 1996, vice chmn, 1996-, chmn, 1998-2001, 1996-; vice chmn, Best Choice Ctr, mkt & pub rels comm chmn, 1996-; chmn, Piedmont Jazz Festival, 2000-; bd dir & chmn, Carolina Christian Col; bd dir & chmn, Winston-Salem Masonic Order; bd dir, Bookmarks; Nat Asn Advan Colored People; Omega Psi Phi; Prince Hall Mason; Scottish Rite Mason; Royal Arch Mason. **Home Addr:** 1676 Quillmark Rd, Winston Salem, NC 27127, **Home Phone:** (336)784-9985. **Business Addr:** President, Chief Executive Officer, Black Business Media LLC, 138 S Cherry St Suite 400, Winston Salem, NC 27101, **Business Phone:** (336)723-5121.

### WILLIAMS, DR. RICHARD LENWOOD
Dentist. **Personal:** Born Mar 11, 1931, Schenectady, NY; married Martha E; children: Brian Lenwood, Kevin Allyn, Darren Wayne & Lori Elaine. **Educ:** Fisk Univ, BA, 1953; Howard Univ, DDS, 1957. **Career:** Queens Gen Hosp, 1958-73; self employed dent, 1977. **Orgs:** Clinical Soc Queens; Alpha Phi Alpha; Les Amis Queens. **Business Addr:** Dentist, 12027 Guy R Brewer Blvd, Jamaica, NY 11434-2428, **Business Phone:** (718)276-4644.

### WILLIAMS, RICKY, JR. (ERRICK LYNNE WILLIAMS)
Football coach, broadcaster, football player. **Personal:** Born May 21, 1977, San Diego, CA; son of Sandy; married Kristin Barnes; children: Marley, Asha & Prince. **Educ:** Univ Tex, Austin, BA, educ, 1999; Nova Southeastern Univ, bio, 2010. **Career:** Football player (retired), executive, coach; New Orleans Saints, running back, 1999-2000, running back, fullback, 2001; Miami Dolphins, running back, 2002-03, 2005, 2007, 2008-10; Ricky Williams Found, founder, 2002-; Toronto Argonauts, 2006; Baltimore Ravens, 2011-12; Access Consciousness, facilitator, 2012-; Errick Williams LLC, chief exec officer, 2012-; ESPN, analyst, 2012-; Univ Incarnate Word, asst football coach, 2013-. **Honors/Awds:** Doak Walker Award, 1997-98; Heisman Trophy, 1998; Maxwell Award, 1998; Walter Camp Award, 1998; AP College Player of the Year, 1998; Player of the Year Award, Walter Camp Found; National Player of the Year Award, Assoc Press; Offensive Player of the Year, Football News; Player of the Year Award, The Sporting News; Pro Bowls, 2002; William Morris Endeavor, Hall of Fame, 2015. **Special Achievements:** Cameo role in the feature film Stuck on You. **Business Addr:** Assistant Football Coach, University of the Incarnate Word, 4301 Broadway St, San Antonio, MD 78209, **Business Phone:** (210)829-6000.

### WILLIAMS, RITA
Basketball player. **Personal:** Born Jan 14, 1976. **Educ:** Univ Conn, sociol, 1998. **Career:** Wash Mystics, guard, 1998-99, 2007; Ind Fever, guard, 2000-02; Houston Comets, 2002; Seattle Storm, guard, 2003-04; Charlotte Sting, guard, 2004; Chicago Sky, guard, 2006.

### WILLIAMS, ROBERT B.
Lawyer. **Personal:** Born Aug 10, 1943, Washington, DC. **Educ:** Univ Md, BA, 1966, Sch Law, JD, 1972. **Career:** Williams & Hanson, atty, currently. **Orgs:** Howard City Bar Asn; Am Bar Asn; pres, Ellicott City Rotary Club MD; Sigma Phi Epsilon; Baltimore Rubgy Football Club. **Honors/Awds:** Dean's list, Univ Md. **Home Addr:** 13105 Greenberry Lane, Clarksville, TN 21029. **Business Addr:** Attorney, Williams & Hanson, 8386 Ct Ave Suite 1, Ellicott City, MD 21043-4514, **Business Phone:** (410)465-5366.

### WILLIAMS, DR. ROBERT H.
Physician, educator, geriatrician. **Personal:** Born Dec 1, 1938, Washington, DC; married Judy R. **Educ:** Howard Univ, BS, 1959, MS, 1960; Howard Univ Col Med, MD, 1964; Am Bd Family Pract, cert. **Career:** Howard Univ Col Med, Family Pract, asst prof; Comm Group Health Found Inc, med dir; Walter Reed Army Hosp & Med Officer, intern, 1964-65, resident, 1965-67; DeWitt Army & Hosp, chief med clinics, 1968-69, 15th inf div vietnam, med officer, 1967-68; Howard Univ Hosp, resident, 1969-73, physician, currently; Harvard Col med, fel, 1970-71; physician pvt pract, currently. **Orgs:** Nat Med Asn; Med Soc DC; chmn, Family Pract Sci Prog; Nat Med Asn, 1971. **Honors/Awds:** Milton K Francis Scholar Award, 1961; bronze star Army Commendation Medal, 1968; combat medic badge, 1968. **Home Addr:** 1222 Edgevale Rd, Silver Spring, MD 20910-1611, **Home Phone:** (301)565-3574. **Business Addr:** Physician, Howard University Hospital, 2041 Ga Ave NW Suite 3200, Washington, DC 20060, **Business Phone:** (202)865-7677.

### WILLIAMS, DR. ROBERT L.
Educator. **Personal:** Born Feb 20, 1930, Biscoe, AR; son of Robert L and Rosie L; married Ava L Kemp; children: Robbie, Julius, Yvonne, Larry, Reva, Dorothy & Robert A Michael. **Educ:** Philadner Smith Col, BA, 1953; Wayne State Univ, MEd, educ psychol, 1955; Wash Univ, PhD, clin psychol, 1961. **Career:** Ariz State Hosp, asst psychologist, 1955-57; Va Hosp, psychol trainee, 1957-61, St Louis asst chief psychol serv, 1961-66; Spokane WA, exec dir hosp improve, 1966-68; Nat Inst Ment Health, 9th region ment health consult psychol, 1968-69; Va Hosp, chief psychol serv, 1969-70; Wash Univ, assoc prof psychol, 1969-70, prof psychol, 1970-92, dir black studies prog, 1970-74, found dir, Dept Psychol, prof emer african & afro am, currently; Robert L Williams Assoc Inc, founder, pres, 1973-; Univ Miss, Columbia, distinguished vis prof, 2001-; Ark State Hosp, staff psychologist. **Orgs:** Bds & comms, Nat Inst Ment Health, 1970-72; nat chmn, Asn Black Psychologists; Am Personel & Guid Asn; chmn bd dir, Inst Black Studies Inc Cognitive Styles Black People, Identity Issues, Personality Develop Black People; dir, Comprehensive Treat Unit & Psychol Consult, Lindell Hosp, St Louis, MO; founding mem, Nat Asn Black Psychologists. **Honors/Awds:** Citizen of the Year, 8th Dist Meeting KC, Mo, 1983; Yes I Can Award, 1984. **Special Achievements:** Author: Ebonics: The True Language of Black Folks, Institute of Black Studies, 1975; The Collective Black Mind: Toward An Afro-Centric Theory of Black Personality. First African-american Psychologist to be Hired at a State Mental Health Facility in Arkansas. **Home Addr:** 8052 Amherst Ave, St Louis, MO 63130-3603, **Home Phone:** (314)862-4120. **Business Addr:** Professor Emeritus, Washington University, 1 Brookings Dr, St. Louis, MO 63130-4899, **Business Phone:** (314)935-0000.

### WILLIAMS, ROBERT L.
Government official. **Educ:** Jackson State Univ. **Career:** Jackson Metrop Crime Comn, community coordr; Jackson, Miss, councilman; Jackson City, asst mayor, currently. **Special Achievements:** Youngest council member ever elected in Jackson, MS. **Business Addr:** Mayoral Assistant, City Jackson, 219 S P St, Jackson, MS 39201, **Business Phone:** (601)960-1084.

### WILLIAMS, ROBERT LEE
Business owner, school administrator, educator. **Personal:** Born Jun 3, 1936, Shreveport, KY; son of M C and Thelma; married Dorothy Young; children: Janis, Jennifer, Ginetta & Tara. **Educ:** Grambling State Univ, BS, 1959; Xavier Univ, attended 1960; La Tech Ruston, attended 1970; Southern Univ Baton Rouge, MS, 1970. **Career:** Pvt Employ Agency, owner, 1964; Southern Univ Shreveport, teacher, 1967-, dir, 1978, chmn speech dept, 1979, dir eve div, assoc prof eng, currently; Prod Co, staff, 1968. **Orgs:** Dixie Janitorial Serv, 1970-85; Restaurant, 1972; bd mem, Caddo Par School Bd, 1975-84; bd dir, Caddo Community Action Agency, 1975-84. **Honors/Awds:** Grant in cont ed Southern Univ New Orleans, 1972. **Home Addr:** 1812 Jewella Ave Apt 3114, Shreveport, LA 71109, **Home Phone:** (318)621-0863. **Business Addr:** Associate Professor of English, Southern University, Rm A-60 L C Barnes Admin Bldg, Shreveport, LA 71107, **Business Phone:** (318)670-6363.

### WILLIAMS, ROBERT M.
Football player. **Personal:** Born May 29, 1977, Shelby, NC. **Educ:** NC Univ. **Career:** Kans City Chiefs, defensive back, 1998; Seattle Seahawks, defensive back, 1999.

**WILLIAMS, ROBERT PETER.** See GUILLAUME, ROBERT.

### WILLIAMS, ROBY SHERRODE
President (organization), association executive, chief executive officer. **Personal:** Born Jun 5, 1949; children: 1. **Educ:** LeMoyne Owen Col, BA, hist. **Career:** Tennessee Bank, banking sales & mkt; mortgage broker; George Flinn, 1988-; Clear Channel Tv, acct exec sales mkt, 1993-99; First Tenn Nat Corp, asst advert dir; Black Bus Asn, Memphis, Tenn, pres, 2002 & chief exec officer, currently. **Orgs:** Bd mem, Nexus Leaders; bd dir, Greater Memphis Chamber Com; Omega Psi Phi Fraternity Inc; bd dir, Memphis Conv & Visitors Bur; bd dir, Emerge Memphis; bd dir, Memphis Better Bus Bur; Shelby Farms Pk Conservancy; bd dir, Coalition a Better Memphis; bd dir, Lifeblood Mid S Regional Blood Ctr; Miss Blvd Christian Church; co-chair, Local Rebuild Govt Initiative; vpres, LeMoyne-Owen Col Nat Alumni Asn; co-chair, Spirit Memphis Initiative. **Special Achievements:** First African American to work for the First Tennessee National Corporation. **Home Addr:** 160 Island Pl, Memphis, TN 38103, **Home Phone:** (901)527-3126. **Business Addr:** President, Chief Executive Officer, Black Business Association of Memphis, 555 Beale St, Memphis, TN 38103, **Business Phone:** (901)526-9300.

### WILLIAMS, RODNEY
Marketing executive, vice president (organization). **Educ:** Amherst Col, BA, polit sci; Northwestern Univ, Kellogg Sch Mgt, MBA. **Career:** Procter & Gamble; Johnson & Johnson Consumer Prod, group prod dir; Gen Motors, OnStar, mkt; Chingari; Efficas & Galileo Labs; Robert Mondavi Lifestyle Brands at Constellation Wines, sr vpres; Addis Creson, brand strategy consult; Classics Mkt at Jackson Family Wines, sr vpres; Moet Hennessy USA (div Louis Vuitton Moet Hennesy), sr vpres Hennessy, 2011-15, exec vpres, Spirits Brands, currently. **Orgs:** Dir, African Diaspora, San Francisco, Calif, 2003-10; charter bd mem, United Movement to End Child Soldiering, Wash, DC, 2004-09; bd mem, Nat Econ Develop & Law Ctr, 2004-10; bd mem, P'kolino, 2008-; bd mem, Calif Coun Humanities, 2010-14; bd mem, Asn Nat Advertisers, 2014-; bd mem, Int Amateur Athletic Asn, 2015-.

### WILLIAMS, RODNEY ELLIOTT

Police chief, executive, government official. **Personal:** Born Nov 14, 1928, San Francisco, CA; son of Nelson and Ruby; married Joyce Gray; children: Rodney II, Brian & Vivian. **Educ:** San Francisco City Col, AA, 1956; San Francisco State Univ, BA, 1972; Golden Gate Univ, MA, 1973. **Career:** Police chief (retired); San Francisco Police Dept, dir, 1969-77; Golden Gate Univ, guest lectr, 1973; City & County San Francisco, insp police, 1983; Peralta Community Col Dist, chief police, 1983-88; 9th Circuit Us Ct Appeals, spec dep US marshal. **Orgs:** Bd dir, Westside Community Ment Health Ctr, 1971-75; Reality House W, 1972-76; bd dir, Comn Streetwork Ctr, 1972-76; Life teaching credential State Calif Comm Col Dist Pub Admin. **Honors/Awds:** Cert Hon, bd supvr, 1968; Liberty Bell Award, SF Bar Asn, 1974; commendation, Calif State Assembly, 1983; commendation, Calif State Senate, 1983. **Home Addr:** 1207 Naples St, San Francisco, CA 94112-4446, **Home Phone:** (415)333-6285.

### WILLIAMS, ROGER L.

Automotive executive, chief executive officer. **Career:** Roger Williams Auto Sales Ltd, founder & owner, 1985-; Southwest Ford Sales Inc, pres & chief exec officer, 1990. **Honors/Awds:** Co is ranked No 68 on Black Enterprise's list of top 100 auto dealers, 1994. **Business Addr:** Founder, Owner, Roger Williams Auto Sales Ltd, 500 Harry Sauner Rd, Hillsboro, OH 45133, **Business Phone:** (937)393-0200.

### WILLIAMS, ROLAND LAMAR

Broadcaster, football player. **Personal:** Born Apr 27, 1975, Rochester, NY. **Educ:** Syracuse Univ, BS, speech commun, 1997, MS, pub rels, 1998; Nat Football League, PhD, championship team bldg & high performance, 2006. **Career:** Football player (retired), analyst; St Louis Rams, tight end, 1998-2000, 2005, quarterback, 1999; Oakland Raiders, tight end, 2001-02, wide receiver, 2004; Tampa Bay Buccaneers, 2003; Atlanta Falcons, 2005; CBS Corp, sports analyst, 2007-10; ESPN, football color commentator, 2009-11; NBC Sports, col football analyst, 2009-11; Roland Williams Int Llc, performance & sales trainer, 2009-, team bldg coach, 2010-, chief exec officer, 2015-; Col Football Vs, studio analyst, currently. **Orgs:** Founder, Youth Lifeline Am, 1999-2011. **Honors/Awds:** Offensive Rookie of the Year, St Louis Rams, 1998; Walter Payton Man of the Year Award, Nat Football League; Man of the Year Award, Oakland Raiders; Unsung Hero Award; Pro Athlete of the Year Award, Press Radio Club; Champion, Super Bowl, XXXIV. **Special Achievements:** Author: "365 Happy Poetry: The Journey", APM Publ, 2012. **Business Addr:** Chief Executive Officer, Team Building Coach, Performance & Sales Trainer, Roland Williams International LLC, 3835 R E Thousand Oaks Blvd Suite 305, Westlake Village, CA 91362, **Business Phone:** (805)409-0622.

### WILLIAMS, RONALD CHARLES

Lawyer. **Personal:** Born Jun 19, 1948, Corsicana, TX; children: Steven & Anita. **Educ:** Colo Sch Mines, BS, 1971; Univ Utah, MBA, 1978; Univ Colo, JD, 1979. **Career:** US Dept Interior, patent coun, 1979-82; Storage Tech Corp, corp & patentcoun, 1982-85; Williams Mgt Group Inc, pvt pract atty, currently. **Orgs:** Pres, Tapestry Films Inc; bd dir, Cadric Drug Rehab Orgn. **Home Addr:** 516 Monaco Pkwy, Denver, CO 80220. **Business Addr:** Attorney, Williams Management Group Inc, 2413 Wash St Suite 260, Denver, CO 80205-3107, **Business Phone:** (303)295-0521.

### WILLIAMS, RONALD D.

Mayor. **Career:** Tuskegee Inst High Sch, prin; aide; City Tuskegee, mayor, 1972-96. **Orgs:** Greenwood Bapt Church; Nat Bus League; Elks, Optimist Int; Masons; Shriners; Alpha Phi Alpha Fraternity; Bd trustee, Tuskegee Univ, 1996-02. **Home Addr:** 1209 Lakeshore Dr, Tuskegee, AL 36083.

### WILLIAMS, RONALD LEE

Government official. **Personal:** Born Aug 31, 1949, Washington, DC; married Fern M; children: Ron II, Nateshia & Natiia M. **Educ:** Univ DC, attended 1977. **Career:** Shaw UM Food & Clothing Bank, vice chmn, 1981-; SE Vicarate Cluster Churches, chmn bd, 1984-85; Adv Neighborhood Comn, chairperson, 1984-; Camp Simms Citizen Adv Task Force, chmn, 1984-; Christian Social Concerns, dir. **Orgs:** Mil personnel tech secy, Army Discharge Rev Bd, 1973-; bd mem, Concerned Citizens Alcohol/Drug Abuse, 1982-, Comt Action Involvement, 1983-; United Way, 1983; UBF, 1983-; chairperson, Hands Across Community, United Methodist Church, 1990-93; coordr, Summer Tent Ministry, 1990-92; exec dir, Black Community Developer Prog Inc. **Honors/Awds:** Letters of Appreciation, Commendations & Plaques, Community Orgn, Mayor, City Coun, 1980. **Home Addr:** 2839 Jasper Rd SE, Washington, DC 20020. **Business Addr:** Director, Church & Soc Christians for Social Concerns, 2525 12th Pl SE, Washington, DC 20020.

### WILLIAMS, ROSA B.

Public relations executive, association executive. **Personal:** Born Sep 29, 1933, Starke, FL. **Educ:** Santa Fe Community Col, AA, 1976. **Career:** Community Action Agency, super Outreach workers, 1965-70; Bell Nursery, supv cook, 1965-70; Community Action Agency, super, 1971-72; Alachua Co Coordr Child Care, eligibility worker, 1972; Sunland Ctr Dept HRS, activ coordr, 1983; Rosa B Williams Community Ctr, owner; Univ Fla, pres; Outreach Cent Fla Community Action Agency, supvr; Tacachale Develop Disability Ctr, currently. **Orgs:** Dir, United Way, 1968-71, 1975-80; chmn, Concerned Citizen Juv Justice; League Women Voters; chmn, Alachua Co Dem Club; Alachua Co Dem Exec Comt; chmn, Debonaire Social Club; bd dirs, Shands Hosp; chmn bd dir, United Gainesville Community Develop Corp; Comn Status Women; Sickle Cell Orgn Alachua Co; Alachua Co Girls Club Am; NW 5th Ave Neighborhood Crime Prev Prog; adv coun Displaced Homemaker Prog; 1st vice chmn Alachua Co Nat Asn Advan Colored People; dir United Way; Alachua Co Coordr Child Care; Alachua Co Econ Develop; Community Policy Adv Comt; chairperson, Black Black Task Force; chmn, Dem Club; Hippodrome State Theater Bd. **Honors/Awds:** Community Service Award, NAACP, 1968; Very Important Citizen Recognition, City Gainesville, 1974; Leadership & Achievement Award, Alpha Phi Alpha Frat, 1974; Outstanding Service to Community Award, Gainesville Rev Issues & Trends, 1978; Community Service Award, Alpha Phi Alpha, 1979; ; Gainesville Sun's Community Service Award, 1982; Distinguished Serv to the Comm in Field of Educ Lodge 1218 IBPOE Elks, 1983; Distinguinshed Service Award, Alachua Co Educ Asn, 1983; Citizen Against Criminal Environ Gainesville Police Dept, 1984; Springhill Baptist Church contribution to Black Community, 1984Recognition Contribution Cult Arts Coalition; Gainesville Sun's Sixth Most Influential Citizen Recognition. **Special Achievements:** First Vice President of the Gainesville branch of the NAACP; First black president of the Gainesville Women for Equal Rights. **Home Addr:** 423 NW 6th Pl, Gainesville, FL 32601, **Home Phone:** (352)372-6573. **Business Addr:** Owner, Rosa B Williams Community Center, 524 NW 1st St, Gainesville, FL 32601, **Business Phone:** (352)339-6674.

### WILLIAMS, ROY LEVY

Public relations executive. **Personal:** married Patricia Ryder; children: Marc & Lauren. **Educ:** Wayne State Univ, MA, urban planning, 1972, PhD, interdisciplinary studies; Univ Manchester, cert, 1974. **Career:** Detroit Urban League, pres & chief exec officer, 1978-84; MSHDA, bd chm, 1984-2000; Daimler-Chrysler, sr mgr community rels, 1984-2001, human resource dir; Highland Pk City Govt, liason, 1980-2011; RML & Assocs, prin consult, 2002-; Gov Milliken, exec asst; State Mich Dept Labor, interim dir. **Orgs:** Vpres, bd mem, 1998-2000; Pres & chief exec officer, Detroit Urban League; chmn, Mich State Housing Develop Authority; bd mem, Detroit City Planning Comn; Steering Comt Detroit Neighborhood Housing Serv; trustee, chmn, nat bd mem, Nat Asn Advan Colored People; Highland Pk Chamber Com; EVP, HR Devco; Wayne State Debating Club; Alpha Phi Alpha Fraternity; dir, State Mich Neighborhood Educ Authority; dir, Automotive Bur Rainbow PUSH; bd dir, Detroit Econ Club; bd dir, Music Hall; bd dir, Detroit Inst Technol; YES Found; HP Devco. **Honors/Awds:** Human Rights Award, Nat Jewish Labor Comt, 1995; WWJ Radio Station's Citizen of the Week. **Business Addr:** Principal Consultant, RML & Associates LLC, 3362 Sherbourne Rd, Detroit, MI 48221, **Business Phone:** (313)862-5062.

### WILLIAMS, RUBY MAI

Association executive. **Personal:** Born Aug 30, 1904, Topeka, KS; married Melvin. **Educ:** Kans State Teachers Col, teaching credential, 1931. **Career:** Real estate sales; Calif State Employ, coun & placement, 1932-36; Golden State Life Ins Co, cashier & clerk, 1936-43. **Orgs:** Nat Youth Work Comt, 1962-69; Nat Asn Advan Colored People, 1966; pres, Pasadena Dem Womens Club, 1967-68; pres, Interracial Womens Club, 1969-70; pres, NW Citizens Pasadena, 1978; chmn, Pasadena Recreation Comn, 1971-72; adv Comt, Citizens Urban Renewal, Pasadena, 1977; mayors comt, Pasadena City, 1979-; adv comt, Kid Space Mus C, 1979-. **Home Addr:** 545 Westgate St, Pasadena, CA 91103.

### WILLIAMS, RUDY V.

School administrator, vice president (organization), association executive. **Personal:** Born Waxahachie, TX; married Ora Ruth Pitts; children: Keith W, Derwin B, Cedric L & Risha V. **Educ:** Huston-Tillotson Col, bus admin; Univ Ariz, MEd, 1964; Fla Atlantic Univ, EdS, 1975. **Career:** Miami-Dade Community Col, assoc dean, 1970-, admin asst, 1969-70; Comm Action Agency EOPI Miami FL, prog admin, 1966-69; Sears Roebuck & Co, salesman, 1967-69; Tucson Pub Sch, teacher, 1963-66; Bur Indian Affairs, prin teacher, 1956-63; Southern Asn Col & Sch, consult, 1972-; Fla Int Univ, Miami, adj prof, 1975-. **Orgs:** Phi Beta Sigma Frat, 1952-; vpres, St Albans Day Nursery, 1970-; Phi Delta Kappa, 1972-. **Honors/Awds:** Unemployment Waste Away, Fla, Voc Jour, 1978; "FL Comm Col Occupational Deans & Dir Competencies" un pub, 1979; "Viable Guidance for the Minority Student" Minority Educ, 1979. **Business Addr:** Adjunct Professor, Director, Miami Dade Community College, 1101 SW 104 St, Miami, FL 33176.

### WILLIAMS, RUNETTE FLOWERS. See FLOWERS, DR. RUNETTE.

### WILLIAMS, RUSSELL, II

Television producer, music producer. **Personal:** Born Oct 14, 1952, Washington, DC; son of Russell and Lillie Mae (deceased); married Rosalind B; children: Myles Candace & Khemet Ellison; married Renee; children: 2. **Educ:** Am Univ, BA, film prod & lit, 1974; Univ Sound Arts, electronics cert,1979. **Career:** WRC/NBC-TV, audio engr, 1973-75, 1977-78; WMAL-TV, audio engr, 1975-76; Sound Is Ready, motion picture sound rec owner; Intersound Studios, studioengr, 1981; Univ Calif, Sch Radio, TV, Film, assoc prof, 1990; Am Univ, Columbia Univ, Howard Univ, UCLA & others, masters class lectr, 1990-; Univ Southern Calif, assoc prof, 1995; Am Univ, artist-in-residence, 2002; sound & sound mixer, currently; Films: Valley Girl, boom operator, 1983; Making the Grade, 1984; Doctor Duck's Super Secret All-Purpose Sauce, 1986; Good to Go, 1986; Invaders from Mars, 1986; Number One with a Bullet, 1987; In the Mood, 1987; The In Crowd, 1988; Field of Dreams, 1989; Glory, 1989; A Gnome Named Gnorm, 1990; Dances with Wolves, 1990; True Identity, 1991; Jungle Fever, 1991; Boomerang, 1992; Mo' Money, 1992; The Distinguished Gentleman, 1992; Drop Zone, 1994; It's Pat, 1994; The Brady Bunch Movie, 1995; How to Make an American Quilt, 1995; Waiting to Exhale, 1995; B.A.P.S, 1997; The Dinner, 1997; The Players Club, 1998; The Negotiator, 1998; Life, 1999; Rules of Engagement, 2000; Training Day, 2001; Kingdom Come, 2001; Golden Dreams, 2001; The Sum of All Fears, 2002; Martin Lawrence Live: Run teldat, 2002; Deliver Us from Eva, 2003; Incident at Loch Ness, 2004; Funeral for a Friend, 2007; Festivale, actor & exec producer, 2007; TV series: Television Parts Home Companion, 1985; "Sledge Hammer!", 1986; Billionaire Boys Club, 1987; Terrorist on Trial: The United States vs.Salim Ajami, 1988; Inherit the Wind, 1988; The Women of Brewster Place, 1989; Heat Wave, 1990; Percy & Thunder, 1993; "The Parent 'Hood", 1995; "Moesha", 1996; Run for the Dream: The Gail Devers Story, 1996; 12 Angry Men, 1997; The Temptations, 1998; Little Richard, 2000; Rules of Engagement, 2000; The American Experience, 2006. **Orgs:** Acad Motion Picture Arts & Sci Sound Br; Acad TV Arts & Sci Sound Br; Alliance Black Entertainment Technicians; Int Alliance Theatrical Stage Employes, Local 695. **Honors/Awds:** Two Emmy Awards, 1988; Oscar Award, 1990 & 1991. **Special Achievements:** First African American multi-Academy Award winner. **Home Addr:** PO Box 50747, Los Angeles, CA 90050. **Business Addr:** Sound Recordist, c/o William Morris Agency LLC, 1 William Morris Pl, Beverly Hills, CA 90212, **Business Phone:** (310)859-4000.

### WILLIAMS, SAMM-ART (SAMUEL ARTHUR WILLIAMS)

Playwright, actor, administrator. **Personal:** Born Jan 20, 1946, Burgaw, NC; son of Samuel and Valdosia. **Educ:** Morgan State Col, BA, polit sci & psychol, 1968. **Career:** Plarwright; Freedom Theatre, co mem, 1968-73; Negro Ensemble Co, 1973-78; Nc Cent Univ, artist-in-residence; Theater appearances: Nowhere to Run, Nowhere to Hide, 1974; Liberty Call, 1975; Waiting for Mongo, 1975; The First Breeze of Summer, 1975; Mark's Playhouse, 1975; Eden, 1976; The Brownsville Raid, 1976-77; Night Shift, 1977; Black Body Blues, 1978; Nevis Mountain Dew, 1978-79; Old Phantoms, 1979; Home, 1982-83; Films: The Wanderers, 1979; Dressed to Kill, 1980; Night of the Juggler, 1980; The Color of Friendship, 1981; Blood Simple, 1984; Hot Resort, 1985; A Rage in Harlem, 1991; TV appearances: "227", 1987; "Frank's Place, " story ed & actor, 1987; "A Rage in Harlem", 1991; "All My Children"; "Search for Tomorrow"; "Mike Hammer"; writings: "Welcome to Black River", 1975; "The Coming", 1976; "Do Unto Ots", 1976; "A Love Play", 1976; "The Last Caravan", 1977; "Brass Birds Don't Sing", 1978; "Home", 1979-80; "Sophisticated Ladies", contribr, 1981; "Friends", 1983; "Eyes of the American", 1985; "Cork", 1986; "Fresh Prince of Bel-Air", writer & producer, 1990; "Marting", 1997; "The Good News", 1997; Writings Stage: Welcome to Black River, Season-Within-a-Season, 1975; The Coming & Do Unto Others, 1976; The Last Caravan, 1977; Brass Birds Don't Sing, 1978; Home, 1979; The Sixteenth Round, 1980; Friends, 1983; Eyes of the American, 1985; "Eve of the Trial" in Orchards, 1986; Cork, 1986; The Waiting Room, 2006; The Montford Point Marine, 2011; NC Cent Univ, artist residence, currently. **Orgs:** Omega Psi Phi Frat, 1967-; Screen Actors Guild; Writers Guild Am; Dramatists Guild. **Honors/Awds:** John Gassner Playwriting Award, Home, Outer Critics Circle, 1980; AudelcoRecognition Award, Home, 1980; North Carolina Governor's Award, 1981; Outstanding Writing in a Variety or Music Program, 1985. **Special Achievements:** Antoinette Perry Award, nomination, Best Play, Home, 1980; Tony Award nomination, Home, 1980; Drama Desk Award nomination, Home; Emmy Award Nomination, 1985, 1988. **Business Addr:** Actor, William Morris Agency, 1350 Avenue of the Americas, New York, NY 10019, **Business Phone:** (212)586-5100.

### WILLIAMS, SANDRA K.

Executive, lawyer. **Personal:** Born Mar 17, 1954, Houston, TX; daughter of Joe and Claretha Bradley; children: Katherine A. **Educ:** Smith Col, Northampton, MA, AB, govt, 1975; Univ Mich, Ann Arbor, MI, JD, law, 1978. **Career:** Nat Labor Rels Bd, Wash, DC, staff atty, 1978-81, Los Angeles, Calif, field atty, 1981-82; CBS Broadcasting Inc, Los Angeles, Calif, labor atty, 1982-89, broadcast coun, 1989-90, dep w coast coun, 1990-95, asst gen coun, 1995-99, vpres sr corp coun, 1999, sr vpres, dep gen coun w coast, currently. **Orgs:** Tex St Bar Asn, 1974-; La County Bar Asn, 1983-; bd mem, Black Women Lawyers Asn Los Angeles, 1985-; Calif Asn Black Lawyers, 1986-; Wash State Bar Asn; DC State Bar Asn; Calif St Bar Asn; bd mem, Alliance C Rights; bd mem, Agape Int Spiritual Ctr; State Bar Calif. **Home Addr:** 6619 Wooster Ave, Los Angeles, CA 90056, **Home Phone:** (310)645-1917. **Business Addr:** Senior Vice President, Deputy General Counsel of West Coast, CBS Broadcasting Inc, 51 W 52nd St 35th Fl, New York, NY 10019, **Business Phone:** (212)975-4321.

### WILLIAMS, SANDRA ROBERTS

Educator. **Personal:** Born Nov 2, 1940, Houston, TX; daughter of Brownie and Thelma; children: David & Michele. **Educ:** Tex Southern Univ, Houston, BM, educ, 1961; Univ NMex, Albuquerque, MA, 1980. **Career:** Houston Independent Sch, music & classroom teacher, 1962-64; Albuquerque Pub Schs, classroom teacher, 1964-70; Univ New Mexico, acad adv & counr, 1973-81; Univ Texas, Med Br, prog coord, 1982-, Internal Med/Div Infectious Dis, coordr, dir recruitment, currently. **Orgs:** Consult, Saturday Bio med Sci Forum; Nat Asn Med Minority Educ; Sci Inc; Sch Health Progs, adv Comt; Delta Sigma Theta Inc; Galveston Alumni; Nat Tech Asn; Residentswap. **Home Addr:** 10201 Schaper Dr, Galveston, TX 77554, **Home Phone:** (512)266-3462. **Business Addr:** ID Fellowship Coordinator, Coordinator, University of Texas Medical Branch, 6431 Fannin MSB 2 112, Houston,, TX 77030, **Business Phone:** (713)500-6767.

### WILLIAMS, SAUL STACEY

Poet, musician, actor. **Personal:** Born Feb 29, 1972, Newburgh, NY; married Persia White; children: Saturn; married Anisia Uzeyman. **Educ:** Morehouse Col, BA; Tisch Sch Arts, NY Univ, MFA. **Career:** Books: Sorcery of Self, 2001; She, 1999; The Seventh Octave, 1998; Films: K-Pax, 2001; The N-Word, 2004; Lackawanna Blues, 2004; Ajourdhui, 2012; Voice: Origin of Cotton, 2000; Kings of LA, 2000; star & co-author, Slam, 1998; Recordings: "Penny For A Thought & Purple Pigeons", 2000; Amethyst Rock Star, 2001; TV: "Street Time", 2002; "Snoop, There It Is", 2003; "Not in My Name", 2003; "Saul Williams", 2004; "The Inevitable Rise & Liberation of Niggy Tardust!", 2007; NGH WHT The Dead Emcee Scrolls with The Arditti Quartet, 2009; New York, I Love You, 2009; Albums: Penny for a Thought / Purple Pigeons, 2000; Amethyst Rock Star, 2001; Not in My Name, 2003; Saul Williams, 2004; The Inevitable Rise & Liberation of Niggy-Tardust!, 2007; NGH WHT-The Dead Emcee Scrolls with The Arditti Quartet, 2009; Volcanic Sunlight, 2011. **Business Addr:** Author, c/o Moore Black Press, PO Box 1865, New York, NY 10032.

### WILLIAMS, SCOTT CHRISTOPHER

Basketball coach, basketball player, television broadcaster. **Personal:** Born Mar 21, 1968, Hacienda Heights, CA; married Lisa; children: Benjamin Sinclair. **Educ:** Univ NC. **Career:** Basketball player (retired), basketball coach, TV analyst; Chicago Bulls, ctr forward, 1990-94; Philadelphia 76ers, 1994-98; Milwaukee Bucks, 1999-2001, asst coach, 2013-14; Denver Nuggets, 2001-02; Phoenix Suns, 2002-04, color commentator, 2008; Dallas Mavericks, 2003-04; Cleveland Cavaliers, 2004-05, tv color commentator, 2005-06; FSN Ohio, color analyst, 2006-07; Milwaukee Bucks, color analyst, 2008; Idaho Stampede, asst coach, 2012-13; NBA Develop League, asst coach, 2012-13; Grand Canyon Antelopes Men's Basketball, analyst, 2014-15, color analyst, currently. **Business Addr:** Television Color Analyst, Phoenix Suns, 201 E Jefferson St, Phoenix, AZ 85004, **Business Phone:** (602)379-7900.

### WILLIAMS, DR. SCOTT W.
Educator, association executive. **Personal:** Born Apr 22, 1943, Staten Island, NY; son of Roger K and Beryl E; married Glo Aniebo; children: Rachael, Rebekah & Eve. **Educ:** Morgan State Col, BS, math, 1964; Lehigh Univ, MS, math, 1967, PhD, math topology, 1969; George Ivanovich Gurdjieff. **Career:** Int Bus Mach, 1964; Pa State Univ, Allentown Ctr, instr, 1968-69; Morgan State Col, instr, 1969; Pa State Univ, Univ Pk, res assoc, 1969-71; State Univ NY, Buffalo, asst prof, 1971-77, assc prof math, 1977-85, prof, 1985-; Inst Med & Math, vis assoc prof, 1980-81; Charles Univ, Prague, fulbright lectr, 1986-97; Beijing Teacher Col, Beijing, China, adj prof, 1988-91; Summer Sch Math Biol Young Scholars, Villanova Univ, Philadelphia PA, 1992-97; Rochester Folk Art Guild, instr; Am Math Soc Notices, ed; Topology Atlas, regular columnist, 1997-2001. **Orgs:** Am Math Soc; Rochester Folk Art Guild; chmn, Balck Uhuru Soc, 1967-69; Ford Found, 1980-81; res grant, Nat Sci Found, 1983-87; Nat Res Coun; Nat Security Agency; Nat Pub Radio; Circle Brotherhood asn; bd mem coun, Afro Am Res; founder, African Am Researchers Math Sci. **Honors/Awds:** Ford Foundation Senior Research Fellow, 1980-81; Chancellor of SUNY Award, 1981; Chancellor's Award for Excellence in Teaching, State Univ New York, 1982; National Science Foundation research grant, 1983-87; Fatherhood and Family Award of the Year, 1997. **Special Achievements:** Paint in acrylics, 1983-96; Played saxophone, piano & congas professionally, 1959-69; Selected to be one of the 50 Most Important Blacks in Res Sci by Sci Spectrum Mag and Career Commun Group; Published 33 papers in Topology & Set Theory; Pubicationsl: Paracompactness and products. General Topology and Appl 6, 1976; Coabsolutes with homeomorphic dense subspaces, 1981; Orderable subspaces of ech-remainders Proceedings of Topology Conference, 1982; Rings of continuous functions, 1982; Handbook of set-theoretic topology, 1984; On box products of small families of spaces of ordinal numbers, 1987; On the multiple Birkhoff recurrence theorem in dynamics, 1987; Paracompact C-scattered spaces, 1987; On box products of small ordinal spaces, 1988; The paracompactness of spaces related to uncountable box products, 1990; Examples of recurrence; Some dynamics on the irrationals, 1997; Order-like structure of monotonically normal spaces, 1998; Black research mathematicians in the United States, 1998; Compact! A tutorial, 2001; Million-buck problems, 2002; Strong versions of normality; Special points arising from self-maps; On the countable box product of compact ordinals; Paracompactness in box products; Proceedings of the 12th winter school on abstract analysis. **Home Addr:** 44 Highgate Ave, Buffalo, NY 14214-1409, **Home Phone:** (716)836-8948. **Business Addr:** Professor of Mathematics, University at Buffalo, 244 Mathematics Bldg 3435 Main St, Buffalo, NY 14260-2900, **Business Phone:** (716)829-2144.

### WILLIAMS, SERENA (SERENA JAMEKA WILLIAMS)
Tennis player, actor, fashion designer. **Personal:** Born Sep 26, 1981, Saginaw, MI; daughter of Richard and Oracene. **Educ:** Art Inst Fl. **Career:** Prof tennis player, 1995-; Aneres, owner & fashion designer, 2004-; HairTech, nail technician, 2010; UNICEF, int goodwill ambassador, 2011. TV Series: "My Wife & Kids", 2002; "Street Time", 2003; "Law & Order: Special Victims Unit", 2004; "The Division", 2004; "Higglytown Heroes", 2005; "ER", 2005; "Loonatics Unleashed", 2007; "Avatar: The Last Airbender", 2007; "The Bernie Mac Show", 2006; "The Game", 2008; "MADtv", 2008; "Keeping Up with the Kardashians", 2011; "Drop Dead Diva", 2012; "Venus and Serena", 2012; "The Legend of Korra", 2013; "7 Days in Hell", 2015; "Pixels", 2015; "Lemonade", 2016. **Orgs:** Women's Sports Found; Serena Williams Found. **Honors/Awds:** Received numerous awards including: Champion Singles, Grand Slam Cup, 1999; Champion singles, Los Angeles, 1999; Champion singles, Indian Wells, 1999; Champion singles, Paris Indoors, 1999; Champion doubles, French Open, 1999, 2002; Champion singles & doubles, US Open, 1999, 2002; Champion doubles, Olympics, 2000; Championdoubles, Wimbledon, 2000, 2003; Champion, Australian Open, 2001, 2003, 2005; Champion singles, Indian Wells, 2001; Sanex Championship, singles, 2001; Champion, State Farm Tennis Classic, 2002; Champion, Nasdaq-100 Open, 2002, 2004; Champion, Italian Open, 2002; Champion singles & doubles, Wimbledon, 2002; Champion, Princess Cup, 2002; Champion, Sparkassen Cup, 2002; Female Athlete of the Year, Assoc Press, 2003; Sportswoman of the Year, Laureus World Sports Acad; Female Athlete of the Year, ESPY; Female Tennis Player of the Year, 2003; Young Heroes Award, Big Bros Big Sisters, Greater L.A., 2003; Celebrity Role Model, Avon Found, 2003; Champion, China Open, 2004; BET Award for Female Athlete of the Year, 2011; Forbes The Celebrity 100 (No.84), 2011; TIME Magazine 30 Legends of Women's Tennis, 2011; Best Female Tennis Player ESPY Award, 2011; Forbes Most Powerful Black Women In The U.S. (No.10), 2011; Sportsperson of the Year, Sports Illus Mag, 2015; WTA Tour Championship. **Special Achievements:** First sisters (Serena & Venus) to win the Olympic doubles event in 2000; Became the first ranked player in the world on July 8, 2002; First African American to win the US Open since 1958; By winning the 2003 Australian Open achieved an historic Serena Slam-winning all four Grand Slam tournaments in a row; ranks 7 female tennis player in the world; Book: Venus & Serena: Serving From The Hip: 10 Rules For Living, Loving and Winning, 2005. On the Line; First African-American women to hold ownership in an NFL franchise. **Business Addr:** Owner, Fashion Designer, Aneres, 4199 Maya Cay, Jupiter, FL 33458, **Business Phone:** (561)630-9400.

### WILLIAMS, SHAUN LEJON
Executive, football player. **Personal:** Born Oct 10, 1976, Oakland, CA; son of Kenneth and Sheliah; children: Tyson, Jordan & Cameron. **Educ:** Univ Calif, Los Angeles, BS, pre-psychol. **Career:** Football player (retired), exec; New York Giants, 1998-99, 2005, free safety, 2000-01, strong safety, 2002-04; Carolina Panthers, strong safety, 2006; William Paterson Univ, part-time asst coach, defensive coordr, currently. **Honors/Awds:** All-American Honors, Blue Chip; All-Pac 10, 1996. **Special Achievements:** Featured in Prep Football Report & Super Prep magazines; named to the Super Prep All-Far West team & Long Beach Press-Telegram's "Best of the West" squad. **Business Addr:** Defensive Coordinator, William Paterson University, 300 Pompton Rd, Wayne, NJ 07470, **Business Phone:** (973)720-2000.

### WILLIAMS, SHERMAN
Editor. **Personal:** Born Jan 1, 1961?, Ft. Benning, GA; son of Thomas and Addie. **Educ:** Ohio State Univ, Columbus, OH, BA, 1983. **Career:** Pub Opinion, Chambersburg, PA, staff photogr, 1984-85; Stand-Examr, Ogden, UT, staff photogr, 1985-87; Hartford Courant, Hartford, CT, staff photogr, 1987, picture ed, 1990-92; Philadelphia Inquirer, picture ed, 1992-2000; Milwaukee Jour Sentinel, Asst Managing Ed, visual journalism & sr ed visuals, 2000-; Am Press Inst, guest fac. **Orgs:** Nat Press Photogr Asn, Fel, 1985-, stud clip contest chair, 1990-91; Nat Asn Black Journalists, 1986-; vpres, Conn Asn Black Communicators, 1987-; Historians Double Diamonds Ski Club, 1989-90; co-prog dir & bd dir, Greater Hartford Minority Jour Prog, 1990-91; pres, Assoc Press Photo Mgr, 2004; dir & chair, Nat Asn Black Journalists Visual Task Force. **Honors/Awds:** Photographer of the Year, 1988; 4th Region 1, NPPA Contest, 1988; Honorable Mention & 3rd place, Nat Asn of Black Journalists Photo Contest, 1989; 1st & 3rd Place Photo Awards, Conn News Photogs, 1991; First Place News Photo, Northern Short Course. **Special Achievements:** One of ten participants in The James K. Batten Leadership Prog. **Home Addr:** 215 S Chancellor St, Newtown, PA 18940-2175. **Business Addr:** Senior Editor Visuals, Assistant Managing Editor, Milwaukee Journal Sentinel, 333 W State St, Milwaukee, WI 53201-0371, **Business Phone:** (414)224-2685.

### WILLIAMS, DR. SHIRLEY YVONNE
Psychologist, physician. **Personal:** Born Washington, DC. **Educ:** Howard Univ, attended 1959. **Career:** New York Med Ctr, resident neurol, 1962; Henry Ford Hosp, psychiat, 1965, Outpatient Ambulatory Serv, dir; Norwalk Hosp, Ambulatory Psychiat, chief, 1966-98. **Orgs:** St Bd Ment Health; St Coun Alcohol & Drugs; chmn, Asn Conn Out patient Clinics; Asn Nerv & Ment Disease; Am Psychol Asn; Am Acad Sci; Nat Med Asn; AMA; Fair field Co Asn; life mem, Nat Asn Advan Colored People; chmn, Keystone House; mem bd, Carver Found Father Looney, 1977; bd mem, Norwalk Hosp; bd mem, Med Examiners St Conn; fel Am Psychiat Asn. **Home Addr:** 5208 Colo Ave NW, Washington, DC 20011, **Home Phone:** (202)723-5571.

### WILLIAMS, SIDNEY B., JR.
Lawyer, football player. **Personal:** Born Dec 31, 1935, Little Rock, AR; son of Sidney B Sr and Eloise Gay Cole; married Carolyn. **Educ:** Univ Wis, BS, 1961; George Washington Univ, Law Sch, JD, 1967. **Career:** Football player, 1956-58; Upjohn Co, patent atty, exec dir, Domestic Patents & Worldwide Trademark Opers, 1990-95; US Patent Off, patent examr; Gen Am Transp Corp, res develop engr; Montreal Alouettes, prof football player; Flynn Thiel Boutell & Tanis PC, atty, currently. **Orgs:** Mich DC Bar Asn; Kalamazoo County Mich Am Nat Patent Law Asn; bd trustee, Borgess Hosp; regional bd dir, Comerica Bank; bd dir, Douglas Community Asn; All Am Football Team Chem & Eng News, 1957-58; Iron Cross Hon Soc, 1958; bd dir, Univ Wis Found; officer & comt chair, Intellectual Property Sect, Am Bar Asn; officer, comt chair & fel Am Intellectual Property Law Asn; pres, Nat Inventors Hall Fame, 1987-88. **Honors/Awds:** Ivan Williamson Scholastic Award; University of Wisconsin's Distinguished Alumnus Award, 1994. **Home Addr:** 2237 Lorraine Ave, Kalamazoo, MI 49008-3931, **Home Phone:** (269)345-5113. **Business Addr:** Attorney, Flynn Thiel Boutell & Tanis PC, 2026 Rambling Rd, Kalamazoo, MI 49008, **Business Phone:** (269)381-1156.

### WILLIAMS, SIMBI KALI. See KHALI, SIMBI.

### WILLIAMS, STANLEY KING
Government official. **Personal:** Born Jan 25, 1948, Columbus, GA; son of Robert and Lucille Willis; married Judy Chichester; children: Lanita L & Malik K. **Educ:** Shaw Univ, Raleigh, NC, BA, 1970. **Career:** Shaw Univ, stud counr, 1967-70; COPE Newark, youth job develop specialist, 1968-69; NC Dept Corrections, classification specialist, 1970; AUS Ger, neuro psychiat tech drug coun, 1970-72; Prog Gales Maternity Clin, coordr, 1972-74; Dept Manpower, job develop specialist, 1972; Veterans Employ DC Dept Labor Veterans Admin Regional Off, supvr & coordr, 1976-86; DC Dept Employ Serv, supvr, 1986-89, opers mgr, NE Employ Ctr, 1989-94; S Capital Employ Ctr, opers mgr, 1994-95; US Dept Labor, dir veterans employ & training serv, 1995-2014. **Orgs:** Chmn, Mt Pleasant Adv Neighborhood Comn, 1976-80; consult sex educ prog, Dept HR, 1973; adv, DC Govt ANC Citizens Neighborhood Coun Coord Comnr, 1975; pres, King Enterprises Inc; Am Legion WA Alliance Neighborhood Govts; del, DC Black Assembly; Shaw Univ Alumni Asn; Sch Without Walls PTA; Econ & Polit Trends; S African Self-determination; Smithsonian Fel Smithsonian Inst; coordin & supvr, Veterans Employ Ctr VA Regional Off, 1976; pres, King Enterprises, 1976; vice chmn, Shiloh Baptist Church, Wash DC, 2001; Am Legion, Carter G Woodson Chap, Asn Study African Am Life & Hist; vice chmn, Brotherhood Shiloh Men, Shiloh Baptist Church, 1996; AMVETS; bd dir, Shiloh Family Life Ctr Found; bd dirs, DC Pvt Indust Coun, 1997; Bachelor Benedict Inc, 2000. **Honors/Awds:** Appreciation Award, ANC 70, 1977; Congressional Appreciation Award, Congressman Fountroy, 1978; Outstanding Service Award, Mt Pleasant Adv Neighborhood Comn, 1978; Meritorious & Distinguished Service Award, VFW, 1978; Commend Award, Vietnam Veteran Civic Coun, 1978; Community Service Award, Nat Black Veteran Orgn, 1979; promoter & sponsor, promoted largest gospel convention given in Washington, DC, 1983; Community Service Award, DC City Coun, 1982; Man of the Year Award, Shiloh Baptist Church, 1998. **Home Addr:** 1806 Lawrence St NE, Washington, DC 20018-2732, **Home Phone:** (202)526-8521. **Business Addr:** Director, US Department of Labor, 64 New York Ave N E Rm 3156, Washington, DC 20002, **Business Phone:** (202)671-2143.

### WILLIAMS, STEVEN
Vice president (organization). **Educ:** Univ Okla, 1987; Univ Cent Okla, Col Bus Admin, BA, econs, 1996; Harvard Bus Sch, PLD, gen mgt, 2006. **Career:** Fleming Co, asst store mgr, 1987-91, buyer, 1991-97; Quaker Oats, broker field mgr, 1997-98, customer mkt mgr, 1998-99, nat customer mkt mgr, 1999-2001; PepsiCo, sr nat acct mgr, 2001-03, dir customer mkt & develop, 2003-04, vpres sales Bentonville, Ark, 2004-09, div vpres, 2009-11, sr vpres W div, 2011-12, sr vpres sales, 2012-13, sr vpres GM Global Walmart, 2013-. **Orgs:** Bd dir, Big Bros, Big Sisters Metrop Chicago; bd dir, Jr Achievement-Chicago Area; adv bd, Enactus USA; Exec Leadership Coun. **Business Addr:** Senior Vice President, PepsiCo Inc, 700 Anderson Hill Rd, Purchase, NY 10577, **Business Phone:** (914)253-2000.

### WILLIAMS, T. JOYCE
Educator. **Personal:** Born Jan 24, 1930, Muskogee, OK; married Paul Jr; children: Cheryl Elizabeth Jackson, Jacquelyn Elaine Miller & Starla P Potts. **Educ:** Wichita State Univ, BA, 1965, EdM, 1974. **Career:** Educator (retired); Bd Educ, USD, 259, teacher, 1965-85. **Orgs:** Local State Nat Rep Assemblies NEA, 1974, 1975, 1979, 1980; Leadership Acad, trainer local bldg dir, Kans Nat Educ Asn, 1975-76; Ethnic Minority Caucus NEA Wichita, 1975-76; Pub Affairs TV Prog, NEA Wichita, 1975; PR & R Com NEA Wichita, 1979; Sigma Gamma Rho Sorority; Nat Asn Advan Colored People; Polit Action Com, 1979; Holy Savior Cath Ch Wichita; Vol God's Food Pantry-Holy Savior Church, 1986-88; Elected Human Resources Bd, City Wis, 1989; CPO, NE Wichita, 1994-; Nominated Int soci Poets, 1996-97; eucharist adorer, St Paul Newman Ctr, 2001; eucharist minister, Holy Savior, 2002-03. **Honors/Awds:** Wichita's Teacher of the Year, 1975; Letter of Appreciation, CPO Coordinator, 1995; Poetry.com Award, 2000; Best Poems & Poets Millenium Award. **Special Achievements:** Speaker-rep address House Reps, Topeka, Kans, 1995; Poem, Entry "Through the Hourglass My Vision," Mama Joyce Williams, nat lib poetry, 1996-; poems published in "Best Poems of 1997," and "Best Poems of 1998;" exhibiton at www.poets.com; book of poetry, Pearls of Life, 2000; poem entry, Amer at the Millenium; Entry, Best Poems and Poets, 2001, 2002; Honored, coun elders, 2003; tutor students, USO-259. **Home Addr:** 4025 Christy St, Wichita, KS 67220-2539, **Home Phone:** (316)685-9804.

### WILLIAMS, TARA
Basketball player. **Personal:** Born Jul 23, 1974, Newport News, VA; daughter of Thomas Nelson and Ethel. **Educ:** Auburn Univ. **Career:** Phoenix Mercury, forward, 1997, guard; Detroit Shock, 1998-2001; Portland Fire, guard, 2001; Eagles, guard, 2003-06; 2008-09.

### WILLIAMS, TAVARES MONTGOMERY. See WILLIAMS, MONTY ELI, JR.

### WILLIAMS, TENETRIA MICHELLE. See WILLIAMS, MICHELLE.

### WILLIAMS, DR. TERRI L.
School administrator, executive. **Personal:** Born May 18, 1958, Bridgeton, NJ. **Educ:** Howard Univ, BS, psychol, 1981, MEd, Stud Coun & Personnel Serv, 1984; Univ SC, Columbia, PhD, coun psychol, 2005. **Career:** Wash Alcohol Coun Ctr, admin asst, 1980-82; Howard Stud Spec Servs, educ specialist, 1984-85; Howard Upward Bound, sr counr, 1985-86; St Lawrence Univ, asst dir admis, 1986-; Univ SC, dir upward bound, 1991-98, Training Consult, 2003-10; Webster Univ, Adj Prof, 2005-; Triple P Int Pty Ltd, Sr Training Consult Triple P Am, 2010-13; Triple P Am, dep head training US, 2013-. **Orgs:** Delta Sigma Theta Inc, 1978-; pub rels coordr, BOF Howard Univ Alumnae, 1983-; vol, DC Mayor's Re-election Comn, 1986; exhibitors coordr, Mid-Eastern Asn Educ Opport Prog Personnel, 1986, US Trainer Yr, 2012. **Honors/Awds:** Outstanding Young Women of America, 1982, 1985; MEAEOPP Conference Service Award, 1986; US Trainer of the Year, Triple P Am, 2012; Triple P International Trainer of the Year, 2012; Mayor's Summer Youth Employment Program Contribution Award. **Home Addr:** RD 2 Russell Rd, PO Box 166, Canton, NY 13617, **Home Phone:** (315)386-8788. **Business Addr:** Adjunct Professor, Webster University, 470 E Lockwood Ave, St. Louis, MO 63119, **Business Phone:** (800)981-9801.

### WILLIAMS, TERRIE MICHELLE
Philanthropist, consultant, executive. **Personal:** Born May 12, 1954, Mt. Vernon, NY; daughter of Charles (deceased) and Marie; children: Rocky. **Educ:** Brandeis Univ, BA, psychol & sociol, 1975; Columbia Univ NY, MA, social work, 1977. **Career:** New York Hosp, med social worker, 1977-80; Black Filmmaker Found, prog admin, 1980-81; Black Owned Comn Alliance, exec dir, 1981-82; World Inst Black Commun, exec dir, 1982; Essence Commun Inc, vpres & dir corp commun, 1982-87; Terrie Williams Agency, pres, 1988-. **Orgs:** Founder, Stay Strong Found, 2001-; Brandeis Univ Alumni Asn; Nat Corp Adv Bd; Communs Community Am Heart Asn; Women Communs. **Honors/Awds:** D Parke Gibson Award, Pub Rels Soc Am, 1981; Building Brick Award, NewYork Urban League, 1987; Matrix Award in Public Relations, Women Communs, 1991; Vernon C. Schranz Distinguished Lectureship, Ball State Univ, 1996; Phillip Dorf Mentoring Award, NY Chap, Pub Rels Soc Am; Eagle Fly Free Award, Inst Advan Multicultural & Minority Med, 2006; Marietta Tree Award, Citizen's Comt NY, 2009; Power 150, Ebony mag; Dr. David Satcher Mental Health Trailblazer Award, Jackson State Univ, 2009; Listed in 50-Women Who Are Changing The World, 2009; PR Executive of the Year, 2011; Heart & Soul Award, 2011; Full Circle Health Award, 2011; Woodie King, Jr. Award, New Fed Theatre, 2011; Woman of Courage Award, Emmett Till Legacy Found, 2011; The Khary Orr Leadership Award, African Am Heritage Parade Comt, 2011; SCLC Women Drum Major for Justice Award, 2012; NYC Social Work Image Award, Nat Asn Social Workers, 2012. **Special Achievements:** Co-author: The Personal Touch, Warner Books, 1994; author: Stay Strong: Simple Life Lessons for Teens, 2001; A Plentiful Harvest: Creating Balance & Harmony Through the Seven Living Virtues, 2003; Black Pain: It Just Looks Like We're Not Hurting, 2008. **Business Addr:** President, The Terrie Williams Agency, 382 Central Park W Suite 17U, New York, NY 10025, **Business Phone:** (212)220-4333.

**WILLIAMS, THEARTRICE T.**
Consultant. **Personal:** Born May 16, 1934, Indianola, MS; son of Fred Mack and Ollie Gray; married Mary Louise Sales; children: Christopher, Jeffrey & Laurie. **Educ:** Univ Ill, BA, sociol, 1956; Univ Pa, MSW, 1962; Northwestern Univ, attended 1971. **Career:** Phyllis Wheatley Comm Ctr Mpls, exec dir, 1965-72; Ombudsman Corrections State Minn, exec dir, 1972-83; Minneapolis Comm Develop Agency, dir pub housing, 1983-85; Humphrey Inst Pub Affairs Univ Minn, sr fel, 1985-91; Rainbow Res Inc, sr proj assoc, 1991-2006; independent consult, 2006-; Minneapolis Pub Sch, Bd Educ, dir & treas, 2007-11. **Orgs:** Chmn, Minority Scholar & Grants Prog Am Luth Ch, 1970-87; trustee, Minneapolis Fdn, 1974-83; dir, Citizens League, 1980-83; pres bd, OperDe Novo; sr fel Humphrey Inst Pub Affairs Univ Minn; comnr, Minn Sentencing Guidelines Comn, 1986-. **Honors/Awds:** Leadership flow, Bush Federaion MN, 1970; Distinguished Service, NASW MN Chap, 1977; Distinguished Service, Nat Chap, 1983; Outstanding Achievement, Nat Asn Blacks Criminal Justice, 1978; Polemarch, St Paul-Minneapolis Alumni Chap & Kappa Alpha Psi Fraternity, 1988-; Achievement Award North Central Province, Kappa Alpha Psi Fraternity. **Special Achievements:** First vpres Nat Assn of Social Workers 1981-83. Special Report for Venture Capital Job Develop Strategies for The Black Community, Humphrey Inst of Public Affairs, 1987. Special report for Church as Partner in Community Economic Development Humphrey Inst Pub Affairs, 1990. **Home Addr:** 1310 Washburn Ave N, Minneapolis, MN 55411-2841, **Home Phone:** (612)522-4994.

**WILLIAMS, DR. THEODORE R**
Educator. **Personal:** Born Jan 17, 1931, Palestine, TX; married Louise M Pogue; children: Wayne R, Darrell R, Brian K, Marica L & Thea Elaine. **Educ:** Tex Southern Univ, BS, 1952, MS, 1954; Ore State Univ; St Lawrence Univ; Univ Wash; Ariz State Univ; Univ Iowa, PhD, 1972. **Career:** St Philips Col, Biol Dept, chmn, 1954-75, prof, asst, assoc dean, 1972-82, actg pres, 1982, interim pres, 1982-, vpres acad affairs, vpres acad affairs emer, 1986 & prof emer biol, currently; Nat Med Fel, grant, 1959-60; Nsf, grant, 1959, 1961, 1963, 1967. **Orgs:** Phi Beta Sigma Fraternity, 1951; fel Southern Fel Found, 1969-71; bd trustee, San Antonio Mus Assoc, 1973-82; adv bd mem, United Col San Antonio, 1973-; dir, Bexar Co Anemia Assoc, 1978-80; appraisal rev bd mem, Bexar Appraisal Dist, 1985-; dir, Guardianship Adv Bd, 1985-; Sigma Pi Phi Fraternity; prog officer, Tex Higher Edu Coord Bd, 1991-. **Home Addr:** 1315 Virginia Blvd, San Antonio, TX 78203, **Home Phone:** (210)532-8955. **Business Addr:** Professor Emeritus, St Philip's College, 1801 Martin Luther King Dr, San Antonio, TX 78203.

**WILLIAMS, THEODORE W., JR. (TED WILLIAMS)**
Automotive executive, chief executive officer. **Personal:** Born Jul 6, 1951, Chicago, IL; son of Theodore Sr and Shirley; married Olivia; children: Theodore III & Brandon N. **Educ:** Trinadad State Col, attended 1973. **Career:** Bob Neal Pontiac, Toyota, sales mgr, 1972-84; Jarrell Pontiac, Toyota, sales mgr, 1984-85; Bonnie Brook Ford, Ford Motor Co, 1985-88; Shamrock Lincoln-Mercury Inc, pres & chief exec officer, 1987-2004; T Williams Enterprises Inc, owner & operator, 2007-. **Orgs:** Rotary Club S Bend, 1989-; Crime Stoppers, 1989-92; Nat Asn Advan Colored People, 1992-; Nissan Dealer, adv coun, 1992-; Minority Bus Dev Coun, 1992-; St Joseph Chamber Com, 1992-; Michiana Community Hosp, 1992-; Lincoln-Mercury Dealer Asn, 1993-. **Honors/Awds:** Entrepreneur of the Year, Minority Bus Develop Coun, 1993. **Home Addr:** 51843 Trowbridge Lane, South Bend, IN 46637-1366. **Business Addr:** Owner, Operator, T Williams Enterprises Inc, 830 Main St Suite 200, Cincinnati, OH 45202.

**WILLIAMS, TINA BYLES**
Founder (originator), chief executive officer, investment banker. **Educ:** NY Univ, BS; Harvard Univ, MS, pub policy & finance. **Career:** WHP Inc, prin & sr consult, 1994-96; FIS Group, founder, chief exec officer, chief investment officer, prod mgr, 1996-; Caribbean Pvt Equity Partners LLC, partner, 2000-; Prudential Ins Co, financial analyst; Philadelphia Gas Works Pension Fund, chief investment officer; City Philadelphia's Bd Pensions & Retirement, chief investment officer. **Orgs:** Bd mem, State Pa's Pub Schs Employees' Retirement Syst; bd mem, Methodist Home C Found; ICMA Retirement Corp; Nat Women's Bus Coun; former chair, Coun's Res Comt. **Honors/ Awds:** New York City National Association of Securities Professionals (NASP) Wall Street Hall of Fame, Inductee, February, 2007; NASP Maynard Jackson Entrepreneur of the Year Award Recipient, 2008; African & Caribbean Business Council's Entrepreneurship Award, Recipient, 2010; "Black Enterprise", 75 Most Powerful Blacks on Wall Street, 2011; Thurgood Marshall Award for Excellence in Business, Recipient. **Special Achievements:** Publications: "Assessing the Chinese counter trend relief rally", Pension & Investments, 2015; "Lessons from Brexit: economic, political impact on investors", Pension & Investments, 2016. **Business Addr:** Founder, Chief Executive Officer, FIS Group, 1818 Mkt St Suite 3205, Philadelphia, PA 19103, **Business Phone:** (212)567-1100.

**WILLIAMS, TONY. See WILLIAMS, ANTHONY ALLEN.**

**WILLIAMS, TONY (ANTHONY DEMETRIC WILLIAMS)**
Football player. **Personal:** Born Jul 9, 1975, Germantown, TN; married Cherilyn; children: Tony Christopher. **Educ:** Memphis Univ, BS, educ. **Career:** Football player (retired); Minn Vikings, defensive tackle, 1997, right defensive tackle, 1998, defensive tackle, Nose Tackle, 1999-2000; Cincinnati Bengals, defensive tackle, right defensive tackle, 2001-04; Jacksonville Jaguars, defensive tackle, 2006. **Honors/ Awds:** Defensive Lineman of the Year, Memphis Univ.

**WILLIAMS, TONYA LEE (TONYA MAXINE WILLIAMS)**
Actor. **Personal:** Born Jul 12, 1958, London; married Robert Simpson. **Educ:** Ryerson Col, Toronto, attended 1979. **Career:** Films: Polka Dot Door, host, 1980-83; Skull Duggery, 1983; Spaced Invaders, 1990; The Borrower, 1991; Seventeen Again, 2000; Maple, exec producer, 2001; Poor Boy's Game, Finding Fathers Toe, 2007; My Name is Khan, news anchor, 2010; TV series: Check It Out, 1985-86; As Is, 1986; Captain Power & the Soldiers of the Future", "Falcon Crest", "Hill Street Blues", "Street Legal", The Liberators, "What's Happening Now!", 1987; A Very Brady Christmas, "A Very Brady Christmas", 1988; "Matlock", Nasty Boys, A Peaceable Kingdom, Generations, 1989; "The Young & the Restless", 1990-2007; Piece of Cake, 1990; "Getting By", Counterstrike", 1993; "Silk Stalkings", 1994; "PSI Factor: Chronicles of the Paranormal", 1998; "Tonya Lee Williams: Gospel Jubilee", exec producer, 2004; Kink in My Hair, exec producer & dir, 2004; "A Perfect Note", 2005; Poor Boy's Game, Finding Father's Toe, 2007; The Border, 2009-10; She's the Mayor, 2011. **Orgs:** Founder, ReelWorld Film Festival; hon mem, Sigma Gamma Rho Sorority. **Honors/Awds:** Crowned Miss Black Ontario, 1977; Image Award, Nat Asn Advan Colored People, 2000 & 2002; Dr Bird Award; TV Cases, Ribbon of Hope Award; Nominated for Image Award, 2009. **Business Addr:** Actress, c/o William Morris Agency, 151 El Camino Dr, Beverly Hills, CA 90212, **Business Phone:** (310)859-4000.

**WILLIAMS, DR. TRINA RACHAEL (TRINA R SHANKS)**
Research scientist, college teacher, activist. **Personal:** Born Nov 6, 1970, New Orleans, LA; daughter of Dwight Nichols and Sheila A. **Educ:** Wash Univ, John M Olin Sch Bus, BS, bus admin, 1992; Wash Univ, George W Brown Sch Social Work, St Louis, MO, MSW, 2000, PhD, 2003; Oxford Univ, MPhil, comparative social res, 1996. **Career:** Fun Ctr Inc, found & dir, 1990-92; Nat Community Educ Asn, intern, 1991; Minority Youth Entrepreneurship Prog, dir, 1992; US Peace Corps, small bus consult, 1992-94; Milwaukee Village Sch, consult, 1995-96; Stand C, Wash, DC, consult, 1996-97; Christian Community Serv Inc, Nashville, TN, exec dir, 1997-98; Chancellor's Fel, 1998; Wash Univ, Grad Stud Senate, Secy, 2002-03; Univ Mich, asst prof social work, 2003-, Good Neighborhoods Initiative, proj coordr, 2005-; SEED Impact Assessment study, co investr, 2004-. **Orgs:** Coun Social Work Educ, 1999-2003; Asn Am Rhodes Scholars, 1995-03; vol, Centennial Olympic Games, 1996; Vol & Staff, US Olympic Festival, St Louis, 1994; vol & informal counr, Coalition Homeless, Wash, DC, 1991; vol, Pan-Am Games, Indpolis, IN, 1987; Vol Staff, US Olympic Festival, 1994; Schrader Lane Day Care Ctr, 1997; N Am Asn Christians Social Work, 1999-2003; Mo state selection comt, Rhodes Scholar competition, 2001-03; exec dir, Christian Community Serv; Co-chair, R I S E N, 2005-. **Home Addr:** 14414 Mansfield St 2nd Fl, Detroit, MI 48227, **Home Phone:** (313)273-2836. **Business Addr:** Assistant Professor Social Work, Project Coordinator, University of Michigan, Rm 3726 SSWB 1080 S Univ, Ann Arbor, MI 48109, **Business Phone:** (734)764-7411.

**WILLIAMS, TYRONE M., JR.**
Football player. **Personal:** Born Oct 22, 1972, Philadelphia, PA; married Amy T; children: Deshon, Amandre, Teryn & Tayvian. **Educ:** Univ Wyo. **Career:** Football player (retired); Chicago Bears, defensive end, 1997; Philadelphia Eagles, 1999-2000; Kans City Chiefs, 2000-01; Wash Redskins, 2001; BC Lions, defensive tackle, 2002-08; Winnipeg Blue Bombers, 2009. **Honors/Awds:** CFL All-Stars, 2006, 2007. **Home Addr:** 18912 NW 23 Rd Ct, Miami Gardens, FL 33056. **Business Addr:** Defensive Lineman, British Columbia Lions, Shepherd Sta765 Pacific Blvd, Vancouver, BC V6B 4Y9, **Business Phone:** (604)661-3626.

**WILLIAMS, ULYSSES JEAN**
Educator, counselor. **Personal:** Born Sep 15, 1947, Memphis, TN; daughter of Ann Moton Warren and Ulysses Warren; married Foster Sr; children: Tasha A, Foster, LaQuentin D & AnQuentin T. **Educ:** Philander Smith Col, 1967; Univ Cent Ark, BSE, 1969, MSE, 1973; Ark State Univ, cert behav dis, 1980, gifted & talented cert, 1985; Ark State Univ, elem principalship cert, 1987, counr cert, 1992; Sch Scripture, BRE. **Career:** Cotton Plant Elem Sch, secy, 1969-70; Helena-West Helena Pub Schs, 1970-78, 1988-89; East Ark Regional Mental Health Ctr, educ specialist, 1978-81; Lucilia Wood Elem Sch, educr, 1982-88; Holly Grove Pub Schs, 1989-; MSE, counr educ, 1993; direct instr coordr; asst elem prin; Sch of the Scripture, instr, currently. **Orgs:** Ark Educ Asn, 1970-; Nat Educ Asn, 1970-; PTA, 1970-; Arkansas Counr Asn, 1989-; Ark Multicultural Asn, 1989-; Ark Voc Asn, 1989-; pres, Theta Gamma Zeta; Theta Gamma Zeta, founding pres, 4 years; adv to Amicae; regional & state coordr S Cent Region; chmn Oper, Big Vote:Nat Asn Advan Colored People; Second Baptist Church; chmn Christian Bd Ed; secy, Matrons; dir, church choir; Gifted & Talented, adv comt; Helena-West Helena Bd Educ, 1980-86; state dir, Ark Zeta Phi Beta Sor Inc, 1987-92; Elaine Six Yr Plan Comn; comt mem, Gov's Rural Develop Action Prog, 1987-88; Laubach bd mem, tutor, 1988-. **Home Addr:** 239 Desota St, West Helena, AR 72390-2822, **Home Phone:** (870)572-2857.

**WILLIAMS, VANESSA A.**
Actor. **Personal:** Born May 12, 1963, Brooklyn, NY; married Andre Wiseman; children: Omar Tafari; married John Marshall Jones; children: Andrea Wiseman, John Marshall Jones Jr & William Jones. **Educ:** Marymount Manhattan Col, BA. **Career:** Films: New Jack City, 1991; Fatal Bond, 1992; Candyman, 1992; Drop Squad, 1994; Mother, 1996; Boogie Nights, 1997; Breakdown, 1997; Punks, 2000; Our America, 2002; Like Mike, 2002; Baby of the Family, 2002; Like Mike, 2002; Black Listed, 2003; Santa, Baby!, 2003; Happy to Be Nappy and Other Stories of Me, 2004; Johnson Family Vacation, 2004; Gift for the Living, 2005; Ice Spiders, 2007; And Then Came Love, 2007; Hummingbird, 2008; Flirting with Forty, 2008; Contradictions of the Heart, 2009; Imagine That, 2009; Tim Alexander's A Mother's Love, 2011; Men, Money & Gold Diggers, 2014; TV series: 227, 1988; "Melrose Place", 1992-93; "Murder One", 1995-96; NYPD Blue, 1995; Buddies, 1996; Chicago Hope, 1996; Malcolm & Eddie, 1996; A Woman of Color, 1997; Between Brothers, 1997; The Pretender, 1998; The Steve Harvey Show, 1998; Total Recall 2070, 1999; "Incognito", 1999; "Playing With Fire", 2000; Our America, 2002; "Soul Food", 2000-04; Afrocentricity, 2000; "Heavy Gear", animated, 2001; Allergic to Nuts, exec producer, 2003; "Dense", exec producer, 2004; Driving Fish, co-exec producer, 2004; South Beach, 2006; Drawing Angel, 2007; Cold Case, 2007; "Lincoln Heights", 2008; "Knight Rider", 2009; "Everybody Hates Chris", 2009; "Sugar Mommas", 2012; "Raising Izzie", 2012. **Honors/Awds:** Image Award, Nat Asn Advan Colored People, 2003. **Business Addr:** Actress, c/o Showtime Networks Inc, 1633 E Broadway, New York, NY 10019, **Business Phone:** (212)708-1600.

**WILLIAMS, VANESSA LYNNE**
Actor, singer. **Personal:** Born Mar 18, 1963, Tarrytown, NY; daughter of Milton and Helen; married Ramon Hervey II; children: Melanie, Jillian & Devin; married Rick Fox; children: Sasha Gabriella. **Educ:** Syracuse Univ, BFA, musical theater. **Career:** Actress, singer, fashion model; Former Miss Am; Albums: The Right Stuff, 1988; The Comfort Zone, 1991; The Sweetest Days, 1994; Star Bright, 1996; Next, 1997; Greatest Hits - the first ten years, 1998; Silver & Gold, 2004; Everlasting Love, 2005; Singles: The Right Stuff, 1988; Dreamin, 1988; (He's got) The Look, 1988; Darlin I, 1988; The Comfort Zone, 1991; Running back to you, 1991; Save the Best for Last, 1991; Just fortnight, 1991; Work to do, 1991; For all the children, 1994; Betcha Never, 1994; You can't run, 1994; The Way that you love?, 1994; The Sweetest Days, 1994; Hostess, Showtime At The Apollo; Soul Train, Live!, Dick Clark Presents, Club MTV, BET's Video Soul, & Live at the Improv; Readings from the Slave Narratives; TV series: "Full Exposure: The Sex Tapes Scandal", 1989; "The Kid Who Loved Christmas", 1990; "Stompin' at the Savoy", 1992; "The Jacksons: An American Dream", 1992; "Kiss of the Spider Woman", 1994; "Bye Bye Birdie", 1995; "Nothing Lasts Forever", 1995; "Vanessa Williams & Friends: Christmas in New York", exec producer, 1996; "The Odyssey", 1997; "Future sport", 1998; "L.A. Doctors", 1999; "Don Quixote", 2000; "The Courage to Love", exec producer, 2000; "A Diva's Christmas Carol", 2000; "WW3", 2001; "Ally McBeal", 2002; "Keep the Faith", 2002; "Baby", 2002; "Boomtown", 2003; "Beck & Call", 2004; "Vanessa Williams Christmas: Live by Request", exec producer, 2004; "South Beach", 2006; "Ugly Betty", 2006-08; "The Beautiful World of Ugly Betty", 2007; "Mama Mirabelle's Home Movies", 2007-08; "Desperate Housewives", 2010-12; "Phineas and Ferb", 2012; "666 Park Avenue", 2012-13; "The Trip to Bountiful", 2014. Films: The Pick Up Artist, 1987; Under the Gun, 1988; Eraser, 1996; Hoodlum, 1997; Soul Food, 1997; Dance With Me, 1998; Another You, 1991; Light It Up, 1999; The Adventures of Elmo in Grouchland, 1999; Shaft, 2000; Johnson Family Vacation, 2004; My Brother, 2006; And Then Came Love, exec producer, 2007; Hannah Montana: The Movie, 2009; Temptation: Confessions of a Marriage Counselor, 2013. **Honors/Awds:** Numerous awards and honors including Miss America, 1983; Billboard Music Award, 1993; Theatre World Award, 1994; Academy Award, 1995; Soul Train Awards, 1996; Image Award, Nat Asn Advan Colored People, 1998, 2007, 2008, 2011 & 2013; MTV Video Music Award, 5 New York Music Awards; Mother Hale Award; Golden Satellite Award, 2003, 2007, 2010 & 2011; Humanitarian Award; Hollywood Walk of Fame, 2007; Jacobi Children's Arts Award, 2007; Teen Choice Award, 2007; Muse Award, 2010. **Special Achievements:** First African American contestant in the hot seat on "Who Wants to Be a Millionaire", 1999; Ranked #56 on VH1's 100 Sexiest Artists; First black woman to be crowned "Miss America"; Grammy, Emmy, and Tony Award nominee; First African-American spokesmodel for L'Oreal cosmetics in the late 1990s. **Home Addr:** 1350 Sixth Ave, New York, NY 10019. **Business Addr:** Actress, William Morris Agency, 1 William Morris Pl, Beverly Hills, CA 90212, **Business Phone:** (310)859-4000.

**WILLIAMS, VENUS EBONE STARR**
Tennis player, business owner. **Personal:** Born Jun 17, 1980, Lynwood, CA; daughter of Richard and Oracene Price. **Educ:** Art Inst Ft Lauderdale, AA, fashion design, 2007. **Career:** V Starr Interiors, owner, 2003-; prof tennis player, currently. **Honors/Awds:** Sports Image Foundation Award, 1995; WTA Newcomer of the Year, 1997; September's Olympic Committee Female Athlete, 1997; Tennis Magazine's Most Improved Player, 1998; Grand Slam Cup, singles, Champion, 1998; Australian Open, doubles, Champion, 1998, 2001, 2003, 2009 & 2010, mixed doubles, 1998; Miami, singles, Champion, 1998; Okla City, singles & doubles, Champion, 1998; Zurich, singles, Champion, 1999; New Haven, singles, Champion, 1999; Italian Open, singles, Champion, 1999; Hamburg, singles, Champion, 1999; Fed Cup, Champion, 1999; Miami, singles, Champion, 1999; Okla City, singles, Champion, 1999; US Open, doubles, Champion, 1999, 2009, singles, Champion, 2000, 2001; French Open, doubles, Champion, 1999, 2010, mixed doubles, 1998; WTA Doubles Team of the Year Award, 2000 & 2008; Sports Illustrated for Women's Sportswoman of the Year, 2000; Womens Tennis Asn Player of the Year, 2000; Teen Awards Achievement Award, 2000; Women's Sports Foundation's Athlete of the Year Award, 2000; Wimbledon, singles, Champion, 2000, 2001, 2005, 2007 & 2008, doubles, Champion, 2000, 2002, 2008, 2009 & 2012; Gold Medal, singles, Olympics, 2000, doubles, 2000, 2008 & 2012; ESPY Award Best Female Tennis Player, 2001, 2002 & 2006; EMMA Best Sport Personality Award, 2001; Ericsson Open, singles, Champion, 2001; Thalgo Australian Womens Hardcourts, singles, Champion, 2002; ESPY Award Best Female Athlete, 2002; 34th Nat Asn Advan Colored People Image Awards' President's Award, 2003; Gaz De France, singles, Champion, 2002; Proximus Diamond Games singles, Champion, 2002; Bausch & Lomb, singles, Champion, 2002; Family Circle Cup, singles, Champion, 2004; Harris Poll Most Favorite Female Sports Star, 2004 & 2006; J & S Cup, singles, Champion, 2004; Istanbul Cup, singles, Champion, 2005; Glamour Magazine's Women of the Year Award, 2005; BET's Best Female Athlete of the Year, 2006; Gitanjali Diamond Award, 2007; Whirlpool Sixth Sense Player of the Year Award, 2008; WTA Fan Favorite Doubles Team of the Year, 2008 & 2010 & 2012; Doha 21st Century Leaders Awards-Outstanding Leadership, 2008 Anti-Defamation League Americanism Award, 2009; Caesars Tennis Classic Achievement Award, 2010; YWCA GLA Phenomenal Woman of the Year Award, 2010; World TeamTennis Finals Most Valuable Player, 2012; WTA Player Service Award, 2012 & 2013; BET Black Girls Rock! Star Power Award, 2013; US Open Sportsmanship Award, 2015; WTA February Best Dressed Player, 2015; WTA Roland Garros Best Dressed Player, 2015; WTA October Best Dressed Player, 2015; WTA Comeback Player of the Year, 2015; WTA Social Fan Favorite - #TBT of the Year, 2015. **Special Achievements:** First African American woman to reach the first ranking on the WTA Tour; first African-American player to garner World No 1 spot since the computer rankings began in 1975; First African American woman to achieve this feat during the Open Era. **Home Addr:** 6466 Emerald Dunes Dr Apt 105, West Palm Beach, FL 33411-2766. **Business Addr:** Professional Tennis Player, US Tennis Association, 70 W Red Oak Lane, White Plains, NY 10604-3602, **Business Phone:** (914)696-7000.

### WILLIAMS, VERNICE LOUISE
Auditor, manager. **Personal:** Born Aug 13, 1934, Indianapolis, IN; daughter of Herman S Whitelaw Sr and Laura Chubbs Guthrie; married Andrew I; children: Crystal B Thomas, Andrea J, Marlon I, Sherman A, Dewayne M & Karen R. **Educ:** Ind Univ-Purdue Univ Indpolis, attended 1972. **Career:** Manager (retired); Army Finance C&R, Ft Benjamin, Harrison Ind, auditor, 1952-67; Ind Bell, Indianapolis, Ind, mgr, 1974-92. **Orgs:** Bd mem & vice chair, Ind Black Expo, 1974-; mem steering comt, United Negro Col Fund, 1982-; bd mem, Dialogue Today, 1985-; bd mem, Police Chief Adv Coun, 1987-; chair, IBE Youth Corp, 1988-. **Honors/Awds:** Minorities Engineering, Indiana Bell, 1984; Leadership Award, Chamber Com, 1986; Outstanding Volunteerism, United Way, 1988; Mount Summitt Award, Ind Bell, 1989; Presidents Club Award, Ind Bell, 1989; Prog coord, admin asst, off mgr, 100 Black Men Indianapolis Inc. **Special Achievements:** Two Hundred Most Influential Blacks In Indiana; Outstanding Women In Indiana. **Home Addr:** 6136 N Meridian W Dr, Indianapolis, IN 46204, **Home Phone:** (317)255-4216.

### WILLIAMS, VERNON R.
Automotive executive. **Career:** Greenville Ford Lincoln-Mercury Inc, pres & chief exec officer, 1997-. **Business Addr:** President, Chief Executive officer, Greenville Ford Lincoln-Mercury Inc, 4001 State St Hwy 30, Greenville, TX 75403, **Business Phone:** (903)455-7222.

### WILLIAMS, W. BILL
Executive, vice president (organization). **Personal:** Born Aug 19, 1939, Chicago, IL; son of William Sr and Ellen Brassfield; married Syleste Tillman; children: Karen, Kevin & Keyth. **Educ:** Chicago State Univ, Chicago, IL, BS, bus mgt; Loading Supr's Course, London, eng. **Career:** United Airlines, Chicago, Ill, cert meeting prof & oper supr, 1960-63; Butler Aviation, Chicago, Ill, oper supr, 1963-70; Sullair Corp, Mich City, Ind, sales engr, 1970-75; Chicago Conv & Tourism Bur, Chicago, Ill, trainee, dir sales, 1975-89, asst vpres, vpres, 1989, consult; K & J Shoe Repair & Shine Parlors, Chicago, Ill, owner, 1985-. **Orgs:** Life mem, Kappa Alpha Psi Fraternity, 1982-; life mem, Mt Calvary Baptist Church; bd mem, Nat Coalition Black Meeting Planners, 1985-89; vpres, Soc Gov Meeting Planners; mkt dir, IBPOEW, 1985-; pres, int vip & conv chmn, Rat Pack Int, 1985-; sovereign grand inspector gen, United Sup Coun, PHA, 1987-; State Ill Compensation Rev Bd; vice chmn, Westside Asn Community Action; bd mem, Shoop Sch; bd mem, Black Metropolis Conv & Tourism Coun; founding bd mem, Chicago Chap Soc Govt Meeting Professionals; Quarter Century Club Kappa Alpha Psi Fraternity; Relig Conf Mgt Asn; Int Asn Hisp Meeting Professionals;Nat Asn Advan Colored People; Christian Meetings & Conv Asn; Nat Urban League; Rainbow Push Coalition; bd trustee, Chicago Baptist Inst; bd mem, Acad Travel & Tourism Chicago Pub Schs; City Clubs Chicago; Montford Pt Marines Asn, currently. **Home Addr:** 12531 S Mich Ave, Chicago, IL 60628, **Home Phone:** (773)821-6438. **Business Addr:** Owner, K & J Shine Parlor, 1340 W 111th St, Chicago, IL 60643, **Business Phone:** (773)445-7525.

### WILLIAMS, W. CLYDE
School administrator, clergy. **Personal:** Born Cordele, GA; married Elaine; children: Joyce, Clyde, John & Gregory. **Educ:** Holsey Cobb Inst, attended 1951; Paine Col, BA, 1955; Howard Univ, MDiv, 1959; Interdenom Theol Ctr, MRE, 1961; Atlanta Univ, MA, 1969; Univ Ala, PhD, 1976. **Career:** Bethlehem Ctr, Augusta, Ga, dir boys work, 1954-56; NY St Coun Church, chaplain, 1957-58; Howard Univ, asst dir stud act, 1959-; Christ Meth Epis Church, exec secy & dir youth work & adult educ, 1960-63; Interdenom Theol Ctr, dir, 1963-67, registr & dir admin, 1967-69, dir of Recruiting & fac; Asn Christ Train & Serv, staff assoc, 1969; Church Union, assoc gen secy consult, 1969-71; Miles Col, pres, 1971-86; Coun Trenholm State Tech Col, Montgomery, inter pres; W. Clyde William Neighborhood Networks Ctr, founder; city Greenville, Dep Asst to Mayor & dir Community Develop. **Orgs:** Adv comt, US Dept State; mem stud fin aid coun, US Dept HEW; res adv panel, US Off Educ Sch Monitor & Consum Prot Proj; Sickle Cell Dis adv com, NIH; co-chmn Comt Aff Com Oper New Birmingham; vice chmn, Ala Comt Human & Pub Policy; bd dir, Unit Negro Col Fund; bd dir, Birmingham Cable Comn; bd dir, Birmingham Urban League; bd dir, Nat Comn Black Chmn; bd dir, Am Nat Red Cross; bd trustee, Birmingham Symphony Asn; exec bd, BSA; exec comt, Jefferson Co Child Develop Coun; City Adv Coun, Jefferson Co; Birmingham Manpower Area Plan Coun; Lay Adv Coun, St Vincent's Hosp; NAACP; YMCA; Alpha Phi Alpha Frat Educ; Hon Soc Kappa Delta Pi, 1975; clergy, St. John CME Church, Trinity CME Church, Noble Chapel CME Church, Bethel CME church, Oak Grove/Cogar Hill CME Church, Moody Temple & First CME Church; Kirkendoll Learning Resources Ctr; Miles Law Sch & Life-Long Learning Ctr Ministries & Christian Workers; Chief exec officer, founder, Nat Inst Human Develop, currently. **Honors/Awds:** Man of Year, Omega Psi Phi Frat; Alumni Achievment Award, Paine Col, 1971; Outstanding Educ Soc Beauty Cong, 1972; hon Ddiv, Paine Col, 1972; City of Birmingham Mayor's Cit, 1974; Outstanding Educ Fed Soc Coop, 1975. **Special Achievements:** Author of books, papers & publications. **Home Addr:** 6301 Myron Massey Blvd, Fairfield, AK 35064, **Home Phone:** (205)925-2153. **Business Addr:** Chief Executive Officer, Founder, National Institute for Human Development, 2805 Shoreland Dr SW, Atlanta, GA 30331, **Business Phone:** (404)346-1167.

### WILLIAMS, WALLACE C.
Executive. **Personal:** Born Jan 1, 1921?, Kannapolis, NC; children: Wallace Jr & Joyce. **Educ:** Boro-Hall Acad, NY, attended 1946; Pace Col, NY, attended 1948; Columbia Univ, attended 1950; Detroit Inst Tech, BS, bus technol, 1958; Wayne State Univ, attended 1970; Univ Detroit BS, bus technol. **Career:** NY State Employ Serv, interviewer, 1947-53; US Bur Prisons, correctional aid prison fiscal officer, 1953-58; Mich Employ Securities Comn, interviewer, 1958-65, employ sec exec, 1965-69; State Mich, Off Minority Bus Enterprise Mich Dept Com, dir, 1959-78; Mich Dept Com, econ develop exec, 1969-; CCAC-ICBIF, dir, 1979; Mich Dept Labor, coordr Manpower Prog; J L Dumas Construct Co, bus develop mgr, consult; Detroit Econ Growth Corp, dir City Detroit; Univ Mich's Econ Develop Admin, spec consult; METCO Eng Servs Inc, vpres bus develop; Royal Oak Twp Planning Comn, chmn; Univ Mich, Sch Bus, lectr, consult, res assoc Spec Proj Div, dir minority bus progs, 1986-96. **Orgs:** Trustee, Exec Coun Trade Union Ldrshp Coun; past pres, Booker T Wash Bus Asn, chmn bd; charter mem & vpres, Univ-Govt-Bus Comt; exec bd, Inner City Bus Improv Forum; chmn, Minority Bus Oppor Com; ed & publ, Minority Bus Newsletter; bd mem, HOPE Inc; New Detroit Minority Adv Com; Wayne Co Bd Comnr Minority Adv Co; serv officer, VFW TF Burns Post 5793; bd mem, Lewis Bus Col; bd dir, People's Comm Civic League; Bus Adv Com Detroit Chamber Com; Tr Bd Orchestra Hall Found; golden heritage, Nat Asn Advan Colored People; coordr, Christian Prison fel Prog; asst reg vpres, Nat Bus League; vice chmn, Highland Pk YMCA; Adv Planning Coun Wayne Co; dir, Minority Bus Serv, Univ Mich, Ann Arbor; rep, White House Conf Small Bus; Detroit E Inc; Community Ment Health Ctr; Cotillion Club Detroit. **Honors/Awds:** Community Service Award, Booker T Wash Bus Asn; Businessman of the Year Award, Wayne County Bd Comnrs & Gamma Phi Delta, 1984; Outstanding Public Service Award, Mich Lupus Found; Outstanding Service Award, State Mich; Spirit of Detroit Award, City Detroit; Appreciation Award, US Dept Com; City Flint, Mich Proclaimations from Mayor Woodrow Stanley; City Coun, Mayor Coleman Young, City Detroit; Appreciation Award, City Coun, Royal Oak Township; Bethel AME Church Missionary Soc. **Home Addr:** 1425 Battlefield Blvd N, Chesapeake, VA 23320. **Business Addr:** Director, University of Michigan Business School, 701 Tappan Ave, Ann Arbor, MI 48109, **Business Phone:** (734)763-5796.

### WILLIAMS, WALLY JAMES, JR.
Football player, radio broadcaster. **Personal:** Born Feb 20, 1971, Tallahassee, FL; children: Bronson. **Educ:** Fla A&M Univ, grad. **Career:** Football player (retired), analyst; Cleveland Browns, 1993, left guard, 1994-95; Baltimore Ravens, ctr, right guard, 1996, ctr, 1997, ctr, left guard, 1998; New Orleans Saints, left guard, 1999-2003; CBS Radio, analyst, currently. **Honors/Awds:** Ed Block Courage Award, 1997; All-City; All-State; Hall of Fame, Fla A&M Univ, 2015. **Home Addr:** 2243 Falkirk Dr, Finksburg, MD 21048. **Business Addr:** Analyst, CBS Radio, 1423 Clarkview Rd Suite 100, Baltimore, MD 21209, **Business Phone:** (410)825-1065.

### WILLIAMS, HON. WALTER
Executive, judge, teacher. **Personal:** Born Jun 13, 1939, Yazoo City, MS; son of Walter Sr and Mary Lee Knight; married Helen M Hudson; children: Toni Marshea. **Educ:** Univ Wis, cert, 1961; Jackson State Univ, attended 1962; John Marshall Law Sch, JD, 1970. **Career:** Williams Slaughter & Williams, partner; Malcolm X Col, asst prof; Circuit Ct Cook County, assoc judge, 1999-2003, supervising judge, 2012. **Orgs:** Am Bar Asn; Chicago Bar Asn; pres, Cook County Bar Asn; Ill State Bar Asn; Nat Bar Asn; Alpha Phi Alpha Frat; pres, Jackson State Univ Alumni Asn; John Marshall Law Sch Alumni; Ill Judicial Coun; Ill Judges Asn; Am Judges Asn; Circuit Ct Cook County Comt, currently. **Home Addr:** 5555 S Everett, Chicago, IL 60637. **Business Addr:** Supervising Judge, Circuit Court of Cook County, Richard J Daley Ctr 50 W Wash St, Chicago, IL 60602, **Business Phone:** (312)603-2600.

### WILLIAMS, WALTER ANDER, JR. (WALT WILLIAMS)
Executive, basketball player, basketball coach. **Personal:** Born Apr 16, 1970, Washington, DC; married April; children: Ty. **Educ:** Univ Md, BA, mgt & consumer studies, 1992. **Career:** Basketball player (retired), exec; Sacramento Kings, guard-forward, small forward, 1992-96; Miami Heat, 1995-96; Toronto Raptors, small forward, 1996-98; Portland Trail Blazers, small forward, 1998-99; Houston Rockets, small forward, 1999-2002; Dallas Mavericks, small forward, 2002-03; UBS, financial advisor, currently; Sherwood High Sch, asst coach, Currently. **Orgs:** Active supporter, March Dimes, currently; bd mem, Walt Williams Found, currently. **Honors/Awds:** Bronze Medal, Pan Am Games, 1991. **Special Achievements:** Film appearance: Eddie, 1996; Appeared in the music video for number one song "Only Wanna To Be With You" by Hootie & the Blowfish; Established $125, 000 scholarship fund at Maryland which benefits minority students in honor of his late father, Walter Sr. **Business Addr:** Financial Advisor, UBS, 307 Int Cir 4th Fl, Hunt Valley, MD 21031, **Business Phone:** (410)771-3140.

### WILLIAMS, WAYNE ALLAN
Research scientist. **Personal:** Born Oct 8, 1964, Brooklyn, NY; son of Isreal and Rose. **Educ:** Davidson Col, BA, class studies, 1989; Boston Col, MEd, statist anal & measurement, 1991; Harvard Univ, technol & human develop. **Career:** Educr, statistician & technologist; Philadelphia Pub Schs Testing Reform, statist consult, 1990-91; Boston Col, Develop Off, res asst, 1990-91; Educ Develop Ctr, res intern, 1991; Boston Col, Career Ctr, statist consult, 1991-94; Boston Col, Ctr Study Testing, Eval & Educ Policy, fac res asst, 1991-93; Basic Plus Math Proj Eval, co-eval, 1992-93; Lesley Col, Algebra Proj Eval, statist consult, 1993-95; Grad Sch Educ Career Ctr, statist consult, 1993-95; Harvard Univ Divinity Sch, statist res assoc; Mass Inst Technol, Reflective Community, prac fel, 2001-03; Empowering Technol Inc, chief exec officer, currently. **Orgs:** Am Educ Res Asn, 1991-; Phi Delta Kappa, 1992-; Baker fel Harvard Univ, 1993-95; co-founder, initial bd trustee, 1994-96, Benjamin Banneker Charter Sch; Black Data Processing Asn; Asn Comput Mach; Seasure Shipping Ltd, Mass Impact. **Honors/Awds:** Cumberland County Med Soc Award, 1983; Fayetteville Chap Links Honoree, 1983; Eumenean Literary Soc Cert, Davidson Col, 1987; AME Zion Church, North Charlotte Dist Outstanding Service Award, 1987; Academic Awareness Certificate for Academic Achievement, Davidson Col, 1989; Nat Hon Soc, 1992. **Special Achievements:** Author: "Developing a Multi-tiered Database for Measuring Systemic School Reform", 1995. **Home Addr:** 22 Peabody Ter, Cambridge, MA 02138, **Home Phone:** (617)384-1128. **Business Addr:** Chief Executive Officer, Empowering Technology Inc, 400 W Cummings Pk Suite 725, Woburn, MA 02138.

### WILLIAMS, WENDY (WENDY WILLIAMS HUNTER)
Radio host, writer, television talk show host. **Personal:** Born Jul 18, 1964, Asbury Park, NJ; daughter of Thomas Williams Sr. and Shirley Williams; married Kevin Hunter Sr., Nov 30, 1997; children: Kevin Hunter Jr.. **Educ:** Northeastern University (Boston), B.A. in Communications and a minor in Journalism, 1989. **Career:** Radio talk show host, St. Croix (WVIS), New York City (then-WRKS, later WQHT), 1989-98, Philadelphia (WUSL), 1998-01, and New York City (WBLS), 2001-09; "The Wendy Williams Show," TV show host, 2008-; QVC apparel line "Adorn"; Wendy Williams Hair World, wig line; TV show "Drop Dead Diva," Judge, 2011; "Queen of Media" movie, Executive Producer, 2011; Wendy Williams Productions, Founder, with husband/manager Kevin Hunter Sr., 2013-. **Honors/Awds:** "Billboard," Best On-Air Personality, 1993; National Radio Hall of Fame, Inductee, 2008. **Special Achievements:** Co-author of "Wendy's Got the Heat" with Karen Hunter, Atria, 2003; author of "The Wendy Williams Experience," 2005, and "Ask Wendy: Straight-Up Advice for All the Drama in Your Life," 2013.

### WILLIAMS, WESLEY S., JR. (WESLEY SAMUEL WILLIAMS, JR.)
Lawyer, association executive, executive director. **Personal:** Born Nov 13, 1942, Philadelphia, PA; married Karen Roberta Hastie; children: Amanda, Bo & Bailey. **Educ:** Harvard Univ, BA, 1963, JD, 1967; Woodrow Wilosn Fel Fletcher Sch Law, dipl, MA, 1964; Columbia Univ, LLM, 1969, JSD, 1969. **Career:** DC Coun, legal coun, 1967-69; Columbia Univ, assoc-in-law, 1968-69; US Sen Com DC, counr, legal coun, 1969-70; Hasty Pudding Inst, mem, 1970; Georgetown Univ Law Ctr, adj prof law, 1971-73; Covington & Burling, assoc, 1970-75, partner, 1975-2005; Lockhart Co Inc, co-chmn, 1978-, pres & chief operating officer, 2003-; Broadcast Capital Inc, chmn & bd dir, 1979-92; Black Star Commun Inc, bd dir, 1987-; CarrAmerica Realty Corp, lead non mgt dir, 1993-; Carramerica Realty LP, gen partner, 1993; CarrAmerica Realty GP Holdings Inc, dir, 1993; Fed Res Bank Richmond, bd dir, 1997-2005, chmn, 2003-04; Guardian Ins Co Inc, co-chmn; Citigroup Global Markets Holdings Inc, dir. **Orgs:** Circuit Judicial Conf, 1971-; Exec Ecom Wash Lawyers Com Civil Rights Under Law, 1972-; bd dir, Nat Symphony Orch Asn, 1972-; Com Legis Bar, 1973-; bd dir, Nat Symphony Orchestra, 1973-91; pres, Bd trustee, Family & Child Serv Wash, 1974-; US Circuit Judge Nominating Comn, 1977-; bd dir, Salomon Inc, 1997-;coun, DC Bar, 1979-81; bd trustee, pres, Nat Child Res Ctr, 1978-82, 1980-82; bd dir, Harvard Alumni Asn, 1979-82; bd dir, Honourable Soc Lincoln's Inn; life mem, Wash Urban League; sr trustee, Exec Comt, bd trustee, Pa Mutual Life Ins Co, Philadelphia, Pa; exec comt, Wash Lawyers Comt Civil Rights Under Law; Am Law Inst; life fel Am Bar Found; NY Bar Asn; coun pres, Harvard Law Sch Asn, 1992-94; dir, World Affairs Coun Wash; Alpha Phi Alpha Fraternity; Sigma Pi Phi Fraternity; St Thomas Yacht Club; City Club Wash; Metrop Club Wash; Waltz Group Wash; bd dir, Nat Prostate Cancer Coalition, 2004-; chmn, Smithsonian Inst; bd trustee, Penn Mutual Life Ins Co. **Home Addr:** 1201 Pa Ave NW, PO Box 7566, Washington, DC 20004, **Home Phone:** (202)662-5628. **Business Addr:** President, Chief Operating Officer, Lockhart Companies Inc, 44 Estate Thomas, St Thomas, VA 00801, **Business Phone:** (340)776-1900.

### WILLIAMS, WILBERT EDD
Engineer, software developer, naval officer. **Personal:** Born Sep 13, 1948, Fayetteville, NC; son of Edd and Mary Moore; married Yolanda Faye DeBerry; children: Danica Michelle & Donata Merie. **Educ:** Fayetteville State Univ, BS, comput info, 1977; Univ MI-Ann Arbor, MS, 1978; Duke Univ, MBA, 1986. **Career:** USN, digital display tech, 1967-74; Bell Labs, mem tech staff, 1977-79; Westinghouse, Metering & Control Div, 1979, corp minority spokesperson, 1983-, sr syst & software engr; ABB T&D Co, syst & software engr, 1979-86, mgr prod software, 1986. **Orgs:** Am Soc Naval Engrs, 1978-; Jack & Jill Am, 1982-; comm ambassador, Westinghouse Elec, 1983-; St Matthew Budget & Finance Comt, 1984-; vpres, St Matthew Scholar Comt, 1986-87. **Honors/Awds:** Fel, Univ MI Bell Labs, 1977-78; Distinguished Corporate Alumni, NAFEO, 1983; Tuition Support for Duke MBA Westinghouse Electric, 1984-86; Corporate Community Service, Westinghouse Elec, 1988. **Home Addr:** 1985 Landing Way, Weston, FL 33326, **Home Phone:** (954)384-0194.

### WILLIAMS, REV. WILBERT LEE
Educator, clergy, association executive. **Personal:** Born Aug 25, 1938, Corsicana, TX; son of Calvin Sr and Mamie; married Catherine L Lemons; children: Sheila, Stuart & Cynthia. **Educ:** Prairie View A&M Col, BS, 1960; Howard Univ Sch Law, JD, 1971; Inst New Govt Attorneys, 1971; Howard Univ Sch Divinity, MDiv, 1990; Faith Christian Univ & Sch, DHL, 2001. **Career:** US Dept Agr, farm mgt supvr, 1965-68; United Planning Org, Wash DC, exec officer, 1968-71; US Dept Agr, Off Gen Coun, Wash DC, atty, 1971-84; US Dept Agr, equal opportunity officer; First New Horizon Baptist Church, founder, pastor, bishop, 1988-. **Orgs:** Past vpres & founding mem, CHASE Inc; DC Neighborhood Reinvestment Comn; bd dir, Neighborhood Legal Serv Prog, Wash DC; bd trustee, United Planning Org, Wash DC; pres & founder, First New Horizon Comt Develop Ctr. **Honors/Awds:** First Annual Achievement Award, OEO Nat Adv Comt, Legal Serv Prog, 1968; Asst Secy Agr Award for Excellence, 1980; USDA Agricultural Award. **Home Addr:** 7908 Old Br Ave, Clinton, MD 20735, **Home Phone:** (301)856-9177. **Business Addr:** Bishop, Pastor, The First New Horizon Baptist Church, 9511 Piscataway Rd, Clinton, MD 20735-4440, **Business Phone:** (301)856-9177.

### WILLIAMS, WILLIAM DECEMBER, JR. See WILLIAMS, BILLY DEE, JR.

### WILLIAMS, PROF. WILLIAM THOMAS, JR.
Educator. **Personal:** Born Jul 17, 1942, Cross Creek, NC; son of William Thomas Sr and Hazel Davis; married Patricia A DeWeese; children: Nila & Aaron. **Educ:** NY Community Col, AAS, 1962; Skowhegan Sch Painting & Sculpture, 1965; Pratt Inst, BFA, 1966; Yale Univ Sch Art & Archit, MFA, 1968. **Career:** Pratt Inst, painting fac, 1970; Sch Visual Arts, painting fac, 1970; City Univ New York, Brooklyn Col, prof art, 1971-; Skowhegan Sch Painting & Sculpture, res painting fac, 1971, 1974, 1978, dir pro tem, 1979; Va Commonwealth Univ, distinguished vis commonwealth prof art, 1984-85; John Simon Guggenheim fel, John Simon Guggenheim Memorial Found,

1987; Mid-Atlantic Found, fel, 1994. **Orgs:** Govenor Skowhegan Sch Painting & Sculpture, 1972-90; artistic bd, Cinque Gallery, 1978-90; bd trustee, Grace Church Sch, 1984-87; hon mem, Golden Key Nat Hon Soc, 1998. **Honors/Awds:** Artist-in-residence, Virginia Commonwealth University, University of Wisconsin, Fisk University; Individual Artist Award, Painting Nat Endowment Arts & Humanities, 1965, 1970; Faculty Research Award, City Univ New York, 1973, 1984, 1987; Annual Award for Lifetime Achievement, Studio Mus, Harlem, 1992; Grant Award, Joan Mitchell Found, 1996; James Van Der Zee Award, Brandywine Workshop, Philadelphia, 2005; North Carolina Award, 2006. **Special Achievements:** First Black Artist Included In H.W. Jansons History Of Art Textbook In 1986 & 1987. **Home Addr:** 654 Broadway, New York, NY 10012-2327. **Business Addr:** Professor of Art, City University of New York, 5122 Boylan Hall, Brooklyn, NY 11210, **Business Phone:** (718)951-5181.

## WILLIAMS, DR. WILLIE, JR.

Educator, association executive. **Personal:** Born Mar 24, 1947, Independence, LA; son of Willie Sr and Leanner Booker; married Deborah A Broady; children: Willie III. **Educ:** Southern Univ, BS, 1970; Iowa State Univ, MS, 1972, PhD, 1974. **Career:** Lincoln Univ, asst prof, 1974-, chmn sci math div, prof & chmn physics, 1978-80, assoc prof, 1979-84, Dept Defense, phys scientist, 1980-82, prin investr, prof, physics, 1984-; Lincoln Adv Sci & Eng Reinforcement Prog, LASER, 1981-96. **Orgs:** Consult, Mobil Oil Co, 1977; PRIME Bd Dir, 1977-; phys scientist, Nat Bur Stands, 1979; fel Nat Aeronaut & Space Admin, 1979; ONR Fel Naval Res Lab, 1980; chmn, Cheyney Lincoln Temple Cluster, 1978-80; Am Asn Univ Professors; NY Acad Sci; Sigma Xi; dir, Lincoln Adv Sci & Eng Reinforcement Prog, 1981-96; Oxford Rotary, 1986-89; Am Phys Soc; Math Asn Am; Am Asn Physics Teachers; AAAS; Sigma Pi Sigma; Lincoln Univ Chap, Am Asn Univ Professors. **Honors/Awds:** CLT Award, Cheyney Lincoln Temple Cluster, 1974-78; Lindback Award, Lincoln Univ, 1976; Excellence in Science & Technology; White House Initiative on HBCU's, 1988; Participaton in Science Symposium, Physics Dept, Southern Univ, 1991; Participation in African-American History Month. **Home Addr:** 448 W Baltimore Pke, West Grove, PA 19390. **Business Addr:** Professor, Lincoln University, 125 Wright Hall 1570 Baltimore Pke, Lincoln University, PA 19352, **Business Phone:** (484)365-8000.

## WILLIAMS, WILLIE, JR.

Executive. **Personal:** married Nellie Redmond; children: Willease Nellitta & Jahsiri Moyenda. **Educ:** Benedict Col, BA; Rutgers Univ, grad study; Mich State Univ; SC St Col; Univ SC. **Career:** Willie Williams Real Estate Inc, pres & founder; Richland Co, inst pub schs; Upward Bound Univ SC, couns; Midland Tech Ctr; Benedict Col, placement dir; SC Chap NAREB, pres. **Orgs:** City chmn, 1974 UNCF Campaign; Omicron Phi Chap Omega Psi Phi; Columbia Bd Realtors; St Manufacturings Housing Comn; Richland Co Planning Comn; Bd Dir Columbia Urban League; adv bd, Columbia Opportunities Industrialization Ctr SC; bd trustees, Benedict Col; Friendship Jr Col; life mem, Nat Asn Advan Colored People; chmn bd, Palmetto Home Coun Inc & Success Investment Co. **Home Addr:** 128 Meadow Lake Dr, Columbia, SC 29203, **Home Phone:** (803)714-6532. **Business Addr:** President, Willie Williams Real Est Inc, 6023 2 Notch Rd, Columbia, SC 29223.

## WILLIAMS, DR. WILLIE ELBERT

Educator, mathematician. **Personal:** Born Jun 6, 1927, Jacksonville, TX; married Doris Lee Matlock; children: Lois E, Willys E, Donald A, Linda W & Dorwyl L. **Educ:** Huston Tillotson Col Austin, Tex, BS, math, 1952; Tex S Univ, Houston, MS, math, 1953; Mich State Univ, PhD, math, 1972. **Career:** Educator, mathematician (retired); Lufkin Independent Sch Dist, teacher, 1953-59; Cleveland Bd Educ, 1960-73; Case-Western Res Univ, 1964-68; Deep Accelerated Math Prog, 1973-78; Fla Intl Univ, assoc prof, prof mathematics, prof emer. **Orgs:** Consult, Nat Follow Through Prog, 1974-75; Second Bapt Ch, 1975-80; Omega Psi Phi Frat State Fla, 1979-80; Concerned Black Educ Higher Educn Fla, 1980-81; evaluator, Col Title III Progs; vpres, chair anti crime comm, PULSE; Black Fac Fla Int Univ; lectr, BAM; recruiter, Black Fac & Black Students. **Honors/Awds:** Outstanding Teacher Award, Univ Colo, 1954; Master Teacher Award, Martha Holden Jennings Found, 1973; Willie E Williams Endowment Award, Fla Intl Univ, named in honor, 1995. **Home Addr:** 9781 SW 148 St, Miami, FL 33176-7838, **Home Phone:** (305)251-8486.

## WILLIAMS, WILLIE J.

Educator. **Personal:** Born Jan 8, 1949, Chester, SC; married Louvenia Brooks. **Educ:** Voorhees Col, BS. **Career:** Indust Educ Develop Corp, proj dir Jobs 70 prog, 1970-73; Custom Packagers & Processors Inc, Atlanta, GA, personnel dir, 1973-74; Colquitt County Bd Educ, Moultries GA, teacher, 1974-. **Orgs:** Hon Soc Finley Sr High Sch, 1964-66; Sigma Theta Chap Omega Psi Phi Fraternity, 1968-; Free Accepted Masons, 1973-; Colquitt County Civil Defense Rescue Team, 1973-; Nat St & Local Educ Asn, 1974-75; Steering Comt Quarter Sys Colquitt County Sch, 1974-75; Amateur Softball Asn Umpires, 1975-; regist, Emer Med Tech St Ga; St Ga Dept Defense Rescue Workers. **Honors/Awds:** Dale Carnegie Certificate of Appreciation, 1973. **Home Addr:** 1219 6th St SW, Moultrie, GA 31768-5303, **Home Phone:** (229)616-7743. **Business Addr:** Teacher, Colquitt County Board of Education, 710 28th Ave SE, Moultrie, GA 31768, **Business Phone:** (229)985-1550.

## WILLIAMS, WILLIE JAMES

Athletic coach, educator. **Personal:** Born Sep 12, 1931, Gary, IN; son of Orrie (deceased) and Elnora; married Barbara, Dec 31, 1955; children: Darla & Margot. **Educ:** Univ Ill, BS, phys educ, 1955; Ind Univ, MS, 1971. **Career:** Athletic coach (retired), consultant; Sch City Gary Ind, teacher-coach, 1958-82; Univ Ill, assoc head men's track coach, sprint coach, 1982-2000; Saudi Arabian Olympic track team, trainer, 1988; Ogden Pk, athletics dir; W Side High Sch, head track coach; Sprintmaster, consult, currently. **Orgs:** NCAA Track & Field Asn, 1982-. **Honors/Awds:** Gold medal, 4 X 100 relay, Pan Am Games, Mex City, 1955; World's Fastest Man, 1956; Inducted into Indiana High School Coaches Track & Field Hall of Fame, 1980. **Special Achievements:** Set world record in 100 meter dash, Int Track & Field Fed, 1956, also racked up nine individual Big Ten Championships during his career, winning the 60 yard dash twice, the 70 yard hurdles twice, two titles in the 100yard dash, and three more in the 220 yard dash, published Track Article on Sprinting, The Coaching Clinic, Prentice Hall, February 1980. Book: "Remembering the Race: Memoirs of a track and field champion". **Home Addr:** 1607 Trails Dr, Urbana, IL 61801, **Home Phone:** (217)337-6616.

## WILLIAMS, WILLIE JAMES, JR.

Football player, executive. **Personal:** Born Dec 26, 1970, Columbia, SC; married Melissa; children: Dominique. **Educ:** Western Carolina Univ, BS, 1993. **Career:** Football player (retired), executive; Pittsburgh Steelers, defensive back, 1993-94, left cornerback, 1995, right corner back, 1996, left cornerback, 2004, right cornerback, 2005; Seattle Sea hawks, right cornerback, 1997-2003, cornerback, 1999, left cornerback, 2002; XPRO Training Consults, owner, 2008-; XPRO Group LLC, owner, 2010-. **Honors/Awds:** Super Bowl champion; AFC Champion, 1995, 2005. **Business Addr:** Owner, XPRO Gear, 8648 Dakota Dr, Gaithersburg, MD 20877, **Business Phone:** (301)330-6029.

## WILLIAMS, WILLIE L.

Law enforcement officer. **Personal:** Born Oct 1, 1943, Philadelphia, PA; son of Willie L Sr and Helen S; married Evelina; children: Lisa, Willie L Jr & Eric. **Educ:** Northwestern Univ, cert, police admin, 1978; Philadelphia Col Textiles & Sci, ABA, 1982; Pub Safety Media Inst, 1986; Ctr Creative Leadership, Eckerd Col, sr leadership, 1986; Harvard Univ, Police Exec Research Forum, cert, 1987; FBI Nat Exec Inst, attended 1989; St Joseph Univ, MS, attended 1991. **Career:** Law enforcement officer (retired); Fairmont Park Guards, police officer, 1964-72; City Philadelphia, police detective, 1972-74, police sgt, 1974-76, Juv Aid Div, police lt, 1976-84, 22nd & 23rd Police Dist, police capt, comdr, 1984-86, Training Bur, Civil Affairs Div, N Police Div, police inspector, head, 1986, dep comnr admin, 1988, police comnr, 1988-92; City Los Angeles, Police Dept, chief police, 1992-97; Dallas-based Argus Servs Corp, vpres & cheif exec officer; Hartsfield Atlanta Int Airport, Transp Security Admin, fed security dir, 2002-08. **Orgs:** Nat Orgn Black Law Enforcement Execs; Int Asn Chiefs Police; Alpha Signian Lambda Nat Hons Soc; Pa Juv Officers Asn; Southeastern Pa Chiefs Police; Los Angeles County Chiefs Asn; James Memorial Methodist Church, W Oak Lane Youth Asn; Boy Scouts Am. **Special Achievements:** Williams was the first African-American police commissioner of both the Philadelphia Police Department and the Los Angeles Police Department.

## WILLIAMS, DR. WILLIE S.

Psychologist. **Personal:** Born May 8, 1932, Prattville, AL; married Marva R Flowers; children: Kevin, Keith & Karla. **Educ:** Wichita State Univ, AB, Chem & Math, 1958; Xavier, MEd, Admin & Personnel Serv, 1960; Mich State Univ, PhD, Coun Psychol, 1970. **Career:** Case Western Res Univ Sch Med, assoc dean stud affairs; NIMH Min Ctr, asst chief psychol res & training prog; Univ Cincinnati, sr counr & asst prof psychol; Cincinnati Police Dept, psychol counr; Willie S Williams PhD Inc, owner, pres, currently. **Orgs:** Pres, Phi Delta Kappa ANWC; Am Personnel & Guild Asn; treas, past pres, Asn Black Psychologists, 2003-04; Am Psychol Asn; Kappa Alpha Psi.Kappa; Ohio Psychol Asn. **Home Addr:** 2690 Green Rd, Shaker Heights, OH 44122-2120, **Home Phone:** (216)831-8009. **Business Addr:** President, Willie S Williams PhD Inc, 20310 Chagrin Blvd Suite 2, Shaker Heights, OH 44122-4913, **Business Phone:** (216)491-9405.

## WILLIAMS, YARBOROUGH, JR.

Government official, teacher. **Personal:** Born Mar 24, 1950, Warrenton, NC; married Carolyn M; children: Consherto V, Yarborough & Juroid C. **Educ:** NC State Univ, voc; Vance Granvillco Col, drafting. **Career:** Franklinton City Schs, teacher, 17 yrs; Warren County Pub Sch Dist, sch bdmem. **Orgs:** Nat Asn Advan Colored People; pres, Warren County Polit Action Coun; pres, Boys Club; Warren County Bd Election; Warren County Dem Party; NC Sch BdAsn. **Honors/Awds:** Teacher of the Year, Asn Gen Contractors Am, 1986. **Home Addr:** 571 Shocco Spring Rd, Warrenton, NC 27589-8726, **Home Phone:** (252)257-2620.

## WILLIAMS, PROF. YVONNE CARTER

Educator. **Personal:** Born Feb 12, 1932, Philadelphia, PA; daughter of Patterson H (deceased) and Evelyn Lightner (deceased); married Theodore; children: Lynora A, Alison P, Meredith J & Lesley Y. **Educ:** Pa State Univ, BA, 1953; Harvard Law Sch, attended 1954; Univ Conn, MA, 1955; Case Western Res Univ, PhD, polit sci, 1981. **Career:** Univ Conn, Dept Educ, admin asst; Ashland Wayne Community Action Comn, dir res, 1964-66; Wayne County Head start, social worker, 1967-68; Wooster Pub Schs, vis teacher, 1968-69; Ohio State Univ, lectr, 1971-72; Lilly Endowment, consult, evaluator; NEH, Mid States & N Cent Assocs; Col Wooster, asst to dean, asst prof pol sci, Dept Black Studies, dir, 1973-74, assoc prof, Dept Pol Sci & Black Studies, prof, dir, 1983, dean fac, 1989-95, prof, emer, black studies, 2000-; DePauw Univ, Greencastle, Ind, hampton & esther boswell distinguished univ prof black studies, currently. **Orgs:** Wayne County Bd Ment Health & Retardation, 1969-76; Wooster City Charter Comn, 1971-72; League Women Voters deleg to Nat Conv, 1972; Head Start Parents Adv Coun, 1970-73; Col Hills Retirement Village, 1973; Mayor's Alt to NEFCO, 1974-75; City Wooster Human Rels Coun, 1978; Wooster City Charter Rev Comn, 1980; Wooster Community Hosp, 1981; Health Trustee Inst, 1986-88; adv bd, Wayne County Adult Basic Educ, 1987-89; Ohio Humanities coun, 1989-96. **Honors/Awds:** John Hay Whitney Fel; Case Western Reserve Univ; Alumni, AHS Fel; Jessie Smith Noyes Found Scholarship; Faculty Develop Grant, Col Wooster, Morris Fund; ATHENA Award, chambers com women's orgn & univs, 2008. **Special Achievements:** Inducted in Ohio Women's Hall of Fame, 2003; First female physician Elizabeth Blackwell. **Home Addr:** 570 Forest Creek Dr, Wooster, OH 44691-1780. **Business Addr:** Professor Emerita Of Black Studies, College of Wooster, 1189 Beall Ave, Wooster, OH 44691, **Business Phone:** (330)263-2000.

## WILLIAMS, YVONNE LAVERNE

Lawyer. **Personal:** Born Jan 7, 1938, Washington, DC; daughter of Smallwood E and Verna L Rapley. **Educ:** Barnard Col, BA, 1959; Boston Univ, MA, 1961; Georgetown Univ, JD, 1977. **Career:** US Info Agency, foreign serv officer, 1961-65; African-Am Inst NY, dir womens Africa comn, 1966-68; Benedict Col, Columbia, SC, assc prof African Am studies, 1968-70; US Cong Wash, press sec Hon Walter Fauntroy, 1970-72; African-Am Scholars Coun Wash, DC, dir, 1972-73; Leva Hawes Symington Martin, assoc atty, 1977-79; Brimmer & Co Wash, DC, asst vpres, 1980-82; Tuskegee Univ, vpres Fed & Int Rel & Legal Coun, 1983-96; Acad Educ Develop Pub Policy & Int Affairs Fel Prog, vpres & nat dir, 1996-. **Orgs:** Oper Crossroads Africa, 1960-, Barnard-in-Wash, 1960-; Am Bar Asn, 1980-, Nat Bar Asn, 1980-, Dist Columbia Bar, 1980-; trustee, Barnard Col, 1988-92; bd dir, Golden Rule Apt Inc, 1986-; Partic Leadership Am, 1988; Overseas Develop Coun, 1988; chair bd trustee, Bible Way Church; DC Housing Authority; Overseas Develop Coun. **Honors/Awds:** Boston Univ, Africa Res & Studies Prog Fel, 1959-60. **Special Achievements:** Author, "William Monroe Trotter, 1872-1934"; in Reid "The Black Prism", New York, 1969. **Home Addr:** 4600 Conn Ave NW Suite 429, Washington, DC 20008-5728, **Home Phone:** (202)244-1791. **Business Addr:** Vice President, National Director, Academy for Educational Development, 1825 Conn Ave NW, Washington, DC 20009-5721, **Business Phone:** (202)884-8000.

## WILLIAMS-BRIDGERS, JACQUELYN L.

Government official. **Personal:** Born Feb 27, 1956, WA; married Daniel; children: 2. **Educ:** Syracuse Univ, BA, 1977; Maxwell Sch Pub Affairs & Citizenship, MPA, 1978. **Career:** Gen Acct Off, assoc dir housing & community develop, mgt analyst; US State Dept, inspector gen, 1995-2001; US Govt Accountability Off, Int Affairs & Trade, managing dir, 2003-11; Mgt Systs Int, chief party, 2011-12; JaDa Int LLC, int develop consult, 2011-12; Deloitte Consult, LLP, chief of party, integrity investments initiative, 2012-15. **Orgs:** Chair, Bd External Auditors, Orgn Am States; adv bd, Maxwell Sch Pub Affairs & Citizenship; fed dir, Surface Transp Infrastructure Issues.

## WILLIAMS-DOTSON, DARYL

Architect. **Personal:** Born Dec 14, 1958, Daytona Beach, FL; daughter of Ernest J and Arnita Green; children: Michael S Burrows, Chloe W & Lyle W. **Educ:** Southern Univ & A&M Col, B Arch, 1984. **Career:** Varney Sexton Lunsford Aye Architects, 1985-89; Clark Tribble Harris Li Architects, 1989-90; Clyde E Woods & Assoc Inc, assoc, 1991-98; Williams-Dotson Assoc Inc, 1995; WDI Archit Inc, prin architect, owner & pres, 1991-2009. **Orgs:** Nat Coun Architects Regist Bd; Prof Am Inst Architects; Nat Asn Women Bus Owners; Nat Orgn Minority Architects; Alpha Chi Nat Hon Scholar Soc. **Home Addr:** 5774 Grandiose Dr, Indianapolis, IN 46228, **Home Phone:** (317)253-3142. **Business Addr:** Owner, WDI Architecture Inc, 15 W 28th St, Indianapolis, IN 46208, **Business Phone:** (317)251-6172.

## WILLIAMS-DOVI, JOANNA

School administrator. **Personal:** Born Apr 16, 1953, Harrisburg, PA; daughter of Thomas Edison Sr and Bertha Manervia Brown; married Sewar M. **Educ:** Cheyney Univ, Cheyney, PA, BA, 1977; Pa State Univ, Middletown, PA, MEd, 1997. **Career:** Penn State Univ, Middletown, Pa, admin asst, EET Prog, 1984-88, Off Multicultural Recruitment & Community Affairs, asst dir admis, 1988-, mkt coordr & admis counr. **Orgs:** Leader, Girl Scouts Coun Am, 1979-83; Penn Asn Col Admis Counr, 1987-; Am Asn Col Registrars & Admin Off, 1987-; Nat Asn Col Admin Counr, 1987-; Delta Sigma Theta Sorority Inc, 1990-; Penn Col Personnel Asn, 1990-. **Business Addr:** Assistant Director of Admissions, Pennsylvania State University, 312 Old Main, University Park, PA 16802-1505, **Business Phone:** (814)865-7517.

## WILLIAMS-GARNER, DEBRA

Writer, consultant, association executive. **Personal:** Born Feb 9, 1957, Washington, DC; daughter of Ernest E Sr and Sadie Lark; married David; children: Brooke N Garner & Evan D Garner. **Educ:** Univ Bridgeport, Bridgeport, CT, BA, 1979; Am Univ, MA, jour & commun, 1999; Maple Springs Baptist Bible Col & Sem, Mdiv, Christian coun, 2008. **Career:** Wash Star Newspaper, Wash, DC, freelance writer, 1979-81; Libr Cong, Wash, DC, ed & writer, 1981-85; Environ Defense Fund, Wash, DC, media specialist, 1985-89; Providence Hosp, Wash, DC, pub rels specialist, 1987-89; Am Heart Asn, Wash, DC, dir communs, 1989-92; freelance writer & prom consult, 1993-; Wash Hosp Ctr, Media rels specialist, 1993-95; MD Asn HMOs, dir commun, 1996-98; Md State Educr Asn, pub rels specialist & spokeswoman, ESP organizer & spec proj coordr, 1998-. Books: Pipe dreams, 1988; Sister Spirit, 1999. Poems: "Poet on Fire for Jesus"; "Words on the Wall". **Orgs:** AFA Writers Guild, 1989-; Delta Sigma Theta, Ft Wash Alumnae Chap, 1990-92; Am Acad Poets, 1994-; vppres & co-founder, Something Inspirational Prods; Poetic Voices, publicity coord. **Home Addr:** 6606 Lansdale St, District Heights, MD 20747, **Home Phone:** (301)967-8235. **Business Addr:** Public Relations Specialist, Spokeswoman, ESP Organizer and Special Projects Coordinator, Maryland State Educators Association, 140 Main St, Annapolis, MD 21401, **Business Phone:** (443)433-3644.

## WILLIAMS-GREEN, JOYCE F.

School administrator, educator. **Personal:** Born Sep 6, 1948, Sanford, NC; daughter of Joseph A Williams; married Edward W. **Educ:** NC Cent Univ, BS, 1970; Herbert H Lehman Col, MS, 1977; Va Polytech Inst & State Univ, EdD, 1984. **Career:** New York Pub Sch, teacher, 1971-76; Livingstone Col, dir learning ctr, 1976-80; Va Polytech Inst & State Univ, Cunningham res fel, 1983, dir & asst provost, 1987-2005; UNC Syst, assoc provost, 2004-. **Orgs:** Citizen rep, Blacksburg 80's, 1984-86; consult, Janus Learning Ctr, 1986, NC A&T, 1986; co-chair, Phi Kappa Phi, 1986-87; mem res comn, NACADA, 1986; bd mem, Warm Hearth Fdn, 1986-; bd mem, New River Community Sentencing Inc; Govs Monitoring Comt, 1990-. **Home Addr:** 205 Oakmont Dr, Kernersville, NC 27284-7469, **Home Phone:** (336)992-9833. **Business Addr:** Director, Virginia Polytechnic Inst & State University, 256/255 Lane Hall, Blacksburg, VA 24061-0227, **Business Phone:** (703)231-5812.

## WILLIAMS-HARRIS, DIANE BEATRICE

School administrator. **Personal:** Born Feb 1, 1949, Newark, NJ; children: Karl & Elayne. **Educ:** Boston Univ, BA, 1971; Rutgers Univ,

Grad Sch Educ, MEd, 1977. **Career:** Prudential Ins Co, pension admin, 1971-73; Rutgers Univ, Undergrad Admis, asst to dir, 1973-76, asst dir, 1976-78, dir, 1978-82, assoc dir, currently, admis officer. **Orgs:** Nat Assoc Col Admis Counrs; Delta Sigma Theta; 100 Black Women. **Honors/Awds:** Sponsored participant in Women in Higher Educ, 1977; Rutgers Univ Merit Awd, 1986, 1993. **Home Addr:** 4 King Rd, Somerset, NJ 08873, **Home Phone:** (732)249-4634. **Business Addr:** Associate Director of Undergraduate Admissions, Rutgers University- New Brunswick Campus, Rm 202 65 Davidson Rd, Piscataway, NJ 08854-8097, **Business Phone:** (732)445-4636.

### WILLIAMS-HAYES, DR. THEA

Educator. **Personal:** Born Jun 19, 1974, Gulfport, MS; daughter of Rosemary and Theodore. **Educ:** Tougaloo Col, BA, 1997; William Carey Col, cert, 1999, MEd, 1999; Univ Southern Miss, PhD, 2003. **Career:** Pass Christian Pub Schs, third grade teacher, 1997-98, gifted educ teacher, 1998-2000, 2002-03; Univ Southern Miss, grad asst, 2000-02; Nicholls State Univ, asst prof educ, 2003; Col William & Mary, Dir, 2005-06; Univ Miss, Asst Prof, 2006-10, Assoc Prof, 2010-14; Jackson State Univ, Dept Chair & Prof, 2014-. **Orgs:** Alpha Kappa Alpha Sorority Inc, 1993-; Kappa Delta Pi, 1996; Int Reading Asn, 2000-; Col Reading Asn, 2000-; Phi Kappa Phi, 2001-; Nat Coun Teachers Eng, 2002-; Int Reading Asn; Kappa Delta Pi; Col Reading Asn. **Home Addr:** 110 Saxony Dr, Houma, LA 70364, **Home Phone:** (985)580-2482. **Business Addr:** Department Chair and Professor, Jackson State University, 1400 John R Lynch St, Jackson, MS 39217, **Business Phone:** (601)979-2121.

### WILLIAMS-MYERS, ALBERT J.

Educator, writer. **Personal:** Born Mar 10, 1939, Edison, GA; son of C Kilmer and Bessie Irene; married Janice Diane Redmond; children: M Maluwa & Plaisimwana Renee. **Educ:** Wagner Col, BA, 1962; Univ Calif, Los Angeles, life-time teaching cert, 1969, MA, 1971, PhD, hist, 1978. **Career:** Mobilization Youth, work group leader, 1962-63; All Saints Parish Sch, teacher 8th through 11th grade, 1963-64; Col Vi, head resident & dir activ, 1964-65; Ford Found, res Africa & mid E grad fel, 1973-74; Carleton Col, prof, 1976-79; State Univ New York Albany African Am Inst, exec dir, 1990-91; SUNY Col New Paltz, prof, currently. **Orgs:** St club worker, NYC Youth Bd, 1965-66; vol, US Peace Corps, Malawi, Africa, 1966-68; African Studies Asn, 1971-80; pres, NY African Studies Asn, 1985-88; NCP, Ellenville, Chap, 1985-. **Home Addr:** 9 Partington Pl, New Paltz, NY 12561, **Home Phone:** (845)255-4606. **Business Addr:** Professor, State University of New York, FOB W11, New Paltz, NY 12561, **Business Phone:** (845)257-2761.

### WILLIAMS-STANTON, DR. SONYA DENISE

Educator, consultant. **Personal:** Born May 31, 1963, Birmingham, AL; daughter of Sam L and Carolyn W; married Tom; children: Thomas & Jasmine. **Educ:** Brown Univ, BA (hons), 1984; Univ Mich, Bus Sch, MBA (hons), 1986, PhD, 1994. **Career:** Irving Trust Co, acct rep, 1986-88; Ohio State Univ, asst prof finance, 1993-2000; JAT Anal, consult. **Orgs:** Pres, Brown Univ Chap, Alpha Kappa Alpha, 1982-83; Nat Black MBA Assoc; Financial Mgt Assoc; vip, Univ Mich Black Bus Stud Asn; Am Fin Asn; Nat Econ Asn; St Philips Episcopal Church; fel Consortium Grad Study Mgt, 1984-86. **Home Addr:** 15217 Redgate Dr, Silver Spring, MD 20905.

### WILLIAMS-TAITT, PATRICIA ANN

School administrator, administrator. **Personal:** Born Jul 3, 1947, Toledo, OH; daughter of Charles Matthews and Nettie; married Arthur R; children: Jason C. **Educ:** Wayne State Univ, BS, elem educ, 1969, grad studies educ admin; Dale Carnegie Inst, Ctr Corp & Comm Rels, effective speaking, 1985; Leadership Detroit XII, cert, 1991; IBM Leadership Develop, 1993. **Career:** Detroit Pub Sch Syst, 2nd grade teacher, 1969-70; Singer Career Syst, Cetroit Job Corps, dir educ, 1972-86; Mercy Health Systs, dir external communs, 1986-89; Pub Rels consult, 1986-; Greater Detroit Chamber Comm, Detroit Compact, dep dir, 1989-; Advert & Specialty Markets, dir; City Connect Detroit, mkt & commun officer, currently. **Orgs:** Exec bd, Am Red Cross, 1994-; chairperson, Booker T Wash, assoc publicity, 1984-90; ed comt, Partners Tabloid, 1986-89; vpres, Winship Community Coun, 1986-89; co-chair, Black Family Develop, publicity chair, 1987-88; vpres, pub info, Am Cancer Soc, 1988-89; exec bd, Friends Southwest, 1990-; Nat Asn Advan Colored People; bd mem, Detroit Br NCP, 1997-2000. **Home Addr:** 19171 Bretton Dr, Detroit, MI 48223. **Business Addr:** Marketing & Communication Officer, City Connect Detroit, 163 Madison Ave 3rd Fl, Detroit, MI 48226, **Business Phone:** (313)887-6503.

### WILLIAMS-WARREN, JANE E.

Government official. **Personal:** Born Jul 19, 1947, Paterson, NJ; daughter of John D and Mae J Jenkins. **Educ:** Passaic County Community Col; Paterson State Col; Seton Hall Univ; Rutgers Univ, Municipal clerk cert, int municipal clerk cert. **Career:** City Paterson, City Clerk's Off, various secretarial titles, 1966-78; Paterson Planning Bd, comnr, 1971-72; City Paterson, dep city clerk, 1978-89, munic clerk, 1990-; Paterson Pub Schs, city clerk. **Orgs:** Recording secy, Municipal Clerks Asn Passaic County; New Jersey State Municipal Clerk's Asn; Intl Clerk's Asn; vice chairperson, Passaic County Mental Health Asn; treas, Municpal Clerk's Asn; New AME Zion Church, numerous positions; Nat Coun Negro Women; Nat Asn Advan Coloured People; bd trustee, St Joseph Hosp & Med Ctr; Fidelity Chapter 16 Order Easter Star; bd mem, Int Inst Munic Clerks; pres, Munic Clerks Asn NJ; bd mem, Region II. **Home Addr:** 468 E 34th St, Paterson, NJ 07504, **Home Phone:** (973)279-1685. **Business Addr:** Municipal Clerk, City Paterson, 155 Market St 3rd FL, Paterson, NJ 07505, **Business Phone:** (973)321-1310.

### WILLIAMS-WITHERSPOON, KIMMIKA L. H.

Writer, educator, playwright. **Personal:** Born Jan 7, 1959, Philadelphia, PA; daughter of Samuel S Hawes Jr and Lillian Yvonne Curry Hawes; children: Essence & Tenasha. **Educ:** Howard Univ, Wash, DC, BA, jour, 1980; Temple Univ, MFA, theater, playwriting, MA, anthrop, PhD, cult anthrop, 2002; Grad Cert, women's studies, BA, jour. **Career:** Philadelphia Tribune, Philadelphia, Pa, reporter & columnist, 1984-86; Pa Prison Soc, Philadelphia, Pa, instr, 1985-89; Bob Lott Prod, Philadelphia, Pa, scriptwriter, 1986-89; WXPN-FM, Philadelphia, Pa, arts host & producer, 1989-90; Village Arts Ctr, Philadelphia, Pa, instr, 1990-; Walnut St Theatre, Philadelphia, Pa, outreach instr & actress, 1990-; Temple Univ, Theatre Dept, post grad teaching fel, adj, 1996-2000, asst prof, lectr & head undergrad advising, 2000, currently; Published books: Negro Kinship to the Park, Halley's Comet, It Ain't Easy to be Different, God Made Men Brown, Selrahc Publication, 1982-90, Published Books: Envisioning a Sea of Dry Bones, 1994, Epic Memory: Places & Spaces I've Been, 1995, Signs of the Time: Culture Pop, Three-Goat Press, 1999, Darby, Pa, Spoken Word Poetry Compact Disc, Three Goat Press & Productions, 2001, They Never Told Me Thered Be Days Like This, Three Goat Press, 2002, Brother Love, Three Goat Press & Productions, Darby, Pa, 2005; Author: Through Smiles and Tears: The History of African American Theater-from Kemet to the Americas; Saarbrucken, Germany: LAP LAMBERT Academic Publishing GmbH & Co. KG. 2011; The Secret Messages in African American Theater: Hidden Meaning Embedded in Public Discourse, 2006. **Orgs:** Future Fac fel, Anthrop Dept, Temple Univ; Int Womens League Peace & Freedom, 1988-; Nat Black Auth Tour, 1989-; Nat Black Storytellers, 1988-; Theater Asn Pa, 1994; Philadelphia Dramatist Ctr, 1993; Lila Wallace Creative Arts fel, Am Antiquarian Soc, 1995-96; Am Anthropolgist Asn, 1997-. **Home Addr:** 423 Pine St, Darby, PA 19023, **Home Phone:** (610)586-1669. **Business Addr:** Associate Professor, Head of Undergraduate Advising, Temple University, 207 Tomlinson Hall, Philadelphia, PA 19122, **Business Phone:** (215)204-8417.

### WILLIAMSON, CARL VANCE

Government official. **Personal:** Born Oct 3, 1955, Portsmouth, VA; son of Carolyn and Shelton. **Educ:** Va Commonwealth Univ, BS, 1977; Univ S Fla, MBA, mgt & finance, 1984. **Career:** Group W Cable Inc, financial analyst, 1983-85; MCI Telecommunications, supvr acct & anal, 1985-86; Hampton Redevelop & Housing Authority, housing mgt supvr, 1986-; Newport News Redevelop & Housing Authority, dir pub & assisted housing, currently. **Orgs:** Omega Psi Phi Frat, 1974-; Am Asn MBA Execs, 1984-; Nat Black MBA Asn, 1985-; Nat Asn Advan Colored People; pres, Va Asn Housing & Community Develop Officials, past pres, 2003-05. **Home Addr:** 475 Water St Apt 206, Portsmouth, VA 23704, **Home Phone:** (804)851-4431. **Business Addr:** Director of Public & Assisted Housing, Newport News Redevelopment & Housing Authority, 227 27th St, Newport News, VA 23607, **Business Phone:** (757)928-2658.

### WILLIAMSON, CARLTON

Football player, executive. **Personal:** Born Jun 12, 1958, Atlanta, GA; married Donna; children: Kevin & Joshua. **Educ:** Univ Pittsburgh, BS, 1981. **Career:** Football player (retired), executive; San Francisco 49ers, Defensive Back, 1981-87; Waffle House Inc, sr vpres, currently; Univ Pittsburgh, safety. **Business Addr:** Senior Vice President, Waffle House Inc, 5986 Financial Dr, Norcross, GA 30071, **Business Phone:** (770)729-5700.

### WILLIAMSON, CLARENCE W., JR.

Manager. **Personal:** Born Oct 15, 1949, Ft. Benning, GA; son of Clarence Sr and Edda R Farmer; children: Tannis Jenine & Clarence Todd. **Educ:** Morris Brown Col, BA, 1971; Emory Univ, mgt cert, 1979; Clark Atlanta Univ, MPA, 1993; Ga Inst Technol, ec dev cert, 2000. **Career:** Citizens & Southern Nat Bank, vpres, 1971-83; Com-Med Corp, vpres, 1983-94; Sweet Auburn Improv Asn, mgt specialist, 1995; Morris Brown Col, alumni affairs dir, 1996-98; Morehouse Sch Med, adminr, 1998; Edinburr LLC, corp consult, managing partner, Atlanta Tech Col, econ develop, edu prog spec, 1998-2002, vpres, currently; Automatic Data Processing Inc, tax credit mgr; Com bank, vpres; W Ray Wallace & Assoc, proj mgr. **Orgs:** Alpha Phi Alpha Fraternity, 1968-; vpres, Morris Brown Col Nat Alumni Asn, 1980-; NABEO Corp Roundtable, 1980-85; 100 Black Men Atlanta, 1992-; bd mem, S Fulton Chamber Com, 1999-; steering comt, Red Oak Network Ctr, 1999-; bd mem, S Fulton Dollars Scholars, 1999-; bd mem, chmn, United Way Fulton County, 2002; life mem, Purple & Black; S Metro Chap; dir, Alumni Affairs; Bank Am Found. **Honors/Awds:** Certified Economic Developer, Ga Dept Tech & Adult Educ, 2000; Achievement Award, South Fulton Chamber Com, 2001. **Special Achievements:** Author: C & S Commercial Credit Documentation Manual, 1975; Morris Brown Nat Alumni Asn Handbook, 1997. **Home Addr:** 115 Green Mountain Trail, College Park, GA 30349, **Home Phone:** (404)761-8169. **Business Addr:** Vice President Economic Development, Atlanta Technical College, 1560 Metrop Pkwy SW, Atlanta, GA 30310, **Business Phone:** (404)225-4511.

### WILLIAMSON, CORLISS MONDARI

Basketball player, basketball coach. **Personal:** Born Dec 4, 1973, Russellville, AR; son of Jerry and Bettye; married Joan Michelle White; children: 3. **Educ:** Ark Univ, attended 1995. **Career:** Basketball player (retired), basketball coach; Sacramento Kings, forward, 1995-2000, 2005-07, 2013-; Toronto Rapters, 2000-01; Detroit Pistons, 2001-04; Philadelphia 76ers, 2004-05; Ark Baptist Col, asst coach, 2007-09, 2009-10; Univ Cent Ark, head coach, 2010. **Business Addr:** Assistant Coach, Sacramento Kings, 1 Sports Pkwy, Sacramento, CA 95834, **Business Phone:** (916)928-3400.

### WILLIAMSON, ETHEL W.

Educator, museum director. **Personal:** Born Nov 28, 1947, Hallandale, FL; daughter of Harvey and Essie L; married Daniel A; children: Jason D. **Educ:** Cent State Univ, BS, eng, 1969; Teachers Col, Columbia Univ, MA, MEd, guid, 1973; Rutgers State Univ, NJ, mus studies cert, 1992. **Career:** Huntington Nat Bank, training asst, 1969-71; NJ Inst Technol, asst dir, 1973-79, dir educ opportunity prog, 1978-79; Douglass Col, Rutgers Univ, asst dean stud, 1979-81; Union County Col, counsr generalist, 1986-90; Cooper-Hewitt Nat Mus Design, Smithsonian Inst, proj coord, AFA design archive, 1991-. **Orgs:** Delta Sigma Theta Sorority, 1968-; historian, North Jersey Chapter Jack & Jill AME, 1985-91; historian, Union County Cult & Hist Comn, City-Plainfield, 1986-89; AFA Mus Asn, 1991-; Sisters United NJS, 1992-; prog comt chair, NJS Chapter Cent State Univ Alumni Asn, 1992-. **Home Addr:** 901 Grant Ave, Plainfield, NJ 07060, **Home Phone:** (908)561-4088. **Business Addr:** Project Coordinator, Cooper-Hewitt National Museum Design Smithsonian Institution, 2 E 91st St, New York, NY 10128, **Business Phone:** (212)849-8400.

### WILLIAMSON, DR. HANDY, JR.

School administrator, consultant. **Personal:** Born Oct 24, 1945, Louin, MS; son of Handy Sr and Lilla M Nobles; married Barbara Jean Herndon; children: Lilla-Marie Juliana. **Educ:** Pineywood Jr Col, Pineywood, MS, AA, gen educ, 1964; Alcorn State Univ, Lorman, MS, BS, voc agr, 1967; Tenn State Univ, Nashville, TN, MS, agr educ, 1969; Univ Miss, Columbia, MO, MS, agr econs, 1971, PhD, agr econs, 1974; Univ Calif, higher educ admin, 1998. **Career:** Tenn State Univ, Nashville, TN, res asst, 1967-69, res dir, assoc prof, 1977-85; Univ Miss, Columbia, Mo, grad res asst, 1969-74; Tuskegee Univ, Tuskegee, AL, assoc dir res & asst prof 1974-77; US Agency Int Develop, dep & interim agency dir, 1985-88; Univ Tenn, Knoxville, TN, dept head & prof, 1988-2001; Tuskegee Univ Prof Agr workers conf, lectr, 2000; Miss Univ, vice provost, 2001-, prof agr econ, currently. **Orgs:** Gamma Sigma Delta, 1971; bd mem, 1972-73, sec chair, comm chair, Univ Mo, 1974-; Black Cult Ctr, Univ Mo; AAEA; Title V Comt Rural Develop, 1975-77; pres, Phi Beta Sigma, Tuskegee chap, 1975-77; charter mem, Optimist Club Tuskegee, 1975-77; Task Force Energy, 1976-77; Southern Region's Small Farm Functional Network, 1976-77; United Methodist Men, 1977; Am Agr Econs Asn; Soc Agr Econs Asn; secy-treas, Asn Res dir, 1977-85; chmn, Tenn Coun Agri Deans, 1977-85; consult, Tenn Valley Authority, 1979-80; consult, Bd Int Food & Agric Develop, 1981-85; legisl subcomn, ESCOP, 1981-84; Paster Parish Comn, Clark UMC Church, 1981-85; US Joint Coun Food & Agri, 1982-83; bd dir, Asn Int dir, 1982-87; bd mem, Asn Int Prog dir, 1984-88; bd dir, Asn State Univ dir Int Agri Develop prog, 1984-88; chmn, Tenn Coun Agr Deans, 1984; NASULGC; White House Comm liaison, USAID, 1985-88; dir, Va Bus Develop Ctr, 1987-; SAEA Hon Life Mem Comt, 1990-93; chmn, AAEA Comt Status Blacks, 1991-93; exec fel, Am Coun Educ, off chancellor, Univ Calif, 1997-98; vice chmn, Southern Agr Econ Dept Heads Asn; pres, Asn Int Agr & Rural Develop; bd, Nat Consortium Continuous Improv, Asn Int Educ Adminr, Higher Educ Develop Edgar Snow Memorial Found Peking Univ; exec comt, Nat Asn Pub Land Grant Univ's Comn Int Progs; longstanding mem, Collab Res Support Prog external adv bd. **Home Addr:** 12108 E Ashton Ct, Knoxville, TN 37922, **Home Phone:** (423)675-4565. **Business Addr:** Vice Provost for International Programs, Professor, University of Missouri-Columbia, 211 Jesse Hall, Columbia, MT 65211, **Business Phone:** (573)882-9061.

### WILLIAMSON, HENRY M., SR.

Association executive, clergy. **Personal:** Born AR; son of Alma J Carvin; married Doris Yvonn; children: Henry Jr & Kelli Daonne. **Educ:** Purdue Univ Calumet Campus, BA, sociol; Garrett-Evangelical Theol Sem, Evanston, IL, Mdiv, advan work clin pastoral educ. **Career:** Israel CME Church, assoc minister, 1967-69, pastoral ministry, 1969-2002; St. Paul CME Church, assoc pastor, 1972-73; Oper People United Serve Humanity, nat pres, chief exec officer, 1991-93; Carter Temple, Rev; Christian Methodist Episcopal Church, Atlanta, Bishop, chair, 2002-, First Episcopal Dist, Bishop, gen conf, 2014-. **Orgs:** Founder & chief exec officer, One Church One Sch Community Partnership Prog; trustee, Phillips Sch Theol ITC, Atlanta, Ga; chmn, Comn Social Justice & Human Concerns CME Church; bd mem, Northern Trust Bank; World Methodist Coun Churches; chmn, Dept Publ Serv. **Business Addr:** Bishop, Christian Methodist Episcopal Church, 4466 Elvis Presley Blvd, Memphis, TN 38116, **Business Phone:** (901)345-4114.

### WILLIAMSON, KEITH H.

Executive, lawyer. **Personal:** Born May 16, 1952, St. Louis, MO; son of Irving A; married Addie; children: 1. **Educ:** Brown Univ, BA, econs & sociol, 1974; Harvard Univ, JD & MBA, 1978; NY Univ Law Sch, LLM, taxation. **Career:** Covington & Burling, tax lawyer, 1978-81; Revis & McGrath & Fulbright Jaworski, dir tax, 1981-88; Pitney Bowes Capital Corp, Capital Serv Div, dir, 1988-99, pres, 1999-2006, Global Credit Serv Div, leader, 2002-04, chief exec officer, currently; Centene Corp, sr vpres, exec vpres, secy & gen co, 2006-. **Orgs:** Exec Leadership Coun; Delta Nu Boule; bd mem, Stamford Mus; bd dir, PPL Corp, 2005-. **Home Addr:** 160 Guinea Rd, Stamford, CT 06903. **Business Addr:** Senior Vice President, Secretary, Centene Corp, Centene Plz 7700 Forsyth Blvd, St. Louis, MO 63105, **Business Phone:** (314)725-4477.

### WILLIAMSON, DR. LIONEL L., JR.

Educator, administrator. **Personal:** Born Aug 6, 1943, Louin, MS; son of Handy and Lilla N; married Mae I; children: Keschler S Love & Lionel LeMarc. **Educ:** Alcorn State Univ, BS, agr educ, 1967; Univ Mo, MS, agr econs, 1974, PhD, agr econs, 1977. **Career:** Miss Pub Schs, voc agr educ teacher, 1967-72; Univ Mo, grad res asst, 1972-77; Nc A & T State Univ, Agr Exten Progs, exten specialist & prog leader, 1977-81; Ky State Univ, Coop Exten Progs, asst exten adminr, 1981-82, Agr Res Prog, res dir, 1982-85; Univ Ky, Dept Agr Econ, ext prof, 1985-, Exten Coordr, 1993-97, asst dean diversity, 2003-. **Orgs:** Southern Agr Econs Asn, 1977-; Am Agr Econs Asn, 1977-; Asn Coop Educ, 1985-; Nat Asn Cols & Teachers Agr, 1986-; Nat Econs Asn, 1989-90; Gamma Sigma Delta; Asn Ky Exten Specialists; Coun Agr Sci & Tech CAST. **Home Addr:** 77 Candlewood Dr, Nicholasville, KY 40356-9174, **Home Phone:** (859)223-1266. **Business Addr:** Assistant Dean for Diversity, Extension Professor, University of Kentucky, 306 Charles E Barnhart Bldg, Lexington, KY 40546-0276, **Business Phone:** (859)257-1637.

### WILLIAMSON, MYKELTI (MICHAEL T WILLIAMSON)

Actor. **Personal:** Born Mar 4, 1957, St. Louis, MO; son of Elaine; married Olivia Brown, Jul 2, 1983?, (divorced 1985); married Cheryl Chisholm, Jan 1, 1989, (divorced 1991); children: Phoenix; married Sondra Spriggs, Apr 26, 1997; children: Nicole & Maya. **Career:** Films: Streets of Fire, 1984; Wildcats, 1986; You Talkin' to Me?, 1987; Number One with a Bullet, 1987; Miracle Mile, 1988; The First Power, 1990; Free Willy, 1993; Forrest Gump, 1994; Waiting to Exhale, 1995; Heat, 1995; How to Make an American Quilt, 1995; Free Willy 2: The Adventure Home, 1995; Con Air, 1997; Truth or Consequences, N.M.,

1997; Double Tap, 1997; Species II, 1998; Primary Colors, 1998; Gideon, 1999; Three Kings, 1999; Ali, 2001; The Assassination of Richard Nixon, 2004; After the Sunset, 2004; Get Rich or Die Tryin', 2005; Lucky Number Slevin, 2006; Kidnapped-13 Tage Hoffnung, 2006-07; Fatwa, 2006; ATL, 2006; Spinning Into Butter, 2007; August Rush, 2007; Vice, 2007; Ball Don't Lie, 2008; Psych, 2009; Black Dynamite, 2009; Final Destination 4, 2009; 24, 2010; High School, 2010; Repatriate, 2011; Have a Little Faith, 2011; Justified, 2012. TV series: "Starsky & Hutch", 1978; "The White Shadow", 1979-80; "The Righteous Apples", 1981; "The White Shadow", 1981; "Father Murphy", 1981; "The Righteous Apples", 1981; "Desperate Lives", 1982; "Alice", 1983; "Hill Street Blues", 1983-86; "Bay City Blues", 1983; "Miami Vice", 1984-85; "Cover Up", 1984-85; "Gimme a Break!", 1984; "MiamiVice", 1985; "The Bronx Zoo", 1987; "JJ Starbuck", 1987; "The Bronx Zoo", 1988; "Police Story: Monster Manor", 1988; "Psywars", 1989; "China Beach", 1989; "Midnight Caller", 1988-91; "A Killer Among Us", 1990; "The New WKRPin Cincinnati", 1991-93; "Other Women's Children", 1993; "Forrest Gump", 1994; "Time Trax", 1994; "The Outer Limits", 1995; "Soul of the Game", 1996; Buffalo Soldiers, 1997; 12 Angry Men, 1997; Soul of the Game, 1996; Having Our Say: The Delany Sisters' First 100 Years, 1999; "The Hoop Life", 1999; Holiday Heart, 2000; "The Fugitive", 2000-01; Our America, 2002; "Touched by an Angel", 2002; "Boomtown", 2002-03; The Secret Service, 2004; Monk, 2004; "Third Watch", 2005; Justice, 2006; Kidnapped", 2006-07; "CSI: NY", 2007; Raines, 2007. **Honors/Awds:** Nominated for Humanities Prize, Image Award, 2003, MTV Movie Award, 1995. **Business Addr:** Actor, c/o William Morris Agency Incorporation, 1325 Ave of the Americas, New York, NY 10019, **Business Phone:** (212)586-5100.

## WILLIAMSON, SAMUEL P.

Government official. **Personal:** Born Mar 5, 1949, Somerville, TN; son of Julius Jr and Izoula Smith; married Brenda Joyce Lee; children: Keith Ramon W & Yulanda Marie W. **Educ:** Tenn State Univ, BS, math & meteorol, 1971; NC State Univ, BS, meteorol, 1972; Webster Univ, St Louis, MO, MA, mgt, 1976, Am Univ, post grad studies engineering technol mgt. **Career:** Atomic Energy Comn, Oak Ridge, TN, res stud, 1969; Dept Com, Nat Oceanic & Atmospheric Admin, Nat Weather Serv, Silver Spring, Md, dir, Next Generation Weather Radar, 1977-, fed coor dr meteorol, currently; African Sci Inst, fel. **Orgs:** Am Meteorol Soc, 1980-; Nat Guard Asn, 1980-; officer, bd trustee & finance, Mt Calvary Baptist Church, 1986-; Sr Execs Serv Asn, 1988-; Am Mgt Asn, 1989-; Int Elec/Electronics Engrs Soc, 1989-; chair, Interdepartmental Comt Meteorol Serv & Supporting Res; chairperson, mem, prin advisor, Fed Coordr Meteorol Serv & Supporting Res; sr advisor, US House Representatives Comt. **Home Addr:** 19121 Barksdale Ct, Germantown, MD 20874, **Home Phone:** (301)972-4229. **Business Addr:** Federal Coordinator for Meteorology, National Weather Service, 8455 Colesville Rd Suite 1500, Silver Spring, MD 20910, **Business Phone:** (301)427-2002.

## WILLIAMSON, SAMUEL R.

Lawyer. **Personal:** Born Nov 22, 1943, Ellaville, GA; son of Joseph S and Mittie M; married Barbara Ann Elliott; children: Patricia & Michael. **Educ:** Hampton Univ, BS, 1965; Seton Hall Univ, JD, 1975; Army Command & Gen Staff Col, grad, 1982. **Career:** AT&T Bell Lab, elec engr, 1968-75, sr patent atty, 1976-95; Lucent Technols Inc, corp coun, 1995-. **Orgs:** Asn Black Lab Employees, 1970-85, Garden State Bar Asn, 1976-, Nat Bar Asn, 1976-, New York Urban League Inc, 1982-; Nj Wing Civil Air Patrol, 1983-; bd mem, Nat Patent Law Asn, 1988-89, pres, 1989-91; BEEP lectr; BPA Inc, Alliance Inc, AUSA, Am Legion, YMCA, Phi Alpha Delta, Scabbard & Blade, Explorers; Prince Hall Mason. **Honors/Awds:** Electronics Asn Honor Award for Miliary Leadership; Award for Unselfish Devotion to ABLE Inc; Perseverance Award, OPP. **Home Addr:** 13 Barge Lane, Somerset, NJ 08873-7361, **Home Phone:** (732)940-0102. **Business Addr:** Corporate Counsel, Attorney, Lucent Technologies Inc, 600 Mountain Ave, Murray Hill, NJ 07974, **Business Phone:** (908)582-5890.

## WILLIE, DR. CHARLES VERT

Sociologist, vice president (organization), educator. **Personal:** Born Oct 8, 1927, Dallas, TX; son of Louis J and Carrie S; married Mary Sue Conklin; children: James T, Martin C & Sarah S. **Educ:** Morehouse Col, BA, 1948; Atlanta Univ, MA, 1949; Syracuse Univ, PhD, sociol, 1957. **Career:** Professor (retired), professor emeritus; Syracuse Univ, from asst prof to prof sociol, 1952-74, chmn dept sociol, 1967-71, vpres stud affairs, 1972-74; Upstate Med Ctr, Syracuse, NY Dept Prev Med, instr, 1955-60; Pres Comt Delinq Wash DC Proj, res dir, 1962-64; Harvard Med Sch, Dept Psychiat, vis lectr, 1966-67; Episcopal Divinity Sch, Cambridge, vis lectr, 1966-67; Harvard Univ, prof educ & urban studies, 1974-98; Harvard Univ, Charles William Eliot prof educ, 1998-2000; Harvard Univ, Charles William Eliot prof emer educ, 2000-; Books: A New Look at Black Families, 1976; The Education of African-Americans, 1991; Theories of Human Social Action, 1994; Mental Health, Racism and Sexism, 1995. **Orgs:** Tech Adv Comt, Falk Fund; UNCF; pres, Eastern Sociol Soc; Am Sociol Asn; bd mem, Soc Sci Res Coun; hon trustee, Episcopal Div Sch; vpres, House Deputies, Gen Conv Episcopal Church USA; sr warden, Christ Episcopal Church, Cambridge, 1984-86; bd mem & chair, Dana McLean Greeley Found Peace & Justice; Press Comn Ment Health, USA; Asn Black Sociologists; vpres, Am Sociol Asn; Am Educ Res Asn; Sociologists Women Soc; Soc Study Social Probs; Alpha Phi Alpha Fraternity; bd dir, Social Sci Res Coun. **Home Addr:** 41 Hillcrest Rd, Concord, MA 01742-4615, **Home Phone:** (978)369-2363. **Business Addr:** Charles William Eliot Professor Emeritus of Education, Harvard University, Gutman Libr, Cambridge, MA 02138, **Business Phone:** (617)495-4678.

## WILLIFORD, STANLEY O.

Editor, businessperson, publisher. **Personal:** Born Jan 3, 1942, Little Rock, AR; son of Claude Theophilus and Mary Esther; married Corliss M; children: Steven D Woods, Nicole O Woods, Brian M & Brandon A. **Educ:** Calif State Univ, BA, jour, 1968. **Career:** Los Angeles Times, reporter & editor, 1969-72; E Los Angeles Col, asst prof jour, 1970-71; Los Angeles Sentinel, reporter, 1972-75; Calif St Univ, asst prof jour, 1973-76; Entrepreneur Mag, ed-in-chief, 1975-76; Los Angeles Herald Examr, copy ed, 1975-76; Travel & Art Mag, ed-in-chief, 1975-76, co-publ, 1977-78; Ichthus Rec/Productions, staff; Los Angeles Times, copy ed, 1976-93; Los Angeles City Col, jour instr, 1989-99; Crenshaw Christian Ctr, dir publ, 1993-94; Vision Publ, pres & founder, 1996-; Books: How Blood Works. **Orgs:** Sigma Delta Chi, 1968; bd mem, Crenshaw Christian Ctr, 1991-95. **Honors/Awds:** Fel, Wash Jour Ctr, 1968; Nat Asn Media Women Award, 1974; Award for General Excellence in Reporting, Michele Clark Found, Columbia Univ, 1974. **Special Achievements:** Participated in a range of post graduate seminars, interviews and policy forums during fellowship studies at the WASHINGTON JOURNALISM CENTER, Washington, DC Interacted with Cabinet-level government officials and nationally known media experts.

## WILLINGHAM, DR. GLORIA J.

Dean (education), health services administrator. **Educ:** Regents Col, Univ State NY, Albany, NY, BS, nursing; Univ Ark, MS, nursing; Claremont Grad Univ, PhD, educ. **Career:** VA Med Ctr, Long Beach, Calif, chief, Nursing Educ & Res; Calif State Univ, fac; King Faisal Specialist Hosp & Res Ctr, Head Svc. Nursing Acad Affairs & Dir Ctr Res Distance Educ, 2000-02; Fielding Grad Univ, assoc dean, 2003-10; Fielding Grad Univ, interim provost & sr vpres, 2010-11; Univ W Los Angeles, adj prof, 2012-; Diversity Consult, consult, 2012-. **Orgs:** Founder, Village Proj; Bellflower Coun Race; African Am Exchanges Partnership, bd dir, 2010; Green Found, bd dir, 2011; Faith & Justice Community, bd dir, 2011; Afram Global Orgn Inc, pres, bd dir, 2013; Psi Eta Chap, Chi Eta Phi Sorority Inc, chap founder, current asst southwest regional dir, 2014; Bd Gov, Calif State Univ, Long Beach, bd dir, 2015. **Business Addr:** Associate Dean, Fielding Graduate University, 2112 Santa Barbara St, Santa Barbara, CA 93105-3538, **Business Phone:** (805)687-1099.

## WILLINGHAM, JAMES EDWARD, SR.

Association executive. **Personal:** Born Jun 15, 1948, Philadelphia, PA; son of Rubin and Ruth; married Dawn M; children: Lynette Wesley, Lynore, Andrea, Tiffany & James Jr. **Educ:** Philadelphia Community Col, AA, 1974; Temple Univ, studied Urban Affairs, 1975; Empire State Col NY Univ, BA, 1980. **Career:** Mailing clerk, US Post Off, Los Angeles, 1968-71; Hartford, conn staff; pre-prof staff, Boy Scouts Am, 1971-74; New York, sr dist exec, 1978-80, field dir, 1985-89; bor scout exec, 1985-89, dir field serv, Pittsburgh, 1989-93; Scout Exec & chief exec officer, 1993; Urban League Greater Hartford, sr pres, chief exec officer, 1991-2009; Low Country Restaurant, owner, partner, currently. **Orgs:** Chair, Kappa Alpha Psi Frat, Youth Progs, 1990-, bd dir, Hartford Alumni Chap, currently; Greater Hartford Urban League, 1993-; pres, bd dir, Community Health Serv Inc, 1992-96; Greater Hartford Chamber Com, 1993-; Sigma Pi Phi Frat, 1995-97; bd dir, St Francis Hosp & Med Ctr, 1995-97; adv bd, Capital Community Col, 1995-97; Workforce Develop Bd, 1999; founder, Ludlow Crusaders Athletic Asn; bd dir, Greek Lett Org Hartford; Capital Community Col; Salvation Army Adv Bd; bd dir, Am Red Cross; Greater Hartford Conv & Visitors Bur; Conn Fair Housing Ctr; Workforce Develop Bd; fel Am Leadership Forum; State Conn Task Force; Job Corps Ctr Community Rels Coun, Metro Hartford Regional Econ Alliance Bd; trustee, Hartford Sch Bd, 2001-03; Hate Crimes Adv Comm; Long Island Sound Fund Adv Comm; Sovereign Bank New Eng Community Adv Bd; bd dir, Channel 3 Kids Camp. **Honors/Awds:** William H. Gray Outstanding Man of the Year Award, Bright Hope Baptist Church, 1971; Outstanding Service to All People Award, Four Chaplains Legion Hon, 1972; Community Service to Youth Award, New York Urban League, 1988; Achievement Award, Kappa Alpha Psi Frat Inc, 1991; AME Zion Church, Role Model for African American Males, 1992; Man of the Year Award, Shiloh Baptist Church, 1999; Whitney M Young Jr Leadership Award; The SANK OF Award; WKND Radio Black History Celebration Award. **Home Addr:** 16 Cliffmount Dr, Bloomfield, CT 06002, **Home Phone:** (860)242-7945. **Business Addr:** Board of Director, Kappa Alpha Psi Fraternity Inc, PO Box 2181, Hartford, CT 06145-2181.

## WILLINGHAM, LIONEL TYRONE. See WILLINGHAM, TYRONE.

## WILLINGHAM, TYRONE (LIONEL TYRONE WILLINGHAM)

Football coach, football player. **Personal:** Born Dec 30, 1953, Kinston, NC; married Kim; children: Cassidy, Kelsey & Nathaniel. **Educ:** Mich State Univ, BS, phys educ, 1977. **Career:** Football player, coach (retired); Mich State Univ, wide receiver, 1975-77, asst coach, 1977, 1980-82; Cent Mich Univ, asst coach, 1978-79; NC State Univ, asst coach, 1983-85; Rice Univ, asst coach, 1986-88; Stanford Univ, asst coach, 1989-91, head football coach, 1995-2001; Minne Vikings, asst coach, 1992-94; Univ Notre Dame, head football coach, 2002-04; Univ Wash, head football coach, 2005-08. **Orgs:** Nat adv bd mem Haas Ctr Pub Serv Stanford; bd trustee & vpres, pres, Am Football Coaches Asn, 2001-08; bd mem, Opportunities Industrialization Ctr W, currently. **Honors/Awds:** Pac-10 Coach of the Year, 1995, 1999; National Coach of the Year, Black Coaches Asn, 1995, 1996; George Munger Award, 2002; Sportsman of the Year, Sporting News, 2002; Coach of the Year, 2002; District-5 Coach of the Year, Am Football Coaches Asn. **Business Addr:** Head Football Coach, University of Washington, Graves Bldg, Seattle, WA 98195, **Business Phone:** (206)543-2223.

## WILLINGHAM, VONCILE

Government official. **Personal:** Born Nov 9, 1935, Opp, AL; daughter of L K Lee and Ida Lee Liggins Lee; married Anderson Jr; children: Donna Marie & Doretta Monique. **Educ:** Ala State Univ, BS, 1957; Univ DC, MS, 1977; Am Univ, MS, personnel & human resources mgt, 1987. **Career:** Greene Co Bd Educ, bus educ instr, 1957-58; US Agency Int Develop, exe casst, 1961-69, employee dev specialist, 1970-77, equal employ mgr, 1978-. **Orgs:** Delta Sigma Theta Sor, 1955-; Sargent Memorial Pres by Chancel Choir, 1975-; Southern Md Choral Soc, 1983-; mem bd dir, Foreign Affairs Recreation Asn, 1985-; Interagency Comn Martin Luther King Fed Holiday Comm, 1986; mem bd dir, Univ DC Sch Bus Educ; USAID Adminr's Adv Comn Women. **Home Addr:** 6107 Wood Pointe Dr, Glenn Dale, MD 20769-2124, **Home Phone:** (301)352-4041. **Business Addr:** EEO Manager, United States Agency for International Development, 21st St & Va Ave NW, Washington, DC 20523, **Business Phone:** (202)712-4810.

## WILLIS, ANDREW

Executive director. **Personal:** Born Oct 5, 1938, Jamesville, NC; married Shirley; children: LaShirl & Anqileena. **Educ:** NC A&T State Univ, BS, 1964; Kent State Univ, MA, 1967; Univ NY, Buffalo. **Career:** Pub Welfare Dept Norfolk, Va, caseworker, 1964; Kent State Univ, grad asst, 1964-67; State Univ NY, Buffalo, teaching asst, 1964-67; Health & Welfare Buffalo Urban League, assoc dir, 1967-68; Buffalo Urban League, dep dir, 1968-72; State Univ Col, Buffalo, pt instr, 1969-72; Buffalo Urban League, actg exec dir, 1972; Erie Community Col, asst prof, 1972-73; Urban League Onondaga County, exec dir, 1973-79, pres, chief exec officer. **Orgs:** Bd dir, PEACE Inc; NY Health Plng Adv Coun; bd dir, Int Ctr Syracuse; adv Coun Equal Opportunity; Manpower Adv Plng Coun; Equal Opportunity Prog Comt; Educ Opportunity Ctr; exec coun, Nat Eastern Reg State; Nat Asn Advan Colored People. **Home Addr:** 109 Wilson Pl, Syracuse, NY 13214.

## WILLIS, CECIL B., SR.

Automotive executive. **Career:** Peninsula Pontiac Inc, Torrance, Calif, chief exec officer & founder, 1979. **Business Addr:** Chief Executing officer, Founder, Peninsula Pontiac Inc, 2909 Pac Coast Hwy, Torrance, CA 90505, **Business Phone:** (310)530-3954.

## WILLIS, CHARLES L.

Judge. **Personal:** Born Sep 11, 1926, New York, NY; married Judith Lounsbury; children: Lisa, Michael Elliott, Susan Elliott, Christopher & John Elliott. **Educ:** NY Univ, attended 1951; City Col NY, attended 1951; St John Univ Sch Law, LLB, 1955. **Career:** Monroe County Dist Atty Off, asst dist atty, 1967-68; Monroe County, pub defender, 1968-70; City Rochester, corp coun, 1970-71, city ct judge, 1971-72; McKay Comn, first dep coun, 1972; State New York, Family Ct, supv judge, 1980-88, Supreme Ct Justice, 1989-96; Seventh Judicial Dist, admin judge, 1991; Law Firm Harris, Beach & Wilcox LLP, spec coun, coun; Fla Acad Prof Mediators Inc, mediator. **Orgs:** Trustee, Monroe County Bar Asn, 1970-72; adv, Fourth Judicial Dept, New York Adv common Law Guardians; Asn Family Ct Judges; dir, Urban League, Rochester C's Convalescent Hosp, 1980-83, SPCC, 1981-83, Ctr Govt Res, 1981-84. **Business Addr:** Mediator, The Florida Academy of Professional Mediators Inc, 751 Pinella Bayway Suite 302, Tierra Verde, FL 33715, **Business Phone:** (727)865-6729.

## WILLIS, DEBORAH

Photographer, college teacher, curator. **Personal:** Born Feb 5, 1948, Philadelphia, PA; daughter of Thomas and Ruth. **Educ:** Temple Univ, BA, 1972; Philadelphia Col Art, BFA, 1975; Pratt Inst, MFA, 1980; George Mason Univ, PhD, cult studies, 2003. **Career:** Worked art centers & non-profit orgn; New York Pub Libr's Schomburg Ctr Res Black Cult, exhibs coordr & cur photographs & prints, 1980-92; prof photogr; Smithsonian's Ctr African Am Hist & Cult, exhibs cur, 1992-2000; New York Univ's Tisch Sch Arts, prof & chair, 2000-. **Special Achievements:** Organized exhibits of work by James VanDerZee, Doris Ullman, and Anthony Barboza; curator of traveling exhibitions, "Posing Beauty: African American Images from the 1890s to the Present"; exhibited photographs at the Smithsonian, the Steinbaum Krauss Gallery, and the Bernice Steinbaum Gallery; author, "Illustrated Bio-Bibliography of Black Photographers, 1840-1988", "Reflections in Black: A History of African American Photographers, 1840-Present", "Posing Beauty: African American Images from the 1890s to Present", "Out [o] Fashion Photography: Embracing Beauty", "A Small Nation of People: W.E.B. DuBois and African American Portraits of Progress", "Let Your Motto Be Resistance", "Obama: The Historic Campaign in Photographs", "Michelle Obama: The First Lady in Photographs", and biographical works on Lorna Simpson, J.P. Ball, and James VanDerZee; co-author, he Black Female Body in Photography", "Envisioning Emancipation: Black Americans and the End of Slavery". **Business Addr:** New York University, 721 Broadway 8th Fl, New York, NY 10003, **Business Phone:** (212)998-1930.

## WILLIS, FRANK B.

Government official, publisher. **Personal:** Born Mar 13, 1947, Cleveland, MS; son of Harry and Mattie; married Bobbie M Henderson; children: Oji-Camara Khari. **Educ:** Rochester Bus Inst, AA, 1968; Dyke Col, BS, 1971. **Career:** Benjamin Franklin High Sch, prin, 1971-80; Communicade newspaper, founder, 1972-86; City Urban Renewal Dept, family relocation aide, 1972-74; Okang Commun Corp, pres, 1973-; City Dept Soc Serv, eligibility examr, 1974; State Univ New York, supv prin, 1975; Communicade Newspaper, publ & ed, 1981-; Rochester City Urban Renewal, 1972-74; County Monroe Dept Social Serv, 1974; Rochester City Sch Dist, sch bd mem, comnr, 1980-95. **Orgs:** Legis intern, Rapic Community Network Judicial Process Comn, 1977-78; Coalition Chap I Parents, 1978-; ed & writer, Horambee Parents Newsletter Chap I Prog, 1979-80; Nat Alliance Black Sch Educrs, 1980-; Caucus Black Sch Bd, 1983-. **Honors/Awds:** Outstanding Personality, Afro-Am Soc, Dyke Col, 1971; Service Award, Greater Rochester Tougaloo Col Alumni Asn Inc, 1983; Outstanding Serv, Rochester City Schs Dist Adv Coun Chap I, 1983; Serv Urban League Rochester, 1984. **Home Addr:** 67 Elba St, Rochester, NY 14608-2918, **Home Phone:** (585)235-3332. **Business Addr:** Commisioner of School, Rochester City School District, 131 W Broad St, Rochester, NY 14608.

## WILLIS, FREDERIC L.

Educator. **Personal:** Born May 14, 1937, Handley, WV. **Educ:** La City Col, AA, 1961; Calif State Univ, BS, 1970; Univ Calif, Los Angeles, grad study, 1971; Pepperdine Univ, attended 1973. **Career:** Educator (retired), consultant; Los Angeles Sheriff, dep sheriff, 1964-67, community expert, 1960-64; Los Angeles, dist atty, community affairs rep, investr, 1967-71; Los Angeles Dist Atty, supvr lt, 1971-93; W LosAngeles Col Admin Justice, instr, 1972-; SW Los Angeles Col Admin Justice Dept, coordr, 1973-; CSAN/Nev, Child Support Asst Network, dir, 1993-; Pre-Paid Legal Servs Inc, dir, vpres, independent assoc; Emergency Travel Assurance Inc, dir mkt; Clark County, Southern Nev, Chamber Com, pres; Contraflow Inc, dir & resident agt; consult, currently. **Orgs:** Chmn, Los Angeles Brotherhood Crusade Campaign, 1971; chmn, Sons Watts Ore Prog Adv Coun, 1972; Men Tomorrow; Nat Asn Advan Colored People; NewFrontier Dem Club; bd mem, Rotary Int. **Home Addr:** 3024 Pismo Beach Dr, Las Vegas, NV 89128.

**WILLIS, GLADYS JANUARY**
Educator. **Personal:** Born Feb 29, 1944, Jackson, MS; daughter of John January and Emily Young January; married Ampere-hour Willis Junior; children: Juliet Christina & Michael Lamont. **Educ:** Jackson State Univ, BA, 1965; Bryn Mawr Col, independent study, 1966; Mich State Univ, MA, 1967; Princeton Univ, PhD, 1973; Lutheran Theol Sem, Philadelphia, PA, Mdiv, 1996. **Career:** Woodrow Wilson Nat Fel, Princeton Univ, 1966-67; Cheyney State Univ, instr, Eng, 1967-68; Rider Col, instr, Eng, 1968-70; Princeton Univ Fel, Princeton Univ, 1970-73; City Univ New York, asst prof, Eng, 1973-76; Pa Human Rel Comn, educ rep, 1976-77; Lincoln Univ, assoc prof, chair, 1977-85, prof, dept chair, 1985-, dean, Sch Humanities & Grad Studies, 2002-; First Redemption Evangel Church, asst pastor, 1992-; Lincoln Univ, Dean Humanities & Grad Studies, currently. Books: Introduction to Third World Literature, ed, 1981; The Penalty of Eve, auth, 1985. **Orgs:** Founder, dir, Col Prep Tutorial, 1974; bd dir, Philadelphia Christian Acad, 1977-; Nat Coun Teachers Eng; reviewer, Mid States Asn, 1985-; bd trustee, Required Writing Proficiency; Nat Coun Negro Women; bd dir, Arts Alliance Oxford. **Home Addr:** 232 Wiltshire Rd, Wynnewood, PA 19096-3333, **Home Phone:** (610)649-5449. **Business Addr:** Dean of Humanities & Graduate Studies, Lincoln University, Lincoln Plz, Philadelphia, PA 19104, **Business Phone:** (215)387-2405.

**WILLIS, JAMES EDWARD, III**
Football player, football coach, executive. **Personal:** Born Sep 2, 1972, Huntsville, AL; married Shalane; children: Jade, Jasselya, Jalen & Jordan. **Educ:** Auburn Univ, BS, adult, continuing educ & teaching, 1993. **Career:** Football player (retired), coach, coordinator; Green Bay Packers, linebacker, 1993-94; Philadelphia Eagles, 1995, mid linebacker, 1996-98; Seattle Seahawks, linebacker, 1999; Birmingham Thunderbolts, linebacker, 2001; Auburn Tigers Football, stud asst, 2001-02, defensive grad asst, 2003-06, asst coach, 2006-09; Univ Ri, asst coach, 2003-05; Cotton Bowl, coach, 2007-09; Ala Crimson Tide, assoc head coach & outside linebackers coach, 2009-10; Tex Tech Univ, defensive coordr, 2010; Va Destroyers, United Football League, defensive coordr, 2011-; 3ANDOUT LLC, owner, chief exec officer, 2011-; Univ La, defensive coordr, 2012-, New Orleans Saints, defensive asst & linebackers coach, 2015-. **Honors/Awds:** SEC Co-Defensive Freshman of the Year, 1990; Rookie of the Year, 1993; Most Valuable Player, 2001. **Home Addr:** 4010 E Adm Doyle Dr, New Iberia, LA 70560-9788, **Home Phone:** (337)560-9583. **Business Addr:** Defensive Coordinator, University of Louisiana, 104 E Univ Ave, Lafayette, AL 70504, **Business Phone:** (337)482-1000.

**WILLIS, JILL MICHELLE**
Lawyer. **Personal:** Born Jan 4, 1952, Atlanta, GA; daughter of Louis Bell Sr and Annette James Strickland; married Paul Hugh Brown; children: Bryant Alexander Brown. **Educ:** Wellesley Col, BA, psychol & sociol, 1973; Columbia Univ Sch Social Work, MS, social work, 1975; Univ Chicago Law Sch, JD, 1984. **Career:** United Charities Chicago Family Serv Bur, 1975-79; Chapman & Cutler, assoc, 1984-86; Allstate Ins Co, asst coun, 1986-2003; Law Office of Jill M. Willis, owner, currently; Sears Holdings Corp, sr coun, 2005-09. **Orgs:** Waddell Wellesley Col Study E Africa, 1972; Adv bd, Thresholds S, 1977-78; bd dir, Howe Develop Ctr, 1984-86; Am Bar Asn, 1984-; Chicago Bar Asn, 1984-; Cook Co Bar Asn, 1984-. **Honors/Awds:** Henry R Luce Scholar Asia Internship, 1979-80; Chairmans Award, Allstate Ins Co, 1988. **Home Addr:** 8012 S Saginaw Ave, Chicago, IL 60617. **Business Addr:** Owner, Law Office of Jill M Willis, 3628 S King Dr, Chicago, IL 60653, **Business Phone:** (847)826-5284.

**WILLIS, KATHI GRANT**
Lawyer. **Personal:** Born Dec 2, 1959, Knoxville, TN; daughter of Lorenzo D Grant and Henrietta Arnold Grant; married Henry W; children: Elizabeth Danielle. **Educ:** Univ VA, BA, foreign affairs, 1981; Univ Tenn Col Law, JD, 1984. **Career:** Provident Life & Accident Ins Co, Chattanooga, TN, mgr, contracts & claims, 1986-88, atty, 1988-89, asst coun, 1989, assoc coun, 1992-95 sr coun, 1984-95; Health source Inc, Chattanooga, TN, coun, 1995-97; Blue Cross & Blue Shield Tenn, sr coun, dir & chief employ coun, 1997-2010; independent law pract prof, currently; Community Health Alliance, gen coun, 2012-; Consumers' Choice Health Plan, gen coun, 2012-. **Orgs:** Tenn Bar Asn; Chattanooga Bar Asn; Am Bar Asn; Am Health Lawyers Asn; Erlanger Baroness Found; pres, Chattanooga Chap Links Inc. **Home Addr:** 308 Willow Glen Rd, Chattanooga, TN 37421-3205, **Home Phone:** (423)893-8069. **Business Addr:** General Counsel, Consumers' Choice Health Plan, 4995 Lacross Rd Suite 1300, North Charleston, SC 29406, **Business Phone:** (800)580-8736.

**WILLIS, KEVIN ALVIN**
Basketball player, businessperson. **Personal:** Born Sep 6, 1962, Los Angeles, CA. **Educ:** Jackson Community Col, attended 1981; Mich State Univ, fashion design, 1984. **Career:** Basketball player (retired), businessman; Atlanta Hawks, forward-ctr, 1984-94, 2004-05; Miami Heat, 1994-96; Golden State Warriors, 1996; Houston Rockets, 1997-98, 2001-02; Toronto Raptors, 1998-2001; Denver Nuggets, 2001; San Antonio Suprs, forward-ctr, 2002-04; Dallas Mavericks, 2006-07; Nat Basketball Asn, dean; Willis & Walker, owner, 1988-. **Orgs:** Heal World Found; Boys & Girls Club; Am Kidney Found. **Business Addr:** Owner, Willis & Walker - It's In The Jeans, 2300 Peachtree Rd, Atlanta, GA 30309, **Business Phone:** (404)352-2555.

**WILLIS, MIECHELLE ORCHID**
Athletic director, administrator. **Personal:** Born Feb 12, 1954, Lakewood, NJ; daughter of M Agnes Garland and Vernon. **Educ:** Grambling State Univ, Grambling, LA, BS, 1976, health & phys educ, 1976, MS, 1978. **Career:** Montclair State Col, Upper Montclair, NJ, head women's track coach, 1978-87; Grambling State Univ, athletic adminr; Temple Univ, Philadelphia, Pa, asst dir athletics, assoc dir athletics, 1987-94; Stud Athlete Support Serv, depts liaison; Ohio State Univ, Dept Athletics, assoc dir, 1994-, sr woman adminr, Ohio State Buckeyes, dep dir athletics, 2014-. **Orgs:** Delta Sigma Theta Sorority Inc, 1975-78; Delta Psi Kappa Fraternity, 1976-78; chair, Field Hockey Comt, Atlantic 10 Conf, 1988-; Coun Col Womens Athletic Adminr, 1990-; Big Ten Legis Rev Comt; Nat Asn Col Women Athletic Adminr; Nat Asn Col dir Athletics; Nat Col Athletic Asn, currently. **Home Addr:** 2991 Sch House Lane, Philadelphia, PA 19144, **Home Phone:** (215)849-9352. **Business Addr:** Deputy Director of Athletics, Associate Director, Ohio State University, 2400 Olentangy River Rd, Columbus, OH 43210, **Business Phone:** (614)688-3280.

**WILLIS, DR. ROSE W.**
Beautician, photographer. **Personal:** Born Jan 2, 1939, Columbus, GA; daughter of Leonard Wright and Christine Wright; children: Gwendolyn D Hunt & Sherry Ancrum. **Educ:** Nat Inst Cosmetology, BA, 1971, MA, 1974, PhD, 1978. **Career:** Lovely Lady Beauty Salon, Hollywood, Fla, mgr & owner, 1967-; Orange Blossom Cosmetologists Asn, local pres unit 24, 1969-78, parade state chmn, 1970-80, state photogr, 1980; Nat Beauty Culturists League, chmn finance & registr, 1984-; Dillard High Sch, Ft Lauderdale, 1992-94; Columbus Times News Paper, freelance photogr, currently. **Orgs:** Pres, Fla State Nat Beauty Culturists League, N Miami Beach, FL, 1978-94; Nat Coun Negro Women, 1979-94; treas, Theta Nu Sigma, Mu chap, 1983-92; fin secy, S Fla Bus Asn, 1988-93; Dade County Sch Bd Cosmetology, 1988-94; co-chmn, Dade County Sch Cosmetology Adv Comt; vpres, Antioch Baptist Church Choir; Nazareth Baptist Church. **Honors/Awds:** Woman of the Year, Theta Nu Sigma Sorority, 1984; Outstanding Service Award, Bahamian Cosmetologists Asn, 1989; Revlon Leadership Award, 1991; Cordelia G Johnson Pioneer Award, NBCL, 1991; No 1 for Thirty-Six Years, Outstanding Service & Dedication, Antioch Baptist Church & Choir, Miami; Outstanding Service, Fla Coun, Thela Nu Sigma, Mu-Chapter & Natl Beauty Culturist's, Miami. **Business Addr:** Freelance Photographer, Columbus Times Newspaper, PO Box 2845, Columbus, GA 31902-2845, **Business Phone:** (706)324-2404.

**WILLOCK, DR. MARCELLE MONICA**
Educator, dean (education). **Personal:** Born Mar 30, 1938, Georgetown; son of George and Renee W. **Educ:** Col New Rochelle, BA, 1958; Howard Univ, MD, 1962; Columbia Univ, MA, 1982; Boston Univ, MBA, 1989. **Career:** Educator, dean (retired); NY Univ Sch Med, asst clin prof, 1968-72, assoc clin prof, 1972-74; Columbia Univ Col Physicians & Surgeons, asst prof, clin anesthesiol, 1978-82; Boston Univ Med Ctr, chief anesthesiol, 1982-98, asst provost external affairs, prof & chmn, 1998; Charles R Drew Univ Med & Sci, dean, 2002-05, prof psychiat & family med. **Orgs:** Pres, Louis & Mar Deveaux Found, 1965; pres, Am Med Womens Asn Mass, 1985-86; pres, Mass Soc Anessiologists, 1988-89, 1987-89; deleg, Am Soc Anessiologists, 1986-94, alt dir, 1990-94, bd dir, 1994-, asst secy, 1999-2001; Asn Univ Anestists; sec & treas, Soc Acad Anessia Chmn, 1989-91, pres, 1994-96; secy bd dir, Med Found, Boston, MA, 1991-94; trustee, Col New Rochelle, 1976-82; Alpha Omega Alpha; co-dir, UTHSCSA Nat Ctr Excellence Womens Health. **Home Addr:** 85 E India Row Apt 31F, Boston, MA 02110-3394, **Home Phone:** (617)720-1314.

**WILLOUGHBY, DR. SUSAN MELITA FENTON. See Obituaries Section.**

**WILLRICH, DR. E. JAMES**
Scholar. **Personal:** Born Sep 16, 1959, Dallas, TX; son of Theodis Sr and Margie Crew. **Educ:** Univ Tex, Arlington, BBA, mkt, 1983; Tex A&M Univ Sch Law, JD, law, 1994. **Career:** Harte-Hanks Direct Mkt, sales consult, 1986-87; Advan Telemarketing Corp, mkt agt, 1987; United Advert, data mgmt supvr, 1987-88; Consol Freightways Inc, sales exec, 1988-99; Willrich Scott Consult Group Inc, dir bus develop, 1999-2000; CLD Solutions Inc, dir mkt & bus develop, 2000; Arlington Independent Schl Dist, Substitute Teacher, 2001; Bruskin Audits & Surveys Worldwide, Mkt Researcher, 2001; US Small Bus Admin, Law Clerk, 2001; US Chamber Com, mem dir, 2002-03; Pearson Educ Measurement, prof scorer & supvr, 2003-11; Tex Atty Gen, child support officer, 2004-06; Off Atty Gen, Arlington, Tex, staff, currently; Wolters Kluwer Law & Bus, acct exec, 2006-07; Schneider Logistics Inc, sales acct exec, 2007-08; Amin Law Firm, law firm mkt mgr, 2009-11; JPMorgan Chase, bus develop, 2016-. **Orgs:** Am Mkt Asn, 1982-87; Charter Mem, Metroplex Egyptian Hist Soc; Univ Tex Arlington Alumni Asn, Phonathon, 1985, bd mem, vpres, 2003-08; Hands Across Am, 1986; Black Enterprise Prof Network Exchange, 1987; Nat Asn Advan Colored People, Grand Prairie, 1989; Dallas Urban League, 1989; African Am Men Endangered Species; NBA, 1990; Delta Theta Phi Int Law Fraternity; Tex Wesleyan Univ Stud Bar Asn; Nat Bar Asn; UT Arlingtons Planetarium; Nat Space Socs; Tex Wesleyan Law Sch Alumni Asn; Tex Aggie Bar Asn; Asn Former Students Tex A&M Univ; Nat Space Soc N Tex; Nat Soc Black Physicists. **Honors/Awds:** UTA Academic Achievement Award, 1981, 1982; UTA Alumni Leadership Scholar Acad Excellence & Campus Involvement, 1982; Jesse Jackson Delegate State Convention, 1988; Wests Law & Technology Essay Winner, 1993; Outstanding American Award; Top Performer Award. **Home Addr:** 701 Manning St, Grand Prairie, TX 75051-2606, **Home Phone:** (972)660-5651. **Business Addr:** Business Development Specialist, JPMorgan Chase, Dallas, TX.

**WILLRICH, PENNY**
Judge, educator. **Personal:** Born Aug 12, 1954, Dallas, TX; daughter of Theodis and Margie; children: Amaya Maria. **Educ:** Univ Tex, Arlington, BA, polit sci, 1974, BA, hist, 1976; Antioch Sch Law, JD, 1982; Springfield Col, MS, human serv-community psychol, 2001; Capella Univ, PhD, pub serv leadership-criminol, 2012. **Career:** Judge, educator; US Dist Ct, Phoenix; Fifth Circuit Ct Appeals; Ninth Circuit Ct Appeals; Reginald Heber Smith Community Law Fel, 1982-85; W Tex Legal Servs, managing atty, 1984-87; Community Legal Serv, litigation dir, 1987-92; Ariz Dept Econ Security, asst dir, 1992-94; Law Off Penny Willrich, priv pract, 1994-95; Super Ct, Maricopa County, comnr, 1995-99; supr ct judge, 1999-2005; Ariz State Univ, Col Law, adj prof, 2001; Phoenix Sch Law, assoc prof law & dir lawyering process, assoc dean acad affairs, 2005-. **Orgs:** Alpha Kappa Alpha Sor; Phi Eta Sigma Hon Soc; Black Women's Task Force; Maricopa County Bar Asn; Nat Women Judges Asn; Thur good Marshall Inn Ct; Ariz Women Lawyers Asn; Hayzel B Daniels Bar Asn; Nat Asn Advan Colored People; Nat coun Negro Women; Phi Delta Phi Legal Frat; Parent Teacher Orgn; bd mem, New Life Battered Women Shelter, 1989-94; Supreme Ct's Comn Minorities, 1990-00; adv bd, US Civil Rights Comn, 1991-98; bd mem, Friends Phoenix Pub Libr, 1992-94; Ariz Supreme Ct Domestic Violence Comm, 1992-96; vol, Maricopa County Modest Means Proj, 1994-95; orientation trainer, Ct App Spec Advocates, 1995-; co chair, ADES, Multi Ethnic Adv comm, 1997-98; chair, liaison to State Bar Bd Gov, H B Daniels Bar Asn, Bar Issues Comm, 1998; presiding comnr, Juv Div, 1998-99; Maricopa County Model Ct Comt, 1998-99; trainer, COLORBLIND Justice Conf, AZ Supreme Ct, 1998-99; Phoenix Violence Prev Initiative; State Bar Ariz Ed Bd, 1998-2000; State Bar Ariz Ethics Comt; Phoenix Fire Dept Community Adv Bd; vol, Gilbert Jr High, Art Master's Prog; C's Voices; 1999 trainer, Ariz New Judge Orientation; minister & teacher, First New Life Missionary Baptist Church, Bd dir, Ariz Black Women Lawyers Ass. **Home Addr:** 1372 N McKenna Lane, Gilbert, AZ 85233-2016, **Home Phone:** (480)926-3034. **Business Addr:** Associate Professor of Law, Associate Dean of Academic Affairs, Phoenix School of Law, 1 N Central Ave 14th Fl, Phoenix, AZ 85004, **Business Phone:** (602)682-6833.

**WILLS, DR. CORNELIA**
Administrator. **Personal:** Born Jul 21, 1973, Talladega, AL. **Educ:** Austin Peay State Univ, Clarksville, Tenn, BS; Tenn State Univ, Nashville, Tenn, MEd, 1992, EdD, 1997. **Career:** Tenn Bd Regents, Nashville, Tenn, res analyst, 1988-89; Mid Tenn State Univ, Murfreesboro, Tenn, Stud Success, dir, dir instnl res, currently. **Orgs:** Delta Sigma Theta Sorority Inc; consult, Fac Res Comt, 1989-95; consult, Univ Plng Comt; Asn Instnl Res; elect, 19 Women Higher Educ Tenn, Tenn Asn Instnl Res, 1990-, pres, 1998-2000; Status Women Acad, 1991-; Task Force Performance Funding, 1991-; Exec Comn Instnl Effectiveness, 1992-; Southern Asn Instnl Res, 1996-; Phi Delta Kappa Int; Tenn State Univ Chap, vpres, 1998-99. **Honors/Awds:** Nat Beta Club, 1970; Outstanding Student Teacher Award, Austin Peay State Univ Ambassador, Austin Peay State Univ, 1978; Listed in PCSW, 2009. **Special Achievements:** First African American & first female director of institutional research at Middle Tennessee State. Author of book: Mama Said: A Word to the Wise is Sufficient. **Business Addr:** Author, Educational Administrator, Middle Tennessee State University, 153 Jones Hall 1301 E Main St, Murfreesboro, TN 37132, **Business Phone:** (615)898-5025.

**WILLS, DOROTHY**
Nurse. **Personal:** Born Oct 17, 1942, Eastaboga, AL; daughter of Willie Jr and Rosa Lee. **Educ:** Homer G Phillips Hosp Sch Nursing, regist nurse, 1964; Webster Univ, BSN, 1998; Covenant Theol Sem, MAC, 2001. **Career:** Barnes-Jewish Hosp, nurse, 1965-2008; Meier New Life Clinics, St Louis, counr, 2001-09, therapist; Alpha Omega Christian Clin, therapist, 2009-10; Bodenheimer Psychol & Coun Ctr, therapist, 2013-. **Orgs:** Sigma Theta Tau Int Soc, 1998-. **Honors/Awds:** Certified, psychiatric & mental health nurse, 1994; Nat Hon Soc, 1998. **Special Achievements:** Travelled to all seven continents, 1965-95. **Home Addr:** 1130 Martha Lane, St Louis, MO 63119-1145, **Home Phone:** (314)962-2938. **Business Addr:** Counselor/Therapist, Meier New Life Clinics, 9717 Landmark Pkway Dr Suite 208, St Louis, MO 63127, **Business Phone:** (888)725-4642.

**WILLS, DR. JAMES WILLARD**
Physician. **Personal:** Born Jan 23, 1933, Aquasco, MD; son of Rossie H and Clara Wright; married Waltine; children: Phyllis, John & Cecil. **Educ:** Morgan State Col, BS, 1954; Howard Univ, MD, 1961. **Career:** Westland Med Ctr, internship, 1961-62; Dc Gen Hosp, fel pulmonary disease, 1964-65; Howard Univ, resident internal med, 1962-64; Glenn Dale Hosp, exec dir, 1973-77; Glenn Dale Hosp, chief, med serv; pvt pract physician, 1975-; Area "C" Chest Clin, Washinton, DC, chief med officer, 1981-; Southern Md Hosp Ctr. **Orgs:** Alpha Phi Alpha, Medico-Chirurgical Soc, DC, Nat Med Asn. **Home Addr:** 11303 Earlston Dr, Mitchellville, MD 20721-2426, **Home Phone:** (301)464-3745. **Business Addr:** Physician, 14310 Old Marlboro Pke, Upper Marlboro, MD 20772, **Business Phone:** (301)627-1448.

**WILMORE, REV. GAYRAUD STEPHEN, JR.**
Writer, educator, historian. **Personal:** Born Dec 20, 1921, Philadelphia, PA; son of Patricia Gardner (deceased); married Lee Wilson; children: Stephen, Jacques & Roberta Wilmore-Hurley. **Educ:** Lincoln Univ, BA, 1947; Lincoln Univ Theol Sem, BD, 1950; Temple Univ Sch Relig, 1952; Drew Theol Sem, 1963. **Career:** Educator (retired); 2nd Presby Church W Chester, PA, pastor, 1950-53; Mid-Atlantic Stud Christian Movement, regional secy, 1953-56; United Presby Church, assoc exec, 1958-; Pittsburgh Theol Sem, asst prof, social ethics, 1959-63; United Presby Coun Church & Race, exec dir, 1963-72; Boston Univ Sch Theol, prof soc ethics, 1972-74; Colgate Rochester Div Sch, ML King Jr prof, 1974-83; NY Theol Sem, MD IV Prog, dean, prof afro-am relig studies, 1983-87; Inter denominational Theol Ctr, distinguished vis scholar, 1986-87; United Theol Sem, Dayton, Ohio, adj prof, 1995-98; Bks: Black Theol: A Doc Hist, 1996-79; Black Relig & Black Radicalism, 1998; Pragmatic Spirituality, 2004. **Orgs:** Am Soc Christian Ethics, 1961-78; bd mem, Faith & Order Comn, World Coun Church, 1973-89; Ecum Asn Third World Theol, 1976-; bd dir, Black Theol Proj Inc, 1977-; consult, Eli Lilly Endowment, 1979-80; pres, Soc Study Black Relig, 1979-80; ed, J Info Technol Ctrs, 1989-94; founding mem, Nat Conf Black Churchmen; Am Theol Soc. **Honors/Awds:** DD, Lincoln Col, 1965; Bruce Klunder Award, Presbyterian Interracial Coun, 1968; DD, Tusculum Col, 1972; innumerable awards. **Home Addr:** 3050 Mil Rd NW Apt 423, Washington, DC 20015-1361, **Home Phone:** (202)686-1643.

**WILMOT, DAVID WINSTON**
Educator, lawyer, businessperson. **Personal:** Born Apr 26, 1944, Panama City, FL; son of David and Bertha; married Mary Elizabeth Mercer; children: Michele, Kristy & David II. **Educ:** Univ Ark, BA, 1970; Georgetown Univ Law Ctr, JD, 1973. **Career:** Little Rock, asst city mgr, 1968-70; Dolphin Branton Stafford & Webber, legal asst, 1970-72; DC Proj Comm Legal Asst, dep dir, 1972-73; Georgetown Univ, asst dean, dir, 1973-92; Harmon & Wilmot, partner, 1992-; Georgetown Univ Law Ctr, res asst; OEO Legal Servs, intern; David W Wilmot & Assocs, owner; DC Conv Ctr, bd dir, gen coun; Hotel Assoc Wash DC, gen coun. **Orgs:** Pres, Stud Equality, 1967-68; vpres, GULC Legal Aid Soc, 1972-73; pres, Black Am Law Stud Assoc, 1972-73; adv bd, DC Bds & Comms Adv Bd Georgetown Today, 1973-76; DC Bar; Pa Bar; US Supreme Ct Appeals; DC Ct Appeals; Supreme Ct PA; Assoc Am Law Schs; Law Sch Admin Coun; Am Bar Assoc; Trial

Lawyers Assoc; Nat Bar Assoc; Nat Conf Black Lawyers; Alpha Kappa Psi; Lawyers Study Group; Potomac Fiscal Soc; Firemens & Policement Retirement Bd; mem bd dir, Fed City Nat Bank, Wash Waterfront Restaurant Corp; mem bd gov, Georgetown Univ Alumni Assoc; mem bd dir, Dist Cable vision Inc; Wash Tennis & Educ Found. **Home Addr:** 1653 Kalmia Rd NW, Washington, DC 20012-1125, **Home Phone:** (202)829-8272. **Business Addr:** Partner, Harmon & Wilmot LLP, 1010 Vt Ave NW Suite 810, Washington, DC 20005, **Business Phone:** (202)783-9100.

## WILSON, ALVA L.

Clergy. **Personal:** Born Nov 21, 1922, Lake City, SC; son of Malichi and Hattie Mayes; married Carrie Williams; children: Allesia Muldrow, Charles K & Benita F. **Educ:** Allen Univ, AB, 1949; Gammon Theol Sem, 1961. **Career:** Owner & farmer, 1950; freelance horticulturist, landscaper, 1979-; UMSC Conf, clergyman. **Orgs:** Barber Shaw AFB, 1949-75; vice chmn, Health Educ & Welfare Minister, 1972-78; secy, trustee bd, Florence County Dist third Sch Bd, 1974-91. **Honors/Awds:** Leadership Training Institute Award, SC Sch Bd Asn, 1975. **Home Addr:** 1454 Eastland Ave, Kingstree, SC 29556-6036.

## WILSON, ANGELA BROWN

Government official. **Personal:** Born Mar 31, 1961, Detroit, MI; daughter of Bunnie Brown Sr (deceased) and Lillie M Brown; married Errol S. **Educ:** Wayne State Univ, BSW, 1984; MSW, 1988; Develop Training Inst, cert, 1989. **Career:** Warren/Conner Dev Coalition, prog dir, 1985-87, dep dir, 1987-94; City Detroit, exec asst mayor, 1994; Communities In Sch Detroit Inc, dir innovation & enterprise, currently. **Orgs:** Minister faith, Sacred Heart Church, 1982-; spokesperson, Save Our Spirit Coalition, 1986-93; chairperson, Dept Catholic Pastoral Alliance, 1992-; chairperson, Nat Community Rels Div Am Friends Serv Comt, 1993; Dominican High Sch Bd Assocs, 1994-; Am Friends Serv Comt, 1995-; Nat Asn Advan Colored People; Wayne State Univ Alumni Asn; Knight & Ladies, St Peter Claver; Develop Practitioners, Develop Leadership Network; bd trustee, Detroit Cristo Rey High Sch; bd dir, Young Detroit Builders; Mich Legal Serv. **Home Addr:** 5016 Seneca, Detroit, MI 48213, **Home Phone:** (313)922-2339. **Business Addr:** Director of Innovation & Enterprise, Communities In School of Detroit Inc, 5575 Conner St, Detroit, MI 48213, **Business Phone:** (313)571-3402.

## WILSON, BARBARA JEAN

Executive, president (organization). **Personal:** Born Jun 5, 1940, Dallas, TX; married Porterfield; children: Porterfield Christopher. **Educ:** Prairie View A&M Univ, BS, 1964; Gen Motors Inst Flint Mich, attended 1975; Hadley Dealer Acct Sch Royal Oak Mich, attended 1975; Reynolds & Reynolds Comput Sch Dayton Ohio, attended 1980. **Career:** TC Hassell Sch Dallas Tex, exec secy, 1964-73; Chrysler Corp Mound Rd Engine Detroit, bookkeeper, 1965-73; Porterfield Wilson Pontiac GMC Truck Mazda-Honda, exec secy, 1973-79; Mazda Honda, pres oper, 1979-84; Ferndale Honda, pres, 1984-96; Porterfield's Marina Village, pres, 1989-. **Orgs:** Pres, Carats Inc Detroit Chap Nat Club, 1969; Women's Econ Club, 1975-; life mem, Nat Asn Advan Colored People, 1975; Palmer Woods Asn, 1976; Am Imported Auto Dealers, 1979; Detroit Auto Dealers Asn, 1979; Negro Bus & Prof Women, 1979; Coalition 100 Black Women Detroit, 1980. **Honors/Awds:** Special Recognition Award, Carats Inc Detroit Chap, 1979; Candace Award, Business Woman of the Year, 1987; Candice Award for Businesswomen of the Year, 1987; Michigan's Top 50 Business Owned & Operated by Women, Crain's Detroit Bus. **Special Achievements:** First African-American automobile dealer in the world. **Home Addr:** 19481 Gloucester Dr, Detroit, MI 48203.

## WILSON, BERNARD (RAPHAEL BERNARD WILSON)

Football player. **Personal:** Born Aug 17, 1970, Nashville, TN; married Roslyn; children: Khandi. **Educ:** Tenn State Univ, grad. **Career:** Football player (retired); Detroit Lions, 1993; Tampa Bay Buccaneers, defensive tackle & linebacker, 1993-94; Ariz Cardinals, right defensive tackle, 1994-97, defensive tackle, 1998. **Honors/Awds:** Intercept Return TD, Nat Football League, 1997; Long Intercept Return, Nat Football League, 1997.

## WILSON, DR. BLENDA JACQUELINE

School administrator. **Personal:** Born Jan 28, 1941, Perth Amboy, NJ; daughter of Horace Lawrence and Margaret Brogsdale; married Louis Fair Jr. **Educ:** Cedar Crest Col, BA, Eng, 1962; Seton Hall Univ, MA, educ, 1965; Boston Col, PhD, higher educ admin, 1979. **Career:** Middlesex County Econ Opportunities Corp, exec dir, 1968-69; Rutgers Univ, asst provost, 1969-71, exec asst pres, 1969-72; Harvard Univ, Grad Sch Educ, sr assoc dean; lectr educ, 1976-82, sr assoc dean, 1972-82; Independent Sector, vpres, 1982-84; Colo Comn Higher Educ, colo state off, exec dir, 1984-88; Univ Mich, chancellor, 1988-92; Calif St Univ, Northridge, pres, 1992-99; Cedar Crest Col, actg pres, 2007-08. **Orgs:** Chairperson, Am Asn Higher Educ, 1990-; bd dir, Alpha Ctr, 1988-91; adv comm, Int Found Educ & Self-Help, 1986-; bd trustee, Boston Col; Found Ctr; bd trustee, Sammy Davis Jr Nat Liver Inst, 1989; exec bd, Detroit Area Boy Scouts Am; Detroit Chap Nat Coalition 100 Black Women; Dearborn Rotary; Asn Gov Bds; United Way SE Mich, 1989; Women's Econ Club Detroit, 1989; bd dir, Commonwealth Fund, 1981-; dir, James IrvineFound; trustee, J Paul Getty Trust; dir, C's TV Workshop; pres & chief executive officer, Nellie Mae Educ Found, 1999-2006; bd mem, Boston After Sch & Beyond; Boston Col; Federated Dorchester Neighborhood Houses; dir, Union Bank Calif, 1993-99; Fed Res Bank, 2002-06, chmn, 2006; dir, Medco Health Solutions, 2003-; Partners Health Care Systs; dir. **Honors/Awds:** Doctor of Educ, Eastern Mich Univ, 1990; Doctor of Laws, Rutgers Univ, 1989, Doctor of Humane Letters, Univ Detroit, 1989; Women on the Move Award, Renaissance Chapter of Links, 1989; Michigan Bell Living Dream Award, Michigan Bell, 1989; Distinguished Leader, Washtenaw Comm Col, 1990. **Special Achievements:** One of 100 Emerging Leaders in America, Higher Educ Change magazine, 1978, 90 for the 90's, Crain's Detroit Business Magazine, 1990. **Home Addr:** 18 Windy Hill Rd, Cohasset, MA 02025, **Home Phone:** (912)234-0240.

## WILSON, DR. BOBBY L.

Educator. **Personal:** Born Sep 30, 1942, Columbus, MS; son of Johnnie B and Lillie Coleman; married Mary; children: Anthony, Melanie, Malissa & Melinda. **Educ:** Ala State Col, BS, chem, 1966; Southern Univ, MS, chem, 1972; Mich State Univ, PhD, chem, 1976. **Career:** Booker T Wash HS, instr, 1966-70; Jefferson Davis HS, instr, 1970-71; Mich State Univ, grad asst, 1971-76; Tex Southern Univ, asst prof, 1976-80, assoc prof, 1980-82; Exxon Res & Engineering, vis prof, 1982-83; Tex Southern Univ, assoc prof, 1983-85, prof, 1985-, Col Arts & Sci, assoc dean, 1986-87, dept head, 1987-89, interim dean arts & sci, 1989-90, vpres, acad affairs, 1990-92, provost, 1992-, prof, 1994, sr vpres, acad affairs, currently, L. Lloyd Woods Distinguished prof, currently; Nat Sci Found, prog dir, 1995-97. **Orgs:** Am Chem Soc; Beta Kappa Chi Hon Soc; Kappa Alpha Psi Frat; Nat Asn Advan Colored People; Nat Geog Soc; exec bd chmn, Nat Org Prof Advan Black Chemists & Chem ENRs; Nat Urban League; Smithsonian Inst; Tex Acad Sci; Tex Asn Col Teachers; Tri-County Civic Asn; Tex Fac Asn; ForumClub Houston; Sigma Xi; Tex Inst Chemists; Am Inst Chemists, stud awards Comm, 1988; Sci Res Soc, 1988; Bylaws Comm, 1988; pres, C Against Drugs & Drinking Inc. **Home Addr:** 3503 Senova Dr, Pearland, TX 77584-7059, **Home Phone:** (281)412-2621. **Business Addr:** Distinguished Professor, Senior Vice President, Texas Southern University, 3100 Cleburne St Rm SB 403L, Houston, TX 77004, **Business Phone:** (713)313-7011.

## WILSON, BRYAN

Gospel singer. **Personal:** Born Nov 3, 1983, Danville, IL; son of Sheila and Lowell Briggs. **Educ:** Claflin Univ, BA, theol, 2004; Princeton Univer, MDiv. **Career:** Albums: Malaco Records, rec artist, 1994; Growing Up, 1998. Bryan Wilson Ministries, founder & chmn, currently. **Orgs:** UNCF Pre-Alumni Coun, 2002. **Honors/Awds:** Gospel Music Asn, Dove Award Nomination, for "Bryan's Songs, " 1996; Don Jackson Productions, Stellar Awards, for "Bryan's Songs, " 1996. **Home Phone:** (803)387-4647. **Business Addr:** Gospel Singer, c/o Capital Entertainment, 217 Seaton Pl NE, Washington, DC 20002, **Business Phone:** (202)636-7028.

## WILSON, CARROLL LLOYD

Educator, association executive. **Personal:** Born Jul 9, 1937, Jamaica, NY; married Barbara Ellen Jones; children: Mark, Eric Theodore & Ellen Clarice. **Educ:** Univ Maine, Orono, BA, 1962; Kean Col, NJ, MA, 1969; Rutgers Univ, grad studies. **Career:** Pub Health Educ State ME, from asst to dir, 1962-63; Plainfield Pub Sch, Plainfield, NJ, teacher & asst track coach, 1963-69; Job Corps, Camp Kilmer NJ, res specialist, 1966-67; Somerset Community Col & Annandale Youth Correctional Inst, coord spec prog, 1973-74; Raritan Valley Community Col, prof, prof emer eng, currently. **Orgs:** Cub Master Pack, 1776; bd dir, Somerset Comn Ment Health Asn, 1978-81; bd trustee, Correctional Inst Women, Clinton, NJ, 1978-82; NJ Asn Devel Educ, 1980-; coach, Hillsborough NJ Recreation Soccer, 1981-; Boy Scouts Am, 1982-85; Nat Coun Black Am Affairs, 1983-; evaluator, Mid States Asn Cols & Univs, 1986-; chair, Paul Robeson Youth Achievement. **Honors/Awds:** Special Faculty Service Award, Somerset Community Col, 1975; Black Student Union Advisory Service Award, 1975-76; Special Faculty Service & Admin Award, 1976. **Home Addr:** 558 Montgomery Rd, PO Box 43, Hillsborough, NJ 08844-3211, **Home Phone:** (908)369-6478. **Business Addr:** Professor Emeritus of English, Raritan Valley Community College, 118 Lamington Rd, Branchburg, NJ 08876, **Business Phone:** (908)526-1200.

## WILSON, CASSANDRA

Singer. **Personal:** Born Dec 3, 1955, Jackson, MS; daughter of Herman B Fowlkes Jr and Mary McDaniel; married Isaach de Bankole; married Anthony; children: Jeris. **Educ:** Jackson State Univ, BA, mass commun; Millsaps Col, PhD, 2007. **Career:** Albums: Point of View, 1985; Days Aweigh, 1987; Blue Skies, 1988; Jumpworld, 1989; She Who Weeps, 1990; Live, 1991; After the Beginning Again, 1991; Dance to the Drums Again, 1992; Blue Light 'Til Dawn, 1993; New Moon Daughter, 1995; Songbook, 1996; Rendezvous, 1998; Traveling Miles, 1999; Belly of the Sun, 2002; Sings Standards, 2002; Glamoured, 2003; Love Phases Dimensions: From the JMT Years compilation, 2004; Thunderbird, 2006; Loverly, 2008; Closer to You: The Pop Side compilation, 2009; Silver Pony, 2010; Another Country, 2012. Filmography: Junior, 1994; The Score, 2001. **Orgs:** Alpha Kappa Alpha Sorority Inc. **Honors/Awds:** Female Jazz Vocalist of the Year, Down Beat mag, 1994-96; Grammy Award, 1996, 2009; Miles Davis Prize, Montreal Int Jazz Festival, 1999; honorary doctorate, Millsaps Col, 2003; Time Magazine, 2001; Down Beat, 1994-96; Grammy Award, 1996; 2009; Miles Davis prize, 1999; Mississippi Blues Trail, 2010; BET Soul Train Award, 2011. **Business Addr:** Vocalist, Blue Note Records, 150 5th Ave 6th Fl, New York, NY 10001, **Business Phone:** (212)786-8610.

## WILSON, CHANDRA DANETTE

Actor. **Personal:** Born Aug 27, 1969, Houston, TX; children: Joy, Serena & Michael. **Educ:** NY Univ, Tisch Sch Arts, BFA, drama, 1991; Lee Strasberg Theatre Inst. **Career:** Films: Mad Dog & Glory, 1993; Philadelphia, 1993; Lone Star, 1996; Head of State, 2003; Strangers with Candy, 2005; A Single Woman, 2008; Accidental Friendship, 2008; Frankie & Alice, 2010; TV series: "The Cosby Show", 1989; "Law & Order", 1992; "CBS School break Special", 1992; "Cosby", 2000; "Third Watch", 2001; "100 Centre Street", 2001; Bob Patterson, 2001; Sex & the City, 2002; "Queens Supreme", 2003; "Law & Order: Special Victims Unit", 2002-05; "The Sopranos", 2004; "Grey's Anatomy", 2005-14, dir, 2009-14; "Accidental Friendship", 2008; "Private Practice", 2009; Theatres: The Good Times are Killing Me; The Miracle Worker; Paper Moon: the Musical; The Family of Mann; Believing; Little Shop of Horrors. **Honors/Awds:** Theatre World Award for Outstanding Debut Performance; Reel Stars of TexasAward, Houston Chap Women in Film TV, 2006; Satellite Award, 2006; Screen Actors Guild Award, 2007; People's Choice Awards, 2008; Image Award, Nat Asn Advan Colored People, 2007, 2008, 2010; Prism Award, 2009; 2014. **Business Addr:** Actress, c/o William Morris Agency Inc, 151 El Camino Dr, Beverly Hills, CA 90212, **Business Phone:** (310)859-4000.

## WILSON, CHARLES LEE, SR.

Chief executive officer, executive. **Personal:** Born Oct 25, 1941, Atlanta, GA; son of William Fred Sr and Ethel; children: Charles Lee Jr & Angela Y. **Educ:** Bethune Cookman Col, BS, psychol; Temple Univ, MS, coun guid & admin; Rutgers Univ, educ admin. **Career:** Camden NJ Sch Syst, teacher, guid counr; Philadelphia Col Art, registr; Howard Univ, dir admis, Dept Educ, consult; Enterprises New Directions Inc, chief exec officer & pres. **Orgs:** Dist Multicultural Tourism Comt; State Md Minority Adv Comt. **Special Achievements:** Author of numerous reports and publications. **Business Addr:** President, Enterprises for New Directions Inc, 4550 Montgomery Ave Suite 955N, Bethesda, MD 20814, **Business Phone:** (301)469-3301.

## WILSON, DR. CHARLES Z., JR.

Educator, association executive, executive. **Personal:** Born Apr 21, 1929, Greenville, MS; son of Charles Zachary and Ora Lee; married Doris; children: Charles Zachary III, Joyce Lynne, Joanne Catherine & Gary Thomas; married Kelly Freeman; children: Amanda Fox & Walter Bremond. **Educ:** Univ Ill, BS, 1952, PhD, econs & statist, 1956; Carnegie Mellon Univ, attended 1961. **Career:** De Paul Univ, asst prof econs, prof econs, bus & educ, 1959-61; State Univ New York, assoc prof bus, 1961-67, prof econs & bus, 1967-68; Educ Planning Prog, spec asst adminr vice chancellor, 1968-70; Univ Calif Los Angeles, prof mgt & educ, 1968-84, vice chancellor acad prog, 1985-87, prof emer & vice chancellor, currently; Cent News-Wave Publs, LA, chief exec officer, publ & pres, 1985-96; Czand Assocs, Pac Palisades, Calif, pres, founder, managing partner, chief exec officer, 1994-; Wave Comt Newspapers, LA, pres & chief exec officer, 1997-; Mayor's Charter Reform Comn, comnr. **Orgs:** Bd dir, Black Econ Res Ctr New York, 1970-; AAAS; bd trustee, Teachers Inst & Annuity Asn Col Retirement Equities Fund, 1971-; chmn, bd trustees, Joint Cntgr Comm Studies, 1971-72; Los Angeles Co Mus Art, 1971-; Adv Bd Educ & Human Resources, Rand Corp, 1972-; pres adv coun, Minority Bus Enterprise, 1972-76; UNA Panel Advan US Japan Rels, 1972-; consult, Nat Inst Educ, Dept HEW, 1973-; Am Educ Res Asn; Inst Mgt Sci; Am Econs Asn; Am Asn Univ Profs; founder, Nat Econ Asn; consult, City Los Angeles; consult, MTA; consult, Ford Found; consult, Ewing Marion Kauffman Found; bd mem, Los Angeles County Mus Arts; bd mem, Golden State Minority Found; bd mem, Los Angeles Philharmonic Adv Comt; bd mem, Mayor's 2000 Comt. **Honors/Awds:** American Men of Science Recipient, Am Coun Educ, 1967-68; Junior Children Outstanding Young Man of the Year, 1965. **Special Achievements:** Published book: "Organizational Decision-Making"; "Crossing Organizational Boundaries By Choice", 2007. **Home Addr:** 1053 Tellem Dr, Pacific Palisades, CA 90272-2243, **Home Phone:** (310)454-0463. **Business Addr:** Professor Emeritus, Vice Chancellor, University of California, 1147 Murphy Hall, Los Angeles, CA 90024-1436, **Business Phone:** (310)825-7906.

## WILSON, CHARLIE KENT (CHARLES KENT WILSON)

Singer. **Personal:** Born Jan 29, 1953, Tulsa, OK; son of Oscar and Irma; married Mahin. **Career:** The Gap Band, 1972-2010.Albums: Magician Holiday, 1974; The Gap Band, 1977; The Gap Band II, 1979; The Gap Band III, 1980; The Gap Band IV, 1982; The Gap Band V, 1983; The Gap Band VI, 1985; The Gap Band VII, 1986; Straight from the Heart, 1987; Rap House, 1989; Round Trip, 1989; You Turn My Life Around, 1992; Best of the Gap Band, 1994; Testimony, 1994; Ain't Nothin' but a Party, 1995; I'm Gonna Git You Sucka, 1998; Bridging the Gap, 2000; Bridging The Gap, 2004; Charlie, Last Name Wilson, 2005; Magic, 2005; Uncle Charlie, 2009; Just Charlie, 2010; Love, Charlie, 2013; Forever Charlie, 2015; Interscope Recs, rec artist, currently. **Business Addr:** Recording Artist, Interscope Records, 2220 Colorado Ave, Santa Monica, CA 90404-3574, **Business Phone:** (310)865-1000.

## WILSON, CHRISTOPHER A.

Journalist. **Personal:** Born Mar 22, 1961, Shelby, NC; married Gwendolyn; children: Evan & Grant. **Educ:** Winston Salem State Univ, bus admin, 1983. **Career:** Ebony Investor.com, ed; Wall Streetwise Newsletter, ed, currently. **Orgs:** Regional pres, Cent NC Investors Coun; founder, New Freedom Investment Club. **Honors/Awds:** Investor of the Year, New Freedom Inv Group, 1991; Growth Stock of Year Winner, NAIC, 1992. **Special Achievements:** Publisher of 20 Most Commonly Asked Questions For Investment Clubs. **Business Addr:** Head, Wall Streetwise Newsletter, PO Box 12451, Durham, NC 27709, **Business Phone:** (800)419-1318.

## WILSON, CLARENCE A.

Executive. **Personal:** Born Aug 27, 1943, Talladega, AL; son of Lara Montgomery Pruitt (deceased) and Philip Monroe (deceased); married Sue Carol Cottman; children: Brian & Eric. **Educ:** Ind Univ, Bloomington, Ind, BS, bus mkt, 1967, MBA, finance, 1981. **Career:** Director (retired); Marathon Oil Co, Findlay, Ohio, sr planner, 1967-69; Du Pont Co, Wilmington, Del, dir finance, 1981; York-James City-Williamsburg NAACP. **Orgs:** Kappa Alpha Psi Frat, 1965-; Fin Exec Inst, 1989-; Dean Bus Sch Adv Bd, Ind Univ, 1990-; bd dir, Neighborhood House, 1990; bd trustee mem, pres, Williamsburg Community Health Found; pres, York-James City-Williamsburg NAACP. **Home Addr:** 121 Huntercombe, Williamsburg, VA 23188-7431, **Home Phone:** (757)229-1076.

## WILSON, CLARENCE S., JR.

Lawyer, educator. **Personal:** Born Oct 22, 1945, Brooklyn, NY; son of Clarence S Sr and Thelma Louise Richards; married Helena Chapellin Iribarren. **Educ:** Williams Col, BA, 1967; Foreign Serv Inst US, attended 1969; Northwestern Univ, Sch Law, JD, 1974. **Career:** US Dept St, Caracas, Venezuela, third secy, vice coun, 1969-71; Friedman & Koven, assoc atty, 1974-76; Us Gypsum Co, legaldept, 1976-79; sole practr, 1979-81; Law Offices Jewel S Lafontant, partner, 1981-83; Chicago-Kent Col Law, adj prof, 1981-94; Boodell, Sears, Sugrue, Giambalvo & Crowley, assoc atty, 1983-84; pvt practr & coun, 1984-; Columbia Col, adj prof, 1996-2000; Law Off Clarence S. Wilson Jr, lawyer, currently. **Orgs:** Trustee, Chicago Symphony Orchestra, 1987-96; bd mem, Implementation Cmsn Lawyers Trust Fund Ill, 1983-85; Art Inst Chicago, Comm Twentieth Century Painting, Sculpture, Develop, 1989-, trustee, 1990-; Citizens Info Serv Ill; bd mem, Harold Wash Found, 1989-92; bd mem, Northwestern Univ Sch Law Alumni Asn; gov bd, Ill Arts Coun, panel, Estab Regional Arts Inst; Ill rep, Arts Midwest; Chicago & Cook County Bar Asn; trustee, Merit Music Prog, 1991-96; Chicago Dept Cult Affairs, Mayor's Adv Bd; Bd Gov, Sch Art Inst Chicago; vis comt mem, Dept Music & Comt Visual Arts, Univ Chicago, 1992-; Ministry Cult, Repub Venezuela, spec legal coun; DuSable Mus African Am Hist; vice chmn, 1994-97, Jazz Mus Chicago. **Special Achievements:** Author, "Visual Arts and the Law," in Law and the Arts--Art and the Law, 1979; author of several copyright/art law articles. **Business Addr:** Lawyer, Law Office of Clarence S Wilson Jr, 25 E Wash Suite 1500, Chicago, IL 60602-1708, **Business Phone:** (312)984-0399.

**WILSON, CLEO FRANCINE**
Association executive, businessperson. **Personal:** Born May 7, 1943, Chicago, IL; daughter of Frances Page Watson and Cleo Chancey; children: David Patrice Silbar (deceased) & SuLyn Silbar. **Educ:** Univ Ill, Chicago, BA, Eng, 1976. **Career:** Playboy Enterprises Inc, supv, 1976-82, grants mgr, 1982-84, exec dir, 1982-2008, dir pub affairs, 1989, vpres pub affairs, 2000; Playboy Found, exec dir; Intuit: Ctr Intuitive & Outsider Art, pres, 2002-06, exec dir, 2006-12; Hugh M Hefner First Amendment Awards, consult, 2011-. **Orgs:** Vpres, Donors Forum Chicago, 1986-88; secy, Chicago Women Philanthrophy, 1986-87, task force, Ill Interdisciplinary AIDS Adv Coun, 1986-87; pres, Emergency Loan Fund, 1987-89; chmn, Chicago Funders Concerned AIDS, 1989-99; founder, Intuit: Ctr Intuitive & Outsider Art; adv coun, Chicago Dept Cult Affairs, 1988-90; pres, AIDS Found Chicago; vpres, Am Civil Liberties Union Ill; bd dir, Nat Coalition Against Censorship, 1997-2000; Planned Parenthood, Chicago, 2000- . **Honors/Awds:** Kizzy Image Award, Black Woman Hall of Fame, 1984; Chicago's Up & Coming, Dollars & Sense Magazine, 1985; Phenomenal Woman Award, Expo Today's Black Woman, 1997; Handy L Lindsey Jr Award, 2004; Edwin A. Rothschild Award, 2006; Friend for Life, Howard Brown Med Ctr; Community Engagement, Community Service, and Community Organizing Award, Univ Ill Chicago, 2011. **Home Addr:** 6571 N Glenwood Ave, Chicago, IL 60626-5121, **Home Phone:** (773)743-2407. **Business Addr:** Consultant, Hugh M Hefner First Amendment Awards, 10236 Charing Cross Rd, Los Angeles, CA 90024.

**WILSON, DANTON THOMAS**
Editor. **Personal:** Born Dec 21, 1958, Houston, TX; son of Thomas Henry and Ann Elizabeth Briscoe; married Janis A; children: SeKou J, Khari T & Ayanna I. **Educ:** Grambling State Univ, Grambling, BA, 1981; Wayne State Univ, JD, 1989. **Career:** Detroit Free Press, Detroit, reporter, 1981; Mich Chronicle, Detroit, reporter, 1982-86, exec ed, 1987; City Detroit Pub Info, Detroit, publicist, 1986-87; Detroit News, ed staff, 1989-. **Orgs:** Black Law Studs Asn, 1985-90; Black United Fund Ann Dinner Comt, 1989-90; chmn, Orchard's C's Serv Media Asn, 1990-; bd, Be Best You Can Be Org, 1990-; bd, Rosa Parks Scholar Fund, 1990-. **Honors/Awds:** James Wadsworth Community Serv Award, Fel Chapel United Church, 1987; 1st place Community Serv Award, 1986. **Home Addr:** 18050 Muirland St, Detroit, MI 48221-2755, **Home Phone:** (313)863-1454.

**WILSON, DANYELL ELAINE**
Military leader. **Personal:** Born Jul 16, 1974, Montgomery, AL; daughter of Shirley Rucks. **Educ:** Northern Va Community Col. **Career:** AUS Mil Police Co, 3rd U.S. Inf, mil police officer, sargent, 1993-98; Walter Reed Army Med Ctr, med supply specialist, 1998-. **Honors/Awds:** Army Achievement Medal, 1996; Tomb Guard Badge, 1997; Army Accomadation Medal; Good Conduct Medal; Silver emblem. **Special Achievements:** First African American female to receive the "Tomb Guard Identification Badge," its the second most least awarded military badge, 1997; First African American female to earn the prestigious badge and guard the Tomb of the Unknowns; She was the second woman to receive the privilege of wearing the sacred symbol. **Home Addr:** 2077 Walden Ct, Bryans Rd, MD 20616, **Home Phone:** (301)375-7759. **Business Addr:** Sergeant, HQCO Walter Reed Army Medical Center, Washington, DC 20307, **Business Phone:** (202)782-5991.

**WILSON, DR. DAVID**
Educator. **Personal:** Born Nov 2, 1954, Thomaston, AL; son of Henry and Minnie; children: Nyere. **Educ:** Tuskegee Univ, BS, polit sci, 1977, MS, educ, 1979; Harvard Univ, EdM, educ planning & admin, 1984, EdD, admin, planning & social policy, 1987. **Career:** Res & Develop Inst Philadelphia, proj dir, 1979-82; Ky State Univ, exec asst, vpres bus affairs, 1984-85; Woodrow Wilson Nat Fel Found, 1985-88; Rutgers Univ, assoc provost, 1988-94; Auburn Univ, vpres univ outreach, assoc provost, 1994-2006; Ayers & Assoc, consult; Univ Wis Col, chancellor, 2006-10; Univ Wis Ext, chancellor, 2006-10; Morgan State Univ, pres, 2010-. **Orgs:** Alpha Phi Alpha Fraternity Inc, 1975-; Woodrow Wilson Fel Woodrow Wilson Nat Fel Found, 1984-85; Optimist Club Lower Bucks, 1986-91; bd dir, Afro-Am Hist & Cult Mus, 1988-; Walt Whitman Asn, 1988-; Princeton Ballet, 1988-; Kellogg Fel WK Kellogg Found, 1988-92; bd dir, United Way Cent Md; gov bd, Md Longitudinal Data Syst Ctr; Md Humanities Coun; Nat Inst Stand & Technol Vis Comt Advan Technol; Md Cybersecurity Coun; boards dirs, Greater Baltimore Comt; Asn Pub & Land Grant Univs; pres, Historically Black Cols & Univs, 2011. **Honors/Awds:** One of America's Best & Brightest Young Business & Professional Men, Dollars & Sense Mag, 1987; Certificate of Appreciation, Gov Ala, 1987; Certificate of Appreciation, Gov Tenn, 1988; Legacy Award, Auburn Univ, 2005; Top 100 leaders in higher education, Am Asn Higher Educ, 1998; Influential Marylanders, Daily Rec Newspaper, 2011; Outstanding Leadership Award, Univ Ala, 2011. **Special Achievements:** First African-American vice president at Auburn University; first chancellor to lead two UW System institutions simultaneously. **Home Addr:** PO Box 2053, Auburn, AL 36830, **Home Phone:** (334)844-5700. **Business Addr:** President, Morgan State University, Rm 400 Truth Hall, Baltimore, MD 21251, **Business Phone:** (443)885-3333.

**WILSON, DAVID**
Chief executive officer, founder (originator). **Career:** HyLife Productions LLC, prin, chief exec officer, founder & dir, 1999-. **Business Addr:** Founder, Director, HyLife Productions LLC, 44 W 24th St, New York, NY 10010, **Business Phone:** (727)821-3303.

**WILSON, DEBRA (DEBRA RENEE WILSON SKELETON)**
Actor, comedian. **Personal:** Born Apr 26, 1962, Queens, NY; married Cliff Skelton. **Educ:** Syracuse Univ. **Career:** Pre-School teacher, Sunnyside, NY; Films: Cracking Up, 1994; New Jersey Drive, 1995; Blue in the Face, 1995; Girl 6, 1996; Asylum, 1997; Soulmates, 1997; B.A.P.S, 1997; Grid lock'd, 1997; Sleeping Together, 1997; Star Trek the Experience: The Klingon Encounter, 1998; Rubbernecking, 2000; Jane White Is Sick & Twisted, 2002; Skin Deep, 2003; Target, 2004; That's So Raven, 2004; Nine Lives, 2004; The Chosen One, 2004; CSI: Crime Scene Investigation, 2004; Knight to F4, 2005; Bringing Up BayBay, writer & actor, 2005; Rockin' Meera, 2006; Shut Up & Shoot!, 2006; Mandingo in a Box, 2006; Scary Movie 4, 2006; Whitepaddy, 2006; Danny Roane: First Time Director, 2006; The Adventures of Brer Rabbit, 2006; Cordially Invited, 2007; Super Sweet 16: The Movie, 2007; If I Had Known I Was a Genius, 2007; Cuttin Da Mustard, 2008; Friends & Lovers: The Ski Trip 2, 2008; Knight to F4, 2009; The Haunted World of El Superbeasto, 2009; Avatar, 2009; Perfect Combination, 2010; Hoodwinked Too! Hood vs. Evil, 2011; Division III: Football's Finest, 2011; Back Then, 2012; Midlife, 2013; Cordially Invited- the Wedding Day of Alton & Kenya, 2013; Jungle Shuffle, 2014; Knock 'em Dead, 2014; Naked Angel, 2014; 10 Year Plan, 2014; Untold, 2014. TV series: "Uptown Comedy Club", writer, 1992-93; "New York Undercover", 1995; "Mad TV", 1995-2007; "Girl 6", 1996; "Asylum", 1997; "Grid lock'd", 1997; "BAPS", 1997; "Soulmates", 1997; "Sleeping Together", 1997; "Star Trek: Deep Space Nine", 1998; "The MrPotato Head Show", 1998; "Family Guy", 2000-11; "The Proud Family", 2002-03; "Clone High", 2002-03; "The Parkers", 2003; "Hawks & Handsaws", 2004; "CSI: Crime Scene Investigation", 2004-07; "Without a Trace", 2004; "That's So Raven", 2004; "I'm with Her", 2004, "Spa Day Afternoon", 2004; "You're Fired", 2005, "Studio House", 2005; "Second Time Around", 2005; "American Dad!", 2005, "Amazing Animal Inventions", 2005, "In Justice", 2006; City Girls, 2007; "Reno 911!", 2008; "Terminator: The Sarah Connor Chronicles", 2008; "90210", 2009; "Scrubs", 2009; "Friends & Lovers", 2010; "The Fresh Beat Band", 2011; "2 Broke Girls", 2013; "The First Family", 2013; "Save Me", 2013; "Mad", 2013; "Super-Pets", 2013-14; "Fatal Acquittal", 2014; GSN Live Co-host, currently; CSI: Crime Scene Investigation, 2004; Knight to F4, 2005; Bringing Up BayBay, writer & actor, 2005; Rockin' Meera, 2006; Shut Up & Shoot!, 2006; Mandingo in a Box, 2006; Scary Movie 4, 2006; Whitepaddy, 2006; Danny Roane: First Time Director, 2006; The Adventures of Brer Rabbit, 2006; Cordially Invited, 2007; Super Sweet 16: The Movie, 2007; If I Had Known I Was a Genius, 2007; Cuttin Da Mustard, 2008; Friends & Lovers: The Ski Trip 2, 2008. **Honors/Awds:** Audience Award, San Francisco Int Lesbian & Gay Film Festival, 2003. **Special Achievements:** First African-American woman performer on "Mad TV", 1995. **Business Addr:** Actress, c/o William Morris Agency Inc, 1325 Avenue of the Americas, New York, NY 10019, **Business Phone:** (212)586-5100.

**WILSON, DR. DONALD**
Dean (education), physician. **Personal:** Born Jan 1, 1936?, Worcester, MA. **Educ:** Harvard Univ; Tufts Univ, MD. **Career:** Univ Ill Med Sch, prof, chief gastroenterol; State Univ NY, Health Sci Ctr, Dept Med, prof & chmn; nat advocate, equality in health care & med educ; Univ Hosp, physician-in-chief; Kings Co Hosp Ctr, Brooklyn, physician-in-chief; Univ MD, Sch of Med, dean, 1991-2006, dir prog minority health & health disparities educ & res, dean emeritus, currently; Howard Univ Wash, DC, sr vpres health sci, 2007-10. **Orgs:** Md Emergency Med Serv bd, 1993-; chmn, Md Health Care Comn, 1994-04; chmn, AAMC Coun Deans; Inst Med Nat Acad Sci; co-founder, Asn Acad Minority Physicians, 1986; chair, NIH Digestive Dis Adv Comt; chair, FDA Gastrointestinal Drugs Adv Comt; chair, Agency for Health Care Policy and Res Adv Coun; Am Clin and Climat Asn; chmn, Asn Am Med Col, 2004; bd dir, vpres, Alpha Omega Alpha, 2004-11. **Business Addr:** Dean Emeritus, University of Maryland, School of Medicine, Rm 14-029 Bressler Res Bldg HSFII S441 655 W Baltimore St, Baltimore, MD 21201-1559, **Business Phone:** (410)706-7410.

**WILSON, DONALD K., JR.**
Lawyer, educator. **Personal:** Born Mar 5, 1954, Lancaster, PA; son of Donald Sr and Gloria; married Lauren, Sep 3, 1977; children: Donald Ray, Tameka, Veronica & Matthew. **Educ:** Univ Southern Calif, BS, 1976; NY Law Sch, JD, 1979. **Career:** Mason & Sloane, assoc atty, 1979-83; Quincy Jones Productions, pres, 1984-89; Law Offices Johnnie L Cochran, coun, 1992-2000; Law Offices Donald K Wilson, Jr, 2000-; Univ Calif Los Angeles, guest lect; Univ Southern Calif, guest lect; OBN Holdings Inc, sr vpres. **Orgs:** Nat Bar Asn; Black Entertainment & Sports Lawyers Asn; Nat Asn Advan Colored People; trustee, First AME Church; pres, Eclectic Entertainment Inc. **Honors/Awds:** Community Service Award, LA Entertainment Community; Outstanding Young Men Am. **Special Achievements:** Executive producer of Frank Sinatra documentary, Portrait of an Album; featured panelist for various entertainment and sports law symposiums; published "The Effect of Termination Rights on Buying and Selling Copyrights", The Los Angeles Daily Journal; "Settlements in the Entertainment Industry", published in Los Angeles Daily Journal; selected participant, Oxford Round table, Oxford university, Oxford, England. **Home Addr:** 4220 Angeles Vista Blvd, Los Angeles, CA 90008-4404, **Home Phone:** (323)290-0248. **Business Addr:** Attorney at Law, Law Offices of Donald K Wilson Jr, 4322 Wilshire Blvd Suite 200, Los Angeles, CA 90010-3792, **Business Phone:** (323)982-7087.

**WILSON, HON. DONALD P.**
Manager, association executive. **Career:** Improved Benevolent Protective Order Elks World, grand exalted ruler, 2003; Elks Lodge, mgr, currently. **Business Addr:** Manager, Elks Lodge, 101 HR Reynolds Dr, Winton, NC 27986, **Business Phone:** (252)358-7661.

**WILSON, DR. DONELLA JOYCE**
Educator, administrator. **Personal:** Born Jul 28, 1951, Milwaukee, WI; daughter of Paul Lawrence and Emily Frenchie Bailey. **Educ:** Johnston Col, Redlands Univ, BA, 1973; Tex Southern Univ, MS, 1977; Purdue Univ, MS, 1979, PhD, molecular biol, 1981. **Career:** Purdue Univ, res asst, 1977-81; Wash Univ, res assoc, 1981; Harvard Sch Dent Med, assoc oral pathol, 1981-83; Radcliffe Col, Bunting fel, 1983-85; vis prof, Univ Mass, Boston, 1983-84; Meharry Med Col, asst prof, 1985-91, assoc prof, 1991-95; Bio Career Ctr, columnist, currently; Res Systs & Commun Int LLC, pres, 2011-. **Orgs:** AAAS, 1982-; Am Soc Cell Biol, 1983-; Harvard Health Prof Admis Comn, 1985; Fedn Am Socs Exp Biol, 1986-; Beta Kappa Chi; Beta Beta Beta; sci prog dir, Dept Res, Am Cancer Soc, dir, Res Prom & Commun, 1993-2009. **Home Addr:** 300 Cross Timbers Dr, Nashville, TN 37221, **Home Phone:** (615)646-7424. **Business Addr:** Director of Research Promotion & Communication, American Cancer Society, 1599 Clifton Rd, Atlanta, GA 30329, **Business Phone:** (404)329-7717.

**WILSON, DONNA SIMS**
President (organization). **Educ:** Yale Univ, BS, polit sci, 1983. **Career:** Lehman Bros Kuhn Loeb, corp finance; Bear Stearns, vpres, 1985-89; MR Beal & Co, exec vpres & head equity sales & trading; Fed Finance Group at MR Beal & Co, sr vpres & dir; Loop Capital Markets, founder & managing dir, 1997-2005; MR Beal & Co., pres, 2005-11; CastleOak Securities, exec vpres, 2011-. **Orgs:** Nat Asn Securities Professionals, Legis Comt, chair; Kohl C's Mus Greater Chicago, vice chmn; John G Shedd Aquarium Bd Trustees; Econ Club Chicago; Execs' Club Chicago. **Honors/Awds:** "Black Enterprise", 75 Most Powerful Women in Business, 2010; National Association of Securities Professionals (NASP) Joyce Johnson Award, Honoree, 2010. **Business Addr:** 222 W Adams St Suite 1900, Chicago, IL 60606, **Business Phone:** (312)577-2500.

**WILSON, EARL LAWRENCE**
Law enforcement officer, consultant. **Personal:** Born Jul 16, 1923, Philadelphia, PA; son of James R and Helen. **Educ:** Villanova Univ, criminal justice courses, attended 1973; PA State Univ, cert, 1970; St Joseph Univ. **Career:** Law enforment officer (retired), consultant; Philadelphia Prison Syst, corrections officer, sgt, lt, capt, dep warden, prison security coord, warden, 1951-79; corrections consult, currently; Pub Health Mgt Corp, Bridge, bd dir, currently. **Orgs:** Examr, Pa Civil Serv Comn, 1974-; Pa Warden's Asn, 1978-; Am Correctional Asn, 1978-; consult & adv, Criminal Justice Syst; Pa Prison Wardens Asn; pres, bd dir, Therapeut Ctr Fox Chase; Am Jail Asn; Pa County Prison Wardens Asn. **Honors/Awds:** Lifetime Achievement Award, PA Prison Wardens Asn, 1993. **Special Achievements:** Article on crime published in Ebony Magazine, 1979. **Business Addr:** Corrections Consultant, 700 Lower State Rd, Horsham, PA 19044, **Business Phone:** (215)542-6859.

**WILSON, ERNEST L, II.** See Obituaries Section.

**WILSON, F. LEON**
Writer. **Personal:** Born Sep 20, 1953, Akron, OH. **Educ:** Ohio State Univ, BS, 1975, MBA, 1983. **Career:** The Black Agenda, Regional coordr, 1983-; Code One Communs Inc, prin agent, 1990-, sr proj mgr, new bus mgr, pres & chief exec officer, currently; Central Control Systems, publisher/principal writer, 2009-; Author: "Dream & Wings", CCS Press, 1994; "White Supremacy: Sources & Uses", CCS Press, 1995; "The Net of My Conversations", Code One Communication Inc, 2000; "Black Pioneers of the Internet". **Orgs:** Chmn, Ams Against Aparid, 1985-87; Nat Black Wholistic Soc, 1989-; corresp secy, bd mem, Nat Black Pub Soc; US Chess Fedn; founder, Chess Learn; nat dir, Black Agenda; chairperson, Black Male Black Female Relationships. **Business Addr:** President, Chief Executive Officer, Code One Communications Inc, 2785 Castlewood Rd, Columbus, OH 43209-3140, **Business Phone:** (614)338-0321.

**WILSON, FLOYD EDWARD, JR.**
Government official, executive director, teacher. **Personal:** Born Nov 22, 1935, Lake Charles, LA; son of Floyd Edward Sr and Leada R; married Dorothy Lyons; children: J Keith & Tanya R Derryck M. **Educ:** Dillard Univ, BA, 1959. **Career:** Dc Sch Syst, Biol/Chem teacher, 1962-72; Hallmark Acad C Ctr, owner & admin, 1968-78; Glenarden MD, councilman vice mayor, 1969-74; Prince George's County Coun, councilman, 1974, Econ Develop Corp, dir; Md Dept Human Resources, Social Serv Admin, dir, 1999; Minority Bus Opportunities Comn, exec dir, 2004; Prince George's County Exec Jack B. Johnson, spec asst, 2010-. **Orgs:** PG Bd Dir Social Serv, 1976-; vice chrmn, NACO Criminal Justice Comn, 1983-; chrmn, COG Air Qual Comn, 1984; mem Alpha Phi Alpha Frat; life mem, Nat Asn Advan Colored People; Prince George's Women's Comn; chmn & bd dir, Prince George's State Bank; chmn & vice chmn, Air Qual Planning Comt; Reorganization Wash's Nat; Dulles Int Airports; Gov's Spec Comn Prof Sports & Econ; United Community Against Poverty; Am Auto Asn Potomac Adv Bd. **Special Achievements:** First African American Elected to Prince George's County Counc, 1974. **Home Addr:** 8909 Pkwy, Cheverly, MD 20785, **Home Phone:** (301)341-1489. **Business Addr:** Director, Minority Business Development Division, 1400 McCormick Drive Suite 282, Largo, MD 20774, **Business Phone:** (301)883-6480.

**WILSON, DR. FRANK FREDRICK, III**
Physician, obstetrician, gynecologist. **Personal:** Born Jun 14, 1936, Oklahoma City, OK; son of Frank F III and Thelma Boyd; married Jacquelyn; children: Frank IV, Nathan, Yolanda & Coreen. **Educ:** Fisk Univ, BA, 1956; Univ Okla; Howard Univ Sch Med, MD, 1961. **Career:** Univ Mo, Gen Hosp & Med Ctr, intern spec educ, 1961-65; Truman Med Ctr W, internship, 1961-62, resident, obstet & gynec, 1962-65; Physician Obstet-Gynec; Univ Okla, Sch Med, clin assoc prof, currently; pvt pract, currently; fel Univ Okla; Okla Univ Med Ctr, physician. **Orgs:** Dir Bd, Park Comnr, 1971-74; Eastside YMCA, 1972-73; Collins Garden Housing Corp, 1972-74; Okla City Obstet-Gynec Soc, sec treas, 1973-74, exec bd, 1974-77, pres, 1975-76, vpres, 1976-77, pres, 1977-; Touchstone Montessori Sch, 1973-74; Okla County Med Soc, Okla State Med Asn, AMA, Nat Med Asn; dipl, Nat Bd Med Examiners; Am Fertility Soc; Am Bd Obstet-Gynec; fel Am Col Obstet-Gynec; Central Asn Obstet-Gynec; chmn, admission bd, Univ Okla Sch Med; bd trustees, OU Med Ctr, 2005-. **Special Achievements:** First African American to receive fellowship from

University of Oklahoma. **Home Addr:** 5408 N Stonewall Dr, Oklahoma City, OK 73111. **Business Addr:** Physician, Oklahoma University Medical Center, 1200 Everett Dr 4th Fl, Oklahoma City, OK 73104, **Business Phone:** (405)271-3900.

### WILSON, GRADY DEMOND

Evangelist, actor, clergy. **Personal:** Born Oct 13, 1946, Valdosta, GA; married Cicely Loise Johnston; children: 6. **Educ:** Hunter Col. **Career:** Sanford & Son, actor, 1972-77; Demond Wilson Ministries, evangelist; Films: All in the Family, 1971; The Organization, 1971; Mission: Impossible, 1971; Dealing: Or the Berkeley-to-Boston Forty-Brick Lost-Bag Blues, 1972; Sanford and Son, 1977; Baby, I'm Back, 1978; Full Moon High, 1981; The Love Boat, 1981; The New Odd Couple, 1982; Me and the Kid, 1993; Hammerlock, 2000; Biography, 2000; American Soundtrack: Rhythm, Love and Soul, 2003; Praise the Lord, 2004; Girlfriends, 2005; Faith Ties, ordained minister, 1984. **Orgs:** Founder & chief exec officer, Restoration House Am. **Special Achievements:** Books: Grady D.Wilson and Avaneda D. Hobbs, 1998; The New Age Millennium: An Expose of Symbols, 1998; Slogans and Hidden Agendas, 1998; John Neuman Smith, 1999; Lil' Mowande, 1999; Mr. Fish Takes a Wife, 1999. "The O'Reilly Factor", playing Lynn's biological father, 2009; Second Banana: The Bittersweet Memoirs of the Sanford & Son Years, 2009. **Business Addr:** Evangelist, Demond Wilson Ministries, Suite C 322, Laguna Hills, CA 92654, **Business Phone:** (714)582-2249.

### WILSON, DR. HARRISON B.

Executive, educator. **Personal:** Born Apr 21, 1925, Amsterdam, NY; married Lucy; children: Benjamin, Harrison, John, Richard, Jennifer & Marquarite; married Anna. **Educ:** Ky State Univ, BS; Ind Univ, MS, PhD, DHS, health sci & admin. **Career:** Educator, executive (retired); Norfolk State Col, pres, 1975; Jackson State Univ, prof, adminr, head basketball coach, 1951-60, chmn dept health & phys educ, 1960-67; Fisk Univ, exec asst pres; Tenn State Univ, chmn & prof health & phys educ. **Orgs:** Bd dir, Va Nat Bank; lay adv bd, DePaul Hosp; Va State Adv Coun Voc Educ; bd dir, Health Welfare Rec Planning Coun; Alpha Kappa Mu Fraternity; bd dir, Va Health, Welfare & Recreation Planning Coun; Kappa Alpha Psi Fraternity. **Honors/Awds:** Honoree, Dominion, 1997, "Male Most Likely to Succeed", "Most Scholarly Athlete", sr class; KY State Univ. **Special Achievements:** Old Dominion University as one of their Strong Men and Women Excellence in Leadership series. **Home Addr:** 416 Mill Stone Rd, Chesapeake, VA 23322-4355, **Home Phone:** (757)482-2760. **Business Addr:** President, Norfolk State University, 700 Park Ave, Norfolk, VA 23504-8003, **Business Phone:** (757)823-8600.

### WILSON, HAZEL FORROW SIMMONS

Executive, educator, association executive. **Personal:** Born Jun 21, 1927, Houston, TX; daughter of Sam W and Summie Lee Whittington; married Jerrimiah; children: David Jerome & James (deceased); married Jesse L. **Educ:** Prairie View A&M Col, attended 1946; Tex So Univ, BA, 1954, MA, 1974. **Career:** Educator (retired); BH Grimes Elem Sch, teacher, 1954-59; J R Reynolds Elem Sch, teacher, 1959-68; Camp Fire Girls, field dir, 1960-68; G.W. Carver Elem. Sch, teacher, 1968-72; Ft Worth Independant Pub Sch, Maude I Logan Elem, first Black coordr reading improv ctr, 1972-; Springdale Elem Sch, Chap I resource teacher. **Orgs:** So reg dir, Amicae, 1960-64; charter mem, Houston League Negro Bus & Prof Women's Club, 1962-68; exec secy, Houston Classroom Teachers Asn, 1964-66; dir, Southern region Zeta Phi Beta, 1965-72; nat trustee, Zeta Phi Beta, 1972-76; chmn, Zeta Phi Beta So Reg Exec Bd, 1972-78; charter & first vpres, Gr Ft Worth Area Negro Bus & Prof Women's Club, 1975-81; nat dir, Stork's Nest Proj Zeta Phi Beta, 1976-82; pres, Kappa Silhouettes, 1976-80; Tex State Teachers Asn; Tex Classroom Teacher's Asn; Ft Worth Classroom Teachers Asn; YWCA, YMCA; Golden life mem, Zeta Phi Beta; ruling elder, St Peter Presb Church, 1980-87; pres, prin, Psi Zeta Chap Zeta Phi Beta Sor, 1981-; pres, Greater Ft Worth Area Negro Bus & Prof Women, 1981-84; sponsor, Zeta Amicae, 1981-; pres, Zeta Chap, 1981-93; presbytery, fin secy, St Mark Cumberland Presby Church, 1986-. **Honors/Awds:** Outstanding Service Award, Tex Southern Univ, 1962, 1963; Zeta of the Year, 1964; Five Years Service Award, Zeta Amicae, 1965; Outstanding Service, Zeta Phi Beta, 1965-72; Southern Regional Zeta of the Year, 1974; March Dimes Volume Service Award, 1974-75; First National Zeta Phi Beta Legacy Award, 1976; Lambda Zeta Service Award, 1984; Phi Beta Sigma Zeta of the Year, 1986; Psi Zeta's Zeta of the Year Award, 1987; Graduate Leadership Award, Phi Beta Sigma/Zeta Phi Beta, 1988; Citizen of the Year, Omega Psi Phi, 1996; Wind Beneath Our Wings Award, Phi Beta Sigma, 1997; 45 Years Extraordinary Service Award, ZPB, 1998; Phenom Woman Community Volunteer Award, ZPB, 1998; Outstanding Leadership Award, Bus & Prof Women, 2000; Outstanding Woman of Ft Worth Volunteer Award, Ft Worth Comm Status Women, 2000; Nat Volunteer Service Award, Nat Bus & Prof Women's Club, 2001; Ft Worth Citizen of the Month, 2001; Named Honor: "The Hazel Wilson Award". **Home Addr:** 2801 Sarah Jane Lane, Ft Worth, TX 76119-4723, **Home Phone:** (817)881-9594. **Business Addr:** Presbytery, Mt. Pelier Presbyterian Church, 4839 NC 130 W, Rowland, NC 28383, **Business Phone:** (910)422-8226.

### WILSON, DR. HELEN TOLSON

Executive. **Personal:** Born New Franklin, MO; daughter of A A Tolson; married Jesse. **Educ:** Kans City Conserv Music; Dale Carnegie Inst Charm & Voice, grad med tech; Mich Univ; Wayne State Univ, BA, humanities, 1957; Urban Bible Col, Detroit, MI, DH, 1984. **Career:** Executive (retired); KC Young Matrons, pres, founder, 1939; Detroit Soc Charm Sch, dir, 1973-; US Govt, acct tech, 26 yrs; DSACE Coord Coun Arts, pres, founder. **Orgs:** Founder, ZONTA Bus & Prof Women's Club, 1944; presidency elder, ME Med Conf, Kans City dist, 1954-; chmn, CineramaFashions Ford's Auditorium, 1957; gen chrmn, dir, organizer, Alpha Theta Chap, 1960; gen chrmn, Detroit Urban League 4th Ann Gala Dinner Ball, 1968; chmn Nat Founders Day Gamma Phi Delta Sor, 1969-; founder, pres, dance coordr CounArts, 1972-85; pres, founder, Youth Assembly Detroit Urban League, 1973-78; bd trustee, Gamma Phi Delta Sor; gen chrmn & dir, Gamma Phi Delta Sor's Exec Staff; gen chrmn, dir publicity, N Region Gamma Phi Delta Sr Inc; nat boule chmn, Gamma Phi Delta Sor Inc; Wheatley Provident Hosp Aux; dir, Civic Fashion Show; supr, KC MO HS Press. **Home Addr:** 2278 W Philadelphia 2nd Fl, Detroit, MI 48206, **Home Phone:** (313)895-7811.

### WILSON, HENRY, JR.

Executive. **Personal:** Born Nov 10, 1938, Taylor, TX; married Carrie L Twyman; children: Peggy Annette & Pamela Ann. **Educ:** Univ Cincinnati, engineering, 1968. **Career:** Cincinnati Water Work, engr tech, 1957-64; Kaizer Engrs, engr, 1964-68; Turner Construct Co, engr, 1968-71; Wilson & Asn Arch & Engrs, pres, 1971-. **Orgs:** Nat Soc Prof Engrs, 1968-; dir, Hamilton County State Bank, 1980-; trustee, Univ Cincinnati Found, 1981-; secy, Zoning Bd Appeals Silverton, 1980-; pastor, Cornerstone missionary Baptist Church, 1984-; instr, Cornerstone Bible Inst, 1985; trustee, Greater Cincinnati C C, 1985-88. **Home Addr:** 6737 Elwynne Dr, Cincinnati, OH 45236, **Home Phone:** (513)791-6417. **Business Addr:** President, Wilson & Association Inc, 4439 Reading Rd, Cincinnati, OH 45229-1282, **Business Phone:** (513)641-2006.

### WILSON, DR. HUGH A.

Educator. **Personal:** Born Jun 20, 1940, Kingston; son of John and Ola. **Educ:** Howard Univ, BA, 1963; Fordham Univ Sch Social Serv, MSW, 1967; Adelphi Univ, DSW, 1995. **Career:** Inst Suburban Studies, assoc prof, dir, 1975-85; Adelphi Univ, NY, Dept Polit Sci, prof & chair, prof emer, currently. **Orgs:** Comt organizer, Comt Coord Coun Long Beach, NY, 1966-67; dir, Welfare Tenants Coord Com Mineola NY, 1968-70; co-founder & sec, Alliance Minority Group Leaders Nassau-Suffolk, 1970; Yonkers Comt Action Prog, 1971-72; consult, Westchester Urban League, 1973; Addiction Serv Agency NY, 1973. **Special Achievements:** Awarded $45000 by N Shore Unitarian Ch to set up Inst for Suburban Studies at Adelphi Univ, 1973. **Home Addr:** 245 W 107th St, New York, NY 10025, **Home Phone:** (212)864-6678. **Business Addr:** Professor Emeritus, Adelphi University, Rm 202D Blodgett Hall, Garden City, NY 11530-0701, **Business Phone:** (516)877-4592.

### WILSON, J. RAY

Executive, association executive. **Personal:** Born Apr 16, 1937, Leesville, LA; son of Emmitt and Florence; married Dorothy Ellison; children: Taleia Appral & Marcus Ray. **Educ:** Tex Southern Univ, Houston, TX, BBA, 1965. **Career:** Relations manager (retired); United Calif Bank, opers officer, 1965-67; Conoco Inc, mgr, employee rels, 1967-93. **Orgs:** Bd mem, Houston Area Urban League, 1979-86; Amigo De Ser, 1979-; vpres, Chase Wood Civic Club, 1980-82; adv exec bd, Network Group, 1982-; Julia C Hester House; Ft Bend Independent Sch Dist; SER-Jobs Progress; United Way Tex Gulf Coast; Houston Livestock Show & Rodeo. **Honors/Awds:** Community Service Award. **Home Addr:** 4203 King Cotton Lane, Missouri City, TX 77459, **Home Phone:** (713)437-5690.

### WILSON, JACI LAVERNE

Government official. **Personal:** Born Dec 9, 1961, Houston, TX; daughter of Mae Ola McKinley-Dogan. **Educ:** Tex Southern Univ, BA. **Career:** Clinton-Gore campaign, dem nat conv, 1996; US Senate, Carol Moseley-Braun; US Trade Rep, EOP; US Dept State, secy al bright; Dem Nat Conv Comt, dep dir, conv housing, dir conv housing, currently. **Home Addr:** 1515 Jefferson Davis Hwy Suite 503, Arlington, VA 22202, **Home Phone:** (703)418-4028. **Business Addr:** Director of Convention Housing, Democratic National Convention Committee, 515 S Flower St 42nd Fl, Los Angeles, CA 90071, **Business Phone:** (202)863-8000.

### WILSON, JAMES REINARD. See WILSON, REINARD.

### WILSON, DR. JEFFREY R.

College teacher. **Personal:** children: Rhonda, Roxanne & Rochelle. **Educ:** Univ Wis, St Augustine, BA, math & econ, 1977; Iowa State Univ, Ames, IA, MS, statist, 1980, PhD, statist, 1984. **Career:** Univ Wi, Dept Mathematics, teaching asst, 1977-78; Iowa State Univ, Ames, IA, Dept Math, teaching asst, 1980-83, Minority Stud Affairs, consult & dir tutorial serv, 1981-83, teaching asst, Statist Lab, dept statist, 1982, 1983; Okla State Univ, Still water, OK, vis asst prof statist, 1983-84; Ariz State Univ, Tempe, AZ, Dept Decision & Info Syst, from asst to assoc prof statist, 1985-95, dir, interdisciplinary prog statist, 1991-96, Sch Health & Admin Policy, assoc prof, biostatistics, 1994-2006, Dept Econ, assoc prof, biostatistics, 1996-, Ariz Col Pub Health, assoc prof biostatistics, 2000-04, interim dir, 2002-03, W P Carey Sch Bus, dir, 2003-06, NIH Ctr Alzheimer, Data Mgt & Biostatistics Core, co-dir, 2006-09; Univ Colo, assoc prof, biostatistics, Dept Sci Health Admin, 1990-94; Charles Drew Univ Med & Sci, Los Angeles, CA, Dept Surg, adj prof surg, 1992-93, Drew Surg Res Group, co-dir, 1993-96; Grad Interdisciplinary Progs, assoc prof epidemiol, 2001-04, HAP Mel & Enid Zuckerman Col Pub Health, div dir & concentration dir, 2002-03; J of Minimally Invasive Gynec, statist assoc ed. **Orgs:** Past pres, Am Statist Asn, 1980; Royal Statist Soc, 1985; chair, Am Pub Health Asn, 2011-12; Biomet Soc; Western N Am Region; Biometrika; Am United Prog Health Asn; chair, Intercollegiate Athletic Bd, Ariz State Univ. **Home Addr:** 1170 N Mallard Pl, Chandler, AZ 85226, **Home Phone:** (602)961-3924. **Business Addr:** Associate Professor of Biostatistics, Associate Professor of Statistics, Arizona State University, BAC 600, Tempe, AZ 85287-4506, **Business Phone:** (480)965-5628.

### WILSON, JERRY LEE, JR.

Football player. **Personal:** Born Jul 17, 1973, Alexandria, LA; children: Trittney, Tanner & Jerry III. **Educ:** Southern Univ, BS, rehab coun, 1994. **Career:** Football player (retired); Tampa Bay Buccaneers, 1995-96; Miami Dolphins, 1996-98, defensive back, 1999, linebacker, 2000; New Orleans Saints, 2001-02; San Diego Chargers, free safety, 2003-05.

### WILSON, ESQ. JIMMIE L.

Lawyer, state government official. **Career:** Lawyer, pvt pract; farmer; State Ark, rep. **Orgs:** Pres, Phillips Co Br Nat Asn Advan Colored People. **Home Addr:** RR 2 PO Box 333, Lakeview, AR 72642. **Business Addr:** Lawyer, Private Practice, 521-523 Plaza St, West Helena, AR 72390.

### WILSON, JIMMY L.

Law enforcement officer. **Personal:** Born Jan 1, 1946, Durham, NC. **Educ:** Am Univ, BS, admin justice, 1974; Va State Univ, MS, educ. **Career:** Police Chief (retired); Wash, DC Police Dept, int affairs investr, 1968-86, dep chief, 1987-92; City Jackson, police chief, 1992-94; City Canton, Miss, police chief, 1994-97; City Suffolk, Va, chief police, 1997-2001; Va State Univ, Dept Police & Pub Safety, chief police, 2003-07. **Orgs:** Pres, NOBLE; Nat Org Black Law Enforcement Exec, 2002-03. **Business Addr:** Chief Police, City of Suffolk, 111 Henley Pl, Suffolk, VA 23434, **Business Phone:** (757)514-7915.

### WILSON, JOHN SYLVANUS, JR.

Government official, college president. **Personal:** married Dr. Carol Espy-Wilson; children: Ayana and Ashia, twin daughters; son John (Jay) Sylvanus III. **Educ:** Morehouse College, B.A., 1979; Harvard University, Master's in Theological Studies and Education, Doctorate in Education with a focus on Administration, Planning, and Social Policy. **Career:** Massachusetts Institute of Technology, various positions, 1985-01, including Director of Foundation Relations; George Washington University (GWU), various positions, including Executive Dean and Associate Professor at the Graduate School of Education; White House Initiative on Historically Black Colleges and Universities (HBCUs), Executive Director, 2009-12; Morehouse College, President, 2013-. **Orgs:** Greater Boston Morehouse College Alumni Association (GBMCAA), former President; United Negro College Fund's Institute for Capacity Building, Consultant; Kresge Foundation's Black College Advisory Board; Samaritans, Trustee Board; Andover Newton Theological School, Trustee Board; Spelman College, Trustee Board. **Honors/Awds:** Morehouse College, Benjamin Elijah Mays Leadership Award, 1998. **Special Achievements:** Appointed to White House Initiative by President Barack Obama; the GBMCAA established the John Wilson Leadership Award in his honor.

### WILSON, DR. JOHN W.

Administrator, educator, executive director. **Personal:** Born Jun 10, 1928, St. Marys, GA; son of Albert and Ora; children: John Jr, Larry & Dwaughn. **Educ:** Albany State Col, BS, elem educ, 1951; Univ Akron, MA, educ admin, 1970, EdD, 1983. **Career:** Albany State Col, employee, 1951; Cleveland Pub Schs, elem teacher, 1957-69; Univ Akron, dir, Black Cult Ctr & Afro-Am Studies. **Orgs:** Nat Asn Advan Colored People, Omega Psi Phi, 1947-; overseas ext teacher, Univ Wis, (English), Korea, 1952; Phi Delta Kappa, 1970-; pres, Nat Black Alliance Grad Educ, 1972-; Higher Educ Comn, Nat Alliance Black Sch Educ, 1984-. **Honors/Awds:** Certificate & plaque, Martha Holden Jennings Scholar, 1966-67; Certificate, Reg Coun Int Educ, 1970-71, Ivory Coast & Lome, West Africa Workshop & Tour Lagos, Dakar, Benin, 1980. **Home Addr:** 11511 Martin Luther King Jr Dr, Cleveland, OH 44105-2549, **Home Phone:** (216)441-3782.

### WILSON, DR. JOHNNY LEAVERNE

Educator. **Personal:** Born Sep 17, 1954, Wilmington, NC; son of William E and Mary; children: Lynnezy Alorida & Johnny Allen. **Educ:** Winston Salem State Univ, BA, polit sci, 1976; Cent Mo State Univ, MA, polit sci, 1979; Atlanta Univ, Atlanta, GA, PhD, polit sci, 1988. **Career:** Cent Mo State Univ, Warrensburg, Mo, work study asst, 1976-78; Oper PUSH, Kans City, Mo, assoc dir int affairs comn, 1978-80; Atlanta Univ, Atlanta, Ga, work study asst, 1980-84; Morehouse Sch Med, Atlanta, Ga, circulation asst, 1984-88; Atlanta Bd Educ, supply teacher, 1984-88; Clark Atlanta Univ, Atlanta, Ga, asst prof, 1988-. **Orgs:** Nat Conf Black Polit Scientist, 1980-; pres, JW Mgt & Assoc, 1988-; bd dir, Ment Health Asn Metro Atlanta Inc, 1989-90; Atlanta Employer Comn Atlanta Fields Serv Off, 1990-91; dir, internship prog, Clark Atlanta Univ, Dept Polit Sci. **Home Addr:** 2518 Springdale Rd SW, Atlanta, GA 30315, **Home Phone:** (404)763-5072. **Business Addr:** Assistant Professor of Political Science, Clark Atlanta University, 223 James P Brawley Dr SW, Atlanta, GA 30314, **Business Phone:** (404)880-8245.

### WILSON, JON

Executive. **Personal:** Born Sep 29, 1955, Canton, OH. **Educ:** Ohio Sch Broadcast Tech Cleveland, attended 1974. **Career:** WKNT Radio Kent OH, asst news dir, 1974; WHBC Radio, combo announcer & engr, 1974-76, prod spec, 1976-77, Black music dir, 1977-84; United Companies Life Ins Baton Rouge, regional dir, 1976-77; WHBC AM & FM, acct exec, res dir & co-op coordr. **Orgs:** Soc Broadcast Engrs, 1975; Black Music Asn, 1979; bd dir, Canton Black United Fund Pub Rels Div, 1979; bd dir, Stark Co, Nat Asn Advan Colored People, 1980 & 1983; bd mem, Metrop Off Canton; youth comt, youth coach, YMCA; dir, Presenters Bur Com Div United Way. **Home Addr:** 1508 Fulton Rd NW, Canton, OH 44703, **Home Phone:** (216)455-5510. **Business Addr:** Account Executive, WHBC AM & FM, 550 Mkt Ave S, Canton, OH 44701, **Business Phone:** (216)456-7166.

### WILSON, JONATHAN CHARLES

Artist, educator. **Personal:** Born Nov 4, 1949, Buffalo, NY; son of Jonathan C Sr and Jean Jimison; married Nan Withers. **Educ:** Daeman Col, BA, theatre & drama, 1971; Rosary Hill Col, BFA, 1971; Univ Cincinnati, MA, theatre, 1972; Univ Wis, Madison, ABD, 1976; Northwestern Univ, MFA, theatre, 1983. **Career:** Loyola Univ, Chicago, prof theatre, 1976-; actor: Fraternity, The Death of Bessie Smith, Union Boys, Burning Bright; dir: Fraternity From the Miss Delta, A Raisin in the Sun, 1987, Jump for Joy, A Midsummer Nights Dream, 2006, Guys & Dolls, 2008; Director: Pantomime; Desire Under the Elms, 1994, Seven Guitars, 1997; Long Days Journey Into Night; Two Trains Running; Fraternity; Electra, 2003; Ma Raineys Black Bottom, 2005. Production: A View from the Bridge, 2001; The Madwoman of Chaillot, 2004; Joe Turner's Come and Gone, 2005; A Midsummer Night's Dream, 2006; Guys and Dolls, 2008; Intimate Apparel, 2009; A Streetcar Named Desire, 2012. **Orgs:** Chmn bd, Playwrights' Ctr, Chicago, 1980-; Asn Theatre Higher Educ, 1981-; Ill Theatre Asn, 1985-; Soc Stage dir & Choreographers, 1991-. **Home Addr:** 923 Wesley Ave, Evanston, IL 60202, **Home Phone:** (847)475-2507. **Business Addr:** Professor of Theatre, Loyola University, Mundelein 1304 1020 W Sheridan Rd, Chicago, IL 60626, **Business Phone:** (773)508-3838.

**WILSON, JOSEPH**
Chief executive officer. **Career:** Integrated Packaging Corp, chief exec officer & co founder, chmn emer, owner, currently. **Business Addr:** Chairman Emeritus, Integrated Packaging Corp, 6400 Harper Ave, Detroit, MI 48211, **Business Phone:** (313)925-1800.

**WILSON, DR. JOSEPH F.**
Educator. **Personal:** Born Dec 2, 1951, Chicago, IL; son of Charles and Ida; married Maria Vazquez; children: Leslie. **Educ:** Columbia Univ, NY, BA, 1973, MA, polit sci, 1976, MPhil, philos, 1978, PhD, polit sci, 1980; Harvard Univ, MDP, instnl develop, 1998. **Career:** Rutgers Univ, Nb, NJ, asst prof, 1980-86; Brooklyn Col, Brooklyn, New York, assoc prof, 1986-94, Dept Polit Sci, prof, 1994-, Ctr Diversity & Multicultural Educ, dir, currently, Grad Ctr Worker Educ Prog, dept chmn, dir, currently; NY City Coun, grant, 2006-07; ERIS, grant, 2007-08; Co-PI ERIS, grant, 2009. Books: Race & Labor Matters in the New US Economy, ed, 2006; International Encyclopedia of Revolution and Protest, assoc ed & contribr, 2009; Encyclopedia of African American History, contribr, 2009. **Orgs:** Exec comt, Black Fac & Staff Asn, 1987-95; dir, Brooklyn Col Multicultural Ctr, 1990-95; Univ Affirmative Action Comt, 2003-09; Univ Diversity Grants Comt, 2003-09; deleg, Prof Staff Cong, 2009. **Home Addr:** 215 W 91st, New York, NY 10024-1321, **Home Phone:** (212)496-8969. **Business Addr:** Professor, Brooklyn College, 3608 James Hall 2900 Bedford Ave, Brooklyn, NY 11210, **Business Phone:** (718)951-3846.

**WILSON, DR. JOSEPH HENRY, JR.**
Dentist. **Personal:** Born Jan 29, 1966, Washington, DC; son of Frankie Jones and Joseph Sr. **Educ:** St Louis Univ, BA, biol, 1987; Univ Ma, Col Dent Surg, Baltimore, MD, DDS, 1991. **Career:** St Elizabeth's Hosp, dent resident, 1991-92; Hamilton Ctr, dentist, 1992-2000; Co Dent Assoc PC, dentist, secy, partner, 1992-2000; River Hill Dent Group, dentist, 2000-; pvt pract dentist, currently. **Orgs:** Am Dent Asn, 1992-; Pa Dent Asn, 1992-2000; Harrisburg Dent Soc, 1992-2000; Md State Dent Asn, 2000-; Bio-Response Solutions Inc. **Home Addr:** 11087 Little Patuxent Pkwy, Columbia, MD 21044, **Home Phone:** (410)730-3323. **Business Addr:** Dentist, River Hill Dental Group, 5005 Signal Bell Lane Suite 101, Clarksville, MD 21029-2606, **Business Phone:** (443)535-8940.

**WILSON, JOY JOHNSON**
Health services administrator, government official. **Personal:** Born Jul 12, 1954, Charleston, SC; daughter of Everett W and Martha L; married Ronald E; children: Devon & Trevon. **Educ:** Keene State Col NH, BS, social sci, 1976; Univ NC, Chapel Hill, MRP, urban planning, 1978. **Career:** Nat Conf State Leg, res assoc, 1978-79, staff assoc, 1979-82, sr staf assoc, 1982-83, staff dir, 1983-89, sr comm dir, health, 1990-96, dir, health policy & fed affairs coun, 1996, dir health & human serv policy, 2013-; Medicaid Comn, non voting mem; US Bipartisan Comn Comprehensive Health Care, prof staff mem, 1989-90. **Orgs:** Treas comn, Adv Neighborhood Comn, 1982-83; treas, Women & Health Round table, 1986-87; Women Govt Rels, 1986-; Am League Lobbyists, 1987-89. **Home Addr:** 6413 Hollins Dr, Bethesda, MD 20817, **Home Phone:** (301)530-8810. **Business Addr:** Director Health and Human Services Policy, Federal Affairs Counsel, National Conference of State Legislatures, 444 N Capitol St NW Suite 515, Washington, DC 20001, **Business Phone:** (202)624-5400.

**WILSON, KEN**
Executive. **Career:** Arista Rec; Columbia Rec, vpres black music prom, 1996; MCA Rec, pres, black music, 1999; J Rec, sr vpres prom; Warner Bros Rec, sr vpres; music exec & consult, currently. **Orgs:** Bd mem & event chmn, Living Legends Found. **Business Addr:** Los Angeles, CA.

**WILSON, KIM ADAIR**
Lawyer. **Personal:** Born Sep 4, 1956, New York, NY; daughter of Walter (deceased) and Rosa J. **Educ:** Boston Col, BA, polit sci, 1978; Hofstra Univ Sch Law, JD, 1982. **Career:** Attorney (retired), judge; New York, Dept Invest, investigative atty, 1986-89, Civil Law Dept, prin & sr ct atty, 1989-2013; Bronx County Supreme Ct, 1989-2013; New York Civil Ct, Bronx County, 2nd Dist, judge, 2013-; NY State Supreme Ct, Bronx Supreme Ct, spec referee election matters. **Orgs:** House deleg, NY State Bar Asn, 1994-96; pres, Metrop Black Bar Asn, 1994-96; bd gov, Nat Bar Asn, 1995-99; Delta Sigma Theta Sorority. **Honors/Awds:** Nelson Mandela International Citizen of the Year Award, NY Asn Black Psychologists, 1994; Outstanding Bar Association Affiliate Chapter Award, Nat Bar Asn, 1995; Jane Matilda Bolin Award, Judicial Friends, 1996; Member of the Year, Women Lawyers Div, Nat Bar Asn, 1998. **Special Achievements:** Co-author: "Affirmative Action Can Help Create Tradition of Excellence,"New York Law Journal, May 1995; "US Constitution and its Meaning to the Afa Ct", Nat Bar Assn Magazine, Volume 10, No 4, pp 3 & 30; Author of book review, Affirmative Action, Race & Am Values, published my book review, New York Law Journal, Jan 10, 1997. **Business Addr:** Judge, New York City Civil Court, 265 E 161st St Suite 924, Bronx, NY 10451-3503, **Business Phone:** (718)618-3100.

**WILSON, LANCE HENRY**
Banker, lawyer. **Personal:** Born Jul 5, 1948, New York, NY; son of William H and Ruth Thomas; married Deirdre Jean Jenkins; children: Jennifer Lee. **Educ:** Hunter Col, AB, 1969; Univ Pa Law Sch, JD, 1972. **Career:** Univ Pa Law Sch, legal writing teaching fel, 1971; Mudge Rose Guthrie & Alexander, atty, 1972-77; Equitable Life Assurance Soc US, assoc coun, 1977-81; US Dept Housing & Urban Develop, exec asst secy, 1981-84; New York Housing Develop Corp, pres, 1984-86; Paine Webber Inc, first vpres, 1986-91; Pvt Bus Ventures & Pract Law, 1991-95; Greystone & Co, 1995-99; Ziegler & Co, sr vpres, co-dir, Housing Finance, 1999-2001; Am Property Financing Inc, sr vpres, 2001-08; Oppenheimer Multifamily Housing & Healthcare Finance Inc, sr vpres, 2008-. **Orgs:** NY State Bar Asn; Finance Comt NYS Repuban Party; vpres, NY Co Repuban Comn, 1984-90; pub mem, Admin Conf US, 1984-86; dir, Vis Nurse Serv NY, 1984-90; trustee, St Luke's Roosevelt Hosp Ctr, 1984-90; dir, Nat Housing Conf, 1986-93; Fed Nat Mortgage Asn Adv Coun, 1986-88; gov, Nat Realty Club; assoc mem, Assoc Builders & Owners Greater New York; trustee, Metrop Col New York; dir, Faith Ctr Community Develop Inc, 2000-; mem adv coun, Atlantic Legal Found; Community Investment Comt. **Honors/Awds:** Outstanding Leadership Award, Ill Coun Black Repubicans, 1982; Outstanding Leadership Award, NY State Coun Black Repubicans, 1982; Secretary Award for Excellence, US Dept Housing & Urban Develop, 1984; Outstanding Public Service Award, Nat Asn Home Builders, 1984; Exemplary Leadership Award, Nat Black Republican Coun, 1984; Housing Man of the Year, Nat & NY Housing Conf, 1985; Humanitarian Award, Southern Brooklyn Comn, Org, 1985; Private Sector Initiative Commendation, White House, 1986. **Home Addr:** 200 Riverside Blvd Suite 23 E, New York, NY 10069, **Home Phone:** (212)579-2444. **Business Addr:** Senior Vice President, Oppenheimer Multifamily Housing & Healthcare Finance Inc, 85 Broad St 23rd Fl, New York, NY 10004-2456, **Business Phone:** (212)667-7443.

**WILSON, DR. LAVAL S.**
School administrator. **Personal:** Born Nov 15, 1935, Jackson, TN; married Constance Ann; children: Laval Jr, Holly, Shawn & Nicole. **Educ:** Chicago Teachers Col, BEd, 1958; Univ Chicago, MA, 1962; Northwestern Univ, PhD, 1967. **Career:** Chicago Sch, teacher, counsr, 1958-64; Northwestern Univ Inst, asst dir, 1965, 1966; Evanston, Ill, asst prin, 1966-67, dir, integration inst & follow-up prog, 1967-70; Cent Sch Evanston, Ill, prin, 1967-70; Philadelphia & Detroit Sch, supt's intern prog, 1970-71; Hempstead, NY, asst supt curric & instr, 1971-72 & 1973-74, actg supt schs, 1972-73; Berkeley, Calif, supt schs, 1974-80; Rochester, NY, supt sch, 1980-85; Univ Rochester, adj prof, 1984-85; Boston Pub Schs, Ma, supt sch, 1985-90; Boston, Massachusetts, educ consult, 1990-91; Paterson, NJ, supt, 1991-97; Columbia Univ, adj prof, 1993; Newburgh, New York, supt, 1997-2000; Newburgh Hist Cemetery Comt, 1998-2000; Paterson, NJ, educ consult, 2001-03; E Orange Sch Dist, supt, 2003-06; Poughkeepsie City Sch Dist, supt, 2006-. **Orgs:** Am Asn Sch Admin; Asn Supvsn & Curric Develop; Kappa Alpha Psi Frat; Nat Asn Advan Colored People; Phi Delta Kappa; New York Coun Sch Dist Admin; League Women Voters; ed consult, Phi Delta Kappan publn Phi Delta Kappa, 1974-78; Berkeley Rotary, 1977-80; mem bd dirs, Berkeley Red Cross, 1975-79; Otetiana Coun Exec Bd Boy Scouts Am, 1981-85; bd trustee, Rochester Mus & Sci Ctr, 1981-85; Rochester Rotary, 1981-85; bd dir, Jr Achieve, Rochester, 1983-; Adv Bd Girl Scouts Genesee Valley, 1984-85f; bd dir, Rochester Area Found, 1984-85; bd dir, Ctr Govt Res Inc, 1984-85; bd dir, Buffalo Br Fed Res Bank, NY, 1984-85; mem bd dirs, Boston Pvt Indust Coun, 1985-90; Boston Chamber Coms Educ Comt, 1985-90; mem greater boston coun, Boy Scouts Am, 1985-90; mem bd trustees, Boston Mus Fine Arts, 1985-90; mem bd overseers, New Eng Med Ctr, 1987-90; mem bd dirs, Mass Blue Cross & Blue Shield, 1987-90; Paterson Educ Collab, 1992-97; bd dir, Passaic Valley Boy Scouts Coun, 1994-97; bd dir, Hudson Valley Boy Scouts Coun, 1997-98; chairperson, Leadership Adv Comt, Am Asn Sch Adminr, 2000-01; Bd Educ, Roosevelt, New York, 2002-06; consult, NY Univ; Common Pa Act 101 Western Reg; Am Asn Sch Admin; Race Deseg Inst Univ Pittsburgh; Nat Inst Educ; Nat Sch Bds Asn; Off Educ; Far W Lab, Los Angeles Conty Sch Dist, San Francisctate Univ; NY Sch Dist, New York Sch Dist 12, Encycl Brittanica. **Honors/Awds:** Received numerous awards from various organizations including: Appreciation Plaque, Phi Delta Kappa, 1978; Resolution of Appreciation, Berkeley Bd Educ, 1980; Congressional Award, Cong Ronald Dellums; Legislative Resolution of Spec Publ Recognition and Commend, Assemblyman Elihu Harris & Sen Nicholas Petris, 1980; Appreciation Plaque, Nat Conf Parent Involvement, 1981; Appreciation Plaque, Dist Adv Council to Chap 1, 1982; Recognition Plaque, Berkeley Black principals, 1980; Special Service Award, Rochester WEB Du Bois Acad, 1983; Community Service Award, Rochester Asn Black Communicators, 1983, 1986; Appreciation Award, Grad School Educ & Human Dev Univ Rochester, 1984; Certification Appreciation, Mason Eureka Lodge No 36, 1984; Top Executive Educator Award, 1984; Certification of Recognition for contributions, Rochester community, United Church Ministry, 1985; Dr. Charles T. Lunsford Award, 1985; Citizen of the Year Award, 1985; Leadership Award, Rochester Chapter, Phi Delta Kappa, 1985; Boston Business Journal Award, 1987; Theodore Storer Memorial Award, 1987; Vision Award, 1989; Urban Emphasis Good Scout Award, 1996; Donald J. Vanderbeck Leadership Paterson Annual Memorial Award, 1996; Faith in Paterson Award, 1996; Presidents Recognition Award, 1997; Parent Appreciation Award, 1997; Dr. Martin L. King, Jr. Distinguished Service Award, 1998; Pillar of the Community Excellence in Education Award, 2000; Superintendent's Award Plaque, 2003. **Special Achievements:** First African American superintendent of Boston's public school system. **Home Addr:** 120 Ward St Apt 1, Paterson, NJ 07505. **Business Addr:** Superintendent, Poughkeepsie City School District, 11 Col Ave, Poughkeepsie, NY 12603, **Business Phone:** (845)451-4950.

**WILSON, LAWRENCE C.**
Executive. **Personal:** Born May 16, 1932, Kansas City, KS; son of John R and Alfretta; children: Stacey Marie. **Educ:** La Col; Cert Pub Housing Mgr, 1983. **Career:** Executive (retired); Gen machinist, 1955-68; Human Resources Corp KC, Mo, area coordr, 1963-69, dir, 1971-72; Greater KC Coun Relig & Race, proj dir, 1969-71; Topeka Daycare Inc, chmn; Shawnee Co Community Asst & Action Inc, Topeka, Kans, exec dir, 1972-80; Nat Ctr Community Action Inc, pres, 1980-82; Topeka Housing Authority, dep dir, 1982-95. **Orgs:** Topeka Opt Club; Nat Asn Comn Develop; Lawrence C Wilson Assoc; chmn, Topeka Human Rels Comn; chmn, Kans Comn Civil Rights; advr, Kans Sec Social Rehab Ser; Topeka-Shawnee Co Metro Planning Comn; League Kans Munic Human Resources Comn; pres, Nat Asn Advan Colored People; Black Econ Union; Kans Asn Comm Action; vice chmn, Arts Coun Topeka; dir, OEO; exec comn & bd dir, Shawnee Co Comn Asst & Action Inc; Shawnee Co Coun Advocacy Aging; outspoken mem & vice chmn, Cong Racial Equality. **Home Addr:** 2906 SW Arrowhead Rd, Topeka, KS 66614-4143, **Home Phone:** (785)273-7833.

**WILSON, LEON E., JR.**
Banker. **Personal:** Born Mar 12, 1945, ME; son of Ollie H Taylor and Leon E Sr; married Sharon Clements; children: Erika & Erin. **Educ:** Boston Univ, Boston, MA, BS, 1975; Williams Col, Williamstown, MA, 1975; Univ Va, Grad Sch Retail Bank Mgt, Charlottesville, VA, 1978; Harvard Bus Sch, Cambridge, MA, PMD, 1986. **Career:** Shawmut Bank, Boston, Mass, vpres, 1966-83; Bank Boston, Boston, Mass, sr vpres, 1983; Pvt Bank, risk mgt & compliance, nat dir, vpres & div head, Consumer Finance Div, Massachusetts Residential Mortgage Div, dir; Fleet Financial Group, exec vpres, 1992; Capital City Capital Group LLC, chief exec officer, exec vpres & managing dir, currently; First Community Bank, chmn; BancBoston Mortgage Corp, sr vpres & dir; GMAC Residential, GMAC Mortgage, corp sr vpres & managing dir; Capital City Ventures, gen partner & investment mgr, currently; Mid-Mkt Instnl Asset Mgt, exec vpres & managing dir, currently. **Orgs:** Pres, Am Inst Banking, 1982-83; commr, Plymouth Redevelop, 1984; Harvard Univ Task Force, 1985; adv bd, Boston Univ, 1990-; chair, Roxbury Comn Col Found, 1990-; Comn Mass Employee Inv & Ownership Comn, 1990-; bd mem, Boston Ballet, 1994; Urban League Eastern Ma; United Negro Col Fund; Bell Found; Dimock Health Care; Fannie Mae's Regional Adv Bd; Philadelphia Safe & Sound; exec mem, GMAC Residential; sr vpres & regional mgr, Fleets; bd mem, Cambridge Cols Bd Trustees. **Honors/Awds:** Black Achievement Award, YMCA; Professional Achievement Award, Boston Urban Bankers. **Home Addr:** 47 Old Farm Rd, Milton, MA 02186, **Home Phone:** (617)696-1590. **Business Addr:** Chief Executive Officer, Capital City Capital Group LLC, 1400 L St NW Suite 400, Washington, DC 20005.

**WILSON, LEROY, JR.**
Lawyer. **Personal:** Born Jun 16, 1939, Savannah, GA; son of Leroy Sr and Mary Louise (Frazier); married Helen Odum; children: Andrea; married Jane Marie Beaver (deceased); children: Jason & Christopher. **Educ:** Univ Vienna, Austria, 1960; Morehouse Col, BS, chem & math, 1962; Univ Calif, MS, phys chem, 1965, JD, 1968. **Career:** IBM, atty, off vpres & gen coun, 1968-74; Covington Grant Howard, atty, 1972; Pvt pract, atty, 1974; Union Carbide Corp, atty & Linde Div, asst div coun, 1974-82; NY Supreme Ct, referee, 1988; Westchester County Surrogates Ct, actg surrogate, 1999; Wilson Jacobson PC, pres, currently. **Orgs:** Hon Woodrow Wilson Fel, 1962; dir, Asn Black Lawyers Westchester County Inc, 1978-87, chmn, 1987-88; gov mem, exec comn & bd dir, Nat Bar Asn, 1979-81, 1984-85, vpres, 1983-84; Am Bar Asn; vpres, Nat Bar Asn; pub mem, NY State Banking Bd, 1983-87; NY Litigator, 1995-96; chmn, Civil Rights Comt, 1997-2000; chmn, Awards Comt, 1998-99; Spec Comt Cameras Courtroom, 2000; Soc African Am Law Firms; NY Trial Lawyers Asn; Asn Trial Lawyers Am; Nat Employ Lawyers Asn; Metrop Black Bar Asn. **Honors/Awds:** Cadet Saber Award, 1972; Pathfinders Award Legal Legends, 1992; Thayer Award, Civil Coun Sickle Cell Anemia Benefit, US Mil Acad; Personal Counsel to His Excellency, Godfrey Lukongwa Binaisa, Fifth Pres Repub Uganda; Haywood Burns Award, NYSBA; Outstanding Lawyer Award, The Asn Black Lawyers Westchester County, Inc, 2002; The W.C. Handy Heritage Master & Legend Award, 2006; Founders Award, Westchester Black Bar Asn, 2008. **Home Addr:** 350 Stratton Rd, New Rochelle, NY 10804-1315, **Home Phone:** (914)576-5157. **Business Addr:** President, Wilson Jacobson PC, 99 Ct St Suite 2, White Plains, NY 10601-4264, **Business Phone:** (914)997-0825.

**WILSON, MABEL O.**
Architect, college teacher. **Educ:** Univ Va, BS, 1985; Columbia Univ Grad Sch Archit, Planning & Preserv, MArch, 1991; NY Univ, PhD, 2007. **Career:** Univ Ky, asst prof, 1991-98; Ohio State Univ, vis asst prof, 1994; Parsons Sch Design, 1997; Princeton Univ, vis asst prof, 1998; Calif Col Arts, assoc prof, 1999-2007; Studio &, archit pract, 2007-; Columbia Univ Grad Sch Archit, Planning & Preserv, prof, 2007-; Inst Res African Am Studies, sr fel, 2009-. Solo exhibs: KW:A, DDC Gallery, 1998; (a)way sta-Archit Spaces Urban Migration, 1999; Listening There-Stories from Ghana, Studio X, 2010. **Orgs:** Am Studies Asn; Col Art Asn; Orgn Am Historians; Soc Archit Historians. **Honors/Awds:** New York State Council for the Arts, Independent Project Award, 1997; Graham Foundation for Advanced Studios in the Fine Arts, 1999; LEF Foundation Artist Grant, 2001; Getty Research Institute visiting scholar fellowship, 2002; United States Artists Ford Fellow, 2011; Ailsa Mellon Bruce Senior Fellow, Nat Gallery Arts Ctr Advan Study Visual Arts, 2015-16. **Special Achievements:** Author, "Negro Building: Black Americans in the World Fairs and Museums", 2012. Contributor, Design Observer Places, Elastic, ANY, Assemblage, and Public. Work featured at Wexner Center for the Arts, the Cooper Hewitt National Design Museum's Triennial, the Storefront for Art and Architecture, and SF Cameraworks. **Business Addr:** Columbia University Graduate School of Architecture, Planning and Preservation, 1172 Amsterdam Ave, New York, NY 10027, **Business Phone:** (212)854-3414.

**WILSON, MARKLY**
Administrator, executive director. **Personal:** Born Mar 30, 1947, Bridgetown; married Gonul Mehmet; children: 2. **Educ:** St Clair Col, Ont, Can; Adelphi Univ, NY. **Career:** Barbados Bd Tourism, US mgr, recept & clerk, 1967-74, pub rel officer, 1974, sales rep, 1974-78, mgr, 1978-79; Skinner Sec Sch, bus Eng teacher, 1967-74; Ministry Civil Aviation, clerical officer, 1967; NY Univ, fac; consult; NY State Tourism, dir int mkt, currently; Int Inst Peace Through Tourism, chmn, mkt & prom, currently; Wilson Co consultancy, pres. **Orgs:** Photog Soc Lind field Sch, 1959-62; pres, Christ Church HS Debating Soc, 1963; sec, Christ Church High Sch Old Scholars Assoc, 1967; Toastmasters Intl Bridgetown Chap, 1968; Gray bar Toastmasters Club, 1974-; bd dir, CTA, 1981-82; chmn, Assembly Nat Tourist Off Rep NY, 1982-83; NY Skal Club; dir, Travel & Tourism Res Asn; bd adv, Tourism Dept New Sch Social Res; dir mkt, Caribbean Tourism Orgn; dir, Big Apple Greeter Inc; dir, I Love NY; dir, Lori Solomon-Duell; dir, Heritage Tourism; dir, Erie Canalway Nat'l Heritage Corridor. **Business Addr:** Chairman of Marketing & Promotion, International Institute for Peace Through Tourism, 13 685 Cottage Club Rd Suite 13, Stowe, VT 05672, **Business Phone:** (802)253-2658.

**WILSON, MARY**
Singer. **Personal:** Born Mar 6, 1944, Greenville, MS; daughter of Sam and Johnnie Mae; married Pedro Ferrer; children: Turkessa, Pedro Antonio Jr, Rafael (deceased) & Willie. **Educ:** NY Univ, AA, 2001. **Career:** Mem Supremes, 1959-77; solo vocalist, 1979-. Albums with the Supremes: Meet the Supremes, 1963; A Bit of Liverpool, 1964; Where Did Our Love Go, 1965; Sing Country Western & Pop, 1965; More Hits By the Supremes, 1965; We Remember Sam Cooke, 1965; At the Copa, 1965; Merry Christmas, 1965; IHear a Symphony, 1966; A Go-Go, 1966; Sing Holland-Dozier-Holland, 1967; Sing Rodgers &

Heart, 1967; 70's Greatest Hits & Rare Classics, 1991; Supremes, 2000. Albums with Diana Ross & the Supremes: Greatest Hits Volumes I, II & III, 1967, 1969; Reflections, 1968; Love Child, 1968; Sing & Perform Funny Girl, 1968; Live at the Talk of the Town, 1968; Join the Temptations, 1968; TCB, 1968; Let the Sunshine In, 1969; Together, 1969; Cream of the Crop, 1969; On Broadway, 1969; Farewell, 1970; Anthology, 1974; Great Songs & Performances, 1985; Motown Legends, 1985; Sing Motown, 1986. Solo: Mary Wilson, 1979. guest appearances: Billboard Top Dance Hits: 1976; Hold up the Light, 1987; Walk the Line, 1992; Love Lessons, 1992; Soul Talkin', 1993; Best of Diana Ross & the Supremes, Diana Ross & the Supremes, 1995; River of Song: A Musical Journey, 1998; Mary Wilson Live at the Sands, 2002; Up Close: Live from San Francisco, 2007; Mary Wilson Enterprises Inc, singer, chief exec officer, currently. **Business Addr:** Singer, Chief Executive Officer, Mary Wilson Enterprises Inc, 2654 W Horizon Ridge Pkwy B-5 Suite 138, Henderson, NV 89052, **Business Phone:** (702)492-6718.

## WILSON, MICHAEL

Basketball player, executive. **Personal:** Born Jul 22, 1972; married Allyson; children: 2. **Educ:** Univ Memphis, BA, educ, 1996. **Career:** Basketball player (retired), executive; Harlem Globetrotters, forward, 1997-2001; Univ Memphis; World Rec Basketball, chief exec officer, currently; Edmund Burke Sch, from asst coach to head coach, 2008-2010; Skills & Scrimmages, founder & chief exec officer, 2008-. **Orgs:** Dir, Headfirst Basketball, 2006-08; founder, World Rec Basketball, 2000. **Home Addr:** 3551 Bishops Gt Dr, Memphis, TN 38115. **Business Addr:** Founder, Chief Executive Officer, Skills and Scrimmages, 1505 Delmont Lane Takoma Pk, Bethesda, MD 20815, **Business Phone:** (240)475-7200.

## WILSON, MITSY

Executive. **Personal:** Born Dec 13, 1950, Georgetown; married Greg James; children: Meisha & Alia. **Educ:** Mt St Vincent Col, BA, social & social work. **Career:** WPIX-TV, NY, com coordr, 1972; NY Bd Educ, Coun & Spec Proj, dir; New York Airlines, mgr consumer affairs & baggage serv, 1981-86; Continental Airlines, dir consumer affairs & training, 1986-88; Times-Mirror Co, Leadership & Orgn Develop, vpres, 1995-2000; Fox Entertainment Group, sr vp, diversity develop, 2000-12; Nielsen Media Res Inc, mem african am adv coun, 2006-; ForAfrica, founding partner, 2011-. **Orgs:** Bd mem, Workplace Hollywood; bd mem, Univ Calif Los Angeles Med Ctr; Nat Asn Advan Colored People; Nat Latino Media Coun; Asian Pac Am Coalition; Am Indians Film & TV; bd mem, Kids Sports, Los Angeles; Nat Asn Minority Media Exec. **Home Addr:** 10201 W Pico Blvd Bldg 100 Rm 5075, Los Angeles, CA 90020. **Business Addr:** Founding Partner, ForAfrica, 21712 Lanar Mission, Viejo, CA 92692, **Business Phone:** (949)470-9758.

## WILSON, MOOKIE (WILLIAM HAYWARD WILSON)

Sports manager, baseball player. **Personal:** Born Feb 9, 1956, Bamberg, SC; married Rosa Gilbert; children: 3. **Educ:** Mercy Col, NY, attended 1996. **Career:** Baseball player (retired), baseball coach, sports mgr; Jackson Generals, 1978; New York Mets, outfielder, 1980-89, coach, 1996-2002, base coach, 2011; Toronto Blue Jays, outfielder, 1989-91; Rookie League Kingsport Mets team, mgr, 2003-04; Brooklyn Cyclones, mgr, 2005; US Team, mgr, 2013. **Home Addr:** , Lakewood, NJ 08701.

## WILSON, NANCY

Singer, actor. **Personal:** Born Feb 20, 1937, Chillicothe, OH; daughter of Olden and Lillian (Ryan); married Rev Wiley Burton; children: Samanthia & Sheryl; married Kenneth C Dennis; children: Kenneth Jr. **Educ:** Cent State Col, teacher training prog, 1955. **Career:** Singer & actress; Rusty Bryant Band, singer, 1956; Midwest & Canada, singing tour, 1958; Capitol Rec, rec artist; EMI Rec, rec artist; Nippon Columbia Japan, rec artist; Interface Japan, rec artist; Epic Sony/CBS, rec artist; TV series: "Burke's Law", 1965; "I Spy", 1966; "Room 222", 1970; "Hawaii Five-O", 1970; "O'Hara, U.S. Treasury", 1972; "The Tonight Show Starring Johnny Carson", 1973; "Search", 1973; "The F.B.I.", 1973; "Police Story", 1974; "The Cosby Show", 1989; "The Sinbad Show", 1993; "The Parent 'Hood", 1995-97; "The Parkers", 2001; Films: The Killers, 1964; The Big Score, 1983; The Meteor Man, 1993; Albums: Like in Love, 1960; Something Wonderful, 1960; The Swingin's Mutual, 1961; Nancy Wilson/Cannonball Adderley, 1962; Hello Young Lovers, 1962; Broadway--My Way, 1963; Hollywood--My Way, 1963; Yesterday's Love Songs, 1963; Today, Tomorrow, Forever, 1964; The Nancy Wilson Show at the Coconut Grove, 1965; Nancy Wilson Today--My Way, 1965; Today My Way, 1965; Gentle Is My Love, 1965; From Broadway With Love, 1966; A Touch of Love Today, 1966; Tender Loving Care, 1966; Nancy--Naturally, 1966; From Broadway with Love, 1966; Just for Now, 1967; Nancy Naturally, 1967; Tender Loving Care, 1967; Lush Life, 1967; A Touch of Today, 1967; Welcome to My Love, 1968; Easy, 1968; The Best of Nancy Wilson, 1968; Sound of Nancy Wilson, 1968; Nancy, 1969; Son of a Preacher Man, 1969; Close Up, 1969; Hurt So Bad, 1969; Can't Take My Eyes Off You, 1970; Now I'm a Woman, 1970; Double Play, 1971; Right to Love, 1971; Kaleidoscope, 1971; But Beautiful, 1971; Right to Love, 1971, Who Can I Turn To, 1971; For Once In My Life, 1971, Double Play, 1971; Free Again, 1972; I Know I Love Him, 1973; All in Love Is Fair, 1974; All In Love Is Fair, 1974; Come Get to This, 1975; This Mother's Daughter, 1976; Music on My Mind, 1978; Life, Love & Harmony, 1979; Take My Love, 1980; At My Best, 1981; Echoes of an Era, 1982; What's New, 1982; I'll Be a Song, 1984; (with R Lewis) The Two of Us, 1986; Keep You Satisfied, 1986; Forbidden Lover, 1987; Nancy Now!, 1990; With My Lover Beside Me, 1991; The Best of Nancy Wilson, 1992; (with G Washington) Next Exit, 1992; Color & Light, 1994; (with Boston Pops Orchestra) It Don't Mean a Thing, 1994; Joyful Christmas, 1994; Love, Nancy, 1994; (with Q Jones & others) Jook Joint, 1995; Spotlight on Nancy Wilson, 1995; Ballads, Blues & Big Bands, 1996; If I Had My Way, 1997; A Nancy Wilson Christmas, 2001; (with R Lewis)Meant To Be, 2002; (with R Lewis) Simple Pleasures, 2003; RSVP, 2004; Live From Las Vegas, 2005; Great Women Singers of the 20th Century - Nancy Wilson, 2005; Turned To Blue, 2006; Music for Lovers, 2007. Singles: "Save Your Love for Me", 1962; "Tell Me the Truth", 1963; "How Glad I Am", 1964; "I Wanna Be with You", 1964; "And Satisfy", 1964; "Don't Come Running Back to Me", 1965; "Welcome, Welcome", 1965; "Where Does That Leave Me", 1965; "I'll Only Miss Him When I Think of Him", 1965; "Uptight (Everything's Alright)", 1966; "You've Got Your Troubles", 1966; "Face It Girl, It's Over", 1968; "Peace of Mind", 1968; "In a Long White Room", 1968; "You'd Better Go", 1969; "Got It Together", 1969; "Can't Take My Eyes Off You", 1969; "This Girl Is a Woman Now", 1970; "Now I'm a Woman", 1971; "Streetrunner", 1974; "You're as Right as Rain", 1974; "He Called Me Baby", 1975; "Don't Let Me Be Lonely Tonight", 1975; "Now", 1976; "In My Loneliness", 1976; "I've Never Been to Me", 1977; "I'm Gonna Get Ya", 1978; "Life, Love and Harmony", 1979; "Don't Ask My Neighbors", 1990; "Do You Still Dream About Me", 1991; "Love Won't Let Me Wait", 1994; "I Can't Make You Love Me", 1994. **Orgs:** Presidential Coun Minority Bus Enterprises; Nat Asn Advan Colored People; Southern Christian Leadership Conf; chairperson, Oper PUSH; United Negro College Fund; Comt Kennedy Ctr Performing Arts. **Honors/Awds:** Numerous honors& awards including Paul Robeson Award, Urban League; Ruby Ring Award, Johnson & Johnson Co; 2 Emmy Awards; Black Book Award; Best Female Vocalist Award, Playboy, Downbeat Jazz Polls; Grammy for Best Rhythm & Blues Recording, 1964; Emmy for The Nancy Wilson Show; named Jazz Master, Nat Endowement Arts, 2004; UNCF Trumpet Award, 2005; Lifetime Achievement Award, NAACP; Oprah Winfrey's Legends Awaand rd; Grammy Award, 2006. Best Jazz Vocal Album, 2005; 2007. **Business Addr:** Singer, c/o John Levy Enterprises Inc, 1828 Coolidge Ave, Altadena, CA 91001, **Business Phone:** (626)398-8179.

## WILSON, NATALIE

Music arranger or orchestrator, composer, singer. **Personal:** Born Jan 1, 1972, Newark, NJ; daughter of Nathaniel Simmons and Johnnie Mae Simmons; married Joseph. **Career:** Sounds Of Praise Chorale, dir, 1992-; Film: What's Love Got to Do with It, 1993; Kingdom Come, 2001. Albums: Not the Same, 1996; Girl Director, 2000; The Good Life, 2004. **Honors/Awds:** Stellar Award, 2002; Stellar's Hall of Fame. **Home Addr:** 689 Sanford Ave, Newark, NJ 07106. **Business Addr:** Director, Sound of Praise Chorale, 662 S 18th St, Newark, NJ 07103.

## WILSON, NATARSHA JULIET

Salesperson. **Personal:** Born Oct 22, 1961, Atlanta, GA. **Educ:** Berry Col, BS, 1982. **Career:** Continental Distribr, sales consult; Soft Sheen Prod Inc, territorial sales merchandiser; Redken Labs Inc, dist sales mgr. **Home Addr:** 1084 Deckner Ave SW, Atlanta, GA 30310-4136, **Home Phone:** (404)753-6981. **Business Addr:** District Sales Manager, Redken Labs Inc, 6625 Variel Ave, Canoga Park, CA 91303, **Business Phone:** (213)349-6563.

## WILSON, DR. OLLY WOODROW, JR.

Educator, composer. **Personal:** Born Sep 7, 1937, St. Louis, MO; son of Olly W Sr and Alma Grace Peoples; married Elouise Dolores Woods; children: Dawn Lynn & Kent Alan. **Educ:** Wash Univ, St Louis, MO, BM, 1959; Univ Ill, MM, music compos, 1960; Univ Iowa, PhD, 1964. **Career:** Musician with local jazz groups St Louis; played bass violin with St Louis Philharmonic Orchestra; St Louis Summer Chambers Players & Cedar Rapids Symphony Orch; Fla Agri & Mech Univ, educr; Oberlin Conserv Music Univ Calif, educr; auth compositions incl chamber works, orchestral works & works electronic media; conducted num concerts contemp music; orchestral compositions performed by maj orchestras incl Boston, Cleveland, San Francisco, St Louis, Houston, Oakland, Detroit Symphony Orchestras; Fla Agr & Mech Univ, Oberlin Conserv Music, teacher, 1965-70; Univ Calif, Berkeley, CA, prof music, asst chancellor, int affairs, prof & chair music, 1993-97, prof emer, 2002-; Univ Ghana, vis scholar. **Orgs:** Consult, Nat Endowment Arts, Nat Endowment Humanities; bd dir, Meet Composer; Univ Calif, Berkeley, Young Musicians Prog; bd overseer, vis comt Harvard Dept Music; ASCAP; Nat Asn Advan Colored People; Nat Urban League; Alpha Phi Alpha; Sigma Pi Phi; World Affairs Coun; Inst Int Educ; fel Rockefeller Found; Am Acad Arts & Lett, 1995; Creative Work Fund; Jerry & Evelyn Hemmings Chambers Chair Music, 1995-98. **Home Addr:** 500 Alameda, Berkeley, CA 94707-1616, **Home Phone:** (510)527-3604. **Business Addr:** Professor Emeritus, University of California, Berkeley, 104 Morrison Hall Suite 1200, Berkeley, CA 94720-1200, **Business Phone:** (510)642-2678.

## WILSON, ORA BROWN

School administrator. **Personal:** Born Austin, TX; children: Evelyn J Jones. **Educ:** Huston-Tillotson Col, BA, bus admin, 1960; Prairie View Agr & Mech Univ, MEd, 1979; St Edwards Univ; Univ Tex, Austin, TX. **Career:** Elem Schs, teaching prof; Pub Sch, teacher, 1964-67; Austin Community Col, part-time instr, 1977-79; Huston-Tillotson Univ, teacher & admin asst, 1967-79, Title III coord, 1979-. **Orgs:** Austin-Travis Co MH-MR Adv Comt, 1981-86; Lic Prof Counr, State Tex, 1983; vol, Austin Hospice 1983-; bd dir, Family Elde Care Inc, 1986; Alpha Kappa Alpha Sor; Nat Asn Historically Black Col Univ; bd mem, Mt Zion Baptist Church; Hospice Found Am; vol, Local Community Serv. **Home Addr:** 1801 Loreto Dr, Austin, TX 78721, **Home Phone:** (512)476-7970. **Business Addr:** Title III Coordinator, Huston-Tillotson University, 900 Chicon St, Austin, TX 78702-2795, **Business Phone:** (512)505-3000.

## WILSON, PATRICIA A.

Educator. **Personal:** Born Feb 1, 1948, Conway, SC. **Educ:** Univ Mich, BA, MA, PhD. **Career:** Univ Mich, asst dir undergrad admis. **Home Addr:** 6930 Cranwood Dr, Flint, MI 48505. **Business Addr:** Faculty, University of Michigan, 1220 SAB, Ann Arbor, MI 48109.

## WILSON, DR. PATRICIA I.

Educator. **Personal:** Born Jun 7, 1940, Belmont, CA; daughter of Hiawatha and Blondine Henderson; married Robert Erwin; children: Geoffrey Keith & Gary Stephen. **Educ:** NC A&T State Univ, Greensboro, NC, BS, bus educ, 1961; Univ Kent, Lexington, KY, MA, 1979, EdD, voc educ, 1984. **Career:** Educator (retired); Morris Twp Jr High Sch, Morristown, NJ, teacher, 1963-65; Roxbury High Sch, Succasunna, NJ, teacher, 1965-67; Morris Hills Regional High Sch, Rockaway, NJ, teacher, 1968-71; Cent High Sch, Joliet, Ill, teacher, 1972-73; Davenport W High Sch, Davenport, IA, teacher, 1974-77; Univ Ky, Lexington, KY, instr, 1979-81; Eastern Ky Univ, Richmond, KY, asst prof, 1981-85; Univ Ky, Col Educ, Lexington, KY, asst prof, 1985-92; Ala A&M Univ, Sch Bus, assoc prof. **Orgs:** Treas, Cent Ky Bus Edn Asn, 1986-87; awards chmn, Ky Bus Educ Asn, 1987; pres, Asn Rec Mgrs Adminrs, 1987-88; pres, Delta Pi Epsilon, 1988-90, treas, Gamma Nu Chap, 1997-99, nat secy, 2002-03; secy/treas, Phi Delta Kappa, 1990-91, vpres, 1991-92; secy, Ala Bus Ed Asn, 1994-, pres, 1998-2000; ed, Southern Bus Educ Asn, Newsletter, 1999-2000, pub rels comn, 1988-89; Nat Bus Educ Asn. **Home Addr:** 105 McNaron Dr, Madison, WI 35758-8182, **Home Phone:** (256)830-5524.

## WILSON, PRESTON JAMES RICHARD

Baseball player, baseball executive. **Personal:** Born Jul 19, 1974, Bamberg, SC; son of Mookie; children: Taya. **Career:** Baseball outfielder (retired), analyst; NY Mets, 1998; Fla Marlins, 1998-2002; Colo Rockies, 2003-05; Wash Nationals, 2005; Houston Astros, 2006; St Louis Cardinals, 2006-07; Long Island Ducks, 2009; FOX Sports Fla, analyst, currently. **Orgs:** African Am Coun Christian Clergy; Adopt-A-Classroom; Make-A-Wish Found; founder, Preston's Pride & Preston's Oper. **Business Addr:** Analyst, Fox Sports Florida, 500 E Broward Blvd Suite 1300, Ft. Lauderdale, FL 33394, **Business Phone:** (954)375-3634.

**WILSON, RAPHAEL BERNARD.** **See WILSON, BERNARD.**

**WILSON, DR. RAY FLOYD.** **See Obituaries Section.**

## WILSON, REINARD (JAMES REINARD WILSON)

Football player, football coach. **Personal:** Born Dec 17, 1973, Gainesville, FL. **Educ:** Fla State Univ. **Career:** Football player (retired), coach; Cincinnati Bengals, linebacker & right linebacker, 1997-2002; Tampa Bay Buccaneers, 2003; Scouts Inc, currently. **Honors/Awds:** Consensus All-American, 1996; Hall of Fame, Fla State Univ, 2009.

## WILSON, RITA P.

Executive. **Personal:** Born Oct 4, 1946, Philadelphia, PA; daughter of Leroy Parker and Julia Phoenix Parker; married Harold; children: Marc. **Educ:** St Paul Col, Lawrenceville, VA, BS, educ, 1968; Temple Univ, Philadelphia, Pa. **Career:** C's Serv Inc, Philadelphia, PA, social worker, 1968-70; Dept Defense, Misawa, Japan, elem sch teacher, 1971-73; Allstate Ins Co, Northbrook, Ill, opers supvr trainee, asst regional mgr, regional vpres, 1983-87, vpres corp human resource admin, 1987-88, territorial vpres, 1988-90, sr vpres, 1990-94, sr vpres corp rels, 1996-99; Northern Ill Univ, Col Bus, bd exec Advs, mem, 1988-; LeaderShape Inc, bd Dir, mem, 1990-; Ameritech, Chicago, sr vpres corp commun, 1994-96; Allstate Indemnity Co, pres, 1999-2000; Darden Restaurants, bd Dir, mem. **Orgs:** Pub rels comt, Nat Asn Independent Insurers, 1990-; trustee, Found Am Commun, 1990-; trustee, Nat Ctr Neighborhood Enterprise, 1991-; bd mem, Allstate. **Business Addr:** Board of Director, Daren Restaurants, PO Box 593330, Orlando, FL 32859-3330, **Business Phone:** (407)245-4000.

## WILSON, ROBERT

Football player. **Personal:** Born May 23, 1974, Tallahassee, FL. **Educ:** Fla A&M Univ, grad. **Career:** Football player (retired); Seattle Seahawks, wide receiver, 1997-99; New Orleans Saints, 2000, wide receiver, 2001.

## WILSON, ROBERT H.

Executive, president (organization), labor activist. **Personal:** Born Columbia, SC; son of Alex and Marian M; married Elizabeth C. **Educ:** Benedict Col. **Career:** Butchers Union Greater New York, pres; NJ Local 174, pres, currently. **Orgs:** Adv bd, Voc Ed New York, 1969; exec bd, Coalition Black Trade Unionist, 1972; chmn, Polit, Civil Polit & Civil Rights Comn Tst, Calvary Baptist Church; life mem, Nat Asn Advan Colored People; exec coun, A Philip Randolph Leaders Tomorrow Scholar Fund Inc; adv coun, Benedict Col Alumni Asn Inc, Nj Chap; exec bd, Ny Coalition Black Trade Unionist; bd educ, New York Youth Employ &Training Prog; bd trustee, Myopia Int Res Found Inc; chmn, bd trustee, UFCW Local 174 Health & Pension Funds; chmn, bd trustee, Com Health & Pension Funds; chmn, bd Trustee, Local 174 Retail Health & Pension Funds; bd trustee, Benedict Col. **Honors/Awds:** Deborah Hospital Founder's Award, 1978; Easter Seal Society Award, 1981; State Israel Bonds Award, 1984; Humanitarian Award, ACRMD, 1985; United Way Award, 1990; Consumer Assembly Award, 1990; Proclamation, City New York, 1990; Comnr Plainfield Housing Authority, New Jersey; Proclamation, City Newark. **Home Addr:** 903 Central Ave, Plainfield, NJ 07060-2310, **Home Phone:** (908)754-2353. **Business Addr:** President, UFCW Local 174, 540 W 48th St, New York, NY 10036, **Business Phone:** (212)307-7007.

## WILSON, RONALD M.

Association executive. **Personal:** Born Feb 19, 1949, Norfolk, VA; son of Guy and Wilhelmena Luster; married Katherine Stewart. **Educ:** Evergreen State Col, Olympia, Wash, BA, 1984; City Univ NY, Baruch Col, MPA, 1985. **Career:** Metro Devel Coun, Tacoma, Wash, prog mgr, 1975-81; House Reps, Olympia, Wash, legis asst, 1981-84; Nat League Cities, Wash, DC, spec asst exec dir, 1984-85; Harrisburg, PA, exec policy specialist, 1985; United Way PA, dir pub policy, 1992, vpres pub policy, 1997; Robert Half Mgt Resources, consult, 2001-. **Orgs:** Local pres, Omega Psi Phi Fraternity, 1969-; Nat Forum Black Pub Adminrs, 1984-; Int City Mgt Asn, 1985-88; Am Soc Pub Admn, 1986-88; vpres pub policy, Am Soc Asn Execs. **Home Addr:** 392 S John Young Pkwy Apt 18, Orlando, FL 32808. **Business Addr:** Consultant, Robert Half Management Resources, 245 Pk Ave 25th Fl, New York, NY 10167, **Business Phone:** (212)687-2610.

## WILSON, RONALD RAY

Lawyer, president (organization). **Personal:** Born Sep 24, 1953, Galveston, TX; son of Carrie and Henry; married Treina; children: Erik & Colby. **Educ:** Univ Tex, Plan II Prog, BS, 1977; Univ Tex Law Sch, JD, 1988. **Career:** Comm State Pension Sys, vice chmn; Sub comm Energy Resources, chmn; Calendars Energy Resources & Finance

Inst, com, 1976; House Rep 65th Session, state rep, 1976-77, 66th session, 1978-80, 67th session, 1980-81; Liquor Regulation 70th, 71st, 72nd Sessions, chmn; Fisher Gallagher & Lewis; Ronald R. Wilson & Assocs, pres, 2005-. **Orgs:** Harris Co Coun Organ, 1976-80; liaison com, Comning Battleship USS TX, 1976; chmn, Select Comm Jr Col Funding, 1980. **Home Addr:** 5039 Reed, Houston, TX 77033. **Business Addr:** President, Ronald R Wilson and Associates, 5777 E Evans Ave # 103, Denver, CO 80222-5309, **Business Phone:** (303)691-0706.

## WILSON, RUDOLPH GEORGE

Educator, administrator, association executive. **Personal:** Born Jun 17, 1935, River Rouge, MI; married Sandra Lavernn; children: Trent Duron, James Aaron, Dana Nicole & Amy Lynette. **Educ:** Los Angeles State Col, BA, 1962, MA, 1964; Wash Univ, PhD. **Career:** Juv Hall Col, counr, 1961-63; Claremont High Sch, eng dept chmn, 1964-69, master teacher eng, 1967-69; Second Educ, lectr, 1969-72; Southern Ill Univ Edwardsville, Dept Curric & Instr, assoc prof sec educ, 1975-, Off Provost, Cult & Soc Diversity, asst provost, currently, vice chancellor acad affairs, currently; US Off Educ, consult. **Orgs:** Pres, Nat Asn African Educ, 1970-71; pres, mem, Edwardsville Dist 7 Bd Educ, 1972-; pres fac Sen, Southern Ill Univ, 1975-76; Kappa Alpha Psi; founder & pres, Southern Ill Adoptive Parents Asn; bd mem, Sr Citizens Inc; bd mem, SW Ill Area Agency Aging; elected mem, Pres Search Com; Southern Ill Univ Edwardsville; vpres, Bus Affairs Search Com; coordr, Johnette Haley Scholar Acad; chair, Financial Oversight Panel; pres, Piasa Health Care; Paul Harris fel Rotary Int. **Honors/Awds:** Teaching Excellence Award, Southern Ill Univ, 1971; Art pub Harcourt-Brace, 1971; Great Teacher Award, 1974; Danforth Leadership Award, Danforth Fel; Kimmel Leadership Center Award; Martin Luther King Jr. Award; St Louis American Outstanding Educator Award; Hudlin Award for Humanistic Teaching; Educator of the Year, St. Louis American; Humanitarian Award. **Special Achievements:** First elected African American to serve on the Edwardsville School Board; First African American to teach in an all-white school; First chairperson of the newly reorganized Department of Curriculum and Instruction at SIUE. **Home Addr:** 1237 Gerber Rd, Edwardsville, IL 62025-3113, **Home Phone:** (618)656-2614. **Business Addr:** Associate Professor, Assistant Provost, Southern Illinois University Edwardsville, 1 Hairpin Dr, Edwardsville, IL 62025, **Business Phone:** (618)650-2000.

## WILSON, RUSSELL (RUSSELL CARRINGTON WILSON)

Football player, baseball player. **Personal:** Born Nov 29, 1988, Cincinnati, OH; son of Harrison Benjamin III (deceased) and Tammy T; married Ciara Princess Harris, Jul 6, 2016; married Ashton Meem, Jan 14, 2012, (divorced 2014). **Educ:** NC State Univ, attended 2010; Univ Wis, 2011. **Career:** NC State Univ Football Team, quarterback, 2007-10; NC State Wolfpack, 2008-10; Univ Wis Football Team, quarterback, 2011; NFL Seattle Seahawks, quarterback, 2012-; Good Man Brand, co-founder, 2016-; Eat The Ball, co-owner. **Honors/Awds:** FedEx Air Player of the Week; NFC Offensive Player of the Week; ACC Rookie of the Year, 2008; Steve Largent Award, Recipient, 2012; NFC Pro Bowl, Selected, 2012; Pepsi Max NFL Rookie of the Year, 2012; Sports Illustrated Offensive Rookie of the Year, Recipient, 2012; Pepsi NFL Rookie of the Week, 2012; Super Bowl Champion, XLVIII, 2014; Lombardi Trophy, 2014; PFWA Good Guy Award, 2014. **Special Achievements:** Drafted with the 12th pick in the third round (75th overall) of the 2012 NFL Draft; first quarterback to throw for more than 300 yards and rush for more than 100 yards in the same game; featured on covers of "Sports Illustrated," "ESPN The Magazine," "Men's Fitness," and "Men's Health" and TV shows "Late Show with David Letterman," "Late Night with Seth Meyers," and "Charlie Rose". **Home Addr:** , Bellevue, WA. **Business Addr:** Quarterback Player, Seattle Seahawks, 12 Seahawks Way, Renton, WA 98056, **Business Phone:** (425)203-8000.

## WILSON, SANDRA E.

Educator, college teacher, association executive. **Personal:** Born Jun 13, 1944, Abington, PA; daughter of James O Walton and Frances Walton; married John H Wilson Jr; children: John III & Shawn. **Educ:** Cheyney Univ, BS, Educ, 1966; Montclair St Col, MS, soc sci, 1971; Beaver Col, MA, 1984; Temple Univ, PhD, 1993. **Career:** Abington Sch Dist, teacher, 1966-67, 1969-80; Endicott Sch Dist, teacher, 1967-68; ment gifted prog, teacher, 1981-86; Abinton Sch Dist, teacher, 1986-99; Montgomery Co Community Col, adj prof; Temple Univ, adj instr, currently. **Orgs:** Cheyney Alumni; Nat Asn Advan Colored People; Abington Educ Asn; Nat Conf Artists; Alpha Kappa Alpha; Black Women's Educ Alliance, 1980-86; Prog dir, Comn Opportunity Coun, 1982-84; region rep, PSEA Minority Affairs Comn, 1984; pres, Montgomery Co Chap; Pa Asn Gifted C; St rep, PSEA; NEA Nat Rep Assembly, 1986; secy, Am Asn Univ Women, 1986; vpres, Nat Chap, Coordr; youth Coun, Nat Asn Advan Colored People, Willow Grove Br; teacher testing comm PSEA Educ Testing Serv, 1987; pres-elect, Nat Chap, Black Women's Educ Alliance, 1988-; youth choir organist, Bethlehem Baptist Church; pres, Black Women's Educ Alliance Nat, 1991; Nat Asn Advan Colored People Youth Dir Eastern PA; Nat Asn Advan Colored People, exec bd, WG Chap; dir, Sandra Wilson Dramatic Ensemble, 1995; charter mem, Phi Beta Omega Chap, 1998. **Honors/Awds:** Phi Delta Scholar, 1962; Richard Humphrey's Scholar, 1962-66; Student Teacher of the Year, Cheyney Univ, 1966; Art Award, Jenkintown Festival Arts, 1980; vol serv, NAACP Youth Job Conf, 1983; Outstanding Service Dedication Award, Citizen Progress, 1983; Distinctive Service Award, Black Women's Educ Alliance, 1985; Black Women's Educ Alliance Leadership, 1986; NAACP Serv to Youth Award, 1988, 1999; Optimist of American Youth Service Award, 1989; poem published Poetic Voices Am, 1990; BWEA Pres Award, 1993, BWEA, Mong Chapter, Newsletter Ed, 1993-; Nominated for Pennsylvania Teacher of the Year, 1995; Temple Univ, Cooperating Teacher of the Year, 1999. **Special Achievements:** Play: We Are, Int Journal of Black Drama, 1995; ed, Antioch Baptist, News From the Pews; teacher, contrib, editor, Silver Burdett Science curric, second grade, 1992; author: "The Taboo Childhood of Jesus", 2014. **Home Addr:** 3106 Ori Pl, Dresher, PA 19025, **Home Phone:** (215)659-1520. **Business Addr:** Professor, Montgomery County Community College, 340 Dekalbo Pke, Blue Bell, PA 19422, **Business Phone:** (215)641-6300.

## WILSON, SHAWN-TA

Government official. **Personal:** Born Mar 31, 1967, Bridgeport, CT; daughter of Robert and Valerie Sterns; married Warren; children: Jordan Janae. **Educ:** Radford Univ, attended 1988; Northern Va Community Col, attended 1991; Millsborough Community Col, attended 1996. **Career:** Graphic Arts Show Co, show coordr, 1989-93; Tampa Conv Ctr, event coordr, 1994, sr conv serv mgr, asst dir conv serv, currently; Tampa Police Dept, house mgr; asst dir conv serv. **Home Addr:** 6915 Jamestown Manor Dr, Riverview, Hillsborough County, FL 33578, **Home Phone:** (813)886-0820. **Business Addr:** Assistant Director, City of Tampa, 333 S Franklin St, Tampa, FL 33602, **Business Phone:** (813)274-7767.

## WILSON, SIDNEY, JR.

Automotive executive, president (organization), chief executive officer. **Career:** Wilson Buick-Pontiac-GMC Truck Inc, pres & chief exec officer, currently. **Business Addr:** Chief Executive Officer, President, Wilson Buick-Pontiac-GMC Inc, 1639 US Hwy 45 Byp, Jackson, TN 38305-4413, **Business Phone:** (901)422-3426.

## WILSON, DR. SODONIA MAE

Educator. **Personal:** Born Galveston, TX; daughter of Rev Jasper Moore and Willie Mae Reed Moore; married James; children: Demetrius D. **Educ:** Fr Hosp Sch Nursing, RN, 1957; San Francisco City Col, AS, 1961; San Francisco State Univ, BA, 1963, MA, 1965; Calif Sch Prof Psycholgy, PhD, 1973. **Career:** Fr Hosp SF CA, RN, 1956-57; Ft Miley Va Hosp SF CA, RN, 1957-60; SF Youth Guid Ctr, counr, 1966, probation off, 1967; Off Econ Opportunities, head start analyst, 1968; SF Redevelop Agency, soc serv rep, 1969; Sequoia Union High Sch Dist, coun coordr, 1969-72; Contra Costa Col, San Pablo, CA, counr, 1972-73, dir spec prog, 1973-83, dir spec prog, serv finance aid officer, 1983-85, mgr instr, tech support serv, 1985-86, dir spec progs & serv, 1986-; Sch Bd San Francisco Unified Sch Dist, pres. **Orgs:** Pres, Calif Comn Col Admin, 1977-78; SF Bus & Prof Women's Club, 1978-; Black Women Polit Action, 1979-; Women Higher Educ Assoc, 1980-84; Nat Women's Polit Caucus, 1981-86; vpres, SF Bd Educ, 1982-84, pres, 1986-88; comnr, Calif Stud Aid Comn, 1982-85; Bay Area Black Women United, 1982-84; stud aid comn, 1982-85; pres, Contra Costa Community Col Dist Mgt Coun Exec Bd, 1992; Nat Asn Advan Colored People. **Honors/Awds:** Merit of Honor, Ernest Kay Hon Gen Ed Int Biography, 1973-; Certificate Distinguished Serv, San Francisco Unified Sch Dist Bd Edu, 1982-90; Certificate Outstanding Serv Rendered, San Francisco Alliance Black School Educrs, 1982-90; Cert Outstanding Serv, San Francisco African Am Hist & Cult Soc Inc, 1982-90; Cert Merit Form, Calif Community Col EOPS Assoc, 1985; Certificate of Appreciation, 1985; Cert Award, Marina Middle Sch, 1985; Certificate of Appreciation, Support Math Eng & Sci Achievement, 1986; Educational Acad Achievement Award, 1987; Cert Commendation, Nat Asn Negro Bus & Prof Women's Clubs Inc, 1987; Cert Award, 1989; Woman of the Year Award, 1989; Education Award, 1989. **Special Achievements:** Books: "A Research Study on Special College Counseling for Non-White and Disadvantaged Students", 1971. **Home Addr:** 101 Dalewood Way, San Francisco, CA 94127-1606, **Home Phone:** (415)242-1199. **Business Addr:** Director of Special Programs & Services, Contra Costa College, 2600 Mission Bell Dr, San Pablo, CA 94806, **Business Phone:** (510)235-7800.

## WILSON, SONALI BUSTAMANTE (Z SONALI BUSTAMANTE)

Lawyer. **Personal:** Born May 31, 1958, Cleveland, OH; daughter of John H and F Joy Simmons; married N Stephen II; children: Martine Celeste, Joy & Julian. **Educ:** Boston Univ, Boston, MA, BA, hist, 1980; Harvard Univ, Boston, MA, ALM, govt studies, 1983; Georgetown Univ Law Ctr, WA, DC, JD, 1986. **Career:** Off Chief Compliance, DC, Dept Consumer & Regulatory Affairs, law clerk, 1984-86; Ohio Supreme Ct Justice, law clerk, 1987; Arter & Hadden, Cleveland, Ohio, assoc, 1986, litigation, 1988-94; pvt pract, 1994-97; Cleveland State Univ, lectr, 1996, asst univ legal coun, 1997, chief legal coun & bd secy, 2000-11, gen coun, 2004-. **Orgs:** Am Bar Asn, Pre-Law Coun Com, Young Lawyers Div; bd trustee, Cleveland Bar Asn, Young Lawyer's Exec Coun, 1988-; corresp sec, Links Inc Cleveland; co-chair, Nat Trends, 1988-; bd trustee, Women space, 1988-91; Citizen's League Greater Cleveland, 1990-; Girlfriends Cleveland, 1990-; United Way, Govt Rels Comt, 1991-; pres, Cleveland Chap, Links Inc; bd trustee, Cuyahoga Co Bd Ment Retardation & Develop Disabilities; legal advisor, Greater Cleveland Alumnae Chap, Delta Sigma Theta Sorority Inc; bd trustee, Cleveland Inst Music; Nat Legal Comt; Nat Asn Col & Univ Atty; Cleveland Metrop Bar Asn; Norman S. Minor Bar Asn; Cleveland Inst Music Bd, 2009-; Univ Hosps McDonald's Women's Hosp Leadership Coun 2009-; United Way Greater Cleveland Bd, 2016-. **Honors/Awds:** Citation for Achievement, Massachusetts House of Representatives, 1979; Citation in Recognition of Service, Governor of King of Massachusetts, 1979; Alumni Association Hall of Fame, Shaker Heights school, 2009; Trail Blazer Award, Norman S Minor Bar Assoc, 2013; Women of Color Foundation Professional Woman of the Year 2014; Woman of Achievement, YWCA, 2015. **Home Addr:** 28279 Red Raven Rd, Cleveland, OH 44124-4552, **Home Phone:** (216)595-0070. **Business Addr:** General Counsel, Cleveland State University, 2121 Euclid Ave AC 327, Cleveland, OH 44115-2214, **Business Phone:** (216)687-3543.

## WILSON, PROF. STANLEY CHARLES

Educator. **Personal:** Born Feb 2, 1947, Los Angeles, CA; son of Ernest and Eleanor Mae Reid; married Jacquelyn Patricia Bellard; children: Jendayi Asabi. **Educ:** Chouinard Art Sch, 1965; Calif State Polytech Univ, Pomona, 1966; Calif State Univ, Los Angeles, Calif, 1967; Otis Art Inst, Los Angeles, Calif, BFA, 1969, MFA, sculpture, 1971. **Career:** Jr Art Ctr, Los Angeles, Calif, instr, 1969-72; Southwestern Col, Chula Vista, Calif, asst prof, 1972-73; Otis Art Inst, Parsons Watts Towers, instr, 1981; Calif State Polytech Univ, Pomona, Calif, prof visual art, 1973-2002, prof emer, 2002-; Univ Art Gallery, dir, 1988-94. **Orgs:** Gallery cur dir, Calif State Polytech Univ, Pomona, Calif, 1975-85; planning & dir, Los Angeles Weave, Los Angeles Olympic Exhib, 1984 planning bd, w coast black artist Exhib, 1976; Brand Art Ctr, Glendale, Calif; bd adv, Watts Towers Art Ctr, Los Bd artists, Brockman GalleryProd, Los Angeles, Calif, 1980-85; bd adv, Africa Quarter, Calif State Polytech Univ, 1984-85; awards panelist, New Genre Fel Calif Arts Coun, Sacramento, Calif, 1989; bd adv, Latin Am Quarter, Calif Polytech Univ, Pomona, Calif, 1989; award panelist, sculpture, Calif Arts Coun, Sacramento, Calif, 1990; bd adv, gallery comt, Armony Art Cen, Pasadena, Calif, 1990-91; awards panelist, sculpture, Colo Coun Arts & Humanities, 1991; fel awards panelist, Ill Arts Coun, 1991-; chmn, City Pasadena, Arts Comn, 1997; chair, Pasadena Arts Comn, 1997-2000; co-chair, sculputure panel, Col Art Asn, 1999; panel, Contemp Sculpture, Calif African Am Mus, 1999; nat develop comn, studio art, advan placement, Princeton, NJ; bd dir, Armory Ctr Arts, Pasadena. **Honors/Awds:** Works publ Black Artist Art, Vol 2, Lewis & Waddy, 1971, Afro-Am Artist, Boston Pub Libr, 1973; Vis Artist Residence Aberdeen, SD, 1975; Nominated Fulbright Fel, West & East Africa, 1984-85; Artist Residence, Studio Mus Harlem, NY, 1986-87; Meritorious & Prof Promise Award, Calif Polytech Univ, Pomona, Calif, 1986; Six African Am Artist, Calif State Univ, Dominquez Hills, Calif, 1989; Calif Art Rev, second ed, Chicago, Ill, 1989; Calif Art Rev, third ed Chicago, Ill, 1991; Two Man Exhibition, Sparc Gallery, Venice, Calif, 1990; Vis Artist, Univ Nevada-Las Vegas, 1990; Calif Polytech Univ, Pomona, Outstanding Pro, 1991; One Man Exhibition, San Antonio Art Inst, San Antonio, Tex, 1992; Pasadena Arts Com, Visual Arts Award, 1998; Vis Artist & Grad Rev, Memphis Col Art, Memphis Tenn, 2001; Invited Lectr, Calif State Univ, North Ridge, Art Dept, 2001; AP Rev Panel Princeton, New Jersey; Nat Endowment Art; Nat Endowment Panel; Awarded Visual Arts Fellowship, Pasadena Arts Comn; Outstanding Professor Award, Col Arts, Cal Poly Univ; Received Numerous Honors & Awards. **Special Achievements:** Curated selected art works Bakerfield Col Exhibition, Local, Space Gallery, Los Angeles, Calif, 1995; Appointed Arts Comn, City Pasadena, Calif; Calif Community Found, Brody fel, 1998; Artist Against the Spreadof Aids in Africia-Auction, 2001; co-curated Exhibition, "The Story is in the Telling," Armoney Center for the Arts, 2002; Two Man Exhibitional,"Method Meaning" Calif State Univ-Bakersfield, 2002: Numerous Publications. **Home Addr:** 2704 W Ave 34, Los Angeles, CA 90065, **Home Phone:** (323)256-2997. **Business Addr:** Professor Emeritus, California State Polytechnic University, 3801 W Temple Ave Bldg 13, Pomona, CA 91768, **Business Phone:** (909)869-7659.

## WILSON, DR. STEPHANIE Y.

Economist. **Personal:** Born Feb 16, 1952, Pittsburgh, PA. **Educ:** Goddard Col, BA, 1973; State Univ NY, Stonybrook, MA, 1975, PhD, 1978; Astridge Sch Mgt, Int Bus Mgt; Harvard Univ, Ctr Int Affair, Dissertation Res. **Career:** Abt Assocs, Wash, DC, analyst, 1977-80, proj dir & sr analyst, 1981-86, managing vpres, 1983-93, vpres & area mgr, 1985-86, group vpres int, 1992-2001; Joint Ctr Econ & Polit Studies, Consult, 2002; Heinz Endowments, Educ Officer, 2 003-05; Carnegie Mellon Univ, Adj Prof, 2 005; Independent Consult, 2005-08; Asn for the Study & Develop Community, Prin Assoc, 2008-. **Orgs:** Pres, Nat Econ Asn; Prof Serv Coun; US-Africa Bus Coun; Bd mem, Soc Int Develop; US-S Africa Bus Coun; US-Russ Bus Coun; Corp Coun Africa; Asn Women Develop; Am Eval Asn; Keynote speaker, Eval Cohort Symp. **Special Achievements:** Third woman to become a President of the Nat Econ Asn; recognized in the Who's Who among African Americans, The Inter Global Who's Who, Strathmores Who's Who, the Who's Who of Women Executives & Sterling Who's Who; published "A Different Vision: African American Economic Thought". **Home Addr:** 11400 Cedar Ridge Dr, Potomac, MD 20854-3762, **Home Phone:** (240)403-7141. **Business Addr:** Principal Associate, Association for the Study and Development of Community, 438 N Frederick Ave Suite 315, Gaithersburg, MD 20878.

## WILSON, THOMAS A., JR.

Banker. **Personal:** Born Sep 25, 1951, Baltimore, MD; son of Thomas A Sr and Margaret R Stokes; married Diane P Freeman; children: Cedric T & Dexter N. **Educ:** Morgan State Univ, BS, 1973. **Career:** Nat Bank, examr; Ind Bank Wash, comptroller currency, nat bank examr, 1974-86, vpres, loan rev officer, 1986-88, controller, sr vpres, 1988-, chief finance officer, currently. **Home Addr:** 1605 Tredegar Ave, Catonsville, MD 21228, **Home Phone:** (410)719-0119. **Business Addr:** Senior Vice President, Chief Finannce Officer, Industrial Bank of Washington, 4812 Ga Ave NW, Washington, DC 20011, **Business Phone:** (202)722-2000.

## WILSON, TREVOR

Basketball player, police officer. **Personal:** Born Mar 16, 1968, Los Angeles, CA. **Educ:** Univ Calif, Los Angeles, CA, attended 1990. **Career:** Basketball player (retired), police; Phoenix Suns, 1990-91; Atlanta Hawks, 1991-92; Glaxo Verona, Italy, 1991; OAR Ferrol, Spain, 1991-93; Los Angeles Lakers, 1993-94; Sacramento Kings, 1993-95; Somontano Huesca, Spain, 1995; Olympique Antibes, France, 1995; Philadelphia 76ers, forward, 1995; Chicago Rockers, 1996; Sioux Falls Skyforce, CBA, 1996-97; Aisin Seahorses, Japan, 1997-98; Caja Cantabria, Spain, 1998; Turk Telekom Ankara, Turkey, 1998-99; Seattle Supersonics, 1995; Los Angeles Lakers, free agt, 1996; Los Angeles Police Departmen, police officer, currently. **Business Addr:** Police Officer, Los Angeles Police Department, 100 W 1st St, Los Angeles, CA 90012, **Business Phone:** (213)486-1000.

## WILSON, VALERIE PETIT

Health services administrator, scientist, educator. **Personal:** Born Jan 24, 1950, New Orleans, LA; daughter of Alvin Joseph and Lorraine Kelly Petit; married Melvin; children: Daniel & Craig. **Educ:** Xavier Univ, BS, pre-med, chem, 1970; Johns Hopkins Univ, PhD, molecular biol, genetics, 1976. **Career:** Mt Sinai Hosp, Dept Human Genetics, researcher, 1976-77; Nat Inst Health, Lab Molecular Virol, NIAMDD, 1977-79, Lab Molecular Hemat, res, 1979-81, Sci Prog Admin, asst Diabetes Br, 1981-82, asst diabetes prog dir, 1982-83, Diabetes, Endocrinol & Metab, asst div dir, 1983-86, off asst secy Health, Bio Med Res, desk officer, 1986-88; Pub Health Serv, AIDS Policy Analyst, 1988-90, dir policy anal & coord, 1990-91, actg dir, 1992-93; Nat Acad Sci, Div Health Scis Policy, dir, 1993-97; Nat AIDS Prog Off, Howard Univ Sch Med, Dept Family & Community Med, adj appointment, 1994-97; Tulane Univ, Sch Pub Health Trop Med, Dept Environ Health Sci, clin assoc prof, 1998-2003, Tulane/Xavier Ctr Bioenvironmental Res, dep dir, 1998-2003; Brown Univ, Leadership Alliance, exec dir, 2003-, Brown Tougaloo Partnership, univ coordr, 2003-, clin prof community health, assoc dean grad sch, 2005-09, assoc provost & dir inst diversity, 2009-. **Orgs:** Am Soc Biochemists & Molecular Biologists; adv bd, 1989-92, bd mem, 1993-96, vpres bd, 1994-96, chmn bd, 1996-97, Jr League Wash; Nat Asn People AIDS; Alpha Kappa Alpha. **Home Addr:** 2433 Lark St, New Orleans, LA 70122. **Business Addr:** Associate Dean, Clinical Professor of Community Health, Brown University, Univ Hall Rm 114 One Prospect St, Providence, RI 02912-1963, **Business Phone:** (401)863-2706.

## WILSON, VELMA J.

Manager, president (organization), educator. **Personal:** Born Aug 28, 1934, Chicago, IL; daughter of Joseph C and Rubye Therkeld; married John E; children: Ginger Renee & Kelly JoAnne. **Educ:** Chicago Teachers Col Chicago State Univ, BS, educ, 1958, MS, educ, 1963. **Career:** Bd Educ, Chicago, primary teacher, 1958-68; Woodlawn Orgn, dir family focus, 1977; Chicago Urban League, consult young parents prog, 1979-83; Harold WAS Mayor, scheduler, 1982-83; City Chicago, dir tourism, 1984-89; Wilson GRP, pres, 1989-. **Orgs:** Delta Sigma Theta, 1958-; Bd mem, Oper Push, 1976-; bd mem, Dusable Mus Bd, 1977-85; tres, secy, ETA Bd, 1978-83; pres, Women's Bd Chicago Urban League, 1985-87; sustaining mem, Univ Chicago Lying Hosp, 1979-; Jesse Owens FND, friend com chair, 1991-92; Links Inc, Windy City, chair, nat trends com, 1995-; pres, Parents Resource Inc; Delta Sigma Theta, 1958-; bd mem, Oper Push, 1976-; bd mem, Dusable Mus Bd, 1977-85; tres, secy, ETA Bd, 1978-83; pres, Women's Bd Chicago Urban League, 1985-87; sustaining mem, Univ Chicago Lying Hosp, 1979-; Jesse Owens FND, friend com chmn, 1991-92; chmn, Links Inc, Windy City, nat trends com, 1995-; pres, Parents Resource Inc. **Honors/Awds:** Oper Push, Salute to Excellence, Women's Deleg To Lebanon, 1979; Community Consciousness, 1977; Outstanding Serv, Chicago Urban League, 1985; Woman of the Yr, Norman LaHarry Scholar Found, 1987; Outstanding Serv, City of Chicago, 1989. **Home Addr:** 1031 E Hyde Pk Blvd 2nd Fl, Chicago, IL 60615-2807, **Home Phone:** (773)752-6680.

## WILSON, WALTER JAMES

Football player. **Personal:** Born Oct 6, 1966, Baltimore, MD. **Educ:** E Carolina Univ, BA, criminal justice. **Career:** Football player (retired); San Diego Chargers, wide receiver & tight end, 1990; Miami Dolphins, wide receiver, 1992. **Honors/Awds:** Honorable Mention of All-America, Sporting News. **Special Achievements:** Set E Carolina University Record with 91 receptions for 1670 yards & 16 touchdowns. **Business Addr:** Wide Receiver, Miami Dolphins, Sun Life Stadium, Miami Gardens, FL 33056.

## WILSON, WENDY L.

Journalist, periodical editor. **Educ:** Skidmore College (Saratoga Springs, NY), Bachelor's in English with a concentration in Creative Writing, 1996; New York University, Master's in Journalism, 2000. **Career:** "George," 2000; "InStyle," Editorial Internship, 2000-01; "Teen People," Editorial Asst., 2001-03, Asst. Editor, 2003-04, Staff Writer, 2004-05; "Essence" Magazine, Staff Writer, 2005-07; Essence.com, News Editor, 2008-09; "Essence" Magazine, News Editor, 2009-13; "Jet" Magazine, Managing Editor, 2013-. **Orgs:** National Association of Black Journalists, Member; American Society of Magazine Editors, Member. **Honors/Awds:** Time Inc. President's Award, Recipient, 2001; National Association of Black Journalists, Best Magazine Business Story Award for "12-Month Home-Ownership Campaign," 2007; New York Association of Black Journalists, Magazine Public Affairs Award and Online/New Media Category for Public Affairs, 2010.

## WILSON, WESLEY CAMPBELL

Vice president (organization), business owner. **Personal:** Born Nov 29, 1931, Philadelphia, PA; son of Wesley and Emily; married Elaine Epps; children: Carl B, Wayne K, Michael K & Eric W. **Educ:** Morgan State Univ, BS, 1954; Col William & Mary, MEd, 1974, adv cert educ, 1978, EdD, 1986. **Career:** Col William & Mary, asst pres, 1974-76; C & W Assocs Inc, co-owner, vpres, 1976-. **Orgs:** Newport News Dem Comn, 1974-; exec bd, First Dist Black Caucus, 1975-; pres, Alpha Alpha Chap Omega Psi Phi, 1975-76; chmn, Gov comn Adv Gov Va EEO, 1975-79; chmn sch bd, Newport News Va Pub Sch, 1977-; bd trustees, Peninsula United Way, 1979-. **Honors/Awds:** Citizen of the Year, Omega Psi Phi Newport News Va, 1977, 1978; Man of the Year, Peninsula Negro Bus & Prof Women, 1979; Educ & Polit Strange Bedfellows, 1979. **Business Addr:** Vice President, C & W Associates Incorporation, 825 Diligence Dr Suite 116, Newport News, VA 23606, **Business Phone:** (804)873-4735.

## WILSON, WILLIAM HAYWARD. See WILSON, MOOKIE.

## WILSON, DR. WILLIAM JULIUS

Sociologist, educator, association executive. **Personal:** Born Dec 20, 1935, Derry Township, PA; son of Esco and Pauline Bracy; married Mildred Mary Hood; married Beverly Huebner; children: Colleen, Lisa, Carter & Paula. **Educ:** Wilberforce Univ, BA, sociol & hist, 1958; Bowling Green State Univ, MA, sociol & hist, 1961; Wash State Univ, PhD, sociol & hist, 1966. **Career:** Univ Mass, Amherst, asst prof social, 1965-69, assoc prof social, 1969-71; Univ Chicago, vis assoc prof, 1971-72, asso prof social, 1972-75, prof social, 1975-80, chmn, Sociol Dept, 1978-81, 1984-96, univ prof, 1990-96; Lucy Flower Univ, prof urban sociol, 1980-84, Distinguished serv prof, social, 1984-90, prof social & pub policy, 1990-96, Sch Pub Policy, Ctr Study Urban, dir, 1990-96; Fr-Am Found, vis prof, Am studies, Ecole des Hautes Etudes eng soc sci, Paris, 1989-90; Col de France, Paris, lectr, soc sci, 1990; Joblessness & Urban Res Prog, Malcolm Wiener Ctr Social Policy, dir, 1996-; Harvard Univ, Malcolm Wiener prof soc policy, prof Afro-Am studies, 1996-98, Lewis P & Linda L Geyser Univ prof, 1996-. **Orgs:** Chmn, res adv comn, Chicago Urban League, 1976-85; bd dir, Soc Sci Res Coun, 1979-85; nat bd, A Philip Randolph Inst, 1981-; bd dir, Chicago Urban League, 1983-97; nat bd, Inst Res Poverty, 1983-87; George M Pullman Found, 1986-93; Carnegie Coun Adoloscent Devel, 1986-95; William TGrant Founds Comn Youth & Am Future, 1986-88; Ctr Budget & Policy Priorities, 1987-; Spencer Founf, 1987-96; bd dir, Ctr Advan Study Behav Scis, 1988-2002; bd dir, Russell Sage Found, 1989-98; bd trustee, Spelman Colm, 1989-98; Nat Humanities Ctr, 1990-95; Consortium Soc Sci Asn, 1991-95; bd trustee, Bard Col, 1992-2001; trustee, Twentieth Century Fund, 1992-2001; bd, Manpower Demonstration Res Corp, 1993-; Pres's Comn White House Fel, 1994-2001; Bd, Pub/Pvt Ventures, 1994-2002; Pres's Comn Nat Med Sci, Nat Sci Found, 1994-98; Adv bd, Ctr Pub Integrity, 1995-; Bd trustee, Wilberforce Univ, 1995-; Bd dir, Nat Urban League, 1995-98; Nat Acad Sci, Comt Sci, Engineering & Pub Policy, 1995-2001; bd adv, Frederick D Patterson Res Inst, 1996-; bd dir, Policylink, 2000-; Scholar's Coun, Libr Cong, 2001; Bd trustee, Bard Col, 2001-; Bd gov, Levy Found Econ Inst, 2001-; AAAS; Am Acad Arts & Sci; Int Sociol Asn; pres, Am Sociol Asn. **Honors/Awds:** Received several honorary degrees from various Universities; Dr Humane Letters, Honoris Causa: Univ Mass, Amherst, 1982; MacArthur Prize Fellow, The John D and Catherine T MacArthur Found, 1987-92; Distinguished Alumnus Award, Washington State Univ, 1988; C Wright Mills Award for the truly disadvantaged, Soc Study Soc Problems, 1988; North Central Sociological Asn Achievement Award, 1988; Washington Monthly's Annual Book Award, 1988; Dr Laws Honoris Causa, Mt Holyoke Col, 1989, Marquette Univ, 1989; Dubois, Johnson, Frazier Award, Am Sociol Asn, 1990; New Sch Soc Res, 1991; Doctor of Humane Letters, Tulane Univ, Bard Col, John Jay ColCriminal Justice, 1992; Univ Penn, Southern Ill Univ, Edwardsville, 1993; Doctor of Laws, Honoris Causa, Northwestern Univ, 1993; Bowling Green State Univ, State Univ NY, Binghamton, Princeton Univ, 1994; Frank E Seidman Distinguished Award Political Economy, Rhodes Col, Memphis, TN, 1994; Doctor of Humane Letters, Honoris Causa, Haverford Col, 1995; Martin Luther King Jr, National Award, 1998; Doctor of Laws, Clarion Univ, Penn, Colgate V Clark Univ, 1999, Bates Col, 1999; Doctor of Social Science, Northeastern Univ, 1999; Doctor Of Humane Letters, Macalester Col, St Paul, Ohio State Univ, Columbus, 2000; Occidental Col, Reusselars Polytechnic Inst, Lawrence Univ, 2001; Sidney Hillman Found Award; Winner of Talcott Parson Prize, 2003; Golden Plate Achievement Award; Burton Gordon Feldman Award. **Special Achievements:** Selected as one of the America's 25 Most Influential People, Time mag, 1991; Recipient of National Medal of Science, 1998; Author of various books and articles; He is the First & only non economist to receive Seidman Award. **Business Addr:** Linda L Geyser University Professor, Harvard University, Malcolm Wiener Ctr Social Policy, Cambridge, MA 02138, **Business Phone:** (617)496-4514.

## WILSON, REV. WILLIE FREDERICK (KWADWO I BOAFO)

Clergy, educator. **Personal:** Born Mar 8, 1944, Newport News, VA; son of Samuel B and Lovey E; married Mary Lewis; children: Anika, Kalilia, Bashiri & Hamani. **Educ:** Ohio Univ, BS, jour, 1966; Howard Univ, Divinity Sch, MDiv, 1969; Doctoral Studies, 1971. **Career:** Union Temple Baptist Church, pastor, 1973-. **Orgs:** Nat exec dir, Millions More Movement; exec prog dir, Hist Million Man March. **Honors/Awds:** Top 10 Most Valuable People in USA, USA Today, 1985; US Presidential Service Award, 1997; One of 100 Model African American Churches in America, Nat Congress Black Churchmen; Outstanding Orator & Preacher; Rockefeller Protestant Fellowship Award; Vernon Johns Preaching Award; Recipient Of Several Awards. **Special Achievements:** Author: "The African American Wedding Manual"; Releasing the Power Within, The Genius of Jesus Revealed; How African Religion Changed the American Church; Ordained as WOLOF priest in Gambia, West Africa, 1980; Enstated as Ashanti subchief in Ghana, 1993; Authored Numerous Publications. **Home Addr:** 3664 Highwood Dr SE, Washington, DC 20020, **Home Phone:** (202)581-5059. **Business Addr:** Pastor, Union Temple Baptist Church, 1225 W St SE, Washington, DC 20020, **Business Phone:** (202)678-8822.

## WILSON, WILLIE MAE

Executive director, association executive, executive. **Personal:** Born Mar 18, 1942, Birmingham, AL; married William L; children: Bertrand LaMarr & Pelina. **Educ:** Knoxville Col, BA; Univ Minn, MA. **Career:** Minn St Comn Discrim, res clerk, 1964; St Paul Bpu Lib, asst librn, 1965-66; Urban League Comn, organizer proj, 1966-67; Econ Develop & Employ St Paul Urban League, actg dir & pres, 1967; Urban Leag, housing dir, 1967-69; St Paul Urban Coal, housing coord, 1969, chief exec officer, 1972-74, pres, adminr dept; Twin Cities Met Coun, 1971. **Orgs:** Chmn bd comt, St Paul Housing & Redev Auth & Comn, 1972-76; co-chmn, Summit Univ, 1973; vpres, Urban N Nonprof Housing Corp, 1973; deleg, St Paul Dem Farm Labor, 1974; pres, Coun EXD Nat Urban Leag, 1980-82; chmn, Unit Way Coun Agency Dir; vpres, St Paul Ramsey Coun Agency Dir; bd dir, First Nat Bank St Paul; Cit Leag; bd dir, Comn Develop Corp; Oper 85 Planning Comn; Minn Met Orgn Displaced Women; tri-chmn, St Paul Publ Sch Sec Educ Adv Comm Desegrat; DST Sor; Lota Phi Lambda Bus & Prof Womens Sor; Am Soc Planning Off; Am Soc Pub Admin; St Paul Urban League; Nat Asn Advan Colored People. **Honors/Awds:** Samuel Ullman Scholar Award, 1960; Woodrow Wilson Enrichment Scholar, Col Univ, 1964. **Home Addr:** 168 N Lexington Pkwy, St Paul, MN 55104.

## WILSON, WILSON W.

Military leader, real estate agent. **Personal:** Born May 31, 1942, Quachita Parish, LA; son of Phillip and Christel Jones; married Georgia Crawford; children: Suzzon E, Ellen M, Warren M & Gladys C. **Educ:** Southern Univ, BA, 1964; McNeese State Univ; Roosevelt Univ; Univ Ky, grad study; Western Ky Univ, MPA, 1975; Northeast State Univ. **Career:** Military leader, real estate agent (retired); AUS, min army off procurement; rep Vietnam joint US staff for mil assistance, 1969-70, supply part officer 5H inf div, Ft Polk, LA, 1978, 5th AUS hq staff off dep chief staff ROTC, equal opportunity officer 5th inf div, Ft Polk, LA, dep comn comdr Wertheim Mil comn Wertheim Gery; self employed, Monroe, LA, real estate broker, 1988-; Monroe City Sch Syst, sci teacher, 1989-91; high sch adminr, 1999-. **Orgs:** Minority Bus Asn, Alpha Phi Alpha Fraternity, 1963; YMCA, 1963; Asn AUS, 1965-73; Prince Hall Masonic, 1967; Off holder Hardin Co, Ky Br, Nat Asn Advan Colored People, 1973-75; Monroe Nat Asn Advan Colored People, Ouachita Br, 1988-. **Honors/Awds:** Numerous military decor; rec'd numerous commend for part in educ seminars MW U's; part in lecture series at these same MW Univs; numerous TV appearances disc the role of black soldier in AUS & black military hist; Legion of Merit Award, US Army, 1989. **Home Addr:** PO Box 265, Monroe, LA 71210.

## WILSON-GEORGE, SYBIL

Football player, executive, actor. **Educ:** Pace Univ, grad. **Career:** Miami Heat Inst, dir corp educ, dir customer rels, admin asst, spec asst to exec vpres, currently. **Honors/Awds:** Exemplary Partnership Award, Dade Co Pub Sch. **Home Addr:** 7833 Plantation Blvd, Miramar, FL 33023-2451. **Business Addr:** Special Assistant to the Executive Vice President, Miami Heat Institution, 1 SE 3rd Ave Suite 2300, Miami, FL 33131, **Business Phone:** (305)577-4328.

## WILSON-KNOX, SHANICE LORRAINE

Singer. **Personal:** Born May 14, 1973, Pittsburgh, PA; daughter of Crystal; married Flex Alexander; children: Imani Shekinah & Elijah. **Career:** Albums: Discovery, 1987; Inner Child, 1991; 21 Ways To Grow, 1994; Shanice, Ultimate Collection, 1999; Every Woman Dreams, 2006; Grand' 88; The Collection, 2009; TBA, 2011. Singles: "(Baby Tell Me) Can You Dance", 1987; "This Time", 1988; "I Love Your Smile", "I'm Cryin'", 1991; "Silent Prayer", "Saving Forever for You", 1992; "It's for You", 1993; "Somewhere", "Turn Down the Lights", "I Wish", "I Like", 1994; "When I Close Eyes", "Yesterday", 1999; "You Need A Man", 1999; "Love is the Gift", 2000; "Every Woman Dreams", 2001; "Take Care of U", 2002; "So Sexy", 2003; "Chasing Fever", 2003; "Tomorrow", 2004; "I Got This", 2005; "Kryptonite", 2006; "Gotta Blame Me", 2007. **Honors/Awds:** Winner, vocal category, Star Search, 1985; Golden Lion Award, 1993; Special Jahruba Atkinson Award for Music, 2005. **Business Addr:** Singer, c/o Motown Record Co, 6255 Sunset Blvd, Los Angeles, CA 90028.

## WILSON-SMITH, WILLIE ARRIE (WILLIE A SMITH)

Educator. **Personal:** Born Jan 12, 1929, Charlotte, NC; daughter of Booker T and Katie A Vance; married Jack. **Educ:** Johnson C Smith Univ, BA, 1956; Western Reserve Univ, Med, 1962. **Career:** Educator (retired); JB Iveys Millinery Shoe Repairing, 1951-54; Belks Shoe Repairing, 1954-57; Charlotte Mecklenburg Sch Syst, teacher, 1957-80. **Orgs:** Dep dir 9th Dist Dem Women, 1977-79; past mem, Charlotte CRC, 1974-82; Appt Study Comt Rel Between Prof Employ Asn & Sch Bd, 1973-75; apptd NC Adv Comt Teacher Educ, 1974-76; soror yr, AKA, 1965; bd trustee, Cent Piedmont Community Col, 1979-87; vol, Charlotte Bus League, 1986, 1987; treas, New Emannuel Congl UCC, 1989-97; dem cand, Charlotte City Coun Dist, 1997; chair, 12th US Cong Dist-NC, 1997-2003; bd trustee, NC Col Found, 1997-; NC High Sch vol, 1997-; life mem, NEA; life mem, NCAE; life mem, NCACT; Alpha Kappa Alpha Sor Inc; Mecklenburg County Dem Womens Club; NC Dem Exec Comt; Womens Forum NC; Charlotte BPC; life mem, New Emmanuel Congregational United Church Christ; past mem, Charlotte Mecklenburg NCCJ; PTA; Girl Scout Adv; Friends Hammocks & Bear Island Inc. **Honors/Awds:** Graduate Advisory Award, 1967; Oper Cir, 1966; Appreciation Award, Gamma Delta, 1965-74; Appreciation Award, Alpha Lambda Omega, 1965-74; Service & Plaque New Emmanuel Congregational UCC, 1987; Service & Plaque Central Piedmount Community Col, 1987. **Home Addr:** 1822 Grier Ave, Charlotte, NC 28216-5043, **Home Phone:** (704)334-1293.

## WILSON-THOMPSON, KATHLEEN

Vice president (organization). **Educ:** Univ Mich, Ann Arbor, Mich, BA, Eng lit, 1979; Wayne State Univ Law Sch, JD, 1982, LLM, 1996. **Career:** Kellogg, sr atty, corp coun, human resources mgr, vpres & chief coun labor & employ, 1992-05, sr vpres global human resources, 2005-09; Walgreen Co, sr vpres & chief human resources officer, 2010-. **Orgs:** Bd dir, Vulcan Mat Co, 2009-; bd trustee, Nat Asn Advan Colored People. **Honors/Awds:** "Black Enterprise", 100 Most Powerful Executives in Corporate America, 2009; "Black Enterprise", 75 Most Powerful Women in Business, 2010. **Business Addr:** Chief Human Resources Officer, Senior Vice President, Walgreen Co, 108 Wilmot Rd, Deerfield, IL 60015, **Business Phone:** (847)315-2500.

## WILTZ, DR. CHARLES J.

Dentist. **Personal:** Born Oct 18, 1934, New Orleans, LA; married Vivianne Carey; children: Charles Jr & Cary E. **Educ:** Xavier Univ, BS, 1956; Howard Univ, Sch Dent, DDS, 1967. **Career:** MA Gen Hosp, asst hematologist, 1959-61; Am Polymer & Chem Corp, jr org chemist, 1962-63; W side VA Hosp, staff dent, 1968-69; Mile Sq Health Ctr, Chicago staff dentist, 1970-71; pvt pract dentist, 1970-. **Orgs:** Consult Ill Dent Serv; Acad Gen Dent; Chicago Dent Soc; Ill State Dent Soc; Am Dent Asn, Nat Dent Asn; Chi Delta Mu; Lincoln Dent Soc; Billiken World Arts & Scis; Alpha Phi Alpha. **Honors/Awds:** City & State High Sch Basketball Los Angeles, 1952; Outstanding Merit of Achievement Va Hosp, 1968; Ten Best Dressed Black Men of Chicago, 1974-76. **Home Addr:** 843 E Drexel Sq, Chicago, IL 60615. **Business Addr:** Dentist, 8701 S Racine Ave, Chicago, IL 60620, **Business Phone:** (773)233-5510.

## WILTZ, DR. PHILIP G., JR.

Physician, orthopedic surgeon. **Personal:** Born Jun 5, 1930, New Orleans, LA; married Barbara Allen; children: Teresa, Phyllis & Yvette. **Educ:** Savannah State Col, BS, 1952; NY Univ, MA, 1956; Howard Univ, MD, 1968. **Career:** Pub Schs, teacher, 1957-60, 1961-64; USPHS, internship, 1968-69, resident orthop surg, 1969-73; pvt pract physician orthop surg; Columbia Univ, fel; Atlanta Med Ctr, surgeon; Emory Crawford Long Hosp. **Orgs:** Alpha Phi Alpha Fraternity; Sigma Phi Fraternity; Phi Delta Kappa Hon Soc, NY Univ, 1957; Ga State Med Asn Inc; bd trustee, Morehouse Sch Med; Atlanta Med Asn; Nat Med Asn; pres, Composite State Bd Med Examiners GA; chmn, Med Adv Comt Morehouse Sch Med. **Home Addr:** 3430 Somerset Trail SW, Atlanta, GA 30331. **Business Addr:** Physician, Orthopaedic Surgery, 285 Blvd NE Suite 110, Atlanta, GA 30312, **Business Phone:** (404)265-6701.

## WIMBERLEY, FRANK

Artist. **Personal:** Born Aug 31, 1926, Pleasantville, NJ; son of Frank Howell and Edythe Carolyn; married Juanita Olga; children: Walden. **Educ:** Howard Univ. **Career:** Exhibitions: African Am Mus, Charleston, NC, 1998; Different Directions Nese Alpan Gallery, Roslyn, NY, 1999; Then & Now, Ctr Gallery, Adel phi Univ, 2000; Omni Gallery, Uniondale, NY, 2001; Compositions Matter, June Kelly Gallery, New

York, 2001; Gestures, Port Wash Libr Gallery, 2002; An Exhib Hon Black Hist Month, Rensselaer Polytech Inst, Shelnutt Gallery, Troy, NY, 2002, 2004; Biennale Internazionale, Florence, Italy, 2003; artist; Spanierman Mod, artist, currently; Southampton Hist Mus, Southampton, NY, 2007; Heckscher Mus, Huntington, NY, 2004; Sage Cols, Albany, NY, 2004; Deborah Davis Fine Art Inc, 2004; Alpan Gallery, 2004; Ferregut Tower Gallery, Southampton, NY, 2005, 2006, June Kelly Galler, New York, NY, 2006; Spanierman Gallery, 2008; Spanierman Mod, 2009. **Orgs:** Bd mem, E Hampton Ctr Contemp Art, 1986; panel mem, Selecting Artist & Art Work US Courthouse, Art-In-Archit Prog, Islip, NY, 1997. **Honors/Awds:** Pollock-Krasner Found Award, 1998; Best In Show, 36th Juried Exhib, Parrish Art Mus, S Hampton, NY. **Home Addr:** 9911 35th Ave, Corona, NY 11368-1834, **Home Phone:** (718)335-3929. **Business Addr:** Artist, Spanierman Modern, 53 E 58th St, New York, NY 10022, **Business Phone:** (212)832-1400.

### WIMBISH, GARY LYNN

College administrator, clergy. **Personal:** Born Oct 13, 1953, Warren, OH; married Cecelia T Lester; children: Khalea, Brennan Jevon & Kyle Jameson. **Educ:** Oakwood Col, BA, 1975; Andrews Univ, Mdiv, 1977; Western State Univ Sch Law, JD, 1984. **Career:** Southeast SDA Church, asst pastor, 1974; Allegheny W Conf SDA, sr clergymen, 1975-80; Southeastern Calif Conf SDA, sr clergyman, 1980-84; Oakwood Col, dir admis & recruitment, 1984-; Emmanuel-Brinklow Seventh-day Adventist Church, exec pastor admin, currently; Columbia Community Ctr Seventh-day Adventists, pastor, currently. **Orgs:** Chaplain vol Orange County Hosp Syst, 1982-84; bus mgr, Viewpoint, A TheolJour, 1983-85. **Home Addr:** 1358 Camden Walk, Decatur, GA 30033-3203. **Business Addr:** Pastor, Columbia Community Center of Seventh-day Adventists, 7277 Eden Brook Dr, Columbia, MD 21046-5623, **Business Phone:** (410)418-4340.

### WIMBUSH, FREDERICK BLAIR

Real estate executive. **Personal:** Born Jul 24, 1955, Halifax, VA; son of Freddie B and Sue Carol Lovelace; married Jane Seay. **Educ:** Univ Rochester, BA, polit sci, 1977; Univ Va, JD, 1980; Duke Univ, Fuqua Sch Bus, Norfolk Southern Mgt Dev Prog, 1996; Advan Mgt Prog, Harvard Buss Sch, 2004. **Career:** Norfolk & Western Rwy Co, atty, 1980-83; Norfolk Southern Corp, solicitor, 1983-85, asst gen solicitor, 1985-89, gen atty, 1989-96, gen solicitor, 1996-2000, gen coun, opers, 2000-02, sr gen coun, 2002-04, vpres, real estate & corp sustainability officer, 2004-15. **Orgs:** Pres, Roanoke Mus Fine Arts, 1981-, secy, 1982-84, vpres, 1984-86, pres, 1986-87; Legal Aid Soc Roanoke Valley, 1982-86; United Way Spec Study Agencies, 1983; Roanoke Co Transp Safety Comn, 1984-85; Leadership Roanoke Valley, Roanoke Valley Chamber Com, 1984-85; Roanoke City Arts Comn, 1984-87; adv panel, VA Comn Arts Area III, 1985-87, Area VI Adv Panel, 1988-90; nat bd dir, Big Bros/Big Sisters Am, 1986-92; Western VA Found Arts & Sci, 1986-87; Am Red Cross, Tidewater, 1990-93; Am Heart Asn, Tidewater, 1990-92; pres, Va Comn Women & Minorities Legal Syst, 1992-93; bd dir, vpres, pres, Va Law Found, 1994-95, pres, 1996-97; fel Va Law Found, 1998; fel Am Bar Found, 2005; chmn & bd dir, exec comt, Va Symphony Orchestra, 2005; exec bd mem, VA, 2015; bd mem, Va Port Authority bd, 2016-; Univ Va Law Sch Alumni Coun; Univ Va Law Sch Bus Adv Coun; Va State Bar Prof Course Fac; bd gov, sect educ, Va State Bar; Civic Leadership Inst; Am, Nat, VA, Old Dom & Norfolk-Portsmouth Bar Asn; Asn Transp Practitioners, VA State Bar; bd trustee, Va Hist Soc; Hampton Roads Asn Com Real Estate; Hampton Roads Econ Develop Alliance; Monarch Bank Norfolk City Bd; Supreme Ct Va Task Force Gender Bias; Va Bar Asn Comt; alumni coun pres, Univ Va Sch Law; Univ Va Sch Law Bus Adv Coun; Univ Va Law Sch Found Bd Trustees; Big Bros Big Sisters Am; Twin City Bar Asn; Am Bar Asn; Nat Bar Asn; Va Comn Women & Minorities Legal Profession; Big Bros Big Sisters Am; Williams Ctr Adv Bd. **Home Addr:** 1330 Baffy Loop, Chesapeake, VA 23320-9457, **Home Phone:** (757)436-2772. **Business Addr:** Vice President, Norfolk Southern Corp, 3 Com Pl, Norfolk, VA 23320, **Business Phone:** (757)629-2608.

### WIMP, EDWARD LAWSON

Business owner. **Personal:** Born Feb 12, 1942, Chicago, IL. **Educ:** Roosevelt Univ, BS & BA, 1966. **Career:** DEW Rlty, vpres, broker, 1961-69; King Terco McDonald's Franchises, owner & operator; Edward L Wimp, principal. **Orgs:** Pres, Black McDonald's Operator's Asn, 1985; bd mem, Chicagoland McDonald's Operators Asn, 1985; exec bd mem, Nat Black McDonald's Operators Asn; bd mem & chmn, Wabash YMCA, 1985; bd Mgrs, Met YMCA'S, 1985; Sigma Pi Phi Frat, 1985. **Honors/Awds:** Nat Champion & World Speed Record Holder, Am Hot Rod Asn, 1963; Philanthropic World Community Islam, 1978; Outstanding Young Am US, 1979; James H Tilehman Award, YMCA, 1979. **Home Addr:** 7700 S Mich Ave, Chicago, IL 60619. **Business Addr:** Principal, Edward L Wimp, 7700 S Mich Ave, Chicago, IL 60619-2315, **Business Phone:** (773)994-6822.

### WIMS, WARNER BARRY

Management consultant. **Personal:** Born Apr 1, 1945, Philadelphia, PA; son of Calvin and Minnie; married Greta F Clark; children: Leslie & Richard Clark. **Educ:** Pa State Univ, BA, philos, 1975; Columbia Univ, MA, educ, 1979, MBA, 1981, PhD, orgn studies, 1982. **Career:** Hay Group, sr consult, 1980-84; Bank Boston, dir orgn develop & corp training, 1984-87; WBW & Assoc, pres, 1987-; Bank Am, sr vpres orgn effectiveness & innovation, 1995-2002; WBW & Assocs LLC, pres, 1992-. **Special Achievements:** Provided Team & organization development for over 50 major corporations; Japanese, French, Spanish proficiency. **Home Addr:** 2449 Lake St, San Francisco, CA 94121, **Home Phone:** (415)346-1697. **Business Addr:** President, WBW & Associates LLC, 2449 Lake St, San Francisco, CA 94121, **Business Phone:** (415)387-4040.

### WINANS, ANGELIQUE

Singer. **Personal:** Born Mar 4, 1968, Detroit, MI; daughter of David and Delores; married Cedric Caldwell. **Career:** Albums with Debbie Winans: "Angie & Debbie Winans", 1993; "Bold", 1998; Solo albums: "Melodies of My Heart", 2001; "The Lord's Prayer", "Changing My Whole Life", "He Loves Me", "Lady Wisdom", "Roses Again" & "Come Go With Me"; Spirit of a Champion"; "Farewell", "Send Me," Film: Follow the Star, actress, 2004. **Honors/Awds:** Grammy Awards; Soul Train Music Awards. **Special Achievements:** Book: What Manner of Love is This?: A Diary of God's Love in Times of Mourning, 2005; Co-author of the book, Never Alone; Nominated for a Grammy Award. **Business Addr:** Singer, Capital Entertainment, 826 S Victory Blvd, Burbank, CA 91502, **Business Phone:** (818)557-8200.

### WINANS, BEBE (BENJAMIN WINANS)

Gospel singer. **Personal:** Born Sep 17, 1962, Detroit, MI; son of David Sr and Delores; married Debra Denise; children: Miya Destiny & Benjamin. **Career:** Vocalist, songwriter, producer, talk show host & actor; Mt Zion Church God & Christ, Detroit, MI, choir; PTL Rec, 1984-87; Sparrow/Capitol, 1987-98; Atlantic Rec, 1997-98; Motown Rec, 1999-2003; Still Waters/Hidden Beach, 2004-06; Movement Group, 2004-; Album: Lord Lift Us Up, 1984; BeBe & CeCe Winans, 1987; Heaven, 1988; Different Lifestyles, 1991; First Christmas, 1993; Relationships, 1994; Greatest Hits, 1996; BeBe Winans, 1997; Love & Freedom, 2000; Live and Up Close, 2002; My Christmas Prayer, 2004; Dream, 2005; Greatest Hits, 2006; Cherch, 2007; Still, 2009; America America, 2012. **Business Addr:** Gospel Singer, The Movement Group Records, 2000 Glenn Echo Rd Suite 104, Nashville, TN 37215, **Business Phone:** (615)844-6288.

### WINANS, CECE (PRISCILLA MARIE WINANS LOVE)

Gospel singer, actor. **Personal:** Born Oct 8, 1964, Detroit, MI; daughter of David Sr and Delores; married Alvin Love; children: Alvin III, Ashley & Aaliyah. **Career:** People That Love Club, gospel singer, 1982-85; Brother BeBe Winans, gospel singer; Lord Lift Us Up, 1985; albums as CeCe Winans, 1987; Heaven, 1988; Different Lifestyles, 1991; First Christmas, 1993; Relationships, 1994; Alone In His Presence, 1995; Count on Me, 1996; His Gift, 1998; Everlasting Love, 1998; Alabaster Box, 1999; CeCe Winans, 2001; Throne Room, 2003; Purified, 2005; CeCe Winans Presents Kingdom Kidz; 2007; Thy Kingdom Come, 2008; CeCe Winans Presents Pure Worship, 2008; Songs of Emotional Healing, 2010; For Always: The Best Of CeCe Winans, 2010; Beauty Parlor, co owner. TV Series: "Christmas in Washington", 2005-06; "National Memorial Day Concert", 2006-07; "Celebration of Gospel", 200-10; "Touched By an Angel", 1994-97 & 2011-12; "Sunday Best", 2011-12; "Martin", 1994-97 & 2011-12; "Living Single", 1996-97 & 2011-12; "We Will Always Love You: A Grammy Salute to Whitney Houston", 2012-13; "Macy's 4th of July Fireworks Spectacular", 2014-15. **Home Addr:** , TN. **Business Addr:** Gospel Singer, PureSprings Gospel, 115 Penn Warren Dr Suite 300 377, Brentwood, TN 37027, **Business Phone:** (615)371-1575.

### WINANS, MARIO

Music producer, singer. **Personal:** Born Aug 27, 1974, Orangeburg, SC; son of Ronald Brown and Vickie. **Career:** Rec producer & vocalist; Album: Story of My Heart, Motown, 1995-97; Forever, 1999; Hurt No More, 2001-05; We Invented the Remix Vol. 1, 2002; Loon, 2003; Back Again!, 2003; Guerilla City, 2005; Loves Highway, 2006-; Press Play, 2007; The Declaration, 2007; The Boss, SWAGG, 2008; Meine Zeit, 2009; My Purpose; Mine, 2010; Prince of Belvedair, 2012; Bad Boy Records, song writer, producer & singer, currenlty. **Honors/Awds:** MOBO Awards, 2004. **Business Addr:** Producer, Singer, Bad Boy Records, 8 W 19th St, New York, NY 10036-4039, **Business Phone:** (212)741-7070.

### WINANS, PASTOR MARVIN L.

Singer, clergy. **Personal:** Born Mar 5, 1958, Detroit, MI; son of David and Delores; married Vickie Bowman; children: Mario, Marvin Jr & Josiah. **Career:** Producer, lyricist, composer & recording artist, 1976-; Perfecting Church, pastor, 1989-; Albums: Introducing the Winans, 1981; Long Time Coming, 1984; Tomorrow, 1984; Let My People Go, 1985; Decisions, 1987; Don't Get God Started, starrer, 1987; The Winans Live At Carnegie Hall, 1988; Live at Carnegie Hall, 1988; Return, 1990; Introducing Perfect Praise, solo, 1992; All Out, 1993; Heart & Soul, 1995; Marvin L Winans Acad Performing Arts, pres sch bd, 1997-; Christmas: Our Gifts To You, 2000; The Songs of Marvin Winans, 2006; Alone but Not Alone, 2007. **Orgs:** I Care Int; Gospel group The Winans. **Honors/Awds:** Dove Award, Gospel Music Asn, 3 times; Stellar Award, Best Gospel Group, 8 times; 6 Grammy Awards. **Special Achievements:** Author of Marvin Winans: Image is Everything, 1996; foreword writer, Who's Who among African Americans, 9th ed, 1996. **Business Addr:** Pastor, Perfecting Church, 7616 E Nev St, Detroit, MI 48234-3131, **Business Phone:** (313)365-5578.

### WINANS, VICKIE (VIVIANE BOWMAN)

Gospel singer, business owner. **Personal:** Born Oct 18, 1953, Detroit, MI; daughter of Aaron Bowman and Mattie; married Joe E McLemore; married Marvin Sr; children: Marvin Jr Mario; married Ronald Brown. **Career:** Albums: Be Encouraged, 1985; Total Victory, 1989; Lady, 1991; Best All, 1991; Vicki Winans, 1995; Live Detroit, 1997; Live Detroit, II, 1999; Share Laughter, 1999; Feel Passion, 1999; Best Vickie Winans, 2002; Bringing It All Together, 2003; My Christmas Gift to You, 2004; Greatest Hits, 2005; Woman to Woman: Songs Life, 2006; Happy Holidays from Vickie Winans, 2007; Praise & Worship, 2008; How I Got Over, 2009; How I Got Over Remix, 2010; Radio One Family Comdedy Tour, 2010; Thy Kingdom w/The Clark Sisters, forthcoming, 2016. Singles: "Don't Throw Your Life Away", 1991; "Just When (featuring Marvin Winans)", 1992; "Work It Out", 1995; "Shake Yourself Loose", 2003; "It's Alright", 2006; "Special Day", 2007; "The Rainbow"; "Kids Love Jesus Too"; "Release it"; "Long As I Got King Jesus"; Winans, mem legendary gospel group; Viviane Inc, pres & owner, currently. **Business Addr:** Singer, President, Viviane Inc, 6689 Orchard Lake Rd Suite 256, West Bloomfield, MI 48322, **Business Phone:** (248)253-3203.

### WINANS-LOWE, DEBBIE RENEE

Singer. **Personal:** Born Sep 3, 1972, Detroit, MI; daughter of David and Delores; married James; children: James Jr, Jayson & Jackson. **Career:** LoweKey Entertainment, exec producer & owner, currently; Renee Image Agencies, owner; Albums: Angie & Debbie, 1993; Bold, 1997. **Special Achievements:** Has been in major magazines, newspapers, political arenas, and television mediums. **Business Addr:** Singer, PO Box 66661 Washington Sq Sta, Washington, DC 20035, **Business Phone:** (202)986-0693.

### WINBUSH, ANGELA LISA

Singer, composer. **Personal:** Born Jan 18, 1955, St. Louis, MO; married Ronald Isley. **Educ:** Howard Univ, music educ. **Career:** Composer; Back-up vocalist Stevie Wonder, 1977-80; Rene & Angela duo, 1980-87; solo artist, 1987; songwriter & producer Isley Bros, LalahHathaway, Klymaxx, Sheena Easton; Sharp, 1987; It's Real Thing, 1989; Angela Winbush, 1994; composed: Gr& Theft Auto: Vice City, 2002; Album:Rene & Angela, 1980; Wall To Wall #15 Billboard Chart, 1981; Rise #33Billboard Chart, 1983; St Called Desire #5 Billboard Chart, 1985; TheBest Rene & Angela: Come My Way, 1996; A St Called Desire & More, 1997; Classic Masters, 2002; Solo Albumns: Sharp #7 Billboard Chart, 1987; It's Real Thing #12 Billboard Chart, 1989; Angela Winbush #11Billboard Chart, 1994; Ultimate Collection, 2001; Greatest Love Songs, 2004.

### WINBUSH, DR. RAYMOND ARNOLD (TIKARI BIOKO)

Educator, administrator. **Personal:** Born Mar 31, 1948, Pittsburgh, PA; son of Harold and Dorothy; children: Omari, Sharifa & Faraji. **Educ:** Oakwood Col, BA, psychol, 1970; Univ Chicago, MS, psychol, 1973, PhD, psychol, 1976. **Career:** Oakwood Col, asst prof & chmn behav sci, 1973-77; Ala A&M Univ, assoc prof, psychol, 1977-80; Vanderbilt Univ, asst prof human develop coun, 1980-84, asst provost, 1986-94, Johnson Black Cult Ctr, assoc prof human devel & dir, 1991-95; United Press Int, vpres corp res, 1984-86; Encyclopaedia Africana Proj, Accra, Ghana, W Africa, consult; Fisk Univ, Benjamin Hooks Prof Social Justice, dir Race Rels Inst, 1995-2002; Morgan State Univ, Inst Urban Res, dir, 2002-. **Orgs:** Treas & exec bd mem, Nat Coun Black Studies, 1992-; Asn Black Psychologists, 1992-; Am Psychol Asn, 1993-; Girl Scouts Am, 1993-; prof consult, Asn Black Cult Ctr, pres, Southern Region; Encyclopaedia Africana Proj; grant writer; tech consult; ed bd, J Black Studies. **Home Addr:** 1190 W Northern Pkwy, Baltimore, MD 21210. **Business Addr:** Director, Morgan State University, Rm D216 Montebello Complex, Baltimore, MD 21251, **Business Phone:** (443)885-4800.

### WINCHESTER, KENNARD NORMAN, JR.

Executive, basketball player. **Personal:** Born Sep 3, 1966, Chestertown, MD. **Educ:** James Madison Univ, BS, social sci, 1988; Averett Univ, attended 1989. **Career:** Basketball player (retired), executive; Atenas de Cordoba, 1989-90; Houston Rockets, 1990-93; NY Knickerbockers, 1991-92; Rapid City Thrillers, 1993-94; Columbus Horizon, 1994; Olimpia de Venado Tuerto, 1994-95; Le Mans Sarthe, 1995-96; Carolina Cardinals, 1996; Treasure Coast Tropics, 1996; RAAST NC Recovery, assoc prof, 2005-; Basement to Attic Mobile Storage, pres & chief exec officer, 2010-. **Home Addr:** 2809 Carriage Meadows Dr, Wake Forest, NC 27587-7048, **Home Phone:** (919)761-8251. **Business Addr:** President, Chief Executive Officer, Basement to Attic Mobile Storage, 702 W Acad St, Fuquay-Varina, NC 27526, **Business Phone:** (919)767-2267.

### WINDER, ALFRED M.

Executive, transport worker. **Educ:** Allan Hancock Jr Col, AA, 1966; Rockhurst Col, BA, indust rel, 1969. **Career:** Kans City Area Transp Authority, mgr equal employ & minority bus enterprise, 1978-80; Saudi Pub Tranps Co, mgr admin personnel, 1981-82; ATB & Ryder Mgt Serv Co, Cincinnati, vpres & gen mgr, 1981-85; Bi-State Develop Agency, dep gen mgr admin, 1983-84; Transp Kans City, Mo Sch Dist, assoc supt, 1991-96; Div Transp DC Pub Schs, gen mgr, 1999-2003, transp dir; Suburban Bus & W Towns, gen mgr; City & Co, San Francisco, CA, dir recreation; Gary Pub Transp Corp, pres & gen mgr; Large Inc, bd mem, vpres & gen mgr. **Orgs:** Conf Minority Transp Officials, 1983-85, exec vpres, 1986-; bd mem, Anderson Boys Club, 1986-; exec bd, Ind Transp Asn; policy comt mem, Northern Ind Regional Planning Comn; Gary Ind C C; Nat Asn Intercollegiate Athletics. **Honors/Awds:** Volunteer of the Year, Boys Clubs Greater Kans City, 1977-79; Outstanding Citizen's Award, Black United Appeal, Mo, 1978; Contractor of the Year Award, MO-KS Contractors Asn, 1978; Volunteer of the Year Award, St Louis, Mo Sch Dist, 1984; Prestigious Presidents Award, 1986; Superintendent's Award of Excellence, DC Pub Schs, 2000. **Home Addr:** 5044 Call Pl SE, Washington, DC 20075.

### WINDHAM, RHONDA

Sports manager, athletic director. **Career:** Los Angeles Sparks, WNBA, Lakers' Team, gen mgr, 1997-99; Univ Southern Calif, all-pac 10 conf guard; Los Angeles Summer Showcase, Womens Summer Basketball League, league dir, currently. **Special Achievements:** WNBA's first Black general manager. **Business Addr:** League Director, Los Angeles Summer Showcase, PO Box 561278, Los Angeles, CA 90056, **Business Phone:** (323)295-7690.

### WINE, DONALD GARY

Automotive executive. **Personal:** Born Aug 16, 1951, Benton, AR; son of James (deceased) and Margaret; married Dorothy; children: Donald II & Steven Gary. **Educ:** Wayne State Univ, BA, lib arts, 1984; Cent Mich Univ, MSA, admin, 1986. **Career:** Gen Motor Corp, asst plant mgr, 1990-92, prod mgr, 1991-92, actg plant mgr, 1992-94, plant mgr, 1994-95, Ohio, Mich & Tex plant mgr, 1994-2009, assembling plant mgr, 1995-99, Cadillac/Luxury Car Div, plant mgr, 1994-2009, Pontiac Metal Ctr, GM Fabricating Div, plant mgr, 1999-2005; Boy Scouts Am Detroit Area Coun, vpres oper, 1996-2005; DGW Mgt Consult, sr exec mgt consult, 2010-; Android Industs, Arlington, Tex, plant mgr, 2010-12, mfg dir, 2010-15; DGW Mgt Consult, sr exec mgt consult, 2010-. **Orgs:** Bd dir, City Ypsilanti Mich Chamber Com, 1992-93; bd dir, Arlington Ind Sch, 1994-95; bd dir, Longhorn Coun, Boy Scouts Am, 1994-95, exec bd, Detroit Coun, 1996; bd dir, City Arlington, Tex, Chamber Com, 1994-; adv bd, Wayne State Univ, 1997. **Honors/Awds:** Socius Collegi Award. **Home Addr:** 27185 Pembridge St, Farmington Hills, MI 48331, **Home Phone:** (248)426-6679. **Business Addr:** Senior Executive, DGW Management Consulting LLC, 816 Battenburg Trl, Pflugerville, TX 78660, **Business Phone:** (419)512-1455.

**WINFIELD, ARNOLD F. See Obituaries Section.**

**WINFIELD, DAVID MARK (DAVE WINFIELD)**
Baseball player, baseball executive. **Personal:** Born Oct 3, 1951, St. Paul, MN; son of Frank and Arline; married Tonya Turner; children: Shanel, Arielle & David Mark II. **Educ:** Univ Minn, polit sci, 1973. **Career:** Baseball player (retired), baseball executive; San Diego Padres, outfielder, 1973-80, exec vpres & sr adv, 2001-13; New York Yankees, outfielder, 1981-90; Calif Angels, outfielder, 1990-91; Toronto Blue Jays, outfielder, 1992; Minn Twins, outfielder, 1993-94; Cleveland Indians, outfielder, 1995; Winfield & Winfield Ltd, chief exec officer & pres, Keynote Speaker, Auth, Baseball Analyst & Communicator, 1995-, prof athlete & consult, 2013-; FOX-TV, analyst; ESPN SportsCenter, baseball analyst, radio contribr, studio analyst, 2009-12; Baseball Music Proj, host & narrator. **Orgs:** Screen Actors Guild, 1982-; Morehouse Sch Med, trustee, 1982-92; Am Fedn Tv & Radio Artists, 1982-; Sponsor & founder, David M Winfield Found; San Diego Padres, 2001-12; Oxford Rec Ctr; ambassador, Ritz Carlton Destination Clubs; Hackensack Univ Med Ctr, trustee, 1984-90; ambassador, Ritz Carlton Destination Clubs, 2004-12; bd mem, Authentify Inc, 2007-; int trustee, Am Acad Hospitality Sci, 2012-. **Home Addr:** 367 W Forest, Teaneck, NJ 07666. **Business Addr:** Vice President, Senior Advisor, San Diego Padres, PETCO Pk 100 Pk Blvd, San Diego, CA 92101, **Business Phone:** (619)795-5000.

**WINFIELD, ELAYNE HUNT**
Counselor. **Personal:** Born Feb 9, 1925, Waco, TX; married Walter Lee; children: Daryl Lynn & Kevin Ren. **Educ:** Paul Quinn Col, BS, 1954; Univ Tex, MA, 1975; cert Educ Admin, 1977. **Career:** Midland Tex, teacher, 1955-56; Odessa L/LD, res teacher, teacher; Big Springs Tex, teacher, 1957-58; Spec Educ Dept, Odessa, elem counsr; Ector Co PubSch, elem counsr, 1977; testing & measurement, dir, 1984-. **Orgs:** Tex St Teacher Asn, Human Rel Com, 1974-78; adj instr, Univ Tex Permian Basin, 1975; bd dir, Nat Educ Asn, 1976-79; Tex Ed Agency Eval Team, 1976; Alpha Kappa Alpha Sor; Am Asn Univ Women; Delta Kappa Gamma Soc; First vpres Qepa Kappa Chap, 1976-79; Phi Delta Kappa Frat. **Honors/Awds:** Outstanding Elementary Teachers of America, 1973; Odessa Classroom Teachers HR Award, 1974; TSTA Hum Rel Award, 1974; Child Dev Profl. **Home Addr:** PO Box 60024, Midland, TX 79711-0024. **Business Addr:** Director, Ector Co Independent School District, PO Box 3912, Odessa, TX 79762.

**WINFIELD, DR. LINDA FITZGERALD**
Educator. **Personal:** Born Dec 9, 1948, Wilmington, DE; daughter of William L Fitzgerald and Bertha Mason Fitzgerald (deceased); children: Kenneth Jr & David. **Educ:** Univ Del, BA (hons) 1975, MA, 1981, PhD, 1982. **Career:** New Castle County Sch Dist Consortium, supvr res, 1981-85; Educ Testing Serv, NAEP vis scholar, 1985-86; Temple Univ, asst prof educ, 1986-89; Temple & Johns Hopkins Univs, Baltimore, Md, Ctr Study Effective Sching Disadvantaged Students; Univ Calif, Los angeles, Grad Sch Educ, vis prof, 1989-, CRESST, res staff, currently. **Orgs:** Am Educ Res Assoc, 1977-; Nat Coun Measurement Educ; Phi Delta Kapp; Am Psychol Asn. **Business Addr:** Research Staff, University of California, 300 Charles E Young Dr N GSE&IS Bldg 3rd Fl, Los Angeles, CA 90095-1522, **Business Phone:** (310)206-1532.

**WINFIELD, HON. SUSAN REBECCA HOLMES**
Judge. **Personal:** Born Jun 13, 1948, East Orange, NJ; daughter of Thomas S Holmes and Mildred L Holmes; children: Jessica L & Heather B. **Educ:** Univ Pa, BA, math, 1970; Boston Col Law Sch, JD, 1976. **Career:** Law Off Salim R Shakur, assoc atty, 1976-78; Dept Justice, Criminal Div, staff atty, 1978-79; US Atty Off, asst US atty, 1979-84; DC Super Ct, assoc judge, 1984-90, Civil, Criminal & Family Div, from dep presiding judge to presiding judge, 1990-94, assoc judge, sr judge, currently; George Wash Univ, Coloumbia Law Sch, adj prof; Harvard Univ, Trial Advocacy Prog, fac; Georgetown Med Sch, Psychiat Dept, ac; Foreign Serv Grievance Bd, mem, 2007-. **Orgs:** Mass Bar Asn, 1976; DC Bar Asn, 1978; Asst US Attys Asn, 1979-; Womens Bar Asn DC, 1984-; Am Judges Asn, 1984-; Nat Asn Women Judges, 1984; bd dir, Bar Asn DC, currently. **Business Addr:** Senior Judge, Superior Court of District of Columbia, Moultrie Courthouse 500 Ind Ave NW, Washington, DC 20001, **Business Phone:** (202)879-1997.

**WINFIELD, THALIA BEATRICE**
Executive, chief executive officer, president (organization). **Personal:** Born Oct 17, 1924, Surry, VA. **Educ:** Va State Univ, BS, 1947. **Career:** Executive, chief executive officer (retired); Storer Col Harpers Ferry, secy to pres, 1947-49; Morehouse Col Atlanta, secy tobursar, 1949-54; Columbia savings & Loan Asn, pres & chief exec officer, 1974-92. **Orgs:** Dir, Carter Child Develop Ctr, 1976-; trustee, CitizensGovt Res Bur, 1977-; Christ Presby Church elder, 1978-, treas, 1984; trustee, Presbytery Milwaukee, 1984. **Home Addr:** 4934 N 52nd St, Milwaukee, WI 53218-4308, **Home Phone:** (414)438-9660.

**WINFIELD, WILLIAM T.**
Administrator, association executive, engineer. **Personal:** Born Oct 24, 1944, Baton Rouge, LA; son of Leander Sr and Alice Simmons; married Rita Gurney; children: William Gurney, Darlene Teresa & Paul Tyrone. **Educ:** Southern Univ; La State Univ. **Career:** WT & Assocs Inc, Eng Firm, chief exec officer & munic planning & zoning comnr, pres, 2000-13; E Baton Rouge Parish Sch, bd dir, 2008-10. **Orgs:** Capitol Class Regeneration Club, 1962; Capitol Region Planning Comn, 1973-76; Coun Mem Dist 3, City Parish, 1973-76; pres, First Ward Voters League; Winborne Ave Boys & Girls Club; Nat AsnAdvan Colored People; Eden Pk Action Comt; pres, First Ward Voters Asn; pres, Neighborhood Orgn; pres, Mid-City Hist Cemetary Coalition; Belfair Elem adv comt; Long Range Planning Comt; Sch Opers Comt; pres, Sweet Olive African Am Hist Cemetary; EBR Planning & Zoning Comn, comnr, vice chmn, 2002-13; dem mem, E Baton Rouge Bd Election Supervisors; chmn, Capitol High Sch Alumni Asn, 2013-. **Honors/Awds:** Hon Dist Atty, 1973; Badge of Courage, Louisiana Police Jury Black Caucus, 2011. **Special Achievements:** First Baton Rougean to participate in a Southern Univ cooperative program with NASA at the Marshall Space Flight Center; First African American employed in engineering in the industrial complexes of LA. **Home Addr:** 1240 N 29th St, Baton Rouge, LA 70802-2511, **Home Phone:** (225)344-7584. **Business Addr:** President, W T & Associates Inc, 2622 N St, Baton Rouge, LA 70802, **Business Phone:** (225)883-0822.

**WINFREY, COL. AUDREY THERESA**
Nurse. **Personal:** Born Houston, TX; daughter of Arthur W and E Agatha McIntyre; children: Jennifer Holland. **Educ:** Grant Hosp, dipl, 1962; DePaul Univ, BSN, 1969, MSN, 1973; Univ Ill Sch Pub Health, MPH, 1976. **Career:** Nurse (retired); Chicago Health Dept, nurse, 1963-66; USAID Vietnam Bur, nurse adv, 1966-68; One Mile Sq Health Ctr, pub health nurse, 1968-70; Michael Reese Med Ctr Sch Nursing, instr 1970-73; Univ Ill Col Nursing, instr, 1973-74; Chicago City Col, asst prof, 1974-77; Va Westside Med Ctr, coordr adm amb care nursing, 1977; Vet Admin Hosp, Chicago, Ill, nurse specialist hosp base home care, 1987-90; US Postal Serv, Chicago, Ill, indust nurse, 1988-90; Univ Ill, Col Nursing, Chicago, researcher, 1988-90; Halsted Terr, Nursing Home, Chicago, Ill, supvr, 1988-90; Amb Care Clinics, primary nurse surg serv, 1990. **Orgs:** Zeta Phi Beta; Am Nursing Asn; Nat League Nurse; Am Pub Health Asn; DePaul Univ Alumni Asn; Univ Ill Alumni Asn; bd mem, Plano Child Develop Ctr, 1978-; Variety Club C Charities, 1980-; St James Cath Church, 1986-; mem comt, Women Achievement, 1987-; planning bd, VIA; Nat Black Nurses Asn. **Honors/Awds:** Civilian Govt Award; Medal of Achievement; Recog Award; Volunteer Service Award, Plano Child Develop Ctr, 1983; CAHMCP Recognition Award, Ill Inst Technol, 1982. **Special Achievements:** Published article: "Maximum Amount of Medication: How Much Is Too Much Injected into One Site" Nursing, July, 1985; Published article w/ Dr Eva D Smith of U of I, College of Nursing "Church Based Hypertension Education Program", 1990. **Home Addr:** 3703 Culloden St, Flossmoor, IL 60422, **Home Phone:** (708)922-9663.

**WINFREY, OPRAH GAIL**
Television talk show host, television producer, entrepreneur. **Personal:** Born Jan 29, 1954, Kosciusko, MS; daughter of Vernon and Vernita Lee; married Stedman Graham. **Educ:** Tenn State Univ, BA, speech, drama. **Career:** WVOL Radio Sta, news reporter, 1971-72; WTVF-TV, reporter, newsanchorperson, 1973-76; WJZ-TV, news anchorperson, 1976-78, host morningtalk show "People Are Talking", 1978-83; WLS-TV, host talk show "AMChicago", 1984; Oprah Winfrey Show, host, 1985-, Nat syndication, 1986-; Harpo Prods, owner, producer, 1986-; ABC Aftersch Specs, 1991-93; Oprah Winfrey Network, host; Eccentric Restaurant, owner, currently; Oprah & Friends, owner, currently; host, supv producer, ser celebrity interview spec, incl: "Oprah: Behind Scenes", 1992; host, exec producer: "Michael Jackson TalksTo Oprah, 90 Prime-Time Minutes With King Pop", 1993; Films: Color Purple, actress, 1985; Native Son, actress, 1986; Ellen, actress, 1997; Beloved, actress, co-author, 1998; Our Friend, Martin, actress, 1999; Charlotte'sWeb, actress, 2006; The Great Debaters, 2007; Bee Movie, actress, 2007; The Princess & the Frog, 2009; The Butler, 2013; Selma, 2014; The Immortal Life of Henrietta Lacks, 2016; A Wrinkle In Time, 2017. Co-author: "You Make Connection", 1997; "You Make Connection", home video, prod, host, 1997; Our Friend, Martin, 1999; Charlotte's Web, 2006; TV:"The Oprah Winfrey Show", 1986-2008; "The Women of Brewster Place", actress, 1989; "Brewster Place", actress, 1990; "Lincoln", actress, 1992; "Nine", 1992; "Overexposed", 1992; "ABC Afterschool Specials", 1993; "There are no Children Here", actress, 1993; "Shades of a Single Protein", 1993; "Before Women Had Wings", 1997; "The Wedding", 1998; "David & Lisa", 1998; "Tuesdays with Morrie", 1999; "Amy & Isabelle", 2001; "Oprah After the Show", 2002; "Entertainment Tonight", 2003-08; "Larry King Live", 2003-07; "Their Eyes Were Watching God", 2005; "Emmanuel's Gift", narrator, 2005; "36th NAACP Image Awards", 2005; "Signe Chanel", 2005; "Late Show with David Letterman", 2005; "Corazon de", 2005; "TheKennedy Center Honors: A Celebration of the Performing Arts", 2005; "Legends Ball", 2006; "Inside Edition", 2006; "The 2006 Black MovieAwards", 2006; "Rachael Ray", 2006; "Forbes Celebrity 100: Who MadeBank?", 2006; "The 60th Annual Tony Awards", 2006; "Legends Ball", 2006; "Showbiz Tonight", 2006; "Oprah Winfrey Presents: Mitch Album's For One More Day", 2007; "Building a Dream: The Oprah Winfrey Leadership Academy", 2007; "The Oprah Winfrey Oscar Special", 2007; "The Big Give", 2007; "Larry King Live: The Greatest Interviews", 2007; "Charlotte's Web: Some Voices", 2007; "Building a Dream: The Oprah Winfrey Leadership Academy", 2007; "Film '72", 2007; "Oprah's Roots: An African American Lives Special", 2007; "Forbes 20 Richest Women in Entertainment", 2007; "Ocean's Thirteen", 2007; "Oprah Winfrey", 2007; "We Have a Dream", 2008; "The Insider", 2008. **Orgs:** SafricA's Zulu Nation. **Honors/Awds:** Academy Award & Golden Globe Award nominee, The Color Purple, 1985; Woman of Achievement Award, 1986; Emmy Award, Best Daytime Talk Show Host, 1987, 1991, 1992, 1998; Broadcaster of the Year, Intl Radio & TV Soc, 1988; Image Awards, Nat Asn Advan Colored People, 1989-92; Entertainer of the Year Award, Nat Asn Advan Colored People, 1989; CEBA Awards, 1989-91; America's Hope Award, 1990; Industry Achievement Award, Broadcast Promotion Mkt Execs/Broadcast Design Asn, 1991; Television Academy Hall of Fame; Daytime Emmy Awards, Lifetime Achievement Award, 1998; 50th Anniversary Gold Medal, Nat Book Awards, 1999; Bob Hope Humanitarian Award; Emmy Awards, 2002; Marian Anderson Award, 2003; Outstanding Community Service Award, Nat Urban League, 2003; The greatest Black philanthropist in American history, Business Week, 2005; Presidental Medal of Freedom, 2013. **Special Achievements:** First African American woman named to Forbes magazine's billionaire list, 2003; Publishes two magazines: O, The Oprah Magazine & O at Home; Richest African American of the 20th century; Named to the list of Greatest Chicagoans of the Century. **Home Addr:** 35 E Wacker Dr Suite 1782, Chicago, IL 60601, **Home Phone:** (312)591-9222. **Business Addr:** Owner, Producer & Actress, Harpo Productions, 110 N Carpenter St, Chicago, IL 60607-2101, **Business Phone:** (312)633-1000.

**WING, PROF. ADRIEN KATHERINE**
Educator. **Personal:** Born Aug 7, 1956, Oceanside, CA; daughter of John E and Katherine; children: Willie, Brooks, Charles, Che & Nolan. **Educ:** Princeton Univ, AB, 1978; Univ Calif, Los Angeles, MA, 1979; Stanford Law Sch, JD, 1982. **Career:** Upward Bound, Univ Calif, Los Angeles, teacher & counr, 1979; Rosenfeld, Meyer & Susman, law clerk, 1980; Un, intern, 1981; Curtis, Mallet, et al, lawyer, 1982-86; Rabinowitz, Boudin, et al, lawyer, 1986-87; Univ Iowa Law Sch, prof law, 1987-, Iowa-France, dir summer abroad prog, 2000-, Bessie Dutton Murray Dist Prof 2001-, assoc dean fac develop 2006-09, dir, London Law Consortium, 2010-12, Ctr Human Rights, dir, 2013-, assoc dean Int & Comparative law progs, 2015-; Univ Mich Law Sch, vis prof, 2002; Chapman Law dist vis prof, 2011. **Orgs:** Bd dir, Nat Black Law Students Asn, 1981-82; Asn Black Princeton Alumni Bd, 1982-87; int chair, Nat Conf Black Lawyers, 1985-95; Palestine Human Rights Campaigns Bd, 1986-91; Am Soc Int Law Exec Coun, 1986-89, 1996-99, 2007-2009, 2014-, exec comt, 1998-99, vpres, Am Soc Int Law, 2007-2009, Co-chair Blacks ASIL Task force 2014-; Iowa City Foreign Rels Coun Bd, 1989-94; Iowa Peace Inst Bd, 1993-95; Transafrica Forum Scholars Coun, 1993-95; bd visitors, Stanford Law Sch, 1993-96; life mem, Coun Foreign Rel, 1993-; chair, Am Soc Int Law, Southern Africa Interest Group, 1994-95; Princeton Alumni Coun, 1996-2000; Int Third World Legal Studies Asn Bd, 1996-; Am Asn Law Schs Minority Sect Exec Comt, 1997-2002, chmn, 2002; Princeton Comn Nominate trustee, 1997-2000; Am Friends Serv Comn; Mid E Progs Bd, 1998-; Am Asn Law Schs Africa sect exec comn, 2000-; Princeton African Am Studies Adv Coun, 2000-10; Princeton Exec Comn Alumni Coun, 2002-04; Am Bar Asn Law Sch Site Inspector, 2002-; Am Bar Asn; Am Br Int Law Asn; Nat Bar Asn; Soc Am Law Teachers; bd ed, Am Jour Comp Law; Univ Iowa's interdisciplinary African Studies fac; Am Law Inst, 2009; Am Bar Asn Accreditation Comt, 2012-; New York Bar. **Special Achievements:** Author or editor of over 100 scholarly publications. **Home Addr:** 819 Southlawn Dr, Iowa City, IA 52245, **Home Phone:** (319)621-7674. **Business Addr:** Bessie Dutton Murray Professor, Associate Dean for International & Comparative Law programs, The University of Iowa, 410 Boyd Law Bldg, Iowa City, IA 52242-1113, **Business Phone:** (319)335-9129.

**WING, THEODORE W, II. See Obituaries Section.**

**WINGATE, DAVID GROVER STACEY, JR.**
Actor, basketball player. **Personal:** Born Dec 15, 1963, Baltimore, MD; married Tyra Holland; children: Howard Sr Brandie, Bryce & Brittney. **Educ:** Georgetown Univ, sociol, 1986. **Career:** Basketball player (retired); Philadelphia 76ers, guard forward, 1986-89; Cleveland Cavaliers, 1987; San Antonio Spurs, 1989-91; Wash Bullets, 1991-92; Charlotte Hornets, 1992-95; Seattle Supersonics, 1995-98 & 2000-01; New York Knicks, 1998-2000; TV Series: "The 1996 NBA Finals", 1996; Movie: Eddie, 1996; Remember Reggie: The Reggie Lewis Story, 2013.

**WINGATE, DR. JAMES G.**
President (organization). **Educ:** Allen Univ, BS, chem & math; State Univ NY Col, Oswego, MS & cert advan studies, 1975; Syracuse Univ, PhD, educ leadership & admin, 1979. **Career:** Winston-Salem State Univ, exec asst to chancellor, 1997-2002, Interim Univ Col, dean, currently; Alpha Phi Alpha Fraternity Inc, col pres; LeMoyne-Owen Col, TN, pres, 2002-06; consult & analyst, 2007-. **Business Addr:** Dean, Winston-Salem State University, 601 S Martin Luther King Jr Dr, Winston-Salem, NC 27110, **Business Phone:** (336)750-2000.

**WINGFIELD, DONTONIO B.**
Basketball player. **Personal:** Born Jun 23, 1974, Albany, GA; children: Dontonio Jr. **Educ:** Univ Cincinnati, BA, 1994. **Career:** Basketball player (retired); Seattle Supersonics, forward & Small forward, 1994-95; Portland Trail Blazers, forward & Small forward, 1995-98; Toronto Raptors, 1995, Leon, Spain, 1998. **Orgs:** Save Our Sons. **Special Achievements:** The Blazersedge "Dontonio Wingcast" podcast is named after Wingfield.

**WINGFIELD, DR. HAROLD LLOYD**
Educator. **Personal:** Born Sep 22, 1942, Danville, VA. **Educ:** Fisk Univ, BA, 1970; Univ Ore, MA, 1973, PhD, 1982. **Career:** Sonoma State Univ, vis asst prof, 1976-77; Tenn State Univ, vis asst prof, 1977-78; Ariz State Univ, vis instr, 1979-80; Univ Rhode Island, vis asst prof, 1980-84; Kennesaw State Univ, Dept Polit Sci & Int Affairs, from asst prof to assoc prof, 1985-98, prof, 1999-. **Orgs:** Am Polit Sci Asn; Western Polit Sci Asn; Southern Polit Sci Asn; Nat Conf Black Polit Scientists; Nat Asn Advan Colored People; Am Civil Liberties Union; Common Cause, People Am Way; Ga State Democratic Comm; elected, Polk Sch District Bd Educ. **Home Addr:** 133 Pinecrest Rd, PO Box 960, Cedartown, GA 30125, **Home Phone:** (770)748-5049. **Business Addr:** Professor, Kennesaw State University, 1000 Chastain Rd, Kennesaw, GA 30144-5591, **Business Phone:** (470)578-6000.

**WINGO, ROBERT V.**
Executive. **Educ:** Univ Tex, El Paso, BBA, 1973. **Career:** Sanders/Wingo Advert Inc, pres & chief exec officer, 1983-; Valcent Prod Inc, bd dir, customer serv officer, asst nat sales mgr & vpres advert sales; SWK Partners, co-founder, pres & chief exec officer, currently. **Orgs:** Chmn, Tex Econ Develop Coun, 2004-; adv bd, Tex Rare Earth Resources Corp, 2014-chmn, Del Sol Med Ctr; dir, Martin Luther King Jr Memorial Found Bd; dir, UnitedHealthcare & Cancer Prev &Res Inst; dir, Wells Fargo Community Bank; co-chmn, YWCA Capital Campaign Steering Comt Campaign; dir, Alterrus Systs, Inc, 2006-08; dir, Advert Coun, 2015-; Finance Comn; Tex Higher Educ Coord Bd. **Honors/Awds:** Gold Nugget Award, Univ Tex El Paso, Col Bus Admin, 2002; Distinguished Alumni Award, Univ Tex, 2013. **Home Addr:** 1021 Los Jardines Cir, El Paso, TX 79912-1942, **Home Phone:** (915)584-4000. **Business Addr:** President, Chief Executive Officer, SWK Partners, 10 E 40th St 26th Fl, New York, NY 10016, **Business Phone:** (212)796-8365.

**WINLEY, REV. DIANE LACEY**
Hospital administrator, clergy, mayor. **Personal:** Born New York, NY; daughter of William and Esther Jackson; married Ronald. **Educ:** Univ Conn, Storrs, BA, 1960; NY Theol Sem, MDIV, 1994. **Career:** Hunts Pt Multi-Serv Compre Health Ctr, dir, 1968-70; City New York, spec asst mayor, 1970-71; John Hay Whitney Ford Found, grantee, 1971-73; New York Health Hosp Corp, asst pres, 1974-76, bd mem; Sydenham Hosp, dirpatient rels & vol serv, 1977-78; Radio Sta

WWRL AM, dir pub affairs, 1978-81; United ChurchSpring Valley, assoc pastor, 1994; Wellness Ctr, Riverside Church, dir, 1996-, coordr; Spirit Landscapes & Interiors, pres; Good-Shepherd-Faith Presby Church, bd mem, co-pastor, currently. **Orgs:** Organizer, First Nat Conf Drug Abuse Policy Minority Leaders, 1972; John Hay Whitney Found, 1973-74; fel Revson Found, 1981-82; bd dir, New York Health Hosp Corp, 1982-; New York exec dir, Physicians Social Responsibility, 1986-88; fel Ellen Lurie Distinguished Serv, Community Serv Soc, 1988; founding mem, Asn Black Social Workers; cand, State Leg. **Honors/Awds:** Twice Elected Dem Dist Leader. **Home Addr:** 10 W 135th St, New York, NY 10037, **Home Phone:** (212)862-3176.

**WINN, CAROL DENISE**
Television director, television producer. **Personal:** Born Mar 18, 1962, San Francisco, CA; daughter of Edward Jr and Mae Willie Baskins. **Educ:** Howard Univ, Wash, DC, BA, 1987. **Career:** WJLA TV Ch 7, Washington, DC, news asst, 1986-87; KBHK TV, San Francisco, Calif, admn asst pres & insurance claims admn, 1987-88, assoc producer & dir, 1988-89, producer & dir, 1989-. **Orgs:** Recording secy, Bay Area Black Journalists Asn, 1989-90, scholar chair, 1990-91, prog chair, 1991-92. **Home Addr:** 2658 San Jose Ave, San Francisco, CA 94112-3027. **Business Addr:** Producer, Director, KBHK-TV, 650 Calif St 6th Fl, San Francisco, CA 94108, **Business Phone:** (415)249-4444.

**WINN, DWIGHT RANDOLPH. See WINN, RANDY.**

**WINN, JOAN TARPLEY**
Lawyer, real estate agent. **Personal:** Born Apr 11, 1942, Dallas, TX; children: Elbert Ikoyi. **Educ:** Dillard Univ, BA, psychol, 1962; S Methodist Univ, JD, 1968. **Career:** Durham & Winn Dallas, atty, 1968-70; US Dept Labor, Off Solicitor, trial atty, 1970-73, atty; Fed Appeals Auth US Civil Serv Comn, asst appeals officer, 1973-75; Danas Co Ct Law No 2, judge, 1975-78; 191st St Judicial Dist Ct, judge, 1978-80; Honeymill & Gunn Realty Co Inc, pres, currently. **Orgs:** St Bar TX; Am Bar Asn; Dallas Bar Asn; JL Turner Legeau Soc; Delta Sigma Theta; Links Inc Dallas Chap. **Honors/Awds:** Woman of the Year, Zeta Phi Beta, 1978; Women Helping Women Award, 1980; Women in Business, Iota Phi Lambda, 1986. **Special Achievements:** First African American woman to practice law in Dallas County, 1969; First African American woman appointed Dallas district judge (191st District Court). **Business Addr:** President, Honeymill & Gunn Realty Co Inc, 7509 Inwood Rd Suite 202, Dallas, TX 75209.

**WINN, RANDY (DWIGHT RANDOLPH WINN)**
Baseball player. **Personal:** Born Jun 9, 1974, Los Angeles, CA; son of Damon Buford; married Blessings Robertson. **Educ:** Santa Clara Univ. **Career:** Baseball player (retired); Tampa Bay Devil Rays, 1998-2002; Seattle Mariners, 2003-05; San Francisco Giants, 2005-09; left wing & ctr-forward, 2005-09; New York Yankees, 2010; St Louis Cardinals, 2010. **Business Addr:** Analyst, CSN Bay Area, 360 3rd St 2nd Fl, San Francisco, CA 94107, **Business Phone:** (415)296-8900.

**WINNINGHAM, HERMAN SON, JR. (HERM WINNINGHAM)**
Baseball player, baseball manager. **Personal:** Born Dec 1, 1961, Orangeburg, SC; son of Herman Son Sr and Lucille Brizz; married Jane Moorman; children: Kevin A. **Educ:** De Kalb Community Col. **Career:** Baseball player (retired), baseball coach; New York Mets, outfielder, 1984; Montreal Expos, 1985-88; Cincinnati Reds, 1988-91; Boston Red Sox, 1992; Orangeburg-Wilkinson High Sch, head coach, currently. **Home Addr:** 1542 Belleville Rd, Orangeburg, SC 29115, **Home Phone:** (803)534-7369. **Business Addr:** Head Coach, Orangeburg-Wilkinson Senior High School, 601 Bruin Dr, Orangeburg, SC 29118, **Business Phone:** (803)534-6180.

**WINSLOW, CLETA MERIS**
City council member, government official. **Personal:** Born Jul 18, 1952, Rockford, IL. **Educ:** Tenn State Univ, BS, social work, 1973; Atlanta Univ Sch, social work, MS, 1975. **Career:** Vanderbilt Univ Res Ctr, psychotherapist social worker's aide, 1972-73; Atlanta Univ Sch Social Work, res asst, 1974; Morehouse Col Pub Rels, secy, 1975-76; Carrie Steele Pitts C's Home, chief social worker, 1976-79; Fulton Co Bd Comnr, admin asst; City Atlanta, Neighborhood Planning Unit, coordr; City Atlanta, Dist 4, city coun mem, 1994-. **Orgs:** Chmn, W End Neighborhood Dev Inc, 1977-; Nat Asn Neighborhoods; bd, Christian Coun Church, 1983-; W End Parents Action Youth Anti-Drug, 1985-; Nat treas, Delta Sigma Theta, 1985-; bd, Boatrock Family Serv Ctr; bd Ment Health Ment Retardation, 1985; Joel Chandler Harris Asn, 1986-; Brown HS PTSA Magnet Prog & Voc Adv Coun, 1986-; Black Women's Coalition, 1987-; mem, Atlanta City Coun. **Home Addr:** 1123 Oglethorpe Ave SW, Atlanta, GA 30310-2609, **Home Phone:** (404)752-8992. **Business Addr:** City Council Member, City of Atlanta, 55 Trinity Ave SW Suite 2900, Atlanta, GA 30303-3584, **Business Phone:** (404)330-6047.

**WINSLOW, KELLEN BOSWELL (KELLEN WINSLOW, SR.)**
Football player, executive. **Personal:** Born Nov 5, 1957, St. Louis, MO; married Katrina McKnight; children: Kellen II. **Educ:** Univ Mo, BS, coun psychol; Univ San Diego, LLB. **Career:** Football player (retired), football exec; San Diego Chargers, tightend, 1979-87; Fox Sports Net, football announcer, 1998-; Cent State Univ, dir athletics & stud wellness, 2008-; Lakeland Col, Wis, vpres athletics & wellness, 2013; Fla A&M Univ, dir athletics. **Orgs:** Comnr, Kellen Winslow Flag Football League, 1982; San Diego Police Deptres prog; Pro Football Hall of Fame. **Honors/Awds:** All-Am; Most Valuable Player, Co-Pro Bowl, 1981; Offensive Player of the Game, Pro Bowl, 1981; Pro Football Hall Fame, 1995; Col Football Hall Fame, 2002; San Diego Chargers Hall of Fame. **Special Achievements:** Films: 1980 AFC Championship Game, 1981; 1981 AFC Championship Game, 1982. TV Series: Who Made You?, 2008. **Business Addr:** Director of Athletics, Fla A&M University, 1601 S Martin L King Jr Blvd, Tallahassee, OH 32307, **Business Phone:** (850)599-3000.

**WINSLOW, KENNETH PAUL**
Investment banker. **Personal:** Born Jul 22, 1949, Chicago, IL; son of Eugene and Rose Rieras. **Educ:** Univ Ill, BA, econs, 1971; Harvard Grad Sch Bus Admin, MBA, finance, 1976; New York Univ, advan prof cert, 1987. **Career:** Harvard Grad Sch Bus Admin, fac res asst; Fed Deposit Ins corp, asst examr, 1972-74; Harvard Univ, res asst, 1976-77; NY Chem Bank, Corp Finance Dept, vpres, 1978-87; Found Enterprise Develop, pres; Benefit Capital Southwest Inc, staff, 1988-89, pres, 1989-. **Orgs:** ESOP Asn, 1985-; Nat Ctr Employee Ownership, 1985-. **Home Addr:** 6011 Village Glen Dr Suite 4127, Dallas, TX 75206, **Home Phone:** (214)368-8512. **Business Addr:** President, Benefit Capital Southwest Inc, 15851 Dallas Pkwy Suite 500, Dallas, TX 75001-6016, **Business Phone:** (214)991-3767.

**WINSLOW, REYNOLDS BAKER**
Administrator. **Personal:** Born Jul 25, 1933, Auburn, NY; son of George M and Mary Baker; married Ovetra Russ; children: Reynolds, Danielle, Christopher & Ericka. **Educ:** Syracuse Univ, BID, indust design, 1961. **Career:** Adminr (retired); Thomas L Faul Assoc, Skaneateles New York, indust designer, 1962-63; Crouse Hinds Co, indust designer, 1963-69; Gen Elec Co, indust designer, 1969-75; Syracuse Univ, minority eng prog coord, 1976-83; Nat Asn of Multicultural Engineering Prog Advocates, mfg exten partnership, 1976-95; Univ Mass Col Eng, dir Minority eng prog & develop officer, 1983-95; Univ of Massachusetts Amherst, mfg exten partnership, dir & develop officer, 1983-2002. **Orgs:** Allocation panel United Way Cent New York, 1980-82; bd dir, Univ Mass Comn Col Educ Blacks & Minorities, 1983-; bd dir, Mass Pre-Eng Prog, 1984-; reg chair, Nat Asn Minority Eng Prog Adminrs, 1985-86; nat treas, Nat Asn Minority Eng Prog Admin, 1986-89; vpres, Nat Asn Advan Colored People, 1989-91, pres, 1991-; bd mem, Roots Int, Univ Mass, 1993-; bd mem, Western Mass Coun, Girl Scouts Am, nomin comm, 1994-98; bd mem, Amherst Area Educ Alliance, 1994-; Human Rights Comn (Amherst). **Home Addr:** 1040 N Pleasant St Suite 219, Amherst, MA 01002, **Home Phone:** (413)549-2770.

**WINSTEAD, DR. VERNON A., SR.**
Lawyer, executive, social worker. **Personal:** Born Sep 15, 1937, Roxboro, NC; married Claudette McFarland; children: Vernon Jr & Claudette. **Educ:** NC Cent Univ, BS & BA, social sci & health educ, 1960, LLB, 1963; Univ Ill, MSW, 1969, AM, 1971, PhD, 1972. **Career:** NC Dept Pub Aid, social worker, 1962-63; NC Redevelop Comn, relocation & contract spec, 1963-65; US Labor Dept Manpower Admin, manpower devel specialist, 1965-83; John H. Johnson Publ Co, contractor, 1969-73; Loyola Univ Press, contractor, 1979-95; VAW Indust Inc, labor rel specialist, pres, currently; consult; arbitrator; Winstead Rest & Convalescent Homes, co-owner. **Orgs:** Nat Asn Advan Colored People; Nat Educ Asn; Nat Conf Black Lawyers; Nat Bar Asn; SE Kiwanis, S Shore Ministerial Asn; Bravo Chap Chicago Lyric Opera, Male Affil; life mem Nat Coun Negro Women; life mem Alpha Phi Alpha; S Shore Community; Joint Negro Appeal; chair St Philip Neri Parish Sch Bd; pres, S Shore Econ Develop Community; found, exec co-dir, Connecting Link, McFarland-Winstead Conf Ctr; found, asst ed, Chicago S Shore Scene Newspaper. **Honors/Awds:** Outstanding Leadership Award, Danforth Found; Monarch Award for public service, Alpha Kappa Alpha, 1991. **Home Addr:** 7433 S Constance Ave, Chicago, IL 60649-3609, **Home Phone:** (773)363-0441. **Business Addr:** President, Labor Relations Specialist, VAW Industries Inc, 7433 S Constance Ave, Chicago, IL 60649-3609, **Business Phone:** (773)643-0939.

**WINSTON, BONNIE VERONICA**
Journalist. **Personal:** Born Mar 13, 1957, Richmond, VA. **Educ:** Northwestern Univ, BSJ, 1978. **Career:** Southern Illinoisan, reporting intern, 1976; Richmond Va Times-Dispatch, reporting intern, 1977, reporter, 1979-86; Huntington WVa Advertiser, reporting intern, 1978; Boston Globe, state house bur reporter, 1986-. **Orgs:** Minority journalist-in-residence, Tougaloo Col Am Soc Newspaper Eds, 1980; bd dir, Va Press Women Nat Fed Press Women, 1982-86; stringer, NY Times, 1983-86; bd dir, Richmond Chap Sigma Delta Chi, Soc Prof Journalists, 1983-86; planning comn, staff mem, Urban Jour Workshop, 1984-85; Nat Asn Black Journalists, 1985-; free-lance writer, Black Engr Mag, 1986-. **Honors/Awds:** National Achievement Award, Northwestern Univ, 1974; Alpha Lambda Delta Hon Soc, Northwestern Univ, 1975; Outstanding Young Women in America Award, 1982; Achievement Award, Miles W Conner Chap, Va Union, Univ Alumni Asn, 1982; First Place, Va Press Asn Writing Contest, VPA, 1983; United Press International Best Writing Award, United Press Int, VA, 1983. **Home Addr:** 21 Dwight St, Boston, MA 02118, **Home Phone:** (617)542-1260. **Business Addr:** State House Bureau Reporter, The Boston Globe, 135 Morrissey Blvd, Boston, MA 02121, **Business Phone:** (617)929-2990.

**WINSTON, GEORGE B., III**
Computer executive. **Personal:** Born Feb 16, 1943, Richmond, VA; son of George B Jr and Gertrude B. **Educ:** Hampton Inst, BS, bus admin & mgt, 1965; Univ Del, MBA, 1972. **Career:** Wilmington Trust Co, 1968-72; GBW Inc, 1972-73; Del State Banking Comn, 1973-75; Bank Am Com Corp, vpres, 1975-82; GBW Int Inc, pres, 1983-; self employed, owner, 2005-. **Orgs:** Pres, Wilmington Chap Hampton Alumni, 1987-98; secy, Monday Club, 1991-01; bd mem, Better Bus Bur, 1993-; Nu Upsilon Chap. **Honors/Awds:** MBE Service Award, Del Minority Bus, 1985; Entrepreneurship Award, Nu Upsilon Chap Omega Psi Phi, 1987; Excellence Award, Independence Blue Cross Vendor, 2000. **Home Addr:** 3212 Strawflower Way, PO Box 542464, Lake Worth, FL 33467. **Business Addr:** President, GBW International Inc, 101 E 13th St, Wilmington, DE 19801-3203, **Business Phone:** (302)658-1315.

**WINSTON, HATTIE**
Actor. **Personal:** Born Mar 3, 1945, Lexington, MS; married Harold Wheeler; children: Samantha. **Educ:** Howard Univ, grad; Group Theatre Workshop, New York. **Career:** Films: Uns et les autres, Les, 1981; Without a Trace, 1983; A Show of Force, 1990; Beverly Hills Cop III, 1994; Sunset Park, 1996; Jackie Brown, 1997; Meet the Deedles, 1998; Living Out Loud, 1998; The Rugrats The Movie (voice), 1998; Unbowed, 1999; True Crime, 1999; The Battle of Shaker Heights, 2003; Death dealer: A Documentary, 2004. TV series: "The Electric Company", 1973-77; Ann in Blue, 1974; Out to Lunch, 1974; "The Dain-Curse", 1978; Hollow Image, 1979; "3-2-1 Contact", 1980; Nurse, 1980; "Unset lesautres, Les", 1983; "Home front", 1991; "One Woman's Courage", 1994; "The Cherokee Kid", 1996; "Port Charles", 1997; "Becker", 1998-2004; "Port Charles", 1997; "To Tell the Truth", 2000; Scrubs, 2002-04; "My Old Man", 2002; "Chock Full O'Nuts", 2003; "Twas the Night", 2004; "With a Twist", 2005; Girlfriends, 2005; "Numb3rs", 2008; "The Game", 2008; "Cold Case", 2009; "Castle", 2009; "Reed Between the Lines", 2011; "Mike & Molly", 2012; "The Soul Man", 2012-14. **Orgs:** Co-chairperson, AFTRA's Equal Employ Opportunities Comm; Negro Ensemble Company. **Honors/Awds:** Hattie Winston Day, Nat Black Theater Festival NC, named in honor, 1993, 1997; AAFCA Award, African-Am Film Critics Asn, 2011. **Business Addr:** Actress, Pakula/King & Associates, 9229 W Sunset Blvd Suite 315, Los Angeles, CA 90069, **Business Phone:** (310)281-4866.

**WINSTON, DR. HUBERT**
Executive director, chemical engineer, educator. **Personal:** Born May 29, 1948, Washington, DC; son of Hubert and Helen Simmons Vincent. **Educ:** NC State Univ, BS, 1970, MS, 1973, PhD, chem engineering, 1975. **Career:** Assoc prof (retired); NC State Univ, Dept Chem Eng, asst prof, 1975-77, Undergrad Admin, Dept Chem Eng, assoc prof chem eng, 1983-86, Col Eng, dir acad affairs, 1985-86; Exxon Prod Res Co, res specialist, 1977-83; NC State Univ, Biomanufacturing Training & Educ Ctr, exec asst dir, 2003-2013. **Home Addr:** 4316 19th Pl NE, Washington, DC 20018, **Home Phone:** (202)526-8932.

**WINSTON, JAMEIS**
Football player. **Personal:** Born Jan 6, 1994, Bessemer, AL; son of Antonor. **Educ:** Fla State Univ, 2015. **Career:** Football player, Florida State University, 2012-15; Tampa Bay Buccaneers, quarterback, 2015-. **Special Achievements:** Drafted by the Texas Rangers in the Major League Baseball first-year player draft, 2012; named to the USA Football National Team (U19) for the International Bowl, 2012; youngest player to ever win a Heisman Trophy, 2013; set NCAA Division I record by winning first 26 starts, 2013-14; first overall pick in the NFL Draft, 2015. **Business Addr:** Tampa Bay Buccaneers, 1 Buccaneer Pl, Tampa, FL 33607.

**WINSTON, JANET E.**
Commissioner, business owner. **Personal:** Born Feb 7, 1937, Morristown, NJ; married Shurney II; children: Shurney III. **Career:** Ernestine McClendon Agency, prof model, 1960-65; Belafonte Enterprises, secy & recpt, 1960-61; Music Corp Am, secy to vpres, 1961-62; Johnson Publicity Co, Ebony fashion fair model, 1963-64; Janet Winston Charm Sch, owner & dir, 1966-70; Winston's Taxi Serv, owner, 1970-72; Winston's Family Tree Bar Club, owner; Morristown Housing Authority, comnr, 1972-91. **Orgs:** Pres, Morris Co Urban League Guild, 1967-68; bd dir, Morristown Neighborhood House; vol, Morristown Memorial Hosp, 1975-76. **Home Addr:** 8 Hazel St, Morristown, NJ 07960-3122, **Home Phone:** (973)539-0213.

**WINSTON, JEANNE WORLEY**
Teacher, school administrator. **Personal:** Born May 27, 1941, Washington, DC; daughter of Gordon Sr and Rosetta Curry; married Reuben Benjamin; children: Kimberly L, Kandace W, Kia L & Reuben B II. **Educ:** DC Teachers Col, BS, elem educ, 1963; George Washington Univ, MA, elem admin, 1967; Univ Wash, DC & Maryland Univ, admin post masters, 1978. **Career:** Educator(retired); Dist Columbia Pub Schs, teacher, 1963-67, grade chairperson, 1965-, supv instr, 1967-69, teacher, 1969-76, actg asst prin, 1976-77, staff devel coord, 1977-86, competence based curric comt chairperson, 1977, teacher, 1977-88, teacher's conv bldg coord, 1984, AIMS coord, 1985, residential supvry support prog, 1985, math, sci minorities prog, 1985, mentors prog, 1986; PGCPS, educator, 1963-2014; Dist Columbia Alliance Black Sch Educ, 1984-; Dist Columbia Pub Schs, Brightwood Elem, Wash, DC, asst prin, 1963-99. **Orgs:** Delta Sigma Theta, 1960-; Parent Teacher Asn, 1963-; Gethsemane Baptist Church, 1966-; Nat Asn Advan Colored People, 1969-; Geo Wash Alumni Asn, 1970-; Wash Teachers Union, 1970-; Urban League, 1975-; vol, Ann Toy Dr Brookland Sch, 1980-; Nat Coun Negro Women, 1980; Dist Columbia Asn Retarded Citizens, 1980-; Dist Columbia Govt Employees Recreation Asn, 1985-; congributor walk-a-thon partic, March Dimes, 1985-; vol, Dist Columbia Village, 1986-, c, 1986-; Dist Columbia Asn Supv Curric Develop, 1986-. **Home Addr:** 1930 Kearney St NE, Washington, DC 20018-2438, **Home Phone:** (202)635-8061.

**WINSTON, JOHN H., JR.**
Physician, surgeon. **Personal:** Born Aug 7, 1928, Montgomery, AL; married Bertha Moore; children: Georgette, Joni Canty, Diva Dotson & Terri. **Educ:** Ala State Univ, BS, 1949; Columbia Univ, MA, 1951; Meharry Med Col, MD, 1956. **Career:** Va Med Ctr, president; Ctr Physician, pvt pract, currently. **Orgs:** Am Col Surgeons; Am Med Asn; Nat Med Asn; bd mem, Young Men's Christian Asn; Montgomery County Bd Educ; Red Cross. **Honors/Awds:** HealthGrades Honor Roll. **Home Addr:** 1521 Robert Hatch Dr, Montgomery, AL 36106, **Home Phone:** (205)262-4095. **Business Addr:** Physician, 1156 Oak St, Montgomery, AL 36108, **Business Phone:** (334)262-1627.

**WINSTON, LAMONTE**
Sports manager, chief executive officer. **Personal:** Born Apr 10, 1959, Oakland, CA; son of Henry C and Georgia R; married Claire L; children: Cameron L & Alanah Nicole. **Educ:** Merritt Jr Col, attended 1977; Westminster Col, 1978; Long Beach City Col, AA, 1980; San Francisco State Univ, BA, phys educ, 1985; Stanford Univ, NFL exec training prog. **Career:** Kaiser Engrs, fitness trainer, 1982-85; Albany High Sch, asst coach, 1982; Westminster Col; Merritt Jr Col, asst football coach, 1983-85; San Francisco State Univ, receivers coach, 1986-88, asst football coach, 1986-90, recruiting coordr & football camp coordr, 1986-89, defensive coordr, 1988-89, offensive coordr, 1989-90; Univ Nev, asst football coach, 1990-93; Atlanta Falcons, sr dir player develop; Kans City Chiefs, exec dir player develop, 1993-2010, exec dir player develop, 2006-10; Christian Athletes, fel; Winston Group, pres, chief exec officer, 2010-; Oakland Raiders, dir player engage-

ment, 2012-. **Orgs:** Bd dir, Youth Ftd, 1996-; NFL Player Progs, adv comm, 1996-; Genesis Sci, spec adv, 1996-; Am Football Coaches Asn; Women's Found Greater Kans City; United Way Leadership Comt; Kans City Sports & Bus Alliance; Derrick Thomas Third & Long Found. **Honors/Awds:** Special Service Award, 1998-99, Innovative Programming Award, 1999-2000, Outstanding Program Award, 2000-01, Award of Distinction, 2003, Steering Committee Recognition of Service, 2005, Outstanding Program Award, 2007, NFL Player Development; San Francisco State Football Hall of Fame, San Francisco State Univ, 2000; San Francisco State Athletic Hall of Fame; San Francisco State Gator Hall of Fame. **Home Addr:** 14448 England, Overland Park, KS 66221. **Business Addr:** Director of Player Engagement, The Oakland Raiders, 1220 Harbor Bay Pkwy, Alameda, CA 94502, **Business Phone:** (510)864-5000.

### WINSTON, MARY A.
Executive, chief financial officer. **Personal:** Born Jan 1, 1961?; children: 2. **Educ:** Univ Wis, BBA, acct & info systs; Northwestern Univ, Kellogg Grad Sch Mgt, MBA. **Career:** Pfizer Inc, 1995-2002; Global Fin Opers Pharmaceut Bus, vpres, 2000-02; Pfizer & Arthur Andersen& Co, sr auditor; Warner-Lambert, sr fin mgt; Baxter Int, Biotech Div, dir bus develop & strategy; Visteon Corp, vpres & treas, 2002-03, vpres & controller, 2003-04; Scholastic Corp, exec vpres & chief fin officer, 2004-07, prin acct officer, 2006-; WinsCo Financial LLC, founder & chief exec officer, 2007-08; Giant Eagle Inc, sr vpres & chief financial officer, 2008-; Family Dollar Stores Inc, chief financial officer, chief acct officer & exec vpres, 2012-. **Orgs:** Dir, Dover Corp, 2005-; Bd dir, Plexus Corp, 2008-; treas, Visteon Corp. **Business Addr:** Chief Financial Officer, Executive Vice President, Family Dollar Stores Inc, PO Box 1017, Charlotte, NC 28201-1017.

### WINSTON, DR. MICHAEL RUSSELL
Educator. **Personal:** Born May 26, 1941, New York, NY; son of Charles Russell and Jocelyn Anita Prem Das; married Judith A Marianno; children: Lisa M & Cynthia A. **Educ:** Howard Univ, BA, 1962; Univ Calif, MA, Fr hist, 1964, PhD, 1974. **Career:** Howard Univ, instr, 1964-66; Inst Serv Educ, exec asst & assoc dir, 1965-66; Educ Assoc Inc, educ consult, 1966-68; Langston Univ, develop consult, 1966-68; Howard Univ, asst dean lib arts, 1968-69, dir reshist dept, 1972-73, vpres acad affairs, 1983-90; Moorland-Spingarn Res Ctr, dir, 1973-83; fel Woodrow Wilson Int Ctr Scholars-Smithsonian Inst, 1979-80; Alfred Harcourt Found, vpres, 1992-93, pres, 1993-. **Orgs:** Am Historical Asn; Asn Study Afro-Am Life & Hist; Orgn Am Historians; Nat Geog Soc; Soc Am Archivists; Phi Beta Kappa. **Special Achievements:** Co-author, Negro US; Co-Editor, Dict Am Negro Biography, Historical Judgements Reconsidered, 1988. **Home Addr:** 1371 Kalmia Rd NW, Washington, DC 20012-1444, **Home Phone:** (202)829-4085. **Business Addr:** President, Administration Bldg, 2400 6 St NW, Washington, DC 20059, **Business Phone:** (202)806-6100.

### WINSTON, DR. NEIL EMERSON
Physician, association executive, president (organization). **Educ:** Rush Med Col, MD. **Career:** Ill Dept Pub Health & Human Servs, physician team leader; Wright State Univ, Dayton, Ohio, resident emergency med; Cook County Dept Pub Health, med dir, 2004-06; Jackson Pk Hosp & Med Ctr, emergency physician, currently. **Orgs:** Ill State Med Soc House Delegates, 1994-; Ama House, 1996-; pres, Chicago Med Soc; Am Col Emergency Physician; Nat Med Asn; bd dir, Ill Med Polit Action Comt, 2002-; Ill St Med Soc, trustee, 2002-; End Health Care Disparities, 2005-; bd dir, Am Med Polit Action Comt, 2006-; trustee, Am Asn Pub Health Physicians, 2006-; chair, Polit Educ Comt, 2008; bd dir, Ill Channel. **Business Addr:** Board of Director, American Medical Political Action Committee, 25 Massachusetts Ave N W Suite 600, Washington, DC 20001, **Business Phone:** (202)789-7400.

### WINSTON, SHERRY E.
Diplomat, musician, broker. **Personal:** Born Feb 15, 1947, New York, NY. **Educ:** Howard Univ, BMus, 1968. **Career:** Flutist; Columbia Rec, Jazz Prom, nat dir; Arista Rec, nat prom dir; Grp & Elektra Rec, nat prom dir; Rec Rotating Host: BET-TV'S "Jazz Cent" with Lou Rawls; Albums: Do It For Love, 1986; Love Madness; Love Is, 1991; Life is Love & Love is You, 2000; For Lovers Only, 2002; For Your Love, 2009; Pepsi Cola, Coca Cola, Anheuser Busch, Nat Asn Advan Colored People LDI, AT&T, corp performances; Sherry Winston Enterprises, owner. **Orgs:** Nat Asn Market Developers, Black MBA's; nat dir, jazz prom, Columbia Rec, 1987-89. **Honors/Awds:** Howard Univ Alumni Award, 1984; Grammy Nominee, 1991; Sally Award, 1991; Serwa Award 100 Black Women, 1993; WBLS Quiet Storm Award. **Special Achievements:** Honor of performing for two sitting presidents, for President & Mrs. Clinton, White House & former President George H Bush at the Waldorf Astoria Hotel in NYC; Featured guest on the Today Show, "Emeril Live," and has co-hosted and performed on 8 shows for Bet TV. **Home Addr:** 1939 Hudson St, Bethel, CT 06801-2026. **Business Addr:** Owner, Sherry Winston Enterprises, 19-39 Hudson St, Bethel, CT 06801, **Business Phone:** (203)790-4111.

### WINT, ARTHUR VALENTINE NORIS
School administrator, college teacher. **Personal:** Born Oct 26, 1950, Kingston; son of Noris and Gwendolyn Nelson; married Carlotta Jo Bradley; children: Tsenia, Jhason, Llarehnn & Khirrah. **Educ:** Wash State Univ, Pullman, Wash, BA, 1973; Univ Wash Sch Law, Seattle, Wash, JD, 1976; Harvard Univ, Inst Educ Mgt, 1993. **Career:** Evergreen Legal Servs, Seattle, Wash, legal asst, 1976-77; City Seattle, Seattle, Wash, eo investr, 1977-79; Wash St Univ, Pullman, Wash, diraff action, 1979-86; Calif St Univ, Fresno, Fresno, Calif, asst pres, dir, affirmative action, 1986-92; Calif St Univ, Fresno, exe asst pres, 1992-, assoc prof criminol, 1991, prof criminol, currently, coordr, Prace & Conflict Prog, Col Social Sci, prof emer, 1986-, prof emer criminol, currently. **Orgs:** Church Christ, 1975-; Nat Asn Advan Colored People, 1976-; Pub Info Comt, 1988-90, dir Region X, 1985-86; Calif Asn AA Offrs, 1986-; bd mem, Golden Valley Girl Scouts, 1987-90; Cent Calif Employ, round table, 1989-; Acad Criminal Justice Scis, Am Asn Affirmative Action, dir Region IX, 1990-91; bd mem, mediator, Fresno Victim Offender Reconciliation Prog; ethics comt, Cent Valley C's Hosp; Fresno County Juv Justice Comn; fac mem, Nat Victim Assistance Acad, 1997-2006; elder, Col Church Christ, 1994-. **Honors/Awds:** Senate Intern, Wash State Senate, 1972; Teaching Leadership Award, NAACP, Fresno, 1989; Pew Teaching Award, Univ Wash, 1989. **Home Addr:** PO Box 5172, Fresno, CA 93755, **Home Phone:** (209)225-9955. **Business Addr:** Professor of Criminology, California State University at Fresno, 2576 E San Ramon MS/ST104, Fresno, CA 93740, **Business Phone:** (559)278-2305.

### WINTER, DARIA PORTRAY
Educator, government official. **Personal:** Born Sep 7, 1949, Washington, DC; daughter of James Michael Portray Jr and Susie Lillian Alston Portray; children: Michael Alan. **Educ:** Hampton Inst, BS, eng sec educ, 1971; Univ Va, MA, eng, 1973; Howard Univ, PhD, African Am lit. **Career:** DC Off Bicentennial Progs, asst to exec dir, 1975-76; Univ DC, Coop Exten Prog, housing specialist, 1976-77, asst prof Eng, 1977-97; Off Mayor, gen asst to DC mayor, 1992-95; Southeastern Univ, asst prof Eng; Univ DC Lorton Col Prison Prog, fac, 1998; Howard Univ, Dept Eng, Col Arts & Sci, Eng prof, 1999-. **Orgs:** Alt Nat Comt Woman; DC Dem State Com, 1980-92; Nat Educ Asn Standing Comt Higher Educ, 1981-87; vice chair, DC Dem State Comt, 1984-92; Dem Nat Comt, 1984-92; deleg, Dem Conv, 1984, 1988 & 1992; Mod Lang Asn; Col Lang Asn; Nat Coun Teachers Eng; ed, Newsletter Nat Educ Asn Black Caucus 1987-89; comnr, Pub Defender Serv, 1987-; Pub Defender Serv Bd trustee, 1988-92; vice chair, DNC Eastern Region Caucus, 1988-92; Dist Statehood Com, 1988-92; bd mem, DC Juv Justice Adv Group; bd mem, United Planning Orgn; pres Rank Comt, 1994; chmn, Univ DC Advocacy Comt, 1996; chmn, DC Juv Justice Adv Group, 1998-; chmn, NE Coalition, Deaconess & Class Leader Metrop Wesley AME Zion Church. **Home Addr:** 1355 Underwood St NW, Washington, DC 20012, **Home Phone:** (202)882-5178. **Business Addr:** English Master Instructor, Howard University, B-16 Locke Hall, Washington, DC 20059, **Business Phone:** (202)806-6235.

### WINTERS, DIANE
School principal. **Career:** Weisser Pk Elem Sch, asst prin; Luella Elem Sch, teacher. **Home Addr:** 6734 Orial Pl, Ft. Wayne, IN 46835, **Home Phone:** (260)492-0016. **Business Addr:** Teacher, Luella Elementary School, 575 Walker Dr, Locust Grove, GA 30248, **Business Phone:** (770)288-2035.

### WINTERS, JACQUELINE F. (JACKIE F WINTERS)
Government official, executive. **Personal:** Born Apr 15, 1936, Topeka, KS; daughter of Forrest V Jackson and Catherine L Green Jackson; married Marc P; children: Anthony, Marlon, William & Brian McClain. **Educ:** Ore State Univ, Syst Continuing Educ. **Career:** Portland Model Cities, vol coordr, 1967-68; Pac NW Bell, serv adv, 1968-69; Ore House Reps, staff, 1999-; State Ore, field mgr, 1969-70, prog exec, 1971-79, asst gov, 1979-, rep, 1999-2002, Ore State Senate, sen, dep leader, 2002-; Gov Tom McCalls Econ Opportunity, Offsupvr; Gov Vic Atiyeh, asst; Ore State Exec Serv; Pub Agency Admin; Ore State House Representatives, rep, 1998-2002; Gov Vic Atiyeh, asst; Jackie's Ribs, owner, operator, pres. **Orgs:** State exec serv dir, Marion-Polk United Way, 1975; vpres & pres, Salem Br Nat Asn Advan Colored People, 1975-78; vpres, Salem Hum Rights Comn, 1975; campaign chair, United Way, 1981-82, pres, 1982-83; bd mem, Goodwill Indust Ore, 1991-; bd dir, Ore Col Ed Found Bd Trustees; Ways & Means Comt; conduct, vice chair, Joint Ways & Means Comt; subcomt, Human Serv & Pub Safety; United Way Polk & Marion Counties; bd trustee, Chemeketa Community Col Found; Marion County Environ Health Adv Comt; Marion Pub Safety Coord Coun; Human Serv Subcomt; Ways & Means; co-chair, Pub Safety; dir, Ore Restaurant Asn; pres, Bones & Brew; Chemeketa Col Found Bd; bd dir, Goodwill Industs Ore; bd, dir, Salem Chamber Com; campaign chair, United Way Polk & Marion Counties; Salem-Keiser Sch Dist Blue Ribbon Comt Excellence; Howard St Charter Sch Bd; Coun mem, Marion Pub Safety Coord; Ore State Managers Asn; Mid Valley Econ Develop Dist; Nat Fedn Independent Bus; Ore Northwest Black Pioneers; co-chair, Pub Safety Subcomt; vice chair, Salem Human Rights Comn; bd dir, Salem Chamber Com; Emergency Bd Subcomt, Human Serv & Rural Health Policy, 2009, 2010. **Honors/Awds:** Distinguished Service Award, City Salem, 1976-77; Presidential Award, Salem, Nat Asn Advan Colored People, 1977; Outstanding Community Service Award, United Way, 1979; Outstanding Leadership, Ore Woman Color, 1979; Martin Luther King Jr Community Service Award, Willamette Univ, 1990; Freshman of the Year, Nat Conf State Legis, 1999; Belka Koyuyomn Legislator Appreciation Award, 2003; Charles E Cannefax Legislative Award, Ore Disabilities Comn, 2003; Ore Health Care Achievement, Ore Health Forum, 2005; Ore Health Care Achievement, NOBEL & Women Leadership Inst, 2005; Policy Leader Award, Ore Comn C & Families; Distinguished Service Award, City Salem; Freshman of the Year Award, Nat Republican Legislators Asn. **Home Addr:** PM 1334676 Com SE, Salem, OR 97302. **Business Addr:** State Senator, State of Oregon, 900 Ct St NE S-212, Salem, OR 97301, **Business Phone:** (503)986-1710.

### WINTERS, JAMES
Executive, chief executive officer. **Educ:** Oregon State Univ, BS, 1986. **Career:** United Energy Inc, pres & chief exec officer, 1990-. **Orgs:** Treas, Urban League. **Business Addr:** Chief Executive Officer, President, United Energy Inc, 8040 NE Sandy Blvd Suite 300, Portland, OR 97213, **Business Phone:** (503)287-4000.

### WINTERS, JAMES ROBERT
Government official. **Personal:** Born Aug 26, 1937, Pittsburgh, PA; married Diane Herndon; children: Angela, Richard, Lisa & Ryan. **Educ:** Fayetteville State Univ, BS, 1965; Univ Pittsburgh, social work, 1972. **Career:** Young Mens Christian Asn Prog Ctr Pittsburgh, caseworker, 1966-67, prog dir, 1967-70, exec dir, 1970-72; Old Ft & Kiwanis Young Mens Christian Asn, Ft Wayne, IN, urban dir, 1972-78; Wayne Twp Trustee's Off, trustee, 1978-90. **Orgs:** Adv comt mem, Univ Pittsburgh Learn Leisure Prog, 1967-70; organizer, Grambling-Morgan St Football Game, 1970; organizer, Pittsburgh Pirate Baseball Wives Benefit Pittsburgh, Young Mens Christian Asn Capital Campaign Fund Dr, 1971; bd mem, Ind Criminal Justice Planning, 1980; bd mem, Ind St Black Assembly, 1980. **Home Addr:** 708 Candlelite Ct, Ft. Wayne, IN 46807-3606, **Home Phone:** (219)745-4403. **Business Addr:** Staff, Chemical Waste Management, 4636 Adams Ctr Rd, Ft. Wayne, IN 46806, **Business Phone:** (260)441-9477.

### WINTERS, JAMES W., II
Executive. **Career:** United Energy Inc, pres, chief exec officer & prin, currently. **Business Addr:** Principal, President, Chief Executive Officer, United Energy Inc, 8040 NE Sandy Blvd Suite 300, Portland, OR 97213, **Business Phone:** (503)287-4000.

### WINTERS, KENNETH E.
Financial manager, real estate executive, executive director. **Personal:** Born Oct 22, 1959, Gonzales, TX; married Wendy C Gordon. **Educ:** St Mary's Univ, BA, finance; Golden Gate Univ, MA, finance. **Career:** United Serv Automobile Asn, financial reporting analyst, 1979-83; USAA Real Estate Co, real estate analyst, 1983; real estate asset mgr, 1983-87; Real Estate Acquisitions, 1987; Port San Francisco, dir real estate, 2002-; AEW Capital Mgt, prin. **Orgs:** Nat Asn Bus Economists; Am Finance Asn; tutor, Eng & Reading, San Antonio Literacy Coun. **Home Addr:** 1924 Middlefield Rd, Redwood City, CA 94063-2241, **Home Phone:** (650)369-8996. **Business Addr:** Director of Real Estate, Port of San Francisco, Pier 1 The Embarcadero, San Francisco, CA 94111, **Business Phone:** (415)274-0400.

### WINTERS, WENDY GLASGOW (WENDY G WINTERS)
School administrator. **Personal:** Born Jun 26, 1930; married Irving J; children: Allison Lenore & Roger DeCourey Jr. **Educ:** Cent Conn State Col, BS, elem educ, 1952; Columbia Univ, Sch Social Work, MS, psychol social work, 1954; Yale Univ, PhD, sociol, 1975. **Career:** Community Serv Soc, fel, 1952-54; Herrick House Bartlett, Ill, dir girls unit, 1954; Community Serv Soc, NY, family caseworker & intake admin, 1954-65; Norwalk Bd Educ, social worker, 1965-68; Univ Conn, Sch Social Work, field instr, 1967-80, assoc prof, asst dean acad affairs, 1975-78; Yale Univ, Child Study Ctr, chief social worker, 1968-75, instr, 1968-71, asst prof social work, 1971, fel, 1971-74, res assoc, 1975-82; Col Lib Arts, dean; Atlanta Univ, Sch Social Work, field instr, 1970-71; Ethel BMorgan, fel, 1972-73; Smith Col, N Hampton, adj assoc prof social work, assoc prof sociol & anthrop, dean, 1979-84; J Educ Studs Placed At Risk, assoc ed, currently; Yale Univ, teacher; Howard Univ, emer prof urban sociol, currently; Baldwin King Sch Prog, chief social worker; BWA Report Newsletter, ed. **Orgs:** Adv bd, Proj Upward Bound Cherry Lawn Sch, 1966-68; adv comn, Norwalk Community Col, Educ Voc Resource Ctr, 1967-68; Norwalk-Wilton Ed Proj, 1967-68; Greater New Haven Urban League, 1969-71; ed cult adv comn, Yale Off Community Affairs Develop, 1974-75; Am Ortho psychiat Asn; reg adv coun, 1975-78; bd dir, Leila Day Nurseries, 1975-78; sub-comt, community serv grants adv comn, Comn Higher Educ, 1976-77; chmn, Eval sub-comt, 1977-78; Conn State, Dept C & Youth Servs; juv justice adv comt, Conn Justice Comn, 1977; bd mem, Bd Managers Casey Family Serv, 1997-; bd corps, N Hampton Inst Savings, 1979-, bd dir, 1977-80, exec comt, 1977-79 Ctr Res Educ Studs Placed At Risk, Johns Hopkins Univ; Sociol Dept; Nat Bd Dirs Parents Pub Schs; bd mem, Annie E. Casey Found; bd mem, Black Womens Agenda; bd mem, La State Bd Educ; Am Orthopsychiat Asn; Am Asn Univ Women; Am Ortho psychiat Asn; Am Sociol Asn; Black Anal Inc; Nat Asn Social Workers; New Eng Deans Asn; New Eng Minority Women Admins; assoc ed, JESPAR, J Educ Students Placed at Risk; oper arm Annie E. Casey Found; ed, Black Womens Agenda; Alpha Kappa Alpha. **Honors/Awds:** National Institute of Mental Health Research Award, 1974; Md Governor Citation, 1996. **Special Achievements:** Taped film on "Excellence", Gen Elect Corp, 1983; "The Practice of Social Work in Schools", workshop Baton Rouge, 1984; Co-author, The Practice of Social Work in Schools: An Ecological Perspective, Free Press, 1983; Author: African American Mothers and Urban Schools: The Power of Participation, Lexington Books, 1993. **Business Addr:** Emerita Professor of Urban Sociology, Associate Editor, Johns Hopkins University, 3003 N Charles St Suite 200, Baltimore, MD 21218, **Business Phone:** (410)516-8270.

### WISDOM, DR. KIMBERLYDAWN
Educator, surgeon. **Personal:** married Garth A Sr; children: 3. **Educ:** Univ Pa, BS, biol, 1978; Univ Mich Sch Pub Health, MD, 1982. **Career:** Henry Ford Hosp, emergency med physician, currently; Univ Mich Med Ctr, asst prof med educ, currently; Henry Ford Health Syst, Inst Multicultural Health, founder & dir, vpres community health, educ & wellness, 2007-11, sr vpres community health & equity & chief wellness officer, 2011-; US Dept Health & Human Serv Nat Inst Health Study, sect reviewer, 2002-04; Mich Dept Community Health, surgeon gen, 2003-10; Univ Mich Med Ctr, asst prof med educ; Univ Mich Sch Pub Health, Dept Health Behav & Health Educ, adj asst prof. **Orgs:** Founder & dir, African-Am Initiative Male Health Improv; Adv Group Prev, Health Prom, & Integrative & Pub Health, 2012-; chair, Gail & Lois Warden Endowment Multicultural Health. **Business Addr:** Senior Vice President of Community Health & Equity, Chief Wellness Officer, Henry Ford Health System, 1 Ford Pl Suite 4C, Detroit, MI 48202, **Business Phone:** (313)874-6500.

### WISE, C. ROGERS
Physician. **Personal:** Born Apr 8, 1930, Ft. Worth, TX; married Margaret. **Educ:** Fisk Univ, BA; Univ de Lausanne, MD, PhD. **Career:** Anesthesiologist (retired); DePaul Hosp, 1971-75; Memorial Hosp, Dept Anesthesia, chief, 1972-74; Self-Employed, physician. **Orgs:** Int Anesthesia Res Soc; Am Soc Anesthesiologists; mem bd trustee, 1968, vice chmn, 1973-77, chmn bd, 1974, Laramie Co Community Col. **Home Addr:** 2406 Omega Rd, Cheyenne, WY 82009. **Business Addr:** PO Box 1144, Cheyenne, WY 82602.

### WISE, FRANK P.
Government official, executive director. **Personal:** Born Oct 28, 1942, Norfolk, VA; son of Frank P Sr (deceased) and Marian C Williams; children: Terri Lynn & Dawne Shenette. **Educ:** Ohio Univ, BBA, acct, econs, 1965; Howard Univ, MUA, city mgt, 1972. **Career:** US Nat Stand Asn, res asst, 1966-67; Eastern Airlines, coordr, 1967-68; Prince Geo Co, admin asst, 1970-72; City Cincinnati, mgt analyst, 1972; asst to city mgr, 1973-74; City Savannah, asst city mgr, 1975-78; City E Cleveland, city mgr, 1979-83; City Dallas, admin finance, asst dir, 1984-87, Pk & Recreation Bd, dir, 1987-92; Cruise & Travel Arrangement, owner, 1992-. **Orgs:** Fel ICMA Urban, 1970; chmn, Minority Coalition, 1972-73; vpres at large, Financil Comt, Conf

Planning Comn, 1973, 1975-76; vpres at-large, Am Soc Pub Admin, Conf Minority Pub Admin Sect Human Res Admin, 1978-79; Nat Develop Dir Asn; Nat Recreation & Pk Asn, 1984-; Tex Recreation & Pk Soc, 1984-; bd mem, Western Revenue Sources Mgt Sch, 1990-; Int City Mgt Asn; Ford Found. **Honors/Awds:** Citations, YMCA, 1973; Mayoral Proclamation, 1974; Award of Merit, Ohio Parks & Recreation Asn. **Special Achievements:** Article "What Role for Minority Assistance? The Second Dilemma", Pub Mgmt Mag, 1972; "The Art of Serving Two Masters", Pub Mgmt Mag, 1975; "Toward Equity of Results Achieved One Approach", Pub Mgmt Mag, 1976. **Home Addr:** 2837 Bonnywood Lane, Dallas, TX 75233. **Business Addr:** Director, City Dallas, 1500 Marilla St Suite 6FN, Dallas, TX 75201.

### WISE, WILLIAM CLINTON, SR.

Executive, government official, manager. **Personal:** Born Jan 14, 1941, Steubenville, OH; son of Robert and Vivian Doggett; married Linda Rayam; children: Shawn, Sharon, Sandra & William Jr. **Educ:** Eastern Mich Univ, labor law; US Armed Forces Inst, bus admin; Washtenaw Community Col, psychol; Univ Mich Labor Sch. **Career:** City Ann Arbor, Ann Arbor, personnel dir, 1973-77; Ford Motor Co, Dearborn, spec prog coord, 1977-84; Martin Marietta Corp, Bethesda, mgr, mgt training, 1984-. **Orgs:** Exec adv, Nat Technol Univ, 1991; Am Soc Training & Develop, 1984-. **Home Addr:** 18354 Hallmark Ct, Gaithersburg, MD 20879, **Home Phone:** (301)963-1182. **Business Addr:** Corporate Manager, Martin Marietta Corp, 6801 Rockledge Dr, Bethesda, MD 20817, **Business Phone:** (301)897-6210.

### WISE-HARRISON, PAMELA DORSEY

Pianist, composer. **Personal:** Born Jan 8, 1956, Steubenville, OH; daughter of Robert C and Eloise D; married Wendell. **Educ:** Univ Steubenville; Cuyahoga Community Col; Kent State Univ. **Career:** Jazz pianist & composer, 1980-; Albums: Songo Festividad, 1994; Wise Tells, 1995; Pamela Wise & the Afro Cuban Project I, 1999; Pamela Wise & the Afro Cuban Project II, 2000; Latin Wise, 2001; "Negre Con Leche, Black with Cream"; Pamela's Club. **Orgs:** Exec dir, Rebirth, 1983-; Detroit Fed Musicians Union, 2000-. **Honors/Awds:** Art Serve of Michigan Commission Award; Michigan Council For The Arts Creative Artist; Creative Artist Grant Award, Arts Found Mich, 1994, 1996, 1998, 2000. **Home Addr:** 81 Chandler St, Detroit, MI 48202, **Home Phone:** (313)875-0289. **Business Addr:** Pianist, Composer, Rebirth Inc, 81 Chandler St, Detroit, MI 48202, **Business Phone:** (313)875-0289.

### WISE-LOVE, KAREN A. See LOVE, KAREN ALLYCE.

### WISHAM, CLAYBRON OSCAR

Executive. **Personal:** Born Dec 28, 1932, Newport, OH; son of Charlie and Willie (deceased); married Evelyn Bailey; children: Deshay Appling, Lorna, Julian Andrew, Evan Clay & Karen Hudson. **Educ:** Philander Smith Col, BA, 1954; Univ Ark, MEd, 1963. **Career:** Executive (retired); AR Baptist Col, dir athletics, 1956-59; E End Boys Club, exec dir, 1957-59; Jones High Sch, guid counr, 1959-61; Union Com Bank, asst vpres personnel, 1970-72; Cleveland State Univ, affirmative action officer, 1972-74; personnel admin, 1974-83; Cleveland Elec Illum Co, gen mgr Opers, 1983-90; Centerior Energy Corp, mgr, training & develop, 1990. **Orgs:** Alpha Phi Alpha, 1952; Blacks Mgt, 1970-; Nat Asn Advan Colored People; Greater Cleveland Growth Asn; charter mem, Am Asn Blacks Energy; sr arbitrator, Cleveland Better Bus Bur; bd trustee, Ctr Rehab Serv, Miles Ahead Inc; Marymount Hosp Civic Adv Bd; Urban League Cleveland; United Way Servs Allocations Panel; Delta Alpha Lambda Chap, Alpha Phi Alpha Fraternity; Minton Legacy Soc; ML Harris Soc. **Honors/Awds:** Inducted, AB Calvin Athletic Hall of Fame, SA Jones High School. **Special Achievements:** First African American Personnel Recruiter Corp Position, City Cleveland, Ohio, 1965; First Black Asst VP, Union Commerce Bank Personnel Dept, 1970; First Black Conf Chmn of EEO, Nat Sem for Edison Elec Inst, 1979; First Black Operations Manager at Cleveland Election Illuminating Co. **Home Addr:** 3626 Sutherland Rd, Shaker Heights, OH 44122, **Home Phone:** (216)295-2276.

### WITCHER, VEROMAN D., JR.

Law enforcement officer. **Personal:** married Marion. **Career:** OH State Hwy Patrol, field training officer, driving instr, police instr, background investr, state trooper, 1985; Churchs Spec Olympics team, founder, coach; Xenia Post; Dayton Post, 2000; Piqua Post, 2005, 2011; Springfield Post, asst post comdr, 2009. **Business Addr:** Highway Patrol Sergeant, Public Safety Department.

### WITHERSPOON, ADDELLE

Artist. **Career:** Fiber Art by Rondell, artist, 2003-; Simply Art Inc, artist, currently. **Business Addr:** Artist, Fiber Art by Rondell, 19220B 67th Ave, Fresh Meadows, NY 11365, **Business Phone:** (718)454-5189.

### WITHERSPOON, AUDREY GOODWIN

School administrator, real estate agent, association executive. **Personal:** Born Aug 19, 1949, Greenwood, SC; daughter of Hudson and Essie Lue Chenault; children: Jacintha Dyan & Andre LaVern. **Educ:** Lander Univ, BA, sociol, 1971; Clemson Univ, MEd, admin & supv, 1975; Vanderbilt Univ, grad study, educ leadership, 1983. **Career:** McCormick County Sch Dist, teacher, 1971-72; GLEAMNS Head Start Prog, social worker, parent coordr, 1972-74, educ dir, 1974-75; GLEAMNS Human Resource Comn, child develop, founder & dir, 1972-2005; Generational Treasures, LLC, Educational Consultant; 2004-11; A-Z Realty, Realtor, 2006-currently. **Orgs:** Nat Asn Educ Young C, 1975-93; vice chairperson, bd trustees, Greenwood Sch Dist, 50, 1977-93; chart mem, SC Child Develop Providers Inc, bd mem, 1978-96, pres, 1987; treas, Greenwood Br, Nat Asn Advan Colored People, 1979-96; vice chairperson, region coordr, Gov Task Force, 1979-82; Negro Bus & Prof Womens Club, 1981-87; Gov Riley's Ed Transition Team, 1983-84; proj coordr, Region V, SC Voices C, 1984-85; planning comn, Effective Schs, SC, 1985; Mt Moriah Baptist Church; State Adv Comt, Day Care Regulations, 1987-89; Lander Univ Class Agt, 1988-96; SC Pub Pvt Child Care Coun, 1990; Early Childhood Educ, Interagency Adv Comt, 1990-93; Nat Coun Negro Women, 1989-93; SC Sch Bds Asn, 1990, 1992; bd trustees, Lander Univ, 2007-. **Honors/Awds:** Distinguished Alumni of the Year, Lander Univ, 1971; Female Citizen of the Year, 1982; Various State & Nat Community Awards, 1982-92; Distinguished Alumni Award, Lander Univ, 1989; Distinguished Service Award, Greenwood Rotary Int, 1993. **Home Addr:** 101 Stafford Dr, Greenwood, SC 29649-8922, **Home Phone:** (803)223-1617. **Business Addr:** Member, Lander University, 320 Stanley Ave, Greenwood, SC 29649-2099, **Business Phone:** (864)388-8000.

### WITHERSPOON, JOHN

Actor, comedian. **Personal:** Born Jan 27, 1942, Detroit, MI; married Angela Robinson; children: John David & Alexander. **Career:** Films: Kidnapped, 1986; Ratboy, 1986; Hollywood Shuffle, 1987; Bird, 1988; I'm Gonna Git You Sucka, 1988; Killer Tomatoes Strike Back!, 1990; House Party, 1990; The Five Heartbeats, 1991; Talkin' Dirty After Dark, 1991; Boomerang, 1992; The Meteor Man, 1993; Fatal Instinct, 1993; Vampire in Brooklyn, 1995; Friday, 1995; A Delicatessen Story, 1996; Fakin' Da Funk, 1997; Sprung, 1997; High Frequency, 1998; Ride, 1998; Bulworth, 1998; I Got the Hook Up, 1998; Next Friday, 2000; Little Nicky, 2000; The Ladies Man, 2000; Friday After Next, 2002; Pryor Offenses, 2004; Soul Plane, 2004; Little Man, 2006; After Sex, 2007; The Hustle, 2008; Hopelessly in June, 2009; A Thousand Words, 2012; TV series: "The Incredible Hulk", 1978; "What's Happening!!", 1978; "Good Times", 1979; "Barnaby Jones", 1979; The Jazz Singer?, 1980; "WKRP in Cincinnati", 1982; "Hill Street Blues", 1982; "You Again?", 1986; "227", 1987; "What's Happening Now!", 1987; "Frank's Place", 1987; "Amen", 1988; "L.A. Law", 1990; Sunday in Paris?, 1991; "Martin", 1993; Cosmic Slop, 1994; "The Fresh Prince of Bel-Air", 1994; "The Wayans Bros.", 1995-99; "Wayne head", 1996-97; "Living Single", 1997; "Happily Ever After: Fairy Tales for Every Child", 2000; "The Proud Family", 2003; "The Tracy Morgan Show", 2003-04; "Kim Possible", 2004; "Weekends at the DL", 2005; "The Boondocks", 2005-14; Thugaboo: A Miracle on D-Roc's Street, 2006; "The Super Rumble Mix show", 2008; exe producer, "John Witherspoon: You Got to Coordinate", exec producer, 2008; "Tosh.0 Episode 58: Fart Bus Kid:, 2011; "The First Family", 2012-13; "Randy Cunningham: 9th Grade Ninja", 2013; "Anger Management", 2014; "Black Jesus", 2014. **Business Addr:** Actor, c/o International Creative Management Inc, 8942 Wilshire Blvd, Beverly Hills, CA 90211, **Business Phone:** (310)550-4000.

### WITHERSPOON, NAOMI. See MADGETT, DR. NAOMI LONG.

### WITHERSPOON, R. CAROLYN

Executive. **Personal:** Born Detroit, MI; married William C; children: W Roger, L Courtney & David J. **Educ:** City Col NY, BS, 1951, MS, 1956. **Career:** Executive (retired); Town Hall NY, acct, 1945-48; Foreign Rels Libr, treas; Coun Foreign Rels Inc, asst treas & comptroller, 1952-87. **Orgs:** Nat financial secy; pres, Nat Asn Negro Bus & Prof Women's Clubs Inc, 1975-79; Community Rel Bd; adjust com Teaneck; Kappa Delta Pi; Beta Alpha Psi; Teaneck Pub Libr. **Home Addr:** 134 Voorhees St, Teaneck, NJ 07666.

### WITHERSPOON, SOPHIA L.

Basketball player. **Personal:** Born Jul 6, 1969, Ft. Pierce, FL. **Educ:** Univ Fla, BS, health & human performance, 1991. **Career:** Basketball player (retired); Providencia Nyon, Switz, 1991-92; Hawthorne High Sch, asst coach, 1992-94; SPD Rouenm, france, 1994-95; FTC Budapest, Hungary, 1995-96; Galatasaray, Turkey, 1997-98; New York Liberty, guard, 1997-99; Ferencvarosi, Hungary, 1998-99; Portland Fire, 2000-01; Los Angeles Sparks, guard, 2002-03; Charlotte Sting, free agt, 2004-07.

### WITHERSPOON, WILLIAM ROGER

Journalist, writer. **Personal:** Born Mar 3, 1949, New York, NY; son of William C and Ruth C; married Cynthia O Bedford; children: Kir & Brie. **Educ:** Univ Mich, attended 1967; Rider Col, attended 1973; Rutgers Univ, Livingstone Col, attended 1975; Fairleigh-Dickinson Univ, attended 1976. **Career:** Star-Ledger, investment reporter, columnist, op-ed page, st house corresp, columnist senate, assembly, banking, transp & agr, gen; assignment reporter, 1970-75; NY Daily News, Sunday assignment ed, health & environ reporter, Pasaic City reporter, ed gen assignment reporter, 1975-79; Atlanta Const, columnist, health & sci writer, 1979-82; Time Mag, SE Bur, Cable News Network, writer/producer; Black Enterprise Mag, Newsweek, GQ Mag, Fortune, Essence Mag, Nat Leader, freelance writer, 1982-85; Dallas Times Herald, ed bd, 1985-. **Orgs:** Atlanta African Film Soc, Nat Asn Black Journalists, Black Perspective, 1970-73; contrib ed, Essence Mag; ed adv bd, Nat Asn Advan Colored People; Crisis Mag, 1979-80; Dallas-Ft Worth Asn Black Communicators. **Honors/Awds:** UPI Ga Newspaper Awards, Second place column writing, third place spot news coverage, Three Mile Island, 1979; First place energy series Media Award for Econ Understanding Series Amos, Tuck Sch Bus Admin Dartmouth Col, 1980; First place outstanding news feature, Atlanta Asn Black Journalists, 1980; Nat Headliners Club Award for Consistently Outstanding Special/Feature Column Writing, 1981; Journ Acolade Award, Ga Conf on Social Welfare, 1981; Special Citation, Reporting Awards Ed Writers Asn, 1982; First place Reg 5, Nat Asn Black Journalists, 1982; Katie Award Best Ed Press Club Dallas, 1986; First Place Editorial Writing Tex Asn Press Managing Eds, 1987. **Special Achievements:** Author, "Martin Luther King Jr To The Mountaintop", Doubleday & Co, 1985. **Home Addr:** 2802 Dukeswood Dr, Garland, TX 75040, **Home Phone:** (214)495-3647. **Business Addr:** Editorial Writer, Dallas Times Herald, 1101 Pacific Ave, Dallas, TX 75202, **Business Phone:** (214)720-6633.

### WOFFORD, CHLOE ANTHONY. See MORRISON, TONI.

### WOLFE, ALLEN, JR.

Nurse. **Career:** Wash Hosp Ctr, clin supvr, critical care clin specialist, currently; Medstar Health, clin supvr & chief flight nurse, currently. **Honors/Awds:** Medical Transport Leadership Institute Scholarship, MedEvac Found Int, 2010. **Business Addr:** Flight Nurse, Medstar Health, 110 Irving St NW, Washington, DC 20010, **Business Phone:** (202)744-6125.

### WOLFE, GEORGE COSTELLO

Television producer, administrator, writer. **Personal:** Born Sep 23, 1954, Frankfort, KY; son of Costello and Anna Lindsey. **Educ:** Pomona Col, BA, directing, 1976; NY Univ, MFA, play writing, musical theatre, 1983. **Career:** Actor, Director, Writer, Producer. Actor: "Great Performances", 1991; "The Colored Museum", 1991; Fresh Kill, 1994; TV Garden State, 2004; The Devil Wears Prada, 2006; Ramona and Beezus, 2010. Director: "Great Performances", 1991; "The Colored Museum", 1991; "Fires in the Mirror", 1993; "The WIN Awards", 2005; "Lackawanna Blues", 2005; Nights in Rodanthe, 2008; You're Not You, 2014. Self: The Papp Project, 2001; "Stage on Screen: The Top dog Diaries", 2002; The 58thAnnual Tony Awards, 2004; Elaine Stritch at Liberty, 2004; "Broadway: The American Musical", 2004; 2006 Independent Spirit Awards, 2006; Show Business: The Road to Broadway, 2007; Theater of War, 2008; Inner City Cult Ctr, exec dir; Director: Nights In Rodanthe, 2008; Untitled Kanye West Project, 2009; Mother Courage & Her Children; Rosenwald, 2015. **Orgs:** Artistic assoc, producer, New York Shakespeare Festival, 1993-04; bd dir, Young Playwrights Festival, 1992-93; exec coun, Dramatist Guild, 1992-93. **Business Addr:** Director, Home Box Office Inc, 1100 Ave of the Americas, New York, NY 10036, **Business Phone:** (212)512-1000.

### WOLFE, DR. JOHN THOMAS, JR.

College administrator, chancellor (education). **Personal:** Born Feb 22, 1942, Jackson, MS; son of John and Jeanette; children: Wyatt, John T & David A. **Educ:** Chicago State Univ, BSEd, 1964; Purdue Univ, MS, engineering educ, 1972, PhD, ling, 1976. **Career:** Purdue Univ, mgr employee rels, 1975-77; Fayetteville State Univ, eng dept chair, 1977-79, div head humanities & fine arts, 1979-83, acad dean, 1983-85; Nat Endowment Humanities fel, 1979; Am Coun Educ fel, 1982-83; Bowie State Univ, provost & vpres acad affairs, 1985-90; KY State Univ, Frankfort, KY, pres, 1990-91; Savannah State Univ, pres, 1993-97; Univ Syst Ga, assoc vice chancellor fac affairs, 1997-2005; Univ Syst Md, assoc vice chancellor, acad affairs, 2006-; Higher Educ Group Wash, pres, 2008-09; Wash Regional Taskforce Against Campus Prejudice, co-chair, 2008-10; HBCU Regional Summit Retention, chair, 2009-10. **Orgs:** Pres, Black Caucus Nat Coun Teacher Eng, 1982-88; standing comn teacher, Prep Nat Coun Teachers Eng, 1984-87; bd dir, Bowie New Town Ctr Minority Adv Bd, 1985-; steering comt mem, Prince Georges Co, Md Univ High Sch, 1985-87; chair, adv bd, Prince Georges County, Md Entrepreneurial Develop Prog; Leadership & Mentoring Inst. **Home Addr:** 9929 Greenbelt Rd Suite 201, Lanham, MD 20706. **Business Addr:** Associate Vice Chancellor for Academic Affairs, University System of Maryland, 3300 Metzerott Rd, Adelphi, MD 20783-1690, **Business Phone:** (301)445-2740.

### WOLFMAN, DR. BRUNETTA REID

School administrator. **Personal:** Born Clarksdale, MS; married Burton I; children: Andrea C & Jeffrey Allen. **Educ:** Univ Calif, Berkeley, BA, 1957, MA, 1968, PhD, 1971. **Career:** Univ Calif, Berkeley, teaching fel, 1969-71; Dartmouth Col, Calif coordr, 1971-72, asst dean fac & asst prof, 1972-74; Univ Mass, asst vpres, 1974-76; Wheelock Col Boston, acad dean, 1976-78; Mass Dept Educ, exec planner, 1978-82; Rox bury Community Col, pres, 1983-; George Washington Univ, assoc vpres acad affairs, 1990-91, prof educ emer; Roxbury Community Col, pres. **Orgs:** Prog dir, Young Women's Christian Asn, Oakland & Berkeley, Calif, 1959-63; exec dir, Camp Fire Girls Berkeley, 1963-67; consult, Arthur D Little Inc, 1977-78; pres, New Eng Minority Women Admins, 1977-78; bd dir, Nat Ctr Higher Educ Mgt Systs, 1978-; bd dir, Boston Fenway Prog, 1979-; overseer, Boston Symphony Orchestra, 1984; Mus Fine Arts, 1984; overseer, Stone Ctr, Wellesley Col; bd, Nat Conf Christians & Jews; bd, US Trust Bank; bd, Boston Pvt Indust Coun; bd, Am Coun Educ; counr, Coun Educ Pub Health; urban comn, Am Asn Community & Jr Cols; Provice Town Coun, 2000; chair bd, secy bd, bd trustee, Provincetown Art Asn & Mus; Nat Asn Women; George Wash Univ Soc Emeritae, Am Sociol Asn, bd mem, Cape Cod Found. **Honors/Awds:** Nat Inst Educ grant Superwomen Study, 1978-79; "Roles", W minister Press, 1983; hon degree, Regis Col; hon degree, Suffolk Univ; hon degree, Boston Univ. **Special Achievements:** Publ, two articles in black separatism & social reality, Pergamon Press, 1977; paper presented & publ, OECD, Paris, 1978; papers presented annual meeting, Am Educ Res Asn, 1980; Author, 'Black Women in America: Social Science Perspectives', 1991; Amelia Earhart Award, Women's Educ & Indust Union. **Home Addr:** 108 Beacon St, Boston, MA 01608. **Business Addr:** Professor, George Washington University Graduate School of Education and Human Development, 2134 G St NW, Washington, DC 20037, **Business Phone:** (202)994-8860.

### WOMACK, ANTHONY DARRELL. See WOMACK, TONY.

### WOMACK, CHRISTOPHER CLARENCE

Executive director, association executive, executive. **Personal:** Born Feb 26, 1958, Greenville, AL; son of Ruby; married Sabrina Shannon; children: Shannon Ashley & Christopher Michael. **Educ:** Western Mich Univ, BS, polit sci, 1979; Am Univ, MPA, 1985. **Career:** US House Rep, legis aide Rep Leon E Panetta, 1979-84; Subcomt Personnel & Police, Comn House Adminr, staff dir, 1984-87; Ala Power Co, govt affairs rep, 1988-89, asst pub affairs, 1989-91, dir community rels, 1991-93, vpres pub rels, 1993-95, sr vpres pub rels & corp serv, sr vpres, sr prod officer, 1995-98; Southern Co, sr vpres human resources, 1988, chief people officer, vpres, 1998-2001, sr prod officer, pres external affairs, 2009-; Ga Power, sr prod officer, sr vpres fossil & hydro generation, 2001-06, exec vpres, external affairs, 2006-08. **Orgs:** Ala Ballet; exec dir, Ala Bus Charitable Trust Fund; chair, Alpha Phi Alpha Educ Found; treas, Birmingham Cult & Heritage Found, City Stages; Birmingham Community Olympic Football; bd deacons, Sixth Ave Baptist Church; bd dir, US Chamber Com; chmn, Atlanta Sports Coun. **Honors/Awds:** Silver Knight of Management Award, 1994. **Special Achievements:** Top 40 Under 40 Designation, Birmingham Business Journal, 1993; Leadership Birmingham, 1990. **Home Addr:** 2109 Christina Cove, Birmingham, AL 35244, **Home Phone:** (205)985-8784. **Business Addr:** President External Affairs,

Southern Co, 30 Ivan Allen Jr Blvd NW, Atlanta, GA 30308, **Business Phone:** (404)506-5000.

### WOMACK, JOE NEAL, JR.

Executive. **Personal:** Born Oct 5, 1950, Mobile, AL; son of Joe N Sr and Annie Laura Brown Pressley; married Juliette F; children: Joe Neal III; married Mary B. **Educ:** St Paul's Col, Lawrenceville, BS, bus, 1972. **Career:** Metropolitan Life, Mobile, sales rep, 1972; Marine Corps, maj, 1973-94; Shell Chem, DuPont, Mobile, financial analyst, 1973-90; Prudential, Mobile, sales rep, 1990-95. **Orgs:** Alpha Phi Alpha Fraternity, 1972; comn chair, Mobile Area Mardi Gras Asn, 1987-; Mardi Gras Maskers, 1988-; co-founder & pres, African-Am Summit Steering Comt, 1989-; co-founder & pres, Black Mil Workers Am Inc; co-founder & bd mem, Mobile Chap Montford Pt Marines. **Special Achievements:** First African American professional to be promoted at the Shell/DuPont Chemical Plant in Axis, Alabama. **Home Addr:** 2816 Westmoor Ct, Mobile, AL 36695, **Home Phone:** (251)666-5108.

### WOMACK, REV. DR. JOHN H., SR.

Executive. **Personal:** Born Jul 8, 1944, Lunenburg, VA; son of George and Elnora; married Bertha; children: Tonya, John Jr & Monica. **Educ:** Fisher Jr Col; Gordon-Conwell Theol Sem, master, relig educ, 1990, doctorate ministry, 2001. **Career:** Pastor (retired); Rec Wagon, sls rep, 1967-70; Prof Maintenance Co, Maintenance Supvr, 1969-76; McGarrahan Steel Erection, iron worker, 1970-77; Salem Fire Dept, Salem, firefighter, 1977-80; JJS Serv & Peabody Paper, Peabody, founder & pres, chief exec officer, 1977-98; TJM Apparel, 1998-; Metrop Baptist Church, pastor, 1993-2010; Warren Bancorp Inc, dir; St John's Baptist Church, Woburn, MA, deacon. **Orgs:** Pres, Black Corp Pres New Eng; bd dir, Bldg Serv Contractors Asn Int, 1986; bd mem, Job Youth, 1990-; pres, Greater Boston Deacon's Union; bd dir, Harvard St Neighborhood Health Ctr; bd trustee, Gordon-Conwell Theol Sem; bd advisor, Ctr Urban Ministerial Educ; bd dir, Minority Bus Enterprise Legal Defense & Educ Fund Inc; bd dir, N Shore Community Col Found Bd; bd dir, Warren Five Cents Savings Bank; bd dir, New Eng Adv Coun, Fed Res Bank Boston. **Home Addr:** 103 St Andrew Rd, Boxford, MA 02128-1251. **Business Addr:** Senior Chairperson, St. Johns Baptist Church, 38-40 Everett St, Woburn, MA 01801.

### WOMACK, RICHARD GILBERT, SR.

Executive, association executive. **Personal:** Born Nov 18, 1939, Danville, VA; son of Gilbert and Louise Patrick. **Career:** A. Philip Randolph Inst, northeast regional pres; Am Fedn Labor-Cong Indust Orgn, Human Resources Develop Inst, asst dir, 1971, Dept Civil Rights, dir, 1986, asst to pres, 2003-. **Orgs:** Bd dir, Nat Asn Advan Colored People; chair, nat bd dir, Labor Comt; chmn bd, Nat Coalition Black Civic Participation; actg exec dir, Leadership Conf Civil Rights; bd mem, Fed Prison Indust, 1996; bd mem, Southern Automotive Wholesalers Inc. **Business Addr:** Assistant to the President, American Federation of Labor, 815 16th St NW, Washington, DC 20006, **Business Phone:** (202)637-5000.

### WOMACK, TONY (ANTHONY DARRELL WOMACK)

Baseball player. **Personal:** Born Sep 25, 1969, Danville, VA; married Janet; children: Jessica & Alsander. **Educ:** Guilford Col, BA, 1992; Univ NC, MA, Greensboro, sports mgt. **Career:** Baseball player (retired); Pittsburgh Pirates, infielder, 1993-94, 1996-98; Ariz Diamondbacks, 1999-2003; Colo Rockies, 2003; Chicago Cubs, infielders, 2003, 2006, free agt, 2006; St Louis Cardinals, 2004; NY Yankees, 2005; Cincinnati Reds, 2006. **Orgs:** Founder, Stealing Hearts, Charlotte.

### WOMBLE, JEFFERY MAURICE

Public relations executive, editor. **Personal:** Born Apr 4, 1964, Fayetteville, NC; son of Charles Leo Sr and Corine McLean. **Educ:** Fayetteville State Univ, Fayetteville, NC, BA, Eng, 1986. **Career:** Fayetteville Observer, Fayetteville, NC, reporter & ed, 1982-2004; Fayetteville State Univ, Pub Rels & Telecommunications, dir, currently, asst vice chancellor, 2004-; LaShanta McCorkle, dir Pub Rels. **Orgs:** Nat Asn Black Journalists, 1988-; ed Sphinx, Alpha Phi Alpha Fraternity, 1990-; Big Bros Prog, 1990-; comm adv bd, Jr League Fayetteville; adv bd, Find-A-Friend; adv bd, Upward Bound, FSU; teen adv bd, Women's Ctr Fayetteville; bd dir, Fayetteville Scholar Pageant Assoc. **Honors/Awds:** Media Award, VFW Post 6018, 1987; Outstanding African-American Male Award, Alpha Kappa Alpha Sorority; Community Resource Specialist, Cumberland County Schs; Outstanding Journalist Award, Omar Ibyn Syiid; Community Service Award, Cumberland County Minority AIDS Speaker's Bur; 1st place, Profiles, NC Working Press; 1st place Profiles, 2nd place Fashion Writing, Teen Adv Bd, Women's Ctr Fayetteville, NC Working Press; Alpha Phi Alpha Man of Merit Award; Ashton Lilly Spirit Award, 2006. **Home Addr:** 629 Deep Creek Rd, Fayetteville, NC 28312, **Home Phone:** (910)483-3951. **Business Addr:** Public Relations Director, Fayetteville State University, 1200 Murchison Rd Helen T Chick Bldg, Fayetteville, NC 28301-4298, **Business Phone:** (910)672-1474.

### WOMBLE, REP. LARRY W.

School administrator, government official, educator. **Personal:** Born Jun 6, 1941, Winston-Salem, NC; son of Luchion and Dorothy Gwyn; married Lonnie Hamilton; children: Jamaal. **Educ:** Winston-Salem State Univ, BS, 1963; Univ NC, cert, 1968; Univ NC, Greensboro, MEd, admin, 1977; Appalachian State Univ, EdS, admin, 1979. **Career:** Educator (retired), state representative; Winston-Salem/Forsyth County Sch, Diggs Intermediate, Winston-Salem, NC, dept chmn, instr, 1971-74; Wake Forest Univ, Winston-Salem, NC, supv, dir, 1974-75; Winston-Salem/Forsyth County Sch, Old Town Sch, Winston-Salem, NC, asst prin, 1975-86; Dem Party, dir vols, 1976; Precinct Chair, 1977-1981; City Winston-Salem, alderman, 1981-93; City Winston-Salem, Coun Mem, 1981-93; Mineral Springs, Winston-Salem, WI, asst prin, 1986-89; Cook Mid Sch, asst prin, 1989-90, Kennedy Mid Sch, Winston-Salem, NC, asst prin, 1990-91; Paisley Mid Sch, Winston-Salem, NC, asst prin, 1992-93; NC Gen Assembly, 1995; NC State House, rep, 1994-2012; co-comdr, Black Leadership Roundtable, 1998; NC House Rep, state rep, currently; State Personnel, chair, 2000; NC Legis Black Caucus, vpres, 2002-04. **Orgs:** Bd mem, Alpha Phi Alpha Fraternity, 1963-; trustee, Bethlehem Baptist Church, 1981-; pres, NC Black Elected Munic Off, 1985-90; bd dir, N Carolina League Munic Officials, 1986; Nat Asn Adv Colored People; Nat Black Caucus Local Elected Off, 1987-; Human Develop Policy Comt, 1989-; chmn, Community Develop Housing & Gen Govt Comt, 1989-; trustee, Friends Winston-Salem State Libr, 1998-; Pub Works Comt, 1989-; Oper Christmas Tree; League Women Voters, 1997-; Old Hickory Boy Scouts Am, 1998-; co-comdr, Black Leadership Roundtable, 1998; chair, Triad Legis Caucus, 2002-04. **Home Addr:** 1294 Salem Lake Rd, Winston Salem, NC 27107-1547, **Home Phone:** (336)784-9373. **Business Addr:** State Representative, North Carolina House of Representatives, 514 Legislative Office Bldg, Raleigh, NC 27603-5925, **Business Phone:** (919)733-5777.

### WONDER, STEVIE (STEVLAND HARDAWAY MORRIS)

Musician, singer, songwriter. **Personal:** Born May 13, 1950, Saginaw, MI; son of Lula Mae Morris (deceased); married Kai Millard; children: Kailand & Mandla Kadjay Carl; married Syreeta Wright; children: Aisha, Keita Sawandi, Kwame, Sophia & Mumtaz Ekow. **Educ:** Mich Sch Blind, grad, 1968. **Career:** Performances Eng, Europe, Japan, Okinawa, Nigeria; Black Bull Music, founder & pres, 1970-; Wondirection Recs, founder & pres, 1972-; singer & songwriter & pianist, currently; Recordings: "The Ringer", writer, 2006; "Glory Road", writer, 2006; "Bobby", performer, 2006. Albums: Tribute to Uncle Ray, 1963; With A Song In My Heart, 1963; The Twelve-Year-Old-Genius, 1963; The Jazz Soul Of Little Stevie, 1962; Stevie At The Beach, 1964; Down To Earth, 1966; Uptight, 1966; Someday At Christmas, 1967; I Was Made To Love Her, 1967; Eivets Rednow, 1968; For Once In My Life, 1968; My Cherie Amour, 1969; Signed, Sealed And Delivered, 1970; Live In Person, 1970; Where I'm Coming From, 1971; Talking Book, 1972; Music Of My Mind, 1972; Innervisions, 1973; Fulfillingness' First Finale, 1974; Songs In The Key Of Life, 1976; Stevie Wonder's Journey Through The Secret Life Of Plants, 1979; The Woman In Red, 1984; In Square Circle, 1985; Characters, 1987; Jungle Fever, 1991; Natural Wonder, 1995; Conversation Peace, 1995; Song Review, 1996; At The Close Of a Century, 1999; Bamboozled, 2000; Hotter Than July, 2000; The Definitive Collection, 2002; Conception: An Interpretation of Stevie Wonder's Songs, 2003; A Time To Love, 2005; TV: "Ed Sullivan"; "Mike Douglas"; "Tom Jones"; "Am Bandstand"; "Dinah Shore"; "Tony Bennett: An American Classic", 2006. **Orgs:** Parent ambassador, Breithaupt Voc Tech Ctr. **Honors/Awds:** Twenty five Grammy Awards including Lifetime Achievement Award; Songwriters Hall of Fame, 1983; Academic Award, 1984; Rock and Roll Hall of Fame, 1989; Kennedy Center for the Performing Arts Award, 1999; Polar Music Prize, 1999; Sammy Khan Lifetime Achievement Award, Songwriters Hall of Fame, 2002; George and Ira Gershwin Lifetime Achievement Award, 2002; Grammy Award, with Take 6 for Love's in Need of Love Today, 2003; Billboard Music Award, 2004; Billboard Century Award, 2004; Michigan Walk of Fame, 2004; numerous awards includes Polar Music Prize, 1999, Gershwin Prize, 2009, Messenger of Peace, 2009, Montreal Jazz Festival Spirit Award, 2009. **Special Achievements:** Participant in numerous social projs, including the creation Martin Luther King Day Nat Holiday, AIDS awareness, anti-Apartheid demonstrations, and campaigns against drunk driving. **Business Addr:** Singer, Black Bull Record Co, 4616 Magnolia Blvd, Burbank, CA 91505, **Business Phone:** (323)877-8383.

### WOOD, ANTON VERNON

Executive. **Personal:** Born Jun 7, 1949, Washington, DC. **Educ:** Montgomery Col, AA, 1969; Shepherd Col, BS, 1971. **Career:** DC Off Consumer Prot, community educ spec, serv area mgr; DC Power Inc, pub affairs dir; Wash Ecol Cen, prog dir; Wash Area Mil & Draft Law Panel, couns. **Orgs:** Chmn, Neighborhood c 6a; publ mem, DC Neighborhood Reinvestment Community; chmn, com Employ prac; Metro Wash Planning & Housing Asn; past chmn, treas, DC Statehood Party. **Home Addr:** 522 3rd St NE, Washington, DC 20002.

### WOOD, BOB. See WOOD, ROBERT L.

### WOOD, BRENDA BLACKMON

Television news anchorperson. **Personal:** Born Sep 8, 1955, Washington, DC; daughter of Henry Blackmon Jr and Alma Montgomery Blackmon (deceased); married Keith Anthony; children: Kristen Brooke & Kandis Brittany. **Educ:** Oakwood Col, Huntsville, AL, 1975; Loma Linda Univ, Riverside CA, BA, Speech Commun & Mass Media, 1977. **Career:** WAAY-TV, Huntsville, AL, broadcaster, 1977-78; WSM-TV, Nashville, Tenn, gen assignment reporter, 1978; WAAY-TV, Huntsville, AL, news reporter, 1977-80; WMC-TV, Memphis, TN, news anchor & reporter, 1980-88; WAGA-TV, Atlanta, GA, news anchor & reporter, 1988-96; 11Alive News, anchor, 1997-; adv bd, Kate's Club. **Orgs:** Nat Acad TV Arts & Sci, 1989-; pres, Southern Soc Adventist Communrs, 1990-; Nat Asn Black Journalists, 1986-; Atlanta Asn Black Journalists; Atlanta Press Club; Am Women Film; active leader, Berean Seventh-Day Adventist Church. **Honors/Awds:** Gabriel Award of Merit, "Ramses the Great", The Cath Denomination, 1986; Ace of Diamond Award, Women in Commun, Ga, Chap, 1990; Two Southern Reg Emmys, Best News Anchor; Four-Time Emmy Winner, Prime Time Spec; Emmy, Ser Reporting; Emmy, News Team Coverage; Ga Asn Broadcasters, News Personality of the Yr, 1996; Phoenix Award, NAACP, 1998; Woman of the year, 1998; Atlanta Asn Black Journalist Award, Doc & Spec Reporting; Best Show Award, AABJ; 15 Emmy Awards. **Home Addr:** 8525 Sharpsburg Ct, Jonesboro, GA 30238, **Home Phone:** (770)703-6220. **Business Addr:** Anchor, 11Alive News, 1611 W Peachtree St NE, Atlanta, GA 30309, **Business Phone:** (404)892-1611.

### WOOD, CURTIS A.

Lawyer, executive. **Personal:** Born Jul 31, 1942, Memphis, TN; son of Curtis and Lou Lee; married Claire O. **Educ:** Columbia Col, BA, 1964; Columbia Law Sch, JD, LLB, 1967. **Career:** Bedford Stuyvesant Restoration Corp, pres, 1977-82, gen coun, 1972-77; Wood, Williams, Rafalsky & Harris, managing partner, 1982; Wood, Rafalsky & Wood LLP, founder & managing partner, currently. **Orgs:** NY Bar Asn; Ill Bar Asn; Dist Columbia Bar; Bar State New York, mem. **Home Addr:** 401 Clinton Ave, Brooklyn, NY 11238-1601, **Home Phone:** (718)638-4817. **Business Addr:** Managing Partner, Wood Rafalsky & Wood LLP, 394 - 396 Waverly Ave, Brooklyn, NY 11238, **Business Phone:** (718)636-8000.

### WOOD, DAISY M. See Obituaries Section.

### WOOD, HAROLD LEROY

Judge, lawyer. **Personal:** Born Dec 6, 1919, Bridgeport, CT; married Thelma Anne Cheatham; children: Gregory Lance & Laverne Jill Wertz. **Educ:** Lincoln Univ, AB, 1942; Cornell Univ Law Sch, JD, 1948; NY Univ Law Sch, LLM, 1952. **Career:** Westchester, Bd Supers, supvr, 1957-67, family ct judge, 1969-71; co ct judge, 1971-74; NY Senate Albany, leg asst, 1964; Mt Vernon City Common Coun, alderman, 1968-69; Supreme Ct, NY, justice supreme ct, 1974-95; Kent Hazzard Wilson Conroy Verni & Freeman LLP, coun, atty, currently. **Orgs:** Pres, Nat Asn Advan Colored People; bd dir, Mt Vernon Hosp; bd dir, Urban League White Plains NY. **Home Addr:** 10 David Rd, Somers, NY 10589-3008, **Home Phone:** (914)248-7579. **Business Addr:** Attorney, Kent, Hazzard, Wilson, Conroy, Verni & Freeman LLP, 111 Church St, White Plains, NY 10601-1505, **Business Phone:** (914)948-4700.

### WOOD, JUANITA WALLACE

Administrator, social worker. **Personal:** Born Jun 30, 1928, Waycross, GA. **Educ:** Cent State Univ, BA; Northeastern Ill Univ, Mass Inner City Studies; John Marshall Sch Law; Loyola Grad Sch Soc Work. **Career:** Cook Co Pub Aid, caseworker, 1952-53; Cook Co Juv Ct, probation officer, 1953-58; caseworker C div, 1958-64; Dept Human Resources Div Corrections Youth Serv, comn unit dir corrections soc work, 1969-; coun youths & families involved Correctional Syst; neighborhood worker comn youth welfare. **Orgs:** NASW Law Sor, 1958-61; Sensitivity Training Sessions & Seminars; managerial training with present agency, US Civil Serv Comn; Cook Co Comon Crime Justice. **Honors/Awds:** Recip Award, Develop Group Progs to deal with Youths & Families involved Juv Justice Syst. **Home Addr:** 604 E 33rd Pl, Chicago, IL 60616-4142, **Home Phone:** (312)326-2408.

### WOOD, DR. LAWRENCE ALVIN

Ophthalmologist. **Personal:** Born Jan 5, 1949, New York, NY; son of Lawrence and Lillian Miller; married Yvette Marie Binns; children: Aaron J Clark, Lawrence A, Alan R Clark & Seth P; married Vanessa Dale Smith. **Educ:** City Univ NY, Bronx Community Col, BS, phys ther & therapist, 1970; City Univ NY, Hunter Col, BS, phys ther, 1972; Meharry Med Col, MD, 1979; Naval Regional Med Ctr San Diego, certificate achievement, ophthal residency, 1985. **Career:** Columbia Univ Med Ctr, staff phys therapist, 1972-75; Harlem Hosp, phys therapist, 1972-75; Howard Univ Hosp, intern, 1979-80; Pub Health Serv, gen practr, 1980-82; Millington Naval Hosp, dept head ophthal; Sky2Sea Travel, owner, 2006-; Productions2BE, auth, 2007-; pvt pract, 2007-; Grifols/Biomat, physician, 2008-; Nat Bd Med Examiners, diplomat; Eyecare San Diego, ophthalmologist, 2008-09; Optical Express USA, surgeon, 2008-09, opthalmic surgeon, currently; Fan Feather Inc, co-founder & pres, 2009-. **Orgs:** Acad Ophthal, 1985; AMA, 1986; Dramatists Guild, 1986; fel Am Acad Ophthal; San Diego Co Med Soc; Calif Med Soc. **Honors/Awds:** Flight Surgeon of the Year, 1984. **Special Achievements:** Production of play "No Marks, Just Memories" 1986. **Home Addr:** 852 Via Barquero, San Marcos, CA 92069, **Home Phone:** (760)725-6641. **Business Addr:** Co-founder, President, Fan of the Feather Inc, 310 S Twin Oaks Valley Rd Suite 107-334, San Marcos, CA 92078-4387, **Business Phone:** (323)225-2221.

### WOOD, LEIGH C.

Executive. **Personal:** children: 4. **Educ:** Williams Col, BA, 1979; NY Univ, MBA, acct, 1985. **Career:** Peat Marwick Mitchell & Co; Int CableTel Inc, chief oper officer; Cellular Commun Inc, vpres, opers, 1984, chief exec officer, 1984; AirTouch, chief exec officer, 1993-96; Cellular one, chief exec officer, 1993-96; NTL Inc, sr vpres, 1996, chief operating officer, 1997-2000; Startup Voice over IP telecom bus, investor & chief operating officer, 2004; RealWinWin, investor & chief operating officer, chief financial officer, 2006-14; Atris Inc, chief financial officer; Gen Atlantic Corp, dep chief officer, 1982-84. **Orgs:** Bd mem, Digital Impact Group; bd chair, treas, Wireless Philadelphia. **Business Addr:** Chief Operating Officer, Chief Financial Officer, RealWinWin Inc, 1926 Arch St, Philadelphia, PA 19103, **Business Phone:** (215)732-4480.

### WOOD, LEON. See WOOD, OSIE LEON, III.

### WOOD, MARGARET BEATRICE

Government official. **Personal:** Born Charleston, WV; daughter of John D and Ivory B; married Alvin B; children: Alvin B Jr, Irene B & Llewellyn. **Educ:** Howard Univ, BA, cum laude, 1934; Cent Conn State Univ, Elementary Educ, 1949; Univ Hartford, MEd, 1964; Bank St Col NY, NDEA Inst, 1969. **Career:** Hartford Pub Sch, teacher, 1948-60, reading consult, 1960-66, asst supvr reading & dir IRIT, 1966-75, coord reading & communiction arts, 1975-80; Hartford Sem St Croix & St Thomas, adj prof, 1978; Town Bloomfield, Bloomfield, CT, counman, 1969-75, dep mayor, 1974-75, town treas, 1987-90. **Orgs:** Dir, Summer Sch, 1974; Develop Lang Arts Generalist, 1972; pres, Community Assoc Reading Res, 1976. **Honors/Awds:** Sojourner Truth Award, Nat Coun Negro Women, 1972; Distinguished Service Award, Hartford Chapter Delta Sigma Theta, 1981. **Home Addr:** 131 Wadhams Rd, Bloomfield, CT 06002, **Home Phone:** (203)242-5190.

### WOOD, DR. MICHAEL HOWARD (MIKE WOOD)

Surgeon, physician. **Personal:** Born Mar 28, 1942, Dayton, OH; married Florentina Serquina; children: Mark, Anthony & Michael Jr. **Educ:** Ind Inst Tech, BS, 1968; Meharry Med Col, MD, 1972. **Career:** Harper Hosp, resident, 1972-73; Westland Med Ctr, chief dept surg, 1984; Wayne State Univ Sch Med, resident, 1973-77, Dept Surg, instr, 1977-78, clin asst prof, 1978-88, clin assoc prof, 1988-; Detroit Riverview Hosp, chief, dept surg; Cain-Wood Surg Assocs, physician; Harper Univ Hosp, Bariatric Surg Servs, dir, currently; Centers Obesity Related Illness, med dir & co-founder, currently; pvt pract, currently; Am Bariatric Med inst, surg, currently. **Orgs:** Chmn bd, Detroit Med

Group, 1985-86; Am Soc Bariatric Surg; fel Am Col Surgeons. **Honors/Awds:** Biomed Res Grant, 1979-80; Res Award Prog, 1980-81, Biomed Research Support Grant, 1981-82 Wayne State Univ; sponsor Frederick Coller Award, Am Col Surgeons, MI Chap, 1980; Theodore McGraw Clinical Faculty Teaching Award, Wayne State Univ Dept Surg, 1990; Obesity Surg, Best Author's Award, for "Marginal Ulcer After Gastric Bypass", 1998; Best Doctor, HOUR Magazine. **Special Achievements:** Co-author: "Marginal Ulcer After Gastric Bypass: A Prospective Three-Year Study of 173 Patients". **Home Addr:** 4555 Cherokee, Bloomfield Hills, MI 48301-1424, **Home Phone:** (810)737-0749. **Business Addr:** Bariatric Surgeon, Medical Director, American Bariatric Medicine Institute, 1385 E 12 Mile Rd Suite 200, Madison Heights, MI 48071, **Business Phone:** (248)284-1760.

### WOOD, OSIE LEON, III (LEON WOOD)
Basketball player, government official. **Personal:** Born Mar 25, 1962, Columbia, SC; children: Ladera Ranch. **Educ:** Univ Ariz, attended 1980; Calif State Univ, Fullerton, CA, attended 1984. **Career:** Basketball player (retired), refree; Philadelphia 76ers, 1984-86; Wash Bullets, 1986; NJ Nets, 1986-87, 1989-90; San Antonio Spurs, 1987-88; Atlanta Hawks, 1988; CAI Zaragoza, 1988-89; Santa Barbara Islanders, 1989-90; Sacramento Kings, 1990-91; Rapid City Thrillers, 1990-92; Pallacanestro Varese, 1991; Gieben 46ers, 1991; CRO Lyon, 1992-93; Fargo-Moorhead Fever, 1993-94; Onyx Caserta, 1994; Nat Basketball Asn, referee, currently. **Orgs:** Nat Basketball Asn. **Business Addr:** Referee, National Basketball Association, Olympic Tower 645 5th Ave 15th Fl, New York, NY 10022-5986, **Business Phone:** (212)407-8000.

### WOOD, ROBERT L. (BOB WOOD)
Executive. **Educ:** Univ Mich, BA, hist. **Career:** Dow Chem Co, staff, 1977-95, vp engrg plastics, 1995-97, vp polyurethanes, 1997-2000, grp pres thermosets & dow automotive, 2000-04; Jarden Corp, bd dir, 2000-; Crompton Corp, pres & chief exec officer, 2004-05; Praxair, bd dir, 2004-; Chemtura Corp, chmn, pres, chief exec officer, 2005-08; Jarden Corp, dir, chmn Nominating & Policies Comt & Mem Audit Comt, currently. **Orgs:** Past chmn, Big Bros/Big Sisters Am; treas, bd mem, exec comt, bd dir, USA Gymnastics; vice chmn, Am Ch Coun. **Business Addr:** Chairman & President, Jarden Corporation, 555 Theodore Fremd Ave, Rye, NY 10580, **Business Phone:** (914)967-9400.

### WOOD, TOMMIE
Manager, basketball executive. **Career:** NBA, referee, currently. **Orgs:** Nat Basketball Referees Asn; Nat Asn Advan Colored People. **Business Addr:** Referee, National Basketball Association, 645 5th Ave 15th Fl, New York, NY 10022-5986, **Business Phone:** (212)407-8000.

### WOOD, VIVIAN FRANCES
Librarian. **Personal:** Born Jan 28, 1945, Plainfield, NJ; daughter of L Cassell Sr and Sarah Frances. **Educ:** Howard Univ, BA, 1967; Cath Univ, MA, 1969; Rutgers Univ, MLS, 1974. **Career:** DC Pub Schs, teacher, 1969-71; Prince Georges County, MD, pub libr, asst librn, 1971-73; Rutgers Univ, ref librn, asst prof, 1974-81; Hofstra Univ, colction develop librn, asst prof libr servs & asst prof emer, currently. **Orgs:** Nassau County Econ Opportunity Comn-92; NJ Libr Asn, Acad Libr Div, vpres, 1979-80; secy, exec bd mem, Asn Black Women in Higher Educ, Nassau Suffolk Chap, 1994-97; vpres, Nassau City Libr Asn, Acad & Spec Libr Div, 1993; Nassau County Libr Asn, Acad & Spec Libr Div, pres, 1994. **Honors/Awds:** United Nations Fourth World Conf on Women NGO Forum in Beijing, China, deleg, 1995; deleg, Res Librns Deleg to SAfrica, 1997. **Special Achievements:** Conf Paper, "Bibliographic Overview Harlem Renaissance," Nat Endowment for Humanities & Hofstra Univ; "Iceland" Read More About It, vol 3 An Encyclopedia Information Sources on Hist Figures & Events, Pierian Press, 1989; Conf Paper "Colction Develop for Africana Studies," Assoc Col & Res Libraries, 1993; Panelist: Race, Gender & Academe, United Nations Fourth World Conf on Women NGO Forum, Beijing, China, 1995. **Home Addr:** 726 Ctr Dr, Baldwin, NY 11510-1102, **Home Phone:** (516)486-4229. **Business Addr:** Assistant Professor Emerita of Library Services, Hofstra University Axinn Library, Axinn Libr 902C, Hempstead, NY 11550, **Business Phone:** (516)463-6431.

### WOOD, HON. WILLIAM S. See Obituaries Section.

### WOOD, WILLIAM VERNELL, SR. (WILLIE WOOD)
Executive, football player. **Personal:** Born Dec 23, 1936, Washington, DC; son of John and Amanda; married Sheila Peres; children: LaJuane, Andre & William Jr. **Educ:** Coalinga Jr Col, attended 1956; Univ Southern Calif, BS, 1960. **Career:** Football player (retired), Coach, President; Green Bay Packers, Nat Football League, free safety, 1960-71; Philadelphia Bell WFL, head coach, 1973-77; Toronto Argonauts Football Team, asst coach, 1979-80, head coach, 1980-82; Woodrow Wilson High Sch, coach; Arena Football League, Ind Firebirds, coach; Willie Wood Mech Syst Inc, pres, 1983-; Arena Football League, Cleveland Gladiators, wide receiver/defensive backs coach, currently. **Orgs:** Bd dir, Police Boys & Girls Club, 1984-. **Special Achievements:** First African American head coach in the modern era of professional football. **Business Addr:** Owner, President, Willie Wood Mechanical Systems, 7941 16th St NW, Washington, DC 20012, **Business Phone:** (202)746-3315.

### WOODALL, DR. JOHN WESLEY
Physician. **Personal:** Born May 24, 1941, Cedartown, GA; son of Japheus P and Estherlena Harris; married Janet Carol Nunn; children: John Wesley Jr, Japheus Clay & Janita Carol. **Educ:** Ball State Univ, BS, med tech, 1964; Ind Univ Sch Med, MD, 1969. **Career:** William N Wishard Memorial Hosp, St Johns Hosp, intern med tech, 1964-65, chief Obstet-Gynec, 1974, chief family pract, 1977; William N Wishard Memorial Hosp, rotating intern, 1969-70; Bridges-Campbell-Woodall Med Corp, physician, owner; pvt pract, currently; St Vincent Heart Ctr Ind, family pract; St Johns Health Syst, family pract; Community Hosp Anderson, physician; St. Vincent Anderson Regional Hosp, physician. **Orgs:** Diplomat, Am Acad Family Pract; fel Am Acad Family Pract, Aesculapian Med Soc, Am Med Dir Asn; Am Geriatric Soc; Nat Med Asn; Urban League; Friendship Baptist Church; life mem, Nat Asn Advan Colored People; Am Bd Family Med. **Special Achievements:** First African American to establish a health clinic in Anderson; First African American to become the president of staff in Anderson community hospital. **Home Addr:** 299 E County Rd 306N, Anderson, IN 46012. **Business Addr:** Family Practitioner, Owner, Bridges Campbell Woodhall Medical Corp, 1302 S Madison Ave, Anderson, IN 46016, **Business Phone:** (765)644-3673.

### WOODARD, ALFRE
Actor. **Personal:** Born Nov 8, 1952, Tulsa, OK; daughter of Marion H and Constance; married Roderick Spencer; children: Duncan & Mavis. **Educ:** Boston Univ, BFA. **Career:** Films: Extremities, 1986; Scrooged, 1988; Grand Canyon, 1991; Passion Fish, 1992; The Gun in Betty Lou's Handbag, 1992; Heart & Souls, 1993; Crooklyn, 1994; How to Make an American Quilt, 1995; The Piano Lesson, 1995; Star Trek: First Contact, 1996; Primal Fear, 1996; Miss Firecracker, 1989; Miss Evers' Boys, 1997; Down in the Delta, co producer, 1998; Mumford, 1999; Love & Basketball, 2000; K-PAX, 2001; The Wild Thorn berrys Movie, 2002; The Singing Detective, 2003; The Core, 2003; Radio, 2003; A Wrinkle In Time, 2003; The Forgotten, 2004; Beauty Shop, 2005-06; Something New, 2006; Take the Lead, 2006; Reach for Me, 2008; AmericanEast, 2008; 12 Years a Slave, 2013; Annabelle, 2014; Mary Lou Williams: The Lady Who Swings the Band, 2015; Mississippi Grind, 2015; Captain America: Civil War, 2016; So B. It, 2016; Burning Sands. 2016; Knucklehead, 2016; Haunted, 2017-. TV Series: "Tucker's Witch", 1982; "Hill Street Blues", 1983; "Sara", 1985; "St. Elsewhere", 1985-87; "L.A. Law", 1986; "Frasier", 1994; "The Practice", 2003; "Desperate Housewives", 2005; "Pictures of Hollis Woods", 2007; "My Own Worst Enemy", 2008; "Maggie Hill", 2009; "Three Rivers", 2009; "Memphis Beat", 2010; "Black Panther", 2010; "True Blood", 2010-12; "Grey's Anatomy", 2011; "Steel Magnolias", 2012; "Private Practice", 2012; "Copper", 2013; "The Last Ship", 2014. **Orgs:** Founder & bd mem artists, New S Africa. **Honors/Awds:** Miss KAY Chi Chap, Boston Univ, 1974; Emmy Award, 1984, 1987, 1997, 2003; Golden Apple Award, Best new comer, 1984; Image Award, Nat Asn Advan Colored People, 1984, 1989-90, 1992, 1996, 1998, 2001, 2004, 2013; Cable ACE Awards, 1989, 1997; Joe A. Callaway Award, 1989; Independent Spirit Awards, 1993; Screen Actors Guild, 1996, 1998, 2006; Women in Film Crystal Award, 1995; Emmy Award, Outstanding Lead Actress in a Miniseries or A Special, Miss Evers' Boys, 1997; Golden Globe, 1998; Golden Satellite Award, Satellite Awards, 1998; Muse Award,New York Women Film & Tv, 2002; Character and Morality Awards, 2005; Black Movie Awards, 2007; Gracie Allen Awards, 2011; Black Reel Award, Best Supporting Actress, 2013; Oklahoma Hall of Fame, 2014. **Special Achievements:** Oscar Award, nominee. **Business Addr:** Actress, Block-Korenbrat, 8271 Melrose Ave, Los Angeles, CA 90046, **Business Phone:** (323)655-0593.

### WOODARD, DR. CHARLES JAMES
School administrator. **Personal:** Born Jun 9, 1945, Laurel, MS; children: Andrea, Craig, Ashley, Adeena & Ataya. **Educ:** PA, BS, 1968; Wayne State Univ, MA, guid & coun higher educ, 1972; Univ Mich, PhD, guid & coun higher educ, 1975. **Career:** Univ Mich Flint, asst, asst dean spec proj, 1973-75; Allegheny Col, assoc dean stud, 1975-82; Coppin State Col, dean stud serv, 1982-85; Ind Univ Northwest, vice chancellor stud Serv, assoc prof educ, 1985-87; Savannah State Col, Stud Affairs, vpres dean, 1987-90; Cheyney Univ, Stud Affairs, vpres, app loaned exec, 1992; Kutztown Univ Penn, Stud Affairs, vpres & dean, 1990-; Family Educ Rights & Privacy Act, emer, coordr, currently; Chick Woodard Enterprises, pres, chief exec officer, 2011-. **Orgs:** Nat Asn Financial Aids Minority Stud, 1972-75; Am Personnel & Guid Asn, 1975-; Non-White Concerns Guid, 1975-; Unity Inst Human Develop, 1976-80; Boy Scouts Am, 1977-82; race rels consult, Penn State Educ Asn, 1978-81; Am Higher Educ Asn, 1985-; Salvation Army, 1986. **Home Addr:** 465 W Main St, Kutztown, PA 19530-1607. **Business Addr:** Vice President, FERPA Coordinator, Kutztown University, 15200 Kutztown Rd 319 Stratton Admin Bldg, Kutztown, PA 19530, **Business Phone:** (610)683-4000.

### WOODARD, FREDRICK
School administrator, poet, educator. **Personal:** Born Jan 29, 1939, Kingfisher, OK; son of Ralph and Rosetta Reed Bishop; married Barbara; children: Jon & Jarilyn. **Educ:** Iowa Wesleyan Col, Mt Pleasant, BA, 1961; Univ Iowa, Iowa City, MA, 1972, PhD, 1976. **Career:** W High Sch, Davenport, IA, teacher, 1961-66; Black Hawk Community Col, Moline, IL, instr, 1967-69; Cornell Col, Mt Vernon, IA, instr, 1972-76; Univ Iowa, Iowa City, from instr to assoc prof, 1973-80, prof, actg assoc dean fac, Off Acad Affairs, 1981-83, assoc dean fac, Off vpres, acad affairs, 1983-90, assoc vpres, acad affairs, 1990-, Mus Art, interim dir, 1990-92, emer fac; Univ Calif, San Diego, vis assoc prof, 1980; Iowa Rev, co-ed, assoc vpres. **Orgs:** Chair session, Midwest Mod Lang Asn, 1970, 1972, 1973, 1977-79, 1981-83; chair session, Coun Col Compos, 1975, 1977, 1981, 1983, 1985; Am Libr Asn, 1980-; Mod Lang Asn, 1980-; chair session, Nat Coun Teachers Eng, 1985; comt mem, Big 10 Acad Personnel Officers, 1985; comt mem, Prof & Orgn Develop Network Higher Educ, 1985-. **Special Achievements:** Book: "Reasons to Dream; Editor:True Poems", 1978; "Love Songs and New Spirituals", 1980; "Human Rights/Human Wrongs: Art and Social Change", 1986. **Home Addr:** 53 Cottage St, Dorchester, MA 52240, **Home Phone:** (617)427-2144. **Business Addr:** Associate Vice President, Professor of English, University of Iowa, 436 Epb, Iowa City, IA 52240, **Business Phone:** (319)335-0317.

### WOODARD, KENNETH EMIL
Football player. **Personal:** Born Jan 22, 1960, Detroit, MI. **Educ:** Tuskegee Univ. **Career:** Football player (retired); Denver Broncos, linebacker, 1982-86, right outside linebacker, 1985; Pittsburgh Steelers, 1987; San Diego Chargers, linebacker, 1988-89. **Special Achievements:** Film: 1986 AFC Championship Game, 1987.

### WOODARD, LOIS MARIE
Systems analyst. **Personal:** Born Porter, TX; married Laverne V; children: Alesia, Erica & Cheryl. **Educ:** Los Angeles Trade Tech Col, AA, 1970; Cal Poly State Univ, San Luis Obispo, BS, 1975. **Career:** Cal Poly San Luis Obispo CA, data processor, 1972-76; Burroughs Corp, programmer, 1976-77; Long Beach Col Bus, instr, 1977-80; Nat Auto & Casualty Ins, syst analyst, 1980-. **Orgs:** Bus woman Esquire Cleaners, 1979-87; pres, Stewardess Bd 2 1st AME Ch, 1980-82; Nat auto co coord Youth Motivation Task Force, 1984-87; conductress, Order Eastern Stars, 1985-86; corresp secy, Zeta Phi Beta Sor, 1986; Nat Asn Advan Colored People, 1986-87. **Honors/Awds:** Appreciation Award, 1st AME Church, Pasedena, CA, 1981. **Home Addr:** 804 W Figueroa Dr, Altadena, CA 91001-5252, **Home Phone:** (626)798-9807. **Business Addr:** System Analyst, National Auto & Casualty Ins, 150 So Los Robles Suite 900, Pasadena, CA 91101, **Business Phone:** (818)577-0600.

### WOODARD, LYNETTE
Basketball player, basketball coach, financial manager. **Personal:** Born Aug 12, 1959, Wichita, KS. **Educ:** Univ Kans, BA, speech commun & human rels, 1981. **Career:** Basketball player, basketball coach (retired), financial consult; Italy, 1987; Japan, 1990-93; Cleveland Rockers, guard, 1997; Detroit Shock, 1998; New York, stockbroker; Univ Kans, asst coach, 1999; Marian Wash, interim head coach, 2004; Kans City, athletics dir, 1992-94; PFS Investments Incorporation, financial rep, 2004; Magna Securities Corp, vpres mkt; A.G. Edwards & Sons Inc, financial consult, currently. **Business Addr:** Financial Consultant, A G Edwards & Sons Inc, 1 N Jefferson Ave, St. Louis, MO 63103, **Business Phone:** (314)955-3000.

### WOODARD, RHONDA MARIE
Insurance executive. **Personal:** Born Jul 14, 1949, Kansas City, MO; daughter of Allen and Zelma; children: Nicole & Jeremy. **Educ:** George Williams Col, BS, 1971. **Career:** Allstate Ins Co, underwriting opers mgr, 1984, reg underwriting mgr, 1984-88, field support dir, 1988-90, personal lines dir, 1990-92, personal lines mkt dir, 1992-93, asst vpres, 1993-95, vpres, underwriting vp, 1995-98, vpres prod, 1999-2002, vpres policy, compliance & homeowners, 2002-, vpres, retired, 2009-. **Orgs:** Nat Black Womens Health Proj, 1988-; bd dir & bd trustee, Neighborhood Housing Servs Am, 1993-; Leadership Ill, 1997-. **Honors/Awds:** Chicago YMCA, Black & Hispanic Achievers; Dollars & Sense, Best & Brightest; YMCA of NY, Acad Women Achievers. **Business Addr:** Product Vice President, Product Operations, Allstate Insurance Co, 2775 Sanders Rd Suite E1N, Northbrook, IL 60062, **Business Phone:** (847)402-5000.

### WOODARD, DR. SAMUEL L.
Educator. **Personal:** Born May 26, 1930, Fairmont, WV; married Linda Waples; children: Mary Ellen, Charlene, Gail & Dana. **Educ:** Mansfield State Univ, BS, sec educ, 1953; Canisius Col, MS, 1959; Lincoln Univ, Buffalo, EdD. **Career:** Buffalo & LA, teacher, 1954-66; Genesee-Humboldt Jr High Buffalo, vice prin, 1966-67; Temple Univ, asst prof educ, 1967-68; Philadelphia Sch Dist, dir prog implementation, 1968-70; Ill State Univ, assoc prof educ admin, 1970-73; Howard Univ, prof educ admin, prof emer, currently. **Orgs:** Intl Asn Appl Soc Sci; Int Transactional Anal Asn; Phi Delta Kappa; Nat All Black Sch Educ; life mem, Nat Asn Advan Colored People; life mem, Alpha Phi Alpha; founder, Naomi Woodard-Smoot Scholar. **Honors/Awds:** The Alumni Citation Award, Mansfield Univ Pa, 1997; Distinguished Pennsylvania Educator, Pa Col Alumni Asn; Role Model for American Youth, Pa Col Alumni Asn. **Special Achievements:** First African American student to receive the Phoenician Trophy, 1948; First African American at the State University of New York, Buffalo to receive a doctorate in educational administration from SUNY Buffalo, 1966; First Black to teach on Educ TV in NY State, Buffalo, WNED-TV, 1961-62. **Home Addr:** 300 Beaumont Rd, Silver Spring, MD 20904, **Home Phone:** (804)693-3748. **Business Addr:** Professor Emeritus, Howard University, 2400 Sixth St NW, Washington, DC 20059, **Business Phone:** (202)806-6100.

### WOODBECK, FRANK RAYMOND
Media executive, executive director. **Personal:** Born Feb 2, 1947, Buffalo, NY; son of George and Avil; married Virginia Ann Carter; children: Harrison, Terry & Frank Raymond II. **Educ:** State Univ NY Buffalo, BS, bus mgt, 1973; Harvard Univ, cert achievement, broadcast mgt, 1982. **Career:** Capital Cities Comm WKBW Radio, gen sales mgr, 1977-80, pres & gen mgr, 1980-84; Capital Cities Cable Inc, vpres advert, 1985-86; Post-Newsweek Cable Inc, advert vpres, 1986-91; ABC Radio Networks, Desert Sky Media, broadcast exec, 1991-2006, vpres affil rel, 1991-2000, ABC Radio Networks/Walt Disney, vpres affil rel, 1992-2000; One Media Pl, sr vpres, radio, 2000-01; SVP-Radio, 2000-01; Silver State Angel Investments LLC, owner, 2004-09; Lakeshore Media LLC, regional gen mgr, 2006-08; Nev Comn Econ Develop, comnr, 2007-09, Las Vegas Opers & Workforce Initiatives, dir, 2009-11; Adaven Consult LLC, pres, 2008-09; Nev Dept Employ Training & Rehab, strategic consult, 2009-11; Nev Comn Econ Develop, Las Vegas Opers & Workforce Initiatives, dir, 2009-; State Nev Dept Employ, Training & Rehab, Nev Dept Employ Training & Rehab, dir, 2011-14; Nev Syst Higher Educ, Nev Col Collab, exec dir, 2014-. **Orgs:** Omega Psi Phi Frat, 1976-; ticket chmn, Dunlop Pro Am Awards Dinner, 1979-84; vice chmn, chmn, Humboldt Br YMCA, 1979-84; Sigma Pi Phi Frat, 1981-; treas, ABC Radio Dir Affil Bd, 1983-84; pres, Buffalo Radio Asn, 1983-84; founding chair, Alpha Epsilon Boule Educ Found; bd dir, Three Sq Food Bank; bd dir, Las Vegas Global Econ Alliance; bd dir, Nev Ctr Excellence. **Home Addr:** 500 E 77 St Apt 239, New York, NY 10162. **Business Addr:** Executive Director, Nevada System of Higher Education, 4300 S Md Pkwy, Las Vegas, NV 89119, **Business Phone:** (702)889-8426.

### WOODBURY, DR. DAVID HENRY, JR.
Scientist. **Personal:** Born Mar 29, 1930, Camden, SC; son of David and Arline; married Margaret Jane Claytor; children: Arline E, Brenda L, Laura R, Kathryn L, Larry D & David H. **Educ:** Johnson C Smith Univ, BS, 1951; Va State Col, MS, 1952; Univ Mich, Md, 1961. **Career:** Atomic Energy Comn, biologist, 1955-57; Westland Med Ctr, dir, nuclear med, 1968-90; Univ Mich, asst prof, internal med, 1968-90; USPHS, dir, nuclear med, 1967-68. **Orgs:** Consult, FDA Radiopharmaceuticals Advisor, 1978-82, med officer, 1990-95, NRC Adv Comm, 1979-; vpres, Johnson C Smith Alumni Asn, 1978; bd regents, Am Col Nuclear Physicians, 1980-87; chief med staff, Wayne County Hosp, 1984-85; pres, club Johnson C Smith Univ, 1984; pres,

Am Col Nuclear Physicians, 1987. **Honors/Awds:** Robert C Wood Scholar, Johnson C Smith Univ, 1950; Fel, Am Col Nuclear Physicians, 1982. **Home Addr:** 1715 Arbordale Dr, Ann Arbor, MI 48103, **Home Phone:** (734)663-1222.

## WOODBURY, DR. MARGARET CLAYTOR

Executive, physician. **Personal:** Born Oct 30, 1937, Roanoke, VA; daughter of John Bunyan Claytor Sr (deceased) and Roberta Morris Woodfin Claytor (deceased); married David Henry Woodbury Jr; children: David Henry III; married Lawrence DeWitt Young; children: Laura Ruth & Lawrence DeWitt Jr. **Educ:** Mt Holyoke Col, AB, 1958; Meharry Med Col, MD, 1962. **Career:** Physician, educator (retired); US Pub Health Serv Hosp, Staten Island, NY, asst chief med/endo, 1967-68; US Pub Health Serv Hosp, Detroit, Mich chief outpatient clin, 1968-69; US Pub Health Serv Outpatient Clin, Detroit, Mich med officer in charge, 1969-71; Univ Mich Med Sch, instr med endo, 1969-80, asst prof internal med, 1980-2002, HCOP proj dir, 1984-90, asst dean student & minority affairs, 1983-90, asst prof emer, 2002. **Orgs:** Co-chair, Ann Arbor Dem Party, 1972-73; admis comn, Univ Mich Med Sch, 1978-83; chmn, ACAAP, Univ Mich Med Sch, 1983-91; chair steering comdr, MLKCHC Ser, 1984-85; bd alumnae, nominating comn, 1981-85, bd trustee, 1985-97, former pres, Mt Holyoke Col; pres, Alumnae Asn Mt Holyoke Col, 1994-97; parent rep, Eng Indust Support Prog, 1978-82; founding mem, Ann Arbor Alliance Achievement, 1981-89. **Honors/Awds:** Dean's List, Albany & Meharry Med Col, 1959-62; First Biochemistry Award, Albany Med Col, 1959; Pediat Prize, Meharry Med Col, 1961; Alpha Omega Alpha Hon Med Soc, Meharry Med Col, 1962; Outstanding Young Woman Am, 1967; Alumnae Asn Medal, 1982; Alumnae Medal Hon, Mt Holyoke Col, 1983; Outstanding Woman for the 21st Century, 1986; Consortium Doctors Inc, 1993. **Special Achievements:** Publisher: has published numerous articles in field, "Quantitative Determination Cysteine in Salivary Amylase," Mt Holyoke Col, 1958; "Hypopituitarism in Current Therapy," WB Saunders Co, 1967; "Cushing's Syndrome in Infancy, A Case Complicated by Monilial Endocarditis," Am JDis Child, 1971; "Three Generations Familial Turner Syndrome," Annals Int Med 1978; "Virilizing Syndrome Associated With Adrenocortical Adenoma Secreting Predominantly Testosterone," Am J Med 1979; "Hormones in Your Life From Childbearing (Or Not) to Menopause," Mt Holyoke Alumnae Quarterly, 1980; "Scintigraphic Localization Ovarian Dysfunction," J Nuc Med, 1988; Co-author: Virginia Kaleidoscope: The Claytor Family of Roanoke & Some of its Kinships, from First Families of Virginia & their former Slaves, 1995. **Home Addr:** 1715 Arbordale Dr, Ann Arbor, MI 48105, **Home Phone:** (734)663-1222.

## WOODEN, SHAWN ANTHONY

Football player, financial manager, executive. **Personal:** Born Oct 23, 1973, Philadelphia, PA; married Marcia Charise Reeves. **Educ:** Notre Dame Univ, BS, comput sci, 1995. **Career:** Football player (retired), exec; Anjon Systs, Comput Systs Consult, 1993-96; Miami Dolphins, safety & free safety & strong safety, 1996-99, linebacker & defensive back, 2001-04; Chicago Bears, safety, 2000; MetLife, financial planner, 2005-08; AXA Advisors, financial advisor, 2008-09; Garrido & Wooden Financial Strategies, pres, 2008-09; Wooden Wealth Mgt, financial advisor & financial serv rep, 2009-12, pres & financial advisor, 2013-Currently; Prin Financial Group, prin securities regist rep & financial advisor & financial Rep, 2012-Currently; Veriteq Acquisition Corp, bd mem; Digital Angel Corp, bd dir, currently. **Orgs:** Habitat Humanity; Big Bros & Big Sisters; Miami Dolphins Found; Broward Boys & Girls Club; Cystic Fibrosis Found; Prudential No Passing Zone; FAD orgn; Bd Dir, Maxwell Football Club; Past Bd Mem, Vita Nova Inc; Past Ambassador Bd Mem, Nova Southeastern Univ. **Honors/Awds:** Dolphins Community Service Award, 1997; Walter Payton NFL Man Of The Year Award, 2003. **Business Addr:** President, Financial Advisor, Wood Wealth Management, 3663 N Laughlin Rd Suite 203, Santa Rosa, CA 95403, **Business Phone:** (707)578-4535.

## WOODEN, TERRY TYLON

Football player, scout. **Personal:** Born Jan 14, 1967, Hartford, CT; married Cindy; children: Tea, Maya & Brock. **Educ:** Syracuse Univ, sociol. **Career:** Football player (retired), scout; Seattle Seahawks, left linebacker, 1990-96; Kans City Chiefs, left inner linebacker, 1997; Oakland Raiders, left linebacker, 1998; Buffalo Bills, scout, 2003-06; New Orleans Saints, scout, 2007-. **Honors/Awds:** All-Rookie Team, Football Digest, 1990; Ed Block Courage Award, 1992; Steve Largent Award, 1995. **Home Addr:** 314 239th Ct SE, Sammamish, WA 98074-3687, **Home Phone:** (425)313-4700. **Business Addr:** Scout, New Orleans Saints, 5800 Airline Dr, Metairie, NY 70003, **Business Phone:** (504)733-0255.

## WOODFOLK, JOSEPH O.

Educator, association executive. **Personal:** Born Mar 4, 1933, St. Thomas. **Educ:** Morgan State Col, AB; NM Highlands Univ, ME, 1955; Morgan State Col, MA; Indian Cult Univ, Mysore, India, cert grad studies, 1973. **Career:** Baltimore Co Pub Schs, teacher, 1955-, Bd Educ, chmn social studies dept, 1969-; State Univ NJ, fac; Johns Hopkins Univ; Woodlawn Sr High Sch, fac, currently. **Orgs:** Develop, curric K-12 soc stud prog Baltimore county, 1969-; dir, Fulbright Alumni India summer stud prog; Teacher Asn, Baltimore County; Md State Teacher Asn; Nat Educ Asn; Phi Alpha Theta; Fulbright fel 1973; Gamma Theta Upsilon; Am Hist Soc; Md Hist Soc; Org Am Historians; Soc Hist Educ; Nat Asn Advan Colored People; Friends Kenya; Asn Foreign Stud Alumni Asn; NM Highlands Univ; Phi Delta Kappa, John Hopkins Univ; eastern reg dir, publ Phi Beta Sigma Frat; Am Heart Asn Minority Comm Affairs; Phi Beta Sigma. **Honors/Awds:** Special Recognition Award, Eta Omega chap Phi Alpha Theta. **Home Addr:** 4008 Deepwood Rd, Baltimore, MD 21218-1403, **Home Phone:** (443)835-4559. **Business Addr:** Faculty, Woodlawn Sr High School, 1801 Woodlawn Dr, Baltimore, MD 21207-4075, **Business Phone:** (410)887-1309.

## WOODFORD, JOHN NILES

Journalist, editor. **Personal:** Born Sep 24, 1941, Chicago, IL; son of Hackley E and Mary Steele; married Elizabeth Subeva Duffy; children: Duffy, Maize & Will. **Educ:** Harvard Univ, BA, eng lit, 1964, MA, 1968. **Career:** Ebony Mag, asst ed, ed-in-chief, 1967-68; Jet Mag; Ann Arbor Observer; Muhammad Speaks Newspaper, ed-in-chief, 1968-72; Chicago Sun Times, copy ed, 1972-74; New York Times, copy ed nat desk, 1974-77; Ford Motor Co, Ford Times, sr ed, 1977-80; Univ Mich, exec ed, 1981-04, Mich Today, exec ed; Med Campus news & publ off, exec ed, 1981; U-M alumni publ Mich Today, exec ed, 1985-2004; freelance writer & ed, currently. **Orgs:** Fac, Univ Mich Asn Black Professionals; essayist & reviewer, Black Scholar J. **Home Addr:** 1922 Lorraine Pl, Ann Arbor, MI 48104.

## WOODHOUSE, ENOCH O'DELL, II

Lawyer. **Personal:** Born Jan 14, 1927, Boston, MA. **Educ:** Yale Univ, attended 1952; Univ Paris, France, attended 1951; Yale Law Sch; Boston Univ Law Sch, LLB, 1955; Acad Int Law Peace Palace, Hague, Neth, attebded 1960. **Career:** Pvt pract, atty; US State Dept, diplomatic courier; City Boston, asst corp coun; Int Fr & Ger, Trial couns corp law. **Orgs:** Int Bar Asn; Boston Bar Asn; exec comt, Mass Trial Lawyers Asn; Yale Club Boston; Res Officers Asn; Am Trial Lawyers Asn bd Govs Yale, 1975; app Liaison Officer AF Acad; Judge Adv Gen; coun mem, dir, Uso Coun New Eng, Inc, currently. **Home Addr:** 650 Huntington Ave Apt 22L, Boston, MA 02115-5910, **Home Phone:** (617)734-7052. **Business Addr:** Council Member, Director, Uso Council Of New England Inc, 427 Com St, Boston, MA 02109, **Business Phone:** (617)223-3171.

## WOODHOUSE, DR. JOHNNY BOYD

Clergy. **Personal:** Born Nov 9, 1945, Elizabeth City, NC; son of Charles and Helen; married Darlyn Blakeney; children: Yolanda, Johnny Jr, Fletcher & Touray. **Educ:** Elizabeth City State, BS, 1967; Shaw Divinity, MD, 1973; Va Sem, DD, 1983. **Career:** PW Moore High Sch, teacher, 1970; NC, Dept Corrections, instr, 1977; Johnston Community Col, instr, 1978, Human Resources Develop, dir; Women Correctional Ctr, Raleigh, NC, instr; Red Oak Grove Baptist Church, sr minister, 1980. **Orgs:** Nat Asn Advan Colored People; MichZ-PAH Temple Suite 66, Goldsboro, NC; Master Mason Prince Hall; Nat Bapt Conv Inc; treas, Smithfield Ministerial Conf; chmn bd, NC Child & Day Care Ctr; vpres, Smithfield Minister's Conf, 1975; vice moderator, Tar River Missionary Baptist Asn, 1980; moderator, Tar River Asn, 1988. **Honors/Awds:** NAACP Award, 1970; Pastor of the Year, 1972; Martin Luther King Jr Award, 1991. **Home Addr:** PO Box 2103, Smithfield, NC 27577-2103. **Business Addr:** Director, Human Resource Development, Johnston Community College, 245 College Rd, Smithfield, NC 27577, **Business Phone:** (919)934-3051.

## WOODHOUSE, ROSSALIND YVONNE

Entrepreneur, manager, chief executive officer. **Personal:** Born Jun 7, 1940, Detroit, MI; daughter of Allen Venable and Pereditha Venable; married Donald; children: Joycelyn & Justin. **Educ:** Univ Wash, BA sociol, 1963; Univ Wash, MSW 1970, PhD, educ policy, governance, & admin, 1983. **Career:** Entrepreneur, manager, chief executive officer (retired); New Careers Proj Seattle, prog cord guide consult, 1968; Seattle Housing Auth, comm org specialist, 1969-70; Central Area Motiv Prog Seattle, exec dir, 1971-73; Edmonds Community Col Lynnwood, instr cord, 1973-77; Wash State Dept Licensing Olympia, dir, 1977-81; Rainier Ban corp, vpres employee rel, 1981-84; Urban League Metropolitan Seattle, Wash, pres & chief exec officer, 1984-98; Woman Achievement, Women Commun, 1991; Custom Fit Productions Inc, pres, 1998; Univ Alaska, Human Serv Dept, asst prof, 2009-; Univ Wash Sch Social Work, fac; Cascade Corp Alliances, owner; Jr. fel, Whitney M. Young. **Orgs:** Alpha Kappa Alpha Sor, 1958; pres, Seattle Womens Commun, 1971-72, 1975-76; bd mem, Seattle Pvt Indust Coun, 1986-98; bd trustee, Central Wash Univ, 1986-98; charter mem, bd, Nat Asn Minority Trusteeship Higher Educ, 1990; Rotary; Leadership Tomorrow; Links Inc; Seattle Econ Develop Comn; Seattle-King County Pvt Indust Coun; Metro/King County Transition Comn & Meeting Professionals Int; Puget Sound Grantwriters Asn Bd; charter mem, Alliance Educ; mem bd, Gov Va Mason Med Ctr; mem bd trustees, Cent Wash Univ; charter mem bd dir, Nat Asn Minority Trusteeship Higher Educ; World Affairs Fel. **Honors/Awds:** Natalie Skells Memorial Award, 1989; Alumni Legend, Univ Wash, 1987; Distinguished Alumni Award, Univ Wash Col Arts & Sci; Martin Luther King, Jr. Award; Outstanding Woman Leader Award, Seattle Sect Nat Coun Negro Women; National Real Estate Brokers Democracy in Housing Award; Zeta Phi Beta Sorority Finer Womanhood Award; Mentor of the Year Award, Women's Prof & Managerial Network; Matrix Table Woman of Achievement Award; Seattle Chapter of Soroptimist International Woman of Distinction Award; Alpha Kappa Alpha Sorority Talented Tenth Award; Heroes Among Us Award, Seattle SuperSonics; Timeless Achievement Award, Univ Wash; Puget Sound Big Sisters Prof Distinction Award. **Special Achievements:** First female chief Motor Vehicle Dir in US or Canada; only black woman to direct a Cabinet Level Agency in Wash State. **Business Addr:** Faculty, University of Washington, 4101 15th Ave NE, Seattle, WA 98105, **Business Phone:** (206)543-5640.

## WOODIE, HENRY L. See Obituaries Section.

## WOODING, DR. DAVID JOSHUA

Physician. **Personal:** Born Apr 10, 1959, Cleveland, OH; married Karen Aline Rogers; children: Joshua David. **Educ:** Oakwood Col, BA, 1981; Meharry Med Col, MD, 1986. **Career:** Kaiser Permanente Riverside Med Ctr, Riverside, Calif, Physician, currently. **Business Addr:** Physician, Kaiser Permanente Riverside Medical Center, 10800 Magnolia Ave, Riverside, CA 92506, **Business Phone:** (909)353-2000.

## WOODLAND, DR. CALVIN EMMANUEL

College teacher, educator, president (organization). **Personal:** Born Nov 3, 1943, La Plata, MD; son of Mildred and Philip H. **Educ:** Morgan State Univ, BS, 1965; Howard Univ, MA, 1970; Rutgers Univ, EdD, 1975; Southern Calif Prof Studies, PhD, 1997. **Career:** Md Dept Health & Ment Hyg, music & rehab therapist, 1966-70; Essex County Col, counr/dir educ advisement, 1970-74; Morgan State Univ Sch Educ, dir teacher corps, assoc prof educ asst dean, 1974-81; Coppin State Col, dir spec serv, actg dean studies, 1981-82; Charles County Community Col, dean, 1982-86; Northern Va Community Col, dean, 1986; Daytona Beach Community Col, vpres stud develop; Bergen Community Col, vpres stud serv; Capital Community Col, pres, 2005-10; Morgan State Univ, assoc prof, Interim Pres Univ Dc Community Col, 2012-14; Morgan State Univ, MD, Lectr, currently. **Orgs:** Evaluator, Mid States Asn Cols & Schs, 1979-; Am Psychol Asn; Am Asn Coun Develop; Am Asn Rehab Therapists; Nat Comn African-Am; lic ment health counr; Nat Bd Cert Counors; pres, bd dir, Nat Coun Black Am Affairs; fel Asn Community Col Comn Diversity Equity Inclusion; fel Asn Community Cols trustee Awards Comt; pres, AACC; Nat Coun Black Am Affairs; Capital Workforce Investment Bd; adv, Greater Hartford area Urban League; Greater Hartford Arts Coun; Am Psychol Asn; Daytona Beach Econ Develop Comn; vpres, Bergen Community Col; chmn, Juv Justice Bd. **Home Addr:** 102 Meridian Blvd, Newark, NJ 19701-6840, **Home Phone:** (302)832-1272. **Business Addr:** Lecturer, Morgan State University, 1700 E Cold Spring Lane, Baltimore, MD 21251, **Business Phone:** (443)885-1969.

## WOODLAND, STANLEY R. (STAN WOODLAND)

Chief executive officer, president (organization). **Personal:** children: 3. **Educ:** Pierce Col. **Career:** Communs Media Inc, founder, pres, chief exec officer, 1988-; Compas Inc, 1991; MediaChek, ommunications res; InfoCures LLC, founder; SmithKline Beecham, dir, 1998. **Orgs:** Founder, Commun Media Inc; SB & pharmaceut clients; bd advisors mem, LSAN. **Business Addr:** President, Chief Executive Officer, Communications Media Inc, 2200 Renaissance Blvd Suite 160, King of Prussia, PA 19406, **Business Phone:** (484)322-0880.

## WOODLEY, ARTO, JR.

Chief executive officer. **Personal:** Born Aug 12, 1965, Tacoma, WA; son of Arto Sr (deceased) and Patricia E; married Yvette; children: 2. **Educ:** Bowling Green Univ, BS, jour, 1988, MA, col stud personnel, 1990; Widener Univ, EdD, higher educ leadership, 2013-. **Career:** Bowling Green State Univ, grad asst, 1988-90, Univ Rels, asst vp, 1990-92; Wright State Univ, assoc dir corp found rel, 1992-94; dir advan, Sch Med, 1994-97; Goodwill Industs Miami Valley, dir, develop, 1997-98; Frontline Outreach Inc, pres & bd dir, 1998-; LFK Group, prin, 2003-; Fla PIRC, Univ S Fla, consult, 2005-11. **Orgs:** Ed, Visions Newsletter, 1990; dist comnr, Boy Scouts Am, 1994-95; co-chair, Mentoring Coalition, 1994-95; Parity 2000, 1994-; ed, Redeeming Time Newsletter; Orlando Regional Chamber Com; Outstanding Young Men Am; Bowling Green State Univ Alumni Bd; Greater Orlando Leadership Found; founding bd mem, Early Learning Coalition Orange County, 2000-08; emer mem, African Am Community Fund; Fla's Comn Marriage & Families, 2001-03; Orange County Fla Sch Readiness Coalition; founding mem, Gov Faith based Adv Comt, 2002-; coun mem, Coun Social Status African Am Men & Boys, Fla, 2011-13; Fla Bar Asn, 2011-; Rotary Int, 2012-; fel, Ger Marshall Fund Us & HUD, 2012-. **Home Addr:** 2131 Alameda St, PO Box 547011, Orlando, FL 32804-6903. **Business Addr:** President, Frontline Outreach Inc, 3000 C R Smith St, Orlando, FL 32805, **Business Phone:** (407)293-3000.

## WOODRIDGE, CHUCK. See WOODRIDGE, WILSON JACK, JR.

## WOODRIDGE, WILSON JACK, JR. (CHUCK WOODRIDGE)

Architect, administrator. **Personal:** Born Aug 29, 1950, East Orange, NJ. **Educ:** Essex County Col, AAS, archit technol, 1970; Cornell Univ Col Arch, BA, archit, 1975. **Career:** Bernard Johnson Inc, designer, 1976-77; Skidmore Owings & Merrill, designer, 1977-80; Welton Becket Assoc, proj designer, 1981; Grad Partnership, proj architect, 1981-85; Essex County Col, dir archit progs, 1983-2001; Woodridge & Ray Architects, 1985; NJ Inst Technol, adj fac, 1989-94, lectr; Cornell Univ, lectr; Wilson Woodridge Architects, pres, 1991-2006; RMJM Hillier Archit, sr proj exec, 2006-09; Woodridge Chen Architects, prin, partner, 2010-; Nj Performing Arts Ctr, assoc architect. **Orgs:** Off interviewer, Cornell Univ Alumni Sec Comn, 1975; chmn proj comn, Houston Community Design Ctr, 1978-80; sec exec comn, Houston Urban Bunch, 1979-80; chmn finance comn, Essex City Col Alumni Asn, 1982-84; bd dir, Am Inst Architects, AIA NJ Newark & Suburban Chap; Newark Hist Landmarks Comt; Newark Symphony Hall Preserv Comt; Cornell Univ's Sec Schs Comt. **Home Addr:** 20 Evergreen Pl, East Orange, NJ 07018, **Home Phone:** (973)674-2412. **Business Addr:** Principal, Partner, Woodridge Chen Architects, 45 Academy St Suite 507, Newark, NJ 07102, **Business Phone:** (973)424-1100.

## WOODRUFF, CHERYL

Editor, publisher. **Personal:** daughter of Phy Stephens. **Career:** One World, founder & exec ed, 1991; Fawcett Bks, staff; Ballantine Publ Group, founding ed & assoc ed, vpres & exec ed, vpres & assoc publ; Cheryl Woodruff Commun LLC, owner, 2003-; Smiley Bks, pres, assoc publ, currently. **Orgs:** Nat Coun Negro Woman Inc. **Honors/Awds:** Achievement Award, SISTAS MOVIN UP, 1996; Publishing Executive of the Year, Chicago's Black Book Fair, 1998. **Business Addr:** President, Associate Publisher, The Smiley Books, 250 Pk Ave S Suite 201, New York, NY 10003.

## WOODRUFF, JAMES W.

Automotive executive. **Career:** Woodruff Oldsmobile Inc, Detroit, Mich, chief exec, 1988; Pochelon Lincoln Mercury Inc, chief exec, 1988-. **Home Addr:** 636 W Fisher St, Saginaw, MI 48604-1533, **Home Phone:** (989)752-1105. **Business Addr:** Chief Executive, Pochelon Lincoln Mercury, 5815 Bay Rd, Saginaw, MI 48604, **Business Phone:** (517)791-3000.

## WOODRUFF, JEFFREY ROBERT

College teacher, educator. **Personal:** Born Jul 13, 1943, Pittsburgh, PA; son of Robert and Alyce Bailey; married Vickie Hamlin; children: Jennifer Ryan. **Educ:** Springfield Col, BA, 1966; NY Inst Tech, MBA, 1978. **Career:** KQV Radio Inc, dir res & develop, 1968-70; WLS Radio Inc, dir res, 1970-72; Elmhurst Col Mgt Prog, fac; Knoxville Col Sem Prog, vis prof; ABCAM Radio Sta, dir res & develop, 1972-77, dir sales & res, 1977-79; WDAI Radio, nat sales mgr, 1979-80; N Cent Col, asst prof bus admin, 1979, adj asst prof bus admin, currently; Ill Bell Tel Co, acct exec indust consult, 1980-83, mgr promos mkt staff, 1983-91, area mgr channel Opers, 1991-93, staff mgr, customer commun opers, 1993-; Ameritech Sales Prom, dir, 1993-94; Comput Learning Ctr, lead instr, 1994-2001; DeVry Inst Tech, instr, 1994-; Aurora Univ, adj prof, 1995; Northwood Univ; Lewis Univ, 2001; New York Inst Tech, adj fac; Col DuPage; Lincoln Tech Inst, instr & master trainer, asst exec dir & dir educ, 2003. **Orgs:** Radio TV Res Coun; Am Mkg Asn; Delta Mu Delta; Radio Advert Bur; GOALS Com; Black Exec Exchange Prog; Nat Urban League Inc; Youth Motivation Task Force; consult, Network Programming Concepts Inc; indust adv, Arbitron Adv Coun Mensa Ltd. **Honors/Awds:** National Alliance of Business Innovator Award, Am Res Bur, 1972; Black Achievers in Industry Award, Harlem YMCA, 1972; Amirtech Fellow, Northwestern Univ, Inst Learning Servs, 1990; Dissinger Award. **Home Addr:** 4559 Normandy Dr, Lisle, IL 60532-1083, **Home Phone:** (630)995-3598. **Business Addr:** Adjunct Professor of Business Administration, North Central College, 201 30 N Brainard St PPH, Naperville, IL 60540, **Business Phone:** (630)637-4067.

### WOODS, ALISON SCOTT
Executive, executive director. **Personal:** Born Jul 28, 1952, Chicago, IL; daughter of Eugene Scott and Erma; married Charles R; children: Jamel Scott, Jihan & Asia. **Educ:** Carleton Col, BA, 1974. **Career:** Int Bus Mach, staff & Br Mkt Support Mgr, 1974-91; Arco Chem Co, mgr end user comput, 1992-96; Independence Blue Cross, sr dir, 1996-97; Philadelphia Coca-Cola Bottling Co, vpres info technol, chief info officer, 1998-2005; Frito-Lay Inc, dir info technol strategy & bus intelligence, 2005-; PepsiCo, dir it strategy, 2007-09, sr dir bus relationship mgt, 2010-; PepsiCo Bus Solutions Grp, Dir, IT Strategy & Plng, 2007-12. **Orgs:** Bd mem, Urban League Philadelphia; bd mem, Girl Scouts SE Pa; Home & Sch Asn Philadelphia Creative. **Home Addr:** 625 W Phil Ellena, Philadelphia, PA 19119, **Home Phone:** (215)438-7032. **Business Addr:** Senior Director Business Relationship Management, PepsiCo Inc, 700 Anderson Hill Rd, Purchase, NY 10577, **Business Phone:** (914)253-2000.

### WOODS, ALLIE, JR.
Educator, theatrical director, actor. **Personal:** Born Sep 28, 1940, Houston, TX; son of Allie Sr and Georgia Stewart; married Beverly; children: Allyson Beverly & Stewart Jordan. **Educ:** Tex Southern Univ, BA; Tenn State Univ, MS; New Sch, producing TV; NY Univ, film prod/writing film/TV; Ctr Media Arts, TV prod. **Career:** Woodswork Prod, producer & dir; Tony Award-winning Negro Ensemble Co, founding mem; Chelsea Theatre Ctr Brooklyn, Acad Music, actor & dir; LaMama Exp Theatre Club NYC, dir residence; Univ Ibadan, teacherguest artist; Univ Wash, teacher guest artist; Brooklyn Col, teacher guestartist; Sunday Ser NY Shakesphere Festival Pub Theatre, guest dir; NewFedn Theatre NYC, dir; State Univ NY Old Westbury, asst prof; Houston PubSchs, NYC Schs, teacher; PBS-TV, staging consult; Mich State Univ, visdir; Univ Conn, guest dir; Univ Pittsburgh, actg & dir credits; Film: Girlfight, 2000; Thirteen Conversations About One Thing, 2001; Bellclair Times, 2005; Sherry Baby, 2006; Heavy Petting, 2007; Be Kind Rewind, 2008; Everybody's Fine, 2009; Old Dogs, 2009; Tower Heist, 2011; Muhammad Ali's Greatest Fight, 2013; Before We Go, 2014; TV series: "Mother's Day", 2003; "Law & Order", 2003; "The Extra Man", 2001; "Blind Spot", 2006; "Law & Order: Criminal Intent", 2001-06; "A New Light", 2006; "Six Degrees", 2006; "Black Box", 2014; "Unbreakable Kimmy Schmidt", 2015; "Blue Bloods", 2015. **Orgs:** Actors Equity Asn; Screen Actors Guild; Am Fedn TV & Radio Artists. **Home Addr:** 504 W 110th St Apt 4B, New York, NY 10025-2006, **Home Phone:** (212)222-2442.

### WOODS, ANDRE VINCENT, II
Executive. **Personal:** Born Feb 21, 1947, Charleston, SC; son of Delbert Leon and Thelma Ruth; married Karen O Lewis; children: Charity, Andre II & Meridith. **Educ:** St Augustine's Col, BA, 1975. **Career:** ACA State Ports Authority, ade analyst, 1975-80; Handyman Network Inc, pres & chief exec officer, 1981-; Interchange Inc, pres; COT Enterprise Tech Transition Team, pres, currently; HNI Ltd, pres, secy & treas, currently. **Orgs:** Vpres, Neighborhood Legal Servs Corp, 1977-; vpres, Eastside Bus Asn, 1989-; irb bd, Med Univ, 1990-; bd, Jr Achievement, 1990-; Sigma Pi Phi, Grand Blvd, 1990-; Trident 1000, 1990-91; vpres, Trident Chamber Com, 1991-92; bd vis, Charleston Southern Univ, 1991-. **Home Addr:** 4350 Briarstone Ct, North Charleston, SC 29418-5407, **Home Phone:** (843)207-0339. **Business Addr:** President, Secretary & Treasurer, HNI Ltd, 1122 Morrison Dr, Charleston, SC 29403-3111, **Business Phone:** (843)577-8252.

### WOODS, HON. ARLEIGH MADDOX
Judge. **Personal:** Born Aug 31, 1929, Los Angeles, CA; daughter of Benjamin and Ida L; married William T. **Educ:** Chapman Col, BA, 1949; Southwestern Univ Sch Law, LLB, 1952; Univ Va, LLM, 1983; Univ W Los Angeles, LLD, 1984. **Career:** Levy Koszdin & Woods, sr partner, 1957-76, vpres, 1962-76; Judge Los Angeles Super Ct, supv judge, 1976-80; Gen Civil Trials Law & Motion, Settlements, family law & probate, 1977-80; N Cent Dist, supv judge, 1978-80; Civil Trials & Settlement judge; Calif Ct Appeal, assoc justice, 1980-82, admin presiding justice, 1984-87; Div Four, presiding justice, 1982-96; Admin Presiding Justice Ca Ct Appeal second Dist, settlement judge, 1984-87; mediator & settlement judge, currently. **Orgs:** Chair, Super Ct Budget & Personnel Comt, 1977-78; BAJI Comt Los Angeles Super Ct, 1977-78; vpres, Const Rights Found, 1980-; bd dir, Cancer Res Found, 1983-; Calif Judicial Coun, 1985-87; chair, State Comn Judicial Performance, 1986-93; founder, Calif Appellate Proj; chmn bd trustee, Southwestern Univ Sch Law, 1986; Var bar Asn; judicial coun adv comt, Judicial performance Procedures, 1991-96; chair, Calif State Habeas Corpus Comn, 1997-; chair bd trustee, Southwestern Univ Sch Law, 1997-; gov bd, Providence Hosps, 1997-; adv bd, Bernard Witkin Inst, 1997-. **Honors/Awds:** Woman of the Year Business & Professional Women, 1982; Appellate Justice of the Year, CA, 1983; Professional Woman of the Year, YMCA, 1984; Pioneer, Black Women Lawyers Asn, 1984; Silver Medallist Award, YMCA, 1984; Life Commitment Award, Equal Opportunity League, 1985; Bernard Jefferson Award, California Asn Black Lawyers, 1985; Outstanding Judicial Officer, Southwestern Univ Sch Law, 1987; Appellate Justice of the Year, Los Angeles Trial Lawyers, 1989; Appellate Justice of the Year, Los Angeles Trial Lawyers Asn, 1990; Alumna of the Year, Southwestern Univ, 1994; Hall of Fame Award, John M Langston, 1995; American Bar Association Award, 1995; Judicial Achievements Award, Consumer Attorneys Calif, 1995. **Business Addr:** Settlement Judge, Mediator, c/o Deb Leathers, Los Angeles, CA 90005-3992, **Business Phone:** (213)738-6704.

### WOODS, BRYNDA
Executive, president (organization). **Career:** Career Advantage Personnel Serv, owner, career coach, founder, pres, currently. **Business Addr:** President, Career Advantage Personnel Services, 1215 E Airport Dr Suite 125, Ontario, CA 91761, **Business Phone:** (909)466-9232.

### WOODS, CATHERINE ELIZABETH. See HUGHES, CATHERINE LIGGINS.

### WOODS, DR. CLIFTON, III
College administrator, educator. **Educ:** NC Cent Univ, BS, chem & math, 1966; NC State Univ, MS, PhD, chem. **Career:** Univ Tenn, fac, Dept Chem, 1974, assoc dean, arts & sci, 1990, asst vprovost, 1997, prof & assoc vice chancellor inorg chem, 2003-. **Business Addr:** Professor, Associate Vice Chancellor, University of Tennessee, 1321 White Ave 552 Buehler Hall, Knoxville, TN 37996-1950, **Business Phone:** (865)974-2940.

### WOODS, ELDRICK TONT. See WOODS, TIGER.

### WOODS, GENEVA HOLLOWAY
Nurse. **Personal:** Born Sep 16, 1930, Saluda, SC; daughter of Mattie Dozier and Zonnie; married Sylvania Webb Sr; children: Sylvania Jr & Sebrena. **Educ:** Grady Hosp Sch Nursing Atlanta, dipl, 1949; Dillard Univ Sch Anesthesia, New Orleans, LA, cert, 1957; Real Estate Cert - P.G. Comm. Col Largo, MD, 1983. **Career:** Nurse (retired); Grady Memorial Hosp Atlanta, pvt duty polio nurse, 1950-52; Grady Memorial Hosp, Atlanta, asst head nurse, 1952-54; Freedmen Hosp, Howard Univ, Wash, DC, staff nurse, 1955-57; DC Gen, staff nurse anesthetist, 1960-70; DC ANaA, pres, 1968-70; Providence Hosp, Wash, DC, chief nurse anesthetist, 1971-76; DC Lawyers Wives, parliamentarian, 1974-76; St Elizabeth Hosp, Wash, DC, chief nurse anesthetist, 1976-79; DC Gen Hosp, Wash, DC, staff nurse anesthetist, 1979-85; PG Co Lawyers Wives, parliamentarian. **Orgs:** Upper Room Bapt Ch Wash DC, 1961-; parliamentarian & charter Jack & Jills PG Co Chap, 1973-75; chmn, Glenarden Inaugural Ball, 1979; chmn, Saluda Rosen Wald/ Riverside Sch Alumni Asn; chmn, Grady Nurses Alumni Asn D.C; Va. Chap; bd ethics, PG Co. **Honors/Awds:** Recipient Mother of the Year Award, BSA Troop 1017, 1966; Certfied Parliamentarian Parliamentary Procecures, Chicago, IL, 1970; Continued Professional Excellence Award, Am Asn, Nurse, Chicago, 1975&78; Outstanding Performance Award, St Elizabeth Hosp, Wash, DC, 1978. **Home Addr:** 7816 Fiske Ave, Glenarden, MD 20706, **Home Phone:** (301)772-7168.

### WOODS, DR. GEORGE W.
Laboratory technician, executive. **Educ:** BS, chem; MBA. **Career:** Combustion Engineering, lab technician & qual assurance mgr; Quali-Pro-Tech Servs, owner; USA Environ Mgt Inc, chief exec officer & owner, pres, 1994-. **Honors/Awds:** Safety Award, AUS CEngr; Minority Enterprise Development Award, Small Bus Admin; Administrator's Award, Small Bus Admin. **Home Addr:** 127 Dominic Dr, Coatesville, PA 19320. **Business Addr:** President, Chief Executive Officer, USA Environmental Management Inc, 8600 W Chester Pke Suite 103, Upper Darby, PA 19082-2629, **Business Phone:** (610)449-9903.

### WOODS, HENRY, JR.
Vice president (organization), executive. **Personal:** Born May 10, 1954, Clarksdale, MS; son of Henry Neal and Estella Marie; children: John M Hite. **Educ:** Utica Jr Col, AA, 1974; Miss Valley State Univ, BA, 1976. **Career:** United CAL Bank, loan officer, 1977-79; Community Bank, bus develop officer, 1979-81; Crocker Nat Bank, bus develop officer, 1981-83; Golden State Financial, gen partner, 1983-84; Woods & ASC/CERS Group, 1984; Thermo Brique W, sr vpres, partner. **Orgs:** Challenger Boys & Girls Club, 1984-; bd trustee, Crossroad Arts Acad, 1989-; bd mem, Techn Health Career Sch, 1992-; steering comt, Beacon Hope Found, 1992-; Horace Mann Sch, One to One Team Mentoring Prog, 1993. **Home Addr:** 600 W 9th St Suite 1013, Los Angeles, CA 90015, **Home Phone:** (213)488-3548. **Business Addr:** Senior Vice President, Thermo Brique West, 25101 Normandie Ave, Harbor City, CA 90710-2407.

### WOODS, HORTENSE E.
Librarian. **Personal:** Born Mar 17, 1926, Malvern, AR; married Walter F; children: Marcia Laureen. **Educ:** Ark AM & N Col, Pine Bluff, BA, 1950; Cath Univ Wash; Univ Calif, Los Angeles; Pepperdine Univ; Univ Southern Calif. **Career:** Lincoln High Sch, Camden AR, sch librn, 1950-51; Vernon Br Lib, pub librn; Pine Bluff Pub Libr, librn, 1954-59; Wilmington Br Los Angeles Pub Libr, librn, 1961-65; Enterprise Sch Dist Los Angeles County, org librn, 1966-69; ed consult, Saturday Mag, 1979. **Orgs:** Dir, All City Emp Asn, Los Angeles, 1973-; secy, Cent Chamber Com, Los Angeles, 1973-; Am Film Inst; bd mem, Ctr Women Develop, Long Beach, Calif. **Special Achievements:** Co Author, Bibliography of the Negro History Collection of the Vernon Branch Library. **Home Addr:** 618 Laconia Blvd, Los Angeles, CA 90044, **Home Phone:** (323)756-5847. **Business Addr:** Branch Librarian, Vernon Branch Library, 4504 S Cent Ave, Los Angeles, CA 90011.

### WOODS, JACQUI
Executive. **Career:** BAM Local Develop Corp, community mem & chair. **Business Addr:** Chair, Community Member, BAM Local Development Corp, 240 Ashland Pl, Brooklyn, NY 11217, **Business Phone:** (718)907-4418.

### WOODS, JEROME HARLAN
Football player, executive. **Personal:** Born Mar 17, 1973, Memphis, TN; children: Jada & Dylan. **Educ:** Northeast Miss Community Col; Univ Memphis. **Career:** Football palyer (retired), executive; Kans City Chiefs, 1996, 2005, free safety, 1997-2004; Live Popcorn LLC, co-founder, 2010-. **Honors/Awds:** Pro Bowl, 2003. **Special Achievements:** Dallas Texans & Kansas City Chiefs First-Round Draft Picks; National Football League Draft First Round Selections, 1996. Film: "1996 NFL Draft, 1996.

### WOODS, KONDRIA YVETTE BLACK
Writer, association executive. **Personal:** Born May 22, 1971, Ft. Bragg, NC; daughter of Calhoun and Mary; married Fred W Jr. **Educ:** Howard Univ, BBA, mkt, 1993; Temple Univ, Fox Sch Bus & Mgt, MBA, strategic mgt, 1995. **Career:** Howard Univ, Bison Yearbk, bus mgr, 1991-93; Blackberry, retail sales assoc, 1994-95; Nations Bank, banking ctr mgr, 1995-97; Greenville Chamber Com, Small Bus Serv, mgr, 1997-2000; Michelin N Am, pub rels mgr, 2000-04; Gannett, journalist spec assignments, 2004-11; Community 1 Fed Credit Union, vpres Mkt, 2005-06; CopyCrafters, sr acct dir, 2006-07; Gwinnett County Pub Schs, ed specialist, 2007-; Talk Greenville Mag, writer, currently; Media Partners, managing dir, currently. **Orgs:** Golden Key Nat Hon Soc, 1989-; Delta Sigma Pi, 1991-; Beta Gamma Sigma Hon Soc, 1992-; comt mem, United Way Greenville Co, 1996-; bd vpres, YWCA Greenville, 1999-; Minority Women Bus, 1999-; Alpha Kappa Alpha Sorority Inc. **Home Addr:** 2210 Cambridge Hill Ct, Dacula, GA 30019-1623. **Business Addr:** Contributing Writer, Talk Greenville, 305 S Main St, Greenville, SC 29601, **Business Phone:** (864)298-4100.

### WOODS, DR. MANUEL T.
Educator. **Personal:** Born May 10, 1939, Kansas City, KS; son of Mable; married Wanda Emanuel; children: Susan & Daniel. **Educ:** Univ Minn, AA, 1968, BA, 1970, PhD, 1978; Univ Hartford, MEd, 1974. **Career:** Univ Minn, prog counr, 1967-70, asst dir off admis registr 1970-85, asst vpres off stud affairs, 1985-86, dir educ stud affairs off, 1986-92; Turning Pt Inc, exec vpres. **Orgs:** Pres, Minn Counr dir, Minority Prog Asn; pres, Univ Asn Black Employ; prog chmn, Upper Midwest Asn Col Registrs Admis Officers; prog convenor, Minn Counr Dir Minority Prog, Coun Disadvantaged Stud; comt mem, Minneapolis Comn Col Adv Bd; bd chmn, Hennepin Human Serv Network; adv bd, chair, Nat Black Alcoholism Coun; Minn Chap pres; Hennepin Co Mayor's Task Force Drug Abuse. **Home Addr:** 461 Owasso Hills Dr, Roseville, MN 55113-2153.

### WOODS, MELVIN LEROY
Executive. **Personal:** Born May 10, 1938, Lexington, KY; married Elnora; children: Gregory & Alyssa. **Educ:** Jackson State Univ, BS, 1962; Va Hosp, cert, 1962; Univ Ill, MS, 1967; Ind Univ-Purdue Univ, Indianapolis, IN, attended 1975. **Career:** Southern Wis Colony & Union Cp Training Sch, supr therapist, 1966-70; Wis Parks & Recreation, Univ Wis, consult, 1967; St Lukes Hosp, 1969-70; Marion Co Asn Retarded Citz, dior adult serv, 1970-73; Southern Ind Retardation Serv, 1972-73; Eli Lilly & Co, comm rel assoc, sr mgr pub affairs; Lilly Endowment Inc, prog officer, 1973-77; Rubicon Pub Affairs, Sacramento, Calif, pres, currently; Health & Human Serv, secy. **Orgs:** Alpha Kappa Mu, 1962; Wis Parks & Rec Asn, 1966-73; Ind Asn Rehab Facil; bd, Int Asn Rehab Facil, 1972-73; Nat Asn Retarded Citz, 1970-75; Am Asn Ment Deficiency, 1973-77; Kappa Alpha Psi; White House Conf Aging Policy Comt; Whos Who Worldwide Registry Bus Leaders, 1994-95; Medicare Coverage Adv Comt, 2002; White House Conf Aging, 2005. **Home Addr:** 428 Snapdragon Lane, Lincoln, CA 95648-8168, **Home Phone:** (916)409-5206. **Business Addr:** President, Rubicon Public Affairs.

### WOODS, DR. ROBERT LOUIS
Dentist. **Personal:** Born Oct 24, 1947, Charlotte, NC; son of Clifton Jr and Effie E; married Cynthia Dianne Hawkins; children: Sonja Nicole & Cheryl Lynnette. **Educ:** NC Cent Univ, BS, Biol, 1969, MS, Biol, 1971; Univ NC, Sch Dent, DDS, 1977. **Career:** Duke Univ Med Ctr, res tech, 1969; NC Agr & Tech Univ, instr biol, 1971-73; pvt pract, dentist, 1977-; Univ NC, Sch Dent, clin instr, 1979-81; Orange Chatham Comprehensive Health Servs, lead staff dentist, 1982-89. **Orgs:** Am Dent Asn, 1977-; NC Dent Soc, 1977-; Old N State Dent Soc, 1977-; bd dir, fin comt, chairperson, Family Med Ctr, 1979-81; bd dir, Parents Adv Gifted Educ, 1982-83. **Home Phone:** (336)599-0835. **Business Addr:** Dentist, Private Practice, 2242 Burlington Rd, Roxboro, NC 27574-9464, **Business Phone:** (336)575-3070.

### WOODS, SANFORD L. (SANDY WOODS)
Automotive executive. **Educ:** Western NMex Univ, 1971. **Career:** Brandon Dodge Inc, pres, chief exec officer & prin; Sanford L Wood Enterprises Inc, pres, cheif exec officer & owner, currently. **Orgs:** Greater Brandon Chamber Com. **Special Achievements:** Owner of Florida's largest African-American auto dealership. **Business Addr:** President, Sanford L Wood Enterprises Inc, 9207 Adamo Dr E, Tampa, FL 33619, **Business Phone:** (813)620-4300.

### WOODS, SYLVIA. See Obituaries Section.

### WOODS, TIGER (ELDRICK TONT WOODS)
Golfer, columnist. **Personal:** Born Dec 30, 1975, Cypress, CA; son of Kultida and Earl D (deceased); married Elin Nordegren; children: Sam Alexis & Charlie Axel. **Educ:** Stanford Univ. **Career:** Int Mkt Group, prof golfer, 1996-; Golf Dig Mag, golf instr columnist, 1997-2011. **Orgs:** Tiger Woods Found, 1996-; Tiger Woods Learning Ctr, 2006-. **Honors/Awds:** Player of the Year, Am Jr Golf Asn, 1991-92; Rolex, First Team All-American, 1991-92; Jr Golfer of the Year, Golf week, 1991; Nat Junior Amateur Champion, US Golf Asn, 1991-92; Insurance Youth Golf Classic Champion, 1992; Golf World Player of the Year, 1992; US Amateur Golf Championship, 1994; Rookie of the Year, PGA TOUR, 1996; Champion, US Masters Golf Tournament, 1997, 2001-02 & 2005; Player of the Year, PGA, 1997, 1999, 2000-03, 2005-07, 2009 & 2013; Leading Money Winner, PGA Tour, 1997, 1999-2002, 2005-07, 2009 & 2013; Male Athlete of the Year, Asniated Press, 1997; Champion, Johnnie Walker Classic, 1998, 2000; Champion, BellSouth Classic, 1998; Vardon Trophy, 1999-2003, 2005, 2007, 2009 & 2013; Byron Nelson Award, 1999-2003, 2005-07 & 2009; Champion, NEC Invitational, 1999, 2001; Co-champion, WorldCup

of Golf, 1999; PGA Championship, 1999-2000, 2006-07; Winner, US Open, 2000, 2002 & 2008; Winner, British Open, 2000, 2005-06; The Open Championship, 2000, 2005-06; Sportsman of the Year, 2001; Bay Hill Invitational Trophy, 2003; FedEx Cup, 2007, 2009; California Hall of Fame, 2007; Dubai Desert Classic, 2008; Arnold Palmer Invitational, 2008, 2009; World Golf Championships-Bridgestone Invitational, 2009; Buick Open, 2009; AT&T National, 2009; the Memorial Tournament, 2009; BMW Championship, 2009; JBWere Masters, 2009. **Special Achievements:** First African American to win US Amateur Golf Championship; youngest person and first African American to win the US Masters Golf Tournament; mem of 1999 World Cup Team; 8-PGA Tour victories, 1999; Author: How I Play Golf, 2001; youngest person ever to win golf's 4 most prestigious events: PGA Championship, Masters, US Open, British Open; highest paid professional athlete in 2006, 2008; He has been named Associated Press Male Athlete of the Year four times. **Home Addr:** 6155 Rocking Horse Rd, PO Box 7310, Jupiter, FL 33458-3307. **Business Addr:** Professional Golfer, c/o Mark Steinberg, 1360 E 9th St Suite 100, Cleveland, OH 44114, **Business Phone:** (216)522-1200.

### WOODS, WILBOURNE F.
Association executive. **Personal:** Born May 7, 1935, Magee, MS. **Educ:** Roosevelt Univ, BA, 1972. **Career:** City Chicago, police officer. **Orgs:** Chmn, Midwest Reg, Nat Black Police Asn. **Honors/Awds:** Member of the Year, Midwest Reg, Nat Black Police Asn, 1986; Member of the Year, African-American Police League, 1991. **Home Addr:** 8155 S State St, Chicago, IL 60619-4719, **Home Phone:** (312)783-3890. **Business Addr:** IL.

### WOODS, WILLIE
President (organization), executive director, association executive. **Career:** Digital Systs Res, founder, 1988-2001; Digital Systs Int Corp, pres & chief exec officer, 2001-03. **Orgs:** Bd mem, Social & Sci Systs Inc, 2003-09. **Business Addr:** Former Board Member, Social & Scientific Systems Inc, 8757 Ga Ave 12th Fl, Silver Spring, MD 20910, **Business Phone:** (301)628-3000.

### WOODS, WILLIE E., JR.
President (organization), executive, founder (originator). **Educ:** Morehouse Col, BA, acct; Harvard Bus Sch, MBA, 1993. **Career:** Nat Bank Detroit (NBD Bank), corp banker; Lehman Bros Inc, investment banker; Levmark Capital Corp, pvt equity; Deutsche Bank Alex Brown, vpres investment banking; ICV Capital Partners, pres & managing dir, 2000-. **Orgs:** Bd dir, Upper Manhattan Empowerment Zone; bd dir, Apollo Theater Found; bd dir, Initiative a Competitive Inner City; bd dir, Mallet & Co Inc; bd dir, Coverall; bd dir, SirsiDynix; bd dir, OneTouchPoint; bd dir, Stauber; bd dir, Marshall Retail Group; bd dir, Cargo Airport Serv LLC; bd dir, PFM Group; bd dir, Mallet & Co Inc; bd dir, Press A Print Int LLC; bd dir, Entertainment Cruises; bd dir, Sterling Foods; bd dir, Innovative Folding Carton Co; bd dir, Interventional Mgt Serv LLC; bd dir, Am Alliance Dialysis Holdings LLC. **Honors/Awds:** "Crain's New York Business," 40 under Forty, 2002; "Black Enterprise," 75 Most Powerful Blacks on Wall Street, 2011. **Business Addr:** President, Managing Director, ICV Capital Partners LLC, 299 Pk Ave 34th Fl, New York, NY 10171, **Business Phone:** (212)455-9600.

### WOODS, DR. WILLIE G.
School administrator. **Personal:** Born Jan 1, 1943, Yazoo City, MS; daughter of John Wesley and Jessie Turner (deceased). **Educ:** Shaw Univ, Raleigh, NC, BEd, 1965; Duke Univ, Durham, NC, MEd, 1968; Temple Univ, PA; PA State Univ; NY Univ; Ind Univ Pa, Ind, PA, PhD, eng, 1995. **Career:** Berry O'Kelly Sch, lang arts teacher, 1965-67; Preston Sch, 5th gradeteacher, 1967-69, adult educ teacher, 1968-69; Harrisburg Area Community Col, prof eng, educ, 1969-, dir acad found prog, 1983-87, asst dean, Acad Found & Basic Educ Div, 1987-89, asst dean Soc Sci, Pub Servs & Basic Educ Div (SSPSBE), 1989-94, dean, SSPSBE Div, 1994-96, 1998, actg vpres, fac & instr, 1996-98; Chesapeake Col, dean Lib Arts & Sci, 1999-. **Orgs:** Bd mgr, Camp Curtin Br, Harrisburg YMCA, 1971-79; rep coun, 1972-, sec, 1977-79, assoc educt, 1981-, Pa Black Conf Higher Educ; exec bd, Western Reg Act 101 Dir Coun, 1978-, coun chairperson, 1981-82; bd dir, Alternative Rehab Comt Inc, 1978-; bd dir, Pa Asn Develop Educ, 1979-, charter mem sec, 1981-82, treas, 1982-83; bd dir, Dauphin Residences Inc, 1981-, sec, 1984-85; bd adv, 1981-, chairperson, actg chairperson, bd sec, Youth Urban Serv Harrisburg, YMCA; inst rep, Nat Coun Black Am Affairs Am Asn Comt & Jr Col, 1983-; mem bd trustee, Chesapeake Col. **Honors/Awds:** Certificate Merit, Community Serv, Harrisburg, 1971; Meritorious Faculty Contribution, Harrisburg, 1977; Outstanding Service Award, 1980-97, Central Regional Award, 1980, 1997, Penn Black Conf Higher Educ; Alpha Kappa Alpha Sor Outstanding Community Service Award, Harrisburg, 1983; Volunteer of the Year Award, YMCA Youth Urban Ser, 1983, 1997; Alpha Kappa Alpha Sor Basileus' Award for Excellence, Comn Chair, 1985; Administrative Staff Merit Award, Harrisburg Area Community Col, 1986; Outstanding Service Award, Black Student Union, Harrisburg Area Community Col, 1989; Outstanding contributions to Harrisburg Area Community Col & comm-at-large, HACC Minority Caucus, 1989; Alpha Kappa Mu Natl Hon Soc; Brooks Dickens Member Award in Education; Kellogg Fel in Expanding Leadership Diversity Pro, 1994-95. **Home Addr:** 8708 Mulberry Dr, Easton, MD 21601, **Home Phone:** (410)820-5898. **Business Addr:** Dean, Chesapeake College, 1000 Col Circle, Wye Mills, MD 21679, **Business Phone:** (410)827-5847.

### WOODS-BURWELL, CHARLOTTE ANN
Government official. **Personal:** Born Jan 7, 1932, Ft. Wayne, IN; daughter of Beauford Williams and Josephine Gaines; married Lawrence Cornelius Burwell Sr; children: Beauford K, Brenda K Coleman, Parnell L Jr & Jeffry C. **Career:** Government official (retired); Peg Leg Bates Country Club, br mgr, 1976, asst mgr, 1980-86, off mgr 1987; Allen County Bd Voters Regist, Ft Wayne, Ind, chief dep, 1988. **Orgs:** Bd mem, Bd Ethics Kerhonkson, 1969-73; Ulster County Ment Health Asn, 1970-76; chmn, Tower Rochester Dem Club, 1970-; Rondout Valley Sch Bd, 1983-87; Ny Sch Bd Legis Network, 1985-87; Prev Connection Community Drug & Alcohol Abuse; vice chmn, Allen County Dem Party, 1987-; secy, Lillian Jones Brown Club, 1988-; Ultra Art Club, 1988-. **Special Achievements:** Elected to Wayne Township Advisory Board, 1992. **Home Addr:** 31 Northgate Dr, Albany, NY 12203, **Home Phone:** (518)745-9872.

### WOODS-WRIGHT, TOMICA (TOMICA WRIGHT)
Executive. **Personal:** Born Jan 1, 1969?, Los Angeles, CA; married Eric Wright; children: Christopher, Dominick & Daijah. **Educ:** Santa Monica Col; W Los Angeles Community Col. **Career:** Producer; Clarence Avant, receptionist; Tabu Rec, secy; Motown Rec, chmn; Ruthless Records, pres & chief exec officer, currently. **Business Addr:** President, Chief Executive Officer, Ruthless Records, 8201 W 3rd St, Los Angeles, CA 90048, **Business Phone:** (323)782-1888.

### WOODSON, ALFRED F., JR.
Banker. **Personal:** Born Feb 18, 1952, Georgetown, SC; son of Alfred F Sr and Zelda J; married Linda Washington. **Educ:** Princeton Univ, Princeton, NJ, BA, polit sci, 1974. **Career:** Fidelity Bank, Philadelphia, Pa, loan officer, 1974-78; First City, Tex, Houston, Tex, vpres, 1978-89; First Am Bank, Wash, DC, sr vpres, chief credit officer, 1989-93; Chevy Chase Bank, sr vpres & chief credit officer, 1993-2004; San Diego Nat Bank, sr vpres credit adminr, 2004-07; Am Cedars Bank, chief credit officer, 2007-09; First Pvt Bank & Trust, sr vpres & sr credit adminr, 2009-11; Boston Pvt Bank & Trust Co, sr vpres, chief credit officer southern calif, 2011-13, sr vpres, w coast chief credit officer, 2013-. **Home Addr:** 310 Lexington Dr, Silver Spring, MD 20901. **Business Addr:** Senior Vice President, West Coast Chief Credit Officer, Boston Private Bank & Trust Co, 10 Post Off Sq, Boston, MA 02109, **Business Phone:** (617)912-1900.

### WOODSON, CHARLES C.
Football player. **Personal:** Born Oct 7, 1976, Fremont, OH. **Educ:** Univ Mich, grad. **Career:** Football (retired); Oakland Raiders, left cornerback, 1998-2001, 2003-04, cornerback, 1999-2005, free safety, 2005, 2013-14, safety, 2015; Green Bay Packers, left cornerback, 2006-11, strong safety, 2008-09, cornerback, 2010. **Orgs:** Owner, Charles Woodson Found. **Honors/Awds:** Mr. Football Award, 1994; Big Ten Freshman of the Year, 1995; Walter Camp Award, 1997; Chic Harley Award, 1997; National Champion, 1997; Heisman Trophy, 1997; Sporting News Player of the Year, 1997; Jim Thorpe Award, 1997; Chuck Bednarik Award, 1997; Jack Tatum Trophy, 1997; Big Ten Jesse Owens Male Athlete of the Year, 1998; AP Defensive Rookie of the Year, Nat football league, 1998; PFWA Defensive Rookie of the Year, Nat football league, 1998; Pro Bowl, 1998-2001, 2008-11; Seven Times All-Pro, 1999-2001, 2008-11; Champion, Am Football Conf, 2002; Bronko Nagurski Trophy; AP Defensive Player of the Year, Nat Football League, 2009; Defensive Player of the Year, Nat Football Conf, 2009; Super Bowl Champion (XLV); Two Times Interceptions Leader, 2009, 2011; Champion, Nat Football Conf, 2010; Art Rooney Award, 2015. **Special Achievements:** He is the only primarily defensive player to have won the Heisman Trophy; Twentyfour by Charles Woodson. **Business Addr:** Corner Back, Green Bay Packers, Lambeau Field Atrium 1265 Lombardi Ave, Green Bay, WI 54304, **Business Phone:** (920)569-7500.

### WOODSON, CHARLES R.
Health services administrator. **Personal:** Born Feb 22, 1942, Louisville, KY. **Educ:** Lincoln Univ, Mo, BS, 1963; Univ Louisville, MSSW, 1969. **Career:** Smithfield Treat Ctr, supt, 1969-70; Univ Louisville, dir off blackaffairs, 1971-74; Action Comn, dir neighbourhood orgn comn, 1970-71; Asn Cols Osteop Med, dir, 1974-79; Dept Health & Human Servs Pub Health Serv, proj dir, 1979-. **Orgs:** Nat Asn Black Social Workers, 1972-; Am Asn Higher Educ, 1973-; Am Pub Health Asn, 1974-; Kappa Alpha Psi. **Honors/Awds:** Unit Commendation, Pub Health Serv. **Special Achievements:** Public Health Service Citation. **Home Addr:** 2702 Woodedge Rd, Silver Spring, MD 20906. **Business Addr:** Project Director, Department of Health & Human Services Public Health Service, 4350 EWest Hwy 9th Fl, Bethesda, MD 20814, **Business Phone:** (301)594-4430.

### WOODSON, CLEVELAND COLEMAN, III
Auditor, executive. **Personal:** Born Sep 5, 1946, Richmond, VA; son of Cleveland C Jr and Naomi Wilder; married Jannifer Eileen Vaughan; children: Cleveland C IV & Camille C. **Educ:** Va Union Univ, BS, acct, 1970; Case Western Res Univ, MBA. **Career:** Ernst & Whinney, sr auditor, 1970-76; Marathon Oil Co, advan auditor, 1976-78, task force mem, 1978, advan acct analyst, 1979, sr acct analyst, 1979-80, Price Control Div, supvr, 1980-83; Marathon Petrol Co, supvr price control div, Dept Prod Supply Acct, mgr, 1983-86; Marathon Oil Co, mgr, 1987-99. **Orgs:** Bd dir, Nat Asn Black Accountants, 1971-73; Am Inst CPA's, 1973-; chairperson, acct personnel comt, Cleveland Chap, Ohio Soc CPA's, 1975; treas/auditor, Cleveland Jaycees, 1975-76; C Serv Adv Bd, 1975-76; treas, Wilson Vance Parent Teacher Org, 1981-83; Hampton Univ Indust Adv Cluster, 1982-99; Cent JH Parent Teacher Orgn, 1983-84; Am Asn Blacks Energy, 1983-99; treas, Findlay High Citizens Adv Comn, 1984-89; bd trustee, Hancock County Chap Am Red Cross; Multicultural Adv Comt, Univ Findlay. **Honors/Awds:** CPA, State Ohio, 1973. **Home Addr:** 4135 Starboard Shores Dr, Missouri City, TX 77459-1722, **Home Phone:** (281)208-1137.

### WOODSON, DARREN RAY
Football player, broadcaster, executive. **Personal:** Born Apr 25, 1969, Phoenix, AZ; son of Freddie Luke; married Julie; children: 3. **Educ:** Ariz State Univ, BA, criminal justice, 1991. **Career:** Football player (retired), analyst, executive; Dallas Cowboys, safety, 1992-2004; ESPN, football analyst, 2006-; GuideHop, co-founder, 2011-; Vets to Techs, co-founder, 2013-. **Orgs:** Bd mem, Make-a-Wish Found. **Business Addr:** Football Analyst, ESPN Television, ESPN Plz, Bristol, CT 06010, **Business Phone:** (860)766-2000.

### WOODSON, JACQUELINE AMANDA
Novelist. **Personal:** Born Feb 12, 1963, Columbus, OH; daughter of Jack and Mary Ann; children: Toshi Georgianna & Jackson Leroi. **Educ:** Adelphi Univ, BA, eng, 1985. **Career:** Goddard Col, MFA prog, assoc fac, 1993-95; Eugene Lang Col, assoc fac, 1994; Vt Col, MFA Prog, assoc fac, 1996; Nat Bk Found, Writer residence; Auth: Martin Luther King, Jr. & His Birthday, 1990; Last Summer With Maizon, 1990; Dear One, 1991; Maizon At Blue Hill, 1992; Between Madison & Palmetto, 1993; Bk Chase, 1994; Bk Chase, 1993; I Hadn't Meant To Tell You This, 1995; From Notebooks Malanin Sun, 1995; Autobiography A Family Photo, 1995; A Way Out No Way, 1996; House You Pass Way, 1997; If you Come Softly, 1998; We Had A Picnic This Sunday Past, 1998; Lena, 1999; Miracle's Boys, 2000; Sweet, Sweet Memory, 2000; Other Side, 2001; Hush, 2002; Our Gracie Aunt, 2002; Vis Day, 2002; Coming Home Soon, 2003; Show Way, 2005; Film: filmmaker Spike Lee, 2002. **Orgs:** Alpha Kappa Alpha. **Honors/Awds:** Best Book Award, Publ's Weekly, 1994; Kenyon Review Award, Lit Excellence Fiction, 1995; Granta, Fifty Best American Authors Under 40 Award, 1996; Honor Book Award, Coretta Scott King, 1995, 1996; Jane Addams Children's Book Award, 1995, 1996; Editor's Choice Award, Booklist; Best Book Award, Am Libr Asn; American Film Institute Award; Coretta Scott King Award, 2000; Los Angeles Times Book Award, 2000; Booklist Editor's Choice Award, 2001; Best Book Award, Child Mag, 2001; Best Book Award, Sch Libr Jour, 2001; Coretta Scott King Award, 2001; Margaret A Edwards Award, 2005; Newbery Hon Medal, Asn Libr Serv C. **Home Addr:** 53 Haver Rd, Olive, NY 12461, **Home Phone:** (845)657-9620. **Business Addr:** Author, c/o Charlotte Sheedy Lit Agency, New York, NY 10012-2420, **Business Phone:** (212)780-9800.

### WOODSON, JEFFREY ANTHONY
Government official. **Personal:** Born May 21, 1955, Baltimore, MD; son of Alfred C and Evelyn Trent; married Paula Mason; children: Jeffrey Jr & Devon. **Educ:** Va State Univ, BA, 1976; Va Commonwealth Univ, MPA, 1983. **Career:** Southside Va Training Ctr, social worker, 1976-78, asst prog mgr, 1978-83; Richmond City, budget & mgt analyst, 1983-85, sr budget analyst, 1985-91, strategic planning & budget dir, dir mgt & budget, 1990-96, dir parks & recreation, 1996-97; City Dayton, Oh, dir mgt & budget, 1997-2002; City Portsmouth, Va, asst city mgr, 2002; San Diego County Regional Airport Authority, vpres admin, 2002-14; San Diego County Regional Airport Authority, vpres develop, 2014-. **Orgs:** Nat Jr Hon Soc, 1968; Omega Psi Phi, 1973; chmn, Mem ship Comt, Am Soc Pub Admin, 1983-; Conf Minority Pub Admin, 1983-; Nat Forum Black Pub Admin, 1983-; chap coun, Am Soc Pub Admin, 1985-87; bd dir, vice chair SDWP. **Home Addr:** 10211 Duryea Dr, Richmond, VA 23235, **Home Phone:** (804)320-5352. **Business Addr:** Vice President Development, San Diego County Regional Airport Authority, 3225 N Harbor Dr, San Diego, CA 92101, **Business Phone:** (619)400-2404.

### WOODSON, MIKE (MICHAEL DEAN WOODSON)
Basketball player, basketball coach. **Personal:** Born Mar 24, 1958, Indianapolis, IN; married Terri Waters; children: Alexis & Mariah. **Educ:** Ind Univ, attended 1980. **Career:** Basketball player (retired), basketball coach; New York Knicks, 1980-81; NJ Nets, 1982; Kans City Kings, 1982-85; Sacramento Kings, 1985-86; Los Angeles Clippers, 1986-88; Houston Rockets, 1988-90; Cleveland Cavaliers, guard, 1991; Toronto Raptors, scout, 1994-95; Milwaukee Bucks, asst coach, 1996-99; Cleveland Cavaliers, asst coach, 1999-2001; Philadelphia 76ers, asst coach, 2001-03; Detroit Pistons, asst coach, 2003-04; Atlanta Hawks, head coach, 2004-10; New York Knicks, asst coach, 2011-12, head coach, 2012-14; Los Angeles Clippers, asst coach, 2014-. **Business Addr:** Head Coach, New York Knicks, Madison Sq Garden 4 Pa Plz, New York, NY 30303.

### WOODSON, ATTY. RODERIC L.
Lawyer. **Personal:** Born Aug 23, 1947, Philadelphia, PA; son of Eugene (deceased) and A Theresa Moses Woodson Carson (deceased); married Terry; children: Roderic L Woodson II, Devon & Keri Archer Brown. **Educ:** Pa State Univ, BA, 1969; Howard Univ, JD, 1973. **Career:** Wdsn & Wdsn Attys & Coun Law, partner; SEC, atty adv corp finance, 1973-75, spec counr freedom info officer, 1976-79; Dc Housing Finance Agency, gen coun; Dc Pub Serv Comn, elec utility coun dist's consumer advocate & legal adv; Holland & Knight LLP, partner. **Orgs:** PA Bar Asn, 1973; St Bar Asn Ga, 1974; Nat Bar Asn; Am Bar Asn; Fed Bar Asn; Wash Bar Asn; Philadelphia Baraster's Asn; Gate City Bar Asn; bd dir, Secy Wash Bar Asn, 1977-79, 1977-, rec secy, 1979-; DC Bar Asn, 1979; Delta Theta Phi Legal Frat; Kappa Alpha Psi Frat; Skull & Bones Soc; Dc Chamber Com; Greater Wash Bd Trade; DC Polit Action Comt; co-chair; bd trustee, Arena Stage Wash; Leadership Greater Wash, 2004; pres, Howard Law Alumni Asn Greater Wash; Pa State Alumni Asn; chmn, DC Alcoholic Beverage Control Bd; Providence Hosp; bd dir, DC Bus Coalition; bd dir, DC Educ Compact; bd dir, YMCA; bd dir, Robert A. Shuker Memorial Found; bd dir, DC Appleseed Ctr Law & Justice; bd dir, United Bank; US Securities & Exchange Comn; bd dir, DC Bldg Indust Asn; bd dir, DC Hosp Asn. **Home Addr:** 6607 16th St NW, Washington, DC 20012, **Home Phone:** (202)723-6623. **Business Addr:** Attorney, Partner, Holland & Knight LLP, 800 17th St NW Suite 1100, Washington, DC 20006, **Business Phone:** (202)955-3000.

### WOODSON, RODERICK KEVIN
Football player, football coach, executive. **Personal:** Born Mar 10, 1965, Ft. Wayne, IN; son of James and Linda Jo; married Nickie; children: 5. **Educ:** Purdue Univ, BS, criminal justice. **Career:** Football player (retired), football coach, partner; Pittsburgh Steelers, punt returner, 1987, kick returner, punt returner, right ctr back, 1988-91, kick returner, left ctr back, punt returner, 1992-93, left ctr back, punt returner, 1994, defensive back, 1995, left ctr back, 1996; San Francisco 49ers, left ctr back, 1997; Baltimore Ravens, left ctr back, 1998, free safety, 1999-2001; Oakland Raiders, free safety, 2002-03; Oakland Raiders, cornerbacks coach, 2011, asst defensive backs coach, 2015-; Valley Christian Sr High, coach defense; Woodson Motorsports, BMW motorcycle dealership & repair shop, partner; Pittsburgh Steelers, coaching intern, 2013; Denver Broncos, coach, currently. **Honors/Awds:** First-team All-Pro selection, 1989-90, 1992-94 & 2002; First-team All-Conference selection; 1989-90, 1992-94, 2000, 2002; Pro Bowl selection, 1989-94, 1996, 1999-2002; All-Decade Team, Nat Football League, 1990; Second-team All-Conference selection, 1991 & 1996; Second-team All-Pro selection, 1991 & 2000; 75th Anniversary All-Time Team, Nat Football League; National Football League Defensive Player of the Year, Assoc Press, 1993; American Football Conference Defensive Player of the Year, UPI, 1993; American Football Conference Defensive Player of the Year, Nat Football League

PA, 1993, 1994; Super Bowl champion; Ed Block Courage Award, 1994; Ranked number 22 on USA Today list of the 25 best National Football League players of the past 25 years, 2007; Player of all-time, Nat Football League, 2009; Pro Football Hall of Fame, 2009. **Special Achievements:** TV Series: Tavi Smiley, 2011; The Biggest Loser, 2009. **Business Addr:** Assistant Defensive Coach, The Oakland Raiders, 1220 Harbor Bay Pkwy, Alameda, CA 94502, **Business Phone:** (510)864-5000.

**WOODSON, SHIRLEY A. (SHIRLEY WOODSON REID)**
Educator, artist. **Personal:** Born Mar 3, 1936, Pulaski, TN; daughter of Claude Elwood and Celia Trotter; married Edsel B; children: Khari & Senghor. **Educ:** Wayne State Univ, BFA, 1958; Art Inst Chicago, grad study, 1960; Wayne State Univ, MA, 1966. **Career:** Forever Free Art African Am Women, 1962-80; Mac Dowell Colony, fel, 1966; Detroit Pub Schs, art supvr; Exhibs, Childe Hassam Found, NY, 1968; Arts Exended Gallery Detroit, 1969; Howard Univ, 1975; Second World Festival African Cult Lagos Nigeria, 1977; Pyramid Art Gallery, dir, 1979-80; Joslyn Mus Omaha NE, 1981; Your Heritage House Mus, 1984; "Share the Memories", Detroit Inst Arts, 1987; Conn Gallery, Marlborogh, Conn, 1989; Sherry Wash Gallery, 1989; Hughley Gallery, 1992; Corcoran Gallery Art, Wash, DC, 1993; Focus & Black Artists '88, Contemp Art Ctr, Cincinnati, Ohio; Wayne State Univ, art educ prof, 1996-2000. **Orgs:** Arts Extended Group, 1958-72; Nat Conf Artists, 1977; bd mem, Ellington White Proj; Detroit Art Teachers Asn; Col Art Asn; Nat Art Educ Asn; bd mem, Mich Art Educ Asn; pres, Mich chap, 1977. **Honors/Awds:** NCA Award for Artistic Excellence, 1977; Artistic Excellence Award, Nat Commun Asn, 1977; Creative Artists Grant, Mich Coun Arts, 1983, 1987; Purchase Award, Toledo Art Comn, Toledo, OH, 1984; Creative Artists Grant, Detroit Coun Arts, 1987; Visual Arts Award, Mich Women's Found, 1988; Arts Achievement Award, Wayne State Univ Detroit, 1996-2000; DIA Alain Locke Award, 1998; Delta Sigma Theta Sorority Lillian Benbow Award. **Special Achievements:** Paintings of African American Life are a Part of 22 Collections Housed by the Detroit Institute of Arts, The Studio Museum Of Harlem, the Museum of the National Center for Afro American Artists (boston), Detroit Edison the Toledo Art Commission, Florida A&M University and Seagrams. **Home Addr:** 5656 Oakman Blvd, Detroit, MI 48204-3011, **Home Phone:** (313)935-4741.

**WOODSON, THELMA L.**
Educator. **Personal:** Born Rutherford County, TN; daughter of Johnny Evans Pate Sr (deceased) and Della Mae Jackson Pate (deceased); married Theodore B; children: Kevan B. **Educ:** Wayne State Univ, Detroit, MI, BEd, 1955, MEd, 1960. **Career:** Educator (retired); Univ Mich, Ann Arbor Mich, Mich St Univ, Lansing, MI, Wayne St Univ, Detroit Mich, educ specialist; City Nashville TN, recreation leader, 1941-43; Fed Govt, Detroit Mich, statist clerk, 1943-44; City Detroit Mich, recreation leader, 1944-55; bd Educ, Detroit Mich, teacher, 1955-66, admin intern, 1966-68, asst prin, 1968-72, prin, 1972-86; T&T Industries Inc, corp dir, 1964-74, corp pres, 1974-79. **Orgs:** Mem & pres, Rho Sigma Chap, Sigma Gamma Rho, 1954-89; Wayne Univ Alumni, 1955-; bd chmn & pres, Am Bridge Asn, 1966-; Am Asn Univ Women, 1968-86; Nat Asn Elem Sch Prin, 1972-; Urban Prog Health, 1977-81; bd chmn, Kirwood Ment Health Ctr, 1979-; mem & pres, Wolverine Bridge Club, 1962-91. **Home Addr:** 2016 Glynn Ct, Detroit, MI 48206-1743, **Home Phone:** (313)865-8921.

**WOODWARD, AARON ALPHONSO, III**
Manager, executive, association executive. **Personal:** married Joan J; children: Aaron A IV, Allen A, Kelvin & Darnell. **Career:** Citibank Opers Mgt, 1970-73; City Univ NY, Edgar Evers Col Seek Prog Fin Aid & Budget Officer; Var Ins Cos, lic ins broker, 1975-83; Count Basie Enterprises, bus mgr, 1983-84, sec, treas, 1983-84, mgr, Count Basie Orchestra, 1983-, co-trustee, Diane Basie Trust, 1983-, chief exec officer & co-execr, 1983-87; Diane Basie, co-guardian; Musicians Union Contractor, Entertainment Mgt, rec producer, currently; Christ Baptist Church, assoc minister, from asst to pastor, currently; Count Basie Enterprises Inc, chief exec officer, pres, currently. **Orgs:** Chmn, trustee bd Christ Baptist Church Coram, NY; life mem, Nat Asn Advan Colored People; past pres, Cent State Univ Metro Alumni Chapt; Omega Psi Phi Frat Nu Omicron Chap; Local 802 Musicians Union; Nat Alliance Bus Youth Motivation Task Force; consult & chair, Am Mgt Asn; 100 Blackmen New York, YCMSDG; chmn, deacon bd, NARAS, voting mem, bd dirs, Int Jazz Hall Fame, Nat Jazz Serv Orgn. **Honors/Awds:** Harlem YMCA Black Achiever; US Presidential Commend Serv Others; Nat Alliance Bus Youth Motivation Task Force Chairperson Awards; Presidential Medal of Freedom, Pres Reagan; Basie Award Gov Kane, NJ; Numerous other awards worldwide. **Special Achievements:** Grammy 1984 for "88 Basie Street" Nat TV. **Home Addr:** 21 Palm St, Selden, NY 11784, **Home Phone:** (631)698-2538. **Business Addr:** Chief Executive Officer, Count Basie Enterprises Inc, 407 E Main St Suite 7, Port Jefferson, NY 11777, **Business Phone:** (631)473-4944.

**WOODY, JACQUELINE BROWN (JACKIE WOODY)**
Government official. **Personal:** Born Oct 13, 1949, Nansemond County, VA; daughter of William and Ernestine Cowling; married Curtis; children: Jonathan. **Educ:** Va Union Univ, Richmond, VA, BA, 1971; Rutgers Univ, NB, NJ, MLS, 1972. **Career:** Charles Taylor Pub Libr, Hampton, VA, librn, 1972-75; Prince George's County Mem Libr, MD, br mgr, 1975-89; Prince George's County Govt, MD, Off County Exec, sister county Rels coordr, 1989-90, Comn C & Youth, educ coordr, 1990-92, Dept Family Serv, prog developer, 1992-94, proj mgr, currently; Prince George's County Coun, legis asst coun mem, Dorothy Bailey, Dist 7, sr staff advisor, 1994-99; Off County Exec, from spec asst to the chief staff. **Orgs:** Bd mem, Big Sisters, Wash Metro Area, 1978-79; bd dir, young adults serv dir, Am Libr Asn, 1983-86; acad selection bd, US Congmen Steny Hoyer, 1985-; Alpha Kappa Alpha Sorority, Lota Gamma Omega Chap, 1988-; trustee, Greater Mt Nebo AME Church, 1991-; bd dir, Bonnie Johns Children's Fund, 1992-. **Honors/Awds:** Proclamation, Outstanding Library Service, Prince George's County Coun, 1987, Dept of Family Services Director's Award, 1994; Outstanding Educator, Black Dem Coun, 1989; Cornerstone Award, Bonnie Johns Children's Fund, 1994; Food & Friends Outstanding Volunteer, 2001; Community Service Award, J Franklin Bourne Bar Asn, 2002. **Home Addr:** 11323 Kettering Ter, Upper Marlboro, MD 20774, **Home Phone:** (301)350-2862. **Business Addr:** Project Manager, Prince George's County Government, 14741 Gov Oden Bowie Dr, Upper Marlboro, MD 20772, **Business Phone:** (301)883-5985.

**WOOLDRIDGE, DAVID, SR.**
Consultant, executive. **Personal:** Born Dec 6, 1931, Chicago, IL; married Juana Natalie Hampton; children: David Juan, Samuel William & Gregg Wayne. **Educ:** Roosevelt Univ, Chicago, BS, physics, 1961; Mass Inst Tech, MS, mgt sci, 1973; Murray State Univ, jour. **Career:** Hughes Aircrft Co, design engr, 1961-68, mgr GED prog, 1968-72, prog mgr, 1973-74; LA City Col, instr, 1968-74; ARDIS, maj acct mgr; Motorola Inc, prog mgr, 1974-76, prod mgr, 1976-78, vpres, local sales commun & electronics; Motorola Nat, mkt transition mgr, 1990-93; Motorola, sr acct mgr, 1993-98, gen mgr, 1998-2001; Motient, dir sales, corp accounts, 2001-04; Roaming Intelligence LLC, chmn, prin, chief exec officer, 2004-13; Field Life Mastery LLC, core energy coach, 2013-. **Orgs:** Alpha Kappa Alpha Sornity; Mass Inst Technol Sloan Fel; bd mem, Jesse Owens Found; bd mem, One Origin Found. **Honors/Awds:** Outstanding Contrbution Youth Mtv tn Task Force, 1969; Community Service Award, Alpha Kappa Alpha Sornity, 1971; Outstanding Serv & Contrbution, Prairie View A&M Col, 1971; Alfred P Sloan Fel, Hughes Aircraft Co. **Home Addr:** 1171 Twisted Oak, Buffalo Grove, IL 60089, **Home Phone:** (847)459-4309. **Business Addr:** Chairman, Roaming Intelligence LLC, 3808 Ashley Ct, Rolling Meadows, IL 60008-1399, **Business Phone:** (847)670-1100.

**WOOLLEY, HOWARD E.**
Executive director, association executive, executive. **Personal:** Born Jan 1, 1957?, New York, NY; son of Ora Leak; married Gail. **Educ:** Syracuse Univ, Newhouse Sch Pub Commun, BS, tv & radio; Johns Hopkins Univ, Carey Bus Sch, MS, bus admin & mgt, 1986. **Career:** Nat Asn Broadcasters, dir cong liaison, vpres regulatory affairs, 1991-93; Bell Atlantic Corp, asst vpres fed rels, 1993-96, vpres wireless matters, 1996-98, vpres wireless & int matters, 1998-2000; Verizon Commun Inc, vpres fed rels, 2000-02, sr vpres fed & state pub policy, 2004-10, sr vpres wireless policy & strategic allliances, 2010-13; Howard Woolley Group LLC, pres, 2015-. **Orgs:** State Dept Communs & Info Policy Adv Comt; Fed Communs Comn; vpres, Regulatory Affairs, Nat Asn Broadcasters; bd gov, Ford Theatre; adv bd, Newhouse Sch Commun; bd dir, Everybody Wins; Exec Leadership Coun; bd mem, Johns Hopkins Carey Bus Sch Leadership Develop Prog; bd trustee, Community Acad Pub Charter Sch; bd dir, Cong Black Caucus Found Inc, currently; chair, Exec Leadership Coucil, 2011-14; sr corp fel World Affairs Coun, 2013-14, bd mem, 2014-. **Honors/Awds:** Distinguished Alumni Award, S I Newhouse Sch Pub Commun, Syracuse Univ, 2005; Named one of the top corporate lobbyists by The Hill newspaper, 2008; Atlas Award, Wash Govt Rels Group, 2010; Lifetime Achievement Award, Wash Govt Rels Group, 2010; Founders Award, World Affairs Coun, 2010; Minority Business Leaders Award, Wash Bus J, 2011; Award for Distinguished Service, Nat Urban League, 2013. **Special Achievements:** first African American to lead this function for a major wireless company. **Home Addr:** 11004 Larkmeade Lane, Potomac, MD 20854, **Home Phone:** (301)983-9772. **Business Addr:** President, Howard Woolley Group LLC, 11004 Larkmade Lane, Potomac, MD 20854.

**WOOLLEY, PHYLLIS (PHYLLIS WOOLLEY-ROY)**
Executive, marketing executive. **Educ:** Lincoln Univ, BA, eng & fr; Pa State Univ, MA, bus admin & fr studies. **Career:** Colgate-Palmolive Co, dir Af-Am mkt; Coca-Cola, dir Af-Am mkt; Hallmark Cards Inc, dir Af-Am mkt; Whirlpool Corp, dir Af-Am mkt; AstraZeneca PLC, dir consumer brand mkt & multicultural mkt; Genentech Inc, Patient Mktg Group, assoc dir, currently; Sears Holdings Corp, dir mkt, sr exec. **Orgs:** Adv bd, Advert Res Found Minority Media Usage; adv bd, Asn Nat Advertisers; Multicultural Mkt Comt; conf chair, Strategic Res Inst LLC; bd dir, Advert Res Found, currently. **Business Addr:** Associate Director, Genentech Inc, 1 DNA Way, South San Francisco, CA 94080-4990, **Business Phone:** (650)225-1000.

**WOOLLEY-ROY, PHYLLIS.** See WOOLLEY, PHYLLIS.

**WOOTEN, CARL KENNETH, JR.**
Sales manager, newspaper executive, publishing executive. **Personal:** Born Oct 14, 1947, Chester, PA; son of Adam D and Hortensee E Washington; married Barbra J Daniely; children: Tracy & Darryl B. **Educ:** Univ Pittsburgh, BA, hist, 1969, MAT, 1971; Fairleigh Dickinson, MBA, bus admin & mgt gen, 1981. **Career:** Wall St J, advert sales rep, 1971-74, sr sales rep, 1975-83, dist sales mgr, 1984-90, southeast sales mgr, 1990-95; Atlanta Bus Chronicle, assoc publ, 1995-98; Am City Bus Journals, media & publ exec, 1995-2008; St & Smiths, publ, 1998-2001; Nat Acct Dir. **Orgs:** Sec Toast Masters Fairleigh Dickinson, 1980; Bus & Prof AA, 1981-83; Wash Ad Club; Youth Motivational Task Force, Xavier UNIV, 1992-98; bd, Atlanta Ad Club; bd dir, Big Bro & Big Sister, Metro Atlanta, 1995-98; bd dir, AM Cancer SOC, Atlanta Unit, 1995-98; Red Cross Disaster Relief Cabinet, 1996-98; bd dir, Ga Coun Econ Educ, 1995-98; Omega Psi Phi Fraternity, 1967; bd dir, Community Found Metro Atlanta, 1997-98; 100 Black Men Am Inc. **Honors/Awds:** Atlantans Who Made a Difference, 1992; Leadership Atlanta Class, 1997; 100 Black Men, Atlanta, 1997. **Home Addr:** 4512 Binfords Ridge Rd, Charlotte, NC 28226-3441, **Home Phone:** (704)540-1384.

**WOOTEN, EARNEST.** See MASON, JOHN.

**WOOTEN, JOHN B.**
Football player, business owner, football executive. **Personal:** Born Dec 5, 1936, Clarksville, TX; married Beverly; married Juanita; children: Gina, Lynette & John David. **Educ:** Univ Colo, BS, 1959. **Career:** Football player (retired), executive; Cleveland Browns, guard, 1959-60, right guard, 1961-62, left guard, 1963-67; Addison Jr High Sch, 1960-63; Wash Redskins, guard & right, 1967-68; Pro Sports Advisors, dir; Prof Athletes, agt, 1973-75; Dallas Cowboys, scout, contract negotiator, player personnel, 1975-91, dir pro personnel, 1980-91; Nat Football League, dir player progs, 1991-92; Philadelphia Eagles, player personnel, 1992-93, vpres player personnel, 1994-97; Ravens, asst dir pro/col scouting, 1998-2001, consult-player personnel, 2001-04; Wooten Printing Inc, Dallas, Tex, pres, currently. **Orgs:** Bd dir, Big Bros, Cleveland, Ohio; City Planning Comn; Nat Minority Econ Develop Coun; chmn, Fritz Pollard Alliance Found. **Honors/Awds:** Pro Bowls, 1995, 1996; Hall of Fame, Tex Black Sports, 2002; William O Walker Community Excellence Honoree, 2002; Hall of Fame, Univ Colo, 2004. **Special Achievements:** One of the NFL's highest ranking African Am officials at the front-office level; Named to Cleveland Browns All-Time team, 1979. **Home Addr:** , Arlington, TX. **Business Addr:** President, Wooten Printing Inc, 2772 W Commerce St, Dallas, TX 75212-4913, **Business Phone:** (214)689-0707.

**WOOTEN, PRISCILLA A.**
Association executive. **Personal:** Born Mar 31, 1936, Aiken, SC; daughter of James and Estella (Hunt) Corley; married Joseph; children: Deborah M, Diana B & Donald T. **Educ:** NY Univ, attended 1969; NY Community Col, attended. **Career:** Family Worker, 1958-66; Head Start Prog, family asst, 1966; Brooklyn, educ asst, 1967-68, health nutritionist, 1968, educ asst trainer, 1968-69; Comn Liaison Worker, 1969-71; Off Educ & Info Serv, prin neighbourhood sch worker, 1971; Chancellors Action Ctr, pub rel dir; New York Coun, Brooklyn, New York, Higher Educ Comt, chair, councilwoman, 1982-2002. **Orgs:** New York Bd Educ, 1954-82; Parent educ trainer, United Parents Asn, 1967; bd mem, Comn Sch Dist 19k, 1967-; Evaluating Team Dist 19, 1969; vpres, New York Sch Bd Asn, 1973-74, treas, 1974-; trust mem, Luth Hosp Brooklyn; Nat Asn Advan Colored People; first vpres, M S Douglas Soc; Bd Educ Employee; educ rep, Grace Baptist Church; vpres, Dist 19 Comm Sch Bd, 1973-; rep, Cent Bd Educ, 1973-; pres, E Brooklyn Civic Asn, 1973-; United Polit Club, 1974-; Dem Club, E New York Brownsville Com; John F Kennedy Dem Club; Friends Music; secy, Black & Hisp Caucus City New York; vice chmn, Kings County Dem Orgn; liaison, New York's Open Govt Comt; Dem Nat Comt; bd trustees, Lutheran Hosp; Margaret S Douglas Soc; pres, E Brooklyn Civil Asn; vice chairperson, Educ Comt Econ Develop Prog Bor; pres, Brooklyn Bor Hall Restoration Found Comt, Nat Polit Cong Black Women; Empire State Grand Chap; NYC Vicinity Chap Inc. **Honors/Awds:** Local School Board Award, Dist 19k, 1968-70; Parents Teachers Association Award; Church Award, Grace Baptist Church Comn Work, 1972-74; Block Association Award, 1973-75; Commission School Board Award, 1973-75; Educator Award, 1974.

**WORDLAW, CLARENCE, JR.**
Government official. **Personal:** Born Jan 28, 1937, Little Rock, AR; son of Thedora Shivers and Clarence Sr; married Pearlene Stegall; children: Zager, Derrick, Nicole & Thaddeus. **Educ:** Univ Iowa, BS, lib arts, 1959. **Career:** Beacon Neighborhood House, group work supvr, 1959-66; Circuit Ct Cook County, casework supvr, 1966-68; Chicago Urban League, dir w side off, 1969-70; Ill Bell Tel Co, pub/personnel mgr, 1971-92; Youth Campus, 1994-95; Pro Care Ctr, facilitator, 1996-2000. **Orgs:** Bd dir, Malcolm X Col Mid Mgt Intern Prog; bd mgr, Dr Martin Luther King Jr Unit Chicago Boys & Girls Clubs; Chicago Urban Affairs Coun; bd dir, Midwest Community Coun; Natl Assn Advan Colored People; adv bd, Career Training Inst Woodlawn Org Chicago; community develop bd, Off Spec Progs Univ Chicago; SCLC; Kappa Alpha Psi Frat Inc; Police Comn Rels Comt Maywood Human Rels Comn; bd dir, Proviso E High Sch Booster Club, Maywood Chamber Com; bd mem, Austin Career Educ Ctr; bd dir, St Joseph High Sch; Oper PUSH; sch bd mem, Cook County Sch Dist 89, 1983-; bd dir, Found Stud Athletes, 1990. **Honors/Awds:** Outstanding Graduate Award, Crane High Sch, 1955; All Big Ten & Hon Mention All Am Basketball selection col, 1958-59; Black Achievers of Industry Award, Metro Chicago YMCA; Hall of Fame, Chicago Sports Found, 1982; Community Oscar Award, Midwest Community Coun; African American Male Image Award, Archbishop Lykes, OFM, 1995; Hall of Fame, Chicago Pub League Basketball Coaches Assn, 1999; Hall of Fame, Ill High Sch Basket ball Coaches Assn, 2000. **Home Addr:** 1245 S Wood Suite 220, Chicago, IL 60608, **Home Phone:** (312)850-9519. **Business Addr:** School Board Member, Cook County School, 1133 S 8th Ave, Maywood, IL 60153, **Business Phone:** (708)450-2000.

**WORFORD, CAROLYN KENNEDY**
Broadcaster. **Personal:** Born Apr 6, 1949, Kansas City, MO; daughter of Lester and Sarah; married Thomas E Jr; children: Roger & Ashleigh. **Educ:** Metrop Jr Col, Kans City, Mo, attended 1967; Penn Valley, attended 1971. **Career:** Southwestern Bell, Kans City, Mo, long distance operator, 1967; Hallmark Cards, Kans City, Mo, code analyst, 1968-74; KMBC-TV, Kans City, Mo, prom asst, 1974-77; Allis-Chalmers, Kans City, Mo, personnel rec clerk, 1977; KSHB-TV, Kans City, Mo, prog dir, 1977-84; WJBK-TV, Southfield, Mich, prog mgr, 1984, dir opers, 1995, dir prog & audience develop, 1989-93, dir prog & audience develop, 1993, sta mgr, vpres, prog develop, 1995; WMYD-TV, prog & news dir, ed, news, opers & prog mgr, 1998-. **Orgs:** Corp leader, Boys & Girls Club SE Mich, 1985-; BUF, 1986-; BART; alumni mem, Leadership Detroit, 1988-; lifetime mem, Nat Asn Advan Colored People, 1988-; bd mem, 1989-, chairperson, 1995, Nat Asn TV Prog Execs. **Honors/Awds:** Leadership Detroit, Detroit Chamber Com, 1987; Certificate of Appreciation, United Negro Col Fund, 1987; Certificate of Appreciation, Detroit Pub Schs, 1988; Outstanding Woman in Television, Top Management Award, Detroit Chap Am Women Radio & TV; Lifetime Achievement Award; Thomas S. Murphy Educational Foundation Award; Kay Koplovitz 29th annual Iris Awards; President/Chairmans Award. **Special Achievements:** First African-American woman to head the National Association of Television Program Executives. **Home Addr:** 5155 Baywood Ct, W Bloomfield, MI 48323-1374, **Home Phone:** (248)926-6450. **Business Addr:** Operations Manager, Program Manager, WMYD-TV, 27777 Franklin Rd Suite 1220, Southfield, MI 48037-0020, **Business Phone:** (248)355-2020.

**WORKMAN, ANTONIO F. D.**
Executive. **Personal:** married Valerie; children: Marcus Xavier, Desmond David & Rawle James. **Career:** Paracentral, pres & chief exec officer, 1985-. **Orgs:** Alpha Phi Alpha Fraternity; founder, coach,

Morris County Track Club; Nj Asn; sub-comt mem chief info officer, Fed; dist sports dir, Amateur Athletic Union, currently. **Business Addr:** District Sports Director, Amateur Athletic Union of the United States Inc, c/o 29 Brookside Rd, Leonardo, NJ 07737, **Business Phone:** (973)243-1736.

## WORKMAN, AURORA FELICE ANTONETTE

Educator. **Personal:** Born May 24, 1962, New York, NY; daughter of Earthalee LaBoard Layne and Rawle Francisco Fredrico (deceased); children: Jayden Taylor, Xavier Thomas & Michele Thomasina. **Educ:** State Univ NY, Nassau Community Col, NY, AA, 1983; C W Post & Long Island Univ, Greenvale, NY, BS, 1987; Concordia Univ, Portland, OR, MA, 2013. **Career:** NY News Day, Melville, NY, ed asst, 1980-; Roosevelt Jr & Sr High Sch, eng teacher, 1984-90; Here Comes Dawn, Hempstead, NY, founder, 1989-, pres, 1991-; Title I Prog, educr, lectr, acad enrichment & comput tutor; Life Skills Appl Prog, prev specialist youth & young adults; 21st Century Commun Media, pres; DAWN, publ, ed; NASSAU Community Col, journalist, asst dir, human resources, Off Human Resources, Spec Progs, dir, Off Equity Inclusion & Affirmative Action, 2014. **Orgs:** Vice chmn, Black Unity Day, NY, 1990-91; Tabernacle One Accord Deliverance Ctr; educ dir, Harambee Ctr; victims rights advocate, Domestic Violence & C & Youth; transitional counr Incarcerated Men & Women; exec admin, Million Man March, Local Organizing Comt Long Island. **Home Addr:** 730 Charter Ct, Uniondale, NY 11553-3020, **Home Phone:** (516)728-4469. **Business Addr:** Assistant Director Equity, Inclusion, & Affirmative Action, NASSAU Community College, 365 Rice Cir, Garden City, NY 11530-6793, **Business Phone:** (516)572-0056.

## WORKMAN, HAYWOODE WILVON

Basketball executive, basketball player. **Personal:** Born Jan 23, 1966, Charlotte, NC; son of Charles and Priscilla Funderburk; married Nicole; children: Chasity. **Educ:** Winston-Salem State Univ, attended 1985; Oral Roberts Univ, attended 1989. **Career:** Basketball player (retired), basketball official; Topeka Sizzlers, CBA, guard, 1989-90; Atlanta Hawks, 1990; Ill Express, CBA, 1990; Wash Bullets, 1990-91; Scavolini Pesaro, 1991-93; Ind Pacers, 1993-99; Milwaukee Bucks, 1999-2000; Toronto Raptors, guard, 2000; NBA referee roster, 2006-08; NBA, referee, 2008-09. **Orgs:** Big Brothers; 100 Black Men Indianapolis; Continental Basketball Asn. **Home Addr:** , Tampa, FL. **Business Addr:** Referee, NBA, 195 Wash Ave, Albany, NY 12210, **Business Phone:** (518)694-0100.

## WORMLEY, CYNTHIA L.

Educator, singer. **Personal:** Born Jan 15, 1953, Philadelphia, PA. **Educ:** Hartt Col Music, BM, music. **Career:** Philadelphia Bd Pub Educ, music teacher; Univ Hartford Spiritual Choir, soloist; Hartt Col Chamber Singers, soloist, 1970-74. **Orgs:** Chap pres, Epsilon Upsilon Chap Delta Sigma Theta Sor, 1973-74; Delta SigmaTheta Sor; Nat Coun Negro Women. **Home Addr:** 2616 W Ingersoll St, Philadelphia, PA 19121.

## WORMLEY, DIANE-LOUISE LAMBERT

Educator. **Personal:** Born Apr 28, 1948, Hartford, CT. **Educ:** William Smith Col, BA, eng, 1970; Bryn Mawr Col, Summer Inst Women Higher Educ, attended 1989. **Career:** Mary Wash Col, admis coun, 1970-71; Wheaton Col, asst dir admis, 1971-73; Simmons Col, asst dir admis, 1973-74; Stanford Univ, asst dir lib arts, 1974-76, dir, 1976-78; Fisk Univ, dir career planning & placement, 1978-81; Atlanta Univ, dir corp assoc, 1981-84; Cornell Univ, Admin Mgt Inst, instr, 1993-95; Penn Plan, sr counr, 1984; Univ Penn, asst dir, 1984-88, dir prod develop & mkt, 1988-94, dir process mgt, div finance, 1992-94; Community Housing, Off Exec vpres, managing dir, currently. **Orgs:** Assoc mem, Nat Black MBA Asn, 1982-84; Southern Col Placement Asn, 1978-84; Vol Pub Serv, 1991; pres, Alumnae Asn, Southern Smith Col, 1994-95; Hobart & William Smith Col, trust, currently; assoc treas, Univ Penn, 1998-. **Home Addr:** 4805 Regent St, Philadelphia, PA 19143, **Home Phone:** (215)727-8025. **Business Addr:** Managing Director, Community Housing, 721 Franklin Bldg Rm 6293, Philadelphia, PA 19107.

## WORRELL, DR. AUDREY MARTINY

Educator, chef. **Personal:** Born Aug 12, 1935, Philadelphia, PA; daughter of Francis A Martiny and Dorothy Rawley Martiny; married Richard V; children: Philip & Amy. **Educ:** Fisk Univ, attended 1955; Whittier Col, attended 1956; Meharry Med Col, MD, 1960. **Career:** Physician (retired), educator, executive; Mercy Hosp Philadelphia, internship, 1960-61; State univ New York-Buffalo Affiliated Hosp, resident, 1961-63; Erie County Med Ctr, resident, 1961-63; Buffalo Psychiat Ctr, resident, 1963-64; Haverford State Hosp, chief serv, 1965-68; Univ Pa, Sch Med, asst prof, 1967; Erie County Ment Health Unit IV, Buffalo Psychiat Ctr, chief, 1970-74; Univ Conn, Sch Med, asst prof psychiat, 1974-81, dir div, 1980-81, clin prof psychiat, 1984-87, Dept Orthopaedics, chair; VA Med Ctr, asst chief psychiat, 1977-78, actg chief psychiat, 1978-79, chief psychiat, 1978-80; State Dept Ment Health, comnr, 1981-86; Vista Sandia Hosp, chief exec officer & med dir, 1986-88; Univ NMex, assoc prof, 1986; Conn Dept Ment Health, comnr; Lovelace Med Ctr, geriat psychiat, 1989-93; St Joseph Med Ctr, dir geriat servs, 1993-2002; pvt pract, 1996-2003; Albuquerque VA Hosp, part-time cons, 2003-08; St Joseph Hosp, chief exec officer; Asn Ment Health Adminr, adminr. **Orgs:** Dir, Ment Health Ctr, 1974-77, actg dir, 1976-77; dir, Regional Ment Health Facil, 1980-87; dir, Lovelace Med Ctr, 1988-90; dir geriat psychiat, Charter Hosp, 1993-96; dir geriat psychiat, St Joseph Med Sys, 1994; Am Psychiat Asn; Conn State Psychiat Asn; Nat Asn Ment Health Prog; Am Pub Health Asn; Am Col Psychiat; Am bd Psychiat & Neurol. **Honors/Awds:** Diplomate Am Bd Psychiat & Neurol, 1970. **Special Achievements:** First director of psychiatric services, St. Joseph, 1993. **Home Addr:** 13112 Canyon Edge Trail N E, Albuquerque, NM 87111, **Home Phone:** (505)857-9669.

## WORRELL, KAYE SYDNELL

Nurse. **Personal:** Born Aug 18, 1952, Axton, VA; married Cleveland D. **Educ:** Petersburg Gen Hosp Sch Nursing, dipl, 1973; Hampton Inst, BS, nursing, 1975. **Career:** Petersburg Gen Hosp Sch Nursing, instr, 1975-78; Southside Community Col, part-time nursing instr, 1983; Poplar Springs Hosp, unit coordr. **Orgs:** Waverly Improv Asn, 1974-; secy, Sussex Co Red Cross, 1982-83 Petersburg Gen Hosp Sch Nursing Alumnae, 1984-85; mem & Waverly Town Coun, 1978-86. **Home Addr:** 8154 Beaverdam Rd, Waverly, VA 23890. **Business Addr:** Unit Coordinator, Poplar Springs Hospital, 350 Wagner Rd, Petersburg, VA 23805, **Business Phone:** (804)732-9585.

## WORRELL, RICHARD VERNON

Orthopedist, physician, educator. **Personal:** Born Jun 4, 1931, Brooklyn, NY; son of John Elmer and Elaine; married Audrey Frances Martiny; children: Philip & Amy Elizabeth. **Educ:** NY Univ, BA, 1952; Meharry Med Col, MD, orthopaedics, 1958; State Univ NY, Buffalo, Affiliated Hosp, Residency Training Orthop Surg, 1964. **Career:** Meharry Med Col, internship, 1959; Mercy-Douglass Hosp, resident, gen surg, 1961; State Univ New York Buffalo Sch Med Affiliated Hosps, orthop surg, 1961-64; Temple Univ, resident, orthopaedics, 1967; Pvt pract, orthop surg, 1967-68; Univ Penn, instr Orthop Surg, 1968-70; Univ Conn Sch Med, Orthop Surg, from asst prof to assoc prof, 1968-83, Stud Affairs, asst dean, 1980-83; State Univ NY, resident orthopaedics, Clin Surg, prof, 1983-86; Univ NMex, Med Ctr, prof orthop, 1986, Sch Med, Dept Orthop, prof & vice chair, 1997-2000, prof emer & vice chmn emer, currently. **Orgs:** Fel Am Acad Orthop Surgeons, 1970-; fel Am Col Surgeons, 1970-; Royal Soc Med, London, affil, 1973-; fel Int Col Surgeons, 1981-; State Univ NY, Clin Surg, prof, 1983-86; dir, Dept Orthop Surg, Brookdale Hosp Med Ctr; Am Orthop Asn, 1990-; Acad Orthop Soc, 1991-. **Home Addr:** 900 Camino De Salud NE, Albuquerque, NM 87131, **Home Phone:** (505)272-4947. **Business Addr:** Professor Emeritus, Vice Chairman Emeritus, University of New Mexico Health Sciences Center, 1 University of New Mexico, Albuquerque, NM 87131, **Business Phone:** (505)272-6240.

## WORRELL, DR. SCOTT P.

Orthopedist. **Educ:** Univ Cent Fla, Orlando, FL, BS; Harvard Univ, Cambridge, MA, MD, 1990. **Career:** Montefiore Med Ctr, internship; Montefiore Med Ctr, resident Orthopaedic Surg; Montefiore Med Ctr, physician; Albert Einstein Hosp, Bronx, NY, physician, 1990-91; Pvt pract, orthop surgeon, 1996-99; Montgomery Gen Hosp; Robinwood Orthop Specialty Ctr, physician, currently; Meritus Med Ctr, staff mem, currently; Waynesboro Hosp, staff mem, currently; Univ Conn HealthCenter fel; Wash County Hosp, chief div Orthop surg, vice chief dept surg, currently. **Orgs:** Md Med Chirological Soc; Am Bd Orthop Surgeons; fel Am Acad Orthop Surg; Am Col Surgeons; Am Orthopaedic Sports Med Soc. **Home Addr:** 11125 Rockville Pkwy Suite 309, Rockville, MD 20852. **Business Addr:** Orthopaedic Surgeon, Robinwood Orthopaedic Specialty Center, 11110 Medical Campus Rd Suite 205, Hagerstown, MD 21742, **Business Phone:** (301)665-4950.

## WORRILL, DR. CONRAD W.

Educator, activist. **Personal:** Born Aug 15, 1941, Pasadena, CA; son of Walter and Anna Bell; married Talibah Collymore; children: Michelle, Femi, Sobenna & Aisha. **Educ:** George Williams Col, BS, 1968; Univ Chicago, MA, 1971; Univ Wis, PhD, 1973. **Career:** Westside YMCA, prog dir, 1968; Northeastern Ill Univ, Carruthers Ctr Inner City Studies Educ, prog coordr & prof, 1976-, adv & dir, 2004-; Chicago Defender, weekly columnist, 1983-. **Orgs:** Co-founder, Task Force for Black Polit Empowerment, 1983; chmn, Nat Black United Front, 1985-; bd mem, Ill Black United Fund, 1985-; Kemetic Inst; Asn Study Class African Civilizations; bd mem, Temple African Community Chicago; Nat Black Law Students Asn; econ develop comnr, Nat Coalition Blacks Reparations Am. **Home Addr:** 8115 S Merrill, Chicago, IL 60617, **Home Phone:** (773)375-0454. **Business Addr:** Professor, Advisor, Director, Northeastern Illinois University, 700 E Oakwood Blvd, Chicago, IL 60653, **Business Phone:** (773)268-7500.

## WORSHAIM, KEITH EUGENE

Law enforcement officer. **Personal:** Born Apr 17, 1960, Louisville, KY; son of John Henry Worsham Jr and Mary Lou; married Linda J Miller; children: Bradford D & John W J. **Educ:** Ky State Univ, attended 1979. **Career:** Police officer (retired); Miss Univ Women, campus security officer, 1982-83; Columbus Police Dept, patrolman, 1983-88, narcotic agt, 1986-87, patrol corporal, 1988-92, patrol sgt, 1992-95, patrol lt, 1995-98, Comn Oriented Policing Enforcement, comdr, 1998, accreditation mgr, 2009; Wakaishu Judo Club, dir. **Orgs:** Col, Big Bros & Big Sisters Columbus, MS, 1983-87; Ala & MS Peace Officers Asn, 1989-; founder, Columbus Police Martial Arts, 1991-95; state repstate MS, World Police & Fire Games, 1991; Am Law Enforcement Trainers Asn, 1995; founder, Columbus Police Dept Athletics, 1996; Nat Orgn Black Law Enforcement Execs, 1998; Nat Black Police Officers Asn, 1998; Golden Triangle Chap. **Home Addr:** PO Box 984, Columbus, MS 39703-0984, **Home Phone:** (662)352-6795. **Business Addr:** MS.

## WORSHAM, JAMES E.

Labor activist, postmaster general, government official. **Personal:** Born Jan 31, 1932, Chicago, IL; son of Adolphus E and Minnie L Smith; married Corrine Kelly; children: Valerie L Stephens, Vance E & Adrienne R. **Career:** US Postal Serv, Chicago, Ill, lett carrier, 1963-90, union steward, 1964-76, chief steward, 1976-78, postal employees union, leader; Nat Asn Lett Carriers, Chicago Br 11, pres, 1978-95 & 2001-03, dir, 1995-98, pres emer, 2003-; Emmanuel Baptist Church, deacon. **Orgs:** Nat trustee, US Postal Serv, Wash, DC, Nat Asn Lett Carriers, 1980-94; Amalgamated Bank Labor Coun, 1988-; chmn, Chicago Post Off Credit Union, 1986-; noble, Shriners, 1982-; Mason 32 degree, F&AM, Masonic, 1982-; Mason 3rd degree, F&AM, Masonic, 1959-; pres, Douglas Aircraft Co. **Special Achievements:** Union building named in honor of James E Worsham; Korean War, received several medals, 1952; Grand Crossing Postal Facility was renamed James E. Worsham Postal Facility by act of congress in honor of President Worshams lifetime achievements, 2005. **Home Addr:** 1430 Joyce Dr, Flossmoor, IL 60422-1784, **Home Phone:** (708)798-5826. **Business Addr:** President Emeritus, National Association of Letter Carriers, 1411 S Michigan Ave, Chicago, IL 60605, **Business Phone:** (312)427-2717.

## WORSLEY, GEORGE IRA, JR.

Executive. **Personal:** Born Apr 3, 1927, Baltimore, MD; married Gloria M Morris; children: Mary Elizabeth Cunningham & Gayll Annette. **Educ:** Howard Univ, BSME, 1949. **Career:** Genl Engineering Asn, engr, 1949-59; Dollar Bltz Assocs, engr, 1959-64; George Ira Worsley Jr & Assocs, owner, 1964-. **Orgs:** Adv bd, United Comt Nat Bank; CEC; MW; ASHRAE; Nat Treat Agency; BOCA; WBA; NFPA. **Business Addr:** President, George Ira Worsley & Associates, 7705 Georgia Ave NW Fl 3, Washington, DC 20012-1618, **Business Phone:** (202)291-1666.

## WORTH, CHARLES JOSEPH

Government official, chief executive officer, auditor. **Personal:** Born Jun 6, 1948, Raleigh, NC; son of James H and Rosa M; married Laurie Gray; children: Kellye N, Kimberlye N & Kourtnye N. **Educ:** NC A&T State Univ, BS, acct, 1970; NC Cent Univ, MPA, 1987. **Career:** Coopers & Lybrand, sr auditor, 1970-74; Gen Signal Corp, sr internal auditor, 1974-76; Bausch & Lomb, sr internal auditor, 1976-79; Soul City Co, dir finance, 1979-80; Charles J Worth & Assoc Inc, pres 1980-; Warren City, county mgr 1984; Vance Warren Comprehensive Health Plan Inc, chief exec officer. **Orgs:** Am Soc Pub Admin; Nat Forum Black Pub Admin; Nat Asn Black County Offs; Conf Minority Pub Admin; bd mem, NC City/Cty Mgmt Asn; Nat Asn City Admin; dist rep, Omega Psi Phi Fraternity Inc; pres, Vance-Warren Chap SCLC; chmn, Kerr-Tar Pvt Indust Coun; Kerr Lake Bd Realtors; treas, Second Congional Dist Black Caucus; Warren County Polit Action Coun; NC A&T State Univ Alumni Assoc; Int City Mgmt Asn; NC Asn Minority Bus Inc; Nat Asn Advan Colored People; Soul City Rural Vol Fire Dept; Int City Mgt Asn. **Home Addr:** 24 Macon Cir, PO Box 411, Manson, NC 27553. **Business Addr:** Chief Executive officer, Vance-Warren Comprehensive Health Plan Inc, 986 Manson-Axtell Rd, Manson, NC 27553, **Business Phone:** (252)456-2181.

## WORTH, JANICE LORRAINE

Business owner, registered nurse. **Personal:** Born Apr 2, 1938, St. Louis, MO; daughter of Oscar Eugene Farrar (deceased) and Beatrice Farrar; married J Quentin; children: Quentin E, Sean Shannon & Jason Evan. **Educ:** St Marys Hosp Sch Nursing, nursing dipl, 1962; Forest Pk Community Col, AA, 1973; Wash Univ, attended 1990. **Career:** Prestige Prod Co, secy & treas, 1982; St Mary's Health Ctr, regist nurse & supvr, 1991. **Orgs:** St Louis Minority Bus Develop Ctr, 1983; MENA, 1985; Black Nurses Asn; Nat Asn Advan Colored People; Million Women March Com St Louis; Zeta Phi Beta Sorority; League Women Voters. **Honors/Awds:** Volunteer of the Year, Mideast Agency Aging, 1994. **Home Addr:** 522 Holland Ave, St Louis, MO 63119, **Home Phone:** (314)963-9669. **Business Addr:** .

## WORTH, STEFANIE PATRICE

Journalist. **Personal:** Born Nov 8, 1962, St. Louis, MO; daughter of Calvert Lee and Patrice Ann Dandridge; married Kevin Rene Gibbs; children: Denmark Sebastian Gibbs. **Educ:** Univ Mo, Columbia, MO, BA, 1985. **Career:** KBIA Radio, Columbia, Mo, reporter, anchor, 1983-84; KOMU-TV, Columbia, Mo, reporter, anchor, 1985; WJLB-FM Radio, Detroit, Mich, reporter, anchor, 1985-86; Mich Chronicle, Detroit, Mich, staff writer, 1987 & 1990-; Off Detroit City Councilman John Peoples, Detroit, Mich, spec proj consult, 1987-89; Wayne County Neighborhood Legal Servs Detroit St, Detroit, Mich, law proj admin consult, 1990. **Honors/Awds:** African American Literary Awards, 2008. **Special Achievements:** Writings under progress: "Where Souls Collide", (A completed work formerly titled Inkling. WC approx. 93, 000), A contemporary paranormal romance; "Secrets to Tell", (A work in progress. Projected WC approx. 95, 000), A contemporary paranormal romance. **Home Addr:** PO Box 31-2456, Detroit, MI 48231, **Home Phone:** (248)893-4553. **Business Addr:** Staff Writer, Michigan Chronicle, 479 Ledyard St, Detroit, MI 48201, **Business Phone:** (313)963-5522.

## WORTHAM, BARRON WINFRED

Football player. **Personal:** Born Nov 1, 1969, Ft. Worth, TX; married Caledra. **Educ:** Univ Tex, El Paso. **Career:** Football player (retired); Houston Oilers, linebacker, 1994, mid linebacker, 1995-96; Tenn Oilers, linebacker, mid linebacker, 1997-98; Tenn Titans, linebacker, 1999; Dallas Cowboys, linebacker & mid line backer, 2000. **Honors/Awds:** Freshman of the Year, Western Athletic Conf, 1990; Defensive Player of the Year, Western Athletic Conf, 1993; Ed Block Courage Award, 1995. **Home Addr:** 1428 Glasgow Rd, Ft Worth, TX 76134-2313, **Home Phone:** (817)293-2973.

## WORTHAM, RUSSEAL

Educator. **Educ:** Sul Ross State Univ, BS, psychol, MEd, coun, 1997. **Career:** Jarvis Christian Col, dir stud develop, 2000-08, Career Mgt Serv, dir, adj prof & instr, currently; Tex Col, head volleyball coach & instr, 2008-. **Orgs:** Nat Asn Advan Colored People; Tex Univ & Col Coun dir Asn. **Home Addr:** , Big Sandy, TX. **Business Addr:** Adjunct Professor, Instructor, Jarvis Christian College, PO Box 1470, Hawkins, TX 75765-1470, **Business Phone:** (903)769-5738.

## WORTHEY, RICHARD E.

Engineer, manager. **Personal:** Born Aug 11, 1934, Greensboro, NC; married Peggie J McTier. **Educ:** NC Agr & Tech State Univ, BSEE, 1960; USAF Inst Tech, MSSE, 1964; Ohio St Univ, PhD, 1969. **Career:** Manager (retired); USAF Aeronaut Syst Div, oper res analyst, prog mgr; ASD Wright-Patterson AFB, elec engr SEG, 1960-66, elec engr, 1966-70; Supvry Oper, res analyst, 1970-80; Oper Res Div, chief, 1980-86; Advan Syst Anal, dir, 1986-89. **Orgs:** Inst Elec & Electronics Engrs, 1964-; Dayton Area Chap, A&T St Univ Almn Asn, 1971-; chmn, ASD Incentive Awards Comn, 1972-78; AF Smelter Adv Group, 1975-78; past pres, mem, Fwy Golf Club, 1973-; Am Inst Aeronaut & Astronaut, 1976; Am Mgt Asn, 1975; Dept Defense NASA Working Group Smelter Tech, 1976-78; one yr exec develop assignment Off Under Secy Def Res & Engr, 1979-80. **Honors/Awds:** Outstanding Performance Awards, 1968, 1971, 1972, 1973 & 1976; Letter Commend Performance, 1978; Outstanding Performance Awards, 1981-84, 1986-88; Meritorious Civilian Service Award, 1986; Outstanding Civilian Career Service Award, 1989. **Special Achievements:** Book:

"Air Force Aircrew Training Devices: Master Plan". **Home Addr:** 4738 Coulson Dr, Dayton, OH 45417-5974, **Home Phone:** (937)263-9562.

### WORTHY, DR. BARBARA ANN

Founder (originator), educator. **Personal:** Born Nov 1, 1942, Thomaston, GA; daughter of Laura Bell Jones and S T. **Educ:** Morris Brown Col, Atlanta, GA, BA, 1964; Atlanta Univ, Atlanta, GA, MA, 1970; Tulane Univ, New Orleans, LA, PhD, 1983. **Career:** Camilla High Sch, Camilla, Ga, social sci teacher, 1964-69; Southern Univ, New Orleans, LA, hist teacher, 1970-, social sci dept chair, Ctr African & African Am Studies, founder, 1989-, Col Arts & Soc Sci, interim dean, currently. **Orgs:** Southern Hist Asn, 1983-; Asn Study Afro-Am Life & Hist, 1984-85; Friends Amistad, 1986-; bd dir, Soc Study Afro-LA & Hist, 1988-; New Orleans League Women Voters, 1988-; Delta Sigma Theta. **Home Addr:** 101 Teton Pl, Thomaston, GA 30286-4634. **Business Addr:** Interim Dean, Southern University at New Orleans, 6400 Press Dr, New Orleans, LA 70126, **Business Phone:** (504)286-5000.

### WORTHY, KYM L.

Judge, lawyer. **Personal:** Born Jan 1, 1957?; children: 1. **Educ:** Univ Mich, BA, polit sci & econ; Univ Notre Dame Law Sch, JD, 1984. **Career:** Wayne County, Mich, asst prosecutor, 1984-94; Recorder's Ct, judge, 1994; Wayne Co Circuit Ct, judge, 1994-2004, prosecutor, 2004-; University of Detroit/Mercy, adjunct professor, criminal law. **Orgs:** Am Bar Asn; bd dir, Wayne County Criminal Advocacy Prog; pres, Asn Black Judges Mich, 2001-02; Wolverine Bar Asn; Mich Judges Asn; United Way; Sickle Cell DisAsn Am; Lead Poisoning Task Force Mich; Optimist Club; Delta Sigma Theta Sorority. **Special Achievements:** First African American and the first female to hold the position, Wayne County Prosecutor in the Wayne County Prosecutor's Office. **Home Addr:** , MI. **Business Addr:** Prosecutor, Wayne County Circuit Court, 1200 Frank Murphy Hall Justice 1441 St Antoine, Detroit, MI 48226, **Business Phone:** (313)224-5777.

### WORTHY, LARRY ELLIOTT (LARRY DOC ELLIOTT)

Radio host. **Personal:** Born Aug 18, 1953, Kosciusko, MS; son of Allie B Carter and Saul T; children: Larry Jr & Sincerely. **Educ:** Career Acad Broadcasting, Milwaukee, Wis, 3rd Class FCC Lic, 1972. **Career:** WAWA, Milwaukee, Wis, announcer, pub serv dir & music dir, 1972-81; WOAK, Atlanta, Ga, announcer, 1981-82; WVEE, Atlanta, Ga, announcer, 1982-83; WJLB, Detroit, Mich, announcer, music dir, 1983-88; WHYT, Detroit, Mich, announcer, 1988-89; WGPR, host, currently; WJZZ, Detroit, Mich, announcer, prom dir. **Honors/Awds:** Testimonial Resolution, Detroit City Coun, 1984; First Honor Award, Best Radio Personality, Mich Lottery Black Music Month, 1986; Big Mac Award, Best Announcer, Detroit News, 1986-88, 1990; Cert Merit, State Mich, 1987; Radio Announcer Year, Metro Area Artists & Songwriters Asn, 1991. **Home Addr:** 13240 Irvine, Oak Park, MI 48237, **Home Phone:** (313)838-7995. **Business Addr:** Host, WGPR, 3146 E Jefferson Ave, Detroit, MI 48207, **Business Phone:** (313)259-8862.

### WOW, BOW (SHAD GREGORY MOSS)

Rap musician, actor. **Personal:** Born Mar 9, 1987, Columbus, OH; son of Alfonso and Teresa Caldwell. **Career:** Albums: Beware of Dog, 2000; Doggy Bag, 2001; Unleashed, 2003; Wanted, 2005, The Price of Fame, 2006, Face Off, 2007; New Jack City II, 2009; Underrated, 2012; Films: Carmen: A Hip Hopera, MTV, 2001; All About the Benjamins, 2002; Like Mike, 2002; Johnson Family Vacation, 2004; Roll Bounce, 2005; The Fast & the Furious: Tokyo Drift, 2006; Hurricane Season, 2009; Lottery Ticket, 2010; Who Is Shad Moss?, 2011; Madeas Big Happy Family, 2011; Recalled, 2012; TV: "Smallville", 2006; 96 Minutes, 2008; Mr. Prez, 2008; Hurricane Season, 2009; Lottery Ticket, 2009; Driving Lessons, 2009; TV appearences: Smallville, 2006; Ugly Betty, 2008; Entourage, 2008; The Secret Life of the American Teenager, 2011; "Real Husbands of Hollywood", 2013; Columbia Records, recording artist, currently; LBW Entertainment, pres & chief exec officer. **Business Addr:** Recording Artist, Columbia Records, 550 Madison Ave 24th Fl, New York, NY 10022-3211, **Business Phone:** (212)833-8000.

### WRENN, DR. THOMAS H., III

Dentist. **Personal:** Born Oct 11, 1942, Mineola, TX; married Joel J Porter. **Educ:** Univ Mo, DDS, 1967; Univ Kans City. **Career:** Pvt pract dentist. **Orgs:** Nat Dent Soc, 1967; Am Dent Soc, 1970; Nat Asn Advan Colored People, 1973; Soc Action Com Univ Mo Kans City Dent Sch, 1974; pres, Heart Am Dent Soc, 1974; Alpha Phi Alpha Frat; Jaycees Kans City, 1975; Southern Christian Leadership Conf. **Home Addr:** 4014 Brooklyn Ave, Kansas City, MO 64130-1213. **Business Addr:** Dentist, 2120 E 63rd St, Kansas City, MO 64130, **Business Phone:** (816)444-9091.

### WRICE, DR. SHELDON B.

College administrator. **Personal:** Born Apr 9, 1966, Orangeburg, SC. **Educ:** SC State Univ, BA, eng, 1988; Atlanta Univ, MLS, 1990; Univ Akron, MA & MS, 1994, EdD, 1995, MPA, 2014. **Career:** Univ Akron, Buchtel Col Arts & Sci, Akron, Ohio, dir Pan-African Studies, 2012-, assoc dean multidisciplinary studies & diversity, 2013-; interim chair, Dept Eng, 2015-. **Orgs:** Akron, Area Int Reading Asn; Am Libr Asn; Asn Supv & Curric Develop; Col Lang Asn; Ga Libr Asn; Int Alliance Teacher Scholars Inc; Kappa Alpha Psi Inc; Nat Alliance Black Educr; Nat Coun Teachers Eng; Ohio Libr/Media Asn; Phi Theta Kappa; Phi Delta Kappa; Pi Lambda Theta; Toni Morrison Soc; chmn, Two-Yr Col Eng Asn-Midwest. **Home Addr:** 1479 Delia Ave, Akron, OH 44320-1601, **Home Phone:** (330)836-6593. **Business Addr:** Associate Dean for Multidisciplinary Studies & Diversity, Professor of Technical Writing & Composition, University of Akron, BCA&S Rm 448 302 Buchtel Common, Akron, OH 44325-1906, **Business Phone:** (330)972-6023.

### WRICE, PROF. VINCENT J.

Computer scientist, educator, business owner. **Personal:** Born Feb 20, 1963, Paterson, NJ. **Educ:** Fla A&M Univ, BS, technol, 1986; Rutgers Univ Sch Law, JD; Univ Phoenix, MS, comput info systs. **Career:** Mid States Comn on Higher Educ, evaluator; NJS Transit, syst analyst, 1986-88; Union Co Col, sr programmer analyst, adj instr, assoc prof, comput sci/Info systs, currently; Proper Gander, pres, currently; Newark Boys Chorus Sch, pres, 2010-11. **Orgs:** Nat Soc Black Engrs; Kappa Alpha Psi; Nat Black Data Processing Asn; Black Filmmaker Found; vice chair, Acad Affair Master Plan's Technol Comt; adv, Haitian Students Asn. **Home Addr:** 489 Jersey Ave, Jersey City, NJ 07302, **Home Phone:** (201)433-1378. **Business Addr:** Associate Professor, Union County College, H 105 Cranford Campus 1033 Springfield Ave, Cranford, NJ 07016-1528, **Business Phone:** (908)709-7000.

### WRIGHT, ALONZO GORDON

Executive. **Personal:** Born Jul 19, 1930, Cleveland, OH; married Patronella Ross; children: Cheryl, Joyce & Gordy. **Educ:** Hiram Col, BA, 1948; Western Res Univ, Cleveland, LLB, 1956. **Career:** Cleveland, atty, 1957-58; Univ Euclid Urban Renewal Proj, dir, 1963-65; Midwest Area Econ Develop Admin, dir, 1965-67; Wright Dev Co, pres, 1975-. **Orgs:** Vpres, Venice C, 1974-; pres, chmn, Econ Res Corp; pres, Bay Dist Motor Car Dealers; dir, Santa Monica Nat Conf Community & Justice. **Home Addr:** 9638 High Ridge Dr, Beverly Hills, CA 90210, **Home Phone:** (310)275-2544.

### WRIGHT, ANTOINETTE D.

Museum director. **Educ:** DePaul Univ, BS bus; Mundelein Col, BS; Univ Colo, cert mus mgt; Boston Univ, cert, fund raising, 2010. **Career:** DuSable Mus African Am Hist, pres, chief exec officer, 1997-09; Midwest African Am Heritage Preserv Network, founder, 2009-. **Orgs:** Bd mem, Asn African Am Mus; bd mem, After Sch Matters; Arts Midwest Arts Admin Fel, Columbus Mus Art & Cin Mus Natural Hist; Dir Fin & Admin, Donors Forum Chicago, 1994-97; Consult, Jabez Cult Mgt Grp, 2010-. **Business Addr:** Founder, Midwest African American Heritage Preservation Network, 7251 S Champlain Ave, Chicago, IL 60619-1219.

### WRIGHT, DR. ARCHON WILSON, JR.

Educator, dentist. **Personal:** Born Apr 27, 1948, Prattville, AL; son of Wilson and Mary Debardelabon; married Malera Traylor; children: Ursula, Karla & Tray. **Educ:** Ala State Univ, Montgomery, AL, BA, 1969; Birmingham Southern Col, Birmingham, AL, 1970; Univ Ala, Birmingham, DMD, 1974; Army Command Gen Staff Col, attended 1989. **Career:** Fisk Univ, Nashville, TN, Biol, instr, 1969-70; Univ Ala, Sch Dent, Birmingham, AL, instr, 1974-77, asst prof, assoc prof, 1977-93, prof dent, 1993-, dir, OD-OR-UC Clin, currently, dir, Stud Dent Health, currently, dir, Dent Assisting Prog, currently; 650th Med Det, comdr, 1995; Am Col Dentists, fel, 2007; Ala Army Nat Guard, chief dent officer; UAB Dent Group. **Orgs:** Pres, Ala Dent Soc, 1975-; Nat Dent Asn, 1975-; Univ Ala Sch Denistry Alumni Asn, 1974-; Int Asn Dent Res, 1982-; Phi Phi Chap, Omicron Kappa Upsilon, Nat Dent Hon Soc, 1985-; fel, Acad Gen Dent, 1994-; Beta Kappa Boule; Am Dent Asn; fel, Acad Dent Int Asn; bd dir, New Pilgrim Baptist Church Towers. **Special Achievements:** First African American graduates of the School of Dentistry, 1974. **Home Addr:** 1801 Univ Blvd, Birmingham, AL 35233, **Home Phone:** (205)934-2340. **Business Addr:** Professor, Restorative Dentistry, UAB Dental Group, 1919 7th Ave S Rm 521, Birmingham, AL 35294, **Business Phone:** (205)934-4532.

### WRIGHT, BILL. See WRIGHT, WILLIAM A.

### WRIGHT, DR. C. T. ENUS

Educator. **Personal:** Born Oct 4, 1942, Social Circle, GA; daughter of George and Carrie Mae; married Mary Stevens. **Educ:** Ft Wayne State Univ, BS, 1964; Atlanta Univ, MA, 1967; Boston Univ, PhD, 1977; Mary Holmes Col, LHD, 2000. **Career:** Ga Pub Sch Social Circle, teacher, 1965-67; Morris Brown Col, fac, 1967-73, div chmn, 1973-77; Eastern Wash Univ, prog dir asst provost, 1977-81; Talladega Col, vpres acad affairs, 1981-82; Cheyney Univ, pres, 1982-86; Fla Memorial Col, vpres acad affairs & provost, 1985-89; Int Found & Coord African-African Am Summit, pres, 1989-2001; Light Hope Inst, chmn & founder, 2000; IFESH, chief exec officer & pres, 2001-04. **Orgs:** Dean pledgees, Phi Beta Sigma Ft Valley State, 1963-64; pres, Madison Bapt Sunday Sch & Training Union Cong, 1967-78; worshipful master, lt community Prince Hall Masons F & AM, 1973-75; del, Nat Dem Conv, 1980; Pub Broadcasting Commn State Wash; vpres, Cheney Lions Club; exec comn, Boy Scouts Am Philadelphia; Nat Asn Equal Opportunity Higher Educ; Am Hist Asn; Am Baptist Club; Am Asn Col & Univ; Asn Studt Afro-Am Life & Hist; Kiwanis Club Fountain Hills; dir, Ariz Nat Day Prayer. **Honors/Awds:** Human Rels Scholar, Boston Univ, 1969-71; Phi Alpha Theta Hist Hon, Soc Boston Univ, 1971. **Special Achievements:** Book: "A History of Black & Educ in Atlanta; Atlanta Hist Bull", 1977; "Black History Week, A Time to Reflect & Eastern Wash Univ", 1979; "The History of Black Historical Mythology", 1980. **Home Addr:** 17420 E Dull Knife Dr, Fountain Hills, AZ 85268, **Home Phone:** (480)837-5534.

### WRIGHT, CARL JEFFREY

Publishing executive, lawyer. **Personal:** Born Nov 18, 1954; son of Alvin Sr (deceased) and Lottie Mae Thomas; married Lakita Garth; children: Stephen, Amanda & Natalie. **Educ:** Fisk Univ, Nashville, TN, BA, polit sci, 1975; Georgetown Univ, Law Ctr, Wash, DC, MBA, 1978, JD, law, 1978; Columbia Univ, New York, NY, MBA, finance, 1982; Trinity Theol Sem Ind, relig studies & church admin. **Career:** Trans World Airlines, int tariff's analyst, 1976-80; Johnson & Johnson, int bus develop, 1982-84; Bristol-Myers Squibb, sr dir planning & admin, Corp Develop Dept, Consumer Health & Personal Care Groups, vpres corp develop, 1984-94; Baptist church, minister, 1988-; Urban Ministries Inc, pres & chief operating officer, 1995-; Univ Evansville In, jurisp & ethics fac. **Orgs:** Trustee, Black Stud Fund, 1976-80; adj prof, Univ Evansville Grad Sch, 1986-89; trustee, Am Red Cross, SW Ind Chap, 1988-90; trustee, bd pres & chief exec officer, Circle YRanch, Bangor, MI; Am Bar Asn; Pen Bar; trustee, Payne Theol Sem; Am United Life; Christian Film & TV Comn; Evangel Christian Publs Asn; Fuller Theol Sem; Urban Outreach Found; US Supreme Ct bar; Baker Publ Group; CareNet; Evangel Christian Publishers Asn. **Honors/Awds:** Johnson & Johnson Leadership Award, Johnson & Johnson Co, 1980; One of America's Best & Brightest Business & Professional Men, Dollars & Sense Mag, 1989. **Special Achievements:** Author: God's Vision or Television? How Television Influences What We Believe. Contributing Author: Nonprofit Leadership in a For Profit World. **Home Addr:** 51 Graymoor Lane, Olympia Fields, IL 60461-1218, **Home Phone:** (708)747-2059. **Business Addr:** President, Chief Operating Officer, Urban Ministries Inc, 1551 Regency Ct, Calumet City, IL 60409-5448, **Business Phone:** (708)868-7100.

### WRIGHT, CAROLYN ELAINE

Educator, administrator. **Personal:** Born Apr 22, 1951, Dayton, OH. **Educ:** Wright State Univ, BS, bus, 1973, MBA, finance & Gen, 1978. **Career:** Educator (retired), administrator; Bolinga Black Cult Resources Ctr, asst dir, 1973-77, dir, 1977-81; Cent State Univ, Col Bus, exec dir, human resources & purchasing, 1986-95, adj prof, 1986-2011; Mat Mgt, dir; Human Resources & Organisational devplop, exec dir; Col Bus & Indust, adj prof; Camp Fire USA Greater Dayton Area Coun, proj adminr, currently. **Orgs:** vpres, Day-Mont W Community Ment Health Ctr, 1984-85; first vpres, pres, emer bd mem, Mary Scott Nursing Ctr, 1984-85; chairperson, Citizen's Adv Coun, 1984-85; secy, Dayton Youth Golf Acad; Camp Fire USA; pres, secy, Dayton Chap, Nat Forum Black Pub Adminr; comt mem, Dayton Urban League Capital Campaign, 2003-05; prog Mgr & dir Scholar Progs, Parents Advancing Choice Educ, 2006-; pres, founding mem, African Am Alumni Socs, Wright State Univ; vpres, Andrews Family Union; mem adv bd, Black Cult Resources Ctr, Wright State Univ; bd dir, Wright State Univ Alumni; chair, Wright State Univ Alumni, Endowment Comt. **Honors/Awds:** Professional internship Cleveland Scholarship Foundation, 1983; graduate Black Leadership Program, Dayton Urban League, 1983-84; African American Award Excellence, Wright State Univ Alumni Asn, 2004; Distinguished Alumni Award, Orgn Black Fac & Staff, Wright State Univ, 2005; Legacy Award, Mary Scott Nursing Ctr, 2007. **Special Achievements:** Hosted Black Achievement on WAVI radio in Dayton. **Home Addr:** 5626 Elgin Roof Rd, Trotwood, OH 45426, **Home Phone:** (937)277-0411. **Business Addr:** Project Administrator, Camp Fire USA Greater Dayton Area Council, 4301 Powell Rd, Dayton, OH 45424, **Business Phone:** (937)236-6115.

### WRIGHT, CHARLOTTE A.

Administrator. **Personal:** Born Jan 1, 1951?. **Career:** Gary Community Sch Corp, Emerson Visual and Performing Arts High Ability Academy, asst prin & dean, Lew Wallace, asst prin; Dunbar-Pulaski Mid Sch, prin, currently; Roosevelt High Sch, prin, 2006-12. **Home Addr:** 6011 Hemlock Ave, Gary, IN 46403, **Home Phone:** (219)939-0249.

### WRIGHT, CLARENCE, SR.

Vice president (organization). **Educ:** Tenn State Univ, BS, Am hist, 1971. **Career:** LIMRA Int's Diversity Mkt Comt, chair, 2000-01; AXA Advisor, vpres, AXA Fin Inc, sr vpres opportunity mkt, 1975-2007. **Orgs:** Bd trustee, Excelsior Col; Adv bd, African Am Chamber com; Exec Leadership Coun; Chair Diversity Marking Comt; Nat Asn Life Underwriters; Gen Agents/Managers Asn; Life Ins & Mkt Res Asn.

### WRIGHT, CLINTON L. A.

Lawyer. **Personal:** Born Oct 24, 1951, Kingston; son of Clinton and Jemima Webster; married Antoinette Green; children: Nia, Challa & Calvin. **Career:** State Con, asst pub defender, 1977-79; CIGNA Corp, Kennedy & Sullivan, sr litigation coun, 1979-83; City New Haven, Con, asst corp coun, 1981-84, corp coun, 1990-91; James, Turner & Wright, law partner, 1983-89; Cooper, Liebowitz, Royster, Wright, law partner, 1990-91. **Orgs:** George Crawford Law Soc, 1976-91; bd mem, Am Cancer Soc, 1988-91; bd mem, Am Red Cross, 1989-91; United Way Greater New Haven, 1989-91; chair, Con Bar Asn Com Minority Participation, 1989-91; exec com, New Haven County Bar Asn, 1989-91. **Home Addr:** 25 Rockview Terr, New Haven, CT 06511-1619.

### WRIGHT, CRYSTAL ANDREA

Business owner, publisher. **Personal:** Born Jan 13, 1958, Los Angeles, CA; daughter of Sharon Lewis and Ray Morrow; married Michael Stradford; married Bill Richardson. **Educ:** Seattle Univ, mkt, 1978; Fashion Inst Design & Merchandising, attended 1979; Univ Wash, mkt, 1982; Univ Calif, pub speaking professionals, 2006. **Career:** Xerox Corp, acct exec, 1980-85; Bobby Holland Photog, artist rep, 1985-86; Crystal Agency Inc, pres, 1986-, artistic dir, 1986-08; Crystal Wright Live, auth, 1995-, pres, 2009-; Set Pace Publ Group, owner, 1994-; MAC Cosmetics, educr/motivational speaker, 2002-04; 1st HOLD Mag, founder & publ. **Orgs:** Womens Econ Develop Corp, 1994-; Nat Asn Women Bus Owners, 1996-; Women, 1996-; Jenesse Ctr Domestic Violence; adv bd mem, Makeup Designory, Burbank; cosmetology adv bd mem, Los Angeles Trade Tech Sch. **Honors/Awds:** Entrepreneur in Action Award, Womens Econ Dev Corp, 1998. **Special Achievements:** The Hair Makeup & Styling Career Guide, 1995, 1997; First Hold Magazine for freelance hair, makeup and fashion stylists, 1997-; Author: "30 DAYS AT 100 PERCENT: Changing Your Life 30 Days at a Time". **Business Addr:** President, Director, Crystal Agency Inc, 4237 Los Nietos Dr, Los Angeles, CA 90027-2911, **Business Phone:** (323)906-9600.

### WRIGHT, DAWIN LYRON

Manager. **Personal:** Born Nov 24, 1951, Chicago, IL; son of Adell and Ruby L; married Carolyn; children: Dedra & Denita. **Educ:** Kennedy King Col, AAS, automotive, 1970; Chicago State Univ, BS, indust educ, 1973, MS, occup educ, 1976. **Career:** Kennedy King Col, asst prof, 1971-77; GM Corp, Chevrolet Motor Div, area serv mgr, 1976-78, personnel coordr, 1978-80, asst serv mgr, 1981-85, zone serv mgr, 1986-88, acct mgr, 1988-90, br mkt mgr, 1990-93, zone mgr, 1993-94, asst regional mgr, 1994-96; dir, bus opers, 1996-2002; Dealer Integration, dir, 2002-05, Dealer Develop, exec dir, 2005; Gen Motors Corp, exec dir, 2007-09. **Orgs:** Black Exec Forum; pres, 4 US Investment. **Home Addr:** 3668 Edinborough, Rochester Hills, MI 48306, **Home Phone:** (248)377-2920. **Business Addr:** Executive Director, General Motors Corp, 100 Renaissance Ctr, Detroit, MI 48265-1000, **Business Phone:** (313)667-9037.

**WRIGHT, DEBORAH C.**
President (organization), chief executive officer, executive. **Personal:** Born Jan 1, 1958, Bennettsville, SC; daughter of Harry C. **Educ:** Radcliffe Col, BA, 1979; Harvard Univs Sch Bus & Sch Law, MBA, JD, 1984. **Career:** First Boston Bank, assoc corp finance, 1984-87; NewYork City Partnership (bus advocacy group), dir mkt, 1987-92; New York Housing Authority Bd, 1990-92; New York Planning Comn, mem, 1992-94; Dept Housing Preserv & Develop, comnr, 1994-96; Upper Manhattan Empowerment Zone Develop Corp, pres & chief exec officer, 1996-99; Carver Bancorp, bd dirs; Carver Bancorp Inc, pres & chief exec officer, 1999-, chmn, 2005-; Carver Fed Savings Bank, pres & chief exec officer, 1999-, chmn, 2005-. **Orgs:** Bd dir, Kraft Foods, 2001-; Time Warner, 2005-; bd dir, C's Defense Fund; trustee, Memorial Sloan-Kettering Cancer Ctr; bd Overseers, Harvard Univ; Ny Tax Reform & Fairness Comn. **Business Addr:** President, Chief Executive Officer, Carver Bancorp Inc, 75 W 125th St, New York, NY 10027, **Business Phone:** (718)230-2900.

**WRIGHT, DMITRI**
School administrator, artist. **Personal:** Born Oct 17, 1948, Newark, NJ; son of John and Ruth; married Karen E Shields; children: Odin L. **Educ:** Newark Sch Fine Arts, cert, valedictorian, 1970; Max Beckman Int Fel Brooklyn Mus Art Sch, fine & studio arts, 1972; Cooper Union Advan Sci & Art, fine & studio arts, 1973; NYACK Col, BS, org mgt, 1993. **Career:** Dmitri Wright Fine Art, master artist/instr, 1970-; Newark Sch Fine & Indust Arts, fine arts instr, 1971-81; Conn Inst Art, class drawing instr, 1971-81, painting & drawing instr, 1981-82; Brooklyn Mus Arts Sch, arts educr, 1972-82; Dmitri's Renaissance Workshops, founder, prin master fine artist & instr, 1982-2001; master fine art instr, 1983-94, dean, dir educ, 1994-2000, fine & applied art, dir spec progs; The Historical Soc Greenwich, artist, 2002-03, instr, 2003-08; Silvermine Sch Art, master artist instr, 2003-; Greenwich Artist Soc, instr, 2006-; Weir Farm Nat Hist Site, impressionist master artist instr, 2009-; Weir Farm Art Acad, master artist & instr, 2014-. **Orgs:** Creative dir, Conn Inst Art, High Touch & High Tech Pigments Pixels Progs; artist residence, Hist Soc Greenwich, 2002-03, master instr, 2003-. **Home Addr:** 106 Hunting Ridge Rd, Greenwich, CT 06831, **Home Phone:** (203)661-0105. **Business Addr:** Master Artist, Instructor, Weir Farm Art Academy, 106 Hunting Ridge Rd, Greenwich, CT 06831-3135, **Business Phone:** (203)832-3325.

**WRIGHT, DR. EARL LEE**
School administrator. **Personal:** Born Jul 5, 1941, Sinton, TX; son of Nola Beatrice Vaughn and Earilee; married Susan; children: Arlene, Darius, Adrian & Laura. **Educ:** St Mary's Univ, BA, 1965, MA, 1970; Univ Tex, Austin, PhD, 1975. **Career:** San Antonio Independent Sch Dist, teacher, 1965-68; Swift & Co, mgt, 1968-70; San Antonio Col, prof & dean, 1970-82, vpres, 1982-95, full prof, psychol, human serv, geront & sociol, 1995-; Prairie View A & M Univ, vis prof, 1973-75; ES Wright Investments Inc, pres & chief exec officer. **Orgs:** Antioch Baptist Church, 1951-; vol serv Northwest YMCA, 1973-78; natl consult, Nova Univ, 1978-90; bd dir, San Antonio Boys Club Am, 1981-82; United Way Comn Adv Bd, 1981; consult Kelly AFT Mgt Org, 1982; Jr Col Stud Personnel Asn Tex, 1982-86, Tex Asn Col & Univ Stud Personnel Adminr; Fed Exec Awards Panel, 1984-85; hon mem, Mayor's Martin Luther King Mem Community, 1986; NCP; Phi Delta Kappa; speaker, State & Natl Conferences & Convs. **Home Addr:** 100 Bikeway Lane, Shavano Park, TX 78231-1401. **Business Addr:** Professor Psychology, Human Services, Gerontology and Sociology Department, San Antonio College, MLC 670 1300 San Pedro Ave, San Antonio, TX 78212-4299, **Business Phone:** (210)486-0000.

**WRIGHT, ELEASE**
Vice president (organization). **Personal:** married Dana; children: 2. **Educ:** Univ Conn, BS, educ; Stanford Univ, Women & Leadership Further Studies. **Career:** Aetna Inc, sr vpres human resources, 1997-2012. **Orgs:** Bd dir, Conn Cs Med Ctr; bd adv, Univ Conn Sch Bus; bd advisors, Cornell Univs Ctr Advan Human Resource Studies; pres bd dir, Hartford Region Ywca; bd dir, Human Resource Policy Asn; Exec Leadership Coun; fel Nat Acad Human Resources; bd dir, Univ Conn Found Inc; bd adv, Cornell Univs Ctr Advan Human Resource Studies; bd trustee, Nat Acad Human Resources. **Business Addr:** Senior Vice President of Human Resources, Aetna Inc, 151 Farmington Ave, Hartford, CT 06156, **Business Phone:** (860)273-0123.

**WRIGHT, ERICA ABI.** **See BADU, ERYKAH.**

**WRIGHT, FALISHA**
Basketball player. **Personal:** Born Jan 28, 1973; daughter of Brady. **Educ:** San Diego State Univ, BS, 1995. **Career:** Basketball player (retired), basketball coach; Portland Power, guard, 1992-95; Portland State Univ, asst coach.

**WRIGHT, HON. GEOFFREY (GEOFFREY D S WRIGHT)**
Judge. **Educ:** Union Col, BA, 1971; Albany Law Sch, JD, 1975. **Career:** John L Edmonds, assoc, 1976-83; Seavey Fingerit Vogel Oziel & Skoller, assoc, 1984-90; Wright & Fingerit, partner, 1991-97; New York Civil Ct, New York County, judge, 1998-. **Business Addr:** Judge, Civil Court Of The City of New York, 80 Centre St Rm 128, New York, NY 10013, **Business Phone:** (646)386-3771.

**WRIGHT, GEORGE C., JR.**
Mayor, executive. **Personal:** Born Mar 9, 1932, Chesapeake City, MD; son of George C and Alice Brooks; married Mary Guy; children: Terun Palmer, George C III, Sharon & Lisa. **Educ:** Md State Col, BS, 1953. **Career:** Dover A&B, Dover, Del, chief staffing, 1956-89; Town Smyrna Del, mayor, 1984-95; Del League Local Govt, league dir, exec dir, 1989-, pres, 1990-92. **Orgs:** Coun Police Training, DE, 1986-; vpres, steward bd, Bethel Am Church, 1987-; Kent Sussex Indust, 1987-; worshipful master, St John's Lodge 7; 33rd Degree Mason. **Honors/Awds:** Received Defense Acquisition Program Administration Award, Distinguished Public Administration, St Del, 1994. **Home Addr:** 31 Locust St, Smyrna, DE 19977-1521, **Home Phone:** (302)659-1769. **Business Addr:** Executive Director, Delaware League of Local Governments, PO Box 484, Dover, DE 19903-0484, **Business Phone:** (302)678-0991.

**WRIGHT, DR. GEORGE C.**
Educator. **Personal:** Born Lexington, KY. **Educ:** Univ Ky, BA, hist, MA, hist, DHL, 2004; Duke Univ, PhD, hist. **Career:** Univ Ky, asst prof, 1977-80; Univ Tex, Austin, asst prof, assoc prof, prof, vice provost undergrad educ, exec vpres, 1980-93; Duke Univ, Afro-Am Studies Prog, dir & vice provost, 1993-95; Univ Tex, Arlington, vpres acad affairs & provost, 1995-98, exec vpres acad affairs & provost, 1998-2002; Prairie View A&M Univ, pres, 2003-; Andrew W Mellon Fac fel Harvard Univ. **Orgs:** Bd dir, City Arlington Chamber Found; Med Ctr Arlington; Southern Hist Asn Prog Comt; Univ Ky Col Arts & Sci Adv Bd; Comn Col Southern Asn Col & Sch; Comn Advan Racial & Ethnic Equity Am Coun Educ & Tex Humanities; teaching fel Silver Spurs Centennial; fel Lillian & Tom B Rhodes Centennial Teaching, Univ Tex. **Business Addr:** President, Prairie View A&M University, PO Box 519 MS 1001, Prairie View, TX 77446-0519, **Business Phone:** (936)261-3311.

**WRIGHT, HOWARD GREGORY**
Basketball player, executive. **Personal:** Born Dec 20, 1967, San Diego, CA; children: Alyssa & Eden. **Educ:** Stanford Univ, BA, economet & quant econs, 1989. **Career:** Basketball player (retired), executive; Atlanta Hawks, 1990; Orlando Magic, 1991, 1992-93; Dallas Mavericks, 1991; Atletico Madrid Villalba, Spain, 1991; Pinturas Bruguer Badalona; Reims Champagne Basket, France, 1991-92; Tri-City Chinook, 1992; Auxilium Torino, Italy, 1992-93; Andorra, Spain, 1993-94; Joventut Badalona, Spain, 1994-95; Murcia, Spain, 1995-96; Japan Energy Griffins, Japan, 1996-98; Toyota Motors Pacers, Japan, 1998-2000; Qualcomm, sr vpres bus develop, 2001-2014; Intel Corp, vpres & dir wireless mkt develop, 2015-. **Orgs:** Chmn, Pro Kids, First Tee San Diego, 2007-. **Business Addr:** Vice President, Director, Intel Corporation, 2200 Mission Col Blvd RNB 4-148, Santa Clara, CA 95054, **Business Phone:** (408)765-5050.

**WRIGHT, DR. JACKSON THOMAS, JR.**
Physician, educator. **Personal:** Born Apr 28, 1944, Pittsburgh, PA; son of Jackson T Sr and Lillian Doak; married Mollie L Richardson; children: Adina. **Educ:** Ohio Wesleyan Univ, Del, OH, BA, 1967; Univ Pittsburgh, Pittsburgh, PA, MD, 1976, PhD, pharmacol, 1977; FACP; FASH; FAHA. **Career:** Woodrow Wilson, Martin Luther King fel, 1971-73; Univ Mich, Ann Arbor, Mich, resident internal med, 1977-80; Med Col Va, Va Commonwealth Univ, Richmond, Va, asst prof, 1980-86, assoc prof med & pharmacol, 1986-90; Case Western Res Univ, dir clin hypertension prog, 1990-, prof med, 1995-, Clin Res Ctr, prog dir, Hypertension Sect, chief, currently; UH Case Med Ctr, William T Dahms Clin Res Unit, prog dir, Clin Hypertension Prog, dir, currently. **Orgs:** Chmn, Va State Affil Hypertension Subcomt, Am Heart Asn, 1984-86; vice chmn, Hypertension Sci Subsection, Am Soc Clin Pharmacol & Therapeut, 1985-87; vpres, Richmond Med Soc, 1985-87; fel Am Physicians, 1987; Am Fed Clin Res; Am Col Physicians; chmn, Internal Med Sect, Nat Med Asn; exec comt mem, Old Dom State Med Soc; exec comt mem, Asn Black Cardiologists; pres, Black Educ Asn; Nat High Blood Educ Prog Coord Comt; chair, Exec Comt; vice chair, Steering Comt; co-chair, Joint Nat Comt; co-chair, NHLBI, currently. **Home Addr:** 2668 Wrenford Rd, Shaker Heights, OH 44122, **Home Phone:** (216)360-0348. **Business Addr:** Director Clinical Hypertension Program, Program Director William T Dahms Clinical Research Unit, UH Case Medical Center, 11100 Euclid Ave, Cleveland, OH 44106-4982, **Business Phone:** (216)844-5174.

**WRIGHT, JAMES E.**
Educator, college administrator. **Educ:** Va Union Univ, BS; Va State Univ, MED. **Career:** Richmond Pub Schs, sci instr; J Sargeant Reynolds Community Col, instr; Goochland County Pub Schs, sci instr & dept chair; Va Union Univ, asst prof; Univ Richmond, Col Arts & Sci, dir MSI, currently. **Orgs:** Founder, African Am Inventors Inst, 1995-. **Home Addr:** 1805 Claiborne St, Richmond, VA 23220-6306, **Home Phone:** (804)359-1916. **Business Addr:** Director, University of Richmond, 311 N Ct 28 Westhampton Way, Richmond, VA 23173, **Business Phone:** (804)289-8245.

**WRIGHT, BISHOP JAMES R., SR.**
Clergy, librarian. **Personal:** Born May 12, 1941, Fayette, AL; son of Elvertis and Corine Henry; married Mary A Law; children: James jr, Coretta & Jason. **Educ:** Ala State Univ, BS, 1962; State Univ NY, MLS, 1970; Union Inst Cincinnati, OH, PhD. **Career:** St Judes Educ Inst, teacher, librn, 1962-66; Gary Pub Libr, 1966-68; AL A&M Univ, from asst libr to libr, 1968-69; Pub Focus, libr, 1968; Libr Jour, 1969; Rochester Pub Libr, dir, Phillis Wheatley libr, 1969-88; Col & Res librn, 1979; Wilson Libr Bull, 1971; Youth Adv Comn, Rochester Urban League, lectr & speaker probs librarianship; Progressive Church God Christ, pastor & founder, 1981; Church God Christ Inc, bishop, currently. **Orgs:** Bd dir, Mont Neighborhood Ctr; Black Res Info Ctr; Black-O-Media; chmn, Black Caucus Am Libr Asn, 1973-74. **Home Addr:** 896 Friar Tuck Lane, Webster, NY 14580-2561, **Home Phone:** (585)671-8344. **Business Addr:** Bishop, Church of God in Christ Incorporation, 384 Chili Ave, Rochester, NY 14611, **Business Phone:** (585)355-2823.

**WRIGHT, JEANNE JASON (JEANNE JASON)**
Editor. **Personal:** Born Jun 24, 1934, Washington, DC; daughter of Robert S Sr (deceased) and Elizabeth Gaddis; married Benjamin Hickman; children: Benjamin Jr (deceased), Deborah, David & Patricia. **Educ:** Radcliffe Col, BA, 1956; Univ Chicago, MA, 1958. **Career:** Editor (retired); Psychiat social worker, var ment health facil, Psychiat & Psychosom Inst, Michael Reese Hosp, Chicago, Jewish Child Care Asn, New York, 1958-70; Black Media Inc, gen mgr, 1970-74, pres, 1974-75; Black Resources Inc, pres, dir, 1975-98; Nat Black Monitor, exec ed, Syndicator weekly ed features Black Resources, pres, exec ed, 1975-99, publ, 1977-99. **Orgs:** Nat Asn Media Women; Newswomans Club; Nat Asn Social Workers; Alpha Kappa Alpha Sorority; Gamma Zeta Omega Chap; Harvard Club; Am Asn Advan Sci. **Home Addr:** 18255 NW 68th Ave Apt 307, Hialeah, FL 33015.

**WRIGHT, REV. JEFFERSON W.**
Clergy, college teacher. **Personal:** Born Jul 24, 1935, Bluefield, WV. **Educ:** Marshall Univ, AB, 1959; Boston Univ Sch Theol, STB, 1963; Boston Univ Sch Theol, MDiv, 1973; Va State Col; WVa Univ Law Sch; WVa Univ; Southern Calif. **Career:** Hebrew C Home, youth counr, 1959; Calvary Baptist Church, stud pastor, 1959-60; Los Angeles Pub Sch Syst, sch teacher, 1960-61; Tremont State Church, asst stud minister, 1961; Sheldon State Church, pastor, 1961-64; Second Baptist Church, Harrisburg, pastor, 1964-; Pa State Univ, fac, 1969-73. **Orgs:** Co-founder, OIC Harrisburg; Nat Baptist Church, Am Baptist Conv; Harrisburg Uptown Neighbors Together; adv comt, Pa Dept Health & Welfare; Urban Strat Comt Coun Christ; Nat Bd Black Churchmen; founder, First Black Sr Citizens Organ Cent Pa; bd mem, Nat Asn Adv Colored People; moderator, WITF-TV prog, A Time to Act; Urban Coalition & Black Coalition Harrisburg; Mayors Cits; adv comt chmn, Sub comt Housing; bd dir, Family & C Serv; Tri-Co Planned Parenthood Asn; adv bd, Harrisburg Sch Dist. **Home Addr:** 2129 Boas St, Harrisburg, PA 17103-1610.

**WRIGHT, REV. DR. JEREMIAH A., JR.**
Educator, clergy, executive. **Personal:** Born Sep 22, 1941, Philadelphia, PA; son of Jeremiah Sr (deceased) and Mary Elizabeth Henderson; married Ramah Reed; children: Janet Marie Moore, Jeri Lynne, Nikol D, Nathan D & Jamila Nandi. **Educ:** Howard Univ, BA, 1968, MA, english, 1969; Univ Chicago Sch Divinity, MA, 1975; United Theol Sem, DMin, 1990. **Career:** Zion Church, interim pastor, 1968-69; Beth Eden Church, asst pastor, 1969-71; Am Asn Theol Schs, researcher, 1970-72; Rockefeller fel, 1970, 1972; Trinity United Church Christ, pastor to sr pastor, 1972-2008, pastor emer, 2008-, Ministers Training Prog, nat leader; Chicago Ctr Black Relig Studies, exec dir, 1974-75; Chicago Cluster Theol Schs, lectr, 1975-77; United Theol Sem, prof, 1991-97; Sem Consortium Pastoral Educ, adj prof; Howard Univ, teaching asst fel; Chicago Theol Sem, prof & bd trustees; Garrett-Evangel Theol Sem, prof. **Orgs:** Omega Psi Phi Frat, 1960-77; United Black Christians, 1972-; Black Clergy Caucus United Church Christ, 1972-; bd dir, Centers New Horizons, 1976-; Doric Lodge 77 F & AM, 1976-; Western Consistory 28, 1983-; bd dir, Malcolm X Col, Sch Nursing; bd dir, Off Church Soc; comnr, Comn Racial Justice; Ill Conf Churches; Urban League Ministerial Alliance; Ecumenical Strategy Comm; Ill Conf United Church Christ; Great Lakes Regional Task Force Churches Transitional Comn; Alpha Kappa Mu Hon Soc; bd trustee, Va Union Univ; bd trustee, City Cols Chicago; bd dir, Evangel Health Systs; bd dir, Ctr New Horizons, Black Theol Proj; bd dir, Malcolm X Sch Nursing. **Honors/Awds:** Three Presidential Commendations, LB Johnson, 1965-66; First Carver Medal, Simpson Col, 2008; Honorary doctorate: Northwestern Univ, 2008; Colgate Univ; Lincoln Univ, PA; Valparaiso Univ; United Theol Sem; Chicago Theol Sem; Starr King Sch Ministry. **Special Achievements:** Publications: "God Will Answer Prayer", "Jesus is His Name"; article publ: "Urban Black Church Renewal", Helen Ujvarosy Chicago Covenant Press, 1984. Book: "A Sankofa Moment: The History of Trinity United Church of Christ", 2010. Published numerous articles, books & academic journals based on sermons which is used in seminaries. **Home Addr:** 9167 S Pleasant Ave, Chicago, IL 60620-5512, **Home Phone:** (773)962-5691. **Business Addr:** Pastor Emeritus, Trinity United Church of Christ, 400 W 95th St, Chicago, IL 60628, **Business Phone:** (773)962-5650.

**WRIGHT, DR. JOHN AARON**
Educator, executive director, photographer. **Personal:** Born May 22, 1939, St. Louis, MO; married Sylvia Henley; children: John Jr, David & Curtis. **Educ:** Harris Teachers Col, BA, 1962; St Louis Univ, MEd, 1968, PhD, 1978; Atlanta Univ; Mo Univ; Teachers Col Columbia Univ. **Career:** Educator (retired); John Griscom Sch, prin, 1965-70; Steger Jr High Sch, asst prin, 1970-73; Kinloch Sch Dist, supt, 1973-75; Ferguson-Florissant Sch Dist, supt, 1975-; St Louis Citizens Educ Task Force, exec dir, 1977-79; Normandy Sch Dist, Interim Supt; trainee, US Dept Justice, Community Rels Div. **Orgs:** Sal Army del Int Corps Cadet Conf London, 1956; pres, Univ City Sch Bd, 1976; bd trustee & elected mem, St Louis Community Col, 1994-2002; Phi Delta Kappa; Anniversary Club; Grace Meth Church; co-chair, St Louis CtrInt Rels; chmn, St Louis, Mo, Senegal Sister Cities Comn; vice chmn, chmn, bd dir, Mo Humanities Coun, 1998-2000; chmn, Gov's Voc Educ Adv Coun. **Honors/Awds:** Man of the Year, Omega Psi Phi Fraternity, 1959, 1967; Danforth Leadership Fel, 1977; Fulbright Scholar, India, 1982; Service to Education Award, Harris-Stone State Col; St Louis Book Award; Julia Davis Award. **Special Achievements:** Author: Discovering African-American St Louis: A Guide to Historic Sites, Missouri Historical Society Press, 1994; Kinloch, Mo, 2000; The Ville of St Louis, 2001; University City, 2002, St. Louis, Disappearing Black Communities, 2005; Extraordinary Black Missourians, Pioneers, Leaders, Performers, Athletes, 2013. **Home Addr:** 5290 Waterman Blvd, Saint Louis, MO 63108-1160, **Home Phone:** (314)726-5612. **Business Addr:** Board of Director, Missouri Humanities Council, 543 Hanley Industrial Ct Suite 201, St. Louis, MO 63144-1905, **Business Phone:** (314)781-9660.

**WRIGHT, JOSEPH (JOBY WRIGHT)**
Basketball player, basketball coach. **Personal:** Born Sep 5, 1950, Savannah, GA; married Cathy; children: Shay, Jenay, Cara, Joby III & Jesse. **Educ:** Ind Univ, BS, phys educ, 1972. **Career:** Basketball player (retired), basketball coach; Seattle Supersonics, 1972-73; Memphis Tams, 1973-74; Berck, 1974-75; San Diego Sails, 1975; Va Squires, 1976; Turun NMKY, 1977-78; Ind Univ, asst basketball coach, 1980-90; Miami Univ, head basketball coach, 1990-93; Univ Wyo, head basketball coach, 1993; Cincinnati Stuff, coach; Harlem Globetrotters, coach, 2000; Ind Univ, coach, currently. **Orgs:** Select team comt, USA Basketball, 1993-96. **Business Addr:** Coach, Indiana University, 107 S Ind Ave, Bloomington, IN 47405, **Business Phone:** (812)855-3089.

**WRIGHT, DR. JOSEPH L.**
Pediatrician, educator. **Educ:** Wesleyan Univ, BA, biol psychol, 1979; NJ Med Sch, MD, med, 1983; George Washington Univ, Sch Pub Health, MPH, adminr med & mgt, 1993; FAAP. **Career:** Child Health Advocacy Inst, exec dir, sr vpres; State EMS Med Dir Pediat; C's Res Inst, prin investr; Pediat Child Advocacy, vice chair; C's Nat Med Ctr, Emergency Med & Prev & Community Health, fac, 1993-, assoc prof

pediat, currently, Ctr Prehospital Pediat, med dir & founder, currently, minority recruitment officer, currently; George Wash Univ Sch Med, assoc prof pediat; Md Inst Emergency Med Serv Syst, State med dir; Howard Univ Col Med, prof & chmn pediat, currently. **Orgs:** Chair, Am Acad Pediat Comt Injury, Violence & Poison Prev; Delta Omega; adv bd, Inst Med; adv bd, Nat Asn Cs Hosps & Related Insts; adv bd, Am Acad Pediat; found dir, Inst Prehospital Pediat & Emergency Res; Pediat Adv Comt Food & Drug Admin; Prince Georges Hosp Authority; bd trustee, Nat Cs Mus; Pub Policy Adv Coun; March Dimes; Consumer Health Found Bd; programming adv, Sesame St Workshop; Am Hosp Asns Maternal & Child Health Coun. **Home Addr:** 111 Mich Ave NW, Washington, DC 20010, **Home Phone:** (202)884-5000. **Business Addr:** Medical Director, Childrens National Medical Center, 111 Mich Ave NW, Washington, DC 20010-2970, **Business Phone:** (202)476-5000.

### WRIGHT, DR. JOSEPH MALCOLM
School administrator, government official, attorney general (U.S. federal government). **Personal:** Born Sep 27, 1944, Toomsboro, GA; son of Ed and May O Dixon; married Sheilah Delores Broome; children: Joseph Oliver, Tiffany Michele & Jennifer Nicole. **Educ:** Eastern Mich Univ, BS, 1969; Wayne State Univ, JD, 1974; Harvard Univ, educ mgt dipl, 1983; Columbia State Univ, PhD, 1997. **Career:** GM-Buick, stat control asst, 1965-67; GM-Chev, sr acct, 1967-69; Univ Mich, suprv payroll, 1969-70, Col Arts Sci & Lett, admin mgr, 1970-72, dean stud affairs, 1973-88, chmn minority affaris, 1975-77; Detroit Col Bus, adj prof, 1975-77; United Motors Corp, pres, 1983-88; 36th Dist Ct, assoc judicial atty & chief dep ct adminr, 1988-; Wayne State Univ, adj prof, 1996; pvt pract, atty, currently. **Orgs:** Bd dir, Washtenaw Co Black Contr & Tradesmen Asn, 1967-72; citizen rep, Oak Pk Urban Renewal Coun, 1969-74; pres, JM Wright & Asn Detroit, 1972-; pres, dir, Asn Urban Legal Ed, 1973-76; bd, Barrino Entertainment Corp, 1973-79; adj prof, Wayne Cty Comt Col, 1975-; bd, Metamorphosis Inc NY, 1975-79; New Detroit Inc MNY Bus Devel Comt, 1978-80; Am Arbit Asn, 1979-; bd dir, Pink Ltd Allen Pk Mich, 1979-85; Am Bar Asn, NBA; Wolverine Bar Asn; bd, Inner-City Bus Improv, Southeastern Mich Bus Devel Ctr; NCP; bd, Western Wayne & Oakland County Comt Housing Resource Bd, Fair Housing Ctr Detroit, 1985-88; bd, E-W Airlines Inc, 1990-; bd, Worldwide Entertainment Ltd, 1991-; partner, Pontchartrain Hotel Group LLC; bd dir, Cent City Investment Corp; Fla Bar Asn; Nat Asn Stud Personnel Adminr. **Home Addr:** PO Box 760193, Lathrup Village, MI 48076. **Business Addr:** Chief Deputy Court Administrator, 36th District Court, 421 Madison Ave Suite 5028, Detroit, MI 48226, **Business Phone:** (313)965-2200.

### WRIGHT, JOYCE C.
Librarian, educator. **Personal:** Born Dec 17, 1951, Charleston, SC; daughter of Rhunette G Crawford. **Educ:** Voorhees Col, Denmark, SC, BA, hist, 1973; Univ Mich, Ann Arbor, MI, AMLS, libr sci, 1974; Univ Ill, Urbana-Champaign, CAS, 1986. **Career:** Trident Tech Col, Charleston, SC, ref/doc librn, 1974-76; Hampton Pub Libr, Hampton, VA, outreach librn, 1976-78; Memphis Pub Libr, Memphis, TN, head ref, 1978-80; Voorhees Col, Denmark, SC, admin librn, 1980-85; Univ Ill, Urbana, IL, head undergrad libr, assoc prof & libr admin, 1985-. **Orgs:** Exec comt, Ill Asn Col & Res Libr, 1992-95, exec bd, 1993-95; Ref & User Serv Div Louis Shores-Oryx Press Award Comt, 1995-97; bd dir, Libr Admin Mgt Sect, 1995-97; chair, Ref & User Serv Div Mem Comt, 1997-99; Am Libr Asn; Ill Libr Asn; Asn Col & Res Libr; Am Asn Univ profs; Am Asn Univ Women; AKA Sorority; Libr Admin Mgt Sect; Staff Orgn Round table; Black Caucus Am Libr Asn; Am Cancer Soc; Midwest Fedn Libr Asn; Sem Acquisition Latin Am Libr Mat; Undergrad Librarians Discussion Group. **Honors/Awds:** Undergraduate Instructional Award, Univ Ill, Urbana, 1987. **Home Addr:** 4112 Amherst Dr, Champaign, IL 61822, **Home Phone:** (217)359-2748. **Business Addr:** Head, Associate Professor, University of Illinois, 1408 W Gregory MC 522, Urbana, IL 61801, **Business Phone:** (217)333-3489.

### WRIGHT, DR. KATIE HARPER
Historian, educator, journalist. **Personal:** Born Oct 5, 1923, Crawfordsville, AR; daughter of James Hale Harper and Connie Mary Locke Washington; married Marvin; children: Virginia Jordan. **Educ:** Univ Ill, AB, 1944, MEd, 1959; St Louis Univ, EdD, 1979. **Career:** E St Louis Pub Schs, elem teacher, 1944-57, spec educ teacher, 1957-65, media dir, 1966-71, spec educ dir, 1971-78, asst supt spec progs, 1977-79; St Louis Argus Newspaper, columnist, 1979, 1984-85, 1986-, writer; Harris-Stowe State Col, assoc prof, 1980-99, adj prof emer; St Louis Univ, learning specialist, 1989-, dir spec educ, learning specialist; TLOD Crown Jour, nat ed, 1991-95, nat second vpres, 1996-; E St. Louis Sch Dist, interim supt, 1993-94; Harris-Stowe State Col, prof emer, 1999; Daniels State Rep, campaign mgr; Dayton Daily News, gen assignment reporter, contribr; Times-Gazette, city ed, columnist, reporter, sports stringer. **Orgs:** DST Sorority, 1949-; bd mem, United Way; past pres, E St Louis Libr Bd, 1964-81; past pres, Delta Pi Hon Soc, 1968-; pres bd dirs, St. Clair County Ment Health Ctr, 1970-72; pres bd trustees, E St. Louis Pub Libr, 1972-77; vice chmn, Ill Comn C, 1973-85; MENSA, proctor, 1973-; pres, Phi Delta Kappa, 1976-; past pres, Pi Lambda Theta Hon Soc, 1978-; secy, E St Louis Election Bd, 1978-88; nat bd dir, 1981-84, vice chmn, 1979-, River Bluffs Girl Scout Coun; assoc dir, Magna Bank Edgemont, 1981-; Girl Scout Nat Bd, 1981-84; fel Study Peoples Rep China, 1983; bd mem, Ment Health; bd mem, Urban League; charter mem, Gateway Chap Links Inc, 1987-; pres, St Clair County Ment Health Bd, 1987-; bd dir, Jackie Joyner-Kersee Youth Ctr Found, 1991-; Ill Minority/Female Bus Coun, 1991-; regional vpres, 1978-79, nat secy, 1979-80, 1992, Am Libr Trustees Asn; exec comt, Urban League & United Way St Louis; organizer, Am Inst Parliamentarians, E St Louis Chap, 1992-; Ill Dept Corrections Sch Bd, 1995-; Educ Deleg S Africa, 1996; E St Louis Financial Adv Auth, 1999-; Pres's Comn Excellence Spec Educ, 2001-; St Louis Delta Sigma Theta Sorority; St Louis Nat Asn Advan Colored People Presidents Comn Excellence Spl Educ; E St Louis Bd Elections; bd mem, exec adv bd, Southern Ill Univ Edwardsville, Sch Educ, Health & Human Behav, 2009-. **Honors/Awds:** Woman of Achievement, St Louis Globe Dem Newspaper, 1974; Girl Scout Thanks Badge, River Bluffs Girl Scout Coun, 1982; Woman of Achievement, St Louis Globe Dem Newspaper, 1974; Girl Scout Thanks Badge, River Bluffs Girl Scout Coun, 1982; Outstanding YWCA Alumnae, UnivIll, 1984; Woman of the Year, St Clair County YWCA, 1987; Top Ladies of Distinction Inc, Nat Br, Nat Top Lady Distinction, 1988-; Vaskon High School Hall of Fame, Vashon High Sch-St Louis, 1989; World of Difference Award, World Difference Orgn, 1990; Phenomenal Woman Award, Spelman Col Alumni-St Louis, 1990; Leadership Award, 1991; Kimmel Award, 1991; St Cr County Ment Health Ctr Award, 1992; Media Award, 1992; ESL Business & Professional Women's Award, 1992; Distinguished Alumnus, Univ Ill, 1996; Ill Sr Hall of Fame, 1997; Ill Women Adminr Award, 1998; Urban League Award, 2002; Ill State Bd Educ Award, 2002; more than 100 other awards, Pelman Col Alumni-St Louis, 1990; Leadership Award, 1991; Kimmel Award, 1991; St CrCounty Ment Health Ctr Award, 1992; Media Award, 1992; ESL Business & Professional Women's Award, 1992; Distinguished Alumnus, Univ Ill, 1996; Ill Sr Hall of Fame, 1997; Ill Women Adminr Award, 1998; Urban League Award, 2002; Ill State Bd Educ Award, 2002, more than 100 other awards; listed, Who's Who in America; listed, Who's Who of American Women; listed, Who's Who Among America's Teachers; listed, Who's Who in Education; listed, Who's Who Among Black Americans; National Black Women Leadership Award; Lifetime Achievement Award. **Home Addr:** 733 N 40th St, East St. Louis, IL 62205-2138, **Home Phone:** (618)271-5174. **Business Addr:** Columnist, The St Louis Argus Newspaper, 4595 Dr Martin Luther King Dr, St. Louis, MO 63113, **Business Phone:** (314)531-1323.

### WRIGHT, KEITH DEREK, SR.
Computer scientist, executive. **Personal:** Born Jun 2, 1953, Orange, NJ; son of Lola Hunt and Clarence Samuel Williams; children: Keisha, Keith & Khalid. **Educ:** Rutgers Univ, BA, 1979, MLA; Univ Md, MA, gen admin; Harvard Bus Sch, exec prog mgt develop. **Career:** Customer tech serv, vpres; MORNETPlus Customer Care, customer care; MORNETPlus Tech Serv, vpres; Nabisco Brands Inc, comput shift supvr; Hoffman-La Roche Inc, sr comput ctr supvr; Port Authority NY & NJ, asst mgr comput oper; Fannie Mae Corp, dir comput oper, Regional Mgt & Housing Partnerships, vpres, 1992-2005; CitiBank, vice pres & dir community rels, 2005-07; Cong Black Caucus Found Inc, exec vpres, chief operating officer, 2007-14; Realtor at Keller Williams, realtor, 2014-. **Orgs:** Chairperson, Black Data Processing Assoc Newsletter, 1983-85; pres, Black Data Processing Assoc, 1984-86; chmn, Parking Authority E Orange, 1984-; counr, YMCA Linkage Prog, 1985; bd dir, Econ Develop E Orange, 1986-; chairperson, Pub Rels Black Data Processing Assoc, 1987; chmn, E Orange Econ Develop, 1988-; dir, Tri-City Citizens Progress, 1988-. **Home Addr:** PO Box 773, East Orange, NJ 07019, **Home Phone:** (201)675-4016. **Business Addr:** Executive Vice President, Congressional Black Caucus Foundation Inc, 1720 Mass Ave NW, Washington, DC 20036, **Business Phone:** (202)263-2801.

### WRIGHT, KENNY D., II (KENNETH DEWAYNE WRIGHT)
Football player. **Personal:** Born Sep 14, 1977, Ruston, LA; children: DyQuon Roberts. **Educ:** Northwestern State Univ, LA, BS, physical educ. **Career:** Minn Vikings, defensive back, cornerback, left cornerback, right cornerback, 1999, corner back, left cornerback, 2000, left cornerback, right cornerback, 2001; Houston Texans, 2002, 2004, left cornerback, right cornerback, 2003; Jacksonville Jaguars, right cornerback, 2005; Wash Redskins, left cornerback, right cornerback, 2006; Cleveland Browns, defensive back, 2007-08; free agt, currently.

### WRIGHT, DR. LARRY L.
Educator. **Personal:** Born Jun 20, 1954, FL; son of Dennis and Gertrude Robinson. **Educ:** Chipola Jr Col, Marianna, FL, AA, 1974; Fla State Univ, Tallahassee, FL, BS, 1976, MS, 1978, PhD, 1980. **Career:** Fla House Representatives, Tallahassee, Fla, res asst, 1976; Fla State Univ, Tallahassee, Fla, res asst, 1977-78, teaching asst, 1978-80; Ctr Pub Affairs & Govt Serv, Tallahasse, Fla, consul, 1982-84; Fla A&M Univ, Tallahassee, Fla, assoc prof, poli sci & pub admin, 1988-; Andrew W Mellonfel, 1996. **Orgs:** Fla Polit Sci Asn; Am Soc Pub Admin; Ga Polit Sci Asn; Southern Polit SciAsn; Asn Social & Behav; Pi Sigma Alpha; Nat Asn Advan Colored People; Scholarly Publ Comt; Univ Fac Senate. **Home Addr:** PO Box 6856, Tallahassee, FL 32314, **Home Phone:** (850)386-5242. **Business Addr:** Associate Professor of Political Science, Public Administration, Florida A&M University, 326 Tucker Hall, Tallahassee, FL 32307, **Business Phone:** (850)576-2067.

### WRIGHT, LINNEL N.
School administrator. **Career:** Executive (retired); Camden City Pub Schs, actg asst supt, Dept Prof Develop, dir, asst supt support serv. **Orgs:** Vice chair, Inst Dev Educ Arts. **Business Addr:** Director, Assistant Superintendent, Camden City Public Schools, 201 N Front St, Camden, NJ 08102, **Business Phone:** (856)966-2000.

### WRIGHT, LINWOOD CLINTON
Scientist, manager, aeronautical engineer. **Personal:** Born Mar 24, 1919, Augusta, GA; son of Leon and Maria; married Ernestine Louise McIver; children: Linda Wright Moore & Linwood Jr. **Educ:** Wayne State Univ, BS, aero engr, 1944; Univ Cincinnati, MS, aero engr, 1960. **Career:** Aeronautical engineer (retired); Nat Adv Comt Aeronaut, aeronaut res scientist, 1943-56; Gen Elec Aircraft Engine Bus Gr, mgr adv compressorres, 1956-66, mgr, adv tech mktg, 1974-83; Garrett Ai Res Mfg Co, LA, chief aerodynamics, 1966-72; Putnam Financial, part-time security salesman, 1971-72; Pratt & Whitney Aircraft Co, asst gas turbine mgr, 1972-74; NASA, actg dir propulsion, power & energy, 1983-85; Ai Res Mfg Co, chief aerodynamics. **Orgs:** Am Inst Aeronaut & Astronaut, 1941-; Tech Mktg Soc Am, 1975; chappres, Sigma Pi Phi Prof Fraternity, Cincinnati, 1978-; Mayor's Task Force Zoning, Forest Pk, OH, 1986; Econ Devel Comn, Forest Pk, OH, 1986-. **Honors/Awds:** Distinguished Alumni Award, Wayne State Univ, 1958; Guest Lecturer, Univ Tenn, Space Inst, 1974; Distinguished Alumni Award, Univ Cincinnati, 1984. **Special Achievements:** Author/Co-Author, 21 published technical papers, 1946-72; Co-author: Investigation of an Experimental Supersonic Axial-Flow Compressor, 1947. **Home Addr:** 303 Ironwood Cir, Elkins Park, PA 19027-1336, **Home Phone:** (215)481-0146.

### WRIGHT, LOUIS DONNEL
Executive, football player, football coach. **Personal:** Born Jan 31, 1953, Gilmer, TX; son of Glover and Verbena; married Vicki; children: Summer Marie, Kyla Lynn & Evan Louis. **Educ:** San Jose State Univ, bus mgt. **Career:** Football player (retired), exec, football coach; Denver Broncos, corner back, left corner back, 1975-86; L Wright Enterprises, sec & treas, 1990; Rangeview High Sch, asst coach, currently; Mrachek Mid Sch, phys educ teacher, currently; GateWay High Sch, teacher & asst football coach, currently. **Orgs:** Conf Champ Track Team, 1973-74. **Honors/Awds:** Col All-Star Game, 1975; East-West Shrine Game, 1975; All-Coast Football Selection, 1975; Football Digest NFL Defensive Back of the Year, 1977; Pro Bowl, 1977-79, 1983 & 1985; NEA All-Pro Team; Denver Broncos Team, capt, 1985-86; Named All NFL by Sporting News and Pro Football Weekly; NFL Pro Football Team, 1986; Denver Broncos Ring of Fame, 1993. **Home Addr:** 11197 E Ky Ave, Aurora, CO 80012-3127. **Business Addr:** Physical Education Teacher, Mrachek Middle School, 1300 S Sable Blvd, Aurora, CO 80012, **Business Phone:** (303)755-7160.

### WRIGHT, LOYCE PIERCE
Government official, executive director. **Personal:** Born Dec 24, 1943, New Orleans, LA; daughter of Frank Pierce and Victoria Martin Pierce; married Louis Clifton Jr; children: Kiana Tamika. **Educ:** Southern Univ, Baton Rouge, LA, BS, 1965; Univ New Orleans, LA, MEd, 1976. **Career:** Orleans Parish Sch Bd, New Orleans, La, fr/span teacher, 1965-76; New Orleans Sickle Cell Anemia Found, assoc dir, 1976-81; Communirep Inc, New Orleans, La, mgt consult, 1980-86; Mayor's Off, City New Orleans, La, dir, 1986-92; Excelth Inc, dir human resources, 1992-97; Southern Univ New Orleans, asst vice chancellor acad affairs, 1997-99; Gov's Off, La Comn Human Rights, exec dir, 1999-. **Orgs:** Pres/founding mem, New Orleans Sickle Cell Anemia Found, 1972-76; campaign coordr state, local & presidential candidates, 1981-88; consult & mkt dir, Educ Jour SENGA; coordr, Martin Luther King Jr Fed Holiday Comn, New Orleans, LA, 1987-; vpres, bd dir, Ment Health Asn, New Orleans, LA, 1988; nominating comn, YWCA-USA, 1988-91; pres, bd dir, YWCA New Orleans, 1989-; planning comn, Agency Rels Comt; Admis/Growth Comt; United Way New Orleans, 1989-; Delta Sigma Theta Sorority Inc, New Orleans Alumnae Chap; founder, Phenomenal Women; bd dir, YWCA USA, 1992-. **Honors/Awds:** Award for outstanding service, Gov La, 1986; Second Mile Award, Nat Asn Neighborhoods, 1987; Certificate of Merit, Mayor New Orleans, 1988; Role Model Award, YWCA New Orleans, 1989. **Home Addr:** 4290 Cabretta Dr SE, Smyrna, GA 30080-6479, **Home Phone:** (504)245-6222. **Business Addr:** Executive Director, Louisiana Commission of Human Rights, 1001 N 23rd St Suite 262, Baton Rouge, LA 70802, **Business Phone:** (225)342-6969.

### WRIGHT, MARILYN N.
Entrepreneur, business owner. **Personal:** Born May 25, 1965, Philadelphia, PA; daughter of Willie and Rachel Bond; married Thomas; children: Marcello & Bianca. **Educ:** Elizabeth City State Univ, BA, 1987. **Career:** Allstate Ins Co, sr staff claims rep, 1987-99; Marilyn's Fashions Inc, owner, chief exec officer & founder, 1994-. **Orgs:** New Castle County Chamber Com, 1999-; Wilmington Women Bus, 2000; Asn Image Consults Int; Nat Asn Female Execs. **Business Addr:** Chief Executive Officer, Owner, Marilyn's Fashions Inc, 4 Moonlight Ct, Newark, DE 19702, **Business Phone:** (302)366-0812.

### WRIGHT, MARK ADRIAN
Executive, sales manager. **Personal:** Born Jan 29, 1957, Philadelphia, PA; son of Richard and Vera Lennon; married Sheela; children: Kyle & Adrian. **Educ:** Drexel Univ, BSME, mech engineering, 1979; Wash Univ, MBA, 1990. **Career:** Monsanto, sales rep, 1979-83, ford motor develop mgr, 1983-86, world wide mkt mgr, 1986-87, regional sales mgr, 1987-90; Advan Elastomer Systs, auto mkt mgr Europe, 1990-93, sales mgr, Ger, 1993-94, dir n am automotive sales, 1994-. **Orgs:** Soc Automotive Engrs, 1983-; bd dir, Soc Plastic Engrs, 1994-95. **Special Achievements:** Lang Skills, French & German; Published in numerous plastic & Eng books; Presentations to SPE, SAE & Trade Groups. **Business Addr:** Director of Automotive, Advanced Elastomer Systems LP, 388 S Main St, Akron, OH 44331, **Business Phone:** (330)849-5000.

### WRIGHT, DR. MELVIN, SR.
Dentist. **Personal:** married Georgia Ann Robinson; children: Melinda & Melvin Jr. **Educ:** Tenn State Univ, BS, 1958; Meharry Med Col, DDS, 1965. **Career:** AUS, dent asst, 1961; US Dent Corps, officer; Jackson Madison Co Hosp, staff mem; Regional Hosp Jackson, Tenn, staff mem; pvt pract dentist, 2005-; Dr. Melvin Wright Sr Gen Family Dent, owner, currently. **Orgs:** Pres, Pan-Tenn Dent Asn, 1977; Tenn Supreme Ct Comn; bd regents, Union Univ; secy, Tenn Dent Asn Found; Am Soc Agron; life mem, Alpha Phi Alpha Fraternity; Meharry Nat Alumni Asn; life mem, Am Dent Asn; pres, Jackson Dent Study Club; Seventh Dist Dent Soc; Nat Dent Asn; vpres, Nat Dent Asn Found; Tenn Univ Alumni Asn; chmn, United Way Campaign; exec comt, Nat Asn Advan Colored People; founding mem, 100 Black Men W Tenn; past pres, Jackson Symphony Asn; past pres, Jackson Rotary Club; trustee, Lane Col; St Paul CME Church. **Honors/Awds:** Meritorious Award, Lane Col; Mason of the Year; Distinguished Fellowship Service Award, Tenn Dent Asn; Distinguished Service Award, Tenn State Gov; Outstanding Service Award, Tenn State Univ; Outstanding Service Award, Jackson Area Chamber Com; Henomenal Achievement & Leadership Award, Nat Dent Asn. **Special Achievements:** First African-American Chairman of the Jackson-Madison County Chamber of Commerce. **Home Addr:** 72 Regency Dr, Jackson, TN 38301, **Home Phone:** (731)424-4862. **Business Addr:** Dentist, Owner, Dr Melvin Wright Sr General Family Dentistry, 340 N Hays Ave, Jackson, TN 38302, **Business Phone:** (731)424-4351.

### WRIGHT, MICHAEL
Actor. **Personal:** Born Apr 30, 1956, New York, NY; son of Alberta; married Mitzie Lau; children: 1. **Educ:** Lee Strasberg Theater. **Career:** Films: The Wanderers, 1979; Streamers, 1983; Bedtime Eyes, 1987; The Principal, 1987; The Five Heartbeats, 1991; Confessions of a Hitman, 1994; Sugar Hill, 1994; Confessions of a Hitman, 1994; The Cottonwood, 1996; Money Talks, 1997; Point Blank, 1998; Rage,

1999; Pinero, 2001; Downtown: A Street Tale, 2002, 2004; Light & the Sufferer, 2004; Coalition, 2004; The Interpreter, 2005; Blood on the Wall, 2005; El Cantante, 2006; Raving, 2007; "Hard Rock", 2007; Diminished Capacity, 2008; "Before I self Destruct", 2009; The Gift, 2010; Passages from Miles, actor & producer, 2011; Jesse, 2011; Beto! The Bad Boy of Thompson Street, 2011; D'Curse, 2013; Good Brutha Bad Brutha, 2013. TV movies: "We're Fighting Back", 1981; "Dream House", 1981; "Benny's Place", 1982; " V", 1983; "V: The Final Battle", 1984; "V", 1984-85; "The Laundromat", 1985; "Miami Vice", 1987; "Private Times", 1991; "Shake, Rattle & Roll: An American Love Story", 1999; "New York Undercover", 1996; "Oz", 2001-03; Video Game: Batman, 2003. **Honors/Awds:** Volpi Cup Award for Best Actor, 1983. **Home Addr:** 594 9th Ave Suite 3, New York, NY 10036. **Business Addr:** Actor, c/o Access Talent, 37 E 28th St Suite 500, New York, NY 10016, **Business Phone:** (212)331-9595.

### WRIGHT, MICHAEL A.

Public utility executive, vice president (organization). **Educ:** NC State Univ, Raleigh, NC, BS, indust engineering, 1984; Columbia Univ, MBA, finance, 1996. **Career:** Kraft Foods, area human resources dir, 1984-97; PM USA, dir human resources, 1997-2002; Altria Corp Serv Inc, vpres human resources & technol, 2002-09; Wright Group Inc, pres & founder, 2008-09; Covanta Energy, sr vpres & chief human resources officer, 2009-. **Orgs:** Exec Leadership Coun; exec adv coun, Del State Univ, Sch Mgt. **Business Addr:** Covanta Holding Corporation, 445 South St, Morristown, NJ 07960, **Business Phone:** (862)345-5000.

### WRIGHT, MICHAEL L.

Lawyer, association executive, founder (originator). **Personal:** Born Jan 1, 1969. **Educ:** Univ Cincinnati, BS, mech engineering, JD. **Career:** Gen Motors Corp, mfg engr; Cincinnati Pub Defenders Off, intern; Mich Bar Intellectual Property Firm, Harness, Dicker & Pierce, intern; Lexis-Nexis Corp, res ref atty; Wright & Vannoy, LPA Inc, search case law, managing partner, sr partner, founder & atty, 2000-; Cochran Firm; Wright & Schulte LLC, host legal side; Wright Choice Homes Inc, bus owner, founder; Am Trial Lawyers Asn, atty. **Orgs:** Ohio State Bar Asn; Thurgood Marshall Law Soc; African Am Chamber Com; Am Trial Lawyer Asn; Dayton Bar Asn; search case law, bd trustee, chair, Ohio Asn Justice. **Honors/Awds:** Best Bachelor of the Year, EBONY, 2003. **Business Addr:** Attorney, Founder, Wright & VanNoy LPA Inc, 130 W 2nd St Suite 1600, Dayton, OH 45402, **Business Phone:** (937)222-7477.

### WRIGHT, HON. MILTON L., JR.

District court judge. **Personal:** Born Miami, FL; children: Kavayah. **Educ:** Princeton Univ, critical lang prog, 1965; Morehouse Col, BA, span lang & lit, 1966; Boston Univ Law Sch, JD, int law & legal studies, 1971. **Career:** Judge, singer, writer, music dir; Comm Ma, CPCS Roxbury Defenders, 1980-93; Boston Munic Ct, First Justice, 1998-2004; City Boston, Comnr Licensing Bd, 2011-; Music Dir: Roxbury Defenders, regional Supvr; Roxbury Dist Ct, first justice, 1999-; Theres A Meeting Here Tonight, Langston Hughes Black Nativity; singer: "The Gallop", "I Belong To You". **Orgs:** Lectr, Mass Continuing Legal Educ; bd dir, Nat Ctr Afro-Am Artists, currently. **Honors/Awds:** Judicial Excellence Award, Mass Judges Conf, 2004. **Business Addr:** Board of Director, National Center for Afro-American Artists, 300 Walnut Ave, Roxbury, MA 02119, **Business Phone:** (617)442-8614.

### WRIGHT, N'BUSHE (BRUKLIN HARRIS)

Actor, television actor. **Personal:** Born Sep 20, 1970, New York, NY; daughter of Suleiman-Marim; children: jazzman Stanely. **Educ:** Stella Adler's studio; Alvin Ailey Sch; Stella Adler Conserv; Martha Graham Sch Dance; Manhattan High Sch Performing Arts, New York, attended 1987. **Career:** Films: Zebrahead, 1992; Fresh, 1994; Dead Presidents, 1995; Johns, 1996; A Woman Like That, 1997; His & Hers, 1997; Squeeze, 1997; Blade, 1998; Three Strikes, 2000; Civil Brand, 2002; MVP, 2003; Joy Road, 2004; He Say She Say But What Does GOD Say?, 2004; God's Forgotten House, 2005; Restraining Order, 2006; A Talent for Trouble, 2011; TV Series: "I'll Fly Away", 1992-93; "Am Gothic", 1995; "New York Undercover", 1996; "Swift Justice", 1996; "Close to Danger", 1997; "Third Watch", 1999; "UC: Undercover", 2001; "Widows", 2002; "The Award Show Awards Show", 2003; "Platinum", 2003, "Chappelle's Show", 2004. **Honors/Awds:** Won the recurring role of Claudia. **Business Addr:** Actress, Innovative Arts, 1505 Tenth St, Santa Monica, CA 90401, **Business Phone:** (310)656-5172.

### WRIGHT, PANDIT F.

Vice president (organization), executive. **Educ:** Univ Conn, BA, 1974; New Sch, New York, Orgn Mgt. **Career:** Aetna Corp; Salomon Bros Inc, vpres employ, 1981-95; Discovery Networks Asia, interim gen mgr, Discovery Commun Inc, Human Resouce & Admin, vpres, sr exec vpres, 1995-2007. **Orgs:** Discovery Channel Global Educ Partnership; Walter Kaitz Found Diversity Coun; chmn, Silver Spring Town Ctr Inc; pres, Cable TV Human Resources Asn; bd mem, Women Cable & Telecommunications Found; past pres, Cable & Telecommunications Human Resources Asn; Bd Cinderella Found; founder, Saturday Spa; pres & chief exec officer, Boys & Girls Clubs Greater Wash, 2009-16. **Honors/Awds:** Named one of Top 50 Women in Cable, CableFax Mag; One of Cableworlds Most Influential Minorities in Cable; President's Award, Family & Child Serv DC; Honorary Commander for the Air Force, 2011; Chief Prof Officer Rookie Yr, Boys & Girls Clubs Am, 2010. **Special Achievements:** Named to Discovery's Exec Comm, 1999, responsible for Discovery's nationally recognized Life Works at Discovery initiative, headed to South Africa to tour the Soweto Learning Center a product of the Discovery Channel Global Educational Partnership, keynote speaker, WICT Forum, 2003. **Business Addr:** Senior Executive Vice President, Discovery Communications Inc, Fl 5 7700 Wis Ave, Bethesda, MD 20814, **Business Phone:** (301)986-1999.

### WRIGHT, RALPH EDWARD

Executive, broker. **Personal:** Born Dec 29, 1950, Newark, NJ; married Sallie Riggins Williams; children: Galen & Garnel. **Career:** New York Stock Exchange, reporter, 1969-77, broker; Carl H Pforzheimer & Co, clerk, stockbroker, 1977-89; JJC Specialist Corp, stockbroker, 1981-95; Doley sec, vpres, 1995-96; Christopher Frank Corp, two-dollar floor broker, 1999-2001; Drexel Burnham, stockbroker, 1989-90; W&P Securities Inc, chair, chief exec officer, 1996-; Exeter & Co, 1996-98; Stratatec LLC, exec dir, 1998-; AFC Partners, New York Stock Exchange Mkt, staff, 1998-99; Caria Group, exec vpres, 1999; Onyx Financial Serv, managing dir, 2004-05; King & Wright LLC, partner & exec vpres, 2005-; Bennett Yarger LLC, pres & chief exec officer, 2009-. **Orgs:** Bd mem, George Jr Republic; bd mem, Clearpool Camps; Borkers United Youth Scholar Fund; New York Sock Exchange. **Honors/Awds:** Plaque, Tau Gamma Delta Sorority, 1991; Community Leader of the Year, Wheelchair Charities of New York, 1995. **Special Achievements:** First African Specialist in New York Stock Exchange, 1981; appeared in TV program "Profiles in Accomplishment", 1984; Profiled in Col textbook, Introduction to Business, Chap 19, 1987; Appeared in Business in a Changing World, 1991; One of the main subjects in Pictorial Songs of My People, A Life Magazine Publication, p 34, Feb 1992; First African-American & American dealer at the Johannesburg Stock Exchange in South Africa, 1995. **Home Addr:** 470 Sandford Ave, Newark, NJ 07106. **Business Addr:** Partner, Executive Vice President, King and Wright LLC, 607 Westport Rd Suite 300, Kansas, MO 64111, **Business Phone:** (816)756-2111.

### WRIGHT, DR. RAYMOND LEROY, JR.

Dentist. **Personal:** Born May 7, 1950, Ft. Dix, NJ; children: Raymond III. **Educ:** Univ Ill, cert periodont, 1970; Univ Ill Col Dent, DDS, 1974. **Career:** Cert Periodont, 1974-76; Cermack Memorial Hosp, staff dentist, 1975-84; Chicago Bd Health, dentist, 1976-77; Dr Clarence Mc Nair, dentist periodontist, 1976-77; Dr Roger Berkley, dentist periodontist, 1977-80; McHarry Med Col, asst prof, 1978-83; Univ Ill Col Dentist, asst prof, 1977-85; pvt pract, 1980-; Pac Dent Serv, periodontist, 2012-; Western Dent, periodontist, 2014-; Smile Brands Inc, periodontist, 2014-. **Orgs:** Prog chmn, Lincoln Dent Soc, 1980-84, parliamentarian, 1984-85, treas, 1985-86, secy, 1986-87; scholar chmn, Nat Dent Asn, 1982; treas, Forum Evolution Progressive Arts; prog chmn, Kenwood Hyde Pk Br, Chicago Dent Soc, 1986-87. **Honors/Awds:** Nomination Outstanding Young Men of America, 1980; Service Award, Lincoln Dental Soc, 1982; Service Award, Nat Dent Soc, 1982. **Home Addr:** 4891 Xanthia St Apt 301, Denver, CO 80238-3611. **Business Addr:** Periodontist, Smile Brands Inc, 8105 Irvine Ctr Dr Suite 1500, Irvine, CA 92618, **Business Phone:** (714)668-1300.

### WRIGHT, DR. ROBERTA V. HUGHES

Lawyer, writer. **Personal:** Born Detroit, MI; daughter of Robert Greenidge; married Charles H (deceased); children: Barbara & Wilbur B. **Educ:** Univ Mich, PhD, behav sci educ, 1973; Wayne State Univ, JD, 1979, MEd. **Career:** Detroit Pub Sch, past sch social worker; Detroit Comn C & Youth, dir; Shaw Col, vpres acad affairs; County Pub Admin, practicing lawyer; Mich Ct, atty; DC & Supreme Ct, USA, pract atty; Lawrence, prof; First Independence Nat Bank, inst organizer & dir; Charro Bk Co Inc, vpres, currently; writer. **Orgs:** Am Bar Asn; Mich Bar Asn; past mem Am & Mich Trial Lawyers Asn; Oakland County Bar Asn; Detroit Bar Asn; Wayne State Univ Law Alumni; Univ Mich Alumni Asn; AKA Sorority; life mem, Nat Asn Advan Colored Peopl; Renaissance Club; million dollar mem, Mus African Am Hist. **Honors/Awds:** NAACP Freedom Award; Harriet Tubman Award; Alpha Kappa Alpha Sorority Recognition Award; Quality Quintet Award Detroit Skyliner Mag. **Special Achievements:** Author: LAY DOWN BODY : Living History in African American Cemeteries, Visible Ink, 1996; The Wright Man: A Biography, Charro Books, 1999. First Lady of the Charles H. Wright Museum of African American History. **Home Addr:** 25266 Larkins, Southfield, MI 48034. **Business Addr:** Vice President, Charro Book Co Inc, 29777 Tel Rd Suite 2500, Southfield, MI 48034.

### WRIGHT, ROOSEVELT RICK, JR.

Educator. **Personal:** Born Jul 24, 1943, Elizabeth City, NC; son of Roosevelt R Sr and Lillie Mae Garrett. **Educ:** Elizabeth City State Univ, BS, indust arts technol, 1964; NC Cent Univ, MA, educ media & com, 1969; Va State Univ, CGS, 1970; Syracuse Univ, PhD, instrnl technol & radio broadcasting, 1993. **Career:** Elizabeth City State Univ, assoc dir ed media, 1968-69; DC State Col Dover, dir ed media, 1969-70; WNDR Radio Syracuse, announcer radio engr, 1970-72; Nc Cent Univ, asst prof educ media radio & tv; Howard Univ, adj prof radio; Del State Univ, dir educ media; Elizabeth City State Univ, Av Ctr, assoc dir; Syracuse Univ, fel, 1970-72, prof, radio, tv & film/naval liaison officer, broadcast consult, 1975-; NC Cent Univ, asst prof ed media, 1972-73; WDNC-AM & FM Durham, NC, announcer radio engr, 1972-73; WTNJ Radio, Trenton, NJ, gen mgr, 1973-74; WLLE Radio Raleigh, NC, prog dir, 1973-74; Nat Broadcasting Co, Radio Div WRC & WKYS Wash, acct exec, 1974-75; Howard Univ Wash, DC, adj prof, radio & TV, 1974-75; SI Newhouse Sch Comm, assoc prof radio & TV, 1975-; WAER FM, fac mgr, 1975-80; WOLF Radio Syracuse, NY, chief engr, 1980-84; WJPZ-FM Syracuse, NY, chief exec officer; Clear Channel Radio Syracuse, broadcast consult, announcer, wphr-fm, 1995-. **Orgs:** Historian Chi Pi Chap Omega Psi Phi Frat, 1975-95; radio com mem, Nat Asn Educ Broadcasters, 1976-80; adv, Nat Acad TV Arts & Scis Syracuse Chap, 1976-80; US naval liaison Officer, Syracuse Univ, 1981-; pub affairs Officer, Nat naval Officers Asn, 1983-85; chmn, Communs Comt, Am Heart Asn, NY, 1985-87; steward AME Zion Church; pub affairs Officer, USN, Great Lakes Cruise, 1985-; commun comt, United Way Onondaga County, 1988-; bd mem, Hiawatha Coun Boy Scout Am, 1992-; Nat Asn Adv Colored People; Nat Coun Negro Women; Navy League Cent New York; Socs Broadcast Engrs; Socs Motion Picture & Tv Engrs; Nat Naval Officers Asn; Res Officers Asn Am; Nat Asn Col Broadcasters; Am Legion. **Home Addr:** 310 W Matson Ave, Syracuse, NY 13205, **Home Phone:** (315)492-4836. **Business Addr:** Professor, Syracuse University, 222 Waverly Ave, Syracuse, NY 13244, **Business Phone:** (315)443-5727.

### WRIGHT, RUSSELL T.

Chief executive officer. **Educ:** Morehouse Col, BA; Keller Grad Sch, MBA; George Washington Univ Sch Bus & Pub Mgt, masters cert govt contracting. **Career:** Dimensions Int Inc, chmn & chief exec officer, currently. **Orgs:** Northern Va Technol Coun; Fairfax Chamber Com; adv bd, George Mason Univ Diversity Adv Bd. **Business Addr:** Chairman, Chief Executive Officer, Dimensions International Inc, 2800 Eisenhower Ave Suite 300, Alexandria, VA 22314, **Business Phone:** (703)998-0098.

### WRIGHT, DR. SAMUEL LAMAR, SR.

School administrator. **Personal:** Born Jul 7, 1953, Boynton Beach, FL; son of Samuel Louis and Rovina Victoria Deal; children: Samuel Lamar Jr & Samaria Elizabeth. **Educ:** Univ Fla, BS, psychol, 1974, MEd, 1975; Fla Atlantic Univ, pub admin, 1981; Univ S Fla, DEd, 1999. **Career:** Palm Beach County Bd Co Comnrs & Action Com, emp & personnel mgr, 1975-76, dir, Delray BchTAC, 1976-77, adm asst & planner, 1977-79, asst dir, 1979-84, head startdir, 1984-85; Boynton Beach FL, city councilman, 1981-85; Univ S Fla, Minority Stud Orgn, adv, 1985-86, Multicult Admis, asst dir, 1987-2000, adj prof, assoc dean stud rels & interim coordr, 2000-, Comt Black Affairs, chmn, dir multicultural affairs, Africana Studies Dept, adj prof, stud ombudsman, 2008-13; Greater Tampa Urban League, Clerical & Word Processing Training Prog, ctr mgr, 1986-87; Dr Samuel L Wright Consult LLC, pres & chief exec officer, 2013-. **Orgs:** Kappa Alpha Psi Fraternity Inc, 1972-; Fla Asn Comm Action, 1975-85; Fla Agr & Mech Univ Alumni Asn PBC, 1979-85; Univ Fla Alumni Asn, 1979-; City Boynton Beach Black Awareness Comm, 1981-85; bd dir, Nat Black Caucus Local Elected Off, 1982-84; State Fla Comm Serv Block Grant Adv Comm, 1982-84; Fla Assoc Comm Rel Prof, 1982-84; bd dir, Southern County Drug Abuse Found, 1982-84; bd dir, Dem Black Caucus Fla, 1982-84; Boynton Beach Kiwanis Sunrisers, 1982-85; bd mem, Selective Serv Syst, 1983-85; vpres, Fla Black Caucus Local Elected Officials, 1983-85; vpres Comm Affairs Suncoast C of C, 1983-85; elected Dem Exec Comm Palm Beach, 1983-85; Gr Boynton Beach C C, 1983-85; Nat Asn Black Social Workers Inc, 1983-85; Fla Head Start Asn, 1984-85; chmn, Inter gov Rel Comm, 1984-85; chmn, Legmm Boynton & Ocean Ridge Bd Realtors, 1984-85; 100 Black Men Tampa Inc, 1988-89; ambassador, Ctr Excellence Inc, 1988-; Tampa Male Club, 1989-; Concerned Voters Coalition, 1991-; Revealing Truth Ministries; Hillsborough Alliance Black Sch Educrs, 1993-; Hillsborough Co C's Serv Adv Bd, 1993-; bd dir, Tampa Bay Conv & Visitors Bur, 1998-; Supt Sch Diversity Round table, 1999-; Tampa's Black Heritage Festival, 1999-; prog judge, Miss Am Scholar Pagent, 1999-; C's Bd Hills bor Co, comm rev team, 1999-; Afro-Am Men's HTH Forum, 2000-; exec comt, Nat Asn Advan Colored People; adv comt, Onyx Mag; sch bd, Village Excellence Acad; sch bd, Walton Acad Performing Arts; Fla Asn Multicultural Educ; Nat Asn Stud Personnel; speaker, The Bailey Group. **Honors/Awds:** Outstanding & Dedicated Service Award, Concerned Citizens Voter's League Boynton Beach, 1981; Citizen of the Year, Omega Psi Phi Frat, 1982; Outstanding Civic Leadership Award, West boro Bus & Prof Women's Club of the Palm Beaches, 1983; participant Leadership Palm Beach County, 1984-85; Pole march's Award, Kappa Alpha Psi Frat, 1988-90; Outstanding Service Award Religion, 1988; Outstanding Service Award for Academic Affairs, Univ S Fla, 1988; Martin Luther King Jr Award, Outstanding Leadership, 1989; Community Service Award, 1989; State of Florida Notary Public; Tampa-Hillsborough Urban League Milestone Award; hon membership, Florida Blue Key, Univ Fla. **Special Achievements:** First Black City Councilman in Boynton Beach, 1980. **Home Addr:** 3402 03 Pk Sq S, Tampa, FL 33613, **Home Phone:** (813)972-7707. **Business Addr:** President, Chief Executive Officer, Dr Samuel L Wright Consulting LLC, 3445 Pk Sq E Apt Suite 1, Tampa, FL 33613, **Business Phone:** (813)789-7714.

### WRIGHT, SHARONE ADDARYL

Basketball player, basketball coach. **Personal:** Born Jan 30, 1973, Macon, GA. **Educ:** Clemson Univ, attended 1994. **Career:** Basketball player (retired), basketball coach; Philadelphia 76ers, ctr forward, 1994-96; Toronto Raptors, ctr forward, 1996-98; Hong Kong Flying Dragons, China, 2002-03; Anwil Wloclawek, Poland, 2003-04; Forum Filatelico, Spain, 2004-05; Yakama Sun Kings, Continental Basketball Asn, 2005-06; Jeonju KCC Egis, S Korea, 2005-06; EiffelTowers, Hertogenbosch, 2006-08, asst coach, 2009-; Hoop Camps, coach. **Honors/Awds:** McDonald's All American, 1991; Gold Medal, Summer Universiade, 1993; NBA All-Rookie, 1995; Holland's best coach, 2007. **Special Achievements:** Film: Space Jam, 1996. **Business Addr:** Assistant Coach, EiffelTowers 's-Hertogenbosch.

### WRIGHT, SHEENA

Administrator, president (organization). **Personal:** Born Bronx, NY; daughter of Debra Fraser-Howze; married Gregg Walker; children: 3. **Educ:** Columbia Col, attended 1990; Columbia Law Sch, BA, law, 1994. **Career:** New York Times Wash Bur, ed asst; law firm Wachtell, Lipton, Rosen & Katz, assoc, 1994-99; law firm Reboul, Mac Murray, Hewitt, Maynard & Kristol, sr assoc, 1999-2000; Crave Technologies, gen counr & exec vpres bus develop; Abyssinian Develop Corp, chief operating officer, pres & chief exec officer, 2002-; United Way of New York City, pres & chief exec officer, 2012-. **Orgs:** Numerous mem incl founding mem, Pan-African House; Ny Bar; Mayor Bloomberg's Neighborhood Investment Adv Panel; bd dir, Citizens Union Found; chair, Sustained Excellence Alliance Corp. **Business Addr:** President, Chief Executive Officer, Abyssinian Development Corp, 4 W 125th St, New York, NY 10027, **Business Phone:** (646)442-6599.

### WRIGHT, SORAYA M.

Insurance executive, manager, executive. **Personal:** Born Dec 24, 1961, Oakland, CA; married Karl; children: Dania & Deidre. **Educ:** Holy Names Col, BA, bus admin & econs, 1985. **Career:** CNA Ins Co; Alexsis Risk Mgt, claim supvr, managing nat acct progs, 1989-91; United Airlines; Clorox Co Found, E Oakland Youth Develop Ctr claim mgr, 1991-94, risk mgr, 1994-2000, dir corp risk mgr, 2000-08, sr dir, 2008-12, vpres-global risk mgt, 2012-14, vpres enterprise risk mgt, 2014-16; Target, vpres-enterprise risk, 2016-. **Orgs:** Risk & Ins Mgt Soc; trustee, E Oakland Youth Develop Found; E Oakland Youth Develop Ctr; Assumption Sch Bd; bd trustee, Clorox Co Found, 2000-07; Nat Black MBA Asn; Alameda County Adv Bd; bd dir, Childrens Hosp Found, 1999-2004; trustee, Holy Names Univ, 2013-. **Honors/Awds:** Outstanding Business & Professional Leader, Dollar & Sense, 1993; Adele Corvin Outstanding Agency Board Volunteer Award, United Way, 1998; Chairman's Award, The Clorox Co, 2000; Achiever Award, Western Asn Educ Opportunity Personnel, 2000; Clorox Leadership Award - Humility, 2013. **Home Addr:** 3656 La Mesa Dr, Hayward, CA 94542. **Business Addr:** Vice President, Target Corp, 1000 Nicollet Mall, Minneapolis, MN 55403, **Business Phone:** (612)304-6073.

**WRIGHT, STEPHEN CALDWELL**
Educator. **Personal:** Born Nov 11, 1946, Sanford, FL; son of Joseph Caldwell and Bernice I. **Educ:** St Petersburg Jr Col, AA, 1967; Fla Atlantic Univ, BA, 1969; Atlanta Univ, MA, 1972; Ind Univ Pa, PhD, 1983. **Career:** Seminole County Sch Bd, teacher, 1969-70; Seminole Comm Col, prof, 1972-. **Orgs:** Gwendolyn Brooks Writers Asn Fla, founder & pres, 1987-; Revelry Poetry J, ed, 1987-; Zora Festival Arts & Humanities, nat planning comn, 1989-99; Boys & Girls Club, chmn, adv coun, 1993-96; Fla Div Cult Affairs Lit Orgns Panel, panelist, 1996-98. **Home Addr:** 127 Langston Dr, Sanford, NC 32771, **Home Phone:** (407)323-7184. **Business Addr:** Professor, Seminole Community College, 100 Weldon Blvd, Sanford, NC 32773-6199, **Business Phone:** (407)708-2442.

**WRIGHT, TANYA**
Entertainer, actor. **Personal:** Born Bronx, NY. **Educ:** Vassar Col. **Career:** TV series: "The Cosby Show", 1986; "Professor Poopsnaggle", 1986; "Parker Lewis Can't Lose", 1991; "Beverly Hills, 90210", 1994; "Living Single", 1995; "Family Matters", 1995; "The Wayans Bros", 1996; "Buddies", 1996; "Mama Flora's Family", 1998; "Mutiny", 1999; "Moesha", 1999; "The District", 2000-01; "24", 2001-02; "NYPD Blue", 2002; "The Handler", 2003-04; "Strong Medicine", 2004; "ER", 2007; "Standoff", 2007; "To Love is to Worry", 2008; "Nothing but the Blood", 2009; "Shake and finger Prop", 2009; "Time Bomb", 2009; "True Blood", 2008-14; "The Good Wife", 2014. Films: Mama Flora's Family, 1998; Mutiny, 1998; The Brothers, 2001; Ralph & Stanley, 2005; Ralph & Stanley, 2005; Angels Can't Help But Laugh, 2007; Butterfly Rising, 2010; Why Stop Now?, 2012. **Orgs:** Los Angeles Mission. **Special Achievements:** Author of Butterfly Rising, 2010. **Business Addr:** Actress, c/o Schiowitz Connor Ankrum Wolf Inc, 1680 Vine St Suite 1016, Los Angeles, CA 90028, **Business Phone:** (323)463-8355.

**WRIGHT, TOBY LIN**
**Personal:** Born Nov 19, 1970, Phoenix, AZ. **Educ:** Univ Nebr. **Career:** Football player (retired); Los Angeles Rams, defensive back, 1994-98; St Louis Rams, defensive back, 1995-98; Washington Redskins, 1999; San Francisco Demons, strong safety, 2001.

**WRIGHT, TOMICA.** **See WOODS-WRIGHT, TOMICA.**

**WRIGHT, VERLYN LAGLEN**
Journalist. **Personal:** Born Aug 2, 1963, Saginaw, MI; daughter of Leeunice Calloway and Louis. **Educ:** Southern Univ, Baton Rouge, LA, BA, 1983; Univ Mo, Columbia, Mo, MA, 1986. **Career:** Dallas Times Herald, Dallas, Tex, reporter, 1987-88; Patriot Ledger, Quincy, Mass, copy ed, 1988. **Orgs:** Nat Asn Black Journalists, 1986-; Boston Asn Black Journalists, 1988-. **Home Addr:** 26 Sch St, Hull, MA 02045, **Home Phone:** (617)925-1090.

**WRIGHT, VERNON S., JR.**
Executive, vice president (organization). **Career:** SFX Radio Networks, sr vpres & gen sales mgr; Am Urban Radio Networks, top mkt & advert exec, sr vpres sales dir, 2000-04, exec vpres sales & new bus develop, 2004-. **Business Addr:** Executive Vice President of Sales, New Business Development, American Urban Radio Networks, 432 Pk Ave S 14th Fl, New York, NY 10016, **Business Phone:** (212)883-2100.

**WRIGHT, WILL J.**
Executive, business owner, educator. **Personal:** Born Sep 9, 1950, Brooklyn, NY; son of Gerard and Mildred; married Patricia Ann; children: Patricia Antoinette. **Educ:** Fordham Univ, BA, jour, commun, 1972; Columbia Univ, Grad Sch Jour, 1974. **Career:** CBS Network News, ed, exec producer, writer & producer, 1972-80 & 2001-03; Cable News Network, sr producer, 1980-84, producer, 1981-87; KYW-TV, asst news dir, 1984-87; KRIV Fox TV News, vpres & news dir, 1987-92; WWOR-TV, news dir, 1992-2002; Upper Saddle River Vol Ambulance Corps, emt & ambulance driver, 1993-94; FOX Tv Stas Inc, vp news dir, 2000-02; BET Nightly News, exec producer, 2002-03; XS Momentum Ltd, pres news exec, 2003-; Will Wright Broadcast Found, founder, 2003-; HDNews, mgr, channel gen mgr, 2003-09; Cablevision, gen mgr, 2003-09; Rainbow Media, gen mgr, 2003-09; NBC News, digital journalism consult, 2009-10, mgr digital prod, 2009-12, sr news ed, 2012-. **Orgs:** Mem & bd mem, RNTDA & RTNDF, 1978-2008; bd dir, bd mem, trustee, Radio-Television News Dir's Asn, 1993-98 & 1986-2004; bd trustee, Fordham Univ, 1995-98; chmn, bd dir, Will J Wright Broadcast Jour Coaching Found, 1997-; dir, Broadcast Journalism Coaching Found. 2009-. **Home Addr:** , New York, NY. **Business Addr:** Founder, Will J Wright Broadcast Journalism Coaching Found, 112 Sunken Meadow Rd, Northport, NY 11768-2727, **Business Phone:** (631)269-2128.

**WRIGHT, WILLIAM A. (BILL WRIGHT)**
Teacher, automotive executive, business owner. **Personal:** Born Apr 4, 1936, Kansas City, MO; son of Robert B and Madeline S; married Ceta D. **Educ:** Western Wash State, Bellingham, WA, BEd, 1961. **Career:** Golf player (retired); entrepreneur; Amateur Athletic Union, player, 1954-55; Los Angeles Sch Dist, teacher, 1961-68; US Amateur Pub Links, player, 1963; Pro Golf Tour, prof golfer, 1964-77; Pasadena Lincoln-Mercury, Pasadena, Calif, owner, currently. **Orgs:** Black Ford Lincoln Mercury Dealers, 1978-; Nat Asn Advan Colored People, Pasadena Br. **Special Achievements:** First African-American to win United States Golf Association title. **Home Addr:** 3502 Mt Vernon Dr, Los Angeles, CA 90008, **Home Phone:** (323)296-3468. **Business Addr:** Owner, Pasadena Lincoln Mercury Inc, 1339 E Green St, Pasadena, CA 91106, **Business Phone:** (818)793-0645.

**WRIGHT-BOTCHWEY, ROBERTA YVONNE**
Lawyer, educator. **Personal:** Born Oct 9, 1946, York, SC. **Educ:** Fisk Univ, BA, 1967; Yale Univ, ISSP cert, 1966; Univ Mich, Sch Andrew III, JD. **Career:** Pvt pract; NC Cent Univ, Sch Law, asst prof corp coun, Tanzania Legal Corp Dar, Salaam Tanzania; Zambia Ltd Lusaka Zambia, sr legal asst, Rural Develop Corp. **Orgs:** NC Asn Black Lawyers; Nat Bar Asn; Nat Conf Black Lawyers; SC & DC Bar Asn; hon mem, Delta Theta Phi; consult, EPA, 1976; lectr, Sci Jury Sel & Evidence Workshop; legal adv, Zambian Corp Del, Tel Aviv, Israel, 1971; Atty Gen Zambia Select Comt Investigate Railways, 1972; Delta Sigma Theta Sorority; consult, Women's Prison Group, 1975; consult, EPA Environ Litigation Workshop, 1976; NCBL Comn Invest Discrim Prac Law Schs, 1977; dir, Councon Legal Educ Opport Summer Inst, 1977; Phi Beta Kappa, 1967. **Home Addr:** PO Box 817, York, SD 29745. **Business Addr:** Lawyer, 339 E Main, Rock Hill, SC 29730.

**WYATT, REV. DR. ALFONSO**
Vice president (organization), executive. **Personal:** married Ouida. **Educ:** Howard Univ, BA; Columbia Teacher Col; Ackerman Inst Family Ther; NY Theol Sem. **Career:** Educator, counr, prog developer, adminr, mentor and advocate; NY Bd Educ, teacher & adminr; Nonprofit consultancy Strategic Destiny, founder;Casey Family Progs Faith-Based Child Welfare Initiative, consult; Valley Inc, dep exec dir, 1982-89; Fund City, NY, vpres, proj dir, 1990-2011; Strategic Destiny LLC, reverend, auth, pub speaker, 2012-; Jericho Faith-Based Tech Assistance Proj, vpres & proj dir. **Orgs:** Adv bd, NY Black Leadership Comn AIDS; Correctional Asn & Osborne Asn; chmn, Fountain Youth; ministerial staff, Greater Allen Cadral, NY; vpres, Lower Manhattan Emergency Preserv Fund; bd mem, 21CF; trustee, 21st Century Found; trustee, New York ol Sem; Casey Family Found, ACS, Fedn Protestant Welfare Agencies; Child welfare ministries; Social Work and Relig Diversity; bd mem, Harlem C's Zone Promise Acad. **Business Addr:** Vice President, Project Director, Fund for City of New York, 121 Avenue of the Americas 6th Fl, New York, NY 10013-1590, **Business Phone:** (212)925-6675.

**WYATT, GAIL E.**
Physiologist, executive director. **Educ:** Univ Calif Los Angeles, Dept Psychol & Bio-Behav Sci, PhD, 1973; Am Bd Sexology, dipl. **Career:** Univ Calif Los Angeles AIDS Inst, assoc dir, currently; Univ Calif Los Angeles, Semel Inst, prof psychiat & biobehavioral sci; Univ Calif Los Angeles Sexual Health Prog, dir; Ctr Cult Trauma & Ment Health Disparities, dir. **Orgs:** Fel Am Psychol Asn & Am Acad Clin Sexologists; CTSI. **Special Achievements:** First African-American woman to be licensed as a psychologist, California. **Business Addr:** Associate Director, UCLA AIDS Institute, 10940 Wilshire Blvd Suite 960, Los Angeles, CA 90024-1678, **Business Phone:** (310)794-4419.

**WYATT, JULI M.**
Association executive, executive. **Personal:** Born Jul 20, 1964, Chester, VA. **Educ:** James Madison Univ, Harrisonburg, VA, BA, polit sci, 1986; Dc Sch Law, JD, 1995. **Career:** Jam Sports & Entertainment LLC, owner, pres, chief exec officer & founder, 1993-; JAM Enterprises, pres & chief exec officer. **Orgs:** DC Law Rev; founder & chair women, Jr Achievers Motivated Succeed Found; founder, Sports & Entertainment Law Soc; founder, Juli's Kids Motivated To Succeed; founder, Greater Mt Calvary Holy Church Legal Ministry. **Business Addr:** Founder, President & Chief Executive Officer, Jam Sports & Entertainment LLC, 13812 Amberfield Ct, Upper Marlboro, MD 20772, **Business Phone:** (301)627-3706.

**WYATT, DR. LANCE EVERETT**
Surgeon. **Personal:** Born Jan 19, 1967, Nashville, TN; son of Lewis and Gail. **Educ:** Howard Univ, BS, 1988; Univ Calif, Los Angeles Sch Med, MD, 1992. **Career:** Nat Inst Health, summer res fel, 1989; Unic Calif, Los Angeles Med Ctr, internship, 1992-93, Div Gen Surg, resident, 1992-99, div gen surg, jr resident, 1993-94, Plastic & Reconstr Surg, sr res fel, 1994-97, Div Plastic & Reconstructive Surg, res fel, 1994-97, sr resident, 1997-99; Lyndon Peer fel, Plastic Surg Educ Found, 1996; Harvard Combined Plastic Surg Residency Training Prog, chief resident, 2003; pvt pract, currently; Wyatt Ctr Plastic Surg, dir, currently. **Orgs:** Co-founder, Surg Resident Forum, 1995; Am Col Surgeons; William P Longmire Surg Soc; Soc Black Acad Surgeons; Nat Med Asn, Morestin Soc; Am Soc Plastic Surgeons; Am Med Asn; New Leaders; Youth Empowerment Comt; Am Soc Bone & Mineral Res; co-founder, organizer, vpres, Health Relief Int; fel White House, 1999-2000; clin fel Harvard Med Sch, 2000-03. **Honors/Awds:** 50 Leaders of Tomorrow, Ebony Mag, 1995; Individual National Research Service Award, Nat Inst Health, 1995-97; Best Basic Science Research, Unic Calif, Los Angeles Div Plastic & Reconstruction Surgery, 1996; Ralph Goldman Basic Research Award, Unic Calif, Los Angeles Div Geriatric Med, 1996; Ralph Goldman Basic Research Award, 1996; Best Plastic Surgery Research & Individual National Research Service Award, Nat Insts Health, 1996; Leadership Award, AMA Found, 2003. **Special Achievements:** Plastic Surgery Educational Foundation Res Grant, 1995, 1997; Book chap "Lymphedema" in Grabb & Smith's Plastic Surgery, 1997; Book chap "Lymphedema & Tumors of the Lymphatics", 1997; Vascular Surgery: A Comprehensive Review, Nat Presentations and Peer Reviewed publication; mentor, Angel City Links, 1990, 1995-98; KACE-Radio, Sunday Morning Live,"Teen Sexuality", 1995. **Home Addr:** 110 Lanark Rd Apt 4, Brighton, MA 02135-7223. **Business Addr:** Surgeon, Director, Wyatt Center for Plastic Surgery, 8631 W 3rd St E Twr Suite 1130, Los Angeles, CA 90048, **Business Phone:** (310)855-8010.

**WYATT, DR. RONALD MICHAEL**
Physician, health services administrator. **Personal:** Born Mar 6, 1954, Selma, AL; son of James and Gladys; married Pamela; children: Michael, Scott & Christopher. **Educ:** Univ Ala, Birmingham, BS, 1976, MD, 1985, MSHA. **Career:** St Louis Univ Sch Med, asst prof, chief resident, 1987-88, clin instr; St Louis Va Med Ctr, dir ER, 1988-89; Peoples Health Ctr, med dir, 1989-93; US Pub Health Servs, assoc recruitor, 1990-; White Wilson Med Ctr, assoc; Cent N Ala Health Servs, dir clin servs, 1993-; Fed Drug Admin; Centers Medicare & Medicaid Serv, mentor; Dept Defense Mil Health Syst, Patient Safety Anal Ctr, dir; Univ Ala, Birmingham Sch Med, asst dean, asst prof. **Orgs:** Adv, Nat Coord Comt Clin Prev Servs, 1992-; chair health policy comn, Nat Asn Community Health Ctrs, 1993-94; Vascular biol working group; George W Merck fel Inst Healthcare Improv, 2009-10; rep, Nat Coord Coun; med dir, Joint Comn, 2012-. **Home Addr:** 115 Lake Crest Dr, Madison, AL 35758, **Home Phone:** (205)722-7973. **Business Addr:** Medical Director, The Joint Commission, 1 Renaissance Blvd, Oakbrook Ter, IL 60181, **Business Phone:** (630)792-5800.

**WYATT, S. MARTIN, III (JAMAL ABDUL-KABIR)**
Journalist. **Personal:** Born Jul 31, 1941, Memphis, TN; son of Nadine Bragg Poindexter and S Martin II; married Joyce Hanson; children: Marcus, Sabriya, Jamila & Aisha. **Educ:** Vallejo Jr Col, Vallejo, Calif, 1960; Univ Wash, Seattle, Wash, 1962. **Career:** Journalist (retired); Huskies Running Back; KYAC Radio, Seattle, Wash, sales mgr, 1966-72; KING-TV, Seattle, Wash, sports anchor & writer, 1972-76; WRC-TV, Wash, DC, sports anchor & writer, 1976-80; KGO-TV, San Francisco, Calif, sports anchor/writer, 1980-85; ABC7 news, weekend sports anchor, 1980-85; ABC-TV's col football games, play-by-play announcer, 1981-82; WMAR-TV, Baltimore, Md, sports anchor & writer, 1986-88; Black Entertainment TV, Wash, DC, producer, a nchor & writer, 1986-89; KGO-TV, San Francisco, Calif, sports anchor & writer, 1989; Calif Black Sports Hall Fame, 1999; ABC7 news, sports anchor & sports dir, 2007. **Orgs:** Nat Asn Black Journalists; Bay Area Black Journalists. **Honors/Awds:** Emmy Award, Acad Tv Arts & Sci, 1976; Access Award Finalist, 1987; Sigma Delta Chi Winner for Ser, 1987; Martin Wyatt Day Declared in Seattle, WA, King County, 1976; Leaders in Action Award, 100 Black Men, 1994; Image Award for Journalism, Delta Sigma Theta Sorority, 1995; Ann St Soldier Award Winner, Omega Boys & Girls Club, 1996; Solano Col Athletic Hall of Fame, Vallejo Jr Col, 1996; Calif Black Sports Hall of Fame, 1999; 100 Black News Community Serv Award, 1999; Man of the Year Award, 100 Black Men of California; Humanitarian of the Year Award, Athletes United for Peace, 1999. **Home Addr:** 547 Merritt Ave, Oakland, CA 94610, **Home Phone:** (510)835-3460.

**WYCHE, LENNON DOUGLAS, JR.**
Physician, radiologist. **Personal:** Born Jul 13, 1946, Washington, DC; married Judith. **Educ:** Howard Univ, attended 1966; George Wash Univ, BS, 1969; Meharry Med Sch, MD, 1973. **Career:** USPHS, intern, 1973-74; USPHS Clin, gen med officer, 1974-46; Resd diag radiol, 1976; Appling Health Care Syst, physician, chatham radiologists, currently. **Orgs:** Alpha Phi Alpha Frat; Am Col Radiol; Nat Med Asn; jr mem, Am Roentgen Ray Soc; Eleven Black Men Liberty County. **Honors/Awds:** Personal Service Award, USPHS. **Home Addr:** 3831 Cloverbrook, Houston, TX 77045. **Business Addr:** Physician, Chatham Radiologists, Appling Health Care System, 5354 Reynolds St Suite 102, Savannah, GA 31405, **Business Phone:** (912)355-7554.

**WYCHE, PAUL H.**
Executive. **Personal:** Born Oct 16, 1946, Miami, FL; son of Paul Howard and Gracie Thompson; married Louise Everett; children: Shaina Nicole & Kimberly Elise. **Educ:** Miami Dade Jr Col; Univ Miami; Southeastern Univ, BS, pub admin; Univ Southern Calif; Southeastern Univ, grad study bus & pub. **Career:** Miami News, reporter, 1965-68; Econ Opportunity Prog Miami, dir pub affairs, 1968-70; WPLG-TV Miami, prog moderator, 1970-71; Fla Mem Col, pub rel dir, 1970-71; The Miami Times, assoc ed, 1970-71; US Rep Pepper, legis asst, 1971-73; Nat Black News Serv Inc, pres dir, 1972-84; US Rep Moakley, sr legis asst, 1973-75; US Environ Protection Agency, assoc pub affairs dir, 1978-80, constituent develop & coord, 1977-78, exec asst pub affairs dir, 1975-77; E I du Pont de Nemours Co, pub affairs rep, 1980-82, pub affairs consult, 1982-88, pub affairs mgr, 1988-91; Safety-Kleen Corp, vpres, corp pub affairs & gov rel, 1991-93, dir, community rel & gov affairs; Safety-Kleen Corp, 1993-98; Whirlpool Corp, vpres global commun & community affairs, 1998; NorthWestern Corp, vpres commun, chief commun officer; Wyche & Assoc, founder, prin & pres, currently. **Orgs:** Life mem, Nat Asn Advan Colored People; bd mem, Mt Vernon-Lee Enter Inc; Nat Urban League; PUSH; Sigma Delta Chi, 1968; Nat Capital Press Clubs; Nat Young Demo Clubs; bd mem, Coun Cath Laity; pres, Good Shepherd Parish Coun; Cong Staff Club; Admin Asst Asn; bd mem, S Fla Econ Opportunity Coun; Dade Co Drug Abuse Adv Bd; Jaycees; founding pres, bd, NW Miami Jaycees; vpres, United Blck Fedn Dade Co; pres, Fla Pub Affairs dir; bd mem, Black Coc; pres, Caths Shared Responsibility; pres, Good Shepherd Coun Laity; dir, Am Heart Asn, 1982-85; trustee, W End City Day Care Nursery, 1983-85; chmn, Brandywine Prof Asn, 1984-91; dir, Del Alliance Prof Women, 1984-86; pres, Civic Asn Surrey Park, 1985-86; dir, Boy Scouts Am, 1985-90; pres, Opportunity ter Inc, 1986-90; vice chmn, Govt Rel, bd dir, United Way DE, 1987-90, chmn Govt Rel, United Way, 1987-89; dir, Ment Health Asn, 1988-90; dir, Layton Home Aged, 1988-90; trustee, Med Ctr Del Found, 1988-93; exec comt, Human Serv Partnership, 1989-91; dir, Del Community Investment Corp, 1989-91; bd dir, 1994, vpres, 1995-, Nat Asn Chem Recyclers; Nat Asn Mfrs, Nat Pub Affairs Steering Comte, 1994; pres, bd dir Nat Asn Chem Recyclers, 1996; bd dir, Pub Affairs Coun, 1997; Conf Bd Corp Strategies Coun, 1997; State Gov Rel Coun, 1995; bd, African Am Chamber Com; chmn, Cent Fla African Am Bus Alliance; fel Metro Orlando Econ Develop Comn; bd dir, Jr Achievement Orlando; bd dir, Orlando Reg Chamber Com; fel WESH-TV's African Am Adv Panel, fel Nat Socs Prof Journalists; Exec Comt NorthWestern Corp. **Home Addr:** 30 Wildflower Lane Apt 3928, Schaumburg, IL 60173-6528, **Home Phone:** (708)487-2046. **Business Addr:** Founder, Principal, President, Wyche & Associates Inc, 2920 Lowell Ct, Casselberry, FL 32707, **Business Phone:** (407)388-1811.

**WYCLIFF, NOEL DON**
Journalist. **Personal:** Born Dec 17, 1946, Liberty, TX; son of Wilbert A and Emily A; married Catherine A; children: Matthew William & Grant Erdmann. **Educ:** Univ Notre Dame, BA, 1969; Univ Chicago, 1970. **Career:** Chicago Sun-Times, reporter; The New York Times, ed writer, 1985-90; Chicago Tribune, dep ed page ed, 1990-91, ed page ed, 1991-2000, pub ed & columnist, 2000-06; Loyola Univ Chicago, clin prof journalism, 2008-, prof journalism, 2008-. **Orgs:** Adv coun, Univ Notre Dame, Col Arts & Lett, 1989-; Nat Asn Minority Media Execs, 1991-; Nat Asn Black Journalists; ASNE Writing Awards Comt, 1995-97; bd mem, Am Soc Newspaper Eds, 2003-06. **Honors/Awds:** Pulitzer Prize juror Finalist for the Pulitzer Prize for Ed Writing, 1996; Chicago Journalism Hall of Fame, Inductee, 1996; ASNE Distinguished Writing Award for Eds, 1997. **Special Achievements:** Contributor to Commonwealth Mag, 1990-; Third black person to serve on the New York Times Editorial Board. **Business Addr:** Professor Journalism, Clinical Professor of Journalism, Loyola University, 1052 W Loyola Ave, Chicago, IL 60626, **Business Phone:** (773)508-2530.

**WYKE, JOSEPH HENRY**
Executive director. **Personal:** Born Jan 9, 1928, New York, NY; married Margaret Elaine Whiteman. **Educ:** City Col NY, BSaS, 1949; NY Univ, MA, 1958. **Career:** Urban League Greater Nb, exec dir, 1966-70; Urban Coalition Met Wilmington, DE, exec vpres, 1970-75; Col M Ed Dent NJ, asst adminr, 1975-76; Westchester Coalition Inc, exec dir, 1976-88. **Orgs:** Bd mem, Afro-Am Cult Found, 1977-; chmn bd dir, Aspire Indust Inc, 1978-; Edges, 1978-; Julius A Thomas Soc, 1978; bd mem, Westchester Community Serv Coun, 1979-; bd trustee, New Heights Acad Charter Sch. **Honors/Awds:** Appreciation for Service Paul Robeson Award, Urban League Greater New Brunswick, 1980; Martin Luther King Jr Award, Greenburgh Community Ctr, 1980. **Home Addr:** 790 Riverside Dr, New York, NY 10032-7459. **Business Addr:** Executive Director, Westchester Coalition Inc, 235 Main St, White Plains, NY 10601.

**WYKLE, MAY LOUISE HINTON**
Educator, dean (education), school administrator. **Personal:** Born Feb 11, 1934, Martins Ferry, OH; daughter of John R and Florence A Randall; married William Lenard; children: Andra Sims & Caron. **Educ:** Ruth Brant Sch Nursing, dipl RN, 1956; Western Res Col, Cleveland, BSN, 1962; Case Western Res Univ, MSN, psych nursing, 1969, PhD, educ, 1981. **Career:** Cleveland Psychiat Inst, staff nurse, head nurse, suprv, 1956-64, dir, nursing educ, 1964; Univ Hosp Cleveland, admin assoc, dir nursing, Hanna Pavilion; Ctr Aging & Health, dir, assoc dean community affairs; Res Psychiat Inst, MD Self-Style-compliance, Nat Inst Aging Res Rev Comt, black & white caregiver intervention, NIH; Case Western Res Univ, asst prof, psych nursing, 1975, prof chairperson, dir psych nursing, adminr assoc, geront nursing; Frances Payne Bolton Sch Nursing, dean, chairperson, Psychiat Ment Health Nursing & Florence Cellar prof Geront Nursing, currently. **Orgs:** Clin nurse spec Fairhill Ment Health Ctr, 1970; nursing consult, Va Med Ctr, 1980-85; bd mem, Eliz Bryant Nursing Home, 1983; proj dir, Robert Wood Johnson Teaching Nursing Home; Res-Self Care among Elderly; chairperson res comm Margaret Hagner House Nursing Home; Prof Adv Bd-ARDA Org Cleveland OH; bd dir, Judson Retirement Ctr, 1989-; bd mem, Golden Age Ctr, Cleveland, 1991; ed bd, Generations Mag, 1991; Nat Panel Alzheimers Dis, 1992; fel Am Acad Nursing; Geront Soc Am; pres, Hon Socs Nursing; fel Geront Socs Am; del, Planning Comt White House Conf Aging, 1993; Pres Friends, Nat Inst Nursing Res; bd dir, Rosalynn Carter Inst Caregiving. **Home Addr:** 34552 Summerset Dr, Cleveland, OH 44139-5635, **Home Phone:** (440)542-0475. **Business Addr:** Dean, Florence Cellar Professor of Gerontological Nursing, Case Western Reserve University, 2121 Abington Rd, Cleveland, OH 44106-4904, **Business Phone:** (216)368-2545.

**WYLIE, ARTHUR**
Chief executive officer. **Educ:** Univ NC, BS, financial mgt, 1999. **Career:** Arthur Wylie Wealth Mgt Group, founder & chief exec officer, 1999-; Global Renaissance Entertainment Holdings, chief exec officer, currently. **Orgs:** Arthur Wylie Found; Wylie Initiative Study Entrepreneurship. **Business Addr:** Chief Executive Officer, Founder, Arthur Wylie Wealth Management Group, 5009Beattis Ford Rd Suite 107-202, Charlotte, NC 28216, **Business Phone:** (866)416-3479.

**WYMAN, DEVIN EDWARD**
Football player, football coach. **Personal:** Born Aug 29, 1973, East Palo Alto, CA; married Shelby McQueen; children: Maria, Sunday & Kaitie. **Educ:** Ky State Univ, grad. **Career:** Football player (retired), coach; New Eng Patriots, defensive tackle, 1996-98; Kans City Chiefs, 2002; Arena Football League, San Jose SaberCats, 2003-05; Arena Football League, Dallas Desperados, 2006-07; Utah Blaze, 2008; Tex Revolution, head coach, 2015-. **Special Achievements:** Part of SaberCats team won Arena Bowl XVIII, 2006. **Home Addr:** , San Jose, CA. **Business Addr:** Head Football Coach, Tex Revolution, 190 E Stacy Rd Suite 1312, Allen, TX 75002.

**WYNN, DR. ALBERT RUSSELL**
Government official, lawyer. **Personal:** Born Sep 10, 1951, Philadelphia, PA; married Gaines Clore; children: Meredith & Gabrielle; married Jessie. **Educ:** Univ Pittsburgh, BS, polit sci, 1973; Howard Univ, MS, pub admin, 1974; Georgetown Law Sch, JD, 1977. **Career:** Prince George's County Consumer Protection Comn, Md, dir, 1979-82; Albert R Wynn & Assocs, founder, 1982-; Md House Deleg, mem, 1983-87; Md State Senate, mem, 1987-93; US House Rep, 4th Cong Dist Md, congressman, 1992-2008; Dickstein Shapiro, sr advisor & partner, 2008-. **Orgs:** Kappa Alpha Psi Fraternity; Dem Message Group; Dep Dem Whip; chmn, Cong Black Caucus Polit Action Comt; chair, Cong Black Caucus Task Force Campaign Fin Reform; Caucus Minority Bus Task Force; Maple Springs Baptist Church; Md Bar Asn; House Energy & Com Comt. **Honors/Awds:** Award for Leadership, Small Bus Admin, 2002. **Business Addr:** Senior Advisor, Partner, Dickstein Shapiro LLP, 1825 Eye St NW, Washington, DC 20006-5403, **Business Phone:** (202)420-2200.

**WYNN, ALMA MCKINNEY.** **See MCKINNEY, ALMA SWILLEY.**

**WYNN, LAMETTA K.**
Government official. **Personal:** Born Jan 1, 1933?, Galena, IL; married Thomas H; children: 10. **Educ:** Grad St Luke's Hosp Sch Nursing, Cedar Rapids, IA. **Career:** Nurse (retired), govt off; Mercy Hosp, nurse; City Clinton, Iowa, mayor, 1995-2007. **Orgs:** Rotary Int; trustee, Mt Clare Col; Nat Asn Advan Colored People; Bethel AME Church; hon mem, Delta Kappa Gamma Soc Int; Clinton Community Sch Bd; chmn, Iowa Comn Status African-Am; bd dir, African Am Mus. **Special Achievements:** First Black Mayor of The City & State. **Home Addr:** 322 3rd Ave N, Clinton, IA 52732-4022, **Home Phone:** (563)242-7018. **Business Addr:** IA.

**WYNN, LINDA T.**
Historian, college teacher, lecturer. **Educ:** Tenn State Univ, BS, MS, MPA. **Career:** Tenn Hist Comn, asst dir state progs, 1974-; Nashville Conf African-Am Hist & Cult, co-founder, 1981-; Fisk Univ, Dept Hist & Polit Sci, lectr, 1993-; Lipscomb Univ, adj instr, 2012-. **Orgs:** Metrop Hist Comn, Civil War Sesquicentennial Comt, markers comt mem; Local Conf African Am Hist & Cult, co-chair. **Special Achievements:** Co-editor of "Freedom Facts and Firsts: 400 Years of the African American Civil Rights Experience" (Visible Ink Press, 2009); Author of "Journey to Our Past: A Guide of African-American Markers in Tennessee" (Tennessee Historical Commission, 1999); contributor to numerous publications on African-American history. **Business Addr:** Lecturer, Fisk University, Park Johnson 228, Nashville, TN 37208, **Business Phone:** (615)329-8529.

**WYNN, RENALDO LEVALLE**
Football player, executive. **Personal:** Born Sep 3, 1974, Chicago, IL. **Educ:** Univ Notre Dame, BA, sociol, 1996. **Career:** Football player (retired) executive; Jacksonville Jaguars, left defensive tackle, 1997, right defensive tackle, right defensive end, 1998, defensive end, 1999-2001; Wash Redskins, defensive end, 2002-06, left defensive tackle, 2004, 2009; New Orleans Saints, defensive tackle, 2007; New York Giants, 2008; Omaha Nighthawks, 2010; Family Faith Found, co-founder & dir, 2003-; Joe Gibbs Racing, bus develop, 2012-; Joe Gibbs Racing, exec dir game plan life: inner city & prison ministries, 2012-. **Orgs:** Hon chmn, Cystic Fibrosis Found, Winner's Cir prog, 1999. **Honors/Awds:** Honorable mention All-American, 1995; PFW All-Rookie Team, 1997. **Business Addr:** Director, Co-Founder, Faith and Family Foundation, 1605 Rte 11, Kirkwood, VA 13795.

**WYNN, SYLVIA J.**
Executive. **Personal:** Born Sep 30, 1941, New York, NY; daughter of Frank and Lucinda Townes. **Educ:** Hunter Col, City Univ NY, attended 1970; Simmons Mid Mgt Prog, cert, 1979. **Career:** Gillette Co, prod mgr, 1978-81; Int Playtex Inc, prod mgr, 1981-83; Johnson Prod Co Inc, group prod mgr, 1983-87, dir mkt, 1985-86, vpres mkt & sales, 1986-87; Women's Bus Develop Ctr, bus counr, 1991-; SJW Enterprises, Chicago, Ill, pres, owner, 1987-. **Orgs:** AMA; tutor Boston Half-Way House, 1978-81; founding mem & chairperson, Target Advert Professionals. **Home Addr:** 333 E Ont St, Chicago, IL 60611, **Home Phone:** (312)943-3117. **Business Addr:** President, SJW Enterprises, 333 E Ont St Suite 1003B, Chicago, IL 60611, **Business Phone:** (312)642-9720.

**WYNN, DR. VALREE FLETCHER**
Educator. **Personal:** Born May 9, 1922, Rockwall, TX; daughter of Will and Alice; married Phail Sr; children: Phail Jr, Patricia Phaye (deceased) & Michael David. **Educ:** Langston Univ, BA, 1943; Okla State Univ, MA, 1951, PhD, eng, 1976. **Career:** Professor (retired), professor emeritus; Lawton Bd Educ, elem & high sch teacher, 1944-48, 1960-66; Cameron Univ, asst prof, assoc prof, prof, 1966-85, prof emer, 1985-. **Orgs:** AKA, 1942-; Phi Delta Kappa Hon Soc, 1973-; cha basileus, Int Const Comn, 1978-82; Int Phi Kappa Phi Hon Soc, 1985-; pres, Bd Regents Okla Cols, 1985-93; bd mem, US Sen David Boren's Found Excellence, 1985-; bd mem, Hospice, 1985-; adv coun, Okla Comn Status Women; hon mem, Awards Com, 1990-93; State Martin Luther King Jr Holiday CMS, 1992-; bd mem, Lawton Pub Schs Found, 1992-; Alpha Kappa Alpha. **Special Achievements:** First African-American professor at Cameron University, 1966-85; first African-American to serve on the Board of Regents of Oklahoma Colleges. **Home Addr:** 6901 Sprucewood Dr, Lawton, OK 73505, **Home Phone:** (580)536-6114. **Business Addr:** Professor Emeritus, Cameron University, 2800 W Gore Blvd, Lawton, OK 73505-6377, **Business Phone:** (580)581-2200.

**WYNNE, DANA SH-NIECE**
Basketball player, basketball coach. **Personal:** Born Feb 2, 1975, Orange, NJ; daughter of Natalie. **Educ:** Seton Hall Univ, BA, advert art & minor sociol, 1997. **Career:** Basket player (retired), basketball coach; Colo Xplosion, forward, beginning, 1996-98; Sacramento Monarchs, forward, 2001; Wash Mystics, forward, 2004; Seton Hall Women's Basketball, asst coach; Seton Hall Pirates, asst coach, 2004-08; Nutley High Sch, coach, 2009-. **Home Addr:** , Irvington, NJ. **Business Addr:** Coach, Nutley High School, 300 Franklin Ave, Nutley, NJ 07110, **Business Phone:** (973)661-8832.

**WYNNE, DIANA S.**
Executive. **Educ:** Spelman Col, BS, polit sci & acct; Wright State Univ, MS, finance. **Career:** Cracker Barrel, sr vpres; sr vpres, Cracker Barrel Old Country Store Inc; Price Waterhouse Coopers; Metromedia Restaurant Group, sr vpres & treas; Blockbuster Inc, vpres treas; CBRL Group Inc, sr vpres corp affairs, 2006-. **Orgs:** Bd mem, Am Dietetic Asn; chmn, Women's Food service Forum; dir, Nat Restaurant Asn. **Home Addr:** 305 Hartmann Dr, Lebanon, TN 37088, **Home Phone:** (615)444-5533. **Business Addr:** Senior Vice President Corporate Affairs, CBRL Group Inc, PO Box 787, Lebanon, TN 37088-0787, **Business Phone:** (615)443-9869.

**WYNNE, MARVELL**
Baseball player. **Personal:** Born Dec 17, 1959, Chicago, IL; son of Marvell Sr; children: Marvell II. **Career:** Baseball player (retired); Pittsburgh Pirates, outfielder, 1983-85; San Diego Padres, outfielder, 1986-89; Chicago Cubs, outfielder, 1989-90; Hanshin Tigers, Japanese Baseball League, 1991. **Orgs:** Cubs Team. **Home Addr:** 8052 S Calumet, Chicago, IL 60619.

**WYNNS, CORYLISS LORRAINE**
Journalist. **Personal:** Born Jan 17, 1958, St. Louis, MO; daughter of Rufus and Helen De Wanda Foree. **Educ:** Ind Univ, BA, tele commun, 1983. **Career:** WKXI-AM, Jackson, Miss, chief reporter, 1982; AP radio network, Wash, DC, news clerk, 1984; KEEL-AM, Shreveport, La, producer, reporter, anchor, 1984-85; KDKS-FM, Shreveport, La, news dir, 1985; Sheridan Broadcasting Network, Pittsburgh, Pa, freelance corresp, 1985-87; WAWA-AM, Milwaukee, Wis, anchor, 1985-86; news dir, 1986-87; WMAQ-AM, outside reporter, 1988-90, inside reporter, writer, 1990-92, ed, 1992-97; WVPE-FM, independent producer, 1998; Mkt Strategies Inc, res technician, 1998, support supvr, 1998-2000, ed, 1999-2003, sr supvr/qual assurance coordr, 2000-03; Morning Star Publicity Serv, owner, 2000-04; Pt Productions, publicity dir/unit publicist, 2000; Feed C Inc, donor rels rep, 2005; Agi Teleperformance, tel sales rep, 2006-09; Liberty Mutual Ins Co, personal claims cutomer serv rep, 2007. **Orgs:** Nat Asn Black Journalists, 1979-; co-founder, Ind Univ Black Telecommunications Asn, 1980; vpres, Milwaukee Sec Nat Coun Negro Women, 1988; WFIU-FM, Newsroom Vol. **Honors/Awds:** Image Award, Milwaukee, Wisconsin, Career Youth Development, 1986; Journalism Award, Radio Series, What About the Father, Nat Asn Black Journalists, 1987, 1991; InterNat Radio & Television Society, Col Conference, 1987; Nat Assn Black Journalists, InterNat Reporting, Radio Series, South Africa Referendum, 1992. **Home Addr:** 1302 Chalfant St, South Bend, IN 46617, **Home Phone:** (219)262-0916.

**WYRE, ESQ. STANLEY MARCEL**
Educator, school administrator. **Personal:** Born Mar 31, 1953, Detroit, MI; son of Nathaniel and Mervell; married Jerri Kailimai; children: Stanley III. **Educ:** Lawrence Inst Technol, BS, 1976; Mich State Univ Col Law, JD, 1984. **Career:** Walbridge Aldinger Co, proj estimator, 1976-78; Palmer Smith Co, sr construct estimator & dir, 1979-83; Charfoos, Christensen & Archer PC, atty-at-law, 1984; Barton-Malow Co, construct mgr, 1984-87; prof photogr; Detroit Col Law, adj prof, 1985-; Lawrence Inst Technol, asst prof, 1985-; Detroit Pub Schs, asst supt, 1992-95; Chez Corp, consult; Rider Levett Bucknall, legal consult, 2007-10; Stanley M. Wyre Assocs, atty, 2011-. **Orgs:** Arbitrator, Am Arbitrator Asn; State Bar Ga; State Bar Mich; Nat Bar Asn; Am Bar Asn. **Business Addr:** Attorney, Stanley M Wyre Associates, 12260 Edgewater Dr, Hampton, GA 30228-3304.

**X, QUANELL (QUANELL RALPH EVANS)**
Community activist. **Personal:** Born Dec 7, 1970, Los Angeles, CA; son of Brian Chris Evans; married Tabitha Stewart. **Career:** Community activist; New Black Panther Party, info minister, currently. **Orgs:** Nation Islam; Ment Freedom Obtains Independence. **Business Addr:** Information Minister, New Black Panther Party, 2428 Southmore, Houston, TX 77004, **Business Phone:** (281)472-5589.

**YAMBA, DR. ZACHARY**
Executive, president (organization). **Educ:** Seton Hall Univ, BS, MS; Pac States Univ, PhD; Brunel Univ, PhD. **Career:** President (retired), president emeritus; Mid States Asn Cols Schs, comnr; Seton Hall Univ, regent; Essex County Col, dir humanities, dean fac, dean lib arts, interim pres, pres, 1980-2010, pres emer, currently. **Orgs:** Trustee, Victoria Found; bd mem, Proj GRAD; bd mem, Newark Workforce Investment Bd; County Community Col Pres Asn NJ; New Community Corp Found, NJ Communities Sch; Int Youth Orgn; Nat Asn Advan Colored People; Seton Halls bd regents; founding mem, Presidents Round Table; Newark Downtown Core Redevelop Corp; Christ King Prep Sch; Two Hundred Club Essex County; Am Conf Diversity. **Business Addr:** President Emeritus, Essex County College, 303 Univ Ave, Newark, NJ 07102, **Business Phone:** (973)877-3022.

**YANCEY, DR. CAROLYN LOIS**
Physician, pediatrician. **Personal:** Born Tuskegee, AL; daughter of Asa G Sr (deceased) and Carolyn E Dunbar (deceased). **Educ:** Atlanta Univ, Spelman Col, BS, 1972; Univ Edinburgh Scotland, UK, attended 1972; Howard Univ Col Med, MD, 1976. **Career:** Univ Penn Childrens Hosp Philadelphia, resident, 1976-79, fel pediat rheumatol, 1979-81, instr pediat, 1980-81, clin asst prof pediat, 1981-82; Howard Univ, Dept Pediat & Child Health, model pract, coordr, 1982-83, clin asst prof pediat, 1982-, assoc clin prof, 1983-; Walter Reed Army Med Ctr, clin asst prof pediat, 1985-; George Wash Univ Sch Med, asst clin prof child health & develop, 1987; Ped Rheum, Kaiser Permanente, Mid Atlantic, dir, 1983-94; Uniformed Serv Univ Health Sci, pediatrician, 1988-; CIGNA Health Care, Mid Atlantic, assoc med dir, 1994-98, sr med dir, 1998-2000; Carolyn L Yancey LLC, pres; KPMG Consult Inc Health Care Pract, 2000-03; FDA/CDER, med officer, 2003-; pvt practr, currently. **Orgs:** Sect Rheumatol, Am Acad Pediat, 1983; diplo & fel Am Acad Pediat, 1984; NMA & Am Rheumatism Asn, 1979; nominating comm, Sect Rheumatol, AAP, 1987; med adv comt, Arthritis Found, Wash Metrop Chap, 1990; exec comt, Sect Pediat Rheumatol, Am Acad Pediat, 1987-90; Jr League Wash, DC, 1990-93; chmn, Sect Rheumatol, Am Acad Pediat, 1991-94; fel Am Col Rheumatology; DAARP. **Honors/Awds:** Department of Medical Award, Howard Univ Col Medicine, 1976; Distinguished Alumni Citation of the Year, Nat Asn Equal Opportunities Higher Educ, 1985; Professionalism Award, Kaiser Permanente Med Group, 1993. **Home Addr:** 8819 Woodland Dr, Silver Spring, MD 20910-2708, **Home Phone:** (301)585-6643. **Business Addr:** Physician, Medical Officer, Food & Drug Administration, 10903 NH Ave, Silver Spring, MD 20993, **Business Phone:** (888)463-6332.

**YANCEY, CHARLES CALVIN**
Government official. **Personal:** Born Dec 28, 1948, Boston, MA; son of Howell T Sr and Alice White; married Marzetta Morrissette; children: Charles, Derrick, Sharif & Ashley. **Educ:** Tufts Univ, BA, econs, 1970; Harvard Univ, MPA, 1991. **Career:** Boston City Coun, Commonwealth, MA, dir admin, 1977-79, Dist 4, councilman, 1983-, pres, 2001; Metro Area Planning Coun, dir finances 1979-82; CCY & Assoc, pres 1977-84; Legis Br City Govt, city coun, 1984-. **Orgs:** Nat Asn Advan Colored People; Greater Roxbury Community Develop Corp, 1978-82; Transafrica1979-; Cod man Sq Community Develop Corp,

1981-83; pres, Black Polit Task Force, 1982-83; Coastal Resources Adv Bd, 1983-; bd mem, Boston African-Am Nat Hist Site, Taxpayers Equity Alliance Mass, Roxbury YMCA, Boston Harbor Assocs; bd mem, Am Lung Asn, Boston, 1990-; bd mem, Amns Dem Action, 1991-; adv coun, Nat League Cities; pres, Nat Black Caucus Local Elected Officials, 1999. **Honors/Awds:** Elected vpres, N Am Region Action Against Apartheid Community United Nations, 1984; Citizen of the Year, Omega Psi Phi, 1984; Meritorious Community Service Award, Kappa Alpha Psi, 1984; Passage Boston S Africa Divestment Legis City Coun, 1984. **Home Addr:** 3 Hooper St, Boston, MA 02124. **Business Addr:** Councilman, Boston City Council, 1 City Hall Plz 5th Fl, Boston, MA 02201, **Business Phone:** (617)635-3131.

### YANCEY, PRENTISS QUINCY
Lawyer. **Personal:** Born Aug 20, 1944, Atlanta, GA; son of Prentiss Q; children: Prentiss III, Cristian & Schuyler. **Educ:** Villanova Univ, BS, polit sci, 1966; Emory Univ, Sch Law, JD, 1969. **Career:** Smith, Cohen, Ringel, Kohler & Martin, assoc, 1969; Smith, Gambrell & Russell LLP, assoc, 1969-73, partner, 1969-98, Corp Sect, coun, atty law, 2002-11; Broadcast Corp, founder, dir & pres; Am Golf Atlanta, Prin, 1986-; Africom Telecommunications Ltd, pres & chief exec officer, 1994-98, dir, exec vpres & gen coun, 1998-2000; Starchase Adv, managing partner, 2012-. **Orgs:** Gen coun, Am Basketball Asn, 1972-76; Trustee, Clark Atlanta Univ, 1978-; Soc Int Bus Fels, 1986-; bd dir, United Way Atlanta; bd mem, Sears Found; bd mem, Child Serv; bd mem, Family Coun Serv; bd mem, Lovett Sch; Atlanta Ballet; Discovery Learning Inc; Atlanta Chamber Com; Int Bus Coun; bd mem, Gov Comn Higher Educ; bd mem, Gov Comn Criminal Justice; dir, Southern Ctr Int Studies; Atlanta Charter Comn; bd mem, Africom Telecommunications Ltd; bd mem, Atlanta Univ. **Home Addr:** 5790 Stonehaven Dr, Stone Mountain, GA 30087-5715.

### YANCY, DR. DOROTHY COWSER
College president, educator, labor activist. **Personal:** Born Apr 18, 1944, Cherokee Cty, AL; daughter of Linnie Bell Covington and Howard; married Robert James; children: Yvonne. **Educ:** Johnson C Smith Univ, BA, hist, 1964; Univ Mass, Amherst, MA, hist, 1965; Atlanta Univ, PhD, polit sci, 1978; Harvard Univ, cert, mgt develop. **Career:** Albany State Col Albany, GA, instr, hist, 1965-67; Hampton Inst, Hampton VA, instr hist, 1967-69; Evanston Twp High Sch, teacher, 1969-71; Barat Col Lake Forest IL, dir black studies, 1971-72; Ga Inst Tech, asst prof, 1972-78, assoc prof, 1978-88, prof, 1988-94; Johnson C Smith Univ, pres, 1994-2008. **Orgs:** Labor panel Am Arbit Asn, 1980; mediator, Mediation Res & Educ Proj, Northwestern Univ, 1988-; Arbit Panel, Bd Regents State Univ Syst Fla & AFSCME, 1988-; chair women, Woman Power Comn, Links Inc, 1990-94; bd trustees, Johnson C Smith Univ, 1991-94; Asn Study Afro-Am Life & Hist; Indust Rels Res Asn; Soc Prof Dispute Resolutions; mem exec comt, Asn Soc & Behav Sci; So Pol Sci Asn; spec master, Fla Pub Employees Rels Comn; bd mem, Asn Study Afro-Am Life & Hist; Labor Arbit Panel Fedn Mediation & Conciliation Serv; bd, Charlotte Coun; Charlotte Urban League; Metro Charlotte YMCA. **Honors/Awds:** Fulbright-Hayes Scholar, 1968; Distinguished Alumnus, Johnson C Smith Univ, 1981; Outstanding Teacher Yr, Ga Inst Technol, 1985; People to People Delegation of Labor Experts, Soviet Union & Europe, 1988, London, Berlin, & Moscow, 1990; The Acad Polit & Social Sci Small Hural, Ulan Bator, Mongolia, lecturer and consultant, 1991; Nat Black Col Alumni Hall of Fame in Educ, inducted; named Black Issues of the 20th Century Educator; Lifetime Achievement Award; Asn Social Change & Behavior Scientists; Maya Angelou Tribute to Achievement, UNCF; named Person of Prominance, Charlotte Post, 2000; Harold E Delaney Exemplary Educational Leadership Award, Am Asn Higher Educ, 2004; Old North State Award, State of North Carolina, 2005; Sisters Delany Honor Society Achievement Award, NC Women of Distinction, 2007; Horizon Award, Leadership Charlotte, 2007; William J Stanley Award, Ga Inst Technol, 2007; Women's History Hall of Fame, Nat Asn Negro Bus, 2008. **Special Achievements:** First female black president of Johnson C. Smith University; First female to be elected President of the Central Intercollegiate Athletic Association; First African American to be promoted and tenured as a full professor at Georgia Tech. **Home Addr:** 1723 Washington Ave, Charlotte, NC 28216-5427, **Home Phone:** (704)334-8317. **Business Addr:** President, Johnson C Smith University, 100 Beatties Ford Rd, Charlotte, NC 28216, **Business Phone:** (704)378-1000.

### YANCY, EARL J.
Executive. **Personal:** children: 3. **Educ:** Southern Univ & Agr & Mech Col, Baton Rouge, BA, archit & engineering; Hoch Schule fur Bildende Kunste, advan col study cert, 1970; Universitat der Kunste Berlin, MArch, advan study archit, 1971; Yale Univ, MCP, city planning, 1972; Harvard Univ, PhD, archit/planning, 1976. **Career:** Yale Univ, fac, asst prof, 1972-75; Harvard Univ, grad sch design, Loeb fel, 1975; Yancy Minerals Inc, founder, pres, 1977-; Peak Electronics Inc, founder, pres, 1990-98; Yancy Van Clief Partners LLC, founder, managing dir, prin, dir, partner, 1999-. **Orgs:** Dir, New Eng Minority Purchasing Coun, 1981; Young Pres Orgn, 1986-93; founder, chair, Black Young Pres Orgn, 1992-; World Pres Orgn, 1993-; Beta Tau Boule Fraternal Group, 1998-; bd dir, Ctr Bank; bd dir, Middlesex Mutual Ins Co; Loeb Alumni Asn; bd advisor mem, Yancy Minerals LLC; bd mem, Auto & Truck Glass LLC. **Business Addr:** Founder, YVC Partners LLC, 2 Enterprise Dr Suite 303, Shelton, CT 06484, **Business Phone:** (203)926-8575.

### YANCY, DR. PRESTON MARTIN
Educator. **Personal:** Born Oct 18, 1938, Sylvester, GA; son of Preston Martin Sr and Margaret Elizabeth Robinson; married Marilyn Leonard; children: Robert James & Grace Elizabeth. **Educ:** Morehouse Col, BA, 1959; Univ Richmond, MH, 1968; Syracuse Univ, MSS, 1974, PhD, 1979. **Career:** Va Union Univ, prof, 1969, vpres acad affairs, 1994-97, Eng & Humanities, dept head, prof, currently; Richmond Free Press, columnist, 1991-94, 1997-2001. **Orgs:** Columnist, Richmond Afro-Am Newspaper, 1967-71, 1974-82; Langston Hughes Soc, 1981-91; Asn Study Afro Am Life & Hist. **Honors/Awds:** Doctoral Grants, Ford Found, 1973-75; Emory O Jackson Best Column Awards, 1975-78, 1980; Doctoral Grants, 1978-79, Post Doctoral Grants, 1981-84, United Negro Col Fund. **Special Achievements:** Author: The Afro-American Short Story: A Comprehensive, 1986. **Home Addr:** 4519 Brook Rd, Richmond, VA 23227-3705, **Home Phone:** (804)266-6168. **Business Addr:** Professor, Virginia Union University, 208 E Ellison Hall, Richmond, VA 23220-1711, **Business Phone:** (804)257-5757.

### YANCY, DR. ROBERT JAMES
Educator. **Personal:** Born Mar 10, 1944, Tifton, GA; son of Preston Martin and Margaret Elizabeth Robinson; married Dorothy Cowser; children: Yvonne. **Educ:** Morehouse Col, Atlanta, GA, BA, bus admin, 1964; Atlanta Univ, MBA, 1966; Northwestern Univ, PhD, mgt, 1973; JL Kellogg Sch Mgt, strategic mgt. **Career:** Hampton Inst, Hampton, Va, asst prof, 1967-69; Atlanta Univ, Atlanta, Ga, asst prof & assoc prof, 1971-82; Zebra Corp, Atlanta, Ga, pres & chief exec officer, 1972-82; WGa Col Carrollton, Ga, asst prof, 1982; Southern Tech Inst, Marietta, Ga, prof, 1983-86; Southern Poly tech State Univ, Marietta, Ga, Sch Mgt, founding dean & prof, 1983-2000, prof, prof emer, currently; RJ Yancy Co, pres & chief exec officer; Woodline Solutions, vpres bus develop, 2011-12; Yancy's Pl LLC, Home Healthcare Network, pres, 2011-14, chief exec officer, 2011-. **Orgs:** Chairperson, Univ Syst Ga, Admin Comm Grad Work, 1990-91; chairperson, Univ Syst Ga, Acad Rev Comm Bus Admin, Ft Valley State Col, 1989; chairperson, Ann Mem Campaign, Butler St Young Mens Christian Asn, 1977; Leadership Cobb Alumni asn; Leadership Atlanta Alumni asn; Soc Intl Bus Fels; Acad Mgt; 100 Black Men Atlanta; Omega Psi Phi Fraternity; chmn, SCORE, Atlanta Chap, 2013-. **Home Addr:** 1525 New Hope Rd SW, Atlanta, GA 30331-7451, **Home Phone:** (404)349-9187. **Business Addr:** Professor Emeritus, Southern Polytechnic State University, 1100 S Marietta Pkwy SE, Marietta, GA 30060, **Business Phone:** (678)915-7778.

### YANCYY, ROBERT (L YANCYY)
Entertainer, entrepreneur. **Personal:** Born Feb 13, 1971, St. Thomas; son of Keith and Lenora. **Educ:** Univ Mich, BMA, 1995. **Career:** CCS Inst Arts, teacher, 1996-98; Three Y Entertainment, chief exec officer, owner, 1995-. **Orgs:** Phi Mu Alpha, 1992. **Home Addr:** 16203 Bentler, Detroit, MI 48219, **Home Phone:** (313)865-9631. **Business Addr:** Chief Executive Officer, Three y Entertainment, 16203 Bentler, Detroit, MI 48219, **Business Phone:** (313)790-0924.

### YARBORO, DR. THEODORE LEON, SR.
Physician. **Personal:** Born Feb 16, 1932, Rocky Mount, NC; married Deanna Marie Rose; children: Theodore L Jr, Deanna R & Theresa L. **Educ:** NC Cent Univ, BS, 1954, MS, 1956; Meharry Med Col, MD, 1963; Univ Pittsburgh Grad Sch Pub Health, MPH, 1979. **Career:** US Bur Mines, chem, anal & org, 1956-59; Penn St Univ, Shenango Valley Campus lectr; Theodore L Yarboro MD Inc, family practr, 1965-; Med Ctr GA, family med. **Orgs:** Three publs J Org Chem, J Chem, Eng Data, 1959-61; Nat Med Asn, 1965-; Am Acad Family Physicians, 1965-; AMA, 1965-; bd dir, Mercer Co Br; Nat Asn Advan Colored People, 1965-; founder, Shenango Valley Urban League, 1968; bd dir, Shenango Valley Urban League, 1968-78; founder & adv, Dr Maceo E Patterson Future Physician Soc, 1969-; charter diplo, Am Bd Family Pract, 1970-; charter fel Am Acad Fam Pract, 1972-; mem bd trustee, Nat Urban League, 1973-78; Gov Adv Com Mult Health Screening, 1975-76; Gov's Com Health Educ, PA, 1975-76; life mem, Nat Asn Advan Colored People, 1976-. **Honors/Awds:** Distinguished Service Award Midwestern PA Chap, Am Heart Asn, 1970 & 75; Distinguished Service Award, Shenango Valley Urban League, 1972; Man of the Year, Shenango Valley Jaycees, 1972; Community Service Award, Mercer Co Br, NAACP, 1976. **Home Addr:** 2920 Crosswhite Dr, West Middlesex, PA 16148, **Home Phone:** (724)347-5950. **Business Addr:** Family Practitioner, Theodore Leon Yarboro MD Inc, 755 Division St, Sharon, PA 16146, **Business Phone:** (724)346-4124.

### YARBOROUGH, PROF. RICHARD A.
Teacher. **Personal:** Born May 24, 1951, Philadelphia, PA; son of John W III and Yvonne K Newby. **Educ:** Mich State Univ, E Lansing, MI, BA, eng high hons, 1973; Stanford Univ, PhD, eng & Am lit, 1980. **Career:** Stanford Univ, Whiting fel humanities, 1977-78; Univ Calif, Los Angeles, Calif, Dept Eng, asst prof, 1979-86, assoc prof, 1986-2010, prof, 2010-, African-Am Studies, fac res assoc, 1979-, chair, 1990-94, assoc dir, 1993-94, Ralph J. Bunche Ctr African Am Studies, interim dir, 1997-2001, 2006-07; Libr Black Lit Ser, UPr N Eng, gen ed, 1988-; Ford Found, fel, 1988-89; Stanford Univ, Ctr Advan Study Behav Sci, fel, 1992-93. **Orgs:** Bd ed adv, Am Quart, 1987-91; nat coun, Am Studies Asn, 1988-91; ed bd, African Am Rev, 1989-2001; chair, Div Black Am Lit & Cult, Mod Lang Asn, 1989-90, exec comt; bd supvr, Eng Inst, 1992-95; Calif Coun Humanities, 1992-96; mng bd, Am Quart, 2012-; Alice Childress Soc; Charles Waddell Chesnutt Asn; Col Lang Asn; Collegium African Am Res; George Moses Horton Soc; Soc Study Multi-Ethnic Lit Us. **Home Addr:** PO Box 49937, Los Angeles, CA 90049-0937, **Home Phone:** (310)670-8565. **Business Addr:** Managing Board, American Quarterly, 2715 N Charles St, Baltimore, MD 21218-4319, **Business Phone:** (410)516-6988.

### YARBRO, WILLIAM E., JR.
Business owner. **Career:** The 95th & Columbus Prod, producer & co owner. **Business Addr:** Producer, Co-Owner, 95th & Columbus Production Co, 1401 Ocean Ave Suite 301, Santa Monica, CA 90401.

### YARBROUGH, DELANO
School administrator, educator, association executive. **Personal:** Born Sep 20, 1936, Thornton, AR; son of Roy and Sadie; married Samella O; children: Delano, Desiree & Darryl. **Educ:** Univ Ark, Pine Bluff, BS, math; AZUSA Pacif Col, MA, 1973; Marquette Univ; Univ Calif, Los Angeles; Univ San Francisco, doct; Pepperdine Univ, ABO. **Career:** School administrator (retired); E HS Lilbourn, teacher, 1961-63; USn, mathematician, 1963-65; Pasadena Unified Sch Dist, teacher, 1964-94, desegregation proj dir, 1967-77; Del Yarbrough & Assocs, consult, 1990; Eliot Mid Sch, prin, 1981-94. **Orgs:** Pres, Pasedena Br, Nat Asn Advan Colored People, 1999-2002; ASCD; CSCD; Am Polit Sci Asn; Phi Delta Kappa; Nat Asn Advan Colored People; Univ Ark-Pine Bluff Alumni Asn; Pasadena Educ Found; consult Afro-Am Educ Cult Ctr; consult Jet Propulsion Lab; vice chmn ESAA; bd dir, Day One, currently; BCDI; Calif State Math Framework Comt, 1984-86; pres & bd dir, Diversified Educ Serv, Inc, 1981; Independent Primary/Sec Educ Prof, bd dir, 1994-. **Honors/Awds:** New Teacher of the Year Pasadena, 1964; Commendation in educ for serv rendered in reducing racial isolation; Pasadena & Altadena Branches; Nat Asn Advan Colored People, Community Service Awards; Nat Parents of the Year Award, Tuskegee Univ, 1988; PTA Service Award, 1994; Commendation from Pres Clinton, 1995. **Business Addr:** Principal, Diversified Educational Services Inc, 555 E Wash Blvd, Pasadena, CA 91104, **Business Phone:** (626)791-4352.

### YARBROUGH, KAREN
Government official, founder (originator), president (organization). **Personal:** married Henderson Sr. **Educ:** Chicago State Univ, BA, bus admin; Northeastern Ill Univ, MA, inner city studies. **Career:** Hathaway Ins Agency, founder & pres; Maywood Chamber Com, pres, 8yrs; Proviso Twp, dem committeeman; State Govt, state rep 7th dist, currently. **Orgs:** Bd mem, United Way Suburban Chicago; bd mem, Oak Pk, YMCA; founder, Maywood's live theater; Maywood Youth Mentoring prog; supporter, var scholar progs; Gold Card Prog; chairwomen, Housing & Urban Develop; vice chairwoman, House Ins Comt; Environ Health Comt. **Special Achievements:** Illinois House Joint Resolution 125, 2006; First Female President of the Maywood Chamber of Commerce. **Business Addr:** State Representative, Illinois, District 7, 272-S Stratton Off Bldg, Springfield, IL 62706, **Business Phone:** (217)782-8120.

### YARBROUGH, MAMIE LUELLA
Government official, real estate executive. **Personal:** Born Sep 19, 1941, Benton Harbor, MI; married Charles; children: Dawn Zoppi & Nyles Charles. **Educ:** Western Mich Univ, attended 1960; Cert Housing Mgt, CHM, ARM, SHS. **Career:** NBD F&M Bank, banking, 1966-75; Berrien Homes Apts, housing mgr, 1975-81; River Terr Apts, housing mgr, 1981-; Benton Harbor Area Sch Bd, vpres & secy; Berrien County, vice chairperson, 4th Dist, comnr, currently; Harbor Pointe Apt, mgr; Benton Harbor & Benton Twp Housing Comns. **Orgs:** Bd mem, SW Mich Comn; bd mem, Mich Works Bd; pres, Benton Harbor Libr Bd; Krasl Art Ctr Bd Dirs; Scholar Comt, New Territory Arts Asn; Lory Pl Bd Dirs; CWCC Arts, Cult & Leisure Comt; Natural Sistas Literacy Soc; bd mem, St Joseph River Harbor Authority Counties Human Serv Comt; adminr, Mich State Housing Develop Authority; pres, Benton Harbor Homecoming Inc; pres, Coming Home Coming Together Concert Comt Second Baptist Church; Berrien County Land Bank Authority. **Honors/Awds:** Golden Acorn Grantee Award, Berrien Community Found, 2009. **Home Addr:** 1086 Monroe St, Benton Harbor, MI 49022, **Home Phone:** (269)925-2669. **Business Addr:** Commissioner, Benton County 4th District, 228 Territorial Rd Suite 2, Benton Harbor, MI 49022, **Business Phone:** (269)925-5699.

### YARBROUGH, NANA CAMILLE
Educator, writer, singer. **Personal:** Born Jan 8, 1938, Chicago, IL. **Career:** Actress, Composer, Singer, Teacher, Writer & Dancer; S Ill Univ, prof; City Col NY, fac mem, prof African dance & diaspora; WWRL-AM, talk show host; MNN, show host, currently; Ancestor House Productions, founder; Albums: The Iron Pot Cooker, 1975, Take Yo' Praise, 1975; Books: Cornrows (poems for children), 1979; The Shimmershine Queen (juvenile), 1989; Tamika & the Wisdom Rings (juvenile), 1994; Little Tree Growing in the Shade (juvenile), 1996; Ancestor House, 2003; Nat Endowment Arts fel. **Business Addr:** Actress, Poet, Activist, African American Traditions Workshop, 80 St Nicholas Ave Suite 4G, New York, NY 10026, **Business Phone:** (212)252-3152.

### YARBROUGH, PATRICIA NICHOLSON
Business owner. **Personal:** Born May 16, 1951, San Francisco, CA; daughter of Bernice; married Herbert; children: Kevin & Martin. **Educ:** Univ San Francisco, BA, 1973. **Career:** Blue World Travel Corp, founder & pres, 1978-; Doris Easly Sch C, pres, currently. **Orgs:** UNCF, Our Festival Sea Prog. **Honors/Awds:** Top Producer Award, Royal Caribbean Cruise Line, 1994, 1995; Outstanding Support Award, Celebrity Cruise Lines, 1996; Best Travel Promotion, Travel Weekly, 1998; Top 50 Producers, Travel Savers, 2000. **Special Achievements:** Founded Festival at Sea African American Theme Cruises and Friends of Festival at Sea, African Americans Cruising the World. **Business Addr:** President, Blue World Travel Corp, 50 1st St Suite 411, San Francisco, CA 94105-2413, **Business Phone:** (415)882-9444.

### YARBROUGH, ROBERT ELZY
Lawyer. **Personal:** Born Dec 16, 1929, Atlanta, GA. **Educ:** Boston Col, BS, 1951; Boston Univ, Law Sch, LLB, 1958. **Career:** US Post Off, clerk, 1954-61; atty law, 1961-; US Cust Serv, impt specialist, 1963-; US Cust Serv, Dept Treas, sr impt specialist, 1975-. **Orgs:** Bd trustee, Boston Latin Sch Alumni Asn, 1980; Am Bar Asn; Mass Bar Asn; Prince Hall Grand Lodge F & AM, Mass; Syria Temple No 31 AEAONMS. **Home Addr:** 22 Mayfair St, Roxbury, MA 02119, **Home Phone:** (617)427-2276. **Business Addr:** Attorney, 22 Mayfair St, Boston, MA 02119, **Business Phone:** (617)427-2276.

### YARBROUGH, ROOSEVELT
Accountant, executive. **Personal:** Born Jan 11, 1946, Pattison, MS. **Educ:** Chapman Col, attended 1968; Miss Valley State Univ, BS, 1973; John Marshall Law Sch, attended 1981; Am Mgt Asn Ctr, mgt develop cert, 1982. **Career:** Ernst & Ernst, staff acct, 1975; Bailey Meter Co, budget analyst, 1976; SW Miss Legal Serv, dir admin, 1982; First Entry Serv, acct; Miss dem Party, Claiborne County, chair, currently. **Orgs:** Bd mem, Claiborne City Sch; Claiborne City Bldg; Supvy & Curric Develop, Black Ed & Econ Proj; Nat Asn Advan Colored People; Miss Cult Arts Coalition; Claiborne City Family Reunion. **Home Addr:** 153 Pattison Tillman Rd, PO Box 141, Pattison, MS 39144, **Home Phone:** (601)437-4413. **Business Addr:** Chair, Claiborne County, 153 Pattison Tillman Rd, Pattison, MS 39144, **Business Phone:** (601)437-4413.

### YARN, DR. BARBARA LYNNE IVEY
Physician. **Personal:** Born Knoxville, TN; daughter of Boyd S (deceased) and Geraldine Celestine Harris; married Tyrone Von; children: Tiffany Nicole & Roan. **Educ:** Knoxville Col, BS, 1963; Univ Tenn, attended 1963; Univ Minn, MPH, 1969; Meharry Med Col,

Sch Med, MD, 1973. **Career:** Knoxville City Sch, sci teacher, 1963-64; Oak Ridge Nat Lab, res asst, 1964-67; Minn Head Start Prog, pub health educr & consult, 1968; Univ Minn Community Pub Health Care Ctr, stud health adv, 1968-69; Pub Health & Safety Admin, 1969; Greely Sch Dist Community Health Ctr, instr/pub health adv, 1969; Matthew Walker Health Care Ctr, 1972-73; Munich Mil Hosp, physician, 1974-75; Cuban-Haitian Refugee Howard Univ Hosp, internship, 1974; Emory Univ Affiliated Hosps, anesthesiol resident, 1975-78; Grady Memorial Hosp, anesthesiologist, 1975-78; US Pub Health Serv, sr surgeon, regional med consult; Dept Health & Human Serv, 1978-82; Camp, chief med officer, 1981-82; Univ Louis, anesthesiol fel, 1982-83; Humana Hosp, Dept Anesthesiol & Dept Respiratory Ther, chair & div head, 1982-91; Atlanta Outpatient Peachtree Dunwoody, anesthesiologist, 1991-; Howard Univ Hosp, internal med, resident; Univ Louisville, Sch Med, anesthesiol, resident; pvt pract, currently. **Orgs:** Am Med Asn; Nat Med Asn; Med Asn Ga; Knoxville Col Alumni Asn, 1963-; Alpha Kappa Alpha Sorority, Pi Alpha Omega chap; Links, Buckhead Cascade City Chap, pres, 1995-01; Atlanta Symphony, bd dir, 1999-; Goodworks Int, co-sponsor, 1999-. **Honors/Awds:** Alpha Kappa Alpha Sorority, Acad Scholar Award, 1959-63; Pub Health Scholar Award, 1968-69; Jesse Smith Noyes Obstet & Gynec Fel, 1969-72; Sloan Found, Med Scholar Award, 1969-73; Univ Louis, Fel Anesthesiology, 1982-83; Pub Health Serv, Citation & Commendation Medal for Distinguished Serv, 1978-82; United States Pub Health Serv, Spec Assignment Ribbon Award, 1979; Habitat Humanity, Knoxville Chap, Plaque, 1992; Knoxville Col, Distinguished Alumnus Award, 1993; Int Yr of the Older Persons, 1999; selected one of 100 Most Powerful & Influential Women of Georgia, 2000. **Home Addr:** 111 Stonington Dr, Peachtree City, GA 30269, **Home Phone:** (404)847-0893. **Business Addr:** Physician, 1077 S Main St, Madison, GA 30650, **Business Phone:** (770)217-5111.

## YATES, ANTHONY J. (TONY YATES)

Basketball coach, president (organization), executive. **Personal:** Born Sep 15, 1937, Lawrenceburg, IN; married Maxine; children: Anthony & Brianna. **Educ:** Univ Cincinnati, BS, 1963. **Career:** Basketball coach (retired), exec; Univ Ill, asst basketball coach, 1974; Univ Cincinnati, asst basketball coach, 1971-74, head coach, 1983-89; Cincin Royals Prof Basketball Team, part time scout, 1966-71; Fin Mgt Corp, salesman, 1968-71; Drake Mem Hosp, asst to admin, person, dir, 1966-68; Shillitos Dept Store, asst employ mgr, 1963-66; Tony Yates Caring Kids Found, pres & founder, currently. **Orgs:** Nat Asn Sec Deal; bd dir, Nat AAU Basktbl League; bd dir, Greater Cincin Jr Basketball Asn; mem, Cincin Plan Parenthd; mem, Cincin Sch Found; mem, Baseball "Kid Gloves" game; mem, Cincin Met AAU. **Business Addr:** President, Founder, Tony Yates Caring For Kids Foundation, 9879 Forest Glen Dr, Montgomery, OH 45242, **Business Phone:** (513)984-6799.

## YATES, PASTOR LEROY LOUIS, SR.

Clergy. **Personal:** Born Dec 8, 1929, Terry, MS; son of Clarence and Mary Ella Summers (deceased); married Beverly Joanne Pannell; children: Sara Doreen, Jonathan Allen, Joyce Ellen, Mary Francis Coultman & LeRoy Louis Jr. **Educ:** Moody Bible Inst, Chicago, grad dipl, 1956; Chicago State Univ, BA, 1971, MS, 1979; Detroit Bible Col, hon doctor humanities, 1981. **Career:** Westlawn Gospel Chapel, Chicago, IL, sr pastor, 1957-; Hektoen Inst, Cook County Hosp, chief tech supvr, 1964-76; Chicago Med Sch, microbiologist, 1968-79; Circle Youth Ranch, Bangor, MI, exec dir, 1978-80. **Orgs:** Exec bd mem, Leukemia Soc Am, 1961-80; exec bd mem, Int Mag Publ, 1967-80; draft bd mem, Local Bd 58, 1968-74; exec bd secy, PACE Inst, Cook County Jail Chicago, 1969-80; adv bd mem, Univ Ill Med Ctr, 1978-80; vol counr, Westside Holistic Family Ctr, 1978-80, counr, currently; secy bd, W African Christian Ministries, currently. **Home Addr:** 555 E 167th St, South Holland, IL 60473-2911. **Business Addr:** Secretary of the Board, West African Christian Ministries, 900 Jefferson St, Valparaiso, IN 46383, **Business Phone:** (219)465-1825.

## YATES, LLOYD

President (organization), chief executive officer, association executive. **Personal:** married Monica; children: 2. **Educ:** Univ Pittsburgh, BS, mech engineering; St Joseph Univ, Philadelphia, MBA; Univ Pa Wharton Sch, advan mgt prog; Advan Mgt Prog, exec mgt prog. **Career:** PECO Energy, exec; Carolina Power & Light, vpres fossil generation, 1998; Progress Energy Carolinas, vpres, pres & chief exec officer, 2007-12; Duke Energy's Carolinas Region, exec vpres regulated utilities, 2012, exec vpres, mkt solutions & pres, 2014-, exec vpres customer opers, sr vpres energy delivery; Duke Energy Florida, LLC, dir; Duke Energy Ohio Inc, exec vpres; Marsh & McLennan Co Inc, dir, 2011-. **Orgs:** Bd mem, NC Econ Develop; bd mem, NC Community Col Found; bd mem, Inst Nuclear Power Opers Accreditation; bd mem, Asn Edison Illum Co; bd mem, NC Chamber Com; Sc Palmetto Bus Forum; Exec Leadership Coun; bd dir, WakeMed; dir, Fla Power Corp. **Honors/Awds:** "Black Enterprise," The 100 Most Powerful Executives in Corporate America, 2010. **Business Addr:** Executive Vice President, Marsh & McLennan Companies Inc, 1166 Avenue of the Americas, New York, NY 10036-2774, **Business Phone:** (212)345-5000.

## YATES, LLOYD M.

President (organization), chief executive officer. **Personal:** married Monica; children: 2. **Educ:** Univ Pittsburgh, BS, mech engineering; St Joseph's Univ, Philadelphia, Pa, MBA; Univ Pa Wharton Sch, advan mgt prog; Harvard Bus Sch, exec mgt prog. **Career:** PECO Energy, gen mgr opers; Progress Energy, vpres fossil generation, 1998-2003, vpres transmission, 2003-04, sr vpres, 2005-07, pres & chief exec officer, 2007-; Duke Energy, exec vpres, currently; Edison Illum Co, pres & chmn, 2014. **Orgs:** Bd mem, Greater Raleigh Conv & Visitors Bur; bd mem, The Triangle Urban League; bd mem, Am Heart Asn; dir, Fla Power Co; dir, Marsh & McLennan Co Inc, 2011-; dir, Duke Energy Carolinas LLC; dir, Duke Energy Fla LLC. **Business Addr:** Executive Vice President, Duke Energy, 400 S Tryon St, Charlotte, NC 28202, **Business Phone:** (704)373-4782.

## YATES, MARK

Vice president (organization), banker, investment banker. **Personal:** Born Sep 15, 1966, Memphis, TN; son of Andres N and Mary F; children: 2. **Educ:** Howard Univ, BA, econs, finance, 1989; Vanderbilt Univ, Owen Grad Sch Mgt, MBA, econs, finance, 1996. **Career:** First Tenn bank, vpres comm loan officer, sr vpres investor rels, 1984-2007; US Rep Harold Ford Jr, chief staff, 1996-98; Morgan Keegan & Co, Memphis, investment banker & vpres, 1998-2001; Univ Memphis, adj prof, Finance, 2004-05; First Horizon Nat Corp, sr vpres, Financial Capital Mkt Div, sr vpres, 2004-07; A & H Contractors, consult, 2007-08; Rice Financial Prod Co, Memphis, managing dir, sr vpres, 2007-09; Le Bonheur C's Med Ctr, exec dir, 2009-; Comer Capital Group LLC, spec adv, currently; LES-TN, pres & chief exec officer, 2011-. **Orgs:** Howard Univ Alumni Asn, 1988-; bd mem, Boys Club, 1993-; keeper finance, Omega Psi Phi Frat, 1993-94; Shelby County Health Educ Bd; bd mem, Juv Ct Foster Care Rev. **Home Addr:** 890 Summer Shade Lane, Memphis, TN 38116-4018, **Home Phone:** (901)398-3519. **Business Addr:** Executive Director, Le Bonheur Childrens Medical Center, 50 N Dunlap St, Memphis, TN 38103, **Business Phone:** (901)287-5437.

## YATES, TONY. See YATES, ANTHONY J.

## YEARWOOD, DAVID MONROE, JR.

Executive. **Personal:** Born Nov 15, 1945, Barbados; son of David M and Una U Holder; children: Edward & David III. **Educ:** Pace Univ, BBA, 1978; Keller Grad Sch Mgt, MBA, 1982, cert human resources, 1983. **Career:** Nat Broadcasting Co, NY, financial analyst, 1970-75, mgr budgets, 1975-77; Nat Broadcasting Co, Chicago, mgr acct, 1977-80, dir finance & admin, 1980; WDRB-TV, Louisville, exec vpres & sta mgr, currently; FOX & UPN Stas, exec vpres & sta mgr; NBC, New York; U.S. Govt, agt cashier; WUSF Pub Media, dir bus, finance, human resources, currently; IntellisMedia, interim dir engineering, opers & tv spec proj, currently. **Orgs:** Leadership Louisville; Bingham Fels; Stage One; Louisville Sci Ctr; Hundred Black Men; Univ Louisville Int Servs Learning Prog; pres, Ill Broadcasters Asn. **Business Addr:** Interim Director, IntellisMedia, 4202 E Fowler Ave TVB100, Tampa, FL 33620, **Business Phone:** (813)396-9850.

## YEARWOOD, REV. DR. KIRTLEY

Clergy, pathologist. **Personal:** Born Oct 12, 1961, Barbados. **Educ:** Tuskegee Inst, BS; Univ Okla, MPh; Univ Ark, Gen Theol Sem, MDiv, 1998; George Wash Med Ctr, MD. **Career:** St Mary's Episcopal Church, Wash, DC, rector; St Paul's, Wash, DC, 2004; Med Univ Sc, path fel; Trinity Cathedral, Pittsburgh, Pa, priest assoc & curate; Grace Episcopal Church, vicar, 2007-08; St Clement Rome Episcopal Church, Seattle, Wash, priest-in-charge, 2009-10; St Andrew's Episcopal Church, Lawton, Okla, interim rector, 2010-11; Seeing the Word, consult; Church St Alban the Martyr, interim priest-in-charge, 2012-. **Orgs:** Diocesan Comt Liturgy & Music. **Honors/Awds:** He is one of more than 100 medical doctor-priests in the Episcopal Church. **Special Achievements:** The only black person at Grace. **Business Addr:** Interim Priest in Charge, Church of Saint Alban the Martyr, 116-42 Farmers Blvd, St Albans, NY 11412, **Business Phone:** (718)528-1891.

## YELDING, ERIC GIRARD

Baseball executive, baseball player. **Personal:** Born Feb 22, 1965, Montrose, AL. **Career:** Baseball player (retired), baseball coach; Houston Astros, shortstop, ctr fielder & second baseman, 1989-92; Cincinnati Reds, shortstop, ctr fielder & second baseman, 1992; Chicago Cubs, shortstop, ctr fielder & second baseman, 1993; Ft Bend Texans, coach, currently. **Honors/Awds:** NL in stolen bases, 1990. **Business Addr:** Coach, The Fort Bend Texans, 8523 Old Quarry Dr, Sugar Land, TX 77479, **Business Phone:** (832)444-2307.

## YELITY, STEPHEN C.

Executive. **Personal:** Born Oct 25, 1949, Littleton, NC; son of Stephen Jackson and Martha Ella Pitchford; married Matlyn Joyce Alston; children: Scott Carnelle. **Educ:** Norfolk State Univ, Norfolk, VA, BS, acct & bus admin, 1973. **Career:** Am Cyanamid, Wayne NJ, acct, 1973-76; Johnson & Johnson, Chicopee & Nb, sr acct & financial analyst, 1976-78; Johnson & Johnson Baby Prod, Skillman, NJ, acct supvr & mgr, 1978-84; Accurate Info Systs, S Plainfield, NJ, pres & chief exec officer, 1984-98; Failure Free Reading, regional dir; Creative Bus Develop LLC, sr consult, currently. **Orgs:** New York/NJ Minority Purchasing Coun, 1986-; Black Data Processing Asn, 1987-; Int Network Unix Syst Uses, 1988-; S Plainfield Chamber Com, 1988-; NJ Brain Trust, 1989-; Nat Urban League, 1989-; Nat Asn Advan Colored People, 1989-. **Home Addr:** 5 Doyle Ct, Piscataway, NJ 08854. **Business Addr:** Senior Consultant, Creative Business Development LLC, 55 Intervale Rd, Boonton, NJ 07005-1052, **Business Phone:** (973)257-7336.

## YERGAN, ERIC

Stockbroker. **Personal:** Born Long Island, NY. **Educ:** Marist Col, Poughkeepsie, NY, BS, bus, 1975; Harvard Bus Sch, MBA, mkt/finance, gen mgt, 1982. **Career:** Paine Webber, sr vpres, 1984-94; Donaldson, Lufkin & Jenrette, sr vpres, 1994-99; Yergan Agency, owner, 1998-2011; Merrill Lynch, financial advisor, 2011-12; NYC Fast Tax & NJ Fast Tax, partner, 2005-; Mutual Omaha, financial advisor, 2013-. **Orgs:** Manhattan Chamber Com; CoachCougar Soccer Club. **Honors/Awds:** National Conference Award, Honor Ring. **Special Achievements:** One of 25 "Hottest Blacks on Wall Street" listed in Black Enterprise, October, 1992. **Business Addr:** Financial Advisor, Mutual of Omaha, Mutual of Omaha Plaza, Omaha, NE NE 68175.

## YERGER, BEN. See Obituaries Section.

## YIZAR, DR. JAMES H., JR.

Educator, school administrator. **Personal:** Born Los Angeles, CA; son of James H and Gladys. **Educ:** Idaho State Univ, BA, 1983; M Coun, 1990; EdD, higher educ admin, 2010. **Career:** Recreational Coordr, 1981-82; Upward Bound Prog, asst dir, 1982-84; Stud Support Serv, coordr, 1984-90; Coun Learning Specialist, 1984-94; Asst Trio Prog, dir, 1990-94; Spec Olympics Idaho, game coordr, 1992-93; Trio Prog Dir, 1994-2007; asst dean students, 2000-07; assoc dean students, 2007-10; Assoc Dir Stud Success Ctr/Asst Athletics Dir Stud Support, 2010-. **Orgs:** Kappa Alpha Psi, 1977-; adv, Epsilon Theta Chap, 1984-; adv, Black Stud Alliance, 1984-86; bd dir, Access Idaho, 1985-97, bd pres, 1988-92; Nat Asn Advan Colored People, 1986-, local br pres, 1994-98; Phi Kappa Phi, 2000-; Rotary Club mem, 2001-; Kappa Delta Pi, 2002-. **Special Achievements:** ISU Sports Hall of Fame, Inducted, 2013. **Home Addr:** 2790 Kootenai St, Pocatello, ID 83201-1870, **Home Phone:** (208)238-7490. **Business Addr:** Assistant Athletics Director for Student Success, Associate Director of Student Success Center, Idaho State University, 921 S 8th Ave PO Box 8010, Pocatello, ID 83209-8010, **Business Phone:** (208)282-3662.

## YOBA, ABDUL-MALIK KASHIE. See YOBA, MALIK.

## YOBA, MALIK (ABDUL-MALIK KASHIE YOBA)

Actor, singer. **Personal:** Born Sep 17, 1967, Bronx, NY; son of Erutan Abdullah and Mahmoudah Young Lanier; married Trisha Mann; children: Josiah, Josiah & Mann; married Cat Wilson; children: Pria. **Career:** Films: Cool Runnings, 1993; Smoke, 1995; Blue in the Face, 1995; Cop Land, 1997; Soul Food, 1997; Ride, 1998; Personals, 1999; Harlem Aria, 1999; His Woman, His Wife, 2000; Dreaming in Black & White, 2002; Oh Happy Day, 2004; Arrested Development, 2004; Oh Happy Day, 2004; The Days, 2004; Criminal, 2004; Kids in America, 2005; Slur, 2005; Girlfriends, 2003-07; They're Just My Friends, 2006; Why Did I Get Married?, 2007; Feel the Noise, 2007; Rockaway, 2007; Caught on Tape, post-production, 2009; My Girlfriend's Back, post-production, 2009; My Girlfriend's Back, 2010; Aluna: The Motion Comic Animation, 2010; Allegiance, 2012; The Assault, 2014; Why Did I Get Married Too, currently; Tonsure, exec producer, 2014. TV appearances: City Kids Found, vpres, 1988-93; "Law & Order", 1994; Universal TV ser, actor, "New York Undercover", 1994; Nature Boy Enterprises, pres & chief exec officer, 1994-; "Where I Live"; "That's So Raven", 2006; "Thief", 2006; "Raines", 2007; TNT ser, actor, "Bull", "Thief", 2005; "To Be Determined", 2007; "Inseparable", 2008; "CSI: Miami", 2008; "Eve Ate the Apple", 2009; "déjà vu", 2009; "Solitary", 2009; "Venus", 2009; "Kiss", 2009; "Defying Gravity", 2009; "Tyler Perry's Why Did I Get Married Too", 2010; "Justified", 2010; "Alphas", 2011-12; "Nikita", 2011; "The Celibate Nympho Chronicles: The Web Series", 2011; "Person of interest", 2012; "NYC 22", 2012; "Betty and Coretta", 2013; "Revolution", 2013; "The Good Wife", 2013; "Turks & Caicos", 2014; "Empire", 2015. **Orgs:** Bd mem, REACH, 1992-; adv & vpres, City Kids Found, 1993; Childrens Peace, 1994; community mem, Hale House, 1995; Phi Beta Sigma Fraternity Inc.

## YOHANNES, DANIEL W.

Banker. **Personal:** Born Sep 22, 1952, Addis Ababa; married Saron; children: Tsedeye, Michael & Rebecca. **Educ:** Claremont McKenna Col, BA, econ; Pepperdine Univ, MBA. **Career:** US Bancorp, 1998-2003; US Bank, vice chmn; Security Pac Bank, exec vpres, 1977-92; US Bank & Firstar, 1992-99; Colo Nat Bank, pres & chief exec officer, 1992-98; M&R Investments LLC, pres & chief exec officer, currently; Millennium Challenge Corp, pres & chief exec officer, 2009-. **Orgs:** Bd mem, Nat Jewish Med & Res Ctr, 1995, bd dir, currently; Denver Art Mus; Univ Med Sch; Proj CURE; mem, Nat Bd Smithsonian Inst; mem, Media One Group Inc; Mgt Comt US Bank; bd mem, First Western Trust Bank; bd dir, Boy Scouts Am; trustee, Denver Art Mus; bd dir, Nat Jewish Hosp; Univ Wash Michael G Foster Sch Bus; Pac Coast Banking Sch; Proj Comn Urgent Relief & Equip. **Home Addr:** 18 Cherry Hills Farm Dr, Englewood, CO 80113-7165. **Business Addr:** President, Chief Executive Officer, Millennium Challenge Corp, 875 Fifteenth St NW, Washington, DC 20005-2221, **Business Phone:** (202)521-3600.

## YORK, DR. RUSSEL HAROLD

Physician. **Personal:** Born May 6, 1952, Chicago, IL; married Yvonne Taylor; children: Damion, Renee & Marucs A. **Educ:** Kalamazoo Col, BA, 1974; Howard Univ, MD, 1978. **Career:** Henry Ford Hosp, intern, resident, 1978-81; Wayne State Univ, fel, 1982-84, fac mem, instr, 1984-86; pvt pract, 1986-; Beals Inst, med doc, currently. **Orgs:** Am Rheumatism Asn, 1986-; Mich Rheumatism Soc; assoc mem, Am Col Physicians; Am Bd Internal Med. **Honors/Awds:** Dipl Am Bd Internal Med, 1982; Am Bd Rheumatology, 1984; Minority Faculty Research Award, Wayne State Univ, 1984, 1985, 1986. **Home Addr:** 19625 Renfrew Rd, Detroit, MI 48221-1891, **Home Phone:** (313)341-7009. **Business Addr:** Medical Doctor, Beals Institute, 4333 W St Joe Hwy Suite 1, Lansing, MI 48917, **Business Phone:** (517)321-1525.

## YORK, VINCENT

Musician, jazz musician. **Personal:** Born Jun 25, 1952, Jacksonville, FL; son of George and Lillie Evans; married Kathleen; children: Natasha & Cedric. **Educ:** Southern Univ, BA, 1974; Univ Mich, MA, 1976. **Career:** Jazz musician, 1975-; Vincent York's NY Force, founder & saxophonist, 1977-; Ann Arbor Community High Sch, artist-in-residence, 1996-2000; Mich Coun for Arts & Cult Affairs Artist-in-Residence Community High Sch, active educr, 1996-2001; Vincent Yorks Jazzistry, founder & perfomer, artistic dir, 1999-; Albums: Blending Forces, 1990; Focusing the Vision, 1998; Washtenaw Community Col, jazz orchestra dir. **Orgs:** Ann Arbor Fed Musicians; Detroit Fed Musicians; Am Fed Musicians. **Business Addr:** Founder, Performer, Vincent York's Jazzistry, 730 Miller Ave, Ann Arbor, MI 48107, **Business Phone:** (734)761-6024.

## YOUNG, AHMEENAH

Executive. **Career:** Philadelphia's Independence Visitor Ctr, gen mgr, 2002; Pa Conv Ctr Authority, gen mgr, exec vpres external affairs, 2004, pres & chief exec officer, 2008; Tourism & hospitality indust, sr exec; Greater Philadelphia Tourism Mkt Corp; SearchWide LLC, vpres corp diversity; Temple Univ, dir & vpres; N by Northwest restaurant, co-owner; Sch Tourism & Hospitality Mgt, currently. **Orgs:** Greater Philadelphia Hotel Asn; Nat Asn Black Meeting Planners; Int Asn Assembly Managers; Nat Speakers Asn; bd, Sunoco Welcome Am, currently; N Philadelphia Health Systs; bd, Temple Univ's Sch Tourism & Hospitality Mgt; bd, Art Sanctuary; bd, Nat Forum Black Pub Adminr; bd, Mt Airy USA; bd, Philadelphia Airport; African Am Mus Philadelphia; Greater Philadelphia Urban Affairs Coalition; Prof Conv Mgt Asn; exec comt, Philadelphia Conv & Visitors Bur. **Business Addr:** President, Temple University's School Tourism & Hospitality Management, 1810 N 13 St Speakman Hall 111, Philadelphia, PA 19122, **Business Phone:** (215)204-8701.

### YOUNG, ALAN C.
Certified public accountant. **Personal:** Born Jan 16, 1953, Inkster, MI; son of Anderson and Sarah; married Colette Brooks; children: Aaron C, Adam C & Austen C. **Educ:** Mich State Univ, BA, 1976; Walsh Col, MA, tax, 1985. **Career:** Deloitte Haskins & Sells, sr consult, 1977-81; Deloitte & Touche, sr consult, 1977-81; Keith Warlick & Co, mgr, 1981-83; Alan C Young & Assoc PC, founder, pres, cheif exec officer, managing dir, 1983-; Fisher Body Co Livonia & Gen Motors Assembly Div, supvr acct. **Orgs:** Vpres, alumni founder, 1972-, Kappa Alpha Psi Fraternity; pres, Nat Asn Black Acct; Detroit Econ Club, 1990-; exec comm, Detroit Chamber Com, treas, bd dir, 1992-; pres, past chmn, Booker T Wash Bus Asn, 1992-94, chmn bd, 1995-; past adv, Fed Res Bd Chicago, 1999; Mich State Bd Acct, 2000-; bd dir, First Independence Bank; trustee bd, Henry Ford Hosp; bd mem, Detroit Regional Chamber Com. **Honors/Awds:** Corp Achievement Award, Nat Asn Black Acct, 1987; One of Detroit's five emerging Black leaders, Greater Detroit Chamber Com, Detroiter Mag, 1993. **Special Achievements:** Frequent interviewee on tax matters, WDIV-TV News, Detroit News. **Home Addr:** 4253 Old Dominion Dr, West Bloomfield, MI 48323, **Home Phone:** (248)683-2865. **Business Addr:** Managing Director, President & Chief Executive Officer, Alan C Young & Assocs PC, 7310 Woodward Ave Suite 740, Detroit, MI 48202, **Business Phone:** (313)873-7500.

### YOUNG, ALAN JOHN
Automotive executive. **Personal:** Born May 25, 1945, Chicago, IL; son of John M and Marion E Bradley Campbell; children: Jeffrey, Kimberly & Christopher. **Educ:** Univ Ill, BS, mkt, 1968. **Career:** AY Shell Serv Sta, owner, 1969-77; GM Dealer Develop Acad, trainee, 1977-79; Alan Young Pontiac Buick GMC, owner & pres, 1979-2008. **Orgs:** Bd mem, NE Motor Vehicle Licensing bd; Lincoln Found; Univ Nebr Found. **Home Addr:** 1000 Clearlake Ct, Colleyville, TX 76034-2822.

### YOUNG, ALBERT JAMES
Writer, publisher. **Personal:** Born May 31, 1939, Ocean Springs, MS; son of Albert James and Mary Campbell Simmons; married Arlin Belck; children: Michael James. **Educ:** Univ Mich, attended 1961; Univ Calif, BA, span, 1969. **Career:** Berkeley Neighborhood Youth Corps, writing instr & lang consult; Loveletter, founder & ed, 1966-68; Wallace Stegner Writing fel, 1966-67; Nat Endowment Arts fel, 1968, 1969, 1975; Guggenheim Memorial Found, Fel, 1974; Stanford Univ, Edward H Jones lectr creative writing, 1969-74; Yardbird, 1972-76; Univ Wash, Seattle, writer, 1981-82; Writer: Nigger, Sparkle, 1972; Bustin Loose, 1981; Yardbird Lives, 1978; The California Poetry, 1979. **Orgs:** E Bay Negro Hist Soc; Authors Guild; Authors League; Writers Guild Am; San Francisco Press Club. **Honors/Awds:** National Arts Council Awards, 1968-70; Joseph Henry Jackson Award, San Francisco Found, 1969; California Association of Teachers of English Special Award, 1973; Pushcart Prize, 1980; Before Columbus Foundation Award, 1982. **Business Addr:** 514 Bryant St, Palo Alto, CA 94301.

### YOUNG, ALENE MARIE
Writer. **Personal:** Born Nov 18, 1952, Tuskegee, AL; daughter of Pleze and Laurae; children: Andre L Brooks. **Educ:** SF City Col. **Career:** American Poultry, 1970; Pacific Bell Yellow Pages, administrative asst, 1970-01; freelance writer, currently; Author: Survival The Will & the Way, 1999; Penny For Your Thoughts, volume one, 1999-2002; Penny For Your Thoughts, volumes one & two, 2001. **Honors/Awds:** Editors Choice Award, InterNat Library of Poetry, 1999-2002. **Home Addr:** 253 Charter Oak Ave, San Francisco, CA 94124, **Home Phone:** (415)468-3004. **Business Addr:** Author/Owner, The Will and the Way Pub Co, PO Box 347068, San Francisco, CA 94134-7075, **Business Phone:** (415)468-3004.

### YOUNG, PROF. ALFRED
Educator, writer. **Personal:** Born Feb 21, 1946, New Orleans, LA; son of Mattie Rayno and Landry Sr; married Angela Marie Broussard; children: Tomara, Marcus, Malcolm & Miles Thurgood. **Educ:** La State Univ, New Orleans, LA, BA, 1972; Syracuse Univ, MA, 1972; Syracuse Univ, Maxwell Sch Citizenship & Pub Affairs, PhD, social sci, 1977. **Career:** Syracuse Univ, lectr, Afro-Am fel, 1970-72, Afro-Am studies, 1971, instr, hist, 1971-72, asst prof, hist, 1972-82, assoc prof, hist, 1982-88; Nat Fel Fund, fel, 1975-77; Colgate Univ, Hamilton, NY, A Lindsay OConnor Chair, 1988-89; Ga Southern Univ, assoc prof, 1989-94, prof hist, 1994-, dir, African Studies prog, 1991; Hist & AFA Studies, vis prof, 1995-97; State Univ New York, Oswego. **Orgs:** Keeper finance, Omega Psi Phi Frat Inc Chi Pi chap, 1980-85, chap hist, 1988-89; adj prof hist, Syracuse Univ & Univ Col Auburn Correctional Facil prog, 1981-89; consult, fac adv, Nat Model OA Univ, Howard Univ, 1982-; bd mem, Friends Syracuse Univ, Alumni Orgn, 1987-; bd, Nat Coun Black Studies, 1992-; Acad Coun Univ Syst GEO Regents' Global Ctr, 1992-; Community Engagement Comt. **Home Addr:** 41 Angel Oaks Dr, Savannah, GA 31410, **Home Phone:** (315)445-0096. **Business Addr:** Professor Emeritus of History, Georgia Southern University, 1143 Forest Bldg, Statesboro, GA 30460-8054.

**YOUNG, ANDRE RAMELLE. See DRE, DR.**

### YOUNG, ANDREW
Association executive, mayor, chairperson. **Personal:** Born Mar 12, 1932, New Orleans, LA; son of Andrews J Sr and Daisy Fuller; married Jean Childs; children: Andrea, Lisa, Paula & Andrew III; married Carolyn McClain. **Educ:** Howard Univ, BS, 1951; Hartford Theol Sem, BDiv, 1955. **Career:** United Church Christ, pastor, 1955-57; Nat Coun Churches, assoc dir youth work, 1957-61; United Church Christ Christian Educ Prog, adminr, 1961-64; Southern Christian Leadership Conf, staff mem, 1961-70, exec dir, 1964-67, exec vpres, 1967; US House Rep, mem, 1972-76; Atlanta Community Rels Comn, 1970-72; 5th Dist Ga, congressman, 1973-77; Un, US ambassador, 1977-79; City Atlanta, mayor, 1982-89; Metro Atlanta Chamber Com, chmn, 1996; Nat Coun Churches, pres, 2000-01; Atlanta Comn Olympic Games, co-chmn, currently; Law Int Inc, chmn, currently. **Orgs:** Bd mem, Freedom House; co-chair, Good Works Int; dir, Drum Maj Inst; Alpha Phi Alpha; Alpha Kappa Alpha; chmn, Global Initiative Advan Nutrit Ther; founder, Andrew Young Found, 2003. **Honors/Awds:** Pax-Christi Award, St John's Univ, 1970; Spingarn Medal; Presidential Medal of Freedom, 1981; Peace & Justice Award, Alpha Kappa Alpha, 1991; Eagle Award, United States Sports Academy, 1995; ROBIE Award, 1998; received numerous hon degrees chair, Southern Africa Enterprise Develop Fund. **Special Achievements:** First African-American Congressman from Georgia since Jefferson Long; United States First African-American Ambassador to the United Nations. **Business Addr:** Founder, Andrew J Young Foundation, 260 14th St NW, Atlanta, GA 30318, **Business Phone:** (404)685-2786.

### YOUNG, ANGELA LYNN
Government official, consultant, founder (originator). **Personal:** Born Dec 1, 1968, Buffalo, NY; daughter of Charles and Carrie Phillips. **Educ:** Dillard Univ, BA, communs, 1990. **Career:** A Weight Life, consult & founder, 1994-; City New Orleans, communs & spec event coord, 1994-; Spears & Young Commun Inc, dir; ALY Media Rels LLC, lead consult & pres, currently. **Orgs:** City New Orleans Gumbo Holiday Com, 1994-; Fr Quartee Festivals, 1995-; coord pub rels, Women Excellence, 1996-; dir pub rels, Full Gospel Baptist Church Fel, 1996-. **Home Addr:** 14101 Michoud Blvd Suite 606, New Orleans, LA 70129, **Home Phone:** (504)254-5399. **Business Addr:** Chief Operating Officer, Special Events Co-Ordinator, City of New Orleans Mayor, 1300 Perdido St Suite 2 E 10, New Orleans, LA 70112, **Business Phone:** (504)658-4000.

### YOUNG, ARLENE H.
Executive. **Personal:** Born Orangeburg, SC; daughter of Louis Hanton and Nina Seaberry Hanton; married Eddie L; children: Eddie, Christopher & Patrick. **Educ:** Bennett Col, BS, 1968; St Joseph's Sch Med Tech, MT, cert, 1969; Oakland Col, ARDMS, 1983; Cent Mich Univ, MSA, 1989. **Career:** Georgetown Univ Hosp, med technologist, 1969; Walter Reed Army Med Ctr, med technologist, 1971; Midwest Med Clin, diag med sonographer, 1983; Hanton Industs Inc, pres & treas, 1984-. **Orgs:** Delta Sigma Theta, 1968-; Arts & Lett Comm, 1992-94; Mich State Coun, Delta Sigma Theta, sec, 1992-94; immediate pres & treas, S Field Alumnae Chap, 1990-94; vpres, Jack & Jill Oakland County Mich Chap, 1992-93; Nat Coun Negro Women, 1986; Nat Asn Women Bus Owners, 1987; Nat Asn Female Execs, 1992; Nat Chair Heritage & Arch, Midwest Regional Leadership Team, 2001-03. **Home Addr:** 23378 Coventry Woods Lane, Southfield, MI 48034, **Home Phone:** (248)354-4325. **Business Addr:** President, Treasurer, Hanton Industries Inc, 22138 Fenkell St, Detroit, MI 48223, **Business Phone:** (313)535-2345.

### YOUNG, DR. ARTEE FELICITA
Educator, college teacher, judge. **Educ:** Southern Univ, BA, speech & theater, 1967; Eastern Mich Univ, MA, ct heater, 1970; Univ Puget Sound Sch Law, JD, 1987; Univ Mich, PhD, speech commun & theater. **Career:** Wash State Supreme Ct, judicial clerk; US Forest Serv, consult; Southern Univ; Ind Univ; Univ Wash; Evergreen State Col, prof law & lit, currently. **Orgs:** Nat Ctr Minority Health & Health Disparities; Nat Insts Health; Western Instnl Rev Bd; pres, St Edward Parish Coun; vol, Nat Asn Advan Colored People Acad Cult Technol Sci Olympics Youth; adv comt, Group Health Coop; adv comt, Pierce County Leadership Adv Group; Nat Bar Asn; Wash State Bar Asn; Pierce County Bar Asn. **Business Addr:** Professor, Evergreen State College, Tacoma Campus, Tacoma, WA 98405, **Business Phone:** (360)867-3026.

### YOUNG, B. ASHLEY
Journalist. **Personal:** Born Danville, IL; daughter of Will Roy Smith and Annette Lewis Alexander; married G Steven; children: Jessica M. **Educ:** Ky State Univ, BA, journ, 1980; Cincinnati Bible Col & Sem, working towards master's degree theol; Miami Univ, MA, speech commun & orgn commun. **Career:** Am Cong Gov Ind Hyg, Cincinnati, Ohio, copy ed, 1986-87; Cincinnati, Ohio, freelance, 1990-; J News, Hamilton, Ohio, reporter & copy ed, 1988-; Macys Inc, mgr & corp commun, currently. **Orgs:** Nat Asn Black Journ; Ohio Newspaper Women's Asn; Ohio Prof Writers. **Honors/Awds:** Journalism Award, Ohio Vet Med Asn, 1989. **Home Addr:** 707 Cloverdale Ave, Cincinnati, OH 45246, **Home Phone:** (513)742-4818. **Business Addr:** Journalist, J News, 228 Ct St, Hamilton, OH 45011, **Business Phone:** (513)863-8200.

### YOUNG, DR. BARBARA J.
Educator, college teacher. **Personal:** Born Nov 2, 1937, Muskogee, OK; daughter of Alonzo Dossett and Idessa Hammond Dossett; married Douglas Charles Jr; children: Crystal Marion Humphrey, Hammond George Bouldin & Danielle Humphrey. **Educ:** Calif State Univ, Sacramento, BA, psychol, 1977, MS, coun, 1981, EdD, admin, 1990. **Career:** Fresno State Univ, sec, 1967-69; Calif State Univ, Sacramento, exec asst pres, 1969-74, employ counr, 1974-77, financial aid officer, 1977-83, stud affairs officer, asst dir, sch rels, 1983-86, asst adj prof, asst dean, 1986-90, assoc dean, acad affairs, Alumni Rels & Community Rels, Div Univ Advan, dir, Sch Bus & Pub Admin, univ adj prof, fac mem; Young Enterprises, founder, chief exec officer & pres, 1983; CSU African Am Initiative, consult; BJY Enterprises Inc, pres, chief exec officer, consult, life empowerment speaker, success coach & leadership trainer, transformation expert, life coach, success trainer, 2003-; calif state univ, chancellor's off, consult, 2003-. **Orgs:** Sacramento Urban League, 1970-; WASFA, 1977-; Black Prof Asn; SPAC; Delta Sigma Theta Sorority, Nu Lambda Chap, 1977-; PACROW; Lambda Kappa Mu Sorority, basileus, 1990; bd mem, CAL-SOAP Adv Bd, 1991-; bd mem, Calif Respiratory Care, 1993; Leadership Calif, partic, 1994; pres, Pan African Doctoral Scholars Inc; United Way, Harbor City; bd mem, Nat Bd Respiratory Care; bd mem, Leadership Am, 1997; founder, Long Beach Nu Lambda Chap Lambda Kappa Mu Sorority; Nat Strengthening & Conditioning Asn (NSCA) Cert Comn, 2002-; Nat Inst Advan Multicultural & Minority Med, 2003-; Success 4 U Foundation, founder, pres & chief exec officer, 2003-. **Home Addr:** 22640 Blue Teal Dr, Canyon Lake, CA 92587-6908. **Business Addr:** Chief Executive Officer, President, Young Enterprise, 31566 Rr Canyon Rd Suite 640, Canyon Lake, CA 92587-9446, **Business Phone:** (951)244-4700.

### YOUNG, DR. BETTY BIGBY
Educator. **Personal:** Born New York, NY; daughter of Dorothy Bigby and Lucius Bigby; married Haskell I; children: Haskell I II & Jessica Melissa Bigby. **Educ:** City Univ NY, Brooklyn Col, BA, 1970, MS, 1972; Nova Univ, EdD, 1987. **Career:** Dept State Foreign Serv Corps, admin asst, foreign serv staff, 1959-67; Off Mayor, NYC, community rels specialist, 1968-71; CUNY, Brooklyn Col, dir, model city, TV training prog, 1972-73; Model City Prog, community rels specialist, 1974-77; Fla Int Univ, dir, univ rels & develop, 1977-83; dir, acad support prog, 1983-89; Fla Mem Col, dir, AIDS & drug abuse prev prog, 1990-92, coordr, Dewitt Wallace, Reader's Dig Fund Pathways to Teaching Careers Prog, 1992-99; Lagos Christian Col, adj prof; Fla Mem Col, Div Humanities, adj prof speech, asst prof speech, 2002-. **Orgs:** Alpha Epsilon Rho Radio TV Frat; Am Asn Univ Women; Sigma Gamma Rho Sorority; Am Coun Educ; Southeast Dist Liaison Minority Affairs, PRSA; YWCA Women's Network; Fla State Sickle Cell Found Inc, 1978-; White House Conf Arts Testimony Cong Hearing, 1978; Pub Rels Soc Am, Accredited Coun Advan & Support Educ, 1978-80; founder, FIU Black Stud Union Adv, 1978-89; Kappa Delta Pi Int Hon Soc Educ, 1980-; pres, Dade County Sickle Cell Found, 1980-82, 1992-94; founder, counr, Omicron Theta Chap KDP FIU, 1981-89; bd mem, Art Pub Places Trust; pres, Scott Lake ElemSch, PTA, Pk view Elem, Greynolds Pk Elem; Ment Health Asn, 1981-82; radio talk show host WMBM Miami, 1981-82; Cong Black Scholars Dade County, 1982; KDP Int Hon Soc const & bylaws chairperson, 1982-84; S Fla Ctr Fine Arts; nat mem, Smitnian Asn; Nat Asn Female Execs, 1984-89; Int Platform Asn; chief adv, Fla Black Stud Asn Inc, 1988-89; bd mem, DCPS Magnet Adv Comt; bd dir, Ctr Haitian Studies, currently; founder, counr, Phi Eta Chap KDP, FMC, 1995-; pres, FIUs Black Employees Asn. **Home Addr:** 17135 NW 12th Ct, Miami Gardens, FL 33169, **Home Phone:** (305)624-8670. **Business Addr:** Board of Director, Center For Haitian Studies, 8260 NE 2nd Ave, Miami, FL 33138, **Business Phone:** (305)757-9555.

### YOUNG, BRYANT COLBY
Football coach, football player. **Personal:** Born Jan 27, 1972, Chicago Heights, IL; married Kristen; children: Kai, Colby, Kennedy, Bryce & Kamille. **Educ:** Univ Notre Dame, BA, mktg, 1994. **Career:** Football player (retired); San Francisco 49ers, left defensive tackle, 1994-2002, defensive tackle, 1999, 2007, right defensive tackle, 1999, 2003-04, defensive end, 2005-07; Univ Notre Dame, defensive grad asst coach, 2009; San Jose State, defensive line coach, 2010; Univ Fla Gators football team, defensive line coach, 2011-13. **Honors/Awds:** Defensive Rookie of the Year, United Press Int, Nat Football League, 1994; Len Eshmont Award, 1996, 1998; Comeback Player of the Year, Nat Football League, 1999; Champion, Super Bowl XXIX. **Special Achievements:** Film: Super Bowl XXIX, 1995; Where's My Man, 2010. TV Series: NFL Monday Night Football. Holding one Super Bowl ring. **Business Addr:** Defensive Line Coach, University Of Florida Gators Football Team, 121 Gale Lemerand Dr, Gainesville, FL 32604, **Business Phone:** (352)375-4683.

### YOUNG, DR. CARLENE HERB
Psychologist, educator. **Personal:** Born Selma, AL; children: Howard & Loren. **Educ:** Univ Detroit, MA, 1960; Wayne State Univ, Detroit, EdD, sociol & educ specialist, 1967; Wright Inst Berkeley, CA, PhD, social clin psychol, 1976. **Career:** Detroit Pub Sch, teacher, 1955-67; Univ Detroit, lectr, physiol dept, 1966-69; Wayne State Univ, lectr, physiol dept, 1966-69; Natl Teacher Corp, team leader, 1966-67; Title III Lincoln Child Devel Ctr, proj dir, 1967; Oakland Co Community Col, dept chmn soc, 1968; San Jose State Univ, prof African Am Studies, 1969-92, prof emer, 1992-; San Jose Police Dept, consult, Law Enforcement Psychol Serv, psychol, 1985-97; mediator, 1998-; Carlene Young & Assoc, clin psychologist & forensic, founder, currently; Mediation Consult, founder, currently. **Orgs:** Bd, Cath Social Serv, 1976-87; exec secy & chmn, Nat Coun Black Studies, 1982-84; fel Am Col Forensic Examrs, 1996; Phi Kappa Phi Hon Soc; Alpha Kappa Alpha Sorority Inc; vpres, Calif Black Fac & Staff Asn, 1997; consult psych, Assessment Pub Safety; adv comt, Calif State Personnel Bd Psychol; Am Psy Asn; Am Soc Clin Hypn Asn Black Psych; Calif Psychol Asn; World Fedn Ment Health; co-chair, Forensic Comt, Santa Clara County Psychol Asn. **Honors/Awds:** Distinguished Alumna, Wayne State Univ, 1991. **Special Achievements:** Editor: "Black Experience analysis & synthesis," Leswing Press, 1972; Traveled: Africa (Cameroon, Senegal, Ivory Coast, Ghana, Mali, Somalia, Egypt); Europe; Mexico; guest editor, Journal Negro Educ, 1984; co-editor: "Out of the Revolution: African American Studies, The Development & Significance of A Discipline", Lexington Press, 2000. **Business Addr:** Clinical Psychologist, Carlene Young and Associates, 1550 S Winchester Blvd Suite 216, Campbell, CA 95008-0553, **Business Phone:** (408)374-1884.

### YOUNG, DR. CHARLES, JR.
School administrator, association executive, army officer. **Personal:** Born Aug 5, 1934, St. Louis, MO; married Jessie Dolores Howell; children: Karen. **Educ:** Lincoln Univ, BS Ed, 1957; Univ Ill, MEd, 1962, EdD, 1972. **Career:** St Louis Pub Sch, teacher, 1957-66, from asst prin to prin, 1966-72; Urbana Comt Sch, prin, 1972-84; Joliet Pub Sch, asst supt, 1984-. **Orgs:** Kappa Alpha Psi, 1952-; Phi Delta Kappa, 1964-; Am Assc Sch Adminr; Rotary Int, 1985; bd mem, Joliet Grade Schs Found Educ Excellence. **Honors/Awds:** Service Award, National Asn Secondary Sch Prin, 1966; Leadership Award, Champaign Co boys Club, 1978. **Home Addr:** 2650 Black Rd, Joliet, IL 60435, **Home Phone:** (815)744-3114. **Business Addr:** Assistant Superintendent, Joliet Public School, 420 N Raynor, Joliet, IL 60435, **Business Phone:** (815)740-3196.

### YOUNG, DR. COLEMAN MILTON, III
Executive, physician. **Personal:** Born Nov 13, 1930, Louisville, KY; son of Colman Milton Jr and Hortense Houston; married Waltraud Schuessler; children: C Milton IV, Lloyd M & Christopher H. **Educ:** Univ Louisville, AB, 1952; Meharry Med Col, MD, 1961. **Career:** Louisville Genl Hosp, intern, 1961-62; Humana Hosp Audubon, resident; St Joseph's Infirmary, res, 1962-65; Methadone Treat Prog, founder & dir, 1968-72; Pk Duvalle Community Health Ctr, physi-

cian; pvt pract physician internal med, currently. **Orgs:** Chmn bd mem, Pk DuValle Neighborhood Health Ctr, 1966-69; Gov Young Kentuckian's Adv Comn, 1967-70; Louisville Jeffers Co Air Pollution Ctrl Bd, 1968-77, chmn, 1968-72; Adv SSS, 1968-73; Hon Order KY Col, 1972; dir, Drug Abuse Prog River Region Ment Health Bd, 1972-73; med dir, Comm Hosp, 1972-75; consult, drug prog River Region Ment Health Bd, 1973-74; Govt Coun Alcohol & Drug Abuse, 1973; consult, Senate Com Juv Prob, 1973; Alpha Phi Alpha; AMA; life mem, Nat Asn Advan Colored People; ed, bd chmn, Black Scene Mag, 1974-76; pres, Falls City Med Soc, 1982-85; Govs Oxycontin Task Force, 2001-; KY Med Asn, patient safety task force, 2001-03. **Honors/Awds:** Louisville Man of the Year Award, WHAS TV, 1970; Nat Adv Am Asn Med Ast, 1976-77; Distinguished Citizen Award, Key to City Mayor Harvey I Sloane, 1977. **Special Achievements:** First African American undergraduate student at the University Louisville, 1950; First African American medical intern, Louisville Gen Hospital, 1961-62; First African American medical resident trained, pvt inst, KY, St Joseph's Infirmary, Louisville, KY. **Home Addr:** 740 Zorn Ave Suite 4-A, Louisville, KY 40206. **Business Addr:** Physician, Park Duvalle Community Health Center, 1015 W Chestnut St, Louisville, KY 40203, **Business Phone:** (502)584-2992.

## YOUNG, COURTNEY LOUISE

President (organization), library administrator, librarian. **Educ:** Col Wooster, BA, Eng, 1996; Simmons Col, MLS, 1997. **Career:** Pa State Univ, Greater Allegheny Campus, prof women's studies; J. Clarence Kelly Libr, head librn; Am Libr Asn, pres, 2014-. **Orgs:** ALA Task Force Electronic Mem Participation, 2007-09; New Mem Round Table (NMRT), pres, 2009-10, Counr, 2005-08, diversity comt chair, 2003-04, Stud Chap Yr Award chair, 2004-05; ALA Resolutions Comt, 2008-09; ALA Counr-at-large, 2008-11, 2012-15, Awards Comt, 2012-14, Planning & Budget Assembly, 2012-14, ALA-APA Fundraising Comt, 2012-13; ALA Exec Bd, mem, 2009-12. **Honors/Awds:** Library Journal, Mover Shaker, 2011. **Special Achievements:** First Penn State librarian to be elected as ALA's president.

## YOUNG, DMITRI DELL

Radio host, baseball player. **Personal:** Born Oct 11, 1973, Vicksburg, MS; son of Larry and Bonnie (deceased); married Rebecca; children: Owen. **Career:** Baseball player (retired); St Louis Cardinals, infielder, 1996-97; Tampa Bay Devil Rays, 1997; Cincinnati Reds, 1998-2001; Detroit Tigers, 2002-06; Wash Nationals, 2007-08; Oakland County Cruisers, vpres, sr advisor baseball opers & spec hitting & fielding instr, 2010; Card Corner Club Radio, co host, 2010-11. **Orgs:** Pres, Dmitri D Young Found Inc, currently. **Honors/Awds:** Reds Ernie Lombardi MVP Award, 2001; Reds Joe Nuxhall Good Guy Award, 2001; Two times All-Star selection, 2003, 2007; National League Comeback Player of the Year, 2007. **Business Addr:** Co-Host, Card Corner Club Radio, 1072 Madison Ave, Lakewood, NJ 08701.

## YOUNG, DONALD (DONALD OLIVER YOUNG, JR.)

Athlete. **Personal:** Born Jul 23, 1989, Chicago, IL; son of Donald Sr and Illona. **Career:** Professional tennis player, 2004-. **Orgs:** US Tennis Asn. **Honors/Awds:** Winner: Aptos Challenger, 2007; Sacramento Challenger, 2008; Calabasas Challenger, 2009; Carson Challenger, 2010; Tallahassee Challenger, 2011; Leon Challenger, 2013; Napa Challenger, 2013; Sacramento Challenger, 2013. **Special Achievements:** Only sports figure in Newsweek's "Who's Next?" feature in December 27, 2004; number one male junior player in the world in 2004-05. **Business Addr:** The United States Tennis Association, 70 West Red Oak Lane, White Plains, NY 10604.

## YOUNG, DONALD OLIVER, JR.

Founder (originator), tennis player. **Personal:** Born Jul 23, 1989, Chicago, IL; son of Donald Sr and Illona. **Career:** Tennis player, currently; Tennis Motion Inc, founder, currently. **Honors/Awds:** Orange Bowl 16s Champion, 2003; Australian Open Junior Champion, 2005; Winner of 26 National and International Junior Championships; Whos Next, Newsweek Mag, 2005. **Special Achievements:** Youngest boy to win a Junior Grand Slam title; Youngest boy to reach the no.1 ITF World Junior Ranking (18 and under) in the history of the sport. **Business Addr:** Founder, Tennis In Motion, 5645 Mason Rd, College Park, GA 30349, **Business Phone:** (770)969-2200.

## YOUNG, PROF. EDITH MAE

Educator. **Personal:** Born Oct 15, 1932, Denison, TX; daughter of Joe C Sr and Pinkie Rambo Franklin (deceased). **Educ:** Tex Col, cert, sec sci, 1951; Lincoln Univ, MO, BSE, 1961, MEd, 1964; Univ Mont, CO, EdD, 1973. **Career:** Educator (retired); Lincoln Univ, sec & admin asst, libr, 1951-66; Educ & Ctr Res Social Behav, Univ Mont, CO, intern & voc teacher, 1973; Ctr Acad Develop UMSL, actg dir, 1977-80; Educ Bus Teacher Educ, instr & asst prof, 1966-70, 1973-77, 1980, actg assoc dean, 1993-94; Univ Mont, St.Louis, assoc prof educ; Univ Miss, St. Louis, chair educ studies, 1995-98. **Orgs:** Nat Bus Educ Asn, 1962-; AVA, 1966-; AAHE, 1967-; Alpha Sor, 1967; Delta Pi Epsilon, 1970-; Kappa Delta Pi, 1972-; Pi Lambda Theta, 1973-; Alpha Kappa edur examr, Nat Accrediting Comn Cosmetology Arts & Sci, 1985-; ed adv bd, Col Press, 1989-90. **Home Addr:** 1630 Summer Run Dr Suite 32, Florissant, MO 63033, **Home Phone:** (314)921-7999.

## YOUNG, EDWARD HIRAM, JR.

Meteorologist. **Personal:** Born Dec 10, 1950, Berkeley, CA; son of Edward Hiram Sr (deceased) and Grace Jean King (deceased); married Doris Kathleen Jackson. **Educ:** San Jose State Univ, BS, meteorol, 1973; grad work meteorol, 1975; N Harris County Col, course, mgt & bus, 1984; Delgado Community Col, course, comput, 1988. **Career:** Nat Weather Servs, meteorologist intern Portland, 1975-78; Riverside CA, agricult meteorologist, 1978-81; Ctr Weather Serv FAA Houston, aviation meteorologist, 1981-84; Nat Weather Serv Southern Region, prog mgr, 1981-87; Ft Worth Tex S Region, spec serv met, 1984-86; Nat Weather Serv, agri, forestry meteorologist, 1986-; Nat Oceanic & Atmospheric Admin, Nat Weather Serv Pac Region, Honolulu, Tech Serv Div, chief, 1988-, dep dir, 1988-. **Orgs:** Bd dir, San Jose Chap Amer Red Cross, 1970-72; Am Meteorol Soc, 1970-; Nat Col Stud Adv Coun Am Red Cross, 1971-72; black prog mgr, Nat Weather Serv Wrn Reg, 1978-81; bd dirs, Great Outdoors, 1980-81; AAAS, 1980; black prog mgr, Nat Weather Serv Srn Region, 1981-; bd, Women & Minorities Am Meteorol Soc, 1985-87, chmn, 1989-90; subcomt, Ft Worth United Way Allocations, 1986; consult, Sci, Math, Aeronaut, Res, Technol & Black Family, 1989; aux bd asst, Bahai Faith Hawaiian Islands, 1988, staff; chair, subcomt, Hawaii Martin Luther King Jr Interim Comn, 1990-95; US China Peoples Friendship Asn, 1995-; Nat Spiritual Assembly Bahais Hawaiian Islands, 1997. **Honors/Awds:** Elks Leadership Award, Oakland CA Elks Club, 1968; EEO Award, Nat Oceanic & Atmospheric Admin, 1984; EEO Award, Dallas-Ft Worth Fed Exec Bd, 1986; Doer of Good Deeds Award, Hawaii Chap, B'Nai Brith, 1995; Outstanding Community Service Award, Honolulu-Pac Fed Exec Bd, 1996; NOAA Unit Citation; Diversity Spectrum Award, 2004. **Home Addr:** 605 N Kainalu Dr, Kailua, HI 96734-1958, **Home Phone:** (808)262-1200. **Business Addr:** Deputy Director, National Oceanic & Atmospheric Administration, 737 Bishop St Suite 2200, Honolulu, HI 96813-3213, **Business Phone:** (808)532-6412.

## YOUNG, DR. ELIZABETH BELL

Government official. **Personal:** Born Jul 2, 1929, Franklinton, NC; daughter of Joseph H (deceased) and Eulalia; married Charles A Jr. **Educ:** NC Cent Univ, BA, 1948, MA, 1950; Ohio State Univ, PhD, 1959. **Career:** Univ DC, Dept Speech Sci Comun & Eng, univ prof & chmn, 1949-84; Catholic Univ, grad sch prof, 1966-79; Barber Scotia Col, NC; Talladega Col, AL; Virg State Col; Ohio State Univ; Florida Agri & Mech Univ; Fayetteville State Univ, NC; Howard Univ, Wash DC; Univ Md, Eastern Shore; Princess Anne, MD; Congressional Staff Aide, 1980, 1987-91, Staff aide; US House Reps Off Congressman Walter E Fauntroy, 1980, 1987-91; US State Dept promotion panelist, field reader & team reviewer, 1980-; Nat & Int Org & Univ, consult & lectr, 1981-; US Govt Off Educ, lectr & consult, 1981-87; Va Bd Audiol & Path, exec dir. **Orgs:** Alpha Kappa Alpha Sor, 1946-; bd mem, Pub Mem Asn, 1973-; bd dir, Handicapped Intervention Prog High Risk Infants Wash DC, 1978-87; bd dir, Wash Ctr Music Ther Clin; adv brd, Negro College Fund, 1979-82; Congressional Adv brd Educ, 1979-82; bd mem, Clin Cert Am Speech-L & H Asn, 1979-83; fel Am Speech Lang Hearing Asn. **Honors/Awds:** Outstanding Alumni Award, Ohio State Univ, 1976; Pub: Journal Articles in Field of Communications & Made Over 450 Speeches in US. **Special Achievements:** First African American to receive PhD in Speech Science; First African American to obtain certification in Speech Pathology & Audiology; First African American to obtain PhD from Ohio State Univ in communications & speech science; First certified speech & learning clinics in historically black colleges & universities.

## YOUNG, ELWANDA

Executive, association executive. **Educ:** York Col, BS, biol. **Career:** Elmcor Youth & Adult Activ, exec dir; United Way New York, chief operating officer & sr vpres prog integration & strategic planning, 1992-2012, interim pres & chief exec officer, 2012-. **Orgs:** Bd mem, Black Agency Execs; Black Women Black Girls Giving Circle. **Honors/Awds:** Outstanding Contributions To The Community, A Better Bronx Youth; Outstanding Contributions To The Community, Nat Coun Negro Bus & Prof Women; The Network Journal: Black Professionals and Small Business Magazine, 25 Influential Black Women in Business, 2006. **Business Addr:** Senior Vice President, Chief Operating Officer, United Way of New York, 2 Pk Ave, New York, NY 10016, **Business Phone:** (212)251-2500.

## YOUNG, ERIC ORLANDO, SR.

Baseball player, media executive. **Personal:** Born May 18, 1967, New Brunswick, NJ; married MaLika Hakeem; children: Erick Jr. **Educ:** Rutgers Univ, bus mgt, 1989. **Career:** Baseball player (retired), media executive; Los Angeles Dodgers, infielder & outfielder, 1989-92, 1997-99; Colo Rockies, infielder & outfielder, 1993-97; Chicago Cubs, infielder & outfielder, 2000-01; Milwaukee Brewers, infielder & outfielder, 2002-03; San Francisco Giants, 2003; Tex Rangers, infielder, 2004, 2006; San Diego Padres, pinch runner, 2005-06; Tex Rangers, 2006; Ariz Diamondbacks, first base coach, 2010-12; Houston Astros, roving instr; ESPN, analyst, currently. **Business Addr:** Analyst, ESPN, ESPN Plz, Bristol, CT 06010, **Business Phone:** (860)766-2000.

## YOUNG, ERNEST WESLEY (ERNIE YOUNG)

Baseball player, athletic coach, manager. **Personal:** Born Jul 8, 1969, Chicago, IL. **Educ:** Lewis Univ. **Career:** Baseball player (retired), baseball coach, manager; Oakland Athletics, outfielder, 1994-97; Kans City Royals, 1998; Ariz Diamondbacks, 1999; Yokohoma Bay Stars, 2002; Detroit Tigers, 2003; Cleveland Indians, 2004; Minor league, Cleveland Indians, 2005-07; Chicago White Sox, hitting coach, currently; Kannapolis Intimidators, mgr, 2009; W Mich Whitecaps, 2011; BASH Sports Acad, vis master instr, currently. **Orgs:** Bd dir, USA Baseball. **Business Addr:** Hitting Coach, Chicago White Sox, US Cellular Field 333 W 35th St, Chicago, IL 60616, **Business Phone:** (312)674-1000.

## YOUNG, FLOYD ALEXANDER

Football player. **Personal:** Born Nov 23, 1975, New Orleans, LA; married Michelle; children: Ostin Giovanni. **Educ:** Tex A&M Univ, Kingsville; Scottsdale Comm Col. **Career:** Tampa Bay Buccaneers, 1998-2000, defensive back, 1997; Orlando Predators, 2006-07. **Honors/Awds:** Rookie of the Year, 1997.

## YOUNG, FRANCES CAMILLE

Executive, manager. **Personal:** Born Sep 3, 1928, Boston, MA; married Virgil J. **Educ:** Howard Univ, BS, 1949; Howard Univ, DDS, 1958; Univ Mich, MPH, 1974. **Career:** Manager (retired); Pvt Pract, Wash, DC, 1962; DC Dept Pub Health, dent officer, 1964-69; Comm Group Health Found, staff dentist, 1969-71; Howard Univ Col Dent, asst prof; Comn Group Health Found, chief dent serv; Am Found for Dent Health, bd trustee; Div Dent Health Bur Health Resources Develop Dept HEW, consult, 1971-74. **Orgs:** Chmn, chmn, Social Com, 1966-70; exec sec, Howard Univ Dental Alumni Asn, 1967-69; exec bd, 1967-69; Budget & Auditing Comn, 1968-70; secy, Dental Health Care Com, 1968; chmn, Speakers Bureau, 1968-72; Nat Dental Asn; pres, 1968-73; area dir Dentistry, Career Prog Recruit Com, 1968-73; chmn, Protocol Com, 1968, 1973; del, Lse Dels, 1969-73; Nat Dental Asn Am & Dental Asn Liaison com, 1968-73; vpres, Robert T Freeman Dental Soc, 1970-72; chmn, Awards Com, 1970; DC Dental Soc; chmn, Table Clinic Com, 1970; chmn, Travel com, 1970-73; Am Dental Asn; Am Pub Health Asn; Nat Asn nNeighborhood Health Ctrs; Asn Am Women Dentists. **Honors/Awds:** President Award, Nat Dental Asn, 1969; Special Award, Nat Dental Asn, 1973. **Special Achievements:** First woman attain off mem Exec Bd, 1966-72. **Home Addr:** 1728 Verbena St NW, Washington, DC 20012, **Home Phone:** (202)291-0193.

## YOUNG, GEORGE, JR. (TOBY YOUNG, JR.)

Broadcaster, media executive, state government official. **Personal:** Born Jan 1, 1933, Gadsden, AL; children: Kathy Ann, Carrie Vernell Marie & Dorthy Louise. **Educ:** Lincoln Univ, MHS, 1984. **Career:** Harrisburg Glass Inc, affirm act coord, 1952-68; Toby Young Show, Echos Glory, Jazz Today WKBO Radio, staff announcer, host, producer, 1965-71; Toby Young Enterprise, affirm act coord, 1971-; TY Rec, affirm act coord, 1971-72; Toby Young Show, Party Line, Echoes Glory, Proj People, WCMB Radio, comm rel spec, 1971-; Where I Sit, True Gospel, WTPA TV, writer producer, MC; Gospel Announcers Guild, founder & pres; WCMB-WMIX Echoes Glory; Dimes Telethon, co-host & talent coordr; PN Civil Serv Comn, affirmative action, PR contract compliance coordr, currently; WTKT 1460 AM, host, currently. **Orgs:** Life mem, Nat Asn Advan Colored People; mem bd, Camp Curtin YMCA, Harristown Community Complex; Tri-County March Dimes; chair person, 1976 Edgemont Fire House; pres, Pa Chap Nat Assoc Radio & TV Artists; bd mem, Gaudinzia House; past co-chair person, Cong Affirm Action; past chmn, bd mgr, owners, Soulville & Jay Walking Rec; bd mem, Nat Progressive Affirm Action Officers Daughin Cty Exec Comm Drug & Alcohol Inc, past master, dir PR Cent; Chosen Friend Lodge 43 F&AM Prince Hall Club 21 Harrisburg, PA; life mem, St Paul Missionary Baptist Church; Cent Pa's Gospel Music Workshop Am; Pa Chap Nat Asn Radio & TV Artists. **Honors/Awds:** People's Choice Gb Award, 1991-92; Gospel DJ of the Year; Meritorious Service Award. **Special Achievements:** Winner of two Glow Awards. **Home Addr:** 1726 N St, Harrisburg, PA 17103. **Business Addr:** Host, WTKT 1460 AM, 600 Corp Cir, Harrisburg, PA 17110.

## YOUNG, GODFREY

Writer, movie producer. **Educ:** Northern Nash, cert, 1976. **Career:** Nashville Gen Hosp, med, 1979-85; N Hollywood, Youngs Prod, 2008-11. **Special Achievements:** Author of "The Heart of a Good Man" (AuthorHouse, 2008).

## YOUNG, IRA MASON

Association executive, lawyer. **Personal:** Born Sep 20, 1929, St. Louis, MO; son of Nathan B and Mamie Mason; married Lillie T. **Educ:** Oberlin Col, AB, 1951; WA Univ, JD, 1957. **Career:** Pvt pract atty, 1957-; Mo State Bd Law, examr, 1979-84; Young & Thompson LLC, atty, prin, currently. **Orgs:** Nat Bar Asn; Am Bar Asn; Am Trial Lawyers Asn; Lawyers Asn St Louis; St Louis Metro Bar Asn; vpres bd dir, Legal Aid Soc, 1965-70; pres, Mound City Bar Asn, 1970-72; bd mem, Law.com; Family & C Serv Greater St Louis; adv coun, Legal Serv Corp Mo; bd dir, Girl Scout Coun St Louis; Gateway Boat Club; vpres, Wash Univ Law Alumni Asn, 1984. **Honors/Awds:** Twenty Five Years Service Award, Mound City Bar Asn, 1982. **Home Addr:** 9201 Lewis & Clark, St Louis, MO 63136. **Business Addr:** Principal, Attorney, Young & Thompson LLC, 1015 Locust St Suite 1038, St Louis, MO 63101, **Business Phone:** (314)436-9603.

## YOUNG, JAMES ARTHUR, III

Teacher, executive. **Personal:** Born Jan 6, 1945, Augusta, GA; son of James A Jr and Pauline Elim; married Felisa Perez; children: Alvin Renato. **Educ:** Claflin Col, BA, 1967; Gable Sch Art Advert, cert, 1975. **Career:** Burke County Bd Educ Waynesboro, teacher, 1967; Montgomery County Bd Educ, Ailey, GA, teacher, 1967-68; CSRA Econ Opportunity Auth Inc, task force leader, 1970-71; Laney-Walker Mus Inc, Augusta, exec dir, 1976-; Jct Inc, sr staff, Video Poker Indust, 1998; Early Intervention Prog Youth Inc, regist agt, 1998-2001. **Orgs:** Second Shilo Baptist Church, Augusta, 1957; Augusta Cult Arts Asn, 1977-80; Nat Trust Hist Preserv, 1979-80; Augusta-Richmond Co Mus, 1979-80; Greater Augusta Arts Coun, 1980; judge, pub sch art contest, Richmond Co Bd Educ, Augusta, 1980; Seven-Thirty Breakfast Club Columbia, SC, 1980. **Home Addr:** 938 Wrightsboro Rd, Augusta, GA 30901, **Home Phone:** (706)724-5614.

## YOUNG, DR. JAMES E., JR.

Association executive, lawyer. **Personal:** Born Jul 18, 1931, New Orleans, LA; married Eddie Mae Wilson; children: James III, Adrienne & Darrin. **Educ:** Southern Univ, BA, 1958, Law Sch, JD, 1960. **Career:** Parish New Orleans, notary pub, 1962-; pvt pract atty, 1960-68; Va Reg Off, adjudicator, 1966-68; New Orleans Legal Asst Corp, neighborhood staff atty, 1968-69, sr staff atty, 1969-70, asst dir, 1970-71; atty & notary pub, 1971-. **Orgs:** La State Bar Asn; Am Bar Asn; Am Judicature Soc; Louis A Martinet Legal Soc; spec consult & guest lectr, Southern Univ New Orleans Eve Div; Poverty & Consumer Law Panelist & Symp Partic Tulane Univ; pres & charter mem, Heritage Sq Develop Corp; pres & mem, Lake Area Pub Sch Improv Asn; pres & officer, Edward Livingston Mid Sch; lifetime mem, Nat Bar Asn; Kappa Alpha Psi Frat; mem & former officer, Acad Pk Devel Asn; pres, New Orleans Pan-Hellenic Coun; gen coun & exec comt mem, Control City Econ Opportunity Corp. **Honors/Awds:** Gold Keys Awards, Nat Art Competition, Nat Scholastic, 1949 & 1950; Hon, La State Bar Asn, 2010. **Special Achievements:** Graduate in top ten percent NCO Leadership & Motor Mechanics School, USMC; contribution & special features editor coll newspaper. **Home Addr:** 3443 Esplanade Ave, New orleans, LA 70119, **Home Phone:** (504)822-6040. **Business Addr:** Attorney at Law, 4624 Lafon Dr, New Orleans, LA 70126, **Business Phone:** (504)242-8181.

## YOUNG, JAMES EDWARD

Educator, consultant. **Personal:** Born Jan 18, 1926, Wheeling, WV; son of James E (deceased) and Edna (Thompson); married E Elaine Hunter; children: James E III. **Educ:** Howard Univ, BS, physics, 1946, MS, physics, 1951; Mass Inst tech, MS, PhD, physics, 1953; Harvard

Univ, Div Med Sci, attended 1986. **Career:** Hampton Inst, instr physics, 1946-49; Gen Atomics, consult, 1957-58; Los Alamos Sci Lab, staff mem, 1956-59; Univ Minn, vis assoc prof, 1964; Sir Rudy Peierls Oxford, res asst, 1965-66; Harvard, vis res sci, 1978; Tufts Univ Med Sch, res assoc neuroscience dept anat & cell boil, 1986-; Mass Inst tech, prof physics, 1970, prof emer physics, currently. **Orgs:** Am Physiol Soc, 1960-; Sigma Xi Hon Soc Mass Inst tech, 1953; post-doctoral fel Mass Inst tech Acoust Lab, 1953-55; Shell BP fell, Aeronaut Dept, Southampton, Eng, 1956; NAS-NRC Ford fel Niels Bohr Inst, Copenhagen, 1961-62; pres, JEY Asn; chief oper officer, MHT Ltd; tech dir, CADEX; partner, Escutcheon Inc; Sigma Pi Sigma; Beta Kappa Chi; Sigma Xi. **Honors/Awds:** US Patent no 4, 564, 798, 1986. **Special Achievements:** First African American Physics Professor in MIT. Books: The Texture of Memory: Holocaust Memorials and Meaning, 1993. **Home Addr:** 24 Puddingstone Lane, Newton, MA 02159. **Business Addr:** Professor Emeritus of Physics, Massachusetts Institute of Technology, 77 Massachusetts Ave, Cambridge, MA 02139-4307, **Business Phone:** (617)253-1000.

### YOUNG, JAMES M., II
Marketing executive. **Personal:** Born Oct 29, 1946, Washington, DC; married Barbara Ann Johnson; children: Julie Elizabeth & Jason Michael. **Educ:** Fisk Univ, Nashville, BA, biol, 1968. **Career:** Xerox Corp, mkt rep, 1971-74; F Serv Bur Co, proj adminr educ, 1977-78; Serv Bur Co, Div Control Date Corp, mkt mgr, 1978-. **Orgs:** Alpha Phi Alpha Frat, 1965. **Home Addr:** 1609 Arlington Dr, Hanover Park, IL 60103. **Business Addr:** Marketing Manager, Service Bureau Co, 222 S Riverside Plz Suite 23, Chicago, IL 60606.

### YOUNG, REV. JIMMY RAY
Clergy. **Personal:** Born Apr 9, 1941, Natchitoches, LA; son of Booker T and Maggie; married Sylvia; children: Tarris, Linda, Lisa, LaShawn, John, Latrice & LaDonna. **Career:** Ford Motor Co, supv, 1965-95; Greater St John Baptist Church, pastor, currently. **Home Addr:** 15793 Snowden St, Detroit, MI 48227, **Home Phone:** (313)836-4732. **Business Addr:** Pastor, Greater St John Baptist Church, 7433 Northfield St, Detroit, MI 48204, **Business Phone:** (313)895-7555.

### YOUNG, DR. JOSEF A.
Psychotherapist, vice president (organization). **Personal:** Born Mar 24, 1941, Memphis, TN; married Joyce Lynom; children: Jorald (deceased). **Educ:** Tenn State Univ, BS, 1962; Mich State Univ, masters, attended 1967; Univ Tenn, masters, attended 1972; Southern Ill Univ Carbondale, PhD, 1981. **Career:** Mason, 1974-; Alpha Phi Alpha, vpres, 1980; Ctr Devel Growth, pres, 1980; Optimist Club Int, Comt Chmn, 1985; SW Tenn Community Col, sr counr, currently. **Orgs:** Bd dir, Int Coun Asn, 1970; pres, W Tenn Personnel & Guid, 1972-73; Black Psychologist Asn, 1983; Asn Black Psychologist, 1984-; State Bd Regents; Tenn Asn Coun; Am Asn Ethical Hypn. **Home Addr:** 5131 Ravensworth Dr, Memphis, TN 38109. **Business Addr:** Senior Counselor, Southwest Tennesse Community College, 737 Union Ave, Memphis, TN 38101-0780, **Business Phone:** (901)333-5000.

**YOUNG, DR. JOYCE HOWELL. See Obituaries Section.**

### YOUNG, KATYE H. MCLAUGHLIN
Chief executive officer. **Personal:** Born Jan 31, 1943, Richland Parish, LA; daughter of Johnnie Sr and Etta Stephens; married Joseph C; children: Brian David & Bridget Diane. **Educ:** DC Teachers Col, Wash, DC, BS, 1963; Antioch Grad Sch Educ, Wash, DC, MA, 1975; Kensington Univ, Glendale, CA, PhD, 1983. **Career:** DC Bd Educ, Wash, DC, teacher, 1976-89; McLaughlin Oldsmobile Inc, owner, pres & chief exec officer, 1985-95; Penguin Unity Enterprises Inc, Penguin Greeting Cards, Wash, DC, pres & chief exec officer. **Orgs:** Phi Delta Kappa Sorority, 1980-; chairperson, United Negro Col Fund Telethon, Wash Metrop Area, 1985 & 1986; Int Club, 1991; bd dir, Langston Univ, 1992; Nat Polit Cong Black Women, 1992; Bd Gov, NDHMAA, 2009-.

### YOUNG, KEVIN
Curator, librarian, writer. **Personal:** Born Nov 8, 1970, Lincoln, NE. **Educ:** Harvard Col, BA, 1992; Brown Univ, MFA, 1996. **Career:** Poet/writer, 1995-; Emory Univ, prof creative writing & Eng & cur Raymond Danowski Poetry Libr at Emory Univ, 2005-, cur Lit Collections, 2008-; Schomburg Ctr Res Black Cult, cur, 2016-. **Orgs:** Am Acad Arts & Sci, 2016-. **Honors/Awds:** Stenger Fellowship, Stanford University, 1992; National Poetry Series, 1995; Zacharis First Book Award, 1995; Paterson Poetry Prize, 2003; Guggenheim Foundation Fellowship, 2003-04; Quill Award in Poetry, 2007; Paterson Poetry Prize for Sustained Literary Achievement, 2008; Southern Independent Bookseller Award, 2009; American Book Award, 2011; Graywolf Press Nonfiction Prize, 2012; PEN Open Book Award, 2012; Lenore Marshall Prize for Poetry, Academy of American Poets, 2014; MacDowell Colony Fellowship; honorary doctorate from Beloit University. **Special Achievements:** Author, Most Way Home, 1995; To Repel Ghosts (the double album), 2001; To Repel Ghost: The Remix, 2006; Jelly Rolls: A Blue, 2003; Black Maria, 2005; For the Confederate Dead, 2007; Dear Darkness, 2008; Ardency: A Chronicle of the Amistad Rebels, 2011; The Grey Album: On the Blackness of Blackness, 2012; Book of Hours, 2014; Blue Laws: Selected & Uncollected Poems 1995-2015, 2016. Editor of collections, The Collected Poems of Lucille Clifton, 1965-2010, 2012; The Hungry Ear: Poems of Food and Drink, 2012. Contributor, New Yorker, New York Times Book Review, Kenyon Review, Ploughshares, and Callaloo. **Business Addr:** Emory University Department of English, 876 Woodruff Library, Atlanta, GA 30322.

### YOUNG, KEVIN CURTIS
Track and field athlete, executive. **Personal:** Born Sep 16, 1966, Los Angeles, CA; son of William and Betty Champion. **Educ:** Univ Calif, Los Angeles, BA, sociol, 1989. **Career:** Athlete (retired), olympic track athlete; Flavours Co Inc; motivational speaker, currently. **Orgs:** Alpha Phi Alpha Frat Inc, 1987-. **Honors/Awds:** Silver Medal, Pan American Games, 1987; Male Athlete of the Year, Int Amateur Athlete Found, 1992; Athlete of the Year, Track & Field News, 1992; Harrison Dilliard Award, 1992; Jesse Owens Award, 1992; Male Athlete of the Year, USOC Track & Field, 1992; Gold Medal, Olympic Games, Barcelona, Spain, 400m Hurdles, 1992; ESPY Award; Gold Medal, World Championships Games, Stuttgart, Germany, 1993; National Track & Field Hall of Fame, 2006. **Special Achievements:** First ever ESPY award winner. **Home Addr:** 127 Fabyan Pl, Newark, NJ 07112, **Home Phone:** (973)371-5503.

### YOUNG, KEVIN STACEY
Baseball player, athletic coach. **Personal:** Born Jun 16, 1969, Alpena, MI; married Kelly; children: Kaleb. **Educ:** Univ Southern Miss. **Career:** Baseball player (retired); Pittsburgh Pirates, infielder, 1992-95, 1997-2003; Kans City Royals, 1996; Protege Sports Inc, dir & coach, currently. **Business Addr:** Director, Coach, Protege Sports Inc, Bldg 1 7077 E Marilyn Ave, Scottsdale, AZ 85254, **Business Phone:** (866)403-4880.

### YOUNG, KORLEONE (SUNTINO KORLEONE YOUNG)
Basketball player. **Personal:** Born Dec 31, 1978, Wichita, KS. **Career:** Basketball player (retired); Detroit Pistons, forward, 1998-99; Sichuan Panda; Richmond Rhythm, 1999-2000; Rockford Lightning, 2000-01; Canberra Cannons, 2001-02; Sioux Falls Skyforce, 2002; BC Avtodor Saratov, 2003; Heilongjiang Zhaozhou Fengshen, 2003-05; Lokomotiv Rostov na Donu, 2003-04; LidoRose Roseto Basket, 2005-06; Bnei HaSharon, Israel, 2006.

### YOUNG, DR. LADONNA R.
Executive director. **Personal:** Born Dec 14, 1972, Demopolis, AL; daughter of Eugene B and Ella M. **Educ:** Christian Bros Univ, BA (magna cum laude), hist, 1995; Univ Memphis, MA, teaching, 2000, EdD, 2006. **Career:** SW Tenn Community Col, MAPS-GEAR-UP dir, Lib Studies & Educ, interim dept chair & assoc prof, 2000-; Walden Univ, fac mentor & instr, 2007-; LeMoyne-Owen Col, adj prof, 2009-12; Univ Miss, adj prof, 2010-11. **Orgs:** YMCA; Achievement Sch Dist; Stand C; Black Alliance Educ Options; Arete Christian Sch; Life Issues Community Develop Ctr Excellence. **Home Addr:** 3258 Duncan Williams Rd, Memphis, TN 38119, **Home Phone:** (901)752-0966. **Business Addr:** Department Chair, Associate Professor, Southwest Tennessee Community College, Ua 209a 737 Union Ave Bldg A220, Memphis, TN 38103, **Business Phone:** (901)333-5350.

### YOUNG, LARRY
Government official. **Personal:** Born Nov 25, 1949, Baltimore, MD; son of Mable Payne. **Educ:** Univ Md College Park, attended 1971. **Career:** Young Beat Afro-Am Newspaper, columnist, 1975-77; Md House Del, 1975-87; Nat Black Caucus State Legislators, acitng exec dir, 1979-82; Md Gen Assembly 39th Legis Dist, chmn house environ matters comn, state sen, 1988-94; LY Group, pres, chief exec officer; Baltimore Times, radio host, columnist. **Orgs:** Dir, Urban Environ Affairs Nat Off Izaak Walton League Am, 1970-77; Md House Delegates, 1975-88; Chmn bd dirs, Citizen's Dem Action Orgn, 1976; pres, Ctr Urban Environ Studies, 1978-83; chair, Environ Matters Comt, 1983-87; chair, Baltimore City Deleg, 1987-88; Md Senate, 1988-98; Baltimore Leadership; chmn, Md Health Convocation; chmn, Health Round table; Isaak Walton League Am; co-chmn, Md Conf Black Aged; Legis Adv Baltimore City Area Agency Aging; New Shiloh Baptist Church; Energy & Environ Study Conf; bd dir, Univ Md Med Systs; Senate Judicial Proc Comt, 1988-90; Baltimore City Dist 39, 1988-92; Senate Finance Comt, 1990-98; bd dir & founder, Black Health Study Group, 1990-; Baltimore City Dist 44, 1992-98; State Adv Coun Hereditary & Congenital Dis, 1992-98; Gov's Task Force Community Health Networks, 1994-95; State Comn Neighborhoods, 1994-96; deleg, Dem Party Nat conv, 1996; chmn, Exec Nominations Comt; chmn, Legis Black Caucus; chmn, Senate Exec Nominations Comt; Nat Asn Advan Colored People; co-chair, Gov's Comn Summer Youth Employ, 1996. **Honors/Awds:** Community Service Award, We Need Prayer Headquarters; Afro-American Newspaper Honor Roll Award, 1971; Distinguished Citizenship Award, State Md, 1972; Annual Award, Nat Asn Environmental Educ, 1976; Statesman Award, Baltimore Baptist Ministers' Conf, 1977; Legislator of the Year, 1978; Community Service Award, Gamma Chap Chi Eta Phi Sor Inc, 1979; MPHA Award, Md Pub Health Asn Your Support Health Legislation, 1980; Concerned Citizens Award, Am Cancer Soc Md State Div, 1980; Statesman Award, Bethel African Methodist Episcopal Church, 1980. **Home Addr:** 601 N Eutaw St Suite 102, Baltimore, MD 21201, **Home Phone:** (410)245-0531.

### YOUNG, LAWRENCE W., JR.
Educator, administrator. **Personal:** Born Dec 30, 1942, Cleveland, OH; son of Lawrence W Sr and Maggie Fuggs; married Eddye. **Educ:** Miami Univ, Oxford, OH, BA, 1965, MEd, 1974. **Career:** Adminr (retired); Cleveland Bd Educ, teacher Eng, 1965-69; Miami Univ, Oxford, dir minority affairs, 1969-82; Pa State Univ, Univ Pk, Pa, dir, Paul Robeson Cult Ctr, 1982-2004; Afromart Mag, US corresp. **Orgs:** Alpha Phi Alpha, 1965; Nat Asn Advan Colored People, 1969-; Nat Coun Black Studies, 1985; chair, steering comt, Asn Black Cult Ctrs, 1989; bd dir, Centre County United Way; bd dir, Cent Pa Festival Arts; bd dir, Easter Seals Soc; bd dir, Miami Univ Alumni Coun; Am Col Personnel Asn; Nat Asn Stud Personnel Adminr. **Home Addr:** PO Box 251, State College, PA 16804, **Home Phone:** (814)234-1922.

### YOUNG, LEE
Vice president (organization), educator. **Educ:** Jackson State Univ, BS, MS. **Career:** Ind State, staff; Augusta State Univ, staff; Tuskegee Univ, staff; Wichita State Univ, staff; Ind State Univ, assoc vpres enrollment serv; NC A&T State Univ, vice chancellor acad affairs & enrollment mgt, dir admis & assoc vice provost enrollment mgt; Nev State Col, assoc vice provost, 2008-12. **Orgs:** Nat Asn Col Adms Counselors; Nat Asn Stud Financial Aid Admrs; Nat Asn Stud Personnel Adminrs & Am Mkt Asn. **Business Addr:** Associate Vice Provost for Enrollment Management, Nevada State College, 1125 Nev State Dr, Henderson, NV 89002, **Business Phone:** (702)992-2000.

### YOUNG, LEE R.
Law enforcement officer, executive. **Personal:** Born Jan 8, 1947, Del Rio, TX; son of Leroy and Abbylean A Ward Nunley; married Mary Sanchez; children: Anthony & Kristen Marie. **Educ:** St Edwards Col, Austin, TX, 1973; Sam Houston State Univ, Huntsville, TX, 1973; Southwest Tex Jr Col, AA, 1973; Univ Tex, Austin, TX, BA, 1975. **Career:** Law Enforcement Officer (retired), executive; Nat Pk Serv, Amistad Rec Area, Del Rio, Tex, 1971-73; Tex Dept Pub Safety, Bryan, Tex, trooper Tex hwy patrol, 1975-77, Eagle Pass, Tex, trooper Tex hwy patrol, 1977-80, Del Rio, Tex, trooper Tex hwy patrol, 1980-88, San Antonio, Tex, criminal intelligence investr, 1988, Garland, Tex, sgt Tex ranger, forensic hypnotist, 1994, comput forensics, 1995; Lee Young & Assoc, pres, 2005-. **Orgs:** Nat Hon Soc, SW Tex Jr Col; Nat Police Officers Asn; Homocide Investr Tex; Tex Police Asn; dir, Tex Asn Investigative Hypn, 1994; Seminole Indian Scout Cemetary Asn; dir region one, Tex Asn Lic Investr's; N Tex Pvt Investr's Asn; Nat Coun Invest& Security Serv; Tex Rangers Asn; adv dir, Kiwanis Club McKinney Tex; ambassador, McKinney Tex Chamber Com; investigative hypnotist, Tex Comn Law Enforcement Officer Stand & Educ, master peace officer; process serv, Tex Supreme Ct; spec tex rang, Tex Dept Pub Safet, Pub Safety Comn. **Honors/Awds:** Trail Blazer Award, So Dallas Bus Women, 1989; Grand Marshal, Black Hist Parade, 1989. **Business Addr:** President, Lee Young & Associates, 6401 W Eldorado Pkwy Suite 119, McKinney, TX 75070, **Business Phone:** (972)548-1182.

### YOUNG, LEON D.
State government official. **Personal:** Born Jul 4, 1967. **Educ:** Univ Wis-Milwaukee. **Career:** Police aide & police officer; 16th Assembly Dist, Milwaukee, WI, state rep, currently. **Orgs:** Dem Party; Harambee Ombudsman Proj; Milwaukee Police Asn; League Martin; House Peace; Nat Asn Advan Colored People; Urban League; Social Develop Comn Minority Male Forum Corrections; Nat Black Caucus State Legislators Task Force African Am Males; 100 Black Men; Milwaukee Metrop Fair Housing; Boy Scouts Am; Martin Luther King Community Ctr; Comt Urban & Local Affairs; Comt Interstate Affairs; Comt Consumer Protection; Comt Housing & Real Estate; Comt Ins. **Business Addr:** State Representative, Wisconsin House of Representatives, Rm 123 W State Capitol, Madison, WI 53708, **Business Phone:** (608)266-3786.

### YOUNG, LIAS CARL
Lawyer. **Personal:** Born Nov 21, 1940, Big Sandy, TX; son of W L and Myrtle Davis; married Rose Breaux, Sep 20, 1943; children: Victor, Kimberly & Phyllis. **Educ:** Tex Southern Univ, AB, Law Sch, JD, 1965; Tyler Jr Col. **Career:** Lawyer (retired); Off Regional Coun US Dept HUD, atty advisor, 1968-76; Fed Nat Mortgage Asn, assoc regional couns, 1976-97. **Orgs:** pres, Ft Worth Chap Fed Bar Asn, 1970-71; Nat Bar Asn; Fed Bar Asn; Tex Bar Asn. **Home Addr:** 4309 Stardust Lane, Fort Worth, TX 76119-3120, **Home Phone:** (817)534-8459.

### YOUNG, DR. LIONEL WESLEY
Pediatrician, radiologist. **Personal:** Born Mar 14, 1932, New Orleans, LA; son of Charles Henry and Ethel Johnson; married Florence Inez Brown; children: Tina I, Lionel T & Owen C. **Educ:** Benedictine Col, BS, 1953; Howard Univ Col Med, MD, 1957. **Career:** Univ Rochester NY, radiol resident, 1958-61; Detroit Gen Hosp Wayne Univ, intern, 1958; Cincinnati C's Hosp, fel, 1965; Univ Pittsburgh, Pa, profradiol & pediat, 1975-86; C's Med Ctr Akron, chmn radiol; Northeastern Ohio Univ Col Med, chmn radiol, 1986-91; Loma Linda Univ Med Ctr, head pediat radiol div & prof radiol, currently; Loma Linda Univ C's Hosp, pediat radiol fac, currently. **Orgs:** Pres, Soc Pediat Radiol, 1984-85; pres, Pittsburgh Roentgen Soc, 1985-86; pres, Akron Pediat Radiologists Inc, 1986-91; Sigma Pi Phi; Alpha Omega Alpha; Royal Soc Med, 2010-. **Honors/Awds:** Caffey Award, Soc Pediat Radiol, 1970; Distinguished Service Award, Howard Univ Col Med, 1987; Distinguished Alumnus Award, Howard Univ, 1989. **Home Addr:** 1472 Rosehill Crest, Redlands, CA 92373. **Business Addr:** Professor, Head, Loma Linda University School of Medicine, 11234 Anderson St, Loma Linda, CA 92350, **Business Phone:** (909)558-4281.

### YOUNG, MARY E.
Educator. **Personal:** Born Jun 5, 1941, Harlan, KY. **Educ:** Detroit Bible Col, BRE, 1966; Eastern Mich Univ, BA, 1969, MA, 1972; Univ Mich, ABD, 1975. **Career:** Eastern Ky Univ, counr, 1969-72; Univ Mich, coun, lab practi cum asst, 1973-74, grad teaching asst, 1974-75; Washtenaw Community Col, counr, 1975. **Orgs:** Nat Educ Asn, 1975; Mich Educ Asn, 1975; Washtenaw Community Col Educ Asn, 1975; Circle Y Ranch Camp, 1983-85; Nat Cert Career Counr, 1985; Nat Asn Advan Colored People, 1985; Nat Black Child Inc, 1985-86; Mich Community Col Counr Acad, 1990-91; Washtenaw Counr's Asn, 1992-93. **Honors/Awds:** Alumni of the Year, Detroit Bible Col, 1978; Outstanding Faculty Award, Wash tenaw Community Col, 1984. **Special Achievements:** Licd Prof Counr. **Home Addr:** 2827 Beechwood Dr, Durham, NC 27707, **Home Phone:** (919)686-0074.

### YOUNG, DR. MICHAEL
Research scientist, educator. **Personal:** Born Mar 28, 1950, Muskogee, OK; son of Robert and Betty Brady; married Tamera Whitely; children: Betsy, Brandon, Bethany, Ricky & Devin. **Educ:** Bacone Col, AA, 1970; Southwest Baptist Univ, BA, 1972; Univ Ark, MEd, 1973; Tex A&M Univ, PhD, 1975. **Career:** Campbellsville Col, Campbellsville, KY, asst prof, 1975-78; Auburn Univ, Auburn, AL, asst prof, 1978-80; Univ Ark, prof health sci, Health Educ Proj Off, dir, currently, Univ prof health sci, currently; New Mex State Univ, interim assoc dean res, col health & social serv, 2008-12; Univ Tex at Arlington, 2012-. **Orgs:** Bd dir, Soc Sci Study Sexuality; founding mem, fel, Am Acad Health Behav; Am Sch Health Asn; Am Alliance Health, Phys Educ Recreation & Dance; Am Pub Health Asn. **Home Addr:** 4101 Meadow View, Fayetteville, AR 72701. **Business Addr:** Associate Dean for Research, College of Nursing, University of Texas at Arlington, 701 S Nedderman Dr, Arlington, TX 76019, **Business Phone:** (817)272-2011.

**YOUNG, DR. NANCY WILSON**
Educator. **Personal:** Born May 1, 1943, Orangeburg, SC; married R Paul; children: Ryan Paul. **Educ:** Clafin Col, BS, 1965; SC State Col, attended 1966; George Peabody Col, attended 1968; Univ Miami, MEd, 1970; Barry Univ, grad courses. **Career:** Wateree Elem Sch Lugoff, SC, grade teacher, 1965-67; Ford Found fel, 1968-69; Univ Miami, grad adv, 1969-70, asst dir admin, 1970-80; Interval Int, personnel dir, 1980-83; Miami-Dade Community Col, employ adv, 1983-91, fac, 1991-, prof. **Orgs:** Consult, CEEB Summer Inst Col Bd, 1975-80; chmn, TOEFL Res Comm ETS, 1977-80; vice chmn, TOEFL Policy Coun ETS, 1977-80; exec comm, TOEFL Policy Coun ETS, 1977-80; consult, US State Dept Visits W Africa & Trinidad, 1979; adv bd, Epilepsy Found S Fla, 1984-85; Comm Total Employ Comm, 1984-85; bd dir, Univ Miami Alumni, 1984-87; Dades Employ Handicapped Comm, 1984-; bd dir, 11th judicial nominating comn, 1991-94; exec comm, Healthy People, 1995, 2000; life mem, Clafin Col Alumni Asn; Dade County Chap, Links; Jack & Jill Am; adv bd mem, coord comt, Miami-Dade Comm Col. **Honors/Awds:** Alumni of the Year, Claflin Col, 1991; Outstanding Alumnus of Claflin Col, 1995. **Home Addr:** 6825 SW 64th St, South Miami, FL 33143-3103, **Home Phone:** (305)665-2685. **Business Addr:** Professor, Miami-Dade Community College, 11011 SW 104th St Bldg 6319, Miami, FL 33176-3393, **Business Phone:** (305)237-2178.

**YOUNG, OLLIE L.**
Executive. **Personal:** Born Feb 8, 1948, Philadelphia, PA; daughter of Samuel B Sr and Mary Huggins; married Reginald B; children: Stephanie D. **Educ:** Tarkio Col, BA, 1970; Temple Univ, MBA, bus & managerial econs, 1977. **Career:** Temple Univ Health Sci Ctr, asst personnel dir; Consol Rail Corp, personnel super; Ducat Assoc, consult; New York Times Reg, employee rel mgr; Gannett Co Inc, human resources dir; Rutgers Univ, asst dir, personnel serv; Valic, financial planner, consult; N Philadelphia Health Syst, asst vpres, human resources, 1993-2003; Mercer County, dep dir, 2008-. **Orgs:** Am Mgt Asn, 1984-; volunteer, New Geth Bapt Church Tutorial Prog, 1985-; prog chmn, Newspaper Personnel Rel Assocs, 1986-87; adv bd, Somerset YMCA, 1986-; mgt consult, Somerset United Way; CUPA, 1988-; Black MBA Asn; SHRM, 1998; Big Brother, Big Sister, 1998. **Home Addr:** PO Box 7211, Princeton, NJ 08543. **Business Addr:** Deputy Director, Mercer County, 640 S Broad St, Trenton, NJ 08650, **Business Phone:** (609)989-6160.

**YOUNG, PAMELA THORPE**
Commissioner. **Personal:** married Reuben F; children: 2. **Educ:** Univ NC, Chapel Hill, NC, BA, 1980; NC Cent Univ Sch Law, JD, 1985. **Career:** Travis County, Tx, asst dist atty & asst county atty; Coun Tex Ethics Comn, asst gen; James E Pete Laney Tex House Representatives, ethics advisor, coun speaker; Teague Campbell Dennis & Gorham LLP, vice chair; NC Off State Budget & Mgt, policy analyst, 1987-90; NC Indust Comn, dep comnr, 1996-02, Legal Coun Dept Cult Resources, dep secy, comnr, 2003-04, vice chair, 2004-07, chair, 2007-13. **Orgs:** NC State Bar; Tex State Bar; NC Bar Asn; NC Workers Compensation Sect NC Bar Asn; Wake County Bar Asn. **Business Addr:** Chair, North Carolina Industrial Commission, 4336 Mail Serv Ctr, Raleigh, NC 27699-4338, **Business Phone:** (919)807-2508.

**YOUNG, RAYMOND, JR.**
Sales manager. **Personal:** Born Aug 22, 1960, Mobile, AL; son of Raymond and Tenner; married Lanie L Johnson. **Educ:** Ala A&M Univ, BS acct & comput sci, 1982; Mt St Mary's Col, MBA, mgt & mkt, 1989; Emory Univ, cert; London Bus Sch, cert; Ind Dept Ins, cert, life, accident & health. **Career:** JC Penney Co, mgt trainee, 1981; Super Oil Co, jr acct, 1982; Int Bus Mach Corp, staff financial analyst, 1982-87; Mt Calvary Bapt Church, sunday sch instr, 1983-; Digital Equip Corp, financial planning mgr, 1988-92, sales mgr, 1992-; Compaq Comput Corp, dir & gm sales & serv, 1994-98, dir customer bus dist, 1990-2000, dir e-serv, N Am, 1999-2001; Roche Diagnostics Corp, Prof & Tech Serv, vpres, 2001-07, vpres prof serv, 2001-08; Cientivegroup Inc, dir sales, mkt & serv, independent med device consult, 2009-12; Raymond Young & Assocs LLC, med device bus prin consult, 2008-; Horizon Planning Group Inc, financial rep, 2014-. **Orgs:** Montgomery County Chap Nat Asn Advan Colored People, 1985-, Nat Black MBA Asn, 1987-; bd dir, Titan Prof Serv, 2009-; bd dir, Little Red Door Cancer Agency, 2010-, bd mem, 2014-15; Greater Indianapolis Area Alumni Chap - Ala A&M, chap pres, 2010-16; chmn, 100 Black Men Indianapolis, Health & Wellness Comt, 2011-15. **Honors/Awds:** Delta Mu Delta Nat Honor Soc Bus Admin, 1982-; Outstanding Young Men Am, 1990; Sales Decathalon, 1993, 1994, 1996; Pacesetter of the Year, 1996; Light House Award, 1999. **Home Addr:** 10705 Club Chase, Fishers, IN 46037, **Home Phone:** (317)459-0797. **Business Addr:** Sales Manager, Digital Equipment Corp, 6406 Ivy Lane, Greenbelt, MD 20770, **Business Phone:** (301)459-7900.

**YOUNG, RICHARD EDWARD, JR.**
Executive. **Personal:** Born Dec 30, 1941, Baltimore, MD; married Carol Emile Gette; children: Joyce Ann & Jeffrey Wendel; married Carol Emile Gette; children: Joyce Ann & Jeffrey Wendel. **Educ:** Univ Md, BA, 1971; Rutgers Univ, MCRP, 1973; Seton Hall Univ, JD, 1978. **Career:** Cty Baltimore Dept Housing & Community Develop, housing inspector, 1967-71; NJ Dept Community Affairs, 1971-72; Fed Govt US Dept HUD, urban planner, 1972-73; United Way Essex & W Hudson, Community Planning & Develop, assoc dir, 1973-74; City Newark, evltns chief, 1974-79; Econ Develop Planning, dir, 1979. **Orgs:** Am Inst Planners Asn, 1970; Am Soc Planning Officials, 1970; NJ Soc Prof Planners, 1973; NJ Prof Planner Lic, 1973; 100 Black Men Inc, 1974; bd trustee, vpres, Joint Conn Inc, 1976; pres, Centennial Commun Inc; pres, RE Young Assoc; pres, ARTEP Inc; bd trustee, NJ Neuro psychiat Inst, 1977. **Home Addr:** 7 Bartle Rd, Somerset, NJ 08873, **Home Phone:** (732)873-3783.

**YOUNG, RICKEY DARNELL**
Executive, salesperson, football player. **Personal:** Born Dec 7, 1953, Mobile, AL; son of Nathanial and Deloris Echols; married Gloria Waterhouse; children: Micah Cole & Colby Darnell. **Educ:** Jackson State Col, BS, 1975. **Career:** Football player (retired), sales representative, executive; San Diego Chargers, running back, full back, 1975-77; Minn Vikings, running back, 1978-83; Edina Realty; Jeff Belzer's Todd Chevrolet, sales rep; Forest Lake Ford-Jeep & Eagle, Forest Lake Minn, sales rep; Eden Prairie Ford, sales rep; Courtesy Ford, vpres & dealer, currently. **Orgs:** Chmn, Heart & Lung Asn, 1981; C fund Viking, 1982. **Honors/Awds:** Pass Receiver Award, Viking's, 1978. **Home Addr:** 13670 Valley View Rd Apt 112, Eden Prairie, MN 55344-1977, **Home Phone:** (612)442-6162. **Business Addr:** Vice President, Dealer, Courtesy Ford, 3401 Coon Rapids Blvd, Coon Rapids, MN 55433-2739, **Business Phone:** (612)427-1120.

**YOUNG, ROSE S.**
Government official, army officer. **Personal:** Born Sep 18, 1943, Wadesboro, NC; daughter of Lester W Sturdivant (deceased) and Ethel R Sturdivant; married Charles M; children: Robin D & Charles M Jr. **Educ:** A&T Univ, attended 1960; Cortez Peters Bus Col, attended 1961. **Career:** Walter Reed Med Ctr, Army Med Dept, personnel spt, 1976-85; US Ct Admin Off, retirement spt, personnel mgt spt, 1985-86; Navy Recruitment Command, pub affairs, mgt analyst; Dept Navy, utilities bus line team leader. **Orgs:** Fed Women, steering com, 1982-85, Fed Women, prog, 1987-; ITC, 1988; Sixth Church, deacon bd mem, ordained elder; NCP; Dist. **Home Addr:** 4728 Eastern Ave NE, Washington, DC 20017-3127, **Home Phone:** (202)269-0819.

**YOUNG, SARAH DANIELS**
Government official. **Personal:** Born Sep 25, 1926, Wetumpka, AL; daughter of Thomas Daniels II (deceased) and Novella Saxton Johnson (deceased); married Anderson Crutcher; children: Saundrea Shillingford & Alan Cla. **Educ:** Detroit Inst Com, dipl sec sci, 1946; Wayne State Univ, attended 1964. **Career:** Government official (retired); Detroit Inst Com Bus Col, from sec to pres, 1946-48; Fed Govt, med sec, 1949-54; County Wayne, admin sec off mgr, labor rel anal, 1954-79; Public Housing Auth, comnr, 1979-99; Episcopal Diocese Mich Finance Comt, secy, 1987-91. **Orgs:** St Clements Epis Chap, 1948-; bd canvassers, City Inkster, 1966-89; bd dir, Chateau Cherry Hill Housing Corp, 1973-89; chairperson, FriendsLibrary City Inkster, 1979-99; bd dir, nat ed chief, nat tamias, trustee, Gamma Phi Delta Sor Inc; treas, Diocese Mich Episcopal Church Women Exec Bd, 1983-91; bd dir, NW Guid Clin, 1984-87; Top Ladies Distinction Inc; Mich Metro Chap Exec Bd; Nat Coun Negro Women; Youth Womens Christian Asn; Nat Asn Advan Colored People. **Home Addr:** 27164 Kitch St, Inkster, MI 48141-2518, **Home Phone:** (313)563-4502.

**YOUNG, SUNTINO KORLEONE.** **See YOUNG, KORLEONE.**

**YOUNG, TERRENCE ANTHONY**
Banker. **Personal:** Born Feb 21, 1954, St. Louis, MO; children: Terrence A Jr. **Educ:** Univ Ill, Champaign, BA, 1977, MBA, 1979; State Ill, CPA, 1980. **Career:** Inland Steel Co, finance, 1979-83; First Nat Bank Chicago, unit mgr, vpres, 1983-92; Peal Develop Co, pres, 1992-95; Fund Community Redevelop, develop specialist, 1993-95; Fannie Mae, regional exec dir, lead dir, currently. **Orgs:** Am Inst Cert Pub Accts; Alpha Phi Alpha Fraternity; bd pres, Covenant Develop Corp; bd mem, Hisp Housing Develop Corp; bd mem, Black Pearl Gallery; Metro Bd, Chicago Urban League; founding mem, Network Real Estate Prof; life mem, Univ Ill Alumni Asn; Fed Nat Mortgage Asn. **Honors/Awds:** Outstanding Young Men of America, 1985. **Home Addr:** 4119 S Drexel Blvd, Chicago, IL 60653, **Home Phone:** (773)548-7607. **Business Addr:** Lead Director, Fannie Mae, 1 S Wacker Dr Suite 1300, Chicago, IL 60606-4667, **Business Phone:** (312)368-6200.

**YOUNG, TERRI JONES**
School administrator, educator. **Personal:** Born May 11, 1957, Laurel, MS; daughter of Heywood and Betty Jean Sanders; married James Keith. **Educ:** Eastern Ill Univ, Charleston, IL, BS, human resources mgt & personnel admin, gen, 1979; Ill Inst Tech, Chicago, IL, MBA, mkt, 1989. **Career:** Ill Inst Tech, Chicago, Ill, dir, minority eng prog, 1980-87; Chicago State Univ, Chicago, Ill, dir, engineering studies, 1987-. **Orgs:** Nat Black MBA Asn; Phi Gamma Nu, 1977-; Nat Asn Advan Colored People, 1988-; NTA, 1989-; nat pres, Nat Asn Minority Eng Prog Advocates, 1992-94. **Home Addr:** 15247 Waterman Dr, South Holland, IL 60473-1178, **Home Phone:** (708)331-6119. **Business Addr:** Director of Engineering Studies Program, Chicago State University, 9501 S King Dr HWH129, Chicago, IL 60628-1598, **Business Phone:** (773)995-2357.

**YOUNG, THOMAS**
Singer, educator. **Personal:** married Soprano Susan Eichhorn. **Career:** Singer, actor & conductor; Opera singer& symphony orchestras, 1969-2012; Sarah Lawrence Col, prof music, 1989-; Cleveland Music Sch Settlement; Cleveland Inst Music; San Francisco Opera, Royal Opera House, Opera La Monnaie, Neth Opera, Opera de Lyon, New York Opera & Houston Grand Opera, prin. Albums: X: The Life & Times of Malcolm X; Tania-Anthony Davis; Blue Monday; Marco Polo; The Death of Klinghoffer; Too Hot to Handel; Black Christmas; A Star in the E; Cook Dixon & Young: Vol 1; Three Mo Tenors, 2001; William Bolcom's Songs of Innocence & Experience. Series:"The Days and Nights of Molly Dodd"; "Aida's Brothers and Sisters"; "Mitch Miller Show"; "Mighty Mouse". **Orgs:** Founder & conductor, Los Angeles Vocal Ensemble. **Home Addr:** 460 W 155th St, New York, NY 10032, **Home Phone:** (212)926-3030. **Business Addr:** Professor of Music, Sarah Lawrence College, 1 Mead Way, Bronxville, NY 10708, **Business Phone:** (914)337-0700.

**YOUNG, TOBY, JR.** **See YOUNG, GEORGE, JR.**

**YOUNG, TOMMY SCOTT**
Executive, founder (originator). **Personal:** Born Dec 12, 1943, Blair, SC; son of John Robert and Nancy Lee Thompson; children: Tamu Toliver & Lee Thompson; children: Lee Thompson. **Educ:** Calif State Univ, BA, 1968, post grad; LA Community Col; Benedict Col. **Career:** IBM Corp, customer eng, 1963-66; Raspberry Recordings, creative performing artist, 1965-; Meat & Theatre Inc, founder, pres, 1969-72; Watts Writers Workshop, instr, 1969-71; Kitani Found Inc, exec dir, bd mem, founder, chmn bd, 1977-83; Equitable Life Assurance Soc US, financial planner, 1984; SC Arts Comn, artist res; Lincoln Ctr Inst, Storyteller-in-Residence, currently; Lord Baltimore Press, printers asst. **Orgs:** NC Cult Arts Com, 1973; dir, Timia Enter, 1974; chmn, Educ Com Shel-Blair Fed Credit Union, 1974-75; Gov Int Yr, Child Com; Artistically Talented & Gifted Spcl Proj Adv Bd, 1977-; Mann-Simons Adv Comm, 1979-; SC Educ TV Adv Bd, 1979-; Bro & Sisters Adv Bd, 1979-; Southern Arts Fed Prog Sel Comt, 1979-80; chmn, SC Arts Comn 5 yr Planning Com Richland Co, 1979-80; SC Arts Comn Adn Adv Com; treas SC Com Arts Agencies, 1979-; Govrs Cult Arts Com, 1979-; Govs Int Yr, Child Com; consult, Media Serv Nat Endow Arts, 1979-; Spoleto Midlands Comm, 1980; Nat Asn Life Underwriters, 1985-; Nat Asn Preserv & Perpetuation Storytelling, 1986-; Asn Bl Storytelling, 1987-; Toastmasters Int, 1987-; chmn, Christ Unity Columbia, 1988-, Youth Encouraged Succeed, 1989-; Columbia Youth Collab, 1989-; Southern Order Storytellers, SC Storytellers Guild; GA Coun Arts; Columbia C C; Nat Lit Soc; Int Platform Asn; Gospel Music Workshop Am; Nat Entertainment Conf. **Honors/Awds:** Elizabeth O'Neil Verner Award for Outstanding contributions to the arts in South Carolina, Kitani Foundation, 1979. Distinguished Performance Citation, The Equitable Financial Companies, 1988; Billings Education Found Award. **Special Achievements:** Author of: "Black Blues & Shiny Songs", Crazy Half Sings a Crazy Wolf Song, Red Clay Books 1977; Recipient "10 for the Future" Columbia Newspapers Inc, 1978; Tommy Scott Young Spins Magical Tales, Raspberry Recordings, 1985. **Home Addr:** PO Box 11247, Columbia, SC 29211-1247. **Business Addr:** Storyteller, Center for the Performing Arts Inc, 70 Lincoln Center Plz, New York, NY 10023, **Business Phone:** (212)875-5000.

**YOUNG, WALLACE L., JR.**
Association executive, executive. **Personal:** Born Oct 5, 1931, New Orleans, LA; married Myra Narcisse. **Educ:** Loyola Univ; So Univ. **Career:** New Orleans Pub Libr, chmn bd, 1976-79; Sr Citizen Ctr, asst dir. **Orgs:** Exec sec, Knights Peter Claver, 1964-72; pres & bd mem, Nat Asn Advan Colored People, 1969-70; Dryades St YMCA; Free So Thtr; Nat Cath ConfInter racial Justice; LA State Lib Devel Com; coord, Cath Com Urban Ministry; Nat Off Black Catholics, Nat Black Lay Cath Caucus. **Honors/Awds:** TX Farmworker Award Human Rights, 1977; Human Relation Catholic Award, 1978; Black Catholic Man of Vision, 1978; Dryades YMCA Man of the Year Award, 1979; NOBC Outstanding Service, 1980. **Home Addr:** 7225 Chef Menteur Hwy, New Orleans, LA 70126-5366, **Home Phone:** (504)302-1659. **Business Addr:** Assistant Director, Senior Citizen Center, 219 Loyola Ave, New Orleans, LA 70112.

**YOUNG, DR. WALTER FULLER**
Consultant, dentist, general. **Personal:** Born Aug 18, 1934, New Orleans, LA; son of Andrew Jackson and Daisy Valentine; married Sonjia W; children: 5. **Educ:** Baldwin Wallace Col, BA, 1955; Howard Univ Dent Sch, DDS, 1959; Harvard Sch Bus, spec prog, 1976. **Career:** Osaka Am Club Japan, consult; Am Comput Technol, Atlanta, consult; Gulfstream Aerospace, consult; Grady Healthcare, consult; Iberville Parish, Community Action; St Laudry Parish; St James Parish; St Helena Parish, dent dir; Datacom Int Inc, dir; Health Mgt Decisions, dir; Jamaica Commun, dir; Nev State Penal Inst, 1964; Nev State Ment Hosp, dent dir, 1969; Young Int Develop Corp, pres & owner, 1975-; pvt pract dentist, 1977-; hon consul gen Liberia, 2003-04; Dillard Univ, fac. **Orgs:** Southern Christian Leadership Conf; bd mem, Nat Asn Advan Colored People; bd mem, Fulton County Hosp Authority; bd trust, GA Econ Task Force; N Ga Dent Soc; bd mem, Int Fel Prog; N Ga Dent Soc; Am Dent Asn; bd dir, 100 Black Men Atlanta Inc; bd trustees, Morris Brown Col; City Atlanta Blue Ribbon Comt Equal Bus Opportunity. **Home Addr:** 2717 Cascade Rd SW, Atlanta, GA 30311-3132, **Home Phone:** (404)755-8539. **Business Addr:** President, Owner, Young International Development Co, 2265 Cascade Rd SW, Atlanta, GA 30311-2861, **Business Phone:** (404)753-4753.

**YOUNG, WILLIAM**
Executive. **Educ:** Calif State Univ, Long Beach, BS, bus admin & investments. **Career:** Inroads Inc, pres & chief operating officer; A G Edwards & Sons Inc, staff; Buford Dickson Harper & Sparrow Inc, vpres & dir mkt, pres & chief operating officer, cheif compliance officer, 2000-. **Orgs:** Pres, Inroads Inc; bd mem, St Louis Empowerment Zone; treas, Bd Police Comnrs city St Louis; treas, St Louis Zoo Friends Asn; chmn, Health & Safety Fair St Louis; pres & chmn invest comt, Buford, Dickson, Harper & Sparrow Inc Invest; bd dir, Dollar Gen Corp; chmn bd, Urban League Metrop St Louis; trustee, Exec Comt Fontbonne Col. **Business Addr:** President, Chief Operating Officer, Buford Dickson Harper & Sparrow Inc, 1 Metrop Sq 211 N Broadway Suite 2080, St. Louis, MO 63102, **Business Phone:** (314)725-5445.

**YOUNG, WILLIAM ALLEN**
Actor, movie director. **Personal:** Born Jan 1, 1953?, Washington, DC; married Helen. **Career:** Films: A Soldier's Story, 1984; Jagged Edge, 1985; Wisdom, 1986; Spies Inc, 1988; Lock Up, 1989; The Waterdance, 1992; Drop Squad, Almost Dead, 1994; Fear X, 2003; District 9, 2009; Fatal Consequences, 2011; TV series: "Freedom Road", 1979; "The Jeffersons", 1980; "Fame", 1982; "Women of San Quentin", "Cagney & Lacey", "The Day After", 1983; "Victims for Victims: The Theresa Saldana Story", Boys in Blue, The Dukes of Hazzard, 1984; "Scarecrow & Mrs. King", Hotel, "The Atlanta Child Murders", 1985; "Sins", "Outrage!", "Johnnie Mae Gibson: FBI", 1986; "Mariah", "The Twilight Zone", 1987; 227, Amen, "Tour of Duty", 1988; "Knots Landing", "My Past Is My Own", "The Women of Brewster Place", CBS Schoolbreak Special, 1989; "Cop Rock", Without Her Consent, "Without Her Consent", 1990; "Matlock", 1990-93; "Lies Before Kisses", Father Dowling Mysteries, "L.A. Law", 1991; "Knots Landing", 1992-93; "Matlock: The Vacation", 1992; "Simple Justice", "Home Improvement", "Sisters", "Renegade", I Can Make You Love Me, "The American Experience", 1993; "Diagnosis Murder", The Sinbad Show, Love & War, "Sweet Justice", 1994; "Babylon 5", 1994-95; "Serving in Silence: The Margarethe Cammermeyer Story", "Chicago Hope", "Fast Company", "Murphy Brown", 1995; "Moesha", actor, 1996-2001, dir, 1999-2000; "Sister, Sister", 1998; "The Parkers", actor & dir, 2000-02; "Soul Food", 2001; "Any Day Now", 2001-02; "The Agency", 2003; "The District", 2003; "CSI: Miami", 2004-06; JAG, 2004; Fielder's Choice, 2005; Detective, 2005; "CSI: Crime Scene Investigation", 2005-07; "Commander in Chief",

2006; "Nip/Tuck", 2006; Murder 101, 2006; Primal Doubt, "Saving Grace", 2007; Depth Charge, "The Mentalist", 2008; "Navy NCIS: Naval Criminal Investigative Service", Medium, 2009; Castle, 2010; Detroit 1-8-7, 2010; "Rock the House", 2011; "Good Luck Charlie", 2011-14; "The Game", 2013. **Orgs:** Kappa Alpha Psi Fraternity. **Business Addr:** Actor, c/o Marc Bass Agency, 9255 Sunset Blvd Suite 727, Los Angeles, CA 90069, **Business Phone:** (310)278-1900.

### YOUNG, DR. WILLIAM FREDERICK, JR.

Physician. **Personal:** Born Aug 10, 1956, Cleveland, OH; son of William F Sr and Amy E; married Doris E; children: Lauren E. **Educ:** Dartmouth Col, BA, 1978; Univ Minn, Minneapolis, MN, MS; Cornell Univ Med Col, MD, 1982; Columbia Sch Pub Health, 1985; Mich State Univ, E Lansing, MI. **Career:** William Beaumont Hosp, Royal Oak, Mich, resident; Georgetown Univ Hosp, intern & gen surg, 1982-83; Nat Health Serv Corps, gen med officer, 1983-85; Georgetown Univ Hosp, resident gen surg, 1985-86; Suburban Hosp, surg house officer, 1986-87; Temple Univ Hosp, resident neurosurg, 1987-92; Temple Univ Sch Med, assoc prof, 1992-2001; Ind Univ, Sch Med-Ft Wayne Ctr, clin prof, 2002-; Mayo Grad Sch Med, resident; Mayo Clin & Found Med Educ & Res, prof, chair, currently. **Orgs:** Am Med Asn, 1992-; Cong Neurol Surgeons, 1992-; N Am Spine Soc, 1994-; Am Asn Neurol Surgeons, 1995-; Am Col Surgeons, 1996-; Nat Neuro Trauma Soc, 1997-; Cervical Spine Res Soc, 1998-; Int Soc Hypertension Blacks, 1999; Am Bd Internal Med. **Honors/Awds:** Research Award, Paralyzed Veterans Am, 1996; Research Award, Cervical Spine Res Soc, 1996; Research Award, N Am Spine Soc, 1996; Distinction in Clinical Endocrinology Award, Col Endocrinol, 2006; Endocrine Teaching Award, Am Asn Clin Endocrinologists, 2008; Distinguished Physician, Endocrine Soc, 2011. **Special Achievements:** Numerous publications. **Business Addr:** Professor, Chair, Mayo Clinic & Foundation for Medical Education & Research, 200 1st St SW, Rochester, MN 55905, **Business Phone:** (507)284-2511.

### YOUNG-SALL, DR. HAJAR

Physician. **Personal:** Born Jan 6, 1952, Asheville, NC; daughter of Curtis and Gladys Young; married El Hadji Sall; children: Muhammad, Sulaiman & Khadijah. **Career:** Out Africa, owner, 1990-92; Int Massage Ther Asn, cert massage therapist, 1992-; Yes inc, Found & Exec Dir. **Orgs:** Am Massage Ther Asn, vpres, 1993-95; Sisters United Network, 1992-95; pres, Soc Against Subtle Racist Acts. **Honors/Awds:** Healing Arts Honoree, Int Masseuse Fed. **Home Addr:** 1650 Eastern Pky, Louisville, KY 40204. **Business Addr:** Founder, Executive Director, YES Inc, 2506 Summer ct Dr, Jonesboro, GA 30236, **Business Phone:** (404)438-1991.

### YOUNGBLOOD, REV. DR. JOHNNY RAY

Clergy. **Personal:** Born Jun 23, 1948, New Orleans, LA; son of Palmon and Ottie May; married Joyce Terrell; children: Johnny Jernell, Joel & Jason. **Educ:** Dillard Univ, New Orleans, La, BA, 1970; Colgate Rochester Divinity Sch, Rochester, MDiv, 1973; United Theol Sem, Dayton, OH, DMin, 1990; Boston Univ, hon master divinity, 1993. **Career:** Bethany Baptist Church, Brooklyn, NY, asst pastor, 1973; Mt Pisgah Baptist Church, Bedford Stuyvesant, Brooklyn, sr pastor, 1974-; St Paul Community Baptist Church, sr pastor & exec organizer, currently. **Orgs:** E Brooklyn Congregations; Progressive Nat Baptist Conv. **Honors/Awds:** Honorary master of divinity, Boston University, 1993; Inducted, Martin Luther King Jr Hall of Preachers, Morehouse College. **Special Achievements:** Recognized in the Congressional Record for his work with the Nehemiah Housing Project. **Business Addr:** Senior Pastor, St Paul Community Baptist Church, 859 Hendrix St, Brooklyn, NY 11207, **Business Phone:** (718)257-1300.

### YOUNGBLOOD, KNEELAND

Physician, founder (originator), executive. **Personal:** Born Dec 13, 1955, Galena Park, TX. **Educ:** Princeton Univ, BA, polit sci human affairs, 1978; Warnborough Col Oxford, Eng, attended 1977; Univ Stockholm, attended 1977; Univ Tex Health Sci Ctr, MD, 1982. **Career:** Emory Univ Sch Med, Grady Memorial Hosp, resident emergency med, 1983-85; Med Ctr Plano, emergency med physician, 1985-97; Teacher Retirement Syst Tex, chmn & trustee, 1993-99; Pharos Capital Group LLC, founding partner, 1997-; Energy Future Holdings Corp, dir; Burger King Holdings Inc, dir, 2004-10; Starwood Hotels & Resorts Worldwide Inc, dir; Task Force Nat Health Care Reform (led by First Lady Hillary Rodham Clinton). **Orgs:** Bd dir, dir emer, US Enrichment Corp (USEC); bd mem, AMR Investments; bd mem, City Dallas Employee Retirement Syst; dir emer, iStar Financial; Coun Foreign Rels; chmn, Am Beacon Funds; bd dir, Gap Inc; bd mem, Egenera & Reel FX; bd mem, Pace Holdings Corp. **Honors/Awds:** "Black Enterprise," 75 Most Powerful Blacks on Wall Street, 2011. **Special Achievements:** Nominated to the USEC by President Bill Clinton; wrote the essay, "From Sit-in to Soweto" after meeting Nelson Mandela. **Business Addr:** Founding Partner, Pharos Capital Group LLC, 3889 Maple Ave Suite 400, Dallas, TX 75219, **Business Phone:** (214)855-0194.

### YOUNGBLOOD, SHAY

Writer. **Personal:** Born Jan 1, 1959, Columbus, GA. **Educ:** Clark-Atlanta Univ, BA, mass commun, 1981; Brown Univ, MFA, creative writing, 1993. **Career:** Creative Writing Workshop Instr & Lectr var univs, 1987-; Peace Corps, Cominican Repub, agr info officer; WETV, Atlanta, Ga, pub info asst; Syracuse Community Writer's Proj, lectr; RI Adult Correctional Inst Women, play wrighting instr; Brown Univ, lectr; Wheaton Col, Col vis prof, 1995-97; Univ Miss, John & Renee Grisham Writer-in-Residence, 2002-03; New Sch Social Res, lectr, currently; Tex A&M Univ, Writer-in-Residence, currently; Riverhead Bks, auth, currently; Plays: Communism Killed My Dog; Shakin' Mess Outta Misery, 1994; Talking Bones, 1994; Sq Blues; Black Power Barbie in Hotel de Dream; fiction: Big Mama Stories, 1989; Novels: Soul Kiss, 1997; Black Girl in Paris, 2000. **Orgs:** Dramatists Guild; Authors Guild; Nat Writers Union; Writers Guild Am; bd mem, Yaddo Artists Colony. **Home Addr:** PO Box 300772, Jamaica Plain, MA 02130. **Business Addr:** Author, Riverhead Books, 200 Madison Ave, New York, NY 10016.

### YOUNGE, IDA

President (organization). **Personal:** married Fitzroy Jr. **Career:** Jack & Jill Am Inc, pres, nat pres, 2002-04, pomona area chapter, regional dir.

### YOUNGER, CELIA DAVIS

Educator. **Personal:** Born Aug 24, 1939, Gretna, VA; married James Arthur; children: Felicia A & Terri E. **Educ:** Va State Univ, BS, 1970, MEd. **Career:** VA State Univ, prog coordr stud union, 1971-73, asst dir financial aid, 1973-75, bus devel specialist & procurement officer, 1974-78; J Sargeant Reynolds Comm Col, adj fac sch bus, 1974-75; Ocean County Col, adj fac sch bus, 1982-83; Georgian Ct Col, dir, learning resource ctr, 1978-83, dir, educ oppor fund prog, 1983-05, dir stud support servs prog, currently. **Orgs:** Alpha Kappa Alpha Sor, 1968-; financial secy & exec bd mem, Educ Opportunity Fund Prof Asn, 1978-; chairperson, affirmative action comm workshop facilitator OC Adv Comm Status Women, 1980-; exec bd mem, Ocean County Girl Scouts, 1983-; Am Asn Univ Women; NJ Asn Devel Educ; NJ Asn Stud Financial Aid Adminrs; Nat Asn Female Execs. **Home Addr:** 32 Chelsea Rd, Jackson, NJ 08527, **Home Phone:** (732)730-1857. **Business Addr:** Director, Educational Opportunity Fund, Georgian Court University, 900 Lakewood Ave, Lakewood, NJ 08701, **Business Phone:** (732)987-2700.

### YOUNGER, KENNETH C.

Automotive executive, business owner, chief executive officer. **Personal:** Born MO. **Career:** McDonnell Douglas Aircraft Corp CA, engr; Ford Motor Co; Landmark Ford Sales Inc, Fairfield, OH, owner, chief exec officer, 1977-. **Orgs:** Founding mem, pres & co-founder, Ford Lincoln-Mercury Black Dealers Asn; pres, Nat Assoc Minority Automobile Dealers. **Honors/Awds:** Quality Dealers Award. **Business Addr:** Chief Executive Officer, Owner, Landmark Ford Sales Inc, 5221 Dixie Hwy, Fairfield, OH 45014, **Business Phone:** (513)829-8000.

### YOUSSEF, SITAMON MUBARAKA

Publisher, writer. **Personal:** Born Nov 21, 1951, Greenwood, MS; daughter of Ellen Mae Dailey and Hurie Lee; children: Meahason Baldwin. **Educ:** Calif Univ, BA, 1987; William Carey Col, MEd, 1993. **Career:** Los Angeles Community Col, instr, 1989-90; Fla A&M Univ, instr, 1994-97; Tallahassee Community Col, instr, 1997-99; Tillman Sims Communs, pres, currently; Author: Mail From Jail: A Glimpse Into A Mother's Nightmare, 2001; Reflections: A Bk of Poetry, 2001; Editor: Marcus Garvey: The FBI File, 2001. **Orgs:** Author's Guild, 1998-. **Home Addr:** 1300 Exec Ctr Dr Suite 537, Tallahassee, FL 32301, **Home Phone:** (850)562-3800. **Business Addr:** President, Tillman Sims Communications, 1300 Exec Ctr Dr Suite 537, Tallahassee, FL 32311, **Business Phone:** (850)251-1606.

### YUILL, ESSIE MCLEAN-HALL

Educator. **Personal:** Born Jan 31, 1923, Wise, NC; daughter of Edward and Lucy; married Lorenzo; children: Lester Slade. **Educ:** Shaw Univ, BA, 1946; Capital Univ, reading specialist cert, 1964; Ohio State Univ, MEd, 1970. **Career:** Educator (retired); Johnsonville High Sch, eng, 1950-55; Kent Elem, 1961-67; Zeta Phi Beta Sorority Inc, chap pres, 1962-64; Franklin Mid Sch, 1967-70; Barrett Mid, coor dr, supvr reading prog, 1971-77; Berry Mid Sch, reading, commun, 1971-77; Briggs High Sch, reading commun skills, 1977-79; Zeta Phi Beta Sorority Inc, chap pres, 1978-79; Cent High Sch, reading commun skills, 1979-80; E High Sch, reading, commun skills, 1980-88. **Orgs:** Zeta Phi Beta; charter mem, Qual Sharing; King Performing Arts; FriendsArts Cult Enrichment; Univ Women; Helen Jenkins Davis Scholar Award Group; Columbus Symphony Orchestra, east unit; Child Develop Coun; hostess, Martin Luther King Breakfast. **Home Addr:** 354 Rhoads Ave, Columbus, OH 43205, **Home Phone:** (614)252-0190.

### YUILLE, DR. BRUCE

Dentist. **Personal:** Born NJ. **Educ:** Hampton Univ, BA, chem, 1968; Univ at Buffalo, grad studies, 1970; Univ Va, grad studies, 1976; Univ Md Sch Dent, DDS, 1976. **Career:** Acad Gen Dent, master, 1989-2011; St Agnes Health Care Ctr, Catonsville, Md, dentist; Pvt pract, dentist, 2008-. **Orgs:** Pres, Univ Md Dent Sch, 2001; Am Dent Asn; Md Acad Gen Dent; pres, Baltimore City Dent Soc; pres, Alumni Asn; pres, Baltimore City Component Md; pres, Acad Gen Dent. **Honors/Awds:** Master dentist status, Md Acad Gen Dent, 1995; Inter Nat Honor Dental Organization, Pierre Fauchard Acad, 2001. **Special Achievements:** First African American to receive master dentist status from Maryland Academy of General Dentistry. **Home Addr:** 9637 Woodland Rd, New Market, MD 21774, **Home Phone:** (310)865-4811. **Business Addr:** Dentist, Private Practice, 700 Geipe Rd Suite 270, Catonsville, MD 21228, **Business Phone:** (410)566-1550.

## Z

### ZACHARY, STEVEN W.

Educator, government official, lawyer. **Personal:** Born Apr 24, 1958, St. Paul, MN; son of Percy J and Martha A; children: Steven Jr & James. **Educ:** Mankato State Univ, BS, 1981; Univ Minn Sch Law, JD, 1984. **Career:** City St Paul, human rights, 1984-92; William Mitchell Col Law, adj prof, 1989-92; State Minn, diversity & equal opportunity dir, 1992-97; Brauer Law Offices, managing atty, currently. **Orgs:** Sch bd pres, St Peter Claver Sch, 1987-88; MN Minority Lawyer's Asn, 1987-93; pres, Nat Car Pk St Paul Br, 1990-93; bd mem, MCLU, 1990-93; criminal justice task force chairperson, Joint Relig Legis Coalition, 1991-92. **Home Addr:** 1360 University Ave W 324, St. Paul, MN 55104-4086, **Home Phone:** (612)510-0926. **Business Addr:** Managing Attorney, Brauer Law Offices, 16430 N Scottsdale Rd Suite 120, Phoenix, AZ 85254, **Business Phone:** (480)621-3535.

### ZACHARY-PIKE, ANNIE R.

Farmer. **Personal:** Born May 12, 1931, Marvell, AR; daughter of Cedel Davidson (deceased) and Carrie Davidson (deceased); married Lester Pike. **Educ:** Homer G Phillips Sch Nursing; St Christian Col, Hon PhD, 1972. **Career:** Farmer, owner & mgr; Marvell Sch Dist, chapter I parent coord, 1990-91. **Orgs:** Eastern Star; Nat Asn Advan Colored People; AR Asn Colored Women; Phillips Co Extnsn Hmmkrs Coun; IPA; Ark Coun Human Rels; Ark Asn Crppld Inc; Wildlife Federation; EAME; Emergency Sch Asst Proj; Pta; 4-H; Farm Bureau; Farmers Home Admin; adv coun, FHA; USDA Civil Rights Comn; Coun Aging; Fair Bd; Small Bus Asn; Nat Coun Christians & Jews; bd, Election Law Inst; Eastern Arkansas Mental Health; Delta Area Devel Inc; Workshop Inc; Rep, Ark St Com Farm; district deputy, Eastern Ark Order Eastern Star; deleg, Republican Nat Conv, 1972. **Honors/Awds:** Family Year Award, 1959; 4-H Friendship, 1959; Home Demonstration Woman Year, 1965; Queens Womens Federated Club Inc, 1969; GOP Conv Women of the Year, Alpha Kappa Alpha, 1971. **Home Addr:** 2700 Phillips 125, Marvell, AR 72366-8918.

### ZAKARI, DR. TATA MOHAMMED

Physician. **Educ:** Ahmadu Bello Univ, MD, 1986. **Career:** Wayne State Univ, resident; Henry Ford Health Syst, physician; Laz Med Group, physician, currently; Wayne State Univ Detroit, adj clin prof family med; Mich State Univ Lansing, adj clin prof family med. **Orgs:** Fel Royal Col, Ireland; Mich Acad-Family Physicians; Am Soc Bioethics & Humanities. **Home Addr:** , MN. **Business Addr:** Physician, Laz Medical Group PC, 29425 Northwestern Hwy Suite 125, Southfield, MI 48034-1080, **Business Phone:** (248)569-7550.

### ZAMBRANA, DR. RAFAEL

Educator. **Personal:** Born May 26, 1931, Santa Isabel; married Laura E Alvarez; children: Gloria, Ralph (deceased), Aida, Magda, Wallace, Olga & Daphne. **Educ:** Cath Univ PR, BA, hist, 1958; Hunter Col, attended 1962; Columbia Univ, psychol, 1965; MSW, 1974; City Univ NY, PhD, 1982. **Career:** Educator (retired); Bd Educ, NY, jr high sch teacher, 1958-62; Rabbi Jacob Joseph High Sch, teacher, 1962-65; Mobilization Youth, social worker, 1965-67; PR Community Develop Proj, dir training & block orgn prog, 1967-68; Lower E Side Manpower Neighborhood Serv Ctr, dir, 1968-69; Williamsburg Community Corp, exec dir, 1969-71; Community Develop Agency, asst comnr, 1971-74; Medgar Evers Col, City Univ NY, prof pub admin, 1974; City Univ NY, Social Sci Div, chairperson, 1982-89; City Univ NY, chairperson pub admin, 1990-95; City Univ NY, Sch Bus & Pub Admin, dean, 1995-98; City Univ NY, asst pres, 1998-2000. **Orgs:** Consult, Coney Island Community Corp, 1969-78; bd mem, Community Coun Greater New York, 1969-76; inst rep, Nat Asn Schs Penn, 1974-98; local sch bd mem, Dist 12 New York, 1975-85; consult, NY State Dept Corrections, 1976; adv bd mem, Mgt Adv Coun, US Dept Labor, Region II, 1980-82; pres, Coun PR & Hisp Orgn. **Home Addr:** 3600 Paseo Condado Levittown, Toa Baja, PR 00949-3015.

### ZANDER, JESSIE MAE REASOR

School administrator. **Personal:** Born Jul 31, 1932, Inman, VA; married Johnny W. **Educ:** Berea Col, BA, Elem Educ, 1954; Univ Ariz, MA, elem educ, 1966, MA, counguid, 1976; supvry & admin cert, 1978. **Career:** School administrator, educator (retired); Benham Elem High Sch, Ky, teacher, 1954-58; Tucson Indian Training Sch, Ariz, teacher jr high, 1956-58; Tucson Unified Sch Dist, teacher, 1958-76; Tucson Unified Sch Dist, counr, 1976-79; Miles Explor Learning Ctr Tucson Unified Sch Dist, prin, 1979-80; Lin weaver Sch, Tucson Unified Sch Dist, prin, 1980-89; vis prof, Brea Col Dept Educ Spring term, 1991; educ consult, Carter G. Woodson Inst; Bereas Pres Coun, Alumni Asn. **Orgs:** Consult, Control Awareness Adminr Retreat, 1975-76; Educ Div Am Cancer Soc, 1975; Tamiochus Alpha Kappa Alpha Sor Eta Epsilon Omega Chap, 1976-81; coordr poetry, Sch Ariz St Poetry Soc, 1977-80; bd mem, Pima Coun Community Serv, 1978-79; vpres, Ariz St Poetry Soc, 1978; conf chair, Ariz St Poetry Soc, 1978-79; facilitator, Y's racial justice prog; coordr, Funeral Consumers Alliance Speakers Bur; prog chair & secy, State Poetry Soc. **Honors/Awds:** The Phenomenal Woman Award, Univ Ariz Black Alumni, 1954; Arizona State Poetry Award, 1977; Outstanding Pres Coun Black Educr, 1978-79, 1979-80; Newspaper Article Open Educ Miles Exploratory Learning Ctr, 1980; AKA Regional Poetry Award, 1985; Berea College Alumni Loyalty Award, 1991; Berea College Service Award, 1992; Black Alumni Phenomenal Woman Award, Univ Ariz, 2002; Lifetime Achievement Award, YWCA, 2008; C.H. Shorter Lifetime Achievement Award, Appalachia Training Cent Bland Alumni Asn, 2013. **Special Achievements:** First African American to graduate from Berea College since the repeal of the Day Law. Works published in: Brush the Mind Gently, PEN Women, Appalachia Independent & other chap books. **Home Addr:** 5835 E 3rd St, Tucson, AZ 85711-1519, **Home Phone:** (520)745-2729.

### ZANGO-HALEY, LINDA

President (organization), vice president (organization). **Personal:** Born NJ; married William Freeman. **Educ:** Long Island Univ, BA, mkt & jour, 1971; City Univ NY, Baruch Col, mkt mgt, gen. **Career:** Elizabeth Arden, mkt develop mgr; Flori Roberts Cosmetics, vpres, mkt; Matchstix Cosmetics, founder; Cosmetics Int, Del Labs Inc, vpres; Links Inc sponsor workshops Cyper Bullying Teens, New York, vol, pres, 2013-; Haley Group LLC Strategic Mkt & Commun Consults, pres, currently. **Orgs:** Pres, Greater New York Chap Links; bd dir, Manhattan Theatre Club; pres's adv comt mem, Metrop Mus Art; officer bd dir, New York Women's Forum Inc; New York affil bd mem, Am Heart Asn; Multi-Cult Adv Comt, Metrop Mus Art; Cosmetic Exec Women; Fashion Group Int New York. **Home Addr:** , Newyork, NY, **Home Phone:** (646)259-2085. **Business Addr:** Vice President, Del Laboratories Inc, 726 Reckson Plz, Uniondale, NY 11553, **Business Phone:** (516)844-2020.

### ZEALEY, DR. SHARON JANINE

Lawyer. **Personal:** Born Aug 30, 1959, St. Paul, MN; daughter of Marion Edward and Freddie Ward. **Educ:** Xavier Univ La, BS, bus admin, 1981; Univ Cincinnati, Col Law, JD, 1984. **Career:** Star Bank, corp trust adminr, 1984-86; UAW Legal Servs, atty, 1986-88; Manley, Burke & Lipton, assoc, 1988-90; Ohio Atty Gen, dep atty gen, 1991-95; Southern Judicial Dist Ohio, Asst US Atty, 1995-97,

US Atty, 1997-2001; Univ Calif Col Law, adj prof law; Blank Rome LLP, partner, 2001-06; Coca-Cola Co, litigation & int arbit, 2006-08, chief ethics & compliance officer, 2008-15, assoc gen coun, 2015. **Orgs:** Alpha Kappa Alpha Sorority; Alpha Kappa Mu Hon Soc; Am Bar Asn; Ohio Bar Asn; bd mem, Cincinnati Bar Asn; Fed Bar Asn; bd trustee, Legal Aid Soc, Cincinnati, 1987-92, secy, 1990-92; pres, Black Lawyers Asn, Cincinnati, 1989-91; bd govs, Nat Bar Asn, 1989-91; City Cincinnati Equal Employ Opportunity Adv Rev Bd, 1989-91; bd trustee, Cincinnati Bar Asn, 1990-94; City Cincinnati, Tall Stacks Comn, comnr, 1991-96; Mayor's Comn, C, comnr, 1992-94; Greater Cincinnati Found Task Force, Affordable Home Ownership, 1992-93; Merit Selection Comt, US Sixth Circuit Ct Appeals, 1992-93; co-chmn, Greater Cincinnati Minority Coun Prog, 2005; Legal Aid Soc; bd visitors, Univ Cincinnati Col Law; bd mem, Playhouse Pk; Nat Asn US Attorneys; Nat LGBT Bar Asn Found; Ethics & Compliance Officers Asn; founding mem, NextGen Compliance LLC, 2015. **Business Addr:** Chief Ethics Officer, Compliance Officer, Coca-Cola Co, PO Box 1734, Atlanta, GA 30301.

### ZEITLIN, JIDE J.
Investment banker, executive. **Personal:** Born Ibadan; son of Arnold and Marian. **Educ:** Amherst Col, AB, econ & eng, 1985; Harvard Univ, MBA, 1987. **Career:** Executive (retired); Goldman Sachs & Co, summer assoc, 1983-86, assoc, 1987-91, vpres, 1991-96, sr investment banker, partner & managing dir, 1996-2005; pvt investor; Independent Mobile Infrastructure Ltd, founder, 2005; Keffi Group, founder. **Orgs:** Chmn, bd trustee, Amherst Col, 1993-; trustee, bd mem, Milton Acad, 1996-; dir, Common Ground Community HDFC, 1996-; dir, Teach Am New York, 1997-; trustee, bd mem, Montefiore Med Ctr, 1998-; bd mem, Harvard Bus Sch Vis Comm; bd mem, Playwrights Horizons & Common Ground Community; bd dir, Affiliated Mgrs Group Inc, 2006-; dir, Coach Inc; bd mem, Doris Duke Charitable Found; bd mem, Cogentus Pharmaceut Inc. **Home Addr:** 147 W 15th St, New York, NY 10011-6749, **Home Phone:** (212)627-3745. **Business Addr:** Board of Directors, Affiliated Managers Group Inc, 600 Hale St, Prides Crossing, MA 01965, **Business Phone:** (617)747-3300.

### ZELIS, KAREN DEE (KAREN ZELIS HOLDER)
Attorney general (U.S. federal government), lawyer. **Personal:** Born Oct 21, 1953, Washington, DC; daughter of Jeanne Rivoire; children: Jason Christopher & Erika Nikole. **Educ:** Univ Calif, BA, 1975; Armstrong Law Sch, JD, 1979. **Career:** Alameda County Family Ct Servs, secy, 1982-83; Contra Costa Dist Atty Off, dep dist atty, sr dep dist atty, 1983-; Zelis Consults LLC, currently. **Orgs:** Calif State Bar Asn, 1982-; Calif Dist Atty Asn, 1983-; Charles HoustonBar Asn, 1990-; Am Bar Asn, 1990-; Contra Costa Bar Asn, 1990-. **Business Addr:** Attorney, Zelis Consultants LLC, 911 San Simeon Dr, Concord, CA 94518, **Business Phone:** (925)705-0740.

### ZELLNER, HUNNDENS GUISEPPI. See ZELLNER, PEPPI.

### ZELLNER, PEPPI (HUNNDENS GUISEPPI ZELLNER)
Football player. **Personal:** Born Mar 14, 1975, Forsyth, GA. **Educ:** Ft Valley State Univ. **Career:** Football player (retired); Dallas Cowboys, defensive end, 1999-2002; Wash Redskins, 2003-04; Ariz Cardinals, defensive end, 2004-05.

### ZEMAN, PAULA REDD
County government official. **Career:** Westchester County, Dept Human Resources, comnr, cur, dir tech serv; City Yonkers, comnr; Westchestergov, human Resources Comnr, vice-chair, chief staff; Nat Gay, vice chair; Lesbian Task Force, vice chair. **Orgs:** Vice chair & chief-of-staff, Westchester County Dem Comt; Women Dem Westchester; Dem nat Conv & Electoral Col; Harriman Soc; Westchester Arts Coun; Downtown Musc Grace Church; bd dir & vice chair, Empire State Pride Agenda; co-chair, Task Force Found; chair, Task Force Action Fund; co-chair, Task Force's New York Leadership Awards; exec bd mem, Jazz Forum Arts Inc; bd mem, Nat Gay. **Business Addr:** Commissioner, Westchester County, 148 Martine Ave Suite 100, White Plains, NY 10601, **Business Phone:** (914)995-2114.

### ZENO, HON. MELVIN COLLINS
Judge. **Personal:** Born Jul 14, 1945, Jonesboro, LA; son of Ruth Doyle and Nathaniel Sr; married Margie Loud; children: Monica Lureen & Micah. **Educ:** Southern Univ, BS, 1967; Loyola Univ S, JD, 1974. **Career:** Judge(retired); Red Ball Motor Freight Co, dock worker, 1966; Iberville Parish, speech & hearing therapist, 1968; Jefferson Parish, spec educ teacher, 1968-75; atty law, 1974-92; Jefferson Parish, asst dist atty, 1975-92, 24th Judicial Dist Ct, div p, chief judge, 1992-; Xavier Univ, bus law instr, 1986-88. **Orgs:** Dir, La State Spec Olympics, 1969-; co-founder, vpres, bd dir, Martin L King Jr Task Force, 1979-; int bd dir, Omega Psi Phi Frat, 1983-90; adv bd, Hope Haven Madonna Manor Home Boys, 1984-; co-founder, pres, bd dir, Jefferson Black Chamber Com Inc, 1989-92; bd dir, March Dimes Birth Defects Found, 1991; life sustaining mem, Nat Asn Advan Colored People; chmn, Jefferson Parish Econ Develop Comn, Bus Develop Abbr Adv Comt; Am Bar Asn; La State Bar Asn; Louis Martinet Legal Soc; Nat Bar Asn; Am Judges Asn; La Dist Judges Asn; Fourth & Fifth Circuit Judges Asn. **Home Addr:** 754 Terry Pkwy, Terrytown, LA 70056, **Home Phone:** (504)393-2792. **Business Addr:** Chief Judge, Jefferson Parish Courthouse, 2nd Derbigny St Fl 4 Suite P, Gretna, LA 70053, **Business Phone:** (504)364-3975.

### ZENO, WILLIE D., SR.
Executive. **Personal:** Born Mar 28, 1942, Dallas, TX. **Educ:** Bus Bishop Col, MBA, 1968; Univ OK, MSEE, 1972. **Career:** Hank Moore & Assoc; Goodyr Aerospace, personal dir; EOC US Dept Labor, dir; Eng & Design Eng Soc Am Leap, dir. **Orgs:** Urban Leg Nat Businessman. **Honors/Awds:** Goodyear, Weak Design Eng Month. **Home Addr:** 4900 3rd Ave, Los Angeles, CA 90043.

### ZIEGLER, DR. LADY DHYANA
Educator, school administrator. **Personal:** Born May 5, 1949, New York, NY; daughter of Ernest and Alberta A Guy. **Educ:** City Univ NY, Baruch Col, BS, jour & music, 1981; Southern Ill Univ, Carbondale, MA, 1983, radio & TV, PhD, higher educ & acad admin, 1985. **Career:** Essence Mag, mkt researcher, 1972-75; Rosenfeld Sirowitz & Lawson, copywriter & radio producer, 1974-75; Patten & Guest Productions NY, regional mgr, 1976-79; WNEW TV, internship desk asst & prod asst; Seton Hall Univ, counr high sch studs, 1979-81; Baruch Col CUNY, Eng tutor& instr writing workshops, 1979-81; Westside Newspaper, reporter; CBS TV Network, prod intern, 1980-81; Southern Ill Univ, Dept Radio & Tv, lab instr, 1981-83; Jackson State Univ, dept Mass Commun, asstprof, 1984-85; Univ Tenn, Knoxville, dept Broadcasting, asst profbroadcasting, 1985-90, prof broadcasting, 1990-97, assoc dir diversity resources & educ serv; Fla A&M Univ, prof jour, 1997-, actg vpres res & dir, Univ Planning & Anal, 2002-03, asst vpres instrnl technol & acad affairs, currently; Int Educ Develop, interim dir, 2006-07. **Orgs:** Nat Pol Cong Black Women; Delta Sigma Theta Sor Inc; Phi Delta Kappa; Post Doctoral Acad Higher Educ, grad fel; Speech Comm Asn; Blacks Commun Alliance; Nat Coun Negro Women Inc; Southern Ill Univ Alumni Asn; Metro Black Media Coalition Conf, 1984, Southern Ill Univ &Blacks Commun Alliance, 1985, Nat Black Media Coalition Conf, 1985; US Armed Forces Azores Port, speaker & consult, 1986; Kiwanis Club Knoxville, 1988-; Southern Regional Develop Educ Proj Coordr, Delta Sigma Theta, 1988-; Soc Prof Journalists, 1988; Women Commun Inc, vpres develop, pres-elect, 1989, pres, 1990-91; Oxford Roundtable; bd mem, Fla Virtual Sch. **Special Achievements:** First African-American to be elected as President of the University of Tennessee-Knoxville Faculty Senate. **Home Addr:** 423 Alps Way, Knoxville, TN 37919. **Business Addr:** Professor of Journalism, Florida Agricultural & Mechanical University, 1601 S Martin Luther King Blvd Suite 100, Tallahassee, FL 32307, **Business Phone:** (850)599-3276.

### ZIMMERMAN, DR. EUGENE
Physician. **Personal:** Born Jul 7, 1947, Orangeburg, SC; married Sheila Beth Hughes; children: Brian & Monica. **Educ:** Jersey City St Col, BA, 1969; Howard Univ Med Sch, MD, 1973. **Career:** Harlem Hosp Ctr, intern, 1973-74; Howard Univ Hosp, resident, 1974-76; Stud Health Serv Gallanhet Col, actg med dir, 1977-81; SENAB, med dir, 1979-84; Dept Forensic Psychiat, staff physician. **Orgs:** Med Soc DC, 1976-; NY Acad Sci, 1984-. **Honors/Awds:** Board Certified Internist, Am Bd Internal Med, 1985. **Home Addr:** 4621 Sargent Rd NE, Washington, DC 20017, **Home Phone:** (202)269-3360. **Business Addr:** Staff Physician, Department of Forensic Psychiatry, 1905 E St SE Bldg 22, Washington, DC 20003, **Business Phone:** (202)724-4387.

### ZIMMERMAN, MATTHEW AUGUSTUS, JR.
Clergy, military leader. **Personal:** Born Dec 9, 1941, Rock Hill, SC; son of Matthew Augustus and Alberta Loretta Brown; married Barbara Ann Boulware; children: Tina, Dana & Meridith. **Educ:** Benedict Col, BS, 1962; Duke Univ, MDiv, 1965; Long Island Univ, MSEd, 1975; AUS Command & Gen Staff Col; AUS War Col. **Career:** Hq, third inf div, staff chaplain, 1980-82; Training Doctrine Command, dep staff chaplain, 1983-85; US Forces Command, command chaplain, 1985-89; USY, dep chief chaplains, 1989-90, chief chaplains, 1990-94; Vet Affairs Med Ctr, Dept Veterans Affairs Chaplain Serv, dir, 1994-98; First Baptist Church, Warrenton, Va, pastor, 1998-; Morris Col, campus pastor & instr; Idaho State Univ, campus pastor. **Orgs:** Mil Chaplains Asn; Asn USY; bd gov, USO; Kiwanis Int; Opp Fraternity Inc; chair, bd visitor, Howard Univ Sch Divinity; bd dir, Coalition Spirit-filled Churches; Nat Asn Advan Colored People; Omega Psi Phi fraternity. **Honors/Awds:** Roy Wilkins Meritorious Service Award, Nat Asn Advan Colored People, 1990; Doctor of Humane Letters, Benedict Col, 1991; Distinguished Alumni Award, Duke Univ Divinity School, 1991; Black Hall of Fame, 1992; Legion Merit, Bronze Star, 3 Meritorious Service Medals, Army Commendation Medal, Vietnam Honor Medal First Class; Distinguished Service Medal; The Defense Superior Service Medal; Legion of Merit. **Special Achievements:** First African-American student to graduate with a master of divinity degree from Duke University; First African director of the Department of Veterans Affairs National Chaplains Center in 1965; First African-American to earn a Master of Science degree in Guidance and Counseling from Long Island University, Brooklyn, New York, 1975; First African-American to serve as Chief of Chaplains of any military service. **Home Addr:** 2661 Centennial Ct, Alexandria, VA 22311-1303, **Home Phone:** (703)671-4833. **Business Addr:** Pastor, First Baptist Church, 39 Alexandria Pke, Warrenton, VA 20188, **Business Phone:** (540)347-2775.

### ZIYAD, KARIM
President (organization). **Career:** TYT Inc, pres. **Orgs:** Bd mem, Youth VIBE Inc. **Business Addr:** Board Member, Youth VIBE Inc, 5240 Snapfinger Pk Dr Suite 125, Decatur, GA 30035, **Business Phone:** (770)593-8800.

### ZOLA, NKENGE (TERESA KRISTINE NKENGE ZOLA BEAMON)
Broadcaster. **Personal:** Born Apr 11, 1954, Detroit, MI; daughter of Maya Beamon-Dean and Henry Edward Moscow Beamon. **Educ:** Univ Mich, Ann Arbor, MI, 1975; Rec Inst Det, E Detroit, MI, 1987; Wayne State Univ, Detroit, MI, 1977, 1989; Wayne County Community Col; Univ detroit mercy, digital media studies, 2010. **Career:** Tribe Mag, Detroit, Mich, copy ed, 1976-77; WJLB AM/FM, Detroit, Mich, continuity dir, 1977-78, news anchor, reporter, 1978-81; Christopher Pitts, Birmingham, Mich, host, Jazzmasters: Keepers Flame, 1989-90; WDET-FM, Detroit, Mich, producter, host, writer, Nkenge Zola Prog, news anchor, reporter, 1981-2000; Arts & Soc, Witness Mag, ed, 1995; Mich citizen newspaper, ed, arts, writer, 2002-05; Oakland Univ, spec lectr, 2001-. **Orgs:** Proj BAIT (Black Awareness TV), 1976-; Afrikan Libr Singers, 1989-; chair, Afrikan Child Enrichment Asn, 1989-; bd mem, Women's Justice Ctr, 1991-; bd mem, Creative Arts Collective, 1990-; forum coordr, Creative Community Artist Support Group, 1990-; Advocators, Nat Org Am Revolution, 1977-87; nat bd mem, Youth Coun Pres, Detroit; co-founder, U M Br National Association for the Advancement of Colored People, 1970-76; James & Grace Lee Boggs Ctr Nuture Community Develop, 1996-; Casa de Unidad Cult & Media Arts Ctr, bd; founding bd, Detroit Women's Coffee House, 1996-. **Honors/Awds:** Subject of tribute, "A Celebration of the Life of a Spiritual Warrior", Committee for Community Access to WDET, 1990; Exceptional Media Artist Award, Beatty & Asn, 1990; Outstanding Supporter of Jazz Artists, Success Academy of Fine Arts, 1985; Spirit of Detroit Award, City of Detroit, 1985; editor, Loving Them to Life, New Life Publishers, 1987; Miss NAACP Detroit, NAACP, 1970; Mich Asn Broadcasters First Place Award, Temple Confessions, Detroit Press Club Award, 1995; Asniated Press Award, 1992, 1995; Recipient Governor's Arts Award, 1995; Media Honor Roll, Arts Reporting; Recipient, Cultural Warrior Award, Societie Culturally Concerned; Pride Banquet Media Award; Success Jazz Academy. **Home Addr:** 91 E Philadelphia, Detroit, MI 48202, **Home Phone:** (313)873-4160. **Business Addr:** Special Lecturer, Oakland University, 2200 N Squirrel Rd, Rochester Hills, MI 48309, **Business Phone:** (248)276-0450.

### ZOLLAR, ALFRED
Executive. **Personal:** Born Jan 1, 1954?, Kansas City, MO; married Alicia Underwood; children: Al Jr & Keisha. **Educ:** Mills High Sch; Univ Calif, San Diego, MA, appl math, 1976. **Career:** Executive (retired); IBM, systs engr, 1977-86, corp staff mem, 1986-89, DB2 prod mgr, 1989-93, Software Group lab mgr, 1993-96, Tivoli sr vpres, 1996-98, Network Comput Software Div gen mgr, 1998-2000, Lotus Develop Corp, dir, pres & chief exec officer, 2000-03, iSeries gen mgr, 2003-04, IBM Tivoli Software, gen mgr, 2004-11; Carnegie Speech Co Inc, dir; AWZ Tech, founder & managing partner, 2011-; Siris Capital Group, exec partner, 2014. **Orgs:** Bd mem, Chubb Group Ins; Bd mem, PSEG Inc; mem Exec Leadership Coun & lifetime mem, Nat Soc Black Engrs; co-chmn, IBM Black Family Technol Awareness; bd mem, Alexian Bros Hosp Found, San Jose, Calif; Leadership Coun Ctr Bus & Govt, John F Kennedy Sch Govt, Harvard Univ; Nc Black Achievers Prog Adv Bd; fel Harvard Univ, 2001. **Business Addr:** Managing Partner, Founder, AWZ Tech LLC, 7014 13th Ave Suite 202, Brooklyn, NY 11228.

### ZOLLAR, DORIS L.
Executive, educator. **Personal:** Born Dec 7, 1930, Little Rock, AR; married Lowell M; children: Nikki Michele & Lowell M Jr. **Educ:** Talladega Col, BA, 1951; Univ Calif, Grad Sch, MA, 1952; DePaul Univ, attended 1954. **Career:** Chicago Pub Sch, teacher, 1952-67; C Haven Residential Sch Mult Handicapped C, founder, org, sch dir, 1973-; Woodlawn Orgn, exec asst to dir, 1974-76, dir develop, 1976; Independent Bull Newspaper, womens ed, 1976-77; Triad Consult Serv, pres, 1977-. **Orgs:** Community leader, Mid-W Conf Pres Lyndon B Johnsons Community Equal Oppty, 1964; Chicago Urban League, 1965-, Lois R Lowe Womens Div UNCF, 1966-, Jackson Pk Highlands Asn, 1966-; vpres, Bravo Chap Lyric Opera Chicago, 1966; chmn, Ebony Fashion Fair, 1968-69; corr sec, Ill Childrens Home & Aid Soc, 1968-70; pub rel fund raising consult, Nat Med Asn Proj, 1973-75; S Shore Community, 1974-; vpres, XXI bd Michael Reese Hosp, 1974-76; Cook Cty Welfare Serv Community, 1975-; Chicago Pub Sch Art Soc Chicago Art Inst, 1975-; org & coordr, Minority Constr Workers, 1975; adv, Midwest Asn Sickle Cell Anemia, 1976-; adv, Black United Fund, 1976-; Art Pub Places Bd, 1976-; Coun Foreign Affaris, 1976; Int Visitors Ctr, Bd, 1976-; dir Ill, International Po Authority, 1986-; dir, fung devel, Woodlawn Org World Serv Counl Nat YWCA, 1976-; Chicago Heart Asn; Women's Bd Oper PUSH; United Negro Col Fund; Chicago Acad Performing Arts; Chicago Port Authority; Women's Bd United Negro Col Fund. **Honors/Awds:** AKA Scholarship, competitive exam, 1947; Exchange student from Talladega College to Cedar Crest College, 1948-49; Florina Lasker Fellowship Award, 1951; Will Rogers Meml Fellowship toward PhD in History, 1952; "Ed Motivation of the Culturally Disadvantaged Youth" Chicago Bd of Ed, 1958-60; National Medical Association Award, Womens Aux, 1966; Person of the Day Award, Radio Stations WAIT, WBEE, 1969, 1976; The Pittsburgh Couriers National Ten Best Dressed, 1972-74; Honour Librarian of the Chicago Public Library City of Chicago, 1974; The Commercial Bread basket Association Award, 1975; Institute for Health Resources Devel Award, 1975; Oper PUSH Award, 1975-76; Annual Merit Award for Civic Achievement, Beatrice Caffrey Youth Serv Inc, 1976; Alpha Gamma Pi, Iota Phi Lambda Sor Bus & Professional Award, 1977. **Special Achievements:** First African American president of the United Nations Children's Fund Chicago. **Home Addr:** 1700 E 56th St Suite 701, Chicago, IL 60637, **Home Phone:** (773)667-4249. **Business Addr:** President, TRIAD Consulting Services, 6901 S Constance Ave, Chicago, IL 60637, **Business Phone:** (773)908-2928.

### ZOLLAR, JAWOLE WILLA JO
Teacher, dancer, choreographer. **Personal:** Born Dec 21, 1950, Kansas City, MO; daughter of Alfred Jr and Dorothy Delores; children: Elizabeth Herron. **Educ:** Univ Miss, BA, dance, 1975; Fla State Univ, MFA, dance, 1979. **Career:** Educr & social activist; Fla State Univ, fac mem, 1977-80; Urban Bush Women dance troupe, founder & artistic dir, 1984-; NEA Choreography fel, 1992, 1993, 1994; Makato State Univ Worlds Thought prog, resident scholar, 1993-94; Univ Calif, LosAngeles, Dept Dance & Worlds Cult, Regents lectr, 1995-96; Ohio State Univ, guest teacher, 1996; Mass Inst Technol, Abramowitz Memorial Lectr, 1998; Fla State Univ, artist-in-residence & prof dance, 1997-, Robert O Lawton Distinguished Prof Dance, 2011; Wynn Fel, US Artists. **Orgs:** Asn Am Cult; Int Asn Blacks Dance; founder, Urban Bush Women, 1984. **Honors/Awds:** NY Dance & Performance Award, 1992; Outstanding Alumni, Univ Miss, 1993; Capezio Award for outstanding Achievement in Dance, 1994; Alumna of the Year Award, Fla State Univ, 1997; Doris Duke Award, Am Dance Festival, 1997; Hon Dr, Columbia Col, Chicago, 2002; New York Dance & Performance Award, A BESSIE, 2006; Martin Luther King Distinguished Service Award, Fl State Univ; United States Artist Fellow, 2008; Guggenheim Fellow, John Simon Guggenheim Memorial Found, 2009; Robert O. Lawton Distinguished Professor of Dance, 2011; Otto Rene Castillo Award for Political Theatre, 2012; Doris Duke Performing Artist Award, 2013; Arthur L. Johnson Memorial Award, 2013; Meadows Prize, Southern Methodist Univ's Meadows Sch Arts, 2014; Dance Magazine Award, 2016; Dance USA Honor Award, 2016. **Special Achievements:** She was prominently featured in the PBS Documentary "Free to Dance", which chronicles the African American influence on modern dance. She is also the choreographer & creator,

"Walking With Pearl...Southern Diaries,". **Business Addr:** Founder, Urban Bush Women, 138 S Oxford St Suite 4B, Brooklyn, NY 11217, **Business Phone:** (718)398-4537.

### ZOLLAR, ESQ. NIKKI MICHELE

Lawyer, chief executive officer, president (organization). **Personal:** Born Jun 18, 1956, Chicago, IL; daughter of Lowell M and Doris J; married William A von Hoene Jr; children: William Lowell von Hoene & Branden Tracey. **Educ:** Johns Hopkins Univ, Baltimore, MD, BA, 1977; Georgetown Univ Law Ctr, JD, 1980. **Career:** US Dist Ct Northern Dist Ill, judicial law clerk, 1980-81; Wilkins, Jones & Ware, assoc lafontant,, Chicago, Ill, assoc, 1981-83; Kirkland & Ellis, Chicago, Ill, assoc, 1983-85; Chicago Bd Election Commissioners, chmn & secy, 1987-90; Ill Dept Prof Regulation, dir, 1991-99; Gemini Electronics Inc, sr vpres & gen coun; Occup Safety & Health Admin, gen indust outreach trainer; Triad Consult Serv Inc, pres & chief exec officer, currently. **Orgs:** Co-chair, Telethon Night Event, UNCF, 1980-90; Chicago Comn Solidarity Southern Africa, 1986-; County Outreach Comn, Field Mus Natural Hist, 1987-90; alumni bd, Georgetown Univ Law Ctr, 1987-90; Lois R Lowe Women's Bd, UNCF, 1987-; chair educ comt, Chicago Archit Found Bd, 1987-90; Alpha Gamma Pi, 1987-; co-chair, Law Exploring Comn, Young Lawyers Sect Chicago Bar Asn, 1988-90; bd trustee, Woodland's Acad Sacred Heart, 1988-; Chicago Urban League, 1988-; trustee, County Youth Creative Learning Experience; trustee, Hektoen Inst Med; bd mem, Proj Explor; Chicago Heart Asn, Women's Coun; bd mem, bd dir, Pro-Literacy Worldwide; bd mem, Ill Dept Prof Regulation; Nat Coalition 100 Black Women; Women's Bd Jackson Pk Hosp; Ill Women Govt; Women Execs State Govt. **Business Addr:** Chief Executive Officer, President, Triad Consulting Services Inc, 118 N Clinton Suite 200, Chicago, IL 60661, **Business Phone:** (312)863-2500.

### ZOOK, KRISTAL BRENT

Writer, educator. **Personal:** Born Los Angeles, CA. **Educ:** Univ Calif, Santa Barbara, BA, eng, 1987; Univ Calif, Santa Cruz, PhD, 1994. **Career:** Univ Calif Santa Barbara, reader, 1986, EOP/SAA Prog, acad adv & tutor, 1986; Pvt Eng teacher, Madrid, Spain, 1986-87; Univ Calif Santa Cruz, Span lit & compos, tutor, 1988-89, instr 1990, Ctr Cult Studies, assoc, 1990-91, teacher's asst, 1991; Black Women Writers, teacher's asst, 1989; Univ Calif Irvine, Humanities Res Inst, resident scholar, 1993; Univ Calif Los Angeles, vis asst prof, African Am Studies, 1995-96; Murdoch Univ, Sch Humanities, vis lectr, 1996; Univ Nev, Reno, Spring, vis hilliard scholar, 1996; Washington Post, feature writer, arts/style sect; Essence, Working Mother, contrib ed; New York Times Mag, feature writer; USA Weekend, features writer; Los Angeles Times Mag, features writer; LA Weekly, features writer; The Village Voice, features writer; Vibe, features writer; Essence, features writer; O: Oprah Mag, features writer; Calif State Univ Northridge, asst prof; Columbia Univ, Grad Sch Jour, assoc adj prof; Hofstra Univ, assoc prof jour, media studies & pub rels, currently; Women's Media Ctr, writer. Books: Color by Fox: the Fox Network & the Revolution in Black Television, 1999; Black Women's Lives: Stories of Power & Pain, 2006; I See Black People: The Rise & Fall of African American-Owned Television & Radio, 2008; Nat Pub Radio, producer & on-air commentator; Op-Ed Proj, mentor. **Orgs:** Bd dir, Alicia Patterson Found. **Home Addr:** , Manhattan, NY 10026. **Business Addr:** Associate Professor of Journalism, Media Studies, & Public Relations, Hofstra University, 409 New Acad Bldg, Hempstead, NY 11549-1000, **Business Phone:** (516)463-4304.

### ZOW, DR. JAMES ALLEN, SR.

Lawyer. **Educ:** Bethune-Cookman Col, BA, polit sci, 1980; Univ Fla Col Law, JD, 1983. **Career:** Bethune-Cookman Col, exec asst pres & legal coun & assoc prof; Savannah State Univ, chief legal officer, dir admin affairs, exec asst pres & gen coun, currently; Heal Global Inc, founder & chief exec officer; Minority Health Adv Coun, Ga Dept Community Health, chmn. **Orgs:** Am Asn State Col & Univ Millennium Leadership Initiative; founder, African Am Health Info; founder, Inst Minority Health, Savannah State Univ. **Honors/Awds:** Innovator Role Model Award, 2000; Healthcare Hero Award, 2002; E-Health & Technology Pacesetter Award, 2002. **Home Addr:** 19 Myrtlewood Dr, Savannah, GA 31405, **Home Phone:** (912)236-9679. **Business Addr:** Executive Assistant to the President, General Counsel, Savannah State University, 3219 Col St, Savannah, GA 31404, **Business Phone:** (912)356-2507.

### ZULU, ITIBARI M.

Librarian, editor. **Personal:** Born Apr 24, 1953, Oakland, CA; married Simone N Koivogui; children: Akiba, Itibari Jr, Togba & Kadiatou. **Educ:** Merritt Col, Oakland, Calif, AA, 1974; Calif State Univ, Hayward, BA, 1976; San Jose State Univ, San Jose, Calif, MLS, libr & info sci, african-am & black studies, 1989; Amen-Ra Theol Sem, Los Angeles, ThD, 1999, PhD. **Career:** Fresno Unified Sch Dist, Fresno, Calif, teacher, 1981-89; Calif State Univ, Fresno, Calif, lectr, 1988-89, ref librn, 1989-92; Univ Calif, Los Angeles, Ctr African-Am Studies, chief librn, 1992, dir & head librn, 1992-2006; Calif Inst Pan African Studies, exec dir, currently; J Pan African Studies, founder & sr ed, 1987-; Mesa Comm Coll, librn, 2006-. **Orgs:** Vpres, African Diaspora Found; African Am Libr & Info Sci Asn; Former chair, African Am Studies, Black Caucus Am Libr Asn; Univ Calif Los Angeles Black Fac & Staff Asn; Am Libr Asn; founding provost, Amen-Ra Community Assembly Calif Inc; Asn Study Class African Civilizations, 1995-; Librarians Sect Asn Col & Res Libr Am Libr Asn, 1996-99; Provisional dir, King-Luthuli Transformation Centre Peace Libr & Distance Learning Centre; Nat Coun Black Studies, Inc. **Honors/Awds:** Jomo Kenyatta Dedication Award, African Stud Union, Calif State Univ, Fresno, 1984; Outstanding Support & Guidance Faculty Award, Calif State Univ, Fresno, African Am Orgn Coun, 1991. **Special Achievements:** Author, Ancient Kemetic Roots Library & Information Science, 1992-; Editor, Multicultural Review, African & African American Studies, 1993-; Co-Editor Lexicon African American Subject Headings, 1994; Contributing Editor: The Black Church Review, 1994; Author, Exploring the African Centered Paradigm: Discourse and Innovation in African World Community Studies, 1999. **Home Addr:** 38610 Annette Ave, Palmdale, CA 93551-5401. **Business Addr:** Senior Editor, The Journal of Pan African Studies, PO Box 24194, Los Angeles, CA 90024-0194.

# Obituaries

### ADAMS, BETTY PHILLIPS

Foundation executive, consultant, executive. **Personal:** Born Apr 9, 1944, Washington, DC; died Jul 5, 2013; daughter of Charles Willis III and Mary Ellen Russell. **Educ:** Howard Univ, BA; Stanford Univ, Grad Sch Bus, MS. **Career:** Nat Asn Advan Colored People Legal Defense & Educ Fund & Fedn Protestant Welfare Orgn, consult, 2003-13; Nat Urban League, vpres admin, Nat Planning & Eval, dir; Jackie Robinson Found, pres, chief exec officer & sr adv. **Orgs:** Bd dir & exec comt, Nat Black Leadership Comn AIDS; vpres, YWCA New York; Spelman Corp, Women's Round Table; YWCA Acad Achievers; Rockefeller Found fel; Sloan fel. **Honors/Awds:** Rev Dr Martin Luther King Jr Living the Dream Award, New York Gov, 1998; Seagrams Vanguard Award. **Home Addr:** 2166 Broadway, New York, NY 10024, **Home Phone:** (212)362-5721.

### ADAMS, DON L. (DONALD L ADAMS)

Financial manager, basketball player. **Personal:** Born Nov 27, 1947, Atlanta, GA; died Dec 25, 2013, Troy, MI; married Mary Wilson; children: Don Jr & Damar. **Educ:** Northwestern Univ, attended 1970. **Career:** Basketball player (retired), executive; consult; San Diego Houston Rockets, 1970-71; Atlanta Hawks, 1971-71; Detroit Pistons, 1972-75; St Louis Spirits, 1975; Buffalo Braves, 1975-77; Sagemark Cosult Lincoln Fin, Mich, investment adv. **Orgs:** Northwestern Univ MEN Club; 4x4 Golf Club; TPC Mich. **Honors/Awds:** Co MVP Northwestern Univ; All-Rookie Team, 1971; Won 2 TPC. **Home Addr:** 17257 Goldwin Dr, Southfield, MI 48075.

### ADAMS, FLOYD, JR.

Newspaper publisher, politician, consultant. **Personal:** Born May 11, 1945, Savannah, GA; died Feb 1, 2014, Savannah, GA; son of Floyd Sr and Wilhelmina; children: Kenneth & Khristi. **Educ:** Armstrong Atlantic State Univ, BA, bus. **Career:** The Herald, ed, 1968-2014, publ & pres, 1983-2014; Savannah City Coun, councilman, 1982, alderman at large, 1992-96; Savannah Mayor Pro Term, mayor, 1996-2003; Savannah Chatham County Bd Educ, pres, 2006. **Orgs:** Pvt Indust Coun; GA Munic Asn; Ga Black Elected Officials Asn; Finance & Inter-Govt Rels Comt Nat League Cities; Pvt Indust Coun; Ga Black Elected Officials Asn; Nat Black Coun Local Elected Officials; Ga Munic Asn; Savannah's Printers Asn; Nat Asn Advan Colored People; Savannah Br; Prince Hall Masons. **Special Achievements:** First African-American to be elected mayor of Savannah; First African-American to win alderman-at-large post 1 in his own right; first African-Am mayor pro-tem of Savannah. cand for GA Dist 12 Race, 2002.

### AGGREY, HON. ORISON RUDOLPH GUGGISBERG

Ambassador, executive. **Personal:** Born Jul 24, 1926, Salisbury, NC; died Apr 6, 2016, Alexandria, VA; son of James Emman Kwegyir and Rose Douglass; married Francoise C Fratacci; children: Roxane Rose. **Educ:** Hampton Inst, BS, 1946; Syracuse Univ, MS jour, 1948. **Career:** Ambassador (retired); United Negro col Fund, publ asst, 1947 & 1950; Cleveland Call & Post, news reporter, 1948-49; Chief Defender, corresp, 1948-49; Bennett Col, publ dir, 1950; Dept State Lagos, Nigeria, vice consult & info officer, 1951-53; USIA, Lille, France, asst pub affairs officer, 1953-54; USIA, Paris, France, asst cult officer & dir cult ctr, 1954-60; Dept State, dep pub affairs adv African Affairs, 1961-64; Voice Am, chief Fr batch, 1965; Am Embassy Kinshasa Zaire, first secy & dep pub affairs, 1966-68; US Info Agency, prog mgr motion picture & TV serv, 1968-70; Dept State, dir off W African Affairs, 1970-73; State Dept's Off, W African Affairs, 1971; US, ambassador to Senegal & Gambia, 1973-77, ambassador to Romania, 1977-81; Georgetown Univ, dept State Foreign Affairs, sr fel, res prof diplomacy & res asn; Georgetown Univ, 1981-83; Bur Res & Intelligence Dept State, spec asst, 1983-84; intl rels consult, 1984; Howard Univ, Patricia Robert Harris Pub Affairs Prog, dir, 1987-90; Howard Univ Press, dir, 1988-90, consult, 1990-94; Us Dept State, Off Historian, Bur Pub Affairs, foreign serv officer. **Orgs:** Fel Ctr Intl Affairs, Harvard Univ, 1964-65; bd dir, Asn Black Am Ambassadors, Wash Asn Diplomatic Studies; consult, Dept State Nat Geog, Howard Univ, USAID, 1984-87; Phelps-Stoke Fund, 1990; Atlantic Coun USA, exec comn; Soc Prodigal Sons State NC; Fed City Club; Alpha Phi Alpha; Sigma Delta Chi; Alpha Kappa Mu; Sigma Pi Phi. **Honors/Awds:** Meritorious & Super Service Awards, USIA, 1950, 1955; Honorable mem, French Acad Jazz Paris, 1960; Alumni Award Hampton Inst, 1961; Harvard Univ, fel, Ctr Intl Affairs, 1964-65; Presidential Meritorious Award, US Govt, 1984; Syracuse Univ Chancellor's Medal, 1984; FL A&M Univ Meritorious Achievement Award, 1985; Distinguished Achievement Award, Dillard Univ, 1987; LLD, Livingstone Col, 1977; Grand Officer, Senegalese Nat Order Lion; Am Acad Diplomacy. **Special Achievements:** Author of comprehensive study leading to establishment of Howard Univ's Ralph J Bunche Intl Affairs Ctr, 1987. **Home Addr:** 2301 Jefferson Davis Hwy, Arlington, VA 22202, **Home Phone:** (703)415-2501.

### ALEXANDER, HUBBARD LINDSAY

Football coach. **Personal:** Born Feb 14, 1939; died Aug 28, 2016; married Gloria; children: Todd, Chad & Bard. **Educ:** Tenn State Univ. **Career:** Tenn State Univ, coach, 1962; high sch coach; Vanderbilt Univ, asst coach, 1974-78; Univ Miami, tight ends football coach, 1979-84, wide receivers, 1985-88; Dallas Cowboys, receivers coach, 1989-97, 2000; Minn Vikings, receivers coach, 1997-99; New Orleans Saints, receivers coach, 2001-03; Melrose High Sch, football head coach, 2006-. **Business Addr:** Football Head Coach, Melrose High School, 2870 Deadrick Ave, Memphis, TN 38114, **Business Phone:** (901)416-5974.

### ALLEN, BENJAMIN P., III

Financial manager, executive. **Personal:** Born Feb 27, 1942, Washington, DC; died Jan 31, 2016, Charlotte, NC; son of Benjamin (deceased) and Elizabeth (deceased); married Francesca M Winslow; children: Nicole & Camille. **Educ:** Howard Univ, BS, zool & allied sci, 1967; Rutgers Univ, MBA, mkt & finance, 1976. **Career:** Marine Midland Bank, proj officer, 1970-78, asst br mgr to br mgr, 1978-84, opers, 1985, corp mgr employee rels, 1986-87, asst vpres br mgr, 1987-88; HSBC, asst vpres, 1970-88; Riggs Bank NA, vpres, pvt banking officer, 1988-89, vpres, regional mgr, 1988-97, vpres br mgr, 1990-91; Prudential Securities, financial advisor, 1997-99; Br Banking & Trust, financial ctr, br mgr, vpres, leader, 1999-2007; consult, 2007; Charlotte Mecklenburg Schs, substitute teacher, 2008. **Orgs:** Treas Edges Group, 1984-88; Urban Bankers Coalition, 1984-88; Nat Black MBA Asn, 1984-88; vestry mem, St Andrews Church, 1985; Wash Urban Bankers Asn, 1988; treas, Edges Group, Metrop Wash DC Chap, 1989; bd dir, Mentors, 1989-94; neighborhood organizer, Obama Am, 2008-12; Charlotte Urban League; Charlotte Social Connection; Kappa Alpha Psi Fraternity; Collab Ventures. **Honors/Awds:** Black Achiever, Harlem Br YMCA, 1974. **Home Addr:** 5451 Ashleigh Rd, Fairfax, VA 22030, **Home Phone:** (703)818-9187. **Business Addr:** Branch Manager, Branch Banking & Trust Co, 8200 Greensboro Dr, McLean, VA 22102-3803, **Business Phone:** (703)442-4035.

### ALLEN, BETTIE JEAN

Executive, government official. **Personal:** Born Oct 21, 1926, Springfield, IL; died Feb 15, 2015, Springfield, IL; daughter of Frank and Florence. **Educ:** Springfield Col; Moody Bible Inst; Lincoln Col Law, Univ Ill; Sangamon State Univ. **Career:** Young Women Christian Asn, Kenya, int div, vol, 1967-68; Springfield Human Rel Comn, exec dir, 1969-70; entrepreneur, 1970-74; Assoc Gen Contractors Ill, training dir, 1971-72; State Ill, Capital Devel Bd, coordr. **Orgs:** Pres, Nat Asn Advan Colored People; Serv Bur Colored C; supvr, Zion Bapt Church Sch; trustee bd mem, Young Women Christian Asn, 1954-70; bd mem, United Way; RR Relocation Auth; pres, Assoc Gen Contractors Am; Human Rels Comn; Phyllis Wheatley Club. **Honors/Awds:** Webster Plaque Award, Springfield Nat Asn Advan Colored People, 1957; Achievement Award, Urban League, 1964; Affirmative Action Award, 1975; Breadbasket Commercial Achievement Award, 1977. **Home Addr:** 1845 S 19th St, Springfield, IL 62703-3316, **Home Phone:** (217)241-1845.

### ALLEN, SAMUEL WASHINGTON

Educator. **Personal:** Born Dec 9, 1917, Columbus, OH; died Jun 27, 2015, Norwood, MA; son of Alexander Joseph and Jewett Washington; children: Marie-Christine Catherine. **Educ:** Fisk Univ, AB, 1938; Harvard Law Sch, JD, 1941; New Sch Soc Res, grad study, 1948; Sorbonne, 1950. **Career:** New York, dep asst dist atty, 1946-47; USAF, Europe, historian, claims officer & civilian atty, 1951-55; New York, gen pract, 1956-57; Tex Southern Univ, assoc prof, 1958-60; US Info Agency, asst gen coun, 1961-64; US Community Rels Serv, chief coun, 1965-68; Tuskegee Inst, avalon prof humanities, 1968-70; Wesleyan Univ, vis prof, 1970-71; Boston Univ, Col Arts & Sci, prof eng, 1971-81, prof emer, 1981-2015; Poems: Presence Africaine, 1949; Elfenbeinzahne, 1956; Ivory Tusks & Other Poems, 1968; Poems from Africa, ed, 1973; Paul Vesey's Ledger, 1975; Every Round, 1987. **Orgs:** Vpres & bd dirs, Southern Educ Found, Atlanta, 1969-76; bd dir, Afrikan Heritage Inst, Roxbury, MA, 1974-78; bd dir, Old S Meeting House, 1984-2000; bd, New Eng Mus African-Am Hist, 1986-2000; bd mem, Boston Partners Educ, 1986-91; comnr, Mass Hist Comn, 1986-92; bd dirs, Blackside, 1988-97; African Studies Asn; NY Bar Asn; New Eng Poetry Club. **Honors/Awds:** NEA Award for Poetry, 1979. **Special Achievements:** Translated Orphee Noir (Jean Paul Sartre), 1960. **Home Addr:** 1155 N Miranda St D7, Las Cruces, NM 88005, **Home Phone:** (505)647-2597. **Business Addr:** .

### ARCHER, DR. CHALMERS, JR.

School administrator, educator. **Personal:** Born Apr 21, 1938, Tchula, MS; died Feb 24, 2014, Manassas, VA; son of Chalmers Sr (deceased) and Eva Alcola Rutharford (deceased). **Educ:** Saints Jr Col; Tuskegee Inst, Ala, BS, 1972, MEd, 1973; Auburn Univ, Ala, PhD, 1979; Univ Ala, post doctorate cert, 1979; Mass Inst Technol, cert, 1982. **Career:** Saints Jr Col, asst to pres, 1968-70; Tuskegee Inst, asst vres & asst prof, 1970-83; Northern Va Community Col, admin & prof, 1983-2000, prof emer, 2000; Jackson Advocate, contrib ed; US Dept Educ, consult; Jennie Dean Proj, pres. **Orgs:** Consult, Dept Educ Retention, 1990-92; Nat Asn Col Deans, Registrars & Admis Officers; Phi Delta Kappa; Kappa Delta Pi; Am Pub Gardens Asn; lifetime mem, Nat Asn Advan Colored People; charter mem, Kiwanis Int Macon Col; Am Asn Univ Professors; Am Asn Col Registrars & Admis Officers; Southeastern Assoc Community Col; Coop Educ; vpres, Saints Jr Col Alumni; bd mem, Nat Consortium Recruitment Black Students Northern Cities; chmn, St Ala's Steering Comm Advan Placement High Sch Studs; charter mem, Pres Clinton's Task Force, Americans Chg. **Honors/Awds:** Hon Doctorate Lett, Saints Jr Col, Lexington, Mass, 1970; Phi Delta Kappa Leadership Award; Exemplary Res & Prog Develop, 1981; lectured at Cambridge Univ, Eng; Architect of Comp Counseling Ctr & Weekend Col Tuskegee Inst; Architect Reading & Language Arts Special Emphasis Curriculum Public schs; Developed successful multi-level Educ Alliance to Adv Equal Access with public schs; Democratic Nat Committee; Clinton/Gore Rapid Response Team; Award, Miss Inst Arts & Letters Award, 1992; Afro-Achievement Award, Dale City Afro-Achievement Comt, 1994. **Special Achievements:** Author: Growing Up Black in Rural Mississippi, 1992; On the Shoulders of Giants, in progress; Growing up With the Green Berets, 1999; Green Berets In the Vanguard: Inside Special Forces, 1953-63, 2000; 22 educational & other publications. **Home Addr:** 4522 Commons Dr Suite 40, Annandale, VA 22003-4959. **Business Addr:** Professor Emeritus, Northern Virginia Community College, 3001 N Beauregard St, Alexandria, VA 22311.

### ATCHISON, LEON H.

Executive. **Personal:** Born Feb 27, 1928, Detroit, MI; died Jun 22, 2015, Detroit, MI; son of A R and Rosy Lee; children: Aleta, Terrance & Erika. **Educ:** Mich State Univ, BA, 1960, MA, 1962. **Career:** US Congressman John Conyers, admin asst, 1965-71; Univ Detroit, dir urban studies, 1971-74; City Detroit under Mayor Coleman A. Young, dir purchasing, 1974-75; dir parks & recreation, 1975-79; Mich Consol Gas Co, dir civic & govt affairs, 1979-94; Ultimed HMO Mich, vpres pub affairs, 1994-. **Orgs:** Bd chmn gov, Wayne State Univ, State Wide Election, 1970-78; bd dir, Cent Bus Dist, 1981; bd dir, Greater Detroit Chamber Com, 1987-15; Am Asn Blacks Energy; Wayne State Univ Bd Gov; bd dir, Omni HMO; bd mem & chair Detroit Med Ctr. **Honors/Awds:** Man of the Year Award, Nat Asn Negro Bus & Prof

Women's Clubs, 1976; Outstanding Service Award, United Cerebral Palsy Asn, 1978; Testimonial Resolution Outstanding Public Service, Detroit City Coun, 1979; Proclamation, Outstanding Public Service, Mayor Detroit City, 1979; Named honor: Leon H. Atchison Hall, Wayne State Univ, 2008. **Home Addr:** 17514 Parkside Dr, Detroit, MI 48221.

### BAKER, ROLAND CHARLES

Executive. **Personal:** Born Aug 12, 1938, Chicago, IL; died Sep 29, 2015, Hilton Head Island, SC; son of William T and Ruth Carrington; married Addie Scott; children: Scott, Stephen & Stefanie. **Educ:** Univ Calif, Los Angeles, BS, bus admin, 1961; Univ Southern Calif, MBA, 1962; CPA licensed, 1971. **Career:** N Am Rockwell Corp, CA, budget admin, 1962-64; Ampex Corp Culver City, financial analyst, 1964-65; Beneficial Stand Life Ins Co, staff asst, controller, 1965-67, mgr corp acct, 1967-68, asst controller, 1968-69, vpres, controller, 1969-71, admin vpres, controller, 1973-75, sr vpres, 1975-77, bd mem; Colonial Penn Ins Co & Colonial Penn Franklin Ins Co & Colonial Penn Life Ins Co, exec vpres bd dir; Colonial Penn Group Inc, sr vpres, 1977-80; Signature Group, chmn, pres, chief exec officer; independent dir, chmn audit comt, Quanta Capital Holdings Ltd; Northeastern Ill Univ, adj prof finance; Am Ins Mgt Group Inc, exec dir; First Penn Pac Life Ins Co, chief exec officer; Allstate Financial Investment Trust; Henderson Global Funds, audit chair, 2001-15; N Am Co Life & Health Ins; Mutual Assurance; Quanta Capital Holdings Ltd; Baker, founder, chief exec officer; Rakich, founder, chief exec officer; Shipley, founder, chief exec officer; Politzer, founder, chief exec officer; EDGAR Online, dir, 2006-. **Orgs:** Bd dir, Philadelphia Zool Soc, 1979-80; bd dir, Fund Open Socs OPEN, 1979-2015; com mem, Cent Allocations Com United Way Fund, 1979-2015; fel Life Ins Mgt Inst; bd mem, Am Inst Cert Pub Accountants; bd mem, Am Socs Chartered Life Underwriters; bd mem, LOMA; bd mem, Nat Asn Independent Insurers; bd mem, Am Inst Property & Liability; bd mem, Am Coun & Life Ins; bd dir, Quanta Capital Holdings Ltd; Henderson Global Funds, independent trustee, chmn audit comt, mem governance comt & mem valuation comt, trustee, 2001-2015; Calif State Teacher's Retirement Bd; bd dir, Am Col; dir, mem audit comt, mem nominating, governance comt, Ceres Group Inc, 2003-. **Honors/Awds:** CLU Bryn Mawr, PA, 1976. **Home Addr:** 307 Weatherford Ct, Lake Bluff, IL 60044.

### BANFIELD, ANNE L.

Public relations executive. **Personal:** Born May 27, 1925, Detroit, MI; died Jun 12, 2008, Ocala, FL; daughter of Albert Tucker (deceased) and Jessie (deceased); married William J; children: DuVaughn, Bruce & William Credric. **Educ:** Detroit Inst Com Sec Sci, attended 1945; Wayne State Univ; HP Col; Univ Mich; Wayne Community Col. **Career:** AUS Signal Corps, tech sec & chief engr; Dr HM Nuttall, med sec; Julian Rodgers & Julian Perry, legal sec; Anne's Secretarial Serv, self-employed; Youth Women's Christian Asn, sec exec dir; Detroit Inst Com, asst adminr officer, asst mgr; MI Chronicle, pub rels dir; Anna Lue Enterprise, pres. **Orgs:** Bd mem, Nat Media Women; bd mem, Mayor's Keep Detroit Beautiful Community; Women's Econ Club Detroit; Women's Conf Concerns; Women's Community United Negro Col Fund; bd mem, Randolph Wallace Kidney Found; Urban League; Nat Tech Asn Auxiliary; Concerned Boaters. **Home Addr:** 20906 Botsford Dr, Farmington, MI 48336, **Home Phone:** (248)476-5472.

### BANKSTON, ARCHIE M.

Lawyer, executive. **Personal:** Born Oct 12, 1937, Memphis, TN; died Jan 18, 2016, Sarasota, FL; son of Archie M Sr and Elsie Shaw; married Emma Ann DeJan; children: Alice DeJan & Louis Shaw. **Educ:** Fisk Univ, BA, 1959; Wash Univ Sch Law, LLB, 1962; Wash Univ Grad Sch Bus Admin, MBA, 1964. **Career:** Gen Foods Corp, asst div coun, 1964-67, prod mgr Maxwell House Div, 1967-69; Pepsico Inc, asst sec & corp coun, 1969-72; Xerox Corp, div coun, 1972-73; Consol Edison Co NY, sec & asst gen coun, 1974-89; sec & assoc gen coun, 1989, secy, 1997-2002; Col New Rochelle, exec-in-residence, 2002-16. **Orgs:** Phi Delta Phi Legal Fraternity, 1960-2016; Securities Indu Comm; adv group, New York Chap, Corp Practices Comn; budget comm, Am Soc Corp Sec, 1974-2016; Stockholder Relat Soc New York; Am Bar Asn; NY State Bar Asn; Asn Black Lawyers Westchester Co; dir, Beth Israel Med Ctr NYC; Ment Health Asn Westchester Co; Am Mgmt Asn; Assoc Black Charities; trustee, Col New Rochelle; 100 Black Men Inc; Beta Zeta Boule; Alpha Phi Alpha Fraternity; Westchester Clubmen; Westchester County African Am Adv Bd. **Honors/Awds:** Recipient Black Achievers in Industry Award, Harlem Branch YMCA, 1971; Merit Award, Nat Urban League, 1974; Distinguished Service Commendation Award, Mental Health Asn, 1987; Corp Award, Red Cross, 2001; Bracebridge H Young Distinguished Service Award, Am Soc Corporate Secretaries, 2001. **Special Achievements:** First Black atty/product mgr Gen Foods, 1964-67; First Black Sr Exec Officer Consolidated Edison, 1974; First Black Corp Sec of a major US Co, 1974. **Home Addr:** 3 Oak Lane, Scarsdale, NY 10583-1621, **Home Phone:** (941)365-5057.

### BAREFIELD, DR. OLLIE DELORES

Educator. **Personal:** Born Dec 19, 1930, Teague, TX; died May 7, 2015, Denver, CO; married Henry B Barefield Sr; children: John Anthony. **Educ:** Huston-Tillotson Col, BA, 1950; Univ Northern Colo, MA, 1966, EdS, 1970. **Career:** Educator (retired); Teague Independent Sch Dist, Eng teacher, 1950-55; Bur Indian Affairs, Ariz, Bilingual teacher, 1955-60; Denver Pub Schs, elem teacher, 1960-70, elem prin; Whittier & John Amesse Elem Schs, prin. **Orgs:** Am Asn Univ Women, 1980, Ministers Wives Asn, 1980; Nat Asn Elem Prin, 1980; bd dir, Nat Asn Advan Colored People, Denver, 1980; Delta SigmaTheta, 1980, Nat Coun Negro Women, 1980; guest lectr, Rocky Mountain Bk Festival, 1970. **Honors/Awds:** Teacher of the Year, Denver Pub Schs, 1969; Distinguished Teacher Award, 1969; Woman of the Year, Kappa Omega Chi Beauticians Sorority, 1980. **Home Addr:** 2979 Monaco Pkwy, Denver, CO 80207-2850.

### BARRETT, DR. RONALD KEITH

Psychologist, educator. **Personal:** Born Aug 17, 1948, Brooklyn, NY; died May 31, 2015, Santa Monica, CA; son of Cyril and Dorothy. **Educ:** Morgan State Univ, Baltimore, BS, psychol, 1970; Univ Pittsburgh, MS, social psychol, 1974, PhD, social psychol, 1977. **Career:** Calif State Univ, Dominguez Hills, asst prof psychol, 1977-78; Open Soc Inst, consult; Philadelphia Co coroner's offs, consult; Mayor's Off City, Baltimore, consult; Loyola Marymount Univ, Dept Psychol, Los Angeles, from asst prof to assoc prof, 1977-96, prof, psychol, 1996-2015, actg chair, 2004-08, chair; Acad Int Educ via Univ Bonn, Ger, assoc prof psychol, 1995. **Orgs:** Asn Death Educ & Coun; Int Asn Trauma Counrs; Int Work Group Death, Dying & Bereavement; Asn Black Psychologists; Am Psychol Asn; Asn Traumatic Stress Specialists; Psi Chi Nat Hon Soc Psychol. **Honors/Awds:** Elected Psi Chi Natl Honor Soc, Psychol, 1969; Optimist Club, Man of the Year, 1991; Lay Man of the Year, 1991; numerous scholarly publs & citations; Recognized & hon, Expert in Residence, Kellogg Foundation, 1998. **Special Achievements:** Author, "Urban Adolescent Homicidal Violence: An emerging public health concern", 1986, "Urban Adolescent Homicidal Violence: An emerging publichealth concern", 1993, "Contemporary African-American Funeral Rites and Traditions" In DeSpelder & Strickland's, 1995, "It's How You Play theGame: Amazing things happen when a community reaches out to youth who areat risk", 1996, "Sociocultural Considerations for working Blacks Experiencing Loss and Grief", 1998, "Unresolved Grief and Urban Youth Violence", 2000, "Recommendations for Culturally Competent End-of-life Care Giving", 2001, "Can We Provide Better Aftercare to Blacks?". **Home Addr:** 240 W Queen St Suite 3, Inglewood, CA 90301, **Home Phone:** (310)677-8414.

### BARROW, REV. WILLIE T.

Association executive, activist. **Personal:** Born Dec 7, 1924, Burton, TX; died Aug 12, 2016, Chicago, IL; married Clyde; children: 1. **Educ:** Univ Monrovia, DD; Harvard Univ, cert leadership; Warner-Pac Theol Sem. **Career:** First Black Church God Portland, organizer; Langley Ave Church God, youth minister; Malcolm X Col, bd dir, 1976; Vernon Pk Church God, assoc min/bd trustee; Rev Jackson Pres Campaign, nat dep campaign & mgr; Oper PUSH, Chicago, IL, chmn bd; Rainbow/PUSH Coalition Inc, co-chairperson, chmn emer, currently; Vernon Pk Church God, assoc minister, minister justices, currently; Southern Christian Leadership Conf, field organizer. **Orgs:** Chairperson, Nat World Peace Coun; Nat Polit Congr Black Women; Nat Urban League, 1943; Nat Coun Negro Women, 1945; commr, Int Women's Yr, 1978; vice chair, Nat Polit Cong Black Women; bd dir, Doctors Hosp Hyde Pk; bd trustees, Bennett Col; bd dir, Core Found; founding mem, Oper BREADBASKET. **Honors/Awds:** Human Service Award, Chicago Firefighters; Woman of the Year, City Chicago, 1969; Image Award, League Black Women, 1972; DHL, Bennett Col, 1991; DDiv, Southern Calif Sch Ministry, 1992; Adv Award, Willie T Barrow Wellness Ctr Doctors Hosp, 1998; History Makers Award, Christian Women's Conf, 1998; Trailblazer Award, Ameritech, 1998; Hall of Fame Award, Victor Goodell Memorial Golf Classic, 1998; Legend Award, Rainbow/PUSH Coalition, 1998; Humanitarian of the Year Award, Indo-American Democratic Organization's Humanitarian of the Year Award, 1999; Who's Who in Chicano Bus, Crain's Mag, 1999; Dr, Adler Sch; Willie Barrow St, Named in Honor. **Home Addr:** 7736 S Euclid Ave, Chicago, IL 60649-4612, **Home Phone:** (773)374-2164. **Business Addr:** Chairman Emeritus, Rainbow/PUSH Coalition Inc, 930 E 50th St, Chicago, IL 60615-2702, **Business Phone:** (773)373-3366.

### BARRY, MARION SHEPILOV, JR.

Mayor, politician. **Personal:** Born Mar 6, 1936, Itta Bena, MS; died Nov 23, 2014, Washington, DC; son of Marion S (deceased) and Mattie Cummings (deceased); married Mary M Treadwell, Jan 1, 1972, (divorced 1977); married Effi Slaughter, Jan 1, 1978, (divorced 1993); children: Marion Christopher; married Cora Masters, Jan 1, 1994. **Educ:** Le Moyne Col, BS, 1958; Fisk Univ, MS, org chem, 1960; Univ Kans, attended 1961; Univ Tenn, chem studies, 1964. **Career:** Pride Inc, dir opers, 1967; Pride Econ Enterprises, co-founder, chair, dir, 1968; Wash DC Sch Bd, mem, 1971-74; Wash City Coun, mem-at-large, 1975-79; Wash, DC, mayor, 1979-91, 1995-99, city councilman, 1992-94; City Wash, DC, mayor, 1994-98; Coun DC Ward 8, rep, 1993-95, coun mem. **Orgs:** Pres, Wash DC Bd Educ, 1972-2006; first nat chmn & pres, Stud Nonviolent Coord Comt; Third World Coalition Against War; Alpha Phi Alpha Fraternity; pres, Nat Conf Black Mayors; pres, Nat Asn Advan Colored People; Comt Finance & Rev, chair. **Special Achievements:** Film appearance: Slam, 1998. **Business Addr:** Council Member, Council of the District of Columbia, 1350 Pa Ave Suite 400, Washington, DC 20004, **Business Phone:** (202)724-8045.

### BASKERVILLE, PENELOPE ANNE

Labor relations manager. **Personal:** Born Jul 9, 1946, South Orange, NJ; died Jul 7, 2014, Plainsboro, NJ; daughter of Robert L and Yolanda Reaves; children: Dylan Craig & Ailey Yolanda. **Educ:** Brown Univ, BA, 1968. **Career:** NJ Div Civil Rights, field rep, 1975-77; NJ Dept Pub Advocate Off Citizen Complaints, field rep, 1977-80; Princeton Univ, personnel admin, 1980-86; Peterson's Guides Inc, personnel mgr, 1986-89; Rider Col, benefits mgr, 1989; Summit Bank, benefits spec, 1998, cebs, 2005-14. **Orgs:** Brown Univ Alumni Sch Comt, 1971; pres, Bd Trustees Princeton Nursery Sch, 1977-82; Intergovernmental Drug Comn; Corner House, 1982-94; Bd Educ Princeton Region Sch, 1982-85, ET Byrd Scholar Fund, 1983-87; bd trustee, Princeton YWCA, 1985-90; Nat Asn Advan Colored People Legal Defense Fund, Princeton comn, 1992; bd mem, Princeton Young Achievers, 1993; bd mem, Princeton Zoning Bd Adjust. **Honors/Awds:** Volunteer Award, Zoning Board, 2006. **Home Addr:** 210 Birch Ave, Princeton, NJ 08542, **Home Phone:** (609)924-8355.

### BATES, WILLIE EARL

Salesperson, executive. **Personal:** Born Feb 19, 1940, Shaw, MS; died Memphis, TN; son of Magnolia Gossett; married JoEllen; children: Roman Earl II & Patrice Simone. **Educ:** Tenn State Univ, BS, 1963. **Career:** Universal Life Ins Co, salesman, asst mgr, dist mgr, asst vpres, dir ordinary mkt; B&B Associaes, partner. **Orgs:** Capital Investment Club; Met Bapt Church; Omega Psi Phi; bd dir, Jr Achievement, 1984-91; chmn, bd dir, Goodwill Boys Club, 1989-91; vice basileus, Omega Epsilon Phi Chap, 1989-91. **Honors/Awds:** Manager of the Year, 1968; Cox Trophy, Nat Ins Asn, 1969; Omega Man of the Year, Omega Psi Phi, 1989. **Home Addr:** 1870 E Alcy Rd, Memphis, TN 38114-5829, **Home Phone:** (901)743-9692.

### BEACH, WALTER G., II

Executive. **Personal:** Born Cataula, GA; died Dec 28, 2014, Milwaukee, WI; married Marian C; children: Pennie, Pamela, Walter III & Bradford S. **Educ:** Univ Wis, BS, educ, 1975; Marquette Univ Law Coloquium, attended 1975; Univ Wis Law Sch. **Career:** Restaurant owner, 1963-64; news dir; spec agt ins; Harambee Newspaper, managing ed; Milwaukee Torch Newspaper, adv mgr; Echo Mag, feature writer; Dept Store, actg asst mgr; Channel 18 TV, news reporter; New Image Concept Inc, pres & founder; WAWA AM & FM Radio, news & pub affairs dir. **Orgs:** Chmn, State Polit Action; pres, Criminal Justice Asn Univ Wis; chmn, Nat Asn Advan Colored People; bd mem, State Police Exam Bd; TV producer & vice chmn, Soc Black Drama Heritage; co-founder, Comt Twenty-One; Steering Comt Model Cities; Midtown Kiwanis Club; Sickle Cell Anemia Found. **Honors/Awds:** Man of the Year, 1971; Youth Image Maker, 1973; Congress Award, 1974. **Home Addr:** 2940 N Buffum St, Milwaukee, WI 53212-2514, **Home Phone:** (414)265-6888. **Business Addr:** News & Public Affairs Director, WAWA AM & FM Radio, PO Box 2385, Milwaukee, WI 53212.

### BEAVERS, REV. NATHAN HOWARD, JR.

Clergy, executive. **Personal:** Born Aug 6, 1928, Alexander City, AL; died Jan 6, 2015; married Velma C; children: Vincent, Norman, Stephany, Rhonda & Lyrica. **Educ:** Howard Univ Sch Law, JD, 1952; Hamma Sch Theol, MDiv, PhD, 1975. **Career:** Gen pract civil & criminal law, 1955-62; Ohio Eagle Newspaper, 1963-65; Cleveland, real estate develop & gen contr & consult, 1966-71; FHA St Univ Col, Buffalo, Nat Acad Sci, lectr, 1969; Affil Contractors Am Inc, founder & nat exec dir, 1971; Faith Baptist Church, Springfield, co-pastor, 1974. **Orgs:** Pres, Beta Chap, 1949; founder & pres, Omicron Lambda Alpha Chap, 1950; Sigma Delta Tau Legal Fraternity, 1951; founder & pres, Zeta Delta Lambda Chap, Alpha Phi Alpha Fraternity, 1957; pres, Soc Regist Contractors, 1968-70; World Bank, 1973; consult, Urban League, 1973-75; Planned Parenthood, 1975; Prince Hall Masons, Shriners, Knights Pythias, Elks, Am Legion; charter mem, Frontiers Int; bd dir, YMCA; Nutrit Elderly. **Honors/Awds:** First & Outstanding FHA, Multi-Fam Housing Proj, HUD, 1968; Outstanding Businessman of the Year, Urban League, 1969; Outstanding Serv Affil, Contractors Am, 1971-72; Outstanding Serv, Mayor Roger Baker, 1976; Outstanding Contrib, Minority Econ Develop, State Ohio, 1977. **Home Phone:** (937)323-2164. **Business Addr:** Co-Pastor, Faith Baptist Church, 328 W Clark St, Springfield, OH 45506.

### BELL, REV. KENNETH M., SR.

Minister (clergy), teacher, executive. **Personal:** Born Apr 17, 1941, Bayboro, NC; died Sep 3, 2016, Grantsboro, NC; married Geraldine P; children: Kenneth Jr, Sonji & Marcel. **Educ:** Livingstone Col, BA, 1964; NC State Univ; Duke Univ, MEd, 1975. **Career:** NC Manpower Devel Corp Bayboro, dep dir; Pamlico Jr High Sch, teacher, social studies, sch guidance counsr; Ashley Assocs, gen partner; Mt Shiloh Baptist Church, New Bern, NC, minister, 1990-. **Orgs:** Nat Asn Advan Colored People, 1964-; pres, Local NC Teachers Asn, 1966; NCEd Asn; Asn Classroom Teachers; Nat Educ Asn; founder, City Youtharama Prog, 1966; dir, Local ABC-TV Gospel Music Show, 1972-73; chmn exec bd, Pamlico Co Voter League, 1974-; bd comnr, Democratic Party Nominee Pamlico Co, 1982. **Special Achievements:** First African American elected in Pamlico City as town alderman, 1969; Audition for Dick Cavett Show, 1971. Recognised in Pamlico County Centen Cele Year book as one of most outstanding blacks in Pamlico County. **Home Addr:** PO Box 131, Bayboro, NC 28515, **Home Phone:** (252)745-4585. **Business Addr:** Guidance Counselor, Pamlico Jr High School, 15526 NC Hwy 55, Bayboro, NC 28515-9400.

### BENJAMIN, DR. TRITOBIA HAYES

School administrator, educator, art historian. **Personal:** Born Oct 22, 1944, Brinkley, AR; died Jun 21, 2014, Arlington, VA; married Donald S; children: Zalika Aminah, Aminah Liani & Anwar Salih. **Educ:** Howard Univ, BA, art hist, 1968, MA, art hist, 1970; Univ Md, College Park, PhD, art hist, 1991. **Career:** Georgetown Univ, instr, 1970; Howard Univ, fac, instr, 1970-73, Art Dept, from asst prof to assoc prof, 1973-93, Cafritz guest lectr, 1978, prof art, 1993-2014, Col Arts & Sci, Div Fine Arts, dir art gallery, assoc dean; Afro-Am Inst, African Artists Am, guest cur; Nat Endowment Humanities, fel, 1984-85; United Negro Col Fund, Humanities Fel Prog Pvt Black Cols, PEW Humanities fel Grant, 1986-87; Wash-Moscow Cult Exchange, Moscow, Russia, cult consult, 1989. **Orgs:** Nat Conf Artists; Col Art Asn; Nat Museum Am Art. **Honors/Awds:** Recipient, Nat Endowment for the Humanities; Fellowships-in-Residence Col Teachers, 1975-76; Spencer Foundation Research Award; Howard Univ Sch Educ, 1975-77; hon mem, Eta Phi Sigma, 1986; Faculty Research Grant in the Social Sciences, Humanities & Education, Off VP Acad Affairs, Howard Univ, 1988-89. **Special Achievements:** Author: "Color,

Structure, Design: The Artistic Expressions of Lois Mailou Jones"; The International Review of African-American Arts, 1991; Biographies on: "Selma Hortense Burke, American Sculptor"; "Lois Mailou Jones, American Painter"; Black Women in America, An Historical Encyclopedia, Brooklyn, New York: Carlson Publishing Inc, 1992; Biography on: "Annie EA Walker, Painter"; Dictionary of American Negro Biography, New York: WW Norton Publishing, 1993; The Awesome Image of James Phillips: Old and New visions; Two summer publications: Haitian Art Newsletter; Africa Reports Magazine; Bearing Witness: Art by Contemporary African American Women; From Academic Representation to Poetic Abstraction: The Art of Alma Thomas; co-author: Three Generations of African American Women Sculptors: A Study in Paradox; The Life & Art of Lois Mailou Jones; San Francisco: Pomegranate Art books, 1994. **Home Addr:** 3525 16 St NW, Washington, DC 20010, **Home Phone:** (202)387-4495.

## BENTON, NELKANE O.

Executive. **Personal:** Born Jun 15, 1935, Kansas City, MO; died Jan 23, 2016; married Thomas J Hill; children: Donna M. **Career:** KABC & KLOS Radio, dir pub affairs, community affairs dir; Bing Crosby, pub rel, rec promo; STEP Inc, counr; NKB Prod Hollywood, exec dir; KABC-AM/KLOS-FM Am Broadcasting Co Inc, dir community rel, dir, ombudsman ser; KABC Talk radio, asst dir, dir, community rel, 2016; ABC News, asst dir community rels. **Orgs:** Consumer Credit Counors; Los Angeles County Community Resource Serv Corp. **Honors/Awds:** Unity Award for Human Relation, 1974; Mayors Award Public Service, 1974; Outstanding Award, Pres Carter, Sen Alan Cranston, Supvr Kenneth Hahn, State Sen Nate Holden, 1976; Outstanding Employee, America Broadcasting Co, Los Angeles Mayor Tom Bradley, 1977, 1978; United Way Media Award for Public Service, 1989, 1990; Crystal Award, Nat Broadcasting Associationn Award Outstanding Community Rels, 1989, 1990; La County Media Volunteer Award, 1990; Community Relations Award, Am Cancer Soc, 1993, 1994; Public Service Spirit Award, Southern Calif Broadcasters Asn, 2003. **Home Addr:** 3646 Potomac Ave, Los Angeles, CA 90016.

## BERRYMAN, ESQ. MATILENE S.

Lawyer, educator. **Personal:** Born Dec 8, 1920, Prince Edward County, VA; died May 6, 2003; children: D'Michele & Sherrill Diane Miller. **Educ:** Bluefield State Univ, WVa; Howard Univ, attended 1946; Pa State Univ; Univ Calif, Los Angeles; George Washington Univ, attended 1965; Am Univ, Wash, DC, BMath, 1957; Howard Univ, Wash, DC, JD, 1973; Univ RI, MS, marine affairs, 1979. **Career:** US Naval Oceanog Off, Suitland, phys oceanog, 1955-63, oceanog instr, 1963-68; Exec Off Pres & Defense Doc Ctr, Alexandria, Va, phys sci admin, 1968-70; Consortium DC, dir marine sci, 1973-76; Univ Dist Columbia, prof marine sci, 1970, Wash Tech Inst, asst prof marine sci & oceanog, head dept environ sci; pvt pract atty. **Orgs:** Chmn, Environ Sci Dept, Univ DC, 1971-78; financial secy, Nat Asn Black Women Atty, 1975-2003; vis prof, Purdue Univ; Pa State Bar, 1974-2003; Bar Dc Ct Appeals, 1975-2003; trustee, Shiloh Baptist Church, Washington, DC; bd dir, DC Ment Health. **Honors/Awds:** Nominated vice pres, Marine Tech Soc, 1978-79; Outstanding Service to Marine Science & Law, Nat Asn Black Women Atty, 1978. **Home Addr:** 2003 Bunker Hill Rd NE, Washington, DC 20018-3223, **Home Phone:** (202)832-5687.

## BLACKWELL, FAYE BROWN

Educator, government official. **Personal:** Born May 10, 1942, Monroe, LA; died Jan 21, 2015, Paradise, CA; married Fred. **Educ:** Southern Univ, BA, 1964. **Career:** Educr, Calcasieu parish sch syst, 1978-82; Coalition Comm Prog, pres, bd dir, 1983-85; Calcasiew Dem Asn, pres, 1984-85; Lake Charles City Coun, vpres, 1984-85; Lake Charles City Coun, coun mem dist B, 2015; KZWA-FM radio sta, owner, gen mgr, 2015. **Orgs:** Owner, oper Faye Brown Rental Inc, 1968-85; pres, Brown Enterprises PMonse LA, 1978-85; secy, Independent Invert Corp, 1980-85; Women League Voters, Nat Asn Advan Colored People, Top Ladies Distinction, Nat Asn Univ Women; founder & exec dir, MLK & Juneteenth Festivals. **Honors/Awds:** Community Serv Zeta Sor; Ed Exal Nat Asn Univ Women; Woman of the Year, Martin L King Found, Los Angeles Municipal, Sch Los Angeles Municipal Asn; Faye B. Blackwell has received numerous awards. **Special Achievements:** The first African-American woman elected to the Lake Charles City Council, she is the first African-American to own and operate an FM urban radio station in Southwest Louisiana. **Home Addr:** 2321 Elaine St, Lake Charles, LA 70601-4871, **Home Phone:** (337)436-2852.

## BLAYTON-TAYLOR, BETTY

Executive, artist, arts administrator. **Personal:** Born Jul 10, 1937, Newport News, VA; died Oct 2, 2016, Bronx, NY; daughter of James Blain Blayton and Alleyne Houser. **Educ:** Syracuse Univ, BA, 1959; City Col, educ psychol, 1961; NY Art Stud's League; Brooklyn Mus Sch, sculptor minoria & nizuma, 1970. **Career:** Maj exhibs, 1959-2016; St Thomas, Virgin Island, art teacher, 1959-60; City New York, recreation leader, 1960-64; Haryou Art, Graphics & Plastics, art supvr, 1964-67; C Art Carnival, exec dir, 1969-98, artistic dir, bd mem, 1998-99, founder spec proj, bd mem, 2000-16; City Col, Elem Educ Dept, prof, 1974; NYS Bd Educ, consult, 1977-2016; New York Bd Educ, consult, 1977-2016; C Art Carnival, artist & founder, currently; Work included following collections: Metrop Mus, Studio Mus, Philip Morris Corp, Chase Manhattan Bank. **Orgs:** Mem bd, Maj Exhib, 1959-84; bd secy, founding mem, Studio Mus, Harlem, 1965-77; bd mem, Printmakers Workshop, 1975-98, adv, 1998-2016; bd mem, Arts & Bus Coun, 1978-97; Comt Cult Affairs, 1979-89; Nat Black Child Develop Inst, 1980-2016; David Rockefeller Jr, Art Educ Res Comt, 1984-85; founding mem, Harlem Textile Works, 1992-2016; NY's Educ's Art & Humanities Curriculm Div Comt, 1992-94; co-founder & exec dir, Harlem C's Art Carnival. **Honors/Awds:** Artist in Residence, Fisk Univ, TN, 1978; Artist in Residence, Norfolk State Col, VA, 1980; Honorary Citizen/ Teacher Training/ Arts in Education, City New Orleans, 1980; National Council of Negro Women of New York Achievement Award, 1980; Artist in Residence, Tougaloo Col, 1982; Apple Polisher Award, 1982; Empire State Woman of the Year in the Arts NYS Governor's Award, 1984; Empire State Woman of the Year in the Arts, 1984; Who's Who in American Art, 1985; Black Women in the Arts Award, Gov New York, 1988; The Governor's Art Award, State New York, 1989; Eugene Grisby Award, Nat Arts Educ Asn's, 1990; CBS, Martin Luther King Jr Fulfilling the Dream Award, 1995; Lifetime Achievement Award, Women's Caucus for Art, 2005. **Home Addr:** 2001 Creston Ave, Bronx, NY 10453, **Home Phone:** (718)716-6266.

## BOND, HORACE JULIAN. See BOND, JULIAN.

## BOND, HOWARD H.

Business owner, executive. **Personal:** Born Jan 24, 1938, Stanford, KY; died Apr 27, 2015, Cincinnati, OH; son of Frederick D and Edna G Coleman; married Ruby L Thomas; children: Sherman, Howard Jr, Anita Warr, John, James, Edward & Alicia. **Educ:** Eastern Mich Univ, Ypsilanti, MI, BS, econ & polit sci, 1965; Pace Univ, New York NY, MBA, 1974. **Career:** US Govt, Detroit, MI, 1959-65; Ford Motor Co, Detroit, MI, labor supvr, 1965-68, mgr labour rels, 2003; Gen Elec Co, personnel mgr, 1968-69; Xerox Corp, personnel dir, 1969-75; Playboy Enterprises Inc, vpres, 1975-77; Phoenix Exec tech Group, pres, managing dir & prin, 1977-2015, chief exec officer; Ariel Capital Mgt Inc, corp dir, 1983-98; Bond Promotions & Apparel Co, chmn & chief exec officer. **Orgs:** Planning bd, United Way; Cincinnati Bd Educ, 1988-91; Salvation Army; Red Cross; Urban League Greater Cincinnati; Trans Africa; Kappa Alpha Psi; Aleikum Temple; Alpha Delta Boule; founder, 100 Black Men Am, Cincinnati Chap; life mem, Nat Asn Advan Colored People. **Honors/Awds:** Developed & implemented Xerox AA & EEO Strategies for Excellence, 1969; Special Recognition, Crusade Mercy, 1976; Board Member of the Year, Lake County Urban League, 1976; Role Model, Cincinnati Friends of Amistad Inc, 1987; Black Business & Professional Award, Quinn Chapel AME Church, 1987; Achievers Award, Robert A Taft High Sch, 1988; Five receive Lions awards from Urban League, The Cincinnati Enquirer, 2006. **Home Addr:** 3900 Rose Hill Ave, Cincinnati, OH 45229, **Home Phone:** (513)861-4920.

## BOND, JULIAN (HORACE JULIAN BOND)

Government official, educator, activist. **Personal:** Born Jan 14, 1940, Nashville, TN; died Aug 15, 2015, Fort Walton Beach, FL; son of Horace Mann and Julia Louise Washington; married Pamela Sue Horowitz; married Alice Clopton; children: Phyllis Jane, Horace Mann Jr, Michael Julian, Jeffrey Alvin & Julia Louise. **Educ:** Morehouse Col, BA, 1971. **Career:** GA House & Senate, 1965-86; Am Univ, distinguished prof, 1991-2015; Univ VA, Dept Hist, prof, 1990-2015; Harvard Univ, Dept Afro-Am Studies, vis prof, 1989; Drexel Univ, prof hist & polits, 1988-89; Am's Black Forum, syndicated tv news show, host & commentator, 1980 & 1990; Stud Nonviolent Coord Comn, founding mem, commun dir, 1960-66; Atlanta Inquirer, managing ed, 1964; Am Univ, Wash, Sch Pub Affairs, distinguished adj prof; Univ Va, Hist Dept, Hist Civil Rights Movement, prof, 1990-2015. **Orgs:** Pres, Atlanta Nat Asn Advan Colored People, 1974-89; pres emer, Southern Poverty Law Ctr; chmn, Nat Asn Advan Colored People, 1998-2010, chmn emer; fac mem, Univ Va. **Honors/Awds:** Nat Freedom Award, 2002; Honorary LLD, Bates Col; Received 25 honorary degrees. **Special Achievements:** Commentator on America's Black Forum, the oldest black-owned show in television syndication; poetry & articles have appeared in numerous publications; narrated numerous documentaries, including the Academy Award winning "A Time For Justice" & the prize-winning & critically acclaimed series "Eyes On The Prize"; First African American President of Lincoln University. **Home Addr:** 5435 41st Pl NW, Washington, DC 20015-2911, **Home Phone:** (202)244-1213.

## BOYCE, CHARLES N.

Executive. **Personal:** Born Jun 9, 1935, Detroit, MI; died Oct 28, 2015, Marquette, MI; married Delma Cunningham; children: Terralyn, Tracy, Charles & LaShawn. **Educ:** Wayne State Univ, attended 1962; Univ Mich, Grad Sch Bus, attended 1981. **Career:** Mich Bell Tel Co, com oper asst, 1966-69, order unit mgr, 1969-71, dist com mgr, 1971-76, gen customer rels mgr, 1976-78, dir pub affairs, 1979-83, asst vpres urban affairs, 1983-; Jim Boyce Found, founder, 2001-. **Orgs:** Bd trustee, New Detroit Inc, 1972-75, 1978-; bd dir, Asn Black Bus & Eng Studs, 1973-; comnr, Detroit Housing Comn, 1976-; bd dir, Nat Asn Advan Colored People, Detroit, 1978-, Million Dollar Club, 1978, 1979, vpres, 1985-86; bd dir, Mich League Human Serv, 1979-; Soc Consumer Affairs Bus, 1979-; bd dir, Inner City Bus Improv Forum, 1987-89; African-Am Heritage Asn; Booker T Wash Bus Asn; Bus Policy Rev Coun; bd dir, Black Family Devel Inc; bd dir, Concerned Citizens Coun; bd dir, Jazz Devel Workshop; bd dir, March Dimes SE Mich Chap, Neighborhood Serv Orgn; vchmn, Metrop Affairs Corp. **Honors/Awds:** Outstanding Service Award, Oakland Co Urban League, 1974; Service Award, Nat Asn Advan Colored People, Detroit, 1979; Outstanding Citizen Service Award, Detroit Housing Comn, 1979; Minority Achievers in Industry Award, YMCA, 1980; Excellence in Marketing Award, AT&T, 1982; Anthony Wayne Award for Leadership, Wayne State Univ, 1983. **Home Addr:** 19450 Shrewsbury Rd, Detroit, MI 48221, **Home Phone:** (313)864-7818. **Business Addr:** Assistant Vice President for Urban Affairs, Michigan Bell Telephone Co, 444 Mich Ave, Detroit, MI 48226, **Business Phone:** (313)223-9900.

## BOYD, EVELYN SHIPPS

Educator. **Personal:** Born Jan 1, 1917, Birmingham, AL; died Jan 1, 2015; daughter of Geneva White and Perry; married Gilbert M. **Educ:** Baldwin-Wallace Col, BEd, 1959; Cleveland Inst Music, MEd, 1970. **Career:** Educator (retired); Cleveland Pub Schs, secy, 1942-55, teacher, 1959-71; Cleveland Inst Music, teacher, 1970-76; Cuyahoga Comm Col, asst prof music, 1971-80, dept head performing arts, 1977-81. **Orgs:** OH Music Teachers Asn; Music Educ Nat Conf, 1961; organist, Western Res Psychiat Hosp, 1981-88; tape recorder, Cleveland Soc Blind, 1984; organist, Miles Pk Pres, byterian Church, 1988-2000; chaplain staff, Univ Hosps Vol, 1992-; ombudsman off vol, Cleveland Clin Found, 1993. **Honors/Awds:** Besse Award, Cuyahoga Com Col, 1980; Alumni Merit Award, Baldwin-Wallace Col, 1983; Award for 2000 Hours Volunteer, Univ Hosp SICU Unit, 1987; Phi Kappa Lambda Music Honorary, Soc Cleveland Inst Music; Baldwin-Walla Mu Phi Music Honorary, Sorority Dayton C Miller Hon Soc; Elizabeth Downes Award, Univ Hosps, 1989; Ten Year Voluntary Service Award, Cleveland Clin. **Home Addr:** 3942 E 123rd St, Cleveland, OH 44105-4549, **Home Phone:** (216)991-6210.

## BRADSHAW, LAWRENCE A., SR.

Educator. **Personal:** Born Sep 23, 1932, Philadelphia, PA; died Jun 25, 2015, Chambersburg, PA; married Mary Ellen Osgood. **Educ:** Shippensburg St Col, BS, MEd; Bucknell Univ; Univ Vt; Ball State Univ; Am Univ, PhD. **Career:** Educator (retired); Shippensburg Area Jr High Sch, teacher, 1961-62; Shippensburg Area Sr High Sch, teacher eng & humanities, 1962-69; Shippensburg State Col, asst dean admis, 1970-72, Acad Affairs Off, asst vpres, 1972-73, Rockefeller fel, Univ Admin, 1973-74, Dept Eng, asst pres, 1974-75, assoc prof, 1999, prof emer. **Orgs:** Phi Delta Kappa; Am Guild Organists; Nat Coun Teacher Eng; Col Eng Asn; Pa Coun Eng Teachers; Am Asn Univ Admin; Pa St Educ Asn; Nat Educ Asn; Kiwanis Club Chambersburg PA; bd dir, United Fund Chambersburg PA; bd dir, Franklin County Sunday Sch Asn; trustee, Chambersburg Hosp; pres, Canterbury Club, Shippensburg State Col; pres, Am Field Serv; Comn Concerts Asn, vestryman & organist, St Andrews Episcopal Church. **Honors/Awds:** Outstanding Educator of America, 1974-75. **Home Addr:** 167 Norlo Dr, Fayetteville, PA 17222-9553, **Home Phone:** (717)352-3323.

## BRAITHWAITE, GORDON L.

Executive. **Personal:** Born Atlantic City, NJ; died Nov 21, 1999, Arlington, TX. **Educ:** Hunter Col; Univ Calif, Los Angeles, Calif; Herbert Berghof Actg Studios. **Career:** City New York Dept Cult Affairs, prog specialist; Nat Endowment Arts, dir spec proj, spec asst minority affairs. **Orgs:** Adv com, comm Gallery Brooklyn Mus, 1970-72; 100 Black Men Inc; Nat Asn Advan Colored People.

## BRANCH, B. LAWRENCE

Labor relations manager, executive. **Personal:** Born Sep 13, 1937, New York, NY; died Nov 21, 2015, West Orange, NJ; married Elva C; children: Erica Danielle & Gabrielle Angelique. **Educ:** Univ Ill, attended 1959; Southern Ill Univ, BS, 1961. **Career:** Traveler's Ins Co, underwriter, 1963-64; Chesebrough-Ponds Inc, wage & salary analyst, 1964-66; Merck & Co Inc, employ supvr, 1966-68, asst to vpres personnel, 1968-72, dir equal employ affairs, dir, diversity/EEA; Nat Urban League, BEEP Prog, vis prof, 1972; EEO Cornell Univ Sch Ind & Labor Rel, prof; Ramapo Col, NJ, secy; BL Br & Assocs, founder & pres; Landmark Faith Based Adv Group, pres. **Orgs:** Bd mem, Coun Concerned Black Exec, 1968-70; bd mem, Asn Integration Mgt, 1970-74; bd & co-chmn, Interracial Coun Bus Opportunity, NY, 1973-78; bd trustee, Ramapo Col, NJ, 2002; bd advisor, UMDNJ Med Sch; bd trustee, S Orange Performance Arts Ctr; Twp S Orange Village Planning Bd; bd trustee, Ursuline Sch New Rochelle, NY; bd dir, Crossroads Theatre Nb, Nj; 100 Black Men Nj; EDGES Group; Sigma Pi Phi Fraternity. **Home Addr:** 56 Sullivan Dr, West Orange, NJ 07052-2259, **Home Phone:** (973)669-8101.

## BRANDON, DR. IDA GILLARD

School administrator. **Personal:** Born Jun 27, 1936, Snow Hill, NC; died Nov 14, 1997, Bowie, MD; daughter of Closton and Emily; married Joseph; children: Cynthia Michelle. **Educ:** NC Agr & Tech State Univ, BS, 1958; Va State Univ, MS, 1970; George Washington Univ, educ specialist, 1975, EdD, 1976. **Career:** Teacher, 1958-69, adminr, 1969-70; Univ Va, NDEA fel, 1969; Bowie State Univ, Career Planning & Placement, dir, 1970-76, part-time fac mem, 1975-76; Continuing Educ, dir, 1976-82; Grad Sch & Cont Educ Ctr, dean, 1982-90, 1991-96, interim provost, vpres acad affairs, 1990-91; SCEES, asst provost & dean, 1996-97; George Washington Univ, adj fac mem, 1978-81; Higher Educ Admin Inst, Harvard Univ. **Orgs:** Coun Historically Black Grad Schs, 1970-97; Am Asn Cols Teacher Educ; Am Asn Higher Educ; Am Asn Higher Continuing Educ; Am Asn State Cols & Univs; Asn Career Devel Higher Educ; Adult Educ Asn USA; Am Asn Univ Profs; Leadership Inst Asn Cont Higher Educ, 1993. **Honors/Awds:** BSU SGA Award, Adminstrator of the Year, 1971; Distinguished Alumni, NC A&T State Univ, 1988; Presidential Citation, Bowie State Univ, 1991-92, Inst Found Legacy Excellence Award, 1992; Meritorious Civic Service Award, Seagram Am, 1997. **Special Achievements:** PG County Woman's Hall of Fame, inductee.

## BRANDT, LILLIAN B.

Executive. **Personal:** Born Jul 4, 1916, New York, NY; died May 30, 2010, New York, NY; married George W Sr; children: Rev Canon George W Jr & Judyie Ellen. **Educ:** City Col NY. **Career:** James Daugherty Ltd, partner, vpres & secy; Teal Traing Inc; Sam Friedlander Inc; Capri Frocks Inc; Ben Reig Inc. **Orgs:** Fashion Sales Guild; Fashion Coun NY Inc. **Home Addr:** 845 W End Ave Apt 10C, New York, NY 10025-8437, **Home Phone:** (212)222-5451.

## BRISKER, LAWRENCE W.

School administrator. **Personal:** Born Oct 5, 1934, St. Louis, MO; died Feb 8, 2014, Cleveland, OH; married Flossie Richmond. **Educ:**

Southern Ill Univ, BA, 1959; Univ NMex, MA, 1966; Case Western Res Univ, PhD, 1977. **Career:** Cleveland Pub Sch Syst, teacher & adminr, 1962-64; Ohio Bell Tel Co Cleveland, employ supvr & traffic mgr, 1964-70; Cleveland Munic Ct, chief dep clerk, 1975-76; Cuyahoga Community Col, coord stud assistance prog, 1976-77, spec asst-chancellor, 1977-78, dean stud life unit, 1978, Finincial Aid, dir. **Orgs:** Bd trustee, Cleveland TB & Respiratory Fed, 1966; bd mem Glenwood Oak Pvt Sch Girls, 1968-; Urban League's Employ & Econs Comn, 1968; Citizen'sLeague, 1978-2014; bd dir, Cleveland Pub Radio, 1979-2014; United Area Citizens Agency, 1979-2014. **Honors/Awds:** Spinix Award, Southern Ill Univ, 1958; Phi Delta Kappa, Univ Nmex, 1960; Nat Defense Educ Act Fel, 1970, Fel Award, Case-Western Res Univ, 1972. **Home Addr:** 17116 Talford Rd, Cleveland, OH 44128.

### BROACH, S. ELIZABETH JOHNSON

School administrator, consultant. **Personal:** Born May 15, 1921, Little Rock, AR; died May 6, 2014, Oakland, CA; daughter of Iris Addie and Nelvia; married Hughes M; children: Jacqueline Johnson Moore, David M Johnson & Anita M. **Educ:** Dunbar Jr Col, teachers cert, 1940; Philander Smith Col, BA, music educ, 1950; Univ Ark, MS, 1953; Calif State Univ, Hayward, Ed, psycho, 1974. **Career:** Little Rock & Pulaski County Pub Sch, music instr, 1955-65; SFUSD, music specialist, 1967-69; Pelton Jr High Sch, dean women, 1969-70, asst prin, 1970-72; Ben Franklin Jr High Sch, asst prin, 1973-74; Wilson High Sch, asst prin, 1975-77; McAteer High Sch, asst prin, 1978-84; San Fran Unified Sch Dist, admin consult. **Orgs:** Organist Beebe Meth Church, 1967-85, 1998; organist, Europ Tour Voices Beebe, 1982; Phi Delta Kappa Ed, 1978; Nat Asn Negro Musicians, 1984-85; educ comt, Nat Asn Advan Colored People, 1984-85; organist, Nat CME Women's Missionary Coun, 1987-2014; founding bd, Okla E Bay Symphony, 1988-2014; Nat Bus & Prof Women; dir instr, Creative Arts Ctr, San Fran; epistoleus, Sigma Gamma Rho Sor; Nat Coun Negro Women; Oakland Symphony Guild; music dir, Mt Pleasant Baptist Church, Little Rock, Ark. **Honors/Awds:** Diagnostic Counseling Learning Ctr SFUSD, 1973; Commendation Merit Letter Bay Area Rapid Transit; Certificate of Merit, Calif Conf 9th Episcopal Dist; organ performance Bristol England, Chippenham Methodist Church, Wesley Chapel, London England; Outstanding Bay Area Organist, Nat Asn Black Musicians, Golden Gate Branch. **Home Addr:** 7615 Hansom Dr, Oakland, CA 94605, **Home Phone:** (510)562-4598.

### BROCKINGTON, EUGENE ALFONZO

Salesperson, football coach, financial manager. **Personal:** Born Jun 21, 1931, Darien, GA; died Jan 20, 2004, Dover, DE; married Mable M; children: Eugene Jr & Karyn L. **Educ:** Comm Col Philadelphia, attended 1968. **Career:** DeMarco Printer Philadelphia, printing press oper, 1951; Am Fiber-Velop Co, printing press oper, 1954; Jones & Johnson Soft Ice Co, salesman, 1956; US Postal Serv Philadelphia, postal source data tech, 1958; Philadelphia Police Athleitc League, football coach, 1969; Nat Alliance Postal & Fed Employees, treas, comptroller, data proc mgr, 1976-2004. **Orgs:** Fin secy, Nat Alliance Postal & Fed Employees, 1966; scout master, Boy Scouts Am Philadelphia Coun, 1968; lay leader, Sayre Meml United Meth Church, Philadelphia, 1969; treas, bd dir, Nat Alliance Postal & Fed Employees, Fed Credit Union Wash DC, 1977; treas, bd dir, Nat Alliance Postal & Fed Employees, Housing Corp Wash DC, 1979. **Honors/Awds:** Legion of Merit, Chapel Four Chaplins Philadelphia, 1969; Merit Service Award, Dist Five Nat Alliance Postal & Fed Employees, 1973. **Home Addr:** 593 Blue Heron Rd, Dover, DE 19904.

### BROOKE, EDWARD WILLIAM, III

Businessperson, law enforcement officer. **Personal:** Born Oct 26, 1919, Washington, DC; died Jan 3, 2015, Coral Gables, FL; son of Edward W Jr and Helen Seldon; married Ann Fleming; children: Edward; married Remigia Ferrari-Scacco; children: Remi & Edwina. **Educ:** Howard Univ, BS, 1941; Boston Univ Law Sch, LLB, 1948, LLM, 1950. **Career:** Senator (retired), business person, board member; law pract, 1948; Commonwealth Mass, atty gen, 1963-66; US Senate, sen, 1967-79; Csaplar & Bok, coun, 1979-90; O'Connor & Hannan, partner, 1979; Bear & Stearns, ltd partner, 1979-; Meditrust Inc, bd dir, currently. **Orgs:** Chmn, Boston Fin Comn, 1961-62; Nat Coun BSA; Nat Bd Boys Clubs Am; fel Am Bar Asn; Mass Bar Asn; Boston Bar Asn; AMVETS; chmn bd, Opera Co Boston; chmn & bd dir, Boston Bank Com; fel Am Acad Arts & Sci; Spingarn Medal Comn; pub mem, Admin Conf US; bd dir, Wash Performing Arts Soc; chair, Nat Low-Income Housing Coalition, 1979-; chmn, World Policy Coun, Alpha Phi Alpha, 1996, chmn emer. **Honors/Awds:** Distinguished Service Award, AMVETS, 1952; Spingarn Medal, Nat Asn Advan Colored People, 1967; Charles Evans Hughes Award, Nat Conf Christians & Jews, 1967; Mary Hudson Onley Achievement Award Recipient, 2001; Presidential Medal of Freedom, 2004; 33 Hon deg from various col & univ; Jeremy Nicholson Negro Achievement Award, 2004; Edward Brooke Award; Congressional Gold Medal, 2009; European-African-Middle Eastern Campaign Medal; American Campaign Medal. **Special Achievements:** First African-American popularly elected to the United States Senate to serve since Reconstruction and the first to be re-elected; First elected African-American Attorney General of any state in American history. Author: The Challenge of Change, 1966. **Home Addr:** 6437 Blantyre Rd, Warrenton, VA 20187, **Home Phone:** (540)347-5656. **Business Addr:** Partner, O'Connor & Hannan LLP, 1666 K St NW Suite 500, Washington, DC 20006-2803, **Business Phone:** (202)887-1400.

### BROWN, DR. ABENA JOAN P.

Foundation executive, movie producer, businessperson. **Personal:** Born May 8, 1928, Chicago, IL; died Jul 12, 2015, Chicago, IL; daughter of Lueola Reed and Rufus Phillips. **Educ:** Roosevelt Univ, BA, 1950; Univ Chicago, MA, community orgn & mgt, 1963. **Career:** YWCA Metrop Chicago, area dir, 1963-65, consult human rel, 1965-70, dir prog serv, 1970-82; ETA Creative Arts Found, founder, 1971, pres & producer, 1971-2011. **Orgs:** Pres, Black Theatre Alliance Chicago, Ill, 1978-84; pres, Midwest Theatre Alliance, 1982-86; chmn, City Arts Policy Comt, 1985-90; chmn, Subcomt Prog, Mayor's Dept Cult Affairs, 1985; Women's Bd, Chicago Urban League; vice chmn, bd dir, Muntu Dance Theatre; chair adv bd, Chicago Dept Cult Affairs, 1998; S Shore Chamber Com; bd dir, Shorebank Neighborhood Inst; bd dir, Ill Arts Alliance Found. **Honors/Awds:** Recipient of over 100 awards; Paul Robeson Award, Black Theatre Alliance Chicago, 1978; Governor's Award, 1981; Hazel Joan Bryant Award, Midwest African Am Theatre Alliance, 1988; Black Rose Award, League Black Women, 1988; Finalist Kool Achiever Award, 1988; Outstanding Achievement Award, Young Exec Polit, 1987; Outstanding Business Award, Iota Phi Lambda, Chicago, 1990; Award of Excellence, Arts & Theatre, Nat Hook Up Black Women, Chicago chap, 1990; Garvey, Muhammed, King Culture Award, Majestic Eagles, 1990; Women's Hall of Fame, City Chicago, 1991; DHL, Chicago State Univ, 1993; Arts Entrepreneurial Award, Columbia Col Chicago, 1995; Black Theatre Alliance Award; Lifetime Achievement Award, Joseph Jefferson Comt, 1996; Paul Robeson Award, Chicago African Am Arts Alliance; African American Theatre Alliance's Hazel Joan Bryant Award; League of Black Women's Black Rose Award; Muntu Dance Theatre's Alyo Award; culpture Chicago's Full Circle Project Award; Edward J Sparling Alumni Award, Roosevelt Univ; Lorraine Hansberry Award; Award of Merit, Black Theater Alliance; Arts Entrepreneurship Lifetime Achievement Award. **Special Achievements:** Produced more than 175 theatrical productions; Director: "Shango Diaspora"; "Witness a Voice Anthology When the Wind Blows", 1981; "Passenger Past Midnight"; Only black theater company that owns its theater space. **Home Addr:** 7637 S Bennett Ave, Chicago, IL 60649, **Home Phone:** (773)731-7414. **Business Addr:** Founder, ETA Creative Arts Foundation, 7558 S South Chicago Ave, Chicago, IL 60619-2644, **Business Phone:** (773)752-3955.

### BROWN, REV. DR. BEATRICE S.

Educator, executive. **Personal:** Born Jul 14, 1950, Louisville, KY; died Jan 1, 2013?; daughter of Thomas J Sr and Irene. **Educ:** Addis Ababa Univ, Ethiopia, psychol, 1990; Cornell Univ, Coop Nutrit Prog, PhD, cert, 1991; Postgrad Ctr Ment Health, New York, cert, 1995. **Career:** Upper Manhattan Ment Health Ctr, c day treat unit dir, 1989-91; City Col, City Univ, NY, adj prof, 1990; Jewish Bd Family & C Serv, residential treat facil girls unit, dir; Cent Brooklyn Coord Coun Inc, ment health unit psychol, 1997; BSB holistic Consult Group Wellness Inc, founder, 1997; Daughters Zion Int 'Women Prayer', founder & pres. **Orgs:** Am Psychol Asn; Am Asn Pastoral Counr; Nat Guild Hypnotists Inc; Ky Asn Hypnotherpists; Nat & Int Bd Missionaries; Sigma Gamma Rho. **Honors/Awds:** Letter of Award, Univ Louisville, 1970; Songwriter Award, St WLOU, Louisville, 1971; Certificate, Univ Louisville, 1974; Appreciation Award, African-Am Music Arts Festival Comn, 1984. **Home Addr:** 425 W Ormsby Ave Suite 7, Louisville, KY 40203-3078. **Business Addr:** Founder, Chief Executive Officer, Daughters of Zion International, PO Box 2731, Louisville, KY 40201, **Business Phone:** (502)636-9183.

### BROWN, CLAUDINE K.

Lawyer, executive. **Personal:** Born Jan 1, 1949; died Mar 17, 2016. **Educ:** Pratt Inst, BA; Bank St Col, MA, mus educ; Brooklyn Law Sch, JD. **Career:** Brooklyn Mus, staff, 1976, mus educr, 1977-82, mgr sch & community prog, 1982-84, asst dir govt & community rels, 1985-90; Smithsonian Insts, dep asst secy mus, 1991, asst secy educ & access, 2010-16; Nathan Cummings Found, atty, dir arts & cult prog; New York Pub Schs, art & drama teacher. **Orgs:** Am Asn Mus; Nat Pk Serv Fund; Asn Black Found Execs; pres bd, Grantmakers Arts; arts admin prog, NY Univ; Mus Leadership Prog, Bank St Col; founding mem, Art & Social Justice Funders Group.

### BRYANT, R. KELLY, JR. (ROBERT K BRYANT, JR.)

Executive. **Personal:** Born Sep 22, 1917, Rocky Mount, NC; died Dec 6, 2015, Durham, NC; son of R Kelly and Maggie Poole; married Artelia Tennesse; children: Robert Kelly III & Sandra Artelia (Yubwannie). **Educ:** Hampton Inst, BS, bus admin, 1940; NC Cent Univ, attended 1942. **Career:** Executive (retired); Peoples Bldg & Loan Asn, bookkeeper, 1940; Mutual Savings & Loan, bookkeeper, 1941-44; NC Mutual Life Ins Co, Ordinary Dept, chief clerk, 1944-56, mgr, 1956-60, asst secy, 1965-81; Hampton Univ, treas. **Orgs:** Durham Chamber Com; pres, Chain Investment Corp; registr, Burton Sch Voting Precinct No 3, 1951-2015; secy, Hunter Lodge No 825 Free & Accepted Masons & First Worshipful Master, 1961-2015; bd dir, Goodwill Indust Inc, 1968-76; bd dir, Vol Serv Bur Inc; chmn, Sch Improv Comm-Burton Sch PTA, 1968-70; chmn, Educ Comm-Durham Human Rels Comn, 1968-76; adv bd, Emergency Sch Assistance Act Prog-Oper Breakthrough Inc, 1972-77; grandsecy, Prince Hall Grand Lodge Masons, NC, 1981-98; educ comm, Durham Comm Negro Affairs; Nat & Durham Chap Nat Hampton Alumni Asn; treas, NC Region; trustee, Auditing Comm, White Rock Baptist Church; leader, Friends Geer Cemetery, currently; trustee, White Rock Baptist Church; secy-treas, Selective Buying Campaign; secy-treas, Black Solidarity Comt; secy-treas, Black Christmas; life long mem, Nat Asn Advan Colored People. **Honors/Awds:** NC Hamptonian of the Year, 1957; Man of the Year, Durham Housewives League, 1958; Silver Beaver Award; Alumni Merit Award, Nat Hampton Alumni Asn, 1969; Appreciation for Service Award, AS Hunter Lodge No 825 Free & Accepted Masons, 1974; Most Outstanding Secretary, AS Hunter Lodge No 825 Free & Accepted Masons, 1976; Special Certificate, Durham Human Rels Comn, Durham City Coun, 1977; Appreciation for Service Award, Nat Hampton Alumni Asn, 1979; Plaque for 38 years of service, Durham Bus & Prof Chain, 1981; NAACP Freedom Fund Dinner Award, 1987. **Home Addr:** 618 Bernice St, Durham, NC 27703-5012, **Home Phone:** (919)596-7100.

### BURDEN, DR. WILLIE JAMES

Educator, football player. **Personal:** Born Jul 21, 1951, Longwood, NC; died Dec 4, 2015, Atlanta, GA; son of John and Emily H; married Velma Stokes; children: Courtney, Willie James Jr & Freddie Hamilton. **Educ:** NC State Univ, BA, econs, 1974; Ohio Univ, MA, sports admin, 1983; Tenn State Univ, EdD, 1990. **Career:** Football player (retired), educator; Calgary Stampeders CFL, prof athlete, 1974-81; NC State Univ, asst football coach, 1974-76, asst to athletics dir, 1976-82; Ohio Univ, asst football coach, 1982-84, asst athletic dir, 1988-90; Tenn Tech Univ, asst athletic dir, 1984-88; NC Agr & Tech State Univ , athletics dir, 1998-98; Ga Southern Univ, assoc prof, 1999, prof sport mgt, 2015. **Orgs:** Sr counr, Am Legion Boys State Tenn, 1984, 1986; pres, Friends Distinction NC, 1969-2015; big bro counr, PHD Prevent High Sch Drop Outs Prog Raleigh, NC, 1973-74; Phi Delta Kappa, 1987-2015; Civitan Civic Org, 1988-90; Nat Greene Kiwanis, 1993-2015. **Honors/Awds:** Atlantic Coast Conf Football Player of the Year, 1973; all-star Can Football League, 1975-79; mvp Canadian Football League, 1975; Athletic endowment scholarship honoree Univ Calgary, Alberta, Can, 1983-2015; Calgary Stampeders, "Wall of Fame, " 1992; Men of Valor Award, Ga Southern Univ, Nat Asn Advan Colored People; Canadian Football League Hall of Fame, 2001; Award, Boys & Girls Clubs of America, 2005. **Home Addr:** 1800 Biscayne Ave, Greensboro, NC 27410.

### BURROUGHS, JOHN ANDREW, JR.

Government official, educator, football player. **Personal:** Born Jul 31, 1936, Washington, DC; died Sep 11, 2014, Washington, DC; son of John A and Yeasavale; married Audrey C Shields. **Educ:** Univ Iowa, BA, polit sci, 1959; George Washington Univ, post grad, 1962; Stanford Univ, attended 1974; Lincoln Univ, dipl-in-residence, 1991. **Career:** Football player, educator, government official (retired); Forest Evashevski, player, 1956-58; Philadelphia Eagles, 1958; Dept State Wash, passport examr, 1960-63; Dept State Bur Econ Affairs, Passport Off, admin asst, 1963-70; Dept Navy Wash, employ rels spec, 1970-77; Dept Navy Wash, spec asst equal employ, 1970-77; Stanford Univ Exec Prog, Merrill Trust Fel; Dept State Wash, asst sec equal employ oppor, 1977-81; Repub Malawi, US ambassador, 1981-84; Joint Ctr Polit Studies, sr res fel, 1984-85; US State Dept, dep asst secy, Am consult gen, 1985-88; Repub Uganda, US ambassador, 1988-91; Lincoln Univ, teacher african polit; Sudan, spec coordr, 1993-94. **Orgs:** Pres & bd dir, Ridge crest Condominium, 1964-70; Kappa Alpha Psi; life mem, Univ Iowa Alumni Asn. **Honors/Awds:** Civilian Superior Service Award, Dept Navy Wash DC, 1977; Superior Honor Award, Dept State Wash DC, 1980; Distinguished Alumni Award, Univ iowa Alumni Asn, 1996. **Special Achievements:** First African-American assigned US Consul General in Cape Town, South Africa. **Home Addr:** , Temple Hills, MD.

### BYRD, HARRIETT ELIZABETH

Politician, government official. **Personal:** Born Apr 20, 1926, Cheyenne, WY; died Jan 27, 2015, Cheyenne, WY; daughter of Robert C Rhone and Sudie E Smith; married James W; children: Robert C, James W II & Linda C. **Educ:** WVa State Col, BS, educ, 1949; Univ WY, MA, elem educ, 1976. **Career:** Dept Admin Training & Supply, Ft Francis E Warren, civilian instr, 1949; Cheyenne's Sch Dist, elem teacher, 1959; WY Educ Asn, WY TEPS Comt, 1970-73; Marshall Scholar Comt, comt mem, 1972-79; NEA Albuquerque, inserv training ctrsl, 1979; Wyo State Legis, House Reps, state rep, comt mem, 1973-80, 1981-88, sen, 1988-92; Dept Educ's Int Youth Yr Awards comt, staff, 1985. **Orgs:** Life mem, Kappa Delta Pi; Delta Kappa Gamma; Kappa Kappa Iota; Laramie Co Coll Booster Club; adv bd, Laramie Co Sr Citizens; vpres, pres, 1992-95, Laramie Co Dem Women's Club; United Med Ctr Cheynne; Univ WY Alumni; St Mary's Cath Church; League Women Voters; WY State Mus; state contact, State WY Dr Martin Luther King Jr State & City King Holiday Fed Comt; Love & Charity Club. **Honors/Awds:** Instructor of Excellence Award, Instr mag, 1967; Distinguished Citizen Award by the Boy Scouts of America, Cheyenne, 1990; Wash, DC, forher efforts toward peace, justice, freedom and dignity for all people, YWCA, 1990; Volunteer Award, Churchill-Corlett Elementary Sch, 1990; Special Recognition Award, Colorado Black Women for Political Action, 1990. **Special Achievements:** First African American legislator in Wyoming; First African American woman to serve in the Wyoming State Legislature; First African American to serve in the Wyoming State Senate; Listed in Who's Who of American Women. **Home Addr:** 6400 Antelope Ave, Cheyenne, WY 82009-3240.

### CARTER, CHESTER C.

Executive. **Personal:** Born Feb 14, 1921, Emporia, KS; married Claudia; children: Chester Jr, Marise & Carol. **Educ:** Univ SC, BA, 1944, MA, philos, 1952; Loyola Law Sch, JD, 1958. **Career:** Sup Ct LA Co, juv traffic hearing officer, 1956-62; US State Dept, Peace Corps, ambassador, 1962-68, cong Rels, dep asst secy; Capitol City Liquor Co Wholesale, pres chmn bd. **Home Addr:** 4233 42 St NW, Washington, DC 20016. **Business Addr:** , 645 Taylor St NE, Washington, DC 20017-2063.

### CHAMBERS, JOHN CURRY, JR.

Lawyer, manager. **Personal:** Born May 22, 1956, Newark, NJ; died Dec 22, 2000, Bowie, MD; son of John and Naomi McGriff; married Georgette Sims; children: John Curry III & Candace Dane. **Educ:** Univ Pa, BA; Am Univ, Wash Col Law, JD. **Career:** Am Petrol Inst, prin RCRA atty, 1981-84; CONOCO, in-house coun, 1985; McKenna & Cuneo, partner, 1986-97; Arent, Fox, Kintner, Plotkin & Kahn, partner; Brownfields Bus Info Network, founder; Wash Govt Rels Group, pres. **Orgs:** DC Bar; Am Bar Asn; Nat Bar Asn; Environ Law Ed Inst; adv bd, J Environ Permitting; adv comt, Am Bar Asn; Conf Minority Partners; comt, Nat Inst Environ; vchair, Am Bar Asn Teleconference & Video Prog Sonreel; vchair, Am Bar Asn Sonreel Diversity Comt; guest commentator, Nat Pub Radio; founder, Brown fields

Bus Info Network; co chair, Am Bar Asn Video Teleconferences Comt; EPA NACEPT Title VI Fed Adv Comn Implementation Environ Justice. **Special Achievements:** First African American equity partner in its history; Book: Of Color and Love, 1997; Appears as a television and radio commentator. **Home Addr:** 14009 Tollison Dr, Bowie, MD 20720, **Home Phone:** (301)464-3960.

### CHAPMAN, DR. MELVIN

Association executive. **Personal:** Born Mar 16, 1928, Detroit, MI; died Aug 16, 2015, Marquette, MI; married Elizabeth Patton; children: Carolyn & Melvin. **Educ:** Wayne State Univ, BA, 1949, MEd, 1953, ed spec, 1965, EdD, 1973. **Career:** Detroit, teacher, 1949; Northwestern High Sch, counr, 1962; Wayne State Univ, High Educ Opportunity Comn, dir, 1964; Cent High Sch, asst prin, 1966; Northwestern High Sch, prin, 1967; Detroit Pub Schs, asst supt, 1970-2015, exec dir. **Orgs:** Corp Body Mich Blue Shield; Trio Adv Comn; Nat Alliance Black Sch Educ; Mich Asn C Learning Disabilities; Met Detroit Soc Black Educ Adminr; Am Asn Sch Adminr; Nat Asn Advan Colored People; Kappa Alpha Psi USC C; founder & pres, Diversified Educ Serv Inc, 2002-15, vpres; Nonprofit Welfare-To-Work Prog, dir. **Honors/Awds:** Leadership Award, Chrysler Corp & NW HS, 1968. **Home Addr:** 19709 Roslyn Rd, Detroit, MI 48221-1893.

### CLARK, DR. AUGUSTA ALEXANDER

Lawyer, government official. **Personal:** Born Mar 5, 1932, Uniontown, AL; died Oct 13, 2013, Wynnewood, PA; son of Harrison and Lula B; married Leroy W; children: Mark & Adrienne. **Educ:** Rosemont Col; WVa State Col, BS, bus admin, 1954; Drexel Univ, MLS, 1958; Temple Univ, Sch Law, JD, 1976. **Career:** Fed Defense Installations & Free Libr Philadelphia, librn, 1958-66; GenElect Co RESD, mkt res analyst, 1967-69; Auerbach Corp, consult, 1970-71; Philadelphia Model Cities Prog, admin, 1971-73; Gen Elect Co, affirmaction requirement mgr, 1973-75; Majority Whip City Coun Philadelphia, councilwoman-at-large & atty (retired); Mayor's Bus Action Team, vice chmn, 2000; Mayor John St's Cabinet, secy agencies, authorities, bds & comns. **Orgs:** Bd dir, Friends Free Libr Philadelphia; city coun mem, Philadelphia Conv & Visitors Bur; New Horizons Res Inst; Horizon House; Shalom Inc; N Cent Br Young Women's Christian Asn; Orgn Women & Girls Offenders, PILCPO; bd trustee, Philadelphia Col Arts; advy bd, Pa Women's Campaign Fund; law comn, Am Baptist Churches USA Inc; founder & co-chair, Bright Hope Survival Prog; sponsor, Month Woman, 1983; delegate, Nat Women's Conf, Houston; co-chair, Pa Int Women's Year Coord Comn; Barristers, Pa Bar Asn; Alpha Kappa Alpha Sorority; W Broad St Coalition; WVa State Alumni; Steering Comt Chess fest; Black Women's Network; organizer, Jefferson Manor Tenant Asn; coun, Minority Contractors Adv Comn; Philadelphia City Coun; Bright Hope Baptist Church; chair, Educ Comt City Coun; bd dir, Philadelphia Mus Art; Del Valley Chap Links, Inc. **Honors/Awds:** Outstanding Service in the Community, Nu Sigma Nat Sorority, 1980; Alumnus of the Year & Outstanding Citizen & Humanitarian, WVa State Col, Theta Chap Theta, 1981; Support to Delta, Iota Chap, Alpha Kappa Alpha Sorority Inc, 1983; Sponsored a number of Bills & Resolutions to assist in improving the quality of life; Honorary Doctorates Degree, Drexel Univ, 1985. **Home Addr:** 1313 Lafayette Pl, Philadelphia, PA 19122. **Business Addr:** Secretary of Agencies Authorities Boards & Commissions, Mayor John Street's Cabinet, Philadelphia, PA 19102.

### COBB, ETHEL WASHINGTON

Government official, manager, executive. **Personal:** Born Jun 10, 1925, Ravenel, SC; died Feb 9, 2012, Charleston, SC; married Shedrick; children: Geneva Nelson, Carolyn C, Shedrick, Sidney, Joan C, Shedricka C & Linda C. **Career:** City Ravenel, bd execs, 1970-; mem & exec comt mem, Dem Party; Primary & Pres Elections, Dem Party, poll mgr; Charleston Co Sch Dist, St Paul's Constituent Dist 23, vice chairperson, currently. **Orgs:** Rec secy & pres pulpit aid bd, St John Baptist Church; founder/chmn, St John Day Care Ctr; Yonges Island Headstart Bd; Daycare Ctr Bd; Rural Mission Coun; Biracial Comt Charleston Co Community Develop Bd; vol fire fighter, Sea Island Prog; Clemson Univ Ext Community Develop Progs; chmn, Polit Action Comt Dist 116; Dem Coun, 1984; Budget Proposal Comt; rep Ravenel, Charleston Berkley & Dorchester Comt; rep ravenel, Firemen Asn; Eastern Star. **Honors/Awds:** Civil Defense Award; 5 Year Recognition Award, Clemson Univ Ext Prog; Outstanding Assistance Award, Who's Who Among Southern Am; Outstanding Assistance Award, Baptist Hill High Sch Athletic Dept; Outstanding Democratic Female; Certificate, Gov's Rural Sch. **Special Achievements:** First African American Woman to be elected to the Bd of Execs in Ravenel. **Home Addr:** 5527 Ellington Rd, Ravenel, SC 29470, **Home Phone:** (843)889-2474. **Business Addr:** Vice Chairperson, Charleston County School District, 7226 Hwy 162, Hollywood, SC 29449-5606.

### COLE, NATALIE (STEPHANIE NATALI MARIA COLE)

Singer, actor. **Personal:** Born Feb 6, 1950, Los Angeles, CA; died Dec 31, 2015, Los Angeles, CA; daughter of Nat King (deceased) and Maria Hawkins; married Marvin J Yancy, Jul 31, 1976, (divorced 1980); children: Robert Adam; married Andre Fischer, Sep 16, 1989, (divorced 1995); married Kenneth H Dupree, Oct 12, 2001, (divorced 2004). **Educ:** Univ Mass, german & child psychol, 1972. **Career:** Capitol Recs, rec artist, 1975-; Big Break, tv show, host & performer, 1990-. Films: "De-Lovely", 2004. TV series: "Lily in Winter", 1994; "Abducted; A Father's Love", 1997; "Concert of Hope", 1997; Always Outnumbered, 1998; "Livin For Love: The Natalie Cole Story", exec producer, 2000; "Natalie: A Woman Who Knows", exec producer, 2002; "Great Performances", exec producer, 2002; "Law & Order: Special Victims Unit", 2006; "Greys Anatomy", 2006; "Frosted Pink", 2007. Albums: Inseparable, 1975; Our Love, 1978; Someone That I Used to Love; Good To Be Back, 1989; Unforgettable With Love, 1991; Everlasting, 1991; I'm Ready, 1992; Take a Look, 1993; Holly & Ivy, 1994; I've Got Love On My Mind, 1995; Stardust, 1996; Snowfall On the Sahara, 1999; Sing Like Natalie Cole, 2000; Livin' For Love, 2001; Ask A Woman Who Knows, 2002; The Easter Egg Adventure, composer, 2004; Eclectic Soul, 2005; Leavin', 2006; Love Songs, 2007; Still Unforgettable, 2008; Caroling, Caroling: Christmas with Natalie Cole, 2008; Natalie Cole en Espanol, 2013. Others: Comic Relief, 1990; A Tribute To Nat King Cole, 1992; Cats Don't Dance, 1997; Freak City, 1999; De-Lovely, 2004; Grey's Anatomy, 2006; The Real Housewives of Miami, 2011; The Real Housewives of New York City, 2011-13. **Orgs:** Afghan World Found. **Honors/Awds:** Gold Rec, "Inseparable"; Grammy Award, 1976-77, 1992, 1994, 1997 & 2009; four gold albums; two platinum albums; Image Award, 1976, 1977; American Music Award, 1977-78 & 1991; The George and Ira Gershwin Award, 1993; Hitmaker Award, 1999; Image Award, Nat Asn Advan Colored People, 2000, 2002 & 2009; Am Music Award, 1977, 1978 & 1991; Cowboy Award, 2004. **Special Achievements:** Author: Angel on My Shoulder, 2000; Love Brought Me Back, 2009. **Home Addr:** 10100 Santa Monica Blvd Fl 16, Los Angeles, CA 90067. **Business Addr:** Singer, Actress, c/o Capitol Recs Inc, 1750 N Vine St, Hollywood, CA 90028, **Business Phone:** (323)462-6252.

### COLE, STEPHANIE NATALI MARIA. See COLE, NATALIE.

### COLLINS, DAMON JAMAL. See COLLINS, MO.

### COLLINS, MO (DAMON JAMAL COLLINS)

Football player, football coach, executive. **Personal:** Born Sep 22, 1976, Charlotte, NC; died Oct 26, 2014, Charlotte, NC. **Educ:** Univ Fla, BS, sports admin, 1998. **Career:** Football player (retired), executive, coach; Oakland Raiders, tackle, 1998-2003; CSA Prepstar, regional scouting dir, 2008-14; Prepstar Football, nat camp dir, 2009-14; Momentum Sports Group LLC, owner & chief exec officer, 2009-14; W Charlotte High Sch, W Charlotte Lions Football Team, head coach, 2014. **Honors/Awds:** SEC Championship, 1995 & 1996; Bowl Alliance National Championship, 1996.

### CONE, DR. CECIL WAYNE

School administrator. **Personal:** Born May 21, 1937, Bearden, AR; died Apr 8, 2016, Atlanta, GA; married Juanita Fletcher; children: Cecil Wayne, Leslie Anita & Charleston Alan. **Educ:** Shorter Col, AA, 1955; Philander Smith, BA, 1957; Garrett Theol Sem, M Div, 1961; Emory Univ, PhD, 1974. **Career:** Union AME Little Rock, pastor, 1964-69; OIC Little Rock, exec dir, 1964-69; Turner Theol Sem, dean, 1969-85; Edward Waters Col, pres, Jacksonville, Fla, 1977-2007. **Orgs:** Soc Study Black Rel; Black Theol Proj Theol Am; Nat Asn Advan Colored People; Alpha Phi Alpha Fraternity; Nat Urban League; bd govr, Cof C Jacksonville, Fla, 1978-81; St Ethics Comn, State Fla, 1979-81; bd dir, Jacksonville Symphony Asn, 1984-85, Mayor's Comn High Tech, 1984-85; Gamma Beta Boule. **Honors/Awds:** Distinguished Service Award, United Negro Col Fund, 1984; Outstanding Educator of the Year, Jacksonville Jaycees, 1985; hon doctorates, Temple Bible Col, Sem; hon doctorates, Philander Smith Col. **Special Achievements:** Author, "Identity Crisis Black Theology", 1975. **Home Addr:** 8787 Southside Blvd Suite 415, Jacksonville, FL 32256.

### COOPER, LOIS LOUISE

Civil engineer. **Personal:** Born Nov 25, 1931, Vicksburg, MS; died Jan 1, 2014; children: Wyatt E & Christopher. **Educ:** Tougaloo Col, MS, 1949; Los Angeles State Col, Los Angles, Calif, BA, math, 1954; Calif State Univ, Los Angeles, Calif, civil engineering, 1975. **Career:** Civil engineer (retired); Div Hwys, Caltrans, eng aid, 1953-58, jr civil engr, 1958-61; Caltrans, asst transp engr, 1961-84, assoc transp engr, 1984-88, sr transp engr, 1988-91, proj mgr. **Orgs:** Past bd dir, sec, Los Angeles Coun Engr Sci; adv bd, Minority Engr Prog Calif State Univ, Los Angles; pres, vpres, sec & treas, La Coun Black Prof Engrs, 1975-76; stud mem, career guid Soc Women Engrs, 1985; Am Soc Civil Engrs; Nat Soc Prof Engrs. **Honors/Awds:** Trail Blazer, Nat Asn Negro Bus & Prof Womens Inc, 1964; Fel Inst Advan Engineering, 1982; Fel Soc of Women Engrs, 1989. **Special Achievements:** First Black Woman to attain a Profl Engrs Lic in Civil Engineering in California, 1978; First Black Woman to achieve all positions at Caltrans, 1983; First Black women hired in the engineering field for the Division of Highways (currently Caltrans) in Los Angeles. **Home Addr:** 14324 S Clymar Ave, Compton, CA 90220-1115, **Home Phone:** (310)639-0293.

### CRAWLEY, DR. OSCAR LEWIS, SR.

Labor relations manager. **Personal:** Born May 19, 1942, Lafayette, AL; died Oct 6, 2015, Lanett, AL; son of Katie and Carlton; married Clemestine Clausell; children: Deitra Phernam & Oscar Lewis III. **Educ:** Ala State Univ, BS, psychol, 1963; Univ S Ala, grad study. **Career:** Marengo High Sch & Dixon Mills, Ala, teacher, 1963-72; Westpoint Pepperell Inc, Fairfax Towel Oper, asst personnel dir, 1972, personnel dir, 1975-2015; W Pt Pepperall Inc, indust rel mgr, 1988-2015; Bath Prod, Westpoint Stevens, mgr human resources, div human resources dir, 1994-2015, corp dir human resources & security; City Lanett, mayor, 2004-15. **Orgs:** Alpha Phi Alpha Inc, 1974; dist comt man, George H Lanier Coun Boy Scouts, 1975; comnr, Goodwill Inds, 1976; gov staff, State Ala Gov George C Wallace, 1977; chmn, bd comnr, Lanett City Housing Auth, 1978; chmn, Indust Com Chambers Co Ment Health, 1978; chmn, Aux Com Chambers Co Bd Educ, 1979; bd mem, Chambers County Heart Asn, 1990; bd dir, Chambers County Libr, 1994; bd dir, Valley Crime Stoppers, 1994. **Honors/Awds:** Chair of the Year, Am Heart Asn, Jailbail, 1992-93. **Home Addr:** 611 N 14th St, Lanett, AL 36863, **Home Phone:** (334)644-2518.

### CROSBY, FRED CHARLES

Lawyer. **Personal:** Born Dec 12, 1959, Cleveland, OH; died Aug 20, 2016; son of Fred and Phendalyne; married Carla; children: Monique Kaitlyn. **Educ:** Northwood Univ, BS, 1982; Cleveland Marshall Col Law, JD, 1987. **Career:** City Cleveland, asst prosecutor, 1988-93; David I Pomerantz, campaign mgr; Pomerantz & Crosby Co, LPA, partner & atty, 1995-2016; Shaker Heights Munic Ct, actg judge, 2016. **Orgs:** Bd dir & pres, Cuyahoga County Criminal Defense Lawyers Asn; Cuyahoga County Cert Grievance Comm; Ohio State Bar Asn; Cleveland Bar Asn; vpres, Cuyahoga County Bar Asn; Am Acad Trial Lawyers Asn; Norman S Minon Bar Asn; Ohio Asn Criminial Defense Attys; chmn, Fenn Found; bd dir, Ohio Motorsist Asn; City News Newspaper; Crosby Furniture; adv bd, Universal Heights Recreation; Cleveland Metrop Bar Asn; bd dir, Ohio Mororists' Asn. **Special Achievements:** Legal Editor for City News Newspaper, 1999.

### CROUCH, PASTOR ANDRAE EDWARD

Gospel singer, clergy, songwriter. **Personal:** Born Jul 1, 1942, San Francisco, CA; died Jan 8, 2015, Los Angeles, CA; son of Benjamin Jerome and Catherine Dorthea Hodnett. **Educ:** Life Bible Col, Los Angeles, CA, religious studies. **Career:** Gospel ginger, 1954-2015; The Disciples, organizer, 1968-2015; Light records, singer, 1971-84; Christ Memorial Church God Christ, sr pastor, 1995-. Singles: "My Tribute"; "Soon & Very Soon"; "Jesus Is the Answer". Albums: Take the Message Everywhere, Light records, 1971; Andrae Crouch & the Disciples; His Best; Just Andrae, 1973; Don't Give Up, Warner Bros, 1981; Finally, 1982; No Time to Lose, 1984; Mercy, 1994; Pray, 1997; Take the Message Everywhere, 2005; Gift of Christmas, 1998; Mighty Wind, 2006; The Journey, 2011; Live in Los Angeles, 2013. **Honors/Awds:** Numerous Grammy Awards; Gold Record for "Jesus is the Answer"; Soul Gospel Artist, Billboard Mag, 1975, 1977; Dove Award, 1978; Daviticus Awards, 1979; Grammy Award for Best Soul Gospel Performance, 1984; Gospel Music Hall of Fame, Gospel Music Asn, 1998; Hollywood Walk of Fame, 2004; Inaugural Salute to Gospel Music Lifetime Achievement Award, Nat Acad Rec Arts & Sci; NARAS Inaugural Salute to Gospel Music Lifetime Achievement Award, 2005. **Special Achievements:** Author, Through It All, 1974. **Home Addr:** 3300 Warner Blvd, Burbank, CA 91510.

### DARITY, DR. WILLIAM ALEXANDER, SR.

Educator, lecturer, army officer. **Personal:** Born Jan 15, 1924, Flat Rock, NC; died Nov 29, 2015, Northampton, MA; son of Aden Randall (deceased) and Elizabeth Smith (deceased); married Evangeline Royall; children: William Jr & Janki Evangelia; married Trudy L Whisonant. **Educ:** Shaw Univ, BS, 1948; NC Cent Univ, MS, public health, 1949; Univ NC, PhD, 1964. **Career:** World Health Orgn, regional adv, 1953-64, consult, 1971-80; Peace Corps Training Progs, consult dir, 1962-67; Headstart Training Progs, consult lectr, 1965-67; Univ Mass, assoc prof, prof, 1965, prof pub health & dean, Sch Health Sci, 1973-89, prof pub health, 1989-91, prof emer pub health, 1989, prof emer & dean emer; Univ NC, vis prof, 1973; Univ SC, vis prof, 1980; Univ Ibadan, Nigeria & Univ Wi, external examr, 1973-2015; Nat Cancer Inst, dir & prin investr, Res Cancer & Smoking Black Populations, 1986-91; Pop Coun, NY, sr assoc, posted Cairo, Egypt, 1991-93; Univ NC, decision-maker, 2001; NC Fund Inc, dir prog develop. **Orgs:** Fel Am Pub Health Asn; fel Soc Pub Health Educ; fel Am Sch Health Asn; Am Nat Coun Health Educ; Int Union Health Educ; Delta Omega; assoc Danforth Found; bd dir, Drug Abuse Coun, 1972-79; bd dir, Planned Parenthood Fed Am, 1967-73; bd dir, SIECUS, 1967-71; pres, Mass Asn Ment Health, 1967-69; pres, Hampshire Pub Health Asn, 1967-70; bd trustee, Univ NC-Chapel Hill, 1985-91; bd sci counrs, Nat Cancer Inst, 1986-90; bd dir, Mass Water Resources Authority, 1989-91; Phi Kappa Phi; Sigma Xi; Sigma Pi Phi, Boule, 1986-2015; Omega Psi Phi 1946-; SASL; mem & off many other civic orgns. **Honors/Awds:** Recipient Fel World Health Orgn; Hildrus Poindexter Pub Health Service Award, BCHW/APHA, 1975; Distinguished Lecture/Chancellor's Medal, Univ Mass, 1989; Dist Alumnus Award, Univ NC, 1996; Alumni Achievement Award, Shaw Univ, 1997. **Special Achievements:** First African American to receive a PhD from Univ NC, Chapel hill, 1964. **Home Addr:** 105 Heatherstone Rd, Amherst, MA 01002, **Home Phone:** (413)253-9861.

### DAVIS, REV. ARNOR S.

Educator, clergy. **Personal:** Born Dec 30, 1919, Patterson, GA; died Aug 10, 2013, Washington, DC; married Virginia; children: 3. **Educ:** Savannah State Col, BS; Howard Univ Sch Relig, Wash DC, BD; Howard Univ, MA. **Career:** Zion Baptist Church, Wash, DC, asst minister, 1950-52; New Bethel Baptist Church, Wash, DC, dir relig educ, 1960-75; Inst Rels DC Redevel Land Agency, Wash, DC, asst area dir; Antioch Baptist Church, Wash, DC, asst minister, 1975, assoc. **Orgs:** Exec dir, Second Precinct Clergymens Asn, 1948-74; Savannah State Alumni Asn DC Chap, 1948-74; Howard Univ Alumni Asn; Bapt Ministers Conf, 1960-74; pres, bd dir, Nat Med Asn Found, 1967-74; bd dir, Mt Ethel Bapt Training Union, 1969-74; bd dir, Lincoln-Westmoreland Non-Profit Housing Corp; bd dir, DC Citizens Better Educ, 1970-74; Nat Asn Advan Colored People, 1970-74; bd dir, Hillcrest C Ctr, 1971-74; bd dir, local coun Churches; Housing Task Force Coun Churches. **Honors/Awds:** Publs A Guide to Chs & Institutions in the Shaw & Urban Renewal Area, 1974; A Guide SAC Area Schs & Non-profit Sponsorships, 1975. **Special Achievements:** Author of "The Pentecostal Movement in Black Christianity". **Home Addr:** 631 Jefferson St NE, Washington, DC 20011, **Home Phone:** (202)526-9380.

### DAVIS, DR. CARRIE LOUISE FILER

Educator. **Personal:** Born Oct 19, 1924, Marianna, AR; married Wm; children: Arthur, Norma, Helen & Gina. **Educ:** Univ Ark, BA, 1948; NE Ill Univ, MA, 1971; NW Univ, grad study; Univ Sarasota, EdD, 1982. **Career:** Educator (retired); Robert Morton High Sch, educr, 1948-55; Crest Finishing Sch, co dir, 1956-60; Englewood High Sch

Chicago, counr, 1961-72; Chicago Bd Educ, co compiler curric guide drama, admin dist 19, instrnl serv coord dist 27, adminr dist 19, 1973; Chicago Schs, educ consult, 1997. **Orgs:** Sigma Gamma Rho Sorority, 1943; campus coord, Cent Region, 1972-74, dir, 1974; grand epistoleus, Sigma Gamma Rho Sorority, 1980-84; pres, Roseland Community Hosp; chmn, Calumet Dist United Charities Educ Comt; Good Citizenship Club Inc; Nat Scholar Comt; Altgeld Urban Prog Ctr Educ Com; com chairperson, Afro-Am Family Serv; Quinn Chapel AME Church; S shore YMCA; sub com, White House Conf Youth; St Luke AME Ch; nat pres, Nat Women Achievement Inc; bd trustees, Univ Sarasota. **Honors/Awds:** Citizenship Award, 1971; Woman of the Year, Creast Finishing School, 1973; Outstanding Drama Coordr, 1978; Outstanding Admin, 1979; Government of Arkansas Award, 1986; Outstanding Alumni Award, Robert Moton High Sch, Marianna Ar, 1997; Community Service Award, Roseland Comt Hosp, 1997; Senior Citizen Hall of Fame Award, Mayor Daley, Chicago, 1997; LeMoyne Col Alumni Award, Community Educ Serv to Youth, 1997; Outstanding Service to Community Award, Sigma Gamma Rho Sorority; Judge IL Speech Association Award. **Special Achievements:** Co-author, Curriculum Guide & Activities for Proficiency in Basic Skills, 1977; co-author, Curriculum Guide for Drama Classes. **Home Addr:** 6922 S Jeffery Blvd Apt 2N, Chicago, IL 60649.

## DAVIS, FR. CYPRIAN

Educator, clergy. **Personal:** Born Sep 9, 1930, Washington, DC; died May 18, 2015, Harrison, IN; son of Clarence William and Evelyn Theresa Jackson. **Educ:** St Meinrad Col, BA, 1953; Cath Univ Am, STL, 1957; Univ Louvain, LicSciHist, 1963, DrSciHist, 1977. **Career:** St Meinrad Archabbey, benedictine monk; St Meinrad Sem & Sch Theol, instr, 1963-68, assoc prof, 1971-82, prof church hist, prof emer, currently. **Orgs:** Archivist & founding mem, Nat Black Cath Clergy Caucus, 1968-; archivist, Swiss-Am Congregation Benedictine abbeys; archivist, St Meinrad Archabbe; archivist, Nat Black Cath Clergy Caucus. **Honors/Awds:** Doctorate Sci Hist, 1977; John Gilmary Shea Award, Am Cath Hist Asn, 1991; Johannes Quasten Medal, Cath Univ, 2002; Univ Notre Dame, hon degree, 2001, Catholic Theological Union, 2002, St. Vincent's Col, 2003, Cath Univ Am, 2006; Distinguished Alumnus Award, St Meinrad Alumni Asn, 2004. **Special Achievements:** Author of several articles, Black Cath hist, Black spirituality; Author: Church Hist, "The Church a Living Heritage," The Hist of Black Catholics in the USS", "Black Spirituality, a Roman Cath Perspective," rev & expositor, "Black Catholics in Nineteenth-Century Am," US Cath Historian "Evangelization Us Since Vatican Coun II," Cath Evangelization Today New Pentecost Us; "The Holy See & Am Blacks, A Forgotten Chap Hist Am Church", US Cath Historian, 7 157-181, 1988; auth, Hist Black Catholics US, Crossroad, 1990; "The Didache & Early Monasticism E & W," The Didache Context, Essays Text, Hist & Transmission, edited Clayton N Jefford, Leiden: EJ Brill, p 352-367, 1995; first African-Am to make final vows in the monastic community at St Meinrad.

## DAVIS, LEONARD HARRY

Manager. **Personal:** Born Sep 3, 1927, Indianapolis, IN; died May 17, 2011, San Diego, CA; married Virginia Mae Griffin; married Erla Darling Robinson; children: Kevin L, Gail D, Janna L, Aaron L (deceased) & Barry C. **Educ:** Univ Ill, Sch Fine & Appl Arts, Champaign, BS & BA, 1952. **Career:** Executive (retired); Naval Ordinance Facil Indianapolis, asst art dir, 1952-57; Indust Arts & Engg Co San Diego, asst dir, 1957-62; Cubic Corp, mgr graphic & promotional arts. **Orgs:** Indus photogr Indus Art & Engg Co San Diego, 1957-62; past secy, Kappa Alpha Psi Champaign, 1949-52; pres, Cubic Mgt Assoc, 1977-79; past pres, San Diego Area Coun, 1980-81. **Honors/Awds:** Numerous 1st through 3rd places art exhibits, 1948-65; Member of the Year, Cubic Mgt Assoc, 1979. **Home Addr:** 5520 Olvera Ave, San Diego, CA 92124, **Home Phone:** (858)277-8879.

## DAVIS, MELVIN LLOYD, SR.

Executive. **Personal:** Born Mar 29, 1917, Richmond, VA; died Feb 20, 2006; son of Adelaide Turner and Thornton F (deceased); married Helen Randolph; children: Melvin Jr, Langston, Adelaide Flamer, Carolyn Harris, Wendell F, Kermit M, Nancy Elam, Anna Hudson, Leon V, Revell R & Deborah N. **Educ:** John Tyer Community Col, attended 1949. **Career:** Thorton F Davis, laborer, 1931-35; Thornton J Davis Jr, painter, 1935-42; USN, painter, 1942-45; Davis & Myers Bldg Co, painter, 1945-60; Melvin L Davis Gen Contractor, owner, 1960-68; Davis Bros Construct Co Inc, pres, 1968-2006. **Orgs:** Sunday Sch Supt, Troop Providence Baptist Church, 1945-50. **Home Addr:** 471 E Ladies Mile Rd, Richmond, VA 23222, **Home Phone:** (804)321-1012.

## DAVIS, PRESTON AUGUSTUS

Administrator, association executive. **Personal:** Born Jan 1, 1925, Norfolk, VA; died Dec 7, 2014; son of Charles Adam Sr and Mattie E Johnson; married Mary Elizabeth Pierson (Deceased); children: Gwendolyn Dyess, Preston A Jr, Karen Heggs & June Kimbrugh; married Helen G. **Educ:** WV State Col, BS, bus admin, 1949; Command & Gen Staff Col, MS, exec mgt, 1965; George Washington Univ, MS, adminr, 1974. **Career:** Executive (retired); Fairmicco Indust, vpres & gen mgr, 1969-70; Morgan State Univ, vpres develop, 1970-71; USDA, sr mgt analyst, 1971-78, spec asst to asst sec adminr, 1978-79, dir small & disadvantaged bus utilization, 1979-87; Grad Sch & N VA Community Col, prof, 1974-94; Davis & Davis Consult Asn, 1989. **Orgs:** Omega Psi Phi Fraternity, 1947; Masonic Lodge, 1949; bd dir & com chmn, Agr Fed Credit Union, 1972-99; Phi Delta Kappa, 1978-92; Kiwanis: gov, 1988-89 (first blacks), int chmn, young c's priority one progs, 1990-93, Kiwanis Int UNICEF, cabinet chmn worldwide serv prog, 1993-95, ambassador worldwide serv proj, 1995-2000, trustee, Kiwanis Found, 1998-2001. **Honors/Awds:** Distinguished Mil Graduate WV State Col, 1949; Outstanding Achievement Award, Salvation Army Wash, DC, 1976; Certificate of Merit for Outstanding Performance, USDA, 1979; NAFEO Distinguished Alumni Award, 1983; Hall of Fame, West VA State Col, 1983; Small Business Administration's Award for Excellence, 1984; Alumnus of the Year, West VA State Col, 1990. **Business Addr:** Chief Executive Officer, Davis & Davis Consultant Associates, 600 6th Pl SW, Washington, DC 20024.

## DAWSON, DR. MARTHA E.

Educator, executive. **Personal:** Born Jan 21, 1924, Richmond, VA; died Jul 18, 2015; daughter of John Eaton (deceased) and Sarah Eaton; children: Greer Dawson Wilson, Martina M & James M. **Educ:** Va State Col, BS, 1943; Ind Univ, MS, 1954, EdD, 1956. **Career:** Educator, provost (retired), executive; Van De Vyer Cath Sch, teacher; Richmond Pub Schs, teacher, supr; Multi-Cult Educ Ctr, dir; Ind Univ, speaker, writer, cons, numerous publs field; Hampton Univ, Dept Elem Educ, chmn, 1960-70, vpres acad affairs, exec leadership summit coordr, Living Hist Res Proj, dir; Va State Univ, Sch Educ, dean, provost & vpres acad affairs, 1993-99, provost emer; 4M Exec Coaching Team Inc, chief exec officer. **Orgs:** Delta Kappa Gamma Hon Soc, 1971; Phi Delta Kappa, 1975; bd visitors, Defense Opportunity Mgt Inst, 1987-90; pres, Ind Univ Sch Educ Alumni Bd, 1989-90; bd visitor, Sch Educ, Ind Univ, 1990-93. **Honors/Awds:** Distinguished Teacher, Hampton Inst, 1967; Cert, Nat Council of Negro Women, 1970; Harbison Distinguished Teacher, finalist Danforth Found, 1970; Outstanding Women of the 70s, 1972; visiting scholar, Southern Univ, 1974; Outstanding Achievement Award in Higher Educ, Zeta Phi Beta Sorority, 1984; Old Masters Honoree, Purdue Univ, 1984; Distinguished Alumni Service Award, Ind Univ, 1980; Brother/Sisterhood Award, Nat Conference Christians & Jews, 1991; President's Citizenship Award, 2001; Delta Sigma Theta Sorority; Peninsula YWCA. **Home Addr:** 13 Howe Rd, Hampton, VA 23669-1012, **Home Phone:** (757)827-5158.

## DAYS, ROSETTA HILL

School administrator. **Personal:** Born Gibsland, LA; married James; children: Yanise & Regiuel. **Educ:** Grambling Col, BS, 1957; Univ Mich, MS, 1965. **Career:** Wilerson's Home srv Inst, home econ lectr, 1957-60; Webster Parish Sch, teacher, 1960-65, counr, 1965-67; Grambling Col, chief counr, 1967, asstprof & acad counr, 1967-70, asst prof & dir, prof Rescue, 1970; La & USCols, grants admin & equal opportunity officer; Grambling St Univ, chmn Coun & Testing Dept, 1972-73, dean & dir, 2001; La Asn Stud AsstProgs, 1974-75. **Orgs:** Bd dir, S W Asn Stud Asst Progs, 1974-75; vice chmn, La State Adv Coun, Ment Health; bd dir, Nat Asn Women Criminal Justice; reg adv coun, Emergency Med Serv Sys; Am Personnl Guid Asn; Asn Counr Ed & Supv; Asn Non-White Counr; Am Col Personnel Asn; La Educ Asn; La Asn Measrement & Eval Guid Admin, Grambling, La; sec-treas League Womn Voters, 1972; chap vp, MentelHealth Asn, 1973-74, pres, 1974-75; Chap pres Delta Sigma Theta Inc, 1971-73; Nat Coun Negro Women; bd dir, Lincoln Sickle Cell Asn, 1974-75; vp, Lincoln Parish Black Elected Coord Comt, 1974-75; Grambling St Univ. **Honors/Awds:** Scroll of Honor Omega Psi Phi Frat, 1973-74; Lewis Temple CME Church Womn's Day Citation, 1972; Alpha Kappa Mu Nat Hon Soc. **Home Addr:** 608 E Grand Ave, Grambling, LA 71245.

## DE RUSSELL, MILICENT

School administrator. **Personal:** Born Jul 10, 1950, Chicago, IL; died Jan 1, 2004?; daughter of Robert Richard and Mildred Iles; married Clifford M; children: Clifford, Corey & Kimberly. **Educ:** Chicago State Univ, BS, educ, 1972; Roosevelt Univ, MA, admin & sup, 1984; Nova Univ, EdD, early mid & childhood, 1989. **Career:** Chicago Bd Educ, teacher, 1972-90, actg asst prin, 1985-86, asst prin, 1990-96, prin, 1996-2004; Kennedy King Col, lectr, 1988-89; Woodlawn Org, consult, 1992; lavizzo elem, prin. **Orgs:** Alumni, Roosevelt Univ, 1984-2004; NAEYC, 1986-89; coord, Parent Vol Prog, 1988-89; secy, Local Sch Coun, 1989-2004; alumni, Nova Univ, 1989-; CAEYC, 1992; Asn Sup & Curric Develop, 1992. **Special Achievements:** Author: Improved Math Skills of Second Grade Students, Resources in Educ, 1988; Increased Home and School Involvement of Parents of Primary Grade Students, 1989. **Home Addr:** 8936 S Leavitt St, Chicago, IL 60643-6426, **Home Phone:** (773)239-3890.

## DEAN, WALTER R., JR.

School administrator. **Personal:** Born Dec 12, 1934, Baltimore, MD; died Sep 18, 2015, Randallstown, MD. **Educ:** Morgan State Col, BA, 1962; Univ Md, MSW, 1969. **Career:** Afro-Am Newspapers Baltimore, reporter, 1962-64; St Club Worker Bur Recreation, 1964-66; Health & Welfare Coun Baltimore, assoc soc res, 1968-69; Legis Dist 41, house rep, 1971-82; Baltimore City Community Col, chairperson, soc & behav sci affairs, coord human serv asst, 1969-2015, asst prof soc & behav sci, 1998-2015. **Home Addr:** PO Box 11967, Baltimore, MD 21207, **Home Phone:** (410)462-7675.

## DEE, RUBY (RUBY ANN WALLACE)

Actor, screenwriter, activist. **Personal:** Born Oct 27, 1922, Cleveland, OH; died Jun 11, 2014, New Rochelle, NY; daughter of Marshall Edward Nathaniel Wallace and Gladys Hightower; married Frankie; married Ossie Davis; children: Nora Day, Guy & Hasna Muhammad. **Educ:** Hunter Col, BA, 1945; Am Negro Theatre, apprentice, 1944. **Career:** Films: That Man of Mine, 1946; What a Guy, 1948; The Fight Never Ends, 1949; Jackie Robinson Story, 1950; The Tall Target, 1951; The St Louis Blues, 1958; Take a Giant Step, 1959; A Raisin in the Sun, 1961; Gone Are the Days, 1963; Uptight, co-producer & writer, 1968; Buck & the Preacher, 1972; Black Girl, 1972; Wattstax, 1973; Do the Right Thing, 1989; Jungle Fever, 1991; Cop & a Half, 1993; Just Cause, 1995; A Simple Wish, 1997; Baby Geniuses, 1999; Baby of the Family, 2002; Naming Number Two, 2006; The Way Back Home, 2006; All About Us, 2007; American Gangster, 2007; Steam, 2007; The Perfect Age of Rock 'n' Roll, 2009; Dream Street, 2010; Red & Blue Marbles, 2011; Video Girl, 2011; Politics of Love, 2011; A Thousand Words, 2012; 1982, 2013. TV series: "The Stand", 1994; "Having Our Say: The Delany Sisters' First 100 Years", 1999; "PassingGlory", 1999; "My One Good Nerve: A Visit With Ruby Dee", 1999; "A Stormin Summer", 2000; "Finding Buck McHenry", 2000; "Taking Back Our Town", 2001; Baby of the Family, 2002; "Their Eyes Were Watching God", 2005; "CSI: Crime SceneInvestigation", 2007; "America", 2009; "Betty and Coretta", 2013. **Orgs:** Nat Asn Advan Colored People; Southern Christian Leadership Conf; Delta Sigma Theta Sorority Inc. **Honors/Awds:** NBR Award, 1961; Obie Award, 1971; Martin Luther King Jr Award, Operation PUSH, 1972; Frederick Douglass Award, NY Urban League, 1970; Drama Desk Award, 1974; Theater Hall of Fame, 1988; Image Award, Nat Asn Advan Colored People, 1989, 1991, 1999, 2008; Literary Guild Award, 1989; Monarch Award, 1990; Crystal Award, 1991; Emmy Award, Best Supporting Actress, Decoration Day, 1991; Silver Circle Award, Acad Tv Arts Sci, 1994; National Medal of Arts, 1995; Muse Award, 1997; Screen Actors Guild Awards, Lifetime Achievement Award, 2001; Kennedy Center Honor, 2004; Lifetime Achievement Freedom Award, Nat Civil Rights Mus, 2006; Jury Award, Atlanta Film Festival, 2006; New Zealand Screen Award, 2006; Westchester County Womens Hall of Fame, 2007; EDA Female Focus Award, Alliance Women Film Journalists, 2007; AAFCA Award, African-Am Film Critics Asn, 2007; Grammy Award, 2007; Screen Actors Guild Award, 2008; Hon Degree, Princeton Univ, 2009. **Special Achievements:** Author: "Take It From the Top; My One Good Nerve"; "Two Ways to Count to Ten"; "Tower to Heaven"; "Glowchild"; co-author: With Ossie & Ruby: "In This Life Together". **Home Addr:** PO Box 1318, New Rochelle, NY 10801. **Business Addr:** Actor, The Artist Agency, 10000 Santa Monica Blvd, Los Angeles, CA 90067.

## DOBBS, MATTIWILDA

Educator, opera singer. **Personal:** Born Jul 11, 1925, Atlanta, GA; died Dec 8, 2015, Atlanta, GA; daughter of John Wesley and Irene; married Luis Rodriguez (deceased); married Bengt Janzon (deceased). **Educ:** Spelman Col, Atlanta, Ga, BA, 1946; Teachers Col, Columbia, MA, 1948; Mme Lotte Leham, New York City, 1950; Mannes Music Col, attended 1949; Berkshire Music Festival, 1949; French Music Pierre Bernac, Paris, France, 1952. **Career:** Opera singer, educator (retired); Appeared Dutch Opera Holland Festival, 1952; numerous recitals Paris, Stockholm, Holland & La Scala, 1953; concerts Scand, Austria, Eng, France, Italy & Belg; Covent Garden, London, command performance, 1954; concert tour, US, 1954; concert tour, Australia, 1955, 1959, 1972; concert tour, Israel, 1957, 1959; concert tour, USSR, 1959; Hamburg State Opera, concert tour, 1961-62; Amoperatic debut, San Francisco Opera, 1955; Metrop Opera debut, 1956; recitals Philadephia, PA, NC, Fla, Al, Ga, La, New York, & Midwest, 1972-75; Univ Tex, performing voice prof, 1973-74; Howard Univ, prof voice; Univ IL Champaign-Urbana, fac mem; Spelman Col, artist-in-residence; released recs, most recent, Arias & Songs, 2000. **Orgs:** Metropolitan Opera Asn, Order N Star Sweden, 1954. **Honors/Awds:** Recipient, second prize, Marian Anderson Award, 1947; John Hay Whitney Fellowship Award, Paris, 1950; first prize, Int Competition Music, Geneva Conservatory Music, 1951; James Weldon Johnson Award Fine Arts, Nat Asn Adv Colored People, 1983; Spelman Col, honorary doctor fine arts degree. **Special Achievements:** Libr Cong, exhibit about career; First African American to sing a romantic lead at the Metropolitan Opera; First African American to sing at La Scalain Milan, Italy; First African American faculty on the faculty of University of Texas. **Home Addr:** 1101 S Arlington Ridge Rd Apt 301, Arlington, VA 22202-1923, **Home Phone:** (703)892-5234.

## DOTSON, BETTY LOU

Management consultant, president (organization). **Personal:** Born Jun 29, 1930, Chicago, IL; died Jun 10, 2013; daughter of Heber T and Christine Price. **Educ:** Ohio Wesleyan Univ, BA, 1950; Lincoln Univ, JD, 1954. **Career:** Dept Urban Renewal, 1963; Cook County Dept Pub Welfare, caseworker-cons, 1964-66; First Nat Bank Chicago, legal serv trust dept, 1966-68; US Dept Agr Food & Nutrit Serv, dir civil rights, 1970-75; Dept Health & Human Serv, Wash, DC, dir off civil rights, 1981-87; BLD & Assoc, pres, currently; Houston Community Col, instr. **Orgs:** From asst dir to dir, Equal Oppty Action, 1975-79; sr staff assoc, Joint Ctr Polit Studies, 1979-80; chief adjudications USDA Equal Oppty Off, 1980-81; bd dir, Nat Capital YWCA, 1981-84; Alpha Kappa Alpha; steeering comm Black Am Nixon/Agnew, 1968; adv bd, Arneson Inst Practical Polit, Ohio Weslegan Univ, 1989-2013; bd trustee, Ohio Wesleyan Univ, Del, trustee, 1994-03. **Honors/Awds:** Administration Assistant Office of President elect Nixon, 1969. **Home Addr:** 5942 S Acres Dr, Houston, TX 77048-1206, **Home Phone:** (713)734-1807. **Business Addr:** President, BLD & Associates, PO Box 331143, Houston, TX 77233-1143, **Business Phone:** (713)734-1807.

## DOVE, DR. PEARLIE C.

Educator. **Personal:** Born Atlanta, GA; died Aug 19, 2015, Atlanta, GA; daughter of Dan Cecile and Lizzie Dyer; married Chaplain Jackson B; children: Carol Ann Kotcha. **Educ:** Clark Col, BA, 1941; Atlanta Univ, MA, 1943; Univ Colo, EdD, 1959. **Career:** Phyllis Wheatley Br, Young Men's Christian Asn, Atlanta, bus & prof secy, 1943-45; Clark Col, dir, stud teaching, 1949-62, chmn, Dept Educ, 1963-85, dist prof, 1975-86; Clark Atlanta Univ, Consol Steering Comt, assoc chair, 1988-89, chair div educ, prof emer, currently; Atlanta Proj, cluster coordr, 1992-96. **Orgs:** Pres, Atlanta Pan-Hellenic Coun, 1960-64; pres, Atlanta Alumni Delta Sigma Theta Sor, 1962-63; nat exe comn, Asn Teacher Educrs, 1970-73; bd dir, Am Asn Col Teacher Educ, 1972-75; elem comn, Southern Asn Col & Schs, 1975-81; pres, Clark Col, Am Assoc Univ Profs, 1978-80, 1983-87; bd dir, Ga Stud Fin Comn, 1981-87; adv coun, Fulton High Sch, Ctr Teaching, 1990-91; bd dir, Helping Teens Succeed Inc, 2000-. **Honors/Awds:** Woman of the Year Education, Iota Phi Lambda Sorority, 1962; Service Award, Atlanta Alumnae, Delta Sigma Theta Sorority, 1963; Chairman's Award, State Comn Life & Hist Black Georgians, 1979; Delta Torch Award, Delta Sigma Theta Sorority Inc, 1989; Distinguished Alumni Achievement

Award, Clark Col, 1989; Included, 1990-91, Calendar Atlanta Black History, Southern Bell: A Bell South Co, 1990-91; lt colonel, Aide De Camp, Govs Staff, 1991; Honorary Rosalynn Carter Fel, Inst Women's Studies, Emory Univ, 1993-95; Local Community Service Award, Spelman Col, 2001; Neighborhood Planning Unit K Legacy Award, 2002. **Home Addr:** 1053 Wash Heights Terr, PO Box 92632, Atlanta, GA 30314, **Home Phone:** (404)522-4445. **Business Addr:** Professor Emeritus, Clark Atlanta University, 223 James P Brawley Dr SW, Atlanta, GA 30314, **Business Phone:** (404)880-8000.

## DOZIER, MORRIS, SR.

Insurance executive, military engineer. **Personal:** Born Nov 30, 1921, Americus, GA; died Jul 24, 2014, Manhattan, NY; son of Charlie and Minnie M; married Mary Lois Strawn; children: Morris Jr & Yolonda Maria. **Educ:** KS State Univ, attended 1963; Brown Mackie Bus Col, 1965; Atlanta Univ, Army/Air Corps Adj Gen Basic Admin Course. **Career:** Military (retired); ins exec; Civilian Conserv Clerk, admin clerk, 1941-42; Aus, sr clerk typist, 1942-44, command sgt maj, 1944-51, mil personnel off, 1951-62; Universal Ins Serv, owner & operator, 1965-80; US Govt Ft Riley, independent contractor, 1967-78; Jct City, comnr; Geary Co, comm, 1973-85. **Orgs:** Pres, PTA Westwood Elem Sch, 1966; vpres, Kawanis S, Jct City, 1970; chmn, Adv Comn Sickle Cell Anemia Educ & Screening Prog; lay leader, Ch Our Savior United Methodist; bd dir, chmn, Geary County Sr Citizens; treas, Hunger Comn, Kans E Conf, United Methodist Ch. **Honors/Awds:** Comm Medal, 1957; 1st Oak Leaf Cluster 1962 US Army; Disting Citizen of the Yr Awd Omega Psi Phi Frat, 1979; Plaque of Recognition for Outstanding Serv of State JTPA Prog Honorable John Carlin Gov State of KS, 1983. **Home Addr:** 1701 W 17th St, Junction City, KS 66441, **Home Phone:** (785)238-3933.

## DRAKES, MURIEL B.

State government official, educator. **Personal:** Born Nov 25, 1935, Bronx, NY; died Nov 12, 2015, Albany, NY; daughter of Alphonso and Frances. **Educ:** Del State Col, BS, 1958; Columbia Teacher Col, MA, 1963. **Career:** NY City Childrens Aid Soc, vis lectr, 1957-60; Farming dale Pub Sch, teacher, 1958-65; Bedford Stuyvesant Comn Corp, dir, educ explt prog, 1965-69; NY Sch Social Res, vis guest speaker, 1968; Comn Corp, assoc dir prog, 1969-72; Dahomey W Africa, vis guest lectr, 1971; Manpower Develop Com Labor Ind Corp, asst vpres, 1972-74; Dept Com & Ind, dep comnr, 1974-75; NY State Lottery Pub Rels, consult, 1976; NY State Off Gen Serv, dir prom & pub affairs, 1976-2015; NY State Environ Conserv, dir EEO, 1987-2015. **Orgs:** Delta Sigma Theta Sor; NEA; vpres, Brooklyn Kings Co Judiciary Sect Comn Bldg; C C Brooklyn Managerial Club; Int Ind Mkt Club; Albany Womens Press Club; pres, Eleanor Roosevelt Educ Action Prog. **Honors/Awds:** Achievement Excellence, Black Photographers Asn, 1974; Outstanding Leadership Civic Asn Jersey City, 1974; Brooklyn Distinguished Coun, Negro Women, 1975; Outstanding effort & Achievement, Inter Ethnic Civic Asn, 1975; Distinguished Citizen Award, Concord Bapt Church; Willoughy Walk Tenants Coun Recipient; Woman of the Year, Albany, YWCA, 1987; Outstanding Leadership, Albany Cap Dist Ethnic Heritage Orgs (28), 1987. **Special Achievements:** Author "1965 Proposal of Bed ford Stuyvesant Comm Corp on the Homework Study Program". **Home Addr:** Oxford Heights Apts Sheffield 7 Johnston Rd, Albany, NY 12203, **Home Phone:** (518)869-7147.

## DULIN, JOSEPH

School administrator. **Personal:** Born Aug 10, 1935, Evansville, IN; died Oct 23, 2014, Ann Arbor, MI; son of Charles and Alberta Cooksey; married Yvonne; children: Tierre Porter, Charles, Joseph II, Doris Fields & Kasner L Will. **Educ:** St Josephs Col, BS, 1957; Ind State Univ, MS, admin, 1963; Eastern Mich Univ; Western Ill Univ. **Career:** St Marys High Sch, W Pt, IA, teacher-coach, 1958-64; St Martin De Porres High Sch, prin, 1967-72; Detroit Pub Schs, teacher, 1964-67; Friends Sch, Detroit, asst headmaster, 1972-73; Neighborhood Serv Orgn, community organizer, 1973-74; Roberto Clemente, Stud Develop Ctr, Ann Arbor Pub Schs, founder, prin, 1974. **Orgs:** Founding Pres, Nat Black Lay Cath Caucus, 1970; United Comm Negro Hist Inc, Educ & Comm Serv, 1971; pres & bd dir, Saturday Acad African Am Studies, 1992; bd mem, Ann Arbor Comm Found, 1993; Founder, NAAPID, 1995-2014; life mem, NABSE; MDABSE; adv bd, Ann Arbor African Am Festival, 1996; vpres, Washte naw Co Comm Ment Health, 1996; vice chairperson, Cope OBrien, 1996-2014; bd trustee, Huron Valley Ambulance; co-chairperson, Ann Arbor Black Adminrs Asn; co-chairperson, Ann Arbor Achievement Initiatives; bd mem, Ann Arbor Hands-Mus; bd mem, Washte naw Housing Alliance. **Honors/Awds:** Hall of Fame, NABSE; Distinguished Achievement Award Parenting, Nat Parent Day Coalition, 1996; UNCF Eugene Powers Comm Service Award, 1993; Distinguished Alumni Merit, St Josephs Col, 1969; Black Lay Catholic Caucus Leadership Award, 1973; Hall of Fame, Nat Alliance Black Sch Educrs, 1997; Alumni Achievement Award, St Joseph Col, 1998; Distinguished Alumni Award, Ind State Univ, 1998; Leadership Award, COPE OBrien Ctr; Appreciation Award, NAAPID Initiative, Washte naw Co Comm Action Bd. **Special Achievements:** First African American Lay Prin Catholic School Nation, 1967, TV & Press appearances, NBC, CBS, ABC & BET, 1995, spec advisor, presidential and AlGore, 2000; Consult Motivational Speaker, 1996. **Home Addr:** 439 Sumark Way, Ann Arbor, MI 48103, **Home Phone:** (313)747-6671.

## EDWARDS, DOROTHY WRIGHT

Educator. **Personal:** Born Jan 13, 1914, Jacksonville, FL; died Sep 14, 2016; daughter of John and Julia Peterson; married Oscar J; children: Oscar J Jr. **Educ:** Fla A&M Univ, BS, phys educ, 1935; NY Univ, MA, guid & coun, 1952. **Career:** Educator (retired); Phys educ instr, 1935-40; BTW, bus instr, 1940; Miami Housing Authority, cashier-booker, 1940-41; Dorsey Jr-Sr High, sec & phys instr, 1941-47, dean girls, 1947-55; Miami Northwestern Sr High Sch, asst prin guid, 1955-71, jr col assistance prog adv; Miami Spgs, asst prin guid, 1970-71; Edward Waters Col, dean women, 1971-72; Proj Upward Bound, counr, 1972-76; Fla Mem Col, counr women, 1976-78. **Orgs:** Bd dir, OIC; bd dir, Dade Mt Zion Fed Credit Union, Am Asn Univ Women, Coun Int Visitors; life mem, Young Women Christian Asn, Alpha Kappa Alpha Sorority; Kappa Delta Pi; 100 Women Fla Mem Col; church clerk, Mt Zion Baptist Church; Docent, Jackson Mem Hosp Alamo; bd dir, Family Health Ctr Inc. **Honors/Awds:** Outstanding Service to Youth Award, Phi Delta Kappa; Star Teacher, Miami NW Sr HS, 1966-67; Certificate of Appreciation, Young Women Christian Asn, 1975; Outstanding Citizen Award, 1984; Outstanding Service Award, Econ Opportunity Family Health Ctr Inc, 1994; Act of Kindness Award, Miami Dade Community Col, 1996; Outstanding Service Award, Commitment & Leadership Educ Excellence, Algonguin Club, 1999; Certificate of Merit, Eta Phi Beta Sorority Inc, 1999; Special Recognition Award, Fla A & M Univ, 2002; Book of Life Certificate of Appreciation by the Black Archives, History & Res Found S Fla, 2002; Sports Hall of Fame, Florida A & M Univ, 2004. **Home Addr:** 3200 NW 49th St, Miami, FL 33142-3332, **Home Phone:** (305)634-0408.

## EDWARDS, GEORGE REGINALD

Executive. **Personal:** Born Feb 1, 1938, New York, NY; died Nov 19, 2015, Derby, CT; son of John and Olga; children: Lisa, Veronica & George Drew. **Educ:** City Col NY, BA, Eng, 1959. **Career:** Brit Airways New York, sales mgr, 1959-63; Pepsi-Cola, Brooklyn, New York, gen sales mgr, 1964-65, gen mgr, 1968-70; Heublein Spirits Div, vpres, group mkt dir, 1974-78; Hartford Grad Ctr, vis prof mkt, 1975-78; Nat Black Network, vpres mkt & sales, pres & chief operating officer, 1983-2015; Venture Mkt Co, Heublein Inc, vpres mkt. **Orgs:** Chmn, Mkt Community, Greater Hartford Arts Coun, 1976-78. **Special Achievements:** An African American owned radio news & feature network. **Home Addr:** 111 Pinebrook Blvd, New Rochelle, NY 10804, **Home Phone:** (914)633-7348.

## EDWARDS, DR. JOHN W., JR.

Educator, physician. **Personal:** Born Apr 9, 1933, Ferndale, MI; died May 31, 2015, Hilton Head Island, SC; son of John W (deceased) and Josephine Wood (deceased); married Ella Marie Law; children: Joella Marie & John W III. **Educ:** Alma Col, attended 1950; Univ Mich, Ann Arbor, BS, 1954; Wayne State Univ, attended 1956; Howard Univ Col Med, MD, 1960. **Career:** Walter Reed Gen Hosp, internship, 1960-61, surg resident, 1962-63, urol resident, 1963-66; Straub Clin Inc, urologist, 1970-74, chief dept surg, 1973; pvt pract urologist, 1974-2015; asst chief dept surg, Queen's Med Ctr, 1977-79; chief dept clin serv, active staff, Kapiolani Women's & C's Med Ctr, 1981-83; active staff, Kuakini Hosp; consult staff, Rehab Hosp Pac; consult urol, Tripler Army Med Ctr; John Burns Sch Med, Univ Hawaii, assoc clin prof, chief surg; Queen's Med Ctr, Honolulu, vpres, med staff servs, 1993-94; Queens Health Sys, Physician Rels, vpres, 1994-96; Diag Lab Servs, actg admin, 1995-96, pres, 1996-2015. **Orgs:** Am Bd Urol; fel Am Col Surgeons; Am Urol Asn, Western Sec Am Urol Asn; Hawaii Urol Asn; Am Med Asn; Honolulu County Med Soc; Hawaii Med Asn; Nat Med Asn; Alpha Phi Alpha; Chi Delta Mu; Waialae Country Club; life mem, Nat Asn Advan Colored People; fel Am Col Surgeons; comnr, chmn, City County Honolulu Liquor Comn, 1987-89; gov Hawaii, Am Col Surgeons, 1987-93; pres, Western Sect Am Urol Asn, 1989-90. **Honors/Awds:** Alpha Omega Alpha Honor Medical Soc, 1959; The Links Inc, Hawaii Chap, Hawaii African Am Humanitarian of the Year, 1991; Howard Gray Award, Urol Sect, Nat Med Asn, 1988; citation, City Honolulu, 1992; Outstanding Physician Award, Queen's Med Ctr, 1992. **Special Achievements:** Co-author: "Anuria Secondary to Bilateral Ureteropelvic Fungus Balls", Urology, 1974; "Representive Causes of Ambiguous Genitalia",Journal of Urology, 1967; "Herpes Zoster with Neurogenic Bladder Dysfunction, "Archives of Dermatology, 1974, Journal of AMA, 1973, 1974; co-author", Anuria Secondary to Bilateral Ureteropelvic Fungus Balls",Urology, Feb, 1980. **Home Addr:** 139 Makaweli St, Honolulu, HI 96825, **Home Phone:** (808)395-1775.

## ELLIS, CALVIN H., III

Educator. **Personal:** Born Jun 9, 1941, Whitesboro, NJ; died Nov 11, 2014, Pomona, NJ. **Educ:** Glassboro St Col, BA, 1970, MA, 1972. **Career:** Atlantic Human Res, training officer, 1968-69; Glassboro State Col, Univ Yr Action, dir, 1969-2014. **Orgs:** Pres & bd trustees, Atlantic Human Res, 1975; Nat Asn Community Develop, 1975; Glassboro St Col Community Human & Res, 1975. **Home Addr:** 103 N Virginia Ave, Atlantic City, NJ 08401-4948, **Home Phone:** (609)348-0877.

## ELLISON, CHESTER LAUGHTON

Lawyer, association executive. **Personal:** Born Jul 2, 1928, Streetman, TX; died Mar 16, 2015, Cincinnati, OH; married Judith K; children: Gregory, Bradford, Jefferson, Jan, Brent & Judy-Lee. **Educ:** Chicago Teachers Col, BEd, 1952; John Marshall Law Sch, JD, 1959. **Career:** Chicago Pub Sch, teacher, 1952-54, 1956-59; pvt pract atty, 1959-2015; 7th Cong Dist Ill, legal counr, 1974-78; Blair & Cole, founding partner, 1974-2015; Asn Trial Lawyers Am, ectr & prof, 1984-98; Chicago Daily Defender, writer, 1984-88. **Orgs:** Ill Supreme Ct Comt Prof Stand, 1977-84; pres, Cook County Bar Asn, 1978; rev bd, Atty Regist & Disciplinary Comn, 1978-84, chmn, 1984-89; bd mgr, Chicago Bar Asn, 1985-87; fel Am Bar Found, 1987; bd dir, Ill Inst Continuing Legal Educ, 1988-91; pres, Chicago Bar Asn, 1989; bd visitors, John Marshall Law Sch, 1993-2015; pres, Ill State Bar Asn, pres, Ill Trial Lawyers Asn; Am Bar Asn, Tort & Ins Pract Sect. **Honors/Awds:** Black Awareness Award, Col St Thomas Min Prog, 1977; Earl H Wright Award, Cook County Bar Asn, 1989; guest speaker, Nat Asn Bar Exec Annual Meeting, 1990; guest instr, Nat Col Advocacy, Advanced Trial Practice, 1991; Earl Burrus Dickerson Award, The Chicago Bar Association, 2009. **Special Achievements:** Author, Chapter 13, "Return of the Verdict," ICCLE Ill Civil Pract Series, 1988, 1992, 1999, 2002; First African American president of the Chicago Bar Association; served on numerous advisory committees for the Illinois Supreme Court and the American Bar Association.

## EURE, DEXTER D., SR.

Executive. **Personal:** Born Nov 20, 1923, Suffolk, VA; died Jul 8, 2015, Boston, MA; son of Luke and Sarah; married Marjorie A; children: Dexter Jr, David & Philip. **Educ:** WVa State Col, BSME, 1946. **Career:** Executive (retired); PRAC Assoc, vpres, 1960-61; Boston Globe, asst circulation mgr, 1963-68, asst ed, 1968-70, dir community rels, 1972-88; Bradlee Div Stop Shop, advert prod mgr. **Orgs:** Boston Globe Found, 1980-90; first act dir, Boston Comm Media Comm; Pub Affairs Coun Greater Boston Chamber Com; former mem, Large United Way MA Bay; Cong Black Caucus Comm Braintrust Comm; adv com, Nat Asn Advan Colored People; panelist Nieman Found, Journalism Harvard Univ, Media Racism. **Honors/Awds:** Distinguished Service Award, Union United Methodist Church, 1984; Presidents Award, 1986; MA Black Legislative Caucus Eight Annual Award, 1986. **Special Achievements:** First undergraduate elected to Omega Psi Phi Fraternity Supreme Council. **Home Addr:** PO Box 459, Sharon, MA 02067-0459.

## EVANS, DR. ARTHUR L.

Educator. **Personal:** Born Jul 26, 1931, Macon, GA; died Jan 5, 2016; married Hattie Fears; children: Ivan Hugh. **Educ:** Morehouse Col, AB, 1953; Columbia Univ, MA, 1957; Univ Miami, PhD, 1972; Union Theol Sem Sch Soc Music. **Career:** Educator (retired); Ballard-Hudson High Sch Macon, band dir, 1953-54; Vohelweh Chapel, Kaiserslautern, Ger, organist & choir dir, 1956; Miami Northwestern Sr High Sch, 1957-69; Miami-Dade Jr Col, prof humanities, 1967-69; Hialeah-Miami Lakes Sr High Sch, chmn, choral dir, 1970-72; Sc State Univ, Bishop Col, Music Dept, prof music & choir dir, 1978-2000; SC State Col, Orangeburg, dir concert choir, Dept visual & performing arts, chmn. **Orgs:** Chmn, Fine Arts Lyceum Comn, 1973; conductor Col Concert Choir, 1974-75; chmn, vice chmn, Col Div SC Music Educrs Asn, 1991; Kappa Delta Phi fraternities; Phi Mu Alpha Sinfonia; Nat Mus Eds Conf; Am Choral Dir Asn; SC Music Ed Asn; Phi Beta Sigma; pres, SC State Am Choral Dirs Asn; chmn, Multi-Cult Comt Southern Div Am Choral Dirs Asn; mem bd dir, SC Philharmonic Orchestra; Am Guild Organists; Am Dirs Asn; organist & choir dir, active mem, treas, St. Paul's Episcopal Church; Am Asn Negro Musicians. **Honors/Awds:** Ed Award, Phi Beta Sigma, 1972; Outstanding Achievement Award, Phi Beta Sigma, 1987; Hall of Fame, Sc Music Educr Asn, 1991. **Home Addr:** 449 Meadowlark Dr, Orangeburg, SC 29118, **Home Phone:** (803)534-3269.

## EVANS, DR. WEBB

Manager, association executive, president (organization). **Personal:** Born Nov 20, 1913, Greensboro, AL; died Feb 23, 2015, Portland, MI; married Cora Golightly. **Educ:** Tenn State Col, attended 1937; Cortez Peters Bus Sch, attended 1943. **Career:** Wells Consumers Coop Inc, mgr, 1945-47; Evans Food Mart Chicago, owner, 1949-74; House Saunders Chicago, mgr, 1974. **Orgs:** Bd dir, Southside Comm Com-Juv Delinq Prev, 1949-65; pres, United Am Progress Asn, 1961; bd dir, Cosmo C C, 1961-65; treas, Forrestville Civic Improve League, 1963-74; trustee, Cathedral Bapt Church, 1964; pres, Layman Dept Prog Bapt State Conv, 1966-68; treas, Fel Bapt Dist Asn, 1971-73; pres, 41st & 42nd Wells St Block Club; Chatham Avalon Pk Community Coun. **Honors/Awds:** Recipient Top Male Volunteer Award, Vol Bur of Met Chicago, 1961; Award Outstanding Serv Civil Rights Movement, Christian Religious Builders, 1964; Civil Progress Award, Inter-Denom Min Civ League IL, 1964; Citizen of Week, WBEE Radio, 1969; Hon Citizen State of TN, Gov Frank Clement, 1966; citation, United Am Prog Asn, 1972. **Home Addr:** 4155 S Wells St, Chicago, IL 60609. **Business Addr:** President, United American Progress Association, 1716 W 79th St, Chicago, IL 60619, **Business Phone:** (773)268-1873.

## FARLEY, WILLIAM HORACE, JR.

Lawyer. **Personal:** Born Feb 20, 1950, Skowhegan, ME; died Apr 22, 2016; son of William H Sr and Laura C; married Gale Foster; children: William Foster & Royal Chase. **Educ:** Yale Univ, BA, 1972; Oxford Univ Eng, MA, 1974; Yale Law Sch JD, 1977. **Career:** McDermott, Will & Emery, atty, 1977-86; City Chicago, First Asst, corp coun, 1987-89; Chicago Transit Authority, gen coun, 1989-92; Jenner & Block, partner, 1992-2000; Atty's Liability Assurance Soc, sr claims atty, 2000-16; Gonzalez Saggio & Harlan LLP, corp coun, atty, Litigation Pract Group, partner, 2006. **Orgs:** Bd mem, Const Rights Found; Pub Interest Law Initiative; Lawyers' Trust Fund ILL; Chicago Bar Asn; Am Bar Asn; Cook County Bar Asn; Markey Inns Ct; trans pres bd, Comt Transit & Inst Transp Law; chmn, Legal Affairs Comt, Am Pub Transit Asn; Affirmative Action Cook County Bd Comnrs; bd dir, Urban Gateways, 2012-; Nat Asn Minority & Women Owned Law Firm; Bus & Prof People. **Honors/Awds:** Rhodes Scholarship, 1972. **Home Addr:** 1023 Oak Pk Ave, Oak Park, IL 60302, **Home Phone:** (708)524-5283.

## FARMER, CLARENCE, SR.

Businessperson, executive. **Personal:** Born Jun 19, 1915, Rochester, PA; died Jan 30, 2014, Wynnefield, PA; son of Francis A and Margaret Artepe; married Marjorie; children: Clarence Jr (deceased) & Franklin. **Educ:** Geneva Col, PA, AB, 1940. **Career:** Philadelphia Police Adv Bd, exec secy, 1965-67; Comn Human Rels, chmn, 1967-82; Comn Human Rels, exec dir & chmn, 1967-82; Self-employed, bus consult, Clarence Farmer & Assocs Inc, pres, owner, 1984-; Stadium Enterprise Inc, pres; Ctr Adult Training, pres; Farmer Commun Inc, pres; First Loan Co & Farmer Press Inc, pres. **Orgs:** Bd, Philadelphia Urban Coalition Inc; bd dir, Wissahick Boys Club; bd dir, Founders Club; Greater Philadelphia Chamber Com; United Fund; Phila Housing Develop Corp; pres, Options Women Inc; Philadelphia Civic Ballet Co; Cape May Tennis Club; St Paul Epis Chap; Nat Asn Advan Colored People; Urban League Phila; Geneva Col Alumni Asn; Alpha Phi Alpha; Benjamin Lodge F & A M; bd trustee, Geneva Col, Beaver Falls, PA; chmn emer, bd dir, Afro-Am Hist & Cult Mus; chmn, Phila Housing Develop Corp; chmn & founder, Greater Philadelphia Enterprise Develop Corp. **Honors/Awds:** N City Congr Award, 1965; Bapt Ministers Conf, 1965; Travelers Club Award, 1967; Gardian Civic Leag Award, 1967; Legion Cornelius, 1967; Distinguished Serv Award, Geneva Col, 1969; Achievement Award, Philadelphia Bar Asn, 1969; Coun of Clergy Award, 1972; 100000 Pennsylvanians Award Community Serv, 1972; Cardinals Comn Human Rel Award, 1972; Distinguished Serv Award, Alpha Phi Alpha, 1971; Richard Allen Award; Mother Bethel Am Chap, 1974; DHL, Tex Col, 1989; Chamber Com Award, 1991. **Home Addr:** 260 S Broad St Suite 901, Philadelphia, PA 19102, **Home Phone:** (215)985-0505. **Business Addr:** Owner, Clarence Farmer Associates Inc, 260 S Broad St Suite 901, Philadelphia, PA 19102-5021, **Business Phone:** (215)985-0505.

## FARR, MELVIN, SR.

Automotive executive, football player, business owner. **Personal:** Born Nov 3, 1944, Beaumont, TX; died Aug 3, 2015, Detroit, MI; son of Miller Sr and Dorthea; married Mae R Forbes; children: Mel Jr, Michael A & Monet A; married Linda Johnson Rice; married Jasmine Rozier. **Educ:** UCLA, 1967; Univ Detroit, BS, polit sci, 1970. **Career:** Football player (retired), entrepreneur; Detroit Lions, prof football player, 1967-73; Mel Farr Ford Inc, co-owner, 1968-75, pres, 1978-2015; Mel Farr Lincoln Mercury, pres, 1986-2015; Mel Farr Imports, pres, 1986-2015; Mel Farr Ford, Ohio, pres, 1991-2015; Mel Farr Ford Grand Blanc, pres, 1993-2015; Mel Farr Lincoln Mercury, Ohio, pres, 1995-2015; Mel Farr Ford-Houston, pres, 1996-2015; Flint, MI 7-Up franchise, co-owner, 1985-87; Farr's football team, owner; Mel Farr Automotive Group, pres. **Orgs:** Co-founder, Minority Ford-Lincoln Mercury Dealers Asn; dir, Nat Asn Minority Auto Dealers; bd mem, Sinai Hosp Health Care Found; bd dir, Better Bus Bur Detroit & SE Mich; Pub Adv Comt Judicial Candidates; life mem, Nat Asn Advan Colored People; bd dir, Metrop Detroit YMCA; Oak Pk, Mich Chamber Com. **Honors/Awds:** NFL Rookie of the Year, 1967; UCLA Athletic Hall of Fame, 1988; Entrepreneur of the Year, Michigan Black MBA Asn, 1992; Meg Mallon Sportsmanship Achievement Award, Mercy High School, 1992; Auto Dealer of the Year, Black Enterprise Magazine, 1992; Executive of the Year, Oakland County, 1993; MVP of the Year. **Special Achievements:** First 100% Black-owned major soft drink franchise. **Home Addr:** 5000 Town Ctr Apt 2803, Southfield, MI 48075-1117.

## FARROW, MAJ. WILLIE LEWIS

Executive, military leader, pilot. **Personal:** Born Nov 26, 1941, Wetumpka, AL; died Feb 28, 2016, Montgomery, AL; married Oneita Boyd; children: Stephen Michael. **Educ:** Knoxville Col, BS, 1965; Central Mich Univ, MA, 1979. **Career:** Military leader, pilot (retired); Dover AFB, squadron training mgr, 1974-75, opers exec officer, 1975-76, aircraft maintainence officer, 1976-77, pilot resource mgr, 1977-79, wing flying training mgr, 1979-81; Budget & Financial Adv, 1981-87; St Jude High Sch, asst prin, 1992-2000; Lt Col, C-5 pilot & air opers staff officer. **Orgs:** Omega Psi Phi Frat; master mason Prince Hall; Sigma Iota Epsilon Hon Mgt Frat; Chi Gamma Iota Hon Mgt Frat. **Honors/Awds:** Recipient, Distinguished Flying Cross USAF, 1967; USAF Air Medal; featured, Ebony Mag, 1979; USAF Meritorious Service Medal; USAF Commendation Medal. **Home Addr:** 128 Saccapatoy Dr, Montgomery, AL 36117, **Home Phone:** (334)277-1680.

## FAUCETT, BARBARA J.

Educator, school administrator, executive director. **Personal:** died Aug 8, 2016, Fox Point, WIdaughter of Wesley Murphy and Reonia Armstead Murphy; married Michael; children: Cynthia Mock & James Mock. **Educ:** Univ Wis, Milwaukee, BS, soc welfare, 1968, MS, 1973. **Career:** School administrator, educator (retired); Univ Wis, Milwaukee, acad adv rels, 1971-72, dir, 1972-76, asst dean ed, 1976-79, dep asst chancellor, 1979-80, dir human resources, sr spec asst chancellor, 1998; Malaika Early Learning Ctr, bd dir, 2009-16. **Orgs:** Nat Forum Black Pub Adminr; TEMPO, 1981-2016; Phi Kappa Phi, 1985-2016; Am Red Cross, Milwaukee; bd, YWCA, Milwaukee; bd mem, Girl Scouts, Milwaukee; Harabee Sch Develop Bd; bd dir, Penfield C's Ctr. **Honors/Awds:** Black Achievement Award, YMCA, 1988; Academic Staff Outstanding Performance Award, Univ Wis, 1989. **Home Addr:** 7837 N Boyd Way, Fox Point, WI 53217, **Home Phone:** (414)351-3592.

## FERGUSON, ROSETTA A.

Manager, government official. **Personal:** Born Jul 1, 1920, Florence, MS; daughter of Gaberil Sexton and Earnie; children: 4. **Educ:** Detroit Inst Tech. **Career:** Mich State Const Conv, 5th Dist, 1961; Mich St House Res, mem 9th Dist, 1965-72, mem 20th dist, 1973-78; Loyalty Invest Community, mgr real estate firm. **Orgs:** Dem State Cent; exec bd & precinct Deleg10 Yrs; rec sect, 13th Cong Dist; Wayne Co Dem Rep Human Rels Coun Civil Rights; Gray Lady Red Cross; PTA; Nat Asn Advan Colroed People; TULC; Women's Pub Affairs Comm1000 Inc; Orgn Youth Civic Eagles; founder & fin, Sec Peoples Community Civil League; Missionary Soc Peoples Bapt Ch; Mich Right Life Community & People Taking Action Against Abortion Community. **Special Achievements:** Featured in Ebony Magazine as one of the Black Women Leaders in State of Michigan, Alpha Kappa Alpha Sorority's Heritage Series No 1, Black Women in Politics, was in Michigan House of Rep, 1970. **Home Addr:** 2676 Arndt, Detroit, MI 48207.

## FIELDING, HERBERT ULYSSES

State government official, funeral director. **Personal:** Born Jul 6, 1923, Charleston, SC; died Aug 10, 2015, Charleston, SC; son of Julius P L and Sadie E Gaillard; married Thelma Erenne Stent; children: Julius PL II, Herbert Stent & Frederick Augustus. **Educ:** WVa State Col, BS, 1948. **Career:** Politics (retired); Fielding Funeral Home Serv, pres, chief exec officer, dir, owner, vpres, currently; SC House Representatives, rep, 1971-74, 1983-84; SC State Senate, Dist 42, sen, 1984, 1985-92. **Orgs:** SC Comt Voc Rehab; Trident Chamber Com; Univ SC Budget Bd; Bd McClennan Banks Hosp; SC Human Affairs Comt; SC Coastal Coun, 1987; chair, Charleston County Sen Deleg, 1989; pres, Robert Gould Shaw Boys Club; bd mem, McClennan Banks Hosp; Trident Coun Alcoholism; Omega Psi Phi Frat; founder & past co chmn, Charleston County Polit Action Comt; Nat Funeral Dir & Morticians Asn Inc; chmn, Sc Senate Deleg, 1989-92; chmn, Sc Legis Black Caucus, 1990-92; Human Resources Comt; Southern Legis Conf; Joint Comt; Calvary Episcopal Church; Sc Human Affairs Comn; Sc Coastal Coun; Sc Comn Voc Rehab; Trident Coun Alcoholism; bd dir, Sea Island Comprehensive Health Care Corp; Univ Sc Budget Bd. **Honors/Awds:** Man of the Year Award, Chas Bus & Prof Mens Asn, 1966; Silver Beaver Award, Boy Scouts Am, 1971; Man of the Year Award, Mu Alpha Chap, 1972; SC Legislative Black Caucus Award, 1975; Harvey Gantt Triumph Award, 1985; Citizens Comt Charleston County Award, 1985; Outstanding Legislator Award, 1987; Royal Arch Masons Award, 1988; SC Farm Cooperatives Award, 1988. **Special Achievements:** First African American legislator elected to the South Carolina House of Representatives. **Home Addr:** PO Box 994, Charleston, SC 29402. **Business Addr:** Owner, Vice President, Fielding Funeral Home, 7173 S Carolina 162, Yonges Island, SC 29449-5603, **Business Phone:** (843)889-9181.

## FIELDS, ALVA DOTSON

School administrator, teacher. **Personal:** Born May 29, 1929, Athens, TN; died Feb 20, 2014, Atlanta, GA; daughter of Walter E Dotson and Estella Vaught; married James Henry III; children: Gordon, James & Sherri L Weathers. **Educ:** Knoxville Col, Tenn, BA, 1958; Univ Tenn, MSW, 1966. **Career:** School administrator (retired); Tenn Dept Human Serv, caseworker & field supv, 1958-68, asst dir, 1968-73, dir, 1973-75; Florence Ala City Sch, sch soc worker, 1976-78; Univ N Ala, instr, 1976-78; Chattanooga State Tech Community Col, dept head, 1978-94, coordr minority affairs, counr. **Orgs:** Title XX Regional Adv Comt, 1979-82; Comn Serv Greater Chattanooga Inc, 1979-82; panelist, Tenn Gov Conf Families, 1980; bd mem, Metro Coun Comn Serv, 1980-91; pres, Tenn Conf Soc Welfare, 1984; vpres, Chatt Links Inc, 1989-91; adv bd, Univ Chattanooga SE Inst Educ Theatre, 1989-2014; pres, Metrop Coun Community Serv, 1991-2014; pres, Chattanooga Links Inc, 1991-2014; curric consult ethnic content, Univ N Ala; bd mem, Chattanooga Area Urban League Inc, Family & C Serv Inc, Presby Homes Chattanooga, VENTURE, Friends Black C; chmn, Consortium Adolescent Pregnancy, Venture Task Force Adolescent Pregnancy; Gov Task Force Healthy C, Infant Mortality Sub-Comt; Tenn Child Welfare Serv Comn; Delta Sigma Theta; Tenn Conf Soc Welfare; Nat Asn Soc Workers. **Honors/Awds:** Nominated Soc Worker of the Year, Muscle Shoals NASW, 1974; Big Brothers-Big Sisters Int, Chattanooga Chap, 1975; Tenn NASW Soc Worker of the Year, 1984; Hall of Fame, Delta Sigma Theta, 1985; Knoxville's Black Achievers, 1986; Outstanding AA Woman of Influence, Girls Club Chattanooga, 1996; Chattanooga Woman Distinction, 1996. **Home Addr:** 1407 Shawhan Terr, Chattanooga, TN 37411-2222, **Home Phone:** (423)622-1565.

## FIGURES, THOMAS H.

Lawyer, chairperson. **Personal:** Born Aug 6, 1944, Mobile, AL; died Jan 22, 2015, Mobile, AL; son of Coleman and Augusta Mitchell; married Janice; children: Nora & Thomas Anthony. **Educ:** Bishop State Jr Col, assoc sci, 1964; Ala State Univ, BS, bus admin, 1966; Ind Univ, MBA, 1968; Univ Ill, JD, 1971. **Career:** Exxon Corp, atty & asst secy, 1971-75; Westchester City, NY, asst dist atty, 1975-76; Mobile Co, AL, asst dist atty, 1976-78; temp probate judge, 1999-2015; Southern Dist AL, asst US atty, 1978-85; Figures, Ludgood & Figures, partner, 1985-88; Thomas H Figures, atty law, 1988-2015; munic judge, 1988; Mobile Co Circuit Ct, referee, 1988-89; State Ala, spec asst atty gen, 1992. **Orgs:** State Bars Ala & NY, Fed Bars; US Supreme Ct; US Ct Appeals; US Dist C; Bar Asns AL State Bar; Nat Bar Asn Mobile Co Ala; vice chmn, Mobile Co Dem Conf, 1976-78, chmn, 1989-2015; Mobile Comm Action Inc, 1976-80; grad, Leadership Mobile, 1978; Nat Asn Advan Colored People; Omega Psi Phi; Nat Asn Bond Attys, 1985-2015; Am Judges Asn, 1995-2015; bd trustees, Ala State Univ, 1998-2015. **Honors/Awds:** Outstanding Young Men Am, 1973; Community Leaders & Noteworthy Am, 1977; Outstanding Community Service Award, 1977; Christian Community Award, 1984; Citizen of the Year, Omega Psi Phi Fraterity, 1990. **Home Addr:** 6120 Palomino Dr N, Mobile, AL 36693, **Home Phone:** (251)666-4927.

## FLINT, MARY FRANCES

Manager. **Personal:** Born Jan 28, 1950, Rustburg, VA; died Jun 4, 2012, Lynchburg, VA; daughter of Cleveland James and Virginia James; married William B; children: JeVonda & RaShonda. **Educ:** Fla A&M Univ, BS, 1974; Xavier Univ, MBA, 1979. **Career:** Am Elec Power Co, acct, 1974-77, supvr, planning & budgeting, 1977-86, admin asst, off pres, 1986-89, customer serv mgr, 1989-93, community serv mgr, 1993-2012; cert pub acct, 1985. **Orgs:** Treas, Power Co Credit Union, rec secy, 1992-2012; Ohio Soc CPA's, 1985-2012; bd trustee, Gahanna Events Inc. **Home Addr:** 1593 Foxhall Rd, Blacklick, OH 43004-9543, **Home Phone:** (614)863-1449.

## FLORES, JOSEPH R.

Artist, educator. **Personal:** Born Oct 22, 1935, New York, NY; died Jan 27, 2014, Dundee, NY; son of Joseph L and Margaret Saunders Gray; children: Sam, Monique, Grace, Joe & Sean. **Career:** Model Cities Prog, Rochester, NY, dir commun, 1968-72; Action Better Community, Rochester, NY, artist, 1972-74; Rochester, NY, artist self-employed, 1974-86; Rochester City Sch Dist, Rochester, NY, instraide, 1986-2014; artist. **Orgs:** Exec Dir, Monroe County. **Honors/Awds:** First place, Mother Earth, Joseph Ave Art Show, 1987; First place, MartinLuther King Jr, Black Am Artists Inc, 1987; Second place, Tired, Letchworth State Park, 1988; First place, Roots & Wings, Waterfront Art Show, 1989; First place, Whole World in His Hands, St John Fisher Col, 1990. **Home Addr:** 67 Rosalind St, Rochester, NY 14619-2121, **Home Phone:** (585)436-4319.

## FLOWERS, RALPH LORENZO

Lawyer. **Personal:** Born Jan 23, 1936, Palatka, FL; died Jan 1, 2014?. **Educ:** Fla A&M Univ, BS, 1957, EdM, 1968, JD, 1968. **Career:** Lincoln Pk Acad, band dir, 1959-65; atty, 1968; Riviera Beach, prosecutor ad litem, 1971-73; City Ft Pierce, judge, prosecutor, 1972-73; Pvt law pract. **Orgs:** Exalted Ruler, Pride St Lucie Lodge IBPOE W, 1970; bd dir & legal adv, Indian Rvr Investment Corp Pioneer Investment Capital Corp; bd dir, Fla Rural Legal Serv; chmn, Judicial Coun Fla Chap Nat Bar Asn; Alpha Phi Alpha; Am Bar Asn; Fla Asn Trial Lawyers. **Honors/Awds:** St Lucie County C C Flowers for the Living Award, Radio Station WIRA, 1973; Public Safety Award, St Lucie County Safety Coun, 1974; Alpha Phi Alpha Man of the Year, 1976. **Home Addr:** 5104 San Diego Ave, Ft Pierce, FL 34946.

## FORD, AILEEN W.

School administrator. **Personal:** Born Apr 28, 1934, Shelby, NC; died Feb 26, 2016, Shelby, NC; daughter of John Watson and Rosa Watson; married Charles; children: Valerie Journeane & Regina Antoinette. **Educ:** Fayetteville State Univ, BS, 1954; Howard Univ, Western Carolina Univ, Appalachian Univ; Univ NC, Charlotte, MA, 1978, CAS, 1982. **Career:** School administrator (retired); Shelby City Sch, Shelby, NC, teacher, 1954-80, elem prin, 1980-89, dir testing & chap I, supvr, 1989-96; Shelby City Coun, Ward six. **Orgs:** Pres, local chap NCAE; dist dir, NCAE; dist pres, NC All City Times; pres, Gastonia Chap Delta; organizer & sec Cleveland Co Civic League; YMCA; Girl Scouts; youth adv ch; Delta Sigma Theta Sorority; NC Asn Educ; NC Asn Classroom Teacher; Nat Educ Asn; Am Asn Univ Women; Int Reading Asn; bd dir, Cleveland Co Orgn Drug Abuse Prev, 1974; bd dir, Cleveland Co Comn Concert Asn; Shelby Human Rels Coun; pres, PTA Shelby Jr HS, 1974; treas, Shelby Negro Woman's Club; pres, Audacian Club, 1974; Nat Advan Asn Colored People; Nat Coun Negro Women; Sunday sch tchr, Mt Calvary Bapt Ch; pres, Shelby Alumnae Chap; Delta Sigma Theta Soroity, Inc; pres, NC Fed Negro Women Inc; Shelby City Coun. **Honors/Awds:** Citizen of the Year, 1984; Elected Official Award, 1987; Outstanding Service Award, 1989; Woman of the Year, 1998. **Home Addr:** 1316 Frederick St, Shelby, NC 28150-3506, **Home Phone:** (704)482-9541.

## FOSTER, IVADALE MARIE FOULKS

Government official, association executive. **Personal:** Born Mar 30, 1922, Sidney, IL; died Nov 13, 2015; daughter of Warren T and Edwarda C Martin; married Wardell; children: Wardella Marie Rouse & Christina Jo. **Educ:** Danville Area Community Col, BS, elem educ, 1966. **Career:** Laura Lee Fel House, jr activ super, 1958-66; City Danville, Recreation Dept, Lincoln Pk, recreation dir, 1968-73; Vermilion County, Health Dept, homemaker/home health aide, 1970-73; Sch Dist 118, teachers aide, 1973-74; Herb Crawford Multi Agency Inc, sr citizens dir & asst dir, 1974-78; E Cent Ill Area Aging, trainee, 1976-77; Vermilion County, bd mem dist 8, 1980-89, chmn, 1988-91; E Cent Ill Area Agency, sr citizen employ specialist, 1981-82; Vermilion County, Health & Educ Chaplain Comn, bd chair, 1994-2015, Pct 26 Comn Woman, 1996, dist 8 bd rep, currently; Health Dept, bd rep, 1996. **Orgs:** Pres, secy, Bradley-Maberry Am Legion Auxiliary 736, 1962-2015; pres, Vermilion County Coun Am Legion Auxiliary, 1972-90; secy, bd mem, Pioneer Ctr Substance Abuse, 1973-2015; secy, Neighborhood House Inc, 1975-2015; precinctcomt woman, Precinct 26, 1978-2015; pres, Sr Citizens Adv Group, Neighborhood House Inc, 1980-90; bd rep, Vermelion County, E Cent Ill, Area Agency Aging, 1988-94; bd rep, Vermilion County Health Dept Bd, 1991-94; chaplain, Vermilion County Bd; Union Missionary Baptist Church; chairwoman, Health & Educ Comt. **Honors/Awds:** Most Outstanding Church Pianist, Faithful Worker & Pianist, 30 Yrs Allen Chapel AME Church, Union Missionary Baptist Church, 1976 & 1984; Hon Banquet, Letter Writers Ed Page Ed, Danville Com News, 1979 & 1980; Outstanding Community Contrib, Danville Br, Nat Asn Advan Colored People, 1981; Athena Award, Women Distinction, Girl Scouts Am, 2002; Hall of Fame, Danville High Sch, 2002; 21st Century Award. **Special Achievements:** One of 3 of Danville's Outstanding Women nominated by readers & sel by comm of Danville Commercial News 1964; First Black woman elected to serve on the Vermilion Co Bd, 1980; 10 Most Outstanding Leaders Danville, Danville Com News Ser & Pictures, 1981. **Home Addr:** 516 Anderson St, Danville, IL 61832-4804, **Home Phone:** (217)442-7872.

## FOSTER, REV. JAMES HADLEI

Educator, clergy. **Personal:** Born Apr 29, 1938, Valdosta, GA; died Mar 27, 2015, Williamsport, MD; son of Arthur Sr and Willie Mae Wright; married Delores Jackson; children: Mark Darnell & Arthur. **Educ:** Morris Brown Col, BA, 1960; Pittsburgh Theol Sem, attended 1970; Union Col, LHD, 1971; United Theol Sem, Dayton, Ohio, MDiv, 1973; Vanderbilt Univ, Nashville, Tenn, DMin, 1981. **Career:** Mass Coun Churches, Boston, Mass, dept pastoral serv, 1962-63; Albany State Col, Albany GA, dean chapel & instr, 1962-66; Alcorn State Univ, Lorman, Miss, chaplain & asst prof, 1966-68; Christian Assoc Metro Erie, Erie, Pa, assoc dir, 1970-73; Wilberforce Univ, Wilberforce, Ohio, chaplain & assoc prof, 1973-80; Dartmouth Col, Hanover, NH, assoc chaplain & lectr, 1980-84; A Better Chance, Boston, Mass, Northern New Eng regional dir, 1980-82; Mercy Col, Dobbs Ferry, NY, prof relig, 1984-2015; St Marks AME Church, E Orange, NJ, assoc pastor, 1985; Tudor Gothic church, pastor; Antioch Church Christ, pastor; Quinn Chapel AME Church, pastor. **Orgs:** Optimist Club, 1975-2015; Community Rels Comn, NJ Coun Churches, 1985-88;

Spec Task Force, E Orange Bd Educ, 1985-86; pres, Jersey Chap, Morris Brown Col Alumni Asn, 1988-2015. **Home Addr:** 89 Hawthorne Ave, East Orange, NJ 07018, **Home Phone:** (973)678-3431.

### FOSTER, DR. ROSEBUD LIGHTBOURN

School administrator, educator. **Personal:** Born Nov 13, 1934, Miami, FL; died Jul 20, 2014, Miami, FL; daughter of Carol Allenmore and Dorothy Bernell; married Harris E; children: Harris Emilio II, Sheila Rosebud, Byron Edward & Lorna Lightbourn. **Educ:** Fisk Univ, attended 1953; Meharry Med Col, Nashville, BS, nursing, 1956; Wayne State Univ, MS, nursing ed, 1960; Univ Miami, EdD, higher educ admin, 1976; Bryn Mawr Col, cert post grad Residency Inst, 1981. **Career:** Detroit Gen Hosp, head nurse, 1956-58, 1969-72; Henry Ford Hosp Sch Nursing, Detroit, instr, 1960-62; Holy Cross Hosp, asst admin, 1960-72; Providence Hosp, Southfield, Mich, asst dir, 1962-65; Kirkwood Gen Hosp, dir nursing, 1967-69; Olivia & Bancroft Extended Care Facil, consult, 1969-72; Univ Miami, prof nursing, 1972-73; Sch Health & Social Serv, assoc dean, 1973-77, dean, 1977-78; Fla Int Univ, vice provost Bay Vista Campus, prof, health serv admin, 1978-90, prof nursing, 1982-2014, proj dir, area health educ ctr, 1990-2014; Nova S eastern Univ, Col Osteop Med, prof pub health, 2001-14, from spec asst to chancellor, asst dir, prof, Doctor Osteop Med. **Orgs:** Bd mem, exec bd secy, Fair Havens Nursing & Retirement Ctr, 1974; bd mem & exec bd officer, Health Systs Agency Southern Fla, 1976; Am Pub Health Asn, 1976; Pub Health Trust Dade City Citizens Adv Coun, 1977; Health Educ & Qual Life Comn N Miami, 1980; bd dir mem, Young Men's Christian Asn Greater Miami; bd mem, New Horizons Community Ment Health Ctr, 1981; Mayor's Econ Task Force N Miami, 1981; bd dir, Ruth Foreman Theatre, 1981; bd dir, N Dade Chamber Com, 1982; N Miami Chamber Com, 1982; chair person, Delta Sigma Theta Task Force Econ Develop Bulk Community, 1983; adv bd mem, Health Planning Coun Dade & Monroe Counties, 1983; dir, Cult Fest, 1983; Art Music, Drama N D Proj, 1983; bd mem, Concerned Citizens NE DadeInc, 1983; Am Pub Health Asn, 1983; adv coun, Delta Int; AfricanDiaspora; Nat Planning Comt & Adv Coun, 1984; Metro Dade County Coun Arts& Sci, 1984; bd dir, United Home Care Serv; vpres, AllianceAging, Area Agency on AgingDade & Monroe Counties, 1990-2014. **Honors/Awds:** JC Holman Microbiology Award, Meharry Med Col Sch Nursing, 1955; Recognition of Outstanding Service Certificate, Meharry Med Col; President Award, 25 Years, Outstanding Service to Mankind, 1956-81; Outstanding Nurse Alumni Award, Col Med Dent Nursing, Meharry Col, 1972; Certificate of Appreciation, Health Syst Agency S Fla, 1979; Certificate of Appreciation, Am Hosp Miami Inc, 1980; Certificate of Appreciation, Lutheran Service for the Elderly, 1982; Outstanding Professional Achievement Award, Miami Alumnae Chap, Delta Sigma Theta, 1983; Person of the Year Award, N Miami Chamber Com, 1984; Public Service Award, Outstanding Professional Achievement; Outstanding Women 12 honors, 1986; Miami Ballet Soc; Am Coun Educ; Outstanding Person for Quarter, North Dade Chamber Com, 1987; Lifetime Achievement Award, AXA Advisors, 2001; Sherman Winn "I Care" Award, 2004. **Home Addr:** 11041 SW 128th Ave, Miami, FL 33186, **Home Phone:** (305)387-1118.

### FOSTER, WILLIAM K., SR.

Salesperson, executive. **Personal:** Born Jun 10, 1933, Pittsburgh, PA; died Jan 20, 2015, Douglasville, GA; married Dolores J Porter; children: Kimberly Anne & William K. **Educ:** Duquesne Univ, Pittsburgh, BA, 1963; Univ Wis-Madison, Grad Sch Banking, 1977, Post Grad Sch Banking, 1978. **Career:** Nat Biscuit Co, sales rep, 1963-67; Pittsburgh Nat Bank, com banking officer, 1967-77; New & World Nat Bank, pres & chief exec officer, 1977-79; Franklin Fed Savings & Loan Asn, vpres, 1979-, community reinvestment officer. **Orgs:** Treas, Home wood-Brushton Med Ctr, 1975-76; bd mem, Governor's Coun Small Bus, 1977; treas, Prog Aide Citizens Enterprise, 1978-2015. **Honors/Awds:** Athlete of the Year, Pittsburgh Optimist Club, 1948; airman of the month, USAF, 1955; good conduct National Service, USAF, 1956. **Home Addr:** 423 Graham St, Pittsburgh, PA 15206, **Home Phone:** (412)441-1923.

### FRANCE, DOUG. See FRANCE, FREDERICK DOUG, JR.

### FRANCE, FREDERICK DOUG, JR. (DOUG FRANCE)

Financial manager, football player, executive. **Personal:** Born Apr 26, 1953, Dayton, OH; died Apr 8, 2016, Las Vegas, NV; son of Fred Sr and Waldine M Sr; married Lawrene Susan Hind; children: Kristin Renee, Jason Kenneth & Kari Lynn. **Educ:** Ohio State Univ, elem educ, 1975. **Career:** Football player (retired), actor; Film: Rose Bowl, 1973; Super Bowl XIV, 1980; Prof football player, Los Angeles Rams, 1975-82; Houston Oilers, 1983; real estate agt; A Plus Off Prod, pres; La Qunita high sch offensive line coach. TV Series: "North Dallas Forty", 1979; "BJ and the Bear", 1981; "The Misadventures of Sheriff Lobo", 1981; "The Greatest American Hero", 1982; "Riptide", 1984. **Orgs:** Marathon runner; Stain Glass Artist. **Honors/Awds:** Hon mention All-Am Tight End Time Mag; 2nd team NEA; 1st team All-Bag TenAP; NFC Championship Game, 1975-76, 1978-79; Pro Bowl, 1977-78; SportingNews NFC All-Stars, 1978; Superbowl XIV, 1980. **Home Addr:** 10939 Spyglass Dr, Rancho Cucamonga, CA 91730, **Home Phone:** (714)837-5070.

### FRANCIS, HENRY MINTON

Consultant. **Personal:** Born Dec 23, 1922, Washington, DC; died Jul 7, 2014, Washington, DC; son of John Richard Jr and Alice King Wormley; married Doris Elizabeth Hall; children: Marsha, Henry, Peter, M Kim Ferris & John. **Educ:** Univ Pa, 1941; US Mil Acad West Point, BS, Eng, 1944; Syracuse Univ, MBA, hons, 1960. **Career:** Dept Housing & Urban Develop, 1965-67, exec asst to first secy, Off Postmaster Gen, Off Planning & Syst Anal, dep plans, Richmond Orgn, 1967-70, exec vpres; AVCO Corp, Printing & Publ, vpres, 1970-73; Dept Defense, dep asst secy, Defense Human Goals Prog, 1973-77; Howard Univ, 1979-81; Univ Planning Dir, Univ-Wide Self-Study Task Force, exec dir, Presidential Search Comt, exec secy, 1981-89, spec asst to pres, Govt Affairs Dir; Secy Army, civilian aide, 1984-92; Black Revolutionary War Patriots Found, pres, 1992-96; Howard Univ, dir univ res & planning; Francis & Francis Inc, pres & chief exec officer, currently. **Orgs:** Vol, Cath Charities, Archdiocese Wash; dir, Share; dir, Christ Child Soc; life mem, Disabled Am Veterans; Veterans Foreign Wars; Asn Grad US Mil Acad, trustee emer; Wash Inst Foreign Affairs; bd mgrs, Wash Hist Soc; dir, USO-Metro in Wash; Nat Press Club; Army & Navy Club Wash. **Honors/Awds:** Distinguished Civilian Service Medal, Dept Defense; Cert Appreciation Patriotic Civilian Service, Dept Army; Cert Appreciation, Urban League; Cert Appreciation, Distinguished Service Award, NAACP; Cert Appreciation, LDF; Beta Gamma Sigma; Knight Soverign Military Order Malta, 1996. **Home Addr:** 1800 Sudbury Rd NW, Washington, DC 20012-2227, **Home Phone:** (202)723-1842.

### FRANKLIN, WILLIAM B.

Consultant. **Personal:** Born May 2, 1948, Brooklyn, NY; died Jan 21, 2016, Birmingham, AL; married Barbara J Burton; children: Gerald R & Alyce M. **Educ:** NY City Community Col, AAS, acct, 1971. **Career:** Bache & Co Inc, supvr, 1966-71; Daniels & Bell Inc, opers mgr, 1971-75; WB Franklin & Assoc, owner, 1975-80; Davis & Franklin Planning Group, vpres, 1980-83; Franklin Planning Group, pres, 1983-2016. **Orgs:** Nat Asn Advan Colored People, 1975; coun mem, S Belmar, 1982-; Int Assoc Finan Planners, 1982-; bd dir, Monmouth County Black United Fund, 1983; Monmouth Co; Check Mate Inc; Comn Action Agency, 1984; pres, Kiwanis Club Belmar, 1984; arbitrator, New York Stock Exchange, 1988; dir, Japan Am Soc, 2006. **Honors/Awds:** Outstanding President Award, Belmar Kiwanis Club, 1984; Professional Achievement Award, Cent Jersey Club NANB & PW ClubsInc, 1985; Professional Award Bus, Excellence Nat Asn Negro Bus & Prof Women's Club Cent NJ. **Home Addr:** 53 Knollwood Dr, Tinton Falls, NJ 07724-2740, **Home Phone:** (732)219-9112.

### FREISEN, GIL

Association executive, movie producer, founder (originator). **Personal:** Born Mar 19, 1937, Pasadena, CA; died Dec 13, 2012, Brentwood, CA. **Career:** Kapp Rec, pres; A&M Rec, pres; Classic Sports, founding partner; Digital Entertainment Network, dir; Painted Turtle, co-founder, currently; Films: Love It or Leave It, 1971; The Breakfast Club, 1985; Better Off Dead, 1985; One Crazy Summer, 1986; The Beast of War, 1988; Worth Winning, 1989; Blaze, 1989; Crooked Hearts, 1991. **Orgs:** Pres, Mus Contemp Art; adv bd, Akamai. **Business Addr:** Co-Founder, The Painted Turtle, 1300 4th St Suite 300, Santa Monica, CA 90401, **Business Phone:** (310)451-1353.

### GALVIN, DR. EMMA CORINNE BROWN

Educator. **Personal:** Born May 2, 1909, Richmond, VA; died Jan 1, 1988, Ithaca, NY; married Alx MD. **Educ:** Shaw Univ, BA, 1929; Univ Pa, MA, 1931; Cornell Univ, PhD, 1943. **Career:** Educator (retired); Ithaca Col, prof; Ithaca Sch Dist, acad counsult; S side Ctr, teacher; Tompkins Co Med Aux, lectr, writer, pres. **Orgs:** Nat Comt Am Asn Univ Women; pres, Pi Lambda Theta & Phi Gamma Delta; Alpha Kappa Alpha; Citizens Adv Comn Environ Qual, State NY; del Nat Conv League Women Voters; chairperson, Tompkins County Comm Chirst; pres, Ithaca PTA; Ithaca B & P W Club; bd chmn & bd trustees, Ithaca's Southside Community Ctr; organizer, Ithaca Women's Comm Bldg; First Baptist Church. **Honors/Awds:** Women of the Year, Shaw Univ, 1924; Women of the Year, Ithca B & PW, 1959; Community Service Award, Black Mem of Ithaca, 1974; achievement comm for a better Am black pub Eisenhower Admin.

### GARNER, JOHN W.

Executive, manager. **Personal:** Born Dec 29, 1924, Franklin, TN; died Oct 9, 2015, Saint Paul, MN; married Leslie Olga Abernathy; children: Reginald J & Paul L. **Educ:** Fisk Univ, BA, chem, 1950, MS, 1952; Ill Inst Tech, MS, phys chem, 1955; Univ Minn, MS. **Career:** Manager (retired); Percy L Julian Labs, chemist, 1952-53; Ill Inst Tech Res Inst, res chemist, 1954-66; 3M Co Dent Prod Lab, sr res chemist, 1966-70; 3M Co Med Prods Div, sr clin res coordr, 1974-75, acad & prof rel mgr; 3M Health Care Group, acad rels mgr, 1976-85; Riker Labs Int & 3M Co, mgr licensing adm, 1985-89. **Orgs:** Bd dir, Big Bros Sis Greater St Paul, 1972-87; life mem, Alpha Phi Alpha Fraternity, 1976-2015; bd trustee, Fisk Univ, 1977-89; human rel adv comt, 3m Co, 1978-86; adv bd, Biomed Eng Dept Tulane Univ, 1979-2015; Omicron Boule Sigma Pi Phi Fraternity Inc, 1979-2015; Minn Metro Golf League, 1980; Am Chem Soc, AAMI Nat Tech Asn, 1985; vpres, Sterling Club, 1985; bd dir, City Walk Condo Assoc, 1985-87; Nat Org Black Chemist & Chem Engrs; Urban League; Nat Asn Advan Colored People. **Honors/Awds:** Christian Father of the Year Award, Trinity United Church, Chicago, IL, 1966; Think Higher Award, 3M Health Care Group, 1972; Nat Life Mem Prog Award, Alpha Phi Alpha Fraternity, 1978; Distiguished Black Col Alumnus Award, Fisk Univ, 1983. **Home Addr:** 66 9th St E Suite 2015, St. Paul, MN 55101-2256, **Home Phone:** (651)224-1499.

### GILLIAM, JAMES H., SR.

Executive, consultant. **Personal:** Born Aug 6, 1920, Baltimore, MD; died Sep 10, 2015, Wilmington, DE; son of James E and Pocahontas; married Louise Hayley; children: James Jr & Patrice G. **Educ:** Morgan State Univ, BA, sociol, 1948; Howard Univ Sch Social Work, MSW, 1950; Yale Univ Summer Sch Alcohol Studies. **Career:** Director (retired); Greater Wilmington Dev Coun Inc, dir neighborhood & housing serv, 1965-67; Greater Wilmington Housing Corp, chmn, pres, 1967-70, founder, first exec dir; Leon N Weiner & Assoc Inc, vpres, 1970-71; Family Ct State Del, admin & dir treat servs, 1971-72, vpres, 1972-74; Del Community Housing Inc, pres, chmn, 1974-90; Wesley Col, trustee; mgt consult. **Orgs:** Dir, Med Ctr Del; bd parole, Del State; Nat Asn Advan Colored People; Sigma Pi Phi Fraternity; exec comn, Grand Opera House, Del; chmn, Metro Wilm Urban League; Kappa Alpha Psi Fraternity; pres, trustee, Nat Asn Housing Orgn; trustee, Wesley Col; dir, Nat Tuberc Asn; dir, New Castle County, chmn, currently; Del Adv Comt, US Comn Civil Rights; Judicial Eval Comt; Supreme Ct Del's Prof Responsibility Comt; Magistrate's Steering Comt; trustee, Nat Urban League; founder, Metro-Wilmington Urban League; mem bd gov, United Way Del; pres, Nat Asn Non-Profit Housing Orgn; spokesperson, Del Cancer Soc. **Honors/Awds:** Alumni Award, Howard Univ Sch Soc Work, 1952; Social Worker of the Year, Nat Asn Social Workers Del Chap, 1969; Distinguished Delawarean Award, 1982; NAHRON Ambassador Award, 1985; Regional Ambassador Award, MARC/NAHRO, 1985; BPA Achievers Award, 1985; State Ambassador Award, Del NAHRO, 1985; Conf Christian & Jews-Del Region Wallace M Johnson Award, 1986; Hon Doctorate, Bus Admin Goldey Beacom Col, 1989; Community Service Award, Kiwanis Club, Wilmington, Del, 1990; J. Caleb Boggs Commission Service Award, Order First State, 1990; Brotherhood Award, 1992; Josiah Marvel Cup Award, Del State Chamber of Com, 1994; Liberty Bell Award, 1997; Hon Doctorate, Univ Del, 1999; Hon Doctorate, Del State Univ; James H Gilliam Community Services Building, New Castle County, named in honor. **Home Addr:** 900 N Broom St Apt 35, Wilmington, DE 19806-4545, **Home Phone:** (302)656-1066. **Business Addr:** Chairman, New Castle County, 77 Reads Way, New Castle, DE 19720-1648, **Business Phone:** (302)395-5613.

### GODETTE, FRANKLIN DELANO ROOSEVELT

Lawyer. **Personal:** Born Nov 3, 1932, Harlowe, NC; died Feb 23, 2015, Hampton, VA; son of Henderson and Lucinda; married Eunice; children: Flondezia, Arturo & Felicia. **Educ:** Howard Univ, BA, 1955, JD, 1958. **Career:** Atty, 1958-2015. **Orgs:** NC State Bar, 1958. **Honors/Awds:** Certificateof Appreciation assoc ed, Howard Univ Law Sch, 1958; Certificate of Outstanding Accomplishments Criminal Justice Syst, Ebenezer Presby Church, 1984. **Special Achievements:** Published articles as assoc editor, Howard Law Journal, 1957-58. **Home Addr:** 1140 Adams Creek Rd, Havelock, NC 28532-9120, **Home Phone:** (252)447-1459.

### GOLDEN, ARTHUR IVANHOE

Lawyer, insurance executive, clergy. **Personal:** Born Jan 14, 1926, New York, NY; died Aug 30, 2015; married Thelma O Eastmond (deceased); children: Thelma Ann & Arthur E. **Educ:** NY Univ, BS, 1959; Brooklyn Law Sch, JD, 1973. **Career:** Golden & Golden Ins, pres, 1957-2015; Dept Social Serv, Harlem, 1960-63; Dept Licensing, NY, 1963-66; Jackson High Sch, instr, 1966-69; Mayor's Off Develop, proj dir, 1969-70; Harlem Br New York County Dist Atty's Off, mem legal staff, 1973-2015; First Presbytarian Church in Jamaica, NY, lay pastor. **Orgs:** Pres, United Ins Brokers Asn; Moot court hon soc Brooklyn Law Sch; Iota Nu Sigma ins hon soc NYU; Neighborhood Sponsor Queens DA Comn Crime Prev Bur; Black Am Law Students Asn; Mayor's High Sch Career Guid Conf, 1966-72; mem adv coun, SBA; One Hundred Black Men; pres, bd dir, Prof Ins Agents NY State; vpres, bd dir, Coun Ins Brokers Greater NY; state app pub mem, gov comt; Automobile Underwriting Asn; chmn, Anti-Arson Comt; chmn, Property Mgt Div, Presby NY; ruling elder, First Presby Church Jamaica, clerk session; Producer Liaison Comt, Ins Serv Off. **Honors/Awds:** Distinguished Serv & Lifetime achievement, CIBGNY, 1996; Brooklyn Law Sch, 50 yr alumni, 1999. **Home Addr:** , Jamaica, NY.

### GOUGH, DR. WALTER C.

Physician, administrator. **Personal:** Born Apr 24, 1943, Pittsburgh, PA; died Feb 16, 2016, Mound Bayou, MS; son of Walter C Sr and Kathryn Scott Grinage; married May Ella Bailey; children: Wanda, Marcus, Henry, Lynette, Kathryn & Nora. **Educ:** Tarkio Col, AB, 1965; Meharry Med Col, MD, 1970. **Career:** UPMC Mercy, intenship; Taboman Hosp, dir, 1972-75; Black Belt Family Health Ctr, med dir, 1973; Mound Bayou, Miss, med dir, 1974-2016; Delta Comm Hosp & Health Ctr, physician, 1974-2016; Choctaw Indian Hosp, med dir, 1976-78; Nat Health Serv, med dir, 1978-81; Spectrum ER Care, dir, 1981-84; Gough's Family & Pediats Clin, owner, 1984-2016; N Sunflower Med Ctr. **Orgs:** Allegheny County Med Co, 1971-72; AMA; NMA, 1973-74; Omega Psi Phi, 1967-2016; Miss Heart Asn, 1974; bd trustee, Delta Health Ctr, 1986-89; WQSZ, 1989-2016; pres, ACEP, Miss Chap, 1999; Miss State Bd Health, 2000-16. **Honors/Awds:** Bronze Medal Tarkio Col, 1965; Best Scientific Article, Meharry Col, 1966; Stud Christian Med Soc, 1967; Jaycee's Man of the Year, 1970; Man of the Year Award, Pittsburgh Jaycees, 1972; Outstanding Alumnus 15yrs, Tarkio Col, 1974; Distinguished Alumni, Tarkio Col, 1974; Board Certified, Am Bd Physicians, 1977, 1983, 1989; Bd Certified, Am Bd Emergency Med, 1983, 1989; Man of the Year, Omega Psi Phi, 1986; No 1 Award Iota Omicron Charter, 1986. **Special Achievements:** First African American graduate at Tariko Col; First African-American physician in Sunflower County, MS; First African American physician on the MS State bd of health. **Home Addr:** PO Box 107, Mound Bayou, MS 38762, **Home Phone:** (601)741-2026.

### GRAHAM, PROF. PRECIOUS JEWEL

Lawyer, social worker, educator. **Personal:** Born May 3, 1925, Springfield, OH; died Nov 30, 2015, Yellow Springs, OH; daughter of Robert Lee Freeman and Lulabelle Malone; married Paul Nathaniel; children: Robert & Nathan. **Educ:** Fisk Univ, BA, 1946; Case Western Res Univ, MSSA, 1953; Univ Dayton, JD, 1979. **Career:** Educator (retired); YWCA, prog dir, 1946-53; Antioch, other positions, 1964-69; 1992-94; Antioch Col, prof soc welfare, 1969-92, fac lectr, 1979-80, Inst Human Develop, dir, 1984-89, social welfare & legal studies, emer prof, 1986. **Orgs:** Pres, YWCA USA, 1979-85; pres, Yellow Springs

Community Found, 1980; Am Bar Asn; Ohio bar asn; Acad Cert Social Workers; dir, Yellow Springs Instrument Co, 1981-93; bd dir, Meadville Lombard Theol Sch, 1983-87; pres, World YWCA1987-91; bds, Unitarian Universalist Serv Comt; Vernay Found; Alpha Kappa Alpha sorority; Nat Asn Social Workers. **Honors/Awds:** Social Worker of the Year, Miami Valley NASW, 1975; Greene County Women's Hall Fame Greene City, OH, 1982; Ten Top Women Miami Valley, Dayton Daily News, 1987; Ohio Women's Hall Fame, 1988; J.D. Dawson Award, 2006. **Home Addr:** 1475 Corry St, Yellow Springs, OH 45387, **Home Phone:** (937)767-7612.

### GREEN, DENNIS

Football coach, football player, executive. **Personal:** Born Feb 17, 1949, Harrisburg, PA; died Jul 21, 2016, San Diego, CA; married Margie; children: Patty & Jeremy. **Educ:** Iowa State Univ, BA, finance, 1971. **Career:** Football player (retired), football coach, executive; BC Lions Can Football League, starting tailback; Iowa State, grad asst, 1972, quarterbacks/receivers coach, 1974-76; Dayton, offensive backs/receivers coach, 1973; Stanford Univ, runing back, 1977-78, offensive coord, 1980, football coach, 1989; N Western Univ, head coach, 1981-85; San Francisco 49ers, receivers coach, 1986-88; Stanford Cardinals, head coach, 1989-91; Minn Vikings, head coach, 1992-2001; NFL Competition Comt, chair, 2000; Entertainment & Sports Programming Network, Nat Football League, analyst, 2002; Ariz Cardinals, head coach, 2004-07; Dennis Green Sports Mkt, currently; San Francisco franchise, head coach, 2009; Sacramento Mountain Lions, head coach, 2010-11. **Honors/Awds:** Big 10 Coach of the Year, 1982; NFC Coach of the Year, Col & Pro Football News Weekly, 1992; NFC Coach of the Year, United Press Int, 1992; NFL Coach of the Year, Wash Touchdown Club, 1992; Pop Warner's Golden Football Award, 1993; Professional Coach of the Year, Upper Midwest, Midwest Sports Channel, 1998; Boys and Girls Club Hall of Fame, 1998; Coach of the Year, Sports Illus, 1998; Coach of the Year, Maxwell Club, 1998; Community Coach of the Year, World Sports Humanitarian Hall Fame, 2001. **Special Achievements:** Autobiography: No Room For Crybabies; Season Record ever by an African-American coach in the NFL.

### GREEN, RUTH A.

Administrator. **Personal:** Born Feb 2, 1907, Oklahoma City, OK; died Jan 1, 1995. **Educ:** Langston Univ, BS, 1936. **Career:** Social worker, Probation officer; Step Parent Adoption; Social Serv, dir; Sr Citizens Prev Health Care Serv Elderly Minority, clin adminr. **Orgs:** All prof jobs San Diego Pres Comn Hosp San Diego Aux, 1973-74; Gov Calif Intergovernmental Rels Coun & Calif St Community Aging, 1974-75; Past coun Youth, Free Clinics Vol; bd dir, Pres Nixon to Small Bus Bur San Diego; past reg pres, Calig Probation & Parole Asn; bd supervisors charter, Rev Comt; past pres, Nat Asn Advan Colored People; second vpres, Urban League; past grand sec, Charity; Order Eastern Star; Orgn San Diego Chap; Links Inc; founder, Civic Orgn Women; Housing Adv Bd. **Honors/Awds:** Probation Officer of the Year Award, 1971; Service Awards, Youth Men's Christian Asn, Nat Asn Advan Colored People, Bus & Prof Womens Clubs. **Home Addr:** 5415 Bonita Dr, San Diego, CA 92114.

### GREENE, NELSON E., SR.

Educator, funeral director. **Personal:** Born May 20, 1914, Danville, VA; died Nov 13, 2014, Alexandria, VA; married Gloria Kay; children: Nelson Jr & Terry F. **Educ:** Shaw Univ, AB, 1941; Renourd Sch Embalming, NY, attended 1948. **Career:** Langston High Sch, Danville, teacher, 1941-42; Greene Funeral Home, Alexandria, Va, funeral dir, owner & pres. **Orgs:** Omega Psi Phi Fraternity, 1938-2014; Comnr, Alexandria Redevelop & Housing & Authority, 1966-69; sr warden, Meade Episcopal Church, 1969-72; bd dir, Alexandria Hosp, 1970; Va Bd Funeral Dirs & Embalmers, 1972; Va City Coun, Alexandria, 1979-82; Nat Funeral Dir Asn; bd dir, Va Mortician Asn; Nat Asn Advan Colored People; Urban League, Masons, Elks, Shrine; bd dirs, Alexandria Bd Trade. **Home Addr:** 814 Franklin St, Alexandria, VA 22314-4106, **Home Phone:** (703)549-0090.

### GRIGGS, HARRY KINDELL, SR.

School administrator. **Personal:** Born Mar 26, 1910, Reidsville, NC; died Sep 13, 1995, Reidsville, NC; son of Jessie P and Alica B; married Mary Swan; children: Harry Kindell Jr & Gary Maurice. **Educ:** Shaw Univ, BS, 1934; Univ Mich, MA, 1948, 1952. **Career:** School administrator (retired); Roanoke Inst, teacher, 1934-36; Yanceville Sch, teacher, 1936-40; Riedsville City Elem & High Schs, teacher, 1940-48, high sch prin, 1948-59, sr high sch prin, 1959-74. **Orgs:** Bd dir, United Fund, 1960-70; Reidsville C C, 1968-87; Nat Lib Trustee Asn, 1968-87; NC Pub Lib, trustee, 1968-87; NC Libr Asn, 1983; trustee, County Pub Lib Prin Sect, 1987; Boy Scouts. **Honors/Awds:** The "Education of Blacks From Slavery to Covert Enforced Integration", 1987. **Home Addr:** 1713 Courtland Ave, Reidsville, NC 27320, **Home Phone:** (336)342-7405.

### GROVES, HARRY EDWARD

School administrator, dean (education). **Personal:** Born Sep 4, 1921, Manitou Springs, CO; died Aug 24, 2013, Chapel Hill, NC; son of Harry (deceased) and Dorothy Cave (deceased); married Evelyn Frances Apperson; children: Sheridon Hale. **Educ:** Univ Colo, BA, 1943; Univ Chicago, JD, 1949; Harvard Univ, LLM, 1959. **Career:** School administrator (retired); Tex Southern Univ, dean sch law, 1956-60; Univ Singapore, dean fac law, 1960-64; Univ Malaya, dean, 1962-64; Cent St Univ, pres, 1965-68; Sch Law Cincinnati, prof, 1968-70; NC Cent Univ, Durham, dean sch law, 1976-81; Univ NC, Brandis Prof Law, 1981-86, Henry Brandis Prof Law Emer; Memphis State Univ, Herbert Heff, vis prof law, 1989-90; Univ Minn, vis prof law, 1992; US Olympic Comt, Ethics Comt, chmn, 1993-96. **Orgs:** Elected mem, City Coun, Fayetteville, NC, 1951-52; chmn, Gov's Task Force Secy & Privacy, 1979-; bd dir, Mutual Savings & Loan Asn, 1979-80; pres, NC Prisoner Legal Serv Inc, 1979-81; bd dir, Law Sch Admis Coun, 1980-82; pres, Legal Serv NC, 1983-85; SigmaPi Phi, Alpha Phi Alpha Frat; NC Bar Asn; Tex Bar Asn; Ohio Bar Asn; vpres bd gov, NC Bar Asn, 1986-87; bd dir, Am Bar Found, 1986-90; Am Bar AsnCoun Sec Legal Educ & Admis Bar, 1989-95. **Honors/Awds:** Judge John J Parker Award, North Carolina Bar Association, 1986; Robert L Kutak Award, American Bar Association, 1997. **Special Achievements:** Comparative Constitutional Law Cases & Materials Oceana Publs Inc, 1963; The Constitution of Malaysia, Malaysia Publs Ltd, 1964; pub more than 30 other books & articles; Phi Beta Kappa; Phi Delta Kappa; Kappa Delta Pi; The Constitution of Malaysia, 4th ed (with Sheridan) 1979; Tun Abdul RazakMemorial Lecture, Kuala Lumpur Malaysia 1983; sire archon, Alpha Tau Chapter of Sigma Pi Phi 1986-88; pres, Wake County North Carolina Phi Beta Kappa 1989-90; Malayan Law Journal Ltd. **Home Addr:** 3050 Mil Rd NW Apt 601, Washington, DC 20015.

### GUNTER, LAURIE

Business owner, nurse, educator. **Personal:** Born Mar 5, 1922, Navarro County, TX; died Jun 15, 2015, Seattle, WA; daughter of Lewis Marion Martin and Hollie Myrtle Carruthers; children: Margo Alyce Gunter Toner & Lara Elaine Bonow. **Educ:** Tenn A&I State Univ, Meharry Med Col Sch Nursing, BS, home Sci, 1948; Univ Toronto, cert, nursing educ, 1949; Fisk Univ, MA, 1952; Cath Univ Am, 1956; Univ Cailf, Berkeley, 1959; Univ Chicago, PhD, 1959. **Career:** George W Hubbard Hosp, staff nurse, 1943-44, head nurse, 1945-46, supvr, 1947-48; Meharry Med Col Sch Nursing, asst instr, 1948-50, instr, 1950-55, asst prof, 1955-57, actg dean, 1957-58, dean, 1958-61; Univ Calif, asst prof nursing, Los Angles, 1961-63, assoc prof, 1963-65; Ind Univ Med Ctr, prof nursing, 1965-66; Univ Wash, prof, 1969-71; Pa State Univ, prof & head nursing human develop, 1971-75, interim dept head, 1984-85, prof emer nursing & human develop, 1987-; Allegheny Hosp, prof nursing; Univ Pk, prof nursing; Blue Bell Bed & Breakfast, owner; Hershey Med Ctr, prof nursing; prof emer, currently. **Orgs:** Am Nurses Asn, 1948-; fel Rockefeller Found, 1948-49; Nat League Nursing, 1948-87; Am Asn Univ Profs, 1949-87; Gerontological Soc, 1959-91; res projgrants, 1965-; Am Asn Col Nursing, 1971; Am Pub Health Asn, 1974-87; consult, HRA/Nat Ctr Health Serv Res, 1976-89; reviewer, HEW, 1976-89; steering comt, Pa Nurses Asn; Coun Nurse Res; Am Nurses Asn; ad hoc ed, adv comt, Div Geriatric Nursing Pract, Am Nurses Asn; proj dir, Composite Ed Prog Geriatric Nursing, 1976-77; Am Acad Nursing, 1979-, Inst Med Nat Acad Sci, 1980-; Univ Wash Sch Nursing, dean's vis comt. **Honors/Awds:** Charles Nelson Gold Medal, Meharry Med Col, Sch Nursing, 1943; Foster Memorial Prize, Meharry Med Col, Sch Nursing, 1943; Alpha Kappa Mu Hon Soc, Tenn A&I St Univ, 1948; Rockefeller Found, 1953-55; Training Inst Soc Geront, Univ Calif, 1959; Golden Annual Citation for Special Competence in Nursing, Tenn A&I Univ, 1963; invitee, White House Conf Food Nutrition & Health, 1969; guest lectr, Japanese Nurses First Res Conf, 1971. **Special Achievements:** First African American women to receive a PhD in human development from the University of Chicago, 1959; author and co-author for numerous articles & audio visual productions, 1949-. **Home Addr:** 4008 47th Ave S, Seattle, WA 98118-1218, **Home Phone:** (206)723-4279. **Business Addr:** Professor Emeritus, Pennsylvania State University, 201 Health Human Develop E, University Park, PA 16802, **Business Phone:** (814)863-0245.

### HADLEY, ERMA C JOHNSON. See JOHNSON, ERMA CHANSLER.

### HALEY, GEORGE WILLIFORD BOYCE

Lawyer, ambassador. **Personal:** Born Aug 28, 1925, Henning, TN; died May 13, 2015, Silver Spring, MD; son of Simon and Bertha Palmer; married Doris Elaine Moxley; children: David Barton & Anne Palmer. **Educ:** Morehouse Col, BA, 1949; Univ Ark, JD, 1952. **Career:** Kans City KS, dep city atty, 1954-64; State KS, KS state senate, 1964-68; US Urban Mass Trans Admin, chief coun, 1969-73; Us Info Agency, Equal Employ Opportunity, assoc dir, 1973-76; US Info Agency, gen coun & cong liasion, 1975-76; George W Haley Prof Corp, pres; Postal Rate Comn, chmn, 1990-94, comnr, 1994-97, vice chmn, 1997-; Repub Gambia, ambassador, 1998-2001. **Orgs:** Lay leader, Methodist-KS-MO-CO Conf, 1956-68; pres, Wyandotte Cty Kans Young Republicans, 1959-60; legal advisor, Econ Community W African States, 1978-84; Un Educ, Sci & Cult Orgn monitoring panel US State Dept, 1984; bd dir, Universal Bank, 1985; bd dir, Antioch Sch Law, 1985; US envoy Gambia, 1998; fel Bar Asns Ark, life mem, Nat Asn Advan Colored People; Un Educ, Sci & Cult Orgn. **Honors/Awds:** Comments editor AR Law Review, 1951-52; Outstanding Alumni Award, Univ Ark, 1988; Man of the Year, Morehouse Col, 1991; Honorary chair, 2nd anniv Kunta Kinte Day, Annapolis, MD, 1988. **Special Achievements:** President Clinton named him Ambassador to the Republic of The Gambia in West Africa.

### HAMBRICK, HAROLD E., JR.

Association executive. **Personal:** Born Feb 17, 1943, New Orleans, LA; died Oct 8, 2014, Los Angeles, CA; married Margaret; children: Tyra, Jeffery & Sharon. **Educ:** Pepperdine Univ, BS, bus admin, 1974; Univ Santa Clara, cert, organ mgt, 1980; Univ Calif, Prof Desig, pub rel, 1987. **Career:** IBM Corp, off mgr, Trn, 1966-67; New Communicators Inc, bus mgr, 1967-69; Watts Health Found Inc, sr acct, 1969-75; Nat Asn Tax consult, 1972-2014; Calif Asn Tax consult, 1972-2014; Western Asn Community Health Ctrs Inc, exec dir, vpres, 1974-2014; Black Bus Expo, founder, pres; Los Angeles Black Bus Expo & Trade Show, exec dir, pres. **Orgs:** Nat Notary Asn, 1972-2014; pres, Employees Serv Asn, 1972-74; Am Pub Health Asn, 1973-2014; founding pres, Western Asn Community Health Ctr Inc, 1973-75; bd mem, Watts United Credit Union Inc, 1974-75; Treas Nat Asn Community Health Ctrs Inc, 1974-76; vpres, Hambricks Mort Inc, 1975-2014; Am Soc Asn Exec, 1976-; State Calif, Dept Health Adv Coun; Greater La Press Club; Nat Press Club; Los Angeles World Affairs Coun; chmn & bd dir, Watts United Credit Union; vpres, pres community adv coun, Charles R Drew Univ Med & Sci; pres, Calif Black Health Network Inc; pres, Black Health Leadership Coun, Los Angeles; Latino/Black Roundtable; cur, co-founder, River Rd African-Am Mus & Gallery; Nat Black Bus Coun Inc; FAMLI. **Honors/Awds:** Selected as one of the Young Men of America, 1978. **Home Addr:** 3936 Sutro Ave, Los Angeles, CA 90008.

### HARDIN-DIGGS, MARIE D.

Administrator. **Personal:** died Mar 3, 2007, Columbus, OHdaughter of Harrison Ridley and Emma; married Granville N; children: Oliver Harrison Sr (deceased) & Alyce Cook. **Educ:** Capital Univ, attended 1984; Wayne State Univ; Ind Univ. **Career:** City Columbus, div mgt coordr, 1970-74, dep dir CDA, 1974-76, dir div CDA, 1975-77, equal employ opportunity adminr, 1977-; Ohio Sen, legal secy, 1977-78. **Orgs:** Am Asn Affirmative Action; bd dir, Amethysts; Cent Ohio EEO Coun; Centenary United Methodist Church; Personnel Soc Columbus; Columbus AreaCol Placement Consortium; Cent Ohio Personnel Asn; United Methodist Ministers Wives; Interdenominational Ministers' Wives Asn; Friend Action; Century Found; Nat Asn Advan Colored People; Nat Coun Negro Women; Columbus Urban League; St Paul Methodist Church; co-founder, Ebondy House; Bethune Ctr Gov Bd; Phillis Wheatley Club. **Honors/Awds:** Outstanding Youth Counr of the Year; Exec of the Month, Nat Mgt Inst. **Special Achievements:** Development of an EEO training manual for supervisors & managers in city; First EEO administrator to be appointed to serve directly under the office of the mayor; First chosen to represent the city at World Conference Decade for Women; Instituted the first Women's Week in Government; Outstanding recognition advancing the cause of equality in employ & housing; recognition human rights serv. **Home Addr:** 3833 Dehner Dr, Columbus, KY 43227, **Home Phone:** (614)236-8947. **Business Addr:** Administrator, City of Columbus Ohio, 90 W Broad St, Columbus, OH 43215, **Business Phone:** (614)645-8292.

### HARDISON, RUTH INGE

Administrator, sculptor, photographer. **Personal:** Born Mar 3, 1914, Portsmouth, VA; died Mar 23, 2016, New York, NY; daughter of William Lafayette and Evelyn Jordan; children: Yolande. **Educ:** Tenn State A&I Univ, attended 1935; Art Stud League, attended 1935; Vassar Col, attended 1944. **Career:** Comn Sculptor By Old Taylor Whiskies, "Ingenious Am", 1966; New York City Bd Educ, "New Generation", 1975; New York City Dept Cult Affairs, Jackie Robinson Portrait, 1980; Black Alumni, Princeton Univ, Frederick Douglass Portrait, 1982; creator of on-going portrait series "Negro Giantsin History", began 1963 includes, Harriet Tubman, "The Slave Woman, "Frederick Douglass, Dr WEB DuBois, Dr Mary McLeod Bethune, 1965; Dr Geo Washin Carver, Sojourner Truth, 1968, Dr Martin Luther King Jr, 1968, 1976, Paul Robeson, 1979; Sojourner Truth head, 1976; Sojourner Truth Pin, 1980; Phillis Wheatley, 1989; new series "Our Folks". began in 1985, collectible sculptures of ordinary people doing ordinary things; Portrait of Al Diop, pres, Local 1549 NYC, commissioned by the Women's Comt, on his 20th yr serv; "Mother & Child", 1957, Klingenstein Pavillion, Mt Sinai Hosp; Hardison Works, owner & sculptor, currently. **Orgs:** Founding mem, Harlem Cult Coun, 1964; founding mem, Black Acad Arts & Letters, 1969. **Honors/Awds:** Self Discovery Workshops, Harlem Cult Coun, 1975; Sch C studio visits Cottonwood Found, 1980; Cultural Achievement Award, Riverside Club Nat Bus& Prof Women's Clubs, 1987; exhib of 26 photographs, "Views From Harlem, "Portsmouth Museum, Portsmouth, Va, 1988; Sojourner Truth figure presented by NY Gov, Cuomo to Nelson Mandela, 1990. **Special Achievements:** Included in "Call Them Heroes", a social studies textbook, published by the Board of Education of NY; One Hundred Successful Blacks, Book 2, Ebony Success Libr. **Home Addr:** 444 Cent Pk W Suite 4B, New York, NY 10025, **Home Phone:** (212)865-7371. **Business Addr:** Sculptor, Owner, Hardison Works, 444 Cent Pk W Suite 4B, New York, NY 10025, **Business Phone:** (866)243-7495.

### HARMON, JOHN H.

Lawyer. **Personal:** Born Feb 10, 1942, Windsor, NC; died Oct 30, 2014, New Bern, NC. **Educ:** BA, 1963; BL, 1965. **Career:** US Dept Labor, solictor's off, 1965-66; US House Rep Com Educ & Labor, asst coun, 1966-67; Harmon & Raynor, owner, 1967-2014. **Orgs:** Pres, Craven County Bar Asn, 1985-86; Fed Bar Asn; Craven Co Bar Asn; Nat Conf Black Lawyers; NC Acad Trial Lawyers; Omega Psi Phi Frat; pres, NC Asn Black Lawyers; Nat Asn Advan Colored People; SCLC; Black Prog Businessmen Inc; pres, New Bern Chap NC Cent Univ Alumni Asn. **Honors/Awds:** Merit Award, NC Cent Univ Sch Law, 1974. **Home Addr:** 526 Thurman Rd, New Bern, NC 28560, **Home Phone:** (919)637-6804.

### HARPER, CURTIS

Research scientist, educator. **Personal:** Born May 13, 1937, Auburn, AL; died Nov 19, 2014. **Educ:** Tuskegee Inst, BS, chem, 1959, MS, org chem, 1961; IA State Univ, MS, biochem, 1965; Univ Miss, PhD, biochem, 1969; Postdoctorate, Yale Univ, biochem, 1970. **Career:** Univ NC Sch Med, Res Assoc & Instr, Dent Res Ctr, 1971-72, Dept Biochem & Moleculr Biophys, resrch assoc, 1970-71, instr, 1971-73, Dept Pharamacol, assoc prof, 1976-2014, Adj Asst Prof, 1973-76, prof, prof emer, co dir, dir grad studies; Yale Univ, resch assoc, 1969-70; Nat Inst Environ Health Sci, sr staff fel, 1972-76. **Orgs:** Am Chem Soc; Am Asn Advan Sci; Soc Sigma Xi; Soc Toxicol; Am Soc Pharmacol & Exp Therapeut Human Rel Comn, 1970-74; Drug Act Comt, 1971-73; Interch Coun Soc Act Comt, 1971-74; bd mem, NC Civ Lib Union, 1976-2014; bd mem, Interch Coun Housing Auth, 1977-2014. **Home Addr:** 166 Ridge Trail Village W, Chapel Hill, NC 27516, **Home Phone:** (919)929-2521.

### HARPER, MICHAEL STEVEN
Educator, poet. **Personal:** Born Mar 18, 1938, Brooklyn, NY; died May 7, 2016, Barrington, RI; son of Walter Warren and Katherine Johnson; married Shirley Ann Buffington; children: Roland Warren, Patrice Cuchulain & Rachel Maria. **Educ:** Los Angeles City Col, AA, 1959; Los Angeles St Col, Los Angeles, BA, 1961, MA, 1963; Univ Iowa, MFA, 1963; Brown Univ, attended 1972. **Career:** Contra Costa Col, Eng instr, 1964-68; Lewis & Clark Col, poet residence, 1968-69; Calif State Col, assoc prof Eng, 1970; Brown Univ, prof Eng, 1970, Israel J Kapstein prof Eng, 1983-90, prof emer lit arts; Univ Ill, Ctr Advan Study fel, 1970-71; Harvard Univ, vis prof, 1974-77; Yale Univ, vis prof, 1976; Carleton Col, Northfield, MN, benedict prof, 1979; Univ Cincinnati, Elliston poet, 1979; Univ Del, distinguished minority prof, 1988; Macalester Col, MN, distinguished vis prof creative writing, 1989. **Orgs:** Fel Poetry John Simon Guggenheim Found, 1976; bicentennial poet Bicentennary Exchange, Brit & USA, 1976; coun mem, Mass Coun Arts & Humanities, 1977-80; Am spec ICA State Dept tour Africa, 1977; judge, Nat Black Award Poetry, 1978; lectr Ger Univ ICA Tournine Univ, 1978; bd mem, Yaddo Artists Colony Saratoga Springs NY; ed bd, Tri Quart, Ga Rev, Obsidian; ed, Collected Poems Sterling A Brown; pub Am Jour by Robert Hayden, 1978; Am Acad Arts & Lett; fel Am Acad Arts & Sci. **Honors/Awds:** Black Academy of Arts & Letters Award, 1971; Black Acad Arts & Lett Award, History Is Your Own Heartbeat, 1972; Nat Inst Arts & Lett Award & Am Acad Award Lit, both 1972; NEA Creative Writing Award, 1977; Poetry Soc Am, Melville-Cane Award for Images of Kin New & Selected Poems, Univ Ill Press, 1978; Nat Book Award nomination for Images of Kin, 1978; Carleton Miscellany, on Ralph Ellison, co-ed, 1980; Obsidian, specialissue on Robert Hayden, guest ed, 1981; Nat Humanities Distinguished Professor, Colgate Univ, 1985; Healing Song of the Inner Ear, 1985; Hon Doctorate Lett, Trinity Col, CT, 1987; First Poet Laureate, State of RI, 1988-93; DHL, Coe Col, 1990; Robert Hayden Mem Poetry Award, United Negro Col Fund, 1990; Phi Beta Kappa, vis scholar, 1991; Hon Amendments, 1995; Collected Poems, 1996; George Kent Poetry Award, 1996; Claiborne Pell Award for excellence in the Arts, 1997; Songlines in Michaeltree, 1998; Robert Hayden Poetry Award, United Negro Col Fund. **Special Achievements:** Published first book of poetry, Dear John, Dear Coltrane, 1970; eight full-length Books of poetry plus other poems and collections; edited stand collections of African-Am poetry; Books of poems: "Dear John, Dear Coltrane" 1970, History Is Your Own Heartbeat 1971, Song, I Want A Witness, 1972, History As Apple Tree 1972, Debridement 1973, Nightmare Begins Responsibility 1975, Images of Kin, 1977, Healing Song For The Inner Ear, 1985, Chant of Saints 1979; Songlines: Mosaics, 1991; Every Shut Eye Aint Asleep, 1994. **Home Addr:** 116 Chestnut St Suite G, Providence, RI 02903-4157, **Home Phone:** (401)273-4773.

### HARPER, RUTH B.
Administrator, state government official. **Personal:** Born Dec 24, 1927, Savannah, GA; died Feb 13, 2006, Philadelphia, PA; daughter of Rev Thomas DeLoach and Sallie; married James; children: Catherine Brown & Deloris (deceased). **Educ:** Beregan Inst Philadelphia, grad; Flamingo Modeling Sch, grad; LaSalle Univ, grad. **Career:** One Hundred & Ninety Sixth Legis Dist, state legislator, 1977-92; Philadelphia, state rep, 1976-92; Gratz HS, instr; Strawberry Mansion Jr HS, instr; Miss Ebony Pa Scholar Pageant, producer; Ruth Harper's Modeling & Charm Sch, owner, 1963-2006, dir. **Orgs:** Nat Dem Comm; Pa Coun Arts; founder & pres, N Cent Philadelphia Women's Pol Caucus; bd mem, YMCA Columbia Br; bd mem, ARC SE Chap; pres, Zion BCCh Womens Serv Guild; life mem, Nat Asn Advan Colored People; Urban League; HOGA Civic League; bd mem, Philadelphia Univ; bd mem, Nat Polit Cong Black Women; Continental Socs Inc; bd dir, Afro Am Museum; life mem, Nat Coun Negro Women; Logan Assistance. **Honors/Awds:** Recipient, Citation of Honor, Philadelphia Tribune Newspaper, 1963; Service Award, Nat Asn Advan Colored People, 1964; Bright Hope BC Ch Award, 1965; Cosmopolitan Club Award, 1969; Achievement Award, LaMode Mannequins Inc, 1969; Black Expo Award, 1972; Women in Politics, Cheynew State Univ, 1978; Freedom Award, Nat Asn Advan Colored People, 1978; Service Award, YMCA, 1979. **Special Achievements:** First lady of the Pennsylvania House of Representatives. **Home Addr:** 1427 W Erie Ave, Philadelphia, PA 19140-4134, **Home Phone:** (215)225-4268.

### HARRELL, ERNEST JAMES
Consultant, military leader. **Personal:** Born Oct 31, 1936, Selma, AL; died Mar 31, 2015, Tuscon, AZ; son of William (deceased) and Arrilla Moorer (deceased); married Paola Boone; children: Ernest J II & Jolene. **Educ:** Tuskegee Inst, Tuskegee, AL, BS, 1960; Ariz State Univ, Tempe, AZ, MS, 1972. **Career:** Military leader (retired); AUS, various locations, gen officer, commissioned officer, 1960; EH & Assocs, consulting engr. **Orgs:** Dean pledges, Omega Psi Phi Fraternity, 1958-60; vice chair, discipline comt, Ariz State Univ, 1967-70; regional vpres, Soc Am Mil Engrs, 1986-91. **Honors/Awds:** Distinguished Service Medal, 1995; Legion of Merit, 1986, Bronze Star Medal, 1967, Meritorious Service Medal (3), 1971, 1979, 1982, Army Commendation Medal, 1970, Combat Infantryman Badge, Airborne Badge. **Home Addr:** 8051 N Como Dr, Tucson, AZ 85742-4321, **Home Phone:** (520)575-7086.

### HARRIS, CHARLES F.
Manager, executive. **Personal:** Born Jan 3, 1934, Portsmouth, VA; died Dec 16, 2015, New York, NY; son of Ambrose Edward and Annie Eula Lawson; married Sammie Jackson; children: Francis & Charles. **Educ:** Va State Univ, BA, 1955; NY Univ Grad Sch, attended 1963. **Career:** Doubleday & Co Inc, rsch analyst to ed, 1956-65; John Wiley & Sons Inc, vpres gen mgr Portal Press, 1965-67; Random House Inc, managing ed & sr ed, 1967-71; Howard Univ Press, exec dir, 1971-86; Amistad Press, founder, dir, 1986-99; HarperCollins Publishers, vpres ed dir, 1999-2003; Alpha Zenith Media, owner, 2003-15; BET Interactive LLC, auth, 2003-15; Jour Howard Univ, adj prof; HarperCollins Gen Bks Group, exec ed. **Orgs:** Nat Press Club; bd dir, Reading Fundamental; Asn Am Publishers; Asn Int Scholarly Publishers; Wash Area Bk Publishers; bd dir, Asn Am Univ Presses, 1984; dir, Laymen's Nat Bible Comt, 1985. **Home Addr:** 607 F St NE, Washington, DC 20002.

### HARRIS, REP. EARL L.
Entrepreneur, state government official. **Personal:** Born Nov 8, 1941, Kerrville, TN; died Mar 23, 2015, East Chicago, IN; son of Collins and Magnolia Hall; married Donna Jean Lara. **Educ:** Ind Univ, attended 1962; Purdue Univ, Calumet, Ind, 1967; Ill Inst Technol. **Career:** Inland Steel Co; Am Maize Prod Co, lab tester; Ky Liquors & Ky Snack Shop, owner & operator; Ind House Rep, 2nd Dist, legis rep, 1982-2015; City E Chicago Schs, fixed asset admin, currently. **Orgs:** Nat Asn Advan Colored People; pres, E Chicago Black Coalition, E Chicago Homeowners Asn; vice chmn, Ways & Means Comt, Ind House Rep; chmn, Ind House Statutory Comt Interstate & Int Coop; chmn, Ind House Statutory Comt Ethics; Ind House Standing Comt; Ind House Rules & Legis Procedures Comt; chair, African Am Leadership Forum; bd mem, Northwest Ind League; pres, Sunnyside Homeowners Asn. **Home Addr:** 4114 Butternut St, East Chicago, IN 46312, **Home Phone:** (219)398-4058.

### HARRIS, JAMES ALEXANDER
Teacher, association executive. **Personal:** Born Aug 25, 1926, Des Moines, IA; died Mar 22, 2015, Derwood, MD; married Jacquelyn; children: James Jr & Jerald. **Educ:** Drake Univ, BA, 1948, MFA, 1955; Drake Div Col, post grad work; Okla A&M Univ. **Career:** Kans City, elem teacher, 1948; Langston Univ, teacher, 1953-54; DesMoines, art, human rel teacher, 1954, mid sch art teacher; Nat Educ Asn, vpres, 1973, pres, 2005. **Orgs:** Speaker, Nat Assembly Educ Res, Yamagata, Japan, 1974; dir, NEA; NEA Budget Com; Steering Com, NEA Const Conv; first deleg, Am Educr Peoples Rep China; co-chmn, NEA Com Am Revolution - Bicen; IA St Educ Asn; DesMoines Educ Asn; dir, Red Cross Refugee Shelter; Am Friends Serv Com; admin com rels, Forest Ave Baptist Church; Mayors Task Forces Educ & Police-Com Rels; NAEA bd dirs liaison, Nat Asn Art Educ; IA Asn Art Educr; Nat Advan Colored People; Kappa Alpha Psi; dir, Des Moines Chap Boys Clubs Am; US Cong Comt Educ & Labor. **Home Addr:** 7215 Reite Ave, Des Moines, IA 50311.

### HARRIS, THOMAS C.
Executive. **Personal:** Born Mar 23, 1933, Paterson, NJ; died Apr 28, 2016, Clarence, NY; married Betty M Kennedy; children: Thomas Jr, Michael, Elaine Jefferson & Brenda. **Educ:** Fairleigh Dickinson Univ, BS, chem, 1970, surface active chem, 1973; Columbia Univ NY, cosmetic sci, 1972. **Career:** Shulton Inc, chemist, 1968; Revlon Inc, sr chemist, 1974; Ame Cyanand Co, group leader res & develop, 1977; Harris Chem Co Inc, pres, 1977-. **Orgs:** Bd dir, Chamber Com; Rotary Club Int; bd trustee, St Joseph's Med Ctr; assoc minister, Mission Church God; nat corresp secy, Nat Mens Orgn; Cosmetic Chem Soc; Sales & Allied Chem Indust; adv, Youth Christ. **Honors/Awds:** Gold Medal Atlantic Richfield Co Prime Sponsor of Olympic, 1984; Excellence in Business, US Olympics Los Angeles. **Home Addr:** 602 14th Ave, Paterson, NJ 07504. **Business Addr:** President, Harris Chemical Co Inc, 546 E 30th St, Paterson, NJ 07504.

### HART, NOEL A.
Government official, educator, firefighter. **Personal:** Born Dec 14, 1927, Jamaica, NY; died Mar 6, 2015, NJ; son of Noel A and Louise Mason; married Patricia Spence Cuffee; children: Noel Jr, Alison, Ira & Jonathan; married Lorraine Booker. **Educ:** NY Univ, BA, 1954; Mt St Mary's, MBA, 1992; Emergency Mgt Inst, educ specialist, computs, admin. **Career:** Government official (retired); Exec Develop Prog Nat Fire Acad, training instr; Peoria Fire Dept, fire marshal, 1977; NY City Fire Dept, 1954-77; John Jay Col, team leader, lectr; Promotional & Career Training Prog, prof; FEMA US Fire Admin, fire prev specialist; Emergency Mgt Inst, educ specialist & group leader, 1987. **Orgs:** Pres, Comus Sch Club; trustee, Port Chester Pub Libr; bd dir, Port Chester Carver Ctr; Int Asn Black Prof Fire Fighters, 1969-2015; ward envestryman, St Peters Episcopal Church; Prince Peace Episcopal Church; Diocese Coun Episcopal Diocese Cent PA; Chief Officers Resource Comt, 1986-2015; Nat Forum Black Pub Adminrs, 1988-2015. **Special Achievements:** First African American to become Peoria's fire chief. **Home Addr:** 2564 Heathrow Lane, Manasquan, NJ 08736-2212, **Home Phone:** (732)223-9184.

### HARTSFIELD, ARNETT L., JR.
Lawyer, educator, firefighter. **Personal:** Born Jun 14, 1918, Bellingham, WA; died Oct 31, 2014, Los Angeles, CA; married Kathleen Bush; children: Maria, Paula Johnson, Charlean Fields, Arnett & Barbara. **Educ:** Univ Southern Calif, BA, econ, 1951; Univ SC, LLB, 1955. **Career:** Lawyer, educator, firefighter (retired); City Los Angeles, fireman, 1940-61; pvt pract, 1955-64; Calif Fair Employ, assoc coun, 1964-65; Los Angeles Neighborhood Legal Serv, exec dir, 1965-67; Comt Mediation Ctr, chief mediator, 1967-69; United Way, asst dir, 1970-71; Calif State Univ, Long Beach, asst prof, 1972-74, assoc prof, 1974. **Orgs:** Bd trustee, S Bay Univ Col Law; pres, Los Angeles City Civil Serv Comn, 1973-76, vpres, 1974-75. **Honors/Awds:** Man of the Year, Comn Rels Conf S Calif, 1962; Lifetime Achievement Award; Eme Award, 2001; Los Angeles City Fire Station No. 46, named in honor. **Special Achievements:** UCLA's first African American member of the ROTC; First blacks to join the Los Angeles fire department with a college education in 1940. **Home Addr:** 8745 S Harvard Blvd, Los Angeles, CA 90047-3316.

### HASKINS, JAMES W., JR.
Public relations executive. **Personal:** Born Dec 1, 1932, Sandusky, OH; died Jun 11, 2014, Tallahassee, FL; married Janie L Moore; children: Lisa, Scott, Karen, Laura, Ronald, Sondra & Iona. **Educ:** Bowling Green State Univ, BA, 1959; Univ Pa, MSEd, 1975, Doct Cand Educ Admin. **Career:** Ctr Providence Hosp Sch Nursing, bctrlgst-tech, 1960-63, sci instr, 1962; Controls Rdtn Inc, tech, 1961-63; US Atomic Enrgy Comn, chem, 1963-66; Chem & Engr & News, asst ed bur head, 1966-69; DuPont Invitation, res sci writer, 1969-71, ed, 1971-2014; IUPAC Bk Org Chem, ed; US Acad Sci Host, mcrmlclr chem, 1971. **Orgs:** Am Chem Soc; AAAS; Nat Asn Sci Writers Inc; Soc Tech Comn; Sigma Delta Chi; Int Asn Bus Comn; Black Educ Forum; Urban League; NAACP; Alpha Phi Alpha; Wynfld Residents Asn; Phi Delta Kappa. **Honors/Awds:** Sci Writer Yr, NY Voice, 1972; Legion Hon; Chap 4 Chap, 1973. **Home Addr:** 5719 Drexel Rd, Philadelphia, PA 19131.

### HEREFORD, DR. SONNIE WELLINGTON, III
Educator, physician, civil rights activist. **Personal:** Born Jan 7, 1931, Huntsville, AL; died Jul 7, 2016, Huntsville, AL; son of Sonnie and Jannie Burwell; married Martha Ann Adams; children: Sonnie IV, Kimela, Lee, Linda, Brenda & Martha. **Educ:** Ala A&M Univ, BS, 1955; Meharry Med Col, MD, 1955. **Career:** Physician (retired); Oakwood Col, campus physician, 1957-73; Ala A&M Univ, prof histol, 1960-68, prof physiol, 1960-68, team physician, 1962-2016, campus physician, 1962-73; Huntsville Civil Rights Movement, leader & photogr, 1962-63; Calhoun Col, adj instr, prof anat & physiol, 1996-2016; Delta Sigma Theta, consult sickle cell anemia, 1971-75; pvt pract physician. **Orgs:** Chmn, Comt Desegregation Huntsville, AL, 1962-63; vol physician, Boy Scouts & Girl Scouts, 1956-93; vol physician, Golden Gloves Huntsville, 1968-88; Omega Psi Phi. **Honors/Awds:** Distinguished Service Award, Voter Coord Com Huntsville, AL, 1962; Distinguished Service Award, Oakwood Coll Huntsville, AL, 1973; Meharry Med Col, Twenty-Five Year Service Award, 1980; Distinguished Service Award, Community Action Agency, 1980; Oakwood Church, Distinguished Service Award, 1980; Distinguished Service Award, Zeta Sorority, 1982; Distinguished Service Award, Madison County Midwives Asn, 1983; Distinguished Service Award, Ala A&M Univ Athletic Dept, 1985; Inducted, Ala Hall of Fame, Huntsville, 1995. **Special Achievements:** Documentary, "A Civil Rights Journey"; guest on Calhoun's 4CTV program "Calhoun Review"; Book: " Beside the Troubled Waters: A Black Doctor Remembers Life, Medicine, and Civil Rights in an Alabama Town", 2011. **Home Addr:** 1810 Lydia Dr NW, Huntsville, AL 35816-1436, **Home Phone:** (256)837-1575.

### HERRING, MARSHA K. CHURCH
Entrepreneur, marketing executive. **Personal:** Born Jun 23, 1958, Detroit, MI; died Sep 3, 2008; daughter of Rogers and Muriel; married Cedric; children: Christopher Earle & Kiara Nicole. **Educ:** Univ Mich, Ann Arbor, BA, gen studies, 1980, MA, pub policy, 1983. **Career:** US Sen Carl Levin, pres asst, 1980-85; Humana Hosp Brazos Valley, dir mktg, 1985-89; Greenleaf Hosp, dir mkt, 1989-90; Christ Hosp, dir ment health mkt, 1991-93; UIC Med Ctr, dir mkt, 1993-2001; M'Powered Commun, prin & chief exec officer, 2001-08; MusXcellence, dir mkt, currently; ACCESS Community Health Network, dir prog implementation, currently. **Orgs:** Am Mkt Asn, 1988-2008; chmn, S Suburban Chamber Com, Ill, 1992-2008, health servs comt, 1992-94; adv bd mem, Crisis Ctr S Suburbia, 1992-93; adv bd, Alliance Healthcare Strategy & Mkt, 1993-2008, 1998-2001; adv bd, Expo Today's Black Woman, 1997-2008; HIV adv comt, Ill Dept Pub Health, 2001. **Honors/Awds:** Agape Award, HCA Greenleaf Hosp, 1990; Employee of the Month, Gold Star Award, Christ Hosp, 1993; Recognition Award, Acad Black Women Health Professions, 1994; Phenomenal Woman Award, 1998; Children of the Storm Award, 2003. **Home Addr:** 6 Richwood Terr, Flossmoor, IL 60422, **Home Phone:** (708)957-5025.

### HILL, RAYMOND
Football player. **Personal:** Born Aug 7, 1975, Detroit, MI; died Aug 6, 2015. **Educ:** Mich State Univ, grad. **Career:** Football player (retired); Buffalo Bills, defensive back, 1998, 2000; Miami Dolphins, defensive back, 1998-2000; New England Patriots, 2001.

### HOLLIMAN, DAVID L.
Executive, business owner. **Personal:** Born Sep 13, 1929, Denver, CO; died Sep 3, 2016; son of Ernest W Jr (deceased) and Dorothy Taylor; married Mildred Helms; children: Rhoda, Lisa & Michael. **Educ:** Regis Col, Denver, Colo, BS, admin, econs, & bus, 1990. **Career:** Continental Air Lines, Denver, Colo, passenger serv opers, 1966-86; United Maintenance Inc, pres, 1972-89; Primalon Int Enterprise Ltd, chief exec officer, 1989; Queen City Servs, vpres. **Orgs:** Past trustee, Campbell Chapel AME Church Steward Bd, 1942; Mayor's Bd Appeals; Mayors Black Adv Comn; Colo Black Roundtable; Colo Centennial Ethnic Minority Cou Bi-Centennial Comn; Imp Coun, 1988-90; Adv group, Colo Pub Serv Co; pres, PTA, Barrett Elem Sch; pres, Barrett Elem Schs Parent & Teacher Asn. **Honors/Awds:** Grand Inspector General, 330 United Supreme, Coun, NJ, PHA, 1973, 1988; Legion of Honor, Charter Mem, 1974; Hall of Fame, Ira C Meadows, Knights Templar, 1985; Man of the Year, Knights Templar, 1985; Past Imperial Potentate, Ancient Egyptian Arabic Order Noble Majestic Shrine Jurisdiction, 1988-90; Joseph E Seagram Vanguard Award; Honorary Past Grand Master, Ill, Ark, Tenn & Prov Ont, Texas Jurisdiction; Hon Captain, Syrian Temple No 49, Arabic Foot Patrol; Hon Lieutenant, Denver Police Dept. **Special Achievements:** First African Americans to gain long term employment with Continental Airlines. **Home Addr:** 2030 E 11th Ave, PO Box 6844, Denver, CO 80206-0844, **Home Phone:** (303)329-6324.

### HOLMES, DR. HENRY SIDNEY, III
Business owner, lawyer. **Personal:** Born Apr 10, 1944, New York, NY; died Apr 15, 2013; son of Henry Sidney II and Annie; married Albertha C Middleton; children: Monique Elizabeth. **Educ:** Columbia Univ, BA, 1976; Hofstra Univ Sch Law, JD, 1979. **Career:** Lever Bros Co, acct mgr, 1969-72; Black Life Discount Stores, owner, 1970-76; Mudge Rose Guthrie Alexander & Ferdon, partner, 1987-95; Winston & Strawn, partner. **Orgs:** Mem NY Bar Asn, 1979-2013; 100 Black Men Inc, 1983-2013; bd dirs, Nat Asn Securities Prof, 1985-91; Port Authority Bd comnr, 2008-13. **Home Addr:** 138-42 228 St, Laurelton, NY 11413.

### HOOD, HON. HAROLD
Judge, educator. **Personal:** Born Jan 14, 1931, Hamtramck, MI; died May 5, 2015; son of W Sylvester Sr and Lenore Elizabeth Hand; married Lottie Jones; children: Harold Keith, Kenneth Loren, Kevin Joseph & Karen Teresa. **Educ:** Univ Mich, BA, 1952; Wayne State Univ, JD, 1959. **Career:** Judge (retired), educator; Hood, Rice & Charity, atty, 1959-61; City Detroit, asst corp coun, 1961-69; E Dist Mich, chief asst US atty, 1969-73; Common Plea Ct, Detroit, judge, 1973-77; Recorders Ct, Detroit, judge, 1977-78; Cent Mich Univ, adj prof; Mich Judicial Inst, fac; Nat Judicial Col, fac; Third Judicial Circuit Mich, judge, 1978-82; Mich Ct Appeals, judge, 1982-2004; BABESWORLD Inc, founder & pres; Cooley Law Sch, adj prof; Oakland Univ, adj prof. **Orgs:** Am Bar Asn; St Mich Bar Asn; Detroit Bar Asn; dir Am Judicature Soc; Nat Bar Asn; Judicial Coun NBA; Asn Black Judges Mich; trustee/vice chmn, Kirwood Gen Hosp, 1974-79; bd mem, Old Newsboys-Good fels, 1974, pres, 1987-89; Detroit Renaissance Lions, 1975; bd mem, NCA/DD Greater Detroit Area, 1976; bd mem & chmn, Nat Coun Alcoholism, 1979; Nat Judicial Col, fac, 1980-82; comnr, Mich Judicial Tenure Comn, 1986-94, chmn, 1988-90; chmn, Mich Supreme Ct Comt Stand Civil Jury Instructions, 1987; chmn, Mich Supreme Ct Task Force Race/Ethnic Issues Courts, 1987; chmn, 1987; comner, Off Substance Abuse Serv, St Mich, 1987-92; dir, Thomas M Cooley Law Sch, 1988-96; Golden Heritage Life; Nat Asn Advan Colored People; trustee, First Congregational Chair Detroit; trustee, Mich St Bar Found, 1992; trustee, Am INNS Ct Found, 1992; Nat Adv Coun Alcohol Abuse & Alcoholism; trustee, Johnson Inst Found; chair, Ecumenical Theol Sem; chair, Glass Scholar Found; co-chair, Open Justice Comn St Bar Mich; bd trustee, Mich St Bar Asn, 2006. **Honors/Awds:** Ted Owens Award, Detroit Alumni Kappa Alpha Psi, 1971; Service Award, Fed Exec Bd, 1972; Northern Province Achievement, Award Kappa Alpha Psi, 1972; City of Inkster Merit Award, City Inkster, Mich, 1976; Distinguished Alumni, Wayne St Univ Law Sch, 1984; "Exec Alcoholism-A Special Problem, " Labor-Management Journal, 1988; Judicial Servant Award, Mich Corrections Comn, 1989; Augustus D Straker Distinguished Jurist Award, 1989; Champion of Justice Award, St Bar Mich, 1990; Phillip A Hart Award, Mich Women's Hall Fame, 1991; Martin Luther King Award, Washtenaw County Bar, 1992; Silver Key Award, NCADD, 1996. **Home Addr:** 300 Riverfront Pk Suite 14K, Detroit, MI 48226. **Business Addr:** Adjunct Professor, Thomas M Cooley Law School, 300 S Capitol Ave, Lansing, MI 48901, **Business Phone:** (517)371-5140.

### HORNE, DR. EDWIN CLAY
Dentist, executive. **Personal:** Born Feb 16, 1924, Greensboro, NC; died Jun 18, 2016, Englewood, NJ; son of Ellis Clay (deceased) and Annie Slade (deceased); married Gene Ann; children: Carol Anne Penn & Edwin Christian. **Educ:** NC Agr & Tech State Univ, BS, 1947; Univ Pa, Sch Dent, DDS, 1952. **Career:** Harlem Hosp, assoc attend dentist, 1954-95; Upper Harlem Comprehensive Care Ctr, attend dentist & attend dent supvr, 1985-89; N Cent Bronx-Montefiore Hosp Affil, from clin assoc supvr to adj prof clin dent; Columbia Univ Sch Dent & Oral Surg; Univ Pa, Sch Dent Med, adj prof; N Cent Bronx Dent Clin, attend & assoc prof; pvt pract dentist, currently; African Coffee Cocoa Tea & Spices Inc, chief financial officer. **Orgs:** Fel Am Col Dentists; First Dist Dent Soc NY; Omega Psi Phi Frat; Sigma Pi Phi Frat; Reveille Club NY; Lions Int Englewood; corp mem; Schomburg Corp, Schomburg Ctr Res Black Cult; sire archon, NE Region Sigma Pi Phi Fraternity, 1987-88; NC A&T State Univ Alumni; bd dirs, Univ Pa-Metro, NJ Alumni Asn, 1987; exec bd, Univ Pa Dent Sch Alumni Soc, 1989-90; comm mem, visualaids, Ann November Dent Conv, NY City; pres, Univ Pa Dent Sch Alumni Soc Adv Dean, 1998; mem bd trustees, Schomberg Corp, 1998. **Honors/Awds:** Man of the Year Award, Kappa Omicron Chap Omega Psi Phi Fraternity, 1970; Honored for 40 yrs Meritorious Membership, Omega Psi Phi Frat, 1986; Fifty Year Membership Award, Los Angeles Grand Conclave Omega, 1996. **Home Addr:** 374 Miller Ave, Englewood, NJ 07631. **Business Addr:** Dentist, 2255 5th Ave, New York, NY 10037-2001, **Business Phone:** (212)368-3912.

### HORNE, GENE-ANN POLK. See POLK, DR. GENE-ANN.

### HORTON, CARL E.
Marketing executive, chief executive officer, president (organization). **Personal:** Born Apr 11, 1944, Philadelphia, PA; died Nov 5, 2015; son of W S and Dorothy L; married Phyllis Sims; children: Meredith & Carl Jr. **Educ:** Morgan State Col, BA, 1967; Univ Pa, Wharton Grad Div, MBA, 1972. **Career:** Seagrambrand; Gen Foods Corp, asst prod mgr, 1972-73; Xerox Corp, sr mkt consult, 1973-76; Heublein Inc, prod mgr, 1976-80; Jos E Seagram, sr prod mgr, 1980-86, group mkt dir, 1986-87, vpres group mkt dir, 1987-92, dir bus dev, 1992-94; Absolut Vodka, vpres mkt, 1994; Absolut Spirits Co, chief exec officer, 2001-06, pres. **Orgs:** Kappa Alpha Psi Fraternity, Stamford Alumni, Morgan State Col, 1965-2015; advbd, CEBA Awards, 1989-2015; bd dir, Cigna, NY, 1990-2015. **Honors/Awds:** Black Achievers Award, NY City YMCA, 1985; Blackbook Awards, Dollars & Sense Mag, 1990. **Special Achievements:** Industrys top-ranking African American as well as one of the most powerful black executives in corporate America.

### HOWARD, MILTON L.
Architect, executive. **Personal:** Born Sep 3, 1927, Hurtsboro, AL; died Aug 30, 2015, Bloomfield, CT; married Dolores Allen; children: Mark & James. **Educ:** Ky State Col; Univ Ill. **Career:** Milton Lewis Howard Assocs Inc, chief exec officer, architect & owner. **Orgs:** Am Inst Archits; Nal Coun Archit Regis Bds; Guild Relig Archit 1; Bldg Bd Appeals City Hartford; asst treasr, Bloomfield Housing Authority; Am Inst Architects, S Arsenal Everywhere Sch, Hartford, CT; Am Asn Sch Admin, S Arsenal Everywhere Sch, Hartford, Conn. **Honors/Awds:** Bus Leadership Award, Greater Hartford Chamber Com. **Home Addr:** 21 Banbury Lane, Bloomfield, CT 06002-2501, **Home Phone:** (860)243-0812.

### HUDSON, WILLIAM THOMAS
Manager, government official. **Personal:** Born Dec 14, 1929, Chicago, IL; died May 14, 2013; son of Cornelius and Mary. **Educ:** NWS Univ, BS, 1953; Univ Chicago, MA, 1954; Harvard Univ, MPA, 1982. **Career:** Bur Retirement & Survivors Ins Balt, claims authorizer, 1963-64; Hders Retirement & Survivors Ins, employee devel officer; Comn EEO WA, detail edto pres; Ret & Survivors Ins, spec asst EEO dir, 1964-65; Off Sec Dept HEW WA, dep EEO officer, 1966-67; Off Secy Dept Transp WA, cons, prog mgr internal EEO prog, Nat Urban league Conv, resource, 1967-70; Off Civil Rights USCG WA, chief, 1970-83; US Dept Transp, dept dir civil rights, 1983-. **Orgs:** Sr Exec Asn; Phi Delta Kappa; Hon Soc Men Ed. **Honors/Awds:** Silver Medal for Meritorious Achievement, 1974. **Home Addr:** 1006 G St SE, Washington, DC 20003-2820.

### HUNTER, PATRICK J., SR.
Educator. **Personal:** Born Oct 29, 1929, Elberton, GA; died Mar 15, 2015, Bridgeport, CT; married Mildred R Powell; children: Patrick J Jr, Kim M Brown, Michael A & Jeffrey M. **Educ:** Univ Bridgeport Conn, BA, 1958, MS, 1959; NY Univ, PhD. **Career:** Conn Dept Social Serv, caseworker, 1960-62; Birdgeport Inter-Group Coun Conn, exec dir, 1963-66; Community Training & Employ, Stamford, conn, exec dir, 1966-68; Housatonic Community Col, dept chmn, 1975-81, prof emer. **Orgs:** Rotary Int Bridgeport Conn, 1963-66; pres, SW Regional Ment Health Bd, 1986-87; Conn State Ment Health Bd, 1987; planning coun, United Way Greater Bridgeport; bd mem, SW Conn Ment Health; Greater Bridgeport Catchment Area; adv bd, Greater Bridgeport Regional Ment Health; vpres, Ment Health Social Club Greater Bridgeport Area. **Honors/Awds:** Citizen of the Year, College Charles Young Post, 1963; Achievement Award, Radio Station WICC, 1963; Outstanding Educator, 1972. **Home Addr:** 939 Wilcoxson Ave, Stratford, CT 06614-4242, **Home Phone:** (203)378-6669.

### HUNTLEY, LYNN JONES
Lawyer, president (organization). **Personal:** Born Jan 24, 1946, Petersberg, VA; died Aug 30, 2015, Atlanta, GA; daughter of Lawrence Neale and Mary Ellen. **Educ:** Fisk Univ, attended 1965; Columbia Univ, Barnard Col, AB, 1967; Columbia Univ Sch Law, JD, 1970. **Career:** Bernard Baruch Col, teaching asst, 1969-70; Judge Motley US Dist Ct NY, law clerk, 1970-71; Nat Asn Advan Colored People Legal Defense & Educ Fund Inc, asst coun, 1971-73, staff atty; NY City Comn Human Rights, gen coun, 1973-75; Nat Asn Advan Colored People Legal Defense Fund Inc, asst coun, 1975-78; US Dept Justice Civil Rights Div, sect chief spec litigation sec, 1978-81, dep asst atty gen, 1981-82; Ford Found, prog officer, 1982-87, dep dir charge human rights & social justice prog, 1987-91, Rights & Social Justice Prog, dir, 1991-; Southern Educ Found, exec dir, exec vpres & dir, pres, 2002-, chief exec officer. **Orgs:** Nat Bar Asn; NY State Bar; chair, Fed Women's Prog Adv Comn US Dept Justice; Black Affairs Prog Adv Comn; bd dir, Sheltering Arms C's Serv; Nat Asn Advan Colored People; columnist, Essence Mag; NY State Sentencing Guidelines Comn; secy, Black Am Law Studs Asn; Columbia Law Rev; bd mem, Legal Aid Soc; NYS Govs Adv Comt Black Affairs; bd trustee, Barnard Col; bd mem, Am Const Soc; bd mem, CARE; bd mem, Grantmakers Educ; bd mem, Ga Stud Finance Comn. **Honors/Awds:** First Black Woman on Columbia Law Rev; Spl Commendation Award, US Dept Justice; Sr Exec Serv Outstanding Performance Award & bonus, US Dept Justice; Outstanding Performance, Ford Found; Thurgood Marshall Award, Asn Bd NY; Lucy Terry Prince Award, Lawyer's Comt Civil Rights. **Special Achievements:** Co-editor, Beyond Racism: Embracing an Interdependent Future in 2000 & Beyond Racism: Race and Equality in Brazil, South Africa & the US in 2001. **Business Addr:** President, Southern Education Foundation, 135 Auburn Ave NE 2nd Fl, Atlanta, GA 30303, **Business Phone:** (404)523-0001.

### JACKSON, HAROLD BARON, JR.
Lawyer. **Personal:** Born Dec 28, 1939, Washington, DC; died Feb 14, 2016, Milwaukee, WI; son of Harold and Julia; children: Julie, Tiffany & Jaime. **Educ:** Marquette Univ, BA, 1964; Marquette Univ Law Sch, JD, 1967. **Career:** Milwaukee County, asst dist atty, 1968; Milwaukee Bd Sch Dir, pres, 1970-72; Jackson & Clark Atty, partner, 1970-73; Marquette Univ Law Sch, prof law, 1972-73; circuit ct judge; Milwaukee Metrop Sewerage Dist, srcoun, 1986, sr staff atty. **Orgs:** Exec bd, Milwaukee Jr Bar Asn, 1970; chmn, Criminal Law Sect Milwaukee Bar Asn, 1972; pres bd dir, Sojourner Truth House; chmn bd dir, Benedict Ctr Criminal Justice; bd dir, Athletes Youth. **Honors/Awds:** Man of the Year, Milwaukee Theol Inst, 1978; Outstanding Jurist Award, Friends in Law, 1982; Winner of American Jurisprudence Awards Constitutional Law, Criminal Law & Jurisprudence. **Home Addr:** 1756 N Hi Mt Blvd, Milwaukee, WI 53208-1719, **Home Phone:** (414)476-4708.

### JACKSON, HAROLD LEONARD, JR.
Financial manager. **Personal:** Born Sep 26, 1955, Columbia, SC; died Jan 1, 2014; son of Harold L Sr and Orion Virginia Meaders; married Deborah Ann Knox; children: Matthew G & Jennifer E. **Educ:** Tex A&M Univ, College Station, BBA, finance, 1977. **Career:** Dresser Atlas, Houston, TX, off supvr, 1977-83; Macy's, Houston, TX, assoc, 1984; Continental Airlines, Houston, TX, rev acct supvr, 1984-85; City Houston, Houston Tex, fin analyst, div mgr grants, 1985-2014. **Orgs:** Nat Forum Black Pub Admin, 1987-88; Govt Finance Officers Asn, 1988-. **Home Addr:** 7622 Ashton Dr, Houston, TX 77095-3921, **Home Phone:** (281)550-3027.

### JAMES, DR. FELIX
Clergy, educator. **Personal:** Born Nov 17, 1937, Hurtsboro, AL; died Feb 23, 2014; son of Leroy Sr and Blanche Clark; married Florence Bernard. **Educ:** Ft Valley State Col, GA, BS, 1962; Howard Univ, DC, MA, 1967; Ohio State Univ, Columbus, PhD, 1972; New Orleans Baptist Theol Sem, New Orleans, MA, christian educ, 1991. **Career:** Columbia Pub Sch, SC, instr social studies, 1962-64; Howard Univ, DC, res bk librn, 1965-67; Tuskegee Inst, instr hist, 1967-70; Southern Ill Univ, Carbondale, asst prof hist, 1972-74; Southern Univ New Orleans, chmn hist dept, 1974-75, prof hist, 1979-2014; Salvation Baptist Church, pastor, moderator; Mt Zion Miss Baptist, assoc. **Orgs:** State dir, Asn Study Afro-Am Life & Hist, 1973-2014, co-chair prog comm, 1979-80, exec bd; New Orleans Martin Luther King Steering Comm, 1977-2014; fac coun, Southern Univ New Orleans, 1980-85; vice-chair arrangement comm, ASBS Ann Meeting New Orleans, 1983; exec bd, La Hist Asn, 1984-86; adv bd, Ann City-Wide Black Heritage Celebration, 1985-2014; comnr, New Orleans Bicentennial Comm, 1987-91; consult, Ethnic Minorities Cult Ctr, Univ N Iowa, 1988; sr warden, DeGruy Lodge, Prince Hall Free & Accepted Masons, 1989; bd dir, S Christian Leadership Conf, 1983-2014; worshipful master, DeGruy Lodge No 7, Prince Hall Free & Accepted Masons, 1991-2014; Illustrious Comman Kadosh, Eureka Consistory, No 7-Masons. **Honors/Awds:** Community Service Award, Southern Univ New Orleans; Departmental Award for Teaching Excellence. **Special Achievements:** Author: The American Addition: History of a Black Community, Univ Press of America, 1978; Contributor to Dict of American Negro Biography, 1982; Dict of Louisiana Biography, 1986; Black Leadership in the 20th Century, 1989; Edn of the Black Adult in the US, 1989; Twentieth Century Black Leaders, 1989. **Home Addr:** PO Box 871195, New Orleans, LA 70187-1195, **Home Phone:** (504)218-7177.

### JAMES, DR. HERMAN DELANO
School administrator, educator. **Personal:** Born Feb 25, 1943, St. Thomas, VI; died Oct 2, 2010, Voorhees, NJ; son of Henry O and Frances Smith; married Marie Gray; children: Renee, Sybil & Sidney. **Educ:** Tuskegee Inst, BS, educ, 1965; St Johns Univ, MA, sociol, 1967; Univ Pittsburgh, PhD, sociol, 1972. **Career:** Distinguished prof (retired); Univ Pittsburgh, asst prof, 1971-72; Univ Mass, asst prof, 1972-78, assoc provost, 1975-76, asst chancellor, 1976-78; Calif St Univ, vice provost, 1978-82; Rowan Univ, acad vpres, 1982-84, pres, 1984-98, dir, 1990, distinguished prof, 1998-2007. **Orgs:** Cherry Hill Minority Civic Asn, 1982-84; bd mem, NJ Educ Comput Network, 1983; chaircols, Gloucester County United Way, 1985; bd dir, Am Asn State Cols & Univs; bd trustee, Mid States Asn; vice chair, Pres Coun, 1996; bd dir, S Jersey Industs; bd dir, NJ St Chamber Com; hon trustee, NJ Symphony Orchestra; Am Coun Educ Comn Leadership Dev; Labor/Higher Educ Forum; Am Coun Educ; adv comt, Am Asn St Cols & Univs; Camden Educ Alliance; bd trustee, NJ Futures; Martin Luther King Comn. **Honors/Awds:** Fellowship, NIH, 1968-71; Young Black Achiever, Boston YMCA, 1977; Outstanding Educator, Williamstown Civic Asn, 1984; Eileen Tosney Award, Am Asn Univ Adminr, 1994; Honorary Doctor of Laws, Tuskegee Univ, 1996. **Home Addr:** 6 Brownstone Blvd, Voorhees, NJ 08043, **Home Phone:** (856)435-7173.

### JEFFERS, CLIFTON R.
Lawyer, president (organization). **Personal:** Born Feb 8, 1934, Roxboro, NC; died Dec 6, 2013, Fresno, CA; son of Theron and Clara; married Mary R Lloyd; children: Kwame. **Educ:** Tenn St Univ, AB, 1956; Univ Calif, Hastings Col Law Univ, Calif, JD, 1964. **Career:** St Calif, state dep atty, 1964-69; US Dept Housing & Urban Develop, reg admin, 1969-76; St Calif, chief asst state pub defender, 1976-84; James & Jeffers, pres, 2002, sr partner; Univ Calif, Berkeley, guest lectr criminal; Stanford Univ Law Sch, guest lectr; Univ Southern Calif Sch Law, guest lectr. **Orgs:** Pres, San Francisco Nat Asn Advan Colored People, 1966-69; San FranciscoCoun Churches, 1967-72; San Francisco Econ Opportunities Coun, 1967-68; bddir, Am Civil Liberties Union Northern Calif, 1969-73; bd dir, LawyersClub, San Francisco, 1981-82; bd dir, Bar Asn San Francisco, 1984-2013; founding pres, William Hastie Lawyers Asn; bd dir, Frederick DouglasHaynes Gardens; gen coun, 3rd Baptist Church; bd dir, Calif Rural LegalAssistance Found; founding mem, San Francisco Black Leadership Forum; trustee, 3rd Baptist Church; bd dir, Nat Asn Advan Colored People; bd dir, First Dist Appellate Proj; co-founder, State Bar Standing Comn Legal ServCriminal Defendants; Calif Asn Black Lawyers; co-founder & dir, ThirdBaptist Gardens Inc; Afro-Am Agenda Coun; Nat Calif & San Francisco BarAsn; Charles Houston Bar Asn; Am Judicature Soc. **Honors/Awds:** Outstanding Pres Award, Nat Asn Advan Colored People, 1967, 1969; AmJurisprudence Award; Equal Employ Opportunities Award, US Dept Housing & Urban Develop; Cert of Fair Housing Achievement, US Dept Housing & UrbanDevelop; Meritorious Service Award, Nat Asn Advan Colored People; Outstanding Performance Award, US Dept Housing & Urban Develop; Cert of Honor, SanFrancisco Bd Supervisors. **Home Addr:** 1883 14th Ave, San Francisco, CA 94122, **Home Phone:** (415)566-0248.

### JENKINS, DR. MELVIN E., JR.
Physician, educator. **Personal:** Born Jun 24, 1922, Kansas City, MO; died Oct 3, 2015, Silver Spring, MD; son of Melvin and Marguerite; married Maria Parker; children: Janis, Carol, Lore & Ingrid. **Educ:** Univ Kans Col Med, AB, 1944, MD, 1946. **Career:** Freedman's Hosp, internship, 1946-47, pediat residency, 1947-50, from asst pediatrician

to assoc pediatrician, 1950-69; Howard Univ Col Med, clin instr, 1951-54, clin asst prof, 1954-55, from asst prof to assoc prof, 1957-69, Dept Pediat & Child Health, prof chmn, 1973-86, prof emer; Johns Hopkins Univ, pediat endocrinol, 1963-65, lectr, dept pediat, 1974; Univ Nebr Med Ctr, pediatrician, 1969-73, dir pediat endocrine clin, 1969-73, prof & vice chmn, dept pediat, 1971-73; George Wash Univ, profial lectr child health & develop, 1973-2015; Hosp Sick C, attend staff, 1973-91; Childrens Hosp Nat Med Ctr, DC, sr attend pediatrician, 1973-2015; Freedmen's Hosp, chief pediatrician, 1973-86; NIH, consult, 1973-2015. **Orgs:** Chmn pediat sect, Nat Med Asn, 1966-69; chmn med rec comt, Freedmen's Hosp, 1966; med sch rep, Howard Univ Coun Admin, 1967, 1974; ed chief, Pediat Newsletter, Nat Med Asn, 1970-83; adv bd, Human Growth Inc, 1971; Policy Adv Comn Ctr Urban Affairs, 1971-73; bd dir, Urban League Nebr, 1971-73; med dir, Parent Ctr, 1971-73; pres bd dir, Comprehensive Health Asn Omaha Inc, 1972-73; bd mem, Howard Univ Hosp, 1974-88; campus rep, Endocrine Soc, 1974-80; med adv comt, Nat Found March Dimes, 1974-78; Nat Adv Res Resources Coun, NIH, 1974-78; med adv comt, Nat Pituitary Agency, 1975-78; examr, Am Bd Pediat, 1975-88, bd mem, 1983-89; Pediat Surg Comn, Am Bd Surg, 1984; chmn, Health Task Force; Sigma Xi; Med Chirurgicalc DC; AAAS; Black Child Develop Inst Inc; Alpha Omega Alpha US Dept Health & Human Serv Residency Training Rev Comt. **Honors/Awds:** Golden Apple Award, South African Med Asn, 1963; Recognition for Outstanding Contributor to Growth of Pediatric Section, Nat Med Asn, 1966-69; Outstanding Achievement Award, Southern Christian Leadership Conf, 1972; Outstanding Scholar-Teacher Award, Howard Univ, 1984; Outstanding Contributor, Citation City Coun, DC, 1984; Leadership in Medicine Award, Univ Kans, 1989. **Home Addr:** 10401 Grosvenor Pl Suite 504, North Bethesda, MD 20852.

## JOHNS, STEPHEN ARNOLD

Marketing executive, insurance executive. **Personal:** Born Aug 21, 1920, Chicago, IL; died Mar 22, 2015, Los Angeles, CA; son of Stephen and Bennie F Shannon; married Tanis Fortier; children: Brenda Johns Penney. **Educ:** Roosevelt Col, BA, 1947; FLMI Life Off Mgt Asn, 1959; Calif Lutheran Univ Am Col Life Underwriters, 1964. **Career:** Jackson Mutual Life, Chicago, 1942-47; methods analyst, 1957; Agency Educ & Tn, dir, 1960; asst agency off, 1962; Asso Agency, dir, 1964; asn agency, dir, 1970; Golden St Mutual Life Ins Co, vpres agency, dir, 1974-80; sr vpres & chief mkt officer, 1980-83. **Orgs:** Mem bd dir, Golden St Mutual Life Ins Co; Life Underwriters' Asn LA LANCCP; Urban League; Kappa Alpha Psi. **Honors/Awds:** FLMI Key, Golden St Mutual Life Ins Co. **Home Addr:** 5221 Angeles Vista Blvd, Los Angeles, CA 90043, **Home Phone:** (213)294-3193.

## JOHNSON, DR. ARTHUR J.

Vice president (organization), association executive, educator. **Personal:** Born Nov 5, 1925, Americus, GA; son of Arthur Allen and Clara Stewart. **Educ:** Morehouse Col, BS, sociol & polit sci, 1948; Atlanta Univ, MS, sociol. **Career:** Fisk Univ, res fel, 1949-50; Wayne State Univ, sociol fac, 1965, dir community rels dept, 1979, vpres univ rels, 1992-95, prof emer, currently; Mich Civil Rights Comn, dep dir; Detroit Pub Sch Syst, dep supt; Univ Detroit, fac. **Orgs:** Bd mem, Pub Broadcasting Serv; bd mem, Am Symphony Orchestra League; bd mem, Detroit Sci Ctr; bd mem, Detroit Symphony Orchestra; bd mem, Detroit Inst Arts; exec secy, Nat Asn Advan Colored People, 1950-61, pres, dir, 1992. **Honors/Awds:** DHL, Wayne State Univ, 1998; Honored with Arthur L Johnson Endowed Scholar, Sch Social Work, Detroit, 2002; Hall of Fame, Inter Nat Heritage; Hon Doctorate, Morehouse Col; Hon Doctorate, Univ Detroit. **Special Achievements:** Articles: "Stock Pickers Up Yonder"; "The Canadian Market: So Familiar, So Different", New York Times Magazine, June 12, 1988, "Is Your City Ready for the Big Leagues", Nation's Cities Weekly, January 25, 1988, p. 6, "The Pennsylvania Challenge", Maclean's, April 23, 1984, p. 26, "Israel's Broken Coalition", Maclean's, April 2, 1984, "A Barometer of Violence", Maclean's, March 5, 1984, "The Collapse of a Nation", Maclean's, February 20, 1984; Author: Breaking the Banks, 1986; Trials to Triumph, 2011. **Business Addr:** Professor Emeritus, Wayne State University, 3222 Fac Admin Bldg, Detroit, MI 48202, **Business Phone:** (313)577-2150.

## JOHNSON, CHARLES H.

Educator. **Personal:** Born Mar 5, 1932, Conway, SC; died Mar 30, 2015, Orangeburg, SC; married Vermelle J; children: Temple & Charles H Jr. **Educ:** SC State Col, BS, 1954; SC State Col, MEd, 1969. **Career:** Educator (retired); Claflin Col, Orangeburg, SC, dean stud, educr & prin pub sch, 1962-67, 1967-96. **Orgs:** SC Stud Personnel Asn; Southern Col Personnel Asn; Nat Stud Personnel Adminrs; Nat Educ Asn; Prof Club; bd dir, Orangeburg Co Coun Aging; Veterans Foreign Wars; bd dir, Orangeburg United Fund; bd trustees, Trinity United Methodist Church; Omega Psi Phi; IBPO Elks World; SC State Univ Alumni; life mem, NCP; vis, Chaflin Col; life mem, PTA; bd dirs, United Way; bd dirs, Palmetto Lou City Health Systs; comn mem, Orangeburg Area Develop Ctr; charter mem, Hon Alumni Asn, Africa Univ, 2000. **Honors/Awds:** Various Naval Awards & Citations; Honorary Doctorate Aspen, Univ, 1997; Hall of Fame, Chaplin Col, 1998; Presidential Citation, Chaplin Col, 1999. **Home Addr:** 691 Bramble Lane, Orangeburg, SC 29115-2640, **Home Phone:** (803)534-8783.

## JOHNSON, ERMA CHANSLER (ERMA C JOHNSON HADLEY)

School administrator, president (organization). **Personal:** Born Jun 6, 1942, Leggett, TX; died Oct 1, 2015; married Bill J Hadley; children: Ardenia Gould. **Educ:** Prairie View A&M Univ, BS, 1963; Bowling Green State Univ, MEd, 1968. **Career:** Turner High Sch, teacher, 1963-67; Bowling Green State Univ, grad asst, 1967-68; Tarrant County Jr Col, Dist Ft Worth, Tex, assoc prof, 1968-72, asst dir personnel, 1973-74, dir personnel, 1974-81, humr consult, vice chancellor human resources, vice chancellor admin, currently; Tex gov, Trinity River Authority Tex & Tex Govs Comt, vol. **Orgs:** Consult, Col & Univ US Civil Comn Serv, 1972-2015; pres, Fannie M Heath Cult Club, 1974-75, 1978-80; Ft Worth Am Revolution Bicentennial Comt, 1974-76; bd dir, 1974-78, treas, 1977-78, Ft Worth-Tarrant County Supportive Outreach Serv; Task Force 100, 1976; vpres, Ft Worth Minority Leaders & Citizens Coun, 1976-78; Ft Worth Pub Transp Adv comt, 1976-80; bd dir, Community Devel Fund, 1976-80; Ft Worth Girls Club, 1976-81, pres, 1979-81; Ft Worth Keep Am Beautiful Task Force, 1977-78; comm vice chairperson, bd dir, United Way Metrop Tarrant County, 1979; Ft Worth Cent Bus Dist Planning Coun, 1979-81; sem leader Col & Univ Personnel Asn, 1980-2015; pres, Tex asn Black personnel Higher Educ, 1981-83; Ft Worth Citizens Move, 1983; chmn, Dallas/Ft Worth Int Airport Bd, 1987; Forum Ft Worth; secy, Mt Rose Baptist Church; bd dir, Ft Worth Black Chamber Com; charter mem, Tarrant County Black Hist & Geneal Socs; Rotary Club Ft Worth; pres, Links Inc; secy bd dir, Mt Rose Child Care Ctr; chmn oper comt, Dallas/Ft Worth Airport Bd. **Honors/Awds:** Grad Asstship, Bowling Green State Univ, 1967-68; One Week Ed & Prof Devel Act Grant in Voc Ed, 1969, four week, 1970; Listed in Outstanding Ed Am, 1972; Outstanding Young Women Am, 1975; Fort Worth Black Female Achiever of the Year, 1977; Distinguished Leadership Award, 2009; Texas Womens Hall of Fame, 2010. **Special Achievements:** Nominated for Outstanding Teacher, Tarrant County Jr Coll, 1971; First black student from Leggett to graduate from college; Fourth chancellor and the first woman and first African American to lead Tarrant County College District; First woman and first African American elected as chairman. **Home Addr:** 2362 Faett Ct, Ft Worth, TX 76119-3112, **Home Phone:** (817)534-8228.

## JOHNSON, DR. MARIE LOVE

Consultant, president (organization), executive director. **Personal:** Born Dec 18, 1925, South Bend, IN; died Nov 24, 2014, Indianapolis, IN; married Arthur. **Educ:** Ind Univ, BS, 1951; Univ Hartford, MEd, 1953; Univ Conn, PhD, 1978. **Career:** E Hartford Bd Educ, spch path, 1949-60, supvr, 1960-77; Shadybrook Lang & Learning Ctr, clin dir, 1971-76, exec dir, 1977-78; self-employed, consult, currently. **Orgs:** Pres, Hartford Alumnae Chap Delta Sigma Theta, 1954-56; bd fin, Town Vernon, 1963-65; clin & cert bd, Am Speech & Hearing Asn, 1969-75; pres, Conn Speech & Hearing Asn, 1971-75; pres, JGM Corp, 1971-78; fel Am Speech & Hearing Asn, 1972; chmn bd mgr, YMCA, 1976-78; vpres, Am Speech & Hearing Asn, 1977-78; contrib fel Ind Univ. **Honors/Awds:** Community Service, Delta Sigma Theta, 1966; Honors, Conn Speech & Hearing Asn, 1970; Tribute Luncheon, Conn Speech & Hearing Asn, 1975; Arthur & Marie Johnson Early Childhood Training Ctr in their honor, 1996; Lifetime Achievement Award, 2007. **Special Achievements:** Editor: The Collected Poetry of Arthur Lyman Johnson. **Home Addr:** 78 Warren Ave, PO Box 2026, Vernon Rockville, CT 06066, **Home Phone:** (860)875-7628.

## JOHNSON, SHARON REED

School administrator. **Personal:** Born Aug 25, 1944, Wichita, KS; died Sep 16, 2007, North Bergen, NJ; children: Michael. **Educ:** Northern Ill Univ, BA, sociol, 1972; Roosevelt Univ, MA, urban studies, 1973; Univ Manchester, Eng, cert environ design & social planning, 1973. **Career:** Northeastern Ill Planning Comn, intern, 1972-73; W NY Bd Educ, teacher, 1974, coordr gifted ed & asst prin; PS No 3, prin; Gifted & Bilingual Educ, grants, affirmative action & spec events, prin assigned superindent's off; W New York Sch Dist, Memorial High Sch, prin alternative, Harry L. Bain Elem Sch, prin alternative, currently. **Orgs:** Fin secy, St Nicholas Tennis Club, 1983-84; pres, Mayor's Coun Youth & Sr; commun rep, N Hudson Head start; asst affirm action officer, W NY Bd Educ; bd mem, Hudson City Coor dr Gifted Ed; State Coordr Gifted Ed, W NY Adminr Asn; St James Episcopal Church Vestry; Nat Asn Elem Sch Prin; Montclair Drifters. **Honors/Awds:** Northeastern Ill Planning Comn, Tuition Grant, 1972-73. **Home Addr:** 6600 Kennedy Blvd, West New York, NJ 07093, **Home Phone:** (201)861-7715. **Business Addr:** Principal of Alternative, Harry L Bain Elementary School, 6200 Broadway, West New York, NJ 07093-3008, **Business Phone:** (201)553-4035.

## JONES, DR. ELNETTA GRIFFIN

Educator. **Personal:** Born Jul 7, 1934, Mullins, SC; died Apr 7, 2016, Shippensburg, PA; married Aaron Mullins; children: Aaron Daryl. **Educ:** SC State Col, BS, 1957; Shippensburg State Col, ME, 1972; Am Univ, DEd, 1979. **Career:** Rosenwald High Sch, teacher, 1957-59; AUS & Air Force, Educ Develop Ctr, staff, 1960-63; AUS Inf Ctr, teacher, 1964-66; AUS Inf Ctr, teacher, 1969-70; Shippensburg Univ, Act 101 Prog, from asst dir to dir, 1972-78, acad affairs, asst vpres, 1979-80, spec acad progs, assoc dean, 1980-82, dean spec acad progs, 1982-99. **Orgs:** Penn Asn Develop Educrs; Pa Black Conf Higher Educ; Phi Delta Kappa; Nat Acad Adv Asn; Nat Polit Cong Black Women; Shippensburg Civic Club; Delta Sigma Theta Inc; Nat Asn Develop Educrs; coun trustee, Shippensburg Univ Pa, 2008. **Honors/Awds:** Outstanding Humanist Award, Shippensburg Univ Black Alumni, 1985. **Special Achievements:** Five publications including contributor to "Research in Higher Education", 1983, Amer Univ Press Wash DC. **Home Addr:** 366 Hostetter Ave, Shippensburg, PA 17257, **Home Phone:** (717)532-8497.

## JONES, HAROLD M.

Musician. **Personal:** Born Mar 25, 1934, Chicago, IL; died Jan 14, 2015, New York, NY; son of William Henry and Rosetta; married Wanda J Hudson; children: Ernest Milton, Louis Eugene & Antar Patrice. **Educ:** Sherwood Music Sch, cert; Juilliard Sch Music, dipl, 1959. **Career:** Flutist & educator: Metrop Music Sch; Tremont YMHA; Bronx House Music Sch; Merrywood Music Camp; Juilliard Sch Music; Prep Div, Westchester Sch Music; Westchester Conserv Music; Manhattanville Col; Manhattan Sch Music; Prep Div, City Univ New York; The Antara Ensemble, dir, conductor, founder, currently. Solo performances: Symphony New World; Munic Concerts Orchestra & Am Symphony Orchestra; The Conserv Orchestra Brooklyn Col; Chamber Orchestra Black Am Music Symposium; S Ark Symphony; The Philharmonic Greensboro, NC; Jackson Symphony Orchestra; Recordings include: Vivaldi Concerti, Max Goberman; Island in the Sun, Harry Belafonte; Trio for Flute, Oboe, Piano, Howard Swanson; Poem for Flute & Harp, N Mondello; Robeson; POV, John Lewis; Harold Jones; From Bach to Bazzini; Afternoon Fantasies; Just As I Am, Antara Rec; Let Us Break Bread Together, Leonarda Rec; This Little Light of Mine; numerous recital, orchestra, ensemble & theatrical appearances. **Orgs:** Bd mem, NY Flute Club, 1965-, pres, 1976-79; pres, Nat Flute Asn, 1979; Am Fedn Musicians, Local 802; Chicago Civic Orchestra; fac mem, Brooklyn Col. **Honors/Awds:** Outstanding Woodwind Player Award, Juilliard Sch Music; Key to the City of Jackson, Tennessee, 1991. **Home Addr:** 100 W 94 St, New York, NY 10025, **Home Phone:** (212)866-2545. **Business Addr:** Founder, The Antara Ensemble, 2065 Fifth Ave 127th St, New York, NY 10025, **Business Phone:** (212)866-2545.

## JONES, IDA KILPATRICK. See WHITE, IDA MARGARET.

## JONES, ROBERT WESLEY

Executive. **Personal:** Born Jul 24, 1929, Boston, MA; died Jul 21, 2015, New York, NY; son of John and Lillian Evans; married Elaine S Savory; children: Todd, Stacy & Austin. **Educ:** Howard Univ, attended 1950; NY Univ, BS, 1956; NY Law Sch, NY Bar, cert, 1960. **Career:** City New York, dep comr, 1964-66; Pianta Dosi & Assoc, vpres, 1966-68; Burnett Constr Co, vpres, 1968-70; New York Univ, adj prof, 1972; Robert W Jones & Assoc Inc, pres, 2015. **Orgs:** Citizens Housing & Planning Coun, 1974-2015; mem bd adv, New York Univ Real Estate Inst, Sch Prof Studies Schack Inst, 1974-2015; exec comt, Asn Better New York, 1975-2015; chmn, Tougaloo Col Bd Trustees, 1980-, chmn emer, 1996; pres, Independent Fee Appraisers, 1984-2015; mem bd adv, Fed Nat Meeting Asn, 1985-2015; bd gov, New Sch Soc Res, Milano Grad Sch, 1993; Exec Comt 14th St Local Develop Comt, 1993; sr advr, Columbia Partners Invest Mgt LLC, 1996; dir, Landon Butler Co, 1996; Brown-Tougaloo Rels community, 1999. **Honors/Awds:** DHL, 1996.

## JONES, REV. VERNON ALGIE, JR.

Educator, clergy. **Personal:** Born Sep 19, 1924, Brunswick County, VA; died Nov 14, 2015, Conyers, GA; son of Vernon A and Harriet Rhodes Simmons; married Lillian Clark; children: Cecilia, Harriett & Vernelle. **Educ:** Va Union Univ, AB, 1945; Bishop Payne Div Sch, BD, 1948; Va Theol Sem, MDiv. **Career:** Clergy (retired); St Stephen's Church, rector, 1953-57; St Andrew's Episcopal Church, vicar, 1957-60, Tuskegee Inst, rector, 1960-90. **Orgs:** Secy, Coun Episcopal Diocese, 1975-78; Soc Increase Ministry. **Home Addr:** 6312 Willow Glen Dr, Montgomery, AL 36117-2527, **Home Phone:** (334)272-4290.

## JORDAN, DR. GEORGE LEE, JR.

Dentist, educator. **Personal:** Born Nov 2, 1935, Norfolk, VA; died Oct 5, 2015, Chesapeake, VA; married Marguerite W; children: George III & Bernard. **Educ:** Cent State Univ, BS, 1957; Fisk Univ, MA, 1963; Meharry Med Col, DDS, 1971. **Career:** Protsmouth VA, teacher, 1958-62; Wash, DC, teacher, 1963-64; Phoenix, sci teacher, 1964-67; Meharry Med Col, instr, 1971-72; Mich State Univ, asst prof, 1972-76; Lakeside Health Ctr, dir, 1972-75; Pontiac Sch Dist, consult, 1974-77; Olin Health Ctr, dir, 1975-76; Va Clin, PC, dent dir, 1977-86; pvt pract dentist, 1986-. **Orgs:** Nat Asn Advan Colored People; Pontiac Area Urban League. **Honors/Awds:** Outstanding Teacher Jaycees, WA, DC, 1962; Outstanding Citizen, Omega Psi Phi, 1967; Citation, Pontiac Schs, 1977. **Home Addr:** 2221 Georgetown Blvd, Chesapeake, VA 23325-4725.

## JORDAN, MARJORIE W.

Manager. **Personal:** Born Jan 12, 1924, New Orleans, LA; children: Cornelius & Emmett. **Educ:** Dillard Univ, BA, 1944; Univ Chicago; Univ Cincinnati; Col Comn Serv Comn Health Adminr. **Career:** Cincinnati Health Dept, coordr health progs; Housing Opportunities Made Equal, exec dir, 1968. **Orgs:** Nat Asn Black Soc Workers; Ohio Pub Health Asn; Prof Soc Pub Health Workers Ohio; Nat Conf Soc Welfare; mem bd, Nat Non-Profit Housing Corp; bd mem, sec, exec com mem, 7 Hills Neighborhood Houses Inc; exec com, Easy Riders Inc; bd, Urban League; ARC; Am Cancer Soc; co-chmn, Consumer Affairs Comn Fed; exec bd, chmn, Consumer Forum; exec com, Housing Opportunities Made Equal Inc; Unitarian Universalist Serv Com Bd; Womans City Club; Social Serv Asn. **Honors/Awds:** Recipient Service Award, Am Cancer Society, 1972. **Home Addr:** 1858 Northcut Ave, Cincinnati, OH 45237.

## KEELS, JAMES DEWEY

Manager, executive, mayor. **Personal:** Born Jan 12, 1930, Blackfork, OH; died Jan 28, 2016, Cincinnati, OH; son of G Dewey and Hulda Howell; married Dorothy M Wilmore; children: James Dewey Jr & Tawana Lynn Simons. **Educ:** Univ Cincinnati Eve Col, attended 1971. **Career:** Mayor (retired); US Post Off, postal clerk, 1953-78, supvr del & collection, 1979-80; Village Woodlawn, coun, 1969-71, mayor, 1972-79; Add Info Systs, mgr, 1981-85. **Orgs:** Cmdr, John R Fox No 631 Ame League, 1960-64; Exec officer & treas, Ohio Mayors Asn; Cincinnati Postal Employ Credit Union, 1969; past vpres, Nat All Fed Employ, 1969-72, vpres, 1989-93, 1995-96, pres, 1994; Hamilton County Munic League, 1972-79; finance chmn, Gross Br, Young Men's Christian Asn, 1980-88; pres, Emancipation Celebration Comt, 1989-94; Woodlawn Action Club; Valley Young Men's Christian Asn; New Hope Baptist Church; Gallia Econ Develop Asn; pres, chmn, Gallia County Minority Rep, Ohio Valley Regional Develop Comn. **Honors/**

**Awds:** Ky Colonel Hon, Or KY Col Commonwealth, 1971; Award of Merit, Pride Mag, 1979; Outstanding Community Service, Gen Assembly Ohio Senate, 1979; Elected member, Govs Ohio Exec Comn, Ohio Rural Develop Partnership, 1993. **Special Achievements:** First African-American mayor for the Village of Woodlawn, 1972; First African-American chairman to the Post Office Credit Union, 1974-75; First African-American elected officer treasure of Ohio Mayor Association, 1978. **Home Addr:** 1041 Vaughn Rd, Bidwell, OH 45614, **Home Phone:** (740)245-5418. **Business Addr:** GEDA President, Chairman, Ohio Valley Regional Development Commission, 9329 State Rte 220, Waverly City, OH 45690-9012, **Business Phone:** (740)947-2853.

### KELLMAN, DENIS ELLIOTT

Lawyer, executive. **Personal:** Born Jul 6, 1948, New York, NY; died Jan 15, 2014, Warwick, NY. **Educ:** Yale Col, BA, 1970; Harvard Law Sch, JD, 1975; Harvard Bus Sch, MBA, 1975. **Career:** LeBoeuf, Lamb, Greene & MacRae, adv bd co-chmn; Columbia Pictures Industs Inc, counr; Bertelsmann Music Group, dir legal & bus affairs; Law Off Denis E. Kelman, atty, currently. **Orgs:** Int Fedn Phonogram & Videogram Producers; Brit Phonograpic Indust; Black Music Asn; Harvard Bus Sch Black Alumni Asn; Harvard Law Sch Black Alumni Asn; pres, Black Entertainment & Sports Lawyers Asn. **Honors/Awds:** BESLA Hall of Fame. **Home Addr:** 9A St Peters Sq, LondonW6 9AB. **Business Addr:** President, Black Entertainment & Sports Lawyers Association, PO Box 230794, New York, NY 10023, **Business Phone:** (919)423-7076.

### KING, B. B. (RILEY B KING)

Blues singer, guitarist. **Personal:** Born Sep 16, 1925, Itta Bena, MS; died May 14, 2015, Las Vegas, NV; son of Albert and Nora Ella Farr; married Sue Carol Hall; children: 8; married Martha Lee Denton. **Career:** Singer, songwriter, guitarist; Blues Boys Kingdom, founder. Albums: Anthology of the Blues; Better Than Ever; Boss of the Blues; Doing My Thing; From the; Incredible Soul of BB King; The Jungle; Let Me Love You; Live BB King Onstage; Original Sweet 16; Pure Soul; Turn On With BB King; Underground Blues; Live at the Regal, 1965; Electric BB King, 1969; Completely Well, 1970; Indianola Mississippi Seeds, 1970; Live & Well, 1970; Live in Cook County Jail, 1971; Back in the Alley, 1973; Midnight Believer, 1978; Take It Home, 1979; Guitar Player; Love Me Tender, 1982; Deuces Wild, 1997; Live at the Regal, 1997; Blues on the Bayou, 1998; Riding With The King, 2000; Reflections, 2003; The Ultimate Collection, 2005; BB King & Friends: 80, 2005; Gold, 2006; Rhythm & Blues Christmas, 2006; One Kind Favor, 2008; Memphis Blues, 2010. Videos: Blues Summit Concert, 2005. Singles: Why I Sing the Blues, 1992; Got my Mojo Working, 1994; In London, 2001. Tv Appearances: The Cosby Show; The Young and the Restless; General Hospital; The Fresh Prince of Bel-Air; Sesame Street; Married... with Children; Sanford and Son; Touched by an Angel. Films: Spies Like Us. **Orgs:** Founding mem, John F Kennedy Performing Arts Ctr, 1971; co-founder, Found Advan Inmate Rehab & Recreation. **Honors/Awds:** Golden Mike Award, Nat Asn TV & Radio Artists, 1969, 1974; Academie duJazz Award, France, 1969; Grammy Award for Best Rhythm & Blues Vocal Male for The Thrill Is Gone, 1970; Humanitarian Award, B nai B rith Music & Performance Lodge, 1973; Honorary Doctorate, Tongaloo Col, 1973; Honorary Doctorate, Yale Univ, 1977; Grammy Award for Best Traditional Blues Recording for My Guitar Sings the Blues, 1986; Lifetime Achievement Award, Nat Acad Recording Arts & Sci, 1987; Inducted to Rock & Roll Hall of Fame, 1987; Presidential Medal of the Arts, 1990; Nat Award of Distinction, Univ MS, 1992; Kennedy Center Honors, 1995; Trumpet Awards, spec honoree, 1997; Hollywood Walk of Fame; Grammy Lifetime Achievement Award, 1987; Nat Asn Advan Colored People Image Awards Hall of Fame; Blues Foundation Hall of Fame; 15 Grammy Awards; A Christmas Celebration of Hope, Auld Lang Syne, 2003; 14th Grammy Award; honorary PhD, Univ Miss & Royal Swed Acad Music, 2004; Presidential Medal of Freedom, 2006; honorary doctorate in music, Brown Univ, 2007; presented with the keys to the city of Utica, New York, 2008; May 18, 2008, declared the day B B King Day in the city of Utica, 2008; Sirius XM Radio channel was re-named to B.B. King's Bluesville, 2008. **Special Achievements:** TV commercials for NW Airlines, Greyhound & Wendy's. **Business Addr:** Guitarist, Singer, William Morris Agency, 1325 Avenue of the Americas, New York, NY 10019, **Business Phone:** (212)586-5100.

### KING, RILEY B. See KING, B. B.

### KIRK, ORVILLE, SR.

Educator. **Personal:** Born Mar 5, 1936, St. Louis, MO; died Jun 21, 2016, Saint Louis, MO; married Joyce; children: Orville Jr, Gerald & Ronald. **Educ:** Wiley Col, BA, 1957; Harris Teachers Col, MO, attended 1965; St Louis Univ, MO, spec educ cert, 1967, MEd, 1970, post masters work educ specialist, 1972, resident stud, 1973, supt cert, 1973. **Career:** St Louis Pub Sch Syst, teacher, 1961-72; St Louis Baby Study Proj CEMREL, res teacher, 1968-71; Univ Mo, res tech, 1971-72, Mo Dept Elem & Sec Educ, spec educ consult, 1972-76, supvr, 1976-2016; Urban Behav Res Assco, consult, 1973-77; Acad Urban Serv, consult, 1973-77; St Louis Sci Ctr, sr off site progs asst. **Orgs:** Pres, Chap 103 Coun Except C, 1975-76; Coun Adminr Spec Educ; Coun C Behav Dis; Coun Execpt C; bd dir, Annie Malone C & Family Serv Ctr; Coun Ment Retardation CEC-MR. **Home Addr:** 5247 Northland Ave, St Louis, MO 63113-1018, **Home Phone:** (314)381-9567.

### LADAY, DR. KERNEY, SR.

Executive, consultant. **Personal:** Born Mar 14, 1942, Ville Platte, LA; died Sep 8, 2012, Dallas, TX; son of Sampson and Lillius; married Floradese Thomas; children: Marucs K, Kerney Jr & Anthony D. **Educ:** Southern Univ, Baton Rouge, LA, BS, 1965; La State Univ, MS, coun & psychol, 1970; Southern Methodist Univ, MBA, 1982. **Career:** Southern Univ, asst placement dir, 1968-71; Eltrex Corp, bd dir, 1982-86; Xerox Corp, vpres & regional gen mgr, 1986-91, vpres field opers, Southern Region, US Customer Oper, 1991-95, sr vpres; TXU Corp, dir, 1993; Energy Future Holdings Corp, dir, 1993-2007; Laday Co, owner & pres, 1997; Erwin, Graves & Assoc, managing dir; 21st Century Group LLC, strategic advisor; TD Industs Inc, bd dir, 1998; Beck Group, bd dir; Select Payment Processing Inc, advisor; Rent-A-Ctr Inc, dir, 2008; Southern Methodist Univ, Edwin L Cox Sch Bus, dir. **Orgs:** Life mem, United Way Metrop Dallas, 1987; bd dir, N Tex Community; trustee, Shiloh Baptist Church, Plano Tex; assoc bd dir, Southern Methodist Univ; bd dir, African Am Mus; bd dir, Dallas Chamber Com; bd dir, Dallas Citizens Coun; bd dir, NC Nat Bank Tex; vice chmn, Tex Health Resources Inc, 2010. **Honors/Awds:** Renowned Grad, Southern Univ; Presidential Citation, Nat Educ Equal Opportunities. **Home Addr:** 4609 Bush Dr, Plano, TX 75093-7112. **Business Addr:** Strategic Advisor, 21st Century Group LLC, 200 Cres Ct Suite 1600, Dallas, TX 75201, **Business Phone:** (214)965-7999.

### LAMBERT, BENJAMIN FRANKLIN

Lawyer. **Personal:** Born Mar 6, 1933, Lowell, MA; died Apr 21, 2016, Newburgh, NY. **Educ:** Boston Univ, BA, chem, 1955; Brandeis Univ, MA, org chem, 1959; Seton Hall Univ Sch Law, JD, 1968. **Career:** Atty (retired); Ciba Phar Co Inc, res chem, 1957-66; Ciba Ltd, res asst, 1962-63; Merck & Co Inc, atty, 1966-70; Fitzpatrick, Cella, Harper & Scinto, atty, 1970-72; Johnson & Johnson, patent atty, 1973; Brandeis Univ, teaching fel. **Orgs:** Reg US Patent Off, 1968; US Dist Ct Dist NJ, 1969; Dist Ct So Dist NY, 1972; NY Bar Asn, 1972; Dist Ct Eastern Dist NY, 1972; US Ct Customs & Patent Appeals, 1977; NJ Patent Law Asn; Am Patent Law Asn; Nat Asn Advan Colored People, 1977; Delta Hon Soc; Scarlet Key Hon Soc. **Honors/Awds:** Augustus Howe Buck Scholar. **Home Addr:** 315 W 70th St, New York, OH 10023, **Home Phone:** (212)580-8008.

### LANDER, CRESSWORTH CALEB

Consultant, government official, president (organization). **Personal:** Born May 15, 1925, Tucson, AZ; died Jul 2, 2015, Tucson, AZ; son of James Franklin and Julia Belle Watson; married Linda C Hill; children: Melodie Lynette & Rochelle Elaine. **Educ:** Univ Ariz Los Angeles State Col, BS, bus admin, 1958; MIT Sloan Bus Sch, summer course, 1975; Harvard Bus Sch & Kennedy Sch Govt, 1979. **Career:** Government official (retired); Real estate bus, 1959; Univ Aria Urban Planning Dept, lectr, 1976-78; Civil Aeronaut Bd, managing dir, 1979-81; Comm Dev Training Inst, consult, pres. **Orgs:** Dept assessor, LA Co Assessor's Off Bus Div, 1958-59; dep dir, Pima-Santa Cruz Co, 1968-69; dir, City Tucson's Dept Urban Resource Coord (Model Cities), 1969-74, dir, City Tucson's Dept Human & Comm Dev, 1974-78; bd trustee, Pub Housing Authority Dirs Asn; bd mem, Pima Coun Aging; bd mem, Tucson Airport Authority; vpres & bd mem, chairperson, Tucson Urban League, 1992-; bd, Ariz Multi bank Comm Develop Corp, 1992-; pres, Community Develop Training Inst, 1992-; dir, Dept Housing City Tucson; pres, Dunbar Coalition. **Honors/Awds:** Senior Executive Service, US Govt Charter, 1979; Meritorious Service, Civil Aeronautics Bd, 1981; Par Excellence Award, Ariz Black C of C, 1984; Comm Leadership Award, Jack & Jill Am Tucson Chap, 1985; Founders Award winner, 2006. **Home Addr:** 5232 N Calle Bujia, Tucson, AZ 85718-5223, **Home Phone:** (520)577-7184. **Business Addr:** President, The Dunbar Coalition Inc, PO Box 86132, Tucson, AZ 85754-6132, **Business Phone:** (520)791-7795.

### LANE, DR. EDDIE BURGYONE, SR.

School administrator, clergy. **Personal:** Born Aug 8, 1939, Providence, LA; died Oct 15, 2015, Dallas, TX; son of John and Cleo; married Betty Jo Washington; children: Felicia, Carla & Eddie II. **Educ:** S Bible Inst, Dallas, bible dipl, 1974; Univ Tex, Dallas, BA, 1980; Dallas Theol Sem, MTh, 1980; Denver Sem, Ddiv. **Career:** Bibleway Bible Church, founder & sr pastor, 1967-; Dallas Bible Col, prof, 1975-76; S Bible Inst, prof, 1975-76; Dallas Theol Sem, from admin asst to pres, 1975-80, asst dean studs, 1980-85, asst prof pastoral ministries, 1980-90, assoc dean studs am minorities, 1985-, assoc prof emer, currently. **Orgs:** Co-founder & vpres, Black Evangelistic Enterprise, Dallas, 1974-; bd mem & pres, Dallas Nat Black Evangel Asn, 1974-; dir, Black Christian Lit Am Tract Soc, 1978-85; founder & pres, Inst Black Family Renewal, 1992-; Black Family Press, 1994-; bd mem, Wycliffe Bible Translrs, 2001-; bd dir, Wycliffe Bible Translr. **Special Achievements:** Author: "The African American Christian Single", 1995; "The African American Christian Family", 1996; "The African American Christian Parent", 1997; "The African American Christian Man". **Home Addr:** 914 Greenway Dr, Duncanville, TX 75137, **Home Phone:** (972)296-2675. **Business Addr:** Associate Professor Emeritus, Dallas Theological Seminary Pastoral Ministry, 3909 Swiss Ave, Dallas, TX 75204, **Business Phone:** (214)824-3094.

### LANIER, MARSHALL LEE

Educator. **Personal:** Born Jan 12, 1920, Halifax, VA; died Aug 20, 2015, DeSoto, TX; son of Parish L and Mary S; married Dorothy Copeland; children: Frederick Delano (Ingrid), Adrien Copeland (Maxine) & Vanessa Colleen (Larry). **Educ:** Tuskegee Univ, AL, BSA, 1948, MSA, 1950; Tex A&M Univ, PhD, 1971. **Career:** Marvell Independent Sch Dist, instr vets, 1950-51; Co Agr Agt, Texarkana, Ark, 1951-54; Sparkman Training Sch, Sparkman, AR, prin & teacher, 1957-60; E AR Community Col, dir spec serv, 1976-77; Jarvis Christian Col Hawkins, TX, dir stud teaching, 1977-85. **Orgs:** Asn Supv & Curric Develop; Kappa Delta Pi; Omega Psi Phi Frat. **Honors/Awds:** Recipient plaque Outstanding Adv, Jarvis Christian Col, 1975; Blue & Gold Plaque, Jarvis Christian Col, 1978. **Home Addr:** 18667 Fm 2015, Tyler, TX 75706.

### LAWRENCE, THOMAS R., JR.

Labor relations manager. **Personal:** Born Sep 2, 1929, Waycross, GA; died Nov 10, 2015, Bloomington, MN; son of Thomas Reid and Thelma Sue Williams; married Caroline Barbosa; children: Lisa Frazier, Dwayne, Damon & Renee. **Educ:** Suffolk Univ, BA, 1960, MA, 1962; Am Univ, grad study, 1964. **Career:** Labor relations manager (retired); Off Econ Opportunity, educ specialist, 1963-65; Urban League Springfield, exec dir, 1965-68; Info Syst, mgr eeo, N Am Oper, 1970-73; Honeywell Inc, Corp Employee Rel, mgr corp eeo prog, 1973-75, mgr univ rel & minority recruitment, 1983-92; Info Syst-Field Eng Div, Distrib & Priority Control, mgr, 1975-77, mgr nat accts, 1977-79; Avionics Div-Prod Support Logistics, mgr syst & procedures, 1979-80; Controls Syst-Honeywell Plaza, staff asst, 1980-82. **Orgs:** Nat Asn Advan Colored People, Minneapolis, 1972-2015; Minneapolis Urban League, 1972-2015; bd mem, Indust Adv Coun ACT-SO, 1985-2015; bd mem, Nat Consortium Minority Eng, 1985-2015; bd mem, Nat Soc Black Engs, 1988-2015. **Honors/Awds:** Meritorious Service Award, Fla A & M Univ, 1988; Honeywell Focus Award, 1988; Black Engineer of the Year Award, Affirmative Action, 1989; National Black Heritage Observance Council Award, 1990; Distinguished Service Award, NC A & T Univ, 1992; Awarded Honorary Doctorate of Laws, NC A & T Univ, 1993. **Home Addr:** 10541 Wyo Ave S, Bloomington, MN 55438-2029, **Home Phone:** (952)941-5368.

### LAWSON, QUENTIN ROOSEVELT

Government official, educator. **Personal:** Born Jan 7, 1933, Fayetteville, AR; died Mar 14, 2016, Baltimore, MD; married Helen Louis Betts; children: Rosilend & Quentin II. **Educ:** WVa State Col, BA, 1953; Morgan State, 1958; Vassar Col, attended 1960; State Univ Col, attended 1962; Univ Md, MEd, supv & admin, 1968; Morgan State Col, MS, 1968; Inst, NSF. **Career:** City Baltimore, teacher & sch adminr, 1953-68; Baltimore, mayor; Baltimore City Pub Schs, asst dir, 1968-69; Baltimore City Schs, Md State Dept Edn, teacher unit head, unit prin, dir, dropout prev prog, 1969-71; Accountability Inner City, cons; Am psychol assn conf, 1971; City Baltimore, educ advisor, 1971-75, human develop dir, 1975-81; Pub Tech Inc, Urban Consortium, vpres appl res & dir, 1981-85, exec vpres, 1985-87; Nat Forum Black Pub Adminr, exec dir, 1987-92; Nat Alliance Black Sch Educrs, exec vpres, 1996-; Ohio, Fla, Ala, cons, dropout prev progs; US Conf Mayors, Nat Orgn Human Serv Officials, founder & pres. **Orgs:** PTA; Phi Delta Kappa; Gov Task Force State Sch Constrn; Ment Health Support Syst; Nat League Cities, mayor's rep; Cen MD Health Systs Agy; retail study Soc Serv Commn; John F Kennedy Inst Handicapped C; Med Eye Bank; United Fund CICHA; Bay Col MD; Dept HEW; steering com Met Comms Syst Study; YMCA; Comm Orgn Notable Ams, 1976-77; chmn, Gov's Coun Adolescent Pregnancy Prev, State Md, 1991-99; Cong Black Caucus Found, exec dir, 1992-95; bd dir, Kurron Inc, 1993-; bd mem, Mus Natural Hist, Smithsonian Inst, 1994-2000; Am Soc Asn Execs; chmn, Md Higher Educ Comn, 1995. **Home Addr:** 7902 Audubon Ct, Baltimore, MD 21244-2945, **Home Phone:** (202)608-6310.

### LEDEE, ROBERT

Consultant. **Personal:** Born Aug 20, 1927, Brooklyn, NY; died Jun 1, 2015; son of Reginald and Mary Godfrey; married Victoria Marzan; children: Yvonne Alvarez, Robert Jr, Reginald & Anthony. **Educ:** FBI Nat Acad, attended 1968; John Jay Col, AS, criminal justice, 1971, BA, 1973, MPA, 1976. **Career:** New York Housing Police Dept, apptd, 1955; sgt, 1958-60, lt, 1960-64, capt, 1964-67, dep insp, 1967-70, insp, 1970, dep chief, 1970-78; Sea Gate NY Harbor Police Dept, chief, 1979-81; Fed Funded Comm Serv Officer Prgm, adminr; Hisp Law Enforcement Training Inst Justice, cons; New York Dept Personnel, cons. **Orgs:** Guest lectr, FBI Nat Acad; rep, Housing Pol Dept; Insterst Conf Delinq Control, 1965; Nat Symp Law Enforcement Tech, 1967; 13th Ann Inst Polic & Comm Mich St Univ, 1967; Crive Prev Sem, 1968; adminstr Model Cities Comm Serv Officer Prog. **Honors/Awds:** Upper Pk Ave Bapt Ch, 1963; Fed Negro Civil Serv Orgs, 1964; Bronx Dective Unit, 1965; Counc of Police Orgns, 1966; Hispanic Soc, 1966, 1970; Anti-Crime Com, 1969; Grand Counc of Hispanic Soc, 1971; Nat Police Ofcrs Asn, 1972; Comm Rel Unit, 1973; NY Club, 1974; John Jay Coll Alumni Asn, 1976; Nat Conf of Christians & Jews, 1977. **Special Achievements:** First black member to hold rank of lt, capt, dep insp, dep chief New York City Housing Police Dept; dept commendations for outst police work; Author article FBI Bull, 1975. **Home Addr:** Milton St, Dartmouth, MA 02714, **Home Phone:** (718)525-4264. **Business Addr:** Consultant, PO Box 657, Jamaica, NY 11434.

### LEE, AUBREY WALTER, SR.

Chief executive officer, banker, president (organization). **Personal:** Born Oct 26, 1934, Huntington, WV; died Oct 9, 2015, MI; married Jeane F; children: Aubrey Jr, David & Mark. **Educ:** Morehouse Col, attended 1952; WV State Col, BA, polit sci, econ, 1955; Marshall Univ, MA, polit sci, econ, 1956; Univ Wis Grad Sch Banking, dipl, 1969. **Career:** Banker, pres, chief executive officer (retired); NBD Bank, teller trainee, 1957, asst mgr, br mgr, 1966, personnel staff asst, 1967, asst vpres, reg mgr, vpres, head minority & com lending, 1971, first vpres, reg banking ctr dir, 1983-96, sr vpres, 1997-99; City Detroit, staff dir, 1976-77; NBD Troy Bank, chmn, chief exec officer, pres, 1980-83; Bank one, Munic banking grp, head & sr vpres, 1999; Fifth Third Bank, pres. **Orgs:** Dir, vice chmn, treas, chmn fin comt, William Beaumont Hosp; bd trustee, bd mem, Walsh Col, chmn orgn & compensation comt; Bloomfield Hills Country Club; pres, chmn & ceo, Troy; Econ Club Detroit; Nat Asn Advan Colored People; Bd mem & pres, Outer Dr Faith Lutheran Church; Am Bankers Asn; Nat Bankers Asn; pres, Troy Chamber Com; co-founder & pres, Urban Financial Serv Coalition; Detroit Regional Chamber. **Honors/Awds:** Pi Sigma Alpha Honor Fraternity, Nat Honor Society; YMCA Minority Achiever Award in Industry; City of Detroit, Medallion; Urban Bankers Forum, Distinguished Banker's Award; Marshall Univ, Distinguished Graduate Student Alumnus Award; Distingushed Warriors, Urban League, 2001. received over 20 awards and honors from local, state and national organizations, including the Trailblazer Award, Nat Bankers Asn, Distinguished Warrior Award, Detroit Urban League; Crain's Detroit Business Black Business Leader Award, Distinguish Graduate Student Alumnus Award, Marshall Univ; Jeffery W. Barry Leadership Award. **Special Achievements:** One of the First African American to be chairman, president and CEO of a NDB bank, 1979. **Home Addr:** 5889 Carmen Ct W, Orchard Lake, MI 48324-2915.

### LEONARD, DR. WALTER J.

Educator, scholar, college president. **Personal:** Born Oct 3, 1929, Alma, GA; died Dec 8, 2015, Kensington, MD; married Betty E Singleton; children: Anthony Carlton & Angela Michele. **Educ:** Savannah State Col, attended 1947; Morehouse Col Atlanta, attended 1960; Atlanta Univ Grad Schl Bus, attended 1962; Howard Univ Sch Law, JD, 1968, Inst Educ Mgt, 1974, AMP, 1977. **Career:** Ivan Allen Jr Atlanta, asst campaign mgr, 1961; Leonard Land Co Atlanta, owner, operator, 1962-65; Sam Phillips McKenzie, campaign asst, 1963; Dean Clarence Clyde Ferguson Jr Sch Law, Howard Univ, legal res asst, 1966-67; Wash Tech Inst, admin asst to pres, 1967-68; Howard Univ Sch Law, asst dean, lectr, 1968-69; Harvard Univ Law Sch, asst dean, asst dir admin, fin aid, 1969-71; US Off Econ Opportunity, hearing examr, 1969-70; Univ Calif, visit prof summers, 1969-72; Univ Va, visit prof summers, 1969-72; Harvard Univ, asst to pres, 1971-77; Fisk Univ, pres, 1977-84, pres emer, 1984-2015; Howard Univ, distinguished sr fel, 1984-86; US Vi, exec asst to gov, 1987-89; pvt consult, 1989-90; Cities Schs Inc, exec dir, 1990-94; Oxford Univ, Ctr Socio-Legal Studies, vis scholar, 1995-2015. **Orgs:** Asn Am Law Schs; Coun Legal Educ Opportunity; Law Sch Admis Coun; Am Asn Univ Prof; Howard Univ Law Sch Alumni Asn; bd visitors, USN Acad; bd trustees, Nat Urban League; bd trustees, Nat Pub Radio; Int Asn Y'sMen's Club Inc; Nat Asn Advan Colored People; pres, Nat Bar Asn; consult, Ford Found NY, 1969-71; Omega Psi Phi Fraternity; Sigma Pi Phi Fraternity; bd trustees, US Naval Acad FND; bd dir, Cities Schs Inc Asn Am Law Sch. **Honors/Awds:** Appreciation Award, Harvard Black Students' Asn, 1971; Distinguished Service Award, Asn & Office Pres, 1972; Exemplary Achieve Award, Fac Resolution Grad Sch Educ, Harvard Univ, 1976; First Annual Melnea A Cass Community Award, Boston YWCA, 1977; Paul Robeston Award, Black Am Law Students Asn, 1977; Frederick Douglass Pub Service Award, Greater Boston YMCA, 1977; Alumni Achievement Award, Morehouse Alumni Club New England, 1977; Appreciation Dinner & Award, Urban League Eastern MA, 1977; Service Award & Appreciation Citation, Governor US Virgin Islands. **Special Achievements:** Two books & more than two dozen published articles; numerous published works l, "Our Struggle Continues-Our Cause is Just" The Crisis, 1978; "Reflecting on Black Admissions in White Colleges" The Morning After A Retrospective View, 1974; articles in, The Boston Globe, USA Today, The Harvard Law Sch Bulletin; Holder of more than 300 awards & honors in education; The Kuumba Singers of Harvard College have Named their Annual Arts Festival The Walter J. Leonard Black Arts Festival. **Home Addr:** 3505 Glenmoor Dr, Chevy Chase, MD 20815-5637, **Home Phone:** (301)951-8995. **Business Addr:** Visiting Scholar, University of Oxford, Manor Rd, OxfordOX1 3UQ, **Business Phone:** (441)86528-42.

### LESTER, NINA MARIE

Manager, journalist, broadcaster. **Personal:** Born Oct 16, 1922, Ft. Davis, AL; died Jan 15, 2016, Detroit, MI; married Eugene A; children: Rev Adlai, Valinda & Regina; married Albert Eggleston Mack. **Career:** Consumer Guardian Newspaper, co organizers, 1972; WGPR TV, variety show hostess, 1976; Detroit Courier, secy to managing ed, adv & gen mgr; L & T Advert Specialties Gifts, founder. **Orgs:** Samaritan Hosp Div Brd Qual Assurance; adv brd, Women Comn, United Negro Col Fund; League Women Voters; Adv Comm Exp Negro Hist & Educ; Deaconess emer, Plymouth United Church Christ; Nat & Area Publicist; pres, Top Ladies Distinction; trustee, Met Asn United Church Christ; bd mem, Booker T Wash Bus Asn; Urban League Guild; Chamber Comn; pres, Eta Phi Beta; life mem, Nat Asn Advan Colored People; Million Dollar Club, 1991; Women's Asn Detroit Symphony Orchestra. **Honors/Awds:** Service Award March of Dimes, 1966; Recognition Certificate, Un Comn NegroHist, 1967; Woman of the Year, 1971; Town Crier Bell Award & Citizen of the Year Award, Ford Motor Co; Honorary Doctorate Humanities, Shaw Col, 1983; Top Lady of the Year, 1983; Outstanding Mother of the Year, Highland ParkYMCA, 1983; Detroit Urban League Guild Initiative Award, 1985; DetroitCity Council Testimonial Resolution, 1985; National Top Lady of the Year, 1991-93; Spirit of Detroit Award, 1992; Budweiser Community Award, 1993; Edith Gamble Award, Outstanding Community Service; UNCF, 1993-95; Meritorius Service Award, United Negro Col Fund Inc, 1994; President Award, Eta Phi Beta, 1995; Volunteer Recognition Award, UNCF. **Special Achievements:** First black to work for Ford World in Dearborn. **Home Addr:** 16834 Princeton St, Detroit, MI 48221.

### LISTER, WILLA MAE

Manager, teacher, executive. **Personal:** Born Jan 16, 1940, Charleston, SC; died Sep 23, 2010, Fort Worth, TX; daughter of Willie Coaxum Sr (deceased) and Beatrice M Coaxum; married Luther Venice. **Educ:** Dillard Univ, New Orleans, LA, BA, 1962; N Tex State Univ, MEd, 1978; E Tex State A&M Com TX; Kennedy-Western Univ, Cheyenne, WY, PhD. **Career:** New Orleans Sch, phys educ teacher, 1962-63; Ft Worth Sch, teacher, 1964-73; Highland Pk YWCA, ballet & mod dance instr, 1964-71; Community Action Agency, activ dir, 1967-70; Episcopal Found Youth, dir Top Teens Tune, 1968-70; City Ft Worth, personnel analyst training div HRD, 1986-88, asst city mgr, 1989-90, human serv admin, 1990-91; Lone Star Auctioners Inc, onsite mgr & assets shipping staff, 1984-2010. **Orgs:** Pres, Delta Sigma Theta Sor Ft Worth Chap, 1966-67; Astro Rangers Riding Club, 1980-2010; Nat Forum Black Pub Admin, 1990-2010; secy, Tarrant County Youth Collab, 1991-93; bd mem, Am Heart Asn, 1991-94; pres, US Conf Human Serv Officials; Tex Asn Comm Action Agencies; bd dir, Meals Wheels; policy adv bd, State Tex Weatherization; Ft Worth Comm Develop Fund. **Honors/Awds:** Henry Armstrong Award, Col Sr Dillard Univ, 1962. **Home Addr:** 4008 Freshfield Rd, Ft. Worth, TX 76119-2188, **Home Phone:** (817)535-2429.

### LOCKARD, PROF. JON ONYE

Artist, educator, painter (artist). **Personal:** Born Jan 25, 1932, Detroit, MI; died Mar 25, 2015, Ann Arbor, MI; son of Cecil E and Lilian Jones; married Leslie; children: Robin Dunitz, John C & Carlton E. **Educ:** Wayne State Univ, attended 1955; Univ Toronto; Fields Sch Art, cert, 1952; Meinzinger Art Sch, cert, 1952. **Career:** Palmer Paint Co; Univ Mich Ctr Afro-Am & African Studies, asst prof; Acad Creative Thought, dir; Nat Conf Artists, pres, exec bd, 1972-83; Washtenaw Community Col, fac, 1979-2015, asst prof, emer prof; State Black Am channel, consult; 56 PBS Detroit, consult, 1983-84; Asubuhi Cult Ctr, Univ Mich, artist & cur, 1984; Visions Destiny Inc, founder, 2015; AFROCOBRA group, founder; Barden Cable's Sankofa TV prog, co-producer & host. **Orgs:** Exhibiting artist, Suriname Festival Diaspora, 1980-81; sponsor, Sandy Sanders Basketball League, 1983-85; pres, Nat Conf Artists; assoc dir, Soc Study African Am Cult & Aesthetics. **Honors/Awds:** Three Emmy Awards; African American Mural Continium, Wayne State Univ, 1979; City Detroit Proclamation, Detroit City Coun, 1980; Mural Tallest Tree in the Forest, Cent State Univ, 1981; NCA Distinguished Award of Honor, Nat Conf Artists Dakar, Seneyal, 1985. **Home Phone:** (734)665-0955.

### MACK, FRED CLARENCE

Financial manager, executive. **Personal:** Born Sep 1, 1940, Elloree, SC; married Mildred Elaine Oliver; children: Lennie B, Keith O, Erika L & Fred S. **Educ:** SC state Col, BS, 1973. **Career:** Utica Tool Co, leadman, 1968-72; NC Mutual Ins Co, debit mgr, 1970-73; Family Health Ctr Inc, assoc dir, 1973-85. **Orgs:** Exec bd, Nat Asn Advan Colored Peopel Bowman Br, 1960-85; Treas, Antioch Baptist Church, 1970-85, chmn & Deacon, 1983-85; Polit Action Concerned Citizen Dist 94, 1972-85; Chamber Com, 1980; OCAAB Community Serv Agency, 1983-85; Advisor bd, Orangeburg-Calhoun Tec Col, 1983-85; vice-chmn, Orangeburg County Coun. **Special Achievements:** First African American to serve on Orangeburg County.

### MADDOX, DR. ELTON PRESTON, JR.

Dentist, educator. **Personal:** Born Nov 17, 1946, Kingston, MD; died Mar 12, 2015, Salisbury, MD; son of Virginia and Elton. **Educ:** Morgan State Col, BS, 1968; Univ Md, Dent Sch, DDS, 1972. **Career:** Univ Md Dent Sch, instr, 1973-75, asst prof, 1975-77, clin asst prof, 1977-82; pvt pract, dentist, 1977-2015; Team Clin, clin dir & actg dir, 1976-77. **Orgs:** Chmn, Minority Recruitment Comt, 1974-77; Univ Md Dent Sch, Admis Comt, 1974-77; Clin Competency Comt, 1975-76; Alpha Phi Alpha Fraternity Inc; JrC C; Md State Dent Asn; Eastern Shore Dent Asn; pres, Community Awareness Comt. **Honors/Awds:** The Spirit of Survivorship, Salisbury Univ, 2009. **Special Achievements:** Publications namely "A Guide to Clinical Competency, " Journal of Dental Education, 1976; "Why Not?" University of Maryland, 1976. **Home Addr:** 8391 Hilda Dr, Salisbury, MD 21804-2218, **Home Phone:** (410)546-4418.

### MADISON, SHANNON L.

Engineer. **Personal:** Born Jun 21, 1927, TX; died Jul 1, 2013, St. Joseph, MI; married Ruth Jean; children: Earl Wayne, Michael Denard, Stephanie Annett, Sharon & Maria. **Educ:** Howard Univ, BS. **Career:** York Div Borg Warner Corp, develop engr, 1954-59; Emerson Radio & Phonograph Co, chief test engr, 1959-61; Delco Appliance Div GM, sr proj engr, 1961-65; Whirlpool Corp, sr mfg res engr, 1965. **Orgs:** Human Resources Coun; Tri-Co Comn Action Community; Soc Mfg Engrs; NTA; Am Soc Heating; Refrig & Air-Conditioning Engrs; Sigma Xi; SPE; Homes Berrien Co Families Inc; State Adv Bd Gov Mich; Comprehen State Health Planning Adv Coun, 1971-74; Community Twin City Area Human Rels Coun; Twin Cities Community Forum; Model Cities; Nat Asn Advan Colored People. **Home Addr:** 2900 Morton Ave, St. Joseph, MI 49085-2527. **Business Addr:** Senior Manufacturer Research Engineer, Whirlpool Corp, 2000 N M 63, Benton Harbor, MI 49022-2692, **Business Phone:** (269)923-5000.

### MALONE, DR. J. DEOTHA

School administrator, educator, government official. **Personal:** Born May 27, 1927, Sumner County, TN; died Jan 7, 2016, Gallatin, TN; daughter of Sadie and Harvey. **Educ:** Fisk Univ, Nashville, BA, 1950, MA, 1955; Tenn State Univ, MA, adult educ, 1973; Ala State Univ, Montgomery, EdD, 1974; Univ Ala, Tuscaloosa, PhD, 1981. **Career:** School administrator, educator (retired), government official; Sumner Co Sch Syst, teacher & librn, 1950-70; suprv elem educ, 1969-81; suprv adult educ, instr & supvr sec educ, supvr int stud, 1986-2004; City Gallatin, Tenn, vice-mayor, 1969-; State Community Col, instr, 1976-80; Tenn State Univ, instr, 1982-83. **Orgs:** Dept Elec Power Adv Bd, 1990-; Nat Asn Advan Colored People; Gallatin Voter's League; Beacon Civic Club; Econ Dev Prog; vpres, Dem Women's Club Sumner Co; Notary Pub; Nat Educ Asn; adv bd, Tenn Educ Asn; Mid Tenn Educ Asn; Sumner Co Educ Asn; Tenn Asn Pub Sch Adult Educ; Austin Peay Area Supvr Coun; Tenn Asn Adult Educrs; Phi Delta Kappa; Tenn Asn Supvr & Admin; adv, Gallatin Day Care Ctr; Human Serv Career Educ Adv Comm Vol, State Community Col; adv bd, Tenn Asn Lic Practical Nurses; bd dir, Tenn Educ Asn; adv bd, First & Peoples Bank Gallatin; Gov Mgt Team; Tenn Master Teacher Prog; First Baptist Church; Rotary Club; Rotarian chmn, Community Drug Awareness Prog; Gallatin Planning Comn; Kappa Delta Pi Nat Hon Soc; Sumner County Teachers Asn. **Honors/Awds:** Outstanding Legislator of the Year, 1999; Tennessee Education Associations Humanitarian Award, 2004. **Special Achievements:** First African American female notary public Sumner Co. **Home Addr:** 229 S Pardue Ave, Gallatin, TN 37066, **Home Phone:** (615)452-5546. **Business Addr:** Vice Mayor, City of Gallatin, 132 W Main St, Gallatin, TN 37066, **Business Phone:** (615)451-5961.

### MARR, CARMEL CARRINGTON

Lawyer, consultant. **Personal:** Born Jun 23, 1921, Brooklyn, NY; died Apr 20, 2015; daughter of William P Carrington (deceased) and Gertrude C Lewis Carrington (deceased); married Warren II; children: Charles Carrington & Warren Quincy III. **Educ:** Hunter Col, BA, polit sci, 1945; Columbia Univ Law Sch, JD, 1948. **Career:** Lawyer, consultant (retired); Dyer & Stevens Esqs, law asst, 1948-49; Pvt Pract, atty law, 1949-53; US Mission Un, adv legal affairs, legal advisor, 1953-67; Un Secretariat, sr legal officer, 1967-68; New York State Human Rights Appeal Bd, 1968-71; New York State Pub Serv Comn, commdr, 1971-86; Amistad Res Ctr, co-founder, 1976; US Dept Transp Tech Pipeline Safety Stand Comn, chmn, 1979-85; Gas Res Inst, chmn adv coun, 1979-86; consult, energy, 1987-90. **Orgs:** Human Rights Appeal Bd, 1968; Amistad Res Ctr, Tulane Univ, 1970-, chmn & pres, 1982-95; exec comt, Brooklyn Soc Prevent Cruelty C, 1972; chair, US Dept Transportations Tech Pipeline Safety Stand Comn, 1979-85; chair, Gas Res Inst, 1979-86; Prospect Park Alliance, 1983-97; Nat Coun UN Asn, 1983-94; chair, Nat Asn Regulatory Utilities Commissioners & Gas Comt, 1984-86, pres; Great Lakes Conf Pub Utility Comn; Nat Arts Stabilization Fund, 1984-93; Nat Coun Hampshire Col; President's Coun, Tulane Univ, 1989-96; Alpha Kappa Alpha Sorority; Alpha Phi Alpha. **Honors/Awds:** Outstanding Community Service, Brooklyn Urban League; Hall of Fame, Hunter Col; Honorary Citizen, New Orleans; Sojourner Truth Award, Jamaica Club Nat Bus & Prof Women's Clubs; Distinguished Alumni Award, Columbia Univ Law Sch, 1998. **Special Achievements:** Author United Nations procedures; First African American woman appointed to the New York State Public Service Commission. **Home Addr:** 831 Sherry Dr, Valley Cottage, NY 10989, **Home Phone:** (914)268-5811.

### MARSHALL, JULYETTE MATTHEWS

Association executive. **Personal:** Born Oct 26, 1942, Port Arthur, TX; died Nov 3, 2015; daughter of Dr J B Matthews (deceased); married Robert James; children: Nicole Yvette. **Educ:** Fisk Univ, BA, 1964. **Career:** Mayor's Off, asst dir spec events, 1970-73; Gov's EEO Off, compliance officer, 1973-75; Univ Tex, personnel officer, 1975-77; Houston Community Col, personnel officer, 1977-78; Career Planning Ctr, counr, 1978-80; Concepts Unlimited, dir, founder, 1980-90; Zamaani, cult designer, owner, dir, 1990. **Orgs:** Actor writer, PBS, Channel 8, 1969-70; Tex Harlem Ren Comn, 1973-74; Twz African Art Gallery, 1990; Tex Writer's Guild, 1995; Houston Black Doll Asn, 1995; Houston Culinary Hist Asn, 1995. **Honors/Awds:** Special Series for Texas Newspaper, Tex Writers Asn, 1980; Community Involvement Award, 1983; Special Arts Award, Arts Comn Austin, 1985; Contribution to the Arts, Friends of the Phoenix, 1987; Outstanding Alumni for 25 Years, Fisk Univ, 1989; Excellence Community Service Award, Nat Asn Advan Colored People, 1989. **Special Achievements:** Created a series of "Black History in Port Arthur Texas", 1980; assisted in an 18 part TV series on "Black History in Pt Arthur, Texas", 1980-81; Created & produced, "Tribute to Twenty-Eight Black Women in Pa", 1981-82; created & produced "Tribute to Twenty-Eight Black Women in Austin", 1984; Developed & produced seminars for disabled persons instate of Texas, 1985; developed & designed 25th class reunion, Fisk Univ, 1989. **Business Addr:** Owner, Zamaani, 2111 Holy Hall St, Houston, TX 77054, **Business Phone:** (713)790-0012.

### MASON, ANTHONY (GEORGE DOUGLAS MASON)

Basketball player. **Personal:** Born Dec 14, 1966, Miami, FL; died Feb 28, 2015, Manhattan, NY; married Mary; children: Anthony Jr. **Educ:** Tenn State Univ, BA criminal justice, 1988. **Career:** Basketball player (retired); Efes Pilsen, Turkey basketball club, 1988-89; NJ Nets, power forward, 1989-90; Savannah Spirits, Continental Basketball Asn, 1990-91; Denver Nuggets, power forward, 1990-91; Tulsa Fast Breakers, Continental Basketball Asn, 1990-91; NY Knicks, power forward, 1991-95, small forward, 1995-96; Long Island Surf, 1991; Charlotte Hornets, power forward, 1996-98, small forward, 1999-2000; Miami Heat, power forward, 2000-01; Milwaukee Bucks, power forward, 2001-02, ctr, 2002-03. **Honors/Awds:** Sixth Man of the Year, Nat Basketball Asn, 1995; All-Star, Nat Basketball Asn, 2001. **Special Achievements:** Film: Eddie, 1996; Album: Best Kept Secret; Root Down. **Home Addr:** , TN.

### MASON, GEORGE DOUGLAS. See MASON, ANTHONY.

### MAYS, DR. JAMES ARTHUR

Physician, educator. **Personal:** Born May 1, 1939, Pine Bluff, AR; died Aug 21, 2015, Los Angeles, CA; son of Talmadge and Edna; married Lovella Geans; children: James Arthur Jr, James Anthony, James Ornett & James Eddie. **Educ:** Univ Ark, BS, MD, 1960; Univ Calif Sch Med, intern, 1965; Univ Calif, Los Angeles, cardiol. **Career:** Baptist Hosp, Nashville, TN, internship, 1957; Univ Hosp & Clinics, Okla City, internship, 1958-60; Stud Gov Univ Ark Pine Bluff, vpres, 1960; Merrill High Sch, stud counr, 1965; Los Angeles & Chap Alumni Asn, pres, 1972-73; United High Blood Pressure Found, med dir, 1974; Univ Okla Health Sci Ctr, internship, 1985-89; Martin Luther King Hosp, cardiologist self congestive heart failure comt ed; Charles R. Drew Med Sch, cardiologist, asst prof; John Muir Med Ctr; Pac Alliance Med Cente; Bellflower Med Ctr; Mays Med Clin, Los Angeles, owner. **Orgs:** Publ ed, Los Angeles Times, 1974; State Coun Hypertension Control, CA, 1975; Wash Human Rels Comt, 1977; chmn, Push, LA, 1981; founder, Adopt-a-Family; creator, Black Super Heroes Radian & Radiance; fel Am Col Surgeons; chmn, New York Pub Serv Found; Philantropee Asn; bd dir, Watt & Health Found; Steering Comt, Pres Reagan's Comn Tax Reform; fel African Sci Inst.

**Honors/Awds:** News Maker, Nat Asn Media, 1975; ANA Award, 1975; Citation Calif State Senate, 1976; Senator Nat Holder 50 Award; George Washington Medal, Freedom Found Valley Forge. **Special Achievements:** Written songs: "Baby Coy", 1977, "Resing Wright", 1977, "Disco Bill Happy Birthday", 1977; Appeared on Donahue, Today Show; Publications: "Methods to Make Ethnic Foods Safer" 1976, "Monogram on High Blood Pressure", 1976, "Chameleon Released", 1977, "Circle of Five", "Blink of an Eye", "Doctor Dan-Man of Steel"; write-ups in Washington Post, Jet, Ebony, LA Times, LA Harold, Life, Look, Newsweek, CBS News, CNW News, ABC News,USA Today, AMA News, Christian Serv Monitor; spoke before Commissioner of US Senate and House of Reps. **Home Addr:** 2415 W 233rd St, Torrance, CA 90501-5731.

## MCCLAIN, WILLIAM ANDREW

Lawyer. **Personal:** Born Jan 11, 1913, Sandford, NC; died Feb 4, 2014; son of Frank and Blanche Leslie (deceased); married Roberta White. **Educ:** Wittenburg Univ, AB, 1934; Univ Mich, JD, 1937, Wilberforce Univ, LLD, 1963; Univ Cincinnati, LLD, 1971. **Career:** Lawyer (retired); City Cincinnati, asst city solicitor, 1942-57; Berry & McClain, 1938-58; City Cincinnati, dep city solicitor, 1957-63, city solicitor, 1963-72, actg city mgr, 1968, 1972; Keating, Muething & Klekamp, 1972-73; Cincinnati Br Small Bus Admin, gen coun, 1973-75; Hamilton County Common Pleas Ct, judge, 1975-76; Hamilton County Munic Ct, judge, 1976-80; Manley Burke, coun, 1980-2003; Village Lincoln Heights, dir legal serv, 1980-87, 1994-2003. **Orgs:** Bd dir, Cincinnati Chap Red Cross, 1975-; Nat Conf Christians & Jews Cincinnati, 1975; Cincinnati Bar Asn, 1951; Am Bar Asn; Nat Bar Asn; Am Judicature Soc; life fel Am Bar Found; Cincinnati Bar Found; Fed Bar Asn; Prince Hall Mason 33 Degree; Alpha Phi Alpha; pres & bd dir, Wittenberg Alumni Asn; mem comt visitors, Univ Mich Law Sch; Sigma Pi Phi Fraternity; Alpha Delta Boule; trustee, Urban League Greater Cincinnati; Ohio State Bar Asn; Keating Muething & Klekamp; Black Lawyers Asn Cincinnati; Lawyers Club Cincinnati. **Honors/Awds:** LLD, Wilberforce Univ, 1963; LLD, Univ Cincinnati, 1971; LHD, Wittenberg Univ, 1972; Ellis Island Gold Medal Honor, 1997; History Maker Award, 2001; Univ Mich, hon degree, 2002. **Special Achievements:** First member of the Cincinnati Bar Association, 1951; The First attorney to serve as City Solicitor of any major city in the country; First African American judge of the Hamilton County Common Pleas Court; First member of the Lawyers Club, 1974; First black in the United States to achieve such a high municipal legal post. **Home Addr:** 2101 Grandin Rd Apt 904, Cincinnati, OH 45208, **Home Phone:** (513)871-0965.

## MCDANIEL, PROF. REUBEN R., JR.

Educator. **Personal:** Born Jan 6, 1936, Petersburg, VA; died Feb 7, 2016, Austin, TX; son of Reuben R and Nannie Finney; married Myra Yores Atwell; children: Diane & Reuben R III. **Educ:** Drexel Univ, BS, mech engineering, 1964; Univ Akron, MS, guid & coun, 1968; Ind Univ, EdD, higher educ, 1971. **Career:** Philco Corp, Govt & Indust Div, mech designer, 1956-60; Sperry Rand Corp, Univac Div, mech engr, 1960-65; Baldwin-Wallace Col, Div Educ Serv, dir, asst to dean & asst prof educ, 1965-69; Claremont Grad Sch, vis prof mgt, 1981; Co Bus Adminr, assoc dean, chair fac senate; Baldwin-Wallace Col, asst dean, asst prof educ & dir div educ serv, 1965-69; Ind Univ, fel, assoc instr, 1969-71; Fla State Univ, asst prof, 1971-72; Helsinki Sch Econ & Bus Admin, vis prof, 1989-90, 1992-96; Univ Tex, Austin, assoc dean students, 1973-73, from asst prof mgt to assoc prof mgt, 1972-81, Col Bus Admin, assoc dean anal & planning, 1976-78, prof mgt, 1981-95, Jesse H Jones, prof, 1983-89, Dept Info, Risk, & Opers Mgt, prof, 1995-2016, IC2 Inst, Henry E Singleton res fel, 2009-16, Sch Nursing, adj prof, 2011-16; Tom E. Nelson, Jr. Regents prof, 1989-91, Charles & Elizabeth Prothro Regents, chair heath care mgt, 1991-2016; Pa State Univ, Dept Health Policy & Admin, vis res scholar, 1994-2016; Univ Tex Health Sci Ctr at San Antonio, Tex, Dept Med, adj prof, 2005-16. **Orgs:** Actg dep comnr, Tex Dept Human Resources, 1979; consult, Seton Med Ctr, Austin, 1980-2016; bd trustees, Seton Med Ctr, Austin, 1985-91; Fac Senate Univ Tex, Austin, chmn, 1985-87; Adv Comt, Banaker Hons Col, Prairie View A&M Univ, 1987-91; Priority Schs Comt, Austin Ind Sch Dist, 1989-91; Sci Adv Comt, Plexus Inst; bd dirs, USA Inst Managed Care Inc, 1995-98; Ed bd, Health Care Mgt Rev; Serv Res Rev Comt; Nimh Initial Rev Group, 2003-05; Sci Adv Comt; Plexus Inst, 2000-05. **Honors/Awds:** J D Beasley Graduate Teaching Award, 1982; Key D Award, Outstanding Alumni, Drexel Univ, 1988; Myron D Fottler Exceptional Service Award, Health Care Mgt Div, Acad Mgt, Univ Tex, 2001; Elective Fac Honor Role, McCombs Sch Bus, 2000-02; Civitatis Award, Univ Tex, Austin, 2004; Heman Marion Sweatt Legacy Award, Univ Tex, Austin, 2011; Texas Ten-Ex-Student's Association Most Influential Professors, 2013. **Special Achievements:** Publication: The Academy of Management Journal, Decision Sciences, Health Care Management Review, Health Progress, Health Services Research, the Journal of Family Practice, The Journal of Applied Behavioral Sciences, The Journal of the National Medical Association, Management Science, Organizational Behavior and Human Decision Processes, and Nursing Economics. **Home Addr:** 3910 Knollwood Dr, Austin, TX 78731, **Home Phone:** (512)345-0006.

## MCGRUDER, DR. CHARLES E.

Physician, educator. **Personal:** Born Jul 25, 1925, Wedgeworth, AL; died Feb 26, 2015, Nashville, TN; married Curlie Haslip; children: Charles II & Jeffery. **Educ:** Ala A&M Col; Xavier Univ; Meharry Med Col, MD, 1952. **Career:** Professor (retired), physician; Fel Am Col, Obstet & Gynec, physician, 1956-2015; Am Bd Obstet & Gynec, dipl; Meharry Med Col, assc prof, retired emer. **Orgs:** Asst Scoutmaster Troop 77; Mid Tenn Coun, BSA; Am Bd Obstet & Gynec. **Honors/Awds:** Woodbadge Beads in Scouting; Long Rifle; Silver Beaver. **Home Addr:** 1524 22nd Ave N, Nashville, TN 37208-2343, **Home Phone:** (615)327-1628.

## MCKANDERS, JULIUS A., II

Lawyer, clergy. **Personal:** Born Jun 21, 1941, Jackson, MS; died Nov 5, 2000, MI; married Yvonne Mclittle. **Educ:** Henry Ford Comm Col, attended 1962; Detroit Inst Tech, attended 1962; Eastern Mich, BS, 1964; Univ Mich Med Sch, attended 1966; Wayne State Univ, JD, 1971; Morehouse Sch Relig, ITC, 1976. **Career:** Univ Mich Med Sch, res asst, 1964-66; City Detroit, syst analyst-progmr, 1966-67; IRS Detroit, syst analyst, 1967-69; Price Water house, sr mgr, 1969-70; Detroit Bd Ed, mgr, 1970-71; Coun Leg Ed Opp, dep dir oper, 1971-72; Ebenezer Bapt Ch, assoc minister; Metro Atlanta Rapid Transit & Auth, dir contracts & procur, 1972; Mich Bar, admitted, 1972; Ga Bar, 1974. **Orgs:** Am Bar Asn; Detroit Bar Asn; Atlanta Bar Asn; Phi Alpha Delta; Purch Mgt Asn Ga; Atlanta Jr C C; bd dir, Martin L King Jr Child Develop Ctr; bd dir, Nat Asn Advan Colored People Atlanta Br Prog Comn; Am Pub Transit Asn; adv coun, Martin L King, Jr Handicapped Child Proj; bd mem, Ebenezer Baptist Church Charitable; founder & life mem, Nat Asn Advan Colored People; Ordained Baptist Ministry. **Home Addr:** 1065 Carlo Woods Dr SW, Atlanta, GA 30331-7337, **Home Phone:** (404)699-1212. **Business Addr:** Director of Contracts, Metro Atlanta Rapid Transit & Auth, 2424 Piedmont Rd NE, Atlanta, GA 30324, **Business Phone:** (404)848-5000.

## MCKERSON, MAZOLA

Manager. **Personal:** Born Jan 1, 1921, Bluff, OK; died Oct 14, 2014, Ardmore, OK; married Alfred; children: 5. **Career:** Gourmet restaurant, mgr & owner, 1962-97; Ardmore City, coun, 1975-81, comn, 1977-79, vice mayor, mayor, 1979-80, chmn, pres, 1992-93; Murray State Col; AHEC; Mt. Zion Baptist Church, pres women's missionary union & sunday sch teacher. **Orgs:** Chmn, Gov Comn St Women; munic bd St OK; bd dir, comn, ed St OK, chmn, 1986-88; chmn, Ardmore's 100th Birthday Centennial, 1887-87, adv bd, Higher Educ Ctr; Ardmore YWCA; bd dir, Greater SW Hist Mus Bd, chmn; bd dir, Ardmore Chamber Com. **Honors/Awds:** Lady of Year, Zeta Phi Beta Sor, 1976-77; Hon Serving chmn C of C Bicentennial Com, 1976; Woman of the Year, YMCA, 1976; hon mem Sigma Gamma Rho, 1986; Women of the Year, 1996-1997; Woman of the Year, Pioneer Woman Mus Ponca City. **Special Achievements:** First Black elected to the Ardmore city commission, 1977; First African-American Female mayor of Ardmore; First African American to be elected to a City Council of a municipality. **Home Addr:** 4 Rock Island Ltd St, Ardmore, OK 73401-2925, **Home Phone:** (580)223-8653.

## MCKNIGHT, FR. ALBERT J.

Financial manager, clergy. **Personal:** Born Brooklyn, NY; died Apr 17, 2016, Greentree, PA. **Educ:** St Mary's Sem, BA, BT; Holy Ghost Fathers PA & CT. **Career:** So Coop Develop Fund, pres, 1970-84; Southern Develop Found, novice dir; Univ Fondwa, campus minister. **Orgs:** La Econ Develop Task Forces; So Consumers Coop; La Task Force; US Off Econ Opportunity Task Force; People's Enterprise Inc; diocesan dir, Credit Unions, 1963; assoc, Lady Lourdes; Immaculate Heart Mary & St Martin de Porres Chs La; bd mem, vice chmn, Nat Consumer Coop Bank, 1979; chmn, Consumer Coop Develop Corp; pastor, Holy Ghost Cath Church Opelousas; financial & tech assistance, Southern Coop Develop Prog; financial & tech assistance, Southern Coop Develop Fund. **Honors/Awds:** Inducted, coop Hall of Fame, 1987.

## MCLAUGHLIN, DR. GEORGE W.

Educator. **Personal:** Born Feb 14, 1932, Petersburg, VA; died Aug 30, 2016, Charlottesville, VA; married Sadie Thurston; children: Wesley, George Jr & Avis. **Educ:** St Paul's Col, BS, educ, 1957; Va State Col, attended 1958; Univ Va, MEd, EdD, 1970; Bank St Col, Univ Pa; Am Bible Inst, DD, 1974. **Career:** Del State Col, dir stud teaching, 1966-72, chmn educ, 1972-75; St Paul's Col, chmn educ & psych; Mecklenburg Co Pub Schs, coordr gifted educ. **Orgs:** Asn Blvd Cab Co, 1962-2016; pastor, Wayland Baptist Church, 1974-2016; pres, L&M Const Co, 1976-2016; vice chmn, Alta Child-Care Ctr, 1978-2016; Los Angeles City Law Enforcement Comt, 1980; pres, Epsilon Omicron Lambda; Alpha Phi Alpha, 1980-85; vpres, Lawrenceville Optimist Int, 1982-84. **Honors/Awds:** Outstanding Citizen Award, Los Angeles Emancipation Orgn, 1979; Faculty of the Year, St Paul's Col, 1979; Alpha Man of the Year, Alpha Phi Alpha Fraternity, 1982; Distinguished Service Award, Optimist Int, 1983. **Home Addr:** 37 Thurston Rd, Louisa, VA 23093-4906, **Home Phone:** (540)967-0630.

## MCLAUGHLIN, REV. DR. JACQUELYN SNOW

School administrator. **Personal:** Born Aug 12, 1943, Camden, NJ; died Mar 21, 2015, Macon, GA; daughter of Arlington Reynolds Sr; married Herman; children: Jevon & Jacques. **Educ:** Shaw Univ, Raleigh, NC, BA, sociol, 1965; Univ Bridgeport, Conn, couns cert, 1965; Glassboro St Col, NJ, MA, couns, 1972; Rutgers Univ, NJ, DEd, 1976. **Career:** Div NJ Employ Serv, counr, 1965-66; Wash Elem Sch, teacher, 1966-70; Camden Co Col, counr, 1970-71, dir, EOF prog, 1971-75, dean student affairs, 1975-. **Orgs:** Mid St Accreditation Asn, 1980-; pres, NJ St Deans Stud, 1980-; Juv Resource Ctr, staff, 1986-89; ad comn mem, Affirmative Action, 1989; YWCA, bd dir, 1990-93; Asn Col Admin, 1990-93; New England Accreditation Asn, 1992; Nat Asn Foreign Studs; Asn Col Adminr; Alpha Kappa Alpha Sorority; bd dir, Nat Coun Black Am Affairs. **Honors/Awds:** Plaque of Outstanding Service to Education Opportunity Fund Program, Camden Co Col, 1976; Certification Cited in Bicentennial Vol, Comm Leaders & Noteworthy Am, 1976; Delta Kappa Pi Hon Soc; Exec Leadership Inst, League for Innovations in the Community Col; Leaders for the 80s Inst for Leadership Develop; Honorary Mem of Phi Theta Kappa Honor Fraternity. **Home Addr:** 1 Sturbridge Ct, Medford, NJ 08055-8349, **Home Phone:** (609)953-1363.

## MCPHERSON, JAMES ALAN

Educator, writer. **Personal:** Born Sep 16, 1943, Savannah, GA; died Jul 27, 2016, Iowa City, IA; son of James Allen and Mable Smalls; children: Rachel Alice. **Educ:** Morris Brown Col, BA, Eng & hist, 1965; Harvard Law Sch, LLB, 1968; Univ Iowa, MFA, 1972; Yale Law Sch. **Career:** Atlantic Monthly, contrib ed, 1969-2016; Univ Calif, teacher, 1969-72; Morgan State Univ, Baltimore, MD, asst prof, 1975-76; Univ Va, Charlottes ville, assoc prof, 1976-81; Univ Iowa, Iowa City, prof, 1981-2016, Iowa Writers' Workshop, fac. **Orgs:** Nat Asn Advan Colored People; Writers Guild; panel mem, Giles Whiting Found, 1986; lit panel, McDowell Colony, 1988-89; planning panel, Dewitt Wallace Found, 1989; fiction judge, Pulitzer Prize Panel, 1990; fiction judge, Nat Bk Awards Panel, 1993; Am Acad Arts & Scis. **Honors/Awds:** Guggenheim Fel, 1973; Pulitzer Prize, 1978; Yale Law Sch, vis scholar, 1978; LLB Hon, Morris Brown Col, 1979; MacArthur Prize Fel, 1981; Award for Excellence in Teaching, Univ Iowa, 1991; Green Eyeshades Award for Excellence in Print Commentary, Soc Southern Journalists, 1994; fel, Stanford Univ, Ctr for Advan Studies, 1997-98, 2002-03. **Special Achievements:** Author: Hue and Cry, 1969, Rr, 1976, Elbow Room, 1977, A World Unsuspected, 1987, The Prevailing S, 1988, Confronting Racial Differences, 1990, Crabcakes, 1996, the memoir Crabcakes, 1997; A Region Not Home, 2000; ed: Gold Coast, 1969; essays, stories and reviews published in numerous journals, mag and authologies incl Atlantic, New York Times Mag, Reader's Dig, The Nation, The Best Amer Short Stories, O'Henry Prize Stories and Best Amer Short Stories of the 20th Century. **Home Addr:** 711 Rundell St, Iowa City, IA 52240, **Home Phone:** (319)338-3136.

## MILLENDER, DHARATHULA H.

School administrator, educator, association executive. **Personal:** Born Feb 4, 1920, Terre Haute, IN; died Jan 2, 2015, Gary, IN; daughter of Orestes Hood and Daisy Ernestine Eslick Hood (deceased); married Justyn L; children: Naomi Estelle, Justine Faye & Preston. **Educ:** Ind State Univ, BS, 1941; Purdue Univ, MS, 1967. **Career:** School administrator (retired), Bettis Jr Col, librn, 1941-42; Pmoney HS, librn teacher, 1942-43; Neth Studies Unit Libr Cong, ref asst, 1943-44; Serv Club No 2 Ind Town & Gap Mil Reser, army librn, 1944; Lincoln Jr High Montgomery County, teacher, 1952-53; Houston Jr High Sch Baltimore, librn, 1953-60; Dunbar-Pulaski Sch Gary, librn media specialist, 1960-78; Black Exper Film News Mag, ed, 1973-82; Gary Sch Syst, librn, media specialist, 1960-78, sch radio stn, 1978-83, reading lab coordr, 1979-82; Gary Hist & Cult Soc Inc, founder, chief exec officer, exec dir; councilwoman, Pulaski Jr High Sch, librn. **Orgs:** State chmn; Hist & Cul, 1966-72; libr, Multi-Media Coun Model Cities Dayton, 1969-70; Gary Precinct Comt woman, 1972-80; prog coordr, Cable TV Gary channel 3a, 1973-; State HistBlack Pol Caucus, 1973; hist, Gary Chap Ind State Black Caucus, 1973; mat from Black Exper State dir, Asn Study Afro-Am Life & Hist, 1973; chairperson & founder, Gary Hist & Cult Soc, 1977; organist, St Philip Luth Church; pres, NIMM Educ Media Serv Inc; Louis Armstrong-Rev Simon & Schuster, 1997; libr, Media Consul Model Cities Gary dev media ctr, Community Res Ctr Gary; radio prog, Lift Every Voice & Sing sta, WWCA; chrmn, Gary Nat Asn Advan Colored People Black Hist Com, 1962-72; libr trustee, Gary Pub Libr, 1971-75, 1982-86; Gary Hist & Cult Soc Inc, 1971-; historian, Nat Black Caucus - Nat League Cities, 1984-92; consult, Follow Through Cult Ling Approach, 1989-; Gary City Coun, 1980-92; historian, City Gary; vpres, Gary Sch Bd Trustees, 1992-; organizer & secy, Peace Lutheran Church Gary, 1989-. **Honors/Awds:** Commendable Book by an Indiana Author Award for Crispus Attucks, Indiana Writers Conf, 1966; outstanding serv Rendered to Comm Award, Gary Nat Asn Advan Colored People, 1966; Outstanding Educator, Ind Univ, 1971; Media Women's Award, Natl Asn Media Women, 1974; Outstanding Women of Lake County, Ind, 1984; author: Brief Note on the Early Development of Lake County & Gary, Ind, published by Gary Historical & Cultural Society, Inc, 1988; History of Gary City Council, 1992, revised, 1995. **Special Achievements:** Author, num articles in journ & educ mags, books include, Martin Luther King, Jr.: Young Man With A Dream, 1983 Crispus Attucks: Black Leader of Colonial Patriots, 1986, Louis Armstrong: Young Music Maker, 1997, Gary's Central Business Community, 2003. **Home Addr:** 2409 W 5th Ave, Gary, IN 46404, **Home Phone:** (219)882-6873.

## MILLER, ARTHUR J.

Business owner, management consultant. **Personal:** Born Oct 7, 1934, New York, NY; died Jun 5, 2015, Glen Ridge, NJ; son of Theodore Roosevelt and Rosalie White; married Mary Lee. **Career:** Chase Manhattan Bank, dividend clerk, 1952, supvr, 1961, sys planning off, 1968, vpres, 1970-87; AJM Assoc Inc, owner & pres, 1988-2015; Bus Syst Mgt Inc, prin, 1989, pres, 1990-2003. **Orgs:** Chair bd, Reality House Inc. **Honors/Awds:** Man of the Year, Angel Guardian Family Service, 1997.

## MILLER, JUANITA ELIZABETH JACKSON

Lawyer. **Personal:** Born Jan 2, 1913, Hot Springs, AR; died Jul 7, 1992, Baltimore, MD; daughter of Kieffer Albert Jackson and Lillie Mae Carroll Jackson; married Clarence M Jr; children: 2. **Educ:** Univ Pa, BS, educ, 1931, MA, sociol, 1935; Univ Md Sch Law, LLB, 1950. **Career:** NAACP, nat youth dir, 1935-38. **Orgs:** Nat Asn Advan Colored People. **Honors/Awds:** Juanita Jackson Mitchell Award for Legal Activism is awarded annually on her behalf to a National Association for the Advancement of Colored People unit that shows outstanding legal redress committee activities. **Special Achievements:** First African American woman admitted to the Maryland bar; Fought for school desegregation in Baltimore after the Brown vs. Board of Ed ruling; As a result, Maryland was the first southern state to integrate school system.

### MILLER, WILLIAM O.

Educator, association executive. **Personal:** Born Apr 14, 1934, Philadelphia, PA; died Dec 23, 2015; son of Joseph M (deceased) and Ethel Reed; married Naomi Terri Fisher; children: William C. **Educ:** Temple Univ, BS, 1957; Antioch Univ, ME, 1974. **Career:** LBS, 1957; Opportunity Indus Ctrs Inc, instr, 1965-73; Pa Urban Coalition, instr, 1968-80; Fitzsimons Jr HS, dir publicity, 1968-70; Fel Comn Pa, dir educ, 1975-76; OIC/A Pa, asst dir funds devel, 1976-83, dir, nat org & specevents, 1983-2015. **Orgs:** Temple Univ Downtown Club; Grad Coun Antioch Univ; Pa Tribune Charities; Voters Crusade; Del Valley Chap Nat Soc Fund Raisers; bd dir, PaCivic Ballet; Prince Hall Masons King David No 52 F & A Penna PHA; AlphaPhi Alpha Fraternity; Deacon Bd Zion Baptist Church; Am League Lobbyist, Archival Comm OIC/Temple Univ. **Honors/Awds:** Distinguished Service Award, Pa Chap NAACP, 1965; Legion Honor Award Chapel Four Chaplins, 1967-75; Second Mile Award Prince Hall Masons Pa, 1972. **Home Addr:** 520 A Glen Echo Rd, Philadelphia, PA 19119, **Home Phone:** (215)248-9793.

### MOBLEY, DR. SYBIL COLLINS

School administrator, educator. **Personal:** Born Oct 14, 1925, Shreveport, LA; died Sep 29, 2015, Tallahassee, FL; daughter of Melvin Collins and Cora Collins; married James Otis; children: James Jr, Janet Yolanda Sermon & Melvin. **Educ:** Bishop Col, BA, 1945; Wharton Sch Univ, Pa, MBA, 1961; Univ Ill, PhD, 1963; Fla State Univ, CPA. **Career:** Educator, school administrator (retired); Fla A&M Univ, Sch Bus & Indust, prof, 1963-2003, dept head, 1971-74, dean, 1974-2003, prof & dean emer; Sears, boards dir; Roebuck & Co., boards dir; Hershey Foods Corp, boards dir. **Orgs:** Alpha Kappa Alpha; Int Assoc Black Bus Educr; bd dir, Anheuser-Busch CoInc, Champion Int Corp, Hershey Foods Corp, Sears Roebuck & Co, Southwestern Bell Corp, Dean Witter, Discover Inc. **Honors/Awds:** Hon doctorate, Wharton Sch, Univ Pa, Babson Col, Bishop Col, Hamilton Col, Washington Univ, Princeton Univ, Univ Ill; UI Alumna Achievement Award, 1989. **Home Addr:** 520 Hampton Ave, Tallahassee, FL 32310-6216, **Home Phone:** (850)576-3668. **Business Addr:** Professor, Dean Emeritus, Florida Agricultural & Mechanical University, Rm 105 1 SBI Plz, Tallahassee, FL 32307-5200, **Business Phone:** (850)599-3565.

### MONTGOMERY, OLIVER R.

Administrator. **Personal:** Born May 31, 1929, Youngstown, OH; died Jun 6, 2015, Pittsburgh, PA; married Thelma Howard; children: Darlene, Howard, Brenda, Oliver Jr & Edwin. **Educ:** BS, 1956. **Career:** Administrator (retired); Youngstown Sheet & Tube Co; United Steelworkers Am, assoc res asst. **Orgs:** Chmn labor, Nat Asn Advan Colored People, 1960-63; nat bd mem, Sec Nat Afro-Am Labor Coun, 1970-75; vpres, United Steelworkers Local 3657; nat bd & exec coun mem, Coalition Black Trade Unionist; bd mem, Gr Pittsburgh Am Civil Liberties Union, 1972-75; Kappa Alpha Phi Frat. **Honors/Awds:** A Philip Randolph Award; Award certification Merit, Nat Asn Advan Colored People Urban League; Testimonial Dinner, 1970; Award from Mayor, City Counc CAP officer, Off Equal Opportunities Progs. **Home Addr:** 7886 Mark Dr, Verona, NY 15147.

### MOORE, DR. NATHAN

Educator. **Personal:** Born Jun 26, 1931, Mayaro; died Jun 28, 2016, Douglasville, GA; son of William B and Eugenie Samuel; married Mary Lisbeth Simmons; children: Christina & Serena. **Educ:** Caribbean Union Col, Trinidad, BA, 1958; Rockford Col, Ill, BA, 1963; Carleton Univ, Ottawa, Mass, 1965; Univ BC, PhD, 1972. **Career:** Educator (retired); Barbados Sec Sch, high sch teacher, 1958-61; Carleton Univ, teaching fel, 1963-65, sessional lectr, 1964-65; Barrier Sch Dist Brit Col, high sch teacher, 1966-67; Walla Walla Col, Wash, col teacher, 1967-79; Ala State Univ, prof Eng, 1979-2001, chmn Eng, speech, theatre & foreign lang dept, 1980-2001. **Orgs:** Mod Lang Asn, 1965-2016; Am Soc 18th Century Studies, 1971-2016; S Atlantic MLA, 1980-2016. **Honors/Awds:** Scholar, Rockford Col, 1961; Scholar, Readers Digest, 1962; Carleton Fel, Carleton Univ, 1963-65. **Home Addr:** 2928 Moorcroft Dr, Montgomery, AL 36116, **Home Phone:** (334)281-2883.

### MOORE-CASH, BETTYE JOYCE

Executive, nurse. **Personal:** Born Feb 19, 1936, Ft. Worth, TX; died Nov 30, 2014; children: Ardranae, James Jr, Anthony, Lisa & Janine. **Educ:** Contra Costa Col, attended 1963, AA, 1975. **Career:** Nurse, executive (retired); W Contra Costa Healthcare Dist, dist hosp dir, bd dir & treas, 2002-06. **Orgs:** Nat Womens Polit Caucus; Black Bus & Prof Asn; Church Missionary; Cailf Hosp Asn; med staff, Asn Women Hosp; Am Hosp Asn; Asn Dist Hosps; Robinson Weeks Robinson Found. **Special Achievements:** First & only black elected female West Contra Costa City. **Home Addr:** 2732 Groom Dr, Richmond, CA 94806-2641.

### MORRIS, HORACE W.

Chief executive officer, teacher, association executive. **Personal:** Born May 29, 1928, Elizabeth, NJ; died Jan 1, 2011?; son of Pringle and Evelyn Turner; children: Bradley, JoAnne, Horace Jr & Bryan. **Educ:** Syracuse Univ Sch Educ, BA, 1949; Rutgers State Univ, Grad Sch Educ, MEduc, 1962. **Career:** Labor relations manager (retired); Burlington Pub Sch, teacher, admin, 1956-64; Garm co Inc, pres chief exec officer, 1968-70; Dade County Community Rels Bd, dep dir, 1970; Dade County Model Cities Prog, dir, 1971; New York Urban League, exec dir, 1974-83, pres, chief exec officer; United Way, exec dir, 1983-88, sr fel; United Way New York, exec dir, exec vpres, 1988-91, consult; Greater NY Fund, pres, chief exec officer. **Orgs:** Nat Conf Soc Welfare; Nat Asn Advan Colored People; Alumni Asn Syracuse Univ; Alpha Phi Alpha Frat; Frontiers Int; Charter mem, Civitan Int Springfield, Ohio Chap; AME Zion Ch; bd dir, New York Partnership; chair, pres, chief exec officer, Black Agency Execs New York; trustee, Wesley AME Zion Church; bd mem, boys & girls club; chair, Human Serv Coun. **Honors/Awds:** Four Year Scholar, 1945-49; Father of the Year, Burlington Jr HS PTA, 1960; Pop Warner Service to Youth Award, S Jersey area, 1962; Outstanding Young Man of the Year, Gr Burlington Area Jr C of C, 1962; Letterman of Distinction, Syracuse Univ, 1985; Frederick Douglass Awardee, New York Urban League, 1992. **Home Addr:** 15 Ridgeview Pl, PO Box 3, Willingboro, NJ 08046, **Home Phone:** (609)871-6399.

### MORTON, JAMES A., II

Executive. **Personal:** Born Dec 20, 1929, Ontario, VA; died May 3, 2016, Baltimore, MD; married Juanita; children: James A & David L. **Educ:** Am Acad Mortuary Sci, 1950; Lincoln Univ, grad; Howard Univ, grad. **Career:** Morton & Dyett Funeral Homes Inc, pres; James A Morton & Sons Funeral Homes Inc; pres & owner. **Orgs:** Past pres, Funeral Dir & Morticians Asn MD; past pres, Opportunities Indust Ctr; bd mem, Nat Funeral Dir Mforticians Asn; chmn, Tri-state Conv Comn; mem Adv, com Bus bd; bd mem, Am Red Cross; comt man BSA; chmn, House Hope Financial Com; trustee, Wayland Bapt Ch; adv bd, Advan Fed Sav; bd mem, YMCA; life mem, Nat Asn Advan Colored People; A Phillip Randolph Prince Hall Masons. **Home Addr:** 3417 Callaway Ave, Baltimore, MD 21215. **Business Addr:** Funeral Director, James A Morton & Sons Funeral Homes Inc, 1701 Laurens St, Baltimore, MD 21217, **Business Phone:** (410)728-1100.

### MOSLEY, EDNA WILSON

Administrator, government official, president (organization). **Personal:** Born May 31, 1925, Helena, AR; died Aug 26, 2014, Denver, CO; married John W; children: 4. **Educ:** Univ Northern Colo, attended 1943; Adams State Col, attended 1969; Met State Col, BA, 1969; Univ Colo, attended 1976. **Career:** Univ Denver, affirmative action dir, 1978-2014; Colo State & Dept Personnel, asst state affirmative action coordr, 1974-78; Colo Civil Rights Comn, community rels coordr, 1970-74; Co Civil Rights Comn, civil rights specialist, 1969-70; Women's Bank NA Denver, founder, 1975; Aurora Colo, councilwoman; Colo Bus Bank, pres & chairwoman, 2014; Denver Found, 1st vice chair, 2014. **Orgs:** Women's Forum Colo Inc Best Sustaining Pub Affairs Prog Colo Broadcasting Asn, 1972; co-chmn, Denver/Nairobi Sister-/City Comm, 1976-80; bd dir, Women's Bank NA Denver, 1978-80; life mem, Delta Sigma Theta Sorority, 1979-81; Nat Asn Advan Colored People; Aurora City Coun, 1991-2003; dir, Higher Educ Affirmative Action; Nat Asn Affirmative Action Officers; Colo Black Women Polit Action; Delta Sigma Theta Denver Alumnae Chap; dir, Fitzsimmons Redevelop Authority; dir, Aurora Econ Develop Coun; founding mem, Womens Bank Denver; comnr, Nat Social Action Comn; pres, Denver Sister Cities Int. **Honors/Awds:** Lola M Parker Achievement Award, Iota Phi Lambda Far Western Region, 1977; Headliner Award Women, Commun Inc, 1978; Appreciation Award, Nat Asn Black Accts, 1978; Distinguished Service Award, Int Stud Orgn Univ Denver, 1979; Business Woman of the Year, 1984, Aurora Area Bus & Prof Women; Named distinguished alumnus, Metrop State Col, 1986; Humanitarian Award, Martin Luther King, Jr. Holiday Comn, 1988; Juanita Gray Community Service Award, 1989; hon doctoral degrees, CSU, 2004. **Special Achievements:** The First African American to be elected to the Aurora City Council. **Home Addr:** 2019 S Macon Way, Aurora, CO 80014.

### MYERS, DR. ERNEST RAY

Writer, educator, vice president (organization). **Personal:** Born Middletown, OH; died Sep 29, 2014, Washington, DC; son of David Sr and Alma Harper; married Carole E Ferguson. **Educ:** Howard Univ, BA, 1962, MSW, 1964; Am Univ, PhD, 1974; Union Inst Univ, PhD, 1976. **Career:** US Pres Task Force War Against Poverty, consult, 1964; VISTA, Proj Develop Div, prog officer, 1964-66, sr eval officer, 1964-66, proj develop officer, 1966-67, prog plans & policy develop officer, 1967; Dept Housing & Urban Develop, neighborhood serv prog officer & coordr, 1967-68; Nat Urban League, asst dir, 1968; Westing house Learning Corp, mgr prog develop, 1968-69; Fed City Col, dir col community eval off, 1969-71; Bur Higher Educ US Off Educ, dir servicemen's early educ coun prog, 1971; Fed City Col, asst prof, 1972-77; Univ DC, assoc prof, 1977-86, chmn depthuman resource dev, 1986-94, Dept Psychol & Coun, prof, 1994; TRI-Austin Inc, vpres, defense bus level; E R Myers & Assocs, owner, 1980-. **Orgs:** Nat Asn Social Workers, 1969-; Asn Black Psychologists, 1972-; Acad Cert Soc Workers, Nat Asn Social Workers, 1974-; Am Psychol Asn, 1975-; pres, ERM Consult Corp, 1980-; trustee, Woodley House Rehab, 1982-88; grievance comt, Nat Asn Social Workers, 1984-86; chmn, DC Ment Health Asn Prof Adv Comn, 1984-86; chmn, DC Govt Ment Health Admin Adv Bd, 1984-86; chmn, Howard Univ Alumni Sch Social Work Fund Raising Comn, 1984-86; Ga Br, Kiwanis Club, 1985-86; mem adv, Zest Inc, 1990-; fel APA, 1995-. **Honors/Awds:** Outstanding Leadership, Univ DC Col Educ & Human Ecology, 1981; Outstanding Scholar, Asn Black Psychologists, 1981; Outstanding Alumni Howard Univ Sch Soc Work, 1982; Outstanding Service, Mental Health Asn, 1982; Outstanding Leadership Award, Univ DC, 1985; Outstanding Scholar Award, Univ DC, 1986; Service Recognition Plaque, Nat Asn Advan Colored People, 1993; Outstanding Services Plaque, Grad, SGA Univ DC, 1994; Outstanding Alumni, Union Inst, 1996; Image Award & Faculty Award, Univ DC, 1996. **Special Achievements:** Author: Race & Culture in the Mental Health Service Delivery System, 1981; Challenges of a Changing America, 1994. **Home Addr:** 5315 Colo Ave NW, Washington, DC 20011-3622, **Home Phone:** (202)882-8124.

### NAPPER, JAMES WILBUR

Educator. **Personal:** Born Feb 25, 1917, Institute, WV; died Nov 3, 2015; son of Walter J and Zanphra D Robinson; married Cassie McKenzie; children: Gregory S & David M. **Educ:** WVa State Col, BS, 1937, MS, 1949; Univ Calif, Berkeley, attended 1964. **Career:** Educator (retired); Boyd Sch, Charleston, WV, teacher, coach, 1950; Alameda City Oakland, Calif, dep probation officer, 1954; DeAnza High Sch, Richmond, teacher, 1958; Richmond Unified Sch Dist, guid consult, 1965; Santa Rose Jr Col, counr, 1969-82. **Orgs:** Calif Teacher Asn, 1958-2015; Nat Educ Asn, 1969; Phi Delta Kappa Educ Group, 1976-2015; ed adv, Alpha Phi Alpha; exec bd, Nat Asn Advan Colored People; pres, Kiwanis Club; bd dir, AGAPE. **Home Addr:** 1010 Bristol Lakes Rd Suite 104, Mount Dora, FL 32757-7543, **Home Phone:** (352)735-3745.

### NELSON, PRINCE ROGERS

Television producer, actor, singer. **Personal:** Born Jun 7, 1958, Minneapolis, MN; died Apr 21, 2016, Chanhassen, MN; son of John L (deceased) and Mattie D Shaw; married Manuela Testolini; married Mayte Garcia; children: Gregory (deceased). **Career:** Singer, songwriter, actor, producer, dir, currently; Albums: Summer Lovers, 1982; Still Smokin, 1983; Risky Business, 1983; Purple Rain, 1984; The Slugger's Wife, 1985; Krush Groove, 1985; Band of the Hand, 1986; Fire with Fire, 1986; Under the Cherry Moon, 1986; Sign o the Times, 1987; Bright Lights, Big City, 1988; My Stepmother Is an Alien, 1988; Batman, 1989; Pretty Woman, 1990; Without You Im Nothing, 1990; Graffiti Bridge, 1990; Gett Off, 1991; The Last Boy Scout, 1991; Innocent Blood, 1992; Poetic Justice, 1993; Prince Interactive, 1994; 3 Chains o Gold, 1994; Frauen sind was Wunderbares, 1994; PCU, 1994; Blankman, 1994; Vampire in Brooklyn, 1995; Showgirls, 1995; Waiting to Exhale, 1995; Girl 6, 1996; Striptease, 1996; Romeo Juliet, 1996; Eine unmogliche Hochzeit, 1996; Scream 2, 1997; Down in the Delta, 1998; An Audience with Tom Jones, 1999; Bamboozled, 2000; Jay and Silent Bob Strike Back, 2001; Stella Shorts, 1998-2002, 2002; Head of State, 2003; Are We There Yet?, 2005; Filthy Gorgeous: The Trannyshack Story, 2005; Get Rich or Die Tryin, 2005; Happy Feet, 2006; Her Best Move, 2007; License to Wed, 2007; Rush Hour 3, 2007; Young at Heart, 2007; Dan in Real Life, 2007; P S I Love You, 2007; Forgetting Sarah Marshall, 2008; Nel nome del male, 2009; Songs: "Saturday Night Live", 1981-2006; "Knight Rider", 1984; "Fame", 1984-85; "Lo Kolel Sherut", 1990; "Tiny Toon Adventures", 1992; "Beavis and Butt-Head", 1993-95; "Muppets Tonight", 1997; "Quelli che il calcio", 2001; "Operacion triunfo", 2001; "Fergus's Wedding", 2002; "Ha-Shminiya", 2006; "Verbotene Liebe", 2006; "20 to 1", 2006; "American Idol: The Search for a Superstar", 2007; "Las Vegas", 2007; "La tele de tu vida", 2007; "60/90", 2008; "Sputnik", 2008; "Banda sonora", 2009; "Late Night with Jimmy Fallon", 2009; Films: Purple Rain, 1984; Under the Cherry Moon, 1986; Sign o' the Times, 1987; Graffiti Bridge, 1990. **Honors/Awds:** Three American Music Awards; three Grammy Awards; 3 gold albums; 2 platinum albums; No 1 album of the year Purple Rain; Rhythm & Blues Musician of the Year, down beat Readers Poll, 1984; Academy Award Best Original Song Score for Purple Rain, 1985; Best Soul/Rhythm & Blues Group of the Year, downbeat Readers Poll, Prince & Revolution, 1985; Oscar Award, 1985; Razzie Award, 1987; ASCAP Award, 1990, 1991; Grammy Award, 1995; Special Award, 2004; Rock and Roll Hall of Fame, 2004; Golden Globe Award, 2007. **Business Addr:** The Artist, EMI, 304 Pk Ave S, New York, NY 10010.

### NELSON, RONALD DUNCAN

Police chief, executive. **Personal:** Born Jun 17, 1931, Pasadena, CA; died Mar 29, 2014, Berkeley, CA; son of Harold O and Zenobia D; married Barbara Dorsey; children: Rhonda & Harold. **Educ:** Drake Univ, Des Moines, Iowa, BA, 1956; Calif State Col, attended 1966; Pepperdine Univ, Malibu, Calif, MA, 1977. **Career:** Police chief (retired), corp executive; Los Angeles Police Dept, Los Angeles, Calif, police lt, 1956-77; Compton Police Dept, Compton, Calif, police comdr, 1977-79; China Lake Police Dept, China Lake, Calif, police chief, 1979-80; City Compton, Compton, Calif, city mgr, 1980-82; Berkeley Police Dept, Berkeley, Calif, police chief, 1982-90; Univ Calif, San Francisco, Police Dept, police chief, 1990-2002; Satellite Housing Inc, secy, prin. **Orgs:** Kappa Alpha Psi Fraternity, 1955; Pasadena Planning Comn, 1976-79; Kiwanis Int, 1978-88; Berkeley Boosters Asn, 1983; Berkeley Breakfast Club, 1984; Nat Forum Black Pub Admin, 1987; nat pres, Nat Orgn Black Law Enforcement Exec, 1988-89; pres, Alameda Co Chief Police & Sheriffs Asn, 1989; Berkeley Booster Asn; Nat League Cities; pres, chmn, Comn Accreditation Law Enforcement Agencies; Black Men United Chg; United Black Clergy Berkeley; life mem, Int Asn Chief Police; bd mem, Satellite Affordable Housing Assocs; bd trustee, Alameda County Med Ctr. **Honors/Awds:** Community Service Award, City Berkeley; Community Service Award, Nat League Cities; Community Service Award, Nat Orgn Black Law Enforcement Agencies; Community Service Award, Nat Forum Black Pub Admin, 1988. **Home Addr:** 1460 Lincoln St, Berkeley, CA 94702, **Home Phone:** (510)644-1237. **Business Addr:** Secretary, Principal, Satellite Housing Inc, 1521 Univ Ave, Berkeley, CA 94703-1422, **Business Phone:** (510)647-0700.

### NEWTON, ERIC CHRISTOPHER

Software developer, chief executive officer. **Personal:** Born Apr 5, 1965, Detroit, MI; died Jan 22, 2015; son of John Henry and Willie Bell Duncan; married Kimberly; children: Brittany Delamere, Haley Christine, Naomi Annabelle & Gabrielle Leigh. **Educ:** Mich State Univ, BS, mathand comput sci, 1988. **Career:** Gen Motors, claims processor, programmer analyst, Intern, 1983-84; Unisys Corp, programmer, analyst, 1984-85; Stroh Brewery Corp, programmer, analyst, 1987-88; Alpha II, developer & partner, 1988-93; Info Serv Inc, pres, owner, div mgr, 1993-96, vpres opers, 1998, pres & cheif exec officer, 2001-05; Great Fit Staffing Solutions, opers mgr, 2005-06; Gilbar Engineering, info systs mgr, 1996-98; SDE Bus Partnering LLC, dir sales, 2006-08; Morgan Bradley, LLC, sr consult, 2008-09; Blue Cross Blue Shield Mich, procurement adminr, 2009-15. **Orgs:** Mentor prog, Detroit Pub Schs, 1983-15; Phi Beta Sigma Fraternity Inc, 1985-15; Apple Programmers & Developers Asn, 1988-15; Mich Asn Comput UsersLearning, 1989-15; IBM Developer Assistance Prog, 1991-15. **Honors/Awds:** Local Corporate Buyer of the Year, Michigan Minority Supplier Development Council, 2011. **Home Addr:** 6566 Horncliffe Dr, Clarkston, MI 48346, **Home Phone:** (248)625-5498.

### NEWTON, JAMES DOUGLAS, JR.

Government official, chief executive officer, manager. **Personal:** Born Jun 11, 1949, New Haven, CT; died Jul 8, 2015; children: Bonita, Melissa, Tomeka, James D III & Allen W II. **Educ:** NH Col, BS, human resources mgt & personnel admin, gen, 1979; Yale Univ, Sch Pub Health & Hosp Admin, hospitality admin & mgt, 1980; Southern Conn State Univ, MS, urban studies & econ develop, 1991. **Career:** New Haven City Personnel Dept, rec syst consult, 1979-82; Conn Nat Bank, mgt trainee, 1984-85, temple St Br, mgr, 1984-85, Church St Br, mgr, 1986-87; Youth Men's Christian Asn Youth & Fitness Ctr, gen mgr, 1990-91; New Haven Job Ctr, exec dir & mgr, 1991-99; Action Bridgeport Community Develop, site mgr, 2001-03; JDN & Assocs, chief exec officer, 2004-15. **Orgs:** Chmn black & hisp caucus, New Haven Bd Aldermen, 1983-97; chmn, N & N Construct Co, 1987-2015; chmn, Yale Univ; New Haven City, Sci Pk Dev Corp, 1992-2015; assoc dir, Greater New Haven Chamber Com, Jobs Compact Prog, 1987-88; assoc dir, New Haven City, Bd Educ, 1988-90. **Honors/Awds:** Community Services Award, Rotary Club Int, 1990. **Home Addr:** 100 Osborne Ave, New Haven, CT 06511.

### NIVENS, BEATRYCE THOMASINIA

Writer, lecturer, executive. **Personal:** Born Apr 1, 1948, New York, NY; died Jun 22, 2016; daughter of Thomas J (deceased) and Surluta Bell (deceased). **Educ:** Fisk Univ, Nashville TN, BA, 1969; Univ Ghana Legon, Ghana W Africa, Summer Sch cert, 1970; Hofstra Univ, Hempstead NY, MS, educ, 1971. **Career:** Denison Univ, Granville OH, asst dean women, 1969-71; Hosftra Univ, Hemptead NY, pre-law counr, 1971-73; Queens Col, Flushing NY, counr, 1974-79; Essence Mag, columnist, 1977-90; Dist Coun 37, New York NY, part-time counr, 1979-87; US Dept Health & Human Serv, Bronx NY, expert, 1980-83; Career Mktg Int, New York NY, pres, lectr, writer, 1985-2016; IBM, consult; Verizon, NY, consult; NJ Port Authority, consult; Am Express, consult; JP Morgan Chase, career mgt consult; Smart Biz Coaching Co, chief coach & pres, 2005-16; Beatryce Nivens.com, owner, currently; Books: Black Woman's Career Guide, 1982, 1987; How to Chg Careers, 1990; How to Choose a Career, 1992; How to Re-Enter Work Force, 1992; Success Strategies African Americans, 1998; Careers Women Without Col Degrees; Oportunidades De Carreira Para Mulheres Sem Cursos Universitarious; How to Chg Careers; So You Want To Becomea Career Guide Young People, 2008; How To Become A Black, chief exec officer & Corp Pres: Top Leaders Share Their Wisdom, 2010. **Orgs:** Delta Sigma Theta Sorority, 1987-2016; bd mem, Asn Career Professionals Int. **Honors/Awds:** Nal Madame C.J. Walker Award; Public Service Award, US Dept of Labor, 1982; author: Fel, Virginia Ctr for the Creative Arts, 1985; Winthrop Rockefeller Distinguished Lectr, Univ of AK, 1986; Humanitarian Award, Unityfirst.com; Certificate of Recognition, Ny Assembly; Careers for Women Without Coll Degrees, 1988. **Special Achievements:** Numerous workshops and sem for col and Univ, corps, libr, women's professional assn, Black civic and professional assn, educ conf, and govt agencies; author of six career books and has written more than 170 career articles for major publ. **Home Addr:** 82 Wall St Suite 1105, New York, NY 10005, **Home Phone:** (212)769-8234.

### NOEL, DR. PATRICK ADOLPHUS

Physician, consultant. **Personal:** Born Nov 9, 1940; died Jun 9, 2014, Trinidad and Tobago; married Evelyn Sebro; children: Carlita, Patrick Jr & John. **Educ:** Howard Univ, BS, 1964; Howard Univ Col Med, MD, 1968. **Career:** Wilson Med Ctr, United Health Syst, internship, 1968-69; Howard Univ, residence, 1969-73; John Hopkins Univ, fel, 1972; pvt pract, physician, 1973; Bowie St Col, physician, 1973, Football Team, orth consult, 1973-76; Howard Univ, instr ortho surg, 1973; Univ Md, consult, 1973-76; Howard Univ Hosp, attend surgeon; Leland Hosp; SSE Comm Hosp; Laurel Hosp. **Orgs:** Fel Int Col Surgeons, 1974; Am Bd Orthopaedic Surg, 1974; fel Am Acad Ortho Surg, 1976; treas, Soc Health Prof, 1977; Nat Med Asn. **Honors/Awds:** Meritorious Serv, Bowie State Col, 1976. **Business Addr:** Physician, Private Practice, 1100 Mercentile Lane Suite 135, Upper Malboro, MD 20774-5361, **Business Phone:** (301)322-4848.

### NOLES, EVA MALINDA

Writer, educator, nurse. **Personal:** Born Apr 5, 1919, Cleveland, OH; died Dec 2, 2015, Williamsville, NY; daughter of Charles Bateman (deceased) and Ola Neal (deceased); married Douglas; children: Tyrone M. **Educ:** EJ Meyer Mem Hosp Sch Nursing, RN, 1940; Nursing Univ Buffalo, BS, 1962; State Univ NY, Buffalo, MEd, 1967. **Career:** Nurse (retired); Roswell Pk Memorial Inst, staff nurse & head nurse, 1945-63, instr nursing & asst dir nursing, 1963-68, nursing educr, dir, 1971, chief nursing serv & training, 1971-74; State Univ NY, Buffalo, clin assoc prof nursing, 1970-77; Erie County Med Ctr, Nurses Practr Prog, coord family planning, 1974-77; Med Personnel Pool Inc, home care supvr & staff develop, 1977-84. **Orgs:** Am Nurses Asn, 1941-2015; bd dir, Am Cancer Soc, 1965-2015; NY State Bd Nursing, 1972-92; comt adv coun, State Univ NY, Buffalo, 1975-2015; chmn, Nursing & Health Serv ARC Greater Buffalo Chap, 1978-84; bd govs & chairwoman, Community Ment Health Ctr, Buffalo, NY, 1979-2015; bd dir, Boys & Girls Clubs Buffalo & Erie Co, 1985; bd dir, Greater Buffalo Chap Am Red Cross; bd trustee, Buffalo Gen Hosp; NY State Nurses Asn; bd dir, ARC; bd trustee, Buffalo Gen Hosp; Community Ment Health. **Honors/Awds:** Distinguished Service Award, 1972; Distinguished Award, AAUW, 1972; Community Award, 1986; Culture Keepers Award, Uncrowned Queens Inst, 2002; Cert Merit, ARC Greater Buffalo Chap; Nat Award, American Red Cross. **Special Achievements:** First African American woman to train and graduate as a Registered Nurse in EJ Meyer Mem Hosp, 1936-40; published "Six Decades of Nursing 1914-74", 1975; published Buffalo's Blacks "Talking Proud", 1987; author: Black History "A Different Approach - A Compilation", 1988; The Church Builder: The Life of Bishop Charles NMcCoy, 1990; published Black History-A Different Approach. **Home Addr:** 3356 Baseline Rd, Grand Island, NY 14072-1065, **Home Phone:** (716)773-2102.

### ORR, DR. DOROTHY J.

President (organization), insurance executive. **Personal:** Born Jan 12, 1920, Meadville, PA; died Jan 17, 2015; married Alfonso. **Educ:** Atlanta Univ; Columbia Univ, accelerated grad study. **Career:** Fordham Univ Sch Social Work, assoc prof; Equitable Life Assurance Soc, vpres; Orr DaCosta Balthazar & Orr, pre & sr partner; NY State, Dept Human Rights, comnr; Equitable Life Financial Co, vpres corp social responsibility; Dorothy J Orr Assoc Consult, founder & pres. **Orgs:** Former comnr, NY State Comn Human Rights. **Honors/Awds:** Carter G Woodson Award, Mercy Col, 2003. **Special Achievements:** Organized the first course on "Culture and Social Work" in response to student requests for courses on cultural diversity; First African-American woman corporate vice president in the insurance industry.

### OWENS, DR. JOAN MURRELL

Educator, association executive. **Personal:** Born Jun 30, 1933, Miami, FL; died May 25, 2011, Washington, DC; daughter of William Henry and Leola Peterson; married Frank A; children: Adrienne Johnson-Lewis & Angela. **Educ:** Fisk Univ, BA, 1954; Univ Mich, MA, 1956; George Washington Univ, BS, 1973, MPhil, 1976, PhD, 1984. **Career:** Educator (retired); C's Psychol Hosp Univ MI, reading rapist, 1955-57; Howard Univ Dept Eng, reading specialist, 1957-64; Inst Servs Educ DC & MA, curric Spec, 1964-71; Smithsonian Inst DC, mus technician, 1972-73; Ford Fel NatFellowships Fund, Atlanta, 1973-76; Howard Univ, Wash DC, 1976-95, assoc prof geol, 1976-91, assoc prof biol, 1991-95. **Orgs:** Speaker, 4th Int Symp Fossil Cnidaria, 1983; Minority Affairs Comt, Nat Asn Geol Teacher, 1988-90; geol counr, Coun Undergrad Res, 1990-91. **Honors/Awds:** College Reading Skills, Alfred J Knopf, 1966; "Microstructural Changes in the Micrabaciidae and Their Taxonomic & Ecologic Implications, "Palaeontographica Americana", 1984; Delta Sigma Theta; "Evolutionary Trends in the Micrabaciidae, An Argument in Favor of Pre-Adaptation", 1984, Geologos Vol II No 1; "Rhombopsammia: New Genus Family Micrabaciidae, " 1986, Proceedings Biological Soc Washington Vol 99 No 2; "On the Elevation of the Stephanophyllia Subgenus Letepsammia to Generic Rank, " Proceedings the Biological Soc Wash Vol 99 No 3; Scientist, Black Achievers Sci, Exhibit Chicago's Mus Sci & Indus, 1988; Distinguished African American Scientists of the 20th Century, 1993; "Letepsammia Franki, A New Species Deep-Sea Coral, " 1994; Proceedings Biol Soc Washington, Vol 107, No 4. **Special Achievements:** First African American American Woman to earn a doctorate in Geology.

### PARKER, DORIS S.

Consultant, association executive. **Personal:** Born Aug 24, 1930, Marvell, AR; died Apr 2, 2015, Merrillville, IN; daughter of Earlie Mae Sims (deceased) and Percy L (deceased); children: Karen Parker Stewart & Terri L. **Educ:** Ind Cent Col, BA, 1959. **Career:** AUS, Finance Ctr, mil pay clerk, 1952-66; Veterans Admin Reg Off, adjudicator veteran claims examr, 1966-73; Ind Voc Tech Col, asst dir, stud serv, 1973-75, reg rels coord, 1975-82; YWCA, exec dir, 1982-85; independent consult, 1985; Alpha Kappa Alpha Educ advan Found, Chicago, exec secy, 1987. **Orgs:** Pres, Hoosier Capital Girl Scout Coun, 1978-82; Nat Comt Campaign Human Develop, US Cath Conf, 1973-77, chmn, 1976-77; St Felicitas Roman Cath Church; FundHoosier Excellence, 1983-2015; St Mary Woods Col, bd trustees, 1985-94, trustee emer, 1994-2015; BlacksDevelop, 1990-2015; Asn Black Found Exec, 1993-2015; US CMS Civil Rights, Ind adv cms; Asn Forum Chicago; Alpha Kappa Alpha Sorority. **Honors/Awds:** Brotherhood Award, Ind Chapter, Nat Conf Christians & Jews, 1975; Human Relations Award, Indianapolis Educ Asn, 1976; Harriet Tubman Award, Community Action Against Poverty, 1982; Thanks Badge, Hoosier Capital Girl Scouts Coun, 1982. Achievement Plus Pub Serv, Ctr Leadership Develop, 1985. **Home Addr:** 1900 W 84th Ave F141, Merrillville, IN 46410, **Home Phone:** (219)793-1104.

### PARKER, DR. HERBERT GERALD

School administrator, consultant. **Personal:** Born May 13, 1929, Fayetteville, AR; died Jan 8, 2016, Arlington, VA; son of Otis James and Anna Fisher; married Florida Fisher; children: Christie Lynne. **Educ:** Univ Nebr, Omaha, BS, 1962; NC Agr & Tech State Univ, MS, 1970; Fla State Univ, PhD, 1982. **Career:** School administrator, consultant (retired); Rep China, Taipei, Taiwan, adv ministry nat defense, 1962-65; NC Agr & Tech State Univ, prof milt sci, 1965-68; AUS Spec Forces The Delta Vietnam, comdr, 1968-69; US Army Civil Affairs Sch Fort Bragg, dir, 1969-73; Fla A&M Univ, prof milt sci, 1973-77; State Fla Bur Crimes Compensation, dir, 1979-87; Fla Dept Educ, Tallahassee, Fla, chief internal auditor, 1987-91, dir admin serv, 1991-94; consultant, 1994. **Orgs:** Kappa Alpha Psi, life mem; Sigma Pi Phi Fraternity; Rocks Inc; bd dir, Civil Affairs Asn, 1970-73; Nat Asn Soc Scientist, 1973; bd dir, Three C's Corp, 1974-79; Tallahassee Area C C, 1974-82; bd dir, Opportunity Indust Ctrs, 1975-78; bd dir, United Way Leon Co, 1978-82; bd dir, Tallahassee Urban League, 1981; pres, Nat Asn Crime Victim Compensation Bd, 1984-87; bd dirs Fla Victim & Witness Network, 1984; bd chmn, 1986-88, 2002-04; Tallahassee Nat Asn Advan Colored People, capital chordsmen; pres-elect, Capital City Rotary, 1998-99, pres, 2000-01; Retired Officers Asn; Military OrderWorld Wars; bd dir, Salvation Army, 2002; pres, One Tallahassee s Rotary Clubs. **Honors/Awds:** Distinguished Service Award, Boy Scouts of Am, 1968; Distinguished Service Award, Civil Affairs Asn, 1974; Outstanding Service Award, Col Humanities & Soc Sci, Fla A&M Univ, 1977; Phi Kappa Phi Hon Soc, 1979; Distinguished Service Award, Nat Asn Crime Victim Compensation Bds, 1986; Fla Network Victim Witness Serv; James Fogarty Distingushed Service Award, 1988; Distinguished Black Achiever Award, Tallahassee Nat Asn Advan Colored People, 1991; James Hudson Citizenship Award, 1998; Silver Star Award, 2001; Annual Award, Christian servive, Sunrise Prayer Breakfast Group, Inc, Rotary Ints Paul Harris Fel, Level 2. **Special Achievements:** Youngest African promoted to Col, United Synagogue Youth, 1969; First African American to serve as president of one of Tallahassee Rotary Clubs. **Home Addr:** 3510 Tullamore Lane, Tallahassee, FL 32309, **Home Phone:** (850)893-2671.

### PARKER, JAMES L.

Administrator. **Personal:** Born Oct 29, 1923, Salina, KS; died Apr 7, 2014; son of John Henry and Classie (Meadows); married Berma Jeane; children: Cheri D Ware, Jami L, Kathleen L Sullivan, Beryl J, Rosalind A Crutcher, Donna J, Janice E & Gloria J Shelton. **Educ:** Kans Wesleyan Univ, attended 1949; Brown-Makie Sch Bus, BA, 1950. **Career:** Adminstrator (retired); Salina Recreation Dept, Carver Rec Ctr, Salina, Kans, asst rec dir, 1946-50; E Side Rec Ctr Freeport IL, exec dir, 1951-66; Sund strand Advan Tech Div, contract adminstr, 1967-87; tax acct. **Orgs:** Gov Comn Minority Entrepreneurship; Gov Comn Emancipation Centennial; secy, Freeport Hum Rels Comn; Ill Law Enforcement Comn; Freeport Adult Educ Coun Freeport; treas Northwestern Ill Community Action Agency; Int Toastmasters Club; adv bd, Freeport Jr Col; ML King Jr Comm Ctr Bd N Ill Constr Affirm Act Prog; steward, St James CME Church; Stephenson County Jury Comnr. **Honors/Awds:** Youth Award Freeport Children of Children, 1956. **Home Addr:** 632 E Iroquois St, Freeport, IL 61032, **Home Phone:** (815)235-2154.

### PASSMORE, JUANITA CARTER

Marketing executive. **Personal:** Born Mar 4, 1926, Chicago, IL; died Mar 22, 2016, Chicago, IL; married Maymon. **Educ:** Long Beach City Col; Columbia Col. **Career:** Market executive (retired); Johnson Prod Co, dir, spec promos, exec nat coord, 1990; Johnson Prod Div Cosmetic Consults; Corp Exec, Community Activist, philanthropist; Africare-Chicago, pres; Womens Task Force. **Orgs:** Founder, 69 Choppi Block Club; chmn, Nat Media Women; parliamentarian, Chicago Chap, Women's Bd, Oper PUSH; chmn, Fashion Ther Ment & Health; Oper Snowball; Chicago Chap Oper PUSHs Women's Bd, Chicago Gospel Festival & bd Jazz Unites Congregational Church Pk Manor, Windy City Links & Nat Coun Negro Women. **Honors/Awds:** Media Woman of Yr Award, Chicago Chap, 1974; Outstanding Woman of Yr, Chicago S End Jaycees Women Asn, 1977; Comm Worker Debutante Master AME Ch, 1977. **Special Achievements:** Author, An Autobiography Black Polit; hosted TV program, Totally Beauty You. **Home Addr:** 6939 Crandon, Chicago, IL 60649.

### PATERSON, HON. BASIL ALEXANDER

Lawyer. **Personal:** Born Apr 27, 1926, Harlem, NY; died Apr 16, 2014, New York, NY; son of Leonard James and Evangeline Rondon; married Portia Hairston; children: David & Daniel. **Educ:** St John's Col, BS, biol, 1948; St John's Univ Sch Law, JD, 1951. **Career:** Paterson Michael Jones & Cherot Esqs, partner, 1956-77; Inst Mediation & Conflict Resolution, pres & chief exec officer, 1972-77; City New York, dep mayor labor rels, 1978; State New York, secy state, 1979-82; Meyer, Suozzi, Eng & Klein, PC, partner, mem & co-chair; Hunter Col, vis prof, 1982-2014; Fordham Uni Sch Educ, adj prof; State Univ New Paltz, vis prof, 1982-2014. **Orgs:** NY Senate, 1965-70; NY Temp Comn Rev NY Charter; vice chmn, Dem Nat Comm, 1972-78; chair, Judicial Screening Comn Second Dept, 1985-95; NY Judicial Nominations Comn, 1986-2014; comnr, Port Authority New York & NJ, 1989-95; chmn, Mayor's Comm Judiciary, 1990-93; Comn Promote Confidence Judical Elections, 2003-14; chmn, Keyspan Fund, 2003-14, bd dir. **Honors/Awds:** Eagleton Institute of Politics Award, Excellence in Politics, 1967; Black Expo Award, 1973; Interracial Justice Cath Interracial Coun, 1978; Humanitarian Award, Coalition Black Trade Unionists, 1980; Medal of Excellence, St John's Univ; Kibbee Award for Outstanding Public Service & Achievement, City Univ NY, 1987; PSC Friend of CUNY Award, 1989; Pierre Toussaint Award, Catholic Archdiocese New York; President's Award, St.John's Univ Law Sch, 2003; Community Service Award, North General Hospital, 2006. **Special Achievements:** First elected African American Vice Chairman of the Democratic National Committee in 1972; First African American to serve Secretary of State of New York, 1979-82; Rated "AV" by Martindale-Hubbell, the highest level in professional excellence and ethics. **Home Addr:** 40 W 35th St, New York, NY 10037, **Home Phone:** (212)690-1850.

### PAWLEY, DR. THOMAS D., III (THOMAS DESIRE PAWLEY)

College teacher, educator. **Personal:** Born Aug 5, 1917, Jackson, MS; died Aug 1, 2016, Jefferson City, MO; son of Thomas D and Ethel John Woolfolk; married Ethel Louise Mc Peters; children: Thomas IV & Lawrence. **Educ:** Va State Col, AB, 1937; Univ Iowa, MA, 1939, PhD, theater arts, 1949; Columbia Univ, Post doctoral studies; Univ Mo, Post doctoral studies. **Career:** Atlanta Univ Summer Theatre, teacher & dir, 1939-41, 1943; Prairie View State Col, teacher & dir, 1939-40; Lincoln Univ Mo, fac, 1940, Dept Eng Speech & Theatre, pref & chmn, 1958-77, Div Humanities & Fine Arts, chmn, 1967-77, dean arts & scis, 1977-83, instr, asst prof to prof, writer residence, head dept commun, 1983-85, curators, disting prof speech & theatre, head dept communs, 1985-88, curators, distinguished prof emer, speech & theatre, 1988; Univ Calif, Santa Barbara, vis prof, 1968; Northern IL Univ, vis prof, 1971; Univ Iowa, vis prof, 1976; Univ Mo, 1980; Columbia Univ, 1980. **Orgs:** Pres, Nat Asn Dramat & Speech Arts, 1953-55; adv comt, Am Educ Theatre Asn, 1953-55; deleg, Episcopal Diocesan Conv, St Louis, 1963; pres, J CLibrary bd, 1970-72; treas, Jefferson Reg Libr Bd, 1974; vpres, Alpha Phi Alpha Fraternity, 1975-79; Theatre Educ Am Theatre Asn, 1977-79; pres, Speech & Theatre Asn, Mo, 1977-78; deleg Gov's Conf Libr Serv, 1978, 1990; Theatre Adv Comm Mo Arts Coun, 1979-87; vis prof, Univ Mo, 1980, 1988, 1990; exec Com Black Theatre Prog, Am Theatre Asn, 1980-83; bd dirs, Mid Am Arts Alliance, 1981; consult, Guggenheim Found, 1981-82; Mo Arts Coun, 1981-87; Nat Endowment Arts Theatre Panel, 1986-88; pres, Nat Conf African, 1987-90; Mo Humanities Coun, 1989-95; deleg, White House Conf Libr & Info Serv, 1991; Historian Alpha Phi Alpha Fraternity Inc, 1993-96; Vestry, Grace Episcopal Church, 1994-97; vice chmn, Mayor's Comm Res Stand; Org comn Jefferson City Coun Race & Relig; Univ Iowa Alumni Asn; Dramatists Guild. **Honors/Awds:** Shields-Howard Creative Writing Award, Va State Col, 1934; Nat Theatre Conf Fel, 1947-48; First Prize Jamestown, Va Corp Play writing Contest, 1954; "FFV" Full-length drama, 1963; First production by Stagecrafters Lincoln Univ, 1963; The Tumult and the Shouting Drama Two Acts, 1969; First prod by Inst in Dramatic Arts Lincoln Univ, 1969; Publ Hatch & Shine, 1974; Nat Asn Dramatic & Speechs Outstanding Service Award, 1984; Nat Conf African Am Theatre Mister Brown Award, 1986; Distinguished Alumnus NAFEO, Va State Univ, 1988; Am Theatre Fel, 1989; Distinguished Alumnus Achievement Award, Univ Iowa Alumni Asn, 1990; Award of Merit, Alpha Phi Alpha Fraternity, 1996; Mo Arts Coun Award, 1999; Winona Lee Fletcher Award, Black Theatre Network, 2000. **Home Addr:** 1014 Lafayette St, Jefferson City, MO 65101, **Home Phone:** (573)635-2719.

## PEAGLER, OWEN FAIR

Educator. **Personal:** Born Nov 28, 1931, New Milford, CT; died Nov 13, 2015, Hartford, CT; son of Robert J and Myrtle E Gary; married Joyce Hancock; children: Catherine Ann & Robert G; married Teresa Balough; children: Kirin. **Educ:** Western Conn State Univ, BS, 1954; NY Univ, MA, 1958, prof dipl, 1964; PhD. **Career:** New Milford Pub Sch, teacher, 1954-57; NY Off Econs, dep dir; Weslyan Univ, sci fel, 1956; White Plains Pub Schs, dir, 1959-66; New York Metro Area, dir, 1966-69; NY Off Econ Opportunity, educ consult, 1966-67, dep dir, 1967-69; Pace Univ, dean eve admin, 1967-75, Sch Continuing Educ, dean, 1972-75; Eastern Conn State Univ, Sch Continuing Educ, dean, 1978-99; Dept Commun Affairs Del, secy, 1982-83; Mitchell Col, acad adv; Mohegan Tribe, educ adv, 2004-. **Orgs:** Chmn, Presidents Adv Coun Disadvantaged C, 1973-80; bd dir, 70001 Training & Employ Inst, 1975-; pres, 70001 Develop Found, 1976-88; pres, Conn Asn Continuing Educ, 1985-86; chmn bd dir, WAVE Inc, 1988-96. **Honors/Awds:** Centennial Award, Western Conn State Univ; Young Man of the Year, New York State Jr Chamber Com, 1964; Distinguished Service Award, New York State Jr Chamber Com, White Plains, 1964; Outstanding Educator, Conn Nat Guard, 1988; Association for Continuing Higher Education Emeritus Award, 1998. **Home Addr:** 57 Boughton Rd, Old Lyme, CT 06371, **Home Phone:** (860)434-9567.

## PEETE, CALVIN

Golfer, educator, president (organization). **Personal:** Born Jul 18, 1943, Detroit, MI; died Apr 29, 2015, Atlanta, GA; son of Dennis and Irenia Bridgeford; married Christine; children: Calvin, Rickie, Dennis, Kalvanetta & Nicole; married Elaine; children: Aisha & Aleya. **Educ:** Wayne State Univ, attended 1983. **Career:** Golfer (retired), instructor; farm laborer, FL, 1957-60; itinerant peddler, 1961-71; prof golfer, 1971-2001; PGA Tour Golf Acad, instr; Calvin Peete Enterprises, pres, currently. **Orgs:** Prof Golfers Asn. **Honors/Awds:** Ben Hogan Award, 1983; Jackie Robinson Award, 1983; Vardon Trophy, 1984; Byron Nelson Award, 1984; African American Ethnic Sports Hall of Fame, 2002. **Special Achievements:** Mem, US Ryder Cup team. **Home Addr:** 128 Garden Gate Dr, Ponte Vedra Beach, FL 32082-3668, **Home Phone:** (904)273-7441. **Business Addr:** President, Calvin Peete Enterprises, 2050 Collier Ave, Ft. Myers, FL 33901.

## PETERS, DR. FENTON

School administrator, educator. **Personal:** Born Jul 10, 1935, Starkville, MS; died Sep 26, 2014, Meridian, MS; son of Pellum and Cora Gandy; married Maggie Teresa Malone; children: Avis Campbell Wilcox, Pellum & Alton. **Educ:** Rust Col, AB, 1958; Miss State Univ, MEd, 1969, EdD, 1983. **Career:** Educator (retired); Henderson High Sch, asst prin & choir dir, 1964; Henderson High Sch, prin, 1968-70; Henderson Jr High Sch, prin, 1970-76; Starkville High Sch, prin, 1976-81; Starkville Sch Dist, dir fed progs, 1981-83; Starkville Sch Dist, Asst Supt, 1983; Holly Springs Pub Schs, supt, 1986-91; Christ Missionary & IDL Sch, prin; Miss St Univ, Meridian campus, adj prof, Starkville Sch Dist, elem sch prin. **Orgs:** Presenter Stud Teaching Miss St Univ, 1978; presenter, Continuing Educ Miss St Univ, 1979; bd dir, Starkville Chamber Com, 1983-84; bd trustee, Oktibbeha Co Hosp, 1984-2014; st choir dir, Church Christ, 1983; St Supts Comm 12, St Supt Educ, 1987-88; bd dir, Holly Springs Chamber Com, 1988-89; Arts Educ Task Force, Miss Arts Comn, 1991; Phi Delta Kappa. **Honors/Awds:** NSF Science Fellowship, 1962, 1962-63, 1967; Public Service Award, United Way, 1985; Presidential Citation, Nat Asn Equal Opportunity Educ, 1987; Northeast MS Baptist Convention Hall of Fame, 1995; Chamber of Commerce Education Hall of Fame, 1996; T E Veitch Community Service Award, 2006, Miss Hosp Asn Trustee, 2008. **Home Addr:** 108 Old W Pt Rd, Starkville, MS 39759, **Home Phone:** (662)323-2796.

## PICKETT, ROBERT E.

Executive, educator. **Personal:** Born Sep 8, 1936, Brookhaven, MS; died Nov 10, 2014, Jackson, MS; married Dorothy Owens; children: Deborah Denise & Ritchie Elyot. **Educ:** Alcorn State Univ, BS, 1957; Jackson State Univ, MS, educ admin, 1969; Miss State Univ, Univ Miss & Atlanta Univ. **Career:** Educator (retired); Randolph High Sch Pass Christian, MS, teacher & coach, 1957-59; Weathers High Sch Rolling Pk, MS, teacher, 1959-60; Temple High Sch Vicksburg, MS, teacher, coach & admin asst, 1960-64; Mc Intyre Elem Jr High Sch Vicksburg, MS, prin, 1964-87; Jefferson Jr High Sch Vicksburg, MS, prin, 1966-73; Vicksburg High Sch, admin prin, 1973-77, prin, 1980-87; Vicksburg Jr High Sch, prin, 1977-80; Vicksburg Warren Sch Dist, dep supt, 1987-94, supt, 1994-99. **Orgs:** Bd mem, mgt, chmn, Jackson St YMCA, 1966-70; ETA TAU Chap Omega Psi Phi Frat Basileus, 1969-71; Vicksburg Pk Comm, 1970-80; pres, Warren Co United Fund, 1973; pres, Port City Kiwanis Club, 1975-76; bd dir, Commun Improv Inc WLBT-TV 3; bd dir, Vicksburg Warren County; bd dir, Merchant Bank; Miss Asn Sec Sch Prin; Nat Asn Sec Sch Prin; Phi Delta Kappa; Asn Supv & Curric Develop; Miss Asn Sch Adminr; Miss Asn Sch Bus Officials; Miss Asn Sch Supt & Southeastern Asn Sch Bus Officials; Three Rivers Dist Boy Scouts Am; Vicksburg Teachers Asn; Nat Educ Asn; Am Asn Sch Admin; vice chmn, Elks Fidelity Lodge #507; Vicksburg Chap Am Red Cross; bd dir, Hinds Comm Col; Warren County Port Comn; Nat Staff Develop Coun; bd dir, Warren County Port Comn. **Honors/Awds:** YMCA Service Award, 1969; UGF Service Award, 1973; Golden Lamp Award, MSAsn, 1997. **Home Addr:** 211 Henry Rd, Vicksburg, MS 39183-9569, **Home Phone:** (601)636-0999.

## PIERCE, DR. RAYMOND O., JR.

Educator, physician. **Personal:** Born May 31, 1931, Monroe, LA; died Oct 18, 2014, Indianapolis, IN; son of Raymond Olee and Ollie B; married Geraldine Brundidge; children: Raymond III, Gregory, Leannette, Geralyn & Lori. **Educ:** Fisk Univ Nashville, TN, BA, 1951; Meharry Med Col, attended 1955; Univ Iowa, MD, 1963. **Career:** Self-employed physician, 1963-69; Va Hosp Des Moines, resident; Univ Iowa, resident, 1963; Methodist Hosp, courtesy staff, 1969-2014; Winona Hosp, hon staff, 1969-2014; Ind Univ Med Ctr, asst prof to prof, 1970-2000, dept chair, prof emer orthop surg, 2000-14; AUS Hosp Ft Benjamin Harrison, consult staff, 1976-79; Wishard Hosp, chief orthop surg, 1988-2014, bd dir; Martin Univ, med dir, currently; J Robert Gladden Orthop Soc, chief exec officer, 2002-14; Nat Med Asn, AAOS rep. **Orgs:** House delegates co-chmn, Nat Med Asn, 1963-76; secy & pres, Hoosier State Med Asn, 1968-75; bd trustee, MDDS, 1968-74; Bd dir, Martin Ctr, 1970-; chmn, Ortho Soc, 1970-80; pres, Aesculapian Med Soc, 1972-75; Am Acad Ortho Surg; AAAS; chmn bd, Group Pract Inc, 1973-79; Am Asn Surg Trauma; examnr, cert Am Bd Ortho Surg, 1976-84; pres, secy & treas, Bone & Joint Club, 1980-2014; bd dir, St Elizabeth's Home, 1980-83; bd dir, Flanner House, 1980-2014; credentials comn, Am Col Surgeons, 1983-84; Am Fracture Asn; Am Soc Sports Med; chrtr mem, Am Trauma Soc; Int Col Surgeons; Pan-Pac Surg Soc; Sigma XI-Res Soc. **Honors/Awds:** Summer Furness Award, Outstanding Community Service, 1977; Physical Recogoniton Award, Am Med Asn, 1977-83; Scientific Award, IN State Med Asn Meeting, 1980; Physical Recogoniton Award, NMA, 1981-83; Scientific Award, IN State Med Asn, 1982; Government Award, Coun Sagamore Wabash, 1984; Health Profession Public Health Award, 2003. **Special Achievements:** Publications: Alcohol, Underlying Cause of Many Skeletal Lesions, Ortho News, Vol 6, 2 Mar/Apr, 1984, p3; Treatment of Subtrochanteric Fractures with a Flexible Intramedulla Rod Ortho Transactions, Vol 8, 3 Fall 1984, p441; The Effect of Alcohol on Skeletal System, Ortho Review, Vol XIV, 1 Jan 1985, p45-49. **Home Addr:** 4925 Kessler Blvd N Dr, Indianapolis, IN 46228, **Home Phone:** (317)630-6800.

## PLEASANT, MAE BARBEE BOONE

School administrator. **Personal:** Born Jul 8, 1919, KY; died Apr 14, 2015, Hampton, VA; daughter of Minnie Mae Burks and Zelma Clarence Barbee; married Noel J; children: Eugene Jr; married Eugene Boone. **Educ:** Tenn State Univ, BS, 1941; Hampton Univ, MA, 1962; George Washington Univ. **Career:** School administrator (retired); Va State Sch Deaf & Blind, sec supt, 1944; Hampton Univ, business mgr, 1946-53, admin asst to pres, 1957-63, faculty mem, 1968-71, sec corp beginning, 1973; Clark Col, exec sec pres, 1953-57; African Am Affairs, assoc dir, 1971-73; Univ MD, dean women, 1963-66; OEO, educ specialist, 1966-68. **Orgs:** Alpha Kappa Mu; Girl Scout Leader; area chmn, UNCF; historian, Diocese Southern Va Daughters King; chmn, Human Rels Comm, League Women Voters; pres, Peninsula Pan Hellenic Coun; bd dir, YWCA, 1953-57; vice chmn, Prof Sec, 1955-57; state chmn, Asn Study Negro Life & History, 1973-75; Vestry & Register, St Cyprian's Episcopal Church, 1974, 1984, 1989, 1997; basileus, Alpha Kappa Alpha, Gamma Upsilon Omega, 1977-79; pres, Quarter Century Club Hampton Univ; bd dir, Children's Home Soc; former vice chmn, King St Community Ctr; trustee, Va Theol Seminary; first black lay person, 1979-89; treas, bd mem, Downtown Day Care Ctr; treas, St Anne Chap, Daughters King St Cyprian's Episcopal Church Peninsula Pastoral Counseling, bd finance community & retreat community, Nominating Community; secy, Exec & Prog Co, Miss Peninsula Chap, Nat Conf Community & Justice. **Honors/Awds:** Woman of the Year, Hampton Inst, 1957, 1963; Outstanding Soror, 1978; Community Woman of the Year, Delta Sigma Theta Sorority, 1994; Outstanding Contributions to the Community, Peninsula Pan-Hellenic Coun, 1994; Eula Edmonds Glover Volunteer Community Service Award, Alpha Kappa Alpha Sorority Inc, 1994; Golden Sorority, Alpha Kappa Alpha Inc, 1999; Humanitarian Award, Va Conf Community & Justice, 2007; Lifelong Citizenship Award, Newport News dept of Parks, 2009; Woman of the Year, Hampton Inst. **Special Achievements:** Author of Hampton University: Our Home By the Sea, 1992. **Home Addr:** 11 Mimos Cres, Hampton, VA 23661.

## POLK, DR. GENE-ANN (GENE-ANN POLK HORNE)

Physician, educator. **Personal:** Born Oct 3, 1926, Roselle, NJ; died Jan 3, 2015, Lafayette Hill, PA; daughter of Charles C (deceased) and Olive Bond (deceased); married Edwin C; children: Carol Anne Horne Penn & Edwin Christian Horne. **Educ:** Oberlin Col, BA, 1948; Women's Med Col, PA, MD, 1952; Columbia Univ, MPH, 1968. **Career:** Physician (retired); Dept Pediat, attend physician, 1955-93; Englewood NJ, pvt practr, 1959-68; Columbia Univ, Harlem Hosp Ctr, Pediat Clin, chief, 1968-75, prof clin pediat, 1969-93, actg dir pediat, 1975-77, prof emer clin pediat, 1995-, chairwoman; Ambulatory Care Servs, dir, 1977-88; Susan Smith McKinney Steward Med Soc, historian. **Orgs:** Fel Am Bd Med Examiners, 1952; fel Am Acad Pediat, 1958; Sch phys City Englewood, NJ, 1960-67; UNCF, 1970-92; Basileus Aka Sorority Iota Epsilon Omega Chap, 1971-73; fel Int Col Pediat, 1978; bd mem, Greater Harlem Nursing Home, 1982-84; bd mem, Bergen County Girl Scouts; bd mem, BergenYouth Orchestra; bd mem, Englewood Adult Sch; Links Inc; bd trustee, Found Hist Women Med, secy, currently. **Honors/Awds:** Leadership in Med, Susan Smith McKinney Steward Med Soc, 1980; Outstanding Prof Achievement, Englewood-Teaneck B&P, 1980; Child Advocacy Award, Barristers' Wives of New York Inc, 1985; Proclamation: Dr Gene-Ann Polk Day, by President of the Borough of Manhattan, 1987; UNCF NJ Volunteer Recognition Award for Outstanding Serv, 1990; Proclamation by Mayor of the City of New York, Dr Gene Ann Polk Day, 1993; Second Century Service Award, Harlem Hosp Cent Auxiliary, 1993; Friends of Harlem Hosp Ctr, 1997. **Special Achievements:** First African American med doctor at New York Lenox Hill Hosp in 1955. **Home Addr:** 374 Miller Ave, Englewood, NJ 07631, **Home Phone:** (201)567-4767.

## POLLARD, DR. DIANE MAE STEWART

Educator. **Personal:** Born Oct 31, 1944, Richmond, VA; died Jan 1, 2015?; daughter of Clara Bayton Stewart and Elric; married Scott; children: Amina & Almasi. **Educ:** Wellesley Col, BA, 1966; Univ Chicago, MA, 1967, PhD, educ psychol, 1972. **Career:** Roosevelt Univ, instr, 1969-72; Univ Wis, Dept Educ Psychol, from asst prof to assoc prof, 1972-79, dir ctr study minorities & disadvantaged, 1979-85, prof, prof emer, 1993-2015. **Orgs:** Am Educ Res Asn, 1972-2015; secy, Nat Asn Black Psychologists, 1973-2015; Eta Phi Beta Inc, 1978-2015; Soc Psychol Study Social Issues; Alpha Kappa Alpha; ed bd, J Black Psychol. **Honors/Awds:** Faculty Distinguished Public Service Award, 1993; UW System Outstanding Women of Color In Education Award, The Univ Wis Syst Womens Studies Consortium, 1995; Willystine Goodsell Award, AERA/SIG RES Women & Educ, 1996. **Special Achievements:** Author: "Against the Odds: A Profile of Academic Achieversfrom the Urban Underclass," Journal of Negro Education, 1989; "Reducing the Impact of Racism on Students," in Educational Leadership, 1990; "A Profile of Black Professional Women in Education, Psychology and Sociology"; "Perceptions of Black Parents Regarding the Socialization of their Children"; "Patterns of Coping in Black School Children;" Motivational Factors Underlying Achievement; book chapter, Black Women, Interpersonal Support and Institutional Change in Changing Education: Woman as Radicals and Conservators; He is author and co-author of many books.

## PORTLOCK, DR. CARVER A.

School administrator, executive. **Personal:** Born Jun 8, 1934, Muskogee, OK; died Nov 2, 2014, Daytona Beach, FL. **Educ:** Bethune Cookman Col, BA, relig & philos, 1955; Syracuse Univ, attended 1957. **Career:** Administrator, executive (retired); Bethune Cookman Col, asst instr speech & drama, 1955-56; Dade Cty Jvnl Miami, counr boys, 1959-61; CME Church Paine Col, admin asst, 1960-62; Nat Alumni Assoc & Bethune Cookman Col, exec sec, 1962-66; Smith Kline Corp, info servs coord, 1966-68, mgr community rels, 1968-88; Bethune-Cookman Col, Northeast Regional Off, dir, 1988, Nat Celebrity Ser Event, narrator; Smithkline Corp, mgr. **Orgs:** Pres, Nat Alumni Asn & Bethune Cookman Col, 1982-84; mem bd dir, Big Brother & Big Sister Asn, 1981-; Catholic & Diocese Philadelphia; Omega Psi Phi Fraternity; life mem, B-CC Nat Alumni Asn; Bd Philadelphia Tribute Charities. **Honors/Awds:** Fund Achievement Award, United Negro Col, 1984; Community Service Award, Berean Inst, 1983; Professional Service Award, Crisis Intervention Network, 1981; LLD, Bethune-Cookman Col, 1986; LHD, Orthodox Catholic Archdiocese Philadelphia, 1985; Mary McLeod Bethune Award; Merit Award, City of Philadelphia; Shaft of Light Award. **Home Addr:** 402 E High St, Philadelphia, PA 19144.

## PRESSLEY, SYLVIA. See WOODS, SYLVIA.

## PRYOR, CALVIN CAFFEY

Lawyer. **Personal:** Born Oct 16, 1928, Montgomery, AL; died Jul 5, 2015, Montgomery, AL; children: Linda Elmore & Debra E. **Educ:** Ala State Univ, BS, 1950; Howard Univ, LLB, 1957. **Career:** Lawyer (retired); Sole pract, atty, 1958-70; US Dept Justice, asst atty, 1971-94. **Orgs:** Ala State Bar Asn; Amerzcan Judicature Soc; Minutes Ala State Bar. **Honors/Awds:** Special Achievement Award, Dept Justice, 1975; Special Alumni Award, Ala State Univ. **Home Addr:** 667 W Jeff Saun Ave, PO Box 1213, Montgomery, AL 36102-1213, **Home Phone:** (334)263-1389.

## PUTNAM, GLENDORA M.

Lawyer. **Personal:** Born Jul 25, 1923, Lugoff, SC; died Jun 5, 2016, Boston, MA; daughter of Simon P McIlwain (deceased) and Katherine Stewart McIlwain (deceased). **Educ:** Barber Scotia Jr Col, cert, 1943; Bennett Col, AB, 1945; Boston Univ, JD, 1948. **Career:** MA Off Atty Gen, asst atty gen, 1963-69; MA Comn Against Discrimination, chmn, 1969-75; US Dept Housing & Urban Develop, dep asst secy, 1975-77; MA Housing Finance Agency, equal opportunity officer, 1977-88; Exec Serv Corps New Eng, nat pres. **Orgs:** MA Bar Asn, 1949-2016; Fed Bar 1st Dist, 1956-2016; US Supreme Ct Bar, 1964-2016; bd trustee, Boston Con serv, 1972-2016; pres, YWCA USA, 1985-91; bd mem, Nat Asn Advan Colored People Legal & Educ Defense Fund; Boston Bar Asn; Boston Lawyers Comt Civil Rights Under Law; life mem, Exec Comt Boston Univ Law Sch Alumni Asn; adv bd, Exec Serv Corps New Eng. **Honors/Awds:** Women of the Year Greater Boston Bus & Prof Club, 1969; Humanitarian Award, Boston Br, Nat Asn Advan Colore People, 1973; Woman of Achievement, Boston Big Sisters, 1985; Honarary Doctor of Laws, Southeastern Mass Univ, 1986; Silver Shingle for Distinguished Public Service, Boston Univ Law Sch, 1988; Academy of Distinguished Bostonians, Greater Boston Chamber Com, 1988; LLD, Bennett Col, 1991; LLD, Leslie Col, 1999. **Special Achievements:** First African American woman to serve as pres of the national YWCA. **Home Addr:** 790 Boylston St, Boston, MA 02199, **Home Phone:** (617)262-6688.

**RANDLE, LUCIOUS A., SR.**
Business owner, real estate agent, educator. **Personal:** Born Aug 15, 1927, McGregor, TX; died Feb 12, 2016, Houston, TX; married Berdine C Reese; children: Lydia Louise. **Educ:** BS, 1949; MEd, 1953; Univ Tex. **Career:** OJ Thomas High Sch, 1949-57; Charlie Brown High Sch, 1957-58; Worthing High Sch, sci teacher, 1958-62; Attucks Jr High Sch, teacher, part-time prin, 1962-70; Homefinders Real Estate Inc, co broker, 1965-70; Miss Lucy's Acad & Early Childhood Educ Ctr, owner-dir, 1969; Robert E Lee Sr High Sch, Houston Independent Sch Dist, vice prin, 1970; Friendship Realty Co, owner-broker, 1970; Homestead Road Sch Dance, owner, 1971. **Orgs:** NEA; TSTA Houston Prin Asn; Nat Asn Real Estate Brokers; Houston Realtors Asn; Tex Realtors Asn; N Forst Task Force Orgn; Fontaine-Scenic Woods Civic Club; Masonic Lodge; Lions Club. **Honors/Awds:** Teacher of the Year, 1955; Real Estate Salesman of the Year, 1965; hon mem FFA Award, 1973; Community Service Award, Nat Coun Negro Women, 1974. **Home Addr:** 5203 Long Creek Lane, Houston, TX 77088-4402, **Home Phone:** (281)445-5585.

**RATES, REV. DR. NORMAN M.**
Clergy, educator. **Personal:** Born Jan 1, 1924, Owensboro, KY; died Apr 5, 2015; married Laura Lynem; children: Sondra & Shari. **Educ:** Kent State Col, BA, 1947; Lincoln Univ, BD, 1950; Oberlin Col, MDiv, 1952; Oberlin Col, STM, 1953; Yale Univ, MAR, 1961; Harvard Univ, independent study, 1969; Vanderbilt Univ, DMin, 1974. **Career:** Clergy (retired), administrator; Camac Community Ctr, stud counr, 1947-48; Philadelphia Gen Hosp, asst protestant chaplain, 1948-49; Div Home Missions Nat Coun Christ, USA, NY, FL & DE, missionary agr migrants, 1948-56; St Paul Baptist Church, asst pastor, 1949-50; Morris Col, minister dean men teacher, 1953-54; Spelman Col, GA Dept Relig, col minister, assoc chmn, 1954, dean emer, 1955-2015; Westhills Presby Church, interim pastor, 1963; Morehouse Spelman Col, Pre-Col Prog summers, counr, minister, 1966-67; Interdenom Theol Ctr, guest lectr, part-time teacher, 1971; Cent Brooklyn Model Cities Summer Acad, Spelman Col, counr, 1972. **Orgs:** Nat Asn Col & Univ Chaplains; Ministry BlacksHigher Educ; Am Asn Univ Prof; Nat Asn Bibl Instr; Univ Ctr Ga Div, Teacher Relig; Petit Jr Fulton Co Super Ct, 1971, 1973; Grand Jr Fulton Co Super Ct, 1972; ministerial standing, United Church Christ; fel Conf African & African-Am Studies Atlanta Univ Campus; bd mem, Camping Unlimited Blue Star Camps Inc; bd dir, Planned Parenthood Asn Atlanta; chmn, Relig Affairs Com Planned Parenthood Asn Atlanta; Comn Ministry United Church Christ; Metro Atlanta Christian Coun; Ga-SC Asn United Church Christ SE Conf; Alpha Phi Alpha Frat; bd trustee, Carrie Steele-Pitts Home. **Honors/Awds:** C Morris Cain Prize in Bible, Samuel Dickey Prize in New Testament, Lincoln Univ, 1949; Campus Christian Worker Grant, Danforth Found, 1960-61; Atlanta Univ Ctr Non-Western Studies Prog Grant, Travel & Study Ford Found, 1968-69. **Special Achievements:** Author:May Thy Dear Wall Remain. **Home Addr:** 2514 Elkhorn Dr, Decatur, GA 30034-2720, **Home Phone:** (404)243-4038.

**REINHARDT, JOHN EDWARD**
Diplomat, educator. **Personal:** Born Mar 8, 1920, Glade Spring, VA; died Feb 18, 2016, Silver Spring, MD; son of Edward Vinton and Alice Miller; married Carolyn L Daves; children: Sharman, Alice & Carolyn. **Educ:** Univ Chicago, Eng; Knoxville Col, BA, 1939; Univ Wisc, MS, 1947, PhD, Eng, 1950. **Career:** Va State Col, prof eng, 1950-56; USIS Manila Philippines, cult affairs officer, 1956-58; Am Cult Ctr Kyoto Japan, dir, 1958-63; USIS Tehran Iran, cult attach, 1963-66; Off E Asia & Pac USIA, dept asst, 1966-68; Nigeria, ambassador, 1971-75; Wash, DC, asst sec state, 1975-77; Int Community Agency, dir, 1976-81; US Info Agency, dir, 1977-80; Smithsonian Inst, asst sec, hist & art, 1981-84, dir & directorate Int Activ, 1984-87; Univ Vt, prof polit sci, 1987-91, prof emer, 1991-2016. **Orgs:** Am Foreign Serv Asn, 1969-2016; distinguished fel US Inst Peace, 1988-89; Mod Lang Asn; Int Club; Cosmos Club. **Special Achievements:** First African American ambassadors. **Home Addr:** 3154 Gracefield Rd Apt 417, Silver Spring, MD 20904-0808, **Home Phone:** (301)890-3250.

**RHODES, JEANNE SIMMONS**
Executive. **Personal:** Born Monongahela, PA; died Jan 1, 1990; daughter of Joseph (deceased) and Martha; married E Washington; children: Joseph Simmons Scott & Margaret Herndon. **Educ:** Duffs Bus Sch; Univ Pitts; Duquesne Univ. **Career:** State Dept Labour, specialist; Philadelphia Tribune, vpres pub rels. **Orgs:** Bd mem, Am Red Cross; life mem, Exec Com, Grad Hosp Aux; bd mem, Inglis Hse Home Incurables; bd dir, Philadelphia Tribune Co; bd trustee, Ruth W Hayre Scholar Found; Sponsers Scholar Club; La Cabaneetas Eastern Sea Bd Dinner Club; Finesse Bridge; DCR Birthday Club; bd mem, Philadelphia 76; bd trustee, Dowingtown Agr & Indust Sch; spec Dept Labor; pres, & secy, Pitts Br, Nat Asn Advan Colored People; chmn bd, Lemington Home Aged; nat pres, Iota P Hi Lambda; mem bd, Civil Light Opera Pittsburgh; hon bd mem, Tribune Charities; Adv comn, Afro-am Mus; bd mem, YWCA Belmont Br; Philadelphia Bicentennial Comn; Bethesda United Presby Church; adhoc com, Floyd Logan Arch Temple U; treas, S St W Bus Asn, 1979; lay mem, Fee Disputes Com Philadelphia Bar Asn, 1979; Cenntennial Com Lucretia Mott, 1980; Univ Pa Grad Hosp. **Honors/Awds:** Service Award, Philadelphia Tribune Charities, 1973; Bi-centennial Achievement Award, AME Ch, 1976; Appreciation Award, Bicentennial Comn PA; Recognition Award, Police Athletic Leg, 1977; Service Award, ARC, 1978; Distinguished Service Award, Downingtown A&I Sch, 1979; 50th Anniversary Leadership Award, Iota Phi Lambda Sor, 1979. **Home Addr:** 1708 Addison St, Philadelphia, PA 19146, **Home Phone:** (314)977-3850.

**RICHIE, DR. WINSTON HENRY**
Association executive, dentist, real estate agent. **Personal:** Born Sep 18, 1925, Jersey City, NJ; died Feb 19, 2016, Cleveland, OH; son of William F and Celeste Strode; married Beatrice; children: Winston Jr, Beth E, Laurel L & Anne C. **Educ:** Adebert Col Western Res Univ, BS, 1948; Western Res Univ, DDS, 1952. **Career:** Dentist (retired); Shaker Heights City Coun, 1972-84, vice mayor, 1977; real estate agt; E Suburban Coun Open Communities, exec dir, 1984-90; self-employed dentist; Realty One, real estate agt, currently. **Orgs:** Am Dent Asn; Cleveland Dent Soc; Ohio St Dent Asn; Elder Fairmount Presby Church, 1972-75; pres, Fair Housing Inc; Shaker Heights City Coun, 1972-. **Honors/Awds:** Distinguished Service in Open Housing Award, Cuyahoga Plan Cleveland; invited to Australia to represent the Ford Foundation & Harvard Univ discussing racial integration in the USA; 2007; Honr Roll, Dartmouth Col. **Home Addr:** 2741 Green Rd, Shaker Heights, OH 44122, **Home Phone:** (216)464-1379. **Business Addr:** Real Estate Agent, Realty One, 20515 Shaker Blvd, Shaker Heights, OH 44122, **Business Phone:** (216)991-8400.

**ROBERTS, LORRAINE MARIE PETTIE**
Consultant, educator. **Personal:** Born May 12, 1930, Philadelphia, PA; died Feb 23, 2015, Newburgh, NY; daughter of Willie Pettie and Adele Marie (Simpson) Pettie; married Arthur M; children: Kevin Middleton & Harlan Keith. **Educ:** Hampton Univ, BS, 1952; Bucknell Univ, exchange stud; Columbia Univ, MA, 1954. **Career:** Educator (retired), administrator; Union High Sch, Bowling Green Bd Educ VA, teacher, 1952-53; Rochester City Sch Dist, teacher, 1956-64; NY Univ Syst State Educ Dept, adj prof; Poughkeepsie City Sch Dist, coordr, Bus Educ, part time teacher, 1965-66, dept chmn, Occup educ, 1966-96, SED Curric OE & Tech Studies Comn, co-chmn, 1992-95; CDOS, consult, 1996-98, co-chair. **Orgs:** Basileus, Iota Alpha Omega Chap, Alpha Kappa Alpha Sor, 1969-71; BTA; EBTA; NBEA; PPSTA; NYSUT; AFL-TA; bd trustees, YWCA, Dutchess Co, 1970-75; bd mem, secy, United Way Dutchess County, 1973-80; chmn, Cent Alloc Div United Way Dutchess Co, 1979-80; Bethel Missionary Baptist Church; AFS Poughkeepsie; United Way; Nat Advan Asn Colored People; bd, Dutchess County & Dominica Partnership Am, 1984-92; bd, Friends Greater Poughkeepsie Libr Dist, 1988-94; pres, Bus Teachers Mid-Hudson, 1989-92; bd, treas, DC Girl Scouts, 1993-99; Bus Educ Div NYS Educ Dept; pres, Dutchess Co Hist Soc, 1996-99; Vassar-Warner Home Bd, 1999-2001; KAD; ERVK; chmn, Poughkeepsie Day Sch, Diversity Comt, 2002-15; Boards United Way, YWCA; Catharine St Ctr; Spec Proj Comt March Dimes; Am; Girl Scouts Dutchess County, DCC Off Technologies Comt; Kids Affected with Disabilities Bd; Eleanor Roosevelt Ctr Val-Kill; Community Found DC. **Honors/Awds:** Outstanding Occupational Educator, NYS Educ Dept, 1989; Outstanding educator, Dutchess Beulah Baptist Ch, 1992; YWCA Award, Salute Women, 1993; Outstanding Business Teacher, NYS, 1994; Martin Luther King Honoree, 1997; Presidents Award, Marist Col, 1998; Eleanor Roosevelt Candle Award, 1999; Contributing writer, Pougnkeepsie Journal Millenum Series, 2000; DCHS Award, 2000. **Special Achievements:** Invisible People, co-author; Untold Stories: A Historical Overview of the Black Community in Poughkeepsie (Dutchess County Historical Society Yearbook), 1987. **Home Addr:** 26 Brothers Rd, Wappingers Falls, NY 12590, **Home Phone:** (845)297-5578.

**ROBERTS, REV. DR. SAMUEL KELTON**
Educator. **Personal:** Born Sep 1, 1944, Muskogee, OK; died Feb 24, 2015, Baltimore, MD; son of Foster and Hattie Harper; married Valerie Hermoine Fisher; children: Samuel Kelton Jr & Franklin. **Educ:** Morehouse Col, BA, 1967; Union Theol Sem, MDiv, 1970; Columbia Univ, MPhil, PhD, 1974. **Career:** Educator (retired); Fund Theol Educ, Protestant fel, 1967-70; New York Mission Soc, summer proj dir, 1967-70; Columbia Univ, fel, 1970-72; S Hempstead Cong Church, pastor, 1972-73; Pittsburgh Theol Sem, asst prof, 1973-76; Union Theol Sem, asst prof relig & soc, 1976-80, Presby Sch Christian Educ, Anne Borden & E Hervey Evans prof theol & ethics, prof theol & ethics; VA Union Univ, prof christian ethics, dean; Va Union Univ Sch Theol, prof christian ethics & dir doctor ministry prog; Union Presbyterian Seminary, teacher. **Orgs:** Am Acad Rels; Soc Sci Study Rel; Soc Study Black Relition; Am Theol Soc, 2003. **Honors/Awds:** Merril Overseas Study Award, Morehouse Col, 1965-66. **Special Achievements:** Author, George Edmund Haynes, 1978; African American Christian Ethics & Inthe Path of Virtue: The African American Moral Tradition. **Home Addr:** 6305 Varina Station Dr, Richmond, VA 23231-5233.

**ROBINSON, CHARLOTTE L.**
Consultant, educator. **Personal:** Born Jun 3, 1918, Long Island, NY; died Jan 3, 2011, Philadelphia, PA; married Henry W; children: Barry K & Cherylyn. **Educ:** Univ Pa, BA, 1948, MBA, 1967, PhD, 1976. **Career:** Philadelphia Pub Sch Systs, asst dir curric, instr multimedia instrnl resources; City Univ NY, consult; Sears Roebuck & Co Phila, consult. **Orgs:** Phi Delta Epsilon; Am Women Radio & TV; Media Adv Comn Commonwealth Pa; Asn Educ Commun & Tech; Pa Learning Resources Asn; Philadelphia Unique Commun Proj, 1974. **Home Addr:** 702 St Georges Rd, Philadelphia, PA 19119, **Home Phone:** (215)248-0319.

**ROBINSON, CURTIS**
Educator. **Personal:** Born May 12, 1934, Wilmington, NC; died Nov 1, 2015, Edinboro, PA; married Joan Elenor Williams; children: Debra D, Milton C & Cheryl A. **Educ:** Morgan State Univ, BS, 1960; Howard Univ, MS, 1968; Univ Md, PhD, biol & biomed sci, 1973. **Career:** Lincoln HS, NC, sci & math teacher, 1960-61; Williston Sr HS, NC, sci & math teacher, 1961-62; Radiation Biol Lab, Smithsonian Inst, Rockville, MD, res biologist, 1962-69; Edinboro Univ, PA, prof, 1973, prof emer. **Orgs:** Alpha Phi Alpha, 1959-2015; Am Soc Plant Physiologists, 1970-2015; Nat Educ Asn, 1973-2015; Asn Pa State Col Biologists, 1973-2015; Nat Asn Advan Colored People, 1975; Am Asn Univ Professors, 1978-. **Home Addr:** 221 Shelhamer Dr, Edinboro, PA 16412-2388, **Home Phone:** (814)734-4332.

**ROBINSON, JACKIE. See SIFFORD, DR. CHARLES L.**

**ROBINSON, KENNETH EUGENE**
Insurance agent, educator, football coach. **Personal:** Born Mar 9, 1947, Hannibal, MO; died Liberty, MO; married Cecilia. **Educ:** William Jewell Col, BS; Northwest Mo State Univ, MS, educ; Univ Mo, Kansas City, ed spec, 1980. **Career:** Moberly Pub Schs, social studies instr, 1969-71; Liberty Sr High Sch, psychol & sociol instr, 1972-80; Liberty Pub Schs, asst football & head track coach, 1972-80; Clay Co Juv Justice Ctr, detention officer, 1977-78; Franklin Life Ins, ins agt, 1979-80; State Farm Ins Co, agt. **Orgs:** Parks & Recreation Bd, Liberty, Mo, 1977-80; pres, elect Liberty CTA, 1978-79; pres, Liberty Teachers Asn, 1979-80; Minority Studies Task Force, William Jewell Col, 1979-80; campaign chmn, United Way Liberty Pub Schs, 1979; Pub Rels, Com MSTA, 1980. **Home Addr:** 8154 NW Prairie View Rd, Kansas City, MO 64151-1020, **Home Phone:** (816)587-5466.

**ROOKS, SEAN LESTER**
Basketball player, basketball coach. **Personal:** Born Sep 9, 1969, New York, NY; died Jun 7, 2016, Philadelphia, PA; married Susanne; children: Kameron & Kayla. **Educ:** Univ Ariz, BA, commun, 1992. **Career:** Basketball player (retired), basketball coach, executive; Dallas Mavericks, ctr, 1992-94; Minn Timber wolves, ctr, 1994-96; Atlanta Hawks, ctr, 1995-96; Los Angeles Lakers, ctr, 1996-99; Dallas Mavericks, ctr, 1999-2000; Los Angeles Clippers, ctr, 2000-03; Skoor Inc, pres, 2000; New Orleans Hornets, ctr, 2003-04; Orlando Magic, ctr, 2004; Unicaja Malaga, Spain, 2005; Joventut Badalona, Spain, 2005; Bakersfield JAM, interim head coach, asst coach, 2007-08; Fox Broadcasting, basketball ananlyst, 2008-11; NMex Thunderbirds, asst coach, 2010-11; Los Angeles Slam, 2011-12; Sioux Falls Skyforce, asst coach, 2012. Nat Basketball Asn, coach; Nat Col Athletic Asn, mentor; Nat Basketball Asn Develop League, player develop coach, 2013-14. **Business Addr:** Assistant Coach, Sioux Falls Skyforce, 2131 S Minnesota Ave, Sioux Falls, CA 57105, **Business Phone:** (605)332-0605.

**RUSSELL, HERMAN JEROME**
Chairperson, executive. **Personal:** Born Dec 23, 1930, Atlanta, GA; died Nov 15, 2014, Atlanta, GA; son of Roger and Maggie; married Otelia; children: Donata, Michael & Jerome. **Educ:** Tuskegee Inst, BS, 1953. **Career:** City Beverage Co Inc, Atlanta GA, pres, chmn bd; Atlanta Enquirer Newspaper Inc, chmn bd dir; Enterprise Investments Inc, chmn bd; Concessions Int Inc, pres, chmn bd, 2014; GA Southeastern Land Co Inc, pres & chmn bd; Paradise Apts Mgt Co Inc, pres; HJ Russell Plastering Co & Constr Co, pres & chief exec officer, 1953-2003; HJ Russell & Co, chief operating officer, chmn, 2014; Herman J. Russell Found Inc, founder, 2014. **Orgs:** Chmn bd, DDR Int Inc, Atlanta, Ga; bd dir, World Cong Ctr Authority, Atlanta, Ga; chmn bd dir, Cit Trust Co Bank; bd dir, YMCA; mem bd trustees, Morris Brown Col; life mem, Nat Asn Advan Colored People; Nat adv bd Ga Inst Tech; African Meth Episcopal Church; mem bd trustees, African Episcopal Church; chmn bd Russell/Rowe Commun; bd dir, Prime Cable; mem bd dir, First Atlanta Corp; pres, Atlanta C C; mem bd dir, Ga C C, Cent Atlanta Prog, Tuskegee Inst; Ga Power Co; First Wachovia Corp; Ga Ports Authority. **Honors/Awds:** Nat Asn of Market Developers Award, 1968; Meritorious Business Achievement Award, Atlanta Community Rels, 1969; Equal Opportunity Day Atlanta Urban League, 1972; African Method Episcopal Outstanding Business of the Year, 1973; Winter Conference Award, Affil Contractor Am Inc, 1973; Disting Service Award, Empire Real Estate Bd, 1973; Black Enterpise Magazine Annual Achievement Award, 1978; Junior Achievement Award (Bus & Youth), 1979; Nat Alumni Award, Tuskegee Inst; Entrepreneur of the Year, Nat Black MBA Asn, 1990; Horatio Alger Award, 1991; Junior Achievement Atlanta Business Hall of Fame, 1992. **Special Achievements:** First black member of Atlanta Chamber of Commerce.

**SALTERS, DR. CHARLES ROBERT**
School administrator. **Personal:** Born Nov 1, 1943, St. Stephen, SC; died Jul 16, 2000, Randallstown, MD; son of Willie D and Marie Izzard; married Vivian Governor; children: Bobvita Shawntrea & Dorian Mont. **Educ:** SC State Col, Orangeburg, SC, BS, 1965; Atlanta Univ, Atlanta, Ga, MA, 1971; Morgan State Univ, Baltimore, MS, 1977; Univ Md, EDd, 1985. **Career:** State Md, Henry Welcome fel, 1984; Morgan State Univ, asst dean grad studies & res, mentor, 2000; Atlanta Bd Educ. **Orgs:** Nat Sci Found, 1970-71; Alpha Phi Alpha Fraternity Inc, 1973; Phi Delta Kappa, 1982; Union Bethel AME Church, 1984; Alpha Lamba Delta, 1990; Golden Key, 1995. **Honors/Awds:** Dr Charles Salters Special Achievement Award, honor. **Home Addr:** 9806 Clanford Rd, Randallstown, MD 21133-2508, **Home Phone:** (410)655-7831.

**SAMUELS, RONALD S. (RON SAMUELS)**
Lawyer. **Personal:** Born Jun 17, 1941, Chicago, IL; died Dec 12, 2011; son of Lena and Peter; married Melva; children: 4. **Educ:** Chicago State Univ, BA, 1964; John Marshall Law Sch, JD, 1969. **Career:** Chicago Bd Educ, teacher, 1964-69; atty, 1969-70; Leadership Coun Metro Open Housing, chief trial lawyer, 1970-73; Cook Co States Atty Off, chief fraud div, 1974-77; Cook Co Bar Asn, pres, 1981-82; Legal Serv Corp, bd mem; Cook County Comnr, mgr; Ronald S Samuels & Assoc, managing partner & atty. **Orgs:** Nat Bar Asn; founding mem, Cook Co Bar Asn, Chicago, Ill; State Bar Asn; Am Bar Asns; dir, Legal Opportunities Scholar Prog; chmn, Consumer Task Force; Chicago Urban League; Kappa Alpha Psi Alumni Chap; CSU Alumni Asn; PUSH; Nat Asn Advan Colored People; Progressive Nat Baptist Conv Inc; Church God Christ; United Methodist Church; Black Methodists Church Renewal Inc. **Honors/Awds:** American Jurisprudence Award; William Ming Award; Richard E Westbrooks; PUSH

Outstanding Public Service; Distinguished Service Award, Nat Bar Asn. **Home Addr:** 9957 S Winchester Ave, Chicago, IL 60643, **Home Phone:** (312)502-2600.

### SCOTT, DR. HUGH J.

Educator. **Personal:** Born Nov 14, 1933, Detroit, MI; died Jul 16, 2016, Valhalla, NY; married Florence I Edwards; children: Marvalisa & Hugh. **Educ:** Wayne State Univ, BS, educ, 1956, MS, educ, 1960, specialist cert educ admin, 1964; Mich State Univ, EdD, 1966. **Career:** City Detroit, teacher, 1956, 1958-65; Mich St Univ, instr, 1965-66; Detroit Great Cities Sch Improv Proj, asst dir, 1965, asst prin, 1966-67, asst dep supt sch community rels, 1967-68, region asst supt, 1968-70; Wash, supt sch, 1970-73; Howard Univ, prof educ, 1973-75; Hunter Col, City Univ New York, dean prog educ, 1975-2000, prof emer, 2000-16; Pace Univ, scholar residence, 2001-04, dir & hon scholar residence, 2004-16. **Orgs:** Phi Delta Kappa, 1960-; Nat Asn Advan Colored People, 1967-70; bd dir, Detroit Soc Black Educ Adminr, 1968-70; Am Asn Sch Adminr, 1969-2016; Nat Alliance Black Sch Educr, 1970-2016; Chevel & conf, 1974-2016. **Honors/Awds:** Distinguished Service Certificate, Phi Delta Kappa, 1969; Distinguished Alumni Award, Mich St Univ, 1970; Hall of Fame, Nat Alliance Black Sch Educr, 1990; Distinguished Service President's Medal, 1993; President's Medal for Distinguished Service, Hunter Col, City Univ New York, 1993; Lifetime Achievement Award, Nat Alliance Black Sch Educr, 1996. **Special Achievements:** First African American school superintendent in Howard University; Author of The Black Superintendent: Messiah or Scapegoat?, Howard University Press, 1980; published numerous articles. **Home Addr:** 46 Silverbirch Dr, New Rochelle, NY 10804-3810, **Home Phone:** (914)576-2261.

### SHAW, DR. ANN

Executive, college teacher, social worker. **Personal:** Born Nov 21, 1921, Columbus, OH; died May 5, 2015, Los Angeles, CA; daughter of Pearl Daniel and Sarah Roberts; children: Valerie, Leslie Jr, Rebecca & Dan. **Educ:** Univ Redlands, AB, 1943, LHD, 1971; OH State Univ, MA, 1944; Univ Sothern Calif, MSW, 1968. **Career:** Univ Calif Los Angeles, teacher; Cent State Col, teacher; LA Job Corps Ctr Women, exec asst, 1965-66; LA City Sch, teacher, 1949-51; Cent St Col, asst prof, 1946-48; Va Union Univ, instr. **Orgs:** Bd mem, Calif Community Found, Calif Med Ctr Found; app to serve on Calif Joint Select Task Force onChanging Family; alumni asn; Univ Sothern Calif; Ohio St & Redlands Univ; PTA; Nat Coun Negro Women; Nat Asn Advan Colored People YWCA World Serv Coun; pres, Wilfandel Club; bd dir, Lloyds Bank Calif, 1978-85; charter mem, Am Women Int; chmn bd, Founders Savings & Loan Assoc, 1986-87. **Honors/Awds:** Agency leadership awards & com Women's Div United Way; cert merit, Asn Study Negro Life & Hist, 1964; Univ Redlands, 1964; Woman of the Year LaSentinel Newspaper, 1964; Royal Blue Book; Nat Asn Advan Colored People Legal Defense & Educ Fund Award, Black Women of Achievement, 1985; BigSisters Los Angeles Award, 1986; Calif Senate Woman of the Year Award, Senatorial Dist 30, 1987; United Way's Highest Honor The Gold Key Award; The Athena Award, YWCA, 1989; Community Service Award, YWCA, 1989; The Key Council Award, California Afro-Amer Museum, 1989; Calif Welfare Archives, Lantern of Hope Award, Calif Med Ctr Community Leadership, 1997; Distinguished Aluma Award, USC, 2001. **Special Achievements:** First woman and the first African American to be appointed by Gov. Jerry Brown in 1975 to serve on the state Commission on Judicial Performance. **Home Addr:** 1650 S Victoria Ave, Los Angeles, CA 90019.

### SHAW, LEANDER JERRY, JR.

Judge. **Personal:** Born Sep 6, 1930, Salem, VA; died Dec 14, 2015, Tallahassee, FL; son of Leander J Sr and Margaret W; children: Sean, Jerry, Sherri, Dione & Dawn. **Educ:** WVa State Col, BA, 1952; Howard Univ, JD, 1957. **Career:** Judge (retired); Fla A&M Univ, asst prof, 1957-60; pvt pract, atty, 1960-69; Duval Co, asst pub defender, 1965-69, asst state atty, 1969-72; head capital crimes div & adv grand jury; pvt pract, atty, 1972-74; Fla Indust Rels Comt, comt, 1974-79; State Fla 1st Dist Ct Appeal, judge, 1979-83; Fla Supreme Ct, justice, 1983-2003, chief justice, 1990-92; W&L Sch Law, judge-in-residence. **Orgs:** Chmn, bd elections, Am Bar Asn, Fla Bar Asn, Nat Bar Asn, Fla Gov Bar Asn; dir, Fla Bar Found; adv, Judicial Admin Comn, State Traffic Ct Rev Comn; chmn, State Ct Restructure Comn; Fla Assoc Vol Agencies Caribbean Action, Most Worshipful Union Grand Lodge Free & Accepted Masons Fla PHA Inc, Alpha Phi Alpha; Tallahassee Bar Asn; Am Judicature Soc; mem bd dir, Nat Ctr State Ct; Appointment Mayor Jacksonville; police adv comn, Human Rels Coun; Jacksonville Jetport Authority; bd chmn, Jacksonville Oppotunities Industrialization Ctr, offender, Res Adv Comn; Fla Stand Jury Instrs, Civil Comn; adv, Ethnic Bias Study Comn, Guardian Ad Litem Prog; chmn, Fla Sentencing Guidelines Comn, Gov Chiles' Criminal Justice Task Force; second vpres, Conf Chief Justices; bd visitor, Fla State Univ, Col Law; bd dir, Nat Ctr State Ct; Am Judicature Soc; Judicial Fel Prog Supreme Ct US. **Honors/Awds:** Dedication to Justice, FL Chap Nat Bar Asn, 1977; Community Service, Jacksonville Bar Asn, 1978; Exemplary Achievement in Judicial Service, State Fla Nat Bar Asn, 1984; Hon LD, Wva State Col, 1986; LD, Wash & Lee Univ, 1991; LD, Nova Univ, 1991; hon pub affairs degree, Fla Int Univ, 1990; Fla Humanist of the Year Award, St Petersburg FL, 1991; Ben Franklin Award, St Petersburg, FL, 1992. **Special Achievements:** First African American to head the high court of Florida. **Home Addr:** , Lake Iamonia, FL.

### SHEPARD, LINDA IRENE

Business owner, consultant. **Personal:** Born Dec 13, 1945, St. Louis, MO; died Oct 30, 2006, Oakland, CA; daughter of Woodie McCune and Dorothy Alice McCune; children: Monica, Adrienne Fitts & Alton Fitts III. **Educ:** Merritt Col, Oxford Calif, AA, 1972; Mills Col, Oakland Calif, BA, 1975. **Career:** Assemblyman Bill Lockyear, San Leondio Calif, dist secy, 1975-76; Jimmy Carter Pres, Atlanta Ga, dir campaign oper, 1976; BART, Oakland Calif, affirmative action officer, 1976-85; Mayor Lionel Wilson, Oakland Calif, campaign mgr, 1985-86; Super Consult, owner, 1982-88; AC Transit, dir human resources, vpres. **Orgs:** Nat Coun Negro Women; Nat Asn Advan Colored People; vpres human resources, Am Pub Transit Asn. **Honors/Awds:** Outstanding Business Achievement Award, Nat Coun Negro Women, 1987. **Home Addr:** 25800 Indust Blvd, Hayward, CA 94545, **Home Phone:** (510)786-9024.

### SHEPHERD, GRETA DANDRIDGE

School administrator, educator. **Personal:** Born Aug 15, 1930, Washington, DC; died Dec 19, 2013, West Orange, NJ; daughter of Philip J and Bertha Johnson; married Gilbert A; children: Michele M Murchison. **Educ:** Minor Teachers Col, Wash, DC, BS, 1951; DC Teachers Col, Wash, DC, MA, 1961. **Career:** Educator, school administrator (retired); Banneker Jr High Sch, teacher, counr & asst prin; DC Pub Schs, teacher, 1951-66, from asst prin to prin, 1966-72; Int Christian Univ, Fulbright/Hayes Fel, 1965; E Orange Pub Schs, NJ, dir, 1972-80, supt, 1980-82; Plainfield NJ, supt schs, 1982-84; NJ St Dept Educ, county supt schs, 1984-89; Essex County Voc Schs, NJ, supt, 1989. **Orgs:** Alpha Kappa Alpha Sorority, 1950; assoc, CFK Ltd Found, 1971; pres elect, CADRE Found, 1975-2013; bd dir, YWCA Oranges, 1975-98; bd trustee, E Orange Pub Libr, 1981-83; Zeta Phi Beta, 1983; bd trustee, Mercer Co Community Col, 1984-2013; fed policy comm mem, Am Asn Sch Admin, 1984-2013; Phi Delta Kappa, 1987-2013; bd trustee mem, Univ DC, 1994-2013. **Honors/Awds:** Woman of the Year, NJ Chap Zeta Phi Beta, 1983; 5 Point Education Award, NJ Chap Delta Sigma Theta Sorority, 1984; Award Recognition, Cong Black Caucus Educ, 1984; Educator of The Year, Northeast Coalition Educ Leaders Inc, 1988; Distinguished Alumni Award, Nat Asn Equal Opportunity Higher Educ; Gubnertorial Appointee, NJ Educational Opportunity Fund. **Special Achievements:** NJ State Assembly Citation; Person of the Decade, Black New Jersey Magazine. **Home Addr:** 6 Linden Ave, West Orange, NJ 07052, **Home Phone:** (973)243-1313.

### SHERWOOD, WALLACE WALTER (WALLY SHERWOOD)

Lawyer, college teacher, educator. **Personal:** Born Oct 6, 1944, Nassau; died Jun 10, 2016; son of Walter and Tereceta. **Educ:** St Vincent Col, BA, 1966; George Washington Univ, JD, 1969; Harvard Univ, LLM, 1971. **Career:** Professor (retired); Legal Serv, staff atty, 1969-71; Mass Comn Against Discrimination, comnr, 1971-73; Roxbury Defenders Comt, exec founding dir, 1971-73; OEO, gen coun, 1973-74; Lawyers Comn Civil Rights Under Law, exec div, 1974-76; pvt pract atty, 1976-2016; Northeastern Univ Col Criminal Justice, adj assoc prof, 1978, asst prof, assoc prof, assoc dean acad affairs, chair, prof criminal justice; Community Legal Assistance Off, staff atty; Boston Off Lawyers Comt Civil Rights Under Law, exec dir. **Orgs:** Mass Bar Asn, 1969-2016; Boston Bar Asn, 1969-2016; Mass Coun Pub Justice. **Honors/Awds:** Dulles Fulbright Award, Nat Law Ctr, 1969; Teacher of The Year, Col Criminal Justice, 1987. **Special Achievements:** Book: "Constitutional Requirements in the Administration of Criminal Justice". **Home Addr:** 10 Trowbridge St, Cambridge, MA 02138.

### SHIRLEY, DR. OLLYE L. BROWN

Association executive. **Personal:** Born Mound Bayou, MS; died Sep 10, 2016, Jackson, MS; married Aaron. **Educ:** Tougaloo Col, BA, Eng; Miss Col, MA, guid & coun, 1969; Jackson State Univ, EdS, coun, 1978; Univ Miss, PhD, higher educ & stud personnel, 1988. **Career:** Vicksburg Citizens Appeal, ed; Lanier High Sch, After Sch Prog, coordr & consult; Jackson Pub Schs, Jackson Med Mall Quantum Opportunities Prog, staff. **Orgs:** Miss Civil Rights Educ Comn; Nat Sch Bds Asn; bd dir, First Am Bank; MS Mus Nat Sci Found; Jackson chap, vpres, Serv Youth dir, Links Inc. **Honors/Awds:** Goodman, Chaney, Schwerner Award, 1989; Medgar Evers Award, Nat Asn Advan Colored People, 1999.

### SIFFORD, DR. CHARLES L. (JACKIE ROBINSON)

Golfer. **Personal:** Born Jun 2, 1922, Charlotte, NC; died Feb 3, 2015, Cleveland, OH; married Rose; children: Charles & Craig. **Career:** Pvt golf instr, Singer Billy Eckstine, 1947-53; prof golfer. **Orgs:** Deerwood Country Club. **Honors/Awds:** Winner, Long Beach Open, 1957; winner, Puerto Rico Open, 1963; winner, Greater Hartford Open, 1967; Los Angeles Open, 1969; Sea Pines, 1971; Suntree Classic, 1980; Achievement Award, 2001; World Gold Hall of Fame, 2004; Won Negro National Open; hon degree, Univ St Andrews, 2006; Old Tom Morris Award, Golf Course Superintendents Asn Am, 2007; Presidential Medal of Freedom, 2014. **Special Achievements:** Author: Just Let Me Play, autobiography, 1992; First African American to achieve success on the PGA tour; first African American to win the PGA Sr Championship, 1975; first African American elected to World Gold Hall of Fame, 2004; Won Negro National Open six times; The first African American man to break the color barrier in one of the nation's most elitist sports; First African American golfer to break into another exclusive club in 2004; First black golfer to earn a PGA Tour card. **Home Addr:** PO Box 43128, Highland Heights, OH 44143-0128.

### SIMMONS, DR. S. DALLAS

School administrator, management consultant. **Personal:** Born Jan 28, 1940, Ahoskie, NC; died Jul 5, 2014, Richmond, VA; son of Yvonne Martin; married Mary A; children: S Dallas Jr & Kristie Lynn. **Educ:** NC Cent Univ, BS, 1962, MS, 1967; Duke Univ, PhD, 1977. **Career:** NC Cent Univ, dir data processing, 1962-64; Norfolk State Univ, dir data processing, 1964-66; NC Cent Univ, asst prof bus admin, 1967-71, asst chancellor, 1971-77, vice chancellor univ rels, 1977-81; St Paul's Col, pres, 1981-85, Va Union Univ, pres, 1985-99; Dominions Bd dir, mem; Dallas Simmons & Assocs, pres & chief exec officer, currently. **Orgs:** Durham C C, 1971-81; liaison officer, Moton Col Serv Bur, 1972; competency testing comn, NC State Bd Educ, 1977-81; exec comn, Cent Intercollegiate Athletic Assoc, 1981, coun pres, 1981, bd dir, 1981, fin comn, 1984-85; Brunswick C C, 1981-85; bd dir, Va Polytech Inst & State Univ, 1982-83; bd trust, NC Cent Univ, 1983-85; conf comm, Nat Assoc Equal Opportunity Higher Educ, 1983, chmn leadership awards comm, 1984-85, bd dir, 1985; exec comm, NC Cent Univ, mem bd trust, 1983-85; mem bd dir, Pace Am Bank, 1984; US Zululand Educ Found, 1985; exec bd, John B McLendon Found Inc, 1985; exec com mem bd dir, UNCF; Am Mgt Asn; Kappa Alpha Psi; Data Processing Mgt Assoc; Doric Lodge No 28 Free & Accepted Masons; Kappa Alpha Psi, Tobaccoland Kiwanians; Sigma Pi Phi Frat Alpha Beta Boule; Optimist Club; Am Assoc Sch Admin; Am Assoc Univ Admin; Downtown Club. **Honors/Awds:** Kappa of the Month, Kappa Alpha Psi Fraternity, 1981; Citizen of the Year, Omega Psi Phi Fraternity, 1983-84; Black Am Achievers, 1983-84; Business Associate of the Year, B&G Charter Chap, ABWA, 1984. **Home Addr:** 314 Burnwick Rd, Richmond, VA 23227-1652, **Home Phone:** (804)264-5631. **Business Addr:** President, Chief Executive Officer, Dallas Simmons & Associates, 314 Burnwick Rd, Richmond, VA 23227.

### SINCLAIR, CLAYTON, JR.

Lawyer. **Personal:** Born Jul 4, 1933, Wadesboro, NC; died Feb 10, 2014, Atlanta, GA; married Jeanette B. **Educ:** Univ Maine, BA, 1955; Howard Univ Law Sch, LLB, 1960. **Career:** O'Donald & Schwartz NYC, atty, 1960-68; NY State Banking, Dept NYC, asst coun, 1968-69; Scott Paper Co, 1969-70; Goodis, Greenfield & Mann Phila, atty, 1970-71; Patterson Parks & Franklin Atlanta, atty, 1971-76; Sinclair & Dixon, sr partner, 1976-2014; pvt pract atty. **Orgs:** Am Bar Asn; Nat Bar Asn; Atlanta Bar Asn; Ga Trial Lawyers Asn; State Bar Ga, 1971-2014. **Home Addr:** , Atlanta, GA.

### SKINNER, ROBERT L., JR.

Airline executive. **Personal:** Born Oct 5, 1941, Chicago, IL; died Jan 16, 2014, Chicago, IL; son of Robert L Sr and Willie Louise Jemison. **Educ:** Southeastern City Col, Chicago, IL, attended 1961; Univ Wis, Madison, Wis, attended 1963; Northeastern Univ, Boston, MA, attended 1979. **Career:** Am Airlines, Chicago, Ill, passenger serv rep, 1965-66, passenger serv mgr, 1966-69, sales rep, 1969-77, Boston, MA, supvr flight serv, 1977-80, Chicago, Ill, acct exec, 1980-84, mgr conv & co meeting sales, 1984-88, Rochester, Minn, gen mgr, 1987-91, gen mgr, Indianapolis, Ind, 1991-96; Atlanta, Ga, gen mgr, 1996-2001; Conv/Co Meeting Sales, Chicago, Ill, specialist, 1984-87. **Orgs:** Bd dir, Rochester Conv & Visitors Bur, 1989-91; Chicago Soc Asn Exec; Chicago Area Meeting Planners Int. **Special Achievements:** Recognized with numerous Safety & Dependability Awards. **Home Addr:** 175 N Harbor Dr Suite 3904, Chicago, IL 60601-7348, **Home Phone:** (312)819-0366.

### SMITH, CAROL J.

Consultant. **Personal:** Born Dec 24, 1924, Houston, TX; died Jan 1, 2016, Washington, DC; daughter of Richard T Andrews Sr and Julia Augusta Somerville; children: Julius W Jr & Jean M. **Educ:** Prairie View, BA, 1944; Howard Univ, MA, 1948. **Career:** Howard Univ, grad fel, 1944-45, 1947-48; US Off Educ, dep act asst comn spec concern, 1971-74; US Dept Educ Off Postsecondary Educ, liaison minorities & women higher educ, 1974-84, prog deleg nat adv comt blackhigher educ & black cols & univs, 1976-82; US Dept Educ Off Higher Educ Progs, Div Stud Serv, dir, 1984-86; Howard Univ, conf coordr, 1989-90; pvt pract consult, 2001-16. **Orgs:** Elder Church Redeemer Presby; adv consult, NAFEO Educ Braintrust; Cong Black Caucus; vpres, B May's Res Ctr. **Honors/Awds:** Superior Service Award, US Off Educ, 1970; Certificate for Outstanding Performance, US Dept Educ Off Postsecondary Educ, 1979; Achievement Award, Nat Alliance Black Sch Educs, 1982; Leadership Award, Higher Educ Nat Asn Equal Opportunities Higher Educ, 1983; Honored, Nat Coun Educ Opporortunities Asn, 1986; Phenomenal Woman Tribute, 1997.

### SMITH, DR. CHARLES U.

Educator. **Personal:** Born Jan 1, 1926, Birmingham, AL; died Apr 20, 2015, Tallahassee, FL; children: Shauna. **Educ:** Tuskegee Inst, BA, 1944; Fisk Univ, MA, 1946; WA State Univ, PhD, 1950; Univ Mich, attended 1958. **Career:** Fla A & M Univ, adj prof sociol, 1966, grad dean, 1974, emer distinguished prof. **Orgs:** Pres, Southern Sociol Soc; Am Sociol Asn, 1960-2015; ed, Fla A & M Res Bull, 1960-2015; Am Acad Polit Soc Sci, 1969-2015; Leon Co Dem exec comm, 1969-2015; bd dir, Leon Co CAP, 1972-2015; Nat Soc Study Educ, 1973-2015; WFSU TV adv Com, 1973-2015; ed bd, Jour Soc & Behav Sci, 1973-2015; state committeeman, 1975; ed bd, Negro Ed Rev, 1976-2015; consult, SC Comm Higher Educ, 1984; bd advr, Fla Ment Health Inst; pres, Conf Deans Black Grad Schs; Coun Grad Sch US; Conf Southern Grad Schs. **Honors/Awds:** Col Athletics, 1966; Cert Serv State Fla, 1965, 1972; Silver Mental Health Service, 1966; Gold Medallion, 1970; Fla delegate White House Conf, 1960, 1965, 1970, 1971; Plaque, Serv Dept Sociol, 1970; DuBois Award Scholarship Service, 1973; Fla A & M Univ Merit Achievement Award, 1973; plaque Sociol, 1974; FAMU Martin Luther King Leadership Award, 1995; Distinguished Career Award, Southern Sociol Soc, 1997; Received honors from various societies like: Sigma XI, Alpha Kappa Delta, Pi Gamma Mu, Alpha Kappa Mu, Phi Delta Kappa, Sigma Rho Sigma, Phi Kappa Phi, Lambda Alpha Epsilon; DuBois-Johnson-Frazier Award, Am Sociol Asn, 2000. **Special Achievements:** Author, editor, co-author: 14 books, 8 monographs, approximately 80 scholarly and research journals, 10 book reviews, 12 copyrighted songs and lyrics. **Home Addr:** 3039 Cloudland Dr, Tallahassee, FL 32312.

### SMITH, REGINALD D., SR.

Educator. **Personal:** Born Apr 5, 2016, Baltimore, MD; died Apr 9, 2016; married Euzelle Patterson; children: Andrea, Pamela, Patrice & Regi. **Educ:** Hampton Inst, BS, 1940; NC Agr & Tech State Univ.

**Career:** Hampton Inst, staff, 1940-42; Chapel Hill City Schs, teacher, 1942-80, asst prin, 1970-80, vice prin, 2004, prof emer. **Orgs:** Civitan Chapel Hill; Chapel Hill Planning Bd, 1959-65; bd alderman, 1965-74; Triangle J Coun Govts, 1970-74; NC Asn Educr; Nat Educ Asn; Nat Asn Sec Sch Principals; NC League & Munic. **Honors/Awds:** Smith Middle School, Chapel Hill, named in honor; NC Hamptonian of the Year, 1969; mayor pro-tem Chapel Hill, 1969-74; Chapel Hill Father of the Year, 1970; Masonic Distinguished Service Award, 1971; Outstanding Service Award, Ment Health Asn, 1983; Martin Luther King Community Service Award, 1988; Outstanding Service Award, Am Cancer Soc, 1991; Outstanding Senior Citizen, Chapel Hill Jaycees, 1991-92; Sertoma of the Year Award, Chapel Hill, Cariboro, 1993. **Home Addr:** 200 Caldwell St, Chapel Hill, NC 27516-2006, **Home Phone:** (919)942-5883.

### SPIKES, DR. DELORES RICHARD

College president, mathematician. **Personal:** Born Aug 24, 1936; died Baton Rouge, LA; daughter of Lawrence Granville Richard and Margaret Patterson Richard; married Hermon; children: Rhonda. **Educ:** Southern Univ, BS, maths, 1957; Univ Ill, MS, maths, 1958; Louisana State Univ, PhD, 1971. **Career:** Mossville High Sch, Calcasien Parish, teacher, 1958; Southern Univ, from asst prof to prof mathematics; Southern Univ, Baton Rouge, asst chancellor, exec vchancellor & chancellor academic affairs, 1882-85; Southern Univ A&M Systs, pres, 1988, pres emer, currently; Univ Md, Eastern Shore, pres, 1996-2001, pres emer, currently. **Orgs:** Vice chair, Kellogg Comn. **Honors/Awds:** George Washington Carver Public Service Hall of Fame Lect, 1993; Most influential Black women in America, Ebony, 1990; Thurgood Marshall Educational Achievement Award. **Special Achievements:** First African American, as well as the first Southern University graduate, to receive a doctorate in mathematics from Louisiana State University; First female to lead a public college or university in Louisiana but also the first woman in the United States to head a university system. **Home Addr:** 1315 Balsam Ave, Baton Rouge, LA 70807-2901, **Home Phone:** (225)775-8710. **Business Addr:** President Emeritus, University of Maryland Eastern Shore, 11868 Col Backbone Rd, Princess Anne, MD 21853, **Business Phone:** (410)651-2200.

### SPIVA, DR. ULYSSES VAN

Educator. **Personal:** Born May 6, 1931, New Market, TN; died Mar 29, 2016, Virginia Beach, VA; son of Samuel and Mary Ruth Spiva-Chandler; married Olivia A; children: Vanessa, Valerie & Bruce. **Educ:** Tenn State Univ, Nashville, BS, math & physics, 1954; Case Western Res Univ, Cleveland, Ohio, MA, 1964; Stanford Univ, Palo Alto, Calif, PhD, educ admin & polit sci, 1971. **Career:** Sch Health Sch Serv, Sch Educ Fla, interim dean, exec asst pres, asst dean; Stanford Univ, Grad Sch Educ, Nat Follow Through Prog, US Off Educ, spec asst to dean; Ohio Pub Sch, Cleveland, eve sch prin & math dept chmn, 1955; Union Grad Sch, adj prof; Nova Southeastern Univ, Ft Lauderdale, Fla, Doctoral Prog Educ Leadership, sr nat lectr, 1974-2000, prof emer; Darden Col Educ, prof educ leadership & coun & dean emer, 2016; Norfolk Kiwanis Inc, bd dir; HR 200+ Men Inc; Cleveland, math teacher, dept chair & adult sch prin; Amherst Col, math coordr; Dartmouth Col Summer ABC Prog, math coordr; US Off Educ, Wash Policy fel; Fla Int Univ, Sch Educ, asst dean & asst prof, exec asst to pres, Sch Health & Social Serv, interim dean, Div Continuing Educ, actg dean, Div Sponsored Res & Training, dir, assoc exec vpres; Old Dom Univ, prof educ leadership & serv, dean, 1979-84, prof emer educ leadership & coun, dean emer, 2016; Legis Comt, chmn; Southeastern Tidewater Opportunity Prog, bd dir, pres. **Orgs:** Life mem Alpha Phi Alpha Fraternity; Stanford Alumni Asn; bd trustee, Bd Educ, Va Beach Pub Sch Syst; dir, Va Beach Found, 1990-2016; pres, Va Asn Col Teacher Educ; dir, Nat Sch Bd Asn, 1990-92; mem bd dir, Va Sch Bd Asn; chair, Coun Urban Bd Educ. **Honors/Awds:** Leadership & Eagle Award in Pedagogy, John F Kennedy HS, Alpha Phi Alpha Fraternity, 1969; Phi Delta Kappa Hon Soc; Benjamin Elijah Mays Lifetime Achievement Award, Nat Sch Boards Asns Coun of Urban Boards of Educ, 2008. **Special Achievements:** Published 3 books & numerous papers; First African American dean. **Home Addr:** 705 Southleaf Dr, Virginia Beach, VA 23462-4727, **Home Phone:** (757)467-0819.

### STAMPS, JOE, JR.

School administrator. **Personal:** Born Dec 3, 1939, Houston, TX; died Apr 6, 2016; married Mable Hubbard; children: Jo-Ellen, Bernadette & Joe III. **Educ:** Tex Southern Univ, attended 1962; Labor Studies, attended 1982. **Career:** Pct 371 Harris Co, election judge, 1978-, pres, United Steelworkers Local 7682, 1979-82; Bd Educ, legis rep, 1981; North Forest ISD, bd mem. **Orgs:** Philip Randolf Inst, 1963; NABSE; vpres, Local 7682, 1993-97; NSBA Little Union Baptist Church, deacon, youth Sunday sch teacher; pres, N Forest ISD Bd Trustees; life mem, Tex, PTA; life mem, Texas Cong Parents Teacher Asn. **Honors/Awds:** Outstanding Sch Bd Member, Region IV Tex. **Home Addr:** 8430 Gallahad St, Humble, TX 77078, **Home Phone:** (713)491-3982. **Business Addr:** Vice President, School Board Member, North Forest ISD, 10721 Mesa Rd, Houston, TX 77028, **Business Phone:** (713)633-1600.

### STEVENS, DR. MAXWELL MCDEW

School administrator, dean (education). **Personal:** Born Dec 3, 1942, Savannah, GA; died Oct 8, 2015, New Brunswick, NJ. **Educ:** St Augustine Col, BS, 1964; Atlanta Univ, MBA, 1970; Rutgers Univ, EdD, 1977. **Career:** Glenbrook Labs, chemist & group leader, 1964-68; Allied Chem Corp, mkt analyst, 1970-72; Somerset Co Col, asst dean instr; Raritan Valley Community Col, actg sr vpres acad affairs, interim sr vpres acad affairs, dean acad affairs & dir coop educ. **Orgs:** Pres, Int Coop Ed Asn, 1974; pres, NJ Coop Ed Asn, 1974; adv bd, Ed Opportunity Fund Somerset County Col, 1980; pres, Am Mkt Asn; adv bd, Mid-Atlantic Training Ctr Coop Ed, Temple Univ; adv bd, Somerset Co Day Care Ctr; adv bd, Somerset County Col; serv learning adv, RVCC; NJ Coop Educ & Internship Asn; Acad Officers Asn NJ. **Home Addr:** 15 Llewellyn Pl, New Brunswick, NJ 08901.

### STEWART, RUTH ANN

Manager. **Personal:** Born Apr 4, 1942, Chicago, IL; died May 30, 2014; daughter of Ann M and Elmer A; married David Levering Lewis; children: Allegra, Jason, Allison & Eric. **Educ:** Univ Chicago, attended 1962; Wheaton Col Norton, Mass, BA, 1963; Columbia Univ, MS, 1965; Harvard Univ, attended 1974; John F Kennedy Sch Govt, govt exec prog, 1987. **Career:** Philips Acad Lib, Andover, Mass, 1963-64; Columbia Univ Libr, 1965-68; Macmillan Publ Co, NYC, 1968-70; Schomburg Ctr Res Black Cult NY, 1970-80; New York Pub Libr, 1980-86; Nat Progs, Lib Cong, Wash, DC, 1986-89; Cong Res Serv, Wash, DC, 1989-95; Rutgers Univ, Bloustein Sch Planning & Pub Policy, 1997-2003, founding co-ed; New York Univ, Wagner Grad Sch Pub Policy, clin prof pub policy, 2003-14. **Orgs:** Vis comt, Harvard Univ, 1976-88; trustee, Nat Pk Found, 1978-84; Wheaton Col, 1979-99; Coun Foreign Rel, 1980-2014; Sch Libr & Info Sci, Univ Pittsburgh, 1988-94; Women's Foreign Policy Group, 1992-97; Lab Sch Wash, 1993-95; Studio a Sch, 2000-14; Berkeley Botanic Garden, 2000-14; Smithsonian Inst Cooper- Hewitt Nat Design Mus, 2003-14; res adv coun, Ctr Arts & Cult; Pub Life Arts. **Honors/Awds:** Outstanding Alumnae Award, Wheaton College, 2000. **Home Addr:** 784 Columbus Ave Apt 10-O, New York, NY 10025.

### STOCKTON, CLIFFORD, SR.

Manager, executive director. **Personal:** Born Sep 16, 1932, Memphis, TN; died Oct 12, 2015, Memphis, TN; married Lois J Hampton; children: Angela, Clifford Jr & Brian. **Educ:** Tenn State Univ, BS, educ, 1954; Memphis State Univ; C C Inst; Univ Ga. **Career:** Memphis Pub Schs, teacher, 1956-68; Upward Bound Proj LeMoyne, Owen Col, teacher, 1967-68; NAB Training Prog Goldsmith's Dept Store, coordr, 1967-69; Human Resources C C, assoc mgr, 1969-71, mgr, 1971-72; Bus Res Ctr, exec dir, 1972; Econ Dev Memphis Area C C, assoc mgr; Memphis Regional Chamber, consult, sr adv logistics & pub policy & vpres econ develop & dir mkt & res. **Orgs:** Bd dir, Boys Club Am; OIC; Memphis Vol Placement Prog; Memphis & Shelby County Indust Develop Bd. **Honors/Awds:** Booker T Wash Award, NBL, 1972; Outstanding Service Minority Bus. **Home Addr:** 516 Monteigne Blvd, Memphis, TN 38103-4743, **Home Phone:** (901)525-1882.

### SUTTON, DR. OZELL

Writer, executive, government official. **Personal:** Born Dec 13, 1925, Gould, AR; died Dec 19, 2015, Atlanta, GA; son of Charlie and Lula Belle Dowthard; married Joanna Freeman; children: Angela Martin, Alta Muhammad & Dietre Jo. **Educ:** Philander Smith Col, BA, 1950, HonD, 1962; Fisk Univ, Nashville, TN, attended 1961. **Career:** Government official (retired); Ark Dem, staff writer, 1950-57; Little Rock Housing Authority, relocations supvr, 1957-59; Winthrop Rockefeller, pub rels, 1959-61; Ark Coun Human Rels, exec dir, 1961-66; US Dept Justice, field rep CRS, 1966-68, Commun Rels Serv, state supvr, Ark state dir, 1969-72, reg dir SE region comn, 1972-2003; Govt Winthrop Rockefeller Ark, spec asst, 1968-69; SE region, dir Comm Rels, 1972-2003. **Orgs:** Relocation supvr, Litle Rock Housing Authority, 1959-61; dir, Ark Coun Human Rel, 1961-66; exec bd, Philander Smith Col, 1971; bd trustees, Friendship Baptist Church; exec bd, Atlanta Br Nat Advan Asn Colored People; gen pres, Alpha Phi Alpha Frat, 1980; exec bd, Leadership Conf Civil Rights; exec bd, Black Leadership Forum; chmn, Coun Pres Black Greek lett Orgn; pres, Voter Educ Proj; chmn, Forum Comn Metro-Atlanta Crime Comn; co-chmn, Atlanta Black-Jewish Coalition; pres, Inter-Alumni Coun; chmn, Metro Atlanta Crime Comn; chmn, Voter Educ Proj, 1986; mem bd, Nat Advan Asn Colored People. **Honors/Awds:** Distinguished Service Award, Nat Advan Asn Colored People, 1978; Distinguished Service Award, Alpha Phi Alpha Frat, 1979; Outstanding Performance Award, US Dept Justice, 1979-80; Distinguished Alumnus Award, Philander Smith Col; more than 100 other awards from many orgn; Special Achievement Awards, US Dept Justice; US Attorney General Award; Distinguished Service Award, Nat Ctr Missing & Exploited C, 1994. **Special Achievements:** Book: The Black Experience in America, dramatic portrayal of black struggle; Watch Your Language, commentary on impact of racial & ethnicslurs; Cited as "100 Most Influential African American Leaders", EBONY Magazine; Author: From Yonder to Here: A Memoir of Dr. Ozell Sutton; First African American to serve in the United States Marine Corps in 1944; First African American reporter for the white-owned publication Arkansas Democrat; First African Americans to serve in the United States Marine Corps, 1944. **Home Addr:** 1640 Loch Lomond Tr SW, Atlanta, GA 30331, **Home Phone:** (404)344-0370.

### SWANN, EUGENE MERWYN

Lawyer. **Personal:** Born Aug 1, 1934, Philadelphia, PA; died Oct 1, 2014, Walnut Creek, CA; son of Earl and Doris Burnette; children: Liana, Michael & Elliott. **Educ:** Temple Univ, BS, 1957; Univ Mass, MA, econs, 1959; Univ Calif, Berkeley, Calif, LLB, 1962, JD. **Career:** Contra Costa Co, dep dist atty, 1963-67; Contra Costa Legal Servs, dir, 1967-77; Self Employed, lectr, atty, 1977-83; Off Citzens Complaints, dir, 1983-84; SF Police Dept, 1984-85; Univ Calif, Berkeley, pvt pract; Stanford Grad Sch Bus, pvt pract; Napa Valley Col, asst prof econs & bus law, assoc, Econs & Bus Law, instr. **Orgs:** Mem exec com, Contra Costa Bar, 1965-69. **Honors/Awds:** Outstanding Legal Service Attorney in Nation, 1974. **Home Addr:** 1580 Geary Rd Suite 223, Walnut Creek, CA 94597, **Home Phone:** (925)934-7386.

### TATE, DR. JAMES A.

School administrator. **Personal:** Born Aug 7, 1921, Canton, MS; died Jul 1, 2016; married Barbara; children: Lisa, Jayme & James Jr. **Educ:** Jackson State Col, BS, 1950; Mich State Univ, MA, 1970, PhD, 1975. **Career:** Teacher (retired); Miss, elem teacher, asst prin, 1950-55; Detroit, elem teacher, 1955-57; Mich elem teacher, 1959-70; sci teacher prin, elem schs, 1968-70; Admis & Scholars Mich State Univ, asso dir, 1971-, dir, develop prog admis Off Admis, 1977. **Orgs:** Exec bd, Admin Prof Orgn, 1974-76; Career Planning & Placement Coun; Black Fac Adminr Asn; adv bd, Ypsilanti Area Comm Servs; Phi Beta Sigma; Am Personnel Guid Asn; Mich Counsrs Asn; Nat Cong Parents & Teachers; Nat &Mich Educ Asn; Mich Asn Sec Sch Prin; Mich Asn Col Admis Coun; MAAAO; Mich Asn Col Registr & Admis Officers; Orgn Mich State Univ; YMCA; Urban League; Nat Asn Advan Colored People; Am Asn Col Regist B Admis Officers; exec bd, Admin Prof Orgn, Mich Educ Asn; founder, Wood-Mere Neighborhood Org; trustee, Trinity AME Church, Disciplinary Adv Bd, Lansing Sch Dist. **Home Addr:** 3820 Starlight Lane, Lansing, MI 48911, **Home Phone:** (517)394-4523.

### TAYLOR, GILBERT LEON

Museum curator, consultant, educator. **Personal:** Born May 5, 1937, Indianapolis, IN; died Sep 29, 2015, Indianapolis, IN; son of Hugh Ross and Irene Crystal; children: 7. **Educ:** Univ Indianapolis, BS, 1958; Ind Univ, MS, 1969; Univ Mass, EdD. **Career:** Ind Pub Sch, teacher, 1959-63; Liberia Presby Sch, ed teacher consult, 1963-66; Knoxville Col, adminr, 1966-68; Ind Univ, adminr, 1968-70; Col Holy Cross, adminr, 1970-74; Univ Mass, Ford fel, 1974-76; pvt pract, consult, 1975-; C Mus, adminr, 1976-84; Butler Univ, admin, 1984-86; Indianapolis Pub Sch, Crispus Attucks Ctr Mus, dir, founding cur, 1991-. **Orgs:** Ed & Human Rights Ind Teachers Asn, 1983; co-host, Views & Visions TY Prog WTTV, 1983-; Long range Plan Comn, African-Am Mus Asn, 1983-85; Featured Personality United Press Int, 1983; coord, AFA Exec coun, 1984-; pres, Parent Centered Educ, 1984-85; long range plan comn, Madame Walker Urban Life Ctr, 1984-85; adv comn, Freetown Vill, 1984-85; adv comn, Training Inc, 1984-85; I V Tech Outreach Comt, 1989; trainer, OAR, 1991; fac, Witherspoon Performing Arts Ctr, 1991-; adv bd, 4 H Exten; bd mem, Etheridge Knight Festival; Indianapolis Progress Comn, Vision Indianapolis. **Honors/Awds:** Key to the City Tuskegee City, 1979; Recognition Award, Bahai Faith, 1983; Award for Appreciation, Concerned Males, 1989; Outstanding Leadership, Career Beginnings, 1990; Certificate of Appreciation, Veteran's Admin, 1990; Certificate of Appreciation, African-Am Multicultural Ed, 1992; Certificate of Appreciation, IPS/IEA Multicultural Festival, 1992; Certificate of Appreciation, Indiana Watch Comn Award, 1992; Certificate of Appreciation, Annual 4H Ace Acad, 1993; Service Award, Martin L KingDay IPS Sch 20, 1994; Certificate of Appreciation, US Dept Housing & Devt, 1994; Open Window Award, Positive Change Network, 1995; Certificate of Volunteer Service, OAR, 1995; Indianapolis Indians Sch 26 Reunion Award, 1997; 100 Black Men, 1998; Jr Drum Mayor Award, Dr MLK, 2000. **Home Addr:** PO Box 88341, Indianapolis, IN 46208-0341. **Business Addr:** Curator, Crispus Attucks Center Museum, 1140 Martin Luther King Jr St, Indianapolis, IN 46202, **Business Phone:** (317)226-2432.

### TAYLOR, RUTH SLOAN

Educator. **Personal:** Born Jun 8, 1918, Greenville, SC; died Jan 1, 1999?, Cincinnati, OH. **Educ:** EdD, 1962. **Career:** Summer HS Cairo, Ill, eng teacher, 1946-48; Roosevelt HS Gary, Ind, eng, 1948-66; Title I E SEA Gary, Ind, sup, 1966-68; Ind Univ NW, asst chrmn dived, 1969. **Orgs:** Pres, Nat Sec Delta Sigma Theta Sorority Inc, 1963-65; Coop Ed Res Lab Prog Assoc, N field, IL, 1967; asst prof, Ind Univ NW, 1969; assoc prof, Ind Univ NW, 1972; pres, bd trustee, Gary Community Sch; Nat Soc Act Comm Delta Sigma Theta Sorority, 1973; consult, leec chmn Bi-Cen Comm, Ind Univ NW United Way Camp City Met Chmn, 1974; asst chmn, Div Ed Ind Univ NW, 1974-75. **Honors/Awds:** Outstanding Cit Award, Ed IU Dons Inc, 1974. **Special Achievements:** Author:"Teaching in the Desegregated Classroom", 1974. **Home Addr:** 104 Morningside Ave, Gary, IN 46408.

### TAYLOR, STERLING R.

Buyer, executive, consultant. **Personal:** Born Jan 5, 1942, Philadelphia, PA; died Apr 6, 2016, Anchorage, AK; son of Willie Ray and Ellanora K Bivens; married Sonia E Madden; children: Tiarzha M & Khara D. **Career:** Army & Air Force Exchange Serv, buyer, 1964-70; Equitable Co Inc, life underwriter & regist rep, 1970-2016; AXA Advisors LLC, Seattle Br, financial consult & vice chmn. **Orgs:** Pres, Southern Alaska Life Underwriters, 1974-75; life mem, Million Dollar Round Table, 1986; pres, Alaska State Asn Life Underwriters; life mem, exec comm, Nat Asn Advan Colored People Anchorage Br; founder, Alaska Black Caucus; pres & comt chmn, Alaska Black Leadership Conf; ambassador, Life Underwriters Polit Action Comt; life mem, Alpha Phi Alpha; pres, Nu Zeta Lambda Chap; grand master, Prince Hall Masons, Alaska; bd chmn, Anchorage Community Health Ctr; chmn, Anchorage Transp Comn; bd trustee, Anchorage Sr Activ Ctr; Nat Asn Ins & Financial Advisors. **Honors/Awds:** Nat Sales Achievement Awards; Nat Quality Awards; Hall of Fame, The Equitable Companies Inc, 1982; Nat Community Leadership Award, 1993. **Home Addr:** 200 W 34th Ave Suite 376, Anchorage, AK 99503-3969, **Home Phone:** (907)394-1918.

### TAYLOR, VERONICA C.

School administrator. **Personal:** Born May 17, 1941, Pensacola, FL; died Apr 8, 2015, NJ; married Raymond R. **Educ:** Tenn State Univ, BS, 1962; Trenton State Col, MA, 1970. **Career:** Booker T Wash HS, instr, 1962-67; Trenton Pub Sch, speech therapist, 1967-88; Trenton State Col, co-adj fac, 1985; Jefferson Sch, fac; Robbins & Jefferson, asst prin, 1988-96; Grant Elem Sch, prin, 1998; DST, NJ State, coordr, 1997-99. **Orgs:** Bd dir, NJ Sickle Cell Soc, 1972-74; pres, Trenton Delta Sigma Theta, 1973-75; pres, TABS, 1974-77; vpres, Trenton Ed Assoc; NJ Ed Assoc Pol Action Fund, 1974-75; pres, vpres, Trenton Pan Hellenic Coun; bd dir, chmn, NJ EOF; pres, Womans Steering Comn, Shiloh Bapt Church, Nat Asn Advan Colored People; Nat Scholar Comn Delta Sigma Theta, 1983-88; Gov's Task Force Higher Educ; bd dir,

Merabash Mus; chairperson, NJ State Soc Action; nat exec bd, Delta Sigma Theta, 1988-92; Gov's Rev Comt Minorities Higher Educ; exec bd, Trenton Admins & Supvrs Asn; NJ Coordr Col Adv DST. **Honors/Awds:** Most All Around; Most Outstanding Female Graduate Wash, HS; Outstanding Commission Service Award, Trenton Delta Sigma Theta Inc; Outstanding Service Award, NJ Dept Higher Educ, 1982 & 1985, 1987; Outstanding Service Award, Shiloh Baptist Church; Outstanding Service Award, Tri State Social Action Comn DST; New Jersey Educational Opportunity Fund Leadership Award, Eastern Region DST; Pearl Certificate, Eastern Reg Conf, 1995; Outstanding Service Award-Students, Robbins Sch, 1996. **Home Addr:** 111 La Ave, Ewing, NJ 08638-2132, **Home Phone:** (609)883-3361.

## TERRELL, DR. FRANCIS

Educator. **Personal:** Born Nov 25, 1944, Greensboro, GA; died Jun 27, 2015, Grapevine, TX; son of Carrie and Emery; married Sandra L; children: Ivanna Samal, Amani Shama & Elon Jadhal. **Educ:** Wilmington Col, BS, 1968; Univ Pittsburgh, MS, 1972; Univ Pittsburgh, PhD, clin psychol, 1975. **Career:** Univ Fla, intership, Univ Pittsburgh, post-doctoral fel, 1975-76; Tex Christian Univ, Dept Psychol, asst prof, 1976-80; Univ N Tex, Dept Psychol, dir clin training, 1981-89, assoc prof psychol, 1980-95, prof, 1995-2015. **Orgs:** Am Psychol Asn, 1976-80; Black Psychol Asn, 1976-80; Sigma Xi, 1976-80; regional ment health consult, US Labor Dept, 1978-2015; fel Am Psychol Asn, fel Soc Study Personality, 1984; charter fel Am Psychol Soc. **Special Achievements:** Published "Self Concept of Juveniles Who Commit Black on Blacks Crimes" Corrective & Social Psychiatry, 1980; "Effects of Race of Examiner & Type of Reinforcement on the Intelligence Test of Black Children" Psychology in the Schs, 1980; Over 40 Journals published. **Home Addr:** 501 Doubletree Dr, Highland Village, TX 75077-6969, **Home Phone:** (469)948-0957.

## THOMAS, EARLE FREDERICK, SR.

Manager, executive. **Personal:** Born May 6, 1925, Preston, MD; died Dec 15, 2014, New Bern, NC; son of Rev Henry L and Frances Gore; married Bettie; children: Janice, Denise, Earle Jr, Rodney & Sherri. **Educ:** Morgan State Col Univ, attended 1942; Hampton Inst; Va Bankers Sch, life underwriters. **Career:** Newport New Shipyard, machinist, 1951-59; Am Tobacco Co, state rep, 1959-68; John Hancock Mutual Life Ins Co, underwriter, 1966-68; Atlantic Nat Bank, pres, chief exec officer, dir sec, 1972-74, vpres dir sec, 1971-72, org, 1968-71, asst mgr, 1974-75, mkt officer, 1974; VA Nat Bank, mgr, 1975, loan exec, 1975. **Orgs:** Bd visitors, Norfolk State Col, 1977; bd mem, Retail Merchants Asn, 1977-78; vpres, dir Tidewater Coun Boy Scouts; bd mem, Tidewater Red Cross; dir sec, Tidewater Area Minority Contractors; bd mem, Sickel Cell Anemia; adv coun fourth Club; Sales Mkt & Exec Club; pres, Club; Norfolk CC; budget comn United Fund; treas, Norfolk State Col Found Martin Luther King Comn. **Honors/Awds:** Achievement Award, 1975. **Home Addr:** 6102 Felucca Ct, New Bern, NC 28560-9746, **Home Phone:** (252)635-2879.

## THOMAS, EDWARD S. (EDWARD ST CLAIR THOMAS)

Executive. **Personal:** died Detroit, MImarried Jane; children: 1. **Career:** President (retired); Detroit Receiving Hosp, Univ Health Ctr, pres, 1990. **Orgs:** C's Home Detroit; Mich Hosp Asn; Wayne State Univ Sch Med. **Honors/Awds:** Meritorious Service Key Award, Mich Hosp Asn, 1994. **Business Addr:** Member, Wayne State University, Scott Hall 540 E Canfield, Detroit, MI 48201, **Business Phone:** (313)577-1429.

## THOMAS, JUANITA WARE (JUANITA GLEE WARE)

Educator, elementary school teacher. **Personal:** Born Oct 30, 1923, Little Rock, AR; died Dec 1, 2014, Washington, DC; married Morris E Thomas Sr; children: Roumania T Wiggins, Morris Jr, Veronica T Gray, Etelka & Pearl. **Educ:** Philadners Smith & Dunbar Jr Col, AA, elem ed, 1944; DC Teachers Col, attended 1970; Howard Univ, attended 1974; N Va Community Col, attended 1984. **Career:** George W Carver Elem Sch, elem teacher, 1944; War Dept, typist, 1945; Hibbler & Hibbler Attorneys Law, law firm secy & notary, 1946; USN Dept, cong typist, 1948; USN Dept, examr, 1949-51; DC Pub Schs, elem sub teacher, 1963-2014; Patterson Sch Admin Sch, elem teacher, 1974, 1980-81; Headstart Pre-Sch-United Planning Orgn, teacher, 1982-2014. **Orgs:** Elem secy, Nalle Elem Sch, 1956-63; pres, PTA Buchanan Elem Sch, 1957-65; secy, SE Civic Asn, 1963-65; chmn, SECA Beautification Prog, 1965-68; advcomt mem, Adv Neighbourhood Comn, 1975-85; W&V Womens Clubs-Nat Asn C W Clubs, 1985; red ribbon week chair, Calimesa Elem Sch; Parent Teacher Asn. **Honors/Awds:** Grass Roots Honoree, SE Civic Asn, 1965; Woman of the Year, NE Fedn Womens Clubs, 1976; Adv Neighborhoods Comn Outstanding Serv, 1981-84. **Special Achievements:** Celebrating 10 yrs "Home Rule in DC", 1975-. **Home Addr:** 1528 E St SE, Washington, DC 20003, **Home Phone:** (202)546-9142.

## THOMAS, ORLANDO PAUL

Football coach, football player. **Personal:** Born Oct 21, 1972, Crowley, LA; died Nov 9, 2014, Crowley, LA; married Demetra; children: Alexis & Orlando Jr. **Educ:** Southwestern La Univ; La Lafayette Univ. **Career:** Football player (retired), coach; Minn Vikings, defensive back, 1995-2001; Comeaux High Sch, asst coach. **Honors/Awds:** Rookie of the Year, 1995.

## THOMPSON, DR. LANCELOT C. A., SR.

Educator. **Personal:** Born Mar 3, 1925; died Sep 10, 2016, Toledo, OH; son of Cyril Alfonso (deceased) and Vera Leolyn Reid (deceased); married Naomi E; children: Lancelot Jr, Carol Lynn & Angela Maria. **Educ:** Morgan State Univ, BS, phys inorg chem, 1952; Wayne State Univ, PhD, physics & inorg chem, 1955. **Career:** Educator (retired); Wolmers Boys Sch, teacher, 1955-56; Penn State Univ, res fel, 1957; Univ Toledo, asst prof, 1958, asst dean, 1964, vpres, prof, 1966, dean stud serv, 1966, vpres stud affairs, 1968-88, prof emer chem, 1988-98. **Orgs:** Sigma Xi, 1956; Phi Kappa Phi, 1963; Blue Key, 1964; chmn, local sect Am Chem Soc; NY Acad Sci; exec com, Nat Stud Personnel Adminrs, 1972; ed bd, NASPA Journ, 1972; pres, local group Torch Int, 1974; vice chmn, Toledo Red Cross, 1990-91; pres, Univ Toledo Retirees Asn, 1997-98; pres, Ohio Coun Higher Educ Retirees, 1998-99; George F Hixton fel 1999; Mayor's Com Alcoholism; Toledo Develop Com; life mem, Nat Asn Advan Colored People. **Honors/Awds:** Key to Golden Door Award, Int Inst, 1973; Distinguished Bro Award, Midwestern Reg, Alpha Phi Alpha Frat, 1973; Dr. Lancelot C.A. Thompson Academic Achievement Program, named in honor, Univ Toledo. **Special Achievements:** First African American Vice President of Student Affairs, Univ Toledo. **Home Addr:** 2507 Cheltenham Rd, Toledo, OH 43606-3204, **Home Phone:** (419)536-9754.

## THOMPSON, RICHARD ELLIS

Consultant, educator. **Personal:** Born May 5, 1935, Gary, IN; died Feb 8, 2008, Chicago, IL; son of Elija and Roberta May; children: Kevin. **Educ:** Beatty Memorial Hosp, psych-aide training cert, 1955; Ind Univ, Ala, 1956; Roosevelt Univ, BA, 1963, MA, 1966; DePaul Univ, EdM, 1973; Ill Admins Acad, cert, 1989. **Career:** Educator, consultant (retired); Beatty Memorial Hosp, psychiat aide, 1955-56, 1957-58; Lake County C's Home, child care counr, 1958-63; Harlan HS, Chicago Bd Educ, hist teacher, 1963-70; Ill Dept Labor, employ counr, 1966-67; City Cols Chicago, teacher, registr & admin, 1966-70, 1973-79; Harlan HS, asst prin, 1970-97; Mayor's Summer Youth Prog Chicago, training spec, 1976, 1977, 1980-91; Chicago Pub Schs, consult, 1997-2008. **Orgs:** Phi Delta Kappa, 1968-2008; Chicago Asst Prin Asn, USY, 1973-2008; Nat Asn Sec Sch Princ, 1973-2008; notary pub, Notaries Asn Ill, 1979-2008; trustee, First Church Love & Faith, 1982-2008; Headstart Prog, First Church Love & Faith, 1983-2008; consult, Curric Community Sch Educ, Chicago State Univ, 1984-2008. **Honors/Awds:** Soldier of the Month, USY, 1960; Good Conduct Award, USY, 1961; Certificate of Achievement, USY, 1962; Outstanding Educator of AME, 1975; Outstanding Secondary Educator, AME, 1975; Certificate of Apppreciation, Chicago Asst Prin Asn, 1978; Achievement Award, Roosevelt High Sch, 1978; Service Award, Div Educ Governors, State Univ Chicago, 1982; Distinguished Service Award, Chicago Asst Prin Asn, 1990; "Mr. T", The Richard E. Thompson Fund, named in honor, John M. Harlan High Sch Alumni Asn. **Special Achievements:** Eight articles. **Home Addr:** 500 E 33rd St Apt 1601, Chicago, IL 60616, **Home Phone:** (312)225-5106.

## THOMPSON, DR. WINSTON EDNA

School administrator, educator. **Personal:** Born Apr 9, 1933, Newark, NJ; died Mar 26, 2016, Marblehead, MA; daughter of Dorsey Nelson West and Cora West; married Robert S; children: Darren Eric. **Educ:** Seton Hall Univ, BA, 1965; Columbia Univ, Teachers Col, MS, 1969; Rutgers Univ, EdD, 1980. **Career:** Mother Seton Regional High Sch, guid counr, 1965-68; Essex County Col, dir advising, counr, 1968-72; Rutgers Univ, Livingston Col, assoc dean students, 1972-75; Tomb rock Col, dean stud dev, 1975-76; Tomb rook Col, dean stud develop, 1975-76; AT & T Bell Lab, consult, 1975-77; E Orange Bd Educ, adult educr, 1977-78; Salem State Col, vpres stud servs, 1978-88; Wesley Col, lectr, 1984-89; Univ Mass, designer, 1986-88; Conn State Univ, exec officer acad affairs & res, 1988-2003, asst vpres acad affairs & res, trustee emer, 2003-; State Univ syst, asst provost. **Orgs:** Bd mem, JJS Enterprise, 1979-; consult, Am Coun Educ, 1981-; adv bd mem & faculty, HERS Wellesley Col, 1982; adv bd mem, AAA New England, 1986-88; bd trustee; Morgan Memorial Goodwill Industries, 1986-88; state educ coordr, Nat Coalition 100 Black Women, 1988-89. **Honors/Awds:** Recipient Women's Award, Salem State Col, 1981; Univ MA Amherst, co-designer non-traditional doctoral prog, 1983; Northeastern Univ, Greater Boston Inter Univ Coun report, minority student retention, 1985; Distinguished Educator, Nat Coalition 100 Black Women, 1988; Meritorious Service Award, United Negro Col Fund Inc, 1989; Black Women & Black Men lecture & writing, 1989; Black Feminism, lecture & writing, 1989. **Home Addr:** 1340 E Asylum Ave, Hartford, CT 06105, **Home Phone:** (203)832-0072. **Business Addr:** Trustee Emeritus, Connecticut State University System, 39 Woodland St, Hartford, CT 06105, **Business Phone:** (860)493-0000.

## TOWNSEND, MURRAY LUKE, JR.

Consultant, government official. **Personal:** Born Jul 6, 1919, Indianapolis, IN; died Jun 5, 2016, Middleborough, MA; son of Murray L Sr (deceased) and Novella Foster; married Evelyn; children: Cheryl, Murray III, Norman & Frederick (deceased). **Educ:** Morehouse Col, BA, 1942; Boston Univ, LLB, 1949. **Career:** Government official (retired); PO, 1950-56; IRS, criminal investr, 1956-64; Boston & NY, dep equal employ policy officer, 1963-66; Small Bus Admin, sr compliance officer, 1967-81; consult. **Orgs:** Omega Psi Phi Frat, 1939; deacon, Union Bapt Ch, 1955-62; Prince Hall Mason, 1963-; Middleboro Lakeville Ment Health Comn Coun, 1966; bd deacons, Cent Baptist Church, 1973-; Nat Asn Advan Colored People; 366th Inf Vet Asn; adv comn, bd dir, New Eng Village Human Rights, 1979; Afro Am Vet US, 1980; life mem, Morehouse Col Nat Alumni Asn. **Honors/Awds:** Citz Scholar Found Middleboro, 1968-70; Cits Scholar Found MA, 1970-72; Paul Revere Bowl Citz Scholar Found Am, 1976. **Home Addr:** 95 Thomas St, Middleboro, MA 02346, **Home Phone:** (508)947-1584.

## TRICE, DR. JUNIPER YATES

Educator, clergy, mayor. **Personal:** Born Aug 10, 1921, Verona, MS; died Feb 5, 2016, Cleveland, OH; married Detris Delois Scales; children: Juniper Olyen & Harriman Robert. **Educ:** AB, 1942; BTh, 1950; DD, 1958; MEd, 1961; spl deg, admin, 1972. **Career:** Mayor, educator (retired), executive, clergy; Hall's Chapel New, Albany, Miss, pastor; City Rd Corinth, Miss, pastor; Naylor Chapel, Pontotoc, Miss, pastor; Aberdeen Dist, presided; Jennings Temple, Greenwood, Miss, pastor; Greenwood Dist, pres; Booneville Sch, prin; Carter High Sch, Tishomingo, Miss, staff; E High Sch, Fulton, Miss, staff; W Bolivar High Sch, Rosedale, Miss, staff; Rosedale Miss Sch, asst supt; City Rosedale, mayor, 2001; Bolivar County Coun Aging Inc, founder, cheif exec officer, chmn, exec dir, 2016; Ittawamba & Bolivar Counties Sch Districts, asst supt. **Orgs:** Selective Serv Bd Bolivar County; City Coun; bd dir, S Delta Planning & Develop Dist Inc; exec bd, Delta Area Coun BSA; bd trust, MS Indus Col; presiding elder, Christ Methodist Episcopal Church; Hwy Com Delta Coun; MS Teacher Asn; Nat Educ Asn; 32 degree Mason; secy, MS Educ Fin Comn; So Reglig Educ Bd; MS Adult Educ Asn; bd dir, First Nat Bank Rosedale; bd trustees, Bolivar County Hosp; MS Employ Security Coun; exec dir & chmn, Bolivar County Coun Aging. **Honors/Awds:** BSA Award for Outstanding Service, 1970; Listed in Outstanding Person, 1971; Leader of America, Sec Educ, 1972; Silver Beaver Award for Oustanding Service, 1977; The 2009 Aaron Henry Leadership Award, Community Transp Asn Am, 2010. **Special Achievements:** First black appointed President of the South Delta Economic Planning and Development District; first black Chairman of the State Educational Finance Commission. **Home Addr:** PO Box 819, Rosedale, MS 38769, **Home Phone:** (601)759-3349.

## TRIM, JOHN H.

Educator, air force officer, association executive. **Personal:** Born Apr 19, 1931, Ft. Worth, TX; died Dec 12, 2011, Dallas, TX; married Earnestine E. **Educ:** Bishop Col, BA, social sci; Prairie View A&M Univ, cert voc indust educ. **Career:** Neiman Marcus, 1957-64; Franklin D Roosevelt HS Dallas TX, cvae coordr instr master level, 1964-; GPBN, asst ed. **Orgs:** Prof Teacher Org; vpres, Asn Adv Artists & Writers; Human Interest Colum Post Tribune News, 1970-2011; colum inst, Porters & Quall Ecumenical News, 1975; deacon trust, Morning Star Bapt Ch; Org orginal Dalworth Leadership Coun Grand Prairie TX; dir, community youth mural comt ctr. **Honors/Awds:** Wrote book poetry life; fine arts shows; Airman Mo, 1954; city Mo KNOX, 1954; Service Award, 1969; Youth Award, 1973. **Home Addr:** 2130 Beaumont St, Grand Prairie, TX 75051, **Home Phone:** (972)641-5658.

## TUCKER, JAMES F.

Executive, educator. **Personal:** Born Nov 2, 1924, Brooklyn, NY; died Jul 6, 2016; married Caroline Hamblin; children: Kenneth & Lauren. **Educ:** Howard Univ, AB, 1947, MA, 1948; Univ PA, PhD, 1957. **Career:** WV St Col, chmn dept bus, 1956-62; NC Cent Univ, chmn dept econs, 1962-65; US Dept Labor, dir oper, 1965-68; VA St Col, pres, 1968-70; VA Polytech Inst & State Univ, prof econ dept, 1970-74; Fed Res Bank Richmond, vpres, 1974, sr vpres, 1986-90. **Orgs:** Pres, bd dir Va Coun Econ Educ; Va St Adv Coun Vocat Educ; liason bd Nat Consumer Econs Proj; bd vis VA Polytech Inst & State Univ; bd trustees Howard Univ; adv bd dir, Richmond Mem Hosp. **Honors/Awds:** Auth Essentials Econ Prentice-Hall Inc, 1975; Current Econ Issues & Problems Rand McNally, 1976; Anathomy High-Earning Minor Banks, Am Bankers Asn, 1978; Outstanding Service Award, Va Coun Econ Educ, 1978; various articles published. **Special Achievements:** Richmond Fed's first African-American officer. **Home Addr:** 8596 Ironington Terr, Richmond, VA 23227, **Home Phone:** (804)262-9937.

## TURNER, WINSTON EDWIN

Teacher, educator. **Personal:** Born Aug 23, 1921, Washington, DC; died May 30, 2012, Washington, DC; son of Frederick Finley and Mary Montague; married Helen Smith; children: Lisa & Valerie. **Educ:** Miner Teachers Col, BS, 1947; NY Univ, MA, 1949; St Col Educ Plattsburgh, NY; DC Teachers Col; Georgetown Univ; Univ Bridgeport Ct. **Career:** Educator (retired); DC Pub Sch, teacher, 1947-54; Miner Teachers Col, Monroe Lab Sch, 1954-57; DC Teachers Col, Truesdell Lab Sch, asst prof educ, 1957-59; HD Cooke Elem Sch, Wash, DC, prin, 1959-69; River Terr Elem Sch, Wash, DC, prin, 1976. **Orgs:** Life mem, Nat Educ Asn; Phi Delta Kappa; pres, Nat Asn Elem Sch Prins, 1974-75; DC Elem Sch Prin Asn; Asn Study Negro Life Hist; pres, vpres, treas; bd dirs SE Neighborhood House; bd Columbia Heights Boys Club; Queens Chapel Civic Asn; life mem, Nat Asn Advan Colored People; Omega Psi Phi Frat; Pigskin Club Prins Asn, Wash, DC; exec comt coun officers, DC Pub Schs; Exam Panels Prin & Asst Prins, DC Pub Schs; Mt Horeb Bapt Ch. **Honors/Awds:** Guest lecture, Howard Univ, 1974; Outstanding Principal Award, DC Elem Sch Prin Asn, 1974; Outstanding Ret Teacher Award, Jr Citizens Corps, 1978; Outstanding Public Service: Mayor Baltimore Md, Afro-Am Newspaper, Central Summerfield United Meth Church, 1980; Man of the Year, New Bethel Baptist Church, 1981; publications: The Black Principal Bicentennial, Principal, 1976; Principals Pressure Cooker, Principal, 1977; Expanding Our Horizons through Global Educ, Principal, 1980. **Home Addr:** 1626 Varnum Pl NE, Washington, DC 20017-3141, **Home Phone:** (202)526-4011.

## VEST, DONALD SEYMOUR

Business owner, executive. **Personal:** Born Apr 5, 1930, Ypsilanti, MI; died Jan 17, 2015, Detroit, MI; son of Vida Carter and Eugene L; married Hilda Freeman; children: Karen, Donald Jr & Carl. **Educ:** Mich State Univ, East Lansing, BA, social serv, 1952. **Career:** Detroit Mutual Ins, Detroit, MI, agt, 1954-55; City Detroit, MI, play leader, 1955-56; State Mich, Detroit, MI, interviewer, 1956-57; City Detroit, MI, recreation instr, 1957-60; Boy Scouts Am, Detroit, MI, dist exec, 1960-62; Ford Motor Co, Dearborn, MI, mgr, 1962-87, personnel mgr, 1987; Broadside Press, Detroit, MI, owner & bus mgr, currently. **Orgs:** Pres, Mus African-Am Hist, bd trustees, 1986-87, chair collections comn, 1987-88; pres & bd dir, Brazeal Dennard Chorale, 1989. **Honors/Awds:** Community Service Award, Ford Motor Co, 1968-69; Special Service Award, Detroit Brd Educ, 1977; Sankofa Award, Mus African-Am Hist, 1988; otstanding serv Awrd Admin, 2000. **Home Addr:** 4734 Sturtevant St, Detroit, MI 48204, **Home Phone:** (313)935-8396.

## VINSON, ROSALIND ROWENA

Lawyer, government official. **Personal:** Born Sep 25, 1962, Highland Park, MI; daughter of Roosevelt Massey and Mary S McGhee. **Educ:** Mich State Univ, BA, 1983; Georgetown Univ, Law Ctr, JD, 1987. **Career:** Equal Employ Opportunity Comn, atty, 1989. **Orgs:** Vice magister, Phi Delta Phi, 1986-87; vpres, H Carl Moultrie T Endowment, 1989; secy, Black Law Alumni, Georgetown Univ Law Ctr, 1992. **Honors/Awds:** Second Year Pacesetter, 1985; First Year Pacesetter, 1986; Mary McCloud Bethune Award, Black Law Students Asn, 1987. **Home Addr:** 2134 Martin Ave SE, Grand Rapids, MI 49507-3238.

## WAGNER, DAVID H.

Lawyer. **Personal:** Born Jul 23, 1926, Davidson County, NC; died Jul 13, 2014, Lexington, KY; married Mollie Craig; children: Brenda C & Davida S. **Educ:** NC Agr & Tech State Univ, BS, 1948, MS, 1957; Wake Forest Univ, JD, 1968. **Career:** Pender Co, instr prin, 1954-58; Lexington NC, instr prin, 1958-66; Wachovia Bank, closing atty & housing spec, 1968-69; atty, pvt pract, 1969-. **Orgs:** Gen couns Winston Mutual Life Ins, 1969-; pres, Urban Housing Inc, 1970-; pres, Asn Furniture Inc, 1970-; NBA; NC Black Bar Asn; Forsyth Co Bar Asn; NC Bar treas Goler Met AME Zion Church; vpres, life mem Nat Asn Advan Colored People; bd mem & stockholder, Vanguard Invest Co; Forsyth Econ Develop Corp; life mem, Alpha Phi Alpha; life mem, NEA. **Home Addr:** 3440 Cumberland Rd, Winston-Salem, NC 27105. **Business Addr:** Attorney, Private Practitioner, PO Box 12068, Winston-Salem, NC 27117-2068, **Business Phone:** (336)722-0272.

## WALKER, DR. M. LUCIUS, JR.

Educator. **Personal:** Born Dec 16, 1936, Washington, DC; died Jun 6, 2013, Annapolis, MD; son of Inez and M Lucius Sr; children: Mark & Monique. **Educ:** Morehouse Col, attended 1954; Howard Univ, BS, mech engineering, 1957; Carnegie Inst Technol, MS, mech engineering, 1958, PhD, 1966. **Career:** Howard Univ, Sch Engineering, asst prof, 1963-67, assoc prof, asst dean, 1965-66, Dept Mech Engineering, from actg chmn to chmn, 1966-73, actg dean, 1975-77, dean, 1977-95, prof, 1995-2002, prof emer, 2002-13; Engineering Coalition Schs Excellence Educ & Leadership, dir, 1990-97; Gen Elec; Exxon; Ford Motor Co; Harry Diamond Labs. **Orgs:** Biomed Cardiovasc Renal Res Team, 1966-73; consult, Ford Motor Co, 1971-2013; Engr Manpower Comt Engrs Coun Prof Develop, 1972-95; Biotech Resources Rev Comt, Nat Inst Health, 1980-84; consult, Ctr Naval Anal, 1991-93, bd dir; Am Soc Eng Educ; Am Soc Mech Engrs; Tau Beta Pi; bd trustee, Carnegie Mellon Univ; Am Soc Mech Engrs; Ad Hoc Visitor Accreditation Bd Eng & Technol; pres, Howard Univ Chap Sigma Xi; bd dir, Jr Engineering Tech Socs; MichTs Vis Comt Dept Elec Engineering & Comput Sci. **Honors/Awds:** Lifetime Achievement Award, Nat Action Coun Minorities Engineering; Black Educator of the Year Award for Higher Education; Distinguished Alumni Award, Howard Univ, 2008. **Home Addr:** 703 Twin Holly Lane, Silver Spring, MD 20910-4665, **Home Phone:** (301)588-7478.

## WALLACE, C. EVERETT

Lawyer, government official, executive director. **Personal:** Born Aug 16, 1951, Chicago, IL; died Aug 1, 2016, Durham, NC. **Educ:** Northwestern Univ, BA, 1973, JD, taxation & corp law, 1976; Univ Chicago Sch Law, LLM. **Career:** Clausen Miller & Gorman Caffery & Witous Law Firm, res assoc, 1975-76; Memphis Light Gas & Water Div, Memphis, staff atty, 1976-77; Sen Howard Baker, US Sen, legal asst, 1977-80; Shelby County Black Rep Coun, legal coun & co-founder, 1977; Progressive Assembly Reps, gen coun & co-founder, 1979; US Senate, Budget Comn, sr anal & energy counr, 1980, sr legis asst, Dept Health & Human Serv, head transition & chief staff; Dept Housing & Urban Develop, gen dep asst secy; Wallace Enterprise Int, pres, 1994-2011; Nat Minority Franchising Inst, dir & founder; NC Community Develop Initiative Capital, pres, 2004-08; Access Ment Health LLC, Consult & coun, 2011-16. **Orgs:** Bar Tenn, 1977; vice chmn & co-founder, Black Rep Cong Staffer's Asn, 1979; coun secy, Republican Nat Conv; Nat Bar Asn; Am Bar Asn; pres, Alpha Mu Chap, Alpha Phi Alpha Frat Inc; chmn, Minorities Franchising Comt, Int Franchise Asn. **Honors/Awds:** Top Ten Debator, Northwestern Univ Ill State Contest; Nat Achievement Scholar, Thornton Township High Sch, Harvey, Ill; Nat Merit Scholar; Ill State Scholar; Honors Grad, Northwestern Univ Sch Law. **Home Addr:** 638 G St N E, Washington, DC 20002.

## WALLACE, RUBY ANN. See DEE, RUBY.

## WARD, HORACE TALIAFERRO

Judge. **Personal:** Born Jul 29, 1927, LaGrange, GA; died Apr 23, 2016, Atlanta, GA; married Ruth LeFlore; children: Theodore J (deceased). **Educ:** Morehouse Col, BA, polit sci, 1949; Atlanta Univ, MA, 1950; Northwestern Univ Sch Law, JD, 1959. **Career:** Judge (retired); Social Security Admin, vlaims authorizer, 1959-60; Hollowell, Ward, Moore & Alexander, atty-at-law, 1960-68; State Ga, Atlanta, GA, state sen, 1965-74; City Atlanta, dep city atty, 1969-70; Fulton County, asst county atty, 1970-74, civil ct judge, 1974-77; State Ga, super ct judge, 1977-79; US Dist Ct, judge, 1979; US Dist Ct, Northern Dist Ga, sr judge, 1993; Ga State Senate, mem. **Orgs:** Alpha Phi Alpha Fraternity Inc, 1948; Phi Beta Kappa, Delta Ga; Am Bar Asn; Nat Bar Asn. **Honors/Awds:** Distinguished Alumni Award, Atlanta University; Bennie Service Award, Morehouse Col; Merit Award, Nwestern University, Hall of Fame, National Bar Asn, The Gate City Bar Association; A Heroes, Saints and, Legends Award, The Wesley Woods Foundation, 1976; Hon Doctor Laws, Morehouse Col, La Grange Col; Trumpet Award Civil Rights Advocate, Turner Broadcasting System, 2004. **Special Achievements:** First African American to challenge the racially discriminatory practices at Horace Ward the University of Georgia; Atlanta Magazine listed him as one of 200 people who shaped Atlanta; First African American ever to serve on the federal bench in Georgia; First African-American to sue for admission to an all-white college in Georgia; Second African-American in the state's history to be elected to the Georgia senate; First African-American to become a Superior Court judge in Georgia. **Home Addr:** 215 Piedmont Ave NE, Atlanta, GA 30303, **Home Phone:** (404)588-0641.

## WARE, JUANITA GLEE. See THOMAS, JUANITA WARE.

## WESTBROOK, DR. JOSEPH W., III

Educator, school superintendent. **Personal:** Born Jul 13, 1919, Shelby County, TN; died Nov 13, 2006, Memphis, TN; son of Joseph W II and Clara Nelson; married Dorothy Greene; children: 4. **Educ:** BA, attended 1943; MA, attended 1961; PhD, 1970. **Career:** Educator, school superintendent (retired); Melrose High Sch, teacher, 1942; Devel Plan Decentralization, dir; supvr sec instr; sr hs, asst prin; class rm teacher athletic coach; area asst supt; Memphis City Schs, Memphis, TN, dir, presiding officer, 1971-81. **Orgs:** Sigma Pi Phi Fraternity; Nat Educ Asn; Asn Supv & Curric Devel; Phi Delta Kappa Ed Frat; Nat Sci Supvrs Asn; pres, Tenn Educ Asn; Memphis Educ Asn; Nat Sci Teachers Asn; Am Asn Sch Adminrs; Nat Asn Sec Sch Prins; Exec Comt Nat Coun Teachers Retirement; bd dir, Memphis Urban League; bd dir, Dixie Homes Goodwill Boys Club; Glenview YMCA; Frontiers Club Int; Memphis Reg Sickle Cell Coun; pres, Alpha Phi Alpha Frat; Local Chap; Exec Comt United Way Memphis; Exec Comt LeBonheur Hosp; bd dir, Nat Urban League, 1978-82; bd dir, Nat Asn Sickle Cell Dis, 1979-83; bd dir, Nat Educ Asn, 1984-90; pres, Nat Educ Asn, 1984-90. **Honors/Awds:** Academy of Professional Devel Award, Nat Acad Sch Execs; Outstanding Alumnus, LeMoyne-Owen Col, 1973; Greek of the Year, Alpha Phi Alpha Fraternity Memphis Chap, 1973; Melrose Schlorship fund, Community Found Greater Memphis, 2002. **Special Achievements:** In Honor Dedicated the Field at Melrose Stadium. **Home Addr:** 1711 Glenview Dr, Memphis, TN 38106, **Home Phone:** (901)276-6458.

## WHITE, DR. ARTIS ANDRE

Dentist, executive. **Personal:** Born Sep 13, 1926, Middletown, OH; died May 14, 2015, Inglewood, CA. **Educ:** Morehouse Col, BS, 1951; Howard Univ, DDS, 1955; Univ Calif, Los Angeles, cert, 1970. **Career:** Dentist (retired), executive; Unic Calif Los Angeles, lectr, 1969-72; Drew Postgrad Med Sch LA, lectr; Martin Luther King Hosp, Maxillofacial Prosthetic Div, LA, dir, 1972-; pvt pract maxillofacial prosthetics dentist, 1972; Univ Guadalajara Mex, lectr, 1975-. **Orgs:** Fel Royal Soc Health Engr; fel Acad Dent Int; Am Prosthdontic Soc, Am Cleft Palate Asn, Am Dent Asn, Nat Dent Asn; fel Acad Dent Handicapped, Am Asn Hosp Dentists; Acad Maxillofacial Dent; mem bd trustee, Morehouse col, 1991-. **Honors/Awds:** Distinguished Alumnus Award, Howard Univ; Outstanding Service Award, Morehouse Col Nat Alumni Assoc; Bennie Achievement Award, Morehouse College, 2002; ScD, Morehouse College, 2002. **Home Addr:** 333 Crown Dr, Los Angeles, CA 90049, **Home Phone:** (213)673-4490.

## WHITE, IDA MARGARET (IDA KILPATRICK JONES)

Government official, manager. **Personal:** Born Aug 1, 1924, Atlanta, GA; died Mar 19, 2016; married Luther Randolph; children: Victor A Jones & Russell C Jones. **Educ:** Spelman Col Atlanta, AB, 1945; Atlanta Univ, MA, sociol, 1946; Fed Exec Inst, attended 1973; Brookings Inst, attended 1979. **Career:** Government official, manager (retired); NY Dept Welfare, case work supvr, 1958-61; Dept HUD, NY, Regional Off, dir relocation, 1966-70; Practicing Law Inst, guest lectr, 1970; Dept HUD, NY, Area Off, dir housing mgmt, 1970-74; NYU, lectr, 1971; Cleveland Dept Community Develop, dep dir, 1974-77; Cleveland State Univ, lectr, 1976; Case Western Res & Kent State Univ, lectr, 1977; Cleveland City Coun, exec asst to pres, 1977-78; Builders Inst, VPI, lectr; Dept HUD, Richmond Off, mgr, 1989; independent consult, housing, community develop, beginning 1990. **Orgs:** Am Soc Pub Admin; bd mem, Eliza Bryant HomeAged Kathryn Tyler Neighborhood Ctr; Real Property Inventory; Neighborhood Housing Servs. **Honors/Awds:** First Black Woman NY Area Office Dept HUD, 1970-74; Award Salute to Black Clevelanders The Greater Cleveland Inter church Coun & Cleveland Call & Post, 1979. **Home Addr:** 6016 26th St, Arlington, VA 22207.

## WHITE, LUTHER J.

Business owner, automotive executive. **Personal:** Born Feb 10, 1936, Gary, IN; died Nov 30, 1996; son of Luther and Viarda; married Archousa Bobbie; children: Keith, Kelli, Eric, Alan & Scott. **Educ:** Drake Univ. **Career:** Westfield Ford Inc, Westfield, Mass, owner & chief exec officer. **Home Addr:** 11 Highland Cir, Westfield, MA 01085.

## WILLIAMS, CLYDE, JR.

Lawyer. **Personal:** Born Feb 23, 1939, SC; died Dec 10, 2011, Richmond, IN; children: 2. **Educ:** JD, BA, 1965. **Career:** Williams, DeLaney & Simkin, partner, atty. **Orgs:** Gen Coun Off Staff, Fed Housing Admin DC; Wayne Twp Bd Richmond; elected pub off mem, Rep Party IN; vpres, Hoosier State Bar Asn; ABA Asn; Nat Bar Asn. **Home Addr:** 131 S 16th St, Richmond, IN 47374-5619, **Home Phone:** (765)962-4714.

## WILLIAMS, JOHN ALFRED

Writer, educator, actor. **Personal:** Born Dec 5, 1925, Jackson, MS; died Jul 3, 2015, Paramus, NJ; son of John Henry and Ola Mae Jones; married Carolyn Clopton; children: Gregory D & Dennis A; married Lorrain Isaac; children: Adam J. **Educ:** Syracuse Univ, BA, 1950. **Career:** Educator (retired), writer, actor; Work foundry & supermarket, 1951; Onondaga County Welfare Dept, caseworker, 1952; Gold State Mutual, CBS, NBC-TV, 1954; Comet Books Press, publicity dir, 1955; Abelard-Schuman, asst pub, 1957-58; Amer Comm Africa, dir info, 1957; spec events WOV NY, 1957; contributed Herald-Tribune Book Week, 1963-65; Holiday Mag Europe, 1965-66; Teaching: Col Virgin Islands, lectr black lit, 1968; City Univ NY, lectr, creative writing, 1968-69; Macalester Col, visiting prof, 1970; Audience Mag, ed bd. 1970-72; Amer J, 1972-74; Univ Calif Santa Barbara, regent slectr, 1973; LaGuardia Comm Col, visting prof, 1973-78; Univ Hawaii, visiting prof, 1974; Boston Uni, visiting prof, 1978-79; Rutgers Univ, prof, 1979-94; New York Univ, visiting prof, 1986-87; WNET-TV writer, bd dir Coord Coun Lit Mags, 1983-85; Paul Robeson prof Eng, 1990-93; Bard Col, visiting prof, 1994-95; Univ Houston, visiting prof, 1994; Bard Col, fel, 1994-95; Novels & Poems: The Angry Ones, 1960; Night Song, 1961; Sissie, 1963; Africa, Her History, Lands & People, 1963; This is My Country, Too, 1965; Beyond the Angry Black, 1966; The Man Who Cried I Am, 1967; Sons of Darkness, Sons of Light: A Novel of Some Probability, 1969; The King God Didn't Save: Martin Luther King, Jr, 1970; The Most Native of Sons: Richard Wright, 1970; Amistad 1, 1970, Amistad 2, 1971; Captain Blackman, 1972; Flashbacks: A 20-Year Diary of Article Writing, 1973; Minorities in the City, 1975; Mothersill & the Foxes, 1975; Junior Bachelor Soc, 1975; Yardbird No. 1., editor, 1979; Drama: Last Flight from Ambo Ber, 1981; Click Song, 1982; The Berhama Account, 1985; The McGraw-Hill Intro to Lit, 1st ed, 1985, 2nd ed, 1994; Jacob's Ladder, 1987; Bridges: Literature across Cultures, editor, 1994; Approaches to Literature, editor, 1994; Safari West: Poems, 1998; Clifford's Blues, 1999; If I Stop I'll Die: The Comedy & Tragedy of Richard Pryor (with Dennis A. Williams), 1991; August Forty-Five, 1991: Vanqui (libretto), 1999; Safari West, 1998; Transform, 2003; Ways In: Approaches to Reading and Writing about Literature. **Orgs:** Nat Inst Arts & Lett. **Honors/Awds:** National Inst Arts & Letters, 1962; Centenial Medal, Outstanding Achievement, Syracuse Univ, 1970; J Richard Wright Jacques Romain Award, 1973; National Endowment, 1977; American Book Award, 1983, 1998; US Observer, 23rd Premio Casa Award, 1985, Distinguish Writer Award, Middle Atlantic Writers, 1987; Michael Award, NJ Literature Hall of Fame, 1987; Carter G. Woodson Award Mercy Col, 1989; Lind back Award Distinguished Teaching, Rutgers Univ, 1993; Black Writers Hall of Fame, 1998; name sake of the John A. Williams Lecture Series, Rutgers Univ, 1999; President's Award, Hartwick Col, 2001; ohn Oliver Killens Award for Fiction, 2002; QBR Phyllis Wheatley Award, 2002. **Special Achievements:** February 2 proclaimed John Williams Day in the City of Syracuse, NY, 1988. **Home Addr:** 693 Forest Ave, Teaneck, NJ 07666, **Home Phone:** (201)692-9157.

## WILLIAMS, NOVELLA STEWART

Association executive. **Personal:** Born Jul 13, 1927, Johnston County, NC; died Mar 20, 2015, Philadelphia, PA; daughter of Charlie and Cassie; married Thomas; children: Charles, Frank, Willis, Thomas, Kim, Michelle & Pam. **Educ:** Rutgers Univ, attended 1971; Univ Pa Wharton Sch, 1974. **Career:** Citizens Prog, founder, chief exec officer & pres, 1964. **Orgs:** Chmn, bd dir, W Philadelphia Comt Free Sch, 1969; Harcourt-Brace-World-Measurement & Conf, 1969; dir, Philadelphia Anti Poverty Comn, 1970; vice chmn, YMCA, 1970; coordr, 513 Women's Comt Carter-Mondale Camp; White House Conf Hunger, 1970; Red Bk, 1970; pres, House Foreign Aff Sub-com Congressnal Rec, 1970; Seven Sch, 1971; prin, Nat Ed Asn, 1972; Peoples Health Serv, 1973; partner & consult, Ed Mgt Asn, 1973; consult, US Consumer Prod Safety Comn, 1975-76; secy, bd dir Health Sys Agency SE PA, 1976; bd dir, RCHPC; bd dir, SE Pa Am Red Cross, 1976; person & consumer affil Comt Philadelphia Health Mgt Corp, 1976-; del, Dem Nat Conv, 1976; Dem Rules Com, 1976; Dem Del Whip, 1976; bd dir, Philadelphia Urban Coalitiion, 1977; Bd trustees, Lincoln Univ, 1977; trustee, United Way, 1981, co-chairperson, Philadelphia Urban Coalition, 1989. **Honors/Awds:** Human Rights Award, Philadelphia Comn Human Rels, 1968; Community Organization Award, OIC, 1970; Outstanding Service Award, White House Conf Small Bus, 1980; Woman of the Year, Nat Asn Pub Accountants; Cultural Advancement Award, Bronze Asn; Humanitarian Award, Nat Opportunities Industrialization Ctr; Community Service Award, Nat Asn Univ Women; The Achievement Award, Philadelphia Health & Welfare Coun. **Home Addr:** 5308 Spruce St, Philadelphia, PA 19139, **Home Phone:** (215)471-6507. **Business Addr:** Founder, President, Citizens Progress Inc, 5236 Market St, Philadelphia, PA 19139, **Business Phone:** (215)474-8633.

## WILLOUGHBY, DR. SUSAN MELITA FENTON

School administrator. **Personal:** Born Nov 25, 1925; died May 4, 2016, South Lancaster, MA; children: Gerald M & Juliette M. **Educ:** Atlantic Union Col, S Lancaster, Mass, BA, chem, 1956; Clark Univ Worcester, Mass, MA, educ, 1969; Harvard Univ, Cambridge, EdD, admin, 1972; Boston Univ, Sch Social Work, Mass, MSW, 1984; Boston Univ Sch Med, MPH, 1985; Andrews Univ, PedD, 2004. **Career:** Worcester Found Exp Biol, sr res chemist, 1961-68; Ctr Urban Studies Harvard Univ, dir coun serv, 1970-72; Mass Consumer Coun, Gov Sargent, gubernatorial appointee, 1973-75; Mass Pub Health Coun, Gov Dukakis, gubernatorial appointee, 1975-79; Atlantic Union Col, Dept Sociol & Social Work, prof educ & behav sci, instr, 1972-2016, tenured prof & chmn, 1983-2016, prof emerita & distinguished lectr, 2016. **Orgs:** Phi Delta Kappa & Pi Lambda Theta, AAUP, 1972-2016; chmn, Health Task Force Mass State Consumer Coun, 1974-75; chmn, Centennial Comn Atlantic Union Col S Lancaster, Mass, 1978-82; mem bd trustee, Atlantic Union Col, 1986-2016; comnr, SDA Educ, W Africa, 1994. **Honors/Awds:** Scholar, Clark Univ, 1968, 1971; scholar, Harvard Univ, 1968, 1971. **Special Achievements:** Published numerous articles in Atlantic Union Gleaner (local), 1974-78; Author, "The Go-Getter" Pacific Press Publishing Assoc Boise ID, 1985. **Home Addr:** 1029 George Hill Rd, PO Box 482, South Lancaster, MA 01561, **Home Phone:** (978)365-9782.

### WILSON, ERNEST L., II

Manager. **Personal:** Born Nov 4, 1930, New York, NY; died Feb 16, 2003, Highland, CA; son of Ernest and Bessie; children: Ernest Jr, Steven & Patricia. **Educ:** NY Univ, BA; cert, mediation/conflict resolution, 1997; Super Ctr, comput training, 1997. **Career:** Freight Liner Corp, personnel mgr, 1966-71; MBM Corp, personnel dir, 1971-72; TRW Corp, personnel admin, 1972-74; Commutronx Corp, personnel dir, 1974-75; City San Bernardino, dir affirmative action & community affairs, 1975-85, dir safety, community affairs, 1985-88, dir affirmative action, 1991-2003; Calif St Legis, field rep, 1989-90. **Orgs:** Vol, leg adv assembly man, 67th Dist St Calif, 1979-80; Kiwanis Int; Mex/Am Personnel Asn; Urban League; Nat Asn Advan Colored People; Am Soc Training & Develop; Kiwanis Club San Bernardino; bd mem, Black Hist Found; Econ Round Table; Westside Action Group; Calif Asn Affirmative Action Officers; Am Asn Affirmative Action; vpres, Easter Seal Soc. **Honors/Awds:** Outstanding Achievement, OSC Comn Org, 1975; Outstanding Achievement, JustX Club, 1976; Cert of Outstanding Achievement, Mex/Am Mgt Asn, 1978; Cert of Outstanding Participation & Contrib, Calif Poly Univ, 1979; Cert of Appreciation, Dr Martin Luther King Mem & Scholar Fund Inc, 1980; Good Will Ambassador, City of San Bernardino, 1982; Scroll of Hon, Omega Psi Phi Frat, 1983; Cert of Achievement, San Bernardino Black Hist, 1983; We Serve Award, Highland Dist Lions Club; Commendation, Dept Fair Employ & Housing State, CA; Cert of Achievement, Equal Employ Opportunity Comn; Cert of Recognition, Civil rgency Mgt, 34th Senate Dist State, CA, 1990; Cert of Recognition, Ruben S Ayala, Calif State Sen, 1990; Cert of Award, Provisional Accelerated Learning Ctr, 1991; Cert of Appreciation, San Bernardino Nat Forest, 1992; Cert of Appreciation, Am Heart Asn, 1992; Cert of Recognition, San Bernidino C C, 1992; Community Service Award, 1994; Cert of Recognition, Nat Asn Advan Colored People, 1996. **Special Achievements:** Citation for Community Service, San Bernardino Light House of the Blind, 1982; Resolution by Mayor & Council City of San Bernardino Commending Leadership of the Affirmative Action Program. **Home Addr:** 7786 Bobcat Lane, Highland, CA 92346.

### WILSON, DR. RAY FLOYD

Educator. **Personal:** Born Feb 20, 1926, Giddings, TX; died Jun 10, 2015; son of Fred; married Faye; children: Ray Jr, Freddie, Roy & Mercedes. **Educ:** Huston Tillotson, BS, chem & math, 1950; Tex S Univ, MS, chem & math, 1951; Univ Tex, PhD, chem & math, 1953; Tex Univ, JD, law, 1973. **Career:** Educator (retired); Univ Tex, Austin, res scientist, 1951-53; Tex S Univ, prof chem, 1972, grad & res adv; owner; cong counr; Houston Comm Col, part time instr chem, 1972. **Orgs:** Vpres, SW Regional Meeting Am Chem Soc, 1955; dir, SE Tex, Sect Am Chem Soc, 1967-68, 1969-70; counr, SE Tex Sect Am Soc, 1968-69; Phi Alpha Delta Law Frat; Phi Beta Sigma Frat; Legis Couns US Congresswoman; Supt Pilgrim Congregational Ch; Comm Consult & Adv; pres, TSU-TACT Chap; pres, PUC Credit Union. **Honors/Awds:** Academic Achievement Award, Huston-Tillotson Col, 1953; Beta Kappa Chi Achievement Awards, TSU, 1965; Faculty Forum Achievement Award, 1969; Faculty Forum Post Doctoral Certificate Achievement, TSU, 1970; Huston-Tillotson Alumni Asn Sci Achievement, 1971; Human Resource US, 1974. **Special Achievements:** First African Am stud to receive a Ph.D from the Univ of Tex at Austin in 1953; Authored eighty-three different articles that have appeared in nat or int sci journals; The First African American Female From A Southern State to Serve In the U.S. House Of Representatives and Congressman Mickey Leland. **Home Addr:** 3506 Arbor Ave, Houston, TX 77004-6423, **Home Phone:** (713)522-7413.

### WINFIELD, ARNOLD F.

Chemist, executive. **Personal:** Born Sep 29, 1926, Chicago, IL; died Feb 23, 2012; married Florence Frye; children: Michael A & Donna Winfield-Terry. **Educ:** Howard Univ, BS, 1949; Wayne State Univ, Grad Study, biochem, 1951. **Career:** Executive (retired); Ordinance Corp, chemist, 1952-59, biochemist, 1969-71; Abbott Labs, reg prod mgr, 1953-71, Admin Consumer Div, mgr regulatory affairs, 1971-83; 2nd Ward Evanston, alderman, 1963-77; Winfield & Assoc, consult, 1983; Colfield Foods Inc, corp secy, 1983. **Orgs:** Nat Asn Advan Colored People; Urban League; Alpha Phi Alpha; Evanston Neighbors at Work; bd mem, Victory Gardens Theater, 1979-. **Honors/Awds:** Youth Alliance Scholar, 1943; Jr Chamber of Commerce Man of the Year, 1964; Service Award Ebenezer Church, 1966. **Home Addr:** 2640 Summit Dr, Glenview, IL 60025, **Home Phone:** (847)998-1037.

### WING, THEODORE W., II

Executive, artist. **Personal:** Born Jul 12, 1948, Philadelphia, PA; died Oct 15, 2013, Philadelphia, PA; son of Theodore W and Mardie Phillip; married Denise; children: Hillary Allen. **Educ:** Howard Univ, BA, hist, film & govt, 1970; Syracuse Univ, MS, pub commun, 1972; Temple Univ, REL, 1981, cert educ leadership, 2002; George Washington Univ, MCCP, bus, 1991; St Joseph's Univ, MS, educ, 1998, MS, instrnl technol, 2005. **Career:** White House, spec asst vpres, 1970-71; Howard Univ, Wash, DC, spec asst pres, 1971-72; Commonwealth Pa, Harrisburg, Pa, prin, 1972-74; City Philadelphia, Philadelphia, Pa, dir fed funding & youth prog, 1974-78, dep comnr, 1991-93; AT&T Fed Syst, 1978-91, div dir, 1978-93; Ray Commun, vpres, 1993-98; Wing Films, owner, 1999-2011; Prime Bldg Corp, dir; Theodore W Wing Productions, founder & prin; Camden High Sch, IEP, case mgr, 2001-04; US Small Bus Admin, consult, 2006-13; Hillary House Found, pres, 2011-13. **Orgs:** Pres, Howard Univ Alumni Club, 1978-81; pres, Philadelphia Sch Syst, Day Care Ctr, 1979-81; dir, Downtown Indust Sch, 1981-83; chmn, Boys & Girls Clubs, Philadelphia, 1989-91; dir, Tender Care Inc, Philadelphia, 1989-91; founder, Syracuse Challenger Newspaper; educ hon soc, Kappa Delta Pi; founder, Media Charter Sch K-7 grades. **Honors/Awds:** Outstanding Youth, John Wanamaker, 1970; Alumni Award, Howard Univ, 1986; Ben Franklin Award, Philadelphia Free Libr, 1987; Trustee Award, Bennet Col, 1988; President's Award, Univ Md, 1990. **Special Achievements:** Author, "Urban Education from the Bedlands to the Classroom;" Winner of numerous awards & fellowships, public speaker, involved with several movie & TV productions & author of many scholarly papers. **Home Addr:** 1700 Baird St, Camden, NJ 08103, **Home Phone:** (856)966-5100.

### WOOD, DAISY M.

Executive. **Personal:** Born Jan 5, 1942, Raleigh, NC; died Sep 26, 2014. **Educ:** SC State Univ. **Career:** Raytheon Systs Co, global diversity & recruiting dir, currently. **Orgs:** Pres, Nat Pan-Hellenic Coun Inc; bd dir, Urban League. **Honors/Awds:** Soror of the Year, 1976-82; Achievers Award, Nat Asn Advan Colored People, 1978; Citizen of the Year, Urban League, 1979; Undergraduate Award, 1980; Outstanding Soror, National Pan-Hellenic Coun, 1980; Volunteer of the Year, 1983; Award Dinner Recognition, United Negro Col Fund, 1983; Founders Day Award, 1983; Community Service Award, 1984, Delta; Community Achiever, 1984; Reclamation Award, 1984; Volunteer of the Year, 1985; Outstanding Volunteer, 1986; Presidential Award, 1987; Soror of the Year, 1987; Outstanding Prog Award, 1988; National Interfraternity Coun Achievement Award, 1992; NC A&T Univ Recruiting Award, 1995. **Home Addr:** PO Box 9507, Arlington, VA 22219.

### WOOD, HON. WILLIAM S.

Lawyer, judge. **Personal:** Born Dec 3, 1926, Chicago, IL; died May 1, 2015; married Rosita; children: William Jr & Eugene T. **Educ:** Univ Iowa, BA, 1947, LLD, 1950. **Career:** State Atty Off, asst atty, 1956-60; pvt pract, 1960-83; Circuit Ct Cook County, assoc judge, 1995-99, presiding judge. **Orgs:** Chicago Bar Asn; Ill Judicial Coun; Ill Judges Asn. **Home Addr:** 4800 S Chicago Beach Dr Apt 1301N, Chicago, IL 60615-2057.

### WOODIE, HENRY L.

Engineer, clergy. **Personal:** Born Oct 24, 1940, Tallahassee, FL; died May 2, 2016; son of Albert and Willie Mae Simmons Stephens; married Kathey Curry; children: Henry LaSean, Dorian Small, Aaron Jones & Travis Jones. **Educ:** Fla A&M Univ, BS, 1963; Stetson Univ, BBA, 1974; Rollins Col, MSM, 1979. **Career:** African Methodist Episcopal Church, minister, 1991-2016; Brevard Co Sch Syst Fla, teacher; RCA Patrick AFB Fla, mathematician; Auditor Gen Off Fla, auditor; Daytona Beach Community Col, internal auditor; Bellsouth Telecommunications, engr mgr. **Honors/Awds:** Keeper of peace, Omega Psi Phi Fraternity, 1990-91. **Home Addr:** 1067 Marlin Dr, Rockledge, FL 32955, **Home Phone:** (321)632-2911.

### WOODS, SYLVIA (SYLVIA PRESSLEY)

Restaurateur, executive, cosmetics executive. **Personal:** Born Feb 2, 1926, Hemingway, SC; died Jul 19, 2012, Mount Vernon, NY; daughter of Van and Julia Pressley; married Herbert K; children: Van, Bedelia, Kenneth & Crizette. **Educ:** La Robert Cosmetology Sch. **Career:** Sylvia's Restaurant, founder & owner, 1962-; Sylvia's Atlanta, owner, 1997-; Sylvia's Beauty Products & Sylvia's Express, owner, NY, 2001-. **Orgs:** Share Our Strength; City Meals on Wheels; Women's Roundtable. **Honors/Awds:** Woman of the Year Award, NAACP, 1978; Women's Day Award, Cert Appreciation, 1988; Bus Award, The Riverside Club, 1991; African American Award, Bus Award, 1990; Mayor NY City, Cert Appreciation, 1992; Lifetime Achievement Award, NY Metro Roundtable, 1993; Bus Award, The NY State Dept Econ Develop, 1994; Featured in Ebony Magazine. **Special Achievements:** US Air Force, Cert Appreciation, 1989; US Army, Cert Appreciation, 1991; Sylvia's Soul Food Cookbook, William Morrow Co, 1992; Sylvia's Family Soul Food Cookbook, 1999. **Home Addr:** 581 E Lincoln Ave, Mount Vernon, NY 10552-3715, **Home Phone:** (914)667-4446. **Business Addr:** Founder, Owner, Sylvia's Restaurant, 328 Malcolm X Blvd, New York, NY 10027, **Business Phone:** (212)996-0660.

### YERGER, BEN

School administrator. **Personal:** Born Dec 8, 1931, Hope, AK; died Feb 5, 2014; married Charlene A; children: Valerie B & Benjamin Jr. **Educ:** Philander Smith Col, BS, 1951; San Fran Univ, MA, 1969; Univ Calif, PhD, 1975. **Career:** Pub Sch Far West Educ Lab, sci educ res, 1955-68; Merritt & Col, admin asst pres, 1968-71, fac emer; Grove St Col, pres, 1971; Merritt & Vista Col, dir comm serv, 1972-78; Vista Col, dean stud serv. **Orgs:** Bd dir, Berkeley Area Comn Found; vpres, Res Develop Ctr Soc Redes; chmn, Youth Employ Coun Berkeley, Calif; chapter mem, Asn Calif Comn Col Admin; Congregational Christian Church Coun Soc Action; CCJCA; NASPA; Am Asn Health Educ; Asn Advan Educ Res; NCCSCE; Alpha Kappa Mu Hon Soc; Phil Smith Col, 1949-50; Beta Kappa Chi Sci Hon Soc Phil Smith Col, 1949-50; Alpha Phi Alpha & Cum Laude Phil Smith Col, 1949-50. **Honors/Awds:** Outstanding educator in America Higher Education Award, 1971; Outstanding Dissert Award, Inst Res Plan Comn Calif Asn Community & Jr Col, 1976-77. **Home Addr:** 51 Bonnie Lane, Berkeley, CA 94708, **Home Phone:** (510)524-5928.

### YOUNG, DR. JOYCE HOWELL

Consultant, physician. **Personal:** Born Mar 22, 1934, Cincinnati, OH; died Sep 17, 2015, Louisville, KY; daughter of Lloyd Marion and Addiebelle Foster; married Coleman Milton Young III; children: C Milton IV, Lloyd M & Christopher H. **Educ:** Fisk Univ, BA, zool, 1954; Womans Med Col Pa, MD, 1958; Meharry Med Col, Hubbard Hosp, cert, pediat, 1960, cert, int med, 1961; Univ Louisville Child Eval Ctr, cert, growth & develop, 1973. **Career:** Miami Valley Hosp, intern, 1959; Louisville St Joseph Hosp, 1960; Louisville, KY, pvt med pract, 1961-67; Lou Links Inc, 1965-80, finan sec, 1980-; Univ Louisville Child Eval Ctr, pediat develop specialist, 1973-74; Pk Duvalle Neighbourhood Health Ctr, med dir, 1974-76; KY Dept Human Resources, med consult, 1984-; Falls City Med Soc, pres, currently. **Orgs:** Alpha Kappa Alpha Sorority, 1952-; Falls City Med Soc, 1961-, Jefferson County Med Soc, 1962-; KY Med Asn, 1962-; Shawnee Presby Church; chmn, Louis Bd Educ, 1971-74, 1974, 1973-, mem session, 1988-, Lou Links Inc; bd mem, Lincoln Found, 1974-; dir, Pk DuValle Neighborhood Health Ctr Pres, 1974-76; dir, Continental Nat Bank KY, 1974-86; KY Human Rights Comn, 1983-; AMA; Syn Covenant Cabinet Ethnic Church Affairs, 1983-86; treas, KBPU, 1983-; chmn, Comn Representation, 1985-86; Exec Coun Presbytery Louisville, 1986-91; bd mem, Jefferson City Med Soc Bus Bur, 1990-. **Honors/Awds:** Appointment by gov KY Colonel, 1962; Community Service Award, Lou Links Inc, 1973-74, Alpha Kappa Alpha Sor, 1974, Zeta Phi Beta, 1975; diplomate, Am Bd Disability Consults, 1989-. **Special Achievements:** Series of articles on health, Black Scene Mag, 1975; First African American woman to serve on the Louisville board of education, 1971. **Business Addr:** President, Falls City Medical Society, 739 S Wern Pkwy, Louisville, KY 40211, **Business Phone:** (502)595-4404.

# Geographic Index

### Clopton
Scott, Hosie L.

### Colbert County
Herd, Rev. John E.
West, Edward Lee, III

### Columbia
Chavous, Mildred L.

### Conecuh County
Starks, Doris Nearror

### Consul
Pettway, Jo Celeste

### Corona
Rice, Susie Leon

### Cortelyou
Pogue, Rev. Richard James

### Courtland
Hampton, Grace
Redding, Gloria Ann

### Crenshaw
Person, Wesley Lavon, Sr.

### Cuba
LeFlore, Dr. Larry

### Cypress
Jackson, Dr. Franklin D. B.

### Dallas County
Reese, Rev. Dr. Frederick Douglas

### Daphne
Howze, Rev. Joseph Lawson
Washington, Rose Wilburn

### Decatur
Blanks, Wilhelmina E.
Burton, Kendrick Duran
Holmes, Major Gen. Arthur, Jr.
Jemison, Dr. Mae Carol
Rice, Derica W.
Rogers, Charles Leonard
White, Ralph L., Jr.

### Demopolis
Basil, Richard
Boddie, Algernon Owens
Jones, Dr. Herbert C.
Owens, Sen. William
Owens-Hicks, Shirley
Ratliff, Theo
Todd, Thomas N.
Young, Dr. LaDonna R.

### Dixons Mills
Grayson, George Welton

### Dora
Hubbard, Amos B., II

### Dothan
Anderson, Dr. Benjamin Stratman, Jr.
Dawsey, Lawrence Leneir
King, Naomi Ruth
McCain, Ella Byrd
Page, Willie F.
Powell, Dr. C. Clayton
Reese, Izell

### Eastaboga
Wills, Dorothy

### Elba
Bullard, Robert Doyle
Tucker, Clarence T.

### Elby
Knox, William Robert, Sr.

### Elrod
Giles, Joe L.

### Enterprise
Gibson, Kenneth Allen
Smith, Cedric Delon

### Eufaula
Bremby, Roderick LeMar
Comer, Jonathan
Cohen, Gwen A.
Reeves, Martha Rose

### Evergreen
Henderson, Dr. John L.
King, W. James
Powell, Dr. Myrtis Hall
Reed, Joe Louis

### Fackler
Timberlake, John Paul

### Fairfield
Cameron, Dr. Joseph A.
Clemon, U. W.
Davis, Dr. Brenda Lightsey-Hendricks
Giles-Gee, Dr. Helen Foster
Grayson, Elsie Michelle
Jackson, Oscar Jerome
Lawson, Jennifer Karen
Lloyd, Dr. Barbara Ann
McWilliams, Esq. James D.
McGinnis, James W.
McKee, Dr. Adam E., II
Ross, Dr. Edward

### Fayette
Davis, Mike
Wright, Bishop James R., Sr.

### Finchburg
Brown, Rev. Dr. George Houston, XIX

### Florala
Bradberry, Dr. Richard Paul
Stone, Dwight

### Florence
Blackburn, Charles Miligan, II
Brewer, Moses
Butler, Tonia Paulette
Bulls, Herman E.
Cole, James O.
DeCosta-Willis, Dr. Miriam
Mullen, Harryette
Nails, John Walker
Reynolds, James W.
Thompson, Hon. Bobby E.

### Forkland
Isaac, Hon. Earlean

### Ft. Davis
Lester, Nina Marie

### Ft. Deposit
Metcalf, Dr. Zubie West, Jr.
Mitchell, Sharon

### Ft. McClelland
Davis, Nathaniel Alonzo

### Ft. Mitchell
Johnson, Theodore, Sr.

### Ft. Rucker
Barlow, William B.
McKinnon, Ronald

### Gadsden
Chambers, Pamela S.
Croft, Wardell C.
Foster, Dr. Portia L.
Goddard, Rosalind Kent
Howard, Dr. Lillie Pearl
Hughes, Dr. Joyce A.
Irving, Ophelia McAlpin
James, Dr. Betty Harris
Jennings, Margaret Elaine
Lawrence, Edward
Lowe, Jack, Jr.
Patrick, Dr. Jennie R.
Peoples, Erskine L.
Sandridge, Dr. John Solomon
Thomas, Spencer
Young, George, Jr.

### Gallion
Brown, Dr. Frank

### Geiger
Thompson, Sharon

### Goshen
Saulsberry, Charles R.

### Grady
Cummings, Annette Merritt

### Greene County
Byrd, Dr. Taylor, Jr.

### Greensboro
Evans, Dr. Webb
Jackson, Grady O'Neal
Johnson, Alexander Hamilton
King, Dr. Arthur Thomas

### Greenville
Brown, Janice Rogers
Gamble, Dr. Wilbert
Scott, Veronica J.
Waters, Mary D.
Womack, Christopher Clarence

### Grove Hill
Martin, Rev. Edward, Jr.

### Hanceville
Staton, Canzetta Maria

### Harpersville
Kidd, Warren Lynn

### Hatchechubbee
Fortson, Walter Lewis

### Hayneville
Smith, Rev. George Walker

### Headland
Greene, Charles Lavant
Gray, JoAnne S.

### Helena
Briggins, Charles E.

### Hollywood
Robinson, John E.
Scott, R. Lee

### Huntsville
Bransford, Dr. Paris
Bradford, Andrea
Cashin, Sheryll D.
Cooper, Ronald
Crutcher, Sihon Heath
Cross, Howard Edward, Jr.
Hereford, Dr. Sonnie Wellington, III
Lacy, Hugh Gale
Lacy, Walter
Lowery, Rev. Dr. Joseph E.
Peoples, Dr. Joyce P.
Rice, William E.
Rice, Dr. Horace Warren
Shelton, Bryan
Sheridan, Edna K.
Steger, Dr. C. Donald
Timmons-Toney, Rev. Deborah Denise
Williams, James
Willis, James Edward, III

### Hurtsboro
Henderson, Dr. George
Howard, Milton L.
James, Dr. Felix

### Jackson
Mayfield, JoAnn M.
Powers, Dr. Runas, Jr.

### Jacksonville
Levell, Col. Edward, Jr.

### Kinterbish
Portis, Kattie Harmon

### Lafayette
Crawley, Dr. Oscar Lewis, Sr.
Matthews, Dr. Virgil E.

### Lanett
Copeland, John
Pollard, Marcus LaJuan

### Langdale
Evans, Josh

### Lawrence County
Smith, Dorothy O.

### Leeds
Barkley, Charles Wade
Germany, Albert

### Linden
Rogers, Roy Lee, Jr.

### Lisman
Kennedy, Callas Faye

### Livingston
Arrington, Richard, Jr.
Hatter, Henry
Simmons, Robert L.
Smith, William Xavier

### Loxley
Jerkins, Rev. Jerry Gaines

### Macon
Chancey, Robert Dewayne

### Madison
Burgess, Linda Gail

### Malcom
Brown, Dr. James Harvey, Sr.

### Mantua
Harris, Dr. Trudier

### Maplesville
Agee, Bobby L.
Foster, Edward, Sr.
Morrow, Harold, Jr.

### Marion
Billingsley, Andrew
Coleman, Donald
Melton, Bryant
Steele, Dr. Ruby L.

### Midway
Rutledge, Dr. Essie Manuel
Thomas, Wilbon
Turner, Robert, Jr.

### Millbrook
Smith, Antowain Drurell

### Millry
Atchison, Br. Calvin O.
May, James F.

### Mobile
Aaron, Henry Louis
Abston, Dr. Nathaniel, Jr.
Anderson, Willie Aaron
Anthony, Vernice Davis
Benjamin, Dr. Regina M.
Bell, Hubert Thomas
Bishop, Sanford Dixon, Jr.
Bivins, Hon. Sonja F.
Byrd, Dr. Katie W.
Cafritz, Peggy Cooper
Caffey, Jason Andre
Chatman, Ronald Dean
Chapman, Diana Cecelia
Chestang, Dr. Leon Wilbert
Clayton, Lloyd E.
Coleman, Derrick D.
Cox, LaVerne
Craig, Dameyune Vashon
Crenshaw, Dr. Reginald Anthony
Davis, Charles A.
Davis, Dr. Bertha Lane
Days, Bertram Maurice
Day, Eric Therander, Jr.
Figures, Vivian Davis
Figures, Thomas H.
Freeman, Lauretta
Gavin, Dr. James Raphael, III
Gibson, Dr. Harris, Jr.
Guyton, Patsy
Hazzard, Dr. Terry Louis
Hawthorne, Kenneth L.
Herman, Alexis Margaret
Holloway, Dr. Joaquin Miller, Jr.
Hope, Rev. Julius Caesar
Hudson, Dr. Robert Lee
James, Frank Samuel, III
Johnson, Rev. Clinton Lee
Jones, Elvin R.
Johnson, Lonnie G.
Jones, Orlando
Jones, Benjamin A.
Lang, Antonio Maurice
Lee, Clara Marshall
Malone, Jeffrey Nigel
Matchett, Johnson
Madison, Yvonne Reed
Marshall, Anthony Dewayne
McCants, Keith
McWhorter, Dr. Grace Agee
McMillian, Dr. Frank L.
McCovey, Willie Lee
Mitchell, William Grayson
Myers, Peter Eddie
Packer, Daniel Fredric, Jr.
Perine, Martha Levingston
Pogue, Frank G., Jr.
Porter, Dr. Charles William
Powell, Kenneth Alasandro
Rainey, Timothy Mark
Reese, Albert A., Jr.
Scott, Dr. Windie Olivia
Simmons, Dr. Howard L.
Smith, Ozzie
Smith, Elaine Marie
Smith, Dr. Barbara Wheat
Stallworth, Yolanda W.
Stallworth, Oscar B., Sr.
Taylor, Mary Quivers
Taylor, Andre Jerome
Thrower, Julius B.
Vivians, Nathaniel Roosevelt
Wallace, Dr. Jeffrey J.
Watson, Michael A.
Wallace, Darrell, Jr.
White, Joseph Councill
Williams, Dr. Daniel Edwin
Womack, Joe Neal, Jr.
Young, Raymond, Jr.
Young, Rickey Darnell

### Monroeville
Sainte-Johnn, Don
Tucker, Cynthia Anne

### Montgomery
Abernathy, Rev. Ralph David, III
Alexander, Willie James
Anderson, Marlon Ordell
Arrington, Lloyd M., Jr.
Arrington, Dr. Pamela Gray
Bailey, Richard
Barlow, Reggie Devon
Beasley, Frederick Jerome
Bibb, Dr. T. Clifford
Boyd, Gwendolyn Elizabeth
Bruce, Aundray
Carter, Billy L.
Daniels, Jesse
Davis, Artur
Daniels, Lemuel Lee
Delaney, John Paul
Dukes, Hazel Nell
Elmore, Stephen A., Sr.
Gibson, Dr. John Thomas
Gray, Esq. Fred David, Sr.
Gray, Karen G.
Hagan, Willie James
Hamlar, Portia Yvonne Trenholm
Hardy, Charlie Edward
Henderson, Theresa Crittenden
Hogan, Dr. William E., II
Holmes, Alvin Adolf
James, Dr. Stephen Elisha
Jackson, Lillian
Jackson, Dr. Andrew
Jenkins, Dr. Herman Lee
Jenkins, Carol Ann
Jones, Alma Wyatt
Jones, Merlakia Kenyatta
King, Martin Luther, III
Knott, Mable M
Knight, Dr. Robert S.
Knight, John F., Jr.
Lofton, Michael
Long, Terrence Deon
Mathews, George
McPherson, Vanzetta Penn
McKinnon, Dr. Isaiah
McCorvey, Dr. Everett D.
Norman, Georgette M.
Oliver, Gary Dewayne
Oliver, Kenneth Nathaniel
Plummer, Dr. Diane Loretta
Price, Judge Charles
Pryor, Calvin Caffey
Rich, Wilbur C.
Rich, Isadore A.
Richards, Leon
Sanders, Rhonda Sheree
Sanders, Dr. Isaac Warren
Smiley, Dr. Emmett L.
Smitherman, Rodger M.
Spencer, Octavia
Stewart, Charles J.
Thomas, Dr. Marvette Jeraldine
Walton, Dr. Edward D.
Williams, Dr. James Hiawatha
Wilson, Danyell Elaine

## ALASKA



## ARIZONA



## ARKANSAS

# CALIFORNIA

Cherry, Lee Otis
Coogler, Ryan
Cooper, Earl
Curry, Mark G.
Curry, Dr. James H.
Davis, Antonio Lee
Dellums, Ronald Vernie
Drummond, William Joe
Foster, Gregory Clinton
Fulgham, Roietta Goodwin
Gaines, Cassandra Jean
Gibson, Roger Allan
Goodwin, Curtis LaMar
Gravenberg, Dr. Eric Von
Hawkins, Edwin
Harris, Kamala Devi, Jr.
Hammer, M. C.
Howard, Glen
Humphrey, Margo
Jensen, Marcus Christian
Jones, Victoria Gene
Johnson, Wayne J.
Kenoly, Samuel
Kenoly, Bingo
Lars, Byron
Laird, Rev. Alan
Lange, Ted W.
Lowery, Quenton Terrell
Lynch, Marshawn
McCoy, Jelani Marwan
McKissack, Perri Alette
Moore, Shemar F.
Payton, Gary Dwayne
Pettis, Gary George
Pierce, Paul Anthony
Pines, Darryll J.
Richardson, Valerie K.
Rider, Isaiah, Jr.
Saadiq, Raphael
Shaw, Brian K.
Smith, Danyel
Smith, Bobby
Stewart, David Keith
Valentine, Diann
White, Donald R.
Williams, Shaun LeJon
Winston, Lamonte
Wright, Soraya M.
Zulu, Itibari M.

### Oaktown
Hayes, Laura

### Oceanside
Bosley, Thad
Wing, Prof. Adrien Katherine

### Ontario
Fielder, Prince Semien
Munoz, Anthony

### Orange
Gipson, Charles Wells, Jr.
Pitts, Leonard, Jr.

### Orange County
Bell, Coby Scott

### Orangeburg
Evans, Etu

### Palmdale
Nash, Niecy

### Panorama City
Good, Megan Monique

### Pasadena
Al-Mateen, Dr. Kevin Bakeer
Augmon, Stacey Orlando
Clark, Mario Sean
Freisen, Gil
Griffin, Ples Andrew
Hines, Kingsley B.
Holmes, Darick Lamon
Jones, Tamala R.
Murray, Lamond Maurice
Nelson, Ronald Duncan
Robertson, Marcus Aaron
White, Jaleel Ahmed
Worrill, Dr. Conrad W.

### Pittsburg
Allen-Jones, Patricia Ann

### Pomona
McWilliams, Johnny E.

### Rancho Cucamonga
Manuel, Lionel, Jr.

### Redwood City
Bass, Kevin Charles

### Richmond
Loud, Kamil Kassam
Plummer, Glenn E.

### Riverside
Bayne, Chris
Baker, Dusty
Bonds, Barry Lamar
Clemons, Duane Anthony
Cooper, Drucilla Hawkins
Gray, Edward, Jr.
Ivey, Phil
Miller, Cheryl De Ann
Miller, Reginald Wayne
Patterson, Andrae Malone
Russell, Beverly Ann
Stephens, Joseph

### Sacramento
Best, Dr. Sheila Diane
Brown, Angela Yvette
Clifford, Charles H.
Colley, Nathaniel S., Jr.
Dungey, Merrin
Galbraith, Alan Scott
Hayes, Jim
Henderson-Nocho, Audrey J.
James, Wynona Yvonne
Jordan, Ricky
Johnson, Kevin Maurice
Knowles, Dr. Em Claire
Lee, Derrek Leon
Mann, Charles Andre
McNeal, Timothy Kyle
Newfield, Marc Alexander
Nelson, Darrin Milo
Oldham, Christopher Martin
Phillips, Ralph Leonard
Reynolds, Robert James
Reynolds, Ricky Scott
Robinson, Carol Evonne
Taylor, Hon. Eric Charles
Vaughn, Gregory Lamont
Ward, Ronald R.

### Salinas
Boutte, Ernest John
Cooper, Josephine H.
Toney, Anthony

### San Bernardino
Blakely, Dr. Edward James
Bohannon, Etdrick
Coles, Darnell
Hayes, Chris
Johnson, Charles Everett
Jobe, Shirley A.
Ramsey, Dr. Jerome Capistrano
Russell, Bryon Demetrise
Thomas, J. T.
Walker, Wesley Darcel

### San Diego
Allen, Marcus LeMarr
Anderson, Barbara Louise
Anthony, Eric Todd
Banks, Tony
Barnes, Adia Oshun
Brown, Jurutha
Cathey, Leon Dennison
Cannon, Nick
Charles, RuPaul Andre
Claiborne, Chris
Cook, Rashard
Davis, Terrell Lamar
Dimry, Charles Louis, III
Dunn, David Leon
Edwards, Donnie Lewis, Jr.
Ethridge, Raymond Arthur, Jr.
Fortier, Dr. Theodore T., Sr.
Glover, La'Roi
Harkey, Michael Anthony
Jones, Jacque Dewayne
Lewis, Sarasvati Ananda
Lewis, Ananda
Levingston, Clifford Eugene
Marshall, Donald James
McBeth, Hon. Veronica Simmons
McGill, Michele Nicole Johnson
McNeil, Lori Michelle
McLemore, Mark Tremell
Milligan, Randy
Moore, Larry Maceo
Moss, Robert C., Jr.
Pearson, Bishop Carlton Demetrius
Richardson, Lita Renee
Sanders, Brandon Christopher
Salaam, Rashaan Iman
Stokes, Jerel Jamal
Williams, Cheryl L.
Williams, Ricky, Jr.
Wright, Howard Gregory

### San Fernando
Fontenot-Jamerson, Berlinda

### San Francisco
Baker, Althea R.
Bell, Sandra Watson
Bobino, Dr. Rita Florencia
Bryant, Anthony
Brooks, Golden Ameda
Bridges, Todd Anthony
Collins, Charles Miller
Coleman, Dr. Ronald Gerald
Crouch, Pastor Andrae Edward
Darkins, Christopher Oji
Floyd, Malcolm Gregory Ali
Fregia, Darrell Leon
Furlough, Joyce Lynn
Gaston, Linda Saulsby
Gant, Richard E.
Glover, Danny Lebern
Goss-Seeger, Debra A.
Graves, Clifford Wayne
Hall, Dr. David Anthony, Jr.
Hawkins, Tramaine
Herron-Braggs, Cindy Ann
Hundon, James Henry
Jenkins, Monica
Jones, Charisse Monsio
Jordan, Kevin
Kaslofsky, Thor
Kidd, Jason Fredrick
Lacy, Aundrea
Lelaind, Detra Lynette
Loville, Derek Kevin
Malveaux, Julianne
Malveaux, Antoinette Marie
Matthews, Gary Nathaniel, Jr.
McGee, Willie Dean
Mills, Lois Terrell
Moore, Chante Torrane
Nicholas, Gwendolyn Smith
Reed, Brandy Carmina
Rhodes, John K.
Scott, Robert Jerome
Scott, Samuel N.
Sewell, Steven Edward
Sinkford, Rev. William George
Simon, Dr. Kenneth Bernard
Spears, Stephanie
Taylor, Aaron Matthew
Thompson, Art
Winn, Carol Denise
Williams, Paul S.
Williams, Rodney Elliott
Yarbrough, Patricia Nicholson

### San Jose
Andrews, James
Hodgins, James William
Ribbs, William Theodore, Jr.

### San Mateo
Haysbert, Dennis Dexter

### San Pablo
Farr, D'Marco Marcellus

### San Pedro
Bibbs, Charles

### Santa Ana
Jordan, Michael B.

### Santa Barbara
Cunningham, Randall

### Santa Clara
Ross, Adrian

### Santa Cruz
Hill, Glenallen
Slaughter, Atty. Fred L.

### Santa Monica
Green, Sean Curtis
Smith, Dennis
Williams, Gary C.

### Santa Rosa
Whiting, Brandon Renee

### Seaside
Levingston, Bashir A.

### Stockton
Carver, Shante Ebony
McElvane, Pamela Anne
Slaughter, Webster Melvin
Walker, Kara

### Sun Valley
Kelly, Joseph Winston, Jr.
Mixon, Kenneth Jermaine

### Sylmar
Martin, Kevin

### Torrance
Gonzalez, Tony
Holbert, Ray Arthur, III
Hunter, Brian Ronald

### Upland
Hempstead, Hessley James, II

### Vacaville
Dye, Jermaine Terrell

### Vallejo
Anderson, Richard Charles
E-40, E.
Pierce, Dr. Gregory W.
Terrell, Reginald V.
Tyson, Bernard J., Sr.

### Watsonville
DeLeon, Priscilla

### West Covina
Martin, Albert Lee

### Westlake Village
Carroll, Jason

## COLORADO

### Adams
West, George Ferdinand, Jr.

### Aurora
Adams, Vashone LaVey

### Colorado Springs
Boatman, Michael Patrick
Hall, Dr. Christine C. Iijima
Mallory, Glenn Oliver, Jr.
Vereen, Dixie Diane
Walker, Brian

### Denver
Allen, Ty W.
Bailey, Philip
Bennett, Rev. Gordon D.
Billups, Chauncey Ray
Brewer, Gregory Alan
Cason, Marilynn Jean
Chambers, Olivia Marie
Cooper, Kenneth Joseph
Darling, James Jackson
Elliott, Darrell Stanley, Sr.
Harrison, Dr. Mernoy Edward, Jr.
Harris, Dr. Gary Lynn
Harris, Corey
Hart, Dr. Christopher Alvin
Heard, Herman Willie, Jr.
Hilliard, Patsy Jo
Holliman, David L.
Jackson, Gary Monroe
Jones, Greg Phillip
Jones, Victoria C.
Johnson, Stephen L.
Knight, Rev. Dr. Carolyn Ann
Lee, Tamela Jean
Lewis, William Henry
Martin, Darrick David
McConnell, Conrad
Mouton, James Raleigh
Morrison, Dr. Trudi Michelle
Owens, Keith Alan
Parker, Anthony E.
Rabouin, Esq. E. Michelle
Rice, Hon. Norman Blann
Robinson, Cleo Parker
Sanders, Christopher Dwayne
Simpson, India Arie
Simpson, Diane Jeannette
Tate, David Fitzgerald
Thrash, James Ray
Tuggle, Rev. Reginald
Walls, Rev. Fredric T.
Washington, Marvin Andrew
Webb, Wilma J. Gerdine

### Jasper
Rambo, Bettye R.

### Louisville
McMillan, Regina Ellis

### Mancos
Elliss, Luther John

### Manitou Springs
Groves, Harry Edward

### Pueblo
Benjamin, Rose Mary
Hamilton, Dr. Paul L.
Jones, Hon. Raymond Dean
Perkins, Myla Levy

### Sequndo
Hunn, Myron Vernon

### Trinidad
London, Dr. Clement B. G.

## CONNECTICUT

### Bloomfield
Rose, Anika Noni

### Branford
Slie, Pastor Samuel N.

### Bridgeport
Butts, Calvin Otis, III
Clarke, Kenton
Clinkscales, Keith
Edwards, Theodore Thomas
Harris, Jeanette
James, Rev. Darryl Farrar
Petrick, Dr. Jane Allen
Smith, Charles Daniel
Smith, Christopher Gerard
Thomas, Prof. Nina M.
Ward, Keith Lamont
Walters, George W., Jr.
Wilson, Shawn-Ta
Wood, Harold Leroy

### Danbury
Bush, Evelyn
Smith, Dr. Ian K.

### Derby
Walker, Lula Aquillia

### Greenwich
Merchant, Esq. John F.

### Hartford
Borders, Michael G.
Carr, Kurt
Camby, Marcus D.
Cannon, Tyrone Heath
Closs, Keith Mitchell, Jr.
Copes, Ronald Adrian
Crawford, Jayne Suzanne
Daniels, Jerome Alvonne
Dixon, Dr. Benjamin
Freeman, Walter Eugene
Freeman, Brian M.
Gramby, Shirley Ann
Gray, Christine
Hendon, Lea Alpha
Holt, Melonie R.
Hodgson-Brooks, Gloria J.
Johnson, Wayne Lee
Jones, Dr. Meredith J.
Knight, Dr. Muriel Bernice
Lane, Eleanor Tyson
LaSalle, Eriq
Lightfoot, Jean Drew
Martin, Arnold Lee, Jr.
Mahorn, Rick
Milner, Thirman L.

## DELAWARE



## DISTRICT OF COLUMBIA

Morris, Dr. Archie M., III
Morris, Marlene C.
Monagan, Dr. Alfrieta Parks
Moore-Stovall, Dr. Joyce
Montgomery, Sonsyrea Tate
Morgan, Michael
Moragne, Maurice S.
Morton, Norman
Mumford, Prof. Jeffrey Carlton
Murphy, Daniel Howard
Mumford, Thaddeus Quentin, Jr.
Murray, Dr. James Hamilton
Nash, Dr. Daniel Alphonza, Jr.
Newhouse, Dr. Quentin, Jr.
Newkirk, Dr. Gwendolyn
Nix, Dr. Theophilus Richard, Jr.
Norton, Eleanor Holmes
O'Bryant, Beverly J.
Oates, Wanda Anita
Ogden, Jonathan Phillip
Owens, Bishop Alfred A., Jr.
Oyewole, Dr. Saundra Herndon
Padgett, Prof. James A.
Payne, Dr. Norma Joyce
Parris, Rev. Alvin, III
Pailen, Donald, Sr.
Peal, Dr. Regina Randall
Perkins, Daniel T.
Pinkney, Andrea Davis
Pinkett, Allen Jerome
Pinson, Margo Dean
Pitcher, Capt. Frederick M. A.
Powell-Jackson, Rev. Dr. Bernice
Porter-Esmailpour, Carol D.
Pollard, Alfonso McInham
Price, Pamela Anita
Pride, Curtis John
Price, Hugh Bernard
Puryear, Martin
Quander, Esq. Rohulamin
Raveling, George Henry
Rand, A. Barry
Ray, Rosalind Rosemary
Rashad, Johari Mahasin
Randolph, Laura B.
Reason, J. Paul
Reid, Don
Reaves, E. Fredericka M
Reed, Dr. Daisy Frye
Rhines, Jesse Algeron
Richards, Jaime Augusto, III
Rice, Ambassador Susan Elizabeth
Richmond, Rodney Welch
Robinet, Harriette Gillem
Robinson, Carl Cornell
Robbins, Austin Dion
Rogers, Chris
Robinson, Harry G., III
Robinson, Peter Lee, Jr.
Ruffner, Raymond P.
Russ, Timothy Darrell
Saunders, David J.
Scott, Seret
Scott, Judith Sugg
Scott, Robert Cortez
Scott, Dr. Helen Madison Marie Pawne Kinnard
Seay, Dawn Christine
Searcy, Leon, Jr.
Shepherd, Leslie Glenard
Shannon, Odessa M.
Shakoor, Dr. Waheedah Aqueelah
Shepherd, Greta Dandridge
Siler, Brenda Claire
Silva, Dr. Omega C. Logan
Sims, Lowery Stokes
Sims, Carl W.
Simpkins, LuBara Dixon
Simmons, Maurice Clyde
Smith, Dr. Clifford V., Jr.
Smith, Debbie A.
Smith, Rodney Stacey
Smith, Michael John
Smith, Dr. Roland Blair, Jr.
Smothers, Ronald Eric
Smith, Dr. Alonzo Nelson
Snyder, Vanessa W.
Sockwell, Oliver R., Jr.
Southern, Herbert B.
Stent, Madelon Delany
Stewart, Kenneth C.
Stone, William T.
Stanley, Major Gen. Clifford Lee
Streeter, Denise Williams
Sullivan, Emmet G.
Swiner, Dr. Connie C., III
Taylor, Anna Diggs
Taylor, Dr. Estelle Wormley
Taylor, Tyrone Curtis
Taylor, Joseph
Taylor, Jeanine Y. Cooper
Teasley, Michelle Nicole
Thompson, John, III
Thompson, Ronald Anthony
Thompson, Carol Belita
Thompson, Milt
Thomas, Ralph Albert
Thompson, Bette Mae
Thornton, Cora Ann Barringer
Thomas, Dr. John Henderson, III
Thomas, Carol M.
Thomas, Dr. Audria Acty
Thompson, Portia Wilson
Thompson, John Robert, Jr.
Tucker, Karen
Turner, Winston Edwin
Vann, Gregory Alvin
Vertreace-Doody, Martha Modena
Vertreace, Walter Charles
Wade, Dr. Eugene Henry-Peter
Ware, Omego John Clinton
Waters, Neville R., III
Walker, Dr. George T., Jr.
Walker, Kenneth R.
Walker, Dr. M. Lucius, Jr.
Walker-Slocum, Frances
Washington, Adrienne Terrell
Ward, Dr. Jerry Washington, Jr.
Watkins, Dr. Michael Thomas
Waddy, Jude Michael
Wagner, Annice M.
Wells, Theodore V., Jr.
Westray, Rev. Kenneth Maurice
Webb, Dr. Harvey, Jr.
Weeks, Hon. Renee Jones
Weaver, Gary W.
White, Sylvia Kay
Winston, Jeanne Worley
Winter, Daria Portray
Williams, Karen Hastie
Williams, Deborah Ann
Wilbon, Joan Marie
Wideman, John Edgar
Williams, Ronald Lee
Williams, Herman
Winston, Dr. Hubert
Williams, Robert B.
Williams, Dr. Robert H.
Williams, Dr. Shirley Yvonne
Williams, Yvonne LaVerne
Williams-Garner, Debra
Williams, Russell, II
Williams, Hon. Alexander, Jr.
Wilson, Dr. Joseph Henry, Jr.
Williams, Walter Ander, Jr.
Wilkerson, Isabel
Williams, Larry
Williams, Jerome
Williams, Jay Omar
Williams, Hon. Carolyn H.
Williams, Jamal
Williams, Elvira Felton
Wood, Brenda Blackmon
Wood, William Vernell, Sr.
Wood, Anton Vernon
Wright, Jeanne Jason
Wyche, Lennon Douglas, Jr.
Young, James M., II
Young, William Allen
Zelis, Karen Dee

# FLORIDA

## Altamonte Springs
Hastings, Rep. Alcee Lamar

## Alturas
Reddick, Alzo Jackson, Sr.

## Apalachicola
Adams, Dr. Willie, Jr.
Hawkins, James C.
Humphries, Dr. Frederick S., Sr.
Kornegay, Br. William F.

## Apopka
Brown, Eddie C.
Lawrence, Rodell

## Arcadia
Blanden, Lee Ernest
Owens, Dr. Robert Leon, III

## Archer
Cotman, Dr. Henry Earl

## Aucilla
Hamilton, Dr. Franklin D.

## Avon Park
Cox, Dr. Arthur James, Sr.
McRae, Harold Abraham
Seigler, Dexter E.

## Barton
Smith, Voydee

## Bartow
Blake, Dr. Wendell Owen
Carroll, Robert F.
Davidson, Cleatus Lavon
Gray, Torrian
Grace, George H.
Highsmith, Alonzo Walter
Lewis, Raymond Anthony, Jr.
McGrady, Tracy Lamar, Jr.
Riley, Kenneth Jerome, II
Stewart, James, Jr.
Thompson, Rhonda Denise

## Bascom
Bowers, Dr. Mirion Perry
Sorey, Hilmon S., Jr.

## Belle Glade
Anthony, Clarence Edward
Harrold, Lawrence A.
Johns, Dr. Jackie C.
Oliver, Louis, III

## Blountstown
Barnwell, Dr. Henry Lee
English, Dr. Perry T., Jr.

## Boynton Beach
Simon, Corey Jermaine
Thorpe, Otis Henry
Wright, Dr. Samuel Lamar, Sr.

## Bradenton
Rozier, Clifford Glen, II

## Bunnell
Koch, Francena Jones

## Carrabelle
Patterson, Lydia R.

## Carver Ranches
Curry, Rev. Victor Tyrone

## Caryville
Gibson, Johnnie Mae

## Casselberry
Smith, Marquette

## Century
Hayes, Donald Ross, Jr.
Pleasant, Anthony Devon

## Chipley
Horne, Dr. Aaron, Sr.
Lee, Amp

## Clearwater
Harris, Calvin D.
Hatchett, Joseph Woodrow
Hatchett, Paul Andrew
Rowe, Christa F.

## Clermont
Johnson, Julia L.

## Clewiston
Boston, Archie, Jr.

## Cocoa
Folston, James Edward
Smith, Dr. Joe Lee

## Coconut Creek
Carter, Nigea

## Coconut Grove
Green, Walter

## Crescent City
Carey, Dr. Addison, Jr.
Williams, Clarence

## Crystal River
Bunche, Curtis J.

## Dade City
Dorsett, Mary Alice

## Dania
Brown, Diana Johnson

## Daytona Beach
Bartley, Dr. William Raymond
Blake, Jeff Bertrand Coleman
Carter, Vince
Crockett, Delores Loraine
Gaskins, Percell McGahee
Horton, Dr. Carrell Peterson
Long, William H., Jr.
Mack, Dr. Astrid Karona
McCloud, George Aaron, III
McNorton, Bruce Edward
Moore, Annie Jewell
Primus-Cotton, Dr. Bobbie J.
Stalling, Ronald Eugene
Williams-Dotson, Daryl

## De Land
Dunn, Marvin

## Deerfield
Hicks, Leon Nathaniel

## Deerfield Beach
Battle, Gloria Jean

## DeLand
Avery, Byllye Y.
Gordon, Bridgette C.
Ivey, Horace Spencer
Roper, Richard Walter
Thomas, Tra
Williams, Reginald Clark

## Delray Beach
Patrick, Vincent Jerome
Wallace, Al

## Dunnellon
Churchwell, Charles Darrett
Mills, Ernie

## East Palatka
Ellis, Benjamin F., Jr.

## Eglin AFB
Gordon-Dillard, Joan Yvonne
Jefferson, Karen L.

## Escambia County
Shannon, Marian L. H.

## Eustis
Coney, Loraine Chapell
Poe, Dr. Booker

## Evinston
Cabrera-White, Eloise J.

## Fernandina Beach
Allen, Dr. William Barclay
Kennedy, Howard E.

## Fort Lauderdale
Bruce, Isaac Isidore
Connell, Albert Gene Anthony

## Fort Meade
McCutchen, Andrew Stefan

## Ft. Lauderdale
Barton, Wayne Darrell
Bennett, Donnell, Jr.
Blue, Octavia LaDawn
Blades, Bennie, Sr.
Dudley-Washington, Loise
Files, Lolita
Hair, Princell
Irvin, Michael Jerome
Jones, Albert C.
Marshall, Reese
McCloud, Tyrus Kamall
Parham, Brenda Joyce
Richmond, Mitch
Sanders, Frank Vondel
Sudarkasa, Niara
Taylor, Daisy Curry
Taylor, Johnny C., Jr.
Weatherspoon, Jimmy Lee

## Ft. Meade
Franklin, Audrey Demps
Gillis, Theresa McKinzy

## Ft. Myers
German, Jammi Darnell
Henry, Anthony Daniel
Lucas, Rubye
Sanders, Deion Luwynn
Shoemaker, Veronica Sapp

## Ft. Pierce
Bailey, Harry Augustine, Jr.
Blackshear, Jeffery Leon
Brock, Roslyn McCallister
Gaines, Dr. Samuel Stone
Johnson, Charles Edward, Jr.
McNeil, Ryan Darrell, II
Strong-Kimbrough, Dr. Blondell M.
Witherspoon, Sophia L.

## Ft. Walton Beach
Hammonds, Tom

## Gainesville
Bynum, Kenneth Bernard
Ham-Ying, Dr. John Michael
Hart, Dr. Jacquelyn D.
Holley, Sharon Yvonne
Jackson, Terry
Jackson, Tammy Eloise
Jackson, Willie Bernard, Jr.
Marion, Fred Donald
Maxwell, Vernon
Nattiel, Richard Rennard
Rawls, Dr. George H.
Rawls, Raleigh Richard
Rudolph, Maya Khabira
Solomon, Freddie Lee, Jr.
Wilson, Reinard

## Gifford
Holmes, Kenny

## Goulds
Waters, Willie Anthony

## Graceville
Mack, Lurene Kirkland

## Green Cove Springs
Chase, Arnett C.

## Greenville
Washington, Leroy

## Gretna
Colston, Dr. Freddie C.
Davis, Esq. Marva Alexis

## Haines City
Gandy, Wayne Lamar
Jones, Margaret B.
Neal, Mario Lanza

## Hallandale
Terrell, Dorothy A.
Williamson, Ethel W.

## Hawthorne
Middleton, John Allen

## Hialeah
Jackson, Greg Allen
Mateen, Malik Abdul

## Hines
Reynolds, Ida Manning

## Holiday
Vickers, Kipp Emmanuel

## Homestead
Barrow, Micheal Colvin
Sands, Dr. Rosetta F.

## Jacksonville
Alexander, Gary Roberts
Alexander, Derrick L.
Badger, Dr. Leonard Michael
Baety, Edward L., Sr.
Best, Jennings H.
Belton, C. Ronald
Bennett, Edgar, III
Betha, Mason Durrell
Bowens, Dr. Johnny Wesley
Bragg, Robert Henry, Jr.
Bruton, Bertram A.

Lewis, Dr. Henry L., III
Lee, Fred D., Jr.
McFadden, Dr. Gregory L.
Meeks, Hon. Perker L., Jr.
Meek, Carrie P.
Moore, Nathaniel
Smith, Dr. Judith Moore
Stickney, Janice L.
Sullivan, Dr. Zola Jiles
Tatum, Dr. Beverly Daniel
Thompson, Tawana Sadiela
Vanover, Tamarick T.
Williams, Wally James, Jr.
Wilson, Robert
Williams, Dorothy Payne
Woodie, Henry L.

### Tampa
Abrams, Kevin R.
Alfonso, Pedro
Aldridge, Dr. Delores Patricia
Bell, Derek Nathaniel
Bolden, Juran T.
Campbell, Dr. Otis, Jr.
Colleton, Katrina Yvette
Culpepper, Louis S.
Cutler, Donald
Dennis, Dr. Rodney Howard
Footman, Dan Ellis, Jr.
George, Dr. Hermon, Jr.
Gonzalez, Cambell
Gooden, Dwight Eugene
Grist, Arthur L.
Hammond, James A.
Haggins, Jon
Horton, Earle Chico, III
Hubbard, Josephine Brodie
Jacobs, Ennis Leon, Jr.
James, Jerome Keith
Jordan, Bettye Davis
King, Marcellus, Jr.
Lafayette, Dr. Bernard, Jr.
Lillard, Kwame Leo
Loyd, Walter, Jr.
McDonald, Dr. Charles J.
McGriff, Frederick Stanley
Miller, Gwendolyn Martin
Mutcherson, Dr. James Albertus, Jr.
Oglesby, Joe
Purdee, Nathan
Scrivens, Dr. John J.
Sheffield, Gary Antonian
Small, Torrance Ramon
Smith, Torrance
Smith, Dr. Walter L.
Smith, Esq. Jeraldine Williams
Stone, Dr. John S.
Staley, Duce
Timmons, Ozzie
Vance, Eric Devon
Washington, Theodore, Jr.

### Titusville
Campbell, Melanie L.
Marshall, Wilber Buddyhia

### Vero Beach
Davis, Ben Jerome
Lane, Prof. Johnny Lee, Jr.
Sharpton, Denise

### Wabasso
Cromartie, Eugene Rufus

### Wauchula
Mowatt, Zeke

### Webster
Pennington, Dr. Leenette Morse

### Weirsdale
Johnson, Frank

### West Palm Beach
Billingslea, Dr. Monroe L.
Goldwire, Anthony
Harper, Esq. Ronald J.
Harris-Jones, Yvonne
Jones, Christopher Todd
Kinsey, Bernard W.
Maloney, Charles Calvin
Mitchell, Robert Lee, Sr.
Noble, John Pritchard
Rozier, Gilbert Donald
Smith, Bobby Antonia
Wester, Richard Clark

### West Tampa
Hargrett, James T., Jr.

### Wildwood
Johnson, Ellis Bernard

### Winter Garden
Long, Hon. James L.

### Winter Haven
Gibson, Derrick Lamont
Hendry, Gloria
Johnson, Ulysses Johann, III
Kennedy, Dr. Theodore Reginald
Lawrence, Merlisa Evelyn
Rollins, Tree

### Winter Park
Boyer, James Buchanan
English, Dr. Richard Allyn
Parrish, James Nathaniel

### Yulee
Martin, Dr. Joanne Mitchell

## GEORGIA

### Adel
Beady, Dr. Charles H., Jr.
McDonald, Ella Seabrook

### Albany
Bolden, Frank Augustus
Brown, Dr. Ola M.
Dixon, Leonard Bill
Jones, Dr. Joseph, Jr.
King, Dr. William Carl
King, Preston
King, Alonzo B.
Marshall, Ameila
Marshall, Dr. Edwin Cochran
McBride, Shelia Ann
Moore, Derrick C.
Payton-Noble, JoMarie
Reynolds, Charles McKinley, Jr.
Rush, Bobby Lee
Slaughter-Titus, Rev. Linda Jean
Travis, Rep. Geraldine W.
Weather, Dr. Leonard, Jr.
Wingfield, Dontonio B.

### Allentown
Hogges, Dr. Ralph

### Alma
Leonard, Dr. Walter J.

### Americus
Allen-Noble, Prof. Rosie Elizabeth
Anderson, William Gilchrist
Cooper, Albert, Sr.
Dozier, Morris, Sr.
Fuse, Bobby LeAndrew, Jr.
Green, Victor Bernard
Hopkins, William A.
Howard, Rev. Moses William, Jr.
Johnson, Waldo Emerson, Jr.
Johnson, Dr. Arthur J.
Mathis, Dr. Thaddeus P.
Paschal, Willie L.
Scott, Artie A.

### Andersonville
Anderson, Mary Elizabeth

### Arlington
Jacobs, Rev. Larry Ben
Jones, Nettie Pearl

### Ashburn
Taylor, Dr. Robert, III

### Athens
Broderick, Johnson
Burgess, Tituss
Clark, Walter H.
Green, Willie Aaron
Harris, Rev. Dr. Michael Neely
Hardeman, James Anthony
James, Dr. Betty Nowlin
Jackson, Dr. Burnett Lamar, Jr.
McBride, Frances E.
Pope, Dr. Henry
Smith, Charles Henry, III
Turner, Dr. Moses

### Atlanta
Adams, Don L.
Adams, Judge Gregory Albert
Adams, Eugene Bruce
Allen, Charles Edward, Jr.
Ali, Tatyana Marisol
Allen, Robert Lee
Alford, Brenda
Anderson, Shandon Rodriguez
Arnold, Monica Denise
Arrington, Judge Marvin S., Sr.
Arnold, David
Beasley, Victor Mario
Bell, Karl I.
Black, Harold Alonza
Boyd, Valerie
Bryant, Gregory Alexander
Brown, Thomas Edison, Jr.
Bradford-Eaton, Zee
Bridgewater, Dr. Rev. Herbert Jeremiah, Jr.
Byrd, Dr. Marquita L.
Cato, Kelvin T.
Carmichael, Benjamin G.
Cantrell, Forrest Daniel
Caviness, Lorraine F.
Catchings, Dr. Yvonne Parks
Challenor, Herschelle Sullivan
Chennault, Dr. Madelyn
Clement, William A., Jr.
Clark, Laron Jefferson, Jr.
Coombs, Fletcher
Cook, Tonya Denise
Conwill, Kinshasha
Collier, Dr. Millard James, Jr.
Craft, Dr. Guy Calvin
Culbreath-Manly, Tongila M.
Davis, Clarence
Davis, Dr. Ernestine Bady
Davis, Stacey H.
Days, Drew Saunders, III
Dean, James Edward
Dent, Richard Lamar
Doanes-Bergin, Sharyn F.
Dobbs, Mattiwilda
Dove, Dr. Pearlie C.
Drennen, Gordon, Jr.
Dye, Dr. Clinton Elworth, Jr.
Espy-Wilson, Carol
Evans, Albert
Fernandez, Denise Burse
Foster, Robert Leon
Frazier, Walt, Jr.
Free, World B.
Fuse-Hall, Rosalind
Gay, Birdie Spivey
Glover, Hamilton
Green, Gloria J.
Grissom, Marquis Dean
Grantley, Robert Clark
Green, Liller
Guthrie, Carlton Lyons
Guest, William, II
Harden, Cedric Bernard
Hastings, Andre Orlando
Hammonds, Evelynn M.
Hatchett, Glenda A.
Harris, Sidney E.
Haskins, Esq. Yvonne B.
Harper, Eugene, Jr.
Hawkins, Walter L.
Harvey, Maurice Reginald
Harris, Hon. Barbara Ann
Hawk, Charles Nathaniel, III
Hill, William Bradley, Jr.
Hill, James A., Jr.
Hightower, Anthony
Hicks, Robert Otis, Jr.
Hodges, Dr. David Julian
Hornsby, Dr. Alton, Jr.
Hope, Dr. Richard Oliver
Jackson, Bishop Wiley, Jr.
Jervay, Paul Reginald, Jr.
Jennings, Dr. Robert Ray
Jones, Dr. Michael Andrea
Jordan, Robert A.
Jordan, Vernon Eulion, Jr.
Johnson, Henry
Johnson, Dr. Carrie Clements
Jordan, Dr. Robert Howard, Jr.
Jones, Sen. Emanuel Davie
Jones, Milton H., Jr.
Karangu, David M.
King, Dexter Scott
King, Rev. Dr. Bernice Albertine
Kimbrough, Walter M.
Kirby, Dr. Jacqueline
Knight, Gladys Maria
Knox, Wayne Harrison
Knight, Bubba
Lee, E. Jacques
Lewis, Mo
Lee, Spike
Lombard, George Paul
Mason, Rev. Herman Skip, Jr.
Mayo, James Wellington
Mann, Dr. Marion
Major, Dr. Clarence
McLin, Rev. Lena Johnson
McZier, Arthur
McKenzie, Miranda Mack
McKinney, Dr. Cynthia Ann
McNeil, Robert Lawrence
McDougall, Dr. Gay J.
Meyers, Lisa Anne-Marie
Merideth, Charles Waymond
Miller, Helen Sullivan
Milner, Michael Edwin
Miller, George Carroll, Jr.
Mickelbury, Penny
Molette-Ogden, Dr. Carla
Moore, Shameik
Mosley, Christopher D.
Morris, Christopher Vernard
Moore, Howard, Jr.
Murphy, Hon. Harriet Louise M.
Newton, Cam
Norman, Wallace
Parham, Johnny Eugene, Jr.
Page, Harrison Eugene
Parks, Karen Elaine Webster
Payne, Jacqueline LaVerne
Parks, Bernard, Jr.
Pender, Mel
Pope, Derrick Alexander
Powell, Arthur F.
Poussaint-Hudson, Dr. Ann Ashmore
Pritchett, Stanley Jerome, Jr.
Pritchett, Kelvin Bratodd
Prothro, Gerald Dennis
Reid, Robert Keith
Richardson, LaTanya
Rowland, Kelly Trene
Roye, Monica R Hargrove
Robinson, Angela Yvonne
Roberts, Tara Lynette
Robinson, Jeannette
Robinson, Jontyle Theresa
Russell, Herman Jerome
Russell, Michael
Samples, Jared Lanier
Sadler, Dr. Wilbert L., Jr.
Scott, Marian Alexis
Scott, Alexis
Shanks, Wilhelmina Byrd
Shopshire, Dr. James Maynard, Sr.
Sims, Dr. Edward Hackney
Slocumb, Jonathan
Smallwood, Richard
Smith, Dr. Jane E.
Smith, C. Miles
Smith-Epps, E. Paulette
Smith, Carol Barlow
Snipes, Lolita Walker
Stephens, Brooke Marilyn
Strickland, Mark
Stafford, Derrick
Stewart, Brittanica
Stith, Antoinette Freeman
Sullivan, Dr. Louis Wade
Sutton, Clyde Avery, Sr.
Symone, Raven
Tanner, Hon. Gloria Travis
Thomas, Joan McHenry Bates
Threatt, Sedale Eugene
Thomas, Mable
Thomas, Rozonda
Torrence-Waller, Gwendolyn Lenna
Tucker, Christopher
Wallace, Steve
Ward, Hon. Christopher Evan
Ward, Sandra L.
Ward, Dr. Calvin Edouard
Wade, Hon. Lyndon Anthony
Warren, Nagueyalti
Washington, Mary Parks
Wardlaw, Alvin Holmes
Waters, John W.
Watkins, Lottie Heywood
Wells, James A.
White, Wendell F.
White, Ida Margaret
Willis, Jill Michelle
Wilson, Natarsha Juliet
Wilkins, Gerald Bernard
Williamson, Carlton
Wilson, Charles Lee, Sr.
Yancey, Prentiss Quincy
Yarbrough, Robert Elzy

### Augusta
Bell, Kendrell Alexander
Bigham, Rita Lacy
Bland, Glenn W.
Booker, John P., III
Boozer, Emerson
Carey, Claire Lamar
Cain, Simon Lawrence
Curry, Rev. Dr. Mitchell L.
Cunningham, William
Davis, James Edgar
Dawson, Horace Greeley
Dawson, Dr. Leonard Ervin
Ellison, Jerry Ernest
Evans, W. Franklin
Evans, Elizabeth
Fishburne, Laurence John, III
Flono, Fannie
Fowler, Bennie W., II
Grant, Harvey
Grant, Horace Junior
Harris, Rev. H. Franklin, II
Hasan, Aqeel Khatib
Hobbs, Dr. Joseph
Hunt, Eugene
James, Prof. William
Jordan, Dr. Carolyne Lamar
Johnson, Jimmie Olden, Jr.
Jones, Annie Lee
Kelly, Thomas, Jr.
Lanier, Horatio Axel
Mitchell, Joann
Norman, James H.
Norman, Jessye Mae
Patterson, James C.
Paschall, Evita Arneda
Perry-Holston, Waltina D.
Rice, Dr. Louise Allen
Roundtree, Raleigh Cito
Russell, Keith Bradley
Settles, Darryl Stephen
Smith, Matt Jermaine
Spikes, Takeo Gerard
Steele, Carolyn Odom
Stallings, James Raiford
Tillman, Dr. Joseph Nathaniel
Toby, William, Jr.
Vaughn, Dr. Janice S.
Walker, Herschel
Williams, Dr. Edward M.
Williams, Milton Lawrence
Wright, Linwood Clinton
Young, James Arthur, III

### Bainbridge
Black, Charles E.
Canson, Fannie Joanna
Davis, Rev. Willie Floyd, Jr.
Pruitt-Logan, Dr. Anne Smith
Turnquest, Sandra Close

### Barnesville
Hicks, Michael

### Bartow County
Phillips, Delores

### Baxley
Martin, Clarence L.
Nails, Jamie Marcellus
Timpson, Michael Dwain

### Berria County
Lewis, Virginia Hill

### Bethlehem
Bell, Robert Wesley

### Blakely
Jacobs, Hazel A.
Pittman, Dr. Marvin B.
Washington, Robert Benjamin, Jr.

### Bloomingdale
Adams, Lucinda Williams

### Bluffton
King, William Frank

Griffin, Floyd Lee, Jr.
Hogan, Dr. James Carroll, Jr.
Monroe, Annie Lucky
Washington, Rico
White, Rondell Bernard

### Miller
Hollis, Mary Lee

### Millhaven
Martin, Blanche W.

### Monroe
Harris, James Larnell
Locklin, James R.
Roberts, Trish

### Montezuma
Martin, Hosea L.

### Morris Station
Clayton, Robert L.

### Moultrie
Edwards, Antonio
Harris, Dr. MaryAnn
Hooker, Odessa Walker
Hooker, Douglas Randolf
Myers, Dr. Bernard Samuel
Wilkinson, Brenda Scott

### Musella
Campbell, Dr. Margie

### Nashville
Richardson, Leon T.

### Newnan
Harris, Dr. Sarah Elizabeth
Hendricks, Dr. Marvin B.
Jordan, Dr. Harold Willoughby
Smith, Dr. Frank, Jr.
Ware, Carl H.

### Newton
Churchwell, Dr. Caesar Alfred
Trice, Dr. William Benjamin

### Ogeechee
Anderson, Henry L. N.

### Patterson
Chatman, Dr. Jacob L.
Davis, Rev. Arnor S.

### Pavo
King, Dr. Reatha Clark

### Peach County
Lucas, David Eugene, Sr.
Smith, Rev. Elijah, Sr.

### Perry
Imhotep, Akbar
Miller, William Nathaniel
Newberry, Cedric Charles
Roberts, Deborah
Simmons, Ron

### Pin Point
Thomas, Hon. Clarence

### Pine Mountain
Jones, Dr. Rena Talley

### Quitman
Holsendolph, Ernest
King, Mary Booker
McIntosh, Dr. Frankie L.
Pearson, Dr. Stanley E.
Stevens, Reatha J.
Williams, Dr. Howard Copeland
Wilfork, Andrew Louis

### Reynolds
Jones, Dr. Michael Bozelly

### Riceboro
Jones, DeLisha Milton

### Richland
Jones, Bertha Diggs

### Rincon
Small, Israel G.

### Roberta
Jackson, James E., Sr.

### Rochelle
Clark, Joe Louis

### Rome
Askew, Bonny Lamar
Brown, Tommie Florence
Holsey, Bernard
Irvin, Kenneth Pernell
Kinnebrew, Lawrence D.
Mitchell, Dr. Julius P.

### Royston
Jones, Tony Edward
Walker, Gary Lamar

### Sale City
Whitlow, Barbara Wheeler

### Sandersville
Boardley, Curtestine May
Houston, Dr. Johnny L.
Minor, Greg Magado
Taylor, Stacey Lorenzo

### Sapelo Island
Hall, Charles Harold

### Savannah
Adams, Floyd, Jr.
Bontemps, Dr. Jacqueline Marie Fonvielle
Brant, Charles Tyrone
Branch, Dr. Geraldine Burton
Bynes, Dr. Frank Howard, Jr.
Cash-Rhodes, Winifred E.
Cannida, James Thomas, II
Campbell, Alma Porter
Christophe, Cleveland A.
Clayton, Hon. Eva M.
Colbert, Benjamin James
Curtis-Rivers, Susan Yvonne
Day, John H.
Daughtry, Rev. Herbert Daniel
Denmark, Robert Richard
El-Kati, Mahmoud
Ellison, Pervis
Hall, David
Harmon, James F., Sr.
Harris, Dr. Horatio Preston
Harper, Ruth B.
Hardwick, Clifford E., III
Jamerson, Dr. John W., III
Johnson, Lester B., III
Jones, Esq. Ernest Edward
Johnson, Paul Lawrence
Johnson, Hon. Otis Samuel
Louard, Agnes Anthony
Martin, Shedrick M., Jr.
Martin, Gertrude S.
McPherson, James Alan
McIver, John Douglas
Milledge, Dr. Luetta Colvin Upshur
Mills, Alan Keith
Patton, Antwan Andre
Perry, Gerald June
Pino, Rev. Jerome King Del
Rivers, Dr. Louis
Riley, Shaunce R.
Seabrook, Rev. Bradley Maurice
Smith, William Fred
Stevens, Dr. Maxwell McDew
Strickland-Hill, Dr. Marva Yvonne
Thomas, Dr. Priscilla D.
Williams, Dr. Hubert
Wilson, Leroy, Jr.
Wright, Joseph

### Screven
Frazier, Jordan

### Screven County
Thomas, James O.

### Sharon
Lewis, Dr. Lonzy James

### Shellman
King, Edgar Lee

### Social Circle
Wright, Dr. C. T. Enus

### Soperton
Allen, Bernestine

### Sparta
Ingram, Hon. Edith J.
Wiley, Leroy Sherman

### St. Marys
Hicks, Doris Morrison
Wilson, Dr. John W.

### St. Simons Island
Brown, James Nathaniel

### Statesboro
Campbell, Dr. Charles Everett
Clifton, Dr. Ivery Dwight
Hall, Alfonzo Louis
Lewis, Reta Jo
Lewis, Sharma
Mincey, W. James, Jr.

### Summerville
Knox, Stanley

### Sycamore
Kendrick, Tommy L.

### Sylvania
Burgest, Rev. Dr. David Raymond
Roberts, Bryndis Wynette

### Sylvester
Butts, Marion Stevenson, Jr.
Crutchfield-Baker, Verdenia
Yancy, Dr. Preston Martin

### Taccoa
Wheeler, Leonard Tyrone

### Talbotton
Culpepper, Dellie L.
Persons, W. Ray

### Tallapoosa
Rosser, Dr. Samuel Blanton

### Tattnall County
White, Margarette Paulyne Morgan

### Tennille
Edwards, Robert Lee, III

### Thomaston
Carter, Dr. John H.
Kendall, Robert, Jr.
Walker, Dr. Eugene P., Sr.
Worthy, Dr. Barbara Ann

### Thomasville
Banks, Dr. William Maron, III
Curry, Eric Felece
Gilchriest, Lorenzo
Hardy-Hill, Edna Mae
Madison, Samuel Adolfus, Jr.
Traylor, Prof. Eleanor W.
Ward, Charlie
Williams, Dr. Rev. Earl, Jr.

### Thompson
Jackson, Millie

### Thomson
Parks, Dr. Edward Y. A.

### Tifton
Adams, Eula L.
Brown, Evelyn
Mott, Stokes E., Jr.
Yancy, Dr. Robert James

### Tignall
Moore, Cornell Leverette

### Tingnall
Stripling, Dr. Luther

### Toccoa
Davis, Dale
Dortch, Thomas W., Jr.
Johnson, Kalanos Vontell

### Toombs County
Fuller, Jack Lewis

### Toomsboro
Deese, Manuel
Wright, Dr. Joseph Malcolm

### Valdosta
Asante, Dr. Molefi Kete
Bridges, Dr. James Wilson
Carter, Dr. Lawrence
Foster, Rev. James Hadlei
Godfrey, Randall Euralentris
Herring, Leonard, Jr.
McCluskey, Audrey Thomas
McMillan, Dr. Joseph Turner, Jr.
Mobley, Emily Ruth
Register, Dr. Jasper C.
Relaford, Desi
Roberts, J. Edgar
Wilson, Grady Demond

### Vidalia
Blount, Melvin Cornell
Sanders, Dr. George L.
Simpson, Carl Wilhelm

### Vienna
Kingdom, Roger Nona

### Warner Robins
Anderson, Eddie Lee, Jr.
Brooks, James Robert
Ferguson, Ralph
Granville, William, Jr.
Smith, Benjamin Joseph

### Warrenton
Brooks, Tyrone L., Sr.
Caroline, James C.

### Washington
Davis, Frank Allen
Hargrave, Thomas Burkhardt, Jr.
Harden, Dr. Robert James, Sr.

### Waycross
Adams, Samuel Levi, Sr.
Davis, Norman Emanuel
Dyson, William Riley
English, Kenneth
Lawrence, Thomas R., Jr.
Mayes, Helen M.
Mayes, Nathaniel H., Jr.
McCray, Christopher Columbus
Smith, Vernel Hap
Taylor, Reginald Redall, Jr.
Williams, Gerald
Wood, Juanita Wallace

### Waynesboro
Byrd, Dr. Helen P. Bessent
Gainer, Dr. Frank Edward
Godbee, Thomasina D.
Herrington, Perry Lee
Howard, Paul Lawrence, Jr.
Majors, Mattie Carolyn
McCloud, Rev. Dr. J. Oscar

### West Point
Canady, Blanton Thandreus
Davidson, Lurlean G.
Dismuke, Mary Eunice
Lovelace, John C.

### Wilcox County
Jordan, Dr. Abbie H.

### Wilkes County
Davis, Clarence

### Woodland
Carter, Hon. James

## HAWAII

### Honolulu
Anderson, Granville Scott
Chamberlain, Byron Daniel
McGee, Sherry
McKandes, Darnell Damon
Obama, Dr. Barack Hussein, II
Palms, Sylvia J.

### Kailua
Naeole, Chris

### Maui
Ceballos, Cedric Z.

## IDAHO

### Coeur d'Alene
Latham, Christopher Joseph

### Pocatello
Johnson, Dr. Pompie Louis, Jr.
Purce, Dr. Thomas Les

## ILLINOIS

### Alton
Haley, Prof. Johnetta Randolph
Johnson, Alvin Roscoe
Taylor, T. Shawn
White, Jesse C.

### Arlington
Payton, Jarrett Walter

### Aurora
Bownes, Fabien Alfranso
Compton, James W.
Pool-Eckert, Marquita Jones
Thomas, Carl

### Belleville
Collons, Ferric Jason
Syler, M. Rene
Wiley, Gerald Edward

### Bellwood
McElroy, Raymond Edward

### Bloomington
Ebo, Antona

### Cairo
Bates, Louise Rebecca
Hall, Jack L.
Morris, Dr. Frank Lorenzo, Sr.
Robichaux, Jolyn H.
Thomas, Dr. William
Trotter, Donne E.

### Canton
Pickett, Cecil Bruce

### Carbondale
Hudson, Troy

### Centerville
Covington, Kim Ann
Hudlin, Reginald Alan

### Centralia
Burris, Roland W.
Coleman, Cecil R.
Coleman, Kenneth L.
Norwood, William R.
Saunders, Dr. Elizabeth Ann
Taylor, Mildred E. Crosby
Welch, Harvey

### Champaign
Hale, Kimberly Anice
Ludacris
Whitner, Donna K.

### Chicago
Abdullah, Dr. Samella Berry
Adams, Flozell Jootin
Adkins, William
Adams, Dr. Sheila Mary
Addams, Robert David
Adair, Andrew A.
Aguirre, Mark Anthony
Aikens, Alexander E., III
Allen, Mark S.
Allen, Eugene, Jr.
Allison, Verne
Albert, Charles Gregory
Anderson, Ronald Gene
Anderson, George A.
Anderson, Dr. Barbara Stewart Jenkins
Anderson, Miller R.
Anderson, Nick
Atwater, Stephen Dennis
Bates, Barbara Ann
Bailey, Duwain
Ball-Reed, Hon. Patrice M.
Banks, Paula A.
Barksdale, Chuck
Baisden, Michael
Baiocchi, Regina A. Harris
Barnett, Amy DuBois
Banks, Alicia
Bailey, Dr. Adrienne Yvonne
Baker, Roland Charles
Ball, Dr. Wilfred R.
Banks, Ronald
Bailey, Ronald T.
Bell, Janet Sharon
Bell, Dr. Carl Compton
Belle, Charles E.

Robinson, Jack A, Jr.
Rogers, George
Roper, Bobby L.
Robinson, Renault Alvin
Rodez, Andrew LaMarr
Robinson, Kenneth
Rockett, Damon Emerson
Robinson, Robin
Roberts, Angela Dorrean
Robinson-Jacobs, Karen Denise
Rogers, John W., Jr.
Rodgers, Carolyn Marie
Robinson, Malcolm S.
Savage, Janet Marie
Salaam, Ephraim Mateen
Savage, William Arthur
Saunders, Vincent E., III
Sawyer, Roderick Terrence
Salone, Marcus R.
Salter, Roger Franklin, Sr.
Samuels, Ronald S.
Sagers, Rudolph, Jr.
Scott-Clayton, Dr. Patricia Ann
Scott, Michael W., Sr.
Sengstacke, Bobby
Seals, Theodore Hollis
Segree, E. Ramone
Shaw, Bernard
Shepherd, Malcolm Thomas
Sharpe, Shannon
Shepherd-Tarpley, Sherri
Shackelford, William G., Jr.
Short, Prof. Kenneth L.
Simmons, James Richard
Simpson, Carole
Singleton, Harold, III
Singleton, Rickey
Sims, Robert
Simmons, Tony DeAngelo
Simmons, Geraldine Crossley
Skinner, Robert L., Jr.
Smith, Robert D.
Smith, Rev. Harold Gregory
Smith, Fronse Wayne, Sr.
Smith, Tangela Nicole
Smith, Kellita
Smith, Dr. Donald Hugh
Smith, LeRoi Matthew-Pierre, III
Smith, Dr. Allen Joseph, Sr.
Smith, Dr. Elmer G., Jr.
Smith, Lonnie
South, Leslie Elaine
Soliunas, Francine Stewart
Spurlock, Dr. Oliver M.
Spivey, Dr. Donald
Stokes, Dr. Gerald Virgil
Stevens, Sharon A.
Stricklin, James
Stewart, Ruth Ann
Stewart, Dr. Donald Mitchell
Steele, Dr. Claude Mason
Stevens, Michelle
Stepto, Robert Burns
Steele, Dr. Shelby
Sterling, Dr. Jeffrey Emery
Staples, Mavis
Strautmanis, Michael A.
Steward, David L.
Staggers, Robin L.
Sutton, Norma J.
Tarpley, Natasha Anastasia
Tate, Larenz
Terrell, Dr. Melvin Cleveland
Terrell, Frederick O.
Teruel, Lauren
Thompson, Donald
Thomas, Deon La Velle
Thurman, Cedric Douglas
Thomas, Isiah Lord, III
Thompson, Lowell Dennis
Thurston, William A.
Tillman, Paula Sellars
Townsel, Ronald P.
Townsend, Andre S.
Townsend, Robert
Todd, Beverly
Truitt, Kevin
Turner, Harry Glenn
Turner, Dr. Castellano Blanchet
Tureaud, Lawrence
Tyler, Selma L. Dodson
Vance, Lawrence N.
Vargus, Bill
Vaughans, Kirkland Cornell
Valentine, Darnell Terrell
Van Peebles, Melvin
Vincent, Marjorie Judith
Watley, Jody Vanessa
Ward, Calvin
Warmack, Kevin Lavon
Wade, Joyce K.
Washington, James A.
Walker, Charles
Waller, Ruby Larry
Warfield, Marsha Francine
Washington, William
Watson, Tony J.
Walters, Ronald L., Jr.
Washington, Ben James, Jr.
Wayne, Nate
Walker, Antoine Devon
Washington, Robin
Warren, Dorian T.
Wade, Dwyane
Walker, Grover Pulliam
Washington, Consuela M.
Walker, Stanley Michael
Ward, Hon. Doris Margaret
Wallace, C. Everett
Watson, Dr. Clyniece Lois
Walker, Darrell
Washington, Dr. Earl Melvin
Ware, Dyahanne
Walker, Allene Marsha
Weiss, Dr. Joyce Lacey
Welsing, Dr. Frances Cress
Webb, Wellington E.
West, Cheryl L.
Webb, Dr. Joseph G.
White, Richard H.
White, Deidre R.
Whitehurst, Steven Laroy
Wheelan, Belle Smith
Wilson, Cleo Francine
Wiley, Dr. Fletcher Houston
Wimp, Edward Lawson
Winfield, Arnold F.
Williams, Edward Joseph
Williams, Dr. David George
Williams, Donald H.
Williams, Theodore W., Jr.
Wilson, Velma J.
Winslow, Kenneth Paul
Wilkins, David Brian
Williams, Herb E.
Wilson, Dr. Joseph F.
Williams, W. Bill
Williams, Dr. Eddie Robert
Williams, Hope Denise Walker
Williams, Deborah A.
Williams, Cynda
Williams, Carol H.
Williams, Frank James
Woods, Alison Scott
Worsham, James E.
Wood, Hon. William S.
Wooldridge, David, Sr.
Woodford, John Niles
Wright, Dawin Lyron
Wynn, Renaldo Levalle
Wynne, Marvell
Yarbrough, Nana Camille
Young, Donald Oliver, Jr.
Young, Donald
Young, Ernest Wesley
York, Dr. Russel Harold
Young, Alan John
Zollar, Esq. Nikki Michele

### Chicago Heights
Gavin, L. Katherine
McIntosh, Rhodina Covington
Pate, John W., Sr.
Penn, Algernon H.
Whittler, Dr. Tommy E.
Young, Bryant Colby

### Colp
Bowen, Richard, Jr.

### Corapeake
Eure, Dr. Herman Edward

### Danville
Brooks, Rev. Clyde Henry
Clark, Keon Arian
Hutchins, Jan Darwin
Weaver, Reginald Lee
Wilson, Bryan
Young, B. Ashley

### Decatur
Day, Todd Fitzgerald
Ford, Deborah Lee
Jones, Dr. Marcus Earl
McClendon, Bishop Clarence E.

### DuQuoin
Livingston-White, Dr. Deborah J. H.

### E Moline
Posten, Hon. William S., Sr.

### East Chicago
Jackson, Raymond DeWayne

### East St. Louis
Bush, Homer Giles
Cox, Bryan Keith
Daniel, Mary Reed
Ellis, LaPhonso Darnell
Higgins, Clarence R., Jr.
Hunt, Dr. Portia L.
Joyner-Kersee, Jackie
King, Hulas H.
Lawrence, Archie L.
Manager, Vada O.
Pleas, Dr. John Roland
Powell, Debra A.
Randolph, Dr. Robert Lee
Redmond, Dr. Eugene B.
Rosser, Dr. James M.
Scaggs, Dr. Edward W.
Smith, Marie F.
Thompson, Derrick

### Edwardsville
Van Trece, Jackson C.

### Elgin
Smith, Donald M.

### Elmhurst
Gavin, Mary Ann

### Eureka
Albers, Kenneth Lynn

### Evanston
Cheeks, Darryl Lamont
Ellis-Simon, Amy
Green, Lisa R.
Johnson, Charles Richard
Johnson, Bennett J.
Jones, Damon S.
Moore, Ralph G.
Moragne, Lenora
Moragne, Dr. Rudolph
Posey, John R., Jr.
Roy, Jan S.
Thomas, Charles Richard
Williams, Aaron

### Freeport
Johnson, Jerry L.
Pearson, Preston James

### Galena
Wynn, LaMetta K.

### Galesburg
Forney, Mary Jane
Hendricks, Leta

### Glenwood
Walker, Derrick Norval

### Great Lakes
Chase, Debra Martin

### Greater Lakes
Chase, Debra Martin

### Harrisburg
Jordan, Thurman

### Harvey
Curry, Eddy Anthony, Jr.
Gardner, Barry Allan
Smith, Anthony Edward
Whack, Rita Coburn

### Highland Park
Bateman, Paul E.
Thomas, Rodolfo Rudy

### Jacksonville
Berry, Fredrick Joseph
White, Nan Elizabeth
Williams, Paul

### Joliet
Nesby, Ann

### Kankakee
Morrow, Laverne

### Kewanee
Davis, Robert N.

### Lake Cormorant
Varner, Dr. Nellie M.

### Lake Forest
Richards, DeLeon Marie

### Lockport
Smith, Dolores J.

### Markham
Harrison, Rodney Scott

### Matteson
Streets, Tai Lamarr

### Maywood
Brewer, Jim
Dillenberger, R. Jean
Kunes, Kenneth R.
Linyard, Richard

### Melrose Park
Finley, Michael Howard

### Metropolis
Blackwell, Patricia A.
McGuffin, Dorothy Brown
Stalls, Dr. Madlyn A.

### Moline
Collins, James H.
Johnson, Geraldine Ross

### Monmouth
Wallace, Charles Leslie

### Mound City
Coatie, Robert Mason
Jackson, Frank

### Mounds
England, Dr. Rodney Wayne
Frazier, Dr. Wynetta Artricia

### Murphysboro
Jordan, Leroy A.
Sutton, Wilma Jean

### Naperville
Hairston, Jerry Wayne, Jr.
Parker, Anthony Michael

### North Chicago
Coleman, Dennis

### Park Forest
Hodges, Craig Anthony

### Peoria
Alexander, Dr. Drew W.
Arbuckle, John Finley, Jr.
Ashmore, Darryl Allan
Earl, Acie Boyd
Leatherwood, Larry Lee
Ransom, Dr. Preston L.
Todd, Cynthia Jean

### Phoenix
Buckner, Quinn

### Plainfield
Morton, Karen Victoria

### Quincy
Bryson, Seymour L.
Robinson, Denauvo M.

### Rantoul
McCaa, John K.

### Robbins
Montgomery, Joseph, Jr.
Nichols, Nichelle

### Rock Island
Keys, Madison
Lomas, Dr. Ronald Leroy
Washington, Dr. Thomas

### Rockford
Blevins, Tony
Blake, John Patrick
Box, Dr. Charles
Gentry, Nolden I., Jr.
Renick, Dr. James Carmichael
Roby, Kimberla Lawson
Williams, Michelle
Winslow, Cleta Meris

### Sidney
Foster, Ivadale Marie Foulks

### Springfield
Allen, Bettie Jean
Ball, Richard E.
Brown, Dr. Ronald Edward
Cummings, Theresa Faith
Gothard, Dr. Barbara Wheatley
Hill, Dr. Bonnie Guiton
Hickman, Frederick Douglass
Jackson, Keith M.
Logan, Willis Hubert
Meek, Dr. Russell Charles
Morrison, Dr. Rev. Juan LaRue, Sr.
Stewart, John Ogden
Trees, Candice D.
Williams, Annie

### St. Louis
Crawford, Rainey James
McHenry, Donald F.
O'Flynn-Pattillo, Patricia

### Streator
Jaynes, Dr. Gerald David

### Urbana
Sievers, Eric Scott

### Venice
Williams, Rev. John Henry

### Waukegan
Brown, Jarvis Ardel
Hankins, Dr. Andrew Jay, Jr.
Massey, Brandon
McKinney, Billy
Morris, Earl Scott
Pickles, Dr. Patricia L.
Taylor, Dr. Jerome
Thomas, Hon. Mary Maxwell

### Woodlawn
Jones, Jennie Y.

## INDIANA

### Anderson
Allensworth, Jermaine LaMont
Greenwood, Dr. Charles H.
Landers, Naaman Garnett, Jr.
Steans, Edith Elizabeth

### Bedford
Brashear, Donald Maynard

### Bloomington
Bradley, Philip Poole

### Booneville
Harvey, Rev. Dr. Wardelle G., Sr.

### Brazil
White, Paul Edward

### East Chicago
Biblo, Mary
Blalock, Marion W.
Bridgeman, Junior
Brandford, Napoleon, III
Brownlee, Dr. Geraldine Daniels
Comer, Dr. James Pierpont
Comer, Dr. Norman David, Sr.
Davis, Reginald Francis
Holt, Deloris Lenette
Lee, Dr. Guy Milicon, Jr.
Lofton, Kenny
Pettis, Bridget
Simpson-Watson, Dr. Ora Lee
Thomas, Kendall

### Elkhart
Kemp, Shawn T.
Vinson, Chuck Rallen

### Nicodemus
Switzer, Veryl A., Sr.

### Oakley
Henderson, Frank S., Jr.

### Olathe
Davis, Donald Earl, Jr.

### Oskaloosa
Reynolds, James

### Parsons
Tipton, Dr. Dale Leo
Watkins, Donald V.

### Pittsburg
Hutton, Gerald L.

### Salina
Newman, Terence
Parker, James L.

### Tonganoxie
Matthews, Robert L.

### Topeka
Anderson, Joseph B., Jr.
Bugg, Robert L.
Douglas, Joe, Jr.
Evans, Patricia P.
Ewing, Samuel Daniel
Henderson, Cheryl Brown
Hill, Jacqueline R.
Kluge, Pamela Hollie
Nightingale-Hawkins, Monica R.
Phelps, Constance Kay
Powers, Ray
Slaughter, Dr. John Brooks
Taylor, Dr. Dale B.
Williams, Ruby Mai
Winters, Jacqueline F.

### Weir City
King, Dr. Delutha Porter Harold, Jr.

### Wichita
Bacon-Bercey, June Esther
Coleman, Barbara Sims
Davis, Wendell
Eubanks, Dayna C.
Evans, Kamiel Denise
James, Kevin Porter
Johnson, Sharon Reed
Pitts, Dr. Vera L.
Sayers, Gale Eugene
Sanders, Barry David
Terry, Adeline Helen
Wesley, Barbara Ann
Woodard, Lynette
Young, Korleone

## KENTUCKY

### Almo
Washington, Edith Stubblefield

### Ashland
Lee, Aubrey Walter, Jr.
Lottier, Patricia Ann

### Barbourville
Gregory, Michael Samuel

### Beaver Dam
Baugh, Florence Ellen

### Benham
Bickerstaff, Bernard Tyrone, Sr.
McDonald, Jeffrey Bernard

### Bowling Green
Austin, Dr. Bobby William
Denning, Joe William
Hayden, Rev. Dr. John Carleton
Haskins, Clemette L.
Nichols, George

### Campbellsville
Haskins, Clem Smith

### Christian County
Richardson, Dr. Mary Margaret

### Clinton
Dillard, Howard Lee

### Covington
McCrimon, Audrey L.

### Danville
Griffin, Dr. Betty Sue

### Earlington
Johnson, Arthur T.
Owens, Dr. Jerry Sue
Washington, Rev. Henry L.

### Frankfort
Fields, William I., Jr.
Wolfe, George Costello

### Franklin
Neal, Dr. Homer Alfred

### Ft. Campbell
Jordan, Dr. Eddie J., Jr.
Massey, Dr. Rev. Selma Diane Redd

### Ft. Knox
Brown, Dr. Glenn Arthur
Caldwell, Dr. Sandra Ishmael
Parks, Suzan-Lori

### Garrard County
Smith, Joshua Isaac

### Georgetown
Mason, Luther Roscoe

### Glasgow
Murrell, Dr. Peter C., Sr.

### Greenup
Hunter, Cecil Thomas

### Guthrie
Warfield, Robert N.

### Hardinsburg
Beard, Butch, Jr.

### Harlan
Meeks, Willis Gene
Young, Mary E.

### Harrodsburg
Dunn, Jason Adam

### Hazard
Olinger, David Y., Jr.

### Hickman
Daniels, Lincoln S., Sr.

### Hopkinsville
Burse, Dr. Luther, Sr.
Burse, Raymond Malcolm
Coleman, Robert A.
Davie, Timothy M.
Luney, Percy R., Jr.
McCombs, Tony
Pettigrew, Dr. L. Eudora
Whitney, Christopher Antoine

### Horse Cave
Golightly, Lena Mills

### Jenkins
Cummings, Dr. Jay R.

### Lancaster
Francis, Delma J.

### Lexington
Cook, Elizabeth G.
Finn, John William
Gay, Tyson
Higgins, Chester Archer, Jr.
Jefferson, Robert R.
Jones, Gayl
Lyons, Donald Wallace, Sr.
Merchant, Esq. John Cruse
Ray, Prof. William Benjamin, Sr.
Smith, Rev. Otis Benton, Jr.
Smith, Prof. Andrew W.
Smith, Dr. Gerald Lamont
Wilkinson, Dr. Doris
Woods, Melvin LeRoy
Wright, Dr. George C.

### Logan County
Washington, Edward, Jr.

### Louisville
Abernathy, Ronald Lee
Adams, Dr. Carol Laurence
Alexander, Dr. Estella Conwill
Ali, Muhammad
Anderson, Carey Laine, Jr.
Anderson, Derek Lamont
Appleton, Clevette Wilma
Baker, Dr. Houston Alfred, Jr.
Baldon, Janice C.
Brazley, Dr. Michael Duwain
Bright, Kirk
Brown, Beverly J.
Brummer, Chauncey Eugene
Brown, Rev. Dr. Beatrice S.
Caldwell, James E.
Carter, Kenneth Gregory
Chatmon, Linda Carol
Clay, Timothy Byron
Cowden, Michael E.
Conwill, Giles
Conwill, Dr. William Louis
Conwill, Dr. Houston Eugene
Davidson, Rudolph Douglas
Daniel, Hon. Wiley Young
Dishman, Cris Edward
Elmore, Dr. Ronn
Garnett, Ronald Leon
Grundy, Chester
Griffith, Darrell Steven
Harrison, Lisa Darlene
Haines, Charles Edward
Hardin, Dr. John
Henderson, Angelo B.
Hines, Carl R., Sr.
Holmes, Robert Kathrone, Jr.
Hopkins, Telma Louise
Houston, Allan Wade
House, Michael A.
Jackson, Pamela J.
Johnson, John J.
Johnson, Jay
Lanier, Shelby, Jr.
Lanier, Anthony Wayne
Lewis, Sherman Paul
Lomax, Janet E.
Majozo, Estella Conwill
Malone, Claudine Berkeley
McReynolds, Elaine A.
McClain, Dr. Paula Denice
McDonald, Larry Marvin
Meaux, Ronald
Meeks, Reginald Kline
Payne, Margaret Ralston
Paris, William H., Jr.
Richardson, Rhonda Karen
Robinson, Ronnie W.
Robinson, Dr. Sharon Porter
Shockley, Ann Allen
Shannon, John William
Smith, Carson Eugene
Spencer, Felton LaFrance
Summers, William E., IV
Sumner, Thomas Robert
Taylor, Kimberly Hayes
Thornton, Dr. John C.
Unseld, Wes
Upshaw, Sam, Jr.
Wheat, DeJuan Shontez
Wilkins, Charles O.
Williams, Harold L., Jr.
Williams, Dr. Jamye Coleman
Woodson, Charles R.
Worshaim, Keith Eugene
Young, Dr. Coleman Milton, III

### Lynch
Jackson, Lee Arthur
Turner, Mark Anthony
Turner, Dr. William Hobert

### Madisonville
Lowery, Michael Douglas
Sharp, Charles Louis

### Mayfield
Thurman, Alfonzo

### Mays Lick
Franklin, Dr. Herman

### Middlesboro
Martin, Charles Wesley

### Monticello
Craft, Dr. Thomas J., Sr.
Kendrick, L. John, Sr.

### Morganfield
Martin, Hon. Janice R.

### Nickolasville
Jarrett-Jackson, Mary Francis

### Noraville
Hampton, Kym

### Owensboro
Moore, George Thomas
Rates, Rev. Dr. Norman M.

### Paducah
Shumpert, Terrance Darnell
Williams, Dr. Lea E.

### Paris
Ecton, Virgil E.
Jackson, Earl, Jr.
Russell, Dr. Leonard Alonzo

### Pembroke
Archer, Susie Coleman

### Princeton
Bumphus, Dr. Walter Gayle
Edwards, Dr. Abiyah, Jr.

### Providence
Moss, Estella Mae

### Richmond
Dudley, Herman T.

### Russellville
Cage, Athena

### Scottsville
Starks, Rick H.

### Shelby County
Groves, Dr. Delores Ellis

### Shelbyville
Payne, Mitchell Howard
Seals, Rupert Grant

### Shreveport
Williams, Robert Lee

### Somerset
Lewis, James R.

### Springfield
Powers, Georgia M.

### Stanford
Bond, Howard H.

### Sturgis
Chivers, Gwendolyn Ann

### Versailles
Branch, Calvin Stanley
Stepp, Marc
Steppe, Cecil H.

### Waverly Hills
Ballard, Dr. Bruce Laine

### West Bend
Gatewood, Dr. Wallace Lavell

### Winchester
Bell, Dr. Winston Alonzo
Hackett, Wilbur L.

## LOUISIANA

### Abbeville
Mitchell, Brandon

### Alexandria
Breda, Dr. Malcolm J.
Desselle, Natalie
Fontenot, Rev. Albert E., Jr.
Hayward, Olga Loretta Hines
Isadore, Dr. Harold W.
Merenivitch, Jarrow
Newell, Kathleen W.
Ollee, Mildred W.
Smith, Heman Bernard, Jr.
Venson, Clyde R.
Wilson, Jerry Lee, Jr.

### Amite
Atkins, James Curtis
Porter, Rufus
Reed, Clarence Hammit, III

### Archie
Martin, Rev. Dr. Lawrence Raymond

### Basile
LeDay, John Austin

### Bastrop
Bell, Dr. Robert L.
Coleman, Ronnald Dean
Davis, Nigel S.
Hamlin, Arthur Henry
John, Dr. Mable
Johnson, Walter Louis, Sr.
Love, Robert Earl
Sawyer, Talance Marche
Simmons, Thelma M.
Smith, John L., Jr.

### Baton Rouge
Baranco, Dr. Raphael Alvin
Bernard, Donald L.
Bradford, Corey Lamon
Breaux, Timothy
Brown, Reginald Royce, Sr.
Butler, Michael Keith
Byrd, Camolia Alcorn
Carter, Alphonse Haley
Carpenter, Dr. Barbara West
Chaney, Donald Ray
Cox, Dr. Sandra Hicks
Davis, Dr. Donald Fred
Daniel, Eugene, Jr.
Delpit, Dr. Lisa Denise
Delpit, Joseph A.
Dunn, Warrick De'Mon
Fields, Cleo
Green, Brenda Kay
Hamilton, Roy L.
Hall, Delilah Ridley
Hebert, Stanley Paul, III
Hicks, Dr. Rev. H. Beecher, Jr.
Hollins, Prof. Joseph Edward
Houston, Dr. Alice Vivian
Jackson, Randy
Judge, Dr. Paul Qantas
Kelly, Marion Greenup
Kraft, Dr. Benjamin F.
Lemon, Don
Mencer, Dr. Ernest James
Moody, Dr. Charles David, Sr.
Mullen, Roderick Louis
Northern, Gabriel O' Kara
Norwood, Dr. Tom
Patin, Dr. Joseph Patrick
Patin, Jude W. P.
Pitcher, Judge Freddie, Jr.
Posey, Bruce Keith
Poindexter, Hon. Gammiel Gray
Profit, Eugene A.
Raby, Clyde T.
Ricard, Rev. John Huston
Rotan, Dr. Constance S.
Robinson, Dr. Rufus E.
Shine, Theodis
Sowell, Jerald Monye
Spears, Marcus Raishon
Stampley, Gilbert Elvin
Whitfield, Lynn C.
Wiley, Chuck, Jr.
Winfield, William T.
Williams, Elynor A.
Williams, Dr. Karen Renee

### Belle Rose
Larvadain, Edward, Jr.

### Benton
Jones, Dr. Howard James
Smith, Prof. Robert Charles

### Bernice
Montgomery, Rev. Payne

### Bogalusa
Komunyakaa, Yusef
Mims, Pastor Raymond Everett, Sr.

### Bon Ami
Cade, Harold Edward

### Bossier City
Ballard, Dr. Billy Ray

Robinson, Larry

### Boyce
Metoyer, Rosia G.

### Breaux Bridge
Alexander, Dr. Livingston
Marsalis, Branford
Thibodeaux, Sylvia Marie, Sr.

### Bunkie
Clark, Leon Stanley
Durand, Winsley O., Jr.
Sheppard, Stevenson Royrayson

### Burnside
Ward, Douglas Turner

### Charenton
Pierre, Dr. Dallas

### Claiborne Parish
Johnson, John Will

### Clinton
London, Gloria D.
Talbert, Melvin George

### Collinston
Jones, Dr. Vida Yvonne
Williams, Brandon D.

### Columbia
Rush, Sonya C.

### Cotton Port
Jackson, Dr. Roy Joseph, Jr.

### Cotton Valley
Underwood, Maude Esther

### Coushatta
Johnson, Vickie Annette

### Crowley
Jackson, W. Sherman
Paddio-Johnson, Dr. Eunice Alice
Thomas, Orlando Paul

### Cullen
Mendenhall, John Rufus

### Curtis
Nelson, Dr. Ivory V.

### Delhi
Salter, Kwame S.

### DeQuincy
Brown, Abner Bertrand
Dorsey, Ivory
Pattillo, Roland A.
Warner, Isiah Manuel

### Deridder
Morris, Elise Lenoir

### Donaldsonville
Buggage, Cynthia Marie
Johnson, Bernette Joshua
Morgan, Robert, Jr.

### Duboc
Wilks, Gertrude

### Dubuisson
Brooks, Lonnie

### Ethel
Taylor, William Henry, Sr.

### Eunice
James, Eldridge M.

### Farmerville
Roberts, Charles L.

### Ferriday
Johnson, Ernest L.

### Fort Polk
Mitchell, Brian Keith

### Franklin
Marshall, Leonard Allen, Jr.
Middleton, Dr. Ernest J.
Nelson, Dr. Wanda Lee

### Franklin Parish
Williams, Moses, Sr.

### Franklinton
Martin, Rayfus

### Gibsland
Days, Rosetta Hill

### Gibson
Smith, Dr. John Raye

### Gilbert
Johnson, Hermon M., Sr.
Watson, Genevieve

### Grambling
Watts, Dr. Anne Wimbush

### Gramercy
Harvey, Jacqueline V.

### Grand Coteau
Malbroue, Joseph, Jr.

### Hammond
Chester, Larry Travis
Robinson, Dr. Edward Ashton, III
Sanders, Larry Kyle

### Haughton
Baker, Myron Tobias

### Heflin
Bolen, David B.

### Hodge
Perry, Emma Bradford

### Homer
Barnes, Matthew Molena, Jr.
Davis, Bettye J.
Ford, Cheryl
Moss, Wilmar Burnett

### Houma
Gray, Valerie Hamilton

### Independence
Ross, Emma Jean
Williams, Dr. Willie, Jr.

### Iota
Jones, Zoia L.

### Jena
Walker, Dwayne M.

### Jones
Smith, Gloria Dawn

### Jonesboro
Bradford, James Edward
Wilber, Ida Belinda
Zeno, Hon. Melvin Collins

### Jonesville
Welch, Jesse Roy

### Keatchie
Ransburg, Frank S.

### Kelly
Moorehead, Bobbie Wooten

### Lafayette
Benoit, David
Belson, Jerry
Caillier, James Allen
Clement, Anthony George
Cooper, Jerome Gary
Edgar, Jacqueline L.
Francis, Dr. Norman C.
Johnson-Blount, Theresa
Mouton, Lyle Joseph
Paddio, Gerald James
Prudhomme, Dr. Nellie Rose
Rose, Bessie L.
Rubin, Chanda
Sam, Sheri Lynette
Senegal, Rev. Nolton Joseph, Sr.
Skipper, Clarence, III
Smith, Judy Seriale
St Julien, Marlon
Taylor, Vanessa Gail

### Lake Charles
Anderson, Rosaland Guidry
Boutte, Marc Anthony
Brown-Guillory, Elizabeth
Carrier, Mark Anthony, III
Charles, Joseph C.
Clemons, James Albert, III
Gray, Johnnie Lee
Guillory, Linda Semien
Harris, J. Robert
Johnson, Norman B.
Kennison, Eddie Joseph, III
Kirk-Duggan, Rev. Dr. Cheryl Ann
LeDoux, Rev. Jerome G.
Pappillion, Glenda M.
Richardson, Odis Gene
Schexnider, Dr. Alvin J.
Shelton, Harold Tillman
Wilson, Floyd Edward, Jr.

### Lake Providence
Atlas, Dr. John Wesley
Calvin, Dr. Virginia Brown
Frazier, Ray Jerrell
Griffin, Leonard James, Jr.
Jefferson, Hon. William Jennings
Marshall, H. Jean
Scott, Dr. Elsie L.

### Laplace
Bernard, Dr. Louis Joseph

### Laurel Hill
Jones, Johnnie Anderson, Sr.

### Lawtell
LaVergne, Hon. Luke Aldon
Rideau, Wibert

### LeCompte
Sykes, Ray A., III
Webster, Dr. Charles L.

### Leesville
Wilson, J. Ray

### Lemoine
Hegger, Wilber L.

### Lettsworth
Guy, Buddy

### Lincoln Parish
Reed, Willis, Jr.

### Lisbon
Davis, William Delford

### Longstreet
Lofton, Andrew James
Simton, Chester

### Louisiana
Foster, Ezola Broussard

### Lutcher
Steptoe, Sonja
Wilderson, Dr. Frank B., Jr.

### Mansfield
Blue, Vida Rochelle, Jr.
Cox, Corine G.
Durant, Dr. Thomas James
Lewis, Albert Ray
Paul, Vera Maxine
Simpkins, Dr. Cuthbert Ormond, Sr.

### Mansura
Lehman, Dr. Paul Robert

### Many
Hadden, Eddie Raynord
Joiner, Charles, Jr.

### Maringouin
Scott, Benjamin
Stewart, Joseph M.

### Marion
Sims-Davis, Edith R.

### Marksville
Cadoria, Brigadier Gen. Sherian Grace

### Marthaville
Fisher, Lloyd B.
Mack, Ally Faye

### Martinville
Garrett, Aline Mae

### Melrose
Williams, Dr. E. Faye

### Milton
Landry, L. Bartholomew

### Minden
Moore, Rev. Dr. Jerry Alexander, Jr.
Pierce, Walter J., Sr.

### Monroe
Anderson, Stevie Darrell
Blackwell, Faye Brown
Boyd, Barbara Jean
Carson, Irma
Davis, Belva
Garrett, Louis Henry
Grigsby, Alice Burns
Haynes, Dr. John Kermit
Harris, Dr. Betty Wright
Higgins, Roderick Dwayne
Lewis, Dr. Lyn Etta
Mills, Rev. Dr. Larry Glenn
Natt, Kenny
Peoples, VerJanis Andrews
Petett, Dr. Freddye J. Webb
Pierce, Dr. Raymond O., Jr.
Pierce, Abe E., III
Powell, Elaine
Richardson, Dr. Elisha Roscoe
Turner, Ervin
Williams, Patrick

### Montgomery
Brossette, Alvin, Jr.

### Moreauville
Duper, Mark Super

### Morgan City
Dar, Kirby David Dar
Johnson, Dave M.
London, Eddie

### Mt. Hermon
Cryer, Dr. Linkston T., Jr.

### Napoleonville
Jones, Dr. Leslie Faye
King, Dr. Wesley A.

### Natchitoches
Braxton, Rev. Steve
Young, Rev. Jimmy Ray

### New Iberia
Borders, Florence Edwards
Brooks, Norward J.
Jackson, Dr. Edward R.
Joseph, Kerry
LeMelle, Tilden J.
Lowery, Carolyn T.

### New Orleans
Adams, Bennie
Allain, Stephanie
Allen, Charles Edward
Alexander, Dr. Laurence Benedict
Albert, Donnie Ray
Allen, Percy, II
Ambrose, Ashley Avery
Armstrong, Joan Bernard
Augustus, Franklin J. P.
Batiste, Kimothy Emil
Barrois, Lyndon J.
Barnes, Lionel, Jr.
Bates, Lionel Ray, Sr.
Ballard, Dr. Harold Stanley
Barnes, Fannie Burrell
Barthelemy, Sidney John
Bacon, Dr. Gloria Jackson
Bechet, Ronald
Bishop, Esq. Wesley T.
Birch, Willie
Birchette-Pierce, Dr. Cheryl L.
Block, Carolyn B.
Blanc, Eric Anthony-Hawkins
Bocage, Esq. Ronald Joseph
Boyce, Joseph Nelson
Bouie, Tony Vanderson
Bonner, Alice A.
Borden, Harold F., Jr.
Broussard, Arnold Anthony
Brown, Brigadier Gen. Dallas C., Jr.
Bremer, Charles E.
Bronz, Hon. Lois Gougis Taplin
Brown, Warren Aloysius
Brazile, Donna L.
Brister, Bishop Darryl Sylvester
Butler, Dr. John Sibley
Burchell, Dr. Charles R.
Butler, Oliver Richard
Cates, Hon. Sidney Hayward, IV
Cayou, Nontsizi Kirton
Carter, Troy A.
Chatman, Dr. Donald Leveritt
Charbonnet, Louis, III
Clanton, Dr. Lemuel Jacque
Clark, Edward
Coulon, Burnel Elton, II
Copelin, Sherman Nathaniel, Jr.
Collins, Robert Frederick
Coaston, Shirley Ann Dumas
Coleman, Rev. Dr. DeeDee M.
Crusto, Mitchell Ferdinand
Davis, Darlene Rose
Davis, Harold
Davis, Anthony R.
Dalferes, Edward R., Jr.
Davis, Bunny Coleman
Dejoie, Carolyn Barnes Milanes
Dejoie, Michael C.
Dillon, Vermon Lemar
Donald, Arnold Wayne
Douglas, Omar
Doan, Lurita Alexis
Donald, Arnold W.
Dorsey, John L., Jr.
Doley, Ambassador Harold E., Jr.
Domino, Fats, Jr.
Drexler, Clyde Austin
Dupre, Dr. John Lionel
Earles, Dr. Rene Martin
Eaton, Thelma Lucile
Edwards, Preston Joseph, Sr.
Edwards, Monique Marie
Ellis, Johnell A.
Epps, Anna Cherrie
Eugere, Edward J.
Faulk, Marshall William
Ferdinand, Dr. Keith C.
Fletcher, Milton Eric
Foster, Janice Martin
Francis, Dr. Cheryl Margaret
Francisco, Joseph Salvadore
Francis, Patrick John
Gaspard, Dr. Patrice Theresa
Garnier, Thomas Joseph
Garibaldi, Dr. Antoine Michael
Germany, Sylvia Marie Armstrong
Gilbert, Dr. Fred D., Jr.
Gibson, Betty M.
Glapion, Michael J.
Glover, Andrew Lee
Goins, Atty. Richard Anthony
Green, Hydia Lutrice
Green, Alexander N.
Graves, Curtis M.
Gumbel, Bryant Charles
Guillory, Dr. William A.
Guillaume, Dr. Alfred Joseph, Jr.
Gumbel, Greg
Haynes, Michael David
Hayes, Melvin Anthony
Hambrick, Harold E., Jr.
Harris, William H., Jr.
Henderson, Dr. Lenneal Joseph
Hilliard, Randy
Higginbotham, Dr. Eve Juliet
Holden, Melvin Lee
Howard, Jules Joseph, Jr.
Hoard, Leroy J.
Hogan, Carolyn Ann
Houze, Jeneice Carmel Wong
Hollowell, Johnny Laveral
Hughes, Tyrone Christopher
Hypolite, Dr. Christine
Irons, Hon. Paulette R.
James, Tory Steven
Jackson, Jaren
Jackson, Garnet Nelson
Jackson, Ronald G., Jr.
Jackson, Johnny, Jr.
Jackson, Audrey Nabors
Jefferson, Dr. Frederick Carl, Jr.
Jefferson, Dr. Andrea Green
Jefferson-Bullock, Jalila Eshe
Jordan, Atty. Eddie Jack, Jr.
Johnson, Ervin, Jr.
Jolivet, Linda Catherine
Johnson, Avery
Jolly, Mary B.
Johnson, Troy Dwan

Jones, Nathaniel, Sr.
Jordan, Marjorie W.
Jones, Albert Allen
Johnson, Dr. Lucien Love
Johnson, Dr. Joseph B.
Johnson, Dr. Cage Saul
Jupiter, Clyde Peter
Kazi, Abdul-Khaliq Kuumba
Keller, Dr. Edmond Joseph
Kelly, John Paul, Jr.
King, Dr. Richard Devoid
King, Gerard
Laneuville, Eric Gerard
Lawson, Bruce Benjamin
LaCour, Nathaniel Hawthorne
Lambert, Dr. Violet Theresa Early
Lee, Dr. Silas H., III
LeCesne, Terrel M.
Lewis, Dr. Felton Edwin
Lewis, Dr. Samella Sanders
Lee, Robert Emile
LeCesne, Alvarez, Jr.
Livingston, Randy Anthony
Lipps, Louis Adam, Jr.
Lundy, Larry
Marsalis, Ellis Louis, Jr.
Marchand, Melanie Annette
Martin-Ogunsola, Dellita Lillian
Marts, Lonnie, Jr.
Mackie, Dr. Calvin
Massey, Dr. Janelle Renee
Marsalis, Delfeayo
Mackie, Timothy
Marsalis, Jason
Matthews, Leonard Louis
Magee, Dr. Robert Walter
Marsalis, Wynton Learson
McKenna, Dr. George J., III
McDonald, Alden J., Jr.
McPherson, Rosalyn J.
Miller, Percy Romeo, Jr.
Miller, Percy Robert
Mitchell, Melvin Lester
Mitchell, Dr. Earl Douglass, Jr.
Morris, Garrett Gonzalez
Morial, Sybil Haydel
Morial, Dr. Marc Haydel
Moore, Juliette R.
Mosley, Carolyn W.
Morgan, Dolores Parker
Nagin, Clarence Ray, Jr.
Neville, Aaron
Pack, Robert John, Jr.
Payton, Nicholas
Patterson, Rev. Alonzo B., Jr.
Patnett, John Henry
Perkins, Charles Windell
Peters, Charles L., Jr.
Perry, Tyler
Pittman, Michael
Polk, Anthony Joseph
Pryor, Lillian W.
Reid, Hon. Inez Smith
Reed, Dr. Rodney J.
Recasner, Eldridge David
Rhodes, Dr. Paula R.
Riley, Dr. Wayne Joseph
Richard, Alvin J.
Rideau, Iris
Rogers, Desiree Glapion
Roche, Joyce M.
Robinson, Eddie Joseph, Jr.
Robinson, Dr. Harry, Jr.
Royal, Donald Adam
Roux, Dr. Vincent J., Sr.
Robinson, Dr. Sandra Lawson
Ruffin, John
Ryan, Marsha Ann
Sanders, Barbara A.
Sergent, Ernest E., Jr.
Sergeant, Carra Susan
Sigur, Wanda Anne Alexander
Singleton, Ernie
Singleton, Nate, III
Smith, Otis, III
Smith-Smith, Peola
Smith, Guy Lincoln
Smith, Leonard Phillip
Smith, Neil
Smith, Dr. Robert P., Jr.
Smith, George Bundy
Smith, Norman Raymond
Snowden, Frank Walter
Stephens, William Haynes
Stewart, Kordell
St Etienne, Gregory Michael
Sutton, William W., Jr.
Surtain, Patrick Frank
Sylvester, Melvin R.
Sylvas, Dr. Lionel B.
Tarver, Marie Nero
Temple, Dr. Jacqueline B.
Thompson, Bennie
Tropez-Sims, Dr. Susanne
Turner, Diane Young
Tyler, Michael Lawrence
Vaughn, Dr. Percy Joseph, Jr.
Verrett, Joyce McKee
Vincent, Daniel Paul
Watson, Carole M.
Washington, Betty Lois
Warner, Dr. Neari Francois
Walker, May E.
Washington, Lionel
Webster, Lenny
Wells, Roderick Arthur
Weathers, Carl
Webb, Dr. Shelia J.
Williams, Dr. Trina Rachael
Williams, Aeneas Demetrius
Williams, Gerald Floyd
Wiley, Morlon David
Wilson, Valerie Petit
Wicker, Dr. Henry Sindos
Wiltz, Dr. Charles J.
Wiltz, Dr. Philip G., Jr.
Williams, Leroy Joseph
Wilderson, Thad
Wright, Loyce Pierce
Young, Floyd Alexander
Youngblood, Rev. Dr. Johnny Ray
Young, Prof. Alfred
Young, Andrew
Young, Dr. James E., Jr.
Young, Dr. Lionel Wesley
Young, Wallace L., Jr.
Young, Dr. Walter Fuller

### New Roads
Paul, Dr. Alvin

### Newellton
Durham, Rev. Eddie L., Sr.
Travis, Jack
Troutman, Dr. Porter Lee, Jr.

### Oak Grove
Harper, Tommy
Peagler, Dr. Richard C.

### Opelousas
Aubespin, Mervin R.
Brown, Dr. Lillie Richard
Harris, Alonzo
Haynes, Willie C., III
Joseph, James Alfred
Lemelle, Ivan
Malveaux, Dr. Floyd Joseph
Pitre, Prof. Merline
Richard, Dr. Floyd Anthony

### Paincourtville
Melancon, Norman, Sr.

### Palmetto
Guidry, David

### Patterson
Hilliard, Ike

### Pineville
Anderson, Betty Keller
Lewis, Rashard Quovon
Talley, Rev. Dr. Clarence, Sr.
White, Sharon Brown

### Plaquemine
Dawson, Dr. Peter Edward

### Pointe Coupee Parish
Gaines, Ernest James

### Ponchatoula
Thomas, Irma

### Port Allen
Wiggins, William H., Jr.

### Providence
Lane, Dr. Eddie Burgyone, Sr.

### Quachita Parish
Wilson, Wilson W.

### Raceland
Lawless, Earl

### Rayville
Hayes, Elvin Ernest
Potts, Roosevelt Bernard

### Richland Parish
Young, Katye H. McLaughlin

### Ridge
McZeal, Alfred, Sr.

### Ruston
Atkins, Pervis R., Jr.
Chaffers, James Alvin
Hicks, Augusta M. Gale
Mumford, Esther Hall
Wright, Kenny D., II

### Shreveport
Abdul-Rahman, Tahira Sadiqa
Ashford, Evelyn
Baker, LaVolia Ealy
Ballard, Myrtle Ethel
Bennett, Charles James
Belle, Albert Jojuan
Bryant, Edward Joe, III
Carter, Margaret Louise
Chalmers, Thelma Faye
Christopher, John A.
Collins, Rev. Dr. Paul L.
Daniels, Terry L.
Dumars, Joe, III
Dyas, Patricia Ann
Edmond, Paul Edward
Epps, Dolzie C. B.
Evans, Douglas Edwards
Fuller, Dr. Howard L.
Glover, Rev. Clarence Ernest, Jr.
Graham, Ladell
Hardy, Timothy W.
Henderson, Hon. Thelton Eugene
Holt, Dr. James Stokes, III
Holt, Dr. Dorothy L. Thomas
Holt, Dr. Edwin J.
Honeycutt, Jerald DeWayne
Howard, Wardell Mack
Hudson, Don R..
Hull, Akasha Gloria
Jamison, Antawn Cortez
Johnson, Ezra Ray
Joseph-McIntyre, Mary
Kinchen, Dennis Ray
Langston, Dr. Esther J.
LaMotte, Jean Moore
Lovett, Mack, Jr.
Malry, Dr. Lenton, Sr.
Mobley, Dr. Sybil Collins
Patterson, Curtis Ray
Patton, Joyce Bradford
Parish, Robert Lee
Peters, Aulana Louise
Penn, Dr. Nolan E.
Pennywell, Phillip, Jr.
Smith, Lee Arthur
Snowden, Phillip Ray
Stewart, Carl E.
Taylor, Rev. Dr. Martha C.
Tarver, Gregory Williams, Sr.
Tramiel, Kenneth Ray, Sr.
Warmly, Leon
Walker, Mary L.
Washington, Ada Catherine
Walker, Joseph W., III
Wells, Vernon Michael, III
White, Randy
Williams, Clarence

### Sicily Island
Atkins, Hon. Edna R.
Holt, Dr. Essie W.

### Simsboro
Lee, Pauline W.

### Sorrento
Williams, John

### St. Francisville
Collier, Clarence Marie

### St. James
Pierre, Dr. Percy Anthony

### St. Joseph
Brown, Joseph Davidson, Sr.
Hart-Holifield, Emily B.
Hymes, Jesse
Johnson, Caliph
Turner, Isiah

### St. Martinville
Pratt, Alexander Thomas
Richard, Dr. Arlene Castain

### St. Maurice
Anthony, Bernard Winston

### Sterlington
McHenry, Dr. James O.
Perkins, Edward Joseph
Talley, John Stephen

### Summerfield
Buggs, James Ferdinand
Malone, Karl Anthony

### Sweetville
Walter, Mildred Pitts

### Swords
Gallot, Richard Joseph, Sr.

### Tallulah
McLean, Dr. Zarah Gean
Nash, Curtis
Robinson, Dr. Carl Dayton
Washington, Dr. Arthur Clover

### Thibodaux
Davis, Mark Anthony
Hardy, Eursla Dickerson

### Trout
Jacob, John Edward

### Tullos
Riggs, Gerald Antonio

### Vacherie
Louis, Joseph
Steib, Rev. James Terry

### Vidalia
Sanders, Michael Anthony

### Ville Platte
Alfred, Rayfield
Laday, Dr. Kerney, Sr.
Thomas, Arthur Ray

### Washington
Doomes, Dr. Earl

### Weeks Island
Carrier, Clara L. DeGay
Small, Stanley Joseph

### West Monroe
King, Shawn
Russell, Bill

### Winnfield
Smith, James Charles
Thomas, Anthony J.

### Winnsboro
Ellis, Ladd, Jr.
McFarland, Anthony Darelle
Myles, Wilbert

### Wisner
Boone, Dr. Zola Ernest

### Zachary
Hughes, Isaac Sunny
Williams, Doug Lee

## MAINE

### Augusta
Burney, William D., Jr.

### Baltimore
Roane, Dr. Philip Ransom, Jr.

### Bangor
Harris, Alfred Carl, III
Talbot, Gerald Edgerton
Taylor, S. Martin
Walbey, Theodosia Emma Draher

### Bar Harbor
DuBois, Col. Joshua

### Kittery
Davis, Sidney Louis

### Lewistown
Santos, Henry Joseph

### Portland
Rice, Lois Dickson
Rowell, Victoria Lynn

### Skowhegan
Farley, William Horace, Jr.

## MARYLAND

### Aberdeen
Howard, Leslie Carl
Jackson, Brenda
Moore, Dr. Milton Donald, Jr.
Vannaman, Madi T.

### Annapolis
Daley, Thelma Thomas
Gatling, Patricia Lynn
Hoyle, Dr. Classie G.
West, Hon. Royce Barry

### Aquasco
Wills, Dr. James Willard

### Baltimore
Abrams, Kenneth Rodney
Adams, Jean Tucker
Adams, Dr. Russell Lee
Andrews, Mark Althavean
Arnez, Dr. Nancy L.
Armstead, Wilbert Edward, Jr.
Banfield, Dr. Edison H.
Baker, Shana V.
Bailey, Carlton Wilson
Bennett, Rev. Robert Avon, Jr.
Black, Barry C.
Booth, Keith Eugene
Bogues, Tyrone Curtis
Boyd, Wilhemina Y.
Booth, Rev. Dr. Charles E.
Bond, Dr. Louis Grant
Boone, Frederick Oliver, Jr.
Booker, Simeon Saunders, Jr.
Boyd, Linda F. Wharton
Brunt, Samuel Jay
Brown, Dr. Marsha Jeanette
Bryant, Bishop John Richard
Brooks, Rodney Alan
Bryant, Jamal Harrison
Brown, Paulette
Buford, Damon Jackson
Burke, Gary Lamont
Buckson, Toni Yvonne
Byrd, Albert Alexander
Carroll, Dr. Constance Marie
Callum, Agnes Kane
Carroll, Beverly A.
Cassell, Samuel James, Sr.
Chase, Sonia Lynn
Chapman, Nathan A., Jr.
Chideya, Farai
Charles, Dr. Roderick Edward
Clark, Walter L.
Clash, Kevin
Coates, Ta-Nehisi
Cole, Harriette
Collier, Dr. Eugenia W.
Cruise, Esq. Warren Michael
Curtis, Rev. Dr. William H.
Curbeam, Robert Lee, Jr.
Cummings, Elijah Eugene
Curtis, Mary C.
Dates, Dr. Jannette Lake
Davis, Samuel C.
Dailey, Thelma
Davis, Hon. Arrie W.
Davis, Dr. Elaine Carsley
Dean, Walter R., Jr.
Dixon, Ardena S.
Dixon, Sheila Ann
Doss, Dr. Juanita King
Dorsey, Joseph A., Jr.
Draper, Rev. Frances Murphy
Durant, Bishop Naomi C.
Dutton, Charles Stanley
Easter, Eric Kevin

## MASSACHUSETTS

### Gay Head
Smalley, Paul

### Greenfield
Whitsett, James A., Jr.

### Greenville
Brown, Vivian

### Holyoke
Spears, Richard James

### Lowell
Lambert, Benjamin Franklin
Person, Robert Alan
Prior, Anthony Eugene

### Lynn
Gilton, Dr. Donna L.
Hill, Kenneth Wade

### Malden
Bailey, Dr. Randall Charles

### Medford
Carrington, Terri Lyne
Vargus, Dr. Ione D.

### Nantucket
Browning, Rev. Dr. Jo Ann

### Natick
Thomas, Dr. Gerald Eustis

### Nettleton
Ferguson, Jason O.

### New Bedford
Araujo, Dr. Norman
Barboza, Anthony
Barboza, Steven Alan
Dash, Prof. Leon DeCosta
Hayden, William Hughes
Hayden, Robert C., Jr.
Hillman, Gracia M.
Leighton, Hon. George Neves
O'Connor, Thomas F., Jr.
Stone, Harold Anthony

### North Hampton
Walker, Ian Robin

### Northampton
Walker, Dr. Gregory T. S.

### Norwood
Potter, Judith Diggs

### Roxbury
Beach, Michael Anthony
Bell, Ricky
Curwood, Stephen Thomas

### Springfield
Ali, Dr. Kamal Hassan
Battle, Dr. Stanley F.
Best, Travis Eric
Brouhard, Deborah Taliaferro
Cleage, Pearl Michelle
Denniston, Prof. Dorothy L.
Freeman, Diane S.
Heacock, Dr. Don Roland
Ireland, Hon. Roderick Louis
Isaacs, Cheryl Boone
Jackson, Dr. Reginald Leo
Johnson, Rebecca M.
Johnson, Brent E.
Johnson, Lillian Mann
Johnson, Wayne Alan
Lee, Kermit J., Jr.
Mapp, Dr. John Robert
Phifer, B. Janelle Butler
Webb, Schuyler Cleveland

### Stoneham
Allston, Thomas Gray, III

### Wareham
Pena, Robert Bubba

### Williamstown
Hart, Brenda G.

### Worcester
Osborne, Dr. William Reginald, Jr.
Wilson, Dr. Donald

## MICHIGAN

### Albion
Boggan, Daniel A., Jr.
Holland, Robert, Jr.
Scott, Ruth Elaine Holland
Washington, Dr. Von Hugo, Sr.
Williams, Karl Danell

### Alpena
Young, Kevin Stacey

### Ann Arbor
Baker, Dr. Gwendolyn Calvert
Brown, Carol Ann
Cherot, Esq. Nicholas Maurice
Chappell, Michael James
Cooley, Keith Winston
Eaglin, Fulton B.
Finley, Skip
Hall, Pamela Vanessa
Henderson, Major Gen. William Avery
Jackson, Eric Scott
Jackson, Earl W
Patterson, Dr. Willis Charles
Smith, Dr. Phillip M.
Spann, Rev. Paul Ronald
Teeuwissen, Pieter

### Battle Creek
Daniel, Griselda
Gaither, James W., Jr.
Miller, Oliver O.
Walker, Dr. Manuel Lorenzo

### Benton Harbor
Barnes, William L.
Barnes, Quacy
Cooper, Duane
Cooke, Wilce L.
Hudson, Ernie
Miller, Anthony
Walker, Chester
Yarbrough, Mamie Luella

### Berrien Springs
Upshaw, Regan Charles

### Columbus
Mathis, Walter Lee, Sr.

### Detroit
Adams, Dr. Charles Gilchrist
Ahart, Thomas I.
Ahmad, Jadwaa W.
Alexander, Derrick Scott
Aldridge, Markita
Alexander, Brent
Allen, Byron
Anderson, Dr. Marjorie
Arrington, Dr. Harold Mitchell
Archer, Dennis Wayne
Arnold, Dr. John Russell, Jr.
Armstrong, Vanessa Bell
Armstrong, B. J., Jr.
Atkins, Hon. Marylin E.
Atchison, Leon H.
Banfield, Anne L.
Baker, Dr. Darryl Brent, Sr.
Baxter, Hon. Wendy Marie
Baker-Kelly, Dr. Beverly
Bell, Edna R.
Benyard, William B.
Bernoudy, Monique Rochelle
Berry, Charles F., Jr.
Bettis, Jerome Abram, Sr.
Bernard, Sharon Elaine
Berry, Paul Lawrence
Black, Frank S.
Blackwell, Arthur Brendhal, II
Bowron, Eljay B.
Boyd, Dr. Melba Joyce
Bowens, Gregory John
Boyce, Charles N.
Boykin, A. Wade, Jr.
Bowie, Oliver Wendell
Brooks, Arkles Clarence, Jr.
Bryant, Donnie L.
Brown, Sharon Marjorie Revels
Brown, Dr. Leroy Bradford, Sr.
Brown, Reuben D.
Brown, Helen E.
Brown, P. J.
Brown, Gilbert Jesse
Bruce, Adriene Kay
Brooks, Rosemarie
Bridgforth, Glinda
Brown-Philpot, Stacy
Bryant, Kathryn Ann
Bridgforth, Walter, Jr.
Branham, George, III
Broughton, Christopher Leon
Butler, Keith Andre
Burton, David Lloyd
Butler, Gwendolyn L.
Butler, Rosalind Marie
Burrell, Kenneth Earl
Carreker, William, Jr.
Cabbil, Lila
Campbell, Sandra Pace
Cadwell, Rev. Harold H., Jr.
Carter, Regina
Carson, Dr. Benjamin Solomon, Sr.
Carpenter, Dr. Vivian L.
Calhoun, Gregory Bernard
Chaney, Alphonse
Chandler, Dr. Mittie Olion
Chambers, Caroline E.
Chenevert-Bragg, Irma J.
Charles, Daedra Janel
Chisholm, Dr. Joseph Carrel, Jr.
Chapman, Dr. Melvin
Clark, Dr. Harry Westley
Clarke, Dr. Greta Fields
clark, Karen
Clemons, Sandra L.
Clarke, Judge Hugh Barrington, Jr.
Clark-Taylor, Kristin
Clingman, Kevin Loren
Coleman, Michael Victor
Cole, Patricia A.
Coleman-Burns, Dr. Patricia Wendolyn
Cole, Dorinda Clark
Cornwell, Dr. JoAnne
Conner, Gail Patricia
Conyers, Nathan G.
Combs, Dr. Julius V.
Collins, Barbara-Rose
Cole, Dr. Edyth Bryant
Coffee, Dr. Lawrence Winston
Conyers, John James, Jr.
Cooper, Evelyn Kaye
Cotman, Dr. Ivan Louis
Cross, Rev. Haman
Craig, Carl
Croel, Michael
Curtis-Hall, Vondie
Cureton, Earl
Cushingberry, George, Jr.
Daniels, Melvin J.
Davidson, Arthur B.
Davis, John Wesley
Davis, Diane Lynn
Davis, Johnny Reginald
Davis, Robert Alan
Davie, Damon Jonathon
Dean, Terrance
Dennis, Karen
Dean, Diane D.
Diggs, Dr. Roy Dalton, Jr.
Dickson, Daryl M.
Dozier, Lamont
Dotson, Albert E., Jr.
Donawa, Dr. Maria Elena
Drew, Stephen Richard
Drain, Gershwin Allen
Dunmore, Gregory Charles
Dumas, Karen Marie
Dyson, Rev. Dr. Michael Eric
Edwards, Carl Ray, II
Eisley, Howard Jonathan
Ellis, Michael G.
Ellison, Keith Maurice
Evans, Elinor Elizabeth
Evans, Warren Cleage
Fears, Harding H., Jr.
Ferrebee, Thomas G.
Fields, Dr. Dexter L.
Fletcher, Robert E.
Floyd, Christopher Michael
Flowers, Dr. Sally A.
Ford, Darryl
Fort, Dr. Edward Bernard
Frohman, Roland H.
Franklin, Eugene T., Jr.
Frierson, Dr. Michael Anthony
Frazier, Cliff
Fuller, Curtis D.
Gaskin, Jeanine
Garner, Nathan Warren
Gant, Crystal M.
Gardner, Loman Ronald
Gervin, George
Gist, Carole Anne-Marie
Gilford, Vera Elaine
Gibson, JoAnn
Givens, Lawrence
Givhan, Robin Deneen
Gillum, Roderick D.
Gibson, Dr. Cheryl Dianne
Glover, Chester Artis
Gordon, Edward Lansing, III
Goodwin, Donald Edward
Gordy, Berry, Jr.
Godbold, Dr. Donald Horace
Grier, David Alan
Green, Robert Lee
Green, Dennis O.
Gregory, Karl Dwight
Gragg, Lauren Andrea
Graves, Dr. Leslie Theresa
Grier, Bobby
Grier, Michael James
Greely, M. Gasby
Granderson, LZ
Guice, Rev. Gregory Charles
Guyton, Tyree
Guilford, Diane Patton
Guilmenot, Richard Arthur
Gullattee, Alyce C.
Hamilton, Phanuel J.
Harper, Conrad Kenneth
Harris, Dr. Geraldine E.
Haney, Don Lee
Hanson, John L., Jr.
Hall-Keith, Jacqueline Yvonne
Harris, Dr. Robert Allen
Hall, Dr. Perry Alonzo
Harrington, Gerald E.
Hall, Elliott Sawyer
Hamilton, Rainy, Jr.
Harlan, Carmen
Harrison, Boyd G., Jr.
Hathaway, Cynthia Gray
Hall-Turner, Deborah
Haugabook, Dr. Terrence Randall
Hazel, Janis D.
Hamilton, Arthur Lee, Jr.
Hart, Phyllis D.
Harvey, Linda Joy
Hall, Darnell Kenneth
Harrison, Wendell Richard
Hale, Derrick F.
Harris, Ona C.
Hayden, Aaron Chautezz
Hamilton, Ruffin, III
Hardwick, Gary C.
Harvey, Dana Colette
Hammond, Fred
Henry, Alaric Anthony
Herring, Marsha K. Church
Hilliard, Amy Sharmane
Higgins, Sean Marielle
Hill, Raymond
Hill, George Hiram
Howze, Karen Aileen
Hollowell, Dr. Melvin Laverne
Hollowell, Kenneth Lawrence
Holland, Edward, Jr.
Holland, Brian
Howard, Glen L.
Howell, Rachel
Hope, Marie H. Saunders
Hogue, Leslie Denise
Hurst, Robert
Hunter, Teola P.
Humphries, Esq. James Nathan
Hutchison, Dr. Harry Greene
Hunt, Jeffrey C.
Hughes, Allen
Hughes, Albert
Hutchison, Dr. Peyton S.
Hudson, Lester Darnell
Ice, Dr. Anne-Mare
Ingram, Phillip M.
Irmagean, U.
Jackson, Dr. James Sidney
Jackson, Beverly Joyce
Jackson, Gregory
Jacques, Cornell
Jaggers, Garland
Jenkins, Jim
Jenkins, Pastor Kenneth Joe
Jeff, Gloria Jean
Jefferson-Ford, Charmain
Jefferson, Dr. Horace Lee
Johnson, Davis
Johnson, Frederick E., Sr.
Jones, James McCoy
Johnson, Donna Alligood
Johnson, Nancy Aline Flake
Johnson, Charles Bernard
Jones, Ingrid Saunders
Johnson, Dr. James Kenneth
Jones, Cobi N'Gai
Johnson, Michael
Jones, Rev. Robert Bernard
Johnson, Cynthia Ann
Johnson, Cynthia L. M.
Jones, Mable Veneida
Jones, Donna L.
Jones, Dr. Lewis Arnold
Johnson, Pepper
Jones, Rodrek Edward
Johnson, Robert E.
Jones, Dr. Toni Stokes
Keith, Luther
Kendall, Michelle Katrina
Keith, Hon. Damon Jerome
Kilpatrick, Carolyn Jean Cheeks
King, Anita
Kispert, Dorothy Lee
King, John Thomas
King, John L.
King, Lawrence Patrick
Knight, Negele Oscar
Langford, Hon. Denise Morris
Lawson, Debra Ann
Lasley, Phelbert Quincy, III
Langford, Rev. Victor C., III
Lee, Dr. Andre L.
Lester, Donald
Lewis, David Baker
Lemon, Michael Wayne, Sr.
Lee, Helen Elaine
Lewis, Carmen Cortez
Lee, Otis Knapp
Lewis, Alonzo Todd
Lewis, Michael Ward
Lewis-Langston, Hon. Deborah
Lenard, Voshon Kelan
Lightfoot, Simone Danielle
Lipscomb, Curtis Alexander
Lloyd, Hon. Leonia Jannetta
Lockard, Prof. Jon Onye
Locke, Dr. Hubert G.
Lofton, Ernest
Lowery-Jeter, Dr. Renecia Yvonne
Love, Loni
Lyle, Percy H., Jr.
Maddox, Jack H.
Martin, Carol
Mays, William, Jr.
Malone, Maurice
May, Derrick
Mathews, Maj. K. Kendall
Mallory, James A.
Malone, Rosemary C.
Mathis, Gregory
Martin, Dr. Kimberly Lynette
Mallett, Dr. Conrad L., Jr.
Mack, Nathan Wesley
Mayberry, Dr. Claude A., Jr.
Mausi, Shahida Andrea
McTyre, Robert Earl, Sr.
McWhorter, Sharon Louise
McSwain, Michael Crittenden
McBurrows, Gerald
McKenzie, Keith Derrick
McKenzie, Reginald
McDonald, William Emory, Sr.
McNeil, DeeDee
McKee, Lonette
McRipley, Dr. Gil Whitney
Metcalf, Dr. Michael Richard, Jr.
Merkerson, Sharon Epatha
Mercer-Pryor, Diana
Miller-Holmes, Cheryl
Miller-Lewis, S. Jill
Minor, DeWayne
Mitchell, Charles, Jr.
Moore, Gwen
Moore, Evelyn K.
Moore-Poole, Jessica Care
Morton, Capt. Benjamin
Morris, Laticia
Moore, Alfred
Morgan, Monica Alise
Morris, William Howard
Moore, Kerwin Lamar
Molden, Alex M.
Moore, Kenya Summer
Munson, Robert H.
Napoleon, Benny Nelson

**Baldwyn**
Moore, Helen D. S.

**Bassfield**
Posey, Jeffery Lavell

**Batesville**
Austin, Lucius Stanley
Berhe-Hunt, Annette
Blakely, Charles
Herring, Dr. Larry Windell, Sr.
Rudd, Dwayne Dupree

**Battles**
Ladner, Joyce Ann

**Bay Springs**
Lang, Dr. Marvel
Smith, Greg

**Bay St. Louis**
Labat, Eric Martin

**Belzoni**
Watson, Anne

**Benoit**
Cooper, Maudine R.

**Bentonia**
Cheatham, Henry Boles

**Beulah**
Gaters, Dorothy L.
Silas, Dennis Dean

**Biloxi**
Cook, Charles A.
Rhodeman, Clare M.

**Bogue Chitto**
Owens, Dr. Charles Edward

**Bolton**
Cooper, Dr. Bobby G.
Nichols, Dr. Walter LaPlora
O'Brien, Mary Nell
Sanders, Dr. Lou Helen
Thompson, Bennie G.

**Booneville**
McGee, Benjamin Lelon

**Brandon**
Glenn, Patricia Campbell
Locke, Dr. Mamie Evelyn

**Brookhaven**
Cox, Warren E.
Kimbrough, Marjorie L.
Markham, Houston, Jr.
Pickett, Robert E.
Washington, Earlene

**Bruce**
Thomas, Fred L.

**Bryant**
Harris, Loretta K.

**Bude**
Walker-Gibbs, Shirley Ann

**Byhalia**
Calloway, Laverne Fant
Nichols, Dimaggio

**Calhoun**
Parker, David Gene

**Cambridge**
Freelon, Nnenna

**Canton**
Blackmon, Edward, Jr.
Esco, Fred, Jr.
Foster, Dr. E. C.
Moore, Lewis Calvin
Moore, Cleotha Franklin
Payton, Jeff
Porter, Lionel
Pruitt, Dr. George Albert
Tate, Dr. James A.
Williams, Jewel L.

**Carlisle**
Argrett, Loretta Collins

**Carp**
Holland, Dr. Loys Marie

**Carthage**
Crouther, Dr. Betty Jean
Dotson, Phillip Randolph

**Cedar Bluff**
Petty-Edwards, Lula Evelyn

**Centerville**
Ray, Dr. Andrew A.

**Charleston**
Bullock, James N.
Johnson, Roy Lee
Keglar, Shelvy Haywood
Phillips, W. Thomas

**Chicora**
Millender, Hon. B. Pennie

**Claiborne County**
Davis, Frank

**Clarksdale**
Bennett, Lerone, Jr.
Carter, Mary Louise
Childs, Josie L.
Gipson, Dr. Lovelace Preston, II
Hemmingway, Dr. Beulah S.
Jones, Wilbert
Martin, Myron C.
Martin, Dr. McKinley C.
Mickens, Maxine N.
Moore, Johnny Belle
Netters, Rev. Tyrone Homer
Noah, Leroy Edward
Outlaw, John L.
Patton, Robert
Smith, Aubrey Carl
Woods, Henry, Jr.
Wolfman, Dr. Brunetta Reid

**Cleveland**
Richardson, Johnny L.
Steele, Bobbie L.
Willis, Frank B.

**Clinton**
Johnson, Niesa Evett
Plumpp, Prof. Sterling Dominic

**Clyde**
Holloway, Dr. Ernestine

**Collins**
Eubanks, W. Ralph
Keys, Randolph

**Columbia**
Hamilton, Bobby Jerome
Hildreth, Dr. Gladys Johnson
Irvin, Regina Lynette
Johnson, Kenneth Lavon

**Columbus**
Brown, Dr. William T.
Givins, Abe, Jr.
Hackman, Luther Gean
Hester, Arthur C.
Irby, Mary
Munson, Eddie Ray
Nabors, Jesse Lee
Peters, Dr. Sheila Renee
Ryan-White, Jewell
Turner, Rep. Robert Lloyd
Williams, James R.
Wilson, Dr. Bobby L.

**Conehatta**
Clay, Ross Collins
Overstreet, Harry L.
Smith, Marzell L.

**Copiah County**
Catchings, Howard Douglas
Hill, Annette Tillman

**Corinth**
Eddings, John R.
McLeod, Dr. Gustavus A.

**Crawford**
Rice, Jerry Lee
Weatherspoon, Clarence, Sr.

**Crenshaw**
Pride, William L., Jr.

**Crystal Springs**
Calhoun, Prof. Thomas C.
Hogan, Beverly Wade
Smith, Dr. Estus
Wilkes, Dr. Shelby R.

**Darling**
Scales, Alice Marie

**De Kalb**
Clayborne, Oneal N.
Overstreet, Dr. Everett Louis

**Decatur**
Evers, James Charles

**DeSoto County**
Donald, Dr. Bernice Bouie

**Doddsville**
Edwards, Shirley Jean
Journey, Lula Mae
Smith, Willie B.

**Drew**
Parker, G. John, Sr.

**Durant**
Bell, Victory
Harris, Dr. Percy G.
McGee, Buford Lamar
Mims, Dr. Robert Bradford
Teague, Robert

**Ebenezer**
Clark, Robert G., Jr.

**Edwards**
Allen, Dr. Van Sizar
Currie, Betty
Morrison, Dr. K. C
Thompson-Moore, Ann

**Enterprise**
Hill, Dr. Obie Cleveland
Hunter, Rev. David

**Escatawpa**
Mass, Edna Elaine

**Eupora**
Ford, Vernon N.

**Farmhaven**
Brown-Wright, Flonzie B.
Dennis, Dr. Evie Garrett

**Fayette**
Collins, Dr. Lenora W.
Guice, Leroy
Harris, Burnell
Hamberlin, Dr. Emiel
King, Virgie M. Dunlap

**Florence**
Ferguson, Rosetta A.

**Forest**
Bennett, Patricia W.
Hunt, Betty Syble
Perry, Marlo
Thomas, Roy L.

**Forrest**
Epting, Marion Austin

**Friars Point**
Rodgers, William M., Jr.

**Gautier**
McCorvey, Kez

**Glen Allen**
Taulbert, Clifton LeMoure

**Glendora**
Thomas, Johnny B.
Washington, James Lee, Sr.

**Gloster**
Feltus, Bishop James, Jr.
Neyland, Leedell Wallace

**Goodman**
Scarborough, Charles S.
Scott, Melvina Brooks

**Greenville**
Campbell, Gertrude Sims
Dancy, Rev. William F.
Gill, Dr. Walter A.
Grigsby, David P.
Hudson, Heather McTeer
Jackson, Angela
Mudiku, Mary Esther Greer
Nelson, Dr. Dorothy J. Smith
Powell, William S., Sr.
Richardson, Gloster Van
Sutherland, Dr. Frankie
Wicker, Lisa J. Lindsay
Wilson, Mary
Wilson, Dr. Charles Z., Jr.

**Greenwood**
Adams, Dr. Afesa M.
Beck, Saul L.
Brisco-Hooks, Valerie Ann
Brooks, John S.
Clay, Cliff
Emmons, Carlos Antoine
Glass, Gerald Damon
Gordon, Dr. Sherman A.
Gray, Earnest L.
Hodges, Dr. John O.
Jones, Thomas L.
Johnson, Wyneva
King, Clarence Maurice, Jr.
Mitchell, George L.
Pool, Vera C.
Reaves, Ginevera N.
Shelton, Rep. O. L.
Ware, Dr. William Levi
Youssef, Sitamon Mubaraka

**Grenada**
Dobbs, Dr. John Wesley
Pittman, Winston R., Sr.
Starks, Robert Terry

**Gulfport**
Abdul-Rauf, Mahmoud
Barney, Lemuel Jackson
Lawton, Matthew, Jr.
Smiley, Tavis
Williams-Hayes, Dr. Thea

**Gunnison**
Barnett, Fred Lee, Jr.
Finley, Dr. D. Linell, Sr.

**Hattiesburg**
Cameron, Rev. John Earl, Sr.
Collier, Willye
Fielder, Dr. Fred Charles
Harris, Daisy
Hayes, Charles Dewayne
Hill, Vonciel Jones
James, Dr. Robert Earl
James, Dr. Jimmie, Jr.
Magee, Wendell Errol, Jr.
Manning, Daniel Ricardo
Massey, Walter Eugene
McGee, Waddell
Miller, Melvin Allen
Sartin, Johnny Nelson, Jr.
Smotherson, Rev. Dr. Melvin
Spriggs, Marcus
Whigham, Larry Jerome

**Hazlehurst**
Anderson, Dr. Amel L.
Ephriam, Esq. Mablean Deloris
Singleton, James Milton
Smith, Mary Levi
Williams, Edward Ellis

**Heidelberg**
Thomas, Dr. Johnny D.
Thomas, Dr. Dennis E.

**Helm**
Thompson, Rep. Betty Lou

**Hernando**
Kimmons, Dr. Willie James
Meriweather, Melvin, Jr.

**Hickory**
Johnson, Robert Louis

**Hillhouse**
Phillips, Rev. Acen L.

**Hinds County**
Lee, Aaron

**Hollandale**
Jones, Jake
Smith, Dr. Edgar Eugene

**Holly Springs**
Elliott, Cathy
Jones, Gwendolyn J.
Marsh, Ben Franklin
Rankin, Hon. Michael Lee
Rankin, Dr. Edward Anthony
Taylor, John L.
Talley, Curtiss J.

**Houlka**
Bean, Dr. Bobby Gene

**Indianola**
Alice, Mary
Bell, Jimmy
Featherstone, Karl Ramon
Hixon, Mamie Webb
Matthews, Rev. David
Randle, Carver A.
Williams, Theartrice T.

**Inverness**
Robinson, Virgil, Jr.

**Isola**
Pollard, Muriel Ransom
Reed, Clara Taylor

**Itta Bena**
Barry, Marion Shepilov, Jr.
King, B. B.

**Jackson**
Banks, Fred L., Jr.
Blackburn, Dr. Benjamin Allan, II
Blackmon, Barbara Martin
Bobbitt, Leroy
Bracey, Willie Earl
Brown, Rev. Dr. Amos Cleophilus
Bryant, N. Z., Jr.
Catching-Kyles, Sharron Faye
Colbert, Virgis W.
Dampier, Erick Trevez
Debro, Dr. Julius
Donald, Major Gen. James E.
Ellis, Dr. Tellis B., III
Faulding, Juliette J.
Freeman, Shirley Walker
Gates, Jimmie Earl
Gibbs, Robert Lewis
Gordon, Lancaster
Hayes-Giles, Joyce V.
Harper, Earl
Harrington, Othella
Hickman, Elnor B. G.
Hicks, Dr. Arthur James
Hollingsworth, Alfred Delano
Jenkins, Melvin
Johnson, David E.
Jones, Chester Ray
Johnson, C. Christine
Johnson, Mertha Ruth
Kennedy, James E.
Khali, Simbi
Lofton, Dr. Barbara
Manley, Dr. Audrey Forbes
Massey, Jacquelene Sharp
McKanders, Julius A., II
McNeil, Freeman, III
McDonald, Jon Franklin
Middleton, Rev. Dr. Richard Temple, III
Myles, Toby L.
Nichols, Alfred Glen
Odom, Dr. John Yancy
Patrick, Hon. Isadore W., Jr.
Palmer-Hildreth, Barbara Jean
Pawley, Dr. Thomas D., III
Samkange, Dr. Tommie Marie
Sampson, Dr. Henry Thomas, Jr.
Scott, Dr. Mona Vaughn
Slater, Jackie Ray
Taylor, Mildred D.
Veal, Howard Richard, Sr.
Watson, Jackie
Wesley, Joseph
Wilson, Cassandra
Willacy, Hazel M.
Willis, Gladys January
Williams, John Alfred
Wolfe, Dr. John Thomas, Jr.

Cooper, Lois Louise
Dunbar, Dr. Joseph C.
Evers-Williams, Dr. Myrlie Louise
Gardner, Dr. Bettye J.
Howard, Dalton J., Jr.
Johnson, Harvey, Jr.
Lacey, Dr. Bernardine M.
Lawyer, Cyrus Jefferson, III
Lassiter, Rev. Dr. Wright Lowenstein, Jr.
McRoy, Dr. Ruth Gail
Myers, Michael
Otis, Clarence, Jr.
Pritchard, Daron
Scott, Joseph M.
Shelton, Joseph B., Jr.
Smith, Mark Anthony
Stewart, Ella
Warfield, Eric Andrew
Young, Dmitri Dell

### Victoria
Royston, Evelyn Ross

### Walls
McLemore, Leslie Burl

### Water Valley
Davidson, Ezra C., Jr.
Davidson, Dr. Kerry
Mix, Bryant Lee

### Webb
Haynes, Dr. Worth Edward
Wheeler, Primus, Jr.

### Weir
Kennedy, Rev. James E.

### Wesson
Newsome, Rev. Burnell, Sr.

### West Point
English, Henry L.
Gladney, Dr. Marcellious
Harris, Carol R.
Perkins, Bernice Perry
Robinson, Dr. Kitty Kidd

### Wilkinson County
Moody, Anne

### Winona
Alexander, Cornelia
Bibbs-Sanders, Angelia

### Woodville
Ashford, L. Jerome
Jackson, Felix W.
Johnson, Charles E.
Shepherd, Benjamin Arthur
Tolliver, Thomas C., Jr.
Tolliver, Ned, Jr.

### Yazoo City
Brown, Willie
Clarke, Alyce Griffin
Espy, Alphonso Michael
Hamilton, Lynn
Kelly, Ida B.
Morgan, Robert Lee
Muhammad, Askia
White, Frankie Walton
Williams, Hon. Walter
Woods, Dr. Willie G.

## MISSOURI

### Armstrong
Shade, Dr. Barbara J.

### Boonville
Jackson, John H.

### Canalou
Henry, William Arthur, II

### Canton
Tate, Eleanora Elaine

### Charleston
Ealy, Mary Newcomb
Williams, Dr. Charles Thomas

### Clayton
Stevens, Dr. Joyce West

### Columbia
Anderson, Gary Wayne
Lewis, Leo E., III
Lee, Dorothy A. H.
Logan, Lloyd
Ridgeway, Dr. Bill Tom
Washington, William Montell

### Creve Coeur
Green, Scarborough

### DeSoto
Bentley, Herbert Dean

### East St. Louis
Bush, Dwight L., Sr.

### Glasgow
Cason, Udell, Jr.
Hayes, Curtiss Leo

### Hannibal
Robinson, Kenneth Eugene
Teasley, Marie R.
Thompson, Esq. Larry D.

### Harveil
Bailey, Dr. Weltman D., Sr.

### Hayti
Cooper, Dr. Charles W.
Russell, Dorothy Delores

### Hermondale
Barnes, Dr. Joseph Nathan

### Higginsville
Seals, George Edward

### Howard County
Vivian, Dr. Cordy Tindell

### Hunnewell
Scott, Dr. Donald LaVern

### Illmo
Jackson, Mannie L.

### Ironton
Carr, Chris Dean

### Jefferson City
Entertainer, Cedric The

### Joplin
Landrum, Tito

### Kansas
Simmons, Kelvin

### Kansas City
Adams, Joseph Lee
Anderson, Dr. Carol Byrd
Andrews, William Phillip
Baker, Gregory D.
Baskett, Kenneth Gerald
Benton, Nelkane O.
Belser, Jason Daks
Brooks, Sheila Dean
Brown, Conella Coulter
Brooks, Joyce Renee Ward
Burrows, Clare
Caro, Ralph M.
Cheadle, Donald Frank, Jr.
Clemmons, Clifford R.
Copeland, Misty
Collins, Joanne Marcella
Cunningham, Dr. William Dean
Dunson, Dr. Carrie Lee
Emanuel, Bert Tyrone
Fitchue, M. Anthony
Gaston, Patricia Elaine
Griffin, Eddie
Gray, Marcus J.
Hampton, Phillip Jewel
Harris, Dr. Jasper William
Henderson, Prof. Stephen McKinley
Henderson, Ruth Faynella
Hill, Julia H.
Jackson, Ronald Lee
Jackson, Dr. Julius Hamilton
Jenkins, Wanda Joyce
Jenkins, Dr. Melvin E., Jr.
Jerome, Curtis
Jones, Frank Benson
Jones, Michael Anthony
Lange, LaJune Thomas
May, Floyd O.
McMurry, Merley Lee
McClain, Andre
McCord, LaNissa Renee
Myles, William, Jr.
Nash, Troy
Oliver, Darren Christopher
Parker, Stafford W.
Peeler, Anthony Eugene
Powell, Clarence Dean, Jr.
Ponder, Eunice Wilson
Richardson, Robert Eugene
Richardson, Joseph
Riley, Rosetta Margueritte
Robinson, Dr. Genevieve
Sanders, Dr. Reliford Theopolis, Jr.
Scroggins, Bobby
Shivers, P. Derrick
Smith, Rev. Dr. J. Alfred, Sr.
Stephenson, Dama F.
Swift, Karen A.
Swindell, Dr. Warren C.
Thomas, David Anthony
Turner, Sharon V.
White, Evelyn M.
Williams, Margaret Ann
Wilkins, Roger Wood
Worford, Carolyn Kennedy
Woodard, Rhonda Marie
Wright, William A.
Zollar, Jawole Willa Jo
Zollar, Alfred

### Keytesville
McKissack, Leatrice Buchanan

### Kinloch
Lewis, Jenifer Jeanette

### Liberty
Blake, Carl LeRoy
Houston, Seawadon L.

### Malden
Jones-Grimes, Dr. Mable Christine

### Marshall
Gamble, Kenneth L.

### Mexico
Lue, Tyronn Jamar
Vance, Dr. Irvin Elmer

### Morley
Hine, Darlene Clark

### Neelyville
Dukes, Ronald

### New Franklin
Wilson, Dr. Helen Tolson

### New Madrid
Costa, Annie Bell Harris
Shoffner, James Priest

### Oak Ridge
Bell, Doris E.

### Parma
Ige, Dr. Dorothy W. K.
Ige, Dr. Dorothy W.

### Poplar Bluff
Chapman, Dr. Joseph Conrad, Jr.
Cheeks, Dr. Carl L.
Johnson, Joseph David
Jones, Rev. Bishop Spencer
Ridgel, Dr. Gus Tolver
Smith, Dr. Ann Elizabeth
Townsend, Br. Prentice A.

### San Bernardino
Collins, Mark Anthony

### Sedalia
Kitchen, Wayne Leroy, Jr.
Riley, Hon. Eve Montgomery

### Springfield
Estes, Elaine Rose Graham

### St. Joseph
Crouther, Betty M.
Crouch, Robert Allen
Richards, Dr. Hilda

### St. Louis
Addei, Arthella Harris
Adkins, Leroy J.
Alligood, Douglass Lacy
Anderson, Dr. Carl Edwin
Anthony, Rev. Dr. Wendell
Anderson, Nathaniel
Bailey, Antoinette M.
Banks, Richard Edward
Barber, Ornetta M.
Bailey, Myrtle Lucille
Ballentine, Krim Menelik
Berry, Chuck
Billingsly, Dr. Marilyn Maxwell
Blackwell, Willie
Bonner, Anthony
Boykin, Keith
Boykins, Amber
Bolden, Betty A.
Boon, Ina M.
Bouie, Dr. Merceline H.
Bouie, Preston L.
Bosley, Freeman Robertson, Jr.
Brown, Lloyd
Brisker, Lawrence W.
Brownlee, Jack M.
Brooks, Barrett Charles
Buford, James Henry
Byrd, Isaac, III
Carter, Jandra D.
Carter, Thomas J., II
Calvert, Dr. Wilma Jean
Carter, Hon. Geoffrey Norton
Chapman, Sharon Jeanette
Clarke, Hon. Anne-Marie
Clifton, Rosalind Maria
Clay, William Lacy, Sr.
Clay, William Lacy, Jr.
Collins, Rev. Dr. William, Jr.
Conrad, Dr. Cecilia Ann
Coleman, Robert Earl, Jr.
Crawley, Darline H.
Dave, Alfonzo, Jr.
Davis, Billy, Jr.
Daggs, Leon, Jr.
Dennis, Dr. Philip H.
Diuguid, Lewis Walter
Dorsey, Elbert
Draper, Dr. Frederick Webster
Easley, Billy Harley
Edwards, Dr. Harry
Evanzz, Karl Anderson
Fisher, E. Carleton
Fletcher, Terrell Antoine
Fowler, Dr. Queen Dunlap
Frazer, Dr. Eva Louise
Gatewood, Esq. Diane Ridley
Gaines, Richard Kendall
Gilkey, Bernard
Golden, Ronald Allen
Gregory, Richard Claxton
Green, Darlene
Guillaume, Robert
Hall, Fred, III
Harris, Dr. Terea Donnelle
Harrington, Zella Mason
Harding, Michael S.
Harmon, Clarence
Herndon, Gloria E.
Henry, Thomas
Henry, Joseph King
Hill, Mervin E., Jr.
Hines, Dr. William E.
Howard, Raymond
Holmes, Michael R.
Horne, Gerald Charles
Hughes, Larry
Ingrum, Adrienne G.
Jackson, Suzanne Fitzallen
Jackson, Oliver L.
Jackson, Carol E.
Jackson, Larron Deonne
Jenkins, Ella Louise
Jenkins, DeRon Charles
Jones, Henry Louis
Jones, William Barnard
Johnson, Esq. Harry E., Sr.
Johnson, Lavera
Johnson, Donn S.
Johnson, Dr. Willard Raymond
Johnson, Dr. John Thomas
Jones, Hardi Liddell
Kaiser, James Gordon
Kennedy, Dr. Joyce S.
Kent, Deborah Stewart
Kirk, Orville, Sr.
Lathen, Deborah Ann
Lamaute, Denise
Lester, Julius
LeFlore, Lyah Beth
Lemmons, Kasi
LeCompte, Peggy Lewis
Little, Dr. Monroe Henry, Jr.
Lowe, Victoria
May, Dr. Gary Stephen
Mabrey, Vicki L.
Marshall, Dr. Joseph Earl, Jr.
Mayberry, Patricia Marie
Matthews, Dorothy
McDaniel, Elizabeth B.
McNeil, Frank, Sr.
McElroy, Dr. Colleen J.
McClelland, Marguerite Marie
McPherson, David
Miller, Kevin
Milloy, Lawyer Marzell
Mitchell, Cranston J.
Mitchell, Stanley Henryk
Miller-Jones, Dr. Dalton
Murphy, Raymond M., Jr.
Nelson, Mary Elizabeth
Nobles, Dr. Patricia Joyce
Nutt, Rev. Maurice Joseph
Officer, Carl Edward
Osby, Gregory Thomas
Otis-Lewis, Alexis D.
Parker, Candace
Parks, Dr. Arnold Grant
Perry, Lee Charles, Jr.
Person, Leslie Robin
Peoples, Dr. Veo
Peterson, Alphonse
Perine, James L.
Ray, Dr. Judith Diana
Randolph-Jasmine, Carol Davis
Ratcliffe, Dr. Alfonso F.
Redon, Leonard Eugene
Reece, Guy L., II
Reed, Dr. Vincent Emory
Reeves, Louise
Roberts, Michael V., Sr.
Rodgers, Vincent G. J.
Russell, Mark
Sanford, Mark
Sanders, Dr. Gwendolyn W.
Sanderson, Randy Chris
Scott, James Henry
Scott, Darnay
Seay, Norman R.
Shipp, Dr. Pamela Louise
Shelton, Esq. Reuben Anderson, III
Shaw, Booker Thomas
Shelton, Hilary O.
Shepard, Linda Irene
Shead, Ken
Shelton, Millicent Beth
Simmons, Kimora Lee
Simms, Dr. Margaret Constance
Smith, Dr. Earl Bradford
Smith, Dr. Luther Edward, Jr.
Smith, Dr. James Almer, III
Smith, Esq. Wayman F., III
Spinks, Michael
Stith, Dr. Charles Richard
Sweets, Ellen Adrienne
Terry, Clark
Thomas, Calvin Lewis
Thomas, Lillie
Thomas, Raymond A.
Torry, Guy
Troupe, Quincy Thomas, Jr.
Troupe, Rep. Charles Quincy
Troupe-Frye, Betty Jean
Turner, Dr. Doris J.
Vincent, Irving H.
Vickers, Eric K.
Walker, Eugene Kevin
Walker-Thoth, Daphne LaVera
Ward, Ronnie V.
Walker, Darnell Robert
Walker, Marquis Roshe
Wattleton, Alyce Faye
Walton, Elbert Arthur, Jr.
Walls, Melvin
Waters, Maxine
West, Dr. Gerald Ivan
Westbrook, Peter Jonathan
Whitfield, Kennard O.
White, Jahidi
Whittington, Bernard Maurice
White, Jo Jo
White-Ware, Grace Elizabeth
Wharton, Hon. Milton S.
White, Arthur W., Jr.

Jones, Dr. Lee
Knight-Pulliam, Keshia
Lewis, Byron E., Sr.
Lewis, Kenneth Dwight
Little, Benilde Elease
Marrow, Tracy Lauren
Marshall, Anita
McDaniel, Karen Cotton
O'Neal, Shaquille Rashaun
Okantah, Mwatabu S.
Payne, William D.
Palmore, Lynne A. Janifer
Peoples, Sesser Randall
Petty, Oscar, Jr.
Queen Latifah
Randolph, Leonard Washington
Redman, R.
Reid, Joel Otto
Richardson, George C.
Salaam, Dr. Abdul
Singleton, Alshermond Glendale
Stanley, Craig A.
Stokes, Herb
Stalks, Larrie W.
Staats, Dr. Florence Joan
Strickland, Dorothy S.
Taylor, Norman Eugene
Terrell, Stanley E.
Thompson, Dr. Mavis Sarah
Thorburn, Dr. Carolyn Coles
Thompson, Dr. Winston Edna
Tucker, Geraldine Jenkins
Way, Dr. Gary Darryl
Washington, Zenobia
Wesley, Dr. Herman Eugene, III
White, Edward Clarence, Jr.
White, Raymond Rodney, Sr.
Wiggins-Obie, Rev. Daphne Cordelia
Williams-Harris, Diane Beatrice
Williams, Reginald T.
Williams, Charles Mason, Jr.
Williams, Eric C.
Wilson, Natalie
Wright, Ralph Edward
Wright, Dmitri

### Newton
Pope, Harold D.

### Ocean City
Davis, Esq. Nathan W., Jr.
Lee, Margaret S.

### Orange
Austin, Mary Jane
Baugh, Esq. Edna Y.
Burrell, Dr. Joel Brion
Davis, Lance Roosevelt
Jones, Bobby M.
Kafele, Baruti Kwame
Marshall, David
Miles, George L., Jr.
Miles, Frank J. W., Jr.
Reid, Malissie Laverne
Scott, Donnell
Williams, Dr. Kenneth Herbert
Wright, Keith Derek, Sr.
Wynne, Dana Sh-Niece

### Palmyra
Cherry, Deron Leigh

### Parsippany
Singleton, Chris

### Passaic
Bolles, A. Lynn
Davis, Edith G. Williams
Tucker, Sheryl Hilliard
Wethers, Dr. Doris Louise

### Paterson
Benson, Gilbert O.
Clark, Pastor James Irving, Jr.
Copeland, Barry B.
Davis, Anthony Eboney
Garner, Dr. Mary E.
Harris, Thomas C.
Henderson, Henry Fairfax, Jr.
Howell, Robert L.
Jones, Maxine
Jones, Ben F.
Kline, William M.
Lyde, Jeanette S.
Moore, Trudy S.
Stewart, W. Douglas
Swinger, Rashod Alexander
Thomas, Timothy Mark
Wade, James Nathaniel
Williams-Warren, Jane E.
Wrice, Prof. Vincent J.

### Paulsboro
Anderson, Willie Lee, Jr.

### Pequannock
Jeter, Derek Sanderson

### Perth Amboy
Bellamy, Jay
Wilson, Dr. Blenda Jacqueline

### Plainfield
Beane, Dorothea Annette
Cary, Rev. William Sterling
Farrow, Sallie A.
Ganey, Dr. James Hobson
Heyward-Garner, Ilene Patricia
Letson, Alfred, Jr.
Morrison, Jacqueline
Reed, Hon. Kasim
Wood, Vivian Frances

### Pleasantville
Darden, Dr. Joseph Samuel, Jr.
Jerkins, Rodney
Wimberley, Frank

### Port Norris
Milbourne, Lawrence William

### Princeton
Coy, John T.
Lewis, W. Arthur
Rivers, Dr. Robert Joseph, Jr.

### Red Bank
Dawkins, Sean Russell
Nelson, Dr. Robert Wales, Sr.

### Riverside
Collins, Andre Pierre
Simmons, Craig, Sr.

### Roebling
Hodges, Dr. Carolyn Richardson

### Roselle
Bowles, Howard Roosevelt
Polk, Dr. Gene-Ann
Riley, Barbara P.

### Salem
Berry, Eric
Ford, Evern D.
Ibn McDaniels-Noel, Muhiyyaldin
Malak Abd Al Muta'ali
Nicholas, Brenda L.
Watson, Solomon B., IV

### Scotch Plains
Hammonds, Jeffrey Bryan
Howe, Prof. Ruth-Arlene W.

### Somers Point
Summerour-Perry, Lisa

### Somerset
Lister, David Alfred

### Somerville
Mines, Raymond C.
Monroe, Robert Alex
Murdock, Eric Lloyd

### South Orange
Baskerville, Penelope Anne
Hill-Marley, Lauryn Noelle
Michel, Samuel Prakazrel

### South River
Pearson, Drew

### Stratford
Hall, Tanya Evette

### Summitt
Knight, Thomas Lorenzo

### Swedesboro
Clark, Douglas L.

### Tarrytown
Whitely, Donald Harrison

### Teaneck
Campbell, Tony
Christian-Christensen, Donna-Marie
LaGarde, Rev. Frederick H., Jr.

### Trenton
Bagley, Rev. Stanley B.
Bauldock, Gerald, Sr.
Cook, Prof. William Wilburt
Dinkins, David Norman
Dix, Henry
Evers, William Preston
Fitzgerald, Herbert H.
Geary, Reggie
Granville, Billy
Harper, Arthur H.
Hayling, Dr. William Hartley
Hinson, Roy Manus, Jr.
Holmes, William B.
Hopkins, Dr. John David
Joyner, Rubin E., Jr.
Marrow-Mooring, Barbara A.
Morrow, Dr. John Howard, Jr.
Palmer, Douglas Harold
Pendergraft, Michele M.
Rodman, Dennis Keith
Robinson, Rev. Harold Oscar
Schenck, Frederick A.
Shange, Ntozake
Shepard, Gregory
Smith, Irvin Martin
Thomas, Arthur Lafayette, III
Vincent, Troy Darnell
Williams, Paul T., Jr.
Williams, Bisa

### Vauxhall
Kearse, Amalya Lyle
Lambert, Joseph C.

### Westfield
Campbell, Esq. Christopher Lundy

### Whitesboro
Ellis, Calvin H., III
Graham, Stedman

### Willingboro
Hemsley, Nate

### Winslow
Freeman, Hon. Ronald J.

### Woodbury
Buck, Ivory M., Jr.

## NEW MEXICO

### Alamagordo
McMillon, Billy

### Albuquerque
Buckhanan, Rev. Shawn L.
Hutchinson, Dr. George
Lott, Ronnie
Siglar, Ricky Allan

### Aragon
Jacobs, Dr. Rev. Daniel Wesley, Sr.

### Carlsbad
Johnson, Kelley Antonio

### Clovis
Large, Jerry D.

### Hobbs
Evans, Robert Oran

### Las Cruces
Potter, Myrtle Stephens

### Roswell
Brogden, Robert, Jr.
Lewis, James B.

### Vado
Boyer, Marcus Aurelius

## NEW YORK

### Albany
Durr, Dr. Marlese
Greene, Jerry Louis
Jackson, Frederick Leon
Marion, Dr. Phillip Jordan
Merriweather, Michael Lamar
Queen, Evelyn E. Crawford
Tucker, Michael Kevin
Walton, James Donald
West, Prof. Pheoris

### Amityville
Benymon, Chico
Mayhew, Richard

### Amsterdam
Wilson, Dr. Harrison B.

### Astoria
Holdsclaw, Chamique Shaunta

### Auburn
Fletcher, Glen Edward
Winslow, Reynolds Baker

### Babylon
Lee, Cheryl Taylore

### Bath
Robinson, Beverly Jean

### Bay Shore
LL Cool J
Sermon, Erick

### Beacon
Dugger, Clinton George
Perdreau, Cornelia Whitener

### Bethpage
Dowell-Cerasoli, Patricia R.

### Binghamton
Haskins, William J.

### Bronx
Alexander, Preston Paul
Alston, Derrick Samuel
Alexander, Arika
Banks, Carlton Luther
Betty, Lisa C.
Beckford, Tyson Craig
Blige, Mary Jane
Blake, Dr. B. David
Bouldes, Ruth Irving
Bolden, Aletha Simone
Bonilla, Bobby
Bradley, Jeffrey
Brown, Anthony Maurice
Bryant, Joy
Brown, Rushia
Brown, Dermal Bram
Bynum, Valerie Collymore
Carroll, Diahann
Champion, James A.
Clark, Vincent W.
Cornelius, Charles Henry
Dash, Stacey Lauretta
Davis, John Alexander
De Veaux, Stuart Samuel
Drakes, Muriel B.
Dyer, Bernard Joel
Edwards, Dr. Claudia L.
Epps, Dr. C. Roy
Farrakhan, Louis
Gaither, Katryna Renee
Garnes, Sam Aaron
Gooding, Cuba M., Jr.
Hall, Aaron
Hansen, Joyce Viola
Harris, Thomas Walter
Hammock, Esq. Edward R.
Henson, Darrin Dewitt
Hicks, D'Atra
Holder, Eric Himpton, Jr.
Jackson, Arthur Howard
Jackson, Alterman
Jennings, Bernard Waylon-Handel
Johnson, Robert T.
Jones, Cullen
Jones, Charles
Kitt, Sandra Elaine
King, Stanley Oscar
Kroon, Marc Jason
Lamar, Jake V., Sr.
Lewis, Edward T.
Lester, Dr. Elton J.
Lumpkin, Adrienne Kelly
Martin, Darnell
Mardenborough, Leslie A.
Martin, Robert E.
Mayo, Barry Alan
McClain, William L.
McCray, Darryl K.
Mitchell, Daryl
Micks, Deitra Handy
Miller, Lawrence A., Jr.
Morgan, Tracy Jamal
Monroe, Dr. Anthony E.
Morton, Joe, Jr.
Munroe, Dr. Anthony E.
Murray, James P., Jr.
Owens, Victor Allen
Patton, Jean E.
Payne, Cecilia
Pease, Denise Louise
Pinckney, Edward Lewis
Porter, Michael Anthony
Reid, Desiree Charese
Reid, Dr. Pamela Trotman
Reid, Christopher
Scott, Nelson
Seymore, Stanley
Simpson, Valerie
Smith, Clarence O.
Sobers, Waynett A., Jr.
Spaulding, Esq. Lynette Victoria
Speede-Franklin, Wanda A.
Stamps, Leon Preist
Strickland, Rodney
Tigger, Big
Tobias, Randolf A.
Vaughan, Gerald R.
Wansley, Lisa Payne
Washington, Kerry
Watson, Justin Sean
Walker, Jimmie
Williams, Gayle Terese Taylor
Wright, Sheena
Wright, Tanya
Yoba, Malik

### Bronxville
Green, Thomas E.

### Brooklyn
Abramson, Dr. John J., Jr.
Addison, Caroline Elizabeth
Alexis, Doris Virginia
Alleyne, Rev. Edward D.
Ali, Shahrazad
Allotey, Victor P.
Anderson, Antonio Kenneth
Andrews, Phillip
Anthony, Dr. David Henry, III
Applewhaite, Leon B.
Austin, Dr. Ernest Augustus
Barrett, Dr. Ronald Keith
Bazil, Ronald
Baxter, Dr. Charles F., Jr.
Baye, Betty Winston
Bell, Gordon Philip
Bembry, Jerry E.
Benson, Romona Riscoe
Billue, Zana
Blake, Neil
Bolden, Veronica Marie
Bowe, Riddick Lamont
Boyce, William M.
Bramwell, Patricia Ann
Brooks, Carol Lorraine
Bramwell, Dr. Fitzgerald Burton
Brown, Carolyn Thompson
Brown, Dr. Lawrence S., Jr.
Bryant, Connie L.
Burgie, Irving Louis
Caison-Sorey, Dr. Thelma Jann
Carroll, George D.
Carroll, Dr. James S.
Carmichael, Carole A.
Carey, Jennifer Davis
Cave, Dr. Alfred Earl
Carter, JoAnne Williams
Cave, Perstein Ronald
Cameron, Krystol
Carwell, Hattie V.
Carson, Lisa Nicole
Carter, Shawn Corey
Chrichlow, Livingston L.
Clark, Dr. James N.
Clarke, Rep. Yvette Diane
Coles, Kimberley
Davis, Dr. Jewelnel
Daniels, Lloyd
Dash, Dr. Hugh M. H.
Dember, Jean Wilkins
DeGraffenreidt, James Henry, Jr.

Delsarte, Louis J.
Delcy, Ludget
Dingle, Derek T.
Dixon, Dr. Leon Martin
Douglass, Hon. Lewis Lloyd
Doug, Doug E.
Downing, Will
Dorsey, Herman Sherwood, Jr.
Dunston, Shawon Donnell
Dure, Gerard
Eastmond, Joan Marcella
Elizey, Chris William
Elam, Donna
Epps, Omar Hashim
Ericsson, Dr. Aprille Joy
Evans, Alicia
Fareed, Kamaal Ibn John
Fingaz, Sticky
Fillyaw, Leonard David
Fischer, Lisa
Fierce, Hughlyn F.
Fierce, Milfred C.
Fields, Earl Grayson
Flateau, Dr. John
Foster, Gladys M.
Fonrose, Dr. Harold Anthony
Forde, James Albert
Fox, Thomas E., Jr.
Forbes, Marlon Darryl
Frazier, Shirley George
Francis, Livingston S.
Fraser, George C.
Franklin, William B.
Francis, Dr. Gilbert H.
Franklin, Linda Cheryl Kennedy
Gabriel, Benjamin Moses
Gates, Jacquelyn Burch
Gall, Dr. Lenore Rosalie
Gaines, Crystal Monique
Gatlin, Justin
Gittens, Anthony Edgar
Gifford, Dr. Bernard R.
Gill, Samuel A.
Gossett, Louis Cameron, Jr.
Goodloe, Celestine Wilson
Gore, Cedric J.
Gore, James Anthony
Groff, Rev. Regina Coleen
Green, Vincent E.
Graves, John Clifford
Green, Anita Lorraine
Graves, Earl Gilbert, Jr.
Green, Dr. Richard Carter
Green, Sidney
Graves, Earl Gilbert, Sr.
Grayson, John N.
Greene, Dr. Lionel Oliver
Guitano, Anton W.
Hardison, Kadeem
Harris, Jonathan Cecil
Harris, Francis C.
Hardison, Bethann
Harper, Michael Steven
Hawkins, Dr. Calvin D.
Haynes, Ambassador Ulric St. Clair, Jr.
Haynes, Dr. Alphonso Worden, Jr.
Haywoode, M. Douglas
Hall, Dr. Dolores Brown
Hamer, Dr. Judith Ann
Hernandez, Aileen Clarke
Herbert, Bob
Hibbert, Lawrence M.
Hill, Donna
Hicks, Rev. Dr. Sherman G.
Hill, Robert Bernard
Hill, Barbara Ann
Hobson, Charles Blagrove
Howard, Gwendolyn Julius
Howard, Vera Gouke
Holder, Laurence
Hurd, David James
Ince, Dr. Harold Sealy
Irving, Dr. Clarence Larry, Jr.
Jackson, Pazel G., Jr.
Jackson, Hon. Randolph
James, Letitia
James, Cheryl R.
Jackson, Dorothy R.
James, Juanita T.
Jackson, Mark A.
Jackson, Andrew Preston
Jells, Dietrich Davis
Jenkins, Elizabeth Ameta
Jenkins, Andrew James
Jiggetts, Danny Marcellus
Johnson, Sterling, Jr.
Jones, David R.
Johnson, Dr. Anthony Michael
Jordan, Michael Jeffrey
Jones, Marsha Regina
Jones, Kimberly Denise
Jones, Charles Rahmel
John, Daymond G.
Jones, Clarence Thomas
Jones, William James
Joyner, Lauren Celeste
Johnson, Ronald A.
John, Daymond
Johnson, Michele
Joyner, Irving L.
Johnson, Vinnie
Kani, Karl
Kenan, Randall G.
Kellogg, George
Kearse, Gregory Sashi
King, Albert
King, Bernard
Kweli, Talib
Law, Robert Louis
LaVeist, Wilbert Francisco
Latham, Esq. Weldon Hurd
Ledee, Robert
Lewis, Emmanuel
Lewis, Dawnn
Lee, Joie Susannah
Lewis, Harold Thomas
Long, Nia
Love, Mia
Lord, Dr. Clyde Ormond, Sr.
Marshall, Rev. Calvin Bromley, III
Marr, Carmel Carrington
Marshall, Paule Burke
Maynard, Dr. Edward Samuel
Mason, Clifford L.
Matthew, Clifton, Jr.
Mayo, Harry D., III
Maxwell
Majette, Denise L.
Mandulo, Rhea
Martin, Duane
Marchand, Inga Fung
Marbury, Stephon Xavier
Martin, Patricia Elizabeth
McQueen, Kevin Paige
McCormack, Hurvin
Mcknight, Claude V., III
McFadden, Bernice L.
McKnight, Fr. Albert J.
Meridith, Denise Patricia
Miles, Albert Benjamin, Jr.
Moorer, Michael Lee
Morris, Celeste
Morgan, Wayne
Mos Def
Morris, Stanley E., Jr.
Moore, Esq. Emanuel A.
Murphy, Eddie
Muhammad, Ali Shaheed
Myatt, Hon. Gordon J., Sr.
Nelson, Novella C.
Neal, Lia
Nunn, Ronnie
Omolade, Barbara J.
Osborne, Oliver Hilton
Owens, Dr. Debbie A.
Owens, Geoffrey
Paterson, Dr. David Alexander
Patrick, Esq. Diane
Parsons, Richard Dean
Parker, Lawrence Krisna
Parson, Richard Dean
Perrineau, Harold, Jr.
Peek, Gail Lenore
Perkins, Sam Bruce
Phillips, Rev. Dr. F. Allison
Pinn, Dr. Samuel J., Jr.
Powell, Esq. Darlene Wright
Pryce, Trevor Wesley, II
Procope, Ernesta G
Prince, Edgar Oliver
Ray, James R., III
Ransier, Frederick L., III
Reide, Saint Clair Eugene, Jr.
Reynolds, Jerry Ice
Rhymes, Busta
Rivera, Gerald Maxwell
Richardson, Leroy
Rich, Matty
Richards, Dr. Johnetta Gladys
Rice, Dr. Constance Williams
Robinson, John F.
Ross, Tracey
Samuel, Jasper H.
Salley, John Thomas
Sharpton, Rev. Alfred Charles, Jr.
Shamsid-Deen, Waleed
Simpson, Lorna
Singletary, Deborah Denise
Simmons, Esmeralda
Skeene, Linell De-Silva
Smith, Esq. Stanley G.
Soden, Richard Allan
Soaries, Rev. Dr. DeForest Blake, Jr.
Southerland, Ellease
Stewart, Kebu Omar
Stubbs, Dr. George Winston
Taylor, Hon. Janice A.
Terborg-Penn, Dr. Rosalyn M.
Terry, Patricia S.
Thornton, Ivan Tyrone, Sr.
Thackeray, Anjetta McQueen
Thomas, Terence
Thompson, Gail L.
Thomas, Jane Roscoe
Thompson, William Colridge, Jr.
Thomas, Franklin A.
Tomlinson, Dr. Robert
Tucker, James F.
Tyson, Mike
Tyson, Edward Charles
Vanzant, Rev. Dr. Iyanla
Valmon, Andrew Orlando
Vann, Albert
Velez, Lauren
Walker, Bishop Hezekiah Xzavier, Jr.
Watford-McKinney, Yvonne V.
Walker, Dr. Mark Lamont
Whitaker, Louis Rodman, Jr.
Whyte, Amelious N., Jr.
Wheeler, Robyn Elaine
White, Michael Jai
Whitfield, Dondre T.
Williams, Vanessa A.
Williams, Dr. Audrey L.
Williams, Wayne Allan
Wilson, Clarence S., Jr.
Wilkens, Lenny
Wilkinson, Dr. Robert Shaw, Jr.
Williams, Prof. Daniel Salu
Worrell, Richard Vernon
Wright, Will J.

### Buffalo
Adams, Dr. Julius Gregg
Allen-Meares, Paula G.
Alexander, Dr. Lenora Cole
Amin, Karima
Amos, Donald E.
Arthur, George Kenneth
Bell, James L., Jr.
Bishop, Ellen Elizabeth Grant
Bonds, Kathleen
Brown, Denise J.
Carson, Clayborne
Cole, Dr. Arthur
Coles, Robert Traynham
Curry, Levy Henry
Curtin, Hon. John T.
Darden, Calvin Ramarro
Dozier, Dr. Richard K.
Druitt, Beverly F.
Easley, Brenda Vietta
Edwards, Donald Philip
Gayle, Dr. Helene Doris
Glover, Diana M.
Harrison, Carol L.
Halyard, Dr. Michele Yvette
Herman, Kathleen Virgil
Howard, Dr. Keith L.
Johnson, Rev. Dr. Paul Edwin
Johnson, Beverly
Kirkland-Gordon, Dr. Sharon Elaine
Lanier, Rob
Lloyd, Phil Andrew
McKnight, Brian
McKee, Esq. Clarence Vanzant
McGee, Dr. Joann
Mesiah, Raymond N.
Nickson, Sheila Joan
Ojumu, Ayodele
Parker, Vaughn Antoine
Peterson, Prof. Lorna Ingrid
Pipkins, Robert Erik
Price, Prof. Alfred Douglas
Ray, Jacqueline Walker
Richie, Leroy C.
Rice, Florence M.
Robinson, Clifford Ralph
Robinson, Edith B.
Ryce, Sundra L.
Sarmiento, Shirley Jean
Scott, Hugh B.
Sevillian, Clarence Marvin, Sr.
Shelton, John W.
Sims, Barbara Merriweather
Stewart, Dr. Bess
Thomas, Ron
Wilson, Jonathan Charles
Woodbeck, Frank Raymond
Young, Angela Lynn

### Copiague
McClurkin, Donnie

### Cortlandt Manor
Brand, Elton Tyron

### Crown Heights
Jeffries, Hakeem

### Cuba
Biddle, Dr. Stanton F.

### Delhi
Williams, Jeffrey Lem

### Dunkirk
Thompson, Geraldine

### Earlville
Myrick, Svante L.

### East Harlem
Poussaint, Dr. Alvin Francis

### East Meadow
Roberson, Prof. Gloria Grant

### East Patchogue
Eleazer, Dr. George Robert, Jr.

### Elmhurst
Whaley, Charles H.

### Elmira
Givens, Leonard David
Strickland, Clinton Vernal, Jr.

### Flushing
Cobbs, Dr. Winston H. B.
Craig-Rudd, Joan
Drew, Thelma Lucille
Jackson, Kenya Love
Steward, Elaine Weddington
White, June Joyce

### Freeport
Barnett, Teddy
Gaines, Dr. Thurston Lenwood, Jr.

### Glasco
Kithcart, Larry E., Sr.

### Glen Cove
Beckett, Evette Olga
Corley, Todd L.
Douglas, Ashanti Shequoiya
Hendricks, Richard D.
Pierce, Dr. Chester Middlebrook
Washington, MaliVai

### Great Neck
Curry, Dr. William Thomas

### Harlem
Arnold, Hon. Rudolph P.
Austin, Patti
Bath, Dr. Patricia Era
Belafonte, Harry
Blow, Kurtis
Bryan, Ashley F.
Campbell, Carlos Cardozo
Combs, Sean John
Davis, Ronald R.
Dash, Damon
Francis, Dr. Edith V.
Garland, John William
Grimes, Nikki
Harrell, Andre
Hart, Rev. Tony
Henderson, David
Higginson, Vy
Higginsen, Vy
Jackson, Freddie Anthony
Lawrence, James H.
Mahal, Taj
Madison, Paula Williams
Maynard, Valerie J.
McCrimmon, Nicole
McCannon, Dindga Fatima
Nelson, Jill
Payne, Allen
Paterson, Hon. Basil Alexander
Phifer, Mekhi Thira
Riley, Teddy
Ringgold, Faith
Sandler, Joan Delores
Salaam, Abdel R.
Scott, Larry B.
Shaw, Nina L.
Stancell, Dr. Arnold Francis
Strayhorn, Lloyd
Sweat, Keith
Tunstel, Dr. Edward, Jr.
Watson, Dr. Elizabeth Darby
Williams, Keith David

### Haverstraw
Meriwether, Louise Jenkins

### Hempstead
Beaubien, George L.
Harleston, Brigadier Gen. Robert Alonzo
Mereday, Richard F.
Moore, Rob
Rubio, Jacqueline
Smith, Clifford

### Hollis
Gotti, Irv

### Hudson
Coleman, Trevor W.

### Huntington
Carey, Mariah

### Irvington
Ogbogu, Eric O.

### Ithaca
Majors, Richard G.
Miller, Richard Charles

### Jackson Heights
Grant-Bruce, Esq. Darlene Camille

### Jamaica
Adams, Edward Robert
Bolling, Carol Nicholson
Caines, Bruce Stuart
Cassis, Glenn Albert
Collins, Clifford Jacob
DiAna, DiAna
Elmore, Esq. Ernest Eric
Foxx, Nina
Hamilton, Harry Edwin
Hart, Noel A.
Keizs, Marcia V.
McNeill, Cerves Todd
McMillan, Jacqueline Marie
McDonald, Herbert G.
Ross, Dr. Anthony Roger
Shields, Cydney Robin
Slocumb, Heathcliff
Tillman-DeWitt, Lillian G.
Wilson, Carroll Lloyd

### Kings County
Backus, Bradley

### Kingston
Drake, Jerry

### Lackawanna
Coffey, Dr. Gilbert Haven, Jr.
Edwards, Dr. Sylvia

### Long Beach
Graham, Scottie

### Long Island
Allah, Rakim
Brandon, Barbara
Chenault, Kenneth Irvine
Dash, Julie
Gaffney, Michele Elizabeth
Jones, James F.
McClomb, George E.
Robinson, Charlotte L.
Routte-Gomez, Eneid G.
Yergan, Eric

## Manhattan
Brown, Denise Sharon
Brewster, Luther George
Douglass, Dr. Melvin Isadore
El-Amin, Sa'ad
Johnson, Tre, III
Kinniebrew, Robert Lee
Lewis, William Sylvester, Sr.
Marshall, John W.
McCreary, Bill
Pilgrim, Dr. David
Powell, Gayle Lett
Ramseur, Andre William
Wade, Kim Mache
Williams, Barry Lawson

## Mt. Vernon
Barksdale, Rosa Kittrell
Blake, Dr. J. Herman
Gaines, Hon. Adriane Theresa
Keller, Mary Jean
Lawrence, Elliott
Lee, Robinne
Martin, Dr. Juanita K.
Mason, Dr. Donna S.
Maynor, Kevin Elliott
Parker, William Hayes, Jr.
Reed-Humes, Robi
Rolle, Janet
Sealls, Alan Ray
Washington, Dr. Denzel Hayes, Jr.
Williams, Terrie Michelle
Williams, Gus

## New Rochelle
Arnelle, Hugh Jesse
Boddie, Daniel W.
Goulbourne, Donald Samuel, Jr.
Jamar, Lord
James, Dr. Robert D.
Love, Thomas Clifford
Roundtree, Richard
Robinson, Carol W.
Scott, Ruby Dianne
Spradley, Frank Sanford
Staton, Kerry D.
Torian, Edward Torrence
Walker, Vernon David

## New York
Abdul-Jabbar, Kareem
Abdul-Malik, Dr. Ibrahim
Addison, Adele
Adair, Dr. Robert A.
Adolph, Gerald Stephen
Aiken, William
Alexander, Clifford Leopold, Jr.
Allen, Dr. Winston Earle
Allen, Sanford
Allen, S. Monique Nicole
Alexander, Flex
Alexander, Khandi
Alers, Rochelle
Anderson, Bernadine M.
Anderson, Amelia Veronica
Anderson, Harold A.
Andrews, Emanuel Carl
Archibald, B. Milele
Archibald, Nathaniel
Arroyo, Prof. Martina
Argrette, Joseph M.
Artope, William
Aremu, Dr. Aduke
Austin, Dr. Wanda M.
Austin, Joyce Phillips
Bassett, Angela Evelyn
Baylor, Emmett Robert, Jr.
Babb, Dr. Valerie M.
Baker, Shaun
Barnette, Neema
Bagley, Gregory P., Sr.
Bailer, Bonnie Lynn
Bain, Linda Valerie
Barkley, Rufus, Jr.
Baltimore, Ambassador Richard Lewis, III
Banks, Marguerita C.Banks
Bates, Dr. Clayton Wilson, Jr.
Barzey, Dr. Raymond Clifford, II
Baity, Gail Owens
Baldwin, Louis J.
Basri, Gibor
Baker-Parks, Sharon L.
Bailey, Dr. Didi Giselle
Beane, Robert Hubert
Berry, Philip Alfonso
Bellinger, Harold
Bennett, Courtney Ajaye
Besson, Dr. Paul Smith
Bennett, Rev. Debra Quinette
Bedell, Dr. Frederick Delano
Beard, Dr. Lillian McLean
Benjamin, Ronald
Benoit, Edith B.
Belizaire-Spitzer, Julie
Bent-Goodley, Dr. Tricia
Benjamin, Albert W.
Beach, George
Bell, Yvonne Lola
Beraki, Dr. Nailah G.
Beyer, Troy Yvette
Belafonte, Shari Lynn
Beal, Bernard B.
Bludson-Francis, Vernett Michelle
Bolling, Deborah A.
Bonaparte, Norton Nathaniel, Jr.
Bonaparte, Lois Ann
Bostic, Viola W.
Bolden, Tonya
Bourne, Judith Louise
Bowser, Prof. Benjamin Paul
Brown, Lester J.
Braithwaite, Dr. Mark Winston
Brooks, Dr. Todd Frederick
Branch, B. Lawrence
Branch, Prof. Harrison
Brandt, Lillian B.
Brice, Percy A., Jr.
Brewington, Rudolph W.
Brown, Dr. Mortimer
Brown, Kay B.
Bruce, Raymond L.
Brandon, Symra D.
Brown, Chucky
Bristow, Dr. Lonnie Robert
Brown, Joseph Samuel
Brown, Dr. Joyce F.
Brown, Byron William, II
Burley, Dale S.
Butler, Melba
Burns, Ursula M.
Bunte, Doris
Burns, Ronald Melvin
Butler, Michael E.
Butts, Dr. Hugh Florenz
Cade, Walter, III
Callender, Hon. Carl O.
Callender, Dr. Clive Orville
Callender, Leroy N.
Castenell, Dr. Louis Anthony
Camper, Diane G.
Caldwell, Benjamin
Cadogan, Marjorie A.
Chew, Ray
Chance, Dr. Kenneth Bernard, Sr.
Chapman-Minutello, Alice Mariah
Christian, Dolly Lewis
Chisholm, Dr. June E.
Cheek, Donald Kato
Charles, Bernard L.
Clarke, Joseph Lance
Clyne, John Rennel
Cogsville, Donald J.
Cousins, Althea L.
Coshburn, Henry S., Jr.
Cottrol, Robert James
Cornish, Betty W.
Cortada, Dr. Rafael Leon
Cook, Victor Trent
Cook, Dr. Suzan Denise Johnson
Collins-Eaglin, Dr. Jan Theresa
Cross, June Victoria
Crump, Dr. Arthel Eugene (Gene)
Davis, Clarence A.
Davis, Jean E.
Dawkins, Wayne J.
Davis, Earl S.
Davenport, Dr. Christian A.
Dawson, Rosario Isabel
Daniel, Dr. Yvonne
Dash, Darien C.
Davis, Charles
Davis, Guy
Davis, Allison Jeanne
Darden, Edwin Carley
Dehere, Terry
De Veaux, Alexis
DeSousa, Dr. D. Jason
de Passe, Suzanne
Dennard, Darryl W.
De Graff, Jacques Andre
Delany, Samuel Ray, Jr.
deMille, Dr. Valerie Cecilia
DeSandies, Dr. Kenneth Andre
Dilworth, Dr. Mary Elizabeth
Dickerson, Janet Smith
Dixon, T. Troy
Dillard, Victoria
Diesel, Vin
Dorsey, Clinton George
Dowdy, James H.
Drewry, Cecelia Hodges
Driggriss, Daphne Bernice Sutherland
Drake, Michael V.
Dungie, Ruth Spigner
Dunner, Dr. Leslie Byron
Durant-Paige, Beverly
Durant, Karen
Dunbar, Anne Cynthia
Durant, Celeste Millicent
Early, Robert S.
Easley, Damion
Earley, Keith Henry
Easter, Wilfred Otis, Jr.
Eagan, Catherine B.
Eatman, Dr. Timothy K.
Edwards, Delores A.
Edmond, Dr. Janice L. Sumler
Edwards, Hon. Harry Thomas
Edwards, George Reginald
Edwards, Hon. Dennis, Jr.
Edwards, Theodore Unaldo
Ellington, Mercedes
Ellis, Ernest W.
Elie, Mario Antoine
Ellington, E. David
Eve, Arthur O.
Ewing, Esq. William James
Fay, Toni Georgette
Faison, Donald Adeosun
Felton, James A.
Fields, Kim Victoria
Fleming, Alicia DeLaMothe
Fleming, Vern
Flatts, Barbara Ann
Fletcher, William G., Jr.
Flores, Joseph R.
Fournier, Collette V.
Fortune-Maginley, Lois J.
Ford, Dr. Clyde W.
Ford, Hilda Eileen
Ford, Wallace L., II
Friday, Jeff
Frye, Thomas John
Fraser, Thomas Edwards
Frazier-Ellison, Vicki L.
Fuerst, Jean Stern
Gaskin, Dr. Frances Christian
Garrett, Darrell W.
Gaston, Dr. Arnett W.
George, Allen
Gellineau, Victor Marcel, Jr.
Givens, Robin Simone
Giles, Nancy
Gill, Prof. Jacqueline A.
Goodrich, Dr. Thelma E.
Govan, Reginald C.
Goldberg, Whoopi
Golden, Arthur Ivanhoe
Greaves, William
Green, Geraldine D.
Griffith, Reginald Wilbert
Greene, Aurelia
Grant, Claude DeWitt
Greene, Esq. Gabrielle Elise
Grist, Ronald
Graham, Helen W.
Greenidge, Dr. Kevin C.
Gray, Felix Gary
Guinier, Lani
Halliburton, Christopher
Habersham-Parnell, Jeanne
Halliburton, Warren J.
Harrison, Paul Carter
Hazel, Darryl B.
Harvey, Raymond
Harris, Dr. Don Navarro
Harkness, Jerry B.
Harrigan, Rodney Emile
Harris, Jerome C., Jr.
Harris, Dr. Harcourt Glenties
Harrison, Ronald E.
Harvin, Alvin
Heineback, Barbara Taylor
Hines, Dr. Morgan B.
Hibbert, Dorothy Lasalle
Holmes, Dr. Henry Sidney, III
Horne, June C.
Howell, Robert J., Jr.
Howard, Norman Leroy
Holmes, Esq. Robert Ernest
Horsford, Anna Maria
Holland-Calbert, Mary Ann
Holmes, Carlton
Huff, Janice Wages
Hueston, Dr. Oliver David
Hughes, George Vincent
Jackson, Norman A.
James, Olive C. R.
Jackson, John, III
Jackson, Dwayne Adrian
Jenkins, Dr. Chip, Jr.
Jenkins, Augustus G., Jr.
Jensen, Dr. Renaldo Mario
Jeffers, Dr. Sheila B.
Jeffries, Dr. Rosalind Robinson
Jemmott, Hensley B.
Jeffers, Grady Rommel
Johnson, Robert H.
Johnson, Patrice Doreen
Jones, Benjamin E.
Jones, Anthony, Jr.
Jones, Dr. Ferdinand Taylor
Jones, Prof. Shirley Joan
Jones, Dr. Yvonne Vivian
Jones, Dr. Katherine Elizabeth Butler
Johnson, Wendy Robin
Johnson, Michael Anthony
Johnston, Charlene B.
Johnson, John
Jones, Gregory Allan
Jones, Phillip Madison
Johnson, Hon. Jeh Charles
Johnson, Patricia L.
Johnson, Carl Earld
John, Anthony
Jones-Smith, Jacqueline
Jordan, Patricia
Kappner, Dr. Augusta Souza
Kane, Dr. Jacqueline Anne
Kelley, William Melvin
Kendrick, Curtis L.
Kellman, Denis Elliott
Keyes, Alan Lee
Kendrick, Carol Yvonne
Keys, Alicia
King, Dr. Rosalyn Cain
Knowles, Dr. Eddie Ade
Kotto, Yaphet Frederick
Kravitz, Lenny
Lane, Charles
Lacey, Marc Steven
Lathan, Sanaa McCoy
Lawrence, Dr. Margaret Morgan
Lavergneau, Rene L.
Lee, Clifton Valjean
Lewis, Hon. Daniel
Levy, Valerie Lowe
LeGendre, Henri A.
Leacock, Dr. Ferdinand S., Sr.
Levister, Dr. Ernest Clayton, Jr.
Leftwich, Esq. Norma Bogues
Lewis, Arthur W.
Lewis, Diane Y.
League, Cheryl Perry
Lindsay, Horace Augustin
Llewellyn-Travis, Chandra
London, Roberta Levy
Loney, Carolyn Patricia
Lockhart, James Alexander Blakely
Love, Dr. Helen Althia Mendes
Luckey, Dr. Irene
Luis, Dr. William
Lucas, Dr. William
Martinez, Ralph
Marshall, Thurgood, Jr.
Martin, Walter L.
Mason, Ronald Edward
Martin, Christopher
Mask, Dr. Susan L.
Mashburn, Jamal
Makau, Esq. Elena K.
Maitland, Tracy V.
Marius, Dr. Kenneth Anthony
Mapp, Dr. Edward C.
Manning, Dr. Randolph H., Sr.
Martin, Dr. Rosalee Ruth
Marquez, Dr. Camilo Raoul
McClane, Prof. Kenneth Anderson, Jr.
McPhail, Dr. Irving P.
McMillan, Friar Douglas James
McKayle, Donald Cohen
McLeod, Dr. Georgianna R.
McDaniels, Darryl
McLean, Dollie Clarice H.
McBride, James
McLean, Rene
McHenry, Doug
McMichael, Earlene Clarisse
McFerrin, Bobby
McDuffie, Deborah Jeanne
Mercado-Valdes, Frank Marcelino
Merritt, Eleanor L.
Meeks, Gregory Weldon
Miller, Saundra C.
Miller, Donald Lesessne
Miller, Norma Adele
Miller, Robert, Jr.
Miller, Rev. Kevin D.
Mitchell, Brenda K.
Miller, Arthur J.
Miller, Jacqueline Elizabeth
Mills, Stephanie
Mitchell, Arthur
Miller, E. Ethelbert
Mitchell, Carlton S.
Moose, George Edward
Mohamed, Gerald R., Jr.
Morris, Bernard Alexander
Mobley, Dr. Joan Thompson
Montgomery, Evangeline Juliet
Moore, Dr. Jean E.
Moore, Melba
Morris, Dr. Dolores Orinskia
Morisey, Dr. Patricia Garland
Moseley-Davis, Barbara M.
Morton, Marilyn M.
Monteiro, Dr. Thomas
Monteverdi, Mark Victor
Moses, Dr. Charles T.
Moore, Gregory B.
Morsell, Frederick Albert
Mordecai, David K. A.
Mullens, Delbert W.
Muwakkil, Salim
Murrain, Godfrey H.
Napper, Hyacinthe T.
Naylor, Gloria
Nall, Alvin James, Jr.
Nesbitt, Robin Anthony
Newkirk, Dr. Pamela
Nelson, Jonathan P.
Neavon, Joseph Roy
Newkirk, Thomas H.
Nivens, Beatryce Thomasinia
Noguera, Dr. Pedro Antonio
Norwood, Kimberly Jade
Nurse, Richard A.
Nunez, Miguel A., Jr.
O'Banno, Dr. Donna M. Edwards
Oliver, Donald Byrd, Sr.
Orlandersmith, Dael
Ortiz, Victor N.
Osbourne, Maxwell
Owens, James Robert
Palmer, Dr. Edward, Jr.
Parker-Robinson, D. LaVerne
Patterson, Grace Limerick
Perez, Anna
Perry, Richard H.
Perez, Rev. Altagracia
Pemberton-Heard, Dr. Danielle Marie
Peterson, Rocky Lee
Perkins, Tony
Pearce, Richard Allen
Peters, Samuel A.
Perry, Jean B.
Phillips, Mildred Evalyn
Phillips, Lionel Gary
Phillips, Julian Martin
Pile, Michael David McKenzie
Piper, Adrian Margaret Smith
Pinado, Alan E., Sr.
Powell, Gen. Colin Luther
Poussaint, Renee Francine
Powell, Adam Clayton, III
Pope, McCoy S.
Powell, Robert John
Poe, Kirsten Noelle
Preston, George Nelson
Price, Judith
Prince, Richard Everett
Pugh, Robert William, Sr.
Purvis, Archie C.
Quarles, Norma R.
Randall, Ann Knight
Randolph, Dr. Bernard Clyde, Sr.
Rangel, Charles Bernard
Rainsford, Dr. Greta M.
Rawlins, Dr. Sedrick John

## NORTH CAROLINA



Geographic Index

**Belmont**
Biggins, J. Veronica

**Black Mountain**
Proctor, Barbara Gardner

**Bolivia**
Johnson, Douglas H., Jr.

**Bryson City**
Thomas, Dr. Herman Edward

**Burgaw**
Becote, Fohliette W.
Williams, Samm-Art

**Burlington**
Barker, Judy
Cobb, Rev. Harold James, Jr.
Harris, Cynthia Julian
Kendrick, Joy Antoinette
Leath, Verlyn Faye

**Caroleen**
McSwain, Rodney

**Castalia**
Harris, Maj. James E.

**Caswell County**
Hunter, Edwina Earle

**Cerro Gordo**
Gerald, Dr. Melvin Douglas, Sr.

**Chadbourn**
Lewis, Tom
Towns, Edolphus, Jr.

**Chapel Hill**
Farrington, Thomas Alex
Freeman, Melinda Lyons
Fuller, Dr. Vivian L.
Harris, Bernardo Jamaine
Howard, Tanya Millicent
Miller, Dr. Margaret Elizabeth Battle
Roberts, Margaret Ward

**Charlotte**
Alexander, James, Jr.
Alexander-Whiting, Harriett
Alexander, Rep. Kelly Miller, Jr.
Barrett, Jacquelyn Harrison
Burke, Vivian H.
Cherry, Je'Rod L.
Collins, Mo
Crawford, David
Davis, Howlie R.
Dixon, Gerald Scott, Sr.
Durham, Ray
El Wilson, Barbara
Foxx, Anthony
Grier, Marrio Darnell
Grigsby, Jefferson Eugene, III
Grier, John K.
Grier, Johnny
Gray, Andrew Jackson
Grier, Arthur E., Jr.
Grigsby, Dr. Marshall C.
Hanley, J. Frank, II
Hailey, JoJo
Herron, Vernon M.
Hunter, Dr. David Lee
Jordan, Andrew, Jr.
Johnson, Tiffani Tamara
Leeper, Ronald James
Long, Eddie L.
Massey, Ardrey Yvonne
McCray, Almator Felecia
McInnis, Jeff Lemans
Murphy, Dr. John Matthew, Jr.
Nichols, Elaine
Ramsey, Donna Elaine
Roach, Prof. Hildred Elizabeth
Roundtree, Dovey Johnson
Robinson, Alfreda P.
Sifford, Dr. Charles L.
Tidwell, Isaiah
West, William Lionel, II
Westbrook, Bryant Antoine
Wilson-Smith, Willie Arrie
Woods, Dr. Robert Louis
Workman, Haywoode Wilvon

**China Grove**
Hailey, K-Ci

**Clarkton**
McCoy, James F.
Spaulding, William Ridley

**Clayton**
Debnam, Chadwick Basil
Exum, Dr. Wade F.

**Cleveland County**
DeHart, Dr. Panzy H.

**Climax**
Avant, Clarence

**Clinton**
Dixon, Ronnie Christopher
Fowler, John D.
McPhail, Jerris Cornelius
Sampson, Robert R.

**Columbia**
Bennett, Joyce Annette
Colter, Mike
Pettis, Dr. Joyce Owens

**Columbus County**
Simmons, Juanita

**Como**
Barham, Wilbur Stectson

**Concord**
Alston, Betty Bruner
Cannon, Rev. Dr. Katie Geneva
Goodson, Dr. Ernest Jerome
Hitchcock, Jimmy Davis, Jr.
Mathis, Robert Lee, Jr.
Steele-Robinson, Alice Louise
Taylor, Felicia Michelle
Turner, Vivian Love
Wagoner, J. Robert

**Conway**
Morris, Dr. Carole V.

**Corapeake**
Bennett, Arthur T.

**Cornelius**
Stinson, Andrea Maria

**Council**
Bowen, George Walter

**Creedmoor**
Jackson, William E.

**Cross Creek**
Williams, Prof. William Thomas, Jr.

**Cumberland**
McIver, Everett Allen

**Dallas**
Johnson, Dr. Charles Edward

**Davidson County**
Wagner, David H.

**Dover**
Cox, M. Maurice

**Dudley**
McCloud, Anece Faison
Philyaw, Dino

**Dunn**
Brewington, Dr. Thomas E., Jr.
Freeman, Dr. Algeania Warren
Morgan, Debbi
Thomas, Dr. Lucille Cole

**Durham**
Bowden, Dr. Regina George
Bryant, Dr. Willa Coward
Burroughs, Robert A.
Caesar, Shirley Ann
Clay, Eric Lee
Clemons, Alois Ricardo
Collins, Elsie
Cooper, Esq. Almeta E.
Daye, Charles Edward
Dawson, Horace G., III
Evans-Tranumn, Dr. Shelia
Fluellen, Velda Spaulding
Franklin, Costella M.
George-Bowden, Dr. Regina
Harris, Mary Lorraine
Horton, Dr. Stella Jean
Ishman, Dr. Sybil Ray
Kee, John P.
Kee, Marsha Goodwin
King, Warren Earl
Lawrence, John Edward
Lucas, John Harding, II
Marsh, William A., Jr.
Mangum, Ernestine Brewer
Marsh, Hon. William Andrew, III
McKissick, Floyd B., Jr.
McFadden, Cora
Michaux, Eric Coates
Michaux, Henry M., Jr.
Mitchell, Dr. James Winfield
Nelson-Holgate, Gail Evangelyn
Palmer, Dr. Elliott B., Sr.
Parker Jones, April
Quigless, Dr. Milton Douglas, Jr.
Reeves, Carl Donmark, Jr.
Rogers, Rodney Ray, Jr.
Sampson, Thomas Gatewood
Schooler, Dr. James Morse, Jr.
Shipman, Rev. Dr. Sheldon R.
Smith, Andre Raphel
Spaulding, Aaron Lowery
Strudwick, Lindsey H., Sr.
Stephens, Brenda Wilson
Stanley, Carol Jones
Tate, Grady Bernard
Thorpe, Wesley Lee, Sr.
Townes, Emilie M.
Verbal, Claude A.
Washington, Dewayne Neron
Whisenton, Andre C.
Wilson, Jimmy L.

**East Spencer**
Jackson, Bobby

**Eden**
Brown, Hazel Evelyn

**Edenton**
Brinkley, Norman, Jr.
Jordan, Rev. John Wesley
Perry, Rev. Jerald Isaac, Sr.
Williams, Richard Lee

**Elizabeth City**
Boston, McKinley, Jr.
Logan, Hon. George, III
Sharpe, Dr. Audrey Howell
Smith, Dr. Edward Nathaniel, Jr.
Watt, Garland Wedderick
Williams, Kenny Ray
Woodhouse, Dr. Johnny Boyd
Wright, Roosevelt Rick, Jr.

**Elizabethtown**
Corbett, Dr. Doris R.
Lewis, Jimmy
Owens, Lynda Gayle

**Eureka**
Becton, Rudolph

**Evergreen**
Nixon, Otis Junior, Jr.

**Fair Bluff**
Johnson, Robert B.

**Fairmont**
Buie, Pastor Sampson, Jr.
Campbell, Bobby Lamar

**Farmville**
Barnes, Ronald Lewis
Dupree, Edward A.
Hobbs, Dr. Alma Cobb
Parker, Charles McCrae

**Fayetteville**
Andrews-McCall, Dr. Maxine Ramseur
Bowman, William Alton
Carpenter, William Arthur
Cade, Brigadier Gen. Alfred Jackal
Coram, Willie Mae
Dailey, Lenora Shell
Hales, Dr. Mary A.
McNeill-Huntley, Esther Mae
McEachern, D. Hector
McPherson, Roosevelt
McPherson, James R.
Murrell, Adrian Bryan
Murphy, Michael McKay
Puryear, Dr. Alvin Nelson
Tatum, Kinnon Ray, II
Williams, Harold David
Williams, Wilbert Edd
Womble, Jeffery Maurice

**Flat Rock**
Darity, Dr. William Alexander, Sr.

**Fletcher**
Allen, Ottis Eugene, Jr.

**Franklinton**
Jones, Rev. Dr. Robert Earl
Perry, Wilmont Darnell
Young, Dr. Elizabeth Bell

**Ft. Bragg**
Logan, Ernest Edward, II
Morris, Joe
Powell, Marvin, Jr.
Tose, Maurice B.
Woods, Kondria Yvette Black

**Fuquay**
McLean, Dennis Ray

**Garner**
McCullers, Eugene

**Garysburg**
Garner, James A.
Powell, Bettye Boone

**Gaston County**
Anderson, Nicholas Charles
Moses, Dr. Henry A.

**Gastonia**
Armstrong, Darrell Eugene
Floyd, Eric Augustus
Hamilton, Leonard
Latimer, Jennifer Ann
Miller, James S.
Sadler, Dr. Kenneth Marvin
Sowell, Thomas

**Gates County**
Edwards, Bessie Regina
Smith, Thomas Lee, Jr.

**Goldsboro**
Bass, Marshall Brent
Coley, Malcomb
Evans, Mike
Forte, Dr. Minnie T.
Gordon, Dr. Edmund W.
Hairston, William
Howell, Amaziah, III
House, James E.
Silver, Dr. Joseph Howard, Sr.
Summers, Retha
Waters, Brenda Joyce
Ward, Frances Marie
Williams, Dr. Clarence G.

**Gratham**
Martin, Wanda C.

**Greensboro**
Anderson, Norman Bruce
Austin, Raymond Demont
Burns, Lamont Antonio
Butler, Pinkney L.
Cotton, Joseph Craig
Davis, Reuben Cordell
Davis-McFarland, Dr. E. Elise
Foulks, Dr. Carl Alvin, Jr.
Free, Kenneth A., Sr.
Garrett, James F.
Hackett, Barry Dean
Harris, John Clifton
Henry, John Wesley, Jr.
Horne, Dr. Edwin Clay
Holt, Torry Jabar
Ingram, Gregory Lamont
Johnson, Walter Thaniel, Jr.
Lynch, Loretta E.
McKinney-Johnson, Eloise
McAdoo, Bob, Jr.
Moone, Wanda Renee
Neal, Frederic Douglas
Perry, Dr. Patsy Brewington
Scantling, Wayne Lamar
Shoffner, Garnett Walter
Sharpe, Prof. Calvin William
Smith, Dr. Jessie Carney
Stewart, Dr. William H.
Strachan, Lloyd Calvin, Jr.
Tasco, Hon. Marian B.
Towns, Dr. Myron B., II
Waden, Fletcher Nathaniel, Jr.
Welch, D. Michelle Flowers
Webb, Harold H.
Wiggins, Edith Mayfield
Worthey, Richard E.

**Greenville**
Cherry, Edward Earl, Sr.
Crumpler, Carlester T., Jr.
Hemby, Dorothy Jean
Hines, Dr. Wiley Earl, Jr.
Highsmith, Carlton L.
James, Dr. David Phillip
Jenkins, Emmanuel Lee
McLawhorn, James Thomas, Jr.
Robinson, Ann Garrett
Stokes, Dr. Lillian Gatlin
Streeter, Dr. Elwood James
Tyson, Andre
Walters, Rev. Hubert Everett
Williams, Dr. Harry Lee

**Gregory**
Perkins, William O., Jr.

**Halifax**
Jenkins, Dr. Melvin Lemuel

**Hamlet**
Bethea, Gregory Austin
Douglas, Walter Edmond, Sr.
Fisher, Ronald L., Sr.
Fletcher, Winona Lee
Quick, Mike Anthony

**Hampstead**
Sharpless, Hon. Mattie R.
Sidbury, Harold David

**Harlowe**
Godette, Franklin Delano Roosevelt

**Harrellsville**
Revelle, Robert, Sr.

**Harrisburg**
Means, Natrone Jermaine

**Havelock**
Carter, Edward Earl
Mitchell, Dennis Allen

**Henderson**
Alston, Gerald
Baskerville, Hon. Randolph
Evans, Dr. Therman E.
Gregg, Lucius Perry, Jr.
Hawkins, Dr. Gene
Lewis, Robert Alvin, Jr.
Person, Dr. William Alfred
Scott, Dr. Marvin Bailey

**Hendersonville**
Evans, Hon. Carole Yvonne Mims
Gash, Samuel Lee, Jr.

**Henrico**
Edwards, Grover Lewis, Sr.

**Herdford**
Vaughan, Rev. Dr. James Edward

**Hertford**
Barnes, Dr. Delorise Creecy
Gregory, Robert Alphonso

**Hickory**
Barrett, Iris Louise Killian
Dennis, Carolyn K.

**High Point**
Adams, Alma
Brown, Robert Joe
Carter, Martin Joseph
Chess, Eva L.
Davis, Harold R.
Harris, Helen B.
Hutton, Dr. Ronald Irving
Jackson, Fred James, Sr.
Jeffries, Greg
Kelly, James Johnson
Matthews, Claude Lankford, Jr.
McNeil, Frank William
Price, Ray Anthony
Truesdale, Dr. Carlton Maurice

### Tryon
Carson, Dr. Warren Jason, Jr.

### Vanceboro
Bryan, Dr. Curtis Eugene, Sr.
Edwards, Dr. Thomas Oliver

### Vass
Sellars, Harold Gerard

### Wadesboro
DeBerry, Virginia
Gatewood, Dr. Algie C.
Hilliard, Alicia Victoria
Kersey, Elizabeth T.
Kirby-Davis, Montanges
Little, Herman Kernel
Little, General T.
Miller, Dr. Maposure T.
Sinclair, Clayton, Jr.
Young, Rose S.

### Wagram
Gholston, Betty J. Blue

### Wake County
Gill, Rep. Rosa Underwood

### Wake Forest
Billingsley, Ray C.
Mitchell, LeMonte Felton

### Wallace
Carr, Michael Leon

### Walnut Cove
Golden, Donald Leon

### Warrenton
Tunstall, Richard Clayton
West, Dr. Herbert Lee, Jr.
Williams, Yarborough, Jr.

### Warsaw
Bass, Dr. Herbert H.
Lowe, Dr. James Edward, Jr.
Smith, Janice Evon

### Washington
Gray-Little, Dr. Bernadette
Moore, Alice Evelyn
Rasby, Walter Herbert, III
White, Jack E., Jr.
Williams, Hilda Yvonne

### Wayne County
Cogdell, D. Parthenia
Harris, Marion Rex
Williams, Dr. Charles J., Sr.

### Weldon
Cheek, King Virgil, Jr.
Cooke, Leonard G
Dell, Willie J.
Wiley, Forrest Parks

### Wendell
Ellis, Gregory Lemont

### Whiteville
Hall, Dr. Reginald Lawrence
Lawrence, Dr. William Wesley
Lennon, Patrick Orlando
Maultsby, Rev. Dr. Sylvester
Singletary, Reggie Leslie
Spaulding, Romeo Orlando
Thurman, Marjorie Ellen

### Williamston
Smith, Frances C.

### Willow Springs
Adams-Ender, Clara Leach

### Wilmington
Bell, Dr. Joseph N.
Bowen, Dr. Blannie E.
Childs, Joy B.
Clemmons, Major Gen. Reginald G.
Davis, Esq. Morris E.
Hill, Robert J., Jr.
Jones, Samuel
Jones, Anthony Ward
Lemon, Meadowlark, III
McLaren, Douglas Earl
McCracken, Quinton Antoine
Newsome, Dr. Paula Renee
Robinson, Curtis
Robinson, James Waymond
Solomon, David
Tatem, Dr. Patricia Ann
Waddell, Ruchadina LaDesiree
Wilson, Dr. Johnny Leaverne

### Wilson
Baines, Dr. Rev. Henry T., Sr.
Barnes, Dr. Boisey O., Jr.
Butterfield, George Kenneth, Jr.
Conaway, Mary Ward Pindle
Fitch, Milton Frederick Toby, Jr.
Hagood, Henry Barksdale
Moore, Floreese Naomi
Muhammad, Marian
Sherrod, Ezra Cornell
Tayari, Kabili

### Windsor
Bond, Vernon, Jr.
Harmon, John H.
Moore, Christine James
Smith, William Gene
Speller, Dr. Charles K.

### Winston Salem
Miller, Jones Sandy

### Winston-Salem
Agnew, Raymond Mitchell, Jr.
Anderson, Rev. Dr. Al H., Jr.
Andrews, Nelson Montgomery
Atkins, Edmund E.
Black, Veronica Correll
Cox, Otis Graham, Jr.
Cockerham, Haven Earl
Cook, Dr. Nathan Howard
Crawford, H. R.
Crews, Rev. William Hunter
Cribb, Juanita Sanders
Crowell, Germane L.
Davis, Hubert Ira, Jr.
Dye, Hon. Luther V.
Eller, Carl Lee
Ewers, Dr. James Benjamin, Jr.
Fair, Talmadge Willard
Feemster, John Arthur
Frasier, Ralph Kennedy
Grier, Pamela Suzette
Harry, Jackee
Howard, Brian Eugene
Jones, Randy
Lattimore, Dr. Caroline Louise
Martin, Harold L., Sr.
Morton, Lorraine H.
Pritchard, Robert Starling, II
Quivers, Dr. Eric Stanley
Reynolds, Andrew Buchanan
Rogers, Dr. Bernard Rousseau
Sarreals, E. Don
Scales, Dr. Manderline Elizabeth Willis
Scales-Trent, Prof. Judy
Shell, Dr. Juanita
Sprinkle-Hamlin, Sylvia Yvonne
Stallings, Ramondo Antonio
Thompson, Kevin Lamont
Watts, Rolanda
West, Dr. Togo Dennis, Jr.
Womble, Rep. Larry W.

### Winterville
Hammond, Rev. Kenneth Ray

### Winton
Christian, John L.

### Wise
Yuill, Essie McLean-Hall

### Woodland
Majete, Dr. Clayton Aaron

### Yanceyville
Edwards, Hon. Donna F.
Jeffries, Fran M.

### Youngsville
Jeffreys, John H.

### Zebulon
Ivery, James A.

## NORTH DAKOTA

### Grand Forks
Baugh, Dr. Reginald F.

### Minot
Bradford, Ronnie

### Valley City
Burd, Steven A.

## OHIO

### Akron
Banton, Linda Wheeler
Blake, Rev. William J.
Bryant, Leon Serle
Carter, Tracy L.
Chapman, Esq. David Anthony
Clark, Dr. Theotis, Jr.
Curry, Stephen
Davis, Diana L.
Davison, Edward Larry
Dove, Rita Frances
Fowler, Judge William E., Jr.
Hannah, Johnnie, Jr.
Hewett, Howard
Heflin, Marrion
Ingram, James Edward
James, LeBron Raymone
Lane, Jerome
Lane, Allan C.
Lewis, Thomas A.
Marsh, Doug Walter
McClenic, Patricia L.
McClain, Andrew Bradley
McIlwain, Toni
Minter, Steven Alan
Paschal, Trisa Long
Satterwhite, Dr. Frank Joseph Omowale
Scruggs, Cleorah J.
Scruggs, Sylvia Ann
Simon, Matt
Thomas-Richardson, Dr. Valerie Jean
Thurmond, Nate
Wallace, Linda Skye
Wilson, F. Leon

### Alliance
Watts, Hon. Lucile A.

### Ashtabula
Ball, Roger

### Barberton
Sims, Esau, Jr.

### Batavia
Parham, Marjorie B.

### Bellaire
Galloway, Joseph Scott
Scott, Dr. John Sherman
Speights, Esq. Nathaniel H.

### Berea
Binford, Henry C.

### Blackfork
Keels, James Dewey

### Bowling Green
Hill, James L.

### Bratenahl
Chancellor, Carl Eugene

### Caledonia
Terrell, Francis D'Arcy

### Canton
Danzy, Patricia Lynn
Grant, Gary
Gray, Macy
Hawkins, Steven Michael
Hughley, Stephanie S.
Hudgeons, Louise Taylor
Hubbard, Philip Gregory
Kennard, Patricia A.
Lacy, Donald E., Jr.
Mack, C.
McDaniels, Jeaneen J.
McIlwain, Nadine Williams
Monroe, Kevin A.
Page, Hon. Alan Cedric
Snow, Eric
Snow, Percy Lee
Wilson, Jon

### Chillicothe
Beard, James William, Jr.
Boxill, John Hammond
Menefee, Juan F.
Shatteen, Westina Matthews
Wilson, Nancy

### Cincinnati
Adams, Sheila J.
Al'Uqdah, William Mujahid
Anderson, Judge David Turpeau
Anderson, Darren Hunter
Anderson, Tyfini Chence
Anderson, Dr. David Atlas
Axam, John Arthur
Beaver, Joseph T., Jr.
Bellinger, Rev. Mary Anne Allen
Blackwell, John Kenneth
Booker, Vaughn Jamel
Booker, Michael
Brunson, Frank
Brasey, Henry L.
Bronson, Rev. Dr. Fred James, Sr.
Bryant, Dr. Napoleon Adebola, Jr.
Bryson, Dr. Ralph J.
Burlew, Ann Kathleen
Burgin, Bruce L.
Carpenter, Ronald, Jr.
Carroll, Rocky
Carruthers, Dr. George Robert
Carter, Thomas Allen
Chenault, John
Clarke, Bryan Christopher
Clarke, Raymond R.
Collins, Bootsy
Cross, Judge Denise L.
Crutcher, Dr. Ronald Andrew
Cross, Fr. William Howard
Cureton, Michael
Davis, Michael James
Daniel, Colene Yvonne
Davis, William R.
Davis, John W., III
Doddy, Reginald Nathaniel
Durham, Leon
Edwards, Leo Derek
Edwards, Dixon Voldean, III
Fox, Ambassador Richard K., Jr.
Fornay, Alfred R., Jr.
Francis, James L.
Garrett, Kathryn
Gaston, Dr. Marilyn Hughes
George, Dr. Theodore Roosevelt, Jr.
Grant, Judge Cheryl Dayne
Gray, Carlton Patrick
Grauer, Gladys Barker
Hardy, Darryl Gerrod
Hansford, Louise Todd
Hamilton, Edward N.
Hargraves, Col. William Frederick, II
Henderson, Leon C.
Hilson, Dr. Arthur Lee
Hill, Tyrone
Holmes, Emma Selean
Hubbard, Paul Leonard
Hutton, Marilyn Adele
Hunter, Tony Wayne
Isley, Ernie
Johnson, Lance
Johnson, Melvin Carlton, III
Johnson-Helton, Karen
Jones, Lafayette Glenn
Justice, David Christopher
Kearney, Eric Henderson
Killens, Terry Deleon
Larkin, Barry Louis
Larkin, Michael Todd
Lawson, Lawyer
Logan-Tooson, Linda Ann
Maryland, Mary Angela
Maxey, Dr. Randall W.
Maddox, Garry Lee
Merriweather, Robert Eugene
Meadows, Cheryl R.
Morgan, Clyde Alafiju
Morris, Elizabeth Louise
Morris, Major
N'Namdi, Carmen Ann
Orr, Louis McLaughlin
Parker, Rev. Matthew
Perry, Margaret
Penny, Dr. Robert
Pleasant, Albert E., III
Pryor, Dr. Chester Cornelius, II
Qamar, Nadi Abu
Reece, Steven, Sr.
Reid, Antonio
Rhodes, Karl Derrick
Shepherd, Veronika E.
Smiley-Robertson, Carolyn
Stewart, Dr. Gregory
Stroud, Louis Winston
Stewart, Shannon Harold
Summers, Loretta M.
Sutton, Dr. Sharon Egretta
Thompson, LaSalle, III
Thompson, Sylvia Moore
Thompson, Herman G.
Tillery, Dwight
Tucker, Geraldine Coleman
Van Johnson, Rodney
Ward, Rev. Dr. Daryl
Washington, Dr. Michael Harlan
West, John Andrew
Weathersby, Joseph Brewster
White, Janice G.
Wilson, Russell
Wiggins, Lillian Cooper
Williams, Harold Louis
Wiles, Dr. Leon E.
Young, Dr. Joyce Howell

### Circleville
Smith, Dr. Eleanor Jane

### Cleveland
Abercrumbie, Dr. Paul Eric
Ackerman, Dr. Patricia A.
Adams, Armenta Estella
Adrine, Ronald Bruce
Adams, H. Leslie, Jr.
Allen, Jerry Ormes
Alexander, Major Gen. Richard C.
Anglen, Reginald Charles
Atkins, Russell
Barrett, James A.
Baker, Robert N.
Barnes, Yolanda L.
Bailey, Prof. Gary
Baldwin, Olivia McNair
Baker, Jacqueline J.
Beverly, Eric R.
Berry, Halle Maria
Beasley, Arlene A.
Billings, Earl William
Blount, Heidi Lynne
Boykins, Earl Antoine
Boyd, Terry A.
Boone, Alexandria Johnson
Brown, Norman E.
Brown, Lewis Frank
Bradley, Dr. James George
Butler, Annette Garner
Bustamante, J. W. Andre
Carter, Marva Griffin
Carter, Kevin Antony
Calloway, Vanessa Bell
Carter, Robert T.
Carter, Robert Thompson
Carlton, Pamela Gean
Chriss, Henry Thomas
Chapman, Tracy
Chambers, Christopher J.
Clemons, Linda K.
Clark, Dr. Sanza Barbara
Cloud, William Eric
Clouden, LaVerne C.
Cooper, Michael Gary
Coleman, Dr. Melvin D.
Connally, C. Ellen
Crosby, Fred Charles
Craven, Judith B.
Crosby, Dr. Edward Warren
Crosby, Fred McClellen
Daniels, Frederick L., Jr.
Davis, Jacklean Andrea
Derryck, Vivian Lowery
Dee, Ruby
Dorman, Hattie Lawrence
Doss, Conya
Draper, Dr. Sharon Mills
Dunnigan, Jerry A.
Duncan, Geneva
Easler, Michael Anthony
Eatman-Williams, Janice A.
Edwards, Ruth McCalla

Taylor, Dr. Carol Ann
Watkins, Wynfred C.
Warren, Roland C.
Williams, Dr. Lisa R.
Williams-Taitt, Patricia Ann

### Trotwood
Butler, Duane

### Troy
Carter, Cris

### Union City
Enis, Curtis D.

### Urbana
Honore, Stephan LeRoy
Mike, Daedra Anita Von
Stevens, Warren Sherwood

### Warren
Browner, Ross D.
Browner, Joey Matthew
Carter, Etta F.
Daniels, LeShun Darnell, Sr.
Thomas, Prof. Nate
Wimbish, Gary Lynn

### Warrensville Heights
Johnson, Luther E.
Williams, Barbara Ann

### Wellsville
Carter, Dr. Joye Maureen

### Westerville
Carter, Ki-Jana

### Woodstock
Mayo, Blanche Irene

### Wyoming
Lowry, James E.

### Xenia
Callender, Lucinda R.

### Youngstown
Allen, Clyde Cecil
Ashe, Dr. Clifford, III
Bacon, Barbara Crumpler
Borom, Lawrence H.
Bryant-Ellis, Paula D.
Brown, Ernestine
Bright, Alfred Lee
Carter, Dr. Raymond Gene, Sr.
Cobbin, W. Frank, Jr.
Dillard, Dr. June White
Doxie, Marvin Leon, Sr.
Echols, Mary Ann
Graham, Donald
Holloway, Ardith E.
Jennings, Dr. Lillian Pegues
Johnson, Andrew L., Jr.
Johnson-Odim, Dr. Cheryl
Jones, Nathaniel R.
Jones, Nathaniel R.
Luten, Thomas Dee
Marshall, Betty J.
Montgomery, Oliver R.
Neal-Barnett, Dr. Angela M.
Payne, Wilford Alexander
Penn, Derek
Pegues, Francine
Powell, Craig Steven
Pride, John L.
Revish, Jerry
Robinson, Myron Frederick
Spencer, Brenda L.
Williams, Annalisa Stubbs

### Zanesville
Anderson, Dr. George Allen
Ball, Richard Erwin
Burke, Dr. William Arthur
Coates, Dr. Janice Eula
Farmer, Forest Jackson, Sr.
Morse, Barbara Lyn
Newman, Paul Dean
Preston, Eugene T.

## OKLAHOMA

### Ada
McKinzie, Barbara Anne

### Altus
Gildon, Jason Larue

### Anadarko
Huskey, Butch

### Arcadia
Parks, Dr. Gilbert R.

### Ardmore
Douglas, Dr. Samuel Horace
Foreman, Doyle

### Atoka
Robinson, Crystal LaTresa

### Bixby
Billups, Mattie Lou

### Bluff
McKerson, Mazola

### Boley
Lee, Forrest A., Sr.
Matthews, Mary Joan Holloway
Walker, Ronald Plezz

### Boswell
Mitchell, Jacob Bill

### Bristow
Tillman, Dr. Mary Anne

### Checotah
Dorn, Dr. Rev. Roosevelt F.
Scroggins, Tracy L.

### Cherokee County
Rogers, Charles D.

### Chickasha
Benton, Leonard D.
Crowell, Dr. Bernard Gene
Hiatt, Dana Sims

### Chouteau
Ray, Johnny

### Claremore
Goodwin, Della McGraw
Supernaw, Kywin

### Cushing
Cornwell, W. Don

### Depew
Goode, Calvin Coolidge

### El Reno
Cook, Wallace Jeffery

### Elmore City
Gigger, Nathaniel Jay

### Enid
Mitchell, Leona Pearl
Strother, Dr. Germaine D.

### Erin
Smith, Elsie Mae

### Eufaula
Watts, Julius Caesar, Jr.

### Fallis
Epps, George Allen, Jr.

### Frederick
Acrey, Autry
Miller, Constance Joan

### Ft. Gibson
Douglass, M. Lorayne

### Ft. Sill
Gardner, Ava Maria

### Goodnight
Jones, Viola W.

### Guthrie
Adams, Dr. Eugene William
Black, Dr. James Tillman, Sr.
Greene-Thapedi, Dr. Llwellyn L.
Kelso-Watson, Angela R.
Miller, Camille Louise Stearns

### Hartshorne
Hopper, Dr. Cornelius Lenard
Webber, William Stuart

### Haskell
Rowe, Jimmy L.

### Hennessey
Williams, Dr. Everett Belvin

### Henryetta
Tunley, Naomi Louise

### Holdenville
Brown, James Marion
Jordan, Richard Lamont

### Hugo
Hill, Clara Grant
Raye, Vance Wallace

### Hulbert
Blackwell, Dr. Harvel E.
Irons, Dr. Edward Davis

### Idabel
Burris, Bertram Ray
Counts, Dr. George W.
Johnson, Bill Wade
Vaughn, Countess Danielle

### Kingfisher
Nelson, Dr. Wanda Jean
Woodard, Fredrick

### Langston
Henry, Dr. Marcelett Campbell
House, Millard L., II

### Lawton
Anderson, Sunny
Green, John M.
Griggs, Anthony G.
King, Stacey
Love, Dr. Ruth Burnett

### Lone Tree
Hill, Anita Faye

### Marietta
Howard, Samuel Houston

### McAlester
Mason, Dr. Cheryl Annette
Porter, Dr. Clarence A.
Thomas, Charles Columbus

### Meridian
McKinney, Venora Ware

### Midwest City
Kemp, Matthew Ryan
Ponder-Nelson, Debra

### Muskogee
Belton, Howard G.
Busby, Everett C.
Carter, Kenneth Wayne
Chisum, Dr. Gloria Twine
Clayton, Xernona
Davis, Dr. Bennie L.
Davis, Denyvetta
Garner, Dr. La Forrest Dean
Hardeman, Dr. Carole Hall, Sr.
Hamilton, Charles Vernon
Herbert, Dr. Adam W., Jr.
Hooker, Dr. Olivia J.
Jones, George H.
Ledbetter, Charles Ted
McDaniels, Alfred F.
McClinton, Curtis R., Jr.
Owens, Dr. Wallace, Jr.
Parks, Thelma Reece
Portlock, Dr. Carver A.
Porter, Dr. Temille
Richardson, DeRutha Gardner
Roberts, Rev. Dr. Samuel Kelton
Shipp, Howard J., Jr.
Stewart, Loretta A.
Tollett, Dr. Charles Albert, Jr.
Tucker, Norma Jean
Twigg, Dr. Lewis Harold, Jr.
Wallace, Arthur, Jr.
Williams, T. Joyce
Young, Dr. Barbara J.
Young, Dr. Michael

### Newalla
Clardy, William J.

### Newby Creek
Tottress, Dr. Richard Edward

### Newkirk
Brooks, William P.

### Nowata
Penn, Christopher Anthony

### Oklahoma City
Boone, Ronald Bruce
Brown-Francisco, Teresa Elaine
Carter, Joseph Christopher
Campbell-Martin, Tisha Michelle
Clark, Beverly Gail
Corlette, Edith Parker
Cox, Kevin C.
Easter, Dr. Marilyn K.
Ferguson, Renee
Fry, Darrell
Fuller, Dr. Harold David
Green, Ruth A.
Harvey, Rev. Dr. William James, III
Henderson, Joyce Ann
Holmes, Prof. Carl
Huggins, Linda Johnson
Jones, Dr. Barbara Ann Posey
Kennedy, Sandra Denise
Kimbrough, Donna L.
Lacy-Pendleton, Stevie A.
Lennox, Betty Bernice
Mayes, Alonzo Lewis, Jr.
Matthews, Albert D.
McCollum, Judge Alice Odessa
Moore, Etta R.
Newton, Jacqueline L.
Parker, Maryland Mike
Payne-Nabors, Colleen J.
Sparks, Phillippi Dwaine
Stewart, Rayna Cottrell, II
Thompson, Linda Jo
Todd, Melvin R.
Wilson, Dr. Frank Fredrick, III
Williams, Norris Gerald
Williams, Jennifer J. Scott

### Okmulgee
Porter, Edward Melvin
Thompson, David Farrod
Walker, Wilbur P.

### Oktaha
King, Ruby Dean

### Pauls Valley
Franklin, Dr. Grant L.

### Ponca City
Coleman, Dr. Don Edwin
Thomas, Joyce Carol

### Poteau
See, Dr. Letha A.

### Sallisaw
Hankins, Hesterly G., III

### Seminole
Frelow, Dr. Robert Dean

### Shamrock
Moland, Willie C.

### Shawnee
Gordon, Darrien X. Jamal

### Slick
Hare, Dr. Nathan

### Soper
Armstrong, Ernest W., Sr.

### Spencer
Moore, Ronald
Tipton, Danell

### Stillwater
Arnold, Ethel N.

### Taft
Davis, Lelia Kasenia
Wilkins, Rillastine Roberta

### Tatums
Patrick, Dr. Opal Lee Young

### Tulsa
Baylor, Helen
Berry, Jay
Bryant, Hubert Hale
Brewer, Dr. Rose Marie
Davis, Frederick D.
Fletcher, James Andrew
Goodwin, James Osby
Goodwin, Martin David
Goodwin, Pastor Robert Kerr
Hall, Melvin Curtis
Hare, Dr. Julia
Hare, Julia Reed
Hopkins, Donald Ray
Hopkins, Dr. Gayle P.
Hughes, Hollis Eugene, Jr.
Johnson, Jerry Calvin
Johnson, Roy Steven
Kimble, Bettye Dorris
Lockett, Kevin Eugene
Mabson, Glenn T.
Madison, Eddie L., Jr.
McLeod, Dr. Michael Preston
McQuarters, Robert William, II
Monday, Sabrina Goodwin
Nash, Marcus DeLando
Parker, De'Mond Keith
Perara, Dr. Mitchell Mebane
Sanders, Patricia Roper
Samuels, Everett Paul, Sr.
Starks, John Levell
Troupe, Dr. Marilyn Kay
Vaughn, David, III
Walker, Dr. Ethel Pitts
West, Cornel Ronald
Wilson, Charlie Kent
Woodard, Alfre

### Vernon
Hill, Curtis T., Sr.

### Waukomis
Jackson, Eugene D.

### Weeletka
Williams, Dr. Leon Lawson

### Wewoka
Brown, Dr. Lee Patrick
McWilliams, Dr. Alfred E., Jr.
Ponder, Dr. Henry

### Wynnewood
Allen, James

## OREGON

### Klamath Falls
Black, Gail M.

### La Grande
Marsh, Dr. Pearl-Alice

### Portland
Benton, Phyllis Clora
Brown, Cindy
Brandon, Terrell
Brown, Sherman L.
Davidson, Fletcher Vernon, Jr.
Daniels, Richard Bernard
Green, A. C., Jr.
Hunter, Brian Lee
Leonard, Carolyn Marie
Rashad, Dr. Ahmad
Smith, Wilson Washington, III
Stoudmaire, Damon
Thomas, Liz A.
Washington, Dr. Warren Morton

## PENNSYLVANIA

### Abington
Dickerson, Tyrone Edward
Hopson, Harold Theodore, Jr.
Wilson, Sandra E.
Williams, Hon. Louise Bernice

### Aliquippa
Denson, Damon Michael
Dorsett, Anthony Drew, Jr.
Gilbert, Sean
Law, Ty
Mann, Richard
Myers, L. Leonard
Thornton, Dozier W.

### Allentown
Felton, Zora Martin
Linton, Jonathan C.
Reed, Andre Darnell
Williams, Janice L.

### Altoona
Harris, Joseph John, III
Harris, Dr. John, III
Moore, John Brian
West, Doug

### Avondale
Hodge, Marguerite V.

### Bedford
Bradley, David Henry, Jr.

### Bellefonte
Luckey, Dr. Evelyn F.

### Berwyn
Welburn, Ronald Garfield

### Bethlehem
Kelly, Rev. James Clement
Smith, Dr. Ernest Howard

### Blairsville
Watkins, Aretha La Anna

### Blythedale
Kirkland, Prof. Jack A.

### Braddock
Blair, Dr. George Ellis, Jr.
Wilkins, Betty

### Bristol
Lester, Betty J.

### Brownsville
Gary, Dr. Melvin Lee
Kirksey, M. Janette

### Bryn Mawr
Becton, Lt. Gen. Julius Wesley, Jr.
Cordell, LaDoris Hazzard
Hill, Kenneth D.
Saunders, John Edward, III
Turner, George R.
Wansel, Dexter Gilman

### Camp Hill
Jaycox, Mary Irine

### Canonsburg
Bates, William J.

### Carlisle
Gilbert, Albert C.
Myers, Lewis Horace
Owens, Dr. Judith Myoli
Owens, Billy Eugene

### Chester
Bond, Ronald A.
Bond, Cecil Walton, Jr.
Brown, Rev. William Rocky, III
Campbell, Lamar
Collins, Audrey B.
Cuff, George Wayne
Dale, Clamma Churita
Dodson, Howard, Jr.
Dotson, Howard, Jr.
Mobley, John Ulysses
Mobley, Stacey J.
Nicholas, Philip
Oliver-Simon, Gloria Craig
Riley, William Scott
Staton, Donna Hill
Thompson, Garland Lee
Wooten, Carl Kenneth, Jr.

### Clairton
Cooper, Walter, Sr.

### Coatesville
Anderson, Dr. Thomas Jefferson
Baxter, Rev. Nathan Dwight
Jacks, Ulysses
Johnson, Paul Lawrence
Rhoden, Dr. Richard Allan, Sr.
Suber, Tora
Walls, Gen. George Hilton, Jr.
Washington, John Calvin, III

### Coraopolis
Latimer, Esq. Allie B.
Miller-Perry, Rosetta

### Darby
Tyler, Robert James, Sr.
Walker, Dr. Valaida Smith

### Derry Township
Wilson, Dr. William Julius

### Donora
Griffey, Ken, Sr.
Griffey, Ken, Jr.
Payne, Ulice, Jr.
Walton, Reggie Barnett

### DuBois
Matthews, Dolores Evelyn

### Duquesne
Castleman, Elise Marie
Coleman, Audrey Rachelle
Jordan, J. Paul

### Edenborn
Stringer, Charlaine Vivian

### Eerie
Blanks, Billy

### Ellwood City
Kirklin, Dr. Perry William

### Erie
Hicks, Eric David
Jones, Theresa Diane
Moore, Richard Baxter
Wilcher, Dr. Shirley Jean

### Ford City
Lovelace, Dean Alan

### Gates
Gillum, Dr. Ronald M., Sr.

### Germantown
Cosby, Dr. William Henry
Coleman, William T., Jr.

### Greensburg
Frye, Nadine Grace
Griffith, John A.

### Grindstone
Pratt, A. Michael

### Gum Tree
Middleton, Rose Nixon

### Harrisburg
Cannon, Paul L., Jr.
Dawson, Lumell Herbert
Drayton, Troy Anthony
Gadsden, Rev. Dr. Nathaniel J., Sr.
Gist, Karen Wingfield
Green, Dennis
Gumby, Dr. John Wesley
Hargrove, Dr. Trent
Johnson, Prof. Stephanie Anne
Robinson, William A.
Tate, Robert Lee
Temple, Edward Stanley
Thornton, Wayne T.
Watters, Ricky
Waters, Paul Eugene, Jr.
Williams-Dovi, Joanna

### Homestead
Batch, Charlie
Baker, Maxine Beatrice
Blackmon, Hon. Mosetta Whitaker
Fergerson, Miriam N.

### Homewood
Tanksley, Ann Graves

### Johnstown
Daniel, Jack L.
Hawkins, Artrell, Jr.
Murphy, Dr. Donald Richard, II
Richardson, Rev. Louis M., Jr.

### La Mott
Littlepage, Craig

### Lancaster
Anderson, Madeline
Hopkins, Leroy Taft, II
Wilson, Donald K., Jr.

### Langhorne
Franklin, James E.

### Latrobe
Haile, Annette L.

### Leechburg
Hales, Edward Everette

### Malvern
Lewis, Ida Elizabeth

### McDonald
Gilbert, Jean P.
Lewis, Matthew Marvin
Lewis, Marvin Ronald

### McKeesport
Abif, Khafre Kujichagulia
Alford, Thomas Earl
Baldwin, Cynthia A.
Crutchfield, James N.
Curry, Major Gen. Jerry Ralph
Dickerson, Prof. Dennis Clark, Sr.
Griffin, Michael D.
Hayes, James Harold, Jr.
James, Toni-Leslie
Jefferies, Charlotte S.
Johnson, Sheila Crump
Mason, Major Albert, III
Mikell, Dr. Charles Donald
Montgomery, Esq. Gregory B.
Rhinehart, June Acie
Rogers, Dr. George
Smith, Bruce L.
Tunie, Tamara Renee

### Meadville
Orr, Dr. Dorothy J.
Patterson, Evelynne R.
Singleton, Esq. Harry M.

### Monongahela
Graves, Autumn Adkins
Procter, Harvey Thornton, Jr.
Rhodes, Jeanne Simmons
Simmons, Paul A.

### New Brighton
Denson, Fred L.
Matthews, Candace Sheffield

### New Castle
Gaither, Israel L.
Gunn, Dr. Arthur Clinton
Hewitt, Vivian Ann Davidson
Jones, Dr. Anne R.
Mauney, Donald Wallace, Jr.
McClendon, Kellen
Miller, Thomasene

### New Kensington
Preston, Joseph, Jr.

### Norristown
Brown, Simon F.
Campbell, Thomas W.
LeRoy, Charles
Robinson, Hon. Rosalyn Karen

### Panama
Jonas, Dr. Ernesto A.

### Philadelphia
Abel, Renaul N.
Abdullah, Sharif
Ackridge, Florence Gateward
Adderley, Herb Anthony
Adams, Gregory Keith, Sr.
Albright, Dr. Robert, Jr.
Allen, Dr. Claude Alexander, Jr.
Alston, Kwaku
Anderson, Kenneth Richard
Anderson, Dr. Bernard E.
Archie, Shirley Franklin
Ausbrooks, Beth Nelson
Bagby, Rachel L.
Ballard, Shareese Renee
Baltimore, Charli
Battle, Dr. Conchita Y.
Banks, Gene
Bailey, Curtis Darnell
Balthrope, Dr. Jacqueline Morehead
Ballard, Dr. Allen Butler, Jr.
Barnett, Dr. Samuel B.
Beckett, Sydney Ann
Beckham, Barry Earl
Best, John T., Jr.
Bethel, Dr. Leonard Leslie
Benson, Rubin Author, Jr.
Beverly, Frankie
Bell, Lawrence F.
Billings, Cora Marie
Bishop, Dr. Alfred A.
Bluford, Col. Guion Stewart, Jr.
Bozeman, Bruce L.
Boyd, Thomas
Booker, Rev. Vaughan P. L.
Bowser, Kyle Damon
Bogle, Donald
Browne, Dr. Craig C.
Brown, Christine James
Brown, Cherie Greer
Bryant, Kobe Bean
Brown, James Lamont
Bridges, Sheila
Brown, Marie Dutton
Brooks, Carl
Brown, Gilbert David, III
Brown, Clifton George
Brooks, Suzanne R.
Branche, Gilbert M.
Bradshaw, Lawrence A., Sr.
Braxton, Hon. John Ledger
Brooker, Moe Albert
Brown, Tyrone W.
Brown, William H., III
Bunyon, Ronald S.
Burton-Lyles, Blanche
Butler, Esq. Frederick Douglas
Burton-Shannon, Dr. Clarinda
Bullins, Ed
Burrell, Leroy Russell
Butler, Kathleen Jean
Campbell, Edna
Carroll, Rodney J.
Calhoun, Monica
Cary, Lorene
Case, Dr. Arthur M.
Campbell, Dr. Mary Schmidt
Carter, Fredrick James
Carter, William Beverly, III
Chappell, Emma Carolyn
Chase-Riboud, Dr. Barbara DeWayne
Cheek, Donna Marie
Childs, Oliver Bernard
Chisholm, Samuel Jackson
Chandler, Alton H.
Clarke, Stanley Marvin
Clark, Patricia Ann
Clayton, Dr. Constance Elaine
Clark, Claude Lockhart
Clark, Jesse B., III
Clayton, Matthew D.
Collins, Dr. Patricia Hill
Crawford, Betty Marilyn
Crutchfield, Lisa
Cuyjet, Cynthia K.
Daniels, Alfred Claude Wynder
Davis, Brownie W.
Davis, Dr. Marianna White
Davis, Emanual
Dawson, Shed, Jr.
Daniels, Lee Louis
Days, Michael Irvin
Davenport, Ronald R., Sr.
DeFrantz, Dr. Anita L.
Dent, Dr. Preston L.
Dickerson, Dr. Bette Jeanne
Dixon, Valena Alice
Dourdan, Gary Robert
Domingo, Colman
Driver, Richard Sonny, Jr.
Dunmore, Charlotte J.
Dyer-Goode, Dr. Pamela Theresa
Early, Dr. Gerald
Echols, Alvin E., Jr.
Edmunds, Dr. Walter Richard
Edwards, Lewis
Edmunds, Allan L.
Ellis, Bishop J. Delano, II
Ellis, Benjamin F., Jr.
Emmons, Rev. Rayford E.
Erving, John, Jr.
Essoka, Gloria Corzen
Essien, Dr. Francine
Eubanks, Kevin Tyrone
Evans, Rep. Dwight
Everett, Charles Roosevelt
Fattah, Hon. Chaka
Fain, Constance Frisby
Fattah, Falaka
Faulcon, Dr. Clarence Augustus, II
Falana, Lola
Fernandez-Smith, Wilhelmenia
Fields, Lynn M.
Flamer, John Henry
Fleming, Patricia Stubbs
Ford, Antoinette
Ford, Donald A.
Foote, Yvonne
Foard, Frederick Carter
Fordham, Cynthia Williams
Fortson, Danny
Frazier, Kenneth C.
Frazier, Frances Curtis
Frazier, Herman Ronald
Franklin, Shirley Clarke
Fuller, Charles
Gamble, Kenneth
Gaither, Dr. Cornelius E.
Garner, Dr. Melvin C.
George, Eddie, Jr.
Golson, Benny
Goode, Wilson, Jr.
Goss, Clayton
Gordon, Levan
Green, William Ernest
Grantham, Prof. Regina B.
Grundy, Dallas A.
Gray, Brian Anton
Graves, Denique
Gregory, Judge Roger L.
Graham, Paul, Jr.
Gundy, Roy Nathaniel, Jr.
Guillebeaux, Tamara Elise
Hayward, Ann Stewart
Harley, Philip A.
Harrington, Elaine Carolyn
Harris, Jeanette G.
Hall, Dr. Julia Glover
Harris, Barbara Clementine
Hagins, Ogbonna
Harrison, Marvin Daniel
Heath, Dr. James E.
Hendricks, Barkley L.
Henry, Brent Lee
Henry J, Thelma Preyer
Hilton, Stanley William, Jr.
Hill, William Randolph
Hill, Jeffrey Ronald
Hill, Dr. Rosalie A.
Hoagland, Everett H.
Holley, Rev. Jim
Hopkins, Bernard
Hooks, Kevin
Horton, Carl E.
Hughes, Sen. Vincent J.
Hunter Hayes, Tracey Joel
Hunter, Kim L.
Ingram, Kevin
Jackson, Ricardo C.
Jackson, Lisa P.
Jasper, Lawrence E.
Jamison, Judith Ann
James, Marquita L.
Jackson, Dr. Russell A., Jr.
Jackson, Beverly Anne
James, Dion
Jenkins, Andrew M., Jr.
Jeter, Joseph C., Jr.
Jeffers, Eve Jihan
Jeff, D J Jazzy
Johnson, Mathew
Johnstone, Lance
Jordan, Prof. Sandra D.
Jones, Thomas Wade
Johnson, Nathaniel J., Sr.
Jones, William Allen
Jordan, Josephine E. C.
Jones, Hon. Bonnie Louise
Jordan, Dr. J. St. Girard
Johnson, Warren S.
Kane, Eugene A.
Keene, Sharon C.
King, Jeanne Faith
Kimble, Bo
Lawson, Jason L.
Lathan, Dr. William Edward
Lassiter, Prof. Chad Dion
Lahr, Dr. Charles Dwight
Landry, Dolores Branche
LaBelle, Patti
Lawes, Verna
Lewis, Dr. Samuel L., Jr.
Leonard, Jeffrey
Lewis, Ronald C.

Lewis, Dr. William A.
Lee, Edward S.
Lehman, Dr. Christopher Paul
Lewis, Karen A.
Lee, William Thomas
Lee, Kevin Brian
Linton, Gordon J.
Linton, Sheila Lorraine
Lloyd, Lewis Kevin
Lloyd, Rev. Dr. J. Anthony
Love, Edward Tyrone
Lowman, Carl D.
Lownes-Jackson, Dr. Millicent Gray
Lomax, Michael Wilkins
Long, John Edward
Long, Steffan
Lockwood, James Clinton
Lyons, A. Bates
Mayes, Doris Miriam
Mallette, Carol L.
Maddox, Julius Arnell
Mack, John L.
Mansfield, Dr. Carl Major
Martin, Dr. Richard Cornish
Manning, Dr. Eddie James
Mayo, Dr. Julia A.
McLaurin, Daniel Washington
McFadden, Nathaniel James
McCoullum, Dr. Valarie Ena Swain-Cade
McKie, Aaron Fitzgerald
McAndrew, Anne E. Battle
McFaddin, Theresa Garrison
McCrary, Michael
McKinney-Whetstone, Diane
Mercer, Valerie June
Meeks, Stephen Abayomi Obadele
Merriweather, Barbara Christine
Mixon, Veronica
Miller, William O.
Mills, Joey Richard
Miller, Dr. M. Sammye
Miller, Frederick A.
Mitchell, Rev. Dr. Sadie Stridiron
Minor, Tracey L.
Miller, Jamir Malik
Morrow, W. Derrick
Morris, Valerie Coleman
Morris, Nathan Bartholomew
Morris, Wanya Jermaine
Montgomery, Dr. Toni-Marie
Mosley, Elwood A.
Morris, Valerie Dickerson Coleman
Monroe, Earl
Moore, Acel
Murray, Fr. J-Glenn
Myers, Andre
Nearn, Arnold Dorsey, Jr.
Neal, Charlie
Nissel, Angela
Okore, Cynthia Ann
Oliver, Bilal Sayeed
Overton, Douglas M.
Owens, Rich Darryl
Owens, Curtis
Owens, David Kenneth
Parnell, Arnold W.
Page, Dr. Gregory Oliver
Pate, Alexs D.
Palmer, Stephanie
Palmer, Bishop Gregory Vaughn
Parks, Dr. Donald B.
Paul, Wanda D.
Peete, Holly Robinson
Pennick, Janet
Peguese, Herman A.
Perry, Leonard Douglas, Jr.
Peguese, Charles R.
Pettaway, Charles
Phillips, Dr. Frederick Brian
Pierce, Hon. Lawrence Warren
Pindell, Howardena D.
Pittman, Dr. Audrey Bullock
Pilot, Ann Hobson
Pinkett, Dr. Randal D.
Pinkney, Jerry
Pope, Bishop Courtney A.
Powell, Mike
Poellnitz, Fred Douglas
Polk, Dr. William C.
Questlove
Ramey, Dr. Felicenne H.
Rasberry, Rev. Robert Eugene
Reid-Merritt, Dr. Patricia Ann
Reed, Esq. Michael H., Jr.
Rhone, Sylvia M.
Richardson, Jerome, Jr.
Rich, Betty
Richards, Dr. Germaine Gail Branch
Richardson, Linda Waters
Ridley, Dr. Charles Robert
Richardson, Wayne Michael
Roberts, Lorraine Marie Pettie
Robinson, Dr. Randall S.
Roney, Raymond George
Roebuck, Rep. James Randolph, Jr.
Robinson, Charles
Robinson, Dr. William Andrew
Robinson, Dr. Malcolm Kenneth
Robbins, Carl Gregory Cuyjet
Roberts, Troy
Rose, Malik Jabari
Robinson, John Moses
Rush, Otis
Salmons, John Rashall
Saddler, Dr. Elbert M., II
Sanders, Steven LeRoy
Samuels, Charlotte
Scott, Marvin Wayne
Scott, Jill
Sealy, Dr. Joan Rice
Shamwell, Prof. Ronald L.
Simpson, Stephen Whittington
Singleton, Dr. Robert
Sloan, Maceo Kennedy
Slaton, Gwendolyn C.
Smith, Will
Smith, Dr. Rev. Gregory Robeson, Sr.
Smith, Dr. Marie Evans
Smith, Rev. Dr. Wallace Charles
Soulchild, Musiq
Spence, Dr. Donald Dale
Spencer, Prof. Margaret Beale
Stokes, Carolyn Ashe
Stockman, Shawn Patrick
St. Patrick, Matthew
Stokes, Shereitte Charles, III
Staley, Dawn Michelle
Stewart, Larry A., Jr.
Staley, Pastor Kenneth Bernard
Staten, Everett R.
Stevens, Dr. George Edward
Summers, Dr. Rodger
Swygert, Prof. H. Patrick
Swann, Eugene Merwyn
Swain, James H.
Swayne, Harry Vonray
Taylor, Dr. Susan Charlene
Tann, Esq. Daniel J.
Taylor, Sterling R.
Temple, Esq. Donald Melvin
Thompson, Dr. Deborah Maria
Thompson, Benjamin Franklin
Thompson, Hon. Anne Elise
Thompson, DeHaven Leslie
Thompson, Gloria Crawford
Thomas, Roderick
Thomas, Hon. W. Curtis
Thompson, Aaron A.
Thomas, Blair
Thornton, Leslie
Tolliver, Rev. Dr. Joel
Traynham, Robert Lee, II
Turner, Marvin Wentz
Turner, Jean Taylor
Tucker, Dr. Wilbur Carey
Tyler, Shirley Neizer
Tyner, Alfred McCoy
Tyree-Walker, Ida May
Tyree, Omar
Tyson, Ron
Vaughn, Dr. Alvin
Vaughn, Clarence B.
Waites-Howard, Shirley Jean
Walker, Tanya Rosetta
Waiters, Dr. Ann Gillis
Washington, Ukee
Washington, LeAnna M.
Way, Charles Christopher
Wallace, Rasheed Abdul
Waters, Crystal
Weston, Martin V.
Welmon, Dr. Vernis M.
Weaver, Aissatou Mijiza
Welborn, Edward Thomas, Jr.
Whitaker, William Thomas, Jr.
Whitney, Dr. W. Monty
White, William Joseph
Whitten, Eloise Culmer
Williams, Martha S.
Wilson, Earl Lawrence
Wilson, Wesley Campbell
Williams, Wesley S., Jr.
Wilmore, Rev. Gayraud Stephen, Jr.
Williams, Prof. Yvonne Carter
Williams, Willie L.
Wilson, Rita P.
Williams, Jerome D.
Wing, Theodore W., II
Williams-Witherspoon, Kimmika L. H.
Williams, Dr. Anita Spencer
Williams, Judith Byrd
Wims, Warner Barry
Willis, Deborah
Williams, Clarence J., III
Williams, Tyrone M., Jr.
Willingham, James Edward, Sr.
Williams, Alvin Leon
Wooden, Shawn Anthony
Woodson, Atty. Roderic L.
Wormley, Cynthia L.
Worrell, Dr. Audrey Martiny
Wright, Rev. Dr. Jeremiah A., Jr.
Wright, Marilyn N.
Wright, Mark Adrian
Wynn, Dr. Albert Russell
Yarborough, Prof. Richard A.
Young, Ollie L.

### Pittsburgh

Adams, Jonathan, III
Adams, Richard Melvin
Adams, Katherine J.
Allen, Cheryl L.
Arties, Lucy Elvira Yvonne
Arties, Walter Eugene, III
Atkins, Sharif
Baeza, Della Britton
Benson, George
Bell, George
Bell, Sheila Trice
Bobonis, Regis Darrow, Jr.
Brown, Geoffrey Franklin
Bradford, Gary C.
Bridgeforth, Arthur Mac, Jr.
Brown, Ralph Benjamin
Brown, Dr. Ruby Edmonia
Bush, Esther L.
Buckley, Gail Lumet
Burley, Jack L., Sr.
Carter, Norman L.
Cash, Swintayla Marie
Clancy, Sam, Jr.
Clay, Willie James
Clark, John Joseph
Clowney, Audrey E.
Copeland, Kevon
Conley, Martha Richards
Cunningham, Dr. James J.
DeAnda, Peter
Dilday, Hon. Judith Nelson
Douglas, Herbert Paul, Jr.
Doss, Rod
Drake, Lawrence M., II
Eskridge, Rev. John Clarence
Foster, William K., Sr.
Gough, Dr. Walter C.
Griffith, John H.
Griggs, Judith Ralph
Gresham, Darryl Wayne
Hamlin, David W.
Harris, Eugene Edward
Harrison, James, Jr.
Harris, Dr. Arthur Leonard, III
Higgins, Stann
Howard, Leon W., Jr.
Holloway, Douglas V.
Hubbard, Lawrence Ray
Hunter, Dr. Frederick Douglas, Sr.
Jamal, Ahmad
Jackson, Hon. Marie Oliver
Jefferson, Gary Scott
Kennedy, Adrienne Lita
Knott, Dr. Albert Paul Lowe, Jr.
Lauderback, Brenda Joyce
Littlejohn, Dr. Edward J.
Lowry, Donna Shirlynn
Mason, Felicia Lendonia
Martin, Curtis James, Jr.
Marshall, Brandon Tyrone
Malone, Dr. Gloria S.
Mabrey, Prof. Marsha Eve
Marbury, Rev. Donald Lee
McNairy, Dr. Francine G.
McDonald, Dr. R. Timothy
McDaniel, Dr. James Berkley, Jr.
Michel, Harriet Richardson
Mitchell, Dean Lamont
Motley, David Lynn
Nelson, Ramona M.
Nixon, James I., Jr.
Oliver, Dr. Melvin L.
Palmore, Roderick A.
Page, Solomon
Pegues, Dr. Wennette West
Phillips, Frank Edward
Pittman, Darryl E.
Porter, Billy
Porter, Karl Hampton
Price, Sr. Fred L.
Pratt, Awadagin
Ramey, Dr. Melvin R.
Richardson, Munro Carmel
Richardson, Julieanna
Roberts, Margaret Mills
Roberts, Dr. Grady H., Jr.
Rodgers, Edward
Robinson-Walker, Mary P.
Saunders, Prof. Raymond Jennings
Smith, Dr. Joanne Hamlin
Taylor, Jason Paul
Taylor, Carole Lillian
Taylor, Dr. Jack Alvin
Titus, LeRoy Robert
Tibbs, Edward A.
Tomlin, Josephine D.
Utley, Richard Henry
Watson, Hon. J. Warren
Washington, Leonard, Jr.
Weaver, Herbert C.
Wheeler, Shirley Y.
Winters, James Robert
Williams, Maxine Broyles
Williams, Dr. McDonald
Williams, Dr. Melvin Donald
Williams, James Otis
Williams, Lauryn
Wilson, Dr. Stephanie Y.
Wilson-Knox, Shanice Lorraine
Winbush, Dr. Raymond Arnold
Woodruff, Jeffrey Robert
Wright, Dr. Jackson Thomas, Jr.

### Pittston

Cousin, Rev. Philip R.

### Pottstown

Beasley, Aaron Bruce

### Reading

Jackson, Robert E.
Jackson, Stuart Wayne
Marshall, Donyell Lamar
Miller, Wade Thomas
Moore, Lenny Edward

### Ridley Park

Hutchins, Dr. Francis L., Jr.

### Rochester

Douglas, Elizabeth (Betty) Asche
Dorsett, Tony Drew
Farmer, Clarence, Sr.
Farmer, Dr. Robert Clarence, Sr.
Fuget, Dr. Charles Robert
Haynes, Barbara Asche
Sessoms, Dr. Frank Eugene

### Sewickley

Person, Dr. Dawn Renee

### Sharon

James, Dava Paulette
McCall, Rev. Dr. Emmanuel Lemuel, Sr.
Norman, Dr. William H.
O'Connor, Dr. Rodney Earl
Phillips, Dr. James Lawrence

### South Fayette

Hayes, Jonathan Michael

### Steelton

Cornish, Jeannette Carter

### Tarentum

Howell, Rev. Chester Thomas

### Uniontown

Hooper, Michele J.
Hunt, Ronald Joseph
Lawson, Rev. James Morris, Jr.
Poole, Dr. Rachel Irene
Trent, James Eugene

### Washington

Henderson, Barrington
Spencer, Gregory Randall
Tucker, Dr. M. Belinda

### West Chester

Boyer, Spencer H.
Mehreteab, Ghebre-Selassie
Washington, Marian E.
Welburn, Edward Thomas, Jr.
Westmoreland, Samuel Douglas

### West Grove

Rivero, Marita

### West Reading

Knox, Wayne D. P.

### Wilkes-Barre

Patterson, Dr. Elizabeth Ann
Patterson, Christine Ann

### Wilkinsburg

Bailey, Arthur
Johnson, Esq. Livingstone M.
Johnson, Justin Morris

### Williamsport

Andrews, Carl R.
Brown, Gary Leroy
Davis, Anita Louise
Thurston, Dr. Paul E.
Tremitiere, Chantel Ruth

### Wyncote

Jackson, Reggie Martinez

### Wynnefield

Armstrong, Robb

### Yeadon

Lee, Andrea
Reed-Miller, Rosemary E.

### York

Armstrong, William F.
Brown, Omar Lamont
Claiborne, Loretta
Grayson, Rev. Dr. Byron J., Sr.
Ham, Dr. Debra Newman
Hartzog, Ernest E.
Hairston, Dr. Eddison R., Sr.
Kennedy, Lincoln
Peters, Rev. Dr. Pamela Joan
Price, Glenda Delores
Smallwood, William Lee

## PUERTO RICO

### Boqueron

Carlo, Nelson

### San Juan

Williams, Bernie

### Santurce

Batine, Dr. Rafael

## RHODE ISLAND

### East Providence

Lopes, David Earl
Walker, Dr. Kenneth R., Sr.

### Newport

Gaines, Hon. Paul Laurence
Suggs, Dr. Robert Chinelo

### Providence

Blunt, Roger Reckling, Sr.
Cantrell, Blu
Castro, George A.
Evans, Charlotte A.
Harris, William Allen
Jackson, Dr. Raymond Thompson
Noonan, Dr. Allan S.
Osborne, Jeffrey Linton
Pryde, Arthur Edward
Santos, Mathies Joseph
Smith, Wayne Franklin
Taylor, Stuart A.

### Quonset Point

Allen, Quincy L.

# SOUTH CAROLINA

### Hardeeville
Robinson, Eunice Primus
Williams, Daniel Louis

### Hartsville
Davis, Major
Johnson, Shannon Regina
McClain-Thomas, Dorothy Mae
Myers, Emma McGraw
Paschal, Eloise Richardson
Richardson, Dr. Luns C.

### Heath Springs
Michael, Dr. Charlene Belton

### Hemingway
Barr-Davenport, Leona
Cooper, Joseph
Montgomery, Joe Elliott
Weaver, Dr. John Arthur
Woods, Sylvia

### Hilton Head Island
Campbell, Emory Shaw
Driessen, Daniel
Driessen, Henry, Jr.

### Hodges
Goggins, Dr. Horace

### Holly Hill
Morant, Mack Bernard
Randolph, Willie Larry, Jr.
Washington, Dr. Sarah M.

### Hopkins
Burroughs, Tim
Lowman, Dr. Isom D.
Neal, Dr. Green Belton, II
Prioleau, Dr. Sara Nelliene
Prioleau, Peter Sylvester

### Horry County
Gore, David L.

### Islandton
Johnson, Dr. Vermelle Jamison

### Jenkinsville
Owens, Mercy P.

### Johns Island
Saunders, William Bill

### Johnsonville
Moore, Albert

### Jonesville
Jones, Alfredean

### Kathwood
Larke, Charles G.

### Kershaw
Mickle, Hon. Andrea Denise
Roscoe, Dr. Wilma J.

### Kingstree
Hamiter, Uhuru A.
Mack, John W.
Miller, Ward Beecher
Smith-Gaston, Linda Ann
Tisdale, Dr. Henry Nehemiah

### Ladson
Green, Harold, II
Washington, Arnic J.

### Lake City
Burgess, Robert E., Sr.
Cross-McClam, Deloris Nmi
Hannah, Mosie R.
Jones, Ervin Edward
Wilson, Alva L.

### Lamar
Kirkland, Levon
Pollard, Raymond J.

### Lancaster
Caldwell, Dr. Esly Samuel
Duncan, Dr. Louis Davidson, Jr.
Harris, Pep
Pelote, Dorothy Barnes
Williams, Brian O'Neal

### Lane
Simmons, Clyde, Jr.

### Laurens
Atkinson, Eugenia Calwise
Carter, John R.
Coleman, Marian M.
Cunningham, Malena Ann
Floyd, Dr. Jeremiah
Floyd, James T., Sr.
Hamill, Margaret Hudgens
Hall, Benjamin Lewis, III
Irby, Galven

### Leesville
Etheredge, James W., Jr.

### Lexington
Sewell, Isiah Obediah

### Lincolnville
Seele, Pernessa C.

### Loris
Floyd, Dr. Dean Allen

### Lugoff
Putnam, Glendora M.

### Lynchburg
Jowers, Johnnie Edward, Sr.

### Manning
Canty, George
Ellerby, William Mitchell
Spencer, Jimmy, Jr.

### Marion
Davis, James F.
McCummings, Dr. LeVerne
McClellan, Frank Madison
Richardson, Dr. Leo O.
Williams, Armstrong

### Marlboro County
Bostic, Dr. James Edward, Jr.

### Matthews
Golden, Louie

### Mauldin
Garnett, Kevin Maurice

### McBee
Mack, Levorn

### McClellanville
Ball, Drexel Bernard
Smalls, Marcella E.

### McCormick
Carter, Dr. Judy L.

### Moncks Corner
Mitchum, Dorothy M.
Stewart, Ryan Evan

### Mt. Pleasant
Meyers, Dr. Rose M.

### Mullins
Faulkner, Carolyn D.
Jones, Dr. Elnetta Griffin
Reaves, Rev. Franklin Carlwell
Williams, Jean Carolyn

### Myrtle Beach
Smalls, O'Neal

### Nesmith
Butts, Janie Pressley

### Newberry
Caldwell, John Edward
Coleman, Hon. Claude M.
Davenport, Hon. Horace Alexander
Hailstock, Shirley
Lawlah, Gloria Gary
Taylor, Reggie

### North Augusta
Britton, Ambassador Theodore R., Jr.

### Orangeburg
Abraham, Nathaniel Donnell
Bodrick, Leonard Eugene
Brunson, Dr. Debora Bradley
Davis, Dr. Leroy, Sr.
Dorman, Dr. Linneaus C.
Everett, Esq. Ralph B.
Frazier, Dr. Leon
Glover, Agnes W.
Goodwin, Mac Arthur
Harper, Dwayne Anthony
James, Carrie Houser
Johnson, Doris Elayne
Payton, Dr. Benjamin Franklin
Pendergrass, Emma H.
Quick, George Kenneth
Rackley, Lurma M.
Rhodes, Dr. Robert Shaw
Robinson, Rev. Joseph, Jr.
Robinson, Eugene Harold
Spigner, Dr. Clarence
Switzer, Lou
Thompson, William L.
Winans, Mario
Winningham, Herman Son, Jr.
Wrice, Dr. Sheldon B.
Young, Arlene H.
Young, Dr. Nancy Wilson
Zimmerman, Dr. Eugene

### Pacolet
Means, Dr. Fred E.

### Pageland
Miller, Patina

### Pawleys Island
Reid, Dr. Irvin D.

### Pelzer
Reid, Janie Ellen

### Pendleton
Anderson, Carl Edward

### Pinesville
Ravenell, Rev. Joseph Phillip

### Port Royal
Robinson, Henry

### Prosperity
James, Frederick C.

### Ravenel
Cobb, Ethel Washington

### Rembert
Wade, Terrell

### Richburg
Douglas, John Daniel
Greene, Dr. William Henry L.

### Ridgeland
Barnes, Diane
Hickson, Dr. Sherman Ruben
Newton, Gen. Lloyd W.

### Ridgeway
Brunson, David
Johnson, Mamie Peanut
Peay, Hon. Samuel

### Ritter
Williams, Jayson

### Rock Hill
Agurs, Donald Steele
Burris, Jeffrey Lamar
Fewell, Richard
Gaines, John A., Sr.
Mack, Gladys Walker
McDaniel, Rev. Paul Anderson
McDaniel, Dr. Adam Theodore
Roach, Lee
Zimmerman, Matthew Augustus, Jr.

### Ruffin
Grant, James

### Salley
Corbitt, Dr. John H.

### Salters
Tisdale, Prof. Celes

### Saluda
Graham, Dr. Patricia G.
Woods, Geneva Holloway

### Sellers
Jones, Gen. Frank

### Seneca
Gunn, Willie Cosdena Thomas
Maxwell, Bertha Lyons
Williams, Larry C.

### Shaw AFB
Pritchard, Michael Robert

### Sheldon
Black, Daniel L., Jr.

### Spartanburg
Booker, Anne M.
Brewton, Dr. Butler E.
Davis, Stephen Lamont
Dominic, Irwing
Gilmore, Dr. Al Tony
Hill, Robert Lewis
Johnson, Robert L.
Perkins, Louvenia Black
Saunders-Henderson, Martha M.
Simmons, Anthony Lamont
Smith, Anne Street
Tanner, James W., Jr.
Talley, James Edward
Townes, Hon. Sandra L.
Tucker, Dr. Dorothy M.

### Spring Gulley
Evans, Ernest

### St. Matthews
Davis, Viola
Haynes, Dr. Walter Wesley
Hewing, Dr. Pernell Hayes

### St. Stephen
Salters, Dr. Charles Robert
Twiggs, Dr. Leo Franklin

### Sumerton
Hammett, Willie Anderson

### Summerville
Singleton, Benjamin, Sr.

### Sumpter
Hall, Sydney Jay, III
Johnson, Joshua

### Sumter
Blanding, Larry
Buckhanan, Dorothy Wilson
Canty, Dr. Ralph Waldo, Sr.
Clyburn, James Emos
Clyburn, John B.
Conyers, Dr. James Ernest, Sr.
Davis, Dr. Sheila Parham
Felder, Dr. Loretta Kay
Heyward, James Oliver
King, Dr. Talmadge Everett, Jr.
Martin, Dr. Edward Williford
Martin, Frank C., II
Pogue, Brent Daryl
Reuben, Dr. Lucy J.
Reynolds-Brown, Blondell
Reuben, Dr. Lucy Jeanette
Richardson, Desmond
Stephen, Joyce A.
Talley, William B.
Weston, Larry Carlton

### Swansea
Riley, Victor Allan

### Timmonsville
Williams, Dr. Helen Elizabeth

### Townville
Thompson, Dr. Beatrice R.

### Union
Grayson, Jennifer A.
Jeter, Delores DeAnn
Jenkins, Barbara Williams
Talley, Dianne W.
Thomas, Rev. Dr. Latta Roosevelt, Sr.

### Varnville
Burns, Jeff, Jr.
Folk, Dr. Frank Stewart

### Wagener
Benjamin, Arthur J., Jr.

### Walterboro
Lewis, Andre
Thompson, Johnnie

### Wando
Porcher, Robert, III

### Waverly
Cromartie, Ernest W., III

### Westminster
Johnson, Dr. Martin Leroy

### Williston
Brown, Rep. Charles
Norris, Rev. Charles L., Sr.

### Winnsboro
Floyd, Hon. Marquette L.
McCants, Dr. Odell

### Woodruff
Pulliam, Rev. Betty E.

### Yonges Island
Archie-Hudson, Marguerite

### York
Dixon, Ernest James
Portee, Rev. Dr. Frank, III
Sanders, Dori
Walker, John Leslie
Wright-Botchwey, Roberta Yvonne

## SOUTH DAKOTA

### Sioux Falls
Jackson, William R.

## TENNESSEE

### Adams
Miller, Mattie Sherryl

### Alamo
Kindall, Dr. Alpha S.
Nance, Jesse J., Jr.

### Alcoa
Goss, Linda
Houston, Allan Wade, Sr.
Mitchell, Shannon Lamont
Swann, Lynn Curtis

### Arlington
Jones, Lorean Electa

### Athens
Fields, Alva Dotson

### Atoka
Tripp, Dr. Luke Samuel

### Bellwood
Rucks, Alfred J.

### Bethel Springs
Garrett, Cheryl Ann

### Bluff City
Wells, Billy Gene

### Bolivar
Fentress, Shirley B.
Norment, Lynn Aurelia

### Braden
Glass, Dr. Ernestine W McCoy Pickens

### Brentwood
Harper, Thelma Marie

### Brighton
Williams, Dr. Bertha Alston

### Bristol
Butler, John O.

### Brownsville
Bond, Dr. Lloyd
Bond, Charles Cynthia V.
Crews, Victoria Wilder
Dickerson, Dr. Warner Lee
Evans, Rev. Clay
Mann, Thomas J., Jr.
Mabry, Edward L.
Rawls, Mark Anthony
Rhodes, Jacob Alexander
Roxborough, Mildred Bond
Smitherman, Dr. Geneva
Taylor, Dr. Quintard, Jr.

Quarles, Shelton Eugene, Sr.
Ramsey, Freeman, Jr.
Ridley, Dr. May Alice
Roddy, Howard W.
Roberts, Prof. Kay George
Stickney, William Homer
Stamps, Spurgeon Martin David
Stuart, Reginald A.
Swinney, Dr. T. Lewis
Taylor, Dr. Henry Louis, Jr.
Thomas, Jacqueline Marie
Voorhies, Lark
Watts, Beverly L.
Watson, Constance A.
Washington, Dr. Sandra Beatrice
Watley, Margaret Seay
Webster, Winston Roosevelt
Williams, Hon. Marcus Doyle
Wilson, Bernard
Wyatt, Dr. Lance Everett

### New Market
Spiva, Dr. Ulysses Van

### Newbern
Nolan, Daniel Kaye

### Nutbush
Turner, Tina

### Oak Ridge
Caldwell, Mike Isaiah, Jr.

### Oakland
Dickson, Reginald D.

### Palmersville
Payne, Ronnie E.

### Portland
Brewer, Corey

### Prospect
Griffin, Bobby L.
Kimbrough, Charles Edward

### Pulaski
Woodson, Shirley A.

### Ripley
Murray, Albert R.

### Rockwood
Locke-Mattox, Bernadette

### Rutherford County
Woodson, Thelma L.

### Shelby County
Westbrook, Dr. Joseph W., III

### Shelbyville
Bright, Dr. Herbert L.

### Smyrna
McKissack, Patricia Carwell

### Somerville
Coleman, Dr. Harry Theodore, Jr.
Pierce, Aaronetta Hamilton
Williamson, Samuel P.

### South Fulton
Hillard, Terry

### South Pittsburg
Jordan, Kenneth Ulys
Pope, Dr. Isaac S.

### Springfield
Chatman, Melvin E., Sr.

### Stanton
Burgess, Dr. Norma J.
Giles, Henrietta

### Sumner County
Malone, Dr. J. Deotha

### Sweetwater
Davis, Antone Eugene

### Toone
Cooper, Ernest, Jr.

### Union City
Spratlen, Thaddeus H.

### Wilmington
Stewart, William

### Winchester
Fraser, Dr. Leon Allison
Johnson, LaTonya
Robertson, Evelyn Crawford, Jr.

## TEXAS

### Abilene
Stubblefield, Raymond M.
Thomas, Hollis, Jr.

### Alice
Johnson, Dr. Raymond Lewis

### Amarillo
Harkins-Carter, Dr. Rosemary Knighton
Maxie, Peggy Joan
Moore, Thelma LaVerne Wyatt Cummings
Thomas, William Harrison, Jr.

### Angleton
Harris, Derrick

### Anson
Waynewood, Dr. Freeman Lee

### Arlington
Jones, Seth

### Atlanta
Epps, Phillip Earl
Stanmore, Dr. Roger Dale

### Austin
Alexander, Marcellus Winston, Jr.
Baylor, Donald Edward
Bacon, Dr. William Louis
Clemons, Rev. Earlie, Jr.
Collins, Bert
Foster, Lloyd L.
Freeman, Louis Lawrence
Harvey, Kenneth Ray
Harden, Marvin
Hammond, Dr. Benjamin Franklin
Hammond, Dr. Melvin Alan Ray, Jr.
Hill, James O.
Kirk, Ambassador Ronald
Lee, Dr. William H.
McMillan, Dr. Mae F.
Medearis, Victor L.
Neal, Sylvester
Nelly
Richards-Alexander, Billie J.
Roberts, Dr. Alfred Lloyd, Sr.
Shaw, Sedrick Anton
Waters, Dianne E.
Wilson, Ora Brown

### Bagwell
Williams, Dr. Euphemia Goodlow

### Bastrop
Moore, Dr. Lois Jean
Piper, Elwood Arthur
Sanders, Glenn Carlos

### Bay City
Simien, Tracy Anthony
Smith, William French

### Baytown
Messiah-Jiles, Sonceria
Pringle, Dr. Nell Rene

### Beaumont
Auguste, Donna M.
Ball, Jerry Lee, Jr.
Baptiste, Hansom Prentice, Jr.
Banks, Dr. Waldo R., Sr.
Cormier, Dr. Rufus P., Jr.
Collins, Calvin Lewis
Dotson, Earl Christopher
Edwards, Kenneth J., Sr.
Farr, Melvin, Sr.
Frazier, Dr. Jimmy Leon
Fregia, Ray, Sr.
Goodman, Harold
Graham, Larry, Jr.
Lartigue, Roland E.
LeFebvre, Dale
Lynn, Barbara
McElroy, Leeland Anthony
McElroy, Dr. Lee A., Jr.
Middleton, Frank, Jr.
Odom, Clifton Lewis
Parks, Bernard C.
Pinson, Hermine Dolorez
Robinson, Frank, Jr.
Stanton, Janice D.
Wade, Dr. Joseph Downey
White, Dr. Dezra

### Belton
Harrison, Roscoe Conklin, Jr.

### Big Lake
Thompson, Alicia Rachelle

### Big Sandy
Young, Lias Carl

### Billville
McDade, Joe Billy

### Bivins
Gipson, Dr. Bernard Franklin, Sr.
Mitchell, Huey P.

### Blanco
Upshaw, Willie Clay

### Bloomburg
Mothershed, Spaesio Willar

### Bonham
Hurd, Dr. James L. P.
Morgan, Joe Leonard

### Bouthwyn
Johnson, William Arthur

### Brady
Porter, John T.

### Bremond
Ray, Rev. Patricia Ann

### Brenham
Cooper, Cecil Celester
Thomas, Gloria V.

### Broaddus
Teagle, Terry Michael

### Brookshire
Cockrell, Mechera Ann

### Brownfield
Swoopes-Jackson, Sheryl

### Brownwood
Crawford, Odel

### Bryan
Boone, Clarence Wayne, Sr.
Harris, Lee
Mahomes, Patrick Lavon
McGowan, Atty. Clarence Roy
Tennant, Melvin, II

### Buffalo
Cunningham, E. Brice

### Burkeville
Brailsford, Marvin Delano

### Burton
Barrow, Rev. Willie T.

### Calvert
Gibson, Elvis Sonny
Gooden, Cherry Ross
Hearne, Earl

### Carthage
Carter, Dr. Lamore Joseph
Knox-Benton, Dr. Shirley
Perkins, Dr. Robert E. L.
Roberts, Roy J.

### Cary
Cary, Reby

### Cason
Bates, Nathaniel Rubin

### Cedar Lake
Harkless-Webb, Mildred
Hawkins-Russell, Hazel M.

### Celeste
Enis, Shalonda Mochea

### Center
White, Billy Ray

### Centerville
Stewart, Dorothy Nell

### Childress
Jones, Jimmie Dene, II

### Clarksville
Boston, Dr. Horace Oscar, Sr.
Guyton, Rev. Booker T., Sr.
Smith, Dr. Tommie
Wooten, John B.

### Cleburne
Cash, Pamela J.

### Clifton
Sadler, Donnie Lamont

### College Station
Groce, Clifton Allen

### Columbus
Hill, Leo

### Commerce
Franklin, Dr. Curtis U., Jr.

### Corsicana
Hicks, Skip LaVell
Waters, Sylvia Ann
Williams, Rev. Wilbert Lee
Williams, Ronald Charles

### Crockett
Adams, Cecil Ray
Biggers, Dr. Samuel Loring, Jr.
Lockhart, Eugene, Jr.
Ratcliff, Wesley D.
Sherman, C. A.
Watkins, Mozelle Ellis

### Crossroads
Allen, Billy R.

### Cuero
Goodson, James Abner, Jr.
Mathis, Dedric Ronshell
Moore, Johnnie Adolph

### Cushing
McClearn, Billie Marie

### Daingerfield
Everett, Thomas Gregory

### Dallas
Abraham, Clifton Eugene, Jr.
Armstead, Jessie Willard
Aycock, Angela Lynnette
Badu, Erykah
Battie, Tony
Barnes, Esq. Willie R.
Blanford, Dr. Colvin
Black, Albert, Jr.
Bowden, Joseph Tarrod, III
Brown, Timothy Donell
Brown, Floyd A.
Campbell, Gertrude M.
Campbell, Tevin Jermod
Carr, William
Clark, Rosalind K.
Coleman, Marcus Le'Sha
Crockett, Ray
Cullors, Derrick Shane
Divins, Charles
Duncan, Sydney Ree
Early, Ida H.
Fleming, George
Garcia, Dr. William Burres
Giddings, Rep. Helen
Grayson, Mel
Gray, Rev. Maceo
Handy, John Richard, III
Haugstad, May Katheryn
Hanspard, Byron Courtenay, Sr.
Harris, Johnnie Frances
Hadley, Dr. Sybil Carter
Henry, Herman
Hill, Grant Henry
Hill, Gregory LaMonte
Howard, Stephen
Hubbard, Calvin L.
Jackson, Lurline Bradley
Jacox, Kendyl
Jackson, Tomi L.
Jones, Jill Marie
Joyner, Oscar Albert
Johnson, Michael Duane
Kirven, Mythe Yuvette
Lister, Alton Lavelle
Maxwell, Anita
McDonald, Ramos
McGrier, Hon. Jerry, Sr.
Mitchell, Sally Ruth
Montgomery, Monty
Moore, Will Henry, III
Morris, Wayne Lee
Murray, Calvin Duane
Nayman, Dr. Robbie L.
Norman, Bobby Don
Ogletree, Dr. John D., Jr.
Oliver, Pam
Pegram, Erric Demont
Pierce, Ricky Charles
Preston, Dr. Swanee H. T., Jr.
Robertson, Quindonell Stinson
Robinson, Dr. Cecelia Ann
Robinson, Damien Dion
Rossum, Allen Bonshaca Lamont
Scott, Candace Yvette Willrich
Seale, Bobby
Smith, Detron Negil
Smith, Stevin L.
Taylor, Dr. Regina
Thomas, Kurt Vincent
Usher
Walker, Denard Antuan
Watkins, Hon. Craig
Wattley, Thomas Jefferson, Jr.
Webb, Richmond Jewel, Jr.
Webb, Spud
Williams, Michael Douglas
Williams, Brian Marcee
Willrich, Penny
Williams, Kevin Ray
Williams, Michael Deshaun
Willrich, Dr. E. James
Willie, Dr. Charles Vert
Wilson, Barbara Jean
Winn, Joan Tarpley
Zeno, Willie D., Sr.

### De Kalb
Stallworth, Annie P.

### Deerpark
Chelsi, Chelsi

### Del Rio
Young, Lee R.

### Denison
Bunkley, Lonnie R.
Carreathers, Dr. Kevin R.
McDonald, Katrina Bell
Young, Prof. Edith Mae

### Denton
Brown, Ellen Rochelle
Perry, Prof. Wayne D., Sr.

### Devern
McFarland, Roland C.

### Deweyville
Prestage, Dr. James Jordan

### Dickinson
Ware, Andre

### Eagle Lake
Dogins, Kevin Ray

### East Bernard
Bankston, Michael Kane

### El Paso
Ali-Jackson, Kamil
Brooks, Cornell William
Davis, William Augusta, III
Floyd, Mark Stephen
Lee, Barbara Jean
McWilliams-Franklin, Taj
Richardson, Nolan, Jr.
Thompson, Dr. Robert Farris

### Elgin
Greene, Joe

Tatum, James
Wrenn, Dr. Thomas H., III

### Mineral Wells
Connor, Dolores Lillie

### Miniola
Richard, Stanley Palmer

### Moddy
Thompson, Bobbie Fay

### Montgomery
Robinson, Dr. Rev. Frank James, Jr.

### Mount Pleasant
Minter, Barry Antoine

### Mt. Pleasant
Hawkins, Dr. Dorisula Wooten
Jones, Larry W.
Ollison, Ruth Allen

### Mt. Vernon
Rogers, Ormer, Jr.

### Nacogdoches
Collins, Dorothy Lee
Collier, Dr. Troy L.
Franklin, Martha Lois
Rison, Dr. Faye
Sanders, Prentice Earl
Skillern, Gwendolyn D.

### Naples
Hervey, Billy T.

### Nashville
Wainwright, Hon. J. Dale

### Navarro County
Gunter, Laurie

### Navasota
Minor, Willie

### New Braunfels
Ball, Clarence M., Jr.

### Newton County
Harris, Dr. Zelema M.

### Oakwood
Echols, Doris Brown

### Odessa
Hicks, Maryellen

### Onalaska
Douglas, Dr. James Matthew

### Orange
Cane, Kathryn T. Singleton
Gant, Travesa Evette
Goins, Mary G.
Robertson, Andre Levett
Smith, Kevin Rey

### Palestine
Brown, Carrye Burley
Brady, Charles A.
Crawford, Keith
Harris, Vera Dial
Henry, Dr. Charles E.
Wheeler, Beverly
Williams, Dr. Theodore R

### Paris
Anderson, Elizabeth M.
Rollins, Ethel Eugenia
Washington, Rev. Johnnie M.

### Pineland
Weatherspoon, Teresa Gaye

### Pittsburg
Johnson, Ralph C.
Mabrey, Harold Leon
Mitchell, Basil Mucktar

### Plainview
McCutcheon, Lawrence P.

### Port Arthur
Harris, Carla Ann
James, Ronald
Jacket, Barbara Jean
Marshall, Julyette Matthews
Mack, Donald J.
McElroy, Charles Dwayne, Sr.
Price, Marcus Raymond

### Porter
Woodard, Lois Marie

### Prairie View
Dickerson, Col. Harvey G., Jr.
Richardson, Dr. Madison Franklin

### Redwater
Dickey, Bernestine D.

### Richards
Kennedy, Nathelyne Archie

### Richardson
Turner, Eric Scott

### Richland
Ray, Francis

### Rockwall
Wynn, Dr. Valree Fletcher

### Rusk
Stafford, Don A.

### San Angelo
Holmes, Rev. Zan W., Jr.
McFall, Mary
Thomas, Reginald Maurice
Williams, Rev. A. Cecil

### San Antonio
Andrews, Dr. Charles Clifton, Jr.
Ball, William Batten
Berry, Gemeral E., Jr.
Brewington, Donald Eugene
Brown, Eric Jon
Caldwell, Marion Milford, Jr.
Crawford, Deborah Collins
Cumber, Victoria Lillian
Daniel, Dr. Jessica Henderson
Davis-Wrightsil, Clarissa
Eason, Oscar J., Jr.
Gardner, Cedric Boyer
Gray, Derwin Lamont
Hamilton, Bishop Wilburn Wyatt
Hilliard, Dr. Robert Lee Moore
Hines, Alice Williams
Hudspeth, Gregory Charles
Lindsay, Sam A.
McGarity, Wane Keith
McEwen, Mark
McNary, Oscar Lee
Mooring, Dr. Kittye D.S.
Moore, Dr. Harold Earl, Jr.
Morris, Vernon R.
Outlaw, Charles
Peterson, Lloyd, Jr.
Rodgers, Johnathan Arlin
Sears, Corey Alexander
Thomas, Matthew W., Jr.
Trotter, Andrew Leon
Warren, Dr. Rueben Clifton
Webb, Joe, Sr.
Wesley, David Barakau
Wheat, Hon. Alan Dupree
Wiley, Dr. Kenneth LeMoyne, Sr.

### San Augustine
Hoyt, Hon. Kenneth M.
Jones, Gary DeWayne
Pualani, Gloria

### San Benito
Cormier, Lawrence J.

### San Marcos
Wheeler, Mark Anthony

### Sanger
Crisp, Dr. Robert Carl, Jr.

### Sealy
Dickerson, Eric Demetric

### Seguin
Hodge, Dr. Charles Mason

### Sherman
Howard, Sherri
McElroy, Dr. Njoki

### Shiner
Greenwood, Edna Turner

### Sinton
Wright, Dr. Earl Lee

### Smithville
Owens, Dr. Charles Clinton

### Somerville
Chapman, Dr. George Wallace, Jr.

### Sour Lake
Johnson, Milton D.

### Spring
Lee, Vivian Booker

### Streetman
Ellison, Chester Laughton

### Sulphur Springs
Hicks, Doris Askew

### Tatum
Centers, Larry Eugene

### Taylor
Jones, K. C.
Nance, Herbert Charles, Sr.
Wilson, Henry, Jr.

### Teague
Barefield, Dr. Ollie Delores
Burnim, Mellonee Victoria
Burnim, Dr. Mickey L.

### Temple
Dixon, Tynna G.
Flakes, Rev. Garland KaZell
Harris, Dr. Bernard A., Jr.
Leak, Virginia Nell
Powell, Dorothy A.
Sanders, Ricky Wayne
Skinner, Brian

### Terrell
Anderson, Abbie H.
Foxx, Jamie
Johnson, Darrius Dashome
Newman, Miller Maurice

### Texarkana
Bradley, Melvin LeRoy
Brannon, James R.
Favors, Dr. Steve Alexander, Jr.
Gray-Morgan, Dr. LaRuth H.

### Texas City
Crawford, Vernon Dean, Jr.
Murdock, Dr. Nathaniel H.

### Thelma
Foreman, Joyce Blacknall

### Thompsons
Solomon, Jimmie Lee

### Timpson
Deramus, Bill R.
Grace, Horace R.

### Trinity
Seals, Maxine Lane

### Troup
Hodge, Dr. Cynthia Elois
Jones, Dr. Jesse W.

### Troy
Dearman, John Edward

### Tyler
Allen, Shirley Jeanne
Butler, Roy
Carter, Chris
Clark, Della L.
Houston, Lillian S.
Jasper, Edward Videl
Johnson, Larry Demetric
Johnson, Dr. Lectoy Tarlington
Mack, Tremain Ferrell
McPhail, Dr. Christine Johnson
Mumphrey, Jerry Wayne
Rheams, Leonta DeMarkel
Ross, Martha Erwin
Sanders, Sally Ruth
Spigner, Dr. Donald Wayne
Wallace, Milton De
Warren, Herman Lecil
Waits, Rev. Va Lita Francine

### Uvalde
Kinchlow, Ben

### Valley Mills
Means, Hon. Bertha Elizabeth

### Van Alstyne
Totten, Dr. Herman Lavon

### Vernon
Cole, Dr. Thomas Winston, Jr.

### Victoria
Bates, Michael Dion
Gant, Ronald Edwin
Herron, Bruce Wayne
Hobbs, Daryl Ray
Prince, Andrew Lee
Sanders, Laura Green
Tillmon, Joey

### Waco
Anderson, Alfred Anthony
Johnson, Rep. Eddie Bernice
Jones, Marilyn Elaine
Johnson, Lawrence E.
Mills, Billy G.
Mohr, Dr. Paul B., Sr.
Rhodes, Arthur Lee, Jr.
Sterling, H. Dwight, Sr.
Walker, Ronald Wayne
Watkins, Ira Donnell
Wilkins, Rayford, Jr.
Wilkins, Ray
Winfield, Elayne Hunt

### Wallisville
Cooper, Gordon R., II

### Waskom
Cornelius, Rev. Ulysses S., Sr.
Gaines, Grady
Vance, Vera R.

### Waxahachie
Butler, Douthard Roosevelt
Cleaver, Emanuel, II
Williams, Rudy V.
Williams, Ada L.

### Weatherford
Hopkins, Edna J.

### Weimar
Kea, Arleas Upton

### Wellington
Childs, Dr. Francine C.

### Wharton
Coleman, Columbus E., Jr.
Gray, Dr. Carol Coleman
Lathon, Lamar Lavantha

### Whitewright
Orr, Clyde Hugh

### Willis
Straughter, Edgar, Sr.

### Yoakum
Hicks, William L.
Neal, Curtis Emerson, Jr.

## UTAH

### Dragerton
Crump, Janice Renae

### Hill AFT
Flack, Dr. John M.

### Ogden
Scott, Byron Antom

### Salt Lake City
Lake, Carnell Augustino

## VERMONT

### Burlington
Caldwell, Lisa Jeffries

### Halifax
Jennings, Sylvesta Lee

## VIRGIN ISLANDS

### Christiansted
Roberts, Dr. Rona Dominique

### St. Croix
Coryatt, Quentin John
Cummings, Midre Almeric
Duncan, Tim
Innis, Roy Emile Alfredo
Ngongba, Tajama Abraham
Thomas, Maurice McKenzie

### St. Thomas
Coakley, H. M.
James, Dr. Herman Delano

## VIRGINIA

### Accomac
Thomas, Philip S.

### Alexandria
Barber, James W.
Brooks, Bernard W.
Brooks, Brigadier Gen. Leo Austin, Sr.
Cowans, Alvin Jeffrey
Dual, Dr. Peter Alfred
Ruffin, Paulette Francine
Stewart, Paul Allen

### Altavista
Futrell, Dr. Mary Alice Franklin Hatwood

### Amelia County
Johnson, Ronald Cornelius
Thompson, Joseph Isaac

### Amherst
Douglas, Willard H., Jr.

### Amonate
Hairston, Raleigh Daniel

### Arlington
Brittain, Bradley Bernard, Jr.
Jackson, Esther Cooper
Johnson, Rita Falkener

### Arno
Horton, Willie Wattison

### Axton
Hairston, Joseph Henry
Worrell, Kaye Sydnell

### Ballsville
Lambert, Lillian Lincoln

### Beaverdam
Gilpin, Clemmie Edward

### Big Stone Gap
Morris, Dr. Charles Edward, Jr.

### Blackridge
Person, Dr. Waverly J.

### Blackstone
Gray, Dr. Ronald A.
Jones, Robert Lee

### Bluefield
Dillard, Wanda J.
Haynes, Farnese N.

### Boykins
Harris, Gladys Bailey

### Branchville
Parker, Dr. Walter Gee, Jr.
Parker, Claude A., Jr.

### Bristol
Harrell, Oscar W., II

### Brunswick County
Jones, Rev. Vernon Algie, Jr.
Parham, Dashton Daniel
Powell, Rev. Dr. Grady Wilson, Sr.

### Buckingham
Brown, Charles Edward

White-Parson, Willar F.
Wilson, Ronald M.
Wiggins, Joseph L.
Wise, Frank P.

### North Holston
Brown, Agnes Marie

### Oak Grove
Bankett, William Daniel

### Ontario
Morton, James A., II

### Orange
Williams, Dr. Eugene, Sr.

### Ornancock
Bohannan-Sheppard, Barbara

### Painter
Bailey, Eugene Ridgeway

### Palmer Springs
Robinson, Dr. Joyce Russell

### Petersberg
Huntley, Lynn Jones

### Petersburg
Ballard, Dr. James M., Jr.
Bland, Dr. Robert Arthur
Boone, Dr. Elwood Bernard, Jr.
Brown, Rodger L., Jr.
Crocker, Wayne Marcus
Crawford, Vanessa Reese
Dark, Okianer Christian
Haughton, Dr. Ethel Norris
Hardy, Michael Leander
Holland, Darius Jerome
Holland, Dr. Antonio Frederick
Kaiser, Ernest Daniel
Martin, Harold B.
McLaughlin, Dr. George W.
McDaniel, Prof. Reuben R., Jr.
Mickens, Dr. Ronald Elbert
Moody, Eric Orlando
Odom, Stonewall
Perry, Dr. Aubrey M.
Powell, Wayne Hugh
Remy, Esq. Donald M.
Robinson, Catherine
Sherrod, Rev. Charles M.
Tate, Valencia Faye
Watkins, Dr. Charles B.
West, Mark Andre

### Phoebus
Downing, Dr. John William, Jr.

### Pittsylvania County
Adams, Dr. Howard Glen

### Pocahontas
Lowe, Martha P.

### Portsmouth
Allen, Dr. Maxine Bogues
Bugg, Mayme Carol
Copeland, Dr. Leon L., Sr.
Corbett, Dr. Alexander E., III
Colyer, Dr. Sheryl Lynn
Earles, Dr. Julian Manly
Earls, Dr. Julian Manly
Eley, Randall Robbi
Elliott, Missy
Franklin, Prestonia D.
Goodman, Dr. James Arthur
Hampton, Cheryl Imelda
Hardie, Robert L., Jr.
Hardison, Ruth Inge
Harris, Charles F.
Harrison, Dr. A. B.
Hudson, Cheryl Willis
James, Kay Coles
Jackson, Gordon Martin, Jr.
Jones, Cheryl Arleen
Jones, Helen Hampton
Josey-Herring, Anita Marie
Jordan, Dr. Dedra R.
Knight, Athelia Wilhelmenia
Lucas, L. Louise
McGriff, Dr. Deborah M.
McCall, Nathan
Merritt, LaShawn
Morrison, Hon. Johnny Edward, Jr.
Myrick, Bismarck
Randall, Marlene West
Smith, Dr. Henry Thomas
Steele, Tommy
Sykes, Wanda Y'vette
Todd, William S.
Walker, Bracey Wordell
White, Debra Y.
Whitehead, Andre
Whitehurst, Charles Bernard, Sr.
Williamson, Carl Vance

### Powhatan
Swainson, Sharon C.
Taylor, Iris

### Prince Edward County
Berryman, Esq. Matilene S.

### Princess Anne County
Brockett, Charles A.
Morris, Margaret Lindsay

### Prospect
Walker, Laneuville V.

### Pulaski
Russell, Leon W.

### Quantico
Hayden, Frank F.

### Radford
Casey, Rev. Carey Walden, Sr.
Charlton, Rev. Charles Hayes
Clark, Gary C., Jr.

### Reedville
Jackson, Robert Andrew

### Regina
Taylor, Dr. Arnold H.

### Richmond
Adams, Robert Eugene
Andrews, William Pernell
Archer, Michael Eugene
Barber, Shawn William
Barrett, Audra
Barnes, Melody
Barnes, Wilson Edward
Banks, Dr. William Jasper, Jr.
Barrett, Rev. Walter Carlin, Jr.
Bennett, Karen
Biggs, Dr. Shirley Ann
Bledsoe, Carolyn E. Lewis
Boatwright, Dr. Joseph Weldon, III
Boone, Melanie Lynn
Brooks, Dr. Carolyn Branch
Bullock, Thurman Ruthe
Butts, Carlyle A.
Burton, Dr. Charles Howard, Jr.
Cameron, Dr. Wilburn Macio, Jr.
Carter, Dr. Wesley Byrd
Campbell, Dr. George, Jr.
Cartwright, Brenda Yvonne
Cain, Dr. Rudolph Alexander Kofi
Chapman, Roslyn C.
Cheatham, Linda Moye
Clay, Dr. Reuben Anderson, Jr.
Clevert, Hon. Charles Nelson, Jr.
Copeland, Margot James
Davis, Melvin Lloyd, Sr.
Dawson, Dr. Martha E.
Dandridge, Robert L., Jr.
Dandridge, Prof. Rita Bernice
Dance, Dr. Daryl Cumber
Dungee, Margaret R.
Edwards, Dr. Rondle E.
Eggleston, Neverett A., Jr.
Farrar, Moses
Ferguson, Sherlon Lee
Foster, T. Eloise
Freeman, Dr. Thomas F.
Freeman, Dr. Paul D.
Galvin, Dr. Emma Corinne Brown
Gray, Wilfred Douglas
Gray, Dr. Earl Haddon
Hansbury, Vivien H.
Harris, Dr. William McKinley, Sr.
Harvell, Dr. Valeria Gomez
Harris, Charles Somerville
Henley, Vernard W.
Hewlett, Everett Augustus, Jr.
Henderson, Leroy W., Jr.
Henderson, Gerald, Sr.
Henderson, William Terrelle
Hicks, Jessie Yvette
Hood, Charles McKinley, Jr.
Horne, Marvin L. R., Jr.
Jackson, Charles N., II
Jackson, Isaiah Allen
Jackson, Dr. Rudolph Ellsworth
Jackson, Giles B.
Jackson, Miles M.
Jewell, Curtis T.
Jones, Dr. William C.
Jones, Dr. Percy Elwood
Kenney, Walter T., Sr.
Lewis, William M., Jr.
Lipscomb, Dr. Wanda Dean
Logue-Kinder, Joan
Marsh, Sen. Henry Leander, III
Mitchell, Michelle Burton
Moore, Dr. Roscoe Michael, Jr.
Morgan-Washington, Dr. Barbara
Morgan, Alice Johnson Parham
Murdock, Patricia Green
Newman, Hon. William Thomas, Jr.
Norrell-Thomas, Sondra L.
Oxendine, Kenneth Qwarious
Payne, Allison Griffin
Perry, Edward Lewis, Jr.
Peyton, Rev. Jasper E.
Pollard, Dr. Diane Mae Stewart
Poindexter, Rev. Charles L. L.
Pressey, Paul Matthew
Robinson, Dr. Randall M.
Robertson, Delores W.
Scott, Gilbert H., Sr.
Scott, Albert Nelson
Shakir, Dr. Adib Akmal
Simms, Rev. James Edward
Spurlock, LaVerne Beard
Story, Charles Irvin
Stallings, Gregory Ralph
Thompson-Wright, Dr. Brenda Smith
Thomas, Sherri
Thomas, Dr. Harry Lee
Tillman, Christine L.
Townes, Clarence Lee, Jr.
Walker, Dr. Edwin L.
Warden, George W.
White, Robert C.
White, D. Richard
Wilder, Lawrence Douglas
Williams, Dr. Patricia Hill
Winston, George B., III
Winston, Bonnie Veronica
Woodson, Cleveland Coleman, III

### Roanoke
Barrett, Matthew Anderson
Barber, Ronde
Barber, Tiki
Blair, Curtis
Butler, Dr. Johnnella E.
Carroll, Sally G.
Coles, John Edward, Sr.
Goode, Fr. James Edward
Hackley, Dr. Lloyd Vincent
Hale, Rev. Cynthia Lynnette
Hopson, Kevin M.
Lynch, George DeWitt, III
Meadows, Dr. Richard H.
Miller, Dr. Dennis Weldon
Moorman, Holsey Alexander
Perry, Gary W.
Powell, Juan Herschel
Robinson, Steve
Sample, William Amos
Saunders, Barbara Ann
Spurlock, Dr. James B., Jr.
Staples, Robert E.
Thomas, Ralph Charles, III
Woodbury, Dr. Margaret Claytor

### Rock Castle
Gray, Moses W.

### Rocky Mount
Martin, Jesse Lamont
Wade, William Carl

### Roseland
Rouse, Jacqueline Anne

### Rustburg
Flint, Mary Frances

### Salem
Shaw, Leander Jerry, Jr.

### Skippers
Garner, Edward, Jr.
Williams, Dr. Ella O.

### Smithfield
Brown, Jenever H.
Delk, James F., Jr.
Finney, Ernest A., Jr.

### South Boston
Edmunds, Ferrell, Jr.
Lee, Jefferi Keith
Sargent, Dr. Virginia Hightower
Shiver, Jube
Tucker, Michael Anthony

### South Hill
Jackson, Waverly Arthur, Jr.

### Spotsylvania County
Burnett, Arthur Louis, Sr.

### Staunton
Carter, Dr. Gene Raymond
Early, Sybil Theresa
Venable, Andrew Alexander, Jr.

### Suffolk
Barnes, Johnnie Darnell
Britt, L. D.
Briscoe, Gayle
DeLoatch, Dr. Sandra J.
Earl, Dr. Archie, Sr.
Eure, Dexter D., Sr.
Glover, Dr. Bernard Ellsworth
Hart, Ronald O.
Montgomery, Annette
Sparrow, Rory Darnell
Valentine, J. T.
Williams, Esq. Junius W.

### Surry
Winfield, Thalia Beatrice

### Sussex
Hamlin, Ernest Lee
Massenburg, Tony Arnel

### Tabb
Whiting-Wright, Barbara E.

### Tappahannock
Robinson, Dr. Luther Dabney

### Tidewater
Cortor, Eldzier

### Virginia Beach
Darby, Matthew Lamont
Douglas, Gabrielle Christina Victoria
George, Jason Winston
Holley, John Clifton
Reid, Herman, Jr.
Williams, Pharrell

### Warrenton
Campbell, Carlos, Sr.
Davis, Johnetta Garner
Mosley, Benita Fitzgerald

### Warwick
Holmes, Willie A.

### Waverly
Bailey, Dr. Gracie Massenberg
Sconiers, Hon. Rose H.

### Waynesboro
Alexander, Cory Lynn
Harris, Reggie

### Wightman
Howard, Donald R.

### Williamsburg
Bogger, Dr. Tommy
Farris, Esq. Deborah Ellison
Gray, Mel
Springs, Shawn
Taylor, Lawrence Julius
Wallace, Thomas Albert

## WASHINGTON

### Bellingham
Hartsfield, Arnett L., Jr.
Newman, Anthony Q.

### Bremerton
Powe, Joseph S.

### Georgetown
Pitt, Dr. Clifford Sinclair

### Kennewick
Davis, Anthony D.

### Moses Lake
Warrick, Bryan Anthony

### Seattle
Adams, Oleta Angela
Alex, Gregory K.
Arkhurst, Joyce Cooper
Arnold, Alison Joy
Brown, Carolyn M.
Christie, Douglas Dale
Davis, Charles
Devers, Yolanda Gail
Dillon, Corey James
Gayton, Esq. Gary D.
Hasty, James Edward
Harris-Perry, Melissa
Holton, Michael David
Jones, Dr. Edward L.
Lavizzo-Mourey, Dr. Risa Juanita
Leonard, Gloria Jean
Lombard, Ken
McKissack, Cheryl Mayberry
Metcalf, Eric Quinn
Mitchell, Brian Stokes
Peoples, John Derrick, Jr.
Pierce, Aaron
Raines, Franklin D.
Richardson, Clint Dewitt, Jr.
Saulter, Gilbert John
Tate, Brett Andre

### Spokane
Bellegarde-Smith, Dr. Patrick
Ferguson, Elliott LaRoy, II
McGough, Robyn LaTrese
Roseman, Jennifer Eileen
Sims, Ronald Cordell

### Tacoma
Conley, James Sylvester, Jr.
Edwards, Audrey Marie
Fields, Brenda Joyce
Horton, Raymond Anthony
Mobley, Singor A.
Pichon, Rise Jones
Underwood, Blair Erwin
Woodley, Arto, Jr.

### Washington
Parker, Barrington Daniels, Jr.

### Yakima
Frye, Reginald Stanley

## WEST VIRGINIA

### Barrackville
Cherry, Robert Lee
Hinton, Dr. Gregory Tyrone

### Beard
Lee, Ivin B.

### Beckley
Chambers, Madrith Bennett
Dodson, William Alfred, Jr.
Dodson, Angela Pearl
Gwynn, Florine Evayonne
Haynes, Philip R.
Knight, W. H., Jr.
Thompson, Regina

### Belle
Moss, Eric

### Bluefield
Adams, Dr. Billie Morris Wright
Jackson, Dr. Deborah Byard Campbell
Morrison, James W., Jr.
Smith, Janet Maria
Stephens, Booker T.
Wright, Rev. Jefferson W.

### Burnwell
Harris, Robert D.

### Charleston
Baskerville, Dr. Samuel J., Jr.
Baugh, Lynnette B.
Bowman, Dr. Janet Wilson

### Whitby
Santiago, O. J.

### Windsor
Bluford, James F.
Hill, Tamia Marilyn
Johnson, Harold R.
Stinson, Constance Robinson
White, Gary Leon

### Winnipeg
Jerrard, Paul

## CHILE

### Santiago
Clark, Dr. Granville E., Sr.

## CONGO

### Kinshasa
Biakabutuka, Tim
Kazadi, Muadianvita Machez

## COSTA RICA

### Puerto Limon
Samuels, Dr. Wilfred D.

## CUBA

### Havana
Dalley, George Albert
Leon, Dr. Tania Justina
Rodriguez, Argelia Velez
Valdes, Pedro H.

### Santiago de Cuba
Garbey, Barbaro
Love, Faizon

## DENMARK

### Copenhagen
Esposito, Giancarlo Giuseppe Alessandro

## DOMINICAN REPUBLIC

### Hato Mayor
Franco, Julio Cesar Robles

### Kinshasa
Mutombo, Dikembe

### Montecristi
Pena, Tony

### Rancho Viejo
DeLeon, Jose Chestaro

### San Cristobal
Rijo, Jose Antonio

### San Pedro de Macoris
Bell, George Antonio
Fernandez, Tony
Isaac, Telesforo Alexander
Joseph, Hon. Raymond Alcide
Sosa, Samuel Peralta

### Santo Domingo
Bautista, Danny
Cedeno, Cesar Encarnacion
Guzman, Juan Andres Correa
Martinez, Ramon Jaime

## EGYPT

### Alexandria
Aman, Dr. Mohammed

## ENGLAND

### Epsom
Congreaves, Andrea Fiona

## ESTONIA

### London
Edwards, Trevor A.

## ETHIOPIA

### Addis Ababa
Samara, Noah Azmi
Samuelsson, Marcus
Tessema, Tesfaye
Yohannes, Daniel W.

### Asmara
Checole, Prof. Kassahun

### Monoxeito
Sebhatu, Dr. Mesgun U.

### Nedjio
Isaac, Dr. Ephraim

### Tig-Ray
Birru, Dr. Mulugetta

## FRANCE

### Chateauroux
Fairley, Juliette S.
Neizer, Meredith Ann

### Cucq
Stewart, Michael Curtis

### Evreux
Hagan, Gwenael Stephane

### Paris
Beal, Lisa Suzanne
Mallebay-Vacqueur Dem, Jean Pascal
Wilkins, Jacques Dominique

### Val de Marne
Abdul-Wahad, Tariq

### Verdun
Romes, Charles Michael

## GERMANY

### Aschaffenburg
Marshall, Marvin Ali

### Augsburg
Moody, Dominique Faye

### Berlin
McDonald, Audra Ann
McDonald, Audra

### Bonn
Johnson, Michael L.

### Frankfurt
Boose, Dorian Alexander
English, Stephen
Jones, Esq. Rosalyn Evelyn
McGriggs-Jamison, Imogene
Mickens, William Ray
Pittman, Kavika Charles
Richardson, Tony
Steed, Joel Edward
Vinson, Anthony Cho
White, Beverly Anita

### Furstenfeldbruck
McKnight, Reginald

### Heidelberg
Dozier, Morris Cicero
George, Ronald Lawrence
Mosby, Dr. Carla Mane

### Landstuhl
Burton, Levar, Jr.

### Mainz
Karpeh, Enid Juah Hildegard

### Munich
Monroe, Bryan K.
Walters, Frank E.

### Nuremberg
Watts, Andre

### Pfungstadt
Scott, Werner Ferdinand

### Schwabach
Hodges, Dr. Helene

### Stuttgart
Booker, Corliss Voncille
Ragland, Sherman Leon, II
Staten, Mark Eugene

### Teisendorf
Cooper, Irmgard M.

### Wiesbaden
Autry, Harrington Darnell
Harris, Tricia R.
Laisure, Sharon Emily Goode

### Wurzburg
Mayberry, Tony

## GHANA

### Aburi
Apea, Joseph Bennet Kyeremateng

### Accra
Adom, Dr. Edwin Nii Amalai
Mensah, E. Kwaku
Okunor, Rev. Dr. Shiame S.
Opoku, Dr. Evelyn

### Apam
Quansah-Dankwa, Dr. Juliana Aba

### Awate
Hicks, Dr. Veronica Abena

### Ejisu Ashanti
Sarkodie-Mensah, Dr. Kwasi

### Kukurantumi
Ohene-Frempong, Prof. Kwaku

### Kumasi
Addy, Dr. Tralance Obuama

### Oda
Bempong, Dr. Maxwell A.

### Tegbi
Sogah, Dr. Dotsevi Yao

## GRENADA

### Grenada
Bonaparte, Dr. Tony Hillary
Bridgeman, Dexter Adrian

### Grenville
Bridgeman, Donald Earl

### St. Georges
Crosse, Rev. St George Idris Bryon, III
Maitland, Dr. Conrad Cuthbert

## GUAM

### Georgetown
Thomas, Edward Arthur

## GUINEA

### Conakry
Diane, Mamadi

## GUYANA

### Ann's Grove Village
Liverpool, Charles Eric

### Berbice
Moore, Colin A.

### Georgetown
Ali, Dr. Grace L.
Forsythe, Hazel Waldron
Harris, Prof. E. Nigel
Hintzen, Percy Claude
Isaacs-Greene, Patricia
Liverpool, Rev. Herman Oswald
Pounder, C. C. H.
Thorne, Dr. Cecil Michael
Willock, Dr. Marcelle Monica
Wilson, Mitsy

### Mahaicony
Phillips, Eric McLaren

### McKenzie
Subryan, Carmen Barclay

### New Amsterdam
Bone, Rev. Winston S.
Joseph, Jennifer Inez

### Wismar Demerara
Ally, Dr. Akbar F.

## HAITI

### Arcahaie
Alexandre, Dr. Journel

### Cap Haitien
Delphin, Dr. Jacques Mercier
Ferere, Dr. Gerard Alphonse

### Croix-des-Bouquets
Jean, Nelust Wyclef

### Jacmel
Chicoye, Etzer

### Jeremie
Clermont, Dr. Volna

### Pont Sonde
Simeus, Dumas M.

### Port-au-Prince
Audain, Dr. Linz
Behrmann, Serge T.
Danticat, Edwidge
Dreyfuss, Joel P.
Duffoo, Dr. Frantz Michel
Fleurant, Gerdes
Francois, Dr. Emmanuel Saturnin
Gaston, Patrick Reginald
Jerome, Rev. Joseph D.
Kernisant, Dr. Lesly J.
Louis, Dr. Suchet Lesperance
Nicholson, Gemma
Polynice, Olden
Prezeau, Louis E.
Prezeau, Dr. Maryse P.
Racine, Karl A.
Richard, Dr. Henri-Claude
Saint-Louis, Rudolph Anthony
Toussaint, Dr. Rose-Marie

### St. Marc
Beauvais, Garcelle
Molaire, Michel Frantz
Mortel, Dr. Rodrigue M.

## HONDURAS

### Puerto Cortes
Aviles, Dora

## INDIA

### Calcutta
Biswas, Dr. Prosanto K.

### Chandigarh
Suneja, Dr. Sidney Kumar

## IRAN

### Shiraz
Jarrett, Dr. Valerie B.

## ITALY

### Livorno
Collins, LaVerne Vines

### Rome
Fales, Susan Marya

## JAMAICA

### Annotto Bay
Cummings, Aeon L.

### Clarendon
Reid, Dr. Leslie Bancroft
Sawyers, Dorret E.

### Crooked River
Johnson, Dr. Edward Elemuel

### Darliston
Salmon, Dr. Jaslin Uriah

### Half Way Tree
Brown, Dr. Malore Ingrid

### Jamaica
Gordon, Esq. Claudia Lorraine
Grant, Dr. Augustus O.
Meade, Dr. Alston B., Sr.
Patterson, Dr. Orlando Horace
Simpson, Rev. Dr. Samuel G.
Thomson, Dr. Thelma B.
Walters, Curla Sybil

### Kingston
Auld, Albert Michael
Bell, Thom Randolph
Blackwood, Ronald A.
Carney, Lloyd A.
Channer, Colin
Cliff, Michelle
Clarke, Dr. Donald Dudley
Creary, Ludlow Barrington
Davis, Chili
Denton, Sandra
Downie, Dr. Winsome Angela
Ewing, Patrick Aloysius, Sr.
Francis, Charles S. L.
Francis, Rev. Dr. James N.
Griffiths, Errol D.
Handwerk, Jana D.
Hankin, Noel
Hewitt, Christopher Horace
Hunter, Bryan C.
Isaacs-Lowe, Arlene Elizabeth
McCullough, Rev. Dr. Jacqueline E.
McDonald, Ricardo Milton
Palmer, Dr. Doreen P.
Ridley, Dr. Alfred Dennis
Rodney, Karl Basil
Sherwood, Hon. O. Peter
Shakespeare, Easton Geoffrey
Taylor, Karin Katherine
Thompson, Dr. Lloyd Earl
Waite, Dr. Norma Lillia Polyn
Watson, Prof. Denton L.
Wedderburn, Dr. Raymond
White, Devon Markes
Whitworth, Dr. E. Leo, Jr.
Wilson, Dr. Hugh A.
Wint, Arthur Valentine Noris
Wright, Clinton L. A.

### Linstead
Morrison, Prof. Keith Anthony

# SOMALIA

**Mogadishu**
Abdulmajid, Iman Mohamed

# SOUTH AFRICA, REPUBLIC OF

**Alexandra Township**
Mathabane, Mark

**Calendon**
Philander, Dr. S. George H

**Cape Town**
Ibrahim, Abdullah
Pathon, Jerome

**Johannesburg**
Noah, Trevor

**Port Elizabeth**
Nagan, Winston Percival

# ST. LUCIA

**St. Lucia**
Flemming, Dr. Charles Stephen
St. Omer, Dr. Vincent V. E.

# ST. VINCENT

**Canouan**
Foyle, Adonal David

**St. Vincent**
Cox, Keith
King-Gamble, Marcia
Niles, Alban I.

# SURINAME

**Paramaribo**
Comvalius, Dr. Nadia Hortense

# SWEDEN

**Stockholm**
Jennings, Dominique
Simon, Miles Julian

# SWITZERLAND

**Geneva**
Primm, Annelle Benee

**Lausanne**
Hermanuz, Prof. Ghislaine

# TANZANIA, UNITED REPUBLIC OF TRINIDAD AND TOBAGO

**Barataria**
Headley, Heather

**Chaguanas**
Richards, Dr. Winston Ashton

**El Dorado**
Rambison, Dr. Amar B.

**Mayaro**
Moore, Dr. Nathan

**Port-of-Spain**
Alexis, Dr. Carlton Peter
Clarke, LeRoy P.
Cooper, Winston Lawrence
Dowdy, Dr. Joanne Kilgour
Hinds, Prof. Lennox S.
Lynch, Hollis Ralph
Phillip, Dr. Michael John
Prout, Patrick M.
Rampersad, Arnold
Rauch, Esq. Doreen E.
Williams, Dr. Hugh Hermes

**San Fernando**
Morancie, Horace L.
Natta, Clayton Lyle

**Tacarigua**
Cudjoe, Dr. Selwyn Reginald

**Trinidad**
Barnett, Dr. Lorna
Dottin, Dr. Robert Philip
Leon, Jean G.
Palmer, Dr. Annette
Toussaint, Lorraine

**Tunapuna**
Kadree, Dr. Margaret Antonia

# TURKS AND CAICOS ISLANDS

**Grand Turk**
Swan, Dr. Llewellyn Alex

# UGANDA

**Entebbe**
Okino, Elizabeth Anna

**Gulu**
Abe, Dr. Benjamin Omara A.

**Kabale**
Bisamunyu, Jeanette

**Kampala**
Serwanga, Wasswa Kenneth

# UNITED KINGDOM

**Braintree**
Newsome, Vincent Karl

**Burton-On-Trent**
Dennis, Andre L.

**Charleston**
Fryson, Sim E.

**Hampshire**
Gladwell, Malcolm

**Heachem**
Donaldson, James Lee, III

**Laken Heath**
Freeman, Kimberley Edelin

**Leicester**
Dummett, Dr. Jocelyn Angela

**London**
Ejogo, Carmen
Elba, Idris
Jones, Quincy Delight, III
Levychin, Richard
Lindo, Delroy George
Reid, Vernon Alphonsus
Samuel, Seal Henry Olusegun Olumide Adeola
Smith, Dawn C. F.
White, Constance C. R.
Williams, Tonya Lee

**Middlesex**
Laine, Dame Cleo

**Oakhampton Devon**
Carby, Hazel V.

**Scotland**
Agwunobi, Dr. Andrew C.

**Swindon**
Clarke, Priscilla

# UNITED REPUBLIC OF TANZANIA

# URUGUAY

**Birmingham**
Hill, Rev. Dr. Robert Lee

# VENEZUELA

**Curacao**
Robertson, Dr. Marilyn Anita

# VIRGIN ISLANDS (US)

**Charlotte Amalie**
Nibbs, Alphonse (Allie), Sr.
Olugebefola, Dr. Ademola
Turnbull, Dr. Charles Wesley

**Christiansted**
Belardo de O, Lilliana

**Frederiksted**
Bryan, Adelbert M.

**St. Croix**
Aska, Joseph
Browne, Jerry
Garcia, Kwame N., Sr.
Petersen, Hon. Eileen Ramona
Rivera, Eddy
Terrell, Dr. Catherine Milligan
Wadsworth, Andre L.

**St. Thomas**
Boschulte, Alfred F.
Bryant, Homer Hans
Brown, Dr. Walter E.
Brady, Julio A.
Christian, Dr. Cora LeEthel
Dawson, Dr. Eric Emmanuel
de Jongh, Prof. James Laurence
Francis, Dr. E. Aracelis
Frazer, Victor O.
Greaves, McLean
Hendricks, Beatrice E.
James, Dr. Herbert I.
Krigger, Dr. Marilyn Francis
Meyers, Ishmael Alexander
Moorehead, Justin Leslie
Sprauve, Dr. Gilbert A.
Stapleton, Marylyn A.
Turnbull, Renaldo Antonio
Watlington, Janet Berecia
Williams, Lloyd L.
Woodfolk, Joseph O.
Yancyy, Robert

# VIRGIN ISLANDS, BRITISH

**Tortola**
Boschulte, Dr. Joseph Clement
Christian, Eric Oliver, Jr.
Dennis, Hugo, Jr.

# WALES

**Laurel**
Davis, Dr. John Wesley, Sr.

# WESTERN SAMOA

**Lake County**
Northern, David A., Sr.

# ZIMBABWE

**Essexvale**
Dube, Thomas M. T.

**Harare**
Kumbula, Dr. Tendayi Sengerwe

# Occupation Index

## Activism, Political/Civil/ Social Rights

### Actuarial Science



### Advertising/Promotion (*See Also* Management/ Administration—Advertising/Marketing/ Public Relations)



### Aerospace (*See* Engineering—Aerospace)

### Agribusiness



### Agricultural Science



### Airline Industry



### Anthropology



### Architecture



### Art, Visual—Animation



### Art, Visual—Commercial Art/Graphic Design

Benson, Rubin Author, Jr.
Black, David Eugene, Sr.
Blow, Charles M.
Brown, Tony
Dabbs, Henry Erven
deJongh, Monique Evadne Jellerette
Dorsey, Denise
Ferguson, Dr. Robert Lee, Sr.
Ferguson, Cecil L.
Gainer, Prof. John F.
Grant, Claude DeWitt
Graham, Mariah
Higgins, Stann
Hill, Jacqueline R.
Hudson, Cheryl Willis
Jackson, Dr. Reginald Leo
James, Dr. Synthia Saint
Jones, William James
Johnson, Jeh Vincent, Sr.
Johnson, Edward M.
Johnson, Kerry Gerard
Jones, Richmond Addison
Johnson, Timothy Julius, Jr.
Lipscomb, Curtis Alexander
Logan, Juan Leon
McGill, Michele Nicole Johnson
Mitchum, Dorothy M.
Payne, Cecilia
Parham, Dashton Daniel
Porter-Esmailpour, Carol D.
Pryde, Arthur Edward
Prelow, Arleigh
Ross, N. Rodney
Robinson, Peter Lee, Jr.
Samuel, Jasper H.
Smith, Robert D.
Vereen, Dixie Diane
Williams, Donald
Williams, Judith Byrd
Wright, Dmitri

## Art, Visual-Illustration (*See Also* Art, Visual—Painting)

Armstrong, Robb
Barkley, Rufus, Jr.
Blaylock, Ronald Edward
Brooks, Bernard W.
Bryan, Ashley F.
Crews, Donald
Cummings, Pat
Granger, Edwina C.
James, Dr. Synthia Saint
Jones, William James
Johnson, Kerry Gerard
Johnson, Timothy Julius, Jr.
Mitchell, Rhonda Alma
Mitchell, Dean Lamont
Pinkney, Jerry
Ross, N. Rodney
Ruffins, Reynold
Sandoval, Dolores S.
Smith, Robert D.
Steptoe, Javaka
Taylor, Michael Loeb
Walker, George Edward
Walker, Kara
Young, Tommy Scott

## Art, Visual—Not Elsewhere Classified

Adams, Esq. John Oscar
Adair, James E.
Allain, Stephanie
Anderson, William
Bell, Ngozi O.
Bechet, Ronald
Bernard, Donald L.
Benjamin, Dr. Tritobia Hayes
Billingsley, Ray C.
Bontemps, Dr. Jacqueline Marie Fonvielle
Boutte, Rhonda
Brown, Kay B.
Bright, Alfred Lee
Branch, Prof. Harrison
Byrd, Joan Eda
Carter, Yvonne Pickering
Catchings, Dr. Yvonne Parks
Clarke, LeRoy P.
Claye, Charlene Marette
Cortor, Eldzier
Conway, Curtis LaMont
Crouther, Dr. Betty Jean
Curtis-Rivers, Susan Yvonne
Dash, Julie
Dalton, Raymond Andrew
Davis, Dr. Donald Fred
Dickerson, Amina J.
Diggs, Lawrence J.
Douglas, Elizabeth (Betty) Asche
Driskell, David Clyde
Dunnigan, Jerry A.
Epting, Marion Austin
Franklin, Prestonia D.
Gilliam, Sam J., Jr.
Gittens, Anthony Edgar
Goodwin, Mac Arthur
Green, Jonathan
Hall, Horathel
Harrison, Pearl Lewis
Henry, Alicia
Hilton, Stanley William, Jr.
Hogu, Barbara J. Jones
Humphrey, Margo
Imhotep, Akbar
Ingram, Gregory Lamont
Irmagean, U.
Jackson, Dr. Reginald Leo
Jackson, Earl W
Jackson, Suzanne Fitzallen
Jones-Henderson, Napoleon
Johnson, Prof. Stephanie Anne
Johnson, Rita Falkener
Jones, Grace
Kamau, Mosi
Kent, Herb
Kinsey, Shirley
Ligon, Doris Hillian
Lockard, Prof. Jon Onye
McGruder, Aaron Vincent
McCray, Almator Felecia
McElrath-Frazier, Wanda Faith
Mercer, Valerie June
Meaux, Ronald
Mills, Joey Richard
Miller-Lewis, S. Jill
Morgan-Welch, Beverly Ann
Moody, Dominique Faye
Mudiku, Mary Esther Greer
Newton, Dr. James Elwood
Nengudi, Senga
Nixon, Norman Ellard
Owens, Andi
Patterson, Curtis Ray
Patton, Leroy
Parham, Dashton Daniel
Pearson, Dr. Clifton
Pindell, Howardena D.
Pinckney, Stanley
Piper, Adrian Margaret Smith
Rabb, Madeline Murphy
Richardson, Frank
Rico, Dr. Tracey
Robinson, Jontyle Theresa
Robinson, John E.
Robinson, Anthony W.
Sandridge, Dr. John Solomon
Saar, Betye Irene
Simpson, Lorna
Stewart, Jacqueline Najuma
Styles, Freddie L.
Staats, Dr. Florence Joan
Sutton, Dr. Sharon Egretta
Tessema, Tesfaye
Thompson, Lowell Dennis
Thomas, Matthew W., Jr.
Todd, Charles O.
Utley, Richard Henry
Walker, George Edward
Washington, Mary Parks
Washington, Zenobia
Weaver, Aissatou Mijiza
Whitfield, Jenenne
White, Clarence Dean
Williams, Prof. Daniel Salu
Wilson, Dr. Helen Tolson
Wiley, Kehinde

## Art, Visual—Painting

Andrews, Sharony S.
Ashford, John
Banks, Ellen
Barboza, Anthony
Beckett, Sydney Ann
Beasley, Arlene A.
Birch, Willie
Blayton-Taylor, Betty
Bowles, Joyce Germaine
Borders, Michael G.
Bright, Alfred Lee
Brooks, Bernard W.
Brooker, Moe Albert
Brown, Malcolm McCleod
Burns, Ronald Melvin
Cade, Walter, III
Carter, Ora Williams
Catchings, Dr. Yvonne Parks
Carter, JoAnne Williams
Carter, Nanette Carolyn
Camp, Kimberly
Carroll, Joe Barry
Clark, Claude Lockhart
Clark, Edward
Clay, Cliff
Cortor, Eldzier
Collins, Paul
Dabbs, Henry Erven
Daniel, Mary Reed
Davis, Donald
Delsarte, Louis J.
Dotson, Phillip Randolph
Edmunds, Allan L.
Ferguson, Dr. Robert Lee, Sr.
Flores, Joseph R.
Gilliam, Sam J., Jr.
Gilchriest, Lorenzo
Gibbs, Nathaniel K.
Goodnight, Paul D.
Green, Jonathan
Grauer, Gladys Barker
Greenfield, Mark Steven
Granger, Edwina C.
Guyton, Tyree
Hampton, Phillip Jewel
Harden, Marvin
Harris, Virginia R.
Hendricks, Barkley L.
Henderson, Leroy W., Jr.
Hinton, Alfred Fontaine
High-Tesfagiorgis, Freida W.
Hicks, Leon Nathaniel
James, Dr. Synthia Saint
Jackson, Suzanne Fitzallen
Jackson, Oliver L.
Johnson, Luther E.
Johnson, John
Jones, Ben F.
Johnson, Timothy Julius, Jr.
Jones, Richmond Addison
Knox, Simmie
Laird, Rev. Alan
Lewis, Dr. Samella Sanders
Lindsay, Dr. Arturo
Mayhew, Richard
Martin, Ionis Bracy
McDonald, Jon Franklin
McCoullum, Dr. Valarie Ena Swain-Cade
McMillan, Friar Douglas James
McNary, Oscar Lee
McMillan, James C.
Merritt, Eleanor L.
Mitchell, Dean Lamont
Mitchell, Rhonda Alma
Morrison, Prof. Keith Anthony
Morgan, Tracy Jamal
Nelson, Eileen F.
Norman, Bobby Don
Norwood, Dr. Tom
Olugebefola, Dr. Ademola
Onli, Turtel
Owens, Dr. Wallace, Jr.
Padgett, Prof. James A.
Painter, Dr. Nell Irvin
Pinckney, Stanley
Pindell, Howardena D.
Pitts, George Edward
Rickson, Gary Ames
Ringgold, Faith
Rogers, Charles D.
Sandoval, Dolores S.
Saunders, Prof. Raymond Jennings
Sheats, Jamaal B.
Singletary, Deborah Denise
Smith, Robert D.
Smythe, Victor N.
Snowden, Sylvia Frances
Sprout, Prof. Francis
Talley, Rev. Dr. Clarence, Sr.
Tanksley, Ann Graves
Tomlinson, Dr. Robert
Twiggs, Dr. Leo Franklin
Watkins, Ira Donnell
Walker, Larry Moore
Walker, Kara
West, Prof. Pheoris
White, Paul Edward
Wimberley, Frank
Williams, Frank James
Wiley, Kehinde
Williams, Katherine S.
Wilson, Prof. Stanley Charles
Williams, Prof. William Thomas, Jr.
Wilson, Sandra E.
Woodson, Shirley A.
Wright, Dmitri

## Art, Visual—Sculpting

Anderson, William
Auld, Albert Michael
Birch, Willie
Blayton-Taylor, Betty
Chase-Riboud, Dr. Barbara DeWayne
Clark, Edward
Conwill, Dr. Houston Eugene
Douglas, Elizabeth (Betty) Asche
Foreman, Doyle
Guyton, Tyree
Harris, William Joseph, II
Hardison, Ruth Inge
Hamilton, Edward N.
Hodgson-Brooks, Gloria J.
Hubbard, Calvin L.
Hunt, Richard Howard
Johnson, Prof. Stephanie Anne
Maynard, Valerie J.
McMillan, James C.
McNary, Oscar Lee
McMillan, Friar Douglas James
Meeks, Larry Gillette
Montgomery, Evangeline Juliet
Nengudi, Senga
Owens, Dr. Wallace, Jr.
Padgett, Prof. James A.
Pugh, Robert William, Sr.
Puryear, Martin
Scroggins, Bobby
Sherman, C. A.
Sheats, Jamaal B.
Talley, Rev. Dr. Clarence, Sr.
Williams, Prof. William Thomas, Jr.
Wilson, Prof. Stanley Charles

## Association Management (*See Also* Banking/Financial Services)

Abrams, Kenneth Rodney
Abdul-Malik, Dr. Ibrahim
Abernathy, Ronald Lee
Adair, Andrew A.
Addison, Caroline Elizabeth
Adolph, Gerald Stephen
Adams, Gregory Keith, Sr.
Adams, V. Toni
Addams, Robert David
Adams, Sheila J.
Airall, Dr. Guillermo Evers
Akbar, Dr. Na'im
Allen, W. George
Alford, Brenda
Alexander, Dr. Lenora Cole
Allen, Dr. Edna Rowery
Allen, Terrell Allison, III
Allen, Mark S.
Aldridge, Karen Beth
Allen, Charles Edward, Jr.
Alexander, Vic
Allen, Charles Edward
Alexander, Hon. Joyce London
Ambrose, Dr. Ethel L.
Anderson, Helen Louise
Anderson, Doreatha Madison
Anderson, Dr. Marjorie
Anderson, J. Morris
Anderson, Michael Wayne
Andrews, Carl R.
Anderson, Nicholas Charles
Anderson, Elizabeth M.
Anthony, Rev. Dr. Wendell
Anderson, William Gilchrist
Anderson, Rev. Dr. Al H., Jr.
Anderson, Rosaland Guidry
Arnold, Alison Joy
Arnold, Clarence Edward, Jr.
Arnold, Wallace C.
Armstead, Wilbert Edward, Jr.
Askew, Bonny Lamar
Baxter, Hon. Wendy Marie
Baines, Dr. Tyrone Randolph
Barnes, Dr. Delorise Creecy
Barnes, Rev. Anne T.
Baldwin, Louis J.
Barksdale, Mary Frances
Bates, Barbara Ann
Baskette, Ernest E., Jr.
Barnes, Dr. Joseph Nathan
Banks, Caroline Long
Bagneris, Esq. Michele Christine Beal
Barrett, Jacquelyn Harrison
Ball, Brenda Louise
Bagley, Gregory P., Sr.
Bailey, Dr. Clarence Walter
Banks, Cecil James
Banks, Dr. William Maron, III
Bain, Linda Valerie
Barnett, Teddy
Barthelemy, Sidney John
Barrow, Rev. Willie T.
Bates, Dr. Clayton Wilson, Jr.
Baugh, Florence Ellen
Baskerville, Dr. Lezli
Barner, Sharon R.
Battle-Bumpers, Katrina
Badejo, Dr. Diedra L.
Beal, Lisa Suzanne
Benford-Lee, Alyssia
Bell, James A.
Betty, Michael W., Sr.
Bernard, Nicole A.
Bethel, Nikki
Beard, Darryl H.
Beshah, Esq. Guenet M. M.
Beasley, Arlene A.
Bell, Thom Randolph
Bellegarde-Smith, Dr. Patrick
Bennett, Ivy H.
Beckett, Justin F.
Bell, Lawrence F.
Bettis, Anne Katherine
Becton, Rudolph
Belardo de O, Lilliana
Billups, Mattie Lou
Bingham, Rebecca Taylor
Bickham, Dr. Luzine B.
Black, Dr. Frederick Harrison
Blackwood, Ronald A.
Blanford, Dr. Colvin
Blanks, Wilhelmina E.
Blue, Dr. Gene C.
Blackmon, Joyce McAnulty
Bostic, Viola W.
Bond, Charles Cynthia V.
Bofill, Angela
Bogle, Robert W.
Bolton, Hon. Julian Taylor
Bobino, Dr. Rita Florencia
Bowman, Dr. Janet Wilson
Boyd, Audrey B. Rhodes
Boyd, Rev. Marsha Foster
Bond, Norman
Bostic, Dr. James Edward, Jr.
Bouie, Dr. Merceline H.
Bourne, Judith Louise
Bolden, Raymond A.
Bolden, Betty A.
Booker, Anne M.
Bowman, Phillip Jess
Broadwater, Tommie, Jr.
Bronson, Dr. Oswald Perry, Sr.
Brown, A. Sue
Brown, Dr. Abena Joan P.
Brown, Franchot A.
Brown, Claudell, Jr.
Bryant, Jesse A.
Bryant, R. Kelly, Jr.
Bryant, Dr. William Jesse
Brown, Dr. Malore Ingrid
Brazile, Donna L.
Bryant, Damon K.
Brown, Andrea Molette
Brooks, Brian A.
Brown-Ellen, Kimi L.
Brewington-Carr, Sherese
Brown, Michele Courton
Brown, Thomas K.
Brown, Mary Boykin
Brown, Joyce
Bryant, Wayne R.
Bruce, Dr. Preston, Jr.
Brockington, Donella P.

Jobe, Ben W.
Johnson, Marjorie Lynn
Johnson, John E., Jr.
Kaalund, Sekou H.
Kenny, James A.
Kennedy, Ray C.
Kennedy, Teresa Kay-Aba
Kelly, Marion Greenup
Kelley, William E.
Kendrick, L. John, Sr.
Keith, Luther
Kemp, Leroy Percy, Jr.
King, Dexter Scott
Kispert, Dorothy Lee
Kidd, Herbert C., Jr.
King, Ruby E.
King-Poynter, Marva
Kington, Raynard S.
Kinsey, Shirley
Knox, Marshall
Knight, Walter R.
Knuckles, Kenneth J.
Koch, Francena Jones
Kunes, Kenneth R.
LaCour, Nathaniel Hawthorne
Lafayette, Dr. Bernard, Jr.
Lancaster, Herman Burtram
Lassiter, Dr. James Edward, Jr.
Latham, Esq. Weldon Hurd
Lavergneau, Rene L.
Lawrence, Edward
Lawrence, John Edward
Lawson, Dr. Cassell Avon, Sr.
Lawyer, Vivian Moore
Lawrence, Charles, Jr.
Lawrence, Elliott
Lawson, Charles J.
Lawrence, Hon. Brenda L.
Lacey, Dr. Bernardine M.
Lathen, Deborah Ann
Lanier, Horatio Axel
Ladd, Florence Cawthorne
Lee, Margaret S.
Lee, Jefferi Keith
Leigh, Major Gen. Fredric H.
Lee, Ivin B.
Lewis, Karen A.
Lewis, Dr. Bettye Davis
Lewis, Carol J.
LeGrand, Yvette Marie
Lee, Oliver B.
Leffall, Dr. LaSalle Doheny, Jr.
Lee, Howard N.
LeCesne, Terrel M.
Lewis, Ora Lee
Lewis, Dr. Jesse J.
Lewis, Lillian J.
Levy, Valerie Lowe
Lewis, Edward T.
Lewis, Floyd Edward
Little, Reuben R., Sr.
Lindsay, Horace Augustin
Livingston-Wilson, Karen E.
Linton, Sheila Lorraine
Llewellyn-Travis, Chandra
Lloyd, Dr. Raymond Anthony
Lofton, Mellanese S.
Lockwood, James Clinton
Love, Roosevelt Sam
Lovett, Mack, Jr.
Lowe, Victoria
Logan, Harold James
Lowery, Carolyn T.
Lue-Hing, Dr. Cecil
Lytle, Marilyn Mercedes
Martin, Gertrude S.
Mayes, Dr. McKinley
Maddox, Julius Arnell
Marshall, Dr. Joseph Earl, Jr.
Matthis, James L., III
Martin, Hosea L.
Mariel, Serafin U
Martin, Arnold Lee, Jr.
Marshall, Jonnie Clanton
Mason, Dr. Cheryl Annette
Mahoney, Keith Weston
Martin, Dr. McKinley C.
Mack, Sylvia Jenkins
May-Pittman, Ineva
Mack, Pearl Willie
Mack, John W.
Malone, Dr. Gloria S.
Martin, Dr. Edward Williford
Martin, Rev. Dr. Lawrence Raymond

Marrs, Dr. Stella
Mansfield, W. Ed
Mansfield, Dr. Carl Major
Mathis, Sharon Bell
Massey, Walter Eugene
Mason, Major Albert, III
Maitland, Tracy V.
Mason, Mark
Malveaux, Antoinette Marie
Manuel, Jerry
Manson, Richard
Madison, Yvonne Reed
McLeod, Roshown
McNeil, Robert Lawrence
McCammon, Marques
McMorris, Lamell
McClendon, Bishop Clarence E.
McLean, Dollie Clarice H.
McGee, Adolphus Stewart
McGee, Eva M.
McClinton, Curtis R., Jr.
McClung, Rev. Willie David, II
McPhail, Dr. Irving P.
McKee, Esq. Clarence Vanzant
McGoodwin, Dr. Roland Caryle
McHenry, Dr. James O.
McIver, John Douglas
McDonald, Dr. R. Timothy
McRoy, Dr. Ruth Gail
McNairy, Dr. Francine G.
McGuire, Jean Mitchell
McCloud, Thomas Henry
McCollum, Anita LaVerne
McKay-Davis, Monique Dionne
McCloud, Anece Faison
McWhorter, Dr. Grace Agee
McKissack, Leatrice Buchanan
McClammy, Dr. Thad C.
Merritt, William T.
Metters, Dr. Samuel
Merenivitch, Jarrow
Merideth, Charles Waymond
Meaux, Ronald
Means, Dr. Fred E.
Mesa, Dr. Mayra L.
Metoyer, Rosia G.
Meyers, Dr. Rose M.
Menogan, Annita M.
Meyers, Dr. Carolyn W.
Mims, Rhonda
Miller, Jones Sandy
Miller, Kevin
Mills, Alan Keith
Michael, Dr. Charlene Belton
Miller, Frederick A.
Millender, Dharathula H.
Milton, LeRoy
Mims, Dr. George L.
Milner, Thirman L.
Miller, Rev. Dr. Telly Hugh
Miller, Thomasene
Miller, Dr. Jeanne-Marie Anderson
Miller, Mattie Sherryl
Mitchell, William Grayson
Mitchem, Dr. Arnold Levy
Mitchell, Iverson O., III
Minter, Steven Alan
Miller, E. Ethelbert
Mims, Marjorie Joyce
Miller, William Nathaniel
Minter, Wilbert Douglas, Sr.
Miller, Marquis David
Miller, Rev. Anthony Glenn
Miller-Pope, Consuelo Roberta
Millett, Dr. Ricardo A.
Mitchell, George L.
Miller, Major Gen. Frank Lee, Jr.
Miller, Rev. Kevin D.
Mills, Lois Terrell
Moore, Dr. Elizabeth D.
Moss, Wayne B.
Moore, Dr. Harold Earl, Jr.
Montague, Christina P.
Moss-Buchanan, Tanya Jill
Morrison, Jacqueline
Moseley, Frances Kenney
Monroe, Robert Alex
Montgomery, Elder Oscar Lee
Morgan, Robert, Jr.
Moaney, Eric R.
Montgomery, Evangeline Juliet
Montgomery, Catherine Lewis
Monroe, Annie Lucky
Moore, Cleotha Franklin

Mooring, Dr. Kittye D.S.
Moore, Evelyn K.
Mortel, Dr. Rodrigue M.
Morning, John
Moo-Young, Louise L.
Moore, Minyon
Morris, Margaret Lindsay
Muhammad, Akbar A.
Muse, J. Melvin
Murrain, Godfrey H.
Murray, James P., Jr.
Murphy, Hon. Harriet Louise M.
Muhammad, Shirley M.
Murphy, Laura W.
Murphy, Daniel Howard
Muhammad, Benjamin Chavis
Mwamba, Dr. Zuberi I.
Nabors, Jesse Lee
Nance, Herbert Charles, Sr.
Nelson, Richard Y., Jr.
Newsome, Dr. Emanuel T.
Newton, Oliver A., Jr.
Nelson, Dr. Wanda Jean
Newbille, Cynthia I.
Newell, Daryl
NeSmith, Winifred L. Acosta
Neal, Langdon D.
Nichols, George
Nix, Rick
Nichols, Dr. Owen Douglas
Nixon, James Melvin
Nix, Dr. Theophilus Richard, Jr.
Nnolim, Charles Ekwusiaga
Norman, Dr. Moses C., Sr.
Nowlin, Frankie L.
Northern, David A., Sr.
O'Neal, Stanley
O'Brien, Mary Nell
Ohene-Frempong, Prof. Kwaku
Oliver, Kenneth Nathaniel
Orr, Ray
Orticke, Leslie Ann
Otis, Clarence, Jr.
Overstreet, Morris L.
Owens, Dr. Joan Murrell
Owens, Kelly D.
Parker, Anthony L.
Patterson, Kevin L.
Palmer, Stephanie
Paschal, Trisa Long
Palmer, Dr. Elliott B., Sr.
Patterson, Kay
Parks, Bernard, Jr.
Parker, Paul E.
Parker, H. Wallace
Patton, Robert
Parker, Bernard F., Jr.
Parker, Jacquelyn Heath
Paschal, Eloise Richardson
Patterson, Barbara Ann
Person, Dr. William Alfred
Peterson, Rev. Dr. Alan Herbert
Peeples, Audrey Rone
Pegues, Dr. Wennette West
Peoples, Sesser Randall
Peguese, Charles R.
Perkins, Charles Windell
Perkins, John M.
Perry, Prof. Wayne D., Sr.
Pender, Mel
Philander, Dr. S. George H
Phillips, Rev. Acen L.
Phillips, June M. J.
Philpott, Ethel
Phifer, B. Janelle Butler
Pinkney, Dr. Enid C.
Pickrum, Michael
Pinn, Dr. Vivian
Pinn, Dr. Samuel J., Jr.
Pierre-Louis, Dr. Constant
Polk, Richard A.
Powell, Dr. C. Clayton
Polk, Dr. William C.
Ponder, Eunice Wilson
Porter, Dr. Michael LeRoy
Porter, Dr. Charles William
Pounds, Dr. Augustine Wright
Pogue, D. Eric Rick
Pratt, Mable
Procter, Harvey Thornton, Jr.
Preston, Eugene T.
Pryor, Dr. Chester Cornelius, II
Price, Hugh Bernard
Pride, John L.

Price, Brenda G.
Price, Andrea R.
Priestley, Marilyn
Procope, Ernesta G
Ray, Rev. Patricia Ann
Rankin, Marlene Owens
Rasheed, Fred H.
Raveling, George Henry
Rayford, Brenda L.
Reaves, E. Fredericka M
Reed, Joe Louis
Reid, Joel Otto
Reid, Malissie Laverne
Reed-Clark, Larita Diane
Reed, Derryl L.
Reaves, Rev. Dr. Benjamin Franklin
Rhodes, Jacob Alexander
Rhea, Michael
Rice, Lois Dickson
Rivers, Dorothy
Richardson, Dr. Luns C.
Richards, Dr. Hilda
Richards, Dr. Johnetta Gladys
Richardson, Linda Waters
Richardson, Timothy Lee
Rice, Sandra Dorsey
Ribeau, Dr. Sidney A.
Riley, Shaunce R.
Robertson, Frankie George
Robinson, Malcolm S.
Royston, Evelyn Ross
Roshell, Pamela P.
Robinson, Verneda Bachus
Rodgers-Rose, Dr. LaFrances Audrey
Romney, Edgar O.
Roscoe, Dr. Wilma J.
Robinson, Carl Cornell
Robinson, Myron Frederick
Rogers, Rev. Dr. Victor Alvin
Robinson, Dr. Sharon Porter
Rodgers, Pamela E.
Robinson, Thomas Donald
Rodney, Karl Basil
Robertson, Quincy L.
Roach, Lee
Rodriguez, Doris L.
Rose, Shelvie, Sr.
Robinson, Renault Alvin
Robinson, Dr. Samuel
Robinson, Dr. Thelma Maniece
Robinson, Jack E.
Robinson, Kenneth Eugene
Robinson, Harry G., III
Roberts, Michael V., Sr.
Robertson, Quindonell Stinson
Robinson, Albert M.
Robinson, Denauvo M.
Rotan, Dr. Constance S.
Rowe, Jimmy L.
Robinson, Kenneth
Rucks, Alfred J.
Rutledge, Dr. Essie Manuel
Russell, Joseph J.
Rush, Sonya C.
Russell, Dian Bishop
Samples, Jared Lanier
Sailor, Elroy
Sanderson, Randy Chris
Saunders, John Edward, III
Saffold, Dr. Oscar E.
Samkange, Dr. Tommie Marie
Sanders-Johnson, Lina
Sanders, Joseph Stanley
Sampson, Marva W.
Satcher, Dr. Robert Lee, Sr.
Sandler, Joan Delores
Savage, Dr. Edward W., Jr.
Saulny, Cyril B.
Sanders, Dr. Lawrence, Jr.
Salaam, Abdel R.
Scott, Michael W., Sr.
Scanlan, Agnes Bundy
Scales-Trent, Prof. Judy
Scales, Dr. Manderline Elizabeth Willis
Scales, Robert L.
Scott, Joseph Walter
Scott, Ruth Elaine Holland
Scott, James Henry
Scott, Albert Nelson
Scott, Ruby Dianne
Scott, Artie A.
Sessoms, Dr. Frank Eugene
Seale, Bobby
Sevillian, Clarence Marvin, Sr.

Shade, Dr. Barbara J.
Shamwell, Prof. Ronald L.
Sharpe, Dr. Audrey Howell
Sheffey, Dr. Ruthe T.
Sherwood, Hon. O. Peter
Shipley, Rev. Anthony J.
Shuford, Humphrey Lewis
Sheftall, Dr. Willis B., Jr.
Shepphard, Dr. Charles Bernard
Shaw, Booker Thomas
Sheats, Marvin Anthony
Shepard, Gregory
Shelton, Helen C.
Shurney, Dr. Dexter Wayne
Sims, Esau, Jr.
Simmons, Shirley Davis
Siler, Brenda Claire
Simpson-Watson, Dr. Ora Lee
Silva, Dr. Omega C. Logan
Singleton, Esq. Harry M.
Simms, Stuart Oswald
Singleton, Dr. Robert
Simmons, James Richard
Simmons, Dr. Sylvia Q.
Slash, Joseph A.
Slaughter, Carole D.
Smith, Shirley LaVerne
Smith, Alice B
Smiley-Robertson, Carolyn
Small, Israel G.
Smith, Dr. Estus
Small, William
Smith, Dr. Luther Edward, Jr.
Smith, Marzell L.
Smith, Dr. Roulette William
Smith, Fronse Wayne, Sr.
Smith, Debbie A.
Smith, Tubby
Smith, Wilson Washington, III
Smith, Eugene DuBois
Smith, Lafayette Kenneth
Smith, Beverly Evans
Smith, Dr. Joanne Hamlin
Smith, Esq. G. Elaine
Smith, Stevin L.
Smith, Dr. Jane E.
Smith, Marie F.
Smith, Gwendolyn Iloani
Sneed, Michael E.
Snorton, Teresa E.
Sorey, Hilmon S., Jr.
Spriggs, Dr. William
Springs, Lenny F., II
Spand, Rev. Dr. Margot
Spears, Stephanie
Stevenson, Rev. Dr. Jerome Pritchard, Sr.
Stanton, Robert G.
Stewart, Diana Brown
Stone, Aubry L.
Stevens, Warren Sherwood
Styles, Kathleen Ann
Strong, Hon. Craig Stephen
Stubblefield, Raymond M.
Stinson, Donald R., Jr.
Stockton, Clifford, Sr.
Stampley, Gilbert Elvin
Steele, Dr. Claude Mason
Stephenson, Allan Anthony
Stepp, Marc
Stevens, Reatha J.
Stevens, Timothy S.
Staten, Everett R.
Starks, John Levell
Streeter, Denise Williams
Summers, Dr. Rodger
Summitt, Krista E.
Swan, John William David
Sylvester, Melvin R.
Taliaferro, George
Taylor, Howard Francis
Taylor, Felicia Michelle
Taylor, Vivian A.
Tasco, Hon. Marian B.
Taylor, Marie de Porres, Sr.
Tate, David Kirk
Tanner, Craig
Talley, Sarah
Taylor, Johnny C., Jr.
Thomas, Bette
Thompson, Mavis T.
Thomson, Alice G.
Thomas, Barbara Louise
Thompson, Linda Jo
Thompson, Hon. Bobby E.

### Astronomy (*See* Physics/Astronomy)

### Athletics (*See* Sports—Amateur; Sports—Professional/Semiprofessional; Sports—Not Elsewhere Classified; Sports Coaching/Training/Managing/Officiating)

### Automobile Industry (*See* Manufacturing—Motor Vehicles; Retail Trade—Motor Vehicles, Parts, and Services; Wholesale Trade—Motor Vehicles and Parts)

### Banking/Financial Services

Lambert, Joseph C.
Lazard, Betty
Lemon, Ann
Lee, Aubrey Walter, Jr.
Lee, E. Jacques
Lewis, Michael Ward
Lewis, William M., Jr.
Lee, Dr. John Robert E.
Lewis, Andre
Lewis, Willard C.
Lee, John M.
Linyard, Richard
Loving, James Leslie, Jr.
Loney, Carolyn Patricia
Long, Steffan
London, Gloria D.
Lowery, Donald Elliott
Lyons, Dr. Lamar Andrew, Sr.
Lyons, Patrick Alan
Mason, Mark
Maitland, Tracy V.
Macon-Rue, Pamela A.
Malliet, Schone
Mayes, George S., Jr.
Mack, C.
Martin, Prof. Charles Howard
Mariel, Serafin U
Martin, I. Maximillian
Malone, Claudine Berkeley
McLin, Rev. Lena Johnson
McReynolds, Elaine A.
McMullins, Tommy
McQueen, Kevin Paige
McKinney, Norma J.
McBeth-Reynolds, Sandra Kay
McClure, Fredrick H. L.
McEachern, D. Hector
McGuire, Raymond J.
McKenzie, Obie L.
McNeal, Glenda G.
Mensah, Bernard
Mehu, Geraldine
Miller, Phillip M.
Miller, Rodney M., Sr.
Miller, James
Mitchell, Carlton S.
Miller, George Carroll, Jr.
Miller, Ward Beecher
Milner, Michael Edwin
Moorehead, Justin Leslie
Moses, Edwin Corley
Mosley, Edna Wilson
Morris, William Howard
Mosley, Elwood A.
Morse, Dr. Laurence C.
Moss, Lesia Bates
Mosley, Valerie
Mordecai, David K. A.
Mullings, Paul
Myles, Wilbert
Nash, Bob J.
Narcisse, Colbert
Newell, Daryl
Neal, Mario Lanza
Newsome, Ronald Wright
Nichols, George
Nunn, Clarence
Oliver, Kenneth Nathaniel
Otis, Clarence, Jr.
Ourlicht, David E.
Owens, Mercy P.
Patterson, Ronald E.
Parker, George Anthony
Patterson, Rev. Clinton David
Perine, Martha Levingston
Perkins, Charles Windell
Pearce, Richard Allen
Pearson, Michael Novel
Pease, Denise Louise
Pendergraft, Michele M.
Perry-Mason, Gail F.
Perry, Clifford R., III
Penn, Dr. Suzanne Y.
Penn, Derek
Phillips, Wilburn R.
Pierson, Kathryn A.
Plummer, Milton
Powell, Richard Maurice
Pope, Mirian Artis
Powell, Kenneth Alasandro
Powell, Council, Sr.
Powell, Arthur F.
Powell, Kemper O.
Price, JoAnn H.
Profit, Eugene A.
Pryor, Vikki L.
Prioleau, Peter Sylvester
Prestwidge-Bellinger, Barbara Elizabeth
Pryor, Malcolm D.
Prezeau, Louis E.
Prout, Patrick M.
Purnell, Mark W.
Quick, George Kenneth
Ramirez, Richard M.
Raines, Franklin D.
Ray, Michael
Rainford, Valerie I.
Reynolds, James, Jr.
Reynolds, Sandra Michele
Remy, Esq. Donald M.
Rice, J. Donald, Jr.
Richards, George, Jr.
Riddle, R. Lucia
Rice, Hon. Norman Blann
Rodgers, Horace J.
Roland, Benautrice, Jr.
Royster, Don M., Sr.
Rodman, Michael Worthington
Rodgers, Napoleon B.
Rogers, John W., Jr.
Ross, Cathy D.
Robinson-Ivy, Jacqueline
Robinson, Virgil, Jr.
Rushing, Coretha M.
Rucker, Alston Louis
Russell, George Alton, Jr.
Savage, Frank
Sanders, Steven LeRoy
Saunders, Kim D.
Scott, Joseph M.
Seidenberg, Mark
Sellars, Harold Gerard
Shealey, Richard W.
Shank, Suzanne F.
Singleton, Harold, III
Sims-Person, LeAnn Michelle
Simmons, Norbert
Simmons, Craig, Sr.
Simmons, Willie, Jr.
Sloan, Maceo Kennedy
Smith, William Xavier
Smith, Esq. Stanley G.
Smith, Debbie A.
Smith, William Gene
Smith, Voydee
Smith, Thelma J.
Small, Eric
Smith, Gerald B.
Smith, Robert F.
Snowden, Gail
Sobers, Waynett A., Jr.
Sorey, Hilmon S., Jr.
Spaulding, Aaron Lowery
Spencer, Anthony Lawrence
Spooner, Richard C.
Speed, James H., Jr.
Spriggs, Otha T. Skip, III
Stockton, Dmitri
Stephens, Brooke Marilyn
Stith, Antoinette Freeman
St Etienne, Gregory Michael
Stahnke, William E.
Stamper, Henry J.
Stokes, Bunny, Jr.
Stephenson, Dama F.
Strickland, Herman William, Jr.
Staten, Mark Eugene
Sudarkasa, Dr. Michael Eric Mabogunje
Sullivan, Ernest Lee
Sutton, Wilma Jean
Sweat, Sheila Diane
Taylor, William Glenn
Taylor, Sterling R.
Tate, Brett Andre
Taylor, Sandye R.
Taylor, Colleen
Terrell, Frederick O.
Thomas, Shundrawn A.
Thompson, Westley V.
Thurman, Cedric Douglas
Thomas, Ralph Albert
Thomas, Earle Frederick, Sr.
Thornton, Wayne T.
Tidwell, Isaiah
Tomlin, Josephine D.
Toon, Albert Lee, Jr.
Truitt, Kevin
Trotter, Lloyd G.
Turner, Jesse H., Jr.
Turnipseed, Carl Wendell
Utendahl, John O.
Van Amson, George Louis
Vaughan, Gerald R.
Viera, Paul E.
Walker, Monica L.
Washington, Robin L.
Waller, Kathy N.
Watkins, Donald V.
Wade, Joyce K.
Ward, Calvin
Washington, Ada Catherine
Washington, William
Walker, Arman Kennis
Watters, Linda A.
Watson, Daniel
Waters, John W.
Warder, John Morgan
Walker, John Leslie
Weaver, Jeffery Jerome
White, Thurman V., Jr.
Whiteman, Raymond A.
Whitfield, Alphonso, III
White, Edward Clarence, Jr.
Wheat, James Weldon, Jr.
Wilson, Leon E., Jr.
Williams, Joseph Barbour
Winslow, Kenneth Paul
Williams, Walter Ander, Jr.
Wiggins, Paul R.
Wilson, Thomas A., Jr.
Wilcox, Thaddeus
Williams, Joseph Lee, Jr.
Williams, E. Thomas, Jr.
Winters, Kenneth E.
Wilson, Lance Henry
Williams, Edward Joseph
Wilkes, Jamaal
Williams, Christopher J.
Williams, Tina Byles
Wilson, Donna Sims
Williams, Anre D.
Woods, Willie E., Jr.
Woods, Henry, Jr.
Woodson, Alfred F., Jr.
Wright, Deborah C.
Yates, Mark
Young, Tommy Scott
Young, Terrence Anthony
Yohannes, Daniel W.
Youngblood, Kneeland

## Biochemistry

Bargonetti, Jill
Clarke, Dr. Donald Dudley
Crittenden, Raymond C., IV
Davis, Leodis J.
Daley, Thelma Thomas
Daly, Dr. Frederica Y.
Gamble, Dr. Wilbert
Haynie, Sharon
Harris, Dr. Don Navarro
Hogan, Dr. James Carroll, Jr.
Hopson, Kevin M.
Jones, George H.
Martin, William R.
Meade-Tollin, Dr. Linda C.
Mitchell, Dr. Earl Douglass, Jr.
Pointer, Dr. Richard H.
Sanders, Dr. Robert B.
Schooler, Dr. James Morse, Jr.
Scott, Dr. Kenneth Richard
Smith, Dr. Edgar Eugene
Sudbury, Leslie G.
Washington, Dr. Linda Phaire
Ward, Velma Lewis
West, William Lionel, II

## Biology/Microbiology

Ampy, Dr. Franklin R.
Bass, Harry S., Jr.
Bargonetti, Jill
Cameron, Dr. Joseph A.
Christopher, John A.
Coleman, James William
Cobb, Dr. Jewel Plummer
Cook, Dr. Nathan Howard
Craft, Dr. Thomas J., Sr.
Dottin, Dr. Robert Philip
Emeagwali, Dale Brown
Essien, Dr. Francine
Eure, Dr. Herman Edward
Foster, Lloyd L.
Fuller, Almyra Oveta
Hammond, Dr. Benjamin Franklin
Harris, Dr. Mary Styles
Harris, Dr. Geraldine E.
Henderson, Dr. Nannette Smith
Hendricks, Dr. Marvin B.
Hildreth, James
Hopkins, Thomas Franklin
Hollingsworth, John Alexander
Hogan, Dr. James Carroll, Jr.
Holt, Dr. James Stokes, III
Jackson, Earl, Jr.
Jackson, Dr. Julius Hamilton
Johnson, Dr. Charles Edward
Jones, George H.
Kinde, Isaac
Madu, Dr. Anthony Chisaraokwu
Meade, Dr. Alston B., Sr.
Nance, Jesse J., Jr.
Newberry, Cedric Charles
Patton, Dr. Curtis Leverne
Parker, Charles McCrae
Pickett, Cecil Bruce
Porter, Dr. Clarence A.
Richo, Anna
Salters, Dr. Charles Robert
Sanders, Dr. Robert B.
Watkins, Dr. Michael Thomas
Washington, Robin L.
Wells, Roderick Arthur

## Botany

Haugstad, May Katheryn
Hicks, Dr. Arthur James
Hill, Dr. Ray Allen
Hodge, William Anthony
Warren, Herman Lecil

## Building/Construction (*See Also* Retail Trade—Building/Construction Materials; Wholesale Trade—Building/ Construction Materials)

Apea, Joseph Bennet Kyeremateng
Argrette, Joseph M.
Bates, William J.
Bell, Robert Wesley
Bowser, Hamilton Victor, Sr.
Brown, Raymond Madison
Brown, Rodney W.
Burges, Melvin E.
Byrd, Lumus, Jr.
Bynam, Sawyer Lee, III
Cargile, William, III
Carter, Thomas Allen
Chapman, Cleveland M.
Chigbu, Gibson Chuks
Copeland, Richard Allen
Cooke, Hon. Thomas H., Jr.
Coles, John Edward, Sr.
Coleman, John H.
Cotton, Garner
Davis, Ronald U.
Davis, Melvin Lloyd, Sr.
Davis, Frank Allen
Dickerson, Dr. Warner Lee
Edmonds, Campbell Ray
Edwards, Grover Lewis, Sr.
Ethridge, John E., Jr.
Floyd, James T., Sr.
Frye, Reginald Stanley
Gibson, Kenneth Allen
Henson, Daniel Phillip, III
Irons, Hon. Paulette R.
Jackson, James Holmen
Jennings, Everett Joseph
Jenkins, Jim
Jett, Arthur Victor, Sr.
Johnson, Edward M.
Johnson, Jared Modell
Keeler, Vernes
Khadar, Mohamed A.
King, Richard L., Jr.
King, W. James
Lee, John C., III
Lee, Charles Gary, Sr.
Leigh, William A.
London, Roberta Levy
Mabin, Joseph E.
Mack, Cleveland J., Sr.
Merritt, Wendy Warren
Moore, Thomas L.
Overstreet, Dr. Everett Louis
Ozanne, Dominic L.
Ozanne, Leroy
Pierson, Randy
Pierson, Derron
Platt, Richard A.
Powell, Juan Herschel
Robbins, Leonard
Rowe, Dr. Nansi Irene
Robinson, James L.
Royston, Evelyn Ross
Russell, Herman Jerome
Russell, Jerome
Sidbury, Harold David
Stanley, Thornton, Sr.
Thermilus, Jacques Evens
Turner, Linda Darnell
Vann, Gregory Alvin
Waller, Ruby Larry
Warren, Otis, Jr.
Washington, Edith Stubblefield
Webster, Theodore E.
Weaver, Gary W.
Williams, Yarborough, Jr.
Williams-Dotson, Daryl
Woods, Henry, Jr.

## Cable Broadcasting Industry (*See* Television/ Cable Broadcasting Industry)

## Chemistry

Adesuyi, Dr. Sunday Adeniji
Alexander, Dr. Edward Cleve
Barefield, Dr. James E., II
Bramwell, Dr. Fitzgerald Burton
Cannon, Dr. Charles Earl
Cannon, Paul L., Jr.
Clarke, Dr. Donald Dudley
Clark, Dr. Theotis, Jr.
Cooper, Walter, Sr.
Dent, Dr. Anthony L.
Dixon, Dr. Louis Tennyson
Dorman, Dr. Linneaus C.
Eduok, Dr. Etim Effiong
Eseonu, Dr. Dorothy N.
Evans, Dr. Billy Joe
Foster, Lloyd L.
Ford, Lisa Denise
Francisco, Joseph Salvadore
Gainer, Dr. Frank Edward
Goodwin, Dr. Jesse Francis
Harris, Dr. Betty Wright
Hargrave, Charles William
Herrell, Dr. Astor Yeary
Hogan, Dr. James Carroll, Jr.
Innis, Roy Emile Alfredo
Jackson, Dr. Roy Joseph, Jr.
Johnson, Dr. William Randolph, Jr.
Kirklin, Dr. Perry William
King, William Frank
Lee, Dr. Charlotte O.
Lester, Prof. William Alexander, Jr.
Lewis, Virginia Hill
Macklin, Dr. John W.
Matthews, Dr. Virgil E.
Madison, Jacqueline Edwina
McBee, Vincent Clermont
Mitchell, Dr. James Winfield
Morris, Marlene C.
Morris, Vernon R.
Molaire, Michel Frantz
Nelson, Dr. Ivory V.
Onyejekwe, Dr. Chike Onyekachi
Sanders, Dr. Robert B.
Schooler, Dr. James Morse, Jr.
Shoffner, James Priest
Shavers, Dr. Cheryl L.
Smith, Fronse Wayne, Sr.
Sogah, Dr. Dotsevi Yao
Spurlock, Dr. Langley Augustine
Sudbury, Leslie G.
Thompson, Dr. Lancelot C. A., Sr.
Thurston, Dr. Paul E.
Truesdale, Dr. Carlton Maurice
Warner, Isiah Manuel
Walters, Dr. Marc Anton

## Chiropractic

Barnett, Dr. Lorna
Ford, Dr. Clyde W.
Pulliam, Rev. Betty E.

Freeman, Dr. Thomas F.
Gaines, Ava Canda
Gadsden, Rev. Dr. Nathaniel J., Sr.
Gainer, Prof. John F.
George, Constance P.
Gilbert, Shedrick Edward
Githiga, Rev. Dr. John Gatungu
Gill, Rev. Laverne McCain
Gibson, Rev. William M.
Gilmore, Rev. Marshall B.
Givens-Little, Aurelio Dupriest
Glover, Rev. Clarence Ernest, Jr.
Gordon, Pastor Alexander H., II
Grigsby, Dr. Marshall C.
Groff, Rev. Regina Coleen
Grant, Rev. Dr. Jacquelyn
Grayson, Rev. Dr. Byron J., Sr.
Grant, Rev. Debora Felita
Greene, Rev. William
Guyton, Rev. Booker T., Sr.
Hammond, Dr. James Matthew
Hall, Dr. Addie June
Hardman-Cromwell, Dr. Rev. Youtha Cordella
Hammond, Rev. Kenneth Ray
Hall, Kirkwood Marshal
Harvey, Dr. Louis-Charles
Hale, Rev. Cynthia Lynnette
Harris, Barbara Clementine
Hairston, Raleigh Daniel
Harvin, Rev. Durant Kevin, III
Harris, Rev. Dr. Michael Neely
Harvey, Rev. Errol Allen
Hardin, Dr. Henry E.
Harvey, Rev. Dr. Wardelle G., Sr.
Harrold, Rev. Austin Leroy
Hayden, Rev. Dr. John Carleton
Hawkins, Dr. Calvin D.
Haynes, Dr. Rev. Michael E.
Hemphill, Rev. Dr. Miley Mae
Herd, Rev. John E.
Hewitt, Rev. Basil
Herron, Vernon M.
Higgins, Sammie L.
Hill, Vonciel Jones
Hicks, Rev. Dr. Sherman G.
Hilson, Dr. Arthur Lee
Hicks, Dr. Rev. H. Beecher, Jr.
Howard, Glen
Holmes, Rev. James Arthur
Hope, Rev. Julius Caesar
Holley, Rev. Jim
Holmes, Rev. Zan W., Jr.
Horton, Pastor Larnie G., Sr.
Howard, Rev. Moses William, Jr.
Hughes, Rev. Carl D.
Humphrey, Marion Andrew
Hunter, Rev. David
James, Frederick C.
James, Dr. Felix
James, Rev. Darryl Farrar
Jackson, Dr. Rev. Earl J.
Jackson, Rev. Henry Ralph, Sr.
James, Dr. Gillette Oriel
Jakes, Bishop Thomas Dexter, Sr.
Jefferson, Dr. Rev. Austin, Jr.
Jerkins, Rev. Jerry Gaines
Jerome, Rev. Joseph D.
Johnson, Rev. Clinton Lee
Johnson, Rev. Dr. Leroy
Jones, Rev. Bishop Spencer
Jordan, Charles Wesley
Joyner, Claude C.
Johnson, Pastor James H.
Jones, Rev. Vernon Algie, Jr.
Jones, Dr. William O.
Jones, Rev. Dr. Robert Earl
Jordan, Rev. John Wesley
Jordan, Rev. Dr. Ternae T., Sr.
Kee, John P.
Kenoly, Ron
Kelly, Rev. Dr. Herman Osby, Jr.
Kelly, Rev. James Clement
Kimbrough, Charles Edward
Kirk-Duggan, Rev. Dr. Cheryl Ann
King, Rev. Dr. Bernice Albertine
Kinchlow, Ben
Knight, Rev. Dr. Carolyn Ann
Lane, William Keith
LaGarde, Rev. Frederick H., Jr.
Langford, Rev. Victor C., III
Lawson, Rev. James Morris, Jr.
Lewis, Rev. Dr. Alvin, Jr.
Lewis, Sharma
Lewis, Harold Thomas
Lewis, Dr. Lloyd Alexander
Lewis, Rev. Theodore Radford, Jr.
Lewis, Kenneth Dwight
Lemmons, Herbert Michael
Liverpool, Rev. Herman Oswald
Lloyd, Rev. Dr. J. Anthony
Lowe, Eugene Yerby, Jr.
Lovett, Dr. Rev. Leonard
Lowery, Rev. Dr. Joseph E.
Long, Eddie L.
Lynch, Rev. Lorenzo A., Sr.
Lyles, James V.
Martin, B. Herbert, Sr.
Manley, Rev. John Ruffin
Mack, Charles Richard
Massey, Dr. James Earl
Marshall, Rev. Calvin Bromley, III
Martin, Rev. Dr. Lawrence Raymond
Martin, Dr. James Tyrone
Martin, Dr. Richard Cornish
Martin, Rev. Edward, Jr.
Mayes, Clinton, Jr.
Marshall, Anita
McGuire, Raymond J.
McNeal, Rev. John Alex, Jr.
McNorriell, Mozell M.
McCall, H. Carl
McClendon, Bishop Clarence E.
McKenzie, Bishop Vashti Murphy
McNeill, Cerves Todd
Medford, Isabel
Middleton, Rev. Dr. Richard Temple, III
Mickle, Hon. Andrea Denise
Mitchell, Rev. Dr. Sadie Stridiron
Mims, Pastor Raymond Everett, Sr.
Montgomery, Elder Oscar Lee
Moore, Oscar William, Jr.
Morrison, Dr. Rev. Juan LaRue, Sr.
Moore, Helen D. S.
Montgomery, Rev. Dwight Ray
Montgomery, James C.
Montague, Nelson C.
Murray, Rev. Cecil Leonard
Muhammad, Benjamin Chavis
Nabors, Rev. Dr. Michael C.R.
Newman, Nathaniel
Nelson, Otha Curtis, Sr.
Neighbors, Rev. Dolores Maria
Newbold, Rev. Simeon Eugene, Sr.
Newsome, Dr. Clarence Geno
Newsome, Rev. Burnell, Sr.
Nicholson, Rev. Aleathia Dolores
O'Neal, Rev. Eddie S.
Okunor, Rev. Dr. Shiame S.
Ollison, Ruth Allen
Oliver, Donald Byrd, Sr.
Oldham, Dr. Lloyd
Outlaw, Dr. Patricia Anne
Patterson, Rev. Clinton David
Patterson, Rev. Alonzo B., Jr.
Paddio-Johnson, Dr. Eunice Alice
Pannell, William E.
Parker, Rev. Matthew
Patrick, Pastor Charles Namon, Jr.
Palmer, Bishop Gregory Vaughn
Peete, Nan Arrington
Pearson, Bishop Carlton Demetrius
Perkins, Dr. Rev. James Connelle
Perry, Rev. Jerald Isaac, Sr.
Pearson, Herman B.
Pinder, Rev. Nelson W.
Pino, Rev. Jerome King Del
Powell-Jackson, Rev. Dr. Bernice
Porter, Rev. Dr. Kwame John R.
Pollard, Dr. Alton Brooks, III
Portee, Rev. Dr. Frank, III
Poindexter, Rev. Charles L. L.
Porter, Bishop Henry Lee
Pruitt, Fr. Alonzo Clemons
Price, Dr. Joseph L.
Pruitt, Rev. Eddie Jay Delano
Pulliam, Rev. Betty E.
Rasberry, Rev. Robert Eugene
Ratliff, Dr. Joe Samuel
Rambison, Dr. Amar B.
Reed, Kwame Osei
Rhodes, Lisa D.
Richardson, Rev. Dr. Lacy Franklin
Ricard, Rev. John Huston
Richardson, Rev. Louis M., Jr.
Robinson, Dr. Rev. Frank James, Jr.
Robinson, Rev. Joseph, Jr.
Rowe, Dr. Nansi Irene
Rogers, Rev. Dr. Victor Alvin
Roye, Monica R Hargrove
Rucker, Rev. Raleigh
Sandidge, Dr. Oneal C.
Scott, Dr. Leonard Stephen
Shipley, Rev. Anthony J.
Shopshire, Dr. James Maynard, Sr.
Shaw, Rev. Martini
Sheard, Rev. John Drew
Simpson, Rev. Dr. Samuel G.
Smith, Rev. Elijah, Sr.
Smith, Rev. Dr. Paul
Smith, Dr. Luther Edward, Jr.
Smith, Rev. Dr. J. Alfred, Sr.
Smith, Rev. George Walker
Smith, Rev. Dr. Wallace Charles
Smith, Rev. Harold Gregory
Smith, Dr. Rev. Gregory Robeson, Sr.
Smith, Kelly Miller, Jr.
Snead, Dr. Willie T., Sr.
Spann, Rev. Paul Ronald
Stewart, Dr. Warren Hampton, Sr.
Stotts, Rev. Dr. Valmon D., Sr.
Stamps, Rev. Lynman A., Sr.
Stewart, Dr. William H.
Steele, Tommy
Sutton, Gloria W.
Swain, Dr. Ronald L.
Taylor, Rev. Dr. Martha C.
Talley, Rev. Dr. Clarence, Sr.
Thompson, Rev. Carl Eugene, Sr.
Thomas, Byron E.
Thomas, Bishop Walter Scott, Sr.
Timmons-Toney, Rev. Deborah Denise
Tolliver, Dr. Richard Lamar
Torain, Rev. Dr. Tony William
Tolliver, Rev. Dr. Joel
Tottress, Dr. Richard Edward
Trice, Dr. Juniper Yates
Turner, Dr. Eugene A., Sr.
Tuggle, Rev. Reginald
Turman, Rev. Dr. Kevin
Tyner, Rev. Charles R., Sr.
Underwood, King James, Sr.
Vaughan, Rev. Dr. James Edward
Venable, Rev. Robert Charles
Vivian, Dr. Cordy Tindell
Washington, Rev. Johnnie M.
Warner, Rev. Edward L.
Washington, Rev. Henry L.
Waits, Rev. Va Lita Francine
Washington, Rev. Dr. Emery, Sr.
Walker, Joseph W., III
Wesley, Howard-John
Weathersby, Joseph Brewster
Webb, Joe, Sr.
Weathers, Rev. Dr. J. Leroy
White, Woodie W.
Williams, Dr. Rev. Earl, Jr.
Williams, Deborah Brown
Williams, Dr. Eddie Robert
Williams, Rev. Ellis
Williams, Rev. Dr. Maceo Merton
Williams, Rev. A. Cecil
Williams, Dr. Charles J., Sr.
Wiggins, William H., Jr.
Wilson, Alva L.
Williams, Reginald Clark
Wilson, Grady Demond
Wiggins-Obie, Rev. Daphne Cordelia
Williams, Byron
Williams, Rev. Dr. Curtis Cortez
Winley, Rev. Diane Lacey
Woodhouse, Dr. Johnny Boyd
Wright, Bishop James R., Sr.
Wright, Rev. Jefferson W.
Yates, Pastor LeRoy Louis, Sr.
Zimmerman, Matthew Augustus, Jr.
X, Quanell

## Community Service

Aiken, Kimberly Clarice
Andrews, Phillip
Anderson, Patricia Hebert
Austin, Joyce Phillips
Bailey, Doris Jones
Badger, Brenda Joyce
Bailey, Ronald T.
Baugh, Florence Ellen
Bacoate, Matthew V., Jr.
Belizaire-Spitzer, Julie
Bennett, Rev. Debra Quinette
Bernard, Dr. Michelle Denise
Block, Dr. Leslie S.
Bommer, Minnie L.
Boxill, John Hammond
Booker, Robert Joseph
Bradley, William B.
Brown, Ralph Benjamin
Bradley-Burns, Melissa Lynn
Brooks, Suzanne R.
Bright, Dr. Herbert L.
Browner, Joey Matthew
Burgess, Robert E., Sr.
Byrd, Harriett Elizabeth
Carey, Wilhemina Cole
Castleman, Elise Marie
Christburg, Sheyann Webb
Childs, Josie L.
Clemons, Linda K.
Collins, Joanne Marcella
Comer, Jonathan
Cooper, Earl
Coleman, Frankie Lynn
Crosby, Dr. Willis Herman, Jr.
Crawford, Betty Marilyn
Davis, Preston Augustus
Daniels, Richard D.
Davidson, Dr. Alphonzo Lowell, Sr.
Dailey, Thelma
Dixon, Margaret A.
Dixon, Valena Alice
Dorsey, Herman Sherwood, Jr.
Doby, Allen E.
Dowery, Mary A.
Easton, Earnest Lee
Eatman-Williams, Janice A.
Early, Ida H.
Edmonds, Elaine
Emmons, Rev. Rayford E.
Evers-Williams, Dr. Myrlie Louise
Evans, Elizabeth
Falana, Lola
Fattah, Falaka
Fitts, Dr. Rev. Leroy
Foggs, Rev. Dr. Edward L.
Ford, Rev. Samuel Lee
Francis, Rev. Dr. James N.
Frazier, Cliff
Gates, Jacquelyn Burch
Garrett, Cheryl Ann
Gilbert, Shedrick Edward
Giles, Terri Lynnette
Gillette, Hon. Frankie Jacobs
Gibson, Dr. Cheryl Dianne
Gordon, Dr. Sherman A.
Greene, Mary Ann
Grier, Rosey
Greene, Rev. William
Greene, Grace Randolph
Harris, Dr. Willa Bing
Hardy-Woolridge, Karen E.
Hackey, Rev. George Edward, Jr.
Hamlin, Ernest Lee
Hale, Kimberly Anice
Hasson, Nicole Denise
Harris, Arthur L., Sr.
Hager, Joseph C., Jr.
Harris, James G., Jr.
Henderson, Joyce Ann
Hewitt, Rev. Basil
Henderson, Cheri Kaye
Herring, Marsha K. Church
Hill, Annette Tillman
Hicks, Doris Askew
Holley, John Clifton
Horton, Dollie Bea Dixon
Hughes, Rev. Carl D.
Hughes, Hollis Eugene, Jr.
Hutchins, Jan Darwin
Jeffrey, Ronnald James
Jennings, Devoyd
Johnson, Beverley Ernestine
Johnson, Alexander Hamilton
Jones, Booker Tee, Sr.
Johnson, Hon. Otis Samuel
John, Dr. Mable
Johnson, Dorothy M.
Jordan, Rev. Dr. Ternae T., Sr.
Kelly, Rev. James Clement
Kennedy, Callas Faye
Khadar, Mohamed A.
King, Dr. Earl B.
King-Poynter, Marva
Knox, Wayne D. P.
Lawson, Debra Ann
Langston-Jackson, Wilmetta Ann Smith
LaGarde, Rev. Frederick H., Jr.
Lewter, Rev. Andy C., Sr.
League, Cheryl Perry
Lemon, Michael Wayne, Sr.
Lewis, Peggy
Love, Karen Allyce
Lynch, Rev. Lorenzo A., Sr.
Mack, Melvin
Marshall, Dr. Joseph Earl, Jr.
Martin, Dr. Kimberly Lynette
Marsh, Ben Franklin
McNeil, Freeman, III
McLeod, Dr. Georgianna R.
McDaniel, Rev. Paul Anderson
McCloud, Rev. Dr. J. Oscar
McGuire, Alfred D., Jr.
Medearis, Victor L.
Metters, Dr. Samuel
Miller, Rev. Anthony Glenn
Mitchell, Rev. Dr. Henry Heywood, Jr.
Miller, Lawrence A., Jr.
Miles, Dr. Norman Kenneth, Sr.
Moore, Lenny Edward
Monagan, Dr. Alfrieta Parks
Morrison, Jacqueline
Moore, Etta R.
Nelson, Rex
Newman, Miller Maurice
Nix, Rick
Norris, Rev. Charles L., Sr.
Norris, Fred Arthur, Jr.
Owens, Curtis
Payden, Rev. Henry J., Sr.
Parker, Jacquelyn Heath
Perkins, Prof. Frances J.
Pinder, Rev. Nelson W.
Pittman, Dr. Audrey Bullock
Pino, Rev. Jerome King Del
Powell, Alma Vivian Johnson
Pounds, Elaine
Randolph-Jasmine, Carol Davis
Ray, Rev. Patricia Ann
Richardson, Rev. Dr. Lacy Franklin
Robinson, S. Yolanda
Rockett, Damon Emerson
Rowe, Christa F.
Russell, Dorothy Delores
Saunders-Henderson, Martha M.
Saunders, Jerry, Sr.
Scott, Carstella H.
Sewell, Eugene P.
Shatteen, Westina Matthews
Shaw, Dr. Ann
Shabazz, Kaleem
Simmons, James Richard
Smith, William Fred
Smith, Dr. Alonzo Nelson
Smith, Dr. Richard Alfred
Smith, Marvin Preston
Smith, Fronse Wayne, Sr.
Spencer, Larry Lee
Stewart, Loretta A.
Stewart, Dorothy Nell
Stanyard, Hermine P.
Stalls, Dr. Madlyn A.
Stovall-Tapley, Mary Kate
Suttle, Rhonda Kimberly
Thomas, Joan McHenry Bates
Thomas, Liz A.
Tokley, Joanna Nutter
Turner, Vivian Love
Tyler, Robert James, Sr.
Watkins, Mozelle Ellis
Walker-Thoth, Daphne LaVera
Warren, Gertrude Francois
Watkins, Rolanda Rowe
Watkins, Shirley R.
Washington, MaliVai
Watson, Mary Elaine
Watkins, Rosyln
Weldon, Ramon N.
White, Ralph Lee
Williams, Geneva J.
Williams, Reginald Clark
Williams, Ronald Lee
Williams, Rev. John Henry
Williams, Theartrice T.
Williams, T. Joyce
Williams, Dr. Harriette F.
Willingham, James Edward, Sr.
Williams, Gail
Wordlaw, Clarence, Jr.
Young, Elwanda
Zambrana, Dr. Rafael

## Computer Science—Not Elsewhere Classified



## Computer Science—Programming/Software Development



## Computer Science—Systems Analysis/Design



## Computer Services (*See Also* Management/ Administration—Computer Systems/Data Processing)



## Consulting (*See Also* Management/ Administration—Consultation/Analysis)

## Counseling—Career/ Placement



## Counseling—Marriage/ Family



## Counseling—Mental Health

## Counseling—Not Elsewhere Classified



## Counseling—Rehabilitation



## Counseling—School/ Academic



## Criminology/Corrections



## Dance/Choreography



## Dentistry

White, Dr. Artis Andre
Williams, Dr. Harvey Joseph
Williams, Dr. Henry R., Jr.
Wiltz, Dr. Charles J.
Williams, Dr. Richard Lenwood
Wilson, Dr. Joseph Henry, Jr.
Woods, Dr. Robert Louis
Wright, Dr. Raymond LeRoy, Jr.
Wrenn, Dr. Thomas H., III
Wright, Dr. Melvin, Sr.
Young, Dr. Walter Fuller
Young, Frances Camille
Yuille, Dr. Bruce

## Directing/Producing (Performing Arts)

Albers, Kenneth Lynn
Allen, Debbie
Anderson, Madeline
Anderson, Gary
Barnette, Neema
Billings, Cora Marie
Bolling, Deborah A.
Boseman, Chadwick
Bowser, Yvette Denise Lee
Brown, Reginald DeWayne
Branch, William Blackwell
Brown, Dr. Abena Joan P.
Burnett, Zaron Walter, Jr.
Burton, Levar, Jr.
Carroll, Joe Barry
Caines, Bruce Stuart
Cannon, Reuben
Chase, Debra Martin
Cheatham, Henry Boles
Clay, Stanley Bennett
Collins, Tessil John
Combs, Sean John
Coker, Dr. Adeniyi Adetokunbo, Jr.
Coogler, Ryan
Collie, Kelsey E.
Coleman, Elizabeth Sheppard
Cosby, Dr. William Henry
Collins, Bernice Elaine
Crawford, Deborah Collins
Crudup, Gwendolyn M.
Curtis-Hall, Vondie
Daniels, Lee Louis
Dash, Julie
de Passe, Suzanne
Dickerson, Ernest Roscoe
Diesel, Vin
Dixon, Brandon Victor
Domingo, Colman
Dorn, Michael
DuVernay, Ava
Dunmore, Gregory Charles
Dutton, Charles Stanley
Ellington, Mercedes
Eskridge, Rev. John Clarence
Fales, Susan Marya
Fletcher, Winona Lee
Freisen, Gil
Free, World B.
Frazier, Cliff
Gamble, Kenneth
Giles, Henrietta
Glover, Danny Lebern
Gonzalez, Anita Louise
Gray, Felix Gary
Greaves, William
Gramby, Shirley Ann
Guillaume, Robert
Haddock, Mable J.
Hardison, Kadeem
Halliburton, Christopher
Harrison, Paul Carter
Harris, Helen B.
Harris, Thomas Walter
Head, Helaine
Hendry, Gloria
Hicklin, Dr. Fannie Frazier
Higginson, Vy
Horsford, Anna Maria
Hooks, Kevin
Hughes, Coquie
Hughes, Allen
Hughes, Albert
Hudlin, Reginald Alan
Hudson, Dianne Atkinson
Hudson, Frederick Bernard
Imhotep, Akbar
Ione, Carole
Jam, Jimmy
Jessup, Gayle Louise
Johnson, Nancy Aline Flake
Johnson, Prof. Stephanie Anne
Johnson, Dr. Charles Floyd
Joyner, Lemuel Martin
Khan, Dr. Ricardo M.
King, Woodie, Jr.
Klausner, Willette Murphy
Knight, Gladys Maria
Knowles, Beyonce Giselle
Kotto, Yaphet Frederick
Laneuville, Eric Gerard
Lange, Ted W.
Lane, Charles
Lee, Joie Susannah
LeFlore, Lyah Beth
Lee, Spike
Lemmons, Kasi
Lee, Damon
Lipscombe, Margaret Ann
Livingston-White, Dr. Deborah J. H.
Martin, Darnell
Martin, Jesse Lamont
McCord, LaNissa Renee
McNeill, Cerves Todd
McHenry, Doug
McKayle, Donald Cohen
McKee, Dr. Adam E., II
Meek, Dr. Russell Charles
Merritt, Wendy Warren
Mitchell, Arthur
Morton, Joe, Jr.
Nash, Niecy
Newman, Dr. Geoffrey W.
Nelson, Novella C.
Nelson, Prince Rogers
Nicholas, Donna Denise
Nurse, Richard A.
Nyong'o, Lupita
Patterson, Saladin K.
Palcy, Euzhan
Parsons, Karyn
Page, Harrison Eugene
Pawley, Dr. Thomas D., III
Phifer, Mekhi Thira
Poitier, Sidney L.
Prelow, Arleigh
Preston-Williams, Dr. Rodena
Prince-Bythewood, Gina
Purdee, Nathan
Reid, Timothy L.
Rhimes, Shonda
Rhames, Ving
Ribeiro, Alfonso
Rivera, Lance
Ridley, John
Rich, Matty
Riley, Teddy
Rock, Chris
Rodgers, Nile Gregory
Russ, Timothy Darrell
Ryan-White, Jewell
Sarmiento, Shirley Jean
Schultz, Michael A.
Scott, Seret
Sharp, Saundra Pearl
Shivers, P. Derrick
Singleton, John Daniel
Simmons, Russell Wendell
Snipes, Lolita Walker
Stokes, Chris
Story, Timothy Kevin
Sykes, Wanda Y'vette
Taylor, Almina Roberts
Thomas, Philip S.
Thomas, Prof. Nate
Thomas, Lorna E.
Tillman, George, Jr.
Townsend, Robert
Todd, Beverly
Treadwell, Tina McKinley
Turner-Forte, Diana
Tunie, Tamara Renee
Van Peebles, Mario
Vincent, Irving H.
Vinson, Chuck Rallen
Wagoner, J. Robert
Washington, Dr. Denzel Hayes, Jr.
Wayans, Keenen Ivory, Sr.
Washington, Dr. Von Hugo, Sr.
Walker, Charles
Ward, Douglas Turner
Walker, Dr. Ethel Pitts
Warren, Michael
Wade, Kim Mache
Walker, Phillip Eugene
Wallace, Linda Skye
Wayans, Shawn Mathis
West, Valerie Y.
Whitaker, Mical Rozier
Wilkerson, Prof. Margaret Buford
Winfrey, Oprah Gail
Wilson, Jonathan Charles
Wolfe, George Costello
Woods, Allie, Jr.
Young, William Allen

## Ecology

Crisp, Dr. Robert Carl, Jr.
Hoyte, James Sterling
Jackson, Lisa P.
Lillard, Kwame Leo
Marsh, Esq. Sandra M.
Malcom, Dr. Shirley Mahaley
Meridith, Denise Patricia
Mesiah, Raymond N.
Nelson, Edward O.
Williams, Dr. Howard Copeland

## Economics

Alford, Harry C.
Anderson, Dr. Carol Byrd
Bailey, Thomas R., Jr.
Chapman, Susan
Clifton, Dr. Ivery Dwight
Conrad, Dr. Cecilia Ann
Cunningham, William L.
Davie, Damon Jonathon
Ferguson, Roger W., Jr.
Flood, Eugene, Jr.
Gregory, Karl Dwight
Harris, Prof. Donald J.
Hoxby, Caroline M.
King, Dr. Arthur Thomas
Lemuwa, Ike Emmanuel
Loury, Dr. Glenn Cartman
Love, Carolyn Diane
Mordecai, David K. A.
Myers, Dr. Samuel L., Jr.
Myers, Dr. Samuel L., Sr.
O'Neal, Raymond W., Sr.
Onwudiwe, Ebere C.
Perry-Holston, Waltina D.
Ridgel, Dr. Gus Tolver
Senbet, Prof. Lemma W.
Simms, Dr. Margaret Constance
Spriggs, Dr. William
Stewart, Dr. James Benjamin
Sykes, Dr. Vernon Lee
Sylvester, Dr. Patrick Joseph
Thompson, Carol Belita
Wharton, Dr. Clifton Reginald, Jr.
Wilson, Ronald M.
Wilson, Dr. Stephanie Y.
Williamson, Dr. Lionel L., Jr.
Wordlaw, Clarence, Jr.

## Editing (*See* Writing/Editing—Fiction; Writing/Editing—Nonfiction; Writing/Editing—Plays, Screenplays, TV Scripts; Writing/Editing—Poetry; Writing/Editing—Not Elsewhere Classified)

## Education—Adult/Vocational

Allen, Dr. Brenda Foster
Batten, Rev. Grace Ruth
Banks, Dr. Lula F.
Baugh, Florence Ellen
Bennett, Joyce Annette
Birchette, Dr. William Ashby, III
Block, Dr. Leslie S.
Black, Frank S.
Brooks, Norward J.
Brooks, Rosemarie
Brown, Dr. Bertrand James
Brunson, David
Bryant, William Henry, Jr.
Carey, Wilhemina Cole
Clark-Hudson, Veronica L.
Colvin, Alex, II
Cole, Joyce Bowman
Colbert, George Clifford
Coleman, Avant Patrick
Collins, Tessil John
Davis, Hon. L. Clifford
Dean, Diane D.
Dean, Vyvyan Ardena Coleman
Eastmond, Joan Marcella
Fisher, Edith Maureen
Flowers, Dr. Loma Kaye
Franklin, Clarence Frederick, Jr.
Francis, Dr. Edith V.
Fulgham, Roietta Goodwin
Garrett, James Edward, Jr.
Gibson, JoAnn
Gillum, Dr. Ronald M., Sr.
Goines, Dr. Leonard
Goodman, Ruby Lene
Haynes, Dr. Worth Edward
Harris-Ebohon, Dr. Altheria Thyra
Horton, Dollie Bea Dixon
Hollingsworth, John Alexander
Holt, Dr. Dorothy L. Thomas
Hubbard, Calvin L.
Jones, Esq. Ernest Edward
King, Thomas Lawrence
Lawrence, Dr. Jaquator Hamer
Mack, Melvin
Mack, Dr. Wilhelmena
Martin, Rayfus
McCloud, Anece Faison
Middleton, Rev. Dr. Richard Temple, III
Miller, William O.
Mitchell, Rev. Dr. Henry Heywood, Jr.
Mortimer, Delores M.
Moore, Hazel Stamps
Morant, Mack Bernard
Newhouse, Millicent DeLaine
Nunes Kirby, Mizan Roberta Patricia
Patton, Jean E.
Patrick, Dr. Opal Lee Young
Perry, Felton E.
Pittman, Dr. Audrey Bullock
Price, Brenda G.
Price, Ray Anthony
Pulliam, Rev. Betty E.
Quarles, George R.
Rich, Wilbur C.
Robinson, S. Yolanda
Saunders-Henderson, Martha M.
Sands, George M.
Sarmiento, Shirley Jean
Seams, Francine Swann
Selby, Dr. Cora Norwood
Smith, Willie B.
Thomas, David Anthony
Thompson, Dr. Winston Edna
Troupe, Dr. Marilyn Kay
Vaughn, Dr. Alvin
West, William Lionel, II
White-Ware, Grace Elizabeth
Williams, Katherine S.
Williams, Rev. Dr. Clarence Earl, Jr.
Willingham, Voncile
Woodruff, Jeffrey Robert
Wright, Dmitri

## Education—College/University

Abdullah, Dr. Makola
Abdul-Malik, Dr. Ibrahim
Abe, Dr. Benjamin Omara A.
Abdullah, Dr. Larry Richard Burley
Addison, Terry Hunter, Jr.
Adams, Dr. Afesa M.
Adesuyi, Dr. Sunday Adeniji
Adams, Joseph Lee
Adams, Anne Currin
Adair, Alvis V.
Addei, Arthella Harris
Adams, Dr. Russell Lee
Adams, Samuel Levi, Sr.
Adams, Dr. Elaine Parker
Adams, Dr. Carol Laurence
Adeyiga, Dr. Adeyinka A.
Adams, Robert Eugene
Adams-Gaston, Dr. Javaune
Adams, Dr. Julius Gregg
Adeyemi, Bakari
Adams, Kaweeda G.
Aikens, Alexander E., III
Aikens-Young, Dr. Linda Lee
Akbar, Dr. Na'im
Akinyemi, Dr. Nurudeen B.
Akorede, Ayo
Akins, Dr. Daniel L.
Alonzo, Jenny
Allen, Dr. Mitchell
Allen, Cathy H.
Allen, Dr. Karen M.
Aldridge, Dr. Delores Patricia
Alexander, Dr. Edward Cleve
Alexander, Dr. Drew W.
Allen, Walter R.
Allen, Shirley Jeanne
Allen, Robert Lee
Allen, Samuel Washington
Alfred, Rayfield
Allen, Carole Geneva Ward
Allen, Dr. William Barclay
Alexander, Dr. Lenora Cole
Aldredge, Prof. James Earl
Alexander, Dr. Estella Conwill
Allen, Dr. Maxine Bogues
Allen, Dr. Van Sizar
Alexander-Whiting, Harriett
Al-Mateen, Dr. Cheryl Singleton
Al-Mateen, Dr. Kevin Bakeer
Allen-Meares, Paula G.
Ali, Dr. Kamal Hassan
Alexander, Dr. Laurence Benedict
Amory, Dr. Reginald L.
Aman, Dr. Mohammed
Amiji, Hatim M.
America, Richard F.
Ammons, Dr. James H.
Aman, Mary Jo Parker
Anderson, Marsha C.
Anderson, Dr. Rachell
Anderson, Rachel
Anderson, Dr. Belinda C.
Andrews, William Pernell
Anokwa, Kwadwo
Anderson, Dr. Gloria Long
Anderson, Dr. Bernard E.
Anthony-Perez, Dr. Bobbie M.
Anderson, Dr. Thomas Jefferson
Anderson, Dr. James Alan
Andrews-McCall, Dr. Maxine Ramseur
Anderson, Dr. David Atlas
Anderson, Dr. Avis Olivia
Anthony, Dr. David Henry, III
Anderson, Kenneth Richard
Anderson, William Gilchrist
Applewhaite, Leon B.
Appleby-Young, Sadye Pearl
Archie, Shirley Franklin
Archer, Dr. Juanita A.
Ardrey, Dr. Saundra Curry
Archer, Dr. Chalmers, Jr.
Arrington, Dr. Pamela Gray
Araujo, Dr. Norman
Arterbery, Dr. V. Elayne
Aremu, Dr. Aduke
Armour, Dr. Lawrence
Arnold, Dr. Lionel A.
Arrington, Richard, Jr.
Arroyo, Prof. Martina
Arties, Lucy Elvira Yvonne
Artisst, Robert Irving, Sr.
Asante, Dr. Molefi Kete
Ashford, Mary E.
Atlas, Dr. John Wesley
Atkins, Dr. Carl J.
Audain, Dr. Linz
Ausbrooks, Beth Nelson
Austin, Mary Jane
Austin, Dr. Debra
Azibo, Dr. Daudi Ajani Ya
Bailey, Dr. Darlyne
Barrington, Dr. Eugene L.
Barnes, Dr. Elsie M.
Bailey, Dr. Deryl Flynn
Battle, Prof. Juan
Baraka, Amina
Baker, Dr. Gail F.
Battle, Dr. Stanley F.
Baiocchi, Regina A. Harris
Banks, Jahshuwan-Jessean
Banks, Cerri Annette
Barnette, Neema
Baker, Dr. Beryle I.
Badejo, Dr. Diedra L.
Baxter, Rev. Nathan Dwight
Barnwell, Andre
Battle, Dr. Conchita Y.
Bailey, Dr. Joseph Alexander, II
Bailey, Harry Augustine, Jr.
Bailey, Dr. Adrienne Yvonne
Bagley, Dr. Peter B. E.

Cooper, Ernest, Jr.
Cooper, Iris N.
Copeland, Dr. Leon L., Sr.
Cooper, Joseph
Cooper-Lewter, Rev. Dr. Nicholas Charles
Cropp, Dr. Dwight Sheffery
Creary, Ludlow Barrington
Crosby, Dr. Edward Warren
Cruz, Dr. Iluminado Angeles
Cruzat, Dr. Gwendolyn S.
Cromwell, Adelaide McGuinn
Crumpton, Dr. Lesia
Crosby, Dr. Margaree Seawright
Crawford, Brenita
Crutchfield, James N.
Cross, Dr. Dolores E.
Creighton-Zollar, Dr. Ann
Crusto, Mitchell Ferdinand
Crenshaw, Dr. Reginald Anthony
Craig, Starlett Russell
Cruthird, J. Robert Lee
Crouther, Dr. Betty Jean
Culver, Rhonda
Culpepper, Dr. Lucy Nell
Cunningham, David S., Jr.
Cunningham, Dr. Paul Raymond Goldwyn
Cummings, Annette Merritt
Cummings, Dr. Jay R.
Curry, Jason R.
Curry, Dr. James H.
Cudjoe, Dr. Selwyn Reginald
Cunningham, Dr. James J.
Cunningham, Dr. William Dean
Curry, Sadye Beatryce
Curry, Dr. William Thomas
Cuyjet, Dr. Aloysius Baxter
Curtis, Dr. James L.
Dale, Clamma Churita
Dandridge, Prof. Rita Bernice
Daly, Dr. Frederica Y.
Daley, Thelma Thomas
Dalton, Raymond Andrew
Dalley, George Albert
Davis, Johnetta Garner
Davis, Joseph Solomon
Davis, Dr. Katie Campbell
Davis, Leodis J.
Davis, Dr. John Albert
Davis, George Bernard
Davis, Dr. Marianna White
Davis, Dr. Nathan Tate
Davis, Dr. Edward L.
Davis, Dr. Elaine Carsley
Davis, Etheldra S.
Davis, Rev. France Albert
Davis, Dr. Carrie Louise Filer
Dash, Prof. Leon DeCosta
Dave, Alfonzo, Jr.
Davenport, Calvin A.
Davis, Dr. Abraham, Jr.
Davidson, Ezra C., Jr.
Daniels, A. Raiford
Daniels, Dr. Ron D.
Darden, Dr. Joseph Samuel, Jr.
Dawkins, Stan Barrington Bancroft
Davis, Willis H.
Days, Drew Saunders, III
Davis, Dr. William L.
Davis, William R.
Days, Rosetta Hill
Davis-Haley, Dr. Rachel T.
Davis, Dr. Ernestine B.
Davis, Dr. Bertha Lane
Dawson, Dr. Alma
Dawson, Shed, Jr.
Davenport, Dr. Carol A.
Davis, Diana L.
Davidson, Adenike Marie
Dawson, Dr. Michael C.
Dartson, Dr. Myrna Vanessa
Davis, Joan Yvette
Davis, Dr. Willie
Davis-Millin, Dr. Myrtle A.
Davis, Dr. Jewelnel
Davenport, Dr. Christian A.
Davis, Willie Clark
Davenport, Ronald R., Sr.
Davis, Earl S.
Dawson, Dr. Rev. B. W.
Davis, Jean E.
Davis, Denice Faye
Damper, Ronald Eugene
Davis, Angela Yvonne
Daniel, Simmie Childrey
Davis, Lelia Kasenia
Davis, Dr. Marilyn Ann Cherry
Daniels, Dr. William James
Davis, Dr. Sheila Parham
Dark, Okianer Christian
Davis, Erroll B., Jr.
Davis, Donald
Davis, Lance Roosevelt
Davis, Dr. Ernestine Bady
Dates, Dr. Jannette Lake
Davis, Dr. Russell Andre
Davis, Robert N.
Darby, Dr. Emma Turner Lucas
Dawkins, Tammy C.
Dandy, Dr. Roscoe Greer
Dansby, Jesse L., Jr.
Daniel, Griselda
Davis-McFarland, Dr. E. Elise
Delany, Samuel Ray, Jr.
DeCosta-Willis, Dr. Miriam
de Jongh, Prof. James Laurence
Dean, Diane D.
Derricotte, Toi
De Veaux, Alexis
Delpit, Dr. Lisa Denise
DeLauder, Dr. William B.
DeLoatch, Dr. Eugene M.
DeSassure, Charles
Dent, David J.
Delsarte, Louis J.
DeLoatch, Dr. Sandra J.
Dejoie, Carolyn Barnes Milanes
Dean, Walter R., Jr.
Delco, Wilhelmina R.
Derricotte, Dr. Eugene Andrew
Denniston, Prof. Dorothy L.
Dent, Dr. Preston L.
Dempsey, Rev. Dr. Joseph Page
Dennis, Hugo, Jr.
Dennis, Dr. Rutledge M.
Dickerson, Janet Smith
Diggs, Rev. Dr. William P., Jr.
Dillard, Dr. Martin Gregory
Dixon, Dr. Leon Martin
Dixon, Dr. Ruth F.
Dixon, Dr. Armendia P.
Dickson, Dr. Charlie Jones
Dill, Dr. Bonnie Thornton
Dickerson, Ron, Jr.
Dinkins, David Norman
Dickerson, Dr. Bette Jeanne
Dixon, Dr. Benjamin
Dickerson, Lowell Dwight
Dickerson, Prof. Dennis Clark, Sr.
Dorman, Hattie Lawrence
Douglass, M. Lorayne
Douglas, Dr. Janice Green
Dove, Rita Frances
Downs, Crystal
Downie, Dr. Winsome Angela
Dobard, Dr. Raymond G., Jr.
Dowdy, Dr. Joanne Kilgour
Donaldson, Dr. Shawn Riva
Doggett, John Nelson
Dodson, Howard, Jr.
Dorsey, Joseph A., Jr.
Douglas, Herbert Paul, Jr.
Douglas, Dr. James Matthew
Doomes, Dr. Earl
Douglas, Elizabeth (Betty) Asche
Dodson, Dr. Jualynne E.
Donaldson, Dr. Leon Matthew
Donegan, Charles Edward
Dowery, Mary A.
Downing, Dr. John William, Jr.
Douglas, Dr. Samuel Horace
Dove, Dr. Pearlie C.
Douglas, Joseph Francis, Sr.
Draper, Dr. Edgar Daniel
Driskell, David Clyde
Drummond, William Joe
Draper, Dr. Frederick Webster
Drewry, Cecelia Hodges
Drake, Michael V.
Drumming, Saundra T.
Dubroy, Tashni-Ann
Durr, Dr. Marlese
DuPree, Kia
Dube, Thomas M. T.
Dungy, Dr. Claibourne I.
Dunmore, Charlotte J.
Dunn, Marvin
Duster, Troy S.
Durant, Celeste Millicent
Durand, Dr. Henry J., Jr.
Dunlap, Dr. Karen F. Brown
Dugas, A. Jeffrey Alan, Sr.
DuPree, Prof. Sherry Sherrod
Durham, Dr. Joseph Thomas
Dudley-Washington, Loise
Dual, Dr. Peter Alfred
Dupree, David H.
Durant, Dr. Thomas James
Dykes, DeWitt S., Jr.
Dymally, Lynn V.
Dyson, Rev. Dr. Michael Eric
Eastmond, Joan Marcella
Early, Dr. Gerald
Ealy, Mary Newcomb
Earl, Dr. Archie, Sr.
Eaton, Thelma Lucile
Earls, Dr. Julian Manly
Eaves, Dr. John H.
Eady, Cornelius
Eatman, Dr. Timothy K.
Easter, Dr. Marilyn K.
Ebbe, Dr. Obi N. I.
Edley, Christopher Fairchild, Jr.
Edmond, Dr. Janice L. Sumler
Edney, Dr. Norris Allen
Edwards, Theodore Unaldo
Edwards, Dr. John W., Jr.
Edwards, Dr. Thomas Oliver
Edmonds, Bevelyn
Edwards, Dr. Nicole R.
Edwards, Brent Hayes
Edmunds, Dr. Walter Richard
Edwards, Leo Derek
Edwards, Mattie Smith
Edwards, Dr. Harry
Edwards, John L., Sr.
Edwards, Dr. Solomon
Edwards, Ruth McCalla
Ekechi, Felix K.
Eke, Dr. Kenoye Kelvin
Ellis, Benjamin F., Jr.
Elliott, Dr. Derek Wesley
Ellis, Michael G.
Elders, Dr. M. Joycelyn
Ellis, Marilyn Pope
El-Kati, Mahmoud
Elam, Dr. Harry Penoy, Jr.
Elliott, Anthony Daniel, III
Ellison, Nolen M.
Ellison, Rosalind
Elzey, Thomas J.
Emmanuel, Dr. Tsegai
England, Dr. Rodney Wayne
Epps, Dr. Edgar G.
Epting, Marion Austin
Ericsson, Dr. Aprille Joy
Eseonu, Dr. Dorothy N.
Espy-Wilson, Carol
Eskridge, Rev. John Clarence
Esogbue, Dr. Augustine O.
Essiet, Dr. Evaleen Johnson
Estill, Dr. Ann H. M.
Essoka, Gloria Corzen
Essien, Dr. Francine
Ethridge, Dr. Robert Wylie
Eugere, Edward J.
Eure, Dr. Herman Edward
Evans, Dr. Billy Joe
Evans, Mari
Evans, W. Franklin
Evans, Warren Cleage
Evans, Patricia P.
Exum, Thurman McCoy
Farmer, Dr. Robert Clarence, Sr.
Fain, Constance Frisby
Farley, Dr. Jonathan David
Faulcon, Dr. Gaddis J.
Fadulu, Dr. Sunday O.
Faulcon, Dr. Clarence Augustus, II
Faw, Barbara Ann
Fearn-Banks, Kathleen
Felder-Hoehne, Felicia Harris
Ferere, Dr. Gerard Alphonse
Felton, James A.
Felton, Herman J., Jr.
Fentress-Williams, Judy
Felder, Harvey
Felder, Cain Hope
Fears, Emery Lewis, Jr.
Fewell, Richard
Fields, Savoynne Morgan
Fisher, Fr. David Andrew
Finley, Dr. D. Linell, Sr.
Fitchue, M. Anthony
Fields, Dr. Ewaugh Finney
Fitts, Dr. Rev. Leroy
Fields, Alva Dotson
Fierce, Milfred C.
Fisher, Rubin Ivan
Flake, Rev. Dr. Floyd H.
Flateau, Dr. John
Fleming, Dr. Juanita W.
Fluker, Dr. Walter Earl
Fletcher, Dr. Bettye Ward
Flint, Dr. Charley
Floyd, Dr. Samuel A., Jr.
Fletcher, Winona Lee
Fleming, Prof. Raymond Richard
Fleming-Rife, Anita
Fleurant, Gerdes
Ford, Nancy Howard
Ford, Dr. David Leon, Jr.
Fortune, Dr. Gwendoline Y.
Foster, Dr. E. C.
Forrest-Carter, Dr. Audrey Faye
Fogam, Prof. Margaret Hanorah
Fournier, Collette V.
Forbes, Calvin
Fox, Charles Washington
Foxx, Laura R.
Foster, Jennifer K.
Ford, Dr. Robert L.
Foggs, Joyce D.
Fomufod, Dr. Antoine Kofi
Ford, Dr. Albert S.
Ford, Ausbra
Forte, Dr. Minnie T.
Foster, Frances Smith
Foster, Lloyd L.
Foster, Rev. James Hadlei
Foreman, Doyle
Foster, Dr. Rosebud Lightbourn
Foxall, Dr. Martha Jean
Franklin, Allen D.
Freeman, Dr. Thomas F.
Franklin, Dr. Harold A.
Franklin, Dr. Renty Benjamin
Frazier, Dr. Leon
Frye, Nadine Grace
Freeman, Kimberley Edelin
Freeman, Dr. Antoinette Y.
Frederick, Wayne A. I.
Francis, Charles K.
Franklin, Dr. Lance Stonestreet
Francis, Livingston S.
Francisco, Joseph Salvadore
Franklin, Dr. Rev. Robert Michael, Jr.
Fresh, Edith McCullough
Freeman, Diane S.
Fuller, Almyra Oveta
Fuerst, Jean Stern
Fuller, Dr. Vivian L.
Fuse-Hall, Rosalind
Fuller, Dr. Howard L.
Gainous, Fred J.
Gayles, Dr. Jonathan
Gary, Kathye J.
Garland, John William
Gabbin, Dr. Alexander Lee
Gaither, Dr. Thomas W.
Gaines, Ernest James
Gaines, Herschel Davis
Gamble, Dr. Wilbert
Galvin, Dr. Emma Corinne Brown
Gardiner, George L.
Garner, Dr. La Forrest Dean
Garrett, Aline Mae
Garner, Dr. Charles
Gardner, Dr. Bettye J.
Gardner, Dr. Frank W.
Gatewood, Dr. Wallace Lavell
Garrison, Jewell K.
Garrett, Dr. E. Wyman
Garrity, Monique Paul
Gary, Dr. Lawrence Edward
Gary, Dr. Melvin Lee
Gabbin, Dr. Joanne Veal
Gaither, Magalene Dulin
Garcia, Dr. William Burres
Gainer, Prof. John F.
Garner, Dr. Mary E.
Gates, Dr. Henry Louis, Jr.
Gatewood, Dr. Algie C.
Garcia, Kwame N., Sr.
Gadsden, Rev. Dr. Nathaniel J., Sr.
Gallon, Dr. Dennis P.
Gayle-Thompson, Dr. Delores Joyce
Gaspard, Dr. Patrice Theresa
Gayles-Felton, Dr. Anne Richardson
George, Dr. Hermon, Jr.
Gecau, Dr. Kimani James
Gentry, Dr. Atron A.
Gerald, Dr. Melvin Douglas, Sr.
George, Dr. Luvenia A.
George-Bowden, Dr. Regina
Gemeda, Dr. Guluma
Gholson, Dr. General James
Givens, Dr. Donovahn Heston, Jr.
Gilpin, Clemmie Edward
Giovanni, Nikki, Jr.
Gibson, Rev. William M.
Gifford, Dr. Bernard R.
Gilchriest, Lorenzo
Gilbert, Jean P.
Gill, Dr. Wanda Eileen
Gill, Dr. Walter A.
Gittens, Anthony Edgar
Gilyard-Ingraham, Dr. Geraline L.
Gill, Prof. Jacqueline A.
Gilmore, Rev. Dr. Robert McKinley, Sr.
Giddings, Paula Jane
Gilton, Dr. Donna L.
Giles-Gee, Dr. Helen Foster
Givens, Dr. Henry, Jr.
Gillespie, Bonita
Githiga, Rev. Dr. John Gatungu
Giles, Charlotte Emma
Gill, Glenda Eloise
Gibbs, Dr. Jewelle Taylor
Glass, Dr. Ernestine W McCoy Pickens
Glover, Dr. Glenda B.
Gladden, Dr. Major P.
Glasco, Dr. Anita L.
Glasgow, Douglas G.
Glenn, Cecil E.
Goodson, Dr. Martin L., Jr.
Gona, Dr. Ophelia Delaine
Golden, Donald Leon
Gordon, Dr. Edmund W.
Goodwin, Dr. Norma J.
Gould, Prof. William Benjamin, IV
Goudy, Dr. Andrew James
Govan, Ronald M.
Goodwin, Stefan Cornelius
Gonzalez, Anita Louise
Gordon-Reed, Annette
Gomez, Dr. Michael A.
Govan, Dr. Sandra Yvonne
Goins, Atty. Richard Anthony
Golden, Marita
Golden, Dr. Willie L.
Goddard, Rosalind Kent
Golden, Marvin Darnell
Gooden, Cherry Ross
Gravenberg, Dr. Eric Von
Graham, Dr. Patricia G.
Grant, Rev. Dr. Jacquelyn
Griffin, Jean Thomas
Griffin, Dr. Betty Sue
Grace, Dr. Marcellus
Greene, Joann Lavina
Griffin, Dr. Ervin Verome, Sr.
Graham, Dr. Jo-Ann Clara
Grant, Claude DeWitt
Gray, Dr. C. Vernon
Griffin, Gregory O., Sr.
Grayson, George Welton
Graham, Helen W.
Greene, Dr. Beverly A.
Grantham, Charles
Gray, Jon R.
Graves, Autumn Adkins
Grantham, Prof. Regina B.
Grant, Christine S.
Green, Vincent E.
Graham, Mariah
Grant, Judge Cheryl Dayne
Graham, Prof. Precious Jewel
Grant, Dr. Wilmer, Jr.
Graydon, Wasdon, Jr.
Green, Dr. James L.
Green, Robert Lee
Greene, Charles Lavant
Gregory, Karl Dwight
Greer, Dr. Robert O., Jr.
Greenwood, Dr. Charles H.
Griffith, Elwin Jabez
Griffith, Dr. Ezra E. H.
Griffin, Lula Bernice

Kelley, Dr. Delores G.
Kelley, William Melvin
Keith, Dr. Leroy, Jr.
Kennedy, Dr. Theodore Reginald
Kennedy, James E.
Kennedy, Dr. Joyce S.
Kennedy, Adrienne Lita
Kelly, Rev. Dr. Herman Osby, Jr.
Kennedy, Bernice Roberts
Keizs, Marcia V.
Kennedy, Randall L.
Kern-Foxworth, Dr. Marilyn L.
Kennedy, Dr. Karel Ralph
Kelly, Ernece Beverly
Kenyatta, Mary
Kenan, Randall G.
Khan, Dr. Ricardo M.
Kington, Raynard S.
Kimbrough, Walter M.
King, Preston
King-Hammond, Leslie
Kilson, Martin Luther, Jr.
Kilimanjaro, John Marshall
Kirklin, Dr. Perry William
King, Rev. William J.
Kirkland-Holmes, Dr. Gloria
Kirkland, Prof. Jack A.
Kirkland, Theodore
King, Dr. Talmadge Everett, Jr.
King, Lewis M.
King, Mary Booker
King, Patricia Ann
Kindall, Dr. Luther Martin
King, Colbert I.
King, Thomas Lawrence
Kimbro, Dennis Paul
Kirk-Duggan, Rev. Dr. Cheryl Ann
King, Dr. Arthur Thomas
Kitchen, Wayne Leroy, Jr.
King, Dr. Reatha Clark
Kleven, Prof. Thomas E.
Knight, Athelia Wilhelmenia
Knable, Bobbie Margaret Brown
Knight, W. H., Jr.
Knight, Dr. Franklin W.
Knight, Dr. Muriel Bernice
Knight, Dr. Robert S.
Knowles, Dr. Eddie Ade
Koger, Dr. Linwood Graves, III
Kotzin, Dr. Diana
Komunyakaa, Yusef
Krigger, Dr. Marilyn Francis
Kuykendall, Dr. Crystal Arlene
Kumbula, Dr. Tendayi Sengerwe
Kumanyika, Dr. Shiriki K.
Kwame, Paul T.
Ladson, Gwinnett
Lane, Austin A.
Lawson, Erma J.
Lawrence, Dr. Jaquator Hamer
LaPoint, Dr. Velma
Lacey, Wilbert, Jr.
Lanier, Marshall Lee
Langston, Dr. Esther J.
Landry, L. Bartholomew
Lancaster, Herman Burtram
Lairet, Dr. Dolores Person
Lahr, Dr. Charles Dwight
Lawrence, Dr. Leonard Eugene
Lawrence, Annie L.
Latham, Esq. Weldon Hurd
Lawson, Elizabeth Harris
Larkin, Dr. Byrdie A.
Lawrence, Dr. William Wesley
Lattimer, Dr. Agnes Dolores
LaVeist, Dr. Thomas
Langston-Jackson, Wilmetta Ann Smith
Lamaute, Denise
Lacey, Dr. Bernardine M.
Lane, Prof. Johnny Lee, Jr.
Lacy, Walter
Leon, Dr. Tania Justina
Lewis, Charles Michael
Lewis, Harold Thomas
Lewis, Dr. Henry L., III
Lee, M. David, Jr.
Lee, Helen Elaine
Lewis, David Levering
Lee, Dorothy A. H.
Lewis, Kenneth Dwight
Leonard, Carolyn Marie
Lester, Julius
Lewis, Dr. Margaret W.
Lee, Dr. Margaret Carol
Lewis, Leo E., III
Lewis, Therthenia Williams
Lewis, Cleveland Arthur
Leace, Donal Richard
Lewis, Lauretta Fields
Lee, Dr. Charlotte O.
Leacock, Prof. Stephen Jerome
Lehman, Dr. Paul Robert
Leggon, Herman W.
LeFlore, Dr. Larry
Lee, Ritten Edward, II
Lee, Clifton Valjean
Lee, Dr. Guy Milicon, Jr.
Lee, Kermit J., Jr.
Lee, LaVerne C.
LeDoux, Rev. Jerome G.
Lee, Dr. Allen Francis, Jr.
Lede, Dr. Naomi W.
Lewis, William Sylvester, Sr.
Lewis, Ramsey Emanuel, Jr.
Lewis, Ida Elizabeth
Lewis, Dr. Meharry Hubbard
Leonard, Dr. Walter J.
Lester, Donald
LeMelle, Tilden J.
Lester, Prof. William Alexander, Jr.
Lewis, Almera P.
Lewis, David Baker
LeRoy, Charles
LeRoy, Dr. Gary Lewis
Ledbetter, Charles Ted
Leonard, Donis
Lewis, Dr. Lonzy James
Lewis, Dr. Brenda Neumon
Lehman, Dr. Christopher Paul
Lewis, Earl
Lewis, William Henry
Lewis, Dr. Angela K.
Lee, Cheryl Taylore
Lindsay, Dr. Arturo
Lindsey, Jerome W., Jr.
Littlejohn, Dr. Edward J.
Lipscombe, Margaret Ann
Lillie, Dr. Vernell Audrey Watson
Lipscomb, Darryl L.
Linton, Sheila Lorraine
Lister, David Alfred
Little, Dr. Monroe Henry, Jr.
Lide, Dr. William Ernest
Lightfoot, Dr. Sara Lawrence
Liautaud, James
Lloyd, Dr. Barbara Ann
Lloyd, Dr. Raymond Anthony
Lloyd, Wanda
Llewellyn-Travis, Chandra
Lloyd, Rev. Dr. J. Anthony
Love, Dr. Eric Tyrone Lowery
Lownes-Jackson, Dr. Millicent Gray
London, Dr. Harlan
Logan, Dr. Barbara N.
Lofton, Dr. Barbara
Locke, Dr. Hubert G.
Lockwood, James Clinton
Lomas, Dr. Ronald Leroy
London, Dr. Clement B. G.
Lockard, Prof. Jon Onye
Love, Dr. Barbara J.
Louard, Agnes Anthony
Long, Dr. Charles H.
London, Eddie
Love, Thomas Clifford
Lowe, Eugene Yerby, Jr.
Long, John Edward
Lowery, Dr. Birl
Louis, Dr. Suchet Lesperance
Locke, Dr. Mamie Evelyn
Love, Lynnette Alicia
Lockett, Dr. James D.
Locke, Dr. Don C.
Loury, Dr. Glenn Cartman
Lomax, Michael Wilkins
Lucas, Dr. Rev. Dorothy J.
Luckey, Dr. Irene
Lucas, Rubye
Luten, Thomas Dee
Lucas, Dr. John Harding, Sr.
Luis, Dr. William
Luckey, Dr. Evelyn F.
Luke, Dr. Learie B.
Luney, Percy R., Jr.
Lynch, Dr. Rufus Sylvester
Lyons, Donald Wallace, Sr.
Lynch, Hollis Ralph
Mabry, Edward L.
Mack, Ally Faye
Mack, Joan Gladden
Maddox, Dr. Elton Preston, Jr.
Macklin, Dr. John W.
Mack, Pearl Willie
Madgett, Dr. Naomi Long
Major, Dr. Clarence
Mann, Dr. Marion
Manning, Blanche Marie
Manning, Dr. Jean Bell
Malone, Dr. Gloria S.
Massey, Dr. James Earl
Massey, Walter Eugene
Mathis, Walter Lee, Sr.
Maxwell, Dr. Marcella J.
May, James F.
Mayes, Helen M.
Matthews, Dr. Virgil E.
Matthews, Dr. Hewitt William
Martin, Ionis Bracy
Martin, Harold B.
Martin, Dr. Edward Williford
Martin, Maxine Smith
Mansfield, Dr. Carl Major
Mapp, Dr. Edward C.
Marius, Dr. Kenneth Anthony
Mays, David W., III
Mays, Dr. James Arthur
Maynard, Valerie J.
Mayo, James Wellington
Madhubuti, Dr. Haki R.
Mackie, Dr. Calvin
Matthews, Dr. Gerald Eugene
Majozo, Estella Conwill
Malveaux, Julianne
Marks, Dr. John
Maxey, Dr. Randall W.
Martin, Harold L., Sr.
Mangum, Elmira
Martin, Harold L., Sr.
Mason, Derek
May, Dr. Gary Stephen
Martin, Dr. Joanne Mitchell
Mays, Dr. Vickie M.
Mayes, Doris Miriam
Martin, Sylvia Cooke
Martin-Ogunsola, Dellita Lillian
Mallette, Carol L.
Martin, Hoyle Henry
Mason, Ronald Edward
Mazon, Larri Wayne
Mayden, Ruth Wyatt
Maryland, Mary Angela
Mahone, Dr. Charlie Edward, Jr.
Madu, Dr. Anthony Chisaraokwu
Marshall, Dr. Joseph Earl, Jr.
Massey, Ardrey Yvonne
Majors, Richard G.
Martin, Frank C., II
Martin, Dr. Rosalee Ruth
Manning, Dr. Randolph H., Sr.
Majete, Dr. Clayton Aaron
Marriott, Dr. Salima Siler
Maynard, Dr. Edward Samuel
Matthews, Leonard Louis
Matthews, Harry Bradshaw
Maultsby, Dr. Portia K.
Maddox-Simms, Dr. Margaret Johnnetta
Matthews, Mary Joan Holloway
Martin, Prof. Carolyn Ann
Martin, Dr. McKinley C.
Matthews, Dolores Evelyn
Marshall, Dr. Edwin Cochran
Marshall, Paule Burke
Mathis, Dr. Thaddeus P.
Maultsby, Rev. Dr. Sylvester
McAfee, Dr. Leo C., Jr.
McBride, Frances E.
McClendon, Kellen
McClomb, George E.
McClain, William Andrew
McClellan, Frank Madison
McCloud, Aaron Curtis
McDaniels, Alfred F.
McDaniel, Prof. Reuben R., Jr.
McFadden, James L.
McFarlin, Emma Daniels
McFerrin, Sara Elizabeth Copper
McWilliams, Dr. Alfred E., Jr.
McNeil, Dr. Ogretta V.
McReynolds, Elaine A.
McMillian, Dr. Frank L.
McMillan, Friar Douglas James
McKee, Dr. Adam E., II
McKayle, Donald Cohen
McGuire, Dr. Chester C., Jr.
McIntyre, Dianne Ruth
McHenry, Mary Williamson
McHenry, Donald F.
McGlothan, Ernest
McGee, Dr. Joann
McGee, Eva M.
McGee, Prof. Henry W., Jr.
McGhee, Samuel T.
McGinnis, James W.
McKinney, Bishop George Dallas
McKinney, Rufus William
McKinney, Alma Swilley
McLemore, Leslie Burl
McLean, Dr. Helen Virginia
McLaughlin, Rev. Dr. Jacquelyn Snow
McLaughlin, Dr. LaVerne Laney
McCluskey, John A., Jr.
McDonald, Jon Franklin
McLaughlin, Dr. George W.
McIlwain, Nadine Williams
McAdoo, Henry Allen, Sr.
McCummings, Dr. LeVerne
McCall, Barbara Collins
McGuffin, Dorothy Brown
McLaughlin, Dr. Megan E.
McLaughlin, Dr. Andree Nicola
McClane, Prof. Kenneth Anderson, Jr.
McGee, Patricia J. Horne
McWhorter, Dr. Grace Agee
McCloud, Anece Faison
McAndrew, Anne E. Battle
McKinnon, Dr. Isaiah
McMillan, Jacqueline Marie
McClearn, Billie Marie
McKenna, Dr. George J., III
McIntosh, Dr. Frankie L.
McKnight, Reginald
McKandes, Dorothy Dell
McClain, Dr. Paula Denice
McElroy, Dr. Lee A., Jr.
McKanders, Kenneth Andre
McClelland, Marguerite Marie
McCarrell, Clark Gabriel, Jr.
McElroy, Dr. Colleen J.
McElvane, Pamela Anne
McClendon, Bishop Clarence E.
McKinney-Whetstone, Diane
McMorris, Dr. Michael Anthony
McCaskill, Carolyn
McCann, Renetta
McCants, Prof. Jennifer Barnes
McCluskey, Audrey Thomas
McKissack, Cheryl Mayberry
McNeal, William R., Jr.
McDemmond, Dr. Marie Valentine
McDonald, Katrina Bell
McCorvey, Dr. Everett D.
Mevorach, Katya Gibel
Mell, Patricia
Meyers, Dr. Carolyn W.
Menogan, Annita M.
Meadows, Cheryl R.
Means, Donald Fitzgerald
Melton, Bryant
Meridith, Denise Patricia
Merriweather, Barbara Christine
Meriwether, Roy Dennis
Metcalf, Dr. Zubie West, Jr.
Meade-Tollin, Dr. Linda C.
Means, Hon. Bertha Elizabeth
Merideth, Charles Waymond
Mesa, Dr. Mayra L.
Michaux, Eric Coates
Milledge, Dr. Luetta Colvin Upshur
Miles, Dr. Elijah Walter
Miles, Dr. Edward Lancelot
Millender, Mallory Kimerling, Sr.
Middleton, Vertelle D. M.
Middleton, Dr. Ernest J.
Miles, Dr. Carlotta G.
Miller, Frederick A.
Miller, Horatio Cabrere
Mimms, Dr. Maxine Buie
Minor, Billy Joe
Mims, Dr. George L.
Miller, Dr. M. Sammye
Miller, Dr. Margaret Greer
Miller, Jacqueline Elizabeth
Miller, Dr. Jeanne-Marie Anderson
Miller, Louise T.
Miller, Rev. Dr. Telly Hugh
Miller, Dr. Ronald Baxter
Miller, Dr. Russell L., Jr.
Miller, Richard Charles
Mitchell, Rev. Dr. Henry Heywood, Jr.
Mitchell, Dr. Earl Douglass, Jr.
Miller, E. Ethelbert
Mitchell-Kernan, Dr. Claudia Irene
Miller-Jones, Dr. Dalton
Mitchell, Theo W.
Miles, Dr. Norman Kenneth, Sr.
Miller, Dr. Bernice Johnson
Miller, Lawrence A., Jr.
Miller, Dr. Andrea Lewis
Middleton, Rev. Dr. Richard Temple, III
Mitchell, Joann
Mims, Beverly Carol
Miller, Dr. Warren F., Jr.
Miller, Dr. Dorsey Columbus, Jr.
Middleton, John Allen
Minor, Dale Michael
Middleton, Phillip B.
Middleton, Michael A.
Miller, Fayneese
Mitchell, Sharon
Miller, Dr. Ingrid Fran Watson
Moore, Juliette R.
Morris, Dr. Carole V.
Montgomery, Soncerey L.
Morris, Vernon R.
Montgomery, Dr. Clyde, Jr.
Molette-Ogden, Dr. Carla
Morris, Margaret Lindsay
Moore, Beverly
Moreland-Young, Dr. Curtina
Mosley, Carolyn W.
Mosley, Marie Oleatha Pitts
Mosley, Walter
Morris, William Howard
Moore, Dr. Quincy L., Sr.
Mosely, Dr. Kenneth D.
Monteiro, Dr. Thomas
Montgomery, Dr. Toni-Marie
Moses, Dr. Harold Webster
Mock, James Edward, Sr.
Moss, Alfred A., Jr.
Molette, Barbara J.
Morris, Bernard Alexander
Morgan-Cato, Prof. Charlotte Theresa
Moore, Alice Evelyn
Moore, Larry Louis
Moore, Lenard Duane
Moses, Dr. Henry A.
Mobley, Emily Ruth
Morris, Dr. Frank Lorenzo, Sr.
Morrison, Dr. Rev. Juan LaRue, Sr.
Morgan, Hazel C Brown
Morrow, Dr. John Howard, Jr.
Moore, Dr. Jossie A.
Morrison, Toni
Morrison, Dr. K. C
Morial, Sybil Haydel
Molette, Dr. Carlton Woodard
Mobley, Dr. Sybil Collins
Moaney, Eric R.
Monroe, Annie Lucky
Monteith, Dr. Henry C.
Mooring, Dr. Kittye D.S.
Moore, Dr. Nathan
Moore, Dr. Jean E.
Moody, Dr. Charles David, Sr.
Morrison, Prof. Keith Anthony
Morris, Stanley E., Jr.
Morris, Leibert Wayne
Morgan, Dr. Gordon Daniel
Moore, Dr. Robert Frazier
Moreland, Dr. Lois Baldwin
Moo-Young, Louise L.
Morisey, Dr. Patricia Garland
Morgan, Jane Hale
Morris, Dr. Dolores Orinskia
Moss, Robert C., Jr.
Monagan, Dr. Alfrieta Parks
Muwakkil, Salim
Murray, Dr. James Hamilton
Musgrove, Dr. Margaret Wynkoop
Murray, Dr. Mabel Lake
Muhammad, Khalil Gibran
Murphy, Dr. Vanessa A.
Mwamba, Dr. Zuberi I.
Myers, Dr. Samuel L., Sr.
Myers, Dr. Samuel L., Jr.
Myers, Dr. Lena Wright
Myers, Dr. Jacqualine Desmona
Myricks, Dr. Noel
Myrick, Dr. Howard A.

Shotwell, Ada Christena
Showell, Hazel Jarmon
Simmons, Dr. Howard L.
Simmons, Prof. John Emmett, III
Simpkins, J. Edward
Simpson, Carole
Simpson, Dr. Willa Jean
Singleton, James Milton
Sims, Genevieve Constance
Simmons, Dr. Sylvia Q.
Siler, Dr. Joyce B.
Singley, Yvonne Jean
Sinnette, Dr. Calvin Herman
Simmons, Dr. S. Dallas
Simpson-Taylor, Dr. Dorothy Marie
Silver, Dr. Joseph Howard, Sr.
Singleton, Leroy, Sr.
Sinnette, Dr. Elinor DesVerney
Sims, Robert
Simpson, Dr. John Randolph
Sims, Prof. Ronald R.
Skinner, Dr. Ewart C.
Slaughter, Atty. Fred L.
Slade, Phoebe J.
Slie, Pastor Samuel N.
Slaughter, Dr. John Brooks
Smith, Dr. Ann Elizabeth
Smith, Alfred J., Jr.
Smith, Alphonso Lehman
Smith, Prof. Andrew W.
Small, Lily B.
Smalls, O'Neal
Smith, Arthur D.
Smith, Dr. Charles Frank, Jr.
Smith, Dr. Charles U.
Smith, Dr. Donald Hugh
Smith, Dr. Edgar Eugene
Smith, Vernon G.
Smith, Virginia M.
Smitherman, Dr. Geneva
Smith, Joseph F.
Smith, Dr. Jessie Carney
Smith, Dr. James Almer, Jr.
Smith, Dr. Luther Edward, Jr.
Smith, Dr. Joshua L.
Smith, Dr. Judith Moore
Smith, LeRoi Matthew-Pierre, III
Smith, Heman Bernard, Jr.
Smith, Geraldine T.
Smith, Dr. J. Clay, Jr.
Smith, Howlett P.
Smith, Rev. Dr. Paul
Smith, Dr. Nellie J.
Smith, Dr. Phillip M.
Smith, Dr. Quentin Ted
Smith, Dr. Roulette William
Smith, Reginald D., Sr.
Smith, Dr. Robert P., Jr.
Smith, Dr. Roland Blair, Jr.
Smith, Dr. Walter L.
Smith, Mary Levi
Smith, Dr. Edward Nathaniel, Jr.
Smith, Dr. Eleanor Jane
Smith, Keith Dryden, Jr.
Smith, Janice Evon
Smith, Dolores J.
Smith, John L., Jr.
Smith, Dr. Barbara Wheat
Smith, Prof. Robert Charles
Smith, Charles Edison
Smith, Audrey S.
Smith, Dr. Joanne Hamlin
Smitherman, Esq. Carole Catlin
Smith, Dr. Jesse Owens
Smith, Darryl C.
Small, Dr. Clara Louise
Smith, Tracy K.
Smith, Valerie
Smith, Dr. George Edmond
Smith, Dr. Gerald Lamont
Smith, Shirley Hunter
Snowden, Sylvia Frances
Snowden, Frank Walter
Southern, Joseph
Sowell, Thomas
Solomon, Barbara J.
Sommerville, Joseph C.
Sockwell, Oliver R., Jr.
Sogah, Dr. Dotsevi Yao
Soliunas, Francine Stewart
Southerland, Ellease
Southgate, Martha
Spaulding, Jean Gaillard
Spikes, Dr. Delores Richard
Spencer, Dr. Michael Gregg
Spence, Rev. Joseph Samuel, Sr.
Spigner, Dr. Clarence
Spiva, Dr. Ulysses Van
Sprauve, Dr. Gilbert A.
Spencer, Prof. Margaret Beale
Sprout, Prof. Francis
Spaulding, William Ridley
Stewart, Dr. William H.
Strickland, Dorothy S.
Stripling, Dr. Luther
Stubblefield, Jennye Lee Washington
Styles, Kathleen Ann
Stull, Dr. Virginia Elizabeth
Stinson, Dr. Joseph McLester
Stinson, Constance Robinson
Stodghill, Dr. Ronald
Stokes, Dr. Lillian Gatlin
Stewart, Dr. Albert C.
Stewart, Dr. Donald Mitchell
Stewart, Dr. John Othneil
Steele, Dr. Claude Mason
Staples, Robert E.
Stansbury, Dr. Clayton Cresvell, Jr.
Stent, Madelon Delany
Stewart, Dr. Elizabeth Pierce
Stevens, Althea Williams
Stevens, Dr. Maxwell McDew
St. Omer, Dr. Vincent V. E.
Stokes, Dr. Gerald Virgil
Stith, Dr. Melvin Thomas
Stewart, Dr. James Benjamin
Stewart, Dr. Mac A.
Stalls, Dr. Madlyn A.
Stetson, Jeffrey Paul
Starks, Robert Terry
Stockman, Dr. Ida J.
Steele, Dr. Shelby
Stamps, Spurgeon Martin David
Steele, Dr. Ruby L.
Stevens, Dr. George Edward
Stanley, Carol Jones
Stepto, Robert Burns
St. John, Primus
Stewart, Dr. Bess
Starks, Doris Nearror
Stancell, Dr. Arnold Francis
Stewart, Pearl
Stephens, E. Delores B
Stokes, Julie Elena
Strother, Dr. Germaine D.
Stevens, Dr. Joyce West
Strickland-Hill, Dr. Marva Yvonne
Stokes, Shereitte Charles, III
Stewart, Jacqueline Najuma
St-Pierre, Dr. Maurice
Stewart, Ella
Stevenson, Dr. Bryan A.
Suber, Dianne Boardley
Sulton, Dr. Anne Thomas
Summers, Loretta M.
Subryan, Carmen Barclay
Sullivan, Dr. J. Christopher
Sullivan, Dr. Edward James
Suneja, Dr. Sidney Kumar
Sutton, Dianne Floyd
Sutton, Dr. Sharon Egretta
Sullivan, Dr. Allen R.
Sutton, Dr. William Wallace
Sullivan, Dr. Zola Jiles
Suggs, Dr. Robert Chinelo
Swindell, Dr. Warren C.
Swann, Eugene Merwyn
Swan, Dr. Llewellyn Alex
Swanson, Charles
Swan, Dr. George W., III
Sykes, Prof. Rick
Sylvas, Dr. Lionel B.
Sykes, Dr. Vernon Lee
Sylvester, Dr. Patrick Joseph
Sylvester, Melvin R.
Talbot, Gerald Edgerton
Tanner, James W., Jr.
Tarver, Marie Nero
Tate, Dr. James A.
Taylor, Dr. Quintard, Jr.
Taylor, Stuart A.
Taylor, Howard Francis
Taylor, Dr. Jerome
Taylor, Michael Loeb
Taylor, Dr. Patricia E.
Taylor, Dr. Arnold H.
Taylor, Carole Lillian
Taylor, Edward Walter
Taylor, Dr. Dale B.
Taylor, Dr. David Vassar
Taylor, Prof. Paul David
Taylor, Dr. Robert, III
Tanter, Raymond
Taylor, Dr. Ronald Lewis
Taylor, Dr. Henry Louis, Jr.
Taylor-Thompson, Dr. Betty E.
Taylor, Dr. Estelle Wormley
Taylor, Orlando L.
Tarter, Roger Powell
Talley, William B.
Talley, Michael Frank, Sr.
Taylor, Mary Quivers
Taylor, Dr. Charles E.
Tanner, Dr. Tyrone
Tatum, Dr. Beverly Daniel
Tatum, James
Tate, Greg
Tei, Dr. Ebo
Temple, Dr. Jacqueline B.
Teruel, Lauren
Teasley, Ronald
Temple, Edward Stanley
Terrell, Dr. Melvin Cleveland
Terrell, Mary Ann Gooden
Terrell, Francis D'Arcy
Terborg-Penn, Dr. Rosalyn M.
Terrell, Dr. Francis
Terrell, Robert L.
Thomas, Carl Alan
Thomas, Charles Columbus
Thomas, Prof. Nate
Thomas, Dr. Maxine Suzanne
Thomas, Dr. Lucille Cole
Thomas, Mary A.
Thomas, Rev. Dr. Latta Roosevelt, Sr.
Thomas, Dr. Harry Lee
Thomas, Dr. Herman Edward
Thomas, Joyce Carol
Thompson, Francesca
Thompson, Dr. Litchfield O.
Thurston, Dr. Paul E.
Thornton, Dozier W.
Thompson, Marcus Aurelius
Thompson, Regina
Thompson, Dr. Robert Farris
Thompson, Sylvia Moore
Thomson, Gerald Edmund
Thornell, Richard Paul
Thompson, Dr. Winston Edna
Thomas, Althea Shannon Lawson
Thurman, Alfonzo
Thorburn, Dr. Carolyn Coles
Thomas, Jacqueline Marie
Thomas, Robert Lewis, Jr.
Thornton, Dr. Maurice M.
Thomas, Dr. Gerald Eustis
Thomas, Eula Wiley
Thomas, Prof. Nina M.
Thompson, Dr. Joseph Earl, Sr.
Thomas, Kendall
Thomas, Jacquelyn Small
Thelwell, Michael M. Ekwueme
Thomas, Dr. Pamella D.
Thompson, Dr. Sidney A.
Thomas, Rodolfo Rudy
Thompson, Dr. Charles
Thomas, Dr. Dennis E.
Thomas, Stephen
Thomas, Matthew W., Jr.
Thomas, David Anthony
Thomas, Jane Roscoe
Thomas, David
Thompson, Dr. Betty Taylor
Thomson, Dr. Thelma B.
Thompson, Evelyn Maria
Thompson, Clifford
Titus-Dillon, Dr. Pauline Y.
Tisdale, Prof. Celes
Tillman, Dr. Talmadge Calvin, Jr.
Tipton, Dr. Dale Leo
Tidwell, John Edgar
Tillis, Dr. Frederick Charles
Tobias, Randolf A.
Tolbert, Dr. Herman Andre
Tollett, Dr. Charles Albert, Jr.
Tottress, Dr. Richard Edward
Tomlinson, Dr. Robert
Tolbert, Jacquelyn C.
Towns, Dr. Sanna Nimtz
Tolliver, Dr. Richard Lamar
Townes, Emilie M.
Torrence-Thompson, Juanita Lee
Tropez-Sims, Dr. Susanne
Troutman, Dr. Adewale
Troupe, Quincy Thomas, Jr.
Troupe, Dr. Marilyn Kay
Traylor, Prof. Eleanor W.
Tripp, Dr. Luke Samuel
Trice, Dr. William Benjamin
Traylor, Dr. Horace Jerome
Treadwell, David Merrill
Troutman, Dr. Porter Lee, Jr.
Trottman, Charles Henry
Trimiar, Dr. Sinclair J.
Tucker, Dr. Dorothy M.
Tucker, James F.
Turner, Dr. Castellano Blanchet
Tucker, Norma Jean
Tucker, Geraldine Jenkins
Turner-Givens, Ella Mae
Turner, Dr. Doris J.
Turner, Winston Edwin
Turner, Dr. William Hobert
Turner, Dr. Moses
Turner, Marvin Wentz
Tukufu, Dr. Darryl S.
Turner, Jean Taylor
Turner, Geneva
Tuckson, Reed V.
Tucker, Dr. M. Belinda
Tufon, Chris
Turnbull, Dr. Charles Wesley
Tucker-Allen, Dr. Sallie
Turner, Margaret Dodson
Twiggs, Dr. Leo Franklin
Twigg, Dr. Lewis Harold, Jr.
Tyler, Rev. Gerald DeForest
Ulmer, Bishop Kenneth C.
Unaeze, Felix Eme
Uzoigwe, Dr. Godfrey N.
Valdes, Pedro H.
Vance, Dr. Irvin Elmer
Van Trece, Jackson C.
Varner, James, Sr.
Varner, Dr. Nellie M.
Vaughans, Kirkland Cornell
Vaughn, Dr. Janice S.
Verret, C. Reynold
Vernon, Francine M.
Vessup, Dr. Aaron Anthony
Vertreace-Doody, Martha Modena
Via, Thomas Henry
Vivians, Nathaniel Roosevelt
Violenus, Dr. Agnes A.
Vogel, Dr. Roberta Burrage
Walker, Dr. Melvin E., Jr.
Washington, Dr. Sarah M.
Walker, Charles
Ward, Dr. Perry W.
Ward, Dr. Jerry Washington, Jr.
Walls, Gen. George Hilton, Jr.
Walker, Dr. Valaida Smith
Watson, Genevieve
Washington, Dr. Von Hugo, Sr.
Walker, Eugene Kevin
Walton, Dr. Edward D.
Watts, Dr. Anne Wimbush
Walker, Dr. Sandra Venezia
Walker, Hon. Charles Ealy, Jr.
Wade, William Carl
Walters, Dr. Marc Anton
Watson, John Clifton
Washington, Adrienne Terrell
Wade, Achille Melvin
Waiguchu, Dr. Julius Muruku
Washington, Dr. Roosevelt, Jr.
Washington, Josie B.
Washington, Joseph R., Jr.
Waters, John W.
Washington, Dr. Thomas
Watts, Dr. Roberta Ogletree
Watson, Dr. Bernard C.
Watson, Joseph W.
Wayne, George Howard, Sr.
Wardlaw, Alvin Holmes
Ward, Daniel
Walters, Rev. Hubert Everett
Walton, Reggie Barnett
Washington, Elmer L.
Washington, Gladys J.
Washington, James Lee, Sr.
Warren, Herman Lecil
Warren, Dr. Stanley
Walker, Stanley Michael
Walker, Wilbur P.
Walter, Dr. John C.
Walters, Curla Sybil
Walker, Dr. Kenneth R., Sr.
Walker, Larry Moore
Walker, Dr. Lewis
Washington, Dr. Linda Phaire
Walton, Dr. Harriett J.
Wade, Dr. Joseph Downey
Walker, Cynthia Bush
Ware, Dr. William Levi
Walker, Dr. Sheila Suzanne
Ward, Dr. James Dale
Watkins, Dr. Charles B.
Wallace, Milton De
Wallace, Dr. Renee C.
Watson, Dennis Rahiim
Washington, Dr. Michael Harlan
Ward, Arnette Scott
Washington, Dr. Earl Melvin
Washington, Dr. Sandra Beatrice
Warren, Nagueyalti
Walton, R. Keith
Ward, Velma Lewis
Wallace, John M., Jr.
Walker, Dr. Gregory T. S.
Wafer, Deborah
Walker, Margie
Warner, Isiah Manuel
Ware, Leland Brett
Warren, Dorian T.
Watkins, Faye
Ware, Leland
Ware, Dr. John E.
Watson, Dr. Elizabeth Darby
Wasow, Omar Tomas
Watson, Dr. Janice
Wade-Gayles, Dr. Gloria Jean
Weaver, Afaa Michael
Weddington, Bill
Wesley, Howard-John
West, Roderick K.
Weaver, Dr. John Arthur
West, Dr. Herbert Lee, Jr.
Webster, Niambi Dyanne
Welch, Dr. Olga Michele
Weiss, Dr. Joyce Lacey
Wead, Dr. Rodney Sam
Weaver, Reginald Lee
Webb, Melvin Richard
Welsh, Dr. Kariamu
West, George Ferdinand, Jr.
West, Dr. John Raymond
Wells, Fr. Patrick Roland
Welch, Harvey
Webster, Winston Roosevelt
Weber, Dr. Shirley Nash
West, William Lionel, II
West, Prof. Pheoris
Westmoreland, Samuel Douglas
Wethers, Dr. Doris Louise
West, Valerie Y.
West, Cornel Ronald
Welmon, Dr. Vernis M.
Webb, Georgia Houston
Weddington, Dr. Wilburn Harold, Sr.
Welburn, Ronald Garfield
White, Dr. Katie Kinnard
Whitely, Donald Harrison
White, Dr. Yolanda Simmons
White, Sharon Brown
Whittaker-Davis, Dr. Sharon Elaine
White-Parson, Willar F.
Whitehurst, Steven Laroy
Wharton, A. C., Jr.
Whitaker, Mical Rozier
White, Dr. Augustus A., III
White, Dr. Clayton Cecil
Whiting, Dr. Albert Nathaniel
White, Dr. Tommie Lee
White, Dr. Sandra LaVelle
White, Dr. Barbara Williams
White, Frederic Paul, Jr.
Wheelan, Belle Smith
White, Frankie Walton
Whitehead, Joe B., Jr.
Whittler, Dr. Tommy E.
White, Dr. Keith L.
Wheeler, Beverly
Whaley, Edward I.
White, Paul Edward
White, Dr. Marilyn Elaine
Willrich, Penny
Williams, Dr. Carolyn Grubbs
Williams, Dr. Trina Rachael
Williams, Dr. Audrey L.

## Education—Elementary/ Secondary

Johnson, Rebecca M.
Jones, Sherman J.
Jones, Gary DeWayne
Jowers, Johnnie Edward, Sr.
Jones, Nettie Pearl
Johnson, Carroll Jones
Kafele, Baruti Kwame
Kennedy, Callas Faye
Kelley, William Melvin
Kimmons, Carl Eugene
Kimble, Bettye Dorris
King, Virgie M. Dunlap
Knox-Benton, Dr. Shirley
Kuykendall, Dr. Crystal Arlene
Lawson, Quentin Roosevelt
Langston-Jackson, Wilmetta Ann Smith
Lewis, Green Pryor, Jr.
Lewis, Carmen Cortez
Levermore, Claudette Madge
Lee, Clara Marshall
Lee, LaVerne C.
Lee, Dr. Guy Milicon, Jr.
LeGrand, Robert C., Jr.
Leggette, Violet Olevia Brown
Lee, Dr. Gwendolyn B.
Leath, Verlyn Faye
Lister, Willa Mae
Lowery, Michael Douglas
Lorthridge, Dr. James E.
Lyles, Marie Clark
Lyde, Jeanette S.
Madison, Yvonne Reed
Mandulo, Rhea
Marks, Lee Otis
Martin, Rosetta P.
Matthews, Robert L.
Maxwell, Dr. Marcella J.
Malone, Dr. J. Deotha
Malry, Dr. Lenton, Sr.
Marshall, Patricia Prescott
Mayberry, Dr. Claude A., Jr.
Maddox, Julius Arnell
Mack, Lurene Kirkland
Matthews, Rev. David
Matthews, Leonard Louis
Martin, Rayfus
Mangum, Ernestine Brewer
May-Pittman, Ineva
McBride, Shelia Ann
McAlpine, Robert
McMillan, Friar Douglas James
McKay-Davis, Monique Dionne
McMillan, Wilton Vernon
McAndrew, Anne E. Battle
McElrath-Frazier, Wanda Faith
McPherson, Roosevelt
McCrackin, Olympia H.
McCannon, Dindga Fatima
McGuire, Alfred D., Jr.
McGowan, Atty. Clarence Roy
Melendez-Rhinehart, Carmen M.
Mitchell, Connie R Cohn
Mills, Mary Elizabeth
Minor, Emma Lucille
Miles, Ruby A. Branch
Miller, Mattie Sherryl
Miller, William O.
Micks, Deitra Handy
Mickens, Maxine N.
Michael, Dr. Charlene Belton
Moore, Cleotha Franklin
Montgomery, Rev. Payne
Moore, Helen D. S.
Moore, Lenny Edward
Morris, Horace W.
Moorehead, Bobbie Wooten
Morston, Gary Scott
Moore, Katherine Bell
Montgomery, Joe Elliott
Moss, James Edward
Motley, J. Keith
Moss, Yolanda M.
Murray, Dr. Mabel Lake
Murray, Anna Martin
N'Namdi, Carmen Ann
Nabors, Jesse Lee
Nance, Herbert Charles, Sr.
Nathan, Rev. Timothy Eric
Nettles, Willard P., Jr.
Nellums, Michael Wayne
Northern, Robert A.
Oates, Wanda Anita
Orr, Marlett Jennifer
Owens, Isaiah Hudson
Oyeshiku, Dr. Patricia Delores Worthy
Patrick, Pastor Charles Namon, Jr.
Paul, Vera Maxine
Palmer, Dr. Elliott B., Sr.
Parms, Edwin L.
Patrick, Dr. Opal Lee Young
Patton, Robert
Palmer-Hildreth, Barbara Jean
Parker, Lee
Pelote, Dorothy Barnes
Perkins, William O., Jr.
Pearce, Oveta W.
Perry, Steve
Petty, Jervie Scott, Sr.
Pines, Darryll J.
Piggee, James M.
Pinkney, Dr. Enid C.
Pickett, Robert E.
Pitts, Dr. Vera L.
Piper, Elwood Arthur
Pinckney, Stanley
Pinkney, Dr. Betty Kathryn
Porter, Bishop Henry Lee
Polk, Dr. William C.
Porter, Lionel
Pratt, Mable
Pritchett, Stanley Jerome, Jr.
Pullen-Brown, Stephanie D.
Rayford, Lee Edward
Rambo, Bettye R.
Randall, Marlene West
Reaves, E. Fredericka M
Reddick, Alzo Jackson, Sr.
Reavis, John William
Reese, Mamie Bynes
Reese, Rev. Dr. Frederick Douglas
Reed, Joe Louis
Reed, Caroliese Ingrid Frink
Rhodeman, Clare M.
Richardson, DeRutha Gardner
Rivers, Vernon Frederick, Jr.
Richardson, Odis Gene
Robinson, Charles
Roberts, Lorraine Marie Pettie
Robertson, Quindonell Stinson
Robinson, Charlotte L.
Robinson, Kenneth Eugene
Robinson, Carol W.
Rogers, Earline S.
Ross, Emma Jean
Roberts, Margaret Ward
Roberts, Dr. Rona Dominique
Rochester, Dr. Mattilyn T.
Robinson, Rev. Harold Oscar
Robinson, Dr. Joyce Russell
Robertson, Delores W.
Rudd, Charlotte Johnson
Russell, Dian Bishop
Russell, John Peterson, Jr.
Saunders, Dr. Elizabeth Ann
Saunders-Henderson, Martha M.
Sandidge, Dr. Oneal C.
Sanders, Gladys N.
Scroggins, Bobby
Scott-Johnson, Roberta Virginia
Selby, Dr. Cora Norwood
See, Dr. Letha A.
Shanks, Wilhelmina Byrd
Shakoor, Dr. Waheedah Aqueelah
Sharpe, Dr. Audrey Howell
Shifflett, Lynne Carol
Sheard, Rev. John Drew
Simpkins, J. Edward
Singley, Yvonne Jean
Simpson, Dr. John O.
Smith, John B., Sr.
Smith-Gregory, Deborah P.
Smith, Dr. Donald Hugh
Smalls, Dorothy M.
Smotherson, Rev. Dr. Melvin
Smith, Dr. Mildred Beatty
Smith, Rev. Dr. J. Alfred, Sr.
Smith, Sherman, Sr.
Small, Stanley Joseph
Smith, Juanita
Smith-Gray, Cassandra Elaine
Smith, Willie B.
Smith-Smith, Peola
Snyder, Vanessa W.
Soares, Bea T.
Spradley, Frank Sanford
Stanislaus, Rev. Gregory K.
Stewart, Loretta A.
Stamps, Rev. Lynman A., Sr.
Stallings, Gregory Ralph
Stanyard, Hermine P.
Steele-Robinson, Alice Louise
Stansbury, Kevin Bradley
Summerville, Willie T.
Switzer, Lou
Taylor, Anderson
Tarver, Marie Nero
Taylor, Dr. Cledie Collins
Taylor, Gilbert Leon
Taylor, Veronica C.
Taylor, Reginald Redall, Jr.
Tate, Matthew
Taylor, John L.
Talley, James Edward
Taylor, Mildred D.
Terrell, Dr. Catherine Milligan
Thurman, Marjorie Ellen
Thomas, Charles Richard
Thomas, Juanita Ware
Thomas, Dr. Dennis E.
Thomas, Matthew W., Jr.
Thomas, Herman L.
Todd, Charles O.
Tolliver, Ned, Jr.
Troupe, Dr. Marilyn Kay
Turner, M. Annette
Turner-Forte, Diana
Turner, Winston Edwin
Turner, Johnnie Rodgers
Turner, Leslie Ford
Tyler, Shirley Neizer
Tyson, Lorena E.
Varner, James, Sr.
Vaughn, Dr. Alvin
Wallace, Milton De
Watley, Margaret Seay
Washington, Mary Parks
Wallace, Helen Winfree-Peyton
Walker, Wesley Darcel
Ward, Daniel
Washington, Rev. Dr. Emery, Sr.
Washington, Dr. Sarah M.
Watkins, Dr. Walter J.
Walker, James, Jr.
Watson, Mary Elaine
Washington, Coquese Makebra
Wells-Davis, Dr. Margie Elaine
West, Valerie Y.
Weathers, Margaret A.
Westbrook, Dr. Joseph W., III
White-Ware, Grace Elizabeth
White-Hunt, Deborah Jean
White, Dr. Marilyn Elaine
Williams, Kelvin Edwin
Williams-Hayes, Dr. Thea
Williams, Gerald
Wiley, Leroy Sherman
Wilson, Dr. John W.
Wilson, Floyd Edward, Jr.
Williams, Ulysses Jean
Wilson-Smith, Willie Arrie
Wilson, Hazel Forrow Simmons
Winston, Jeanne Worley
Williams, Georgianna M.
Williams, E. Thomas, Jr.
Williams, George L., Sr.
Williams, Dr. Carolyn Ruth Armstrong
Wright, William A.
Wright, Linnel N.
Yuill, Essie McLean-Hall
Zollar, Doris L.

## Education—Not Elsewhere Classified

Addison, Rafael
AkanDe, Benjamin Ola
Alexis, Eloise Abernathy
Alexander, Brent
Allen, Dr. Edna Rowery
Anderson, Dr. Carol Byrd
Anderson, Dr. Barbara Stewart Jenkins
Arnold, Wallace C.
Auld, Albert Michael
Barber, William, Jr.
Bain, Linda Valerie
Baker, Dave E.
Balton, Dr. Juanita J.
Barnes, Melody
Belton, Howard G.
Beane, Patricia Jean
Bennett, Courtney Ajaye
Belton, C. Ronald
Bills, Dr. Johnny Bernard, Jr.
Block, Dr. Leslie S.
Blanford, Dr. Colvin
Bogus, Dr. S. Diane Adamz
Boddie, Algernon Owens
Boynton, Asa Terrell, Sr.
Brunt, Samuel Jay
Bryant, Edward Joe, III
Brass, Reginald Stephen
Brooks, Dr. Daisy M. Anderson
Brown, Claudell, Jr.
Brown, Hezekiah
Bridges, Leon
Briggins, Charles E.
Bryan, Glynis A.
Bransford, Patricia
Brice, Dr. Barbara Gohanna
Britton, Dr. Carolyn B.
Brown, Rev. Annie Carnelia
Bryant-Shanklin, Dr. Mona Maree
Burke, Alfreda
Burns, Ursula M.
Burges, Joyce M.
Burse, Dr. Luther, Sr.
Butler, Eula M.
Butler, Dr. John Sibley
Byrd, Camolia Alcorn
Carter, Margaret Louise
Carson, Irma
Carrier, Clara L. DeGay
Carter, Thomas J., II
Carter, J. B., Jr.
Caroline, James C.
Caviness, Lorraine F.
Cafritz, Peggy Cooper
Calloway, Laverne Fant
Chambers, Juanita Clay
Cherry, Edward Earl, Sr.
Charleston, Dr. Gomez, Jr.
Cheatham, Henry Boles
Clayton, Dr. Constance Elaine
Clark, Savanna M. Vaughn
Clark, Dr. Bertha Smith
Clark, Dr. Harry Westley
Cole, Dr. Arthur
Cornish, Betty W.
Collins, Elsie
Cowden, Michael E.
Cooper, Dr. LaMoyne Mason
Council, LaVerne H.
Coleman, Deborah Stewart
Colvin, Alex, II
Collins, Dr. Bobby L.
Coleman, Avant Patrick
Collins, Corene
Cooper, Barbara J.
Cross, Fr. William Howard
Crews, Rev. William Hunter
Davis, Herman E.
Davis, Etheldra S.
Daye, Charles Edward
Davis, Dr. Jackie Sowell
Davis, Esq. Nathan W., Jr.
Darden, Christopher Allen
Davis, Donald
Dale, Robert J.
Deloatch, Myrna Spencer
Dixon, Ardena S.
Diaz, Fruitta Louise
Dixon, Sheila Ann
Dickerson, Amina J.
Didlick, Wells S.
Dobbs, Mattiwilda
Dottin, Dr. Robert Philip
Drakes, Muriel B.
Dungee, Margaret R.
Edwards, Dorothy Wright
Elam, Donna
Ellington, Mercedes
Elliott, John
Estes, Simon Lamont
Fann, Albert Louis
Fears, Emery Lewis, Jr.
Felix, Dr. Dudley E.
Flores, Joseph R.
Floyd, Vircher B.
Floyd, Dr. Jeremiah
Fortier, Dr. Theodore T., Sr.
Fortune, Dr. Gwendoline Y.
Ford, Deborah Lee
Fresh, Edith McCullough
Francis, Patrick John
Freeman, Melinda Lyons
Futrell, Dr. Mary Alice Franklin
Hatwood
Gardner, Loman Ronald
Gaskins, Percell McGahee
George, Dr. Luvenia A.
Gilbert, Jean P.
Gibbs, Dr. Sandra E.
Gibson, JoAnn
Givens, Sr. Clementina M.
Gilmore, Dr. Al Tony
Gordon, Walter Lear, III
Gooden, Dr. Winston Earl
Gordon, Aaron Z., Jr.
Greene, Nelson E., Sr.
Graham, Albertha L.
Greenidge, Dr. Kevin C.
Grayson, Mel
Grant, Rev. Dr. Jacquelyn
Graves, Carole A.
Guyton, Patsy
Harrold, Lawrence A.
Harper, Dr. Walter Edward
Hardy-Woolridge, Karen E.
Haynes, Farnese N.
Harvey-Salaam, Dyane Michelle
Harrison, Dr. Robert Walker, III
Hamill, Margaret Hudgens
Hall, Lamont
Hare, Dr. Julia
Hall, Joel
Harris, Prof. E. Nigel
Hageman, Hans Eric
Hageman, Ivan
Hall, Horathel
Hale, Dr. Janice Ellen
Haywoode, M. Douglas
Hawkins, Mary L.
Hatter, Henry
Harris, Vera Dial
Harrison, Don K., Sr.
Henry, Dr. Charles E.
Henry, Thomas
Henry, Joseph King
Hernandez, Mary N.
Hill, Hattie
Hilton, Tanya
Hill, Robert Lewis
Higgins, Sammie L.
Hines, Dr. Deborah Harmon
Hoxby, Caroline M.
Hopson, Cynthia A. Bond
Holland, Dr. Spencer H.
Hopkins, Edna J.
Holmes, Dr. Barbara J.
Holmes, William B.
Howard, Gwendolyn Julius
Houze, Jeneice Carmel Wong
Hubbard, Calvin L.
Hutton, Gerald L.
Jacobs, Danny Odell
Jackson, Dorothy R.
James, Dr. Betty Harris
Jackson, Frank Donald
Jenkins, Dr. Julius
Jervay-Pendergrass, Dr. Debra
Jor'dan, Dr. Jamilah R.
Johns, David J.
Jones, Lenoy
Johnson, Dr. Fred D.
Johnson, Hermon M., Sr.
Johnson, Joseph A.
Jones, Albert Allen
Johnson, Dr. Lorretta
Johnson, Robert B.
Jones, Brent M.
Jones, Zoia L.
Jones, Sondra Michelle
Joyner, Irving L.
Johnson, Michael Anthony
Johnson, Dr. Edward Elemuel
Jupiter, Clyde Peter
Kimbrough, Thomas J.
King, Ruby Dean
King, Rev. William J.
Kline, William M.
Lawson, Quentin Roosevelt
Lawyer, Cyrus Jefferson, III
Langford, Rev. Victor C., III
Lamb, Sabrina
Lamar, Jake V., Sr.
Lee, Aaron
Levermore, Dr. Monique A.
Lee, Tamela Jean
Lewis, Dr. Samella Sanders
Lightfoot, Jean Harvey
Linton, Sheila Lorraine

## Educational Administration

O'Leary, Hazel R.
O'Neale, Dr. Sondra A.
Okunor, Rev. Dr. Shiame S.
Oliver, Jesse Dean
Oliver, Gary Dewayne
Omolade, Barbara J.
Ortiz, Delia
Osborne, Dr. Alfred E., Jr.
Outlaw, Warren Gregory
Overton-Adkins, Dr. Betty Jean
Owens, Dr. Judith Myoli
Owens, Dr. Robert Leon, III
Palmer, Dr. Elliott B., Sr.
Parker, Dr. Herbert Gerald
Parks, Thelma Reece
Parker, Paul E.
Patrick, Dr. Opal Lee Young
Payne, Margaret Ralston
Payton, Dr. Benjamin Franklin
Patterson, Evelynne R.
Paddio-Johnson, Dr. Eunice Alice
Patterson, Joan Delores
Patton, Joyce Bradford
Parker, Jacquelyn Heath
Parks, Dr. Arnold Grant
Paige, Dr. Roderick Raynor
Paschal, Willie L.
Payne, Dr. Norma Joyce
Pates, Harold
Payne, Mitchell Howard
Palmer, Dr. Annette
Parham, Dr. James B.
Paschal, Trisa Long
Peoples, Dr. L. Kimberly
Peoples, VerJanis Andrews
Peoples, Dr. Gerald C.
Peagler, Dr. Richard C.
Perry, Steve
Peal, Dr. Regina Randall
Petty, Jervie Scott, Sr.
Pennix, James A.
Perry, Dr. Patsy Brewington
Perdreau, Cornelia Whitener
Perdue, Rep. George, Jr.
Pettigrew, Dr. L. Eudora
Pendleton, Florence Howard
Pendleton, Dr. Bertha Mae Ousley
Perdue, Dr. Wiley A.
Petty-Edwards, Lula Evelyn
Peoples, Gregory Allan
Peters, Dr. Fenton
Peoples, Dr. Joyce P.
Peterson, Lloyd, Jr.
Perry, Leonard Douglas, Jr.
Pennington, Dr. Leenette Morse
Penn, Dr. Nolan E.
Pegues, Dr. Wennette West
Peoples, Dr. John Arthur, Jr.
Perine, James L.
Peguese, Charles R.
Peoples, Sesser Randall
Perry, Dr. Aubrey M.
Perkins, Myla Levy
Perry, Dr. Robert Lee
Peyton, Rev. Jasper E.
Pennywell, Phillip, Jr.
Phelps, Constance Kay
Phillip, Dr. Michael John
Pierre, Dr. Percy Anthony
Pitt, Dr. Clifford Sinclair
Pinson, Margo Dean
Pinkard, Dr. Deloris Elaine
Pines, Darryll J.
Pickles, Dr. Patricia L.
Pleasant, Albert E., III
Plummer, Michael Justin
Pleasant, Mae Barbee Boone
Pogue, Frank G., Jr.
Pollard, Raymond J.
Ponder, Dr. Henry
Poole, Dillard M.
Poole, Dr. Rachel Irene
Portlock, Dr. Carver A.
Powell, Dr. Myrtis Hall
Pounds, Dr. Augustine Wright
Powell, Dr. Archie James
Pounds, Dr. Moses B.
Poellnitz, Fred Douglas
Polk, Rev. Dr. Robert L.
Potts, Sammie
Poindexter, Rev. Charles L. L.
Porche-Burke, Lisa
Porter, Bishop Henry Lee
Powell, Paula Livers
Price, Marcus Raymond
Prothrow-Stith, Dr. Deborah Boutin
Price, Dr. Paul Sanford
Prestage, Dr. James Jordan
Price, Glenda Delores
Prater, Dr. Oscar L.
Provost, Marsha Parks
Pratt, Mable
Pruitt-Logan, Dr. Anne Smith
Pratt, Alexander Thomas
Pruitt, Dr. George Albert
Primous, Emma Moore
Purce, Dr. Thomas Les
Pyles, J. A.
Ray, Dr. Andrew A.
Rayford, Lee Edward
Ransburg, Frank S.
Rambo, Bettye R.
Randle, Lucious A., Sr.
Rayburn, Dr. Wendell Gilbert, Sr.
Rampersad, Arnold
Rauch, Esq. Doreen E.
Ransom, Lillie Sharon
Reid, Dr. Irvin D.
Reed, Dr. Charlotte
Redding, Gloria Ann
Renick, Dr. James Carmichael
Reaves, Rev. Dr. Benjamin Franklin
Reed, Dr. James W.
Reid, Janie Ellen
Redmond, Dr. Jane Smith
Reaves, Ginevera N.
Reavis, John William
Reddick, Alzo Jackson, Sr.
Reed, Dr. Vincent Emory
Reed, Dr. Rodney J.
Rhoades, Dr. Samuel Thomas, III
Rigsby, Esther Catherine Martin
Richardson, Odis Gene
Richards, LaVerne W.
Rice, Dr. Constance Williams
Richard, Alvin J.
Richards, Dr. Hilda
Richardson, Dr. Earl Stanford
Richardson, DeRutha Gardner
Richardson, Dr. Luns C.
Richardson, Dr. Mary Margaret
Rivers, Vernon Frederick, Jr.
Rivers, Dorothy
Ridley, Dr. May Alice
Ridgel, Dr. Gus Tolver
Richards, Leon
Richardson, Dr. Roger Gerald
Ribeau, Dr. Sidney A.
Robinson, Dr. Joyce Russell
Robison, Louis
Rogers, Esq. Joyce Q.
Roberson, Dr. Valerie R.
Rochester, Dr. Mattilyn T.
Rodriguez, Argelia Velez
Royster, Philip M.
Ross, Emma Jean
Ross, Lee Elbert
Royster, Dr. Vivian Hall
Rodgers, Dr. Augustus
Ross-Lee, Dr. Barbara
Roscoe, Dr. Wilma J.
Rogers, Dr. Decatur Braxton
Roney, Raymond George
Roper, Bobby L.
Rogers, George
Robinson, Dr. Samuel
Robinson, Dr. Thelma Maniece
Robinson, Dr. Prezell Russell
Robinson, S. Yolanda
Roberts, Dr. Grady H., Jr.
Roberts, Roy J.
Roberts, Edward A.
Roberts, Dr. Alfred Lloyd, Sr.
Robertson, Quindonell Stinson
Robinson, Alfreda P.
Robinson, Dr. Andrew A., Jr.
Robinson, Eunice Primus
Robinson, Harry G., III
Rosser, Dr. James M.
Rockett, Damon Emerson
Roberts, Paquita Hudson
Roulhac, Dr. Edgar Edwin
Robinson, Jeannette
Robinson, Prof. Ella S.
Robertson, Evelyn Crawford, Jr.
Rodgers, Shirley Marie
Russell, John Peterson, Jr.
Russell, Dian Bishop
Rudd, Charlotte Johnson
Ruffin, Paulette Francine
Saxton, Paul Christopher
Salters, Dr. Charles Robert
Sawyers, Dorret E.
Sanders, Dr. Karen Eley
Sardin, James E.
Salmond, Dr. Jasper
Sanders, Dr. Lou Helen
Savage, William Arthur
Sands, Dr. Rosetta F.
Sands, Prof. Mary Alice
Sanders, Dr. Isaac Warren
Saunders-Henderson, Martha M.
Saunders, Dr. Elizabeth Ann
Satcher, Dr. Robert Lee, Sr.
Sanders, Dr. Gwendolyn W.
Samuel, Lois S.
Sanders, Dr. Robert B.
Schexnider, Dr. Alvin J.
Scruggs, Booker T., II
Scott, Veronica J.
Scott, Dr. Marvin Bailey
Scott, Hosie L.
Scott, Dr. Basil Y.
Scott, Dr. Julius S., Jr.
Scott, Dr. Otis L.
Scott-Coleman, Melissa
Scott, Quincy, Jr.
Scroggins, Bobby
Seaton, Dr. Shirley Smith
Seals, Maxine Lane
Seay, Norman R.
Sevillian, Clarence Marvin, Sr.
Sharpe, Dr. Audrey Howell
Shade, Dr. Barbara J.
Shockley, Ann Allen
Shipley, Rev. Anthony J.
Shaw, Talbert Oscall
Sharp, Jean Marie
Short, Prof. Kenneth L.
Sheftall, Dr. Willis B., Jr.
Shepherd, Greta Dandridge
Shakir, Dr. Adib Akmal
Shuford, Humphrey Lewis
Shelton, Roy Cresswell, Jr.
Silver, Dr. Joseph Howard, Sr.
Simmons, Dr. Charles William
Simpson-Taylor, Dr. Dorothy Marie
Simpson, Dr. John O.
Singley, Yvonne Jean
Simmons, Esmeralda
Simmons, Dr. Howard L.
Simmons, Dr. Sylvia Q.
Simpson, Norvell J.
Sims-Davis, Edith R.
Simpson, Dr. John Randolph
Silas, Dennis Dean
Slade, Dr. Priscilla Dean
Smith, Obrie, Sr.
Smith, Dr. Gerald Lamont
Smith, Shirley Hunter
Smith, Dr. Edgar Eugene
Smith, Dr. Estus
Smith, Dr. Donald Hugh
Smith, Arthur D.
Smith, Carol J.
Smith, Dr. Roland Blair, Jr.
Smith, Dr. Joshua L.
Smith, Reginald D., Sr.
Smith, Dr. Phillip M.
Smith, Dr. Mildred Beatty
Smith, Rev. George Walker
Smith, Virginia M.
Small, Stanley Joseph
Smith, Dr. Joe Lee
Smith, Keith Dryden, Jr.
Smith-Surles, Dr. Carol Diann
Smith, Carl William
Smith, Dr. Eleanor Jane
Smith, Dr. Allen Joseph, Sr.
Smith, Carson Eugene
Smith, Mary Levi
Smith, Dr. Walter L.
Smith, Alice B
Smallwood, William Lee
Smith, John B., Sr.
Smith, Dr. Calvert H.
Smith, Dr. Robert H.
Smith, Dr. Joanne Hamlin
Smith, Sundra Shealey
Smith, William French
Smith, Dr. Barbara Wheat
Smith, Dr. Herman Brunell, Jr.
Smith, Dr. Clifford V., Jr.
Smith, Reginald Keith
Snead, Dr. David Lowell
Solomon, Barbara J.
Spurlock, LaVerne Beard
Speight-Buford, Dr. Velma R.
Speede-Franklin, Wanda A.
Spurlock-Evans, Karla Jeanne
Spivey, Dr. Donald
Spradley, Frank Sanford
Spikes, Dr. Delores Richard
Spriggs, Edward J.
Spaulding, Jean Gaillard
Steele-Robinson, Alice Louise
Steele, Tommy
Stamps, Dr. Delores Bolden
Stringfellow, Eric DeVaughn
Stewart, Dr. James Benjamin
Stewart, Dr. Gregory
Stith, Dr. Melvin Thomas
Strickland, Clinton Vernal, Jr.
Stamps, Joe, Jr.
Staats, Dr. Florence Joan
Stallings, James Raiford
Standifer, Ben H.
Stansbury, Markhum L.
Steele, Dr. Claude Mason
Stodghill, Dr. Ronald
Stokes, Johnnie Mae
Styles, Kathleen Ann
Strachan, Dr. Richard James
Straughter, Edgar, Sr.
Sullivan, Dr. Louis Wade
Sutton, Dr. William Wallace
Sudarkasa, Niara
Summers, Dr. Rodger
Summitt, Gazella Ann
Sutherland, Dr. Frankie
Swift, Karen A.
Swygert, Prof. H. Patrick
Switzer, Veryl A., Sr.
Swain, Dr. Ronald L.
Swinton, Dr. David Holmes
Swan, Dr. George W., III
Sylvas, Dr. Lionel B.
Taylor, Dr. Donald Fulton, Sr.
Taylor, Dr. Jack Alvin
Taliaferro, George
Tanner, James W., Jr.
Taylor, Ruth Sloan
Taylor, Veronica C.
Taylor, Dr. David Vassar
Taylor, Reginald Redall, Jr.
Taylor-Archer, Dr. Mordean
Taylor, Dr. Henry Louis, Jr.
Taylor, Orlando L.
Taylor, Dr. Estelle Wormley
Taylor-Thompson, Dr. Betty E.
Tarver, Dr. Leon R., II
Tatum, Dr. Beverly Daniel
Tanner, Dr. Tyrone
Tei, Dr. Ebo
Terrell, Dr. Melvin Cleveland
Terry, Dr. Angela Owen
Terrell, John L.
Teamer, Dr. Charles C., Sr.
Thomas, Maurice McKenzie
Thompson, Jesse M.
Thomas, Dr. Marvette Jeraldine
Thompson-Wright, Dr. Brenda Smith
Thurman, Alfonzo
Thomas, Althea Shannon Lawson
Thornton, Dr. Maurice M.
Theodore, Yvonne M.
Thomas, Janice Morrell
Thrower, Julius B.
Thompson, Dr. Lancelot C. A., Sr.
Thompson, Dr. Cleon Franklyn, Jr.
Thompson, Francesca
Thomas, Dr. William
Thompson, Rosie L.
Thomas, Dr. Arthur E.
Thompson, Dr. Edwin A.
Thomas, Dr. Sheryl Ann Benning
Thompson, Dr. Sidney A.
Thompson, Gayle Ann-Spencer
Thomas, Herman L.
Thompson, Dr. Betty Taylor
Thomas, James Albert
Thomas, Jane Roscoe
Thompson, Rhonda Denise
Tidwell, John Edgar
Timberlake, Dr. Constance Hector
Tisdale, Dr. Henry Nehemiah
Torain, Rev. Dr. Tony William
Tolliver, Ned, Jr.
Todd, Melvin R.
Tolliver, Rev. Dr. Joel
Toran, Kay Dean
Totten, Dr. Herman Lavon
Trice, Dr. Juniper Yates
Trotman, Richard Edward
Troupe, Dr. Marilyn Kay
Trueheart, Dr. William E.
Turner, Diane Young
Tucker, Dr. M. Belinda
Turner, Mikoel
Tuckson, Reed V.
Turner, Richard M., III
Tuggle, Rev. Reginald
Turner, Johnnie Rodgers
Tucker, Norma Jean
Turner, Leslie Ford
Turner, Teresa Ann
Turner, Shirley A.
Tyson, Lorena E.
Tyner, Rev. Charles R., Sr.
Tyler, Shirley Neizer
Uzoigwe, Dr. Godfrey N.
Vargus, Dr. Ione D.
Vance, Vera R.
Varner, Dr. Nellie M.
Vaughn, Dr. Percy Joseph, Jr.
Vaughn, Dr. Alvin
Vaughn, Dr. Janice S.
Verrett, Joyce McKee
Vernon, Francine M.
Vernon-Chesley, Michele Joanne
Viltz, Dr. Stanley
Warner, Dr. Neari Francois
Walker, Dr. Eugene P., Sr.
Watkins, Dr. Walter J.
Warren, Roland C.
Walker, James, Jr.
Waiters, Dr. Ann Gillis
Washington, Herman A., Jr.
Watson, Genevieve
Wallace, Arthur, Jr.
Walburg, Judith Ann
Walker, Dr. Melvin E., Jr.
Ward, Dr. Perry W.
Ward, Rev. Dr. Daryl
Watts, Dr. Anne Wimbush
Walker, Dr. Sandra Venezia
Wade, Achille Melvin
Watson, Dr. Diane Edith
Watts, Dr. Roberta Ogletree
Wayne, George Howard, Sr.
Ward, Daniel
Wardlaw, Alvin Holmes
Washington, Elmer L.
Wallace, Rev. Harold Gene
Wallace, Helen Winfree-Peyton
Walker, Wilbur P.
Walker, Dr. M. Lucius, Jr.
Walker, Larry Moore
Walker, George Raymond
Warren, Nagueyalti
Washington, Dr. Earl Melvin
Washington, Dr. Michael Harlan
Ward, Arnette Scott
Walker, Dr. Mark Lamont
Walker, Ronald Plezz
Walker, Dr. Howard Kent
Ware, Dr. William Levi
Washington, Dr. Arthur Clover
Wallace, Dr. Jeffrey J.
Walker, Dr. Larry Vaughn, Sr.
Webb, Harold H.
Wells, Fr. Patrick Roland
Welch, Harvey
Welch, Jesse Roy
Wells, Dr. Elmer Eugene
West, Dr. Gerald Ivan
Wesley, Barbara Ann
Weber, Dr. Shirley Nash
Westbrook, Dr. Joseph W., III
Wells-Merrick, Lorraine Roberta
West, Cornel Ronald
West, Valerie Y.
Webb, Georgia Houston
Welmon, Dr. Vernis M.
White, Sharon Brown
Whitely, Donald Harrison
White, Dr. Yolanda Simmons
Whitney, Rosalyn L.
White, Richard H.
Whittaker-Davis, Dr. Sharon Elaine

## Electronics (*See* Computer Science—Programming/Software Development; Computer Science—Systems Analysis/Design; Computer Science—Not Elsewhere Classified; Engineering—Electrical/Electronics; Retail Trade—Electrical/Electronics Products; Wholesale Trade—Electrical/Electronics Products)

## Engineering—Aerospace



## Engineering—Chemical



## Engineering—Civil



## Engineering—Electrical/Electronics



## Engineering—Industrial



## Engineering—Mechanical



## Engineering—Metallurgical/Ceramic/Materials



## Engineering—Not Elsewhere Classified

James, Anthony R.
Jenkins, Woodie R., Jr.
Johnson, Marvin R.
Joseph, Lloyd Leroi
Kennedy, Nathelyne Archie
Lue-Hing, Dr. Cecil
Madison, Shannon L.
Martin, Montez Cornelius, Jr.
Metters, Dr. Samuel
Mincey, Karen
Morgan, Robert, Jr.
Munson, Robert H.
Murray, Gary S., Sr.
Neal, Curtis Emerson, Jr.
Owan, Dr. Ransome E.
Porter, Michael Anthony
Porter, John T.
Pollard, Muriel Ransom
Rakestraw, Kyle Damon
Ravenell, Mildred
Ray, Dr. Judith Diana
Ratcliffe, Dr. Alfonso F.
Rucks, Alfred J.
Sanders, Dr. Woodrow Mac
Sawyer, Deborah M.
Shank, Suzanne F.
Sigur, Wanda Anne Alexander
Snowden, Phillip Ray
Stallworth, Oscar B., Sr.
Sutton, Mary A.
Trueblood, Vera J.
Turner, Franklin James
Underwood, Anthony
Webster, Theodore E.
Whiteside, Ernestyne E.
Wilhoit, Carl H.
Winfield, William T.
Williams, Wilbert Edd
Woodie, Henry L.

## Engineering—Nuclear

Johnson, Lonnie G.
Jupiter, Clyde Peter
LeVert, Dr. Francis E., II
Lewis, Kenneth Dwight
Pogue, Brent Daryl
Williams, Dr. Dwight

## Engineering—Petroleum

Coshburn, Henry S., Jr.
Douglas, Nicholas
Ford, Darrell L.
Granville, William, Jr.
Grimes, Darlene M. C.
Hightower, Stephen Lamar, II
Kirklin, Dr. Perry William
Landers, Naaman Garnett, Jr.
Oyekan, Dr. Soni Olufemi
Riddick, Eugene E.
Timbaland

## Entertainment/ Recreation-Not Elsewhere Classified (*See Also* Music—Composing/ Songwriting; Music—Conducting/Directing; Music—Instrumental; Music—Vocal; Music—Not Elsewhere Classified)

Ali, Laila Amaria
Allotey, Victor P.
Amin, Karima
Anderson, Bernadine M.
Anderson, Tony
Ashhurst-Watson, Carmen
Avant, Clarence
Bailey, Kenetta
Bartlett, Lorrie
Bateman, Celeste
Bailey, Thurl Lee
Bellamy, Bill
Bell, Ricky
Bertelsen, Phil
Billops, Camille J.
Blanc, Eric Anthony-Hawkins
Bobbitt, Leroy
Bowser, Yvette Denise Lee
Brown, Reginald DeWayne
Brown, Esq. Ronald Wellington
Brown, Michelle Listenbee
Broderick, Johnson
Brown, Tony
Brown, William T.
Brown, Dr. Abena Joan P.
Broughton, Christopher Leon
Brown, Lomas, Jr.
Burke, Kirkland R.
Buchanan, Raymond Louis
Carter, Regina
Carter, Daisy
Carpenter, Dr. Vivian L.
Chase, Debra Martin
Cherry, Je'Rod L.
Chappelle, Dave
Charles, RuPaul Andre
Chase, Debra Martin
Clark, Prof. Linda Day
Clarke, Priscilla
Clash, Kevin
Cosby, Camille Olivia Hanks
Copeland, Misty
Cole, Dorinda Clark
Cosby, Dr. William Henry
Copage, Marc Diego
Cumber, Victoria Lillian
Cummings, Terry
Dawson, Horace G., III
Davis, Hubert Ira, Jr.
DeBarge, Chico
Deese, Derrick Lynn, Sr.
Douglas, Elizabeth (Betty) Asche
Dupri, Jermaine
Dunlap, Ericka
Duke, Bill
Durant-Paige, Beverly
Eason-Steele, Elaine
Eckstine, Ed
Ellaraino, Baki
Emerson, Melinda
Ervin, Kathryn
Evans, Gregory James
Fay, Toni Georgette
Farrell, Cheryl Layne
Fernandez-Smith, Wilhelmenia
Fearn-Banks, Kathleen
Fox, Rick
Freeman, Antonio Michael
Friday, Jeff
Goodrich, Linda S.
Gordy, Berry, Jr.
Goldberg, Whoopi
Gregory, Richard Claxton
Greene, Joe
Greaves, McLean
Green, Willie Aaron
Gray, Felix Gary
Harris, Tricia R.
Hagins, Ogbonna
Hardwick, Gary C.
Hayes, Laura
Harris, Joyce
Harris, Dr. MaryAnn
Harvey, Kenneth Ray
Harrell, Andre
Haymon, Alan
Hall, Aaron
Harvey, Antonio
Henson, Taraji P.
Hill, Tamia Marilyn
Hopkins, Bradley Donnell
Hopson, Harold Theodore, Jr.
Israel, Steven Douglas
Isaacs, Cheryl Boone
Ivey, Phil
Iverson, Johnathan Lee
J., Ray
Jackson, Tyoka
Jackson, Tomi L.
Jamison, Judith Ann
Jackson, Eugene D.
James, Hawthorne
James, Toni-Leslie
Jackson, Tom
Jeter, Clifton B.
Johnson, Dr. Charles Floyd
Jones, Gary
Jones, Brian Keith
Jones, Donna L.
Jolley, Willie
Jones, Roy Levesta, Jr.
Johnson, Henry Wade
Karpeh, Enid Juah Hildegard
Kennedy, Lincoln
King, Brett
King, Jeanne Faith
Kilgore, Twanna Debbie
King, Gayle
Lacy, Donald E., Jr.
Lawrence, Elliott
Lauren, Green
Lewis, Charles Henry
Lee, Dr. Debra Louise
Lipps, Louis Adam, Jr.
Love, Darlene
Love, Loni
Long, John Eddie
Madison, Samuel Adolfus, Jr.
Martin, Cheryl
Mahoney, Dwayne
Mason, Clifford L.
Mashburn, Jamal
McHenry, Doug
McElvane, Pamela Anne
McKayle, Donald Cohen
McGill, Michael
Medina, Benny
Miller, Tangi
Morrison, Vanessa
Moore, Shemar F.
Moore, Juliette R.
Morgan, Dolores Parker
Morris, Garrett Gonzalez
Mumford, Thaddeus Quentin, Jr.
Nellums, Michael Wayne
Nelson, Novella C.
Nichols, Nichelle
Okino, Elizabeth Anna
Owens, Terrell Eldorado
Parker, James L.
Peete, Holly Robinson
Pinkney, Rose Catherine
Pressley, DeLores
Procope, Jonelle
Prince-Bythewood, Gina
Reed-Humes, Robi
Reeves, Martha Rose
Reid, Daphne Etta Maxwell
Richardson, Timothy Lee
Richards, DeLeon Marie
Riggins, Jean
Richardson, Lita Renee
Rihanna
Roker, Albert Lincoln
Robinson, Wendy Raquel
Ross, Tracey
Rolle, Janet
Ruffin, John Walter, Jr.
Sabree, Clarice Sylla
Savage, Janet Marie
Salaam, Ephraim Mateen
Shaw, Nina L.
Simmons, Kimora Lee
Simmons, Juanita
Sims, Keith Alexander
Simpson, Donnie
Smith, Nick
Sneed, Gregory J.
Strahan, Michael Anthony
Taylor, Tenisha Nicole
Thomas, Hollis, Jr.
Toomer, Amani Askari
Treadwell, Tina McKinley
Varner, Dr. Nellie M.
Walden, Narada Michael
Warmly, Leon
Walker, Chester
Wayans, Marlon
Walker-Kuhne, Donna
Wheaton, Esq. Frank Kahlil
Wing, Theodore W., II
Williams, Armstrong
Williams, Judith Byrd
Wilson, Mitsy
Williams, Roland Lamar
Williams, Ricky, Jr.
Woodward, Aaron Alphonso, III
Wolfe, George Costello

## Fashion Design

Aiken, Kimberly Clarice
Armstrong, Janet
Bailey, Cynthia
Barnwell, Andre
Banks, Jeffrey
Barkley, Rufus, Jr.
Bates, Barbara Ann
Beckford, Tyson Craig
Blake, Jennifer Lynn
Burrows, Stephen
Carter, Ruth E.
Collins, Cornell
Dean, Angela
Delcy, Ludget
Devers, Yolanda Gail
Dunmore, Gregory Charles
Fleetwood, Therez
Fuller, Jack Lewis
Green, Derek
Grayson, Mel
Hankins, Anthony Mark
Haggins, Jon
Hilton, Stanley William, Jr.
Hunter, Gigi
Jones, Genevieve
Johnson, Larry Demetric
Kani, Karl
King, Shaka C.
Kirby, Anthony T.
Kodjoe, Boris
Lars, Byron
Lockett, Bradford R.
Malone, Maurice
McCray, Darryl K.
Miller-Lewis, S. Jill
Michael, B.
Monroque, Shala
Moore, Annie Jewell
Nedd, Cathy
Ogilvie, Lana
Osbourne, Maxwell
Patton, Jean E.
Perkins, Louvenia Black
Pinkney, John Edward
Ralph, Sheryl Lee
Revish, Danielle A.
Rohe, Bernie
Simmons, Kimora Lee
Smith, Wilson Washington, III
Smith, Dorothy O.
Snell, Johnna M.
Steele, Lawrence
Stubblefield, Michael Jerome, Jr.
White, Sylvia Kay
Williams, Serena

## Fire Prevention and Control

Alfred, Rayfield
Blackshear, William
Bouie, Preston L.
Brown, Carrye Burley
Brown, Thomas Edison, Jr.
Burton, Brent F.
Davie, Timothy M.
Douglas, Joe, Jr.
Dyas, Patricia Ann
Edmonds, Curtis
Gladman, Charles R., Jr.
Graham, Charlene G.
Hart, Noel A.
Hairston, Harold B.
Holmes, Prof. Carl
Jackson, Frank Donald
Love, Ch. J. Gregory
Neal, Sylvester
Parker, G. John, Sr.
Seavers, Dean
Spaulding, Romeo Orlando
Stewart, John B., Jr.
Tatem, Dr. Patricia Ann
Thomas, Reginald Maurice
Trotter, Cortez
Watkins, Harold D., Sr.
Wester, Richard Clark
Williams, Charles Earl

## Food and Beverage Industry (*See Also* Restaurant/ Food Service Industry; Retail Trade—Food and Beverages; Wholesale Trade—Food and Beverages)

## Foreign Service

Boldridge, George
Carter, William Beverly, III
Carson, Johnnie
Cooper, Dr. LaMoyne Mason
Davis, Robert N.
Flemming, Dr. Charles Stephen
Fox, Ambassador Richard K., Jr.
Hewan, Clinton George
Jones, Dr. William Bowdoin
LeMelle, Tilden J.
Mack, John L.
Moose, George Edward
Perkins, Edward Joseph
Perry, June Carter
Reinhardt, John Edward
Render, Ambassador Arlene
Spriggs, Edward J.
White, Paul Edward
Williams, Elvira Felton
Williams, Bisa

## Forestry/Forest Industries

Burse, Dr. Luther, Sr.
Dixon, Ora Wright
Gaines, Mary E.
Jackson, Charles N., II
Keene, Sharon C.
Williams, Dr. Carroll Burns, Jr.

## Funeral Service (*See Also* Mortuary Services)

## Gallery/Museum Administration/Education

Aviles, Dora
Bolden, Aletha Simone
Booker, John P., III
Burton, Brent F.
Cabbell, Edward Joseph
Campbell, Dr. Mary Schmidt
Camp, Kimberly
Conwill, Kinshasha
Crew, Spencer R.
Cruz, Patricia
Davis, Dr. Willie
Dickerson, Amina J.
Driskell, David Clyde
Felton, Zora Martin
Fleming, Dr. John Emory
Gaither, Barry
Ghent, Henri Hermann
Gilliam, Sam J., Jr.
Hall, Robert L.
Haymore, Tyrone
High-Tesfagiorgis, Freida W.
Hodges, Dr. David Julian
Houston, Willie Lewis
Jackson, Earl, Jr.
Jeffries, Dr. Rosalind Robinson
John, Daymond G.
Johnson, Patricia Anita
Ligon, Doris Hillian
Martin, Frank C., II
Mack, Dr. Deborah Lynn
Moore, Dr. Marian J.
Morgan-Welch, Beverly Ann
Montgomery, Evangeline Juliet
N'Namdi, Dr. George Richard
Newman, Constance Ernestine Berry
Omogbai, Meme
Parrish, Maurice Drue
Palmer, Dr. Elliott B., Sr.
Peerman-Pledger, Vernese Dianne
Pierce, Aaronetta Hamilton
Pindell, Howardena D.
Pilgrim, Dr. David
Porter, Dr. Michael LeRoy
Robinson, Dr. Harry, Jr.
Saunders-Henderson, Martha M.
Shifflett, Lynne Carol
Sims, Lowery Stokes
Smythe, Victor N.
Stewart, Paul Wilbur
Stewart, Ruth Ann
Stith, Hana L.
Taylor, Dr. Cledie Collins
Taylor, Gilbert Leon
Ward, Hon. Doris Margaret
Washington, Sherry Ann
Walker, Roslyn Adele
Williams, Kathryn
Williamson, Ethel W.
Young, James Arthur, III

## Geography

Jones, Dr. Marcus Earl
King, Thomas Lawrence

## Geology/Geophysics

Brown, Charles Edward
Davis, Edith G. Williams

## Geophysics (*See* Geology/ Geophysics)

## Government Service (Elected or Appointed)/ Government Administration—City

### Government Service (Elected or Appointed)/ Government Administration—County



### Government Service (Elected or Appointed)/ Government Administration—Federal

## Government Service (Elected or Appointed)/ Government Administration—Not Elsewhere Classified

Scott, Melvina Brooks
Scott, Ruth Elaine Holland
Scott, Dr. Donald LaVern
Scott, Anthony R.
Seals, Gerald
Shivers, S. Michael
Shanks, James A.
Sharpton, Rev. Alfred Charles, Jr.
Simmons, Clayton Lloyd
Slater, Rodney E.
Smith, Bobby Antonia
Smithers, Priscilla Jane
Smith-Gray, Cassandra Elaine
Smith, James Russell
Smith, Shirley LaVerne
Smith, Capt. Janet K.
Solomon, David
Soaries, Rev. Dr. DeForest Blake, Jr.
Spencer, Collins Robert, III
Stewart, Jarvis Christopher
Stanton, Robert G.
Stephens, Joseph
Stephen, Joyce A.
Sterling, H. Dwight, Sr.
Steger, Dr. C. Donald
Stanton, Janice D.
Stevens, Dr. Patricia Ann
Stallworth, Annie P.
Straughter, Edgar, Sr.
Stebbins, Esq. Dana Brewington
Talbot, Gerald Edgerton
Tayari, Kabili
Taylor, Felicia Michelle
Tarver, Elking, Jr.
Tate, Dr. Herbert Holmes, Jr.
Thompson, Portia Wilson
Thomas, Joan McHenry Bates
Thomas, Wilbon
Thomas, Roy L.
Thomas, Hon. Samuel Buzz, III
Tillman, Christine L.
Tibbs, Edward A.
Towns, Edolphus, Jr.
Troupe-Frye, Betty Jean
Trotter, Andrew Leon
Turner, Sharon V.
Turner, Leslie Marie
Tyler, Robert James, Sr.
Van Lierop, Robert F.
Washington, John Calvin, III
Waters, Maxine
Watkins, Shirley R.
Ware, Hon. Jewel C.
Wallace, Peggy Mason
Wagner, Annice M.
Washington, Mickey Lin
Webber, William Stuart
White, Michael Reed
White, Robert C.
Wilson, Jaci Laverne
Williams, Joe H.
Williams, Charles C.
Williams, Dr. Leon Lawson
Williams, Earl West
Wiley-Pickett, Gloria
Willingham, Voncile
Williams, Ronald Lee
Wilson, Joy Johnson
Williams, Herman
Williams, Stanley King
Williams, Lloyd L.
Williams, James R.
Wilson, Angela Brown
Williams, Charles Earl
Williams, Margaret Ann
Williamson, Carl Vance
Wilkins, Dr. Kenneth C.
Williamson, Samuel P.
Worsham, James E.
Wordlaw, Clarence, Jr.
Woods-Burwell, Charlotte Ann
Wright, Loyce Pierce
Wynn, Dr. Albert Russell
Young, Sarah Daniels
Young, Leon D.

## Government Service (Elected or Appointed)/ Government Administration—State

Abebe, Ruby
Abramson, Dr. John J., Jr.
Abernathy, Rev. Ralph David, III
Adams, Edward Robert
Adams, Jean Tucker
Adiele, Dr. Moses Nkwachukwu
Aggrey, Hon. Orison Rudolph Guggisberg
Alexis, Doris Virginia
Allen, Dr. Claude Alexander, Jr.
Andrews, Emanuel Carl
Anderson, Eugene
Anthony, Vernice Davis
Applewhaite, Leon B.
Arberry, Morse, Jr.
Baker, Thurbert E.
Babineaux-Fontenot, Claire
Bates, Nathaniel Rubin
Barkley, Mark E.
Barnett, Ethel S.
Bennett, Patricia A.
Benjamin, Stephen K.
Beals, Yvonne
Bernard, Linda D.
Beatty, Otto B., Jr.
Bennett, Maybelle Taylor
Bell, Theron J.
Billingsley, Ray C.
Bishop, Ellen Elizabeth Grant
Black, Leona R.
Blackwell, John Kenneth
Blue, Daniel Terry, Jr.
Blackmon, Barbara Martin
Block, Dr. Leslie S.
Bowron, Eljay B.
Boone, Alexandria Johnson
Bohannan-Sheppard, Barbara
Bonds, Kevin Gregg
Boardley, Curtestine May
Boschulte, Dr. Joseph Clement
Boykins, Amber
Bradley, Jennette B.
Brown, Binta
Brewington-Carr, Sherese
Brooke, Edward William, III
Brown, Reginald Royce, Sr.
Bradley, Melvin LeRoy
Brown, Inez M.
Brooks, Tyrone L., Sr.
Brown, Corrine
Brown-Francisco, Teresa Elaine
Brown, Mary Katherine
Brown, Robert, Jr.
Brady, Julio A.
Brown, Rev. William Rocky, III
Bryant, Wayne R.
Brooks, Carol Lorraine
Bush, Evelyn
Burnette, Dr. Ada Puryear
Buskey, James E.
Burney, William D., Jr.
Burris, Roland W.
Bush, James, III
Burris-Floyd, Pearl
Bully-Cummings, Dr. Ella Mae
Byrd, Harriett Elizabeth
Carter, Margaret Louise
Carey, Jennifer Davis
Carter, Troy A.
Castro, George A.
Carter, Dr. Pamela Lynn
Campbell, William Earl
Carter, Jandra D.
Cane, Rudolph C.
Carter, Pamela Lynn
Cary, Reby
Charbonnet, Louis, III
Chatman, Alex
Christian, Hon. Mary T.
Chambers, Madrith Bennett
Clay, William Lacy, Jr.
Clark-Thomas, Eleanor M.
Clarke, Hon. Anne-Marie
Clayton, Hon. Eva M.
Clarke, Alyce Griffin
Clark, Robert G., Jr.
Cogsville, Donald J.
Conyers, John James, Jr.
Collins, Barbara-Rose
Copelin, Sherman Nathaniel, Jr.
Cotman, Dr. Ivan Louis
Coleman, Bonnie Watson
Cox, Courtland
Collins-Grant, Earlean
Coleman, Eric Dean
Coleman, Andrew Lee
Cooper, Michael Gary
Cox, Kevin C.
Crouch, Robert Allen
Crews, Victoria Wilder
Crawford, Odel
Cummings, Frances McArthur
Cummings, Theresa Faith
Cunningham, William L.
Daniels, Dr. Joseph
Davis, Dr. Bennie L.
Daniels, Randy A.
Davis, Bettye J.
Dawson, Dr. Eric Emmanuel
Dames, Dr. Kathy W.
Delpit, Joseph A.
Delco, Wilhelmina R.
Dean, James Edward
Dix, Henry
Dillon, Vermon Lemar
Dorsett, Dr. Katie Grays
Donald, Major Gen. James E.
Douglass, John W.
Drakes, Muriel B.
Dudley, Herman T.
Dyson, William Riley
Eaves, Dr. John H.
Edwards, Hon. Rev. Al E.
Edwards, Monique Marie
Ellerby, William Mitchell
Ellison, Keith Maurice
Eve, Arthur O.
Evans, Rep. Dwight
Farrell, Herman Denny, Jr.
Farrell, Robert C.
Ferguson, Rosetta A.
Fernandes, Julie A.
Fielding, Herbert Ulysses
Figures, Vivian Davis
Fields, Cleo
Fitch, Milton Frederick Toby, Jr.
Flippins, Gregory L.
Fleming, Gwendolyn R. Keyes
Foster, T. Eloise
Ford, Harold Eugene, Jr.
Ford, John Newton
Fordham, Cynthia Williams
Frazier-Ellison, Vicki L.
Frazier, Frances Curtis
Fregia, Darrell Leon
Frazier, Ray Jerrell
Fuget, Dr. Charles Robert
Gaines, Cassandra Jean
Garner, James A.
Gavin, Mary Ann
Garner, Velvia M.
Gardner, Cedric Boyer
Gadsden, Rev. Dr. Nathaniel J., Sr.
George, Dr. Gary Raymond
Giddings, Rep. Helen
Gillum, Andrew D.
Gillum, Dr. Ronald M., Sr.
Goodson, Annie Jean
Goodman, George D.
Goodall, Hurley Charles
Gore, John Michel
Gorman, Bertha Gaffney
Grayson, George Welton
Gramby, Shirley Ann
Greene, Edith L.
Griffin, Dr. Betty Sue
Greene, Aurelia
Griffin, Ples Andrew
Graham, Saundra M.
Groff, Peter Charles
Hammonds, Garfield, Jr.
Hale, Derrick F.
Harris, Arthur L., Sr.
Harrison, Jaime
Hargrett, James T., Jr.
Harper, Ruth B.
Hammock, Esq. Edward R.
Haynes, Dr. Rev. Michael E.
Haynes, Dr. Worth Edward
Harris, Melvin
Hampton, Thomas Earle, II
Hart, Phyllis D.
Harper, Thelma Marie
Harley, Legrand
Harris, Rep. Earl L.
Hamilton, Art
Harding, John Edward
Hargrove, Dr. Trent
Henderson, Remond
Hendricks, Steven Aaron
Henderson, Hugh C.
Henry, Dr. Marcelett Campbell
Hill, James A., Jr.
Hilliard, Earl Frederick
Hill, Jimmy H.
Hill, Dr. Bonnie Guiton
Hilson, Dr. Arthur Lee
Hightower, Anthony
Higginbotham-Brooks, Esq. Renee
Hogan, Beverly Wade
Holden, Melvin Lee
Hooker, Douglas Randolf
Holmes, Alvin Adolf
Horsford, Steven
Holder, Eric Himpton, Jr.
Howard, Raymond
Horton, Pastor Larnie G., Sr.
Holmes, Dr. Robert A.
Hudson, Heather McTeer
Hughes, Sen. Vincent J.
Hudson, Merry C.
Hynson, Carroll Henry, Jr.
Jackson, Lee Arthur
James, Kay Coles
Jackson, Hon. Darnell
Jackson, Dorothy R.
Jackson, Sandra Stevens
Jackson, Johnny, Jr.
Jacks, Ulysses
Jefferson-Moss, Carolyn
Jeffries, Hakeem
Jeff, Gloria Jean
Johnson, Jon D.
Johnson, Rev. Clinton Lee
Jones, Charles D.
Johnson, Julia L.
Jones, Marilyn Elaine
Jones, Peter Lawson
Johnson, Willie F.
Jones, Daryl L.
Johnson, Bennett J.
Jones, Chester Ray
Jones, Emil, Jr.
Johnson, Rev. Dr. Paul Edwin
Johnson, Justin Morris
Jordan, Frederick E., Sr.
Kane, Dr. Jacqueline Anne
Kelley, Dr. Delores G.
Kennedy, Sandra Denise
King, Martin Luther, III
Kilpatrick, Carolyn Jean Cheeks
Kindall, Dr. Luther Martin
Lawson, Herman Ace
Lawrence, Archie L.
Lawlah, Gloria Gary
Lewis, James B.
Leland, Joyce F.
League, Cheryl Perry
LeFlore, Dr. Larry
Lee, Ivin B.
Linton, Gordon J.
Lockley, Clyde William
Lucas, David Eugene, Sr.
Lyons, A. Bates
Manager, Vada O.
Marsh, Ben Franklin
Marable, Herman, Jr.
Marriott, Dr. Salima Siler
Malry, Dr. Lenton, Sr.
Mann, Thomas J., Jr.
Marshall, Charlene Jennings
Marshall, John W.
McClendon, Rep. Ruth Jones
McKay-Davis, Monique Dionne
McFadden, Nathaniel James
McRipley, Dr. Gil Whitney
McClain-Thomas, Dorothy Mae
McNair, Chris
McCrimon, Audrey L.
Meek, Carrie P.
Melton, Bryant
Meeks, Hon. Perker L., Jr.
Metcalf, Andrew Lee, Jr.
Mehu, Geraldine
Mike, Daedra Anita Von
Michel, Harriet Richardson
Miller, George Carroll, Jr.
Mitchell, Theo W.
Mitchell, Brenda K.
Mitchell, Cranston J.
Moore, Eddie N., Jr.
Montgomery, Velmanette
Morse, Hon. John E., Jr.
Morgan, Alisha Thomas
Mosby, Marilyn
Murphy, Raymond M., Jr.
Murphy, Margaret Humphries
Myers, Lewis Horace
Myers, Victoria Christina
Napoleon, Benny Nelson
Neal, Sylvester
Nicholas, Gwendolyn Smith
Norwood, Calvin Coolidge
Nunnery, Willie James
Oliver, Jesse Dean
Owens, Sen. William
Owens-Hicks, Shirley
Owens, Lynda Gayle
Owens, Arley E., Jr.
Owens, Rissie Louise
Payne, Debra K.
Paterson, Dr. David Alexander
Payne, Mitchell Howard
Patterson, Kay
Pelote, Dorothy Barnes
Peters, Kenneth Darryl, Sr.
Pease, Denise Louise
Perdue, Rep. George, Jr.
Pendleton, Florence Howard
Pennington, Richard J.
Pinckney, Clementa C.
Pickett, Donna A.
Pickering, Robert Perry
Plummer, Ora Beatrice
Powers, Georgia M.
Preston, Joseph, Jr.
Proctor, Sonya T.
Pulliam, Rev. Betty E.
Quince, Kevin
Randolph, Lonnie Marcus
Ramey, Adele Marie
Rayford, Lee Edward
Raye, Vance Wallace
Reddick, Alzo Jackson, Sr.
Reynolds, Dr. Nanette Lee
Reynolds, Melvin Jay, Sr.
Reed, Hon. Kasim
Rhodes, C. Adrienne
Richardson, Dr. Leo O.
Rice, William E.
Rickman, Ray
Ridley, Dr. May Alice
Riley, Antonio
Rogers, Ormer, Jr.
Roberts, Hon. Jacqueline Johnson
Roberts, Janice L.
Rogers, Earline S.
Ross, Dr. Catherine Laverne
Roebuck, Rep. James Randolph, Jr.
Robinson, Dr. Prezell Russell
Rogers, Desiree Glapion
Roberts, Gregory G.
Rushing, Byron D.
Sabree, Clarice Sylla
Savage, Dennis James
Sanders, Hank
Scott, Samuel N.
Scott, Albert J.
Scott, David A.
Settles, Trudy Y.
Sewell, Isiah Obediah
Shepphard, Dr. Charles Bernard
Shelton, Rep. O. L.
Shelton, Ulysses
Simms, Stuart Oswald
Simpkins, Dr. Cuthbert Ormond, Sr.
Singleton, Leroy, Sr.
Simmons, Kelvin
Smith, Diane L.
Smith, Judy Seriale
Smyre, Calvin
Smitherman, Rodger M.
Smitherman, Esq. Carole Catlin
Smith, Vernon G.
Spencer, Anthony Lawrence
Spruce, Dr. Kenneth L.
Spicer, Kenneth, Sr.
Spigner, Marcus E.
Stanley, Craig A.
Sturdivant, Col. Tadarial J.
Steele, Michael Stephen
Stanley-Turner, LaNett L.
Stallworth, Hon. Alma G.
Sykes, Dr. Vernon Lee
Tabor, Lillie Montague
Tarver, Gregory Williams, Sr.
Tanner, Hon. Gloria Travis
Taylor, David Richard, III
Tate, Dr. Lenore Artie

## Health Care-Not Elsewhere Classified (*See Also* Medicine—Anesthesiology; Nursing; Nutrition; Optometry; Podiatry)



## Health Services Administration



## History

Painter, Dr. Nell Irvin
Phillips, Dr. Glenn Owen
Pitre, Prof. Merline
Pinkney, Dr. Enid C.
Ransby, Barbara
Reynolds, Dr. Edward
Roberts, Rev. Wesley A.
Robinson, Dr. Genevieve
Rouse, Jacqueline Anne
Rushing, Byron D.
Smith, Dr. Alonzo Nelson
Smith, Dr. Gerald Lamont
Taylor, Dr. Henry Louis, Jr.
Terborg-Penn, Dr. Rosalyn M.
Thomas, Robert Lewis, Jr.
Troupe, Dr. Marilyn Kay
Turner, Margaret Dodson
Washington, Dr. Michael Harlan
Williams, Dr. Carolyn Ruth Armstrong
Winston, Dr. Michael Russell
Williams, Kathryn
Wright, Dmitri
Wynn, Linda T.

## Horticulture (*See* Landscape/Horticultural Services)

## Hotel/Motel Industry

Alexander, Larry
Ash, Richard Larry
Bolt, Usain St. Leo
Broadwater, Tommie, Jr.
Bright, Kirk
Carter, Harriet LaShun
Childs, Oliver Bernard
Corley, Todd L.
Deramus, Bill R.
Dean, Curtis
DeLeon, Priscilla
Dixon, John M.
Edwards, Daniel
Eggleston, Neverett A., Jr.
Harmon, James F., Sr.
Hudson, Lester Darnell
Isom, Eddie L.
Jenkins, Ozella
Johnson, Sheila Crump
King, Lewis Henry
Littlejohn, Hon. Bill C.
Porcher, Robert, III
Robinson, Deanna Adell
Roy, Jan S.
Shelton, John W.
Walker, Eugene Kevin
Watson, Leighton
Watson, Barbara M.

## Industrial Design

Bates, William J.
Charity, Lawrence Everett
Charles, Lewis
Ellis, Michael G.
Morris, Earl Scott
Winslow, Reynolds Baker

## Information Science (*See* Library/Information Science)

## Insurance

Alexander, Willie James
Anderson, Tony
Ashford, Orlando D.
Ayers, Hon. Timothy F.
Baker, Roland Charles
Baker, LaVolia Ealy
Bates, Willie Earl
Batchelor, Rev. Asbury Collins
Bell, William Jerry
Bennett, Ivy H.
Bluford, James F.
Bond, Charles Cynthia V.
Bonaparte, Dr. Tony Hillary
Bowie, Willette
Britton, Ambassador Theodore R., Jr.
Brannen, James H., III
Brown, Sherman L.
Brown, Leilani M.
Bryant, R. Kelly, Jr.
Brown, Abner Bertrand
Brown, Herbert R.
Bryce, Dr. Herrington J.
Brown, Virgil E., Jr.
Brown, D. Joan
Burges, Melvin E.
Buggs, James Ferdinand
Carr, Gwenn L.
Caldwell, John Edward
Catchings, Howard Douglas
Chaney, Alphonse
Chaplin, C. Edward
Clement, William A., Jr.
Cowart, Sam
Copes, Ronald Adrian
Cockrell, Mechera Ann
Creuzot, Cheryl D.
Croft, Wardell C.
Cunningham, David S., Jr.
Davis, Darlene Rose
Dance, Dr. Daryl Cumber
Davis, Brownie W.
Demeritte, Dr. Edwin T.
Dennis, James Carlos
DeVaughn-Tidline, Donna Michelle
Dixon, Dr. Benjamin
Dillard, Dr. Melvin Rubin
Dozier, Morris, Sr.
Douglas, Gary A.
Duncan, Verdell E.
Duncan, Sandra Rhodes
Easley, Jacqueline Ruth
Elliott, Cathy
Ellis, Benjamin F., Jr.
Esco, Fred, Jr.
Evans, Leon, Jr.
Fontayne, K. Nicole
Ford, John Newton
Fouche, Lori Dickerson
Fouche, Lori Dickerson
Forster, Jacqueline Gail
Gaines, Richard Kendall
Gholson, Robert L.
Givins, Abe, Jr.
Givens, Lawrence
Glapion, Michael J.
Goodrich, Dr. Thelma E.
Gomez, Dennis Craig
Golden, Ronald Allen
Golden, Arthur Ivanhoe
Graddick-Weir, Dr. Mirian M.
Green, Kim M.
Harrison, James C.
Hall, Pamela Vanessa
Hale, Hilton I.
Haugstad, May Katheryn
Harris, Joseph Preston
Harper, Dr. Bernice Catherine
Hardy, Charlie Edward
Haydel, James V., Sr.
Harrison, Delbert Eugene
Handwerk, Jana D.
Herndon, Gloria E.
Howard, Leon W., Jr.
Houston, Ivan J.
Holmes, Willie A.
Howell, Gerald T.
Hopkins, William A.
Hunter, Rev. John Davidson
Hurst, Rodney Lawrence, Sr.
Isaacs, Jessica C.
Jackson, Dwayne Adrian
James, Charles Leslie
Jackson, James E., Sr.
Jenkins, Joseph Walter
Jones, Leonard Warren
Jones, Gregory Wayne
Jones, Thomas Wade
Johnson, Patricia Duren
Johnson, John
Jones, Gregory Allan
Johnson, Hermon M., Sr.
Johns, Stephen Arnold
Kennedy, Lincoln
Kendrick, Carol Yvonne
King, Josephine
Knight, W. H., Jr.
Livingston-Wilson, Karen E.
Lomax, Michael Wilkins
Mateen, Malik Abdul
Mack, Daniel J.
Mackie, Timothy
Martin, Reddrick Linwood
Marsh, McAfee A.
Mauney, Donald Wallace, Jr.
McGinnis, Robert Lawrence
McGrier, Hon. Jerry, Sr.
McReynolds, Elaine A.
Miller, Joseph Herman, Jr.
Miller, Donald Lesessne
Morris, Joe
Morse, Mildred S.
Moses, Milton E.
Morrison, Harold L., Jr.
Murray, J. Ralph
Myers, Andre
Obi, James Esomonu
Olawumi, Bertha Ann
Orr, Dr. Dorothy J.
Palmer, Douglas Harold
Patterson, James C.
Parrish, James Nathaniel
Paul, Tito Jermaine
Pegues, Francine
Pemberton, David Melbert
Peoples, Erskine L.
Pocknett, Lawrence Wendell
Porter, Linsey
Procope, Ernesta G
Pryor, Vikki L.
Rawls, Mark Anthony
Rivers, Alfred J.
Rogers-Grundy, Ethel W.
Roberts, Cecilia
Robinson, Alcurtis
Ruffner, Raymond P.
Ruffin-Barnes, Wendy Yvette
Scott, Artie A.
Shakespeare, Easton Geoffrey
Simms, William E.
Slaughter-Titus, Rev. Linda Jean
Smith, Denver Lester
Smith, James Russell
Smith, Dr. Ann Elizabeth
Snowden, Raymond C.
Sobers, Waynett A., Jr.
Solomon, Donald L., Sr.
Sockwell, Oliver R., Jr.
Steed, Tyrone
Stith, Antoinette Freeman
Stewart, James A., III
Taylor, Dr. Carol Ann
Teasley, Larkin
Thomas, Isaac Daniel, Jr.
Thompson, Joseph Isaac
Thompson, Rev. Carl Eugene, Sr.
Thomas, Edward Arthur
Thompson, Westley V.
Tinsley, Hon. Dwane L.
Turnbull, Horace Hollins
Veney, Marguerite C.
Vincent, Daniel Paul
Watson, Milton H.
Waters, John W.
Ware, William J.
Walker, Laneuville V.
Warden, George W.
Walters, George W., Jr.
Watson, Michael A.
Webb, Dr. Harvey, Jr.
White, Arthur W., Jr.
Wilkes, Jamaal
Williams, Charlotte Leola
Williams, Annalisa Stubbs
Wilson, Rita P.
Williams, Eldredge M.
Woodard, Rhonda Marie
Woodward, Aaron Alphonso, III
Wright, Soraya M.

## Interior Design

Bridges, Sheila
Carter, Vincent G.
Charity, Lawrence Everett
Duckett, Karen Irene
Gainer, Prof. John F.
Grace, Sherry
Hubbard, Lawrence Ray
Johnson, Costello O.
Merritt, Wendy Warren
Reid, Malissie Laverne
Stull, Donald L.
Travis, Jack
Wilder, Jason Barnard

## Interpretation (*See* Translation/Interpretation)

## Journalism—Broadcast

Adams, Katherine J.
Agurs, Donald Steele
Alexander, Marcellus Winston, Jr.
Allen, Ron
Anglen, Reginald Charles
Armstrong, Mario
Bates, Karen Grigsby
Bailey, Lee
Badger, Madelyne Woods
Berry, Col. Ondra Lamon
Bell, Harold Kevin
Berry, Halle Maria
Bennett, Dr. Sybril M.
Blackmon, Brenda
Blanton, Dain
Black, Charles E.
Blount, Charlotte Renee
Boykin, Keith
Bobonis, Regis Darrow, Jr.
Bridgeforth, Arthur Mac, Jr.
Bromery, Keith Marcel
Brown, Angela Yvette
Brown-Francisco, Teresa Elaine
Broome, Sharon Weston
Bryant, Howard
Brewington, Rudolph W.
Bridgewater, Dr. Rev. Herbert Jeremiah, Jr.
Bundles, A'Lelia
Bundy, Kissette L.
Burwell, Bryan Ellis
Burns, Regina Lynn
Burose, Renee
Burns, Diann
Carroll, Lawrence William, III
Carroll, Jason
Calloway, Christopher Fitzpatrick
Casey, Frank Leslie
Christian, Spencer
Covington, Kim Ann
Coward, Onida Lavoneia
Costa, Annie Bell Harris
Cohen, Janet Langhart
Cornish, Audie
Cross, June Victoria
Crockett-Ntonga, Noluthando
Curwood, Stephen Thomas
Cunningham, Malena Ann
Davis, Barbara D.
Daniels, Kysa
Davis, Alisha
Dember, Jean Wilkins
Dee, Merri
Dennard, Darryl W.
Dickerson, Thomas L., Jr.
Drummond, William Joe
Edwards, Delores A.
Ellis, Rehema
Elder, Larry
Estes-Sumpter, Sidmel Karen
Evans, James L.
Ferguson, Renee
Ford, Sam
Franklin, Linda Cheryl Kennedy
French, Mary Ann
Gite, Lloyd Anthony
Gill, Rev. Laverne McCain
Gillum, Andrew D.
Gordon, Edward Lansing, III
Greer, Karyn Lynette
Granderson, LZ
Gumbel, Bryant Charles
Guillory, Keven
Gumbel, Greg
Hayes, James Harold, Jr.
Harlan, Carmen
Hampton, Cheryl Imelda
Harris, Gil W.
Hanson, John L., Jr.
Hare, Julia Reed
Handy, Delores
Haney, Don Lee
Hayward, Dr. Jacqueline C.
Harrison-Sullivan, Jeanette LaVerne
Hall, Tamron
Harris-Perry, Melissa
Herbert, Bob
Heyward, Rev. Dr. Isaac
Hedgspeth, Adrienne Cassandra
Hilliard, Alicia Victoria
Horne, Deborah Jean
Holman, Kwame Kent Allan
Holmes, T. J.
Holt, Melonie R.
Hunter-Gault, Charlayne
Hughes, Catherine Liggins
Ifill, Gwen
Ingram, Valerie J.
Izrael, Jimi
Jenkins, Carol Ann
Jessup, Gayle Louise
Jiggetts, Danny Marcellus
Johnson, Donn S.
Johnson, Iola Vivian
Johnson, Patrice Doreen
Johnson, John
Jones, Star
Jones, Victoria C.
Johnson, Charles Bernard
Jordan, Dr. Robert Howard, Jr.
Jones, Marsha Regina
Jones, Leander Corbin
Kaigler-Reese, Marie Madeleine
Keyes, Alan Lee
Kennedy-Overton, Jayne
King, Emery C.
King, Gayle
Lawson, Debra Ann
Lane, Janis Olene
Lee, Consella Almetter
Lemon, Don
Lewis, Maurice
Lewis, Ida Elizabeth
Lester, Nina Marie
Love, Thomas Clifford
Lomax, Janet E.
Lowry, Donna Shirlynn
Mathis, Deborah F.
Massey, Dr. Rev. Selma Diane Redd
Mack, Joan Gladden
Madison, Eddie L., Jr.
Martin, Robert E.
Martin, Carol
Martin, Wisdom T.
Makupson, Amyre Ann Porter
Mabrey, Vicki L.
Madison, Paula Williams
McMichael, Earlene Clarisse
McTyre, Robert Earl, Sr.
McCreary, Bill
McCovey, Willie Lee
Miles, Steen
Mickelbury, Penny
Morris, Valerie Coleman
Morse, Barbara Lyn
Moore, Cynthia M.
Morris, Valerie Dickerson Coleman
Moore, Dr. Jean E.
Nelson, Debra J.
O'Brien, Soledad
Ollison, Ruth Allen
Owens, Dr. Debbie A.
Owens, Donna M.
Parker, Maryland Mike
Parker, E. Charmaine Roberts
Peoples, John Derrick, Jr.
Petty, Bob
Phillips, Julian Martin
Powell, Darrell Lee
Pool-Eckert, Marquita Jones
Pressley, Condace L.
Quarles, Alicia
Quarles, Norma R.
Randolph-Jasmine, Carol Davis
Revish, Jerry
Reid, Joy-Ann
Rice, Sandra Dorsey
Ridenhour, Carlton Douglas
Rideau, Wibert
Rice, Dr. Horace Warren
Roberts, Robin Rene
Rodgers, Barbara Lorraine
Robinson, Carol Evonne
Robinson, Angela Yvonne
Rodgers, Johnathan Arlin
Roberts, Deborah
Roberts, Troy
Robinson, Shaun
Rojas, Don
Sample, William Amos
Sartin, Johnny Nelson, Jr.
Santiago, Roberto
Saunders, John P.
Scafe, Judith Arlene
Sealls, Alan Ray
Seals, Rupert Grant
Shifflett, Lynne Carol
Shearin, Kimberly Maria
Shaw, Bernard
Simpson, Carole

## Journalism—Not Elsewhere Classified



## Journalism—Photojournalism



## Journalism—Print

Waters, Sylvia Ann
Wade, Kim Mache
Watkins, Rev. Joseph Philip
Washington, Robin
Weathersbee, Tonyaa Jeanine
Wesley, Dr. Herman Eugene, III
Weston, Martin V.
White, George Gregory
White, Jack E., Jr.
White, John Clinton
White, Margarette Paulyne Morgan
Whack, Rita Coburn
Wheeler, Robyn Elaine
Wilkerson, Isabel
Wilson, Wendy L.
Wilkins, Betty
Williams, Dr. McDonald
Williams, Dr. Jamye Coleman
Williams, Armstrong
Wiley, Edward, III
Wilkins, Roger Wood
Winston, Bonnie Veronica
Wickham, DeWayne
Womble, Jeffery Maurice
Woodford, John Niles
Wright, Jeanne Jason
Wright, Dr. Katie Harper
Wright, Carl Jeffrey
Young, B. Ashley
Zola, Nkenge

## Judiciary

Abdus-Salaam, Sheila
Adams, Esq. John Oscar
Adrine, Ronald Bruce
Allen-Rasheed, Jamal Randy
Alexander, Pamela Gayle
Allen, Cheryl L.
Alexander, Hon. Joyce London
Anthony, Emory, Jr.
Anderson, Judge David Turpeau
Argrett, Loretta Collins
Archer, Hon. Trudy DunCombe
Arrington, Judge Marvin S., Sr.
Armstrong, Joan Bernard
Armstrong, Saundra Brown
Atkins, Hon. Marylin E.
Atkins, Hon. Edna R.
Baety, Edward L., Sr.
Banks, Hon. Patricia
Baylor, Hon. Margaret E.
Baskerville, Dr. Lezli
Baranco, Hon. Gordon S.
Baxter, Hon. Wendy Marie
Baker, Althea R.
Benham, Dr. Robert
Bennett, Arthur T.
Bennett, Patricia A.
Benton, James Wilbert, Jr.
Bell, Robert Mack
Bishop, Ronald L.
Blackwell-Hatcher, Hon. June E.
Blackwell, Willie
Boyd, Judge Delores Rosetta
Braden, Everette Arnold
Brewer, Hon. Webster L.
Bransford, Dr. Paris
Braxton, Hon. John Ledger
Brown, Hon. Irma Jean
Brown, George Henry, Jr.
Brown, Helen E.
Brown, Janice Rogers
Brown, Frederick L.
Brown, Judge Joe
Bruce, Raymond L.
Brock, Gerald
Burrell, Garland, Jr.
Bugg, Mayme Carol
Burnett, Arthur Louis, Sr.
Byrd, Jerry Stewart
Byrd, Hon. Isaac, Jr.
Canady, Hon. Herman G., Jr.
Cartwright, Hon. Joan S.
Card, Larry D.
Carroll, George D.
Carroll, Sally G.
Chenevert-Bragg, Irma J.
Clevert, Hon. Charles Nelson, Jr.
Clemon, U. W.
Clark, Hon. Tama Myers
Cooper, Hon. Candace D.
Coleman, Hon. Claude M.
Cooley, Hon. Wendy C.
Coleman, Hon. Veronica F.
Cook, Ralph D.
Collins, Jeffrey G.
Cousins, William, Jr.
Cooper, Evelyn Kaye
Cooper, Clarence
Cook, Hon. Julian Abele, Jr.
Collins, Daisy G.
Collins, Robert Frederick
Coleman, Hon. Rudy B.
Connally, C. Ellen
Collins, Audrey B.
Craig, Rhonda Patricia
Crockett, George W., III
Crider, Edward S., III
Cross, Judge Denise L.
Curtin, Hon. John T.
Culpepper, Dellie L.
Curtis, James
Davenport, Hon. Horace Alexander
Daniel, Hon. Wiley Young
Davis, Rev. Arnor S.
Davis, Lawrence Arnette, Jr.
Davis, Hon. L. Clifford
Davis, Michael James
Delaney, Duane B.
Dearman, John Edward
Dilday, Hon. Judith Nelson
Donald, Dr. Bernice Bouie
Dorse, Earnestine Hunt
Doss, Hon. Theresa
Dorn, Dr. Rev. Roosevelt F.
Douglass, Hon. Lewis Lloyd
Douglas, Willard H., Jr.
Drake, Maggie W.
Drain, Gershwin Allen
Dunn, Reginald Arthur
Dye, Hon. Luther V.
Edwards, Hon. Dennis, Jr.
Edwards, Hon. Harry Thomas
Edwards, Raymond, Jr.
Edwards, Hon. Wilbur Patterson, Jr.
Edwards, Prentis
Ephriam, Esq. Mablean Deloris
Evans, Hon. Carole Yvonne Mims
Farris, Hon. Jerome
Farmer, Nancy A.
Figures, Thomas H.
Finney, Ernest A., Jr.
Floyd, Hon. Marquette L.
Fowler, Judge William E., Jr.
Ford, Hon. Judith Donna
Fordham, Cynthia Williams
Foskey, Hon. Carnell T.
Freeman-Wilson, Karen Marie
Freeman, Hon. Ronald J.
Frye, Hon. Henry E.
Gaitan, Hon. Fernando J., Jr.
Gartin, Claudia L.
Gates, Lee
Garner, Edward, Jr.
Gibson, Dr. Benjamin F.
Gilmore, Hon. Vanessa Diane
Gibbs, Robert Lewis
Gibson, Reginald Walker
Giles, James Tyrone
Glover, Hon. Don Edward
Gordon, Levan
Grimes, Douglas M.
Graves, Ray Reynolds
Grant, Judge Cheryl Dayne
Grante, Jullian Irving
Gray, Jon R.
Green, Alexander N.
Greene-Thapedi, Dr. Llwellyn L.
Guice, Leroy
Haynes, William Joseph, Jr.
Harris, Hon. Barbara Ann
Harbin-Forte, Hon. Brenda F.
Harris, Alonzo
Hathaway, Cynthia Gray
Hatter, Hon. Terry J., Jr.
Hartsfield, Hon. Judy A.
Harris, Hon. Leslie E.
Hall, Sophia H.
Hatchett, Glenda A.
Hall, Hon. L. Priscilla
Harris, Leodis
Harper, Sara J.
Henderson, Hon. Thelton Eugene
Hicks, Maryellen
Hill, Reuben Benjamin
Hill, Vonciel Jones
Hood, Hon. Harold
Holt, Hon. Leo E.
Hoyt, Hon. Kenneth M.
Howard, Raymond
Hood, Denise Page
Humphries, Hon. Paula G.
Humphrey, Marion Andrew
Ingram, Hon. Edith J.
Ireland, Hon. Roderick Louis
Irons, Hon. Paulette R.
Jackson, Carol E.
James, Letitia
Jackson, Hon. Randolph
Jackson, Arthur D., Jr.
Jackson, Harold Baron, Jr.
Jamison, Birdie Hairston
Jackson, Hon. Marie Oliver
Jackson, Hon. Darnell
Jackson, Giles B.
Jackson, Janet E.
Jackson, Ricardo C.
Jackson, Michael W.
Jewell, Tommy Edward, III
Johnson, Dr. Charles Floyd
Johnson, Charles V.
Johnson, Esq. Livingstone M.
Johnson, Justin Morris
Johnson, Clinisson Anthony
Jones, Nathaniel R.
Johnson, Norman B.
Johnson, Sterling, Jr.
Jones, Hon. Raymond Dean
Joy, Daniel Webster
Jones, Nathaniel R.
Jordan, Atty. Eddie Jack, Jr.
Jones, Daryl L.
Josey-Herring, Anita Marie
Johnson, Bernette Joshua
Jordan, Hon. Claudia J.
Jones, Hon. Vera Massey
Johnson, Paul Lawrence
Johnson, Kenneth Lavon
Kearney, Jesse L.
Kennedy, Brenda Picola
Kerr, Stanley Munger
Kendall, Robert, Jr.
Kennedy, Henry Harold, Jr.
Keith, Hon. Damon Jerome
Kearse, Amalya Lyle
Lawrence, Charles, Jr.
Lange, LaJune Thomas
LaVergne, Hon. Luke Aldon
Langford, Hon. Denise Morris
Lay, Clorius L.
Lester, Betty J.
Lewis, Hon. Alexis Otis
Lemelle, Ivan
Lewis, Wilma A.
Lewis, Hon. Jannie M.
Lee, Gerald Bruce
Lee, Helen Shores
Lewis, Dr. William A.
Lewis, Hon. Daniel
Leighton, Hon. George Neves
Lindsay, Sam A.
Logan, Hon. George, III
Long, Hon. James L.
Logan, Judge Benjamin Henry, II
Luke, Sherrill David
Lytle, Judge Alice A.
Lyle, Dr. Freddrenna Margaret
Mallett, Dr. Conrad L., Jr.
Martin, Hon. Janice R.
Marable, Herman, Jr.
Marsh, Esq. Sandra M.
Manning, Blanche Marie
Martin, Hon. Joshua Wesley, III
Marshall, Hon. Consuelo B.
Martin, Baron H.
Mathews, Lawrence Talbert
Mathews, Keith E.
Mathis, Gregory
McGriggs-Jamison, Imogene
McGhee, Odell G., II
McKee, Evelyn Palfrey
McDade, Joe Billy
McPherson, Vanzetta Penn
McBeth, Hon. Veronica Simmons
McDonald, Gabrielle Kirk
McCollum, Judge Alice Odessa
McFarland, Arthur C.
McPherson, William H.
McKee, Hon. Theodore A.
McNairy, Dr. Francine G.
McCollum, Anita LaVerne
McNeal, Pastor Don
Meyers, Ishmael Alexander
Mills, Billy G.
Miller, Loren, Jr.
Mitchell-Rankin, Zinora M.
Miles-LaGrange, Vicki
Miller, Hon. Sheila
Molock, Rev. Guizelous O., Jr.
Morse, Hon. John E., Jr.
Moore, Thelma Wyatt Cummings
Moore, Thelma LaVerne Wyatt Cummings
Morrison, Hon. Johnny Edward, Jr.
Morrow, Hon. Dion Griffith
Moore, Hon. Warfield, Jr.
Murphy, Hon. Harriet Louise M.
Naves, Larry J.
Nelson, Otha Curtis, Sr.
Neals, Felix Ramon
Newman, Dr. Theodore Roosevelt, Jr.
Niles, Alban I.
Nunn, Robinson S.
O'Bryant, Dr. Constance Taylor
O'Banno, Dr. Donna M. Edwards
Ortiz, Victor N.
Otis-Lewis, Alexis D.
Overstreet, Morris L.
Owens, Nathaniel Davis
Page, Hon. Alan Cedric
Patrick, Hon. Isadore W., Jr.
Patterson, Hon. Robert L.
Parker, Barrington Daniels, Jr.
Peavy, Hon. John W., Jr.
Peay, Hon. Samuel
Petersen, Hon. Eileen Ramona
Pettway, Jo Celeste
Pichon, Rise Jones
Price, Judge Charles
Queen, Evelyn E. Crawford
Quince, Peggy A.
Rankin, Hon. Michael Lee
Ransom, Gary Elliott
Reece, Guy L., II
Richardson, Andra Virginia
Riley, Hon. Eve Montgomery
Riggs, Hon. Elizabeth A.
Rodgers, Edward
Rogers, Judith W.
Roberts, Victoria A.
Ruth, James A.
Rucker, Dr. Robert D.
Salone, Marcus R.
Sandoz, John Henry
Satterfield, Hon. Patricia Polson
Saffold, Shirley Strickland
Sconiers, Hon. Rose H.
Scott, Hugh B.
Scott, Richard Eley
Selby, Myra C.
Sherwood, Hon. O. Peter
Shaw, Leander Jerry, Jr.
Shaw, Booker Thomas
Shields, Karen Bethea
Sims, Barbara Merriweather
Simmons, Paul A.
Sleet, Gregory Moneta
Smitherman, Esq. Carole Catlin
Smith, George Bundy
Smith, Hon. Virgil Clark, Jr.
South, Leslie Elaine
Spurlock, Dr. Oliver M.
Spencer, James Randolph
Squire, Carole Renee
Stephens, Booker T.
Stringer, Thomas Edward
Stephens, Cynthia Diane
Strong, Hon. Craig Stephen
Stone, William T.
Stephens, William Haynes
Stewart, Carl E.
Sullivan, Emmet G.
Taliaferro, Viola J.
Taylor, Vernon Anthony
Taylor, Anna Diggs
Terrell, Mary Ann Gooden
Thompson, Hon. Sandra Ann
Thompson, Hon. Anne Elise
Thompson, Hon. William Coleridge, Sr.
Thomas, Hon. Clarence
Thomas, Hon. Mary Maxwell
Thompson, Hon. Myron Herbert
Tinsley, Hon. Dwane L.
Townes, Hon. Sandra L.
Tusan, Hon. Gail S.
Tuffin, Esq. Paul Jonathan
Van Hook, George Ellis, Jr.
Veals, Craig Elliott
Warren, Hon. Joyce Williams
Ward, Horace Taliaferro
Waldon, Hon. Alton Ronald, Jr.
Ware, Charles Jerome
Walton, Reggie Barnett
Watt, Garland Wedderick
Watson, Hon. J. Warren
Watts, Hon. Lucile A.
Wagner, Annice M.
Walker, Hon. Joseph M., III
Walker, Linda T.
Wainwright, Hon. J. Dale
Walker, Adrian
Webber, Hon. Paul R., III
Weeks, Hon. Renee Jones
West, Joseph King
Wharton, Hon. Milton S.
Williams, Patricia Anne
Williams, Hon. Walter
Williams, Hon. Marcus Doyle
Williams, Jewel L.
Willis, Charles L.
Williams, Hon. Louise Bernice
Williams, Hon. Ann Claire
Williams, Milton Lawrence
Williams, Hon. Alexander, Jr.
Wigenton, Susan Davis
Williams, Hon. Carolyn H.
Willrich, Penny
Worthy, Kym L.
Wood, Hon. William S.
Woods, Hon. Arleigh Maddox
Wood, Harold Leroy
Wright, Hon. Geoffrey
Wright, Hon. Milton L., Jr.
Zeno, Hon. Melvin Collins

## Labor Relations (*See* Labor Union Administration)

## Labor Union Administration

Adams, Nelson Eddy
Andrews, James Edward
Baker, Willie L., Jr.
Bolden, Betty A.
Bremer, Charles E.
Bryant, Connie L.
Brown, Louis Sylvester
Brown, Emmett Earl
Burrus, William Henry, Jr.
Davis, Norman Emanuel
Davis, George Bernard
Dixon, Yvonne T.
Dixon, Jimmy
Druitt, Beverly F.
Fletcher, William G., Jr.
Gilliam, Arleen Fain
Glass, James
Graves, Carole A.
Harris, Leon L.
Holmes, Cloyd James
Hollowell, Kenneth Lawrence
Jackson, Lee Arthur
Jackson, Dr. Franklin D. B.
Johnson, Pastor James H.
Johnson, Georgianna
Lee, William Thomas
Lewis, Green Pryor, Jr.
Lucy, William
McMillian, Josie Anderson
Moore, Lewis Calvin
Montgomery, Oliver R.
Murphy, Dr. Donald Richard, II
O'Brien, Mary Nell
Patrick, Esq. Diane
Phillips, Dr. Robert Hansbury
Pollard, Alfonso McInham
Rhett, Michael L.
Richmond, Rodney Welch
Romney, Edgar O.
Roberts, Lillian Davis
Taylor, William Henry, Sr.
Thomas, Ralph Charles, III
Turner, Doris
Worsham, James E.

## Landscape/Horticultural Services

Grace, Horace R.

## Law Enforcement



## Law/Legal Services

Cook, Ralph D.
Coleman, April Howard
Coleman, Michael Bennett
Cooley, Hon. Wendy C.
Cooke, Leonard G
Coleman, Michael Victor
Cole, Ransey Guy, Jr.
Coleman, Hon. Claude M.
Cooper, Drucilla Hawkins
Cole, James O.
Coleman, William T., Jr.
Cox, Warren E.
Collins, Robert Frederick
Collins, Kenneth L.
Collins, Daisy G.
Cook, Frank Robert, Jr.
Cook, Rufus
Conley, Martha Richards
Cooper, Clarence
Cooper, Gordon R., II
Corlette, Edith Parker
Cooper, Joseph
Cousins, William, Jr.
Cormier, Dr. Rufus P., Jr.
Cornish, Jeannette Carter
Cothorn, John A.
Colvin, Cedric B.
Cook, Ronald R.
Corrothers, Garry James
Coar, David H.
Cromer, Ronnie E., Jr.
Crosby, Fred Charles
Crockett, George W., III
Cruise, Esq. Warren Michael
Cross, Judge Denise L.
Crenshaw, Waverly David, Jr.
Cromartie, Ernest W., III
Crump, Dr. Arthel Eugene (Gene)
Cunningham, Courtney
Cunningham, T. J., Sr.
Curtin, Hon. John T.
Cunningham, E. Brice
Curry, Levy Henry
Curtis, James
Cunningham, Joy Virginia
Davis, Denise
Davis, Artur
Dawson, Ralph Curtis
Daniels, John W.
Darden, Anthony Kojo
Darden, Edwin Carley
Dalley, George Albert
Dalferes, Edward R., Jr.
Davis, Willie J.
Davis, Dr. William L.
Days, Drew Saunders, III
Daye, Charles Edward
Dawson, Warren Hope
Davison, Edward Larry
Davis, Dr. Elaine Carsley
Davis, Dr. Doris Ann
Davis, Esq. Morris E.
Davis, Lawrence Arnette, Jr.
Davis, J. Mason, Jr.
Daniel, Hon. Wiley Young
Davenport, Hon. Horace Alexander
Davis, Dr. Alfred C., Sr.
Darity, Janki Evangelia
Davis, Lisa E.
Davis, Esq. Nathan W., Jr.
Davis, Esq. Marva Alexis
Davis, John Wesley
Dawson, Horace G., III
Davis, Robert N.
Darden, Christopher Allen
Daggs, Leon, Jr.
Davis, Milton Carver
Daniels, Earl Hodges
Davidson-Harger, Esq. Joan Carole
Davis, Darlene Rose
Dellums, Dr. Leola Higgs
DeFrantz, Dr. Anita L.
DeGraffenreidt, James Henry, Jr.
Dennis, Andre L.
Dennis, Edward S. G., Jr.
DePriest, Darryl Lawrence
Denson, Fred L.
Deloach, Wendelin W.
Devine, Tameika Isaac
Dixon, Yvonne T.
Dillard, Dr. June White
Donald, Dr. Bernice Bouie
Doss, Hon. Theresa
Douglas, Carl E.
Dorse, Earnestine Hunt
Dotson, Hon. Norma Y.
Dotson, Albert E., Jr.
Donegan, Charles Edward
Douglas, Dr. James Matthew
Dorsey, Elbert
Dorsey, John L., Jr.
Druitt, Beverly F.
Drew, Stephen Richard
Drew-Peeples, Brenda
Dupree, David H.
Dunnings, Stuart J., III
Duckett, Esq. Gregory
Eaglin, Fulton B.
Earley, Keith Henry
Echols, Alvin E., Jr.
Edwards, Hon. Harry Thomas
Edwards, Dr. Sylvia
Edwards, Ruth McCalla
Edmonds, Bobbie Gray
Edmonds, Lisa I.
Edwards, Hon. Wilbur Patterson, Jr.
Edmunds, David L., Jr.
Edwards, Carl Ray, II
Edmond, Dr. Janice L. Sumler
Edwards, Donald Philip
Ellis, Rodney Glenn
Elliott, Darrell Stanley, Sr.
Elliott, Lori Karen
Elmore, Esq. Ernest Eric
Elder, Larry
El-Amin, Sa'ad
Ellison, Chester Laughton
Ephriam, Esq. Mablean Deloris
Epps, Phillip Earl
Espy, Alphonso Michael
Espy, Ben E.
Everett, Cynthia A.
Evans, Warren Cleage
Evans, Timothy C.
Everett, Esq. Ralph B.
Evans, Hon. Carole Yvonne Mims
Evans, Dr. LeRoy Winston
Everett, Esq. J. Richard
Ewing, Esq. William James
Farrow, Sallie A.
Farley, William Horace, Jr.
Farris, Esq. Deborah Ellison
Fain, Constance Frisby
Fearn, James E., Jr.
Feaster, Bruce Sullivan
Ferguson, Roger W., Jr.
Fitzhugh, Benjamin Dewey
Fitch, Harrison Arnold
Fields, Inez C.
Fisher, Lloyd B.
Figures, Thomas H.
Finlayson, Dr. Arnold Robert
Fitzhugh, Kathryn Corrothers
Filer, Hon. Kelvin Dean
Finch, Gregory Martin
Flowers, William Harold, Jr.
Floyd, Mark Stephen
Fletcher, Robert E.
Flowers, Ralph Lorenzo
Flatts, Barbara Ann
Flowers, Michael E.
Flowers, Michael E.
Forster, Jacqueline Gail
Foster, T. Eloise
Foxx, Anthony
Forbes, George L.
Foster, Janice Martin
Foster, Gladys M.
Fox, Thomas E., Jr.
Fortson, Walter Lewis
Ford, Hon. Barry W.
Foreman, Peggy E.
Fordham, Cynthia Williams
Ford, Wallace L., II
Frazer, Victor O.
Fraser, Thomas Edwards
Freeman-Wilson, Karen Marie
Freeman, Frankie Muse
Frasier, Ralph Kennedy
Frazier-Lyde, Hon. Jacqui
Frisby, H. Russell, Jr.
Fuse-Hall, Rosalind
Fugett, Jean Schloss, Jr.
Gaines, John A., Sr.
Gartrell, Bernadette A.
Gatling, Patricia Lynn
Gary, Willie E.
Gardner, Cedric Boyer
Garrett, Dr. Paul C.
Gatewood, Esq. Diane Ridley
Gary, Tanisha Nunn
Gary, Sekou M.
Garland, John William
Gatling, Joseph Theodore
Gaitan, Hon. Fernando J., Jr.
Garner, Dr. Melvin C.
Garnett, Ronald Leon
Gayton, Esq. Gary D.
Garrett, Dr. Nathan Taylor, Sr.
Gentry, Nolden I., Jr.
George, Allen
Gibson, Reginald Walker
Gibson, Warren Arnold
Gigger, Helen C.
Givens, Leonard David
Gillum, Roderick D.
Gibbs, Robert Lewis
Gibbs, Jack Gilbert, Jr.
Gilford, Vera Elaine
Gill, Roberta L.
Gigger, Nathaniel Jay
Glenn, Patricia Campbell
Godette, Franklin Delano Roosevelt
Goins, Atty. Richard Anthony
Goldson, Esq. Amy Robertson
Govan, Reginald C.
Gordy, Desiree D'Laura
Gordon, Walter Lear, III
Gordon, Esq. Claudia Lorraine
Golden, Arthur Ivanhoe
Gore, David L.
Gould, Prof. William Benjamin, IV
Gordon, Helen A.
Goodwin, James Osby
Griffin, Ronald Charles
Grimes, Douglas M.
Groves, Harry Edward
Griffin, Eurich Z.
Gregg, Hon. Harrison M., Jr.
Graves, Ray Reynolds
Gray, Esq. Fred David, Sr.
Graham, Prof. Precious Jewel
Green, Dr. Deborah Kennon
Green, Georgia Mae
Gray, Marvin W.
Gray, Ruben L.
Green, William Ernest
Grady-Smith, Esq. Mattie D.
Greer, Ernest LaMont
Gray, Jon R.
Grant-Bruce, Esq. Darlene Camille
Groff, Peter Charles
Grant, Andre M.
Grant, Esq. Denise M.
Green, Larry A.
Gray, Dr. Ronald A.
Green, Saul A.
Graves, Dr. Leslie Theresa
Green, Gloria J.
Griffin, Gregory O., Sr.
Graves, John Clifford
Gregory, Judge Roger L.
Gray, Kenneth D.
Guinier, Lani
Guthrie, Michael J.
Hart, Dr. Christopher Alvin
Hall, David
Hawk, Charles Nathaniel, III
Haynes, William Joseph, Jr.
Haye, Esq. Clifford S.
Hall-Keith, Jacqueline Yvonne
Hatchett, Elbert L.
Haley, George Williford Boyce
Hadden, Eddie Raynord
Hayes, Charles
Haynes, Farnese N.
Harbin-Forte, Hon. Brenda F.
Hardy, Timothy W.
Hall, Sydney Jay, III
Hall, Benjamin Lewis, III
Hatcher, Lizzie R.
Harlan, Emery King
Hawkins, Steven Wayne
Hamilton, Harry Edwin
Hall, Melvin Curtis
Harris, Gladys Bailey
Haskins, Esq. Yvonne B.
Hall, Elliott Sawyer
Harrell, Adam Nelson, Jr.
Harding, Roberta
Hampton, Phillip G., II
Haugabook, Dr. Terrence Randall
Hadley, Dr. Sybil Carter
Hairston, Abbey Gail
Hall, Hon. L. Priscilla
Harris, Paul Clinton, Sr.
Harrison, Jaime
Hayes, Dennis Courtland
Harris, Kamala Devi, Jr.
Hall, Dr. Morris B., Jr.
Hawkins, Esq. Johnny L.
Harvey, Dr. Peter C.
Hageman, Hans Eric
Hall, Hon. Shelvin Louise Marie
Hatchett, Glenda A.
Hall, Sarah N.
Hales, Edward Everette
Hairston, Joseph Henry
Hamlar, Portia Yvonne Trenholm
Hamilton, Samuel Cartenius
Hanley, J. Frank, II
Harper, Esq. Ronald J.
Harper, Conrad Kenneth
Harmon, John H.
Hart-Nibbrig, Harold C.
Hartsfield, Arnett L., Jr.
Hastings, Rep. Alcee Lamar
Hatcher, Richard Gordon
Hatchett, Joseph Woodrow
Harth, Raymond Earl
Harris, William H., Jr.
Haywoode, M. Douglas
Hayes, Edward, Jr.
Hawkins, Dr. Calvin D.
Hayes, Graham Edmondson
Hebert, Stanley Paul, III
Heiskell, Michael Porter
Henry, Karl H.
Herbert, John Travis, Jr.
Henry, William Arthur, II
Henry, Brent Lee
Henley, Carl R.
Hendricks, Beatrice E.
Hewlett, Everett Augustus, Jr.
Henry, Alaric Anthony
Henderson, Esq. Wade
Henderson, Hon. Thelton Eugene
Hill, Cynthia D.
Hinton, Dr. Gregory Tyrone
Hill, Jacqueline R.
Higginbotham-Brooks, Esq. Renee
Hill, Anita Faye
Hightower, Anthony
Hillard, Terry
Hill, Hon. Deirdre Hughes
Hill, James A., Jr.
Hilliard, Earl Frederick
Hill, William Bradley, Jr.
Hinds, Prof. Lennox S.
Hines, Kingsley B.
Hodges, Melvin Sancho
Howard, Dalton J., Jr.
Howard, Dr. John Robert
Horton, Earle Chico, III
Holmes, Robert C.
Holmes, Esq. Robert Ernest
Honore, Stephan LeRoy
Hopkins, Donald Ray
Hopkins, Dr. Esther Arvilla Harrison
Holt, Donald H.
Howe, Prof. Ruth-Arlene W.
Howze, Karen Aileen
Howard, Raymond
Howard, Esq. John Milton
Holder, Eric Himpton, Jr.
Hoyte, James Sterling
Holden, Melvin Lee
Howard, Paul Lawrence, Jr.
Holmes, Dr. Henry Sidney, III
Howard, Leslie Carl
Hudson, Merry C.
Hutton, Marilyn Adele
Huntley, Lynn Jones
Hunter, James Mackiell
Hughes, Jimmy Franklin, Sr.
Hutchison, Dr. Harry Greene
Humphries, Esq. James Nathan
Hunt, Charles Amoes
Hunter, Rhonda F.
Hudson, Cynthia
Hubbard, Hon. Arnette Rhinehart
Hughes, Dr. Joyce A.
Hughes, Harvey L.
Hunt, Isaac Cosby, Jr.
Hunter, Jerry L.
Hunter, Dr. Frederick Douglas, Sr.
Ifill, Sherrilyn
Ike, Alice Denise
Irving, Dr. Clarence Larry, Jr.
Irons, Hon. Paulette R.
Isadore, Dr. Harold W.
Isaac, Hon. Earlean
Jamison, Birdie Hairston
Jackson, Hon. Marie Oliver
Jackson, Hon. Ava Nicola
Jackson, Gary Monroe
Jackson, Darrell Duane
Jackson, Elijah
Jarrett, Dr. Valerie B.
Jackson-Gillison, Esq. Helen L.
Jacobs, Ennis Leon, Jr.
Jarrett, Gerald I., Sr.
Jacobs, Rev. Gregory Alexander
James, Sherri Gwendolyn
James, Patricia Rea Coleman
Jackson, Ricardo C.
Jacks, Ulysses
Jackson, Gerald Milton
Jackson, Harold Baron, Jr.
Jackson, Hon. Randolph
Jacobs, Patricia Dianne
James, Ronald J.
James, Frank Samuel, III
James, Frederick John
Jefferies, Charlotte S.
Jeffers, Clifton R.
Jewell, Tommy Edward, III
Jervay, Dr. Marion White
Jenkins, Dr. Melvin Lemuel
Jeffries, Hakeem
Jefferson-Bullock, Jalila Eshe
Jefferson, Hon. Wallace Bernard
Jenkins, Nedra
Jenkins, Dr. Chip, Jr.
Johnson, Ernest L.
Jones, Leonard Warren
Jordan, Dr. Eddie J., Jr.
Johnson, Wayne J.
Jordan, Prof. Sandra D.
Jones, Charles D.
Johnson, Cynthia L. M.
Johnson, Michael L.
Jones, Esq. Rosalyn Evelyn
Jones, Randy Kane
Johnson, Patricia L.
Joyner, Irving L.
Jones, Ida M.
Johnson, Robert T.
Joyner, Esq. Gordon L.
Jones, Clyde Eugene
Johnson, Dr. Charles Henry
Jones, William Allen
Jones, Peter Lawson
Jones, David R.
Jones, Dr. William Bowdoin
Jones, Emma Pettway
Jones, Hon. Bonnie Louise
Johnson, Geraldine Ross
Johnson, Raymond L.
Johnson, Hon. J. Leon
Johnson, Esq. Harry E., Sr.
Joyner, Lauren Celeste
Johnson, Stephen A.
Johnson, Kenya
Jones, Nathaniel R.
Johnson, Hon. Jeh Charles
Jones, Dr. Walter, Jr.
Jones, Star
Johnson, Lester B., III
Jordan, B. Delano
Johnson, Almeta Ann
Johnson, Andrew L., Jr.
Johnson, Caliph
Johnson, James Walter
Johnson, John Will
Johnson, Esq. Johnnie Louis, III
Johnson, Justin Morris
Johnson, Lawrence E.
Johnson, Edward C.
Johnson, I. S. Leevy
Johnson, Edmond R., Jr.
Jones, Chester Ray
Jones, Nathaniel R.
Jones, Gerald Winfield
Jones, Johnnie Anderson, Sr.
Johnson, Wyneva
Johnson, William Theolious
Johnson, Wilbur Eugene
Johnson, Walter Thaniel, Jr.
Johnson, Sterling, Jr.

Spooner, Richard C.
Spaulding, Esq. Lynette Victoria
Spain, Dr. Hiram, Jr.
Springer, Eric Winston
Spence, Rev. Joseph Samuel, Sr.
Speights, Esq. Nathaniel H.
Squire, Carole Renee
Staton, Donna Hill
Stiell, Esq. Phelicia D.
Stephens, Cynthia Diane
Stone, William T.
Strong, Hon. Craig Stephen
Stampley, Gilbert Elvin
Stewart, John Ogden
Stancell, Dr. Dolores Wilson Pegram
Strautmanis, Michael A.
Staton, Kerry D.
Stewart, Carolyn House
Sulton, Dr. Anne Thomas
Sumner, Thomas Robert
Sutton, Norma J.
Sudarkasa, Dr. Michael Eric Mabogunje
Swanson, Charles
Swain, James H.
Swann, Eugene Merwyn
Taylor, Dr. Patricia E.
Taylor, Hon. Janice A.
Taylor, Dr. Carol Ann
Taylor, Wilford, Jr.
Talley, Michael Frank, Sr.
Tann, Esq. Daniel J.
Taylor, David Richard, III
Taylor, Eartha Lynn
Taylor, Hon. Eric Charles
Taylor, Atty. Jeffery Charles
Tate, David Kirk
Tate, Dr. Herbert Holmes, Jr.
Taylor, Johnny C., Jr.
Teeuwissen, Pieter
Terrell, Reginald V.
Telfair, Esq. Brian Kraig
Temple, Esq. Donald Melvin
Terrell, Mary Ann Gooden
Terrell, Francis D'Arcy
Terry, Adeline Helen
Terrell, Henry Matthew
Thigpen, Dr. Calvin Herritage
Thomas, James O.
Thomas, Franklin A.
Thompson, Hon. William Coleridge, Sr.
Thompson, Hon. Anne Elise
Thompson, Daniel Joseph, Jr.
Thompson, Esq. Larry D.
Thompson, Herman G.
Thorpe, Josephine Horsley
Thomas, Hon. Clarence
Thompson, Hon. M. T., Jr.
Thomas, Edward Arthur
Thomas, Samuel Haynes, Jr.
Thigpen, Esq. Donald A., Jr.
Thompson, William L.
Thomas, Kendall
Thomas, Maureen A.
Thornton, Leslie
Thomas, Dermond Edwin
Thompson, Mavis T.
Tinsley, Hon. Dwane L.
Tillman, Paula Sellars
Tibbs, Edward A.
Tinsley, Hon. Fred Leland, Jr.
Todd, Thomas N.
Townsend, Br. Prentice A.
Toote, Gloria E. A
Townes, Hon. Sandra L.
Trumbo, George William
Tucker, Karen
Tuffin, Esq. Paul Jonathan
Tucker, Geraldine Jenkins
Tucker, Robert L.
Tucker, Michael Kevin
Turner, Leslie Marie
Tucker, Dr. Walter Rayford, III
Turner, Reginald M., Jr.
Tyson, Lance C.
Uku, Eustace Oris
Underwood, Arthur C.
Ussery, Esq. Terdema Lamar, II
Vance, Lawrence N.
Van Hook, George Ellis, Jr.
Vaaughters-Johnson, Cecilie A.
Van Lierop, Robert F.
Valentine, J. T.
Vertreace, Walter Charles
Veals, Craig Elliott
Venson, Clyde R.
Vickers, Eric K.
Vinson, Rosalind Rowena
Waddell, Ruchadina LaDesiree
Walker, Hon. Charles Ealy, Jr.
Waits, Rev. Va Lita Francine
Ward, Ronald R.
Ward, Sandra L.
Ware, R. David
Wade, Beryl Elaine
Walker-Gibbs, Shirley Ann
Ward, Keith Lamont
Watford-McKinney, Yvonne V.
Watson, Solomon B., IV
Way, Dr. Gary Darryl
Warrick, Dr. Alan Everett
Walton, Elbert Arthur, Jr.
Washington, Valdemar Luther
Walker, Tanya Rosetta
Ware, Dyahanne
Wagner, David H.
Walker, Betty Stevens
Walker, Charles H.
Walker, Grover Pulliam
Walker, Stanley Michael
Wallace, C. Everett
Walker, Woodson DuBois
Ward, Nolan F.
Ware, Charles Jerome
Washington, Consuela M.
Washington, Craig Anthony
Washington, Betty Lois
Watson, Hon. J. Warren
Watt, Garland Wedderick
Washington, Robert Benjamin, Jr.
Washington, Dr. Roosevelt, Jr.
Watkins, Hon. Craig
Walker-Kuhne, Donna
Ware, Leland
Ware, Leland Brett
Watkins, Donald V.
Ward, Hon. Christopher Evan
Wareham, Dr. Roger S.
Walker, Karol Corbin
Washington, Mickey Lin
Watkins, Rosyln
Watson, Esq. Gary A.
West, Roderick K.
Wells, Theodore V., Jr.
Webster, Lesley Douglass
Weeks, Hon. Renee Jones
Webster, William H.
Webster, Winston Roosevelt
West, John Andrew
West, George Ferdinand, Jr.
West, Dr. Togo Dennis, Jr.
Weston, Larry Carlton
West, Joseph King
Webb, Dr. Joseph G.
Weems, Dr. Vernon Eugene, Jr.
Weeks, Deborah Redd
West, Hon. Royce Barry
Wheaton, Esq. Frank Kahlil
White, Richard Thomas
White, Janice G.
White, Frankie Walton
White, Frederic Paul, Jr.
Wharton, A. C., Jr.
White, D. Richard
Whiting-Wright, Barbara E.
Wiley, Dr. Fletcher Houston
Wilbon, Joan Marie
Williams, James R.
Williams, Gregory Howard
Williams, Esq. Junius W.
Williams, Larry C.
Willacy, Hazel M.
Williams, Charles E., III
Williams, Clyde, Jr.
Wilmot, David Winston
Wilson, Leroy, Jr.
Williams, Robert B.
Williams, Philip B.
Williams, Randolph
Williams, Sidney B., Jr.
Williams, Wesley S., Jr.
Williams, Yvonne LaVerne
Williamson, Samuel R.
Willis, Frederic L.
Willis, Jill Michelle
Winn, Joan Tarpley
Winstead, Dr. Vernon A., Sr.
Wilson, Lance Henry
Williams, Annalisa Stubbs
Willis, Kathi Grant
Williams, Karen Hastie
Williams, Dr. E. Faye
Willrich, Dr. E. James
Wilkins, David Brian
Wilder, Kurt
Wing, Prof. Adrien Katherine
Williams, Gary C.
Wilcher, Dr. Shirley Jean
Williams, Hon. Alexander, Jr.
Wilber, Ida Belinda
Wilson, Clarence S., Jr.
Wilson, Esq. Jimmie L.
Wilson, Sonali Bustamante
Williams, Ronald Charles
Williams, Sandra K.
Williams, Bart H.
Wiley, Erleigh Norville
Wiley, Aaron L.
Williams, David, III
Williams, Gail
Williams, Maxine
Williams, Paul S.
Williams, Paul T., Jr.
Wigenton, Susan Davis
Willrich, Penny
Wideman, Jamila
Wilson, Kim Adair
Wilson, Donald K., Jr.
Worthy, Kym L.
Wood, Hon. William S.
Wood, Curtis A.
Woodhouse, Enoch O'Dell, II
Woodson, Atty. Roderic L.
Wright, Dr. Joseph Malcolm
Wright-Botchwey, Roberta Yvonne
Wright, Clinton L. A.
Wright, Hon. Geoffrey
Wright, Michael L.
Wright, Dr. Roberta V. Hughes
Yancey, Prentiss Quincy
Yarbrough, Robert Elzy
Young, Andrew
Young, Lias Carl
Young, Dr. James E., Jr.
Young, Ira Mason
Young, Dr. Artee Felicita
Zachary, Steven W.
Zealey, Dr. Sharon Janine
Zelis, Karen Dee
Zollar, Esq. Nikki Michele

## Library/Information Science

Abif, Khafre Kujichagulia
Adkins, Rodney C.
Adams, Dr. Elaine Parker
Alexander, Dr. Otis Douglas
Allen, Ottis Eugene, Jr.
Alford, Thomas Earl
Aman, Dr. Mohammed
Anderson, Barbara Louise
Arkhurst, Joyce Cooper
Ashford, Mary E.
Avery, Charles E.
Axam, John Arthur
Battle, Dr. Thomas Cornell
Barnes, Fannie Burrell
Beane, Patricia Jean
Best, Vanessa
Bean, Dr. Bobby Gene
Benning, Dr. Emma Bowman
Bethel, Kathleen Evonne
Bell, Dr. Katie Roberson
Birtha, Jessie M.
Blake, Peggy Jones
Boyd, Barbara Jean
Bowens, Dr. Johnny Wesley
Boyce, William M.
Bogger, Dr. Tommy
Bryan, Glynis A.
Brown, Dr. Malore Ingrid
Bradberry, Dr. Richard Paul
Brown, Atlanta Thomas
Burnett, Rev. Bescye P.
Butler, Kathleen Jean
Byrd, Joan Eda
Cannon, Tyrone Heath
Campbell, Sandra
Carlton, Barbara
Carter, Darline Louretha
Calhoun, Dorothy Eunice
Cash, Pamela J.
Chisum, Dr. Gloria Twine
Chapman, Kelly
Clayton, Minnie H.
Cleveland, Granville E., Sr.
Clark, Patricia Ann
Clark, Laron Jefferson, Jr.
Coleman, Dennis
Conner, Dr. Laban Calvin
Coaston, Shirley Ann Dumas
Cooke, Anna L.
Council, LaVerne H.
Coley, Denise
Coleman, Deborah Stewart
Cruzat, Dr. Gwendolyn S.
Cross, Fr. William Howard
Crayton, Dr. James Edward
Crocker, Wayne Marcus
Craft, Dr. Guy Calvin
Curtis, Jean Trawick
Culpepper, Betty M.
Cunningham, Dr. William Dean
Daniel, Celia C.
Davis, Denyvetta
Davis, Bunny Coleman
DuPree, Prof. Sherry Sherrod
Dupree, Sandra Kay
Estes, Elaine Rose Graham
Evans, Meredith
Fancher, Dr. Evelyn Pitts
Felder-Hoehne, Felicia Harris
Fisher, Alma M.
Fitzhugh, Kathryn Corrothers
Fisher, Edith Maureen
Fillyaw, Leonard David
Freeman, Shirley Walker
Fuller, Gloria A.
Gardiner, George L.
Gay, Birdie Spivey
Gill, Prof. Jacqueline A.
Gilton, Dr. Donna L.
Goddard, Rosalind Kent
Grant, Dr. George C.
Gray, Donnee L.
Gray, Beverly A.
Grigsby, Alice Burns
Gunn, Dr. Arthur Clinton
Guilford, Diane Patton
Hardy, Eursla Dickerson
Hart, Mildred
Hayden, Dr. Carla Diane
Hardnett, Carolyn Judy
Ham, Dr. Debra Newman
Hale, Kimberly Anice
Harvell, Dr. Valeria Gomez
Harris, Loretta K.
Hargrave, Charles William
Hawkins, Ernestine L.
Hayward, Olga Loretta Hines
Harris, Thomas Walter
Hewitt, Vivian Ann Davidson
Hendricks, Leta
Hicks, Doris Askew
Hinson, Ann J.
Howard, Dr. Elizabeth Fitzgerald
Holley, Sharon Yvonne
Hopkins, Dr. Dianne McAfee
Hunt, Charles Amoes
Hunter Hayes, Tracey Joel
Hudson-Ward, Alexia
Hylton, Andrea Lamarr
Irving, Ophelia McAlpin
Isadore, Dr. Harold W.
Jackson, Andrea R.
Jackson, Miles M.
Jackson, Andrew Preston
James, Dr. Stephen Elisha
James, Olive C. R.
Jackson, Dr. Ruth Moore
Jefferson, Karen L.
Jefferson, Marcia D.
Jenkins, Dr. Althea H.
Jenkins, Jo Ann
Jenkins, Barbara Williams
Johnson, Edwin T.
Johnson, Sheila Ann
Johnson, Shirley
Jones-Trent, Bernice R.
Jolivet, Linda Catherine
Johnson-Blount, Theresa
Johnson, Sheila Monroe
Jones, Gwendolyn J.
Johnson, Doris Elayne
Jones, Helen Hampton
Jobe, Shirley A.
Kendrick, Curtis L.
King, Thomas Lawrence
Knowles, Dr. Em Claire
Langston-Jackson, Wilmetta Ann Smith
Lanier, Gayle S.
Lee, Pauline W.
Leonard, Gloria Jean
Lewis, Billie Jean
Lockett, Sandra Bokamba
Lockley-Myles, Barbara J.
Martin, Rosetta P.
Marks, Rose M.
Madison, Jacqueline Edwina
Mack, Phyllis Green
Marshall, Anita
Mangum, Ernestine Brewer
McCoy, James F.
McKinney, Wade Hampton, III
McPherson, James Alan
McLaughlin, Dr. LaVerne Laney
McCray, Melvin M.
McLaughlin, Dr. Megan E.
McTyre, Robert Earl, Sr.
McCain, Ella Byrd
McCrackin, Olympia H.
McKinney, Venora Ware
McGill, Michele Nicole Johnson
McDaniel, Karen Cotton
Metcalf, DaVinci Carver
Miller-Holmes, Cheryl
Miller, Constance Joan
Miller, Robert, Jr.
Miles, Ruby A. Branch
Miller, Jacqueline Elizabeth
Miller, Erenest Eugene
Mincey, Karen
Moore, Christopher Paul
Moore, Evia Briggs
Moore, M. Elizabeth Gibbs
Mothershed, Spaesio Willar
Morrison, Samuel F.
Morgan, Jane Hale
Mohr, Diane Louise
Mobley, Emily Ruth
Moore, Hazel Stamps
Mohammad, Sandra B.
Murphy, Paula Christine
Ojumu, Ayodele
Parham, Sandra
Parham, Loretta
Page, John Sheridan, Jr.
Patterson, Grace Limerick
Perry, Emma Bradford
Peterson, Prof. Lorna Ingrid
Peguese, Charles R.
Price, Dr. Paul Sanford
Price, Pamela Anita
Ramsey, Donna Elaine
Randall, Ann Knight
Reese, Gregory Lamarr
Riley, Barbara P.
Richo, Anna
Roney, Raymond George
Roberson, Prof. Gloria Grant
Robertson, Karen A.
Royster, Dr. Vivian Hall
Robinson, Carol W.
Russell, Beverly Ann
Sapp, Lauren B.
Sarkodie-Mensah, Dr. Kwasi
Seunagal, Deborah Evans
Shockley, Ann Allen
Singley, Elijah
Simton, Chester
Sinnette, Dr. Elinor DesVerney
Slaton, Gwendolyn C.
Smythe, Victor N.
Smith-Epps, E. Paulette
Smith, Dr. Jessie Carney
Sprinkle-Hamlin, Sylvia Yvonne
Stinson, Linda
Stephens, Brenda Wilson
Strong-Kimbrough, Dr. Blondell M.
Stewart, Ruth Ann
States, Lauren C.
Stuckey, Sheila Arnetta
Sutton, Gloria W.
Swift, Linda Denise
Sylvester, Melvin R.
Terry, Patricia S.
Thompson, Bette Mae
Thomas, Dr. Lucille Cole
Thomas, Maurice McKenzie
Totten, Dr. Herman Lavon
Towns, Rose Mary

## Management/ Administration— Accounting/Financial



## Management/ Administration— Advertising/Marketing/ Public Relations

## Management/ Administration—Computer Systems/Data Processing



## Management/ Administration—Consultation/Analysis

### Management/ Administration—General

Bryant, Connie L.
Bromery, Keith Marcel
Bright, Kirk
Brooks, Derrick Dewan
Bradshaw, Wayne-Kent A.
Bridgforth, Walter, Jr.
Brandon, Terrell
Brigham, Freddie M.
Brown, Carolyn Thompson
Bryant, N. Z., Jr.
Bramble, Rev. Peter W. D.
Broadnax, Dr. Walter Doyce
Brown, Brian A.
Bryant, Russell Philip
Brown, John E.
Brownlee, Dennis James
Bryant, Franklyn
Brown, Dr. Ronald Paul
Brown, Mary Katherine
Bryant, Donnie L.
Brown, Dr. Lee Patrick
Brooks, Rodney Norman
Bryant, William Henry, Jr.
Broome, Sharon Weston
Brown, Rodger L., Jr.
Brown, Henry H.
Bryan, Dr. Curtis Eugene, Sr.
Bryant, Edward Joe, III
Brown, Bettye Jean
Brown, Stanley Donovan
Brown, Carroll Elizabeth
Bradley, Wayne W., Sr.
Bradley, Melvin LeRoy
Branche, Gilbert M.
Brockington, Eugene Alfonzo
Brinkley, Charles H., Sr.
Bridges, Leon
Brown, Lewis Frank
Brown, Norman E.
Brown, Raymond Madison
Brown, Nancy Cofield
Brown, Dr. Walter E.
Brown, Robert Joe
Brown, Eddie C.
Brown, Carolyn M.
Brown, Booker T.
Brown, Ellen Rochelle
Brown, Dr. Abena Joan P.
Brooke, Edward William, III
Bronson, Dr. Oswald Perry, Sr.
Brooks, Wadell, Sr.
Brooks, Brigadier Gen. Leo Austin, Sr.
Brooks, William C.
Brown, Arnold E.
Bryant, Jesse A.
Bryson, Dr. Ralph J.
Brown, Julia M.
Brown, Shannon A.
Brown-Philpot, Stacy
Bridgeman, Leea Nash
Bransford, Patricia
Brown, Elaine M.
Brown, Tony K.
Bryan, Glynis
Brown, Adriane M.
Brock, Roslyn McCallister
Brooks, Robin C.
Bryant, Anderson B., Jr.
Bryant-Howroyd, Janice
Brock, Lorraine
Brown-Ellen, Kimi L.
Brooks, Brian A.
Bromfield, Cassandra
Brown, Reginald L., Jr.
Brown, Dr. Diane R.
Brown, Barbara L.
Brown, Dr. Carlton E.
Brown, Heather M.
Brown, Claudine K.
Brown, Broadine M.
Bridges, Ruby Nell
Brown, Anthony Maurice
Brazzell, Dr. Johnetta Cross
Brown, Beverly J.
Britton, Barbara
Brooks, Diane K.
Branch, Rochelle
Brooks, Aaron Lafette
Briscoe, Marlin Oliver
Bridgeman-Veal, Judy
Broderick, Johnson
Brooks, Robert Darren
Brown, Gilbert Jesse
Brown, Chadwick Everett
Brown, James B.
Brooks, Pauline C.
Bryant, Homer Hans
Brown, Denise J.
Brown, Todd C.
Brooks, Fabienne
Bradley-Burns, Melissa Lynn
Bridgeman, Dexter Adrian
Brown, Christine James
Brown, Dr. J. Theodore, Jr.
Brown, Cherie Greer
Brown, Rushia
Braxton, Rev. Steve
Brown, Ruben Pernell
Bryant, John Hope
Brown, Gerald
Brown, Jim
Brooks, Joseph
Brown, Roosevelt Lawayne
Bulls, Herman E.
Butler, Duane
Burrell, Judith Ann
Buford, William Ken M., III
Burkett, Gale E.
Burnett, Robert Barry
Butler, LeRoy, III
Buckley, Marcus Wayne
Burd, Steven A.
Burke, Donna M.
Burnett, Dr. Myra N.
Bush, Esther L.
Buchanan, Shawn D.
Burris-Floyd, Pearl
Burrows, Chelsye J.
Burton, Valorie
Buford, Howard
Burgess, Chaka
Butler, Eric L.
Burton, Patricia Lewis
Bush, Dwight L., Sr.
Buckner, Dr. James Lowell
Bunyon, Ronald S.
Bullock, J. Jerome
Burroughs, Hugh Charles
Bush, Nathaniel
Butler, Oliver Richard
Burrell, Thomas J., Jr.
Burse, Raymond Malcolm
Burke, Olga Pickering
Bullard, Keith
Burges, Melvin E.
Butler, Pinkney L.
Buckner, Quinn
Burley, Jack L., Sr.
Burns, Jesse L., Jr.
Bush, Patricia R.
Butler, Mitchell Leon
Burns, Tommie, Jr.
Bullock, Thurman Ruthe
Butler, Joyce M.
Byrd, Manford, Jr.
Byrd, Lumus, Jr.
Byrd, Carolyn H.
Byrd, Lewis E.
Bynum, Dr. Juanita, II
Byers, Susan M.
Byrd, Isaac, III
Carter, Dale Lavelle
Carter, Thomas, III
Capers, James, Jr.
Campbell, Maia
Cameron, Michael Terrance
Carpenter, Dr. Barbara West
Canada, Geoffrey
Calloway-Moore, Doris
Cabbil, Lila
Carter, Shawn Corey
Cartwright, Jonathan, Sr.
Caswell, Rosell R.
Carney, Lloyd A.
Caradine, Tracy
Cadet, Ron
Cator, Johnny
Caldwell, Ardis
Cash, Lisa
Casselberry, James Arthur
Carter, Cecilia K.
Carroll, Dr. Natalie L.
Campbell, Melanie L.
Carroll, Rodney J.
Calhoun, Essie Lee
Carter, Roda Ward
Carr, Gwenn L.
Casey, Carey
Carter, Pamela Lynn
Carr, Gwenn L.
Cane, Rudolph C.
Cade, Brigadier Gen. Alfred Jackal
Caillier, James Allen
Carey, Harmon Roderick
Campbell, Emory Shaw
Campbell, Gertrude M.
Cannon, Reuben
Callaway, Louis Marshall, Jr.
Callender, Leroy N.
Carroll, Robert F.
Carroll, Sally G.
Carter, Arlington W., Jr.
Carter, Chester C.
Carter, Dr. Gene Raymond
Carter, John R.
Carter, Dr. James P.
Carter, Dr. Marion Elizabeth Louise Jackson
Carter, Dr. Raymond Gene, Sr.
Cassis, Glenn Albert
Casey, Rev. Carey Walden, Sr.
Camp, Esq. Marva Jo
Castle, Keith L.
Carter, Will J.
Carlo, Nelson
Campbell, Dr. George, Jr.
Cain, Herman
Carey, Wayne E.
Canady, Blanton Thandreus
Carter, Harriet LaShun
Carter, Kevin Antony
Carter, Kevin Louis
Carter, Ki-Jana
Carter, Troy A.
Cain, Nathaniel Z., Jr.
Castro, George A.
Carter, Anthony Jerome
Carter, Kenneth Wayne
Cadoria, Brigadier Gen. Sherian Grace
Carroll, Charlene O.
Cannon, Calvin Curtis
Campbell, Carlos, Sr.
Carter, Robert Thompson
Cartwright, Bill
Carter, Fredrick James
Cain, Dr. Robert R., Jr.
Carson, Irma
Ceballos, Cedric Z.
Chargois, James M.
Chisholm, Samuel Jackson
Chapman, Diana Cecelia
Chenault, Kenneth Irvine
Chigbu, Gibson Chuks
Childs, Joy B.
Chamberlain, Wesley Polk
Christian, John L.
Chriss, Henry Thomas
Chapman, Willie R.
Cherry, Dr. Cassandra Brabble
Chapman, Lee Manuel
Chambers, Olivia Marie
Channell, Eula L.
Chisholm, Dr. Reginald Constantine
Chrichlow, Livingston L.
Christian, Dolly Lewis
Chennault, Dr. Madelyn
Cherry, Edward Earl, Sr.
Chase, Arnett C.
Chaney, Regmon A.
Chapman, Samuel Otha, Jr.
Chase, Tony
Chase, Anthony R.
Champ-Yerby, Tami
Chaney, Matthew
Chatman, Tyrone
Chew, Vivian Scott
Chappelle, Joseph C.
Chambers, Juanita Clay
Chew, Cheryl
Chambers, Christopher J.
Chambers, Chris
Charna, Daniel A.
Chastine, Robert
Christburg, Sheyann Webb
Chamberlain, Byron Daniel
Clark, David Earl
Clark, Tony
Clemons, Sandra L.
Clark, Ralph A.
Clinkscales, Keith
Clark, Frank M.
Clardy, William J.
Clement, William A., Jr.
Clark, Walter H.
Clayton, Matthew D.
Clayton, Lloyd E.
Claytor, Charles E.
Clayton, Xernona
Clark, Mario Sean
Clark, Edward
Clark, Mildred E.
Clarke, Joseph Lance
Clipper, Milton Clifton, Jr.
Clay, Timothy Byron
Clemons, Duane Anthony
Clemons, Alois Ricardo
Clayborn, Raymond Dewayne
Clark, Gary C., Jr.
Clark, Savanna M. Vaughn
Clarke, Raymond R.
Clarke, Priscilla
Clowney, Audrey E.
Cobb, Cynthia Joan
Cobb, Reginald John
Coffey, Richard Lee
Corbin, Tyrone Kennedy
Coaston, Shirley Ann Dumas
Coleman, Derrick D.
Coleman, Frankie Lynn
Cox, Joseph Mason Andrew
Colbert, Virgis W.
Coleman, Rodney Albert
Connor, Dolores Lillie
Corley, Eddie B., Sr.
Connor, Herman P.
Conley, Mike, Sr.
Counts, Allen W.
Coleman, Leonard S., Jr.
Conyers, Jean Louise
Cohen, Gwen A.
Combs, Sean John
Cook, Levi, Jr.
Cook, Keith Lynn
Coleman, Donald
Coaxum, Harry Lee
Cockerham, Peggy
Copeland, Richard Allen
Collins, Bert
Cooper, Maudine R.
Cooper, Michael Jerome
Cooper, Barbara J.
Cox, Dr. Sandra Hicks
Cockerham, Haven Earl
Cooper, Winston Lawrence
Cobb, Ethel Washington
Cooper, Albert, Sr.
Cobbs, Dr. Price Mashaw
Cogsville, Donald J.
Coleman, Cecil R.
Coleman, Barbara Sims
Coleman, Columbus E., Jr.
Coleman, Elizabeth Sheppard
Cooper, Merrill Pittman
Copelin, Sherman Nathaniel, Jr.
Coombs, Harry James
Cormier, Lawrence J.
Conyers, John James, Jr.
Cook, Dr. Samuel DuBois
Cook, Frank Robert, Jr.
Colston, Dr. Freddie C.
Collins, Dr. Lenora W.
Combs, Samuel, III
Copeland, Margot James
Conner, Steve
Combs, Samuel, III
Conaway, Samuel L.
Council, LaVerne H.
Cotton, Thomasenia Green
Covington, Tarriel Lamont
Coakley, H. M.
Copeland, Robert S.
Corbi, Lana E.
Cofield, Marvis
Cox, Dr. Sandra
Cooper, Warren
Collier-Wilson, Wanda
Cousin, Ertharin
Compton, Charletta Rogers
Cooper, Barry Michael
Collins, Dorothy
Cole, Andrea M.
Coulter, Phyllis A.
Coleman, Robert L.
Collins, Mark Anthony
Collins, Mo
Cooper-Gilstrap, Jocelyn Andrea
Coleman, Rev. Donald LeRoy, Sr.
Coleman, Marcus Le'Sha
Coakley, William Dexter
Cobb, Delmarie L.
Cornelius, Charles Henry
Crusoe-Ingram, Charlene
Crumpton, Dr. Lesia
Cross, Howard Edward, Jr.
Crumpler, Carlester T., Jr.
Crockett, Henri
Crawford, Pam Scott
Crump-Caine, Lynn
Crosbie, Ivan
Crawford, Rainey James
Crosby, James R.
Crawford-Major, Toni
Crawford, Victor L.
Croft, Wardell C.
Crews, William Sylvester
Crawford, H. R.
Crawford, Jayne Suzanne
Crowell, Dr. Bernard Gene
Craven, Judith B.
Crosby, Dr. Willis Herman, Jr.
Crawford, Curtis J.
Crawford, Brenita
Crutchfield, James N.
Crump, Janice Renae
Cunningham, Randall
Curry, Dell
Cunningham, William Michael
Cuyjet, Dr. Aloysius Baxter
Cummings, Theresa Faith
Cuff, George Wayne
Dalley, George Albert
Dandridge, Prof. Rita Bernice
Daniels, A. Raiford
Davidson, Arthur B.
Dave, Alfonzo, Jr.
Davis, Algenita Scott
Davis, Charles A.
Davis, Herman E.
Davis, Ronald Weston
Davis, Preston Augustus
Dallas, H. James
Davidson, Carol Anthony
Davis, Steven A.
Daniels, Greg
Davis, Sonia Y.
Davis, Denise
Daley-Meleschi, Valrine
Davis, Glenn
Davis, Stacey H.
Day, John
Davis, Kery
Davis, Beverly Watts
Davidson, Hezekiah Miles
Daniels, John W.
Daniels-Carter, Valerie
Daniels, Darrell B.
Dash, Darien C.
Days, Bertram Maurice
Dash, Damon
Davis, Dr. James R.
Darden, Edwin Carley
Davis, Marie H.
Davis, Dr. Leroy, Sr.
Davis, Ronald
Davis, Rob Emmett
Daily, Lori Beard
Davis-Wrightsil, Clarissa
Dalton, Dr. David
Daniels, Phillip Bernard
Dawson, Lake
Dar, Kirby David Dar
Dawkins, Brian Patrick
Davis, Antone Eugene
Darden, Calvin Ramarro
Davis, Donald Gene
Darden, Anthony Kojo
Davie, Damon Jonathon
Davis, Thurman M., Sr.
Davis, John Wesley
Davis, James Edgar
Dates, Dr. Jannette Lake
Daniels, Willie L.
Davenport, Chester C.
Davis, William W.
Davenport, Reginald
Dawson, Bobby H.
Davis, Agnes Maria
Davis, Erroll B., Jr.
Davis, Darlene Rose
Daggs, Leon, Jr.

Hamlin, David W.
Hale, Kimberly Anice
Hamilton, Howard W.
Hardin-Diggs, Marie D.
Harris, James Larnell
Hayes-Jordan, Margaret
Harrison, Charles
Handwerk, Jana D.
Hazel, Janis D.
Harris-Diaw, Rosalind Juanita
Hardy, Kevin Lamont
Havis, Jeffrey Oscar
Harding, Michael S.
Hawkins, La-Van
Hagood, Henry Barksdale
Harvey, Maurice Reginald
Hammond, Dr. Pamela V.
Hastick, Roy A., Sr.
Hardman, Artina Tinsley
Hawkins, Ernestine L.
Harris, Ramon
Haynes, Joe A.
Haywood, Dwayne A.
Hayes, Jacquelyn
Harvey, Dr. Peter C.
Harris, Carla Ann
Harris, Dale F.
Harris, Kelly C.
Hampton, Randall C.
Harris, Steve
Haber, Lois E.
Harrison, Dr. Roderick J.
Harrison, James C.
Hamilton, Dean
Hall, Frances White
Hawkins, Paulette
Hamm, Paula
Hartsfield, Hon. Judy A.
Harrington, John M.
Harris, David L.
Harvey, Michael P.
Hancock, Herbie
Harper, Arthur H.
Hazel, Darryl B.
Hammond, Verle B.
Harris, Tricia R.
Harris, Ona C.
Hankins, Anthony Mark
Hayes, Chris
Harris, Corey Lamont
Hall, Dana Eric
Harris, Jackie Bernard
Harris, Raymont LeShawn
Harvey, Richard Clemont, Jr.
Hamilton, Ruffin, III
Hale, Marna Amoretti
Harris, Franco
Hall, Robert L.
Hare, Dr. Julia
Hakim, Az-Zahir
Hammonds, Tom
Harvey, William J.
Hammond, James A.
Hardie, Robert L., Jr.
Hardison, Ruth Inge
Harper, Ruth B.
Harper, Earl
Hargrett, James T., Jr.
Haines, Charles Edward
Hackett, Wilbur L.
Hawkins, James C.
Haynes, Dr. Rev. Michael E.
Haywood, Spencer
Hayward, Ann Stewart
Harris, Lester L.
Harris, Joseph Preston
Harris, Dr. Mary Styles
Harris, Robert Lewis
Harris, Dr. Sarah Elizabeth
Harris, Thomas C.
Harrington, Zella Mason
Harris, Caspa L., Jr.
Harris, J. Robert
Hartaway, Pastor Thomas N., Jr.
Hatchett, Joseph Woodrow
Haskins, Morice Lee, Jr.
Hatter, Henry
Harvin, Alvin
Head, Helaine
Herenton, Dr. Willie Wilbert
Henry, William Arthur, II
Henson, Daniel Phillip, III
Hendricks, Richard D.
Henley, Carl R.
Henderson, Henry Fairfax, Jr.
Hewitt, Ronald Jerome
Heard, Geoffrey A.
Henry, Alaric Anthony
Herbert, Dr. Adam W., Jr.
Henderson, Cheryl Brown
Hegamin, George Russell
Henry, Jo-Ann
Heller, Bridgette P.
Heller, Bridgette P.
Henry, Anthony Daniel
Heywood, Anthony
Henderson, Henry F., Jr.
Henderson, Major Gen. William Avery
Henry-Fairhurst, Ellenae L.
Heard, Marian L.
Herndon, Harold Thomas, Sr.
Heard, Herman Willie, Jr.
Herrington, Perry Lee
Hendon, Lea Alpha
Hedgepeth, Leonard
Henderson, Frank S., Jr.
Hendricks, Steven Aaron
Henry, Dr. Samuel Dudley
Hill, Kenneth D.
Hill, Deborah
Hill, James, Jr.
Hicks-Bartlett, Sharon Theresa
Hill, Cynthia D.
Hicks, Dr. Clayton Nathaniel
Hill, Robert A.
Highsmith, Carlton L.
Hicks, Dr. Veronica Abena
Higgins, Sean Marielle
Hill, Eric
Highsmith, Alonzo Walter
Hightower, Stephen Lamar, II
High, Claude J., Jr.
Hilliard, Amy Sharmane
Hipkins, Conrad
Hines, Jimmie
Hickman, Elnor B. G.
Hill, Bobby L., Sr.
Hill, Marvin Lewis
Hibbert, Lawrence M.
Hicks, Dr. Patricia Larkins
Hill, Colin C.
Hicks, Jimmie, Jr.
Hill, Barbara A.
Hill, George Hiram
Hill, James A., Jr.
Hogges, Dr. Ralph
Hodge, Marguerite V.
Holman, Alvin T.
Hopkins, Dr. Esther Arvilla Harrison
Horton, Pastor Larnie G., Sr.
Horton, Willie Wattison
Horne, Gerald Charles
Howard, Ellen D.
Howard, Aubrey J.
Howell, Amaziah, III
House, Kyla N.
Hollinger, Reginald J.
Howlett, Walter, Jr.
Hovell, Yvonne
Holloman, J. Phillip
Horsford, Steven
Houston, Alice K.
Hopkins, Edward Charles, Jr.
Howard, Anica
Horton, Oscar J.
Howard, Stephen
Howard, Ty L.
Holland, Darius Jerome
Holmes, Clayton Antwan
Hobbs, Daryl Ray
Holliday, Dr. Gayle
Howard, Jules Joseph, Jr.
Houston, Allan Wade
Holmes, Major Gen. Arthur, Jr.
Hodge, Ernest M.
Holman, Karriem Malik
Holland, Robert, Jr.
Holloway, Douglas V.
Holloway, Ardith E.
Holley, Sharon Yvonne
Holliman, David L.
Holmes, Emma Selean
Hornbuckle, Napoleon
Holyfield, Evander
Hooker, Douglas Randolf
Hooper, Michele J.
Howell, Rachel
Hord, Noel Edward
Howell, Rev. Chester Thomas
Howard, Ray F.
Horton, Carl E.
Holmes, Robert Kathrone, Jr.
Howard, Norman H., Jr.
Hollowell, Johnny Laveral
Horne, Dr. Edwin Clay
Howard, Leslie Carl
Holmes, Dr. Henry Sidney, III
Holmes, Larry
Houston, William DeBoise
Horton, Larkin J., Jr.
Hunter, John W.
Hunter, Edwina Earle
Hubbard, Paul Leonard
Hubbard, Josephine Brodie
Hughes, George Vincent
Hunter, Rev. John Davidson
Huntley, Lynn Jones
Hunter, Teola P.
Hutchins, Lawrence G., Sr.
Hudson, Elbert T.
Hubbard, Reginald T.
Hughes, Catherine Liggins
Humphrey, Sonnie
Huyghue, Michael L.
Huggins, Linda Johnson
Hudson, Paul C.
Hunt, Edward
Hunter, Cecelia Corbin
Hughes, Tyrone Christopher
Hughes, Mark
Huggins-Williams, Dr. Nedra
Hughes, Kori
Hurd, Bridget G.
Hunter, Kim L.
Hunter, Bryan C.
Huger, Raymond A.
Hull, Dr. Stephanie J.
Hughley, Stephanie S.
Hutchinson, James J., Jr.
Hymes, Jesse
Hysaw, Guillermo Lark
Hyman, Dr. Mark J.
Hyler, Lora Lee
Hyde, Dr. Maxine Deborrah
Ingram, Phillip M.
Ingrum, Adrienne G.
Ingram, Kevin
Innis, Roy Emile Alfredo
Irvin, Michael Jerome
Irving, Dr. Clarence Larry, Jr.
Ismial, Salaam Ibn
Isom, Eddie L.
Isaacs-Greene, Patricia
Isler, Marshall A., III
Izell, Booker T.
J., Ray
Jackson, Marcus
Jackson, Dr. Russell H.
James, Anthony R.
Jackson, George W., Jr.
Jackson-Bennett, Rosalind
Jackson, Dr. Edison O.
Jackson, Tonya Charisse
James, Lawrence W.
Jackson, Inez Austin
Jackson, Yvonne Ruth
Jackson, Lisa P.
James, Wil
Jackson, Willie Bernard, Jr.
Jackson, Arthur Howard
James, Joseph J.
Jackson, William R.
Jamison, Isaac Terrell
Jackson, Brenda
Jackson, Johnny, Jr.
Jackson, Keith M.
Jackson, Emory Napoleon
Jackson, Donald J.
Jackson, Beverly Anne
James, Alexander, Jr.
James, Kevin Porter
Jackson, William Alvin
Jackson, Clarence A.
Jackson, Gregory
Jackson, Mannie L.
James, John A.
Jackson, Elijah
Jackson, Janet E.
Jacques, Cornell
James, Juanita T.
Jackson-Crawford, Vanella Alise
Jackson, Mary
Jackson, Dr. Horace
Jackson, Kenya Love
Jackson, Gerald E.
Jacobs, Dr. Rev. Daniel Wesley, Sr.
James, Ronald
Jackson, Rickey Anderson
James, Dr. Betty Nowlin
James, Dr. Betty Harris
Jackson, Ronald G., Jr.
Jacob, John Edward
Jennings, Dr. Robert Ray
Jenkins, Monica
Jenifer, Dr. Franklyn Green
Jervay, Paul Reginald, Jr.
Jefferson, Gary Scott
Jean, Kymberly
Jefferson, Dr. Andrea Green
Jennings, Devoyd
Jemmott, Hensley B.
Jefferson, Robert R.
Jeffers, Esq. Jack
Jenkins, Dr. Melvin Lemuel
Jervay, Dr. Marion White
Jeffries, Greg
Jefferson-Jenkins, Dr. Carolyn
Jefferson, Shawn
Jemison, Aj D.
Jenkins, Jim
Jefferson, Linda
Johnson, Kimberly Lynn
Johnson, Robert E.
Johnson, Eartha Jean
Johnson, Mamie Peanut
Johnson, Marvin R., Jr.
Jones, Monique
Johnson, Cheryl P.
Joseph, David E.
Johnson, Willie F.
Johnson, Jonathan F.
Johnson, Sheila Crump
Johnson, Edward E., Jr.
Johnson, Dennis A.
Jordan, Dr. Dedra R.
Jones, Dr. Horace F.
Jones, A. Lorraine
Johnson, Dr. Shirley Bailey
Jones, Benjamin A.
Johnson, John E., Jr.
Jones, Gregory Allan
Johnson, Cynthia Ann
Jones, James Alfie
Jones, Chris
Johnstone, Lance
Jones, Brian Keith
Jones, Dr. Vivian R.
Jones, Nathaniel Jamal
Johnson, Kenneth L.
Jones, Albert C.
Jordan, Kevin
Johnson, Tiffani Tamara
Jones, Phillip Madison
Johnson, Sheila
Jones, Dr. Walter, Jr.
Joseph, Kerry
Johnson, Bennett J.
Johnson, Charles E.
Johns, Stephen Arnold
Johnson, George Ellis, Sr.
Johnson, Davis
Johnson, Edward M.
Johnson, Dr. Joseph Edward, Jr.
Johnson, Ralph C.
Johnson, Dr. Marie Love
Johnson, Walter Thaniel, Jr.
Johnson, Wilbur Eugene
Johnson, William Theolious
Johnson, Dr. William Randolph, Jr.
Jones, Benjamin E.
Jones, Elaine R.
Jones, Emil, Jr.
Johnson, Sidney
Jordan, Thurman
Jordan, Vernon Eulion, Jr.
Joseph, James Alfred
Jordan, Frederick E., Sr.
Jones, Robert Wesley
Jones, Thomas L.
Johnson, Julia L.
Jones, Gus
Jones, James R., III
Johnson, Earl
Johnson, Eunita E.
Jones, Mable Veneida
Jones, Nancy Reed
Jones, David L.
Johnson, Robert B.
Jolley, Dr. Samuel Delanor, Jr.
Johnson, Arthur E.
Johnson, Mark A.
Jones, Cheryl Arleen
Jones, Lester C.
Johnson, Costello O.
Jones, James B.
Johnson, Edward Arnet
Jordan, J. Paul
Jones, Gregory Wayne
Johnson, Carl Earld
Jones, Milton H., Jr.
Jones, Theresa C.
Jones, Michelle
Johnson, T. J.
Johnson, Fran
Jones, Francis R.
Jones, Anthony Ward
Jowers, Johnnie Edward, Sr.
John, Anthony
Jones, Esq. Ernest Edward
Johnson, Roy Lee
Johnson, Juliana Cornish
Jones, Geri Duncan
Johnson, Kevin Maurice
Jones, Ingrid Saunders
Johnson, Cato, II
Johnson, Joan B.
Johnson, Jon D.
Joseph, Lloyd Leroi
Jones, Aaron Delmas, II
Joyner-Kersee, Jackie
Johnson, Rev. William Smith
Johnson, Ray
Johnson, Wayne Lee
Jones, Grover William, Jr.
Jordan, Michael Jeffrey
Johnson, Frank J., Sr.
Jones, William Allen
Jordan, George Washington, Jr.
Johnson, Wilhelmina Lashaun
Jones, Booker Tee, Sr.
Jones, Peter Lawson
Jordan, Dr. Carolyne Lamar
Johnson, Patricia Anita
Jones, David R.
Journey, Lula Mae
Joseph-McIntyre, Mary
Kaiser, James Gordon
Karangu, David M.
Kani, Karl
Kane, Dr. Jacqueline Anne
Kaalund, Sekou H.
Keizs, Marcia V.
Kennedy, Inga D.
Kennison, Eddie Joseph, III
Keels, James Dewey
Kelly, Marion Greenup
Keith, Dr. Leroy, Jr.
Kerr, Walter L.
Kenlaw, Jessie
Kendrick, L. John, Sr.
Kennard, William Earl
Kelly, Joseph Winston, Jr.
Keeler, Vernes
Kennedy, Sandra Denise
Kennedy, Rev. James E.
Kent, Melvin Floyd
King, Dr. Reatha Clark
King, Dr. James, Jr.
Kirchhofer, Dr. Wilma Ardine Lyghtner
King, Hulas H.
Kinsey, Bernard W.
Kirby-Davis, Montanges
Kindle, Archie
King, Dexter Scott
Kirksey, M. Janette
Kidd, Herbert C., Jr.
Kilimanjaro, John Marshall
King, Edgar Lee
King, Marcellus, Jr.
King, Gale V.
Kinchen, Arif S.
King-Poynter, Marva
Kindall, Dr. Alpha S.
Klausner, Willette Murphy
Knight, Gladys Maria
Knowling, Robert E., Jr.
Knowles, Sudani
Knowles, Mathew
Knight, Thomas Lorenzo
Knox, Wayne Harrison

Myers, L. Leonard
Myers, Michael
Nalls, Patricia
Nance, Booker Joe, Sr.
Nash, Henry Gary
Naylor, Gloria
Nanula, Richard D.
Nearn, Arnold Dorsey, Jr.
Neloms, Henry
Nellums, Michael Wayne
Newsome, Ronald Wright
Neal, Frederic Douglas
Nelson, Dr. Wanda Jean
Newberry, Cedric Charles
Nelson, Ronald Duncan
Neizer, Meredith Ann
Nelson, Ronald J.
Nelson, Debra J.
Neal, Brenda Jean
Nelson, Ricky Lee
Newman, Paul Dean
Newkirk, Thomas H.
Newton, Andrew E., Jr.
Newsome, Ozzie, Jr.
Nelson, Jonathan P.
Newton, James Douglas, Jr.
Newton, Ernest E., II
Neal, Brandon
Newell, Daryl
Newman, Anthony Q.
Neal, Lorenzo LaVon
Newton, Gen. Lloyd W.
Nelson, Rex
Nichols, George
Nichols, Dr. Edwin J.
Nixon, Norman Ellard
Nibbs, Alphonse (Allie), Sr.
Nixon, Dr. Harold Lewis
Nicco-Annan, Lionel
Nichols, Dimaggio
Nightingale-Hawkins, Monica R.
Northern, Christina Ann
Norman, William Stanley
Norris, William E.
Norrell-Nance, Rosalind Elizabeth
Norris, Fred Arthur, Jr.
Noble, John Pritchard
Norman, James H.
Nowlin, Frankie L.
Norvell, Dr. Merritt J., Jr.
Northern, Gabriel O' Kara
Northern, David A., Sr.
Nunn, Gregory
Nurse, Richard A.
Nunn, John
Nunery, Dr. Leroy David, II
Nwagbaraocha, Dr. Joel O.
O'Neal, Stanley
O'Connor, Thomas F., Jr.
O'Neal, Malinda King
O'Flynn-Pattillo, Patricia
O'Neal, Rodney
O'Neal, Jermaine Lee
Oben, Roman Dissake
Obama, Michelle LaVaughn Robinson
Odom, Melanie
Odom, Clifton Lewis
Odom, Stonewall
Officer, Carl Edward
Oglesby, Joe
Ogunlesi, Adebayo O.
Ogden, Steven A.
Oglesby, Boris
Ogbogu, Eric O.
Ohuche, Emeka
Okoye, Christian Emeka
Oliver, Albert, Jr.
Oldham, Jawann
Ono, Musashi
Orduna, Dr. Kenneth Maurice
Orr, Ray
Osborne, Gwendolyn Eunice
Otis, Clarence, Jr.
Ourlicht, David E.
Owens, Mercy P.
Owens, Isaiah Hudson
Owens, Curtis
Owens, Treka Elaine
Owens, Brigman
Owens, Rev. Zelba Rene
Oxendine, Kenneth Qwarious
Ozanne, Leroy
Patton, Marvcus Raymond
Parrish, James Nathaniel
Payne, Ronnie E.
Paul, Wanda D.
Parker, Clarence E.
Parkinson, Nigel Morgan, Sr.
Pattillo, Joyce M.
Pailen, Donald, Sr.
Parker, Stafford W.
Parrish, Maurice Drue
Patrick, Pastor Charles Namon, Jr.
Patterson, Gerald William
Parker, George Anthony
Parks, James Clinton, Jr.
Patnett, John Henry
Parker, Kai J.
Patrick, Dr. Jennie R.
Parker, Rev. Matthew
Paige, Emmett, Jr.
Parker, Claude A., Jr.
Patrick, Odessa R.
Parker, H. Wallace
Parker, Doris S.
Parnell, Arnold W.
Parnell, John V., III
Parker, Thomas Edwin, III
Palms, Sylvia J.
Parker, Harry
Palmore, Roderick A.
Parker, Anthony Michael
Pace, Orlando Lamar
Parker, Anthony
Parker, Riddick Thurston, Jr.
Parson, Richard Dean
Parker, Anthony L.
Payne-Nabors, Colleen J.
Parks, Kenneth D.
Payne, Ulice, Jr.
Parham, Loretta
Parker, Mel
Paschall, Jimmie Walton
Palmer, Dr. Annette
Parham, Richelle
Peoples, Alice Leigh
Pearce, Oveta W.
Perry, Betty Hancock
Penn, James T., Jr.
Perryman, Angelo R.
Peck, Dr. Dorothy Adams
Peal, Darryl Alan
Pegram, Erric Demont
Pennington, Richard J.
Petett, Dr. Freddye J. Webb
Peters, Charles L., Jr.
Peterson, Gerard M.
Perkins, Myla Levy
Pearson, Drew
Peoples, Dr. Veo
Peters, Aulana Louise
Perry, Rev. Jerald Isaac, Sr.
Peeples, Audrey Rone
Perkins, Sam Bruce
Perry, Lowell Wesley, Jr.
Perry, Lee Charles, Jr.
Perry, Eugene Calvin, Jr.
Pearson, Michael Novel
Peoples, Harrison Promis, Jr.
Peete, Calvin
Perez, Anna
Peck, Leontyne Clay
Peebles, Daniel Percy, III
Perry, Clifford R., III
Peterson, Coleman Hollis
Peters, Rev. Dr. Pamela Joan
Perry, LaVal
Phillips, Edward Alexander
Phillips, Eric McLaren
Phillips, Rev. Dr. F. Allison
Phillips, W. Thomas
Phillips, Frank Edward
Phillips, Anthony Dwayne
Philyaw, Dino
Phillips, Charles E., Jr.
Pitts, Meagan R.
Pickrum, Lisa M.
Pickard, William F.
Pickard, Vivian R.
Pinkney, Rose Catherine
Pickett, Robert E.
Pinckney, Lewis, Jr.
Pinckney, Andrew Morgan, Jr.
Pinder, Rev. Nelson W.
Pickard, Dr. William Frank
Pinkney, John Edward
Pierce, Ricky Charles
Pickett, Donna A.
Pierre, Jennifer Casey
Pittman, Darryl E.
Pierson, Derron
Pierson, Randy
Plunkett, Raphael Hildan
Pless, Willie
Powell, Michael K.
Powell, Wilma D.
Posey, John R., Jr.
Posey, Deborah
Powers, Ray
Porter, Dr. Temille
Porter, Michael C.
Powell, Arthur F.
Powers, Laura Weidman
Poe, Fred J.
Polk, Don
Potter, Jamie
Potter, Myrtle Stephens
Powell, Juan Herschel
Powell, Adam Clayton, III
Powell, Bettye Boone
Poston, Carl, III
Poston, Kevin D.
Poe, Alfred
Ponder-Nelson, Debra
Powell, Wayne Hugh
Pogue, D. Eric Rick
Pollard, Percy Edward, Sr.
Pollard, Muriel Ransom
Pope, Mirian Artis
Poitier, Sidney L.
Powell, Gen. Colin Luther
Poussaint, Renee Francine
Powell-Jackson, Rev. Dr. Bernice
Porter, Edward Melvin
Porter, John T.
Posey, Bruce Keith
Portis, Kattie Harmon
Preston, Eugene T.
Pruitt, Michael
Prewitt, Dr. Lena Voncille Burrell
Pride, Hemphill P., II
Pride, J. Thomas
Pruitt, Dr. George Albert
Pruitt, Gregory Donald, Jr.
Pruitt, Fred Roderic
Proctor, Barbara Gardner
Prioleau, Dr. Sara Nelliene
Pryde, Arthur Edward
Price, Phillip G.
Prothro, Gerald Dennis
Pryor, Malcolm D.
Primo, Quintin, III
Procope, Jonelle
Prioleau, Oscar Eugene, Jr.
Prince-Bythewood, Gina
Procope, Ernesta G
Prior, Anthony Eugene
Pugh, Mary E.
Puryear, Dr. Alvin Nelson
Quince, Kevin
Quarles, Dr. Nancy L.
Quarles, Shelton Eugene, Sr.
Rankin, Marlene Owens
Rand, A. Barry
Rasheed, Fred H.
Rayford, Brenda L.
Raveling, George Henry
Ransom, Dr. Preston L.
Rann, Dr. Emery Louvelle, Jr.
Ramsey, Dr. Jerome Capistrano
Randall, Dr. Queen Franklin
Reeves, Julius Lee
Reese-Randle, Berdine Caronell
Reed, Cordell
Reaves, Rev. Franklin Carlwell
Reynolds, Andrew Buchanan
Reynolds, Charles McKinley, Jr.
Reed-Miller, Rosemary E.
Reed, Joe Louis
Reeves, Michael Stanley
Reid, Malissie Laverne
Reid, Duane L.
Reddrick, Mark A.
Reagon, Dr. Bernice Johnson
Reynolds, James
Reed, Derryl L.
Reid, Ronda A.
Redon, Leonard Eugene
Reed, Andre Darnell
Reynolds, Ricky Scott
Reese, Izell
Reynolds, Sandra Michele
Reason, J. Paul
Reed, Jake
Reeves, Carl Donmark, Jr.
Renford, Edward J.
Reyes, Ricardo A.
Redmond, DeVera Yvonne
Reeves, Brenda
Reid, Dr. Pamela Trotman
Rhodes, Gerald N.
Rhone, Sylvia M.
Rhinehart, June Acie
Rhea, Michael
Rhodes, Edward Thomas, Sr.
Richards, William Earl
Richards, Dr. Hilda
Richards-Alexander, Billie J.
Richardson, Joseph
Richardson, Gloster Van
Richardson, Rev. Louis M., Jr.
Rickson, Gary Ames
Richardson, Linda Waters
Rice, Linda Johnson
Richardson, Dr. Leo O.
Rich, Matty
Richardson, Otis Alexander, Sr.
Rison, Andre Previn
Richardson, Timothy Lee
Richardson, Valerie K.
Rivers, Glenn Anton
Richardson, Albert Dion
Riley, Rosetta Margueritte
Richardson, Munro Carmel
Richardson, Leon T.
Riggins, Jean
Rice, Ronald
Richmond, Jacqueline
Rice, J. Donald, Jr.
Richards-Ross, Sanya
Rideau, Iris
Rivera, Lance
Ridenour, Lionel
Rojas, Don
Robinson, Rev. Harold Oscar
Robinson, Cleo Parker
Ross, Cathye P.
Robinson, Malcolm S.
Robinson, Rashad
Ross, William R.
Robinson, Dr. JaMuir Michelle
Rogers, Esq. Joyce Q.
Robinson, Dr. Rufus E.
Roberts, Richard Ray, Jr.
Robbins, Austin Dion
Robbins, Carl Gregory Cuyjet
Robertson, Charles E., Jr.
Royster, Scott Robert
Robinson, Jeffrey A.
Romain, Pierre R.
Robinson, Ronnie W.
Roberson, F. Alexis H.
Robinson, Nina
Robinson, Beverly Jean
Rodman, Dennis Keith
Rogers, John W., Jr.
Roberts, J. Edgar
Robinson, John Moses
Rogers, Ormer, Jr.
Rogers, Rodney Ray, Jr.
Rose, Jalen Anthony
Roberts, Cecilia
Robinson, Eugene Harold
Robinson, Anthony W.
Rodgers, Pamela E.
Rochester, Geof
Roberts, Kim
Robinson, Myron Frederick
Rodriguez, Ruben
Robinson, Dr. Harry, Jr.
Rodman, John A.
Roy, John Willie
Rooks, Sean Lester
Rogers-Reece, Shirley
Roberts, Angela Dorrean
Rowe, Marilyn Johnson
Rodney, Karl Basil
Robinson, John E.
Robertson, Quincy L.
Rohadfox, Dr. Ronald Otto
Roberts, Lillian Davis
Robinson, Patricia Wilson
Rodriguez, Doris L.
Rodgers, Horace J.
Rodgers, Johnathan Arlin
Robinson, Sherman
Robinson, Smokey
Robinson, Dr. Edward Ashton, III
Robinson, John F.
Robinson, Peter Lee, Jr.
Roberts, Michael V., Sr.
Robertson, Oscar Palmer
Robichaux, Jolyn H.
Robinson, Catherine
Roxborough, Mildred Bond
Royster, Don M., Sr.
Rozier, Gilbert Donald
Robinson, James Edward
Roach, Deloris
Robinson, Kenneth
Russell, Wesley L., Sr.
Russell, Joseph J.
Russell, Campy
Ruffner, Raymond P.
Russell, John Peterson, Jr.
Rutledge, Jennifer M.
Rutledge, George
Russell, Jerome
Rusk, Reggie
Russell, Mark
Russell, Michael
Rucker, Clyde
Ryan-Cornelius, Stacey
Ryce, Sundra L.
Ryan, Marsha Ann
Salter, Kwame S.
Salter, Roger Franklin, Sr.
Sarreals, E. Don
Sanders, Joseph Stanley
Sampson, Marva W.
Satterwhite, Dr. Frank Joseph Omowale
Sanders, Laura Green
Samuels, Everett Paul, Sr.
Sanderson, Randy Chris
Sanders, Barbara A.
Samuel, Jasper H.
Sailor, Elroy
Sawyer, Deborah M.
Samara, Noah Azmi
Savage, Frank
Samuels, Bryan
Salaam, Abdel R.
Sanders, Jasmine
Saunders, David J.
Saunders, Kim D.
Sampson, James S.
Sanders, Melba T.
Samuel, Antoinette Allison
Scott, Stephen L.
Scott, Candace Yvette Willrich
Scurlock, Michael Lee, Jr.
Scott, Michael W., Sr.
Scott, Marian Alexis
Scott, Gilbert H., Sr.
Scott, Donnell
Scott, Robert Jerome
Scott, Artie A.
Scribner, Arthur Gerald, Jr.
Scott, R. Lee
Schmoke, Kurt Lidell
Scruggs, Cleorah J.
Scott, Dr. Mona Vaughn
Scott, Dr. Gloria Dean Randle
Scott, James Henry
Seals, George Edward
Sewell, Luther Joseph, Jr.
Sewell, Edward C.
Sergent, Ernest E., Jr.
Seals, Maxine Lane
Settles, Darryl Stephen
Seay, Dawn Christine
Sessoms, Glenn D.
Seabrooks, Nettie Harris
Sergeant, Carra Susan
Settles, Trudy Y.
Self, Frank Wesley
Seymore, Stanley
Searcy, Lillie
Sebree-Brown, Claudia
Seavers, Dean
Seymour, Dr. Barbara L.
Seele, Pernessa C.
Shockley, Linda Waller
Shehee, Rashaan A.
Shaw, Carl Bernard
Shelton, Helen C.
Shelton, Hilary O.
Shirley, Dr. Ollye L. Brown
Shamsid-Deen, Waleed
Short, Leslie

## Management/ Administration-Not Elsewhere Classified (*See Also* Association Management)

## Management/ Administration—Operations/Maintenance

Hardy, Michael Leander
Holliman, David L.
Hunigan, Earl
James, Wilbert W., Jr.
Jackson, Frank
Johnson, Miriam B.
Jordan, Carolyn D.
Johnson, Fran
Johnson, Ronald J.
Jordan, Steve Russell
Johnson, Dr. Charles Edward
King, Kelley A.
Lanier, Gayle S.
Lewis, Ronald N.
Lewis, Clinton A., Jr.
Lowry, James E.
Lozada, De Juana
Louis, Joseph
Lowery, Bobby G.
Martin, Walter L.
Marion, Fred Donald
Martin, William R.
Mayes, George S., Jr.
Millegan, Michael H.
Miller, George Carroll, Jr.
Monteverdi, Mark Victor
Mosley, Elwood A.
Morrison, Harold L., Jr.
Moore, Rick
Murrell, Adrian Bryan
Newell, Kevin
Neizer, Meredith Ann
Nearn, Arnold Dorsey, Jr.
Nicholas, Philip
Norwood, Felicia
Omogbai, Meme
Owens, Billy Eugene
Pitchford, Gerard Spencer
Piper, Elwood Arthur
Powers, Ray
Prophet, Tony
Reed, Cordell
Reeves, Julius Lee
Rogers, Elijah Baby
Rogers, George
Rogers-Reece, Shirley
Rogers, Charles Leonard
Sanders, Laura Green
Schenck, Frederick A.
Scranton, Brenda A.
Shavers, Dr. Cheryl L.
Smithers, Priscilla Jane
Smith, Aubrey Carl
Snead, Cheryl Watkins
Springs, Lenny F., II
Sterling, John D.
Stewart, Shelley, Jr.
Suggs, Denis
Taylor, Lorenzo James, Jr.
Taylor, Natalie Manns
Taylor, Susan L.
Thompson, Westley V.
Thornton, Matthew, III
Toney, Frederiek
Troy-Brooks, Patricia
Ukabam, Innocent O.
Verbal, Claude A.
Wade, Unav Opal
Walker, Russell Dewitt
Washington, Stanley E.
Washington, Shaunise A.
Welburn, Edward Thomas, Jr.
White, Winifred Viaria
White, Dr. Alvin, Jr.
White, Valerie D.
Whitfield, Robert Lectress, Jr.
Williams, Barbara Ann
Williams, Eldredge M.
Williams, Stanley King
Williams, Edward Ellis
Wright, Sheena
Yates, Lloyd M.
Young, William

## Management/ Administration—Personnel/ Training/Labor Relations

Adderly, T. C., Jr.
Albright, William Dudley, Jr.
Allen, Billy R.
Alexander, Preston Paul
Arrington, Dr. Pamela Gray
Ashford, Orlando D.
Augustine, Cynthia
Bailey, Lilicia
Bartlett, Lorrie
Bailey, Ronald T.
Barksdale, Mary Frances
Barrett, Iris Louise Killian
Baity, Gail Owens
Baskerville, Penelope Anne
Banks, Paula A.
Bailey, Antoinette M.
Barnes, Diane
Beckles, Benita Harris
Bell, Sandra Watson
Besson, Dr. Paul Smith
Berry, Philip Alfonso
Bethel, Nikki
Berry, Paul Lawrence
Bing, Lisa A.
Blakely, Dr. Edward James
Black, Dr. Frederick Harrison
Block, Dr. Leslie S.
Blackmon, Hon. Mosetta Whitaker
Black, Veronica Correll
Blackmon, Joyce McAnulty
Bolden, Frank Augustus
Boyd, Rozelle
Boyd, Dr. Theophilus B., III
Browder, Anne Elna
Brooks, Wadell, Sr.
Brown, Booker T.
Bradford, Lajuana
Brown, Shannon A.
Brewer, Rosalind G.
Brown, A. David
Bryant-Reid, Johanne
Bridgeman, Donald Earl
Bruce, Carol Pitt
Brown, Jurutha
Burges, Melvin E.
Butler, Gwendolyn L.
Burns, Janice Robinson
Calaway, Tonit M.
Cason, Marilynn Jean
Cates, Hon. Sidney Hayward, IV
Caldwell, Lisa Jeffries
Cammack, Charles Lee, Jr.
Carter, Jandra D.
Carter, Judy Sharon
Caldwell, George Theron, Sr.
Carter, Patrick Henry, Jr.
Caldwell, John Edward
Chalmers, Thelma Faye
Chapman-Minutello, Alice Mariah
Champion, James A.
Chapman-Hughes, Susan Evelyn
Chandler, Kerry D.
Chapman, Kelly
Cissoko, Dr. Alioune Badara
Clark, Pastor James Irving, Jr.
Clemons, Tanya C.
Clark, Della L.
Clarke, Benjamin Louis
Cox, M. Maurice
Copes, Ronald Adrian
Colyer, Dr. Sheryl Lynn
Cornell, Bob
Cooper, Linda G.
Cockerham, Haven Earl
Cooper, Lois
Coley, Denise
Collins, James H.
Crawley, Dr. Oscar Lewis, Sr.
Crusoe-Ingram, Charlene
Crosse, Rev. St George Idris Bryon, III
Cribb, Juanita Sanders
Cummings, Annette Merritt
Cureton, John Porter
Culpepper, Pamela
David, Patricia
Dais, Larry
Davis, Brownie W.
Dent, Gary Kever
Deloatch, Myrna Spencer
Dewberry-Williams, Madelina Denise
Dean, Diane D.
Dickson, Daryl M.
Dickerson, Amina J.
Doanes-Bergin, Sharyn F.
Dominic, Irwing
Douglas, Mae Alice
Dowdell, Dennis, Jr.
Dotson, Betty Lou
Dorsey, Herman Sherwood, Jr.
Dost, Janice H. Burrows
Dortch, Heyward
Dumars, Joe, III
Dungie, Ruth Spigner
Early, Robert S.
Edwards, Verba L.
Edwards, Bessie Regina
Elam, Deborah A.
Enders, Murvin S.
Evans, Gwendolyn
Fisher, Rubin Ivan
Fitzpatrick, Albert E.
Fields, Felicia J.
Finley, Sandra Jean Killingsworth
Fletcher, Milton Eric
Fleming, Alicia DeLaMothe
Flemming, Lillian Brock
Ford, Evern D.
Foster, Jylla Moore
Ford, Hilda Eileen
Ford, Darrell L.
Francis, Dr. E. Aracelis
Franklin, Clarence Frederick, Jr.
Frazier, Ramona Yancey
Gaston, Linda Saulsby
Gaskin, Jeanine
Gaston, Mack Charles
Giscombe, Dr. Katherine
Gibson, JoAnn
Glover, Diana M.
Gordon-Dillard, Joan Yvonne
Gomez, Dennis Craig
Grant, Nathaniel
Greaux, Cheryl Prejean
Green, Allison
Gray-Walker, Tracey
Graddick-Weir, Mirian M.
Graddick-Weir, Dr. Mirian M.
Gray, Brian Anton
Greene, Cecil M., Jr.
Gulliver, Robert E.
Guillory, Linda Semien
Harris, Joseph Elliot, II
Harrison, Shirley Dindy
Hawkins, William Douglas
Harris-Jones, Yvonne
Hardeman, James Anthony
Hayes-Giles, Joyce V.
Hamer, Dr. Judith Ann
Hawthorne, Kenneth L.
Harris, Eugene Edward
Harris, Robert D.
Harris, Robert Eugene Peyton
Harrington, Denise Marion
Hall, Terry L.
Henry, Grace Angela
Heard, Georgina E.
Hightower, Michael
Hill, Leo
Hopson, Melvin Clarence
Holt, Donald H.
Holloway, Cecelia
Holmes, Michael R.
Howroyd, Janice Bryant
Horton, Lemuel Leonard
Huff, Loretta Love
Hunigan, Earl
Isaac, Brian Wayne
Jackson, James E., Sr.
Jackson, Dwayne Adrian
Jackson, Alfred Thomas
James, Dr. Herbert I.
Jackson, Frank
Jackson, Kevin Allen
James, Donna Anita
Jenkins, Monica
Jenkins, Joseph Walter
Jolly, Mary B.
Johnson, Alvin Roscoe
Jones, Ronald Lyman
Johnson, Michael
Johnson, Lavera
Jordan, Dr. Dedra R.
Johnson, Vaneese
Johnson, Milton D.
Johnson, Warren S.
Jordan, Rev. John Wesley
Kenney, James A.
Keizs, Marcia V.
Kee, Linda Cooper
Kellogg, George
Kimbrough, Walter M.
King, Howard O., Sr.
King, Gale V.
King, John L.
Kimbrough, Donna L.
Lawrence, Ollie, Jr.
Lawrence, Thomas R., Jr.
Lane, Nancy L.
Lawson, Herman Ace
Lanier, Gayle S.
Lewis, Floyd Edward
Lewis, Dr. Meharry Hubbard
Leonard, Gloria Jean
Lee, Kevin Brian
Lister, David Alfred
Lister, Willa Mae
Little, Irene Pruitt
Mays, Leslie A.
Mason, William E., Sr.
Mahone, Barbara J.
Marbury, Martha G.
Marsh, Ben Franklin
Mardenborough, Leslie A.
Martin, Sylvia Cooke
McGuire, Raymond J.
McIntosh, Rhodina Covington
McDaniel, Elizabeth B.
Miller, George Carroll, Jr.
Mitchell, LeMonte Felton
Mills, Rev. Dr. Larry Glenn
Mims, Pastor Raymond Everett, Sr.
Miller, Saundra C.
Moss, Nikki
Moody, Carol Baldwin
Moragne, Maurice S.
Morrow, Laverne
Moore, Cleotha Franklin
Newman, Constance Ernestine Berry
Nunn, John
Oliver-Simon, Gloria Craig
Orr, Clyde Hugh
Osborne, Clayton Henriquez
Patton, Jean E.
Peterson, Coleman Hollis
Pearson, Marilyn Ruth
Petties, Carolyn D.
Perry, Beverly L.
Pickett, Donna A.
Powers, Clyde Joseph
Powell, Bettye Boone
Powell, Kenneth Alasandro
Polk, Eugene Steven S., Sr.
Porter, Gloria Jean
Pope, Ruben Edward, III
Powell, Robert John
Powell, Christopher R.
Procter, Harvey Thornton, Jr.
Reid, Ralph D.
Richo, Anna
Richardson, Joseph
Richardson, Ralph H.
Rosenthal, Robert E.
Robinson, Renault Alvin
Robinson, Jeannette
Robinson, John G.
Rogers-Reece, Shirley
Robinson, Ronnie W.
Robinson, Wendy Raquel
Rushing, Coretha M.
Ryan-White, Jewell
Savage, Dr. James Edward, Jr.
Sandidge, Kanita Durice
Saunders, John Edward, III
Saunders, Vincent E., III
Sargent, Dr. Virginia Hightower
Scott, Dr. Helen Madison Marie Pawne Kinnard
Scott, Ruby Dianne
Schutz, Andrea Louise
Shawnee, Laura Ann
Shelton, Charles E.
Shepard, Linda Irene
Simms, Robert H.
Smith, William Fred
Smith, Dolores J.
Somerville, Patricia Dawn
Spencer, Brenda L.
Spearman, Larna Kaye
Spurlock, Dr. Langley Augustine
Spriggs, Otha T. Skip, III
Spencer, Gregory Randall
Staggers, Robin L.
Story, Charles Irvin
Stanley, Carol Jones
Sullivan, Ernest Lee
Sutton, Dianne Floyd
Sunday, Delena Marie
Summers, Loretta M.
Taylor, Johnny C., Jr.
Tabb, Roosevelt
Taylor, Sylvia
Taylor, Mildred E. Crosby
Thomas-Williams, Jovita
Thomson, Cynthia Bramlett
Thomas, Sherri
Thompson, Jesse M.
Thomas, Isaac Daniel, Jr.
Thomas, Samuel C., Sr.
Toliver, Virginia F. Dowsing
Turner, Vivian Love
Turner, Linda Darnell
Turnquest, Sandra Close
Vannaman, Madi T.
Vertreace, Walter Charles
Washington, David Warren
Walker, Dr. William Sonny
Walker, Tracy A.
Washington, Jacqueline Ann
Ward, Lenwood E.
Warren, James Kenneth
Watson, Eric
Walker, Loretta Young
Wells-Davis, Dr. Margie Elaine
Webb, Joseph
Wims, Warner Barry
Wilson-Thompson, Kathleen
Wise, William Clinton, Sr.
Wilkins, Charles O.
Williams, Harold David
Williams, James
Williams, Karen Elaine
Williams, Annalisa Stubbs
Willacy, Hazel M.
Williams, Janice L.
Williams, Stanley King
Williams, Dr. Felton Carl
Womack, Joe Neal, Jr.
Woods, Andre Vincent, II
Wright, Elease
Wright, Michael A.
Yates, Lloyd M.
Young, Ollie L.
Young, Dr. Nancy Wilson

## Management/ Administration—Purchasing

Armstrong, William F.
Banks, Dr. Lula F.
Banks, Charlie
Brown, Thomas K.
Brannon, Deborah Dianne
Brown, Julia M.
Carey, Carnice L.
Cargill, Sandra Morris
Camphor, Michael Gerard
Clarke, Charlotte
Corbett, Dr. Alexander E., III
Connor, Dolores Lillie
Edwards, Lewis
Fleming, Vernon Cornelius
Freeman, Walter Eugene
Gibson, Wayne Carlton
Hayes-Giles, Joyce V.
Horne, June C.
Jackson, Audrey Nabors
Jenkins, Jim
Johnson, Wendy Robin
Keitt, Liz Zimmerman
Knott, Mable M
London, Roberta Levy
Marshall, Betty J.
Mercer-Pryor, Diana
Olds, Lydia Michelle
Payne, Ronnie E.
Reynolds, James W.
Richardson, Johnny L.
Sheridan, Edna K.
Smith, Lafayette Kenneth
Strudwick, Lindsey H., Sr.
Sutton, James Carter
Taylor, Sandye R.
Welch, Lolita

## Management/ Administration—Sales

Abboa-Offei, Abenaa
Alexander, Rep. Kelly Miller, Jr.
Anderson, Nicholas Charles
Baker, Gregory D.
Bassett, Dennis
Barrett, Matthew Anderson

### Manufacturing—Apparel



### Manufacturing—Chemicals and Allied Products



### Manufacturing—Drugs and Toiletries



### Manufacturing—Electrical/ Electronics Products



### Manufacturing—Food/ Beverages



### Manufacturing—Furniture/ Fixtures



### Manufacturing—Industrial/ Commercial Machinery



### Manufacturing— Metalworking Industries



### Manufacturing—Motor Vehicles



### Manufacturing—Not Elsewhere Classified



### Manufacturing—Paper and Allied Products



### Manufacturing—Textile Mill Products



### Mathematics



### Medicine—Anesthesiology



### Medicine—Cardiology

Ferdinand, Dr. Keith C.
Fletcher, Dr. Anthony M.
Fontaine, Dr. John M.
Gibson, Dr. Harris, Jr.
Grant, Dr. Augustus O.
Haywood, Dr. L. Julian
Johnson, Dr. Lucien Love
Jonas, Dr. Ernesto A.
Leggett, Dr. Christopher J. W. B.
Mays, Dr. James Arthur
Pegus, Cheryl
Pearson, Dr. Stanley E.
Quivers, Dr. Eric Stanley
Revis, Dr. Nathaniel W.
Ross, Dr. Edward
Saunders, Dr. Elijah
Sanders, Dr. George L.
Smith, Dr. Ernest Howard
Underwood, Dr. Paul L., Jr.
Watkins, Dr. Anthony E.

## Medicine—Dermatology

Braddock, Dr. Marilyn Eugenia
Earles, Dr. Rene Martin
Garrett, Dr. Jacquelyn Brewer
King, Dr. William Carl
Magee, Dr. Robert Walter
Mack, Sylvia Jenkins
McDonald, Dr. Charles J.
McNeely, Dr. Carol Jean
Melvin, Dr. Alexander A.
Moore, Dr. Milton Donald, Jr.
Peoples, Dr. Danita L.
Taylor, Dr. Susan Charlene

## Medicine—Family Practice

Adegbile, Dr. Gideon Sunday Adebisi
Adiele, Dr. Moses Nkwachukwu
Anderson, Dr. Benjamin Stratman, Jr.
Armour, Dr. Christopher E.
Audain, Dr. Linz
Bass, Dr. Leonard Channing
Bacon, Dr. Gloria Jackson
Benjamin, Dr. Regina M.
Brown, Dr. William, Jr.
Brown, Dr. Ewart F., Jr.
Butler, Dr. Charles H.
Carter, Dr. James Earl, Jr.
Caldwell, Dr. Esly Samuel
Christian, Dr. Cora LeEthel
Creary, Ludlow Barrington
Duncan, Dr. Louis Davidson, Jr.
Floyd, Dr. Dean Allen
Frazer, Dr. Eva Louise
Frazier, Dr. Jimmy Leon
Garvin-Leslie, Dr. Penola M.
Gerald, Dr. Melvin Douglas, Sr.
George, Dr. Theodore Roosevelt, Jr.
George, Dr. Alma Rose
Goodson, Dr. Leroy Beverly
Harris, Dr. Percy G.
Ham-Ying, Dr. John Michael
Hereford, Dr. Sonnie Wellington, III
Hines, Dr. William E.
Hoyte, Dr. Arthur Hamilton
Johnson, Dr. Lucien Love
Johnson, Dr. Mark S.
Johns, Dr. Sonja Maria
Jordan, Dr. Wilbert Cornelious
King, Dr. Delutha Porter Harold, Jr.
LeRoy, Dr. Gary Lewis
Little, Dr. Robert Benjamin
Martin, Dr. James Tyrone
Millett, Dr. Knolly E.
Moore, Dr. Oscar James, Jr.
Pierce, Dr. Gregory W.
Powers, Dr. Runas, Jr.
Randolph, Dr. Bernard Clyde, Sr.
Robinson, Dr. Muriel F. Cox
Robbins, Jessica Dowe
Sessoms, Dr. Frank Eugene
Shields, Dr. Clarence L., Jr.
Slade, Dr. John Benjamin, Jr.
Spigner, Dr. Donald Wayne
Strother, Dr. Germaine D.
Swinney, Dr. T. Lewis
Thompson, Dr. Deborah Maria
Tunstall, Dr. June Rebecca
Vester, Dr. Terary Y.
Wade, Dr. Eugene Henry-Peter
Walker, Dr. Manuel Lorenzo
Wash, Dr. David K.
Weddington, Dr. Wilburn Harold, Sr.
Wilkinson, Dr. Robert Shaw, Jr.
Wills, Dr. James Willard
Winston, John H., Jr.
Woodall, Dr. John Wesley

## Medicine—Internal Medicine

Arterbery, Dr. V. Elayne
Bartley, Dr. William Raymond
Baskerville, Dr. Samuel J., Jr.
Banks, Dr. Tazewell
Ballard, Dr. Harold Stanley
Bethel-Murray, Dr. Kimberly F.
Best, Dr. Sheila Diane
Bouie, Rev. Dr. Simon Pinckney
Bouknight, Dr. Reynard Ronald
Bristow, Dr. Lonnie Robert
Brown, Dr. Lawrence S., Jr.
Brown, Dr. Marsha Jeanette
Brown, Dr. William, Jr.
Brown, Dr. Leroy Bradford, Sr.
Buckhalter, Dr. Emerson R.
Bynes, Dr. Frank Howard, Jr.
Campbell, Dr. Otis, Jr.
Carter, Dr. Ricardo T.D.
Chisholm, Dr. Joseph Carrel, Jr.
Clift, Dr. Joseph William
Cooper, Dr. Edward Sawyer
Counts, Dr. George W.
Cone, Dr. Juanita Fletcher
Corbin, Dr. Angela Lenore
Cobbs, Dr. Winston H. B.
Cook, Charles A.
Curry, Sadye Beatryce
De Loatch, Raven L.
deMille, Dr. Valerie Cecilia
Dixon, Dr. Leon Martin
Dillard, Dr. Martin Gregory
Douglas, Dr. Janice Green
Duffoo, Dr. Frantz Michel
Ellis, Dr. Tellis B., III
England, Dr. Rodney Wayne
Ferdinand, Dr. Keith C.
Floyd, Dr. Winston Cordell
Flack, Dr. John M.
Fontaine, Dr. John M.
Fraser, Dr. Leon Allison
Fredrick, Dr. Earl E., Jr.
Gavin, Dr. James Raphael, III
Grate, Dr. Isaac, Jr.
Hardin, Dr. Eugene
Harris, Dr. Terea Donnelle
Haywood, Dr. L. Julian
Herring, Dr. Bernard Duane
Hewlett, Dr. Dial, Jr.
Hildreth, James
Hoffler, Dr. Richard Winfred, Jr.
Jackson, Dr. Benita Marie
Johnson-Crockett, Dr. Mary Alice
Jonas, Dr. Ernesto A.
Johnson, Dr. Lucien Love
Jones, Dr. Edith Irby
Johnson, Charles
Johnson, Dr. Cage Saul
Jones, Dr. Michael Bozelly
Joshua, Dr. Alexa A.
Kadree, Dr. Margaret Antonia
Kennedy, Dr. Karel Ralph
Kinde, Isaac
King, Dr. Talmadge Everett, Jr.
Kilpatrick, Dr. George Roosevelt, Jr.
Lathan, Dr. William Edward
Lavizzo-Mourey, Dr. Risa Juanita
Levister, Dr. Ernest Clayton, Jr.
Malveaux, Dr. Floyd Joseph
Marius, Dr. Kenneth Anthony
McCuiston, Dr. Stonewall, Jr.
McFadden, Dr. Gregory L.
Mims, Dr. Robert Bradford
Moore, Dr. Oscar James, Jr.
Mosby, Dr. Carla Mane
Nash, Dr. Daniel Alphonza, Jr.
Natta, Clayton Lyle
Neal, Dr. Green Belton, II
Osborne, Dr. William Reginald, Jr.
Owens, Dr. Cynthia Dean
Patin, Dr. Joseph Patrick
Palmer, Dr. Doreen P.
Pearson, Dr. Stanley E.
Powers, Dr. Runas, Jr.
Pruitt, Fred Roderic
Priest, Dr. Marlon L.
Reed, Dr. James W.
Render, Dr. William H., Sr.
Rhodes, Dr. Robert Shaw
Riley, Dr. Wayne Joseph
Robinson, James Waymond
Sanders, Dr. George L.
Sanders, Dr. Lawrence, Jr.
Scott, Veronica J.
Simmons, Dr. Ellamae
Silva, Dr. Omega C. Logan
Smith, Dr. Henry Thomas
Thomas, Dr. Pamella D.
Titus-Dillon, Dr. Pauline Y.
Walker, Dr. Maria Latanya
Wiley, Dr. Kenneth LeMoyne, Sr.
Wills, Dr. James Willard
Wilkinson, Dr. Robert Shaw, Jr.
Williams, Dr. Arthur Love
Woodbury, Dr. Margaret Claytor
Woodbury, Dr. David Henry, Jr.
Wright, Dr. Jackson Thomas, Jr.
Wyatt, Dr. Ronald Michael
Young, Dr. Coleman Milton, III

## Medicine—Neurology

Adams, Dr. Alice Omega
Bethel, Dr. Amiel W.
Biggers, Dr. Samuel Loring, Jr.
Black, Dr. Keith L.
Burrell, Dr. Joel Brion
Carson, Dr. Benjamin Solomon, Sr.
Chapman, Dr. William Talbert
Clayton, Dr. Alfred Bannerman
Dennis, Dr. Philip H.
Hopper, Dr. Cornelius Lenard
Hyde, Dr. Maxine Deborrah
Pierre-Louis, Dr. Constant
Williams, Dr. Hugh Hermes
Wyche, Lennon Douglas, Jr.

## Medicine-Not Elsewhere Classified (*See Also* Pharmacy; Veterinary Medicine)

Adelekan, Dr. Tahira Gittens
Adair, Dr. Robert A.
Adeyiga, Dr. Olanrewaju Muniru
Alston, Dr. Kathy Diane
Alexandre, Dr. Journel
Allen, Dr. Gloria Marie
Allison, Carolyn C.
Anderson, Dr. Arnett Artis
Anderson, Dr. Benjamin Stratman, Jr.
Armour, Dr. Christopher E.
Armstrong, Dr. Earl Magnus
Baugh, Dr. Reginald F.
Bailey, Dr. Joseph Alexander, II
Ballard, Dr. James M., Jr.
Banfield, Dr. Edison H.
Banton, Dr. William C., II
Bataille, Dr. Jacques Albert
Batties, Dr. Paul Terry
Barber, Dr. Hargrow Dexter
Beraki, Dr. Nailah G.
Betty, Dr. Warren Randall
Bell, Dr. Robert L.
Bennett, Karen
Best, Vanessa
Birchette-Pierce, Dr. Cheryl L.
Blake, Milton James
Blake, Dr. Wendell Owen
Blount, Melvin Cornell
Boone, Clarence Wayne, Sr.
Boone, Dr. Elwood Bernard, Jr.
Boschulte, Dr. Joseph Clement
Bowles, Howard Roosevelt
Boyd, Audrey B. Rhodes
Bogus, Dr. Houston, Jr.
Bowles, Dr. James Harold, Sr.
Brannon, Dr. James K.
Bryant, Dr. Patrick L.
Brown, Dr. Diane R.
Branch, Dr. Geraldine Burton
Bransford, Dr. Paris
Bridges, Dr. James Wilson
Butts, Dr. Hugh Florenz
Bugg, Dr. George Wendell, Sr.
Burrell, Dr. Joel Brion
Butts, Dr. Samantha F.
Carter, CDR James Harvey, Jr.
Carter, Dr. James Earl, Jr.
Callender, Dr. Clive Orville
Campbell, Dr. Emmett Earle
Caison-Sorey, Dr. Thelma Jann
Carter, Dr. William Thomas, Jr.
Campbell, Dr. Otis, Jr.
Capel, Dr. Wallace
Chapman, Dr. George Wallace, Jr.
Chisholm, Dr. Reginald Constantine
Chapman, Dr. Joseph Conrad, Jr.
Chambers, Dr. Donald Clive
Clanton, Dr. Lemuel Jacque
Clark, Dr. Granville E., Sr.
Coffey, Dr. Gilbert Haven, Jr.
Coggs, Dr. Granville Coleridge
Cotman, Dr. Henry Earl
Cowell, Dr. Catherine
Cooper, Dr. Charles W.
Combs, Dr. Julius V.
Cooper, Warren
Corbin, Dr. Angela Lenore
Coleman, James William
Crump, Nathaniel L., Sr.
Cruz, Dr. Iluminado Angeles
Curry, Dr. William Thomas
Cuyjet, Dr. Aloysius Baxter
Cummings, Dr. Cary, III
Dawkins, Dr. Stephen A.
Dawson, Dr. Peter Edward
Davis, Dr. Matilda Laverne
Davis-Millin, Dr. Myrtle A.
Demas, Dr. William F.
Delaney, Dallas
Dillard, Wanda J.
Diggs, Dr. Roy Dalton, Jr.
Doomes, Dr. Earl
Drake, Michael V.
Dunmore, Dr. Lawrence Alfred, Jr.
Dugas, A. Jeffrey Alan, Sr.
Duffoo, Dr. Frantz Michel
Edwards, Dr. John W., Jr.
Elders, Dr. M. Joycelyn
Ennix, Dr. Coyness Loyal, Jr.
Epps, Dr. Charles Harry, Jr.
Eugere, Edward J.
Exum, Dr. Wade F.
Farmer, Dr. Robert Clarence, Sr.
Feemster, John Arthur
Fisher, Dr. Edward G.
Fleming, Dr. Arthur Wallace
Floyd, Dr. Dean Allen
Foulks, Dr. Carl Alvin, Jr.
Folk, Dr. Frank Stewart
Fonrose, Dr. Harold Anthony
Frazier, Dr. William James
Frazier, Kenneth C.
Frierson, Dr. Michael Anthony
Funderburk, Dr. William Watson
Gayle, Dr. Helene Doris
Gibson, Dr. Edward Lewis
Givens, Dr. Donovahn Heston, Jr.
Gladney, Dr. Marcellious
Grate, Dr. Isaac, Jr.
Gray, Dr. Joseph William, III
Grant, Ernest J.
Graddick-Weir, Dr. Mirian M.
Grant, Dr. Ellsworth R.
Harris, Dr. Jazmine A.
Harrison, Sarah S.
Harris, Prof. E. Nigel
Harris, Ona C.
Hairston, Dr. Sandra Watson
Hambrick-Dixon, Dr. Priscilla J.
Hammond, Dr. Benjamin Franklin
Hall, Charles Harold
Hamberg, Dr. Marcelle R.
Harris, Dr. Percy G.
Harris, Dr. Harcourt Glenties
Harrison, Dr. A. B.
Harvey, Dr. Harold A.
Hardin, Dr. Eugene
Halyard, Dr. Michele Yvette
Hall, Dr. Reginald Lawrence
Heller, Bridgette P.
Hicks, Dr. Michael L.
Hill, Velma Murphy
Hicks, William James
Hoffman, Dr. Joseph Irvine, Jr.
Hobbs, Dr. Joseph
Hopkins, Dr. John David
Honablue, Dr. Richard Riddick, Jr.
Hosten, Dr. Adrian Oliver
Hopkins, Dr. Donald Roswell
Huggins, Dr. Clarence L.
Hurd, Dr. William Charles
Idewu, Olawale Olusoji
Jackson, Dr. Benita Marie
Jackson, Dr. Arthur James
Jackson, Dr. Rudolph Ellsworth
Jessup, Marsha Edwina
Johnson, Dr. Georgia Anna Lewis
Johnson, Dr. Lectoy Tarlington
Johnson-Carson, Dr. Linda D.
Jones, Dr. Percy Elwood
Johnson, Dr. Melvin Russell
Joyner, Lemuel Martin
Johnson, Marco
Joe, Dr. Lonnie, Jr.
Johnson, Dr. John Thomas
Jones, Dr. Herbert C.
Johnson, Dr. James Kenneth
Kennon, Rozmond H., Sr.
Kirby, Dr. Jacqueline
Koger, Dr. Michael Pigott, Sr.
Lattimer, Dr. Agnes Dolores
Lachman, Dr. Ralph Steven
Lawrence, Dr. Margaret Morgan
Lewis-Hall, Freda
Lee, Cheryl Taylore
LeNoir, Dr. Michael A.
Little, Bryan
Little, General T.
Little, Dr. Robert Benjamin
Littles, Dr. James Frederick, Jr.
Lloyd, Dr. Raymond Anthony
Lowman, Dr. Isom D.
Long, Dr. Irene Duhart
Matthews, Dr. Merritt Stewart
Mason, Dr. Terry
Marion, Dr. Phillip Jordan
Mack, Dr. Wilhelmena
Mapp, Dr. John Robert
Mabrie, Dr. Herman James, III
Maloney, Charles Calvin
Mays, Dr. William O.
Madison, Dr. Romell J.
Manning, Brian
McFaddin, Theresa Garrison
McCall, H. Carl
McKee, Dr. Adam E., II
Metcalf, Dr. Michael Richard, Jr.
Meade-Tollin, Dr. Linda C.
Meeks, Stephen Abayomi Obadele
Menzies-Williams, Dr. Barbara Ann
Mims, Dr. Robert Bradford
Miller, Dr. Russell L., Jr.
Miles, Dr. Carlotta G.
Moragne, Dr. Rudolph
Mowatt, Dr. Oswald Victor
Motley, Dr. Ronald Clark
Moore, Dr. Harold Earl, Jr.
Mutcherson, Dr. James Albertus, Jr.
Natta, Clayton Lyle
Newton, Dr. Pynkerton Dion
Nelson, Dr. Robert Wales, Sr.
Newborn, Dr. Odie Vernon, Jr.
Noel, Dr. Patrick Adolphus
Norris, Dr. James Ellsworth Chiles
Noonan, Dr. Allan S.
Onyejekwe, Dr. Chike Onyekachi
Opoku, Dr. Evelyn
Parks, Dr. Donald B.
Parks, Sonia A.
Perara, Dr. Mitchell Mebane
Penny, Dr. Robert
Phillips, Mildred Evalyn
Pinn, Dr. Melvin T., Jr.
Pierce, Dr. Raymond O., Jr.
Preston, Dr. Swanee H. T., Jr.
Prince, Dr. Joan Marie
Prothrow-Stith, Dr. Deborah Boutin
Raby, Clyde T.
Rankin, Dr. Marc E.
Reed, Kathleen Rand
Reed, Dr. Theresa Greene
Rhetta, Helen Lowe
Richard, Dr. Arlene Castain
Richo, Anna
Rice, Valerie Montgomery
Robinson, Dr. Malcolm Kenneth
Rogers, Dr. Bernard Rousseau
Robinson, Dr. William Andrew
Robinson, Dr. Lawrence Daniel, Jr.
Rosser, Dr. Samuel Blanton
Ross-Lee, Dr. Barbara
Sandridge, Dr. John Solomon
Saffold, Dr. Oscar E.
Satcher, Dr. David
Savage, Dr. Edward W., Jr.
Saffore, Lateef
Scott, Wesley Ellington
Scott, Dr. Deborah Ann
Scipio, Dr. Laurence Harold
Scantlebury-White, Dr. Velma Patricia

## Medicine—Obstetrics/ Gynecology



## Medicine—Ophthalmology



## Medicine—Pathology



## Medicine—Pediatrics



## Medicine—Psychiatry



## Medicine—Radiology



## Medicine—Surgery

## Meteorology



## Military—Air Force



## Military—Army



## Military—Coast Guard



## Military—Marine Corps



## Military—National Guard



## Military—Navy



## Military—Not Elsewhere Classified



## Mining/Quarrying



## Modeling



## Mortuary Services



## Moving Services (*See* Transportation/Moving Services)

## Music—Composing/Songwriting

## Music—Conducting/ Directing



## Music—Instrumental



## Music—Not Elsewhere Classified

Marsalis, Delfeayo
Maxwell
May, Derrick
Mabson, Glenn T.
Maultsby, Rev. Dr. Sylvester
Mc Lyte
McFerrin, Sara Elizabeth Copper
McWright, Carter C.
McCampbell, Ray Irvin
McDaniels, Darryl
Miller, Percy Robert
Mos Def
Moore, Shameik
Morris, Wanya Jermaine
Monet, Jerzee
Morgan, Dolores Parker
Moore, Dorothy Rudd
Moore, Melba
Muhammad, Ali Shaheed
Nelly
Nesby, Ann
Nichols, Nichelle
Nicholas, Philip
O'Flynn-Pattillo, Patricia
Oliver, Bilal Sayeed
Parker, Ray, Jr.
Pharris, Chrystee
Phifer, Mekhi Thira
Powell, Doc
Queen Latifah
Ramseur, Andre William
Reid, Antonio
Reagon, Dr. Bernice Johnson
Reddick, Lance S.
Rodriguez, Ruben
Rock, Chris
Robinson, Dawn Sherrese
Robinson, Smokey
Rihanna
Rush, Otis
Saddler, Joseph
Sermon, Erick
Simmons, Russell Wendell
Singleton, Ernie
Smith, Howlett P.
Stockman, Shawn Patrick
Staples, Mavis
Starr, Fredro
Taylor, Dr. Dale B.
Taylor, Almina Roberts
Thomas, Terence
Thompson, Derrick
Thomas, Carl
Tresvant, Ralph Edward, Jr.
Usher
Washington, Ada Catherine
Watley, Jody Vanessa
Walden, Narada Michael
Walker-Slocum, Frances
Waters, Willie Anthony
Walker, Pastor Terry
Westbrooks, Logan H.
White, Dr. Clayton Cecil
White, Persia
White, Maurice
Wise-Harrison, Pamela Dorsey
Williams, Harvey
Winans, Mario
Wimberley, Frank
Williams, Bernie
Wilson, Ken
Williams, James Arthur
Williams, Hilda Yvonne
Williams, Vanessa Lynne
Williams, Russell, II
Woods-Wright, Tomica

## Music—Vocal

Addison, Adele
Adams, Oleta Angela
Adams, Yolanda Yvette
Allah, Rakim
Allison, Verne
Ali, Tatyana Marisol
Alston, Gerald
Albert, Donnie Ray
Armstrong, Vanessa Bell
Arnold, Monica Denise
Archer, Michael Eugene
Arroyo, Prof. Martina
Arnold, David
Atkins, Erica
Atkins, Tina
Austin, Patti
Baker, Anita Denise
Battle, Kathleen Deanna
Baylor, Helen
Barksdale, Chuck
Ballard, Shareese Renee
Bailey, Philip
Babatunde, Obba
Barcliff, Melvin
Badu, Erykah
Benymon, Chico
Berry, Chuck
Benson, George
Belafonte, Harry
Bell, Ricky
Beverly, Frankie
Blige, Mary Jane
Blow, Kurtis
Blake, Jennifer Lynn
Bodrick, Leonard Eugene
Brooks, Avery Franklin
Braxton, Toni Michelle
Bryson, Peabo
Brown, Bobby
Brooks, Lonnie
Brown, Dr. Uzee, Jr.
Burgess, Tituss
Burke, Alfreda
Butler, Jerry
Carrington, Terri Lyne
Carey, Mariah
Campbell, Tevin Jermod
Caesar, Shirley Ann
Cage, Athena
Cantrell, Blu
Cade, Walter, III
Carroll, Diahann
Chapman, Kelly
Christian, Eric Oliver, Jr.
Chapman, Tracy
clark, Karen
Clouden, LaVerne C.
Clark, Rosalind K.
Clark, Tempy M. Hoskins
Collins, Bootsy
Cook, Victor Trent
Cooper, Bridgett Louise
Costen, Dr. Melva Wilson
Combs, Sean John
Cole, Natalie
Crouch, Pastor Andrae Edward
Cummings, Terry
Day, Morris Eugene
Davis, Guy
Davis, Billy, Jr.
Davis, Clarence A.
Davis, Rev. Clifton Duncan
Desert, Alex
DeBarge, El
Denton, Sandra
DeVoe, Ronald Boyd, Jr.
Digga, Rah
Dixon, Rodrick
Dixon, Brandon Victor
Douglas, Ashanti Shequoiya
Downing, Will
Dobbs, Mattiwilda
Domino, Fats, Jr.
Douglas, Elizabeth (Betty) Asche
Douglas, Suzzanne
Dogg, Snoop
Dre, Dr.
Easton, Earnest Lee
Ellis, Terry Lynn
Elliott, Missy
Estill, Dr. Ann H. M.
Estes, Simon Lamont
Evans, Ernest
Evans, Faith Renee
Falana, Lola
Fischer, Lisa
Flack, Roberta
Freeland, Robert Lenward, Jr.
Franklin, Aretha Louise
Franklin, Kirk Dwayne
Freelon, Nnenna
Gaynor, Gloria
Garrett, Denise Eileen
Gary, Kathye J.
Gamble, Kenneth
Gainer, Prof. John F.
Gist, Carole Anne-Marie
Gill, Johnny, Jr.
Giddens, Rhiannon
Golson, Benny
Gray, Macy
Graves, Denyce Antoinette
Green, Rev. Albert Leornes
Guest, William, II
Guy, Buddy
Harper, Benjamin Chase
Hailey, JoJo
Hailey, K-Ci
Harris, Corey
Hammond, Fred
Hawkins, Edwin
Harris, Shawntae
Hanna, Cassandra H.
Haley, Prof. Johnetta Randolph
Hammer, M. C.
Hardy-Woolridge, Karen E.
Hawkins, Tramaine
Hewett, Howard
Herron-Braggs, Cindy Ann
Hendricks, Barbara
Hendricks, Jon Carl
Headley, Heather
Henderson, Barrington
Hill, Rev. Dr. Robert Lee
Hill-Marley, Lauryn Noelle
Hicks, D'Atra
Hopkins, Telma Louise
Houston, Cissy
Holliday, Jennifer-Yvette
Howard, Wardell Mack
Ighner, Benard T.
Ingram, James Edward
Ivey, Artis Leon, Jr.
Iverson, Johnathan Lee
Jackson, Millie
Jackson, Rebbie
Jarreau, Alwyn Lopez
Jackson, Freddie Anthony
Jackson, La Toya Yvonne
James, Cheryl R.
Jackson, Janet Damita Jo
Jenkins, Ella Louise
Jeffers, Eve Jihan
Jean, Nelust Wyclef
Jones, Kimberly Denise
Jones, Nasir
John, Dr. Mable
Jolley, Willie
Jordan, Montell Dusean
Jones, Donell
Jones, Quincy Delight, Jr.
Jones, Jennifer
Johnson, Willie
Jones, Maxine
Johnson, Beverly
Jones, Grace
Junior-Spence, Rev. Samella E.
Keys, Alicia
Kenoly, Samuel
Kenoly, Bingo
Kee, John P.
Kenoly, Ron
Kelly, Robert Sylvester
Khan, Chaka
King, B. B.
King, Rev. Charles E.
Kirk-Duggan, Rev. Dr. Cheryl Ann
Knight, Bubba
Knight, Gladys Maria
Knowles, Beyonce Giselle
Kravitz, Lenny
Lattimore, Kenny
Laine, Dame Cleo
LaBelle, Patti
LeVert, Eddie, Sr.
Lee, William James Edwards, III
Lewis, Keirston
Legend, John
Lewis-Scott, Aisha
Loc, Tone
Love, Darlene
Lynn, Lonnie Rashid, Jr.
Lynn, Barbara
Madison, Yvonne Reed
Marchand, Inga Fung
Mathis, Johnny
Mayfield, JoAnn M.
Maynor, Vernon Perry
Marrow, Tracy Lauren
Matthews, Denise
Maynor, Kevin Elliott
McCoo, Marilyn
McNeil, DeeDee
McDonald, Audra Ann
McFerrin, Bobby
McClurkin, Donnie
McCorvey, Dr. Everett D.
McKnight, Brian
McNeill, Cerves Todd
McDonald, Audra
McClain, Andre
Mcknight, Claude V., III
Miller, Percy Romeo, Jr.
Minaj, Nicki
Miller, Patina
Mitchell, Brian Stokes
Miller, Percy Robert
Michel, Samuel Prakazrel
Mills, Stephanie
Mitchell, Leona Pearl
Morgan, Meli'sa
Moore, Chante Torrane
Moss, Anni R.
Moore, Samuel David
Monae, Janelle
Moore, Johnny Belle
Moore, Kevin
Murphy, Eddie
Nash, John Lester, Jr.
Nelson, Novella C.
Neville, Aaron
Nicholas, Philip
Nicholas, Brenda L.
Norwood, Brandy
Norton, Cheryl Week
Norman, Jessye Mae
O'Neal, Shaquille Rashaun
Odom, Leslie, Jr.
Osby, Patricia Roberta
Osborne, Jeffrey Linton
Patton, Antwan Andre
Peoples, Dottie
Penniman, Richard Wayne
Peniston, CeCe
Pinkins, Tonya
Porter, Billy
Pride, Rita McKinley
Price, Kelly Cherelle
Price, Leontyne
Pride, Charley Frank
Ray, Prof. William Benjamin, Sr.
Ralph, Sheryl Lee
Reeves, Dianne
Reeves, Martha Rose
Reese, Della
Rhymes, Busta
Ridenhour, Carlton Douglas
Riley, Amber
Rivers, Johnny
Richie, Lionel Brockman, Jr.
Robinson, Smokey
Ross, Diana
Rowland, Kelly Trene
Rucker, Darius
Russell, Sandra Anita
Rushen, Patrice Louise
Sabree, Clarice Sylla
Saddler, Joseph
Saadiq, Raphael
Salter, Sam
Samuel, Seal Henry Olusegun Olumide
Adeola
Scott, Jill
Shirley, Dr. George Irving
Shamborguer, Naima
Simpson, Valerie
Simpson, India Arie
Sims, Robert
Simmons, Earl
Smith, Clifford
Smallwood, Richard
Smith, Prof. Andrew W.
Smith, Howlett P.
Smith, Will
Soulchild, Musiq
Spencer, Tracie Monique
Stripling, Dr. Luther
Studdard, Ruben
Stone, Angie
Staton, Canzetta Maria
Still, Valerie
Sumpter, Tika
Sweat, Keith
Thomas, Rozonda
Thomas, Irma
Tyler, Michael Lawrence
Tyson, Ron
Uggams, Leslie
Walden, Narada Michael
Warwick, Dionne
Watkins, Tionne Tenese
Waters, Crystal
Washington, Keith
Watley, Jody Vanessa
Walker, Bishop Hezekiah Xzavier, Jr.
White, Maurice
White, Karyn Layvonne
Whittaker, Yolanda
White, Dr. Clayton Cecil
Williams, Esq. Junius W.
Williams, Earl
Wilson, Nancy
Wilson, Cassandra
Winans, Pastor Marvin L.
Wilson-Knox, Shanice Lorraine
Winans, CeCe
Winans, BeBe
Williams, Alyson
Williams, Deniece
Wilson, Charlie Kent
Williams, Saul Stacey
Wilson, Bryan
Winans, Angelique
Williams, Douglas LeAllen
Williams, Melvin
Wilson, Mary
Williams, Michelle
Wilds, Tristan Paul Mack
Williams, Pharrell
Winans, Vickie
Winans-Lowe, Debbie Renee
Winans, Mario
Wow, Bow
Wonder, Stevie
Wormley, Cynthia L.
Young, Thomas

## Nursing

Addison, Caroline Elizabeth
Alexander, Josephine
Allen, Dr. Karen M.
Arnold, Nancy
Barksdale, Rosa Kittrell
Bell, Doris E.
Bellamy, Ivory Gandy
Benoit, Edith B.
Bivens, Shelia Reneea
Bolton, Dr. Linda Burnes
Britton, Elizabeth
Brown, Mary Boykin
Brown, Dr. Alyce Doss
Butler, Tonia Paulette
Carey, Audrey L.
Caggins, Dr. Ruth Porter
Calvert, Dr. Wilma Jean
Campbell, Dr. Arthur Ree
Creft, Brenda K.
Davis, Dr. Sheila Parham
Daniel, Dr. Elnora D.
Essiet, Dr. Evaleen Johnson
Essoka, Gloria Corzen
Foster, Dr. Portia L.
Foxall, Dr. Martha Jean
Franklin, Costella M.
Frye, Nadine Grace
Gaskin, Dr. Frances Christian
Goodwin, Della McGraw
Gordon, Bertha Comer
Griffin, Lula Bernice
Grant, Ernest J.
Gunter, Laurie
Harrington, Zella Mason
Haynes, Barbara Asche
Hamilton, Jonnie
Hendricks, Dr. Constance Smith
Hicks, Augusta M. Gale
Holland, Ethel Marie
Holland-Calbert, Mary Ann
Howard-Coleman, Billie Jean
James, Carrie Houser
Johnson, Margie N.
Jordan, Jacquelyn D.
Johnson, Dorothy M.
Kennedy, Bernice Roberts
Lane, Daphene Corbett
Lawrence, Annie L.
Lacey, Dr. Bernardine M.
Leak, Virginia Nell
Lloyd, Dr. Barbara Ann
Maryland, Mary Angela
Martin, Patricia Elizabeth
Martin, Wanda C.

## Nutrition



## Oceanography



## Optometry



## Personnel Management (*See Also* Management/ Administration—Personnel/ Training/Labor Relations)

## Pharmacology



## Pharmacy



## Philanthropy



## Photography (*See Also* Journalism—Photojournalism)



## Physics/Astronomy



## Physiology



## Podiatry



## Political Science



## Printing (*See* Publishing/Printing)

## Psychology

Samkange, Dr. Tommie Marie
Savage, Horace Christopher
Saddler, Dr. Elbert M., II
Shipp, Dr. Pamela Louise
Shell, Dr. Juanita
Smith, Dr. James Almer, III
Smith, Dr. Marie Evans
Spencer, Prof. Margaret Beale
Stokes, Julie Elena
Suite, Dr. Derek H.
Tatum, Dr. Beverly Daniel
Tate, Dr. Lenore Artie
Taylor, Dr. Sandra Elaine
Terrell, Dr. Francis
Thomas, Dr. John Henderson, III
Thornton, Dozier W.
Thompson, Dr. Beatrice R.
Toldson, Ivory A.
Tucker, Dr. Leota Marie
Turner, Dr. Castellano Blanchet
Tucker, Dr. Samuel Joseph
Tucker, Dr. M. Belinda
Vaughans, Kirkland Cornell
Vogel, Dr. Roberta Burrage
West, Dr. Gerald Ivan
White, Dr. Tommie Lee
Whitney, Dr. W. Monty
Whitaker, Von Frances
White, Paul Edward
Williams, Deborah A.
Wilderson, Thad
Winfield, Dr. Linda Fitzgerald
Wilderson, Dr. Frank B., Jr.
Williams, Dr. Daniel Edwin
Williams, Dr. Everett Belvin
Wilson, Dr. Sodonia Mae
Williams, Dr. Robert L.
Williams, Dr. Willie S.
Young, Dr. Carlene Herb
Young, Dr. Josef A.

## Public Utilities

Adderly, T. C., Jr.
Ambeau, Karen M.
Anthony, Bernard Winston
Barney, Lemuel Jackson
Baugh, Lynnette B.
Blackmon, Edward, Jr.
Bryant, Anthony
Bunting, Theo H., Jr.
Crutchfield, Lisa
Daniels, Alfred Claude Wynder
DeGraffenreidt, James Henry, Jr.
Dorsey, Herman Sherwood, Jr.
Doby, Allen E.
Enders, Murvin S.
Flint, Mary Frances
Fontenot-Jamerson, Berlinda
Grantley, Robert Clark
Griffith, John A.
Harris, Robert Lewis
Harrell, William Edwin
Hayes-Giles, Joyce V.
Horton, Dollie Bea Dixon
Jackson, Brenda
Jennings, Devoyd
Jones, Delores
King, Gwendolyn Stewart
Lanier, Gayle S.
Loyd, Walter, Jr.
Lofton, Andrew James
Lucas, Victoria
McCarrell, Clark Gabriel, Jr.
McPherson, James R.
McCraw, Tom
McZier, Arthur
McGhee, Samuel T.
McKinney, Samuel Berry
Morris, Herman, Jr.
Moore, Gregory B.
Moore, Ronald
Penn, Mindell Lewis
Reed, Esq. Jerrildine
Rollins, Lee Owen
Roland, Benautrice, Jr.
Rogers, Alfred R.
Rogers, Desiree Glapion
Taylor, Andre Jerome
Taylor, S. Martin
Tate, Sherman E.
Thomas, Samuel C., Sr.
Thaxton, June E.
Tufon, Chris
Turner, George Cordell, II
Urdy, Dr. Charles E.
Watkins, William, Jr.
Ware, Irene Johnson
Wagoner, J. Robert
Watts, Patricia L.
Washington, Earlene
Washington, Nancy Ann
Whitehead, David William
Williams, James
Wright, Michael A.
Yates, Lloyd
Yates, Lloyd M.

## Publishing/Printing

Abebe, Ruby
Abbott, Leandra
Adams, Floyd, Jr.
Allen, S. Monique Nicole
Bauldock, Gerald, Sr.
Bailey-Thomas, Sheryl K.
Bass, Patrick Henry
Barrett, Audra
Baquet, Dean
Bailey, Harry Augustine, Jr.
Beckham, Barry Earl
Benton, Angela
Bell, Alberta Saffell
Benson, Wanda Miller
Black, David Eugene, Sr.
Blair, Dr. George Ellis, Jr.
Bobb-Semple, Crystal
Booker, Michael
Bowens, Gregory John
Boyd, Terry A.
Brown, Marie Dutton
Brown, Barbara Ann
Bronner, Bernard
Bridgeman, Dexter Adrian
Bronner, Sheila
Buckner, Floyd
Burns-Cooper, Ann
Burton, Ronald J.
Burns, Jeff, Jr.
Carter, Dr. Stephen L.
Carter, Jackie
Canedy, Dana
Chapman, Kelly
Chappell, Kevin
Checole, Prof. Kassahun
Chandler, Alton H.
Conyers, Nathan
Colvin, Alonza James
Cole, Harriette
Cross-White, Agnes
Crosby, James R.
Crawford, Jayne Suzanne
Daly, Ronald Edwin
Doss, Rod
Drayton-Martin, Michelle
Drew, Kenneth R.
Driver, Richard Sonny, Jr.
Driver, David E.
Ducksworth, Marilyn Jacoby
DuPree, Prof. Sherry Sherrod
Dunn, Linda Spradley
Earl, Dr. Archie, Sr.
Eady, Lydia Davis
Easter, Eric Kevin
Ebanks, Michelle
Edwards, Dr. Claudia L.
Edwards, Preston Joseph, Sr.
Edmonds, Tracey E.
Edwards, Audrey Marie
Ellison, Keith
English, Dr. Perry T., Jr.
Enoch, John D.
Erving, John, Jr.
Eubanks, W. Ralph
Fairley, Juliette S.
Farrar, Moses
Ferguson, Dr. Robert Lee, Sr.
Fischer, William S.
Fornay, Alfred R., Jr.
Fountleory, Millicent
Foard, Frederick Carter
Fraser, George C.
Frazier, Shirley George
Gant, Crystal M.
Glover, Robert G.
Graves, Earl Gilbert, Sr.
Grant, Ian
Grant, Dr. Gwendolyn Goldsby
Grant, Dr. George C.
Gray, Wilfred Douglas
Graves, Earl Gilbert, Jr.
Guy-Sheftall, Beverly
Hansford, Louise Todd
Harris-Diaw, Rosalind Juanita
Harris, Peter J.
Hailey, Priscilla W.
Harris, Charles F.
Hartman, Hermene Demaris
Hill, Paul, Jr.
Hines, Courtney
Holt, Deloris Lenette
House, Michael A.
Hudson, Cheryl Willis
James, Juanita T.
Jackson, Karen Denise
Jervay, Paul Reginald, Jr.
Jeffers, Ben L.
Joseph, Hon. Raymond Alcide
John, Dr. Mable
Johnson, R. Benjamin
Johnson, Frank J., Sr.
Kafele, Baruti Kwame
Kelly, Dr. John Russell
Kearney, Eric Henderson
Kearse, Gregory Sashi
Kilimanjaro, John Marshall
Kirksey, M. Janette
Latif, Naimah
Lewis, James D.
Lee, Dr. Debra Louise
Lewis, Ida Elizabeth
Lewis, Edward T.
Lee, Dr. William H.
Light, Alan
Logan, Dr. John C., Jr.
Love, Dr. Ruth Burnett
Lovick, Calvin L.
Lottier, Patricia Ann
Lyons, Charlotte
Mack, Donald J.
McDaniels, Darryl
McPherson, Rosalyn J.
McElroy, Dr. Lee A., Jr.
McClure, Frederick Donald
McKnight, Reginald
McWright, Carter C.
Meyer, Alton J.
Means, Pat
Messiah-Jiles, Sonceria
Minor, Keija
Miller, Mitzi
Miller, Jones Sandy
Minor, Tracey L.
Millender, Mallory Kimerling, Sr.
Moragne, Lenora
Morris, Celeste
Morant, Mack Bernard
Moore-Poole, Jessica Care
Mumford, Esther Hall
Nichols, Alfred Glen
Norment, Lynn Aurelia
O'Flynn-Pattillo, Patricia
Oliver, John J., Jr.
Oliver, Jake
Onli, Turtel
Parham, Marjorie B.
Patterson, Barbara Ann
Paschall, Evita Arneda
Pemberton-Heard, Dr. Danielle Marie
Perry, Rita Eggleton
Peters, William Alfred
Perkins, John M.
Perry, Pam Elaine
Pierce, Ponchitta A.
Porter, Dr. Charles William
Powell, Charles Arthur
Posey, John R., Jr.
Rawls, Mark Anthony
Ray, Walter I., Jr.
Randolph, Laura B.
Rhodes, Jeanne Simmons
Rhinehart, June Acie
Rice, Linda Johnson
Roney, Raymond George
Roebuck-Hayden, Marcia
Robinson, Beverly Jean
Robinson, Nina
Roby, Kimberla Lawson
Rogers, Desiree Glapion
Russell, Mark
Samuel, Jasper H.
Scott, Marian Alexis
Scott, Alexis
Sessoms, Dr. Frank Eugene
Shepphard, Dr. Charles Bernard
Shelton, Charles E.
Shockley, Linda Waller
Smith, Clarence O.
Smith, John B., Sr.
Smith, Janet Maria
Smith, Norman Raymond
Smith, Dr. Charles U.
Sockwell, Oliver R., Jr.
Spight, Benita L.
Spruell, Sakina P.
Sterling, H. Dwight, Sr.
Stewart, Ruth Ann
Tandy, Dr. Mary B.
Tarpley, Natasha Anastasia
Taylor, Susan L.
Tatum, Elinor Ruth
Thompson, Derrick
Thompson, Dr. Charles H.
Trammer, Monte Irvin
Turner, Yvonne Williams
Tucker-Allen, Dr. Sallie
Vance-Cooks, Davita
Vest, Donald Seymour
Vest, Hilda Freeman
Washington, James A.
Washington, Alonzo Lavert
Ware, Janis L.
Ware, William J.
Wesley, Dr. Herman Eugene, III
Wells, Billy Gene
Weathers, Diane
Whitworth, Claudia Alexander
Winston, Dr. Michael Russell
Williford, Stanley O.
Wilmore, Rev. Gayraud Stephen, Jr.
Williams, John Alfred
Willis, Frank B.
Wilson, F. Leon
Williams, Dr. Eddie Nathan
Williams, Karen
Woods, Kondria Yvette Black
Worth, Janice Lorraine
Woodruff, Cheryl
Wooten, Carl Kenneth, Jr.
Wright, Carl Jeffrey
Wright, Crystal Andrea
Youssef, Sitamon Mubaraka
Young, Katye H. McLaughlin
Young, Albert James

## Radio Broadcasting Industry

Anderson, Sunny
Arnold, Dr. John Russell, Jr.
Baisden, Michael
Bambaataa, Afrika
Banks, Alicia
Banks, Carl E.
Bailey, Lee
Benham, Dr. Robert
Berry, Bertand Demond
Beckles, Ian Harold
Beach, Walter G., II
Bishop, Blaine Elwood, Jr.
Blake, Neil
Brownlee, Dennis J.
Brown, Larry, Jr.
Brown, Reginald Royce, Sr.
Brown, Floyd A.
Brooks, Derrick Dewan
Brown, Lomas, Jr.
Brown, Timothy Donell
Butler, Clary Kent
Burley, Dale S.
Burchell, Dr. Charles R.
Burnett, Robert Barry
Campbell, Lamar
Carter, Robert T.
Chretien, Gladys M.
Chideya, Farai
Cole, Lydia
Collinet, Georges Andre
Coles, Bimbo
Coleman, Rev. Donald LeRoy, Sr.
Coleman, Marco Darnell
Covington, Tarriel Lamont
Cornish, Audie
Curry, Rev. Victor Tyrone
Davis, Nathaniel Alonzo
Davenport, Ronald R., Sr.
Daniels, Preston A.
Davis, Gregory T.
Davis, William Delford
Dickerson, Thomas L., Jr.
Durant, Bishop Naomi C.
Ellis, LaPhonso Darnell
Evans, Elizabeth
Fair, Terrance Delon
Finley, Skip
Floyd, Vernon Clinton
Fletcher, Cliff
Floyd, Cliff, Jr.
Frazier, Ray Jerrell
Franklin, Linda Cheryl Kennedy
Freeland, Shawn Ericka
Fuller, William Henry, Jr.
Gaines, Hon. Adriane Theresa
Germany, Albert
Gilliam, Herman Arthur, Jr.
Golightly, Lena Mills
Green, Victor Bernard
Graham, Jeff Todd
Green, Verna S.
Harvey, Linda Joy
Hampton, Cheryl Imelda
Hawkins, Artrell, Jr.
Haines, Charles Edward
Harris, Daisy
Hickson, Dr. William F., Jr.
Hines, Rosetta
Higginson, Vy
Horton, Dollie Bea Dixon
Hopson, Harold Theodore, Jr.
Howard, Samuel Houston
Hodgins, James William
Hughes, Catherine Liggins
Jackson, Keith Jerome
Jackson, Gordon Martin, Jr.
Jones, Rev. Robert Bernard
Johnston, Ernest
Joyner, Thomas
Joyner, Oscar Albert
Johnson, Marlene E.
Kalu, Ndukwe Dike
Kennard, Patricia A.
Lacy, Donald E., Jr.
Law, Robert Louis
Lamb, Sabrina
Lee, Aubrey Walter, Jr.
Long, John Eddie
Logan, Dr. John C., Jr.
Mason, John
Martin, Roland S.
Majors, Jeff
Manney, William A.
Mathews, Keith E.
Marshall, Pluria William, Jr.
Mahorn, Rick
Mayo, Barry Alan
McKee, Lonette
McKinney, Billy
Meek, Dr. Russell Charles
Miles, George L., Jr.
Moncrieffe, Peter
Moss, Anni R.
Muhammad, Askia
Muhammad, James A.
Myrick, Dr. Howard A.
Nightingale-Hawkins, Monica R.
Pritchard, Michael Robert
Rawls, Mark Anthony
Reese, Ike
Rivero, Marita
Royster, Scott Robert
Robinson, Eugene Keefe
Robinson, James Edward
Satchell, Elizabeth
Sainte-Johnn, Don
Sanders, Frank Vondel
Sanders, Jasmine
Saunders, William Bill
Segar, Leslie
Shields, Rev. Del Pierce
Sherrell, Charles Ronald, II
Simpson, Donnie
Smith, Dr. Judith Moore
Smith, Darryl C.
Smith, C. Miles
Smith, J. Thomas
Smith, Charles Henry, III
Smith, Irvin Martin
Stewart, Ryan Evan
Stewart, Kordell
Stansbury, Markhum L.
Sutton, Pierre Monte
Swain, Hampton J., Jr.
Talley, James Edward

## Real Estate



## Regional Planning (*See* Urban/Regional Planning)

## Restaurant/Food Service Industry



## Retail Trade—Apparel and Accessories



## Retail Trade—Building/ Construction Materials



## Retail Trade—Drugs and Toiletries



## Retail Trade—Electrical/ Electronics Products



## Retail Trade—Food and Beverages



## Retail Trade—Furniture/ Home Furnishings



## Retail Trade—General Merchandise



## Retail Trade—Hardware



## Retail Trade—Motor Vehicles, Parts, and Services

Brogden, Robert, Jr.
Bryant, Anderson B., Jr.
Bunche, Curtis J.
Bullard, Keith
Cain, Nathaniel Z., Jr.
Carthen, John, Jr.
Cabell, Enos Milton, Jr.
Carter, Will J.
Callaway, Louis Marshall, Jr.
Chargois, James M.
Cockerham, Peggy
Corley, Eddie B., Sr.
Conyers, Nathan G.
Dapremont, Delmont O., Jr.
Davis, Richard O.
Delk, James F., Jr.
Dillard, Howard Lee
Douglas, Walter Edmond, Sr.
Dukes, Carl R.
Early, Ezzard Dale
Edgar, Jacqueline L.
Eggleston, Neverett A., Jr.
Farr, Melvin, Sr.
Fletcher, Glen Edward
Fregia, Ray, Sr.
Frink, Samuel H.
Frazier, Jordan
Fryson, Sim E.
Gatewood, Dr. Algie C.
Grace, Princeston
Hatcher, Robert L.
Harrell, Charles H.
Harrison, Boyd G., Jr.
Harper, T. Errol
Harris, Randall Owen
Hall, Ronald E.
Hayes, Elvin Ernest
Hill, Robert A.
Hines, Jimmie
Hodge, Ernest M.
Horton, Oscar J.
Hughes, George Vincent
Hysaw, Guillermo Lark
Jackson, Clarence A.
Jackson, Gregory
Jones, Lester C.
Jones, James B.
Johnson, Hester
Jones, Theresa C.
Johnson, T. J.
Johnson, Sam
Jones, Fredrick E.
Jones, James V.
Karangu, David M.
Kemp, Leroy Percy, Jr.
Kindle, Archie
Lewis, Clarence K.
Lee, Chandler Bancroft
Lloyd, Phil Andrew
Long, Monti M.
Majors, Anthony Y.
Matthews, Irving J.
McClain, William L.
McClammy, Dr. Thad C.
Mitchell, George L.
Mitchell, James H.
Moore, Allyn D.
Montgomery, Robert E.
Moore, Jesse A.
Moore, Gary
Newberry, Cedric Charles
Nichols, Dimaggio
Norris, William E.
Parker, Clarence E.
Perry, LaVal
Piper, Elwood Arthur
Pittman, Winston R., Sr.
Price, Phillip G.
Reid, Duane L.
Reeves, Alan M.
Rodgers, Pamela E.
Roberts, John Christopher
Roberts, Roy S.
Rutledge, George
Shamberger, Jeffery L.
Sutton, Nathaniel K.
Sutton, Charles W.
Swain, Hampton J., Jr.
Taylor, Henry F.
Temple, Oney D.
Thompson, Johnnie
Trainer, James E.
Tupper, Leon E.
Turner, George Timothy
Walker, Jimmy L.
Watson, Perry, III
Warren, Clarence F.
Walker, William B.
Weiss, Ed, Jr.
White, Luther J.
White, Bryan
Williams, Brainard
Williams, Theodore W., Jr.
Williams, Roger L.
Wickware, Damon
Willis, Cecil B., Sr.
Williams, Gregory M.
Wilkinson, Raymond M., III
Wilkinson, Raymond M., III
Woodruff, James W.
Woods, Sanford L.
Wright, William A.
Young, Alan John
Younger, Kenneth C.

## Retail Trade—Not Elsewhere Classified

Abraham, Nathaniel Donnell
Allison, Carolyn C.
Banks, Manley E., Sr.
Best, Vanessa
Bing, Lisa A.
Boston, McKinley, Jr.
Brown, Elaine M.
Bransford, Patricia
Brown, Ernestine
Brown, Arnold E.
Burns, Ursula M.
Burns, Tommie, Jr.
Carter, Patrick Henry, Jr.
Carr, Gwenn L.
Capel, Felton Jeffrey, Sr.
Cooper, Joli C.
Cooper, Lois
Cooper, Antoinette
Coleman, Deborah Stewart
Coley, Denise
Connor, Dolores Lillie
Creighton, Lorenzo David
deMille, Dr. Valerie Cecilia
Drayton-Martin, Michelle
Dukes, Lillian A.
Ebanks, Michelle
Edmonds, Elaine
Elam, Deborah A.
Fluellen, Velda Spaulding
Freeman, Brenda
Gardner, Heide
Giscombe, Dr. Katherine
Green, Kim M.
Gray-Walker, Tracey
Guy, Angela E.
Harrison, Sarah S.
Haygood, Marsha
Henry, Grace Angela
Hilton, Stanley William, Jr.
Jackson, James E., Sr.
Jackson, Lurline Bradley
Johnson, Bennett J.
Keizs, Marcia V.
King, Frederick L., Jr.
Meade-Tollin, Dr. Linda C.
Morrison, Paul-David
Moss, Lesia Bates
Moaney, Gail L.
Omogbai, Meme
Paris, Calvin Rudolph
Peterson, Theresa H.
Perry, Beverly L.
Pearson-McNeil, Cheryl
Pinkney, Andrea Davis
Purchase-Owens, Francena
Rainford, Valerie I.
Robinson, Dr. Rev. Frank James, Jr.
Salaam, Dr. Abdul
Sandler, Debra A.
Skillern, Gwendolyn D.
Smashum, Olivia
States, Lauren C.
Stewart, Brittanica
Taylor, Sandye R.
Thompson, Mavis T.
Vaughn, Ed
Walker-Kuhne, Donna
Westbrooks, Logan H.
Whitehurst, Steven Laroy
White, Valerie D.
Williams, Deborah A.
Willis, Dr. Rose W.
Wright, Elease
Young, Elwanda
Zango-Haley, Linda

## Retail Trade—Service Industry

Abboa-Offei, Abenaa
Adkins, Rodney C.
Alves, Paget L.
Allen, Quincy L.
Andrews, Phillip
Barham, Wilbur Stectson
Babineaux-Fontenot, Claire
Beal, Bernard B.
Blaylock, Ronald
Blunt, Roger Reckling, Sr.
Bobo, Cedric L.
Borges, Francisco L.
Brown, Tony K.
Bryan, Glynis
Busumbru, Lisa Opoku
Carter, Jackie
Chapman, Kelly
Cooper, Edith W.
Dixon, T. Troy
Dickerson, Amina J.
Dubroy, Tashni-Ann
Ferguson, Roger W., Jr.
Fisher, Edith Maureen
Fletcher, Alphonse, Jr.
Frazier, Kenneth C.
Frazier, Shirley George
George, Stuart
Gonsalves, Gregg A.
Gomez, Todd A.
Gordon, Joi
Grain, David J.
Green, Isaac H.
Harper, Arthur H.
Harris, Carla
Heller, Bridgette P.
Henry, Lisa Jennifer
Holloway, Cecelia
Holley, Kenneth
Hobson, Mellody
Holt, Ronald Wayne, Jr.
Hughes, Frankie D.
Isaacs, Jessica C.
James, Melissa E.
Jackson, William R.
Johnson, Sheila Crump
Jones, Kim Harris
Johnson, Dennis A.
Johnson, Robert Louis
Johnson, Edward E., Jr.
Jones, Derek K.
Jones, Terry L.
Kindall, Dr. Alpha S.
Lambert, Lillian Lincoln
Lanier, Gayle S.
LaVar, Ellin
Lee, Esq. Debra L.
Lewis-Hall, Freda
Lewis, William M., Jr.
Lucas, Wonya
Mason, Mark
McKenzie, Obie L.
McGuire, Raymond J.
McNeal, Glenda G.
Mensah, Bernard
Miller, Rodney M., Sr.
Mincey, Karen
Mosley, Valerie
Morse, Dr. Laurence C.
Mosley, Elwood A.
Narcisse, Colbert
Norman, Christina
Norwood, Felicia
O'Neal, Rodney
Penn, Derek
Price, JoAnn H.
Profit, Eugene A.
Pryor, Vikki L.
Ray, Michael
Reynolds, James, Jr.
Rice, J. Donald, Jr.
Richo, Anna
Roper, Deidre Muriel
Saunders, Jerry, Sr.
Shank, Suzanne F.
Smith, Gerald B.
Smith, Robert F.
Stockton, Dmitri
Steele, Joyce Yvonne
Taylor, Colleen
Terrell, Frederick O.
Thomas, Shundrawn A.
Torres, Sherice
Trotter, Lloyd G.
Utendahl, John O.
Viera, Paul E.
Walker, Monica L.
Waller, Kathy N.
Warren-Merrick, Gerri
West, Mary Beth
Whiteman, Raymond A.
Williams, Tina Byles
Wilson-Thompson, Kathleen
Wilson, Donna Sims
Williams, Elizabeth
Williams, Rebecca
Williams, Karen
Yates, Lloyd M.
Yates, Lloyd

## Sales Management (*See* Management/ Administration—Sales)

## Science-Not Elsewhere Classified (*See Also* Oceanography; Physiology; Zoology)

Bacon-Bercey, June Esther
Bertley, Frederic
Best, Glenn
Bonham, Vence L.
Brewer, Gregory Alan
Brown, Dr. William T.
Bridgewater, Albert Louis
Chicoye, Etzer
Chapman, Willie R.
Cherry, Lee Otis
Clark, Dr. Theotis, Jr.
Cooper, Walter, Sr.
Cobb, Dr. Jewel Plummer
Curbeam, Robert Lee, Jr.
Davis-Millin, Dr. Myrtle A.
Dean, Dr. Mark E.
Diggs, Lawrence J.
Franklin, Dr. Lance Stonestreet
Franklin, Dr. Renty Benjamin
Gavin, Dr. James Raphael, III
Graham, Rhea L.
Greene, Dr. Lionel Oliver
Hannah, Dr. Marc Regis
Hendricks, Dr. Marvin B.
Henderson, Dr. Nannette Smith
Hicks-Bartlett, Sharon Theresa
Horne, June Merideth
Jackson, Duane Myron
James, Dr. Herbert I.
Jarrett-Jackson, Mary Francis
Jemison, Dr. Mae Carol
Johnson, Michael Anthony
Jones, Van
King, Lewis M.
Kornegay, Dr. Wade M.
Kumanyika, Dr. Shiriki K.
Leeke, Madelyn Cheryl
Malcom, Dr. Shirley Mahaley
Martin, Dr. Patrick M.
Meade-Tollin, Dr. Linda C.
Moore, George Thomas
Nelson, Edward O.
Parnell, John V., III
Philander, Dr. S. George H
Pratt, Alexander Thomas
Rhoden, Dr. Richard Allan, Sr.
Richo, Anna
Roane, Dr. Philip Ransom, Jr.
Shavers, Dr. Cheryl L.
Slaughter, Dr. John Brooks
Smalls, Charley Mae
Smith, Morris Leslie
Smith, Dr. Roulette William
Sogah, Dr. Dotsevi Yao
Tatem, Dr. Patricia Ann
Thomas, Mary A.
UmBayemake-Hayes, Linda
Urdy, Dr. Charles E.
Walton, Dr. Edward D.
Wilson, Valerie Petit
Williams, Ralph O.
Williams, Dr. Carolyn Ruth Armstrong
Wilson, Dr. Donella Joyce
Wilford, Gloria Gantt

## Social Work

Abdullah, Dr. Samella Berry
Adair, Alvis V.
Adams, Anne Currin
Adair, Andrew A.
Ali, Muhammad
Allen, Herbert J.
Aldredge, Prof. James Earl
Allen-Meares, Paula G.
Ambrose, Dr. Ethel L.
Anderson, Marva Jean
Anderson, Barbara Louise
Anderson, Miller R.
Anderson, Stevie Darrell
Appleton, Clevette Wilma
Armstead, Ron E.
Atkinson, Regina Elizabeth
Atkinson, Eugenia Calwise
Auguste, Donna M.
Baxter, Frederick Denard
Baugh, Florence Ellen
Baker-Parks, Sharon L.
Ballard, Myrtle Ethel
Baker, Dr. Gwendolyn Calvert
Barnard-Bailey, Dr. Wanda Arlene
Bennett, Delores M.
Beane, Robert Hubert
Berry, Philip Alfonso
Berry, Paul Lawrence
Beverly, Eric R.
Belizaire-Spitzer, Julie
Beatty, Christine Rowland
Bishop, Ellen Elizabeth Grant
Blake, James Riley
Blakely, Charles
Brooks, Rodney Norman
Brown, Denise Sharon
Brass, Reginald Stephen
Bryant, John Hope
Bramwell, Patricia Ann
Brown, Tommie Florence
Brown, Marva Y.
Bugg, Mayme Carol
Burlew, Ann Kathleen
Busby, Everett C.
Butler, Melba
Carper, Gloria G.
Casey, Frank Leslie
Castleman, Elise Marie
Chambers, Madrith Bennett
Chestang, Dr. Leon Wilbert
Clay, William Lacy, Sr.
Coleman, Barbara Sims
Cox, Dr. Arthur James, Sr.
Crawford, Margaret Ward
Crawford, Cranford L., Jr.
Davidson, Arthur B.
Daniels, Dr. Ron D.
Darden, Anthony Kojo
Dandy, Dr. Roscoe Greer
Davis, Bettye J.
Dale, Robert J.
DeHart, Dr. Panzy H.
Deloatch, Myrna Spencer
Dellums, Ronald Vernie
Dell, Willie J.
Dember, Jean Wilkins
Dinkins, David Norman
Dismuke, Mary Eunice
Dixon, Ardena S.
Dobson, Dorothy Ann
Douglas, Walter Edmond, Sr.
Dunmore, Charlotte J.
Duncan, Sydney Ree
Dudley, Juanita C.
Dugger, Clinton George
Dyer, Bernard Joel
Eaton, Thelma Lucile
English, Dr. Richard Allyn
Eve, Constance B.
Farrakhan, Louis
Fields, Alva Dotson
Fleming, Patricia Stubbs
Floyd, Vircher B.
Forney, Mary Jane
Francis, Dr. E. Aracelis
Funderburke, Lawrence Damon
Fuerst, Jean Stern
Gary, Dr. Lawrence Edward
Garrison, Jewell K.
Gordy, Berry, Jr.
Gossett, Louis Cameron, Jr.

## Sociology



## Sports Coaching/Training/Managing/Officiating

Day, Todd Fitzgerald
Davis, Hubert Ira, Jr.
Davis, Johnny Reginald
Davis, Chili
Dawson, Andre Nolan
Dent, Richard Lamar
Dennis, Karen
Dickerson, Ron, Jr.
Dishman, Cris Edward
Dimry, Charles Louis, III
Dixon, Gerald Scott, Sr.
Dodge, Dedrick Allen
Douglass, Maurice Gerrard
Dorsey, Tredell
Downing, Stephen
Draper, Dr. Frederick Webster
Drew, Larry Donnell
Drexler, Clyde Austin
Driessen, Daniel
Durham, Leon
Dungy, Tony
Durden, Earnel
Dunn, Jason Adam
Dumas, Troy T.
Dumas, Michael Dion
Dunn, Jerry Michael
Easley, Damion
Edwards, Tonya
Edmunds, Ferrell, Jr.
Edwards, Antonio
Edwards, Teresa
Edwards, Michelle
Edwards, Robert Lee, III
Edwards, Herman Lee
Eisley, Howard Jonathan
Elie, Mario Antoine
Elewonibi, Mohammed Thomas David
Ellison, Pervis
Ellerbe, Brian Hersholt
Embry, Wayne Richard
English, Alex
English, Stephen
Enis, Curtis D.
Engram, Bobby
Evans, Mike
Evans, Lee Edward
Evans, Robert Oran
Evans, Gregory James
Ewing, Patrick Aloysius, Sr.
Fair, Terrance Delon
Featherstone, Karl Ramon
Felton, Dennis
Ferrell, Duane Edward
Fisher, Derek Lamar
Floyd, Malcolm Gregory Ali
Floyd, Eric Augustus
Floyd, James T., Sr.
Fleming, Vern
Fonville, Chad Everette
Ford, Henry
Franklin, James E.
Frazier, Charles Douglas
Frank, Tellis Joseph, Jr.
Freeman, Marianna
Free, Kenneth A., Sr.
Fryar, Rev. Irving Dale, Sr.
Fuhr, Grant Scott
Fuller, Dr. Vivian L.
Fuller, Randy Lamar
Gash, Samuel Lee, Jr.
Gaters, Dorothy L.
Garnes, Sam Aaron
Garrett, Cain, Jr.
Gaines, Corey Yasuto
Garbey, Barbaro
Gentry, Alvin Harris
Gervin, George
Gilliam, Frank Delano, Sr.
Gillom, Jennifer
Gildon, Jason Larue
Gibson, Oliver Donnovan
Glenn, Aaron DeVon
Glass, Virginia M.
Glass, Gerald Damon
Goss, Tom A.
Goodwin, Thomas Jones
Golden, Louie
Gordon, Pastor Alexander H., II
Gordon, Bridgette C.
Goodson, Adrienne M.
Green, Jacquez
Green, Scarborough
Grant, Gary
Groce, Clifton Allen
Green, Robert David
Gray, Torrian
Grillo, Luis
Grier, Michael James
Green, Litterial Maurice
Groth, Chad
Green, James
Gray, Johnnie Lee
Griffin, Archie
Gray, Donnee L.
Grier, Johnny
Green, Sean Curtis
Grier, Bobby
Gray, Jerry Don
Greer, Harold Everett
Griffin, Leonard James, Jr.
Grant, Harvey
Griffey, Ken, Sr.
Green, Hugh Donell
Griggs, Anthony G.
Green, Dennis
Gumby, Dr. John Wesley
Guyton, Wanda Marie
Hamblin, Angela
Harris, Al
Hawkins, Steven Michael
Ham, Darvin
Harrington, Othella
Harris, Pep
Hagood, Jay
Hall, Dana Eric
Hall, Lemanski
Hawkins, Courtney Tyrone, Jr.
Hasty, James Edward
Harper, Terry Joe
Harrison, Robert
Hairston, Jerry Wayne, Sr.
Harkness, Jerry B.
Harris, Alfred Carl, III
Harris, Charles Somerville
Haskins, Clem Smith
Haley, Charles Lewis
Hayes, Jonathan Michael
Hatcher, William Augustus
Hardaway, Timothy Duane, Sr.
Harper, Ronald
Hawkins, Hersey R., Jr.
Hamilton, Leonard
Hardaway, Jerry David
Harris, James Larnell
Hardaway, Anfernee Deon
Haskins, Clemette L.
Hardy, Kevin Lamont
Harvey, Antonio
Hecker, Barry
Herndon, Larry Darnell
Henderson, Rickey Nelson Henley
Henderson, Jerome Virgil
Hegamin, George Russell
Heard, Gar
Hewitt, Christopher Horace
Henry, Forest T., Jr.
Hill, Glenallen
Hicks, Jessie Yvette
Hicks, Robert Otis, Jr.
Higgins, Roderick Dwayne
Highsmith, Alonzo Walter
Higgins, Sean Marielle
Hill, Tyrone
Hill, Dennis Odell
Houston, Allan Wade, Sr.
Hopkins, Dr. Gayle P.
Holyfield, Evander
Holmes, Jerry Lee
Howard, Juwan Antonio
Howard, Brian Eugene
Hodges, Craig Anthony
Holton, Michael David
Holbert, Ray Arthur, III
Hodgins, James William
Holcombe, Robert Wayne
Horne, Antonio Tremaine
Hollins, Lionel Eugene
Holsey, Bernard
Holmes, Earl L.
Howard, Sherri
Horton, Willie Wattison
Hunt, Maurice
Hunter, Cottrell James, III
Huskey, Butch
Hughes, Mark
Humphries, Jay
Hubbard, Philip Gregory
Hunter, Lindsey Benson, Jr.
Humphrey, Robert Charles
Huyghue, Michael L.
Ingram, Garey Lamar
Irvin, Kenneth Pernell
Irvin, Sedrick
Ismail, Qadry Rahmadan
Ivery, Eddie Lee
Jackson, Reggie Martinez
Jackson, Steven Wayne
Jackson, Greg Allen
Jackson, Jaren
Jackson, James Arthur
Jackson, Terry
Jackson, Tammy Eloise
Jamison, Antawn Cortez
Jackson, Stuart Wayne
Jackson, Dr. Edgar Newton, Jr.
James, Kevin Porter
Jackson, Kevin Andre
Jacket, Barbara Jean
Jackson, Eric Scott
Jackson, Keith Jerome
Jackson, Willis Randell, II
Jackson, Grant Dwight
Jerrard, Paul
Jeffcoat, James Wilson, Jr.
Jensen, Marcus Christian
Jefferson, Shawn
Jenkins, Billy Leon, Jr.
Jefferson, Greg Benton
Jenkins, James
Jenkins, Ferguson Arthur, Jr.
Johnson, Albert James
Johnson, Earvin, Jr.
Jones, Charles
Joiner, Charles, Jr.
Jones, Samuel
Johnson, Tre, III
Johnson, Jimmie Olden, Jr.
Jones, Michael Anthony
Johnson, William Edward
Johnson, Lonnie Demetrius
Johnson, Pepper
Jones, Lenoy
Jones, Roger Carver
Jones, Damon S.
Jones, Rodrek Edward
Jordan, Randy Loment
Jones, Bobby M.
Johnson, Anthony Scott
Jones, Markeysia Donta
Jones, Charlie Edward
Jordan, Reginald
Jordan, Edward Montgomery
Johnson, Vickie Annette
Jones, Tebucky Shermain
Joseph, Kerry
Johnson, Kevin N.
Johnson, LaTonya
Jones, DeLisha Milton
Joe, William (Billy)
Jones, James F.
Jordan, Richard Lamont
Jones, Freddie Ray, Jr.
Johnson, Rafer Lewis
Johnson, Mamie Peanut
Johnson, Avery
Jordan, Ricky
Jones, Cobi N'Gai
Jones, Gary DeWayne
Jones, Popeye
Jones, Grover William, Jr.
Jones, K. C.
Johnson, Jerry Calvin
Johnson, Frank
Johnson, Ezra Ray
Kazadi, Muadianvita Machez
Keith, Floyd A.
Kenlaw, Jessie
Keith, Karen C.
King, Stacey
Kidd, Jason Fredrick
King, Stanley Oscar
Kingdom, Roger Nona
King, Billy
Kirkland, Levon
Kittles, Kerry
Kinsey, Jim
King, Don
Knight, Sammy D., Jr.
Lassiter, Kwamie
Lamb, Monica
Lanier, Rob
Lavan, Alton
Lang, Antonio Maurice
Lake, Carnell Augustino
Lewis, Albert Ray
Lewis, Leo E., III
Lee, Charlie
Levingston, Clifford Eugene
Lever, Lafayette
Lee, Leron
Lee, Larry Dwayne
Lewis, Sherman Paul
LeGrand, Robert C., Jr.
Lewis, Duane
Lee, Amp
Lester, Tim Lee
Lennon, Patrick Orlando
Lister, Alton Lavelle
Littles, Gene
Love, Lynnette Alicia
Love, Robert Earl
Lowe, Sidney Rochell
Locke-Mattox, Bernadette
Lopes, David Earl
Logan, Ernest Edward, II
Lofton, James
Lucas, John Harding, II
Lyons, Donald Wallace, Sr.
Lynn, Anthony Ray
Lyght, Todd William
Lynch, George DeWitt, III
Macon, Mark L.
Massenburg, Tony Arnel
Manuel, Lionel, Jr.
Malone, Karl Anthony
Markham, Houston, Jr.
Mathews, George
Mann, Richard
Madlock, Bill, Jr.
Martin, Prof. Carolyn Ann
Mahorn, Rick
Malone, Jeffrey Nigel
Martin, Emanuel C.
Marion, Brock Elliot
Marshall, Marvin Ali
Mack, Tremain Ferrell
Marts, Lonnie, Jr.
May, Derrick Brant
Manuel, Jerry
Martin, Darrick David
Manning, Sharon
Mason, Derek
Marks, Lee Otis
May, Lee Andrew
McAdoo, Bob, Jr.
McCray, Nikki
McLeod, Roshown
McLeod, Kevin
McKinnon, Ronald
McGarity, Wane Keith
McCarty, Walter Lee
McCarthy, Gregory O'Neil
McGee, Pamela
McAfee, Fred Lee
McKnight, James Edward
McMillon, Billy
McCorvey, Kez
McDaniel, Emmanuel
McCleon, Dexter Keith
McGill, Lenny
McDonald, Timothy
McDaniel, Randall Cornell
McKenzie, Keith Derrick
McCraw, Tom
McGee, Willie Dean
McRae, Harold Abraham
McCutcheon, Lawrence P.
McGee, Adolphus Stewart
McDaniels, Alfred F.
McDaniel, Xavier Maurice
McClendon, Lloyd Glenn
McGriff, Frederick Stanley
McKandes, Dorothy Dell
McGee, Timothy Dwayne Hatchett
McDonald, Michael, Jr.
McNorton, Bruce Edward
McMillan, Nate
McKinney, Billy
McKandes, Darnell Damon
McElrath-Frazier, Wanda Faith
McCray, Almator Felecia
McKie, Aaron Fitzgerald
McElroy, Dr. Njoki
Means, Natrone Jermaine
Merriweather, Michael Lamar
Mitchell, Sam, Jr.
Mills, Terry Richard
Minor, Greg Magado
Mills, Alan Bernard
Milstead, Roderick Leon, Jr.
Miller, Cheryl De Ann
Mitchell, Robert Cornelius
Miller, Fred Junior, Jr.
Mincy, Charles Anthony
Mills, Ernie
Mills, John Henry
Milliard, Ralph Gregory
Miller, Wade Thomas
Minter, Michael Christopher
Middleton, Frank, Jr.
Mills, Steve
Morgan, Wayne
Moore, Larry Maceo
Moore, Yolanda
Moss, Winston N., Sr.
Mouton, James Raleigh
Moss, Zefross P.
Mobley, Singor A.
Monk, Art
Moore, Oscar William, Jr.
Moore, John Brian
Moore, Rob
Mosley, Benita Fitzgerald
Morton, Johnnie James, Jr.
Moore, Derrick C.
Morris, James Walter
Morgan, Joe Leonard
Murdock, Eric Lloyd
Murray, Tracy Lamont
Murray, Eddie Clarence
Myles, William, Jr.
Myers, Peter Eddie
Nattiel, Richard Rennard
Napper, Hyacinthe T.
Nathan, Tony Curtis
Naeole, Chris
Nails, Jamie Marcellus
Natt, Kenny
Ndiaye-Diatta, Astou
Newman, Anthony Q.
Newsome, Ozzie, Jr.
Nelson, Darrin Milo
Newsome, Vincent Karl
Ngongba, Tajama Abraham
Nichols, Crystal Faye
Nickerson, Hardy Otto
Norton, Kenneth Howard, Jr.
Norrell-Thomas, Sondra L.
Northern, Gabriel O' Kara
Norvell, Dr. Merritt J., Jr.
Nunn, Ronnie
O'Bannon, Edward Charles, Jr.
Oakley, Charles
Oates, Wanda Anita
Odomes, Nathaniel Bernard
Oglivie, Benjamin Ambrosio
Ogden, Jonathan Phillip
Okoye, Christian Emeka
Orr, Louis McLaughlin
Outlaw, John L.
Overton, Douglas M.
Owens, Billy Eugene
Oxendine, Kenneth Qwarious
Patterson, Andrae Malone
Page, Solomon
Patten, David
Palmer, Violet
Pathon, Jerome
Patton, Ricardo Maurice
Parker, Charlie
Parker, Anthony
Parmalee, Bernard A.
Pack, Robert John, Jr.
Paris, William H., Jr.
Paddio, Gerald James
Payne, Kenneth Victor
Parker, David Gene
Perry, Gerald June
Pettis, Gary George
Pendleton, Terry Lee
Pearson, Drew
Perry, Timothy D.
Perryman, Robert Lewis, Jr.
Person, Chuck Connors
Person, Wesley Lavon, Sr.
Pender, Mel
Perry, Darren
Pegram, Erric Demont
Peck, Carolyn Arlene
Perry, Wilmont Darnell

## Sports—Amateur



## Sports—Not Elsewhere Classified



## Sports—Professional/ Semiprofessional

Alford, Brian Wayne
Ali, Laila Amaria
Allen, Will D.
Allen, Marcus LeMarr
Alexander, Charles Fred, Jr.
Ali, Muhammad
Alexander, Willie James
Alomar, Sandy, Sr.
Alexander, Gary Roberts
Alston, Derrick Samuel
Alexander, Derrick Scott
Alomar, Sandy, Jr.
Alomar, Roberto Velazquez
Ambrose, Ashley Avery
Ambers, Monique
Amaker, Harold Tommy
Anthony, Reidel Clarence
Anderson, Derek Lamont
Anderson, Garret Joseph
Anderson, Shandon Rodriguez
Anderson, Willie Aaron
Anderson, Darren Hunter
Anders, Kimble Lynard
Anderson, Eddie Lee, Jr.
Anderson, Richard Darnoll
Anderson, Stevie Darrell
Anderson, Antonio Kenneth
Anderson, Keisha Dawn
Anderson, Jamal Sharif
Anderson, Marlon Ordell
Andrade, Mery
Anthony, Gregory Carleton
Anderson, Kenny
Anderson, Alfred Anthony
Anderson, Willie Lee, Jr.
Anderson, Nick
Anderson, Gary Wayne
Anthony, Eric Todd
Anderson, Gregory Wayne
Anderson, Ronald Gene
Armstrong, B. J., Jr.
Armstrong, Tyji Donrapheal
Armstead, Jessie Willard
Archambeau, Lester Milward, III
Armstrong, Bruce Charles
Arnold, Jahine Amid
Armstrong, Darrell Eugene
Archer, Chris
Artest, Ronald William, Jr.
Arnelle, Hugh Jesse
Archibald, Nathaniel
Aska, Joseph
Ashmore, Darryl Allan
Askins, Keith Bernard
Asbury, William W.
Askew, Vincent Jerome
Ashford, Evelyn
Attles, Alvin Austin, Jr.
Atwater, Stephen Dennis
Atkins, James Curtis
Atkins, Pervis R., Jr.
Austin, Raymond Demont
Autry, Harrington Darnell
Augmon, Stacey Orlando
Austin, Isaac Edward
Aycock, Angela Lynnette
Battie, Tony
Bayne, Chris
Batch, Charlie
Barnes, Quacy
Barnes, Adia Oshun
Ballard, Gregory
Barnes, Lionel, Jr.
Barber, Shawn William
Bass, Anthony Emmanole
Barber, Ronde
Barber, Tiki
Bankston, Michael Kane
Bailey, Robert
Banks, Tony
Bates, Mario Doniel
Baxter, Frederick Denard
Barlow, Reggie Devon
Barber, Michael Lenard
Bailey, Carlton Wilson
Barrow, Micheal Colvin
Baker, Myron Tobias
Bates, Michael Dion
Bartee, Kimera Anotchi
Bautista, Danny
Baldwin, James J., Jr.
Basil, Richard
Barney, Lemuel Jackson
Barnes, Johnnie Darnell

Barnett, Fred Lee, Jr.
Banks, Willie Anthony
Batiste, Kimothy Emil
Baker, Vin
Ball, Jerry Lee, Jr.
Banks, Carl E.
Barros, Dana Bruce
Barkley, Charles Wade
Baylor, Elgin Gay
Banks, Gene
Bailey, Thurl Lee
Baines, Harold Douglas
Baker, Dusty
Bass, Kevin Charles
Bell, George Antonio
Bernstine, Roderick Earl
Berry, Latin Dafonso
Bettis, Jerome Abram, Sr.
Beard, Butch, Jr.
Bell, Derek Nathaniel
Belle, Albert Jojuan
Benoit, David
Bennett, Michael
Bell, Kendrell Alexander
Beasley, Jamar
Bennett, Michael
Best, Travis Eric
Bennett, Cornelius O'landa
Bellamy, Jay
Bell, Myron Corey
Bennett, Donnell, Jr.
Beasley, Aaron Bruce
Berry, Bertand Demond
Belser, Jason Daks
Bennett, Tony Lydell
Bennett, Edgar, III
Benson, Darren
Beckles, Ian Harold
Beasley, Frederick Jerome
Beck, Corey Laveon
Benjamin, Corey Dwight
Beverly, Eric R.
Bennett, Brandon Purrell
Berry, Jay
Bing, Dave
Bibby, Mike
Bishop, Blaine Elwood, Jr.
Biakabutuka, Tim
Billups, Chauncey Ray
Biles, Simone
Blake, James Riley
Blake, John Patrick
Blackshear, Jeffery Leon
Blanton, Dain
Blackmon, Roosevelt, III
Blevins, Tony
Blue, Octavia LaDawn
Bly, Dre'
Blaise, Kerlin
Blue, Vida Rochelle, Jr.
Blackburn, Charles Miligan, II
Blair, Curtis
Blount, Corie Kasoun
Blake, Jeff Bertrand Coleman
Blades, Bennie, Sr.
Blanton, Ricky Wayne
Blaylock, Mookie
Blackman, Rolando Antonio
Bosley, Thad
Bonner, Anthony
Bogues, Tyrone Curtis
Boone, Ronald Bruce
Bolen, David B.
Bonilla, Bobby
Bonds, Barry Lamar
Bonner, Alice Carol
Bowe, Riddick Lamont
Bones, Ricardo
Bowdoin, Robert E.
Boston, Ralph Harold
Boozer, Emerson
Boyd, Judge Delores Rosetta
Boston, David Byron
Boykins, Earl Antoine
Boose, Dorian Alexander
Booker, Karen
Bowden, Joseph Tarrod, III
Bowens, Timothy L.
Booker, Vaughn Jamel
Boutte, Marc Anthony
Bowie, Larry Darnell, Jr.
Bouie, Tony Vanderson
Bownes, Fabien Alfranso
Bolden, Juran T.

Bowen, Bruce, Jr.
Booth, Keith Eugene
Boulware, Peter Nicholas
Booker, Michael
Bolton-Holifield, Ruthie
Breaux, Timothy
Brown, P. J.
Brashear, Donald Maynard
Bryant, Kobe Bean
Brown, Larry, Jr.
Brown, Ray, Jr.
Bryant, Junior
Brown, Gilbert Jesse
Brooks, Robert Darren
Bronson, Robert Zack
Bruce, Isaac Isidore
Brown, Derek Darnell
Brooks, Barrett Charles
Brooks, Macey
Browning, John Edward
Bruce, Aundray
Brown, Gary Leroy
Brown, James B.
Braxton, Tyrone Scott
Broussard, Steven
Brown, Chadwick Everett
Brown, Reggie
Brown, Adrian Demond
Brown, Emil Quincy
Brigance, Orenthial James
Brown, James Lamont
Brown, Corwin Alan
Brown, Cornell Desmond
Brackens, Tony Lynn, Jr.
Brown, Derek Vernon
Brisby, Vincent Cole
Brown, Cindy
Brown, Rushia
Braxton, Janice Lawrence
Brown, Cherie Greer
Bryant, Mark Craig
Brown, Ruben Pernell
Bradford, Corey Lamon
Brown, Cyron DeAndre
Brown, Eric Jon
Brown, Troy Fitzgerald
Bradford, Ronnie
Brown, Omar Lamont
Branch, Calvin Stanley
Bromell, Lorenzo Alexis
Bradford, Paul L.
Broughton, Luther Rashard, Jr.
Brunson, Rick
Brown, Gerald
Brewer, Jim
Brown, Na Orlando
Bradley, Milton Obelle, Jr.
Brown, Dermal Bram
Brown, Roosevelt Lawayne
Brock, Tarrik Jumaan
Briscoe, Marlin Oliver
Brown, Kwame James
Brooks, Aaron Lafette
Brand, Elton Tyron
Brewer, Corey
Brown, Antron
Browner, Ross D.
Brown, Raymond Madison
Brown, John C., Jr.
Brantley, Clifford
Brown, Jarvis Ardel
Brown, Randy
Briggs, Greg
Brooks, Derrick Dewan
Brown, Jamie Shepard, II
Brandon, Terrell
Brown, Michael
Brown, Chucky
Browne, Jerry
Browner, Joey Matthew
Branham, George, III
Brown, Timothy Donell
Brown, Lomas, Jr.
Brown, Dee
Bridgeman, Junior
Brown, Willie
Brooks, James Robert
Brisco-Hooks, Valerie Ann
Bradley, Philip Poole
Butts, Marion Stevenson, Jr.
Burrell, Scott David
Butler, Mitchell Leon
Bush, Devin Marquese
Buford, Damon Jackson

Burroughs, Tim
Burroughs, Jordan
Buchanan, Shawn D.
Bush, Homer Giles
Buckner, Brentson Andre
Burgess, James Paul
Butler, Duane
Burras, Alisa Marzatte
Bullett, Victoria Andrea
Burgess, Linda Gail
Burnett, Robert Barry
Burton, Kendrick Duran
Burns, Lamont Antonio
Buckley, Terrell
Burns, Keith Bernard
Buckley, Marcus Wayne
Burris, Jeffrey Lamar
Butler, LeRoy, III
Buchanan, Raymond Louis
Byrd, Isaac, III
Byears, Latasha Nashay
Bynum, Kenneth Bernard
Byner, Earnest Alexander
Byars, Keith Allan
Caldwell, Adrian Bernard
Causwell, Duane
Casey, Rev. Carey Walden, Sr.
Campbell, Tony
Carter, Joseph Christopher
Cambridge, Dexter Ryan
Campbell, Elden Jerome
Carter, Cris
Carter, Ki-Jana
Carter, Kevin Louis
Cabell, Enos Milton, Jr.
Carr, Michael Leon
Carter, Thomas J., II
Carrier, Mark Anthony, III
Cartwright, Bill
Carroll, Joe Barry
Carter, Fredrick James
Carr, Kenneth Alan
Cage, Michael Jerome, Sr.
Cade, Harold Edward
Campbell, Lamar
Carpenter, Ronald, Jr.
Carr, Cory Jermaine
Carter, Vince
Campbell, Edna
Campbell, Michelle
Cato, Kelvin T.
Carter, Butch
Carter, Chris
Cannida, James Thomas, II
Carswell, Dwayne A.
Carter, Dale Lavelle
Cain, Joseph Harrison, Jr.
Carr, William
Carter, Perry Lynn
Carter, Marty LaVincent
Carter, Thomas, III
Carter, Tony A.
Carter, Nigea
Carver, Shante Ebony
Caldwell, Mike Isaiah, Jr.
Carter, Pat
Calloway, Christopher Fitzpatrick
Caffey, Jason Andre
Carr, Chris Dean
Cassell, Samuel James, Sr.
Camby, Marcus D.
Cameron, Michael Terrance
Canty, Chris
Carter, Quincy
Cash, Swintayla Marie
Centers, Larry Eugene
Cedeno, Cesar Encarnacion
Ceballos, Cedric Z.
Cheaney, Calbert Nathaniel
Cherry, Deron Leigh
Christie, Douglas Dale
Childress, Randolph
Chamberlain, Wesley Polk
Cheeks, Maurice Edward
Cherry, Je'Rod L.
Chamberlain, Byron Daniel
Charles, Daedra Janel
Childs, Chris
Chancey, Robert Dewayne
Chester, Larry Travis
Chase, Sonia Lynn
Chavous, Corey Lamonte
Chandler, Tyson
Chambers, Christopher J.

Chandler, Kerry D.
Chaney, Donald Ray
Clancy, Sam, Jr.
Clement, Anthony George
Claiborne, Chris
Clayton, Royce Spencer
Clarke, Charlotte
Clemons, Charlie Fitzgerald
Clark, Keon Arian
Cleamons, James Mitchell
Closs, Keith Mitchell, Jr.
Clark, David Earl
Clark, Tony
Clay, Willie James
Clark, Willie Calvin, Jr.
Clemons, Duane Anthony
Clark, Gary C., Jr.
Clayborn, Raymond Dewayne
Coleman, Derrick D.
Conner, Lester Allen
Coffey, Richard Lee
Corbin, Tyrone Kennedy
Coles, Bimbo
Collins, Andre Pierre
Coleman, Monte Leon
Cobb, Reginald John
Cofer, Michael Lynn
Cox, Bryan Keith
Cooper, Duane
Coles, Darnell
Cobbins, Lyron Duryea
Coakley, William Dexter
Copeland, Horace Nathaniel
Cox, Ronald Eugene, Sr.
Colon, Harry Lee
Coates, Ben Terrence
Collons, Ferric Jason
Copeland, John
Cook, Anthony Andrew
Coryatt, Quentin John
Coleman, Marcus Le'Sha
Cooper-Dyke, Cynthia
Collier, Louis Keith
Cook, Toi Fitzgerald
Coleman, Marco Darnell
Conway, Curtis LaMont
Cotton, James Wesley
Collins, James
Congreaves, Andrea Fiona
Cowart, Sam
Coleman, Quincy
Coghill, George
Collins, Mark Anthony
Collins, Mo
Collins, Calvin Lewis
Colleton, Katrina Yvette
Connell, Albert Gene Anthony
Cook, Rashard
Coleman, Ronnald Dean
Coleman, Dr. Don Edwin
Cooper, Cecil Celester
Croom, Sylvester, Jr.
Crawford, Rainey James
Crowell, Germane L.
Craig, Dameyune Vashon
Crockett, Henri
Croel, Michael
Crawley, Sylvia
Crittenden, Raymond C., IV
Craver, Aaron LeRenze
Crockett, Ray
Crumpler, Carlester T., Jr.
Crockett, Zack Theopolis
Crawford, Vernon Dean, Jr.
Crawford, Keith
Cross, Howard Edward, Jr.
Cross-Battle, Tara
Cureton, Earl
Curry, Dell
Cunningham, Randall
Cummings, Terry
Curry, Eric Felece
Cunningham, Rick
Cummings, Midre Almeric
Curry, Michael Edward
Custis, Ace
Cullors, Derrick Shane
Cunningham, William
Culpepper, Daunte Rachard
Curry, Eddy Anthony, Jr.
Curry, Stephen
Daley, Trevor
Davis, Mike
Darling, Helen Marie

Hewitt, Christopher Horace
Hemsley, Nate
Hearns, Thomas
Herndon, Larry Darnell
Henderson, Rickey Nelson Henley
Herron, Bruce Wayne
Heard, Herman Willie, Jr.
Henderson, Gerald, Sr.
Henderson, Alan Lybrooks
Henry, Herman
Hill, Grant Henry
Hill, Eric
Highsmith, Alonzo Walter
Hill, Bruce Edward
Higgins, Sean Marielle
Hinson, Roy Manus, Jr.
Hill, Tyrone
Hill, Kenneth Wade
Hicks, Eric David
Hill, Raymond
Hicks, Robert Otis, Jr.
Hicks, Jessie Yvette
Hicks, Foster
Hicks, Skip LaVell
Hill, Glenallen
Hicks, Michael
Hill, Randal Thrill
Hitchcock, Jimmy Davis, Jr.
Hill, Gregory LaMonte
Hilliard, Randy
Hilliard, Ike
Hill, Michael
Hill, Calvin G.
Horton, Willie Wattison
Houston, Kenneth Ray
Hopkins, Bernard
Horton, Andre
Horton, Andreana Suki
Holmes, Kenny
Honeycutt, Jerald DeWayne
Howard, Stephen
Holmes, Earl L.
Horn, Joseph
Houston, Bobby Darin
Holmes, Lester
Hobbs, Daryl Ray
Hopkins, Bradley Donnell
Holmes, Priest Anthony
Hollier, Dwight Leon, Jr.
Holmes, Clayton Antwan
Holmes, Darick Lamon
Holland, Darius Jerome
Howard, Ty L.
Holsey, Bernard
Holbert, Ray Arthur, III
Hodgins, James William
Holt, Torry Jabar
Hollins, Lionel Eugene
Holdsclaw, Chamique Shaunta
Holcombe, Robert Wayne
Horne, Antonio Tremaine
Holland-Corn, Kedra
Holliday, Vonnie
Hopkins, Wesley Carl
Holyfield, Evander
Hoard, Leroy J.
Holmes, Jerry Lee
Holt, Leroy
Horton, Raymond Anthony
Howard, Juwan Antonio
Houston, Allan Wade
Howard, Desmond Kevin
Howard, Brian Eugene
Hodge, Donald Jerome
Horry, Robert Keith, Jr.
Holmes, Larry
Hodges, Craig Anthony
Hudson, Charles Lynn
Hunter, Tony Wayne
Hubbard, Philip Gregory
Humphries, Jay
Hunter, Brian Ronald
Hunter, Lindsey Benson, Jr.
Humphrey, Robert Charles
Hundon, James Henry
Hutson, Tony
Hughes, Larry
Hudson, Troy
Hunter, Torii Kedar
Hunt, Cletidus Marquell
Hughes, Tyrone Christopher
Hudson, Christopher Reshard
Hunter, Brian Lee
Huskey, Butch
Hubbard, Trent
Hughes, Robert Danan
Hughes, Mark
Huckaby, Malcolm J.
Hunter, Cottrell James, III
Iginla, Jarome
Ingram, Garey Lamar
Ingram, Stephen Anthony
Irving, Terry Duane
Irvin, Kenneth Pernell
Irvin, Sedrick
Irvin, Michael Jerome
Ismail, Raghib Ramadian
Israel, Steven Douglas
Ismail, Qadry Rahmadan
Ivery, Eddie Lee
Iverson, Allen Ezail
Jackson, Stanley Leon
Jackson, Mark A.
Jackson, Bo
Jackson, Roy Lee
James, Dion
Jackson, Grant Dwight
Jackson, Rickey Anderson
Jackson, Reggie Martinez
Jackson, Larron Deonne
Jacobs, Timothy, Jr.
Jacquet, Nate
Jackson, Willie Bernard, Jr.
Jackson, Steven Wayne
Jackson, Mike
Jackson, Damian Jacques
Jackson, Waverly Arthur, Jr.
Jackson, Greg Allen
Jackson, John
James, Tory Steven
Jackson, Raymond DeWayne
Jamison, George R., Jr.
Jasper, Edward Videl
Jackson, Tyoka
Jackson, James Arthur
James, Henry Charles
Jackson, Jaren
Jackson, Dexter Lamar
Jackson, Terry
James, Jerome Keith
Jackson, Randell
Jacox, Kendyl
Jamison, Antawn Cortez
Jackson, Tia
Jackson, Tammy Eloise
Jackson, Bobby
Jackson, Grady O'Neal
Jacobs, Regina
James, LeBron Raymone
Jeffries, Greg
Jells, Dietrich Davis
Jenkins, James
Jefferson, Greg Benton
Jenkins, Billy Leon, Jr.
Jett, James
Jeter, Derek Sanderson
Jensen, Marcus Christian
Jenkins, DeRon Charles
Jefferson, Shawn
Jenkins, Ferguson Arthur, Jr.
Jeffcoat, James Wilson, Jr.
Jenkins, Melvin
Jefferson, Reggie
Jordan, Brian O'Neil
Johnson, Larry Demetric
Jones, Gary DeWayne
Jones, Cobi N'Gai
Jordan, Darin Godfrey
Johnson, Dave M.
Johnson, Ervin, Jr.
Jones, Eddie Charles
Jones, Popeye
Johnson, Edward Arnet
Johnson, Joseph Keyshawn
Jones, Cedric Lewis
Johnson, Ellis Bernard
Johnson, Ronald J.
Joyner, Seth
Jones, Aaron Delmas, II
Johnson, Avery
Jordan, Ricky
Johnson, Wallace Darnell
Johnson, Kevin Maurice
Johnson, Vinnie
Jordan, Steve Russell
Jones, Grover William, Jr.
Jones, K. C.
Jordan, Michael Jeffrey
Johnson, Frank
Jones, Charles Gadget
Johnson, Kelley Antonio
Johnson, Troy Dwan
Johnson, Ezra Ray
Joyner-Kersee, Jackie
Johnson, Albert James
Johnson, William Arthur
Johnson, Earvin, Jr.
Joiner, Charles, Jr.
Jones, Edward Lee
Jones, Samuel
Jones, Michael David
Johnson, William Leon
Johnson, Pepper
Jones, Marvin Maurice
Jones, James Alfie
Jones, Rondell Tony
Jones, Lenoy
Jones, Roger Carver
Jones, Damon S.
Jones, Rodrek Edward
Jordan, Randy Loment
Jones, Bobby M.
Jones, Chris
Johnson, Lance
Johnson, Anthony Scott
Johnson, Darrius Dashome
Jones, Ernest Lee
Jones, Selwyn Aldridge
Jones, Charlie Edward
Johnson, Charles Everett
Jones, Markeysia Donta
Jones, Tony Edward
Johnson, Raylee Terrell
Jones, Reggie
Johnstone, Lance
Jones, Michael Anthony
Jones, Robert Lee
Johnson, William Edward
Johnson, Lonnie Demetrius
Jones, Henry Louis
Jones, Brian Keith
Jones, Clarence Thomas
Johnson, Jimmie Olden, Jr.
Jones, Christopher Todd
Jones, Jimmie Sims
Johnson, Tre, III
Johnson, Melvin Carlton, III
Jordan, Andrew, Jr.
Jones, Dontae' Antijuaine
Jordan, Reginald
Jordan, Edward Montgomery
Jones, Marcus Edward
Johnson, Anthony Mark
Johnson, Charles Edward, Jr.
Jones, Andruw Rudolf
Jones, Walter, Jr.
Johnson, Olrick
Jones, Greg Phillip
Jones, Jacque Dewayne
Jordan, Kevin
Johnson, Joseph T.
Jordan, Richard Lamont
Jones, Freddie Ray, Jr.
Jones, Damon Darron
Jones, Charles Rahmel
Johnson, Leslie
Jones, DeLisha Milton
Johns, Pollyanna
Johnson, LaTonya
Joe, William (Billy)
Joseph, Kerry
Jones, Tebucky Shermain
Johnson, Vickie Annette
Johnson, Adrienne
Jones, Merlakia Kenyatta
Johnson, Shannon Regina
Johnson, Niesa Evett
Johnson, Tiffani Tamara
Johnson, Mamie Peanut
Johnson, Dwayne
Jones, Cullen
Jones, Seth
Johnson, Robert Louis
Jones, Randy
Jones, Marion
Jones, Roy Levesta, Jr.
Johnson, Dwayne Douglas
Junior, E. J.
Justice, David Christopher
Kalu, Ndukwe Dike
Kazadi, Muadianvita Machez
Kerner, Marlon Lavelle
Kennedy, Lincoln
Kelly, Mike
Kennison, Eddie Joseph, III
Kelly, Brian Patrick
Kellogg, Clark Clifton, Jr.
Keys, Madison
Kemp, Matthew Ryan
Keys, Randolph
Kemp, Shawn T.
Kennedy, Cortez C.
Kelly, Joseph Winston, Jr.
Kenlaw, Jessie
Kidd, Jason Fredrick
King, Jimmy Hal
Kidd, Warren Lynn
Kinnebrew, Lawrence D.
King, Stacey
Kimble, Bo
King, Albert
King, Bernard
King, Gerard
King, Ray
King, Shaun Earl
Kittles, Kerry
King, Shawn
Kirkland, Levon
Killens, Terry Deleon
Knight, Sammy D., Jr.
Knight, Thomas Lorenzo
Knight, Brevin Adon
Knox, William Robert, Sr.
Knight, Negele Oscar
Koonce, George
Kroon, Marc Jason
Land, Daniel
Langham, Collie Antonio
Langford, Jevon
Lassiter, Kwamie
Latham, Christopher Joseph
Lawton, Matthew, Jr.
Lang, Kenard Dushun
Lauderdale, Priest
Lacy, Venus
Lawson, Jason L.
Lamb, Monica
Lanier, Rob
Lavan, Alton
Lankford, Raymond Lewis
Lang, Antonio Maurice
Law, Ty
Lathon, Lamar Lavantha
Lake, Carnell Augustino
Larkin, Barry Louis
Lane, Jerome
Lang, Andrew Charles, Jr.
Landreaux, Kenneth Francis
Landrum, Tito
Lanier, Willie Edward
Lee, Mark Anthony
Leavell, Allen Frazier
Lewis, Carl
Leonard, Jeffrey
Lever, Lafayette
Lewis, Ronald Alexander
Lewis, Albert Ray
Lee, Carl, III
Levingston, Clifford Eugene
Lee, Leron
Lester, George Lawrence
Lewis, Darren Joel
Lewis, Steve Earl
Leonard, Sugar Ray
Lemon, Meadowlark, III
Lennox, Betty Bernice
Lewis, Marvin Ronald
Leftwich, Byron Antron
Lester, Bill
Lewis, Rashard Quovon
Levingston, Bashir A.
Leslie-Lockwood, Lisa Deshaun
Lewis, Martin
Lenard, Voshon Kelan
Lewis, Raymond Anthony, Jr.
Lennon, Patrick Orlando
Lee, Derrek Leon
Lewis, Thomas A.
Legette, Tyrone Christopher
Lee, Amp
Levens, Dorsey
Lewis, Jermaine Edward
Lewis, Roderick Albert
Lewis, Mo
Lester, Tim Lee
Lincoln, Jeremy Arlo
Livingston, Randy Anthony
Little, Leonard Antonio
Linton, Jonathan C.
Lippett, Ronnie Leon
Lipps, Louis Adam, Jr.
Lister, Alton Lavelle
Lloyd, Lewis Kevin
Lloyd, Gregory Lenard, Sr.
Loville, Derek Kevin
Logan, James Eddie
Lowery, Quenton Terrell
Logan, Ernest Edward, II
Lofton, Steven Lynn
Louchiey, Corey
Lowery, Michael Zantel
Long, John Eddie
Loud, Kamil Kassam
Lockett, Kevin Eugene
Lombard, George Paul
Long, Terrence Deon
Lofton, James
Lott, Ronnie
Lockhart, Eugene, Jr.
Long, Grant Andrew
Lofton, Kenny
Love, Robert Earl
Lowe, Sidney Rochell
Lucas, Raymond J.
Lue, Tyronn Jamar
Lucas, John Harding, II
Lyght, Todd William
Lyle, Keith Allen
Lynn, Anthony Ray
Lynch, Marshawn
Lynch, Eric D.
Lynch, George DeWitt, III
Lyles, Lester Everett
Maxwell, Vernon
Massenburg, Tony Arnel
Mays, Travis Cortez
Mann, Charles Andre
Manuel, Lionel, Jr.
Marion, Fred Donald
May, Mark Eric
Martinez, Ramon Jaime
Manning, Daniel Ricardo
Malone, Karl Anthony
Marshall, Leonard Allen, Jr.
Mack, Kevin
Mackey, Malcolm
Mason, Anthony
Marshall, Donyell Lamar
Mashburn, Jamal
Mack, Shane Lee
Marsh, Michael Lawrence
Macon, Mark L.
Maxey, Marlon Lee
Martin, George Dwight
Marsh, Doug Walter
Madlock, Bill, Jr.
Marve, Eugene Raymond
Marshall, Wilber Buddyhia
Marshall, Henry Howard
Mahorn, Rick
Malone, Jeffrey Nigel
Mason, Derek
Marshall, Brandon Tyrone
Mayers, Jamal David
Martin, Tony Derrick
Martin, Albert Lee
Magee, Wendell Errol, Jr.
Martin, Curtis James, Jr.
Madison, Samuel Adolfus, Jr.
Marts, Lonnie, Jr.
Mack, Tremain Ferrell
Maddox, Mark Anthony
Martin, Emanuel C.
Martin, Steven Albert
Mathis, Dedric Ronshell
Martin, Gerald Wayne
Mayes, Derrick Binet
Marshall, Anthony Dewayne
Marshall, Marvin Ali
Marion, Brock Elliot
Mathis, Kevin Bryant
Marbury, Stephon Xavier
Martin, Darrick David
Mayberry, Jermane Timothy
May, Derrick Brant
Manuel, Jerry
Mahomes, Patrick Lavon
Matthews, Gary Nathaniel, Jr.
Mason, Eddie Lee
Martin, Danyel Cecil

Roundtree, Raleigh Cito
Roberts, Nyree Khadijah
Ross, Oliver Calvin
Rossum, Allen Bonshaca Lamont
Rogers, Chris
Rolison, Nate
Robinson, Crystal LaTresa
Ross, Oliver Calvin, III
Ross, Adrian
Robinson, Marcus
Roberts, Richard Ray, Jr.
Robinson, Damien Dion
Robinson, Eugene Keefe
Roaf, William Layton
Robbins, Austin Dion
Rogers, Sammy Lee, Sr.
Roberts, Bip
Royal, Andre Tierre
Roye, Orpheus Michael
Robertson, Marcus Aaron
Rodgers, Derrick Andre
Roberts, William Harold
Rose, Malik Jabari
Robinson, Christopher Sean
Rogers, Roy Lee, Jr.
Rudd, Dwayne Dupree
Russell, Derek Dwayne
Russ, Bernard Dion
Rutledge, Rod
Rusk, Reggie
Rubin, Chanda
Ruffin, John Walter, Jr.
Russell, Campy
Russell, Bryon Demetrise
Rycraw, Eugenia
Salaam, Ephraim Mateen
Santiago, O. J.
Sadler, Donnie Lamont
Sawyer, Talance Marche
Sanders, Brandon Christopher
Sapp, Patrick
Sam, Sheri Lynette
Sanders, Christopher Dwayne
Sampson, Charles
Salmons, John Rashall
Sapp, Warren Carlos
Salaam, Rashaan Iman
Sanders, Frank Vondel
Sanders, Reginald Laverne
Sanders, Deion Luwynn
Sanders, Barry David
Sanders, Ricky Wayne
Salley, John Thomas
Sayers, Gale Eugene
Sample, William Amos
Sanders, Michael Anthony
Sampson, Ralph Lee, Jr.
Scott, Dennis Eugene
Scott, Chad Oliver
Scott, Shawnelle
Scott, Brent
Scott, Darnay
Scott, Todd Carlton
Scurlock, Michael Lee, Jr.
Scroggins, Tracy L.
Schulters, Lance A.
Scott, Byron Antom
Scott, Olympia Ranee
Sears, Corey Alexander
Serwanga, Wasswa Kenneth
Seals, Raymond Bernard
Seigler, Dexter E.
Seale, Samuel Ricardo
Sewell, Steven Edward
Searcy, Leon, Jr.
Seals, George Edward
Shell, Arthur, Jr.
Shaw, Dr. Willie G.
Shaw, Terrance Bernard
Shackleford, Charles Edward
Shelton, Bryan
Shumpert, Terrance Darnell
Shaw, Brian K.
Sheffield, Gary Antonian
Shields, Will Herthie
Shedd, Kenny
Sharpe, Shannon
Shade, Samuel Richard
Shelton, Daimon
Shaw, Sedrick Anton
Shepherd, Leslie Glenard
Shammgod, God
Shuler, Adrienne
Shaw, Harold Lamar
Shehee, Rashaan A.
Simmons, Anthony Lamont
Simmons, Tony DeAngelo
Simmons, Brian Eugene
Simpson, Darla
Singleton, Christopher Verdell
Simmons, Robert L.
Sims, Keith Alexander
Simpson, Carl Wilhelm
Singleton, Alshermond Glendale
Siglar, Ricky Allan
Simmons, Clyde, Jr.
Singleton, Nate, III
Simien, Tracy Anthony
Sinclair, Michael Glenn
Simon, Corey Jermaine
Sifford, Dr. Charles L.
Singleton, Chris
Silas, Paul Theron, Sr.
Simms, William E.
Simmons, Ron
Sievers, Eric Scott
Simpkins, LuBara Dixon
Singletary, Reggie Leslie
Simpson, Ralph Derek
Skinner, Brian
Slaughter, Webster Melvin
Slade, Christopher Carroll
Slater, Jackie Ray
Slater, Reggie Dwayne
Slocumb, Heathcliff
Smith, Rodney Stacey
Smith, Al Fredrick
Smith, Leonard Phillip
Smith, Neil
Smith, Steven Delano
Smith, Doug
Smith, Christopher Gerard
Small, Torrance Ramon
Smith, Dennis
Smith, Bruce Bernard
Smith, Benjamin Joseph
Smith, Emmitt J., III
Smith, Tony
Smith, Otis Fitzgerald
Smith, Charles Daniel
Smith, Ozzie
Smith, Lonnie
Smith, Lee Arthur
Smith, Dr. Tommie
Smith, Otis, III
Smith, Lamar Hunter
Smith, Marquette
Smith, Rodney Marc
Smith, Detron Negil
Smith, Rod
Smith, Irvin Martin
Smedley, Eric Alan
Smith, Thomas Lee, Jr.
Smith, Vernice Carlton
Smith, Frankie Lee
Smith, Charles Henry, III
Smith, Matt Jermaine
Smith, Fernando Dewitt
Smith, Robert Scott
Smith, Vinson Robert
Smith, Kevin Rey
Smith, Darrin Andrew
Smith, Michael John
Smith, Stevin L.
Smith, Charles Cornelius
Smith, Antowain Drurell
Smith, Michael
Smith, Tangela Nicole
Smith, Joe
Smith, Larry
Smith, Bobby
Smith, Shevin Jamar
Smith, Mark Anthony
Smith, Tarik
Smith, Torrance
Smith, Cedric Delon
Smith, Charlotte
Smith, Lovie Lee
Snow, Eric
Snow, Percy Lee
Sosa, Samuel Peralta
Solomon, Freddie Lee, Jr.
Sowell, Jerald Monye
Spikes, Irving E., Sr.
Spencer, Jimmy, Jr.
Spears, Marcus Raishon
Sparks, Phillippi Dwaine
Spellman, Alonzo Robert
Spriggs, Marcus
Springs, Shawn
Spencer, Felton LaFrance
Spurlock, Racquel
Spikes, Takeo Gerard
Spires, Gregory Tyrone
Sprewell, Latrell Fontaine
Spinks, Michael
Sparrow, Rory Darnell
Stewart, David Keith
Stephenson, Dwight Eugene
Still, Arthur Barry
Strawberry, Darryl Eugene, Sr.
Stith, Bryant Lamonica
Stewart, Larry A., Jr.
Stokes, Jerel Jamal
Stewart, Kordell
Stoudmaire, Damon
Stackhouse, Jerry Darnell
Stewart, James Ottis, III
Strong, Derek Lamar
Strickland, Rodney
Starks, John Levell
Stokes, Eric
Stinson, Andrea Maria
Still, Valerie
Staley, Dawn Michelle
Stewart, Michael Curtis
Stephens, Joseph
Starks, Duane Lonell
Streets, Tai Lamarr
Stewart, Paul Allen
Stull, Everett James
Stephens, Tremayne Raphael
Stewart, Kebu Omar
Strickland, Mark
Strickland, Erick
Stubblefield, Dana William
Styles, Lorenzo
Stargell, Tony
Stewart, Ryan Evan
Stone, Ronald Christopher
Strahan, Michael Anthony
Staley, Duce
Stoutmire, Omar Array
Strickland, Fredrick William, Jr.
Still, Bryan Andrei
Stone, Dwight
Strong, Mack Carlington
Stewart, Shannon Harold
Stallings, Ramondo Antonio
Steed, Joel Edward
Stephens, Jamain
Stewart, Rayna Cottrell, II
Stephens, Sloane
Stewart, James, Jr.
Stevenson, Alexandra Winfield
Stoudemire, Amar'e Carsares
St Julien, Marlon
Suggs, Terrell Raymonn
Sullivan, Jonathon Lamar
Supernaw, Kywin
Suber, Tora
Surtain, Patrick Frank
Swayne, Harry Vonray
Swann, Eric Jerrod
Swinger, Rashod Alexander
Swift, Michael Aaron
Sweatt, Dr. James L., III
Swoopes-Jackson, Sheryl
Swann, Lynn Curtis
Taylor, Charley Robert
Taylor, Lawrence Julius
Taylor, Bobby, III
Talley, Darryl Victor
Taylor, Maurice De Shawn
Taylor, Jason Paul
Tatum, Kinnon Ray, II
Taylor, Aaron Matthew
Tate, David Fitzgerald
Talley, Benjamin Jermaine
Taylor, Reggie
Taylor, Johnny Antonio
Tate, Sonja Patrice
Taylor, Fred
Tate, Robert Lee
Tatum, Mark A.
Teasley, Ronald
Teague, George Theo
Terry, Rick, Jr.
Teasley, Michelle Nicole
Templeton, Garry Lewis
Teagle, Terry Michael
Threatt, Sedale Eugene
Thomas, Isiah Lord, III
Thomas, Calvin Lewis
Thompson, LaSalle, III
Theus, Reggie Wayne
Thurmond, Nate
Thornton, Andre
Thomas, Broderick Lee
Thomas, Eric Jason
Thomas, Rodney Lamar
Thomas, Thurman Lee
Thomas, Frank Edward, Jr.
Thomas, Earl Lewis
Thompson, Ryan Orlando
Thomas, Kurt Vincent
Thomas, Henry Lee, Jr.
Thompson, Kevin Lamont
Thomas, Deon La Velle
Thierry, John Fitzgerald
Thomas, Jim
Thomas, Blair
Thompson, Milt
Thorpe, Otis Henry
Thomas, Debi
Thomas, Anthony J.
Thigpen, Yancey Dirk
Thompson, Bennie
Thomas, Dave Garfield
Thomas, Fred L.
Thomas, Orlando Paul
Thomas, J. T.
Thomas, Hollis, Jr.
Thomas, William Harrison, Jr.
Tharpe, Larry James
Thomas, Chris Eric
Thomas, Timothy Mark
Thomas, John
Thompson, Sharon
Thompson, Tina Marie
Thomas, Robert Lee, IV
Thrash, James Ray
Thomas, Tra
Thompson, David Farrod
Thompson, Alicia Rachelle
Tipton, Danell
Timpson, Michael Dwain
Timmons, Ozzie
Tippett, Andre Bernard
Tillman, Cedric Cornell
Toney, Anthony
Tolbert, Tony
Townsend, Andre S.
Toon, Albert Lee, Jr.
Tongue, Reginald Clinton
Tovar, Steven Eric
Toomer, Amani Askari
Toler, Penny
Trotter, Jeremiah
Trapp, James Harold
Traylor, Keith
Trent, Gary Dajaun
Tuggle, Jessica Lloyd, Jr.
Turnbull, Renaldo Antonio
Tureaud, Lawrence
Turner, Eric Scott
Tubbs, Winfred O'Neal
Tucker, Michael Anthony
Turner, Jim Allen
Tunsil, Necole Monique
Tyson, Mike
Tyus, Wyomia
Tyler, B. J.
Unseld, Wes
Upshaw, Willie Clay
Upshaw, Regan Charles
Vaughn, Mo
Vaught, Loy Stephen
Vaughn, Gregory Lamont
Valentine, Darnell Terrell
Van Embricqs, Alexandra
Vance, Eric Devon
Vaughn, Jacque
Van Exel, Nickey Maxwell
Vaughn, David, III
Vanover, Tamarick T.
Veland, Tony
Venable, Max
Vinson, Anthony Cho
Vickers, Kipp Emmanuel
Vincent, Troy Darnell
Way, Charles Christopher
Watts, Damon Shanel
Washington, Theodore, Jr.
Washington, Mickey Lin
Walker, Darnell Robert
Washington, Marvin Andrew
Walker, Jay
Washington, Dewayne Neron
Walker, Denard Antuan
Walker, Gary Lamar
Ward, Dedric Lamar
Walker, Bracey Wordell
Ward, Ronnie V.
Wallace, Steve
Wade, Terrell
Wallace, Ben Camey
Wallace, John Gilbert
Walker, Samaki Ijuma
Walker, Antoine Devon
Washington, Coquese Makebra
Watson, Justin Sean
Washington, Rico
Wallace, Al
Washington, Eric Maurice
Watkins, Melvin Lenzo
Wadsworth, Andre L.
Walker, Marquis Roshe
Walker, Brian
Warfield, Eric Andrew
Waddy, Jude Michael
Wayne, Nate
Washington, Todd Page
Ware, Andre
Wallace, Darrell, Jr.
Wade, Dwyane
Ward, Joel
Ward, Gary Lamell
Warrick, Bryan Anthony
Walker, Herschel
Wade, Dr. Joseph Downey
Warren, Michael
Walker, Darrell
Walker, Wesley Darcel
Ward, Rev. Melvin Fitzgerald, Sr.
Watson, Robert Jose
Walker, Chester
Walker, Derrick Norval
Washington, Lionel
Walker, Ronald Wayne
Washington, Dante Deneen
Wallace, Rasheed Abdul
Watters, Ricky
Ward, Charlie
Washington, MaliVai
Watson, Perry
Webber, Chris, III
Wesley, David Barakau
Westbrook, Michael Deanailo
Webster, Lenny
Weatherspoon, Clarence, Sr.
West, Doug
Webb, Spud
Welch, Harvey
West, Mark Andre
Wells, Bonzi
Webb, Umeki
Weatherspoon, Teresa Gaye
Wesley, Joseph
Wells, Vernon Michael, III
Weathers, Andre Le'Melle
Westbrook, Bryant Antoine
Webb, Richmond Jewel, Jr.
Webster, Larry Melvin, Jr.
West, Edward Lee, III
Whitfield, Robert Lectress, Jr.
Wheeler, Leonard Tyrone
Whittington, Bernard Maurice
Wheaton, Kenny Tyron
White, Stephen Gregory
Wheeler, Mark Anthony
Whigham, Larry Jerome
Wheat, DeJuan Shontez
White, Rondell Bernard
Whiting, Brandon Renee
White, Jahidi
Whiting, Val
Whatley, Ennis
Whitaker, Louis Rodman, Jr.
White, Jo Jo
White, Devon Markes
White, Randy
White, Bill
Whiten, Mark Anthony
Wheatley, Tyrone Anthony, Sr.
Whitney, Christopher Antoine
Whitaker, Pernell
Whitmore, Darrell Lamont
Williams, Calvin John, Jr.
Wilkinson, Daniel Raymon

## Statistics



## Telegraph Industry (*See* Telephone/Telegraph Industry)

## Telephone/Telegraph Industry



## Television/Cable Broadcasting Industry

Powell, Christopher R.
Prelow, Arleigh
Price, Ray Anthony
Purvis, Archie C.
Quick, Mike Anthony
Randolph-Jasmine, Carol Davis
Rashad, Dr. Ahmad
Rae, Issa
Ready, Stephanie
Revish, Jerry
Reed, Andre Darnell
Rhimes, Shonda
Richardson, Julieanna
Rivero, Marita
Rich, Betty
Rice, Sandra Dorsey
Riley, Glenn Pleasants
Rickman, Ray
Rodgers, Johnathan Arlin
Robinson, Johnathan Prather
Rogers, David William
Robinson, Robin
Rose, Jalen Anthony
Rolle, Janet
Roker, Albert Lincoln
Roberts, Bip
Russell, Sandra Anita
Russell, Bryon Demetrise
Ryan-White, Jewell
Satchell, Elizabeth
Sapp, Warren Carlos
Sanders, Deion Luwynn
Salley, John Thomas
Scott, Robert Jerome
Scafe, Judith Arlene
Scott, Samuel N.
Scott, Byron Antom
Sharpe, Shannon
Singleton, Christopher Verdell
Simons, Eglon E.
Singleton, Kenneth Wayne
Simmons-Edelstein, Dee
Simpson, Donnie
Slocumb, Jonathan
Smith, Rodney Marc
Smith, Vinson Robert
Smith, Salaam Coleman
Smith, Jamil
Smashum, Olivia
Smith, Barbara
Smith, Gerald Wayne
Stewart, Bernard
Stokes, Jerel Jamal
Stackhouse, Jerry Darnell
Stewart, James, Jr.
Stokes, Chris
Strong, Mack Carlington
Stewart, Alison
Suggs, Denis
Swainson, Sharon C.
Syler, M. Rene
Taylor, Ellis Clarence, Sr.
Taylor, Aaron Matthew
Taylor, Sylvia
Terrell, Donna
Thompson, Ronald Anthony
Thoms, Donald H.
Thomas-Samuel, Kalin Normoet
Thomas, Arthur Lafayette, III
Thomas, Terence
Timpson, Michael Dwain
Torres, Sherice
Tobin, Lauren
Townsend, Ronald
Vaughan, Rev. Dr. James Edward
Vanzant, Rev. Dr. Iyanla
Vargus, Bill
Vincent, Irving H.
Waters, Brenda Joyce
Waugh, Judith Ritchie
Washington, Dr. Edith May Faulkner
Watson, Karen Elizabeth
Watts, Rolanda
Walker, Derrick Norval
Wagoner, J. Robert
Washington, Dante Deneen
Walker, Mary L.
Watson, Ben
Warfield, Robert N.
Waters, Paul Eugene, Jr.
Washington, Ukee
Walker, Rhonda
Warren-Merrick, Gerri
Warren, Dorian T.
Wallace, John Gilbert
Walker, Loretta Young
Webb, Spud
Wesley, David Barakau
White, Bill
Whitsett, James A., Jr.
Whack, Rita Coburn
Williams, Judith Byrd
Williams, Wendy
Williams, Marsha E.
Williams, Armon Abdule
Williams, Joanne Louise
Winn, Carol Denise
Wilkins, Gerald Bernard
Williams, Scott Christopher
Williams, Juan
Williams, Montel
Williams, Jayson
Williams, Charlene J.
Williams, Reginald T.
Winfrey, Oprah Gail
Woodbeck, Frank Raymond
Worford, Carolyn Kennedy
Woodson, Darren Ray
Wright, Pandit F.
Yearwood, David Monroe, Jr.
Young, Godfrey
Young, Eric Orlando, Sr.
Zola, Nkenge

## Translation/Interpretation

Hodges, Patricia Ann
Winder, Alfred M.

## Transportation/Moving Services

Aiken, William
Allen, Bernestine
Allen, Stanley M.
Atkinson, Eugenia Calwise
Baker, Robert N.
Barnes, Ronald Lewis
Bledsoe, Melvin
Branker, Julian Michael
Brazil, Dr. Robert D.
Brown, Bishop Edward Lynn
Butler, Eric L.
Burts, Ezunial
Butler, Roy
Buckson, Toni Yvonne
Carter, Will J.
Copeland, Richard Allen
Cooke, Hon. Thomas H., Jr.
Curry, Major Gen. Jerry Ralph
Davis, Ronald R.
DeLibero, Shirley A.
Diane, Mamadi
Duncan, Sandra Rhodes
Farmer, Clarence, Sr.
Ferguson, Sherlon Lee
Ferguson, Elliott LaRoy, II
Garrett, Melvin Alboy
Gabriel, Benjamin Moses
George, Edward
Griffith, John A.
Hall, Brian Edward
Hart, Dr. Christopher Alvin
Heyward-Garner, Ilene Patricia
Henry, I. Patricia
Hogan, Carolyn Ann
Hunter, John W.
Jackson, Fred H.
Jones, Frank Benson
Jordan, Josephine E. C.
Kennard, Patricia A.
Lewis, Dr. Samuel L., Jr.
Lee, Dr. John Robert E.
Lewis, Robert Alvin, Jr.
Medford, Isabel
Merritt, LaShawn
Morris, John P., III
Moore, David Bernard, II
Mohamed, Gerald R., Jr.
Norwood, William R.
Petersen, Arthur Everett, Jr.
Robinson, Albert Arnold
Scott, Dr. Beverly Angela
Sigler, I. Garland
Smith, LeRoi Matthew-Pierre, III
Stewart, Ronald Patrick
Stokes, Rueben Martine
Taylor, Rev. Dr. Martha C.
Thomas, Charles W.
Tyree, Patricia Grey
White, Gary Leon
Williams, Dr. Lisa R.

## Travel Industry

Bennett, Belinda
Bledsoe, Melvin
Bridgewater, Dr. Rev. Herbert Jeremiah, Jr.
Campbell, Franklyn D.
Campbell, Blanch
Davis, Agnes Maria
Dildy, Catherine Greene
Donald, Arnold W.
Gardner, Ava Maria
Gray, Dr. Ronald A.
Grimsley, Ethelyne
Hall, Tanya Evette
Harper, Hoyt H., II
Heard, Georgina E.
Houston, Allan Wade, Sr.
Jackson, Mary
Johnson, Sheila Crump
Moaney, Gail L.
Muhammad, Akbar A.
Norman, William Stanley
Pitcher, Capt. Frederick M. A.
Rochester, Geof
Saunders, Barbara Ann
Spencer, Brenda L.
Strong, Otis Reginald, III
Starks, Rick H.
Taylor, Valerie Charmayne
Wilson, Charles Lee, Sr.
Wilson, Markly
Yarbrough, Patricia Nicholson

## Urban/Regional Planning

Allen, Charles Claybourne
Arbuckle, John Finley, Jr.
Armstead, Ron E.
Bennett, Maybelle Taylor
Best, John T., Jr.
Black, Dr. Malcolm Mazique
Blayton-Taylor, Betty
Bostic, Raphael W.
Brown, Aja
Bridges, Leon
Brown, Norman E.
Cooper, Ernest, Jr.
Coleman, Hurley J., Jr.
Davis, William E., Sr.
Daniels, A. Raiford
Davis, Anita Louise
Dowell-Cerasoli, Patricia R.
Dubose, Cullen Lanier
Earvin, Dr. Larry L.
Gilliam, James H., Sr.
Griggs, John W.
Grigsby, Troy L.
Grigsby, Jefferson Eugene, III
Harris, Dr. William McKinley, Sr.
Harris, Kamala Devi, Jr.
Hernandez, Aileen Clarke
Hill, Robert Bernard
Jackson, Dr. Russell H.
Jeff, Gloria Jean
Johnson, Kalanos Vontell
Knox, Wayne D. P.
Lane, Allan C.
Lang, Dr. Marvel
Lee, Dr. Silas H., III
Lillard, Kwame Leo
Lindsey, Jerome W., Jr.
Maith, Sheila Francine
Meeks, Reginald Kline
Millett, Dr. Ricardo A.
Mock, James Edward, Sr.
Morrison, Jacqueline
Price, Prof. Alfred Douglas
Ross, Dr. Catherine Laverne
Scruggs-Leftwich, Yvonne
Schmiegelow, Toni D.
Shepherd, Malcolm Thomas
Smith, Diane L.
Stull, Donald L.
Wescott, Abraham L., Jr.
Williams, Roy Levy
Williams, Harold Louis
Williams, Reginald Clark

## Veterinary Medicine

Adams, Dr. Eugene William
Bass, Dr. Laurent
Christie, James Albert, Jr.
Kimbrough, Charles Edward
Lee, Dr. Allen Francis, Jr.
Lewis, Clinton A., Jr.
Moore, Dr. Roscoe Michael, Jr.
Myers, Dr. Bernard Samuel
Parker, Charles McCrae
Presley, Dr. Oscar Glen
Raby, Clyde T.
St. Omer, Dr. Vincent V. E.

## Wholesale Trade—Apparel, Piece Goods, and Notions

Brandon, Carl Ray
Browner, Joey Matthew
Clarke, Charlotte
Foster-Grear, Pamela
Jackson, Willis Randell, II
Lauderback, Brenda Joyce
Liggins, W. Anthony
Mohamed, Gerald R., Jr.
Robinson, Ronnie W.
Sockwell, Oliver R., Jr.
Thackeray, Anjetta McQueen
Thornton, Cora Ann Barringer

## Wholesale Trade—Building/ Construction Materials

Dean, Daniel R.

## Wholesale Trade—Chemicals and Allied Products

Coshburn, Henry S., Jr.
Harrison, Charles
Williams, Joseph Lee, Jr.

## Wholesale Trade—Drugs and Toiletries

Bethea, Edwin Ayers
Daurham, Ernest, Jr.
Dudley, Joe Louis, Sr.
Pratt, Dr. Ruth Jones K.
Williams, Dr. E. Faye
Williams, Paul S.

## Wholesale Trade—Electrical/Electronics Products

Davis, Frank Allen
Handy, Lillian B.
Turner, Rep. Robert Lloyd

## Wholesale Trade—Food and Beverages

Beauchamp, Patrick L.
Carter, Chester C.
Diggs, Lawrence J.
Goss, Tom A.
Harvey, Dr. William R.
Henry, I. Patricia
Johnson, Eric G.
Jones, Wilbert
Lara, Edison R., Sr.
Locklin, James R.
Maple, Dennis
McCoy, Jessie Haynes
McCain, Ella Byrd
Price, Judith
Richardson, Johnny L.
Robinson, Richard David, Sr.
Thompson, Albert N.
Watson, Eric
White, Ralph L., Jr.
Woods, Alison Scott

## Wholesale Trade—Hardware

Thornton, Willie
Worth, Janice Lorraine

## Wholesale Trade—Industrial Machinery, Equipment, and Supplies

Anderson, Alfred Anthony
Lewis, Robert Alvin, Jr.
Morrison, Paul-David
Oliver, Everett Ahmad
Thornton, Willie

## Wholesale Trade—Motor Vehicles and Parts

Addison, James David
Brown, Larry T.
Davidson, Fletcher Vernon, Jr.
Dixon, Raymond P
Durden, Earnel
Hovell, Yvonne
Hysaw, Guillermo Lark
Lewis-Kemp, Jacqueline
Lee, Fred D., Jr.
Munson, Robert H.
Statham, Carl
Wright, Dawin Lyron

## Wholesale Trade—Not Elsewhere Classified

Apea, Joseph Bennet Kyeremateng
Arrington, Warren H., Jr.
Bennett, Courtney Ajaye
Benjamin, Floyd G.
Black, Walter Weldon, Jr.
Cowden, Michael E.
Honore, Stephan LeRoy
Howell, Amaziah, III
James, Dr. Synthia Saint
Lewis, Michele
Love, Lamar Vincent
McMillan, Rosalyn A.
Richardson, Otis Alexander, Sr.
Seals, George Edward
Tate, Brett Andre
Taylor, Lorenzo James, Jr.
Thornton, Willie
Turner, Rep. Robert Lloyd
Williams, Joseph Lee, Jr.
Young, Arlene H.

## Wholesale Trade—Paper and Allied Products

Gray, Wilfred Douglas
Thornton, Willie
Williams, Joseph Lee, Jr.

## Writing/Editing—Fiction

Alexander, Dr. Estella Conwill
Ansa, Tina McElroy
Austin, Dr. Bobby William
Avery, Charles E.
Bauldock, Gerald, Sr.
Bates, Karen Grigsby
Baiocchi, Regina A. Harris
Bailey, Richard
Bell, Jimmy
Beckham, Barry Earl
Billingsley, Ray C.
Boyd, Dr. Candy Dawson
Booth, Rev. Dr. Charles E.
Branch, Otis Linwood
Bradley, David Henry, Jr.
Brown, Kay B.
Bryan, Ashley F.
Brown, Elaine M.
Bright, Jean Marie
Bullins, Ed
Burnett, Zaron Walter, Jr.
Bunkley, Anita Richmond
Buchanan, Shonda T.
Carter, Jackie
Cary, Lorene
Channer, Colin
Chase-Riboud, Dr. Barbara DeWayne
Cleage, Pearl Michelle
Coleman, Robert A.
Covin, Dr. David L.
Collier, Dr. Eugenia W.
Curtis, Christopher Paul
Cummings, Pat
Danticat, Edwidge
DeRamus, Betty
De Veaux, Alexis
Delany, Samuel Ray, Jr.
Dean, Terrance
DeBerry, Virginia
Dickey, Eric Jerome
Draper, Dr. Sharon Mills
Due, Tananarive
Evans, Mari
Fewell, Richard
Files, Lolita
Flournoy, Valerie Rose
Fortune, Dr. Gwendoline Y.
Forbes, Calvin
Fry, Darrell
Fuller, Charles
Gaines, Ernest James
Gates, Dr. Henry Louis, Jr.
Goss, Linda
Golden, Marita
Govan, Dr. Sandra Yvonne
Gomez, Jewelle L.
Grimes, Nikki
Haywood, Gar Anthony
Hansen, Joyce Viola
Halliburton, Warren J.
Hairston, William

## Writing/Editing-Nonfiction (*See Also* Journalism—Print)



## Writing/Editing—Not Elsewhere Classified

Foxx, Nina
Gipson, Reve
Givens, Joshua Edmond
Gladwell, Malcolm
Greenfield, Eloise
Greer, Dr. Robert O., Jr.
Green, Lester L.
Haynes, Sue Blood
Harris, Bill
Harrison, Dr. Andolyn B.
Harris, Francis C.
Harris, Johnnie Frances
Haggins, Jon
Harris, William J.
Harris, Jay Terrence
Hamilton, Arthur Lee, Jr.
Hill, Jennifer A.
Higginson, Vy
Hixon, Mamie Webb
Holt, Mikel
Howard, Ellen D.
Howard, Dr. Elizabeth Fitzgerald
Hudgeons, Louise Taylor
Hull, Akasha Gloria
Hutcherson, Dr. Hilda
James, Dr. Synthia Saint
Jackson, Robert, Jr.
James, Frank Samuel, III
Jones, Geraldine J.
Jones, Alexander R.
Johnson, Dr. Georgia Anna Lewis
Johnson, Dinah
Johnson-Helton, Karen
Jonas, Dr. Ernesto A.
Jones, Dr. Howard James
Jones, K. Maurices
Johnson, Henry Wade
Jones, Dr. Katherine Elizabeth Butler
Kazi, Abdul-Khaliq Kuumba
Kaiser, Ernest Daniel
Kelley, William Melvin
King, Anita
King, Colbert I.
King, Howard O., Sr.
Kirkland, Theodore
King, Preston
Knowles, Dr. Eddie Ade
Kunes, Kenneth R.
Lachman, Dr. Ralph Steven
Lewis, Dr. Samella Sanders
LeRoy, Charles
Leavy, Walter
Lewis-Kemp, Jacqueline
Leslie, Marsha R.
LeFlore, Lyah Beth
Lindsay, Gwendolyn Ann Burns
Little, Benilde Elease
Little, Robert E.
Lownes-Jackson, Dr. Millicent Gray
Long, Dr. Charles H.
Luis, Dr. William
Malveaux, Julianne
Mathis, Gregory
Massey, Ardrey Yvonne
Mayberry, Dr. Claude A., Jr.
McConnell, Conrad
McGill, Michele Nicole Johnson
McKissack, Patricia Carwell
McPherson, William H.
McKinney-Johnson, Eloise
McEachin, James
McBride, James
McLeod, Dr. Gustavus A.
McKinney-Whetstone, Diane
McGruder, Aaron Vincent
Meyers, Dr. Rose M.
Meade-Tollin, Dr. Linda C.
Medina, Benny
Mercer, Valerie June
Miller, Norma Adele
Mitchell, Rhonda Alma
Millender, Dharathula H.
Miller, Melvin B.
Miller, Dr. Ronald Baxter
Mixon, Veronica
Moore, Acel
Moore, Dr. Jossie A.
Moore, Katherine Bell
Moore, Derrick C.
Morant, Mack Bernard
Molette-Ogden, Dr. Carla
Montgomery, Sonsyrea Tate
Muwakkil, Salim
Murray, Virgie W.
Neal, LaVelle E., III
Nissel, Angela
Norment, Lynn Aurelia
Orr, Ray
Osborne, Gwendolyn Eunice
Palcy, Euzhan
Phillips, Delores
Pierce, Ponchitta A.
Poole, Tyrone
Prettyman, Prof. Quandra
Prior, Anthony Eugene
Pryce, Trevor Wesley, II
Rainey, Timothy Mark
Randolph, Laura B.
Reed, Sheila A.
Reynolds, Pamela Terese
Redmond, Dr. Eugene B.
Reid, Joel Otto
Robinson, Ann Garrett
Rodgers, Carolyn Marie
Robinson, Eugene Harold
Roebuck-Hayden, Marcia
Russell, Dorothy Delores
Russell, Mark
Sanders, Prentice Earl
Sample, William Amos
Saunders, Barbara Ann
Savage, Frank
Sanders, Rhonda Sheree
Scott, Ruby Dianne
Scott, Col. Eugene Frederick
Seale, Bobby
Sherman, Edward Forrester
Shange, Ntozake
Shelton, Millicent Beth
Sims, Lowery Stokes
Sims, Harold Rudolph
Simpson, Rev. Dr. Samuel G.
Simms, Dr. Margaret Constance
Smith, Barbara
Smith, Danyel
Smith, Dr. George Edmond
Snyder, Vanessa W.
Southgate, Martha
Soaries, Rev. Dr. DeForest Blake, Jr.
Spruell, Sakina P.
Stephens, E. Delores B
Starks, John Levell
Sutton, Dr. Ozell
Summers, Dr. Rodger
Sweets, Ellen Adrienne
Tate, Greg
Teasley, Marie R.
Thomas, Spencer
Thomas, Raymond A.
Thomas, Duane
Timmons-Toney, Rev. Deborah Denise
Toote, Gloria E. A
Torrence-Thompson, Juanita Lee
Troupe, Dr. Marilyn Kay
Tucker, Karen
Tyree, Omar
VelJohnson, Reginald
Washington, Adrienne Terrell
Waters, Mary D.
Washington, Alonzo Lavert
Washington, Jesse
Walker-Thoth, Daphne LaVera
Walton, Anthony Scott
Wayans, Keenen Ivory, Sr.
Watson, Dennis Rahiim
Washington, Joseph R., Jr.
West, George Ferdinand, Jr.
Whitehurst, Steven Laroy
White, Stephen Gregory
Whitehead, Colson
Williams, George R.
Williams, Dr. Eugene, Sr.
Williams, Juan
Wilson, Danton Thomas
Wilson, Ronald M.
Williams, Dr. Everett Belvin
Woods, Kondria Yvette Black
Wright, Dr. Roberta V. Hughes
Yarbrough, Nana Camille
Youngblood, Shay
Young, Prof. Alfred

## Writing/Editing—Plays, Screenplays, TV Scripts

Abney, Robert
Bauldock, Gerald, Sr.
Benson, Dr. James Russell
Bertelsen, Phil
Beckham, Barry Earl
Blake, Jennifer Lynn
Boone, Eunetta T.
Boseman, Chadwick
Brown, Michelle Listenbee
Bradley, David Henry, Jr.
Branch, Otis Linwood
Branch, William Blackwell
Brown-Guillory, Elizabeth
Burns, Khephra
Bullins, Ed
Caldwell, Benjamin
Chenault, John
Clark-Taylor, Kristin
Cleage, Pearl Michelle
Clay, Stanley Bennett
Collins, Tessil John
Cooper, Barry Michael
Coogler, Ryan
Coles, Kimberley
Cowden, Michael E.
Colley, Nathaniel S., Jr.
Collie, Kelsey E.
de Jongh, Prof. James Laurence
Dickey, Eric Jerome
Diesel, Vin
Domingo, Colman
Easton, Earnest Lee
Entertainer, Cedric The
Evans, Mari
Fales, Susan Marya
Fewell, Richard
Fernandez, Denise Burse
Fisher, Antwone Quenton
Franklin, J. E.
Fuller, Charles
Genet, Michael
Goss, Clayton
Gomez, Jewelle L.
Greaves, William
Hairston, William
Harris, Thomas Walter
Hay, Samuel Arthur
Hayes, Teddy
Hardwick, Gary C.
Hamilton, Arthur Lee, Jr.
Harris, William Anthony
Harrison, Paul Carter
Higginsen, Vy
Hill, Donna
Holder, Laurence
Howard, Gregory Allen
Hobson, Charles Blagrove
Hughes, Coquie
Hudlin, Reginald Alan
Ione, Carole
James, Hawthorne
Jackson, Millie
Jackson, Angela
Jackson, Kevin Allen
Jakes, Bishop Thomas Dexter, Sr.
Jefferson, Roland Spratlin
Jones, Orlando
Jones, Sarah
Kennedy, Adrienne Lita
Keymah, Crystal T.
Khan, Dr. Ricardo M.
King, Woodie, Jr.
Kotto, Yaphet Frederick
Lanier, Anthony Wayne
Lee, William James Edwards, III
Lee, Spike
Lemmons, Kasi
Letson, Alfred, Jr.
Lee, Malcolm D.
Lillie, Dr. Vernell Audrey Watson
Mason, Clifford L.
McNeill, Cerves Todd
McNeil, DeeDee
McElroy, Dr. Colleen J.
Mixon, Veronica
Molette, Dr. Carlton Woodard
Moss, Winston
Molette, Barbara J.
Morris, Robert V.
Moore, Christopher Paul
Mumford, Thaddeus Quentin, Jr.
Naylor, Gloria
Nunes Kirby, Mizan Roberta Patricia
Orlandersmith, Dael
Parks, Suzan-Lori
Page, Harrison Eugene
Pawley, Dr. Thomas D., III
Perry, Felton E.
Perry, Tyler
Purdee, Nathan
Rae, Issa
Randall, Alice
Reid, Timothy L.
Rich, Matty
Richardson, Odis Gene
Ridley, John
Sarmiento, Shirley Jean
Scott, Larry B.
Scott, Dr. John Sherman
Seaton, Sandra Cecelia
Shange, Ntozake
Sharp, Saundra Pearl
Shelton, Millicent Beth
Singleton, John Daniel
Smith, Anna Deavere
Snipes, Lolita Walker
Stetson, Jeffrey Paul
Sykes, Wanda Y'vette
Taylor, Dr. Regina
Thomas, Joyce Carol
Torry, Guy
Van Peebles, Melvin
Van Peebles, Mario
Wade, Kim Mache
Wagoner, J. Robert
Wayans, Damon Kyle
Warfield, Marsha Francine
Wayans, Shawn Mathis
Walker, Ian Robin
Weathersbee, Tonyaa Jeanine
West, Cheryl L.
Williams, Samm-Art
Wilson, Sandra E.
Williams, John Alfred
Young, Alene Marie

## Writing/Editing—Poetry

Alexander, Dr. Estella Conwill
Arnez, Dr. Nancy L.
Bandele, Asha
Baiocchi, Regina A. Harris
Bauldock, Gerald, Sr.
Berhe-Hunt, Annette
Bennett, Lerone, Jr.
Blake, Jennifer Lynn
Boyd, Dr. Melba Joyce
Brown, Dr. Barbara Mahone
Brewton, Dr. Butler E.
Bunyon, Ronald S.
Chase-Riboud, Dr. Barbara DeWayne
Chenault, John
Cliff, Michelle
Clark, Beverly Gail
Clarke, Cheryl L.
Clarke, LeRoy P.
Cowden, Michael E.
Cox, Joseph Mason Andrew
Devers, Yolanda Gail
Derricotte, Toi
Dejoie, Carolyn Barnes Milanes
Dember, Jean Wilkins
Dove, Rita Frances
Eady, Cornelius
Evans, Mari
Faust, Dr. Naomi Flowe
Fisher, Antwone Quenton
Fry, Darrell
Gary, Kathye J.
Giovanni, Nikki, Jr.
Golightly, Lena Mills
Gomez, Jewelle L.
Grimes, Nikki
Grosvenor, VertaMae
Hairston, William
Hardy, Dr. Dorothy C.
Harper, Michael Steven
Henderson, David
Hoagland, Everett H.
Howard, Susan E.
Hogue, Leslie Denise
Hord, Dr. Frederick Lee
Holland, Robin W.
Hull, Akasha Gloria
James, Dr. Synthia Saint
Jackson, Angela
Jackson, Fred James, Sr.
Jackson, Suzanne Fitzallen
Jackson, Garnet Nelson
Jeter-Johnson, Sheila Ann
Jones, Patricia Kay Spears
Jones, Gayl
Jones, Sarah
Komunyakaa, Yusef
Lacy, Walter
Lee, William James Edwards, III
Leeke, Madelyn Cheryl
Lester, Julius
Letson, Alfred, Jr.
Liverpool, Charles Eric
London, Dr. Clement B. G.
Major, Dr. Clarence
Madgett, Dr. Naomi Long
Madison, Jacqueline Edwina
Marbury, Rev. Donald Lee
McClane, Prof. Kenneth Anderson, Jr.
McNeil, DeeDee
McElroy, Dr. Colleen J.
Meeks, Larry Gillette
Miller, Erenest Eugene
Miller, E. Ethelbert
Miller, Major Gen. Frank Lee, Jr.
Moore, Lenard Duane
Moore-Poole, Jessica Care
Moss, Thylias
Mullen, Harryette
Nunes Kirby, Mizan Roberta Patricia
Okantah, Mwatabu S.
Orlandersmith, Dael
Pate, Alexs D.
Pawley, Dr. Thomas D., III
Porter, Bishop Henry Lee
Ramseur, Andre William
Ray, Walter I., Jr.
Reed, Ishmael Scott
Russell, Beverly Ann
Sanchez, Dr. Sonia Benita
Skinner, Dr. Ewart C.
Smith, Dr. Dorothy Louise White
Smith, Tracy K.
Southerland, Ellease
Stansbury, Kevin Bradley
Subryan, Carmen Barclay
Taylor, Mildred D.
Tarpley, Natasha Anastasia
Thomas, Joyce Carol
Tillis, Dr. Frederick Charles
Tisdale, Prof. Celes
Torrence-Thompson, Juanita Lee
Troupe, Quincy Thomas, Jr.
Vest, Hilda Freeman
Vertreace-Doody, Martha Modena
Ward, Dr. Jerry Washington, Jr.
Warren, Nagueyalti
Walker, Alice Malsenior
Walker, Bishop Hezekiah Xzavier, Jr.
Wade-Gayles, Dr. Gloria Jean
Weaver, Afaa Michael
Welburn, Ronald Garfield
White, Paul Edward
Williams, Saul Stacey
Wilkinson, Brenda Scott
Williams-Witherspoon, Kimmika L. H.
Williams-Garner, Debra
Williams, John Alfred
Williams, T. Joyce
Wright, Stephen Caldwell
Young, Kevin

## Zoology

Ampy, Dr. Franklin R.
Ball, Dr. Wilfred R.
Ball, Richard Erwin
Delco, Dr. Exalton Alfonso, Jr.
Gaffney, Michele Elizabeth
Hudson, Dr. Roy Davage
Jones, Dr. Joseph, Jr.
Jones, George H.
Mack, Dr. Astrid Karona
Porter, Dr. Clarence A.
Russell, Keith Bradley
Shelby, Khadejah E.
Shepherd, Benjamin Arthur
Stevens, Lisa Maria
Sutton, Dr. William Wallace